Beckett®

THE #1 AUTHORITY ON COLLECTIBLES

BASKETBALL CARD PRICE GUIDE

NUMBER 25

THE HOBBY'S MOST RELIABLE AND RELIED UPON SOURCE™

Founder & Advisor: Dr. James Beckett III • Edited by the staff of Beckett Basketball

Prices in this guide reflect current retail rates determined just prior to printing. They do not reflect for-sale prices by the author, publisher, distributors, advertisers, or any card dealers associated with this guide. Every effort has been made to eliminate errors. Readers are invited to write us noting any errors which may be researched and corrected in subsequent printings. The publisher will not be held responsible for losses which may occur in the sale or purchase of cards because of information contained herein.

BECKETT is a registered trademark of BECKETT MEDIA LLC, DALLAS, TEXAS

Manufactured in the United States of America | Published by Beckett Media LLC

Beckett Media LLC

4635 McEwen Dr. • Dallas, TX 75244

(972) 991-6657 • beckett.com

First Printing ISBN: 978-1-930692-20-6

Basketball **DEALER DIRECTORY**

ALASKA

Don's Sportscards
9900 Old Seward Hwy., Ste 8
Anchorage AK, 99515-2249,
(907) 349-8804
donssports@aol.com

ARKANSAS

HobbyTown USA
2614 S. Shackleford Rd. Suite C
Little Rock AR, 72205
(501) 228-4800
htulittlerock@gmail.com

ARIZONA

Phoenix Card Co-Op
4326 West Bell Rd., Suite# 7
Glendale AZ, 85308-3545,
(602) 548-1254
phoenixcardcoop@cox.net

The Hot Corner
Sportscard Shop
6750 E Main St., Ste 112
Mesa AZ, 85205-9049
(480) 396-0442

CALIFORNIA

Taylor Baseball Cards
8682 Beach Blvd., Ste 101
Buena Park CA, 90620-4808,
(714) 827-7746
taycard@aol.com

Burbank Sportscards
1500 W Burbank Blvd
Burbank CA, 91506
818-843-2600
burbanksportscards.com
Beckett Marketplace

Beverly Hills Baseball Card Shop
1137 So Robertson Blvd
Los Angeles CA, 90035,
310-278-4263
californiasportscards.com

The Bullpen 2.0
13470 Washington Blvd
suite 100
Marina Del Rey CA, 90292,
424-228-2830
bullpensportscards@yahoo.com

Clairemont Sportcards
3949 Clairemont Drive Suite 4
San Diego CA, 92117
(858) 270-4945
clairemontsc@netscape.net

A & N Sports Cards
105 W Arrow Highway,
Suite #7
San Dimas CA, 91773,
(909) 394-2375
ansportscard@yahoo.com

CONNECTICUT

Matt's Sportscards & Comics
169 Elm St
Enfield CT, 06082,
860-741-2522
contact@cardandcomicshop.com

FLORIDA

Big League
920 State Road 436
Casselberry FL, 32707-5563,
(407) 834-2273

Orlando Sportscards South
9476 S Orange Blossom Trl.
Orlando FL, 32837-8321,
(407) 240-0384
orlandosportscards@hotmail.com

Scott's Sportscards
6724 N University Dr
Tamarac FL , 33321,
954-721-7141
scottysportscards@hotmail.com

ILLINOIS

Steven's Collectibles
35 East Plainfield Road #2
Countryside IL, 60525,
708-352-7758
sslustore@aol.com

The Baseball Card King
1552 Ogden Ave
Downers Grove IL, 60515,
630-512-9300
thebaseballcardking@comcast.net

Baseball Card Connection
313 W Jefferson Ave.
Effingham IL, 62401,
(217) 342-2539

Gizmo's Sportscards
111 Harvest Glen Dr
Davis Junction, IL 61020,
815-540-5206
Pirate8@aol.com

INDIANA

K&L Cards
265 S State Road 135
Greenwood IN, 46142-1421,
(317) 883-2240
lscantcard@aol.com

B Card Exchange Inc
8519 Westfield Rd.
Indianapolis IN, 46240-2369,
(317) 254-8681
bce8519@aol.com

Hockeyman's
125 E Maple St.
Jeffersonville IN, 47130,
(812) 285-8806
kenhockeyman@yahoo.com

Baseball Card Exchange
2412 U.S. Highway 41
Schererville IN, 46375,
800-598-8656
bbcexchange.com

KENTUCKY

Readmore Bookstore
63 Glyn View Plz.
Prestonsburg KY, 41653-7958,
(606) 886-2266

MASSACHUSETTS

Baystate Sports Cards
861 Edgell Rd.
Framingham MA, 1701,
(508) 877-2273
baystatesportscards.com

MARYLAND

DugoutZone
10226 Baltimore Nat'l Pike
Ellicott City MD, 21042,
(410) 461-8664
www.dugoutzone.com

MICHIGAN

S & F Sport Cards
26019 Lorelei Dr.
Flat Rock MI, 48134-9422,
(734) 782-5462
frankmio@provide.net

Kruk Cards
210 Campbell St
Rochester MI, 48307,
248-656-6028
krukcards.com

MINNESOTA

A Rising Star
7113 10th St N
Oakdale, MN 55128,
651-756-1379
Arisingstarmn.com

NORTH CAROLINA

Score More Sports Collectibles
4944 Martin View Lane
Winston-Salem NC, 27104,
336-602-2383
scoremorenow.com
BGS Submission Center

NEVADA

John's Grand Slam Collectibles
6115 S Rainbow Blvd
Suite #108
Las Vegas NV, 89118,
(702) 463-9426
jgscollectibles@yahoo.com

Legacy Sports Cards
8125 W Sahara Ave Ste 160
Las Vegas NV, 89117,
(702) 341-6525
marcel@legacysportscards.com

Ultimate Sportscards
450 Fremont #183
Las Vegas NV, 89101,
(702) 363-7999

NEW YORK

BP Sportscards
& Memorabilia
38 N Main St.
Florida NY, 10921-1319,
(845) 651-1660
www.bpsportscards.com

Royal Collectibles
9601 Metropolitan Ave.
Forest Hills NY, 11375-6697,
(718) 793-0542

Montasy Comics
70-17 Austin Street, 2nd floor
Forest Hills NY, 11375,
718-575-8815
montasycomics.com

Chameleon Comics
3 Maiden Ln.
New York NY, 10038-4008,
(212) 587-3411
schameleon@hotmail.com

Montasy Chapter 2
431 5th Avenue, 2nd floor
New York NY, 10016,
212-683-2018
montasycomics.com

Dave & Adam's Card World
2217 Sheridan Dr.
Tonawanda, NY 14223
716-837-4920

Dave & Adam's Card World
8075 Sheridan Dr. (42,000 sq. ft.)
Williamsville, NY 14221
(716) 626-0000

OHIO

T.C.I. Sports Fan
3962 Linden Ave.
Dayton OH, 45432-3004,
(937) 254-8551
tcisportsfan@aol.com

Tallboyz Swap n Shop
127 W Main St.
Hillsboro OH, 45133,
(937) 402-5120
tall_boyz@yahoo.com

Lima Sports Collectibles
1096 N Cable Rd.
Lima OH, 45805,
(567) 371-3090
limasportscollectibles.com

OREGON

The Sports Room
3889 SW Hall Blvd.
Beaverton OR, 97005,
(503) 533-5412
webbsite99@msn.com

Hooker's Sportscards
293 W 7th Ave.
Eugene OR, 97401-2654,
(541) 485-3414
dhooker1@comcast.net

Heaven Sent Sports Cards
7002 SW Nyberg St.
Tualatin OR, 97062-9231,
(503) 692-8894
hvsent@frontier.com

PENNSYLVANIA

Baseball Card Castle
20555 Route 19
Cranberry Twp PA,
16066-7525,
(724) 772-0490
bbcardcas@aol.com

Sports Cards Etc.
110 West McMurray Road
McMurray PA, 15317,
(724) 942-8085

Steel City Collectibles
- Ross Park Mall
1000 Ross Park Mall Drive
Pittsburgh PA, 15237,
412-366-5858
www.steelcitycollectibles.com

RHODE ISLAND

281 sports card
798 Atwood 2
Cranston RI, 2920,
(401) 270-3329
281sportscards@gmail.com

Central Sports Cards
791 Central Ave.
Pawtucket RI, 2861,
(401) 724-2040
www.centralsportscards.com

TENNESSEE

3 R Baseball Cards
55 Flea Market,
4938 New Tullahoma
Hwy Booth 2 & 3
Manchester TN, 37355,
(931) 607-8380
3rstransportinc@bellsouth.net

TEXAS

Superior Sports Investments
PO Box 180488
Arlington TX, 76096,
(817) 557-9196
www.superiorsportsinv.com

Houston Sports Connection
12280 Westheimer Rd.,
Ste 12B
Houston TX, 77077-6055,
(281) 589-9600
hsclau@flash.net

Triple Cards & Collectibles
2452 Ave K
Plano TX, 75074-5911,
(972) 509-5263
triplecard@sbcglobal.net

All American Sports Wear
3903 Eisenhauer Road
San Antonio TX, 78218-3408,
(210) 393-5521
saallamerican@aol.com

Sports Cards Plus
2239 Lock Hill Selma Rd.
San Antonio TX, 78230,
(210) 524-2337
www.sportscardsplussa.com

Whats On Second
4177 Naco Perrin Blvd.
San Antonio TX, 78217-2505,
(210) 590-8444
whatsonsecond@stic.net

VIRGINIA

Blowout Cards
- The Fantastic Store
14508 Lee Rd - Unit F
Chantilly VA, 20151,
Blowoutcards.com

WASHINGTON

DJ's Sports Cards
1630 Duvall Ave NE Suite D
Renton WA, 98059,
425-235-4357
djssportscards.com
Beckett Marketplace

Columbia Sports Card and More
11713 NE 99th Street Suite 1030
Vancouver WA, 98682,
(360) 605-4400
steve@columbiasportscard.com

WISCONSIN

Larry Fritsch Cards
735 Old Wausau Road
Stevens Point WI, 54481,
866-595-8687
fritschcards.com

WEST VIRGINIA

Baseball Cards And More
765 3rd Ave.
Huntington WV, 25701-1421,
(304) 522-1380

Puerto Rico

Collector Corner
192-A NE Rd., Ramey
Aguadilla Puerto Rico, 924,
(787) 612-6944
gonzalesedgardo417@yahoo.com

Collector House
Plaza Las Americas Mall
local 408
San Juan Puerto Rico, 918,
(787) 632-0203

ONLINE

2Bros Sports Collectibles, LLC
2brossports.com

Baseball Card Exchange
bbcexchange.com

Blowout Cards
Blowoutcards.com

Burbank Sportscards
burbanksportscards.com
Beckett Marketplace

Cardboard Memories
cardboardmemories.ca

Dave & Adam's Card World
dacardworld.com

Sport Card Direct
sportscarddirect.com

Steel City Collectibles
steelcitycollect.com

UltimateSportsAuctions.com
UltimateSportsAuctions.com

AUSTRALIA

Just Cards Trading Cards
140 / 33 Prindiville Dr Wangara
Perth,WA AUSTRALIA, 6065,
61.413707587
justin@justdabestcards.com

CONTENTS

HOW TO USE AND CONDITION GUIDE

Isn't it great? Every year this book gets bigger and better with all the new sets coming out. But even more exciting is that every year there are more attractive choices and, subsequently, more interest in the cards we love so much. This edition has been enhanced and expanded from the previous edition. The cards you collect—who appears on them, what they look like, where they are from, and (most important to most of you) what their current values are—are enumerated within. Many of the features contained in the other Beckett Price Guides have been incorporated into this volume since condition grading, terminology, and many other aspects of collecting are common to the card hobby in general. We hope you find the book both interesting and useful in your collecting pursuits.

The Beckett Basketball Card Price Guide has been successful where other attempts have failed because it is complete, current, and valid. This Price Guide contains not just one, but two prices for all the basketball cards listed. These account for most of the basketball cards in existence. The prices were added to the card lists just prior to printing and reflect not the author's opinions or desires, but the going retail prices for each card based on the active market (sports memorabilia conventions and shows, sports card shops, mail-order catalogs, local club meetings, auction results, and other firsthand reports of actual realized prices).

What is the best price guide available on the market today? Of course card sellers will prefer the price guide with the highest prices, while card buyers will naturally prefer the one with the lowest prices. Accuracy, however, is the true test. Use the price guide used by more collectors and dealers than all the others combined because it's not the lowest and not the highest — but the most accurate guide, and is produced with integrity.

To facilitate your use of this book, read the complete introductory section on the following pages before going to the pricing pages. Every collectible field has its own terminology; we've tried to capture most of these terms and definitions in our glossary. Please read carefully the section on grading and the condition of your cards, as you will not be able to determine which price column is appropriate for a given card without first knowing its condition.

HOW TO COLLECT

Each collection is personal and reflects the individuality of its owner. There are no set rules on how to collect cards. Since card collecting is a hobby or leisure pastime, what you collect, how much you collect, and how much time and money you spend collecting are entirely up to you. The funds you have available for collecting and your own personal taste should determine how you collect.

It is impossible to collect every card ever produced. Therefore, beginners as well as intermediate and advanced collectors usually specialize in some way. One of the reasons this hobby is popular is that individual collectors can define and tailor their collecting methods to match their own tastes.

Many collectors select complete sets from particular years, acquire only certain players, some collectors are only interested in the first cards or Rookie Cards of certain players, and others collect cards by team.

Remember, this is a hobby so pick a style of collecting that appeals to you.

CONDITION GUIDE

The most widely used grades are defined to the right. Obviously, many cards will not perfectly fit one of the definitions. Therefore, categories between the major grades known as in-between grades are used, such as Good to Very Good (G-Vg), Very Good to Excellent (VgEx), and Excellent-Mint to Near Mint (ExMt-NrMt). Such grades indicate a card with all qualities of the lower category but with at least a few qualities of the higher category.

The value of cards that fall between the listed columns can also be calculated using a percentage of the top grade. For example, a card that falls between the top and middle grades (Ex, ExMt or NrMt in most cases) will generally be valued at anywhere from 50% to 90% of the top grade.

Similarly, a card that falls between the middle and bottom grades (G-Vg, Vg or VgEx in most cases) will generally be valued at anywhere from 20% to 40% of the top grade.

There are also cases where cards are in better condition than the top grade or worse than the bottom grade. Cards that grade worse than the lowest grade are generally valued at 5-10% of the top grade.

When a card exceeds the top grade by one — such as NrMt-Mt when the top grade is NrMt, or Mint when the top grade is NrMt-Mt — a premium of up to 50% is possible, with 10-20% the usual norm.

When a card exceeds the top grade by two — such as Mint when the top grade is NrMt, or NrMt-Mt when the top grade is ExMt — a premium of 25-50% is the usual norm. But certain condition sensitive cards or sets, particularly those from the pre-war era, can bring premiums of up to 100% or even more.

Unopened packs, boxes and factory-collated sets are considered Mint in their unknown (and presumed perfect) state. Once opened, however, each card can be graded (and valued) in its own right by taking into account any defects that may be present in spite of the fact that the card has never been handled.

GENERAL CARD FLAWS

CENTERING

Current centering terminology uses numbers representing the percentage of border on either side of the main design. Obviously, centering is diminished in importance for borderless cards.

Slightly Off-Center (60/40): A slightly off-center card is one that upon close inspection is found to have one border bigger than the opposite border. This degree once was offensive to only purists, but now some hobbyists try to avoid cards that are anything other than perfectly centered.

Off-Center (70/30): An off-center card has one border that is noticeably more than twice as wide as the opposite border.

Badly Off-Center (80/20 or worse): A badly off-center card has virtually no border on one side of the card.

Miscut: A miscut card actually shows part of the adjacent card in its larger border and consequently a corresponding amount of its card is cut off.

GLOSSARY/LEGEND

Our glossary defines terms frequently used in the card collecting hobby. Many of these terms are also common to other types of sports memorabilia collecting. Some terms may have several meanings depending on use and context.

ABA – American Basketball Association
ACC – Accomplishment
ACO – Assistant Coach Card
AL – Active Leader
ART – All-Rookie Team
AS – All-Star
ASA – All-Star Advice
ASW – All-Star Weekend
AUTO or AU – Autograph.
AW – Award Winner
B – Bronze
BC – Bonus Card
BT – Beam Team or Breakaway Threats
CB – Collegiate Best
CBA – Continental Basketball Association
CL – Checklist card. Older checklist cards in Mint condition that have not been checked off are very desirable and command large premiums.
CO – Coach card
COMMON CARD – The typical card of any set; it has no premium value accruing from subject matter, numerical scarcity, popular demand, or anomaly.
COR – Corrected card. A version of an error card that was fixed by the manufacturer.
CY – City Lights
DIE-CUT – A card with part of its stock partially cut for ornamental reasons.
DISC – A circular-shaped card
DP – Double Print. A card that was printed in approximately double the quantity compared to other cards in the same series.
ERR – Error card. A card with erroneous information, spelling, or depiction on either side of the card.
EXCH – An exchange card that is inserted into packs that can be redeemed.
FIN – Finals
FLB – Flashback
FPM – Future Playoff MVP's
FSL – Future Scoring Leaders
FULL SHEET – A complete sheet of cards that has not been cut into individual cards by the manufacturer. Also called an uncut sheet.
G – Gold
GQ – Gentleman's Quarterly
GRA – Grace
HL – Highlight card
HOF – Hall of Fame, or Hall of Famer (also abbreviated HOFer).
HOR – Horizontal pose on a card as opposed to the standard vertical orientation found on most cards.
IA – In Action card. A special type of card depicting a player in an action photo, such as the 1982 Topps cards.
INSERT – A card of a different type, e.g., a poster, or any other sports collectible contained and sold in the same package along with a card or cards of a major set.
IS – Inside Stuff
JSY – Card contains a jersey swatch
JWA – John Wooden Award
MAG – Magic of SkyBox cards
MC – Members Choice
MEM – Memorial
MO – McDonald's Open
MINI – A small card or stamp (the 1991-92 SkyBox Canadian set, for example)
MVP – Most Valuable Player
NNO – No card number on back
NY – New York
OBVERSE – The front, face, or pictured side of the card
OLY – Olympic card
PANEL – An extended card that is composed of multiple individual cards
PC – Poster card
PF – Pacific Finest

CORNER WEAR

Corner wear is the most scrutinized grading criteria in the hobby.

Corner with a slight touch of wear: The corner still is sharp, but there is a slight touch of wear showing. On a dark-bordered card, this shows as a dot of white.

Fuzzy corner: The corner still comes to a point, but the point has just begun to fray. A slightly "dinged" corner is considered the same as a fuzzy corner.

Slightly rounded corner: The fraying of the corner has increased to where there is only a hint of a point. Mild layering may be evident. A "dinged" corner is considered the same as a slightly rounded corner.

Rounded corner: The point is completely gone. Some layering is noticeable.

Badly rounded corner: The corner is completely round and rough. Severe layering is evident.

CREASES

A third common defect is the crease. The degree of creasing in a card is difficult to show in a drawing or picture. On giving the specific condition of an expensive card for sale, the seller should note any creases additionally. Creases can be categorized as to severity according to the following scale.

Light Crease: A light crease is a crease that is barely noticeable upon close inspection. In fact, when cards are in plastic sheets or holders, a light crease may not be seen (until the card is taken out of the holder). A light crease on the front is much more serious than a light crease on the card back only.

Medium Crease: A medium crease is noticeable when held and studied at arm's length by the naked eye, but does not overly detract from the appearance of the card. It is an obvious crease, but not one that breaks the picture surface of the card.

Heavy Crease: A heavy crease is one that has torn or broken through the card's picture surface, e.g., puts a tear in the photo surface.

ALTERATIONS

Deceptive Trimming: This occurs when someone alters the card in order (1) to shave off edge wear, (2) to improve the sharpness of the corners, or (3) to improve centering — obviously their objective is to falsely increase the perceived value of the card to an unsuspecting buyer. The shrinkage usually is evident only if the trimmed card is compared to an adjacent full-sized card or if the trimmed card is itself measured.

Obvious Trimming: Obvious trimming is noticeable and unfortunate. It is usually performed by non-collectors who give no thought to the present or future value of their cards.

Deceptively Retouched Borders: This occurs when the borders (especially on those cards with dark borders) are touched up on the edges and corners with magic marker or crayons of appropriate color in order to make the card appear to be Mint.

MISCELLANEOUS CARD FLAWS

The following are common minor flaws that, depending on severity, lower a card's condition by one to four grades and often render it no better than Excellent-Mint: bubbles (lumps in surface), gum and wax stains, diamond cutting (slanted borders), notching, off-centered backs, paper wrinkles, scratched-off cartoons or puzzles on back, rubber band marks, scratches, surface impressions and warping.

The following are common serious flaws that, depending on severity, lower a card's condition at least four grades and often render it no better than Good: chemical or sun fading, erasure marks, mildew, miscutting (severe off-centering), holes, bleached or retouched borders, tape marks, tears, trimming, water or coffee stains and writing.

GRADES

Mint (Mt) – A card with no flaws or wear. The card has four perfect corners, 55/45 or better centering from top to bottom and from left to right, original gloss, smooth edges and original color borders. A Mint card does not have print spots, color or focus imperfections.

Near Mint-Mint (NrMt-Mt) – A card with one minor flaw. Any one of the following would lower a Mint card to Near Mint-Mint: one corner with a slight touch of wear, barely noticeable print spots, color or focus imperfections. The card must have 60/40 or better centering in both directions, original gloss, smooth edges and original color borders.

Near Mint (NrMt) – A card with one minor flaw. Any one of the following would lower a Mint card to Near Mint: one fuzzy corner or two to four corners with slight touches of wear, 70/30 to 60/40 centering, slightly rough edges, minor print spots, color or focus imperfections. The card must have original gloss and original color borders.

Excellent-Mint (ExMt) – A card with two or three fuzzy, but not rounded, corners and centering no worse than 80/20. The card may have no more than two of the following: slightly rough edges, very slightly discolored borders, minor print spots, color or focus imperfections. The card must have original gloss.

Excellent (Ex) – A card with four fuzzy but definitely not rounded corners and centering no worse than 70/30. The card may have a small amount of original gloss lost, rough edges, slightly discolored borders and minor print spots, color or focus imperfections.

Very Good (Vg) – A card that has been handled but not abused: slightly rounded corners with slight layering, slight notching on edges, a significant amount of gloss lost from the surface but no scuffing and moderate discoloration of borders. The card may have a few light creases.

Good (G), Fair (F), Poor (P) – A well-worn, mishandled or abused card: badly rounded and layered corners, scuffing, most or all original gloss missing, seriously discolored borders, moderate or heavy creases, and one or more serious flaws. The grade of Good, Fair or Poor depends on the severity of wear and flaws. Good, Fair and Poor cards generally are used only as fillers.

GLOSSARY/LEGEND

POY – Player of the Year

PROMOTIONAL SET – A set, usually containing a small number of cards, issued by a national card producer and distributed in limited quantities or to a select group of people, such as major show attendees or dealers with wholesale accounts. Also called a preview, prototype, promo, or test set.

QP – Quadruple Print. A card that was printed in approximately four times the quantity compared to other cards in the same series.

RC – Rookie Card. A player's first appearance on a regular issue card from one of the major card companies. With a few exceptions, each player has only one RC in any given set. A Rookie Card cannot be an All-Star, Highlight, In Action, League Leader, Super Action or Team Leader card. It can, however, be a coach card or draft pick card.

REGIONAL – A card issued and distributed only in a limited geographical area of the country.

REVERSE – The back or narrative side of the card

REV NEG – Reversed or flopped photo side of the card. This is a common type of error card, but only some are corrected

RIS – Rising Star

ROY – Rookie of the Year

S – Silver

SA – Super Action card. Similar to an In Action card

SAL – SkyBox Salutes

SERIES – The entire set of cards issued by a particular producer in a particular year, e.g., the 1978-79 Topps series. Also, within a particular set, series can refer to a group of (consecutively numbered) cards printed at the same time, e.g., the first series of the 1972-73 Topps set (#1 through #132).

SET – One each of an entire run of cards of the same type, produced by a particular manufacturer during a single season. In other words, if you have a complete set of 1989-90 Fleer cards, then you have every card from #1 up to and including #132; i.e., all the different cards that were produced.

SHOOT – Shooting Star

SKED – Schedules

SP – Single or Short Print. A card which was printed in lesser quantity compared to the other cards in the same series (also see DP).

SS – Star Stats.

STANDARD SIZE – The standard size for sports cards is 2 1/2 by 3 1/2 inches. All exceptions, such as 1969-70 Topps, are noted in card descriptions.

STOCK – The cardboard or paper on which the card is printed.

STY – Style

SY – Schoolyard Stars

TC – Team card or team checklist card

TD – Triple Double. A term used for having double digit totals in three categories.

TEAM CARD – A card that depicts an entire team, notably the 1989-90 and 1990-91 NBA Hoops Detroit Pistons championship cards and the 1991-92 NBA Hoops subset.

TEST SET – A set, usually containing a small number of cards, issued by a national producer and distributed in a limited section of the country or to a select group of people. Also called a promo or prototype set.

TFC – Team Fact card

TL – Team Leader

TO – Tip-off

TR – Traded card

TRIB – Tribune

TRV – Trivia

TT – Team Tickets card

UER – Uncorrected Error card

USA – Team USA

VAR – Variation card. One of two or more cards from the same series, with the same card number (or player with identical pose, if the series is unnumbered) differing from one another in some aspect, from the printing, stock or other feature of the card. This is often caused when the manufacturer of the cards notices an error in a particular card, corrects the error and then resumes the print run.

VERT – Vertical pose on a card

XRC – Extended Rookie Card. A player's first appearance on a card, but issued in a set that was not distributed nationally nor in packs. In basketball sets, this term only refers to the 1983, '84 and '85 Star Company sets.

YB – Yearbook

20A – Twenty assist club

50P – Fifty point club

6M – Sixth Man

! – Condition sensitive card or set

1994 A Question of Sport UK

These cards are part of a British board game "A Question of Sport" in which participants attempt to name an athlete by seeing a picture of them. These white bordered, full color cards measure 2 1/4" by 3 1/2" and have a back that contains only the player's name surrounded by a blue border on white card stock. We've arranged the unnumbered cards alphabetically below.

COMPLETE SET (79) 20.00 50.00
37 Michael Jordan 3.20 8.00

1996 A Question of Sport Who Am I

This 100-card multi-sport set was from a game exclusively sold in England. Each front of the game cards features a blue and yellow border with a small color photo of the featured athlete on the top half. The player's name is listed below in light blue after a series of written clues about the player's identity. The only notable basketball player is Magic Johnson. The cards are not numbered and are checklisted below in alphabetical order.

COMPLETE SET (100) 30.00 75.00
48 Magic Johnson 3.20 8.00

1970-71 ABA All-Star 5x7 Picture Pack

This 12-card set featues black and white photos of ABA All-Stars from 1970-71. Each photo measures 5" by 7". The backs are blank and checklisted below in alphabetical order.

COMPLETE SET (12) 75.00 150.00
1 Rick Barry 20.00 40.00
2 John Brisker 5.00 10.00
3 George Carter 5.00 10.00
4 Mack Calvin 6.00 12.00
5 Joe Caldwell 6.00 12.00
6 Warren Jabali 7.50 15.00
7 Larry Jones 5.00 10.00
8 George Lehmann 5.00 10.00
9 Jim McDaniel 5.00 10.00
10 Bill Melchionni 7.50 15.00
11 John Roche 5.00 10.00
12 George Thompson 5.00 10.00

2012-13 Absolute

COMP.SET w/o SPs (100) 20.00 50.00
RETIRED PRINT RUN 499 SER.#'d SETS
AU RC PRINT RUN 199 TO 399 SER.#'d SETS
UNPRICED BLACK PRINT RUN ONE SET
UNPRICED PLATINUM PRINT RUN 10 SETS
1 Kevin Love .75 2.00
2 Derrick Rose 1.00 2.50
3 LeBron James 3.00 8.00
4 Carmelo Anthony 1.00 2.50
5 Kevin Durant 2.00 5.00
6 Devin Harris .50 1.25
7 Blake Griffin .75 2.00
8 Andre Iguodala .60 1.50
9 Elton Brand .75 2.00
10 Rodney Stuckey .60 1.50
11 Brendan Haywood .50 1.25
12 Stephen Jackson .60 1.50
13 Paul Pierce .75 2.00
14 Ty Lawson .50 1.25
15 Dwight Howard .60 1.50
16 Jeremy Lin .75 2.00
17 Anderson Varejao .50 1.25
18 Derrick Favors .60 1.50
19 Jose Calderon .50 1.25
20 LaMarcus Aldridge .75 2.00
21 Tony Parker .75 2.00
22 Ersan Ilyasova .50 1.25
23 Zach Randolph .60 1.50
24 Kobe Bryant 3.00 8.00
25 Andrew Bogut .60 1.50
26 Andrei Kirilenko .60 1.50
27 Dirk Nowitzki 1.00 2.50
28 Deron Williams .60 1.50
29 Hakim Warrick .60 1.50
30 James Harden 1.25 3.00
31 Hedo Turkoglu .60 1.50
32 Channing Frye .60 1.50
33 Andre Miller .60 1.50
34 Joakim Noah .60 1.50
35 Rashard Lewis .60 1.50
36 Stephen Curry 3.00 8.00
37 Chris Paul 1.00 2.50
38 Wesley Matthews .50 1.25
39 Steve Nash .75 2.00
40 Josh Smith .60 1.50
41 Kevin Martin .60 1.50
42 Emeka Okafor .60 1.50
43 Gordon Hayward .75 2.00
44 Tyson Chandler .60 1.50
45 Russell Westbrook 2.00 5.00
46 Brandon Jennings .50 1.25
47 Marcin Gortat .60 1.50
48 Andrew Bynum .50 1.25
49 Brook Lopez .60 1.50
50 Manu Ginobili .75 2.00
51 Tyrus Thomas .50 1.25
52 Greg Monroe .60 1.50
53 Eric Gordon .60 1.50
54 DeMar DeRozan .75 2.00
55 Dwyane Wade 1.25 3.00
56 David West .60 1.50
57 Rudy Gay .75 2.00
58 Evan Turner .50 1.25
59 Shane Battier .60 1.50
60 Nick Collison .60 1.50
61 Daniel Gibson .60 1.50
62 DeMarcus Cousins .75 2.00
63 Kevin Garnett 1.25 3.00
64 Ricky Rubio .75 2.00
65 Roy Hibbert .60 1.50
66 DeAndre Jordan .75 2.00
67 Nicolas Batum .60 1.50
68 Al Horford .60 1.50
69 Al Jefferson .60 1.50
70 Carlos Boozer .60 1.50
71 Serge Ibaka .60 1.50
72 David Lee .50 1.25
73 Samuel Dalembert .50 1.25
74 Tyreke Evans .50 1.25
75 Jason Richardson .75 2.00
76 Goran Dragic .60 1.50
77 Danny Granger .60 1.50
78 Pau Gasol .75 2.00
79 Chris Bosh .75 2.00
80 Tim Duncan 1.25 3.00
81 Grant Hill 1.00 2.50
82 Jason Kidd .75 2.00
83 Danilo Gallinari .50 1.25
84 O.J. Mayo .50 1.25
85 Ryan Anderson .60 1.50
86 Joe Johnson .60 1.50
87 Marc Gasol .75 2.00
88 Darren Collison .60 1.50
89 Omer Asik .60 1.50
90 John Wall 1.00 2.50
91 Luol Deng .60 1.50
92 Monta Ellis .60 1.50
93 Ben Gordon .60 1.50
94 Thaddeus Young .50 1.25
95 DeShawn Stevenson .50 1.25
96 Ray Allen .75 2.00
97 Andrea Bargnani .60 1.50
98 Tayshaun Prince .60 1.50
99 Rajon Rondo .75 2.00
100 Amare Stoudemire .60 1.50
101 Kareem Abdul-Jabbar 2.00 5.00
102 Larry Bird 3.00 8.00
103 Rick Barry 1.00 2.50
104 David Robinson 2.00 5.00
105 Bob Cousy 2.00 5.00
106 Elgin Baylor 1.25 3.00
107 Scottie Pippen 2.50 6.00
108 Wes Unseld 1.25 3.00
109 Nate Thurmond 1.00 2.50
110 Dominique Wilkins 1.50 4.00
111 George Gervin 1.25 3.00
112 Bill Russell 2.00 5.00
113 James Worthy 1.50 4.00
114 Steve Kerr 1.25 3.00
115 Clyde Drexler 1.50 4.00
116 Sean Elliott 1.25 3.00
118 Kenny Smith 1.00 2.50
119 Shaquille O'Neal 2.50 6.00
120 Allan Houston 1.00 2.50
121 Dave Cowens .75 2.00
122 Karl Malone 1.50 4.00
123 Connie Hawkins 1.25 3.00
125 Yao Ming 1.50 4.00
126 Robert Horry 1.00 2.50
127 Jerry West 1.50 4.00
128 Muggsy Bogues 1.00 2.50
129 Darryl Dawkins .75 2.00
130 Kevin McHale 1.25 3.00
131 Chuck Person 1.00 2.50
132 Patrick Ewing 1.50 4.00
133 Dennis Rodman 2.50 6.00
134 Christian Laettner 1.00 2.50
135 Hakeem Olajuwon 1.50 4.00
136 George Mikan 2.50 6.00
137 John Starks 1.00 2.50
138 Nate Archibald 1.00 2.50
140 Bill Walton 1.25 3.00
141 Earl Monroe 1.25 3.00
142 Alonzo Mourning 1.50 4.00
143 Wilt Chamberlain 2.50 6.00
144 Gary Payton 1.25 3.00
145 Walt Frazier 1.25 3.00
146 Willis Reed 1.25 3.00
147 John Stockton 2.00 5.00
148 Julius Erving 2.00 5.00
149 Oscar Robertson 1.50 4.00
150 Moses Malone 1.25 3.00
151 Kyrie Irving AU/199 RC 50.00 120.00
152 Derrick Williams AU/199 RC 3.00 8.00
153 Quincy Acy AU/399 RC 3.00 8.00
154 Lavoy Allen AU/399 RC 3.00 8.00
155 Harrison Barnes AU/199 RC 15.00 40.00
156 Will Barton AU/399 RC 4.00 10.00
157 Bradley Beal AU/199 RC 20.00 50.00
158 J.Valanciunas AU/199 RC 5.00 12.00
159 B.Biyombo AU/249 RC 3.00 8.00
160 MarShon Brooks AU/299 RC 4.00 10.00
161 Alec Burks AU/249 RC 5.00 12.00
162 Jimmy Butler AU/299 RC 20.00 50.00
163 Norris Cole AU/249 RC 3.00 8.00
164 Jae Crowder AU/399 RC 4.00 10.00
165 Anthony Davis AU/199 RC 100.00 250.00
166 J.Cunningham AU/299 RC 3.00 8.00
167 A.Drummond AU/199 RC 8.00 20.00
168 Festus Ezeli AU/299 RC 4.00 10.00
169 Kim English AU/399 RC 3.00 8.00
170 Kenneth Faried AU/299 RC 5.00 12.00
171 A.Goudelock AU/399 RC EXCH 3.00 8.00
172 D.Green AU/399 RC 15.00 40.00
173 Evan Fournier AU/249 RC 5.00 12.00
174 Jordan Hamilton AU/399 RC 3.00 8.00
175 Jimmer Fredette AU/199 RC 3.00 8.00
176 Tobias Harris AU/249 RC 5.00 12.00
177 J.Harrellson AU/299 RC 3.00 8.00
178 John Henson AU/199 RC 5.00 12.00
179 Tyler Honeycutt AU/399 RC 3.00 8.00
180 Robert Sacre AU/399 RC 3.00 8.00
181 Justin Harper AU/399 RC 3.00 8.00
182 Johnson-Odom AU/399 RC 3.00 8.00
183 Reggie Jackson AU/399 RC 5.00 12.00
184 Bernard James AU/349 RC 3.00 8.00
185 Charles Jenkins AU/399 RC 3.00 8.00
186 John Jenkins AU/299 RC EXCH 3.00 8.00
187 JaJuan Johnson AU/299 RC 3.00 8.00
188 Ivan Johnson AU/399 RC 3.00 8.00
189 O.Johnson AU/399 RC 3.00 8.00
190 Terrence Jones AU/249 RC 4.00 10.00
191 Perry Jones AU/399 RC 3.00 8.00
192 Cory Joseph AU/349 RC 3.00 8.00
193 Kris Joseph AU/399 RC 3.00 8.00
194 Enes Kanter AU/249 RC 4.00 10.00
195 Kidd-Gilchrist AU/199 RC 5.00 12.00
196 Brandon Knight AU/199 RC 5.00 12.00
197 Jeremy Lamb AU/199 RC 5.00 12.00
198 Doron Lamb AU/399 RC 3.00 8.00
199 Malcolm Lee AU/399 RC 3.00 8.00
200 Kawhi Leonard AU/399 RC 60.00 150.00
201 Meyers Leonard AU/199 RC 4.00 10.00
202 Travis Leslie AU/399 RC 3.00 8.00
203 Jon Leuer AU/299 RC 4.00 10.00
204 DeAndre Liggins AU/399 RC 4.00 10.00
205 Shelvin Mack AU/299 RC 4.00 10.00
206 C.Fortson AU/399 RC 3.00 8.00
207 Kendall Marshall AU/249 RC 3.00 8.00
208 Fab Melo AU/249 RC 3.00 8.00
209 Khris Middleton AU/349 RC 5.00 12.00
210 Quincy Miller AU/399 RC 3.00 8.00
211 D.Miller AU/399 RC 3.00 8.00
212 E'Twaun Moore AU/299 RC 3.00 8.00
213 Mark.Morris AU/249 RC EXCH 5.00 12.00
214 Marc.Morris AU/249 RC EXCH 4.00 10.00
215 Darius Morris AU/399 RC 3.00 8.00
216 Arnett Moultrie AU/299 RC 3.00 8.00
217 Kevin Murphy AU/399 RC 3.00 8.00
218 A.Nicholson AU/249 RC 3.00 8.00
219 Kyle O'Quinn AU/399 RC 3.00 8.00
220 C.Parsons AU/249 RC 5.00 12.00
221 Miles Plumlee AU/349 RC 3.00 8.00
222 Austin Rivers AU/199 RC 5.00 12.00
223 T.Robinson AU/199 RC 4.00 10.00
224 Terrence Ross AU/199 RC 5.00 12.00
225 Jeremy Pargo AU/399 RC 3.00 8.00
226 Mike Scott AU/399 RC 3.00 8.00
227 Josh Selby AU/299 RC 3.00 8.00
228 T.Shengelia AU/299 RC 3.00 8.00
229 Iman Shumpert AU/299 RC 5.00 12.00
230 Chris Singleton AU/299 RC 3.00 8.00
231 Nolan Smith AU/249 RC 3.00 8.00
232 Greg Stiemsma AU/299 RC 3.00 8.00
233 Jared Sullinger AU/199 RC 4.00 10.00
234 Jeff Taylor AU/299 RC 3.00 8.00
235 Tyshawn Taylor AU/299 RC 3.00 8.00
236 Marquis Teague AU/299 RC 3.00 8.00
237 Isaiah Thomas AU/399 RC 20.00 50.00
238 Lance Thomas AU/299 RC 3.00 8.00
239 Trey Thompkins AU/249 RC 3.00 8.00
240 T.Thompson AU/199 RC EXCH 5.00 12.00
241 Klay Thompson AU/199 RC 40.00 100.00
242 Jeremy Tyler AU/349 RC 3.00 8.00
243 Jan Vesely AU/249 RC 3.00 8.00
244 Nikola Vucevic AU/299 RC 5.00 12.00
245 D.Waiters AU/199 RC 5.00 12.00
246 Kemba Walker AU/199 RC 10.00 25.00
247 Royce White AU/349 RC 3.00 8.00
248 Gustavo Ayon AU/299 RC 3.00 8.00
249 Tony Wroten AU/249 RC 4.00 10.00
250 Tyler Zeller AU/249 RC 4.00 10.00

2012-13 Absolute Spectrum Gold

*STARS: 2.5X TO 6X BASE HI
*RETIRED: 1.5X TO 4X BASE HI
STATED PRINT RUN 25 SER.#'d SETS
39 Steve Nash 6.00 15.00
81 Grant Hill 8.00 20.00
132 Patrick Ewing 10.00 25.00

2012-13 Absolute Frequent Flyer Autographs

STATED PRINT RUN 25 TO 149 SER.#'d SETS
1 Kobe Bryant/99 100.00 175.00
2 Blake Griffin/25
3 Kevin Durant/25 100.00 200.00
4 Vince Carter/25 15.00 40.00
5 Andre Iguodala/99 8.00 20.00
6 Josh Smith/99 6.00 15.00
7 Roy Hibbert/99 4.00 10.00
8 Russell Westbrook/49 50.00 120.00
9 LaMarcus Aldridge/99 8.00 20.00
10 Brandon Bass/149 4.00 10.00
11 Marcin Gortat/149 6.00 15.00
12 Chase Budinger/149 4.00 10.00
13 DeAndre Jordan/149 4.00 10.00
14 Brook Lopez/149 4.00 10.00
15 Hakim Warrick/149 4.00 10.00
16 Paul George/149 20.00 50.00
17 Carlos Boozer/99 6.00 15.00
18 Stephen Curry/99 125.00 250.00
19 Al Horford/99 4.00 10.00
20 Stephen Jackson/99 EXCH 4.00 10.00
21 Tyson Chandler/49 8.00 20.00
22 Andrew Bynum/49 8.00 20.00
23 Kendrick Perkins/149 EXCH 5.00 12.00
24 DeJuan Blair/149 EXCH 4.00 10.00
25 Anderson Varejao/142 4.00 10.00

2012-13 Absolute Frequent Flyer Materials

STATED PRINT RUN 10 TO 99 SER.#'d SETS
*PRIME: 1.25X TO 3X BASE HI
PRIME PRINT RUN ONE TO 25 SETS
1 Al Jefferson/74 2.00 5.00
2 Marc Gasol/74 2.50 6.00
3 John Wall/74 3.00 8.00
4 Derrick Rose/74 3.00 8.00
5 Rudy Gay/99 2.50 6.00
6 Tim Duncan/99 4.00 10.00
7 Wesley Johnson/99 2.00 5.00
8 Joel Anthony/99 2.00 5.00
9 Stephen Curry/99 6.00 15.00
10 Josh Smith/99 2.00 5.00
11 LeBron James/74 10.00 25.00
12 James Harden/74 4.00 10.00
13 Raymond Felton/74 2.00 5.00
14 Blake Griffin/74 2.50 6.00
15 Wesley Matthews/99 1.50 4.00
16 Nick Collison/99 2.00 5.00
17 Tyreke Evans/74 1.50 4.00
18 DeMar DeRozan/99 2.50 6.00
19 Kevin Martin/99 2.00 5.00
20 Danny Granger/99 2.00 5.00
21 Yao Ming/74 3.00 8.00
23 Anthony Mason/74 2.00 5.00
24 Shawn Kemp/49 15.00 40.00
25 Larry Johnson/49 6.00 15.00

2012-13 Absolute Frequent Flyer Materials Autographs

STATED PRINT RUN 49 TO 149 SER.#'d SETS
1 Al Jefferson/49 EXCH 8.00 20.00
2 Udonis Haslem/149 5.00 12.00
3 Tayshaun Prince/49 6.00 15.00
4 Kevin Love/49 12.00 30.00
5 Richard Hamilton/49 5.00 12.00
6 Channing Frye/99 5.00 12.00
7 LaMarcus Aldridge/74 6.00 15.00
8 Chris Bosh/49 10.00 25.00
9 Stephen Curry/74 125.00 250.00
10 Josh Smith/49 8.00 20.00
11 Brook Lopez/49 5.00 12.00
12 James Harden/49 EXCH 15.00 40.00
13 Chase Budinger/149 5.00 12.00
14 Blake Griffin/49 30.00 80.00
15 Wesley Matthews/74 5.00 12.00
16 DeJuan Blair/149 EXCH 6.00 15.00
17 Tyreke Evans/49 10.00 25.00
18 Zach Randolph/49 10.00 25.00
19 Kevin Martin/99 5.00 12.00
20 Danny Granger/49
21 Yao Ming/25 20.00 50.00
22 Xavier McDaniel/99 5.00 12.00
23 Jalen Rose/99 5.00 12.00
24 Dominique Wilkins/49 12.00 30.00
25 Larry Johnson/99 10.00 25.00

2012-13 Absolute Frequent Flyer Materials Autographs Prime

STATED PRINT RUN ONE TO 25 SER.#'d SETS
SOME UNPRICED DUE TO SCARCITY
3 Tayshaun Prince/25 12.00 30.00
6 Channing Frye/25 8.00 20.00
16 DeJuan Blair/25 EXCH 15.00 40.00
18 Zach Randolph/25 15.00 40.00
19 Kevin Martin/25 8.00 20.00

2012-13 Absolute Heroes Autographs

STATED PRINT RUN 24 TO 99 SER.#'d SETS
UNPRICED RED INK VERSIONS W/IN PRINT RUN
1 Kobe Bryant/99 100.00 200.00
2 Calvin Murphy/49 10.00 25.00
3 Bill Russell/25 50.00 125.00
4 Rolando Blackman/99 6.00 15.00
5 Steve Nash/25 80.00 160.00
6 Steve Kerr/49 10.00 25.00
7 Michael Finley/49 10.00 25.00
8 Hakeem Olajuwon/25 30.00 80.00
9 Alonzo Mourning/25
10 Kevin Durant/49 75.00 150.00
11 Dave Cowens/49 15.00 40.00
12 Kareem Abdul-Jabbar/25 50.00 125.00
13 Robert Horry/49 6.00 15.00
14 James Worthy/25 30.00 80.00
15 David Robinson/25 75.00 150.00
16 John Stockton/25
17 Sam Jones/49 20.00 50.00
18 Derek Fisher/99 EXCH 10.00 25.00
19 Artis Gilmore/49 6.00 15.00
20 Isiah Thomas/49 12.00 30.00
21 Chris Mullin/99 12.00 30.00
22 Stephen Jackson/99 6.00 15.00
23 Gary Payton/25 30.00 80.00
24 Dominique Wilkins/25 25.00 80.00
25 Tyson Chandler/25 15.00 40.00
26 Nick Van Exel/49 10.00 25.00
27 Avery Johnson/99 8.00 20.00
28 Larry Johnson/99 8.00 20.00
29 Anfernee Hardaway/49 40.00 100.00
30 Tony Parker/25 15.00 40.00
31 Oscar Robertson/25 50.00 100.00
32 Magic Johnson/25 75.00 150.00
33 Larry Bird/25 50.00 125.00
34 Bill Laimbeer/99 6.00 15.00
35 Scottie Pippen/25 150.00 300.00
36 Muggsy Bogues/99 12.00 30.00
37 Willis Reed/49 12.00 30.00
38 Tim Hardaway/99 12.00 30.00
39 Dennis Rodman/25 100.00 200.00
40 John Starks/99 6.00 15.00
41 Vlade Divac/99 EXCH 10.00 25.00
42 Julius Erving/25 60.00 120.00
43 Grant Hill/25 50.00 120.00
44 Dikembe Mutombo/49 12.00 25.00
45 Andre Miller/49 6.00 15.00
46 Sean Elliott/99 15.00 40.00
47 Bruce Bowen/99 12.00 30.00
48 Jalen Rose/99 12.00 30.00
49 Bill Walton/49 6.00 15.00
50 Yao Ming/25 EXCH 20.00 50.00

2012-13 Absolute Hoopla Autographs

STATED PRINT RUN 25 TO 99 SER.#'d SETS
1 Blake Griffin/49 12.00 30.00
2 Aaron Brooks/99 4.00 10.00
3 Brook Lopez/49 6.00 15.00
4 Luol Deng/99 EXCH 4.00 10.00
5 Chase Budinger/99 4.00 10.00
6 Kyle Lowry/99 5.00 12.00
7 Ty Lawson/99 4.00 10.00
8 Greg Monroe/99 6.00 15.00
9 Antawn Jamison/99 4.00 10.00
10 Danny Granger/49 EXCH 4.00 10.00
11 Tyson Chandler/49 8.00 20.00
12 James Harden/99 EXCH 12.00 30.00
13 Rudy Gay/99 EXCH 4.00 10.00
14 Al Horford/49 5.00 12.00
15 Andre Miller/99 4.00 10.00
16 Monta Ellis/49 8.00 20.00
17 Tony Parker/25 12.00 30.00
18 DeMarcus Cousins/49 12.00 30.00
19 Josh Smith/49 6.00 15.00
20 DeAndre Jordan/99 5.00 12.00
21 Pau Gasol/25 20.00 50.00
22 Eric Gordon/49 5.00 12.00
23 Darren Collison/99 EXCH 4.00 10.00
24 Kobe Bryant/49 100.00 200.00
25 Ryan Anderson/99 4.00 10.00
26 Deron Williams/25 12.00 30.00
27 Marcin Gortat/99 6.00 15.00
28 Russell Westbrook/25
29 DeJuan Blair/99 EXCH 4.00 10.00
30 Avery Bradley/99 EXCH 5.00 12.00
31 Al Jefferson/49
32 Chris Paul/25 EXCH 30.00 80.00
33 Roy Hibbert/99 6.00 15.00
34 Joakim Noah/49 10.00 25.00
35 Kevin Love/25 15.00 40.00
36 Serge Ibaka/99 6.00 15.00
37 Derrick Favors/49 4.00 10.00
38 Andrew Bynum/25 6.00 15.00
39 Evan Turner/25 10.00 25.00
40 LaMarcus Aldridge/49 6.00 15.00
41 O.J. Mayo/99 8.00 20.00
42 Jrue Holiday/99 6.00 15.00
43 Steve Nash/25 30.00 60.00
44 Shane Battier/49 12.00 30.00
45 Kevin Martin/99 6.00 15.00
46 Goran Dragic/99 8.00 20.00
47 Chris Kaman/49 4.00 10.00
48 Arron Afflalo/99 4.00 10.00
49 Grant Hill/49 25.00 60.00
50 Ray Allen/25 30.00 80.00

2012-13 Absolute Iconic Autographs

STATED PRINT RUN 25 TO 99 SER.#'d SETS
1 Blake Griffin/25 EXCH
2 Steve Nash/25 15.00 40.00
3 Gerald Wallace/49 4.00 10.00
4 Chase Budinger/99 4.00 10.00
5 James Harden/49 20.00 50.00
6 Kevin Martin/99
7 Aaron Brooks/99 4.00 10.00
8 Luol Deng/99 EXCH 4.00 10.00
9 David Lee/99 4.00 10.00
10 Mario Chalmers/99 4.00 10.00
11 Boris Diaw/99
12 Paul George/99 25.00 50.00
13 Kendrick Perkins/99 4.00 10.00
14 Chris Paul/25 EXCH 30.00 80.00
15 Grant Hill/49 25.00 60.00
16 Ray Allen/25 60.00 120.00
17 Ty Lawson/49 4.00 10.00
18 Landry Fields/99 4.00 10.00
19 Carlos Boozer/99
20 Jason Kidd/25 25.00 60.00
21 DeAndre Jordan/99
22 Rodrigue Beaubois/99 4.00 10.00
23 Arron Afflalo/99 4.00 10.00
24 Kobe Bryant/99 75.00 150.00
25 Roy Hibbert/99
26 Deron Williams/25
27 O.J. Mayo/99 4.00 10.00
28 Jeff Teague/99 4.00 10.00
29 Andrew Bogut/99 4.00 10.00
30 Jose Calderon/99 4.00 10.00
31 Marcin Gortat/99 8.00 20.00
32 Carl Landry/99 4.00 10.00
33 LaMarcus Aldridge/49 10.00 25.00
34 Goran Dragic/99 8.00 20.00
35 Kevin Durant/25 125.00 250.00
36 Kris Humphries/99 4.00 10.00
37 Andrew Bynum/25 4.00 10.00
38 George Hill/99 4.00 10.00
39 Jrue Holiday/99 4.00 10.00
40 Brandon Bass/99 4.00 10.00
41 Hakim Warrick/99 4.00 10.00
42 Vince Carter/25 25.00 60.00
43 Anderson Varejao/99 4.00 10.00
44 Gordon Hayward/99
45 DeMarcus Cousins/48
46 Eric Bledsoe/99
47 Stephen Curry/99 60.00 150.00
48 Chris Bosh/25 12.00 30.00
49 Kevin Love/25 20.00 50.00
50 Andre Iguodala/49 6.00 15.00

2012-13 Absolute Iconic Materials

STATED PRINT RUN 10 TO 49 SER.#'d SETS
*PRIME: .75X TO 2X BASE HI
PRIME PRINT RUN 5 TO 25 SETS
1 Kevin Garnett/25 6.00 15.00
2 Dirk Nowitzki/25 8.00 20.00
3 David Lee/49 2.50 6.00
4 Derrick Rose/25 5.00 12.00
5 Tayshaun Prince/49 3.00 8.00
6 Serge Ibaka/49 3.00 8.00
7 John Wall/25 5.00 12.00
8 Al Horford/25 3.00 8.00
9 Raymond Felton/25 3.00 8.00
11 Russell Westbrook/25 10.00 25.00
12 Tony Parker/25 6.00 15.00
14 Marc Gasol/49 4.00 10.00
15 Kevin Durant/25 10.00 25.00
16 Tim Duncan/25 6.00 15.00
17 Paul Pierce/25 6.00 15.00
18 Dwyane Wade/25 6.00 15.00
19 Carmelo Anthony/25 6.00 15.00
20 LeBron James/25 12.00 30.00
21 David West/25 3.00 8.00
22 Kirk Hinrich/49 3.00 8.00
23 Amare Stoudemire/25 3.00 8.00
24 Al Jefferson/49 3.00 8.00
25 Linas Kleiza/49 2.50 6.00

2012-13 Absolute Iconic Materials Autographs

STATED PRINT RUN 25 TO 74 SER.#'d SETS
1 Raymond Felton/74 5.00 12.00
2 Kevin Durant/25 100.00 200.00
3 Kevin Love/25 10.00 25.00
4 Blake Griffin/25 50.00 125.00
5 Brandon Jennings/49 12.00 30.00
6 Chris Paul/25 EXCH 30.00 80.00
7 Tyson Chandler/49 8.00 20.00
8 LaMarcus Aldridge/49 10.00 25.00
9 Chris Bosh/25 15.00 40.00
10 James Harden/74 EXCH 12.00 30.00
11 Tony Parker/74 12.00 30.00
12 Al Jefferson/49 EXCH 8.00 20.00
13 Al Horford/74 5.00 12.00
14 Brook Lopez/49 6.00 15.00
15 Josh Smith/49 8.00 20.00
16 Deron Williams/25 12.00 30.00
17 Pau Gasol/25 20.00 50.00
18 Ty Lawson/74 5.00 12.00
19 Luol Deng/74 5.00 12.00
20 Carlos Boozer/74 8.00 20.00
21 Zach Randolph/74 6.00 15.00
22 Kyrie Irving/25 60.00 150.00
23 Danny Granger/74 6.00 15.00
24 Tristan Thompson/74 10.00 25.00
25 Tyreke Evans/74 EXCH 6.00 15.00

2012-13 Absolute Iconic Materials Autographs Prime

STATED PRINT RUN 5 TO 25 SER.#'d SETS
SOME UNPRICED DUE TO SCARCITY
8 LaMarcus Aldridge/25 25.00 60.00
15 Josh Smith/25 20.00 50.00
18 Ty Lawson/25 6.00 15.00
19 Luol Deng/25 EXCH 8.00 20.00
20 Carlos Boozer/25 12.00 30.00

2012-13 Absolute Marks of Fame Autographs

STATED PRINT RUN 25 TO 149 SER.#'d SETS
1 Spud Webb/100 6.00 15.00
2 Dan Majerle/100 4.00 10.00
3 Paul Westphal/100 6.00 15.00
4 Glen Rice/100 4.00 10.00
5 World B. Free/100 4.00 10.00
6 Adrian Dantley/100 6.00 15.00
7 Wes Unseld/49 8.00 20.00
8 Mark Price/105 6.00 15.00
9 Larry Bird/49 50.00 120.00
10 Kenny Smith/49 6.00 15.00
11 Magic Johnson/49 30.00 80.00
12 Jeff Hornacek/100 4.00 10.00
13 Dan Issel/106 4.00 10.00
14 Charles Oakley/96 8.00 20.00
15 Michael Cooper/149 4.00 10.00
16 Fat Lever/108 4.00 10.00
17 Michael Finley/49 6.00 15.00
18 Dikembe Mutombo/128 8.00 20.00
19 Vin Baker/100 4.00 10.00
20 A.C. Green/105 8.00 20.00
21 Zydrunas Ilgauskas/100 4.00 10.00
22 Julius Erving/25 30.00 80.00
23 Jamal Mashburn/100 8.00 20.00
24 Hakeem Olajuwon/25 20.00 50.00
25 Darryl Dawkins/96 5.00 12.00
26 Dominique Wilkins/25 12.00 30.00
27 Detlef Schrempf/100 10.00 25.00
28 Gary Payton/99 8.00 20.00
29 Allan Houston/149 6.00 15.00
30 Mark Aguirre/100 4.00 10.00
31 Mark Jackson/99 4.00 10.00
32 Joe Dumars/100 6.00 15.00
33 Vernon Maxwell/149 4.00 10.00
34 Christian Laettner/25 10.00 25.00
35 Otis Birdsong/96 4.00 10.00
36 Sidney Moncrief/100 4.00 10.00
37 Kurt Rambis/100 5.00 12.00
38 Terry Porter/100 5.00 12.00
39 Lenny Wilkens/100 4.00 10.00
40 Bill Walton/100 8.00 20.00
41 John Paxson/100 4.00 10.00
42 Isiah Thomas/49 10.00 25.00
43 Kiki Vandeweghe/100 4.00 10.00
44 Vinny Del Negro/149 EXCH 5.00 12.00
45 Connie Hawkins/99 8.00 20.00
46 Rex Chapman/149 4.00 10.00
47 Kelly Tripucka/100 4.00 10.00
48 Shawn Bradley/149 EXCH 4.00 10.00
49 Bill Cartwright/100 4.00 10.00
50 Brent Barry/149 4.00 10.00

2012-13 Absolute Panini All-Stars

COMPLETE SET (18) 15.00 40.00
RANDOM INSERTS IN RETAIL PACKS
1 Carmelo Anthony 1.25 3.00
2 LeBron James 4.00 10.00
3 Blake Griffin 1.00 2.50
4 Dwyane Wade 1.50 4.00
5 Dwight Howard .75 2.00
6 Dirk Nowitzki 1.25 3.00
7 Kevin Durant 2.50 6.00
8 Kobe Bryant 4.00 10.00
9 Kevin Love 1.00 2.50
10 Karl Malone 1.25 3.00
11 Larry Bird 2.50 6.00
12 Magic Johnson 2.50 6.00
13 Julius Erving 1.50 4.00
14 Shaquille O'Neal 2.00 5.00
15 Yao Ming 1.25 3.00
16 John Stockton 1.50 4.00
17 Scottie Pippen 2.00 5.00
18 David Robinson 1.50 4.00

2012-13 Absolute Patches

STATED PRINT RUN 4 TO 25 SER.#'d SETS
SOME UNPRICED DUE TO SCARCITY
1 Tony Parker/25 15.00 40.00
3 Amare Stoudemire/25 10.00 25.00
6 Tyrus Thomas/25 12.00 30.00
8 Brook Lopez/25 15.00 40.00
9 Derrick Rose/25 200.00 400.00
12 Manu Ginobili/25 20.00 50.00
13 LaMarcus Aldridge/25 20.00 50.00
16 Metta World Peace/25 40.00 80.00
17 Ty Lawson/25 12.00 30.00
19 Carlos Boozer/25
20 George Hill/25 25.00 60.00
21 John Wall/25 25.00 60.00
22 David Lee/25 25.00 60.00
23 Kemba Walker/25 30.00 80.00
24 Tim Duncan/25 40.00 80.00
27 Zach Randolph/25
29 Deron Williams/25 25.00 60.00
30 Tristan Thompson/25 15.00 40.00
31 Raymond Felton/25 30.00 80.00
32 Danny Granger/25 15.00 40.00

2012-13 Absolute Private Signings

RANDOM INSERTS IN PACKS
PSAM Alonzo Mourning 15.00 40.00
PSBC Billy Cunningham 12.00 30.00
PSBG Blake Griffin 40.00 100.00
PSBL Bob Lanier 10.00 25.00
PSDD Daryl Dawkins 8.00 20.00
PSGP Gary Payton 30.00 80.00
PSKJ Kevin Johnson 25.00 60.00
PSMP Mark Price 40.00 80.00
PSPG Pau Gasol 40.00 100.00
PSRR Rajon Rondo 40.00 100.00

2012-13 Absolute Star Gazing Jersey Number Materials

STATED PRINT RUN 10 TO 99 SER.#'d SETS
*PRIME: .75X TO 2X BASE HI
PRIME PRINT RUN ONE TO 25 SETS
1 Tim Duncan/99 10.00 25.00
2 Vince Carter/74 8.00 20.00
3 Dwyane Wade/99 8.00 20.00
4 Amare Stoudemire/74 5.00 12.00
5 Dirk Nowitzki/74 10.00 25.00
6 Paul Pierce/49 10.00 25.00
7 Derrick Rose/49 8.00 20.00
8 Kevin Garnett/74 10.00 25.00
9 Chris Paul/49 8.00 20.00
10 Kevin Durant/25 15.00 40.00
11 John Wall/99 8.00 20.00
12 Pau Gasol/49 6.00 15.00
14 Ricky Rubio/25 20.00 50.00
15 Marc Gasol/74 6.00 15.00
16 Carmelo Anthony/49 8.00 20.00
17 Joakim Noah/49 5.00 12.00
18 Al Jefferson/49 5.00 12.00
19 David West/49 5.00 12.00
20 Kevin Martin/74 5.00 12.00
21 Linas Kleiza/49 4.00 10.00
22 Manu Ginobili/25 12.00 30.00
23 Raymond Felton/49 5.00 12.00
24 Zach Randolph/49 5.00 12.00
25 LeBron James/49 12.00 30.00

2012-13 Absolute Team Tandem Materials

STATED PRINT RUN 25 TO 49 SER.#'d SETS
1 T.Duncan/T.Parker/49 8.00 20.00
2 D.Wade/L.James/25 20.00 50.00
3 Durant/Westbrook/25 12.00 30.00
4 D.Rose/L.Deng/25 15.00 40.00
5 J.Smith/A.Horford/49 4.00 10.00
6 T.Evans/J.Fredette/25 4.00 10.00
7 B.Griffin/C.Paul/25 12.00 30.00
8 P.Pierce/R.Rondo/25 15.00 40.00
9 Anthony/Stoudemire/25 6.00 15.00
10 D.Williams/B.Lopez/25 4.00 10.00
11 D.Granger/G.Hill/49 4.00 10.00
12 K.Thompson/D.Lee/49 5.00 12.00
13 Z.Randolph/M.Gasol/49 4.00 10.00
14 S.Hawes/J.Holiday/25 4.00 10.00
15 K.Bryant/M.Peace/49 10.00 25.00
16 Cartwright/E.Monroe/25 6.00 15.00
17 A.English/D.Issel/25 4.00 10.00
18 J.Stockton/K.Malone/25 12.00 30.00
19 T.Thompson/K.Irving/25 30.00 80.00
20 D.West/Hansbrough/25 8.00 20.00
21 E.Turner/T.Young/49 4.00 10.00
22 C.Boozer/D.Rose/25 15.00 40.00
23 Mourning/L.Johnson/25 15.00 40.00
24 A.Jefferson/Favors/25 4.00 10.00
25 T.Prince/B.Knight/49 4.00 10.00

2012-13 Absolute Team Tandem Materials Prime

*PRIME: 1X TO 2.5X BASE HI
STATED PRINT RUN 5 TO 25 SER.#'d SETS
SOME UNPRICED DUE TO SCARCITY
12 K.Thompson/D.Lee/25 15.00 40.00

2012-13 Absolute Team Trios Materials

STATED PRINT RUN 5 TO 25 SER.#'d SETS
SOME UNPRICED DUE TO SCARCITY
UNPRICED PRIME PRINT RUN ONE TO 5 SETS
7 Hywrd/Al/Favors/25
8 Manu/Dncn/Prkr/25 10.00 25.00
10 Morris/Frye/Dudley/25
12 Davis/DeMar/Klza/25 8.00 20.00
15 Tyler/Grngr/Hill/25 5.00 12.00
23 Harris/Jennings/Udrih/25 5.00 12.00
24 Miller/Ty/Faried/25 10.00 25.00
25 Nelson/Hedo/Davis/25 5.00 12.00

2009-10 Absolute Memorabilia

101-141 PRINT RUN 499 SER.#'d SETS
JSY AU RC PRINT RUNS LISTED IN CHECKLIST
1 Kobe Bryant 5.00 12.00
2 Dwight Howard 1.00 2.50
3 Rajon Rondo 1.25 3.00
4 Samuel Dalembert .75 2.00
5 LeBron James 5.00 12.00
6 Chris Andersen 1.00 2.50
7 Dwyane Wade 2.00 5.00
8 Chris Bosh 1.25 3.00
9 Steve Nash 1.25 3.00
10 LaMarcus Aldridge 1.25 3.00
11 Danilo Gallinari 1.00 2.50
12 Joakim Noah 1.00 2.50
13 Brook Lopez 1.00 2.50
14 Tony Parker 1.25 3.00
15 Deron Williams 1.00 2.50
16 Marc Gasol 1.25 3.00
17 Joe Johnson 1.00 2.50
18 Dirk Nowitzki 1.50 4.00
19 Chris Paul 1.50 4.00
20 Chris Kaman 1.00 2.50
21 Kevin Love 1.25 3.00
22 Danny Granger 1.00 2.50
23 Antawn Jamison 1.00 2.50
24 Trevor Ariza .75 2.00
25 Carmelo Anthony 1.50 4.00
26 Monta Ellis 1.00 2.50
27 Al Horford 1.25 3.00
28 Kevin Durant 3.00 8.00
29 Brandon Roy 1.25 3.00
30 Corey Maggette 1.00 2.50
31 Andre Iguodala 1.00 2.50
32 Ray Allen 1.25 3.00
33 Shaquille O'Neal 2.50 6.00
34 Jamal Crawford 1.25 3.00
35 Gerald Wallace 1.00 2.50
36 David West 1.00 2.50
37 Zach Randolph 1.00 2.50
38 Rodney Stuckey .75 2.00
39 Derrick Rose 2.00 5.00
40 Tim Duncan 2.00 5.00
41 David Lee .75 2.00
42 Amare Stoudemire 1.00 2.50

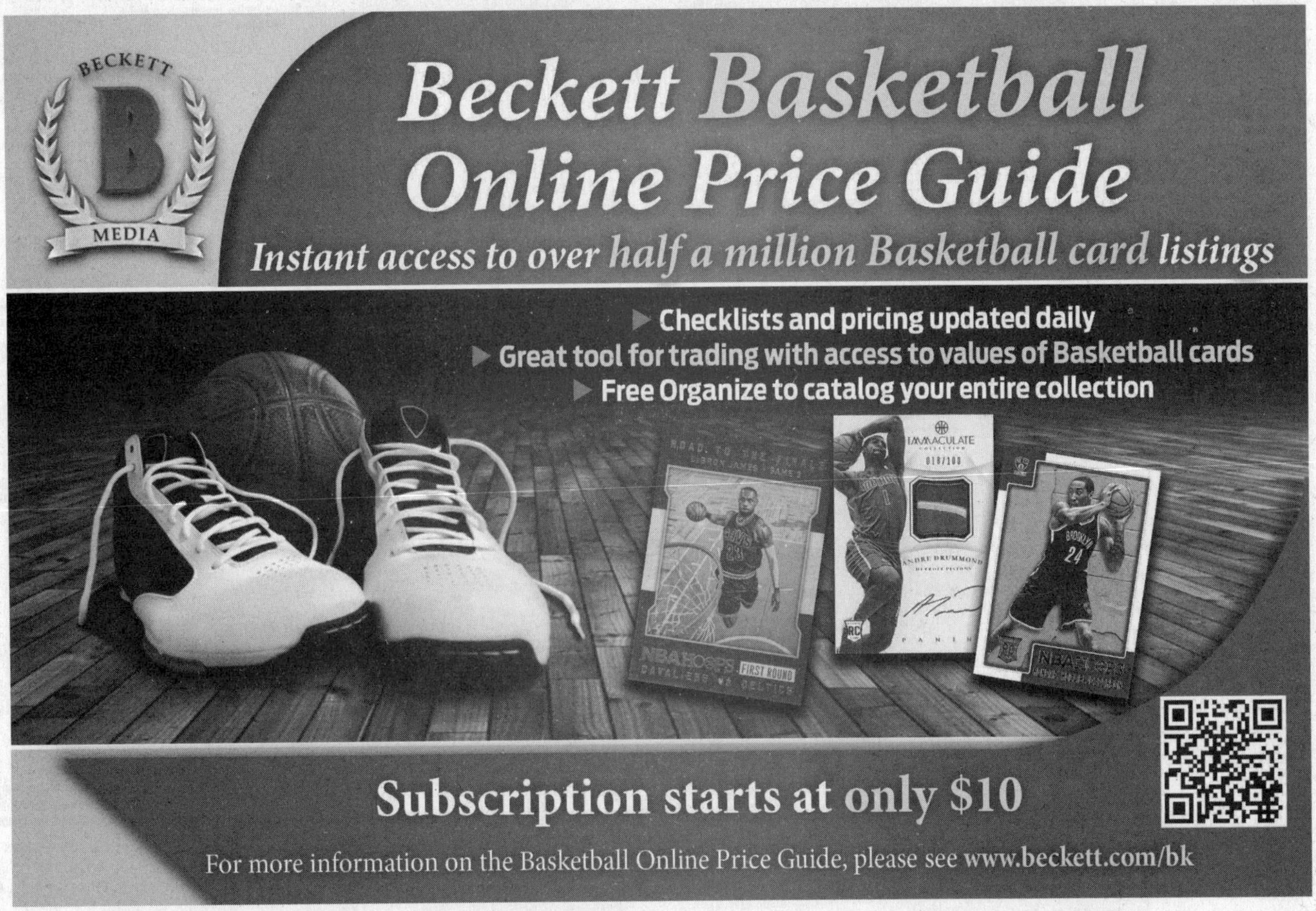
BECKETT
MEDIA
Beckett Basketball
Online Price Guide
Instant access to over half a million Basketball card listings
Checklists and pricing updated daily
Great tool for trading with access to values of Basketball cards
Free Organize to catalog your entire collection
Subscription starts at only $10
For more information on the Basketball Online Price Guide, please see www.beckett.com/bk

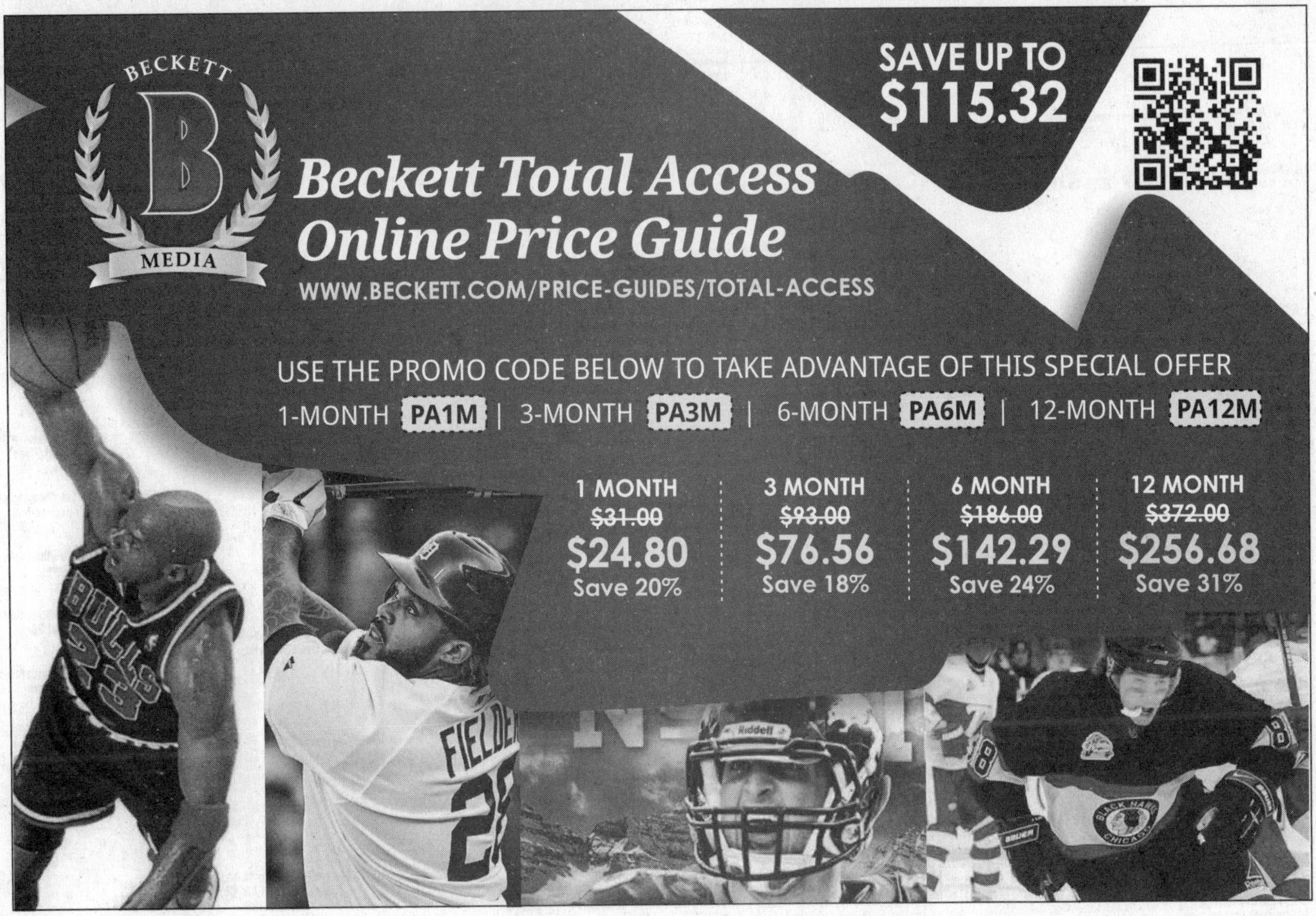
BECKETT
MEDIA
SAVE UP TO
$115.32
Beckett Total Access
Online Price Guide
WWW.BECKETT.COM/PRICE-GUIDES/TOTAL-ACCESS
USE THE PROMO CODE BELOW TO TAKE ADVANTAGE OF THIS SPECIAL OFFER
1-MONTH PA1M | 3-MONTH PA3M | 6-MONTH PA6M | 12-MONTH PA12M
1 MONTH
$31.00
$24.80
Save 20%
3 MONTH
$93.00
$76.56
Save 18%
6 MONTH
$186.00
$142.29
Save 24%
12 MONTH
$372.00
$256.68
Save 31%

43 Aaron Brooks .75 2.00
44 Lamar Odom 1.00 2.50
45 Ben Wallace 1.00 2.50
46 J.J. Barea 1.50 4.00
47 Emeka Okafor 1.00 2.50
48 Brendan Haywood .75 2.00
49 Michael Beasley .75 2.00
50 Allen Iverson 1.50 4.00
51 Andrea Bargnani 1.00 2.50
52 Nene 1.00 2.50
53 Paul Pierce 1.25 3.00
54 Mo Williams 1.00 2.50
55 Jason Thompson .75 2.00
56 Russell Westbrook 3.00 8.00
57 Andrew Bogut 1.00 2.50
58 Al Jefferson 1.00 2.50
59 Devin Harris .75 2.00
60 Vince Carter 1.50 4.00
61 Jason Kidd 1.25 3.00
62 Kevin Garnett 2.00 5.00
63 Rudy Gay 1.25 3.00
64 Stephen Jackson 1.00 2.50
65 Luol Deng 1.00 2.50
66 Carl Landry .75 2.00
67 Baron Davis 1.00 2.50
68 Ben Gordon 1.00 2.50
69 Al Harrington 1.00 2.50
70 Carlos Boozer 1.00 2.50
71 Pau Gasol 1.25 3.00
72 Luke Ridnour 1.00 2.50
73 Josh Smith 1.00 2.50
74 Raymond Felton 1.00 2.50
75 Kendrick Perkins .75 2.00
76 Dahntay Jones .75 2.00
77 Kevin Martin 1.00 2.50
78 Shawn Marion 1.00 2.50
79 Marcus Camby .75 2.00
80 Jermaine O'Neal 1.00 2.50
81 Manu Ginobili 1.25 3.00
82 Richard Hamilton 1.00 2.50
83 Rashard Lewis 1.00 2.50
84 Jason Richardson 1.25 3.00
85 Jeff Green 1.00 2.50
86 Elton Brand 1.25 3.00
87 Mehmet Okur .75 2.00
88 O.J. Mayo .75 2.00
89 Caron Butler 1.00 2.50
90 Rasheed Wallace 1.25 3.00
91 Jason Terry 1.00 2.50
92 Ron Artest 1.25 3.00
93 Jason Williams 1.00 2.50
94 Hedo Turkoglu 1.00 2.50
95 Yao Ming 1.50 4.00
96 Chauncey Billups 1.25 3.00
97 Nate Robinson .75 2.00
98 Mike Dunleavy .75 2.00
99 Louis Williams 1.00 2.50
100 Juwan Howard 1.00 2.50
101 Jalen Rose 1.25 3.00
102 Chris Webber 1.25 3.00
103 David Robinson 2.00 5.00
104 Chuck Person 1.00 2.50
105 Alvan Adams .75 2.00
106 Larry Bird 3.00 8.00
107 Scottie Pippen 2.50 6.00
108 Connie Hawkins 1.25 3.00
109 Magic Johnson 3.00 8.00
110 Bill Laimbeer 1.00 2.50
111 Shawn Bradley .75 2.00
112 Kelly Tripucka .75 2.00
113 Robert Horry 1.00 2.50
114 Spud Webb 1.00 2.50
115 World B. Free 1.00 2.50
116 Tim Hardaway 1.25 3.00
117 Sean Elliott 1.25 3.00
118 Anfernee Hardaway 3.00 8.00
119 Paul Westphal 1.25 3.00
120 Pete Maravich 2.00 5.00
121 Willis Reed 1.25 3.00
122 Nate Thurmond 1.00 2.50
123 Mychal Thompson 1.25 3.00
124 Kenny Anderson 1.00 2.50
125 Jerry West 1.50 4.00
126 Marcus Thornton RC 1.50 4.00
127 Jonas Jerebko RC 2.00 5.00
128 Wesley Matthews RC 2.00 5.00
129 A.J. Price RC 1.25 3.00
130 David Andersen RC 1.25 3.00
131 Serge Ibaka RC 2.00 5.00
132 Garrett Temple RC 2.00 5.00
133 Derrick Brown RC 1.25 3.00
134 Sundiata Gaines RC 1.25 3.00
135 Chris Hunter RC 1.25 3.00
136 Jon Brockman RC 1.25 3.00
137 Danny Green RC 2.50 6.00
138 Marcus Landry RC 1.25 3.00
139 Lester Hudson RC 1.25 3.00
140 Patrick Mills RC 4.00 10.00
141 Dante Cunningham RC 1.25 3.00
142 B.Jennings JSY AU/499 RC 6.00 15.00
143 Jonny Flynn JSY AU/349 RC 4.00 10.00
144 S.Curry JSY AU/499 RC 400.00 800.00
145 Omri Casspi JSY AU/499 RC 5.00 12.00
146 J.Harden JSY AU/499 RC 60.00 150.00
147 Ty Lawson JSY AU/349 RC 6.00 15.00
148 Taj Gibson JSY AU/499 RC 6.00 15.00
149 T.Hansbrough JSY AU/499 RC 5.00 12.00
150 Chase Budinger JSY AU/499 RC 5.00 12.00
151 Sam Young JSY AU/299 RC 4.00 10.00
152 DeJuan Blair JSY AU/499 RC 5.00 12.00
153 Ter.Williams JSY AU/499 RC 4.00 10.00
154 D.Collison JSY AU/499 RC 6.00 15.00
155 T.Douglas JSY AU/499 RC 4.00 10.00
156 Wayne Ellington JSY AU/499 RC 6.00 15.00
157 Jrue Holiday JSY AU/499 RC 8.00 20.00
158 Eric Maynor JSY AU/499 RC 4.00 10.00
159 R.Beaubois JSY AU/349 RC 4.00 10.00
160 Austin Daye JSY AU/499 RC 4.00 10.00
161 Jodie Meeks JSY AU/499 RC 6.00 15.00
162 Jeff Pendergraph JSY AU/499 RC 4.00 10.00
163 Jordan Hill JSY AU/499 RC 5.00 12.00
164 DeMarre Carroll JSY AU/499 RC 5.00 12.00
165 Jeff Teague JSY AU/499 RC 6.00 15.00
166 T.Evans JSY AU/499 RC 5.00 12.00
167 J.Johnson JSY AU/349 RC 5.00 12.00
168 Earl Clark JSY AU/499 RC 5.00 12.00
169 G.Henderson JSY AU/499 RC 5.00 12.00
170 DaJuan Summers JSY AU/499 RC 4.00 10.00
171 Hasheem Thabeet JSY AU/499 RC 4.00 10.00
172 Blake Griffin JSY AU/499 RC 30.00 80.00
173 B.J. Mullens JSY AU/499 RC 4.00 10.00
174 Taylor Griffin JSY AU/499 RC 4.00 10.00
175 J.Taylor JSY AU/299 RC 4.00 10.00
176 D.DeRozan JSY AU/499 RC 30.00 80.00

2009-10 Absolute Memorabilia Spectrum Gold

*GOLD: .6X TO 1.5X BASE HI
PRINT RUN 100 SER.#'d SETS

2009-10 Absolute Memorabilia Spectrum Platinum

*PLATINUM: 1.25X TO 3X BASE HI
PRINT RUN 25 SER.#'d SETS
118 Anfernee Hardaway 20.00 50.00

2009-10 Absolute Memorabilia Frequent Flyer

COMPLETE SET (19) 20.00 40.00
STATED PRINT RUN 100 SER.#'d SETS
1 Devin Harris .75 2.00
2 Elton Brand 1.25 3.00
3 Eric Gordon 1.00 2.50
5 Kobe Bryant 5.00 12.00
6 LeBron James 5.00 12.00
7 Kevin Martin 1.00 2.50
8 Shawn Marion 1.00 2.50
9 Vince Carter 1.50 4.00
10 DeMar DeRozan 3.00 8.00
11 Dwyane Wade 2.00 5.00
12 Nate Robinson .75 2.00
13 Allen Iverson 1.50 4.00
14 Amare Stoudemire 1.00 2.50
15 Gerald Wallace 1.00 2.50
16 Carmelo Anthony 1.50 4.00
17 Kevin Love 1.25 3.00
18 Ron Artest 1.25 3.00
19 Joe Johnson 1.00 2.50
20 Trevor Ariza .75 2.00

2009-10 Absolute Memorabilia Frequent Flyer Materials

STATED PRINT RUN 10 TO 100 SER.#'d SETS
SOME UNPRICED DUE TO SCARCITY
UNPRICED PRIME PRINT RUN 10 SER.#'d SETS
1 Devin Harris/100 2.00 5.00
2 Elton Brand/100 3.00 8.00
3 Eric Gordon/100 2.50 6.00
5 Kobe Bryant/100 10.00 25.00
6 LeBron James/100 10.00 25.00
7 Kevin Martin/100 2.50 6.00
8 Shawn Marion/100 2.50 6.00
9 Vince Carter/100 4.00 10.00
10 DeMar DeRozan/100 8.00 20.00
11 Dwyane Wade/50 5.00 12.00
12 Nate Robinson/100 2.00 5.00
13 Allen Iverson/25 8.00 20.00
15 Gerald Wallace/100 2.50 6.00
16 Carmelo Anthony/100 4.00 10.00
17 Kevin Love/100 3.00 8.00
19 Joe Johnson/100 2.50 6.00

2009-10 Absolute Memorabilia Frequent Flyer Materials Jersey Number

STATED PRINT RUN 5 TO 25 SER.#'d SETS
SOME UNPRICED DUE TO SCARCITY
UNPRICED PRIME PRINT RUN 5 SER.#'d SETS
1 Devin Harris/25 3.00 8.00
2 Elton Brand/25 5.00 12.00
3 Eric Gordon/25 4.00 10.00
5 Kobe Bryant/25 12.50 30.00
6 LeBron James/25 12.50 30.00
7 Kevin Martin/25 4.00 10.00
8 Shawn Marion/25 4.00 10.00
9 Vince Carter/25 6.00 15.00
10 DeMar DeRozan/25 12.00 30.00
11 Dwyane Wade/25 8.00 20.00
12 Nate Robinson/25 3.00 8.00
15 Gerald Wallace/25 4.00 10.00
16 Carmelo Anthony/25 6.00 15.00
17 Kevin Love/25 5.00 12.00
19 Joe Johnson/25 4.00 10.00

2009-10 Absolute Memorabilia Frequent Flyer Materials Jersey Number Signatures

STATED PRINT RUN 10 TO 25 SER.#'d SETS
UNPRICED PRIME PRINT RUN 5 SER.#'d SETS
1 Devin Harris/25 6.00 15.00
3 Eric Gordon/10 12.50 30.00
5 Kobe Bryant/25 100.00 200.00
17 Kevin Love/25 15.00 40.00

2009-10 Absolute Memorabilia Frequent Flyer Materials Signatures

STATED PRINT RUN 5 TO 25 SER.#'d SETS
UNPRICED PRIME PRINT RUN 5 SER.#'d SETS
1 Devin Harris/25 6.00 15.00
3 Eric Gordon/10 12.50 30.00
5 Kobe Bryant/25 100.00 200.00
10 DeMar DeRozan/25 15.00 40.00
17 Kevin Love/25 20.00 50.00

2009-10 Absolute Memorabilia Heroes

COMPLETE SET (14) 15.00 30.00
STATED PRINT RUN 100 SER.#'d SETS
1 Ray Allen 1.25 3.00
2 Rudy Fernandez .75 2.00
4 T.J. Ford .75 2.00
5 Brandon Jennings 1.25 3.00
6 Lamar Odom 1.00 2.50
7 Eric Gordon 1.00 2.50
8 Devin Harris .75 2.00
9 LeBron James 5.00 12.00
10 Russell Westbrook 3.00 8.00
11 Tyler Hansbrough 1.00 2.50
12 David Lee .75 2.00
13 Jason Kidd 1.25 3.00
14 Richard Hamilton 1.00 2.50
15 Kobe Bryant 5.00 12.00

2009-10 Absolute Memorabilia Heroes Materials

STATED PRINT RUN 50 TO 100 SETS
UNPRICED PRIME PRINT RUN 10 SER.#'d SETS
1 Ray Allen/100 3.00 8.00
2 Rudy Fernandez/100 2.00 5.00
4 T.J. Ford/100 2.00 5.00
5 Brandon Jennings/100 3.00 8.00
7 Eric Gordon/100 2.50 6.00
8 Devin Harris/100 2.00 5.00
9 LeBron James/100 8.00 20.00
10 Russell Westbrook/100 8.00 20.00
11 Tyler Hansbrough/100 2.50 6.00
12 David Lee/50 2.00 5.00
13 Jason Kidd/100 3.00 8.00
15 Kobe Bryant/100 8.00 20.00

2009-10 Absolute Memorabilia Heroes Materials Signatures

STATED PRINT RUN 5 TO 25 SER.#'d SETS
SOME UNPRICED DUE TO SCARCITY
UNPRICED PRIME PRINT RUN ONE TO 5 SETS
1 Ray Allen/25 20.00 50.00
4 T.J. Ford/25 6.00 15.00
5 Brandon Jennings/25 15.00 40.00
8 Devin Harris/25 6.00 15.00
10 Russell Westbrook/25 30.00 80.00
11 Tyler Hansbrough/25 10.00 25.00
13 Jason Kidd/25 12.00 30.00
15 Kobe Bryant/25 100.00 200.00

2009-10 Absolute Memorabilia Hoopla

COMPLETE SET (20) 25.00 50.00
STATED PRINT RUN 100 SER.#'d SETS
1 LeBron James 5.00 12.00
2 Dwyane Wade 2.00 5.00
3 Chris Paul 1.50 4.00
4 Kevin Durant 3.00 8.00
5 Dwight Howard 1.00 2.50
6 Gerald Wallace 1.00 2.50
7 Kobe Bryant 5.00 12.00
8 Steve Nash 1.25 3.00
9 Kevin Garnett 2.00 5.00
10 Dirk Nowitzki 1.50 4.00
11 Josh Smith 1.00 2.50
12 Chris Bosh 1.25 3.00
13 Carmelo Anthony 1.50 4.00
14 Brandon Roy 1.25 3.00
15 Derrick Rose 2.00 5.00
16 Tracy McGrady 1.25 3.00
17 Devin Harris .75 2.00
18 Tony Parker 1.25 3.00
19 Allen Iverson 1.50 4.00
20 Chris Andersen 1.00 2.50

2009-10 Absolute Memorabilia Hoopla Materials

STATED PRINT RUN 25 TO 100 SETS
UNPRICED PRIME PRINT RUN 10 SER.#'d SETS
1 LeBron James/100 10.00 25.00
2 Dwyane Wade/50 5.00 12.00
3 Chris Paul/100 4.00 10.00
4 Kevin Durant/100 8.00 20.00
5 Dwight Howard/100 2.50 6.00
6 Gerald Wallace/100 2.50 6.00
7 Kobe Bryant/100 10.00 25.00
9 Kevin Garnett/100 5.00 12.00
10 Dirk Nowitzki/100 4.00 10.00
11 Josh Smith/100 2.50 6.00
12 Chris Bosh/100 3.00 8.00
13 Carmelo Anthony/100 4.00 10.00
14 Brandon Roy/100 3.00 8.00
16 Tracy McGrady/100 3.00 8.00
17 Devin Harris/100 2.00 5.00
18 Tony Parker/50 3.00 8.00
19 Allen Iverson/25 8.00 20.00
20 Chris Andersen/100 2.50 6.00

2009-10 Absolute Memorabilia Hoopla Materials Jersey Number

STATED PRINT RUN 10 TO 25 SER.#'d SETS
SOME UNPRICED DUE TO SCARCITY
UNPRICED PRIME PRINT RUN 5 SER.#'d SETS
1 LeBron James/25 15.00 30.00
2 Dwyane Wade/25 8.00 20.00
3 Chris Paul/25 6.00 15.00
5 Dwight Howard/25 4.00 10.00
6 Gerald Wallace/25 4.00 10.00
7 Kobe Bryant/25 15.00 30.00
11 Josh Smith/25 4.00 10.00
13 Carmelo Anthony/25 6.00 15.00
16 Tracy McGrady/25 5.00 12.00
17 Devin Harris/25 3.00 8.00
18 Tony Parker/25 5.00 12.00

2009-10 Absolute Memorabilia Hoopla Materials Jersey Number Signatures

STATED PRINT RUN 5 TO 25 SER.#'d SETS
SOME NOT PRICED DUE TO SCARCITY
UNPRICED PRIME PRINT RUN 5 SER.#'d SETS
7 Kobe Bryant/25 100.00 200.00
16 Tracy McGrady/25 20.00 40.00
17 Devin Harris/25 6.00 15.00
18 Tony Parker/25 15.00 30.00

2009-10 Absolute Memorabilia Hoopla Materials Signatures

STATED PRINT RUN 25 SER.#'d SETS
UNPRICED PRIME PRINT RUN 5 SER.#'d SETS
7 Kobe Bryant 100.00 200.00
16 Tracy McGrady 15.00 40.00
17 Devin Harris 6.00 15.00
18 Tony Parker 12.00 30.00

2009-10 Absolute Memorabilia Marks of Fame

COMPLETE SET (10) 15.00 30.00
STATED PRINT RUN 100 SER.#'d SETS
1 LeBron James 5.00 12.00
2 Kareem Abdul-Jabbar 2.00 5.00
3 Allen Iverson 1.50 4.00
4 Magic Johnson 3.00 8.00
5 Ray Allen 1.25 3.00
6 Dikembe Mutombo 1.25 3.00
7 Dirk Nowitzki 1.50 4.00
8 Bill Russell 2.00 5.00
9 Kobe Bryant 5.00 12.00
10 Mark Price 1.25 3.00

2009-10 Absolute Memorabilia Marks of Fame Materials

STATED PRINT RUN 25 TO 100 SETS
UNPRICED PRIME PRINT RUN 10 SER.#'d SETS
1 LeBron James/100 8.00 20.00
2 Kareem Abdul-Jabbar/100 6.00 15.00
3 Allen Iverson/25 8.00 20.00
4 Magic Johnson/100 8.00 20.00
5 Ray Allen/100 3.00 8.00
6 Dikembe Mutombo/100 4.00 10.00
7 Dirk Nowitzki/100 4.00 10.00
9 Kobe Bryant/100 8.00 20.00
10 Mark Price/100 4.00 10.00

2009-10 Absolute Memorabilia Marks of Fame Materials Signatures

STATED PRINT RUN 8 TO 25 SER.#'d SETS
SOME NOT PRICED DUE TO SCARCITY
UNPRICED PRIME PRINT RUN 5 SER.#'d SETS
4 Magic Johnson/25 40.00 100.00
5 Ray Allen/25 25.00 50.00
9 Kobe Bryant/25 100.00 200.00

2009-10 Absolute Memorabilia Materials Prime Spectrum

STATED PRINT RUN ONE TO 25 SER.#'d SETS
SOME NOT PRICED DUE TO SCARCITY
1 Kobe Bryant/25 25.00 60.00
2 Dwight Howard/25 5.00 12.00
3 Rajon Rondo/25 10.00 25.00
4 Samuel Dalembert/25 4.00 10.00
5 LeBron James/25 25.00 60.00
6 Chris Andersen/25 6.00 15.00
7 Dwyane Wade/25 10.00 25.00
8 Chris Bosh/25 6.00 15.00
10 LaMarcus Aldridge/25 6.00 15.00
11 Danilo Gallinari/25 5.00 12.00
12 Joakim Noah/25 5.00 12.00
13 Brook Lopez/25 5.00 12.00
15 Deron Williams/25 5.00 12.00
16 Marc Gasol/25 6.00 15.00
17 Joe Johnson/25 5.00 12.00
18 Dirk Nowitzki/25 10.00 25.00
19 Chris Paul/25 8.00 20.00
21 Kevin Love/25 6.00 15.00
22 Danny Granger/25 5.00 12.00
25 Carmelo Anthony/25 8.00 20.00
27 Al Horford/25 6.00 15.00
28 Kevin Durant/25 15.00 40.00
29 Brandon Roy/25 6.00 15.00
30 Corey Maggette/25 5.00 12.00
31 Andre Iguodala/25 5.00 12.00
32 Ray Allen/25 6.00 15.00
33 Shaquille O'Neal/25 20.00 50.00
35 Gerald Wallace/25 5.00 12.00
36 David West/25 5.00 12.00
38 Rodney Stuckey/25 4.00 10.00
40 Tim Duncan/25 10.00 25.00
41 David Lee/25 4.00 10.00
46 J.J. Barea/25 12.50 30.00
47 Emeka Okafor/25 5.00 12.00
51 Andrea Bargnani/25 5.00 12.00
53 Paul Pierce/25 6.00 15.00
56 Russell Westbrook/25 15.00 40.00
57 Andrew Bogut/25 5.00 12.00
58 Al Jefferson/25 5.00 12.00
59 Devin Harris/25 4.00 10.00
60 Vince Carter/25 8.00 20.00
61 Jason Kidd/15 6.00 15.00
62 Kevin Garnett/25 10.00 25.00
63 Rudy Gay/25 6.00 15.00
65 Luol Deng/25 5.00 12.00
67 Baron Davis/25 5.00 12.00
70 Carlos Boozer/25 5.00 12.00
73 Josh Smith/25 5.00 12.00
74 Raymond Felton/25 5.00 12.00
77 Kevin Martin/25 5.00 12.00
79 Marcus Camby/25 4.00 10.00
81 Manu Ginobili/25 8.00 20.00
83 Rashard Lewis/25 5.00 12.00
85 Jeff Green/25 5.00 12.00
86 Elton Brand/25 6.00 15.00
87 Mehmet Okur/25 4.00 10.00
88 O.J. Mayo/25 4.00 10.00
90 Rasheed Wallace/25 6.00 15.00
91 Jason Terry/25 5.00 12.00
94 Hedo Turkoglu/25 5.00 12.00
96 Chauncey Billups/25 6.00 15.00
98 Mike Dunleavy/25 4.00 10.00
102 Chris Webber/25 15.00 40.00
104 Chuck Person/25 5.00 12.00
105 Alvan Adams/25 4.00 10.00
106 Larry Bird/25 15.00 30.00
109 Magic Johnson/25 15.00 30.00
113 Robert Horry/25 10.00 25.00
124 Kenny Anderson/25 5.00 12.00
125 Jerry West/15 15.00 40.00

2009-10 Absolute Memorabilia NBA Icons

COMPLETE SET (15) 40.00 70.00
STATED PRINT RUN 100 SER.#'d SETS
1 Jerry West 4.00 10.00
2 Patrick Ewing 4.00 10.00
3 Scottie Pippen 6.00 15.00
4 Reggie Lewis 3.00 8.00
5 Alonzo Mourning 4.00 10.00
6 Karl Malone 4.00 10.00
7 Dominique Wilkins 4.00 10.00
8 Willis Reed 3.00 8.00
9 Tim Hardaway 3.00 8.00
10 George Mikan 6.00 15.00
11 George Gervin 3.00 8.00
12 John Stockton 5.00 12.00
13 Bob Lanier 2.50 6.00
14 Mark Aguirre 2.50 6.00
15 Mark Eaton 2.00 5.00

2009-10 Absolute Memorabilia NBA Icons Materials

STATED PRINT RUN 5 TO 100 SETS
SOME NOT PRICED DUE TO SCARCITY
UNPRICED PRIME PRINT RUN 5 TO 10 SETS
UNPRICED SIG.MAT PRINT RUN 5 SETS
UNPRICED SIG.MAT PRIME PRINT RUN 5 SETS
2 Patrick Ewing/100 6.00 15.00
4 Reggie Lewis/100 10.00 25.00
6 Karl Malone/100 6.00 15.00
7 Dominique Wilkins/49 6.00 15.00
10 George Mikan/50 20.00 40.00
12 John Stockton/100 8.00 20.00
13 Bob Lanier/100 4.00 10.00
15 Mark Eaton/100 3.00 8.00

2009-10 Absolute Memorabilia Patches Jumbo Prime Spectrum

STATED PRINT RUN 25 SER.#'d SETS
1 Chris Paul 15.00 40.00
2 Danny Granger 10.00 25.00
3 Josh Smith 10.00 25.00
4 Marc Gasol 12.00 30.00
5 Kobe Bryant 50.00 125.00
6 Andre Iguodala 10.00 25.00
7 Kevin Garnett 30.00 80.00
8 Antawn Jamison 10.00 25.00
9 Raymond Felton 10.00 25.00
10 Marcus Camby 8.00 20.00

2009-10 Absolute Memorabilia Redemptions

EXCHANGES FOR FULL SIZE ITEMS
NNO Kobe Bryant Jersey/24 600.00 900.00
NNO Kobe Bryant Bsktbll/24 400.00 800.00

2009-10 Absolute Memorabilia Rookie Materials Jumbo Jersey Numbers Basketball

STATED PRINT RUN 25 SER.#'d SETS
UNPRICED PRIME PRINT RUN 10 SER.#'d SETS
UNPRICED PRIME SPECT.PRINT RUN 5 SETS
142 Brandon Jennings 5.00 12.00
143 Jonny Flynn 3.00 8.00
144 Stephen Curry 200.00 400.00
145 Omri Casspi 4.00 10.00
146 James Harden 25.00 60.00
147 Ty Lawson 5.00 12.00
148 Taj Gibson 5.00 12.00
149 Tyler Hansbrough 4.00 10.00
150 Chase Budinger 4.00 10.00
151 Sam Young 3.00 8.00
152 DeJuan Blair 4.00 10.00
153 Terrence Williams 3.00 8.00
154 Darren Collison 5.00 12.00
155 Toney Douglas 3.00 8.00
156 Wayne Ellington 5.00 12.00
157 Jrue Holiday 6.00 15.00
158 Eric Maynor 3.00 8.00
159 Rodrigue Beaubois 3.00 8.00
160 Austin Daye 3.00 8.00
161 Jodie Meeks 5.00 12.00
162 Jeff Pendergraph 3.00 8.00
163 Jordan Hill 4.00 10.00
164 DeMarre Carroll 4.00 10.00
165 Jeff Teague 5.00 12.00
166 Tyreke Evans 4.00 10.00
167 James Johnson 4.00 10.00
168 Earl Clark 4.00 10.00
169 Gerald Henderson 4.00 10.00
170 DaJuan Summers 3.00 8.00
171 Hasheem Thabeet 3.00 8.00
172 Blake Griffin 20.00 50.00
173 B.J. Mullens 3.00 8.00
174 Taylor Griffin 3.00 8.00
175 Jermaine Taylor 3.00 8.00
176 DeMar DeRozan 12.00 30.00

2009-10 Absolute Memorabilia Rookie Materials Jumbo Jersey Numbers Basketball Signatures

STATED PRINT RUN 25 SER.#'d SETS
UNPRICED PRIME PRINT RUN 5 SER.#'d SETS
UNPRICED PRIME SPECT.PRINT RUN 5 SETS
142 Brandon Jennings 20.00 50.00
143 Jonny Flynn 5.00 12.00
144 Stephen Curry 600.00 800.00
145 Omri Casspi 6.00 15.00
146 James Harden 75.00 200.00
147 Ty Lawson 8.00 20.00
148 Taj Gibson 8.00 20.00
149 Tyler Hansbrough 6.00 15.00
150 Chase Budinger 6.00 15.00
151 Sam Young 5.00 12.00
152 DeJuan Blair 6.00 15.00
153 Terrence Williams 5.00 12.00
154 Darren Collison 8.00 20.00
155 Toney Douglas 5.00 12.00
156 Wayne Ellington 8.00 20.00
157 Jrue Holiday 20.00 50.00
158 Eric Maynor 5.00 12.00
159 Rodrigue Beaubois 5.00 12.00
160 Austin Daye 5.00 12.00
161 Jodie Meeks 8.00 20.00
162 Jeff Pendergraph 5.00 12.00
163 Jordan Hill 6.00 15.00
164 DeMarre Carroll 6.00 15.00
165 Jeff Teague 8.00 20.00
166 Tyreke Evans 25.00 60.00
167 James Johnson 6.00 15.00
168 Earl Clark 6.00 15.00
169 Gerald Henderson 6.00 15.00
170 DaJuan Summers 5.00 12.00
171 Hasheem Thabeet 5.00 12.00
172 Blake Griffin 125.00 250.00
173 B.J. Mullens 5.00 12.00
174 Taylor Griffin 5.00 12.00
175 Jermaine Taylor 5.00 12.00
176 DeMar DeRozan 15.00 40.00

2009-10 Absolute Memorabilia Spectrum Signatures Gold

STATED PRINT RUN 20 TO 249 SETS
1 Kobe Bryant/99 75.00 150.00
14 Tony Parker/49 10.00 25.00
15 Deron Williams/49 10.00 25.00
21 Kevin Love/99 12.00 30.00
22 Danny Granger/49 5.00 12.00
31 Andre Iguodala/49 5.00 12.00
32 Ray Allen/49 15.00 40.00
43 Aaron Brooks/49 5.00 12.00
46 J.J. Barea/49 12.50 30.00
47 Emeka Okafor/49 5.00 12.00
51 Andrea Bargnani/49 5.00 12.00
56 Russell Westbrook/49 40.00 100.00
59 Devin Harris/49 5.00 12.00
61 Jason Kidd/49 10.00 25.00
67 Baron Davis/49 6.00 15.00
70 Carlos Boozer/49 6.00 15.00
80 Jermaine O'Neal/49 6.00 15.00
82 Richard Hamilton/49 5.00 12.00
92 Ron Artest/49 15.00 40.00
96 Chauncey Billups/20 8.00 20.00
101 Jalen Rose/49 10.00 25.00
105 Alvan Adams/49 6.00 15.00
106 Larry Bird/49 30.00 80.00
107 Scottie Pippen/49 100.00 200.00
108 Connie Hawkins/49 8.00 20.00
109 Magic Johnson/49 30.00 80.00
110 Bill Laimbeer/99 6.00 15.00
111 Shawn Bradley/49 8.00 20.00
114 Spud Webb/49 6.00 15.00
115 World B. Free/49 5.00 12.00
116 Tim Hardaway/49 10.00 25.00
117 Sean Elliott/49 15.00 30.00
119 Paul Westphal/40 10.00 25.00
122 Nate Thurmond/99 6.00 15.00
125 Jerry West/49 25.00 50.00
126 Marcus Thornton/249 10.00 25.00
127 Jonas Jerebko/249 6.00 15.00
128 Wesley Matthews/249 5.00 12.00
129 A.J. Price/249 3.00 8.00
131 Serge Ibaka/249 15.00 40.00
133 Derrick Brown/99 3.00 8.00
134 Sundiata Gaines/249 3.00 8.00
136 Jon Brockman/249 3.00 8.00
137 Danny Green/249 6.00 15.00
138 Marcus Landry/249 3.00 8.00
139 Lester Hudson/249 3.00 8.00
140 Patrick Mills/99 10.00 25.00
141 Dante Cunningham/249 3.00 8.00

2009-10 Absolute Memorabilia Spectrum Signatures Platinum

*PLATINUM STARS: .5X TO 1.25X GOLD
*PLATINUM RCs: .6X TO 1.5X GOLD
STATED PRINT RUN 5 TO 25 SER.#'d SETS
SOME UNPRICED DUE TO SCARCITY
1 Kobe Bryant/25 125.00 225.00
3 Rajon Rondo/25 25.00 50.00
71 Pau Gasol/25 25.00 50.00
106 Larry Bird/25 30.00 80.00
107 Scottie Pippen/25 50.00 100.00
108 Connie Hawkins/25 8.00 20.00
121 Willis Reed/25 8.00 20.00
137 Danny Green/25 40.00 100.00
140 Patrick Mills/25 20.00 50.00

2009-10 Absolute Memorabilia Star Gazing

COMPLETE SET (35) 40.00 80.00
STATED PRINT RUN 100 SER.#'d SETS
1 LeBron James 5.00 12.00
2 Kobe Bryant 5.00 12.00
3 Brandon Jennings 1.25 3.00
4 Tyreke Evans 1.00 2.50
5 Carmelo Anthony 1.50 4.00
6 Dwyane Wade 2.00 5.00
7 Chris Bosh 1.25 3.00
8 Pau Gasol 1.25 3.00
9 Jonny Flynn .75 2.00
10 Stephen Curry 125.00 250.00
11 Jason Kidd 1.25 3.00
12 Tony Parker 1.25 3.00
13 Danny Granger 1.00 2.50
14 Deron Williams 1.00 2.50
15 Dwight Howard 1.00 2.50
16 Kevin Durant 3.00 8.00
17 Blake Griffin 10.00 25.00
18 Omri Casspi 1.00 2.50
19 Kevin Garnett 2.00 5.00
20 Ray Allen 1.25 3.00
21 Shaquille O'Neal 2.50 6.00
22 Brandon Roy 1.25 3.00
23 Monta Ellis 1.00 2.50
24 Chris Paul 1.50 4.00
25 Dirk Nowitzki 1.50 4.00
26 David Lee .75 2.00
27 Tim Duncan 2.00 5.00
28 Antawn Jamison 1.00 2.50
29 Joe Johnson 1.00 2.50
30 Amare Stoudemire 1.00 2.50
31 Chris Kaman 1.00 2.50
32 Zach Randolph 1.00 2.50
33 Andrea Bargnani 1.00 2.50
34 Brook Lopez 1.00 2.50
35 Derrick Rose 2.00 5.00

2009-10 Absolute Memorabilia Star Gazing Jumbo Jersey Numbers

STATED PRINT RUN 10 TO 25 SER.#'d SETS
SOME NOT PRICED DUE TO SCARCITY
UNPRICED PRIME PRINT RUN ONE TO 10 SETS
1 LeBron James/25 15.00 40.00
2 Kobe Bryant/25 15.00 40.00
3 Brandon Jennings/25 5.00 12.00
4 Tyreke Evans/25 4.00 10.00
5 Carmelo Anthony/25 6.00 15.00
7 Chris Bosh/25 5.00 12.00
8 Pau Gasol/25 5.00 12.00
9 Jonny Flynn/25 3.00 8.00
10 Stephen Curry/25 200.00 400.00
11 Jason Kidd/25 5.00 12.00
13 Danny Granger/25 4.00 10.00
14 Deron Williams/25 4.00 10.00
15 Dwight Howard/25 4.00 10.00
16 Kevin Durant/25 12.00 30.00
17 Blake Griffin/25 20.00 50.00
18 Omri Casspi/25 4.00 10.00
19 Kevin Garnett/25 8.00 20.00
20 Ray Allen/25 5.00 12.00
21 Shaquille O'Neal/25 12.00 30.00
22 Brandon Roy/25 5.00 12.00
23 Monta Ellis/25 4.00 10.00
24 Chris Paul/25 6.00 15.00
25 Dirk Nowitzki/25 6.00 15.00
27 Tim Duncan/25 8.00 20.00
28 Antawn Jamison/25 4.00 10.00
29 Joe Johnson/25 4.00 10.00
33 Andrea Bargnani/25 4.00 10.00
34 Brook Lopez/25 4.00 10.00

2009-10 Absolute Memorabilia Star Gazing Jumbo Jersey Numbers Signatures

STATED PRINT RUN 10 TO 25 SER.#'d SETS
SOME UNPRICED DUE TO SCARCITY
UNPRICED PRIME PRINT RUN ONE TO 10 SETS
2 Kobe Bryant/25 100.00 200.00
3 Brandon Jennings/25 10.00 25.00
4 Tyreke Evans/25 8.00 20.00
8 Pau Gasol/25 30.00 60.00
9 Jonny Flynn/25 6.00 15.00
10 Stephen Curry/25 300.00 600.00
11 Jason Kidd/25 15.00 40.00
13 Danny Granger/25 10.00 25.00
14 Deron Williams/25 10.00 25.00
17 Blake Griffin/25 150.00 400.00
18 Omri Casspi/25 8.00 20.00
20 Ray Allen/25 25.00 60.00
33 Andrea Bargnani/25 20.00 40.00

2009-10 Absolute Memorabilia Star Gazing Jumbo Materials

STATED PRINT RUN 5 TO 25 SER.#'d SETS
UNPRICED PRIME SPECT.PRINT RUN 1 TO 5 SETS
1 LeBron James/25 15.00 40.00
2 Kobe Bryant/25 15.00 40.00
3 Brandon Jennings/25 5.00 12.00
4 Tyreke Evans/25 4.00 10.00
5 Carmelo Anthony/25 6.00 15.00
7 Chris Bosh/25 5.00 12.00
9 Jonny Flynn/25 3.00 8.00
10 Stephen Curry/25 30.00 80.00
11 Jason Kidd/25 5.00 12.00
13 Danny Granger/25 4.00 10.00
14 Deron Williams/25 4.00 10.00
15 Dwight Howard/25 4.00 10.00
16 Kevin Durant/25 12.00 30.00
17 Blake Griffin/25 20.00 50.00
18 Omri Casspi/25 4.00 10.00
19 Kevin Garnett/25 8.00 20.00
20 Ray Allen/25 10.00 25.00
21 Shaquille O'Neal/25 12.50 30.00
22 Brandon Roy/25 5.00 12.00
24 Chris Paul/25 6.00 15.00
25 Dirk Nowitzki/25 6.00 15.00
27 Tim Duncan/25 8.00 20.00
28 Antawn Jamison/25 4.00 10.00
29 Joe Johnson/25 4.00 10.00
33 Andrea Bargnani/25 4.00 10.00
34 Brook Lopez/25 4.00 10.00

2009-10 Absolute Memorabilia Star Gazing Materials

STATED PRINT RUN 10 TO 100 SER.#'d SETS
SOME NOT PRICED DUE TO SCARCITY
UNPRICED PRIME PRINT RUN 10 SER.#'d SETS
1 LeBron James/100 8.00 20.00
2 Kobe Bryant/100 8.00 20.00
3 Brandon Jennings/100 3.00 8.00
4 Tyreke Evans/100 2.50 6.00
5 Carmelo Anthony/100 4.00 10.00
6 Dwyane Wade/100 5.00 12.00
7 Chris Bosh/100 3.00 8.00
8 Pau Gasol/100 3.00 8.00
9 Jonny Flynn/100 2.00 5.00
10 Stephen Curry/100 75.00 200.00
11 Jason Kidd/100 3.00 8.00
12 Tony Parker/50 3.00 8.00
13 Danny Granger/100 2.50 6.00
14 Deron Williams/100 2.50 6.00
15 Dwight Howard/100 2.50 6.00
16 Kevin Durant/100 8.00 20.00
17 Blake Griffin/100 12.00 30.00
18 Omri Casspi/100 2.50 6.00
19 Kevin Garnett/100 5.00 12.00
20 Ray Allen/100 3.00 8.00
21 Shaquille O'Neal/100 6.00 15.00
22 Brandon Roy/100 3.00 8.00
23 Monta Ellis/100 2.50 6.00
24 Chris Paul/100 4.00 10.00
25 Dirk Nowitzki/100 4.00 10.00
26 David Lee/50 2.00 5.00
27 Tim Duncan/100 5.00 12.00
28 Antawn Jamison/100 2.50 6.00
29 Joe Johnson/100 2.50 6.00
31 Chris Kaman/25 2.50 6.00
33 Andrea Bargnani/100 2.50 6.00
34 Brook Lopez/100 2.50 6.00

2009-10 Absolute Memorabilia Star Gazing Materials Signatures

STATED PRINT RUN 25 SER.#'d SETS
UNPRICED PRIME PRINT RUN 5 SER.#'d SETS
2 Kobe Bryant 100.00 200.00
3 Brandon Jennings 10.00 25.00
4 Tyreke Evans 8.00 20.00
8 Pau Gasol 30.00 60.00
9 Jonny Flynn 6.00 15.00
10 Stephen Curry 300.00 600.00
11 Jason Kidd 15.00 40.00
12 Tony Parker 12.50 30.00
13 Danny Granger 10.00 25.00
14 Deron Williams 10.00 25.00
17 Blake Griffin 150.00 300.00
18 Omri Casspi 8.00 20.00
20 Ray Allen 20.00 50.00
33 Andrea Bargnani 10.00 25.00

2009-10 Absolute Memorabilia Team Quads TEAM Die Cut Materials

STATED PRINT RUN 25 TO 100 SER.#'d SETS
UNPRICED PRIME PRINT RUN 5 TO 10 SETS
1 CP/DW/EO/PS 6.00 15.00
2 AB/CB/HT/JC 6.00 15.00
3 BG/RH/RS/TP 6.00 15.00
4 AM/BR/LA/RF 6.00 15.00
5 KG/PP/RR/RW 15.00 30.00
6 BD/CK/EG/MC 6.00 15.00
7 LJ/MW/SO/ZI 12.00 30.00
8 DH/JN/RL/VC 6.00 15.00
9 CA/CA/JS/N 6.00 15.00

2009-10 Absolute Memorabilia Team Tandems Materials

STATED PRINT RUN 100 SER.#'d SETS
UNPRICED PRIME PRINT RUN 10 SER.#'d SETS
1 D.West/E.Okafor 4.00 10.00
2 H.Turkoglu/J.Calderon 6.00 15.00
3 C.Andersen/Nene 6.00 15.00
4 A.Miller/R.Fernandez 4.00 10.00
5 R.Rondo/R.Wallace 8.00 20.00
6 B.Diaw/R.Felton 4.00 10.00
7 B.Lopez/D.Harris 4.00 10.00
8 S.O'Neal /Z.Ilgauskas 8.00 20.00
9 J.Nelson/R.Lewis 4.00 10.00

2009-10 Absolute Memorabilia Team Trios NBA Materials

STATED PRINT RUN 40 TO 100 SETS
UNPRICED PRIME PRINT RUN ONE TO 10 SETS
1 Atlanta Hawks/100 6.00 15.00
2 Golden State Warriors/100 60.00 150.00
3 Memphis Grizzlies/100 5.00 12.00
4 Philadelphia 76ers/100 5.00 12.00
5 Boston Celtics/100 10.00 25.00
6 Minnesota Timberwolves/60 5.00 12.00
7 Oklahoma City Thunder/100 10.00 25.00
8 Utah Jazz/40 6.00 15.00
9 Houston Rockets/100 5.00 12.00

2009-10 Absolute Memorabilia Tools of the Trade Materials Prime Black Spectrum

STATED PRINT RUN ONE TO 25 SER.#'d SETS
SOME UNPRICED DUE TO SCARCITY
*DOUBLE: .4X TO 1X BASE HI
DOUBLE PRINT RUN ONE TO 25 SETS
*TRIPLE: .6X TO 1.5X BASE HI
TRIPLE PRINT RUN ONE TO 25 SETS
2 Al Jefferson/25 5.00 12.00
3 Baron Davis/20 5.00 12.00
4 Brandon Roy/25 6.00 15.00
5 Carlos Boozer/25 5.00 12.00
8 D.J. Augustin/25 4.00 10.00
9 Elton Brand/25 6.00 15.00
10 Emeka Okafor/25 5.00 12.00
11 Kobe Bryant/25 20.00 50.00
12 LeBron James/25 20.00 50.00
15 Omri Casspi/25 5.00 12.00
16 Rajon Rondo/25 12.00 30.00
17 Ray Allen/25 8.00 20.00
20 Russell Westbrook/25 10.00 25.00
23 Stephen Curry/25 60.00 150.00

2009-10 Absolute Memorabilia Tools of the Trade Materials Prime Black Spectrum Jumbo

PRINT RUNS LISTED IN CHECKLIST
UNPRICED JSY NUMBER PRINT RUN 1 TO 10 SETS
2 Al Jefferson/25 8.00 20.00
3 Baron Davis/25 12.00 30.00
5 Carlos Boozer/25 8.00 20.00
9 Elton Brand/25 10.00 25.00
10 Emeka Okafor/25 8.00 20.00
11 Kobe Bryant/25 40.00 100.00
15 Omri Casspi/25 8.00 20.00
16 Rajon Rondo/25 20.00 50.00
17 Ray Allen/25 15.00 40.00
20 Russell Westbrook/25 30.00 80.00
23 Stephen Curry/25 60.00 510.00

2009-10 Absolute Memorabilia Tools of the Trade Materials Red

STATED PRINT RUN 150 TO 249 SETS
*BLUE: .4X TO 1X BASE HI
BLUE STATED PRINT RUN 30 TO 100 SETS
2 Al Jefferson/249 2.50 6.00
3 Baron Davis/249 2.50 6.00
4 Brandon Roy/249 3.00 8.00
5 Carlos Boozer/249 2.50 6.00
7 Chris Kaman/150 2.50 6.00
8 D.J. Augustin/249 2.00 5.00
9 Elton Brand/249 3.00 8.00
10 Emeka Okafor/249 2.50 6.00
11 Kobe Bryant/249 10.00 25.00
12 LeBron James/249 10.00 25.00
14 Nene/249 2.50 6.00
15 Omri Casspi/249 2.50 6.00
16 Rajon Rondo/249 3.00 8.00
17 Ray Allen/249 3.00 8.00
20 Russell Westbrook/249 8.00 20.00
22 Shane Battier/249 3.00 8.00
23 Stephen Curry/249 40.00 100.00
24 T.J. Ford/249 2.00 5.00

2009-10 Absolute Memorabilia Retail

COMPLETE SET (125) 25.00 60.00
*RETAIL: .2X TO .5X HOBBY

2009-10 Absolute Memorabilia Retail Frequent Flyer

COMPLETE SET (20) 10.00 25.00
*RETAIL: .2X TO .5X HOBBY

2009-10 Absolute Memorabilia Retail Heroes

COMPLETE SET (15) 8.00 20.00
*RETAIL: .2X TO .5X HOBBY

2009-10 Absolute Memorabilia Retail Hoopla

COMPLETE SET (20) 10.00 25.00
*RETAIL: .2X TO .5X HOBBY

2009-10 Absolute Memorabilia Retail Marks of Fame

COMPLETE SET (10) 8.00 20.00
*RETAIL: .2X TO .5X HOBBY

2009-10 Absolute Memorabilia Retail NBA Icons

COMPLETE SET (15) 15.00 40.00
*RETAIL: .2X TO .5X HOBBY

2009-10 Absolute Memorabilia Retail Star Gazing

COMPLETE SET (35) 20.00 50.00
*RETAIL: .2X TO .5X HOBBY
10 Stephen Curry 60.00 150.00

2010-11 Absolute Memorabilia

COMP.SET w/o SPs (100) 25.00 60.00
ROOKIE PRINT RUN 499 SER.#'d SETS
JSY AU RC PRINT RUN 249 TO 499 SETS
UNPRICED SPECT.BLACK PRINT RUN ONE SET
EXCH.EXPIRATION 9/16/2012
1 Kevin Durant 2.00 5.00
2 Derrick Rose 1.00 2.50
3 Blake Griffin .75 2.00
4 Dwight Howard .60 1.50

5 Kobe Bryant 3.00 8.00
6 Dwyane Wade 1.25 3.00
7 Chris Paul 1.00 2.50
8 Deron Williams .60 1.50
9 Paul Pierce .75 2.00
10 Stephen Curry 3.00 8.00
11 Amare Stoudemire .60 1.50
12 Dirk Nowitzki 1.00 2.50
13 Steve Nash .75 2.00
14 LeBron James 4.00 10.00
15 Carmelo Anthony 1.00 2.50
16 Brandon Jennings .50 1.25
17 Kevin Love .75 2.00
18 Joakim Noah .60 1.50
19 Tyreke Evans .50 1.25
20 Monta Ellis .60 1.50
21 Kevin Martin .60 1.50
22 Tim Duncan 1.25 3.00
23 Joe Johnson .60 1.50
24 LaMarcus Aldridge .75 2.00
25 Brook Lopez .60 1.50
26 Ray Allen .75 2.00
27 Stephen Jackson .60 1.50
28 Pau Gasol .75 2.00
29 Michael Beasley .50 1.25
30 Danny Granger .60 1.50
31 Chris Bosh .75 2.00
32 Tony Parker .75 2.00
33 Jrue Holiday .75 2.00
34 Vince Carter 1.00 2.50
35 DeMar DeRozan .75 2.00
36 Daniel Gibson .60 1.50
37 Marc Gasol .75 2.00
38 David West .60 1.50
39 David Lee .50 1.25
40 Ben Gordon .60 1.50
41 Andrew Bogut .60 1.50
42 Rajon Rondo .75 2.00
43 Luis Scola .60 1.50
44 Caron Butler .60 1.50
45 Andray Blatche .50 1.25
46 Antawn Jamison .60 1.50
47 O.J. Mayo .50 1.25
48 Paul Millsap .60 1.50
49 Eric Gordon .60 1.50
50 Andre Iguodala .60 1.50
51 Al Horford .60 1.50
52 Kevin Garnett 1.25 3.00
53 Luol Deng .60 1.50
54 DeJuan Blair .50 1.25
55 Mike Dunleavy .50 1.25
56 Al Thornton .50 1.25
57 Lamar Odom .60 1.50
58 Andrea Bargnani .60 1.50
59 Jason Richardson .75 2.00
60 Russell Westbrook 2.00 5.00
61 Tracy McGrady .75 2.00
62 Gerald Wallace .60 1.50
63 Jamal Crawford .75 2.00
64 Al Jefferson .60 1.50
65 Marcus Camby .50 1.25
66 Jonny Flynn .50 1.25
67 Jeff Green .60 1.50
68 Trevor Ariza .50 1.25
69 Rudy Gay .75 2.00
70 Aaron Brooks .50 1.25
71 Jason Kidd .75 2.00
72 Danilo Gallinari .60 1.50
73 Ty Lawson .50 1.25
74 Elton Brand .75 2.00
75 Terrence Williams .50 1.25
76 Richard Jefferson .60 1.50
77 J.J. Redick .75 2.00
78 Chris Kaman .60 1.50
79 Gerald Henderson .50 1.25
80 Jeff Teague .60 1.50
81 Drew Gooden .60 1.50
82 Juwan Howard .60 1.50
83 Tyler Hansbrough .60 1.50
84 Derek Fisher .60 1.50
85 Boris Diaw .60 1.50
86 Anderson Varejao .50 1.25
87 Toney Douglas .50 1.25
88 Robin Lopez .50 1.25
89 Zach Randolph .60 1.50
90 Carl Landry .50 1.25
91 Rashard Lewis .60 1.50
92 Darren Collison .60 1.50
93 Sasha Vujacic .50 1.25
94 Nene .60 1.50
95 Shaquille O'Neal 1.50 4.00
96 Emeka Okafor .60 1.50
97 Brandon Roy .75 2.00
98 Josh Smith .60 1.50
99 Devin Harris .50 1.25
100 Rodrigue Beaubois .50 1.25
101 M.L. Carr 1.50 4.00
102 Patrick Ewing 2.00 5.00
103 World B. Free 1.25 3.00
104 Tim Hardaway 1.50 4.00
105 Sam Perkins 1.00 2.50
106 Kenny Smith 1.25 3.00
107 Walt Bellamy 1.25 3.00
108 Scott Skiles 1.25 3.00
109 Robert Reid 1.50 4.00
110 Mitch Richmond 1.50 4.00
111 Nick Anderson 1.50 4.00
112 Shawn Kemp 2.50 6.00
113 Gary Payton 1.50 4.00
114 John Stockton 2.50 6.00
115 Ron Harper 1.50 4.00
116 Elgin Baylor 1.50 4.00
117 Darryl Dawkins 1.00 2.50
118 Bernard King 1.25 3.00
119 Bill Laimbeer 1.25 3.00
120 Tree Rollins 1.00 2.50
121 Bill Sharman 1.50 4.00
122 Danny Manning 1.25 3.00
123 Charles D. Smith 1.50 4.00
124 Wilt Chamberlain 3.00 8.00
125 Dan Majerle 1.25 3.00
126 Jeff Hornacek 1.25 3.00
127 George McGinnis 1.00 2.50
128 John Starks 1.25 3.00
129 Toni Kukoc 1.50 4.00
130 Byron Scott 1.25 3.00
131 Gus Williams 1.00 2.50
132 Jalen Rose 1.50 4.00
133 Campy Russell 1.00 2.50
134 Elvin Hayes 1.50 4.00
135 Kurt Rambis 1.00 2.50
136 Jeremy Lin RC 10.00 25.00
137 Terrico White RC 1.00 2.50
138 Timofey Mozgov RC 1.50 4.00
139 Sherron Collins RC 1.00 2.50
140 Ishmael Smith RC 1.50 4.00
141 Pape Sy RC 1.00 2.50
142 Jeremy Evans RC 1.00 2.50
143 Tiago Splitter RC 1.50 4.00
144 Landry Fields RC 1.25 3.00
145 Solomon Alabi RC 1.00 2.50
146 Derrick Caracter RC 1.00 2.50
147 Hamady N'diaye RC 1.50 4.00
148 Gary Neal RC 1.50 4.00
149 Armon Johnson RC 1.00 2.50
150 Omer Asik RC 2.00 5.00
151 John Wall JSY AU/499 RC 30.00 80.00
152 Evan Turner JSY AU/299 RC 3.00 8.00
153 Derrick Favors JSY AU/499 RC 5.00 12.00
154 W.Johnson JSY AU/499 RC 2.50 6.00
155 D.Cousins JSY AU/499 RC 15.00 40.00
156 Ekpe Udoh JSY AU/499 RC 2.50 6.00
157 Greg Monroe JSY AU/499 RC 5.00 12.00
158 Al.Aminu JSY AU/399 RC 4.00 10.00
159 G.Hayward JSY AU/499 RC 25.00 60.00
160 Paul George JSY AU/499 RC 50.00 100.00
161 Cole Aldrich JSY AU/499 RC 3.00 8.00
162 Xavier Henry JSY AU/499 RC 2.50 6.00
163 Ed Davis JSY AU/499 RC 2.50 6.00
164 P.Patterson JSY AU/499 RC 3.00 8.00
165 Larry Sanders JSY AU/299 RC 2.50 6.00
166 Luke Babbitt JSY AU/499 RC 3.00 8.00
167 Kevin Seraphin JSY AU/249 RC 2.50 6.00
168 Eric Bledsoe JSY AU/499 RC 5.00 12.00
169 Avery Bradley JSY AU/499 RC 5.00 12.00
170 J.Anderson JSY AU/499 RC 2.50 6.00
171 Elliot Williams JSY AU/499 RC 2.50 6.00
172 Trevor Booker JSY AU/299 RC 3.00 8.00
173 Damion James JSY AU/299 RC 2.50 6.00
174 D.Jones JSY AU/299 RC 2.50 6.00
175 Q.Pondexter JSY AU/499 RC 2.50 6.00
176 J.Crawford JSY AU/499 RC 3.00 8.00
177 G.Vasquez JSY AU/499 RC 3.00 8.00
178 Daniel Orton JSY AU/499 RC 2.50 6.00
179 Lazar Hayward JSY AU/299 RC 2.50 6.00
180 Dexter Pittman JSY AU/499 RC 2.50 6.00
181 H.Whiteside JSY AU/499 RC 12.00 30.00
182 Andy Rautins JSY AU/499 RC 2.50 6.00
183 L.Stephenson JSY AU/499 RC 4.00 10.00
184 Devin Ebanks JSY AU/299 RC 2.50 6.00
185 Willie Warren JSY AU/299 RC 2.50 6.00

2010-11 Absolute Memorabilia Spectrum Gold

*GOLD 1-100: 1X TO 2.5X BASE HI
*GOLD 101-135: .5X TO 1.25X BASE HI
*GOLD 136-150: .6X TO 1.5X BASE HI
STATED PRINT RUN 100 SER.#'d SETS
136 Jeremy Lin 20.00 50.00

2010-11 Absolute Memorabilia Spectrum Platinum

*PLATINUM 1-100: 2X TO 5X BASE HI
*PLATINUM 101-135: 1X TO 2.5X BASE HI
*PLATINUM 136-150: 1X TO 2.5X BASE HI
STATED PRINT RUN 25 SER.#'d SETS
112 Shawn Kemp 75.00 150.00
113 Gary Payton 8.00 20.00

2010-11 Absolute Memorabilia Absolute Heroes

COMPLETE SET (15) 12.50 25.00
STATED PRINT RUN 399 SER.#'d SETS
*SPECTRUM: 1X TO 2.5X BASE HI
SPECTRUM PRINT RUN 100 SER.#'d SETS
UNPRICED BLACK PRINT RUN ONE SET
1 Adrian Dantley .75 2.00
2 Alonzo Mourning 1.25 3.00
3 Bernard King .75 2.00
4 Bob Lanier .75 2.00
5 Detlef Schrempf 1.00 2.50
6 Glen Rice .75 2.00
7 Hakeem Olajuwon 1.25 3.00
8 Isiah Thomas 1.00 2.50
9 Karl Malone 1.25 3.00
10 Larry Bird 2.50 6.00
11 Larry Johnson 1.25 3.00
12 Magic Johnson 2.50 6.00
13 Mark Aguirre .75 2.00
14 Robert Parish 1.00 2.50
15 Toni Kukoc 1.00 2.50

2010-11 Absolute Memorabilia Absolute Heroes Materials

STATED PRINT RUN 25 TO 49 SER.#'d SETS
UNPRICED PRIME PRINT RUN 10 SETS
2 Alonzo Mourning/25 12.00 30.00
3 Bernard King/25 2.50 6.00
4 Bob Lanier/49 2.50 6.00
5 Detlef Schrempf/49 4.00 10.00
6 Glen Rice/49 2.50 6.00
7 Hakeem Olajuwon/49 4.00 10.00
8 Isiah Thomas/49 3.00 8.00
9 Karl Malone/49 4.00 10.00
10 Larry Bird/49 8.00 20.00
11 Larry Johnson/49 10.00 25.00
12 Magic Johnson/49 6.00 15.00
13 Mark Aguirre/49 2.50 6.00
14 Robert Parish/49 3.00 8.00
15 Toni Kukoc/49 5.00 12.00

2010-11 Absolute Memorabilia Absolute Heroes Materials Signatures

STATED PRINT RUN 5 TO 25 SER.#'d SETS
SOME UNPRICED DUE TO SCARCITY
UNPRICED PRIME PRINT RUN 5 SETS
4 Bob Lanier/25 8.00 20.00
5 Detlef Schrempf/25 8.00 20.00
6 Glen Rice/25 8.00 20.00
8 Isiah Thomas/25 12.00 30.00
10 Larry Bird/25 50.00 120.00
11 Larry Johnson/25 20.00 50.00
13 Mark Aguirre/25 8.00 20.00
14 Robert Parish/25 10.00 25.00
15 Toni Kukoc/25 20.00 50.00

2010-11 Absolute Memorabilia Absolute Patches Jumbo Prime Spectrum

STATED PRINT RUN 5 TO 25 SER.#'d SETS
SOME UNPRICED DUE TO SCARCITY
1 Bernard King/25 12.00 30.00
12 Robert Parish/25 12.00 30.00
13 Toni Kukoc/25 100.00 200.00

2010-11 Absolute Memorabilia Frequent Flyer

COMPLETE SET (20) 15.00 40.00
STATED PRINT RUN 399 SER.#'d SETS
*SPECTRUM: .6X TO 1.5X BASE HI
SPECTRUM PRINT RUN 100 SER.#'d SETS
UNPRICED BLACK PRINT RUN ONE SET
1 LeBron James 5.00 12.00
2 Kobe Bryant 4.00 10.00
3 Blake Griffin 1.00 2.50
4 Nate Robinson .60 1.50
5 Shannon Brown .60 1.50
6 DeMar DeRozan 1.00 2.50
7 Dwight Howard .75 2.00
8 Vince Carter 1.25 3.00
9 Jason Richardson 1.00 2.50
10 Andre Iguodala .75 2.00
11 Josh Smith .75 2.00
12 Rudy Gay 1.00 2.50
13 Derrick Rose 1.25 3.00
14 Gerald Wallace .75 2.00
15 J.R. Smith .75 2.00
16 Amare Stoudemire .75 2.00
17 Corey Brewer .60 1.50
18 David Thompson 1.00 2.50
19 Clyde Drexler 1.50 4.00
20 Dominique Wilkins 1.50 4.00

2010-11 Absolute Memorabilia Frequent Flyer Materials Jersey Number

STATED PRINT RUN 5 TO 25 SER.#'d SETS
SOME UNPRICED DUE TO SCARCITY
UNPRICED PRIME PRINT RUN ONE TO 5 SETS
1 LeBron James/25 15.00 40.00
2 Kobe Bryant/25 15.00 40.00
3 Blake Griffin/25 4.00 10.00
5 Shannon Brown/25 2.50 6.00
6 DeMar DeRozan/25 4.00 10.00
7 Dwight Howard/25 3.00 8.00
11 Josh Smith/25 3.00 8.00
12 Rudy Gay/25 4.00 10.00
15 J.R. Smith/25 3.00 8.00
20 Dominique Wilkins/25 5.00 12.00

2010-11 Absolute Memorabilia Frequent Flyer Materials Jersey Number Signatures

STATED PRINT RUN 5 TO 25 SER.#'d SETS
SOME UNPRICED DUE TO SCARCITY
UNPRICED PRIME PRINT RUN ONE TO 5 SETS
2 Kobe Bryant/25 100.00 200.00
3 Blake Griffin/25 20.00 50.00
6 DeMar DeRozan/25 10.00 25.00
20 Dominique Wilkins/25 15.00 40.00

2010-11 Absolute Memorabilia Frequent Flyer Materials Signatures

STATED PRINT RUN 5 TO 25 SER.#'d SETS
SOME UNPRICED DUE TO SCARCITY
UNPRICED PRIME PRINT RUN ONE TO 5 SETS
2 Kobe Bryant/25 100.00 200.00
3 Blake Griffin/25 40.00 80.00
6 DeMar DeRozan/25 12.00 30.00
20 Dominique Wilkins/25 15.00 40.00

2010-11 Absolute Memorabilia Hoopla

COMPLETE SET (20) 15.00 40.00
STATED PRINT RUN 399 SER.#'d SETS
*SPECTRUM: .6X TO 1.5X BASE HI
SPECTRUM PRINT RUN 100 SER.#'d SETS
UNPRICED BLACK PRINT RUN ONE SET
1 Andrew Bogut .75 2.00
2 Brook Lopez .75 2.00
3 Carmelo Anthony 1.25 3.00
4 Chauncey Billups 1.00 2.50
5 Chris Paul 1.25 3.00
6 Danilo Gallinari .75 2.00
7 Danny Granger .75 2.00
8 David Lee .60 1.50
9 Deron Williams .75 2.00
10 Dirk Nowitzki 1.25 3.00
11 Dwyane Wade 1.50 4.00
12 Gerald Wallace .75 2.00
13 Kobe Bryant 4.00 10.00
14 Kevin Durant 2.50 6.00
15 LeBron James 5.00 12.00
16 Monta Ellis .75 2.00
17 Derrick Rose 1.25 3.00
18 Rajon Rondo 1.00 2.50
19 Steve Nash 1.00 2.50
20 Tyreke Evans .60 1.50

2010-11 Absolute Memorabilia Hoopla Materials

STATED PRINT RUN 25 TO 49 SER.#'d SETS
UNPRICED PRIME PRINT RUN 5 TO 10 SETS
1 Andrew Bogut/49 2.50 6.00
3 Carmelo Anthony/25 5.00 12.00
4 Chauncey Billups/49 3.00 8.00
5 Chris Paul/49 4.00 10.00
6 Danilo Gallinari/49 2.50 6.00
8 David Lee/49 2.00 5.00
9 Deron Williams/49 2.50 6.00
10 Dirk Nowitzki/49 4.00 10.00
11 Dwyane Wade/49 5.00 12.00
13 Kobe Bryant/49 10.00 25.00
14 Kevin Durant/49 8.00 20.00
15 LeBron James/49 10.00 25.00
17 Derrick Rose/49 4.00 10.00
18 Rajon Rondo/49 3.00 8.00
19 Steve Nash/49 3.00 8.00
20 Tyreke Evans/49 2.00 5.00

2010-11 Absolute Memorabilia Hoopla Materials Jersey Number

STATED PRINT RUN 5 TO 25 SER.#'d SETS
SOME UNPRICED DUE TO SCARCITY
UNPRICED PRIME PRINT RUN 5 SETS
1 Andrew Bogut/25 3.00 8.00
3 Carmelo Anthony/25 5.00 12.00
4 Chauncey Billups/25 4.00 10.00
5 Chris Paul/25 5.00 12.00
8 David Lee/25 2.50 6.00
9 Deron Williams/25 3.00 8.00
10 Dirk Nowitzki/25 5.00 12.00
11 Dwyane Wade/25 6.00 15.00
13 Kobe Bryant/25 12.00 30.00
14 Kevin Durant/25 10.00 25.00
15 LeBron James/25 12.00 30.00
17 Derrick Rose/25 5.00 12.00
18 Rajon Rondo/25 4.00 10.00
20 Tyreke Evans/25 2.50 6.00

2010-11 Absolute Memorabilia Hoopla Materials Jersey Number Signatures

STATED PRINT RUN 5 TO 25 SER.#'d SETS
SOME UNPRICED DUE TO SCARCITY
UNPRICED PRIME PRINT RUN ONE TO 5 SETS
1 Andrew Bogut/25 15.00 40.00
13 Kobe Bryant/25 100.00 200.00
14 Kevin Durant/25 100.00 200.00

2010-11 Absolute Memorabilia Hoopla Materials Signatures

STATED PRINT RUN 5 TO 25 SER.#'d SETS
SOME UNPRICED DUE TO SCARCITY
UNPRICED PRIME PRINT RUN ONE TO 5 SETS
13 Kobe Bryant/25 100.00 200.00
14 Kevin Durant/25 100.00 200.00

2010-11 Absolute Memorabilia Marks of Fame

COMPLETE SET (10) 8.00 20.00
STATED PRINT RUN 399 SER.#'d SETS
*SPECTRUM: .75X TO 2X BASE HI
SPECTRUM PRINT RUN 100 SER.#'d SETS
UNPRICED BLACK PRINT RUN ONE SET
1 Magic Johnson 2.50 6.00
2 John Stockton 1.50 4.00
3 Hakeem Olajuwon 1.25 3.00
4 Isiah Thomas 1.00 2.50
5 Kareem Abdul-Jabbar 1.50 4.00
6 Karl Malone 1.25 3.00
7 Moses Malone 1.00 2.50
8 Robert Parish 1.00 2.50
9 Scottie Pippen 2.00 5.00
10 Xavier McDaniel .60 1.50

2010-11 Absolute Memorabilia Marks of Fame Materials

STATED PRINT RUN 49 SER.#'d SETS
UNPRICED PRIME PRINT RUN 10 SETS
1 Magic Johnson 6.00 15.00
2 John Stockton 6.00 15.00
3 Hakeem Olajuwon 5.00 12.00
4 Isiah Thomas 4.00 10.00
5 Kareem Abdul-Jabbar 6.00 15.00
6 Karl Malone 5.00 12.00
7 Moses Malone 4.00 10.00
8 Robert Parish 4.00 10.00
9 Scottie Pippen 8.00 20.00
10 Xavier McDaniel 2.50 6.00

2010-11 Absolute Memorabilia Marks of Fame Materials Signatures

STATED PRINT RUN 5 TO 25 SER.#'d SETS
SOME UNPRICED DUE TO SCARCITY
UNPRICED PRIME PRINT RUN ONE TO 5 SETS
4 Isiah Thomas/25 15.00 40.00
8 Robert Parish/25 10.00 25.00

2010-11 Absolute Memorabilia Materials Prime Spectrum

STATED PRINT RUN ONE TO 25 SER.#'d SETS
SOME UNPRICED DUE TO SCARCITY
3 Blake Griffin/25 6.00 15.00
9 Paul Pierce/25 6.00 15.00
13 Steve Nash/25 8.00 20.00
22 Tim Duncan/25 10.00 25.00
24 LaMarcus Aldridge/25 6.00 15.00
26 Ray Allen/25 8.00 20.00
29 Michael Beasley/25 4.00 10.00
32 Tony Parker/25 6.00 15.00
33 Jrue Holiday/25 6.00 15.00
35 DeMar DeRozan/25 6.00 15.00
38 David West/25 5.00 12.00
41 Andrew Bogut/25 5.00 12.00
43 Luis Scola/25 5.00 12.00
44 Caron Butler/25 5.00 12.00
47 O.J. Mayo/25 4.00 10.00
50 Andre Iguodala/25 5.00 12.00
51 Al Horford/25 5.00 12.00
52 Kevin Garnett/25 10.00 25.00
53 Luol Deng/25 5.00 12.00
54 DeJuan Blair/25 4.00 10.00
55 Mike Dunleavy/25 4.00 10.00
66 Jonny Flynn/25 4.00 10.00
71 Jason Kidd/25 10.00 25.00
73 Ty Lawson/25 4.00 10.00
74 Elton Brand/25 6.00 15.00
75 Terrence Williams/25 4.00 10.00
76 Richard Jefferson/25 5.00 12.00
77 J.J. Redick/25 6.00 15.00
78 Chris Kaman/25 5.00 12.00
79 Gerald Henderson/25 4.00 10.00
80 Jeff Teague/25 5.00 12.00
83 Tyler Hansbrough/25 5.00 12.00
85 Boris Diaw/25 5.00 12.00
87 Toney Douglas/25 4.00 10.00
94 Nene/25 5.00 12.00
95 Shaquille O'Neal/25 20.00 50.00
98 Josh Smith/25 5.00 12.00
99 Devin Harris/25 4.00 10.00
100 Rodrigue Beaubois/25 4.00 10.00
102 Patrick Ewing/25 15.00 40.00
105 Sam Perkins/25 4.00 10.00
110 Mitch Richmond/25 10.00 25.00
111 Nick Anderson/25 6.00 15.00
112 Shawn Kemp/25 75.00 200.00
114 John Stockton/25 15.00 40.00
118 Bernard King/25 5.00 12.00
126 Jeff Hornacek/25 5.00 12.00
129 Toni Kukoc/25 10.00 25.00
132 Jalen Rose/25 8.00 20.00
138 Timofey Mozgov/25 6.00 15.00

2010-11 Absolute Memorabilia NBA Icons

COMPLETE SET (15) 15.00 30.00
STATED PRINT RUN 399 SER.#'d SETS
*SPECTRUM: .75X TO 2X BASE HI
SPECTRUM PRINT RUN 100 SER.#'d SETS
UNPRICED BLACK PRINT RUN ONE SET
1 Larry Bird 2.50 6.00
2 Kareem Abdul-Jabbar 1.50 4.00
3 Patrick Ewing 1.25 3.00
4 David Robinson 1.50 4.00
5 Gary Payton 1.00 2.50
6 John Stockton 1.50 4.00
7 Magic Johnson 2.50 6.00
8 Kevin Durant 2.50 6.00
9 Kobe Bryant 4.00 10.00
10 Amare Stoudemire .75 2.00
11 Rajon Rondo 1.00 2.50
12 Carmelo Anthony 1.25 3.00
13 Chris Bosh 1.00 2.50
14 Steve Nash 1.00 2.50
15 Deron Williams .75 2.00

2010-11 Absolute Memorabilia NBA Icons Materials

STATED PRINT RUN 25 TO 49 SER.#'d SETS
UNPRICED PRIME PRINT RUN 5 TO 10 SETS
1 Larry Bird/49 8.00 20.00
2 Kareem Abdul-Jabbar/49 5.00 12.00
3 Patrick Ewing/49 8.00 20.00
4 David Robinson/49 5.00 12.00
6 John Stockton/49 5.00 12.00
7 Magic Johnson/49 6.00 15.00
8 Kevin Durant/49 8.00 20.00
9 Kobe Bryant/49 10.00 25.00
10 Amare Stoudemire/49 2.50 6.00
11 Rajon Rondo/49 3.00 8.00
12 Carmelo Anthony/25 5.00 12.00
13 Chris Bosh/49 3.00 8.00
14 Steve Nash/49 3.00 8.00
15 Deron Williams/49 2.50 6.00

2010-11 Absolute Memorabilia NBA Icons Materials Signatures

STATED PRINT RUN 5 TO 25 SER.#'d SETS
UNPRICED PRIME PRINT RUN ONE TO 5 SETS
1 Larry Bird/25 50.00 120.00
8 Kevin Durant/25 100.00 200.00
9 Kobe Bryant/25 100.00 200.00

2010-11 Absolute Memorabilia Panini All Stars Rack Pack

RANDOM INSERTS IN RETAIL PACKS
1 Dwight Howard 1.50 4.00
2 Dwyane Wade 3.00 8.00
3 Kevin Garnett 3.00 8.00
4 LeBron James 10.00 25.00
5 Rajon Rondo 2.00 5.00
6 Amare Stoudemire 1.50 4.00
7 Derrick Rose 2.50 6.00
8 John Wall 10.00 25.00
9 Ray Allen 2.00 5.00
10 Chris Bosh 2.00 5.00
11 Paul Pierce 2.00 5.00
12 Shaquille O'Neal 4.00 10.00
13 Joakim Noah 1.50 4.00
14 Carmelo Anthony 2.50 6.00
15 Chris Paul 2.50 6.00
16 Kevin Durant 5.00 12.00
17 Kobe Bryant 8.00 20.00
18 Yao Ming 2.50 6.00
19 Andrew Bynum 1.25 3.00
20 Blake Griffin 2.00 5.00
21 Dirk Nowitzki 2.50 6.00
22 Manu Ginobili 2.00 5.00
23 Tim Duncan 3.00 8.00
24 Nene 1.50 4.00
25 Pau Gasol 2.00 5.00
26 Steve Nash 2.00 5.00
27 Bob Cousy 3.00 8.00
28 Elvin Hayes 2.00 5.00
29 Jerry West 2.50 6.00
30 John Havlicek 2.50 6.00
31 Kareem Abdul-Jabbar 3.00 8.00
32 Karl Malone 2.50 6.00
33 Larry Bird 5.00 12.00
34 Magic Johnson 5.00 12.00
35 Moses Malone 2.00 5.00

2010-11 Absolute Memorabilia Rookie Materials Jumbo Jersey Numbers Basketball

STATED PRINT RUN 25 SER.#'d SETS
UNPRICED PRIME PRINT RUN 10 SETS
151 John Wall 10.00 25.00
152 Evan Turner 4.00 10.00
153 Derrick Favors 6.00 15.00
154 Wesley Johnson 3.00 8.00
155 DeMarcus Cousins 12.00 30.00
156 Ekpe Udoh 3.00 8.00
157 Greg Monroe 6.00 15.00
158 Al-Farouq Aminu 5.00 12.00
159 Gordon Hayward 8.00 20.00
160 Paul George 15.00 40.00
161 Cole Aldrich 4.00 10.00
162 Xavier Henry 3.00 8.00
163 Ed Davis 3.00 8.00
164 Patrick Patterson 4.00 10.00
165 Larry Sanders 3.00 8.00
166 Luke Babbitt 4.00 10.00
167 Kevin Seraphin 3.00 8.00
168 Eric Bledsoe 6.00 15.00
169 Avery Bradley 6.00 15.00
170 James Anderson 3.00 8.00
171 Elliot Williams 3.00 8.00
172 Trevor Booker 4.00 10.00
173 Damion James 3.00 8.00
174 Dominique Jones 3.00 8.00
175 Quincy Pondexter 3.00 8.00
176 Jordan Crawford 4.00 10.00
177 Greivis Vasquez 4.00 10.00
178 Daniel Orton 3.00 8.00
179 Lazar Hayward 3.00 8.00
180 Dexter Pittman 3.00 8.00
181 Hassan Whiteside 10.00 25.00
182 Andy Rautins 3.00 8.00
183 Lance Stephenson 5.00 12.00
184 Devin Ebanks 3.00 8.00
185 Willie Warren 3.00 8.00

2010-11 Absolute Memorabilia Rookie Materials Jumbo Jersey Numbers Basketball Signatures

STATED PRINT RUN 25 SER.#'d SETS
UNPRICED PRIME PRINT RUN 5 SETS
151 John Wall 60.00 150.00
152 Evan Turner 10.00 25.00
153 Derrick Favors 12.00 30.00
154 Wesley Johnson 6.00 15.00
155 DeMarcus Cousins 30.00 80.00
156 Ekpe Udoh 6.00 15.00
157 Greg Monroe 12.00 30.00
158 Al-Farouq Aminu 10.00 25.00
159 Gordon Hayward 15.00 40.00
160 Paul George 150.00 300.00
161 Cole Aldrich 8.00 20.00
162 Xavier Henry 6.00 15.00
163 Ed Davis 6.00 15.00
164 Patrick Patterson 8.00 20.00
165 Larry Sanders 6.00 15.00
166 Luke Babbitt 8.00 20.00
167 Kevin Seraphin 6.00 15.00
168 Eric Bledsoe 12.00 30.00
169 Avery Bradley 12.00 30.00
170 James Anderson 6.00 15.00
171 Elliot Williams 6.00 15.00
172 Trevor Booker 8.00 20.00
173 Damion James 6.00 15.00
174 Dominique Jones 6.00 15.00
175 Quincy Pondexter 6.00 15.00
176 Jordan Crawford 8.00 20.00
177 Greivis Vasquez 8.00 20.00
178 Daniel Orton 6.00 15.00
179 Lazar Hayward 6.00 15.00
180 Dexter Pittman 6.00 15.00
181 Hassan Whiteside 50.00 120.00
182 Andy Rautins 6.00 15.00
183 Lance Stephenson 10.00 25.00
184 Devin Ebanks 6.00 15.00
185 Willie Warren 6.00 15.00

2010-11 Absolute Memorabilia Spectrum Signatures Gold

STATED PRINT RUN ONE TO 199 SER.#'d SETS
SOME UNPRICED DUE TO SCARCITY
1 Kevin Durant/25 100.00 200.00
3 Blake Griffin/99 30.00 80.00
5 Kobe Bryant/25 100.00 200.00
8 Deron Williams/25 10.00 25.00
10 Stephen Curry/49 125.00 250.00
16 Brandon Jennings/99 4.00 10.00
18 Joakim Noah/99 8.00 20.00
19 Tyreke Evans/15 10.00 25.00
24 LaMarcus Aldridge/99 8.00 20.00
30 Danny Granger/99 4.00 10.00
31 Chris Bosh/25 20.00 50.00
33 Jrue Holiday/199 6.00 15.00
35 DeMar DeRozan/199 8.00 20.00
39 David Lee/99 4.00 10.00
40 Ben Gordon/199 4.00 10.00
44 Caron Butler/99 5.00 12.00
47 O.J. Mayo/49 5.00 12.00
51 Al Horford/49 4.00 10.00
54 DeJuan Blair/99 4.00 10.00
55 Mike Dunleavy/99 4.00 10.00
56 Al Thornton/199 4.00 10.00
57 Lamar Odom/99 8.00 20.00
58 Andrea Bargnani/99 4.00 10.00
60 Russell Westbrook/25 25.00 60.00
62 Gerald Wallace/199 4.00 10.00
64 Al Jefferson/25 5.00 12.00
70 Aaron Brooks/199 4.00 10.00
71 Jason Kidd/49 10.00 25.00
73 Ty Lawson/35 10.00 25.00
74 Elton Brand/25 5.00 12.00
75 Terrence Williams/99 4.00 10.00
77 J.J. Redick/99 5.00 12.00
78 Chris Kaman/99 4.00 10.00
79 Gerald Henderson/199 4.00 10.00
80 Jeff Teague/199 4.00 10.00
83 Tyler Hansbrough/99 6.00 15.00
84 Derek Fisher/99 8.00 20.00
85 Boris Diaw/199 4.00 10.00
87 Toney Douglas/199 4.00 10.00
88 Robin Lopez/99 4.00 10.00
89 Zach Randolph/99 4.00 10.00
90 Carl Landry/199 4.00 10.00
96 Emeka Okafor/99 4.00 10.00
97 Brandon Roy/99 6.00 15.00
99 Devin Harris/25 5.00 12.00
100 Rodrigue Beaubois/143 4.00 10.00
104 Tim Hardaway/49 8.00 20.00
105 Sam Perkins/99 4.00 10.00
121 Bill Sharman/99 4.00 10.00
122 Danny Manning/99 5.00 12.00
125 Dan Majerle/99 8.00 20.00
126 Jeff Hornacek/49 5.00 12.00
127 George McGinnis/49 4.00 10.00
128 John Starks/99 12.00 30.00
129 Toni Kukoc/25 20.00 50.00
130 Byron Scott/49 5.00 12.00
131 Gus Williams/99 4.00 10.00
133 Campy Russell/99 4.00 10.00
135 Kurt Rambis/49 6.00 15.00
136 Jeremy Lin/199 60.00 120.00
137 Terrico White/199 2.00 5.00
138 Timofey Mozgov/199 3.00 8.00
139 Sherron Collins/199 2.00 5.00
140 Ishmael Smith/199 3.00 8.00
142 Jeremy Evans/199 2.00 5.00
143 Tiago Splitter/199 10.00 25.00
144 Landry Fields/199 6.00 15.00
146 Derrick Caracter/199 4.00 10.00
149 Armon Johnson/199 2.00 5.00
150 Omer Asik/199 10.00 25.00

2010-11 Absolute Memorabilia Spectrum Signatures Platinum

*PLATINUM STARS: .6X TO 1.5X GOLD
*PLATINUM RCs: .75X TO 2X GOLD
STATED PRINT RUN ONE TO 25 SER.#'d SETS
SOME UNPRICED DUE TO SCARCITY
3 Blake Griffin/25 50.00 120.00
16 Brandon Jennings/25 10.00 25.00
57 Lamar Odom/25 10.00 25.00
64 Al Jefferson/25 6.00 15.00
72 Danilo Gallinari/25 6.00 15.00
77 J.J. Redick/25 10.00 25.00
83 Tyler Hansbrough/25 8.00 20.00
92 Darren Collison/25 8.00 20.00
97 Brandon Roy/25 8.00 20.00
117 Darryl Dawkins/25 6.00 15.00
127 George McGinnis/25 8.00 20.00
128 John Starks/25 15.00 40.00
136 Jeremy Lin/25 350.00 600.00
150 Omer Asik/25 15.00 40.00

2010-11 Absolute Memorabilia Star Gazing

COMPLETE SET (35) 30.00 60.00
STATED PRINT RUN 399 SER.#'d SETS
*SPECTRUM: .6X TO 1.5X BASE HI
SPECTRUM PRINT RUN 100 SER.#'d SETS
UNPRICED BLACK PRINT RUN ONE SET
1 Kobe Bryant 4.00 10.00
2 Kevin Durant 2.50 6.00
3 Dwyane Wade 1.50 4.00
4 Amare Stoudemire .75 2.00
5 Dwight Howard .75 2.00
6 LeBron James 5.00 12.00
7 Pau Gasol 1.00 2.50
8 Rajon Rondo 1.00 2.50
9 Carmelo Anthony 1.25 3.00
10 Monta Ellis .75 2.00
11 Dirk Nowitzki 1.25 3.00
12 Derrick Rose 1.25 3.00
13 Kevin Martin .75 2.00
14 Russell Westbrook 2.50 6.00
15 Eric Gordon .75 2.00
16 Luis Scola .75 2.00
17 Michael Beasley .60 1.50
18 Rudy Gay 1.00 2.50
19 Deron Williams .75 2.00
20 Paul Pierce 1.00 2.50
21 Danny Granger .75 2.00
22 Paul Millsap .75 2.00
23 Kevin Garnett 1.50 4.00
24 Chris Paul 1.25 3.00
25 Brandon Roy 1.00 2.50
26 Kevin Love 1.00 2.50
27 Chris Bosh 1.00 2.50
28 Tony Parker 1.00 2.50
29 Steve Nash 1.00 2.50
30 Tyreke Evans .60 1.50
31 Joe Johnson .75 2.00
32 Ray Allen 1.00 2.50
33 Zach Randolph .75 2.00
34 Gerald Wallace .75 2.00
35 Brandon Jennings .60 1.50

2010-11 Absolute Memorabilia Star Gazing Materials Jumbo Jersey Number

STATED PRINT RUN 2 TO 25 SER.#'d SETS
SOME UNPRICED DUE TO SCARCITY
UNPRICED PRIME PRINT RUN 3 TO 10 SETS
1 Kobe Bryant/25 15.00 40.00
2 Kevin Durant/25 12.00 30.00
3 Dwyane Wade/25 8.00 20.00
5 Dwight Howard/25 4.00 10.00
6 LeBron James/25 15.00 40.00
7 Pau Gasol/25 5.00 12.00
8 Rajon Rondo/25 8.00 20.00
11 Dirk Nowitzki/25 6.00 15.00
12 Derrick Rose/25 6.00 15.00
14 Russell Westbrook/25 12.00 30.00
16 Luis Scola/25 4.00 10.00
19 Deron Williams/25 4.00 10.00
20 Paul Pierce/25 5.00 12.00
23 Kevin Garnett/25 8.00 20.00
24 Chris Paul/25 6.00 15.00
25 Brandon Roy/25 5.00 12.00
26 Kevin Love/25 5.00 12.00
27 Chris Bosh/25 5.00 12.00
28 Tony Parker/25 5.00 12.00
30 Tyreke Evans/25 3.00 8.00
31 Joe Johnson/25 4.00 10.00
35 Brandon Jennings/25 3.00 8.00

2010-11 Absolute Memorabilia Star Gazing Materials Jumbo Jersey Number Signatures

STATED PRINT RUN 5 TO 25 SER.#'d SETS
SOME UNPRICED DUE TO SCARCITY
UNPRICED PRIME PRINT RUN ONE TO 5 SETS
1 Kobe Bryant/25 125.00 250.00
2 Kevin Durant/25 75.00 200.00
14 Russell Westbrook/25 50.00 120.00
25 Brandon Roy/25 10.00 25.00
35 Brandon Jennings/25 12.50 30.00

2010-11 Absolute Memorabilia Star Gazing Materials

STATED PRINT RUN 5 TO 49 SER.#'d SETS
SOME UNPRICED DUE TO SCARCITY
UNPRICED PRIME PRINT RUN ONE TO 10 SETS
1 Kobe Bryant/49 10.00 25.00
2 Kevin Durant/49 8.00 20.00
3 Dwyane Wade/49 5.00 12.00
4 Amare Stoudemire/49 2.50 6.00
5 Dwight Howard/49 2.50 6.00
6 LeBron James/49 10.00 25.00
7 Pau Gasol/49 3.00 8.00
8 Rajon Rondo/49 3.00 8.00
9 Carmelo Anthony/25 5.00 12.00
11 Dirk Nowitzki/49 4.00 10.00
12 Derrick Rose/49 4.00 10.00
14 Russell Westbrook/49 8.00 20.00
16 Luis Scola/49 2.50 6.00
17 Michael Beasley/49 2.00 5.00
18 Rudy Gay/49 3.00 8.00
19 Deron Williams/49 2.50 6.00
20 Paul Pierce/49 3.00 8.00
23 Kevin Garnett/49 5.00 12.00
24 Chris Paul/49 4.00 10.00
25 Brandon Roy/49 3.00 8.00
26 Kevin Love/49 3.00 8.00
27 Chris Bosh/49 3.00 8.00
28 Tony Parker/49 3.00 8.00
29 Steve Nash/49 3.00 8.00
30 Tyreke Evans/49 2.00 5.00
31 Joe Johnson/49 2.50 6.00
32 Ray Allen/49 3.00 8.00
35 Brandon Jennings/49 2.00 5.00

2010-11 Absolute Memorabilia Star Gazing Materials Signatures

STATED PRINT RUN 5 TO 25 SER.#'d SETS
SOME UNPRICED DUE TO SCARCITY
UNPRICED PRIME PRINT RUN ONE TO 5 SETS
1 Kobe Bryant/25 100.00 200.00
2 Kevin Durant/25 60.00 120.00
14 Russell Westbrook/25 40.00 100.00
25 Brandon Roy/25 10.00 25.00
35 Brandon Jennings/25 8.00 20.00

2010-11 Absolute Memorabilia Team Quads TEAM Die Cut Materials

STATED PRINT RUN 100 SER.#'d SETS
UNPRICED PRIME PRINT RUN 10 SETS
1 Los Angeles Lakers 15.00 40.00
2 Boston Celtics 12.00 30.00
3 Dallas Mavericks 8.00 20.00
4 Orlando Magic 6.00 15.00
5 San Antonio Spurs 6.00 15.00

2010-11 Absolute Memorabilia Team Tandems Materials

STATED PRINT RUN 100 SER.#'d SETS
UNPRICED PRIME PRINT RUN 10 SETS
1 L.James/D.Wade 12.00 30.00
2 R.Rondo/P.Pierce 6.00 15.00
3 P.Gasol/K.Bryant 8.00 20.00
4 T.Parker/T.Duncan 4.00 10.00
5 R.Westbrook/K.Durant 10.00 25.00
6 S.Curry/D.Lee 6.00 15.00
7 D.Rose/J.Noah 10.00 25.00
8 B.Jennings/A.Bogut 4.00 10.00
9 C.Anthony/C.Billups 4.00 10.00
10 D.Nowitzki/J.Kidd 6.00 15.00

2010-11 Absolute Memorabilia Team Trios NBA Materials

STATED PRINT RUN 40 TO 100 SER.#'d SETS
UNPRICED PRIME PRINT RUN 10 SETS
1 Bryant/Gasol/Odom 10.00 25.00
2 Wade/James/Bosh 15.00 40.00
3 Pierce/Garnett/Rondo 12.00 30.00
4 Johnson/Smith/Horford 5.00 12.00
5 Anthony/Billups/Nene 5.00 12.00
6 Paul/West/Okafor 5.00 12.00
7 Curry/Biedrins/Lee/40 8.00 20.00
8 Rose/Noah/Deng 12.50 30.00
9 Nowitzki/Kidd/Terry 8.00 20.00
10 Williams/Kirilenko/Jefferson 5.00 12.00

2010-11 Absolute Memorabilia Tools of the Trade Materials Jumbo

STATED PRINT RUN ONE TO 99 SER.#'d SETS
SOME UNPRICED DUE TO SCARCITY
1 Kevin Durant/99 10.00 25.00
2 Brandon Jennings/99 2.50 6.00
3 Derrick Rose/49 5.00 12.00
4 LeBron James/49 15.00 40.00
5 Kobe Bryant/49 15.00 40.00
6 Deron Williams/99 3.00 8.00
7 Amare Stoudemire/49 3.00 8.00
8 Jonny Flynn/99 3.00 8.00
9 Chris Paul/49 5.00 12.00
10 Gary Payton/49 6.00 15.00
11 Anfernee Hardaway/99 12.50 30.00
12 Brook Lopez/99 3.00 8.00
13 Blake Griffin/99 4.00 10.00
14 LaMarcus Aldridge/99 4.00 10.00
15 Rajon Rondo/49 6.00 15.00
16 Dan Majerle/49 6.00 15.00
17 Mark Price/49 8.00 20.00
18 Dwight Howard/99 3.00 8.00
19 Ben Gordon/25 3.00 8.00
20 Stephen Curry/49 15.00 40.00
21 Carmelo Anthony/49 6.00 15.00
22 Dennis Rodman/99 10.00 25.00
23 Paul Pierce/99 4.00 10.00
24 Kevin Love/99 4.00 10.00
25 David Robinson/49 6.00 15.00
26 Hakeem Olajuwon/49 8.00 20.00
27 Joakim Noah/25 5.00 12.00
28 Dwyane Wade/99 6.00 15.00
29 Charles Oakley/99 4.00 10.00
30 Alonzo Mourning/25 15.00 40.00
31 Dirk Nowitzki/99 8.00 20.00
32 Steve Nash/99 5.00 12.00

2010-11 Absolute Memorabilia Tools of the Trade Materials Jumbo Jersey Numbers

STATED PRINT RUN ONE TO 99 SER.#'d SETS
SOME UNPRICED DUE TO SCARCITY
UNPRICED PRIME PRINT RUN 3 TO 10 SETS
1 Kevin Durant/99 10.00 25.00
2 Brandon Jennings/99 2.50 6.00
3 Derrick Rose/25 15.00 40.00
4 LeBron James/49 25.00 60.00
5 Kobe Bryant/49 15.00 40.00
6 Deron Williams/99 3.00 8.00
7 Amare Stoudemire/49 3.00 8.00
8 Jonny Flynn/49 3.00 8.00
9 Chris Paul/25 5.00 12.00
10 Gary Payton/49 6.00 15.00
11 Anfernee Hardaway/99 12.50 30.00
13 Blake Griffin/99 4.00 10.00
14 LaMarcus Aldridge/99 4.00 10.00
15 Rajon Rondo/49 6.00 15.00
16 Dan Majerle/25 10.00 25.00
17 Mark Price/49 10.00 25.00
18 Dwight Howard/99 3.00 8.00
21 Carmelo Anthony/49 6.00 15.00
22 Dennis Rodman/49 10.00 25.00
23 Paul Pierce/99 4.00 10.00
24 Kevin Love/99 4.00 10.00
25 David Robinson/25 8.00 20.00
26 Hakeem Olajuwon/49 8.00 20.00
27 Joakim Noah/25 6.00 15.00
28 Dwyane Wade/99 6.00 15.00
29 Charles Oakley/25 4.00 10.00
30 Alonzo Mourning/25 15.00 40.00
31 Dirk Nowitzki/49 6.00 15.00
32 Steve Nash/99 5.00 12.00

2010-11 Absolute Memorabilia Tools of the Trade Materials Prime Black Double Spectrum

STATED PRINT RUN ONE TO 25 SER.#'d SETS
SOME UNPRICED DUE TO SCARCITY
UNPRICED SIG.PRINT RUN ONE TO 5 SETS
11 Anfernee Hardaway/25 30.00 80.00
13 Blake Griffin/25 25.00 60.00
14 LaMarcus Aldridge/25 8.00 20.00
17 Mark Price/25 15.00 40.00
23 Paul Pierce/25 12.00 30.00
29 Charles Oakley/25 10.00 25.00

2010-11 Absolute Memorabilia Tools of the Trade Materials Prime Black Spectrum

STATED PRINT RUN ONE TO 25 SER.#'d SETS
SOME UNPRICED DUE TO SCARCITY
UNPRICED JUMBO PRINT RUN 3 TO 10 SETS
UNPRICED SIG.PRINT RUN ONE TO 10 SETS
11 Anfernee Hardaway/25 25.00 60.00
13 Blake Griffin/25 25.00 60.00
14 LaMarcus Aldridge/25 8.00 20.00
17 Mark Price/25 10.00 25.00
23 Paul Pierce/25 10.00 25.00
29 Charles Oakley/25 8.00 20.00

2010-11 Absolute Memorabilia Tools of the Trade Materials Prime Black Triple Spectrum

STATED PRINT RUN ONE TO 25 SER.#'d SETS
UNPRICED SIG.PRINT RUN ONE TO 5 SETS
8 Jonny Flynn/25 6.00 15.00
11 Anfernee Hardaway/25 20.00 50.00
13 Blake Griffin/25 30.00 80.00
14 LaMarcus Aldridge/25 10.00 25.00
17 Mark Price/25 15.00 40.00
23 Paul Pierce/25 15.00 40.00
29 Charles Oakley/25 15.00 40.00

2015-16 Absolute Memorabilia

101-160 PRINT RUN 999 SER.#'d SETS
161-200 PRINT RUN 999 SER.#'d SETS
1 Jonas Valanciunas .50 1.25
2 Deron Williams .50 1.25
3 Dwyane Wade 1.00 2.50
4 Harrison Barnes .50 1.25
5 Anthony Davis 1.25 3.00
6 DeAndre Jordan .60 1.50
7 Nikola Vucevic .50 1.25
8 Al Horford .50 1.25
9 Mason Plumlee .50 1.25
10 Kemba Walker .60 1.50
11 Kyle Lowry .50 1.25
12 Dirk Nowitzki .75 2.00
13 Goran Dragic .50 1.25
14 Klay Thompson .75 2.00
15 Jrue Holiday .50 1.25
16 Paul Pierce .60 1.50
17 Tobias Harris .50 1.25
18 Jeff Teague .50 1.25
19 DeMarcus Cousins .60 1.50
20 Nicolas Batum .50 1.25
21 Terrence Ross .50 1.25
22 Wesley Matthews .40 1.00
23 Giannis Antetokounmpo 1.25 3.00
24 Stephen Curry 2.50 6.00
25 Tyreke Evans .40 1.00
26 Jordan Clarkson .60 1.50
27 Victor Oladipo .50 1.25
28 Kyle Korver .50 1.25
29 Rajon Rondo .60 1.50
30 Derrick Rose .75 2.00
31 Gordon Hayward .60 1.50
32 Danilo Gallinari .50 1.25
33 Greg Monroe .50 1.25
34 Dwight Howard .50 1.25
35 Arron Afflalo .40 1.00
36 Kobe Bryant 2.50 6.00
37 Nerlens Noel .50 1.25
38 Evan Turner .50 1.25
39 Rudy Gay .60 1.50
40 Jimmy Butler .60 1.50
41 Rudy Gobert .60 1.50
42 Jusuf Nurkic .40 1.00
43 Jabari Parker .75 2.00
44 James Harden 1.00 2.50
45 Carmelo Anthony .75 2.00
46 Roy Hibbert .50 1.25
47 Robert Covington .40 1.00
48 Jared Sullinger .40 1.00
49 Kawhi Leonard 1.00 2.50
50 Joakim Noah .50 1.25
51 Trey Burke .40 1.00
52 Kenneth Faried .50 1.25
53 Michael Carter-Williams .40 1.00
54 Ty Lawson .40 1.00
55 Robin Lopez .40 1.00
56 Marc Gasol .60 1.50
57 Brandon Knight .50 1.25
58 Marcus Smart .50 1.25
59 LaMarcus Aldridge .60 1.50
60 Pau Gasol .60 1.50
61 Bradley Beal .60 1.50
62 Andre Drummond .60 1.50
63 Andrew Wiggins 1.00 2.50
64 Monta Ellis .50 1.25
65 Kevin Durant 1.50 4.00
66 Mike Conley .60 1.50
67 Eric Bledsoe .50 1.25
68 Bojan Bogdanovic .40 1.00
69 Manu Ginobili .60 1.50
70 Kevin Love .60 1.50
71 John Wall .75 2.00
72 Brandon Jennings .40 1.00
73 Kevin Garnett 1.00 2.50
74 Paul George .75 2.00
75 Russell Westbrook 1.50 4.00
76 Vince Carter .75 2.00
77 Tyson Chandler .50 1.25
78 Brook Lopez .50 1.25
79 Tim Duncan 1.00 2.50
80 Kyrie Irving 1.25 3.00
81 Marcin Gortat .50 1.25
82 Reggie Jackson .50 1.25
83 Ricky Rubio .60 1.50
84 Blake Griffin .60 1.50
85 Serge Ibaka .50 1.25
86 Zach Randolph .50 1.25
87 Damian Lillard 1.25 3.00
88 Joe Johnson .50 1.25
89 Tony Parker .60 1.50
90 LeBron James 2.50 6.00
91 Nene .50 1.25
92 Draymond Green .75 2.00
93 Zach LaVine .60 1.50
94 Chris Paul .75 2.00
95 Elfrid Payton .50 1.25
96 Chris Bosh .60 1.50
97 Gerald Henderson .40 1.00
98 Al Jefferson .50 1.25
99 DeMar DeRozan .60 1.50
100 Chandler Parsons .50 1.25
101 Bill Russell 1.25 3.00
102 Rick Fox .60 1.50
103 Dell Curry .50 1.25
104 Shareef Abdur-Rahim .60 1.50
105 Drazen Petrovic .75 2.00
106 Mitch Richmond .75 2.00
107 James Worthy 1.00 2.50
108 John Stockton 1.25 3.00
109 Allan Houston .60 1.50
110 Magic Johnson 2.00 5.00
111 Bob Cousy 1.25 3.00
112 Rik Smits .60 1.50
113 Dennis Johnson .60 1.50
114 Shawn Kemp 1.25 3.00
115 Elgin Baylor .75 2.00
116 Moses Malone .75 2.00
117 Jason Kidd .75 2.00
118 Julius Erving 1.25 3.00
119 Manute Bol .75 2.00
120 Allen Iverson 1.00 2.50
121 Chauncey Billups .75 2.00
122 Dennis Rodman 1.50 4.00
123 Robert Horry .60 1.50
124 Steve Kerr .75 2.00
125 Elvin Hayes .75 2.00
126 Tracy McGrady .75 2.00
127 Jerry Stackhouse .60 1.50
128 Karl Malone 1.00 2.50
129 Alonzo Mourning 1.00 2.50
130 Muggsy Bogues .60 1.50
131 Clyde Drexler 1.00 2.50
132 Rony Seikaly .50 1.25
133 Dikembe Mutombo .75 2.00
134 Steve Nash .75 2.00
135 Gary Payton .75 2.00
136 Wilt Chamberlain 1.50 4.00
137 Larry Bird 2.00 5.00
138 Jerry West 1.00 2.50
139 Anfernee Hardaway 2.00 5.00
140 Oscar Robertson 1.00 2.50
141 Damon Stoudamire .60 1.50
142 Scottie Pippen 1.50 4.00
143 Dino Radja .50 1.25
144 Michael Redd .60 1.50
145 Grant Hill 1.00 2.50
146 Yao Ming 1.00 2.50
147 John Havlicek 1.00 2.50
148 Latrell Sprewell .60 1.50
149 Antonio McDyess .60 1.50
150 Pete Maravich 1.25 3.00
151 David Robinson 1.25 3.00
152 Shaquille O'Neal 1.50 4.00
153 Dominique Wilkins 1.00 2.50
154 Mike Bibby .60 1.50
155 Hakeem Olajuwon 1.00 2.50
156 Tim Legler .50 1.25
157 John Starks .60 1.50
158 Louie Dampier .75 2.00
159 Baron Davis .60 1.50
160 Richard Hamilton .60 1.50
161 Justin Anderson RC .75 2.00
162 Frank Kaminsky RC 1.00 2.50
163 Jarell Martin RC .75 2.00
164 Devin Booker RC 3.00 8.00
165 Montrezl Harrell RC .75 2.00
166 Rashad Vaughn RC .60 1.50
167 Karl-Anthony Towns RC 5.00 12.00
168 Richaun Holmes RC .75 2.00
169 Nemanja Bjelica RC .75 2.00
170 Mario Hezonja RC .75 2.00
171 Bobby Portis RC 1.00 2.50
172 Justise Winslow RC 1.00 2.50
173 Larry Nance Jr. RC 1.00 2.50
174 Cameron Payne RC .75 2.00
175 Jordan Mickey RC .60 1.50
176 Sam Dekker RC .75 2.00
177 Pat Connaughton RC .60 1.50
178 D'Angelo Russell RC 2.50 6.00
179 Cliff Alexander RC .60 1.50
180 Willie Cauley-Stein RC 1.00 2.50
181 Rondae Hollis-Jefferson RC .75 2.00
182 Myles Turner RC 1.00 2.50
183 R.J. Hunter RC .60 1.50
184 Kelly Oubre Jr. RC .75 2.00
185 Anthony Brown RC .60 1.50
186 Jerian Grant RC .60 1.50
187 Jonathon Simmons RC 1.00 2.50
188 Jahlil Okafor RC 1.25 3.00
189 Joe Young RC .75 2.00
190 Emmanuel Mudiay RC 1.00 2.50
191 Tyus Jones RC 1.00 2.50
192 Trey Lyles RC 1.00 2.50
193 Chris McCullough RC .60 1.50
194 Terry Rozier RC .75 2.00
195 Rakeem Christmas RC .60 1.50
196 Delon Wright RC .75 2.00
197 Walter Tavares RC .60 1.50
198 Kristaps Porzingis RC 2.50 6.00
199 T.J. McConnell RC 5.00 12.00
200 Stanley Johnson RC .75 2.00

2015-16 Absolute Memorabilia Frequent Flyer Material Autographs

RANDOM INSERTS IN PACKS
PRINT RUNS B/WN 40-99 COPIES PER
EXCHANGE DEADLINE 8/5/2017
*PRIME: .5X TO 1.2X BASIC
FRAD Adrian Dantley/65 5.00 12.00
FRAG A.C. Green/99 6.00 15.00
FRAG Aaron Gordon/49 5.00 12.00
FRAR Andre Roberson/99 4.00 10.00
FRBB Bojan Bogdanovic/99 4.00 10.00
FRBL Bill Laimbeer/99 5.00 12.00
FRBM Ben McLemore/49 4.00 10.00
FRCD Clyde Drexler/49 12.00 30.00
FRCL Carl Landry/99 4.00 10.00
FRDC DeMarre Carroll/99 4.00 10.00
FRDE Dante Exum/49 5.00 12.00
FRDM Donatas Motiejunas/99 4.00 10.00
FRDM Dan Majerle/99 5.00 12.00
FRDR Dino Radja/99 12.00 30.00
FRDS Dennis Schroder/99 5.00 12.00
FREK Enes Kanter/99 4.00 10.00
FREP Elfrid Payton/99 5.00 12.00
FRFE Festus Ezeli/99 4.00 10.00
FRGA G. Antetokounmpo/99 25.00 60.00
FRGH Gerald Henderson/99 4.00 10.00
FRGH Grant Hill/49
FRGP Gary Payton/49 8.00 20.00
FRJC Jordan Clarkson/99 6.00 15.00
FRJD Joe Dumars/49 6.00 15.00
FRJE James Ennis/99 4.00 10.00
FRJK Jason Kidd/40 15.00 40.00
FRJN Jusuf Nurkic/99 4.00 10.00
FRJP Jabari Parker/49 12.00 30.00
FRJS John Starks/99 5.00 12.00
FRKA Kyle Anderson/99 4.00 10.00
FRKC Kentavious Caldwell-Pope/49
FRKV Kiki Vandeweghe/99 5.00 12.00
FRKV Keith Van Horn/99 5.00 12.00
FRLG Langston Galloway/99 4.00 10.00
FRMD Matthew Dellavedova/99 5.00 12.00
FRMF Michael Finley/49 6.00 15.00
FRMK Michael Kidd-Gilchrist/49 5.00 12.00
FRMM Mitch McGary/99 4.00 10.00
FRMP Mark Price/99 6.00 15.00
FRMS Marcus Smart/49 8.00 20.00
FRNM Nikola Mirotic/99 5.00 12.00
FRNS Nik Stauskas/99 4.00 10.00
FRNV Noah Vonleh/49
FRPB Patrick Beverley/99 4.00 10.00
FRPT P.J. Tucker/99 4.00 10.00
FRRA Ray Allen/49 10.00 25.00
FRRA Rafer Alston/99 4.00 10.00
FRRG Rudy Gobert/99 6.00 15.00
FRRH Richard Hamilton/49 5.00 12.00
FRRH Roy Hibbert/99 5.00 12.00
FRRK Ryan Kelly/99 4.00 10.00
FRRP Robert Parish/99 6.00 15.00
FRRS Ralph Sampson/49 5.00 12.00
FRSH Solomon Hill/99 4.00 10.00
FRSM Shabazz Muhammad/49 5.00 12.00
FRTA Tony Allen/99 4.00 10.00
FRTB Trey Burke/49 4.00 10.00
FRTG Taj Gibson/99 5.00 12.00
FRUH Udonis Haslem/99 4.00 10.00
FRVD Vlade Divac/99 6.00 15.00
FRVO Victor Oladipo/49 5.00 12.00
FRWC Wilson Chandler/99 5.00 12.00

2015-16 Absolute Memorabilia Frequent Flyer Materials

RANDOM INSERTS IN PACKS
STATED PRINT RUN 99 SER.#'d SETS
*PRIME/20-25: .75X TO 2X BASIC
1 Anthony Davis 6.00 15.00
2 Jeff Teague 2.50 6.00
3 Brook Lopez 2.50 6.00
4 David Lee 2.00 5.00
5 Kemba Walker 3.00 8.00
6 Mason Plumlee 2.50 6.00
7 Elfrid Payton 2.50 6.00
8 Roy Hibbert 2.50 6.00
9 Aaron Gordon 2.50 6.00
10 Tony Allen 2.00 5.00
11 Avery Bradley 2.50 6.00
12 Joe Johnson 2.50 6.00
13 Chandler Parsons 2.50 6.00
14 Kenneth Faried 2.50 6.00
15 David West 3.00 8.00
16 Michael Kidd-Gilchrist 2.50 6.00
17 Eric Bledsoe 2.50 6.00
18 Serge Ibaka 2.50 6.00
19 Al Horford 2.50 6.00
20 Tony Wroten 2.00 5.00
21 Ben McLemore 2.00 5.00
22 Josh Smith 2.50 6.00
23 Chris Andersen 2.50 6.00
24 Kevin Love 3.00 8.00
25 Doug McDermott 2.50 6.00
26 Nick Young 2.50 6.00
27 George Hill 2.50 6.00
28 Shabazz Napier 2.00 5.00
29 Alex Len 2.00 5.00
30 Trey Burke 2.00 5.00
31 Boris Diaw 2.50 6.00
32 Jrue Holiday 2.50 6.00
33 Danilo Gallinari 2.50 6.00
34 Lance Stephenson 2.50 6.00
35 DeMar DeRozan 3.00 8.00
36 Paul Pierce 3.00 8.00
37 T.J. Warren 2.50 6.00
38 Goran Dragic 2.50 6.00
39 Andre Drummond 3.00 8.00
40 Tristan Thompson 2.50 6.00
41 Bradley Beal 3.00 8.00
42 Jusuf Nurkic 2.00 5.00
43 Danny Green 2.50 6.00
44 Deron Williams 2.50 6.00
45 Langston Galloway 2.00 5.00
46 Rajon Rondo 3.00 8.00
47 Taj Gibson 2.50 6.00
48 Greg Monroe 2.50 6.00
49 Andre Iguodala 2.50 6.00
50 Ty Lawson 2.00 5.00
51 Brandon Jennings 2.00 5.00
52 Kelly Olynyk 2.00 5.00
53 Dante Exum 2.50 6.00
54 Marcus Smart 2.50 6.00
55 Draymond Green 4.00 10.00
56 Reggie Jackson 2.50 6.00
57 Jared Sullinger 2.00 5.00
58 Terrence Ross 2.50 6.00
59 Andrew Bogut 2.50 6.00
60 Tyreke Evans 2.00 5.00
61 Toni Kukoc 3.00 8.00
62 Alonzo Mourning 4.00 10.00

2015-16 Absolute Memorabilia Freshman Flyer Jersey Autographs

RANDOM INSERTS IN PACKS
PRINT RUNS B/WN 49-149 COPIES PER
EXCHANGE DEADLINE 8/5/2017
*PRIME: .5X TO 1.2X BASIC
FJAAB Anthony Brown/149 4.00 10.00
FJABP Bobby Portis/149 10.00 25.00
FJACM Chris McCullough/149 4.00 10.00
FJACP Cameron Payne/149 5.00 12.00
FJADB Devin Booker/149 25.00 60.00
FJADR D'Angelo Russell/149 25.00 60.00
FJADW Delon Wright/149 5.00 12.00
FJAEM Emmanuel Mudiay/149 6.00 15.00
FJAFK Frank Kaminsky/149 6.00 15.00
FJAJA Justin Anderson/149 5.00 12.00
FJAJG Jerian Grant/149 4.00 10.00
FJAJH Josh Huestis/149 4.00 10.00
FJAJM Jarell Martin/149 5.00 12.00
FJAJM Jordan Mickey/149 4.00 10.00
FJAJO Jahlil Okafor/149 15.00 40.00
FJAJR Josh Richardson/149 6.00 15.00
FJAJW Justise Winslow/149 10.00 25.00
FJAJY Joe Young/149 5.00 12.00
FJAKL Kevon Looney/149 3.00 8.00
FJAKO Kelly Oubre Jr./149 5.00 12.00
FJAKP Kristaps Porzingis/149 50.00 120.00
FJAKT Karl-Anthony Towns/149 75.00 200.00
FJAMH Mario Hezonja/149 5.00 12.00
FJAMH Montrezl Harrell/149 5.00 12.00
FJAMT Myles Turner/149 6.00 15.00
FJAPC Pat Connaughton/149 4.00 10.00
FJARC Rakeem Christmas/149 4.00 10.00
FJARH Richaun Holmes/149 5.00 12.00
FJARH R.J. Hunter/149 4.00 10.00
FJARH Rondae Hollis-Jefferson/149 5.00 12.00
FJARV Rashad Vaughn/149 4.00 10.00
FJASD Sam Dekker/149 5.00 12.00
FJASJ Stanley Johnson/149 5.00 12.00
FJATJ Tyus Jones/49 6.00 15.00
FJATL Trey Lyles/149 6.00 15.00
FJATR Terry Rozier/149 5.00 12.00
FJAWC Willie Cauley-Stein/149 6.00 15.00
FJAWT Walter Tavares/149 4.00 10.00

2015-16 Absolute Memorabilia Freshman Flyer Jumbo Jerseys

RANDOM INSERTS IN PACKS
STATED PRINT RUN 99 SER.#'d SETS
*PRIME: 1.2X TO 3X BASIC
1 Karl-Anthony Towns 10.00 25.00
2 D'Angelo Russell 6.00 15.00
3 Jahlil Okafor 4.00 10.00
4 Kristaps Porzingis 8.00 20.00
5 Mario Hezonja 2.50 6.00
6 Willie Cauley-Stein 3.00 8.00
7 Emmanuel Mudiay 4.00 10.00
8 Stanley Johnson 2.50 6.00
9 Frank Kaminsky 3.00 8.00
10 Justise Winslow 3.00 8.00
11 Myles Turner 3.00 8.00
12 Trey Lyles 3.00 8.00
13 Devin Booker 10.00 25.00
14 Cameron Payne 2.50 6.00
15 Kelly Oubre Jr. 2.50 6.00
16 Terry Rozier 2.50 6.00
17 Rashad Vaughn 2.00 5.00
18 Sam Dekker 2.50 6.00
19 Jerian Grant 2.00 5.00
20 Delon Wright 2.50 6.00
21 Justin Anderson 2.50 6.00
22 Bobby Portis 3.00 8.00
23 Rondae Hollis-Jefferson 2.50 6.00
24 Tyus Jones 3.00 8.00
25 Jarell Martin 2.50 6.00
26 R.J. Hunter 2.00 5.00
27 Chris McCullough 2.00 5.00
28 Montrezl Harrell 2.50 6.00
29 Jordan Mickey 2.00 5.00
30 Anthony Brown 2.00 5.00
31 Rakeem Christmas 2.00 5.00
32 Richaun Holmes 2.50 6.00
33 Pat Connaughton 2.00 5.00
34 Josh Huestis 2.00 5.00
35 Joe Young 2.50 6.00
36 Josh Richardson 3.00 8.00
37 Walter Tavares 2.00 5.00
38 Kevon Looney 2.50 6.00

2015-16 Absolute Memorabilia Glass

RANDOM INSERTS IN PACKS
EXCHANGE DEADLINE 8/5/2017
1 Kyrie Irving 20.00 50.00
2 James Harden EXCH 15.00 40.00
3 Chris Paul EXCH 12.00 30.00
4 Damian Lillard EXCH 20.00 50.00
5 Blake Griffin EXCH 10.00 25.00
6 Magic Johnson EXCH 25.00 60.00
7 Tim Duncan EXCH 40.00 100.00
8 Julius Erving 25.00 60.00
9 Kobe Bryant EXCH 60.00 150.00
10 Scottie Pippen EXCH 20.00 50.00
11 LeBron James 50.00 120.00
12 Andrew Wiggins EXCH 20.00 50.00
13 Stephen Curry 100.00 200.00
14 Kevin Garnett EXCH 15.00 40.00
15 Dwyane Wade EXCH 60.00 150.00
16 Larry Bird EXCH 25.00 60.00
17 Anthony Davis EXCH 40.00 100.00
18 Allen Iverson 40.00 100.00
19 Kevin Durant 25.00 60.00
20 Pete Maravich EXCH 15.00 40.00

2015-16 Absolute Memorabilia Heroes Autographs

RANDOM INSERTS IN PACKS
PRINT RUNS B/WN 25-149 COPIES PER
EXCHANGE DEADLINE 8/5/2017
1 Rik Smits/149 5.00 12.00
2 Tony Parker/25
3 Steve Kerr/99 8.00 20.00
4 Kobe Bryant/25 125.00 250.00
5 Artis Gilmore/49 5.00 12.00
6 Karl Malone/25 40.00 100.00
7 Rick Fox/49 5.00 12.00
8 Kyrie Irving/25 60.00 150.00
9 Robert Horry/99 5.00 12.00
10 Andrew Wiggins/25 30.00 80.00
11 Antoine Walker/149 5.00 12.00
12 Marcus Smart/49 10.00 25.00
13 Tim Hardaway/149 6.00 15.00
14 Kevin Durant/25
16 Anthony Davis/25 60.00 150.00
17 Jerry Stackhouse/99 5.00 12.00
18 Jabari Parker/25 40.00 100.00
19 Rolando Blackman/99 5.00 12.00
20 Dennis Rodman/25 50.00 120.00
21 Jo Jo White/149 5.00 12.00
22 Christian Laettner/49 5.00 12.00
23 Cedric Ceballos/149 4.00 10.00
24 Oscar Robertson/25 60.00 150.00
25 Robert Parish/49 6.00 15.00
26 Jerry West/25 30.00 80.00
27 Earl Monroe/99 6.00 15.00
28 Tom Chambers/25 12.00 30.00
29 Damon Stoudamire/149 5.00 12.00
30 Vince Carter/25 25.00 60.00

2015-16 Absolute Memorabilia Heroes Materials

RANDOM INSERTS IN PACKS
STATED PRINT RUN 99 SER.#'d SETS
*PRIME/25: .75X TO 2X BASIC
1 Ray Allen 3.00 8.00
2 Dan Majerle 2.50 6.00
3 Shawn Bradley 2.00 5.00
4 Hakeem Olajuwon 4.00 10.00
5 James Harden 5.00 12.00
6 Kareem Abdul-Jabbar 5.00 12.00
7 LeBron James 12.00 30.00
8 Allen Iverson 5.00 12.00
9 Mark Jackson 2.50 6.00
10 Brad Daugherty 2.50 6.00
11 Richard Hamilton 2.50 6.00
12 Danny Manning 2.50 6.00
13 Walter Davis 2.00 5.00
14 Jamal Mashburn 3.00 8.00
15 John Wall 4.00 10.00
16 Kevin Duckworth 2.00 5.00
17 Marcin Gortat 2.50 6.00
18 Anfernee Hardaway 8.00 20.00
19 Michael Redd 2.50 6.00
20 Chris Mullin 3.00 8.00
21 Robert Parish 3.00 8.00
22 Adrian Dantley 2.50 6.00
23 Kobe Bryant 10.00 25.00
24 Jerry Stackhouse 2.50 6.00
25 Kevin Garnett 5.00 12.00
26 Larry Bird 8.00 20.00
27 Stephen Curry 12.00 30.00
28 Baron Davis 2.50 6.00
29 Moses Malone 3.00 8.00
30 Christian Laettner 2.50 6.00
31 Shane Battier 2.50 6.00
32 Gary Payton 3.00 8.00
33 Tim Duncan 5.00 12.00
34 John Starks 2.50 6.00
35 Kyle Lowry 2.50 6.00
36 Manute Bol 3.00 8.00
37 Tony Parker 3.00 8.00
38 Bill Laimbeer 2.50 6.00
39 Rafer Alston 2.00 5.00
40 Clyde Drexler 4.00 10.00

2015-16 Absolute Memorabilia Iconic Autographs

RANDOM INSERTS IN PACKS
PRINT RUNS B/WN 25-149 COPIES PER
EXCHANGE DEADLINE 8/5/2017
1 Dan Issel/149 5.00 12.00
2 Kyrie Irving/25
3 Cliff Hagan/99 5.00 12.00
4 Kareem Abdul-Jabbar/25 20.00 50.00
5 Paul Westphal/149 6.00 15.00
6 Shane Battier/49 5.00 12.00
7 Larry Nance/149 5.00 12.00
8 Kobe Bryant/25 100.00 200.00
9 Glen Rice/99 5.00 12.00
10 Magic Johnson/25 25.00 60.00
11 Dino Radja/149 4.00 10.00
12 John Wall/25 20.00 50.00
13 Zydrunas Ilgauskas/149 5.00 12.00
15 Rafer Alston/149 4.00 10.00
16 Byron Scott/49 5.00 12.00
18 Shaquille O'Neal/25 60.00 150.00
19 Kurt Rambis/149 4.00 10.00
20 Oscar Robertson/25 30.00 80.00
21 Eddie Jones/149 5.00 12.00
22 Andrew Wiggins/25 30.00 80.00
23 Alex English/149 5.00 12.00
24 Gary Payton/25 10.00 25.00
25 Dee Brown/149 4.00 10.00
26 Joe Dumars/49 6.00 15.00
27 Antoine Walker/149 5.00 12.00
28 Kevin Durant/25 50.00 120.00
29 Kenny Walker/149 4.00 10.00
30 Anthony Davis/25 40.00 100.00
31 Rony Seikaly/149 4.00 10.00
32 Kevin McHale/25 10.00 25.00
34 Rick Barry/49 5.00 12.00
35 Antonio McDyess/149 5.00 12.00
36 Dave Cowens/49 4.00 10.00
37 Bill Laimbeer/149 5.00 12.00
38 Dwyane Wade/25 EXCH 25.00 60.00
39 Dan Majerle/99 5.00 12.00

2015-16 Absolute Memorabilia Iconic Materials

RANDOM INSERTS IN PACKS
STATED PRINT RUN 99 SER.#'d SETS
*PRIME/25: .75X TO 2X BASIC
1 Bernard King 2.50 6.00
2 John Stockton 5.00 12.00
3 Chris Webber 3.00 8.00
4 Larry Johnson 4.00 10.00
5 Danny Ainge 3.00 8.00
6 Mike Bibby 2.50 6.00
7 Jalen Rose 3.00 8.00
8 Reggie Lewis 3.00 8.00
9 Alex English 2.50 6.00
10 Shaquille O'Neal 5.00 12.00
11 Bobby Jackson 2.00 5.00
12 Karl Malone 4.00 10.00
13 Clifford Robinson 2.00 5.00
14 Mark Aguirre 2.50 6.00
15 Dikembe Mutombo 3.00 8.00
16 Patrick Ewing 5.00 12.00
17 Jason Kidd 3.00 8.00
18 Rick Fox 2.50 6.00
19 Alonzo Mourning 4.00 10.00
20 Toni Kukoc 3.00 8.00
21 Charles Oakley 2.50 6.00
22 Kevin McHale 3.00 8.00
23 Dan Issel 2.50 6.00
24 Michael Finley 3.00 8.00
25 Grant Hill 4.00 10.00
26 Ralph Sampson 2.50 6.00
27 Joe Dumars 3.00 8.00
28 Scottie Pippen 5.00 12.00
29 Antoine Walker 2.50 6.00
30 Yao Ming 4.00 10.00

2015-16 Absolute Memorabilia Marks of Fame

RANDOM INSERTS IN PACKS
PRINT RUNS B/WN 25-149 COPIES PER
EXCHANGE DEADLINE 8/5/2017
1 Kevin Durant/25 75.00 150.00
2 Kenneth Faried/49 5.00 12.00
3 Kyrie Irving/25
4 Kevin McHale/25
5 Jusuf Nurkic/99 4.00 10.00
6 Ron Harper/149 6.00 15.00
7 Tony Parker/25 15.00 40.00
8 Sean Elliott/125 6.00 15.00
9 Kobe Bryant/25 100.00 200.00
10 Michael Carter-Williams/49 4.00 10.00
11 Magic Johnson/25 25.00 60.00
12 Enes Kanter/99 4.00 10.00
13 John Wall/25 25.00 60.00
14 Dennis Rodman/25 12.00 30.00
15 Marcin Gortat/99 5.00 12.00
16 Adrian Dantley/149 5.00 12.00
17 Klay Thompson/49 25.00 60.00
18 DeMarre Carroll/149 4.00 10.00
19 Shaquille O'Neal/25 60.00 150.00
20 Trey Burke/49
21 Jerry West/25
22 Frank Ramsey/99 6.00 15.00
23 Jabari Parker/25
24 Muggsy Bogues/149 5.00 12.00
26 Larry Nance/149 5.00 12.00
28 Kenny Anderson/149 5.00 12.00
29 Julius Erving/25 25.00 60.00
30 Bradley Beal/49 6.00 15.00

2015-16 Absolute Memorabilia NBA Stars Materials

RANDOM INSERTS IN PACKS
STATED PRINT RUN 99 SER.#'d SETS
*PRIME/20-25: .75X TO 2X BASIC
1 Joakim Noah 2.50 6.00
2 Ricky Rubio 3.00 8.00
3 Chris Bosh 3.00 8.00
4 Victor Oladipo 2.50 6.00
5 DeMarcus Cousins 3.00 8.00
6 Klay Thompson 6.00 15.00
7 Dwight Howard 2.50 6.00
8 Manu Ginobili 3.00 8.00
9 Andrew Wiggins 5.00 12.00
10 Monta Ellis 2.50 6.00
11 Kawhi Leonard 5.00 12.00
12 Russell Westbrook 8.00 20.00
13 Chris Paul 4.00 10.00
14 Zach LaVine 3.00 8.00
15 Derrick Rose 5.00 12.00
16 Kyrie Irving 6.00 15.00
17 Dwyane Wade 5.00 12.00
18 Marc Gasol 3.00 8.00
19 Blake Griffin 4.00 10.00
20 Nicolas Batum 2.50 6.00
21 Kevin Durant 6.00 15.00
22 Tobias Harris 2.50 6.00
23 Damian Lillard 5.00 12.00
24 Zach Randolph 2.50 6.00
25 Dirk Nowitzki 4.00 10.00
26 LaMarcus Aldridge 3.00 8.00
27 Jimmy Butler 3.00 8.00
28 Mike Conley 3.00 8.00
29 Carmelo Anthony 4.00 10.00
30 Nikola Vucevic 2.50 6.00

2015-16 Absolute Memorabilia Next Day Autographs

RANDOM INSERTS IN PACKS
EXCHANGE DEADLINE 8/5/2017
1 Karl-Anthony Towns 250.00 500.00
2 D'Angelo Russell 60.00 150.00
3 Jahlil Okafor 30.00 80.00
4 Kristaps Porzingis 75.00 200.00
6 Willie Cauley-Stein 20.00 50.00
7 Emmanuel Mudiay 20.00 50.00
8 Stanley Johnson 12.00 30.00
9 Frank Kaminsky 15.00 40.00
10 Justise Winslow 25.00 60.00
11 Myles Turner 50.00 120.00
12 Trey Lyles 10.00 25.00
13 Devin Booker 100.00 200.00
14 Cameron Payne 10.00 25.00
15 Kelly Oubre Jr. 10.00 25.00
16 Terry Rozier 12.00 30.00
17 Rashad Vaughn 6.00 15.00
18 Sam Dekker 5.00 12.00
19 Jerian Grant 10.00 25.00
20 Delon Wright 5.00 12.00
21 Justin Anderson 8.00 20.00
22 Bobby Portis 15.00 40.00
23 Rondae Hollis-Jefferson 8.00 20.00
24 Tyus Jones 6.00 15.00
25 Jarell Martin 5.00 12.00
27 R.J. Hunter 4.00 10.00
28 Chris McCullough 4.00 10.00
29 Montrezl Harrell 5.00 12.00
30 Jordan Mickey 4.00 10.00
31 Anthony Brown 4.00 10.00
32 Rakeem Christmas 4.00 10.00
33 Richaun Holmes 5.00 12.00
34 Pat Connaughton 4.00 10.00
35 Joe Young 5.00 12.00
37 Dakari Johnson 4.00 10.00
38 Tyler Harvey 4.00 10.00
40 Walter Tavares 4.00 10.00
46 Josh Richardson 6.00 15.00
47 Kevon Looney 5.00 12.00

2015-16 Absolute Memorabilia Team Quads Materials

RANDOM INSERTS IN PACKS
STATED PRINT RUN 99 SER.#'d SETS
*PRIME/25: 1X TO 2.5X BASIC
TQCHI McDrmtt/Noah/Rose/Gbsn 6.00 15.00
TQCLE Jms/Love/Irvng/Thmpsn 20.00 50.00
TQGSW Brns/Curry/Igdla/Thmpsn 20.00 50.00
TQLAC Grffn/Jrdn/Paul/Rdck 6.00 15.00
TQSAS Dncn/Lnrd/Gnbli/Prkr 12.00 30.00

2015-16 Absolute Memorabilia Team Tandems Materials

RANDOM INSERTS IN PACKS
STATED PRINT RUN 99 SER.#'d SETS
*PRIME/25: 1X TO 2.5X BASIC
TTATL A.Horford/J.Teague 2.50 6.00
TTBRK B.Lopez/J.Johnson 2.50 6.00
TTCHA A.Jefferson/K.Walker 3.00 8.00
TTCHI D.Rose/J.Butler 4.00 10.00
TTCLE K.Irving/L.James 15.00 40.00
TTDAL D.Nowitzki/C.Parsons 4.00 10.00
TTDEN D.Gallinari/K.Faried 2.50 6.00
TTDET A.Drummond/B.Jennings 3.00 8.00
TTGSW K.Thompson/S.Curry 12.00 30.00
TTHOU J.Harden/D.Howard 5.00 12.00
TTLAC C.Paul/B.Griffin 4.00 10.00
TTMEM M.Gasol/M.Conley 3.00 8.00
TTMIA C.Bosh/D.Wade 5.00 12.00
TTMIN A.Wiggins/Z.LaVine 8.00 20.00
TTOKL K.Durant/R.Westbrook 6.00 15.00
TTORL N.Vucevic/E.Payton 2.50 6.00
TTSAN M.Ginobili/T.Duncan 5.00 12.00
TTTOR K.Lowry/D.DeRozan 3.00 8.00
TTWAS B.Beal/J.Wall 4.00 10.00

2015-16 Absolute Memorabilia Team Trios Materials

RANDOM INSERTS IN PACKS
STATED PRINT RUN 99 SER.#'d SETS
*PRIME/25: 1X TO 2.5X BASIC
TTRBOS Bradley/Sullinger/Smart 4.00 10.00
TTRCHI Rose/Butler/Noah 6.00 15.00
TTRCLE Love/James/Irving 40.00 100.00
TTRGSW Iguodala/Curry/Thompson 30.00 80.00
TTRLAL Clarkson/Bryant/Young 8.00 20.00
TTRMEM Conley/Randolph/Gasol 5.00 12.00
TTRMIA Chalmers/Bosh/Wade 5.00 12.00
TTRORL Harris/Gordon/Vucevic 4.00 10.00
TTRSAC McLemore/Collison/Cousins 5.00 12.00
TTRSAS Leonard/Duncan/Parker 10.00 25.00

2015-16 Absolute Memorabilia Tools of the Trade Jumbo Rookie Material Signatures

RANDOM INSERTS IN PACKS
STATED PRINT RUN 99 SER.#'d SETS
EXCHANGE DEADLINE 8/5/2017
*PRIME: .5X TO 1.2X BASIC
TTJAB Anthony Brown 4.00 10.00
TTJBP Bobby Portis 12.00 30.00
TTJCM Chris McCullough 4.00 10.00
TTJCP Cameron Payne 10.00 25.00
TTJDB Devin Booker 25.00 60.00
TTJDR D'Angelo Russell 30.00 80.00
TTJDW Delon Wright 5.00 12.00
TTJEM Emmanuel Mudiay 6.00 15.00
TTJFK Frank Kaminsky 6.00 15.00
TTJJA Justin Anderson 5.00 12.00
TTJJG Jerian Grant 4.00 10.00
TTJJM Jarell Martin 5.00 12.00
TTJJM Jordan Mickey 4.00 10.00
TTJJO Jahlil Okafor 30.00 80.00
TTJJW Justise Winslow 20.00 50.00
TTJKL Kevon Looney 10.00 25.00
TTJKO Kelly Oubre Jr. 5.00 12.00
TTJKP Kristaps Porzingis 150.00 300.00
TTJKT Karl-Anthony Towns 150.00 300.00
TTJMH Mario Hezonja 10.00 25.00
TTJMH Montrezl Harrell 5.00 12.00
TTJMT Myles Turner 20.00 50.00
TTJPC Pat Connaughton 4.00 10.00
TTJRC Rakeem Christmas 4.00 10.00
TTJRH R.J. Hunter 4.00 10.00
TTJRH Rondae Hollis-Jefferson 5.00 12.00
TTJRV Rashad Vaughn 4.00 10.00
TTJSD Sam Dekker 5.00 12.00
TTJSJ Stanley Johnson 12.00 30.00
TTJTL Trey Lyles 6.00 15.00
TTJTR Terry Rozier 5.00 12.00
TTJWC Willie Cauley-Stein 10.00 25.00
TTJWT Walter Tavares 4.00 10.00

2015-16 Absolute Memorabilia Tools of the Trade Rookie Autograph Materials

RANDOM INSERTS IN PACKS
STATED PRINT RUN 99 SER.#'d SETS
EXCHANGE DEADLINE 8/5/2017
*PRIME: .5X TO 1.2X BASIC
TTJCM Chris McCullough 4.00 10.00
TTJCP Cameron Payne 5.00 12.00
TTJDB Devin Booker 30.00 80.00
TTJDR D'Angelo Russell 25.00 60.00
TTJDW Delon Wright 5.00 12.00
TTJEM Emmanuel Mudiay 10.00 25.00
TTJFK Frank Kaminsky 10.00 25.00
TTJJA Justin Anderson 5.00 12.00
TTJJG Jerian Grant 4.00 10.00
TTJJM Jordan Mickey 4.00 10.00
TTJJM Jarell Martin 5.00 12.00
TTJJO Jahlil Okafor 20.00 50.00
TTJJR Josh Richardson 10.00 25.00
TTJJW Justise Winslow 6.00 15.00
TTJJY Joe Young 5.00 12.00
TTJKL Kevon Looney 5.00 12.00
TTJKO Kelly Oubre Jr. 5.00 12.00
TTJKP Kristaps Porzingis 50.00 120.00
TTJKT Karl-Anthony Towns 75.00 200.00
TTJMH Mario Hezonja 5.00 12.00
TTJMH Montrezl Harrell 5.00 12.00
TTJMT Myles Turner 10.00 25.00
TTJPC Pat Connaughton 4.00 10.00
TTJRC Rakeem Christmas 4.00 10.00
TTJRH Richaun Holmes 5.00 12.00
TTJRH R.J. Hunter 4.00 10.00
TTJRH Rondae Hollis-Jefferson 5.00 12.00
TTJRV Rashad Vaughn 4.00 10.00
TTJSD Sam Dekker 5.00 12.00
TTJSJ Stanley Johnson 5.00 12.00
TTJTL Trey Lyles 6.00 15.00
TTJTR Terry Rozier 5.00 12.00
TTJWC Willie Cauley-Stein 12.00 30.00

2015-16 Absolute Memorabilia Tools of the Trade Rookie Materials Dual

RANDOM INSERTS IN PACKS
STATED PRINT RUN 125 SER.#'d SETS
*PRIME/49: .75X TO 2X BASIC
*PATCH/25: 1.2X TO 3X BASIC
1 Karl-Anthony Towns 12.00 30.00
2 D'Angelo Russell 5.00 12.00
3 Jahlil Okafor 5.00 12.00
4 Kristaps Porzingis 12.00 30.00
5 Mario Hezonja 2.50 6.00
6 Willie Cauley-Stein 3.00 8.00
7 Emmanuel Mudiay 4.00 10.00
8 Stanley Johnson 2.50 6.00
9 Frank Kaminsky 3.00 8.00
10 Justise Winslow 3.00 8.00
11 Myles Turner 3.00 8.00
12 Trey Lyles 3.00 8.00
13 Devin Booker 10.00 25.00
14 Cameron Payne 2.50 6.00
15 Kelly Oubre Jr. 2.50 6.00
16 Terry Rozier 2.50 6.00
17 Rashad Vaughn 2.00 5.00
18 Sam Dekker 2.50 6.00
19 Jerian Grant 2.00 5.00
20 Delon Wright
21 Justin Anderson 2.50 6.00
22 Bobby Portis 3.00 8.00
23 Rondae Hollis-Jefferson 2.50 6.00
24 Tyus Jones 3.00 8.00
25 Jarell Martin 2.50 6.00
26 Kevon Looney 2.50 6.00
27 R.J. Hunter 2.00 5.00
28 Chris McCullough 2.00 5.00
29 Montrezl Harrell 2.50 6.00
30 Jordan Mickey 2.00 5.00
31 Anthony Brown
32 Rakeem Christmas 2.00 5.00
33 Walter Tavares 2.00 5.00

2015-16 Absolute Memorabilia Tools of the Trade Rookie Materials Jumbo

RANDOM INSERTS IN PACKS
STATED PRINT RUN 149 SER.#'d SETS
*PRIME/49: .75X TO 2X BASIC
*PATCH/25: 1.2X TO 3X BASIC
1 Karl-Anthony Towns 10.00 25.00
2 D'Angelo Russell 5.00 12.00
3 Jahlil Okafor 5.00 12.00
4 Kristaps Porzingis 8.00 20.00
5 Mario Hezonja 2.50 6.00
6 Willie Cauley-Stein 3.00 8.00
7 Emmanuel Mudiay 4.00 10.00
8 Stanley Johnson 2.50 6.00
9 Frank Kaminsky 3.00 8.00
10 Justise Winslow 3.00 8.00
11 Myles Turner 3.00 8.00
12 Trey Lyles 3.00 8.00
13 Devin Booker 10.00 25.00
14 Cameron Payne 2.50 6.00
15 Kelly Oubre Jr. 2.50 6.00
16 Terry Rozier 2.50 6.00
17 Rashad Vaughn 2.00 5.00
18 Sam Dekker 2.50 6.00
19 Jerian Grant 2.00 5.00
20 Delon Wright 2.50 6.00
21 Justin Anderson 2.50 6.00
22 Bobby Portis 3.00 8.00
23 Rondae Hollis-Jefferson 2.50 6.00
24 Tyus Jones 3.00 8.00
25 Jarell Martin 2.50 6.00
26 Kevon Looney 2.50 6.00
27 R.J. Hunter 2.00 5.00
28 Chris McCullough 2.00 5.00
29 Montrezl Harrell 2.50 6.00
30 Jordan Mickey 2.00 5.00

31 Anthony Brown 2.00 5.00
32 Rakeem Christmas 2.00 5.00
33 Walter Tavares 2.00 5.00

2015-16 Absolute Memorabilia Tools of the Trade Rookie Materials Quad

RANDOM INSERTS IN PACKS
STATED PRINT RUN 75 SER.#'d SETS
*PRIME/49: .75X TO 2X BASIC
*PATCH/25: 1.2X TO 3X BASIC
TTMAB Anthony Brown 2.00 5.00
TTMBP Bobby Portis 3.00 8.00
TTMCM Chris McCullough 2.00 5.00
TTMCP Cameron Payne 2.50 6.00
TTMDB Devin Booker AU/99 10.00 25.00
TTMDR D'Angelo Russell 6.00 15.00
TTMDW Delon Wright 2.50 6.00
TTMEM Emmanuel Mudiay 4.00 10.00
TTMFK Frank Kaminsky 3.00 8.00
TTMJA Justin Anderson 2.50 6.00
TTMJG Jerian Grant 2.00 5.00
TTMJM Jordan Mickey 2.00 5.00
TTMJM Jarell Martin 2.50 6.00
TTMJO Jahlil Okafor 5.00 12.00
TTMJW Justise Winslow 3.00 8.00
TTMKL Kevon Looney 2.50 6.00
TTMKO Kelly Oubre Jr. 2.50 6.00
TTMKP Kristaps Porzingis 12.00 30.00
TTMKT Karl-Anthony Towns 12.00 30.00
TTMMH Mario Hezonja 2.50 6.00
TTMMH Montrezl Harrell 2.50 6.00
TTMMT Myles Turner 3.00 8.00
TTMRC Rakeem Christmas 2.00 5.00
TTMRH R.J. Hunter 2.00 5.00
TTMRH Rondae Hollis-Jefferson 2.50 6.00
TTMRV Rashad Vaughn 2.00 5.00
TTMSD Sam Dekker 2.50 6.00
TTMSJ Stanley Johnson 2.50 6.00
TTMTJ Tyus Jones 3.00 8.00
TTMTL Trey Lyles 3.00 8.00
TTMTR Terry Rozier 2.50 6.00
TTMWC Willie Cauley-Stein 3.00 8.00
TTMWT Walter Tavares 2.00 5.00

2015-16 Absolute Memorabilia Tools of the Trade Rookie Materials Six

RANDOM INSERTS IN PACKS
STATED PRINT RUN 60 SER.#'d SETS
*PRIME/49: .6X TO 1.5X BASIC
*PATCH/25: .75X TO 2X BASIC
1 Karl-Anthony Towns 20.00 50.00
2 D'Angelo Russell 10.00 25.00
3 Jahlil Okafor 5.00 12.00
4 Kristaps Porzingis 25.00 60.00
5 Mario Hezonja 3.00 8.00
6 Willie Cauley-Stein 4.00 10.00
7 Emmanuel Mudiay 4.00 10.00
8 Stanley Johnson 3.00 8.00
9 Frank Kaminsky 4.00 10.00
10 Justise Winslow 4.00 10.00
11 Myles Turner 6.00 15.00
12 Trey Lyles 4.00 10.00
13 Devin Booker 10.00 25.00
14 Cameron Payne 3.00 8.00
15 Kelly Oubre Jr. 3.00 8.00
16 Terry Rozier 3.00 8.00
17 Rashad Vaughn 2.50 6.00
18 Sam Dekker 3.00 8.00
19 Jerian Grant 2.50 6.00
20 Delon Wright 3.00 8.00
21 Justin Anderson 3.00 8.00
22 Bobby Portis 4.00 10.00
23 Rondae Hollis-Jefferson 3.00 8.00
24 Tyus Jones 4.00 10.00
25 Jarell Martin 2.50 6.00
26 Kevon Looney 3.00 8.00
27 R.J. Hunter 2.50 6.00
28 Chris McCullough 2.50 6.00
29 Montrezl Harrell 3.00 8.00
30 Jordan Mickey 2.50 6.00
31 Anthony Brown 2.50 6.00
32 Rakeem Christmas 2.50 6.00
33 Walter Tavares 2.50 6.00

2015-16 Absolute Memorabilia Tools of the Trade Rookie Materials Trio

RANDOM INSERTS IN PACKS
STATED PRINT RUN 99 SER.#'d SETS
*PRIME/49: .75X TO 2X BASIC
*PATCH/25: 1.2X TO 3X BASIC
1 Karl-Anthony Towns 12.00 30.00
2 D'Angelo Russell 5.00 12.00
3 Jahlil Okafor 5.00 12.00
4 Kristaps Porzingis 6.00 15.00
5 Mario Hezonja 2.50 6.00
6 Willie Cauley-Stein 3.00 8.00
7 Emmanuel Mudiay 4.00 10.00
8 Stanley Johnson 2.50 6.00
9 Frank Kaminsky 3.00 8.00
10 Justise Winslow 3.00 8.00
11 Myles Turner 3.00 8.00
12 Trey Lyles 3.00 8.00
13 Devin Booker 4.00 10.00
14 Cameron Payne 2.50 6.00
15 Kelly Oubre Jr. 2.50 6.00
16 Terry Rozier 2.50 6.00
17 Rashad Vaughn 2.00 5.00
18 Sam Dekker 2.50 6.00
19 Jerian Grant 2.00 5.00
20 Delon Wright 2.50 6.00
21 Justin Anderson 2.50 6.00
22 Bobby Portis 3.00 8.00
23 Rondae Hollis-Jefferson 2.50 6.00
24 Tyus Jones 3.00 8.00
25 Jarell Martin 2.50 6.00
26 Kevon Looney 2.50 6.00
27 R.J. Hunter 2.00 5.00
28 Chris McCullough 2.00 5.00
29 Montrezl Harrell 2.50 6.00
30 Jordan Mickey 2.00 5.00
31 Anthony Brown 2.00 5.00
32 Rakeem Christmas 2.00 5.00
33 Walter Tavares 2.00 5.00

2016-17 Absolute Memorabilia

101-160 PRINT RUN 999 SER.#'d SETS
161-200 PRINT RUN 999 SER.#'d SETS
1 Kevin Durant 1.25 3.00
2 Dirk Nowitzki .60 1.50
3 Harrison Barnes .40 1.00
4 DeMar DeRozan .50 1.25
5 Khris Middleton .40 1.00
6 Will Barton .30 .75
7 Michael Carter-Williams .30 .75
8 Dennis Schroder .40 1.00
9 DeMarre Carroll .30 .75
10 Draymond Green .60 1.50
11 LaMarcus Aldridge .50 1.25
12 Kenneth Faried .40 1.00
13 Klay Thompson .60 1.50
14 Giannis Antetokounmpo 1.00 2.50
15 T.J. McConnell .30 .75
16 J.J. Barea .40 1.00
17 Willie Cauley-Stein .40 1.00
18 Andrew Wiggins .75 2.00
19 Cody Zeller .30 .75
20 Dwight Howard .40 1.00
21 Kyle Lowry .40 1.00
22 Rudy Gobert .50 1.25
23 Emmanuel Mudiay .40 1.00
24 Stephen Curry 2.00 5.00
25 Paul George .60 1.50
26 Wesley Matthews .30 .75
27 Robert Covington .30 .75
28 Rudy Gay .50 1.25
29 Karl-Anthony Towns 1.25 3.00
30 Kemba Walker .50 1.25
31 Paul Millsap .50 1.25
32 Dwyane Wade .75 2.00
33 Kawhi Leonard .75 2.00
34 Rodney Hood .40 1.00
35 Marcin Gortat .40 1.00
36 Blake Griffin .50 1.25
37 Myles Turner .40 1.00
38 Clint Capela .30 .75
39 Nerlens Noel .40 1.00
40 DeMarcus Cousins .50 1.25
41 Zach LaVine .50 1.25
42 Marvin Williams .40 1.00
43 Tony Parker .50 1.25
44 Isaiah Thomas .50 1.25
45 Jimmy Butler .50 1.25
46 Gordon Hayward .50 1.25
47 John Wall .60 1.50
48 Chris Paul .60 1.50
49 Monta Ellis .40 1.00
50 James Harden .75 2.00
51 Kristaps Porzingis 1.00 2.50
52 Tyson Chandler .40 1.00
53 Ricky Rubio .50 1.25
54 Chris Bosh .50 1.25
55 Tyreke Evans .30 .75
56 Jae Crowder .40 1.00
57 Rajon Rondo .50 1.25
58 Evan Turner .30 .75
59 Bradley Beal .50 1.25
60 J.J. Redick .50 1.25
61 Reggie Jackson .40 1.00
62 Patrick Beverley .30 .75
63 Derrick Rose .60 1.50
64 Eric Bledsoe .40 1.00
65 Enes Kanter .30 .75
66 Goran Dragic .40 1.00
67 Tyler Zeller .40 1.00
68 Kevin Love .50 1.25
69 Damian Lillard 1.00 2.50
70 Serge Ibaka .40 1.00
71 Paul Pierce .50 1.25
72 Kentavious Caldwell-Pope .40 1.00
73 Courtney Lee .40 1.00
74 Chandler Parsons .40 1.00
75 Devin Booker .75 2.00
76 Solomon Hill .30 .75
77 Russell Westbrook 1.25 3.00
78 Justise Winslow .40 1.00
79 Brook Lopez .40 1.00
80 Kyrie Irving 1.00 2.50
81 C.J. McCollum .40 1.00
82 Evan Fournier .40 1.00
83 D'Angelo Russell .60 1.50
84 Andre Drummond .50 1.25
85 Carmelo Anthony .60 1.50
86 Mike Conley .40 1.00
87 Luol Deng .40 1.00
88 Steven Adams .40 1.00
89 Aaron Gordon .40 1.00
90 Jeremy Lin .50 1.25
91 LeBron James 2.00 5.00
92 Victor Oladipo .40 1.00
93 Elfrid Payton .40 1.00
94 Jordan Clarkson .40 1.00
95 Richard Jefferson .40 1.00
96 Zach Randolph .40 1.00
97 Trevor Booker .30 .75
98 Anthony Davis 1.00 2.50
99 Julius Randle .50 1.25
100 Manu Ginobili .50 1.25
101 Kobe Bryant 2.50 6.00
102 Jon McGlocklin .50 1.25
103 Joe Dumars .60 1.50
104 Dave DeBusschere .60 1.50
105 Damon Stoudamire .50 1.25
106 Andrei Kirilenko .50 1.25
107 Alonzo Mourning .75 2.00
108 Spencer Haywood .40 1.00
109 Shawn Marion .50 1.25
110 Oscar Robertson .75 2.00
111 Muggsy Bogues .50 1.25
112 John Salley .40 1.00
113 Jerry Lucas .60 1.50
114 Dave Twardzik .40 1.00
115 Connie Hawkins .60 1.50
116 Anfernee Hardaway 1.50 4.00
117 Allen Iverson .75 2.00
118 Stacey Augmon .40 1.00
119 Shareef Abdur-Rahim .50 1.25
120 Nate Archibald .50 1.25
121 Mitch Richmond .60 1.50
122 John Stockton 1.00 2.50
123 Jason Kidd .60 1.50
124 David Thompson .50 1.25
125 Chris Webber .60 1.50
126 Ben Wallace .50 1.25
127 Willis Reed .60 1.50
128 Steve Kerr .60 1.50
129 Shaquille O'Neal 1.50 4.00
130 Patrick Ewing .75 2.00
131 Mack Calvin .40 1.00
132 Julius Erving 1.00 2.50
133 Jamal Mashburn .60 1.50
134 Derek Harper .50 1.25
135 Chauncey Billups .60 1.50
136 Bill Bradley .75 2.00
137 Wilt Chamberlain 1.25 3.00
138 Tim Hardaway .60 1.50
139 Sean Elliott .60 1.50
140 Pete Maravich 1.00 2.50
141 Lucius Allen .60 1.50
142 Horace Grant .60 1.50
143 Dikembe Mutombo .60 1.50
144 Byron Scott .50 1.25
145 Bill Walton .60 1.50
146 Wes Unseld .60 1.50
147 Toni Kukoc .60 1.50
148 Scottie Pippen 1.25 3.00
149 Rick Barry .50 1.25
150 Latrell Sprewell .50 1.25
151 Larry Bird 1.50 4.00
152 Gary Payton .60 1.50
153 Fat Lever .50 1.25
154 Brian Grant .40 1.00
155 Brent Barry .40 1.00
156 Walt Frazier .60 1.50
157 Tracy McGrady .60 1.50
158 Robert Parish .60 1.50
159 Nick Van Exel .60 1.50
160 Robert Horry .50 1.25
161 Brandon Ingram RC 4.00 10.00
162 Jaylen Brown RC 2.50 6.00
163 Dragan Bender RC .75 2.00
164 Kris Dunn RC 2.00 5.00
165 Buddy Hield RC 1.50 4.00
166 Jamal Murray RC 2.00 5.00
167 Marquese Chriss RC 1.50 4.00
168 Jakob Poeltl RC .75 2.00
169 Thon Maker RC 2.00 5.00
170 Domantas Sabonis RC 1.00 2.50
171 Taurean Prince RC 1.00 2.50
172 Denzel Valentine RC .75 2.00
173 Wade Baldwin IV RC .60 1.50
174 Henry Ellenson RC .75 2.00
175 Malik Beasley RC .60 1.50
176 DeAndre' Bembry RC .60 1.50
177 Malachi Richardson RC .75 2.00
178 T. Luwawu-Cabarrot RC 1.25 3.00
179 Brice Johnson RC .60 1.50
180 Pascal Siakam RC .60 1.50
181 Skal Labissiere RC 1.00 2.50
182 Damian Jones RC .60 1.50
183 Deyonta Davis RC .60 1.50
184 Cheick Diallo RC .60 1.50
185 Tyler Ulis RC 2.00 5.00
186 Patrick McCaw RC 1.25 3.00
187 Isaiah Whitehead RC .60 1.50
188 Kay Felder RC .60 1.50
189 Demetrius Jackson RC .60 1.50
190 Ivica Zubac RC 1.00 2.50
191 Caris LeVert RC .75 2.00
192 A.J. Hammons RC .60 1.50
193 Diamond Stone RC .60 1.50
194 Gary Payton II RC .75 2.00
195 Ben Bentil RC .60 1.50
196 Chinanu Onuaku RC .60 1.50
197 Stephen Zimmerman RC .60 1.50
198 Jake Layman RC .75 2.00
199 Dejounte Murray RC 1.25 3.00
200 Ben Simmons RC 10.00 25.00

2016-17 Absolute Memorabilia Draft Day Ink

RANDOM INSERTS IN PACKS
STATED PRINT RUN 25 SER. #'d SETS
EXCHANGE DEADLINE 8/21/2018
1 Brandon Ingram 100.00 250.00
2 Jaylen Brown 50.00 120.00
3 Dragan Bender 12.00 30.00
4 Kris Dunn 25.00 60.00
5 Buddy Hield 25.00 60.00
6 Jamal Murray 30.00 80.00
7 Marquese Chriss 20.00 50.00
8 Jakob Poeltl 8.00 20.00
9 Domantas Sabonis 12.00 30.00
10 Thon Maker 30.00 80.00
11 Taurean Prince 10.00 25.00
12 Denzel Valentine 10.00 25.00
13 Wade Baldwin IV 8.00 20.00
14 Brice Johnson 8.00 20.00
15 Skal Labissiere 15.00 40.00

2016-17 Absolute Memorabilia Frequent Flyer Material Autographs

RANDOM INSERTS IN PACKS
STATED PRINT RUN 75 SER. #'d SETS
EXCHANGE DEADLINE 8/21/2018
1 Bobby Portis 3.00 8.00
2 Tristan Thompson 8.00 20.00
3 Dirk Nowitzki 50.00 120.00
4 Devin Harris 3.00 8.00
5 Reggie Jackson 4.00 10.00
6 Justise Winslow 6.00 15.00
7 Zach LaVine 12.00 30.00
8 Carmelo Anthony 12.00 30.00
9 Jordan Clarkson 8.00 20.00
10 Tyler Ennis 3.00 8.00
12 Karl-Anthony Towns 30.00 80.00
13 Aaron Gordon 4.00 10.00
14 Alex Len
15 Archie Goodwin 3.00 8.00
16 C.J. McCollum 5.00 12.00
17 Jonathon Simmons 5.00 12.00
18 Kent Bazemore 8.00 20.00
20 Andrew Wiggins

2016-17 Absolute Memorabilia Frequent Flyer Materials

RANDOM INSERTS IN PACKS
STATED PRINT RUN 149 SER. #'d SETS
1 Karl-Anthony Towns 5.00 12.00
2 Stanley Johnson 2.00 5.00
3 DeMar DeRozan 3.00 8.00
4 LeBron James 12.00 30.00
5 James Harden 5.00 12.00
6 Giannis Antetokounmpo 5.00 12.00
7 Kenneth Faried 2.50 6.00
8 Shabazz Muhammad 2.50 6.00
9 Aaron Gordon 2.50 6.00
10 Bobby Portis 2.00 5.00
11 Jusuf Nurkic 2.00 5.00
12 Marcus Morris 2.00 5.00
13 Russell Westbrook 5.00 12.00
14 Enes Kanter 2.00 5.00
15 Kevin Durant 6.00 15.00
16 Tyler Ennis 2.00 5.00
17 Alex Len 2.00 5.00
18 Tristan Thompson 2.50 6.00
19 Emmanuel Mudiay 2.50 6.00
20 J.R. Smith 2.50 6.00
21 Dwyane Wade 5.00 12.00
22 Dwight Powell 2.00 5.00
23 Jimmy Butler 3.00 8.00
24 Jordan Clarkson 2.50 6.00
25 Archie Goodwin 2.00 5.00
26 Dirk Nowitzki 4.00 10.00
27 Anthony Davis 5.00 12.00
28 Michael Beasley 2.00 5.00
29 John Henson 2.50 6.00
30 Reggie Jackson 2.50 6.00
31 Zach LaVine 3.00 8.00
32 Justise Winslow 2.50 6.00
33 Andrew Wiggins 4.00 10.00
34 Carmelo Anthony 4.00 10.00
35 Jonathon Simmons 3.00 8.00
36 Kent Bazemore 2.50 6.00
37 C.J. McCollum 2.50 6.00
39 Devin Harris 2.00 5.00
40 Kawhi Leonard 5.00 12.00
41 LaMarcus Aldridge 3.00 8.00
42 Trevor Ariza 2.00 5.00
43 Nicolas Batum 2.50 6.00
44 Khris Middleton 2.50 6.00
45 Kyle Lowry 2.50 6.00
46 Kobe Bryant 8.00 20.00
47 Larry Nance 2.50 6.00
48 Clyde Drexler 4.00 10.00
49 Steve Francis 2.50 6.00
50 Bernard King 2.50 6.00
51 Julius Erving 5.00 12.00
52 Dan Majerle 2.50 6.00
53 Tom Chambers 2.50 6.00
54 Shaquille O'Neal 5.00 12.00
55 Shawn Marion 2.50 6.00
56 Kenny Smith 2.50 6.00
57 Larry Johnson 4.00 10.00
58 Manu Ginobili 3.00 8.00
59 Rashard Lewis 2.50 6.00
60 Ray Allen 3.00 8.00

2016-17 Absolute Memorabilia Freshman Flyer Jersey Autographs

RANDOM INSERTS IN PACKS
STATED PRINT RUN 75 SER. #'d SETS
EXCHANGE DEADLINE 8/21/2018
1 Brandon Ingram 30.00 80.00
2 Wade Baldwin IV 3.00 8.00
3 Cheick Diallo 3.00 8.00
4 Tyler Ulis 10.00 25.00
5 Jaylen Brown 20.00 50.00
6 Henry Ellenson 4.00 10.00
7 Patrick McCaw 12.00 30.00
8 Dragan Bender 6.00 15.00
9 Malik Beasley 3.00 8.00
10 Kris Dunn 15.00 40.00
11 DeAndre' Bembry 3.00 8.00
12 Isaiah Whitehead 3.00 8.00
13 Demetrius Jackson 3.00 8.00
14 Buddy Hield 20.00 50.00
15 Malachi Richardson 4.00 10.00
16 Kay Felder 3.00 8.00
17 Jamal Murray 20.00 50.00
18 Timothe Luwawu-Cabarrot 10.00 25.00
19 Marquese Chriss 12.00 30.00
20 Brice Johnson 3.00 8.00
21 Ivica Zubac 20.00 50.00
22 Malcolm Brogdon 15.00 40.00
23 Jakob Poeltl 4.00 10.00
24 Pascal Siakam 3.00 8.00
25 Diamond Stone 3.00 8.00
26 Thon Maker 15.00 40.00
27 Skal Labissiere 6.00 15.00
28 Taurean Prince 5.00 12.00
29 Dejounte Murray
30 Damian Jones 3.00 8.00
31 Gary Payton II 4.00 10.00
32 Caris LeVert 4.00 10.00
33 Denzel Valentine 8.00 20.00
34 Deyonta Davis 10.00 25.00
35 Chinanu Onuaku 3.00 8.00
36 Juan Hernangomez 4.00 10.00
37 Georgios Papagiannis 3.00 8.00
38 Stephen Zimmerman 3.00 8.00

2016-17 Absolute Memorabilia Freshman Flyer Jumbo Jerseys

RANDOM INSERTS IN PACKS
STATED PRINT RUN 75 SER. #'d SETS
1 Brandon Ingram 6.00 15.00
2 Jaylen Brown 6.00 15.00
3 Dragan Bender 2.50 6.00
4 Kris-Dunn 4.00 10.00
5 Buddy Hield 5.00 12.00
6 Jamal Murray 5.00 12.00
7 Marquese Chriss 5.00 12.00
8 Jakob Poeltl 2.50 6.00
9 Thon Maker 5.00 12.00
11 Taurean Prince 3.00 8.00
12 Denzel Valentine 2.50 6.00
13 Wade Baldwin IV 2.00 5.00
14 Henry Ellenson 2.50 6.00
15 Malik Beasley 2.00 5.00
16 DeAndre' Bembry 2.00 5.00
17 Malachi Richardson 2.50 6.00
18 Timothe Luwawu-Cabarrot 4.00 10.00
19 Brice Johnson 2.00 5.00
20 Pascal Siakam 2.00 5.00
21 Skal Labissiere 3.00 8.00
22 Damian Jones 2.00 5.00
23 Deyonta Davis 2.00 5.00
24 Cheick Diallo 2.00 5.00
25 Tyler Ulis 6.00 15.00
26 Patrick McCaw 4.00 10.00
27 Isaiah Whitehead 2.00 5.00
28 Demetrius Jackson 2.00 5.00
29 Kay Felder 2.00 5.00
30 Ivica Zubac 3.00 8.00
31 Malcolm Brogdon 5.00 12.00
32 A.J. Hammons 2.00 5.00
33 Diamond Stone 2.00 5.00
34 Gary Payton II 2.50 6.00
35 Caris LeVert 2.50 6.00
36 Chinanu Onuaku 2.00 5.00
37 Juan Hernangomez 2.50 6.00
38 Georgios Papagiannis 2.00 5.00
39 Dejounte Murray 4.00 10.00
40 Stephen Zimmerman 2.00 5.00

2016-17 Absolute Memorabilia Glass

RANDOM INSERTS IN PACKS
EXCHANGE DEADLINE 8/21/2018
1 Ben Simmons 100.00 250.00
2 Brandon Ingram 50.00 125.00
3 Kris Dunn 25.00 60.00
4 Jaylen Brown 30.00 80.00
5 Buddy Hield 30.00 80.00
6 Jamal Murray 20.00 50.00
7 Anthony Davis 25.00 60.00
8 Kyrie Irving 25.00 60.00
9 Kevin Durant 30.00 80.00
10 Chris Paul 15.00 40.00
11 Karl-Anthony Towns 30.00 80.00
12 Russell Westbrook 30.00 80.00
13 Andrew Wiggins 20.00 50.00
14 Stephen Curry 50.00 125.00
15 LeBron James 50.00 125.00
16 Kawhi Leonard 20.00 50.00
17 Dirk Nowitzki 30.00 80.00
18 Jimmy Butler 30.00 80.00
19 James Harden 20.00 50.00
20 Karl Malone 25.00 60.00
21 Kobe Bryant 50.00 125.00
22 Steve Nash 15.00 40.00
23 Patrick Ewing 20.00 50.00
24 Scottie Pippen 25.00 60.00
25 Allen Iverson 25.00 60.00

2016-17 Absolute Memorabilia Heroes Autographs

RANDOM INSERTS IN PACKS
PRINT RUN B/WN 60-75 COPIES PER
EXCHANGE DEADLINE 8/21/2018
3 Kevin Durant/60 60.00 150.00
4 Blake Griffin/60 15.00 40.00
5 Elfrid Payton/75
6 Kevin Love/60 15.00 40.00
7 D'Angelo Russell/60 20.00 50.00
8 Chris Paul/60 25.00 60.00
9 Devin Booker/75 30.00 80.00
10 Bobby Portis/75
11 Jabari Parker/60 12.00 30.00
12 Myles Turner/75 6.00 15.00
13 Anthony Davis/60 25.00 60.00
14 Victor Oladipo/75 4.00 10.00
15 Reggie Jackson/75
16 Andrew Wiggins/60
17 Julius Randle/75
18 Tony Parker/60 20.00 50.00
19 Paul Millsap/75
21 Eric Bledsoe/75
22 LaMarcus Aldridge/75 15.00 40.00
23 Chris Bosh/60 5.00 12.00
24 Karl-Anthony Towns/60 40.00 100.00
25 Kristaps Porzingis/75 20.00 50.00
26 Jahlil Okafor/60 6.00 15.00
27 Draymond Green/75 20.00 50.00
28 Dwyane Wade/60 20.00 50.00
29 Emmanuel Mudiay/75 4.00 10.00
30 Carmelo Anthony/60 20.00 50.00

2016-17 Absolute Memorabilia Heroes Materials

RANDOM INSERTS IN PACKS
PRINT RUNS B/WN 49-149 COPIES PER
1 Alvan Adams/99 2.00 5.00
2 Allen Iverson/99 4.00 10.00
3 Manute Bol/99 3.00 8.00
4 Kevin McHale/99 3.00 8.00
5 Danny Ainge/99 3.00 8.00
6 Yao Ming/99 5.00 12.00
7 Kobe Bryant/149 8.00 20.00
8 Shaquille O'Neal/149 5.00 12.00
9 Christian Laettner/149 2.50 6.00
10 Tim Duncan/149 4.00 10.00
11 Stephen Curry/149 12.00 30.00
12 LeBron James/149 12.00 30.00
14 Chris Paul/149 4.00 10.00
16 Steve Nash/90 3.00 8.00
17 Xavier McDaniel/149 2.00 5.00
18 Detlef Schrempf/149 3.00 8.00
19 James Harden/149 5.00 12.00
20 Joe Johnson/149 2.50 6.00
21 Andrei Kirilenko/99 2.50 6.00
22 Manu Ginobili/149 3.00 8.00
23 Walter Davis/149 2.00 5.00
24 Bill Walton/49 3.00 8.00
25 Nate Thurmond/49 2.50 6.00
26 Paul Pierce/149 3.00 8.00
27 Rashard Lewis/149 2.50 6.00
28 Rik Smits/149 2.50 6.00
29 Robert Parish/149 3.00 8.00
30 Reggie Lewis/149 3.00 8.00
31 Mitch Richmond/149 3.00 8.00
32 Kevin Duckworth/149 2.00 5.00
33 Glen Rice/149 2.50 6.00
34 George Mikan/49 8.00 20.00
35 Elgin Baylor/49 3.00 8.00
36 Dwyane Wade/149 5.00 12.00
37 Derrick Rose/149 4.00 10.00
38 Chris Bosh/149 3.00 8.00
39 Walter Berry/149 2.00 5.00
40 Clifford Robinson/149 2.00 5.00

2016-17 Absolute Memorabilia Iconic Autographs

RANDOM INSERTS IN PACKS
PRINT RUN B/WN 60-75 COPIES PER
EXCHANGE DEADLINE 8/21/2018
1 Jason Kidd/60 10.00 25.00
2 Danny Manning/75 4.00 10.00
3 Isiah Thomas/75 8.00 20.00
4 Ray Allen/60 15.00 40.00
5 Robert Parish/75 5.00 12.00
6 Gary Payton/60 10.00 25.00
7 Jalen Rose/75 5.00 12.00
8 Walt Frazier/75 5.00 12.00
9 A.C. Green/75 5.00 12.00
10 Cuttino Mobley/75
11 Hersey Hawkins/75 3.00 8.00
12 Glen Rice/75 4.00 10.00
13 Bob McAdoo/75 8.00 20.00
14 Clyde Drexler/60 12.00 30.00
15 Michael Finley/75 5.00 12.00
16 Mitch Richmond/75 8.00 20.00
17 Joe Dumars/75 5.00 12.00
18 Anfernee Hardaway/60 20.00 50.00
19 Bill Walton/75 8.00 20.00
20 Dominique Wilkins/60 8.00 20.00
21 Tracy McGrady/60 15.00 40.00
22 Grant Hill/60 12.00 30.00
24 Steve Nash/60
25 Dikembe Mutombo/75 8.00 20.00
26 Dan Majerle/75 5.00 12.00
27 Damon Stoudamire/75
28 Steve Smith/75 4.00 10.00
29 Antonio McDyess/75 4.00 10.00
30 Ralph Sampson/75 4.00 10.00
31 Jo Jo White/75
32 Robert Horry/75 6.00 15.00
33 Mark Jackson/75 4.00 10.00
34 John Starks/75 4.00 10.00
35 Horace Grant/75 5.00 12.00
36 Jeff Hornacek/75 4.00 10.00
37 Bob Dandridge/75 3.00 8.00
38 Magic Johnson/60 25.00 60.00
39 Mark Aguirre/75 4.00 10.00
40 Cedric Maxwell/75 3.00 8.00

2016-17 Absolute Memorabilia Iconic Materials

RANDOM INSERTS IN PACKS
PRINT RUNS B/WN 49-149 COPIES PER
1 Kobe Bryant/149 8.00 20.00
2 Clyde Drexler/149 4.00 10.00
3 Hakeem Olajuwon/149 4.00 10.00
4 Patrick Ewing/149 4.00 10.00
5 Shaquille O'Neal/149 5.00 12.00
6 Chauncey Billups/149 3.00 8.00
7 Chris Mullin/149 3.00 8.00
8 Dennis Johnson/149 2.50 6.00
9 Larry Bird/149 6.00 15.00
10 Dikembe Mutombo/149 3.00 8.00
11 Lucius Allen/149 3.00 8.00
12 Wilt Chamberlain/49 30.00 80.00
13 Karl Malone/149 4.00 10.00
14 John Stockton/149 5.00 12.00
15 Tom Chambers/149 2.50 6.00
16 Michael Redd/149 2.50 6.00
17 Jason Kidd/49 3.00 8.00
18 Magic Johnson/149 8.00 20.00
19 Bernard King/149 2.50 6.00
20 Earl Monroe/99 3.00 8.00
21 John Starks/149 2.50 6.00
22 Kelly Tripucka/149 2.00 5.00
23 Jamaal Wilkes/149 3.00 8.00
24 James Worthy/149 4.00 10.00
25 LeBron James/149 10.00 25.00
26 Kevin Garnett/149 5.00 12.00
27 Dirk Nowitzki/149 4.00 10.00
28 Tim Duncan/149 4.00 10.00
29 DeMar DeRozan/149 3.00 8.00
30 Carmelo Anthony/149 4.00 10.00

2016-17 Absolute Memorabilia Marks of Fame

RANDOM INSERTS IN PACKS
PRINT RUN B/WN 60-75 COPIES PER
EXCHANGE DEADLINE 8/21/2018
1 Kobe Bryant/75 75.00 200.00
2 Kevin Durant/60 60.00 150.00
3 Kyrie Irving/60 25.00 60.00
4 Paul Westphal/75
5 Jeff Hornacek/75 4.00 10.00
6 Sean Elliott/75 5.00 12.00
7 Tony Parker/60 12.00 30.00
8 Chris Bosh/60 5.00 12.00
9 Dan Issel/75 4.00 10.00
10 Jamaal Wilkes/75 5.00 12.00
11 Bernard King/60
12 Adrian Dantley/75 4.00 10.00
13 Toni Kukoc/75 5.00 12.00
14 Andrew Wiggins/60
15 Isiah Thomas/60 10.00 25.00
16 Robert Horry/60 6.00 15.00
17 Zach LaVine/75 10.00 25.00
18 Robert Parish/60 5.00 12.00
19 Dennis Schroder/75
20 Giannis Antetokounmpo/75
21 Nick Van Exel/60
22 Bill Laimbeer/75 4.00 10.00
23 Bill Russell/60 75.00 200.00
24 Jim Jackson/75 3.00 8.00
25 Mark Price/75 8.00 20.00
26 Evan Turner/75
27 Kiki Vandeweghe/75 4.00 10.00
28 David Robinson/60 20.00 50.00
29 Tim Hardaway/75 10.00 25.00
30 Kurt Rambis/75 3.00 8.00

2016-17 Absolute Memorabilia NBA Stars Materials

RANDOM INSERTS IN PACKS
STATED PRINT RUN 149 SER. #'d SETS
1 Dirk Nowitzki 4.00 10.00
2 Kyrie Irving 5.00 12.00
3 Eric Bledsoe 2.50 6.00
4 LeBron James 12.00 30.00
5 Karl-Anthony Towns 5.00 12.00
6 Stephen Curry 12.00 30.00
7 DeMar DeRozan 3.00 8.00
8 Isaiah Thomas 3.00 8.00
9 Deron Williams 2.50 6.00
10 James Harden 5.00 12.00
11 Russell Westbrook 5.00 12.00
12 Andrew Wiggins 4.00 10.00
13 Carmelo Anthony 4.00 10.00
14 Damian Lillard 4.00 10.00
15 John Wall 4.00 10.00
16 Anthony Davis 5.00 12.00
17 Blake Griffin 3.00 8.00
18 Kevin Garnett 5.00 12.00
19 Jabari Parker 4.00 10.00
20 Jimmy Butler 3.00 8.00
21 Paul George 4.00 10.00
22 Gordon Hayward 3.00 8.00
23 DeMarcus Cousins 3.00 8.00
24 Draymond Green 4.00 10.00
25 Brandon Knight 2.50 6.00
26 Kenneth Faried 2.50 6.00
27 Myles Turner 2.50 6.00
28 Dwight Howard 2.50 6.00
29 Giannis Antetokounmpo 5.00 12.00
30 Nerlens Noel 2.50 6.00

2016-17 Absolute Memorabilia Rookie Autographs

RANDOM INSERTS IN PACKS
STATED PRINT RUN 99 SER. #'d SETS
EXCHANGE DEADLINE 8/21/2018
1 Brandon Ingram 40.00 100.00
2 Jaylen Brown 12.00 30.00
3 Dragan Bender 6.00 15.00
4 Kris Dunn 20.00 50.00
5 Buddy Hield 15.00 40.00
6 Jamal Murray 15.00 40.00
7 Marquese Chriss 8.00 20.00
8 Jakob Poeltl 4.00 10.00
9 Thon Maker 25.00 60.00
10 Domantas Sabonis 5.00 12.00
11 Taurean Prince 5.00 12.00
12 Denzel Valentine 4.00 10.00
13 Wade Baldwin IV 3.00 8.00
14 Henry Ellenson 4.00 10.00
15 Malik Beasley 3.00 8.00
16 DeAndre' Bembry 3.00 8.00
17 Malachi Richardson 12.00 30.00
18 Timothe Luwawu-Cabarrot 6.00 15.00
19 Brice Johnson 3.00 8.00
20 Pascal Siakam 3.00 8.00
21 Skal Labissiere 12.00 30.00
22 Damian Jones 3.00 8.00
23 Deyonta Davis 3.00 8.00
24 Cheick Diallo 3.00 8.00
25 Tyler Ulis 10.00 25.00
26 Patrick McCaw 12.00 30.00
27 Isaiah Whitehead 3.00 8.00
28 Demetrius Jackson 3.00 8.00
29 Kay Felder 3.00 8.00
30 Ivica Zubac 12.00 30.00
31 Malcolm Brogdon 15.00 40.00
32 A.J. Hammons 3.00 8.00
33 Diamond Stone 3.00 8.00
34 Gary Payton II 4.00 10.00
35 Caris LeVert 10.00 25.00

2016-17 Absolute Memorabilia Team Quads Materials

RANDOM INSERTS IN PACKS
STATED PRINT RUN 25 SER. #'d SETS
1 Wiggins/Towns/Garnett/LaVine 10.00 25.00
2 Love/Irving/James/Thompson 25.00 60.00
3 Mudiay/Nurkic/Faried/Jokic 4.00 10.00
4 Williams/Nowitzki/Anderson/Matthews 5.00 12.00
5 Bradley/Thomas/Crowder/Smart 4.00 10.00

2016-17 Absolute Memorabilia Team Tandems Materials

RANDOM INSERTS IN PACKS
STATED PRINT RUN 149 SER. #'d SETS
*PRIME/25: .75X TO 2X BASIC
1 K.Thompson/S.Curry 10.00 25.00
2 D.Schroder/P.Millsap 3.00 8.00
3 C.Anthony/K.Porzingis 5.00 12.00
4 A.Davis/T.Evans 5.00 12.00
5 E.Kanter/S.Adams 2.50 6.00
6 A.Gordon/E.Payton 2.50 6.00
7 B.Griffin/D.Jordan 3.00 8.00
8 D.Russell/J.Randle 4.00 10.00
9 M.Conley/Z.Randolph 2.50 6.00
10 A.Wiggins/Z.LaVine 5.00 12.00
11 D.DeRozan/K.Lowry 3.00 8.00
12 B.Bogdanovic/B.Lopez 2.50 6.00
13 J.Wall/M.Gortat 4.00 10.00
14 C.Drexler/H.Olajuwon 4.00 10.00
15 K.Bryant/S.O'Neal 10.00 25.00
16 I.Thomas/J.Dumars 3.00 8.00
17 R.Parish/S.Pippen 5.00 12.00
18 A.Mourning/L.Johnson 5.00 12.00
19 J.Kidd/J.Jackson 3.00 8.00

2016-17 Absolute Memorabilia Team Trios Materials

RANDOM INSERTS IN PACKS
STATED PRINT RUN 49 SER. #'d SETS
1 Wiggins/Towns/LaVine 6.00 15.00
2 Love/Irving/James 15.00 40.00
3 Mudiay/Faried/Jokic 4.00 10.00
4 Williams/Nowitzki/Anderson 5.00 12.00
5 Bradley/Thomas/Crowder 8.00 20.00
6 Capela/Brewer/Harden 5.00 12.00
7 Ellis/Turner/George 5.00 12.00
8 Griffin/Paul/Jordan 5.00 12.00
9 Drummond/Caldwell-Pope/Jackson 4.00 10.00
10 Antetokounmpo/Monroe Carter-Williams 5.00 12.00

2016-17 Absolute Memorabilia Tools of the Trade Jumbo Rookie Material Signatures

RANDOM INSERTS IN PACKS
STATED PRINT RUN 49 SER. #'d SETS
EXCHANGE DEADLINE 8/21/2018
1 Brandon Ingram 30.00 80.00
2 Isaiah Whitehead 3.00 8.00
3 DeAndre' Bembry 3.00 8.00
4 Marquese Chriss 8.00 20.00
5 Wade Baldwin IV 3.00 8.00
6 Denzel Valentine 8.00 20.00
7 Dragan Bender 10.00 25.00
8 Deyonta Davis 3.00 8.00
9 Georgios Papagiannis 3.00 8.00
10 Jamal Murray 15.00 40.00
11 Demetrius Jackson 3.00 8.00
12 Kris Dunn 10.00 25.00
13 Brice Johnson 3.00 8.00
14 Tyler Ulis 10.00 25.00
15 Jaylen Brown 20.00 50.00
16 Jakob Poeltl 4.00 10.00
17 Timothe Luwawu-Cabarrot 6.00 15.00
18 Buddy Hield 12.00 30.00
19 Malik Beasley 3.00 8.00
20 Pascal Siakam 3.00 8.00
21 Ivica Zubac 8.00 20.00
22 Henry Ellenson 4.00 10.00
23 Diamond Stone 3.00 8.00
24 Thon Maker 10.00 25.00
25 Skal Labissiere 5.00 12.00
26 Taurean Prince 5.00 12.00
27 Juan Hernangomez 8.00 20.00
28 Dejounte Murray
29 Stephen Zimmerman 3.00 8.00
30 Damian Jones 3.00 8.00
31 Chinanu Onuaku 3.00 8.00
32 Caris LeVert 6.00 15.00
33 Malachi Richardson 4.00 10.00

2016-17 Absolute Memorabilia Tools of the Trade Rookie Autograph Materials

RANDOM INSERTS IN PACKS
STATED PRINT RUN 75 SER. #'d SETS
EXCHANGE DEADLINE 8/21/2018
1 Brandon Ingram 50.00 120.00
2 Isaiah Whitehead 4.00 10.00
3 DeAndre' Bembry 4.00 10.00
4 Marquese Chriss 12.00 30.00
5 Wade Baldwin IV 8.00 20.00
6 Denzel Valentine 10.00 25.00
7 Dragan Bender 10.00 25.00
8 Deyonta Davis 4.00 10.00
9 Georgios Papagiannis 4.00 10.00
10 Jamal Murray 30.00 80.00
11 Demetrius Jackson 4.00 10.00
12 Kris Dunn 20.00 50.00
13 Brice Johnson 8.00 20.00
14 Tyler Ulis 15.00 40.00
15 Jaylen Brown 30.00 80.00
16 Jakob Poeltl 5.00 12.00
17 Timothe Luwawu-Cabarrot 10.00 25.00
18 Buddy Hield 20.00 50.00
19 Malik Beasley 6.00 15.00
20 Pascal Siakam 4.00 10.00
21 Ivica Zubac 10.00 25.00
22 Henry Ellenson 5.00 12.00
23 Diamond Stone 6.00 15.00
24 Thon Maker 40.00 100.00
25 Skal Labissiere 10.00 25.00
26 Taurean Prince 6.00 15.00
27 Juan Hernangomez 8.00 20.00
28 Dejounte Murray
29 Stephen Zimmerman 4.00 10.00
30 Damian Jones 10.00 25.00
31 Chinanu Onuaku 4.00 10.00
32 Caris LeVert 8.00 20.00
33 Malachi Richardson 6.00 15.00

2016-17 Absolute Memorabilia Tools of the Trade Rookie Materials Dual

RANDOM INSERTS IN PACKS
STATED PRINT RUN 149 SER. #'d SETS
*PRIME/49: .5X TO 1.2X BASIC
*PATCH/25: .6X TO 1.5X BASIC
1 Brandon Ingram 6.00 15.00
2 Isaiah Whitehead 2.50 6.00
3 DeAndre' Bembry 2.50 6.00
4 Marquese Chriss 6.00 15.00
5 Wade Baldwin IV 2.50 6.00
6 Denzel Valentine 3.00 8.00
7 Dragan Bender 3.00 8.00
8 Deyonta Davis 2.50 6.00
9 Georgios Papagiannis 2.50 6.00
10 Jamal Murray 5.00 12.00
11 Demetrius Jackson 2.50 6.00
12 Kris Dunn 5.00 12.00
13 Brice Johnson 2.50 6.00
14 Tyler Ulis 8.00 20.00
15 Jaylen Brown 6.00 15.00
16 Jakob Poeltl 3.00 8.00
17 Timothe Luwawu-Cabarrot 5.00 12.00
18 Buddy Hield 6.00 15.00
19 Malik Beasley 2.50 6.00
20 Pascal Siakam 2.50 6.00
21 Ivica Zubac 4.00 10.00
22 Henry Ellenson 3.00 8.00
23 Diamond Stone 2.50 6.00
24 Thon Maker 6.00 15.00
25 Skal Labissiere 4.00 10.00
26 Taurean Prince 4.00 10.00
27 Juan Hernangomez 3.00 8.00
28 Dejounte Murray 5.00 12.00
29 Stephen Zimmerman 2.50 6.00
30 Damian Jones 2.50 6.00
31 Chinanu Onuaku 2.50 6.00
32 Caris LeVert 3.00 8.00
33 Malachi Richardson 3.00 8.00

2016-17 Absolute Memorabilia Tools of the Trade Rookie Materials Jumbo

RANDOM INSERTS IN PACKS
STATED PRINT RUN 149 SER. #'d SETS
*PRIME/25: .75X TO 2X BASIC
1 Brandon Ingram 6.00 15.00
2 Isaiah Whitehead 2.50 6.00
3 DeAndre' Bembry 2.50 6.00
4 Marquese Chriss 6.00 15.00
5 Wade Baldwin IV 2.50 6.00
6 Denzel Valentine 3.00 8.00
7 Dragan Bender 3.00 8.00
8 Deyonta Davis 2.50 6.00
9 Georgios Papagiannis 2.50 6.00
10 Jamal Murray 5.00 12.00

Beverly Hills Baseball Card Shop

est.1983

BUY / SELL / TRADE

Baseball•Basketball•Football•Hockey

Packs, Sets, Singles, Stars, Inserts

Autographs & Memorabilia - Bats, Balls, Pictures, Jerseys, Cards and Jersey Cards... * Custom Framing also available

WE ARE ALWAYS BUYING

1137 So. Robertson Blvd. (between Olympic & Pico) Los Angeles, CA 90035

Ph: 310-278-4263 • Fx: 310-626-9667

HOURS: Tue-Fri: 11-6 • Sat: 11-5 • Closed Sun/Mon.

www.californiasportscards.com

NEW STORE!

Westside Sportscards and Memorabilia

1431 Santa Monica Blvd • Santa Monica CA 90404

Baseball Cards | Basketball Cards
Football Cards | Hockey Cards
Gaming Cards | Boxes and Packs
Birthday Parties | Framing

$ ALWAYS BUYING! $

www.westsidesportscards.com

310-458-8867

BECKETT VINTAGE COLLECTOR

JOE NAMATH'S RC Photo was Taken Where? >>

BRINGING FOCUS TO THE BLACK SOX

Collecting The Eight Men Out

Call 239.280.2380

$9.99

WWW.BECKETTMEDIA.COM

Monthly Premier Sportscards Auctions

brent@pwccauctions.com • 510-725-7853

PWCCAuctions.com

Japan's Largest Trading Card Chain Stores

Online Store: mint-mall.net eBay: team-mint

Twitter: @mint_jpn Waibo: MINT-SportsCard

AUTOGRAPHS ★ SPORTS CARDS ★ COLLECTIBLES

DAILY AUCTIONS!

Hoody's

COLLECTIBLES

Sports Cards Memorabilia Consignment

Twitter: @collecthoodys Phone: 503-536-7692

Instagram: @hoodyscollectibles email: tait@hoodys.us

www.hoodys.us

GW'S SPORTS CARDS

ebay: greatwrighter

Beckett: GW's Sports Cards

Facebook: GW's Sports Cards

Email: greatwrighter@aol.com

★ ★ ★ ★ ★ ★

3431 Pomona Blvd. Suite I,

Pomona CA 91768

YOUR AD HERE for as low as → $100 ←

Contact Priscilla Torres

972.448.9131 or ptorres@beckett.com

The Fantastic Store

Hours of Operation:
Tue-Fri 11am - 7pm
& Sat 10am - 6pm

Email:
thefantasticstore@blowoutcards.com

Twitter:
@afantasticstore

Phone:
(703) 953-3131

blowoutcards.com/thefantasticstore

Fastball Collectibles

fastballcollectibles.com

Since 1975* Buying and Selling Basketball cards 1920s-80s

Sets* Boxes* Autographs* Inserts*Memorabilia

Ship Worldwide

Ebay: fastballplatinum store id • 416.323.0403

fastball@interlog.com

11 Demetrius Jackson 2.50 6.00
12 Kris Dunn 5.00 12.00
13 Brice Johnson 2.50 6.00
14 Tyler Ulis 8.00 20.00
15 Jaylen Brown 6.00 15.00
16 Jakob Poeltl 3.00 8.00
17 Timothe Luwawu-Cabarrot 5.00 12.00
18 Buddy Hield 6.00 15.00
19 Malik Beasley 2.50 6.00
20 Pascal Siakam 2.50 6.00
21 Ivica Zubac 4.00 10.00
22 Henry Ellenson 3.00 8.00
23 Diamond Stone 2.50 6.00
24 Thon Maker 6.00 15.00
25 Skal Labissiere 4.00 10.00
26 Taurean Prince 4.00 10.00
27 Juan Hernangomez 3.00 8.00
28 Dejounte Murray 5.00 12.00
29 Stephen Zimmerman 2.50 6.00
30 Damian Jones 2.50 6.00
31 Chinanu Onuaku 2.50 6.00
32 Caris LeVert 3.00 8.00
33 Malachi Richardson 3.00 8.00

2016-17 Absolute Memorabilia Tools of the Trade Rookie Materials Quad

RANDOM INSERTS IN PACKS
STATED PRINT RUN 125 SER. #'d SETS
*PRIME: .6X TO 1.5X BASIC
1 Brandon Ingram 8.00 20.00
2 Isaiah Whitehead 3.00 8.00
3 DeAndre' Bembry 3.00 8.00
4 Marquese Chriss 8.00 20.00
5 Wade Baldwin IV 3.00 8.00
6 Denzel Valentine 4.00 10.00
7 Dragan Bender 4.00 10.00
8 Deyonta Davis 3.00 8.00
9 Georgios Papagiannis 3.00 8.00
10 Jamal Murray 6.00 15.00
11 Demetrius Jackson 3.00 8.00
12 Kris Dunn 6.00 15.00
13 Brice Johnson 3.00 8.00
14 Tyler Ulis 10.00 25.00
15 Jaylen Brown 6.00 15.00
16 Jakob Poeltl 4.00 10.00
17 Timothe Luwawu-Cabarrot 6.00 15.00
18 Buddy Hield 8.00 20.00
19 Malik Beasley 3.00 8.00
20 Pascal Siakam 3.00 8.00
21 Ivica Zubac 5.00 12.00
22 Henry Ellenson 4.00 10.00
23 Diamond Stone 3.00 8.00
24 Thon Maker 8.00 20.00
25 Skal Labissiere 5.00 12.00
26 Taurean Prince 5.00 12.00
27 Juan Hernangomez 4.00 10.00
28 Dejounte Murray 6.00 15.00
29 Stephen Zimmerman 3.00 8.00
30 Damian Jones 3.00 8.00
31 Chinanu Onuaku 3.00 8.00
32 Caris LeVert 4.00 10.00
33 Malachi Richardson 4.00 10.00

2016-17 Absolute Memorabilia Tools of the Trade Rookie Materials Six

RANDOM INSERTS IN PACKS
STATED PRINT RUN 75 SER. #'d SETS
*PRIME/25: .6X TO 1.5X BASIC
1 Brandon Ingram 8.00 20.00
2 Isaiah Whitehead 3.00 8.00
3 DeAndre' Bembry 3.00 8.00
4 Marquese Chriss 8.00 20.00
5 Wade Baldwin IV 3.00 8.00
6 Denzel Valentine 4.00 10.00
7 Dragan Bender 4.00 10.00
8 Deyonta Davis 3.00 8.00
9 Georgios Papagiannis 3.00 8.00
10 Jamal Murray 6.00 15.00
11 Demetrius Jackson 3.00 8.00
12 Kris Dunn 6.00 15.00
13 Brice Johnson 3.00 8.00
14 Tyler Ulis 10.00 25.00
15 Jaylen Brown 8.00 20.00
16 Jakob Poeltl 4.00 10.00
17 Timothe Luwawu-Cabarrot 6.00 15.00
18 Buddy Hield 8.00 20.00
19 Malik Beasley 3.00 8.00
20 Pascal Siakam 3.00 8.00
21 Ivica Zubac 10.00 25.00
22 Henry Ellenson 4.00 10.00
23 Diamond Stone 3.00 8.00
24 Thon Maker 10.00 25.00
25 Skal Labissiere 5.00 12.00
26 Taurean Prince 5.00 12.00
27 Juan Hernangomez 4.00 10.00
28 Dejounte Murray 6.00 15.00
29 Stephen Zimmerman 3.00 8.00
30 Damian Jones 3.00 8.00
31 Chinanu Onuaku 3.00 8.00
32 Caris LeVert 4.00 10.00
33 Malachi Richardson 4.00 10.00

2016-17 Absolute Memorabilia Tools of the Trade Rookie Materials Trio

RANDOM INSERTS IN PACKS
STATED PRINT RUN 149 SER. #'d SETS
*PRIME/25: .6X TO 1.5X BASIC
1 Brandon Ingram 6.00 15.00
2 Isaiah Whitehead 2.50 6.00
3 DeAndre' Bembry 2.50 6.00
4 Marquese Chriss 6.00 15.00
5 Wade Baldwin IV 2.50 6.00
6 Denzel Valentine 3.00 8.00
7 Dragan Bender 3.00 8.00
8 Deyonta Davis 2.50 6.00
9 Georgios Papagiannis 2.50 6.00
10 Jamal Murray 5.00 12.00
11 Demetrius Jackson 2.50 6.00
12 Kris Dunn 5.00 12.00
13 Brice Johnson 2.50 6.00
14 Tyler Ulis 8.00 20.00
15 Jaylen Brown 6.00 15.00
16 Jakob Poeltl 3.00 8.00
17 Timothe Luwawu-Cabarrot 5.00 12.00
18 Buddy Hield 6.00 15.00
19 Malik Beasley 2.50 6.00
20 Pascal Siakam 2.50 6.00
21 Ivica Zubac 4.00 10.00
22 Henry Ellenson 3.00 8.00
23 Diamond Stone 2.50 6.00
24 Thon Maker 6.00 15.00
25 Skal Labissiere 4.00 10.00
26 Taurean Prince 4.00 10.00
27 Juan Hernangomez 3.00 8.00
28 Dejounte Murray 5.00 12.00
29 Stephen Zimmerman 2.50 6.00
30 Damian Jones 2.50 6.00
31 Chinanu Onuaku 2.50 6.00
32 Caris LeVert 3.00 8.00
33 Malachi Richardson 3.00 8.00

1990 Action Packed Promos Gold

Action Packed produced these cards in order to show the NBA what they could do with basketball cards. These unnumbered cards are numbered alphabetically for convenience in the checklist below. The cards are standard size, 2 1/2" by 3 1/2" with rounded corners. There is some question as to whether this is a legitimate set since Action Packed did not intend these to be sold.
COMPLETE SET (4) 100.00 200.00
*SILVER: .4X TO 1X GOLD
1 Patrick Ewing 10.00 25.00
2 Magic Johnson 15.00 40.00
3 Michael Jordan 100.00 250.00

1993 Action Packed Hall of Fame

In conjunction with the Naismith Memorial Basketball Hall of Fame, Action Packed issued this 84-card standard-size set to honor the greatest basketball players and coaches of all time. The set was released in two separate series of 42 cards each. The first series contains 37 current Hall of Famers and a five-card subset devoted to Larry Bird, a Hall of Famer in waiting. The Julius Erving (72G) autographed card was numbered "x of 2500" on the card and was originally only available as a chiptopper in the second series hobby boxes, approximately found one per 20 boxes. The fronts display color photos featuring embossed, sculptured images of the player. The player's name and position are gold-foil stamped across the bottom. A Basketball Hall of Fame 25th anniversary logo in gold foil runs down the right edge. The backs display career highlights overlaid on a parquet basketball court design. Topical subsets featured are One On One (1-10), Coaches (11-16), and Larry Bird (17-21). The cards are numbered on the back. Card 24A is actually a preview card which was delivered to the hobby during January and February via Chiptoppers packed in every box of All-Madden football cards and Action Packed All-Star Gallery Series II baseball cards; it is distinguished from the regular cards by the fact that it has only black and gold print on the back and is not considered part of the complete set. The second series is subdivided into Hall of Fame players (43-51), Hall of Fame coaches (52-59), Class of 1993 (60-67), Dr.J. (68-72), College Days (74-78), and Players Who Coached (79-84).
COMPLETE SET (84) 8.00 20.00
COMPLETE SERIES 1 (42) 4.00 10.00
COMPLETE SERIES 2 (42) 4.00 10.00
1 Walt Frazier .15 .40
2 Jerry West .30 .75
3 Dave Bing .12 .30
4 Earl Monroe .15 .40
5 Willis Reed .15 .40
6 Dave Cowens .12 .30
7 Bill Bradley .15 .40
8 Elgin Baylor .20 .50
9 Elvin Hayes .15 .40
10 Nate Thurmond .15 .40
11 Red Auerbach CO .20 .50
12 John Wooden CO .20 .50
13 Red Holzman CO .15 .40
14 Lou Carnesecca CO .12 .30
15 Bob Knight CO .15 .40
16 Dean Smith CO .15 .40
17 Larry Bird .40 1.00
18 Larry Bird .40 1.00
19 Larry Bird .40 1.00
20 Larry Bird .40 1.00
21 Larry Bird .40 1.00
22 K.C. Jones .12 .30
23 Slater Martin .15 .40
24 Bob Wanzer .12 .30
25 Bob Davies .12 .30
26 Nate Archibald .15 .40
27 Bill Sharman .15 .40
28 Tom Gola .12 .30
29 Tom Heinsohn .15 .40
30 Clyde Lovellette .15 .40
31 Bob Pettit .15 .40
32 Dolph Schayes .15 .40
33 Jack Twyman .15 .40
34 Hal Greer .15 .40
35 Sam Jones .15 .40
36 Dave DeBusschere .15 .40
37 Connie Hawkins .15 .40
38 Jerry Lucas .15 .40
39 Pete Maravich .30 .75
40 Oscar Robertson .25 .60
41 Lenny Wilkens .15 .40
42 Bob Lanier .15 .40
43 Paul Arizin .15 .40
44 Harry Gallatin .15 .40
45 Frank Ramsey .20 .50
46 Ed Macauley .12 .30
47 Bob Kurland .12 .30
48 Rick Barry .15 .40
49 John Havlicek .20 .50
50 Hank Luisetti .12 .30
51 Wes Unseld .15 .40
52 Al McGuire .15 .40
53 Frank McGuire .12 .30
54 Ray Meyer .12 .30
55 Pete Newell .12 .30
56 Jack Ramsay .15 .40
57 Adolph Rupp .15 .40
58 Clarence Gaines .12 .30
59 Henry Iba .15 .40
60 Dan Issel .15 .40
61 Walt Bellamy .15 .40
62 Dick McGuire .12 .30
63 Calvin Murphy .15 .40
64 Uljana Semjonova .12 .30
65 Bill Walton .20 .50
66 Ann Meyers .12 .30
67 Julius Erving .25 .60
68 Julius Erving .25 .60
69 Julius Erving .25 .60
70 Julius Erving .25 .60
71 Julius Erving .25 .60
72 Julius Erving .25 .60
73 Larry O'Brien .12 .30
74 Bill Bradley .15 .40
75 Pete Maravich .30 .75
76 Elvin Hayes .15 .40
77 Jerry West .30 .75
78 Oscar Robertson .25 .60
79 K.C. Jones .12 .30
80 Tom Heinsohn .15 .40
81 Billy Cunningham .15 .40
82 Red Holzman .15 .40
83 Lenny Wilkens .15 .40
84 Bill Sharman .15 .40
XX Oscar Robertson PROMO 1.25 3.00

1993 Action Packed Hall of Fame 24K Gold

Randomly inserted in packs, these cards parallel the base set. The cards feature extra gold foil and a 24K logo on the card front.
*GOLD: 6X TO 15X VALUE
56G Julius Erving/2500 4.00 10.00
72G Julius Erving AU/2500 100.00 250.00

1995 Action Packed Hall of Fame

1995 Action Packed Hall of Fame Signature series I was released in January, with series II released in time for the playoffs. Except for Pete Maravich, every player in the set autographed at least 500 cards. Bill Russell and Bob Cousy are featured only on signed cards, not unsigned ones; thus, the regular set consists of 38 cards, but the signed set contains 40. Action Packed limited the product to 2,000 cases. "Greats of the Game" autograph cards were inserted one per case. The fronts feature either color or black-and- white embossed player photos inside gold borders. The player's name is reversed out in the top wider gold border. His facsimile autograph is inscribed in gold across the picture. On a ghosted version of the front photo, the backs present biography and career summary. The third series is subdivided as follows: Hall of Fame (1-31), Class of '94 (32-36), and Greats of the Game (37-40). Redeemed autograph cards are valued at 60 times the listed prices below. The autographed Russell and Cousy cards are priced individually below.
COMPLETE SET (38) 4.00 10.00
COMPLETE SERIES 1 (20) 2.00 5.00
COMPLETE SERIES 2 (18) 2.00 5.00
1 Nate Archibald .15 .40
2 Dick McGuire .20 .50
3 Lou Carnesecca .20 .50
4 Red Holzman .20 .50
5 Rick Barry .15 .40
6 Billy Cunningham .20 .50
7 Connie Hawkins .20 .50
8 Dan Issel .15 .40
9 Walt Bellamy .15 .40
10 Elvin Hayes .20 .50
11 Calvin Murphy .15 .40
12 Bob Knight .25 .60
13 Al McGuire .20 .50
14 K.C. Jones .20 .50
15 Jack Ramsay .20 .50
16 John Wooden .25 .60
17 Ray Meyer .20 .50
18 Lenny Wilkens .20 .50
19 Dean Smith .25 .60
20 Ed Macauley .20 .50
21 Nate Thurmond .15 .40
22 Dolph Schayes .20 .50
23 Bill Sharman .20 .50
24 Jerry Lucas .20 .50
25 Frank Ramsey .20 .50
26 Pete Maravich .30 .75
27 Bob Pettit .20 .50
28 Hal Greer .15 .40
29 Bill Walton .20 .50
30 Bill Bradley .25 .60
31 Tom Gola .20 .50
32 Carol Blazejowski .20 .50
33 Denny Crum .20 .50
34 Chuck Daly .20 .50
35 Buddy Jeanette .20 .50
36 Cesare Rubini .20 .50
37 Bill Bradley .25 .60
38 Bill Walton .20 .50

1995 Action Packed Hall of Fame 24K Gold

Inserted one per box, these cards parallel the base set. The cards feature extra gold foil and a "24K" logo on the card front.
*GOLD: 8X TO 20X VALUE

1995 Action Packed Hall of Fame Autographs

Every box contained one autograph redemption card that were randomly inserted. Cousy and Russell only had autographed cards, thus, this set is complete at 40 cards, rather than 38.
COMPLETE SET (40) 400.00 700.00
1 Nate Archibald 6.00 15.00
2 Dick McGuire 8.00 20.00
3 Lou Carnesecca 8.00 20.00
4 Red Holzman 8.00 20.00
5 Rick Barry 6.00 15.00
6 Billy Cunningham 8.00 20.00
7 Connie Hawkins 8.00 20.00
8 Dan Issel 6.00 15.00
9 Walt Bellamy 6.00 15.00
10 Elvin Hayes 8.00 20.00
11 Calvin Murphy 6.00 15.00
12 Bob Knight 10.00 25.00
13 Al McGuire 8.00 20.00
14 K.C. Jones 8.00 20.00
15 Jack Ramsay 8.00 20.00
16 John Wooden 10.00 25.00
17 Ray Meyer 8.00 20.00
18 Lenny Wilkens 8.00 20.00
19 Dean Smith 10.00 25.00
20 Ed Macauley 10.00 25.00
21 Nate Thurmond 6.00 15.00
22 Dolph Schayes 8.00 20.00
23 Bill Sharman 8.00 20.00
24 Jerry Lucas 8.00 20.00
25 Frank Ramsey 8.00 20.00
26 Pete Maravich 12.00 30.00
27 Bob Pettit 8.00 20.00
28 Hal Greer 6.00 15.00
29 Bill Walton 8.00 20.00
30 Bill Bradley 10.00 25.00
31 Tom Gola 8.00 20.00
32 Carol Blazejowski 8.00 20.00
33 Denny Crum 8.00 20.00
34 Chuck Daly 8.00 20.00
35 Buddy Jeanette 8.00 20.00
36 Cesare Rubini 8.00 20.00
37 Bill Bradley 10.00 25.00
38 Bill Walton 8.00 20.00
39 Bob Cousy 20.00 50.00
40 Bill Russell 125.00 300.00

2009-10 Adrenalyn XL

COMPLETE SET (300) 30.00 80.00
1 Arron Afflalo .12 .30
2 Alexis Ajinca .12 .30
3 LaMarcus Aldridge .20 .50
4 Joe Alexander .12 .30
5 Ray Allen .20 .50
6 Rafer Alston .12 .30
7 Chris Andersen .15 .40
8 David Andersen RC .30 .75
9 Ryan Anderson .15 .40
10 Carmelo Anthony .25 .60
11 Joel Anthony RC .50 1.25
12 Gilbert Arenas .15 .40
13 Trevor Ariza .12 .30
14 Hilton Armstrong .12 .30
15 Ron Artest .20 .50
16 Darrell Arthur .15 .40
17 D.J. Augustin .12 .30
18 Kelenna Azubuike .12 .30
19 Renaldo Balkman .12 .30
20 Leandro Barbosa .15 .40
21 J.J. Barea .25 .60
22 Andrea Bargnani .15 .40
23 Matt Barnes .12 .30
24 Brandon Bass .12 .30
25 Tony Battie .12 .30
26 Shane Battier .20 .50
27 Nicolas Batum .15 .40
28 Michael Beasley .12 .30
29 Rodrigue Beaubois RC .30 .75
30 Raja Bell .15 .40
31 Charlie Bell .12 .30
32 Mike Bibby .15 .40
33 Andris Biedrins .12 .30
34 Chauncey Billups .20 .50
35 DeJuan Blair RC .40 1.00
36 Steve Blake .12 .30
37 Andray Blatche .12 .30
38 Andrew Bogut .15 .40
39 Matt Bonner .12 .30
40 Carlos Boozer .15 .40
41 Chris Bosh .20 .50
42 Elton Brand .20 .50
43 Corey Brewer .12 .30
44 Ronnie Brewer .15 .40
45 Primoz Brezec .12 .30
46 Aaron Brooks .12 .30
47 Derrick Brown .12 .30
48 Devin Brown .12 .30
49 Kobe Bryant .75 2.00
50 Rasual Butler .12 .30
51 Caron Butler .15 .40
52 Will Bynum .12 .30
53 Andrew Bynum .12 .30
54 Jose Calderon .12 .30
55 Marcus Camby .12 .30
56 Brian Cardinal .12 .30
57 DeMarre Carroll RC .40 1.00
58 Vince Carter .25 .60
59 Omri Casspi RC .40 1.00
60 Mario Chalmers .15 .40
61 Tyson Chandler .15 .40
62 Darren Collison RC .50 1.25
63 Mike Conley Jr. .15 .40
64 Daequan Cook .12 .30
65 Jamal Crawford .20 .50
66 Joe Crawford .12 .30
67 Stephen Curry RC 8.00 20.00
68 Samuel Dalembert .12 .30
69 Erick Dampier .12 .30
70 Glen Davis .12 .30
71 Baron Davis .15 .40
72 Austin Daye RC .30 .75
73 Luol Deng .15 .40
74 DeMar DeRozan RC 1.25 3.00
75 Boris Diaw .15 .40
76 Dan Dickau .12 .30
77 Travis Diener .12 .30
78 Toney Douglas RC .30 .75
79 Jared Dudley .12 .30
80 Chris Duhon .12 .30
81 Tim Duncan .30 .75
82 Mike Dunleavy .12 .30
83 Kevin Durant .50 1.25
84 Wayne Ellington RC .50 1.25
85 Monta Ellis .15 .40
86 Melvin Ely .12 .30
87 Maurice Evans .12 .30
88 Tyreke Evans RC .40 1.00
89 Reggie Evans .12 .30
90 Jordan Farmar .12 .30
91 Raymond Felton .15 .40
92 Rudy Fernandez .12 .30
93 Michael Finley .20 .50
94 Derek Fisher .15 .40
95 Jonny Flynn RC .30 .75
96 T.J. Ford .12 .30
97 Jeff Foster .12 .30
98 Randy Foye .12 .30
99 Adonal Foyle .12 .30
100 Channing Frye .15 .40
101 Francisco Garcia .12 .30
102 Kevin Garnett .30 .75
103 Pau Gasol .20 .50
104 Marc Gasol .20 .50
105 Rudy Gay .20 .50
106 Devean George .12 .30
107 Taj Gibson RC .50 1.25
108 Daniel Gibson .15 .40
109 Manu Ginobili .20 .50
110 Ryan Gomes .12 .30
111 Ben Gordon .15 .40
112 Eric Gordon .15 .40
113 Danny Granger .15 .40
114 Jeff Green .15 .40
115 Blake Griffin RC 2.00 5.00
116 Taylor Griffin RC .30 .75
117 Richard Hamilton .15 .40
118 Tyler Hansbrough RC .40 1.00
119 James Harden RC 2.50 6.00
120 Matt Harpring .12 .30
121 Al Harrington .15 .40
122 Devin Harris .12 .30
123 Udonis Haslem .12 .30
124 Trenton Hassell .12 .30
125 Spencer Hawes .12 .30
126 Jarvis Hayes .12 .30
127 Brendan Haywood .12 .30
128 Gerald Henderson RC .40 1.00
129 Roy Hibbert .15 .40
130 Jordan Hill RC .40 1.00
131 Grant Hill .25 .60
132 Kirk Hinrich .15 .40
133 Jrue Holiday RC .60 1.50
134 Ryan Hollins .12 .30
135 Al Horford .20 .50
136 Eddie House .12 .30
137 Josh Howard .15 .40
138 Dwight Howard .15 .40
139 Lester Hudson RC .30 .75
140 Larry Hughes .15 .40
141 Othello Hunter .12 .30
142 Lindsey Hunter .12 .30
143 Andre Iguodala .15 .40
144 Zydrunas Ilgauskas .15 .40
145 Didier Ilunga-Mbenga .12 .30
146 Ersan Ilyasova .12 .30
147 Allen Iverson .25 .60
148 Jarrett Jack .15 .40
149 Stephen Jackson .15 .40
150 LeBron James .75 2.00
151 Antawn Jamison .15 .40
152 Marko Jaric .12 .30
153 Al Jefferson .15 .40
154 Richard Jefferson .15 .40
155 Jared Jeffries .12 .30
156 Brandon Jennings RC .50 1.25
157 Yi Jianlian .15 .40
158 Joe Johnson .15 .40
159 Amir Johnson .12 .30
160 Dahntay Jones .12 .30
161 James Jones .20 .50
162 Chris Kaman .15 .40
163 Jason Kapono .12 .30
164 Jason Kidd .20 .50
165 Andrei Kirilenko .15 .40
166 Kyle Korver .15 .40
167 Kosta Koufos .12 .30
168 Nenad Krstic .12 .30
169 Carl Landry .12 .30
170 Acie Law .12 .30
171 Ty Lawson RC .50 1.25
172 Courtney Lee .15 .40
173 David Lee .12 .30
174 Rashard Lewis .15 .40
175 Shaun Livingston .12 .30
176 Brook Lopez .15 .40
177 Robin Lopez .12 .30
178 Kevin Love .20 .50
179 Kyle Lowry .15 .40
180 Corey Maggette .15 .40
181 Shawn Marion .15 .40
182 Kenyon Martin .15 .40
183 Kevin Martin .15 .40
184 Roger Mason .12 .30
185 Jason Maxiell .12 .30
186 Eric Maynor RC .30 .75
187 O.J. Mayo .12 .30
188 Luc Mbah a Moute .12 .30
189 JaVale McGee .15 .40
190 Tracy McGrady .20 .50
191 Dominic McGuire .12 .30
192 Darko Milicic .12 .30
193 Brad Miller .15 .40
194 Andre Miller .15 .40
195 Mike Miller .15 .40
196 Paul Millsap .15 .40
197 Yao Ming .25 .60
198 Jamario Moon .12 .30
199 Anthony Morrow .12 .30
200 B.J. Mullens RC .30 .75
201 Troy Murphy .12 .30
202 Steve Nash .20 .50
203 Jameer Nelson .12 .30
204 Nene .15 .40
205 Joakim Noah .15 .40
206 Andres Nocioni .12 .30
207 Steve Novak .12 .30
208 Dirk Nowitzki .25 .60
209 Patrick O'Bryant .12 .30
210 Greg Oden .15 .40
211 Lamar Odom .15 .40
212 Emeka Okafor .15 .40
213 Mehmet Okur .12 .30
214 Shaquille O'Neal .40 1.00
215 Jermaine O'Neal .15 .40
216 Travis Outlaw .15 .40
217 Zaza Pachulia .12 .30
218 Jannero Pargo .12 .30
219 Anthony Parker .12 .30
220 Tony Parker .20 .50
221 Chris Paul .25 .60
222 Sasha Pavlovic .12 .30
223 Jeff Pendergraph .12 .30
224 Kendrick Perkins .12 .30
225 Johan Petro .12 .30
226 Paul Pierce .20 .50
227 Mickael Pietrus .12 .30
228 James Posey .12 .30
229 Leon Powe .12 .30
230 Tayshaun Prince .15 .40
231 Joel Przybilla .12 .30
232 Chris Quinn .12 .30
233 Vladimir Radmanovic .12 .30
234 Zach Randolph .15 .40
235 Theo Ratliff .12 .30
236 Michael Redd .15 .40
237 J.J. Redick .20 .50
238 Quentin Richardson .15 .40
239 Jason Richardson .20 .50
240 Luke Ridnour .15 .40
241 Nate Robinson .12 .30
242 Rajon Rondo .20 .50
243 Derrick Rose .30 .75
244 Brandon Roy .20 .50
245 Brandon Rush .12 .30
246 John Salmons .15 .40
247 Luis Scola .15 .40
248 Thabo Sefolosha .12 .30
249 Ramon Sessions .15 .40
250 Bobby Simmons .12 .30
251 Josh Smith .15 .40
252 J.R. Smith .15 .40
253 Craig Smith .12 .30
254 Jason Smith .12 .30
255 Marreese Speights .15 .40
256 Peja Stojakovic .20 .50
257 Amare Stoudemire .15 .40
258 Rodney Stuckey .12 .30
259 Jermaine Taylor RC .30 .75
260 Jeff Teague RC .50 1.25
261 Sebastian Telfair .12 .30
262 Jason Terry .15 .40
263 Hasheem Thabeet RC .30 .75
264 Tyrus Thomas .12 .30
265 Kurt Thomas .12 .30
266 Kenny Thomas .12 .30
267 Jason Thompson .12 .30
268 Al Thornton .15 .40
269 Marcus Thornton .15 .40
270 Ronny Turiaf .12 .30
271 Hedo Turkoglu .15 .40
272 Beno Udrih .12 .30
273 Anderson Varejao .12 .30
274 Charlie Villanueva .12 .30
275 Jake Voskuhl .12 .30
276 Sasha Vujacic .12 .30
277 Dwyane Wade .30 .75
278 Rasheed Wallace .20 .50
279 Gerald Wallace .15 .40
280 Ben Wallace .15 .40
281 Luke Walton .12 .30
282 Hakim Warrick .15 .40
283 Kyle Weaver .12 .30
284 Delonte West .12 .30
285 David West .15 .40
286 Russell Westbrook .50 1.25
287 D.J. White .12 .30
288 Chris Wilcox .12 .30
289 Marvin Williams .15 .40
290 Shelden Williams .12 .30
291 Mo Williams .15 .40
292 Shawne Williams .12 .30
293 Terrence Williams RC .30 .75
294 Louis Williams .15 .40
295 Marcus Williams .12 .30
296 Deron Williams .15 .40
297 Julian Wright .12 .30
298 Antoine Wright .12 .30
299 Thaddeus Young .12 .30
300 Nick Young .15 .40

2009-10 Adrenalyn XL Extra

COMPLETE SET (30) 30.00 60.00
STATED ODDS 1:8 PACKS
1 Ron Artest 2.00 5.00
2 Michael Beasley 1.25 3.00
3 Chauncey Billups 2.00 5.00
4 Elton Brand 2.00 5.00
5 Jose Calderon 1.25 3.00
6 Vince Carter 2.50 6.00
7 Jamal Crawford 2.00 5.00
8 Boris Diaw 1.50 4.00
9 Mike Dunleavy 1.25 3.00
10 Monta Ellis 1.50 4.00
11 Kevin Garnett 3.00 8.00
12 Ryan Gomes 1.25 3.00
13 Ben Gordon 1.50 4.00
14 Eric Gordon 1.50 4.00
15 Antawn Jamison 1.50 4.00
16 David Lee 1.25 3.00
17 Brook Lopez 1.50 4.00
18 Andre Miller 1.50 4.00
19 Yao Ming 2.50 6.00
20 Steve Nash 2.00 5.00
21 Andres Nocioni 1.25 3.00
22 Mehmet Okur 1.25 3.00
23 Shaquille O'Neal 4.00 10.00
24 Tony Parker 2.00 5.00
25 Zach Randolph 1.50 4.00
26 John Salmons 1.50 4.00
27 Jason Terry 1.50 4.00
28 Hakim Warrick 1.50 4.00
29 David West 1.50 4.00
30 Russell Westbrook 5.00 12.00

2009-10 Adrenalyn XL Extra Signature

COMPLETE SET (30) 50.00 120.00
STATED ODDS 1:8 PACKS
1 Carmelo Anthony 4.00 10.00
2 Gilbert Arenas 2.50 6.00
3 Chris Bosh 3.00 8.00
4 Kobe Bryant 10.00 25.00
5 Tim Duncan 5.00 12.00
6 Kevin Durant 8.00 20.00
7 Rudy Gay 3.00 8.00
8 Danny Granger 2.50 6.00
9 Blake Griffin 12.00 30.00
10 Richard Hamilton 2.50 6.00
11 Devin Harris 2.00 5.00
12 Dwight Howard 2.50 6.00
13 Andre Iguodala 2.50 6.00
14 Stephen Jackson 2.50 6.00
15 LeBron James 10.00 25.00
16 Al Jefferson 2.50 6.00
17 Joe Johnson 2.50 6.00
18 Kevin Martin 2.50 6.00
19 Tracy McGrady 3.00 8.00
20 Dirk Nowitzki 4.00 10.00
21 Chris Paul 4.00 10.00
22 Paul Pierce 3.00 8.00
23 Michael Redd 2.50 6.00
24 Nate Robinson 2.00 5.00
25 Derrick Rose 5.00 12.00
26 Brandon Roy 3.00 8.00
27 Amare Stoudemire 2.50 6.00
28 Dwyane Wade 5.00 12.00
29 Gerald Wallace 2.50 6.00
30 Deron Williams 2.50 6.00

2009-10 Adrenalyn XL Special

COMPLETE SET (60) 15.00 30.00
STATED ODDS 1:2 PACKS
1 LaMarcus Aldridge .60 1.50
2 Ray Allen .60 1.50
3 Rafer Alston .40 1.00
4 Kelenna Azubuike .40 1.00
5 Andrea Bargnani .50 1.25
6 Shane Battier .60 1.50
7 Raja Bell .50 1.25
8 Mike Bibby .50 1.25
9 Andrew Bogut .50 1.25
10 Carlos Boozer .50 1.25
11 Caron Butler .50 1.25
12 Baron Davis .50 1.25
13 Raymond Felton .50 1.25
14 T.J. Ford .40 1.00
15 Randy Foye .40 1.00
16 Francisco Garcia .40 1.00
17 Marc Gasol .60 1.50
18 Pau Gasol .60 1.50
19 Manu Ginobili .60 1.50
20 Jeff Green .50 1.25
21 Al Harrington .50 1.25
22 Udonis Haslem .40 1.00
23 Spencer Hawes .40 1.00
24 Grant Hill .75 2.00
25 Larry Hughes .50 1.25
26 Zydrunas Ilgauskas .50 1.25
27 Richard Jefferson .50 1.25
28 Yi Jianlian .50 1.25
29 Jason Kidd .60 1.50
30 Andrei Kirilenko .50 1.25
31 Nenad Krstic .40 1.00
32 Rashard Lewis .50 1.25
33 Kevin Love .60 1.50
34 Corey Maggette .50 1.25
35 Shawn Marion .50 1.25
36 Kenyon Martin .50 1.25
37 O.J. Mayo .40 1.00
38 Troy Murphy .40 1.00
39 Jameer Nelson .40 1.00
40 Nene .50 1.25
41 Joakim Noah .50 1.25
42 Greg Oden .50 1.25
43 Lamar Odom .50 1.25
44 Emeka Okafor .50 1.25
45 Jermaine O'Neal .50 1.25
46 Tayshaun Prince .50 1.25
47 Jason Richardson .60 1.50
48 Luke Ridnour .50 1.25
49 Rajon Rondo .60 1.50
50 Luis Scola .50 1.25
51 Ramon Sessions .50 1.25
52 Josh Smith .50 1.25
53 Peja Stojakovic .60 1.50
54 Tyrus Thomas .40 1.00
55 Al Thornton .50 1.25
56 Hedo Turkoglu .50 1.25
57 Charlie Villanueva .40 1.00
58 Mo Williams .50 1.25
59 Louis Williams .50 1.25
60 Thaddeus Young .40 1.00

2009-10 Adrenalyn XL Ultimate Signature

COMPLETE SET (30) 60.00 120.00
STATED ODDS 1:23 PACKS
1 Carmelo Anthony 5.00 12.00
2 Gilbert Arenas 3.00 8.00
3 Chris Bosh 4.00 10.00
4 Kobe Bryant 15.00 40.00
5 Tim Duncan 6.00 15.00
6 Kevin Durant 10.00 25.00
7 Rudy Gay 4.00 10.00
8 Danny Granger 3.00 8.00
9 Blake Griffin 8.00 20.00
10 Richard Hamilton 3.00 8.00
11 Devin Harris 2.50 6.00
12 Dwight Howard 3.00 8.00
13 Andre Iguodala 3.00 8.00
14 Stephen Jackson 3.00 8.00
15 LeBron James 15.00 40.00
16 Al Jefferson 3.00 8.00
17 Joe Johnson 3.00 8.00
18 Kevin Martin 3.00 8.00
19 Tracy McGrady 4.00 10.00
20 Dirk Nowitzki 5.00 12.00
21 Chris Paul 5.00 12.00
22 Paul Pierce 4.00 10.00
23 Michael Redd 3.00 8.00
24 Nate Robinson 2.50 6.00
25 Derrick Rose 6.00 15.00
26 Brandon Roy 4.00 10.00
27 Amare Stoudemire 3.00 8.00
28 Dwyane Wade 6.00 15.00
29 Gerald Wallace 3.00 8.00
30 Deron Williams 3.00 8.00

2010-11 Adrenalyn XL

Released in January 2011, this interactive basketball game features a 300-card base set. Each card also features an online activation code to build a virtual collection.
COMPLETE SET (300) 25.00 60.00
1 Brendan Haywood .12 .30
2 Caron Butler .15 .40
3 Dirk Nowitzki .25 .60
4 Dominique Jones RC .30 .75
5 J.J. Barea .15 .40
6 Jason Kidd .20 .50
7 Jason Terry .15 .40
8 Rodrigue Beaubois .12 .30
9 Shawn Marion .15 .40
10 Tyson Chandler .15 .40
11 Aaron Brooks .12 .30
12 Brad Miller .15 .40
13 Chase Budinger .12 .30
14 Courtney Lee .15 .40
15 Jordan Hill .12 .30
16 Kevin Martin .15 .40
17 Luis Scola .15 .40
18 Patrick Patterson RC .40 1.00
19 Shane Battier .15 .40
20 Yao Ming .25 .60
21 Acie Law .12 .30
22 Darrell Arthur .12 .30
23 DeMarre Carroll .15 .40
24 Hasheem Thabeet .12 .30
25 Marc Gasol .20 .50
26 Mike Conley Jr. .20 .50
27 O.J. Mayo .12 .30
28 Rudy Gay .20 .50
29 Xavier Henry RC .30 .75
30 Zach Randolph .15 .40
31 Chris Paul .25 .60
32 David West .15 .40
33 Emeka Okafor .15 .40
34 Marco Belinelli .12 .30
35 Marcus Thornton .12 .30
36 Peja Stojakovic .20 .50
37 Pops Mensah-Bonsu .12 .30
38 Quincy Pondexter RC .30 .75
39 Trevor Ariza .12 .30
40 Willie Green .12 .30
41 Antonio McDyess .15 .40
42 DeJuan Blair .12 .30
43 Garrett Temple .12 .30
44 George Hill .15 .40
45 James Anderson RC .30 .75
46 Manu Ginobili .20 .50
47 Matt Bonner .12 .30
48 Richard Jefferson .15 .40
49 Tim Duncan .30 .75
50 Tony Parker .20 .50
51 Al Harrington .15 .40
52 Arron Afflalo .12 .30
53 Carmelo Anthony .25 .60
54 Chauncey Billups .20 .50
55 Chris Andersen .15 .40
56 J.R. Smith .15 .40
57 Kenyon Martin .15 .40
58 Nene .15 .40
59 Renaldo Balkman .12 .30
60 Ty Lawson .12 .30
61 Corey Brewer .12 .30
62 Darko Milicic .12 .30
63 Jonny Flynn .12 .30
64 Kevin Love .20 .50
65 Luke Ridnour .15 .40
66 Martell Webster .15 .40
67 Michael Beasley .12 .30
68 Sebastian Telfair .12 .30
69 Wayne Ellington .15 .40
70 Wesley Johnson RC .30 .75
71 Andre Miller .15 .40
72 Brandon Roy .20 .50
73 Dante Cunningham .12 .30
74 Elliot Williams RC .30 .75
75 Greg Oden .15 .40
76 LaMarcus Aldridge .20 .50
77 Luke Babbitt RC .40 1.00
78 Marcus Camby .12 .30
79 Patrick Mills .20 .50
80 Rudy Fernandez .12 .30
81 Cole Aldrich RC .40 1.00
82 Daequan Cook .12 .30
83 Eric Maynor .12 .30
84 James Harden .30 .75
85 Jeff Green .15 .40
86 Kevin Durant .50 1.25
87 Nenad Krstic .12 .30
88 Royal Ivey .12 .30
89 Russell Westbrook .50 1.25
90 Serge Ibaka .15 .40
91 Al Jefferson .15 .40
92 Andrei Kirilenko .15 .40
93 C.J. Miles .15 .40
94 Deron Williams .15 .40
95 Gordon Hayward RC .75 2.00
96 Kyrylo Fesenko .12 .30
97 Mehmet Okur .12 .30
98 Paul Millsap .15 .40
99 Raja Bell .15 .40
100 Ronnie Price .12 .30
101 Andris Biedrins .12 .30
102 Brandan Wright .12 .30
103 Charlie Bell .12 .30
104 Dan Gadzuric .12 .30
105 David Lee .12 .30
106 Ekpe Udoh RC .30 .75
107 Monta Ellis .15 .40
108 Reggie Williams RC .20 .50
109 Stephen Curry .75 2.00
110 Vladimir Radmanovic .12 .30
111 Al-Farouq Aminu RC .50 1.25
112 Baron Davis .15 .40
113 Blake Griffin .20 .50

114 Chris Kaman .15 .40
115 Craig Smith .12 .30
116 Eric Bledsoe RC .60 1.50
117 Eric Gordon .15 .40
118 Randy Foye .12 .30
119 Rasual Butler .12 .30
120 Ryan Gomes .12 .30
121 Andrew Bynum .12 .30
122 Derek Fisher .15 .40
123 Devin Ebanks RC .30 .75
124 Kobe Bryant .75 2.00
125 Lamar Odom .15 .40
126 Luke Walton .12 .30
127 Pau Gasol .20 .50
128 Ron Artest .20 .50
129 Sasha Vujacic .12 .30
130 Theo Ratliff .12 .30
131 Channing Frye .15 .40
132 Earl Clark .12 .30
133 Goran Dragic .15 .40
134 Grant Hill .25 .60
135 Hakim Warrick .15 .40
136 Hedo Turkoglu .15 .40
137 Jared Dudley .12 .30
138 Jason Richardson .20 .50
139 Robin Lopez .12 .30
140 Steve Nash .20 .50
141 Beno Udrih .12 .30
142 Carl Landry .12 .30
143 DeMarcus Cousins RC 1.50 4.00
144 Donte Greene .12 .30
145 Francisco Garcia .12 .30
146 Hassan Whiteside RC 1.00 2.50
147 Jason Thompson .12 .30
148 Omri Casspi .12 .30
149 Samuel Dalembert .12 .30
150 Tyreke Evans .12 .30
151 Avery Bradley RC .60 1.50
152 Glen Davis .12 .30
153 Jermaine O'Neal .15 .40
154 Kendrick Perkins .12 .30
155 Kevin Garnett .30 .75
156 Nate Robinson .12 .30
157 Paul Pierce .20 .50
158 Rajon Rondo .20 .50
159 Ray Allen .20 .50
160 Shaquille O'Neal .40 1.00
161 Anthony Morrow .12 .30
162 Brook Lopez .15 .40
163 Damion James RC .30 .75
164 Derrick Favors RC .60 1.50
165 Devin Harris .12 .30
166 Jordan Farmar .12 .30
167 Quinton Ross .12 .30
168 Terrence Williams .12 .30
169 Travis Outlaw .15 .40
170 Troy Murphy .12 .30
171 Amare Stoudemire .15 .40
172 Andy Rautins RC .30 .75
173 Anthony Randolph .12 .30
174 Danilo Gallinari .15 .40
175 Kelenna Azubuike .12 .30
176 Raymond Felton .15 .40
177 Ronny Turiaf .12 .30
178 Timofey Mozgov RC .50 1.25
179 Toney Douglas .12 .30
180 Wilson Chandler .15 .40
181 Andre Iguodala .15 .40
182 Andres Nocioni .12 .30
183 Elton Brand .20 .50
184 Evan Turner RC .40 1.00
185 Jason Kapono .12 .30
186 Jodie Meeks .20 .50
187 Jrue Holiday .20 .50
188 Louis Williams .15 .40
189 Spencer Hawes .12 .30
190 Thaddeus Young .12 .30
191 Andrea Bargnani .15 .40
192 David Andersen .12 .30
193 DeMar DeRozan .20 .50
194 Ed Davis RC .30 .75
195 Jarrett Jack .15 .40
196 Jose Calderon .12 .30
197 Julian Wright .12 .30
198 Leandro Barbosa .15 .40
199 Linas Kleiza .12 .30
200 Reggie Evans .12 .30
201 C.J. Watson .12 .30
202 Carlos Boozer .15 .40
203 Derrick Rose .25 .60
204 James Johnson .12 .30
205 Joakim Noah .15 .40
206 Keith Bogans .12 .30
207 Kyle Korver .15 .40
208 Luol Deng .15 .40
209 Ronnie Brewer .15 .40
210 Taj Gibson .15 .40
211 Anderson Varejao .12 .30
212 Antawn Jamison .15 .40
213 Anthony Parker .12 .30
214 Daniel Gibson .15 .40
215 J.J. Hickson .12 .30
216 Jamario Moon .12 .30
217 Leon Powe .12 .30
218 Mo Williams .15 .40
219 Ramon Sessions .15 .40
220 Ryan Hollins .12 .30
221 Austin Daye .12 .30
222 Ben Gordon .15 .40
223 Ben Wallace .15 .40
224 Charlie Villanueva .12 .30
225 Greg Monroe RC .60 1.50
226 Jason Maxiell .12 .30
227 Richard Hamilton .15 .40
228 Rodney Stuckey .15 .40
229 Tayshaun Prince .15 .40
230 Tracy McGrady .20 .50
231 Brandon Rush .12 .30
232 Dahntay Jones .12 .30
233 Danny Granger .15 .40
234 Darren Collison .15 .40
235 Jeff Foster .12 .30
236 Mike Dunleavy .12 .30
237 Paul George RC 1.50 4.00
238 Roy Hibbert .15 .40
239 T.J. Ford .12 .30
240 Tyler Hansbrough .15 .40
241 Andrew Bogut .15 .40
242 Brandon Jennings .12 .30
243 Carlos Delfino .12 .30
244 Chris Douglas-Roberts .12 .30
245 Drew Gooden .15 .40
246 Ersan Ilyasova .15 .40
247 John Salmons .15 .40
248 Larry Sanders RC .30 .75
249 Luc Mbah a Moute .12 .30
250 Michael Redd .15 .40
251 Al Horford .15 .40
252 Jamal Crawford .20 .50
253 Jeff Teague .15 .40
254 Joe Johnson .15 .40
255 Jordan Crawford RC .40 1.00
256 Josh Smith .15 .40
257 Marvin Williams .15 .40
258 Maurice Evans .12 .30
259 Mike Bibby .15 .40
260 Zaza Pachulia .12 .30
261 Boris Diaw .15 .40
262 D.J. Augustin .12 .30
263 Derrick Brown .12 .30
264 Eduardo Najera .12 .30
265 Gerald Wallace .15 .40
266 Kwame Brown .12 .30
267 Matt Carroll .12 .30
268 Nazr Mohammed .12 .30
269 Stephen Jackson .15 .40
270 Tyrus Thomas .12 .30
271 Chris Bosh .20 .50
272 Dwyane Wade .30 .75
273 Eddie House .12 .30
274 Joel Anthony .12 .30
275 Juwan Howard .15 .40
276 LeBron James 1.00 2.50
277 Mario Chalmers .15 .40
278 Mike Miller .15 .40
279 Udonis Haslem .12 .30
280 Zydrunas Ilgauskas .15 .40
281 Daniel Orton RC .30 .75
282 Dwight Howard .15 .40
283 J.J. Redick .20 .50
284 Jameer Nelson .12 .30
285 Marcin Gortat .15 .40
286 Mickael Pietrus .12 .30
287 Quentin Richardson .15 .40
288 Rashard Lewis .15 .40
289 Ryan Anderson .15 .40
290 Vince Carter .25 .60
291 Al Thornton .12 .30
292 Andray Blatche .12 .30
293 Gilbert Arenas .15 .40
294 Hamady N'Diaye RC .50 1.25
295 JaVale McGee .15 .40
296 John Wall RC 2.50 6.00
297 Josh Howard .15 .40
298 Kevin Seraphin RC .30 .75
299 Kirk Hinrich .15 .40
300 Yi Jianlian .15 .40

2010-11 Adrenalyn XL Extra

COMPLETE SET (30) 30.00 60.00
STATED ODDS 1:8 PACKS
1 Dirk Nowitzki 2.50 6.00
2 Luis Scola 1.50 4.00
3 Rudy Gay 2.00 5.00
4 Peja Stojakovic 2.00 5.00
5 Manu Ginobili 2.00 5.00
6 Nene 1.50 4.00
7 Martell Webster 1.50 4.00
8 Greg Oden 1.50 4.00
9 Jeff Green 1.50 4.00
10 Andrei Kirilenko 1.50 4.00
11 David Lee 1.25 3.00
12 Baron Davis 1.50 4.00
13 Ron Artest 2.00 5.00
14 Hedo Turkoglu 1.50 4.00
15 Omri Casspi 1.25 3.00
16 Jermaine O'Neal 1.50 4.00
17 Derrick Favors 2.50 6.00
18 Anthony Randolph 1.25 3.00
19 Elton Brand 2.00 5.00
20 DeMar DeRozan 2.00 5.00
21 Derrick Rose 2.50 6.00
22 Ramon Sessions 1.50 4.00
23 Richard Hamilton 1.50 4.00
24 T.J. Ford 1.25 3.00
25 John Salmons 1.50 4.00
26 Joe Johnson 1.50 4.00
27 Boris Diaw 1.50 4.00
28 Chris Bosh 2.00 5.00
29 Rashard Lewis 1.50 4.00
30 Gilbert Arenas 1.50 4.00

2010-11 Adrenalyn XL Extra Signature

COMPLETE SET (30) 60.00 120.00
STATED ODDS 1:8 PACKS
1 Jason Terry 2.50 6.00
2 Kevin Martin 2.50 6.00
3 Zach Randolph 2.50 6.00
4 David West 2.50 6.00
5 Tim Duncan 5.00 12.00
6 Chauncey Billups 3.00 8.00
7 Michael Beasley 2.00 5.00
8 Brandon Roy 3.00 8.00
9 Russell Westbrook 8.00 20.00
10 Al Jefferson 2.50 6.00
11 Monta Ellis 2.50 6.00
12 Blake Griffin 3.00 8.00
13 Pau Gasol 3.00 8.00
14 Jason Richardson 3.00 8.00
15 Carl Landry 2.00 5.00
16 Ray Allen 3.00 8.00
17 Devin Harris 2.00 5.00
18 Danilo Gallinari 2.50 6.00
19 Evan Turner 2.50 6.00
20 Leandro Barbosa 2.50 6.00
21 Joakim Noah 2.50 6.00
22 Antawn Jamison 2.50 6.00
23 Ben Gordon 2.50 6.00
24 Mike Dunleavy 2.00 5.00
25 Andrew Bogut 2.50 6.00
26 Mike Bibby 2.50 6.00
27 Gerald Wallace 2.50 6.00
28 Dwyane Wade 5.00 12.00
29 Vince Carter 4.00 10.00
30 Al Thornton 2.00 5.00

2010-11 Adrenalyn XL Special

COMPLETE SET (60) 20.00 40.00
STATED ODDS 1:2 PACKS
1 Caron Butler .50 1.25
2 Tyson Chandler .50 1.25
3 Aaron Brooks .40 1.00
4 Courtney Lee .50 1.25
5 Marc Gasol .60 1.50
6 Mike Conley Jr. .60 1.50
7 Emeka Okafor .50 1.25
8 Marcus Thornton .40 1.00
9 George Hill .50 1.25
10 Richard Jefferson .50 1.25
11 Chris Andersen .50 1.25
12 Kenyon Martin .50 1.25
13 Darko Milicic .40 1.00
14 Wesley Johnson .40 1.00
15 Andre Miller .50 1.25
16 Rudy Fernandez .40 1.00
17 Cole Aldrich .50 1.25
18 James Harden 1.00 2.50
19 Mehmet Okur .40 1.00
20 Raja Bell .50 1.25
21 Charlie Bell .40 1.00
22 Reggie Williams .60 1.50
23 Eric Gordon .50 1.25
24 Randy Foye .40 1.00
25 Derek Fisher .50 1.25
26 Lamar Odom .50 1.25
27 Channing Frye .50 1.25
28 Robin Lopez .40 1.00
29 DeMarcus Cousins 2.00 5.00
30 Francisco Garcia .40 1.00
31 Kevin Garnett 1.00 2.50
32 Paul Pierce .60 1.50
33 Terrence Williams .40 1.00
34 Troy Murphy .40 1.00
35 Raymond Felton .50 1.25
36 Wilson Chandler .50 1.25
37 Andres Nocioni .40 1.00
38 Louis Williams .50 1.25
39 Ed Davis .40 1.00
40 Jose Calderon .40 1.00
41 Kyle Korver .50 1.25
42 Luol Deng .50 1.25
43 Anderson Varejao .40 1.00
44 Anthony Parker .40 1.00
45 Rodney Stuckey .50 1.25
46 Tracy McGrady .60 1.50
47 Darren Collison .50 1.25
48 Tyler Hansbrough .50 1.25
49 Chris Douglas-Roberts .40 1.00
50 Michael Redd .50 1.25
51 Jamal Crawford .60 1.50
52 Jeff Teague .50 1.25
53 D.J. Augustin .40 1.00
54 Nazr Mohammed .40 1.00
55 Mario Chalmers .50 1.25
56 Udonis Haslem .40 1.00
57 J.J. Redick .60 1.50
58 Jameer Nelson .40 1.00
59 JaVale McGee .50 1.25
60 Kirk Hinrich .50 1.25

2010-11 Adrenalyn XL Ultimate Signature

COMPLETE SET (30) 125.00 250.00
STATED ODDS 1:23 PACKS
1 Jason Kidd 4.00 10.00
2 Yao Ming 5.00 12.00
3 O.J. Mayo 2.50 6.00
4 Chris Paul 5.00 12.00
5 Tony Parker 4.00 10.00
6 Carmelo Anthony 5.00 12.00
7 Kevin Love 4.00 10.00
8 LaMarcus Aldridge 4.00 10.00
9 Kevin Durant 10.00 25.00
10 Deron Williams 3.00 8.00
11 Stephen Curry 15.00 40.00
12 Chris Kaman 3.00 8.00
13 Kobe Bryant 15.00 40.00
14 Steve Nash 4.00 10.00
15 Tyreke Evans 2.50 6.00
16 Rajon Rondo 4.00 10.00
17 Brook Lopez 3.00 8.00
18 Amare Stoudemire 3.00 8.00
19 Andre Iguodala 3.00 8.00
20 Andrea Bargnani 3.00 8.00
21 Carlos Boozer 3.00 8.00
22 Mo Williams 3.00 8.00
23 Tayshaun Prince 3.00 8.00
24 Danny Granger 3.00 8.00
25 Brandon Jennings 2.50 6.00
26 Josh Smith 3.00 8.00
27 Stephen Jackson 3.00 8.00
28 LeBron James 15.00 40.00
29 Dwight Howard 3.00 8.00
30 John Wall 20.00 50.00

2010 Adrenalyn XL All-Star Game

These cards were distributed via a wrapper redemption during the NBA All-Star Jam Session in Dallas in February 2010. The card fronts feature the All-Star logo.

COMPLETE SET (10) 6.00 15.00
1 Carmelo Anthony .60 1.50
2 Kobe Bryant 2.50 6.00
3 Tim Duncan .75 2.00
4 Kevin Garnett 1.00 2.50
5 Dwight Howard .75 2.00
6 Allen Iverson .60 1.50
7 LeBron James 2.50 6.00
8 Steve Nash .50 1.25
9 Amare Stoudemire .60 1.50
10 Dwyane Wade 1.00 2.50

2011 Adrenalyn XL All-Star Game

These cards were distributed via a wrapper redemption during the NBA All-Star Jam Session in Los Angeles in February 2011. The card fronts feature the All-Star logo.

COMPLETE SET (6) 10.00 20.00
AS3 John Wall 6.00 15.00
AS4 Tony Parker .60 1.50
AS5 Stephen Curry .75 2.00
AS6 Blake Griffin 4.00 10.00
AS7 Ron Artest .60 1.50
AS8 Kobe Bryant 3.00 8.00

2009-10 Adrenalyn XL Italian

Released in Italy, this 302-card set is a parallel to the regular American issue, but adds two cards that were exclusively available in the Italian Starter Kit, which are cards #301 and #302. The card fronts are identical to the American issue, but the backs contain both a larger font for the code and both the legal lines and web addresses are different.

COMPLETE SET (302) 75.00 150.00
1 Arron Afflalo .15 .40
2 Alexis Ajinca .15 .40
3 LaMarcus Aldridge .25 .60
4 Joe Alexander .15 .40
5 Ray Allen .25 .60
6 Rafer Alston .15 .40
7 Chris Andersen .20 .50
8 David Andersen .40 1.00
9 Ryan Anderson .20 .50
10 Carmelo Anthony .30 .75
11 Joel Anthony .60 1.50
12 Gilbert Arenas .20 .50
13 Trevor Ariza .15 .40
14 Hilton Armstrong .15 .40
15 Ron Artest .25 .60
16 Darrell Arthur .20 .50
17 D.J. Augustin .15 .40
18 Kelenna Azubuike .15 .40
19 Renaldo Balkman .15 .40
20 Leandro Barbosa .20 .50
21 J.J. Barea .30 .75
22 Andrea Bargnani .20 .50
23 Matt Barnes .15 .40
24 Brandon Bass .15 .40
25 Tony Battie .15 .40
26 Shane Battier .25 .60
27 Nicolas Batum .20 .50
28 Michael Beasley .15 .40
29 Rodrigue Beaubois .40 1.00
30 Raja Bell .20 .50
31 Charlie Bell .15 .40
32 Mike Bibby .20 .50
33 Andris Biedrins .15 .40
34 Chauncey Billups .25 .60
35 DeJuan Blair .50 1.25
36 Steve Blake .15 .40
37 Andray Blatche .15 .40
38 Andrew Bogut .20 .50
39 Matt Bonner .15 .40
40 Carlos Boozer .20 .50
41 Chris Bosh .25 .60
42 Elton Brand .25 .60
43 Corey Brewer .15 .40
44 Ronnie Brewer .20 .50
45 Primoz Brezec .15 .40
46 Aaron Brooks .15 .40
47 Derrick Brown .15 .40
48 Devin Brown .15 .40
49 Kobe Bryant 1.00 2.50
50 Rasual Butler .15 .40
51 Caron Butler .20 .50
52 Will Bynum .15 .40
53 Andrew Bynum .15 .40
54 Jose Calderon .15 .40
55 Marcus Camby .15 .40
56 Brian Cardinal .15 .40
57 DeMarre Carroll .50 1.25
58 Vince Carter .30 .75
59 Omri Casspi .50 1.25
60 Mario Chalmers .20 .50
61 Tyson Chandler .20 .50
62 Darren Collison .60 1.50
63 Mike Conley Jr. .20 .50
64 Daequan Cook .15 .40
65 Jamal Crawford .25 .60
66 Joe Crawford .15 .40
67 Stephen Curry 12.00 30.00
68 Samuel Dalembert .15 .40
69 Erick Dampier .15 .40
70 Glen Davis .15 .40
71 Baron Davis .20 .50
72 Austin Daye .40 1.00
73 Luol Deng .20 .50
74 DeMar DeRozan 1.50 4.00
75 Boris Diaw .20 .50
76 Dan Dickau .15 .40
77 Travis Diener .15 .40
78 Toney Douglas .40 1.00
79 Jared Dudley .15 .40
80 Chris Duhon .15 .40
81 Tim Duncan .40 1.00
82 Mike Dunleavy .15 .40
83 Kevin Durant .60 1.50
84 Wayne Ellington .60 1.50
85 Monta Ellis .20 .50
86 Melvin Ely .15 .40
87 Maurice Evans .15 .40
88 Tyreke Evans .50 1.25
89 Reggie Evans .15 .40
90 Jordan Farmar .15 .40
91 Raymond Felton .20 .50
92 Rudy Fernandez .15 .40
93 Michael Finley .25 .60
94 Derek Fisher .20 .50
95 Jonny Flynn .40 1.00
96 T.J. Ford .15 .40
97 Jeff Foster .15 .40
98 Randy Foye .15 .40
99 Adonal Foyle .15 .40
100 Channing Frye .20 .50
101 Francisco Garcia .15 .40
102 Kevin Garnett .40 1.00
103 Pau Gasol .25 .60
104 Marc Gasol .25 .60
105 Rudy Gay .25 .60
106 Devean George .15 .40
107 Taj Gibson .60 1.50
108 Daniel Gibson .20 .50
109 Manu Ginobili .25 .60
110 Ryan Gomes .15 .40
111 Ben Gordon .20 .50
112 Eric Gordon .20 .50
113 Danny Granger .20 .50
114 Jeff Green .20 .50
115 Blake Griffin 8.00 20.00
116 Taylor Griffin .40 1.00
117 Richard Hamilton .20 .50
118 Tyler Hansbrough .50 1.25
119 James Harden 3.00 8.00
120 Matt Harpring .15 .40
121 Al Harrington .20 .50
122 Devin Harris .15 .40
123 Udonis Haslem .15 .40
124 Trenton Hassell .15 .40
125 Spencer Hawes .15 .40
126 Jarvis Hayes .15 .40
127 Brendan Haywood .15 .40
128 Gerald Henderson .50 1.25
129 Roy Hibbert .20 .50
130 Jordan Hill .50 1.25
131 Grant Hill .30 .75
132 Kirk Hinrich .20 .50
133 Jrue Holiday .75 2.00
134 Ryan Hollins .15 .40
135 Al Horford .25 .60
136 Eddie House .15 .40
137 Josh Howard .20 .50
138 Dwight Howard .20 .50
139 Lester Hudson .40 1.00
140 Larry Hughes .20 .50
141 Othello Hunter .15 .40
142 Lindsey Hunter .15 .40
143 Andre Iguodala .20 .50
144 Zydrunas Ilgauskas .20 .50
145 Didier Ilunga-Mbenga .15 .40
146 Ersan Ilyasova .15 .40
147 Allen Iverson .30 .75
148 Jarrett Jack .20 .50
149 Stephen Jackson .20 .50
150 LeBron James 1.00 2.50
151 Antawn Jamison .20 .50
152 Marko Jaric .15 .40
153 Al Jefferson .20 .50
154 Richard Jefferson .20 .50
155 Jared Jeffries .15 .40
156 Brandon Jennings .60 1.50
157 Yi Jianlian .20 .50
158 Joe Johnson .20 .50
159 Amir Johnson .15 .40
160 Dahntay Jones .15 .40
161 James Jones .25 .60
162 Chris Kaman .20 .50
163 Jason Kapono .15 .40
164 Jason Kidd .25 .60
165 Andrei Kirilenko .20 .50
166 Kyle Korver .20 .50
167 Kosta Koufos .15 .40
168 Nenad Krstic .15 .40
169 Carl Landry .15 .40
170 Acie Law .15 .40
171 Ty Lawson .60 1.50
172 Courtney Lee .20 .50
173 David Lee .15 .40
174 Rashard Lewis .20 .50
175 Shaun Livingston .15 .40
176 Brook Lopez .20 .50
177 Robin Lopez .15 .40
178 Kevin Love .25 .60
179 Kyle Lowry .20 .50
180 Corey Maggette .20 .50
181 Shawn Marion .20 .50
182 Kenyon Martin .20 .50
183 Kevin Martin .20 .50
184 Roger Mason .15 .40
185 Jason Maxiell .15 .40
186 Eric Maynor .40 1.00
187 O.J. Mayo .15 .40
188 Luc Mbah a Moute .15 .40
189 JaVale McGee .20 .50
190 Tracy McGrady .25 .60
191 Dominic McGuire .15 .40
192 Darko Milicic .15 .40
193 Brad Miller .20 .50
194 Andre Miller .20 .50
195 Mike Miller .20 .50
196 Paul Millsap .20 .50
197 Yao Ming .30 .75
198 Jamario Moon .15 .40
199 Anthony Morrow .15 .40
200 B.J. Mullens .40 1.00
201 Troy Murphy .15 .40
202 Steve Nash .25 .60
203 Jameer Nelson .15 .40
204 Nene .20 .50
205 Joakim Noah .20 .50
206 Andres Nocioni .15 .40
207 Steve Novak .15 .40
208 Dirk Nowitzki .30 .75
209 Patrick O'Bryant .15 .40
210 Greg Oden .20 .50
211 Lamar Odom .20 .50
212 Emeka Okafor .20 .50
213 Mehmet Okur .15 .40
214 Shaquille O'Neal .50 1.25
215 Jermaine O'Neal .20 .50
216 Travis Outlaw .20 .50
217 Zaza Pachulia .15 .40
218 Jannero Pargo .15 .40
219 Anthony Parker .15 .40
220 Tony Parker .25 .60
221 Chris Paul .30 .75
222 Sasha Pavlovic .15 .40
223 Jeff Pendergraph .15 .40
224 Kendrick Perkins .15 .40
225 Johan Petro .15 .40
226 Paul Pierce .25 .60
227 Mickael Pietrus .15 .40
228 James Posey .15 .40
229 Leon Powe .15 .40
230 Tayshaun Prince .20 .50
231 Joel Przybilla .15 .40
232 Chris Quinn .15 .40
233 Vladimir Radmanovic .15 .40
234 Zach Randolph .20 .50
235 Theo Ratliff .15 .40
236 Michael Redd .20 .50
237 J.J. Redick .25 .60
238 Quentin Richardson .20 .50
239 Jason Richardson .25 .60
240 Luke Ridnour .20 .50
241 Nate Robinson .15 .40
242 Rajon Rondo .25 .60
243 Derrick Rose .40 1.00
244 Brandon Roy .25 .60
245 Brandon Rush .15 .40
246 John Salmons .20 .50
247 Luis Scola .20 .50
248 Thabo Sefolosha .15 .40
249 Ramon Sessions .20 .50
250 Bobby Simmons .15 .40
251 Josh Smith .20 .50
252 J.R. Smith .20 .50
253 Craig Smith .15 .40
254 Jason Smith .15 .40
255 Marreese Speights .20 .50
256 Peja Stojakovic .25 .60
257 Amare Stoudemire .20 .50
258 Rodney Stuckey .15 .40
259 Jermaine Taylor .40 1.00
260 Jeff Teague .60 1.50
261 Sebastian Telfair .15 .40
262 Jason Terry .20 .50
263 Hasheem Thabeet .40 1.00
264 Tyrus Thomas .15 .40
265 Kurt Thomas .15 .40
266 Kenny Thomas .15 .40
267 Jason Thompson .15 .40
268 Al Thornton .20 .50
269 Marcus Thornton .20 .50
270 Ronny Turiaf .15 .40
271 Hedo Turkoglu .20 .50
272 Beno Udrih .15 .40
273 Anderson Varejao .15 .40
274 Charlie Villanueva .15 .40
275 Jake Voskuhl .15 .40
276 Sasha Vujacic .15 .40
277 Dwyane Wade .40 1.00
278 Rasheed Wallace .25 .60
279 Gerald Wallace .20 .50
280 Ben Wallace .20 .50
281 Luke Walton .15 .40
282 Hakim Warrick .20 .50
283 Kyle Weaver .15 .40
284 Delonte West .15 .40
285 David West .20 .50
286 Russell Westbrook .60 1.50
287 D.J. White .15 .40
288 Chris Wilcox .15 .40
289 Marvin Williams .20 .50
290 Shelden Williams .15 .40
291 Mo Williams .20 .50
292 Shawne Williams .15 .40
293 Terrence Williams .40 1.00
294 Louis Williams .20 .50
295 Marcus Williams .15 .40
296 Deron Williams .20 .50
297 Julian Wright .15 .40
298 Antoine Wright .15 .40
299 Thaddeus Young .15 .40
300 Nick Young .20 .50
301 Marco Belinelli 1.25 3.00
302 Danilo Gallinari 1.25 3.00

1956 Adventure R749

The Adventure series produced by Gum Products in 1956, contains a wide variety of subject matter. Cards in the set measure the standard size. The color drawings are printed on a heavy thickness of cardboard and have large white borders. The backs contain the card number, the caption, and a short text. The most expensive cards in the series of 100 are those associated with sports (Louis, Tunney, etc.). In addition, card number 86 (Schmelling) is notorious and sold at a premium price because of the Nazi symbol printed on the card. Although this set is considered by many to be a topical or non-sport set, several boxers are featured (cards 11, 22, 31-35, 41-44, 76-80, 86-90). One of the few cards of Boston-area legend Harry Agannis is in this set. The sports-related cards are in greater demand than the non-sport cards. These cards came in one-card penny packs where were packed 240 to a box.

COMPLETE SET (100) 225.00 450.00
8 Baskets and Rebounds Makes Points 12.50 25.00

2006-07 Albany Patroons CBA

Produced by the Albany Patroons, this 16-card set features photographs taken by team photographer, Chuck Miller, and a white bordered card stock. The sets were sold at Patroons home games.

COMPLETE SET (16) 2.50 6.00
1 Jamario Moon 2.00 5.00
2 Carl Mitchell .15 .40
3 Felipe Lopez .30 .75
4 Chris Sockwell .15 .40
5 T.J. Thompson .15 .40
6 Kwan Johnson .15 .40
7 Eric Williams .30 .75
8 Reggie Jessie .15 .40
9 Jordan Klaiber .15 .40
10 Kareem Reid .15 .40
11 Marvin Phillips .15 .40
12 Lucious Jordan .15 .40
13 John Strickland .15 .40
14 Michael Ray Richardson CO .40 1.00
15 Derrick Rowland ACO .15 .40
16 Lito The Panda Mascot .15 .40

1995-96 All-Star Jam Session David Robinson

This 4-card standard-size set was a wrapper redemption offer at the NBA All-Star Weekend Jam Session show (February 9-11) in San Antonio. Although each card features a distinctive design, they all carry the "All-Star Weekend, San Antonio '96" emblem on them. According to the backs, just 10,500 of each card were produced.

COMPLETE SET (4) 4.00 10.00
1 David Robinson Upper Deck 1.25 3.00
2 David Robinson Stadium Club 1.25 3.00
3 David Robinson Fleer 1.25 3.00
4 David Robinson SkyBox 1.25 3.00

1996-97 All-Star Jam Session Terrell Brandon

This three-card set was a wrapper redemption offer at the NBA All-Star Weekend Jam Session show (February 7-9) in Cleveland. Although each card features a distinctively different design, they all carry the "All-Star Weekend, Cleveland '97" emblem on them. According to the backs of the Ultra and SkyBox card, only 6,200 of each card were produced. The cards are numbered out of three.

COMPLETE SET (3) 2.00 4.00
1 Terrell Brandon Ultra .60 1.50
2 Terrell Brandon SkyBox .60 1.50
3 Terrell Brandon Stadium Club .60 1.50

1996-97 All-Star Jam Session Terrell Brandon Ticket

This ticket stub was used for admission into the Jam Session show during the 1997 NBA All-Star Weekend. The ticket carries the regular 1996-97 Ultra design.

NNO Terrell Brandon .40 1.00

1997-98 All-Star Jam Session Knicks Sheet A

Given away at the 1998 Jam Session in New York, collector's could receive this sheet by bringing three wrappers from any Fleer or SkyBox 1997-98 NBA product to the Fleer/SkyBox booth. The sheet features six Ultra cards. The sheets had a limited edition of 7500.

1 Knicks All-Star Sheet 2.00 5.00
Patrick Ewing
Larry Johnson
John Starks
Chris Dudley
Charlie Ward
Chris Mills

1997-98 All-Star Jam Session Knicks Sheet B

To obtain sheet B, collectors had to take three wrappers from any 1997-98 Fleer or SkyBox NBA product to a participating hobby dealer (or by mail) from a list that could be obtained at the Fleer/SkyBox booth at Jam Session. The sheet features SkyBox cards of Knick players. The sheet had a limited edition of 7500.

1 Knicks All-Star Sheet 2.50 6.00
Patrick Ewing
Larry Johnson
John Starks
Buck Williams
Chris Childs
Allan Houston

1992 Americana

COMPLETE SET (250) 8.00 20.00
UNOPENED BOX (36 PACKS) 15.00 25.00
UNOPENED PACK (12 CARDS) .75 1.00
COMMON CARD (1-250) .12 .30

2007 Americana

COMPLETE SET (100) 30.00 60.00
COMMON CARD (1-100) .40 1.00
MINOR STARS .40 1.00
SEMISTARS .60 1.50
UNLISTED STARS .75 2.00
*RETAIL: .3X TO .8X BASIC CARDS
*SILVER PROOFS: 1.5X TO 4X BASIC CARDS
*SILVER PROOFS RETAIL: 1.5X TO 4X BASIC CARDS
SILVER PROOFS #'d TO 250
*GOLD PROOFS: 2X TO 5X BASIC CARDS
*GOLD PROOFS RETAIL: 2X TO 5X BASIC CARDS
GOLD PROOFS #'d TO 100
*PLATINUM PROOFS: 3X TO 8X BASIC CARDS
*PLATINUM PROOFS RETAIL: 3X TO 8X BASIC CARDS
PLATINUM PROOFS #'d TO 25
74 Sheryl Swoopes .40 1.00

2007 Americana Sports Legends

RANDOM INSERTS IN PACKS
STATED PRINT RUN 500 SERIAL #'d SETS
3 Walt Frazier 1.50 4.00
10 Larry Bird 4.00 10.00

2007 Americana Sports Legends Material

RANDOM INSERTS IN PACKS
PRINT RUNS B/WN 25-500 COPIES PER
3 Walt Frazier Jsy/500 4.00 10.00

2007 Americana Sports Legends Signature

RANDOM INSERTS IN PACKS
PRINT RUNS B/WN 25-50 COPIES PER
3 Walt Frazier/25 15.00 40.00
10 Larry Bird/25 70.00 120.00

2007 Americana Sports Legends Signature Material

*MTL: .5X TO 1.2X BASIC SIG
RANDOM INSERTS IN PACKS
PRINT RUNS B/WN 25-50 COPIES PER

2008 Americana II

201-270 ONE PER BOX
*RETAIL: .3X TO .8X BASIC CARDS
*SILVER 101-200: 1.5X TO 4X BASIC CARDS
SILVER 101-200 #'d TO 250
UNPRICED SILVER 201-270 #'d TO 25
*GOLD 101-200: 2X TO 5X BASIC CARDS
GOLD 101-200 #'d TO 100
UNPRICED GOLD 201-270 #'d TO 10
*PLATINUM 101-200: 3X TO 8X BASIC CARDS
PLATINUM 101-200 #'d TO 25
UNPRICED PLATINUM 201-270 #'d TO 5
174 John Wooden .75 2.00
239 Lisa Leslie SP 2.00 5.00
242 Dick Vitale SP 2.00 5.00

2008 Americana II Private Signings

RANDOM INSERTS IN PACKS
PRINT RUNS B/WN 1-1200 COPIES PER
NO PRICING ON QTY OF 14 OR LESS
EXCHANGE DEADLINE 01/16/10
174 John Wooden/79 30.00 60.00
239 Lisa Leslie/25 10.00 25.00
242 Dick Vitale/25 10.00 25.00

2008 Americana II Sports Legends

RANDOM INSERTS IN PACKS
STATED PRINT RUN 500 SERIAL #'d SETS
13 Dick Vitale 1.25 3.00
14 John Wooden 1.50 4.00

2008 Americana II Sports Legends Signature

RANDOM INSERTS IN PACKS
PRINT RUNS B/WN 50-100 COPIES PER
13 Dick Vitale/100 15.00 40.00
14 John Wooden/100 50.00 100.00

2008 Americana II Stars Signature Material

RANDOM INSERTS IN PACKS
PRINT RUNS B/WN 5-250 COPIES PER
NO PRICING ON QTY OF 10 OR LESS
239 Lisa Leslie/25 10.00 25.00

2000 American Express Postcards

This 4-card postcard set features Shaquille O'Neal, Walt Frazier, Allan Houston, and Marcus Camby. It was issued by "Max Racks", and distibuted to stores that carry "Max Racks" postcards.

COMPLETE SET (4) 2.50 6.00
1 Marcus Camby .40 1.00
2 M.Camby/A.Houston .80 2.00
3 Walt Frazier .40 1.00
4 Shaquille O'Neal 2.00 5.00

1993 Anti-Gambling Postcards

COMPLETE SET (13) 6.00 15.00
6 Alex English BK .50 1.25
7 Alvin Robertson BK .50 1.25
8 Buck Williams BK .50 1.25

1991 Arena Holograms

The 1991 Arena Hologram cards were distributed through hobby dealers and feature famous athletes. According to Arena, production quantities were limited to 250,000 of each card. The standard-size hologram cards have on the horozontially oriented backs a color photo of the player in a tuxedo. Ken Griffey Jr. Frank Thomas, David Robinson, Joe Montana and Barry Sanders all signed cards with each being serial numbered by hand. A card-sized certificate of authenticity was also issued with each signed card.

COMPLETE SET (5) 3.20 8.00
5 David Robinson .40 1.00
AU5 David Robinson AU/250 40.00 80.00

1991 Arena Holograms 12th National

These standard-size cards have on their fronts a 3-D silver-colored emblem on a white background with orange borders. Though the back of each card salutes a different superstar, the players themselves are not pictured; instead, one finds pictures of a football; hockey stick and puck; basketball; and baseball in glove respectively. The cards are numbered on the front.

COMPLETE SET (4) 4.00 10.00
3 Michael Jordan 2.00 5.00

1979 Arizona Sports Collectors Show

COMPLETE SET (10) 7.50 15.00
8 Dick Van Arsdale 2.00 5.00
9 Tom Van Arsdale 2.00 5.00

2007-08 Artifacts

This 230-card set was released in October, 2007. The set was issued into the hobby in four-card packs which came 10 packs to a box and 20 boxes to a case. Cards numbered 1-100 feature NBA veterans while cards numbered 101-150 feature 2007-08 NBA rookies and cards numbered 151-200 feature retired greats. The cards numbered from 101-150 were issued to a stated print run of 699 serial numbered sets while cards 151-200 were issued to a stated print run of 999 serial numbered sets. The set concludes with cards 201-230 as Artifact Exclusives which were issued four cards per unopened box as a box topper.

COMP.SET w/o SP's (100) 15.00 40.00
101-110 PRINT RUN 699 SER.#'d SETS
111-150 PRINT RUN 1299 SER.#'d SETS
151-200 PRINT RUN 999 SER.#'d SETS
FOUR CARDS AS BOX TOPPER
UNPRICED COPPER PRINT RUN 10 SETS
UNPRICED ARTIFACTS PRINT RUN ONE SET
1 Joe Johnson .30 .75
2 Josh Smith .30 .75
3 Marvin Williams .30 .75
4 Josh Childress .30 .75
5 Al Jefferson .30 .75
6 Paul Pierce .40 1.00
7 Gerald Green .30 .75
8 Adam Morrison .25 .60
9 Gerald Wallace .30 .75
10 Emeka Okafor .30 .75
11 Raymond Felton .40 1.00
12 Ben Gordon .30 .75
13 Luol Deng .30 .75
14 Kirk Hinrich .30 .75
15 Andres Nocioni .25 .60
16 LeBron James 1.50 4.00
17 Larry Hughes .30 .75
18 Zydrunas Ilgauskas .30 .75
19 Dirk Nowitzki .50 1.25
20 Josh Howard .30 .75
21 Jason Terry .30 .75
22 Carmelo Anthony .50 1.25
23 Allen Iverson .50 1.25
24 J.R. Smith .30 .75
25 Richard Hamilton .30 .75
26 Tayshaun Prince .30 .75
27 Chauncey Billups .40 1.00
28 Baron Davis .30 .75
29 Monta Ellis .30 .75
30 Jason Richardson .40 1.00
31 Yao Ming .50 1.25
32 Tracy McGrady .40 1.00
33 Rafer Alston .25 .60
34 Jermaine O'Neal .30 .75
35 Jamaal Tinsley .25 .60
36 Mike Dunleavy .30 .75
37 Elton Brand .40 1.00
38 Cuttino Mobley .30 .75
39 Corey Maggette .30 .75
40 Kobe Bryant 1.50 4.00
41 Lamar Odom .30 .75
42 Jordan Farmar .25 .60
43 Pau Gasol .40 1.00

44 Rudy Gay .40 1.00
45 Mike Miller .30 .75
46 Shaquille O'Neal .75 2.00
47 Dwyane Wade .60 1.50
48 Jason Kapono .25 .60
49 Alonzo Mourning .50 1.25
50 Andrew Bogut .30 .75
51 Michael Redd .30 .75
52 Maurice Williams .30 .75
53 Kevin Garnett .60 1.50
54 Ricky Davis .30 .75
55 Randy Foye .40 1.00
56 Rashad McCants .25 .60
57 Jason Kidd .40 1.00
58 Vince Carter .50 1.25
59 Richard Jefferson .30 .75
60 Peja Stojakovic .40 1.00
61 Chris Paul .50 1.25
62 David West .30 .75
63 David Lee .25 .60
64 Stephon Marbury .30 .75
65 Eddy Curry .25 .60
66 Jamal Crawford .40 1.00
67 Dwight Howard .30 .75
68 Grant Hill .50 1.25
69 Jameer Nelson .25 .60
70 J.J. Redick .40 1.00
71 Andre Iguodala .30 .75
72 Andre Miller .30 .75
73 Samuel Dalembert .25 .60
74 Steve Nash .50 1.25
75 Amare Stoudemire .30 .75
76 Shawn Marion .30 .75
77 Leandro Barbosa .30 .75
78 Zach Randolph .30 .75
79 Brandon Roy .40 1.00
80 LaMarcus Aldridge .50 1.25
81 Jarrett Jack .30 .75
82 Mike Bibby .40 1.00
83 Kevin Martin .30 .75
84 Brad Miller .30 .75
85 Tim Duncan .60 1.50
86 Manu Ginobili .40 1.00
87 Tony Parker .40 1.00
88 Rashard Lewis .30 .75
89 Ray Allen .40 1.00
90 Chris Wilcox .25 .60
91 Chris Bosh .40 1.00
92 Andrea Bargnani .40 1.00
93 T.J. Ford .25 .60
94 Anthony Parker .25 .60
95 Deron Williams .30 .75
96 Carlos Boozer .30 .75
97 Mehmet Okur .25 .60
98 Gilbert Arenas .30 .75
99 Caron Butler .30 .75
100 Antawn Jamison .30 .75
101 Greg Oden RC 1.50 4.00
102 Kevin Durant RC 15.00 40.00
103 Al Horford RC 2.00 5.00
104 Mike Conley Jr. RC 2.00 5.00
105 Jeff Green RC 1.50 4.00
106 Sun Yue RC 1.50 4.00
107 Corey Brewer RC 1.50 4.00
108 Brandan Wright RC 1.50 4.00
109 Joakim Noah RC 1.50 4.00
110 Spencer Hawes RC 1.25 3.00
111 Acie Law RC 1.00 2.50
112 Thaddeus Young RC 1.50 4.00
113 Julian Wright RC 1.00 2.50
114 Al Thornton RC 1.25 3.00
115 Rodney Stuckey RC 1.25 3.00
116 Nick Young RC 2.00 5.00
117 Sean Williams RC 1.00 2.50
118 Marco Belinelli RC 1.50 4.00
119 Javaris Crittenton RC 1.00 2.50
120 Jason Smith RC 1.25 3.00
121 Daequan Cook RC 1.25 3.00
122 Jared Dudley RC 1.25 3.00
123 Wilson Chandler RC 1.25 3.00
124 Morris Almond RC 1.00 2.50
125 Aaron Brooks RC 1.25 3.00
126 Arron Afflalo RC 1.50 4.00
127 Alando Tucker RC 1.00 2.50
128 Petteri Koponen RC 1.50 4.00
129 Carl Landry RC 1.00 2.50
130 Gabe Pruitt RC 1.00 2.50
131 Marcus Williams RC 1.00 2.50
132 Nick Fazekas RC 1.00 2.50
133 Glen Davis RC 1.25 3.00
134 Jermareo Davidson RC 1.00 2.50
135 Josh McRoberts RC 1.25 3.00
136 Chris Richard RC 1.00 2.50
137 Derrick Byars RC 1.00 2.50
138 Adam Haluska RC 1.00 2.50
139 Reyshawn Terry RC 1.00 2.50
140 Jared Jordan RC 1.00 2.50
141 Stephane Lasme RC 1.00 2.50
142 Dominic McGuire RC 1.00 2.50
143 Aaron Gray RC 1.00 2.50
144 JamesOn Curry RC 1.00 2.50
145 Taurean Green RC 1.00 2.50
146 Demetris Nichols RC 1.00 2.50
147 Herbert Hill RC 1.00 2.50
148 Ramon Sessions RC 1.50 4.00
149 Sammy Mejia RC 1.00 2.50
150 D.J. Strawberry RC 1.00 2.50
151 Bernard King 1.00 2.50
152 Bill Laimbeer 1.00 2.50
153 Bill Russell 2.00 5.00
154 Bill Sharman 1.25 3.00
155 Bill Walton 1.25 3.00
156 Billy Cunningham 1.25 3.00
157 Bob Cousy 2.00 5.00
158 Bob McAdoo 1.00 2.50
159 Bob Pettit 1.50 4.00
160 Chris Mullin 1.25 3.00
161 Clyde Drexler 1.50 4.00
162 Dave Bing 1.25 3.00
163 Dave Cowens .75 2.00
164 David Robinson 2.00 5.00
165 David Thompson 1.00 2.50
166 Dennis Rodman 2.50 6.00
167 Dolph Schayes 1.25 3.00
168 Earl Monroe 1.25 3.00
169 Elgin Baylor 1.25 3.00
170 Elvin Hayes 1.25 3.00
171 George Gervin 1.25 3.00
172 George Mikan 2.50 6.00
173 Hakeem Olajuwon 1.50 4.00
174 Hal Greer 1.00 2.50
175 Isiah Thomas 1.25 3.00
176 James Worthy 1.50 4.00
177 Jerry West 1.50 4.00
178 John Havlicek 1.25 3.00
179 John Stockton 2.00 5.00
180 Julius Erving 2.00 5.00
181 Karl Malone 1.50 4.00
182 Kevin McHale 1.50 4.00
183 Larry Bird 3.00 8.00
184 Lenny Wilkens 1.25 3.00
185 Magic Johnson 3.00 8.00
186 Michael Jordan 10.00 25.00
187 Moses Malone 1.25 3.00
188 Nate Archibald 1.00 2.50
189 Nate Thurmond 1.00 2.50
190 Oscar Robertson 1.25 3.00
191 Paul Arizin 1.25 3.00
192 Paul Westphal 1.50 4.00
193 Pete Maravich 2.00 5.00
194 Rick Barry 1.00 2.50
195 Robert Parish 1.25 3.00
196 Sam Jones 1.50 4.00
197 Walt Frazier 1.25 3.00
198 Wes Unseld 1.25 3.00
199 Willis Reed 1.25 3.00
200 Wilt Chamberlain 2.50 6.00
201 Yao Ming EX .60 1.50
202 Steve Nash EX .60 1.50
203 Chris Paul EX .60 1.50
204 Brandon Roy EX .50 1.25
205 Rudy Gay EX .50 1.25
206 Al Horford Uni EX .60 1.50
207 LaMarcus Aldridge EX .60 1.50
208 Tyrus Thomas EX .30 .75
209 Julian Wright EX .30 .75
210 Al Horford Suit EX .60 1.50
211 Corey Brewer EX .50 1.25
212 Joakim Noah EX .50 1.25
213 Mike Conley Jr. EX .60 1.50
214 Jeff Green EX .50 1.25
215 Kevin Durant Suit EX 5.00 12.00
216 Michael Jordan Red EX 4.00 10.00
217 Kobe Bryant Prpl EX 2.00 5.00
218 LeBron James Red EX 2.00 5.00
219 Kevin Durant Ball EX 5.00 12.00
220 Michael Jordan White EX 4.00 10.00
221 Kobe Bryant Yllw EX 2.00 5.00
222 LeBron James Blue EX 2.00 5.00
223 Kevin Durant Uni EX 5.00 12.00
224 Michael Jordan Red EX 4.00 10.00
225 Kobe Bryant Yllw EX 2.00 5.00
226 LeBron James White EX 2.00 5.00
227 Kevin Durant Back EX 5.00 12.00
228 Michael Jordan Black EX 4.00 10.00
229 Kobe Bryant White EX 2.00 5.00
230 LeBron James Orange EX 2.00 5.00

2007-08 Artifacts Blue

*BLUE 1-100: 3X TO 8X BASE HI
*BLUE 101-150: 1.25X TO 3X
*BLUE 151-200: 2X TO 5X BASE HI
BLUE PRINT RUN 10 TO 25 SER.#'d SETS

2007-08 Artifacts Gold

*GOLD 1-100: 1.25X TO 3X BASE HI
*GOLD 101-150: .75X TO 2X BASE HI
*GOLD 151-200: .75X TO 2X BASE HI
GOLD PRINT RUN 100 SER.#'d SETS

2007-08 Artifacts Red

*RED 1-100: 2X TO 5X BASE HI
*RED 101-150: 1X TO 2.5X BASE HI
*RED 151-200: 1.25X TO 3X BASE HI
RED PRINT RUN 50 SER.#'d SETS

2007-08 Artifacts Autofacts

APPROXIMATELY ONE PER BOX
AFAB Andrea Bargnani 5.00 12.00
AFAG Maurice Ager 4.00 10.00
AFAH Al Horford 5.00 12.00
AFAJ Antawn Jamison 4.00 10.00
AFAR Allan Ray 4.00 10.00
AFBA B.J. Armstrong 8.00 20.00
AFBB Bruce Bowen 4.00 10.00
AFBD Brad Daugherty 5.00 12.00
AFBG Ben Gordon 8.00 20.00
AFBJ Bobby Jones 4.00 10.00
AFBL Bill Laimbeer 5.00 12.00
AFBM Brad Miller 4.00 10.00
AFBR Brandon Roy 6.00 15.00
AFBW Bill Walton 8.00 20.00
AFCD Chris Duhon 4.00 10.00
AFCF Channing Frye 4.00 10.00
AFCH Connie Hawkins 8.00 20.00
AFCM Cedric Maxwell 4.00 10.00
AFCO Michael Cooper 5.00 12.00
AFCS Cedric Simmons 4.00 10.00
AFDB Dee Brown 4.00 10.00
AFDG Daniel Gibson 4.00 10.00
AFDL David Lee 5.00 12.00
AFDN David Noel 4.00 10.00
AFDR David Robinson 30.00 60.00
AFDU Kevin Durant 125.00 250.00
AFEC Eddy Curry 4.00 10.00
AFEV Maurice Evans 4.00 10.00
AFFE Raymond Felton 5.00 12.00
AFFG Francisco Garcia 4.00 10.00
AFGG George Gervin 6.00 15.00
AFGR Aaron Gray 6.00 15.00
AFIL Mile Ilic 4.00 10.00
AFJA James Augustine 4.00 10.00
AFJB Josh Boone 4.00 10.00
AFJE Julius Erving 30.00 60.00
AFJG Joey Graham 4.00 10.00
AFJK Jason Kapono 4.00 10.00
AFJM Jamaal Magloire 4.00 10.00
AFJR Jalen Rose 4.00 10.00
AFJS J.R. Smith 4.00 10.00
AFJW Julian Wright 6.00 15.00
AFKB Kobe Bryant 100.00 250.00
AFKI Jason Kidd 20.00 50.00
AFKL Kyle Lowry 4.00 10.00
AFLA LaMarcus Aldridge 8.00 20.00
AFLJ LeBron James 100.00 200.00
AFMA Corey Maggette 4.00 10.00
AFMB Mike Bibby 4.00 10.00
AFMC Mardy Collins 4.00 10.00
AFME Mark Eaton 5.00 12.00
AFMI Mike James 4.00 10.00
AFMJ Michael Jordan 300.00 525.00
AFMP Pops Mensah-Bonsu 4.00 10.00
AFMW Marcus Williams 4.00 10.00
AFNO Steve Novak 4.00 10.00
AFPD Paul Davis 4.00 10.00
AFPM Paul Millsap 5.00 12.00
AFPO Patrick O'Bryant 4.00 10.00
AFPP Paul Pierce 10.00 25.00
AFQR Quentin Richardson 4.00 10.00
AFRE Renaldo Balkman 4.00 10.00
AFRF Randy Foye 4.00 10.00
AFRG Rudy Gay 4.00 10.00
AFRH Ryan Hollins 4.00 10.00
AFRP Robert Parish 6.00 15.00
AFRR Rajon Rondo 15.00 40.00
AFSB Shannon Brown 4.00 10.00
AFSJ Solomon Jones 4.00 10.00
AFSL Shaun Livingston 4.00 10.00
AFSM Sean May 4.00 10.00
AFSN Steve Nash 30.00 80.00
AFSR Sergio Rodriguez 4.00 10.00
AFSS Saer Sene 4.00 10.00
AFST John Stockton 40.00 80.00
AFSW Shawne Williams 4.00 10.00
AFTC Tyson Chandler 4.00 10.00
AFTF T.J. Ford 4.00 10.00
AFTM Tracy McGrady 20.00 50.00
AFTP Tayshaun Prince 5.00 12.00
AFTS Thabo Sefolosha 4.00 10.00
AFTT Tyrus Thomas 5.00 12.00
AFWE Martell Webster 4.00 10.00
AFWF Walt Frazier 8.00 20.00
AFYM Yao Ming 15.00 30.00

2007-08 Artifacts Conference Pairings

PRINT RUN 150 SER.#'d SETS
UNPRICED SILV.PATCH PRINT RUN 5 SETS
UNPRICED GOLD PATCH PRINT RUN ONE SET
CPAH C.Anthony/A.Harrington 6.00 15.00
CPAJ G.Arenas/J.Johnson 3.00 8.00
CPAK N.Krstic/T.Ariza 3.00 8.00
CPAM A.Kirilenko/B.Miller 3.00 8.00
CPAN R.Allen/J.Nelson 3.00 8.00
CPAO L.Aldridge/M.Okur 3.00 8.00
CPAS T.Allen/J.Starks 5.00 12.00
CPBA S.Battier/M.Ager 3.00 8.00
CPBB C.Boozer/S.Battier 3.00 8.00
CPBC C.Bosh/V.Carter 6.00 15.00
CPBE L.Bird/J.Erving 15.00 30.00
CPBG F.Garcia/A.Bynum 3.00 8.00
CPBH C.Billups/L.Hughes 3.00 8.00
CPBI K.Bryant/A.Iverson 10.00 25.00
CPBN A.Bargnani/A.Nocioni 4.00 10.00
CPBR J.Farmar/B.Roy 3.00 8.00
CPCB C.Maggette/C.Boozer 3.00 8.00
CPCC J.Childress/J.Collins 3.00 8.00
CPCD S.Cassell/B.Davis 3.00 8.00
CPCO M.Camby/M.Okur 3.00 8.00
CPCS A.Bargnani/A.Bogut 4.00 10.00
CPDC M.Collins/I.Diogu 3.00 8.00
CPDF B.Davis/J.Farmar 3.00 8.00
CPDM M.Jordan/D.Rodman 25.00 60.00
CPDN A.Nocioni/R.Dupree 3.00 8.00
CPDO C.Drexler/H.Olajuwon 8.00 20.00
CPDR M.Dunleavy/J.Redick 3.00 8.00
CPED M.Ellis/R.Davis 3.00 8.00
CPEJ M.Ellis/J.Jack 4.00 10.00
CPES E.Brand/S.Battier 3.00 8.00
CPFG R.Foye/R.Gay 3.00 8.00
CPFH M.Finley/J.Howard 4.00 10.00
CPFR R.Felton/M.Redd 3.00 8.00
CPGB D.Gooden/C.Butler 3.00 8.00
CPGH M.Ginobili/L.Head 4.00 10.00
CPGS P.Gasol/A.Stoudemire 4.00 10.00
CPGW D.West/R.Gay 3.00 8.00
CPHF J.Howard/M.Finley 3.00 8.00
CPHG B.Gordon/R.Hamilton 3.00 8.00
CPHH K.Hinrich/R.Hamilton 3.00 8.00
CPHM B.Haywood/S.May 3.00 8.00
CPHR J.Howard/J.Rose 5.00 12.00
CPIJ A.Iguodala/R.Jefferson 3.00 8.00
CPJF J.Johnson/R.Felton 3.00 8.00
CPJJ L.James/M.Jordan 40.00 80.00
CPJM M.Johnson/P.Maravich 20.00 40.00
CPJN B.Jones/D.Noel 3.00 8.00
CPJP L.James/T.Prince 8.00 20.00
CPJR J.Jack/J.Rose 3.00 8.00
CPJV L.Jackson/C.Villanueva 3.00 8.00
CPJW A.Jamison/M.Williams 3.00 8.00
CPKA K.Martin/A.Kirilenko 3.00 8.00
CPKM J.Kidd/S.Marbury 6.00 15.00
CPMB T.McGrady/K.Bryant 10.00 25.00
CPMC A.Miller/J.Crawford 3.00 8.00
CPMD M.Bibby/D.Stoudamire 3.00 8.00
CPMH K.Martin/D.Harris 6.00 15.00
CPMK C.Kaman/B.Miller 3.00 8.00
CPMP M.Pietrus/T.Parker 5.00 12.00
CPMW S.May/M.Williams 3.00 8.00
CPNA Nene/H.Armstrong 3.00 8.00
CPNS D.Nowitzki/P.Stojakovic 5.00 12.00
CPOB L.Odom/E.Brand 4.00 10.00
CPOH E.Okafor/D.Howard 5.00 12.00
CPOO S.O'Neal/J.O'Neal 6.00 15.00
CPPD M.Pietrus/B.Diaw 3.00 8.00
CPPH P.Pierce/K.Hinrich 5.00 12.00
CPPL J.Petro/S.Livingston 3.00 8.00
CPPM T.Parker/M.Miller 4.00 10.00
CPPW D.Williams/C.Paul 5.00 12.00
CPRA Q.Richardson/G.Arenas 3.00 8.00
CPRF B.Roy/R.Foye 3.00 8.00
CPRH Q.Richardson/U.Haslem 3.00 8.00
CPRL R.Artest/L.Odom 3.00 8.00
CPRO D.Robinson/H.Olajuwon 6.00 15.00
CPRR Z.Randolph/J.Richardson 3.00 8.00
CPSH J.Smith/D.Harris 3.00 8.00
CPSJ J.Calderon/S.Brown 3.00 8.00
CPSN S.Nash/J.Stockton 8.00 20.00
CPSS C.Simmons/S.Swift 3.00 8.00
CPTW J.Terry/L.Walton 3.00 8.00
CPWD C.Wilcox/B.Diaw 3.00 8.00
CPWK J.Williams/K.Korver 5.00 12.00
CPWM C.Webber/A.Mourning 8.00 20.00
CPWO B.Wallace/S.O'Neal 6.00 15.00
CPWP A.Walker/T.Prince 3.00 8.00
CPWR M.Webster/L.Ridnour 3.00 8.00
CPWW B.Wallace/R.Wallace 4.00 10.00
CPYD Y.Ming/T.Duncan 8.00 20.00

2007-08 Artifacts Divisional Artifacts

PRINT RUN 250 SER.#'d SETS
*BLUE: .6X TO 1.5X BASE HI
BLUE PRINT RUN 50 SER.#'d SETS
*COPPER: 1.25X TO 3X BASE HI
COPPER PRINT RUN 25 SER.#'d SETS
UNPRICED GOLD PRINT RUN ONE SET
*RED: .5X TO 1.25X BASE HI
RED PRINT RUN 100 SER.#'d SETS
UNPRICED SILVER PRINT RUN 10 SETS
*PATCH RED: 1.5X TO 4X BASE HI
PATCH RED PRINT RUN 29 SER.#'d SETS
UNPRICED PATCH SILV.PRINT RUN 5 SETS
UNPRICED PATCH GOLD PRINT RUN ONE SET
DAAB Andrew Bogut 2.50 6.00
DAAI Andre Iguodala 2.50 6.00
DAAJ Antawn Jamison 2.50 6.00
DAAK Andrei Kirilenko 2.50 6.00
DAAL Al Harrington 2.50 6.00
DAAM Alonzo Mourning 4.00 10.00
DAAR Allan Ray 2.00 5.00
DAAS Amare Stoudemire 2.50 6.00
DABC Brian Cardinal 2.00 5.00
DABD Boris Diaw 2.50 6.00
DABG Ben Gordon 2.50 6.00
DABI Chauncey Billups 3.00 8.00
DABJ Bobby Jones 2.00 5.00
DABR Brandon Roy 3.00 8.00
DABU Caron Butler 2.50 6.00
DACA Carmelo Anthony 4.00 10.00
DACB Chris Bosh 3.00 8.00
DACF Channing Frye 2.50 6.00
DACH Josh Childress 2.50 6.00
DACM Corey Maggette 2.50 6.00
DACP Chris Paul 4.00 10.00
DACS Cedric Simmons 2.50 6.00
DACW Chris Wilcox 2.00 5.00
DADA Baron Davis 2.50 6.00
DADH Dwight Howard 2.50 6.00
DADN David Noel 2.00 5.00
DADR David Robinson 5.00 12.00
DADS DeShawn Stevenson 2.00 5.00
DADW Deron Williams 2.50 6.00
DAEB Elton Brand 3.00 8.00
DAEO Emeka Okafor 2.50 6.00
DAGH Grant Hill 5.00 12.00
DAGW Gerald Wallace 2.50 6.00
DAHA Devin Harris 2.00 5.00
DAHO Josh Howard 2.50 6.00
DAIV Allen Iverson 4.00 10.00
DAJC Jose Calderon 2.00 5.00
DAJE Julius Erving 5.00 12.00
DAJH Juwan Howard 2.50 6.00
DAJK Jason Kidd 3.00 8.00
DAJM Jamaal Magloire 2.00 5.00
DAJO Jermaine O'Neal 2.50 6.00
DAJR J.J. Redick 3.00 8.00
DAJS Josh Smith 2.50 6.00
DAJT Jamaal Tinsley 2.00 5.00
DAKB Kobe Bryant 6.00 15.00
DAKE Kenyon Martin 2.50 6.00
DAKG Kevin Garnett 5.00 12.00
DAKT Kenny Thomas 2.00 5.00
DALA LaMarcus Aldridge 4.00 10.00
DALB Larry Bird 8.00 20.00
DALD Luol Deng 2.50 6.00
DALH Larry Hughes 2.50 6.00
DALJ LeBron James 8.00 20.00
DALO Lamar Odom 2.50 6.00
DALR Luke Ridnour 2.50 6.00
DALW Luke Walton 2.00 5.00
DAMA Sean May 2.00 5.00
DAMB Mike Bibby 3.00 8.00
DAMD Mike Dunleavy 2.50 6.00
DAMG Manu Ginobili 3.00 8.00
DAMJ Michael Jordan 25.00 60.00
DAMM Mike Miller 2.50 6.00
DAMO Mehmet Okur 2.00 5.00
DAMP Morris Peterson 2.00 5.00
DAMR Michael Redd 2.50 6.00
DAMW Marvin Williams 2.50 6.00
DANO Dirk Nowitzki 4.00 10.00
DANR Nate Robinson 2.00 5.00
DAPG Pau Gasol 3.00 8.00
DAPI Mickael Pietrus 2.00 5.00
DAPO Patrick O'Bryant 2.00 5.00
DAPP Paul Pierce 3.00 8.00
DAPS Peja Stojakovic 3.00 8.00
DARA Ray Allen 3.00 8.00
DARI Jason Richardson 3.00 8.00
DARJ Richard Jefferson 2.50 6.00
DARL Rashard Lewis 2.50 6.00
DARW Rasheed Wallace 3.00 8.00
DASC Sam Cassell 2.50 6.00
DASD Samuel Dalembert 2.00 5.00
DASH Shawn Marion 2.50 6.00
DASM Stephon Marbury 2.50 6.00
DASN Steve Nash 4.00 10.00
DASO Shaquille O'Neal 6.00 15.00
DAST John Stockton 5.00 12.00
DATD Tim Duncan 5.00 12.00
DATE Jason Terry 2.50 6.00
DATH J.R. Smith 2.50 6.00
DATM Tracy McGrady 3.00 8.00
DATP Tayshaun Prince 2.50 6.00
DAUD Beno Udrih 2.00 5.00
DAUH Udonis Haslem 2.00 5.00
DAVC Vince Carter 4.00 10.00
DAWA Ben Wallace 2.50 6.00
DAWF Walt Frazier 3.00 8.00
DAWR Bracey Wright 2.00 5.00
DAYM Yao Ming 4.00 10.00
DAZI Zydrunas Ilgauskas 2.50 6.00
DAZR Zach Randolph 2.50 6.00

2007-08 Artifacts Triple Jerseys

PRINT RUN 50 SER.#'d SETS
UNPRICED GOLD PRINT RUN ONE SET
BA Andrea Bargnani 5.00 12.00
AB Andrew Bogut 4.00 10.00
AI Allen Iverson 8.00 20.00
AJ Antawn Jamison 4.00 10.00
AK Andrei Kirilenko 4.00 10.00
AM Alonzo Mourning 15.00 40.00
AW Antoine Walker 4.00 10.00
BR Brandon Roy 5.00 12.00
CB Chauncey Billups 5.00 12.00
CD Clyde Drexler 15.00 40.00
DR David Robinson 20.00 40.00
DW Deron Williams 4.00 10.00
GG Gerald Green 4.00 10.00
HO Hakeem Olajuwon 6.00 15.00
JC Josh Childress 4.00 10.00
JE Julius Erving 8.00 20.00
JF Jordan Farmar 3.00 8.00
JK Jason Kidd 5.00 12.00
JO Jermaine O'Neal 4.00 10.00
JS John Stockton 8.00 20.00
JW Jason Williams 4.00 10.00
KB Kobe Bryant 15.00 40.00
KG Kevin Garnett 8.00 20.00
LA LaMarcus Aldridge 6.00 15.00
LB Larry Bird 12.00 30.00
LJ LeBron James 15.00 40.00
MG Manu Ginobili 5.00 12.00
MJ Michael Jordan 25.00 60.00
MA Magic Johnson 12.00 30.00
MR Michael Redd 4.00 10.00
PA Tony Parker 8.00 20.00
PM Pete Maravich 50.00 100.00
RH Richard Hamilton 4.00 10.00
RJ Richard Jefferson 4.00 10.00
RW Rasheed Wallace 5.00 12.00
SB Shane Battier 4.00 10.00
SM Josh Smith 4.00 10.00
TD Tim Duncan 8.00 20.00
TM Tracy McGrady 5.00 12.00
VC Vince Carter 6.00 15.00
YM Yao Ming 6.00 15.00
ZR Zach Randolph 4.00 10.00

1955 Ashland/Aetna Oil

The 1955 Ashland/Aetna Oil Basketball set contains 96 black and white, unnumbered cards each measuring 2 5/8" by 3 3/4". There are two different backs for each card front, one with an Ashland Oil ad, the other with an Aetna Oil ad. Aetna cards are considered to be worth an additional premium of 25 percent above the prices listed below. The backs contain a player's vital statistics, his home town, and his graduation class. These thin-stocked cards are difficult to obtain and have been numbered in the checklist below, by team and alphabetically within each team. The cards were distributed one at a time at Ashland (Kentucky and West Virginia) or Aetna (Ohio) gas stations in the region of the particular college. The set contains 12 players each from eight colleges: Eastern Kentucky 1-12, Kentucky 13-24, Louisville 25-36, Marshall 37-48, Morehead 49-60, Murray 61-72, Western Kentucky 73-84, and West Virginia 85-96. The cards of smaller school players within this set seem to be in shorter supply than the cards of the larger schools. However, the prices below reflect the smaller demand for the cards of players from the smaller schools. The key cards in the set are the first cards of Adolph Rupp, Hall of Famer and legendary coach of the Kentucky Wildcats, Ed Diddle, and Laker player/announcer Hot Rod Hundley. The catalog designation for this set is UO18.

COMPLETE SET (96) 5000.00 8500.00
COMMON CARD (1-36/73-84) 35.00 700.00
COMMON CARD (37-60) 35.00 70.00
COMMON CARD (61-72) 45.00 90.00
COMMON CARD (85-96) 50.00 100.00
1 Jack Adams 35.00 70.00
2 William Baxter 35.00 70.00
3 Jeffrey Brock 35.00 70.00
4 Paul Collins 35.00 70.00
5 Richard Culbertson 35.00 70.00
6 James Floyd 35.00 70.00
7 Harold Fraler 35.00 70.00
8 George Francis Jr. 35.00 70.00
9 Paul McBrayer CO 50.00 100.00
10 James Mitchell 35.00 70.00
11 Ronald Pellegrinon 35.00 70.00
12 Guy Strong 35.00 70.00
13 Earl Adkins 35.00 70.00
14 William Bibb 35.00 70.00
15 Jerry Bird 35.00 70.00
16 John Brewer 35.00 70.00
17 Robert Burrow 35.00 70.00
18 Gerry Calvert 35.00 70.00
19 William Evans 40.00 80.00
20 Phillip Grawemeyer 35.00 70.00
21 Ray Mills 35.00 70.00
22 Linville Puckett 35.00 70.00
23 Gayle Rose 40.00 80.00
24 Adolph Rupp CO 250.00 500.00
25 William Darragh 35.00 70.00
26 Vladimir Gastevich 35.00 70.00
27 Allan Glaza 35.00 70.00
28 Herbert Harrah 35.00 70.00
29 Bernard Peck Hickman CO 50.00 100.00
30 Richard Keffer 35.00 70.00
31 Gerald Moreman 35.00 70.00
32 James Morgan 35.00 70.00
33 John Prudhoe 35.00 70.00
34 Phillip Rollins 35.00 70.00
35 Roscoe Shackelford 35.00 70.00
36 Charles Tyra 50.00 100.00
37 Robert Ashley 35.00 70.00
38 Lewis Burns 35.00 70.00
39 Francis Crum 35.00 70.00
40 Raymond Frazier 35.00 70.00
41 Cam Henderson CO 40.00 80.00
42 Joseph Hunnicutt 35.00 70.00
43 Clarence Parkins 35.00 70.00
44 Jerry Pierson 35.00 70.00
45 David Robinson 35.00 70.00
46 Paul Underwood 35.00 70.00
47 Cebert Price 35.00 70.00
48 Charles Slack 35.00 70.00
49 David Breeze 35.00 70.00
50 Leonard Carpenter 35.00 70.00
51 Omar Fannin 35.00 70.00
52 Donnie Gaunce 35.00 70.00
53 Steve Hamilton 75.00 130.00
54 Bobby Laughlin CO 35.00 70.00
55 Jesse Mayabb 35.00 70.00
56 Jerry Riddle 35.00 70.00
57 Howard Shumate 35.00 70.00
58 Dan Swartz 35.00 70.00
59 Harlan Tolle 35.00 70.00
60 Donald Whitehouse 35.00 70.00
61 Rex Alexander CO 45.00 90.00
62 Jorgen Anderson 45.00 90.00
63 Jack Clutter 45.00 90.00
64 Howard Crittenden 45.00 90.00
65 James Gainey 45.00 90.00
66 Richard Kinder 45.00 90.00
67 Theo. Koenigsmark 45.00 90.00
68 Joseph Mikez 45.00 90.00
69 John Powless 50.00 100.00
70 Dolph Regelsky 45.00 90.00
71 Reinhard Tauck 45.00 90.00
72 Francis Watrous 45.00 90.00
73 Forrest Able 35.00 70.00
74 Tom Benbrook 35.00 70.00
75 Ronald Clark 35.00 70.00
76 Lynn Cole 35.00 70.00
77 Robert Daniels 35.00 70.00
78 Ed Diddle CO 125.00 250.00
79 Victor Harned 35.00 70.00
80 Dencil Miller 35.00 70.00
81 Ferrel Miller 35.00 70.00
82 George Orr 35.00 70.00
83 Jerry Weber 35.00 70.00
84 Jerry Whitsell 35.00 70.00
85 William Bergines 50.00 100.00
86 James Brennan 50.00 100.00
87 Marc Constantine 50.00 100.00
88 Michael Holt 50.00 100.00
89 Hot Rod Hundley 250.00 500.00
90 Clayce Kishbaugh 50.00 100.00
91 Ronald LaNeve 50.00 100.00
92 Gary Mullins 50.00 100.00
93 Fred Schaus CO 150.00 275.00
94 Frank Spadafore 50.00 100.00
95 Peter White 50.00 100.00
96 Paul Witting 50.00 100.00

1997 AT and T NBA PrePaid Phone Cards

These prepaid phone cards were available through advertisements in AT and T and Chevron billing statements, as well as through various mailer coupon packs. The twelve 15-minute cards sold for $5.25 per card. Nine 30-minute cards at $10.50 per card and eight 60-minute cards at $21.00 per card were also available. One could purchase the entire 29 card set for $265.50. The offer was available through 8/31/97, but the prepaid cards have no expiration date. The card fronts have a blue background with a close-up of the player. The left side contains a somewhat blurred color action shot of the player with his name in white font running perpendicular on the side. Prices below are for cards that have unused phone time. Expired cards are 20 percent of the values listed below. The cards are unnumbered and listed below in alphabetical order within each section.

COMPLETE SET (28) 120.00 300.00
COMP.15 MINUTE SET (12) 20.00 50.00
COMP.30 MINUTE SET (8) 30.00 80.00
COMP.60 MINUTE SET (8) 80.00 200.00
1 Vin Baker 15 MIN 2.00 5.00
2 Shawn Bradley 15 MIN 2.00 5.00
3 Dale Ellis 15 MIN 2.00 5.00
4 Tom Gugliotta 15 MIN 2.00 5.00
5 Juwan Howard 15 MIN 2.00 5.00
6 Jim Jackson 15 MIN 2.00 5.00
7 Dikembe Mutombo 15 MIN 2.50 6.00
8 Bobby Phills 15 MIN 2.00 5.00
9 Dino Radja 15 MIN 2.00 5.00
10 Clifford Robinson 15 MIN 2.00 5.00
11 David Robinson 15 MIN 3.00 8.00
12 Latrell Sprewell 15 MIN 2.50 6.00
13 Greg Anthony 30 MIN 4.00 10.00
14 Brent Barry 30 MIN 4.00 10.00
15 Anfernee Hardaway 30 MIN 8.00 20.00
16 Kevin Johnson 30 MIN 5.00 12.00
17 Shawn Kemp 30 MIN 5.00 12.00
18 Karl Malone 30 MIN 8.00 20.00
19 Alonzo Mourning 30 MIN 6.00 15.00
20 Mitch Richmond 30 MIN 5.00 12.00
22 Clyde Drexler 60 MIN 12.00 30.00
23 Grant Hill 60 MIN 12.00 30.00
24 Eddie Jones 60 MIN 10.00 25.00
25 Toni Kukoc 60 MIN 10.00 25.00
26 Reggie Miller 60 MIN 12.00 30.00
27 Charles Oakley 60 MIN 8.00 20.00
28 Glen Rice 60 MIN 8.00 20.00
29 Damon Stoudamire 60 MIN 8.00 20.00

1992 Australian Futera NBL

This standard-size 96-card set was sponsored by Mitsubishi Motors. It consists of 12 teams with eight cards per team. The fronts display white-bordered player action shots with the team name and logo in the upper right corner and a different colored stripe for each team down the left side. The backs carry a color player portrait with biography and career statistics. The cards are unnumbered, arranged alphabetically by player, and checklisted alphabetically according to teams as follows: Adelaide 36ers (1-12), Brisbane Bullets (13-24), Camberra Cannons (25-36), Melbourne Tigers (37-48), North Melbourne Giants (49-60), Perth Wildcats (61-72), Southeast Melbourne Magic (73-84), and Sydney Kings (85-96).

COMPLETE SET (96) 20.00 50.00
1 Mark Bradtke .60 1.50
2 Mike Corkeron .20 .50
3 Mark Davis .40 1.00
4 Jerry Dennard .20 .50
5 Butch Hays .60 1.50
6 Graham Kubank .20 .50
7 Albert Leslie ACO .20 .50
8 Brett Maher .20 .50
9 Michael McKay .20 .50
10 Don Shipway CO .20 .50
11 Kym Taylor .20 .50
12 Brett Wheeler .20 .50
13 Adrian Branch 1.00 2.50
14 Lyndon Brieffies .20 .50
15 Greg Fox .20 .50
16 Luke Gribble .20 .50
17 Shane Heal .75 2.00
18 Brian Kerle CO .20 .50
19 Simon Kerle .20 .50
20 Leroy Loggins .75 2.00
21 Gordie McLeod ACO .20 .50
22 Andre Moore .40 1.00
23 Paul Rees .20 .50
24 Blair Smith .20 .50
25 Lachlan Armfield .20 .50
26 Barry Barnes CO .20 .50
27 Simon Cottrell .20 .50
28 Ian Ellis ACO .20 .50
29 Steve Hood .40 1.00
30 Jamie Kennedy .20 .50
31 Herb McEachin .20 .50
32 Jason Reese .20 .50
33 Phil Smyth .20 .50
34 John Stelzer .20 .50
35 Matt Witkowski .20 .50
36 Mat Zauner .20 .50
37 Lanard Copeland .60 1.50
38 Andrew Gaze 1.25 3.00
39 Lindsay Gaze CO .20 .50
40 Warrick Giddey .20 .50
41 Ray Gordon .20 .50
42 Steven Lunardon .20 .50
43 Nigel Purchase .20 .50
44 Robert Sibley .20 .50
45 David Simmons .40 1.00
46 Dean Vickerman .20 .50
47 Alan Westover ACO .20 .50
48 Steven Whitehead .30 .75
49 Glenn Binnes ACO .20 .50
50 Ray Borner .20 .50
51 Martin Clarke .20 .50
52 Scott Fisher .40 1.00
53 David Graham .20 .50
54 Rod Johnson .20 .50
55 Mark Leader .20 .50
56 Paul Maley .30 .75
57 Bruce Palmer CO .20 .50
58 Darryl Pearce .20 .50
59 Pat Reidy .20 .50
60 Andrew Simons .20 .50
61 Murray Arnold CO .20 .50
62 James Crawford .30 .75
63 Michael Ellis .20 .50
64 Ricky Grace .60 1.50
65 Dave Hancock ACO .20 .50
66 Peter Hansen .20 .50
67 Vince Hinchen .20 .50
68 Griffin Longley .20 .50
69 Tiny Pinder 1.25 3.00
70 Trevor Torrance .20 .50
71 Andrew Vlahov .60 1.50
72 Eric Watterson .20 .50
73 Lucas Agrums .20 .50
74 Bruce Bolden .50 1.25
75 John Dorge .30 .75
76 Brian Goorjian CO .20 .50
77 Andrew Howey .20 .50
78 Darren Lucas .20 .50
79 Milt Newton .75 2.00
80 Scott Ninnis .20 .50
81 Andrew Parkinson .20 .50
82 Darren Perry .30 .75
83 Tony Ronaldson .20 .50
84 Ian Stacker .20 .50
85 Jody Austin .20 .50
86 Brad Dalton .20 .50
87 Mark Dalton .20 .50
88 Tony De Ambrosis .20 .50
89 Peter Hill .20 .50
90 Damian Keogh .20 .50
91 Dwayne McClain .75 2.00
92 Ken McClary .20 .50
93 Tim Morrissey .20 .50
94 Cory Reader .20 .50
95 Bob Turner CO .20 .50
96 Dean Uthoff .75 2.00

1992 Australian Stops NBL

This 92-card standard-size Australian National Basketball League set features black-bordered glossy color player action photos on the card fronts. The player's name appears in white lettering in the margin above each photo. The team name appears in white in the margin below along with "Stops '92" in red. On the white back, the player's name, along with a brief biography, are shown in the top left, and in the top right, the NBL and Stops logos are displayed. A short stat table appears underneath along with some career highlights. The player's team logo at the bottom rounds out the card. The cards are grouped by team as follows: Adelaide 36ers (2-6, 26, 51), Brisbane Bullets (7-12), Canberra Cannons (13-16, 18), Hobart Devils (17, 29-33), Geelong Supercats (19-22, 58), Gold Coast Rollers (23-25, 27, 28), Melbourne Tigers (1, 34-40, 80), Newcastle Falcons (41-44), North Melbourne Giants (45-50), Perth Wildcats (52-57, 59, 91), Illawarra Hawks (60-64), South-East Melbourne Magic (65-71), Sydney Kings (72-79), and Women's NBL (82-87).

COMPLETE SET (92) 35.00 70.00
1 Ken Watson CO .40 1.00
2 Mark Bradtke .75 2.00
3 Mark Davis .50 1.25
4 Butch Hays .75 2.00
5 Michael McKay .20 .50
6 Graham Kubank .20 .50
7 Leroy Loggins .75 2.00
8 Andre Moore .75 2.00
9 Shane Heal 1.25 3.00
10 Simon Kerle .20 .50
11 Greg Fox .20 .50
12 Adrian Branch 1.50 4.00
13 Jamie Kennedy .20 .50
14 Herb McEachin .20 .50
15 Phil Smyth .20 .50
16 Simon Cottrell .20 .50
17 Jason Reese UER .40 1.00
(Card front says Canberra Cannons)
18 Steve Hood .60 1.50
19 Robert Locke .40 1.00
20 Cecil Exum .50 1.25
21 Matthew Alexander .40 1.00
22 Wayne Larkins .20 .50
23 Mike Mitchell .75 2.00
24 Larry Sengstock .20 .50
25 Andre LaFleur .60 1.50
26 Matthew Reece UER .20 .50
(Card front says Gold Coast Rollers)
27 Ron Radliff .20 .50
28 Rodger Smith .20 .50
29 Cal Bruton CO .20 .50
30 Wayne McDaniel .40 1.00
31 Justin Cass .20 .50
32 Shane Froling .20 .50
33 David Stiff .20 .50
34 Lindsay Gaze CO .40 1.00
35 Andrew Gaze 2.00 5.00
36 David Simmons .50 1.25
37 Stephen Whitehead .50 1.25
38 Warrick Giddey .20 .50
39 Lanard Copeland 1.25 3.00
40 Robert Sibley .20 .50
41 Terry Dozier .75 2.00
42 Michael Johnson .20 .50
43 Al Green .20 .50
44 Paul Kuiper .20 .50
45 Bruce Palmer CO .20 .50
46 Scott Fisher .40 1.00
47 Ray Borner .20 .50
48 Paul Maley .40 1.00
49 Pat Reidy .40 1.00
50 Mark Leader .20 .50
51 Darryl Pearce UER .20 .50
(Card front says North Melbourne Giants)
52 Murray Arnold CO .20 .50
53 Ricky Grace .75 2.00
54 Andrew Vlahov .75 2.00
55 Tiny Pinder .75 2.00
56 James Crawford .60 1.50
57 Mike Ellis .20 .50
58 Vince Hinchen UER .40 1.00
(Card front says Perth Wilcats)
59 Perth Team Photo .40 1.00
60 Justin Withers .40 1.00
61 Greg Hubbard .40 1.00
62 Chuck Harmison .75 2.00
63 Melvin Thomas .60 1.50
64 Doug Overton 1.50 4.00
65 Brian Goorjian CO .20 .50
66 Bruce Bolden .60 1.50
67 Darren Lucas .20 .50
68 Darren Perry .40 1.00
69 John Dorge .20 .50
70 Andrew Parkinson .40 1.00
71 Scott Ninnis .40 1.00
72 Bob Turner CO .20 .50
73 Dean Uthoff .75 2.00
74 Damian Keogh .40 1.00
75 Dwayne McClain 1.50 4.00
76 Ken McClary .40 1.00
77 Tim Morrissey .20 .50
78 Mark Dalton .20 .50
79 The Jester .40 1.00
(Sydney Kings mascot)
80 Balmy Melbourne .40 1.00
Tigers mascot)
81 Eddie Crouch REF .20 .50
82 Jim Pappas CO .20 .50
83 Debbie Black .20 .50
84 Joanne Moyle .20 .50
85 Australian Women's Team .40 1.00
86 Annie Burgess .20 .50
87 Dandenong Rangers .40 1.00
Team Photo
88 Eric Cooks .20 .50
Ballarat Miners
89 Knox Raiders .40 1.00
Team Photo
90 Checklist .20 .50
91 Ricky Grace SP 1.25 3.00
James Crawford (Back to Back Champions)
92 Logo Card SP .75 2.00

1993 Australian Futera NBL

The first series of the 1993 Australian Futera NBL set consists of 110 standard-size cards. The fronts display white-bordered glossy color player action shots. Above each photo, the player's name is displayed within a light gray bar. Below the photo, the NBL logo appears along with the Mitsubishi name and logo. The backs sport the player's stats, career highlights and head shot, all within a light gray field. The player's name appears at the top within a darker gray bar. The cards are checklisted below alphabetically according to teams as follows: Adelaide 36ers (1-7), Brisbane Bullets (8-16), Canberra Cannons (17-23), Geelong Supercats (24-30), Gold Coast Rollers (31-36), Illawarra Hawks (37-42), Hobart Devils (43-50), Melbourne Tigers (51-58), Newcastle Falcons (59-67), North Melbourne Giants (68-76), Perth Wildcats (77-84), Townsville Suns (85- 91), South-East Melbourne Magic (92-102), and Sydney Kings (103-110).

COMPLETE SET (110) 20.00 50.00
1 Chris Blakemore .30 .75
2 Brett Maher .20 .50
3 Phil Smyth .20 .50

4 Scott Ninnis .20 .50
5 Mark Davis .40 1.00
6 Mike McKay .20 .50
7 Jerry Dennard .20 .50
8 Nigel Purchase .20 .50
9 Shane Heal .75 2.00
10 Leroy Loggins .40 1.00
11 Dave Colbert .20 .50
12 Andre Moore .40 1.00
13 Rodger Smith .20 .50
14 Luke Gribble .20 .50
15 Shane Froling .20 .50
16 Lachlan Armfield .20 .50
17 John Stelzer .20 .50
18 Simon Cottrell .20 .50
19 Rodney Monroe .75 2.00
20 Fred Herzog .20 .50
21 Matt Witkowski .20 .50
22 Adam Kendrick .20 .50
23 Justin Withers .20 .50
24 Michael Morrison .20 .50
25 Cecil Exum .40 1.00
26 Ray Borner .20 .50
27 Adrian Branch 1.00 2.50
28 Wayne Larkins .20 .50
29 Alex Hetenyi .20 .50
30 Vince Hinchen .20 .50
31 Mike Mitchell .40 1.00
32 Andre LaFleur .40 1.00
33 Andrew Goodwin .20 .50
34 Greg Fox .20 .50
35 Matthew Reece .20 .50
36 Peter Hill .20 .50
37 Chuck Harmison .50 1.25
38 Bruce Hays .40 1.00
39 Melvin Thomas .40 1.00
40 Chris Steele .20 .50
41 Dene MacDonald .20 .50
42 Mike Corkeron .20 .50
43 Wayne McDaniel .30 .75
44 Jim Havrilla .20 .50
45 Donald Whiteside .20 .50
46 David Close .20 .50
47 Neil Turner .20 .50
48 Anthony Stewart .20 .50
49 Justin Cass .20 .50
50 Andrew Svaldenis .20 .50
51 Warrick Giddey .20 .50
52 Andrew Gaze 1.00 2.50
53 Mark Bradtke .50 1.25
54 Lanard Copeland .50 1.25
55 Ray Gordon .20 .50
56 Stephen Whitehead .20 .50
57 Robert Sibley .20 .50
58 David Simmons .30 .75
59 Shawn Dennis .20 .50
60 Michael Johnson .20 .50
61 Everette Stephens .75 2.00
62 Al Green .20 .50
63 Grant Kruger .20 .50
64 Jason Joynes .20 .50
65 Terry Dozier .60 1.50
66 Peter Harvey .20 .50
67 Paul Kuiper .20 .50
68 Terry Johnson .20 .50
69 Darryl Pearce .20 .50
70 Mark Leader .20 .50
71 Larry Sengstock .20 .50
72 Pat Reidy .20 .50
73 Jason Reese .30 .75
74 Rod Johnson .20 .50
75 Paul Rees .20 .50
76 Paul Maley .20 .50
77 Scott Fisher .30 .75
78 James Crawford .20 .50
79 Andrew Vlahov .50 1.25
80 Eric Watterson .20 .50
81 Ricky Grace .40 1.00
82 Chris Carroll .20 .50
83 Trevor Torrance .20 .50
84 Steve Davis .20 .50
85 David Blades .20 .50
86 Rimas Kurtinaitias .30 .75
87 Ricky Jones .40 1.00
88 Lucas Agrums .20 .50
89 Graham Kubank .20 .50
90 Tonny Jensen .20 .50
91 Paul Simpson .20 .50
92 Darren Perry .20 .50
93 Bruce Bolden .40 1.00
94 Robert Rose .40 1.00
95 Darren Lucas .20 .50
96 Andrew Parkinson .20 .50
97 Tony Ronaldson .20 .50
98 Shane Bright .20 .50
99 David Graham .20 .50
100 Simon Kerle .20 .50
101 Andre Lemamis UER .20 .50
(Misspelled Andrej on back)
102 John Dorge .20 .50
103 Dwayne McClain .50 1.25
104 Damian Keogh .20 .50
105 Ken McClary .20 .50
106 Tony De Ambrosis .20 .50
107 Greg Hubbard .20 .50
108 Tim Morrissey .20 .50
109 Dean Uthoff .50 1.25
110 Mark Dalton .20 .50
NNO Melbourne Magic 8.00 20.00
NNO Herb McEachin 12.50 30.00
Legends Card

1993 Australian Futera Best of Both Worlds

The "Best of Both Worlds" redemption cards were randomly inserted in foil packs, and they could be redeemed for four cards featuring basketball players who have played in both the NBA and the NBL. Only 500 of each card were produced. The expiration date to redeem the cards in Australia was December 31, 1993. Each redeemed card was accompanied by a certification card. Inside white borders, the fronts show color action player photos, with the player's name printed across the top. The backs carry a color closeup above a player profile.

COMPLETE SET (4) 40.00 100.00
1 Terry Dozier 12.50 30.00
2 Dwayne McClain 12.50 30.00
3 Adrian Branch 15.00 35.00
4 Doug Overton 12.50 30.00

1993 Australian Futera Honours Awards

1,000 of each of these 11 standard-size cards were inserted in 1993 Futera packs. The fronts display full-color action photos framed by white borders. The top left corner of the picture is cut off and replaced by a set logo displaying the honor received. The backs have a narrowly-cropped closeup photo on the left and season summary on the right.

COMPLETE SET (11) 80.00 200.00
1 Scott Fisher MVP 6.00 15.00
2 Andrew Gaze MVP 10.00 25.00
3 Andrew Svaldenis MIP 3.00 8.00
4 Terry Dozier D-POY 6.00 15.00
5 Lachlan Armfield ROY 3.00 8.00
6 Brian Goorjian COY 3.00 8.00
7 Doug Overton 1st 8.00 20.00
8 Andrew Gaze 1st 10.00 25.00
9 Dwayne McClain 1st 6.00 15.00
10 Andrew Vlahov 1st 8.00 20.00
11 Scott Fisher 1st 6.00 15.00

1993 Australian Futera Super Gold

1,000 of each of these 14 standard-size cards were inserted in 1993 Futera packs. The fronts feature an color action shot surrounded by gold borders. The player's name is printed on a ghosted stripe along the left edge, while the title "Super Gold Card Series" appears across the top. The backs show gold borders and have a color photo, player profile, team logo and career stats.

COMPLETE SET (14) 50.00 125.00
1 John Dorge 3.00 8.00
2 Lanard Copeland 8.00 20.00
3 Pat Reidy 3.00 8.00
4 Cecil Exum 3.00 8.00
5 Melvin Thomas 6.00 15.00
6 Dean Uthoff 4.00 10.00
7 Terry Dozier 8.00 20.00
8 Mark Davis 8.00 20.00
9 Rimas Kurtinaitias 6.00 15.00
10 Shane Heal 10.00 25.00
11 Mike Mitchell 6.00 15.00
12 Justin Withers 3.00 8.00
13 Ricky Grace 10.00 25.00
14 Donald Whiteside 3.00 8.00

1993 Australian Stops NBL

This 92-card standard-size Australian National Basketball League set features white-bordered glossy color player action photos on the card fronts. The player's name appears in black lettering in the margin above each photo. The team name appears in black in the margin below along with "Stops '92" in red. On the white back, the player's name, along with a brief biography, are shown in the top left, and in the top right, the Stops logo is displayed. A short stat table appears underneath along with some career highlights. The player's team logo at the bottom and a picture of the front of the player's Rookie Card rounds out the card.

COMPLETE SET (92) 20.00 50.00
1 Terry Dozier .50 1.25
2 Steve Hood SD .40 1.00
3 Shane Heal 1.25 3.00
4 Tim Morrissey .20 .50
5 Cecil Exum .30 .75
6 Andrew Syaldenis .20 .50
7 Andrew Goodwin .20 .50
8 Al Green .20 .50
9 Wayne McDaniel .30 .75
10 Couch REF .20 .50
Mildenhall REF
11 Cal Bruton CO .20 .50
12 American All-Stars .40 1.00
13 Craig Adams .20 .50
14 Stephen Whitehead .20 .50
15 Michael Johnson .20 .50
16 Everette Stephens .75 2.00
17 Donald Whiteside .20 .50
18 Michael McKay .20 .50
19 Grant Kruger .20 .50
20 James Crawford .30 .75
21 Paul Maley .20 .50
22 Pat Reidy .20 .50
23 Australian Boomers .20 .50
24 Trevor Torrance .20 .50
25 Luc Longley 2.00 5.00
26 Chuck Harmison .60 1.50
27 Tony Ronaldson .20 .50
28 Tony De Ambrosis .20 .50
29 Mark Davis .40 1.00
30 Lanard Copeland SD .50 1.25
31 Darren Perry .40 1.00
32 Everette Stephens SD .50 1.25
33 Checklist .30 .75
34 Andrew Parkinson .20 .50
35 David Simmons .30 .75
36 Warrick Giddey .20 .50
37 Phil Smyth .20 .50
38 Scott Ninnis .20 .50
39 Leroy Loggins .60 1.50
40 Rodney Monroe .75 2.00
41 Lachlan Armfield .30 .75
42 Michael Morrison .30 .75
43 Ray Borner .20 .50
44 Mike Mitchell .60 1.50
45 Andre La Fleur .40 1.00
46 Andrew Vlahov .40 1.00
47 Scott Fisher .40 1.00
48 Dean Uthoff .50 1.25
49 Bruce Bolden .40 1.00
50 Greg Hubbard .30 .75
51 Damian Keogh .30 .75
52 Rimas Kurtinaitas .40 1.00
53 Adrian Branch 1.00 2.50
54 Vince Hinchen .20 .50
55 Ricky Jones .30 .75
56 Paris McCurdy .40 1.00
57 Brett Maher .20 .50
58 Shane Froling .20 .50
59 1992 Magic Champs .20 .50
60 Andre Moore .40 1.00
61 Fred Herzog .20 .50
62 Justin Withers .20 .50
63 Graham Kubank .20 .50
64 Wayne Larkins .20 .50
65 Lucas Agrums .20 .50
66 Matthew Reese .20 .50
67 Jim Havrilla .30 .75
68 Chris Steele .20 .50
69 Ray Gordan .20 .50
70 Mark Bradtke .50 1.25
71 Larry Sengstock .20 .50
72 Darryl Pearce .20 .50
73 Rod Johnson .20 .50
74 Brett Brown CO .20 .50
75 Jason Reese .20 .50
76 Ricky Grace .60 1.50
77 Darren Lucas .20 .50
78 Bruce Palmer CO .20 .50
79 Tigerman .30 .75
80 Robert Sibley .20 .50
81 Robert Rose .40 1.00
82 David Graham .20 .50
83 Ken McClary .20 .50
84 Dwayne McClain .75 2.00
85 Brian Goorjian CO .20 .50
86 Peter Hill .20 .50
87 Butch Hays .40 1.00
88 Andrew Gaze 1.25 3.00
89 Tonny Jensen .20 .50
90 Melvin Thomas .30 .75
91 Lanard Copeland .75 2.00
92 Checklist .40 1.00

1994 Australian Futera NBL Promos

This five-card cello-wrapped promo pack was given away at the 1994 National Sports Collectors Convention in Houston. Measuring the standard size, the fronts display full-bleed color action photos. Each card of the set is serially-numbered out of 5,000 sets produced. The cards are numbered on the back in gold foil in the upper right corner.

COMPLETE SET (5) 2.50 6.00
RC5 Andrew Gaze BK 1.00 2.50

1994 Australian Futera NBL

The 1994 Futera Australian NBL set consists of 220 standard-size cards. Foil packs contained nine cards, with 40 packs per display box and eight boxes per case. Australian and U.S. versions of the set were produced; the latter is distinguished by the silver foil "World Export Edition" seal on the card fronts. The fronts display white-bordered glossy color player action shots. A wooden basketball court stripe that cuts across the bottom of the picture and up the right edge carries the player's name and his team name. On a wooden basketball court background, the backs have a second color action photo, player profile, biography, and statistics. The cards are numbered on the back and checklisted below alphabetically according to teams as follows: Adelaide Sixers (1-6/111-116), Brisbane Bullets (7-13/117-121), Canberra Cannons (14-19/122-126), Geelong Supercats (20-25/127-130), Gold Coast Rollers (26-31/131-135), Hobart Devils (32-37/136-140), Illawarra Hawks (38-43/141-145), Melbourne Tigers (44-50/146-151), Newcastle Falcons (51-57/152-156), North Melbourne Giants (58-65/157-162), Perth Wildcats (66-72/163-167), South East Melbourne Magic (73-80/168-173), Sydney Kings (81-88/174-179), and Townsville Suns (89-96/180-183). The first series closes with NBL Honour Awards (97-106) and checklists (107-110).

COMPLETE SET (220) 30.00 60.00
COMPLETE SERIES 1 (110) 15.00 30.00
COMPLETE SERIES 2 (110) 15.00 30.00
1 Phil Smyth .20 .50
2 Scott Ninnis .20 .50
3 Brett Maher .20 .50
4 Michael McKay .20 .50
5 Mark Davis .40 1.00
6 David Robinson .40 1.00
7 Dave Colbert .20 .50
8 Shane Froling .20 .50
9 Rodger Smith .20 .50
10 Leroy Loggins .40 1.00
11 Andre Moore .30 .75
12 Shane Heal .60 1.50
13 Luke Gribble .20 .50
14 Rodney Monroe .40 1.00
15 Justin Withers .20 .50
16 Matt Witkowski .20 .50
17 Fred Herzog .20 .50
18 Lachlan Armfield .20 .50
19 John Stelzer .20 .50
20 Wayne Larkins .20 .50
21 Adrian Branch .75 2.00
22 Cecil Exum .30 .75
23 Ray Borner .20 .50
24 Michael Morrison .30 .75
25 Vince Hinchen .20 .50
26 Andrew Goodwin .20 .50
27 Andre LaFleur .20 .50
28 John Szigetti .20 .50
29 Matthew Reece .20 .50
30 Mike Mitchell .30 .75
31 Greg Fox .20 .50
32 Justin Cass .20 .50
33 David Close .20 .50
34 Andrew Svaldenis .20 .50
35 Donald Whiteside .30 .75
36 Wayne McDaniel .30 .75
37 Anthony Stewart .20 .50
38 Butch Hays .40 1.00
39 Chris Steele .20 .50
40 Melvin Thomas .30 .75
41 Dene MacDonald .20 .50
42 Chuck Harmison .50 1.25
43 Mike Corkeron .20 .50
44 Lanard Copeland .40 1.00
45 Stephen Whitehead .20 .50
46 Robert Sibley .20 .50
47 Mark Bradtke .50 1.25
48 Andrew Gaze .50 1.25
49 David Simmons .20 .50
50 Warrick Giddey .20 .50
51 Michael Johnson .20 .50
52 Al Green .20 .50
53 Peter Harvey .20 .50
54 Everette Stephens .30 .75
55 Grant Kruger .20 .50
56 Terry Dozier .40 1.00
57 Simon O'Donnell .20 .50
58 Paul Maley .20 .50
59 Darryl Pearce .20 .50
60 Mark Leader .20 .50
61 Jason Reese .20 .50
62 Rod Johnson .20 .50
63 Pat Reidy .20 .50
64 Paul Rees .20 .50
65 Larry Sengstock .20 .50
66 Trevor Torrance .20 .50
67 Andrew Vlahov .30 .75
68 James Crawford .20 .50
69 Ricky Grace .40 1.00
70 Scott Fisher .20 .50
71 Eric Watterson .20 .50
72 Chris Carroll .20 .50
73 Darren Lucas .20 .50
74 Bruce Bolden .30 .75
75 Robert Rose .40 1.00
76 John Dorge .20 .50
77 Andrew Parkinson .20 .50
78 David Graham .20 .50
79 Darren Perry .20 .50
80 Tony Ronaldson .20 .50
81 Greg Hubbard .20 .50
82 Dwayne McClain .40 1.00
83 Ken McClary .20 .50
84 Tim Morrissey .20 .50
85 Damian Keogh .20 .50
86 Tony De Ambrosis .20 .50
87 Dean Uthoff .50 1.25
88 Wayne Womack .20 .50
89 David Blades .20 .50
90 Ricky Jones .40 1.00
91 Rimas Kurtinaitas .20 .50
92 Brian Andrews .20 .50
93 Lucas Agrums .20 .50
94 Tonny Jensen .20 .50
95 Paul Simpson .20 .50
96 Darren Smith .20 .50
97 Robert Rose .30 .75
MVP Award
98 Andrew Gaze .40 1.00
Most Efficient Player
99 Andrew Gaze .40 1.00
Top Point Scorer
100 Terry Dozier .40 1.00
Best Defensive Player
101 Andre LaFleur .30 .75
Good Hands Award
102 Bruce Bolden .20 .50
Top Rebounder
103 Chris Blakemore .20 .50
Rookie of the Year
104 Scott Ninnis .20 .50
Most Improved Player
105 Andrew Vlahov .20 .50
Int'l. POY
106 Alan Black .20 .50
Coach of the Year
107 Checklist 1-37 .20 .50
108 Checklist 38-80 .20 .50
109 Checklist 81-110 .20 .50
110 Checklist Specials .20 .50
111 Robert Rose .40 1.00
112 Mark Davis .30 .75
113 Chris Blakemore .20 .50
114 Phil Smyth .20 .50
115 Brett Maher .20 .50
116 Mike McKay .20 .50
117 Dave Colbert .20 .50
118 Shane Heal .40 1.00
119 Leroy Loggins .40 1.00
120 Andre Moore .30 .75
121 Robert Sibley .20 .50
122 Jason Reese .20 .50
123 Lachlan Armfield .20 .50
124 Fred Herzog .20 .50
125 Justin Withers .20 .50
126 Adam Kendrick .20 .50
127 Everette Stephens .30 .75
128 Ray Borner .20 .50
129 Cecil Exum .30 .75
130 Simon Kerle .20 .50
131 Mike Mitchell .30 .75
132 Matthew Reece .20 .50
133 Tony De Ambrosis .20 .50
134 Andre LaFleur .30 .75
135 Peter Hill .20 .50
136 Calvin Talford .50 1.25
137 Darren Perry .20 .50
138 Wayne McDaniel .30 .75
139 Anthony Stewart .20 .50
140 Keith Nelson .20 .50
141 Butch Hays .30 .75
142 Melvin Thomas .30 .75
143 Chuck Harmison .50 1.25
144 Chris Steele .20 .50
145 Dene MacDonald .20 .50
146 Lanard Copeland .40 1.00
147 David Simmons .20 .50
148 Mark Bradtke .40 1.00
149 Andrew Gaze .50 1.25
150 Warrick Giddey .20 .50
151 Ray Gordon .20 .50
152 Derek Rucker .30 .75
153 Terry Dozier .40 1.00
154 Tonny Jensen .20 .50
155 Grant Kruger .20 .50
156 Paul Kuiper .20 .50
157 Darryl McDonald .60 1.50
158 Paul Maley .20 .50
159 Mark Leader .20 .50
160 Larry Sengstock .20 .50
161 Pat Reidy .20 .50
162 Paul Rees .20 .50
163 Ricky Grace .40 1.00
164 James Crawford .20 .50
165 Andrew Vlahov .30 .75
166 Scott Fisher .20 .50
167 Martin Cattalini .20 .50
168 Adonis Jordan .75 2.00
169 Darren Lucas .20 .50
171 Andrew Parkinson .20 .50
172 Tony Ronaldson .20 .50
173 David Graham .20 .50
174 Mario Donaldson .20 .50
175 Leon Trimmingham .60 1.50
176 Tim Morrissey .20 .50
177 Greg Hubbard .20 .50
178 Dean Uthoff .50 1.25
179 Damian Keogh .20 .50
180 Brendan LeGassick .20 .50
181 Ricky Jones .40 1.00
182 Lucas Agrums .20 .50
183 Graham Kubank .20 .50
184 1993 Finals Series .20 .50
Perth Defeats Brisbane
185 1993 Finals Series .20 .50
Melbourne Defeats SE Melbourne
186 1993 Finals Series .20 .50
Melbourne Leads Perth
187 1993 Finals Series .20 .50
Perth Squares the Series
188 1993 Finals Series .20 .50
Melbourne Defeats Perth
189 1993 Finals Series .20 .50
Grand Final MVP
190 1993 Finals Series .20 .50
Victory At Last
191 Lanard Copeland .40 1.00
Andrew Gaze
192 Ricky Grace .30 .75
James Crawford
193 Andre LaFleur .30 .75
Mike Mitchell
194 Shane Heal .30 .75
Leroy Loggins
195 Melvin Thomas .40 1.00
Butch Hays
196 Leon Trimmingham .30 .75
Mario Donaldson
197 Patrick Reidy .30 .75
Darryl McDonald
198 Sam MacKinnon .60 1.50
199 C.J. Bruton .20 .50
200 Aaron Trahair .40 1.00
201 Brad Williams .20 .50
202 Ryan Knights .20 .50
203 Darren Smith .20 .50
204 Opals Header .20 .50
204A Jenny Whittel .20 .50
205 Annie Burgess .20 .50
206 Sandy Brondello .20 .50
207 Allison Cook .20 .50
208 Michele Timms 1.00 2.50
209 Shelley Gorman .20 .50
210 Robyn Maher .20 .50
211 Trish Fallon .20 .50
212 Rachael Sporn .20 .50
213 Karen Dalton .20 .50
214 Michelle Brogan .20 .50
215 Samantha Thornton .20 .50
216 Tom Maher .20 .50
217 Checklist 111-151 .20 .50
218 Checklist 152-183 .20 .50
219 Checklist 184-220 .20 .50
220 Checklist Specials .20 .50

1994 Australian Futera Best of Both Worlds

Randomly inserted in foil packs, the "Best of Both Worlds" redemption cards feature basketball players who have played in both the NBA and the NBL. The odds of finding these standard-size cards were 1:300 foil packs. 1,000 of each card were produced, and the cards were individually numbered 0001-1000. The expiration date to redeem the first series cards in Australia was December 31, 1994. The second series cards' expiration date in Australia was August 31, 1995. Both the redemption and the certificate fronts show a ball, which displays the Australian and American flags, swishing through the net. The picture card shows an action and a portrait shot on the front, while the back contains biographical information.

COMPLETE SET (12) 125.00 250.00
BW1 Ricky Grace 12.50 30.00
Picture Card
BW2 Lanard Copeland 12.50 30.00
Picture Card
BW3 Andrew Gaze 15.00 40.00
Picture Card
BW4 Adonis Jordan 15.00 50.00
Picture Card
CC3 Andrew Gaze 10.00 20.00
Certification Card
CC4 Adonis Jordan 10.00 20.00
Certification Card
CD1 Ricky Grace 6.00 15.00
Certification Card
CD2 Lanard Copeland 8.00 20.00
Certification Card
RC3 Andrew Gaze 10.00 25.00
Redemption Card
RC4 Adonis Jordan 8.00 20.00
Redemption Card
RD1 Ricky Grace 8.00 20.00
Redemption Card
RD2 Lanard Copeland 8.00 20.00
Redemption Card

1994 Australian Futera Defensive Giants

Randomly inserted in second series foil packs, this seven-card standard-size set features the ABL's better defensive players. Just 3,000 of each card were produced, with each one individually numbered 0001-3000. The fronts display full-bleed color action photos; the letter D appears in the background in lightly ghosted lettering. The player's name is stamped in gold foil in the lower right corner. The backs have full-color photos in the left corner and a career summary on a light blue panel.

COMPLETE SET (7) 20.00 50.00
DG1 Terry Dozier 3.00 8.00
DG2 Robert Rose 5.00 12.00
DG3 Darren Lucas 2.00 5.00
DG4 Melvin Thomas 5.00 12.00
DG5 Derek Rucker 5.00 12.00
DG6 Mark Davis 5.00 12.00
DG7 Mark Bradtke 6.00 15.00

1994 Australian Futera Lords of the Ring

Randomly inserted in foil packs, this six-card standard-size set focuses on the NBL's best slam dunkers. The odds of finding these cards were 1:20 foil packs. Just 5,000 of each card were produced, with each one individually numbered 0001-5000. Against a brick wall (LR1-LR6) or textured (LR7-LR12) design, the fronts show these players dunking. The player's name is gold-foil stamped vertically along the left edge, and the Lords of the Ring logo is in the lower right corner. The backs feature player profiles.

COMPLETE SET (12) 25.00 60.00
LR1 Robert Rose 3.00 8.00
LR2 Lanard Copeland 3.00 8.00
LR3 Ricky Jones 1.50 4.00
LR4 Mark Bradtke 3.00 8.00
LR5 David Simmons 2.00 5.00
LR6 Andrew Vlahov 3.00 8.00
LR7 James Crawford 3.00 8.00
LR8 Bruce Bolden 3.00 8.00
LR9 Mike Mitchell 3.00 8.00
LR10 Darryl McDonald 4.00 10.00
LR11 Paul Maley 3.00 8.00
LR12 Leon Trimmingham 4.00 10.00

1994 Australian Futera NBL Heroes

Randomly inserted in foil packs, this 14-card standard-size set documents the careers of NBL legend Leroy Loggins in the first series and Scott Fisher in the second series. The odds of finding these cards were 1:17 foil packs. Just 5,000 of each card were produced, with each one individually numbered 0001-5000. Cards number NH2-NH7 and NH9-NH14 feature various action shots surrounded by black borders. The bottoms read "NBL 94" in white lettering against the black background while the word "Heroes" is stamped in gold foil. On a gray background, the backs carry a color drawing and summarize the player's career by year.

COMPLETE SET (14) 10.00 25.00
NH1 Leroy Loggins 1.50 4.00
Drawing
NH2 Leroy Loggins 1989 1.25 3.00
NH3 Leroy Loggins 1990 1.25 3.00
NH4 Leroy Loggins 1991 1.25 3.00
NH5 Leroy Loggins 1992 1.25 3.00
NH6 Leroy Loggins 1993 1.25 3.00
NH7 Leroy Loggins 1.25 3.00
Olympic Career
NH8 Scott Fisher 1.50 4.00
Drawing
NH9 Scott Fisher 1988 1.00 2.50
NH10 Scott Fisher 1989 1.00 2.50
NH11 Scott Fisher 1990 1.00 2.50
NH12 Scott Fisher 1991 1.00 2.50
NH13 Scott Fisher 1992 1.00 2.50
NH14 Scott Fisher 1993 1.00 2.50

1994 Australian Futera New Horizons

Randomly inserted in second series foil packs, this six-card standard-size set features young ABL stars. The fronts have the player's photo against their city skyline. In gold foil lettering, the player's first name runs across the left side while their last name is on the top. The words "New Horizons" are on the bottom. The backs feature a player photo and information against a street map of their city. According to the media release, only 3000 of each card was produced.

COMPLETE SET (6) 12.00 30.00
HZ1 Calvin Talford 4.00 10.00
HZ2 Darryl McDonald 5.00 12.00
HZ3 Leon Trimmingham 5.00 12.00
HZ4 Mario Donaldson 2.00 5.00
HZ5 Adonis Jordan 4.00 10.00
HZ6 Keith Jordan 2.00 5.00

1994 Australian Futera Offensive Threats

Randomly inserted in first series foil packs, this 14-card standard-size set features the highest point scorer from each NBL team. The odds of finding these cards were one per nine foil packs. Just 5,000 of each card were produced, with each one individually numbered 0001-5000. The fronts display full-bleed color action photos; the player's last name and scoring average appear in the background in lightly ghosted lettering. The backs have a full-color photo in the left corner and a career summary on a green panel.

COMPLETE SET (14) 20.00 50.00
OT1 Andrew Gaze 4.00 10.00
OT2 Ricky Jones 1.50 4.00
OT3 Adrian Branch 2.50 6.00
OT4 Jason Reese 1.50 4.00
OT5 Melvin Thomas 1.50 4.00
OT6 Rodney Monroe 2.50 6.00
OT7 Dwayne McClain 2.50 6.00
OT8 Scott Fisher 2.50 6.00
OT9 Leroy Loggins 2.50 6.00
OT10 Mike Mitchell 2.50 6.00
OT11 Mark Davis 1.50 4.00
OT12 Bruce Bolden 2.50 6.00
OT13 Everette Stephens 2.50 6.00
OT14 Wayne McDaniel 1.50 4.00

1994 Australian Futera Signature Series

Randomly inserted in second series foil packs, this seven-card standard-size set features signed cards of popular players. According to information provided on the media release, only 500 of each card was produced and each was individually numbered.

COMPLETE SET (7) 175.00 350.00
SS1 Checklist 8.00 20.00
SS2 Calvin Talford 24.00 60.00
SS3 Darryl McDonald 40.00 100.00
SS4 Mario Donaldson 20.00 50.00
SS5 Leon Trimmingham 50.00 125.00
SS6 Andrew Vhalov 24.00 60.00
SS7 Bruce Bolden 20.00 50.00

1995 Australian Futera NBL

The first series of the 1995 Futera Australian NBL set consists of 110 standard-size cards. Each display box contained forty 9-card foil packs. Each pack contains one card from an insert set, and one pack in each box featured only insert set cards. The fronts display full-bleed color action shots, with the player's name and team logo in an orangish-red stripe running along one of the sides. The backs have the player's name, a full-color inset photo, biographical information and NBL seasonal and career stats. All these elements are framed against a purple background on the left, a basketball in the middle and a wrap-around of the front photo on the right.

COMPLETE SET (110) 12.00 30.00
1 Darryl McDonald .40 1.00
2 Ricky Grace .30 .75
3 Fred Cofield .40 1.00
4 Brett Maher .10 .30
5 Lanard Copeland .40 1.00
6 Dean Uthoff .40 1.00
7 Everette Stephens .40 1.00
8 Andre LaFleur .25 .60
9 Graham Kubank .10 .30
10 Luke Gribble .10 .30
11 Darryl Johnson .20 .50
12 Mike Corkeron .10 .30
13 Keith Nelson .10 .30
14 Greg Hubbard .10 .30
15 Robert Rose .30 .75
16 Andrew Vlahov .30 .75
17 Paul Kuiper .10 .30
18 Wayne McDaniel .20 .50
19 Jason Reese .10 .30
20 Justin Cass .10 .30
21 Butch Hays .30 .75
22 Paul Maley .20 .50
23 Dave Simmons .10 .30
24 Mike Mitchell .30 .75
25 Bruce Bolden .30 .75
26 David Colbert .10 .30
27 Pat Reidy .10 .30
28 Mark Dalton .10 .30
29 Chris Blakemore .20 .50
30 Checklist 1-44 .10 .30
31 Simon Kerle .10 .30
32 Chris Steele .10 .30
33 Paul Rees .10 .30
34 Warrick Giddey .10 .30
35 Doug Peacock .10 .30
36 Damian Keogh .10 .30
37 Michael Johnson .10 .30
38 Justin Withers .10 .30
39 Aaron Trahair .20 .50
40 Leroy Loggins .30 .75
41 Mark Leader .10 .30
42 Anthony Stewart .10 .30
43 Adonis Jordan .75 2.00
44 Scott Ninnis .15 .40
45 Leon Trimmingham .50 1.25
46 David Blades .10 .30
47 Grant Kruger .10 .30
48 Robert Sibley .10 .30
49 Vince Hinchen .10 .30
50 Chuck Harmison .40 1.00
51 Matthew Alexander .10 .30
52 Simon Cottrell .10 .30
53 Tony De Ambrosis .10 .30
54 Calvin Talford .40 1.00
55 Sam MacKinnon .30 .75
56 Martin Cattalini .10 .30
57 Mike McKay .10 .30
58 Larry Sengstock .10 .30
59 Andrew Gaze .75 2.00
60 Checklist 45-88 .10 .30
61 Rodger Smith .10 .30
62 Melvin Thomas .20 .50
63 Peter Hill .10 .30
64 Mario Donaldson .10 .30
65 Darren Perry .10 .30
66 Matt Witkowski .10 .30
67 Derek Rucker .30 .75
68 Cecil Exum .30 .75
69 Lucas Agrums .10 .30
70 Darren Lucas .10 .30
71 Mark Bradtke .30 .75
72 Mark Davis .30 .75
73 Peter Harvey .10 .30
74 Ray Borner .10 .30
75 Dene MacDonald .10 .30
76 John Dorge .10 .30
77 Ricky Jones .30 .75
78 Shane Heal .40 1.00
79 Terry Dozier .40 1.00
80 Paul Crombie .10 .30
81 Stephen Whitehead .15 .40
82 Lachlan Armfield .10 .30
83 James Crawford .15 .40
84 Cameron Dickinson .10 .30
85 Tony Ronaldson .10 .30
86 Scott Fisher .15 .40
87 Andrew Parkinson .10 .30
88 Ray Gordon .10 .30
89 Checklist 89-110 .10 .30
90 Giants vs Magic .10 .30
Semi-Finals
91 Sixers vs Tigers .10 .30
Semi-Finals
92 Sixers vs Giants .10 .30
Semi-Finals
93 Giants vs Sixers .10 .30
Semi-Finals
94 N Melbourne Giants .10 .30
Championship Team
95 Paul Rees .10 .30
96 Shane Heal .50 1.25
97 Derek Rucker .20 .50
98 Shane Heal .40 1.00
99 Mark Bradtke .30 .75
100 Keith Nelson .10 .30
101 Andrew Gaze .75 2.00
102 Darryl McDonald .30 .75
103 Sam MacKinnon .20 .50
104 Brett Brown .10 .30
105 Andrew Gaze .75 2.00
106 Darren Lucas .10 .30
107 Chris Blakemore .20 .50
108 Mark Bradtke .30 .75
109 Checklist .10 .30
110 Checklist Specials .10 .30

1995 Australian Futera Airborne

Randomly inserted in first series foil packs, this nine-card standard-size set features players with exceptional jumping ability. The fronts show the featured player in the air against a speckled blue background. The player is identified in the lower left corner with set title above his name. The back is dedicated to a description of the player's leaping capabilities.

COMPLETE SET (9) 2.00 5.00
NA1 Sam MacKinnon .60 1.50
NA2 Butch Hays .30 .75
NA3 Paul Maley .30 .75
NA4 Calvin Talford .40 1.00
NA5 Mike Mitchell .40 1.00
NA6 Dave Simmons .20 .50
NA7 Ricky Jones .30 .75
NA8 Darryl McDonald .75 2.00
NA9 Checklist .20 .50

1995 Australian Futera Clutchmen

Randomly inserted in first series foil packs, this 15-card standard-size set features players who are considered "go-to" players. The fronts feature a color action shot framed by a brown geometric design. The identification of NBL Clutchmen runs vertically down either side while his name is printed across the bottom. The backs contain a player profile on the left, while the right side has a narrowly-cropped color photo.

COMPLETE SET (15) 5.00 12.00
CM1 Robert Rose .40 1.00
CM2 Leroy Loggins .75 2.00
CM3 Fred Cofield .40 1.00
CM4 Cecil Exum .30 .75
CM5 Doug Peacock .20 .50
CM6 Darren Perry .20 .50
CM7 Butch Hays .40 1.00
CM8 Andrew Gaze 1.00 2.50
CM9 Derek Rucker .75 2.00
CM10 Darryl McDonald .75 2.00
CM11 Ricky Grace .60 1.50
CM12 Tony Ronaldson .20 .50
CM13 Leon Trimmingham .30 .75
CM14 Cameron Dickinson 1.00 2.50
CM15 Checklist .20 .50

1995 Australian Futera Head To Head

Randomly inserted in first-series foil packs, these six die-cut double-sided cards feature 12 NBL stars. They were individually numbered out of 5000 and were inserted at a rate of one in every 23 packs. Each side features a color action photo, with a circular headshot gracing the top of the card and extending beyond the upper border. On each side the player's name is gold foil-stamped across the photo.

COMPLETE SET (6) 30.00 80.00
H1 Andrew Gaze 12.50 30.00
Darren Lucas
H2 Leroy Loggins 10.00 25.00
Robert Rose
H3 Leon Trimmingham 10.00 25.00
Ricky Jones
H4 Melvin Thomas 6.00 15.00
Keith Nelson
H5 Fred Cofield 5.00 12.00
Tonny Jensen
H6 Peter Hill 4.00 10.00
Simon Kerle

1995 Australian Futera Instant Impact

Randomly inserted in first series foil packs, this six-card standard-size set highlights players new to the NBL who have made a significant impact on the league. These cards are individually numbered out of 2,500 and were inserted one per 53 packs. The fronts show the player in action against a watercolor background. The set subtitle and the player's name are gold foil stamped on the fronts. The backs have player profile on the left with a narrowly-cropped closeup photo on the right.

COMPLETE SET (6) 25.00 60.00

II1 Darryl McDonald	6.00	15.00
II2 Sam MacKinnon	6.00	15.00
II3 Leon Trimmingham	8.00	20.00
II4 Chris Blakemore	4.00	10.00
II5 Derek Rucker	6.00	15.00
II6 Calvin Talford	4.00	10.00

1995 Australian Futera MVP/Rookie Redemption

Randomly inserted into first series foil packs, this three-card standard-size set features 1994-95 Australian MVP Andrew Gaze and 1994-95 Australian Rookie of the Year Sam MacKinnon. One in every 3,200 packs contained a redemption card for the special card signed by both players. Only 250 of these cards were produced. After a collector mailed in the redemption card, he received the special card, a certification card and the redemption card returned stamped.

COMPLETE SET (3)	125.00	250.00
MR1 Redemption Card	10.00	25.00
MR2 Andrew Gaze	100.00	250.00
Sam MacKinnon		
MR3 Certification Card	10.00	25.00

1995 Australian Futera Star Challenge

Randomly inserted into first series foil packs, this ten-card standard-size set comprises of players who participated in the 1994 All-Star Challenge in Sydney. The cards were inserted one in every 16 packs and are individually numbered out of 5,000. The fronts have action shots in their all-star uniforms against a multi-colored background. The backs feature on the right side a color photo of the player in their all-star uniform, with game performance information directly beneath the picture.

COMPLETE SET (10)	15.00	40.00
NBL1 Tony Ronaldson	1.50	4.00
NBL2 Paul Rees	1.00	2.50
NBL3 Mark Bradtke	1.50	4.00
NBL4 Andrew Gaze	4.00	10.00
NBL5 Shane Heal	3.00	8.00
NBL6 Derek Rucker	2.50	6.00
NBL7 Butch Hays	1.50	4.00
NBL8 Mario Donaldson	1.00	2.50
NBL9 Leon Trimmingham	4.00	10.00
NBL10 Lanard Copeland	2.50	6.00

1995 Australian Futera 300 Club

Randomly inserted in first series foil packs, this 17-card standard-size set features players who have played in 300 or more NBL games. The fronts have player portraits which roll back in the lower right corner to reveal how many games each player appeared in. The backs show an action shot and a brief description of their career against a royal blue background.

COMPLETE SET (17)	2.50	6.00
GC1 Larry Sengstock	.20	.50
GC2 Leroy Loggins	.40	1.00
GC3 Damian Keogh	.20	.50
GC4 Herb McEachin	.20	.50
GC5 James Crawford	.30	.75
GC6 Al Green	.20	.50
GC7 Ray Borner	.20	.50
GC8 Darryl Pearce	.20	.50
GC9 Michael Johnson	.20	.50
GC10 Phil Smyth	.20	.50
GC11 Chuck Harmison	.40	1.00
GC12 Mike Ellis	.20	.50
GC13 Tim Morrissey	.20	.50
GC14 Simon Cottrell	.20	.50
GC15 Eric Waterson	.20	.50
GC16 Mike McKay	.20	.50
GC17 Checklist	.20	.50

1995 Australian Futera Abdul-Jabbar Adidas Promo

This four-card standard-size set covers the career of NBA great Kareem Abdul-Jabbar. This set was issued to promote the 1995 Adidas streetball challenge. These cards are numbered individually out of 5,000. The fronts feature various color action shots of Kareem. The backs have descriptions of his career as well as a photo. Each card also has one line with his complete point totals.

COMPLETE SET (4)	15.00	40.00
COMMON CARD (K1-K4)	5.00	12.00

1996 Australian Futera NBL

This 100-card Series 1 set features big-name players and their respective teams on cards numbered 1-84. Cards numbered 85-89 honor women basketball players in the "Best of Both Worlds" subset. Cards numbered 90-98 feature the 1995 NBL Awards and the Finals Champions. The fronts feature full bleed borderless color action player photos. The backs carry player biographical and career information and statistics.

COMPLETE SET (100)	10.00	25.00
1 Mark Davis	.40	1.00
2 Brett Maher	.10	.30
3 Chris Blakemore	.10	.30
4 Scott Ninnis	.10	.30
5 Robert Rose	.30	.75
6 Mike McKay	.10	.30
7 Leroy Loggins	.50	1.25
8 Mike Mitchell	.20	.50
9 Robert Sibley	.15	.40
10 Andrew Goodwin	.10	.30
11 Shane Heal	.30	.75
12 John Rillie	.10	.30
13 Ray Borner	.10	.30
14 Jamie Pearlman	.10	.30
15 David Close	.10	.30
16 Simon Dwight	.10	.30
17 Lachlan Armfield	.10	.30
18 Jervaughn Scales	.20	.50
19 Andrew Svaldenis	.10	.30
20 Cecil Exum	.30	.75
21 Joey Wright	.10	.30
22 Simon Kerle	.10	.30
23 Greg Smith	.10	.30
24 Justin Cass	.10	.30
25 Trevor Torrance	.10	.30
26 John Szigeti	.10	.30
27 Peter Harvey	.10	.30
28 Doug Peacock	.10	.30
29 Tony De Ambrosis	.10	.30
30 Steve Woodberry	.60	1.50
31 Darren Smith	.10	.30
32 Mark Nash	.10	.30
33 Darren Perry	.10	.30
34 David Stiff	.10	.30
35 Andre Moore	.30	.75
36 Jerome Scott	.10	.30
37 Chuck Harmison	.40	1.00
38 Terry Johnson	.10	.30
39 Dene MacDonald	.10	.30
40 Melvin Thomas	.20	.50
41 Andre LaFleur	.10	.30
42 Marc Brandon	.10	.30
43 Andrew Gaze	.75	2.00
44 Mark Bradtke	.30	.75
45 Lanard Copeland	.40	1.00
46 Blair Smith	.10	.30
47 Dave Simmons	.10	.30
48 Stephen Whitehead	.10	.30
49 Butch Hays	.30	.75
50 Michael Johnson	.10	.30
51 Tonny Jensen	.10	.30
52 Grant Kruger	.10	.30
53 Martin McClean	.10	.30
54 Matthew Alexander	.10	.30
55 Darryl McDonald	.10	.30
56 Paul Rees	.10	.30
57 Larry Sengstock	.10	.30
58 Paul Maley	.10	.30
59 Pat Reidy	.10	.30
60 Rod Johnson	.10	.30
61 Andrew Vlahov	.30	.75
62 Aaron Trahair	.10	.30
63 Anthony Stewart	.10	.30
64 Ricky Grace	.40	1.00
65 Scott Fisher	.50	1.25
66 James Crawford	.30	.75
67 John Dorge	.10	.30
68 Darren Lucas	.10	.30
69 Tony Ronaldson	.10	.30
70 Chris Anstey	1.25	3.00
71 Andrew Parkinson	.10	.30
72 Sam MacKinnon	.10	.30
73 Bruce Bolden	.30	.75
74 Leon Trimmingham	.30	.75
75 Justin Withers	.10	.30
76 Brad Williams	.10	.30
77 Greg Hubbard	.10	.30
78 Mark Dalton	.10	.30
79 Derek Rucker	.10	.30
80 Clarence Tyson	.15	.40
81 Shane Froling	.10	.30
82 Cameron Dickinson	.10	.30
83 David Blades	.10	.30
84 Jason Cameron	.10	.30
85 Michele Timms	.60	1.50
86 Allison Cook	.10	.30
87 Trish Fallon	.10	.30
88 Sandy Brondello	.10	.30
89 Shelley Gorman	.10	.30
90 Andrew Gaze MVP	.40	1.00
91 John Rillie ROY	.20	.50
92 Darren Lucas	.10	.30
93 Reggie Smith	.20	.50
94 Tonny Jensen	.10	.30
95 Darryl McDonald	.10	.30
96 Andrew Gaze	.40	1.00
97 Alan Black	.10	.30
Tom Wisman CO		
98 Championship Team	.10	.30
Perth Wildcats		
99 Checklist 1	.10	.30
100 Checklist 2	.10	.30

1996 Australian Futera NBL All-Stars

Randomly inserted in packs at a rate of one in 20, this 10-card set features the five starting players from the North vs South All-Star game. The fronts display a color player action cut-out on a metallic background that changes when the card is tilted slightly. The backs carry a small color player action photo with information about the player's performance in the All-Star game. Only 1,500 of each card was made and it's individual number is printed on the back.

COMPLETE SET (10)	25.00	60.00
ASN1 Shane Heal	6.00	15.00
ASN2 Derek Rucker	2.00	5.00
ASN3 Leroy Loggins	6.00	15.00
ASN4 Leon Trimmingham	2.00	5.00
ASN5 Clarence Tyson	2.00	5.00
ASS1 Andrew Gaze	10.00	25.00
ASS2 Darryl McDonald	2.00	5.00
ASS3 Mark Davis	2.00	5.00
ASS4 Andrew Vlahov	2.00	5.00
ASS5 John Dorge	2.00	5.00

1996 Australian Futera NBL Futera Dream Team

Randomly inserted in packs at a rate of one in 24, this 5-card set features five composite teams. Each team member contributed to his team's overall score by either points, rebounds, assists, steals or blocks. At the end of the season, the team's final score was calculated by using each player's '96 season average in his nominated category. The card with the winning team could be redeemed by mail for an uncut Series 1 sheet and was automatically entered into a drawing for a trip to the NBL Grand Final. The fronts display color action photos of each of the five members of the team indicated on the card with their names and categories below. The backs carry the instructions on how to arrive at the team's final score. The cards are listed below according to the team number on each card.

COMPLETE SET (5)	8.00	20.00
1 Andrew Gaze	5.00	12.00
Ray Borner		
Peter Harvey		
Brett Maher		
Paul Rees		
2 Derek Rucker	1.50	4.00
Andrew Vlahov		
Butch Hays		
Mike Mitchell		
Blair Smith		
3 Leon Trimmingham	1.50	4.00
David Simmons		
Andre LaFleur		
Leroy Loggins		
Simon Dwight		
4 Melvin Thomas	1.50	4.00
Bruce Bolden		
Ricky Grace		
Jamie Pearlman		
Clarence Tyson		
5 Lanard Copeland	2.50	6.00
Mark Davis		
Darryl McDonald		
Sam MacKinnon		
John Dorge		

1996 Australian Futera NBL Future Forces

Randomly inserted in packs at a rate of one in 12, this 10-card set features the five starting players from the Bucks vs Colts Coca-Cola Future Forces game. The fronts feature a color action player cut-out on a metallic blue, aqua, and silver-colored basketball background. The backs carry a color action player photo with information about the player's performance during the game. Only 2,500 of each card were printed and are individually numbered on the back.

COMPLETE SET (10)	15.00	40.00
FFB1 Chris Blakemore	2.00	5.00
FFB2 David Stiff	2.00	5.00
FFB3 John Rillie	2.00	5.00
FFB4 Jason Smith	2.00	5.00
FFB5 Rupert Sapwell	2.00	5.00
FFC1 Brett Maher	2.00	5.00
FFC2 Chris Anstey	8.00	20.00
FFC3 Terry Johnson	2.00	5.00
FFC4 Brad Williams	2.00	5.00
FFC5 Martin Catallini	2.00	5.00

1996 Australian Futera NBL Outer Limits

Randomly inserted in packs at a rate of one in 7, this 8-card set features the best three-point shooters in the league. The fronts display a color action player cut-out on a purple background which sparkles when tilted slightly. The backs carry information about the player over a faded player photo. Only 6,000 of each card was produced and are individually numbered on the back.

COMPLETE SET (8)	8.00	20.00
OL1 Shane Heal	1.50	4.00
OL2 Andrew Gaze	3.00	8.00
OL3 Aaron Trahair	1.25	3.00
OL4 Simon Kerle	1.25	3.00
OL5 Chris Jent	1.50	4.00
OL6 Derek Rucker	1.25	3.00
OL7 Terry Johnson	1.25	3.00
OL8 Andrew Parkinson	1.25	3.00

1996 Australian Futera NBL Ten Thousand Point Card

This one-card set commemorates the great achievement of Andrew Gaze and Leroy Loggins for reaching the milestone of scoring 10,000 points. Only 1,000 of the cards were produced, plus the first 150 redemption cards feature a gold seal entitling the holder to a rare dual-autograph version. The cards were randomly inserted at the rate of one in 300 packs with the rate of insertion for the dual-autograph redemption cards being one in 2,000 packs.

TTP2 Andrew Gaze	30.00	80.00
Leroy Loggins		

1993-94 Avia Clyde Drexler

This six-card set was cosponsored by Avia and G.I.Joe's (The Sports and Auto Store). Inside white borders, the fronts display color action photos, with "Drexler" gold-foil stamped across the top. All team logos have been airbrushed off the photos. In black print on white background, the backs summarize milestones in Drexler's career. Biographical information on each card rounds out the back. The cards are numbered "X of 6." Between February 26 and March 5, 1994, the redemption card could be exchanged for three Drexler cards.

COMPLETE SET (6)	3.00	8.00
COMMON CARD	1.00	2.50
NNO Redemption Card	.40	1.00

1993 Charles Barkley Collector's Edition

This unsightly 14-card set showcases NBA power forward Charles Barkley at various stages of his career. The set was printed by BD Production and Marketing Co. and was licensed by Barkley but not by the NBA as all league logos are removed. The cards full-color measure the standard size and was intended to be updated each year. We have yet to see any cards issued after 1993.

COMPLETE SET (14)	2.00	5.00
COMMON CARD (1-14)	.20	.50

1994-95 Basketball USA

These cards were issued in the now defunct German Magazine entitled "Basketball USA". The cards are very similar in size and thickness as 5 Majuer however these cards seem to be a bit harder to locate. The cards have the same layout as 5 Majuer as well, but with purple borders on the front, and the backs are written in German. A few of the cards were issued with white borders and purple stars on the front. All cards have the Basketball USA logo on the bottom of the backs. Eight cards were issued in each bi-monthly magazine with four to a page perforated on the edge. The checklist below is believed to cover only half of the cards in existence. The cards listed are from issues #8 (July 1994) through #15 (September 1995). We hope to be able to provide a more complete listing in future price guides. The cards are unnumbered and listed below in alphabetical order.

COMPLETE SET (64)	150.00	300.00
1 Mahmoud Abdul-Rauf	1.50	4.00
2 Danny Ainge	2.50	6.00
3 Kenny Anderson	2.00	5.00
4 Nick Anderson	1.50	4.00
5 B.J. Armstrong	1.50	4.00
6 Stacey Augmon	2.00	5.00
7 Charles Barkley	6.00	15.00
8 Dana Barros	1.50	4.00
9 Muggsy Bogues	2.00	5.00
10 Cedric Ceballos	1.50	4.00
11 Derrick Coleman	2.00	5.00
12 Vlade Divac	2.50	6.00
13 Clyde Drexler	5.00	12.00
14 Joe Dumars	2.50	6.00
15 Sean Elliott	2.50	6.00
16 Patrick Ewing	5.00	12.00
17 Kendall Gill	1.50	4.00
18 Horace Grant	2.00	5.00
19 Anfernee Hardaway	4.00	10.00
20 Tim Hardaway	2.50	6.00
21 Carl Herrera	1.50	4.00
22 Jeff Hornacek	2.00	5.00
23 Robert Horry	2.50	6.00
24 Kevin Johnson	2.50	6.00
25 Larry Johnson	2.50	6.00
26 Michael Jordan	20.00	50.00
27 Shawn Kemp	2.50	6.00
28 Toni Kukoc	3.00	8.00
29 Christian Laettner	2.00	5.00
30 Dan Majerle	2.50	6.00
31 Karl Malone	5.00	12.00
32 Anthony Mason	1.50	4.00
33 Vernon Maxwell	1.50	4.00
34 Derrick McKey	1.50	4.00
35 Nate McMillan	1.50	4.00
36 Reggie Miller	5.00	12.00
37 Alonzo Mourning	5.00	12.00
38 Tracy Murray	1.50	4.00
39 Dikembe Mutombo	2.50	6.00
40 Charles Oakley	2.00	5.00
41 Hakeem Olajuwon	5.00	12.00
42 Shaquille O'Neal	6.00	15.00
43 Shaquille O'Neal	6.00	15.00
44 Billy Owens	1.50	4.00
45 Gary Payton	2.50	6.00
46 Sam Perkins	1.50	4.00
47 Ricky Pierce	1.50	4.00
48 Scottie Pippen	6.00	15.00
49 Mark Price	2.50	6.00
50 Glen Rice	2.50	6.00
51 Mitch Richmond	2.50	6.00
52 David Robinson	5.00	12.00
53 Dennis Rodman	5.00	12.00
54 Detlef Schrempf Dribbling	2.50	6.00
55 Detlef Schrempf Passing	2.50	6.00
56 Charles Smith	1.50	4.00
57 Rik Smits	2.00	5.00
58 Latrell Sprewell	3.00	8.00
59 John Starks	2.00	5.00
60 John Stockton	6.00	15.00
61 Rod Strickland	1.50	4.00
62 Otis Thorpe	1.50	4.00
63 Dominique Wilkins	4.00	10.00
64 Kevin Willis	1.50	4.00

1984-85 Bay State Bombardiers

This oversized blank-backed card was released during the 1984-85 CBA season. The card features many of the Bay State Bombardiers players and coaches. This black and white card measures 8 3/4" x11".

1 John Ligums	4.00	10.00
Dave Cowens		
Eddie Chavez		
Joe Dawson		
Pete DeBisschop		
Mark Halsel		
Kirk Richards		
Kevin Springman		
Kevin Williams		
Leon Wilson		

2003-04 Bazooka

Released in January 2004, Bazooka features 288 cards where numbers 1-220 are base veterans, some of which have two uniform versions. Card numbers 221-275 feature rookies, some of which have two uniform versions, and are inserted at the rate of one in three. Cards 276-288 feature rookie players along with Bazooka Joe and are inserted at one in six. Bazooka was packaged in 24-pack boxes where packs contained six cards, one mini parallel card, one regular parallel card (eight total) and one stick of gum. Packs carried a suggested retail price of $2.

COMP.SET w/o RC's (220)	15.00	30.00
221-275 RC STATED ODDS: 1:3		
276-288 BAZ. JOE STATED ODDS 1:6		
SOME CARDS HAVE HOME AND AWAY VERSION		
B (AWAY) VERSION SAME VALUE AS A (HOME)		
1A Tracy McGrady Home	.30	.75
1B Tracy McGrady Away	.30	.75
2 DaJuan Wagner	.15	.40
3A Allen Iverson Home	.40	1.00
3B Allen Iverson Away	.40	1.00
4 Stromile Swift	.15	.40
5 Jalen Rose	.20	.50
6 Morris Peterson	.15	.40
7 Lamar Odom	.20	.50
8 Kobe Bryant	1.00	2.50
9 Chauncey Billups	.25	.60
10 Jason Kidd	.40	1.00
11 Yao Ming	.50	1.25
12 Stephon Marbury	.20	.50
13 Ricky Davis	.20	.50
14 Andrei Kirilenko	.25	.60
15 Courtney Alexander	.15	.40
16 Brad Miller	.20	.50
17 Bobby Jackson	.15	.40
18 Rashard Lewis	.25	.60
19 Juwan Howard	.20	.50
20 Allan Houston	.20	.50
21 Kevin Garnett	.40	1.00
22 Jason Terry	.20	.50
23A Jason Richardson Home	.25	.60
23B Jason Richardson Away	.25	.60
24 Jerry Stackhouse	.20	.50
25 Tyson Chandler	.20	.50
26 Drew Gooden	.20	.50
27 Jason Williams	.20	.50
28 Eddie Jones	.20	.50
29 Quentin Richardson	.20	.50
30 Rasheed Wallace	.25	.60
31A Shawn Marion Home	.20	.50
31B Shawn Marion Away	.20	.50
32 Malik Rose	.15	.40
33 Ben Wallace	.20	.50
34 Paul Pierce	.25	.60
35 Matt Harpring	.15	.40
36 Eddie Griffin	.15	.40
37 Toni Kukoc	.25	.60
38 Mike Bibby	.25	.60
39 Kwame Brown	.15	.40
40 Kurt Thomas	.15	.40
41 Dirk Nowitzki	.40	1.00
42 Theo Ratliff	.15	.40
43 Ray Allen	.25	.60
44 Michael Finley	.25	.60
45 Lucious Harris	.15	.40
46 Anfernee Hardaway	.40	1.00
47 Christian Laettner	.20	.50
48 Manu Ginobili	.30	.75
49 Tayshaun Prince	.20	.50
50 Shaquille O'Neal	.60	1.50
51 Vladimir Radmanovic	.15	.40
52 Calbert Cheaney	.15	.40
53 Eric Snow	.15	.40
54A Pau Gasol Home	.25	.60
54B Pau Gasol Away	.25	.60
55 Dikembe Mutombo	.25	.60
56 Alvin Williams	.15	.40
57 Corliss Williamson	.15	.40
58 Kedrick Brown	.15	.40
59 Jamaal Tinsley	.15	.40
60 Chris Webber	.25	.60
61 Donyell Marshall	.15	.40
62 Darrell Armstrong	.15	.40
63 Kenny Thomas	.15	.40
64 Mehmet Okur	.20	.50
65 Carlos Boozer	.20	.50
66A Kenyon Martin Home	.20	.50
66B Kenyon Martin Away	.20	.50
67 Speedy Claxton	.15	.40
68 Brent Barry	.15	.40
69 Ron Artest	.25	.60
70 Elton Brand	.25	.60
71 Troy Hudson	.15	.40
72A Steve Nash Home	.30	.75
72B Steve Nash Away	.30	.75
73 Tony Parker	.25	.60
74 Earl Boykins	.15	.40
75 Kerry Kittles	.15	.40
76 Shawn Bradley	.15	.40
77 Tony Delk	.15	.40
78 Zydrunas Ilgauskas	.20	.50
79 Doug Christie	.15	.40
80 Amare Stoudemire	.30	.75
81 Rick Fox	.15	.40
82 Brian Skinner	.15	.40
83 Jamal Mashburn	.20	.50
84 Qyntel Woods	.15	.40
85 Rafer Alston	.15	.40
86 Derek Anderson	.15	.40
87 Andre Miller	.20	.50
88 Antoine Walker	.25	.60
89 Frank Williams	.15	.40
90A Vince Carter Home	.40	1.00
90B Vince Carter Away	.40	1.00
91 Donnell Harvey	.15	.40
92 Raef Lafrentz	.15	.40
93 Desmond Mason	.20	.50
94 Rodney Rogers	.15	.40
95 Juan DixonA•	.15	.40
96 Kareem Rush	.15	.40
97 Bryon Russell	.15	.40
98 Shandon Anderson	.15	.40
99 Gordan Giricek	.15	.40
100 Tim Duncan	.40	1.00
101 Zach Randolph	.20	.50
102 Malik Allen	.15	.40
103 Richard Hamilton	.20	.50
104 Maurice Taylor	.15	.40
105 Marko Jaric	.15	.40
106 Joe Smith	.20	.50
107 Peja Stojakovic	.25	.60
108 Othella Harrington	.15	.40
109 Anthony Carter	.15	.40
110 Wally Szczerbiak	.20	.50
111 Troy Murphy	.15	.40
112 Shareef Abdur-Rahim	.20	.50
113 Reggie Miller	.25	.60
114 Vin Baker	.15	.40
115 Brian Scalabrine	.15	.40
116 Eric Piatkowski	.15	.40
117 Cuttino Mobley	.15	.40
118 Erick Dampier	.15	.40
119 Walter Mccarty	.15	.40
120 Caron Butler	.20	.50
121 Keyon Dooling	.15	.40
122 Michael Redd	.25	.60
123 Kenny Anderson	.20	.50
124 P.J. Brown	.15	.40
125 Devean George	.15	.40
126 Joe Johnson	.20	.50
127 Adrian Griffin	.15	.40
128 Bonzi Wells	.15	.40
129 Rasual Butler	.15	.40
130 Baron Davis	.20	.50
131 Wesley Person	.15	.40
132 Shammond Williams	.15	.40
133 Tyronn Lue	.15	.40
134 Brian Grant	.15	.40
135 Elden Campbell	.15	.40
136 Glen Rice	.15	.40
137 Michael Olowokandi	.15	.40
138 Anthony Peeler	.15	.40
139 Steven Hunter	.15	.40
140 Eddy Curry	.15	.40
141 Jerome James	.15	.40
142 Travis Best	.15	.40
143 Nazr Mohammed	.15	.40
144 Tony Battie	.15	.40
145 Scot Pollard	.15	.40
146 Stanislav Medvedenko	.15	.40
147 Jim Jackson	.15	.40
148 Marcus Camby	.20	.50
149 Marcus Haislip	.15	.40
150 Glenn Robinson	.20	.50
151 Jerome Williams	.15	.40
152 Greg Ostertag	.15	.40
153 Stephen Jackson	.20	.50
154 David Wesley	.15	.40
155 Sam Cassell	.20	.50
156 Hedo Turkoglu	.20	.50
157 Al Harrington	.20	.50
158 John Salmons	.20	.50
159 Nikoloz Tskitishvili	.15	.40
160 Samaki Walker	.15	.40
161 Jake Tsakalidis	.15	.40
162 Tim Thomas	.15	.40
163 Ronald Murray	.15	.40
164 Alonzo Mourning	.30	.75
165 Chris Jefferies	.15	.40
166 Darius Miles	.15	.40
167 Kendall Gill	.15	.40
168 Lonny Baxter	.15	.40
169 Jonathan Bender	.15	.40
170 Antawn Jamison	.20	.50
171 Keon Clark	.15	.40
172 Chris Wilcox	.15	.40
173 Brendan Haywood	.15	.40
174 Predrag Drobnjak	.15	.40
175 Nene	.20	.50
176 Casey Jacobsen	.15	.40
177 Marcus Fizer	.15	.40
178 Howard Eisley	.15	.40
179 Damon Stoudamire	.20	.50
180 Gary Payton	.25	.60
181 Shane Battier	.20	.50
182 Desagana Diop	.15	.40
183 Antonio Davis	.15	.40
184 Keith Van Horn	.20	.50
185 Corey Maggette	.20	.50
186 Jarron Collins	.15	.40
187 James Posey	.15	.40
188 Latrell Sprewell	.20	.50
189 Aaron McKie	.15	.40
190 Vlade Divac	.20	.50
191 Pat Garrity	.15	.40
192 Eric Williams	.15	.40
193 Radoslav Nesterovic	.15	.40
194 Dan Gadzuric	.15	.40
195 Moochie Norris	.15	.40
196 Clifford Robinson	.15	.40
197 Richard Jefferson	.20	.50
198 Lorenzen Wright	.15	.40
199 Nick Van Exel	.20	.50
200 Gilbert Arenas	.20	.50
201 Robert Horry	.20	.50
202 Scottie Pippen	.40	1.00
203 Jon Barry	.15	.40
204 Derrick Coleman	.20	.50
205 Ron Mercer	.15	.40
206 DeShawn Stevenson	.15	.40
207 Ruben Patterson	.15	.40
208 Rodney White	.15	.40
209 Jamal Crawford	.25	.60
210 Jermaine O'Neal	.20	.50
211 Eduardo Najera	.15	.40
212 Dan Dickau	.15	.40
213 Antonio McDyess	.20	.50
214 J.R. Bremer	.15	.40
215 Dion Glover	.15	.40
216 Lamond Murray	.15	.40
217 Larry Hughes	.20	.50
218 Mike Miller	.20	.50
219 Mike Dunleavy	.20	.50
220 Karl Malone	.30	.75
221 David West RC	.60	1.50
222 Steve Blake RC	.50	1.25
223A LeBron James Home RC	6.00	15.00
223B LeBron James Away RC	6.00	15.00
224 Keith Bogans RC	.40	1.00
225 Josh Howard RC	.60	1.50
226A Chris Kaman Home RC	.60	1.50
226B Chris Kaman Away RC	.60	1.50
227A Marcus Banks Home RC	.40	1.00
227B Marcus Banks Away RC	.40	1.00
228A Chris Bosh Home RC	1.00	2.50
228B Chris Bosh Away RC	1.00	2.50
229 Troy Bell RC	.40	1.00
230 Luke Walton RC	.60	1.50
231 Francisco Elson RC	.40	1.00
232 Ndudi Ebi RC	.40	1.00
233 Maurice Williams RC	.60	1.50
234 Kendrick Perkins RC	.50	1.25
235 Dahntay Jones RC	.50	1.25
236 Jason Kapono RC	.40	1.00
237 Kyle Korver RC	.75	2.00
238 Josh Moore RC	.40	1.00
239 Travis Hansen RC	.40	1.00
240A Carmelo Anthony Blue RC	2.00	5.00
240B Carmelo Anthony White RC	2.00	5.00
241 Keith McLeod RC	.40	1.00
242 Zoran Planinic RC	.40	1.00
243A Jarvis Hayes Home RC	.40	1.00
243B Jarvis Hayes Away RC	.40	1.00
244A Mickael Pietrus Home RC	.50	1.25
244B Mickael Pietrus Away RC	.50	1.25
245A Mike Sweetney Home RC	.40	1.00
245B Mike Sweetney Away RC	.40	1.00
246 Jerome Beasley RC	.40	1.00
247 Zaza Pachulia RC	.60	1.50
248 Ben Handlogten RC	.40	1.00
249 Torraye Braggs RC	.40	1.00
250A Nick Collison White RC	.50	1.25
250B Nick Collison Green RC	.50	1.25
251 Reece Gaines RC	.40	1.00
252A Dwyane Wade Dribble RC	2.00	5.00
252B Dwyane Wade Layup RC	2.00	5.00
253 Devin Brown RC	.40	1.00
254 Leandro Barbosa RC	.60	1.50
255 Boris Diaw RC	.60	1.50
256 Aleksandar Pavlovic RC	.50	1.25
257 Udonis Haslem RC	.50	1.25
258 Brian Cook RC	.40	1.00
259 Maciej Lampe RC	.40	1.00
260A T.J. Ford Home RC	.50	1.25
260B T.J. Ford Away RC	.50	1.25
261 Matt Carroll RC	.40	1.00
262 James Jones RC	.40	1.00
263 Brandon Hunter RC	.40	1.00
264 Luke Ridnour RC	.50	1.25
265 Theron Smith RC	.40	1.00
266 Jon Stefansson RC	.40	1.00
267 Zarko Cabarkapa RC	.40	1.00
268 Marquis Daniels RC	.50	1.25
269 Willie Green RC	.40	1.00
270A Kirk Hinrich Left RC	.60	1.50
270B Kirk Hinrich Right RC	.60	1.50
271 Linton Johnson RC	.40	1.00
272 Travis Outlaw RC	.50	1.25
273 James Lang RC	.40	1.00
274 Slavko Vranes RC	.40	1.00
275A Darko Milicic Home RC	.50	1.25
275B Darko Milicic Away RC	.50	1.25
276 LeBron James BAZ	8.00	20.00
277 Darko Milicic BAZ	.40	1.00
278 Carmelo Anthony BAZ	1.50	4.00
279 Chris Bosh BAZ	.75	2.00
280 Dwyane Wade BAZ	1.50	4.00
281 Chris Kaman BAZ	.50	1.25
282 Kirk Hinrich BAZ	.50	1.25
283 T.J. Ford BAZ	.40	1.00
284 Mike Sweetney BAZ	.30	.75
285 Jarvis Hayes BAZ	.30	.75
286 Mickael Pietrus BAZ	.40	1.00
287 Nick Collison BAZ	.40	1.00
288 Marcus Banks BAZ	.30	.75

2003-04 Bazooka Parallel

*PARALLEL SINGLES: .5X TO 1.25X BASE HI
*PARALLEL RCs: .6X TO 1.5X BASE HI
*PARALLEL BAZ. JOE: .75X TO 2X BASE HI
STATED ODDS: 1:1

2003-04 Bazooka Mini

*MINI SINGLES: .6X TO 1.5X BASE HI
*MINI RCs: .5X TO 1.25X BASE HI
*MINI BAZ. JOE: .6X TO 1.5X BASE HI
STATED ODDS: 1:3

2003-04 Bazooka Beginnings

Randomly inserted in packs at the rate of one in 26, this 24-card set features the new rookies on a white background with a swatch of memorabilia in the shape of the letter "B."

STATED ODDS 1:26		
*PARALLEL: .75X TO 2X BASE HI		
PARALLEL PRINT RUN 25 SER.#'d SETS		
BC Brian Cook	1.50	4.00
CA Carmelo Anthony UER	8.00	20.00
CB Chris Bosh	4.00	10.00
CK Chris Kaman	2.50	6.00
DJ Dahntay Jones	2.00	5.00
DW Dwyane Wade	8.00	20.00
DWE David West	2.50	6.00
JH Jarvis Hayes	1.50	4.00
JHO Josh Howard	2.50	6.00
JK Jason Kapono	1.50	4.00
KH Kirk Hinrich	2.50	6.00
KP Kendrick Perkins	2.00	5.00
LB Leandro Barbosa	2.50	6.00
LR Luke Ridnour	2.00	5.00
LW Luke Walton	2.50	6.00
MB Marcus Banks	1.50	4.00
MP Mickael Pietrus	2.00	5.00
MS Mike Sweetney	1.50	4.00
NC Nick Collison	2.00	5.00
NE Ndudi Ebi	1.50	4.00
RG Reece Gaines	1.50	4.00
TB Troy Bell	1.50	4.00
TF T.J. Ford	2.00	5.00
TO Travis Outlaw	2.00	5.00

2003-04 Bazooka Blasts

Randomly inserted in packs at the following rates, Group A one in 850, Group B one in 143, Group C one in 72, and Group D one in 15, this 59-card set is horizontally designed and looks like a comic strip. The letters "oo" in the word Bazooka are replaced with a memorabilia swatch. A Parallel set was also produced with cards sequentially numbered to 25.

ODDS: GROUP A 1:850, GROUP B 1:143		
*PARALLEL: 1X TO 2.5X BASE HI		
PARALLEL PRINT RUN 25 SER.#'d SETS		
SOME PARALLEL NOT PRICED DUE TO SCARCITY		
JK Jason Kidd D	4.00	10.00
AG Adrian Griffin D	2.00	5.00
AHO Allan Houston C	2.00	5.00
AJ Avery Johnson D	2.00	5.00
AW Antoine Walker D	2.50	6.00
BD Baron Davis C	2.00	5.00
CB Caron Butler D	2.00	5.00
CM Cuttino Mobley C	1.50	4.00
CW Chris Wilcox D	2.00	5.00
DF Derek Fisher B	2.00	5.00
DM Dikembe Mutombo D	2.50	6.00
DW DaJuan Wagner D	2.00	5.00
EN Eduardo Najera D	2.00	5.00
FW Frank Williams D	2.00	5.00
GA Gilbert Arenas B	2.00	5.00
GP Gary Payton B	2.50	6.00
GR Glenn Robinson C	2.00	5.00
HT Hedo Turkoglu D	2.00	5.00
JD Juan Dixon B	2.00	5.00
JJ Joe Johnson B	2.00	5.00
JM Jamal Mashburn D	2.00	5.00
JO Jermaine O'Neal C	2.00	5.00
JR Jason Richardson D	2.50	6.00
JT Jamaal Tinsley D	2.00	5.00
KG Kevin Garnett C	4.00	10.00
KM Karl Malone D	3.00	8.00
KMA Kenyon Martin C	2.00	5.00
KR Kareem Rush D	2.00	5.00
LS Latrell Sprewell D	2.00	5.00
MB Mike Bibby D	2.50	6.00
MF Marcus Fizer B	2.00	5.00
MH Marcus Haislip C	2.00	5.00
MJ Marko Jaric/112 A	2.00	5.00
MP Morris Peterson B	1.50	4.00
MR Michael Redd D	2.50	6.00
N Nene D	2.00	5.00
NT Nikoloz Tskitishvili D	2.00	5.00
PP Paul Pierce D	2.50	6.00
PS Peja Stojakovic B	2.50	6.00
QR Quentin Richardson C	2.00	5.00
QW Qyntel Woods D	2.00	5.00
RA Ray Allen B	2.50	6.00
RJ Richard Jefferson D	2.00	5.00
RW Rasheed Wallace D	2.50	6.00
SAR Shareef Abdur-Rahim B	2.00	5.00
SF Steve Francis C	2.00	5.00
SM Stephon Marbury D	2.00	5.00
SMA Shawn Marion C	2.00	5.00
SN Steve Nash C	3.00	8.00
SO Shaquille O'Neal C	6.00	15.00
TAP Tayshaun Prince/182 A	2.00	5.00
TAW Tariq Abdul-Wahad D	2.00	5.00
TP Tony Parker D	2.50	6.00
VD Vlade Divac C	2.00	5.00
VR Vladimir Radmanovic C	2.00	5.00
WS Wally Szczerbiak B	2.00	5.00
YM Yao Ming D	5.00	12.00
ZI Zydrunas Ilgauskas D	2.00	5.00
ZR Zeljko Rebraca D	2.00	5.00

2003-04 Bazooka Boo-Yah

Randomly inserted at the following rates, Group A one in 850, Group B one in 143, Group C one in 72 and Group D one in 15, this 50-card set places a full-color player action photo on the left and the words BOO-YAH, where the letter "A" has been replaced with a swatch of jersey, along the right from top to bottom. A Parallel set was also produced and these cards are sequentially numbered to 25.

ODDS: GROUP A 1:850, GROUP B 1:143		
*PARALLEL: 1X TO 2.5X BASE HI		
PARALLEL PRINT RUN 25 SER.#'d SETS		
SOME PARALLEL NOT PRICED DUE TO SCARCITY		
AI Allen Iverson/156 A		
AK Andrei Kirilenko/97 A		
AM Alonzo Mourning D	3.00	8.00
AS Amare Stoudemire D	3.00	8.00
AW Antoine Walker C	2.50	6.00
BD Baron Davis B	2.00	5.00
BW Ben Wallace B	2.00	5.00
CB Caron Butler C	2.00	5.00
CW Chris Webber B	2.50	6.00
DAM Darius Miles D	2.00	5.00
DG Devean George C	2.00	5.00
DM Dikembe Mutombo B	2.50	6.00
DN Dirk Nowitzki D	4.00	10.00
DW DaJuan Wagner B	2.00	5.00
EC Elden Campbell D	2.00	5.00
EG Eddie Griffin D	2.00	5.00
GA Gilbert Arenas D	2.00	5.00
JO Jermaine O'Neal B	2.00	5.00
JR Jason Richardson C	2.50	6.00
JS Jerry Stackhouse D	2.00	5.00
JT Jason Terry B	2.00	5.00
JW Jerome Williams D	2.00	5.00
KG Kevin Garnett C	4.00	10.00
KM Karl Malone B	3.00	8.00
KMA Kenyon Martin C	2.00	5.00
LO Lamar Odom B	2.00	5.00
LS Latrell Sprewell C	2.00	5.00
MF Michael Finley D	2.50	6.00
MFZ Marcus Fizer C	2.00	5.00
MO Michael Olowokandi D	2.00	5.00
N Nene D	2.00	5.00
NVE Nick Van Exel B	2.00	5.00
PG Pau Gasol D	2.50	6.00
PP Paul Pierce C	2.50	6.00
QR Quentin Richardson B	2.00	5.00
RA Ray Allen B	2.50	6.00
RJ Richard Jefferson C	2.00	5.00
RL Rashard Lewis C	2.50	6.00
RLA Raef Lafrentz A	2.00	5.00
RW Rasheed Wallace D	2.50	6.00
SB Shawn Bradley B	2.00	5.00
SF Steve Francis C	2.00	5.00
SM Shawn Marion C	2.00	5.00
SMA Stephon Marbury C	2.00	5.00
SN Steve Nash B	3.00	8.00
SO Shaquille O'Neal B	6.00	15.00
TC Tyson Chandler/164 A	2.00	5.00
TD Tim Duncan D	4.00	10.00
TMG Tracy McGrady B	3.00	8.00
YM Yao Ming D	5.00	12.00

2003-04 Bazooka Comics

Inserted at the rate of one in three, this set features 24 mini comics of NBA players.

COMPLETE SET (24)	8.00	20.00
STATED ODDS: 1:3		
1 Tracy McGrady	.30	.75
2 Paul Pierce	.25	.60
3 Allen Iverson	.40	1.00
4 Amare Stoudemire	.30	.75
5 Jason Kidd	.40	1.00
6 Allan Houston	.20	.50
7 Shaquille O'Neal	.60	1.50
8 Kobe Bryant	1.00	2.50
9 Yao Ming	.50	1.25
10 Tim Duncan	.40	1.00
11 Ben Wallace	.20	.50
12 Karl Malone	.30	.75
13 Kevin Garnett	.40	1.00
14 Jason Richardson	.25	.60
15 LeBron James	5.00	12.00
16 Darko Milicic	.20	.50
17 Carmelo Anthony	.75	2.00
18 T.J. Ford	.20	.50
19 Kirk Hinrich	.25	.60
20 Nick Collison	.20	.50
21 Chris Bosh	.40	1.00
22 Mike Sweetney	.15	.40
23 Reece Gaines	.15	.40
24 Luke Walton	.25	.60

2003-04 Bazooka Four on One Stickers

Inserted at the rate of one in four, this 55-card set places four player stickers on each front. The stickers themselves are done in the same design as the base Bazooka set.

COMPLETE SET (55)	15.00	40.00
STATED ODDS 1:4		
1 Duncan/Yao/Shaq/KG	1.25	3.00

2 T-Mac/Kobe/Vince/Al 1.50 4.00
3 Pierce/Dirk/C-Web/Mash .50 1.25
4 Kidd/J-Will/Marb/Payton .50 1.25
5 Tinsley/Terry/Nash/Andre .50 1.25
6 B.Wall/J.O'Ne/Grant/Murphy .50 1.25
7 Butler/Amare/Wagnr/Goodn .50 1.25
8 Giricek/Nene/Boozer/J.R. .50 1.25
9 J-Rich/Marian/Mason/Jeffer .50 1.25
10 Houston/Allen/Hudson/Reg .50 1.25
11 Redd/Person/Wesley/Wally .50 1.25
12 Artest/Martin/Christie/Pipp .50 1.25
13 Malone/Juwan/Rash/Brand .50 1.25
14 Parker/Baron/Cassel/Vexel .50 1.25
15 Horn/Bradley/Harpr/Laettnr .50 1.25
16 Gasol/Jaric/Peja/Kirilenko .50 1.25
17 Billi/B.Jack/Rogers/Thomas .50 1.25
18 Theo/Bradley/Ilgas/Griffin .50 1.25
19 M.Mill/Dunl/E.Jones/Finley .50 1.25
20 Swift/Rose/Mo/Odom .50 1.25
21 R.Davis/C.Alex/Lewis/Stack .50 1.25
22 Tyson/Kwme/Woods/Rasho .50 1.25
23 QRich/Rose/Kukoc/Bibby .50 1.25
24 Thomas/Harris/Anf/Gino .50 1.25
25 Prince/Rad/Cheaney/Snow .50 1.25
26 Mutom/A.Will/C.Will/Perkins .50 1.25
27 BArmstr/Speed/Barry/D.Stod .50 1.25
28 Alston/F.Willims/Dixon/Delk .50 1.25
29 Donyell/Ke.Thom/Raef/Fox .50 1.25
30 AWalk/Hamilt/Bonzi/G.Rob .50 1.25
31 Alonzo/Hayw/Divac/Olowo .50 1.25
32 Rush/Randl/George/Curry .50 1.25
33 Rice/Peeler/Horry/Spree .50 1.25
34 Coles/Gadzur/Keon/Wilcox .50 1.25
35 C.Jacob/Sketa/Battier/McDy .50 1.25
36 Arenas/Magg/Miles/Crawfrd .50 1.25
37 Najera/Hedo/Nazr/Tsakilid .50 1.25
38 J.Smith/P.Brwn/Rahim/Jwill .50 1.25
39 Jamison/Fizer/Taylor/Hunter .50 1.25
40 J.John/Diop/Pollard/Salmon .50 1.25
41 Noris/R.Pat/L.Hugh/Keyon .50 1.25
42 Mercer/Eric/Derek/Cutt .50 1.25
43 Boyk/Lue/Eis/Best .50 1.25
44 Battie/James/C.Rob/Damp .50 1.25
45 Piatk/McCar/Garr/Harr .50 1.25
46 Haislip/Gill/Murray/Wright .50 1.25
47 DeShawn/Kitt/Posey/McKie .50 1.25
48 Scalb/K.And/Oster/Shandon .50 1.25
49 A.Dav/J.Coll/A.Griff/J.Jones .50 1.25
50 LeBron/Darko/Melo/Bosh 4.00 10.00
51 Wade/Kaman/Hinr/Ford 1.25 3.00
52 Sweet/Hayes/Pietrus/Collisn .50 1.25
53 Banks/Ridnour/Gaines/Bell .50 1.25
54 West/D.Jones/Outlaw/Cook .50 1.25
55 Ebi/Perkins/Barb/Josh .50 1.25

2003-04 Bazooka Piece of Americana

Inserted in packs at the following rate: Group A one in 850, Group B one in 143, Group C one in 72 and Group D one in 15, this 27-card set features a horizontal design with black borders along the top and bottom, a copper background, color player photos on the left and a swatch of memorabilia on the right. A Parallel of this set was also inserted and those cards are sequentially numbered to 25.

ODDS: GROUP A 1:850, GROUP B 1:143
*PARALLEL: 1X TO 2.5X BASE HI
PARALLEL PRINT RUN 25 SER.#'d SETS
SOME PARALLEL NOT PRICED DUE TO SCARCITY
AD Antonio Davis B 2.00 5.00
AH Allan Houston B 2.00 5.00
AM Alonzo Mourning C 3.00 8.00
AS Amare Stoudemire C 3.00 8.00
BH Brendan Haywood D 2.00 5.00
BM Brad Miller D 2.00 5.00
BW Ben Wallace C 2.00 5.00
CB Carlos Boozer D 2.00 5.00
DA Darrell Armstrong C 2.00 5.00
DD Dan Dickau/150 A 2.00 5.00
DM Darius Miles C 2.00 5.00
DW David Wesley D 2.00 5.00
ES Eric Snow B 2.00 5.00
GH Grant Hill D 3.00 8.00
JJ Jared Jeffries B 2.00 5.00
JT Jamaal Tinsley B 2.00 5.00
LO Lamar Odom/150 A 2.00 5.00
MD Mike Dunleavy D 2.00 5.00
MP Morris Peterson/150 A 1.50 4.00
PG Pat Garrity D 2.00 5.00
SB Shane Battier/44 A 2.00 5.00
SC Sam Cassell B 2.00 5.00
SO Shaquille O'Neal D 6.00 15.00
SS Steve Smith D 2.00 5.00
TD Tim Duncan D 4.00 10.00
TM Troy Murphy B 1.50 4.00
WP Wesley Person D 2.00 5.00

2003-04 Bazooka Signs

Inserted at the following rates: Group A one in 5840, Group B one in 4328 and Group C at one in 2000, this four card set features a full-color player photo that fades to white towards the bottom for authentic player autographs.

ODDS: GROUP A 1:5840; B 1:4328, C 1:2000
CA Carmelo Anthony/100 A 50.00 120.00
FW Frank Williams B 5.00 12.00
KH Kirk Hinrich/100 A 20.00 50.00
SO Shaquille O'Neal C 30.00 80.00

2003-04 Bazooka Stand Ups

One pop-up card was perforated on each box of Bazooka. Each has a full-color player photo and a two-tone colored background.

COMPLETE SET (4) 1.25 3.00
ONE PERFORATED CARD PER HOBBY BOX
PRICES GIVEN FOR SEPARATED CARDS
NNO Carmelo Anthony 1.00 2.50
NNO T.J. Ford .25 .60
NNO Kirk Hinrich .30 .75
NNO Nick Collison .25 .60

2003-04 Bazooka Tattoos

Randomly inserted in packs at the rate of one in three, this 34-card set features temporary tattoos of team logos, the NBA logo, the Bazooka Logo and the Eastern and Western Conference logos.

COMPLETE SET (34) 5.00 12.00
STATED ODDS 1:3
1 Bazooka Logo .30 .75
2 Eastern Conference .30 .75
3 Western Conference .30 .75
4 NBA .30 .75
5 Atlanta Hawks .30 .75
6 Boston Celtics .30 .75
7 Charlotte Bobcats .30 .75
8 Chicago Bulls .30 .75
9 Cleveland Cavaliers .30 .75
10 Dallas Mavericks .30 .75
11 Denver Nuggets .30 .75
12 Detroit Pistons .30 .75
13 Golden State Warriors .30 .75
14 Houston Rockets .30 .75
15 Indiana Pacers .30 .75
16 Los Angeles Clippers .30 .75
17 Los Angeles Lakers .30 .75
18 Memphis Grizzlies .30 .75
19 Miami Heat .30 .75
20 Milwaukee Bucks .30 .75
21 Minnesota Timberwolves .30 .75
22 New Jersey Nets .30 .75
23 New Orleans Hornets .30 .75
24 New York Knicks .30 .75
25 Orlando Magic .30 .75
26 Philadelphia 76ers .30 .75
27 Phoenix Suns .30 .75
28 Portland Trailblazers .30 .75
29 Sacramento Kings .30 .75
30 San Antonio Spurs .30 .75
31 Seattle Supersonics .30 .75
32 Toronto Raptors .30 .75
33 Utah Jazz .30 .75
34 Washington Wizards .30 .75

2004-05 Bazooka

This 220-card set was released in January, 2005. The set was issued in eight-card packs with an $2 SRP and came 24 packs to a box. The first 165 cards feature active veterans while cards 166-220 feature Rookie Cards.

COMP.SET w/o RC's (165) 10.00 25.00
2 Marquis Daniels .15 .40
1 Shaquille O'Neal .60 1.50
3 Ben Wallace .20 .50
4 Jarvis Hayes .15 .40
5 Gerald Wallace .20 .50
6 Fred Jones .15 .40
7 Pau Gasol .25 .60
8 Latrell Sprewell .20 .50
9 Steve Francis .20 .50
10 Mike Bibby .25 .60
11 Chris Bosh .25 .60
12 Steve Nash .30 .75
13 Kirk Hinrich .20 .50
14 Richard Jefferson .20 .50
15 Zach Randolph .20 .50
16 Willie Green .15 .40
17 Al Harrington .20 .50
18 Rashard Lewis .25 .60
19 Ricky Davis .20 .50
20 Dwyane Wade .40 1.00
21 Tim Duncan .40 1.00
22 Eddy Curry .15 .40
23 Andre Miller .20 .50
24 Chris Wilcox .15 .40
25 Bobby Jackson .15 .40
26 Stephen Jackson .20 .50
27 Shane Battier .20 .50
28 Antawn Jamison .20 .50
29 Brent Barry .15 .40
30 Stephon Marbury .20 .50
31 Gordan Giricek .15 .40
32 Jamal Mashburn .20 .50
33 Allen Iverson .40 1.00
34 Paul Pierce .25 .60
35 Mike Dunleavy .20 .50
36 Gary Payton .25 .60
37 Brad Miller .20 .50
38 Eric Snow .15 .40
39 Theo Ratliff .15 .40
40 Richard Hamilton .20 .50
41 Dirk Nowitzki .40 1.00
42 Elton Brand .25 .60
43 Reggie Miller .25 .60
44 Baron Davis .20 .50
45 Jerome Williams .15 .40
46 Stromile Swift .15 .40
47 Andrei Kirilenko .20 .50
48 Jason Richardson .25 .60
49 Larry Hughes .20 .50
50 Yao Ming .50 1.25
51 Tim Thomas .15 .40
52 Erick Dampier .15 .40
53 Keith Van Horn .20 .50
54 Grant Hill .30 .75
55 Shareef Abdur-Rahim .20 .50
56 Amare Stoudemire .20 .50
57 David Wesley .15 .40
58 Chris Kaman .20 .50
59 Caron Butler .20 .50
60 Kenyon Martin .20 .50
61 Ray Allen .25 .60
62 Jerry Stackhouse .20 .50
63 Jason Kapono .15 .40
64 Mark Blount .15 .40
65 Hedo Turkoglu .20 .50
66 Carlos Boozer .20 .50
67 Kenny Thomas .15 .40
68 Manu Ginobili .30 .75
69 Kobe Bryant 1.00 2.50
70 Vince Carter .40 1.00
71 Troy Murphy .15 .40
72 Maurice Taylor .15 .40
73 Earl Boykins .15 .40
74 Boris Diaw .20 .50
75 Kerry Kittles .15 .40
76 Jamaal Tinsley .15 .40
77 Lamar Odom .20 .50
78 Jamaal Magloire .15 .40
79 Wally Szczerbiak .20 .50
80 Tayshaun Prince .20 .50
81 Mehmet Okur .20 .50
82 Eddie Jones .20 .50
83 Voshon Lenard .15 .40
84 Jamal Crawford .25 .60
85 Marko Jaric .15 .40
86 Ron Mercer .15 .40
87 Steve Smith .20 .50
88 Antoine Walker .25 .60
89 Kurt Thomas .15 .40
90 Primoz Brezec .15 .40
91 Luke Walton .15 .40
92 Dajuan Wagner .15 .40
93 Luke Ridnour .20 .50
94 Nene .20 .50
95 Josh Howard .25 .60
96 Juwan Howard .20 .50
97 David West .20 .50
98 Jonathan Bender .15 .40
99 Tony Parker .25 .60
100 LeBron James 1.50 4.00
101 Chris Webber .25 .60
102 Cuttino Mobley .15 .40
103 Rasheed Wallace .25 .60
104 Marcus Banks .15 .40
105 Ronald Murray .15 .40
106 Quentin Richardson .20 .50
107 Antonio McDyess .20 .50
108 Sam Cassell .20 .50
109 Allan Houston .20 .50
110 Leandro Barbosa .25 .60
111 Joe Smith .20 .50
112 Jason Kidd .40 1.00
113 Aleksandar Pavlovic .15 .40
114 Bruce Bowen .15 .40
115 Carmelo Anthony .50 1.25
116 Kwame Brown .15 .40
117 Mickael Pietrus .20 .50
118 Tony Battie .15 .40
119 Joe Johnson .20 .50
120 Damon Stoudamire .20 .50
121 Kevin Garnett .40 1.00
122 Michael Redd .20 .50
123 Doug Christie .15 .40
124 Darrell Armstrong .15 .40
125 James Posey .15 .40
126 Jim Jackson .15 .40
127 Udonis Haslem .15 .40
128 Drew Gooden .15 .40
129 Rasho Nesterovic .15 .40
130 Jermaine O'Neal .20 .50
131 Shawn Marion .20 .50
132 Samuel Dalembert .15 .40
133 Marcus Camby .20 .50
134 Devean George .15 .40
135 Darius Miles .15 .40
136 Michael Olowokandi .15 .40
137 Mike Miller .20 .50
138 Kareem Rush .15 .40
139 Jalen Rose .20 .50
140 Chauncey Billups .25 .60
141 Jason Williams .20 .50
142 Derek Fisher .20 .50
143 Donyell Marshall .15 .40
144 Alonzo Mourning .30 .75
145 T.J. Ford .15 .40
146 Tony Delk .15 .40
147 Gilbert Arenas .20 .50
148 Glenn Robinson .20 .50
149 Peja Stojakovic .25 .60
150 Tracy McGrady .30 .75
151 Rafer Alston .15 .40
152 Nazr Mohammed .15 .40
153 Corey Maggette .20 .50
154 Michael Doleac .15 .40
155 Zydrunas Ilgauskas .20 .50
156 Troy Hudson .15 .40
157 Vladimir Radmanovic .15 .40
158 Jason Collins .15 .40
159 Dikembe Mutombo .25 .60
160 Bonzi Wells .15 .40
161 Jason Terry .20 .50
162 Tyson Chandler .20 .50
163 Desmond Mason .20 .50
164 Carlos Arroyo .15 .40
165 Darko Milicic .15 .40
166 Ben Gordon RC .60 1.50
167 Kevin Martin RC .75 2.00
168 Jackson Vroman RC .40 1.00
169 Delonte West RC .60 1.50
170 Dorell Wright RC .60 1.50
171 Erik Daniels RC .50 1.25
172 Josh Childress RC .50 1.25
173 Anderson Varejao RC .50 1.25
174 Andre Emmett RC .40 1.00
175 Chris Duhon RC .60 1.50
176 Bernard Robinson RC .50 1.25
177 D.J. Mbenga RC .50 1.25
178 Kirk Snyder RC .40 1.00
179 Damien Wilkins RC .50 1.25
180 Andre Iguodala RC .75 2.00
181 Nenad Krstic RC .60 1.50
182 Pape Sow RC .50 1.25
183 Maurice Evans RC .60 1.50
184 John Edwards RC .40 1.00
185 Andres Nocioni RC .60 1.50
186 Arthur Johnson RC .60 1.50
187 Beno Udrih RC .50 1.25
188 Andris Biedrins RC .40 1.00
189 Kris Humphries RC .60 1.50
190 Trevor Ariza RC .60 1.50
191 Devin Harris RC .50 1.25
192 J.R. Smith RC .60 1.50
193 Romain Sato RC .40 1.00
194 Lionel Chalmers RC .60 1.50
195 Al Jefferson RC .75 2.00
196 Josh Smith RC .60 1.50
197 Antonio Burks RC .50 1.25
198 Matt Freije RC .50 1.25
199 Justin Reed RC .40 1.00
200 Emeka Okafor RC .50 1.25
201 Sebastian Telfair RC .50 1.25
202 Sasha Vujacic RC .60 1.50
203 Royal Ivey RC .50 1.25
204 Rafael Araujo RC .40 1.00
205 Ibrahim Kutluay RC .60 1.50
206 Pavel Podkolzin RC .40 1.00
207 Jared Reiner RC .60 1.50
208 Luis Flores RC .50 1.25
209 Robert Swift RC .40 1.00
210 Shaun Livingston RC .60 1.50
211 Peter John Ramos RC .40 1.00
212 Luke Jackson RC .40 1.00
213 Luol Deng RC .60 1.50
214 Jameer Nelson RC .60 1.50
215 Tony Allen RC .60 1.50
216 Josh Davis RC .60 1.50
217 Yuta Tabuse RC .60 1.50
218 Donta Smith RC .40 1.00
219 David Harrison RC .40 1.00
220 Dwight Howard RC 1.25 3.00

2004-05 Bazooka Gold

*GOLD: .75X TO 2X BASE CARD HI
STATED ODDS ONE PER PACK

2004-05 Bazooka Mini

*MINI SINGLES: .5X TO 1.25X BASE HI
*MINI RC's: .6X TO 1.5X BASE HI
STATED ODDS ONE PER PACK

2004-05 Bazooka 4-on-1 Stickers

Randomly inserted into packs, these 55 stickers feature four-players each.

COMPLETE SET (55) 12.50 30.00
RANDOM INSERTS IN PACKS
1 Shaq/Okafor/Kobe/Iggy .75 2.00
2 B.Wall/Duncan/Yao/Damp .75 2.00
3 Brand/Duhon/Battier/Dunlvy .50 1.25
4 Marbry/Livingstn/Kidd/Bassy .50 1.25
5 Webb/Rose/Howrd/Crawfrd .50 1.25
6 Garnett/T-Mac/Bron/J.O'N 1.50 4.00
7 Vince/Jones/J-Rich/Mason .75 2.00
8 Gasol/Dirk/AK47/Peja .50 1.25
9 Melo/Artest/Dalem/Rip .50 1.25
10 Boozer/Redd/Mobley/Lewis .50 1.25
11 Alston/Arroyo/Williams/Nash .50 1.25
12 RJeff#/Waltn/DStoud/Bibby .50 1.25
13 Wilcox/Frncis/Jamisn/Stack .50 1.25
14 Wade/Hinrich/Al/Arenas 1.00 2.50
15 S.Abdur/Nazr/Hedo/Okur .50 1.25
16 Wallace/Martin/Spree/Glove .50 1.25
17 Wright/Daniels/L.Rid/Nelson .50 1.25
18 Howard/Brown/Kandi/Smith .75 2.00
19 Miller/Mash/Cassell/Jackson .50 1.25
20 Amare/Curry/Z.Rand/Prince .50 1.25
21 Magl/Kaman/Chand/Camby .50 1.25
22 Wilkins/Swift/Harrisn/Ramos .50 1.25
23 Parker/Gordon/Miller/Harris .75 2.00
24 Bosh/Odom/Miles/Marion .50 1.25
25 L.Jack/Vrmn/B.Jack/S.Jack .50 1.25
26 Pierce/Davis/Magg/Terry .50 1.25
27 Thomas/Deng/Miller/Walker .60 1.50
28 K.Hum/Murphy/Araujo/Miller .50 1.25
29 Johnsn/Hayes/Green/Butler .50 1.25
30 Thomas/Nene/BigAl/Varejao .60 1.50
31 T-Hud/Fllip/Banks/Boykins .50 1.25
32 Blount/Battie/Rasho/Ilgausk .50 1.25
33 Emmett/Allen/Houston/Childr .50 1.25
34 Q-Rich/Hughes/Davis/Wall .50 1.25
35 K.Van-H/Darko/Swift/McDy .50 1.25
36 Hwrd/Al Har/Bender/Pietrus .50 1.25
37 Smith/Allen/Vujacic/Martin .75 2.00
38 Snyder/Smith/Ber.Rob/West .50 1.25
39 Rush/Ariza/Podkolz/ZO .50 1.25
40 Szcz./Barry/Giricek/Kapono .50 1.25
41 Bowen/Snow/Kittles/Tinsley .50 1.25
42 Thmas/Haslm/Goodn/Manu .50 1.25
43 Jaric/Wagner/Sato/Chalmer .50 1.25
44 George/Willims/West/Posey .50 1.25
45 Robnsn/C.Billp/Fish/Donyell .50 1.25
46 Doleac/Theo/Krstic/Mbenga .50 1.25
47 Barbosa/Wsley/Jones/Diaw .50 1.25
48 Biedrins/Johnson/Udrih/Yuta .75 2.00
49 Vo/Christie/Armstrng/Ford .50 1.25
50 Wells/Taylor/Smith/Delk .50 1.25
51 Reiner/Flores/Burks/Freije .50 1.25
52 Zaur/Mercr/Ncioni/VladRad .50 1.25
53 Sow/Evans/Edwards/Ivey .50 1.25
54 Hill/Collins/Mutombo/Davis .50 1.25
55 Reed/Kutluay/Daniels/Smith .50 1.25

2004-05 Bazooka Admissions

Randomly inserted into packs, these 23 cards featuring game-used swatches of leading rookies in the shape of an A. Since the players in group A and group B are inserted at different odds, we have notated which group they are a part of next to the player's name.

GROUP A ODDS 1:927
GROUP B ODDS 1:46
AE Andre Emmett B 1.25 3.00
AI Andre Iguodala A 2.50 6.00
AJ Al Jefferson B 2.50 6.00
AV Anderson Varejao B 1.50 4.00
BG Ben Gordon B 2.00 5.00
DH Devin Harris A 1.50 4.00
DW Dorell Wright B 2.00 5.00
EO Emeka Okafor B 1.50 4.00
JC Josh Childress B 1.50 4.00
JN Jameer Nelson B 2.00 5.00
JS Josh Smith B 2.00 5.00
KH Kris Humphries B 2.00 5.00
KM Kevin Martin B 2.50 6.00
KS Kirk Snyder B 1.25 3.00
LD Luol Deng B 2.00 5.00
LJ Luke Jackson B 1.25 3.00
SL Shaun Livingston B 2.00 5.00
ST Sebastian Telfair B 1.50 4.00
TA Tony Allen B 2.00 5.00
DHA David Harrison B 1.25 3.00
DHO Dwight Howard B 4.00 10.00
DWE Delonte West B 2.00 5.00
JRS J.R. Smith B 2.00 5.00

2004-05 Bazooka Adventures

Randomly inserted into packs, these 23 cards featuring game-used swatches of leading veterans. Since the players in group A and group B are inserted at different odds, we have notated which group they are a part of next to the player's name.

GROUP A ODDS 1:515
GROUP B ODDS 1:52
BD Baron Davis B 2.00 5.00
CA Carmelo Anthony B 5.00 12.00
CB Carlos Boozer A 2.00 5.00
CM Cuttino Mobley B 1.50 4.00
FM Frank Williams B 2.00 5.00
GP Gary Payton B 2.50 6.00
JK Jason Kidd B 4.00 10.00
JM Jamaal Magloire A 2.00 5.00
JM2 Jamal Mashburn B 2.00 5.00
JO Jermaine O'Neal A 2.00 5.00
JS Joe Smith B 2.00 5.00
KH Kirk Hinrich B 2.00 5.00
MB Mike Bibby B 2.50 6.00
MG Manu Ginobili A 3.00 8.00
MP Morris Peterson B 2.00 5.00
PS Peja Stojakovic B 2.50 6.00
RJ Richard Jefferson B 2.00 5.00
SF Steve Francis B 2.00 5.00
SO Shaquille O'Neal B 6.00 15.00
TD Tim Duncan B 4.00 10.00
YM Yao Ming B 5.00 12.00
ZR Zach Randolph B 2.00 5.00

2004-05 Bazooka Back-Up

Randomly inserted into packs, these 24 cards featuring game-used relics of leading veterans who normally don't start. Since the players in group A and group B are inserted at different odds, we have notated which group they are a part of next to the player's name.

GROUP A ODDS 1:849
GROUP B ODDS 1:43
N Nene B 2.50 6.00
AM Antonio McDyess B 2.50 6.00
AP Aleksandar Pavlovic B 2.00 5.00
BD Boris Diaw B 2.50 6.00
CK Chris Kaman B 2.50 6.00
DC Derrick Coleman B 2.50 6.00
DF Derek Fisher B 2.50 6.00
DM Dikembe Mutombo B 3.00 8.00
DW David Wesley B 2.00 5.00
GR Glenn Robinson B 2.50 6.00
HG Horace Grant B 2.00 5.00
JC Jason Collins B 2.00 5.00
JJ Jim Jackson B 2.00 5.00
JK Jason Kapono B 2.00 5.00
MJ Marko Jaric B 2.00 5.00
MM Mike Miller B 2.50 6.00
PG Pat Garrity B 2.00 5.00
SP Scot Pollard B 2.00 5.00
TC Tyson Chandler B 2.50 6.00
VL Voshon Lenard B 2.00 5.00
VR Vladimir Radmanovic B 2.00 5.00
DWE David West B 2.50 6.00

2004-05 Bazooka Breakaway

Randomly inserted into packs, these 31 cards featuring game-used swatches of leading veterans. Since the players in group A and group B are inserted at different odds, we have notated which group they are a part of next to the player's name.

GROUP A ODDS 1:363
GROUP B ODDS 1:18
AF Anfernee Hardaway B 6.00 15.00
AI Allen Iverson B 4.00 10.00
AS Amare Stoudemire A 2.00 5.00
AW Antoine Walker B 2.50 6.00
BD Baron Davis B 2.00 5.00
BW Ben Wallace B 2.00 5.00
CA Chris Andersen B 2.50 6.00
CB Chris Bosh B 2.50 6.00
DM Desmond Mason B 2.00 5.00
DN Dirk Nowitzki B 4.00 10.00
EB Elton Brand A 2.50 6.00
JR Jason Richardson B 2.50 6.00
JS Jerry Stackhouse A 2.00 5.00
KH Kirk Hinrich B 2.00 5.00
LS Latrell Sprewell B 2.00 5.00
MJ Marko Jaric B 2.00 5.00
MR Michael Redd B 2.00 5.00
PG Pau Gasol B 2.50 6.00
PP Paul Pierce B 2.50 6.00
RA Ray Allen B 3.00 8.00
RH Richard Hamilton B 2.00 5.00
RJ Richard Jefferson B 2.00 5.00
SF Steve Francis B 2.00 5.00
SO Shaquille O'Neal B 6.00 15.00
TD Tim Duncan B 4.00 10.00
TM Tracy McGrady A 3.00 8.00
TP Tayshaun Prince B 2.00 5.00
UH Udonis Haslem B 1.50 4.00
YM Yao Ming B 5.00 12.00
SMA Stephon Marbury B 2.00 5.00
TOP Tony Parker B 2.50 6.00

2004-05 Bazooka Comics

Randomly inserted into packs, these 24 comics, done in the style of the old Bazooka comics, feature leading NBA superstars.

COMPLETE SET (24) 4.00 10.00
RANDOM INSERTS IN PACKS
1 Tracy McGrady .25 .60
2 Peja Stojakovic .20 .50
3 Kevin Garnett .30 .75
4 Ben Wallace .15 .40
5 Stephon Marbury .15 .40
6 Michael Redd .15 .40
7 Kenyon Martin .15 .40
8 Carmelo Anthony .40 1.00
9 Jermaine O'Neal .15 .40
10 LeBron James 1.25 3.00
11 Zach Randolph .15 .40
12 Vince Carter .30 .75
13 Andrei Kirilenko .15 .40
14 Pau Gasol .20 .50
15 Steve Francis .15 .40
16 Dwight Howard .40 1.00
17 Emeka Okafor .15 .40
18 Ben Gordon .20 .50
19 Shaun Livingston .20 .50
20 Devin Harris .15 .40
21 Luol Deng .20 .50
22 Andre Iguodala .25 .60
23 Sebastian Telfair .15 .40

2004-05 Bazooka Signs

Randomly inserted into packs, these 24 cards feature autograph of leading NBA players. Since the players in group A and group B are inserted at different odds, we have notated which group they are a part of next to the player's name.

NO ODDS GIVEN
SOME UNPRICED DUE TO SCARCITY
AB Andris Biedrins B 2.50 6.00
AJ Al Jefferson B 5.00 12.00
BG Ben Gordon B 4.00 10.00
DH Devin Harris B 3.00 8.00
EO Emeka Okafor C 3.00 8.00
JC Josh Childress B 3.00 8.00
JS Josh Smith B 4.00 10.00
LD Luol Deng B 4.00 10.00
ST Sebastian Telfair B 3.00 8.00
TD Tim Duncan A 40.00 100.00

2005-06 Bazooka

Released in November 2005, Topps Bazooka boasts a 220 card set where cards 1-165 feature veteran players, cards 166-215 feature rookies and cards 216-220 feature celebrities. Base cards have white borders and a red name box at the bottom of the card. Bazooka was packaged in 24-pack boxes containing eight cards each and carrying a SRP of $2.00.

COMPLETE SET (220) 15.00 40.00
UNPRICED BLUE PRINT RUN 5 SETS
1 Gilbert Arenas .20 .50
2 Josh Smith .20 .50
3 Carlos Boozer .20 .50
4 Al Jefferson .20 .50
5 Jalen Rose .25 .60
6 Primoz Brezec .15 .40
7 Rashard Lewis .25 .60
8 Ben Gordon .20 .50
9 Tony Parker .25 .60
10 Drew Gooden .20 .50
11 Mike Bibby .25 .60
12 Josh Howard .25 .60
13 Sebastian Telfair .20 .50
14 Earl Boykins .15 .40
15 Joe Johnson .20 .50
16 Rasheed Wallace .25 .60
17 Marc Jackson .15 .40
18 Baron Davis .20 .50
19 Dwight Howard .20 .50
20 Tracy McGrady .30 .75
21 Trevor Ariza .15 .40
22 David Harrison .15 .40
23 J.R. Smith .20 .50
24 Chris Kaman .20 .50
25 Richard Jefferson .20 .50
26 Chris Mihm .15 .40
27 Sam Cassell .20 .50
28 Mike Miller .20 .50
29 Joe Smith .20 .50
30 Dwyane Wade .40 1.00
31 Tony Allen .15 .40
32 Antawn Jamison .20 .50
33 Eddy Curry .15 .40
34 Rafael Araujo .15 .40
35 Jerry Stackhouse .20 .50
36 Manu Ginobili .25 .60
37 Antonio McDyess .20 .50
38 Zach Randolph .20 .50
39 Mike James .15 .40
40 Chris Webber .25 .60
41 Bobby Simmons .15 .40
42 Jamal Crawford .25 .60
43 Pau Gasol .25 .60
44 Brian Scalabrine .15 .40
45 Desmond Mason .15 .40
46 Tyronn Lue .15 .40
47 Andrei Kirilenko .20 .50
48 Luke Ridnour .20 .50
49 Gerald Wallace .20 .50
50 LeBron James 1.00 2.50
51 Peja Stojakovic .25 .60
52 Andre Miller .20 .50
53 Quentin Richardson .20 .50
54 Mike Dunleavy .20 .50
55 Steve Francis .20 .50
56 Stephen Jackson .20 .50
57 P.J. Brown .15 .40
58 Caron Butler .20 .50
59 Keith Van Horn .20 .50
60 Shaquille O'Neal .50 1.25
61 Josh Childress .20 .50
62 Michael Doleac .15 .40
63 Lamar Odom .20 .50
64 Stephon Marbury .20 .50
65 Chris Duhon .15 .40
66 Shaun Livingston .15 .40
67 Eric Snow .15 .40
68 Travis Outlaw .20 .50
69 Ron Artest .25 .60
70 Emeka Okafor .20 .50
71 Chauncey Billups .25 .60
72 Jason Williams .20 .50
73 Jameer Nelson .15 .40
74 Eduardo Najera .15 .40
75 Speedy Claxton .15 .40
76 Kirk Snyder .15 .40
77 Rafer Alston .15 .40
78 Kobe Bryant 1.00 2.50
79 Michael Redd .20 .50
80 Tim Duncan .40 1.00
81 Tayshaun Prince .20 .50
82 Brendan Haywood .15 .40
83 Kyle Korver .20 .50
84 Tony Delk .15 .40
85 Luol Deng .20 .50
86 Elton Brand .25 .60
87 Jason Richardson .25 .60
88 Antoine Walker .20 .50
89 Ray Allen .25 .60
90 Yao Ming .30 .75
91 Damon Jones .15 .40
92 Anderson Varejao .15 .40
93 Kurt Thomas .15 .40
94 Latrell Sprewell .20 .50
95 Cuttino Mobley .15 .40
96 Chris Wilcox .15 .40
97 Devin Harris .15 .40
98 Jared Jeffries .15 .40
99 Nenad Krstic .15 .40
100 Steve Nash .30 .75
101 Reggie Evans .15 .40
102 Ben Wallace .20 .50
103 Allen Iverson .40 1.00
104 Bruce Bowen .15 .40
105 Paul Pierce .25 .60
106 Shareef Abdur-Rahim .20 .50
107 Vladimir Radmanovic .15 .40
108 Michael Finley .25 .60
109 Brent Barry .15 .40
110 Carmelo Anthony .50 1.25
111 Andre Iguodala .20 .50
112 Shane Battier .20 .50
113 Richard Hamilton .20 .50
114 Kenny Thomas .15 .40
115 Tyson Chandler .20 .50
116 Jim Jackson .15 .40
117 David Wesley .15 .40
118 Grant Hill .30 .75
119 Wally Szczerbiak .20 .50
120 Dirk Nowitzki .40 1.00
121 Udonis Haslem .15 .40
122 Jason Hart .15 .40
123 Marcus Camby .20 .50
124 Kirk Hinrich .20 .50
125 Jermaine O'Neal .20 .50
126 Derek Fisher .20 .50
127 Donyell Marshall .15 .40
128 Darius Miles .15 .40
129 Kenyon Martin .20 .50
130 Jason Kidd .40 1.00
131 Marquis Daniels .15 .40
132 Kevin Garnett .40 1.00
133 Juwan Howard .20 .50
134 Shawn Marion .20 .50
135 Morris Peterson .15 .40
136 Kevin Martin .20 .50
137 Gary Payton .25 .60
138 Maurice Williams .20 .50
139 Eddie Jones .20 .50
140 Vince Carter .40 1.00
141 Lorenzen Wright .15 .40
142 Dan Dickau .15 .40
143 Chucky Atkins .15 .40
144 Mike Sweetney .15 .40
145 Corey Maggette .20 .50
146 Hedo Turkoglu .20 .50
147 Jamaal Tinsley .15 .40
148 Samuel Dalembert .15 .40
149 Bob Sura .15 .40
150 Amare Stoudemire .20 .50
151 Troy Murphy .15 .40
152 Joel Przybilla .15 .40
153 Carlos Arroyo .15 .40
154 Brad Miller .20 .50
155 Jason Terry .20 .50
156 Beno Udrih .15 .40
157 Zydrunas Ilgauskas .20 .50
158 Nick Collison .20 .50
159 Andres Nocioni .15 .40
160 Chris Bosh .25 .60
161 Brevin Knight .15 .40
162 Mehmet Okur .15 .40
163 Ricky Davis .20 .50
164 Larry Hughes .20 .50
165 Al Harrington .20 .50
166 Chris Paul RC 2.50 6.00
167 Danny Granger RC .75 2.00
168 Jarrett Jack RC .60 1.50
169 Wayne Simien RC .40 1.00
170 Deron Williams RC .75 2.00
171 Ryan Gomes RC .50 1.25
172 Daniel Ewing RC .50 1.25
173 Sean May RC .40 1.00
174 Alan Anderson RC .40 1.00
175 Hakim Warrick RC .50 1.25
176 Francisco Garcia RC .50 1.25
177 Nate Robinson RC .60 1.50
178 Luther Head RC .50 1.25
179 Joey Graham RC .50 1.25
180 Marvin Williams RC .60 1.50
181 Antoine Wright RC .50 1.25
182 Andrew Bynum RC .50 1.25
183 Johan Petro RC .40 1.00
184 Louis Williams RC .60 1.50
185 Andray Blatche RC .60 1.50
186 Sarunas Jasikevicius RC .60 1.50
187 Ike Diogu RC .40 1.00
188 Channing Frye RC .60 1.50
189 Julius Hodge RC .40 1.00
190 Rashad McCants RC .50 1.25
191 Yaroslav Korolev RC .40 1.00
192 C.J. Miles RC .60 1.50
193 Brandon Bass RC .50 1.25
194 Travis Diener RC .40 1.00
195 Monta Ellis RC .75 2.00
196 Linas Kleiza RC .40 1.00
197 Gerald Green RC .60 1.50
198 Jason Maxiell RC .50 1.25
199 David Lee RC .60 1.50
200 Andrew Bogut RC .75 2.00
201 Salim Stoudamire RC .50 1.25
202 Raymond Felton RC .60 1.50
203 Martell Webster RC .50 1.25
204 Chris Taft RC .50 1.25
205 Charlie Villanueva RC .60 1.50
206 Lawrence Roberts RC .40 1.00
207 Ersan Ilyasova RC .60 1.50
208 Martynas Andriuskevicius RC .40 1.00
209 Bracey Wright RC .40 1.00
210 Von Wafer RC .40 1.00
211 Eddie Basden RC .40 1.00
212 Dijon Thompson RC .40 1.00
213 Robert Whaley RC .40 1.00
214 Matt Walsh RC .60 1.50
215 Ricky Sanchez RC .60 1.50
216 Jay-Z .75 2.00
217 Shannon Elizabeth .75 2.00
218 Christie Brinkley .75 2.00
219 Jenny McCarthy .75 2.00
220 Carmen Electra .75 2.00

2005-06 Bazooka Gold

*1-165 GOLD: .6X TO 1.5X BASE HI
*166-220 GOLD: .75X TO 2X BASE HI
STATED ODDS ONE PER PACK

2005-06 Bazooka 4-on-1 Stickers

Inserted in packs at the rate of one in four, this 55-card set features mini stickers that are designed to parallel the best set design. Each sticker showcases four players, hence the 4-on-1 set name.

STATED ODDS 1:4
1 Nash/Okafor/Gordn/BigBen .50 1.25
2 J.O'Neal/Arena/Smmns/Rndlph .50 1.25
3 JshSmith/J-Rich/B.Barry/Mason .50 1.25
4 Al/Kobe/LeBron/Amare 1.50 4.00
5 Dirk/T-Mac/Pierce/Wade .75 2.00
6 R.Allen/Q-Rich/Redd/D.Jones .50 1.25
7 Shaq/Duncan/KG/Yao 1.25 3.00
8 Parker/Marbury/Hinrich/Telfair .50 1.25
9 Bosh/R.Lewis/Sheed/Jamison .50 1.25
10 May/Felton/Mv.Wllms/McCants .50 1.25
11 Webb/Big Al/D.Howard/Brand .50 1.25
12 R.Davis/Artest/Spree/K-Martin .50 1.25
13 Prince/Marion/Manu/AK-47 .50 1.25
14 Scala/Brezec/Araujo/Kaman .50 1.25
15 Rose/M.Millr/G.Wllce/SJcksn .50 1.25
16 K.Thomas/Reef/Wilcox/Boozer .50 1.25
17 A.Hrrngtn/Magg/Donyell/Kn.Thomas .50 1.25
18 Dunlvy/Varjao/Chldrss/Lvngstn .50 1.25
19 B.Davis/Bibby/A.Mllr/Francis .50 1.25
20 Peja/Billups/A.Wlkr/Szcz .50 1.25
21 JayZ/Vince/Kidd/R.Jeffrsn 1.00 2.50
22 Paul/Deron/N.Rbnsn/J.Jack 1.25 3.00
23 Przy/Z.Ilg/Brd.Miller/Krstic .50 1.25
24 Bogut/Frye/Bynum/Blatche .75 2.00
25 Battier/Goodn/Evans/Sweet .50 1.25
26 Wesley/Hughes/Glove/Bowen .50 1.25
27 Marquis/Jeffries/Snydr/Ariza .50 1.25
28 Boykins/Lue/Alston/Arroyo .50 1.25
29 Chandlr/Collisn/Okur/L.Wright .50 1.25
30 Haywd/Haslem/Ju.Hwrd/Jjax .50 1.25
31 Hill/Melo/Iggy/Jo.Johnson .50 1.25
32 Camby/Dalemb/Taft/Villnva .50 1.25
33 S.Eliz/C.Brink/J.McCr/Elektra 1.25 3.00
34 Green/Hodge/An.Wright/F.Garcia .50 1.25
35 Crawf/Stack/JDub/Jameer .50 1.25
36 Rip/E.Jones/JR.Smith/T.Allen .50 1.25
37 Eddy/M.Jackson/Mihm/Harrison .50 1.25
38 Odom/McDyess/Pau/Deng .50 1.25
39 Miles/Mobley/Finley/Butler .50 1.25
40 Jo.Smth/Ncni/Jo.Hwrd/Korver .50 1.25
41 Martell/Salim/Head/D.Ewing .50 1.25
42 Ridnour/Cssll/M.Jms/Duhon .50 1.25
43 Lee/Warrick/Grangr/Graham .50 1.25
44 Terry/Beno/Dickau/Atkins .50 1.25
45 Devin/Speed/Kv.Mrtn/Mc.Will .50 1.25
46 A.And/Kleiza/Maxiell/Simien .60 1.50
47 Gomes/Jasik/Korolv/Diener .50 1.25
48 T.Murphy/VanH/Doleac/Hedo .50 1.25
49 Fisher/Snow/Sura/Knight .50 1.25
50 Delk/L.Wllms/C.Miles/Ellis .75 2.00
51 Outlaw/Hart/MoPete/Tinsley .50 1.25
52 P.Brown/Radman/Najera/Krstic .50 1.25
53 May/Petro/Diogu/Bass .40 1.00
54 Bogut/Duncn/Shaq/Mv.Willms .60 1.50
55 Wade/Al/JayZ/Amare 1.50 4.00

2005-06 Bazooka All-Access Relics

Inserted in packs at the rate of one in 24, this 25-card set places small player photos and a circular swatch of memorabilia on a card with a blue and red background design.

STATED ODDS 1:24
AW Antoine Wright 2.00 5.00
CF Channing Frye 2.50 6.00
CP Chris Paul 8.00 20.00
CV Charlie Villanueva 2.50 6.00
DG Danny Granger 3.00 8.00
DL David Lee 2.50 6.00
DW Deron Williams 3.00 8.00
FG Francisco Garcia 2.00 5.00
GG Gerald Green 2.50 6.00
HW Hakim Warrick 2.00 5.00
JG Joey Graham 2.00 5.00
JH Julius Hodge 1.50 4.00
JJ Jarrett Jack 2.50 6.00
JM Jason Maxiell 2.00 5.00
LH Luther Head 2.00 5.00
ME Monta Ellis 3.00 8.00
MW Martell Webster 2.00 5.00
NR Nate Robinson 2.50 6.00
RF Raymond Felton 2.50 6.00
RG Ryan Gomes 2.00 5.00
RM Rashad McCants 2.00 5.00
SJ Sarunas Jasikevicius 2.50 6.00
SM Sean May 1.50 4.00
WS Wayne Simien 1.50 4.00
ABO Andrew Bogut 3.00 8.00

2005-06 Bazooka All-Star Relics

Seeded in packs at the rate of one in 46, this 20-cards set features NBA All-Stars along with a star-shaped swatch of memorabilia from All-Star Weekend. Backgrounds are blue and red and utilize several different star background elements.

STATED ODDS 1:46
AJ Antawn Jamison Shirt 2.50 6.00
BU Beno Udrih Shirt 2.00 5.00
BW Ben Wallace Warm 2.50 6.00
CA Chris Andersen Shorts 3.00 8.00
DH Dwight Howard Warm 2.50 6.00
EB Earl Boykins Warm 2.00 5.00

EO Emeka Okafor Shorts 2.50 6.00
GH Grant Hill Warm 4.00 10.00
JH Josh Howard Shorts 3.00 8.00
KH Kirk Hinrich Warm 2.50 6.00
KK Kyle Korver Shorts 2.50 6.00
LR Luke Ridnour 2.50 6.00
MG Manu Ginobili Warm 3.00 8.00
RA Ray Allen Shirt 3.00 8.00
RD Ronald Dupree 2.00 5.00
SM Shawn Marion Warm 2.50 6.00
SO Shaquille O'Neal Shorts 6.00 15.00
UH Udonis Haslem Shirt 2.00 5.00
YM Yao Ming Warm 4.00 10.00
AJE Al Jefferson Shorts 2.50 6.00

2005-06 Bazooka Blog Squad Relics

Inserted in packs at the rate of one in 37, this 25-card set features player photos and "B" shaped memorabilia swatches in the lower left hand corner.

STATED ODDS 1:37
AJ Al Jefferson 2.50 6.00
AN Andres Nocioni 2.00 5.00
AV Anderson Varejao 2.00 5.00
CA Carlos Arroyo 2.00 5.00
CB Caron Butler 2.50 6.00
CW Chris Wilcox 2.00 5.00
DW Dwyane Wade 6.00 15.00
GW Gerald Wallace 2.50 6.00
JC Josh Childress 2.50 6.00
JJ Joe Johnson 2.50 6.00
MD Marquis Daniels 2.00 5.00
NC Nick Collison 2.50 6.00
RA Ray Allen 3.00 8.00
RJ Richard Jefferson 2.50 6.00
SL Shaun Livingston 2.00 5.00
SO Shaquille O'Neal 6.00 15.00
ST Sebastian Telfair 2.50 6.00
UH Udonis Haslem 2.00 5.00
YM Yao Ming 4.00 10.00
DWE Delonte West 2.00 5.00
DWR Dorell Wright 2.00 5.00
MDU Mike Dunleavy 2.50 6.00
RAL Rafer Alston 2.00 5.00
RAR Ron Artest 3.00 8.00
SAR Shareef Abdur-Rahim 2.50 6.00

2005-06 Bazooka Comics

Inserted in packs at the rate of one in four, this 24-card set features NBA player themed comic cards.

COMPLETE SET (24) 10.00 25.00
STATED ODDS 1:4
1 Dwyane Wade .75 2.00
2 Steve Nash .60 1.50
3 Josh Smith .40 1.00
4 Emeka Okafor .40 1.00
5 Gilbert Arenas .40 1.00
6 Tim Duncan .75 2.00
7 Grant Hill .60 1.50
8 Ben Gordon .40 1.00
9 Dirk Nowitzki .75 2.00
10 Shaquille O'Neal 1.00 2.50
11 Ray Allen .50 1.25
12 Chris Bosh .50 1.25
13 Jason Richardson .50 1.25
14 Allen Iverson .75 2.00
15 Amare Stoudemire .40 1.00
16 LeBron James 2.00 5.00
17 Carmelo Anthony 1.00 2.50
18 Manu Ginobili .50 1.25
19 Andrew Bogut .60 1.50
20 Marvin Williams .50 1.25
21 Deron Williams .60 1.50
22 Raymond Felton .50 1.25
23 Channing Frye .50 1.25
24 Sean May .30 .75

2005-06 Bazooka Minis

*MINI STARS: .4X TO 1X BASE HI
*MINI RCs: .6X TO 1.5X HI
STATED ODDS ONE PER PACK

2005-06 Bazooka Power Relics

Randomly seeded in packs at the rate of one in 29, this 30-card set features full color player photos, a yellow name box along the bottom of the card and a circular swatch of memorabilia.

STATED ODDS 1:29
AK Andrei Kirilenko 2.50 6.00
BG Ben Gordon 2.50 6.00
BJ Bobby Jackson 2.00 5.00
BW Bonzi Wells 2.00 5.00
CA Carmelo Anthony 6.00 15.00
CB Carlos Boozer 2.50 6.00
DG Drew Gooden 2.50 6.00
DH Dwight Howard 2.50 6.00
DM Desmond Mason Shirt 2.00 5.00
EB Elton Brand 3.00 8.00
EO Emeka Okafor 2.50 6.00
JK Jason Kidd 5.00 12.00
JM Jamaal Magloire 2.00 5.00
JO Jermaine O'Neal 2.50 6.00
JR Jalen Rose 3.00 8.00
JS Josh Smith 2.50 6.00
LD Luol Deng 2.50 6.00
LH Larry Hughes 2.50 6.00
PG Pau Gasol 3.00 8.00
PS Peja Stojakovic 3.00 8.00
RA Rafael Araujo 2.00 5.00
RL Rashard Lewis 3.00 8.00
RM Ronald Murray 2.00 5.00
SF Steve Francis 2.50 6.00
SO Shaquille O'Neal 6.00 15.00
TD Tim Duncan 5.00 12.00
ZR Zach Randolph 2.50 6.00
CBO Chris Bosh 3.00 8.00
JRS J.R. Smith 2.50 6.00
KBR Kobe Bryant 8.00 20.00

2005-06 Bazooka Signs

Inserted in packs at the rate of one in 236, this 20-card set is designed to appear as though it's been printed on a page from a lined notebook. Cards are enhanced with silver autograph stickers.

STATED ODDS 1:236
AB Andrew Bogut 6.00 15.00
AI Allen Iverson 75.00 150.00
CA Carmelo Anthony 20.00 50.00
CB Christie Brinkley 40.00 80.00
DW Dwyane Wade 30.00 80.00
EO Emeka Okafor 5.00 12.00
GG Gerald Green 6.00 15.00
JM Jenny McCarthy 60.00 120.00
JN Jameer Nelson 5.00 12.00
JZ Jay-Z 30.00 80.00
ME Monta Ellis 8.00 20.00
RF Raymond Felton 6.00 15.00
SE Shannon Elizabeth 60.00 120.00
SM Stephon Marbury 8.00 20.00
SO Shaquille O'Neal 40.00 100.00
DWI Deron Williams 12.00 30.00
SMA Sean May 5.00 12.00

2005-06 Bazooka Window Clings

Inserted in packs at the rate of one in four, these clear plastic window clings feature NBA team logos.

STATED ODDS 1:4
1 Atlanta Hawks .60 1.50
2 Boston Celtics .60 1.50
3 Charlotte Bobcats .60 1.50
4 Chicago Bulls .60 1.50
5 Cleveland Cavaliers .60 1.50
6 Dallas Mavericks .60 1.50
7 Denver Nuggets .60 1.50
8 Detroit Pistons .60 1.50
9 Golden State Warriors .60 1.50
10 Houston Rockets .60 1.50
11 Indiana Pacers .60 1.50
12 Los Angeles Clippers .60 1.50
13 Los Angeles Lakers .60 1.50
14 Memphis Grizzlies .60 1.50
15 Miami Heat .60 1.50
16 Milwaukee Bucks .60 1.50
17 Minnesota Timberwolves .60 1.50
18 New Jersey Nets .60 1.50
19 New Orleans Hornets .60 1.50
20 New York Knicks .60 1.50
21 Orlando Magic .60 1.50
22 Philadelphia 76ers .60 1.50
23 Phoenix Suns .60 1.50
24 Portland Trail Blazers .60 1.50
25 Sacramento Kings .60 1.50
26 San Antonio Spurs .60 1.50
27 Seattle SuperSonics .60 1.50
28 Toronto Raptors .60 1.50
29 Utah Jazz .60 1.50
30 Washington Wizards .60 1.50

1951 Berk Ross

The 1951 Berk Ross set consists of 72 cards (each measuring approximately 2 1/16" by 2 1/2") with tinted photographs, divided evenly into four series (designated in the checklist as 1, 2, 3 and 4). The cards were marketed in boxes containing two card panels, without gum, and the set includes stars of other sports as well as baseball players. The set is sometimes still found in the original packaging. Intact panels command a premium over the listed prices. The catalog designation for this set is W532-1. In every series the first ten cards are baseball players; the set has a heavy emphasis on Yankees and Phillies players as they were in the World Series the year before. The set includes the first card of Bob Cousy as well as a card of Whitey Ford in his Rookie Card year.

COMPLETE SET (72) 900.00 1500.00
1-11 Bob Cousy Basketball 100.00 200.00
1-12 Dick Schnittker Basketball 5.00 10.00
2-11 Sherman White Basketball 5.00 10.00
3-11 Paul Unruh Basketball 5.00 10.00
4-11 Bill Sharman Basketball 20.00 40.00

1998-99 Black Diamond

The inaugural 120-card Black Diamond set was released in six-card packs with a suggested retail price of $3.99. The cards feature light f/x foil treatment with each sporting a single black diamond. The first 13 cards in the set commemorate Michael Jordan. The rookie card subset was inserted at one in four.

COMPLETE SET (120) 40.00 80.00
COMPLETE SET w/o RC (90) 20.00 40.00
RC STATED ODDS 1:4 HOB/RET
1 Michael Jordan 1.25 3.00
2 Michael Jordan 1.25 3.00
3 Michael Jordan 1.25 3.00
4 Michael Jordan 1.25 3.00
5 Michael Jordan 1.25 3.00
6 Michael Jordan 1.25 3.00
7 Michael Jordan 1.25 3.00
8 Michael Jordan 1.25 3.00
9 Michael Jordan 1.25 3.00
10 Michael Jordan 1.25 3.00
11 Michael Jordan 1.25 3.00
12 Michael Jordan 1.25 3.00
13 Michael Jordan 1.25 3.00
14 Dikembe Mutombo .30 .75
15 Steve Smith .25 .60
16 Mookie Blaylock .20 .50
17 Antoine Walker .30 .75
18 Kenny Anderson .25 .60
19 Ron Mercer .25 .60
20 Glen Rice .30 .75
21 Derrick Coleman .25 .60
22 Michael Jordan 1.25 3.00
23 Toni Kukoc .30 .75
24 Brent Barry .25 .60
25 Brevin Knight .20 .50
26 Derek Anderson .20 .50
27 Shawn Kemp .30 .75
28 Shawn Bradley .20 .50
29 Michael Finley .30 .75
30 Nick Van Exel .25 .60
31 Chauncey Billups .40 1.00
32 Antonio McDyess .25 .60
33 Grant Hill .50 1.25
34 Jerry Stackhouse .30 .75
35 Bison Dele .20 .50
36 John Starks .25 .60
37 Chris Mills .20 .50
38 Scottie Pippen .50 1.25
39 Hakeem Olajuwon .40 1.00
40 Charles Barkley .50 1.25
41 Antonio Davis .20 .50
42 Reggie Miller .40 1.00
43 Mark Jackson .25 .60
44 Eddie Jones .30 .75
45 Shaquille O'Neal .75 2.00
46 Kobe Bryant 1.25 3.00
47 Rodney Rogers .20 .50
48 Maurice Taylor .20 .50
49 Tim Hardaway .30 .75
50 Jamal Mashburn .25 .60
51 Alonzo Mourning .40 1.00
52 Ray Allen .40 1.00
53 Terrell Brandon .20 .50
54 Glenn Robinson .25 .60
55 Joe Smith .25 .60
56 Stephon Marbury .40 1.00
57 Kevin Garnett .50 1.25
58 Kerry Kittles .20 .50
59 Jayson Williams .20 .50
60 Keith Van Horn .30 .75
61 Patrick Ewing .40 1.00
62 Allan Houston .25 .60
63 Latrell Sprewell .30 .75
64 Anfernee Hardaway .50 1.25
65 Horace Grant .25 .60
66 Allen Iverson .60 1.50
67 Tim Thomas .30 .75
68 Jason Kidd .50 1.25
69 Danny Manning .25 .60
70 Tom Gugliotta .20 .50
71 Damon Stoudamire .25 .60
72 Rasheed Wallace .30 .75
73 Isaiah Rider .25 .60
74 Corliss Williamson .20 .50
75 Chris Webber .30 .75
76 Tim Duncan .60 1.50
77 David Robinson .50 1.25
78 Sean Elliott .30 .75
79 Gary Payton .30 .75
80 Vin Baker .25 .60
81 John Wallace .20 .50
82 Tracy McGrady .50 1.25
83 Jeff Hornacek .25 .60
84 Karl Malone .40 1.00
85 John Stockton .40 1.00
86 Bryant Reeves .20 .50
87 Shareef Abdur-Rahim .30 .75
88 Rod Strickland .20 .50
89 Juwan Howard .25 .60
90 Mitch Richmond .30 .75
91 Michael Olowokandi RC 1.00 2.50
92 Dirk Nowitzki RC 5.00 12.00
93 Raef LaFrentz RC 1.00 2.50
94 Mike Bibby RC 1.25 3.00
95 Ricky Davis RC 1.25 3.00
96 Jason Williams RC 2.00 5.00
97 Al Harrington RC 1.25 3.00
98 Bonzi Wells RC .75 2.00
99 Keon Clark RC .75 2.00
100 Rashard Lewis RC 2.00 5.00
101 Paul Pierce RC 3.00 8.00
102 Antawn Jamison RC 1.25 3.00
103 Nazr Mohammed RC .75 2.00
104 Brian Skinner RC .75 2.00
105 Corey Benjamin RC .50 1.25
106 Peja Stojakovic RC 2.00 5.00
107 Bryce Drew RC .50 1.25
108 Matt Harpring RC .75 2.00
109 Toby Bailey RC .75 2.00
110 Tyronn Lue RC .75 2.00
111 Michael Dickerson RC .75 2.00
112 Roshown McLeod RC .50 1.25
113 Felipe Lopez RC .50 1.25
114 Michael Doleac RC .60 1.50
115 Ruben Patterson RC .75 2.00
116 Robert Traylor RC .75 2.00
117 Sam Jacobson RC .60 1.50
118 Larry Hughes RC 1.50 4.00
119 Pat Garrity RC .60 1.50
120 Vince Carter RC 4.00 10.00

1998-99 Black Diamond Double Diamond

*STARS: 1X TO 2.5X BASE CARD HI
*RCs: .5X TO 1.25X BASE HI
STARS: PRINT RUN 3000 SERIAL #'d SETS
RCs: PRINT RUN 2500 SERIAL #'d SETS

1998-99 Black Diamond Triple Diamond

COMMON MJ (1-13/22) 6.00 15.00
*STARS: 1.5X TO 4X BASE CARD HI
*RCs: 1X TO 2.5X BASE CARD HI
STARS: PRINT RUN 1500 SERIAL #'d SETS
RCs: PRINT RUN 1000 SERIAL #'d SETS
92 Dirk Nowitzki 15.00 40.00

1998-99 Black Diamond Quadruple Diamond

COMMON MJ (1-13/22) 30.00 80.00
*STARS: 15X TO 40X BASE CARD HI
*RCs: 4X TO 10X HI
STARS: PRINT RUN 150 SERIAL #'d SETS
RCs: PRINT RUN 50 SERIAL #'d SETS
92 Dirk Nowitzki 75.00 200.00
96 Jason Williams 75.00 200.00
120 Vince Carter 75.00 200.00

1998-99 Black Diamond Diamond Dominance

Randomly inserted in packs, this 30-card set features the most dominant players in the NBA. The cards are set against a bronze foil background. The cards are also serially numbered to 1000. Card backs carry a "D" prefix.

STATED PRINT RUN 1000 SERIAL #'d SETS
*EMERALD: 4X TO 10X HI COLUMN
EMERALD: PRINT RUN 100 SERIAL #'d SETS
D1 Steve Smith .75 2.00
D2 Paul Pierce 4.00 10.00
D3 Glen Rice 1.00 2.50
D4 Toni Kukoc 1.00 2.50
D5 Shawn Kemp 1.00 2.50
D6 Michael Finley 1.00 2.50
D7 Antonio McDyess .75 2.00
D8 Grant Hill 1.50 4.00
D9 Antawn Jamison 1.50 4.00
D10 Scottie Pippen 1.50 4.00
D11 Reggie Miller 1.25 3.00
D12 Michael Olowokandi 1.25 3.00
D13 Shaquille O'Neal 2.50 6.00
D14 Alonzo Mourning 1.25 3.00
D15 Ray Allen 1.25 3.00
D16 Stephon Marbury 1.25 3.00
D17 Keith Van Horn 1.00 2.50
D18 Allan Houston .75 2.00
D19 Anfernee Hardaway 1.50 4.00
D20 Allen Iverson 2.00 5.00
D21 Jason Kidd 1.50 4.00
D22 Damon Stoudamire .75 2.00
D23 Chris Webber 1.00 2.50
D24 Tim Duncan 2.00 5.00
D25 Gary Payton 1.00 2.50
D26 Vince Carter 5.00 12.00
D27 Karl Malone 1.25 3.00
D28 Mike Bibby 1.50 4.00
D29 Mitch Richmond 1.00 2.50
D30 Michael Jordan 15.00 40.00

1998-99 Black Diamond MJ Sheer Brilliance

Randomly inserted in hobby packs, this 30-card set focuses on Michael Jordan. The cards are serially numbered to 230 on the back. Card backs also contain a "B" prefix.

COMMON CARD (B1-B30) 25.00 60.00
STATED PRINT RUN 230 SERIAL #'d SETS

1998-99 Black Diamond MJ Sheer Brilliance Extreme

COMMON CARD (B1-B30) 100.00 250.00
STATED PRINT RUN 23 SERIAL #'d SETS

1998-99 Black Diamond UD Authentics

Randomly inserted in packs, this five-card set features autographs from some of the top rookies in 1999. The cards are numbered out of 475.

STATED PRINT RUN 475 SETS
AJ Antawn Jamison 10.00 25.00
BW Bonzi Wells 6.00 15.00
LH Larry Hughes 12.00 30.00
MB Mike Bibby 10.00 25.00
RT Robert Traylor 6.00 15.00

1999-00 Black Diamond

Upper Deck produced this year's Black Diamond with six-cards per pack that carried a suggested retail price of $3.99. The base set was made up of 120 cards, consisting of 90 veterans and a 30-card rookie subset that was inserted one in three packs.

COMPLETE SET (120) 25.00 50.00
COMPLETE SET w/o RC (90) 12.50 25.00
91-120 STATED ODDS 1:3 H/R
MJ FINAL FLOOR LISTED UNDER 99-00 UD
1 Dikembe Mutombo .30 .75
2 Alan Henderson .20 .50
3 Roshown McLeod .20 .50
4 Kenny Anderson .25 .60
5 Paul Pierce .40 1.00
6 Antoine Walker .30 .75
7 Eddie Jones .30 .75
8 Elden Campbell .20 .50
9 David Wesley .20 .50
10 Toni Kukoc .30 .75
11 Randy Brown .20 .50
12 Dickey Simpkins .20 .50
13 Shawn Kemp .30 .75
14 Zydrunas Ilgauskas .25 .60
15 Brevin Knight .20 .50
16 Michael Finley .30 .75
17 Dirk Nowitzki .60 1.50
18 Robert Pack .20 .50
19 Antonio McDyess .25 .60
20 Nick Van Exel .25 .60
21 Ron Mercer .25 .60
22 Grant Hill .40 1.00
23 Lindsey Hunter .20 .50
24 Jerry Stackhouse .30 .75
25 Antawn Jamison .30 .75
26 John Starks .25 .60
27 Donyell Marshall .20 .50
28 Hakeem Olajuwon .40 1.00
29 Charles Barkley .50 1.25
30 Cuttino Mobley .20 .50
31 Reggie Miller .30 .75
32 Rik Smits .30 .75
33 Jalen Rose .25 .60
34 Maurice Taylor .20 .50
35 Tyrone Nesby RC .25 .60
36 Michael Olowokandi .20 .50
37 Shaquille O'Neal .75 2.00
38 Kobe Bryant 1.25 3.00
39 Glen Rice .30 .75
40 P.J. Brown .20 .50
41 Tim Hardaway .30 .75
42 Alonzo Mourning .40 1.00
43 Jamal Mashburn .25 .60
44 Glenn Robinson .25 .60
45 Ray Allen .30 .75
46 Tim Thomas .25 .60
47 Kevin Garnett .50 1.25
48 Joe Smith .25 .60
49 Terrell Brandon .20 .50
50 Stephon Marbury .25 .60
51 Jayson Williams .20 .50
52 Keith Van Horn .25 .60
53 Latrell Sprewell .30 .75
54 Allan Houston .25 .60
55 Patrick Ewing .40 1.00
56 Marcus Camby .25 .60
57 Darrell Armstrong .20 .50
58 Bo Outlaw .20 .50
59 Michael Doleac .20 .50
60 Allen Iverson .60 1.50
61 Theo Ratliff .25 .60
62 Larry Hughes .25 .60
63 Anfernee Hardaway .50 1.25
64 Jason Kidd .50 1.25
65 Tom Gugliotta .20 .50
66 Brian Grant .20 .50
67 Damon Stoudamire .25 .60
68 Rasheed Wallace .30 .75
69 Jason Williams .40 1.00
70 Chris Webber .30 .75
71 Vlade Divac .30 .75
72 Tim Duncan .60 1.50
73 David Robinson .50 1.25
74 Avery Johnson .25 .60
75 Sean Elliott .30 .75
76 Gary Payton .30 .75
77 Vin Baker .25 .60
78 Brent Barry .25 .60
79 Vince Carter .60 1.50
80 Tracy McGrady .50 1.25
81 Doug Christie .25 .60
82 Karl Malone .40 1.00
83 John Stockton .40 1.00
84 Bryon Russell .20 .50
85 Shareef Abdur-Rahim .25 .60
86 Mike Bibby .30 .75
87 Felipe Lopez .20 .50
88 Juwan Howard .25 .60
89 Rod Strickland .20 .50
90 Mitch Richmond .30 .75
91 Elton Brand RC 1.00 2.50
92 Steve Francis RC 1.00 2.50
93 Baron Davis RC 1.00 2.50
94 Lamar Odom RC 1.00 2.50
95 Jonathan Bender RC .40 1.00
96 Wally Szczerbiak RC .75 2.00
97 Richard Hamilton RC .75 2.00
98 Andre Miller RC .75 2.00
99 Shawn Marion RC .75 2.00
100 Jason Terry RC .60 1.50
101 Trajan Langdon RC .40 1.00
102 A.Radojevic RC .25 .60
103 Corey Maggette RC .60 1.50
104 William Avery RC .30 .75
105 Ron Artest RC .75 2.00
106 Adrian Griffin RC .40 1.00
107 James Posey RC .40 1.00
108 Quincy Lewis RC .25 .60
109 Dion Glover RC .30 .75
110 Jeff Foster RC .40 1.00
111 Kenny Thomas RC .40 1.00
112 Devean George RC .40 1.00
113 Tim James RC .25 .60
114 Vonteego Cummings RC .25 .60
115 Jumaine Jones RC .30 .75
116 Scott Padgett RC .30 .75
117 Obinna Ekezie RC .30 .75
118 Ryan Robertson RC .25 .60
119 Chucky Atkins RC .40 1.00
120 A.J. Bramlett RC .40 1.00

1999-00 Black Diamond Diamond Cut

COMPLETE SET (120) 40.00 100.00
*STARS: .75X TO 2X BASE CARD HI
*RCs: .6X TO 1.5X BASE HI
STARS: STATED ODDS 1:6 H/R
RCs: STATED ODDS 1:12 H/R

1999-00 Black Diamond Final Cut

*STARS: 10X TO 25X BASE CARD HI
*RCs: 6X TO 12X BASE HI
STARS: PRINT RUN 100 SERIAL #'d SETS
RCs: PRINT RUN 50 SERIAL #'d SETS

1999-00 Black Diamond A Piece of History

Randomly inserted in packs at one in 336 for regular cards and one in 144 for hobby-only, this 25-card set features a "single" piece of a game-used basketball that was used by that particular player.

STATED ODDS 1:144 H; 1:336 H/R
*DOUBLE: 1.25X TO 3X BASE HI
DOUBLE STATED ODDS 1:864 H; 1:1008 H/R
*TRIPLE: 2.5X TO 6X HI
TRIPLE: PRINT RUN 25 SER.#'d SETS
AH Allan Houston H/R 2.50 6.00
AW Antoine Walker H 3.00 8.00
BD Baron Davis H 8.00 20.00
CB Charles Barkley H/R 15.00 40.00
CM Corey Maggette H/R 5.00 12.00
CW Chris Webber H 10.00 25.00
DG Devean George H 3.00 8.00
DR David Robinson H/R 5.00 12.00
GP Gary Payton H 6.00 15.00
HO Hakeem Olajuwon H 4.00 10.00
JB Jonathan Bender H 3.00 8.00
JS John Stockton H/R 4.00 10.00
JT Jason Terry H/R 5.00 12.00
JW Jason Williams H 8.00 20.00
KG Kevin Garnett H 5.00 12.00
KM Karl Malone H 4.00 10.00
KT Kenny Thomas H/R 3.00 8.00
MF Michael Finley H/R 3.00 8.00
PP Paul Pierce H/R 4.00 10.00
RM Reggie Miller H 3.00 8.00
SA Shareef Abdur-Rahim H/R 2.50 6.00
SF Steve Francis H 8.00 20.00
SO Shaquille O'Neal H/R 8.00 20.00
TB Terrell Brandon H 2.00 5.00
WS Wally Szczerbiak H/R 6.00 15.00

1999-00 Black Diamond Diamonation

Randomly inserted in packs at one in eight, this 10-card set features elite players who can take control of the game with their dominant play. Card backs carry a "D" prefix.

COMPLETE SET (10) 5.00 12.00
STATED ODDS 1:8 HOB/RET
D1 Vince Carter 1.00 2.50
D2 Tim Duncan 1.00 2.50
D3 Kobe Bryant 2.00 5.00
D4 Stephon Marbury .40 1.00
D5 Ron Mercer .40 1.00
D6 Allen Iverson 1.00 2.50
D7 Shareef Abdur-Rahim .40 1.00
D8 Kevin Garnett .75 2.00
D9 Jason Kidd .75 2.00
D10 Allan Houston .40 1.00

1999-00 Black Diamond Jordan Diamond Gallery

Randomly inserted in packs at one in 12, this 10-card set featured candid portrait photography of Michael Jordan. Card backs carry a "DG" prefix.

COMPLETE SET (10) 15.00 30.00
COMMON CARD (DG1-DG10) 2.00 5.00
STATED ODDS 1:12 HOB/RET
UNPRICED GOLD VERSION SERIAL #'d TO 1

1999-00 Black Diamond Might

Randomly inserted in packs at one in three, this 20-card set features some of the top powerhorses in the NBA. Card backs carry a "DM" prefix.

COMPLETE SET (20) 4.00 10.00
STATED ODDS 1:3 HOB/RET
DM1 Shaquille O'Neal 1.00 2.50
DM2 Allan Houston .30 .75
DM3 Keith Van Horn .30 .75
DM4 Antonie Walker .40 1.00
DM5 Latrell Sprewell .40 1.00
DM6 Hakeem Olajuwon .50 1.25
DM7 David Robinson .60 1.50
DM8 Antonio McDyess .30 .75
DM9 Shawn Kemp .40 1.00
DM10 Ray Allen .40 1.00
DM11 Karl Malone .50 1.25
DM12 Tim Hardaway .40 1.00
DM13 Mike Bibby .40 1.00
DM14 Antawn Jamison .40 1.00
DM15 Dikembe Mutombo .40 1.00
DM16 Michael Finley .40 1.00
DM17 Juwan Howard .30 .75
DM18 Maurice Taylor .25 .60
DM19 Gary Payton .40 1.00
DM20 Shareef Abdur-Rahim .30 .75

1999-00 Black Diamond Myriad

Randomly inserted in packs at one in 24, this 10-card set highlights the NBA's biggest stars in action. Card backs carry a "M" prefix.

COMPLETE SET (10) 10.00 25.00
STATED ODDS 1:24 HOB/RET
M1 Kobe Bryant 4.00 10.00
M2 Tim Duncan 2.00 5.00
M3 Kevin Garnett 1.50 4.00
M4 Keith Van Horn .75 2.00
M5 Vince Carter 2.00 5.00
M6 Grant Hill 1.25 3.00
M7 Anfernee Hardaway 1.50 4.00
M8 Karl Malone 1.25 3.00
M9 Allen Iverson 2.00 5.00
M10 Jason Williams 1.25 3.00

1999-00 Black Diamond Skills

Randomly inserted in packs at one in 24, this 10-card set takes a look at some of the most versatile athletes in the NBA. Card backs carry a "DS" prefix.

COMPLETE SET (10) 6.00 15.00
STATED ODDS 1:24 HOB/RET
DS1 Stephon Marbury .75 2.00
DS2 Grant Hill 1.25 3.00
DS3 Reggie Miller 1.00 2.50
DS4 Jason Kidd 1.50 4.00
DS5 Mike Bibby 1.00 2.50
DS6 John Stockton 1.25 3.00
DS7 Jason Williams 1.25 3.00
DS8 Shaquille O'Neal 2.50 6.00
DS9 Antonio McDyess .75 2.00
DS10 Hakeem Olajuwon 1.25 3.00

2000-01 Black Diamond

The 2000-01 Black Diamond product was released in March, 2001 and featured a 132-card base set that ws broken into tiers as follows: Base Veterans (1-90), and Rookies (91-132) that were broken into five groups. Group 1 (91-100) were serial numbered to 2000, Group 2 (101-110) were serial numbered to 1000, Group 3 (111-120) were serial numbered to 750, Group 4 (121-126) had a swatch of jersey and were serial numbered to 1750, and Group 5 (127-132) had a swatch of jersey and were serial numbered to 900. Each pack contained five cards, and carried a suggested retail price of $2.99.

COMP.SET w/o SP's (90) 8.00 20.00
91-100 PRINT RUN 2000 SER.#'d SETS
101-110 PRINT RUN 1000 SER.#'d SETS
111-120 PRINT RUN 750 SER.#'d SETS
121-126 PRINT RUN 1750 SER.#'d SETS
127-132 PRINT RUN 900 SER.#'d SETS
1 Dikembe Mutombo .30 .75
2 Alan Henderson .20 .50
3 Jason Terry .30 .75
4 Paul Pierce .30 .75
5 Antoine Walker .25 .60
6 Kenny Anderson .25 .60
7 Jamal Mashburn .25 .60
8 Derrick Coleman .25 .60
9 Baron Davis .30 .75
10 Elton Brand .30 .75
11 Ron Artest .30 .75
12 Ron Mercer .20 .50
13 Lamond Murray .20 .50
14 Andre Miller .25 .60
15 Matt Harpring .20 .50
16 Michael Finley .30 .75
17 Dirk Nowitzki .50 1.25
18 Steve Nash .50 1.25
19 Antonio McDyess .25 .60
20 Nick Van Exel .25 .60
21 Raef LaFrentz .20 .50
22 Jerry Stackhouse .25 .60
23 Joe Smith .25 .60
24 Chucky Atkins .20 .50
25 Antawn Jamison .30 .75
26 Larry Hughes .25 .60
27 Chris Mills .20 .50
28 Steve Francis .25 .60
29 Hakeem Olajuwon .40 1.00
30 Cuttino Mobley .20 .50
31 Reggie Miller .30 .75
32 Jalen Rose .25 .60
33 Jermaine O'Neal .25 .60
34 Austin Croshere .20 .50
35 Lamar Odom .25 .60
36 Corey Maggette .25 .60
37 Jeff McInnis .20 .50
38 Kobe Bryant 1.25 3.00
39 Shaquille O'Neal .75 2.00
40 Ron Harper .25 .60
41 Isaiah Rider .25 .60
42 Eddie Jones .30 .75
43 Tim Hardaway .30 .75
44 Brian Grant .20 .50
45 Glenn Robinson .25 .60
46 Sam Cassell .25 .60
47 Ray Allen .30 .75
48 Kevin Garnett .50 1.25
49 Terrell Brandon .20 .50
50 Wally Szczerbiak .25 .60
51 Stephon Marbury .25 .60
52 Keith Van Horn .25 .60
53 Kendall Gill .20 .50
54 Latrell Sprewell .25 .60
55 Allan Houston .25 .60
56 Marcus Camby .25 .60
57 Grant Hill .40 1.00
58 Tracy McGrady .50 1.25
59 Darrell Armstrong .20 .50
60 Allen Iverson .60 1.50
61 Toni Kukoc .30 .75
62 Theo Ratliff .20 .50
63 Jason Kidd .50 1.25
64 Shawn Marion .25 .60
65 Anfernee Hardaway .50 1.25
66 Scottie Pippen .50 1.25
67 Rasheed Wallace .30 .75
68 Damon Stoudamire .25 .60
69 Steve Smith .25 .60
70 Chris Webber .30 .75
71 Jason Williams .30 .75
72 Peja Stojakovic .30 .75
73 Tim Duncan .60 1.50
74 David Robinson .50 1.25
75 Derek Anderson .20 .50
76 Gary Payton .30 .75
77 Patrick Ewing .40 1.00
78 Rashard Lewis .30 .75
79 Vince Carter .60 1.50
80 Mark Jackson .25 .60
81 Antonio Davis .20 .50
82 Karl Malone .40 1.00
83 John Stockton .40 1.00
84 Bryon Russell .20 .50
85 Shareef Abdur-Rahim .25 .60
86 Michael Dickerson .20 .50
87 Mike Bibby .30 .75
88 Mitch Richmond .25 .60
89 Richard Hamilton .25 .60
90 Juwan Howard .25 .60
91 Eduardo Najera RC 1.25 3.00
92 Eddie House RC 1.00 2.50
93 Michael Redd RC 3.00 8.00
94 Ruben Wolkowyski RC .75 2.00
95 Dan Langhi RC .75 2.00
96 Mark Madsen RC 1.25 3.00
97 Speedy Claxton RC 1.25 3.00
98 Iakovos Tsakalidis RC .75 2.00
99 Dragan Tarlac RC .75 2.00
100 Donnell Harvey RC 1.00 2.50
101 Etan Thomas RC 1.50 4.00
102 Hedo Turkoglu RC 2.50 6.00
103 Mike Penberthy RC 1.50 4.00
104 Paul McPherson RC 1.00 2.50
105 Jason Collier RC 1.50 4.00
106 Hanno Mottola RC 1.00 2.50
107 A.J. Guyton RC 1.00 2.50
108 Daniel Santiago RC 1.50 4.00
109 Lavor Postell RC 1.00 2.50
110 Erick Barkley RC 1.00 2.50
111 Chris Porter RC 1.00 2.50
112 Mateen Cleaves RC 1.25 3.00
113 Marc Jackson RC 1.25 3.00
114 Joel Przybilla RC 1.25 3.00
115 Courtney Alexander RC 1.25 3.00
116 Khalid El-Amin RC 1.00 2.50
117 Keyon Dooling RC 1.50 4.00
118 Desmond Mason RC 2.00 5.00
119 Stephen Jackson RC 2.50 6.00
120 Morris Peterson RC 1.50 4.00
121 Jerome Moiso JSY RC 2.00 5.00
122 Jamal Crawford JSY RC 8.00 20.00
123 D.Stevenson JSY RC 3.00 8.00
124 Q.Richardson JSY RC 3.00 8.00
125 Marcus Fizer JSY RC 3.00 8.00
126 Mike Miller JSY RC 5.00 12.00
127 Jamaal Magloire JSY RC 4.00 10.00
128 Chris Mihm JSY RC 3.00 8.00
129 DerMarr Johnson JSY RC 3.00 8.00
130 Stromile Swift JSY RC 4.00 10.00
131 Darius Miles JSY RC 4.00 10.00
132 Kenyon Martin JSY RC 10.00 25.00

2000-01 Black Diamond Gold

*STARS 1-90: 1.5X TO 4X BASE HI
1-90 PRINT RUN 500 SERIAL #'d SETS
*GEMS 91-100: 1X TO 2.5X BASE HI
*GEMS 101-120: .8X TO 2X BASE HI
91-120 PRINT RUN 250 SERIAL #'d SETS
*JERSEY 121-126: .6X TO 1.5X BASE HI
*JERSEY 127-132: .5X TO 1.25X BASE HI
121-132 PRINT RUN 100 SERIAL #'d SETS

2000-01 Black Diamond Gold Jersey Autographs

Randomly inserted in packs at the rate of one in 280, this 12-card set parallels the Gold Rookie Jersey cards, numbers 121-132, and are enhanced with player autographs. Card print runs vary, and are all sequentially numbered to either 100, 150, or 200. Jamaal Magloire, card number 122A, and Kenyon Martin, card number 132A, were initially released as exchange cards.

STATED ODDS 1:280
121A Jerome Moiso/150 8.00 20.00
122A Jamal Crawford/200 15.00 40.00
123A DeShawn Stevenson/200 6.00 15.00
124A Quentin Richardson/150 6.00 15.00
125A Marcus Fizer/150 6.00 15.00
126A Mike Miller/150 6.00 15.00
130A Stromile Swift/100 6.00 15.00
131A Darius Miles/100 6.00 15.00

2000-01 Black Diamond Diamonation

Randomly inserted into packs at one in 10, this 14-card insert features players that dominate the game. Card backs carry a "D" prefix.

COMPLETE SET (14) 6.00 15.00
STATED ODDS 1:10
D1 Kobe Bryant 1.50 4.00
D2 Steve Francis .30 .75
D3 Allen Iverson .75 2.00
D4 Kevin Garnett .60 1.50
D5 Tracy McGrady .60 1.50
D6 Michael Finley .40 1.00
D7 Paul Pierce .40 1.00
D8 Shaquille O'Neal 1.00 2.50
D9 Vince Carter .75 2.00
D10 Larry Hughes .30 .75
D11 Grant Hill .50 1.25
D12 Latrell Sprewell .30 .75
D13 Jerry Stackhouse .30 .75
D14 Tim Duncan .75 2.00

2000-01 Black Diamond Gallery

Randomly inserted into packs at one in 18, this 6-card insert features a gallery of talented players. Card backs carry a "DG" prefix.

COMPLETE SET (6) 3.00 8.00
STATED ODDS 1:18
DG1 Kobe Bryant 1.50 4.00
DG2 Vince Carter .75 2.00
DG3 Kevin Garnett .60 1.50
DG4 Shaquille O'Neal 1.00 2.50
DG5 Tim Duncan .75 2.00
DG6 Steve Francis .30 .75

2000-01 Black Diamond Game Gear

Randomly inserted into hobby packs at one in 20, this 28-card insert features swatches of actual game-used memorabilia. Card backs carry the player's initials as numbering.

STATED ODDS 1:20 HOBBY
AH Anfernee Hardaway 5.00 12.00
AW Antoine Walker 2.50 6.00
BD Baron Davis 3.00 8.00
CP Chris Porter 2.00 5.00
DM Dikembe Mutombo 3.00 8.00
DN Dirk Nowitzki 5.00 12.00
DS DeShawn Stevenson 3.00 8.00
GH Grant Hill 4.00 10.00
GR Glen Rice 2.50 6.00
IR Isaiah Rider 2.50 6.00
JM Jamal Mashburn 2.50 6.00
KB Kobe Bryant 12.00 30.00
KE Khalid El-Amin 2.00 5.00
KG1 Kevin Garnett 5.00 12.00
KG2 Kevin Garnett 5.00 12.00
KM Karl Malone 4.00 10.00
LH Larry Hughes 2.50 6.00
LS Latrell Sprewell 2.50 6.00
MC Marcus Camby 2.50 6.00
MF Michael Finley 3.00 8.00
MM Mike Miller 5.00 12.00
PP Paul Pierce 3.00 8.00
RA Ron Artest 3.00 8.00
SM Stephon Marbury 2.50 6.00
TB Terrell Brandon 2.00 5.00
TG Tom Gugliotta 2.00 5.00
TM Tracy McGrady 5.00 12.00
WS Wally Szczerbiak 2.50 6.00

2000-01 Black Diamond Might

Randomly inserted into packs at one in 8, this 11-card insert features players that have the will to win. Card backs carry a "DM" prefix.

COMPLETE SET (11) 4.00 10.00
STATED ODDS 1:8
DM1 Shaquille O'Neal 1.00 2.50
DM2 Allen Iverson .75 2.00
DM3 Vince Carter .75 2.00
DM4 Chris Webber .40 1.00
DM5 Elton Brand .40 1.00
DM6 Karl Malone .50 1.25
DM7 Rasheed Wallace .40 1.00
DM8 Antawn Jamison .40 1.00
DM9 Kevin Garnett .60 1.50
DM10 Antonio McDyess .30 .75
DM11 Kobe Bryant 1.50 4.00

2000-01 Black Diamond Skills

Randomly inserted into packs at one in 8, this 11-card insert features some of the NBA's most skilled players. Card backs carry a "DS" prefix.

COMPLETE SET (11) 4.00 10.00
STATED ODDS 1:8
DS1 Kevin Garnett .60 1.50
DS2 Jason Kidd .60 1.50
DS3 Allen Iverson .75 2.00
DS4 Gary Payton .40 1.00
DS5 Tim Duncan .75 2.00
DS6 Eddie Jones .40 1.00
DS7 Grant Hill .50 1.25
DS8 Andre Miller .30 .75
DS9 Jason Williams .40 1.00
DS10 Kobe Bryant 1.50 4.00
DS11 Ray Allen .40 1.00

2003-04 Black Diamond

Released in December 2003, Black Diamond boasts a 198-card set divided up as follows: Single Diamond veterans are featured on card numbers 1-84; Double Diamond veterans, card numbers 85-117, are inserted at the rate of one in two; Double Diamond rookies, card numbers 118-126, are inserted at the rate of one in two, Triple Diamond veterans, card numbers 127-147, are inserted at the rate of one in eight; Triple Diamond rookies, card numbers 148-168, are inserted at the rate of one in eight; Quadruple Diamond veterans, card numbers 169-183, are inserted at the rate of one in 48; and Quadruple Diamond rookies, card numbers 184-198, are inserted at the rate of one in 48. Two players, Kyle Korver and Kerry Kittles are featured on two different cards in the set. All cards are printed on foil, feature full-color player action photos, and have diamonds in the lower right-hand corner for quick

refernce to see if the card is a Single, Double, Triple or Quadruple Diamond Version. Black Diamond was packaged in 24-pack boxes of five-card packs and carried a suggested retail price of $3.99.
COMP.SET w/o SP's (84) 6.00 15.00
85-126 STATED ODDS 1:2
127-168 STATED ODDS 1:8
169-198 STATED ODDS 1:48
KORVER AND KITTLES HAVE 2 CARDS
UNPRICED RAINBOW PRINT RUN 10 SETS
1 Carlos Boozer .25 .60
2 Dajuan Wagner .20 .50
3 Steve Francis .25 .60
4 Michael Finley .30 .75
5 Jalen Rose .25 .60
6 Kenyon Martin .25 .60
7 Quentin Richardson .25 .60
8 Antoine Walker .30 .75
9 Drew Gooden .25 .60
10 Mike Bibby .30 .75
11 Zydrunas Ilgauskas .25 .60
12 Dan Dickau .20 .50
13 Steve Nash .40 1.00
14 Eduardo Najera .20 .50
15 Joe Smith .25 .60
16 Pau Gasol .30 .75
17 Anthony Mason .20 .50
18 Lamar Odom .25 .60
19 Sam Cassell .25 .60
20 Marko Jaric .20 .50
21 Marcus Fizer .20 .50
22 Jay Williams .20 .50
23 Jason Richardson .30 .75
24 Richard Jefferson .25 .60
25 Gerald Wallace .25 .60
26 Reggie Evans .20 .50
27 Jerome Williams .20 .50
28 Grant Hill .40 1.00
29 Darrell Armstrong .20 .50
30 Rasheed Wallace .30 .75
31 Shane Battier .25 .60
32 Richard Hamilton .25 .60
33 Antonio Davis .20 .50
34 Ray Allen .30 .75
35 Terrell Brandon .20 .50
36 Tim Thomas .20 .50
37 Al Harrington .25 .60
38 Brian Grant .20 .50
39 Zeljko Rebraca .20 .50
40 Kerry Kittles .20 .50
41 Maurice Taylor .20 .50
42 Jerry Stackhouse .25 .60
43 Nikoloz Tskitishvili .20 .50
44 Derrick Coleman .25 .60
45 Raef LaFrentz .20 .50
46 Dale Davis .20 .50
47 Andrei Kirilenko .30 .75
48 Melvin Ely .20 .50
49 Speedy Claxton .20 .50
50 Mike Miller .25 .60
51 Scot Pollard .20 .50
52 Popeye Jones .20 .50
53 Wesley Person .20 .50
54 Chris Wilcox .20 .50
55 Dikembe Mutombo .30 .75
56 Toni Kukoc .30 .75
57 Eddie Griffin .20 .50
58 Kedrick Brown .20 .50
59 Eddie Jones .25 .60
60 Jon Barry .20 .50
61 Jonathan Bender .20 .50
62 Larry Hughes .25 .60
63 Rodney White .20 .50
64 Eddy Curry .20 .50
65 Theo Ratliff .20 .50
66 Jamaal Tinsley .20 .50
67 Zach Randolph .25 .60
68 Alvin Williams .20 .50
69 Derek Fisher .25 .60
70 Vin Baker .20 .50
71 Juan Dixon .20 .50
72 Devean George .20 .50
73 Damon Stoudamire .25 .60
74 Joe Johnson .25 .60
75 Jared Jeffries .20 .50
76 Cuttino Mobley .20 .50
77 Vladimir Radmanovic .20 .50
78 Ron Mercer .20 .50
79 Kenny Thomas .20 .50
80 Nazr Mohammed .20 .50
81 Donyell Marshall .20 .50
82 Lorenzen Wright .20 .50
83 Nick Van Exel .25 .60
84 Jason Terry .25 .60
85 Ben Wallace .30 .75
86 Glenn Robinson .30 .75
87 Gilbert Arenas .30 .75
88 Caron Butler .30 .75
89 Marcus Camby .30 .75
90 Jason Kidd .60 1.50
91 Antawn Jamison .30 .75
92 Rashard Lewis .40 1.00
93 Juwan Howard .30 .75
94 Andre Miller .30 .75
95 Hedo Turkoglu .30 .75
96 Jason Williams .30 .75
97 Chauncey Billups .40 1.00
98 P.J. Brown .25 .60
99 Tyson Chandler .30 .75
100 Jamal Mashburn .30 .75
101 Bonzi Wells .25 .60
102 Brad Miller .30 .75
103 Gordan Giricek .25 .60
104 Nene .30 .75
105 Mike Dunleavy .30 .75
106 Kerry Kittles .25 .60
107 Jamaal Magloire .25 .60
108 Desmond Mason .30 .75
109 Corey Maggette .30 .75
110 Michael Olowokandi .25 .60
111 Tayshaun Prince .30 .75
112 Earl Boykins .25 .60
113 Allan Houston .30 .75
114 Morris Peterson .25 .60
115 Ricky Davis .30 .75
116 Keith Van Horn .30 .75
117 Shareef Abdur-Rahim .30 .75
118 Willie Green RC .75 2.00
119 Kyle Korver RC 1.50 4.00
120 Brandon Hunter RC .75 2.00
121 Keith Bogans RC .75 2.00
122 Maurice Williams RC 1.25 3.00
123 James Lang RC .75 2.00
124 Zaur Pachulia RC 1.25 3.00
125 Slavko Vranes RC .75 2.00
126 Theron Smith RC .75 2.00
127 Paul Pierce .75 2.00
128 Alonzo Mourning 1.00 2.50
129 Elton Brand .75 2.00
130 Manu Ginobili 1.00 2.50
131 Peja Stojakovic .75 2.00
132 Latrell Sprewell .60 1.50
133 Baron Davis .60 1.50
134 Stephon Marbury .60 1.50
135 Darius Miles .50 1.25
136 Antonio McDyess .60 1.50
137 Jermaine O'Neal .60 1.50
138 Scottie Pippen 1.25 3.00
139 Wally Szczerbiak .60 1.50
140 Chris Webber .75 2.00
141 Reggie Miller .75 2.00
142 Tony Parker .75 2.00
143 Karl Malone 1.00 2.50
144 David Robinson 1.25 3.00
145 Matt Harpring .50 1.25
146 Shawn Marion .60 1.50
147 Tim Duncan 1.25 3.00
148 Dwyane Wade RC 5.00 12.00
149 Chris Kaman RC 1.50 4.00
150 Chris Bosh RC 2.50 6.00
151 Mickael Pietrus RC 1.25 3.00
152 Boris Diaw RC 1.50 4.00
153 Marcus Banks RC 1.00 2.50
154 Troy Bell RC 1.00 2.50
155 Zarko Cabarkapa RC 1.00 2.50
156 David West RC 1.50 4.00
157 Zoran Planinic RC 1.00 2.50
158 Aleksandar Pavlovic RC 1.25 3.00
159 Jerome Beasley RC 1.00 2.50
160 Kyle Korver 2.00 5.00
161 Travis Hansen RC 1.00 2.50
162 Steve Blake RC 1.25 3.00
163 Leandro Barbosa RC 1.50 4.00
164 Kendrick Perkins RC 1.25 3.00
165 Kirk Penney RC 1.50 4.00
166 Maciej Lampe RC 1.00 2.50
167 Jason Kapono RC 1.00 2.50
168 Luke Walton RC 1.50 4.00
169 Gary Payton 1.50 4.00
170 Wilt Chamberlain 3.00 8.00
171 Tracy McGrady 2.00 5.00
172 Amare Stoudemire 2.00 5.00
173 Vince Carter 2.50 6.00
174 Shaquille O'Neal 4.00 10.00
175 Larry Bird 4.00 10.00
176 Julius Erving 2.50 6.00
177 Magic Johnson 4.00 10.00
178 Dirk Nowitzki 2.50 6.00
179 Yao Ming 3.00 8.00
180 Allen Iverson 2.50 6.00
181 Kevin Garnett 2.50 6.00
182 Kobe Bryant 6.00 15.00
183 Michael Jordan 12.00 30.00
184 LeBron James RC 60.00 150.00
185 Darko Milicic RC 2.50 6.00
186 Carmelo Anthony RC 10.00 25.00
187 T.J. Ford RC 2.50 6.00
188 Mike Sweetney RC 2.00 5.00
189 Kirk Hinrich RC 3.00 8.00
190 Nick Collison RC 2.50 6.00
191 Travis Outlaw RC 2.50 6.00
192 Jarvis Hayes RC 2.00 5.00
193 Luke Ridnour RC 2.50 6.00
194 Reece Gaines RC 2.00 5.00
195 Ndudi Ebi RC 2.00 5.00
196 Dahntay Jones RC 2.50 6.00
197 Brian Cook RC 2.00 5.00
198 Josh Howard RC 3.00 8.00
NNO Lebron James PROMO 6.00 15.00
with product information

2003-04 Black Diamond Bronze

*1-84 SINGLES: 4X TO 10X BASE HI
*85-117 SINGLES: 3X TO 8X BASE HI
*118-126 RCs: 1.5X TO 4X BASE HI
*127-147 SINGLES: 1.5X TO 4X BASE HI
*148-168 RCs: 1.25X TO 3X BASE HI
*169-183 SINGLES: .75X TO 2X BASE HI
*184-198 RCs: .6X TO 1.5X BASE HI
148 Dwyane Wade 25.00 60.00

2003-04 Black Diamond Gold

*1-84 SINGLES: 10X TO 25X BASE HI
*85-117 SINGLES: 8X TO 20X BASE HI
*118-126 RCs: 2.5X TO 6X BASE HI
*127-147 SINGLES: 4X TO 10X BASE HI
*148-168 RCs: 2X TO 5X BASE HI
*169-183 SINGLES: 2.5X TO 6X BASE HI
*184-198 RCs: 1X TO 2.5X BASE HI
GOLD PRINT RUN 25 SER.#'d SETS
148 Dwyane Wade 50.00 120.00

2003-04 Black Diamond 24 Karat Signatures

Inserted in packs at the rate of one in 72, this 42-card set features a full color player action photo and a holofoil autograph sticker on a white and gold background.
STATED ODDS 1:72
AJ Antawn Jamison 5.00 12.00
BA Marcus Banks 2.50 6.00
BE Jerome Beasley 2.50 6.00
BI Chauncey Billups 8.00 20.00
CA Carmelo Anthony/100 40.00 80.00
CB Caron Butler 8.00 20.00
CK Chris Kaman 4.00 10.00
CM Corey Maggette 4.00 10.00
CM Cuttino Mobley 4.00 10.00
DD Dan Dickau 4.00 10.00
DJ DerMarr Johnson 4.00 10.00
DM Darko Milicic/100 10.00 25.00
EB Earl Boykins 4.00 10.00
EG Eddie Griffin 4.00 10.00
GA Gilbert Arenas 8.00 20.00
GI Manu Ginobili 12.50 30.00
GP Gary Payton 12.50 30.00
JH Jarvis Hayes 2.50 6.00
JK Jason Kidd 15.00 40.00
JM Jerome Moiso 4.00 10.00
JR Jason Richardson 6.00 15.00
JS Jerry Stackhouse 6.00 15.00
KA Jason Kapono 2.50 6.00
KB Kobe Bryant/100 100.00 200.00
KE Keith Bogans 2.50 6.00
LJ LeBron James/100 500.00 1000.00
LW Luke Walton 4.00 10.00
MB Mike Bibby 8.00 20.00
MJ Michael Jordan/23 300.00 600.00
ML Maciej Lampe 2.50 6.00
MS Mike Sweetney 2.50 6.00
PP Paul Pierce 15.00 40.00
PS Peja Stojakovic 8.00 20.00
RE Reggie Evans 4.00 10.00
RG Reece Gaines 2.50 6.00
RH Richard Hamilton 4.00 10.00
RJ Richard Jefferson 4.00 10.00
SB Shane Battier 5.00 12.00
SM Shawn Marion 5.00 12.00
TM Tracy McGrady/100 30.00 80.00
TP Tony Parker/100 12.50 30.00
YM Yao Ming/100 20.00 50.00

2003-04 Black Diamond Jerseys

Inserted in packs at the rate of one in 14, this 63-card set features a horizontal design with player photos on the left and jersey swatches on the right. The card backgrounds look like broken glass and accent colors are set to match the player's team. A gold version was also inserted with gold background highlights and cards sequentially numbered to 100.
STATED ODDS 1:14
*GOLD: .6X TO 1.5X BASE JSY HI
GOLD PRINT RUN 100 SER.#'d SETS
BDAD Antonio Davis 2.00 5.00
BDAH Anfernee Hardaway 4.00 10.00
BDAI Allen Iverson 4.00 10.00
BDAM Aaron McKie 2.00 5.00
BDAW Antoine Walker 2.50 6.00
BDBA Lonny Baxter 2.00 5.00
BDBW Ben Wallace 2.00 5.00
BDCB Caron Butler 2.00 5.00
BDCM Corey Maggette 2.00 5.00
BDCW Charlie Ward 2.00 5.00
BDDF Derek Fisher 2.00 5.00
BDDM Darius Miles 2.00 5.00
BDDN Dirk Nowitzki 4.00 10.00
BDDW David Wesley 2.00 5.00
BDEB Elton Brand 2.50 6.00
BDEC Eddy Curry 1.50 4.00
BDEG Manu Ginobili 3.00 8.00
BDEJ Eddie Jones 2.00 5.00
BDES Eric Snow 2.00 5.00
BDFW Frank Williams 2.00 5.00
BDGH Grant Hill SP 5.00 12.00
BDGR Glenn Robinson 2.00 5.00
BDHO Allan Houston 2.00 5.00
BDHO Robert Horry 2.00 5.00
BDJA Mark Jackson 2.50 6.00
BDJB Jonathan Bender 2.00 5.00
BDJF Joe Forte 2.00 5.00
BDJJ Joe Johnson 2.00 5.00
BDJK Jason Kidd 4.00 10.00
BDJM Jamaal Magloire 2.00 5.00
BDJR Jason Richardson 2.50 6.00
BDKB Kobe Bryant SP 15.00 40.00
BDKG Kevin Garnett 4.00 10.00
BDKM Karl Malone 3.00 8.00
BDKR Kareem Rush 2.00 5.00
BDKV Keith Van Horn 2.00 5.00
BDKY Kenyon Martin 2.00 5.00
BDLH Larry Hughes 2.00 5.00
BDLO Lamar Odom 2.00 5.00
BDLS Latrell Sprewell 2.00 5.00
BDMA Jamal Mashburn 2.00 5.00
BDMB Mike Bibby 2.50 6.00
BDMC Marcus Camby 2.00 5.00
BDMF Marcus Fizer 2.00 5.00
BDMJ Michael Jordan SP 40.00 100.00
BDMM Mike Miller 2.00 5.00
BDMO Michael Olowokandi 2.00 5.00
BDMO Alonzo Mourning 4.00 10.00
BDMU Dikembe Mutombo 2.50 6.00
BDPG Pau Gasol 2.50 6.00
BDPP Paul Pierce 2.50 6.00
BDPS Peja Stojakovic 2.50 6.00
BDQW Qyntel Woods 2.00 5.00
BDRA Ray Allen 2.50 6.00
BDRL Rashard Lewis 2.50 6.00
BDRM Reggie Miller 2.50 6.00
BDRW Rasheed Wallace 2.50 6.00
BDSM Joe Smith 2.00 5.00
BDST Stephon Marbury 2.00 5.00
BDTM Tracy McGrady 3.00 8.00
BDWE Chris Webber 2.50 6.00
BDWI Chris Wilcox 2.00 5.00
BDYM Yao Ming 5.00 12.00

2003-04 Black Diamond Jerseys Double Diamond

Randomly seeded, this 26-card set parallels the base Jerseys set enhanced with two diamonds in the lower right-hand corner of the card and sequential numbering to 250. A Gold version sequentially numbered to 75 was also produced and is noticably different by its gold background.
PRINT RUN 250 SER.#'d SETS
*GOLD: .6X TO 1.5X JSY HI
GOLD PRINT RUN 75 SER.#'d SETS
BD2AW Antoine Walker 4.00 10.00
BD2CA Carmelo Anthony 12.00 30.00
BD2CB Caron Butler 3.00 8.00
BD2DM Darius Miles 2.50 6.00
BD2EB Elton Brand 4.00 10.00
BD2EG Manu Ginobili 5.00 12.00
BD2GA Gilbert Arenas 3.00 8.00
BD2GH Grant Hill 5.00 12.00
BD2JR Jason Richardson 4.00 10.00
BD2KB Kobe Bryant 15.00 40.00
BD2KM Kenyon Martin 3.00 8.00
BD2LJ LeBron James 50.00 120.00
BD2LS Latrell Sprewell 3.00 8.00
BD2MB Mike Bibby 4.00 10.00
BD2MI Darko Milicic 3.00 8.00
BD2MJ Michael Jordan 50.00 120.00
BD2MM Mike Miller 3.00 8.00
BD2PG Pau Gasol 4.00 10.00
BD2PP Paul Pierce 4.00 10.00
BD2RA Ray Allen 4.00 10.00
BD2RL Rashard Lewis 4.00 10.00
BD2RM Reggie Miller 4.00 10.00
BD2RW Rasheed Wallace 4.00 10.00
BD2SM Stephon Marbury 3.00 8.00
BD2SO Shaquille O'Neal 10.00 25.00
BD2TP Tony Parker 4.00 10.00

2003-04 Black Diamond Jerseys Quadruple Diamond

Randomly seeded, this 6-card set parallels the base Jerseys set enhanced with four diamonds in the lower right-hand corner of the card and sequential numbering to 50. A Gold version sequentially numbered to 25 was also produced and is noticably different by its gold background.
PRINT RUN 50 SER.#'d SETS
*GOLD: .6X TO 1.5X BASE HI
GOLD PRINT RUN 25 SER.#'d SETS
BD4AI Allen Iverson 12.00 30.00
BD4KB Kobe Bryant 40.00 100.00
BD4LJ LeBron James 80.00 200.00
BD4MJ Michael Jordan 100.00 225.00
BD4TM Tracy McGrady 10.00 25.00
BD4YM Yao Ming 15.00 40.00

2003-04 Black Diamond Jerseys Triple Diamond

Randomly seeded, this 10-card set parallels the base Jerseys set enhanced with three diamonds in the lower right-hand corner of the card and sequential numbering to 100. A Gold version sequentially numbered to 50 was also produced and is noticably different by its gold background.
PRINT RUN 100 SER.#'d SETS
*GOLD: .6X TO 1.5X BASE JSY HI
GOLD PRINT RUN 50 SER.#'d SETS
BD3AS Amare Stoudemire 6.00 15.00
BD3CW Chris Webber 5.00 12.00
BD3DN Dirk Nowitzki 8.00 20.00
BD3JK Jason Kidd 8.00 20.00
BD3KB Kobe Bryant 20.00 50.00
BD3KG Kevin Garnett 8.00 20.00
BD3LJ LeBron James 80.00 200.00
BD3MJ Michael Jordan 60.00 150.00
BD3SN Steve Nash 6.00 15.00
BD3TD Tim Duncan 8.00 20.00

2004-05 Black Diamond

Released in March, Black Diamond consists of a 198-card set that features four tiers for the veteran players and two for the rookies. The card design places a player on a card that is bordered only on the bottom and about a third of the way up on the left and right that contains the player's name, the card's highlight color and the diamond logo that indicates what tier the card falls into. Highlight colors are as follows: Single Dimond cards have blue highlights, Double Diamond cards have red highlights, Triple Diamond cards have green highlights and Quadruple Diamond cards have black highlights. The tiers break down as follows: cards 1-84 feature single Diamond Veterans, cards 85-126 are inserted at the rate of one in two packs and feature Double Diamond veterans, cards 127-147 are inserted at the rate of one in eight packs and feature Triple Diamond veterans, cards 148-162 are inserted at the rate of one in 30 packs and feature Quadruple Diamond veterans, cards 163-183 are inserted at the rate of one in eight packs and feature Triple Diamond rookies, and cards 184-198 are inserted at the rate of one in 30 packs and feature Quadruple Diamond rookies.
COMP.SET w/o SPs (84) 8.00 20.00
85-126 DOUBLE STATED ODDS 1:2
127-147 TRIPLE STATED ODDS 1:8
148-162 QUAD STATED ODDS 1:30
163-183 TRIPLE RC STATED ODDS 1:8
184-198 QUAD RC STATED ODDS 1:30
UNPRICED BLACK PRINT RUN 5 SETS
1 Tony Delk .20 .50
2 Boris Diaw .25 .60
3 Chris Crawford .20 .50
4 Ricky Davis .25 .60
5 Jiri Welsch .20 .50
6 Raef LaFrentz .20 .50
7 Jason Kapono .20 .50
8 Brevin Knight .20 .50
9 Bernard Robinson RC 1.00 2.50
10 Jahidi White .20 .50
11 Tyson Chandler .25 .60
12 Antonio Davis .20 .50
13 Andres Nocioni RC 1.25 3.00
14 Dajuan Wagner .20 .50
15 Zydrunas Ilgauskas .25 .60
16 Jeff McInnis .20 .50
17 Josh Howard .30 .75
18 Marquis Daniels .20 .50
19 Jason Terry .25 .60
20 Andre Miller .25 .60
21 Earl Boykins .20 .50
22 Carlos Delfino .20 .50
23 Ben Wallace .25 .60
24 Tayshaun Prince .25 .60
25 Mickael Pietrus .25 .60
26 Mike Dunleavy .25 .60
27 Speedy Claxton .20 .50
28 Jim Jackson .20 .50
29 Juwan Howard .25 .60
30 Maurice Taylor .20 .50
31 Tyronn Lue .20 .50
32 Jamaal Tinsley .20 .50
33 Stephen Jackson .25 .60
34 Fred Jones .20 .50
35 Kerry Kittles .20 .50
36 Marko Jaric .20 .50
37 Chris Kaman .25 .60
38 Caron Butler .25 .60
39 Kareem Rush .20 .50
40 Mike Miller .25 .60
41 James Posey .20 .50
42 Stromile Swift .20 .50
43 Eddie Jones .25 .60
44 Udonis Haslem .20 .50
45 Matt Freije RC 1.00 2.50
46 T.J. Ford .20 .50
47 Toni Kukoc .30 .75
48 Joe Smith .25 .60
49 Michael Olowokandi .20 .50
50 Wally Szczerbiak .25 .60
51 Troy Hudson .20 .50
52 Aaron Williams .20 .50
53 Alonzo Mourning .40 1.00
54 Nenad Krstic RC 1.25 3.00
55 Jamal Mashburn .25 .60
56 David Wesley .20 .50
57 Tim Pickett RC 1.25 3.00
58 Trevor Ariza RC 1.25 3.00
59 Tim Thomas .20 .50
60 Grant Hill .40 1.00
61 Hedo Turkoglu .25 .60
62 Kelvin Cato .20 .50
63 Kenny Thomas .20 .50
64 Aaron McKie .20 .50
65 Joe Johnson .25 .60
66 Quentin Richardson .25 .60
67 Damon Stoudamire .25 .60
68 Derek Anderson .20 .50
69 Nick Van Exel .25 .60
70 Doug Christie .20 .50
71 Bobby Jackson .20 .50
72 Malik Rose .20 .50
73 Rasho Nesterovic .20 .50
74 Romain Sato RC .75 2.00
75 Ronald Murray .20 .50
76 Luke Ridnour .25 .60
77 Pape Sow RC 1.00 2.50
78 Rafer Alston .20 .50
79 Morris Peterson .20 .50
80 Matt Harpring .20 .50
81 Mehmet Okur .25 .60
82 Larry Hughes .25 .60
83 Jarvis Hayes .20 .50
84 Kwame Brown .20 .50
85 Antoine Walker .50 1.25
86 Al Harrington .40 1.00
87 Gary Payton .50 1.25
88 Gerald Wallace .40 1.00
89 Eddy Curry .30 .75
90 Kirk Hinrich .40 1.00
91 Drew Gooden .30 .75
92 Michael Finley .50 1.25
93 Jerry Stackhouse .40 1.00
94 Kenyon Martin .40 1.00
95 Nene .40 1.00
96 Chauncey Billups .50 1.25
97 Richard Hamilton .40 1.00
98 Derek Fisher .40 1.00
99 Reggie Miller .50 1.25
100 Ron Artest .50 1.25
101 Corey Maggette .40 1.00
102 Lamar Odom .40 1.00
103 Karl Malone .60 1.50
104 Jason Williams .40 1.00
105 Bonzi Wells .30 .75
106 Desmond Mason .40 1.00
107 Sam Cassell .40 1.00
108 Jamaal Magloire .30 .75
109 Jamal Crawford .50 1.25
110 Allan Houston .40 1.00
111 Cuttino Mobley .30 .75
112 Glenn Robinson .40 1.00
113 Shawn Marion .40 1.00
114 Darius Miles .30 .75
115 Zach Randolph .40 1.00
116 Chris Webber .50 1.25
117 Mike Bibby .50 1.25
118 Brad Miller .40 1.00
119 Manu Ginobili .60 1.50
120 Rashard Lewis .50 1.25
121 Jalen Rose .40 1.00
122 Chris Bosh .50 1.25
123 Carlos Boozer .40 1.00
124 Carlos Arroyo .30 .75
125 Gilbert Arenas .40 1.00
126 Antawn Jamison .40 1.00
127 Paul Pierce 1.00 2.50
128 Dirk Nowitzki 1.50 4.00
129 Rasheed Wallace 1.00 2.50
130 Jason Richardson 1.00 2.50
131 Jermaine O'Neal .75 2.00
132 Elton Brand 1.00 2.50
133 Pau Gasol 1.00 2.50
134 Dwyane Wade 1.50 4.00
135 Michael Redd .75 2.00
136 Latrell Sprewell .75 2.00
137 Richard Jefferson .75 2.00
138 Baron Davis .75 2.00
139 Stephon Marbury .75 2.00
140 Steve Francis .75 2.00
141 Steve Nash 1.25 3.00
142 Shareef Abdur-Rahim .75 2.00
143 Peja Stojakovic 1.00 2.50
144 Tony Parker 1.00 2.50
145 Ray Allen 1.00 2.50
146 Vince Carter 1.50 4.00
147 Andrei Kirilenko .75 2.00
148 Larry Bird 3.00 8.00
149 Michael Jordan 10.00 25.00
150 LeBron James 8.00 20.00
151 Carmelo Anthony 2.50 6.00
152 Tracy McGrady 1.50 4.00
153 Yao Ming 2.50 6.00
154 Kobe Bryant 5.00 12.00
155 Magic Johnson 3.00 8.00
156 Shaquille O'Neal 3.00 8.00
157 Kevin Garnett 2.00 5.00
158 Jason Kidd 2.00 5.00
159 Allen Iverson 2.00 5.00
160 Julius Erving 2.00 5.00
161 Amare Stoudemire 1.00 2.50
162 Tim Duncan 2.00 5.00
163 Andris Biedrins RC 1.50 4.00
164 Robert Swift RC 1.50 4.00
165 Al Jefferson RC 3.00 8.00
166 Kirk Snyder RC 1.50 4.00
167 Dorell Wright RC 2.50 6.00
168 Pavel Podkolzin RC 1.50 4.00
169 Viktor Khryapa RC 1.50 4.00
170 Delonte West RC 2.50 6.00
171 Tony Allen RC 2.50 6.00
172 Kevin Martin RC 3.00 8.00
173 Sasha Vujacic RC 2.50 6.00
174 Beno Udrih RC 2.00 5.00
175 David Harrison RC 1.50 4.00
176 Anderson Varejao RC 2.00 5.00
177 Jackson Vroman RC 1.50 4.00
178 Peter John Ramos RC 1.50 4.00
179 Lionel Chalmers RC 2.50 6.00
180 Andre Emmett RC 1.50 4.00
181 Yuta Tabuse RC 2.50 6.00
182 Trevor Ariza RC 2.50 6.00
183 Chris Duhon RC 2.50 6.00
184 Dwight Howard RC 6.00 15.00
185 Emeka Okafor RC 2.50 6.00
186 Ben Gordon RC 3.00 8.00
187 Shaun Livingston RC 3.00 8.00
188 Devin Harris RC 2.50 6.00
189 Josh Childress RC 2.50 6.00
190 Luol Deng RC 3.00 8.00
191 Andre Iguodala RC 4.00 10.00
192 Luke Jackson RC 2.00 5.00
193 Sebastian Telfair RC 2.50 6.00
194 Kris Humphries RC 3.00 8.00
195 Josh Smith RC 3.00 8.00
196 J.R. Smith RC 3.00 8.00
197 Jameer Nelson RC 3.00 8.00
198 Rafael Araujo RC 2.00 5.00

2004-05 Black Diamond Green

*1-84 SINGLE: 6X TO 15X BASE HI
*1-84 SINGLE RC: 2.5X TO 6X BASE HI
*85-126 DOUBLE: 4X TO 10X BASE HI
*127-147 TRIPLE: 2X TO 5X BASE HI
*148-162 QUAD: 1.5X TO 4X BASE HI
*163-183 RC TRIPLE: .75X TO 2X BASE HI
*184-198 RC QUAD: .6X TO 1.5X BASE HI
PRINT RUN 25 SER.#'d SETS
134 Dwyane Wade 20.00 50.00
149 Michael Jordan 50.00 125.00

2004-05 Black Diamond Red

*1-84 SINGLE: 3X TO 8X BASE HI
*1-84 SINGLE RC: 1X TO 2.5X BASE HI
*85-126 DOUBLE: 2X TO 5X BASE HI
*127-147 TRIPLE: 1X TO 2.5X BASE HI
*148-162 QUAD: .75X TO 2X BASE HI
*163-183 RC TRIPLE: .5X TO 1.25X BASE HI
*184-198 RC QUAD: .4X TO 1X BASE HI
PRINT RUN 100 SER.#'d SETS
149 Michael Jordan 50.00 80.00

2004-05 Black Diamond UD Promos

*PROMOS: .75X TO 2X BASIC

2004-05 Black Diamond Die Cuts

Inserted in packs at the rate of one in ten, this 42-card set features players in action on a card that is die cut on all four corners and a blue strip. This first die cut set is the single diamond version and a blue strip runs along the left side of the card. The double diamond version is inserted at one in 20 packs, utilizes the same card design but has a red strip along the left. The Triple Diamond version is inserted at one in 100 and has a green strip along the left side, and the quad version is inserted at one in 400 and has a black strip along the left.
STATED ODDS 1:10
*DC DOUBLE: .5X TO 1.25X BASE HI
DC DOUBLE STATED ODDS 1:20
*DC TRIPLE: .6X TO 1.5X BASE HI
DC TRIPLE STATED ODDS 1:100
*DC QUAD: 2X TO 5X BASE HI
DC QUAD STATED ODDS 1:400
DC1 LeBron James 8.00 20.00
DC2 Michael Jordan 10.00 25.00
DC3 Kobe Bryant 5.00 12.00
DC4 Dwight Howard 2.50 6.00
DC5 Tracy McGrady 1.50 4.00
DC6 Kevin Garnett 2.00 5.00
DC7 Emeka Okafor 1.00 2.50
DC8 Ben Gordon 1.25 3.00
DC9 Shaun Livingston 1.25 3.00
DC10 Devin Harris 1.00 2.50
DC11 Josh Childress 1.00 2.50
DC12 Luol Deng 1.25 3.00
DC13 Andre Iguodala 1.50 4.00
DC14 Sebastian Telfair 1.00 2.50
DC15 Josh Smith 1.25 3.00
DC16 J.R. Smith 1.25 3.00
DC17 Jameer Nelson 1.25 3.00
DC18 Larry Bird 3.00 8.00
DC19 Carmelo Anthony 2.50 6.00
DC20 Yao Ming 2.50 6.00
DC21 Magic Johnson 3.00 8.00
DC22 Shaquille O'Neal 3.00 8.00
DC23 Jason Kidd 2.00 5.00
DC24 Allen Iverson 2.00 5.00
DC25 Julius Erving 2.00 5.00
DC26 Amare Stoudemire 1.00 2.50
DC27 Tim Duncan 2.00 5.00
DC28 Paul Pierce 1.25 3.00
DC29 Dirk Nowitzki 2.00 5.00
DC30 Dwyane Wade 2.00 5.00
DC31 Baron Davis 1.00 2.50
DC32 Stephon Marbury 1.00 2.50
DC33 Steve Francis 1.00 2.50
DC34 Steve Nash 1.50 4.00
DC35 Peja Stojakovic 1.25 3.00
DC36 Tony Parker 1.25 3.00
DC37 Ray Allen 1.25 3.00
DC38 Vince Carter 2.00 5.00
DC39 Andrei Kirilenko 1.00 2.50
DC40 Mike Bibby 1.25 3.00
DC41 Ben Wallace 1.00 2.50
DC42 Manu Ginobili 1.50 4.00

2004-05 Black Diamond GemoGRAPHy

Seeded in packs at the rate of one in 20, this 36-card set is printed on foil board with a player image along the top of the card and an autograph box along the bottom. The autograph box is colored to match the feature player's team colors.
STATED ODDS 1:20
AH Al Harrington 4.00 10.00
AI Andre Iguodala 5.00 12.00
AK Andrei Kirilenko 4.00 10.00
AS Amare Stoudemire SP 12.50 30.00
BG Ben Gordon 4.00 10.00
BR Bernard Robinson 3.00 8.00
CA Carmelo Anthony SP 20.00 50.00
CB Carlos Boozer 6.00 15.00
DE Devin Harris 3.00 8.00
DH Dwight Howard 12.00 30.00
JC Josh Childress 3.00 8.00
JN Jameer Nelson 4.00 10.00
JR J.R. Smith 4.00 10.00
JS Josh Smith 4.00 10.00
KB Kobe Bryant SP 125.00 300.00
KG Kevin Garnett SP 20.00 50.00
KH Kris Humphries 4.00 10.00
LD Luol Deng 4.00 10.00
LJ LeBron James SP 100.00 200.00
LU Luke Jackson 2.50 6.00
MB Mike Bibby 4.00 10.00
MF Matt Freije 3.00 8.00
MJ Michael Jordan SP 250.00 500.00
PG Pau Gasol 6.00 15.00
PS Pape Sow 3.00 8.00
RA Rafael Araujo 2.50 6.00
RJ Richard Jefferson 4.00 10.00
RM Reggie Miller 75.00 200.00
RO Romain Sato 2.50 6.00
RS Robert Swift 2.50 6.00
SE Sebastian Telfair 3.00 8.00
SL Shaun Livingston 4.00 10.00
ST Stephon Marbury 6.00 15.00
TA Trevor Ariza 4.00 10.00
TM Tracy McGrady SP 20.00 50.00
ZR Zach Randolph 4.00 10.00

2004-05 Black Diamond Jerseys

Inserted in packs at one in 13, this 42-card set is horizontally designed with a player photo on the left and a swatch of jersey on the right. The base level of this set is considered the single diamond, has the single diamond logo and highlight colors along the top and bottom of the card are in blue. There are three parallels to this set, Double Diamond, Triple Diamond and Quadruple Diamond, and for each progressive set, the jersey swatch gets larger. Doubles are highlighted with red, contain the double diamond logo and are squentially numbered to 250. Triples are highlighted with green, contain the double diamond logo and are squentially numbered to 100. Quads are highlighted with black, contain the double diamond logo, are squentially numbered to 10 and contain player autographs.
STATED ODDS 1:13
*DOUBLE: .5X TO 1.25X BASE HI
DOUBLE PRINT RUN 250 SER.#'d SETS
*TRIPLE: .6X TO 1.5X BASE HI
TRIPLE PRINT RUN 100 SER.#'d SETS
UNPRICED QUAD AU PRINT RUN 10 SETS
AI Allen Iverson 6.00 15.00
AN Andre Iguodala 3.00 8.00
AS Amare Stoudemire 2.00 5.00
AV Anderson Varejao 2.00 5.00
BD Baron Davis 2.00 5.00
BG Ben Gordon 2.50 6.00
CA Carmelo Anthony 5.00 12.00
CB Chauncey Billups 2.50 6.00
CD Chris Duhon 2.50 6.00
DA David Harrison 1.50 4.00
DB Elton Brand 2.50 6.00
DE Devin Harris 2.00 5.00
DH Dwight Howard 5.00 12.00
DN Dirk Nowitzki 4.00 10.00
DW Dajuan Wagner 2.00 5.00
EG Manu Ginobili 3.00 8.00
JC Jamal Crawford 2.50 6.00
JK Jason Kidd 4.00 10.00
JO Josh Childress 2.00 5.00
JR J.R. Smith 2.50 6.00
JS Josh Smith 2.50 6.00
JV Jackson Vroman 1.50 4.00
KB Kobe Bryant SP 10.00 25.00
KG Kevin Garnett 4.00 10.00
KM Kevin Martin 3.00 8.00
LC Lionel Chalmers 2.50 6.00
LD Luol Deng 2.50 6.00
LJ LeBron James SP 15.00 40.00
LU Luke Jackson 1.50 4.00
MJ Michael Jordan SP 30.00 80.00
RJ Richard Jefferson 2.00 5.00
RW Rasheed Wallace 2.50 6.00
SE Sebastian Telfair 2.00 5.00
SF Steve Francis 2.00 5.00
SL Shaun Livingston 2.50 6.00
SO Shaquille O'Neal 6.00 15.00
TA Tony Allen 2.50 6.00
TD Tim Duncan 4.00 10.00
TM Tracy McGrady 3.00 8.00
WE Delonte West 2.50 6.00
YT Yuta Tabuse 2.50 6.00
AU Andre Emmett 1.50 4.00

1994 Bleachers 23 Karat Promos

These standard-size promo cards were issued to promote two products licensed by Classic but produced by Bleachers, the 23K all-gold sculptured cards and Bleachers prototypical gold border cards. One promo card was included in each gold foil-stamped box that contained the all-gold sculptured card. These promo cards read "Original 23 Karat Genuine All-Gold Sculptured Trading Cards" at the bottom. Some of these card fronts have Bleachers logos while others have Classic logos. The other promo cards read "The Original 23 Karat Genuine Gold Border Basketball Cards" at the bottom. The fronts of show full-bleed color action player photos with an advertisement across the bottom. On a wood-grain background, the backs carry player profile and a facsimile autograph. The cards are unnumbered and checklisted below in alphabetical order.
COMPLETE SET (7) 1.00 2.50
1 Alonzo Mourning .08 .25
2 Shaquille O'Neal .20 .50
3 Shaquille O'Neal .20 .50
4 Shaquille O'Neal .20 .50
5 Shaquille O'Neal .20 .50
6 Chris Webber .08 .25
7 Class of '93 .20 .50

1997 Bleachers/Fleer Gold Promos

This 2-card promo set was first released at the 1997 18th National Sports Collectors Convention in Cleveland, Ohio. The standard size cards are sculpted in Genuine 23 karat gold and are crafted to parallel these players' 1993-94 Fleer rookie cards. The backs have a "23 KT Gold Card" logo and are numbered "Prototype of 10,000". The cards were distributed individually in CD jewel cases. The actual set of 12 different Fleer rookie card parallels was not live at press time. Scheduled for release of 100,000 each are Michael Jordan, Karl Malone, Charles Barkley, Patrick Ewing, Hakeem Olajuwon, Clyde Drexler, Dennis Rodman, Scottie Pippen, Shawn Kemp, Shaquille O'Neal, Anfernee Hardaway and Grant Hill. The promo cards are unnumbered and listed below in alphabetical order.
COMPLETE SET (2) 2.00 5.00
1 Anfernee Hardaway 1.25 3.00
2 Grant Hill 1.25 3.00

1997 Bleachers/Fleer Gold

This 12-card set features embossed player images on 23 Karat all-gold sculptured cards. Each card was sold individually with a suggested retail price of $24.95 and packaged in a CD jewel case. The cards were packaged as six boxes per case with eight cards per box. The cards are unnumbered and checklisted below in alphabetical order. Each card is serially numbered with only 10,000 of each card produced. 17 matching serial number sets were also offered. These redemption cards were inserted at one in 2400 packs. The continuation line states the year of the player's original Fleer rookie card.
COMPLETE SET (12) 40.00 100.00
1 Charles Barkley 1986-87 5.00 12.00
2 Clyde Drexler 1986-87 4.00 10.00
3 Patrick Ewing 1986-87 4.00 10.00
4 Anfernee Hardaway 1993-94 5.00 12.00
5 Grant Hill 1994-95 5.00 12.00
6 Michael Jordan 1986-87 12.00 30.00
7 Shawn Kemp 1990-91 4.00 10.00
8 Karl Malone 1986-87 4.00 10.00
9 Hakeem Olajuwon 1986-87 4.00 10.00
10 Shaquille O'Neal 1992-93 8.00 20.00
11 Scottie Pippen 1988-89 5.00 12.00
12 Dennis Rodman 1988-89 6.00 15.00

1997 Bleachers/Fleer Gold Black Foil

COMPLETE SET (12) 60.00 150.00
1 Charles Barkley 1986-87 8.00 20.00
2 Clyde Drexler 1986-87 6.00 15.00
3 Patrick Ewing 1986-87 6.00 15.00
4 Anfernee Hardaway 1993-94 8.00 20.00
5 Grant Hill 1994-95 8.00 20.00
6 Michael Jordan 1986-87 20.00 50.00
7 Shawn Kemp 1990-91 6.00 15.00
8 Karl Malone 1986-87 6.00 15.00
9 Hakeem Olajuwon 1986-87 6.00 15.00
10 Shaquille O'Neal 1992-93 12.00 30.00
11 Scottie Pippen 1988-89 8.00 20.00
12 Dennis Rodman 1988-89 10.00 25.00

1997 Bleachers/Fleer Gold Holographic Foil

COMPLETE SET (12) 150.00 300.00
1 Charles Barkley 1986-87 12.00 30.00
2 Clyde Drexler 1986-87 10.00 25.00
3 Patrick Ewing 1986-87 10.00 25.00
4 Anfernee Hardaway 1993-94 12.00 30.00
5 Grant Hill 1994-95 12.00 30.00
6 Michael Jordan 1986-87 30.00 80.00
7 Shawn Kemp 1990-91 10.00 25.00
8 Karl Malone 1986-87 10.00 25.00
9 Hakeem Olajuwon 1986-87 10.00 25.00
10 Shaquille O'Neal 1992-93 20.00 50.00
11 Scottie Pippen 1988-89 12.00 30.00
12 Dennis Rodman 1988-89 15.00 40.00

1996-97 Blockbuster NBA at 50 Postcards

Distributed exclusively through Blockbuster music locations, this 5-card set features a colorful front with a post-card back. Collector's could mail in their postcard for a chance to win a trip for two to the 1997 NBA Conference Finals. The cards were available when purchasing the NBA at 50 - A Musical Celebration tapes or CD's. The cards are not numbered and listed in alphabetical order below.
COMPLETE SET (5) 4.00 10.00
1 Shareef Abdur-Rahim 1.50 4.00
2 Grant Hill 1.50 4.00
3 Hakeem Olajuwon 1.25 3.00
4 Scottie Pippen 1.50 4.00
5 Damon Stoudamire .75 2.00

1948 Bowman

The 1948 Bowman set of 72 cards was the company's only basketball issue. Five cards were issued in each pack. It was also the only major basketball issue until 1957-58 when Topps released a set. Cards in the set measure 2 1/16" by 2 1/2". The set is in color and features both player cards and diagram cards. The player cards in the second series are sometimes found without the red or blue printing on the card front, leaving only a gray background. These gray versions are more difficult to find, as they are printing errors where the printer apparently ran out of red or blue ink that was supposed to print on the player's uniform. The key Rookie Card in this set is George Mikan. Other Rookie Cards include Carl Braun, Joe Fulks, William Red Holzman, Jim Pollard, and Max Zaslofsky.
COMPLETE SET (72) 4000.00 6000.00
CARDS PRICED IN EX-MT CONDITION
1 Ernie Calverley RC 60.00 120.00
2 Ralph Hamilton 40.00 60.00
3 Gale Bishop 40.00 60.00
4 Fred Lewis RC 40.00 60.00
5 Basketball Play 30.00 50.00
Single cut off post
6 Bob Feerick RC 50.00 75.00
7 John Logan 40.00 60.00

8 Mel Riebe 40.00 60.00
9 Andy Phillip RC 50.00 100.00
10 Bob Davies RC 60.00 120.00
11 Basketball Play 30.00 50.00
Single cut with return pass to post
12 Kenny Sailors RC 50.00 75.00
13 Paul Armstrong 40.00 60.00
14 Howard Dallmar RC 50.00 75.00
15 Bruce Hale RC 50.00 75.00
16 Sid Hertzberg 50.00 75.00
17 Basketball Play 30.00 50.00
Single cut
18 Red Rocha 40.00 60.00
19 Eddie Ehlers 40.00 60.00
20 Ellis(Gene) Vance 40.00 60.00
21 Fuzzy Levane RC 50.00 75.00
22 Earl Shannon 40.00 60.00
23 Basketball Play 30.00 50.00
Double cut off post
24 Leo (Crystal) Klier 40.00 60.00
25 George Senesky 40.00 60.00
26 Price Brookfield 40.00 60.00
27 John Norlander 40.00 60.00
28 Don Putman 40.00 60.00
29 Basketball Play 30.00 50.00
Double post
30 Jack Garfinkel 40.00 60.00
31 Chuck Gilmur 40.00 60.00
32 Red Holzman RC 125.00 225.00
33 Jack Smiley 40.00 60.00
34 Joe Fulks RC 90.00 150.00
35 Basketball Play 30.00 50.00
Screen play
36 Hal Tidrick 40.00 60.00
37 Don (Swede) Carlson 60.00 90.00
38 Buddy Jeanette CO RC 80.00 135.00
39 Ray Kuka 60.00 90.00
40 Stan Miasek 60.00 90.00
41 Basketball Play 50.00 75.00
Double screen
42 George Nostrand 60.00 90.00
43 Chuck Halbert RC 75.00 125.00
44 Arnie Johnson 60.00 90.00
45 Bob Doll 60.00 90.00
46 Bones McKinney RC 80.00 135.00
47 Basketball Play 50.00 75.00
Out of bounds
48 Ed Sadowski 75.00 125.00
49 Bob Kinney 60.00 90.00
50 Charles (Hawk) Black 60.00 90.00
51 Jack Dwan 50.00 75.00
52 Connie Simmons RC 75.00 125.00
53 Basketball Play 50.00 75.00
Out of bounds
54 Bud Palmer RC 100.00 150.00
55 Max Zaslofsky RC 125.00 200.00
56 Lee Roy Robbins 60.00 90.00
57 Arthur Spector 60.00 90.00
58 Arnie Risen RC 90.00 150.00
59 Basketball Play 50.00 75.00
Out of bounds play
60 Ariel Maughan 60.00 90.00
61 Dick O'Keefe 60.00 90.00
62 Herman Schaefer 60.00 90.00
63 John Mahnken 60.00 90.00
64 Tommy Byrnes 60.00 90.00
65 Basketball Play 50.00 75.00
Held ball
66 Jim Pollard RC 125.00 250.00
67 Lee Mogus 60.00 90.00
68 Lee Knorek 60.00 90.00
69 George Mikan RC 1500.00 2500.00
70 Walter Budko 60.00 90.00
71 Basketball Play 50.00 75.00
Guards Play
72 Carl Braun RC 200.00 400.00

2003-04 Bowman

Released in October 2003 and marketed as two brands in one pack, Bowman and Bowman Chrome cards shared the same packs and boxes. The Bowman version features a 156-card set divided up into 110 base veteran cards with a red border around a centered picture surrounded by silver borders on the left and right and black borders on the top and the bottom. Cards 111-147 feature rookie players and have a blue border around their pictures and share the rest of the design elements with the base cards. Cards 148-157 are autographed rookie cards sequentially numbered to 250. Upon issue, card number 147 was not released. Bowman was packaged in 24-pack boxes with packs containing seven cards, four Bowman cards, four Bowman Chrome Cards and one Parallel, and carried a suggested retail price of $4.

COMP.SET w/o RC's (110) 15.00 40.00
1 Yao Ming .60 1.50
2 Glenn Robinson .25 .60
3 Antoine Walker .30 .75
4 Jalen Rose .25 .60
5 Ricky Davis .25 .60
6 Juwan Howard .25 .60
7 Kwame Brown .20 .50
8 Mike Bibby .30 .75
9 Wally Szczerbiak .25 .60
10 Allen Iverson .50 1.25
11 Shareef Abdur-Rahim .25 .60
12 Jamal Mashburn .25 .60
13 Stephon Marbury .25 .60
14 Desmond Mason .25 .60
15 Gordan Giricek .20 .50
16 Caron Butler .25 .60
17 Jermaine O'Neal .25 .60
18 Kenyon Martin .25 .60
19 Andrei Kirilenko .30 .75
20 Dirk Nowitzki .50 1.25
21 Richard Hamilton .25 .60
22 Troy Murphy .20 .50
23 Shawn Marion .25 .60
24 Allan Houston .25 .60
25 Keith Van Horn .25 .60
26 Brian Grant .20 .50
27 Mike Miller .25 .60
28 Chris Webber .30 .75
29 Brent Barry .20 .50
30 Elton Brand .30 .75
31 Juan Dixon .20 .50
32 Karl Malone .40 1.00
33 Darrell Armstrong .20 .50
34 Rasheed Wallace .30 .75
35 Michael Redd .30 .75
36 Rashard Lewis .30 .75
37 Ron Artest .30 .75
38 P.J. Brown .20 .50
39 Eddie Griffin .20 .50
40 Tim Duncan .50 1.25
41 Kurt Thomas .20 .50
42 Raef Lafrentz .20 .50
43 Ben Wallace .25 .60
44 Lamar Odom .25 .60
45 Vince Carter .50 1.25
46 Derek Anderson .20 .50
47 Stromile Swift .20 .50
48 Bobby Jackson .20 .50
49 Richard Jefferson .25 .60
50 Shaquille O'Neal .75 2.00
51 Calbert Cheaney .20 .50
52 Troy Hudson .20 .50
53 Ray Allen .30 .75
54 Howard Eisley .20 .50
55 Alonzo Mourning .40 1.00
56 Sam Cassell .25 .60
57 Derrick Coleman .25 .60
58 Andre Miller .25 .60
59 Antawn Jamison .25 .60
60 Kevin Garnett .50 1.25
61 Steve Francis .25 .60
62 Tyson Chandler .25 .60
63 Drew Gooden .25 .60
64 Scottie Pippen .50 1.25
65 Pau Gasol .30 .75
66 Steve Nash .40 1.00
67 DaJuan Wagner .20 .50
68 Jason Terry .25 .60
69 Reggie Miller .30 .75
70 Tracy McGrady .40 1.00
71 Nene Hilario .25 .60
72 Morris Peterson .20 .50
73 Peja Stojakovic .30 .75
74 Eddie Jones .25 .60
75 Tony Parker .30 .75
76 Corliss Williamson .20 .50
77 Vladimir Radmanovic .20 .50
78 Amare Stoudemire .40 1.00
79 Tony Delk .20 .50
80 Jason Kidd .50 1.25
81 Gary Payton .30 .75
82 Corey Maggette .25 .60
83 Darius Miles .20 .50
84 Cuttino Mobley .20 .50
85 Eric Snow .20 .50
86 Matt Harpring .20 .50
87 Manu Ginobili .40 1.00
88 Latrell Sprewell .25 .60
89 Alvin Williams .20 .50
90 Paul Pierce .30 .75
91 Anfernee Hardaway .50 1.25
92 Gilbert Arenas .25 .60
93 Jerry Stackhouse .25 .60
94 Tim Thomas .20 .50
95 Nikoloz Tskitishvili .20 .50
96 Doug Christie .20 .50
97 Zydrunas Ilgauskas .25 .60
98 Jamaal Tinsley .20 .50
99 Theo Ratliff .20 .50
100 Kobe Bryant 1.25 3.00
101 Chauncey Billups .30 .75
102 Michael Finley .30 .75
103 Jason Williams .25 .60
104 Bonzi Wells .20 .50
105 Voshon Lenard .20 .50
106 Jason Richardson .30 .75
107 Baron Davis .25 .60
108 Radoslav Nesterovic .20 .50
109 Eddy Curry .20 .50
110 Michael Olowokandi .20 .50
111 Josh Howard RC 1.50 4.00
112 Mario Austin RC 1.50 4.00
113 Rick Rickert RC 1.00 2.50
114 Tommy Smith RC 1.50 4.00
115 Dahntay Jones RC 1.25 3.00
116 Ndudi Ebi RC 1.00 2.50
117 Maurice Williams RC 1.50 4.00
118 Kendrick Perkins RC 1.25 3.00
119 Steve Blake RC 1.25 3.00
120 David West RC 1.50 4.00
121 Chris Kaman RC 1.50 4.00
122 Keith Bogans RC 1.00 2.50
123 LeBron James RC 40.00 100.00
124 Devin Brown RC 1.00 2.50
125 Jason Kapono RC 1.00 2.50
126 Zoran Planinic RC 1.00 2.50
127 Zaur Pachulia RC 1.50 4.00
128 Malick Badiane RC 1.50 4.00
129 Kyle Korver RC 2.00 5.00
130 Darko Milicic RC 1.25 3.00
131 Troy Bell RC 1.00 2.50
132 Luke Walton RC 1.50 4.00
133 Mike Sweetney RC 1.00 2.50
134 Jarvis Hayes RC 1.00 2.50
135 Leandro Barbosa RC 1.50 4.00
136 Carlos Delfino RC 1.25 3.00
137 Sofoklis Schortsanitis RC 1.00 2.50
138 Slavko Vranes RC 1.00 2.50
139 Travis Hansen RC 1.00 2.50
140 Carmelo Anthony RC 3.00 8.00
141 Reece Gaines RC 1.00 2.50
142 Maciej Lampe RC 1.00 2.50
143 Travis Outlaw RC 1.25 3.00
144 Jerome Beasley RC 1.00 2.50
145 Mickael Pietrus RC 1.25 3.00
146 Brian Cook RC 1.00 2.50
148 Kirk Hinrich AU RC 4.00 10.00
149 Dwyane Wade AU RC 30.00 80.00
150 Marcus Banks AU RC 4.00 10.00
151 Nick Collison AU RC 4.00 10.00
152 Boris Diaw AU RC 6.00 15.00
153 Chris Bosh AU RC 8.00 20.00
154 T.J. Ford AU RC 4.00 10.00
155 Luke Ridnour AU RC 5.00 12.00
156 A.Pavlovic AU RC 5.00 12.00
157 Z.Cabarkapa AU RC 4.00 10.00

2003-04 Bowman Gold

*1-110 GOLD: 1.25X TO 3X BASE HI
*111-146 GOLD RCs: .5X TO 1.25X BASE HI
*148-157 GOLD RCs: .1X TO .3X BASE HI
148-157 GOLD NOT AUTOGRAPHED
CARD 147 NOT RELEASED
149 Dwyane Wade 4.00 10.00

2003-04 Bowman Fabric of the Future

Inserted in packs at the rate of one in 37, this 25-card set places rookies in front of their new team logo with a swatch of memorabilia.

STATED ODDS 1:37
BC Brian Cook 1.50 4.00
CA Carmelo Anthony 8.00 20.00
CB Chris Bosh 4.00 10.00
CK Chris Kaman 2.50 6.00
DJ Dahntay Jones 2.00 5.00
DW Dwyane Wade 8.00 20.00
JH Jarvis Hayes 1.50 4.00
KB Keith Bogans 1.50 4.00
KH Kirk Hinrich 2.50 6.00
KP Kendrick Perkins 2.00 5.00
LB Leandro Barbosa 2.50 6.00
LR Luke Ridnour 2.00 5.00
LW Luke Walton 2.50 6.00
MB Marcus Banks 1.50 4.00
MP Mickael Pietrus 2.00 5.00
MS Mike Sweetney 1.50 4.00
NC Nick Collison 2.00 5.00
RG Reece Gaines 1.50 4.00
SB Steve Blake 2.00 5.00
SV Slavko Vranes 1.50 4.00
TB Troy Bell 1.50 4.00
TF T.J. Ford 2.00 5.00
TO Travis Outlaw 2.00 5.00
DWE David West 2.50 6.00
JHO Josh Howard 2.50 6.00

2003-04 Bowman Remembering Rookies

Inserted at the rate of one in 1282, this two card set features Elton Brand and Shaquille O'Neal with their authentic autographs.

STATED ODDS 1:1282
RREB Elton Brand 6.00 15.00
RRSO Shaquille O'Neal 50.00 120.00

2003-04 Bowman Rookie Recalls

Inserted at the rate of one in 46, this 15-card set places players in action on a brown background with a circular swatch of memorabilia towards the bottom of the card.

STATED ODDS 1:46
RREAM Andre Miller 2.00 5.00
RREDM Darius Miles 2.00 5.00
RREEB Elton Brand 2.50 6.00
RREGH Grant Hill 3.00 8.00
RREGP Gary Payton 2.50 6.00
RREGR Glenn Robinson 2.00 5.00
RREKG Kevin Garnett 4.00 10.00
RREKM Karl Malone 3.00 8.00
RRELH Larry Hughes 2.00 5.00
RRERH Richard Hamilton 2.00 5.00
RRESF Steve Francis 2.00 5.00
RRETD Tim Duncan 4.00 10.00
RRETM Tracy McGrady 3.00 8.00

2003-04 Bowman Signs of the Future

Seeded in packs at the rate of one in 171, this 37-card set features a white-out towards the bottom part of the card front for autographs of the 2003-04 Rookie Draft Class.

STATED ODDS: A 1:171 B 1:43
AP Aleksandar Pavlovic 3.00 8.00
BC Brian Cook 2.50 6.00
CA Carmelo Anthony 25.00 50.00
CB Chris Bosh 8.00 20.00
CD Carlos Delfino 3.00 8.00
DJ Dahntay Jones 3.00 8.00
DW Dwyane Wade 30.00 80.00
JB Jerome Beasley 2.50 6.00
JH Josh Howard 4.00 10.00
JK Jason Kapono 2.50 6.00
KB Keith Bogans 2.50 6.00
KH Kirk Hinrich 6.00 15.00
KP Kendrick Perkins 3.00 8.00
LB Leandro Barbosa 2.50 6.00
LR Luke Ridnour 3.00 8.00
LW Luke Walton 4.00 10.00
MA Mario Austin 4.00 10.00
MB Marcus Banks 2.50 6.00
ML Maciej Lampe 2.50 6.00
MP Mickael Pietrus 3.00 8.00
MS Mike Sweetney 2.50 6.00
NE Ndudi Ebi 2.50 6.00
NV Nick Collison 3.00 8.00
RG Reece Gaines 2.50 6.00
SB Steve Blake 3.00 8.00
SS Sofoklis Schortsianitis 2.50 6.00
SV Slavko Vranes 2.50 6.00
TB Troy Bell 2.50 6.00
TH Travis Hansen 2.50 6.00
TJ T.J. Ford 3.00 8.00
TO Travis Outlaw 3.00 8.00
TS Tommy Smith 4.00 10.00
ZP Zaur Pachulia 4.00 10.00
DWE David West 4.00 10.00
JHA Jarvis Hayes 2.50 6.00
MBA Malick Badiane 4.00 10.00
ZOP Zoran Planinic 2.50 6.00

2003-04 Bowman Sophomore Strands

Seeded at one in 46, this 10-card set focuses on players from the previous year's draft class. Each card places a full-color action photo above a square-shaped swatch of memorabilia.

STATED ODDS 1:46
AS Amare Stoudemire 3.00 8.00
CB Carlos Boozer 2.00 5.00
DG Drew Gooden 2.00 5.00
DW DaJuan Wagner 2.00 5.00
EG Manu Ginobili 3.00 8.00
JD Juan Dixon 2.00 5.00
MD Mike Dunleavy Jr. 2.00 5.00
MH Marcus Haislip 2.00 5.00
NH Nene Hilario 2.00 5.00
RH Ryan Humphrey 2.00 5.00
TP Tayshaun Prince 2.00 5.00
YM Yao Ming 5.00 12.00
CBU Caron Butler 2.00 5.00
JRB J.R. Bremer 2.00 5.00

2004-05 Bowman

Released in October of 2004 under the name Bowman Rookies and Stars again this year, packs contained an assortment of cards from both Bowman and Bowman Chrome, therefore they have been designated as such. Both sets contain 156 cards where cards 1-110 feature veteran players, cards 111-146 feature rookies, and card numbers 147-156 feature autographed rookie cards inserted at one in 105 packs for Bowman and are sequentially numbered to 250 for Bowman Chrome. All cards have gray borders, but the veteran players have red accents along the side borders and the rookies have blue accents. Boxes contained 24 packs of seven cards (four Bowman, two Bowman Chrome and one Bowman Gold Parallel) that carried a SRP of $4.00.

COMP.SET w/o RC's (110) 15.00 40.00
147-156 RC STATED ODDS 1:105
1 Yao Ming .60 1.50
2 Eddy Curry .20 .50
3 Stephon Marbury .25 .60
4 Chris Webber .30 .75
5 Jason Kidd .50 1.25
6 Cuttino Mobley .20 .50
7 Jermaine O'Neal .25 .60
8 Kobe Bryant 1.25 3.00
9 Tony Parker .30 .75
10 Gary Payton .30 .75
11 T.J. Ford .20 .50
12 Tim Duncan .50 1.25
13 Glenn Robinson .25 .60
14 Jason Richardson .30 .75
15 Carmelo Anthony .60 1.50
16 Pau Gasol .30 .75
17 Kirk Hinrich .25 .60
18 Kenyon Martin .25 .60
19 Jamal Crawford .30 .75
20 Elton Brand .30 .75
21 Kevin Garnett .50 1.25
22 Michael Redd .25 .60
23 LeBron James 2.00 5.00
24 Andre Miller .25 .60
25 Peja Stojakovic .30 .75
26 Jarvis Hayes .20 .50
27 David Wesley .20 .50
28 Jason Kapono .20 .50
29 Corey Maggette .25 .60
30 Rasheed Wallace .30 .75
31 Nene .25 .60
32 Amare Stoudemire .25 .60
33 Allen Iverson .50 1.25
34 Shaquille O'Neal .75 2.00
35 Mike Dunleavy .25 .60
36 Steve Nash .40 1.00
37 Brad Miller .25 .60
38 Chris Bosh .30 .75
39 Boris Diaw .25 .60
40 Steve Francis .25 .60
41 Dirk Nowitzki .50 1.25
42 Jason Williams .25 .60
43 Gilbert Arenas .25 .60
44 Keith Van Horn .25 .60
45 Jamal Mashburn .25 .60
46 Derek Fisher .25 .60
47 Andrei Kirilenko .25 .60
48 Ricky Davis .25 .60
49 Gerald Wallace .25 .60
50 Tracy McGrady .40 1.00
51 Zach Randolph .25 .60
52 Rafer Alston .20 .50
53 Bobby Jackson .20 .50
54 Desmond Mason .25 .60
55 Tim Thomas .20 .50
56 Jamaal Tinsley .20 .50
57 Kwame Brown .20 .50
58 Chauncey Billups .30 .75
59 Brandon Hunter .20 .50
60 Reggie Miller .30 .75
61 Samuel Dalembert .20 .50
62 James Posey .20 .50
63 Erick Dampier .20 .50
64 Carlos Arroyo .20 .50
65 Reece Gaines .20 .50
66 Darko Milicic .20 .50
67 Sam Cassell .25 .60
68 Dwyane Wade .50 1.25
69 Allan Houston .25 .60
70 Ray Allen .30 .75
71 Tyson Chandler .25 .60
72 Bonzi Wells .20 .50
73 Jalen Rose .25 .60
74 Marquis Daniels .20 .50
75 Zydrunas Ilgauskas .25 .60
76 Tayshaun Prince .25 .60
77 Lamar Odom .25 .60
78 Luke Ridnour .25 .60
79 Joe Johnson .25 .60
80 Vince Carter .50 1.25
81 Antoine Walker .30 .75
82 Shareef Abdur-Rahim .25 .60
83 Richard Jefferson .25 .60
84 Maurice Taylor .20 .50
85 Chris Kaman .25 .60
86 Marcus Banks .20 .50
87 Mike Bibby .30 .75
88 Latrell Sprewell .25 .60
89 Rashard Lewis .30 .75
90 Baron Davis .25 .60
91 Caron Butler .25 .60
92 Michael Finley .30 .75
93 Mike Miller .25 .60
94 Al Harrington .25 .60
95 Quentin Richardson .25 .60
96 Jamaal Magloire .20 .50
97 Darius Miles .20 .50
98 Jeff Foster .20 .50
99 Karl Malone .40 1.00
100 Shawn Marion .25 .60
101 Antawn Jamison .25 .60
102 Manu Ginobili .40 1.00
103 Ben Wallace .25 .60
104 Paul Pierce .30 .75
105 Mike Sweetney .20 .50
106 Ron Artest .30 .75
107 Michael Olowokandi .20 .50
108 Jason Terry .25 .60
109 Gordan Giricek .20 .50
110 Carlos Boozer .25 .60
111 Romain Sato RC .60 1.50
112 Chris Duhon RC 1.00 2.50
113 Ben Gordon RC 1.00 2.50
114 Matt Freije RC .75 2.00
115 Al Jefferson RC 1.25 3.00
116 Beno Udrih RC .75 2.00
117 Kirk Snyder RC .60 1.50
118 Anderson Varejao RC .75 2.00
119 Devin Harris RC .75 2.00
120 Tony Allen RC 1.00 2.50
121 Ha Seung-Jin RC 1.00 2.50
122 J.R. Smith RC 1.00 2.50
123 Blake Stepp RC 1.00 2.50
124 Jameer Nelson RC 1.00 2.50
125 Kris Humphries RC 1.00 2.50
126 Josh Childress RC .75 2.00
127 Tim Pickett RC 1.00 2.50
128 Delonte West RC 1.00 2.50
129 Dwight Howard RC 2.00 5.00
130 Luke Jackson RC .60 1.50
131 Rickey Paulding RC .60 1.50
132 Andre Emmett RC .60 1.50
133 Josh Smith RC 1.00 2.50
134 Antonio Burks RC .75 2.00
135 Ricky Minard RC .75 2.00
136 Lionel Chalmers RC 1.00 2.50
137 Shaun Livingston RC 1.00 2.50
138 Trevor Ariza RC 1.00 2.50
139 Sergei Lishouk RC .75 2.00
140 Pape Sow RC .75 2.00
141 Rashad Wright RC .75 2.00
142 Jackson Vroman RC .60 1.50
143 Luis Flores RC .75 2.00
144 Royal Ivey RC .75 2.00
145 Kevin Martin RC 1.25 3.00
146 Andre Iguodala RC 1.25 3.00
147 Andris Biedrins AU RC 3.00 8.00
148 Pavel Podkolzin AU RC 3.00 8.00
149 Luol Deng AU RC 5.00 12.00
150 Robert Swift AU RC 3.00 8.00
151 Sebastian Telfair AU RC 4.00 10.00
152 Emeka Okafor AU RC 4.00 10.00
153 Dorell Wright AU RC 5.00 12.00
154 Sasha Vujacic AU RC 5.00 12.00
155 Rafael Araujo AU RC 3.00 8.00
156 David Harrison AU RC 3.00 8.00

2004-05 Bowman Gold

*1-110 GOLD:1.25 X TO 3X BASE HI
*111-146 GOLD: .6X TO 1.5X BASE HI
STATED ODDS ONE PER PACK
147 Andris Biedrins 1.00 2.50
148 Pavel Podkolzin 1.00 2.50
149 Luol Deng 1.50 4.00
150 Robert Swift 1.00 2.50
151 Sebastian Telfair 1.25 3.00
152 Emeka Okafor 1.25 3.00
153 Dorell Wright 1.50 4.00
154 Sasha Vujacic 1.50 4.00
155 Rafael Araujo 1.00 2.50
156 David Harrison 1.00 2.50

2004-05 Bowman Cityscape Relics

Inserted in packs at the rate of one in 150, this 29-card set is horizontally designed with one player with a swatch of jersey on the left side, one player with a swatch of jersey on the right, a black border on the bottom of the card, and a city skyline background.

STATED ODDS 1:150
AR R.Allen/L.Ridnour 3.00 8.00
BK E.Brand/C.Kaman 3.00 8.00
CH E.Curry/K.Hinrich 3.00 8.00
DG T.Duncan/M.Ginobili 12.50 30.00
FG S.Francis/D.Gooden 3.00 8.00
GJ P.Gasol/D.Jones 3.00 8.00
GO K.Garnett/M.Olowokandi 6.00 15.00
IB Z.Ilgauskas/C.Boozer 3.00 8.00
IG A.Iverson/W.Green 6.00 15.00
KJ J.Kidd/R.Jefferson 6.00 15.00
MA A.Miller/C.Anthony 6.00 15.00
MF D.Mason/T.Ford 3.00 8.00
MM T.McGrady/Y.Ming 8.00 20.00
MO R.Miller/J.O'Neal 6.00 15.00
MS S.Marbury/M.Sweetney 3.00 8.00
MW J.Mashburn/D.West 3.00 8.00
NH D.Nowitzki/J.Howard 3.00 8.00
OW L.Odom/D.Wade 6.00 15.00
PB P.Pierce/M.Banks 3.00 8.00
PR G.Payton/K.Rush 3.00 8.00
RP J.Richardson/M.Pietrus 3.00 8.00
TD J.Terry/B.Diaw 3.00 8.00
WP B.Wallace/T.Prince 3.00 8.00
WS C.Webber/P.Stojakovic 3.00 8.00
MAS S.Marion/A.Stoudemire 5.00 12.00
OWA S.O'Neal/L.Walton 8.00 20.00
PEB M.Peterson/C.Bosh 3.00 8.00

2004-05 Bowman Instant Impact Relics

Inserted in packs at one in 120, this 15-card set places full-color player action photos on a borderless card with a circular swatch of game worn memorabilia in the upper left corner.

STATED ODDS 1:120
AI Allen Iverson 4.00 10.00
AK Andrei Kirilenko 2.00 5.00
AS Amare Stoudemire 2.00 5.00
AW Antoine Walker 2.50 6.00
CA Carmelo Anthony 5.00 12.00
EB Elton Brand 2.50 6.00
JK Jason Kidd 4.00 10.00
JR Jason Richardson 2.50 6.00
PG Pau Gasol 2.50 6.00
SF Steve Francis 2.00 5.00
SM Stephon Marbury 2.00 5.00
SO Shaquille O'Neal 6.00 15.00
TD Tim Duncan 4.00 10.00
TP Tony Parker 2.50 6.00
YM Yao Ming 5.00 12.00

2004-05 Bowman Original Rookies

Serially numbered to 100, unless noted in the checklist, these are buybacks of each player's original Topps RC card and are enhanced by an embossed crimp stamp.

COMPLETE SET (8) 50.00 100.00
PRINT RUN 50 TO 100 SER.#'d SETS
115 T.Duncan 97-98T 5.00 12.00
138 K.Bryant 96-97T 25.00 60.00
171 A.Iverson 96-97T 6.00 15.00
185 Y.Ming 02-03T 5.00 12.00
199 V.Carter 98-99T 5.00 12.00
221 L.James 03-04T/50 50.00 100.00
225 D.Wade 03-04T 8.00 20.00
237 K.Garnett 95-96T 5.00 12.00
362 S.O'Neal 92-93T 12.50 30.00

2004-05 Bowman Remembering Rookies Autographs

Inserted at one in 658 packs for Group A and one in 1579 packs for Group B, this 13-card set features players and autographs on the Bowman card design for that year. If Bowman wasn't produced for basketball that year, Topps used the design from Bowman baseball.

STATED ODDS: GROUP A 1:658, B 1:1579
AS Amare Stoudemire A 12.00 30.00
BD Baron Davis B 6.00 15.00
CA Carmelo Anthony A 12.00 30.00
JK Jason Kidd A 15.00 40.00
JO Jermaine O'Neal A 6.00 15.00
LO Lamar Odom A 6.00 15.00
PS Peja Stojakovic A 6.00 15.00
RH Richard Hamilton A 8.00 20.00
SM Shawn Marion A 6.00 15.00
SO Shaquille O'Neal A 40.00 80.00
TD Tim Duncan A 200.00 400.00
TM Tracy McGrady A 15.00 40.00
SMA Stephon Marbury B 12.00 30.00

2004-05 Bowman Rookie Registration Relics

Inserted in packs at the rate of one in 44, this 25-card set features the 2004-05 rookie class on a horizontally designed card with a portrait photo on the left, a player worn jersey on the right and a white background.

STATED ODDS 1:44
AE Andre Emmett 1.50 4.00
AI Andre Iguodala 3.00 8.00
AJ Al Jefferson 3.00 8.00
AV Anderson Varejao 2.00 5.00
BG Ben Gordon 2.50 6.00
CD Chris Duhon 2.50 6.00
DH Dwight Howard 5.00 12.00
DW Dorell Wright 2.50 6.00
EO Emeka Okafor 2.00 5.00
JC Josh Childress 2.00 5.00
JN Jameer Nelson 2.50 6.00
JS Josh Smith 2.50 6.00
KH Kris Humphries 2.50 6.00
KM Kevin Martin 3.00 8.00
KS Kirk Snyder 1.50 4.00
LD Luol Deng 2.50 6.00
LJ Luke Jackson 1.50 4.00
RA Rafael Araujo 1.50 4.00
SL Shaun Livingston 2.50 6.00
ST Sebastian Telfair 2.00 5.00
TA Tony Allen 2.50 6.00
DEH Devin Harris 2.00 5.00
DHA David Harrison 1.50 4.00
DWE Delonte West 2.50 6.00
JRS J.R. Smith 2.50 6.00

2004-05 Bowman Signs of the Future

Seeded in packs at one in 38, this 34-card set features the 2004-05 NBA draft class on a background set to match their new team's colors and has an autograph on a foil sticker.

STATED ODDS 1:38
DREJER AND MONIA NEVER ISSUED
AB Antonio Burks 2.50 6.00
AE Andre Emmett 2.00 5.00
AJ Al Jefferson 4.00 10.00
AV Anderson Varejao 2.50 6.00
BG Ben Gordon 3.00 8.00
BR Bernard Robinson 2.50 6.00
BS Blake Stepp 3.00 8.00
BU Beno Udrih 2.50 6.00
CD Chris Duhon 3.00 8.00
DH Devin Harris 2.50 6.00
DW Delonte West 3.00 8.00
EO Emeka Okafor 2.50 6.00
JN Jameer Nelson 3.00 8.00
JO Josh Childress 2.50 6.00
JR Justin Reed 2.00 5.00
JS Josh Smith 3.00 8.00
JV Jackson Vroman 2.00 5.00
KM Kevin Martin 4.00 10.00
KS Kirk Snyder 2.00 5.00
KY Kris Humphries 3.00 8.00
LJ Luke Jackson 2.00 5.00
MF Matt Freije 2.50 6.00
PS Pape Sow 2.50 6.00
RM Ricky Minard 2.50 6.00
RP Rickey Paulding 2.00 5.00
RS Romain Sato 2.00 5.00
RW Rashad Wright 2.50 6.00
SL Sergei Lishouk 2.50 6.00
TA Trevor Ariza 3.00 8.00
TP Tim Pickett 3.00 8.00
HSJ Ha Seung-Jin 3.00 8.00
JRS J.R. Smith 3.00 8.00
SLI Shaun Livingston 3.00 8.00
TAI Tony Allen 3.00 8.00

2004-05 Bowman Twice As Nice Relics

Inserted in packs at one in 207, this nine card set features colored background, a scale-colored portrait photo in the background, a full-color photo in the foreground and a memorabilia swatch in the shape of the number 2.

STATED ODDS 1:207
CB Carlos Boozer 2.50 6.00
CM Cuttino Mobley 2.00 5.00
EN Eduardo Najera 2.00 5.00
GA Gilbert Arenas 2.50 6.00
MG Manu Ginobili 4.00 10.00
MJ Marko Jaric 2.00 5.00
MR Michael Redd 2.50 6.00
RL Rashard Lewis 3.00 8.00

2005-06 Bowman

Released as a two-in one product (Bowman Draft Picks and Prospects) featuring both Bowman and Bowman Chrome cards, the Bowman portion of the set includes 162-cards where cards 1-110 picture veterans, cards 111-146 feature rookies, cards 147-151 feature celebrities and cards 152-161 feature autographed rookie cards. Also included and randomly inserted is card #DSBS featuring the NBA's Andrew Bogut and the NFL's Alex Smith (both from Utah) along with their autographs and sequential numbering to 100. Base cards feature white borders and red highlights on veteran cards and blue highlights on rookie cards. The rookie autographs showcase silver autograph stickers and stated odds of one in 63. Each pack contains seven cards, four bowman cards, two bowman chrome cards and a thick gold parallel and carried a suggested retail price of four dollars.

COMP.SET w/o RC's (110) 15.00 40.00
AU RC STATED ODDS 1:63
1 Steve Nash .40 1.00
2 Primoz Brezec .20 .50
3 Baron Davis .25 .60
4 Al Harrington .25 .60
5 Caron Butler .25 .60
6 Marcus Camby .25 .60
7 Carlos Boozer .25 .60
8 Ben Gordon .25 .60
9 Stephen Jackson .25 .60
10 Dirk Nowitzki .50 1.25
11 Nenad Krstic .20 .50
12 Jason Richardson .30 .75
13 Brendan Haywood .20 .50
14 Chauncey Billups .30 .75
15 Corey Maggette .25 .60
16 Peja Stojakovic .30 .75
17 Grant Hill .40 1.00
18 Pau Gasol .30 .75
19 Vladimir Radmanovic .20 .50
20 Jason Kidd .50 1.25
21 Tim Duncan .50 1.25
22 David Harrison .20 .50
23 LeBron James 1.25 3.00
24 Udonis Haslem .20 .50
25 Dan Dickau .20 .50
26 Cuttino Mobley .20 .50
27 Chris Bosh .30 .75
28 Sebastian Telfair .25 .60
29 Latrell Sprewell .25 .60
30 Emeka Okafor .25 .60
31 Mike James .20 .50
32 Trevor Ariza .20 .50
33 Larry Hughes .25 .60
34 Desmond Mason .20 .50
35 Tayshaun Prince .25 .60
36 Manu Ginobili .30 .75
37 Mike Bibby .30 .75
38 Andre Iguodala .25 .60
39 Jamaal Magloire .20 .50
40 Amare Stoudemire .25 .60
41 Rafer Alston .20 .50
42 Elton Brand .30 .75
43 Steve Francis .25 .60
44 Rashard Lewis .30 .75
45 Lorenzen Wright .20 .50
46 Kirk Hinrich .25 .60
47 Andrei Kirilenko .25 .60
48 Brad Miller .25 .60
49 Jamal Crawford .30 .75
50 Shaquille O'Neal .60 1.50
51 Shaun Livingston .20 .50
52 Troy Murphy .20 .50
53 Drew Gooden .25 .60
54 Paul Pierce .30 .75
55 Vince Carter .50 1.25
56 Wally Szczerbiak .25 .60
57 Antawn Jamison .25 .60
58 Marquis Daniels .20 .50
59 Gerald Wallace .25 .60
60 Ray Allen .30 .75
61 Jamaal Tinsley .20 .50
62 Shane Battier .25 .60
63 Zydrunas Ilgauskas .25 .60
64 Mehmet Okur .20 .50
65 Rasheed Wallace .30 .75
66 Maurice Williams .25 .60
67 Josh Howard .30 .75
68 Zach Randolph .25 .60
69 Kobe Bryant 1.25 3.00
70 Tracy McGrady .40 1.00
71 Luke Ridnour .25 .60
72 Damon Jones .20 .50
73 Tony Allen .20 .50
74 Mike Miller .25 .60
75 Sam Cassell .25 .60
76 Ben Wallace .25 .60
77 Mike Sweetney .20 .50
78 Eddy Curry .20 .50
79 Michael Redd .25 .60
80 Carmelo Anthony .60 1.50
81 Dwight Howard .25 .60
82 Josh Smith .25 .60
83 Richard Jefferson .25 .60
84 Richard Hamilton .25 .60
85 Chris Webber .30 .75
86 Shawn Marion .25 .60
87 Jalen Rose .30 .75
88 Bob Sura .20 .50
89 Mike Dunleavy .25 .60
90 Dwyane Wade .50 1.25
91 Gary Payton .30 .75
92 Luol Deng .25 .60
93 Kenyon Martin .25 .60
94 Beno Udrih .20 .50
95 J.R. Smith .25 .60
96 Lamar Odom .25 .60
97 Andre Miller .25 .60
98 Jermaine O'Neal .25 .60
99 Yao Ming .40 1.00
100 Allen Iverson .50 1.25
101 Quentin Richardson .25 .60
102 Gilbert Arenas .25 .60
103 Stephon Marbury .25 .60
104 Antoine Walker .25 .60
105 Jameer Nelson .20 .50
106 Joel Przybilla .20 .50
107 Devin Harris .20 .50
108 Tony Parker .30 .75
109 Josh Childress .25 .60
110 Kevin Garnett .50 1.25
111 Chris Paul RC 4.00 10.00
112 Danny Granger RC 1.25 3.00
113 Antoine Wright RC .75 2.00
114 Joey Graham RC .75 2.00
115 Wayne Simien RC .60 1.50
116 Channing Frye RC 1.00 2.50
117 Charlie Villanueva RC 1.00 2.50
118 Francisco Garcia RC .75 2.00
119 Ike Diogu RC .60 1.50
120 Jarrett Jack RC 1.00 2.50
121 Robert Whaley RC .60 1.50
122 C.J. Miles RC 1.00 2.50
123 Ryan Gomes RC .75 2.00
124 Nate Robinson RC 1.00 2.50
125 Daniel Ewing RC .75 2.00
126 Andray Blatche RC 1.00 2.50
127 Luther Head RC .75 2.00
128 Julius Hodge RC .60 1.50
129 Lawrence Roberts RC .60 1.50
130 Jason Maxiell RC .75 2.00
131 Martynas Andriuskevicius RC .60 1.50
132 Ersan Ilyasova RC 1.00 2.50
133 Martell Webster RC .75 2.00
134 Andrew Bynum RC .75 2.00
135 Louis Williams RC 1.00 2.50
136 Johan Petro RC .60 1.50
137 Brandon Bass RC .75 2.00
138 Travis Diener RC .60 1.50
139 Bracey Wright RC .60 1.50
140 Marvin Williams RC 1.00 2.50
141 Eddie Basden RC .60 1.50
142 Von Wafer RC .60 1.50
143 David Lee RC 1.00 2.50
144 Linas Kleiza RC .60 1.50
145 Luke Schenscher RC .60 1.50
146 Yaroslav Korolev RC .60 1.50
147 Carmen Electra 2.50 6.00
148 Christie Brinkley 2.50 6.00
149 Shannon Elizabeth 2.50 6.00
150 Jenny McCarthy 2.50 6.00
151 Jay-Z 2.50 6.00
152 Raymond Felton AU RC 4.00 10.00
153 Gerald Green AU RC 4.00 10.00
154 Rashad McCants AU RC 3.00 8.00
155 Andrew Bogut AU RC 5.00 12.00
156 Chris Taft AU RC 3.00 8.00
157 Sarunas Jasikevicius AU RC 4.00 10.00
158 Hakim Warrick AU RC 3.00 8.00
159 Deron Williams AU RC 15.00 30.00
160 Sean May AU RC 2.50 6.00
161 Monta Ellis AU RC 5.00 12.00
DSBS A.Bogut/A.Smith AU/100 60.00 120.00

2005-06 Bowman Gold

*1-110 GOLD: 1X TO 2.5X BASE HI
*111-151 GOLD: .6X TO 1.5X BASE HI
152-161 CARDS ARE NOT AUTOGRAPHED
STATED ODDS ONE PER PACK

2005-06 Bowman Back to the Future Autographs

Inserted at the rate of one in 511 for group A and one in 8263 for group B, this 10-card set features top NBA players with full color action photos and a silver autograph sticker in the lower right-hand corner.

GROUP A ODDS 1:511, GROUP B 1:8263
AI Allen Iverson B 40.00 100.00
BD Baron Davis B 6.00 15.00
BW Ben Wallace A 10.00 25.00
JK Jason Kidd B 15.00 40.00
LO Lamar Odom A 6.00 15.00
RH Richard Hamilton B 6.00 15.00
SM Stephon Marbury B 6.00 15.00
SO Shaquille O'Neal B ERR 30.00 80.00
TD Tim Duncan A 75.00 150.00

2005-06 Bowman Beginnings Relics

Inserted at the rate of one in 324, this cards showcases two players, one on the top and one on the bottom along with a "B" shaped swatch of memorabilia. Several different memorabilia swatches were used, see checklist for details.

STATED ODDS 1:324
AA C.Anthony/R.Artest 5.00 12.00

AI G.Arenas Warm/A.Iguodala 5.00 12.00
BM C.Bosh/S.Marbury 5.00 12.00
DH Luol Deng/Grant Hill Warm 10.00 25.00
GH B.Gordon/R.Hamilton Warm 5.00 12.00
HF D.Harris Shirt/M.Finley 5.00 12.00
JW A.Jamison/R.Wallace 5.00 12.00
OA E.Okafor/R.Allen 5.00 12.00
PH P.Pierce/K.Hinrich Shirt 10.00 25.00
DHO Duncan Shirt/Howard Shorts 6.00 15.00

2005-06 Bowman Bravo Relics

Inserted at the rate of one in 60, this 27-card set features both NBA players and celebrites on a card where full color photos appear on the top, and the word "Bravo!" appears on the bottom in big letters. The letter "A" from the word is actually a swatch of memorabilia. An autographed version sequentially numbered to nine was also products, but these cards are not priced due to scarcity.

STATED ODDS 1:60
UNPRICED AUTO PRINT RUN 9 SETS
AI Andre Iguodala 2.50 6.00
AK Andrei Kirilenko 2.50 6.00
AS Amare Stoudemire Shirt 2.50 6.00
AV Anderson Varejao 2.00 5.00
BG Ben Gordon 2.50 6.00
CA Carmelo Anthony 6.00 15.00
CB Christie Brinkley Jeans 8.00 20.00
CE Carmen Electra Jeans 10.00 25.00
DH Dwight Howard 2.50 6.00
DW Dwyane Wade 5.00 12.00
EO Emeka Okafor 2.50 6.00
GA Gilbert Arenas Shirt 2.50 6.00
JM Jenny McCarthy Jeans 10.00 25.00
JS Josh Smith 2.50 6.00
JZ Jay-Z Jeans 8.00 20.00
KB Kobe Bryant 10.00 25.00
KH Kirk Hinrich Shorts 2.50 6.00
LD Luol Deng 2.50 6.00
PG Pau Gasol 3.00 8.00
RL Rashard Lewis 3.00 8.00
RW Rasheed Wallace 3.00 8.00
SE Shannon Elizabeth Jeans 8.00 20.00
SO Shaquille O'Neal 6.00 15.00
TD Tim Duncan Warm 5.00 12.00
YM Yao Ming 4.00 10.00
ZR Zach Randolph 2.50 6.00
DHA Devin Harris 2.00 5.00

2005-06 Bowman Signs of the Future

Seeded in packs at the rate of one in 41, this 21-card set profiles some of the NBA's current-year rookies with full color photography and silver autograph stickers.

STATED ODDS 1:41
AB Andrew Bynum 3.00 8.00
AW Antoine Wright 3.00 8.00
BB Brandon Bass 3.00 8.00
CV Charlie Villanueva 4.00 10.00
DE Daniel Ewing 3.00 8.00
DG Danny Granger 5.00 12.00
DL David Lee 4.00 10.00
FG Francisco Garcia 3.00 8.00
ID Ike Diogu 2.50 6.00
JG Joey Graham 3.00 8.00
JH Julius Hodge 2.50 6.00
JJ Jarrett Jack 4.00 10.00
JM Jason Maxiell 3.00 8.00
JP Johan Petro 2.50 6.00
LH Luther Head 3.00 8.00
MW Martell Webster 3.00 8.00
RU Roko Ukic 4.00 10.00
SJ Sarunas Jasikevicius 4.00 10.00
TD Travis Diener 2.50 6.00
VW Von Wafer 2.50 6.00
WS Wayne Simien 2.50 6.00

2005-06 Bowman Skills Nation Relics

Randomly inserted at the rate of one in 81, this 20-card set places color player photos on the right side of the card and a red and black border on the left. Centered towards the bottom of the card is an "N" shaped swatch of memorabilia.

STATED ODDS 1:81
AI Allen Iverson 5.00 12.00
AM Andre Miller 2.50 6.00
BW Ben Wallace Warm 2.50 6.00
DM Desmond Mason 2.00 5.00
DW Dwyane Wade 5.00 12.00
FJ Fred Jones 2.00 5.00
JK Jason Kidd 5.00 12.00
JR Jason Richardson 3.00 8.00
JS Josh Smith 2.50 6.00
MB Mike Bibby 3.00 8.00
MC Marcus Camby 2.50 6.00
MR Michael Redd 2.50 6.00
PS Peja Stojakovic 3.00 8.00
QR Quentin Richardson 2.50 6.00
RA Ray Allen 3.00 8.00
SM Stephon Marbury 2.50 6.00
SN Steve Nash 4.00 10.00
SO Shaquille O'Neal 6.00 15.00
VL Voshon Lenard 2.00 5.00
DMU Dikembe Mutombo 4.00 10.00

2005-06 Bowman Welcome to the Show Relics

Found in packs at the rate of one in 41, this 27-card set features full-color player photos and a swatch of memorabilia worn at the NBA rookie photo shoot. Each card is horizontally designed with player photos on the left and memorabilia on the right. An autographed version sequentially numbered to five was also produced but is not priced due to scarcity.

STATED ODDS 1:41
UNPRICED AUTO PRINT RUN 5 SER.#'d SETS
AW Antoine Wright 2.50 6.00
BB Brandon Bass 2.50 6.00
CF Channing Frye 3.00 8.00
CP Chris Paul 10.00 25.00
CV Charlie Villanueva 3.00 8.00
DE Daniel Ewing 2.50 6.00
DG Danny Granger 4.00 10.00
DL David Lee 3.00 8.00
DW Deron Williams 4.00 10.00
EI Ersan Ilyasova 3.00 8.00
FG Francisco Garcia 2.50 6.00
GG Gerald Green 3.00 8.00
HW Hakim Warrick 2.50 6.00
JG Joey Graham 2.50 6.00
JH Julius Hodge 2.00 5.00
JJ Jarrett Jack 3.00 8.00
JM Jason Maxiell 2.50 6.00
LH Luther Head 2.50 6.00
MW Martell Webster 2.50 6.00
NR Nate Robinson 3.00 8.00
RF Raymond Felton 3.00 8.00
RM Rashad McCants 2.50 6.00
SJ Sarunas Jasikevicius 3.00 8.00
SM Sean May 2.00 5.00
WS Wayne Simien 2.00 5.00
ABO Andrew Bogut 4.00 10.00
CJM C.J. Miles 3.00 8.00

2006-07 Bowman

Packaged together with Bowman Chrome, Bowman features a 165-card set, showcasing veteran players on card numbers 1-110, NCAA coaches on card numbers 111-115 and rookie players on cards 116-165. All cards feature black borders, silver foil highlights and red color accents on veteran player cards and blue color accents on rookie player cards. Released late November 2006 under the product name of Bowman Rookies and Stars, boxes contain 18 packs where each pack has four Bowman cards, two Bowman Chrome cards and carried an original suggested retail price of $4.00 per pack.

COMPLETE SET (165) 20.00 50.00
COMP.SET w/o RC'S (115) 8.00 20.00
1 Gilbert Arenas .25 .60
2 Delonte West .20 .50
3 Gerald Wallace .25 .60
4 Ike Diogu .20 .50
5 Mike Miller .25 .60
6 Kobe Bryant 1.25 3.00
7 Richard Hamilton .25 .60
8 Vince Carter .40 1.00
9 Elton Brand .30 .75
10 Boris Diaw .25 .60
11 Carmelo Anthony .40 1.00
12 Jermaine O'Neal .25 .60
13 Al Harrington .25 .60
14 Dwight Howard .25 .60
15 Chris Bosh .30 .75
16 Ben Gordon .25 .60
17 Josh Howard .25 .60
18 Yao Ming .40 1.00
19 David West .25 .60
20 Tim Duncan .50 1.25
21 Andre Iguodala .25 .60
22 LeBron James 1.25 3.00
23 Channing Frye .25 .60
24 Antoine Walker .25 .60
25 Ricky Davis .25 .60
26 Lamar Odom .25 .60
27 Amare Stoudemire .25 .60
28 Mike Bibby .30 .75
29 Allen Iverson .40 1.00
30 Marvin Williams .25 .60
31 Wally Szczerbiak .25 .60
32 Ben Wallace .25 .60
33 Nenad Krstic .20 .50
34 Deron Williams .25 .60
35 Troy Murphy .20 .50
36 Raymond Felton .25 .60
37 Jason Terry .25 .60
38 Zach Randolph .25 .60
39 Pau Gasol .30 .75
40 Larry Hughes .25 .60
41 Luol Deng .25 .60
42 Steve Francis .25 .60
43 Chauncey Billups .30 .75
44 Smush Parker .20 .50
45 Shareef Abdur-Rahim .25 .60
46 Andrei Kirilenko .25 .60
47 Shawn Marion .25 .60
48 Darko Milicic .20 .50
49 Shaquille O'Neal .60 1.50
50 Kevin Garnett .50 1.25
51 Michael Finley .30 .75
52 Peja Stojakovic .30 .75
53 Michael Redd .25 .60
54 Desmond Mason .20 .50
55 Luke Ridnour .25 .60
56 Kenyon Martin .25 .60
57 Morris Peterson .20 .50
58 Chris Kaman .25 .60
59 Jason Richardson .30 .75
60 Jason Kidd .50 1.25
61 Carlos Boozer .25 .60
62 Rashad McCants .20 .50
63 Nate Robinson .20 .50
64 Devin Harris .20 .50
65 Andrew Bogut .25 .60
66 Chris Duhon .20 .50
67 Drew Gooden .25 .60
68 Manu Ginobili .30 .75
69 Jameer Nelson .20 .50
70 Corey Maggette .25 .60
71 Charlie Villanueva .20 .50
72 Shane Battier .25 .60
73 Udonis Haslem .20 .50
74 Tracy McGrady .40 1.00
75 Bobby Simmons .20 .50
76 Baron Davis .25 .60
77 Zydrunas Ilgauskas .25 .60
78 Danny Granger .25 .60
79 Hakim Warrick .25 .60
80 Josh Smith .25 .60
81 Tayshaun Prince .25 .60
82 Rashard Lewis .30 .75
83 Luther Head .25 .60
84 Andre Miller .25 .60
85 T.J. Ford .20 .50
86 Sebastian Telfair .20 .50
87 Dirk Nowitzki .50 1.25
88 Kwame Brown .20 .50
89 Antawn Jamison .25 .60
90 Ron Artest .30 .75
91 Mehmet Okur .20 .50
92 Emeka Okafor .25 .60
93 Sam Cassell .25 .60
94 Chris Paul .40 1.00
95 Chris Webber .30 .75
96 Richard Jefferson .25 .60
97 Dwyane Wade .50 1.25
98 Tony Parker .30 .75
99 Paul Pierce .30 .75
100 Marcus Camby .25 .60
101 Ray Allen .30 .75
102 Stephon Marbury .25 .60
103 Rasheed Wallace .30 .75
104 Brad Miller .25 .60
105 Kirk Hinrich .25 .60
106 Steve Nash .40 1.00
107 Sarunas Jasikevicius .25 .60
108 Darius Miles .20 .50
109 Joe Johnson .25 .60
110 Caron Butler .25 .60
111 John Wooden CO 1.25 3.00
112 Ben Howland CO 1.00 2.50
113 Jim Calhoun CO 1.00 2.50
114 Jim Boeheim CO 1.00 2.50
115 Roy Williams CO 1.00 2.50
116 LaMarcus Aldridge RC 2.50 6.00
117 Marcus Vinicius RC .60 1.50
118 Sergio Rodriguez RC 1.00 2.50
119 Will Blalock RC .60 1.50
120 Paul Millsap RC 1.25 3.00
121 Leon Powe RC .75 2.00
122 Rudy Gay RC 1.25 3.00
123 Tyrus Thomas RC .75 2.00
124 Brandon Roy RC 1.00 2.50
125 J.R. Pinnock RC .60 1.50
126 Kevin Pittsnogle RC .75 2.00
127 Mile Ilic RC .60 1.50
128 Mardy Collins RC .60 1.50
129 Craig Smith RC .75 2.00
130 Jordan Farmar RC 1.00 2.50
131 Quincy Douby RC .60 1.50
132 James Augustine RC .60 1.50
133 Josh Boone RC .60 1.50
134 Shannon Brown RC .60 1.50
135 David Noel RC .60 1.50
136 Kyle Lowry RC 1.25 3.00
137 Ryan Hollins RC .75 2.00
138 Renaldo Balkman RC .75 2.00
139 James White RC .60 1.50
140 Damir Markota RC .60 1.50
141 Paul Davis RC .60 1.50
142 Alexander Johnson RC .60 1.50
143 Steve Novak RC .75 2.00
144 P.J. Tucker RC .75 2.00
145 Saer Sene RC .60 1.50
146 Bobby Jones RC .60 1.50
147 Cedric Simmons RC .60 1.50
148 Allan Ray RC .60 1.50
149 Solomon Jones RC .60 1.50
150 Ronnie Brewer RC 1.00 2.50
151 Thabo Sefolosha RC 1.00 2.50
152 Maurice Ager RC .60 1.50
153 Daniel Gibson RC .75 2.00
154 Shawne Williams RC .60 1.50
155 Dee Brown RC .60 1.50
156 Andrea Bargnani RC 1.00 2.50
157 Patrick O'Bryant RC .60 1.50
158 Shelden Williams RC .75 2.00
159 Hilton Armstrong RC .60 1.50
160 Adam Morrison RC 1.00 2.50
161 Rodney Carney RC .60 1.50
162 Randy Foye RC 1.00 2.50
163 Rajon Rondo RC 1.50 4.00
164 Marcus Williams RC .60 1.50
165 J.J. Redick RC 1.25 3.00

2006-07 Bowman Bronze

*BRONZE 1-115: 4X TO 10X BASE HI
*BRONZE 116-165: 1.5X TO 4X BASE HI
STATED PRINT RUN 50 SER.#'d SETS

2006-07 Bowman Silver

*SILVER 1-115: 1.25X TO 3X BASE HI
*SILVER 116-165: .75X TO 2X BASE HI
STATED PRINT RUN 379 SER.#'d SETS

2006-07 Bowman McDonald's All-American Rookie Relics

STATED ODDS 1:60
1 Jordan Farmar 2.50 6.00
2 Rajon Rondo 8.00 20.00
3 Shannon Brown 1.50 4.00
4 Dee Brown 1.50 4.00
5 Paul Davis 1.50 4.00
6 J.J. Redick 3.00 8.00

2006-07 Bowman McDonald's All-American Rookie Relics Autographs

PRINT RUN 50 SER.#'d SETS
UNPRICED SUPER PRINT RUN ONE SET
1 Jordan Farmar 6.00 15.00
2 Rajon Rondo 30.00 80.00
3 Shannon Brown 4.00 10.00
4 Dee Brown 4.00 10.00
5 Paul Davis 4.00 10.00
6 J.J. Redick 8.00 20.00

2006-07 Bowman Power of 2 Autographs

PRINT RUN 10 TO 25 SER.#'d SETS
SOME NOT PRICED DUE TO SCARCITY
POWER OF 3 UNPRICED DUE TO SCARCITY
MW A.Morrison/D.Wade B 50.00 125.00

2006-07 Bowman Relics

GROUP A STATED ODDS 1:107
GROUP B STATED ODDS 1:19
*DUAL: .5X TO 1.25X BASE HI
DUAL PRINT RUN 249 SER.#'d SETS
*TRIPLE: .6X TO 1.5X BASE HI
TRIPLE PRINT RUN 50 SER.#'d SETS
AB Andrew Bogut B 2.00 5.00
AI Allen Iverson A 3.00 8.00
AJ Antawn Jamison A 2.00 5.00
AM Adam Morrison B 2.50 6.00
BJ Bobby Jones B 1.50 4.00
BW Ben Wallace A Shorts 2.00 5.00
CA Carmelo Anthony B 3.00 8.00
CB Chris Bosh B Shirt 2.50 6.00
CP Chris Paul B Shorts 3.00 8.00
CS Cedric Simmons B 1.50 4.00
CW Chris Webber A 2.50 6.00
DH Dwight Howard A 2.00 5.00
DN Dirk Nowitzki A Shorts 4.00 10.00
DW Dwyane Wade B 4.00 10.00
GA Gilbert Arenas B Shirt 2.00 5.00
HA Hilton Armstrong B 1.50 4.00
JB Josh Boone B 1.50 4.00
JF Jordan Farmar B 2.50 6.00
JS Josh Smith A 2.00 5.00
KB Kobe Bryant B 10.00 25.00
KG Kevin Garnett A Warm 4.00 10.00
LA LaMarcus Aldridge B 6.00 15.00
MB Mike Bibby B 2.50 6.00
MC Mardy Collins B 1.50 4.00
MW Marcus Williams B 1.50 4.00
PD Paul Davis B 1.50 4.00
PO Patrick O'Bryant B 1.50 4.00
PP Paul Pierce A Warm 2.50 6.00
QD Quincy Douby B 1.50 4.00
RA Ray Allen B 2.50 6.00
RB Renaldo Balkman B 2.00 5.00
RC Rodney Carney B 1.50 4.00
RF Randy Foye B 2.50 6.00
RG Rudy Gay B 3.00 8.00
RR Rajon Rondo B 6.00 15.00
RW Rasheed Wallace B 2.50 6.00
SJ Solomon Jones B 1.50 4.00
SM Shawn Marion A 2.00 5.00
SN Steve Nash A Warm 3.00 8.00
SO Shaquille O'Neal B 5.00 12.00
SW Shelden Williams B 2.00 5.00
TD Tim Duncan B 4.00 10.00
YM Yao Ming B 3.00 8.00
CSM Craig Smith B 2.00 5.00
DNO David Noel B 1.50 4.00
JJR J.J. Redick B 3.00 8.00
PJT P.J. Tucker B 2.00 5.00
RAR Ron Artest A 2.50 6.00
RBR Ronnie Brewer B 2.50 6.00
SNO Steve Novak B 2.00 5.00

2006-07 Bowman Rookie Snapshots Relics

PRINT RUN 199 SER.#'d SETS
AM Adam Morrison 3.00 8.00
CS Cedric Simmons 2.00 5.00
DB Dee Brown 2.00 5.00
HA Hilton Armstrong 2.00 5.00
JB Josh Boone 2.00 5.00
JF Jordan Farmar 3.00 8.00
JW James White 2.00 5.00
KL Kyle Lowry 4.00 10.00
KP Kevin Pittsnogle 2.50 6.00
LA LaMarcus Aldridge 8.00 20.00
MA Maurice Ager 2.00 5.00
MW Marcus Williams 2.00 5.00
PO Patrick O'Bryant 2.00 5.00
QD Quincy Douby 2.00 5.00
RB Renaldo Balkman 2.50 6.00
RC Rodney Carney 2.00 5.00
RF Randy Foye 3.00 8.00
RG Rudy Gay 4.00 10.00
RR Rajon Rondo 8.00 20.00
SB Shannon Brown 2.00 5.00
SW Shelden Williams 2.50 6.00
CSM Craig Smith 2.50 6.00
JJR J.J. Redick 4.00 10.00
RBR Ronnie Brewer 3.00 8.00
SWI Shawne Williams 2.00 5.00

2007-08 Bowman

This 160-card set was released in November, 2007. The set was issued into the hobby in six-card packs (2 of which were Bowman Chrome cards), with an $4 SRP, which came 18 packs per box and 12 boxes per case. Cards numbered 1-110 feature veterans while cards numbered 111-160 feature 2007-08 NBA rookies which were issued to a stated print run of 2999 serial numbered sets.

COMPLETE SET (160) 30.00 60.00
COMP.SET w/o SP's (110) 15.00 30.00
RC PRINT RUN 2999 SER.#'d SETS
UNPRICED PLATE PRINT RUN ONE SET
1 Gilbert Arenas .25 .60
2 Dwight Howard .25 .60
3 Dwyane Wade .50 1.25
4 Chris Bosh .30 .75
5 Josh Smith .25 .60
6 Andrew Bogut .25 .60
7 Ben Gordon .25 .60
8 Deron Williams .25 .60
9 Tony Parker .30 .75
10 Mike Bibby .30 .75
11 Yao Ming .40 1.00
12 Raymond Felton .30 .75
13 Steve Nash .40 1.00
14 Jameer Nelson .20 .50
15 Carmelo Anthony .40 1.00
16 Pau Gasol .30 .75
17 Rashard Lewis .25 .60
18 Eddy Curry .20 .50
19 Luol Deng .25 .60
20 Kevin Garnett .50 1.25
21 Tim Duncan .50 1.25
22 Michael Redd .25 .60
23 LeBron James 1.25 3.00
24 Kobe Bryant 1.25 3.00
25 Al Jefferson .25 .60
26 Mike Dunleavy .25 .60
27 Tyson Chandler .25 .60
28 Zach Randolph .25 .60
29 Jason Richardson .30 .75
30 Rasheed Wallace .30 .75
31 Shawn Marion .25 .60
32 Shaquille O'Neal .60 1.50
33 Allen Iverson .40 1.00
34 Paul Pierce .30 .75
35 Adam Morrison .20 .50
36 Mike Miller .25 .60
37 Larry Hughes .25 .60
38 Kevin Martin .25 .60
39 Charlie Villanueva .20 .50
40 Vince Carter .40 1.00
41 Dirk Nowitzki .40 1.00
42 Elton Brand .30 .75
43 Ray Allen .30 .75
44 Luke Walton .20 .50
45 Chris Paul .40 1.00
46 Marcus Camby .20 .50
47 Andrei Kirilenko .25 .60
48 J.J. Redick .30 .75
49 Richard Hamilton .25 .60
50 Emeka Okafor .25 .60
51 Manu Ginobili .30 .75
52 Monta Ellis .25 .60
53 Jorge Garbajosa .25 .60
54 Kyle Korver .25 .60
55 Jason Kidd .30 .75
56 Randy Foye .30 .75
57 Shane Battier .25 .60
58 Shaun Livingston .20 .50
59 Jason Terry .25 .60
60 Joe Johnson .25 .60
61 Lamar Odom .25 .60
62 Tayshaun Prince .25 .60
63 Chris Wilcox .20 .50
64 Leandro Barbosa .25 .60
65 Al Harrington .25 .60
66 Jamal Crawford .30 .75
67 Caron Butler .25 .60
68 Chauncey Billups .30 .75
69 Ricky Davis .25 .60
70 Andrea Bargnani .30 .75
71 Samuel Dalembert .20 .50
72 LaMarcus Aldridge .40 1.00
73 Mehmet Okur .20 .50
74 Marcus Williams .20 .50
75 Andre Miller .25 .60
76 Rudy Gay .30 .75
77 Jermaine O'Neal .25 .60
78 Boris Diaw .25 .60
79 Ryan Gomes .20 .50
80 Gerald Wallace .25 .60
81 Udonis Haslem .20 .50
82 Mo Williams .25 .60
83 Jarrett Jack .25 .60
84 Chris Webber .30 .75
85 Trevor Ariza .20 .50
86 Kirk Hinrich .25 .60
87 Rafer Alston .20 .50
88 Danny Granger .25 .60
89 David West .25 .60
90 Drew Gooden .25 .60
91 Stephon Marbury .25 .60
92 Antawn Jamison .25 .60
93 Ron Artest .30 .75
94 Richard Jefferson .25 .60
95 Carlos Boozer .25 .60
96 Hakim Warrick .25 .60
97 T.J. Ford .20 .50
98 Desmond Mason .20 .50
99 Andre Iguodala .25 .60
100 Amare Stoudemire .25 .60
101 Tracy McGrady .30 .75
102 Jason Kapono .20 .50
103 Ben Wallace .25 .60
104 Marvin Williams .25 .60
105 Baron Davis .25 .60
106 Andrew Bynum .20 .50
107 Brandon Roy .30 .75
108 David Lee .20 .50
109 Corey Maggette .25 .60
110 Josh Howard .25 .60
111 Kevin Durant RC 30.00 80.00
112 Al Horford RC 2.00 5.00
113 Mike Conley Jr. RC 2.00 5.00
114 Jeff Green RC 1.50 4.00
115 Corey Brewer RC 1.50 4.00
116 Joakim Noah RC 1.50 4.00
117 Julian Wright RC 1.00 2.50
118 Ramon Sessions RC 1.50 4.00
119 Sammy Mejia RC 1.00 2.50
120 Luis Scola RC 2.00 5.00
121 Yi Jianlian RC 2.00 5.00
122 Arron Afflalo RC 1.50 4.00
123 Carl Landry RC 1.00 2.50
124 Alando Tucker RC 1.00 2.50
125 Gabe Pruitt RC 1.00 2.50
126 Marcus Williams RC 1.00 2.50
127 Spencer Hawes RC 1.25 3.00
128 Acie Law RC 1.00 2.50
129 Thaddeus Young RC 1.50 4.00
130 Nick Fazekas RC 1.00 2.50
131 Al Thornton RC 1.25 3.00
132 Rodney Stuckey RC 1.25 3.00
133 Nick Young RC 2.00 5.00
134 Glen Davis RC 1.25 3.00
135 Jermareo Davidson RC 1.00 2.50
136 JamesOn Curry RC 1.00 2.50
137 Jason Smith RC 1.25 3.00
138 Daequan Cook RC 1.25 3.00
139 Jared Dudley RC 1.25 3.00
140 Derrick Byars RC 1.00 2.50
141 Josh McRoberts RC 1.25 3.00
142 Adam Haluska RC 1.00 2.50
143 Reyshawn Terry RC 1.00 2.50
144 Aaron Gray RC 1.00 2.50
145 Herbert Hill RC 1.00 2.50
146 Jared Jordan RC 1.00 2.50
147 Wilson Chandler RC 1.25 3.00
148 Morris Almond RC 1.00 2.50
149 Aaron Brooks RC 1.25 3.00
150 Petteri Koponen RC 1.50 4.00
151 Dominic McGuire RC 1.00 2.50
152 Greg Oden RC 1.50 4.00
153 Stephane Lasme RC 1.00 2.50
154 D.J. Strawberry RC 1.00 2.50
155 Sean Williams RC 1.00 2.50
156 Marco Belinelli RC 1.50 4.00
157 Javaris Crittenton RC 1.00 2.50
158 Demetris Nichols RC 1.00 2.50
159 Taurean Green RC 1.00 2.50
160 Brandan Wright RC 1.50 4.00

2007-08 Bowman Copper

*COPPER: .5X TO 1.25X BASE HI
COPPER PRINT RUN 399 SER.#'d SETS
111 Kevin Durant 75.00 200.00

2007-08 Bowman Gold

*GOLD 1-110: 1.25X TO 3X BASE HI
*GOLD 111-160: 1.5X TO 4X BASE HI
GOLD PRINT RUN 99 SER.#'d SETS
111 Kevin Durant 200.00 500.00

2007-08 Bowman Silver

*SILVER: .75X TO 2X BASE HI
SILVER PRINT RUN 199 SER.#'d SETS
111 Kevin Durant 100.00 250.00

2007-08 Bowman Relics

*BRONZE: .6X TO 1.25X BASE HI
BRONZE PRINT RUN 50 SER.#'d SETS
*SILVER: .6X TO 1.5X BASE HI
SILVER PRINT RUN 25 SER.#'d SETS
UNPRICED GOLD PRINT RUN ONE SET
*DUAL: .5X TO 1.25X BASE HI
DUAL PRINT RUN 199 SER.#'d SETS
*DUAL BRONZE: .6X TO 1.5X HI
DUAL BRONZE PRINT RUN 50 SETS
*DUAL SILVER: .75X TO 2X HI
DUAL SILVER PRINT RUN 25 SETS
UNPRICED DUAL GOLD PRINT RUN ONE SET
*TRIPLE: .6X TO 1.5X BASE HI
TRIPLE PRINT RUN 99 SER.#'d SETS
TRIPLE BRONZE: .75X TO 2X BASE HI
TRIPLE BRONZE PRINT RUN 50 SETS
*TRIPLE SILVER: 1X TO 2.5X BASE HI
TRIPLE SILVER PRINT RUN 25 SETS
UNPRICED TRIPLE GOLD PRINT RUN ONE SET
AH Al Horford 3.00 8.00
AIG Andre Iguodala 2.00 5.00
AL Acie Law 1.50 4.00
AM Adam Morrison 1.50 4.00
AS Amare Stoudemire 2.00 5.00
AT Al Thornton 2.00 5.00
BG Ben Gordon 2.00 5.00
BR Brandon Roy 2.50 6.00
BWR Brandan Wright 2.50 6.00
C Corey Brewer 2.50 6.00
CA Carmelo Anthony 3.00 8.00
CB Chris Bosh 2.50 6.00
DH Dwight Howard 2.00 5.00
DN Dirk Nowitzki 3.00 8.00
DW Dwyane Wade 5.00 12.00
DWI Deron Williams 2.00 5.00
EB Elton Brand 2.50 6.00
GO Greg Oden 2.50 6.00
GW Gerald Wallace 2.00 5.00
JC Javaris Crittenton 1.50 4.00
JG Jeff Green 2.50 6.00
JK Jason Kidd 2.50 6.00
JN Joakim Noah 2.50 6.00
JR Jason Richardson 2.50 6.00
JS Josh Smith 2.00 5.00
JSM Jason Smith 2.00 5.00
JW Julian Wright 1.50 4.00
KB Kobe Bryant 6.00 15.00
KG Kevin Garnett 4.00 10.00
LB Larry Bird 6.00 15.00
LD Luol Deng 2.00 5.00
MB Mike Bibby 2.50 6.00
MC Mike Conley Jr. 3.00 8.00
MJ Magic Johnson 6.00 15.00
NY Nick Young 3.00 8.00
PG Pau Gasol 2.50 6.00
RA Ray Allen 2.50 6.00
RH Richard Hamilton 2.00 5.00
RS Rodney Stuckey 2.00 5.00
SH Spencer Hawes 2.00 5.00
SM Shawn Marion 2.00 5.00
SN Steve Nash 3.00 8.00
SO Shaquille O'Neal 5.00 12.00
SW Sean Williams 1.50 4.00
TD Tim Duncan 4.00 10.00
TM Tracy McGrady 2.50 6.00
TP Tony Parker 2.50 6.00
TY Thaddeus Young 2.50 6.00
VC Vince Carter 3.00 8.00
YM Yao Ming 3.00 8.00

2008-09 Bowman

This set was released on October 29, 2008. The base set consists of 150 cards. Cards 1-110 feature veterans, and cards 111-150 are rookies.

COMPLETE SET (150) 25.00 60.00
UNPRICED PRESS PLATE PRINT RUN ONE SET
UNPRICED RED PRINT RUN ONE SET
1 Tracy McGrady .30 .75
2 Jason Kidd .30 .75
3 LeBron James 1.25 3.00
4 Chris Bosh .30 .75
5 Kevin Garnett .50 1.25
6 Josh Smith .25 .60
7 Richard Hamilton .25 .60
8 Monta Ellis .25 .60
9 Yi Jianlian .30 .75
10 Danny Granger .25 .60
11 Richard Jefferson .25 .60
12 Elton Brand .30 .75
13 Rudy Gay .30 .75
14 Andres Nocioni .20 .50
15 Carmelo Anthony .40 1.00
16 Pau Gasol .30 .75
17 Corey Brewer .25 .60
18 Hedo Turkoglu .25 .60
19 Andre Iguodala .25 .60
20 Raymond Felton .25 .60
21 Tim Duncan .50 1.25
22 Michael Redd .25 .60
23 Chris Paul .40 1.00
24 Kobe Bryant 1.25 3.00
25 Brandon Roy .30 .75
26 Carlos Boozer .25 .60
27 Jeff Green .25 .60
28 Luis Scola .25 .60
29 Al Thornton .25 .60
30 Gilbert Arenas .25 .60
31 Brandan Wright .25 .60
32 Shaquille O'Neal .60 1.50
33 Allen Iverson .40 1.00
34 Paul Pierce .30 .75
35 Ben Gordon .25 .60
36 Jamal Crawford .30 .75
37 Andrew Bynum .20 .50
38 Gerald Wallace .25 .60
39 Mike Conley Jr. .25 .60
40 Ben Wallace .25 .60
41 Dirk Nowitzki .40 1.00
42 David Lee .20 .50
43 Mo Williams .25 .60
44 Al Jefferson .25 .60
45 Tayshaun Prince .25 .60
46 Jameer Nelson .20 .50
47 Andrei Kirilenko .25 .60
48 David West .25 .60
49 Al Horford .30 .75
50 Steve Nash .30 .75
51 Ron Artest .30 .75
52 Greg Oden .25 .60
53 Sean Williams .25 .60
54 Jamario Moon .20 .50
55 Baron Davis .25 .60
56 Udonis Haslem .20 .50
57 Mike Dunleavy .25 .60
58 Shane Battier .25 .60
59 Andrew Bogut .25 .60
60 Ray Allen .30 .75
61 Nick Young .25 .60
62 Manu Ginobili .30 .75
63 Jason Richardson .30 .75
64 Mike Miller .25 .60
65 Leandro Barbosa .25 .60
66 Luol Deng .25 .60
67 Shawn Marion .25 .60
68 Peja Stojakovic .30 .75
69 Kevin Durant .75 2.00
70 Corey Maggette .25 .60
71 Chauncey Billups .30 .75
72 Josh Howard .25 .60
73 Kevin Martin .25 .60
74 Anderson Varejao .20 .50
75 Craig Smith .20 .50
76 Antawn Jamison .25 .60
77 Marcus Camby .20 .50
78 Andre Miller .25 .60
79 Zach Randolph .25 .60
80 Deron Williams .25 .60
81 Devin Harris .20 .50
82 Rashard Lewis .25 .60
83 Damien Wilkins .20 .50
84 LaMarcus Aldridge .30 .75
85 Larry Hughes .25 .60
86 Brad Miller .25 .60
87 Jermaine O'Neal .25 .60
88 Caron Butler .25 .60
89 Tyson Chandler .25 .60
90 Joe Johnson .25 .60
91 Amare Stoudemire .25 .60
92 Dwight Howard .25 .60
93 Rajon Rondo .30 .75
94 T.J. Ford .20 .50
95 Rodney Stuckey .25 .60
96 Samuel Dalembert .20 .50
97 Tony Parker .30 .75
98 Vince Carter .40 1.00
99 Yao Ming .40 1.00
100 Dwyane Wade .50 1.25
101 Dominique Wilkins .40 1.00
102 Rick Barry .25 .60
103 John Stockton .50 1.25
104 Magic Johnson .75 2.00
105 George Gervin .40 1.00
106 Bill Russell .50 1.25
107 David Robinson .50 1.25
108 Dennis Rodman .60 1.50
109 Larry Bird .75 2.00
110 Jerry West .40 1.00
111 Derrick Rose RC 3.00 8.00
112 Michael Beasley RC .75 2.00
113 O.J. Mayo RC .75 2.00
114 Russell Westbrook RC 12.00 30.00
115 Kevin Love RC 2.50 6.00
116 Danilo Gallinari RC 1.25 3.00
117 Eric Gordon RC 1.25 3.00
118 Joe Alexander RC .50 1.25
119 D.J. Augustin RC .60 1.50
120 Brook Lopez RC 1.00 2.50
121 Jerryd Bayless RC .60 1.50
122 Jason Thompson RC .50 1.25
123 Anthony Randolph RC .50 1.25
124 Robin Lopez RC .75 2.00
125 Marreese Speights RC .60 1.50
126 Roy Hibbert RC .75 2.00
127 JaVale McGee RC 1.00 2.50
128 J.J. Hickson RC .60 1.50
129 Alexis Ajinca RC .50 1.25
130 Ryan Anderson RC .60 1.50
131 Courtney Lee RC .60 1.50
132 Kosta Koufos RC .60 1.50
133 Donte Greene RC .50 1.25
134 George Hill RC .75 2.00
135 D.J. White RC .60 1.50
136 J.R. Giddens RC .50 1.25
137 Joey Dorsey RC .50 1.25
138 Mario Chalmers RC .75 2.00
139 DeAndre Jordan RC 1.00 2.50
140 Chris Douglas-Roberts RC .50 1.25
141 Malik Hairston RC .50 1.25
142 Sean Singletary RC .50 1.25
143 Kyle Weaver RC .50 1.25
144 Patrick Ewing Jr. RC .50 1.25
145 Walter Sharpe RC .50 1.25
146 Sonny Weems RC .50 1.25
147 Shan Foster RC .50 1.25
148 Nicolas Batum RC 1.00 2.50
149 Brandon Rush RC .60 1.50
150 Darrell Arthur RC .60 1.50

2008-09 Bowman Blue

*BLUE 1-110: .75X TO 2X BASE HI
*BLUE 111-150: 1X TO 2.5X BASE HI
BLUE PRINT RUN 499 SER.#'d SETS
3 LeBron James 4.00 10.00
114 Russell Westbrook 50.00 120.00

2008-09 Bowman Gold

*1-110 GOLD: 3X TO 8X BASE
*111-150 GOLD RC: 2X TO 5X BASE
GOLD PRINT RUN 50 SER.#'d SETS
3 LeBron James 40.00 100.00
114 Russell Westbrook 125.00 300.00

2008-09 Bowman Orange

*1-110 ORANGE: 1.25X TO 3X BASE
*111-150 ORANGE: 1.25X TO 3X BASE
ORANGE PRINT RUN 299 SETS
3 LeBron James 20.00 50.00
114 Russell Westbrook 60.00 150.00

2008-09 Bowman Draft Day Issue Relics

PRINT RUN 399 SER.#'d SETS
*BLUE: .5X TO 1.25X BASE HI
BLUE PRINT RUN 50 SER.#'d SETS
UNPRICED GOLD PRINT RUN 10 SER.#'d SETS
*ORANGE: .6X TO 1.5X BASE HI
ORANGE PRINT RUN 25 SETS
UNPRICED RED PRINT RUN ONE SET
DDIRAR Anthony Randolph 1.50 4.00
DDIRBL Brook Lopez 3.00 8.00
DDIRBR Brandon Rush 2.00 5.00
DDIRDG Danilo Gallinari 4.00 10.00
DDIRDJA D.J. Augustin 2.00 5.00
DDIRDR Derrick Rose 12.00 30.00
DDIREG Eric Gordon 4.00 10.00
DDIRJA Joe Alexander 1.50 4.00
DDIRJB Jerryd Bayless 2.00 5.00
DDIRJD Joey Dorsey 1.50 4.00
DDIRKL Kevin Love 15.00 40.00
DDIRMB Michael Beasley 2.50 6.00
DDIROJM O.J. Mayo 2.50 6.00
DDIRRL Robin Lopez 2.50 6.00
DDIRRW Russell Westbrook 20.00 50.00

2008-09 Bowman Draft Day Issue Relics Autographs

PRINT RUN 75 SER.#'d SETS
*BLUE: .5X TO 1.25X BASE HI
BLUE PRINT RUN 50 SER.#'d SETS
UNPRICED GOLD PRINT RUN 10 SETS
*ORANGE: .6X TO 1.5X BASE HI
ORANGE PRINT RUN 25 SER.#'d SETS
UNPRICED RED PRINT RUN ONE SET
DDIABL Brook Lopez 12.00 30.00
DDIADJA D.J. Augustin 8.00 20.00
DDIADR Derrick Rose 40.00 100.00
DDIAEG Eric Gordon 15.00 40.00
DDIAJA Joe Alexander 6.00 15.00
DDIAJB Jerryd Bayless 8.00 20.00
DDIAKL Kevin Love 30.00 80.00
DDIAMB Michael Beasley 10.00 25.00
DDIAOJM O.J. Mayo 10.00 25.00
DDIARW Russell Westbrook 100.00 250.00

2008-09 Bowman Draft Day Issue Relics Combos

PRINT RUN 99 SER.#'d SET
*BLUE: .5X TO 1.25X BASE HI
BLUE PRINT RUN 50 SER.#'d SETS
UNPRICED GOLD PRINT RUN 10 SER.#'d SETS
*ORANGE: .6X TO 1.5X BASE HI
ORANGE PRINT RUN 25 SETS
UNPRICED RED PRINT RUN ONE SET
DDICAR Anthony Randolph 2.50 6.00
DDICBR Brandon Rush 3.00 8.00
DDICDG Danilo Gallinari 6.00 15.00
DDICJD Joey Dorsey 2.50 6.00
DDICRL Robin Lopez 4.00 10.00

2008-09 Bowman Draft Day Issue Relics Combos Autographs

PRINT RUN 75 SER.#'d SETS
*BLUE: .5X TO 1.25X BASE HI
BLUE PRINT RUN 50 SER.#'d SETS
UNPRICED GOLD PRINT RUN 10 SER.#'d SETS
*ORANGE: .6X TO 1.5X BASE HI
ORANGE PRINT RUN 25 SER.#'d SETS
UNPRICED RED PRINT RUN ONE SET
DDICABL Brook Lopez 12.00 30.00
DDICADJA D.J. Augustin 8.00 20.00
DDICADR Derrick Rose 125.00 300.00
DDICAEG Eric Gordon 15.00 40.00
DDICAJA Joe Alexander 6.00 15.00
DDICAJB Jerryd Bayless 8.00 20.00
DDICAKL Kevin Love 30.00 80.00
DDICAMB Michael Beasley 10.00 25.00
DDICAOJM O.J. Mayo 10.00 25.00
DDICARW Russell Westbrook 80.00 200.00

2008-09 Bowman Relics

STATED ODDS 1:13
*BLUE: .75X TO 2X BASE HI
BLUE PRINT RUN 50 SER.#'d SETS
UNPRICED GOLD PRINT RUN 10 SER.#'d SETS
*ORANGE: 1X TO 2.5X BASE HI
ORANGE PRINT RUN 25 SETS
UNPRICED RED PRINT RUN ONE SET
BRAH Al Horford 2.50 6.00
BRAI Allen Iverson 3.00 8.00
BRAJ Al Jefferson 2.00 5.00
BRAJA Antawn Jamison 2.00 5.00
BRAT Al Thornton 2.00 5.00
BRBR Brandon Roy 2.50 6.00
BRBW Ben Wallace 2.00 5.00
BRCA Carmelo Anthony 3.00 8.00
BRCB Chris Bosh 2.50 6.00
BRCBO Carlos Boozer 2.00 5.00
BRCBU Caron Butler 2.00 5.00
BRCM Corey Maggette 2.00 5.00
BRCP Chris Paul 3.00 8.00
BRDH Devin Harris 1.50 4.00
BRDHO Dwight Howard 2.00 5.00
BRDN Dirk Nowitzki 3.00 8.00
BRDW Dwyane Wade 4.00 10.00
BRDWI Deron Williams 2.00 5.00
BRJJ Joe Johnson 2.00 5.00
BRJO Jermaine O'Neal 2.00 5.00
BRJR Jason Richardson 2.50 6.00
BRKB Kobe Bryant 8.00 20.00
BRKG Kevin Garnett 4.00 10.00
BRLO Lamar Odom 2.00 5.00
BRMB Mike Bibby 2.00 5.00
BRMC Mike Conley Jr. 2.00 5.00
BRMG Manu Ginobili 2.50 6.00
BRMR Michael Redd 2.00 5.00
BRPG Pau Gasol 2.50 6.00
BRPP Paul Pierce 2.50 6.00
BRPS Peja Stojakovic 2.50 6.00
BRRA Ray Allen 2.50 6.00
BRRH Richard Hamilton 2.00 5.00
BRRL Rashard Lewis 2.00 5.00
BRRW Rasheed Wallace 2.50 6.00
BRSN Steve Nash 2.50 6.00
BRSO Shaquille O'Neal 5.00 12.00
BRTD Tim Duncan 4.00 10.00

BRTM Tracy McGrady 2.50 6.00
BRYM Yao Ming 3.00 8.00

2009-10 Bowman 48

COMPLETE SET (121) 25.00 50.00
COMP.SET w/o SP's (100) 10.00 25.00
101-114 RC PRINT RUN 2009 SER.#'d SETS
115-121 PRINT RUN 1948 SER.#'d SETS
UNPRICED RED PRINT RUN ONE SET
1 Al Horford .25 .60
2 Joe Johnson .20 .50
3 Josh Smith .20 .50
4 Paul Pierce .25 .60
5 Kevin Garnett .40 1.00
6 Ray Allen .25 .60
7 Rajon Rondo .25 .60
8 Gerald Wallace .20 .50
9 Emeka Okafor .20 .50
10 Ben Gordon .20 .50
11 Derrick Rose .40 1.00
12 John Salmons .20 .50
13 Mo Williams .20 .50
14 LeBron James 1.00 2.50
15 Anderson Varejao .15 .40
16 Dirk Nowitzki .30 .75
17 Jason Kidd .25 .60
18 Jason Terry .20 .50
19 Chauncey Billups .25 .60
20 Carmelo Anthony .30 .75
21 Richard Hamilton .20 .50
22 Allen Iverson .30 .75
23 Rasheed Wallace .25 .60
24 Monta Ellis .20 .50
25 Corey Maggette .20 .50
26 Anthony Randolph .15 .40
27 Tracy McGrady .25 .60
28 Yao Ming .30 .75
29 Ron Artest .25 .60
30 Danny Granger .20 .50
31 T.J. Ford .15 .40
32 Eric Gordon .20 .50
33 Baron Davis .20 .50
34 Marcus Camby .15 .40
35 Pau Gasol .25 .60
36 Kobe Bryant 1.00 2.50
37 Andrew Bynum .15 .40
38 Rudy Gay .25 .60
39 O.J. Mayo .15 .40
40 Michael Beasley .15 .40
41 Dwyane Wade .40 1.00
42 Jermaine O'Neal .20 .50
43 Michael Redd .20 .50
44 Richard Jefferson .20 .50
45 Al Jefferson .20 .50
46 Kevin Love .25 .60
47 Mike Miller .20 .50
48 Vince Carter .30 .75
49 Devin Harris .15 .40
50 David West .20 .50
51 Chris Paul .30 .75
52 Nate Robinson .15 .40
53 David Lee .15 .40
54 Kevin Durant .60 1.50
55 Russell Westbrook .60 1.50
56 Dwight Howard .20 .50
57 Jameer Nelson .15 .40
58 Hedo Turkoglu .20 .50
59 Andre Iguodala .20 .50
60 Elton Brand .25 .60
61 Andre Miller .20 .50
62 Shaquille O'Neal .50 1.25
63 Amare Stoudemire .20 .50
64 Steve Nash .25 .60
65 Rudy Fernandez .15 .40
66 Brandon Roy .25 .60
67 LaMarcus Aldridge .25 .60
68 Spencer Hawes .15 .40
69 Kevin Martin .20 .50
70 Tony Parker .25 .60
71 Tim Duncan .40 1.00
72 Manu Ginobili .25 .60
73 Jose Calderon .15 .40
74 Chris Bosh .25 .60
75 Shawn Marion .20 .50
76 Carlos Boozer .20 .50
77 Deron Williams .20 .50
78 Caron Butler .20 .50
79 Antawn Jamison .20 .50
80 Gilbert Arenas .20 .50
81 Dominique Wilkins .30 .75
82 Bill Russell .40 1.00
83 Bob Cousy .40 1.00
84 Larry Bird .60 1.50
85 Rick Barry .20 .50
86 Elgin Baylor .25 .60
87 Jerry West .30 .75
88 Magic Johnson .60 1.50
89 Oscar Robertson .25 .60
90 George Mikan .50 1.25
91 Pete Maravich .40 1.00
92 Patrick Ewing .30 .75
93 Willis Reed .25 .60
94 Julius Erving .40 1.00
95 Moses Malone .25 .60
96 Wilt Chamberlain .50 1.25
97 Bill Walton .25 .60
98 Clyde Drexler .30 .75
99 Bob Pettit .25 .60
100 Karl Malone .30 .75
101 Blake Griffin RC 5.00 12.00
102 Jonny Flynn RC .75 2.00
103 Hasheem Thabeet RC .75 2.00
104 James Harden RC 20.00 50.00
105 DeMar DeRozan RC 3.00 8.00
106 Stephen Curry RC 60.00 150.00
107 Brandon Jennings RC 1.25 3.00
108 Jordan Hill RC 1.00 2.50
109 Earl Clark RC 1.00 2.50
110 Gerald Henderson RC 1.00 2.50
111 Tyreke Evans RC 1.00 2.50
112 Jrue Holiday RC 1.50 4.00
113 Tyler Hansbrough RC 1.00 2.50
114 Terrence Williams RC .75 2.00
115 Play Card 1.25 3.00
116 Play Card 1.25 3.00
117 Play Card 1.25 3.00
118 Play Card 1.25 3.00
119 Play Card 1.25 3.00
120 Play Card 1.25 3.00
121 Play Card 1.25 3.00

2009-10 Bowman 48 Black

*1-100 BLACK: 5X TO 12X BASE HI
*101-114 RC BLACK: 2.5X TO 6X BASE
*115-121 BLACK: 1X TO 2.5X BASE HI
BLACK PRINT RUN 48 SER.#'d SETS
106 Stephen Curry 300.00 600.00

2009-10 Bowman 48 Blue

*1-100 BLUE: 1.5X TO 4X BASE HI
*101-114 RC BLUE: .4X TO 1X BASE HI
*PLAY CARDS SAME VALUE AS BASE
BLUE PRINT RUN 1948 SER.#'d SETS

2009-10 Bowman 48 Autographs

ATED ODDS 1:9
*BLACK: .5X TO 1.25X BASE HI
BLACK PRINT RUN 48 SER.#'d SETS
48AAB Andrew Bynum 5.00 12.00
48AAJ Antawn Jamison 5.00 12.00
48ABG Ben Gordon 5.00 12.00
48ABR Bill Russell 50.00 120.00
48ABW Bill Walton SP 60.00 150.00
48ACA Carmelo Anthony 20.00 50.00
48ACM Corey Maggette 5.00 12.00
48ACP Chris Paul 15.00 40.00
48ADG Danny Granger 6.00 15.00
48ADH Dwight Howard 12.00 30.00
48ADL David Lee 5.00 12.00
48ADR Derrick Rose 15.00 40.00
48ADW Dwyane Wade 15.00 40.00
48AGO Greg Oden 5.00 12.00
48AJJ Jarrett Jack 5.00 12.00
48AJS Josh Smith 5.00 12.00
48AJW Jerry West 20.00 50.00
48AKH Kirk Hinrich 5.00 12.00
48AKL Kevin Love 8.00 20.00
48ALB Larry Bird SP 75.00 150.00
48ALD Luol Deng 5.00 12.00
48AMJ Magic Johnson 30.00 80.00
48AMW Mo Williams 5.00 12.00
48ARB Rick Barry 6.00 15.00
48AABA Andrea Bargnani 5.00 12.00
48AAIG Andre Iguodala 5.00 12.00
48ABRO Brandon Roy 5.00 12.00
48ADWI Dominique Wilkins 12.00 30.00
48AOJM O.J. Mayo 5.00 12.00
48ATJF T.J. Ford 5.00 12.00

2009-10 Bowman 48 Locker Room Collection Autograph Relics

PRINT RUN 41 SER.#'d SETS
UNPRICED BLACK PRINT RUN 8 SETS
*PATCHES: .75X TO 2X BASE HI
PATCH PRINT RUN 24 SER.#'d SETS
DRCARJW Jerry West 30.00 80.00
LRCARBR Bill Russell 50.00 125.00
LRCARCA Carmelo Anthony 25.00 50.00
LRCARCP Chris Paul 25.00 60.00
LRCARDG Danny Granger 10.00 25.00
LRCARDH Dwight Howard 15.00 40.00
LRCARDR Derrick Rose 100.00 250.00
LRCARDW Dwyane Wade 25.00 60.00
LRCARJS Josh Smith 10.00 25.00
LRCARLB Larry Bird 40.00 100.00
LRCARMJ Magic Johnson 40.00 100.00
LRCARAIG Andre Iguodala 10.00 25.00
LRCARBRO Brandon Roy 20.00 40.00
LRCARDWI Dominique Wilkins 20.00 50.00
LRCAROJM O.J. Mayo 20.00 40.00

2003-04 Bowman Chrome

Released in October 2003 and marketed as two brands in one pack, Bowman and Bowman Chrome cards shared the same packs and boxes. The Bowman version features a 156-card set divided up into 110 base veteran cards with a red border around a centered picture surrounded by silver borders on the left and right and black borders on the top and the bottom. Cards 111-147 feature rookie players and have a blue border around their pictures and share the rest of the design elements with the base cards. Cards 148-157 are autographed rookie cards sequentially numbered to 250. Upon issue, card number 147 was not released. Bowman was packaged in 24-pack boxes with packs containing seven cards, four Bowman cards, four Bowman Chrome Cards and one Parallel, and carried a suggested retail price of $4.

COMP.SET w/o RC's (110) 30.00 80.00
148-157 AU RC STATED ODDS 1:385
148-157 AU PRINT RUN 250 SER.#'d SETS
1 Yao Ming 1.00 2.50
2 Glenn Robinson .40 1.00
3 Antoine Walker .50 1.25
4 Jalen Rose .40 1.00
5 Ricky Davis .40 1.00
6 Juwan Howard .40 1.00
7 Kwame Brown .30 .75
8 Mike Bibby .50 1.25
9 Wally Szczerbiak .40 1.00
10 Allen Iverson .75 2.00
11 Shareef Abdur-Rahim .40 1.00
12 Jamal Mashburn .40 1.00
13 Stephon Marbury .40 1.00
14 Desmond Mason .40 1.00
15 Gordan Giricek .30 .75
16 Caron Butler .40 1.00
17 Jermaine O'Neal .40 1.00
18 Kenyon Martin .40 1.00
19 Andrei Kirilenko .50 1.25
20 Dirk Nowitzki .75 2.00
21 Richard Hamilton .40 1.00
22 Troy Murphy .30 .75
23 Shawn Marion .40 1.00
24 Allan Houston .40 1.00
25 Keith Van Horn .40 1.00
26 Brian Grant .30 .75
27 Mike Miller .40 1.00
28 Chris Webber .50 1.25
29 Brent Barry .30 .75
30 Elton Brand .50 1.25
31 Juan Dixon .30 .75
32 Karl Malone .60 1.50
33 Darrell Armstrong .30 .75
34 Rasheed Wallace .50 1.25
35 Michael Redd .50 1.25
36 Rashard Lewis .50 1.25
37 Ron Artest .50 1.25
38 P.J. Brown .30 .75
39 Eddie Griffin .30 .75
40 Tim Duncan .75 2.00
41 Kurt Thomas .30 .75
42 Raef Lafrentz .30 .75
43 Ben Wallace .40 1.00
44 Lamar Odom .40 1.00
45 Vince Carter .75 2.00
46 Derek Anderson .30 .75
47 Stromile Swift .30 .75
48 Bobby Jackson .30 .75
49 Richard Jefferson .40 1.00
50 Shaquille O'Neal 1.25 3.00
51 Calbert Cheaney .30 .75
52 Troy Hudson .30 .75
53 Ray Allen .50 1.25
54 Howard Eisley .30 .75
55 Alonzo Mourning .60 1.50
56 Sam Cassell .40 1.00
57 Derrick Coleman .40 1.00
58 Andre Miller .40 1.00
59 Antawn Jamison .40 1.00
60 Kevin Garnett .75 2.00
61 Steve Francis .40 1.00
62 Tyson Chandler .40 1.00
63 Drew Gooden .40 1.00
64 Scottie Pippen .75 2.00
65 Pau Gasol .50 1.25
66 Steve Nash .60 1.50
67 DaJuan Wagner .30 .75
68 Jason Terry .40 1.00
69 Reggie Miller .50 1.25
70 Tracy McGrady .60 1.50
71 Nene Hilario .40 1.00
72 Morris Peterson .30 .75
73 Peja Stojakovic .50 1.25
74 Eddie Jones .40 1.00
75 Tony Parker .50 1.25
76 Corliss Williamson .30 .75
77 Vladimir Radmanovic .30 .75
78 Amare Stoudemire .60 1.50
79 Tony Delk .30 .75
80 Jason Kidd .75 2.00
81 Gary Payton .50 1.25
82 Corey Maggette .40 1.00
83 Darius Miles .30 .75
84 Cuttino Mobley .30 .75
85 Eric Snow .30 .75
86 Matt Harpring .30 .75
87 Manu Ginobili .60 1.50
88 Latrell Sprewell .40 1.00
89 Alvin Williams .30 .75
90 Paul Pierce .50 1.25
91 Anfernee Hardaway .75 2.00
92 Gilbert Arenas .40 1.00
93 Jerry Stackhouse .40 1.00
94 Tim Thomas .30 .75
95 Nikoloz Tskitishvili .30 .75
96 Doug Christie .30 .75
97 Zydrunas Ilgauskas .40 1.00
98 Jamaal Tinsley .30 .75
99 Theo Ratliff .30 .75
100 Kobe Bryant 2.00 5.00
101 Chauncey Billups .50 1.25
102 Michael Finley .50 1.25
103 Jason Williams .40 1.00
104 Bonzi Wells .30 .75
105 Voshon Lenard .30 .75
106 Jason Richardson .50 1.25
107 Baron Davis .40 1.00
108 Radoslav Nesterovic .30 .75
109 Eddy Curry .30 .75
110 Michael Olowokandi .30 .75
111 Josh Howard RC 3.00 8.00
112 Mario Austin RC 3.00 8.00
113 Rick Rickert RC 2.00 5.00
114 Tommy Smith RC 3.00 8.00
115 Dahntay Jones RC 2.50 6.00
116 Ndudi Ebi RC 2.00 5.00
117 Maurice Williams RC 3.00 8.00
118 Kendrick Perkins RC 2.50 6.00
119 Steve Blake RC 2.50 6.00
120 David West RC 3.00 8.00
121 Chris Kaman RC 3.00 8.00
122 Keith Bogans RC 2.00 5.00
123 LeBron James RC 75.00 200.00
124 Devin Brown RC 2.00 5.00
125 Jason Kapono RC 2.00 5.00
126 Zoran Planinic RC 2.00 5.00
127 Zaur Pachulia RC 3.00 8.00
128 Malick Badiane RC 3.00 8.00
129 Kyle Korver RC 4.00 10.00
130 Darko Milicic RC 2.50 6.00
131 Troy Bell RC 2.00 5.00
132 Luke Walton RC 3.00 8.00
133 Mike Sweetney RC 2.00 5.00
134 Jarvis Hayes RC 2.00 5.00
135 Leandro Barbosa RC 3.00 8.00
136 Carlos Delfino RC 2.50 6.00
137 Sofoklis Schortsanitis RC 2.00 5.00
138 Slavko Vranes RC 2.00 5.00
139 Travis Hansen RC 2.00 5.00
140 Carmelo Anthony RC 10.00 25.00
141 Reece Gaines RC 2.00 5.00
142 Maciej Lampe RC 2.00 5.00
143 Travis Outlaw RC 2.50 6.00
144 Jerome Beasley RC 2.00 5.00
145 Mickael Pietrus RC 2.50 6.00
146 Brian Cook RC 2.00 5.00
148 Kirk Hinrich AU RC 6.00 15.00
149 Dwyane Wade AU RC 100.00 250.00
150 Marcus Banks AU RC 5.00 12.00
151 Nick Collison AU RC 6.00 15.00
152 Boris Diaw AU RC 8.00 20.00
153 Chris Bosh AU RC 12.00 30.00
154 T.J. Ford AU RC 5.00 12.00
155 Luke Ridnour AU RC 6.00 15.00
156 A.Pavlovic AU RC 6.00 15.00
157 Zarko Cabarkapa AU RC 5.00 12.00

2003-04 Bowman Chrome Refractors

*1-110: 1.5X TO 4X BASE CARD HI
*111-146: 1.25X TO 3X BASE HI
*148-157 AU RC REF: .75X TO 2X BASE HI
148-157 AU RC REF PRINT RUN 50 SETS
CARD 147 NOT RELEASED
100 Kobe Bryant 15.00 40.00
123 LeBron James 500.00 800.00

2003-04 Bowman Chrome Refractors Gold

*1-110: 8X TO 20X BASE HI
*111-146 RC: 2X TO 5X BASE HI
1-146 REF.GOLD PRINT RUN 50 SETS
CARD 147 NOT RELEASED
100 Kobe Bryant 60.00 150.00
123 LeBron James 2000.00 4000.00
140 Carmelo Anthony 150.00 300.00

2003-04 Bowman Chrome X-fractors

*1-110: 4X TO 10X BASE CARD HI
*111-146 RCs: 2X TO 5X BASE HI
1-146 X-FRACTOR PRINT RUN 150 SETS
*148-157 RCs: 1.25X TO 3X BASE HI
CARD 147 NOT RELEASED
100 Kobe Bryant 30.00 80.00
123 LeBron James 1000.00 1500.00

2004-05 Bowman Chrome

Released in October of 2004 under the name Bowman Rookies and Stars again this year, packs contained an assortment of cards from both Bowman and Bowman Chrome, therefore they have been designated as such. Both sets contain 156 cards where cards 1-110 feature veteran players, cards 111-146 feature rookies, and card numbers 147-156 feature autographed rookie cards inserted at one in 105 packs for Bowman and are sequentially numbered to 250 for Bowman Chrome. All cards have gray borders, but the veteran players have red accents along the side borders and the rookies have blue accents. Boxes contained 24 packs of seven cards (four Bowman, two Bowman Chrome and one Bowman Gold Parallel) that carried a SRP of $4.00.

COMP.SET w/o RCs (110) 25.00 60.00
147-156 PRINT RUN 250 SER.#'d SETS
1 Yao Ming 1.00 2.50
2 Eddy Curry .30 .75
3 Stephon Marbury .40 1.00
4 Chris Webber .50 1.25
5 Jason Kidd .75 2.00
6 Cuttino Mobley .30 .75
7 Jermaine O'Neal .40 1.00
8 Kobe Bryant 2.00 5.00
9 Tony Parker .50 1.25
10 Gary Payton .50 1.25
11 T.J. Ford .30 .75
12 Tim Duncan .75 2.00
13 Glenn Robinson .40 1.00
14 Jason Richardson .50 1.25
15 Carmelo Anthony 1.00 2.50
16 Pau Gasol .50 1.25
17 Kirk Hinrich .40 1.00
18 Kenyon Martin .40 1.00
19 Jamal Crawford .50 1.25
20 Elton Brand .50 1.25
21 Kevin Garnett .75 2.00
22 Michael Redd .40 1.00
23 LeBron James 3.00 8.00
24 Andre Miller .40 1.00
25 Peja Stojakovic .50 1.25
26 Jarvis Hayes .30 .75
27 David Wesley .30 .75
28 Jason Kapono .30 .75
29 Corey Maggette .40 1.00
30 Rasheed Wallace .50 1.25
31 Nene .40 1.00
32 Amare Stoudemire .40 1.00
33 Allen Iverson .75 2.00
34 Shaquille O'Neal 1.25 3.00
35 Mike Dunleavy .40 1.00
36 Steve Nash .60 1.50
37 Brad Miller .40 1.00
38 Chris Bosh .50 1.25
39 Boris Diaw .40 1.00
40 Steve Francis .40 1.00
41 Dirk Nowitzki .75 2.00
42 Jason Williams .40 1.00
43 Gilbert Arenas .40 1.00
44 Keith Van Horn .40 1.00
45 Jamal Mashburn .40 1.00
46 Derek Fisher .40 1.00
47 Andrei Kirilenko .40 1.00
48 Ricky Davis .40 1.00
49 Gerald Wallace .40 1.00
50 Tracy McGrady .60 1.50
51 Zach Randolph .40 1.00
52 Rafer Alston .30 .75
53 Bobby Jackson .30 .75
54 Desmond Mason .40 1.00
55 Tim Thomas .30 .75
56 Jamaal Tinsley .30 .75
57 Kwame Brown .30 .75
58 Chauncey Billups .50 1.25
59 Brandon Hunter .30 .75
60 Reggie Miller .50 1.25
61 Samuel Dalembert .30 .75
62 James Posey .30 .75
63 Erick Dampier .30 .75
64 Carlos Arroyo .30 .75
65 Reece Gaines .30 .75
66 Darko Milicic .30 .75
67 Sam Cassell .40 1.00
68 Dwyane Wade .75 2.00
69 Allan Houston .40 1.00
70 Ray Allen .50 1.25
71 Tyson Chandler .40 1.00
72 Bonzi Wells .30 .75
73 Jalen Rose .40 1.00
74 Marquis Daniels .30 .75
75 Zydrunas Ilgauskas .40 1.00
76 Tayshaun Prince .40 1.00
77 Lamar Odom .40 1.00
78 Luke Ridnour .40 1.00
79 Joe Johnson .40 1.00
80 Vince Carter .75 2.00
81 Antoine Walker .50 1.25
82 Shareef Abdur-Rahim .40 1.00
83 Richard Jefferson .40 1.00
84 Maurice Taylor .30 .75
85 Chris Kaman .40 1.00
86 Marcus Banks .30 .75
87 Mike Bibby .50 1.25
88 Latrell Sprewell .40 1.00
89 Rashard Lewis .50 1.25
90 Baron Davis .40 1.00
91 Caron Butler .40 1.00
92 Michael Finley .50 1.25
93 Mike Miller .40 1.00
94 Al Harrington .40 1.00
95 Quentin Richardson .40 1.00
96 Jamaal Magloire .30 .75
97 Darius Miles .30 .75
98 Jeff Foster .30 .75
99 Karl Malone .60 1.50
100 Shawn Marion .40 1.00
101 Antawn Jamison .40 1.00
102 Manu Ginobili .60 1.50
103 Ben Wallace .40 1.00
104 Paul Pierce .50 1.25
105 Mike Sweetney .30 .75
106 Ron Artest .50 1.25
107 Michael Olowokandi .30 .75
108 Jason Terry .40 1.00
109 Gordan Giricek .30 .75
110 Carlos Boozer .40 1.00
111 Romain Sato RC 1.25 3.00
112 Chris Duhon RC 2.00 5.00
113 Ben Gordon RC 2.00 5.00
114 Matt Freije RC 1.50 4.00
115 Al Jefferson RC 2.50 6.00
116 Beno Udrih RC 1.50 4.00
117 Kirk Snyder RC 1.25 3.00
118 Anderson Varejao RC 1.50 4.00
119 Devin Harris RC 1.50 4.00
120 Tony Allen RC 2.00 5.00
121 Ha Seung-Jin RC 2.00 5.00
122 J.R. Smith RC 2.00 5.00
123 Blake Stepp RC 2.00 5.00
124 Jameer Nelson RC 2.00 5.00
125 Kris Humphries RC 2.00 5.00
126 Josh Childress RC 1.50 4.00
127 Tim Pickett RC 2.00 5.00
128 Delonte West RC 2.00 5.00
129 Dwight Howard RC 4.00 10.00
130 Luke Jackson RC 1.25 3.00
131 Rickey Paulding RC 1.25 3.00
132 Andre Emmett RC 1.25 3.00
133 Josh Smith RC 2.00 5.00
134 Antonio Burks RC 1.50 4.00
135 Ricky Minard RC 1.50 4.00
136 Lionel Chalmers RC 2.00 5.00
137 Shaun Livingston RC 2.00 5.00
138 Trevor Ariza RC 2.00 5.00
139 Sergei Lishouk RC 1.50 4.00
140 Pape Sow RC 1.50 4.00
141 Rashad Wright RC 1.50 4.00
142 Jackson Vroman RC 1.25 3.00
143 Luis Flores RC 1.50 4.00
144 Royal Ivey RC 1.50 4.00
145 Kevin Martin RC 2.50 6.00
146 Andre Iguodala RC 2.50 6.00
147 Andris Biedrins AU RC 5.00 12.00
148 Pavel Podkolzin AU RC 5.00 12.00
149 Luol Deng AU RC 5.00 12.00
150 Robert Swift AU RC 5.00 12.00
151 Sebastian Telfair AU RC 6.00 15.00
152 Emeka Okafor AU RC 6.00 15.00
153 Dorell Wright AU RC 8.00 20.00
154 Sasha Vujacic AU RC 8.00 20.00
155 Rafael Araujo AU RC 5.00 12.00
156 David Harrison AU RC 5.00 12.00

2004-05 Bowman Chrome Refractors

*1-110 REFRACTORS: 1.5X TO 4X BASE HI
*111-146 REFRACTORS: 1.25X TO 3X BASE HI
STATED PRINT RUN 300 SER.#'d SETS
*147-156 REFRACTOR AU: 1X TO 2.5X BASE HI
STATED PRINT RUN 50 SER.#'d SETS
23 LeBron James 40.00 100.00

2004-05 Bowman Chrome Refractors Gold

*1-110 GOLD: 6X TO 15X BASE HI
*111-146 GOLD: 3X TO 8X BASE HI
STATED PRINT RUN 50 SER.#'d SETS
23 LeBron James 300.00 600.00
129 Dwight Howard 60.00 150.00

2004-05 Bowman Chrome X-Fractors

*1-110 X-FRACTORS: 4X TO 10X BASE HI
*111-146 X-FRACTORS: 2X TO 5X BASE HI
STATED PRINT RUN 150 SER.#'d SETS
*147-156 X-FRACTORS AU: 1.5X TO 4X BASE HI
147-156 PRINT RUN 25 SER.#'d SETS
23 LeBron James 125.00 300.00

2005-06 Bowman Chrome

Randomly seeded in packs at the rate of two per, this 161-card set parallels the base set design and numbering of Bowman. Each card is finished in chrome and rookie autographs are sequentially numbered to 250.

COMP.SET w/o RC's (110) 25.00 60.00
AU RC PRINT RUN 250 SER.#'d SETS
UNPRICED SUPERFR.PRINT RUN ONE SET
1 Steve Nash .75 2.00
2 Primoz Brezec .40 1.00
3 Baron Davis .50 1.25
4 Al Harrington .50 1.25
5 Caron Butler .50 1.25
6 Marcus Camby .50 1.25
7 Carlos Boozer .50 1.25
8 Ben Gordon .50 1.25
9 Stephen Jackson .50 1.25
10 Dirk Nowitzki 1.00 2.50
11 Nenad Krstic .40 1.00
12 Jason Richardson .60 1.50
13 Brendan Haywood .40 1.00
14 Chauncey Billups .60 1.50
15 Corey Maggette .50 1.25
16 Peja Stojakovic .60 1.50
17 Grant Hill .75 2.00
18 Pau Gasol .60 1.50
19 Vladimir Radmanovic .40 1.00
20 Jason Kidd 1.00 2.50
21 Tim Duncan 1.00 2.50
22 David Harrison .40 1.00
23 LeBron James 2.50 6.00
24 Udonis Haslem .40 1.00
25 Dan Dickau .40 1.00
26 Cuttino Mobley .40 1.00
27 Chris Bosh .60 1.50
28 Sebastian Telfair .50 1.25
29 Latrell Sprewell .50 1.25
30 Emeka Okafor .50 1.25
31 Mike James .40 1.00
32 Trevor Ariza .40 1.00
33 Larry Hughes .50 1.25
34 Desmond Mason .40 1.00
35 Tayshaun Prince .50 1.25
36 Manu Ginobili .60 1.50
37 Mike Bibby .60 1.50
38 Andre Iguodala .50 1.25
39 Jamaal Magloire .40 1.00
40 Amare Stoudemire .50 1.25
41 Rafer Alston .40 1.00
42 Elton Brand .60 1.50
43 Steve Francis .50 1.25
44 Rashard Lewis .60 1.50
45 Lorenzen Wright .40 1.00
46 Kirk Hinrich .50 1.25
47 Andrei Kirilenko .50 1.25
48 Brad Miller .50 1.25
49 Jamal Crawford .60 1.50
50 Shaquille O'Neal 1.25 3.00
51 Shaun Livingston .40 1.00
52 Troy Murphy .40 1.00
53 Drew Gooden .50 1.25
54 Paul Pierce .60 1.50
55 Vince Carter 1.00 2.50
56 Wally Szczerbiak .50 1.25
57 Antawn Jamison .50 1.25
58 Marquis Daniels .40 1.00
59 Gerald Wallace .50 1.25
60 Ray Allen .60 1.50
61 Jamaal Tinsley .40 1.00
62 Shane Battier .50 1.25
63 Zydrunas Ilgauskas .50 1.25
64 Mehmet Okur .40 1.00
65 Rasheed Wallace .60 1.50
66 Maurice Williams .50 1.25
67 Josh Howard .60 1.50
68 Zach Randolph .50 1.25
69 Kobe Bryant 2.50 6.00
70 Tracy McGrady .75 2.00
71 Luke Ridnour .50 1.25
72 Damon Jones .40 1.00
73 Tony Allen .40 1.00
74 Mike Miller .50 1.25
75 Sam Cassell .50 1.25
76 Ben Wallace .50 1.25
77 Mike Sweetney .40 1.00
78 Eddy Curry .40 1.00
79 Michael Redd .50 1.25
80 Carmelo Anthony 1.25 3.00
81 Dwight Howard .50 1.25
82 Josh Smith .50 1.25
83 Richard Jefferson .50 1.25
84 Richard Hamilton .50 1.25
85 Chris Webber .60 1.50
86 Shawn Marion .50 1.25
87 Jalen Rose .60 1.50
88 Bob Sura .40 1.00
89 Mike Dunleavy .50 1.25
90 Dwyane Wade 1.00 2.50
91 Gary Payton .60 1.50
92 Luol Deng .50 1.25
93 Kenyon Martin .50 1.25
94 Beno Udrih .40 1.00
95 J.R. Smith .50 1.25
96 Lamar Odom .50 1.25
97 Andre Miller .50 1.25
98 Jermaine O'Neal .50 1.25
99 Yao Ming .75 2.00
100 Allen Iverson 1.00 2.50
101 Quentin Richardson .50 1.25
102 Gilbert Arenas .50 1.25
103 Stephon Marbury .50 1.25
104 Antoine Walker .50 1.25
105 Jameer Nelson .40 1.00
106 Joel Przybilla .40 1.00
107 Devin Harris .40 1.00
108 Tony Parker .60 1.50
109 Josh Childress .50 1.25
110 Kevin Garnett 1.00 2.50
111 Chris Paul RC 4.00 10.00
112 Danny Granger RC 2.50 6.00
113 Antoine Wright RC 1.50 4.00
114 Joey Graham RC 1.50 4.00
115 Wayne Simien RC 1.25 3.00
116 Channing Frye RC 2.00 5.00
117 Charlie Villanueva RC 2.00 5.00
118 Francisco Garcia RC 1.50 4.00
119 Ike Diogu RC 1.25 3.00
120 Jarrett Jack RC 2.00 5.00
121 Robert Whaley RC 1.25 3.00
122 C.J. Miles RC 2.00 5.00
123 Ryan Gomes RC 1.50 4.00
124 Nate Robinson RC 2.00 5.00
125 Daniel Ewing RC 1.50 4.00
126 Andray Blatche RC 2.00 5.00
127 Luther Head RC 1.50 4.00
128 Julius Hodge RC 1.25 3.00
129 Lawrence Roberts RC 1.25 3.00
130 Jason Maxiell RC 1.50 4.00
131 Martynas Andriuskevicius RC 1.25 3.00
132 Ersan Ilyasova RC 2.00 5.00
133 Martell Webster RC 1.50 4.00
134 Andrew Bynum RC 1.50 4.00
135 Louis Williams RC 2.00 5.00
136 Johan Petro RC 1.25 3.00
137 Brandon Bass RC 1.50 4.00
138 Travis Diener RC 1.25 3.00
139 Bracey Wright RC 1.25 3.00
140 Marvin Williams RC 2.00 5.00
141 Eddie Basden RC 1.25 3.00
142 Von Wafer RC 1.25 3.00
143 David Lee RC 2.00 5.00
144 Linas Kleiza RC 1.25 3.00
145 Luke Schenscher RC 1.25 3.00
146 Yaroslav Korolev RC 1.25 3.00
147 Carmen Electra 4.00 10.00
148 Christie Brinkley 4.00 10.00
149 Shannon Elizabeth 4.00 10.00
150 Jenny McCarthy 4.00 10.00
151 Jay-Z 4.00 10.00
152 Raymond Felton AU RC 6.00 15.00
153 Gerald Green AU RC 6.00 15.00
154 Rashad McCants AU RC 5.00 12.00
155 Andrew Bogut AU RC 8.00 20.00
156 Chris Taft AU RC 5.00 12.00
157 S.Jasikevicius AU RC 6.00 15.00
158 Hakim Warrick AU RC 5.00 12.00
159 Deron Williams AU RC 20.00 50.00
160 Sean May AU RC 4.00 10.00
161 Monta Ellis AU RC 8.00 20.00

2005-06 Bowman Chrome Refractors

*1-110: 1.5X TO 4X BASE HI
*111-151: 1X TO 2.5X BASE HI
*152-161: 1X TO 2.5X BASE HI
152-161 AU PRINT RUN 50 SER.#'d SETS
23 LeBron James 40.00 100.00
69 Kobe Bryant 15.00 40.00
111 Chris Paul 15.00 40.00

2005-06 Bowman Chrome Refractors Gold

*1-110 GOLD: 3X TO 8X BASE HI
*111-146 GOLD: 2X TO 5X BASE HI
152-161 AU PRINT RUN FIVE SETS
23 LeBron James 200.00 500.00
69 Kobe Bryant 40.00 100.00
90 Dwyane Wade 20.00 50.00
111 Chris Paul 50.00 120.00

2005-06 Bowman Chrome X-Fractors

*1-110: 2X TO 5X BASE HI
*111-146: 1.25X TO 3X BASE HI
*152-161 AU: 1.5X TO 4X BASE HI
152-161 AU PRINT RUN 25 SER.#'d SETS
23 LeBron James 100.00 250.00
69 Kobe Bryant 20.00 50.00
111 Chris Paul 20.00 50.00

2006-07 Bowman Chrome

Packaged together with Bowman, Bowman Chrome features a 165-card set, showcasing veteran players on card numbers 1-110, NCAA coaches on card numbers 111-115, rookies on cards 116-125, and autograph sticker rookies on cards 126-165. All cards feature chromium foil card stock, black borders, and red color accents on veteran player cards and blue color accents on rookie player cards. Released late November 2006 under the product name of Bowman Rookies and Stars, boxes contain 18 packs where each pack has four Bowman cards, two Bowman Chrome cards and carried an original suggested retail price of $4.00 per pack.

COMP.SET w/o SP's (115) 30.00 60.00
116-125 RC APPROXIMATE ODDS 1:9
126-165 AU RC GROUP A ODDS 1:140
126-165 AU RC GROUP B ODDS 1:34
126-165 AU RC GROUP C ODDS 1:63
UNPRICED SUPERFR.PRINT RUN ONE SET
1 Gilbert Arenas .50 1.25
2 Delonte West .40 1.00
3 Gerald Wallace .50 1.25
4 Ike Diogu .40 1.00
5 Mike Miller .50 1.25
6 Kobe Bryant 2.50 6.00
7 Richard Hamilton .50 1.25
8 Vince Carter .75 2.00
9 Elton Brand .60 1.50
10 Boris Diaw .50 1.25
11 Carmelo Anthony .75 2.00
12 Jermaine O'Neal .50 1.25
13 Al Harrington .50 1.25
14 Dwight Howard .50 1.25
15 Chris Bosh .60 1.50
16 Ben Gordon .50 1.25
17 Josh Howard .50 1.25
18 Yao Ming .75 2.00
19 David West .50 1.25
20 Tim Duncan 1.00 2.50
21 Andre Iguodala .50 1.25
22 LeBron James 2.50 6.00
23 Channing Frye .50 1.25
24 Antoine Walker .50 1.25
25 Ricky Davis .50 1.25
26 Lamar Odom .50 1.25
27 Amare Stoudemire .50 1.25
28 Mike Bibby .60 1.50
29 Allen Iverson .75 2.00
30 Marvin Williams .50 1.25
31 Wally Szczerbiak .50 1.25
32 Ben Wallace .50 1.25
33 Nenad Krstic .40 1.00
34 Deron Williams .50 1.25
35 Troy Murphy .40 1.00
36 Raymond Felton .50 1.25
37 Jason Terry .50 1.25
38 Zach Randolph .50 1.25
39 Pau Gasol .60 1.50
40 Larry Hughes .50 1.25
41 Luol Deng .50 1.25
42 Steve Francis .50 1.25
43 Chauncey Billups .60 1.50
44 Smush Parker .40 1.00
45 Shareef Abdur-Rahim .50 1.25
46 Andrei Kirilenko .50 1.25
47 Shawn Marion .50 1.25
48 Darko Milicic .40 1.00
49 Shaquille O'Neal 1.25 3.00
50 Kevin Garnett 1.00 2.50
51 Michael Finley .60 1.50
52 Peja Stojakovic .60 1.50
53 Michael Redd .50 1.25
54 Desmond Mason .40 1.00
55 Luke Ridnour .50 1.25
56 Kenyon Martin .50 1.25
57 Morris Peterson .40 1.00
58 Chris Kaman .50 1.25
59 Jason Richardson .60 1.50
60 Jason Kidd 1.00 2.50
61 Carlos Boozer .50 1.25
62 Rashad McCants .40 1.00
63 Nate Robinson .40 1.00
64 Devin Harris .40 1.00
65 Andrew Bogut .50 1.25
66 Chris Duhon .40 1.00
67 Drew Gooden .50 1.25
68 Manu Ginobili .60 1.50
69 Jameer Nelson .40 1.00
70 Corey Maggette .50 1.25
71 Charlie Villanueva .40 1.00
72 Shane Battier .50 1.25
73 Udonis Haslem .40 1.00
74 Tracy McGrady .75 2.00
75 Bobby Simmons .40 1.00
76 Baron Davis .50 1.25
77 Zydrunas Ilgauskas .50 1.25
78 Danny Granger .50 1.25
79 Hakim Warrick .50 1.25
80 Josh Smith .50 1.25
81 Tayshaun Prince .50 1.25
82 Rashard Lewis .60 1.50
83 Luther Head .50 1.25
84 Andre Miller .50 1.25
85 T.J. Ford .40 1.00
86 Sebastian Telfair .40 1.00
87 Dirk Nowitzki 1.00 2.50
88 Kwame Brown .40 1.00
89 Antawn Jamison .50 1.25
90 Ron Artest .60 1.50
91 Mehmet Okur .40 1.00
92 Emeka Okafor .50 1.25
93 Sam Cassell .50 1.25
94 Chris Paul .75 2.00
95 Chris Webber .60 1.50
96 Richard Jefferson .50 1.25
97 Dwyane Wade 1.00 2.50
98 Tony Parker .60 1.50
99 Paul Pierce .60 1.50
100 Marcus Camby .50 1.25
101 Ray Allen .60 1.50
102 Stephon Marbury .50 1.25
103 Rasheed Wallace .60 1.50
104 Brad Miller .50 1.25
105 Kirk Hinrich .50 1.25
106 Steve Nash .75 2.00
107 Sarunas Jasikevicius .50 1.25
108 Darius Miles .40 1.00
109 Joe Johnson .50 1.25
110 Caron Butler .50 1.25
111 John Wooden CO 2.50 6.00
112 Ben Howland CO 2.00 5.00
113 Jim Calhoun CO 2.00 5.00
114 Jim Boeheim CO 2.00 5.00
115 Roy Williams CO 2.00 5.00
116 LaMarcus Aldridge RC 5.00 12.00
117 Marcus Vinicius RC 1.25 3.00
118 Sergio Rodriguez RC 2.00 5.00
119 Will Blalock RC 1.25 3.00
120 Paul Millsap RC 2.50 6.00
121 Leon Powe RC 1.50 4.00
122 Rudy Gay RC 2.50 6.00
123 Tyrus Thomas RC 1.50 4.00
124 Brandon Roy RC 2.00 5.00
125 J.R. Pinnock RC 1.25 3.00
126 Kevin Pittsnogle B AU RC 4.00 10.00
127 Mile Ilic C AU RC 3.00 8.00
128 Mardy Collins B AU RC 3.00 8.00
129 Craig Smith C AU RC 4.00 10.00
130 Jordan Farmar B AU RC 5.00 12.00
131 Quincy Douby B AU RC 3.00 8.00
132 James Augustine B AU RC 3.00 8.00
133 Josh Boone B AU RC 3.00 8.00
134 Shannon Brown B AU RC 3.00 8.00
135 David Noel B AU RC 3.00 8.00
136 Kyle Lowry B AU RC 6.00 15.00
137 Ryan Hollins C AU RC 4.00 10.00
138 Renaldo Balkman B AU RC 4.00 10.00
139 James White C AU RC 3.00 8.00
140 Damir Markota C AU RC 3.00 8.00
141 Paul Davis B AU RC 3.00 8.00
142 Alexander Johnson C AU RC 3.00 8.00
143 Steve Novak B AU RC 4.00 10.00
144 P.J. Tucker B AU RC 4.00 10.00
145 Saer Sene B AU RC 3.00 8.00
146 Bobby Jones B AU RC 3.00 8.00
147 Cedric Simmons B AU RC 3.00 8.00
148 Allan Ray C AU RC 3.00 8.00
149 Solomon Jones B AU RC 3.00 8.00
150 Ronnie Brewer A AU RC 5.00 12.00
151 Thabo Sefolosha B AU RC 5.00 12.00
152 Maurice Ager B AU RC 3.00 8.00
153 Daniel Gibson C AU RC 4.00 10.00
154 Shawne Williams B AU RC 3.00 8.00
155 Dee Brown B AU RC 3.00 8.00
156 Andrea Bargnani A AU RC 5.00 12.00
157 Patrick O'Bryant A AU RC 3.00 8.00
158 Shelden Williams A AU RC 4.00 10.00
159 Hilton Armstrong A AU RC 3.00 8.00
160 Adam Morrison A AU RC 3.00 8.00
161 Rodney Carney B AU RC 3.00 8.00

162 Randy Foye A AU RC 5.00 12.00
163 Rajon Rondo B AU RC 12.00 30.00
164 Marcus Williams A AU RC 3.00 8.00
165 J.J. Redick A AU RC 6.00 15.00

2006-07 Bowman Chrome Refractors

*1-115 REFRACTORS: 1X TO 2.5X BASE HI
*116-125 RC's: .75X TO 2X BASE HI
*126-165 RC's: .4X TO .8X BASE HI
REF.PRINT RUN 249 SER.#'d SETS
126-165 REF.RC's NOT AUTOGRAPHED
22 LeBron James 60.00 150.00

2006-07 Bowman Chrome Refractors Gold

*1-110 GOLD: 4X TO 10X BASE HI
*111-125 GOLD: 2.5X TO 6X BASE HI
*125-165 GOLD: 1.25X TO 3X BASE HI
REF.GOLD PRINT RUN 50 SER.#'d SETS
22 LeBron James 250.00 500.00
165 J.J. Redick AU 25.00 60.00

2006-07 Bowman Chrome X-Fractors

*1-110 X-FRACTORS: 2X TO 5X BASE HI
*111-125: 1.25X TO 3X BASE HI
*126-165: .5X TO 1.25X BASE HI
X-FRAC PRINT RUN 150 SER.#'d SETS
126-165 RC's NOT AUTOGRAPHED
6 Kobe Bryant 20.00 50.00
22 LeBron James 100.00 250.00

2007-08 Bowman Chrome

This 160-card set was released in November, 2007. The set which has the same checklist as the basic Bowman set also is broken down into veterans (1-110) and rookies (111-160). The Rookie Cards were issued to a stated print run of 2999 serial numbered sets as well.

COMPLETE SET (160) 50.00 100.00
COMP.SET w/o SP's (110) 20.00 50.00
UNPRICED SUPERFRACT. PRINT RUN ONE SET
UNPRICED PRESS PLATE PRINT RUN ONE SET
1 Gilbert Arenas .50 1.25
2 Dwight Howard .50 1.25
3 Dwyane Wade 1.00 2.50
4 Chris Bosh .60 1.50
5 Josh Smith .50 1.25
6 Andrew Bogut .50 1.25
7 Ben Gordon .50 1.25
8 Deron Williams .50 1.25
9 Tony Parker .60 1.50
10 Mike Bibby .60 1.50
11 Yao Ming .75 2.00
12 Raymond Felton .60 1.50
13 Steve Nash .75 2.00
14 Jameer Nelson .40 1.00
15 Carmelo Anthony .75 2.00
16 Pau Gasol .60 1.50
17 Rashard Lewis .50 1.25
18 Eddy Curry .40 1.00
19 Luol Deng .50 1.25
20 Kevin Garnett 1.00 2.50
21 Tim Duncan 1.00 2.50
22 Michael Redd .50 1.25
23 LeBron James 4.00 10.00
24 Kobe Bryant 2.50 6.00
25 Al Jefferson .50 1.25
26 Mike Dunleavy .50 1.25
27 Tyson Chandler .50 1.25
28 Zach Randolph .50 1.25
29 Jason Richardson .60 1.50
30 Rasheed Wallace .60 1.50
31 Shawn Marion .50 1.25
32 Shaquille O'Neal 1.25 3.00
33 Allen Iverson .75 2.00
34 Paul Pierce .60 1.50
35 Adam Morrison .40 1.00
36 Mike Miller .50 1.25
37 Larry Hughes .50 1.25
38 Kevin Martin .50 1.25
39 Charlie Villanueva .40 1.00
40 Vince Carter .75 2.00
41 Dirk Nowitzki .75 2.00
42 Elton Brand .60 1.50
43 Ray Allen .60 1.50
44 Luke Walton .40 1.00
45 Chris Paul .75 2.00
46 Marcus Camby .40 1.00
47 Andrei Kirilenko .50 1.25
48 J.J. Redick .60 1.50
49 Richard Hamilton .50 1.25
50 Emeka Okafor .50 1.25
51 Manu Ginobili .60 1.50
52 Monta Ellis .50 1.25
53 Jorge Garbajosa .50 1.25
54 Kyle Korver .50 1.25
55 Jason Kidd .60 1.50
56 Randy Foye .60 1.50
57 Shane Battier .50 1.25
58 Shaun Livingston .40 1.00
59 Jason Terry .50 1.25
60 Joe Johnson .50 1.25
61 Lamar Odom .50 1.25
62 Tayshaun Prince .50 1.25
63 Chris Wilcox .40 1.00
64 Leandro Barbosa .50 1.25
65 Al Harrington .50 1.25
66 Jamal Crawford .60 1.50
67 Caron Butler .50 1.25
68 Chauncey Billups .60 1.50
69 Ricky Davis .50 1.25
70 Andrea Bargnani .60 1.50
71 Samuel Dalembert .40 1.00
72 LaMarcus Aldridge .75 2.00
73 Mehmet Okur .40 1.00
74 Marcus Williams .40 1.00
75 Andre Miller .50 1.25
76 Rudy Gay .60 1.50
77 Jermaine O'Neal .50 1.25
78 Boris Diaw .50 1.25
79 Ryan Gomes .40 1.00
80 Gerald Wallace .50 1.25
81 Udonis Haslem .40 1.00
82 Mo Williams .50 1.25
83 Jarrett Jack .50 1.25
84 Chris Webber .60 1.50
85 Trevor Ariza .40 1.00
86 Kirk Hinrich .50 1.25
87 Rafer Alston .40 1.00
88 Danny Granger .50 1.25
89 David West .50 1.25
90 Drew Gooden .50 1.25
91 Stephon Marbury .50 1.25
92 Antawn Jamison .50 1.25
93 Ron Artest .60 1.50
94 Richard Jefferson .50 1.25
95 Carlos Boozer .50 1.25
96 Hakim Warrick .50 1.25
97 T.J. Ford .40 1.00
98 Desmond Mason .40 1.00
99 Andre Iguodala .50 1.25
100 Amare Stoudemire .50 1.25
101 Tracy McGrady .60 1.50
102 Jason Kapono .40 1.00
103 Ben Wallace .50 1.25
104 Marvin Williams .50 1.25
105 Baron Davis .50 1.25
106 Andrew Bynum .40 1.00
107 Brandon Roy .60 1.50
108 David Lee .40 1.00
109 Corey Maggette .50 1.25
110 Josh Howard .50 1.25
111 Kevin Durant RC 60.00 150.00
112 Al Horford RC 3.00 8.00
113 Mike Conley Jr. RC 3.00 8.00
114 Jeff Green RC 2.50 6.00
115 Corey Brewer RC 2.50 6.00
116 Joakim Noah RC 2.50 6.00
117 Julian Wright RC 1.50 4.00
118 Ramon Sessions RC 2.50 6.00
119 Sammy Mejia RC 1.50 4.00
120 Luis Scola RC 3.00 8.00
121 Yi Jianlian RC 3.00 8.00
122 Arron Afflalo RC 2.50 6.00
123 Carl Landry RC 1.50 4.00
124 Alando Tucker RC 1.50 4.00
125 Gabe Pruitt RC 1.50 4.00
126 Marcus Williams RC 1.50 4.00
127 Spencer Hawes RC 2.00 5.00
128 Acie Law RC 1.50 4.00
129 Thaddeus Young RC 2.50 6.00
130 Nick Fazekas RC 1.50 4.00
131 Al Thornton RC* 2.00 5.00
132 Rodney Stuckey RC 2.00 5.00
133 Nick Young RC 3.00 8.00
134 Glen Davis RC 2.00 5.00
135 Jermareo Davidson RC 1.50 4.00
136 JamesOn Curry RC 1.50 4.00
137 Jason Smith RC 2.00 5.00
138 Daequan Cook RC 2.00 5.00
139 Jared Dudley RC 2.00 5.00
140 Derrick Byars RC 1.50 4.00
141 Josh McRoberts RC 2.00 5.00
142 Adam Haluska RC 1.50 4.00
143 Reyshawn Terry RC 1.50 4.00
144 Aaron Gray AU RC 1.50 4.00
145 Herbert Hill RC 1.50 4.00
146 Jared Jordan RC 1.50 4.00
147 Wilson Chandler RC 2.00 5.00
148 Morris Almond RC 1.50 4.00
149 Aaron Brooks RC 2.00 5.00
150 Petteri Koponen RC 2.50 6.00
151 Dominic McGuire RC 1.50 4.00
152 Greg Oden RC 2.50 6.00
153 Stephane Lasme RC 1.50 4.00
154 D.J. Strawberry RC 1.50 4.00
155 Sean Williams RC 1.50 4.00
156 Marco Belinelli RC 2.50 6.00
157 Javaris Crittenton RC 1.50 4.00
158 Demetris Nichols RC 1.50 4.00
159 Taurean Green RC 1.50 4.00
160 Brandan Wright RC 2.50 6.00

2007-08 Bowman Chrome Refractors

*REFRACTORS: .6X TO 1.5X BASE HI
PRINT RUN 299 SER.#'d SETS
23 LeBron James 30.00 80.00
24 Kobe Bryant 8.00 20.00
111 Kevin Durant 200.00 500.00

2007-08 Bowman Chrome Refractors Black

*BLACK 1-110: .75X TO 2X BASE HI
*BLACK 111-160: .75X TO 2X BASE HI
BLACK PRINT RUN 199 SER.#'d SETS
23 LeBron James 50.00 120.00
24 Kobe Bryant 10.00 25.00
111 Kevin Durant 400.00 800.00

2007-08 Bowman Chrome Refractors Gold

*GOLD 1-110: 1.5X TO 4X BASE HI
*GOLD 111-160: 1.5X TO 3X BASE HI
GOLD PRINT RUN 99 SER.#'d SETS
3 Dwyane Wade 8.00 20.00
23 LeBron James 75.00 200.00
24 Kobe Bryant 50.00 125.00
111 Kevin Durant 800.00 1200.00

2007-08 Bowman Chrome X-Fractors

*X-FRAC 1-110: 2X TO 5X BASE HI
*X-FRAC 111-160: 1.5X TO 4X BASE HI
X-FRAC PRINT RUN 50 SER.#'d SETS
23 LeBron James 75.00 200.00
111 Kevin Durant 1200.00 2000.00

2007-08 Bowman Chrome Refractors Rookie Autographs

PRINT RUN 599 SER.#'d SETS
UNLESS LISTED IN CHECKLIST
*BLACK: .5X TO 1.25X BASE HI
BLACK PRINT RUN 99 SER.#'d SETS
*GOLD: .75X TO 2X BASE HI
GOLD PRINT RUN 50 SER.#'d SETS
UNPRICED SUPER PRINT RUN ONE SET
UNPRICED X-FRAC PRINT RUN 10 SETS
EXCH EXPIRATION 10/31/09
121 Yi Jianlian AU 8.00 20.00
122 Arron Afflalo AU 5.00 12.00
123 Carl Landry AU 3.00 8.00
124 Alando Tucker AU/479 3.00 8.00
125 Gabe Pruitt AU 3.00 8.00
126 Marcus Williams AU/479 3.00 8.00
127 Spencer Hawes AU/479 4.00 10.00
128 Acie Law AU/479 3.00 8.00
129 Thaddeus Young AU 5.00 12.00
130 Nick Fazekas AU 3.00 8.00
131 Al Thornton AU/479 4.00 10.00
132 Rodney Stuckey AU 4.00 10.00
133 Nick Young AU/479 6.00 15.00
134 Glen Davis AU 4.00 10.00
135 Jermareo Davidson AU 3.00 8.00
136 JamesOn Curry AU 3.00 8.00
137 Jason Smith AU 4.00 10.00
138 Daequan Cook AU 4.00 10.00
139 Jared Dudley AU 4.00 10.00
140 Derrick Byars AU 3.00 8.00
141 Josh McRoberts AU 4.00 10.00
142 Adam Haluska AU 3.00 8.00
143 Reyshawn Terry AU 3.00 8.00
144 Aaron Gray AU 3.00 8.00
145 Herbert Hill AU 3.00 8.00
146 Jared Jordan AU 3.00 8.00
147 Wilson Chandler AU 4.00 10.00
148 Morris Almond AU 3.00 8.00
149 Aaron Brooks AU 4.00 10.00
150 Petteri Koponen AU 5.00 12.00
151 Dominic McGuire AU 3.00 8.00
152 Greg Oden AU/479 5.00 12.00
153 Stephane Lasme AU 3.00 8.00
154 D.J. Strawberry AU 3.00 8.00
155 Sean Williams AU 3.00 8.00
156 Marco Belinelli AU 5.00 12.00
157 Javaris Crittenton AU/479 3.00 8.00
158 Demetris Nichols AU 3.00 8.00
159 Taurean Green AU 3.00 8.00
160 Brandan Wright AU/479 5.00 12.00

2008-09 Bowman Chrome

This set was released on October 29, 2008. The base set consists of 183 cards. Cards 1-110 feature veterans, and cards 111-150 are rookies. Cards 151-183 are autographed cards of most of the rookies.

COMP.SET w/o RC (110) 20.00 40.00
UNPRICED PRESS PLATE PRINT RUN ONE SET
UNPRICED RED PRINT RUN 5 SETS
UNPRICED SUPERFR.PRINT RUN ONE SET
1 Tracy McGrady .60 1.50
2 Jason Kidd .60 1.50
3 LeBron James 2.50 6.00
4 Chris Bosh .60 1.50
5 Kevin Garnett 1.00 2.50
6 Josh Smith .50 1.25
7 Richard Hamilton .50 1.25
8 Monta Ellis .50 1.25
9 Yi Jianlian .60 1.50
10 Danny Granger .50 1.25
11 Richard Jefferson .50 1.25
12 Elton Brand .60 1.50
13 Rudy Gay .60 1.50
14 Andres Nocioni .40 1.00
15 Carmelo Anthony .75 2.00
16 Pau Gasol .60 1.50
17 Corey Brewer .50 1.25
18 Hedo Turkoglu .50 1.25
19 Andre Iguodala .50 1.25
20 Raymond Felton .50 1.25
21 Tim Duncan 1.00 2.50
22 Michael Redd .50 1.25
23 Chris Paul .75 2.00
24 Kobe Bryant 2.50 6.00
25 Brandon Roy .60 1.50
26 Carlos Boozer .50 1.25
27 Jeff Green .50 1.25
28 Luis Scola .50 1.25
29 Al Thornton .50 1.25
30 Gilbert Arenas .50 1.25
31 Brandan Wright .50 1.25
32 Shaquille O'Neal 1.25 3.00
33 Allen Iverson .75 2.00
34 Paul Pierce .60 1.50
35 Ben Gordon .50 1.25
36 Jamal Crawford .60 1.50
37 Andrew Bynum .40 1.00
38 Gerald Wallace .50 1.25
39 Mike Conley Jr. .50 1.25
40 Ben Wallace .50 1.25
41 Dirk Nowitzki .75 2.00
42 David Lee .40 1.00
43 Mo Williams .50 1.25
44 Al Jefferson .50 1.25
45 Tayshaun Prince .50 1.25
46 Jameer Nelson .40 1.00
47 Andrei Kirilenko .50 1.25
48 David West .50 1.25
49 Al Horford .60 1.50
50 Steve Nash .60 1.50
51 Ron Artest .60 1.50
52 Greg Oden .50 1.25
53 Sean Williams .50 1.25
54 Jamario Moon .40 1.00
55 Baron Davis .50 1.25
56 Udonis Haslem .40 1.00
57 Mike Dunleavy .50 1.25
58 Shane Battier .50 1.25
59 Andrew Bogut .50 1.25
60 Ray Allen .60 1.50
61 Nick Young .50 1.25
62 Manu Ginobili .60 1.50
63 Jason Richardson .60 1.50
64 Mike Miller .50 1.25
65 Leandro Barbosa .50 1.25
66 Luol Deng .50 1.25
67 Shawn Marion .50 1.25
68 Peja Stojakovic .60 1.50
69 Kevin Durant 1.50 4.00
70 Corey Maggette .50 1.25
71 Chauncey Billups .60 1.50
72 Josh Howard .50 1.25
73 Kevin Martin .50 1.25
74 Anderson Varejao .40 1.00
75 Craig Smith .40 1.00
76 Antawn Jamison .50 1.25
77 Marcus Camby .40 1.00
78 Andre Miller .50 1.25
79 Zach Randolph .50 1.25
80 Deron Williams .50 1.25
81 Devin Harris .40 1.00
82 Rashard Lewis .50 1.25
83 Damien Wilkins .40 1.00
84 LaMarcus Aldridge .60 1.50
85 Larry Hughes .50 1.25
86 Brad Miller .50 1.25
87 Jermaine O'Neal .50 1.25
88 Caron Butler .50 1.25
89 Tyson Chandler .50 1.25
90 Joe Johnson .50 1.25
91 Amare Stoudemire .50 1.25
92 Dwight Howard .50 1.25
93 Rajon Rondo .60 1.50
94 T.J. Ford .40 1.00
95 Rodney Stuckey .50 1.25
96 Samuel Dalembert .40 1.00
97 Tony Parker .60 1.50
98 Vince Carter .75 2.00
99 Yao Ming .75 2.00
100 Dwyane Wade 1.00 2.50
101 Dominique Wilkins .75 2.00
102 Rick Barry .50 1.25
103 John Stockton 1.00 2.50
104 Magic Johnson 1.50 4.00
105 George Gervin .75 2.00
106 Bill Russell 1.00 2.50
107 David Robinson 1.00 2.50
108 Dennis Rodman 1.25 3.00
109 Larry Bird 1.50 4.00
110 Jerry West .75 2.00
111 Derrick Rose RC 6.00 15.00
112 Michael Beasley RC 1.50 4.00
113 O.J. Mayo RC 1.50 4.00
114 Russell Westbrook RC 60.00 150.00
115 Kevin Love RC 8.00 20.00
116 Danilo Gallinari RC 2.50 6.00
117 Eric Gordon RC 2.50 6.00
118 Joe Alexander RC 1.00 2.50
119 D.J. Augustin RC 1.25 3.00
120 Brook Lopez RC 2.00 5.00
121 Jerryd Bayless RC 1.25 3.00
122 Jason Thompson RC 1.00 2.50
123 Anthony Randolph RC 1.00 2.50
124 Robin Lopez RC 1.50 4.00
125 Marreese Speights RC 1.25 3.00
126 Roy Hibbert RC 1.50 4.00
127 JaVale McGee RC 2.00 5.00
128 J.J. Hickson RC 1.25 3.00
129 Alexis Ajinca RC 1.00 2.50
130 Ryan Anderson RC 1.25 3.00
131 Courtney Lee RC 1.25 3.00
132 Kosta Koufos RC 1.25 3.00
133 Donte Greene RC 1.00 2.50
134 George Hill RC 1.50 4.00
135 D.J. White RC 1.25 3.00
136 J.R. Giddens RC 1.00 2.50
137 Joey Dorsey RC 1.00 2.50
138 Mario Chalmers RC 1.50 4.00
139 DeAndre Jordan RC 2.00 5.00
140 Chris Douglas-Roberts RC 1.00 2.50
141 Malik Hairston RC 1.00 2.50
142 Sean Singletary RC 1.00 2.50
143 Kyle Weaver RC 1.00 2.50
144 Patrick Ewing Jr. RC 1.00 2.50
145 Walter Sharpe RC 1.00 2.50
146 Sonny Weems RC 1.00 2.50
147 Shan Foster RC 1.00 2.50
148 Nicolas Batum RC 2.00 5.00
149 Brandon Rush RC 1.25 3.00
150 Darrell Arthur RC 1.25 3.00
151 Derrick Rose AU A 150.00 300.00
152 Michael Beasley AU A 5.00 12.00
153 O.J. Mayo AU A 5.00 12.00
154 Russell Westbrook AU A 200.00 500.00
155 Kevin Love AU A 40.00 100.00
156 Danilo Gallinari AU A 10.00 25.00
157 Eric Gordon AU A 12.00 30.00
158 Joe Alexander AU A 3.00 8.00
159 D.J. Augustin AU B 4.00 10.00
160 Brook Lopez AU A 6.00 15.00
161 Jerryd Bayless AU A 4.00 10.00
162 Jason Thompson AU B 3.00 8.00
163 Anthony Randolph AU B 3.00 8.00
164 Robin Lopez AU B 5.00 12.00
165 Marreese Speights AU B 4.00 10.00
166 Roy Hibbert AU B 3.00 8.00
167 J.J. Hickson AU B 4.00 10.00
168 Ryan Anderson AU B 4.00 10.00
170 Kosta Koufos AU B 4.00 10.00
171 George Hill AU B 5.00 12.00
172 D.J. White AU B 4.00 10.00
173 J.R. Giddens AU B 3.00 8.00
174 Joey Dorsey AU B 3.00 8.00
175 Mario Chalmers AU B 5.00 12.00
176 DeAndre Jordan AU B 10.00 25.00
177 Chris Douglas-Roberts AU B 3.00 8.00
178 JaVale McGee AU B 6.00 15.00
179 Kyle Weaver AU B 3.00 8.00
180 Patrick Ewing Jr. AU B 3.00 8.00
181 Sonny Weems AU B 3.00 8.00
182 Brandon Rush AU B 4.00 10.00
183 Darrell Arthur AU B 4.00 10.00

2008-09 Bowman Chrome Refractors

*1-110 REF: .6X TO 1.5X BASE HI
*101-150 REF: 75X TO 2X BASE HI
1-150 PRINT RUN 499 SER.#'d SETS
*151-183 AU.REF: .75X TO 2X BASE HI
151-183 AU PRINT RUN 50 SETS
3 LeBron James 30.00 80.00
24 Kobe Bryant 12.00 30.00
69 Kevin Durant 10.00 25.00
154 Russell Westbrook AU 400.00 800.00

2008-09 Bowman Chrome Refractors Blue

*1-110 REF.BLUE: 2.5X TO 6X BASE HI
*111-150 REF.BLUE: 2X TO 5X BASE
PRINT RUN 99 SER.#'d SETS
3 LeBron James 50.00 120.00
100 Dwyane Wade 10.00 25.00
111 Derrick Rose 125.00 250.00
114 Russell Westbrook 300.00 600.00

2008-09 Bowman Chrome Refractors Gold

*1-110 REF.GOLD: 5X TO 12X BASE
*111-150 REF.GOLD: 2.5X TO 6X BASE
1-150 PRINT RUN 50 SER.#'d SETS
*151-183 REF.GOLD: 1.5X TO 4X BASE
151-183 PRINT RUN 25 SER.#'d SETS
3 LeBron James 75.00 200.00
15 Carmelo Anthony 10.00 25.00
24 Kobe Bryant 75.00 200.00
34 Paul Pierce 15.00 40.00
69 Kevin Durant 50.00 125.00
111 Derrick Rose 200.00 400.00
114 Russell Westbrook 400.00 800.00
115 Kevin Love 75.00 150.00
154 Russell Westbrook AU 1200.00 1800.00
155 Kevin Love AU 300.00 600.00
157 Eric Gordon AU 150.00 300.00

2008-09 Bowman Chrome X-Fractors

*X-FRACTORS 1-110: 1X TO 2.5X BASE HI
*X-FRACTORS 111-150: 1.25X TO 3X BASE HI
STATED PRINT RUN 299 SER.#'d SETS
3 LeBron James 40.00 100.00
24 Kobe Bryant 15.00 40.00
69 Kevin Durant 15.00 40.00
114 Russell Westbrook 150.00 400.00

2006-07 Bowman Elevation

Bowman Elevation contains more insert and parallel sets of any product in the history of basketball cards--144 unique inserts and parallels were originally inserted. The base set features all-foil card stock, veteran players on cards 1-90 and rookies on cards 91-130 sequentially numbered to 999. Released in August 2006, Elevation boxes contained 16 packs of five cards each and carried an original suggested retail price of $10.00 per pack.

COMP.SET w/o SP's (90) 25.00 60.00
ROOKIE PRINT RUN 999 SER.#'d SETS
UNPRICED ONE OF ONE PARALLELS EXIST
1 Dwyane Wade 1.00 2.50
2 Elton Brand .60 1.50
3 Dwight Howard .50 1.25
4 Chris Bosh .60 1.50
5 Baron Davis .50 1.25
6 Marcus Camby .50 1.25
7 Rashard Lewis .60 1.50
8 Paul Pierce .60 1.50
9 Jermaine O'Neal .50 1.25
10 Gilbert Arenas .50 1.25
11 Larry Hughes .50 1.25
12 Manu Ginobili .60 1.50
13 Lamar Odom .50 1.25
14 Ron Artest .60 1.50
15 Carmelo Anthony .75 2.00
16 Deron Williams .50 1.25
17 Gerald Wallace .50 1.25
18 Peja Stojakovic .60 1.50
19 Vince Carter .75 2.00
20 Kevin Garnett 1.00 2.50
21 Yao Ming .75 2.00
22 Josh Howard .50 1.25
23 Michael Redd .50 1.25
24 Eddy Curry .50 1.25
25 Shawn Marion .50 1.25
26 Luol Deng .50 1.25
27 Ben Wallace .50 1.25
28 Sam Cassell .50 1.25
29 Steve Francis .50 1.25
30 Ray Allen .60 1.50
31 Andre Iguodala .50 1.25
32 Shaquille O'Neal 1.25 3.00
33 Pau Gasol .60 1.50
34 Jason Richardson .60 1.50
35 Ricky Davis .50 1.25
36 Joe Johnson .50 1.25
37 Dirk Nowitzki 1.00 2.50
38 Richard Hamilton .50 1.25
39 Troy Murphy .40 1.00
40 Charlie Villanueva .40 1.00
41 T.J. Ford .40 1.00
42 Zydrunas Ilgauskas .50 1.25
43 Andrei Kirilenko .50 1.25
44 Chris Paul .75 2.00
45 Grant Hill .75 2.00
46 Kobe Bryant 2.50 6.00
47 Tim Duncan 1.00 2.50
48 Raymond Felton .50 1.25
49 Antawn Jamison .50 1.25
50 Jason Kidd 1.00 2.50
51 Shareef Abdur-Rahim .50 1.25
52 Shane Battier .50 1.25
53 Kirk Hinrich .50 1.25
54 Jason Terry .50 1.25
55 Mehmet Okur .40 1.00
56 Stephon Marbury .50 1.25
57 Steve Nash .75 2.00
58 Mike Bibby .60 1.50
59 Sebastian Telfair .40 1.00
60 Richard Jefferson .50 1.25
61 Andre Miller .50 1.25
62 Delonte West .40 1.00
63 Tracy McGrady .75 2.00
64 Rasheed Wallace .60 1.50
65 Al Harrington .50 1.25
66 Emeka Okafor .50 1.25
67 Caron Butler .50 1.25
68 Andrew Bogut .50 1.25
69 Tony Parker .60 1.50
70 Zach Randolph .50 1.25
71 Allen Iverson .75 2.00
72 David West .50 1.25
73 Chris Webber .60 1.50
74 Ben Gordon .50 1.25
75 Corey Maggette .50 1.25
76 Sarunas Jasikevicius .50 1.25
77 Chauncey Billups .60 1.50
78 Amare Stoudemire .50 1.25
79 Luke Ridnour .50 1.25
80 LeBron James 2.50 6.00
81 Kenyon Martin .50 1.25
82 Marko Jaric .40 1.00
83 Antoine Walker .50 1.25
84 J.R. Smith .50 1.25
85 Mike Miller .50 1.25
86 Channing Frye .50 1.25
87 Smush Parker .40 1.00
88 Wally Szczerbiak .50 1.25
89 Morris Peterson .40 1.00
90 Luther Head .50 1.25
91 Randy Foye RC 2.00 5.00
92 Daniel Gibson RC 1.50 4.00
93 Hassan Adams RC 1.25 3.00
94 Hilton Armstrong RC 1.25 3.00
95 Marcus Williams RC 1.25 3.00
96 Paul Davis RC 1.25 3.00
97 Quincy Douby RC 1.25 3.00
98 Ronnie Brewer RC 2.00 5.00
99 Rodney Carney RC 1.25 3.00
100 Rudy Gay RC 2.50 6.00
101 Adam Morrison RC 2.00 5.00
102 Rajon Rondo RC 3.00 8.00
103 Steve Novak RC 1.50 4.00
104 Craig Smith RC 1.50 4.00
105 Leon Powe RC 1.50 4.00
106 James White RC 1.25 3.00
107 Josh Boone RC 1.25 3.00
108 J.J. Redick RC 2.50 6.00
109 Shelden Williams RC 1.50 4.00
110 Alexander Johnson RC 1.25 3.00
111 Guillermo Diaz RC 1.25 3.00
112 Maurice Ager RC 1.25 3.00
113 Jordan Farmar RC 2.00 5.00
114 Mardy Collins RC 1.25 3.00
115 Ryan Hollins RC 1.50 4.00
116 Kyle Lowry RC 2.50 6.00
117 James Augustine RC 1.25 3.00
118 Shawne Williams RC 1.25 3.00
119 LaMarcus Aldridge RC 5.00 12.00
120 Patrick O'Bryant RC 1.25 3.00
121 Cedric Simmons RC 1.25 3.00
122 P.J. Tucker RC 1.50 4.00
123 Brandon Roy RC 2.00 5.00
124 Tyrus Thomas RC 1.50 4.00
125 Andrea Bargnani RC 2.00 5.00
126 Dee Brown RC 1.25 3.00
127 Denham Brown RC 1.25 3.00
128 Saer Sene RC 1.25 3.00
129 Thabo Sefolosha RC 2.00 5.00
130 Shannon Brown RC 1.25 3.00

2006-07 Bowman Elevation Blue

*1-90 BLUE: .6X TO 1.5X BASE HI
*91-130 BLUE RC's SAME VALUE AS BASE
BLUE PRINT RUN 399 SER.#'d SETS
80 LeBron James 12.00 30.00

2006-07 Bowman Elevation Gold

*1-90 GOLD: 1X TO 2.5X BASE HI
*91-130 GOLD RC's: .6X TO 1.5X BASE HI
GOLD PRINT RUN 99 SER.#'d SETS
80 LeBron James 30.00 80.00

2006-07 Bowman Elevation Red

*1-90 RED: .75X TO 2X BASE HI
*91-130 RED RC's: .5X TO 1.25X BASE HI
PRINT RUN 299 SER.#'d SETS
80 LeBron James 15.00 40.00

2006-07 Bowman Elevation Board of Directors Relics

PRINT RUN 99 SER.#'d SETS
*RELICS BLUE SAME VALUE AS BASE
BLUE PRINT RUN 79 SER.#'d SETS
*RELICS GOLD: .75X TO 2X RELIC HI
GOLD PRINT RUN 25 SER.#'d SETS
*RELICS RED: .5X TO 1.25X RELIC HI
RED PRINT RUN 49 SER.#'d SETS
*RELICS DUAL: .5X TO 1.25 RELIC HI
DUAL PRINT RUN 99 SER.#'d SETS
*REL.DUAL BLUE: .5X TO 1.25X RELIC HI
DUAL BLUE PRINT RUN 79 SER.#'d SETS
*REL.DUAL GOLD: .75X TO 2X RELIC HI
DUAL GOLD PRINT RUN 25 SER.#'d SETS
*REL.DUAL RED: .6X TO 1.5X BASE HI
DUAL RED PRINT RUN 49 SER.#'d SETS
ONE OF ONES EXIST FOR RELICS AND DUAL
*PATCHES: 1.25X TO 3X RELIC HI
PATCH PRINT RUN 10 SER.#'d SETS
UNPRICED PATCH BLUE PRINT RUN 5 SETS
UNPRICED PATCH GOLD PRINT RUN 2 SETS
UNPRICED PATCH RED PRINT RUN 3 SETS
UNPRICED PATCH DUAL PRINT RUN 5 SETS
UNPRICED PATCH DUAL BLUE PRINT RUN 4 SETS
UNPRICED PATCH DUAL GOLD PRINT RUN 2 SETS
UNPRICED PATCH DUAL RED PRINT RUN 3 SETS
PATCH DUAL ONE OF ONE's EXIST
UNPRICED PATCH TRIPLE PRINT RUN 5 SETS
UNPRICED PATCH TRIP.BLUE PRINT RUN 4 SETS
UNPRICED PATCH TRIP.GOLD PRINT RUN 2 SETS
UNPRICED PATCH TRIP.RED PRINT RUN 3 SETS
PATCH TRIPLE ONE OF ONE'S EXIST
RAI Allen Iverson 4.00 10.00
RAM Andre Miller 2.50 6.00
RBB Brent Barry 2.00 5.00
RBM Brad Miller 2.50 6.00
RCB Chauncey Billups 3.00 8.00
RCM Corey Maggette 2.50 6.00
RDW David West 2.50 6.00
RGA Gilbert Arenas 2.50 6.00
RJK Jason Kidd 5.00 12.00
RJR Jason Richardson 3.00 8.00
RJS Josh Smith 2.50 6.00
RJT Jamaal Tinsley 2.00 5.00
RJW Jason Williams 2.50 6.00
RKH Kirk Hinrich 2.50 6.00
RLO Lamar Odom 2.50 6.00
RLR Luke Ridnour 2.50 6.00
RMG Manu Ginobili 3.00 8.00
RPG Pau Gasol 3.00 8.00
RPP Paul Pierce 3.00 8.00
RSM Sean May 2.00 5.00
RSO Shaquille O'Neal 6.00 15.00
RTM Tracy McGrady 4.00 10.00
RTP Tony Parker 3.00 8.00
RDWA Dwyane Wade 6.00 15.00
RDWE Delonte West 2.00 5.00
RSMA Stephon Marbury 2.50 6.00
RTJF T.J. Ford 2.00 5.00
RTPR Tayshaun Prince 2.50 6.00

2006-07 Bowman Elevation Board of Directors Relics Autographs

PRINT RUN 25 SER.#'d SETS
RSO Shaquille O'Neal 40.00 100.00
RTP Tony Parker 20.00 50.00
RDWA Dwyane Wade 75.00 150.00
RDWE Delonte West 12.50 30.00

2006-07 Bowman Elevation Board of Directors Relics Autographs Blue

PRINT RUN 19 SER.#'d SETS
UNPRICED RED PRINT RUN 9 SETS
UNPRICED GOLD PRINT RUN 5 SETS
ONE OF ONE'S EXIST
RLR Luke Ridnour 10.00 25.00
RSO Shaquille O'Neal 60.00 120.00
RTP Tony Parker 12.00 30.00
RDWE Delonte West 12.50 30.00

2006-07 Bowman Elevation Board of Directors Relics Dual Autographs

PRINT RUN 15 SER.#'d SETS
UNPRICED BLUE PRINT RUN 10 SETS
UNPRICED GOLD PRINT RUN 3 SETS
UNPRICED RED PRINT RUN 5 SETS
ONE OF ONE's EXIST
RAI Allen Iverson 75.00 150.00
RLR Luke Ridnour 10.00 25.00
RDWA Dwyane Wade 75.00 200.00
RDWE Delonte West 15.00 40.00
RTJF T.J. Ford 10.00 25.00

2006-07 Bowman Elevation Executive Level Relics

PRINT RUN 99 SER.#'d SETS
*RELICS BLUE SAME VALUE AS BASE
BLUE PRINT RUN 79 SER.#'d SETS
*RELICS GOLD: .75X TO 2X RELIC HI
GOLD PRINT RUN 25 SER.#'d SETS
*RELICS RED: .5X TO 1.25X RELIC HI
RED PRINT RUN 49 SER.#'d SETS
*RELICS DUAL: .5X TO 1.25 RELIC HI
DUAL PRINT RUN 99 SER.#'d SETS
*REL.DUAL BLUE: .5X TO 1.25X RELIC HI
DUAL BLUE PRINT RUN 79 SER.#'d SETS
*REL.DUAL GOLD: .75X TO 2X RELIC HI
DUAL GOLD PRINT RUN 25 SER.#'d SETS
*REL.DUAL RED: .6X TO 1.5X BASE HI
DUAL RED PRINT RUN 49 SER.#'d SETS
ONE OF ONES EXIST FOR RELICS AND DUAL
*PATCHES: 1.25X TO 3X RELIC HI
PATCH PRINT RUN 10 SER.#'d SETS
UNPRICED PATCH BLUE PRINT RUN 5 SETS
UNPRICED PATCH GOLD PRINT RUN 2 SETS
UNPRICED PATCH RED PRINT RUN 3 SETS
UNPRICED PATCH DUAL PRINT RUN 5 SETS
UNPRICED PATCH DUAL BLUE PRINT RUN 4 SETS
UNPRICED PATCH DUAL GOLD PRINT RUN 2 SETS
UNPRICED PATCH DUAL RED PRINT RUN 3 SETS
PATCH DUAL ONE OF ONE's EXIST
UNPRICED PATCH TRIP.PRINT RUN 5 SETS
UNPRICED PATCH TRIP.BLUE PRINT RUN 4 SETS
UNPRICED PATCH TRIP.GOLD PRINT RUN 2 SETS
UNPRICED PATCH TRIP.RED PRINT RUN 3 SETS
PAT.TRIPLE ONE OF ONE'S EXIST
RAB Andrew Bogut 2.50 6.00
RAI Allen Iverson 4.00 10.00
RAK Andrei Kirilenko 2.50 6.00
RBD Baron Davis 2.50 6.00
RBG Ben Gordon 2.50 6.00
RCA Carmelo Anthony 4.00 10.00
RCB Chris Bosh 3.00 8.00
RCP Chris Paul 4.00 10.00
RCV Charlie Villanueva 2.00 5.00
RDN Dirk Nowitzki 5.00 12.00
RDW Dwyane Wade 6.00 15.00
REB Elton Brand 3.00 8.00
REO Emeka Okafor 2.50 6.00
RJO Jermaine O'Neal 2.50 6.00
RKB Kobe Bryant 8.00 20.00
RKG Kevin Garnett 5.00 12.00
RLO Lamar Odom 2.50 6.00
RMB Mike Bibby 3.00 8.00
RNR Nate Robinson 2.00 5.00
RPG Pau Gasol 3.00 8.00
RPP Paul Pierce 3.00 8.00
RRA Ray Allen 3.00 8.00
RRH Richard Hamilton 2.50 6.00
RSB Shane Battier 2.50 6.00
RSM Sean May 2.00 5.00
RSN Steve Nash 4.00 10.00
RSO Shaquille O'Neal 6.00 15.00
RST Sebastian Telfair 2.00 5.00
RTD Tim Duncan 5.00 12.00
RVC Vince Carter 4.00 10.00
RYM Yao Ming 4.00 10.00
RRHO Robert Horry 2.50 6.00

2006-07 Bowman Elevation Executive Level Relics Autographs

PRINT RUN 25 SER.#'d SETS
RCV Charlie Villanueva 10.00 25.00
RDW Dwyane Wade 25.00 50.00
REO Emeka Okafor 10.00 25.00
RJO Jermaine O'Neal 10.00 25.00
RRH Richard Hamilton 10.00 25.00

2006-07 Bowman Elevation Executive Level Relics Autographs Blue

PRINT RUN 19 SER.#'d SETS
UNPRICED RED PRINT RUN 9 SETS
UNPRICED GOLD PRINT RUN 5 SETS
ONE OF ONE'S EXIST
RCV Charlie Villanueva 10.00 25.00
RDW Dwyane Wade 60.00 150.00
REO Emeka Okafor 10.00 25.00
RJO Jermaine O'Neal 10.00 25.00
RRH Richard Hamilton 10.00 25.00
RVC Vince Carter 25.00 50.00

2006-07 Bowman Elevation Executive Level Relics Dual Autographs

PRINT RUN 15 SER.#'d SETS
UNPRICED BLUE PRINT RUN 10 SER.#'d SETS
UNPRICED GOLD PRINT RUN 3 SER.#'d SETS
UNPRICED RED PRINT RUN 5 SER.#'d SETS
ONE OF ONE's EXIST
RDW Dwyane Wade 100.00 200.00
RVC Vince Carter 30.00 60.00

2006-07 Bowman Elevation Power Brokers Relics

PRINT RUN 99 SER.#'d SETS
*RELICS BLUE SAME VALUE AS BASE
BLUE PRINT RUN 79 SER.#'d SETS
*RELICS GOLD: .75X TO 2X RELIC HI
GOLD PRINT RUN 25 SER.#'d SETS
*RELICS RED: .5X TO 1.25X RELIC HI
RED PRINT RUN 49 SER.#'d SETS
*RELICS DUAL: .5X TO 1.25 RELIC HI
DUAL PRINT RUN 99 SER.#'d SETS
*REL.DUAL BLUE: .5X TO 1.25X RELIC HI
DUAL BLUE PRINT RUN 79 SER.#'d SETS
*REL.DUAL GOLD: .75X TO 2X RELIC HI
DUAL GOLD PRINT RUN 25 SER.#'d SETS
*REL.DUAL RED: .6X TO 1.5X BASE HI
DUAL RED PRINT RUN 49 SER.#'d SETS
ONE OF ONES EXIST FOR RELICS AND DUAL
*PATCHES: 1.25X TO 3X RELIC HI
PATCH PRINT RUN 10 SER.#'d SETS
UNPRICED PATCH BLUE PRINT RUN 5 SETS
UNPRICED PATCH GOLD PRINT RUN 2 SETS
UNPRICED PATCH RED PRINT RUN 3 SETS
UNPRICED PATCH DUAL PRINT RUN 5 SETS
UNPRICED PATCH DUAL BLUE PRINT RUN 4 SETS
UNPRICED PATCH DUAL GOLD PRINT RUN 2 SETS
UNPRICED PATCH DUAL RED PRINT RUN 3 SETS
PATCH DUAL ONE OF ONE's EXIST
UNPRICED PATCH TRIP.PRINT RUN 5 SETS
UNPRICED PATCH TRIP.BLUE PRINT RUN 4 SETS
UNPRICED PATCH TRIP.GOLD PRINT RUN 2 SETS
UNPRICED PATCH TRIP.RED PRINT RUN 3 SETS
PAT.TRIPLE ONE OF ONE'S EXIST
RAB Andrew Bogut 2.50 6.00
RAI Allen Iverson 4.00 10.00
RAJ Antawn Jamison 2.50 6.00
RBB Bruce Bowen 2.00 5.00
RBW Ben Wallace 2.50 6.00
RCB Chris Bosh 3.00 8.00
RCF Channing Frye 2.50 6.00
RCK Chris Kaman 2.50 6.00
RCV Charlie Villanueva 2.00 5.00
RCW Chris Webber 3.00 8.00
RDH Dwight Howard 2.50 6.00
RDW Dwyane Wade 6.00 15.00
REB Elton Brand 3.00 8.00
REO Emeka Okafor 2.50 6.00
RHW Hakim Warrick 2.50 6.00
RID Ike Diogu 2.00 5.00
RJO Jermaine O'Neal 2.50 6.00
RKB Kobe Bryant 8.00 20.00
RKG Kevin Garnett 5.00 12.00
RKM Kenyon Martin 2.50 6.00
RLD Luol Deng 2.50 6.00
RMC Marcus Camby 2.50 6.00
RRJ Richard Jefferson 2.50 6.00
RRL Rashard Lewis 3.00 8.00
RRW Rasheed Wallace 3.00 8.00
RSD Samuel Dalembert 2.00 5.00
RSM Shawn Marion 2.50 6.00
RSO Shaquille O'Neal 6.00 15.00
RTC Tyson Chandler 2.50 6.00
RTD Tim Duncan 5.00 12.00
RTP Tayshaun Prince 2.50 6.00
RYM Yao Ming 4.00 10.00
RAIG Andre Iguodala 2.50 6.00
RSAR Shareef Abdur-Rahim 2.50 6.00

2006-07 Bowman Elevation Power Brokers Relics Autographs

PRINT RUN 25 SER.#'d SETS
*BLUE: 4X TO 1X BASE HI
BLUE PRINT RUN 19 SER.#'d SETS
UNPRICED GOLD PRINT RUN 5 SETS
UNPRICED RED PRINT RUN 9 SETS
RAI Allen Iverson 75.00 150.00
RCB Chris Bosh 20.00 50.00
RCV Charlie Villanueva 10.00 25.00
RDW Dwyane Wade 40.00 80.00
REO Emeka Okafor 10.00 25.00
RHW Hakim Warrick 10.00 25.00
RLD Luol Deng 10.00 25.00

2006-07 Bowman Elevation Power Brokers Relics Dual Autographs

STATED PRINT RUN 15 SER.#'d SETS
UNPRICED BLUE PRINT RUN 10 SETS
UNPRICED GOLD PRINT RUN 3 SETS
UNPRICED RED PRINT RUN 5 SETS
ONE OF ONE'S EXIST
RAI Allen Iverson 75.00 150.00
RCB Chris Bosh 20.00 50.00
RCV Charlie Villanueva 10.00 25.00
RDW Dwyane Wade 75.00 150.00
RHW Hakim Warrick 10.00 25.00
RSO Shaquille O'Neal 75.00 150.00

2006-07 Bowman Elevation Rookie Writing Autographs

APPROXIMATE ODDS ONE PER BOX
AJ Alexander Johnson 2.00 5.00
AM Adam Morrison 3.00 8.00
AR Allan Ray 2.00 5.00
BJ Bobby Jones 2.00 5.00
CS Craig Smith 2.50 6.00
DB Denham Brown 2.00 5.00
DG Daniel Gibson 2.50 6.00
DN David Noel 2.00 5.00
GD Guillermo Diaz 2.00 5.00
HA Hassan Adams 2.00 5.00
JA James Augustine 2.00 5.00

JB Josh Boone 2.00 5.00
JF Jordan Farmar 3.00 8.00
KL Kyle Lowry 4.00 10.00
MA Maurice Ager 2.00 5.00
MC Mardy Collins 2.00 5.00
MW Marcus Williams 2.00 5.00
PD Paul Davis 2.00 5.00
QD Quincy Douby 2.00 5.00
RB Ronnie Brewer 3.00 8.00
RC Rodney Carney 2.00 5.00
RF Randy Foye 3.00 8.00
RH Ryan Hollins 2.50 6.00
RR Rajon Rondo 12.00 30.00
SJ Solomon Jones 2.00 5.00
SN Steve Novak 2.50 6.00
SW Shelden Williams 2.50 6.00
ABA Andrea Bargnani 3.00 8.00
CSI Cedric Simmons 2.00 5.00
DBR Dee Brown 2.00 5.00
HAR Hilton Armstrong 2.00 5.00
JJR J.J. Redick 4.00 10.00
PJT P.J. Tucker 2.50 6.00
POB Patrick O'Bryant 2.00 5.00
RBA Renaldo Balkman 2.50 6.00

2006-07 Bowman Elevation Rookie Writing Autographs Blue

*BLUE: .5X TO 1.25X HI COLUMN
STATED PRINT RUN 79 TO 139 SETS
RR Rajon Rondo/99 20.00 50.00

2006-07 Bowman Elevation Rookie Writing Autographs Red

*RED: .6X TO 1.5X HI COLUMN
STATED PRINT RUN 59 TO 99 SETS

2006-07 Bowman Elevation Rookie Writing Autographs Gold

*GOLD: .75X TO 2X HI COLUMN
STATED PRINT RUN 29 TO 79 SETS
RR Rajon Rondo/39 30.00 80.00
JJR J.J. Redick/29 20.09 60.00

2007-08 Bowman Elevation

Released in April 2008, Bowman Elevation boasts a 100-card set where cards 1-100 picture both veteran and retired NBA players and cards 51-100 feature rookie players sequentially numbered to 999. Rather than an all-foil card design that had been used in previous years, 2007-08 Bowman Elevation features a cardboard stock with foil highlights incorporated into the design. Elevation is packaged in 12-pack boxes of five cards each and carried an intial suggested retail price of $9.75 per pack.

COMPLETE SET (100) 25.00 50.00
51-100 RC PRINT RUN 999 SER.#'d SETS
UNPRICED BLACK PRINT RUN ONE SET
UNPRICED GOLD PRINT RUN ONE SET
UNPRICED PLATE PRINT RUN ONE SET
1 Tracy McGrady .40 1.00
2 Shaquille O'Neal .75 2.00
3 Allen Iverson .50 1.25
4 Chris Bosh .40 1.00
5 Jason Kidd .40 1.00
6 Elton Brand .40 1.00
7 Brandon Roy .40 1.00
8 Tony Parker .40 1.00
9 Luol Deng .30 .75
10 Gilbert Arenas .30 .75
11 Amare Stoudemire .30 .75
12 Dwight Howard .30 .75
13 Deron Williams .30 .75
14 Dirk Nowitzki .50 1.25
15 Vince Carter .50 1.25
16 Richard Hamilton .30 .75
17 Baron Davis .30 .75
18 Pau Gasol .40 1.00
19 Kevin Garnett .60 1.50
20 LeBron James 1.50 4.00
21 Tim Duncan .60 1.50
22 Steve Nash .50 1.25
23 Jason Richardson .40 1.00
24 Kobe Bryant 1.50 4.00
25 Josh Smith .30 .75
26 Eddy Curry .25 .60
27 Mike Bibby .40 1.00
28 Ray Allen .40 1.00
29 Andre Iguodala .30 .75
30 Chris Paul .50 1.25
31 Yao Ming .50 1.25
32 Shawn Marion .30 .75
33 Dwyane Wade .60 1.50
34 Paul Pierce .40 1.00
35 Carmelo Anthony .50 1.25
36 Jermaine O'Neal .30 .75
37 Michael Redd .30 .75
38 Gerald Wallace .30 .75
39 Ben Gordon .30 .75
40 Carlos Boozer .30 .75
41 Larry Bird 1.50 4.00
42 Bill Walton .60 1.50
43 Moses Malone .60 1.50
44 John Havlicek .60 1.50
45 David Robinson 1.00 2.50
46 Bill Russell 1.00 2.50
47 Isiah Thomas .60 1.50
48 John Stockton 1.00 2.50
49 Dominique Wilkins .75 2.00
50 Magic Johnson 1.50 4.00
51 Nick Young RC 2.00 5.00
52 Greg Oden RC 1.50 4.00
53 Julian Wright RC 1.00 2.50
54 Dominic Mcguire RC 1.00 2.50
55 Acie Law RC 1.00 2.50
56 Luis Scola RC 2.00 5.00
57 Thaddeus Young RC 1.50 4.00
58 Rodney Stuckey RC 1.25 3.00
59 Jermareo Davidson RC 1.00 2.50
60 Daequan Cook RC 1.25 3.00
61 Josh McRoberts RC 1.25 3.00
62 Aaron Gray RC 1.00 2.50
63 Wilson Chandler RC 1.25 3.00
64 Chris Richard RC 1.00 2.50
65 Stephane Lasme RC 1.00 2.50
66 Kyrylo Fesenko RC 1.00 2.50
67 Taurean Green RC 1.00 2.50
68 Al Thornton RC 1.25 3.00
69 Corey Brewer RC 1.50 4.00
70 Ramon Sessions RC 1.50 4.00
71 Kevin Durant RC 15.00 40.00
72 Alando Tucker RC 1.00 2.50
73 Spencer Hawes RC 1.25 3.00
74 Nick Fazekas RC 1.00 2.50
75 Yi Jianlian RC 2.00 5.00
76 Juan Carlos Navarro RC 1.25 3.00
77 Jared Dudley RC 1.25 3.00
78 Adam Haluska RC 1.00 2.50
79 Herbert Hill RC 1.00 2.50
80 Kosta Perovic RC 1.00 2.50
81 JamesOn Curry RC 1.00 2.50
82 D.J. Strawberry RC 1.00 2.50
83 Javaris Crittenton RC 1.00 2.50
84 Al Horford RC 2.00 5.00
85 Mike Conley Jr. RC 2.00 5.00
86 Joakim Noah RC 1.50 4.00
87 Marco Belinelli RC 1.50 4.00
88 Arron Afflalo RC 1.50 4.00
89 Gabe Pruitt RC 1.00 2.50
90 Carl Landry RC 1.00 2.50
91 Jeff Green RC 1.50 4.00
92 Glen Davis RC 1.25 3.00
93 Jason Smith RC 1.25 3.00
94 Morris Almond RC 1.00 2.50
95 Cheik Samb RC 1.00 2.50
96 Brandon Wallace RC 1.00 2.50
97 Aaron Brooks RC 1.25 3.00
98 Brandan Wright RC 1.50 4.00
99 Sean Williams RC 1.00 2.50
100 Coby Karl RC 1.00 2.50

2007-08 Bowman Elevation Blue

*1-50 BLUE: 1X TO 2.5X BASE HI
*51-100 BLUE RCs: .5X TO 1.25X BASE HI
PRINT RUN 99 SER.#'d SETS

2007-08 Bowman Elevation Green

*1-40 GREEN: 4X TO 10X BASE HI
*41-50 GREEN: 3X TO 8X BASE HI
*51-100 GREEN RCs: 1X TO 2.5X BASE HI
GREEN PRINT RUN 19 SER.#'d SETS
71 Kevin Durant 200.00 400.00

2007-08 Bowman Elevation Red

*1-50 RED: 1.25X TO 3X BASE HI
*51-100 RED RCs: .6X TO 1.5X BASE HI
PRINT RUN 49 SER.#'d SETS

2007-08 Bowman Elevation Autographs Patches

PRINT RUN 15 SER.#'d SETS
UNPRICED BLACK PRINT RUN ONE SET
UNPRICED BLUE PRINT RUN NINE SETS
UNPRICED GOLD PRINT RUN THREE SETS
UNPRICED GREEN PRINT RUN FIVE SETS
UNPRICED RED PRINT RUN SEVEN SETS
AI Andre Iguodala 15.00 30.00
BD Baron Davis 15.00 30.00
BG Ben Gordon 8.00 20.00
BR Bill Russell 100.00 200.00
CA Carmelo Anthony 25.00 60.00
CB Carlos Boozer 8.00 20.00
CBO Chris Bosh 20.00 40.00
CM Corey Maggette 8.00 20.00
DL David Lee 8.00 20.00
DR David Robinson 50.00 100.00
DW Dwyane Wade 50.00 120.00
DWI Deron Williams 20.00 40.00
DWK Dominique Wilkins 25.00 50.00
GW Gerald Wallace 15.00 30.00
IT Isiah Thomas 15.00 30.00
JH Josh Howard 8.00 20.00
JST John Stockton 60.00 150.00
PP Paul Pierce 15.00 30.00
RB Rick Barry 20.00 40.00
SO Shaquille O'Neal 50.00 100.00

2007-08 Bowman Elevation Relics

PRINT RUN 179 SER.#'d SETS
UNPRICED BLACK PRINT RUN ONE SET
*BLUE: .5X TO 1.25X BASE HI
BLUE PRINT RUN 79 SER.#'d SETS
*GOLD: .75X TO 2X BASE HI
GOLD PRINT RUN 19 SER.#'d SETS
*GREEN: .6X TO 1.5X BASE HI
GREEN PRINT RUN 29 SER.#'d SETS
*RED: .5X TO 1.25X BASE HI
RED PRINT RUN 49 SER.#'d SETS
*DUAL: .5X TO 1.25X BASE HI
DUAL PRINT RUN 79 SER.#'d SETS
UNPRICED DUAL BLACK PRINT RUN ONE SET
*DUAL BLUE: .5X TO 1.25X BASE HI
DUAL BLUE PRINT RUN 49 SER.#'d SETS
UNPRICED DUAL GOLD PRINT RUN 9 SETS
*DUAL GREEN: .75X TO 2X BASE HI
DUAL GREEN PRINT RUN 19 SER.#'d SETS
*DUAL RED: .6X TO 1.5X BASE HI
DUAL RED PRINT RUN 29 SER.#'d SETS
*TRIPLE: .6X TO 1.5X BASE HI
TRIPLE PRINT RUN 39 SER.#'d SETS
UNPRICED TRIP.BLACK PRINT RUN ONE SET
*TRIP.BLUE: .6X TO 1.5X BASE HI
TRIP.BLUE PRINT RUN 29 SER.#'d SETS
UNPRICED TRIP.GOLD PRINT RUN 5 SETS
UNPRICED TRIP.GREEN PRINT RUN 9 SETS
*TRIP.RED: .75X TO 2X BASE HI
TRIP.RED PRINT RUN 19 SER.#'d SETS
*PATCHES: 1.25X TO 3X BASE HI
PATCH PRINT RUN 29 SER.#'d SETS
UNPRICED PATCH BLACK PRINT RUN ONE SET
*PAT.BLUE: 1.5X TO 4X BASE HI
PAT.BLUE PRINT RUN 19 SER.#'d SETS
UNPRICED PAT.GOLD PRINT RUN 3 SETS
UNPRICED PAT.GREEN PRINT RUN 5 SETS
UNPRICED PAT.RED PRINT RUN 9 SETS
UNPRICED PAT.DUAL PRINT RUN 9 SETS
UNPRICED PAT.DUAL BLACK PRINT RUN ONE SET
UNPRICED PAT.DUAL BLUE PRINT RUN 5 SETS
UNPRICED PAT.DUAL GOLD PRINT RUN 2 SETS
UNPRICED PAT.DUAL GREEN PRINT RUN 3 SETS
UNPRICED PAT.DUAL RED PRINT RUN 4 SETS
UNPRICED PAT.TRIPLE PRINT RUN 9 SETS
UNPRICED PAT.TRIP.BLACK PRINT RUN ONE SET
UNPRICED PAT.TRIP.BLUE PRINT RUN 5 SETS
UNPRICED PAT.TRIP.GOLD PRINT RUN 2 SETS
UNPRICED PAT.TRIP.GREEN PRINT RUN 3 SETS
UNPRICED PAT.TRIP.RED PRINT RUN 4 SETS
AB Andrea Bargnani 3.00 8.00
AI Andre Iguodala 2.50 6.00
AJ Al Jefferson 2.50 6.00
AJA Antawn Jamison 2.50 6.00
AS Amare Stoudemire 2.50 6.00
BD Baron Davis 2.50 6.00
BRO Brandon Roy 3.00 8.00
BW Ben Wallace 2.50 6.00
CBI Chauncey Billups 3.00 8.00
CBO Chris Bosh 3.00 8.00
CM Corey Maggette 2.50 6.00
CP Chris Paul 4.00 10.00
DH Dwight Howard 2.50 6.00
DL David Lee 2.00 5.00
DN Dirk Nowitzki 4.00 10.00
DR David Robinson 5.00 12.00
DW Dwyane Wade 6.00 15.00
DWI Deron Williams 2.50 6.00
DWK Dominique Wilkins 4.00 10.00
EB Elton Brand 3.00 8.00
GA Gilbert Arenas 2.50 6.00
IT Isiah Thomas 3.00 8.00
JO Jermaine O'Neal 2.50 6.00
JR Jason Richardson 3.00 8.00
JS Josh Smith 2.50 6.00
JST John Stockton 5.00 12.00
KB Kobe Bryant 8.00 20.00
KG Kevin Garnett 5.00 12.00
LB Larry Bird 8.00 20.00
LD Luol Deng 2.50 6.00
LO Lamar Odom 2.50 6.00
MJ Magic Johnson 6.00 15.00
MR Michael Redd 2.50 6.00
PM Pete Maravich 15.00 30.00
PP Paul Pierce 3.00 8.00
RA Ray Allen 3.00 8.00
RH Richard Hamilton 2.50 6.00
RL Rashard Lewis 2.50 6.00
SM Stephon Marbury 2.50 6.00
SN Steve Nash 4.00 10.00
SO Shaquille O'Neal 6.00 15.00
TD Tim Duncan 5.00 12.00
TM Tracy McGrady 3.00 8.00
TT Tyrus Thomas 2.00 5.00
YM Yao Ming 4.00 10.00

2007-08 Bowman Elevation Rookie Relics

PRINT RUN 199 SER.#'d SETS
*RELICS 99: SAME VALUE AS BASE
*RELICS 69: .5X TO 1.25X BASE
*RELICS 49: .5X TO 1.25X BASE
*RELICS 29: .6X TO 1.5X BASE
RELICS 1 UNPRICED DUE TO SCARCITY
*DUAL 99: .5X TO 1.25X BASE
*DUAL 79: .5X TO 1.25X BASE
*DUAL 29: .6X TO 1.5X BASE
*DUAL 19: .75X TO 2X BASE
DUAL 9 UNPRICED DUE TO SCARCITY
DUAL 1 UNPRICED DUE TO SCARCITY
*TRIPLE 49: .6X TO 1.5X BASE
*TRIPLE 39: .6X TO 1.5X BASE
*TRIPLE 29: .75X TO 2X BASE
*TRIPLE 19: 1X TO 2.5X BASE
TRIPLE 9 UNPRICED DUE TO SCARCITY
TRIPLE 1 UNPRICED DUE TO SCARCITY
AA Arron Afflalo 2.50 6.00
AB Aaron Brooks 2.00 5.00
AH Al Horford 3.00 8.00
AHA Adam Haluska 1.50 4.00
AL4 Acie Law 1.50 4.00
AT Al Thornton 2.00 5.00
ATU Alando Tucker 1.50 4.00
BW Brandan Wright 2.50 6.00
CB Corey Brewer 2.50 6.00
CL Carl Landry 1.50 4.00
CR Chris Richard 1.50 4.00
DC Daequan Cook 2.00 5.00
DJS D.J. Strawberry 1.50 4.00
DM Dominic McGuire 1.50 4.00
GD Glen Davis 2.00 5.00
GO Greg Oden 2.50 6.00
GP Gabe Pruitt 1.50 4.00
HH Herbert Hill 1.50 4.00
JC Javaris Crittenton 1.50 4.00
JD Jared Dudley 2.00 5.00
JDA Jermareo Davidson 1.50 4.00
JG Jeff Green 2.50 6.00
JN Joakim Noah 2.50 6.00
JS Jason Smith 2.00 5.00
JW Julian Wright 1.50 4.00
MA Morris Almond 1.50 4.00
MC Mike Conley Jr. 3.00 8.00
NF Nick Fazekas 1.50 4.00
NY Nick Young 3.00 8.00
RS Rodney Stuckey 2.00 5.00
SH Spencer Hawes 2.00 5.00
SW Sean Williams 1.50 4.00
TG Taurean Green 1.50 4.00
TY Thaddeus Young 2.50 6.00
WC Wilson Chandler 2.00 5.00

2007-08 Bowman Elevation Rookie Writings

STATED PRINT RUN 49 TO 299 SER.#'d SETS
UNPRICED BLACK PRINT RUN ONE SET
*BLUE: .5X TO 1.25X BASE
BLUE PRINT RUN 29 SER.#'d SETS
UNPRICED GOLD PRINT RUN NINE SETS
*GREEN: .6X TO 1.5X BASE
GREEN PRINT RUN 15 SER.#'d SETS
*RED: .6X TO 1.5X BASE
RED PRINT RUN 19 SER.#'d SETS
RWAA Arron Afflalo/299 4.00 10.00
RWAB Aaron Brooks/299 3.00 8.00
RWAG Aaron Gray/299 2.50 6.00
RWAH Adam Haluska/299 2.50 6.00
RWAL4 Acie Law/199 2.50 6.00
RWAT Al Thornton/199 3.00 8.00
RWCL Carl Landry/299 2.50 6.00
RWDJS D.J. Strawberry/299 2.50 6.00
RWGO Greg Oden/49 12.00 30.00
RWHH Herbert Hill/299 2.50 6.00
RWJC Javaris Crittenton/299 2.50 6.00
RWJD Jermareo Davidson/299 2.50 6.00
RWJS Jason Smith/199 3.00 8.00
RWMA Morris Almond/299 2.50 6.00
RWMB Marco Belinelli/299 4.00 10.00
RWNF Nick Fazekas/299 2.50 6.00
RWNY Nick Young/49 8.00 20.00
RWRS Rodney Stuckey/299 3.00 8.00
RWSW Sean Williams/299 2.50 6.00
RWTY Thaddeus Young/49 12.00 30.00
RWWC Wilson Chandler/199 3.00 8.00
RWYJ Yi Jianlian/49 12.00 30.00

2007-08 Bowman Elevation Rookie Writings Relics

STATED PRINT RUN 29 TO 169 SER.#'d SETS
UNPRICED BLACK PRINT RUN ONE SET
*BLUE: .5X TO 1.25X BASE HI
BLUE PRINT RUN 19 SER.#'d SETS
UNPRICED GOLD PRINT RUN FIVE SETS
UNPRICED GREEN PRINT RUN NINE SETS
*RED: .6X TO 1.5X BASE HI
RED PRINT RUN 15 SER.#'d SETS
RWAA Arron Afflalo/169 5.00 12.00
RWAB Aaron Brooks/169 4.00 10.00
RWAG Aaron Gray/169 3.00 8.00
RWAH Adam Haluska/169 3.00 8.00
RWAL4 Acie Law/79 3.00 8.00
RWAT Al Thornton/79 4.00 10.00
RWCL Carl Landry/169 3.00 8.00
RWDJS D.J. Strawberry/169 3.00 8.00
RWGO Greg Oden/29 15.00 40.00
RWHH Herbert Hill/169 3.00 8.00
RWJC Javaris Crittenton/169 3.00 8.00
RWJD Jermareo Davidson/169 3.00 8.00
RWJS Jason Smith/79 4.00 10.00
RWMA Morris Almond/169 3.00 8.00
RWMB Marco Belinelli/169 5.00 12.00
RWNF Nick Fazekas/169 3.00 8.00
RWNY Nick Young/29 15.00 40.00
RWRS Rodney Stuckey/169 4.00 10.00
RWSW Sean Williams/169 3.00 8.00
RWTY Thaddeus Young/29 15.00 40.00
RWWC Wilson Chandler/79 4.00 10.00
RWYJ Yi Jianlian/29 15.00 40.00

2007-08 Bowman Elevation Rookie Writings Patches

PRINT RUN 15 SER.#'d SETS
UNPRICED BLACK PRINT RUN ONE SET
UNPRICED BLUE PRINT RUN NINE SETS
UNPRICED GOLD PRINT RUN THREE SETS
UNPRICED GREEN PRINT RUN FIVE SETS
UNPRICED RED PRINT RUN SEVEN SETS
RWAA Arron Afflalo 8.00 20.00
RWAB Aaron Brooks 6.00 15.00
RWAG Aaron Gray 5.00 12.00
RWAH Adam Haluska 5.00 12.00
RWAL4 Acie Law 5.00 12.00
RWAT Al Thornton 6.00 15.00
RWCL Carl Landry 5.00 12.00
RWDJS D.J. Strawberry 5.00 12.00
RWGO Greg Oden 60.00 150.00
RWHH Herbert Hill 5.00 12.00
RWJC Javaris Crittenton 5.00 12.00
RWJD Jermareo Davidson 5.00 12.00
RWJS Jason Smith 6.00 15.00
RWMA Morris Almond 5.00 12.00
RWMB Marco Belinelli 8.00 20.00
RWNF Nick Fazekas 5.00 12.00
RWNY Nick Young 25.00 60.00
RWRS Rodney Stuckey 6.00 15.00
RWSW Sean Williams 5.00 12.00
RWTY Thaddeus Young 10.00 25.00
RWWC Wilson Chandler 6.00 15.00
RWYJ Yi Jianlian 30.00 80.00

2008-09 Bowman Retail Relics

BSRAA Arron Afflalo 1.50 4.00
BSRAB Aaron Brooks 1.50 4.00
BSRAL4 Acie Law IV 2.00 5.00
BSRAT Alando Tucker 1.50 4.00
BSRATH Al Thornton 2.00 5.00
BSRBW Brandan Wright 2.00 5.00
BSRDC Daequan Cook 1.50 4.00
BSRGD Glen Davis 1.50 4.00
BSRGO Greg Oden 2.00 5.00
BSRJC Javaris Crittenton 1.50 4.00
BSRJD Jared Dudley 2.00 5.00
BSRJS Jason Smith 1.50 4.00
BSRMA Morris Almond 1.50 4.00
BSRNY Nick Young 2.00 5.00
BSRRS Rodney Stuckey 2.00 5.00
BSRSW Sean Williams 2.00 5.00
BSRTY Thaddeus Young 2.00 5.00
BSRWC Wilson Chandler 2.00 5.00

2002-03 Bowman Signature Edition

Released in January 2003, Bowman Signature Edition boasts a 100-card set and is numbered to coincide with the featured player's initials. 45 rookie players were issued, numbered to 999, where all cards are autographed with some also containing jersey swatches-all of these cards were issued in uncirculated card holders with an irridescent tamper sticker along the top of the holder. Jay Williams is the only RC in the set who does not have an autographed card and his card is sequentially numbered to 1249. Signature Edition was packaged in six card packs, all containing one rookie autograph, with boxes of six packs each and a suggested retail price of $35 per pack.

RC PRINT RUN 999 SER.#'d SETS
SEAI Allen Iverson 1.25 3.00
SEAJ Antawn Jamison .75 2.00
SEAK Andrei Kirilenko .75 2.00
SEAM Alonzo Mourning 1.00 2.50
SEAS Stoudemire JSY AU RC 5.00 12.00
SEAW Antoine Walker .60 1.50
SEAKM Antonio McDyess .60 1.50
SEALM Andre Miller .60 1.50
SEBD Baron Davis .60 1.50
SEBN Bostjan Nachbar AU RC 3.00 8.00
SEBW Ben Wallace .60 1.50
SECB Curtis Borchardt AU RC 2.50 6.00
SECM Cuttino Mobley .50 1.25
SECO Chris Owens AU RC 2.50 6.00
SECT Cezary Trybanski AU RC 4.00 10.00
SECW Chris Wilcox JSY AU RC 3.00 8.00
SECBO C.Boozer JSY AU RC 4.00 10.00
SECBU Caron Butler JSY AU RC 4.00 10.00
SECJA C.Jacobsen JSY AU RC 3.00 8.00
SECJE C.Jefferies JSY AU RC 2.50 6.00
SEDD Dan Dickau AU RC 3.00 8.00
SEDN Dirk Nowitzki 1.25 3.00
SEDW D.Wagner JSY AU RC 3.00 8.00
SEDGA D.Gadzuric JSY AU RC 3.00 8.00
SEDGO D.Gooden JSY AU RC 4.00 10.00
SEDLM Darius Miles .50 1.25
SEEB Elton Brand .75 2.00
SEEC Eddy Curry .50 1.25
SEEG Manu Ginobili AU RC 30.00 80.00
SEEJ Eddie Jones .60 1.50
SEER E.Rentzias AU RC 2.50 6.00
SEFJ Fred Jones JSY AU RC 3.00 8.00
SEFR Frank Williams AU RC 2.50 6.00
SEGG Gordan Giricek AU RC 4.00 10.00
SEGP Gary Payton .75 2.00
SEGR Glenn Robinson .60 1.50
SEJB J.R. Bremer AU RC 2.50 6.00
SEJD Juan Dixon JSY AU RC 4.00 10.00
SEJJ J.Jeffries JSY AU RC 3.00 8.00
SEJK Jason Kidd 1.25 3.00
SEJM Jamal Mashburn .60 1.50
SEJO Jermaine O'Neal .60 1.50
SEJP Jannero Pargo AU RC 2.50 6.00
SEJS John Salmons JSY AU RC 4.00 10.00
SEJT Jamaal Tinsley .50 1.25
SEJAW Jay Williams/1249 RC 2.50 6.00
SEJDS Jerry Stackhouse .60 1.50
SEJOS John Stockton 1.00 2.50
SEJWE Jiri Welsch AU RC 3.00 8.00
SEJWI Jerome Williams .50 1.25
SEKB Kobe Bryant 3.00 8.00
SEKG Kevin Garnett 1.25 3.00
SEKM Karl Malone 1.00 2.50
SEKR K.Rush JSY AU RC 3.00 8.00
SEKS Kenny Satterfield .50 1.25
SEKLM Kenyon Martin .60 1.50
SELS Latrell Sprewell .60 1.50
SEMB Mike Bibby .75 2.00
SEMD M.Dunleavy JSY AU RC 4.00 10.00
SEME Melvin Ely JSY AU RC 3.00 8.00
SEMH M.Haislip JSY AU RC 3.00 8.00
SEMO Mehmet Okur AU RC 4.00 10.00
SEMCW Chris Webber .75 2.00
SEMJA Marko Jaric AU 4.00 10.00
SEMJJ Michael Jordan 6.00 15.00
SENH N.Hilario JSY AU RC 4.00 10.00
SENT N.Tskitishvili JSY AU RC 2.50 6.00
SEPG Pau Gasol 1.00 2.50
SEPP Paul Pierce .75 2.00
SEPS Peja Stojakovic .75 2.00
SEPSA P.Savovic JSY AU RC 3.00 8.00
SEQR Quentin Richardson .60 1.50
SERA Ray Allen .75 2.00
SERA R.Archibald JSY AU RC 2.50 6.00
SERB Rasual Butler AU RC 4.00 10.00
SERJ Richard Jefferson .75 2.00
SERL Rashard Lewis .75 2.00
SERW Rasheed Wallace .75 2.00
SERCH Richard Hamilton .60 1.50
SERHU R.Humphrey JSY AU RC 3.00 8.00
SERMA Roger Mason JSY AU RC 3.00 8.00
SERMU R.Murray JSY AU RC 4.00 10.00
SESA Shareef Abdur-Rahim .60 1.50
SESC Sam Clancy JSY AU RC 3.00 8.00
SESF Steve Francis .60 1.50
SESM Stephon Marbury .60 1.50
SESN Steve Nash 1.00 2.50
SESO Shaquille O'Neal 2.00 5.00
SESCB Shane Battier .75 2.00
SESDM Shawn Marion .60 1.50
SETC Tyson Chandler .75 2.00
SETD Tim Duncan 1.50 4.00
SETP T.Prince JSY AU RC 6.00 15.00
SETP Tony Parker 1.00 2.50
SETS Tamar Slay AU RC 2.50 6.00
SETLM Tracy McGrady 1.25 3.00
SEVC Vince Carter 1.25 3.00
SEVY V.Yarbrough JSY AU RC 2.50 6.00
SEWS Wally Szczerbiak .60 1.50
SEYM Yao Ming AU RC 40.00 100.00

2002-03 Bowman Signature Edition Parallel

*STARS: 1X TO 2.5X BASE CARD HI
*RCs: .6X TO 1.5X BASE CARD HI
VETERAN PRINT RUN 249 SER.#'d SETS
RC PRINT RUN 99 SER.#'d SETS
SEEG Manu Ginobili AU 60.00 150.00
SEJAW Jay Williams/249 6.00 15.00
SEMJJ Michael Jordan 20.00 50.00
SEYM Yao Ming AU 100.00 250.00

2003-04 Bowman Signature Edition

Released in January 2004, this 118-card set is divided up into 55 veteran player cards (numbers 1-55), five rookie cards sequentially numbered to 1250 (numbers 56-60), 16 autographed rookie cards sequentially numbered to 1250 unless noted in the checklist (numbers 61-76), 29 autograph jersey rookie cards sequentially numbered to 1250 unless noted in the checklist (numbers 77-105) and 13 autographed rookie cards sequentially numbered to 1250 (numbers 106-118). Bowman Signature Edition was packaged in six pack boxes with packs containing six cards, one of them being an uncirculated autograph or relic card, and carried a suggested retail price of $35.

COMP.SET w/o SP's (55) 15.00 40.00
56-60 RC PRINT RUN 1250 SER.#'d SETS
UNPRICED BLUE PRINT RUN ONE SET
1 Tracy McGrady 1.00 2.50
2 Baron Davis .60 1.50
3 Allen Iverson 1.25 3.00
4 Bonzi Wells .50 1.25
5 Tony Parker .75 2.00
6 Morris Peterson .50 1.25
7 Jerry Stackhouse .60 1.50
8 Jason Terry .60 1.50
9 Tyson Chandler .60 1.50
10 Dirk Nowitzki 1.25 3.00
11 Nene .60 1.50
12 Antawn Jamison .60 1.50
13 Richard Hamilton .60 1.50
14 Steve Francis .60 1.50
15 Jermaine O'Neal .60 1.50
16 Elton Brand .75 2.00
17 Mike Miller .60 1.50
18 Caron Butler .60 1.50
19 Gary Payton .75 2.00
20 Shaquille O'Neal 2.00 5.00
21 Kevin Garnett 1.25 3.00
22 Desmond Mason .60 1.50
23 Jamal Mashburn .60 1.50
24 Drew Gooden .60 1.50
25 Eric Snow .50 1.25
26 Shawn Marion .60 1.50
27 Peja Stojakovic .75 2.00
28 Karl Malone 1.00 2.50
29 Shareef Abdur-Rahim .60 1.50
30 Paul Pierce .75 2.00
31 Dajuan Wagner .50 1.25
32 Steve Nash 1.00 2.50
33 Ben Wallace .60 1.50
34 Jason Richardson .75 2.00
35 Yao Ming 1.50 4.00
36 Ron Artest .75 2.00
37 Andre Miller .60 1.50
38 Kobe Bryant 3.00 8.00
39 Pau Gasol .75 2.00
40 Tim Duncan 1.25 3.00
41 Ray Allen .75 2.00
42 Vince Carter 1.25 3.00
43 Andrei Kirilenko .75 2.00
44 Chris Webber .75 2.00
45 Rasheed Wallace .75 2.00
46 Amare Stoudemire 1.00 2.50
47 Latrell Sprewell .60 1.50
48 Kenyon Martin .60 1.50
49 Wally Szczerbiak .60 1.50
50 Jason Kidd 1.25 3.00
51 Eddie Jones .60 1.50
52 Jalen Rose .60 1.50
53 Ricky Davis .60 1.50
54 Antoine Walker .75 2.00
55 Allan Houston .60 1.50
56 LeBron James RC 75.00 200.00
57 Darko Milicic RC 2.00 5.00
58 Chris Kaman RC 2.50 6.00
59 Kyle Korver RC 3.00 8.00
60 Willie Green RC 1.50 4.00
61 James Lang AU RC 2.00 5.00
62 Carl English AU RC 3.00 8.00
63 Devin Brown AU RC 2.00 5.00
64 Theron Smith AU RC 2.00 5.00
65 Rick Rickert AU RC 2.00 5.00
66 Z.Cabarkapa AU RC 2.00 5.00
67 D.Zimmerman AU RC 3.00 8.00
68 A.Pavlovic AU RC 2.50 6.00
69 Malick Badiane AU RC 3.00 8.00
70 Boris Diaw AU RC 3.00 8.00
71 Zaur Pachulia AU RC 3.00 8.00
72 Zoran Planinic AU RC 2.00 5.00
73 Carlos Delfino AU RC 2.50 6.00
74 Maciej Lampe AU RC 2.00 5.00
75 S.Schortsanitis AU RC 2.00 5.00
76 Mario Austin AU RC 3.00 8.00
77 C.Anthony/1170 JSY AU RC 20.00 50.00
78 Chris Bosh JSY AU RC 6.00 15.00
79 D.Wade JSY AU RC 30.00 80.00
80 Kirk Hinrich JSY AU RC 5.00 12.00
81 T.J. Ford JSY AU RC 4.00 10.00
82 D.West/1245 JSY AU RC 6.00 15.00
83 Marcus Banks JSY AU RC 3.00 8.00
84 Dahntay Jones JSY AU RC 4.00 10.00
85 Luke Ridnour JSY AU RC 4.00 10.00
86 Reece Gaines JSY AU RC 3.00 8.00
87 T.Outlaw/1075 JSY AU RC 4.00 10.00
88 B.Cook/1063 JSY AU RC 3.00 8.00
89 Troy Bell JSY AU RC 3.00 8.00
90 Ndudi Ebi JSY AU RC 3.00 8.00
91 K.Perkins/1238 JSY AU RC 4.00 10.00
92 L.Barbosa JSY AU RC 5.00 12.00
93 J.Howard/1111 JSY AU RC 5.00 12.00
94 Slavko Vranes JSY AU RC 3.00 8.00
95 Jason Kapono JSY AU RC 3.00 8.00
96 Luke Walton JSY AU RC 5.00 12.00
97 M.Williams/1172 JSY AU RC 5.00 12.00
98 M.Bonner/960 JSY AU RC 5.00 12.00
99 Travis Hansen JSY AU RC 3.00 8.00
100 Steve Blake JSY AU RC 3.00 8.00
101 Keith Bogans JSY AU RC 3.00 8.00
102 Mike Sweetney JSY AU RC 3.00 8.00
103 Jarvis Hayes JSY AU RC 3.00 8.00
104 Mickael Pietrus JSY AU RC 4.00 10.00
105 Nick Collison JSY AU RC 4.00 10.00
107 James Jones AU RC 2.00 5.00
108 Brandon Hunter AU RC 2.00 5.00
109 Tommy Smith AU RC 3.00 8.00
110 Marcus Hatten AU RC 3.00 8.00
111 Koko Archibong AU RC 3.00 8.00
112 Ime Udoka AU RC 3.00 8.00
113 Eric Chenowith AU RC 3.00 8.00
114 Stephane Pelle AU RC 3.00 8.00
115 Marquis Daniels AU RC 2.50 6.00
116 Paccelis Morlende AU RC 3.00 8.00
117 George Williams AU RC 3.00 8.00
118 Udonis Haslem AU RC 2.50 6.00

2003-04 Bowman Signature Edition Foil

*FOIL 1-55 SINGLES: 1.25X TO 3X BASE HI
*FOIL 56-60 SINGLES: 1X TO 2.5X BASE HI
*FOIL 61-76 SINGLES: .75X TO 2X BASE HI
*FOIL 77-105 SINGLES: .5X TO 1.25X BASE HI
*FOIL 106-118 SINGLES: .75X TO 2X BASE HI
FOIL PRINT RUN 125 SER.#'d SETS
FOIL RC PLAYERS NO JSY OR AUTO
77 Carmelo Anthony 20.00 50.00
79 Dwyane Wade 20.00 50.00

2003-04 Bowman Signature Edition Gold

*GOLD 1-55 SINGLES: 1.5X TO 4X BASE HI
*GOLD 56-60 SINGLES: 1.25X TO 3X BASE HI
*GOLD 61-76 SINGLES: 1X TO 2.5X BASE HI
*GOLD 77-105 SINGLES: .75X TO 2X BASE HI
*GOLD 106-118 SINGLES: 1X TO 2.5X BASE HI
GOLD PRINT RUN 99 SER.#'d.SETS
79 Dwyane Wade 75.00 150.00

2003-04 Bowman Signature Edition Silver

*SLVR 1-55 SINGLES: 1X TO 2.5X BASE HI
*SLVR 56-60 SINGLES: .75X TO 2X BASE HI
*SLVR 61-76 SINGLES: .6X TO 1.5X BASE HI
*SLVR 77-105 SINGLES: .5X TO 1.25X BASE HI
*SLVR 106-118 SINGLES: .6X TO 1.5X BASE HI
SILVER PRINT RUN 249 SER.#'d SETS

2004-05 Bowman Signature Edition

Issued in early November 2004, Bowman Signature Edition consists of a 102-card set divided up into 55 veteran players, two jersey rookies (numbers 56 and 57) sequentially numbered to 100, jersey and autograped rookies (numbers 58-86) sequentially numbered to 399 and autographed rookies (numbers 87-103) sequentially numbered to 399. Veteran cards have red borders, while rookie cards have blue borders, and for the ones that include jerseys and autographs, the jerseys are in the shape of a star and the autographs are on foil stickers. Signature Edition was packaged in six pack boxes of six card packs (where one of the cards was Uncirculated in a sealed holder--all the rookies with jerseys and autographs were delivered sealed) and packs carred a $35.00 SRP. Card number 101 was not issued.

COMP.SET w/o SP's (55) 20.00 50.00
56-57 RC JSY PRINT RUN 100 SER.#'d SETS
58-103 PRINT RUN 399 SER.#'d SETS
UNPRICED PARALLEL PRINT RUN ONE SET
1 Kevin Garnett 1.25 3.00
2 Eddy Curry .50 1.25
3 Ben Wallace .60 1.50
4 Cuttino Mobley .50 1.25
5 Vince Carter 1.25 3.00
6 Bonzi Wells .50 1.25
7 Jermaine O'Neal .60 1.50
8 Kobe Bryant 3.00 8.00
9 Stephon Marbury .60 1.50
10 Mike Bibby .75 2.00
11 Yao Ming 1.50 4.00
12 Richard Jefferson .60 1.50
13 Steve Nash 1.00 2.50
14 Luke Ridnour .60 1.50
15 Carmelo Anthony 1.50 4.00
16 Pau Gasol .75 2.00
17 Amare Stoudemire .60 1.50
18 Chris Webber .75 2.00
19 Sam Cassell .60 1.50
20 Tracy McGrady 1.00 2.50
21 Tim Duncan 1.25 3.00
22 Michael Redd .60 1.50
23 LeBron James 5.00 12.00
24 Baron Davis .60 1.50
25 Zach Randolph .60 1.50
26 Peja Stojakovic .75 2.00
27 Lamar Odom .60 1.50
28 Michael Finley .75 2.00
29 Zydrunas Ilgauskas .60 1.50
30 Rasheed Wallace .75 2.00
31 Mike Sweetney .50 1.25
32 Elton Brand .75 2.00
33 Steve Francis .60 1.50
34 Paul Pierce .75 2.00
35 Ray Allen .75 2.00
36 Tony Parker .75 2.00
37 Gerald Wallace .60 1.50
38 Chris Bosh .75 2.00
39 Desmond Mason .60 1.50
40 Allen Iverson 1.25 3.00
41 Dirk Nowitzki 1.25 3.00
42 Antoine Walker .75 2.00
43 Ron Artest .75 2.00
44 Jamaal Magloire .50 1.25
45 Kirk Hinrich .60 1.50
46 Jason Richardson .75 2.00
47 Andrei Kirilenko .60 1.50
48 Kenyon Martin .60 1.50
49 Carlos Boozer .60 1.50
50 Shaquille O'Neal 2.00 5.00
51 Shawn Marion .60 1.50
52 Kwame Brown .50 1.25
53 Corey Maggette .60 1.50
54 Dwyane Wade 1.25 3.00
55 Jason Kidd 1.25 3.00
56 Dwight Howard JSY RC 4.00 10.00
57 Andre Iguodala JSY RC 2.50 6.00
58 Andre Emmett JSY AU RC 3.00 8.00
59 Al Jefferson JSY AU RC 6.00 15.00
60 A.Varejao JSY AU RC 4.00 10.00
61 Ben Gordon JSY AU RC 8.00 20.00
62 David Harrison JSY AU RC 3.00 8.00
63 Delonte West JSY AU RC 5.00 12.00
64 Devin Harris JSY AU RC 4.00 10.00
65 Dorell Wright JSY AU RC 5.00 12.00
66 Ha Seung-Jin JSY AU RC 5.00 12.00
67 J.R. Smith JSY AU RC 10.00 25.00
68 Jackson Vroman JSY AU RC 3.00 8.00
69 Jameer Nelson JSY AU RC 5.00 12.00
70 Kris Humphries JSY AU RC 5.00 12.00
71 Josh Smith JSY AU RC 6.00 15.00
72 Kevin Martin JSY AU RC 6.00 15.00
73 Kirk Snyder JSY AU RC 3.00 8.00
74 Trevor Ariza JSY AU RC 5.00 12.00
75 Lionel Chalmers JSY AU RC 5.00 12.00
76 Luke Jackson JSY AU RC 3.00 8.00
77 Luol Deng JSY AU RC 5.00 12.00
78 Rafael Araujo JSY AU RC 3.00 8.00
79 Rickey Paulding JSY AU RC 3.00 8.00
80 Sebastian Telfair JSY AU RC 4.00 10.00
81 S.Livingston JSY AU RC 5.00 12.00
82 Tony Allen JSY AU RC 5.00 12.00
83 Josh Childress JSY AU RC 4.00 10.00
84 Emeka Okafor JSY AU RC 4.00 10.00
85 Ber.Robinson JSY AU RC 4.00 10.00
86 Chris Duhon JSY AU RC 5.00 12.00
87 Blake Stepp AU RC 3.00 8.00
88 Andris Biedrins AU RC 2.00 5.00
89 Donta Smith AU RC 2.00 5.00
90 Beno Udrih AU RC 2.50 6.00
91 Justin Reed AU RC 2.00 5.00
92 Pavel Podkolzin AU RC 2.00 5.00
93 Matt Freije AU RC 2.50 6.00
94 Pape Sow AU RC 2.50 6.00
95 Antonio Burks AU RC 2.50 6.00
96 Rashad Wright AU RC 2.50 6.00
97 Ricky Minard AU RC 2.50 6.00
98 Robert Swift AU RC 2.00 5.00
99 Romain Sato AU RC 2.00 5.00
100 Sasha Vujacic AU RC 3.00 8.00
102 Tim Pickett AU RC 3.00 8.00
103 Yuta Tabuse AU RC 3.00 8.00

2004-05 Bowman Signature Edition 169

*1-55 169 SINGLES: 1.25X TO 3X BASE HI
*56-57 JSY 169: .4X TO 1X BASE HI
*58-86 JSY AU 169: .5X TO 1.25X BASE HI
*87-103 AU 169: .5X TO 1.25X BASE HI

2004-05 Bowman Signature Edition 50

*1-55 50 SINGLES: 1.5X TO 4X BASE HI
*56-57 JSY 50 SINGLES: .6X TO 1.5X BASE HI
*58-86 JSY AU 50: .75X TO 2X BASE HI
*87-103 AU 50: .6X TO 1.5X BASE HI
103 Yuta Tabuse AU 5.00 12.00

2004-05 Bowman Signature Edition Foil

FOIL PRINT RUN 50 SER.#'d SETS
ONE PER BOX AS TOPPER
56 Dwight Howard 8.00 20.00
57 Andre Iguodala 5.00 12.00
58 Andre Emmett 2.50 6.00
59 Al Jefferson 5.00 12.00
60 Anderson Varejao 3.00 8.00
61 Ben Gordon 4.00 10.00
62 David Harrison 2.50 6.00
63 Delonte West 4.00 10.00
64 Devin Harris 3.00 8.00
65 Dorell Wright 4.00 10.00
66 Ha Seung-Jin 4.00 10.00
67 J.R. Smith 4.00 10.00
68 Jackson Vroman 2.50 6.00
69 Jameer Nelson 4.00 10.00
70 Kris Humphries 4.00 10.00
71 Josh Smith 4.00 10.00
72 Kevin Martin 5.00 12.00
73 Kirk Snyder 2.50 6.00
74 Trevor Ariza 4.00 10.00
75 Lionel Chalmers 4.00 10.00
76 Luke Jackson 2.50 6.00
77 Luol Deng 4.00 10.00
78 Rafael Araujo 2.50 6.00
79 Rickey Paulding 2.50 6.00
80 Sebastian Telfair 3.00 8.00
81 Shaun Livingston 4.00 10.00
82 Tony Allen 4.00 10.00
83 Josh Childress 3.00 8.00
84 Emeka Okafor 3.00 8.00
85 Bernard Robinson 3.00 8.00
86 Chris Duhon 4.00 10.00
87 Blake Stepp 4.00 10.00
88 Andris Biedrins 2.50 6.00
89 Donta Smith 2.50 6.00
90 Beno Udrih 3.00 8.00
91 Justin Reed 2.50 6.00
92 Pavel Podkolzin 2.50 6.00
93 Matt Freije 3.00 8.00
94 Pape Sow 3.00 8.00
95 Antonio Burks 3.00 8.00
96 Rashad Wright 3.00 8.00
97 Ricky Minard 3.00 8.00
98 Robert Swift 2.50 6.00
99 Romain Sato 2.50 6.00
100 Sasha Vujacic 4.00 10.00
102 Tim Pickett 4.00 10.00
103 Yuta Tabuse 4.00 10.00

2004-05 Bowman Signature Edition Flashback Autographs

Randomly inserted in packs, this 15-card set showcases players with images from earlier in their career and background colors to match their jersey colors. Each card has received the refractor treatment, contains both an autograph and a swatch of jersey and is sequentially numbered to 60. Two parallel versions of this set exist, one sequentially numbered to 10 and one where the cards are all numbered one of one.

PRINT RUN 60 SER.#'d SETS
AS Amare Stoudemire 25.00 60.00
BD Baron Davis 12.50 30.00
CA Carmelo Anthony 25.00 60.00
FJ Fred Jones 12.50 30.00
JK Jason Kidd 25.00 60.00
JO Jermaine O'Neal 12.50 30.00
LO Lamar Odom 12.50 30.00
PS Peja Stojakovic 12.50 30.00
RH Richard Hamilton 15.00 40.00
SM Stephon Marbury 15.00 40.00
SO Shaquille O'Neal 40.00 100.00
TD Tim Duncan 75.00 150.00
TM Tracy McGrady 25.00 60.00
SMA Shawn Marion 12.50 30.00

2006-07 Bowman Sterling

Released in early April 2006, Bowman Sterling features an interesting base set consisting of extra-thick all-foil card stock and an array of memorabilia, autographs and combos of the two. Card numbers 1-30 feature retired and veteran player jersey cards consisting of a player photo and a jersey swatch towards the bottom of the front, card numbers 31-40 feature retired and veteran player jersey/memorabilia combo cards where the card is horizontally designed with a circular jersey swatch and a sticker autograph, card numbers 41-50 feature base rookies, card numbers 51-70 feature jersey rookies, card numbers 71-90 feature autograph rookies which place a sticker autograph below a player photo and card numbers 91-100 feature horizontally designed jersey/autograph combo rookies which showcase a circular swatch of memorabilia along with a sticker autograph. Bowman Sterling carried an initial suggested retail price of $50 per pack and each pack contains two base rookies, one retired/veteran relic, one autograph rookie and one rookie relic.

UNPRICED RED REF.PRINT RUN ONE SET
1 Ben Wallace JSY 2.50 6.00
2 Jason Richardson JSY 3.00 8.00
3 Steve Nash JSY 2.00 5.00
4 Pau Gasol JSY 3.00 8.00
5 Carmelo Anthony JSY 4.00 10.00
6 Kevin Garnett JSY 5.00 12.00
7 Tim Duncan JSY 5.00 12.00
8 Chauncey Billups JSY 3.00 8.00
9 Chris Paul JSY 4.00 10.00
10 Kobe Bryant JSY 10.00 25.00

11 Tony Parker JSY 3.00 8.00
12 Shaquille O'Neal JSY 6.00 15.00
13 Allen Iverson JSY 4.00 10.00
14 Dirk Nowitzki JSY 5.00 12.00
15 Paul Pierce JSY 3.00 8.00
16 Tracy McGrady JSY 4.00 10.00
17 Channing Frye JSY 3.00 8.00
18 Amare Stoudemire JSY 2.50 6.00
19 Dwight Howard JSY 2.50 6.00
20 Dwyane Wade JSY 5.00 12.00
21 Yao Ming JSY 2.00 5.00
22 Andrei Kirilenko JSY 3.00 8.00
23 Gilbert Arenas JSY 2.50 6.00
24 Shawn Marion JSY 2.50 6.00
25 Bob Lanier JSY 2.50 6.00
26 Pete Maravich JSY 15.00 40.00
27 Bill Walton JSY 3.00 8.00
28 Dennis Rodman JSY 6.00 15.00
29 Magic Johnson JSY 8.00 20.00
30 John Stockton JSY 3.00 8.00
31 Larry Bird JSY AU 30.00 80.00
32 Rick Barry JSY AU 8.00 20.00
33 Isiah Thomas JSY AU 10.00 25.00
34 Dominique Wilkins JSY AU 10.00 25.00
35 Ben Gordon JSY AU 8.00 20.00
36 Raymond Felton JSY AU 4.00 10.00
37 T.J. Ford JSY AU 4.00 10.00
38 Josh Howard JSY AU 5.00 12.00
39 Dwyane Wade JSY AU 30.00 60.00
40 Andre Iguodala JSY AU 4.00 10.00
41 Tarence Kinsey RC 1.25 3.00
42 Mickael Gelabale RC 1.25 3.00
43 Kelenna Azubuike RC 2.50 6.00
44 Pops Mensah-Bonsu RC 1.25 3.00
45 Walter Herrmann RC 1.25 3.00
46 Tyrus Thomas RC 1.50 4.00
47 Lynn Greer RC 1.25 3.00
48 Leon Powe RC 1.50 4.00
49 Yakhouba Diawara RC 1.25 3.00
50 Jose Barea RC 6.00 15.00
51 Saer Sene JSY RC 1.50 4.00
52 Steve Novak JSY RC 2.00 5.00
53 Josh Boone JSY RC 1.50 4.00
54 James White JSY RC 1.50 4.00
55 Rudy Gay JSY RC 3.00 8.00
56 David Noel JSY RC 1.50 4.00
57 Allan Ray JSY RC 1.50 4.00
58 Paul Davis JSY RC 1.50 4.00
59 Shawne Williams JSY RC 1.50 4.00
60 LaMarcus Aldridge JSY RC 6.00 15.00
61 Mardy Collins JSY RC 1.50 4.00
62 Solomon Jones JSY RC 1.50 4.00
63 Craig Smith JSY RC 2.00 5.00
64 Rajon Rondo JSY RC 4.00 10.00
65 Jorge Garbajosa JSY RC 2.00 5.00
66 Patrick O'Bryant JSY RC 1.50 4.00
67 Dee Brown JSY RC 1.50 4.00
68 Brandon Roy JSY RC 2.50 6.00
69 Bobby Jones JSY RC 1.50 4.00
70 Kyle Lowry JSY RC 3.00 8.00
71 Paul Millsap AU RC 4.00 10.00
72 Vassilis Spanoulis AU RC 2.50 6.00
73 Daniel Gibson AU RC 3.00 8.00
74 Marcus Vinicius AU RC 2.50 6.00
75 Ronnie Brewer AU RC 4.00 10.00
76 Damir Markota AU RC 2.50 6.00
77 Hilton Armstrong AU RC 2.50 6.00
78 Shannon Brown AU RC 2.50 6.00
79 Mile Ilic AU RC 2.50 6.00
80 Alexander Johnson AU RC 2.50 6.00
81 Will Blalock AU RC 2.50 6.00
82 P.J. Tucker AU RC 3.00 8.00
83 Sergio Rodriguez AU RC 4.00 10.00
84 Jordan Farmar AU RC 4.00 10.00
85 Renaldo Balkman AU RC 3.00 8.00
86 Quincy Douby AU RC 2.50 6.00
87 Hassan Adams AU RC 2.50 6.00
88 Chris Quinn AU RC 2.50 6.00
89 James Augustine AU RC 2.50 6.00
90 Ryan Hollins AU RC 3.00 8.00
91 J.J. Redick JSY AU RC 6.00 15.00
92 Adam Morrison JSY AU RC 5.00 12.00
93 Maurice Ager JSY AU RC 3.00 8.00
94 Shelden Williams JSY AU RC 4.00 10.00
95 Marcus Williams JSY AU RC 3.00 8.00
96 Andrea Bargnani JSY AU RC 5.00 12.00
97 Thabo Sefolosha JSY AU RC 5.00 12.00
98 Randy Foye JSY AU RC 5.00 12.00
99 Cedric Simmons JSY AU RC 3.00 8.00
100 Rodney Carney JSY AU RC 3.00 8.00

2006-07 Bowman Sterling Refractors

*1-30 REF: .5X TO 1.25X BASE HI
*31-40 AU REF SAME VALUE AS BASE
*41-100 RC REF: .5X TO 1.25X BASE HI
PRINT RUN 199 SER.#'d SETS
50 Jose Barea 12.50 30.00

2006-07 Bowman Sterling Refractors Black

*1-30 JSY REF.BLK: .75X TO 2X BASE HI
*31-40 JSY AU REF.BLK: .5X TO 1.25X HI
*42-100 RC REF.BLK: .75X TO 2X HI
PRINT RUN 25 SER.#'d SETS
26 Pete Maravich JSY 40.00 100.00
50 Jose Barea 60.00 150.00

2006-07 Bowman Sterling Refractors Gold

*31-40 REF.GOLD: .5X TO 1.25X BASE HI
91-40 PRINT RUN 25 SER.#'d SETS
*71-90 REF.GOLD: .6X TO 1.5X BASE HI
71-90 PRINT RUN 219 TO 599 SETS
*91-100 REF.GOLD: .6X TO 1.5X BASE HI
91-100 PRINT RUN 25 SER.#'d SETS

2007-08 Bowman Sterling

Released in April 2008, Bowman Sterling features a 125-card set which mixes base cards, Jersey cards, Autograph cards, Autograph Jersey cards and Rookie cards--most cards are sequentially numbered and print runs are listed in the checklist. The card stock features an all-foil finish along with sticker autographs and circular jersey swatches. Sterling is packaged in six-pack boxes of five cards each, each pack contians two base cards, two relic cards and one autograph card, and carried an initial suggested retail price of $50 per pack.
UNPRICED SUPERFR.PRINT RUN ONE SET
UNPRICED X-FR BLACK PRINT RUN 10 SETS
UNPRICED X-FR GOLD PRNT RUN 10 SETS
UNPRICED X-FR RED PRINT RUN 10 SETS
AA Arron Afflalo JSY AU/218 RC 5.00 12.00
AB Andrea Bargnani JSY/385 2.50 6.00
ABR Aaron Brooks JSY AU/218 5.00 12.00
ABY Andrew Bynum JSY/385 2.50 6.00
AG Aaron Gray AU/412 RC 4.00 10.00
AH1 Al Horford RC 2.00 5.00
AH2 Al Horford JSY/975 4.00 10.00
AHA Al Harrington JSY/385 2.50 6.00
AHK Adam Haluska JSY AU/218 RC 5.00 12.00
AI Allen Iverson JSY/385 4.00 10.00
AIG Andre Iguodala JSY AU/190 6.00 15.00
AJ Al Jefferson JSY/385 2.50 6.00
AJA Antawn Jamison JSY/385 2.50 6.00
AL1 Acie Law JSY AU/113 5.00 12.00
AL2 Acie Law AU/412 RC 5.00 12.00
AS Amare Stoudemire JSY/385 4.00 10.00
AT1 Alando Tucker JSY AU/218 3.00 8.00
AT2 Alando Tucker AU/829 RC 2.50 6.00
ATH2 Al Thornton AU/412 RC 3.00 8.00
BD Baron Davis JSY AU/275 6.00 15.00
BG Ben Gordon JSY/385 2.50 6.00
BK Bernard King JSY/385 3.00 8.00
BL Bill Laimbeer JSY/385 3.00 8.00
BR Brandon Roy JSY/385 3.00 8.00
BRU Bill Russell JSY AU/15 100.00 200.00
BWR1 B. Wright JSY AU/21 12.00 30.00
BWR2 Brandan Wright JSY/975 RC 2.50 6.00
CA C. Anthony JSY AU/15 25.00 50.00
CB1 Corey Brewer RC 1.50 4.00
CB2 Corey Brewer JSY/975 3.00 8.00
CBO Chris Bosh JSY AU/89 10.00 25.00
CBZ Carlos Boozer JSY AU/340 6.00 15.00
CD Clyde Drexler JSY/385 4.00 10.00
CK Coby Karl AU/829 RC 2.50 6.00
CL Carl Landry JSY AU/218 RC 3.00 8.00
CM Corey Maggette JSY/385 2.50 6.00
CP Chris Paul JSY/385 4.00 10.00
CR Chris Richard RC 1.00 2.50
CR2 Chris Richard JSY/975 2.50 6.00
DC Daequan Cook JSY AU/113 RC 5.00 12.00
DH Dwight Howard JSY AU/89 20.00 40.00
DJS1 D.J. Strawberry JSY AU/218 3.00 8.00
DJS2 D.J. Strawberry AU/829 RC 2.50 6.00
DM D.McGuire JSY AU/113 RC 5.00 12.00
DN Dirk Nowitzki JSY/385 3.00 8.00
DNI D.Nichols JSY AU/218 RC 5.00 12.00
DR David Robinson JSY AU/15 50.00 120.00
DRO D. Rodman JSY AU/89 20.00 50.00
DW Dwyane Wade JSY AU/15 30.00 80.00
DWI D.Wilkins JSY AU/275 10.00 25.00
EM Earl Monroe JSY/385 3.00 8.00
GA1 Gilbert Arenas JSY/385 2.50 6.00
GD1 Glen Davis JSY AU/218 4.00 10.00
GD2 Glen Davis AU/829 RC 3.00 8.00
GG George Gervin JSY/385 4.00 10.00
GO1 Greg Oden JSY AU/21 5.00 12.00
GO2 Greg Oden JSY/975 RC 4.00 10.00
GP1 Gabe Pruitt JSY AU/218 5.00 12.00
GP2 Gabe Pruitt AU/829 RC 5.00 12.00
HH1 Herbert Hill JSY AU/218 3.00 8.00
HH2 Herbert Hill AU/829 RC 1.00 2.50
IT Isiah Thomas JSY AU/89 15.00 30.00
JC1 J.Crittenton JSY/218 AU 5.00 12.00
JC2 Javaris Crittenton AU/412 RC 5.00 12.00
JCN Juan Navarro AU/129 RC 5.00 12.00
JD Jared Dudley JSY AU/218 RC 5.00 12.00
JDA J.Davidson JSY AU/218 RC 5.00 12.00
JG1 Jeff Green RC 1.50 4.00
JG2 Jeff Green JSY/975 4.00 10.00
JJ Joe Johnson JSY/385 2.50 6.00
JK Jason Kidd JSY/385 2.50 6.00
JMC J.McRoberts JSY AU/218 RC 5.00 12.00
JN1 Joakim Noah RC 1.50 4.00
JN2 Joakim Noah JSY/975 5.00 12.00
JO Jermaine O'Neal JSY/385 2.50 6.00
JOC J.Curry AU/412 RC 5.00 12.00
JR Jason Richardson JSY/385 2.50 6.00
JS Jason Smith JSY AU/113 RC 5.00 12.00
JW1 Julian Wright RC 1.00 2.50
JW2 Julian Wright JSY/975 2.50 6.00
KB Kobe Bryant JSY/385 8.00 20.00
KD Kevin Durant RC 15.00 40.00
KG Kevin Garnett JSY/385 5.00 12.00
KMA Karl Malone JSY/385 5.00 12.00
LB Larry Bird JSY AU/15 60.00 120.00
LD Luol Deng JSY/385 2.50 6.00
LS Luis Scola RC 2.00 5.00
MA Morris Almond JSY AU/113 RC 5.00 12.00
MB Mike Bibby JSY/385 2.50 6.00
MBE Marco Belinelli AU/129 RC 5.00 12.00
MC1 Mike Conley Jr. RC 2.00 5.00
MC2 Mike Conley Jr. JSY/975 4.00 10.00
MCO Michael Cooper JSY/385 3.00 8.00
MG Manu Ginobili JSY/385 3.00 8.00
MG Marcin Gortat AU/829 RC 6.00 15.00
MJ Magic Johnson JSY AU/15 75.00 150.00
MM Mike Miller JSY/385 2.50 6.00
MR Michael Redd JSY/385 2.50 6.00
NF Nick Fazekas JSY AU/218 RC 5.00 12.00
NTA Nate Archibald JSY/385 3.00 8.00
NY2 Nick Young JSY RC 4.00 10.00
PG Pau Gasol JSY/385 2.50 6.00
PP Paul Pierce JSY AU/190 15.00 30.00
RA Ray Allen JSY AU/190 15.00 40.00
RB Rick Barry JSY AU/340 8.00 20.00
RH Richard Hamilton JSY/385 2.50 6.00
RS Ramon Sessions RC 1.50 4.00
RS R.Stuckey JSY AU/218 RC 4.00 10.00
SH Spencer Hawes JSY AU/113 RC 4.00 10.00
SM Stephon Marbury JSY/385 2.50 6.00
SMA Shawn Marion JSY/385 2.50 6.00
SN Steve Nash JSY/385 4.00 10.00
SO Shaquille O'Neal JSY AU/15 60.00 150.00
SW Sean Williams JSY AU/218 RC 5.00 12.00
TD Tim Duncan JSY/385 4.00 10.00
TG T.Green JSY AU/218 RC 3.00 8.00
TM Tracy McGrady JSY/385 2.50 6.00
TY T.Young JSY AU/21 RC 20.00 50.00
VC Vince Carter JSY AU/89 12.00 30.00
WC W.Chandler JSY AU/218 RC 6.00 15.00
YJ Yi Jianlian AU/129 RC 10.00 25.00
YM Yao Ming JSY/385 3.00 8.00

2007-08 Bowman Sterling Refractors

*RC REFRACTORS: .6X TO 1.5X BASE
*AU REFRACTOR: .5X TO 1.25X BASE
AUTO PRINT RUN 99 SER.#'d SETS
*JSY REFRACTOR: .5X TO 1.25X BASE
JSY.REF.PRINT RUN 199 SER.#'d SETS
JSY AU REF.PRINT RUN 10 SETS
JSY AU REF.UNPRICED DUE TO SCARCITY
JW1 Julian Wright 1.50 4.00
KD Kevin Durant/399 100.00 250.00
NY1 Nick Young JSY AU/19 15.00 40.00
RS Ramon Sessions 2.50 6.00
TY T.Young JSY AU/19 20.00 50.00

2007-08 Bowman Sterling Refractors Black

*RC REF.: .75X TO 2X BASE
*AU REF.: .6X TO 1.5X BASE
AUTO PRINT RUN 25 SER.#'d SETS
*JSY REF.: .6X TO 1.5X BASE
JSY.REF.PRINT RUN 199 SER.#'d SETS
JSY AU REF.PRINT RUN 5 SETS
JSY AU REF.UNPRICED DUE TO SCARCITY
KD Kevin Durant 100.00 250.00

2007-08 Bowman Sterling Refractors Gold

*RC REF.: 1.25X TO 3X BASE
UNPRICED AU.REF.PRINT RUN 10 SETS
*JSY REF.: 1X TO 2.5X BASE
JSY.REF.PRINT RUN 25 SETS
JSY AU REF.PRINT RUN ONE SET
JSY AU REF.UNPRICED DUE TO SCARCITY
KD Kevin Durant 200.00 500.00

2007-08 Bowman Sterling Refractors Red

*RC REF.: 1.25X TO 3X BASE
REF.AU/JSY PRINT RUN ONE SET
REF.AU/JSY UNPRICED DUE TO SCARCITY
KD Kevin Durant 200.00 500.00

2007-08 Bowman Sterling X-Fractors

*RC X-FRAC: 1.5X TO 4X BASE
PRINT RUN 25 SER.#'d SETS
KD Kevin Durant 200.00 400.00

2007-08 Bowman Sterling Box Loaders

*REFRACTORS: .75X TO 2X BASE
REF.PRINT RUN 50 SER.#'d SETS
*REF.BLACK: 1.5X TO 4X BASE
REF.BLACK PRINT RUN 25 SER.#'d SETS
*REF.GOLD: 2X TO 5X BASE
REF.GOLD PRINT RUN 15 SER.#'d SETS
UNPRICED REF.RED PRINT RUN ONE SET
BL1 Acie Law/199 1.00 2.50
BL2 Yi Jianlian/199 2.00 5.00
BL3 Brandan Wright/99 1.50 4.00
BL4 Corey Brewer/99 1.50 4.00
BL5 Greg Oden/199 1.50 4.00
BL6 Javaris Crittenton/99 1.00 2.50
BL7 Nick Young/199 2.00 5.00
BL8 Julian Wright/99 1.00 2.50
BL9 Thaddeus Young/199 1.50 4.00
BL10 Kevin Durant/199 30.00 80.00
BL11 Al Horford/199 2.00 5.00
BL12 Mike Conley Jr./199 2.00 5.00
BL13 Joakim Noah/99 1.50 4.00
BL14 Jeff Green/199 1.50 4.00

2007-08 Bowman Sterling Relics Autographs Dual

REFRACTOR PRINT RUN FIVE SETS
REF.BLACK PRINT RUN FIVE SETS
REF.GOLD PRINT RUN ONE SET
REF.RED PRINT RUN FIVE SETS
REFRACTORS UNPRICED DUE TO SCARCITY
SOME UNPRICED DUE TO SCARCITY
BC C.Bosh/V.Carter/25 30.00 80.00
BJ Billups/Johnson/85 12.50 30.00
BW C.Boozer/D.Williams/85 20.00 50.00
CJ V.Carter/A.Jamison/85 15.00 40.00
HB J.Havlicek/E.Baylor/15 50.00 100.00
HM D.Howard/M.Malone/85 30.00 60.00
IW A.Iguodala/L.Walton/85 12.50 30.00
JO Y.Jianlian/G.Oden 30.00 80.00
LM D.Lee/M.Miller/85 12.50 30.00
PA P.Pierce/R.Allen/25 40.00 80.00
RR D.Robinson/D.Rodman/15 100.00 200.00
WB J.West/E.Baylor/15 100.00 200.00
WW S.Webb/D.Wilkins/85 25.00 60.00

1996-97 Bowman's Best

The premier edition of 1996-97 Bowman's Best set was issued in one series totalling 125 cards. The basic set consists of 80 veterans on a gold foil card background, 25 rookies on a silver foil card background and 20 throwback cards on a black and white card background. Each six-card pack had a suggested retail price of $3.99.
COMPLETE SET (125) 12.00 30.00
1 Scottie Pippen .60 1.50
2 Glen Rice .40 1.00
3 Bryant Stith .25 .60
4 Dino Radja .25 .60
5 Horace Grant .30 .75
6 Mahmoud Abdul-Rauf .25 .60
7 Mookie Blaylock .25 .60
8 Clifford Robinson .25 .60
9 Vin Baker .30 .75
10 Grant Hill .60 1.50
11 Terrell Brandon .25 .60
12 P.J. Brown .25 .60
13 Kendall Gill .25 .60
14 Brent Barry .30 .75
15 Hakeem Olajuwon .50 1.25
16 Allan Houston .30 .75
17 Elden Campbell .25 .60
18 Latrell Sprewell .40 1.00
19 Jerry Stackhouse .50 1.25
20 Robert Horry .30 .75
21 Mitch Richmond .40 1.00
22 Gary Payton .40 1.00
23 Rik Smits .30 .75
24 Jim Jackson .25 .60
25 Damon Stoudamire .30 .75
26 Bobby Phills .25 .60
27 Chris Webber .50 1.25
28 Shawn Bradley .25 .60
29 Arvydas Sabonis .30 .75
30 John Stockton .50 1.25
31 Anfernee Hardaway .60 1.50
32 Christian Laettner .30 .75
33 Juwan Howard .30 .75
34 Anthony Mason .25 .60
35 Tom Gugliotta .25 .60
36 Avery Johnson .30 .75
37 Cedric Ceballos .25 .60
38 Patrick Ewing .50 1.25
39 Joe Smith .30 .75
40 Dennis Rodman .75 2.00
41 Alonzo Mourning .50 1.25
42 Kevin Garnett 1.00 2.50
43 Antonio McDyess .40 1.00
44 Detlef Schrempf .40 1.00
45 Reggie Miller .50 1.25
46 Charles Barkley .60 1.50
47 Derrick Coleman .30 .75
48 Brian Grant .30 .75
49 Kenny Anderson .30 .75
50 Otis Thorpe .25 .60
51 Rod Strickland .25 .60
52 Eric Williams .25 .60
53 Rony Seikaly .25 .60
54 Danny Manning .30 .75
55 Karl Malone .50 1.25
56 B.J. Armstrong .25 .60
57 Greg Anthony .25 .60
58 Larry Johnson .40 1.00
59 Loy Vaught .25 .60
60 Sean Elliott .40 1.00
61 Dikembe Mutombo .40 1.00
62 Clarence Weatherspoon .25 .60
63 Jamal Mashburn .30 .75
64 Bryant Reeves .25 .60
65 Vlade Divac .40 1.00
66 Shawn Kemp .40 1.00
67 LaPhonso Ellis .25 .60
68 Tyrone Hill .25 .60
69 David Robinson .60 1.50
70 Shaquille O'Neal 1.00 2.50
71 Doug Christie .25 .60
72 Jayson Williams .25 .60
73 Michael Finley .50 1.25
74 Tim Hardaway .40 1.00
75 Clyde Drexler .50 1.25
76 Joe Dumars .40 1.00
77 Glenn Robinson .30 .75
78 Dana Barros .25 .60
79 Jason Kidd .60 1.50
80 Michael Jordan 3.00 8.00
R1 Allen Iverson RC 3.00 8.00
R2 Stephon Marbury RC 1.50 4.00
R3 Shareef Abdur-Rahim RC 1.00 2.50
R4 Marcus Camby RC 1.00 2.50
R5 Ray Allen RC 2.50 6.00
R6 Antoine Walker RC 1.00 2.50
R7 Lorenzen Wright RC .50 1.25
R8 Kerry Kittles RC .60 1.50
R9 Samaki Walker RC .50 1.25
R10 Tony Delk RC .60 1.50
R11 Vitaly Potapenko RC .50 1.25
R12 Jerome Williams RC .50 1.25
R13 Todd Fuller RC .40 1.00
R14 Erick Dampier RC .60 1.50
R15 Derek Fisher RC .75 2.00
R16 Donald Whiteside RC .60 1.50
R17 John Wallace RC .60 1.50
R18 Steve Nash RC 3.00 8.00
R19 Brian Evans RC .60 1.50
R20 Jermaine O'Neal RC 1.00 2.50
R21 Roy Rogers RC .50 1.25
R22 Priest Lauderdale RC .40 1.00
R23 Kobe Bryant RC 8.00 20.00
R24 Martin Muursepp RC .40 1.00
R25 Zydrunas Ilgauskas RC 1.00 2.50
TB1 Avery Johnson RET .15 .40
TB2 Chris Webber RET .25 .60
TB3 Sean Elliott RET .20 .50
TB4 Joe Dumars RET .20 .50
TB5 Grant Hill RET .30 .75
TB6 Gary Payton RET .20 .50
TB7 Shawn Kemp RET .20 .50
TB8 Shaquille O'Neal RET .50 1.25
TB9 Eddie Jones RET .20 .50
TB10 John Wallace RET .30 .75
TB11 Patrick Ewing RET .25 .60
TB12 Jerry Stackhouse RET .25 .60
TB13 Allen Iverson RET 1.50 4.00
TB14 Latrell Sprewell RET .20 .50
TB15 Dino Radja RET .12 .30
TB16 David Wesley RET .12 .30
TB17 Joe Smith RET .15 .40
TB18 Damon Stoudamire RET .15 .40
TB19 Marcus Camby RET .50 1.25
TB20 Juwan Howard RET .15 .40

1996-97 Bowman's Best Refractors

*STARS: 4X TO 10X BASE CARD HI
*RCs/RET RCs: 2X TO 5X BASE HI
*RETRO STARS: 8X TO 20X BASE HI
STATED ODDS 1:12 HOBBY, 1:20 RETAIL
79 Jason Kidd 8.00 20.00
80 Michael Jordan 60.00 150.00

1996-97 Bowman's Best Atomic Refractors

*STARS: 8X TO 20X HI COLUMN
*RCs/RET RCs: 4X TO 10X HI
*RETRO STARS: 15X TO 40X HI
STATED ODDS 1:24 HOBBY, 1:40 RETAIL
79 Jason Kidd 12.00 30.00
80 Michael Jordan 150.00 400.00
R23 Kobe Bryant 250.00 500.00

1996-97 Bowman's Best Cuts

Randomly inserted in packs at a rate of one in 24, this 20-card set features the best in the NBA against a die-cut chromium background. Each card front also contains a facsimile autograph of the player. Card backs are numbered with a "BC" prefix.
COMPLETE SET (20) 40.00 100.00
STATED ODDS 1:24 HOBBY, 1:40 RETAIL
*ATOMIC REFRACTORS: 2X TO 5X HI
ATO: STATED ODDS 1:192 HOB, 1:320 RET
*REFRACTORS: 1.5X TO 4X HI COLUMN
REF: STATED ODDS 1:96 HOB, 1:160 RET
BC1 Karl Malone 2.00 5.00
BC2 Michael Jordan 10.00 25.00
BC3 Juwan Howard 1.25 3.00
BC4 Charles Barkley 2.50 6.00
BC5 Jerry Stackhouse 2.00 5.00
BC6 Anfernee Hardaway 2.50 6.00
BC7 Shaquille O'Neal 4.00 10.00
BC8 Alonzo Mourning 2.00 5.00
BC9 Shawn Kemp 1.50 4.00
BC10 Scottie Pippen 2.50 6.00
BC11 David Robinson 2.50 6.00
BC12 Kevin Garnett 4.00 10.00
BC13 Patrick Ewing 2.00 5.00
BC14 Hakeem Olajuwon 2.00 5.00
BC15 Damon Stoudamire 1.25 3.00
BC16 Grant Hill 2.50 6.00
BC17 Dennis Rodman 3.00 8.00
BC18 Chris Webber 2.00 5.00
BC19 Gary Payton 1.50 4.00
BC20 John Stockton 2.00 5.00

1996-97 Bowman's Best Honor Roll

Randomly inserted in packs at a rate of one in 48, this 10-card set showcases some of the top draft pick combos all the way back to 1984. Card backs are numbered with a "HR" prefix.
COMPLETE SET (10) 30.00 80.00
STATED ODDS 1:48 HOBBY, 1:80 RETAIL
*REFRACTORS: 1.25X TO 3X HI COLUMN
REF: STATED ODDS 1:192 HOB, 1:320 RET
HR1 C.Barkley/J.Stockton 4.00 10.00
HR2 M.Jordan/H.Olajuwon 12.00 30.00
HR3 P.Ewing/K.Malone 3.00 8.00
HR4 D.Rodman/A.Sabonis 2.50 6.00
HR5 S.Pippen/D.Robinson 5.00 12.00
HR6 G.Rice/S.Kemp 2.00 5.00
HR7 S.O'Neal/A.Mourning 6.00 15.00
HR8 A.Hardaway/C.Webber 3.00 8.00
HR9 G.Hill/J.Howard 3.00 8.00
HR10 K.Garnett/J.Stackhouse 2.50 6.00

1996-97 Bowman's Best Honor Roll Atomic Refractors

*STARS: 2.5X TO 6X VALUE
STATED ODDS 1:384
HR2 M.Jordan/H.Olajuwon 125.00 250.00

1996-97 Bowman's Best Picks

Randomly inserted in packs at a rate of one in 24, this 10-card set features some of the best players from the class of 1996. Card fronts also contain a facsimile autograph of each player. Card backs are numbered with a "BP" prefix.
COMPLETE SET (10) 20.00 50.00
STATED ODDS 1:24 HOBBY, 1:40 RETAIL
*REFRACTORS: .6X TO 1.5X HI COLUMN
REF: STATED ODDS 1:96 HOB, 1:160 RET
BP1 Stephon Marbury 2.50 6.00
BP2 Marcus Camby 1.50 4.00
BP3 Lorenzen Wright .75 2.00
BP4 John Wallace 1.00 2.50
BP5 Ray Allen 4.00 10.00
BP6 Kerry Kittles 1.00 2.50
BP7 Shareef Abdur-Rahim 1.50 4.00
BP8 Todd Fuller .60 1.50
BP9 Allen Iverson 5.00 12.00
BP10 Kobe Bryant 12.00 30.00

1996-97 Bowman's Best Picks Atomic Refractors

*ATOMIC: 1.2X TO 3X VALUE
STATED ODDS 1:96
BP10 Kobe Bryant 200.00 400.00

1996-97 Bowman's Best Shots

Randomly inserted in packs at a rate of one in 12, this 10-card set features some of the top NBA superstars on crystal clear chromium cards. Card backs are numbered with a "BS" prefix.
COMPLETE SET (10) 12.00 30.00
STATED ODDS 1:12 HOBBY, 1:20 RETAIL
*ATOMIC REFRACTORS: 2X TO 5X HI
ATO: STATED ODDS 1:96 HOB, 1:160 RET
*REFRACTORS: 1.2X TO 3X HI COLUMN
REF: STATED ODDS 1:48 HOB, 1:80 RET
BS1 Scottie Pippen 1.25 3.00
BS2 Gary Payton .75 2.00
BS3 Shaquille O'Neal 2.00 5.00
BS4 Hakeem Olajuwon 1.00 2.50
BS5 Kevin Garnett 2.00 5.00
BS6 Michael Jordan 8.00 20.00
BS7 Anfernee Hardaway 1.25 3.00
BS8 Grant Hill 1.25 3.00
BS9 Shawn Kemp .75 2.00
BS10 Dennis Rodman 1.50 4.00

1997-98 Bowman's Best

The 1997-98 Bowman's Best set was issued in one series totalling 125 cards. The basic set consists of 90 veterans, a 10 card Best Performances subset and 25 rookie cards. Each six-card pack had a suggested retail price of $3.99.
COMPLETE SET (125) 15.00 40.00
BP SUBSET CARDS HALF VALUE
1 Scottie Pippen .50 1.25
2 Michael Finley .30 .75
3 David Wesley .20 .50
4 Brent Barry .25 .60
5 Gary Payton .30 .75
6 Christian Laettner .25 .60
7 Grant Hill .50 1.25
8 Glenn Robinson .25 .60
9 Reggie Miller .40 1.00
10 Tyus Edney .20 .50
11 Jim Jackson .20 .50
12 John Stockton .40 1.00
13 Karl Malone .40 1.00
14 Samaki Walker .20 .50
15 Bryant Stith .20 .50
16 Clyde Drexler .40 1.00
17 Danny Ferry .20 .50
18 Shawn Bradley .20 .50
19 Bryant Reeves .20 .50
20 John Starks .25 .60
21 Joe Dumars .30 .75
22 Checklist .20 .50
23 Antonio McDyess .25 .60
24 Jeff Hornacek .25 .60
25 Terrell Brandon .20 .50
26 Kendall Gill .20 .50
27 LaPhonso Ellis .20 .50
28 Shaquille O'Neal .75 2.00
29 Mahmoud Abdul-Rauf .20 .50
30 Eric Williams .20 .50
31 Lorenzen Wright .20 .50
32 Shareef Abdur-Rahim .30 .75
33 Avery Johnson .25 .60
34 Juwan Howard .25 .60
35 Vin Baker .25 .60
36 Dikembe Mutombo .30 .75
37 Patrick Ewing .40 1.00
38 Allen Iverson .60 1.50
39 Alonzo Mourning .40 1.00
40 Travis Knight .20 .50
41 Ray Allen .40 1.00
42 Detlef Schrempf .30 .75
43 Kevin Johnson .30 .75
44 David Robinson .50 1.25
45 Tim Hardaway .30 .75
46 Shawn Kemp .30 .75
47 Marcus Camby .30 .75
48 Rony Seikaly .20 .50
49 Eddie Jones .30 .75
50 Rik Smits .25 .60
51 Jayson Williams .20 .50
52 Malik Sealy .20 .50
53 Chris Mullin .30 .75
54 Larry Johnson .30 .75
55 Isaiah Rider .25 .60
56 Dennis Rodman .60 1.50
57 Bob Sura .20 .50
58 Hakeem Olajuwon .40 1.00
59 Steve Smith .25 .60
60 Michael Jordan 2.50 6.00
61 Jerry Stackhouse .30 .75
62 Joe Smith .25 .60
63 Walt Williams .20 .50
64 Anthony Peeler .20 .50
65 Charles Barkley .50 1.25
66 Erick Dampier .20 .50
67 Horace Grant .25 .60
68 Anthony Mason .20 .50
69 Anfernee Hardaway .50 1.25
70 Elden Campbell .20 .50
71 Cedric Ceballos .20 .50
72 Allan Houston .25 .60
73 Kerry Kittles .20 .50
74 Antoine Walker .30 .75
75 Sean Elliott .30 .75
76 Jamal Mashburn .25 .60
77 Mitch Richmond .30 .75
78 Damon Stoudamire .25 .60
79 Tom Gugliotta .20 .50
80 Jason Kidd .50 1.25
81 Chris Webber .30 .75
82 Glen Rice .30 .75
83 Loy Vaught .20 .50
84 Olden Polynice .20 .50
85 Kenny Anderson .25 .60
86 Stephon Marbury .40 1.00
87 Calbert Cheaney .20 .50
88 Kobe Bryant 1.50 4.00
89 Arvydas Sabonis .25 .60
90 Kevin Garnett .50 1.25
91 Grant Hill BP .25 .60
92 Clyde Drexler BP .20 .50
93 Patrick Ewing BP .20 .50
94 Shawn Kemp BP .15 .40
95 Shaquille O'Neal BP .40 1.00
96 M.Jordan BP UER 1.25 3.00
97 Karl Malone BP .20 .50
98 Allen Iverson BP .30 .75
99 Shareef Abdur-Rahim BP .15 .40
100 Dikembe Mutombo BP .15 .40
101 Bobby Jackson RC .40 1.00
102 Tony Battie RC .30 .75
103 Keith Booth RC .25 .60
104 Keith Van Horn RC .50 1.25
105 Paul Grant RC .20 .50
106 Tim Duncan RC 1.50 4.00
107 Scot Pollard RC .30 .75
108 Maurice Taylor RC .30 .75
109 Antonio Daniels RC .30 .75
110 Austin Croshere RC .25 .60
111 Tracy McGrady RC 1.25 3.00
112 Charles O'Bannon RC .30 .75
113 Rodrick Rhodes RC .25 .60
114 Johnny Taylor RC .25 .60
115 Danny Fortson RC .30 .75
116 Chauncey Billups RC 1.00 2.50
117 Tim Thomas RC .40 1.00
118 Derek Anderson RC .30 .75
119 Ed Gray RC .30 .75
120 Jacque Vaughn RC .25 .60
121 Kelvin Cato RC .25 .60
122 Tariq Abdul-Wahad RC .25 .60
123 Ron Mercer RC .40 1.00
124 Brevin Knight RC .30 .75
125 Adonal Foyle RC .25 .60

1997-98 Bowman's Best Refractors

*STARS: 4X TO 10X BASE CARD HI
*SUBSET: 6X TO 15X BASE HI
*RCs: 1.5X TO 4X BASE HI
STATED ODDS 1:12 HOB, 1:20 RET
60 Michael Jordan 30.00 80.00
96 Michael Jordan BP UER 25.00 60.00
Stoudamire date on back should be '96
106 Tim Duncan 50.00 120.00

1997-98 Bowman's Best Atomic Refractors

*STARS: 6X TO 15X BASE CARD HI
*SUBSET: 10X TO 25X BASE HI
*RCs: 3X TO 8X BASE HI
STATED ODDS 1:24 HOB, 1:40 RET
1 Scottie Pippen 10.00 25.00
60 Michael Jordan 100.00 250.00
88 Kobe Bryant 30.00 80.00
96 Michael Jordan BP UER 50.00 120.00
Stoudamire date on back should be '96
106 Tim Duncan 100.00 250.00

1997-98 Bowman's Best Autographs

Randomly inserted into packs at a rate of one in 373, this 11-card set features autographs on the regular player cards. The only exception is Karl Malone, who has a regular autograph and a special MVP card autograph. There is no special insertion rate for the MVP card.
STATED ODDS 1:373 HOB, 1:745 RET
*REFRACTORS: .75X TO 2X HI COLUMN
REF: STATED ODDS 1:1,987 H, 1:3,974 R
*ATOMIC REFRACTORS: 2.5X TO 6X HI
ATO: STATED ODDS 1:5,961 H, 1:11,922 R
8 Glenn Robinson 10.00 25.00
13 Karl Malone 75.00 150.00
36 Dikembe Mutombo 12.00 30.00
59 Steve Smith 6.00 15.00
77 Mitch Richmond 12.50 25.00
102 Tony Battie 6.00 15.00
104 Keith Van Horn 10.00 25.00
116 Chauncey Billups 8.00 20.00
123 Ron Mercer 8.00 20.00
125 Adonal Foyle 6.00 15.00
KM Karl Malone MVP 75.00 150.00

1997-98 Bowman's Best Cuts

Randomly inserted into packs at one in 24, this 10-card laser cut set features ten of the hottest players in the game today. Card backs feature a "BC" prefix.
COMPLETE SET (10) 20.00 50.00
STATED ODDS 1:24 HOB, 1:40 RET
*ATOMIC REFRACTORS: 1.25X TO 3X HI
ATO: STATED ODDS 1:96 HOB, 1:160 RET
*REFRACTORS: .6X TO 1.5X HI COLUMN
REF: STATED ODDS 1:48 HOB, 1:80 RET
BC1 Vin Baker 1.50 4.00
BC2 Patrick Ewing 2.50 6.00
BC3 Scottie Pippen 3.00 8.00
BC4 Karl Malone 2.50 6.00
BC5 Kevin Garnett 3.00 8.00
BC6 Anfernee Hardaway 3.00 8.00
BC7 Shawn Kemp 2.00 5.00
BC8 Charles Barkley 3.00 8.00
BC9 Stephon Marbury 2.50 6.00
BC10 Shaquille O'Neal 5.00 12.00

1997-98 Bowman's Best Mirror Image

Randomly inserted into packs at a rate of one in 48, this 10-card set features two veterans and two rookies together on double-sided cards. The cards look similar to "playing cards". Card backs carry a "MI" prefix.
COMPLETE SET (10) 30.00 80.00
STATED ODDS 1:48 HOB, 1:80 RET
*ATOMIC REFRACTORS: 1.25X TO 3X HI
ATO: STATED ODDS 1:192 HOB, 1:320 RET
*REFRACTORS: .6X TO 1.5X HI COLUMN
REF: STATED ODDS 1:96 HOB, 1:160 RET
MI1 MJ/Mercer/Marbry/Pay 6.00 15.00
MI2 Thom/Web/O'Neal/Foyle 2.00 5.00
MI3 THard/Ivrsn/BJack/Kidd 1.50 4.00
MI4 Pip/VnHorn/Kobe/Ceblls 4.00 10.00
MI5 Hill/McGrady/Rahim/KG 3.00 8.00
MI6 Kemp/Cmby/Dncn/Rob 4.00 10.00
MI7 Allen/Smith/Andrsn/Elliott 1.00 2.50
MI8 Billups/Brndn/Daniels/KJ 2.50 6.00
MI9 Kittles/Miller/Battie/Olaj 1.00 2.50
MI10 LJ/Walker/Taylor/Baker .75 2.00

1997-98 Bowman's Best Picks

Randomly inserted into packs at a rate of one in 24, this 10-card set features some of the top rookies from the 1997 class. Card backs carry a "BP" prefix.
COMPLETE SET (10) 8.00 20.00
STATED ODDS 1:24 HOB, 1:40 RET
*ATOMIC REFRACTORS: 1.5X TO 4X HI
ATO: STATED ODDS 1:96 HOB, 1:160 RET
*REFRACTORS: .75X TO 2X HI COLUMN
REF: STATED ODDS 1:48 HOB, 1:80 RET
BP1 Adonal Foyle .40 1.00
BP2 Maurice Taylor .50 1.25
BP3 Austin Croshere .40 1.00
BP4 Tracy McGrady 2.00 5.00
BP5 Antonio Daniels .50 1.25
BP6 Tony Battie .50 1.25
BP7 Chauncey Billups 1.50 4.00
BP8 Tim Duncan 4.00 10.00
BP9 Ron Mercer .60 1.50
BP10 Keith Van Horn .75 2.00

1997-98 Bowman's Best Techniques

Randomly inserted into packs at a rate of one in 12, this 10-card set focuses on some of the NBA's top players at their positions. Card backs carry a "T" prefix.
COMPLETE SET (10) 12.50 30.00
SEMISTARS .50 1.25
UNLISTED STARS .60 1.50
STATED ODDS 1:12 HOB, 1:20 RET
*ATOMIC REFRACTORS: 2.5X TO 6X HI
ATO: STATED ODDS 1:96 HOB, 1:160 RET
*REFRACTORS: 1.2X TO 3X HI COLUMN
REF: STATED ODDS 1:48 HOB, 1:80 RET
T1 Dikembe Mutombo .60 1.50
T2 Michael Jordan 5.00 12.00
T3 Grant Hill 1.00 2.50
T4 Kobe Bryant 3.00 8.00
T5 Gary Payton .60 1.50
T6 Glen Rice .60 1.50
T7 Dennis Rodman 1.25 3.00
T8 Hakeem Olajuwon .75 2.00
T9 Allen Iverson 1.25 3.00
T10 John Stockton .75 2.00

1998-99 Bowman's Best

Released as a 125-card set, this product was distributed in six card packs with a suggested retail price of $5.00. The set was broken up into 100 veterans and 25 rookies. The veterans were issued against gold backgrounds, while the rookies were issued against silver backgrounds. The rookies were also inserted one in four packs.
COMPLETE SET (125) 50.00 100.00
COMPLETE SET w/o SP (100) 10.00 20.00
ROOKIES STATED ODDS 1:4
1 Jason Kidd .50 1.25
2 Dikembe Mutombo .30 .75
3 Chris Mullin .30 .75
4 Terrell Brandon .20 .50
5 Cedric Ceballos .20 .50
6 Rod Strickland .20 .50
7 Darrell Armstrong .20 .50
8 Anfernee Hardaway .50 1.25
9 Eddie Jones .30 .75
10 Allen Iverson .60 1.50
11 Kenny Anderson .25 .60
12 Toni Kukoc .30 .75
13 Lawrence Funderburke .20 .50
14 P.J. Brown .20 .50
15 Jeff Hornacek .25 .60
16 Mookie Blaylock .20 .50
17 Avery Johnson .25 .60
18 Donyell Marshall .25 .60
19 Detlef Schrempf .25 .60
20 Joe Dumars .30 .75
21 Charles Barkley .50 1.25
22 Maurice Taylor .20 .50
23 Chauncey Billups .40 1.00
24 Lee Mayberry .20 .50
25 Glen Rice .30 .75
26 John Stockton .40 1.00
27 Rik Smits .25 .60
28 LaPhonso Ellis .20 .50
29 Kerry Kittles .20 .50
30 Damon Stoudamire .25 .60
31 Kevin Garnett .50 1.25
32 Chris Mills .20 .50
33 Kendall Gill .20 .50
34 Tim Thomas .30 .75
35 Derek Anderson .30 .75
36 Billy Owens .20 .50
37 Bobby Jackson .20 .50
38 Allan Houston .25 .60
39 Horace Grant .25 .60
40 Ray Allen .40 1.00
41 Shawn Bradley .20 .50
42 Arvydas Sabonis .25 .60
43 Rex Chapman .20 .50
44 Larry Johnson .30 .75
45 Jayson Williams .20 .50
46 Joe Smith .25 .60
47 Ron Mercer .25 .60
48 Rodney Rogers .20 .50
49 Corliss Williamson .20 .50
50 Tim Duncan .60 1.50
51 Rasheed Wallace .30 .75
52 Vin Baker .25 .60
53 Reggie Miller .40 1.00
54 Patrick Ewing .40 1.00
55 Michael Finley .30 .75
56 Bryant Reeves .20 .50
57 Glenn Robinson .25 .60
58 Walter McCarty .20 .50
59 Brent Barry .25 .60
60 John Starks .25 .60
61 Clarence Weatherspoon .20 .50
62 Calbert Cheaney .20 .50
63 Lamond Murray .20 .50
64 Zydrunas Ilgauskas .30 .75
65 Anthony Mason .20 .50
66 Bryon Russell .20 .50
67 Dean Garrett .20 .50
68 Tom Gugliotta .20 .50
69 Dennis Rodman .60 1.50
70 Keith Van Horn .30 .75
71 Jamal Mashburn .25 .60
72 Steve Smith .25 .60
73 David Wesley .20 .50
74 Chris Webber .30 .75
75 Isaiah Rider .25 .60
76 Stephon Marbury .40 1.00
77 Tim Hardaway .30 .75
78 Jerry Stackhouse .30 .75
79 John Wallace .20 .50
80 Karl Malone .40 1.00
81 Juwan Howard .25 .60
82 Antonio McDyess .25 .60
83 David Robinson .50 1.25
84 Bobby Phills .20 .50
85 Scottie Pippen .50 1.25
86 Brevin Knight .20 .50
87 Alan Henderson .20 .50
88 Kobe Bryant 1.25 3.00
89 Shawn Kemp .30 .75
90 Antoine Walker .30 .75
91 Tracy McGrady .50 1.25
92 Hakeem Olajuwon .40 1.00
93 Mark Jackson .25 .60
94 Bison Dele .20 .50
95 Gary Payton .30 .75
96 Ron Harper .25 .60

97 Shareef Abdur-Rahim .30 .75
98 Alonzo Mourning .40 1.00
99 Grant Hill .50 1.25
100 Shaquille O'Neal .75 2.00
101 Michael Olowokandi RC 1.25 3.00
102 Mike Bibby RC 1.50 4.00
103 Raef LaFrentz RC 1.25 3.00
104 Antawn Jamison RC 1.50 4.00
105 Vince Carter RC 5.00 12.00
106 Robert Traylor RC 1.00 2.50
107 Jason Williams RC 2.50 6.00
108 Larry Hughes RC 2.00 5.00
109 Dirk Nowitzki RC 6.00 15.00
110 Paul Pierce RC 4.00 10.00
111 Bonzi Wells RC 1.00 2.50
112 Michael Doleac RC .75 2.00
113 Keon Clark RC 1.00 2.50
114 Michael Dickerson RC 1.00 2.50
115 Matt Harpring RC 1.00 2.50
116 Bryce Drew RC .60 1.50
117 Pat Garrity RC .75 2.00
118 Roshown McLeod RC .60 1.50
119 Ricky Davis RC 1.50 4.00
120 Brian Skinner RC 1.00 2.50
121 Tyronn Lue RC 1.00 2.50
122 Felipe Lopez RC .60 1.50
123 Al Harrington RC 1.50 4.00
124 Corey Benjamin RC .60 1.50
125 Nazr Mohammed RC 1.00 2.50

1998-99 Bowman's Best Refractors

*STARS: 5X TO 12X BASE CARD HI
*RCs: 1.25X TO 3X BASE HI
STATED PRINT RUN 400 SERIAL #'d SETS
STATED ODDS 1:25
105 Vince Carter 30.00 80.00
109 Dirk Nowitzki 50.00 120.00
110 Paul Pierce 25.00 60.00

1998-99 Bowman's Best Atomic Refractors

*STARS: 15X TO 40X BASE CARD HI
*RCs: 3X TO 8X BASE HI
STATED PRINT RUN 100 SERIAL #'d SETS
STATED ODDS 1:100
1 Jason Kidd 25.00 60.00
8 Anfernee Hardaway 25.00 60.00
21 Charles Barkley 25.00 60.00
26 John Stockton 20.00 50.00
31 Kevin Garnett 40.00 100.00
40 Ray Allen 25.00 60.00
69 Dennis Rodman 40.00 100.00
85 Scottie Pippen 25.00 60.00
88 Kobe Bryant 60.00 150.00
89 Shawn Kemp 20.00 50.00
91 Tracy McGrady 40.00 100.00
95 Gary Payton 15.00 40.00
99 Grant Hill 60.00 150.00
100 Shaquille O'Neal 60.00 150.00
105 Vince Carter 125.00 300.00
107 Jason Williams 75.00 200.00
109 Dirk Nowitzki 200.00 500.00
110 Paul Pierce 100.00 250.00

1998-99 Bowman's Best Autographs

Randomly inserted in packs, this 9-card set features autographs of five current favorties and five future superstars. The veterans were inserted at one in 628, while the rookies were inserted at one in 598. Card backs carry an "A" prefix. Card "A7" does not exist.
STATED ODDS VET 1:628; RC 1:598
A1 Kobe Bryant 75.00 150.00
A2 Tim Duncan 150.00 400.00
A3 Eddie Jones 6.00 15.00
A4 Gary Payton 12.00 30.00
A5 Antoine Walker 6.00 15.00
A6 Antawn Jamison 10.00 25.00
A8 Mike Bibby 6.00 15.00
A9 Vince Carter 40.00 100.00
A10 Michael Doleac 5.00 12.00

1998-99 Bowman's Best Autographs Atomic Refractors

*ATO.REF: 2X TO 5X VALUE
VETERAN STATED ODDS 1:10073
RC STATED ODDS 1:12515
A9 Vince Carter 600.00 1200.00

1998-99 Bowman's Best Autographs Refractors

*REF: .75X TO 2X VALUE
VETERAN STATED ODDS 1:3358
RC STATED ODDS 1:4172
A9 Vince Carter 125.00 250.00

1998-99 Bowman's Best Franchise Best

Randomly inserted in packs at one in 23, this 10-card set highlights some of the best to ever play in the NBA. The cards are printed on 26-pt. stock and carry a "FB" prefix.
COMPLETE SET (10) 10.00 25.00
STATED ODDS 1:23
FB1 Michael Jordan 6.00 15.00
FB2 Karl Malone 1.00 2.50
FB3 Antoine Walker .75 2.00
FB4 Grant Hill 1.25 3.00
FB5 Kevin Garnett 1.25 3.00
FB6 Shaquille O'Neal 2.00 5.00
FB7 Gary Payton .75 2.00
FB8 Keith Van Horn .75 2.00
FB9 Tim Duncan 1.50 4.00
FB10 Allen Iverson 1.50 4.00

1998-99 Bowman's Best Mirror Image

Randomly inserted in packs at one in 12, this 20-card set features a player from both the Western Conference and Eastern Conference on a die cut design. Card backs carry a "MI" prefix.
COMPLETE SET (20) 20.00 40.00
STATED ODDS 1:12
*REF: 6X TO 15X HI COLUMN
REF: PRINT RUN 100 SERIAL #'d SETS
*ATO.REF: 25X TO 60X HI
ATO.REF: PRINT RUN 25 SERIAL #'d SETS
ATO.REF: STATED ODDS 1:2504
MI1 T.Hardaway/B.Knight .75 2.00
MI2 G.Payton/D.Stoudamire .75 2.00
MI3 A.Hardaway/A.Iverson 2.00 5.00
MI4 J.Stockton/S.Marbury 1.00 2.50
MI5 R.Allen/K.Kittles 1.00 2.50
MI6 E.Jones/K.Bryant 3.00 8.00
MI7 S.Smith/R.Mercer .60 1.50
MI8 I.Rider/M.Finley .75 2.00
MI9 L.Sprewell/A.Walker .75 2.00
MI10 D.Schrempf/S.A-Rahim .75 2.00
MI11 G.Hill/T.Thomas 1.25 3.00
MI12 S.Pippen/K.Garnett 2.00 5.00
MI13 J.Williams/J.Howard .60 1.50
MI14 V.Baker/A.McDyess .60 1.50
MI15 S.Kemp/K.Van Horn .75 2.00
MI16 K.Malone/T.Duncan 1.50 4.00
MI17 A.Mourning/Z.Ilgauskas 1.00 2.50
MI18 S.O'Neal/B.Reeves 2.00 5.00
MI19 D.Mutombo/T.Ratliff .75 2.00
MI20 D.Robinson/G.Ostertag 1.25 3.00

1998-99 Bowman's Best Performers

Randomly inserted at one in 12, this 10-card set highlights five veterans with some of last season's best stats, plus five rookies with the best collegiate stats. Card backs carry a "BP" prefix.
COMPLETE SET (10) 10.00 20.00
STATED ODDS 1:12
*REF: 4X TO 10X HI COLUMN
REF: PRINT RUN 200 SERIAL #'d SETS
*ATO.REF: 12X TO 30X HI
ATO.REF: PRINT RUN 50 SERIAL #'d SETS
ATO.REF: STATED ODDS 1:2504
BP1 Shaquille O'Neal 2.00 5.00
BP2 Kevin Garnett 1.25 3.00
BP3 Dikembe Mutombo .75 2.00
BP4 Grant Hill 1.25 3.00
BP5 Tim Duncan 1.50 4.00
BP6 Antawn Jamison .60 1.50
BP7 Raef LaFrentz .50 1.25
BP8 Mike Bibby .60 1.50
BP9 Paul Pierce 1.50 4.00
BP10 Jason Williams 1.00 2.50

1999-00 Bowman's Best

This year's version of Bowman's Best was issued as a 133-card set. Each pack contained five regular cards and one rookie card and carried a suggested retail price of \$5. The set was broken into the following categories: 90 veterans, 10 Best Performers (subset) and 33 rookies.
COMPLETE SET (133) 30.00 60.00
1 Vince Carter .60 1.50
2 Dikembe Mutombo .30 .75
3 Steve Nash .50 1.25
4 Matt Harpring .20 .50
5 Stephon Marbury .25 .60
6 Chris Webber .30 .75
7 Jason Kidd .50 1.25
8 Theo Ratliff .25 .60
9 Damon Stoudamire .25 .60
10 Shareef Abdur-Rahim .25 .60
11 Rod Strickland .20 .50
12 Jeff Hornacek .25 .60
13 Vin Baker .25 .60
14 Joe Smith .25 .60
15 Alonzo Mourning .40 1.00
16 Isaiah Rider .25 .60
17 Shaquille O'Neal .75 2.00
18 Chris Mullin .30 .75
19 Charles Barkley .50 1.25
20 Grant Hill .40 1.00
21 Chris Mills .20 .50
22 Antonio McDyess .25 .60
23 Brevin Knight .20 .50
24 Toni Kukoc .30 .75
25 Antoine Walker .30 .75
26 Eddie Jones .30 .75
27 Tim Thomas .25 .60
28 Latrell Sprewell .30 .75
29 Larry Hughes .25 .60
30 Tim Duncan .60 1.50
31 Horace Grant .25 .60
32 John Stockton .40 1.00
33 Mike Bibby .30 .75
34 Mitch Richmond .30 .75
35 Allan Houston .25 .60
36 Terrell Brandon .20 .50
37 Glenn Robinson .25 .60
38 Tyrone Nesby RC .25 .60
39 Glen Rice .30 .75
40 Hakeem Olajuwon .40 1.00
41 Jerry Stackhouse .30 .75
42 Elden Campbell .20 .50
43 Ron Harper .20 .50
44 Kenny Anderson .25 .60
45 Michael Finley .30 .75
46 Scottie Pippen .50 1.25
47 Lindsey Hunter .20 .50
48 Michael Olowokandi .20 .50
49 P.J. Brown .20 .50
50 Keith Van Horn .25 .60
51 Michael Doleac .20 .50
52 Anfernee Hardaway .50 1.25
53 Rasheed Wallace .30 .75
54 Nick Anderson .20 .50
55 Gary Payton .30 .75
56 Tracy McGrady .50 1.25
57 Ray Allen .30 .75
58 Kobe Bryant 1.25 3.00
59 Ron Mercer .25 .60
60 Shawn Kemp .30 .75
61 Anthony Mason .20 .50
62 Tim Hardaway .30 .75
63 Antawn Jamison .30 .75
64 Mark Jackson .25 .60
65 Tom Gugliotta .20 .50
66 Marcus Camby .25 .60
67 Kerry Kittles .20 .50
68 Vlade Divac .30 .75
69 Avery Johnson .25 .60
70 Karl Malone .40 1.00
71 Juwan Howard .25 .60
72 Alan Henderson .20 .50
73 Hersey Hawkins .20 .50
74 Darrell Armstrong .20 .50
75 Allen Iverson .60 1.50
76 Maurice Taylor .20 .50
77 Gary Trent .20 .50
78 John Starks .25 .60
79 Paul Pierce .40 1.00
80 Kevin Garnett .50 1.25
81 Patrick Ewing .40 1.00
82 Steve Smith .25 .60
83 Jason Williams .40 1.00
84 David Robinson .50 1.25
85 Charles Oakley .25 .60
86 Bryant Reeves .20 .50
87 Nick Van Exel .25 .60
88 Reggie Miller .30 .75
89 Chris Gatling .20 .50
90 Brian Grant .20 .50
91 Allen Iverson BP .60 1.50
92 Tim Duncan BP .60 1.50
93 Keith Van Horn BP .25 .60
94 Kevin Garnett BP .50 1.25
95 Kobe Bryant BP 1.25 3.00
96 Elton Brand BP .75 2.00
97 Baron Davis BP .75 2.00
98 Lamar Odom BP .75 2.00
99 Wally Szczerbiak BP .60 1.50
100 Jason Terry BP .50 1.25
101 Elton Brand RC 1.00 2.50
102 Steve Francis RC 1.00 2.50
103 Baron Davis RC 1.00 2.50
104 Lamar Odom RC 1.00 2.50
105 Jonathan Bender RC .40 1.00
106 Wally Szczerbiak RC .75 2.00
107 Richard Hamilton RC .75 2.00
108 Andre Miller RC .75 2.00
109 Shawn Marion RC .75 2.00
110 Jason Terry RC .60 1.50
111 Trajan Langdon RC .40 1.00
112 A.Radojevic RC .25 .60
113 Corey Maggette RC .60 1.50
114 William Avery RC .30 .75
115 DeMarco Johnson RC .40 1.00
116 Ron Artest RC .75 2.00
117 Cal Bowdler RC .25 .60
118 James Posey RC .40 1.00
119 Quincy Lewis RC .25 .60
120 Dion Glover RC .30 .75
121 Jeff Foster RC .40 1.00
122 Kenny Thomas RC .40 1.00
123 Devean George RC .40 1.00
124 Tim James RC .25 .60
125 Vonteego Cummings RC .25 .60
126 Jumaine Jones RC .30 .75
127 Scott Padgett RC .30 .75
128 Anthony Carter RC .30 .75
129 Chris Herren RC .30 .75
130 Todd MacCulloch RC .40 1.00
131 John Celestand RC .25 .60
132 Adrian Griffin RC .40 1.00
133 Mirsad Turkcan RC .40 1.00

1999-00 Bowman's Best Atomic Refractors

*STARS: 10X TO 25X BASE CARD HI
*RCs: 5X TO 12X BASE HI
STATED PRINT RUN 100 SERIAL #'d SETS
20 Grant Hill 30.00 80.00
58 Kobe Bryant 75.00 200.00
83 Jason Williams 60.00 150.00

1999-00 Bowman's Best Refractors

*STARS: 3X TO 8X BASE CARD HI
*RCs: 2X TO 5X BASE HI
STATED PRINT RUN 400 SERIAL #'d SETS
58 Kobe Bryant 25.00 60.00
95 Kobe Bryant BP 20.00 50.00

1999-00 Bowman's Best Autographs

Randomly inserted in packs at one in 79, this 11-card set features autographs of top players and rookies. Each card features the Topps "Cerified Autograph Issue" logo and Topps 3M sticker. Card backs carry a "BBA" prefix.
STATED ODDS 1:79
BBA1 Mitch Richmond 5.00 12.00
BBA2 Damon Stoudamire 4.00 10.00
BBA3 Antoine Walker 4.00 10.00
BBA4 Antonio McDyess 4.00 10.00
BBA5 Trajan Langdon 4.00 10.00
BBA6 Jumaine Jones 3.00 8.00
BBA7 Andre Miller 6.00 15.00
BBA8 Richard Hamilton 6.00 15.00
BBA9 Jonathan Bender 4.00 10.00
BBA10 William Avery 3.00 8.00
BBA11 Shawn Marion 6.00 15.00

1999-00 Bowman's Best Class Photo

Randomly inserted in packs at one in 100, this set features the star members of the 1999 NBA Rookie Class on one card. The card was also available as a Refractor (one in 3478 and serially numbered to 125) and as an Atomic Refractor (one in 12420 and serially numbered to 35).
STATED ODDS 1:100
REF: STATED ODDS 1:3478
REF: PRINT RUN 125 SERIAL #'d SETS
AR: STATED ODDS 1:12420
AR: PRINT RUN 35 SERIAL #'d SETS
CS1 Draft Picks 3.00 8.00
CS1 Draft Picks REF 25.00 60.00
CS1 Draft Picks AR 100.00 200.00

1999-00 Bowman's Best Franchise Favorites

Randomly inserted in packs at one in 14, this three-card set honors the 1998-99 NBA Champion San Antonio Spurs. Autographs of all three cards were also available. The Duncan auto was inserted at one in 2174, the Gervin auto was inserted at one in 966 and the combo auto was inserted at one in 8694.
COMPLETE SET (3) 1.50 4.00
STATED ODDS 1:14
DUNCAN AU: STATED ODDS 1:2174
GERVIN AU: STATED ODDS 1:966
COMBO AU: STATED ODDS 1:8694
FR1A Tim Duncan .75 2.00
FR1B George Gervin .40 1.00
FR1C T.Duncan/G.Gervin 1.25 3.00
FRA1A Tim Duncan AU 125.00 250.00
FRA1B George Gervin AU 8.00 20.00
FRA1C T.Duncan/G.Gervin AU 200.00 400.00

1999-00 Bowman's Best Franchise Foundations

Randomly inserted in packs at one in 21, this 13-card set features greats of the game posed against the skyline of their team's home city. The cards are die cut and carry a "FF" prefix.
COMPLETE SET (13) 12.50 30.00
STATED ODDS 1:21
FF1 Allen Iverson 2.00 5.00
FF2 Tim Duncan 2.00 5.00
FF3 Kevin Garnett 1.50 4.00
FF4 Shareef Abdur-Rahim .75 2.00
FF5 Kobe Bryant 4.00 10.00
FF6 Grant Hill 1.25 3.00
FF7 Keith Van Horn .75 2.00
FF8 Vince Carter 2.00 5.00
FF9 Antoine Walker 1.00 2.50
FF10 Shaquille O'Neal 2.50 6.00
FF11 Jason Williams 1.25 3.00
FF12 Stephon Marbury .75 2.00
FF13 Antonio McDyess .75 2.00

1999-00 Bowman's Best Franchise Futures

Randomly inserted at one in 27, this 10-card set showcases the future leaders of their respective franchises. The cards were die cut and carry a "FFT" prefix.
COMPLETE SET (10) 6.00 15.00
STATED ODDS 1:27
FFT1 Elton Brand 1.25 3.00
FFT2 Steve Francis 1.25 3.00
FFT3 Baron Davis 1.25 3.00
FFT4 Lamar Odom 1.25 3.00
FFT5 Jonathan Bender .50 1.25
FFT6 Wally Szczerbiak 1.00 2.50
FFT7 Richard Hamilton 1.00 2.50
FFT8 Andre Miller 1.00 2.50
FFT9 Shawn Marion 1.00 2.50
FFT10 Jason Terry .75 2.00

1999-00 Bowman's Best Rookie Locker Room Collection

Randomly inserted in packs, this nine-card set features jerseys and autographs of the top rookies. All cards feature the Topps 3M sticker to verify authenticity. The autographed cards were inserted at one in 174, while the jersey cards were inserted at one in 197. Card backs carry either a "LRCA" prefix or "LRCJ" prefix.
AU STATED ODDS 1:174
JERSEY STATED ODDS 1:197
LRCA1 Elton Brand AU 8.00 20.00
LRCA2 Steve Francis AU 8.00 20.00
LRCA3 Wally Szczerbiak AU 6.00 15.00
LRCA4 Baron Davis AU 6.00 15.00
LRCA5 Corey Maggette AU 5.00 12.00
LRCJ1 Elton Brand 5.00 12.00
LRCJ2 Steve Francis 5.00 12.00
LRCJ3 Wally Szczerbiak 4.00 10.00
LRCJ4 Baron Davis 5.00 12.00

1999-00 Bowman's Best Techniques

Randomly inserted in packs at one in 21, this 13-card set features the NBA's most spectacular players and their patented moves. Card backs carry a "BT" prefix.
COMPLETE SET (13) 8.00 20.00
STATED ODDS 1:21
BT1 Tim Duncan 2.00 5.00
BT2 Tim Hardaway 1.00 2.50
BT3 Shaquille O'Neal 2.50 6.00
BT4 Vince Carter 2.00 5.00
BT5 Dikembe Mutombo 1.00 2.50
BT6 Grant Hill 1.25 3.00
BT7 Gary Payton 1.00 2.50
BT8 Jason Williams 1.25 3.00
BT9 Stephon Marbury .75 2.00
BT10 Reggie Miller 1.00 2.50
BT11 Scottie Pippen 1.50 4.00
BT12 John Stockton 1.25 3.00
BT13 Karl Malone 1.25 3.00

1999-00 Bowman's Best World's Best

Randomly inserted in packs at one in 30, this nine-card set features nine members of the Men's Team USA squad that competed in the 2000 Summer Olympic Games. Card backs carry a "WB" prefix.
COMPLETE SET (9) 5.00 12.00
STATED ODDS 1:30
WB1 Allan Houston .75 2.00
WB2 Kevin Garnett 1.50 4.00
WB3 Gary Payton 1.00 2.50
WB4 Steve Smith .75 2.00
WB5 Tim Hardaway 1.00 2.50
WB6 Tim Duncan 2.00 5.00
WB7 Jason Kidd 1.50 4.00
WB8 Tom Gugliotta .60 1.50
WB9 Vin Baker .75 2.00

2000-01 Bowman's Best Promos

This six-card standard-size set was sent to dealers as a promotional set for the 2000-01 Bowman's Best issue. The cards carry a "PP" prefix.
COMPLETE SET (6) 1.25 3.00
PP1 Jason Kidd .50 1.25
PP2 Alonzo Mourning .40 1.00
PP3 John Stockton .40 1.00
PP4 Antoine Walker .25 .60
PP5 Scottie Pippen .50 1.25
PP6 Allan Houston .25 .60

2000-01 Bowman's Best

The 2000-01 Bowman's Best product was released in February, 2001 and features a 133-card base set. The set is broken into tiers as follows. Base Veterans (1-100), and Rookies (101-133) that are individually serial numbered to 499. Please note that there are three different versions of each rookie card, and that each version is serial numbered to 499. Please note that version "A" cards are blue, Version "B" cards are black, and Version "C" cards are blue-black. Each pack contains five cards and carries a suggested retail price of 2.99.
COMPLETE SET w/o RC (100) 15.00 30.00
ROOKIE STATED ODDS 1:23
ROOKIE PRINT RUN 499 SERIAL #'d SETS
THREE VERSIONS OF EACH RC SAME VALUE
LCP1: STATED ODDS 1:767
LCP1: PRINT RUN 499 SERIAL #'d SETS
1 Allen Iverson .60 1.50
2 Darrell Armstrong .20 .50
3 Kendall Gill .20 .50
4 Marcus Camby .25 .60
5 Glen Rice .25 .60
6 Eddie Jones .30 .75
7 Wally Szczerbiak .25 .60
8 Antawn Jamison .30 .75
9 Raef LaFrentz .20 .50
10 Steve Francis .25 .60
11 Tracy McGrady .50 1.25
12 Brian Grant .20 .50
13 Vlade Divac .25 .60
14 Gary Payton .30 .75
15 Vince Carter .60 1.50
16 John Stockton .40 1.00
17 Mike Bibby .30 .75
18 Derek Anderson .20 .50
19 Juwan Howard .25 .60
20 Allan Houston .25 .60
21 Kevin Garnett .50 1.25
22 Michael Olowokandi .20 .50
23 Maurice Taylor .20 .50
24 Jerry Stackhouse .25 .60
25 Nick Van Exel .25 .60
26 Andre Miller .25 .60
27 Michael Finley .30 .75
28 Jamal Mashburn .25 .60
29 Ron Mercer .20 .50
30 Jim Jackson .20 .50
31 Kenny Anderson .25 .60
32 Karl Malone .40 1.00
33 Rod Strickland .20 .50
34 Shaquille O'Neal .75 2.00
35 Glenn Robinson .25 .60
36 Keith Van Horn .25 .60
37 Grant Hill .40 1.00
38 Eric Snow .20 .50
39 Anfernee Hardaway .50 1.25
40 Scottie Pippen .50 1.25
41 Jason Williams .30 .75
42 Elton Brand .30 .75
43 Stephon Marbury .25 .60
44 David Robinson .50 1.25
45 Antonio Davis .20 .50
46 Michael Dickerson .20 .50
47 Mitch Richmond .25 .60
48 Rashard Lewis .30 .75
49 Jermaine O'Neal .25 .60
50 Tim Duncan .60 1.50
51 Tom Gugliotta .20 .50
52 Theo Ratliff .20 .50
53 Joe Smith .25 .60
54 Tim Thomas .20 .50
55 Brevin Knight .20 .50
56 Dale Davis .20 .50
57 Cuttino Mobley .20 .50
58 Cedric Ceballos .20 .50
59 Christian Laettner .25 .60
60 Dirk Nowitzki .50 1.25
61 Paul Pierce .30 .75
62 Derrick Coleman .25 .60
63 Dikembe Mutombo .30 .75
64 Lamond Murray .20 .50
65 Antonio McDyess .25 .60
66 Reggie Miller .30 .75
67 Hakeem Olajuwon .40 1.00
68 Corey Maggette .25 .60
69 Lamar Odom .25 .60
70 Larry Hughes .25 .60
71 Anthony Mason .20 .50
72 Sam Cassell .25 .60
73 Terrell Brandon .20 .50
74 Latrell Sprewell .25 .60
75 Kobe Bryant 1.25 3.00
76 Tim Hardaway .30 .75
77 Mark Jackson .25 .60
78 Vin Baker .25 .60
79 Jonathan Bender .20 .50
80 Chris Webber .30 .75
81 Rasheed Wallace .30 .75
82 Shawn Marion .25 .60
83 Toni Kukoc .30 .75
84 Patrick Ewing .40 1.00
85 Ray Allen .30 .75
86 Isaiah Rider .25 .60
87 Danny Fortson .20 .50
88 Jerome Williams .20 .50
89 Shawn Kemp .30 .75
90 Ron Artest .30 .75
91 P.J. Brown .20 .50
92 Baron Davis .30 .75
93 Antoine Walker .25 .60
94 Jason Terry .30 .75
95 Jalen Rose .25 .60
96 Avery Johnson .25 .60
97 Shareef Abdur-Rahim .25 .60
98 Bryon Russell .20 .50
99 Richard Hamilton .25 .60
100 Jason Kidd .50 1.25
101A Kenyon Martin RC 2.50 6.00
101B Kenyon Martin RC 2.50 6.00
101C Kenyon Martin RC 2.50 6.00
102A Stromile Swift RC 1.00 2.50
102B Stromile Swift RC 1.00 2.50
102C Stromile Swift RC 1.00 2.50
103A Darius Miles RC 1.00 2.50
103B Darius Miles RC 1.00 2.50
103C Darius Miles RC 1.00 2.50
104A Marcus Fizer RC 1.00 2.50
104B Marcus Fizer RC 1.00 2.50
104C Marcus Fizer RC 1.00 2.50
105A Mike Miller RC 1.50 4.00
105B Mike Miller RC 1.50 4.00
105C Mike Miller RC 1.50 4.00
106A DerMarr Johnson RC .75 2.00
106B DerMarr Johnson RC .75 2.00
106C DerMarr Johnson RC .75 2.00
107A Chris Mihm RC .75 2.00
107B Chris Mihm RC .75 2.00
107C Chris Mihm RC .75 2.00
108A Jamal Crawford RC 2.50 6.00
108B Jamal Crawford RC 2.50 6.00
108C Jamal Crawford RC 2.50 6.00
109A Joel Przybilla RC .75 2.00
109B Joel Przybilla RC .75 2.00
109C Joel Przybilla RC .75 2.00
110A Keyon Dooling RC 1.00 2.50
110B Keyon Dooling RC 1.00 2.50
110C Keyon Dooling RC 1.00 2.50
111A Jerome Moiso RC .60 1.50
111B Jerome Moiso RC .60 1.50
111C Jerome Moiso RC .60 1.50
112A Etan Thomas RC 1.00 2.50
112B Etan Thomas RC 1.00 2.50
112C Etan Thomas RC 1.00 2.50
113A Courtney Alexander RC .75 2.00
113B Courtney Alexander RC .75 2.00
113C Courtney Alexander RC .75 2.00
114A Mateen Cleaves RC .75 2.00
114B Mateen Cleaves RC .75 2.00
114C Mateen Cleaves RC .75 2.00
115A Jason Collier RC 1.00 2.50
115B Jason Collier RC 1.00 2.50
115C Jason Collier RC 1.00 2.50
116A Hedo Turkoglu RC 1.50 4.00
116B Hedo Turkoglu RC 1.50 4.00
116C Hedo Turkoglu RC 1.50 4.00
117A Desmond Mason RC 1.25 3.00
117B Desmond Mason RC 1.25 3.00
117C Desmond Mason RC 1.25 3.00
118A Quentin Richardson RC 1.00 2.50
118B Quentin Richardson RC 1.00 2.50
118C Quentin Richardson RC 1.00 2.50
119A Jamaal Magloire RC 1.00 2.50
119B Jamaal Magloire RC 1.00 2.50
119C Jamaal Magloire RC 1.00 2.50
120A Speedy Claxton RC 1.00 2.50
120B Speedy Claxton RC 1.00 2.50
120C Speedy Claxton RC 1.00 2.50
121A Morris Peterson RC 1.00 2.50
121B Morris Peterson RC 1.00 2.50
121C Morris Peterson RC 1.00 2.50
122A Donnell Harvey RC .75 2.00
122B Donnell Harvey RC .75 2.00
122C Donnell Harvey RC .75 2.00
123A D.Stevenson RC 1.00 2.50
123B D.Stevenson RC 1.00 2.50
123C D.Stevenson RC 1.00 2.50
124A Dalibor Bagaric RC .75 2.00
124B Dalibor Bagaric RC .75 2.00
124C Dalibor Bagaric RC .75 2.00
125A Iakovos Tsakalidis RC .60 1.50
125B Iakovos Tsakalidis RC .60 1.50
125C Iakovos Tsakalidis RC .60 1.50
126A Mamadou N'Diaye RC .60 1.50
126B Mamadou N'Diaye RC .60 1.50
126C Mamadou N'Diaye RC .60 1.50
127A Lavor Postell RC .60 1.50
127B Lavor Postell RC .60 1.50
127C Lavor Postell RC .60 1.50
128A Erick Barkley RC .60 1.50
128B Erick Barkley RC .60 1.50
128C Erick Barkley RC .60 1.50
129A Mark Madsen RC 1.00 2.50
129B Mark Madsen RC 1.00 2.50
129C Mark Madsen RC 1.00 2.50
130A Khalid El-Amin RC .60 1.50
130B Khalid El-Amin RC .60 1.50
130C Khalid El-Amin RC .60 1.50
131A A.J. Guyton RC .60 1.50
131B A.J. Guyton RC .60 1.50
131C A.J. Guyton RC .60 1.50
132A Stephen Jackson RC 1.50 4.00
132B Stephen Jackson RC 1.50 4.00
132C Stephen Jackson RC 1.50 4.00
133A Michael Redd RC 2.50 6.00
133B Michael Redd RC 2.50 6.00
133C Michael Redd RC 2.50 6.00
LCP1 Draft Picks 4.00 10.00

2000-01 Bowman's Best Elements of the Game

Randomly inserted into packs at one in 12, this 13-card insert features players that have all of the elements to make them superstars. Card backs carry an "EG" prefix.
COMPLETE SET (13) 12.50 25.00
STATED ODDS 1:12
EG1 Shaquille O'Neal 1.50 4.00
EG2 Allen Iverson 1.25 3.00
EG3 Vince Carter 1.25 3.00
EG4 Jason Kidd 1.00 2.50
EG5 Kevin Garnett 1.00 2.50
EG6 Tracy McGrady 1.00 2.50
EG7 Tim Duncan 1.25 3.00
EG8 Gary Payton .60 1.50
EG9 Larry Hughes .50 1.25
EG10 Lamar Odom .50 1.25
EG11 Jason Williams .60 1.50
EG12 Kobe Bryant 2.50 6.00
EG13 Karl Malone .75 2.00

2000-01 Bowman's Best Expressions

Randomly inserted into packs at one in 8, this 20-card insert features players that express themselves very well on the basketball court. Card backs carry an "E" prefix.
COMPLETE SET (20) 12.50 25.00
STATED ODDS 1:8
E1 Shaquille O'Neal 1.50 4.00
E2 Kevin Garnett 1.00 2.50
E3 Allen Iverson 1.25 3.00
E4 Antonio McDyess .50 1.25
E5 Rasheed Wallace .60 1.50
E6 Steve Francis .50 1.25
E7 Kobe Bryant 2.50 6.00
E8 Vince Carter 1.25 3.00
E9 Chris Webber .60 1.50
E10 Gary Payton .60 1.50
E11 Latrell Sprewell .50 1.25
E12 Tracy McGrady 1.00 2.50
E13 Reggie Miller .60 1.50
E14 Antoine Walker .50 1.25
E15 Jason Williams .60 1.50
E16 Michael Finley .60 1.50
E17 Patrick Ewing .75 2.00
E18 Karl Malone .75 2.00
E19 Elton Brand .60 1.50
E20 Lamar Odom .50 1.25

2000-01 Bowman's Best Franchise Favorites

Randomly inserted into packs, this 10-card insert features seven dual-player jersey cards of superstar teammates. The set also includes autographed cards of Shaquille O'Neal, Magic Johnson, and a Shaquille O'Neal/Magic Johnson co-signer. Card backs carry an "FFJ" prefix.
SHAQ AU: STATED ODDS 1:1926
MAGIC AU: STATED ODDS 1:852
COMBO AU: STATED ODDS 1:5488
OVERALL AU: STATED ODDS 1:320
GJ: STATED ODDS 1:637
GJ: PRINT RUN 100 SERIAL #'d SETS
FFA1 Shaquille O'Neal AU 60.00 150.00
FFA2 Magic Johnson AU 40.00 100.00
FFA3 S.O'Neal/Magic AU 150.00 300.00
FFJ1 T.McGrady/G.Hill JSY 10.00 25.00
FFJ2 A.Walker/P.Pierce JSY 12.00 30.00
FFJ3 D.Miles/K.Dooling JSY 8.00 20.00
FFJ4 S.Marbury/K.Martin JSY 8.00 20.00
FFJ5 J.Kidd/A.Hardaway JSY 25.00 60.00
FFJ6 S.A-Rahim/S.Swift JSY 8.00 20.00

2000-01 Bowman's Best Rookie Locker Room Collection

Randomly inserted into packs, this 58-card insert is broken into four tiers. The first tier features (15) rookies from the 2000-01 season (1:4), the second tier features an autographed version of the these (15) cards (1:32), the third tier features (25) rookies with a swatch of jersey worn at the Rookie Photo Shoot. (1:41), and the fourth tier features (3) autographed cards of Steve Francis and Elton Brand (1:274). Card backs carry an "LRC" prefix.
INSERTS: STATED ODDS 1:4
AU: OVERALL STATED ODDS 1:32
FB AU: OVERALL STATED ODDS 1:274
JSY: OVERALL STATED ODDS 1:41
LRC1 Kenyon Martin .75 2.00
LRC2 Stromile Swift .30 .75
LRC3 Darius Miles .30 .75
LRC4 Marcus Fizer .30 .75
LRC5 Mike Miller .50 1.25
LRC6 DerMarr Johnson .25 .60
LRC7 Chris Mihm .25 .60
LRC8 Jamal Crawford .75 2.00
LRC9 Joel Przybilla .25 .60
LRC10 Keyon Dooling .30 .75
LRC11 Jerome Moiso .20 .50
LRC12 Courtney Alexander .25 .60
LRC13 Mateen Cleaves .25 .60
LRC14 Speedy Claxton .30 .75
LRC15 DeShawn Stevenson .30 .75
LRCA1 Jamal Crawford AU 12.00 30.00
LRCA2 Courtney Alexander AU 3.00 8.00
LRCA3 Keyon Dooling AU 4.00 10.00
LRCA4 Mateen Cleaves AU 3.00 8.00
LRCA5 A.J. Guyton AU 2.50 6.00
LRCA6 Khalid El-Amin AU 2.50 6.00
LRCA7 Desmond Mason AU 5.00 12.00
LRCA8 Erick Barkley AU 2.50 6.00
LRCA9 Larry Hughes AU 4.00 10.00
LRCA10 Maurice Taylor AU 4.00 10.00
LRCA11 Tim Thomas AU 4.00 10.00
LRCA12 Antawn Jamison AU 6.00 15.00
LRCA13 Jonathan Bender AU 4.00 10.00
LRCA14 Baron Davis AU 5.00 12.00
LRCA15 Mike Bibby AU 5.00 12.00
LRCF1 Steve Francis AU 6.00 15.00
LRCF2 Elton Brand AU 5.00 12.00
LRCF3 S.Francis/Brand AU 12.50 30.00
LRCR1 Kenyon Martin JSY 6.00 15.00
LRCR2 Stromile Swift JSY 2.50 6.00
LRCR3 Darius Miles JSY 2.50 6.00
LRCR4 Marcus Fizer JSY 2.50 6.00
LRCR5 Mike Miller JSY 4.00 10.00
LRCR6 DerMarr Johnson JSY 2.00 5.00
LRCR7 Chris Mihm JSY 2.00 5.00
LRCR8 Mark Madsen JSY 2.50 6.00
LRCR9 Joel Przybilla JSY 2.00 5.00
LRCR10 Keyon Dooling JSY 2.50 6.00
LRCR11 Jerome Moiso JSY 1.50 4.00
LRCR12 Etan Thomas JSY 2.50 6.00
LRCR13 Courtney Alexander JSY 2.00 5.00
LRCR14 Mateen Cleaves JSY 2.00 5.00
LRCR15 Jason Collier JSY 2.50 6.00
LRCR16 Desmond Mason JSY 3.00 8.00
LRCR17 Quentin Richardson JSY 2.50 6.00
LRCR18 Jamaal Magloire JSY 2.50 6.00
LRCR19 Speedy Claxton JSY 2.50 6.00
LRCR20 Morris Peterson JSY 2.50 6.00
LRCR21 Donnell Harvey JSY 2.00 5.00
LRCR22 DeShawn Stevenson JSY 2.50 6.00
LRCR23 Mamadou N'Diaye JSY 1.50 4.00
LRCR24 Erick Barkley JSY 1.50 4.00
LRCR25 Hedo Turkoglu JSY 4.00 10.00

1974-75 Braves Buffalo Linnett

These three charcoal drawings are skillfully executed facial portraits of Buffalo Braves players. They were drawn by noted sports artist Charles Linnett and measure approximately 8 1/2" by 11". In the lower right corner, a facsimile autograph of the player is written across the portrait. The backs are blank. The drawings are unnumbered and are checklisted below in alphabetical order.
COMPLETE SET (3) 10.00 20.00
1 Ernie DiGregorio 5.00 10.00
2 Garfield Heard 2.50 6.00
3 Jim McMillian 2.50 6.00

1976-77 Braves Team Issue

These 8" by 10" blank-backed black and white glossy photos feature members of the 1976-77 Buffalo Braves. Since these photos are unnumbered, we have sequenced them in alphabetical order.
COMPLETE SET (14) 15.00 30.00
1 Don Adams .75 2.00
2 Bird Averitt .75 2.00
3 Gary Brewster .75 2.00
4 Fred Foster .75 2.00
5 George Jackson .75 2.00
6 Greg Jackson .75 2.00
7 Bob McAdoo 5.00 10.00
8 John Neumann .75 2.00
9 Dale Schlueter .75 2.00
10 Randy Smith 2.50 6.00
11 John Shumate 1.00 2.50
12 Claude Terry .75 2.00
13 Bob MacKinnon GM .75 2.00
Tates Locke CO
14 Charlie Harrison ACO .75 2.00
Ray Melchiorre TR

1951 Bread For Energy

The 1951 Bread for Energy bread end labels set contains 11 known labels of players in the National Football League, professional basketball, pro boxing, and famous actors. Each measures approximately 2 3/4" by 2 3/4" with the corners cut out in typical bread label style. These labels are not usually found in top condition due to the difficulty in removing them from the bread package. While all the bakeries who issued this set are not presently known, Junge's Brand Bread in the New England area is one bakery that has been confirmed. As with many of the bread label sets of the early 1950's, an album to house the set was probably issued. Each label was printed with a red, yellow, and blue background. The cards are unnumbered but are arranged alphabetically within subject below.
28 Bob Davies BK 600.00 1000.00
29 Joe Fulks BK 1000.00 1500.00
30 Dick McGuire BK 600.00 1000.00
31 George Mikan BK 6000.00 8000.00

1950-51 Bread for Health

The 1950-51 Bread for Health basketball set consists of 32 bread end labels (each measuring approximately 2 3/4" by 2 3/4") of players in the National Basketball Association. While all the bakeries who issued this set are not at present known, Fisher's Bread in the New Jersey, New York and Pennsylvania area and NBC Bread in the Michigan area are two of the bakeries that have been confirmed to date. As with many of the bread label sets of the early '50s, an album to house the set was probably issued. Each label contains the B.E.B. copyright found on so many of the labels of this period. Labels which contain "Bread for Energy" at the bottom are not a part of the set but part of a series of movie, western and sports stars issued during the same approximate time period. The American Card Catalog does not designate a number to this series; however, based on its similarity to a corresponding football issue, it is referenced as D290-15A. The set is dated by the fact that 1949-50 was Buddy Jeanette and Bob Kinney's last active year and Vince Boryla, Tony Lavelli, and Vern Mikkelsen's first active year.
COMPLETE SET (32) 18000.00 22000.00
1 Paul Armstrong 250.00 450.00
2 Ralph Beard 400.00 750.00
3 Vince Boryla 300.00 600.00
4 Walter Budko 250.00 450.00
5 Al Cervi 250.00 450.00
6 Bob Davies 600.00 950.00
7 Dwight Eddleman 300.00 600.00
8 Arnold Ferrin 300.00 600.00
9 Joe Fulks 800.00 1200.00
10 Harry Gallatin 400.00 650.00
11 Chuck Gilmur 250.00 450.00
12 Alex Groza 400.00 750.00
13 Bruce Hale 300.00 600.00
14 Paul Hoffman 250.00 450.00
15 Buddy Jeanette 400.00 750.00
16 Bob Kinney 250.00 450.00
17 Tony Lavelli 250.00 450.00
18 Ron Livingstone 250.00 450.00
19 Horace McKinney 400.00 700.00
20 Stan Miasek 250.00 450.00
21 George Mikan 2500.00 3500.00
22 Andy Phillip 300.00 600.00
23 Arnie Risen 400.00 750.00
24 Fred Schaus 400.00 700.00
25 Dolph Schayes 1100.00 1500.00
26 Fred Scolari 250.00 450.00
27 George Senesky 250.00 450.00
28 Paul Seymour 300.00 600.00
29 Cornelius Simmons 300.00 600.00
30 Gene Vance 250.00 450.00
31 Brady Walker 250.00 450.00
32 Max Zaslofsky 350.00 700.00

1976 Buckmans Discs

The 1976 Buckmans Discs set contains 20 unnumbered discs measuring approximately 3 3/8" in diameter. The discs have various color borders containing brief biographical information and feature black and white drawings of the players with fascimile signatures. This set was distributed through Buckmans Ice Cream Village in Rochester, New York. The discs can be found with Buckmans backs or blank backs with the Buckmans backs being harder to find and carrying a 50 percent premium above the prices listed below. The cards are listed alphabetically in the checklist below. The set was also issued with Crane Potato Chips; the Crane Potato Chips advertisement on the backs is printed in red and blue on a white background. The Crane variations show Crane at the top of the disc rather than four stars; the Crane discs are harder to find and are valued at approximately six

times the Buckmans prices listed below.
COMPLETE SET (20) 25.00 50.00
1 Kareem Abdul-Jabbar 4.00 10.00
2 Nate Archibald 2.00 5.00
3 Rick Barry 2.00 5.00
4 Tom Boerwinkle .75 2.00
5 Bill Bradley 2.00 5.00
6 Dave Cowens 2.50 6.00
7 Bob Dandridge 1.00 2.50
8 Walt Frazier 2.50 6.00
9 Gail Goodrich 2.50 6.00
10 John Havlicek 3.00 8.00
11 Connie Hawkins 2.50 6.00
12 Lou Hudson 1.25 3.00
13 Sam Lacey .75 2.00
14 Bob Lanier 2.00 5.00
15 Bob Love 1.50 4.00
16 Bob McAdoo 2.00 5.00
17 Earl Monroe 2.00 5.00
18 Jerry Sloan 2.00 5.00
19 Norm Van Lier 1.25 3.00
20 Jo Jo White 1.25 3.00

1977-78 Bucks Action Photos

These glossy action photos featuring members of the Milwaukee Bucks measure approximately 5" by 7" and are printed on very thin paper. The photos are in full color and borderless. The players are identified only by their facsimile autographs inscribed across the picture. The backs are blank.
COMPLETE SET (10) 6.00 15.00
1 Kent Benson .75 2.00
2 Junior Bridgeman .75 2.00
3 Quinn Buckner 1.00 2.50
4 Alex English 3.00 8.00
5 John Gianelli .60 1.50
6 Ernie Grunfeld 1.00 2.50
7 Marques Johnson 2.00 5.00
8 Dave Meyers .75 2.00
9 Lloyd Walton .60 1.50
10 Brian Winters 1.00 2.50

1985 Bucks Card Night/Star

This 13-card set was given away during the Milwaukee Bucks "Card Night" on January 21, 1985. Card number 10 Larry Micheaux was withdrawn at the request of the Bucks management due to his Free Agent signing after the printing of the cards. Cards measure 2 1/2" by 3 1/2" and have a green border around the fronts of the cards and green printing on the backs. Cards feature Star '85 logo on the fronts.
COMPLETE SET (13) 25.00 60.00
1 Don Nelson CO 1.50 4.00
2 Randy Breuer .75 2.00
3 Terry Cummings 2.00 5.00
4 Charlie Davis .75 2.00
5 Mike Dunleavy 1.50 4.00
6 Kenny Fields .75 2.00
7 Kevin Grevey .75 2.00
8 Craig Hodges 1.25 3.00
9 Alton Lister .75 2.00
10 Larry Micheaux SP 10.00 25.00
11 Paul Mokeski 1.25 3.00
12 Sidney Moncrief 2.50 6.00
13 Paul Pressey 1.25 3.00

1988-89 Bucks Green Border

This 16-card set was issued in sheet form: four rows of four cards each; after perforation, the cards measure approximately 2 3/4" by 4". Each of the four strips was given away at a different Milwaukee Bucks home game. The fronts feature a color action player photo, with a thin black border on medium green background. In white lettering the team and player name are given below the picture. The back has the Milwaukee Bucks logo in the upper left corner and biographical information given in tabular format. Whole sheets carry a slight premium on the set price.
COMPLETE SET (16) 12.50 30.00
1 Kareem Abdul-Jabbar 5.00 12.00
2 Randy Breuer .75 2.00
3 Terry Cummings 1.50 4.00
4 Jeff Grayer .75 2.00
5 Del Harris CO 1.25 3.00
6 Tito Horford .75 2.00
7 Jay Humphries 1.25 3.00
8 Larry Krystkowiak .75 2.00
9 Paul Mokeski .75 2.00
10 Sidney Moncrief 2.00 5.00
11 Ricky Pierce 1.25 3.00
12 Paul Pressey .75 2.00
13 Fred Roberts .75 2.00
14 Jack Sikma 1.50 4.00
15 The Bradley Center .75 2.00
16 Del Harris CO 1.00 2.50
Frank Hamblen ACO
Mack Calvin ACO
Mike Dunleavy ACO
Jeff Snedeker TR

1986 Bucks Lifebuoy/Star

The 1986 Star Lifebuoy Milwaukee Bucks set contains 13 cards, one for each of the 12 players plus a coaching staff card. The set's basic design is identical to those of the Star Company's regular NBA sets. The front borders are lime green, and the backs show each player's NBA statistics (collegiate for number 13 Jerry Reynolds). The cards show a Star '86 logo in the upper right corner. The cards measure approximately 2 1/2" by 3 1/2". The cards are numbered in the upper left corner of the reverse; the numbering corresponds to alphabetical order by player.
COMPLETE SET (13) 6.00 15.00
1 Don Nelson CO 1.25 3.00
2 Randy Breuer .60 1.50
3 Terry Cummings 1.25 3.00
4 Charlie Davis .60 1.50
5 Kenny Fields .60 1.50
6 Craig Hodges .75 2.00
7 Jeff Lamp .75 2.00
8 Alton Lister .60 1.50
9 Paul Mokeski .75 2.00
10 Sidney Moncrief 1.50 4.00
11 Ricky Pierce .75 2.00
12 Paul Pressey .75 2.00
13 Jerry Reynolds .60 1.50

1973-74 Bucks Linnett

Measuring 8 1/2" by 11", these six charcoal drawings are facial portraits by noted sports artist Charles Linnett. The player's facsimile autograph is inscribed across the lower right corner. The backs are blank. Three portraits were included in each package, with a suggested retail price of 99 cents. The portraits are unnumbered and checklisted below in alphabetical order. The set is dated by the fact that 1973-74 is Oscar Robertson's last year with the Bucks and Terry Driscoll's first year with the Bucks.
COMPLETE SET (6) 20.00 40.00
1 Kareem Abdul-Jabbar 12.50 25.00
2 Lucius Allen 1.50 4.00
3 Terry Driscoll 1.25 3.00
4 Russell Lee 1.25 3.00
5 Curtis Perry 1.25 3.00
6 Oscar Robertson 10.00 20.00

1974-75 Bucks Linnett

These ten charcoal drawings are skillfully executed facial portraits of Milwaukee Bucks players. They were drawn by noted sports artist Charles Linnett and measure approximately 8 1/2" by 11". In the lower right corner, a facsimile autograph of the player is written across the portrait. The backs are blank. The drawings are unnumbered and we have checklisted them below in alphabetical order. The set is dated by the fact that 1974-75 was Gary Brokaw and Kevin Restani's first active year and Steve Kuberski and George Thompson's only year with the Bucks.
COMPLETE SET (10) 25.00 50.00
1 Kareem Abdul-Jabbar 12.50 25.00
2 Gary Brokaw 1.25 3.00
3 Bob Dandridge 1.50 4.00
4 Mickey Davis 1.00 2.50
5 Steve Kuberski 1.00 2.50
6 Jon McGlocklin 1.50 4.00
7 Jim Price 1.00 2.50
8 Kevin Restani 1.00 2.50
9 George Thompson 1.00 2.50
10 Cornell Warner 1.00 2.50

1976-77 Bucks Playing Cards

The 55-card deck of playing cards was co-sponsored by White Hen Pantry and Coca-Cola. The cards measure approximately 2 1/4" by 3 1/2" and have rounded corners. The fronts feature black-and-white action shots with coach or player identification, player background and statistics below the picture. The backs have a brown, red and yellow design with a basketball in the center. The two sponsors logos appear twice at opposite diagonal corners of the card. The set is checklisted below as if it was a playing card set. In the checklist, C means Clubs, D means Diamonds, H means Hearts and S means Spades. The cards are checklisted in playing card order by suits and numbers are assigned to Aces (1), Jacks (11), Queens (12), and Kings (13). Two coaches cards that could be used as jokers and a filler card with a color Bucks logo and White Hen Pantry ad are listed at the end. Key cards include the first ever of Quinn Buckner and Alex English.
COMP.FACT.SET (55) 35.00 70.00
C1 Bucks Logo .30 .75
C2 Brian Winters 1.25 3.00
C3 Lloyd Walton .30 .75
C4 Junior Bridgeman .75 2.00
C5 Alex English 5.00 10.00
C6 Quinn Buckner 1.25 3.00
C7 David Meyers .75 2.00
C8 Swen Nater .75 2.00
C9 Scott Lloyd .30 .75
C10 Bob Dandridge 1.00 2.50
C11 Kevin Restani .40 1.00
C12 Rowland Garrett .30 .75
C13 Fred Carter 1.25 3.00
D1 Bucks Logo .30 .75
D2 Fred Carter .75 2.00
D3 Rowland Garrett .30 .75
D4 Kevin Restani .40 1.00
D5 Bob Dandridge 1.00 2.50
D6 Scott Lloyd .30 .75
D7 Swen Nater .75 2.00
D8 David Meyers .75 2.00
D9 Quinn Buckner 1.25 3.00
D10 Alex English 5.00 10.00
D11 Junior Bridgeman 1.00 2.50
D12 Lloyd Walton .75 2.00
D13 Brian Winters 1.00 2.50
H1 Bucks Logo .30 .75
H2 Fred Carter .60 1.50
H3 Rowland Garrett .30 .75
H4 Kevin Restani .40 1.00
H5 Bob Dandridge 1.00 2.50
H6 Scott Lloyd .30 .75
H7 Swen Nater .75 2.00
H8 David Meyers .75 2.00
H9 Quinn Buckner 1.25 3.00
H10 Alex English 5.00 10.00
H11 Junior Bridgeman 1.00 2.50
H12 Lloyd Walton .30 .75
H13 Brian Winters 1.25 3.00
S1 Bucks Logo .30 .75
S2 Brian Winters 1.25 3.00
S3 Lloyd Walton .30 .75
S4 Junior Bridgeman 1.00 2.50
S5 Alex English 5.00 10.00
S6 Quinn Buckner 1.25 3.00
S7 David Meyers .75 2.00
S8 Swen Nater .75 2.00
S9 Scott Lloyd .30 .75
S10 Bob Dandridge 1.00 2.50
S11 Kevin Restani .40 1.00
S12 Rowland Garrett .30 .75
S13 Fred Carter .75 2.00
NNO K.C. Jones ACO 2.00 5.00
NNO Don Nelson CO 2.50 6.00
NNO Bucks Logo .30 .75
White Hen Pantry Ad

1987-88 Bucks Polaroid

The 1987-88 Polaroid Milwaukee Bucks set contains 16 cards each measuring approximately 2 3/4" by 4". There are 14 player cards plus one coaching staff card and one title card. The cards were distributed in sheet form with perforations. The front borders are deep green and the backs feature biographical information. Whole sheets carry a slight premium on the set price.
COMPLETE SET (16) 12.50 30.00
2 Junior Bridgeman 1.25 3.00
3 Pace Mannion .75 2.00
4 Sidney Moncrief 2.50 6.00
10 John Lucas 2.00 5.00
15 Craig Hodges 1.25 3.00
21 Conner Henry 1.00 2.50
25 Paul Pressey 1.25 3.00
34 Terry Cummings 2.00 5.00
35 Jerry Reynolds .75 2.00
42 Larry Krystkowiak 1.25 3.00
43 Jack Sikma 2.00 5.00
44 Paul Mokeski .75 2.00
45 Randy Breuer .75 2.00
54 John Stroeder .75 2.00
NNO Del Harris CO 1.25 3.00
Frank Hamblen ACO
Mack Calvin ACO
Mike Dunleavy ACO
Jeff Snedeker TR

NNO Title Card 1.00 2.50
(discount offer detailed on back)

1979-80 Bucks Police/Spic'n'Span

This set contains 12 standard-size cards measuring featuring the Milwaukee Bucks. Card backs contain safety tips ("Game Plan Tip"). The cards are numbered on the back next to the facsimile autograph. The cards feature full-color fronts and black printing on a white card stock back. The set was sponsored by Spic'N'Span. The cards were available one per cleaning order or were available (originally) for sale as a set from the Wisconsin Sports Collectors Association for 2.25 postpaid. A coupon card was also available which was good for 1.00 discount on cleaning.
COMPLETE SET (13) 40.00 80.00
2 Junior Bridgeman 3.00 8.00
4 Sidney Moncrief 12.50 25.00
6 Pat Cummings 2.00 5.00
7 Dave Meyers 3.00 8.00
8 Marques Johnson 8.00 20.00
11 Lloyd Walton 1.50 4.00
21 Quinn Buckner 2.50 6.00
31 Richard Washington 2.50 6.00
32 Brian Winters 3.00 8.00
42 Harvey Catchings 2.00 5.00
54 Kent Benson 2.50 6.00
NNO Don Nelson CO and John Killilea ACO 5.00 10.00
NNO Coupon Card 10.00 25.00

1972-73 Bucks Ruler

This standard 12" ruler features a head shot of the players from the 1972-3 Milwaukee Bucks. Similar to the ruler, we have identified the rulers using the left to right method.
1 Kareem Abdul-Jabbar 5.00 10.00
Jon McGlocklin
Curtis Perry
Dick Cunningham
Russell Lee
Oscar Robertson
Mickey Davis
Lucius Allen
Terry Driscoll
Bob Dandridge
Bill Bates TR
Hubie Brown ACO
Larry Costello CO

1970-71 Bucks Team Issue

Each of these team-issued photos measure approximately 5" by 7" and feature black and white player portraits. The player's name is listed below the photo. The backs are blank. The photos are unnumbered and listed below alphabetically.
COMPLETE SET (10) 25.00 50.00
1 Lew Alcindor 12.50 25.00
2 Lucius Allen 2.00 5.00
3 Bob Boozer 1.50 4.00
4 Larry Costello CO 1.25 3.00
5 Dick Cunningham .75 2.00
6 Bob Dandridge 2.00 5.00
7 Bob Greacen .75 2.00
8 Jon McGlocklin 1.50 4.00
9 Oscar Robertson 10.00 20.00
10 Greg Smith .75 2.00

1971-72 Bucks Team Issue

Each of these team-issued photos measure approximately 5" by 6 3/4" and feature black and white player portraits. The player's name is listed below the photo. The backs are blank. The photos are unnumbered and listed below alphabetically.
COMPLETE SET (12) 25.00 50.00
1 Kareem Abdul-Jabbar 10.00 20.00
2 Lucius Allen 1.50 4.00
3 John Block .75 2.00
4 Larry Costello CO 1.00 2.50
5 Bob Dandridge 1.50 4.00
6 Toby Kimball .75 2.00
7 Jon McGlocklin 1.25 3.00
8 McCoy McLemore .75 2.00
9 Barry Nelson .75 2.00
10 Oscar Robertson 8.00 20.00
11 Greg Smith .75 2.00
12 Jeff Webb .75 2.00

1992-93 Bullets Crown/Topps

Subtitled "Great Bullets Past and Present," this set of nine standard-size player cards was a promotion only at Crown Gasoline Stations. The cards were distributed one strip for 29 cents with a fill-up of gas. The cards were issued in vertical strips of three players (1-3, 4-6, and 7-9) and a coupon/checklist card. Each strip contained two current Bullets players and one ex-Bullets star. The design was identical to the 1992-93 Topps regular series. The distinctive characteristic of the cards is that they are numbered with a "WB" prefix on their backs.
COMPLETE SET (12) 2.50 6.00
WB1 Tom Gugliotta .75 2.00
WB2 Rex Chapman .30 .75
WB3 Phil Chenier .20 .50
WB4 Pervis Ellison .20 .50
WB5 Brent Price .20 .50
WB6 Wes Unseld .60 1.50
WB7 Michael Adams .20 .50
WB8 Harvey Grant .20 .50
WB9 Elvin Hayes 1.00 2.50
NNO Crown Gasoline Coupon 1 .08 .25
NNO Crown Gasoline Coupon 2 .08 .25
NNO Crown Gasoline Coupon 3 .08 .25

1954-55 Bullets Gunther Beer

This 11-card set of Baltimore Bullets was sponsored by Gunther Beer. These black and white cards measure approximately 2 5/8" by 3 5/8". The fronts feature a black and white posed player photo. The question "What's the good word," is written across the card top. A Gunther Beer bottle cap and the player's name are superimposed on the player's chest. The back has the words "Follow the Bullets with Gunther Beer" at the top, with biographical information and career summary below. A radio and TV notice on the bottom round out the card back. The cards are unnumbered and are checklisted below in alphabetical order. The cards are frequently found personally autographed. The catalog designation for this set is H805.
COMPLETE SET (11) 2000.00 3500.00
1 Leo Barnhorst 150.00 300.00
2 Clair Bee CO 400.00 800.00
3 Bill Bolger 150.00 300.00
4 Ray Felix 250.00 500.00
5 Jim Fritsche 150.00 300.00
6 Rollen Hans 150.00 300.00
7 Paul Hoffman 200.00 400.00
8 Bob Houbregs 250.00 500.00
9 Ed Miller 150.00 300.00
10 Al Roges 150.00 300.00
11 Harold Uplinger 150.00 300.00

1995-96 Bullets Police

Presented by NationsBank, this 6-card standard-size "Kids 'N Cops" set was issued by the Washington Bullets in conjunction with the District of Columbia Metropolitan Police Department. Youths ages 6-16 who introduced themselves to a Metropolitan police officer received a player card. By completing the 6-card set and turning in the Hoops mascot card to any DC precinct, one received a coupon good for two tickets to a Bullets home game. The offer began on February 11 and ran through April 8. The fronts display glossy full-bleed color action photos. A red vertical bar at the upper left carries the set title and NationsBank emblem. On a white card face, the backs carry a circular headshot, biography, facsimile autograph, conflict resolution message, and sponsor logos. The set is designed so that the first letter of each conflict resolution message spells out POWER. The cards are unnumbered and checklisted below in alphabetical order.
COMPLETE SET (6) 4.00 10.00
1 Calbert Cheaney .40 1.00
2 Juwan Howard .75 2.00
3 Gheorghe Muresan .40 1.00
4 Robert Pack .40 1.00
5 Rasheed Wallace 1.50 4.00
6 Chris Webber 2.50 6.00
NNO Hoops Mascot Card .40 1.00

1973-74 Bullets Standups

These 12 player cards were issued by Johnny Pro Enterprises in an album, with six players per 11 1/4" by 14" sheet. Reportedly 6,000 albums were produced for distribution in a promotion at the Bullets' February 16th game at the Capital Centre. After perforation, the cards measure approximately 3 3/4" by 7 1/16". The cards are die cut, allowing the player pictures and bases to be pushed out and displayed as stand-ups. The fronts feature a color photo of the player, either dribbling or shooting the ball. The backs are blank. The cards are unnumbered and are checklisted below in alphabetical order. A card set, still intact in the album, would be valued at double the values listed below.
COMPLETE SET (12) 25.00 50.00
1 Phil Chenier 2.00 5.00
2 Archie Clark 2.00 5.00
3 Elvin Hayes 10.00 20.00
4 Tom Kozelko 1.25 3.00
5 Manny Leaks 1.25 3.00
6 Louie Nelson 1.25 3.00
7 Kevin Porter 1.50 4.00
8 Mike Riordan 1.50 4.00
9 Dave Stallworth 1.50 4.00
10 Wes Unseld 7.50 15.00
11 Nick Weatherspoon 1.25 3.00
12 Walt Wesley 1.25 3.00

1977-78 Bullets Standups

These 11 player cards were issued by Johnny Pro Enterprises in conjunction with Dart Drugs. The cards were issued in a four-page colorful album and were given out at the Bullets game on March 25, 1978. The cards are die cut, allowing the player pictures and bases to be pushed out and displayed as stand-ups. The backs are blank. The cards are unnumbered and are checklisted below in alphabetical order. A card set, still intact in the album, would be valued at double the values listed below.
COMPLETE SET (11) 15.00 30.00
1 Greg Ballard .75 2.00
2 Phil Chenier 1.50 4.00
3 Bob Dandridge 1.25 3.00
4 Kevin Grevey 1.25 3.00
5 Elvin Hayes 7.50 15.00
6 Tom Henderson .75 2.00
7 Mitch Kupchak 1.50 4.00
8 Joe Pace .75 2.00
9 Wes Unseld 5.00 10.00
10 Phil Walker .75 2.00
11 Larry Wright .75 2.00

1964-65 Bullets Team Issue

These blank-backed photos, which measure 8" by 11" and have blank backs, Since these photos are unnumbered, we have sequenced them in alphabetical order.
COMPLETE SET (7) 75.00 150.00
1 Gary Bradds 10.00 20.00
2 Bob Ferry 12.50 25.00
3 SI Green 10.00 20.00
4 Les Hunter 10.00 20.00
5 Wally Jones 12.50 25.00
6 Kevin Loughery 20.00 40.00
7 Don Ohl 10.00 20.00

1968-69 Bullets Team Issue

This set is complete at 12 pieces and is measured at 8 1/2 by 11 1/2. The items were printed on thin paper stock (newsprint type quality, but thicker than ordinary writing paper) in black and white and feature a facsimile signature on the front with a blank back.
COMPLETE SET (12) 150.00 300.00
1 Leroy Ellis 15.00 30.00
2 Bob Ferry 15.00 30.00
3 Gus Johnson 15.00 30.00
4 Kevin Loughery 15.00 30.00
5 Jack Matin 15.00 30.00
6 Earl Monroe 25.00 50.00
7 Barry Orms 15.00 30.00
8 Bob Quick 15.00 30.00
9 Ray Scott 15.00 30.00
10 Gene Shue 15.00 30.00
11 Wes Unseld 20.00 50.00
12 Tom Workman 15.00 30.00

1969-70 Bullets Team Issue

Each of these team-issued photos measure approximately 8" by 10" and feature black and white player portraits. The player's name is listed below the photo. Each photo also contains a facsimile autograph. The backs are blank. The photos are unnumbered and listed below alphabetically.
COMPLETE SET (12) 25.00 50.00
1 Mike Davis .75 2.00
2 Fred Carter 2.00 5.00
3 Leroy Ellis 1.25 3.00
4 Gus Johnson 2.00 5.00
5 Kevin Loughery 2.00 5.00
6 Ed Manning 1.25 3.00
7 Jack Marin .75 2.00
8 Earl Monroe 7.50 15.00
9 Bob Quick .75 2.00
10 Ray Scott .75 2.00
11 Gene Shue CO 2.00 5.00
12 Wes Unseld 6.00 12.00

1975-76 Bullets Team Issue

Each of these 11 team-issued photos measure approximately 5" by 7" and feature black and white player portraits. The backs are blank. The photos are unnumbered and listed below alphabetically.
COMPLETE SET (11) 20.00 35.00
1 Dave Bing 2.50 6.00
2 Bernie Bickerstaff ACO 2.00 5.00
3 Clem Haskins 1.25 3.00
4 Elvin Hayes 6.00 12.00
5 Jimmy Jones .75 2.00
6 K.C. Jones CO 1.25 3.00
7 Tom Kozelko .75 2.00
8 Mike Riordan 1.00 2.50
9 Leonard Robinson 1.25 3.00
10 Nick Weatherspoon .75 2.00
11 Wes Unseld 2.50 6.00

1976-77 Bullets Team Issue

Each of these team-issued photos measure approximately 5" by 7" and feature black and white player portraits. The player's name is listed below the photo. The backs are blank. The photos are unnumbered and listed below alphabetically.
COMPLETE SET (15) 20.00 40.00
1 Bernie Bickerstaff ACO .75 2.00
2 Dave Bing 1.50 4.00
3 Phil Chenier 1.25 3.00
4 Leonard Gray .60 1.50
5 Kevin Grevey 1.25 3.00
6 Elvin Hayes 5.00 10.00
7 Jimmy Jones .60 1.50
8 Mitch Kupchak 1.50 4.00
9 Dick Motta CO .75 2.00
10 Joe Pace .60 1.50
11 Mike Riordan .75 2.00
12 Len Robinson .75 2.00
13 Wes Unseld 2.00 5.00
14 Bob Weiss .75 2.00
15 Larry Wright .60 1.50

1977-78 Bullets Team Issue 5x7

This 5" x7" set was produced for the Washington Bullets during the 1977-78 season. The set features 12 black and white cards of the team's players and coaches.
COMPLETE SET (12) 20.00 40.00
1 Greg Ballard 1.25 3.00
2 Bernie Bickerstaff ACO 1.25 3.00
3 Phil Chenier 1.50 4.00
4 Bob Dandridge 2.00 5.00
5 Elvin Hayes 2.50 6.00
6 Tom Henderson 1.25 3.00
7 Mitch Kupchak 1.25 3.00
8 Dick Motta CO 1.50 4.00
9 Joe Pace 1.25 3.00
10 Wes Unseld 2.00 5.00
11 Phil Walker 1.25 3.00
12 Larry Wright 1.25 3.00

1977-78 Bullets Team Issue

These black and white glossy blank-backed photos, which measure 8" by 10" feature members of the World Championship Washington Bullets team. Since these photos are unnumbered, we have sequenced them in alphabetical order.
COMPLETE SET (13) 15.00 30.00
1 Greg Ballard .75 2.00
2 Dave Corzine .75 2.00
3 Bob Dandridge 1.00 2.50
4 Kevin Grevey 1.00 2.50
5 Elvin Hayes 2.50 6.00
6 Tom Henderson .75 2.00
7 Charles Johnson .75 2.00
8 Mitch Kupchak 1.00 2.50
9 Dick Motta CO 1.00 2.50
10 Roger Phegley .75 2.00
11 Wes Unseld 2.00 5.00
12 Larry Wright .75 2.00
13 Bernie Bickerstaff ACO 1.00 2.50
John Lally TR

1989-90 Bulls Dairy Council

Sponsored by the Dairy Council of Wisconsin Inc., this six-card set was issued to promote the consumption of milk by educating the public to its health benefits. The cards are printed on thin card stock and measure approximately 4" by 8". Each front has a color cartoon drawing of the player posed with a basketball. The size of each player's head is exaggerated, and a plackard overlaying a portion of the picture reads "Grow Like a Pro." At the bottom of each card are pictures of an apple, a glass of milk, a slice of bread, and a steak, representing the four major food groups. As indicated by the subtitles listed below, the backs extol the health benefits of drinking milk. The cards are unnumbered and checklisted alphabetically below.
COMPLETE SET (6) 75.00 150.00
1 Bill Cartwright (Milk is Good for Snacks) 2.50 6.00
2 Horace Grant (Milk is Good for Teeth) 3.00 8.00
3 Michael Jordan (Milk is Good for Breakfast) 50.00 100.00
4 Stacey King (Milk is Good for Skin) 1.50 4.00
5 John Paxson (Milk is Good for Bones) 3.00 7.00
6 Scottie Pippen (Milk is Good for Eyes) 12.50 30.00

1987-88 Bulls Entenmann's

The 1987-88 Entenmann's Chicago Bulls set contains 12 blank-backed cards measuring approximately 2 5/8" by 4". The complete set was given to each attending fan at a specific Bulls home game during the 1987-88 season. There are 11 player cards and one coach card in this set. The cards are unnumbered except for uniform number; they are ordered and numbered below by uniform number. The set features the first professional cards of Horace Grant and Scottie Pippen.
COMPLETE SET (12) 40.00 100.00
2 Rory Sparrow .75 2.00
3 Sedale Threatt 1.25 2.50
5 John Paxson 2.00 5.00
6 Brad Sellers .75 2.00
17 Mike Brown 1.50 4.00
23 Michael Jordan 30.00 60.00
31 Granville Waiters 1.25 3.00
33 Scottie Pippen 12.50 30.00
34 Charles Oakley 1.50 4.00
40 Dave Corzine .75 2.00
54 Horace Grant 4.00 10.00
NNO Doug Collins CO 3.00 8.00

1988-89 Bulls Entenmann's

The 1988-89 Entenmann's Chicago Bulls set contains 12 blank-backed player cards each measuring approximately 2 5/8" by 4". The complete set was given to each attending fan at a specific Bulls home game during the 1988-89 season. The cards are unnumbered except for uniform number; they are ordered and numbered below by uniform number.
COMPLETE SET (12) 40.00 80.00
2 Brad Sellers .75 2.00
5 John Paxson 1.50 4.00
11 Sam Vincent .75 2.00
14 Craig Hodges .75 2.00
15 Jack Haley .75 2.00
22 Charles Davis .75 2.00
23 Michael Jordan 20.00 40.00
24 Bill Cartwright 1.50 4.00
32 Will Perdue .75 2.00
33 Scottie Pippen 8.00 20.00
40 Dave Corzine .75 2.00
54 Horace Grant 2.00 5.00

1989-90 Bulls Equal

This 12-card set was sponsored by Equal Brand sweetener, and its company logo appears in the lower right corner of the card face. It has been reported that 10,000 sets were given away to fans attending the April 17th Chicago Bulls home game, although reportedly additional sets later made their way into the hobby. These oversized cards measure approximately 3" by 4 1/4". The fronts feature a borderless color action photo. The player's number, name, height, and position are given in the white stripe below the picture. Except for the sponsor's trademark notice, the backs are blank. The cards are unnumbered and checklisted below in alphabetical order. The set contains the first professional cards of B.J. Armstrong and Stacey King.
COMPLETE SET (12) 6.00 15.00
1 B.J. Armstrong .75 2.00
2 Bill Cartwright .60 1.50
3 Charles Davis .30 .75
4 Horace Grant 1.00 2.50
5 Craig Hodges .40 1.00
6 Michael Jordan 3.00 8.00
7 Stacey King .60 1.50
8 Ed Nealy .30 .75
9 John Paxson .75 2.00
10 Will Perdue .40 1.00
11 Scottie Pippen 1.50 4.00
12 Jeff Sanders .30 .75

1990-91 Bulls Equal/Star

This 16-card standard-size set was sponsored by Equal brand sweetener and celebrates the 25th anniversary of the Chicago Bulls franchise. The set was produced (reportedly 10,000 complete sets) by Star Company and was distributed at the April 9th Chicago Bulls home game, although additional sets later made their way into the hobby. The fronts feature color action player photos for current Bull players, and blue-tinted photos for past Bull players. The team logo and the words "The Silver Season" overlay the top of the picture. The card background is in silver, and the player's name appears in a gray diagonal stripe traversing the bottom of the picture. The sponsor logo appears in blue print at the card bottom. The back has brief biographical information and statistics, in black print on a pink background. There was also a glossy version reportedly reproduced in 1997 which is valued at two to three times the values listed below.
COMPLETE SET (16) 5.00 12.00
2 Tom Boerwinkle .20 .50
3 Bob Boozer .20 .50
4 Bill Cartwright .30 .75
5 Artis Gilmore .40 1.00
6 Horace Grant .40 1.00
7 Phil Jackson CO .40 1.00
8 Johnny Kerr .40 1.00
9 Bob Love .40 1.00
10 Dick Motta CO .20 .50
11 John Paxson .40 1.00
12 Scottie Pippen .75 2.00
13 Guy Rodgers .20 .50
14 Jerry Sloan .60 1.50
15 Norm Van Lier .20 .50
16 Chet Walker .40 1.00
1 Michael Jordan 1.50 4.00

1970-71 Bulls Hawthorne Milk

This six-card set was issued on the side panels of Hawthorne Milk cartons. The cards were intended to be cut from the carton and measure approximately 3 1/4" by 3 3/8" and feature on the front a posed head shot of the player within a circular picture frame. The second Weiss card measures 4 11/16" by 2 7/8". The backs are blank. The cards are unnumbered and are checklisted below in alphabetical order. The player photo is printed in blue but the outer border of the card is bright red.
COMPLETE SET (6) 1000.00 1800.00
1 Bob Love 250.00 450.00
2 Jerry Sloan 250.00 450.00
3 Jerry Sloan 250.00 450.00
4 Chet Walker 200.00 350.00
5 Bob Weiss 125.00 225.00
6 Bob Weiss 125.00 250.00

1997-98 Bulls Hoops Nabisco Jewel

25 Steve Kerr
26 Toni Kukoc
27 Luc Longley
29 Scottie Pippen
30 Dennis Rodman
219 Ron Harper
220 Michael Jordan
221 Bill Wennington

1985 Bulls Interlake

These glossy color action photos measure approximately 5" by 7" and are printed on thin card stock. The player photo image has rounded corners and a red border on a white card face. Player information appears beneath the picture, between two circles. The left circle has a Boy Scout emblem, while the right one has the words "An Interlake Youth Incentive Program." Supposedly the cards were given out in the fall of 1985 as an incentive to join the Boy Scouts. The Chicago Bulls sponsored a dinner for the Boy Scouts and Michael Jordan was the guest speaker. The backs are blank. The Jordan card has been heavily counterfeited so buyer beware when attempting to purchase one. The counterfeits are very glossy, made with very thin stock and are cut slightly smaller than the real cards.
COMPLETE SET (2) 75.00 150.00
1 Michael Jordan 100.00 175.00
2 Orlando Woolridge 4.00 10.00

1969-70 Bulls Pepsi

Sponsored by Pepsi, this 13-card set measures 8" by 10" and features members of the 1969-70 Chicago Bulls. The fronts have black-and-white player portraits with white borders. The player's name and height appear under the photo, along with team and sponsor logos, and the slogan "You've got a lot to live. Pepsi's got a lot to give." The backs are blank. The cards are unnumbered and checklisted below in alphabetical order.
COMPLETE SET (13) 75.00 150.00
1 Tom Boerwinkle 6.00 12.00
2 Shaler Halimon 2.50 6.00
3 Clem Haskins 5.00 10.00
4 Bob Kauffman 2.50 6.00
5 Bob Love 20.00 40.00
6 Ed Manning 3.00 8.00
7 Dick Motta CO 5.00 10.00
8 Loy Petersen 2.50 6.00
9 Jerry Sloan 15.00 40.00
10 Al Tucker 2.50 6.00
11 Chet Walker 12.50 25.00
12 Bob Weiss 5.00 12.00
13 Walt Wesley 3.00 8.00

1979-80 Bulls Police

This set contains 16 cards measuring approximately 2 5/8" by 4 1/8" featuring the Chicago Bulls. Cards in the set have either rounded or squred corners. Backs contain safety tips and are written in black ink with blue accent. The set was also sponsored by La Margarita Mexican Restaurants and Azteca Tortillas. The card backs are subtitled Kiwanis Cue Cards. Cards are unnumbered except for uniform number; they are checklisted below by uniform number. The cards of Coby Dietrick and (especially) Reggie Theus are considered more difficult to find and are marked as SP in the listings below.
COMPLETE SET (16) 40.00 70.00
1 Delmer Beshore .75 2.00
13 Dwight Jones .75 2.00
15 John Mengelt .75 2.00
17 Scott May 1.25 3.00
20 Dennis Awtrey 1.00 2.50
24 Reggie Theus SP 15.00 30.00
26 Coby Dietrick SP 7.50 15.00
27 Ollie Johnson .75 2.00
28 Sam Smith .75 2.00
34 David Greenwood 2.00 5.00
40 Ricky Sobers 1.25 3.00
53 Artis Gilmore 2.50 6.00
54 Mark Landsberger 1.25 3.00
NNO Jerry Sloan CO 2.50 6.00
NNO Phil Johnson ACO 1.25 3.00
NNO Luv-A-Bull .75 2.00

1976-77 Bulls Team Issue

These black and white blank-backed glossy photos, which measure 8" by 10", feature members of the 1976-77 Chicago Bulls. Since these photos are unnumbered, we have sequenced them in alphabetical order.
COMPLETE SET (17) 17.50 35.00
1 Ed Badger CO 1.00 2.50
2 Leon Benbow .75 2.00
3 Tom Boerwinkle 1.00 2.50
4 Eric Fernsten .75 2.00
5 Mickey Johnson .75 2.00
6 Tom Kropp .75 2.00
7 John Laskowski .75 2.00
8 Bob Love 1.25 3.00
9 Jack Marin 1.00 2.50
10 Scott May 1.00 2.50
11 Cliff Pondexter .75 2.00
12 Jerry Sloan 1.50 4.00
13 Willie Smith .75 2.00
14 Keith Starr .75 2.00
15 Norm Van Lier 1.00 2.50
16 Bob Wilson .75 2.00
17 Doug Atkinson TR .75 2.00
Gene Tormohlen ACO

1985-86 Bulls Team Issue

Each of these team-issued photos measure approximately 8" by 10" and feature black and white player portraits on two sheets. The player's name is listed below the photo. Both sheets contain eight individual player portraits. The backs are blank. The photos are unnumbered and listed below alphabetically.
COMPLETE SET (2) 20.00 50.00
1 Sidney Green 20.00 50.00
Michael Jordan
Kyle Macy
Billy McKinney
Charles Oakley
Jawann Oldham
Mike Smrek
Orlando Woolridge
2 Stan Albeck CO 4.00 10.00
Murray Arnold ACO
Gene Banks
Dave Corzine
George Gervin
Jerry Krause GM
Mike Thibault ACO
Tex Winter ACO

2008-09 Bulls Upper Deck

COMPLETE SET (14) 8.00 20.00
1 Luol Deng .25 .60
2 Ben Gordon .25 .60
3 Kirk Hinrich .25 .60
4 Drew Gooden .25 .60
5 Larry Hughes .25 .60
6 Andres Nocioni .20 .50
7 Thabo Sefolosha .20 .50
8 Joakim Noah .25 .60
9 Tyrus Thomas .20 .50
10 Aaron Gray .20 .50
11 Cedric Simmons .25 .60
12 Derrick Rose 6.00 15.00
13 Vinny Del Negro CO .20 .50
14 Michael Jordan 2.50 6.00

1977-78 Bulls White Hen Pantry

These high gloss player photos are printed on very thin paper and measure approximately 5" by 7". The fronts feature borderless color game action photos with a facsimile autograph; the backs are blank. The photos are unnumbered and we have checklisted them below in alphabetical order.
COMPLETE SET (7) 6.00 12.00
1 Tom Boerwinkle .75 2.00
2 Artis Gilmore 2.00 5.00
3 Wilbur Holland .60 1.50
4 Mickey Johnson .75 2.00
5 Scott May 1.00 2.50
6 John Mengelt .60 1.50
7 Norm Van Lier 1.00 2.50

1932 Briggs Chocolate

This set was issued by C.A. Briggs Chocolate company in 1932. The cards feature 31-different sports with each card including an artist's rendering of a sporting event. Although players are not named, it is thought that most were modeled after famous athletes of the time. The cardbacks include a written portion about the sport and an offer from Briggs for free baseball equipment for building a compete set of cards.
8 Basketball 125.00 250.00

1992 Canadian Kraft Olympic 3D

This set of 10 3D-action cards celebrate various Olympic sports. Through a mail-in offer, collectors could obtain three cards by sending in one UPC symbol and $3.00 for shipping and handling. The cards measure the standard size and consist of three thin sheets attached at the top. The first sheet provides the background. The second sheet is a color player cutout; a tab is inserted into sheet one, thus "locking" the player cutout into action. In a bilingual format, the third sheet discusses the history of the sport as an Olympic event. The front cover consists of a montage of Olympic athletes; the bilingual backs list medal winners for the sport from previous Olympic games. The cards are numbered on the front.

COMPLETE SET (10) 2.00 5.00
1 Basketball .40 1.00

1989 CAO Muflon Yugoslavian

This 73-card set was issued in 2-card packs in Yugoslavia. The cards measure at 2 1/2" by 3 3/16". Aside from the checklist below very little is known about this product. It is believed to have been produced by a company in Belgrade.

COMPLETE SET (73) 4000.00 5200.00
1 Magic Johnson 12.50 30.00
Pat Riley
2 Mitch Richmond 6.00 15.00
3 Mark Jackson 3.00 8.00
4 Moses Malone 3.00 8.00
5 Mark Price 2.00 5.00
6 Vern Fleming 1.25 3.00
7 Spud Webb 2.50 6.00
8 Rumeal Robinson 1.25 3.00
9 Lionel Simmons 1.25 3.00
10 John Stockton 15.00 40.00
11 Michael Adams 1.25 3.00
12 Fat Lever 1.25 3.00
13 Muggsy Bogues 3.00 8.00
14 Maurice Cheeks 2.50 6.00
15 Kenny Smith 25.00 60.00
Jordan in background
16 Larry Bird 15.00 40.00
James Worthy
17 Gerald Wilkins 1.25 3.00
18 Rolando Blackman 1.25 3.00
19 Arijan Komazec 1.25 3.00
20 Kevin Johnson 2.00 5.00
21 Zoran Radovic 1.25 3.00
22 Sarunas Marcilionis 2.50 6.00
23 Mario Primorac 1.25 3.00
24 Clyde Drexler 15.00 40.00
25 Jure Zdovc 1.25 3.00
26 Drazen Petrovic 15.00 40.00
27 Predrag Danilovic 1.50 4.00
28 Dale Ellis 1.50 4.00
29 John Battle 1.25 3.00
30 Nikos Galis 2.50 6.00
31 Antdanelo Riva 1.50 4.00
32 Toni Kukoc 6.00 15.00
33 Zoran Cutura 1.25 3.00
34 Kevin McHale 6.00 15.00
35 Valdemar Homicus 1.25 3.00
36 Charles Barkley 15.00 40.00
37 Detlef Schrempf 2.00 5.00
38 Larry Nance 2.50 6.00
39 Danny Manning 3.00 8.00
40 Mark Aguirre 8.00 20.00
Magic Johnson
41 Chris Mullin 6.00 15.00
Kevin McHale
42 Chuck Person 1.25 3.00
43 A.C. Green 3.00 8.00
Bill Laimbeer
44 Dominique Wilkins 10.00 25.00
45 Jack Sikma 1.25 3.00
46 James Worthy 15.00 40.00
Larry Bird
47 Otis Thorpe 1.25 3.00
48 Adrian Dantley 15.00 40.00
Larry Bird
49 Karl Malone 10.00 25.00
50 Alex English 2.50 6.00
51 Terry Cummings 1.25 3.00
52 Willie Anderson 1.25 3.00
53 Zarko Paspalj 2.00 5.00
54 Robert Parish 3.00 8.00
55 Patrick Ewing 6.00 15.00
56 Dusko Ivanovic 1.25 3.00
57 Pat Cummings 1.25 3.00
58 Bill Laimbeer 3.00 8.00
59 Craig Hodges 1.25 3.00
60 Moses Malone 3.00 8.00
61 Hakeem Olajuwon 10.00 25.00
Karl Malone
62 Julius Erving 20.00 50.00
63 Kareem Abdul-Jabbar 8.00 20.00
64 Manute Bol 3.00 8.00
65 Stefan Ostrowski 1.25 3.00
66 San Epifanio 1.25 3.00
67 Arvydas Sabonis 8.00 20.00
68 Dino Radja 2.50 6.00
69 Isiah Thomas 6.00 15.00
70 Vlade Divac 4.00 10.00
72 Michael Jordan 3000.00 5000.00
73 Magic Johnson 20.00 50.00

1975 Carvel Discs

The 1975 Carvel NBA Basketball Discs set contains 36 unnumbered discs measuring approximately 3 3/8" in diameter. The blank-backed discs have various (five different colors) color borders, and feature black and white drawings of the players with fascimile signatures. There are also white (colorless) border variations, which can be found with or without Carvel at the top, which are very difficult to find. A poster was produced which provided circular places for each of the 36 discs to be taped or glued onto. Since the discs are unnumbered, they are checklisted below in alphabetical order. The set is dated by the fact that 1974-75 was Happy Hairston and Chet Walker's last active year in the NBA.

COMPLETE SET (36) 40.00 80.00
1 Kareem Abdul-Jabbar 4.00 10.00
2 Nate Archibald 2.00 5.00
3 Bill Bradley 2.00 5.00
4 Don Chaney 1.25 3.00
5 Dave Cowens 2.00 5.00
6 Bob Dandridge 1.00 2.50
7 Ernie DiGregorio 1.25 3.00
8 Walt Frazier 2.00 5.00
9 John Gianelli .75 2.00
10 Gail Goodrich 2.00 5.00
11 Happy Hairston 1.25 3.00
12 John Havlicek 3.00 8.00
13 Spencer Haywood 1.25 3.00
14 Garfield Heard .75 2.00
15 Lou Hudson 1.00 2.50
16 Phil Jackson 2.00 5.00
17 Sam Lacey .75 2.00
18 Bob Lanier 2.00 5.00
19 Bob Love 1.50 4.00
20 Bob McAdoo 2.00 5.00
21 Jim McMillian 1.25 3.00
22 Dean Meminger .75 2.00
23 Earl Monroe 2.00 5.00
24 Don Nelson 1.50 4.00
25 Jim Price .75 2.00
26 Clifford Ray .75 2.00
27 Charlie Scott 1.00 2.50
28 Paul Silas 1.50 4.00
29 Jerry Sloan 2.00 5.00
30 Randy Smith 1.25 3.00
31 Dick Van Arsdale 1.25 3.00
32 Norm Van Lier 1.25 3.00
33 Chet Walker 1.25 3.00
34 Paul Westphal 2.00 5.00
35 Jo Jo White 1.25 3.00
36 Hawthorne Wingo .75 2.00

1993-94 Cavaliers Nickles Bread

One card from this 13-card set was inserted in every loaf of Nickles brand bread. The bakery does an annual card promotion in the greater Cleveland area.

COMPLETE SET (13) 6.00 15.00
1 John Battle .40 1.00
2 Terrell Brandon .75 2.00
3 Brad Daugherty .40 1.00
4 Danny Ferry .40 1.00
5 Jay Guidinger .40 1.00
6 Tyrone Hill .40 1.00
7 Gerald Madkins .40 1.00
8 Chris Mills .60 1.50
9 Larry Nance .75 2.00
10 Bobby Phills .40 1.00
11 Mark Price .75 2.00
12 Gerald Wilkins .50 1.25
13 John Williams .40 1.00

1973-74 Cavaliers Postcards

This eight-card set was released during the 1973-74 season, and features many of the Cleveland Cavalier players from that year. Please note that these postcards measure 3 1/2"x5 1/4".

COMPLETE SET (8) 20.00 40.00
1 Lenny Wilkens CO 2.50 6.00
2 Austin Carr 1.50 4.00
3 Barry Clemens 1.25 3.00
4 Bobby Smith 1.25 3.00
5 Jim Brewer 1.25 3.00
6 Dwight Davis 1.25 3.00
7 Steve Patterson 1.25 3.00
8 Fred Foster 1.25 3.00
9 Jim Cleamons 1.50 4.00
10 Luke Witte 1.25 3.00
11 Bob Rule 1.25 3.00
12 John Warren 1.25 3.00

1976 Cavaliers Royal Crown Cola Cans

The 1976 Royal Crown Cola Cleveland Cavaliers Cans team issue contains at least seven standard-sized cans. Each can contains a facsimile autograph, except one - Dick Snyder has cans with and without an autograph. There is no number given, thus the set is listed below alphabetically. Cans opened from the bottom command up to a 25 percent premium over the prices below. The checklist below is thought to be incomplete--any additional input on this series would be appreciated.

COMPLETE SET (7) 20.00 40.00
1 Jim Brewer 2.00 5.00
2 Austin Carr 3.00 8.00
3 Bill Fitch CO 2.50 6.00
4 Jim Chones 2.50 6.00
5 Jim Cleamons 2.50 6.00
6 Dick Snyder 2.00 5.00
with autograph
6A Dick Snyder 2.00 5.00
without autograph
7 Bingo Smith 2.50 6.00

1980-81 Cavaliers Team Issue

This 5 1/2"x 8 1/2" set was produced for the Cleveland Cavaliers during the 1980-81 season. The set features 10 black and white cards of the team's players.

COMPLETE SET (10) 15.00 30.00
1 Kenny Carr 1.25 3.00
2 Mack Calvin 1.50 4.00
3 Mike Bratz 1.25 3.00
4 Geoff Huston 1.25 3.00
5 Walter Jordan 1.25 3.00
6 Bill Laimbeer 2.50 6.00
7 Don Ford 1.25 3.00
8 Mike Mitchell 1.50 4.00
9 Roger Phegley 1.25 3.00
10 Randy Smith 1.50 4.00

2008-09 Cavaliers Upper Deck

COMPLETE SET (14) 2.50 6.00
1 LeBron James 1.25 3.00
2 Delonte West .20 .50
3 Daniel Gibson .25 .60
4 Zydrunas Ilgauskas .25 .60
5 Anderson Varejao .20 .50
6 Ben Wallace .25 .60
7 Aleksandar Pavlovic .20 .50
8 Lorenzen Wright .20 .50
9 Wally Szczerbiak .25 .60
10 Eric Snow .20 .50
11 Mo Williams .25 .60
12 J.J. Hickson .25 .60
13 Mike Brown CO .20 .50
14 Mark Price .50 1.25

2008-09 Cavaliers Upper Deck LeBron James

COMPLETE SET (10) 8.00 20.00
COMMON CARD 1.00 2.50

2007 Cavaliers Upper Deck Rite Aid

COMPLETE SET (16) 5.00 12.00
1 Shannon Brown .60 1.50
2 Daniel Gibson .40 1.00
3 Drew Gooden .40 1.00
4 Larry Hughes .60 1.50
5 Zydrunas Ilgauskas .60 1.50
6 LeBron James 3.00 8.00
7 Damon Jones .40 1.00
8 Dwayne Jones .40 1.00
9 Donyell Marshall .40 1.00
10 Ira Newble .40 1.00
11 Aleksandar Pavlovic .40 1.00
12 Scot Pollard .40 1.00
13 Eric Snow .40 1.00
14 Anderson Varejao .60 1.50
15 David Wesley .40 1.00
16 Mike Brown .40 1.00

2008 Americana Celebrity Cuts

COMPLETE SET (100) 125.00 200.00
STATED PRINT RUN 499 SERIAL #'d SETS
*CENTURY SILVER/50: .6X TO 1.5X BASE
*CENTURY GOLD/25: .75X TO 2X BASE
UNPRICED CENTURY PLATINUM #'d TO 1
47 John Wooden 1.50 4.00
48 Larry Bird 2.00 5.00
92 Walt Frazier 1.50 4.00

2008 Americana Celebrity Cuts Century Material

RANDOM INSERTS IN PACKS
PRINT RUNS B/WN 5-100 COPIES
NO PRICING ON QTY OF 5
48 Larry Bird/100 6.00 15.00
92 Walt Frazier/100 4.00 10.00

2008 Americana Celebrity Cuts Century Material Prime

RANDOM INSERTS IN PACKS
PRINT RUNS B/WN 1-50 COPIES PER
NO PRICING ON QTY OF 12 OR LESS
48 Larry Bird/50 10.00 25.00
92 Walt Frazier/50 6.00 15.00

2008 Americana Celebrity Cuts Century Material Combo

RANDOM INSERTS IN PACKS
PRINT RUNS B/WN 5-50 COPIES PER
NO PRICING ON QTY OF 10 OR LESS
48 Larry Bird/50 10.00 25.00
92 Walt Frazier/50 6.00 15.00

2008 Americana Celebrity Cuts Century Signature Gold

RANDOM INSERTS IN PACKS
PRINT RUNS B/WN 1-200 COPIES PER
NO PRICING ON QTY OF 14 OR LESS
47 John Wooden/25 75.00 150.00
48 Larry Bird/50 40.00 70.00
92 Walt Frazier/50 10.00 25.00

2008 Americana Celebrity Cuts Century Signature Material

RANDOM INSERTS IN PACKS
PRINT RUNS B/WN 1-50 COPIES PER
NO PRICING ON QTY OF 14 OR LESS
48 Larry Bird/50 50.00 80.00
92 Walt Frazier/50 10.00 25.00

2008 Americana Celebrity Cuts Century Signature Material Prime

48 Larry Bird/50 60.00 100.00

1977-78 Celtics Citgo

Sponsored by Citgo Gas, the 17 photos in this set each measure approximately 8 1/2" by 11". The fronts feature full bleed glossy color action pictures. Most card backs carry player information for the featured player including biography, career summary, amd complete statistics. The back of card number 5 exhibits a chart titled "Celtics vs. NBA Opponents Over The Years" (1946-1977), while the back of card number 6 lists the Celtics' roster for the 1977-78 season. Only the Kermit Washington photo is a non-action, portrait shot, suggesting that he may have been added to the set later. The photos are unnumbered and ordered below in alphabetical order.

COMPLETE SET (17) 40.00 75.00
1 Dave Bing 2.50 6.00
2 Tommy Boswell 1.25 3.00
3 Don Chaney 2.00 5.00
4 Dave Cowens 3.00 8.00
5 Dave Cowens 3.00 8.00
6 Dave Cowens 3.00 8.00
7 John Havlicek 7.50 15.00
8 Sam Jones 2.50 6.00
9 Cedric Maxwell 1.50 4.00
10 Curtis Rowe 2.00 5.00
11 Tom Sanders CO 1.50 4.00
12 Fred Saunders 1.25 3.00
13 Kevin Stacom 1.25 3.00
14 Kermit Washington 1.25 3.00
15 Jo Jo White 2.50 6.00
16 Sidney Wicks 2.50 6.00
17 Ballboy Contest 1.25 3.00

1988-89 Celtics Citgo

Sponsored by Citgo Gas, these approximately 10 1/2" by 12 1/2" color illustrations are bordered in white and printed on thin glossy paper. The players are pictured in a color action pose in Boston Garden. Bird is pictured shooting his patented outside jumper; an unidentified Golden State Warrior (uniform number 34) extends his right arm in a vain effort to block the shot. The wider bottom white border carries a facsimile autograph and a brief player profile. The pictures are unnumbered and blank on the back.

COMPLETE SET (7) 20.00 50.00
1 Danny Ainge 3.00 8.00
2 Larry Bird 8.00 20.00
3 Dennis Johnson 3.00 8.00
4 Reggie Lewis 2.00 5.00
5 Kevin McHale 4.00 10.00
6 Robert Parish 2.50 6.00
7 Team Picture 3.00 8.00

1989-90 Celtics Citgo Posters

Sponsored by Citgo Petroleum Corp. of Tulsa, Oklahoma, this set of posters was produced with each player's permission and the cooperation of the Boston Celtics and The Sports Museum of New England. Each poster measures 17" by 11" and is printed on glossy paper stock. The left two-thirds of the poster consists of a color painting of an action scene by artist Mike Wimmer. On the right third are a portrait (in blank ink), biographical information, and career summary. The Citgo emblem in the lower right corner rounds out the front. The backs are blank. The posters are unnumbered and checklisted below alphabetically according to player's last name.

COMPLETE SET (6) 10.00 25.00
1 Bob Cousy 3.00 8.00
1 Dave Cowens 2.50 6.00
2 Tom Heinsohn 2.50 6.00
3 Sam Jones 2.50 6.00
4 Tom Sanders 1.25 3.00
5 Paul Silas 1.50 4.00

1986 Celtics Cups

Issued by Nestle, this set is comprised of four white plastic souvenir cups. Along the top rim of the cups, in red letters, the words "Sharpshooters" appear, and below are color portraits of Celtics players. Each cup features two players, the Celtics logo, the years the Celtics won championships, and the Nestle Crunch and Chunky logos.

COMPLETE SET (4) 8.00 20.00
1 Dennis Johnson 1.25 3.00
Greg Kite
2 Bill Walton 2.00 5.00
Jerry Sichting
3 Larry Bird 4.00 10.00
Danny Ainge
4 Robert Parish 2.50 6.00
Kevin McHale

1974-75 Celtics Linnett

These charcoal drawings are skillfully executed facial portraits of Boston Celtic players. They were drawn by noted sports artist Charles Linnett and measure approximately 8 1/2" by 11". A facsimile autograph of the player is written across the lower right, the Celtics' logo appears in the lower left, and the backs are blank. The drawings are unnumbered and checklisted below in alphabetical order. The set is very similar to the Linnett Milwaukee Bucks set of the same year. A 1969 NBA Properties copyright is printed in the lower left corner of the card and a 1973 NBAPA copyright is printed on the wrapper of the two-card package in which they were sold. The set is dated by the fact that Steve Downing and Phil Hankinson's first year with the Boston Celtics was 1973-74.

COMPLETE SET (9) 30.00 60.00
1 Don Chaney 2.50 6.00
2 Dave Cowens 7.50 15.00
3 Steve Downing 2.00 5.00
4 Henry Finkel 2.50 6.00
5 Phil Hankinson 2.00 5.00
6 John Havlicek 10.00 20.00
7 Don Nelson 5.00 10.00
8 Paul Silas 3.00 8.00
9 Jo Jo White 3.00 8.00

1975-76 Celtics Linnett Green Borders

Packaged in cello wrap, these three cards measure approximately 4" by 6" and feature artwork by Charles Linnett. The fronts feature a charcoal portrait of the player surrounded by a green border displaying players from various sports. The team logo, player's name, and facsimile autograph appear across the lower portion of the front. The backs are blank. The cards are unnumbered and checklisted below in alphabetical order.

COMPLETE SET (3) 8.00 20.00
1 Dave Cowens 3.00 8.00
2 John Havlicek 4.00 10.00
3 Jo Jo White 2.50 6.00

1956-57 Celtics Photos

This ten card oversized blank backed set was released during the 1956-57 season, and features such Celtics stars as Bob Cousy and Bill Sharman. Please note that these black and white cards measure 6.5"x 8".

COMPLETE SET (10) 1000.00 2000.00
1 Bob Cousy 250.00 500.00
2 Tom Heinsohn 200.00 400.00
3 Dick Hemric 75.00 150.00
4 Jim Loscutoff 100.00 200.00
5 Jack Nichols 75.00 150.00
6 Togo Palazzi 75.00 150.00
7 Andy Phillip 100.00 200.00
8 Arnie Risen 100.00 200.00
9 Bill Sharman 150.00 300.00
10 Lou Tsioropoulos 75.00 150.00

1976-77 Celtics Team Issue

These black and white blank-backed photos, which measure 8" by 10" feature members of the 1976-77 Boston Celtics. Since these photos are unnumbered, we have sequenced them in alphabetical order.

COMPLETE SET (12) 15.00 30.00
1 Jerome Anderson .75 2.00
2 Jim Ard .75 2.00
3 Tom Boswell .75 2.00
4 Norm Cook .75 2.00
5 John Havlicek 3.00 8.00
6 Steve Kuberski .75 2.00
7 Glenn McDonald .75 2.00
8 Curtis Rowe 1.00 2.50
9 Fred Saunders .75 2.00
10 Paul Silas 1.50 4.00
11 Kevin Stacom .75 2.00
12 Sidney Wicks 1.00 2.50

2001-02 Celtics Topps

Released by Topps in conjunction with Dunkin' Donuts, this 10-card set is horizontally designed with the Celtics logo in the background and was given away at a game during the 2001-02 season.

COMPLETE SET (10) 2.50 6.00
BC1 Antoine Walker .50 1.25
BC2 Paul Pierce .60 1.50
BC3 Kenny Anderson .50 1.25
BC4 Bryant Stith .40 1.00
BC5 Vitaly Potapenko .40 1.00
BC6 Eric Williams .40 1.00
BC7 Mark Blount .40 1.00
BC8 Tony Battie .40 1.00
BC9 Jerome Moiso .40 1.00
BC10 Randy Brown .40 1.00

1994-95 Celtics Tribute

This set of eight was issued to commemorate tributes in the Boston Garden at various dates during the 1994-95 season. Though each measures 8 1/2" by 11" and is printed on thin glossy paper, Bird and McHale are photos taken by photographer Steve Lipofsky, while the other players and coaches are portrayed by canvas paintings by Boston-based sports artist Paul Balmer. Each picture has a white border and a Boston Celtics "Honor the Tradition" logo superposed at the lower left corner. The backs give the date the player or coach was honored, a detailed career summary, and season-by-season statistics. Only the Bird photo was sponsored by CellularOne, and only McHale's photo includes an anti-smoking message sponsored by the Massachusetts Department of Public Health. The pictures are listed in alphabetical order.

COMPLETE SET (8) 8.00 20.00
1 Red Auerbach CO 2.00 5.00
2 Larry Bird 3.00 8.00
3 Bob Cousy 1.50 4.00
4 Dave Cowens 1.25 3.00
5 John Havlicek 1.50 4.00
6 Tom Heinsohn 1.25 3.00
7 K.C. Jones 1.25 3.00
8 Kevin McHale 1.50 4.00

2008-09 Celtics Upper Deck

COMPLETE SET (14) 2.50 6.00
1 Paul Pierce .30 .75
2 Kevin Garnett .50 1.25
3 Ray Allen .30 .75
4 Rajon Rondo .30 .75
5 Kendrick Perkins .20 .50
6 Leon Powe .20 .50
7 Glen Davis .20 .50
8 Sam Cassell .25 .60
9 Patrick O'Bryant .20 .50
10 Eddie House .20 .50
11 Gabe Pruitt .20 .50
12 J.R. Giddens .20 .50
13 Doc Rivers CO .30 .75
14 Larry Bird .75 2.00

1992-93 Center Court

This 53-card set was produced by Capital Cards and Forgotten Heroes for the Basketball Hall of Fame. The production run was limited to 10,000 (each card of the set is numbered "X of 10,000" on the back). The cards are postcard size measuring approximately 3 1/2" by 5 1/2". Inside white borders, the fronts display glossy color player portraits by noted sports artist Ron Lewis. The horizontally oriented backs have the player's name and the year he was elected to the Hall of Fame. The cards are numbered on the back. A second series (27-52) was issued in 1993, which included a card (PD1) honoring George Mikan as the Player of the Decade of the 40's.

COMPLETE SET (53) 12.00 30.00
COMPLETE SERIES 1 (26) 6.00 15.00
COMPLETE SERIES 2 (27) 6.00 15.00
1 George Mikan 1.50 4.00
2 Bill Bradley .75 2.00
3 Bobby Wanzer .60 1.50
4 Ed Macauley .75 2.00
5 Harry Gallatin .75 2.00
6 William (Pop) Gates .75 2.00
7 Bobby Knight CO 1.25 3.00
8 Dolph Schayes .75 2.00
9 Bob Pettit 1.25 3.00
10 Walt Frazier .75 2.00
11 Elvin Hayes .75 2.00
12 Paul Arizin .75 2.00
13 Forrest (Phog) Allen CO .75 2.00
14 Oscar Robertson 1.25 3.00
15 John Wooden CO 1.25 3.00
16 Red Holzman CO 1.25 3.00
17 Jack Twyman .75 2.00
18 Dean Smith CO 1.25 3.00
19 John Nucatola .60 1.50
20 Elgin Baylor 1.00 2.50
21 Dave Bing .60 1.50
22 Lester Harrison .60 1.50
23 Joe Lapchick .60 1.50
24 Rick Barry .75 2.00
25 Lou Carnesecca CO .75 2.00
26 Checklist Card .75 2.00
27 Red Auerbach 1.25 3.00
28 Dave DeBusschere .75 2.00
29 Clarence Gaines .60 1.50
30 Tom Gola .75 2.00
31 Hal Greer .75 2.00
32 Lusia Harris-Stewart .75 2.00
33 K.C. Jones .75 2.00
34 Sam Jones 1.00 2.50
35 Robert Davies .60 1.50
36 Harry Litwack .60 1.50
37 Clyde Lovellette .75 2.00
38 Slater Martin .75 2.00
39 Al McGuire .75 2.00
40 Ray Meyer .75 2.00
41 Earl Monroe .75 2.00
42 Andy Phillip .75 2.00
43 Jim Pollard .75 2.00
44 Bill Sharman 1.25 3.00
45 J.Dallas Shirley .60 1.50
46 Nate Thurmond .75 2.00
47 Stan Watts .60 1.50
48 Bobby McDermott .60 1.50
49 Clair Bee .75 2.00
50 Willis Reed .75 2.00
51 Larry O'Brien .60 1.50
52 Checklist Card .60 1.50
PD1 George Mikan 1.50 4.00

2009-10 Certified

COMP.SET w/o SPs (150) 50.00 100.00
151-170 PRINT RUN 500 SER.#'d SETS
171-200 RC PRINT RUN 399 SER.#'d SETS
UNPRICED BLACK PRINT RUN ONE SET
UNPRICED EMERALD PRINT RUN 3 TO 5 SETS
1 Dirk Nowitzki 1.00 2.50
2 Jason Kidd .75 2.00
3 Jason Terry .60 1.50
4 J.J. Barea 1.00 2.50
5 Josh Howard .60 1.50
6 Shawn Marion .60 1.50
7 Luis Scola .60 1.50
8 Shane Battier .75 2.00
9 Tracy McGrady .75 2.00
10 Trevor Ariza .50 1.25
11 Yao Ming 1.00 2.50
12 Allen Iverson 1.00 2.50
13 Marc Gasol .75 2.00
14 O.J. Mayo .50 1.25
15 Rudy Gay .75 2.00
16 Zach Randolph .60 1.50
17 Chris Paul 1.00 2.50
18 David West .60 1.50
19 Emeka Okafor .60 1.50
20 James Posey .50 1.25
21 Peja Stojakovic .75 2.00
22 Manu Ginobili .75 2.00
23 Michael Finley .75 2.00
24 Richard Jefferson .60 1.50
25 Tim Duncan 1.25 3.00
26 Tony Parker .75 2.00
27 Carmelo Anthony 1.00 2.50
28 Chauncey Billups .75 2.00
29 Chris Andersen .60 1.50
30 J.R. Smith .60 1.50
31 Kenyon Martin .60 1.50
32 Nene .60 1.50
33 Al Jefferson .60 1.50
34 Kevin Love .75 2.00
35 Ramon Sessions .60 1.50
36 Ryan Gomes .50 1.25
37 Andre Miller .60 1.50
38 Brandon Roy .75 2.00
39 Greg Oden .60 1.50
40 LaMarcus Aldridge .75 2.00
41 Rudy Fernandez .50 1.25
42 Jeff Green .60 1.50
43 Kevin Durant 2.00 5.00
44 Nick Collison .60 1.50
45 Russell Westbrook 2.00 5.00
46 Andrei Kirilenko .60 1.50
47 Carlos Boozer .60 1.50
48 Deron Williams .60 1.50
49 Mehmet Okur .50 1.25
50 Paul Millsap .60 1.50
51 Andris Biedrins .50 1.25
52 Anthony Randolph .50 1.25
53 Corey Maggette .60 1.50
54 Devean George .50 1.25
55 Kelenna Azubuike .50 1.25
56 Stephen Jackson .60 1.50
57 Al Thornton .60 1.50
58 Baron Davis .60 1.50
59 Chris Kaman .60 1.50
60 Eric Gordon .60 1.50
61 Marcus Camby .50 1.25
62 Andrew Bynum .50 1.25
63 Derek Fisher .60 1.50
64 Kobe Bryant 3.00 8.00
65 Lamar Odom .60 1.50
66 Luke Walton .50 1.25
67 Pau Gasol .75 2.00
68 Ron Artest .75 2.00
69 Amare Stoudemire .60 1.50
70 Grant Hill 1.00 2.50
71 Jason Richardson .75 2.00
72 Leandro Barbosa .60 1.50
73 Steve Nash .75 2.00
74 Andres Nocioni .50 1.25
75 Francisco Garcia .50 1.25
76 Kevin Martin .60 1.50
77 Sean May .50 1.25
78 Kevin Garnett 1.25 3.00
79 Paul Pierce .75 2.00
80 Rajon Rondo .75 2.00
81 Rasheed Wallace .75 2.00
82 Ray Allen .75 2.00
83 Brook Lopez .60 1.50
84 Courtney Lee .60 1.50
85 Devin Harris .50 1.25
86 Yi Jianlian .60 1.50
87 Al Harrington .60 1.50
88 Chris Duhon .50 1.25
89 Danilo Gallinari .60 1.50
90 Darko Milicic .50 1.25
91 David Lee .50 1.25
92 Nate Robinson .50 1.25
93 Andre Iguodala .60 1.50
94 Elton Brand .75 2.00
95 Samuel Dalembert .50 1.25
96 Thaddeus Young .50 1.25
97 Andrea Bargnani .60 1.50
98 Chris Bosh .75 2.00
99 Hedo Turkoglu .60 1.50
100 Jarrett Jack .60 1.50
101 Jose Calderon .50 1.25
102 Derrick Rose 1.25 3.00
103 Joakim Noah .60 1.50
104 Luol Deng .60 1.50
105 Tyrus Thomas .50 1.25
106 Anderson Varejao .50 1.25
107 LeBron James 3.00 8.00
108 Mo Williams .60 1.50
109 Shaquille O'Neal 1.50 4.00
110 Zydrunas Ilgauskas .60 1.50
111 Ben Gordon .60 1.50
112 Ben Wallace .60 1.50
113 Charlie Villanueva .50 1.25
114 Richard Hamilton .60 1.50
115 Rodney Stuckey .50 1.25
116 Tayshaun Prince .60 1.50
117 Danny Granger .60 1.50
118 Jeff Foster .50 1.25
119 T.J. Ford .50 1.25
120 Troy Murphy .50 1.25
121 Andrew Bogut .60 1.50
122 Hakim Warrick .60 1.50
123 Luke Ridnour .60 1.50
124 Michael Redd .60 1.50
125 Al Horford .75 2.00
126 Jamal Crawford .75 2.00
127 Joe Johnson .60 1.50
128 Josh Smith .60 1.50
129 Mike Bibby .60 1.50
130 Boris Diaw .60 1.50
131 D.J. Augustin .50 1.25
132 Gerald Wallace .60 1.50
133 Raja Bell .60 1.50
134 Raymond Felton .60 1.50
135 Tyson Chandler .60 1.50
136 Dwyane Wade 1.25 3.00
137 Jermaine O'Neal .60 1.50
138 Mario Chalmers .60 1.50
139 Michael Beasley .50 1.25
140 Quentin Richardson .60 1.50
141 Udonis Haslem .50 1.25
142 Dwight Howard .60 1.50
143 J.J. Redick .75 2.00
144 Jameer Nelson .50 1.25
145 Mickael Pietrus .50 1.25
146 Rashard Lewis .60 1.50
147 Antawn Jamison .60 1.50
148 Caron Butler .60 1.50
149 Gilbert Arenas .60 1.50
150 Randy Foye .50 1.25
151 Isiah Thomas 1.50 4.00
152 Byron Scott 1.25 3.00
153 Frank Ramsey 1.50 4.00
154 Dikembe Mutombo 1.50 4.00
155 Alonzo Mourning 2.00 5.00
156 John Starks 1.25 3.00
157 Adrian Dantley 1.25 3.00
158 Bailey Howell 1.50 4.00
159 Al Attles 1.50 4.00
160 Walt Frazier 1.50 4.00
161 Tim Hardaway 1.50 4.00
162 Pat Riley 1.50 4.00
163 Paul Westphal 1.50 4.00
164 Bill Walton 1.50 4.00
165 Jack Sikma 1.25 3.00
166 Magic Johnson 4.00 10.00
167 Spud Webb 1.25 3.00
168 Wilt Chamberlain 3.00 8.00
169 Wes Unseld 1.50 4.00
170 James Worthy 2.00 5.00
171 Blake Griffin JSY AU RC 30.00 80.00
172 Hasheem Thabeet JSY AU RC 3.00 8.00
173 James Harden JSY AU RC 60.00 150.00
174 Tyreke Evans JSY AU RC 4.00 10.00
175 Jonny Flynn JSY AU RC 3.00 8.00
176 Stephen Curry JSY AU RC 200.00 400.00
177 Jordan Hill JSY AU RC 4.00 10.00
178 Brandon Jennings JSY AU RC 4.00 10.00
179 T.Williams JSY AU RC 3.00 8.00
180 Henderson JSY AU RC 4.00 10.00
181 Tyler Hansbrough JSY AU RC 4.00 10.00
182 Earl Clark JSY AU RC 4.00 10.00
183 Austin Daye JSY AU RC 3.00 8.00
184 James Johnson JSY AU RC 4.00 10.00
185 Jrue Holiday JSY AU RC 6.00 15.00
186 Ty Lawson JSY AU RC 5.00 12.00
187 Jeff Teague JSY AU RC 5.00 12.00
188 Eric Maynor JSY AU RC 3.00 8.00
189 Darren Collison JSY AU RC 5.00 12.00
190 Omri Casspi JSY AU RC 4.00 10.00
191 B.J. Mullens JSY AU RC 3.00 8.00
192 Rodrigue Beaubois JSY AU RC 3.00 8.00
193 Taj Gibson JSY AU RC 5.00 12.00
194 DeMarre Carroll JSY AU RC 4.00 10.00
195 Wayne Ellington JSY AU RC 5.00 12.00
196 Toney Douglas JSY AU RC 3.00 8.00
197 Jeff Pendergraph JSY AU RC 3.00 8.00
198 Jermaine Taylor JSY AU RC 3.00 8.00
199 DeJuan Blair JSY AU RC 4.00 10.00
200 Jodie Meeks JSY AU RC 5.00 12.00

2009-10 Certified Mirror Blue

*BLUE 1-150: 1X TO 2.5X BASE HI
*BLUE 151-170: .6X TO 1.5X BASE HI
BLUE 1-170 PRINT RUN 100 SER.#'d SETS
*BLUE RC 171-200: .6X TO 1.5X BASE HI
BLUE RC PRINT RUN 50 SER.#'d SETS

2009-10 Certified Mirror Blue Materials

STATED PRINT RUN 10 TO 50 SER.#'d SETS
SOME UNPRICED DUE TO SCARCITY
1 Dirk Nowitzki/50 5.00 12.00
2 Jason Kidd/50 4.00 10.00
3 Jason Terry/50 3.00 8.00
4 J.J. Barea/50 10.00 25.00
5 Josh Howard/50 3.00 8.00
6 Shawn Marion/50 3.00 8.00
7 Luis Scola/25 3.00 8.00
8 Shane Battier/50 4.00 10.00
9 Tracy McGrady/50 4.00 10.00
11 Yao Ming/25 5.00 12.00
14 O.J. Mayo/25 2.50 6.00
17 Chris Paul/50 5.00 12.00
18 David West/50 3.00 8.00
25 Tim Duncan/50 6.00 15.00
27 Carmelo Anthony/50 5.00 12.00
28 Chauncey Billups/25 4.00 10.00
29 Chris Andersen/25 3.00 8.00
31 Kenyon Martin/50 3.00 8.00
32 Nene/25 3.00 8.00
33 Al Jefferson/50 3.00 8.00
34 Kevin Love/50 4.00 10.00
36 Ryan Gomes/25 2.50 6.00
38 Brandon Roy/50 4.00 10.00
39 Greg Oden/50 3.00 8.00
40 LaMarcus Aldridge/25 4.00 10.00
46 Andrei Kirilenko/50 3.00 8.00
47 Carlos Boozer/50 3.00 8.00
48 Deron Williams/50 3.00 8.00
49 Mehmet Okur/50 2.50 6.00
50 Paul Millsap/25 3.00 8.00
59 Chris Kaman/50 3.00 8.00
62 Andrew Bynum/50 2.50 6.00
64 Kobe Bryant/50 15.00 30.00
67 Pau Gasol/50 4.00 10.00
74 Andres Nocioni/25 2.50 6.00
78 Kevin Garnett/25 6.00 15.00
79 Paul Pierce/25 4.00 10.00
82 Ray Allen/25 4.00 10.00
87 Al Harrington/25 3.00 8.00
89 Danilo Gallinari/50 3.00 8.00
91 David Lee/50 2.50 6.00
92 Nate Robinson/25 2.50 6.00
93 Andre Iguodala/50 3.00 8.00
94 Elton Brand/25 4.00 10.00
95 Samuel Dalembert/50 2.50 6.00
96 Thaddeus Young/50 2.50 6.00
97 Andrea Bargnani/50 3.00 8.00
98 Chris Bosh/50 4.00 10.00
101 Jose Calderon/50 2.50 6.00
102 Derrick Rose/50 6.00 15.00
107 LeBron James/25 15.00 40.00
108 Mo Williams/25 3.00 8.00
109 Shaquille O'Neal/50 8.00 20.00
110 Zydrunas Ilgauskas/50 3.00 8.00
111 Ben Gordon/50 3.00 8.00
113 Charlie Villanueva/50 2.50 6.00
114 Richard Hamilton/50 3.00 8.00
116 Tayshaun Prince/50 3.00 8.00
118 Jeff Foster/50 2.50 6.00
125 Al Horford/50 4.00 10.00
127 Joe Johnson/25 3.00 8.00
128 Josh Smith/25 3.00 8.00
130 Boris Diaw/25 3.00 8.00
131 D.J. Augustin/50 2.50 6.00
132 Gerald Wallace/50 3.00 8.00
134 Raymond Felton/25 3.00 8.00
136 Dwyane Wade/50 6.00 15.00
137 Jermaine O'Neal/25 3.00 8.00
139 Michael Beasley/25 2.50 6.00
141 Udonis Haslem/25 2.50 6.00
142 Dwight Howard/50 3.00 8.00
146 Rashard Lewis/25 3.00 8.00
147 Antawn Jamison/50 3.00 8.00
149 Gilbert Arenas/50 3.00 8.00
151 Isiah Thomas/50 4.00 10.00
154 Dikembe Mutombo/50 6.00 15.00
157 Adrian Dantley/50 3.00 8.00
166 Magic Johnson/50 10.00 25.00

2009-10 Certified Mirror Gold

*1-150: 2.5X TO 6X BASE HI
*151-170: 1.5X TO 4X BASE HI
*171-200 RC: 1X TO 2.5X BASE HI
STATED PRINT RUN 25 SER.#'d SETS
173 James Harden JSY AU 100.00 250.00
174 Tyreke Evans JSY AU 20.00 50.00
178 Brandon Jennings JSY AU 20.00 50.00
180 Gerald Henderson JSY AU 15.00 40.00
185 Jrue Holiday JSY AU 15.00 40.00

2009-10 Certified Mirror Gold Materials Prime

STATED PRINT RUN 5 TO 25 SER.#'d SETS
SOME UNPRICED DUE TO SCARCITY
1 Dirk Nowitzki/25 10.00 25.00
2 Jason Kidd/25 8.00 20.00
3 Jason Terry/25 6.00 15.00
4 J.J. Barea/25 12.00 30.00
6 Shawn Marion/25 6.00 15.00
8 Shane Battier/25 8.00 20.00
25 Tim Duncan/25 12.00 30.00
33 Al Jefferson/25 6.00 15.00
34 Kevin Love/25 8.00 20.00
46 Andrei Kirilenko/25 6.00 15.00
59 Chris Kaman/25 6.00 15.00
64 Kobe Bryant/25 25.00 60.00
87 Al Harrington/15 6.00 15.00
89 Danilo Gallinari/25 6.00 15.00
91 David Lee/25 5.00 12.00
93 Andre Iguodala/25 6.00 15.00
95 Samuel Dalembert/25 5.00 12.00
96 Thaddeus Young/25 5.00 12.00
109 Shaquille O'Neal/25 20.00 50.00
110 Zydrunas Ilgauskas/25 6.00 15.00
118 Jeff Foster/25 5.00 12.00
125 Al Horford/25 8.00 20.00
131 D.J. Augustin/25 5.00 12.00
151 Isiah Thomas/25 8.00 20.00
154 Dikembe Mutombo/25 10.00 25.00
157 Adrian Dantley/25 6.00 15.00
166 Magic Johnson/25 12.00 30.00

2009-10 Certified Mirror Gold Signatures

STATED PRINT RUN 10 TO 25 SER.#'d SETS
SOME UNPRICED DUE TO SCARCITY
5 Josh Howard/25 6.00 15.00
19 Emeka Okafor/25 6.00 15.00
26 Tony Parker/25 15.00 30.00
34 Kevin Love/25 25.00 60.00
36 Ryan Gomes/25 6.00 15.00
45 Russell Westbrook/25 50.00 120.00
47 Carlos Boozer/25 8.00 20.00
48 Deron Williams/25 8.00 20.00
59 Chris Kaman/25 6.00 15.00
60 Eric Gordon/25 10.00 25.00
64 Kobe Bryant/25 125.00 225.00
80 Rajon Rondo/25 20.00 50.00
82 Ray Allen/25 15.00 40.00
85 Devin Harris/25 10.00 25.00
91 David Lee/15 10.00 25.00
93 Andre Iguodala/25 8.00 20.00
94 Elton Brand/25 8.00 20.00
113 Charlie Villanueva/25 6.00 15.00
117 Danny Granger/25 8.00 20.00
137 Jermaine O'Neal/25 8.00 20.00
150 Randy Foye/25 6.00 15.00
152 Byron Scott/25 8.00 20.00
153 Frank Ramsey/25 6.00 15.00
157 Adrian Dantley/25 8.00 20.00
158 Bailey Howell/25 8.00 20.00
164 Bill Walton/25 12.00 30.00
170 James Worthy/25 20.00 40.00

2009-10 Certified Mirror Red

*1-170: .5X TO 1.25X BASE HI
PRINT RUN 250 SER.#'d SETS
*171-200 RC: .5X TO 1.25X BASE HI
171-200 RC PRINT RUN 100 SER.#'d SETS

2009-10 Certified Champions

COMPLETE SET (25) 20.00 40.00
PRINT RUN 500 SER.#'d SETS
UNPRICED BLACK PRINT RUN ONE SET
*BLUE: .6X TO 1.5X BASE HI
BLUE PRINT RUN 100 SER.#'d SETS
UNPRICED EMERALD PRINT RUN 5 SETS

*GOLD: 1.25X TO 3X BASE HI
GOLD PRINT RUN 25 SER.#'d SETS
*RED: .5X TO 1.25X BASE HI
RED PRINT RUN 250 SER.#'d SETS
1 Kobe Bryant 4.00 10.00
2 Bill Laimbeer .75 2.00
3 Bill Russell 1.50 4.00
4 Bill Walton 1.00 2.50
5 Dwyane Wade 1.50 4.00
6 Hakeem Olajuwon 1.25 3.00
7 Isiah Thomas 1.00 2.50
8 Jerry West 1.25 3.00
9 John Havlicek 1.00 2.50
10 Kevin Garnett 1.50 4.00
11 Magic Johnson 2.50 6.00
12 Oscar Robertson 1.00 2.50
13 Rick Barry .75 2.00
14 Shaquille O'Neal 2.00 5.00
15 Tim Duncan 1.50 4.00
16 Walt Frazier 1.00 2.50
17 Chauncey Billups 1.00 2.50
18 Tony Parker 1.00 2.50
19 Wes Unseld 1.00 2.50
20 Willis Reed 1.00 2.50
21 Kareem Abdul-Jabbar 1.50 4.00
22 Joe Dumars 1.00 2.50
23 Paul Pierce 1.00 2.50
24 Dolph Schayes 1.00 2.50
25 Arnie Risen 1.00 2.50

2009-10 Certified Champions Materials

STATED PRINT RUN 10 TO 99 SER.#'d SETS
SOME UNPRICED DUE TO SCARCITY
*PRIME: .6X TO 1.5X HI COLUMN
PRIME PRINT RUN ONE TO 25 SETS
1 Kobe Bryant/99 10.00 25.00
5 Dwyane Wade/99 5.00 12.00
6 Hakeem Olajuwon/99 5.00 12.00
7 Isiah Thomas/99 4.00 10.00
8 Jerry West/99 5.00 12.00
9 John Havlicek/50 6.00 15.00
10 Kevin Garnett/50 5.00 12.00
11 Magic Johnson/99 8.00 20.00
15 Tim Duncan/99 5.00 12.00
22 Joe Dumars/99 4.00 10.00
23 Paul Pierce/99 3.00 8.00

2009-10 Certified Champions Signatures

STATED PRINT RUN 10 TO 50 SER.#'d SETS
SOME UNPRICED DUE TO SCARCITY
1 Kobe Bryant/50 100.00 200.00
2 Bill Laimbeer/50 8.00 20.00
3 Bill Russell/50 60.00 120.00
4 Bill Walton/50 8.00 20.00
7 Isiah Thomas/50 8.00 20.00
8 Jerry West/35 25.00 50.00
9 John Havlicek/50 15.00 40.00
12 Oscar Robertson/50 30.00 80.00
13 Rick Barry/50 8.00 20.00
18 Tony Parker/50 15.00 30.00
19 Wes Unseld/25 8.00 20.00
20 Willis Reed/50 10.00 25.00
21 Kareem Abdul-Jabbar/25 40.00 100.00
24 Dolph Schayes/50 8.00 20.00
25 Arnie Risen/50 8.00 20.00

2009-10 Certified Fabric of the Game

STATED PRINT RUN 10 TO 250 SETS
*JSY NUMBER: .5X TO 1.25X BASE HI
JSY NUMBER PRINT RUN 10 TO 99 SETS
*JSY NUM.PRIME: .75X TO 2X BASE HI
JSY NUM.PRIME PRINT RUN ONE TO 25 SETS
*NBA DC: .6X TO 1.5X BASE HI
NBA DC STATED PRINT RUN 5 TO 50 SETS
*NBA DC PRIME: 1.5X TO 4X BASE HI
NBA DC PRIME PRINT RUN ONE TO 25 SETS
*PRIME: .75X TO 2X BASE HI
PRIME STATED PRINT RUN ONE TO 25 SETS
*TEAM DC: 1X TO 2.5X BASE HI
TEAM DC STATED PRINT RUN ONE TO 25 SETS
UNPRICED TEAM DC PRIME PRINT RUN 1 TO 10 SETS
1 Dirk Nowitzki/250 4.00 10.00
2 Jason Kidd/250 3.00 8.00
3 Jason Terry/250 2.50 6.00
4 J.J. Barea/250 5.00 12.00
5 Josh Howard/250 2.50 6.00
6 Shawn Marion/250 2.50 6.00
7 Luis Scola/250 2.50 6.00
8 Shane Battier/250 3.00 8.00
9 Tracy McGrady/250 3.00 8.00
11 Yao Ming/250 4.00 10.00
14 O.J. Mayo/100 2.00 5.00
17 Chris Paul/250 4.00 10.00
18 David West/250 2.50 6.00
21 Peja Stojakovic/100 3.00 8.00
25 Tim Duncan/250 5.00 12.00
27 Carmelo Anthony/250 4.00 10.00
28 Chauncey Billups/250 3.00 8.00
29 Chris Andersen/250 2.50 6.00
31 Kenyon Martin/250 2.50 6.00
32 Nene/250 2.50 6.00
33 Al Jefferson/250 2.50 6.00
34 Kevin Love/250 3.00 8.00
36 Ryan Gomes/250 2.00 5.00
38 Brandon Roy/50 3.00 8.00
39 Greg Oden/250 2.50 6.00
40 LaMarcus Aldridge/250 3.00 8.00
46 Andrei Kirilenko/250 2.50 6.00
47 Carlos Boozer/250 2.50 6.00
48 Deron Williams/250 2.50 6.00
49 Mehmet Okur/250 2.00 5.00
50 Paul Millsap/250 2.50 6.00
59 Chris Kaman/250 2.50 6.00
62 Andrew Bynum/100 2.00 5.00
64 Kobe Bryant/250 10.00 25.00
67 Pau Gasol/250 3.00 8.00
74 Andres Nocioni/50 2.00 5.00
78 Kevin Garnett/250 5.00 12.00
79 Paul Pierce/250 3.00 8.00
80 Rajon Rondo/100 3.00 8.00
82 Ray Allen/100 3.00 8.00
87 Al Harrington/25 2.50 6.00
89 Danilo Gallinari/250 2.50 6.00
91 David Lee/250 2.00 5.00
92 Nate Robinson/250 2.00 5.00
93 Andre Iguodala/250 2.50 6.00
94 Elton Brand/250 3.00 8.00
95 Samuel Dalembert/250 2.00 5.00
96 Thaddeus Young/250 2.00 5.00
97 Andrea Bargnani/250 2.50 6.00
98 Chris Bosh/250 3.00 8.00
101 Jose Calderon/250 2.00 5.00
102 Derrick Rose/100 5.00 12.00
107 LeBron James/250 8.00 20.00
108 Mo Williams/250 2.50 6.00
109 Shaquille O'Neal/250 8.00 20.00
110 Zydrunas Ilgauskas/250 2.50 6.00
111 Ben Gordon/250 2.50 6.00
113 Charlie Villanueva/250 2.00 5.00
114 Richard Hamilton/250 2.50 6.00
116 Tayshaun Prince/250 2.50 6.00
118 Jeff Foster/250 2.00 5.00
124 Michael Redd/100 2.50 6.00
125 Al Horford/250 3.00 8.00
127 Joe Johnson/100 2.50 6.00
128 Josh Smith/250 2.50 6.00
129 Mike Bibby/100 2.50 6.00
130 Boris Diaw/250 2.50 6.00
131 D.J. Augustin/250 2.00 5.00
132 Gerald Wallace/250 2.50 6.00
134 Raymond Felton/250 2.50 6.00
136 Dwyane Wade/250 5.00 12.00
137 Jermaine O'Neal/25 2.50 6.00
139 Michael Beasley/250 2.00 5.00
141 Udonis Haslem/250 2.00 5.00
142 Dwight Howard/250 2.50 6.00
146 Rashard Lewis/250 2.50 6.00
147 Antawn Jamison/100 2.50 6.00
149 Gilbert Arenas/250 2.50 6.00
151 Isiah Thomas/250 3.00 8.00
154 Dikembe Mutombo/250 5.00 12.00
157 Adrian Dantley/50 2.50 6.00
160 Walt Frazier/50 3.00 8.00
166 Magic Johnson/250 8.00 20.00
171 Blake Griffin/250 6.00 15.00
172 Hasheem Thabeet/250 1.25 3.00
173 James Harden/250 10.00 25.00
174 Tyreke Evans/250 1.50 4.00
175 Jonny Flynn/250 1.25 3.00
176 Stephen Curry/250 60.00 150.00
177 Jordan Hill/250 1.50 4.00
178 Brandon Jennings/250 2.00 5.00
179 Terrence Williams/250 1.25 3.00
180 Gerald Henderson/250 1.50 4.00
181 Tyler Hansbrough/250 1.50 4.00
182 Earl Clark/250 1.50 4.00
183 Austin Daye/250 1.25 3.00
184 James Johnson/250 1.50 4.00
185 Jrue Holiday/250 2.50 6.00
186 Ty Lawson/250 2.00 5.00
187 Jeff Teague/250 2.00 5.00
188 Eric Maynor/250 1.25 3.00
189 Darren Collison/250 2.00 5.00
190 Omri Casspi/250 1.50 4.00
191 B.J. Mullens/250 1.25 3.00
192 Rodrigue Beaubois/250 1.25 3.00
193 Taj Gibson/250 2.00 5.00
194 DeMarre Carroll/250 1.50 4.00
195 Wayne Ellington/250 2.00 5.00
196 Toney Douglas/250 1.25 3.00
197 Jeff Pendergraph/250 1.25 3.00
198 Jermaine Taylor/250 1.25 3.00
199 DeJuan Blair/250 1.50 4.00
200 Jodie Meeks/250 2.00 5.00

2009-10 Certified Fabric of the Game Jersey Number Signatures

STATED PRINT RUN ONE TO 25 SER.#'d SETS
SOME UNPRICED DUE TO SCARCITY
UNPRICED PRIME SIG. PRINT RUN ONE TO 10 SETS
2 Jason Kidd/25 20.00 50.00
5 Josh Howard/25 8.00 20.00
34 Kevin Love/25 20.00 50.00
36 Ryan Gomes/25 8.00 20.00
48 Deron Williams/25 15.00 40.00
59 Chris Kaman/25 8.00 20.00
64 Kobe Bryant/25 125.00 250.00
67 Pau Gasol/25 25.00 60.00
91 David Lee/25 8.00 20.00
93 Andre Iguodala/25 8.00 20.00
98 Chris Bosh/25 12.00 30.00
113 Charlie Villanueva/25 8.00 20.00
137 Jermaine O'Neal/25 8.00 20.00
139 Michael Beasley/25 10.00 25.00
151 Isiah Thomas/25 15.00 30.00
154 Dikembe Mutombo/25 25.00 60.00
157 Adrian Dantley/25 8.00 20.00
171 Blake Griffin/25 175.00 350.00
172 Hasheem Thabeet/25 5.00 12.00
173 James Harden/25 60.00 150.00
174 Tyreke Evans/25 25.00 60.00
175 Jonny Flynn/25 5.00 12.00
176 Stephen Curry/25 800.00 1000.00
177 Jordan Hill/25 6.00 15.00
178 Brandon Jennings/25 8.00 20.00
179 Terrence Williams/25 5.00 12.00
180 Gerald Henderson/25 6.00 15.00
181 Tyler Hansbrough/25 6.00 15.00
182 Earl Clark/25 6.00 15.00
183 Austin Daye/25 5.00 12.00
184 James Johnson/25 6.00 15.00
185 Jrue Holiday/25 10.00 25.00
186 Ty Lawson/25 8.00 20.00
187 Jeff Teague/25 8.00 20.00
188 Eric Maynor/25 5.00 12.00
189 Darren Collison/25 8.00 20.00
190 Omri Casspi/25 6.00 15.00
191 B.J. Mullens/25 5.00 12.00
192 Rodrigue Beaubois/25 5.00 12.00
193 Taj Gibson/25 8.00 20.00
194 DeMarre Carroll/25 6.00 15.00
195 Wayne Ellington/25 8.00 20.00
196 Toney Douglas/25 5.00 12.00
197 Jeff Pendergraph/25 5.00 12.00
198 Jermaine Taylor/25 5.00 12.00
199 DeJuan Blair/25 6.00 15.00
200 Jodie Meeks/25 8.00 20.00

2009-10 Certified Gold Team

COMPLETE SET (25) 10.00 25.00
PRINT RUN 500 SER.#'d SETS
UNPRICED BLACK PRINT RUN ONE SET
*BLUE: .6X TO 1.5X BASE HI
BLUE PRINT RUN 100 SER.#'d SETS
UNPRICED EMERALD PRINT RUN 5 SETS
*GOLD: 1.25X TO 3X BASE HI
GOLD PRINT RUN 25 SER.#'d SETS
*RED: .5X TO 1.25X BASE HI
RED PRINT RUN 250 SER.#'d SETS
1 Kobe Bryant 4.00 10.00
2 Dwyane Wade 1.50 4.00
3 Chris Paul 1.25 3.00
4 Dwight Howard .75 2.00
5 Danny Granger .75 2.00
6 Deron Williams .75 2.00
7 Carmelo Anthony 1.25 3.00
8 Kevin Durant 2.50 6.00
9 Paul Pierce 1.00 2.50
10 LeBron James 4.00 10.00

2009-10 Certified Gold Team Materials

STATED PRINT RUN 99 SER.#'d SETS
*PRIME: 1X TO 2.5X HI COLUMN
PRIME PRINT RUN ONE TO 25 SETS
1 Kobe Bryant 12.00 30.00
2 Dwyane Wade 5.00 12.00
3 Chris Paul 4.00 10.00
4 Dwight Howard 2.50 6.00
6 Deron Williams 2.50 6.00
7 Carmelo Anthony 4.00 10.00
9 Paul Pierce 3.00 8.00
10 LeBron James 10.00 25.00

2009-10 Certified Gold Team Signatures

STATED PRINT RUN 25 TO 50 SER.#'d SETS
1 Kobe Bryant/50 100.00 200.00
5 Danny Granger/25 8.00 20.00
6 Deron Williams/50 10.00 25.00

2009-10 Certified Imports

COMPLETE SET (15) 7.50 15.00
STATED PRINT RUN 500 SER.#'d SETS
UNPRICED BLACK PRINT RUN ONE SET
*BLUE: .6X TO 1.5X BASE HI
BLUE PRINT RUN 100 SER.#'d SETS
UNPRICED EMERALD PRINT RUN 5 SETS
*GOLD: 1.25X TO 3X BASE HI
GOLD PRINT RUN 25 SER.#'d SETS
*RED: .5X TO 1.25X BASE HI
RED PRINT RUN 250 SER.#'d SETS
1 Andrea Bargnani .75 2.00
2 Andrew Bogut .75 2.00
3 Boris Diaw .75 2.00
4 Dirk Nowitzki 1.25 3.00
5 Hasheem Thabeet .60 1.50
6 Hedo Turkoglu .75 2.00
7 Kelenna Azubuike .60 1.50
8 Manu Ginobili 1.00 2.50
9 Nene .75 2.00
10 Omri Casspi .75 2.00
11 Pau Gasol 1.00 2.50
12 Steve Nash 1.00 2.50
13 Yao Ming 1.25 3.00
14 Zydrunas Ilgauskas .75 2.00
15 Andrei Kirilenko .75 2.00

2009-10 Certified Imports Materials

STATED PRINT RUN 25 TO 99 SER.#'d SETS
*PRIME: .75X TO 2X BASE HI
PRIME PRINT RUN 5 TO 25 SER.#'d SETS
1 Andrea Bargnani/25 2.50 6.00
3 Boris Diaw/50 2.50 6.00
4 Dirk Nowitzki/99 4.00 10.00
5 Hasheem Thabeet/99 2.00 5.00
8 Manu Ginobili/25 3.00 8.00
9 Nene/99 2.50 6.00
10 Omri Casspi/99 2.50 6.00
11 Pau Gasol/99 3.00 8.00
13 Yao Ming/99 4.00 10.00
14 Zydrunas Ilgauskas/99 2.50 6.00
15 Andrei Kirilenko/99 2.50 6.00

2009-10 Certified Imports Signatures

STATED PRINT RUN 10 TO 50 SER.#'d SETS
SOME UNPRICED DUE TO SCARCITY
5 Hasheem Thabeet/50 8.00 20.00
10 Omri Casspi/50 8.00 20.00
11 Pau Gasol/25 25.00 50.00

2009-10 Certified Potential

COMPLETE SET (35)
STATED PRINT RUN 500 SER.#'d SETS
UNPRICED BLACK PRINT RUN ONE SET
*BLUE STARS: .75X TO 2X BASE HI
*BLUE RCs: 1X TO 2.5X BASE HI
BLUE PRINT RUN 50 SER.#'d SETS
UNPRICED EMERALD PRINT RUN 5 SETS
*RED STARS: .6X TO 1.5X BASE HI
*RED RCs: .75X TO 2X BASE HI
RED PRINT RUN 100 SER.#'d SETS
1 Anthony Morrow .60 1.50
2 Anthony Randolph .60 1.50
3 Brook Lopez .75 2.00
4 D.J. Augustin .60 1.50
5 Derrick Rose 1.50 4.00
6 Eric Gordon .75 2.00
7 Greg Oden .75 2.00
8 Jason Thompson .60 1.50
9 Kevin Love 1.00 2.50
10 Marc Gasol 1.00 2.50
11 Mario Chalmers .75 2.00
12 Michael Beasley .60 1.50
13 O.J. Mayo .60 1.50
14 Rudy Fernandez .60 1.50
15 Russell Westbrook 2.50 6.00
16 Brandon Rush .60 1.50
17 Courtney Lee .75 2.00
18 Luc Mbah a Moute .60 1.50
19 Ryan Anderson .75 2.00
20 Blake Griffin 4.00 10.00
21 Brandon Jennings 1.00 2.50
22 DeMar DeRozan 2.50 6.00
23 Earl Clark .75 2.00
24 Gerald Henderson .75 2.00
25 James Harden 5.00 12.00
26 Jordan Hill .75 2.00
27 Stephen Curry 25.00 60.00
28 Tyreke Evans .75 2.00
29 DeJuan Blair .75 2.00
30 Jeff Teague 1.00 2.50
31 Sam Young .60 1.50
32 Taj Gibson 1.00 2.50
33 Chase Budinger .75 2.00
34 Hasheem Thabeet .60 1.50
35 Jonny Flynn .60 1.50

2009-10 Certified Potential Gold

*GOLD STARS: 1.25X TO 3X BASE HI
*GOLD RCs: 1.5X TO 4X BASE HI
STATED PRINT RUN 25 SER.#'d SETS
20 Blake Griffin 75.00 150.00

2009-10 Certified Potential Materials

STATED PRINT RUN 100 TO 599 SETS
*PRIME STARS: .75X TO 2X BASE HI
*PRIME RCs: 1X TO 2.5X BASE HI
PRIME PRINT RUN 5 TO 25 SER.#'d SETS
4 D.J. Augustin/100 2.00 5.00
5 Derrick Rose/100 5.00 12.00
7 Greg Oden/100 2.50 6.00
9 Kevin Love/599 3.00 8.00
12 Michael Beasley/250 2.00 5.00
20 Blake Griffin/599 6.00 15.00
21 Brandon Jennings/599 2.00 5.00
22 DeMar DeRozan/599 5.00 12.00
23 Earl Clark/599 1.50 4.00
24 Gerald Henderson/599 1.50 4.00
25 James Harden/599 10.00 25.00
26 Jordan Hill/599 1.50 4.00
27 Stephen Curry/599 20.00 50.00
28 Tyreke Evans/599 1.50 4.00
29 DeJuan Blair/599 1.50 4.00
30 Jeff Teague/599 2.00 5.00
31 Sam Young/599 1.25 3.00
32 Taj Gibson/599 2.00 5.00
33 Chase Budinger/599 1.50 4.00
34 Hasheem Thabeet/599 1.25 3.00
35 Jonny Flynn/599 1.25 3.00

2009-10 Certified Potential Signatures

STATED PRINT RUN 25 SER.#'d SETS
6 Eric Gordon 8.00 20.00
9 Kevin Love 15.00 40.00
12 Michael Beasley 15.00 30.00
15 Russell Westbrook 30.00 80.00
20 Blake Griffin 40.00 100.00
21 Brandon Jennings 8.00 20.00
23 Earl Clark 6.00 15.00
24 Gerald Henderson 6.00 15.00
25 James Harden 60.00 150.00
26 Jordan Hill 6.00 15.00
27 Stephen Curry 800.00 1200.00
28 Tyreke Evans 6.00 15.00
29 DeJuan Blair 6.00 15.00
30 Jeff Teague 8.00 20.00
31 Sam Young 5.00 12.00
32 Taj Gibson 8.00 20.00
34 Hasheem Thabeet 5.00 12.00
35 Jonny Flynn 5.00 12.00

2009-10 Certified Shirt Off My Back Combos

STATED PRINT RUN 25 TO 99 SER.#'d SETS
1 R.Rondo/R.Allen/99 8.00 20.00
2 J.Kidd/J.Howard/99 5.00 12.00
3 S.Battier/McGrady/99 4.00 10.00
7 J.O'Neal/Beasley/49 4.00 10.00
8 A.Jefferson/Gomes/99 4.00 10.00
9 Iguodala/E.Brand/99 4.00 10.00
10 Bargnani/C.Bosh/99 5.00 12.00
12 McHale/R.Parish/99 8.00 20.00
13 A.Gilmore/Gervin/99 6.00 15.00
14 Drexler/S.Pippen/99 15.00 30.00
15 P.Ewing/Frazier/25 25.00 60.00

2009-10 Certified Shirt Off My Back Combos Prime

*PRIME: .75X TO 2X BASE HI
STATED PRINT RUN 10 TO 25 SER.#'d SETS
SOME UNPRICED DUE TO SCARCITY
UNPRICED SIG.PRIME PRINT RUN ONE SET
UNPRICED SIGNATURE PRINT RUN 5 SETS
14 C.Drexler/S.Pippen/25 30.00 80.00

2010 Certified National Convention

COMPLETE SET (4) 6.00 15.00
ET Evan Turner 1.00 2.50
KB Kobe Bryant 4.00 10.00
LB Larry Bird 3.00 8.00
RR Rajon Rondo 1.00 2.50

2010 Certified National Convention Blue

COMPLETE SET (5) 40.00 80.00
ANNOUNCED PRINT RUN 25 SETS
ET Evan Turner 3.00 8.00
JW John Wall 15.00 40.00
KB Kobe Bryant 8.00 20.00
LB Larry Bird 6.00 15.00
RR Rajon Rondo 2.00 5.00

2010 Certified National Convention Green

COMPLETE SET (5) 15.00 30.00
ANNOUNCED PRINT RUN 50 SETS
ET Evan Turner 1.25 3.00
JW John Wall 6.00 15.00
KB Kobe Bryant 5.00 12.00
LB Larry Bird 4.00 10.00
RR Rajon Rondo 1.25 3.00

1992 Champion HOF Inductees

This ten-card standard-size set honors the 1992 Basketball Hall of Fame Inductees. The fronts feature black-and-white photos on a white face. A wide gray stripe cuts across the side borders, carrying a row of white stars that edge each side of the picture. The set title appears in the top white border, while the player's name is printed in the white border beneath the picture. The horizontal backs present biography, statistics or coaching record, and a list of career highlights. The cards are numbered in the upper right corner.

COMPLETE SET (10) 25.00 60.00
1 Bob Lanier 5.00 12.00
2 Sergei Belov 3.00 8.00
3 Lou Carnesecca CO 3.00 8.00
4 Connie Hawkins 6.00 15.00
5 Al McGuire CO 3.00 8.00
6 Jack Ramsay CO 2.50 6.00
7 Nera White 2.00 5.00
8 Phil Woolpert CO 2.00 5.00
9 Lusia Harris-Stewart 2.50 6.00
10 Title card 3.00 8.00

1989-90 Chicle Metalicas Spanish Stickers

If you have more information on this checklist, please feel free to send it to us at basketballmag@beckett.com

JW James Worthy 20.00 40.00
LB Larry Bird IA
MA Magic Johnson IA
RH Ron Harper
DW1 Dominique Wilkins
DW2 Dominique Wilkins IA
MJ1 Michael Jordan 150.00 300.00
MJ2 Michael Jordan IA 125.00 250.00

1993 Chicle Metalicas Spanish Wrappers

BW Buck Williams with Michael Jordan 100.00 200.00
MJ Michael Jordan guarded by #20 100.00 200.00
MJP Michael Jordan Portrait 100.00 200.00

2006-07 Chronology

100 PRINT RUN 199 SER.#'d SETS
101-142 PRINT RUN 99 SER.#'d SETS
143-148 NOT ISSUED IN PACKS
149-184 PRINT RUN 99 SER.#'d SETS
185-226 PRINT RUN 40 SER.#'d SETS
227-246 PRINT RUN 50 SER.#'d SETS
247-276 PRINT RUN 250 SER.#'d SETS
1 Slick Watts 1.50 4.00
2 Louie Dampier 2.50 6.00
3 Al Attles 2.50 6.00
4 Alvin Robertson 2.50 6.00
5 Detlef Schrempf 2.50 6.00
6 Artis Gilmore 2.00 5.00
7 Austin Carr 2.50 6.00
8 Avery Johnson 2.00 5.00
9 B.J. Armstrong 2.50 6.00
10 Dave Bing 2.50 6.00
11 Bingo Smith 2.50 6.00
12 Bob Dandridge 1.50 4.00
13 Bill Bradley 3.00 8.00
14 Bobby Jones 2.00 5.00
15 Brad Daugherty 2.00 5.00
16 Byron Scott 2.00 5.00
17 Cazzie Russell 2.00 5.00
18 Cedric Maxwell 1.50 4.00
19 Charles Oakley 2.50 6.00
20 Chet Walker 2.00 5.00
21 Chuck Share 2.50 6.00
22 Dan Majerle 2.00 5.00
23 Danny Ainge 2.50 6.00
24 Danny Manning 2.00 5.00
25 Darrell Griffith 1.50 4.00
26 Darryl Dawkins 1.50 4.00
27 Dennis Johnson 2.00 5.00
28 Gheorghe Muresan 1.50 4.00
29 Dick Barnett 2.50 6.00
30 Dick Van Arsdale 2.00 5.00
31 Dominique Wilkins 3.00 8.00
32 Don Buse 2.50 6.00
33 Don Ohl 2.50 6.00
34 Ernie DiGregorio 2.50 6.00
35 Fred Brown 1.50 4.00
36 Julius Erving 4.00 10.00
37 George McGinnis 1.50 4.00
38 Calvin Natt 1.50 4.00
39 Rick Mahorn 1.50 4.00
40 Gus Williams 1.50 4.00
41 Jack Sikma 2.00 5.00
42 Jamaal Wilkes 2.50 6.00
43 James Edwards 2.50 6.00
44 Jerry Sloan 2.50 6.00
45 Jim Loscutoff 3.00 8.00
46 Jo Jo White 2.00 5.00
47 John Johnson 2.50 6.00
48 Johnny Kerr 3.00 8.00
49 Karl Malone 3.00 8.00
50 Junior Bridgeman 1.50 4.00
51 Kiki Vandeweghe 2.00 5.00
52 Kurt Rambis 1.50 4.00
53 Larry Nance 2.00 5.00
54 Lonnie Shelton 1.50 4.00
55 Lou Hudson 2.50 6.00
56 Kevin McHale 3.00 8.00
57 Tree Rollins 1.50 4.00
58 George Karl 3.00 8.00
59 Maurice Lucas 2.50 6.00
60 Mel Daniels 2.50 6.00
61 Michael Cooper 2.00 5.00
62 Mitch Richmond 2.50 6.00
63 Joe Dumars 2.50 6.00
64 Mike Dunleavy Sr. 2.50 6.00
65 Moses Malone 2.50 6.00
66 Muggsy Bogues 2.00 5.00
67 Norm Nixon 1.50 4.00
68 Norm Van Lier 3.00 8.00
69 Oscar Robertson 2.50 6.00
70 Paul Arizin 2.50 6.00
71 Paul Westphal 2.50 6.00
72 Phil Chenier 1.50 4.00
73 Phil Ford 2.50 6.00
74 John Starks 2.00 5.00
75 Richie Guerin 2.50 6.00
76 Rolando Blackman 2.00 5.00
77 World B. Free 2.00 5.00
78 Rudy Tomjanovich 2.00 5.00
79 Sam Perkins 1.50 4.00
80 Sean Elliott 2.50 6.00
81 Ricky Pierce 1.50 4.00
82 Sidney Moncrief 1.50 4.00
83 Horace Grant 2.50 6.00
84 Spencer Haywood 1.50 4.00
85 Steve Kerr 2.50 6.00
86 Terry Dischinger 2.50 6.00
87 Mitch Kupchak 2.50 6.00
88 Tom Chambers 2.00 5.00
89 Tom Sanders 2.50 6.00
90 Michael Ray Richardson 2.00 5.00
91 Terry Cummings 2.00 5.00
92 Spud Webb 2.00 5.00
93 Walter Davis 2.50 6.00
94 Wayman Tisdale 2.50 6.00
95 Wayne Embry 1.50 4.00
96 Wilt Chamberlain 5.00 12.00
97 Jeff Hornacek 2.00 5.00
98 Eddie Johnson 1.50 4.00
99 Xavier McDaniel 1.50 4.00
100 Zelmo Beaty 2.50 6.00
101 Allan Ray JSY AU RC 4.00 10.00
102 A.Bargnani JSY AU RC 15.00 40.00
103 Bobby Jones JSY AU RC 4.00 10.00
104 Brandon Roy JSY AU RC 15.00 40.00
105 Cedric Simmons JSY AU RC 4.00 10.00
106 Craig Smith JSY AU RC 5.00 12.00
107 Daniel Gibson JSY AU RC 5.00 12.00
108 Dee Brown JSY AU RC 4.00 10.00
109 D.Markota JSY AU RC 4.00 10.00
110 Hilton Armstrong JSY AU RC 4.00 10.00
111 James Augustine JSY AU RC 4.00 10.00
112 James White JSY AU RC 4.00 10.00
113 H.Adams JSY AU RC 4.00 10.00
114 J.Garbajosa JSY AU RC 12.00 30.00
115 Josh Boone JSY AU RC 4.00 10.00
116 Kyle Lowry JSY AU RC 8.00 20.00
117 L.Aldridge JSY AU RC 20.00 40.00
118 David Noel JSY AU RC 4.00 10.00
119 M.Williams JSY AU RC 4.00 10.00
120 Mardy Collins JSY AU RC 4.00 10.00
121 Maurice Ager JSY AU RC 4.00 10.00
122 P.J. Tucker JSY AU RC 5.00 12.00
123 P.O'Bryant JSY AU RC 4.00 10.00
124 Paul Davis JSY AU RC 4.00 10.00
125 Paul Millsap JSY AU RC 8.00 20.00
126 Q.Douby JSY AU RC 4.00 10.00
127 Rajon Rondo JSY AU RC 20.00 50.00
128 Randy Foye JSY AU RC 8.00 20.00
129 R.Balkman JSY AU RC 5.00 12.00
130 Y.Diawara JSY AU RC 4.00 10.00
131 Rodney Carney JSY AU RC 4.00 10.00
132 Ronnie Brewer JSY AU RC 6.00 15.00
133 Rudy Gay JSY AU RC 8.00 20.00
134 Saer Sene JSY AU RC 4.00 10.00
135 S.Rodriguez JSY AU RC 6.00 15.00
136 Sh.Brown JSY AU RC 4.00 10.00
137 Sha.Williams JSY AU RC 8.00 20.00
138 She.Williams JSY AU RC 5.00 12.00
139 Solomon Jones JSY AU RC 4.00 10.00
140 T.Sefolosha JSY AU RC 6.00 15.00
141 Tyrus Thomas JSY AU RC 10.00 25.00
142 Steve Novak JSY AU RC 5.00 12.00
149 Al Cervi JSY AU 10.00 25.00
150 Alex English JSY AU 10.00 25.00
151 Arnie Risen JSY AU 10.00 25.00
152 Bailey Howell JSY AU 10.00 25.00
153 Bill Sharman JSY AU 10.00 25.00
154 Don Nelson JSY AU 20.00 50.00
155 Bob Lanier JSY AU 15.00 30.00
156 Bob McAdoo JSY AU 25.00 50.00
157 Bob Pettit JSY AU 15.00 40.00
158 Bobby Wanzer JSY AU 10.00 25.00
159 Calvin Murphy JSY AU 10.00 25.00
160 Clyde Lovellette JSY AU 15.00 40.00
161 Bill Laimbeer JSY AU 25.00 50.00
162 Dave Cowens JSY AU 12.00 30.00
163 David Thompson JSY AU 10.00 25.00
164 Dick McGuire JSY AU 10.00 25.00
165 John Wooden JSY AU 125.00 250.00
166 Ed Macauley JSY AU 20.00 50.00
167 Elgin Baylor JSY AU 25.00 60.00
168 Elvin Hayes JSY AU 15.00 30.00
169 Frank Ramsey JSY AU 25.00 60.00
170 Gail Goodrich JSY AU 15.00 40.00
171 Hal Greer JSY AU 10.00 25.00
172 Adrian Dantley JSY AU 10.00 25.00
173 Jerry Lucas JSY AU 15.00 40.00
174 Reggie Theus JSY AU 10.00 25.00
175 Charlie Scott JSY AU 12.00 30.00
176 Nate Archibald JSY AU 12.00 30.00
177 Nate Thurmond JSY AU 10.00 25.00
178 Rick Barry JSY AU 10.00 25.00
179 Slater Martin JSY AU 25.00 50.00
180 Tom Heinsohn JSY AU 12.00 30.00
181 Vern Mikkelsen JSY AU 25.00 50.00
182 Walt Bellamy JSY AU 10.00 25.00
183 Walt Frazier JSY AU 20.00 50.00
184 Rod Hundley JSY AU 15.00 40.00
185 Ralph Sampson JSY AU 12.00 30.00
186 Bill Russell JSY AU 100.00 200.00
187 Julius Erving JSY AU 80.00 200.00
188 Larry Bird JSY AU 100.00 200.00
189 James Worthy JSY AU 50.00 120.00
190 K.Abdul-Jabbar JSY AU 50.00 100.00
191 Clyde Drexler JSY AU 40.00 80.00
192 Magic Johnson JSY AU 80.00 160.00
193 Wes Unseld JSY AU 12.00 30.00
194 John Stockton JSY AU 100.00 200.00
195 George Gervin JSY AU 15.00 40.00
197 David Robinson JSY AU 50.00 100.00
198 Sam Jones JSY AU 50.00 100.00
199 Bill Walton JSY AU 12.00 30.00
200 Earl Lloyd JSY AU 12.00 30.00
201 Mark Price JSY AU 40.00 80.00
202 John Havlicek JSY AU 50.00 100.00
203 Cliff Hagan JSY AU 12.00 30.00
204 Dolph Schayes JSY AU 12.00 30.00
205 Harry Gallatin JSY AU 12.00 30.00
206 Jerry West JSY AU 50.00 120.00
207 Connie Hawkins JSY AU 12.00 30.00
208 Lenny Wilkens JSY AU 12.00 30.00
209 Michael Jordan JSY AU 500.00 850.00
210 Hakeem Olajuwon JSY AU 50.00 100.00
211 Dan Issel JSY AU 12.00 30.00
212 Robert Parish JSY AU 20.00 50.00
213 Dennis Rodman JSY AU 75.00 150.00
214 Pat Riley JSY AU 30.00 80.00
215 Maurice Cheeks JSY AU 12.00 30.00
216 Bob Houbregs JSY AU 12.00 30.00
217 Tracy McGrady JSY AU 20.00 50.00
218 Yao Ming JSY AU 30.00 80.00
219 Paul Pierce JSY AU 25.00 60.00
220 Ben Gordon JSY AU 30.00 80.00
221 Kobe Bryant JSY AU 200.00 450.00
222 Steve Nash JSY AU 100.00 200.00
223 LeBron James JSY AU 200.00 450.00
224 Carmelo Anthony JSY AU 25.00 60.00
225 Jason Kidd JSY AU 40.00 100.00
226 Chris Paul JSY AU 30.00 80.00
227 Bill Fitch AU 10.00 25.00
228 Jack Ramsay AU 15.00 40.00
229 John Kundla AU 50.00 100.00
230 Dean Smith AU 25.00 60.00
231 Pat Riley AU 15.00 30.00
232 Jerry Sloan AU 15.00 30.00
233 Don Haskins AU 20.00 40.00
234 Rick Pitino AU 20.00 50.00
235 John Chaney AU 15.00 40.00
238 Lenny Wilkens AU 10.00 25.00
239 Chuck Daly AU 25.00 50.00
240 George Karl AU 20.00 40.00
241 John Wooden AU 100.00 200.00
242 Digger Phelps AU 10.00 25.00
243 Jud Heathcote AU 20.00 40.00
244 Dick Motta AU 10.00 25.00
245 Gene Shue AU 30.00 80.00
246 Jim Calhoun AU 12.00 30.00
247 Greg Oden XRC 8.00 20.00
248 Kevin Durant AU XRC 125.00 250.00
249 Al Horford XRC 8.00 20.00
250 Mike Conley Jr. XRC 8.00 20.00
251 Jeff Green XRC 6.00 15.00
252 Yi Jianlian XRC 10.00 25.00
253 Corey Brewer XRC 8.00 20.00
254 Brandan Wright XRC 6.00 15.00
255 Joakim Noah XRC 8.00 20.00
256 Spencer Hawes XRC 6.00 15.00
257 Acie Law XRC 6.00 15.00
258 Thaddeus Young XRC 8.00 20.00
259 Julian Wright XRC 6.00 15.00
260 Al Thornton XRC 6.00 15.00
261 Rodney Stuckey XRC 6.00 15.00
262 Nick Young XRC 10.00 25.00
263 Sean Williams XRC 6.00 15.00
264 Marco Belinelli XRC 6.00 15.00
265 Javaris Crittenton XRC 6.00 15.00
266 Jason Smith XRC 6.00 15.00
267 Daequan Cook XRC 6.00 15.00
268 Jared Dudley XRC 5.00 12.00
269 Wilson Chandler XRC 8.00 20.00
270 Morris Almond XRC 6.00 15.00
271 Arron Afflalo XRC 6.00 15.00
272 Aaron Brooks XRC 6.00 15.00
273 Alando Tucker XRC 6.00 15.00
274 Marcus Williams XRC 6.00 15.00
275 Carl Landry XRC 6.00 15.00
276 Gabe Pruitt XRC 6.00 15.00

2006-07 Chronology 2007-08 Rookie Draft Redemptions Silver

*SILVER: .6X TO 1.5X BASE HI
SILVER PRINT RUN 50 SER.#'d SETS
UNPRICED GOLD PRINT RUN 10 SETS

2006-07 Chronology 20,000 Point Club

PRINT RUN 25 SER.#'d SETS
20KAD Adrian Dantley 12.00 30.00
20KAE Alex English 12.00 30.00
20KBP Bob Pettit 20.00 50.00
20KCD Clyde Drexler 30.00 80.00
20KDR David Robinson 50.00 100.00
20KEB Elgin Baylor 30.00 60.00
20KEH Elvin Hayes 12.00 30.00
20KGG George Gervin 30.00 60.00
20KHG Hal Greer 12.00 30.00
20KHO Hakeem Olajuwon 25.00 50.00
20KJH John Havlicek 30.00 60.00
20KJW Jerry West 60.00 150.00
20KKA Kareem Abdul-Jabbar 50.00 100.00
20KLB Larry Bird 50.00 100.00
20KMJ Michael Jordan 400.00 800.00
20KRP Robert Parish 12.00 30.00
20KTC Tom Chambers 12.00 30.00
20KWB Walt Bellamy 20.00 40.00

2006-07 Chronology Autographs

APPROXIMATELY ONE PER PACK
UNPRICED GOLD PRINT RUN 10 SETS
1 Slick Watts 6.00 15.00
1a Slick Watts Slick only 10.00 25.00
2 Louie Dampier 15.00 40.00
3 Al Attles 6.00 15.00
4 Alvin Robertson 6.00 15.00
6 Artis Gilmore 6.00 15.00
7 Austin Carr 8.00 20.00
8 Avery Johnson 6.00 15.00
9 B.J. Armstrong 10.00 25.00
12 Bob Dandridge 8.00 20.00
14 Bobby Jones 8.00 20.00
15 Brad Daugherty 6.00 15.00
16 Byron Scott 8.00 20.00
16a B.Scott 3 Time Champs 30.00 60.00
17 Cazzie Russell 6.00 15.00
18 Cedric Maxwell 6.00 15.00
20 Chet Walker 8.00 20.00
21 Chuck Share 6.00 15.00
24 Danny Manning 8.00 20.00
25 Darrell Griffith 6.00 15.00
26 Darryl Dawkins Silver 8.00 20.00
29 Dick Barnett 10.00 25.00
30 Dick Van Arsdale 15.00 30.00
30a D.Van Arsdale Orig.Sun 25.00 50.00
32 Don Buse 12.00 30.00
33 Don Ohl 10.00 25.00
34 Ernie DeGregorio 15.00 40.00
35 Fred Brown 6.00 15.00
37 George McGinnis 6.00 15.00
39 Rick Mahorn 8.00 20.00
40 Gus Williams 8.00 20.00
41 Jack Sikma 6.00 15.00
42 Jamaal Wilkes 6.00 15.00
44 Jerry Sloan 12.00 30.00
44a Jerry Sloan Spider 30.00 60.00
45 Jim Loscutoff 6.00 15.00
46 Jo Jo White 8.00 20.00
47 John Johnson 6.00 15.00
48 Johnny Kerr 20.00 50.00
50 Junior Bridgeman 8.00 20.00
51 Kiki Vandeweghe 6.00 15.00
53 Larry Nance 6.00 15.00
54 Lonnie Shelton 8.00 20.00
55 Lou Hudson 6.00 15.00
57 Tree Rollins 6.00 15.00
58 George Karl 20.00 35.00
59 Maurice Lucas 6.00 15.00
60 Mel Daniels 10.00 25.00
61 Michael Cooper 8.00 20.00
61a Michael Cooper Gold 10.00 25.00
66 Muggsy Bogues 8.00 20.00
67 Norm Nixon 6.00 15.00
68 Norm Van Lier 15.00 40.00
71 Paul Westphal 6.00 15.00
72 Phil Chenier 6.00 15.00
73 Phil Ford 8.00 20.00
73a Phil Ford UNC 10.00 25.00
75 Richie Guerin 6.00 15.00
76 Rolando Blackman 8.00 20.00
78 R.Tomjanovich Rudy T. 8.00 20.00
78a R.Tomjanovich signed twice 15.00 30.00
79 Sam Perkins 6.00 15.00
80 Sean Elliott 10.00 25.00
82 Sidney Moncrief 6.00 15.00
83 Horace Grant 25.00 60.00
84 Spencer Haywood 6.00 15.00
85 Steve Kerr 20.00 50.00
85a Steve Kerr 30.00 80.00
86 Terry Dischinger 8.00 20.00
88 Tom Chambers 6.00 15.00
89 Tom Sanders 10.00 25.00
90 Michael Ray Richardson 6.00 15.00
91 Terry Cummings 6.00 15.00
93 Walter Davis 6.00 15.00
94 Wayman Tisdale 8.00 20.00
97 Jeff Hornacek 10.00 25.00
98 Eddie Johnson 6.00 15.00
99 Xavier McDaniel 6.00 15.00
100 Zelmo Beaty 10.00 25.00
100a Zelmo Beaty Big E only 10.00 25.00

2006-07 Chronology Contemporaries

PRINT RUN 25 SER.#'d SETS
COBW R.Barry/J.Wilkes 20.00 40.00
COCE M.Cheeks/J.Erving 50.00 100.00
CODH D.Cowens/J.Havlicek 50.00 100.00
CODO C.Drexler/H.Olajuwon 80.00 160.00
COFA W.Frazier/N.Archibald 30.00 60.00
COFB B.Fitch/L.Bird 100.00 225.00
COGB H.Grant/K.Bryant 100.00 250.00
COGC H.Greer/E.Baylor 40.00 80.00
COGD D.Griffith/D.Dawkins 20.00 40.00
COGT G.Gervin/D.Thompson 20.00 40.00
COGW G.Goodrich/J.West 60.00 150.00
COHL C.Hawkins/B.Lanier 25.00 50.00
COHS T.Heinsohn/B.Sharman 25.00 50.00
COHU E.Hayes/W.Unseld 25.00 50.00
COHW L.Hudson/L.Wilkens 20.00 40.00
COJH M.Johnson/J.Heathcote 75.00 200.00
COKM J.Kundla/V.Mikkelsen 40.00 100.00
COKS J.Kerr/D.Schayes 40.00 80.00
COLW M.Lucas/B.Walton 30.00 60.00
COMM S.Martin/V.Mikkelsen 50.00 100.00
CORE D.Robinson/S.Elliott 80.00 160.00
CORL D.Rodman/B.Laimbeer 40.00 80.00
CORS P.Riley/B.Sharman 75.00 200.00
COSJ D.Smith/M.Jordan 500.00 800.00
COSO R.Sampson/H.Olajuwon 25.00 60.00
COWA J.Wooden/K.Abdul-Jabbar 200.00 350.00

2006-07 Chronology Cut Signatures

ATED PRINT RUN 6 TO 17 SER.#'d SETS
MOST UNPRICED DUE TO SCARCITY
CSDD Dave DeBusschere/17 150.00 300.00

2006-07 Chronology HOF Inscriptions

PRINT RUN 50 SER.#'d SETS
HOFAE Alex English 6.00 15.00
HOFBH Bailey Howell 10.00 25.00
HOFBW Bobby Wanzer 20.00 40.00
HOFCD Clyde Drexler 30.00 60.00
HOFCH Cliff Hagan 8.00 20.00
HOFCL Clyde Lovellette 25.00 60.00
HOFCM Calvin Murphy 6.00 15.00
HOFDI Dan Issel 12.00 30.00
HOFDM Dick McGuire 10.00 25.00
HOFFR Frank Ramsey 25.00 50.00
HOFHG Hal Greer 8.00 20.00
HOFJE Julius Erving 40.00 100.00
HOFKA Kareem Abdul-Jabbar 40.00 80.00
HOFLB Larry Bird 50.00 100.00
HOFMJ Magic Johnson 50.00 100.00
HOFNT Nate Thurmond 6.00 15.00

2006-07 Chronology MVP Winners

PRINT RUN 50 SER.#'d SETS
MVPAG Artis Gilmore 15.00 40.00
MVPBL Bob Lanier 10.00 25.00
MVPBM Bob McAdoo 25.00 50.00
MVPBP Bob Pettit 25.00 60.00
MVPBR Bill Russell 75.00 200.00
MVPBS Bill Sharman 10.00 25.00
MVPBW Bill Walton 15.00 30.00
MVPCM Cedric Maxwell 10.00 25.00
MVPDC Dave Cowens 15.00 30.00
MVPDT David Thompson 15.00 30.00
MVPEB Elgin Baylor 25.00 60.00
MVPEM Ed Macauley 30.00 80.00
MVPGG George Gervin 15.00 40.00
MVPHG Hal Greer 12.50 30.00
MVPHO Hakeem Olajuwon 50.00 120.00

MVPJL Jerry Lucas 25.00 60.00
MVPJS John Stockton 60.00 120.00
MVPJW James Worthy 30.00 80.00
MVPLJ LeBron James 125.00 300.00
MVPLW Lenny Wilkens 10.00 25.00
MVPMJ Michael Jordan 400.00 700.00
MVPNA Nate Archibald 12.50 30.00
MVPRB Rick Barry 12.50 30.00
MVPRS Ralph Sampson 10.00 25.00
MVPSH Spencer Haywood 10.00 25.00
MVPTC Tom Chambers 10.00 25.00
MVPWE Jerry West 30.00 80.00
MVPWF Walt Frazier 15.00 30.00
MVPWH Jo Jo White 15.00 30.00
MVPWU Wes Unseld 15.00 30.00

2006-07 Chronology Retired Numbers

STATED PRINT RUN ONE TO 44 SER.#'d SETS
SOME UNPRICED DUE TO SCARCITY
RNBL Bill Laimbeer/40 20.00 50.00
RNDG Darrell Griffith/35 8.00 20.00
RNGG Gail Goodrich/25 20.00 50.00
RNGM George McGinnis/30 20.00 40.00
RNHG Hal Greer/32 25.00 50.00
RNLB Larry Bird/33 60.00 150.00
RNLN Larry Nance/22 15.00 30.00
RNMP Mark Price/25 25.00 50.00
RNPW Paul Westphal/44 6.00 15.00
RNRB Rolando Blackman/22 8.00 20.00
RNTH Tom Heinsohn/15 20.00 50.00
RNTS Tom Sanders/25 20.00 40.00

2006-07 Chronology Signature Decades

STATED PRINT RUN 50 TO 90 SER.#'d SETS
DAC Al Cervi/50 25.00 50.00
DAE Alex English/80 8.00 20.00
DAM Alonzo Mourning/90 20.00 50.00
DAR Arnie Risen/50 40.00 80.00
DBH Bob Houbregs/50 10.00 25.00
DBL Bob Lanier/70 8.00 20.00
DBM Bob McAdoo/70 25.00 50.00
DBP Bob Pettit/60 20.00 50.00
DBS Bill Sharman/50 10.00 25.00
DBW Bill Walton/80 12.50 30.00
DCD Clyde Drexler/90 20.00 40.00
DCH Cliff Hagan/60 15.00 40.00
DCL Clyde Lovellette/50 25.00 50.00
DCM Calvin Murphy/70 8.00 20.00
DDC Dave Cowens/70 8.00 20.00
DDD Darryl Dawkins/80 8.00 20.00
DDM Dick McGuire/50 10.00 25.00
DDR David Robinson/90 30.00 80.00
DDS Dolph Schayes/50 8.00 20.00
DDT David Thompson/70 10.00 25.00
DEB Elgin Baylor/60 20.00 40.00
DEH Elvin Hayes/70 12.50 30.00
DFR Frank Ramsey/50 20.00 40.00
DGG George Gervin/70 10.00 25.00
DGR Hal Greer/60 8.00 20.00
DHG Harry Gallatin/50 15.00 40.00
DHO Bailey Howell/60 10.00 25.00
DJH John Havlicek/70 20.00 40.00
DJK Jason Kidd/90 15.00 40.00
DJL Jerry Lucas/70 15.00 30.00
DJO Mark Price/90 25.00 60.00
DJW James Worthy/80 25.00 60.00
DLA Bill Laimbeer/80 8.00 20.00
DMA Dan Majerle/90 25.00 50.00
DMC Maurice Cheeks/80 8.00 20.00
DMR Mitch Richmond/90 15.00 30.00
DNA Nate Archibald/70 8.00 20.00
DNT Nate Thurmond/60 15.00 30.00
DOL Hakeem Olajuwon/90 15.00 30.00
DRO Dennis Rodman/90 30.00 80.00
DRP Robert Parish/80 8.00 20.00
DSE Sean Elliott/90 15.00 30.00
DSJ Sam Jones/60 15.00 40.00
DSM Slater Martin/50 25.00 60.00
DTH Tom Heinsohn/60 15.00 30.00
DWB Walt Bellamy/60 8.00 20.00
DWD Walter Davis/80 10.00 25.00
DWF Walt Frazier/70 15.00 30.00

2006-07 Chronology Stitches in Time

PRINT RUN 199 SER.#'d SETS
*GOLD: .5X TO 1.25X BASE HI
GOLD PRINT RUN 75 SER.#'d SETS
SITAB Andrea Bargnani 3.00 8.00
SITAI Allen Iverson 4.00 10.00
SITBR Brandon Roy 3.00 8.00
SITCA Carmelo Anthony 4.00 10.00
SITDR Dennis Rodman 6.00 15.00
SITHO Hakeem Olajuwon 4.00 10.00
SITJE Julius Erving 5.00 12.00
SITJO Magic Johnson 8.00 20.00
SITJR J.J. Redick 4.00 10.00
SITJS John Stockton 5.00 12.00
SITJW Jerry West 6.00 15.00
SITKB Kobe Bryant 8.00 20.00
SITKG Kevin Garnett 5.00 12.00
SITKM Kevin McHale 4.00 10.00
SITLA LaMarcus Aldridge 6.00 15.00
SITLB Larry Bird 8.00 20.00
SITLJ LeBron James 10.00 25.00
SITMJ Michael Jordan 25.00 60.00
SITPM Pete Maravich 20.00 50.00
SITRB Ronnie Brewer 3.00 8.00
SITRF Randy Foye 3.00 8.00
SITRG Rudy Gay 4.00 10.00
SITSO Shaquille O'Neal 6.00 15.00
SITSW Shelden Williams 2.50 6.00
SITTD Tim Duncan 5.00 12.00
SITTM Tracy McGrady 4.00 10.00
SITTS Thabo Sefolosha 3.00 8.00
SITTT Tyrus Thomas 2.50 6.00
SITVC Vince Carter 4.00 10.00
SITYM Yao Ming 4.00 10.00

2006-07 Chronology Stitches in Time Autographs

PRINT RUN 25 SER.#'d SETS
SITSAB Andrea Bargnani 15.00 40.00
SITSBR Brandon Roy 15.00 40.00
SITSCA Carmelo Anthony 30.00 80.00
SITSDR Dennis Rodman 40.00 80.00
SITSHO Hakeem Olajuwon 25.00 50.00
SITSJE Julius Erving 75.00 150.00
SITSJO Michael Jordan 400.00 700.00
SITSJS John Stockton 50.00 100.00
SITSKB Kobe Bryant 150.00 300.00
SITSLA LaMarcus Aldridge 25.00 60.00
SITSLB Larry Bird 75.00 200.00
SITSLJ LeBron James 150.00 300.00
SITSMJ Magic Johnson 60.00 120.00
SITSRF Randy Foye 15.00 40.00
SITSRG Rudy Gay 15.00 40.00
SITSTM Tracy McGrady 25.00 50.00
SITSTT Tyrus Thomas 15.00 40.00
SITSVC Vince Carter 30.00 80.00
SITSYM Yao Ming 30.00 80.00

2006-07 Chronology Stitches in Time Dual

PRINT RUN 75 SER.#'d SETS
SITDAR L.Aldridge/B.Roy 10.00 25.00
SITDBJ L.Bird/M.Johnson 20.00 50.00
SITDIA A.Iverson/C.Anthony 10.00 25.00
SITDJB M.Johnson/K.Bryant 20.00 40.00
SITDJE M.Jordan/J.Erving 30.00 80.00
SITDJJ L.James/M.Jordan 40.00 80.00
SITDMM T.McGrady/Y.Ming 6.00 15.00
SITDOD S.O'Neal/T.Duncan 10.00 25.00
SITDTS T.Thomas/T.Sefolosha 6.00 15.00
SITDWS J.West/J.Stockton 15.00 30.00

2007-08 Chronology

1-100 PRINT RUN 250 SER.#'d SETS
101-130 AU PRINT RUN 25 SER.#'d SETS
131-214 AU PRINT RUN 99 SER.#'d SETS
215-244 AU RC PRINT RUN 99 SER.#'d SETS
245-250 RC PRINT RUN 99 SER.#'d SETS
251-283 XRC PRINT RUN 250 SER.#'d SETS
1 Andrew Toney 2.50 6.00
2 Artis Gilmore 2.00 5.00
3 B.J. Armstrong 2.50 6.00
4 Bernard King 2.00 5.00
5 Bill Cartwright 2.00 5.00
6 Bill Laimbeer 2.00 5.00
7 Bill Russell 4.00 10.00
8 Bill Walton 2.50 6.00
9 Bill Wennington 2.50 6.00
10 Billy Cunningham 2.50 6.00
11 Bob Cousy 4.00 10.00
12 Bob McAdoo 2.00 5.00
13 Brad Davis 2.50 6.00
14 Byron Scott 2.00 5.00
15 Cedric Maxwell 2.50 6.00
16 Charles Oakley 2.50 6.00
17 Clyde Drexler 3.00 8.00
18 Clyde Lovellette 2.50 6.00
19 Dan Issel 2.00 5.00
20 Danny Ainge 2.50 6.00
21 Darrell Walker 2.50 6.00
22 Dave Bing 2.50 6.00
23 Dave Cowens 1.50 4.00
24 Dave DeBusschere 2.50 6.00
25 David Robinson 4.00 10.00
26 Dennis Rodman 5.00 12.00
27 Derrick Coleman 2.50 6.00
28 Dino Radja 1.50 4.00
29 Doc Rivers 2.50 6.00
30 Dominique Wilkins 3.00 8.00
31 Earl Monroe 2.50 6.00
32 Elgin Baylor 2.50 6.00
33 Freddie Lewis 2.50 6.00
34 George Gervin 2.50 6.00
35 George Mikan 5.00 12.00
36 Gheorghe Muresan 2.50 6.00
37 Gus Williams 1.50 4.00
38 Hakeem Olajuwon 3.00 8.00
39 Hal Greer 2.00 5.00
40 Harry Gallatin 2.50 6.00
41 Horace Grant 2.50 6.00
42 Isiah Thomas 2.50 6.00
43 Jack Sikma 2.00 5.00
44 James Worthy 3.00 8.00
45 Jay Vincent 2.50 6.00
46 Jerry Lucas 2.50 6.00
47 Jerry West 3.00 8.00
48 Jim Paxson 2.50 6.00
49 Jim Price 2.50 6.00
50 Joe Dumars 2.50 6.00
51 John Havlicek 2.50 6.00
52 John Paxson 2.00 5.00
53 John Salley 1.50 4.00
54 Julius Erving 4.00 10.00
55 Kareem Abdul-Jabbar 4.00 10.00
56 Karl Malone 3.00 8.00
57 Kenny Smith 2.00 5.00
58 Kermit Washington 2.50 6.00
59 Kevin McHale 3.00 8.00
60 Kurt Rambis 1.50 4.00
61 Larry Bird 6.00 15.00
62 Lenny Wilkens 2.50 6.00
63 Lionel Hollins 2.50 6.00
64 Luc Longley 1.50 4.00
65 Magic Johnson 6.00 15.00
66 Manute Bol 2.50 6.00
67 Mark Aguirre 2.00 5.00
68 Marques Johnson 2.00 5.00
69 Michael Jordan 20.00 50.00
70 Michael Ray Richardson 2.00 5.00
71 Moses Malone 2.50 6.00
72 Nate Archibald 2.00 5.00
73 Oscar Robertson 2.50 6.00
74 Paul Arizin 2.50 6.00
75 Paul Silas 2.50 6.00
76 Paul Westphal 3.00 8.00
77 Pete Maravich 4.00 10.00
78 Phil Jackson 3.00 8.00
79 Pooh Richardson 1.50 4.00
80 Reggie Miller 2.50 6.00
81 Rick Barry 2.00 5.00
82 Ron Harper 2.50 6.00
83 Joe Barry Carroll 2.50 6.00
84 Spencer Haywood 1.50 4.00
85 Stacey Augmon 1.50 4.00
86 Steve Kerr 2.50 6.00
87 Swen Nater 2.50 6.00
88 Lonnie Shelton 2.50 6.00
89 Thurl Bailey 2.50 6.00
90 Tom Chambers 2.00 5.00
91 Tom Sanders 2.50 6.00
92 Toni Kukoc 2.50 6.00
93 Vernon Maxwell 1.50 4.00
94 Vlade Divac 2.50 6.00
95 Walt Bellamy 2.00 5.00
96 Will Perdue 1.50 4.00
97 Reggie Theus 2.00 5.00
98 Willis Reed 2.50 6.00
99 Wilt Chamberlain 5.00 12.00
100 Xavier McDaniel 1.50 4.00
101 James Silas AU 15.00 40.00
102 Steve Nash AU 50.00 125.00
103 Yao Ming AU 25.00 60.00
104 Kevin Durant AU 600.00 1000.00
106 Carmelo Anthony AU 25.00 60.00
108 Chris Paul AU 40.00 100.00
109 Dwight Howard AU 25.00 60.00
110 Vince Carter AU 50.00 120.00
111 Bill Laimbeer AU 12.00 30.00
112 Rick Barry AU 12.00 30.00
113 Spencer Haywood AU 12.00 30.00
114 Paul Pierce AU 20.00 40.00
115 Jason Kidd AU 30.00 80.00
116 Wes Unseld AU 12.00 30.00
117 Artis Gilmore AU 12.00 30.00
118 Tracy McGrady AU 25.00 60.00
119 David Robinson AU 40.00 80.00
120 Moses Malone AU 12.00 30.00
121 Dennis Rodman AU 40.00 100.00
122 Pat Riley AU 15.00 40.00
123 Michael Jordan AU 1000.00 2000.00
124 LaMarcus Aldridge AU 15.00 40.00
125 Randy Foye AU 12.00 30.00
126 Jermaine O'Neal AU 12.00 30.00
127 Brad Daugherty AU 40.00 100.00
128 Muggsy Bogues AU 20.00 50.00
129 Kiki Vandeweghe AU 12.00 30.00
130 Micheal Ray Richardson AU 12.00 30.00
131 David Robinson AU 50.00 100.00
132 Kobe Bryant AU 150.00 300.00
133 Vince Carter AU 50.00 120.00
134 Kobe Bryant AU 250.00 500.00
135 Kevin Durant AU RC 300.00 600.00
136 Michael Jordan AU Blue 400.00 800.00
137 Magic Johnson AU 60.00 150.00
138 Michael Jordan AU 400.00 800.00
139 Jerry West AU 100.00 250.00
140 Tom Chambers AU 10.00 25.00
141 Bill Laimbeer AU 15.00 40.00
142 Julius Erving AU 100.00 200.00
143 Spud Webb AU 20.00 50.00
144 Clyde Drexler AU 60.00 150.00
145 Sean Elliott AU 10.00 25.00
146 Dominique Wilkins AU 30.00 60.00
147 Magic Johnson AU 100.00 200.00
148 John Wooden AU 75.00 150.00
149 Kareem Abdul-Jabbar AU 30.00 80.00
150 L.Bird/Magic Johnson AU 175.00 350.00
151 Steve Kerr AU 40.00 100.00
152 Rick Barry AU 15.00 40.00
153 James Worthy AU 60.00 150.00
154 John Paxson AU 30.00 80.00
155 Baron Davis AU 25.00 60.00
156 Chris Paul AU 60.00 150.00
157 LeBron James AU 700.00 1000.00
158 Kobe Bryant AU 250.00 500.00
159 Kevin Durant AU RC 300.00 600.00
160 Kevin Garnett AU 60.00 150.00
161 Bailey Howell AU 12.00 30.00
162 Bob Love AU 12.00 30.00
162a Bob Love #10 15.00 30.00
163 Norm Nixon AU 12.00 30.00
164 Horace Grant AU 25.00 60.00
165 Darrell Griffith AU 10.00 25.00
165a D.Griffith AU Dr. Dunk 20.00 40.00
166 Dick McGuire AU 10.00 25.00
167 Chet Walker AU 10.00 25.00
168 Clyde Drexler AU 30.00 80.00
169 Gail Goodrich AU 15.00 40.00
170 Walt Frazier AU 20.00 50.00
171 George Gervin AU 15.00 40.00
172 Hal Greer AU 15.00 40.00
173 Sam Jones AU 20.00 50.00
174 Jerry Lucas AU 20.00 50.00
175 Hakeem Olajuwon AU 50.00 120.00
175a H.Olajuwon AU 94 MVP 40.00 100.00
176 Robert Parish AU 15.00 40.00
177 Bob Pettit AU 30.00 80.00
178 Spud Webb AU 25.00 60.00
179 Pat Riley AU 40.00 100.00
180 Bill Sharman AU 40.00 100.00
180a Bill Sharman WW2 Vet
181 John Stockton AU 75.00 200.00
182 Nate Thurmond AU 15.00 40.00
183 Wes Unseld AU 15.00 40.00
184 Bill Walton AU 15.00 40.00
185 Sam Perkins AU 10.00 25.00
186 Lenny Wilkens AU 15.00 40.00
187 Rudy Tomjanovich AU 12.00 30.00
188 Artis Gilmore AU 12.00 30.00
189 Adrian Dantley AU 12.00 30.00
190 David Thompson AU 12.00 30.00
190a D.Thompson AU Skywalker 15.00 30.00
190b D.Thompson AU Wolfpack 15.00 30.00
191 Dominique Wilkins AU 30.00 80.00
192 Dennis Rodman AU 30.00 80.00
193 Kiki Vandeweghe AU 10.00 25.00
194 Bob McAdoo AU 15.00 40.00
195 Alex English AU 10.00 25.00
196 George McGinnis AU 10.00 25.00
196a G.McGinnis AU 75 ABA MVP 15.00 40.00
197 Vern Mikkelsen AU 10.00 25.00
198 Walt Bellamy AU 10.00 25.00
199 Bob Lanier AU 12.00 30.00
199a Bob Lanier AU MVP 25.00 50.00
200 Connie Hawkins AU 10.00 25.00
201 Bobby Wanzer AU 25.00 60.00
202 Tom Heinsohn AU 20.00 50.00
203 Slater Martin AU 20.00 50.00
204 Michael Cooper AU 10.00 25.00
205 Darryl Dawkins AU 12.00 30.00
206 Bobby Jones AU 12.00 30.00
207 Dolph Schayes AU 12.00 30.00
208 Louie Dampier AU 12.00 30.00
209 Don Nelson AU 12.00 30.00
210 Marques Johnson AU 10.00 25.00
211 Moses Malone AU 60.00 150.00
212 Dick Barnett AU 12.00 30.00
213 Cliff Hagan AU 20.00 50.00
214 Meadowlark Lemon AU 75.00 200.00
215 Kevin Durant AU RC 400.00 800.00
216 Al Horford AU RC 8.00 20.00
217 Corey Brewer AU RC 6.00 15.00
218 Mike Conley Jr. AU RC 12.00 30.00
218a M.Conley Jr. AU Go Buckeyes 25.00 50.00
219 Joakim Noah AU RC 25.00 60.00
220 Julian Wright AU RC 4.00 10.00
220a J.Wright AU Go Jayhawks 20.00 40.00
221 Jeff Green AU RC 6.00 15.00
222 Spencer Hawes AU RC 5.00 12.00
222a S.Hawes AU Go Huskies 15.00 30.00
223 Acie Law AU RC 4.00 10.00
224 Al Thornton AU RC 5.00 12.00
225 Rodney Stuckey AU RC 5.00 12.00
226 Sean Williams AU RC 4.00 10.00
226a Sean Williams AU Area 51 4.00 10.00
227 Marco Belinelli AU RC 6.00 15.00
228 Javaris Crittenton AU RC 4.00 10.00
229 Jason Smith AU RC 5.00 12.00
230 Daequan Cook AU RC 10.00 25.00
231 Jared Dudley AU RC 5.00 12.00
232 Wilson Chandler AU RC 5.00 12.00
233 Morris Almond AU RC 4.00 10.00
234 Aaron Brooks AU RC 5.00 12.00
235 Arron Afflalo AU RC 6.00 15.00
235a A.Afflalo AU Go Bruins 20.00 40.00
236 Alando Tucker AU RC 4.00 10.00
237 Jermareo Davidson AU RC 4.00 10.00
239 Gabe Pruitt AU RC 4.00 10.00
240 Dominic McGuire AU RC 4.00 10.00
241 Glen Davis AU RC 5.00 12.00
241a Glen Davis AU Big Baby 5.00 12.00
242 Josh McRoberts AU RC 5.00 12.00
243 Luis Scola AU RC 6.00 15.00
244 Juan Navarro AU RC 5.00 12.00
245 Greg Oden RC 4.00 10.00
246 Yi Jianlian RC 5.00 12.00
247 Brandan Wright RC 4.00 10.00
248 Nick Young RC 5.00 12.00
249 Thaddeus Young RC 4.00 10.00
250 Kyrylo Fesenko RC 2.50 6.00
251 Derrick Rose XRC 8.00 20.00
252 Michael Beasley XRC 4.00 10.00
253 O.J. Mayo XRC 4.00 10.00
254 Russell Westbrook XRC 40.00 100.00
255 Kevin Love XRC 6.00 15.00
256 Danilo Gallinari XRC 6.00 15.00
257 Eric Gordon XRC 8.00 20.00
258 Joe Alexander XRC 2.50 6.00
259 D.J. Augustin XRC 3.00 8.00
260 Brook Lopez XRC 6.00 15.00
261 Jerryd Bayless XRC 3.00 8.00
262 Jason Thompson XRC 4.00 10.00
263 Brandon Rush XRC 3.00 8.00
264 Anthony Randolph XRC 4.00 10.00
265 Robin Lopez XRC 4.00 10.00
266 Marreese Speights XRC 4.00 10.00
267 Roy Hibbert XRC 4.00 10.00
268 JaVale McGee XRC 5.00 12.00
269 J.J. Hickson XRC 4.00 10.00
270 Alexis Ajinca XRC 2.50 6.00
271 Ryan Anderson XRC 5.00 12.00
272 Courtney Lee XRC 5.00 12.00
273 Kosta Koufos XRC 4.00 10.00
274 Kyle Weaver XRC 4.00 10.00
275 Nicolas Batum XRC 5.00 12.00
276 George Hill XRC 6.00 15.00
277 Darrell Arthur XRC 4.00 10.00
278 Donte Greene XRC 4.00 10.00
279 D.J. White XRC 4.00 10.00
280 J.R. Giddens XRC 4.00 10.00
281 Mario Chalmers XRC 5.00 12.00
282 Walter Sharpe XRC 4.00 10.00
283 DeAndre Jordan XRC 8.00 20.00

2007-08 Chronology Rookie Redemptions Gold

GOLD: .75X TO 2X BASE HI
STATED PRINT RUN 25 SER.#'d SETS

2007-08 Chronology Rookie Redemptions Silver

*SILVER: .5X TO 1.25X BASE
STATED PRINT RUN 99 SER.#'d SETS
251 Derrick Rose 30.00 80.00

2007-08 Chronology Autographs

RANDOM INSERTS IN PACKS
UNPRICED GOLD PRINT RUN 10 SER.#'d SETS
2 Artis Gilmore 8.00 20.00
3 B.J. Armstrong 6.00 15.00
4 Bernard King 10.00 25.00
5 Bill Cartwright 10.00 25.00
6 Bill Laimbeer 6.00 15.00
8a Bill Walton Grateful Red 30.00 80.00
9 Bill Wennington 8.00 20.00
12 Bob McAdoo 10.00 25.00
13 Brad Davis 6.00 15.00
14 Byron Scott 8.00 20.00
15 Cedric Maxwell 8.00 20.00
17 Clyde Drexler 15.00 40.00
18 Clyde Lovellette 8.00 20.00
19 Dan Issel 8.00 20.00
21 Darrell Walker 6.00 15.00
23 Dave Cowens 6.00 15.00
25 David Robinson 30.00 60.00
28 Dino Radja 12.00 30.00
28a Dino Radja All Rookie 12.00 30.00
32 Elgin Baylor 15.00 30.00
32a Elgin Baylor 77 HOF 25.00 50.00
32b E.Baylor Kappa Alpha Psi 30.00 60.00
33 Freddie Lewis 6.00 15.00
34 George Gervin 10.00 25.00
36 Gheorghe Muresan 6.00 15.00
37 Gus Williams 6.00 15.00
38 Hakeem Olajuwon 12.50 30.00
39 Hal Greer 8.00 20.00
40 Harry Gallatin 6.00 15.00
41 Horace Grant 10.00 25.00
43 Jack Sikma 6.00 15.00
45 Jay Vincent 6.00 15.00
46 Jerry Lucas 15.00 40.00
47 Jerry West 30.00 60.00
48 Jim Paxson 6.00 15.00
49 Jim Price 6.00 15.00
50 Joe Dumars 15.00 30.00
52 John Paxson 10.00 25.00
53 John Salley 6.00 15.00
54 Julius Erving 30.00 60.00
55 Kareem Abdul-Jabbar 60.00 120.00
57 Kenny Smith 8.00 20.00
58 Kermit Washington 6.00 15.00
61 Larry Bird 75.00 150.00
62 Lenny Wilkens 10.00 25.00
63 Lionel Hollins 6.00 15.00
65 Magic Johnson 40.00 80.00
68 Marques Johnson 6.00 15.00
69 Michael Jordan 300.00 400.00
70 Michael Ray Richardson 6.00 15.00
71 Moses Malone 8.00 20.00
72 Nate Archibald 8.00 20.00
76 Paul Westphal 6.00 15.00
79 Pooh Richardson 6.00 15.00
81 Rick Barry 8.00 20.00
82 Ron Harper 30.00 60.00
84 Spencer Haywood 6.00 15.00
85 Stacey Augmon 6.00 15.00
86 Steve Kerr 10.00 25.00
87 Swen Nater 6.00 15.00
88 Lonnie Shelton 6.00 15.00
89 Thurl Bailey 6.00 15.00
90 Tom Chambers 6.00 15.00
91 Tom Sanders 6.00 15.00
92 Toni Kukoc 8.00 20.00
94 Vlade Divac 12.00 30.00
95 Walt Bellamy 6.00 15.00
96 Will Perdue 8.00 20.00
97 Reggie Theus 6.00 15.00
100 Xavier McDaniel 6.00 15.00

2007-08 Chronology Dedications

PRINT RUN 50 SER.#'d SETS
UNPRICED GOLD PRINT RUN 10 SETS
DAC Al Cervi 6.00 15.00
DAD Adrian Dantley 6.00 15.00
DAE Alex English 6.00 15.00
DAG Artis Gilmore 6.00 15.00
DBL Bob Lanier 8.00 20.00
DBM Bob McAdoo 15.00 30.00
DBP Bob Pettit 15.00 30.00
DBS Bill Sharman 15.00 40.00
DBW Bill Walton 8.00 20.00
DCD Clyde Drexler 30.00 60.00
DCW Chet Walker 6.00 15.00
DDC Dave Cowens 10.00 25.00
DDG Darrell Griffith 6.00 15.00
DDT David Thompson 6.00 15.00
DGE George Gervin 12.00 30.00
DGG Gail Goodrich 8.00 20.00
DHG Hal Greer 8.00 20.00
DJR Jack Ramsay 12.00 30.00
DLA Bill Laimbeer 10.00 25.00
DLW Lenny Wilkens 6.00 15.00
DMC Maurice Cheeks 6.00 15.00
DNN Norm Nixon 6.00 15.00
DRB Rick Barry 10.00 25.00
DRO Rolando Blackman 10.00 25.00
DRP Robert Parish 8.00 20.00
DSM Sidney Moncrief 6.00 15.00
DTH Tom Heinsohn 15.00 40.00
DWU Wes Unseld 20.00 50.00

2007-08 Chronology Era Associates

PRINT RUN 15 SER.#'d SETS
BLGW Lucas/Greer/Wlkns/Gdrch 40.00 100.00
EJBJ Bird/Dr.J/Magic/MJ 800.00 1000.00
GDDE Artis/Glide/Dant/Eng 80.00 200.00
JCHP Jamisn/Vince/Hughs/Pierc 100.00 200.00
MHSD Amare/Durant/Howard/Yao 150.00 300.00
MLAW Kareem/McAd/Wltn/Lanier 150.00 300.00
ORMP Malone/Parish/Olaj/DRob 100.00 250.00
PSHS Pettit/Heinshn/Shrmn/Dolph 40.00 100.00

2007-08 Chronology Freshman Registry

PRINT RUN 25 SER.#'d SETS
BCB Williams/Chambers/Blackman 30.00 60.00
DGC Durant/Green/Conley 60.00 150.00
DHP Daugherty/Harper/Price 50.00 100.00
HBN Horford/Brewer/Noah 30.00 60.00
HWN Havlicek/Walker/Nelson 30.00 60.00
LTC Lanier/Tomjanovich/Cowens 40.00 80.00
MKS King/Sikma/Maxwell 15.00 40.00
PKG Pettit/Kerr/Guerin 30.00 80.00
RHJ Heinsohn/Russell/Jones 200.00 300.00
SSD Sampson/Scott/Drexler 40.00 80.00
WCW Worthy/Cummings/Wilkins 40.00 80.00
WSW West/Wilkens/Sanders 50.00 100.00
WWW Walton/Winters/Wilkes 25.00 60.00

2007-08 Chronology Historically Accurate

PRINT RUN 50 SER.#'d SETS
UNPRICED GOLD PRINT RUN 10 SETS
HAAD Adrian Dantley 6.00 15.00
HAAG Artis Gilmore 6.00 15.00
HABA B.J. Armstrong 10.00 25.00
HACM Cedric Maxwell 10.00 25.00
HADI Dan Issel 6.00 15.00
HAJR Jeff Ruland 6.00 15.00
HAKV Kiki Vandeweghe 6.00 15.00
HAMP Mark Price 25.00 60.00
HASK Steve Kerr 12.00 30.00

2007-08 Chronology My Generation

STATED PRINT RUN 62 TO 75 SER.#'d SETS
UNPRICED GOLD PRINT RUN 10 SETS
MGAG Artis Gilmore/71 8.00 20.00
MGBL Bob Love/67 8.00 20.00
MGBM Bob McAdoo/72 15.00 30.00
MGBW Bill Walton/74 15.00 30.00
MGCW Chet Walker/62 8.00 20.00
MGDI Dan Issel/70 8.00 20.00
MGDT David Thompson/75 8.00 20.00
MGGG George Gervin/72 8.00 20.00
MGGM George McGinnis/71 10.00 25.00
MGJL Jerry Lucas/71 8.00 20.00
MGJS James Silas/72 8.00 20.00
MGJW Jamaal Wilkes/74 8.00 20.00
MGLD Louie Dampier/69 8.00 20.00
MGMD Mel Daniels/67 8.00 20.00
MGMM Moses Malone/74 12.00 30.00
MGRB Rick Barry/65 10.00 25.00
MGSH Spencer Haywood/69 8.00 20.00
MGSN Swen Nater/73 8.00 20.00
MGWF Walt Frazier/67 15.00 40.00

2007-08 Chronology Seriatim

STATED PRINT RUN 8 TO 90 SER.#'d SETS
SOME UNPRICED DUE TO SCARCITY
AM N.Archibald/C.Maxwell/80 8.00 20.00
BH B.Hodges/L.Bird/70 50.00 100.00
BT N.Thurmond/R.Barry/70 12.00 30.00
CA D.Cowens/N.Archibald/70 15.00 40.00
CC M.Conley Sr./M.Conley/80 10.00 25.00
CL Bob Lanier/ML Carr/70 8.00 20.00
DD A.Dantley/W.Davis/80 8.00 20.00
DF W.Davis/P.Ford/80 8.00 20.00
DS D.Wilkins/S.Webb/80 20.00 50.00
FR W.Frazier/C.Russell/60 12.00 30.00
FW Walt Frazier/B.Wanzer/60 10.00 25.00
GA G.Gervin/N.Archibald/80 12.00 30.00
GC H.Grant/B.Cartwright/90 15.00 40.00
GG A.Gilmore/G.Gervin/80 15.00 40.00
GW D.Griffith/D.Williams/80 12.00 30.00
HB S.Haywood/F.Brown/70 15.00 40.00
HH A.Horford/A.Horford/80 8.00 20.00
HK T.Kukoc/R.Harper/90 40.00 100.00
HR R.Guerin/H.Gallatin/50 8.00 20.00
IN G.McGinnis/M.Daniels/80 15.00 40.00
IW B.Walton/D.Issel/70 12.00 30.00
KA S.Kerr/B.Armstrong/90 12.00 30.00
KG K.Garnett/J.Kidd/90 40.00 100.00
KP S.Kerr/J.Paxson/90 20.00 50.00
LC D.Cowens/B.Lanier/70 12.00 30.00
LD B.Laimbeer/A.Dantley/80 12.00 30.00
LH H.Greer/C.Walker/70 12.00 30.00
MK B.McAdoo/G.Karl/70 12.00 30.00
MM V.Mikkelsen/S.Martin/50 15.00 40.00
NN Vandeweghe/Vandeweghe/50 12.00 30.00
OD C.Drexler/Olajuwon/80 30.00 80.00
OR D.Robinson/Olajuwon/90 40.00 100.00
PW Perdue/Wennington/90 15.00 40.00
RB R.Parish/B.Walton/80 15.00 40.00
RG G.Goodrich/C.Russell/70 10.00 25.00
RJ S.Jones/B.Russell/50 75.00 200.00
RL D.Rodman/Laimbeer/80 30.00 80.00
RS B.Sharman/A.Risen/50 10.00 25.00
SH T.Sanders/T.Heinsohn/60 15.00 40.00
SK D.Schayes/J.Kerr/60 12.00 30.00
TE English/D.Thompson/80 15.00 40.00
TG Gervin/D.Thompson/80 15.00 40.00
WC J.Worthy/M.Cooper/80 25.00 50.00
WL J.Lucas/J.West/60 30.00 80.00
WP R.Parish/J.Worthy/80 25.00 60.00
WR L.Wilkens/J.Ramsay/70 12.00 30.00
WS J.Wilkes/B.Scott/80 15.00 40.00

2007-08 Chronology Stitches in Time

PRINT RUN 99 SER.#'d SETS
*STITCH 50: .5X TO 1.25X BASE HI
STITCH 50 PRINT RUN 50 SETS
*STITCH 15: .75X TO 2X BASE HI
STITCH 15 PRINT RUN 15 SETS
STITCH FIVE UNPRICED DUE TO SCARCITY
STITCH ONE UNPRICED DUE TO SCARCITY
AB Aaron Brooks R 3.00 8.00
AD Adrian Dantley L 3.00 8.00
AH Al Horford R 5.00 12.00
AI Allen Iverson V 5.00 12.00
AL Acie Law R 2.50 6.00
AT Al Thornton R 3.00 8.00
BG Ben Gordon V 3.00 8.00
BI Bill Russell L 12.00 30.00
BR Brandon Roy V 4.00 10.00
BW Bill Walton L 4.00 10.00
CA Carmelo Anthony V 5.00 12.00
CB Corey Brewer R 4.00 10.00
CD Clyde Drexler L 5.00 12.00
CK Maurice Cheeks L 2.50 6.00
CM Chris Mullin L 4.00 10.00
CP Chris Paul V 5.00 12.00
DC Daequan Cook R 3.00 8.00
DE Deron Williams V 3.00 8.00
DH Dwight Howard V 3.00 8.00
DR Dennis Rodman L 8.00 20.00
DW Dominique Wilkins L 5.00 12.00
GD Glen Davis R 3.00 8.00
GG George Gervin L 4.00 10.00
HO Hakeem Olajuwon L 6.00 15.00
JA Jason Smith R 3.00 8.00
JC Javaris Crittenton R 2.50 6.00
JD Jared Dudley R 3.00 8.00
JE Julius Erving L 6.00 15.00
JG Jeff Green R 4.00 10.00
JK Jason Kidd V 4.00 10.00
JN Joakim Noah R 4.00 10.00
JO Michael Jordan L 50.00 125.00
JS John Stockton L 6.00 15.00
JW Julian Wright R 2.50 6.00
KA Kareem Abdul-Jabbar L 6.00 15.00
KB Kobe Bryant V 15.00 30.00
KD Kevin Durant R 25.00 60.00
KG Kevin Garnett V 6.00 15.00
KH Kirk Hinrich V 3.00 8.00
LB Larry Bird L 10.00 25.00
LJ LeBron James V 12.00 30.00
MA Morris Almond R 2.50 6.00
MC Mike Conley Jr. R 5.00 12.00
MI Michael Cooper L 3.00 8.00
MJ Magic Johnson L 8.00 20.00
MM Moses Malone L 4.00 10.00
PP Paul Pierce V 4.00 10.00
RO David Robinson L 6.00 15.00
RS Rodney Stuckey R 3.00 8.00
SH Spencer Hawes R 3.00 8.00
SN Steve Nash V 5.00 12.00
SO Shaquille O'Neal V 8.00 20.00
SW Sean Williams R 2.50 6.00
TM Tracy McGrady V 4.00 10.00
TP Tony Parker V 4.00 10.00
VC Vince Carter V 5.00 12.00
WA Dwyane Wade V 6.00 15.00
WC Wilson Chandler R 3.00 8.00
WF Walt Frazier L 4.00 10.00
YM Yao Ming V 5.00 12.00

2007-08 Chronology Stitches in Time Patches Autographs

PRINT RUN 35 SER.#'d SETS
*STITCH AUTO 25: .5X TO 1.25X HI
STITCH AUTO 25 PRINT RUN 25 SER.#'d SETS
*STITCH AUTO 15: .6X TO 1.5X HI
STITCH AUTO 15 PRINT RUN 15 SER.#'d SETS
STITCH AUTO 5 UNPRICED DUE TO SCARCITY
STITCH AUTO 1 UNPRICED DUE TO SCARCITY
AB Aaron Brooks 6.00 15.00
AD Adrian Dantley 20.00 50.00
AH Al Horford 10.00 25.00
AL Acie Law 5.00 12.00
CB Corey Brewer 8.00 20.00
CM Chris Mullin 30.00 80.00
DC Daequan Cook 6.00 15.00
DE Deron Williams 6.00 15.00
GD Glen Davis 6.00 15.00
JA Jason Smith 6.00 15.00
JC Javaris Crittenton 5.00 12.00
JD Jared Dudley 6.00 15.00
JG Jeff Green 8.00 20.00
JN Joakim Noah 8.00 20.00
JW Julian Wright 5.00 12.00
KB Kobe Bryant 300.00 600.00
KD Kevin Durant 500.00 1000.00
KG Kevin Garnett 100.00 175.00
KH Kirk Hinrich 12.00 30.00
LJ LeBron James 250.00 500.00
MA Morris Almond 5.00 12.00
MC Mike Conley Jr. 12.00 30.00
MM Moses Malone 25.00 50.00
RS Rodney Stuckey 6.00 15.00
SH Spencer Hawes 6.00 15.00
SW Sean Williams 5.00 12.00
WC Wilson Chandler 6.00 15.00
WF Walt Frazier 25.00 60.00

2007-08 Chronology The LeBrons

RANDOM INSERTS IN PACKS
LJ LeBron James Blue 6.00 15.00
LJ LeBron James Red 4.00 10.00

2007-08 Chronology Through the Years

PRINT RUN 50 SER.#'d SETS
UNPRICED GOLD PRINT RUN 10 SETS
TEAD Adrian Dantley 10.00 25.00
TEAG Artis Gilmore 10.00 25.00
TEBC Bill Cartwright 20.00 40.00
TEBL Bill Laimbeer 10.00 25.00
TEBM Bob McAdoo 15.00 40.00
TEBO Bob Lanier 10.00 25.00
TECD Clyde Drexler 25.00 60.00
TEDR Dennis Rodman 25.00 60.00
TEDT David Thompson 15.00 40.00
TEDW Dominique Wilkins 20.00 40.00
TEHG Horace Grant 15.00 40.00
TEJE Julius Erving 40.00 100.00
TEJP John Paxson 10.00 25.00
TEJS Jack Sikma 10.00 25.00
TERB Rick Barry 12.00 30.00
TERP Robert Parish 15.00 40.00
TESP Sam Perkins 15.00 30.00
TEVD Vlade Divac 25.00 60.00

2007-08 Chronology Uniformity

STATED PRINT RUN 2 TO 44 SER.#'d SETS
SOME UNPRICED DUE TO SCARCITY
UNPRICED GOLD PRINT RUN 10 SETS
UNBA Abdul-Jabbar/Bird/33 100.00 225.00
UNBJ S.Jones/R.Barry/24 20.00 50.00
UNDS Daugherty/Sikma/43 15.00 30.00
UNFW F.Brown/B.Walton/32 15.00 30.00
UNGH Greer/Heinsohn/15 25.00 60.00
UNGW G.Gervin/J.West/44 40.00 80.00
UNIW D.Issel/Westphal/44 20.00 40.00
UNJB K.Bryant/S.Jones/24 125.00 250.00
UNKM B.King/McGinnis/30 20.00 50.00
UNTW Worthy/Thurmond/42 25.00 50.00
UNWN Nelson/L.Wilkens/19 20.00 40.00

1996 Classic Legends of the Final Four

Sponsored by Sears, official NCAA corporate sponsor, this 32-card set spotlights players and coaches who participated in the Final Four. Each 7-card pack contained six player cards and one "Coaches vs. Cancer" card. The fronts feature full-bleed glossy color action player photos. The set title "Legends of the Final Four"and the player's name are gold foil stamped across the bottom. On a mustard card face accented with orange, the backs carry a profile as well as NCAA Tournament record statistics. The set subdivides into four parts: female players (1-10), male players (11-20), male coaches (MC1-MC5), and female coaches (WC1-WC5). The set concludes with an unnumbered checklist card and a "Coaches vs. Cancer" card. The wrapper itself entitled the holder to 10% off the purchase of Craftsman hand tools. The offer expired 12/31/96.

COMPLETE SET (32) 12.00 30.00
1 Sheryl Swoopes 3.00 8.00
2 Cheryl Miller 3.00 8.00
3 Rebecca Lobo 2.00 5.00
4 Jennifer Azzi 1.50 4.00
5 Dawn Staley 2.00 5.00
6 Charlotte Smith 1.00 2.50
7 Bridgette Gordon .40 1.00
8 Erica Westbrooks .20 .50
9 Tracy Claxton .20 .50
10 Clarissa Davis .20 .50
11 Kareem Abdul-Jabbar .40 1.00
12 Hakeem Olajuwon .40 1.00
13 Bill Walton .40 1.00
14 James Worthy .40 1.00
15 Isiah Thomas .40 1.00
16 Darrell Griffith .20 .50
17 Bobby Hurley .20 .50
18 Glen Rice .20 .50
19 Ed Pinckney .20 .50
20 Danny Manning .20 .50
MC1 John Wooden 1.00 2.50
MC2 Dean Smith .60 1.50
MC3 Nolan Richardson .40 1.00
MC4 Mike Krzyzewski .60 1.50
MC5 John Thompson .40 1.00
WC1 Tara Vanderveer .40 1.00
WC2 Pat Summitt 3.00 8.00
WC3 Marianne Stanley .40 1.00
WC4 Sylvia Hatchell .40 1.00
WC5 Geno Auriemma .40 1.00
NNO Coaches vs. Cancer DP .20 .50
NNO Checklist .20 .50
(Sears Trophy)

2002 Classic Signature Series Shaquille O'Neal

This 2 1/2" by 4 3/4" card shows Shaquille O'Neal dunking a basketball with a silver facsimile signature across the card. The borders are gold, and along the bottom of the card, the stated print run is 24,900 total cards. According to hobbyists, this card was only available through Home Shopping Network.

SS1 Shaquille O'Neal 6.00 15.00

2009-10 Classics

COMP.SET w/o SP's (100) 15.00 30.00
101-160 PRINT RUN 999 SER.#'d SETS
161-200 PRINT RUNS LISTED IN CHECKLIST
1 Kevin Garnett .75 2.00
2 Rasheed Wallace .50 1.25
3 Paul Pierce .50 1.25
4 Kendrick Perkins .30 .75
5 Brook Lopez .40 1.00
6 Devin Harris .30 .75
7 Chris Douglas-Roberts .30 .75
8 Al Harrington .40 1.00
9 David Lee .30 .75
10 Danilo Gallinari .40 1.00
11 Andre Iguodala .40 1.00
12 Louis Williams .40 1.00
13 Elton Brand .50 1.25
14 Chris Bosh .50 1.25
15 Andrea Bargnani .40 1.00
16 Hedo Turkoglu .40 1.00
17 Jose Calderon .30 .75
18 Dirk Nowitzki .60 1.50
19 Shawn Marion .40 1.00
20 Drew Gooden .40 1.00
21 J.J. Barea .60 1.50
22 Shane Battier .50 1.25
23 Aaron Brooks .30 .75
24 Trevor Ariza .30 .75
25 Rudy Gay .50 1.25
26 Zach Randolph .40 1.00
27 O.J. Mayo .30 .75
28 Chris Paul .60 1.50
29 David West .40 1.00
30 Emeka Okafor .40 1.00
31 Tim Duncan .75 2.00
32 Tony Parker .50 1.25
33 Richard Jefferson .40 1.00
34 Manu Ginobili .50 1.25
35 Luol Deng .40 1.00
36 Derrick Rose .75 2.00
37 John Salmons .40 1.00
38 LeBron James 2.00 5.00
39 Mo Williams .40 1.00
40 Shaquille O'Neal 1.00 2.50
41 Anderson Varejao .30 .75
42 Ben Gordon .40 1.00
43 Rodney Stuckey .30 .75
44 Charlie Villanueva .30 .75
45 Danny Granger .40 1.00
46 Mike Dunleavy .30 .75
47 Dahntay Jones .30 .75
48 Andrew Bogut .40 1.00
49 Michael Redd .40 1.00
50 Hakim Warrick .40 1.00
51 Carmelo Anthony .60 1.50
52 Chauncey Billups .50 1.25
53 Nene .40 1.00
54 Chris Andersen .40 1.00
55 Al Jefferson .40 1.00
56 Corey Brewer .30 .75
57 Ryan Gomes .30 .75
58 Brandon Roy .50 1.25
59 LaMarcus Aldridge .50 1.25
60 Andre Miller .40 1.00
61 Kevin Durant 1.25 3.00
62 Russell Westbrook 1.25 3.00
63 Jeff Green .40 1.00
64 Carlos Boozer .40 1.00
65 Deron Williams .40 1.00
66 Andrei Kirilenko .40 1.00
67 Joe Johnson .40 1.00
68 Josh Smith .40 1.00
69 Jamal Crawford .50 1.25
70 Stephen Jackson .40 1.00
71 Raymond Felton .40 1.00
72 Gerald Wallace .40 1.00
73 Dwyane Wade .75 2.00
74 Jermaine O'Neal .40 1.00
75 Michael Beasley .30 .75
76 Udonis Haslem .30 .75
77 Vince Carter .60 1.50
78 Dwight Howard .40 1.00
79 Rashard Lewis .40 1.00
80 J.J. Redick .50 1.25
81 Antawn Jamison .40 1.00
82 Caron Butler .40 1.00
83 Randy Foye .30 .75
84 Monta Ellis .40 1.00

85 Corey Maggette .40 1.00
86 Anthony Randolph .30 .75
87 Chris Kaman .40 1.00
88 Eric Gordon .40 1.00
89 Baron Davis .40 1.00
90 Kobe Bryant 2.00 5.00
91 Andrew Bynum .30 .75
92 Lamar Odom .40 1.00
93 Ron Artest .50 1.25
94 Amare Stoudemire .40 1.00
95 Jason Richardson .50 1.25
96 Steve Nash .50 1.25
97 Grant Hill .60 1.50
98 Kevin Martin .40 1.00
99 Beno Udrih .30 .75
100 Jason Thompson .30 .75
101 Larry Bird 3.00 8.00
102 Gail Goodrich 1.00 2.50
103 Harry Gallatin 1.25 3.00
104 Chris Webber 1.25 3.00
105 Nate McMillan 1.25 3.00
106 George Mikan 2.50 6.00
107 Drazen Petrovic 2.50 6.00
108 Jalen Rose 1.25 3.00
109 Mitch Richmond 1.25 3.00
110 Mark Price 1.25 3.00
111 David Robinson 2.00 5.00
112 Rick Barry 1.00 2.50
113 Lenny Wilkens 1.25 3.00
114 Robert Horry 1.00 2.50
115 Walt Frazier 1.25 3.00
116 Buck Williams .75 2.00
117 Patrick Ewing 1.50 4.00
118 Danny Manning 1.00 2.50
119 Dennis Johnson 1.00 2.50
120 Rony Seikaly .75 2.00
121 Chris Mullin 1.25 3.00
122 Hakeem Olajuwon 1.50 4.00
123 George Gervin 1.25 3.00
124 Rex Chapman 1.25 3.00
125 Bob McAdoo 1.00 2.50
126 Dana Barros .75 2.00
127 B.J. Armstrong 1.25 3.00
128 Danny Roundfield 1.25 3.00
129 Oscar Robertson 1.25 3.00
130 Bill Russell 2.00 5.00
131 Doc Rivers 1.25 3.00
132 Clyde Drexler 1.50 4.00
133 Kareem Abdul-Jabbar 2.00 5.00
134 Bernard King 1.00 2.50
135 Don Nelson 1.25 3.00
136 John Salley .75 2.00
137 Jerry Sloan 1.25 3.00
138 Joe Dumars 1.25 3.00
139 Karl Malone 1.50 4.00
140 Magic Johnson 3.00 8.00
141 Dominique Wilkins 1.50 4.00
142 Jack Sikma 1.00 2.50
143 Wes Unseld 1.25 3.00
144 Sidney Moncrief .75 2.00
145 Sleepy Floyd .75 2.00
146 Spencer Haywood .75 2.00
147 Kevin McHale 1.25 3.00
148 Glen Rice 1.00 2.50
149 Isiah Thomas 1.25 3.00
150 Jerry West 1.50 4.00
151 Willis Reed 1.25 3.00
152 Bob Lanier 1.00 2.50
153 Elgin Baylor 1.25 3.00
154 Scottie Pippen 2.50 6.00
155 Elvin Hayes 1.25 3.00
156 Scott Skiles 1.00 2.50
157 Ed Macauley 1.25 3.00
158 Pete Maravich 2.00 5.00
159 Bob Cousy 2.00 5.00
160 Wilt Chamberlain 2.50 6.00
161 Blake Griffin AU/499 RC 40.00 100.00
162 Hasheem Thabeet AU/499 RC 3.00 8.00
163 James Harden AU/499 RC 125.00 300.00
164 Tyreke Evans AU/499 RC 4.00 10.00
165 Jonny Flynn AU/499 RC 3.00 8.00
166 Stephen Curry AU/499 RC 600.00 1000.00
167 Jordan Hill AU/469 RC 4.00 10.00
168 B.Jennings AU/499 RC 5.00 12.00
169 Terrence Williams AU/499 RC 3.00 8.00
170 Gerald Henderson AU/499 RC 4.00 10.00
171 Tyler Hansbrough AU/499 RC 4.00 10.00
172 Earl Clark AU/571 RC 4.00 10.00
173 Austin Daye AU/598 RC 3.00 8.00
174 James Johnson AU/199 RC 4.00 10.00
175 Jrue Holiday AU/499 RC 6.00 15.00
176 Ty Lawson AU/599 RC 5.00 12.00
177 Jeff Teague AU/553 RC 5.00 12.00
178 Eric Maynor AU/599 RC 3.00 8.00
179 D.Collison AU/799 RC 5.00 12.00
180 Omri Casspi AU/862 RC 4.00 10.00
181 B.J. Mullens AU/872 RC 3.00 8.00
182 R.Beaubois AU/199 RC 3.00 8.00
183 Taj Gibson AU/823 RC 5.00 12.00
184 DeMarre Carroll AU/864 RC 4.00 10.00
185 Wayne Ellington AU/575 RC 5.00 12.00
186 Toney Douglas AU/933 RC 3.00 8.00
187 DeJuan Blair AU/999 RC 4.00 10.00
188 Sam Young AU/249 RC 3.00 8.00
189 A.J. Price AU/999 RC 3.00 8.00
190 Chase Budinger AU/999 RC 4.00 10.00
191 David Andersen AU/99 RC 3.00 8.00
192 Jonas Jerebko AU/999 RC 5.00 12.00
193 Marcus Landry AU/999 RC 3.00 8.00
194 Serge Ibaka AU/99 RC 15.00 40.00
195 Patrick Mills AU/99 RC 40.00 100.00
196 Wesley Matthews AU/99 RC 30.00 80.00
197 Taylor Griffin AU/999 RC 3.00 8.00
198 Jermaine Taylor AU/999 RC 3.00 8.00
199 Jodie Meeks AU/249 RC 5.00 12.00
200 DaJuan Summers AU/999 RC 3.00 8.00

2009-10 Classics Timeless Tributes Gold

*1-100 GOLD: 2X TO 5X BASE HI
*101-160 GOLD: .75X TO 2X BASE HI
*161-200 GOLD: .6X TO 1.5X SILVER HI
GOLD PRINT RUN 50 SER.#'d SETS
161 Blake Griffin 30.00 80.00
166 Stephen Curry 125.00 300.00

2009-10 Classics Timeless Tributes Platinum

*1-100 PLATINUM: 3X TO 8X BASE HI
*101-160 PLATINUM: 1.25X TO 3X BASE HI
*161-200 PLAT: .75X TO 2X SILVER HI
PLATINUM PRINT RUN 25 SER.#'d SETS
166 Stephen Curry 150.00 400.00

2009-10 Classics Timeless Tributes Silver

*1-100 SILVER: 1.25X TO 3X BASE HI
*101-160 SILVER: .5X TO 1.25X BASE HI
SILVER PRINT RUN 100 SER.#'d SETS
161 Blake Griffin 10.00 25.00
162 Hasheem Thabeet 1.50 4.00
163 James Harden 12.00 30.00
164 Tyreke Evans 2.00 5.00
165 Jonny Flynn 1.50 4.00
166 Stephen Curry 75.00 200.00

167 Jordan Hill 2.00 5.00
168 Brandon Jennings 2.50 6.00
169 Terrence Williams 1.50 4.00
170 Gerald Henderson 2.00 5.00
171 Tyler Hansbrough 2.00 5.00
172 Earl Clark 2.00 5.00
173 Austin Daye 1.50 4.00
174 James Johnson 2.00 5.00
175 Jrue Holiday 3.00 8.00
176 Ty Lawson 2.50 6.00
177 Jeff Teague 2.50 6.00
178 Eric Maynor 1.50 4.00
179 Darren Collison 2.50 6.00
180 Omri Casspi 2.00 5.00
181 B.J. Mullens 1.50 4.00
182 Rodrigue Beaubois 1.50 4.00
183 Taj Gibson 2.50 6.00
184 DeMarre Carroll 2.00 5.00
185 Wayne Ellington 2.50 6.00
186 Toney Douglas 1.50 4.00
187 DeJuan Blair 2.00 5.00
188 Sam Young 1.50 4.00
189 A.J. Price 1.50 4.00
190 Chase Budinger 2.00 5.00
191 David Andersen 1.50 4.00
192 Jonas Jerebko 2.50 6.00
193 Marcus Landry 1.50 4.00
194 Serge Ibaka 2.50 6.00
195 Patrick Mills 5.00 12.00
196 Wesley Matthews 2.50 6.00
197 Taylor Griffin 1.50 4.00
198 Jermaine Taylor 1.50 4.00
199 Jodie Meeks 2.50 6.00
200 DaJuan Summers 1.50 4.00

2009-10 Classics Blast From The Past Jerseys

STATED PRINT RUN 25 TO 199 SETS
1 Dan Issel/99 3.00 8.00
2 Adrian Dantley/99 3.00 8.00
3 Anfernee Hardaway/199 10.00 25.00
4 Bernard King/199 3.00 8.00
5 Clyde Drexler/199 5.00 12.00
6 Glen Rice/199 3.00 8.00
7 John Stockton/25 8.00 20.00
8 Robert Horry/199 3.00 8.00
9 Karl Malone/199 5.00 12.00
10 Larry Johnson/199 10.00 25.00
11 Danny Manning/199 3.00 8.00
12 Reggie Lewis/199 10.00 25.00
13 Kevin Johnson/199 4.00 10.00
14 Sleepy Floyd/199 2.50 6.00
15 Tom Heinsohn/99 4.00 10.00
16 Xavier McDaniel/199 2.50 6.00
17 Artis Gilmore/199 3.00 8.00
18 Toni Kukoc/199 4.00 10.00
19 Chuck Person/199 3.00 8.00
20 Bob Lanier/199 3.00 8.00
21 Dominique Wilkins/199 5.00 12.00
22 Hakeem Olajuwon/199 5.00 12.00
23 Sam Perkins/199 2.50 6.00
24 Chris Mullin/199 4.00 10.00
25 Michael Cage/199 2.50 6.00

2009-10 Classics Blast From The Past Jerseys Prime

*PRIME: .6X TO 1.5X HI COLUMN
STATED PRINT RUN 10 TO 30 SER.#'d SETS
5 Clyde Drexler/30 12.00 30.00
6 Glen Rice/30 15.00 30.00
9 Karl Malone/30 15.00 30.00
10 Larry Johnson/30 25.00 60.00
11 Danny Manning/30 15.00 30.00
12 Reggie Lewis/30 30.00 60.00
13 Kevin Johnson/30 8.00 20.00
21 Dominique Wilkins/30 10.00 25.00
22 Hakeem Olajuwon/30 10.00 25.00

2009-10 Classics Blast From The Past Jerseys Signatures

PRINT RUN 25 SER.#'d SETS
1 Dan Issel 8.00 20.00
2 Adrian Dantley 8.00 20.00
3 Anfernee Hardaway 50.00 100.00
4 Bernard King 8.00 20.00
5 Clyde Drexler 20.00 50.00
6 Glen Rice 20.00 50.00
10 Larry Johnson 25.00 60.00
11 Danny Manning 15.00 30.00
13 Kevin Johnson 30.00 80.00
14 Sleepy Floyd 8.00 20.00
16 Xavier McDaniel 8.00 20.00
17 Artis Gilmore 8.00 20.00
18 Toni Kukoc 25.00 60.00
23 Sam Perkins 8.00 20.00

2009-10 Classics Blast From The Past Jerseys Prime Signatures

PRINT RUNS LISTED IN CHECKLIST
2 Adrian Dantley/25 12.50 30.00
3 Anfernee Hardaway/25 75.00 150.00
6 Glen Rice/25 25.00 60.00
10 Larry Johnson/25 50.00 120.00
11 Danny Manning/25 20.00 40.00
13 Kevin Johnson/25 50.00 100.00
14 Sleepy Floyd/25 15.00 40.00
16 Xavier McDaniel/25 12.50 30.00
18 Toni Kukoc/25 30.00 80.00
23 Sam Perkins/25 12.50 30.00

2009-10 Classics Classic Combos

COMPLETE SET (10) 10.00 25.00
*GOLD: .75X TO 2X BASE HI
GOLD PRINT RUN 100 SER.#'d SETS
*PLATINUM: 1.5X TO 4X BASE HI
PLATINUM PRINT RUN 25 SER.#'d SETS
*SILVER: .5X TO 1.25X BASE HI
SILVER PRINT RUN 250 SER.#'d SETS
1 K.Bryant/L.Odom 3.00 8.00
2 L.James/S.O'Neal 3.00 8.00
3 P.Pierce/K.Garnett 1.25 3.00
4 D.Nowitzki/S.Marion 1.00 2.50
5 D.Wade/J.O'Neal 1.25 3.00
6 B.Russell/B.Sharman 1.25 3.00
7 A.Mourning/T.Hardaway 1.00 2.50
8 H.Olajuwon/C.Drexler 1.00 2.50
9 I.Thomas/J.Dumars .75 2.00
10 J.Stockton/K.Malone 1.25 3.00

2009-10 Classics Classic Combos Jerseys

STATED PRINT RUN ONE TO 99 SER.#'d SETS
2 L.James/S.O'Neal/99 10.00 25.00
3 P.Pierce/K.Garnett/99 6.00 15.00
4 D.Nowitzki/S.Marion/99 6.00 15.00
8 H.Olajuwon/C.Drexler/99 6.00 15.00
9 I.Thomas/J.Dumars/99 8.00 20.00
10 J.Stockton/K.Malone/99 6.00 15.00

2009-10 Classics Classic Combos Jerseys Prime

*PRIME: 1X TO 2.5X BASE HI
PRINT RUN 25 SER.#'d SETS
2 L.James/S.O'Neal 30.00 80.00
3 P.Pierce/K.Garnett 12.00 30.00
9 I.Thomas/J.Dumars 10.00 25.00

2009-10 Classics Classic Confrontations

COMPLETE SET (10) 10.00 25.00
*GOLD: ..75X TO 2X BASE HI
GOLD PRINT RUN 50 SER.#'d SETS
*PLATINUM: 1.5X TO 4X BASE HI
PLATINUM PRINT RUN 25 SER.#'d SETS
*SILVER: .5X TO 1.25X BASE HI
SILVER PRINT RUN 250 SER.#'d SETS
1 L.Bird/M.Johnson 2.00 5.00
2 E.Monroe/W.Frazier .75 2.00
3 W.Reed/K.Abdul-Jabbar 1.25 3.00
4 J.Worthy/R.Parish 1.00 2.50
5 K.Bryant/L.James 3.00 8.00
6 D.Nowitzki/T.Duncan 1.25 3.00
7 C.Paul/D.Wade 1.25 3.00
8 K.Garnett/S.O'Neal 1.50 4.00
9 J.Kidd/S.Nash .75 2.00
10 J.West/O.Robertson 1.00 2.50

2009-10 Classics Classic Confrontations Jerseys

STATED PRINT RUN 199 SER.#'d SETS
*PRIME: 1X TO 2.5X BASE HI
PRIME PRINT RUN 25 SER.#'d SETS
1 L.Bird/M.Johnson 12.50 30.00
5 K.Bryant/L.James 12.50 30.00
6 D.Nowitzki/T.Duncan 5.00 12.00
7 C.Paul/D.Wade 5.00 12.00
8 K.Garnett/S.O'Neal 10.00 25.00

2009-10 Classics Classic Confrontations Jerseys Signatures

STATED PRINT RUN 25 SER.#'d SETS
*PRIME: .5X TO 1.25X BASE HI
PRIME PRINT RUN 25 SER.#'d SETS
1 L.Bird/M.Johnson 100.00 200.00

2009-10 Classics Classic Greats

COMPLETE SET (30) 25.00 50.00
*GOLD: .6X TO 1.5X BASE HI
GOLD PRINT RUN 100 SER.#'d SETS
*PLATINUM: 1X TO 2.5X BASE HI
PLATINUM PRINT RUN 25 SER.#'d SETS
*SILVER: .5X TO 1.25X BASE HI
SILVER PRINT RUN 250 SER.#'d SETS
1 Bill Russell 2.00 5.00
2 Bill Sharman 1.25 3.00
3 Bill Walton 1.25 3.00
4 Bob Cousy 2.00 5.00
5 Clyde Drexler 1.50 4.00
6 Dave Cowens .75 2.00
7 Earl Monroe 1.25 3.00
8 Elvin Hayes 1.25 3.00
9 George Gervin 1.25 3.00
10 Hakeem Olajuwon 1.50 4.00
11 Hal Greer 1.00 2.50
12 Isiah Thomas 1.25 3.00
13 James Worthy 1.50 4.00
14 Jerry West 1.50 4.00
15 John Havlicek 1.25 3.00
16 Kareem Abdul-Jabbar 2.00 5.00
17 Karl Malone 1.50 4.00
18 Kevin McHale 1.25 3.00
19 Larry Bird 3.00 8.00
20 Lenny Wilkens 1.25 3.00
21 Magic Johnson 3.00 8.00
22 Moses Malone 1.25 3.00
23 Nate Archibald 1.00 2.50
24 Nate Thurmond 1.00 2.50
25 Oscar Robertson 1.25 3.00
26 Rick Barry 1.00 2.50
27 Robert Parish 1.25 3.00
28 Walt Frazier 1.25 3.00
29 Wes Unseld 1.25 3.00
30 Willis Reed 1.25 3.00

2009-10 Classics Classic Greats Jerseys

STATED PRINT RUN 10 TO 99 SER.#'d SETS
SOME UNPRICED DUE TO SCARCITY
5 Clyde Drexler/99 6.00 15.00
6 Dave Cowens/99 2.50 6.00
7 Earl Monroe/99 4.00 10.00
10 Hakeem Olajuwon/99 5.00 12.00
12 Isiah Thomas/99 4.00 10.00
14 Jerry West/49 5.00 12.00
15 John Havlicek/49 4.00 10.00
16 Kareem Abdul-Jabbar/99 8.00 20.00
17 Karl Malone/99 5.00 12.00
18 Kevin McHale/99 4.00 10.00
19 Larry Bird/99 8.00 20.00
21 Magic Johnson/99 6.00 15.00
22 Moses Malone/25 6.00 15.00
26 Rick Barry/99 3.00 8.00
27 Robert Parish/99 4.00 10.00

2009-10 Classics Classic Greats Jerseys Prime

*PRIME: .6X TO 1.5X HI COLUMN
STATED PRINT RUN 10 TO 25 SER.#'d SETS
SOME UNPRICED DUE TO SCARCITY
6 Dave Cowens/25 8.00 20.00
15 John Havlicek/25 8.00 20.00
19 Larry Bird/25 15.00 40.00
21 Magic Johnson/25 12.50 30.00
26 Rick Barry/25 5.00 12.00

2009-10 Classics Classic Greats Jerseys Signatures

STATED PRINT RUN 5 TO 25 SER.#'d SETS
SOME UNPRICED DUE TO SCARCITY
5 Clyde Drexler/25 25.00 60.00
6 Dave Cowens/25 10.00 25.00
7 Earl Monroe/25 15.00 40.00
12 Isiah Thomas/25 12.50 30.00
16 Kareem Abdul-Jabbar/25 30.00 80.00
18 Kevin McHale/25 40.00 100.00
19 Larry Bird/25 40.00 100.00
21 Magic Johnson/25 40.00 100.00
26 Rick Barry/25 12.50 30.00
27 Robert Parish/25 10.00 25.00

2009-10 Classics Classic Greats Jerseys Prime Signatures

STATED PRINT RUN 5 TO 25 SER.#'d SETS
SOME UNPRICED DUE TO SCARCITY
6 Dave Cowens/25 12.50 30.00
7 Earl Monroe/25 15.00 40.00
12 Isiah Thomas/25 15.00 40.00
16 Kareem Abdul-Jabbar/25 50.00 120.00
18 Kevin McHale/25 50.00 120.00
19 Larry Bird/25 50.00 120.00
21 Magic Johnson/25 40.00 100.00
26 Rick Barry/25 12.50 30.00
27 Robert Parish/25 12.50 30.00

2009-10 Classics Dress Code

COMPLETE SET (25) 20.00 40.00
*GOLD: .6X TO 1.5X BASE HI
GOLD PRINT RUN 100 SER.#'d SETS
*PLATINUM: 1.25X TO 3X BASE HI
PLATINUM PRINT RUN 25 SER.#'d SETS
*SILVER: .5X TO 1.25X BASE HI
SILVER PRINT RUN 250 SER.#'d SETS
1 Al Horford .75 2.00
2 Alex English .60 1.50
3 Andre Iguodala .60 1.50
4 Yao Ming 1.00 2.50
5 Tracy McGrady .75 2.00
6 Tim Duncan 1.25 3.00
7 Thaddeus Young .50 1.25
8 Shawn Marion .60 1.50
9 Samuel Dalembert .50 1.25
10 Sam Perkins .50 1.25
11 David Lee .50 1.25
12 Dwight Howard .60 1.50
13 Erick Dampier .50 1.25
14 Randy Foye .50 1.25
15 Jeff Hornacek .60 1.50
16 Kevin Garnett 1.25 3.00
17 Kobe Bryant 3.00 8.00
18 LeBron James 3.00 8.00
19 Mark Price .75 2.00
20 Mehmet Okur .50 1.25
21 Mitch Richmond .75 2.00
22 Nene .60 1.50
23 Patrick Ewing 1.00 2.50
24 Carlos Boozer .60 1.50
25 Chauncey Billups .75 2.00

2009-10 Classics Dress Code Jerseys

STATED PRINT RUN 49 TO 199 SER.#'d SETS
1 Al Horford/199 3.00 8.00
2 Alex English/199 2.50 6.00
3 Andre Iguodala/199 2.50 6.00
4 Yao Ming/99 4.00 10.00
5 Tracy McGrady/199 3.00 8.00
6 Tim Duncan/199 5.00 12.00
7 Thaddeus Young/199 2.00 5.00
8 Shawn Marion/199 2.50 6.00
9 Samuel Dalembert/199 2.00 5.00
10 Sam Perkins/199 2.00 5.00
11 David Lee/49 2.00 5.00
12 Dwight Howard/199 2.50 6.00
13 Erick Dampier/199 2.00 5.00
14 Randy Foye/199 2.00 5.00
15 Jeff Hornacek/199 2.50 6.00
16 Kevin Garnett/199 5.00 12.00
17 Kobe Bryant/99 10.00 25.00
18 LeBron James/199 8.00 20.00
19 Mark Price/199 6.00 15.00
21 Mitch Richmond/199 3.00 8.00
22 Nene/199 2.50 6.00
23 Patrick Ewing/199 4.00 10.00
24 Carlos Boozer/199 2.50 6.00
25 Chauncey Billups/199 3.00 8.00

2009-10 Classics Dress Code Jerseys Prime

*PRIME: .75X TO 2X BASE HI
STATED PRINT RUN 5 TO 25 SER.#'d SETS
SOME UNPRICED DUE TO SCARCITY

2009-10 Classics Dress Code Jerseys Signatures

STATED PRINT RUN 10 TO 25 SER.#'d SETS
SOME UNPRICED DUE TO SCARCITY
2 Alex English/25 8.00 20.00
3 Andre Iguodala/25 6.00 15.00
10 Sam Perkins/25 6.00 15.00
15 Jeff Hornacek/25 8.00 20.00
17 Kobe Bryant/25 100.00 200.00
24 Carlos Boozer/25 6.00 15.00
25 Chauncey Billups/25 12.50 30.00

2009-10 Classics Dress Code Jerseys Prime Signatures

STATED PRINT RUN 10 TO 25 SER.#'d SETS
SOME UNPRICED DUE TO SCARCITY
2 Alex English/25 10.00 25.00
3 Andre Iguodala/25 8.00 20.00
10 Sam Perkins/25 12.50 30.00
11 David Lee/25 10.00 25.00
15 Jeff Hornacek/25 10.00 25.00
24 Carlos Boozer/25 8.00 20.00
25 Chauncey Billups/25 10.00 25.00

2009-10 Classics Significant Signatures Gold

STATED PRINT RUN 13 TO 50 SER.#'d SETS
6 Devin Harris/50 5.00 12.00
22 Shane Battier/50 5.00 12.00
23 Aaron Brooks/50 5.00 12.00
24 Trevor Ariza/27 5.00 12.00
30 Emeka Okafor/50 6.00 15.00
32 Tony Parker/50 10.00 25.00
44 Charlie Villanueva/50 5.00 12.00
45 Danny Granger/39 10.00 25.00
57 Ryan Gomes/50 5.00 12.00
74 Jermaine O'Neal/13 10.00 25.00
88 Eric Gordon/50 8.00 20.00
90 Kobe Bryant/50 100.00 200.00
101 Larry Bird/50 40.00 100.00
102 Gail Goodrich/50 10.00 25.00
103 Harry Gallatin/50 6.00 15.00
108 Jalen Rose/50 8.00 20.00
110 Mark Price/50
112 Rick Barry/50 8.00 20.00
113 Lenny Wilkens/50 8.00 20.00
114 Robert Horry/50 8.00 20.00
115 Walt Frazier/50 10.00 25.00
118 Danny Manning/50 10.00 25.00
121 Chris Mullin/50 25.00 50.00
123 George Gervin/50 10.00 25.00
125 Bob McAdoo/50 15.00 30.00
129 Oscar Robertson/50 60.00 120.00
130 Bill Russell/50 80.00 160.00
131 Doc Rivers/50 10.00 25.00
132 Clyde Drexler/50 30.00 80.00
133 Kareem Abdul-Jabbar/50 50.00 120.00
134 Bernard King/50 8.00 20.00
138 Joe Dumars/50 15.00 40.00
140 Magic Johnson/49 50.00 120.00
141 Dominique Wilkins/50 15.00 40.00
143 Wes Unseld/45 10.00 25.00
144 Sidney Moncrief/50 8.00 20.00
145 Sleepy Floyd/48 8.00 20.00
146 Spencer Haywood/50 6.00 15.00
147 Kevin McHale/50 30.00 60.00
148 Glen Rice/50 12.50 30.00
149 Isiah Thomas/50 12.50 30.00
150 Jerry West/50 30.00 80.00
151 Willis Reed/50 12.50 30.00
153 Elgin Baylor/50 15.00 40.00
154 Scottie Pippen/50 125.00 250.00
155 Elvin Hayes/50 10.00 25.00
159 Bob Cousy/50 20.00 50.00

2009-10 Classics Significant Signatures Platinum

*PLATINUM: .5X TO 1.25X HI COLUMN
STATED PRINT RUN ONE TO 25 SER.#'d SETS
SOME UNPRICED DUE TO SCARCITY
74 Jermaine O'Neal/25 8.00 20.00
90 Kobe Bryant/25 125.00 225.00
110 Mark Price/25 30.00 80.00
122 Hakeem Olajuwon/25 30.00 80.00
131 Doc Rivers/25 15.00 40.00
141 Dominique Wilkins/25 20.00 50.00

2009-10 Classics Timeless Threads

STATED PRINT RUN ONE TO 265 SETS
SOME UNPRICED DUE TO SCARCITY
1 Kevin Garnett/199 5.00 12.00
3 Paul Pierce/199 3.00 8.00
9 David Lee/49 2.00 5.00
10 Danilo Gallinari/25 2.50 6.00
11 Andre Iguodala/199 2.50 6.00
13 Elton Brand/199 3.00 8.00
14 Chris Bosh/199 3.00 8.00
15 Andrea Bargnani/25 2.50 6.00
17 Jose Calderon/299 2.00 5.00
18 Dirk Nowitzki/199 4.00 10.00
19 Shawn Marion/199 2.50 6.00
21 J.J. Barea/199 5.00 12.00
22 Shane Battier/199 3.00 8.00
23 Aaron Brooks/199 2.00 5.00
27 O.J. Mayo/199 2.00 5.00
28 Chris Paul/199 4.00 10.00
29 David West/199 2.50 6.00
31 Tim Duncan/199 5.00 12.00
32 Tony Parker/25 6.00 15.00
38 LeBron James/199 10.00 25.00
39 Mo Williams/99 2.50 6.00
40 Shaquille O'Neal/199 6.00 15.00
44 Charlie Villanueva/199 2.00 5.00
51 Carmelo Anthony/199 4.00 10.00
52 Chauncey Billups/199 3.00 8.00
53 Nene/299 2.50 6.00
55 Al Jefferson/199 2.50 6.00
57 Ryan Gomes/299 2.00 5.00
58 Brandon Roy/199 3.00 8.00
59 LaMarcus Aldridge/199 3.00 8.00
61 Kevin Durant/199 8.00 20.00
64 Carlos Boozer/199 2.50 6.00
65 Deron Williams/199 2.50 6.00
66 Andrei Kirilenko/199 2.50 6.00
68 Josh Smith/199 2.50 6.00
72 Gerald Wallace/199 2.50 6.00
73 Dwyane Wade/199 5.00 12.00
75 Michael Beasley/99 2.00 5.00
76 Udonis Haslem/199 2.00 5.00
78 Dwight Howard/199 2.50 6.00
79 Rashard Lewis/199 2.50 6.00
81 Antawn Jamison/199 2.50 6.00
83 Randy Foye/199 2.00 5.00
87 Chris Kaman/199 2.50 6.00
90 Kobe Bryant/99 8.00 20.00
109 Mitch Richmond/99 4.00 10.00
110 Mark Price/99 8.00 20.00
112 Rick Barry/99 6.00 15.00
117 Patrick Ewing/99 12.50 30.00
119 Dennis Johnson/99 10.00 25.00
121 Chris Mullin/99 6.00 15.00
122 Hakeem Olajuwon/99 6.00 15.00
132 Clyde Drexler/99 8.00 20.00
133 Kareem Abdul-Jabbar/99 6.00 15.00
138 Joe Dumars/49 4.00 10.00
139 Karl Malone/99 8.00 20.00
140 Magic Johnson/99 6.00 15.00
141 Dominique Wilkins/49 6.00 15.00
147 Kevin McHale/99 6.00 15.00
149 Isiah Thomas/99 4.00 10.00
150 Jerry West/49 6.00 15.00
161 Blake Griffin/265 8.00 20.00
162 Hasheem Thabeet/265 1.25 3.00
163 James Harden/265 10.00 25.00
164 Tyreke Evans/265 1.50 4.00
165 Jonny Flynn/265 1.25 3.00
166 Stephen Curry/265 75.00 200.00
167 Jordan Hill/265 1.50 4.00
168 Brandon Jennings/265 2.00 5.00
169 Terrence Williams/265 1.25 3.00
170 Gerald Henderson/265 1.50 4.00
171 Tyler Hansbrough/265 1.50 4.00
172 Earl Clark/265 1.50 4.00
173 Austin Daye/265 1.25 3.00
174 James Johnson/265 1.50 4.00
175 Jrue Holiday/265 2.50 6.00
176 Ty Lawson/265 2.00 5.00
177 Jeff Teague/265 2.00 5.00
178 Eric Maynor/265 1.25 3.00
179 Darren Collison/265 2.00 5.00
180 Omri Casspi/265 1.50 4.00
181 B.J. Mullens/265 1.25 3.00
182 Rodrigue Beaubois/265 1.25 3.00
183 Taj Gibson/265 2.00 5.00
184 DeMarre Carroll/265 1.50 4.00
185 Wayne Ellington/265 2.00 5.00
186 Toney Douglas/265 1.25 3.00
187 DeJuan Blair/265 1.50 4.00
188 Sam Young/265 1.25 3.00
190 Chase Budinger/265 1.50 4.00
197 Taylor Griffin/265 1.25 3.00
198 Jermaine Taylor/265 1.25 3.00
199 Jodie Meeks/265 2.00 5.00
200 DaJuan Summers/265 1.25 3.00

2009-10 Classics Timeless Threads Prime

*PRIME: .75X TO 2X HI COLUMN
*PRIME RCs: 1X TO 2.5X HI COLUMN
STATED PRINT RUN ONE TO 25 SER.#'d SETS
SOME UNPRICED DUE TO SCARCITY
21 J.J. Barea/25 12.50 30.00
40 Shaquille O'Neal/25 20.00 50.00
73 Dwyane Wade/25 15.00 40.00
161 Blake Griffin/25 20.00 50.00

2010-11 Classics

COMP.SET w/o SPs (100) 15.00 30.00
RETIRED PRINT RUN 999 SER.#'d SETS
AU RC PRINT RUN 199 TO 699 SER.#'d SETS
EXCH.EXPIRATION 10/13/2012
UNPRICED BLACK PRINT RUN ONE SET
1 Dirk Nowitzki .60 1.50
2 Caron Butler .40 1.00
3 Tyson Chandler .40 1.00
4 Ian Mahinmi RC .50 1.25
5 George Hill .40 1.00
6 Tim Duncan .75 2.00
7 Manu Ginobili .50 1.25
8 Chris Paul .60 1.50
9 Marco Belinelli .30 .75
10 David West .40 1.00
11 Marc Gasol .50 1.25
12 Zach Randolph .40 1.00
13 Mike Conley Jr. .50 1.25
14 Aaron Brooks .30 .75
15 Kevin Martin .40 1.00
16 Luis Scola .40 1.00
17 Kobe Bryant 2.00 5.00
18 Derek Fisher .40 1.00
19 Pau Gasol .50 1.25
20 Lamar Odom .40 1.00
21 Eric Gordon .40 1.00
22 Blake Griffin .50 1.25
23 Chris Kaman .40 1.00
24 Steve Nash .50 1.25
25 Vince Carter .60 1.50
26 Channing Frye .40 1.00
27 Stephen Curry 2.00 5.00
28 Monta Ellis .40 1.00
29 David Lee .30 .75
30 Tyreke Evans .30 .75
31 Beno Udrih .30 .75
32 Carl Landry .30 .75
33 Kevin Durant 1.25 3.00
34 Jeff Green .40 1.00
35 Russell Westbrook 1.25 3.00
36 Michael Beasley .30 .75
37 Kevin Love .50 1.25
38 Corey Brewer .30 .75
39 Carmelo Anthony .60 1.50
40 Nene .40 1.00
41 Chauncey Billups .50 1.25
42 Arron Afflalo .30 .75
43 Brandon Roy .50 1.25
44 Wesley Matthews .30 .75
45 LaMarcus Aldridge .50 1.25
46 Rudy Fernandez .30 .75
47 Al Jefferson .40 1.00
48 Deron Williams .40 1.00
49 Andrei Kirilenko .40 1.00
50 Rajon Rondo .50 1.25
51 Paul Pierce .50 1.25
52 Kevin Garnett .75 2.00
53 Ray Allen .50 1.25
54 Amare Stoudemire .40 1.00
55 Raymond Felton .40 1.00
56 Toney Douglas .30 .75
57 Danilo Gallinari .40 1.00
58 Bill Walker .30 .75
59 Andrea Bargnani .40 1.00
60 Sonny Weems .30 .75
61 DeMar DeRozan .50 1.25
62 Jrue Holiday .50 1.25
63 Elton Brand .50 1.25
64 Andre Iguodala .40 1.00
65 Brook Lopez .40 1.00
66 Anthony Morrow .30 .75
67 Devin Harris .30 .75
68 Derrick Rose .60 1.50
69 Luol Deng .40 1.00
70 Carlos Boozer .40 1.00
71 Joakim Noah .40 1.00
72 Danny Granger .40 1.00
73 Darren Collison .40 1.00
74 Roy Hibbert .40 1.00
75 J.J. Hickson .30 .75
76 Antawn Jamison .40 1.00
77 Mo Williams .40 1.00
78 Andrew Bogut .40 1.00
79 Brandon Jennings .30 .75
80 John Salmons .40 1.00
81 Tayshaun Prince .40 1.00
82 Rodney Stuckey .40 1.00
83 Charlie Villanueva .30 .75
84 Dwight Howard .40 1.00
85 Jameer Nelson .30 .75
86 Hedo Turkoglu .40 1.00
87 Jason Richardson .50 1.25
88 Stephen Jackson .40 1.00
89 Boris Diaw .40 1.00
90 Gerald Wallace .40 1.00
91 Jamal Crawford .50 1.25
92 Josh Smith .40 1.00
93 Joe Johnson .40 1.00
94 Dwyane Wade .75 2.00
95 LeBron James 2.50 6.00
96 Chris Bosh .50 1.25
97 Erick Dampier .30 .75
98 Nick Young .40 1.00
99 Andray Blatche .30 .75
100 Kirk Hinrich .40 1.00
101 Bill Walton 1.00 2.50
102 Byron Scott .75 2.00
103 Mark Aguirre .75 2.00
104 Michael Finley 1.00 2.50
105 Nate McMillan 1.00 2.50
106 Nick Anderson 1.00 2.50
107 Artis Gilmore .75 2.00
108 Jamal Mashburn 1.00 2.50
109 Larry Bird 2.50 6.00
110 Julius Erving 1.50 4.00
111 Sidney Moncrief .60 1.50
112 Rony Seikaly .60 1.50
113 Jalen Rose 1.00 2.50
114 Rickey Green 1.00 2.50
115 Robert Horry 1.00 2.50
116 Rex Chapman 1.00 2.50
117 Jack Sikma .75 2.00
118 Nate Thurmond .75 2.00
119 Glenn Robinson 1.00 2.50
120 Doc Rivers 1.00 2.50
121 David Robinson 1.50 4.00
122 Michael Cooper .75 2.00
123 Al Attles 1.00 2.50
124 Alonzo Mourning 1.25 3.00
125 Dave Bing 1.00 2.50
126 Bobby Jones .75 2.00
127 Moses Malone 1.00 2.50
128 Tim Hardaway 1.00 2.50
129 Tom Heinsohn 1.00 2.50
130 Chris Webber 1.00 2.50
131 Gus Williams .60 1.50
132 Campy Russell .60 1.50
133 Charles D. Smith 1.00 2.50
134 Magic Johnson 2.50 6.00
135 Spud Webb .75 2.00
136 Charles Oakley 1.00 2.50
137 Pete Maravich 1.50 4.00
138 Jerry West 1.25 3.00
139 Derek Harper .75 2.00
140 Hakeem Olajuwon 1.25 3.00
141 Luke Babbitt/699 AU RC 4.00 10.00
142 Kevin Seraphin/699 AU RC 3.00 8.00
143 Eric Bledsoe/699 AU RC 5.00 12.00
144 Avery Bradley/699 AU RC 6.00 15.00
145 James Anderson/699 AU RC 3.00 8.00
146 Elliot Williams/699 AU RC 3.00 8.00
147 Trevor Booker/699 AU RC 4.00 10.00
148 Damion James/699 AU RC 3.00 8.00
149 Dominique Jones/689 AU RC 3.00 8.00
150 Quincy Pondexter/699 AU RC 3.00 8.00
151 Jordan Crawford/699 AU RC 4.00 10.00
152 Greivis Vasquez/699 AU RC 4.00 10.00
153 Daniel Orton/699 AU RC 3.00 8.00
154 Lazar Hayward/599 AU RC 3.00 8.00
155 John Wall/199 AU RC 50.00 120.00
156 Evan Turner/299 AU RC 4.00 10.00
157 Derrick Favors/299 AU RC 10.00 25.00
158 Wesley Johnson/299 AU RC 3.00 8.00
159 D.Cousins/349 AU RC 25.00 60.00
160 Ekpe Udoh/399 AU RC 3.00 8.00
161 Greg Monroe/399 AU RC 6.00 15.00
162 Al-Farouq Aminu/699 AU RC 5.00 12.00
163 Gordon Hayward/449 AU RC 12.00 30.00
164 Paul George/449 AU RC 50.00 120.00
165 Cole Aldrich/449 AU RC 4.00 10.00
166 Xavier Henry/449 AU RC 3.00 8.00
167 Ed Davis/449 AU RC 3.00 8.00
168 Patrick Patterson/449 AU RC 4.00 10.00
169 Larry Sanders/699 AU RC 3.00 8.00
170 Luke Harangody/699 AU RC 3.00 8.00
171 Dexter Pittman/699 AU RC 3.00 8.00
172 Hassan Whiteside/699 AU RC 10.00 25.00
173 Andy Rautins/699 AU RC 3.00 8.00
174 L.Stephenson/699 AU RC 5.00 12.00
175 Armon Johnson/699 AU RC 3.00 8.00
176 Terrico White/699 AU RC 3.00 8.00
177 S.Collins/699 AU RC EXCH 3.00 8.00
178 Landry Fields/699 AU RC 4.00 10.00
179 Jeremy Lin/699 AU RC 40.00 80.00
180 Timofey Mozgov/699 AU RC 5.00 12.00

2010-11 Classics Timeless Tributes Gold

*STARS: 1.25X TO 3X BASE HI
*RETIRED: .6X TO 1.5X BASE HI
124 Alonzo Mourning 5.00 12.00

2010-11 Classics Timeless Tributes Platinum

*STARS: 3X TO 8X BASE HI
*RETIRED: 1.5X TO 4X BASE HI
124 Alonzo Mourning 10.00 25.00

2010-11 Classics Timeless Tributes Silver

*STARS: 1X TO 2.5X BASE HI
*RETIRED: .5X TO 1.25X BASE HI

2010-11 Classics Blast From The Past

COMPLETE SET (25) 10.00 25.00
RANDOM INSERTS IN PACKS
1 Amare Stoudemire .60 1.50
2 Al Jefferson .60 1.50
3 LeBron James 4.00 10.00
4 David Lee .50 1.25
5 Carlos Boozer .60 1.50
6 Troy Murphy .50 1.25
7 Kirk Hinrich .60 1.50
8 Kevin Martin .60 1.50
9 Kevin Durant 2.00 5.00
10 Josh Howard .60 1.50
11 Hedo Turkoglu .60 1.50
12 Caron Butler .60 1.50
13 Jason Kidd .75 2.00
14 Michael Beasley .50 1.25
15 John Salmons .60 1.50
16 Vince Carter 1.00 2.50
17 Yi Jianlian .60 1.50
18 Al Harrington .60 1.50
19 Andres Nocioni .50 1.25
20 Antawn Jamison .60 1.50
21 Anthony Randolph .50 1.25
22 Chris Bosh .75 2.00
23 Quentin Richardson .60 1.50
24 Nate Robinson .50 1.25
25 Kareem Abdul-Jabbar 1.25 3.00

2010-11 Classics Blast From The Past Jerseys

STATED PRINT RUN 99 TO 199 SER.#'d SETS
1 Amare Stoudemire/199 2.00 5.00
2 Al Jefferson/199 2.00 5.00
3 LeBron James/199 8.00 20.00
4 David Lee/199 1.50 4.00
5 Carlos Boozer/199 2.00 5.00
6 Troy Murphy/99 2.00 5.00
7 Kirk Hinrich/199 2.00 5.00
8 Kevin Martin/199 2.00 5.00
9 Kevin Durant/199 8.00 20.00
10 Josh Howard/199 2.00 5.00
11 Hedo Turkoglu/199 2.00 5.00
12 Caron Butler/199 2.00 5.00
13 Jason Kidd/199 2.50 6.00
14 Michael Beasley/199 1.50 4.00
15 John Salmons/199 2.00 5.00
16 Vince Carter/199 3.00 8.00
17 Yi Jianlian/199 2.00 5.00
18 Al Harrington/199 2.00 5.00
19 Andres Nocioni/199 2.00 5.00
20 Antawn Jamison/199 2.00 5.00
21 Anthony Randolph/199 1.50 4.00
22 Chris Bosh/199 2.50 6.00
23 Quentin Richardson/199 2.00 5.00
24 Nate Robinson/199 1.50 4.00
25 Kareem Abdul-Jabbar/99 4.00 10.00

2010-11 Classics Blast From The Past Jerseys Prime

*PRIME: 1X TO 2.5X BASE HI
STATED PRINT RUN ONE TO 25 SER.#'d SETS
SOME UNPRICED DUE TO SCARCITY
16 Vince Carter/25 12.00 30.00

2010-11 Classics Blast From The Past Jerseys Signatures

STATED PRINT RUN 5 TO 25 SER.#'d SETS
SOME UNPRICED DUE TO SCARCITY
1 Amare Stoudemire/25 15.00 40.00
2 Al Jefferson/25 6.00 15.00
4 David Lee/25 6.00 15.00
9 Kevin Durant/25 125.00 250.00
12 Caron Butler/25 8.00 20.00
13 Jason Kidd/25 15.00 40.00
21 Anthony Randolph/25 6.00 15.00

2010-11 Classics Blast From The Past Jerseys Prime Signatures

STATED PRINT RUN 5 TO 25 SER.#'d SETS
SOME UNPRICED DUE TO SCARCITY
2 Al Jefferson/25 8.00 20.00
4 David Lee/25 8.00 20.00
9 Kevin Durant/15 200.00 400.00
12 Caron Butler/25 10.00 25.00
13 Jason Kidd/25 20.00 50.00
21 Anthony Randolph/25 8.00 20.00

2010-11 Classics Classic Combos

MPLETE SET (10) 6.00 15.00
RANDOM INSERTS IN PACKS
*GOLD: 1X TO 2.5X BASE HI
GOLD PRINT RUN 100 SER.#'d SETS
*PLATINUM: 1.25X TO 3X BASE HI
PLATINUM PRINT RUN 25 SER.#'d SETS
*SILVER: .5X TO 1.25X BASE HI
SILVER PRINT RUN 250 SER.#'d SETS
UNPRICED BLACK PRINT RUN ONE SET
1 L.Bird/R.Parish 2.00 5.00
2 J.Worthy/M.Johnson 2.00 5.00
3 J.Stockton/K.Malone 1.25 3.00
4 K.Abdul-Jabbar/O.Robertson 1.25 3.00
5 G.Goodrich/J.West 1.00 2.50
6 W.Frazier/W.Reed .75 2.00
7 I.Thomas/J.Dumars .75 2.00
8 N.Thurmond/R.Barry .60 1.50
9 D.Rodman/S.Pippen 1.50 4.00
10 D.Issel/D.Thompson .60 1.50

2010-11 Classics Classic Combos Jerseys

STATED PRINT RUN 99 SER.#'d SETS
*PRIME: 1X TO 2.5X BASE HI
PRIME PRINT RUN 25 SER.#'d SETS
1 L.Bird/R.Parish 10.00 25.00
2 J.Worthy/M.Johnson 12.00 30.00
3 J.Stockton/K.Malone 6.00 15.00
7 I.Thomas/J.Dumars 6.00 15.00
9 D.Rodman/S.Pippen 15.00 40.00

2010-11 Classics Classic Greats

COMPLETE SET (30) 15.00 40.00
RANDOM INSERTS IN PACKS

*SILVER: .6X TO 1.5X BASE HI
SILVER PRINT RUN 250 SER.#'d SETS
UNPRICED BLACK PRINT RUN ONE SET
1 Bill Russell 1.50 4.00
2 Adrian Dantley .75 2.00
3 Nate Archibald .75 2.00
4 Patrick Ewing 1.25 3.00
5 Kevin McHale 1.00 2.50
6 Magic Johnson 2.50 6.00
7 Sam Jones 1.00 2.50
8 Walter Berry .60 1.50
9 Spencer Haywood 1.00 2.50
10 Alonzo Mourning 1.25 3.00
11 Artis Gilmore .75 2.00
12 James Worthy 1.25 3.00
13 Paul Westphal 1.00 2.50
14 Scottie Pippen 2.00 5.00
15 Shawn Kemp 1.50 4.00
16 Larry Bird 2.50 6.00
17 Lenny Wilkens 1.00 2.50
18 Mark Jackson .75 2.00
19 Toni Kukoc 1.00 2.50
20 Dennis Rodman 2.00 5.00
21 Chris Mullin 1.00 2.50
22 Dominique Wilkins 1.25 3.00
23 Rolando Blackman .75 2.00
24 Walt Frazier 1.00 2.50
25 Cliff Hagan .75 2.00
26 Connie Hawkins 1.00 2.50
27 Gary Payton 1.00 2.50
28 George Gervin 1.00 2.50
29 Maurice Cheeks .60 1.50
30 Moses Malone 1.00 2.50

2010-11 Classics Classic Greats Gold

*GOLD: .75X TO 2X BASE HI
STATED PRINT RUN 100 SER.#'d SETS
4 Patrick Ewing 4.00 10.00
10 Alonzo Mourning 5.00 12.00
15 Shawn Kemp 12.50 30.00

2010-11 Classics Classic Greats Platinum

*PLATINUM: 1.5X TO 4X BASE HI
STATED PRINT RUN 25 SER.#'d SETS
4 Patrick Ewing 10.00 25.00
10 Alonzo Mourning 10.00 25.00
15 Shawn Kemp 40.00 100.00

2010-11 Classics Classic Greats Signatures

STATED PRINT RUN 5 TO 99 SER.#'d SETS
SOME UNPRICED DUE TO SCARCITY
2 Adrian Dantley/49 12.00 30.00
3 Nate Archibald/49 8.00 20.00
7 Sam Jones/25 25.00 60.00
8 Walter Berry/99 6.00 15.00
12 James Worthy/25 20.00 50.00
13 Paul Westphal/49 6.00 15.00
17 Lenny Wilkens/49 6.00 15.00
19 Toni Kukoc/25 25.00 60.00
23 Rolando Blackman/25 8.00 20.00
26 Connie Hawkins/99 6.00 15.00
28 George Gervin/25 12.00 30.00
29 Maurice Cheeks/49 6.00 15.00

2010-11 Classics Classic Moments

COMPLETE SET (10) 10.00 25.00
RANDOM INSERTS IN PACKS
*GOLD: .75X TO 2X BASE HI
GOLD PRINT RUN 100 SER.#'d SETS
*PLATINUM: 1.25X TO 3X BASE HI
PLATINUM PRINT RUN 25 SER.#'d SETS
*SILVER: .5X TO 1.25X BASE HI
SILVER PRINT RUN 250 SER.#'d SETS
UNPRICED BLACK PRINT RUN ONE SET
1 Wilt Chamberlain 1.50 4.00
2 Magic Johnson 2.00 5.00
3 Brandon Jennings .50 1.25
4 LeBron James 4.00 10.00
5 Rajon Rondo .75 2.00
6 Kevin Durant 2.00 5.00
7 Kareem Abdul-Jabbar 1.25 3.00
8 John Havlicek 1.00 2.50
9 Kobe Bryant 3.00 8.00
10 Blake Griffin .75 2.00

2010-11 Classics Classic Moments Signatures

STATED PRINT RUN 5 TO 99 SER.#'d SETS
SOME UNPRICED DUE TO SCARCITY
5 Rajon Rondo/25 30.00 60.00
6 Kevin Durant/25 125.00 225.00
9 Kobe Bryant/99 100.00 200.00
10 Blake Griffin/25 50.00 120.00

2010-11 Classics Dress Code

COMPLETE SET (25) 12.00 30.00
RANDOM INSERTS IN PACKS
*GOLD: .75X TO 2X BASE HI
GOLD PRINT RUN 100 SER.#'d SETS
*PLATINUM: 1.25X TO 3X BASE HI
PLATINUM PRINT RUN 25 SER.#'d SETS
*SILVER: .5X TO 1.25X BASE HI
SILVER PRINT RUN 250 SER.#'d SETS
UNPRICED BLACK PRINT RUN ONE SET
1 Kobe Bryant 3.00 8.00
2 Andre Iguodala .60 1.50
3 Nene .60 1.50
4 Mo Williams .60 1.50
5 Tim Duncan 1.25 3.00
6 Jason Kidd .75 2.00
7 Gerald Wallace .60 1.50
8 Dwight Howard .60 1.50
9 David Lee .50 1.25
10 Brandon Jennings .50 1.25
11 Brook Lopez .60 1.50
12 Toney Douglas .50 1.25
13 Shawn Marion .60 1.50
14 Marc Gasol .75 2.00
15 Luol Deng .60 1.50
16 Kevin Love .75 2.00
17 Jrue Holiday .75 2.00
18 Dirk Nowitzki 1.00 2.50
19 Stephen Curry 3.00 8.00
20 Dwyane Wade 1.25 3.00
21 Blake Griffin .75 2.00
22 Amare Stoudemire .60 1.50
23 Joe Johnson .60 1.50
24 Andrea Bargnani .60 1.50
25 Andrew Bogut .60 1.50

2010-11 Classics Dress Code Jerseys

STATED PRINT RUN 25 TO 199 SER.#'d SETS
*PRIME: 1X TO 2.5X BASE HI
PRIME PRINT RUN 5 TO 25 SETS
SOME PRIME UNPRICED DUE TO SCARCITY
1 Kobe Bryant/199 10.00 25.00
2 Andre Iguodala/199 2.00 5.00
3 Nene/199 2.00 5.00
5 Tim Duncan/199 4.00 10.00
6 Jason Kidd/199 2.50 6.00
7 Gerald Wallace/199 2.00 5.00
8 Dwight Howard/199 2.00 5.00
9 David Lee/199 1.50 4.00
10 Brandon Jennings/199 1.50 4.00
11 Brook Lopez/199 2.00 5.00
12 Toney Douglas/199 1.50 4.00
13 Shawn Marion/199 2.00 5.00
14 Marc Gasol/199 2.50 6.00
15 Luol Deng /199 2.00 5.00
16 Kevin Love/199 2.50 6.00
17 Jrue Holiday/199 2.50 6.00
18 Dirk Nowitzki/199 3.00 8.00
19 Stephen Curry/25 10.00 25.00
20 Dwyane Wade/199 4.00 10.00
21 Blake Griffin/199 2.50 6.00
22 Amare Stoudemire/199 2.00 5.00
23 Joe Johnson/199 2.00 5.00
24 Andrea Bargnani/199 2.00 5.00
25 Andrew Bogut/199 2.00 5.00

2010-11 Classics Dress Code Jerseys Signatures

STATED PRINT RUN 10 TO 25 SER.#'d SETS
SOME UNPRICED DUE TO SCARCITY
1 Kobe Bryant/25 100.00 200.00
2 Andre Iguodala/25 6.00 15.00
6 Jason Kidd/25 15.00 40.00
7 Gerald Wallace/25 8.00 20.00
9 David Lee/25 6.00 15.00
10 Brandon Jennings/25 12.00 30.00
12 Toney Douglas/25 6.00 15.00
14 Marc Gasol/25 EXCH 15.00 40.00
16 Kevin Love/25 15.00 40.00
17 Jrue Holiday/25 6.00 15.00
19 Stephen Curry/25 60.00 120.00
21 Blake Griffin/25 75.00 150.00
22 Amare Stoudemire/25 20.00 50.00
24 Andrea Bargnani/25 8.00 20.00
25 Andrew Bogut/25 10.00 25.00

2010-11 Classics Dress Code Jerseys Prime Signatures

STATED PRINT RUN 10 TO 25 SER.#'d SETS
SOME UNPRICED DUE TO SCARCITY
1 Kobe Bryant/25 125.00 225.00
2 Andre Iguodala/25 10.00 25.00
7 Gerald Wallace/25 10.00 25.00
9 David Lee/25 8.00 20.00
11 Brook Lopez/25 8.00 20.00
12 Toney Douglas/25 8.00 20.00
16 Kevin Love/25 15.00 40.00
17 Jrue Holiday/25 8.00 20.00
19 Stephen Curry/25 100.00 250.00
21 Blake Griffin/20 40.00 80.00
23 Joe Johnson/25 10.00 25.00
24 Andrea Bargnani/25 10.00 25.00
25 Andrew Bogut/25 12.00 30.00

2010-11 Classics Hoops Previews

COMPLETE SET (20) 20.00 50.00
RANDOM INSERTS IN RACK PACKS
1 Amare Stoudemire .75 2.00
2 Blake Griffin 1.00 2.50
3 Carmelo Anthony 1.25 3.00
4 Dirk Nowitzki 1.25 3.00
5 Dwight Howard .75 2.00
6 Dwyane Wade 1.50 4.00
7 John Wall 5.00 12.00
8 Kevin Durant 2.50 6.00
9 Kobe Bryant 4.00 10.00
10 LeBron James 5.00 12.00
11 Monta Ellis .75 2.00
12 Derrick Rose 1.25 3.00
13 Eric Gordon .75 2.00
14 Russell Westbrook 2.50 6.00
15 Kevin Love 1.00 2.50
16 Chris Paul 1.25 3.00
17 LaMarcus Aldridge 1.00 2.50
18 Paul Pierce 1.00 2.50
19 Steve Nash 1.00 2.50
20 Stephen Curry 4.00 10.00

2010-11 Classics Membership Materials

STATED PRINT RUN 100 TO 499 SER.#'d SETS
1 Mike Bibby/499 2.00 5.00
2 Paul Pierce/499 2.50 6.00
3 Larry Johnson/499 5.00 12.00
4 Scottie Pippen/499 5.00 12.00
5 Dirk Nowitzki/499 3.00 8.00
6 Nene/499 2.00 5.00
7 Tayshaun Prince/499 2.00 5.00
8 Chris Mullin/250 2.50 6.00
9 Yao Ming/499 3.00 8.00
10 Chuck Person/499 2.00 5.00
11 Blake Griffin/499 2.50 6.00
12 Kobe Bryant/499 8.00 20.00
13 O.J. Mayo/499 1.50 4.00
14 Dwyane Wade/499 4.00 10.00
15 Andrew Bogut/499 2.00 5.00
16 Kevin Love/499 2.50 6.00
17 Derrick Coleman/499 2.50 6.00
18 Chris Paul/499 3.00 8.00
19 Charles Oakley/250 2.50 6.00
20 Jameer Nelson/499 1.50 4.00
21 Andre Iguodala/499 2.00 5.00
22 Anfernee Hardaway/499 6.00 15.00
23 LaMarcus Aldridge/499 2.50 6.00
24 Tyreke Evans/499 1.50 4.00
25 Tim Duncan/499 4.00 10.00
26 Karl Malone/499 3.00 8.00
27 Alex English/499 2.00 5.00
28 Kevin Johnson/499 2.50 6.00
29 Clyde Drexler/499 3.00 8.00
30 John Stockton/250 4.00 10.00
31 Kevin McHale/250 2.50 6.00
32 David West/499 2.00 5.00
33 Dwight Howard/250 2.00 5.00
34 Deron Williams/499 2.00 5.00
35 Pau Gasol/499 2.50 6.00
36 Dominique Wilkins/250 3.00 8.00
37 Robert Parish/499 2.50 6.00
38 Dennis Rodman/100 10.00 25.00
39 Shawn Marion/499 2.00 5.00
40 Carmelo Anthony/250 3.00 8.00
41 Dikembe Mutombo/250 3.00 8.00
42 Richard Hamilton/499 2.00 5.00
43 Magic Johnson/100 8.00 20.00
44 Tim Hardaway/499 2.50 6.00
45 Patrick Ewing/499 3.00 8.00
46 Brandon Roy/100 2.50 6.00
47 Chris Webber/499 2.50 6.00
48 David Robinson/100 4.00 10.00
49 Gary Payton/250 3.00 8.00
50 Kevin Durant/499 6.00 15.00

2010-11 Classics Membership Materials Prime

*PRIME: 1.2X TO 3X BASE HI
STATED PRINT RUN 2 TO 49 SER.#'d SETS
SOME UNPRICED DUE TO SCARCITY
26 Karl Malone/49 12.00 30.00
43 Magic Johnson/25 25.00 60.00
44 Tim Hardaway/49 15.00 40.00
45 Patrick Ewing/49 15.00 40.00

2010-11 Classics Significant Signatures

STATED PRINT RUN 10 TO 99 SER.#'d SETS
SOME UNPRICED DUE TO SCARCITY
1 A.C. Green/99 6.00 15.00
2 Adrian Dantley/99 6.00 15.00
3 Al Jefferson/49 6.00 15.00
4 Alonzo Mourning/49 15.00 40.00
5 Amare Stoudemire/49 20.00 50.00
6 Andre Iguodala/99 6.00 15.00
7 Andre Miller/99 6.00 15.00
8 Andrea Bargnani/99 6.00 15.00
9 Artis Gilmore/99 8.00 20.00
10 Bailey Howell/99 10.00 25.00
11 Bill Cartwright/49 15.00 40.00
12 Bob Lanier/99 10.00 25.00
13 Brandon Jennings/99 12.00 30.00
14 David Lee/99 6.00 15.00
15 Dennis Rodman/49 25.00 60.00
16 Dolph Schayes/99 8.00 20.00
17 Dominique Wilkins/49 20.00 50.00
18 Elvin Hayes/49 8.00 20.00
19 Joakim Noah/99 12.00 30.00
20 Kevin Durant/49 50.00 120.00
21 Kobe Bryant/99 75.00 150.00
22 Larry Johnson/99 20.00 50.00
23 Lenny Wilkens/99 6.00 15.00
24 Marc Gasol/99 20.00 50.00
25 Paul Westphal/99 6.00 15.00
26 Rick Barry/49 12.00 30.00
27 Robert Horry/99 8.00 20.00
28 Rolando Blackman/99 6.00 15.00
29 Sam Perkins/49 8.00 20.00
30 Oscar Robertson/49 50.00 120.00
31 Sean Elliott/99 8.00 20.00
32 Shane Battier/49 6.00 15.00
34 Larry Bird/33 60.00 120.00
35 Sam Jones/49 12.00 30.00
36 Spud Webb/99 8.00 20.00
37 Stephen Curry/49 75.00 150.00
38 Toni Kukoc/49 8.00 20.00
39 Tyreke Evans/49 15.00 40.00
40 Jason Kidd/49 15.00 40.00
41 Andrew Bynum/49 15.00 40.00
42 Andrew Bogut/49 6.00 15.00
43 Blake Griffin/99 30.00 80.00
44 Magic Johnson/32 50.00 120.00
45 Gary Payton/49 12.00 30.00
46 Jerry West/35 40.00 100.00
47 Chris Bosh/99 12.00 30.00
49 Devin Harris/99 8.00 20.00
50 Rajon Rondo/49 15.00 40.00
51 Kareem Abdul-Jabbar/25 40.00 100.00
52 Pau Gasol/99 20.00 50.00
53 Bill Walton/49 10.00 25.00
54 Carmelo Anthony/20 25.00 60.00
55 Derrick Rose/25 200.00 400.00
57 Deron Williams/99 6.00 15.00
58 Darren Collison/99 6.00 15.00
59 Steve Nash/25 30.00 80.00
60 Elgin Baylor/25 20.00 50.00

1989 Cleo Michael Jordan Valentines

COMMON CARD .40 1.00

1991 Cleo Michael Jordan Valentines

These blank-backed red- or pink-bordered valentine cards came in 32- and 38-card boxes of Cleo Valentines and feature action and posed color photos of Michael Jordan. The valentines are printed on thin white card stock, with cards 2-5, 7 and 11 measuring 2 1/2" by 3 1/4" and cards 1, 6, 8-10 measuring 2 1/4" by 5". The cards come in perforated groups of two or three. The back of the box features three bonus cutouts that are otherwise identical to cards 7, 10 and 11 except they are printed on gray cardboard stock. Non-mailable envelopes were included in the boxes. The cards are unnumbered and are listed below alphabetically by the valentine messages that are printed in the red hearts on the cards.
COMPLETE SET (11) 2.00 5.00
COMMON CARD (1-11) .30 .75

1978-79 Clippers Handyman

The 1978-79 San Diego Clippers Handyman set contains nine cards measuring approximately 2" by 4 1/4". The cards are "3-D" and are similar to the 1970s Kelloggs baseball sets. Each card has a coupon tab attached (included in the dimensions given above). Coach Gene Shue's card was apparently not distributed (as it was the grand prize winner of the contest) with the other cards but it does exist. Some veteran collectors and dealers also consider Kunnert to be somewhat tougher to find. In addition there is a second version of the Lloyd Free card with a signature variation. The set price below does not include the Gene Shue card.
COMPLETE SET (9) 25.00 50.00
1 Randy Smith 9 2.50 6.00
2 Nick Weatherspoon 12 2.00 5.00
3 Freeman Williams 20 1.50 4.00
4 Sidney Wicks 21 3.00 8.00
5A Lloyd Free 24 2.50 6.00
5B Lloyd Free 24 (Signature variation) 10.00 20.00
6 Swen Nater 31 2.00 5.00
7 Jerome Whitehead 33 1.25 3.00
8 Kermit Washington 42 1.50 4.00
9 Kevin Kunnert 44 10.00 20.00
NNO Gene Shue CO SP 750.00 1200.00

1990-91 Clippers Star

This 12-card set of Los Angeles Clippers was produced by the Star Company and measures the standard size. The fronts feature color action shots, with red borders that wash out in the middle of the card face. The horizontally oriented backs are printed in red and blue on white and have biographical as well as statistical information. The cards are unnumbered and are checklisted below in alphabetical order. Benoit Benjamin and Mike Smrek were apparently planned for the set but were not released with the other cards listed below.
COMPLETE SET (12) 1.50 4.00
1 Ken Bannister .08 .25
2 Winston Garland .08 .25
3 Tom Garrick .08 .25
4 Gary Grant .08 .25
5 Ron Harper .40 1.00
6 Bo Kimble .08 .25
7 Danny Manning .40 1.00
8 Jeff Martin .08 .25
9 Ken Norman .08 .25
10 Mike Schuler CO .08 .25
11 Charles Smith .08 .25
12 Loy Vaught .40 1.00

2000-01 Clippers Topps

COMPLETE SET (10) 3.00 8.00
NNO AT&T Wireless Sponsor Card .20 .50
LC1 Lamar Odom .40 1.00
LC10 Quentin Richardson .50 1.25
LC2 Michael Olowokandi .30 .75
LC3 Corey Maggette .40 1.00
LC4 Alvin Gentry CO .30 .75
LC6 Eric Piatkowski .30 .75
LC7 Brian Skinner .30 .75
LC8 Darius Miles .50 1.25
LC9 Keyon Dooling .50 1.25

2001-02 Clippers Topps

Issued by Topps, this six-card set was given away at a game during the 2001-02 Clippers season.
COMPLETE SET (6) 2.50 6.00
LC2 Michael Olowokandi .40 1.00
LC3 Corey Maggette .50 1.25
LC4 Alvin Gentry CO .40 1.00
LC6 Eric Piatkowski .40 1.00
LC7 Brian Skinner .40 1.00
LC8 Darius Miles .40 1.00

2005-06 Clippers Topps

Sponsored by Jet Blue Airways, this 15-card set was given away at a 2005-06 Los Angeles Clippers home game.
COMPLETE SET (15) 5.00 12.00
NNO Jet Blue Airways Sponsor Card .40 1.00
LAC1 Elton Brand .60 1.50
LAC10 Vladimir Radmanovic .40 1.00
LAC11 Zeljko Rebraca .40 1.00
LAC12 Quinton Ross .40 1.00
LAC13 James Singleton .40 1.00
LAC14 Mike Dunleavy, Sr. CO .60 1.50
LAC2 Sam Cassell .50 1.25
LAC3 Daniel Ewing .50 1.25
LAC4 Chris Kaman .50 1.25
LAC5 Yaroslav Korolev .40 1.00
LAC6 Corey Maggette .50 1.25
LAC7 Walter McCarty .40 1.00
LAC8 Cuttino Mobley .40 1.00
LAC9 Shaun Livingston .40 1.00

2001-02 Clippers Upper Deck

Released by Upper Deck in conjunction with AT&T Wireless, this 10-card set features the Clippers and was given away during the 2001-02 season.
COMPLETE SET (10) 3.00 8.00
NNO AT&T Wireless Sponsor Card .25 .60
LAC1 Elton Brand .60 1.50
LAC2 Darius Miles .40 1.00
LAC3 Lamar Odom .50 1.25
LAC4 Corey Maggette .50 1.25
LAC5 Quentin Richardson .50 1.25
LAC6 Keyon Dooling .40 1.00
LAC7 Jeff McInnis .40 1.00
LAC8 Eric Piatkowski .40 1.00
LAC9 Michael Olowokandi .40 1.00

2006-07 Clippers Upper Deck JetBlue

COMPLETE SET (14) 3.00 8.00
1 Elton Brand .60 1.50
2 Sam Cassell .50 1.25
3 Paul Davis .40 1.00
4 Daniel Ewing .40 1.00
5 Chris Kaman .50 1.25
6 Shaun Livingston .40 1.00
7 Corey Maggette .50 1.25
8 Cuttino Mobley .40 1.00
9 Quinton Ross .40 1.00
10 James Singleton .40 1.00
11 Tim Thomas .40 1.00
12 Aaron Williams .40 1.00
13 Mike Dunleavy Coach .40 1.00
14 Clipper Nation .20 .50

1994-95 Collector's Choice

These 420 standard-size cards, issued in two separate series of 210-cards each, comprise Upper Deck's '94-95 Collector's Choice set. Cards were issued in 12-card hobby packs (suggested retail of ninety-nine cents), 13-card retail packs (suggested retail of $1.18), and 20-card retail jumbo packs. White bordered fronts feature color player action shots. The player's name, team, and position appear in a lower corner. The back carries another color player action shot at the top, with statistics and career highlights displayed below. The following subsets are included in this set: Tip-Off (166-192), All-Star Advice (193-198), NBA Profiles (199-206), Blueprints (372-398), Trivia (399-406), and Draft Class (407-416). Rookie Cards in this set include Grant Hill, Juwan Howard, Eddie Jones, Jason Kidd and Glenn Robinson.
COMPLETE SET (420) 15.00 40.00
COMPLETE SERIES 1 (210) 8.00 20.00
COMPLETE SERIES 2 (210) 8.00 20.00
1 Anfernee Hardaway .20 .50
2 Mark Macon .07 .20
3 Steve Smith .10 .25
4 Chris Webber .20 .50
5 Donald Royal .07 .20
6 Avery Johnson .10 .25
7 Kevin Johnson .12 .30
8 Doug Christie .07 .20
9 Derrick McKey .07 .20
10 Dennis Rodman .25 .60
11 Scott Skiles UER .07 .20
12 Johnny Dawkins .07 .20
13 Kendall Gill .07 .20
14 Jeff Hornacek .10 .25
15 Latrell Sprewell .15 .40
16 Lucious Harris .07 .20
17 Chris Mullin .12 .30
18 John Williams .07 .20
19 Tony Campbell .07 .20
20 LaPhonso Ellis .07 .20
21 Gerald Wilkins .07 .20
22 Clyde Drexler .15 .40
23 Michael Jordan BB 1.00 2.50
24 George Lynch .07 .20
25 Mark Price .12 .30
26 James Robinson .07 .20
27 Elmore Spencer .07 .20
28 Stacey King .07 .20
29 Corie Blount .07 .20
30 Dell Curry .07 .20
31 Reggie Miller .15 .40
32 Karl Malone .15 .40
33 Scottie Pippen .25 .60
34 Hakeem Olajuwon .15 .40
35 Clarence Weatherspoon .07 .20
36 Kevin Edwards .07 .20
37 Pete Myers .07 .20
38 Jeff Turner .07 .20
39 Ennis Whatley .07 .20
40 Calbert Cheaney .07 .20
41 Glen Rice .12 .30
42 Vin Baker .12 .30
43 Grant Long .07 .20
44 Derrick Coleman .10 .25
45 Rik Smits .10 .25
46 Chris Smith .07 .20
47 Carl Herrera .07 .20
48 Bob Martin .07 .20
49 Terrell Brandon .07 .20
50 David Robinson .20 .50
51 Danny Ferry .07 .20
52 Buck Williams .07 .20
53 Josh Grant .07 .20
54 Ed Pinckney .07 .20
55 Dikembe Mutombo .12 .30
56 Clifford Robinson .07 .20
57 Luther Wright .07 .20
58 Scott Burrell .07 .20
59 Stacey Augmon .10 .25
60 Jeff Malone .07 .20
61 Byron Houston .07 .20
62 Anthony Peeler .07 .20
63 Michael Adams .07 .20
64 Negele Knight .07 .20
65 Terry Cummings .10 .25
66 Christian Laettner .10 .25
67 Tracy Murray .07 .20
68 Sedale Threatt .07 .20
69 Dan Majerle .12 .30
70 Frank Brickowski .07 .20
71 Ken Norman .07 .20
72 Charles Smith .07 .20
73 Adam Keefe .07 .20
74 P.J. Brown .07 .20
75 Kevin Duckworth .07 .20
76 Shawn Bradley UER .07 .20
77 Darnell Mee .07 .20
78 Nick Anderson .07 .20
79 Mark West .07 .20
80 B.J. Armstrong .07 .20
81 Dennis Scott .07 .20
82 Lindsey Hunter .07 .20
83 Derek Strong .07 .20
84 Mike Brown .07 .20
85 Antonio Harvey .07 .20
86 Anthony Bonner .07 .20
87 Sam Cassell .12 .30
88 Harold Miner .07 .20
89 Spud Webb .10 .25
90 Mookie Blaylock .07 .20
91 Greg Anthony .07 .20
92 Richard Petruska .07 .20
93 Sean Rooks .07 .20
94 Ervin Johnson .07 .20
95 Randy Brown .07 .20
96 Orlando Woolridge .07 .20
97 Charles Oakley .10 .25
98 Craig Ehlo .07 .20
99 Derek Harper .10 .25
100 Doug Edwards .07 .20
101 Muggsy Bogues .10 .25
102 Mitch Richmond .12 .30
103 Mahmoud Abdul-Rauf .07 .20
104 Joe Dumars .12 .30
105 Eric Riley .07 .20
106 Terry Mills .07 .20
107 Toni Kukoc .15 .40
108 Jon Koncak .07 .20
109 Haywoode Workman .07 .20
110 Todd Day .07 .20
111 Detlef Schrempf .12 .30
112 David Wesley .07 .20
113 Mark Jackson .10 .25
114 Doug Overton .07 .20
115 Vinny Del Negro .07 .20
116 Loy Vaught .07 .20
117 Mike Peplowski .07 .20
118 Bimbo Coles .07 .20
119 Rex Walters .07 .20
120 Sherman Douglas .07 .20
121 David Benoit .07 .20
122 John Salley .07 .20
123 Cedric Ceballos .07 .20
124 Chris Mills .07 .20
125 Robert Horry .12 .30
126 Johnny Newman .07 .20
127 Malcolm Mackey .07 .20
128 Terry Dehere .07 .20
129 Dino Radja .07 .20
130 Reggie Williams .07 .20
131 Xavier McDaniel .07 .20
132 Bobby Hurley .07 .20
133 Alonzo Mourning .15 .40
134 Isaiah Rider .12 .30
135 Antoine Carr .07 .20
136 Robert Pack .07 .20
137 Walt Williams .07 .20
138 Tyrone Corbin .07 .20
139 Popeye Jones .07 .20
140 Shawn Kemp .12 .30
141 Thurl Bailey .07 .20
142 James Worthy .15 .40
143 Scott Haskin .07 .20
144 Hubert Davis .07 .20
145 A.C. Green .10 .25
146 Dale Davis .07 .20
147 Nate McMillan .07 .20
148 Chris Morris .07 .20
149 Will Perdue .07 .20
150 Felton Spencer .07 .20
151 Rod Strickland .07 .20
152 Blue Edwards .07 .20
153 John Williams .07 .20
154 Rodney Rogers .07 .20
155 Acie Earl .07 .20
156 Hersey Hawkins .07 .20
157 Jamal Mashburn .12 .30
158 Don MacLean .07 .20
159 Micheal Williams .07 .20
160 Kenny Gattison .07 .20
161 Rich King .07 .20
162 Allan Houston .12 .30
163 Hoop-it up .07 .20
164 Hoop-it up .07 .20
165 Hoop-it up .07 .20
166 Danny Manning TO .10 .25
167 Dee Brown TO .07 .20
168 Alonzo Mourning TO .15 .40
169 Scottie Pippen TO .25 .60
170 Mark Price TO .12 .30
171 Jamal Mashburn TO .12 .30
172 Dikembe Mutombo TO .12 .30
173 Joe Dumars TO .12 .30
174 Chris Webber TO .20 .50
175 Hakeem Olajuwon TO .15 .40
176 Reggie Miller TO .15 .40
177 Ron Harper TO .10 .25
178 Nick Van Exel TO .12 .30
179 Steve Smith TO .10 .25
180 Vin Baker TO .12 .30
181 Isaiah Rider TO .12 .30
182 Derrick Coleman TO .10 .25
183 Patrick Ewing TO .15 .40
184 Shaquille O'Neal TO .30 .75
185 Clarence Weatherspoon TO .07 .20
186 Charles Barkley TO .20 .50
187 Clyde Drexler TO .15 .40
188 Mitch Richmond TO .12 .30
189 David Robinson TO .20 .50
190 Shawn Kemp TO .12 .30
191 Karl Malone TO .15 .40
192 Tom Gugliotta TO .07 .20
193 Kenny Anderson ASA .10 .25
194 Alonzo Mourning ASA .15 .40
195 Mark Price ASA .12 .30
196 John Stockton ASA .15 .40
197 Shaquille O'Neal ASA .30 .75
198 Latrell Sprewell ASA .15 .40
199 Charles Barkley PRO .20 .50
200 Chris Webber PRO .20 .50
201 Patrick Ewing PRO .15 .40
202 Dennis Rodman PRO .25 .60
203 Shawn Kemp PRO .12 .30
204 Michael Jordan PRO 1.00 2.50
205 Shaquille O'Neal PRO .30 .75
206 Larry Johnson PRO .12 .30
207 Tim Hardaway CL .12 .30
208 John Stockton CL .15 .40
209 Harold Miner CL .07 .20
210 B.J. Armstrong CL .07 .20
211 Vernon Maxwell .07 .20
212 John Stockton .15 .40
213 Luc Longley .10 .25
214 Sam Perkins .07 .20
215 Pooh Richardson .07 .20
216 Tyrone Corbin .07 .20
217 Mario Elie .07 .20
218 Bobby Phills .07 .20
219 Grant Hill RC .60 1.50
220 Gary Payton .12 .30
221 Tom Hammonds .07 .20
222 Danny Ainge .12 .30
223 Gary Grant .07 .20
224 Jim Jackson .07 .20
225 Chris Gatling .07 .20
226 Sergei Bazarevich RC .12 .30
227 Tony Dumas RC .12 .30
228 Andrew Lang .07 .20
229 Wesley Person RC .12 .30
230 Terry Porter .07 .20
231 Duane Causwell .07 .20
232 Shaquille O'Neal .30 .75
233 Antonio Davis .07 .20
234 Charles Barkley .20 .50
235 Tony Massenburg .07 .20
236 Ricky Pierce .07 .20
237 Scott Skiles .07 .20
238 Jalen Rose RC .30 .75
239 Charlie Ward RC .12 .30
240 Michael Jordan COMM 1.00 2.50
241 Elden Campbell .07 .20
242 Bill Cartwright .10 .25
243 Armon Gilliam UER .07 .20
244 Rick Fox .07 .20
245 Tim Breaux .07 .20
246 Monty Williams RC .10 .25
247 Dominique Wilkins .15 .40
248 Robert Parish .12 .30
249 Mark Jackson .10 .25
250 Jason Kidd RC .60 1.50
251 Andres Guibert .07 .20
252 Matt Geiger .07 .20
253 Stanley Roberts .07 .20
254 Jack Haley .07 .20
255 David Wingate .07 .20
256 John Crotty .07 .20
257 Brian Grant RC .20 .50
258 Otis Thorpe .07 .20
259 Clifford Rozier RC .07 .20
260 Grant Long .07 .20
261 Eric Mobley RC .07 .20
262 Dickey Simpkins RC .10 .25
263 J.R. Reid .07 .20
264 Kevin Willis .07 .20
265 Scott Brooks .07 .20
266 Glenn Robinson RC .25 .60
267 Dana Barros .07 .20
268 Ken Norman .07 .20
269 Herb Williams .07 .20
270 Dee Brown .07 .20
271 Steve Kerr .10 .25
272 Jon Barry .07 .20
273 Sean Elliott .12 .30
274 Elliot Perry .07 .20
275 Kenny Smith .10 .25
276 Sean Rooks .07 .20
277 Gheorghe Muresan .07 .20
278 Juwan Howard RC .20 .50
279 Steve Smith .10 .25
280 Anthony Bowie .07 .20
281 Moses Malone .12 .30
282 Olden Polynice .07 .20
283 Jo Jo English .07 .20
284 Marty Conlon .07 .20
285 Sam Mitchell .07 .20
286 Doug West .07 .20
287 Cedric Ceballos .07 .20
288 Lorenzo Williams .07 .20
289 Harold Ellis .07 .20
290 Doc Rivers .10 .25
291 Keith Tower .07 .20
292 Mark Bryant .07 .20
293 Oliver Miller .07 .20
294 Michael Adams .07 .20
295 Tree Rollins .07 .20
296 Eddie Jones RC .40 1.00
297 Malik Sealy .07 .20
298 Blue Edwards .07 .20
299 Brooks Thompson RC .10 .25
300 Benoit Benjamin .07 .20
301 Avery Johnson .10 .25
302 Larry Johnson .12 .30
303 John Starks .10 .25
304 Byron Scott .10 .25
305 Eric Murdock .07 .20
306 Jay Humphries .07 .20
307 Kenny Anderson .10 .25
308 Brian Williams .07 .20
309 Nick Van Exel .12 .30
310 Tim Hardaway .12 .30
311 Lee Mayberry .07 .20
312 Vlade Divac .12 .30
313 Donyell Marshall RC .12 .30
314 Anthony Mason .07 .20
315 Danny Manning .10 .25
316 Tyrone Hill .07 .20
317 Vincent Askew .07 .20
318 Khalid Reeves RC .10 .25
319 Ron Harper .10 .25
320 Brent Price .07 .20
321 Byron Houston .07 .20
322 Lamond Murray RC .12 .30
323 Bryant Stith .07 .20
324 Tom Gugliotta .07 .20
325 Jerome Kersey .07 .20
326 B.J.Tyler RC .07 .20
327 Antonio Lang RC .12 .30
328 Carlos Rogers RC .10 .25
329 Wayman Tisdale .07 .20
330 Kevin Gamble .07 .20
331 Eric Piatkowski RC .15 .40
332 Mitchell Butler .07 .20
333 Patrick Ewing .15 .40
334 Doug Smith .07 .20
335 Joe Kleine .07 .20
336 Keith Jennings .07 .20
337 Bill Curley RC .07 .20
338 Johnny Newman .07 .20
339 Howard Eisley RC .12 .30
340 Willie Anderson .07 .20
341 Aaron McKie RC .12 .30
342 Tom Chambers .10 .25
343 Scott Williams .07 .20
344 Harvey Grant .07 .20
345 Billy Owens .07 .20
346 Sharone Wright RC .10 .25
347 Michael Cage .07 .20
348 Vern Fleming .07 .20
349 Darrin Hancock RC .10 .25
350 Matt Fish .07 .20
351 Rony Seikaly .07 .20
352 Victor Alexander .07 .20
353 Anthony Miller RC .12 .30
354 Horace Grant .10 .25
355 Jayson Williams .07 .20
356 Dale Ellis .07 .20
357 Sarunas Marciulionis .07 .20
358 Anthony Avent .07 .20
359 Rex Chapman .07 .20
360 Askia Jones RC .12 .30
361 Bo Outlaw RC .12 .30
362 Chuck Person .10 .25
363 Danny Schayes .07 .20
364 Morlon Wiley .07 .20
365 Dontonio Wingfield RC .12 .30
366 Tony Smith .07 .20
367 Bill Wennington .07 .20
368 Bryon Russell .07 .20
369 Geert Hammink .07 .20
370 Eric Montross RC .10 .25
371 Cliff Levingston .07 .20
372 Stacey Augmon BP .10 .25
373 Eric Montross BP .10 .25
374 Alonzo Mourning BP .15 .40
375 Scottie Pippen BP .25 .60
376 Mark Price BP .12 .30
377 Jason Kidd BP .60 1.50
378 Jalen Rose BP .30 .75
379 Grant Hill BP .60 1.50
380 Latrell Sprewell BP .15 .40
381 Hakeem Olajuwon BP .15 .40
382 Reggie Miller BP .15 .40
383 Lamond Murray BP .12 .30
384 Eddie Jones BP .40 1.00
385 Khalid Reeves BP .10 .25
386 Glenn Robinson BP .25 .60
387 Donyell Marshall BP .12 .30
388 Derrick Coleman BP .10 .25
389 Patrick Ewing BP .15 .40
390 Shaquille O'Neal BP .30 .75
391 Sharone Wright BP .10 .25
392 Charles Barkley BP .20 .50
393 Aaron McKie BP .12 .30
394 Brian Grant BP .20 .50
395 David Robinson BP .20 .50
396 Shawn Kemp BP .12 .30
397 Karl Malone BP .15 .40
398 Tom Gugliotta BP .07 .20
399 Hakeem Olajuwon TRIV .15 .40
400 Shaquille O'Neal TRIV .30 .75
401 Chris Webber TRIV .20 .50
402 Michael Jordan TRIV 1.00 2.50
403 David Robinson TRIV .20 .50
404 Shawn Kemp TRIV .12 .30
405 Patrick Ewing TRIV .15 .40
406 Charles Barkley TRIV .20 .50
407 Glenn Robinson DC .25 .60
408 Jason Kidd DC .60 1.50
409 Grant Hill DC .60 1.50
410 Donyell Marshall DC .12 .30
411 Sharone Wright DC .10 .25
412 Lamond Murray DC .12 .30
413 Brian Grant DC .20 .50
414 Eric Montross DC .10 .25
415 Eddie Jones DC .40 1.00
416 Carlos Rogers DC .10 .25
417 Shawn Kemp CL .12 .30
418 Bobby Hurley CL .07 .20
419 Shawn Bradley CL .07 .20
420 Michael Jordan CL .40 1.00

1994-95 Collector's Choice Silver Signature

COMPLETE SET (420) 50.00 100.00
COMPLETE SERIES 1 (210) 20.00 40.00
COMPLETE SERIES 2 (210) 30.00 60.00
*STARS: 1.25X TO 3X BASE CARD HI
*RCs: 1X TO 2.5X BASE HI
*SUBSETS: .6X TO 1.5X BASE HI

1994-95 Collector's Choice Gold Signature

*STARS: 10X TO 25X BASE CARD HI
*RCs: 10X TO 25X BASE HI
*SUBSETS: 10X TO 25X BASE HI
SER.1/2 STATED ODDS 1:35 HOB/RET
1 Anfernee Hardaway 8.00 20.00
4 Chris Webber 8.00 20.00
23 Michael Jordan BB 25.00 60.00
140 Shawn Kemp 6.00 15.00
204 Michael Jordan PRO 30.00 80.00
240 Michael Jordan COMM 30.00 80.00
402 Michael Jordan TRIV 25.00 60.00
420 Michael Jordan CL 30.00 80.00

1994-95 Collector's Choice Blow-Ups

One of these oversized (5" by 7") cards was inserted exclusively into each series 2 hobby box. Each Blow-Up is identical in design and numbering to their corresponding basic issue card. According to information provided by Upper Deck at least 3,000 of these cards were autographed and randomly seeded into boxes. There are far fewer autographed Michael Jordan Blow-Ups than the other four players featured.
COMPLETE SET (5) 5.00 10.00
AU CARDS RANDOMLY INSERTED
23 Michael Jordan BB 3.00 8.00
40 Calbert Cheaney .25 .60
76 Shawn Bradley .25 .60
132 Bobby Hurley .25 .60
140 Shawn Kemp .40 1.00
A23 Michael Jordan AU 3500.00 5000.00
A40 Calbert Cheaney AU 15.00 30.00
A76 Shawn Bradley AU 15.00 30.00
A132 Bobby Hurley AU 15.00 30.00
A140 Shawn Kemp AU 20.00 50.00

1994-95 Collector's Choice Crash the Game Assists

These fifteen standard-size Crash the Game Assists cards were randomly inserted exclusively into first series retail packs at a rate of one in 20. Cards that featured players who tallied 750 or more assists during the 1994-95 campaign were redeemable for a 15-card parallel Crash the Game Assists Redemption set. Only John Stockton eclipsed the mark. The fronts feature a color-action photo with the background of the game in black and white. The top has the player's name in a box the color of his team and the bottom has the words "You Crash The Game" in foil with the player's position behind it in his team's color. The back says 750 assists at the top below his name surrounded by the player's team color. There are instructions on how to redeem your cards if you win. The exchange deadline was June 16th, 1995. The redemption cards were delayed in shipping until late October, 1995.

COMPLETE SET (15) 4.00 10.00
SER.1 STATED ODDS 1:20 RETAIL
*RED.CARDS: .2X TO .5X HI COLUMN
A1 Michael Adams .40 1.00
A2 Kenny Anderson .50 1.25
A3 Mookie Blaylock .40 1.00
A4 Muggsy Bogues .50 1.25
A5 Sherman Douglas .40 1.00
A6 Anfernee Hardaway 1.00 2.50
A7 Tim Hardaway .60 1.50
A8 Lindsey Hunter .40 1.00
A9 Mark Jackson .50 1.25
A10 Kevin Johnson .60 1.50
A11 Eric Murdock .40 1.00
A12 Mark Price .60 1.50
A13 John Stockton .75 2.00
A14 Rod Strickland .40 1.00
A15 Micheal Williams .40 1.00

1994-95 Collector's Choice Crash the Game Rebounds

These fifteen standard-size Crash the Game Rebounds cards were randomly inserted exclusively into second series retail packs at a rate of one in 20. Cards that featured players who grabbed 1,000 or more rebounds during the 1994-95 campaign were redeemable for a 15-card parallel Crash the Game Rebounds Redemption set. The card design is the same as the Assists set except on the back it says 1,000 Rebounds. Only Dikembe Mutombo eclipsed the mark. The exchange deadline was June 30, 1995. The redemption cards were delayed in shipping until late October, 1995.

COMPLETE SET (15) 6.00 15.00
SER.2 STATED ODDS 1:20 RETAIL
*RED.CARDS: .2X TO .5X HI COLUMN
R1 Derrick Coleman .50 1.25
R2 Patrick Ewing .75 2.00
R3 Horace Grant .50 1.25
R4 Shawn Kemp .60 1.50
R5 Karl Malone .75 2.00
R6 Alonzo Mourning .75 2.00
R7 Dikembe Mutombo .60 1.50
R8 Charles Oakley .50 1.25
R9 Hakeem Olajuwon .75 2.00
R10 Shaquille O'Neal 1.50 4.00
R11 Olden Polynice .40 1.00
R12 David Robinson 1.00 2.50
R13 Dennis Rodman 1.25 3.00
R14 Otis Thorpe .40 1.00
R15 Kevin Willis .40 1.00

1994-95 Collector's Choice Crash the Game Rookie Scoring

These fifteen standard-size Crash the Game Rookie Scoring cards were randomly inserted exclusively into second series hobby packs at a rate of one in 20. Cards that featured rookies who scored more than 1,250 points during the 1994-95 campaign were redeemable for a 15-card parallel Crash the Game Rookie Scoring Redemption set. The card design is the same as the Assists set except on the back it says 1,250 Points. Only Grant Hill and Glenn Robinson eclipsed the mark. The exchange deadline was June 30th, 1995. The redemption cards were delayed in shipping until late October, 1995.

COMPLETE SET (15) 4.00 10.00
SER.2 STATED ODDS 1:20 HOBBY
*RED.CARDS: .2X TO .5X HI COLUMN
S1 Tony Dumas .25 .60
S2 Brian Grant .40 1.00
S3 Grant Hill 1.25 3.00
S4 Juwan Howard .40 1.00
S5 Eddie Jones .75 2.00
S6 Jason Kidd 1.25 3.00
S7 Donyell Marshall .25 .60
S8 Eric Montross .20 .50
S9 Lamond Murray .25 .60
S10 Khalid Reeves .20 .50
S11 Glenn Robinson .50 1.25
S12 Jalen Rose .60 1.50
S13 Dickey Simpkins .20 .50
S14 Charlie Ward .25 .60
S15 Sharone Wright .20 .50

1994-95 Collector's Choice Crash the Game Scoring

These fifteen standard-size Crash the Game Scoring cards were randomly inserted exclusively into first series hobby packs at a rate of one in 20. Cards that featured players who posted 2,000 or more points during the 1994-95 campaign were redeemable for a 15-card parallel Crash the Game Scoring Redemption set. The card design is the same as the Assists set except on the back it says 2,000 Points. Karl Malone, Shaquille O'Neal, Hakeem Olajuwon and David Robinson all eclipsed the mark. The exchange deadline was June 30, 1995. The redemption cards were delayed in shipping until late October, 1995.

COMPLETE SET (15) 6.00 15.00
SER.1 STATED ODDS 1:20 HOBBY
*RED.CARDS: .2X TO .5X HI COLUMN
S1 Charles Barkley 1.00 2.50
S2 Derrick Coleman .50 1.25
S3 Joe Dumars .60 1.50
S4 Patrick Ewing .75 2.00
S5 Karl Malone .75 2.00
S6 Reggie Miller .75 2.00
S7 Shaquille O'Neal 1.50 4.00
S8 Hakeem Olajuwon .75 2.00
S9 Scottie Pippen 1.25 3.00
S10 Glen Rice .60 1.50
S11 Mitch Richmond .60 1.50
S12 David Robinson 1.00 2.50
S13 Latrell Sprewell .75 2.00
S14 Chris Webber 1.00 2.50
S15 Dominique Wilkins .75 2.00

1994-95 Collector's Choice Draft Trade

This 10-card set was available only by redeeming a Draft Trade card that was randomly seeded into one in every 36 first series Collector's Choice hobby or retail packs. The fronts have a color-action photo with the top-half having the background of the game in black and white. The bottom of the card has a white background. On the left side of the card are the words "NBA Draft Lottery Picks" with the player's name above it. The backs have the player's name and information set against the colors of his team. The expiration date on the redemption was June 16th, 1995.

COMPLETE SET (10) 2.50 6.00
DT CARD: SER.1 STATED ODDS 1:36
1 Glenn Robinson .40 1.00
2 Jason Kidd 1.00 2.50
3 Grant Hill 1.00 2.50
4 Donyell Marshall .20 .50
5 Juwan Howard .30 .75
6 Sharone Wright .15 .40
7 Lamond Murray .20 .50
8 Brian Grant .30 .75
9 Eric Montross .15 .40
10 Eddie Jones .60 1.50

1995-96 Collector's Choice

These 410-standard size cards, issued in two seperate series of 210 and 200 cards respectively, comprise Upper Deck's 1995-96 Collector's Choice set. Cards were primarily issued in 12-card hobby and retail packs (suggested retail price of ninety-nine cents) and five-card retail mini-packs. In addition, large retail chain stores received complete factory sets around the end of the season (SRP $29.97). Each factory set contains a basic 410 card set, four Collector's Choice Jordan Collection inserts, four Player's Club Platinum inserts and a special 5" by 7" Bulls Commemorative card celebrating their 70 win season. Regular issue cards feature white-bordered fronts with color player action shots. The backs have a color photo and statistics. The following subsets are included: Fun Facts (166-194), Professor Dunk (195-208), Scouting Report (321-349), Playoff Time (350-365), I Love this Team (366-394), Photo Gallery (395-403) and Shawn Kemp's Top 40 (404-408). Special Crash Packs containing only inserts (an assortion of Player's Club, Player's Club Platinum and Crash the Game cards) were randomly inserted into one in every 175 12-card packs. Rookie Cards of note include Michael Finley, Kevin Garnett, Joe Smith, Jerry Stackhouse and Damon Stoudamire.

COMPLETE SET (410) 12.50 30.00
COMP.FACTORY SET (419) 12.50 30.00
COMPLETE SERIES 1 (210) 6.00 15.00
COMPLETE SERIES 2 (200) 6.00 15.00
SUBSET CARDS SAME VALUE AS BASE CARDS
1 Rod Strickland .07 .20
2 Larry Johnson .12 .30
3 Mahmoud Abdul-Rauf .07 .20
4 Joe Dumars .12 .30
5 Jason Kidd .20 .50
6 Avery Johnson .10 .25
7 Dee Brown .07 .20
8 Brian Williams .07 .20
9 Nick Van Exel .12 .30
10 Dennis Rodman .25 .60
11 Rony Seikaly .07 .20
12 Harvey Grant .07 .20
13 Craig Ehlo .07 .20
14 Derek Harper .10 .25
15 Oliver Miller .07 .20
16 Dennis Scott .07 .20
17 Ed Pinckney .07 .20
18 Eric Piatkowski .10 .25
19 B.J. Armstrong .07 .20
20 Tyrone Hill .07 .20
21 Malik Sealy .07 .20
22 Clyde Drexler .15 .40
23 Aaron McKie .07 .20
24 Harold Miner .07 .20
25 Bobby Hurley .07 .20
26 Dell Curry .07 .20
27 Micheal Williams .07 .20
28 Adam Keefe .07 .20
29 Antonio Harvey .07 .20
30 Billy Owens .07 .20
31 Nate McMillan .07 .20
32 J.R. Reid .07 .20
33 Grant Hill .20 .50
34 Charles Barkley .20 .50
35 Tyrone Corbin .07 .20
36 Don MacLean .07 .20
37 Kenny Smith .10 .25
38 Juwan Howard .12 .30
39 Charles Smith .07 .20
40 Shawn Kemp .12 .30
41 Dana Barros .07 .20
42 Vin Baker .10 .25
43 Armon Gilliam .07 .20
44 Spud Webb .10 .25
45 Michael Jordan 1.00 2.50
46 Scott Williams .07 .20
47 Vlade Divac .12 .30
48 Roy Tarpley .07 .20
49 Bimbo Coles .07 .20
50 David Robinson .20 .50
51 Terry Dehere .07 .20
52 Bobby Phills .07 .20
53 Sherman Douglas .07 .20
54 Rodney Rogers .07 .20
55 Detlef Schrempf .12 .30
56 Calbert Cheaney .07 .20
57 Tom Gugliotta .07 .20
58 Jeff Turner .07 .20
59 Mookie Blaylock .07 .20
60 Bill Curley .07 .20
61 Chris Dudley .07 .20
62 Popeye Jones .07 .20
63 Scott Burrell .07 .20
64 Dale Davis .07 .20
65 Mitchell Butler .07 .20
66 Pervis Ellison .07 .20
67 Todd Day .07 .20
68 Carl Herrera .07 .20
69 Jeff Hornacek .10 .25
70 Vincent Askew .07 .20
71 A.C. Green .10 .25
72 Kevin Gamble .07 .20
73 Chris Gatling .07 .20
74 Otis Thorpe .07 .20
75 Michael Cage .07 .20
76 Carlos Rogers .07 .20
77 Gheorghe Muresan .07 .20
78 Olden Polynice .07 .20
79 Grant Long .07 .20
80 Allan Houston .10 .25
81 Bo Outlaw .07 .20
82 Clarence Weatherspoon .07 .20
83 Tony Dumas .07 .20
84 Herb Williams .07 .20
85 P.J. Brown .07 .20
86 Robert Horry .10 .25
87 Byron Scott .10 .25
88 Horace Grant .10 .25
89 Dominique Wilkins .15 .40
90 Doug West .07 .20
91 Antoine Carr .07 .20
92 Dickey Simpkins .07 .20
93 Elden Campbell .07 .20
94 Kevin Johnson .12 .30
95 Rex Chapman .07 .20
96 John Williams .07 .20
97 Tim Hardaway .12 .30
98 Rik Smits .10 .25
99 Rex Walters .07 .20
100 Robert Parish .12 .30
101 Isaiah Rider .12 .30
102 Sarunas Marciulionis .07 .20
103 Andrew Lang .07 .20
104 Eric Mobley .07 .20
105 Randy Brown .07 .20
106 John Stockton .15 .40
107 Lamond Murray .07 .20
108 Will Perdue .07 .20
109 Wayman Tisdale .07 .20
110 John Starks .10 .25
111 John Salley .07 .20
112 Lucious Harris .07 .20
113 Jeff Malone .07 .20
114 Anthony Bowie .07 .20
115 Vinny Del Negro .07 .20
116 Michael Adams .07 .20
117 Chris Mullin .12 .30
118 Benoit Benjamin .07 .20
119 Byron Houston .07 .20
120 LaPhonso Ellis .07 .20
121 Doug Overton .07 .20
122 Jerome Kersey .07 .20
123 Greg Minor .07 .20
124 Christian Laettner .10 .25
125 Mark Price .12 .30
126 Kevin Willis .07 .20
127 Kenny Anderson .10 .25
128 Marty Conlon .07 .20
129 Blue Edwards .07 .20
130 Danny Schayes .07 .20
131 Duane Ferrell .07 .20
132 Charles Oakley .10 .25
133 Brian Grant .10 .25
134 Reggie Williams .07 .20
135 Steve Kerr .10 .25
136 Khalid Reeves .07 .20
137 David Benoit .07 .20
138 Derrick Coleman .10 .25
139 Anthony Peeler .07 .20
140 Jim Jackson .07 .20
141 Stacey Augmon .10 .25
142 Sam Cassell .12 .30
143 Derrick McKey .07 .20
144 Danny Ferry .07 .20
145 Anfernee Hardaway .20 .50
146 Clifford Robinson .07 .20
147 B.J. Tyler .07 .20
148 Mark West .07 .20
149 David Wingate .07 .20
150 Willie Anderson .07 .20
151 Hersey Hawkins .07 .20
152 Bryant Stith .07 .20
153 Dan Majerle .12 .30
154 Chris Smith .07 .20
155 Donyell Marshall .07 .20
156 Loy Vaught .07 .20
157 Reggie Miller .15 .40
158 Hubert Davis .07 .20
159 Ron Harper .10 .25
160 Lee Mayberry .07 .20
161 Eddie Jones .12 .30
162 Shawn Bradley .07 .20
163 Nick Anderson .07 .20
164 Ervin Johnson .07 .20
165 Walt Williams .07 .20
166 Steve Smith FF .10 .25
167 Dino Radja FF .07 .20
168 Alonzo Mourning FF .15 .40
169 Michael Jordan FF 1.00 2.50
170 Tyrone Hill FF .07 .20
171 Jamal Mashburn FF .12 .30
172 Dikembe Mutombo FF .12 .30
173 Grant Hill FF w/Jordan .20 .50
174 Latrell Sprewell FF .12 .30
175 Hakeem Olajuwon FF .15 .40
176 Reggie Miller FF .15 .40
177 Pooh Richardson FF .07 .20
178 Cedric Ceballos FF .07 .20
179 Glen Rice FF .12 .30
180 Glenn Robinson FF .10 .25
181 Isaiah Rider FF .12 .30
182 Derrick Coleman FF .10 .25
183 Patrick Ewing FF .15 .40
184 Shaquille O'Neal FF .30 .75
185 Dana Barros FF .07 .20
186 Dan Majerle FF .12 .30
187 Clifford Robinson FF .07 .20
188 Mitch Richmond FF .12 .30
189 David Robinson FF .20 .50
190 Gary Payton FF .12 .30
191 Oliver Miller FF .07 .20
192 Karl Malone FF .15 .40
193 Kevin Pritchard FF .07 .20
194 Chris Webber FF .15 .40
195 Michael Jordan PD 1.00 2.50
196 Hakeem Olajuwon PD .15 .40
197 Vin Baker PD .10 .25
198 Grant Hill PD .20 .50
199 Clyde Drexler PD .15 .40
200 Chris Webber PD .15 .40
201 Shawn Kemp PD .12 .30
202 Shaquille O'Neal PD .30 .75
203 Stacey Augmon PD .10 .25
204 David Benoit PD .07 .20
205 Rodney Rogers PD .07 .20
206 Latrell Sprewell PD .12 .30
207 Brian Grant PD .10 .25
208 Lamond Murray PD .07 .20
209 Shawn Kemp CL .10 .25
210 Michael Jordan CL .40 1.00
211 Cory Alexander RC .12 .30
212 Vernon Maxwell .07 .20
213 George Lynch .07 .20
214 Terry Mills .07 .20
215 Scottie Pippen .20 .50
216 Donald Royal .07 .20
217 Wesley Person .07 .20
218 Antonio Davis .07 .20
219 Glenn Robinson .10 .25
220 Jerry Stackhouse RC .40 1.00
221 James Robinson .07 .20
222 Chris Mills .07 .20
223 Chuck Person .10 .25
224 Duane Causwell .07 .20
225 Gary Payton .12 .30
226 Eric Montross .07 .20
227 Felton Spencer .07 .20
228 Scott Skiles .07 .20
229 Latrell Sprewell .12 .30
230 Sedale Threatt .07 .20
231 Mark Bryant .07 .20
232 Buck Williams .07 .20
233 Brian Williams .07 .20
234 Sharone Wright .07 .20
235 Karl Malone .15 .40
236 Kevin Edwards .07 .20
237 Muggsy Bogues .10 .25
238 Mario Elie .07 .20
239 Rasheed Wallace RC .40 1.00
240 George Zidek RC .10 .25
241 Cedric Ceballos .07 .20
242 Alan Henderson RC .12 .30
243 Joe Kleine .07 .20
244 Patrick Ewing .15 .40
245 Sasha Danilovic RC .12 .30
246 Bill Wennington .07 .20
247 Steve Smith .10 .25
248 Bryant Stith .07 .20
249 Dino Radja .07 .20
250 Monty Williams .07 .20
251 Andrew DeClercq RC .12 .30
252 Sean Elliott .12 .30
253 Rick Fox .07 .20
254 Lionel Simmons .07 .20
255 Dikembe Mutombo .12 .30
256 Lindsey Hunter .07 .20
257 Terrell Brandon .07 .20
258 Shawn Respert RC .10 .25
259 Rodney Rogers .07 .20
260 Bryon Russell .07 .20
261 David Wesley .07 .20
262 Ken Norman .07 .20
263 Mitch Richmond .12 .30
264 Sam Perkins .07 .20
265 Hakeem Olajuwon .15 .40
266 Brian Shaw .07 .20
267 B.J. Armstrong .07 .20
268 Jalen Rose .15 .40
269 Bryant Reeves RC .10 .25
270 Cherokee Parks RC .10 .25
271 Dennis Rodman .25 .60
272 Kendall Gill .07 .20
273 Elliot Perry .07 .20
274 Anthony Mason .07 .20
275 Kevin Garnett RC 1.00 2.50
276 Damon Stoudamire RC .30 .75
277 Lawrence Moten RC .12 .30
278 Ed O'Bannon RC .10 .25
279 Toni Kukoc .12 .30
280 Greg Ostertag RC .12 .30
281 Tom Hammonds .07 .20
282 Yinka Dare .07 .20
283 Michael Smith .07 .20
284 Clifford Rozier .07 .20
285 Gary Trent RC .12 .30
286 Shaquille O'Neal .30 .75
287 Luc Longley .10 .25
288 Bob Sura RC .10 .25
289 Dana Barros .07 .20
290 Lorenzo Williams .07 .20
291 Haywoode Workman .07 .20
292 Randolph Childress RC .10 .25
293 Doc Rivers .10 .25
294 Chris Webber .15 .40
295 Kurt Thomas RC .12 .30
296 Greg Anthony .07 .20
297 Tyus Edney RC .12 .30
298 Danny Manning .10 .25
299 Brent Barry RC .20 .50
300 Joe Smith RC .15 .40
301 Pooh Richardson .07 .20
302 Mark Jackson .10 .25
303 Richard Dumas .07 .20
304 Michael Finley RC .40 1.00
305 Theo Ratliff RC .20 .50
306 Gary Grant .07 .20
307 Jamal Mashburn .12 .30
308 Corliss Williamson RC .12 .30
309 Eric Williams RC .12 .30
310 Zan Tabak .07 .20
311 Eric Murdock .07 .20
312 Sherrell Ford RC .10 .25
313 Terry Davis .07 .20
314 Vern Fleming .07 .20
315 Jason Caffey RC .12 .30
316 Mario Bennett RC .10 .25
317 David Vaughn RC .12 .30
318 Loren Meyer RC .07 .20
319 Travis Best RC .12 .30
320 Byron Scott .10 .25
321 Mookie Blaylock SR .07 .20
322 Dee Brown SR .07 .20
323 Alonzo Mourning SR .15 .40
324 Michael Jordan SR 1.00 2.50
325 Terrell Brandon SR .07 .20
326 Jim Jackson SR .07 .20
327 Dikembe Mutombo SR .12 .30
328 Grant Hill SR .20 .50
329 Joe Smith SR UER .10 .25
330 Clyde Drexler SR .15 .40
331 Reggie Miller SR .15 .40
332 Lamond Murray SR .07 .20
333 Nick Van Exel SR .12 .30
334 Glen Rice SR .12 .30
335 Glenn Robinson SR .10 .25
336 Christian Laettner SR .10 .25
337 Kenny Anderson SR .10 .25
338 Patrick Ewing SR .15 .40
339 Shaquille O'Neal SR .30 .75
340 Jerry Stackhouse SR .25 .60
341 Charles Barkley SR .20 .50
342 Clifford Robinson SR .07 .20
343 Brian Grant SR .10 .25
344 David Robinson SR .20 .50
345 Shawn Kemp SR .12 .30
346 Damon Stoudamire SR .20 .50
347 Karl Malone SR .15 .40
348 Bryant Reeves SR .05 .15
349 Juwan Howard SR .12 .30
350 N.Anderson/D.Brown PT .07 .20
351 Rik Smits PT .10 .25
352 H.Williams/T.Tolbert PT .07 .20
353 Michael Jordan PT 1.00 2.50
354 David Robinson PT .20 .50
355 T.Porter/K.Johnson PT .12 .30
356 Clyde Drexler PT .15 .40
357 Cedric Ceballos PT .07 .20
358 Horace Grant Group PT .10 .25
359 Reggie Miller PT .15 .40
360 A.Johnson/N.Van Exel PT .12 .30
361 H.Olajuwon/R.Horry PT .15 .40
362 Rik Smits PT .10 .25
363 D.Rob/H.Olajuwon PT .20 .50
364 Robert Horry PT .10 .25
365 Kenny Smith PT .10 .25
366 Stacey Augmon LOVE .10 .25
367 Sherman Douglas LOVE .07 .20
368 Larry Johnson LOVE .12 .30
369 Scottie Pippen LOVE .20 .50
370 Tyrone Hill LOVE .07 .20
371 Jamal Mashburn LOVE .12 .30
372 Mahmoud Abdul-Rauf LOVE .07 .20
373 Grant Hill LOVE .20 .50
374 Latrell Sprewell LOVE .12 .30
375 Sam Cassell LOVE .12 .30
376 Rik Smits LOVE .10 .25
377 Terry Dehere LOVE .07 .20
378 Eddie Jones LOVE .12 .30
379 Billy Owens LOVE .07 .20
380 Vin Baker LOVE .10 .25
381 Isaiah Rider LOVE .12 .30
382 Kenny Anderson LOVE .10 .25
383 John Starks LOVE .10 .25
384 Anfernee Hardaway LOVE .20 .50
385 Sharone Wright LOVE .07 .20
386 Charles Barkley LOVE .20 .50
387 Clifford Robinson LOVE .07 .20
388 Walt Williams LOVE .07 .20
389 Sean Elliott LOVE .12 .30
390 Gary Payton LOVE .12 .30
391 Carlos Rogers LOVE .07 .20
392 John Stockton LOVE .15 .40
393 Greg Anthony LOVE .07 .20
394 Chris Webber LOVE .15 .40
395 Gary Payton PG .12 .30
396 Mookie Blaylock PG .07 .20
397 Charles Barkley PG .20 .50
398 Grant Hill PG .20 .50
399 Anfernee Hardaway PG .20 .50
400 Kenny Anderson PG .10 .25
401 Mark Jackson PG .10 .25
402 Karl Malone PG .15 .40
403 Avery Johnson PG .10 .25
404 Larry Johnson 40 .12 .30
405 Nick Van Exel 40 .12 .30
406 Vin Baker 40 .10 .25
407 Jason Kidd 40 .20 .50
408 David Robinson 40 .20 .50
409 Shawn Kemp CL .08 .25
410 Michael Jordan CL .40 1.00
NNO Bulls Fact.Set Comm. 2.50 6.00

1995-96 Collector's Choice Player's Club

COMPLETE SET (410) 35.00 70.00
COMPLETE SERIES 1 (210) 15.00 30.00
COMPLETE SERIES 2 (200) 20.00 40.00
*STARS: 1.25X TO 3X BASE CARD HI
*RCs: 1X TO 2.5X BASE HI
*SUBSETS: .75X TO 2X BASE HI
ONE PER PACK

1995-96 Collector's Choice Player's Club Platinum

*STARS: 10X TO 25X BASE CARD HI
*RCs: 6X TO 15X BASE HI
*SUBSETS: 6X TO 15X BASE HI
SER.1/2 STATED ODDS 1:35
173 Grant Hill FF w/Jordan 8.00 20.00

1995-96 Collector's Choice Crash the Game Assists/Rebounds

Issued randomly into one in every five second series 12-card packs, cards from this 90-card set feature three separate versions of thirty different player cards. Each player was given three separate specific game dates. If the player depicted on the card tallied 10 or more assists or rebounds on that date, the card was redeemable for a special 30-card Crash the Game Assists/Rebounds Silver Trade set. Losing cards are signified with an "L" and winning cards with a "W". The winning cards are actually in shorter supply than losing cards due to the fact that many of them were mailed in for redemption and then destroyed.

SER.2 STATED ODDS 1:5
*GOLD CARDS: 1.25X TO 3X HI COLUMN
GOLD: SER.2 STATED ODDS 1:49
*SILVER RED.CARDS: .2X TO .5X HI COLUMN
*GOLD RED.CARDS: 1.5X TO 4X SILVER RED.
ONE RED.SET PER WINNER BY MAIL
C1 Michael Jordan 4.00 10.00
C1B Michael Jordan 4.00 10.00
C1C Michael Jordan 4.00 10.00
C2 Tim Hardaway .50 1.25
C2B Tim Hardaway .50 1.25
C2C Tim Hardaway .50 1.25
C3 Juwan Howard .50 1.25
C3B Juwan Howard .50 1.25
C3C Juwan Howard .50 1.25
C4 Shawn Kemp .50 1.25
C4B Shawn Kemp .50 1.25
C4C Shawn Kemp .50 1.25
C5 Nick Van Exel .50 1.25
C5B Nick Van Exel .50 1.25
C5C Nick Van Exel .50 1.25
C6 Mookie Blaylock .30 .75
C6B Mookie Blaylock .30 .75
C6C Mookie Blaylock .30 .75
C7 John Stockton .60 1.50
C7B John Stockton .60 1.50
C7C John Stockton .60 1.50
C8 Scottie Pippen .75 2.00
C8B Scottie Pippen .75 2.00
C8C Scottie Pippen .75 2.00
C9 Vin Baker .40 1.00
C9B Vin Baker .40 1.00
C9C Vin Baker .40 1.00
C10 Lamond Murray .30 .75
C10B Lamond Murray .30 .75
C10C Lamond Murray .30 .75
C11 David Robinson .75 2.00
C11B David Robinson .75 2.00
C11C David Robinson .75 2.00
C12 Jason Kidd .75 2.00
C12B Jason Kidd .75 2.00
C12C Jason Kidd .75 2.00
C13 Rod Strickland .30 .75
C13B Rod Strickland .30 .75
C13C Rod Strickland .30 .75
C14 Glen Rice .50 1.25
C14B Glen Rice .50 1.25
C14C Glen Rice .50 1.25
C15 Anfernee Hardaway .75 2.00
C15B Anfernee Hardaway .75 2.00
C15C Anfernee Hardaway .75 2.00
C16 Hakeem Olajuwon .60 1.50
C16B Hakeem Olajuwon .60 1.50
C16C Hakeem Olajuwon .60 1.50
C17 Kenny Anderson .40 1.00
C17B Kenny Anderson .40 1.00
C17C Kenny Anderson .40 1.00
C18 Sharone Wright .30 .75
C18B Sharone Wright .30 .75
C18C Sharone Wright .30 .75
C19 Dikembe Mutombo .50 1.25
C19B Dikembe Mutombo .50 1.25
C19C Dikembe Mutombo .50 1.25
C20 Muggsy Bogues .40 1.00
C20B Muggsy Bogues .40 1.00
C20C Muggsy Bogues .40 1.00
C21 Reggie Miller .60 1.50
C21B Reggie Miller .60 1.50
C21C Reggie Miller .60 1.50
C22 Danny Manning .40 1.00
C22B Danny Manning .40 1.00
C22C Danny Manning .40 1.00
C23 Christian Laettner .40 1.00
C23B Christian Laettner .40 1.00
C23C Christian Laettner .40 1.00
C24 Eric Montross .30 .75
C24B Eric Montross .30 .75
C24C Eric Montross .30 .75
C25 Patrick Ewing .60 1.50
C25B Patrick Ewing .60 1.50
C25C Patrick Ewing .60 1.50
C26 Damon Stoudamire 1.25 3.00
C26B Damon Stoudamire 1.25 3.00
C26C Damon Stoudamire 1.25 3.00
C27 Bryant Reeves .40 1.00
C27B Bryant Reeves .40 1.00
C27C Bryant Reeves .40 1.00
C28 Joe Dumars .50 1.25
C28B Joe Dumars .50 1.25
C28C Joe Dumars .50 1.25
C29 Tyrone Hill .30 .75
C29B Tyrone Hill .30 .75
C29C Tyrone Hill .30 .75
C30 Brian Grant .40 1.00
C30B Brian Grant .40 1.00
C30C Brian Grant .40 1.00

1995-96 Collector's Choice Crash the Game Scoring

Issued randomly into one in every five first series 12-card packs, cards from this 81-card set features three separate versions of twenty-seven different player cards. Each player is matched up against three different teams (two within their conference and one outside of their conference). If the player depicted on the card scored 30 or more points versus the team depicted on the card, the card was redeemable for a special 30-card Crash the Game Scoring Silver Trade set. Losing cards are signified with an "L" and winning cards are signified with a "W". The winning cards are actually in shorter supply than losing cards due to the fact that many of them were mailed in for redemption and then destroyed.

SER.1 STATED ODDS 1:5
*GOLD CARDS: 1.5X TO 4X HI COLUMN
GOLD: SER.1 STATED ODDS 1:50
*SILVER RED.CARDS: .2X TO .5X HI COLUMN
*GOLD RED.CARDS: 1.5X TO 4X SILVER RED.
ONE RED.SET PER WINNER BY MAIL
C1 Michael Jordan 4.00 10.00
C1B Michael Jordan 4.00 10.00
C1C Michael Jordan 4.00 10.00
C2 Kenny Anderson .40 1.00
C2B Kenny Anderson .40 1.00
C2C Kenny Anderson .40 1.00
C3 Charles Barkley .75 2.00
C3B Charles Barkley .75 2.00
C3C Charles Barkley .75 2.00
C4 Dana Barros .30 .75
C4B Dana Barros .30 .75
C4C Dana Barros .30 .75
C5 Anfernee Hardaway .75 2.00
C5B Anfernee Hardaway .75 2.00
C5C Anfernee Hardaway .75 2.00
C6 Mookie Blaylock .30 .75
C6B Mookie Blaylock .30 .75
C6C Mookie Blaylock .30 .75
C7 Lamond Murray .30 .75
C7B Lamond Murray .30 .75
C7C Lamond Murray .30 .75
C8 Karl Malone .60 1.50
C8B Karl Malone .60 1.50
C8C Karl Malone .60 1.50
C9 Alonzo Mourning .60 1.50
C9B Alonzo Mourning .60 1.50
C9C Alonzo Mourning .60 1.50
C10 Hakeem Olajuwon .60 1.50
C10B Hakeem Olajuwon .60 1.50
C10C Hakeem Olajuwon .60 1.50
C11 Mark Price .50 1.25
C11B Mark Price .50 1.25
C11C Mark Price .50 1.25
C12 Isiah Rider .50 1.25
C12B Isaiah Rider .50 1.25
C12C Isaiah Rider .50 1.25
C13 Glen Rice .50 1.25
C13B Glen Rice .50 1.25
C13C Glen Rice .50 1.25
C14 Mitch Richmond .50 1.25
C14B Mitch Richmond .50 1.25
C14C Mitch Richmond .50 1.25
C15 Chris Webber .60 1.50
C15B Chris Webber .60 1.50
C15C Chris Webber .60 1.50
C16 Nick Van Exel .50 1.25
C16B Nick Van Exel .50 1.25
C16C Nick Van Exel .50 1.25
C17 Mahmoud Abdul-Rauf .30 .75
C17B Mahmoud Abdul-Rauf .30 .75
C17C Mahmoud Abdul-Rauf .30 .75
C18 Dominique Wilkins .60 1.50
C18B Dominique Wilkins .60 1.50
C18C Dominique Wilkins .60 1.50
C19 Patrick Ewing .60 1.50
C19B Patrick Ewing .60 1.50
C19C Patrick Ewing .60 1.50
C20 David Robinson .75 2.00
C20B David Robinson .75 2.00
C20C David Robinson .75 2.00
C21 Shawn Kemp .50 1.25
C21B Shawn Kemp .50 1.25
C21C Shawn Kemp .50 1.25
C22 Jason Kidd .75 2.00
C22B Jason Kidd .75 2.00
C22C Jason Kidd .75 2.00
C23 Glenn Robinson .40 1.00
C23B Glenn Robinson .40 1.00
C23C Glenn Robinson .40 1.00
C24 Reggie Miller .60 1.50
C24B Reggie Miller .60 1.50
C24C Reggie Miller .60 1.50
C25 Joe Dumars .50 1.25
C25B Joe Dumars .50 1.25
C25C Joe Dumars .50 1.25
C26 Latrell Sprewell .50 1.25
C26B Latrell Sprewell .50 1.25
C26C Latrell Sprewell .50 1.25
C27 Clifford Robinson .30 .75
C27B Clifford Robinson .30 .75
C27C Clifford Robinson .30 .75
XC28 Damon Stoudamire 1.25 3.00
XC29 Bryant Reeves .40 1.00
XC30 Michael Jordan 4.00 10.00

1995-96 Collector's Choice Debut Trade

This 30-card set was only available by redeeming the Collector's Choice Debut Trade card, which was randomly seeded into second series 12-card packs at a rate of one in 30. The 30-card set primarily consists of a selection of player's traded during the 1995-96 season. The prices listed below are for the more common regular issue cards. The Debut Trade card program expired on May 8th, 1996. Collectors started receiving their cards around late June, 1996. It's interesting to note that rookies Antonio McDyess and Arvydas Sabonis were left out of the regular issue Collector's Choice set but included here in the Debut Trade set.

TRADE: SER.2 STATED ODDS 1:30
*PLAYER'S CLUB: .75X TO 2X HI COLUM
PC TRADE: SER.2 STATED ODDS 1:144
*PC PLATINUM STARS: 8X TO 20X HI COLUMN
*PC PLATINUM RCs: 6X TO 15X HI
PCP TRADE: SER.2 STATED ODDS 1:720
T1 Magic Johnson .40 1.00
T2 Arvydas Sabonis .30 .75
T3 Kenny Anderson .12 .30
T4 Antonio McDyess .20 .50
T5 Sherman Douglas .10 .25
T6 Spud Webb .12 .30
T7 Glen Rice .15 .40
T8 Todd Day .10 .25
T9 John Williams .10 .25
T10 Chris Morris .10 .25
T11 Shawn Bradley .10 .25
T12 Dan Majerle .15 .40
T13 George McCloud .10 .25
T14 Derrick Coleman .12 .30
T15 Kendall Gill .10 .25
T16 Ricky Pierce .10 .25
T17 Robert Pack .10 .25
T18 Alonzo Mourning .20 .50
T19 Matt Geiger .10 .25
T20 Don MacLean .10 .25
T21 Willie Anderson .10 .25
T22 Oliver Miller .10 .25
T23 Tracy Murray .10 .25
T24 Ed Pinckney .10 .25
T25 Alvin Robertson .10 .25
T26 Anthony Avent .10 .25
T27 Blue Edwards .10 .25
T28 Kenny Gattison .10 .25
T29 Chris King .10 .25
T30 Eric Murdock .10 .25

1995-96 Collector's Choice Draft Trade

This 10-card set was only available by redeeming a Collector's Choice Draft Trade card, which was randomly inserted into series one packs at a rate of one in 144 packs. The 10-card set consists of the top rookies from the 1995-96 season. Card fronts contain a photo with the player's name, draft pick number and position. Card backs contain biographical and statistical information from the player's college/high school year(s) and are numbered with a "D" prefix. The Draft Trade card program expired on June 7, 1996.

COMPLETE SET (10) 6.00 15.00
ONE SET PER DRAFT TRADE CARD VIA MAIL
TRADE: SER.1 STATED ODDS 1:144
D1 Joe Smith .60 1.50
D2 Antonio McDyess .60 1.50
D3 Jerry Stackhouse 1.50 4.00
D4 Rasheed Wallace 1.50 4.00
D5 Kevin Garnett 4.00 10.00
D6 Bryant Reeves .40 1.00
D7 Damon Stoudamire 1.25 3.00
D8 Shawn Respert .40 1.00
D9 Ed O'Bannon .40 1.00
D10 Kurt Thomas .50 1.25

1995-96 Collector's Choice Jordan He's Back

Inserted one per special retail pack, this five-card set commemorates Michael Jordan coming back in the 1994-95 season. Each card focuses on a particular moment/game.

COMMON JORDAN (M1-M5) .60 1.50

1995-96 Collector's Choice Jordan He's Back Jumbos

COMPLETE SET (3) 4.00 10.00
COMMON CARD 2.00 5.00

1995-96 Collector's Choice Jordan Collection

Randomly inserted into one in every 11 first and second series 12-card packs, these eight standard-size cards comprise the first and third parts of a 24-card set, spanning across all of Upper Deck's 1995-96 basketball products, highlighting the career of Michael Jordan. The fronts have a full-color photo with a gold-foil picture of Jordan in the lower left hand corner wearing number 45. The backs have a color photo at the top with information about the highlight and statistics from that year at the bottom.

COMPLETE SET (8) 8.00 20.00
COMPLETE SER.1 SET (4) 4.00 10.00
COMPLETE SER.2 SET (4) 4.00 10.00
COMMON SER.1 (JC1-JC8) 1.50 4.00
COMMON SER.2 (JC9-JC12) 1.50 4.00
STATED ODDS 1:11 PACKS

1996-97 Collector's Choice

These 400-standard size cards, comprise Upper Deck's 1996-97 Collector's Choice series one and two set. Cards were primarily issued in 12-card hobby and retail packs with a suggested retail price of ninety-nine cents. Regular issue cards feature white-bordered fronts with color player action shots. The backs have a color photo and statistics. A Factory Set was also issued in early May 1997. The set contained all the basic cards from both series, five Gold Mini-Cards (randomly inserted) and one of four commemorative cards (measuring 3 1/2" by 5") featuring either Shawn Kemp, Michael Jordan, Anfernee Hardaway or a Jordan/Hardaway dual card. The set was issued as a 406-card factory set with a suggested retail price of $29.99. Also included as an insert in packs (1:4 packs) was a game piece for Upper Deck's Meet the Stars promotion. Each game piece was a multiple choice trivia card about basketball. The collector would scratch off the box next to the answer that they felt best matched the question to determine if they won. Instant win game pieces were also inserted one in 72 packs. Winning game pieces could be sent into Upper Deck for a prize drawing. The Grand Prize was a chance to meet Michael Jordan. Prizes for 2nd through 4th were for Upper Deck Authenticated shopping sprees. The 5th prize was two special Michael Jordan Meet the Stars cards. The blank back cards measure 5" by 7" and are titled Dynamic Debut and Magic Memories. These two cards are priced at the bottom of the base set.

COMPLETE SET (400) 10.00 25.00
COMP.FACT.SET (406) 12.00 30.00
COMPLETE SERIES 1 (200) 6.00 15.00
COMPLETE SERIES 2 (200) 6.00 15.00
COMP.UPDATE SET (30) 4.00 10.00
401-430 ONE UP SET VIA TRADE CARD
401-430 STATED ODDS 1:71
1 Mookie Blaylock .07 .20
2 Grant Long .07 .20
3 Christian Laettner .10 .25
4 Craig Ehlo .07 .20
5 Ken Norman .07 .20
6 Stacey Augmon .10 .25
7 Dana Barros .07 .20
8 Dino Radja .07 .20
9 Rick Fox .07 .20
10 Eric Montross .07 .20
11 David Wesley .07 .20
12 Eric Williams .07 .20
13 Glen Rice .12 .30
14 Dell Curry .07 .20
15 Matt Geiger .07 .20
16 Scott Burrell .07 .20
17 George Zidek .07 .20
18 Muggsy Bogues .10 .25
19 Ron Harper .10 .25

20 Steve Kerr .10 .25
21 Toni Kukoc .12 .30
22 Dennis Rodman .25 .60
23 Michael Jordan 1.00 2.50
24 Luc Longley .10 .25
25 M.Jordan/V.Divac Bulls VT 1.00 2.50
26 Michael Jordan Bulls VT 1.00 2.50
27 Luc Longley Bulls VT .10 .25
28 Scottie Pippen Bulls VT .20 .50
29 T.Kukoc/J.Howard Bulls VT .12 .30
30 Terrell Brandon .07 .20
31 Bobby Phills .07 .20
32 Tyrone Hill .07 .20
33 Michael Cage .07 .20
34 Bob Sura .07 .20
35 Tony Dumas .07 .20
36 Jim Jackson .07 .20
37 Loren Meyer .07 .20
38 Cherokee Parks .07 .20
39 Jamal Mashburn .10 .25
40 Popeye Jones .07 .20
41 LaPhonso Ellis .07 .20
42 Jalen Rose .10 .25
43 Antonio McDyess .12 .30
44 Tom Hammonds .07 .20
45 Mahmoud Abdul-Rauf .07 .20
46 Dale Ellis .07 .20
47 Joe Dumars .12 .30
48 Theo Ratliff .07 .20
49 Lindsey Hunter .07 .20
50 Terry Mills .07 .20
51 Don Reid .07 .20
52 B.J. Armstrong .07 .20
53 Bimbo Coles .07 .20
54 Joe Smith .10 .25
55 Chris Mullin .12 .30
56 Rony Seikaly .07 .20
57 Donyell Marshall .07 .20
58 Hakeem Olajuwon .15 .40
59 Robert Horry .10 .25
60 Mario Elie .07 .20
61 Mark Bryant .07 .20
62 Chucky Brown .07 .20
63 Rik Smits .10 .25
64 Derrick McKey .07 .20
65 Eddie Johnson .07 .20
66 Mark Jackson .10 .25
67 Ricky Pierce .07 .20
68 Travis Best .07 .20
69 Rodney Rogers .07 .20
70 Brent Barry .10 .25
71 Lamond Murray .07 .20
72 Eric Piatkowski .10 .25
73 Pooh Richardson .07 .20
74 Cedric Ceballos .07 .20
75 Eddie Jones .12 .30
76 Anthony Peeler .07 .20
77 George Lynch .07 .20
78 Vlade Divac .12 .30
79 Rex Chapman .07 .20
80 Sasha Danilovic .07 .20
81 Kurt Thomas .07 .20
82 Keith Askins .07 .20
83 Walt Williams .07 .20
84 Vin Baker .10 .25
85 Shawn Respert .07 .20
86 Sherman Douglas .07 .20
87 Marty Conlon .07 .20
88 Johnny Newman .07 .20
89 Kevin Garnett .30 .75
90 Andrew Lang .07 .20
91 Terry Porter .07 .20
92 Sam Mitchell .07 .20
93 Tom Gugliotta .07 .20
94 Spud Webb .10 .25
95 Kendall Gill .07 .20
96 Vern Fleming .07 .20
97 Shawn Bradley .07 .20
98 Yinka Dare .07 .20
99 Jayson Williams .07 .20
100 Kevin Edwards .07 .20
101 Charles Oakley .10 .25
102 Anthony Mason .07 .20
103 John Starks .10 .25
104 J.R. Reid .07 .20
105 Hubert Davis .07 .20
106 Gary Grant .07 .20
107 Nick Anderson .07 .20
108 Donald Royal .07 .20
109 Brian Shaw .07 .20
110 Brooks Thompson .07 .20
111 Anfernee Hardaway .20 .50
112 Dennis Scott .07 .20
113 Anfernee Hardaway PEN .20 .50
114 Anfernee Hardaway PEN .20 .50
115 Anfernee Hardaway PEN .20 .50
116 Anfernee Hardaway PEN .20 .50
117 Anfernee Hardaway PEN .20 .50
118 Derrick Coleman .10 .25
119 Rex Walters .07 .20
120 Sean Higgins .07 .20
121 Clarence Weatherspoon .07 .20
122 Jerry Stackhouse .15 .40
123 Elliot Perry .07 .20
124 Wayman Tisdale .07 .20
125 Wesley Person .07 .20
126 Charles Barkley .20 .50
127 A.C. Green .10 .25
128 Harvey Grant .07 .20
129 Arvydas Sabonis .10 .25
130 Aaron McKie .07 .20
131 Gary Trent .07 .20
132 Buck Williams .07 .20
133 Billy Owens .07 .20
134 Brian Grant .10 .25
135 Corliss Williamson .07 .20
136 Tyus Edney .07 .20
137 Olden Polynice .07 .20
138 Avery Johnson .10 .25
139 Vinny Del Negro .07 .20
140 Sean Elliott .12 .30
141 Chuck Person .10 .25
142 Will Perdue .07 .20
143 Nate McMillan .07 .20
144 Vincent Askew .07 .20
145 Detlef Schrempf .12 .30
146 Hersey Hawkins .07 .20
147 Sharone Wright .07 .20
148 Zan Tabak .07 .20
149 Oliver Miller .07 .20
150 Doug Christie .07 .20
151 Damon Stoudamire .10 .25
152 Jeff Hornacek .10 .25
153 Chris Morris .07 .20
154 Antoine Carr .07 .20
155 Karl Malone .15 .40
156 Adam Keefe .07 .20
157 Greg Anthony .07 .20
158 Blue Edwards .07 .20
159 Bryant Reeves .07 .20
160 Anthony Avent .07 .20
161 Lawrence Moten .07 .20
162 Calbert Cheaney .07 .20
163 Chris Webber .15 .40
164 Tim Legler .07 .20
165 Gheorghe Muresan .07 .20
166 Stacey Augmon FUND .10 .25
167 Dee Brown FUND .07 .20
168 Glen Rice FUND .12 .30
169 Scottie Pippen FUND .20 .50
170 Danny Ferry FUND .07 .20
171 Jason Kidd FUND .20 .50
172 LaPhonso Ellis FUND .07 .20
173 Grant Hill FUND .20 .50
174 Chris Mullin FUND .12 .30
175 Clyde Drexler FUND .15 .40
176 Rik Smits FUND .10 .25
177 Loy Vaught FUND .07 .20
178 Nick Van Exel FUND .12 .30
179 Alonzo Mourning FUND .15 .40
180 Glenn Robinson FUND .10 .25
181 Isaiah Rider FUND .10 .25
182 Ed O'Bannon FUND .07 .20
183 Patrick Ewing FUND .15 .40
184 Shaquille O'Neal FUND .30 .75
185 Derrick Coleman FUND .10 .25
186 Danny Manning FUND .10 .25
187 Clifford Robinson FUND .07 .20
188 Mitch Richmond FUND .12 .30
189 David Robinson FUND .20 .50
190 Shawn Kemp FUND .12 .30
191 Oliver Miller FUND .07 .20
192 John Stockton FUND .15 .40
193 Greg Anthony FUND .07 .20
194 Rasheed Wallace FUND .15 .40
195 Michael Jordan FUND 1.00 2.50
196 M.Jordan/M.Geiger CL .20 .50
197 E.Jones/A.McDyess CL .07 .20
198 A.Hardaway/K.Garnett CL .20 .50
199 D.Stoudamire/A.Johnson CL .07 .20
200 D.Robinson/C.Mullin CL .12 .30
201 Alan Henderson .07 .20
202 Steve Smith .10 .25
203 Donnie Boyce RC .12 .30
204 Priest Lauderdale RC .07 .20
205 Dikembe Mutombo .12 .30
206 Dee Brown .07 .20
207 Junior Burrough .07 .20
208 Todd Day .07 .20
209 Pervis Ellison .07 .20
210 Greg Minor .07 .20
211 Antoine Walker RC .20 .50
212 Rafael Addison .07 .20
213 Tony Delk RC .12 .30
214 Vlade Divac .12 .30
215 Anthony Goldwire .07 .20
216 Anthony Mason .07 .20
217 Dickey Simpkins .07 .20
218 Randy Brown .07 .20
219 Jud Buechler .07 .20
220 Jason Caffey .07 .20
221 Scottie Pippen .20 .50
222 Bill Wennington .07 .20
223 Danny Ferry .07 .20
224 Antonio Lang .07 .20
225 Chris Mills .07 .20
226 Vitaly Potapenko RC .10 .25
227 Terry Davis .07 .20
228 Chris Gatling .07 .20
229 Jason Kidd .20 .50
230 George McCloud .07 .20
231 Eric Montross .07 .20
232 Samaki Walker RC .10 .25
233 Mark Jackson .10 .25
234 Ervin Johnson .07 .20
235 Sarunas Marciulionis .07 .20
236 Eric Murdock .07 .20
237 Ricky Pierce .07 .20
238 Bryant Stith .07 .20
239 Stacey Augmon .10 .25
240 Grant Hill .20 .50
241 Otis Thorpe .07 .20
242 Jerome Williams RC .10 .25
243 Andrew DeClercq .07 .20
244 Todd Fuller RC .07 .20
245 Mark Price .12 .30
246 Clifford Rozier .07 .20
247 Latrell Sprewell .12 .30
248 Charles Barkley .20 .50
249 Clyde Drexler .15 .40
250 Othella Harrington RC .12 .30
251 Sam Mack .07 .20
252 Kevin Willis .07 .20
253 Erick Dampier RC .12 .30
254 Antonio Davis .07 .20
255 Dale Davis .07 .20
256 Duane Ferrell .07 .20
257 Reggie Miller .15 .40
258 Jalen Rose .10 .25
259 Reggie Williams .07 .20
260 Terry Dehere .07 .20
261 Bo Outlaw .07 .20
262 Stanley Roberts .07 .20
263 Malik Sealy .07 .20
264 Loy Vaught .07 .20
265 Lorenzen Wright RC .10 .25
266 Corie Blount .07 .20
267 Kobe Bryant RC 2.00 5.00
268 Elden Campbell .07 .20
269 Derek Fisher RC .15 .40
270 Shaquille O'Neal .30 .75
271 Nick Van Exel .12 .30
272 P.J. Brown .07 .20
273 Tim Hardaway .12 .30
274 Voshon Lenard RC .12 .30
275 Dan Majerle .12 .30
276 Alonzo Mourning .15 .40
277 Martin Muursepp RC .07 .20
278 Ray Allen RC .50 1.25
279 Elliot Perry .07 .20
280 Glenn Robinson .10 .25
281 Stephon Marbury RC .30 .75
282 Cherokee Parks .07 .20
283 Doug West .07 .20
284 Micheal Williams .07 .20
285 Kerry Kittles RC .12 .30
286 Ed O'Bannon .07 .20
287 Robert Pack .07 .20
288 Khalid Reeves .07 .20
289 David Benoit .07 .20
290 Patrick Ewing .15 .40
291 Allan Houston .10 .25
292 Larry Johnson .12 .30
293 Dontae' Jones RC .12 .30
294 Walter McCarty RC .12 .30
295 John Wallace RC .12 .30
296 Charlie Ward .07 .20
297 Brian Evans RC .12 .30
298 Horace Grant .10 .25
299 Jon Koncak .07 .20
300 Felton Spencer .07 .20
301 Allen Iverson RC .60 1.50
302 Don MacLean .07 .20
303 Scott Williams .07 .20
304 Sam Cassell .10 .25
305 Michael Finley .15 .40
306 Robert Horry .10 .25
307 Kevin Johnson .12 .30
308 Joe Kleine .07 .20
309 Danny Manning .10 .25
310 Steve Nash RC .60 1.50
311 John Williams .07 .20
312 Kenny Anderson .10 .25
313 Randolph Childress .07 .20
314 Chris Dudley .07 .20
315 Jermaine O'Neal RC .20 .50
316 Isaiah Rider .10 .25
317 Clifford Robinson .07 .20
318 Rasheed Wallace .15 .40
319 Mahmoud Abdul-Rauf .07 .20
320 Duane Causwell .07 .20
321 Bobby Hurley .07 .20
322 Mitch Richmond .12 .30
323 Lionel Simmons .07 .20
324 Michael Smith .07 .20
325 Dominique Wilkins .15 .40
326 Cory Alexander .07 .20
327 Greg Anderson .07 .20
328 Carl Herrera .07 .20
329 David Robinson .20 .50
330 Charles Smith .07 .20
331 Craig Ehlo .07 .20
332 Sherrell Ford .07 .20
333 Shawn Kemp .12 .30
334 Jim McIlvaine .07 .20
335 Gary Payton .12 .30
336 Sam Perkins .07 .20
337 Eric Snow RC .12 .30
338 David Wingate .07 .20
339 Marcus Camby RC .20 .50
340 Acie Earl .07 .20
341 Carlos Rogers .07 .20
342 Greg Ostertag .07 .20
343 Bryon Russell .07 .20
344 John Stockton .15 .40
345 Jamie Watson .07 .20
346 Shareef Abdur-Rahim RC .20 .50
347 Doug Edwards .07 .20
348 George Lynch .07 .20
349 Eric Mobley .07 .20
350 Anthony Peeler .07 .20
351 Roy Rogers RC .10 .25
352 Juwan Howard .10 .25
353 Harvey Grant .07 .20
354 Tracy Murray .07 .20
355 Rod Strickland .07 .20
356 A.Hardaway/M.Jordan ONE .50 1.25
357 H.Olajuwon/S.O'Neal ONE .25 .60
358 J.Smith/S.Kemp ONE .15 .40
359 D.Schrempf/T.Kukoc ONE .08 .25
360 J.Jackson/Stackhouse ONE .15 .40
361 Bryant/Abdur-Rahim ONE .40 1.00
362 N.Anderson/M.Jordan AJ .30 .75
363 J.Dumars/M.Jordan AJ .30 .75
364 J.Starks/M.Jordan AJ .30 .75
365 R.Miller/M.Jordan AJ .50 1.25
366 G.Payton/M.Jordan AJ .40 1.00
367 Mookie Blaylock PLAY .07 .20
368 D.Radja/Fox/Wesley PLAY .07 .20
369 Glen Rice PLAY .12 .30
370 M.Jordan/S.Pippen PLAY .50 1.25
371 Terrell Brandon PLAY .07 .20
372 Jason Kidd PLAY .20 .50
373 Antonio McDyess PLAY .12 .30
374 Grant Hill PLAY .20 .50
375 Joe Smith PLAY .10 .25
376 Barkley/Olaj/Drexler PLAY .30 .75
377 Reggie Miller PLAY .15 .40
378 L.A. Clippers PLAY .07 .20
379 Nick Van Exel PLAY .12 .30
380 Alonzo Mourning PLAY .15 .40
381 Ray Allen PLAY .25 .60
382 Stephon Marbury PLAY .25 .60
383 Shawn Bradley PLAY .07 .20
384 Patrick Ewing PLAY .15 .40
385 Anfernee Hardaway PLAY .20 .50
386 Jerry Stackhouse PLAY .15 .40
387 Danny Manning PLAY .10 .25
388 Clifford Robinson PLAY .07 .20
389 Tyus Edney PLAY .07 .20
390 San Antonio Spurs PLAY .07 .20
391 Shawn Kemp PLAY .12 .30
392 Toronto Raptors PLAY .07 .20
393 John Stockton PLAY .15 .40
394 Greg Anthony PLAY .07 .20
395 Gheorghe Muresan PLAY .07 .20
396 Checklist .07 .20
397 Checklist .07 .20
398 Checklist .07 .20
399 Checklist .07 .20
400 Checklist .07 .20
401 Henry James TRADE .20 .50
402 Shawn Bradley TRADE .20 .50
403 Sasha Danilovic TRADE .20 .50
404 Michael Finley TRADE .40 1.00
405 A.C. Green TRADE .25 .60
406 Derek Harper TRADE .25 .60
407 Khalid Reeves TRADE .20 .50
408 Aaron McKie TRADE .20 .50
409 Matt Maloney TRADE RC .25 .60
410 Darrick Martin TRADE .20 .50
411 Robert Horry TRADE .25 .60
412 Travis Knight TRADE RC .30 .75
413 Isaac Austin TRADE .20 .50
414 Jamal Mashburn TRADE .25 .60
415 Armon Gilliam TRADE .20 .50
416 Chris Carr TRADE RC .30 .75
417 Dean Garrett TRADE RC .30 .75
418 Shane Heal TRADE RC .30 .75
419 Sam Cassell TRADE .25 .60
420 Chris Gatling TRADE .20 .50
421 Jim Jackson TRADE .20 .50
422 Chris Childs TRADE .20 .50
423 Rony Seikaly TRADE .20 .50
424 Gerald Wilkins TRADE .20 .50
425 Cedric Ceballos TRADE .20 .50
426 Tony Dumas TRADE .20 .50
427 Jason Kidd TRADE .50 1.25
428 Popeye Jones TRADE .20 .50
429 Walt Williams TRADE .20 .50
430 Jaren Jackson TRADE .20 .50
NNO Update Trade Card 2.00 5.00
NNO Michael Jordan 5x7 MM 4.00 10.00
NNO Michael Jordan 5x7 DD 4.00 10.00

1996-97 Collector's Choice Crash the Game Scoring 1

Randomly inserted into first series packs at a rate of one in 5, this 60-card silver set features two separate versions of thirty different player cards. Each player is given two seperate weeks to score 30 points in any given game during that time period. If the player depicted on the card scores 30 or more points in the given week, the card can be redeemed for one premium quality silver card of the depicted player. The expiration date for the cards was May 9, 1997.

COMPLETE SILVER SET (60) 20.00 50.00
SER.1 STATED ODDS 1:5
*GOLD CARDS: 1.25X TO 3X HI COLUMN
GOLD: SER.1 STATED ODDS 1:49
*SILVER RED.CARDS: .5X TO 1.25X SILVER HI
*GOLD RED.CARDS: 1.5X TO 4X SILVER HI
ONE RED.CARD PER WINNER BY MAIL
C1 Mookie Blaylock .40 1.00
C1B Mookie Blaylock .40 1.00
C2 Dino Radja .40 1.00
C2B Dino Radja .40 1.00
C3 Glen Rice .60 1.50
C3B Glen Rice .60 1.50
C4 Scottie Pippen 1.00 2.50
C4B Scottie Pippen 1.00 2.50
C5 Terrell Brandon .40 1.00
C5B Terrell Brandon .40 1.00
C6 Jason Kidd 1.00 2.50
C6B Jason Kidd 1.00 2.50
C7 Antonio McDyess .60 1.50
C7B Antonio McDyess .60 1.50
C8 Joe Dumars .60 1.50
C8B Joe Dumars .60 1.50
C9 Joe Smith .50 1.25
C9B Joe Smith .50 1.25
C10 Hakeem Olajuwon .75 2.00
C10B Hakeem Olajuwon .75 2.00
C11 Reggie Miller .75 2.00
C11B Reggie Miller .75 2.00
C12 Loy Vaught .40 1.00
C12B Loy Vaught .40 1.00
C13 Cedric Ceballos .40 1.00
C13B Cedric Ceballos .40 1.00
C14 Alonzo Mourning .75 2.00
C14B Alonzo Mourning .75 2.00
C15 Vin Baker .50 1.25
C15B Vin Baker .50 1.25
C16 Kevin Garnett 1.50 4.00
C16B Kevin Garnett 1.50 4.00
C17 Ed O'Bannon .40 1.00
C17B Ed O'Bannon .40 1.00
C18 Patrick Ewing .75 2.00
C18B Patrick Ewing .75 2.00
C19 Anfernee Hardaway 1.00 2.50
C19B Anfernee Hardaway 1.00 2.50
C20 Clarence Weatherspoon .40 1.00
C20B Clarence Weatherspoon .40 1.00
C21 Kevin Johnson .60 1.50
C21B Kevin Johnson .60 1.50
C22 Clifford Robinson .40 1.00
C22B Clifford Robinson .40 1.00
C23 Mitch Richmond .60 1.50
C23B Mitch Richmond .60 1.50
C24 Sean Elliott .60 1.50
C24B Sean Elliott .60 1.50
C25 Shawn Kemp .60 1.50
C25B Shawn Kemp .60 1.50
C26 Damon Stoudamire .50 1.25
C26B Damon Stoudamire .50 1.25
C27 John Stockton .75 2.00
C27B John Stockton .75 2.00
C28 Bryant Reeves .40 1.00
C28B Bryant Reeves .40 1.00
C29 Rasheed Wallace .75 2.00
C29B Rasheed Wallace .75 2.00
C30 Michael Jordan 5.00 12.00
C30B Michael Jordan 5.00 12.00

1996-97 Collector's Choice Crash the Game Scoring 2

Randomly inserted into second series packs at a rate of one in five, this 60-card silver set features two separate versions of thirty different player cards. Each player is given two seperate weeks to score 30 points in any given game during that time period. If the player depicted on the card scores 30 or more points in the given week, the card can be redeemed for one premium quality silver card of the depicted player. The expiration date for the cards was July 1, 1997.

SER.2 STATED ODDS 1:5
*GOLD CARDS: 1.25X TO 3X HI COLUMN
GOLD: SER.2 STATED ODDS 1:49
*SILVER RED.CARDS: .5X TO 1.25X SILVER HI
*GOLD RED.CARDS: 1.5X TO 4X SILVER HI
ONE RED.CARD PER WINNER BY MAIL
C1 Steve Smith .50 1.25
C1B Steve Smith .50 1.25
C2 Dana Barros .40 1.00
C2B Dana Barros .40 1.00
C3 Tony Delk .60 1.50
C3B Tony Delk .60 1.50
C4 Toni Kukoc .60 1.50
C4B Toni Kukoc .60 1.50
C5 Bobby Phills .40 1.00
C5B Bobby Phills .40 1.00
C6 Jamal Mashburn .50 1.25
C6B Jamal Mashburn .50 1.25
C7 LaPhonso Ellis .40 1.00
C7B LaPhonso Ellis .40 1.00
C8 Jerome Williams .50 1.25
C8B Jerome Williams .50 1.25
C9 Latrell Sprewell .60 1.50
C9B Latrell Sprewell .60 1.50
C10 Clyde Drexler .75 2.00
C10B Clyde Drexler .75 2.00
C11 Dale Davis .40 1.00
C11B Dale Davis .40 1.00
C12 Brent Barry .50 1.25
C12B Brent Barry .50 1.25
C13 Nick Van Exel .60 1.50
C13B Nick Van Exel .60 1.50
C14 Sasha Danilovic .40 1.00
C14B Sasha Danilovic .40 1.00
C15 Glenn Robinson .50 1.25
C15B Glenn Robinson .50 1.25
C16 Stephon Marbury 1.50 4.00
C16B Stephon Marbury 1.50 4.00
C17 Shawn Bradley .40 1.00
C17B Shawn Bradley .40 1.00
C18 John Wallace .60 1.50
C18B John Wallace .60 1.50
C19 Anfernee Hardaway 1.00 2.50
C19B Anfernee Hardaway 1.00 2.50
C20 Jerry Stackhouse .75 2.00
C20B Jerry Stackhouse .75 2.00
C21 Danny Manning .50 1.25
C21B Danny Manning .50 1.25
C22 Arvydas Sabonis .50 1.25
C22B Arvydas Sabonis .50 1.25
C23 Brian Grant .50 1.25
C23B Brian Grant .50 1.25
C24 David Robinson 1.00 2.50
C24B David Robinson 1.00 2.50
C25 Gary Payton .60 1.50
C25B Gary Payton .60 1.50
C26 Marcus Camby 1.00 2.50
C26B Marcus Camby 1.00 2.50
C27 Karl Malone .75 2.00
C27B Karl Malone .75 2.00
C28 Shareef Abdur-Rahim 1.00 2.50
C28B Shareef Abdur-Rahim 1.00 2.50
C29 Juwan Howard .50 1.25
C29B Juwan Howard .50 1.25
C30 Michael Jordan 5.00 12.00
C30B Michael Jordan 5.00 12.00

1996-97 Collector's Choice Draft Trade

This 10-card set was available by exchanging a Draft Trade card, inserted at a rate of one in 144 in the series one set. The trade card expired May 9, 1997. Each card has a full portrait shot of the player and career information on the back. The cards are numbered with a "DR" prefix.

COMPLETE SET (10) 10.00 20.00
TRADE: SER.1 STATED ODDS 1:144
DRAFT TRADE EXPIRATION: 5/9/97
DR1 Allen Iverson 3.00 8.00
DR2 Marcus Camby 1.00 2.50
DR3 Shareef Abdur-Rahim 1.00 2.50
DR4 Stephon Marbury 1.50 4.00
DR5 Ray Allen 2.50 6.00
DR6 Antoine Walker 1.00 2.50
DR7 Lorenzen Wright .50 1.25
DR8 Kerry Kittles .60 1.50
DR9 Samaki Walker .50 1.25
DR10 Erick Dampier .60 1.50
NNO Expired Trade Card .40 1.00

1996-97 Collector's Choice Factory Blow-Ups

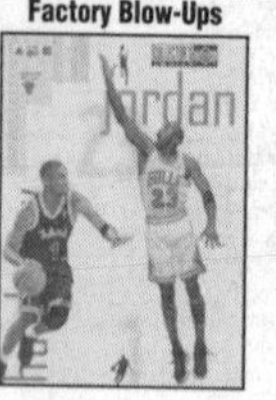

Inserted one per 1996-97 Collector's Choice Factory set, this 4-card set measures 3 1/2" by 5" and features the Upper Deck spokesmen.

COMPLETE SET (4) 2.50 6.00
1 Michael Jordan 2.00 5.00
2 Shawn Kemp .25 .60
3 Anfernee Hardaway .40 1.00
4 Michael Jordan 1.50 4.00
Anfernee Hardaway

1996-97 Collector's Choice Game Face

Inserted one per special retail pack, this 10-card set is standard-sized with white bordered fronts and the logo "Game Face" in gold on the front. Card backs include a inset photo of the player with commentary. Cards are numbered with a "GF" prefix.

COMPLETE SET (10) 4.00 10.00
ONE PER SPECIAL SER.1 RETAIL PACK
GF1 Anfernee Hardaway .60 1.50
GF2 Michael Jordan 3.00 8.00
GF3 Shawn Kemp .40 1.00
GF4 Alonzo Mourning .50 1.25
GF5 Cherokee Parks .25 .60
GF6 Avery Johnson .30 .75
GF7 LaPhonso Ellis .25 .60
GF8 Rasheed Wallace .50 1.25
GF9 Jim Jackson .25 .60
GF10 Larry Johnson .40 1.00

1996-97 Collector's Choice Jordan A Cut Above

One of these ten Jordan ACA cards was inserted into every special Wal-Mart ninety-nine cent series one retail pack. This 10-card set focuses on Michael Jordan's career feats. Each card front is die cut at the top with the set name "A Cut Above" in gold foil. Card backs feature a head shot with a summary of each feat.

COMPLETE SET (10) 8.00 20.00
COMMON JORDAN (CA1-CA10) 1.00 2.50

1996-97 Collector's Choice Jordan A Cut Above Jumbos

Released in complete set form in retail outlets, this 10-card set parallels the A Cut Above insert from 1996-97 Collector's Choice packs. Card backs carry a "CA" prefix.

COMP.FACT SET (10) 8.00 20.00
COMMON CARD (CA1-CA10) 1.00 2.50

1996-97 Collector's Choice Memorable Moments

Inserted one per special series two retail pack, this 10-card set features memorable moments from the 1996 NBA season. The cards have a die cut design on both the top and bottom of the card with gold foil running along each of those die cut borders. Card backs describe the moment.

COMPLETE SET (10) 5.00 12.00
ONE PER SPECIAL SER.2 RETAIL PACK
1 Michael Jordan 3.00 8.00
2 Nick Van Exel .40 1.00
3 Karl Malone .50 1.25
4 Latrell Sprewell .40 1.00
5 Anfernee Hardaway .60 1.50
6 Glenn Robinson .30 .75
7 Shaquille O'Neal 1.00 2.50
8 Damon Stoudamire .30 .75
9 Clyde Drexler .50 1.25
10 Shawn Kemp .40 1.00

1996-97 Collector's Choice Mini-Cards

Inserted in both series at a rate of one per pack, this 60-card set is comprised of 180 different "mini-cards". Three of these mini-cards form one standard-sized card and are issued in that form. Card fronts feature perforated panels of three players with silver foil. Card backs feature a brief commentary on each player. Each card contains it's own individual number, with an "M" prefix and is ordered below by the far left number on the card back. Also, card number M106 was never issued. Both Bob Sura and Bryant Stith were numbered M112.

COMPLETE SET (60) 8.00 20.00
COMPLETE SERIES 1 (30) 3.00 8.00
COMPLETE SERIES 2 (30) 5.00 12.00
*GOLD: 2.5X TO 6X HI COLUMN
GOLD: SER.1/2 STATED ODDS 1:35
SKIP-NUMBERED SET
M2 Walters/Hornacek/Blaylock .15 .40
M5 Schrempf/Kukoc/Radja .20 .50
M6 Amaya/S.Wright/E.Williams .12 .30
M10 Edney/O'Bannon/Zidek .12 .30
M13 Ratliff/Bradley/Longley .15 .40
M22 Phills/A.Johnson/Abdul-Rauf .15 .40
M23 P.Jones/C.Morris/Hammonds .12 .30
M25 Hurley/Laettner/G.Hill .30 .75
M28 Douglas/Coleman/Seikaly .15 .40
M30 Van Exel/Starks/Cassell .20 .50
M33 Geiger/D.Scott/Best .12 .30
M36 Ceballos/Rider/B.Barry .15 .40
M37 Kidd/K.Johnson/L.Murray .30 .75
M38 Mullin/J.Williams/Dehere .20 .50
M39 Sabonis/Danilovic/Divac .20 .50
M43 T.Hill/B.Grant/K.Thomas .15 .40
M44 McKey/Horry/Askins .15 .40
M46 Childress/D.Rob/Respert .30 .75
M49 Day/O.Miller/Lang .12 .30
M56 Curry/Coles/Oakley .15 .40
M57 Wallace/Stackhouse/Reid .25 .60
M66 Dumars/Drexler/Green .25 .60
M67 Gill/N.Anderson/McKie .12 .30
M75 Ferry/M.Jackson/Rivers .15 .40
M78 Jordan/Hardaway/Kemp 1.50 4.00
M79 Rose/Webber/J.King .25 .60
M83 Rodman/Barkley/Malone .75 2.00
M85 Augmon/Johnson/Anthony .20 .50
M86 McMillan/Gugliotta/B.Edwards .12 .30
M90 J.Jackson/G.Rob/Cheaney .15 .40
M92 Norman/West/K.Edwards .12 .30
M93 Smith/T.Hard/Armstrong .20 .50
M99 Rice/Manning/Perkins .20 .50
M102 Kerr/R.Miller/Barros .25 .60
M109 S.Walker/L.Wright/Minor .15 .40
M110 L.Ellis/K.Willis/W'spoon .12 .30
M111 McDyess/Sprewell/Caffey .20 .50
M112A Stith/Del Negro/K.Anderson .15 .40
M112B Sura/R.Rogers/Polynice .12 .30
M113 Hunter/E.Jones/R.Harper .20 .50
M115 Thorpe/Stockton/Carr .25 .60
M125 Smits/Olajuwon/Muresan .25 .60
M129 Bryant/J.O'Neal/Garnett 2.50 6.00
M135 Mourning/Mut/Ewing .25 .60
M137 Baker/Mashburn/Pippen .30 .75
M140 Marbury/Hancock/Person .50 1.25
M146 Houston/Camby/Kittles .30 .75
M148 Wallace/McCarty/Walker .30 .75
M149 H.Grant/Campbell/D.Davis .15 .40
M150 Royal/Legler/Elie .12 .30
M151 Shaw/A.Davis/PJ Brown .12 .30
M152 Iverson/Smith/S.O'Neal 1.00 2.50
M159 Robinson/Burrell/Allen .75 2.00
M161 Richmond/Perdue/Hawk .20 .50
M167 Payton/Brandon/Elliott .20 .50
M170 Christie/Newman/T.Dumas .12 .30
M175 Rahim/Mills/K.Reeves .30 .75
M176 Moten/M.Smith/Russell .12 .30
M177 B.Reeves/Finley/Stoud .25 .60
M178 Howard/Vaught/T.Mills .15 .40

1996-97 Collector's Choice Stick-Ums 1

Randomly inserted into first series packs at a rate of one in 4, this 30-card set features separate removable stickers of the actual player, the player's name and the given statistical categories. Card backs are black and white and feature set information including the complete Stick-Um checklist. Card stock is noticeably thin. Cards are numbered with an "S" prefix.

COMPLETE SET (30) 3.00 8.00
SER.1 STATED ODDS 1:4
S1 Mookie Blaylock .12 .30
S2 Dana Barros .12 .30
S3 Scott Burrell .12 .30
S4 Dennis Rodman .40 1.00
S5 Terrell Brandon .12 .30
S6 Jamal Mashburn .15 .40
S7 LaPhonso Ellis .12 .30
S8 Grant Hill .30 .75
S9 Joe Smith .15 .40
S10 Hakeem Olajuwon .25 .60
S11 Rik Smits .15 .40
S12 Brent Barry .15 .40
S13 Nick Van Exel .20 .50
S14 Sasha Danilovic .12 .30
S15 Vin Baker .15 .40
S16 Kevin Garnett .50 1.25
S17 Shawn Bradley .12 .30
S18 Patrick Ewing .25 .60
S19 Anfernee Hardaway .30 .75
S20 Clarence Weatherspoon .12 .30
S21 Charles Barkley .30 .75
S22 Clifford Robinson .12 .30
S23 Mitch Richmond .20 .50
S24 David Robinson .30 .75
S25 Shawn Kemp .20 .50
S26 Damon Stoudamire .15 .40
S27 Karl Malone .25 .60
S28 Bryant Reeves .12 .30
S29 Gheorghe Muresan .12 .30
S30 Michael Jordan 1.50 4.00

1996-97 Collector's Choice Stick-Ums 2

Randomly inserted into second series packs at a rate of one in 3, this 30-card set features separate removable stickers of the actual player, the player's name and the given statistical categories. Card backs are black and white and feature set information including the complete Stick-Um checklist. Card stock is noticeably thin. Cards are numbered with an "S" prefix.

COMPLETE SET (30) 3.00 8.00
SER.2 STATED ODDS 1:3
S1 Steve Smith .15 .40
S2 Dino Radja .12 .30
S3 Glen Rice .20 .50
S4 Toni Kukoc .20 .50
S5 Bobby Phills .12 .30
S6 Jason Kidd .30 .75
S7 Antonio McDyess .20 .50
S8 Joe Dumars .20 .50
S9 Latrell Sprewell .20 .50
S10 Clyde Drexler .25 .60
S11 Reggie Miller .25 .60
S12 Loy Vaught .12 .30
S13 Eddie Jones .20 .50
S14 Alonzo Mourning .25 .60
S15 Glenn Robinson .15 .40
S16 Tom Gugliotta .12 .30
S17 Ed O'Bannon .12 .30
S18 John Starks .15 .40
S19 Anfernee Hardaway .30 .75
S20 Jerry Stackhouse .25 .60
S21 Kevin Johnson .20 .50
S22 Arvydas Sabonis .15 .40
S23 Brian Grant .15 .40
S24 Sean Elliott .20 .50
S25 Gary Payton .20 .50
S26 Zan Tabak .12 .30
S27 John Stockton .25 .60
S28 Greg Anthony .12 .30
S29 Juwan Howard .15 .40
S30 Michael Jordan 1.50 4.00

1996-97 Collector's Choice Chicago Bulls

Issued with a suggested retail price of $2.99, this set features nine players from the above team. In addition, each team set contained two bonus Collector's Choice Gold Mini-Cards. These differed from the regular Gold Mini-Cards with each having the same card number on each panel and the cards being numbered B1 and B2.

COMP.FACT SET (11) 3.00 8.00
B1 Ron Harper 1.50 4.00
Michael Jordan
Steve Kerr
B2 Toni Kukoc 1.25 3.00
Scottie Pippen
Dennis Rodman
CH1 Jason Caffey .20 .50
CH2 Ron Harper .25 .60
CH3 Michael Jordan 1.50 4.00
CH4 Steve Kerr .25 .60
CH5 Toni Kukoc .30 .75
CH6 Luc Longley .25 .60
CH7 Scottie Pippen .50 1.25
CH8 Dennis Rodman .60 1.50
CH9 Bill Wennington .20 .50

1996-97 Collector's Choice Houston Rockets

Issued with a suggested retail price of $2.99, this set features nine players from the above team. In addition, each team set contained a replica blow-up card of the Building A Winner subset from the 1996-97 Upper Deck set.

COMP.FACT SET (9) 1.50 4.00
HT1 Charles Barkley .50 1.25
HT2 Matt Bullard .20 .50
HT3 Clyde Drexler .40 1.00
HT4 Mario Elie .20 .50
HT5 Othella Harrington .30 .75
HT6 Sam Mack .20 .50
HT7 Matt Maloney .25 .60
HT8 Hakeem Olajuwon .40 1.00
HT9 Kevin Willis .20 .50
NNO Houston Rockets Blow-Up .75 2.00

1996-97 Collector's Choice Los Angeles Lakers

Issued with a suggested retail price of $2.99, this set features nine players from the above team. In addition, each team set contained two bonus Collector's Choice Gold Mini-Cards. These differed from the regular Gold Mini-Cards with each having the same card number on each panel and the cards being numbered L1 and L2.

COMP.FACT SET (11) 8.00 20.00
L1 Kobe Bryant 2.00 5.00
Elden Campbell
Derek Fisher
L2 Eddie Jones .75 2.00
Shaquille O'Neal
Nick Van Exel
LA1 Corie Blount .20 .50
LA2 Kobe Bryant 5.00 12.00
LA3 Elden Campbell .20 .50
LA4 Derek Fisher .40 1.00
LA5 Eddie Jones .30 .75
LA6 Travis Knight .30 .75
LA7 Shaquille O'Neal .75 2.00
LA8 Byron Scott .25 .60
LA9 Nick Van Exel .30 .75

1996-97 Collector's Choice Miami Heat Team Set

Issued with a suggested retail price of $2.99, this set features nine players from the above team. In addition, each team set contained a replica blow-up card of the Building A Winner subset from the 1996-97 Upper Deck set.

COMP.FACT SET (9) 1.50 4.00
MI1 Keith Askins .20 .50
MI2 P.J. Brown .20 .50
MI3 Sasha Danilovic .20 .50
MI4 Tim Hardaway .30 .75
MI5 Voshon Lenard .30 .75
MI6 Dan Majerle .30 .75
MI7 Alonzo Mourning .40 1.00
MI8 Martin Muursepp .20 .50
MI9 Kurt Thomas .20 .50
NNO Miami Heat BW Blow-Up .60 1.50

1996-97 Collector's Choice Orlando Magic Team Set

Issued with a suggested retail price of $2.99, this set features nine players from the above team. In addition, each team set contained two bonus Collector's Choice Gold Mini-Cards. These differed from the regular Gold Mini-Cards with each having the same card number on each panel and the cards being numbered O1 and O2.

COMP. FACT SET (11) 1.50 4.00
O1 Nick Anderson .40 1.00
Horace Grant
Anfernee Hardaway
O2 Dennis Scott .20 .50
Rony Seikaly
Brian Shaw
OR1 Nick Anderson .20 .50
OR2 Brian Evans .30 .75
OR3 Horace Grant .25 .60
OR4 Anfernee Hardaway .50 1.25
OR5 Derek Strong .20 .50
OR6 Rony Seikaly .20 .50
OR7 Dennis Scott .20 .50
OR8 Brian Shaw .20 .50
OR9 Gerald Wilkins .20 .50

1996-97 Collector's Choice Penny! Blow Ups

Inserted one per special series one retail box as chiptoppers, these cards are blown-up parallels of the Penny! 5-card subset from the 1996-97 Collector's Choice series one set. The fronts and backs are identical to that of the regular standard-sized cards.

COMPLETE SET (5) 5.00 12.00
COMMON CARD (113-117) 1.25 3.00

1996-97 Collector's Choice San Antoino Spurs

Issued with a suggested retail price of $2.99, this set features nine players from the above team. In addition, each team set contained a replica blow-up card of the Building A Winner subset from the 1996-97 Upper Deck set.

COMP.FACT SET (9) 1.50 4.00
ST1 Cory Alexander .20 .50
ST2 Vinny Del Negro .20 .50
ST3 Sean Elliott .30 .75
ST4 Carl Herrera .20 .50
ST5 Avery Johnson .25 .60
ST6 Will Perdue .20 .50
ST7 David Robinson .50 1.25
ST8 Charles Smith .20 .50
ST9 Dominique Wilkins .40 1.00
NNO San Antonio Spurs Blow-Up .60 1.50

1996-97 Collector's Choice Seattle Supersonics

Issued with a suggested retail price of $2.99, this set features nine players from the above team. In addition, each team set contained two bonus Collector's Choice Gold Mini-Cards. These differed from the regular Gold Mini-Cards with each having the same card number on each panel and the cards being numbered B1 and B2.

COMP.FACT SET (11) 1.50 4.00
B1 Hersey Hawkins .60 1.50
Shawn Kemp
Nate McMillan
B2 Gary Payton .40 1.00
Sam Perkins
Detlef Schrempf
ST1 Craig Ehlo .20 .50
ST2 Hersey Hawkins .20 .50
ST3 Shawn Kemp .30 .75
ST4 Jim McIlvaine .20 .50
ST5 Nate McMillan .20 .50
ST6 Gary Payton .30 .75
ST7 Sam Perkins .20 .50
ST8 Detlef Schrempf .30 .75
ST9 Eric Snow .30 .75

1997-98 Collector's Choice

The 1997-98 Collector's Choice issue totaled 400 cards with each series containing 200. Each pack contained

14 cards and carried a suggested retail price of $1.29. The set contains the topical subsets: Game Night (156-185), Catch 23 (186-195), Hot Properties (356-385) and Michael's Magic (386-395). The fronts feature color action player photos in a white border. The backs carry player information. Checklist cards 196-200 were Challenge cards which when filled in correctly could be redeemed for a set of the Top 10 Picks in the 1997 NBA Draft. A factory set was also released, which contained not only the 400 basic cards, but also five Miniatures, and 10 special StarQuest cards that were available only in the factory set.

Card	Low	High
COMPLETE SET (400)	12.00	30.00
COMP.FACTORY SET (415)	15.00	40.00
COMPLETE SERIES 1 (200)	6.00	15.00
COMPLETE SERIES 2 (200)	6.00	15.00
1 Mookie Blaylock	.07	.20
2 Dikembe Mutombo	.12	.30
3 Eldridge Recasner	.07	.20
4 Christian Laettner	.10	.25
5 Tyrone Corbin	.07	.20
6 Antoine Walker	.12	.30
7 Eric Williams	.07	.20
8 Dana Barros	.07	.20
9 David Wesley	.07	.20
10 Dino Radja	.07	.20
11 Vlade Divac	.12	.30
12 Dell Curry	.07	.20
13 Muggsy Bogues	.10	.25
14 Tony Smith	.07	.20
15 Glen Rice	.12	.30
16 Anthony Mason	.07	.20
17 Dennis Rodman	.25	.60
18 Brian Williams	.07	.20
19 Toni Kukoc	.12	.30
20 Jason Caffey	.07	.20
21 Steve Kerr	.10	.25
22 Luc Longley	.10	.25
23 Michael Jordan	1.00	2.50
24 Chris Mills	.07	.20
25 Tyrone Hill	.07	.20
26 Vitaly Potapenko	.07	.20
27 Bob Sura	.07	.20
28 Robert Pack	.07	.20
29 Ed O'Bannon	.07	.20
30 Michael Finley	.12	.30
31 Shawn Bradley	.07	.20
32 Khalid Reeves	.07	.20
33 Antonio McDyess	.10	.25
34 Ervin Johnson	.07	.20
35 Dale Ellis	.07	.20
36 Bryant Stith	.07	.20
37 Tom Hammonds	.07	.20
38 Otis Thorpe	.07	.20
39 Lindsey Hunter	.07	.20
40 Grant Long	.07	.20
41 Aaron McKie	.07	.20
42 Randolph Childress	.07	.20
43 Scott Burrell	.07	.20
44 Bimbo Coles	.07	.20
45 B.J. Armstrong	.07	.20
46 Mark Price	.12	.30
47 Latrell Sprewell	.12	.30
48 Felton Spencer	.07	.20
49 Charles Barkley	.20	.50
50 Mario Elie	.07	.20
51 Clyde Drexler	.15	.40
52 Kevin Willis	.07	.20
53 Antonio Davis	.07	.20
54 Reggie Miller	.15	.40
55 Dale Davis	.07	.20
56 Mark Jackson	.10	.25
57 Erick Dampier	.07	.20
58 Pooh Richardson	.07	.20
59 Terry Dehere	.07	.20
60 Brent Barry	.10	.25
61 Loy Vaught	.07	.20
62 Lorenzen Wright	.07	.20
63 Eddie Jones	.12	.30
64 Kobe Bryant	.60	1.50
65 Elden Campbell	.07	.20
66 Corie Blount	.07	.20
67 Shaquille O'Neal	.30	.75
68 Dan Majerle	.12	.30
69 P.J. Brown	.07	.20
70 Tim Hardaway	.12	.30
71 Isaac Austin	.07	.20
72 Jamal Mashburn	.10	.25
73 Ray Allen	.15	.40
74 Glenn Robinson	.10	.25
75 Armon Gilliam	.07	.20
76 Johnny Newman	.07	.20
77 Elliot Perry	.07	.20
78 Sherman Douglas	.07	.20
79 Doug West	.07	.20
80 Kevin Garnett	.20	.50
81 Sam Mitchell	.07	.20
82 Tom Gugliotta	.07	.20
83 Terry Porter	.07	.20
84 Chris Carr	.07	.20
85 Kevin Edwards	.07	.20
86 Jayson Williams	.07	.20
87 Kendall Gill	.07	.20
88 Kerry Kittles	.07	.20
89 Chris Gatling	.07	.20
90 John Starks	.10	.25
91 Charlie Ward	.07	.20
92 Larry Johnson	.12	.30
93 Charles Oakley	.10	.25
94 Chris Childs	.07	.20
95 Allan Houston	.10	.25
96 Horace Grant	.10	.25
97 Darrell Armstrong	.07	.20
98 Rony Seikaly	.07	.20
99 Dennis Scott	.07	.20
100 Anfernee Hardaway	.20	.50
101 Brian Shaw	.07	.20
102 Jerry Stackhouse	.12	.30
103 Rex Walters	.07	.20
104 Don MacLean	.07	.20
105 Derrick Coleman	.10	.25
106 Lucious Harris	.07	.20
107 Clarence Weatherspoon	.07	.20
108 Cedric Ceballos	.07	.20
109 Danny Manning	.10	.25
110 Jason Kidd	.20	.50
111 Loren Meyer	.07	.20
112 Wesley Person	.07	.20
113 Steve Nash	.25	.60
114 Isaiah Rider	.10	.25
115 Stacey Augmon	.10	.25
116 Arvydas Sabonis	.10	.25
117 Kenny Anderson	.10	.25
118 Jermaine O'Neal	.10	.25
119 Gary Trent	.07	.20
120 Michael Smith	.07	.20
121 Kevin Gamble	.07	.20
122 Olden Polynice	.07	.20
123 Billy Owens	.07	.20
124 Corliss Williamson	.07	.20
125 Cory Alexander	.07	.20
126 Vinny Del Negro	.07	.20
127 Sean Elliott	.12	.30
128 Will Perdue	.07	.20
129 Carl Herrera	.07	.20
130 Shawn Kemp	.12	.30
131 Hersey Hawkins	.07	.20
132 Nate McMillan	.07	.20
133 Craig Ehlo	.07	.20
134 Detlef Schrempf	.12	.30
135 Sam Perkins	.07	.20
136 Sharone Wright	.07	.20
137 Doug Christie	.07	.20
138 Popeye Jones	.07	.20
139 Shawn Respert	.07	.20
140 Marcus Camby	.12	.30
141 Adam Keefe	.07	.20
142 Karl Malone	.15	.40
143 John Stockton	.15	.40
144 Greg Ostertag	.07	.20
145 Chris Morris	.07	.20
146 Shareef Abdur-Rahim	.12	.30
147 Roy Rogers	.07	.20
148 George Lynch	.07	.20
149 Anthony Peeler	.07	.20
150 Lee Mayberry	.07	.20
151 Calbert Cheaney	.07	.20
152 Harvey Grant	.07	.20
153 Rod Strickland	.07	.20
154 Tracy Murray	.07	.20
155 Chris Webber	.12	.30
156 Mookie Blaylock/Hawks GN	.12	.30
157 A.Walker/Celtics GN	.12	.30
158 Glen Rice/Hornets GN	.12	.30
159 M.Jordan/Bulls GN	1.00	2.50
160 Tyrone Hill/Cavaliers GN	.07	.20
161 Shawn Bradley/Mavericks GN	.12	.30
162 Antonio McDyess/Nuggets GN	.10	.25
163 G.Hill/Pistons GN	.20	.50
164 Latrell Sprewell/Warriors GN	.12	.30
165 H.Olajuwon/Rockets GN	.20	.50
166 Reggie Miller/Pacers GN	.15	.40
167 Loy Vaught/Clippers GN	.10	.25
168 K.Bryant/Lakers GN	.60	1.50
169 Mourning/Heat GN	.15	.40
170 R.Allen/Bucks GN	.15	.40
171 K.Garnett/T'wolves GN	.20	.50
172 Kendall Gill/Nets GN	.07	.20
173 Patrick Ewing/Knicks GN	.15	.40
174 A.Hardaway/Magic GN	.20	.50
175 A.Iverson/76ers GN	.25	.60
176 J.Kidd/Suns GN	.20	.50
177 Rasheed Wallace/Trail Blazers GN	.12	.30
178 Mitch Richmond/Kings GN	.12	.30
179 D.Robinson/Spurs GN	.20	.50
180 G.Payton/SuperSonics GN	.12	.30
181 D.Stoudamire/Raptors GN	.12	.30
182 Karl Malone/Jazz GN	.15	.40
183 S.Abdur-Rahim/Griz. GN	.12	.30
184 C.Webber/Wizards GN	.12	.30
185 M.Jordan/97 Finals GN	1.00	2.50
186 Michael Jordan C23	.50	1.25
187 Michael Jordan C23	.50	1.25
188 Michael Jordan C23	.50	1.25
189 Michael Jordan C23	.50	1.25
190 Michael Jordan C23	.50	1.25
191 Michael Jordan C23	.50	1.25
192 Michael Jordan C23	.50	1.25
193 Michael Jordan C23	.50	1.25
194 Michael Jordan C23	.50	1.25
195 Michael Jordan C23	.50	1.25
196 Checklist #1	.07	.20
197 Checklist #2	.07	.20
198 Checklist #3	.07	.20
199 Checklist #4	.07	.20
200 Checklist #5	.07	.20
201 Steve Smith	.10	.25
202 Chris Crawford RC	.12	.30
203 Ed Gray RC	.12	.30
204 Alan Henderson	.07	.20
205 Walter McCarty	.07	.20
206 Dee Brown	.07	.20
207 Chauncey Billups RC	.40	1.00
208 Ron Mercer RC	.15	.40
209 Travis Knight	.07	.20
210 Andrew DeClercq	.07	.20
211 Tyus Edney	.07	.20
212 Matt Geiger	.07	.20
213 Tony Delk	.07	.20
214 J.R. Reid	.07	.20
215 Bobby Phills	.07	.20
216 David Wesley	.07	.20
217 Ron Harper	.10	.25
218 Scottie Pippen	.20	.50
219 Scott Burrell	.07	.20
220 Keith Booth RC	.10	.25
221 Bill Wennington	.07	.20
222 Shawn Kemp	.12	.30
223 Zydrunas Ilgauskas	.12	.30
224 Brevin Knight RC	.12	.30
225 Danny Ferry	.07	.20
226 Derek Anderson RC	.12	.30
227 Wesley Person	.07	.20
228 A.C. Green	.10	.25
229 Samaki Walker	.07	.20
230 Hubert Davis	.07	.20
231 Erick Strickland RC	.10	.25
232 Dennis Scott	.07	.20
233 Tony Battie RC	.12	.30
234 LaPhonso Ellis	.07	.20
235 Eric Williams	.07	.20
236 Bobby Jackson RC	.15	.40
237 Anthony Goldwire	.07	.20
238 Danny Fortson RC	.12	.30
239 Joe Dumars	.12	.30
240 Grant Hill	.20	.50
241 Malik Sealy	.07	.20
242 Brian Williams	.07	.20
243 Theo Ratliff	.10	.25
244 Scot Pollard RC	.12	.30
245 Erick Dampier	.07	.20
246 Duane Ferrell	.07	.20
247 Joe Smith	.10	.25
248 Todd Fuller	.07	.20
249 Adonal Foyle RC	.10	.25
250 Othella Harrington	.07	.20
251 Matt Maloney	.07	.20
252 Hakeem Olajuwon	.15	.40
253 Rodrick Rhodes RC	.10	.25
254 Eddie Johnson	.07	.20
255 Brent Price	.07	.20
256 Austin Croshere RC	.10	.25
257 Derrick McKey	.07	.20
258 Chris Mullin	.12	.30
259 Rik Smits	.10	.25
260 Jalen Rose	.10	.25
261 Darrick Martin	.07	.20
262 Lamond Murray	.07	.20
263 Maurice Taylor RC	.12	.30
264 Rodney Rogers	.07	.20
265 James Robinson	.07	.20
266 Rick Fox	.07	.20
267 Nick Van Exel	.10	.25
268 Sean Rooks	.07	.20
269 Derek Fisher	.12	.30
270 Jon Barry	.07	.20
271 Robert Horry	.10	.25
272 Terry Mills	.07	.20
273 Charles Smith RC	.10	.25
274 Alonzo Mourning	.15	.40
275 Voshon Lenard	.07	.20
276 Todd Day	.07	.20
277 Ervin Johnson	.07	.20
278 Terrell Brandon	.07	.20
279 Michael Curry	.07	.20
280 Andrew Lang	.07	.20
281 Tyrone Hill	.07	.20
282 Stephon Marbury	.15	.40
283 Cherokee Parks	.07	.20
284 Stanley Roberts	.07	.20
285 Paul Grant RC	.07	.20
286 David Benoit	.07	.20
287 Lucious Harris	.07	.20
288 Don MacLean	.07	.20
289 Sam Cassell	.10	.25
290 Keith Van Horn RC	.20	.50
291 Patrick Ewing	.15	.40
292 Walter McCarty	.07	.20
293 Chris Dudley	.07	.20
294 Chris Mills	.07	.20
295 Buck Williams	.07	.20
296 Nick Anderson	.07	.20
297 Derek Strong	.07	.20
298 Gerald Wilkins	.07	.20
299 Johnny Taylor RC	.10	.25
300 Derek Harper	.10	.25
301 Anthony Parker RC	.12	.30
302 Allen Iverson	.25	.60
303 Jim Jackson	.07	.20
304 Eric Montross	.07	.20
305 Tim Thomas RC	.15	.40
306 Kebu Stewart RC	.12	.30
307 Rex Chapman	.07	.20
308 Tom Chambers	.10	.25
309 Kevin Johnson	.12	.30
310 John Williams	.07	.20
311 Clifford Robinson	.07	.20
312 Antonio McDyess	.10	.25
313 Rasheed Wallace	.12	.30
314 Brian Grant	.07	.20
315 Dontonio Wingfield	.07	.20
316 Kelvin Cato RC	.10	.25
317 Mahmoud Abdul-Rauf	.07	.20
318 Lawrence Funderburke RC	.12	.30
319 Mitch Richmond	.12	.30
320 Tariq Abdul-Wahad RC	.10	.25
321 Terry Dehere	.07	.20
322 Michael Stewart RC	.12	.30
323 Tim Duncan RC	.60	1.50
324 Avery Johnson	.10	.25
325 David Robinson	.20	.50
326 Charles Smith	.07	.20
327 Chuck Person	.10	.25
328 Monty Williams	.07	.20
329 Jim McIlvaine	.07	.20
330 Gary Payton	.12	.30
331 Eric Snow	.07	.20
332 Dale Ellis	.07	.20
333 Vin Baker	.10	.25
334 Walt Williams	.07	.20
335 Tracy McGrady RC	.50	1.25
336 Damon Stoudamire	.10	.25
337 Carlos Rogers	.07	.20
338 John Wallace	.07	.20
339 Shandon Anderson	.07	.20
340 Jeff Hornacek	.10	.25
341 Howard Eisley	.07	.20
342 Jacque Vaughn RC	.10	.25
343 Bryon Russell	.07	.20
344 Antoine Carr	.07	.20
345 Antonio Daniels RC	.12	.30
346 Pete Chilcutt	.07	.20
347 Blue Edwards	.07	.20
348 Bryant Reeves	.07	.20
349 Chris Robinson RC	.12	.30
350 Otis Thorpe	.07	.20
351 Tim Legler	.07	.20
352 Juwan Howard	.10	.25
353 God Shammgod RC	.12	.30
354 Gheorghe Muresan	.07	.20
355 Chris Whitney	.07	.20
356 Dikembe Mutombo HP	.12	.30
357 Antoine Walker HP	.12	.30
358 Glen Rice HP	.12	.30
359 Scottie Pippen HP	.20	.50
360 Derek Anderson HP	.12	.30
361 Michael Finley HP	.12	.30
362 LaPhonso Ellis HP	.07	.20
363 Grant Hill HP	.20	.50
364 Joe Smith HP	.10	.25
365 Charles Barkley HP	.20	.50
366 Reggie Miller HP	.15	.40
367 Loy Vaught HP	.07	.20
368 Shaquille O'Neal HP	.30	.75
369 Alonzo Mourning HP	.15	.40
370 Glenn Robinson HP	.10	.25
371 Kevin Garnett HP	.20	.50
372 Kendall Gill HP	.07	.20
373 Allan Houston HP	.10	.25
374 Anfernee Hardaway HP	.20	.50
375 Tim Thomas HP	.15	.40
376 Jason Kidd HP	.20	.50
377 Kenny Anderson HP	.10	.25
378 Mitch Richmond HP	.12	.30
379 Tim Duncan HP	.60	1.50
380 Gary Payton HP	.12	.30
381 Marcus Camby HP	.12	.30
382 Karl Malone HP	.15	.40
383 Shareef Abdur-Rahim HP	.12	.30
384 Chris Webber HP	.12	.30
385 Michael Jordan HP	1.00	2.50
386 Michael Jordan MM	.50	1.25
387 Michael Jordan MM	.50	1.25
388 Michael Jordan MM	.50	1.25
389 Michael Jordan MM	.50	1.25
390 Michael Jordan MM	.50	1.25
391 Michael Jordan MM	.50	1.25
392 Michael Jordan MM	.50	1.25
393 Michael Jordan MM	.50	1.25
394 Michael Jordan MM	.50	1.25
395 Michael Jordan MM	.50	1.25
396 Checklist #1	.07	.20
397 Checklist #2	.07	.20
398 Checklist #3	.07	.20
399 Checklist #4	.07	.20
400 Checklist #5	.07	.20

1997-98 Collector's Choice Crash the Game Scoring

Randomly inserted in series one packs at the rate of one in five, this 30-card set features color action player photos in white borders. If the player pictured on the card scored 30 or more points in the week they were designated, the card was a winner and could be redeemed for a complete 30-card redemption set. The expiration date for the game was July 1, 1998. Card backs are numbered with a "C" prefix.

Card	Low	High
COMPLETE SET (60)	25.00	50.00
SER.1 STATED ODDS 1:5		
*RED.CARDS: .25X TO .6X HI COLUMN		
ONE RED.SET PER WINNER BY MAIL		
ONE RED.SET PER 15 NON-WIN BY MAIL		
C1A Dikembe Mutombo	.50	1.25
C1B Dikembe Mutombo	.50	1.25
C2A Dana Barros	.30	.75
C2B Dana Barros	.30	.75
C3A Glen Rice	.50	1.25
C3B Glen Rice	.50	1.25
C4A Scottie Pippen	.75	2.00
C4B Scottie Pippen	.75	2.00
C5A Terrell Brandon	.30	.75
C5B Terrell Brandon	.30	.75
C6A Shawn Bradley	.30	.75
C6B Shawn Bradley	.30	.75
C7A Antonio McDyess	.40	1.00
C7B Antonio McDyess	.40	1.00
C8A Lindsey Hunter	.30	.75
C8B Lindsey Hunter	.30	.75
C9A Joe Smith	.40	1.00
C9B Joe Smith	.40	1.00
C10A Hakeem Olajuwon	.60	1.50
C10B Hakeem Olajuwon	.60	1.50
C11A Reggie Miller	.60	1.50
C11B Reggie Miller	.60	1.50
C12A Rodney Rogers	.30	.75
C12B Rodney Rogers	.30	.75
C13A Nick Van Exel	.40	1.00
C13B Nick Van Exel	.40	1.00
C14A Tim Hardaway	.50	1.25
C14B Tim Hardaway	.50	1.25
C15A Glenn Robinson	.40	1.00
C15B Glenn Robinson	.40	1.00
C16A Kevin Garnett	.75	2.00
C16B Kevin Garnett	.75	2.00
C17A Kerry Kittles	.30	.75
C17B Kerry Kittles	.30	.75
C18A Larry Johnson	.50	1.25
C18B Larry Johnson	.50	1.25
C19A Anfernee Hardaway	.75	2.00
C19B Anfernee Hardaway	.75	2.00
C20A Allen Iverson	1.00	2.50
C20B Allen Iverson	1.00	2.50
C21A Jason Kidd	.75	2.00
C21B Jason Kidd	.75	2.00
C22A Arvydas Sabonis	.40	1.00
C22B Arvydas Sabonis	.40	1.00
C23A Mitch Richmond	.50	1.25
C23B Mitch Richmond	.50	1.25
C24A David Robinson	.75	2.00
C24B David Robinson	.75	2.00
C25A Gary Payton	.50	1.25
C25B Gary Payton	.50	1.25
C26A Marcus Camby	.50	1.25
C26B Marcus Camby	.50	1.25
C27A Karl Malone	.60	1.50
C27B Karl Malone	.60	1.50
C28A Bryant Reeves	.30	.75
C28B Bryant Reeves	.30	.75
C29A Chris Webber	.50	1.25
C29B Chris Webber	.50	1.25
C30A Michael Jordan	4.00	10.00
C30B Michael Jordan	4.00	10.00

1997-98 Collector's Choice Draft Trade

Available only through the checklist challenge redemption from series one, this 10-card set features the top picks from the 1997 Draft.

Card	Low	High
COMPLETE SET (10)	25.00	60.00
1 Tim Duncan	15.00	40.00
2 Keith Van Horn	5.00	12.00
3 Chauncey Billups	10.00	25.00
4 Antonio Daniels	3.00	8.00
5 Tony Battie	3.00	8.00
6 Ron Mercer	4.00	10.00
7 Tim Thomas	4.00	10.00
8 Adonal Foyle	2.50	6.00
9 Tracy McGrady	12.00	30.00
10 Danny Fortson	3.00	8.00

1997-98 Collector's Choice Factory All StarQuest

Inserted into factory sets only, this 10-card set featues some of the top players in the NBA. The set utilizes the same design as the regular StarQuest set, but has "All StarQuest" at the bottom of the card.

Card	Low	High
COMPLETE SET (10)	5.00	12.00
AS1 Kobe Bryant	1.50	4.00
AS2 Gary Payton	.30	.75
AS3 Kevin Garnett	.50	1.25
AS4 Karl Malone	.40	1.00
AS5 Shaquille O'Neal	.75	2.00
AS6 Michael Jordan	2.50	6.00
AS7 Anfernee Hardaway	.50	1.25
AS8 Grant Hill	.50	1.25
AS9 Shawn Kemp	.30	.75
AS10 Dikembe Mutombo	.30	.75

1997-98 Collector's Choice Memorable Moments

Distributed one per series two Anco pack, this 10-card set features some of the most memorable moments for each player from the previous season.

Card	Low	High
COMPLETE SET (10)	6.00	15.00
1 Michael Jordan	3.00	8.00
2 Grant Hill	.60	1.50
3 Anfernee Hardaway	.60	1.50
4 Kobe Bryant	2.00	5.00
5 Kevin Garnett	.60	1.50
6 Jason Kidd	.60	1.50
7 Karl Malone	.50	1.25
8 Hakeem Olajuwon	.50	1.25
9 Gary Payton	.40	1.00
10 Dennis Rodman	.75	2.00

1997-98 Collector's Choice Miniatures

Randomly inserted into series two packs at a rate of one in 3, this 30-card set features one player from all 29 teams on a mini-standee card. Each card is die cut. Each factory set also included five random cards from this set. Card backs carry a "M" prefix.

Card	Low	High
COMPLETE SET (30)	4.00	10.00
SER.2 STATED ODDS 1:3		
M1 Mookie Blaylock	.10	.25
M2 Chauncey Billups	.50	1.25
M3 Glen Rice	.15	.40
M4 Scottie Pippen	.25	.60
M5 Bob Sura	.10	.25
M6 Erick Strickland	.12	.30
M7 Tony Battie	.15	.40
M8 Joe Dumars	.15	.40
M9 Adonal Foyle	.12	.30
M10 Charles Barkley	.25	.60
M11 Dale Davis	.10	.25
M12 Lamond Murray	.10	.25
M13 Kobe Bryant	.75	2.00
M14 Tim Hardaway	.15	.40
M15 Glenn Robinson	.12	.30
M16 Kevin Garnett	.25	.60
M17 Keith Van Horn	.25	.60
M18 Patrick Ewing	.20	.50
M19 Anfernee Hardaway	.25	.60
M20 Tim Thomas	.20	.50
M21 Jason Kidd	.25	.60
M22 Isaiah Rider	.12	.30
M23 Mahmoud Abdul-Rauf	.10	.25
M24 Tim Duncan	.75	2.00
M25 Detlef Schrempf	.15	.40
M26 Damon Stoudamire	.12	.30
M27 John Stockton	.20	.50
M28 Bryant Reeves	.10	.25
M29 Juwan Howard	.12	.30
M30 Michael Jordan	1.25	3.00

1997-98 Collector's Choice MJ Bullseye

Randomly inserted into series two packs at a rate of one in five, this 30-card set features a double Crash the Game theme focused solely on Michael Jordan. Each card had two ways to win, by either matching between the given range Jordan's total points from the 1997-98 season or by having Jordan score 100 points in the given week. Winning cards were redeemable for either individual cards from a 13-card Blow-up Jordan Rewind redemption set or the complete set. The game ended on June 1, 1998.

Card	Low	High
COMMON JORDAN (B1-B30)	2.00	5.00
SER.2 STATED ODDS 1:5		

1997-98 Collector's Choice MJ Rewind Redemption

This 13-card set was available via redemption from winning 1997-98 Collector's Choice Crash the Game MJ Bullseye cards. Each winning card returned either an individual card or a complete set. The cards are oversized and feature key moments and photography from each of Michael Jordan's NBA seasons. Card backs are numbered with a "R" prefix.

Card	Low	High
COMPLETE SET (13)	15.00	40.00
COMMON CARD (R1-R13)	1.50	4.00

1997-98 Collector's Choice Star Attractions

Inserted one per special Collector's Choice series one and two Anco pack, this 20-card set was divided up into two sets of ten cards. The cards feature a silver metallic background on the die cut front with the theme "Star Attractions" logo located at the top. Card backs are numbered with a "SA" prefix.

Card	Low	High
COMPLETE SET (20)	15.00	40.00
COMPLETE SERIES 1 (10)	10.00	25.00
COMPLETE SERIES 2 (10)	6.00	15.00
*GOLD: 2X TO 5X HI COLUMN		
GOLD: SER.1/2 STATED ODDS 1:20 SPEC.		
SA1 Michael Jordan	5.00	12.00
SA2 Joe Smith	.50	1.25
SA3 Karl Malone	.75	2.00
SA4 Chauncey Billups	1.00	2.50
SA5 Charles Barkley	1.00	2.50
SA6 Shaquille O'Neal	1.50	4.00
SA7 Jason Kidd	1.00	2.50
SA8 Chris Webber	.60	1.50
SA9 Allen Iverson	1.25	3.00
SA10 Patrick Ewing	.75	2.00
SA11 Tim Duncan	1.50	4.00
SA12 Kevin Garnett	1.00	2.50
SA13 Tony Battie	.30	.75
SA14 Gary Payton	.60	1.50
SA15 Hakeem Olajuwon	.75	2.00
SA16 Antonio Daniels	.30	.75
SA17 Grant Hill	1.00	2.50
SA18 Anfernee Hardaway	1.00	2.50
SA19 Scottie Pippen	1.00	2.50
SA20 Keith Van Horn	.50	1.25

1997-98 Collector's Choice StarQuest

Randomly inserted both series packs, this 180-card set features color action photos of the top players of the game. Both 90-card series features tiering, containing bronze, silver, gold, and platinum levels. The bronze tier contains 90 players with an insertion rate of 1:1; silver has 40 players with an insertion rate of 1:21; gold contains 30 players with a 1:71 insertion rate; the top twenty stars are in the platinum tier with a 1:145 insertion rate. Card backs are numbered with a "SQ" prefix.

Card	Low	High
1-45/91-135 SER.1/2 STATED ODDS 1:1		
46-65/136-155 SER.1/2 STATED ODDS 1:21		
66-80/156-170 SER.1/2 STATED ODDS 1:71		
81-90/171-180 SER.1/2 STATED ODDS 1:145		
1 Dale Davis	.15	.40
2 Jamal Mashburn	.20	.50
3 Christian Laettner	.20	.50
4 Billy Owens	.15	.40
5 Vlade Divac	.25	.60
6 Sean Elliott	.25	.60
7 Marcus Camby	.25	.60
8 Dana Barros	.15	.40
9 Rod Strickland	.15	.40
10 Jim Jackson	.15	.40
11 Tyrone Hill	.15	.40
12 Ervin Johnson	.15	.40
13 Antoine Walker	.25	.60
14 Lorenzen Wright	.15	.40
15 Shawn Bradley	.15	.40
16 John Starks	.20	.50
17 Corliss Williamson	.15	.40
18 Steve Smith	.20	.50
19 Chris Mills	.15	.40
20 Vinny Del Negro	.15	.40
21 Jayson Williams	.15	.40
22 Anthony Mason	.15	.40
23 Dennis Scott	.15	.40
24 Mark Jackson	.20	.50
25 Dino Radja	.15	.40
26 Greg Ostertag	.15	.40
27 Anthony Peeler	.15	.40
28 Toni Kukoc	.25	.60
29 Michael Finley	.25	.60
30 Brent Barry	.20	.50
31 Wesley Person	.15	.40
32 Horace Grant	.20	.50
33 Walt Williams	.15	.40
34 Bryant Stith	.15	.40
35 Ray Allen	.30	.75
36 Otis Thorpe	.15	.40
37 Rasheed Wallace	.25	.60
38 Charles Oakley	.20	.50
39 Robert Pack	.15	.40
40 Kendall Gill	.15	.40
41 Lindsey Hunter	.15	.40
42 Cedric Ceballos	.15	.40
43 Allan Houston	.20	.50
44 Bryant Reeves	.15	.40
45 Derrick Coleman	.20	.50
46 Isaiah Rider	1.00	2.50
47 Detlef Schrempf	1.25	3.00
48 Antonio McDyess	1.00	2.50
49 Glenn Robinson	1.00	2.50
50 Damon Stoudamire	1.00	2.50
51 Terrell Brandon	.75	2.00
52 Joe Smith	1.00	2.50
53 Tom Gugliotta	.75	2.00
54 Loy Vaught	.75	2.00
55 Kenny Anderson	1.00	2.50
56 Dikembe Mutombo	1.25	3.00
57 Tim Hardaway	1.25	3.00
58 Chris Webber	1.25	3.00
59 Nick Van Exel	1.00	2.50
60 Kerry Kittles	.75	2.00
61 Chris Mullin	1.25	3.00
62 Stephon Marbury	1.50	4.00
63 Juwan Howard	1.00	2.50
64 Larry Johnson	1.25	3.00
65 Shareef Abdur-Rahim	1.25	3.00
66 Dennis Rodman	4.00	10.00
67 Vin Baker	1.50	4.00
68 Clyde Drexler	2.50	6.00
69 Eddie Jones	2.00	5.00
70 Jerry Stackhouse	2.00	5.00
71 Karl Malone	2.50	6.00
72 Mitch Richmond	2.00	5.00
73 Glen Rice	2.00	5.00
74 Jason Kidd	3.00	8.00
75 Latrell Sprewell	2.00	5.00
76 David Robinson	3.00	8.00
77 Charles Barkley	3.00	8.00
78 Gary Payton	2.00	5.00
79 Scottie Pippen	3.00	8.00
80 Reggie Miller	2.50	6.00
81 Alonzo Mourning	3.00	8.00
82 Allen Iverson	5.00	12.00
83 Michael Jordan	12.00	30.00
84 Shawn Kemp	2.50	6.00
85 Kevin Garnett	4.00	10.00
86 Grant Hill	4.00	10.00
87 Anfernee Hardaway	4.00	10.00
88 Shaquille O'Neal	6.00	15.00
89 John Stockton	3.00	8.00
90 Hakeem Olajuwon	3.00	8.00
91 Billy Owens	.15	.40
92 Derek Anderson	.25	.60
93 Hersey Hawkins	.15	.40
94 Bryon Russell	.15	.40
95 Rik Smits	.20	.50
96 Tracy McGrady	1.00	2.50
97 Kendall Gill	.15	.40
98 Tim Thomas	.30	.75
99 Robert Horry	.20	.50
100 Marcus Camby	.25	.60
101 Rodney Rogers	.15	.40
102 Danny Manning	.20	.50
103 John Starks	.20	.50
104 Mahmoud Abdul-Rauf	.15	.40
105 Chris Childs	.15	.40
106 Antonio Davis	.15	.40
107 Lamond Murray	.15	.40
108 Nick Anderson	.15	.40
109 Antoine Walker	.25	.60
110 Christian Laettner	.20	.50
111 Gary Trent	.15	.40
112 Tony Battie	.25	.60
113 Vlade Divac	.25	.60
114 Kevin Johnson	.25	.60
115 Erick Strickland	.20	.50
116 Ray Allen	.30	.75
117 Antonio Daniels	.25	.60
118 Sean Elliott	.25	.60
119 Horace Grant	.20	.50
120 Walt Williams	.15	.40
121 Rony Seikaly	.15	.40
122 Allan Houston	.20	.50
123 Michael Finley	.25	.60
124 Rasheed Wallace	.25	.60
125 Doug Christie	.15	.40
126 Danny Ferry	.15	.40
127 Arvydas Sabonis	.20	.50
128 Shandon Anderson	.15	.40
129 Otis Thorpe	.15	.40
130 Adonal Foyle	.20	.50
131 Bryant Reeves	.15	.40
132 Theo Ratliff	.20	.50
133 Matt Maloney	.15	.40
134 Voshon Lenard	.15	.40
135 Danny Fortson	.25	.60
136 Joe Smith	1.00	2.50
137 Mookie Blaylock	.60	1.50
138 Loy Vaught	.75	2.00
139 Tom Gugliotta	.75	2.00
140 Damon Stoudamire	1.00	2.50
141 Antonio McDyess	1.00	2.50
142 Kobe Bryant	6.00	15.00
143 Juwan Howard	1.00	2.50
144 Tim Hardaway	1.25	3.00
145 Ron Mercer	1.50	4.00
146 Joe Dumars	1.25	3.00
147 Clyde Drexler	1.50	4.00
148 Shareef Abdur-Rahim	1.25	3.00
149 LaPhonso Ellis	.75	2.00
150 Dikembe Mutombo	1.25	3.00
151 Chauncey Billups	4.00	10.00
152 Chris Webber	1.25	3.00
153 Glenn Robinson	1.00	2.50
154 Patrick Ewing	1.50	4.00
155 Stephon Marbury	1.50	4.00
156 Keith Van Horn	3.00	8.00
157 Karl Malone	2.50	6.00
158 Terrell Brandon	1.25	3.00
159 Sam Cassell	1.50	4.00
160 Jerry Stackhouse	2.00	5.00
161 Vin Baker	1.50	4.00
162 Jason Kidd	3.00	8.00
163 Charles Barkley	3.00	8.00
164 Reggie Miller	2.50	6.00
165 Alonzo Mourning	2.50	6.00
166 Scottie Pippen	3.00	8.00
167 Glen Rice	2.00	5.00
168 Allen Iverson	4.00	10.00
169 David Robinson	3.00	8.00
170 Shawn Kemp	2.00	5.00
171 Michael Jordan	20.00	50.00
172 Tim Duncan	12.00	30.00
173 Anfernee Hardaway	4.00	10.00
174 Shaquille O'Neal	6.00	15.00
175 John Stockton	3.00	8.00
176 Gary Payton	2.50	6.00
177 Mitch Richmond	2.50	6.00
178 Kevin Garnett	4.00	10.00
179 Hakeem Olajuwon	3.00	8.00
180 Grant Hill	4.00	10.00

1997-98 Collector's Choice Stick-Ums

Randomly inserted in series one packs at the rate of one in three, this 30-sticker set features color action images of a player from each NBA team in the middle of a dunk and can be stuck anywhere. Card backs carry a checklist for the set and are numbered with a "S" prefix.

Card	Low	High
COMPLETE SET (30)	3.00	8.00
SER.1 STATED ODDS 1:3		
S1 Steve Smith	.12	.30
S2 Antoine Walker	.15	.40
S3 Anthony Mason	.10	.25
S4 Dennis Rodman	.30	.75
S5 Terrell Brandon	.10	.25
S6 Michael Finley	.15	.40
S7 Antonio McDyess	.12	.30
S8 Grant Hill	.25	.60
S9 Joe Smith	.12	.30
S10 Hakeem Olajuwon	.20	.50
S11 Reggie Miller	.20	.50
S12 Loy Vaught	.10	.25
S13 Shaquille O'Neal	.40	1.00
S14 Alonzo Mourning	.20	.50
S15 Vin Baker	.12	.30
S16 Stephon Marbury	.20	.50
S17 Jim Jackson	.10	.25
S18 John Starks	.12	.30
S19 Anfernee Hardaway	.25	.60
S20 Allen Iverson	.30	.75
S21 Jason Kidd	.25	.60
S22 Kenny Anderson	.12	.30
S23 Mitch Richmond	.15	.40
S24 David Robinson	.25	.60
S25 Shawn Kemp	.15	.40
S26 Damon Stoudamire	.12	.30
S27 Karl Malone	.20	.50
S28 Bryant Reeves	.10	.25
S29 Juwan Howard	.12	.30
S30 Michael Jordan	1.25	3.00

1997-98 Collector's Choice Stick-Ums Base Card

Card	Low	High
COMPLETE SET (30)	3.00	8.00
B1 Steve Smith	.12	.30
B2 Antoine Walker	.30	.75
B3 Anthony Mason	.10	.25
B4 Dennis Rodman	.30	.75
B5 Terrell Brandon	.10	.25
B6 Michael Finley	.20	.50
B7 Antonio McDyess	.12	.30
B8 Grant Hill	.25	.60
B9 Joe Smith	.12	.30
B10 Hakeem Olajuwon	.20	.50
B11 Reggie Miller	.20	.50
B12 Loy Vaught	.10	.25
B13 Shaquille O'Neal	.40	1.00
B14 Alonzo Mourning	.20	.50
B15 Vin Baker	.12	.30
B16 Stephon Marbury	.20	.50
B17 Jim Jackson	.10	.25
B18 John Starks	.12	.30
B19 Anfernee Hardaway	.25	.60
B20 Allen Iverson	.75	2.00
B21 Jason Kidd	.25	.60
B22 Kenny Anderson	.12	.30
B23 Mitch Richmond	.15	.40
B24 David Robinson	.25	.60
B25 Shawn Kemp	.15	.40
B26 Damon Stoudamire	.12	.30
B27 Karl Malone	.20	.50
B28 Bryant Reeves	.10	.25
B29 Juwan Howard	.12	.30
B30 Michael Jordan	1.25	3.00

1997-98 Collector's Choice The Jordan Dynasty

Randomly inserted in series one packs, this five-card insert set features color player photos of Michael Jordan and celebrates the five NBA championships he and the Bulls have brought to Chicago. Each card contains a detailed summary of the highlights of each of the five seasons. Only 23,000 of each card was produced.

Card	Low	High
COMPLETE SET (5)	15.00	40.00
COMMON CARD (1-5)	6.00	15.00
STATED PRINT RUN 23,000 EACH		

1997-98 Collector's Choice Catch 23

This 10-card set measures approximately 5" by 7" and features 10 cards that are a larger version of the "Catch 23" subset from 1997-98 Collector's Choice. The cards were inserted one per retail blister package with two 1997-98 Collector's Choice packs. Those blister packs retailed for $2.99. The card backs are numbered with a "C" prefix.

Card	Low	High
COMPLETE SET (10)	10.00	25.00
COMMON CARD (C1-C10)	1.25	3.00

1997-98 Collector's Choice Jumbos

This 15-card set measures approximately 7" by 11" and features color player photos on the fronts. The first 10 cards listed are a jumbo version of the "Catch 23" set and display a Michael Jordan photo with a paragraph on the back explaining the picture. The last five cards honor five top teams from the 1996-97 NBA season and feature color action photos of the top team members with their statistics. The cards were inserted as chiptoppers in retail boxes.

Card	Low	High
COMPLETE SET (15)	15.00	40.00
1 Michael Jordan	2.00	5.00
2 Michael Jordan	2.00	5.00
3 Michael Jordan	2.00	5.00
4 Michael Jordan	2.00	5.00
5 Michael Jordan	2.00	5.00
6 Michael Jordan	2.00	5.00
7 Michael Jordan	2.00	5.00
8 Michael Jordan	2.00	5.00
9 Michael Jordan	2.00	5.00
10 Michael Jordan	2.00	5.00
GN1 Utah Jazz Game Night	1.25	3.00
GN2 Los Angeles Lakers Game Night	1.50	4.00
GN3 Minnesota Timberwolves Game Night	1.25	3.00
GN4 Orlando Magic Game Night	1.25	3.00
GN5 Chicago Bulls Game Night	2.00	5.00

1995-96 Collector's Choice Argentina Stickers

Card	Low	High
1 Golden State Warriors Logo	.10	.25
2 Latrell Sprewell	.40	1.00
3 Ricky Pierce	.25	.60
4 Tim Hardaway	.40	1.00
5 Chris Mullin	.40	1.00
6 Donyell Marshall	.25	.60
7 Clifford Rozier	.25	.60
8 Carlos Rogers	.25	.60
9 Rony Seikaly	.25	.60
10 Los Angeles Clippers Logo	.10	.25
11 Pooh Richardson	.25	.60
12 Terry Dehere	.25	.60
13 Eric Piatkowski	.30	.75
14 Loy Vaught	.25	.60
15 Malik Sealy	.25	.60
16 Lamond Murray	.25	.60
17 Los Angeles Lakers Logo	.10	.25
18 Sedale Threatt	.25	.60
19 Nick Van Exel	.10	.25
20 Cedric Ceballos	.25	.60
21 George Lynch	.25	.60
22 Eddie Jones	.40	1.00
23 Elden Campbell	.25	.60
24 Vlade Divac	.40	1.00
25 Phoenix Suns Logo	.10	.25
26 Kevin Johnson	.40	1.00
27 Wesley Person	.25	.60
28 Dan Majerle	.40	1.00
29 A.C. Green	.30	.75
30 Charles Barkley	.60	1.50
31 Danny Manning	.30	.75
32 Wayman Tisdale	.25	.60
33 Portland Trail Blazers Logo	.10	.25
34 Rod Strickland	.25	.60
35 Terry Porter	.25	.60
36 Aaron McKie	.25	.60

37 Otis Thorpe .25 .60
38 Buck Williams .25 .60
39 Clifford Robinson .25 .60
40 Harvey Grant .25 .60
41 Sacramento Kings Logo .10 .25
42 Randy Brown .25 .60
43 Mitch Richmond .40 1.00
44 Bobby Hurley .25 .60
45 Walt Williams .25 .60
46 Brian Grant .30 .75
47 Olden Polynice .25 .60
48 Duane Causwell .25 .60
49 Seattle Supersonics Logo .10 .25
50 Kendall Gill .25 .60
51 Gary Payton .40 1.00
52 Sarunas Marciulionis .25 .60
53 Nate McMillan .25 .60
54 Detlef Schrempf .40 1.00
55 Shawn Kemp .40 1.00
56 Sam Perkins .25 .60
57 Dallas Mavericks Logo .10 .25
58 Jim Jackson .25 .60
59 Jason Kidd .60 1.50
60 Tony Dumas .25 .60
61 Jamal Mashburn .40 1.00
62 Doug Smith .25 .60
63 Popeye Jones .25 .60
64 Denver Nuggets Logo .10 .25
65 Robert Pack .25 .60
66 Bryant Stith .25 .60
67 Mahmoud Abdul-Rauf .25 .60
68 Jalen Rose .50 1.25
69 Reggie Williams .25 .60
70 LaPhonso Ellis .25 .60
71 Dikembe Mutombo .40 1.00
72 Houston Rockets Logo .10 .25
73 Sam Cassell .40 1.00
74 Kenny Smith .30 .75
75 Clyde Drexler .50 1.25
76 Carl Herrera .25 .60
77 Robert Horry .30 .75
78 Otis Thorpe .25 .60
79 Hakeem Olajuwon .50 1.25
80 Minnesota Timberwolves Logo .10 .25
81 Chris Smith .25 .60
82 Micheal Williams .25 .60
83 Doug West .25 .60
84 Isaiah Rider .40 1.00
85 Christian Laettner .30 .75
86 Tom Gugliotta .25 .60
87 San Antonio Spurs Logo .10 .25
88 Avery Johnson .30 .75
89 Vinny Del Negro .25 .60
90 Dennis Rodman .75 2.00
91 Sean Elliott .40 1.00
92 Chuck Person .30 .75
93 J.R. Reid .25 .60
94 David Robinson .60 1.50
95 Utah Jazz Logo .10 .25
96 Jeff Hornacek .30 .75
97 John Stockton .50 1.25
98 David Benoit .25 .60
99 Karl Malone .50 1.25
100 Tom Chambers .30 .75
101 Antoine Carr .25 .60
102 Felton Spencer .25 .60
103 Atlanta Hawks Logo .10 .25
104 Mookie Blaylock .25 .60
105 Craig Ehlo .25 .60
106 Steve Smith .30 .75
107 Stacey Augmon .30 .75
108 Grant Long .25 .60
109 Ken Norman .25 .60
110 Jon Koncak .25 .60
111 Charlotte Hornets Logo .10 .25
112 Hersey Hawkins .25 .60
113 Dell Curry .25 .60
114 Muggsy Bogues .30 .75
115 Scott Burrell .25 .60
116 Larry Johnson .40 1.00
117 Robert Parish .40 1.00
118 Alonzo Mourning .50 1.25
119 Chicago Bulls Logo .10 .25
120 Michael Jordan 3.00 8.00
121 Ron Harper .30 .75
122 Toni Kukoc .40 1.00
123 Scottie Pippen .60 1.50
124 Dickey Simpkins .25 .60
125 Will Perdue .25 .60
126 Cleveland Cavaliers Logo .10 .25
127 Gerald Wilkins .25 .60
128 Mark Price .40 1.00
129 Terrell Brandon .25 .60
130 Bobby Phills .25 .60
131 Chris Mills .25 .60
132 Tyrone Hill .25 .60
133 John Williams .25 .60
134 Detroit Pistons Logo .10 .25
135 Lindsey Hunter .25 .60
136 Joe Dumars .40 1.00
137 Allan Houston .30 .75
138 Terry Mills .25 .60
139 Grant Hill .60 1.50
140 Mark West .25 .60
141 Indiana Pacers Logo .10 .25
142 Reggie Miller .50 1.25
143 Mark Jackson .30 .75
144 Duane Ferrell .25 .60
145 Derrick McKey .25 .60
146 Dale Davis .25 .60
147 Antonio Davis .25 .60
148 Rik Smits .30 .75
149 Milwaukee Bucks Logo .10 .25
150 Lee Mayberry .25 .60
151 Todd Day .25 .60
152 Vin Baker .30 .75
153 Glenn Robinson .30 .75
154 Marty Conlon .25 .60
155 Johnny Newman .25 .60
156 Eric Mobley .25 .60
157 Boston Celtics Logo .10 .25
158 Sherman Douglas .25 .60
159 Dee Brown .25 .60
160 Rick Fox .25 .60
161 Dino Radja .25 .60
162 Xavier McDaniel .25 .60
163 Dominique Wilkins .50 1.25
164 Eric Montross .25 .60
165 Miami Heat Logo .10 .25
166 Bimbo Coles .25 .60
167 Khalid Reeves .25 .60
168 Glen Rice .40 1.00
169 Billy Owens .25 .60
170 Kevin Willis .25 .60
171 Matt Geiger .25 .60
172 New Jersey Nets Logo .10 .25
173 Kevin Edwards .25 .60
174 Rex Walters .25 .60
175 Kenny Anderson .30 .75
176 Derrick Coleman .30 .75
177 Chris Morris .25 .60
178 Armon Gilliam .25 .60
179 P.J. Brown .25 .60
180 New York Knicks Logo .10 .25
181 Derek Harper .30 .75
182 Charlie Ward .25 .60
183 John Starks .30 .75
184 Charles Smith .25 .60
185 Charles Oakley .30 .75
186 Anthony Mason .25 .60
187 Patrick Ewing .50 1.25
188 Orlando Magic Logo .10 .25
189 Anthony Bowie .25 .60
190 Anfernee Hardaway .60 1.50
191 Nick Anderson .25 .60
192 Dennis Scott .25 .60
193 Donald Royal .25 .60
194 Horace Grant .30 .75
195 Shaquille O'Neal 1.00 2.50
196 Philadelphia 76ers Logo .10 .25
197 Jeff Malone .25 .60
198 Dana Barros .25 .60
199 Clarence Weatherspoon .25 .60
200 Scott Williams .25 .60
201 Sharone Wright .25 .60
202 Shawn Bradley .25 .60
203 Washington Bullets Logo .10 .25
204 Scott Skiles .25 .60
205 Mitchell Butler .25 .60
206 Calbert Cheaney .25 .60
207 Don MacLean .25 .60
208 Juwan Howard .40 1.00
209 Kevin Duckworth .25 .60
210 Gheorghe Muresan .25 .60
211 Toronto Raptors Logo .10 .25
212 Vancouver Grizzlies Logo .10 .25
213 Michael Jordan 3.00 8.00
1985 NBA ROY
214 Michael Jordan 3.00 8.00
1986-87 3,000 Points
215 Michael Jordan 3.00 8.00
1988 NBA Defensive POY
216 Michael Jordan 3.00 8.00
Jordan Collection
217 Michael Jordan 3.00 8.00
He's Back
218 Michael Jordan 3.00 8.00
He's Back
219 Michael Jordan 3.00 8.00
He's Back
220 Michael Jordan 3.00 8.00
He's Back
221 Michael Jordan 3.00 8.00
He's Back

1995-96 Collector's Choice European Stickers

Distributed in 100-pack boxes, this 212-card set utilizes the design of both the 1994-95 Collector's Choice American and the 1995-96 Collector's Choice American (though the 1994-95 design is used primarily throughout the set.) The cards, which are smaller than standard size, feature identical fronts to the American version. The backs feature the NBA Logo, the Collector's Choice/Upper Deck Logo, the card number in a black circle and copyright information. Team logo stickers are also available in the set.

COMPLETE SET (212) 20.00 50.00
1 Golden State Warriors Logo .10 .25
2 Latrell Sprewell .40 1.00
3 Ricky Pierce .25 .60
4 Tim Hardaway .40 1.00
5 Chris Mullin .40 1.00
6 Donyell Marshall .25 .60
7 Clifford Rozier .25 .60
8 Carlos Rogers .25 .60
9 Rony Seikaly .25 .60
10 Los Angeles Clippers Logo .10 .25
11 Pooh Richardson .25 .60
12 Terry Dehere .25 .60
13 Eric Piatkowski .30 .75
14 Loy Vaught .25 .60
15 Malik Sealy .25 .60
16 Lamond Murray .25 .60
17 Los Angeles Lakers Logo .10 .25
18 Sedale Threatt .25 .60
19 Nick Van Exel .40 1.00
20 Cedric Ceballos .25 .60
21 George Lynch .25 .60
22 Eddie Jones .40 1.00
23 Elden Campbell .25 .60
24 Vlade Divac .40 1.00
25 Phoenix Suns Logo .10 .25
26 Kevin Johnson .40 1.00
27 Wesley Person .25 .60
28 Dan Majerle .40 1.00
29 A.C. Green .30 .75
30 Charles Barkley .60 1.50
31 Danny Manning .30 .75
32 Wayman Tisdale .25 .60
33 Portland Trail Blazers Logo .10 .25
34 Rod Strickland .25 .60
35 Terry Porter .25 .60
36 Aaron McKie .25 .60
37 Otis Thorpe .25 .60
38 Buck Williams .25 .60
39 Clifford Robinson .25 .60
40 Harvey Grant .25 .60
41 Sacramento Kings Logo .10 .25
42 Randy Brown .25 .60
43 Mitch Richmond .40 1.00
44 Bobby Hurley .25 .60
45 Walt Williams .25 .60
46 Brian Grant .30 .75
47 Olden Polynice .25 .60
48 Duane Causwell .25 .60
49 Seattle Supersonics Logo .10 .25
50 Kendall Gill .25 .60
51 Gary Payton .40 1.00
52 Sarunas Marciulionis .25 .60
53 Nate McMillan .25 .60
54 Detlef Schrempf .40 1.00
55 Shawn Kemp .40 1.00
56 Sam Perkins .25 .60
57 Dallas Mavericks Logo .10 .25
58 Jim Jackson .25 .60
59 Jason Kidd .60 1.50
60 Tony Dumas .25 .60
61 Jamal Mashburn .40 1.00
62 Doug Smith .25 .60
63 Popeye Jones .25 .60
64 Denver Nuggets Logo .10 .25
65 Robert Pack .25 .60
66 Bryant Stith .25 .60
67 Mahmoud Abdul-Rauf .25 .60
68 Jalen Rose .50 1.25
69 Reggie Williams .25 .60
70 LaPhonso Ellis .25 .60
71 Dikembe Mutombo .40 1.00
72 Houston Rockets Logo .10 .25
73 Sam Cassell .40 1.00
74 Kenny Smith .30 .75
75 Clyde Drexler .50 1.25
76 Carl Herrera .25 .60
77 Robert Horry .30 .75
78 Otis Thorpe .25 .60
79 Hakeem Olajuwon .50 1.25
80 Minnesota Timberwolves Logo .10 .25
81 Chris Smith .25 .60
82 Micheal Williams .25 .60
83 Doug West .25 .60
84 Isaiah Rider .40 1.00
85 Christian Laettner .30 .75
86 Tom Gugliotta .25 .60
87 San Antonio Spurs Logo .10 .25
88 Avery Johnson .30 .75
89 Vinny Del Negro .25 .60
90 Dennis Rodman .75 2.00
91 Sean Elliott .40 1.00
92 Chuck Person .30 .75
93 J.R. Reid .25 .60
94 David Robinson .60 1.50
95 Utah Jazz Logo .10 .25
96 Jeff Hornacek .30 .75
97 John Stockton .50 1.25
98 David Benoit .25 .60
99 Karl Malone .50 1.25
100 Tom Chambers .30 .75
101 Antoine Carr .25 .60
102 Felton Spencer .25 .60
103 Atlanta Hawks Logo .10 .25
104 Mookie Blaylock .25 .60
105 Craig Ehlo .25 .60
106 Steve Smith .30 .75
107 Stacey Augmon .30 .75
108 Grant Long .25 .60
109 Ken Norman .25 .60
110 Jon Koncak .25 .60
111 Charlotte Hornets Logo .10 .20
112 Hersey Hawkins .25 .60
113 Dell Curry .25 .60
114 Muggsy Bogues .30 .75
115 Scott Burrell .25 .60
116 Larry Johnson .40 1.00
117 Robert Parish .40 1.00
118 Alonzo Mourning .50 1.25
119 Chicago Bulls Logo .10 .25
120 Michael Jordan 3.00 8.00
121 Ron Harper .30 .75
122 Toni Kukoc .40 1.00
123 Scottie Pippen .60 1.50
124 Dickey Simpkins .25 .60
125 Will Perdue .25 .60
126 Cleveland Cavaliers Logo .10 .25
127 Gerald Wilkins .25 .60
128 Mark Price .40 1.00
129 Terrell Brandon .25 .60
130 Bobby Phills .25 .60
131 Chris Mills .25 .60
132 Tyrone Hill .25 .60
133 John Williams .25 .60
134 Detroit Pistons Logo .10 .25
135 Lindsey Hunter .25 .60
136 Joe Dumars .40 1.00
137 Allan Houston .30 .75
138 Terry Mills .25 .60
139 Grant Hill .60 1.50
140 Mark West .25 .60
141 Indiana Pacers Logo .10 .25
142 Reggie Miller .50 1.25
143 Mark Jackson .30 .75
144 Duane Ferrell .25 .60
145 Derrick McKey .25 .60
146 Dale Davis .25 .60
147 Antonio Davis .25 .60
148 Rik Smits .30 .75
149 Milwaukee Bucks Logo .10 .25
150 Lee Mayberry .25 .60
151 Todd Day .25 .60
152 Vin Baker .30 .75
153 Glenn Robinson .30 .75
154 Marty Conlon .25 .60
155 Johnny Newman .25 .60
156 Eric Mobley .25 .60
157 Boston Celtics Logo .10 .25
158 Sherman Douglas .25 .60
159 Dee Brown .25 .60
160 Rick Fox .25 .60
161 Dino Radja .25 .60
162 Xavier McDaniel .25 .60
163 Dominique Wilkins .50 1.25
164 Eric Montross .25 .60
165 Miami Heat Logo .10 .25
166 Bimbo Coles .25 .60
167 Khalid Reeves .25 .60
168 Glen Rice .40 1.00
169 Billy Owens .25 .60
170 Kevin Willis .25 .60
171 Matt Geiger .25 .60
172 New Jersey Nets Logo .10 .25
173 Kevin Edwards .25 .60
174 Rex Walters .25 .60
175 Kenny Anderson .30 .75
176 Derrick Coleman .30 .75
177 Chris Morris .25 .60
178 Armon Gilliam .25 .60
179 P.J. Brown .25 .60
180 New York Knicks Logo .10 .25
181 Derek Harper .30 .75
182 Charlie Ward .25 .60
183 John Starks .30 .75
184 Charles Smith .25 .60
185 Charles Oakley .30 .75
186 Anthony Mason .25 .60
187 Patrick Ewing .50 1.25
188 Orlando Magic Logo .10 .25
189 Anthony Bowie .25 .60
190 Anfernee Hardaway .60 1.50
191 Nick Anderson .25 .60
192 Dennis Scott .25 .60
193 Donald Royal .25 .60
194 Horace Grant .30 .75
195 Shaquille O'Neal 1.00 2.50
196 Philadelphia 76ers Logo .10 .25
197 Jeff Malone .25 .60
198 Dana Barros .25 .60
199 Clarence Weatherspoon .25 .60
200 Scott Williams .25 .60
201 Sharone Wright .25 .60
202 Shawn Bradley .25 .60
203 Washington Bullets Logo .10 .25
204 Scott Skiles .25 .60
205 Mitchell Butler .25 .60
206 Calbert Cheaney .25 .60
207 Don MacLean .25 .60
208 Juwan Howard .40 1.00
209 Kevin Duckworth .25 .60
210 Gheorghe Muresan .25 .60
211 Toronto Raptors Logo 1.00 .25
212 Vancouver Grizzlies Logo .10 .25

1995-96 Collector's Choice European Stickers Michael Jordan

Randomly inserted into packs of 1995-96 Collector's Choice European at roughly one in five, this nine-card set is identical in design to the 1995-96 Collector's Choice Jordan Collection and the 1995-96 Collector's Choice He's Back sets. These stickers have a "MJ" prefix on the back.

COMPLETE SET (9) 12.00 30.00
COMMON STICKER (1-9) 1.60 4.00

1996 Collector's Choice Hula Hoops European

This 40-card set was distributed in the United Kingdom under the promoter of KP Foods. The cards are designed like the Collector's Choice set, but are mini in size. Card backs are numbered with a "HH" prefix.

COMPLETE SET (40) 125.00 250.00
HH1 Mookie Blaylock 3.00 8.00
HH2 Dana Barros 3.00 8.00
HH3 Toni Kukoc 5.00 12.00
HH4 Terrell Brandon 3.00 8.00
HH5 Jamal Mashburn 4.00 10.00
HH6 Antonio McDyess 5.00 12.00
HH7 Chris Mullin 5.00 12.00
HH8 Hakeem Olajuwon 6.00 15.00
HH9 Brent Barry 4.00 10.00
HH10 Eddie Jones 5.00 12.00
HH11 Kurt Thomas 3.00 8.00
HH12 Kevin Garnett 12.00 30.00
HH13 Kendall Gill 3.00 8.00
HH14 John Starks 4.00 10.00
HH15 Dennis Scott 3.00 8.00
HH16 Jerry Stackhouse 6.00 15.00
HH17 Arvydas Sabonis 4.00 10.00
HH18 Billy Owens 3.00 8.00
HH19 Avery Johnson 4.00 10.00
HH20 Damon Stoudamire 4.00 10.00
HH21 Christian Laettner 4.00 10.00
HH22 Dino Radja 3.00 8.00
HH23 Dennis Rodman 10.00 25.00
HH24 Jim Jackson 3.00 8.00
HH25 LaPhonso Ellis 3.00 8.00
HH26 Joe Dumars 4.00 10.00
HH27 Joe Smith 4.00 10.00
HH28 Rik Smits 4.00 10.00
HH29 Cedric Ceballos 3.00 8.00
HH30 Sasha Danilovic 3.00 8.00
HH31 Vin Baker 4.00 10.00
HH32 Shawn Bradley 3.00 8.00
HH33 Charles Oakley 4.00 10.00
HH34 Anfernee Hardaway 8.00 20.00
HH35 Derrick Coleman 4.00 10.00
HH36 Wesley Person 3.00 8.00
HH37 Brian Grant 4.00 10.00
HH38 Sean Elliott 5.00 12.00
HH39 Detlef Schrempf 5.00 12.00
HH40 Karl Malone 6.00 15.00

1994-95 Collector's Choice International Australian Coke

COMPLETE SET (41)
1 B.J. Armstrong .40 1.00
2 Stacey Augmon .50 1.25
3 Vin Baker .60 1.50
4 Shawn Bradley .40 1.00
5 Derrick Coleman .50 1.25
6 Dell Curry .40 1.00
7 Vinny Del Negro .40 1.00
8 Clyde Drexler .75 2.00
9 LaPhonso Ellis .40 1.00
10 Kendall Gill .40 1.00
11 Anfernee Hardaway 1.00 2.50
12 Robert Horry .60 1.50
13 Kevin Johnson .60 1.50
14 Shawn Kemp .60 1.50
15 Don MacLean .40 1.00
16 Karl Malone .75 2.00
17 Dan Majerle .60 1.50
18 Jamal Mashburn .60 1.50
19 Reggie Miller .75 2.00
20 Terry Mills .40 1.00
21 Harold Miner .40 1.00
22 Alonzo Mourning .75 2.00
23 Chris Mullin .60 1.50
24 Charles Oakley .50 1.25
25 Hakeem Olajuwon .75 2.00
26 Anthony Peeler .40 1.00
27 Scottie Pippen 1.25 3.00
28 Mark Price .60 1.50
29 Dino Radja .40 1.00
30 Mitch Richmond .60 1.50
31 Isaiah Rider .60 1.50
32 David Robinson 1.00 2.50
33 Dennis Rodman 1.25 3.00
34 Detlef Schrempf .60 1.50
35 Charles Smith .40 1.00
36 Steve Smith .50 1.25
37 Latrell Sprewell .75 2.00
38 Loy Vaught .40 1.00
39 Rex Walters .40 1.00
40 Spud Webb .50 1.25
41 Shawn Kemp CL .60 1.50

1994-95 Collector's Choice International French

This 429-card standard size set was issued in two separate series of 210 and 219 cards by Upper Deck for the French, German and Italian markets. Cards were distributed for all countries in 10-card packs and 30 pack boxes (featuring Michael Jordan on both the wrapper and the box). The first 210 cards are similar in design and numbering to the American 1994-95 Collector's Choice set. The following subsets are included in this set: Tip-Off (166-192), All-Star Advice (193-198), NBA Profiles (199-206), Checklists (207-210, 417-420), Michael Jordan Heroes (211-219), Blueprints (372-398), Trivia (399-406) and Draft Class (407-416). The Michael Jordan Heroes subset cards are believed to be tougher to pull from packs than other regular issue cards. White-bordered fronts feature color player action shots. The player's name, team and position appear in a lower corner. The back carries another color player action shot at the top, with statistics and career highlights displayed below. All cards feature bilingual information. This product has been made readily available to the U.S. market through closeouts.

COMPLETE SET (429) 20.00 50.00
COMPLETE SERIES 1 (219) 10.00 25.00
COMPLETE SERIES 2 (210) 10.00 25.00
1 Anfernee Hardaway .50 1.25
2 Mark Macon .20 .50
3 Steve Smith .25 .60
4 Chris Webber .50 1.25
5 Donald Royal .20 .50
6 Avery Johnson .25 .60
7 Kevin Johnson .30 .75
8 Doug Christie .20 .50
9 Derrick McKey .20 .50
10 Dennis Rodman .60 1.50
11 Scott Skiles .20 .50
12 Johnny Dawkins .20 .50
13 Kendall Gill .20 .50
14 Jeff Hornacek .25 .60
15 Latrell Sprewell .40 1.00
16 Lucious Harris .20 .50
17 Chris Mullin .30 .75
18 John Williams .20 .50
19 Tony Campbell .20 .50
20 LaPhonso Ellis .20 .50
21 Gerald Wilkins .20 .50
22 Clyde Drexler .40 1.00
23 Michael Jordan BB 2.50 6.00
24 George Lynch .20 .50
25 Mark Price .30 .75
26 James Robinson .20 .50
27 Elmore Spencer .20 .50
28 Stacey King .20 .50
29 Corie Blount .20 .50
30 Dell Curry .20 .50
31 Reggie Miller .40 1.00
32 Karl Malone .40 1.00
33 Scottie Pippen .60 1.50
34 Hakeem Olajuwon .40 1.00
35 Clarence Weatherspoon .20 .50
36 Kevin Edwards .20 .50
37 Pete Myers .20 .50
38 Jeff Turner .20 .50
39 Ennis Whatley .20 .50
40 Calbert Cheaney .20 .50
41 Glen Rice .30 .75
42 Vin Baker .30 .75
43 Grant Long .20 .50
44 Derrick Coleman .25 .60
45 Rik Smits .25 .60
46 Chris Smith .20 .50
47 Carl Herrera .20 .50
48 Bob Martin .20 .50
49 Terrell Brandon .20 .50
50 David Robinson .50 1.25
51 Danny Ferry .20 .50
52 Buck Williams .20 .50
53 Josh Grant .20 .50
54 Ed Pinckney .20 .50
55 Dikembe Mutombo .30 .75
56 Clifford Robinson .20 .50
57 Luther Wright .20 .50
58 Scott Burrell .20 .50
59 Stacey Augmon .25 .60
60 Jeff Malone .20 .50
61 Byron Houston .20 .50
62 Anthony Peeler .20 .50
63 Michael Adams .20 .50
64 Negele Knight .20 .50
65 Terry Cummings .25 .60
66 Christian Laettner .25 .60
67 Tracy Murray .20 .50
68 Sedale Threatt .20 .50
69 Dan Majerle .30 .75
70 Frank Brickowski .20 .50
71 Ken Norman .20 .50
72 Charles Smith .20 .50
73 Adam Keefe .20 .50
74 P.J. Brown .20 .50
75 Kevin Duckworth .20 .50
76 Shawn Bradley .20 .50
77 Darnell Mee .20 .50
78 Nick Anderson .20 .50
79 Mark West .20 .50
80 B.J. Armstrong .20 .50
81 Dennis Scott .20 .50
82 Lindsey Hunter .20 .50
83 Derek Strong .20 .50
84 Mike Brown .20 .50
85 Antonio Harvey .20 .50
86 Anthony Bonner .20 .50
87 Sam Cassell .30 .75
88 Harold Miner .20 .50
89 Spud Webb .25 .60
90 Mookie Blaylock .20 .50
91 Greg Anthony .20 .50
92 Richard Petruska .20 .50
93 Sean Rooks .20 .50
94 Ervin Johnson .20 .50
95 Randy Brown .20 .50
96 Orlando Woolridge .20 .50
97 Charles Oakley .25 .60
98 Craig Ehlo .20 .50
99 Derek Harper .25 .60
100 Doug Edwards .20 .50
101 Muggsy Bogues .25 .60
102 Mitch Richmond .30 .75
103 Mahmoud Abdul-Rauf .20 .50
104 Joe Dumars .30 .75
105 Eric Riley .20 .50
106 Terry Mills .20 .50
107 Toni Kukoc .40 1.00
108 Jon Koncak .20 .50
109 Haywoode Workman .20 .50
110 Todd Day .20 .50
111 Detlef Schrempf .30 .75
112 David Wesley .20 .50
113 Mark Jackson .25 .60
114 Doug Overton .20 .50
115 Vinny Del Negro .20 .50
116 Loy Vaught .20 .50
117 Mike Peplowski .20 .50
118 Bimbo Coles .20 .50
119 Rex Walters .20 .50
120 Sherman Douglas .20 .50
121 David Benoit .20 .50
122 John Salley .20 .50
123 Cedric Ceballos .20 .50
124 Chris Mills .20 .50
125 Robert Horry .30 .75
126 Johnny Newman .20 .50
127 Malcolm Mackey .20 .50
128 Terry Dehere .20 .50
129 Dino Radja .20 .50
130 Reggie Williams .20 .50
131 Xavier McDaniel .20 .50
132 Bobby Hurley .20 .50
133 Alonzo Mourning .40 1.00
134 Isaiah Rider .30 .75
135 Antoine Carr .20 .50
136 Robert Pack .20 .50
137 Walt Williams .20 .50
138 Tyrone Corbin .20 .50
139 Popeye Jones .20 .50
140 Shawn Kemp .30 .75
141 Thurl Bailey .20 .50
142 James Worthy .40 1.00
143 Scott Haskin .20 .50
144 Hubert Davis .20 .50
145 A.C. Green .25 .60
146 Dale Davis .20 .50
147 Nate McMillan .20 .50
148 Chris Morris .20 .50
149 Will Perdue .20 .50
150 Felton Spencer .20 .50
151 Rod Strickland .20 .50
152 Blue Edwards .20 .50
153 John S. Williams .20 .50
154 Rodney Rogers .20 .50
155 Acie Earl .20 .50
156 Hersey Hawkins .20 .50
157 Jamal Mashburn .30 .75
158 Don MacLean .20 .50
159 Micheal Williams .20 .50
160 Kenny Gattison .20 .50
161 Rich King .20 .50
162 Allan Houston .30 .75
163 John Stockton .40 1.00
164 Kenny Anderson .25 .60
165 Shaquille O'Neal .75 2.00
166 Danny Manning TO .25 .60
167 Dee Brown TO .20 .50
168 Alonzo Mourning TO .40 1.00
169 Scottie Pippen TO .60 1.50
170 Mark Price TO .30 .75
171 Jamal Mashburn TO .30 .75
172 Dikembe Mutombo TO .30 .75
173 Joe Dumars TO .30 .75
174 Chris Webber TO .50 1.25
175 Hakeem Olajuwon TO .40 1.00
176 Reggie Miller TO .40 1.00
177 Ron Harper TO .25 .60
178 Nick Van Exel TO .30 .75
179 Steve Smith TO .25 .60
180 Vin Baker TO .30 .75
181 Isaiah Rider TO .30 .75
182 Derrick Coleman TO .25 .60
183 Patrick Ewing TO .40 1.00
184 Shaquille O'Neal TO .75 2.00
185 Clarence Weatherspoon TO .20 .50
186 Charles Barkley TO .50 1.25
187 Clyde Drexler TO .40 1.00
188 Mitch Richmond TO .30 .75
189 David Robinson TO .50 1.25
190 Shawn Kemp TO .30 .75
191 Karl Malone TO .40 1.00
192 Tom Gugliotta TO .20 .50
193 Kenny Anderson ASA .25 .60
194 Alonzo Mourning ASA .40 1.00
195 Mark Price ASA .30 .75
196 John Stockton ASA .40 1.00
197 Shaquille O'Neal ASA .75 2.00
198 Latrell Sprewell ASA .40 1.00
199 Charles Barkley PRO .50 1.25
200 Chris Webber PRO .50 1.25
201 Patrick Ewing PRO .40 1.00
202 Dennis Rodman PRO .60 1.50
203 Shawn Kemp PRO .30 .75
204 Michael Jordan PRO 2.50 6.00
205 Shaquille O'Neal PRO .75 2.00
206 Larry Johnson PRO .30 .75
207 Tim Hardaway CL .30 .75
208 John Stockton CL .40 1.00
209 Harold Miner CL .20 .50
210 B.J. Armstrong CL .20 .50
211 Michael Jordan ROY 2.50 6.00
212 Michael Jordan 63-Pt. Game 2.50 6.00
213 Michael Jordan Slam-Dunk 2.50 6.00
214 Michael Jordan MVP 2.50 6.00
215 Michael Jordan All-Star 2.50 6.00
216 Michael Jordan 3,000-Points 2.50 6.00
217 Michael Jordan Champ. 2.50 6.00
218 Michael Jordan 2.50 6.00
1985-94 M.J.'s
Decade of Dominanc
219 Michael Jordan CL 2.50 6.00
220 Gary Payton .30 .75
221 Tom Hammonds .20 .50
222 Danny Ainge .30 .75
223 Gary Grant .20 .50
224 Jim Jackson .20 .50
225 Chris Gatling .20 .50
226 Sergei Bazarevich .30 .75
227 Tony Dumas .30 .75
228 Andrew Lang .20 .50
229 Wesley Person .30 .75
230 Terry Porter .20 .50
231 Duane Causwell .20 .50
232 Shaquille O'Neal .75 2.00
233 Antonio Davis .20 .50
234 Charles Barkley .50 1.25
235 Tony Massenburg .20 .50
236 Ricky Pierce .20 .50
237 Scott Skiles .20 .50
238 Jalen Rose .75 2.00
239 Charlie Ward .30 .75
240 Michael Jordan COMM 2.50 6.00
241 Elden Campbell .20 .50
242 Bill Cartwright .25 .60
243 Armon Gilliam UER .20 .50
Card numbered 372
244 Rick Fox .20 .50
245 Tim Breaux .20 .50
246 Monty Williams .25 .60
247 Dominique Wilkins .40 1.00
248 Robert Parish .30 .75
249 Mark Jackson .25 .60
250 Jason Kidd 1.50 4.00
251 Andres Guibert .20 .50
252 Matt Geiger .20 .50
253 Stanley Roberts .20 .50
254 Jack Haley .20 .50
255 David Wingate .20 .50
256 John Crotty .20 .50
257 Brian Grant .50 1.25
258 Otis Thorpe .20 .50
259 Clifford Rozier .20 .50
260 Grant Long .20 .50
261 Eric Mobley .20 .50
262 Dickey Simpkins .25 .60
263 J.R. Reid .20 .50
264 Kevin Willis .20 .50
265 Scott Brooks .20 .50
266 Glenn Robinson .60 1.50
267 Dana Barros .20 .50
268 Ken Norman .20 .50
269 Herb Williams .20 .50
270 Dee Brown .20 .50
271 Steve Kerr .25 .60
272 Jon Barry .20 .50
273 Sean Elliott .30 .75
274 Elliot Perry .20 .50
275 Kenny Smith .25 .60
276 Sean Rooks .20 .50
277 Gheorghe Muresan .20 .50
278 Juwan Howard .50 1.25
279 Steve Smith .25 .60
280 Anthony Bowie .20 .50
281 Moses Malone .30 .75
282 Olden Polynice .20 .50
283 Jo Jo English .20 .50
284 Marty Conlon .20 .50
285 Sam Mitchell .20 .50
286 Doug West .20 .50
287 Cedric Ceballos .20 .50
288 Lorenzo Williams .20 .50
289 Harold Ellis .20 .50
290 Doc Rivers .25 .60
291 Keith Tower .20 .50
292 Mark Bryant .20 .50
293 Oliver Miller .20 .50
294 Michael Adams .20 .50
295 Tree Rollins .20 .50
296 Eddie Jones 1.00 2.50
297 Malik Sealy .20 .50
298 Blue Edwards .20 .50
299 Brooks Thompson .25 .60
300 Benoit Benjamin .20 .50
301 Avery Johnson .25 .60
302 Larry Johnson .30 .75
303 John Starks .25 .60
304 Byron Scott .25 .60
305 Eric Murdock .20 .50
306 Jay Humphries .20 .50
307 Kenny Anderson .25 .60
308 Brian Williams .20 .50
309 Nick Van Exel .30 .75
310 Tim Hardaway .30 .75
311 Lee Mayberry .20 .50
312 Vlade Divac .30 .75
313 Donyell Marshall .30 .75
314 Anthony Mason .20 .50
315 Danny Manning .25 .60
316 Tyrone Hill .20 .50
317 Vincent Askew .20 .50
318 Khalid Reeves .25 .60
319 Ron Harper .25 .60
320 Brent Price .20 .50
321 Byron Houston .20 .50
322 Lamond Murray .30 .75
323 Bryant Stith .20 .50
324 Tom Gugliotta .20 .50
325 Jerome Kersey .20 .50
326 B.J. Tyler .20 .50
327 Antonio Lang .30 .75
328 Carlos Rogers .25 .60
329 Wayman Tisdale .20 .50
330 Kevin Gamble .20 .50
331 Eric Piatkowski .40 1.00
332 Mitchell Butler .20 .50
333 Patrick Ewing .40 1.00
334 Doug Smith .20 .50
335 Joe Kleine .20 .50
336 Keith Jennings .20 .50
337 Bill Curley .20 .50
338 Johnny Newman .20 .50
339 Howard Eisley .30 .75
340 Willie Anderson .20 .50
341 Aaron McKie .30 .75
342 Tom Chambers .25 .60
343 Scott Williams .20 .50
344 Harvey Grant .20 .50
345 Billy Owens .20 .50
346 Sharone Wright .25 .60
347 Michael Cage .20 .50
348 Vern Fleming .20 .50
349 Darrin Hancock .25 .60
350 Matt Fish .20 .50
351 Rony Seikaly .20 .50
352 Victor Alexander .20 .50
353 Anthony Miller .30 .75
354 Horace Grant .25 .60
355 Jayson Williams .20 .50
356 Dale Ellis .20 .50
357 Sarunas Marciulionis .20 .50
358 Anthony Avent .20 .50
359 Rex Chapman .20 .50
360 Askia Jones .30 .75
361 Bo Outlaw .30 .75
362 Chuck Person .25 .60
363 Danny Schayes .20 .50
364 Morlon Wiley .20 .50
365 Dontonio Wingfield .30 .75
366 Tony Smith .20 .50
367 Bill Wennington .20 .50
368 Bryon Russell .20 .50
369 Geert Hammink .20 .50
370 Eric Montross .25 .60
371 Cliff Levingston .20 .50
372 Stacey Augmon BP .25 .60
373 Eric Montross BP .15 .40
374 Alonzo Mourning BP .40 1.00
375 Scottie Pippen BP .60 1.50
376 Mark Price BP .30 .75
377 Jason Kidd BP 1.00 2.50
378 Jalen Rose BP .50 1.25
379 Grant Hill BP 1.00 2.50
380 Latrell Sprewell BP .40 1.00
381 Hakeem Olajuwon BP .40 1.00
382 Reggie Miller BP .40 1.00
383 Lamond Murray BP .20 .50
384 Eddie Jones BP .60 1.50
385 Khalid Reeves BP .15 .40
386 Glenn Robinson BP .40 1.00
387 Donyell Marshall BP .20 .50
388 Derrick Coleman BP .25 .60
389 Patrick Ewing BP .40 1.00
390 Shaquille O'Neal BP .75 2.00
391 Sharone Wright BP .15 .40
392 Charles Barkley BP .50 1.25
393 Aaron McKie BP .20 .50
394 Brian Grant BP .30 .75
395 David Robinson BP .50 1.25
396 Shawn Kemp BP .30 .75
397 Karl Malone BP .40 1.00
398 Tom Gugliotta BP .20 .50
399 Hakeem Olajuwon TRIV .40 1.00
400 Shaquille O'Neal TRIV .75 2.00
401 Chris Webber TRIV .50 1.25
402 Michael Jordan TRIV 2.50 6.00
403 David Robinson TRIV .50 1.25
404 Shawn Kemp TRIV .30 .75
405 Patrick Ewing TRIV .40 1.00
406 Charles Barkley TRIV .50 1.25
407 Glenn Robinson DC .40 1.00
408 Jason Kidd DC 1.00 2.50
409 Grant Hill DC 1.00 2.50
410 Donyell Marshall DC .20 .50
411 Sharone Wright DC .15 .40
412 Lamond Murray DC .20 .50
413 Brian Grant DC .30 .75
414 Eric Montross DC .15 .40
415 Eddie Jones DC .60 1.50
416 Carlos Rogers DC .15 .40
417 Shawn Kemp CL .30 .75
418 Bobby Hurley CL .20 .50
419 Shawn Bradley CL .20 .50
420 Michael Jordan CL 2.50 6.00
421 Vernon Maxwell .20 .50
422 John Stockton .40 1.00
423 Luc Longley .25 .60
424 Sam Perkins .20 .50
425 Pooh Richardson .20 .50
426 Tyrone Corbin .20 .50
427 Mario Elie .20 .50
428 Bobby Phills .20 .50
429 Grant Hill 1.50 4.00

1994-95 Collector's Choice International French Gold Signatures

COMPLETE SET (72) 55.00 130.00
COMPLETE SERIES 1 (27) 15.00 30.00
COMPLETE SERIES 2 (45) 40.00 100.00
166 Danny Manning TO 1.00 2.50
167 Dee Brown TO .75 2.00
168 Alonzo Mourning TO 1.50 4.00
169 Scottie Pippen TO 2.50 6.00
170 Mark Price TO 1.25 3.00
171 Jamal Mashburn TO 1.25 3.00
172 Dikembe Mutombo TO 1.25 3.00
173 Joe Dumars TO 1.25 3.00
174 Chris Webber TO 2.00 5.00
175 Hakeem Olajuwon TO 1.50 4.00
176 Reggie Miller TO 1.50 4.00
177 Ron Harper TO 1.00 2.50
178 Nick Van Exel TO 1.25 3.00
179 Steve Smith TO 1.00 2.50
180 Vin Baker TO 1.25 3.00
181 Isaiah Rider TO 1.25 3.00
182 Derrick Coleman TO 1.00 2.50

183 Patrick Ewing TO 1.50 4.00
184 Shaquille O'Neal TO 3.00 8.00
185 Clarence Weatherspoon TO .75 2.00
186 Charles Barkley TO 2.00 5.00
187 Clyde Drexler TO 1.50 4.00
188 Mitch Richmond TO 1.25 3.00
189 David Robinson TO 2.00 5.00
190 Shawn Kemp TO 1.25 3.00
191 Karl Malone TO 1.50 4.00
192 Tom Gugliotta TO .75 2.00
372 Stacey Augmon BP 1.00 2.50
373 Eric Montross BP .50 1.25
374 Alonzo Mourning BP 1.50 4.00
375 Scottie Pippen BP 2.50 6.00
376 Mark Price BP 1.25 3.00
377 Jason Kidd BP 3.00 8.00
378 Jalen Rose BP 1.50 4.00
379 Grant Hill BP 3.00 8.00
380 Latrell Sprewell BP 1.50 4.00
381 Hakeem Olajuwon BP 1.50 4.00
382 Reggie Miller BP 1.50 4.00
383 Lamond Murray BP .60 1.50
384 Eddie Jones BP 2.00 5.00
385 Khalid Reeves BP .50 1.25
386 Glenn Robinson BP 1.25 3.00
387 Donyell Marshall BP .60 1.50
388 Derrick Coleman BP 1.00 2.50
389 Patrick Ewing BP 1.50 4.00
390 Shaquille O'Neal BP 3.00 8.00
391 Sharone Wright BP .50 1.25
392 Charles Barkley BP 2.00 5.00
393 Aaron McKie BP .60 1.50
394 Brian Grant BP 1.00 2.50
395 David Robinson BP 2.00 5.00
396 Shawn Kemp BP 1.25 3.00
397 Karl Malone BP 1.50 4.00
398 Tom Gugliotta BP .75 2.00
399 Hakeem Olajuwon TRIV 1.50 4.00
400 Shaquille O'Neal TRIV 3.00 8.00
401 Chris Webber TRIV 2.00 5.00
402 Michael Jordan TRIV 10.00 25.00
403 David Robinson TRIV 2.00 5.00
404 Shawn Kemp TRIV 1.25 3.00
405 Patrick Ewing TRIV 1.50 4.00
406 Charles Barkley TRIV 2.00 5.00
407 Glenn Robinson DC 1.25 3.00
408 Jason Kidd DC 3.00 8.00
409 Grant Hill DC 3.00 8.00
410 Donyell Marshall DC .60 1.50
411 Sharone Wright DC .50 1.25
412 Lamond Murray DC .60 1.50
413 Brian Grant DC 1.00 2.50
414 Eric Montross DC .50 1.25
415 Eddie Jones DC 2.00 5.00
416 Carlos Rogers DC .50 1.25

1994-95 Collector's Choice International French Decade of Dominance

Issued approximately one in every five packs of second series French, German, Italian and Spanish and one in every three second series Japanese packs, these ten standard-size cards are derived from the Decade of Dominance subset within the American 1994 Upper Deck Rare Air boxed set. The card backs are bilingual and the numbering differs from their American counterparts in the Rare Air boxed set. The horizontal fronts feature on the left a photo of Jordan dunking while the right side features various highlights from Jordan's career.

COMPLETE SET (10) 12.00 30.00
J1 Michael Jordan Career Stats 1.50 4.00
J2 Michael Jordan '84 NBA ROY 1.50 4.00
J3 Michael Jordan '87 Slam-Dunk Champion 1.50 4.00
J4 Michael Jordan NBA All-Star Game Stats 1.50 4.00
J5 Michael Jordan Efficient Scorer 1.50 4.00
J6 Michael Jordan '88 NBA Defensive POY 1.50 4.00
J7 Michael Jordan 1991 NBA Title 1.50 4.00
J8 Michael Jordan Unstoppable 1.50 4.00
J9 Michael Jordan All-NBA First Team 1.50 4.00
J10 Michael Jordan Averaging over 30 ppg 1.50 4.00

1994-95 Collector's Choice International German

COMPLETE SET (429) 20.00 50.00
COMPLETE SERIES 1 (219) 10.00 25.00
COMPLETE SERIES 2 (210) 10.00 25.00
*GERMAN: SAME VALUE AS FRENCH

1994-95 Collector's Choice International German Gold Signatures

COMPLETE SET (72) 55.00 130.00
COMPLETE SERIES 1 (27) 15.00 30.00
COMPLETE SERIES 2 (45) 40.00 100.00
*GERMAN: SAME VALUE AS FRENCH

1994-95 Collector's Choice International German Decade of Dominance

COMPLETE SET (10) 12.00 30.00
*GERMAN: SAME VALUE AS FRENCH

1994-95 Collector's Choice International Italian

COMPLETE SET (429) 20.00 50.00
COMPLETE SERIES 1 (219) 10.00 25.00
COMPLETE SERIES 2 (210) 10.00 25.00
*ITALIAN: SAME VALUE AS FRENCH

1994-95 Collector's Choice International Italian Gold Signatures

COMPLETE SET (72) 55.00 130.00
COMPLETE SERIES 1 (27) 15.00 30.00
COMPLETE SERIES 2 (45) 40.00 100.00
*ITALIAN: SAME VALUE AS FRENCH

1994-95 Collector's Choice International Italian Decade of Dominance

COMPLETE SET (10) 12.00 30.00
*ITALIAN: SAME VALUE AS FRENCH

1994-95 Collector's Choice International Japanese I

Collector's Choice Japanese is a two series set where series one is a 219-card standard size set issued by Upper Deck for the Japanese market. Cards were distributed primarily in 10-card packs (with an order form card inserted into each pack) and 30 pack boxes. Suggested retail price per pack was 300 yen (approximately three dollars in American funds). Complete Japanese 1 sets were also available in a glossy binder designed for and distributed in nine-card sheets. The cards are similar in design and numbering to the American 1994-95 Collector's Choice series 1 set. White-bordered fronts feature color player action shots. The player's name, team and position appear in a lower corner. The back carries another color player action shot at the top, with statistics and career highlights displayed below. The following subsets are included in this set: Tip-Off (166-192), All-Star Advice (193-198), NBA Profiles (199-206), Checklists (207-210), and Michael Jordan Heroes (211-219). The last nine cards in the set are derived from the American 1994-95 Upper Deck Michael Jordan Heroes insert set and are believed to be somewhat tougher to pull from packs. All cards feature information only in Japanese except for the subset cards which have information in both English and Japanese.

COMPLETE SET (219) 50.00 100.00
1 Anfernee Hardaway .60 1.50
2 Mark Macon .25 .60
3 Steve Smith .30 .75
4 Chris Webber .60 1.50
5 Donald Royal .25 .60
6 Avery Johnson .30 .75
7 Kevin Johnson .40 1.00
8 Doug Christie .25 .60
9 Derrick McKey .25 .60
10 Dennis Rodman .75 2.00
11 Scott Skiles .25 .60
12 Johnny Dawkins .25 .60
13 Kendall Gill .25 .60
14 Jeff Hornacek .30 .75
15 Latrell Sprewell .50 1.25
16 Lucious Harris .25 .60
17 Chris Mullin .40 1.00
18 John Williams .25 .60
19 Tony Campbell .25 .60
20 LaPhonso Ellis .25 .60
21 Gerald Wilkins .25 .60
22 Clyde Drexler .50 1.25
23 Michael Jordan BB 3.00 8.00
24 George Lynch .25 .60
25 Mark Price .40 1.00
26 James Robinson .25 .60
27 Elmore Spencer .25 .60
28 Stacey King .25 .60
29 Corie Blount .25 .60
30 Dell Curry .25 .60
31 Reggie Miller .50 1.25
32 Karl Malone .50 1.25
33 Scottie Pippen .75 2.00
34 Hakeem Olajuwon .50 1.25
35 Clarence Weatherspoon .25 .60
36 Kevin Edwards .25 .60
37 Pete Myers .25 .60
38 Jeff Turner .25 .60
39 Ennis Whatley .25 .60
40 Calbert Cheaney .25 .60
41 Glen Rice .40 1.00
42 Vin Baker .40 1.00
43 Grant Long .25 .60
44 Derrick Coleman .30 .75
45 Rik Smits .30 .75
46 Chris Smith .25 .60
47 Carl Herrera .25 .60
48 Bob Martin .25 .60
49 Terrell Brandon .25 .60
50 David Robinson .60 1.50
51 Danny Ferry .25 .60
52 Buck Williams .25 .60
53 Josh Grant .25 .60
54 Ed Pinckney .25 .60
55 Dikembe Mutombo .40 1.00
56 Clifford Robinson .25 .60
57 Luther Wright .25 .60
58 Scott Burrell .25 .60
59 Stacey Augmon .30 .75
60 Jeff Malone .25 .60
61 Byron Houston .25 .60
62 Anthony Peeler .25 .60
63 Michael Adams .25 .60
64 Negele Knight .25 .60
65 Terry Cummings .30 .75
66 Christian Laettner .30 .75
67 Tracy Murray .25 .60
68 Sedale Threatt .25 .60
69 Dan Majerle .40 1.00
70 Frank Brickowski .25 .60
71 Ken Norman .25 .60
72 Charles Smith .25 .60
73 Adam Keefe .25 .60
74 P.J. Brown .25 .60
75 Kevin Duckworth .25 .60
76 Shawn Bradley .25 .60
77 Darnell Mee .25 .60
78 Nick Anderson .25 .60
79 Mark West .25 .60
80 B.J. Armstrong .25 .60
81 Dennis Scott .25 .60
82 Lindsey Hunter .25 .60
83 Derek Strong .25 .60
84 Mike Brown .25 .60
85 Antonio Harvey .25 .60
86 Anthony Bonner .25 .60
87 Sam Cassell .40 1.00
88 Harold Miner .25 .60
89 Spud Webb .30 .75
90 Mookie Blaylock .25 .60
91 Greg Anthony .25 .60
92 Richard Petruska .25 .60
93 Sean Rooks .25 .60
94 Ervin Johnson .25 .60
95 Randy Brown .25 .60
96 Orlando Woolridge .25 .60
97 Charles Oakley .30 .75
98 Craig Ehlo .25 .60
99 Derek Harper .30 .75
100 Doug Edwards .25 .60
101 Muggsy Bogues .30 .75
102 Mitch Richmond .40 1.00
103 Mahmoud Abdul-Rauf .25 .60
104 Joe Dumars .40 1.00
105 Eric Riley .25 .60
106 Terry Mills .25 .60
107 Toni Kukoc .50 1.25
108 Jon Koncak .25 .60
109 Haywoode Workman .25 .60
110 Todd Day .25 .60
111 Detlef Schrempf .40 1.00
112 David Wesley .25 .60
113 Mark Jackson .30 .75
114 Doug Overton .25 .60
115 Vinny Del Negro .25 .60
116 Loy Vaught .25 .60
117 Mike Peplowski .25 .60
118 Bimbo Coles .25 .60
119 Rex Walters .25 .60
120 Sherman Douglas .25 .60
121 David Benoit .25 .60
122 John Salley .25 .60
123 Cedric Ceballos .25 .60
124 Chris Mills .25 .60
125 Robert Horry .40 1.00
126 Johnny Newman .25 .60
127 Malcolm Mackey .25 .60
128 Terry Dehere .25 .60
129 Dino Radja .25 .60
130 Reggie Williams .25 .60
131 Xavier McDaniel .25 .60
132 Bobby Hurley .25 .60
133 Alonzo Mourning .50 1.25
134 Isaiah Rider .40 1.00
135 Antoine Carr .25 .60
136 Robert Pack .25 .60
137 Walt Williams .25 .60
138 Tyrone Corbin .25 .60
139 Popeye Jones .25 .60
140 Shawn Kemp .40 1.00
141 Thurl Bailey .25 .60
142 James Worthy .50 1.25
143 Scott Haskin .25 .60
144 Hubert Davis .25 .60
145 A.C. Green .30 .75
146 Dale Davis .25 .60
147 Nate McMillan .25 .60
148 Chris Morris .25 .60
149 Will Perdue .25 .60
150 Felton Spencer .25 .60
151 Rod Strickland .25 .60
152 Blue Edwards .25 .60
153 John S. Williams .25 .60
154 Rodney Rogers .25 .60
155 Acie Earl .25 .60
156 Hersey Hawkins .25 .60
157 Jamal Mashburn .40 1.00
158 Don MacLean .25 .60
159 Micheal Williams .25 .60
160 Kenny Gattison .25 .60
161 Rich King .25 .60
162 Allan Houston .40 1.00
163 John Stockton .50 1.25
164 Kenny Anderson .30 .75
165 Shaquille O'Neal 1.00 2.50
166 Danny Manning TO .30 .75
167 Dee Brown TO .25 .60
168 Alonzo Mourning TO .50 1.25
169 Scottie Pippen TO .75 2.00
170 Mark Price TO .40 1.00
171 Jamal Mashburn TO .40 1.00
172 Dikembe Mutombo TO .40 1.00
173 Joe Dumars TO .40 1.00
174 Chris Webber TO .60 1.50
175 Hakeem Olajuwon TO .50 1.25
176 Reggie Miller TO .50 1.25
177 Ron Harper TO .30 .75
178 Nick Van Exel TO .40 1.00
179 Steve Smith TO .30 .75
180 Vin Baker TO .40 1.00
181 Isaiah Rider TO .40 1.00
182 Derrick Coleman TO .30 .75
183 Patrick Ewing TO .50 1.25
184 Shaquille O'Neal TO 1.00 2.50
185 Clarence Weatherspoon TO .25 .60
186 Charles Barkley TO .60 1.50
187 Clyde Drexler TO .50 1.25
188 Mitch Richmond TO .40 1.00
189 David Robinson TO .60 1.50
190 Shawn Kemp TO .40 1.00
191 Karl Malone TO .50 1.25
192 Tom Gugliotta TO .25 .60
193 Kenny Anderson ASA .30 .75
194 Alonzo Mourning ASA .50 1.25
195 Mark Price ASA .40 1.00
196 John Stockton ASA .50 1.25
197 Shaquille O'Neal ASA 1.00 2.50
198 Latrell Sprewell ASA .50 1.25
199 Charles Barkley PRO .60 1.50
200 Chris Webber PRO .60 1.50
201 Patrick Ewing PRO .50 1.25
202 Dennis Rodman PRO .75 2.00
203 Shawn Kemp PRO .40 1.00
204 Michael Jordan PRO 3.00 8.00
205 Shaquille O'Neal PRO 1.00 2.50
206 Larry Johnson PRO .40 1.00
207 Tim Hardaway CL .40 1.00
208 John Stockton CL .50 1.25
209 Harold Miner CL .25 .60
210 B.J.Armstrong CL .25 .60
211 Michael Jordan ROY 3.00 8.00
212 Michael Jordan 63-Pt. Game 3.00 8.00
213 Michael Jordan Slam-Dunk 3.00 8.00
214 Michael Jordan MVP 3.00 8.00
215 Michael Jordan All-Star 3.00 8.00
216 Michael Jordan 3,000-Points 3.00 8.00
217 Michael Jordan Champ. 3.00 8.00
218 Michael Jordan Decade 3.00 8.00
219 Michael Jordan CL 3.00 8.00

1994-95 Collector's Choice International Japanese II

This 210-card standard size, skip-numbered set was issued by Upper Deck for the Japanese market. Cards were distributed in 10-card packs (with an order form card in each pack) and 30-pack boxes (featuring Michael Jordan on both the wrapper and the box). Suggested retail price per pack was 300 yen (approximately three dollars in American funds). The cards are similar (though not identical) in design and numbering to the American 1994-95 Collector's Choice series 2 set. The following subsets are included in this set: Blueprints (153-179), World of Trivia (399-406), Draft Class (407-416) and Checklists (417-420). Please note that the Blueprints subset is numbered out of order in relation to the rest of the set and may be a source of confusion for collectors assembling both first and second series sets. Also, there are no cards issued between numbers 371 and 399. White-bordered fronts feature color player action shots. The player's name, team and position appear in a lower corner. The back carries another color player action shot at the top, with statistics and career highlights displayed below. All cards feature information only in Japanese except for the subset cards which have information in both English and Japanese. A special Michael Jordan Trade card (T1) was randomly inserted into 1:35 packs. The card was redeemable for a special 3 1/2" by 5" Michael Jordan "C" Sheet jumbo card.

COMPLETE SET (210) 35.00 75.00
220 Gary Payton .40 1.00
221 Tom Hammonds .25 .60
222 Danny Ainge .40 1.00
223 Gary Grant .25 .60
224 Jim Jackson .25 .60
225 Chris Gatling .25 .60
226 Sergei Bazarevich .40 1.00
227 Tony Dumas .40 1.00
228 Andrew Lang .25 .60
229 Wesley Person .40 1.00
230 Terry Porter .25 .60
231 Duane Causwell .25 .60
232 Shaquille O'Neal 1.00 2.50
233 Antonio Davis .25 .60
234 Charles Barkley .60 1.50
235 Tony Massenburg .25 .60
236 Ricky Pierce .25 .60
237 Scott Skiles .25 .60
238 Jalen Rose 1.00 2.50
239 Charlie Ward .40 1.00
240 Michael Jordan COMM 3.00 8.00
241 Elden Campbell .25 .60
242 Bill Cartwright .30 .75
243 Armon Gilliam UER Card numbered 372 .25 .60
244 Rick Fox .25 .60
245 Tim Breaux .25 .60
246 Monty Williams .30 .75
247 Dominique Wilkins .50 1.25
248 Robert Parish .40 1.00
249 Mark Jackson .30 .75
250 Jason Kidd 2.00 5.00
251 Andres Guibert .25 .60
252 Matt Geiger .25 .60
253 Stanley Roberts .25 .60
254 Jack Haley .25 .60
255 David Wingate .25 .60
256 John Crotty .25 .60
257 Brian Grant .60 1.50
258 Otis Thorpe .25 .60
259 Clifford Rozier .25 .60
260 Grant Long .25 .60
261 Eric Mobley .25 .60
262 Dickey Simpkins .30 .75
263 J.R. Reid .25 .60
264 Kevin Willis .25 .60
265 Scott Brooks .25 .60
266 Glenn Robinson .75 2.00
267 Dana Barros .25 .60
268 Ken Norman .25 .60
269 Herb Williams .25 .60
270 Dee Brown .25 .60
271 Steve Kerr .30 .75
272 Jon Barry .25 .60
273 Sean Elliott .40 1.00
274 Elliot Perry .25 .60
275 Kenny Smith .30 .75
276 Sean Rooks .25 .60
277 Gheorghe Muresan .25 .60
278 Juwan Howard .60 1.50
279 Steve Smith .30 .75
280 Anthony Bowie .25 .60
281 Moses Malone .40 1.00
282 Olden Polynice .25 .60
283 Jo Jo English .25 .60
284 Marty Conlon .25 .60
285 Sam Mitchell .25 .60
286 Doug West .25 .60
287 Cedric Ceballos .25 .60
288 Lorenzo Williams .25 .60
289 Harold Ellis .25 .60
290 Doc Rivers .30 .75
291 Keith Tower .25 .60
292 Mark Bryant .25 .60
293 Oliver Miller .25 .60
294 Michael Adams .25 .60
295 Tree Rollins .25 .60
296 Eddie Jones 1.25 3.00
297 Malik Sealy .25 .60
298 Blue Edwards .25 .60
299 Brooks Thompson .30 .75
300 Benoit Benjamin .25 .60
301 Avery Johnson .30 .75
302 Larry Johnson .40 1.00
303 John Starks .30 .75
304 Byron Scott .30 .75
305 Eric Murdock .25 .60
306 Jay Humphries .25 .60
307 Kenny Anderson .30 .75
308 Brian Williams .25 .60
309 Nick Van Exel .40 1.00
310 Tim Hardaway .40 1.00
311 Lee Mayberry .25 .60
312 Vlade Divac .40 1.00
313 Donyell Marshall .40 1.00
314 Anthony Mason .25 .60
315 Danny Manning .30 .75
316 Tyrone Hill .25 .60
317 Vincent Askew .25 .60
318 Khalid Reeves .30 .75
319 Ron Harper .30 .75
320 Brent Price .25 .60
321 Byron Houston .25 .60
322 Lamond Murray .40 1.00
323 Bryant Stith .25 .60
324 Tom Gugliotta .25 .60
325 Jerome Kersey .25 .60
326 B.J. Tyler .25 .60
327 Antonio Lang .40 1.00
328 Carlos Rogers .30 .75
329 Wayman Tisdale .25 .60
330 Kevin Gamble .25 .60
331 Eric Piatkowski .50 1.25
332 Mitchell Butler .25 .60
333 Patrick Ewing .50 1.25
334 Doug Smith .25 .60
335 Joe Kleine .25 .60
336 Keith Jennings .25 .60
337 Bill Curley .25 .60
338 Johnny Newman .25 .60
339 Howard Eisley .40 1.00
340 Willie Anderson .25 .60
341 Aaron McKie .40 1.00
342 Tom Chambers .30 .75
343 Scott Williams .25 .60
344 Harvey Grant .25 .60
345 Billy Owens .25 .60
346 Sharone Wright .30 .75
347 Michael Cage .25 .60
348 Vern Fleming .25 .60
349 Darrin Hancock .30 .75
350 Matt Fish .25 .60
351 Rony Seikaly .25 .60
352 Victor Alexander .25 .60
353 Anthony Miller .40 1.00
354 Horace Grant .30 .75
355 Jayson Williams .25 .60
356 Dale Ellis .25 .60
357 Sarunas Marciulionis .25 .60
358 Anthony Avent .25 .60
359 Rex Chapman .25 .60
360 Askia Jones .40 1.00
361 Bo Outlaw .40 1.00
362 Chuck Person .30 .75
363 Danny Schayes .25 .60
364 Morlon Wiley .25 .60
365 Dontonio Wingfield .40 1.00
366 Tony Smith .25 .60
367 Bill Wennington .25 .60
368 Bryon Russell .25 .60
369 Geert Hammink .25 .60
370 Eric Montross .30 .75
371 Cliff Levingston .25 .60
372 Stacey Augmon BP .30 .75
373 Eric Montross BP .25 .60
374 Alonzo Mourning BP .50 1.25
375 Scottie Pippen BP .75 2.00
376 Mark Price BP .40 1.00
377 Jason Kidd BP 1.50 4.00
378 Jalen Rose BP .75 2.00
379 Grant Hill BP 1.50 4.00
380 Latrell Sprewell BP .50 1.25
381 Hakeem Olajuwon BP .50 1.25
382 Reggie Miller BP .50 1.25
383 Lamond Murray BP .30 .75
384 Eddie Jones BP 1.00 2.50
385 Khalid Reeves BP .25 .60
386 Glenn Robinson BP .60 1.50
387 Donyell Marshall BP .30 .75
388 Derrick Coleman BP .30 .75
389 Patrick Ewing BP .50 1.25
390 Shaquille O'Neal BP 1.00 2.50
391 Sharone Wright BP .25 .60
392 Charles Barkley BP .60 1.50
393 Aaron McKie BP .30 .75
394 Brian Grant BP .50 1.25
395 David Robinson BP .60 1.50
396 Shawn Kemp BP .40 1.00
397 Karl Malone BP .50 1.25
398 Tom Gugliotta BP .25 .60
399 Hakeem Olajuwon TRIV .50 1.25
400 Shaquille O'Neal TRIV 1.00 2.50
401 Chris Webber TRIV .60 1.50
402 Michael Jordan TRIV 3.00 8.00
403 David Robinson TRIV .60 1.50
404 Shawn Kemp TRIV .40 1.00
405 Patrick Ewing TRIV .50 1.25
406 Charles Barkley TRIV .60 1.50
407 Glenn Robinson DC .60 1.50
408 Jason Kidd DC 1.50 4.00
409 Grant Hill DC 1.50 4.00
410 Donyell Marshall DC .30 .75
411 Sharone Wright DC .25 .60
412 Lamond Murray DC .30 .75
413 Brian Grant DC .50 1.25
414 Eric Montross DC .25 .60
415 Eddie Jones DC 1.00 2.50
416 Carlos Rogers DC .25 .60
417 Shawn Kemp CL .40 1.00
418 Bobby Hurley CL .25 .60
419 Shawn Bradley CL .25 .60
420 Michael Jordan CL 3.00 8.00
421 Vernon Maxwell .25 .60
422 John Stockton .50 1.25
423 Luc Longley .30 .75
424 Sam Perkins .25 .60
425 Pooh Richardson .25 .60
426 Tyrone Corbin .25 .60
427 Mario Elie .25 .60
428 Bobby Phills .25 .60
429 Grant Hill 2.00 5.00

1994-95 Collector's Choice International Japanese I Gold Signatures

COMPLETE SET (26) 125.00 250.00
166 Danny Manning 3.00 8.00
167 Dee Brown 2.50 6.00
168 Alonzo Mourning 5.00 12.00
169 Scottie Pippen 8.00 20.00
170 Mark Price 4.00 10.00
171 Jamal Mashburn 4.00 10.00
172 Dikembe Mutombo 4.00 10.00
173 Joe Dumars 4.00 10.00
174 Chris Webber 6.00 15.00
175 Hakeem Olajuwon 5.00 12.00
176 Reggie Miller 5.00 12.00
177 Ron Harper 3.00 8.00
178 Nick Van Exel 4.00 10.00
179 Steve Smith 3.00 8.00
180 Vin Baker 4.00 10.00
181 Isaiah Rider 4.00 10.00
182 Derrick Coleman 3.00 8.00
183 Patrick Ewing 5.00 12.00
184 Shaquille O'Neal 10.00 25.00
186 Charles Barkley 6.00 15.00
187 Clyde Drexler 5.00 12.00
188 Mitch Richmond 4.00 10.00
189 David Robinson 6.00 15.00
190 Shawn Kemp 4.00 10.00
191 Karl Malone 5.00 12.00
192 Tom Gugliotta 2.50 6.00

1994-95 Collector's Choice International Japanese II Gold Signatures

COMPLETE SET (44) 200.00 400.00
372 Stacey Augmon BP 3.00 8.00
373 Eric Montross BP 1.50 4.00
374 Alonzo Mourning BP 5.00 12.00
375 Scottie Pippen BP 8.00 20.00
376 Mark Price BP 4.00 10.00
377 Jason Kidd BP 10.00 25.00
378 Jalen Rose BP 5.00 12.00
379 Grant Hill BP 10.00 25.00
380 Latrell Sprewell BP 5.00 12.00
381 Hakeem Olajuwon BP 5.00 12.00
382 Reggie Miller BP 5.00 12.00
383 Lamond Murray BP 2.00 5.00
384 Eddie Jones BP 6.00 15.00
385 Khalid Reeves BP 1.50 4.00
386 Glenn Robinson BP 4.00 10.00
387 Donyell Marshall BP 2.00 5.00
388 Derrick Coleman BP 3.00 8.00
389 Patrick Ewing BP 5.00 12.00
390 Shaquille O'Neal BP 10.00 25.00
391 Sharone Wright BP 1.50 4.00
392 Charles Barkley BP 6.00 15.00
393 Aaron McKie BP 2.00 5.00
394 Brian Grant BP 3.00 8.00
395 David Robinson BP 6.00 15.00
396 Shawn Kemp BP 4.00 10.00
397 Karl Malone BP 5.00 12.00
398 Tom Gugliotta BP 2.50 6.00
400 Shaquille O'Neal TRIV 10.00 25.00
401 Chris Webber TRIV 6.00 15.00
402 Michael Jordan TRIV 30.00 80.00
403 David Robinson TRIV 6.00 15.00
404 Shawn Kemp TRIV 4.00 10.00
405 Patrick Ewing TRIV 5.00 12.00
406 Charles Barkley TRIV 6.00 15.00
407 Glenn Robinson DC 4.00 10.00
408 Jason Kidd DC 10.00 25.00
409 Grant Hill DC 10.00 25.00
410 Donyell Marshall DC 2.00 5.00
411 Sharone Wright DC 1.50 4.00
412 Lamond Murray DC 2.00 5.00
413 Brian Grant DC 3.00 8.00
414 Eric Montross DC 1.50 4.00
415 Eddie Jones DC 6.00 15.00
416 Carlos Rogers DC 1.50 4.00

1994-95 Collector's Choice International Japanese Silver Signatures

COMPLETE SET (25) 6.00 15.00
166 Danny Manning TO .50 1.25
167 Dee Brown TO .40 1.00
168 Alonzo Mourning TO .75 2.00
169 Scottie Pippen TO 1.25 3.00
170 Mark Price TO .60 1.50
171 Jamal Mashburn TO .60 1.50
172 Dikembe Mutombo TO .60 1.50
173 Joe Dumars TO .60 1.50
174 Chris Webber TO 1.00 2.50
175 Hakeem Olajuwon TO .75 2.00
177 Ron Harper TO .50 1.25
178 Nick Van Exel TO .60 1.50
179 Steve Smith TO .50 1.25
180 Vin Baker TO .60 1.50
181 Isaiah Rider TO .60 1.50
182 Derrick Coleman TO .50 1.25
183 Patrick Ewing TO .75 2.00
184 Shaquille O'Neal TO 1.50 4.00
185 Clarence Weatherspoon TO .40 1.00
187 Clyde Drexler TO .75 2.00
188 Mitch Richmond TO .60 1.50
189 David Robinson TO 1.00 2.50
190 Shawn Kemp TO .60 1.50
191 Karl Malone TO .75 2.00
192 Tom Gugliotta TO .40 1.00

1994-95 Collector's Choice International Japanese Decade of Dominance

COMPLETE SET (10) 30.00 80.00
COMMON CARD 4.00 10.00

1994-95 Collector's Choice International Spanish I

This 219-card standard size set was issued by Upper Deck for the Spanish market. Cards were distributed in 10-card packs and 30 pack boxes (featuring Michael Jordan on both wrappers and boxes). Cards were distributed in 10-card packs and 30 pack boxes (featuring Michael Jordan on both wrappers and boxes). The first 210 cards are similar in design and numbering to the American 1994-95 Collector's Choice set. White-bordered fronts feature color player action shots. The player's name, team and position appear in a lower corner. The back carries another color player action shot at the top, with statistics and career highlights displayed below. The following subsets are included in this set: Tip-Off (166-192), All-Star Advice (193-198), NBA Profiles (199-206), Checklists (207-210), and Michael Jordan Heroes (211-219). The last nine cards in the set are derived from the American 1994-95 Upper Deck Michael Jordan Heroes insert set. All cards feature bilingual information (Spanish and English). This product has been made readily available to the U.S. market through closeouts.

COMPLETE SET (219) 10.00 25.00
*SPANISH: SAME VALUE AS FRENCH

1994-95 Collector's Choice International Spanish II

This 210-card standard-size set was issued by Upper Deck for the Spanish market. Cards were issued in 6-card packs and 50-pack boxes (featuring Shawn Kemp on both the wrapper and box). The cards are similar in design to the American 1994-95 Collector's Choice set. Spanish 2 card sequencing from 1-201 mirrors the American Collector's Choice from 220-420 and Spanish 2 card sequencing from 202-210 mirror the American cards 211-219. The numbering may be a source of confusion for collectors pursuing both first and second series Spanish cards. White-bordered fronts feature color player action shots. The player's name, team, and position appear in a lower corner. The back carries another color player action shot at the top, with statistics and career highlights displayed below. The cards all have bilingual (English and Spanish) information on the back. The following subsets are included in the set: Blueprint for Success (153-179), Dr. Basketball's World of Trivia (180- 187), 1994 Draft Class (188-197), and Checklists (198-201). This product has been made readily available through closeouts.

COMPLETE SET (210) 10.00 20.00
*SPANISH: SAME VALUE AS FRENCH

1994-95 Collector's Choice International Spanish Gold Signatures

COMPLETE SET (72) 55.00 130.00
COMPLETE SERIES 1 (27) 15.00 30.00
COMPLETE SERIES 2 (45) 40.00 100.00
*SPANISH: SAME VALUE AS FRENCH

1994-95 Collector's Choice International Spanish Decade of Dominance

COMPLETE SET (10) 12.00 30.00
*SPANISH: SAME VALUE AS FRENCH

1995-96 Collector's Choice International French I

Consisting of 210 cards, the 1995-96 Collector's Choice International set was distributed in France, Germany, Italy, Latin America, Northern Europe, Portugal and Spain. These cards are identical in design to the 1995-96 Collector's Choice American cards except for bilingual text for the respective countries and the regular card numbering. The first series subsets replicate the exact numbering used for the first series American issue. All countries received 10-card packs and 30-pack boxes. This product has been made available to the U.S. market through closeouts.

COMPLETE SET (210) 8.00 20.00
1 Craig Ehlo .10 .25
2 Tyrone Corbin .10 .25
3 Mookie Blaylock .10 .25
4 Grant Long .10 .25
5 Andrew Lang .10 .25
6 Stacey Augmon .12 .30
7 Dee Brown .10 .25
8 Sherman Douglas .10 .25
9 Pervis Ellison .10 .25
10 Dominique Wilkins .20 .50
11 Greg Minor .10 .25
12 Larry Johnson .15 .40
13 Dell Curry .10 .25
14 Scott Burrell .10 .25
15 Robert Parish .15 .40
16 Michael Adams .10 .25
17 David Wingate .10 .25
18 Hersey Hawkins .10 .25
19 B.J. Armstrong .10 .25
20 Michael Jordan 1.25 3.00
21 Dickey Simpkins .10 .25
22 Will Perdue .10 .25
23 Steve Kerr .12 .30
24 Ron Harper .12 .30
25 Tyrone Hill .10 .25
26 Bobby Phills .10 .25
27 Michael Cage .10 .25
28 John Williams .10 .25
29 Mark Price .15 .40
30 Danny Ferry .10 .25
31 Jason Kidd .25 .60
32 Roy Tarpley .10 .25
33 Popeye Jones .10 .25
34 Tony Dumas .10 .25
35 Lucious Harris .10 .25
36 Jim Jackson .10 .25
37 Mahmoud Abdul-Rauf .10 .25
38 Brian Williams .10 .25
39 Rodney Rogers .10 .25
40 LaPhonso Ellis .10 .25
41 Reggie Williams .10 .25
42 Bryant Stith .10 .25
43 Joe Dumars .15 .40
44 Oliver Miller .10 .25
45 Grant Hill .25 .60
46 Bill Curley .10 .25
47 Allan Houston .12 .30
48 Mark West .10 .25
49 Rony Seikaly .10 .25
50 Chris Gatling .10 .25
51 Carlos Rogers .10 .25
52 Tim Hardaway .15 .40
53 Chris Mullin .15 .40
54 Donyell Marshall .10 .25
55 Clyde Drexler .20 .50
56 Kenny Smith .12 .30
57 Carl Herrera .10 .25
58 Robert Horry .12 .30
59 Sam Cassell .15 .40
60 Dale Davis .10 .25
61 Byron Scott .12 .30
62 Rik Smits .12 .30
63 Duane Ferrell .10 .25
64 Derrick McKey .10 .25
65 Reggie Miller .20 .50
66 Eric Piatkowski .12 .30
67 Malik Sealy .10 .25
68 Terry Dehere .10 .25
69 Bo Outlaw .10 .25
70 Lamond Murray .10 .25
71 Loy Vaught .10 .25
72 Nick Van Exel .15 .40
73 Antonio Harvey .10 .25
74 Vlade Divac .15 .40
75 Elden Campbell .10 .25
76 Anthony Peeler .10 .25
77 Eddie Jones .15 .40
78 Harold Miner .10 .25
79 Billy Owens .10 .25
80 Bimbo Coles .10 .25
81 Kevin Gamble .10 .25
82 John Salley .10 .25
83 Kevin Willis .10 .25
84 Khalid Reeves .10 .25
85 Ed Pinckney .10 .25
86 Vin Baker .12 .30
87 Todd Day .10 .25
88 Eric Mobley .10 .25
89 Marty Conlon .10 .25
90 Lee Mayberry .10 .25
91 Micheal Williams .10 .25
92 Tom Gugliotta .10 .25
93 Doug West .10 .25
94 Isaiah Rider .15 .40
95 Christian Laettner .12 .30
96 Chris Smith .10 .25
97 Armon Gilliam .10 .25
98 P.J. Brown .10 .25
99 Rex Walters .10 .25
100 Benoit Benjamin .10 .25
101 Kenny Anderson .12 .30
102 Derrick Coleman .12 .30
103 Derek Harper .12 .30
104 Charles Smith .10 .25
105 Herb Williams .10 .25
106 John Starks .12 .30
107 Charles Oakley .12 .30
108 Hubert Davis .10 .25
109 Dennis Scott .10 .25
110 Jeff Turner .10 .25
111 Horace Grant .12 .30
112 Anthony Bowie .10 .25
113 Anfernee Hardaway .25 .60
114 Nick Anderson .10 .25
115 Dana Barros .10 .25
116 Scott Williams .10 .25
117 Clarence Weatherspoon .10 .25
118 Jeff Malone .10 .25
119 B.J. Tyler .10 .25
120 Shawn Bradley .10 .25
121 Charles Barkley .25 .60
122 A.C. Green .12 .30
123 Kevin Johnson .15 .40
124 Wayman Tisdale .10 .25
125 Danny Schayes .10 .25
126 Dan Majerle .15 .40
127 Rod Strickland .10 .25
128 Harvey Grant .10 .25
129 Aaron McKie .10 .25
130 Chris Dudley .10 .25
131 Otis Thorpe .10 .25
132 Jerome Kersey .10 .25
133 Clifford Robinson .10 .25
134 Bobby Hurley .10 .25
135 Spud Webb .12 .30
136 Olden Polynice .10 .25
137 Randy Brown .10 .25
138 Brian Grant .12 .30
139 Walt Williams .10 .25
140 Avery Johnson .12 .30
141 Dennis Rodman .30 .75
142 J.R. Reid .10 .25
143 David Robinson .25 .60
144 Vinny Del Negro .10 .25
145 Willie Anderson .10 .25
146 Nate McMillan .10 .25
147 Shawn Kemp .15 .40
148 Detlef Schrempf .15 .40
149 Vincent Askew .10 .25
150 Sarunas Marciulionis .10 .25
151 Byron Houston .10 .25
152 Ervin Johnson .10 .25
153 Adam Keefe .10 .25
154 Jeff Hornacek .12 .30
155 Antoine Carr .10 .25
156 John Stockton .20 .50
157 Blue Edwards .10 .25
158 David Benoit .10 .25
159 Don MacLean .10 .25
160 Juwan Howard .15 .40
161 Calbert Cheaney .10 .25
162 Mitchell Butler .10 .25
163 Gheorghe Muresan .10 .25
164 Rex Chapman .10 .25
165 Doug Overton .10 .25
166 Steve Smith FF .12 .30
167 Dino Radja FF .10 .25
168 Alonzo Mourning FF .20 .50
169 Michael Jordan FF 1.25 3.00
170 Tyrone Hill FF .10 .25
171 Jamal Mashburn FF .15 .40
172 Dikembe Mutombo FF .15 .40
173 Grant Hill FF with Michael Jordan .40 1.00
174 Latrell Sprewell FF .15 .40
175 Hakeem Olajuwon FF .20 .50
176 Reggie Miller FF .20 .50
177 Pooh Richardson FF .10 .25
178 Cedric Ceballos FF .10 .25
179 Glen Rice FF .15 .40
180 Glenn Robinson FF .12 .30
181 Isaiah Rider FF .15 .40
182 Derrick Coleman FF .12 .30
183 Patrick Ewing FF .20 .50
184 Shaquille O'Neal FF .40 1.00
185 Dana Barros FF .10 .25
186 Dan Majerle FF .15 .40
187 Clifford Robinson FF .10 .25
188 Mitch Richmond FF .15 .40
189 David Robinson FF .25 .60
190 Gary Payton FF .15 .40
191 Oliver Miller FF .10 .25

192 Karl Malone FF .20 .50
193 Kevin Pritchard FF .10 .25
194 Chris Webber FF .20 .50
195 Michael Jordan PD 1.25 3.00
196 Hakeem Olajuwon PD .20 .50
197 Vin Baker PD .12 .30
198 Grant Hill PD .25 .60
199 Clyde Drexler PD .20 .50
200 Chris Webber PD .20 .50
201 Shawn Kemp PD .15 .40
202 Shaquille O'Neal PD .40 1.00
203 Stacey Augmon PD .12 .30
204 David Benoit PD .10 .25
205 Rodney Rogers PD .10 .25
206 Latrell Sprewell PD .15 .40
207 Brian Grant PD .12 .30
208 Lamond Murray PD .10 .25
209 Shawn Kemp CL .15 .40
210 Michael Jordan CL 1.25 3.00

1995-96 Collector's Choice International French II

The series two Collector's Choice International set contains 200-cards and was distributed in France, Germany, Italy, Latin America, Northern Europe, Portugal and Spain. Packs contained 10 cards and boxes contained 30 packs. Though player content is the same as the American series two Collector's Choice the order of the cards and numbering is entirely different. Unlike the American cards, basic issue cards were placed in team order alphabetically by the city. Also, unlike the American issue, the cards are not numbered as a continuation of the first series. The second series set was numbered 1-200, which may create some confusion for collectors who have obtained both first and second series cards. This product has been made available to the U.S. market through closeouts.

COMPLETE SET (200) 8.00 20.00
1 Alan Henderson .15 .40
2 Steve Smith .12 .30
3 Ken Norman .10 .25
4 Eric Montross .10 .25
5 Dino Radja .10 .25
6 Rick Fox .10 .25
7 David Wesley .10 .25
8 Dana Barros .10 .25
9 Eric Williams .15 .40
10 George Zidek .12 .30
11 Muggsy Bogues .12 .30
12 Kendall Gill .10 .25
13 Scottie Pippen .25 .60
14 Bill Wennington .10 .25
15 Dennis Rodman .30 .75
16 Toni Kukoc .15 .40
17 Luc Longley .12 .30
18 Jason Caffey .15 .40
19 Chris Mills .10 .25
20 Terrell Brandon .10 .25
21 Bob Sura .12 .30
22 Cherokee Parks .12 .30
23 Lorenzo Williams .10 .25
24 Jamal Mashburn .15 .40
25 Terry Davis .10 .25
26 Loren Meyer .10 .25
27 Bryant Stith .10 .25
28 Dikembe Mutombo .15 .40
29 Jalen Rose .20 .50
30 Tom Hammonds .10 .25
31 Terry Mills .10 .25
32 Lindsey Hunter .10 .25
33 Theo Ratliff .25 .60
34 Latrell Sprewell .15 .40
35 Andrew DeClercq .15 .40
36 B.J. Armstrong .10 .25
37 Clifford Rozier .10 .25
38 Joe Smith .20 .50
39 Mark Bryant .10 .25
40 Mario Elie .10 .25
41 Hakeem Olajuwon .20 .50
42 Antonio Davis .10 .25
43 Haywoode Workman .10 .25
44 Mark Jackson .12 .30
45 Travis Best .15 .40
46 Brian Williams .10 .25
47 Rodney Rogers .10 .25
48 Brent Barry .25 .60
49 Pooh Richardson .10 .25
50 Gary Grant .10 .25
51 George Lynch .10 .25
52 Sedale Threatt .10 .25
53 Cedric Ceballos .10 .25
54 Sasha Danilovic .15 .40
55 Kurt Thomas .15 .40
56 Glenn Robinson .12 .30
57 Shawn Respert .12 .30
58 Eric Murdock .10 .25
59 Kevin Garnett 1.25 3.00
60 Kevin Edwards .10 .25
61 Ed O'Bannon .12 .30
62 Yinka Dare .10 .25
63 Vern Fleming .10 .25
64 Patrick Ewing .20 .50
65 Monty Williams .10 .25
66 Anthony Mason .10 .25
67 Donald Royal .10 .25
68 Brian Shaw .10 .25
69 Shaquille O'Neal .40 1.00
70 David Vaughn .15 .40
71 Vernon Maxwell .10 .25
72 Jerry Stackhouse .50 1.25
73 Sharone Wright .10 .25
74 Richard Dumas .10 .25
75 Wesley Person .10 .25
76 Joe Kleine .10 .25
77 Elliot Perry .10 .25
78 Danny Manning .12 .30
79 Michael Finley .50 1.25
80 Mario Bennett .12 .30
81 James Robinson .10 .25
82 Buck Williams .10 .25
83 Gary Trent .15 .40
84 Randolph Childress .12 .30
85 Duane Causwell .10 .25
86 Lionel Simmons .10 .25
87 Mitch Richmond .15 .40
88 Michael Smith .10 .25
89 Tyus Edney .15 .40
90 Corliss Williamson .15 .40
91 Cory Alexander .15 .40
92 Chuck Person .12 .30
93 Sean Elliott .15 .40
94 Doc Rivers .12 .30
95 Gary Payton .15 .40
96 Sam Perkins .10 .25
97 Sherrell Ford .12 .30
98 Damon Stoudamire .40 1.00
99 Zan Tabak .10 .25
100 Felton Spencer .10 .25
101 Karl Malone .20 .50
102 Bryon Russell .10 .25
103 Greg Ostertag .15 .40
104 Bryant Reeves .12 .30
105 Lawrence Moten .15 .40
106 Greg Anthony .10 .25
107 Byron Scott .12 .30
108 Scott Skiles .10 .25
109 Rasheed Wallace .50 1.25
110 Chris Webber .20 .50
111 Mookie Blaylock SR .10 .25
112 Dee Brown SR .10 .25
113 Alonzo Mourning SR .20 .50
114 Michael Jordan SR 1.25 3.00
115 Terrell Brandon SR .10 .25
116 Jim Jackson SR .10 .25
117 Dikembe Mutombo SR .15 .40
118 Grant Hill SR .25 .60
119 Joe Smith SR .20 .50
120 Clyde Drexler SR .20 .50
121 Reggie Miller SR .20 .50
122 Lamond Murray SR .10 .25
123 Nick Van Exel SR .15 .40
124 Glen Rice SR .15 .40
125 Glenn Robinson SR .12 .30
126 Christian Laettner SR .12 .30
127 Kenny Anderson SR .12 .30
128 Patrick Ewing SR .20 .50
129 Shaquille O'Neal SR .40 1.00
130 Jerry Stackhouse SR .50 1.25
131 Charles Barkley SR .25 .60
132 Clifford Robinson SR .10 .25
133 Brian Grant SR .12 .30
134 David Robinson SR .25 .60
135 Shawn Kemp SR .15 .40
136 Damon Stoudamire SR .40 1.00
137 Karl Malone SR .20 .50
138 Bryant Reeves SR .12 .30
139 Juwan Howard SR .15 .40
140 Nick Anderson .10 .25
Dee Brown PT
141 Rik Smits PT .12 .30
142 Herb Williams .10 .25
Tom Tolbert PT
143 Michael Jordan PT 1.25 3.00
144 David Robinson PT .25 .60
145 Terry Porter .15 .40
Kevin Johnson PT
146 Clyde Drexler PT .20 .50
147 Cedric Ceballos PT .10 .25
148 Horace Grant .12 .30
Group PT
149 Reggie Miller PT .20 .50
150 Avery Johnson .15 .40
Nick Van Exel PT
151 Hakeem Olajuwon .20 .50
Robert Horry PT
152 Rik Smits PT .12 .30
153 David Robinson .25 .60
Hakeem Olajuwon PT
154 Robert Horry PT .12 .30
155 Kenny Smith PT .12 .30
156 Stacey Augmon LOVE .12 .30
157 Sherman Douglas LOVE .10 .25
158 Larry Johnson LOVE .15 .40
159 Scottie Pippen LOVE .25 .60
160 Tyrone Hill LOVE .10 .25
161 Jamal Mashburn LOVE .15 .40
162 Mahmoud Abdul-Rauf LOVE .10 .25
163 Grant Hill LOVE .25 .60
164 Latrell Sprewell LOVE .15 .40
165 Sam Cassell LOVE .15 .40
166 Rik Smits LOVE .12 .30
167 Terry Dehere LOVE .10 .25
168 Eddie Jones LOVE .15 .40
169 Billy Owens LOVE .10 .25
170 Vin Baker LOVE .12 .30
171 Isaiah Rider LOVE .15 .40
172 Kenny Anderson LOVE .12 .30
173 John Starks LOVE .12 .30
174 Anfernee Hardaway LOVE .25 .60
175 Sharone Wright LOVE .10 .25
176 Charles Barkley LOVE .25 .60
177 Clifford Robinson LOVE .10 .25
178 Walt Williams LOVE .10 .25
179 Sean Elliott LOVE .15 .40
180 Gary Payton LOVE .15 .40
181 Carlos Rogers LOVE .10 .25
182 John Stockton LOVE .20 .50
183 Greg Anthony LOVE .10 .25
184 Chris Webber LOVE .20 .50
185 Gary Payton PG .15 .40
186 Mookie Blaylock PG .10 .25
187 Charles Barkley PG .25 .60
188 Grant Hill PG .25 .60
189 Anfernee Hardaway PG .25 .60
190 Kenny Anderson PG .12 .30
191 Mark Jackson PG .12 .30
192 Karl Malone PG .20 .50
193 Avery Johnson PG .12 .30
194 Larry Johnson 40 .15 .40
195 Nick Van Exel 40 .15 .40
196 Vin Baker 40 .12 .30
197 Jason Kidd 40 .25 .60
198 David Robinson 40 .25 .60
199 Shawn Kemp CL .15 .40
200 Michael Jordan CL 1.25 3.00

1995-96 Collector's Choice International French Crash the Game

COMPLETE SET (30) 20.00 50.00
C1 Michael Jordan 8.00 20.00
C2 Kenny Anderson .75 2.00
C3 Charles Barkley 1.50 4.00
C4 Dana Barros .60 1.50
C5 Anfernee Hardaway 1.50 4.00
C6 Mookie Blaylock .60 1.50
C7 Lamond Murray .60 1.50
C8 Karl Malone 1.25 3.00
C9 Alonzo Mourning 1.25 3.00
C10 Hakeem Olajuwon 1.25 3.00
C11 Mark Price 1.00 2.50
C12 Isaiah Rider 1.00 2.50
C13 Glen Rice 1.00 2.50
C14 Mitch Richmond 1.00 2.50
C15 Chris Webber 1.25 3.00
C16 Nick Van Exel 1.00 2.50
C17 Mahmoud Abdul-Rauf .60 1.50
C18 Dominique Wilkins 1.25 3.00
C19 Patrick Ewing 1.25 3.00
C20 David Robinson 1.50 4.00
C21 Shawn Kemp 1.00 2.50
C22 Jason Kidd 1.50 4.00
C23 Glenn Robinson .75 2.00
C24 Reggie Miller 1.25 3.00
C25 Joe Dumars 1.00 2.50
C26 Latrell Sprewell 1.00 2.50
C27 Clifford Robinson .60 1.50
C28 Damon Stoudamire 2.50 6.00
C29 Bryant Reeves .75 2.00
C30 Michael Jordan 8.00 20.00

1995-96 Collector's Choice International French Jordan Collection

Randomly inserted into one in every eleven second series packs of French, German, Italian, Japanese, Latin, Northern European and Portugese packs. These cards are based upon the American second series Collector's Choice Jordan Collection inserts, but were renumbered in the European issue.

COMPLETE SET (4) 5.00 12.00
COMMON CARD (J1-J4) 1.50 4.00

1995-96 Collector's Choice International French NBA Extremes

Randomly inserted into one in every ten second series packs of French, German, Italian, Japanese, Latin, Northern European and Portugese. These cards were exclusive to the International product line and were not derived from any previous American Upper Deck issue.

COMPLETE SET (9) 1.50 4.00
E1 Muggsy Bogues .40 1.00
E2 Spud Webb .40 1.00
E3 Dana Barros .30 .75
E4 Avery Johnson .40 1.00
E5 Vlade Divac .50 1.25
E6 Dikembe Mutombo .50 1.25
E7 Rik Smits .40 1.00
E8 Shawn Bradley .30 .75
E9 Gheorghe Muresan .30 .75

1995-96 Collector's Choice International Special Edition Holograms

Randomly inserted in all first series International foil packs, this set of nine holograms was based upon the American 1994-95 Upper Deck Special Edition inserts. The cards were randomly seeded into 1:5 packs of French, German, Italian and Japanese and 1:10 packs of Latin and Spanish. Unlike the American cards, the fronts display full-bleed holograms except at the upper left, where a black stripe carries the player's name (in gold foil) and position. The backs carry a color action photo and 1994-95 season statistics.

COMPLETE SET (9) 4.00 10.00
H1 Larry Johnson .60 1.50
H2 Scottie Pippen 1.00 2.50
H3 Grant Hill 1.00 2.50
H4 Reggie Miller .75 2.00
H5 Glenn Robinson .50 1.25
H6 Patrick Ewing .75 2.00
H7 Shaquille O'Neal 1.50 4.00
H8 John Stockton .75 2.00
H9 Chris Webber .75 2.00

1995-96 Collector's Choice International German I

COMPLETE SET (210) 8.00 20.00
*GERMAN: SAME VALUE AS FRENCH

1995-96 Collector's Choice International German II

COMPLETE SET (200) 8.00 20.00
*GERMAN: SAME VALUE AS FRENCH

1995-96 Collector's Choice International German Jordan Collection

COMPLETE SET (4) 5.00 12.00
*GERMAN: SAME VALUE AS FRENCH

1995-96 Collector's Choice International German NBA Extremes

COMPLETE SET (9) 1.50 4.00
*GERMAN: SAME VALUE AS FRENCH

1995-96 Collector's Choice International Italian I

COMPLETE SET (210) 8.00 20.00
*ITALIAN: SAME VALUE AS FRENCH

1995-96 Collector's Choice International Italian II

COMPLETE SET (200) 8.00 20.00
*ITALIAN: SAME VALUE AS FRENCH

1995-96 Collector's Choice International Italian Jordan Collection

COMPLETE SET (4) 5.00 12.00
*ITALIAN: SAME VALUE AS FRENCH

1995-96 Collector's Choice International Italian NBA Extremes

COMPLETE SET (9) 1.50 4.00
*ITALIAN: SAME VALUE AS FRENCH

1995-96 Collector's Choice International Northern European

COMPLETE SET (200)
*NORTHERN EUROPEAN: SAME VALUE AS FRENCH

1995-96 Collector's Choice International Northern European NBA Extremes

COMPLETE SET (9) 1.50 4.00
*NORTHERN EUROPEAN: SAME VALUE AS FRENCH

1995-96 Collector's Choice International Japanese

Consisting of 410 cards released in two separate series of 210 and 200 cards respectively, the 1995-96 Collector's Choice Japanese set is identical in design (excexcept for bilingual text) and numbering to the cards released in the 1995-96 American series. The cards were sold in 10-card packs and 30-pack boxes.

COMPLETE SET (410) 110.00 220.00
COMPLETE SERIES 1 (210) 50.00 100.00
COMPLETE SERIES 2 (200) 60.00 120.00
1 Craig Ehlo .40 1.00
2 Tyrone Corbin .40 1.00
3 Mookie Blaylock .40 1.00
4 Grant Long .40 1.00
5 Andrew Lang .40 1.00
6 Stacey Augmon .50 1.25
7 Dee Brown .40 1.00
8 Sherman Douglas .40 1.00
9 Pervis Ellison .40 1.00
10 Dominique Wilkins .75 2.00
11 Greg Minor .40 1.00
12 Larry Johnson .60 1.50
13 Dell Curry .40 1.00
14 Scott Burrell .40 1.00
15 Robert Parish .60 1.50
16 Michael Adams .40 1.00
17 David Wingate .40 1.00
18 Hersey Hawkins .40 1.00
19 B.J. Armstrong .40 1.00
20 Michael Jordan 5.00 12.00
21 Dickey Simpkins .40 1.00
22 Will Perdue .40 1.00
23 Steve Kerr .50 1.25
24 Ron Harper .50 1.25
25 Tyrone Hill .40 1.00
26 Bobby Phills .40 1.00
27 Michael Cage .40 1.00
28 John Williams .40 1.00
29 Mark Price .60 1.50
30 Danny Ferry .40 1.00
31 Jason Kidd 1.00 2.50
32 Roy Tarpley .40 1.00
33 Popeye Jones .40 1.00
34 Tony Dumas .40 1.00
35 Lucious Harris .40 1.00
36 Jim Jackson .40 1.00
37 Mahmoud Abdul-Rauf .40 1.00
38 Brian Williams .40 1.00
39 Rodney Rogers .40 1.00
40 LaPhonso Ellis .40 1.00
41 Reggie Williams .40 1.00
42 Bryant Stith .40 1.00
43 Joe Dumars .60 1.50
44 Oliver Miller .40 1.00
45 Grant Hill 1.00 2.50
46 Bill Curley .40 1.00
47 Allan Houston .50 1.25
48 Mark West .40 1.00
49 Rony Seikaly .40 1.00
50 Chris Gatling .40 1.00
51 Carlos Rogers .40 1.00
52 Tim Hardaway .60 1.50
53 Chris Mullin .60 1.50
54 Donyell Marshall .40 1.00
55 Clyde Drexler .75 2.00
56 Kenny Smith .50 1.25
57 Carl Herrera .40 1.00
58 Robert Horry .50 1.25
59 Sam Cassell .60 1.50
60 Dale Davis .40 1.00
61 Byron Scott .50 1.25
62 Rik Smits .50 1.25
63 Duane Ferrell .40 1.00
64 Derrick McKey .40 1.00
65 Reggie Miller .75 2.00
66 Eric Piatkowski .50 1.25
67 Malik Sealy .40 1.00
68 Terry Dehere .40 1.00
69 Bo Outlaw .40 1.00
70 Lamond Murray .40 1.00
71 Loy Vaught .40 1.00
72 Nick Van Exel .60 1.50
73 Antonio Harvey .40 1.00
74 Vlade Divac .60 1.50
75 Elden Campbell .40 1.00
76 Anthony Peeler .40 1.00
77 Eddie Jones .60 1.50
78 Harold Miner .40 1.00
79 Billy Owens .40 1.00
80 Bimbo Coles .40 1.00
81 Kevin Gamble .40 1.00
82 John Salley .40 1.00
83 Kevin Willis .40 1.00
84 Khalid Reeves .40 1.00
85 Ed Pinckney .40 1.00
86 Vin Baker .50 1.25
87 Todd Day .40 1.00
88 Eric Mobley .40 1.00
89 Marty Conlon .40 1.00
90 Lee Mayberry .40 1.00
91 Micheal Williams .40 1.00
92 Tom Gugliotta .40 1.00
93 Doug West .40 1.00
94 Isaiah Rider .60 1.50
95 Christian Laettner .50 1.25
96 Chris Smith .40 1.00
97 Armon Gilliam .40 1.00
98 P.J. Brown .40 1.00
99 Rex Walters .40 1.00
100 Benoit Benjamin .40 1.00
101 Kenny Anderson .50 1.25
102 Derrick Coleman .50 1.25
103 Derek Harper .50 1.25
104 Charles Smith .40 1.00
105 Herb Williams .40 1.00
106 John Starks .50 1.25
107 Charles Oakley .50 1.25
108 Hubert Davis .40 1.00
109 Dennis Scott .40 1.00
110 Jeff Turner .40 1.00
111 Horace Grant .50 1.25
112 Anthony Bowie .40 1.00
113 Anfernee Hardaway 1.00 2.50
114 Nick Anderson .40 1.00
115 Dana Barros .40 1.00
116 Scott Williams .40 1.00
117 Clarence Weatherspoon .40 1.00
118 Jeff Malone .40 1.00
119 B.J. Tyler .40 1.00
120 Shawn Bradley .40 1.00
121 Charles Barkley 1.00 2.50
122 A.C. Green .50 1.25
123 Kevin Johnson .60 1.50
124 Wayman Tisdale .40 1.00
125 Danny Schayes .40 1.00
126 Dan Majerle .60 1.50
127 Rod Strickland .40 1.00
128 Harvey Grant .40 1.00
129 Aaron McKie .40 1.00
130 Chris Dudley .40 1.00
131 Otis Thorpe .40 1.00
132 Jerome Kersey .40 1.00
133 Clifford Robinson .40 1.00
134 Bobby Hurley .40 1.00
135 Spud Webb .50 1.25
136 Olden Polynice .40 1.00
137 Randy Brown .40 1.00
138 Brian Grant .50 1.25
139 Walt Williams .40 1.00
140 Avery Johnson .50 1.25
141 Dennis Rodman 1.25 3.00
142 J.R. Reid .40 1.00
143 David Robinson 1.00 2.50
144 Vinny Del Negro .40 1.00
145 Willie Anderson .40 1.00
146 Nate McMillan .40 1.00
147 Shawn Kemp .60 1.50
148 Detlef Schrempf .60 1.50
149 Vincent Askew .40 1.00
150 Sarunas Marciulionis .40 1.00
151 Byron Houston .40 1.00
152 Ervin Johnson .40 1.00
153 Adam Keefe .40 1.00
154 Jeff Hornacek .50 1.25
155 Antoine Carr .40 1.00
156 John Stockton .75 2.00
157 Blue Edwards .40 1.00
158 David Benoit .40 1.00
159 Don MacLean .40 1.00
160 Juwan Howard .60 1.50
161 Calbert Cheaney .40 1.00
162 Mitchell Butler .40 1.00
163 Gheorghe Muresan .40 1.00
164 Rex Chapman .40 1.00
165 Doug Overton .40 1.00
166 Steve Smith FF .25 .60
167 Dino Radja FF .20 .50
168 Alonzo Mourning FF .40 1.00
169 Michael Jordan FF 2.50 6.00
170 Tyrone Hill FF .20 .50
171 Jamal Mashburn FF .30 .75
172 Dikembe Mutombo FF .30 .75
173 Grant Hill FF 1.00 2.50
w/Michael Jordan
174 Latrell Sprewell FF .30 .75
175 Hakeem Olajuwon FF .40 1.00
176 Reggie Miller FF .40 1.00
177 Pooh Richardson FF .20 .50
178 Cedric Ceballos FF .20 .50
179 Glen Rice FF .30 .75
180 Glenn Robinson FF .25 .60
181 Isaiah Rider FF .30 .75
182 Derrick Coleman FF .25 .60
183 Patrick Ewing FF .40 1.00
184 Shaquille O'Neal FF .75 2.00
185 Dana Barros FF .20 .50
186 Dan Majerle FF .30 .75
187 Clifford Robinson FF .20 .50
188 Mitch Richmond FF .30 .75
189 David Robinson FF .50 1.25
190 Gary Payton FF .30 .75
191 Oliver Miller FF .20 .50
192 Karl Malone FF .40 1.00
193 Kevin Pritchard FF .20 .50
194 Chris Webber FF .40 1.00
195 Michael Jordan PD 2.50 6.00
196 Hakeem Olajuwon PD .40 1.00
197 Vin Baker PD .25 .60
198 Grant Hill PD .50 1.25
199 Clyde Drexler PD .40 1.00
200 Chris Webber PD .40 1.00
201 Shawn Kemp PD .30 .75
202 Shaquille O'Neal PD .75 2.00
203 Stacey Augmon PD .25 .60
204 David Benoit PD .20 .50
205 Rodney Rogers PD .20 .50
206 Latrell Sprewell PD .30 .75
207 Brian Grant PD .25 .60
208 Lamond Murray PD .20 .50
209 Shawn Kemp CL .30 .75
210 Michael Jordan CL 2.50 6.00
211 Cory Alexander .60 1.50
212 Vernon Maxwell .40 1.00
213 George Lynch .40 1.00
214 Terry Mills .40 1.00
215 Scottie Pippen 1.00 2.50
216 Donald Royal .40 1.00
217 Wesley Person .40 1.00
218 Antonio Davis .40 1.00
219 Glenn Robinson .50 1.25
220 Jerry Stackhouse 2.00 5.00
221 James Robinson .40 1.00
222 Chris Mills .40 1.00
223 Chuck Person .50 1.25
224 Duane Causwell .40 1.00
225 Gary Payton .60 1.50
226 Eric Montross .40 1.00
227 Felton Spencer .40 1.00
228 Scott Skiles .40 1.00
229 Latrell Sprewell .60 1.50
230 Sedale Threatt .40 1.00
231 Mark Bryant .40 1.00
232 Buck Williams .40 1.00
233 Brian Williams .40 1.00
234 Sharone Wright .40 1.00
235 Karl Malone .75 2.00
236 Kevin Edwards .40 1.00
237 Muggsy Bogues .50 1.25
238 Mario Elie .40 1.00
239 Rasheed Wallace 2.00 5.00
240 George Zidek .50 1.25
241 Cedric Ceballos .40 1.00
242 Alan Henderson .60 1.50
243 Joe Kleine .40 1.00
244 Patrick Ewing .75 2.00
245 Sasha Danilovic .60 1.50
246 Bill Wennington .40 1.00
247 Steve Smith .50 1.25
248 Bryant Stith .40 1.00
249 Dino Radja .40 1.00
250 Monty Williams .40 1.00
251 Andrew DeClercq .60 1.50
252 Sean Elliott .60 1.50
253 Rick Fox .40 1.00
254 Lionel Simmons .40 1.00
255 Dikembe Mutombo .60 1.50
256 Lindsey Hunter .40 1.00
257 Terrell Brandon .40 1.00
258 Shawn Respert .50 1.25
259 Rodney Rogers .40 1.00
260 Bryon Russell .40 1.00
261 David Wesley .40 1.00
262 Ken Norman .40 1.00
263 Mitch Richmond .60 1.50
264 Sam Perkins .40 1.00
265 Hakeem Olajuwon .75 2.00
266 Brian Shaw .40 1.00
267 B.J. Armstrong .40 1.00
268 Jalen Rose .75 2.00
269 Bryant Reeves .50 1.25
270 Cherokee Parks .50 1.25
271 Dennis Rodman 1.25 3.00
272 Kendall Gill .40 1.00
273 Elliot Perry .40 1.00
274 Anthony Mason .40 1.00
275 Kevin Garnett 5.00 12.00
276 Damon Stoudamire 1.50 4.00
277 Lawrence Moten .60 1.50
278 Ed O'Bannon .50 1.25
279 Toni Kukoc .60 1.50
280 Greg Ostertag .60 1.50
281 Tom Hammonds .40 1.00
282 Yinka Dare .40 1.00
283 Michael Smith .40 1.00
284 Clifford Rozier .40 1.00
285 Gary Trent .60 1.50
286 Shaquille O'Neal 1.50 4.00
287 Luc Longley .50 1.25
288 Bob Sura .50 1.25
289 Dana Barros .40 1.00
290 Lorenzo Williams .40 1.00
291 Haywoode Workman .40 1.00
292 Randolph Childress .50 1.25
293 Doc Rivers .50 1.25
294 Chris Webber .75 2.00
295 Kurt Thomas .60 1.50
296 Greg Anthony .40 1.00
297 Tyus Edney .60 1.50
298 Danny Manning .50 1.25
299 Brent Barry 1.00 2.50
300 Joe Smith .75 2.00
301 Pooh Richardson .40 1.00
302 Mark Jackson .50 1.25
303 Richard Dumas .40 1.00
304 Michael Finley 2.00 5.00
305 Theo Ratliff 1.00 2.50
306 Gary Grant .40 1.00
307 Jamal Mashburn .60 1.50
308 Corliss Williamson .60 1.50
309 Eric Williams .60 1.50
310 Zan Tabak .40 1.00
311 Eric Murdock .40 1.00
312 Sherrell Ford .50 1.25
313 Terry Davis .40 1.00
314 Vern Fleming .40 1.00
315 Jason Caffey .60 1.50
316 Mario Bennett .50 1.25
317 David Vaughn .60 1.50
318 Loren Meyer .40 1.00
319 Travis Best .60 1.50
320 Byron Scott .50 1.25
321 Mookie Blaylock SR .20 .50
322 Dee Brown SR .20 .50
323 Alonzo Mourning SR .40 1.00
324 Michael Jordan SR 2.50 6.00
325 Terrell Brandon SR .20 .50
326 Jim Jackson SR .20 .50
327 Dikembe Mutombo SR .30 .75
328 Grant Hill SR .50 1.25
329 Joe Smith SR .40 1.00
330 Clyde Drexler SR .40 1.00
331 Reggie Miller SR .40 1.00
332 Lamond Murray SR .20 .50
333 Nick Van Exel SR .30 .75
334 Glen Rice SR .30 .75
335 Glenn Robinson SR .25 .60
336 Christian Laettner SR .25 .60
337 Kenny Anderson SR .25 .60
338 Patrick Ewing SR .40 1.00
339 Shaquille O'Neal SR .75 2.00
340 Jerry Stackhouse SR 1.00 2.50
341 Charles Barkley SR .50 1.25
342 Clifford Robinson SR .20 .50
343 Brian Grant SR .25 .60
344 David Robinson SR .50 1.25
345 Shawn Kemp SR .30 .75
346 Damon Stoudamire SR .75 2.00
347 Karl Malone SR .40 1.00
348 Bryant Reeves SR .25 .60
349 Juwan Howard SR .30 .75
350 Nick Anderson .20 .50
Dee Brown PT
351 Rik Smits PT .25 .60
352 Herb Williams .20 .50
Tom Tolbert PT
353 Michael Jordan PT 2.50 6.00
354 David Robinson PT .50 1.25
355 Terry Porter .30 .75
Kevin Johnson PT
356 Clyde Drexler PT .40 1.00
357 Cedric Ceballos PT .20 .50
358 Horace Grant .25 .60
Group PT
359 Reggie Miller PT .40 1.00
360 Avery Johnson .30 .75
Nick Van Exel PT
361 Hakeem Olajuwon .40 1.00
Robert Horry PT
362 Rik Smits PT .25 .60
363 David Robinson .50 1.25
Hakeem Olajuwon PT
364 Robert Horry PT .25 .60
365 Kenny Smith PT .25 .60
366 Stacey Augmon LOVE .25 .60
367 Sherman Douglas LOVE .20 .50
368 Larry Johnson LOVE .30 .75
369 Scottie Pippen LOVE .50 1.25
370 Tyrone Hill LOVE .20 .50
371 Jamal Mashburn LOVE .30 .75
372 Mahmoud Abdul-Rauf LOVE .20 .50
373 Grant Hill LOVE .50 1.25
374 Latrell Sprewell LOVE .30 .75
375 Sam Cassell LOVE .30 .75
376 Rik Smits LOVE .25 .60
377 Terry Dehere LOVE .20 .50
378 Eddie Jones LOVE .30 .75
379 Billy Owens LOVE .20 .50
380 Vin Baker LOVE .25 .60
381 Isaiah Rider LOVE .30 .75
382 Kenny Anderson LOVE .25 .60
383 John Starks LOVE .25 .60
384 Anfernee Hardaway LOVE .50 1.25
385 Sharone Wright LOVE .20 .50
386 Charles Barkley LOVE .50 1.25
387 Clifford Robinson LOVE .20 .50
388 Walt Williams LOVE .20 .50
389 Sean Elliott LOVE .30 .75
390 Gary Payton LOVE .30 .75
391 Carlos Rogers LOVE .20 .50
392 John Stockton LOVE .40 1.00
393 Greg Anthony LOVE .20 .50
394 Chris Webber LOVE .40 1.00
395 Gary Payton PG .30 .75
396 Mookie Blaylock PG .20 .50
397 Charles Barkley PG .50 1.25
398 Grant Hill PG .50 1.25
399 Anfernee Hardaway PG .50 1.25
400 Kenny Anderson PG .25 .60
401 Mark Jackson PG .25 .60
402 Karl Malone PG .40 1.00
403 Avery Johnson PG .25 .60
404 Larry Johnson 40 .30 .75
405 Nick Van Exel 40 .30 .75
406 Vin Baker 40 .25 .60
407 Jason Kidd 40 .50 1.25
408 David Robinson 40 .50 1.25
409 Shawn Kemp CL .30 .75
410 Michael Jordan CL 2.50 6.00

1995-96 Collector's Choice International Japanese Jordan Collection

COMPLETE SET (4) 8.00 20.00
COMMON CARD (J1-J4) 2.50 6.00

1995-96 Collector's Choice International Japanese NBA Extremes

COMPLETE SET (9) 2.50 6.00
E1 Muggsy Bogues .60 1.50
E2 Spud Webb .60 1.50
E3 Dana Barros .50 1.25
E4 Avery Johnson .60 1.50
E5 Vlade Divac .75 2.00
E6 Dikembe Mutombo .75 2.00
E7 Rik Smits .60 1.50
E8 Shawn Bradley .50 1.25
E9 Gheorghe Muresan .50 1.25

1995-96 Collector's Choice International Portuguese

COMPLETE SET (200) 8.00 20.00
*PORTUGUESE: SAME VALUE AS FRENCH .

1995-96 Collector's Choice International Portuguese Jordan Collection

COMPLETE SET (4) 5.00 12.00
*PORTUGUESE: SAME VALUE AS FRENCH

1995-96 Collector's Choice International Portuguese NBA Extremes

COMPLETE SET (9) 1.50 4.00
*PORTUGUESE: SAME VALUE AS FRENCH

1995-96 Collector's Choice International Spanish I

COMPLETE SET (210) 8.00 20.00
*SPANISH: SAME VALUE AS FRENCH

1995-96 Collector's Choice International Spanish II

COMPLETE SET (200) 8.00 20.00
*SPANISH: SAME VALUE AS FRENCH

1995-96 Collector's Choice International Spanish Jordan Collection

COMPLETE SET (4) 5.00 12.00
*SPANISH: SAME VALUE AS FRENCH

1995-96 Collector's Choice International Spanish NBA Extremes

COMPLETE SET (9) 1.50 4.00
*SPANISH: SAME VALUE AS FRENCH

1996-97 Collector's Choice International English Jordan's Journal

COMPLETE SET (6) 8.00 20.00
COMMON CARD (J1-J6) 2.00 5.00

1996-97 Collector's Choice International French

COMPLETE SET (200) 20.00 40.00
1 Mookie Blaylock .15 .40
2 Grant Long .15 .40
3 Christian Laettner .20 .50
4 Craig Ehlo .15 .40
5 Ken Norman .15 .40
6 Stacey Augmon .20 .50
7 Dana Barros .15 .40
8 Dino Radja .15 .40
9 Rick Fox .15 .40
10 Eric Montross .15 .40
11 David Wesley .15 .40
12 Eric Williams .15 .40
13 Glen Rice .25 .60
14 Dell Curry .15 .40
15 Matt Geiger .15 .40
16 Scott Burrell .15 .40
17 George Zidek .15 .40
18 Muggsy Bogues .20 .50
19 Ron Harper .20 .50
20 Steve Kerr .20 .50
21 Toni Kukoc .25 .60
22 Dennis Rodman .50 1.25
23 Michael Jordan 2.00 5.00
24 Luc Longley .20 .50
25 Michael Jordan VT 2.00 5.00
26 Michael Jordan VT 2.00 5.00
27 Luc Longley VT .20 .50
28 Scottie Pippen VT .40 1.00
29 Toni Kukoc VT .25 .60
30 Terrell Brandon .15 .40
31 Bobby Phills .15 .40
32 Tyrone Hill .15 .40
33 Michael Cage .15 .40
34 Bob Sura .15 .40
35 Tony Dumas .15 .40
36 Jim Jackson .15 .40
37 Loren Meyer .15 .40
38 Cherokee Parks .15 .40
39 Jamal Mashburn .20 .50
40 Popeye Jones .15 .40
41 LaPhonso Ellis .15 .40
42 Jalen Rose .20 .50
43 Antonio McDyess .25 .60
44 Tom Hammonds .15 .40
45 Mahmoud Abdul-Rauf .15 .40
46 Dale Ellis .15 .40
47 Joe Dumars .25 .60
48 Theo Ratliff .15 .40
49 Lindsey Hunter .15 .40
50 Terry Mills .15 .40
51 Don Reid .15 .40
52 B.J. Armstrong .15 .40
53 Bimbo Coles .15 .40
54 Joe Smith .20 .50
55 Chris Mullin .25 .60
56 Rony Seikaly .15 .40
57 Donyell Marshall .15 .40
58 Hakeem Olajuwon .30 .75
59 Robert Horry .20 .50
60 Mario Elie .15 .40
61 Mark Bryant .15 .40
62 Chucky Brown .15 .40
63 Rik Smits .20 .50
64 Derrick McKey .15 .40
65 Eddie Johnson .15 .40
66 Mark Jackson .20 .50
67 Ricky Pierce .15 .40
68 Travis Best .15 .40
69 Rodney Rogers .15 .40
70 Brent Barry .20 .50
71 Lamond Murray .15 .40
72 Eric Piatkowski .20 .50
73 Pooh Richardson .15 .40
74 Cedric Ceballos .15 .40
75 Eddie Jones .25 .60
76 Anthony Peeler .15 .40
77 George Lynch .15 .40
78 Vlade Divac .25 .60
79 Rex Chapman .15 .40
80 Sasha Danilovic .15 .40
81 Kurt Thomas .15 .40
82 Keith Askins .15 .40
83 Walt Williams .15 .40
84 Vin Baker .20 .50
85 Shawn Respert .15 .40
86 Sherman Douglas .15 .40
87 Marty Conlon .15 .40
88 Johnny Newman .15 .40
89 Kevin Garnett .60 1.50
90 Andrew Lang .15 .40
91 Terry Porter .15 .40
92 Sam Mitchell .15 .40
93 Tom Gugliotta .15 .40
94 Spud Webb .20 .50
95 Kendall Gill .15 .40
96 Vern Fleming .15 .40
97 Shawn Bradley .15 .40
98 Yinka Dare .15 .40
99 Jayson Williams .15 .40
100 Kevin Edwards .15 .40
101 Charles Oakley .20 .50
102 Anthony Mason .15 .40
103 John Starks .20 .50
104 J.R. Reid .15 .40
105 Hubert Davis .15 .40
106 Gary Grant .15 .40
107 Nick Anderson .15 .40
108 Donald Royal .15 .40
109 Brian Shaw .15 .40
110 Brooks Thompson .15 .40
111 Anfernee Hardaway .40 1.00
112 Dennis Scott .15 .40
113 Anfernee Hardaway .40 1.00
114 Anfernee Hardaway .40 1.00
115 Anfernee Hardaway .40 1.00
116 Anfernee Hardaway .40 1.00
117 Anfernee Hardaway .40 1.00
118 Derrick Coleman .20 .50
119 Rex Walters .15 .40
120 Sean Higgins .15 .40
121 Clarence Weatherspoon .15 .40
122 Jerry Stackhouse .30 .75
123 Elliot Perry .15 .40

124 Wayman Tisdale	.15	.40
125 Wesley Person	.15	.40
126 Charles Barkley	.40	1.00
127 A.C. Green	.20	.50
128 Harvey Grant	.15	.40
129 Arvydas Sabonis	.20	.50
130 Aaron McKie	.15	.40
131 Gary Trent	.15	.40
132 Buck Williams	.15	.40
133 Billy Owens	.15	.40
134 Brian Grant	.20	.50
135 Corliss Williamson	.15	.40
136 Tyus Edney	.15	.40
137 Olden Polynice	.15	.40
138 Avery Johnson	.20	.50
139 Vinny Del Negro	.15	.40
140 Sean Elliott	.25	.60
141 Chuck Person	.20	.50
142 Will Perdue	.15	.40
143 Nate McMillan	.15	.40
144 Vincent Askew	.15	.40
145 Detlef Schrempf	.25	.60
146 Hersey Hawkins	.15	.40
147 Sharone Wright	.15	.40
148 Zan Tabak	.15	.40
149 Oliver Miller	.15	.40
150 Doug Christie	.15	.40
151 Damon Stoudamire	.20	.50
152 Jeff Hornacek	.20	.50
153 Chris Morris	.15	.40
154 Antoine Carr	.15	.40
155 Karl Malone	.30	.75
156 Adam Keefe	.15	.40
157 Greg Anthony	.15	.40
158 Blue Edwards	.15	.40
159 Bryant Reeves	.15	.40
160 Anthony Avent	.15	.40
161 Lawrence Moten	.15	.40
162 Calbert Cheaney	.15	.40
163 Chris Webber	.30	.75
164 Tim Legler	.15	.40
165 Gheorghe Muresan	.15	.40
166 Stacey Augmon FUND	.20	.50
167 Dee Brown FUND	.15	.40
168 Glen Rice FUND	.25	.60
169 Scottie Pippen FUND	.40	1.00
170 Danny Ferry FUND	.15	.40
171 Jason Kidd FUND	.40	1.00
172 Tom Hammonds FUND	.15	.40
173 Grant Hill FUND	.40	1.00
174 Chris Mullin FUND	.25	.60
175 Clyde Drexler FUND	.30	.75
176 Rik Smits FUND	.20	.50
177 Lamond Murray FUND	.15	.40
178 Nick Van Exel FUND	.25	.60
179 Alonzo Mourning FUND	.30	.75
180 Glenn Robinson FUND	.20	.50
181 Isaiah Rider FUND	.20	.50
182 Ed O'Bannon FUND	.15	.40
183 Patrick Ewing FUND	.30	.75
184 Shaquille O'Neal FUND	.60	1.50
185 Derrick Coleman FUND	.20	.50
186 Danny Manning FUND	.20	.50
187 Clifford Robinson FUND	.15	.40
188 Mitch Richmond FUND	.25	.60
189 David Robinson FUND	.40	1.00
190 Shawn Kemp FUND	.25	.60
191 Oliver Miller FUND	.15	.40
192 John Stockton FUND	.30	.75
193 Greg Anthony FUND	.15	.40
194 Rasheed Wallace FUND	.30	.75
195 Michael Jordan FUND	2.00	5.00
196 Checklist	.40	1.00
197 Checklist	.15	.40
198 Checklist	.40	1.00
199 Checklist	.15	.40
200 Checklist	.25	.60

1996-97 Collector's Choice International French Crash the Game Scoring

COMPLETE SET (60)	40.00	80.00
C1A Mookie Blaylock	.60	1.50
C1B Mookie Blaylock	.60	1.50
C2A Dino Radja	.60	1.50
C2B Dino Radja	.60	1.50
C3A Glen Rice	1.00	2.50
C3B Glen Rice	1.00	2.50
C4A Scottie Pippen	1.50	4.00
C4B Scottie Pippen	1.50	4.00
C5A Terrell Brandon	.60	1.50
C5B Terrell Brandon	.60	1.50
C6A Jason Kidd	1.50	4.00
C6B Jason Kidd	1.50	4.00
C7A Antonio McDyess	1.00	2.50
C7B Antonio McDyess	1.00	2.50
C8A Joe Dumars	1.00	2.50
C8B Joe Dumars	1.00	2.50
C9A Joe Smith	.75	2.00
C9B Joe Smith	.75	2.00
C10A Hakeem Olajuwon	1.25	3.00
C10B Hakeem Olajuwon	1.25	3.00
C11A Reggie Miller	1.25	3.00
C11B Reggie Miller	1.25	3.00
C12A Loy Vaught	.60	1.50
C12B Loy Vaught	.60	1.50
C13A Cedric Ceballos	.60	1.50
C13B Cedric Ceballos	.60	1.50
C14A Alonzo Mourning	1.25	3.00
C14B Alonzo Mourning	1.25	3.00
C15A Vin Baker	.75	2.00
C15B Vin Baker	.75	2.00
C16A Kevin Garnett	2.50	6.00
C16B Kevin Garnett	2.50	6.00
C17A Ed O'Bannon	.60	1.50
C17B Ed O'Bannon	.60	1.50
C18A Patrick Ewing	1.25	3.00
C18B Patrick Ewing	1.25	3.00
C19A Anfernee Hardaway	1.50	4.00
C19B Anfernee Hardaway	1.50	4.00
C20A Clarence Weatherspoon	.60	1.50
C20B Clarence Weatherspoon	.60	1.50
C21A Kevin Johnson	1.00	2.50
C21B Kevin Johnson	1.00	2.50
C22A Clifford Robinson	.60	1.50
C22B Clifford Robinson	.60	1.50
C23A Mitch Richmond	1.00	2.50
C23B Mitch Richmond	1.00	2.50
C24A Sean Elliott	1.00	2.50
C24B Sean Elliott	1.00	2.50
C25A Shawn Kemp	1.00	2.50
C25B Shawn Kemp	1.00	2.50
C26A Damon Stoudamire	.75	2.00
C26B Damon Stoudamire	.75	2.00
C27A John Stockton	1.25	3.00
C27B John Stockton	1.25	3.00
C28A Bryant Reeves	.60	1.50
C28B Bryant Reeves	.60	1.50
C29A Rasheed Wallace	1.25	3.00
C29B Rasheed Wallace	1.25	3.00
C30A Michael Jordan	8.00	20.00
C30B Michael Jordan	8.00	20.00

1996-97 Collector's Choice International French Crash the Game Scoring Gold

*GOLD: .5X TO 1.5X

1996-97 Collector's Choice International French Jordan's Journal

COMPLETE SET (6)	8.00	20.00
COMMON CARD	2.00	5.00

1996-97 Collector's Choice International French Mini-Cards

COMPLETE SET (30)	6.00	15.00
M2 Mookie Blaylock	.30	.75
Jeff Hornacek/Rex Walters		
M5 Dino Radja/Toni Kukoc	.40	1.00
Detlef Schrempf		
M6 Eric Williams/Sharone Wright	.25	.60
Ashraf Amaya		
M10 George Zidek/Ed O'Bannon	.25	.60
Tyus Edney		
M13 Luc Longley/Shawn Bradley	.30	.75
Theo Ratliff		
M22 Mahmoud Abdul-Rauf	.30	.75
Avery Johnson/Bobby Phills		
M23 Tom Hammonds/Chris Morris	.25	.60
Popeye Jones		
M25 Grant Hill/Christian Laettner	.60	1.50
Bobby Hurley		
M28 Rony Seikaly/Derrick Coleman	.30	.75
Sherman Douglas		
M30 Sam Cassell/John Starks	.40	1.00
Nick Van Exel		
M33 Travis Best/Dennis Scott/Matt Geiger	.25	.60
M36 Brent Barry/Isaiah Rider	.30	.75
Cedric Ceballos		
M37 Lamond Murray	.60	1.50
Kevin Johnson/Jason Kidd		
M38 Terry Dehere/Jayson Williams	.40	1.00
Chris Mullin		
M39 Vlade Divac/Sasha Danilovic	.40	1.00
Arvydas Sabonis		
M43 Kurt Thomas/Brian Grant/Tyrone Hill	.30	.75
M44 Keith Askins/Robert Horry	.30	.75
Derrick McKey		
M46 Shawn Respert	.60	1.50
David Robinson/Randolph Childress		
M49 Andrew Lang/Oliver Miller/Todd Day	.25	.60
M56 Charles Oakley/Bimbo Coles	.30	.75
Dell Curry		
M57 J.R. Reid/Jerry Stackhouse	.50	1.25
Rasheed Wallace		
M66 A.C. Green/Clyde Drexler	.50	1.25
Joe Dumars		
M67 Aaron McKie/Nick Anderson	.25	.60
Kendall Gill		
M75 Doc Rivers/Mark Jackson	.30	.75
Danny Ferry		
M78 Shawn Kemp	3.00	8.00
Anfernee Hardaway/Michael Jordan		
M79 Jimmy King/Chris Webber	.50	1.25
Jalen Rose		
M83 Karl Malone/Charles Barkley	.75	2.00
Dennis Rodman		
M85 Greg Anthony/Larry Johnson	.40	1.00
Stacey Augmon		
M86 Blue Edwards/Tom Gugliotta	.25	.60
Nate McMillan		
M90 Calbert Cheaney	.30	.75
Glenn Robinson/Jim Jackson		

1996-97 Collector's Choice International French Stick Ums

COMPLETE SET (30)	8.00	20.00
S1 Mookie Blaylock	.25	.60
S2 Dana Barros	.25	.60
S3 Scott Burrell	.25	.60
S4 Dennis Rodman	.75	2.00
S5 Terrell Brandon	.25	.60
S6 Jamal Mashburn	.30	.75
S7 LaPhonso Ellis	.25	.60
S8 Grant Hill	.60	1.50
S9 Joe Smith	.30	.75
S10 Hakeem Olajuwon	.50	1.25
S11 Rik Smits	.30	.75
S12 Brent Barry	.30	.75
S13 Nick Van Exel	.40	1.00
S14 Sasha Danilovic	.25	.60
S15 Vin Baker	.30	.75
S16 Kevin Garnett	1.00	2.50
S17 Shawn Bradley	.25	.60
S18 Patrick Ewing	.50	1.25
S19 Anfernee Hardaway	.60	1.50
S20 Clarence Weatherspoon	.25	.60
S21 Charles Barkley	.60	1.50
S22 Clifford Robinson	.25	.60
S23 Mitch Richmond	.40	1.00
S24 David Robinson	.60	1.50
S25 Shawn Kemp	.40	1.00
S26 Damon Stoudamire	.30	.75
S27 Karl Malone	.50	1.25
S28 Bryant Reeves	.25	.60
S29 Gheorghe Muresan	.25	.60
S30 Michael Jordan	3.00	8.00

1996-97 Collector's Choice International German

COMPLETE SET (200)	20.00	40.00

*GERMAN: SAME VALUE AS FRENCH

1996-97 Collector's Choice International German Jordan's Journal

COMPLETE SET (6)	8.00	20.00
COMMON CARD	2.00	5.00

1996-97 Collector's Choice International German Mini-Cards

COMPLETE SET (30)	6.00	15.00

*GERMAN: SAME VALUE AS FRENCH

1996-97 Collector's Choice International German Stick Ums

COMPLETE SET (30)	8.00	20.00

*GERMAN: SAME VALUE AS FRENCH

1996-97 Collector's Choice International Italian

Consisting of 200 cards, the 1996-97 Collector's Choice International set was distributed in Italy and possibly other countries. We currently only have a checklist for the Italian. These cards are identical in design to the 1996-97 Collector's Choice American cards except for bilingual text for the respective countries and the regular card numbering.

COMPLETE SET (200)	20.00	40.00

*ITALIAN: SAME VALUE AS FRENCH

1996-97 Collector's Choice International Italian Crash the Game Scoring

Randomly inserted into first series Italian packs, this 60-card silver set features two separate versions of thirty different player cards. Each player is given two separate weeks to score 30 points in any given game during that time period. If the player depicted on the card scores 30 or more points in the given week, the card could be redeemed for one premium quality silver card of the depicted player. The expiration date for the cards was June 7, 1997.

COMPLETE SET (60)	40.00	80.00

*ITALIAN: SAME VALUE AS FRENCH

1996-97 Collector's Choice International Italian Crash the Game Scoring Gold

COMPLETE SET (60)

*ITALIAN: SAME VALUE AS FRENCH

1996-97 Collector's Choice International Italian Jordan's Journal

This six-card set was randomly inserted into packs of 1996-97 Collector's Choice International Italian basketball.

COMPLETE SET (6)	8.00	20.00
COMMON CARD	2.00	5.00

1996-97 Collector's Choice International Italian Mini-Cards

Inserted at a rate of one per series one pack, this 30-card set is comprised of 90 different "mini-cards". Three of these mini-cards form one standard-sized card and are issued in that form. Card fronts feature perforated panels of three players with silver foil. Card backs feature a brief commentary on each player. Each card contains it's own individual number, with an "M" prefix and is ordered below by the far left number on the card back.

COMPLETE SET (30)	6.00	15.00
*ITALIAN: SAME VALUE AS FRENCH		
M2 Mookie Blaylock	.30	.75
Jeff Hornacek		
Rex Walters		
M5 Dino Radja	.40	1.00
Toni Kukoc		
Detlef Schrempf		
M6 Eric Williams	.25	.60
Sharone Wright		
Ashraf Amaya		
M10 George Zidek	.25	.60
Ed O'Bannon		
Tyus Edney		
M13 Luc Longley	.30	.75
Shawn Bradley		
Theo Ratliff		
M22 Mahmoud Abdul-Rauf	.30	.75
Avery Johnson		
Bobby Phills		
M23 Tom Hammonds	.25	.60
Chris Morris		
Popeye Jones		
M25 Grant Hill	.60	1.50
Christian Laettner		
Bobby Hurley		
M28 Rony Seikaly	.30	.75
Derrick Coleman		
Sherman Douglas		
M30 Sam Cassell	.40	1.00
John Starks		
Nick Van Exel		
M33 Travis Best	.25	.60
Dennis Scott		
Matt Geiger		
M36 Brent Barry	.30	.75
Isaiah Rider		
Cedric Ceballos		
M37 Lamond Murray	.60	1.50
Kevin Johnson		
Jason Kidd		
M38 Terry Dehere	.40	1.00
Jayson Williams		
Chris Mullin		
M39 Vlade Divac	.40	1.00
Sasha Danilovic		
Arvydas Sabonis		
M43 Kurt Thomas	.30	.75
Brian Grant		
Tyrone Hill		
M44 Keith Askins	.30	.75
Robert Horry		
Derrick McKey		
M46 Shawn Respert	.60	1.50
David Robinson		
Randolph Childress		
M49 Andrew Lang	.25	.60
Oliver Miller		
Todd Day		
M56 Charles Oakley	.30	.75
Bimbo Coles		
Dell Curry		
M57 J.R. Reid	.50	1.25
Jerry Stackhouse		
Rasheed Wallace		
M66 A.C. Green	.50	1.25
Clyde Drexler		
Joe Dumars		
M67 Aaron McKie	.25	.60
Nick Anderson		
Kendall Gill		
M75 Doc Rivers	.30	.75
Mark Jackson		
Danny Ferry		
M78 Shawn Kemp	3.00	8.00
Anfernee Hardaway		
Michael Jordan		
M79 Jimmy King	.50	1.25
Chris Webber		
Jalen Rose		
M83 Karl Malone	.75	2.00
Charles Barkley		
Dennis Rodman		
M85 Greg Anthony	.40	1.00
Larry Johnson		
Stacey Augmon		
M86 Blue Edwards	.25	.60
Tom Gugliotta		
Nate McMillan		
M90 Calbert Cheaney	.30	.75
Glenn Robinson		
Jim Jackson		

1996-97 Collector's Choice International Italian Stick Ums

This 30-card set was randomly inserted into packs of 1996-97 Collector's Choice International Italian basketball. The checklist mirrors the American 1996-97 Collector's Choice series one Stick-Um set. The card design is the same with different language text on the card back.

COMPLETE SET (30)	8.00	20.00

*ITALIAN: SAME VALUE AS FRENCH

1996-97 Collector's Choice International Japanese Crash the Game Scoring 1

COMPLETE SET (60)

*JAPANESE: SAME VALUE AS FRENCH

1996-97 Collector's Choice International Japanese Crash the Game Scoring Gold 1

COMPLETE SET (60)

1996-97 Collector's Choice International Japanese Crash the Game Scoring 2

COMPLETE SET (60)
C1 Steve Smith 2/17 L
C2 Dana Barros 3/3 L
C3 Tony Delk 2/24 L
C4 Toni Kukoc 3/10 L
C5 Bobby Phills 2/24 L
C6 Jamal Mashburn 3/3 L
C7 LaPhonso Ellis 2/24 W
C8 Jerome Williams 2/17 L
C9 Latrell Sprewell 3/3 L
C10 Clyde Drexler 2/24 L
C11 Dale Davis 3/3 L
C12 Brent Barry 3/3 L
C13 Nick Van Exel 3/10 L
C14 Sasha Danilovic 2/17 L
C15 Glenn Robinson 2/24 L
C16 Stephon Marbury 2/17 L
C17 Shawn Bradley 3/10 W
C18 John Wallace 3/3 L
C19 Anfernee Hardaway 2/24 L
C1B Steve Smith 4/14 W
C20 Jerry Stackhouse 3/10 W
C21 Danny Manning 2/17 L
C22 Arvydas Sabonis 2/24 L
C23 Brian Grant 3/3 L
C24 David Robinson 2/24 L
C25 Gary Payton 3/3 L
C26 Marcus Camby 3/3 L
C27 Karl Malone 2/24 W
C28 Shareef Abdur-Rahim 2/24 L
C29 Juwan Howard 2/17 L
C2B Dana Barros 3/31 L
C30 Michael Jordan 3/9 W
C3B Tony Delk 4/7 L
C4B Toni Kukoc 3/31 L
C5B Bobby Phills 3/17 L
C6B Jamal Mashburn 3/31 L
C7B LaPhonso Ellis 3/31 L
C8B Jerome Williams 4/7 L
C9B Latrell Sprewell 4/7 L
C10B Clyde Drexler 4/7 L
C11B Dale Davis 3/24 L
C12B Brent Barry 4/14 L
C13B Nick Van Exel 4/7 L
C14B Sasha Danilovic 3/17 L
C15B Glenn Robinson 3/17 L
C16B Stephon Marbury 3/31 L
C17B Shawn Bradley 3/24 L
C18B John Wallace 4/14 L
C19B Anfernee Hardaway 4/14 L
C20B Jerry Stackhouse 3/31 W
C21B Danny Manning 3/24 L
C22B Arvydas Sabonis 3/31 L
C23B Brian Grant 3/31 L
C24B David Robinson 3/24 L
C25B Gary Payton 4/14 L
C26B Marcus Camby 4/7 L
C27B Karl Malone 4/14 W
C28B Shareef Abdur-Rahim 3/17 L
C29B Juwan Howard 4/7 L
C30B Michael Jordan 4/14 W

1996-97 Collector's Choice International Japanese Crash the Game Scoring Gold 2

COMPLETE SET (60)

1996-97 Collector's Choice International Japanese Jordan's Journal

COMPLETE SET (6)	8.00	20.00
COMMON CARD	2.00	5.00

1996-97 Collector's Choice International Spanish

COMPLETE SET (200)	20.00	40.00

*SPANISH: SAME VALUE AS FRENCH

1996-97 Collector's Choice International Spanish Crash the Game Scoring

COMPLETE SET (60)	40.00	80.00

*SPANISH: SAME VALUE AS FRENCH

1996-97 Collector's Choice International Spanish Crash the Game Scoring Gold

COMPLETE SET (60)

*SPANISH: SAME VALUE AS FRENCH

1996-97 Collector's Choice International Spanish Jordan's Journal

COMPLETE SET (6)	8.00	20.00
COMMON CARD	2.00	5.00

1996-97 Collector's Choice International Spanish Mini-Cards

COMPLETE SET (30)	6.00	15.00

*SPANISH: SAME VALUE AS FRENCH

1996-97 Collector's Choice International Spanish Stick Ums

COMPLETE SET (30)	8.00	20.00

*SPANISH: SAME VALUE AS FRENCH

1997-98 Collector's Choice International Japanese Michael Jordan Career

COMPLETE SET (9)
COMMON CARD

1998 Collector's Edge Air Apparent Jumbos

NNO Kobe Bryant/1998	4.00	10.00

1971-72 Colonels Volpe Marathon Oil

This set of Marathon Oil Pro Star Portraits consists of colorful portraits by distinguished artist Nicholas Volpe. Each (ABA Kentucky Colonels) portrait measures approximately 7 1/2" by 9 7/8" and features a painting of the player's face on a black background, with an action painting superimposed to the side. A facsimile autograph in white appears at the bottom of the portrait. At the bottom of each portrait is a postcard measuring 7 1/2" by 4" after perforation. While the back of the portrait has offers for a basketball photo album, autographed tumblers, and a poster, the postcard itself could also be used to apply for a Marathon credit card. The portraits are unnumbered and checklisted below in alphabetical order. Tumblers featuring these drawings are valued at 3x the listed prices. The key card in the set is Dan Issel during his Rookie Card year.

COMPLETE SET (11)	50.00	100.00
1 Darrell Carrier	5.00	10.00
2 Bobby Croft	3.00	8.00
3 Louie Dampier	10.00	25.00
4 Les Hunter	3.00	8.00
5 Dan Issel	20.00	40.00
6 Jim Ligon	3.00	8.00
7 Cincy Powell	5.00	12.00
8 Mike Pratt	5.00	10.00
9 Walt Simon	3.00	8.00
10 Sam Smith	3.00	8.00
11 Howard Wright	3.00	8.00

1959 Comet Sweets Olympic Achievements

Celebrating various Olympic events, ceremonies, and their history, this 25-card set was issued by Comet Sweets. The cards are printed on thin cardboard stock and measure 1 7/16" by 2 9/16". Inside white borders, the fronts display water color paintings of various Olympic events. Some cards are horizontally oriented; others are vertically oriented. The set title "Olympic Achievements" appears at the top on the backs, with a discussion of the event below. This set is the first series; the cards are numbered "X to 25."

COMPLETE SET (25)	30.00	60.00
12 Basketball	2.50	5.00

1972-73 Comspec

This 36-card set is printed on thin card stock, and each card measures approximately 2 1/4" by 3 1/2". The fronts display posed color player photos bordered in white. The photos have different color backgrounds (blue, green, orange, pink, red, or yellow). The only card that contains a genuine action shot from a game is that of Chet Walker. The team name, player's name, and his position appear in the white border beneath each picture. The horizontally oriented backs have biography and career statistics. The cards are unnumbered and checklisted below in alphabetical order.

COMPLETE SET (36)	2200.00	2800.00
1 Kareem Abdul-Jabbar	150.00	300.00
2 Rick Adelman	20.00	50.00
3 Nate Archibald	40.00	80.00
4 Rick Barry	40.00	80.00
5 Walt Bellamy	20.00	50.00
6 Dave Bing	30.00	75.00
7 Austin Carr	15.00	40.00
8 Wilt Chamberlain	250.00	500.00
9 Dave Cowens	40.00	80.00
10 Walt Frazier	40.00	80.00
11 Gail Goodrich	30.00	75.00
12 John Havlicek	125.00	250.00
13 Connie Hawkins	45.00	90.00
14 Elvin Hayes	30.00	75.00
15 Spencer Haywood	15.00	40.00
16 John Hummer	12.50	30.00
17 Don Kojis	15.00	40.00
18 Bob Lanier	40.00	80.00
19 Kevin Loughery	15.00	40.00
20 Jerry Lucas	30.00	75.00
21 Pete Maravich	300.00	600.00
22 Jack Marin	15.00	40.00
23 Calvin Murphy	30.00	60.00
24 Geoff Petrie	25.00	50.00
25 Willis Reed	40.00	80.00
26 Oscar Robertson	100.00	225.00
27 Cazzie Russell	20.00	40.00
28 Elmore Smith	15.00	40.00
29 Dick Snyder	15.00	40.00
30 Wes Unseld	40.00	80.00
31 Dick Van Arsdale	25.00	50.00
32 Tom Van Arsdale	15.00	40.00
33 Norm Van Lier	30.00	60.00
34 Chet Walker	30.00	60.00
35 Jerry West	150.00	300.00
36 Lenny Wilkens	45.00	90.00

1971-72 Condors Pittsburgh Team Issue

This set of 11 photos features the Pittsburgh Condors of the American Basketball Association. The cards measure approximately 5 1/2" by 7". The fronts carry black-and-white posed action photos with a white border. The player's name and the team name appear under the picture. The backs are blank. The photos are unnumbered and checklisted below in alphabetical order.

COMPLETE SET (11)	35.00	70.00
1 John Brisker	5.00	10.00
2 George Carter	3.00	8.00
3 Mickey Davis	2.50	6.00
4 Stew Johnson	2.50	6.00
5 Arvesta Kelly	2.50	6.00
6 Dave Lattin	5.00	12.00
7 Mike Lewis	2.50	6.00
8 Jimmy O'Brien	4.00	10.00
9 Paul Ruffner	2.50	6.00
10 Skeeter Swift	3.00	8.00
11 George Thompson	5.00	10.00

1971-72 Condors Pittsburgh Team Photo

Each of these team-issued photos measure approximately 8" by 10" and feature black and white player portraits on two different sheets. The player's name is listed below the photo. Each sheet contains eight player portraits. The backs are blank. The photos are unnumbered and listed below alphabetically.

COMPLETE SET (2)	20.00	40.00
1 John Brisker	12.50	25.00
George Carter		
Mickey Davis		
Mike Lewis		
Jimmy O'Brien		
Paul Ruffner		
Skeeter Swift		
George Thompson		
2 Don Bezahler	10.00	20.00
Mark Binstein		
Stew Johnson		
Arvesta Kelly		
David Lattin		
Jack McMahon		
Ray Melchiorre		
Walt Szczerbiak		

1969-70 Converse Staff

This ten-card set was sponsored by Converse Shoes. The cards measure approximately 2 1/4" by 2 3/4". The fronts feature a drawn player portrait and basketball tip. The backs are blank. The cards are unnumbered and are checklisted below in alphabetical order.

COMPLETE SET (10)	175.00	350.00
1 Bob Davies	40.00	80.00
2 Joe Dean	12.00	30.00
3 Gib Ford	10.00	25.00
4 Bob Houbregs	15.00	40.00
5 Rod Hundley	40.00	80.00
6 Stu Inman	15.00	40.00
7 Bunny Levitt	15.00	40.00
8 Earl Lloyd	15.00	40.00
9 John Norlander	12.00	30.00
10 Phil Rollins	10.00	25.00

1989 Converse

This 15-card standard-size set was sponsored by Converse. The color action player photo on the front of the card is outlined by a thin black border against a white background. At the top, the words "Converse, Official Shoe of the NBA" is printed in blue lettering, as is the player's name and number below the picture. The NBA logo in the upper right corner rounds out the card face. The back presents a brief biography, career highlights, and a tip from the player and Converse in the form of an anti-drug or alcohol message. The cards are unnumbered and checklisted below in alphabetical order. Mark Aguirre is misspelled Aquirre on the checklist card. The set originally included a free video offer card; for 3.95 to cover shipping and handling, the collector could receive a video of Converse basketball tips, featuring Julius Erving, Kevin McHale, and Dale Brown. The cards were reportedly intended for distribution at youth basketball clinics sponsored by Converse but it is apparent that much remainder stock has been made available to the hobby thus greatly increasing the supply.

COMPLETE SET (15)	4.00	10.00
1 Mark Aguirre	.20	.50
2 Larry Bird	2.50	5.00
3 Rolando Blackman	.30	.75
4 Muggsy Bogues	.40	1.00
5 Rex Chapman	.40	1.00
6 Magic Johnson	1.25	3.00
7 Bernard King	.30	.75
8 Bill Laimbeer	.30	.75
9 Karl Malone	1.00	2.50
10 Kevin McHale	.50	1.25
11 Mark Price	.40	1.00
12 Jack Sikma	.20	.50
13 Reggie Theus	.30	.75
14 Title Card	.20	.50
NNO Free Video Offer	.20	.50

1993-94 Costacos Brothers Poster Cards

COMPLETE SET (18)	10.00	20.00
3 Charles Barkley	.60	1.50
Sir Charles		
14 Alonzo Mourning	.30	.75
Zo		
15 Shaquille O'Neal	1.25	3.00
Shaq		

1969-70 Cougars Carolina Team Issue

Each of these team-issued photos measure approximately 8" by 10" and feature black and white player portraits. The player's name is listed below the photo and the fronts feature a facsimile autograph. The backs are blank. The photos are unnumbered and listed below alphabetically.

COMPLETE SET (15)	50.00	100.00
1 Carolina Cougars	5.00	10.00
Team Photo		
2 Bill Bunting	2.50	6.00
3 Cal Fowler	2.50	6.00
4 Steve Kramer	2.50	6.00
5 Gene Littles	3.00	8.00
6 Randy Mahaffey	2.50	6.00
7 Bones McKinney CO	5.00	10.00
8 Larry Miller	3.00	8.00
9 Doug Moe	5.00	10.00
10 Rich Niemann	2.50	6.00
11 George Peeples	2.50.	6.00
12 Ron Perry	2.50	6.00
13 George Sutor	2.50	6.00
14 Bob Verga	3.00	8.00
15 Hank Whitney	2.50	6.00

1970-71 Cougars Team Issue

These photos were issued by the Carolina Cougars. They feature members of the 1970-71 Cougars team. This list may not be complete so any additions are appreciated. Jim McDaniel was signed out of college and was going to be the star rookie the next season. Also please note the Larry Steele never played for the Cougars.

COMPLETE SET	12.50	25.00
1 Gary Bradds	2.00	5.00
2 Jim McDaniels	2.50	6.00
3 Dave Newmark	2.00	5.00
4 George Peeples	2.00	5.00
5 Larry Steele	3.00	8.00

2009-10 Court Kings

COMP.SET w/o RC's (120)	50.00	100.00
1-120 PRINT RUN 450 SER.#'d SETS		
ROOKIE PRINT RUN 649 SER.#'d SETS		
1 Carmelo Anthony	1.25	3.00
2 Chris Andersen	.75	2.00
3 J.R. Smith	.75	2.00
4 Chauncey Billups	1.00	2.50
5 Kevin Love	1.00	2.50
6 Al Jefferson	.75	2.00
7 Corey Brewer	.60	1.50
8 Kevin Durant	2.50	6.00
9 Russell Westbrook	2.50	6.00
10 Jeff Green	.75	2.00
11 Brandon Roy	1.00	2.50
12 LaMarcus Aldridge	1.00	2.50
13 Juwan Howard	.75	2.00
14 Deron Williams	.75	2.00
15 Carlos Boozer	.75	2.00
16 Paul Millsap	.75	2.00
17 Dirk Nowitzki	1.25	3.00
18 Jason Kidd	1.00	2.50
19 Drew Gooden	.75	2.00
20 J.J. Barea	1.25	3.00
21 Trevor Ariza	.60	1.50
22 Aaron Brooks	.60	1.50
23 Carl Landry	.60	1.50
24 Tony Parker	1.00	2.50
25 Richard Jefferson	.75	2.00
26 Tim Duncan	1.50	4.00
27 Marc Gasol	1.00	2.50
28 Rudy Gay	1.00	2.50
29 Zach Randolph	.75	2.00
30 Emeka Okafor	.75	2.00
31 Chris Paul	1.25	3.00
32 David West	.75	2.00
33 Jason Thompson	.60	1.50
34 Kevin Martin	.75	2.00
35 Spencer Hawes	.60	1.50
36 Amare Stoudemire	.75	2.00
37 Channing Frye	.75	2.00
38 Steve Nash	1.00	2.50
39 Pau Gasol	1.00	2.50
40 Kobe Bryant	4.00	10.00
41 Derek Fisher	.75	2.00
42 Andrew Bynum	.60	1.50
43 Monta Ellis	.75	2.00
44 Anthony Morrow	.60	1.50
45 Corey Maggette	.75	2.00
46 Baron Davis	.75	2.00
47 Chris Kaman	.75	2.00
48 Eric Gordon	.75	2.00
49 Kevin Garnett	1.50	4.00
50 Ray Allen	1.00	2.50
51 Paul Pierce	1.00	2.50
52 Kendrick Perkins	.60	1.50
53 Nate Robinson	.60	1.50
54 Chris Duhon	.60	1.50
55 David Lee	.60	1.50
56 Danilo Gallinari	.75	2.00
57 Allen Iverson	1.25	3.00
58 Andre Iguodala	.75	2.00
59 Louis Williams	.75	2.00
60 Elton Brand	1.00	2.50
61 Andrea Bargnani	.75	2.00
62 Chris Bosh	1.00	2.50
63 Hedo Turkoglu	.75	2.00
64 Brook Lopez	.75	2.00
65 Rafer Alston	.60	1.50
66 Devin Harris	.60	1.50
67 LeBron James	4.00	10.00
68 Anderson Varejao	.60	1.50
69 Delonte West	.60	1.50
70 Shaquille O'Neal	2.00	5.00
71 Ben Gordon	.75	2.00
72 Rodney Stuckey	.60	1.50
73 Ben Wallace	.75	2.00
74 Danny Granger	.75	2.00
75 Troy Murphy	.60	1.50
76 Dahntay Jones	.60	1.50
77 Andrew Bogut	.75	2.00
78 Luke Ridnour	.75	2.00
79 Hakim Warrick	.75	2.00
80 Luol Deng	.75	2.00
81 Derrick Rose	1.50	4.00
82 Joakim Noah	.75	2.00
83 John Salmons	.75	2.00
84 Joe Johnson	.75	2.00
85 Al Horford	1.00	2.50
86 Jamal Crawford	1.00	2.50
87 Marvin Williams	.75	2.00
88 Dwyane Wade	1.50	4.00
89 Jermaine O'Neal	.75	2.00
90 Michael Beasley	.60	1.50
91 Gerald Wallace	.75	2.00
92 Stephen Jackson	.75	2.00
93 Raymond Felton	.75	2.00
94 Dwight Howard	.75	2.00
95 Vince Carter	1.25	3.00
96 Rashard Lewis	.75	2.00
97 Jason Williams	.75	2.00
98 Antawn Jamison	.75	2.00
99 Mike Miller	.75	2.00
100 Caron Butler	.75	2.00
101 Harry Gallatin	1.00	2.50
102 Nate Archibald	.75	2.00
103 Elgin Baylor	1.00	2.50
104 Walt Bellamy	.75	2.00
105 Dave Bing	1.00	2.50
106 Louie Dampier	1.00	2.50
107 Clyde Drexler	1.25	3.00
108 Mark Eaton	.60	1.50
109 John Havlicek	1.00	2.50
110 Jerry Lucas	1.00	2.50
111 George McGinnis	.60	1.50
112 Sidney Moncrief	.60	1.50
113 Kurt Rambis	.60	1.50
114 Bill Sharman	1.00	2.50
115 Lenny Wilkens	1.00	2.50
116 Elvin Hayes	1.00	2.50
117 Walt Frazier	1.00	2.50
118 Connie Hawkins	1.00	2.50
119 Spencer Haywood	.60	1.50
120 Dell Curry	.60	1.50
121 Jrue Holiday AU RC	5.00	12.00
122 James Johnson AU RC	3.00	8.00
123 Taj Gibson AU RC	4.00	10.00
124 Brandon Jennings AU RC	4.00	10.00
125 Jeff Teague AU RC	4.00	10.00
126 Earl Clark AU RC	3.00	8.00
127 Jordan Hill AU RC	3.00	8.00
128 Toney Douglas AU RC	2.50	6.00
129 Stephen Curry AU RC	250.00	500.00
130 Austin Daye AU RC	2.50	6.00
131 Jonas Jerebko AU RC	4.00	10.00
132 Jonny Flynn AU RC	2.50	6.00
133 Wayne Ellington AU RC	4.00	10.00
134 Ty Lawson AU RC	4.00	10.00
135 Chase Budinger AU RC	3.00	8.00
136 DeJuan Blair AU RC	3.00	8.00
137 Tyler Hansbrough AU RC	3.00	8.00
138 DeMarre Carroll AU RC	3.00	8.00
139 Hasheem Thabeet AU RC	2.50	6.00
140 Terrence Williams AU RC	2.50	6.00
141 Darren Collison AU RC	4.00	10.00
142 Marcus Thornton AU RC	3.00	8.00
143 Derrick Brown AU RC	2.50	6.00
144 Gerald Henderson AU RC	3.00	8.00
145 James Harden AU RC	50.00	120.00
146 DeMar DeRozan AU RC	20.00	50.00
147 Tyreke Evans AU RC	3.00	8.00
148 Omri Casspi AU RC	3.00	8.00
149 Eric Maynor AU RC	2.50	6.00
150 Blake Griffin AU RC	30.00	80.00

2009-10 Court Kings Bronze

*BRONZE: .5X TO 1.25X BASE HI
STATED PRINT RUN 149 SER.#'d SETS

2009-10 Court Kings Silver

*SILVER: .75X TO 2X BASE HI
STATED PRINT RUN 99 SER.#'d SETS

2009-10 Court Kings Artistry

COMPLETE SET (30)	20.00	40.00
STATED PRINT RUN 249 SER.#'d SETS		
UNPRICED BLACK PRINT RUN ONE SET		
*BRONZE: .5X TO 1.25X BASE HI		
BRONZE PRINT RUN 199 SER.#'d SETS		
*SILVER: .6X TO 1.5X BASE HI		
SILVER PRINT RUN 99 SER.#'d SETS		
1 Josh Smith	.60	1.50
2 Kevin Garnett	1.25	3.00
3 Gerald Wallace	.60	1.50
4 Derrick Rose	1.25	3.00
5 LeBron James	3.00	8.00
6 Jason Terry	.60	1.50
7 Carmelo Anthony	1.00	2.50
8 Rodney Stuckey	.50	1.25
9 Monta Ellis	.60	1.50
10 Carl Landry	.50	1.25
11 Dahntay Jones	.50	1.25
12 Chris Kaman	.60	1.50
13 Kobe Bryant	3.00	8.00
14 Rudy Gay	.75	2.00
15 Dwyane Wade	1.25	3.00
16 Ersan Ilyasova	.50	1.25
17 Al Jefferson	.60	1.50
18 Brook Lopez	.60	1.50
19 David West	.60	1.50
20 Danilo Gallinari	.60	1.50
21 Kevin Durant	2.00	5.00
22 Dwight Howard	.60	1.50
23 Andre Iguodala	.60	1.50
24 Jason Richardson	.75	2.00
25 Brandon Roy	.75	2.00
26 Jason Thompson	.50	1.25
27 Tim Duncan	1.25	3.00

28 Chris Bosh .75 2.00
29 Carlos Boozer .60 1.50
30 Andrew Bogut .60 1.50

2009-10 Court Kings Artistry Materials
PRINT RUN ONE TO 299 SER.#'d SETS
SOME UNPRICED DUE TO SCARCITY
1 Josh Smith/299 2.00 5.00
2 Kevin Garnett/299 4.00 10.00
3 Gerald Wallace/299 2.00 5.00
5 LeBron James/299 8.00 20.00
6 Jason Terry/299 2.00 5.00
7 Carmelo Anthony/299 3.00 8.00
8 Rodney Stuckey/299 1.50 4.00
9 Monta Ellis/299 2.00 5.00
12 Chris Kaman/299 2.00 5.00
13 Kobe Bryant/299 8.00 20.00
14 Rudy Gay/299 2.50 6.00
15 Dwyane Wade/299 4.00 10.00
17 Al Jefferson/299 2.00 5.00
18 Brook Lopez/299 2.00 5.00
19 David West/299 2.00 5.00
20 Danilo Gallinari/49 2.00 5.00
21 Kevin Durant/299 6.00 15.00
22 Dwight Howard/299 2.00 5.00
23 Andre Iguodala/299 2.00 5.00
24 Jason Richardson/299 2.50 6.00
25 Brandon Roy/299 2.50 6.00
27 Tim Duncan/299 4.00 10.00
28 Chris Bosh/299 2.50 6.00
29 Carlos Boozer/299 2.00 5.00
30 Andrew Bogut/299 2.00 5.00

2009-10 Court Kings Artistry Signatures
STATED PRINT RUN 5 TO 99 SER.#'d SETS
SOME UNPRICED DUE TO SCARCITY
13 Kobe Bryant/99 100.00 200.00
23 Andre Iguodala/99 5.00 12.00
25 Brandon Roy/49 8.00 20.00

2009-10 Court Kings Dribble Kings
COMPLETE SET (15) 15.00 30.00
STATED PRINT RUN 149 SER.#'d SETS
UNPRICED BLACK PRINT RUN ONE SET
1 Steve Nash 1.25 3.00
2 Tony Parker 1.25 3.00
3 Chris Paul 1.50 4.00
4 Deron Williams 1.00 2.50
5 Pete Maravich 2.00 5.00
6 John Stockton 2.00 5.00
7 Jerry West 1.50 4.00
8 Carmelo Anthony 1.50 4.00
9 Dwyane Wade 2.00 5.00
10 Bob Cousy 2.00 5.00
11 Rafer Alston .75 2.00
12 Jason Kidd 1.25 3.00
13 Earl Monroe 1.25 3.00
14 Oscar Robertson 1.25 3.00
15 Kobe Bryant 5.00 12.00

2009-10 Court Kings Dribble Kings Materials
STATED PRINT RUN 99 TO 299 SER.#'d SETS
1 Steve Nash/199 2.50 6.00
2 Tony Parker/199 2.50 6.00
3 Chris Paul/299 3.00 8.00
4 Deron Williams/299 2.00 5.00
6 John Stockton/299 4.00 10.00
8 Carmelo Anthony/299 3.00 8.00
9 Dwyane Wade/299 4.00 10.00
11 Rafer Alston/299 2.00 5.00
12 Jason Kidd/299 2.50 6.00
13 Earl Monroe/299 3.00 8.00
15 Kobe Bryant/99 15.00 30.00

2009-10 Court Kings Dribble Kings Signatures
STATED PRINT RUN 5 TO 49 SER.#'d SETS
SOME UNPRICED DUE TO SCARCITY
2 Tony Parker/49 8.00 20.00
12 Jason Kidd/49 12.50 30.00
15 Kobe Bryant/49 100.00 200.00

2009-10 Court Kings Gallery of Stars
COMPLETE SET (20) 15.00 30.00
STATED PRINT RUN 249 SER.#'d SETS
UNPRICED BLACK PRINT RUN ONE SET
*BRONZE: .6X TO 1.5X BASE HI
BRONZE PRINT RUN 149 SER.#'d SETS
*SILVER: .75X TO 2X BASE HI
SILVER PRINT RUN 49 SER.#'d SETS
1 Aaron Brooks .75 2.00
2 Al Jefferson 1.00 2.50
3 Danny Granger 1.00 2.50
4 Devin Harris .75 2.00
5 Chauncey Billups 1.25 3.00
6 David Lee .75 2.00
7 Josh Howard 1.00 2.50
8 Luol Deng 1.00 2.50
9 Lamar Odom 1.00 2.50
10 Marc Gasol 1.25 3.00
11 Rajon Rondo 1.25 3.00
12 Ron Artest 1.25 3.00
13 Russell Westbrook 3.00 8.00
14 Shane Battier 1.25 3.00
15 Stephen Jackson 1.00 2.50
16 Tayshaun Prince 1.00 2.50
17 Vince Carter 1.50 4.00
18 Al Harrington 1.00 2.50
19 Joakim Noah 1.00 2.50
20 Kevin Love 1.25 3.00

2009-10 Court Kings Gallery of Stars Materials
STATED PRINT RUN 25 TO 299 SER.#'d SETS
1 Aaron Brooks/299 1.50 4.00
2 Al Jefferson/299 2.00 5.00
3 Danny Granger/299 2.00 5.00
4 Devin Harris/299 1.50 4.00
5 Chauncey Billups/299 2.50 6.00
6 David Lee/199 1.50 4.00
7 Josh Howard/299 2.00 5.00
8 Luol Deng/299 2.00 5.00
10 Marc Gasol/299 2.50 6.00
11 Rajon Rondo/299 2.50 6.00
12 Ron Artest/299 2.50 6.00
13 Russell Westbrook/299 6.00 15.00
14 Shane Battier/299 2.50 6.00
16 Tayshaun Prince/299 2.00 5.00
17 Vince Carter/299 3.00 8.00
18 Al Harrington/25 3.00 8.00
19 Joakim Noah/299 2.00 5.00
20 Kevin Love/299 2.50 6.00

2009-10 Court Kings Gallery of Stars Signatures
STATED PRINT RUN 49 TO 99 SER.#'d SETS
1 Aaron Brooks/99 4.00 10.00
4 Devin Harris/49 4.00 10.00
5 Chauncey Billups/49 8.00 20.00
7 Josh Howard/49 4.00 10.00
11 Rajon Rondo/49 10.00 25.00
13 Russell Westbrook/49 60.00 150.00
14 Shane Battier/49 5.00 12.00
17 Vince Carter/49 12.50 30.00
20 Kevin Love/49 12.50 30.00

2009-10 Court Kings Hardwood Heroes
COMPLETE SET (20) 20.00 40.00
STATED PRINT RUN 249 SER.#'d SETS
UNPRICED BLACK PRINT RUN ONE SET
1 LeBron James 4.00 10.00
2 Magic Johnson 2.50 6.00
3 Allen Iverson 1.25 3.00
4 Steve Nash 1.00 2.50
5 Patrick Ewing 1.25 3.00
6 Carmelo Anthony 1.25 3.00
7 Kevin Durant 2.50 6.00
8 Oscar Robertson 1.00 2.50
9 Dirk Nowitzki 1.25 3.00
10 Kobe Bryant 4.00 10.00
11 Scottie Pippen 2.00 5.00
12 Deron Williams .75 2.00
13 Dwyane Wade 1.50 4.00
14 Ty Lawson 1.00 2.50
15 Bill Russell 1.50 4.00
16 Shaquille O'Neal 2.00 5.00
17 Chris Paul 1.25 3.00
18 Derrick Rose 1.50 4.00
19 Larry Bird 2.50 6.00
20 Blake Griffin 4.00 10.00

2009-10 Court Kings Hardwood Heroes Materials
STATED PRINT RUN ONE TO 299 SER.#'d SETS
SOME UNPRICED DUE TO SCARCITY
1 LeBron James/299 10.00 25.00
2 Magic Johnson/299 8.00 20.00
3 Allen Iverson/99 4.00 10.00
4 Steve Nash/199 3.00 8.00
5 Patrick Ewing/299 4.00 10.00
6 Carmelo Anthony/299 4.00 10.00
7 Kevin Durant/299 6.00 15.00
9 Dirk Nowitzki/299 4.00 10.00
10 Kobe Bryant/299 8.00 20.00
11 Scottie Pippen/299 6.00 15.00
12 Deron Williams/299 2.50 6.00
13 Dwyane Wade/299 5.00 12.00
14 Ty Lawson/299 3.00 8.00
16 Shaquille O'Neal/299 6.00 15.00
17 Chris Paul/299 4.00 10.00
19 Larry Bird/99 8.00 20.00
20 Blake Griffin/299 10.00 25.00

2009-10 Court Kings Hardwood Heroes Signatures
STATED PRINT RUN ONE TO 49 SER.#'d SETS
SOME UNPRICED DUE TO SCARCITY
10 Kobe Bryant/49 100.00 200.00
11 Scottie Pippen/49 75.00 150.00

2009-10 Court Kings Jumbo Boxtoppers
COMPLETE SET (50) 100.00 200.00
STATED PRINT RUN 349 SER.#'d SETS
1 Ray Allen 2.00 5.00
2 Tracy McGrady 2.00 5.00
3 Bob Cousy 3.00 8.00
4 Pau Gasol 2.00 5.00
5 Dirk Nowitzki 2.50 6.00
6 Alonzo Mourning 2.50 6.00
7 Bill Walton 2.00 5.00
8 Vince Carter 2.50 6.00
9 Tyreke Evans 6.00 15.00
10 David Lee 1.25 3.00
11 Andrew Bogut 1.50 4.00
12 Pete Maravich 3.00 8.00
13 Cedric Maxwell 2.00 5.00
14 Shaquille O'Neal 4.00 10.00
15 Baron Davis 1.50 4.00
16 Kevin Love 2.00 5.00
17 Artis Gilmore 1.50 4.00
18 Connie Hawkins 2.00 5.00
19 Jermaine O'Neal 1.50 4.00
20 Kevin Durant 5.00 12.00
21 Magic Johnson 5.00 12.00
22 Patrick Ewing 2.50 6.00
23 LeBron James 8.00 20.00
24 Jason Kidd 2.00 5.00
25 Rajon Rondo 2.00 5.00
26 Al Attles 2.00 5.00
27 David Thompson 1.50 4.00
28 Chris Bosh 2.00 5.00
29 Lamar Odom 1.50 4.00
30 Tim Duncan 3.00 8.00
31 Dan Majerle 1.50 4.00
32 Isiah Thomas 2.00 5.00
33 Kareem Abdul-Jabbar 3.00 8.00
34 Stephen Curry 125.00 250.00
35 Deron Williams 1.50 4.00
36 Carmelo Anthony 2.50 6.00
37 Darryl Dawkins 1.25 3.00
38 John Thompson
39 Bob McAdoo 1.50 4.00
40 Brandon Jennings 2.00 5.00
41 Trevor Ariza 1.25 3.00
42 Kevin McHale 2.00 5.00
43 Brandon Roy 2.00 5.00
44 Danny Granger 1.50 4.00
45 Jalen Rose 2.00 5.00
46 Devin Harris 1.25 3.00
47 Elton Brand 2.00 5.00
48 Lenny Wilkens 2.00 5.00
49 Larry Bird 5.00 12.00
50 Kobe Bryant 8.00 20.00

2009-10 Court Kings Jumbo Boxtoppers Autographs
STATED PRINT RUN 10 TO 75 SER.#'d SETS
SOME UNPRICED DUE TO SCARCITY
5 Dirk Nowitzki/20 100.00 250.00
6 Alonzo Mourning/49 40.00 80.00
7 Bill Walton/49 12.00 30.00
8 Vince Carter/49 30.00 60.00
9 Tyreke Evans/75 12.00 30.00
10 David Lee/74 10.00 25.00
11 Andrew Bogut/75 10.00 25.00
13 Cedric Maxwell/75 10.00 25.00
15 Baron Davis/75 10.00 25.00
16 Kevin Love/75 15.00 40.00
17 Artis Gilmore/75 15.00 30.00
18 Connie Hawkins/75 15.00 30.00
19 Jermaine O'Neal/49 10.00 25.00
21 Magic Johnson/15 75.00 200.00
24 Jason Kidd/49 20.00 40.00
25 Rajon Rondo/75 25.00 60.00
26 Al Attles/75 10.00 25.00
27 David Thompson/74 10.00 25.00
28 Chris Bosh/49 15.00 40.00
29 Lamar Odom/75 15.00 30.00
31 Dan Majerle/75 20.00 40.00
32 Isiah Thomas/75 10.00 25.00
34 Stephen Curry/64 400.00 800.00
35 Deron Williams/49 15.00 30.00
37 Darryl Dawkins/75 10.00 25.00
39 Bob McAdoo/75 12.00 30.00
40 Brandon Jennings/75 25.00 50.00
41 Trevor Ariza/75 10.00 25.00
42 Kevin McHale/20 30.00 80.00
43 Brandon Roy/49 15.00 30.00
44 Danny Granger/75 10.00 25.00
45 Jalen Rose/75 10.00 25.00
46 Devin Harris/75 10.00 25.00
48 Lenny Wilkens/75 10.00 25.00
49 Larry Bird/15 75.00 150.00
50 Kobe Bryant/75 125.00 225.00

2009-10 Court Kings Kobe Bryant Lithographs
COMMON EXCH (1-5) 250.00 500.00
STATED PRINT RUN 24 SER.#'d SETS

2009-10 Court Kings Le Cinque Piu Belle
COMPLETE SET (5) 40.00 100.00
COMMON CARD (1-5) 12.00 30.00
STATED PRINT RUN 149 SER.#'d SETS

2009-10 Court Kings Le Cinque Piu Belle Signatures
COMMON CARD (1-5) 200.00 400.00
STATED PRINT RUN 24 SER.#'d SETS

2009-10 Court Kings Masterpieces
COMPLETE SET (20) 30.00 60.00
STATED PRINT RUN 149 SER.#'d SETS
UNPRICED BLACK PRINT RUN ONE SET
1 Nate Robinson 1.25 3.00
2 Dwight Howard 1.50 4.00
3 Josh Smith 1.50 4.00
4 Jason Richardson 2.00 5.00
5 Vince Carter 2.50 6.00
6 Kobe Bryant 8.00 20.00
7 Cedric Ceballos 1.25 3.00
8 Dee Brown 1.25 3.00
9 Dominique Wilkins 2.50 6.00
10 Kenny Walker 2.00 5.00
11 Spud Webb 1.50 4.00
12 Larry Nance 1.50 4.00
13 Carmelo Anthony 2.50 6.00
14 Andre Iguodala 1.50 4.00
15 J.R. Smith 1.50 4.00
16 LeBron James 8.00 20.00
17 Larry Johnson 2.00 5.00
18 Kenny Smith 1.50 4.00
19 Clyde Drexler 2.50 6.00
20 Amare Stoudemire 1.50 4.00

2009-10 Court Kings Masterpieces Materials
STATED PRINT RUN 199 TO 299 SER.#'d SETS
2 Dwight Howard/299 2.00 5.00
3 Josh Smith/299 2.00 5.00
4 Jason Richardson/299 2.50 6.00
5 Vince Carter/299 4.00 10.00
6 Kobe Bryant/199 10.00 25.00
9 Dominique Wilkins/299 3.00 8.00
13 Carmelo Anthony/299 3.00 8.00
14 Andre Iguodala/299 2.00 5.00
15 J.R. Smith/299 2.00 5.00
16 LeBron James/299 8.00 20.00
19 Clyde Drexler/299 4.00 10.00
20 Amare Stoudemire/299 2.00 5.00

2009-10 Court Kings Masterpieces Signatures
STATED PRINT RUN 5 TO 49 SER.#'d SETS
SOME UNPRICED DUE TO SCARCITY
5 Vince Carter/49 12.50 30.00
6 Kobe Bryant/49 100.00 200.00
10 Kenny Walker/49 8.00 20.00
11 Spud Webb/49 8.00 20.00
14 Andre Iguodala/49 8.00 20.00
17 Larry Johnson/49 20.00 50.00
19 Clyde Drexler/49 20.00 50.00

2009-10 Court Kings Materials
STATED PRINT RUN 25 TO 149 SER.#'d SETS
1 Carmelo Anthony/149 4.00 10.00
2 Chris Andersen/149 2.50 6.00
3 J.R. Smith/149 2.50 6.00
4 Chauncey Billups/149 3.00 8.00
5 Kevin Love/149 3.00 8.00
6 Al Jefferson/149 2.50 6.00
8 Kevin Durant/149 8.00 20.00
9 Russell Westbrook/149 8.00 20.00
10 Jeff Green/149 2.50 6.00
11 Brandon Roy/149 3.00 8.00
12 LaMarcus Aldridge/149 3.00 8.00
13 Juwan Howard/149 2.50 6.00
14 Deron Williams/149 2.50 6.00
15 Carlos Boozer/149 2.50 6.00
16 Paul Millsap/99 2.50 6.00
17 Dirk Nowitzki/149 4.00 10.00
18 Jason Kidd/149 3.00 8.00
20 J.J. Barea/149 5.00 12.00
22 Aaron Brooks/149 2.00 5.00
24 Tony Parker/149 3.00 8.00
25 Richard Jefferson/149 2.50 6.00
26 Tim Duncan/149 5.00 12.00
27 Marc Gasol/149 3.00 8.00
28 Rudy Gay/149 3.00 8.00
30 Emeka Okafor/149 2.50 6.00
31 Chris Paul/149 4.00 10.00
32 David West/149 2.50 6.00
34 Kevin Martin/149 2.50 6.00
36 Amare Stoudemire/149 2.50 6.00
37 Channing Frye/149 2.50 6.00
38 Steve Nash/149 3.00 8.00
39 Pau Gasol/149 3.00 8.00
40 Kobe Bryant/149 10.00 25.00
41 Derek Fisher/149 2.50 6.00
42 Andrew Bynum/149 2.00 5.00
43 Monta Ellis/149 2.50 6.00
45 Corey Maggette/149 2.50 6.00
46 Baron Davis/149 2.50 6.00
47 Chris Kaman/149 2.50 6.00
48 Eric Gordon/149 2.50 6.00
49 Kevin Garnett/149 5.00 12.00
50 Ray Allen/149 3.00 8.00
51 Paul Pierce/149 3.00 8.00
54 Chris Duhon/149 2.00 5.00
55 David Lee/149 2.00 5.00
56 Danilo Gallinari/49 2.50 6.00
57 Allen Iverson/99 4.00 10.00
58 Andre Iguodala/149 2.50 6.00
60 Elton Brand/149 3.00 8.00
61 Andrea Bargnani/149 2.50 6.00
62 Chris Bosh/149 3.00 8.00
63 Hedo Turkoglu/149 2.50 6.00
64 Brook Lopez/149 2.50 6.00
65 Rafer Alston/149 2.00 5.00
66 Devin Harris/149 2.00 5.00
67 LeBron James/149 10.00 25.00
70 Shaquille O'Neal/149 8.00 20.00
71 Ben Gordon/149 2.50 6.00
72 Rodney Stuckey/149 2.00 5.00
74 Danny Granger/149 2.50 6.00
75 Troy Murphy/149 2.00 5.00
77 Andrew Bogut/149 2.50 6.00
80 Luol Deng/149 2.50 6.00
81 Derrick Rose/149 5.00 12.00
82 Joakim Noah/149 2.50 6.00
83 John Salmons/149 2.50 6.00
84 Joe Johnson/149 2.50 6.00
85 Al Horford/149 3.00 8.00
87 Marvin Williams/149 2.50 6.00
88 Dwyane Wade/149 5.00 12.00
89 Jermaine O'Neal/149 2.50 6.00
90 Michael Beasley/149 2.00 5.00
91 Gerald Wallace/149 2.50 6.00
93 Raymond Felton/149 2.50 6.00
94 Dwight Howard/149 2.50 6.00
95 Vince Carter/149 4.00 10.00
96 Rashard Lewis/149 2.50 6.00
97 Jason Williams/149 2.50 6.00
98 Antawn Jamison/149 2.50 6.00
99 Mike Miller/149 2.50 6.00
100 Caron Butler/149 2.50 6.00
107 Clyde Drexler/149 6.00 15.00
108 Mark Eaton/149 3.00 8.00
109 John Havlicek/99 6.00 15.00
117 Walt Frazier/25 8.00 20.00

2009-10 Court Kings Portraits
COMPLETE SET (20) 15.00 30.00
STATED PRINT RUN 149 SER.#'d SETS
UNPRICED BLACK PRINT RUN ONE SET
1 Chris Andersen .75 2.00
2 Ron Artest 1.00 2.50
3 Kobe Bryant 4.00 10.00
4 LeBron James 4.00 10.00
5 Dirk Nowitzki 1.25 3.00
6 Joakim Noah .75 2.00
7 Dwight Howard .75 2.00
8 Allen Iverson 1.25 3.00
9 Steve Nash 1.00 2.50
10 Tony Parker 1.00 2.50
11 Shaquille O'Neal 2.00 5.00
12 Chris Bosh 1.00 2.50
13 Rasheed Wallace 1.00 2.50
14 Jason Kidd 1.00 2.50
15 Nene .75 2.00
16 Richard Hamilton .75 2.00
17 Zach Randolph .75 2.00
18 Chris Paul 1.25 3.00
19 David Lee .60 1.50
20 Vince Carter 1.25 3.00

2009-10 Court Kings Portraits Materials
STATED PRINT RUN 49 TO 299 SER.#'d SETS
1 Chris Andersen/299 2.50 6.00
3 Kobe Bryant/99 10.00 25.00
4 LeBron James/99 10.00 25.00
5 Dirk Nowitzki/299 4.00 10.00
6 Joakim Noah/299 2.50 6.00
7 Dwight Howard/299 2.50 6.00
8 Allen Iverson/99 4.00 10.00
9 Steve Nash/199 3.00 8.00
10 Tony Parker/199 3.00 8.00
11 Shaquille O'Neal/299 6.00 15.00
12 Chris Bosh/299 3.00 8.00
13 Rasheed Wallace/299 3.00 8.00
14 Jason Kidd/299 3.00 8.00
15 Nene/299 2.50 6.00
16 Richard Hamilton/49 2.50 6.00
18 Chris Paul/299 4.00 10.00
19 David Lee/199 2.00 5.00
20 Vince Carter/299 4.00 10.00

2009-10 Court Kings Portraits Signatures
STATED PRINT RUN 49 SER.#'d SETS
1 Chris Andersen 10.00 25.00
3 Kobe Bryant 125.00 225.00
10 Tony Parker 10.00 25.00
14 Jason Kidd 12.00 30.00
16 Richard Hamilton 6.00 15.00
20 Vince Carter 15.00 40.00

2009-10 Court Kings Signatures
STATED PRINT RUN 5 TO 49 SER.#'d SETS
SOME UNPRICED DUE TO SCARCITY
2 Chris Andersen/49 6.00 15.00
4 Chauncey Billups/49 8.00 20.00
5 Kevin Love/49 20.00 50.00
9 Russell Westbrook/49 60.00 150.00
11 Brandon Roy/49 10.00 25.00
18 Jason Kidd/49 12.00 30.00
20 J.J. Barea/49 15.00 40.00
22 Aaron Brooks/49 5.00 12.00
24 Tony Parker/49 12.00 30.00
30 Emeka Okafor/49 5.00 12.00
40 Kobe Bryant/49 100.00 200.00
42 Andrew Bynum/49 8.00 20.00
46 Baron Davis/49 8.00 20.00
48 Eric Gordon/49 6.00 15.00
58 Andre Iguodala/49 5.00 12.00
61 Andrea Bargnani/49 5.00 12.00
66 Devin Harris/49 5.00 12.00
89 Jermaine O'Neal/49 6.00 15.00
90 Michael Beasley/49 6.00 15.00
95 Vince Carter/49 15.00 40.00
101 Harry Gallatin/49 6.00 15.00
102 Nate Archibald/49 6.00 15.00
111 George McGinnis/49 6.00 15.00
112 Sidney Moncrief/49 6.00 15.00
114 Bill Sharman/49 5.00 12.00
115 Lenny Wilkens/49 6.00 15.00
116 Elvin Hayes/49 10.00 25.00
117 Walt Frazier/49 6.00 15.00
120 Dell Curry/49 5.00 12.00

2009-10 Court Kings Supreme Court
COMPLETE SET (20) 20.00 40.00
STATED PRINT RUN 149 SER.#'d SETS
UNPRICED BLACK PRINT RUN ONE SET
1 Vince Carter 1.25 3.00
2 Carmelo Anthony 1.25 3.00
3 Chris Bosh 1.00 2.50
4 David Lee .60 1.50
5 Tyreke Evans .75 2.00
6 Dirk Nowitzki 1.25 3.00
7 Kevin Durant 2.50 6.00
8 Gerald Wallace .75 2.00
9 Kevin Garnett 1.50 4.00
10 Kobe Bryant 4.00 10.00
11 Dwyane Wade 1.50 4.00
12 Dwight Howard .75 2.00
13 Shaquille O'Neal 2.00 5.00
14 Danny Granger .75 2.00
15 Tony Parker 1.00 2.50
16 Brandon Jennings 1.00 2.50
17 LeBron James 4.00 10.00
18 Chris Paul 1.25 3.00
19 Ray Allen 1.00 2.50
20 Allen Iverson 1.25 3.00

2009-10 Court Kings Supreme Court Materials
STATED PRINT RUN 99 TO 299 SER.#'d SETS
1 Vince Carter/299 4.00 10.00
2 Carmelo Anthony/299 4.00 10.00
3 Chris Bosh/299 3.00 8.00
4 David Lee/199 2.00 5.00
5 Tyreke Evans/299 2.00 5.00
6 Dirk Nowitzki/299 4.00 10.00
7 Kevin Durant/299 6.00 15.00
8 Gerald Wallace/299 2.50 6.00
9 Kevin Garnett/299 5.00 12.00
10 Kobe Bryant/99 10.00 25.00
11 Dwyane Wade/299 5.00 12.00
12 Dwight Howard/299 2.50 6.00
13 Shaquille O'Neal/99 6.00 15.00
14 Danny Granger/299 2.50 6.00
15 Tony Parker/199 3.00 8.00
16 Brandon Jennings/299 2.50 6.00
17 LeBron James/99 10.00 25.00
18 Chris Paul/299 4.00 10.00
19 Ray Allen/299 3.00 8.00
20 Allen Iverson/99 4.00 10.00

2009-10 Court Kings Supreme Court Signatures
STATED PRINT RUN 10 TO 49 SER.#'d SETS
SOME NOT PRICED DUE TO SCARCITY
1 Vince Carter/49 20.00 50.00
4 David Lee/49 8.00 20.00
5 Tyreke Evans/49 20.00 50.00
10 Kobe Bryant/49 100.00 200.00
14 Danny Granger/49 8.00 20.00
15 Tony Parker/49 8.00 20.00
16 Brandon Jennings/49 20.00 50.00
19 Ray Allen/49 25.00 60.00

2013-14 Court Kings
126-150 PRINT RUN 225 SER.#'d SETS
176-200 PRINT RUN 49 SER.#'d SETS
126-150 PRINT RUN 125 SER.#'d SETS
1 Anderson Varejao .60 1.50
2 Roy Hibbert .75 2.00
3 Ricky Rubio 1.00 2.50
4 Jameer Nelson .60 1.50
5 Tony Parker 1.00 2.50
6 Thaddeus Young .60 1.50
7 Tyson Chandler .75 2.00
8 Brandon Knight .75 2.00
9 Blake Griffin 1.00 2.50
10 Steve Nash 1.00 2.50
11 Rodney Stuckey .75 2.00
12 Joakim Noah .75 2.00
13 Gerald Wallace .75 2.00
14 Jeff Teague .75 2.00
15 Al Jefferson .75 2.00
16 Vince Carter 1.25 3.00
17 Mike Conley .75 2.00
18 Nikola Pekovic .60 1.50
19 Serge Ibaka .75 2.00
20 Eric Bledsoe .75 2.00
21 Isaiah Thomas 1.00 2.50
22 Gordon Hayward 1.00 2.50
23 DeMarcus Cousins 1.00 2.50
24 Nikola Vucevic .75 2.00
25 Larry Sanders .60 1.50
26 George Hill .75 2.00
27 Shawn Marion .75 2.00
28 Al Horford .75 2.00
29 Kevin Garnett 1.50 4.00
30 Kyrie Irving 2.00 5.00
31 Lance Stephenson .75 2.00
32 Kevin Love 1.00 2.50
33 Austin Rivers .75 2.00
34 Glen Davis .60 1.50
35 Greivis Vasquez .75 2.00
36 Gerald Green .75 2.00
37 DeMar DeRozan 1.00 2.50
38 Evan Turner .60 1.50
39 Amar'e Stoudemire .75 2.00
40 Dwyane Wade 1.50 4.00
41 Chris Paul 1.25 3.00
42 Andre Drummond 1.00 2.50
43 Luol Deng .75 2.00
44 Paul Millsap 1.00 2.50
45 Paul Pierce 1.00 2.50
46 Ben Gordon .75 2.00
47 Dirk Nowitzki 1.25 3.00
48 Derrick Rose 1.25 3.00
49 Ty Lawson .60 1.50
50 Andre Iguodala .75 2.00
51 Jeremy Lin 1.00 2.50
52 Kobe Bryant 4.00 10.00
53 O.J. Mayo .60 1.50
54 Chris Bosh 1.00 2.50
55 Bradley Beal 1.00 2.50
56 Manu Ginobili 1.00 2.50
57 Damian Lillard 2.00 5.00
58 Kevin Durant 2.50 6.00
59 Marcin Gortat .75 2.00
60 Metta World Peace 1.00 2.50
61 Tyreke Evans .60 1.50
62 Harrison Barnes .75 2.00
63 Dion Waiters .75 2.00
64 Avery Bradley .75 2.00
65 Kemba Walker 1.00 2.50
66 Kenneth Faried .75 2.00
67 James Harden 1.50 4.00
68 Pau Gasol 1.00 2.50
69 Kevin Martin .75 2.00
70 Russell Westbrook 2.50 6.00
71 Goran Dragic .75 2.00
72 Rudy Gay 1.00 2.50
73 John Wall 1.25 3.00
74 Tim Duncan 1.50 4.00
75 LaMarcus Aldridge 1.00 2.50
76 Zach Randolph .75 2.00
77 Carlos Boozer .75 2.00
78 Brandon Jennings .60 1.50
79 Rajon Rondo 1.00 2.50
80 DeAndre Jordan 1.00 2.50
81 Jrue Holiday 1.00 2.50
82 Nicolas Batum .75 2.00
83 Derrick Favors .75 2.00
84 Deron Williams .75 2.00
85 Monta Ellis .75 2.00
86 Andre Miller .75 2.00
87 Stephen Curry 4.00 10.00
88 Paul George 1.25 3.00
89 Dwight Howard .75 2.00
90 Marc Gasol 1.00 2.50
91 LeBron James 4.00 10.00
92 Ersan Ilyasova .60 1.50
93 Anthony Davis 2.00 5.00
94 Carmelo Anthony 1.25 3.00
95 Jason Richardson 1.00 2.50
96 Kawhi Leonard 1.50 4.00
97 Kyle Lowry .75 2.00
98 Brook Lopez .75 2.00
99 Klay Thompson 1.25 3.00
100 J.R. Smith .75 2.00
101 Anthony Bennett RC .75 2.00
102 Cody Zeller RC .75 2.00
103 Ben McLemore RC .75 2.00
104 C.J. McCollum RC 1.50 4.00
105 Kelly Olynyk RC .75 2.00
106 Dennis Schroder RC 1.00 2.50
107 Sergey Karasev RC .60 1.50
108 Gorgui Dieng RC .75 2.00
109 Solomon Hill RC .60 1.50
110 Isaiah Canaan RC .60 1.50
111 Victor Oladipo RC 1.25 3.00
112 Alex Len RC .75 2.00
113 Kentavious Caldwell-Pope RC 1.00 2.50
114 M.Carter-Williams RC 1.00 2.50
115 Shabazz Muhammad RC .75 2.00
116 Shane Larkin RC .60 1.50
117 Tony Snell RC .75 2.00
118 Mason Plumlee RC 1.00 2.50
119 Tim Hardaway Jr. RC 1.00 2.50
120 Glen Rice Jr. RC .60 1.50
121 Otto Porter RC 1.00 2.50
122 Nerlens Noel RC 1.25 3.00
123 Trey Burke RC .75 2.00
124 Steven Adams RC 1.00 2.50
125 G.Antetokounmpo RC 10.00 25.00
126 Anthony Bennett/225 1.00 2.50
127 Cody Zeller/225 1.00 2.50
128 Ben McLemore/225 1.00 2.50
129 C.J. McCollum/225 2.00 5.00
130 Kelly Olynyk/225 1.00 2.50
131 Dennis Schroder/225 1.25 3.00
132 Sergey Karasev/225 .75 2.00
133 Gorgui Dieng/225 1.00 2.50
134 Solomon Hill/225 .75 2.00
135 Isaiah Canaan/225 .75 2.00
136 Victor Oladipo/225 1.50 4.00
137 Alex Len/225 1.00 2.50
138 Kentavious Caldwell-Pope/225 1.25 3.00
139 M.Carter-Williams/225 1.25 3.00
140 Shabazz Muhammad/225 1.00 2.50
141 Shane Larkin/225 .75 2.00
142 Tony Snell/225 1.00 2.50
143 Mason Plumlee/225 1.25 3.00
144 Tim Hardaway Jr./225 1.25 3.00
145 Glen Rice Jr./225 .75 2.00
146 Otto Porter/225 1.25 3.00
147 Nerlens Noel/225 1.50 4.00
148 Trey Burke/225 1.00 2.50
149 Steven Adams/225 1.25 3.00
150 G.Antetokounmpo/225 20.00 50.00
151 Anthony Bennett/125 1.25 3.00
152 Cody Zeller/125 1.25 3.00
153 Ben McLemore/125 1.25 3.00
154 C.J. McCollum/125 2.50 6.00
155 Kelly Olynyk/125 1.25 3.00
156 Dennis Schroder/125 1.50 4.00
157 Sergey Karasev/125 1.00 2.50
158 Gorgui Dieng/125 1.25 3.00
159 Solomon Hill/125 1.00 2.50
160 Isaiah Canaan/125 1.00 2.50
161 Victor Oladipo/125 2.00 5.00
162 Alex Len/125 1.25 3.00
163 Kentavious Caldwell-Pope/125 1.50 4.00
164 M.Carter-Williams/125 1.50 4.00
165 Shabazz Muhammad/125 1.25 3.00
166 Shane Larkin/125 1.00 2.50
167 Tony Snell/125 1.25 3.00
168 Mason Plumlee/125 1.50 4.00
169 Tim Hardaway Jr./125 1.50 4.00
170 Glen Rice Jr./125 1.00 2.50
171 Otto Porter/125 1.50 4.00
172 Nerlens Noel/125 2.00 5.00
173 Trey Burke/125 1.25 3.00
174 Steven Adams/125 1.50 4.00
175 G.Antetokounmpo/125 25.00 60.00
176 Anthony Bennett/49 2.00 5.00
177 Cody Zeller/49 2.00 5.00
178 Ben McLemore/49 2.00 5.00
179 C.J. McCollum/49 4.00 10.00
180 Kelly Olynyk/49 2.00 5.00
181 Dennis Schroder/49 2.50 6.00
182 Sergey Karasev/49 1.50 4.00
183 Gorgui Dieng/49 2.00 5.00
184 Solomon Hill/49 1.50 4.00
185 Isaiah Canaan/49 1.50 4.00
186 Victor Oladipo/49 3.00 8.00
187 Alex Len/49 2.00 5.00
188 Kentavious Caldwell-Pope/49 2.50 6.00
189 M.Carter-Williams/49 2.50 6.00
190 Shabazz Muhammad/49 2.00 5.00
191 Shane Larkin/49 1.50 4.00
192 Tony Snell/49 2.00 5.00
193 Mason Plumlee/49 2.50 6.00
194 Tim Hardaway Jr./49 2.50 6.00
195 Glen Rice Jr./49 1.50 4.00
196 Otto Porter/49 2.50 6.00
197 Nerlens Noel/49 3.00 8.00
198 Trey Burke/49 2.00 5.00
199 Steven Adams/49 8.00 20.00
200 G.Antetokounmpo/49 40.00 100.00

2013-14 Court Kings Gold
*GOLD: 3X TO 8X BASIC
STATED PRINT RUN 25 SER.#'d SETS

2013-14 Court Kings 2 on 2 Quad Memorabilia
PRINT RUNS B/WN 49-99 COPIES PER
1 Brd/Prsh/Jhnsn/Jbbr/49 15.00 40.00
2 Jms/Wde/Hbbrt/Grge/99 20.00 50.00
3 Englsh/Lvr/Adms/Nnce/99 5.00 12.00
4 Wstbrk/Drnt/Gsl/Rndlph/99 8.00 20.00
5 Mlne/Stcktn/Rbnsn/Ellt/49 10.00 25.00
6 Crry/Thmpsn/Lwsn/Frd/99 15.00 40.00
7 Jhnsn/Mrnng/McHle/Lws/49
8 Wllms/Lpz/Anthny/Stdmre/99 8.00 20.00
9 Drxlr/Oljwn/Hrdwy/O'Nl /49 20.00 50.00
10 Brynt/Gsl/Prkr/Dncn/99 20.00 50.00

2013-14 Court Kings 2 on 2 Quad Memorabilia Prime
*PRIME: .75X TO 2X BASIC
PRINT RUNS B/WN 2-25 COPIES PER
NO PRICING ON QTY 3 OR LESS

2013-14 Court Kings 5x7 Box Toppers
1 Magic Johnson 5.00 12.00
2 Grant Hill 2.50 6.00
3 James Harden 3.00 8.00
4 Stephen Curry 8.00 20.00
5 Dikembe Mutombo 2.00 5.00
6 Karl Malone 2.50 6.00
7 Robert Parish 2.00 5.00
8 Clyde Drexler 2.50 6.00
9 Dominique Wilkins 2.50 6.00
10 Adrian Dantley 1.50 4.00
11 Shaquille O'Neal 4.00 10.00
12 Kevin Durant 5.00 12.00
13 Anthony Davis 4.00 10.00
14 Chris Andersen 1.50 4.00
15 Larry Bird 5.00 12.00
16 James Worthy 2.50 6.00
17 Isiah Thomas 2.00 5.00
18 Jason Kidd 2.00 5.00
19 Kyrie Irving 4.00 10.00
20 Dennis Rodman 4.00 10.00
21 Tony Parker 1.50 4.00
22 Anfernee Hardaway 5.00 12.00
23 Kobe Bryant 8.00 20.00
24 Alonzo Mourning 2.50 6.00
25 Blake Griffin 2.00 5.00
26 Bill Russell 3.00 8.00
27 Jeremy Lin 2.00 5.00
28 Russell Westbrook 5.00 12.00
29 John Wall 2.50 6.00
30 Kevin Love 2.00 5.00
31 Vince Carter 2.50 6.00
32 Rajon Rondo 2.00 5.00
33 Dirk Nowitzki 2.50 6.00
34 Steve Nash 2.00 5.00
35 Carmelo Anthony 2.50 6.00
36 Damian Lillard 4.00 10.00
37 Tim Duncan 3.00 8.00
38 Dwyane Wade 3.00 8.00
39 Derrick Rose 2.50 6.00
40 Kevin Garnett 3.00 8.00
41 Dwight Howard 1.50 4.00
42 Ricky Rubio 2.00 5.00
43 Drazen Petrovic 2.00 5.00
44 Deron Williams 1.50 4.00
45 Chris Paul 2.50 6.00
46 Pete Maravich 3.00 8.00
47 Wilt Chamberlain 4.00 10.00
48 LeBron James 8.00 20.00
49 Paul Pierce 2.00 5.00

2013-14 Court Kings 5x7 Box Toppers Autographs
EXCHANGE DEADLINE 9/26/2015
1 Magic Johnson 90.00 150.00
2 Grant Hill 100.00 250.00
3 James Harden
4 Stephen Curry 100.00 200.00
5 Dikembe Mutombo 20.00 50.00
6 Karl Malone 75.00 150.00
7 Robert Parish 15.00 40.00
8 Clyde Drexler 60.00 120.00
9 Dominique Wilkins EXCH 40.00 80.00
10 Adrian Dantley 12.00 30.00
11 Shaquille O'Neal
12 Kevin Durant EXCH 50.00 120.00
13 Anthony Davis 100.00 200.00
14 Chris Andersen EXCH 12.00 30.00
15 Larry Bird 60.00 150.00
16 James Worthy
17 Isiah Thomas 25.00 60.00
18 Jason Kidd 75.00 150.00
19 Kyrie Irving 150.00 300.00
20 Dennis Rodman 50.00 120.00
21 Tony Parker 50.00 120.00
22 Anfernee Hardaway 60.00 150.00
23 Kobe Bryant EXCH 175.00 350.00
24 Alonzo Mourning 100.00 200.00
25 Blake Griffin

2013-14 Court Kings Art Nouveau Jerseys
STATED PRINT RUN 325 SER.#'d SETS
1 C.J. McCollum 4.00 10.00
2 Kelly Olynyk 2.00 5.00
3 Mason Plumlee 2.50 6.00
4 Michael Carter-Williams 2.50 6.00
5 Glen Rice Jr. 1.50 4.00
6 Archie Goodwin 2.00 5.00
7 Tony Mitchell 1.50 4.00
8 Victor Oladipo 3.00 8.00
9 Trey Burke 2.00 5.00
10 Cody Zeller 2.00 5.00
11 Nate Wolters 2.00 5.00
12 Tim Hardaway Jr. 5.00 12.00
13 Ricky Ledo 1.50 4.00
14 Nerlens Noel 3.00 8.00
15 Andre Roberson 1.50 4.00
16 Otto Porter 2.50 6.00
17 Solomon Hill 1.50 4.00
18 Ben McLemore 2.00 5.00
19 Allen Crabbe 2.00 5.00
20 Reggie Bullock 2.00 5.00
21 Shane Larkin 1.50 4.00
22 Isaiah Canaan 1.50 4.00
23 Shabazz Muhammad 2.00 5.00
24 Steven Adams 2.50 6.00
25 Kentavious Caldwell-Pope 2.50 6.00
26 Anthony Bennett 2.00 5.00
27 Giannis Antetokounmpo 12.00 30.00
28 Alex Len 2.00 5.00
29 Ryan Kelly 1.50 4.00
30 Tony Snell 2.00 5.00

2013-14 Court Kings Art Nouveau Jerseys Prime
*PRIME: 2X TO 5X BASIC
STATED PRINT RUN 25 SER.#'d SETS

2013-14 Court Kings Autographs
PRINT RUNS B/WN 20-399 COPIES PER
EXCHANGE DEADLINE 9/26/2015
1 Clyde Drexler/20 40.00 100.00
2 Shane Battier/20 20.00 50.00
3 Greg Anthony/399 3.00 8.00
5 Anthony Mason/399 4.00 10.00
6 Andre Iguodala/20 10.00 25.00
7 Tony Parker/20 50.00 100.00
8 Monta Ellis/20
9 Charlie Scott/399 4.00 10.00
10 Tom Gugliotta/399 3.00 8.00
11 Kemba Walker/20 15.00 40.00
12 Kyrie Irving/35 50.00 120.00
13 Raef LaFrentz/399 3.00 8.00
14 Steve Nash/20 25.00 60.00
15 Andre Drummond/20
16 Kevin Love/20 15.00 40.00
17 Dwight Howard/49 30.00 80.00
18 Eddie Jones/299 8.00 20.00
19 Karl Malone/25 25.00 60.00
20 Scottie Pippen/49 75.00 150.00
21 Zaza Pachulia/349 3.00 8.00
23 Raymond Felton/20 4.00 10.00
24 Magic Johnson/25 40.00 100.00
25 Isiah Thomas/20 15.00 40.00
26 Leonard Truck Robinson/399 3.00 8.00
27 Klay Thompson/99 20.00 50.00
28 Keith Van Horn/249 4.00 10.00
29 Earl Monroe/20 20.00 50.00
30 DeMarcus Cousins/20 10.00 25.00
33 Rick Mahorn/349 3.00 8.00
34 Micheal Ray Richardson/349 4.00 10.00
35 Andrei Kirilenko/20
37 Draymond Green/349 12.00 30.00
38 Alexey Shved/349 3.00 8.00
39 Anthony Davis/35 40.00 80.00
40 Kobe Bryant/35 125.00 250.00
41 Billy Paultz/399 5.00 12.00
42 Jon McGlocklin/349 6.00 15.00
43 Blake Griffin/20 75.00 150.00
44 Dikembe Mutombo/99 12.00 30.00
45 Jrue Holiday/20 15.00 40.00
46 Corey Brewer/399 3.00 8.00
47 Greg Monroe/299 4.00 10.00
48 Kevin Durant/35 50.00 120.00
49 Byron Scott/20 20.00 50.00
50 James Harden/20
RH Ron Harper

2013-14 Court Kings Blacktop Legends
1 Kareem Abdul-Jabbar 2.00 5.00
2 Connie Hawkins 1.25 3.00
3 Kenny Anderson 1.00 2.50
4 Jason Williams 1.00 2.50
5 Nate Archibald 1.00 2.50
6 Vince Carter 1.50 4.00
7 Wilt Chamberlain 2.50 6.00
8 Kevin Durant 3.00 8.00
9 Julius Erving 2.00 5.00
10 Charlie Scott 1.00 2.50
11 Earl Monroe 1.25 3.00

12 Kobe Bryant 5.00 12.00
13 Chris Mullin 1.25 3.00
14 LeBron James 5.00 12.00
15 Satch Sanders 1.25 3.00

2013-14 Court Kings Coast to Coast
1 Magic Johnson 3.00 8.00
2 John Stockton 2.00 5.00
3 Jason Kidd 1.25 3.00
4 Gary Payton 1.25 3.00
5 Chris Paul 1.50 4.00
6 Derrick Rose 1.50 4.00
7 Rajon Rondo 1.25 3.00
8 Steve Nash 1.25 3.00
9 Tony Parker 1.25 3.00
10 Deron Williams 1.00 2.50
11 Isiah Thomas 1.25 3.00
12 Jerry West 1.50 4.00
13 Walt Frazier 1.25 3.00
14 Bob Cousy 2.00 5.00
15 Kyrie Irving 2.50 6.00

2013-14 Court Kings Expressionists
1 LeBron James 5.00 12.00
2 Russell Westbrook 3.00 8.00
3 Blake Griffin 1.25 3.00
4 Chris Bosh 1.25 3.00
5 DeMarcus Cousins 1.25 3.00
6 Joe Dumars 1.25 3.00
7 Alonzo Mourning 1.50 4.00
8 Larry Johnson 1.50 4.00
9 Hakeem Olajuwon 1.50 4.00
10 Bill Laimbeer 1.00 2.50
11 Anderson Varejao .75 2.00
12 Kevin Garnett 2.00 5.00
13 Anthony Davis 2.50 6.00
14 Metta World Peace 1.25 3.00
15 Zach Randolph 1.00 2.50
16 John Starks 1.00 2.50
17 Rick Mahorn .75 2.00
18 Karl Malone 1.50 4.00
19 Magic Johnson 3.00 8.00
20 Dennis Rodman 2.50 6.00
21 Kenneth Faried 1.00 2.50
22 Kobe Bryant 5.00 12.00
23 Kyrie Irving 2.50 6.00
24 Chris Andersen 1.00 2.50
25 J.R. Smith 1.00 2.50
26 Gary Payton 1.25 3.00
27 Darryl Dawkins .75 2.00
28 Shaquille O'Neal 2.50 6.00
29 Larry Bird 5.00 12.00
30 Charles Oakley 1.25 3.00
31 Nate Robinson .75 2.00
32 Joakim Noah 1.00 2.50
33 Dwyane Wade 2.00 5.00
34 Steve Nash 1.25 3.00
35 Udonis Haslem .75 2.00
36 Shawn Kemp 2.00 5.00
37 Dikembe Mutombo 1.25 3.00
38 Tim Duncan 2.00 5.00
39 Moses Malone 1.25 3.00
40 Patrick Ewing 1.50 4.00

2013-14 Court Kings Fresh Paint Autographs
PRINT RUNS B/WN 99-499 COPIES PER
EXCHANGE DEADLINE 9/26/2015
1 Kelly Olynyk/499 4.00 10.00
2 M.Carter-Williams/199 5.00 12.00
3 Tony Mitchell
4 Cody Zeller/99 4.00 10.00
5 Ricky Ledo/499 3.00 8.00
6 Otto Porter/99 10.00 25.00
8 Isaiah Canaan/499 3.00 8.00
10 Alex Len/99 4.00 10.00
11 C.J. McCollum/149 12.00 30.00
12 Glen Rice Jr./299 3.00 8.00
13 Victor Oladipo/199 6.00 15.00
14 Matthew Dellavedova/499 5.00 12.00
15 Nerlens Noel/99 6.00 15.00
17 Peyton Siva/499 3.00 8.00
18 Shabazz Muhammad/99 4.00 10.00
19 Anthony Bennett/99 4.00 10.00
20 Ryan Kelly/499 3.00 8.00
22 Archie Goodwin/499 4.00 10.00
23 Trey Burke/125 4.00 10.00
24 Tim Hardaway Jr./399 8.00 20.00
26 Ben McLemore/99 4.00 10.00
27 Shane Larkin/499 3.00 8.00
28 G.Antetokounmpo/499 60.00 150.00
29 Steven Adams/299 4.00 10.00
30 Nate Wolters/499 4.00 10.00

2013-14 Court Kings Gallery of Stars Jerseys
PRINT RUNS B/WN 10-325 COPIES PER
NO PRICING ON QTY 10
1 Luol Deng/325 3.00 8.00
2 LeBron James/325 10.00 25.00
3 Deron Williams/325 3.00 8.00
4 Manu Ginobili/50 4.00 10.00
5 Kevin Martin/325 3.00 8.00
6 Jose Calderon/325 2.50 6.00
7 Zach Randolph/150 3.00 8.00
8 Dirk Nowitzki/325 5.00 12.00
9 Damian Lillard/325 5.00 12.00
10 Gerald Wallace/325 3.00 8.00
11 Shane Battier/325 3.00 8.00
12 Jrue Holiday/50
13 Serge Ibaka/325 3.00 8.00
14 Andre Miller/50 3.00 8.00
15 Raymond Felton/325 3.00 8.00
16 Chris Paul/150 5.00 12.00
17 Joakim Noah/150 3.00 8.00
18 Ray Allen/325 4.00 10.00
19 Monta Ellis/99
20 Anthony Davis/99 8.00 20.00
21 Kevin Durant/325 8.00 20.00
22 Jeremy Lin/325 8.00 20.00
23 Jameer Nelson/99 2.50 6.00
24 Al Horford/325 3.00 8.00
26 Dwyane Wade/325 5.00 12.00
27 Kobe Bryant/150 10.00 25.00
28 Ty Lawson/325 2.50 6.00
29 Russell Westbrook/325 5.00 12.00
30 Andre Iguodala/325 3.00 8.00
31 Tony Parker/99 4.00 10.00
32 Paul Pierce/325 4.00 10.00
33 Carmelo Anthony/325 5.00 12.00
34 Blake Griffin/99 4.00 10.00
35 Tim Duncan/325 5.00 12.00
36 James Harden/325 5.00 12.00
37 Kevin Garnett/325 5.00 12.00
38 Rajon Rondo/325 3.00 8.00
39 Greivis Vasquez/325 3.00 8.00
40 Tyson Chandler/325 3.00 8.00

2013-14 Court Kings Gallery of Stars Jerseys Prime
*PRIME: 1.2X TO 3X BASIC
PRINT RUNS B/WN 1-25 COPIES PER
NO PRICING ON QTY 10 OR LESS

2013-14 Court Kings Impressionist Ink Autographs
PRINT RUNS B/WN 20-399 COPIES PER
EXCHANGE DEADLINE 9/26/2015
1 Stephen Curry/49 100.00 250.00
2 Anthony Davis/49 50.00 120.00
3 Bradley Beal/99 5.00 12.00
4 Robert Parish/99 5.00 12.00
5 Glen Rice/249 4.00 10.00
6 Kobe Bryant/49 100.00 200.00
7 Artis Gilmore/35 4.00 10.00
8 Tim Hardaway/399 5.00 12.00
9 Steve Blake/399 3.00 8.00
10 Blake Griffin/20 50.00 100.00
12 Adrian Dantley/349 4.00 10.00
13 Kyrie Irving/49 40.00 100.00
14 David Thompson/349 4.00 10.00
15 Kevin Durant/30 60.00 150.00
16 Monta Ellis/25
17 Jeff Hornacek/349 4.00 10.00
18 Al Horford
19 Magic Johnson/25 30.00 80.00
20 Karl Malone/25 60.00 120.00

2013-14 Court Kings Kings of Springfield
1 Bill Russell 3.00 8.00
2 Magic Johnson
3 Larry Bird 30.00 60.00
4 George Mikan 4.00 10.00
5 Dennis Rodman 8.00 20.00
6 Moses Malone
7 Hakeem Olajuwon
8 John Stockton 10.00 25.00
9 Rick Barry
10 Karl Malone 4.00 10.00
11 Julius Erving 3.00 8.00
12 David Robinson
13 Dominique Wilkins 2.50 6.00
14 Scottie Pippen
15 Wilt Chamberlain 6.00 15.00

2013-14 Court Kings Le Cinque Piu Belle
STATED PRINT RUN 35 SER.#'d SETS
1 Kevin Durant 20.00 50.00
2 Kevin Durant 20.00 50.00
3 Kevin Durant 20.00 50.00
4 Kevin Durant 20.00 50.00
5 Kevin Durant 20.00 50.00

2013-14 Court Kings Legacies
1 John Stockton 5.00 12.00
2 Kobe Bryant 12.00 30.00
3 Dirk Nowitzki 4.00 10.00
4 Calvin Murphy 2.50 6.00
5 Dwyane Wade 5.00 12.00
6 Tony Parker 3.00 8.00
7 Larry Bird 8.00 20.00
8 Magic Johnson 8.00 20.00
9 Isiah Thomas 3.00 8.00
10 Alvan Adams 2.00 5.00
11 John Havlicek 4.00 10.00
12 Tim Duncan 5.00 12.00
13 Joe Dumars 3.00 8.00
14 David Robinson 5.00 12.00
15 Wes Unseld 3.00 8.00

2013-14 Court Kings Masterpieces
STATED PRINT RUN 175 SER.#'d SETS
1 Carmelo Anthony 1.50 4.00
2 Dwyane Wade 2.00 5.00
3 Kevin Durant 3.00 8.00
4 Paul George 1.50 4.00
5 Tony Parker 1.25 3.00
6 Kyrie Irving 2.50 6.00
7 Russell Westbrook 3.00 8.00
8 Blake Griffin 1.25 3.00
9 Derrick Rose 1.50 4.00
10 Dirk Nowitzki 1.50 4.00
11 Chris Paul 1.50 4.00
12 Kevin Love 1.25 3.00
13 Rudy Gay 1.25 3.00
14 Tim Duncan 2.00 5.00
15 Andre Iguodala 1.00 2.50
16 LeBron James 10.00 25.00
17 Rajon Rondo 1.25 3.00
18 Damian Lillard 2.50 6.00
19 Stephen Curry 5.00 12.00
20 Manu Ginobili 1.25 3.00
21 Kobe Bryant 5.00 12.00
22 Jrue Holiday 1.25 3.00
23 James Harden 2.00 5.00
24 Deron Williams 1.00 2.50
25 Dwight Howard 1.00 2.50

2013-14 Court Kings Masterpieces Purple
*PURPLE: 2.5X TO 6X BASIC
STATED PRINT RUN 25 SER.#'d SETS

2013-14 Court Kings Next Day Autographs
EXCHANGE DEADLINE 9/26/2015
AB Anthony Bennett 4.00 10.00
AC Allen Crabbe 4.00 10.00
AG Archie Goodwin 10.00 25.00
AL Alex Len 8.00 20.00
AR Andre Roberson 3.00 8.00
BM Ben McLemore 20.00 50.00
CM C.J. McCollum 30.00 80.00
CZ Cody Zeller 4.00 10.00
EM Erik Murphy 3.00 8.00
GA Giannis Antetokounmpo 200.00 500.00
GD Gorgui Dieng 20.00 50.00
GR Glen Rice Jr. 3.00 8.00
IC Isaiah Canaan 3.00 8.00
JF Jamaal Franklin 3.00 8.00
JW Jeff Withey 3.00 8.00
KC Kentavious Caldwell-Pope 15.00 40.00
KO Kelly Olynyk 8.00 20.00
MC Michael Carter-Williams 30.00 80.00
MP Mason Plumlee 5.00 12.00
NN Nerlens Noel 25.00 60.00
NW Nate Wolters 4.00 10.00
OP Otto Porter 12.00 30.00
PS Peyton Siva 3.00 8.00
RB Reggie Bullock 4.00 10.00
RK Ryan Kelly 3.00 8.00
RL Ricky Ledo 3.00 8.00
SA Steven Adams 15.00 40.00
SH Solomon Hill 3.00 8.00
SL Shane Larkin 3.00 8.00
SM Shabazz Muhammad 8.00 20.00
TB Trey Burke 4.00 10.00
TH Tim Hardaway Jr. 12.00 30.00
TM Tony Mitchell
TS Tony Snell 10.00 25.00
VO Victor Oladipo 20.00 50.00

2013-14 Court Kings Performance Art Memorabilia
PRINT RUNS B/WN 49-299 COPIES PER
1 Evan Turner/49 2.50 6.00
2 Kobe Bryant/199 5.00 12.00
3 John Wall/175 5.00 12.00
4 Mario Chalmers/299 3.00 8.00
5 Reggie Evans/299 2.50 6.00
6 LeBron James/299 10.00 25.00
7 Steve Nash/299 4.00 10.00
8 Serge Ibaka/299 3.00 8.00
9 Amar'e Stoudemire/99 3.00 8.00
10 Joe Johnson/150 3.00 8.00
11 Carmelo Anthony/150 5.00 12.00
12 Wesley Matthews/150 2.50 6.00
13 Kevin Durant/299 5.00 12.00
14 Jeremy Lin/299 4.00 10.00
15 J.R. Smith/299 3.00 8.00
16 Andre Miller/299 3.00 8.00
17 Dwyane Wade/150 5.00 12.00
18 Joakim Noah/150 3.00 8.00
19 Ersan Ilyasova/49 3.00 8.00
20 Kobe Bryant/299 4.00 10.00
21 James Harden/299 5.00 12.00
22 Nick Collison/299 3.00 8.00
23 Pau Gasol/299 4.00 10.00
24 Russell Westbrook/299 5.00 12.00
25 Steve Nash/50 5.00 12.00
26 Tim Duncan/299 5.00 12.00
27 Deron Williams/150 3.00 8.00
28 Tony Parker/150 4.00 10.00
29 Matt Barnes/299 2.50 6.00
30 Carmelo Anthony/299 5.00 12.00
31 Rajon Rondo/299 4.00 10.00
32 Chandler Parsons/299 3.00 8.00
33 Chris Paul/299 5.00 12.00
34 Andray Blatche/299 2.50 6.00
35 LeBron James/150 10.00 25.00
36 Luol Deng /150 3.00 8.00
37 David West/150 3.00 8.00
38 Dwyane Wade/150 5.00 12.00
39 Omer Asik/299 3.00 8.00
40 Jamal Crawford/299 4.00 10.00

2013-14 Court Kings Performance Art Memorabilia Prime
*PRIME: 1X TO 2.5X BASIC
PRINT RUNS B/WN 1-25 COPIES PER
NO PRICING ON QTY 25 OR LESS
2 Kobe Bryant/25 40.00 100.00
13 Kevin Durant/18 100.00 200.00
17 Dwyane Wade/25 25.00 60.00
24 Russell Westbrook/15 25.00 60.00
26 Tim Duncan/25 25.00 60.00
35 LeBron James/25 75.00 200.00

2013-14 Court Kings Portraits
1 Klay Thompson 2.00 5.00
2 Jeff Teague 1.25 3.00
3 DeMarcus Cousins 1.50 4.00
4 Kevin Love 1.50 4.00
5 Paul Pierce 1.50 4.00
6 O.J. Mayo 1.25 3.00
7 Avery Bradley 1.50 4.00
8 John Wall 2.00 5.00
9 Deron Williams 1.25 3.00
10 J.R. Smith 1.25 3.00
11 Ricky Rubio 1.50 4.00
12 Al Jefferson 1.25 3.00
13 Nikola Vucevic 1.25 3.00
14 DeMar DeRozan 1.50 4.00
15 Ben Gordon 1.25 3.00
16 Chris Bosh 1.50 4.00
17 Kemba Walker 1.50 4.00
18 Tim Duncan 2.50 6.00
19 Monta Ellis 1.25 3.00
20 Anthony Davis 5.00 12.00
21 Tony Parker 1.50 4.00
22 Vince Carter 1.50 4.00
23 Larry Sanders 1.00 2.50
24 Evan Turner 1.00 2.50
25 Dirk Nowitzki 2.00 5.00
26 Bradley Beal 1.50 4.00
27 Kenneth Faried 1.25 3.00
28 LaMarcus Aldridge 1.50 4.00
29 Stephen Curry 6.00 15.00
30 Carmelo Anthony 2.00 5.00
31 Mike Conley 1.25 3.00
32 Tyson Chandler 1.25 3.00
33 George Hill 1.25 3.00
34 Amar'e Stoudemire 1.25 3.00
35 Derrick Rose 2.00 5.00
36 Manu Ginobili 1.50 4.00
37 James Harden 2.50 6.00
38 Zach Randolph 1.25 3.00
39 Paul George 1.50 4.00
40 Jason Richardson 1.25 3.00
41 Blake Griffin 1.50 4.00
42 Nikola Pekovic 1.25 3.00
43 Shawn Marion 1.25 3.00
44 Dwyane Wade 2.50 6.00
45 Ty Lawson 1.00 2.50
46 Damian Lillard 3.00 8.00
47 Pau Gasol 1.50 4.00
48 Carlos Boozer 1.25 3.00
49 Dwight Howard 1.25 3.00
50 Kawhi Leonard 2.50 6.00
51 Steve Nash 1.50 4.00
52 Serge Ibaka 1.25 3.00
53 Al Horford 1.25 3.00
54 Chris Paul 2.50 6.00
55 Andre Iguodala 1.25 3.00
56 Kevin Durant 4.00 10.00
57 Roy Hibbert 1.25 3.00
58 Brandon Jennings 1.25 3.00
59 Marc Gasol 1.50 4.00
60 Brook Lopez 1.25 3.00
61 Joakim Noah 1.50 4.00
62 Eric Bledsoe 1.50 4.00
63 Kevin Garnett 2.50 6.00
64 Andre Drummond 1.50 4.00
65 Jeremy Lin 1.50 4.00
66 Dion Waiters 1.25 3.00
67 Russell Westbrook 4.00 10.00
68 Rajon Rondo 1.50 4.00
69 LeBron James 10.00 25.00
70 Anderson Varejao 1.00 2.50
71 Gerald Wallace 1.25 3.00
72 Isaiah Thomas 1.50 4.00
73 Kyrie Irving 3.00 8.00
74 Luol Deng 1.25 3.00
75 Kobe Bryant 6.00 15.00

2013-14 Court Kings Portraits Blue Frame
*BLUE FRAME: .5X TO 1.2X BASIC
STATED PRINT RUN 75 SER.#'d SETS

2013-14 Court Kings Portraits Red Frame
*RED FRAME: 1.5X TO 4X BASIC
STATED PRINT RUN 25 SER.#'d SETS

2013-14 Court Kings Renaissance Men
1 James Harden 2.00 5.00
2 Russell Westbrook 3.00 8.00
3 Dwyane Wade 2.00 5.00
4 Josh Smith 1.00 2.50
5 Anthony Davis 2.50 6.00
6 Tim Duncan 2.00 5.00
7 Tyreke Evans .75 2.00
8 Derrick Rose 1.50 4.00
9 Dirk Nowitzki 1.50 4.00
10 Joakim Noah 1.00 2.50
11 LeBron James 5.00 12.00
12 Stephen Curry 5.00 12.00
13 Paul Pierce 1.25 3.00
14 Blake Griffin 1.25 3.00
15 Rajon Rondo 1.25 3.00
16 Ricky Rubio 1.25 3.00
17 Dwight Howard 1.00 2.50
18 Deron Williams 1.00 2.50
19 Damian Lillard 2.50 6.00
20 Kevin Love 1.25 3.00
21 Kevin Durant 3.00 8.00
22 Kobe Bryant 5.00 12.00
23 John Wall 1.50 4.00
24 Kyrie Irving 2.50 6.00
25 Pau Gasol 1.25 3.00
26 Chris Paul 1.50 4.00
27 Steve Nash 1.25 3.00
28 Kevin Garnett 2.00 5.00
29 Tony Parker 1.25 3.00
30 Jeremy Lin 1.25 3.00

2013-14 Court Kings Rookie Portraits
STATED PRINT RUN 125 SER.#'d SETS
1 Anthony Bennett 1.50 4.00
2 Cody Zeller 1.50 4.00
3 Ben McLemore 1.50 4.00
4 C.J. McCollum 3.00 8.00
5 Kelly Olynyk 1.50 4.00
6 Dennis Schroder 2.00 5.00
7 Sergey Karasev 1.25 3.00
8 Gorgui Dieng 1.25 3.00
9 Solomon Hill 1.25 3.00
10 Isaiah Canaan 1.25 3.00
11 Victor Oladipo 2.50 6.00
12 Alex Len 1.50 4.00
13 Kentavious Caldwell-Pope 2.00 5.00
14 Michael Carter-Williams 2.00 5.00
15 Shabazz Muhammad 1.50 4.00
16 Shane Larkin 1.25 3.00
17 Tony Snell 1.50 4.00
18 Mason Plumlee 2.00 5.00
19 Tim Hardaway Jr. 2.00 5.00
20 Glen Rice Jr. 1.25 3.00
21 Otto Porter
22 Nerlens Noel 2.50 6.00
23 Trey Burke 1.50 4.00
24 Steven Adams 2.00 5.00
25 Giannis Antetokounmpo 15.00 40.00

2013-14 Court Kings Rookie Portraits Blue Frame
*BLUE FRAME: .5X TO 1.2X BASIC
STATED PRINT RUN 75 SER.#'d SETS

2013-14 Court Kings Rookie Portraits Red Frame
*RED FRAME: .75X TO 2X BASIC
STATED PRINT RUN 25 SER.#'d SETS

2013-14 Court Kings Royal Performances
STATED PRINT RUN 175 SER.#'d SETS
1 Kobe Bryant 6.00 15.00
2 Rajon Rondo 1.50 4.00
3 Andrew Bynum 1.00 2.50
4 Joakim Noah 1.25 3.00
5 Elgin Baylor 1.50 4.00
6 Deron Williams 1.25 3.00
7 Steve Nash 1.50 4.00
8 Tim Duncan 2.50 6.00
9 Dwyane Wade 2.50 6.00
10 David Robinson 2.50 6.00
11 Brandon Jennings 1.00 2.50
12 Chris Paul 2.00 5.00
13 John Wall 2.00 5.00
14 Wilt Chamberlain 3.00 8.00
15 Tony Parker 1.50 4.00
16 Kevin Love 1.50 4.00
17 Scott Skiles 1.25 3.00
18 Serge Ibaka 1.25 3.00
19 Dirk Nowitzki 2.00 5.00
20 Manute Bol 1.50 4.00

2013-14 Court Kings Royal Performances Purple
*PURPLE: 1X TO 2.5X BASIC
STATED PRINT RUN 25 SER.#'d SETS

2013-14 Court Kings Sketches and Swatches Autographs
PRINT RUNS B/WN 49-199 COPIES PER
EXCHANGE DEADLINE 9/26/2015
1 Andre Drummond/75 15.00 40.00
2 Jason Terry/75
3 Devin Harris/49 3.00 8.00
4 Kawhi Leonard/149 30.00 80.00
5 Luis Scola/149 4.00 10.00
6 Tobias Harris/199 4.00 10.00
7 James Jones/199 3.00 8.00
8 Anthony Davis/49 40.00 100.00
9 Boris Diaw/125 6.00 15.00
10 Tyson Chandler/99 4.00 10.00
11 Enes Kanter/149 3.00 8.00
12 Kevin Durant/49 100.00 200.00
13 Nikola Vucevic/149 4.00 10.00
14 Al Horford/49 4.00 10.00
15 Draymond Green/199 12.00 30.00
16 Tiago Splitter/199 3.00 8.00
17 Iman Shumpert/199 3.00 8.00
18 Udonis Haslem/199 3.00 8.00
19 Danilo Gallinari/99 3.00 8.00
20 Jeff Green/149 6.00 15.00
21 Andrei Kirilenko/99 4.00 10.00
22 Brandon Bass/149 3.00 8.00
23 Kobe Bryant/75 100.00 200.00
24 Raymond Felton/99 4.00 10.00
25 Eric Gordon/99 4.00 10.00
26 Andre Miller/199 4.00 10.00
27 Jared Sullinger/99 5.00 12.00
28 Jrue Holiday/75 5.00 12.00
29 Steve Blake/199 3.00 8.00
30 Kyrie Irving/49 40.00 100.00

2013-14 Court Kings Sketches and Swatches Autographs Prime
*PRIME: .75X TO 2X BASIC
PRINT RUNS B/WN 1-25 COPIES PER
NO PRICING ON QTY 10 OR LESS
EXCHANGE DEADLINE 9/26/2015

2013-14 Court Kings Sovereign Signatures
PRINT RUNS B/WN 20-199 COPIES PER
EXCHANGE DEADLINE 9/26/2015
1 Robert Parish/49 5.00 12.00
2 Anfernee Hardaway/49 15.00 40.00
3 Bill Laimbeer/199 4.00 10.00
4 World B. Free/60 5.00 12.00
5 Joe Dumars/60 5.00 12.00
6 Kelly Tripucka/60 3.00 8.00
7 Bob Lanier/20 4.00 10.00
8 Larry Bird/20 50.00 100.00
9 Eddie Johnson/199 3.00 8.00
10 Jalen Rose/160 5.00 12.00
11 Brad Daugherty/199 4.00 10.00
12 Mark Price/199 5.00 12.00
13 Isiah Thomas/49 10.00 25.00
14 Magic Johnson/30 50.00 100.00
15 John Stockton/25 30.00 80.00
16 Scottie Pippen/49 50.00 120.00
17 Shaquille O'Neal/25 75.00 150.00
18 Jayson Williams/199 3.00 8.00
19 David Robinson/35 15.00 40.00
20 Kevin McHale/20 15.00 40.00
21 Larry Johnson/199 6.00 15.00
22 Karl Malone/35 20.00 50.00
23 Kareem Abdul-Jabbar/35 40.00 80.00
24 Jim Jackson/199 3.00 8.00
25 Alex English/199 4.00 10.00
26 Tracy McGrady/49 20.00 50.00
27 Grant Hill/49 15.00 40.00
28 Artis Gilmore/35 4.00 10.00
29 Clyde Drexler/20 12.00 30.00
30 Robert Horry/99 8.00 20.00

2013-14 Court Kings Sovereign Signatures Prime
*PRIME: .75X TO 2X BASIC
PRINT RUNS B/WN 10-25 COPIES PER
NO PRICING ON QTY 10 OR LESS
EXCHANGE DEADLINE 9/26/2015

2013-14 Court Kings Squires
STATED PRINT RUN 175 SER.#'d SETS
1 Tyreke Evans 1.00 2.50
2 Serge Ibaka 1.25 3.00
3 Ricky Rubio 1.50 4.00
4 John Wall 2.00 5.00
5 DeAndre Jordan 1.50 4.00
6 Kenneth Faried 1.25 3.00
7 Eric Bledsoe 1.25 3.00
8 Ty Lawson 1.00 2.50
9 Brandon Jennings 1.00 2.50
10 Nicolas Batum 1.25 3.00
11 Mike Conley 1.25 3.00
12 Danilo Gallinari 1.00 2.50
13 Greg Monroe 1.25 3.00
14 Larry Sanders 1.00 2.50
15 Ed Davis 1.00 2.50
16 DeMarcus Cousins 1.50 4.00
17 JaVale McGee 1.25 3.00
18 Thaddeus Young 1.00 2.50
19 Brook Lopez 1.25 3.00
20 Anthony Davis 3.00 8.00

2013-14 Court Kings Squires Purple
*PURPLE: .75X TO 2X BASIC
STATED PRINT RUN 25 SER.#'d SETS

2013-14 Court Kings Vintage Materials
STATED PRINT RUN 25-299 SER.#'d SETS
1 Artis Gilmore/35
2 Kiki VanDeWeghe/299 3.00 8.00
3 Calvin Murphy/35 3.00 8.00
4 Chris Mullin/125 4.00 10.00
5 John Lucas/125 4.00 10.00
6 Joe Dumars/299 4.00 10.00
7 Dan Issel/125
8 Robert Horry/75 3.00 8.00
9 Bob Lanier/249 3.00 8.00
10 Scottie Pippen/75 6.00 15.00
11 Patrick Ewing/125 5.00 12.00
12 Isiah Thomas/49 4.00 10.00
13 Earl Monroe/25
14 Danny Manning/150 3.00 8.00
15 Bernard King/75 3.00 8.00
16 Moses Malone/35 4.00 10.00
17 Cazzie Russell/35 3.00 8.00
18 Dominique Wilkins/99 5.00 12.00
19 Spencer Haywood/25
20 Jim Jackson/299 2.50 6.00

2013-14 Court Kings Vintage Materials Prime
*PRIME: .75X TO 2X BASIC
PRINT RUNS B/WN 1-25 COPIES PER
NO PRICING ON QTY 10 OR LESS

2014-15 Court Kings
134-166 PRINT RUN 225 SER.#'d SETS
167-199 PRINT RUN 149 SER.#'d SETS
200-232 PRINT RUN 49 SER.#'d SETS
1A Jared Sullinger .40 1.00
1B LeBron James VAR 5.00 12.00
2A Monta Ellis .50 1.25
2B Kobe Bryant VAR 5.00 12.00
3A DeAndre Jordan .60 1.50
3B Kyrie Irving VAR 2.50 6.00
4A Kawhi Leonard 1.00 2.50
4B Damian Lillard VAR 2.50 6.00
5A Al Horford .50 1.25
5B Kevin Durant VAR 3.00 8.00
6A Ricky Rubio .60 1.50
6B Chris Paul VAR 1.50 4.00
7A Eric Bledsoe .50 1.25
7B Paul George VAR 1.50 4.00
8A Kyrie Irving .75 2.00
8B Anthony Davis VAR 2.50 6.00
9A Brandon Knight .50 1.25
9B Carmelo Anthony VAR 1.50 4.00
10 Tony Parker .60 1.50
11 Jeff Green .50 1.25
12 Nerlens Noel .60 1.50
13 DeMar DeRozan .75 2.00
14 Kemba Walker .60 1.50
15 Roy Hibbert .50 1.25
16 Al Jefferson .50 1.25
17 LaMarcus Aldridge .60 1.50
18 Gerald Henderson .40 1.00
19 Carlos Boozer .50 1.25
20 Tony Wroten .50 1.25
21 Jeff Teague .50 1.25
22 Nicolas Batum .50 1.25
23 DeMarcus Cousins .60 1.50
24 Kenneth Faried .60 1.50
25 Andre Drummond .60 1.50
26 Rudy Gay .60 1.50
27 Giannis Antetokounmpo 1.25 3.00
28 Lance Stephenson .50 1.25
29 Carmelo Anthony .75 2.00
30 Trevor Ariza .40 1.00
31 Jeremy Lin .50 1.25
32 Nikola Vucevic .50 1.25
33 Deron Williams .50 1.25
34 Kevin Durant 1.50 4.00
35 Andre Iguodala .50 1.25
36 Russell Westbrook 1.50 4.00
37 Goran Dragic .50 1.25
38 LeBron James 2.50 6.00
39 Chandler Parsons .50 1.25
40 Trey Burke .50 1.25
41 Joakim Noah .50 1.25
42 O.J. Mayo .40 1.00
43 Derrick Rose .75 2.00
44 Kevin Garnett 1.00 2.50
45 Anthony Davis 1.00 2.50
46 Gordon Hayward .60 1.50
47 Ryan Anderson .40 1.00
48 Luol Deng .50 1.25
49 Channing Frye .50 1.25
50 Ty Lawson .40 1.00
51 Joe Johnson .50 1.25
52 Pau Gasol .60 1.50
53 Dion Waiters .50 1.25
54 Kevin Love .60 1.50
55 Arron Afflalo .50 1.25
56 Serge Ibaka .60 1.50
57 Greg Monroe .50 1.25
58 Manu Ginobili .60 1.50
59 Chris Bosh .60 1.50
60 Tyreke Evans .40 1.00
61 John Wall .75 2.00
62 Paul George .75 2.00
63 Dirk Nowitzki .75 2.00
64 Kevin Martin .40 1.00
65 Ben McLemore .40 1.00
66 Stephen Curry 2.50 6.00
67 Iman Shumpert .40 1.00
68 Marc Gasol .60 1.50
69 Chris Paul .75 2.00
70 Tyson Chandler .50 1.25
71 Jose Calderon .40 1.00
72 Paul Millsap .50 1.25
73 Dwight Howard .60 1.50
74 Klay Thompson .75 2.00
75 Blake Griffin .60 1.50
76 Steve Nash .60 1.50
77 Isaiah Thomas .60 1.50
78 Marcin Gortat .50 1.25
79 Damian Lillard 1.25 3.00
80 Victor Oladipo .60 1.50
81 Josh Smith .50 1.25
82 Rajon Rondo .60 1.50
83 Dwyane Wade 1.00 2.50
84 Kobe Bryant 2.50 6.00
85 Bradley Beal .60 1.50
86 Terrence Ross .50 1.25
87 J.R. Smith .50 1.25
88 Michael Carter-Williams .40 1.00
89 David Lee .40 1.00
90 Vince Carter .75 2.00
91 Jrue Holiday .50 1.25
92 Chris Andersen .50 1.25
93 Enes Kanter .40 1.00
94 Kyle Lowry .50 1.25
95 Brandon Jennings .40 1.00
96 Tim Duncan 1.00 2.50
97 James Harden 1.00 2.50
98 Mike Conley .50 1.25
99 David West .50 1.25
100 Zach Randolph .50 1.25
101 Andrew Wiggins RC 3.00 8.00
102 Jabari Parker RC 1.50 4.00
103 Joel Embiid RC 3.00 8.00
104 Aaron Gordon RC 1.50 4.00
105 Dante Exum RC .60 1.50
106 Marcus Smart RC .60 1.50
107 Julius Randle RC 1.50 4.00
108 Nik Stauskas RC .75 2.00
109 Noah Vonleh RC .75 2.00
110 Elfrid Payton RC 1.00 2.50
111 Doug McDermott RC 1.00 2.50
112 Zach LaVine RC 1.50 4.00
113 T.J. Warren RC 1.00 2.50
114 Adreian Payne RC .75 2.00
115 James Young RC .60 1.50
116 Tyler Ennis RC .60 1.50
117 Gary Harris RC 1.00 2.50
118 Bruno Caboclo RC .75 2.00
119 Rodney Hood RC 1.00 2.50
120 Shabazz Napier RC .75 2.00
121 P.J. Hairston RC .60 1.50
122 Kyle Anderson RC 1.00 2.50
123 K.J. McDaniels RC .75 2.00
124 Markel Brown RC .60 1.50
125 Russ Smith RC .60 1.50
126 Cleanthony Early RC .60 1.50
127 Spencer Dinwiddie RC .75 2.00
128 Damien Inglis RC .60 1.50
129 James Ennis RC .60 1.50
130 Nick Johnson RC .60 1.50
131 C.J. Wilcox RC .60 1.50
132 Jordan Adams RC .60 1.50
133 Mitch McGary RC .75 2.00
134 Andrew Wiggins/225 4.00 10.00
135 Jabari Parker/225 2.00 5.00
136 Joel Embiid/225 4.00 10.00
137 Aaron Gordon/225 2.00 5.00
138 Dante Exum/225 1.25 3.00
139 Marcus Smart/225 1.25 3.00
140 Julius Randle/225 2.00 5.00
141 Nik Stauskas/225 1.00 2.50
142 Noah Vonleh/225 1.00 2.50
143 Elfrid Payton/225 1.25 3.00
144 Doug McDermott/225 1.25 3.00
145 Zach LaVine/225 2.00 5.00
146 T.J. Warren/225 1.25 3.00
147 Adreian Payne/225 1.00 2.50
148 James Young/225 .75 2.00
149 Tyler Ennis/225 .75 2.00
150 Gary Harris/225 1.25 3.00
151 Bruno Caboclo/225 1.00 2.50
152 Rodney Hood/225 1.25 3.00
153 Shabazz Napier/225 1.00 2.50
154 P.J. Hairston/225 .75 2.00
155 Kyle Anderson/225 1.25 3.00
156 K.J. McDaniels/225 1.00 2.50
157 Markel Brown/225 .75 2.00
158 Russ Smith/225 .75 2.00
159 Cleanthony Early/225 .75 2.00
160 Spencer Dinwiddie/225 1.00 2.50
161 Damien Inglis/225 .75 2.00
162 James Ennis/225 .75 2.00
163 Nick Johnson/225 .75 2.00
164 C.J. Wilcox/225 .75 2.00
165 Jordan Adams/225 .75 2.00
166 Mitch McGary/225 .75 2.00
167 Andrew Wiggins/149 12.00 30.00
168 Jabari Parker/149 2.50 6.00
169 Joel Embiid/149 5.00 12.00
170 Aaron Gordon/149 2.50 6.00
171 Dante Exum/149 1.50 4.00
172 Marcus Smart/149 1.50 4.00
173 Julius Randle/149 2.50 6.00
174 Nik Stauskas/149 1.25 3.00
175 Noah Vonleh/149 1.25 3.00
176 Elfrid Payton/149 1.50 4.00
177 Doug McDermott/149 1.50 4.00
178 Zach LaVine/149 2.50 6.00
179 T.J. Warren/149 1.50 4.00
180 Adreian Payne/149 1.25 3.00
181 James Young/149 1.00 2.50
182 Tyler Ennis/149 1.00 2.50
183 Gary Harris/149 1.50 4.00
184 Bruno Caboclo/149 1.25 3.00
185 Rodney Hood/149 1.50 4.00
186 Shabazz Napier/149 1.25 3.00
187 P.J. Hairston/149 1.00 2.50
188 Kyle Anderson/149 1.50 4.00
189 K.J. McDaniels/149 1.25 3.00
190 Markel Brown/149 1.00 2.50
191 Russ Smith/149 1.00 2.50
192 Cleanthony Early/149 1.00 2.50
193 Spencer Dinwiddie/149 1.25 3.00
194 Damien Inglis/149 1.00 2.50
195 James Ennis/149 1.00 2.50
196 Nick Johnson/149 1.00 2.50
197 C.J. Wilcox/149 1.00 2.50
198 Jordan Adams/149 1.00 2.50
199 Mitch McGary/149 1.25 3.00
200 Andrew Wiggins/49 15.00 40.00
201 Jabari Parker/49 8.00 20.00
202 Joel Embiid/49 15.00 40.00
203 Aaron Gordon/49 8.00 20.00
204 Dante Exum/49 5.00 12.00
205 Marcus Smart/49 5.00 12.00
206 Julius Randle/49 8.00 20.00
207 Nik Stauskas/49 4.00 10.00
208 Noah Vonleh/49 4.00 10.00
209 Elfrid Payton/49 5.00 12.00
210 Doug McDermott/49 5.00 12.00
211 Zach LaVine/49 8.00 20.00
212 T.J. Warren/49 5.00 12.00
213 Adreian Payne/49 4.00 10.00
214 James Young/49 3.00 8.00
215 Tyler Ennis/49 3.00 8.00
216 Gary Harris/49 5.00 12.00
217 Bruno Caboclo/49 4.00 10.00
218 Rodney Hood/49 5.00 12.00
219 Shabazz Napier/49 4.00 10.00
220 P.J. Hairston/49 3.00 8.00
221 Kyle Anderson/49 5.00 12.00
222 K.J. McDaniels/49 4.00 10.00
223 Markel Brown/49 3.00 8.00
224 Russ Smith/49 3.00 8.00
225 Cleanthony Early/49 3.00 8.00
226 Spencer Dinwiddie/49 4.00 10.00
227 Damien Inglis/49 3.00 8.00
228 James Ennis/49 3.00 8.00
229 Nick Johnson/49 3.00 8.00
230 C.J. Wilcox/49 3.00 8.00
231 Jordan Adams/49 3.00 8.00
232 Mitch McGary/49 3.00 8.00

2014-15 Court Kings Sapphire
*VETS: 2X TO 5X BASE HI
STATED PRINT RUN 25 SER.#'d SETS

2014-15 Court Kings 2 on 2 Quad Memorabilia
STATED PRINT RUN 99 SER.#'d SETS
*PRIME/25: 1X TO 2.5X BASE HI
QBOLA Grntt/Gsl/Brynt/Alln 12.00 30.00
QBOPH McHle/Brd/Ervng/Mloe 8.00 20.00
QBOTP Wllms/Grntt/DRzn/Ross 5.00 12.00
QCLSA Jms/Pkr/Dncn/Ilgskis 12.00 30.00
QDAHR Nwtzki/Hwrd/Hrdn/Ellis 5.00 12.00
QDAMI Wde/Jms/Mrn/Nwtzki 12.00 30.00
QDELA Thms/Dmrs/Wrthy/Jhnsn 8.00 20.00
QDEPO Lmbr/Dmrs/Drxlr/Dckwrth 4.00 10.00
QGOLA Igdla/Paul/Crry/Grffn 12.00 30.00
QLAPH Irvsn/Brynt/Mtmbo/O'Nl 12.00 30.00
QMIWA Bsh/Wll/Beal/Wade 5.00 12.00
QOKMI Wstbrk/Bsh/Drnt/Jms 12.00 30.00
QOKPO Drnt/Aldrdge/Llrd/Wstbrk 8.00 20.00
QSACL Lnrd/Wde/Jms/Prker 12.00 30.00

2014-15 Court Kings 5x7 Box Toppers Autographs
BTKI Kyrie Irving 60.00 150.00
BTAW Andrew Wiggins 100.00 200.00
BTJP Jabari Parker 150.00 250.00
BTMS Marcus Smart 40.00 100.00
BTDM Doug McDermott 15.00 40.00
BTSN Shabazz Napier 12.00 30.00
BTLA LaMarcus Aldridge 25.00 60.00
BTSC Stephen Curry 100.00 200.00
BTBB Bradley Beal 15.00 40.00
BTEP Elfrid Payton 40.00 100.00
BTJY James Young 15.00 40.00
BTZL Zach LaVine 40.00 100.00
BTJK Jason Kidd 40.00 100.00
BTBW Bill Walton 10.00 25.00
BTJS John Stockton 40.00 100.00
BTWF Walt Frazier 25.00 60.00
BTJR Julius Randle 25.00 60.00
BTJW Jerry West 30.00 80.00

2014-15 Court Kings 5x7 Box Toppers Panoramics
1 Damian Lillard 4.00 10.00
2 Kobe Bryant 6.00 15.00
3 Kevin Durant 5.00 12.00
4 Russell Westbrook 5.00 12.00
5 Kyrie Irving 4.00 10.00
6 James Harden 3.00 8.00
7 Paul George 2.50 6.00
8 LeBron James 6.00 15.00
9 Carmelo Anthony 2.50 6.00
10 Derrick Rose 2.50 6.00
11 Dirk Nowitzki 2.50 6.00
12 Tony Parker 2.00 5.00
13 Rajon Rondo 2.00 5.00
14 Chris Paul 2.50 6.00
15 Blake Griffin 2.50 6.00
16 Ben McLemore 1.25 3.00
17 Michael Carter-Williams 1.25 3.00
18 John Wall 2.50 6.00
19 Bradley Beal 2.00 5.00
20 Terrence Ross 1.50 4.00
21 Ricky Rubio 2.00 5.00
22 Goran Dragic 1.50 4.00
23 Stephen Curry 8.00 20.00
24 Anthony Davis 4.00 10.00
25 Kenneth Faried 1.50 4.00

2014-15 Court Kings 5x7 Box Toppers Rookies
1 Mitch McGary 1.50 4.00
2 Jabari Parker 6.00 15.00
3 Spencer Dinwiddie 2.00 5.00
4 Aaron Gordon 4.00 10.00
5 Cory Jefferson 1.50 4.00
6 Marcus Smart 2.50 6.00
7 Julius Randle 4.00 10.00
8 Nik Stauskas 2.00 5.00
9 Noah Vonleh 2.00 5.00
10 Elfrid Payton 2.50 6.00
11 Doug McDermott 2.50 6.00
12 Zach LaVine 4.00 10.00
13 T.J. Warren 2.50 6.00
14 Adreian Payne 2.00 5.00
15 James Young 1.50 4.00
16 Tyler Ennis 1.50 4.00
17 Gary Harris 2.50 6.00
18 Bruno Caboclo 2.00 5.00
19 Rodney Hood 2.50 6.00
20 Shabazz Napier 2.00 5.00
21 P.J. Hairston 1.50 4.00
22 Kyle Anderson 2.50 6.00
23 K.J. McDaniels 2.00 5.00
24 Russ Smith 1.50 4.00
25 Cleanthony Early 1.50 4.00

2014-15 Court Kings Aficionado
*SAPPHIRE/25: .75X TO 2X BASE HI
1 Kevin Love 1.50 4.00
2 LeBron James 6.00 15.00
3 Joakim Noah 1.25 3.00
4 Russell Westbrook 4.00 10.00

5 DeMarcus Cousins 1.50 4.00
6 Chris Paul 2.00 5.00
7 James Harden 2.50 6.00
8 Kobe Bryant 6.00 15.00
9 Derrick Rose 2.00 5.00
10 Stephen Curry 6.00 15.00
11 LaMarcus Aldridge 1.50 4.00
12 Kevin Durant 4.00 10.00
13 Paul George 2.00 5.00
14 Dwight Howard 1.25 3.00
15 John Wall 2.00 5.00
16 Anthony Davis 3.00 8.00
17 Goran Dragic 1.25 3.00
18 Blake Griffin 1.50 4.00
19 Damian Lillard 3.00 8.00
20 Carmelo Anthony 2.00 5.00

2014-15 Court Kings Also Known As

STATED PRINT RUN 49 SER.#'d SETS
1 Kobe Bryant 30.00 80.00
2 Shawn Marion 5.00 12.00
3 Harrison Barnes 5.00 12.00
4 Paul Pierce 6.00 15.00
5 Chris Andersen 5.00 12.00
6 Danilo Gallinari 8.00 20.00
7 Tim Duncan 20.00 50.00
8 LeBron James 30.00 80.00
9 Marcin Gortat 5.00 12.00
10 Dwight Howard 5.00 12.00
11 Bob Cousy 10.00 25.00
12 Anfernee Hardaway 15.00 40.00
13 Allen Iverson 8.00 20.00
14 Shawn Kemp 10.00 25.00
15 Dennis Rodman 12.00 30.00
16 George Gervin 6.00 15.00
17 Walt Frazier 6.00 15.00
18 Hakeem Olajuwon 20.00 50.00
19 Gary Payton 12.00 30.00
20 Dominique Wilkins 8.00 20.00

2014-15 Court Kings Art Nouveau Jerseys

STATED PRINT RUN 299 SER.#'d SETS
*PRIME/25: 2X TO 5X BASIC
1 Andrew Wiggins 10.00 25.00
2 Jabari Parker 6.00 15.00
3 Joel Embiid 8.00 20.00
4 Aaron Gordon 4.00 10.00
5 Dante Exum 2.50 6.00
6 Marcus Smart 2.50 6.00
7 Julius Randle 4.00 10.00
8 Nik Stauskas 2.00 5.00
9 Noah Vonleh 2.00 5.00
10 Elfrid Payton 2.50 6.00
11 Doug McDermott 2.50 6.00
12 Zach LaVine 4.00 10.00
13 T.J. Warren 2.50 6.00
14 Adreian Payne 2.00 5.00
15 James Young 1.50 4.00
16 Tyler Ennis 1.50 4.00
17 Gary Harris 2.00 5.00
18 Bruno Caboclo 2.00 5.00
19 Mitch McGary 1.50 4.00
20 Jordan Adams 1.50 4.00
21 Rodney Hood 2.50 6.00
22 Shabazz Napier 2.00 5.00
23 P.J. Hairston 1.50 4.00
24 C.J. Wilcox 1.50 4.00
25 Kyle Anderson 2.50 6.00
26 K.J. McDaniels 2.00 5.00
27 Joe Harris 1.50 4.00
28 Cleanthony Early 1.50 4.00
29 Jarnell Stokes 1.50 4.00
30 Spencer Dinwiddie 2.00 5.00
31 Glenn Robinson III 1.50 4.00
32 James Ennis 1.50 4.00
33 Markel Brown 1.50 4.00
34 Cory Jefferson 1.50 4.00
35 Russ Smith 1.50 4.00

2014-15 Court Kings Art Nouveau Jerseys Prime Numbers

*PRIME NUMBERS: 2X TO 5X BASE HI
STATED PRINT RUN 25 SER.#'d SETS

2014-15 Court Kings Artistic Endeavors Jerseys

PRINT RUNS B/WN 99-299 COPIES PER
*PRIME/15-25: 1.5X TO 4X BASE HI
1 LeBron James/299 8.00 20.00
2 Kobe Bryant/299 8.00 20.00
3 Kevin Durant/299 5.00 12.00
4 Dwyane Wade/299 3.00 8.00
5 Russell Westbrook/299 5.00 12.00
6 Blake Griffin/299 2.00 5.00
7 Rajon Rondo/149 2.00 5.00
8 Chris Paul/149 2.50 6.00
9 Kevin Love/299 2.00 5.00
10 Pau Gasol/299 2.00 5.00
11 Damian Lillard/99 4.00 10.00
12 Carmelo Anthony/149 2.50 6.00
13 DeMar DeRozan/149 2.00 5.00
14 John Wall/149 2.50 6.00
15 Kyrie Irving/149 4.00 10.00

2014-15 Court Kings Autographs

STATED PRINT RUN B/WN 35-149 COPIES PER
CKAG Artis Gilmore/50 6.00 15.00
CKBB Bradley Beal/60 10.00 25.00
CKBG Blake Griffin/35 20.00 50.00
CKBW Bill Walton/60 8.00 20.00
CKCC Cedric Ceballos/149 5.00 12.00
CKCL Christian Laettner/50 6.00 15.00
CKCM Chris Mullin/50 8.00 20.00
CKCR Clifford Robinson/149 5.00 12.00
CKDM Dikembe Mutombo/99 8.00 20.00
CKGR Glen Rice/99 6.00 15.00
CKJH Jeff Hornacek/149 6.00 15.00
CKJW John Wall/50 20.00 50.00
CKKB Kobe Bryant/40 100.00 200.00
CKKD Kevin Durant/40 100.00 200.00
CKKI Kyrie Irving/40 25.00 60.00
CKMC Maurice Cheeks/99 5.00 12.00
CKMJ Marques Johnson/149 6.00 15.00
CKNA Nick Anderson/99 6.00 15.00
CKNA Nate Archibald/60 6.00 15.00
CKNT Nate Thurmond/60 6.00 15.00
CKSC Stephen Curry/50 75.00 150.00
CKSM Sidney Moncrief/149 5.00 12.00
CKTH Tim Hardaway/149 5.00 12.00
CKTP Terry Porter/149 5.00 12.00
CKTP Tony Parker/35 12.00 30.00
CKWF Walt Frazier/60 8.00 20.00
CKAH1 Anfernee Hardaway/50 30.00 80.00
CKAH2 Allan Houston/99 6.00 15.00
CKNVE Nick Van Exel/60 25.00 60.00

2014-15 Court Kings Autographs Sapphire

*SAPPHIRE: .5X TO 1.2X BASE HI
STATED PRINT RUN 25 SER.#'d SETS

2014-15 Court Kings Brush Strokes Autographs

PRINT RUNS B/WN 50-149 COPIES PER
*SAPPHIRE/25: .6X TO 1.5X BASE HI
BRAJ Amir Johnson/99 3.00 8.00
BRIS Iman Shumpert/99 3.00 8.00
BRKI Kyrie Irving/50 40.00 100.00
BRJCA Jose Calderon/60 3.00 8.00
BRKL Kyle Lowry/149 4.00 10.00
BRMC Mike Conley/60 4.00 10.00
BRKO Kelly Olynyk/149 3.00 8.00
BRPM Patty Mills/149 5.00 12.00
BRRJ Reggie Jackson/149 3.00 8.00
BRRL Robin Lopez/149 3.00 8.00
BRSC Stephen Curry/40 60.00 150.00
BRTG Taj Gibson/99 4.00 10.00
BRTY Thaddeus Young/149 3.00 8.00
BRJW John Wall/50 20.00 50.00
BRTP Tony Parker/50 15.00 40.00
BRTZ Tyler Zeller/149 4.00 10.00

2014-15 Court Kings Expressionists

*SAPPHIRE/25: 1X TO 2.5X BASE HI
1 Chris Andersen 1.00 2.50
2 Latrell Sprewell 1.00 2.50
3 Kevin Garnett 2.00 5.00
4 Gary Payton 1.25 3.00
5 Patrick Ewing 1.50 4.00
6 Magic Johnson 3.00 8.00
7 Charles Oakley 1.00 2.50
8 Shaquille O'Neal 2.50 6.00
9 DeMarcus Cousins 1.25 3.00
10 David Robinson 2.00 5.00
11 Karl Malone 1.50 4.00
12 Anthony Davis 2.50 6.00
13 Isiah Thomas 1.25 3.00
14 Dwyane Wade 2.00 5.00
15 Bill Laimbeer 1.00 2.50
16 Dwight Howard 1.00 2.50
17 Kevin Durant 3.00 8.00
18 Joe Dumars 1.25 3.00
19 Kyrie Irving 2.50 6.00
20 Dikembe Mutombo 1.25 3.00
21 Blake Griffin 1.25 3.00
22 LeBron James 5.00 12.00
23 Hakeem Olajuwon 1.50 4.00
24 Allen Iverson 1.50 4.00
25 Dennis Rodman 2.50 6.00
26 Larry Johnson 1.50 4.00
27 Chris Bosh 1.25 3.00
28 Kobe Bryant 5.00 12.00
29 Larry Bird 3.00 8.00
30 Chris Webber 1.25 3.00

2014-15 Court Kings Fresh Paint Autographs

PRINT RUNS B/WN 225-260 COPIES PER
FPAG Aaron Gordon/225 8.00 20.00
FPAP Adreian Payne/260 4.00 10.00
FPAW Andrew Wiggins/225 60.00 150.00
FPBC Bruno Caboclo/260 4.00 10.00
FPCE Cleanthony Early/260 3.00 8.00
FPDE Dante Exum/225 12.00 30.00
FPDM Doug McDermott/260 5.00 12.00
FPEP Elfrid Payton/260 5.00 12.00
FPGH Gary Harris/260 5.00 12.00
FPGR Glenn Robinson III/260 3.00 8.00
FPJC Jordan Clarkson/260 15.00 40.00
FPJE Joel Embiid/225 40.00 80.00
FPJG Jerami Grant/260 3.00 8.00
FPJH Joe Harris/260 3.00 8.00
FPJN Jusuf Nurkic/260 5.00 12.00
FPJO Johnny O'Bryant/260 3.00 8.00
FPJP Jabari Parker/225 20.00 50.00
FPJR Julius Randle/225 12.00 30.00
FPJY James Young/260 3.00 8.00
FPKA Kyle Anderson/260 5.00 12.00
FPKM K.J. McDaniels/260 4.00 10.00
FPMB Markel Brown/260 3.00 8.00
FPMS Marcus Smart/225 5.00 12.00
FPNS Nik Stauskas/260 4.00 10.00
FPNV Noah Vonleh/225 4.00 10.00
FPPH P.J. Hairston/260 3.00 8.00
FPRH Rodney Hood/260 5.00 12.00
FPRS Russ Smith/260 3.00 8.00
FPSD Spencer Dinwiddie/260 4.00 10.00
FPSN Shabazz Napier/260 4.00 10.00
FPTA Thanasis Antetokounmpo/260 6.00 15.00
FPTE Tyler Ennis/225 3.00 8.00
FPTW T.J. Warren/260 5.00 12.00
FPZL Zach LaVine/260 15.00 40.00

2014-15 Court Kings Heir Apparent Autographs

STATED PRINT RUN 130 SER.#'d SETS
HAZL Zach LaVine 20.00 50.00
HAEP Elfrid Payton 6.00 15.00
HANS Nik Stauskas 5.00 12.00
HATE Tyler Ennis 4.00 10.00
HANV Noah Vonleh 5.00 12.00
HAJP Jabari Parker 40.00 80.00
HAJE Joel Embiid 50.00 120.00
HAMS Marcus Smart 6.00 15.00
HADM Doug McDermott 6.00 15.00
HAAG Aaron Gordon 10.00 25.00
HADE Dante Exum 6.00 15.00
HAAW Andrew Wiggins 50.00 120.00

2014-15 Court Kings Impressionist Ink Autographs

PRINT RUNS B/WN 35-99 COPIES PER
IIAD Anthony Davis/40 75.00 150.00
IIBM Ben McLemore/49 3.00 8.00
IIDG Danny Green/99 4.00 10.00
IIDG Danilo Gallinari/35 3.00 8.00
IIDS Dennis Schroder/99 4.00 10.00
IIGD Gorgui Dieng/99 3.00 8.00
IIGH Gerald Henderson/35
IIJN Joakim Noah/49 12.00 30.00
IIJT Jason Terry/49 4.00 10.00
IIKB Kobe Bryant/40 100.00 250.00
IIKD Kevin Durant/40 60.00 150.00
IIMC M.Carter-Williams/49 3.00 8.00
IIPA Pero Antic/99 3.00 8.00
IIPP Phil Pressey/99 3.00 8.00
IIRJ Reggie Jackson/99 3.00 8.00
IIRL Robin Lopez/99 3.00 8.00
IIRM Ray McCallum/99 3.00 8.00
IISA Steven Adams/99 4.00 10.00
IISB Steve Blake/99 3.00 8.00
IITB Trey Burke/49 3.00 8.00
IITC Tyson Chandler/35 4.00 10.00
IITH Tim Hardaway Jr./99 3.00 8.00
IITP Tony Parker/49 12.00 30.00
IITP Tayshaun Prince/35 12.00 30.00
IIVO Victor Oladipo/49 10.00 25.00
IIZR Zach Randolph/35 4.00 10.00

2014-15 Court Kings Impressionist Ink Autographs Sapphire

*SAPPHIRE: .6X TO 1.5X BASE HI
STATED PRINT RUN 25 SER.#'d SETS

2014-15 Court Kings Le Cinque Piu Belle

PRINT RUNS B/WN 12-36 COPIES PER
1 Andrew Wiggins/22 150.00 300.00
3 Marcus Smart/36 15.00 40.00
4 Julius Randle/30 25.00 60.00

2014-15 Court Kings New Aesthetic

*SAPPHIRE/25: .75X TO 2X BASE HI
1 Mitch McGary .75 2.00
2 Elfrid Payton 1.25 3.00
3 Andrew Wiggins 10.00 25.00
4 Shabazz Napier 1.00 2.50
5 T.J. Warren 1.25 3.00
6 Aaron Gordon 2.00 5.00
7 Kyle Anderson 1.25 3.00
8 Tyler Ennis .75 2.00
9 Julius Randle 2.00 5.00
10 Glenn Robinson III .75 2.00
11 Jordan Adams .75 2.00
12 Doug McDermott 1.25 3.00
13 Jabari Parker 2.00 5.00
14 P.J. Hairston .75 2.00
15 Adreian Payne 1.00 2.50
16 Dante Exum 1.25 3.00
17 Cleanthony Early .75 2.00
18 Gary Harris 1.25 3.00
19 Nik Stauskas 1.00 2.50
20 Nick Johnson .75 2.00
21 Rodney Hood 1.25 3.00
22 Zach LaVine 2.00 5.00
23 Joel Embiid 4.00 10.00
24 C.J. Wilcox .75 2.00
25 James Young .75 2.00
26 Spencer Dinwiddie 1.00 2.50
27 Marcus Smart 1.25 3.00
28 Bruno Caboclo 1.00 2.50
29 Noah Vonleh 1.00 2.50
30 K.J. McDaniels 1.00 2.50

2014-15 Court Kings Performance Art Jerseys

PRINT RUNS B/WN 49-299 COPIES PER
*PRIME/20-25: 1X TO 2.5X BASE HI
1 Kevin Love/149 3.00 8.00
2 Taj Gibson/99 2.50 6.00
3 Rajon Rondo/110 3.00 8.00
4 Arron Afflalo/199 2.00 5.00
5 George Hill/260 2.50 6.00
6 Eric Bledsoe/299 2.50 6.00
7 Dwight Howard/149 2.50 6.00
8 Mike Conley/249 2.50 6.00
9 Kyle Korver/299 2.50 6.00
10 Tim Duncan/149 5.00 12.00
11 Nene/99 2.50 6.00
12 Blake Griffin/199 3.00 8.00
13 Paul George/49 4.00 10.00
14 Ryan Anderson/199 2.00 5.00
15 Kobe Bryant/299 6.00 15.00
16 Jrue Holiday/99 2.50 6.00
17 Jarrett Jack/99 2.50 6.00
18 Jamal Crawford/99 3.00 8.00
19 David Lee/99 2.00 5.00
20 Kevin Durant/75 6.00 15.00
21 Chris Paul/149 4.00 10.00
22 Jeff Teague/99 2.50 6.00
23 Blake Griffin/149 3.00 8.00
24 Carmelo Anthony/99 4.00 10.00
25 Al Horford/299 2.50 6.00
26 Trey Burke/249 2.00 5.00
27 Brandon Knight/99 2.50 6.00
28 Stephen Curry/149 12.00 30.00
29 Kawhi Leonard/149 5.00 12.00
30 Monta Ellis/149 2.50 6.00
31 James Harden/199 5.00 12.00
32 DeMar DeRozan/99 3.00 8.00
33 Dwight Howard/199 2.50 6.00
34 Dion Waiters/149 2.50 6.00
35 Russell Westbrook/199 8.00 20.00

2014-15 Court Kings Portraits

STATED PRINT RUN 149 SER.#'d SETS
*RUBY/99: .6X TO 1.5X BASE HI
*SAPPHIRE/25: 1.2X TO 3X BASE HI
1 Dwyane Wade 2.00 5.00
2 Carmelo Anthony 1.50 4.00
3 Rajon Rondo 1.25 3.00
4 Nicolas Batum 1.00 2.50
5 Chris Bosh 1.25 3.00
6 Nerlens Noel 1.00 2.50
7 Kyle Lowry 1.00 2.50
8 Al Horford 1.00 2.50
9 Damian Lillard 2.50 6.00
10 Victor Oladipo 1.00 2.50
11 Zach Randolph 1.00 2.50
12 John Wall 1.50 4.00
13 Ty Lawson .75 2.00
14 Luol Deng 1.00 2.50
15 Chris Paul 1.50 4.00
16 Michael Carter-Williams .75 2.00
17 DeMar DeRozan 1.25 3.00
18 Joakim Noah 1.00 2.50
19 LaMarcus Aldridge 1.25 3.00
20 Tobias Harris 1.00 2.50
21 Anthony Davis 2.50 6.00
22 Bradley Beal 1.25 3.00
23 DeMarcus Cousins 1.25 3.00
24 Pau Gasol 1.25 3.00
25 Blake Griffin 1.25 3.00
26 Dirk Nowitzki 1.50 4.00
27 Serge Ibaka 1.00 2.50
28 Jimmy Butler 1.25 3.00
29 Trey Burke .75 2.00
30 Tim Duncan 2.00 5.00
31 Lance Stephenson 1.00 2.50
32 Marcin Gortat 1.00 2.50
33 Kyrie Irving 2.50 6.00
34 Chandler Parsons 1.00 2.50
35 Ben McLemore .75 2.00
36 Steve Nash 1.25 3.00
37 Deron Williams 1.00 2.50
38 Derrick Rose 1.50 4.00
39 Gordon Hayward 1.25 3.00
40 Manu Ginobili 1.25 3.00
41 Paul George 1.50 4.00
42 Goran Dragic 1.00 2.50
43 Kobe Bryant 5.00 12.00
44 Jeremy Lin 1.25 3.00
45 Stephen Curry 5.00 12.00
46 James Harden 2.00 5.00
47 Andrei Kirilenko 1.00 2.50
48 Russell Westbrook 3.00 8.00
49 Roy Hibbert 1.00 2.50
50 Kawhi Leonard 2.00 5.00
51 Kevin Love 1.25 3.00
52 Eric Bledsoe 1.00 2.50
53 LeBron James 5.00 12.00
54 Andre Drummond 1.25 3.00
55 Klay Thompson 1.50 4.00
56 Dwight Howard 1.00 2.50
57 Iman Shumpert .75 2.00
58 Kevin Durant 3.00 8.00
59 Larry Sanders .75 2.00
60 Tony Parker 1.25 3.00
61 Andrew Wiggins 10.00 25.00
62 Jabari Parker 2.00 5.00
63 Joel Embiid 4.00 10.00
64 Aaron Gordon 2.00 5.00
65 Dante Exum 1.25 3.00
66 Marcus Smart 1.25 3.00
67 Julius Randle 2.00 5.00
68 Nik Stauskas 1.00 2.50
69 Noah Vonleh 1.00 2.50
70 Elfrid Payton 1.25 3.00
71 Doug McDermott 1.25 3.00
72 Zach LaVine 2.00 5.00
73 T.J. Warren 1.25 3.00
74 Adreian Payne 1.00 2.50
75 James Young .75 2.00
76 Tyler Ennis .75 2.00
77 Gary Harris 1.25 3.00
78 Bruno Caboclo 1.00 2.50
79 Rodney Hood 1.25 3.00
80 Shabazz Napier 1.00 2.50
81 P.J. Hairston .75 2.00
82 Kyle Anderson 1.25 3.00
83 Markel Brown .75 2.00
84 Russ Smith .75 2.00
85 Cleanthony Early .75 2.00
86 Spencer Dinwiddie 1.00 2.50
87 James Ennis .75 2.00
88 Nick Johnson .75 2.00
89 C.J. Wilcox .75 2.00
90 Jordan Adams .75 2.00
91 Mitch McGary .75 2.00
92 Jusuf Nurkic 1.25 3.00
93 Clint Capela 1.00 2.50
94 Nikola Mirotic 1.50 4.00
95 Johnny O'Bryant .75 2.00
96 Bojan Bogdanovic 1.00 2.50
97 Devyn Marble .75 2.00
98 Joe Harris .75 2.00
99 Kostas Papanikolaou .75 2.00
100 Erick Green .75 2.00

2014-15 Court Kings Remarkable Rookies

*SAPPHIRE/499: .6X TO 1.5X BASE
1 Russ Smith .60 1.50
2 Doug McDermott 1.00 2.50
3 Jarnell Stokes .60 1.50
4 Marcus Smart 1.00 2.50
5 C.J. Wilcox .60 1.50
6 Andrew Wiggins 3.00 8.00
7 Damjan Rudez .60 1.50
8 Jordan Adams .60 1.50
9 Cameron Bairstow .60 1.50
10 James Young .60 1.50
11 Cory Jefferson .60 1.50
12 Zach LaVine 1.50 4.00
13 Spencer Dinwiddie .75 2.00
14 Julius Randle 1.50 4.00
15 Kyle Anderson 1.00 2.50
16 Jabari Parker 1.50 4.00
17 Kostas Papanikolaou .60 1.50
18 Rodney Hood 1.00 2.50
19 Damien Inglis .60 1.50
20 Tyler Ennis .60 1.50
21 Johnny O'Bryant .60 1.50
22 T.J. Warren 1.00 2.50
23 Glenn Robinson III .60 1.50
24 Nik Stauskas .75 2.00
25 K.J. McDaniels .75 2.00
26 Joel Embiid 3.00 8.00
27 Bojan Bogdanovic .75 2.00
28 Shabazz Napier .75 2.00
29 Devyn Marble .60 1.50
30 Gary Harris 1.00 2.50
31 Tarik Black .60 1.50
32 Adreian Payne .75 2.00
33 Nick Johnson .60 1.50
34 Noah Vonleh .75 2.00
35 Joe Harris .60 1.50
36 Aaron Gordon 1.50 4.00
37 Andre Dawkins .60 1.50
38 Clint Capela .75 2.00
39 Nikola Mirotic 1.25 3.00
40 Bruno Caboclo .75 2.00
41 Jordan Clarkson 1.00 2.50
42 Jusuf Nurkic 1.00 2.50
43 Markel Brown .60 1.50
44 Elfrid Payton 1.00 2.50
45 Cleanthony Early .60 1.50
46 Dante Exum 1.00 2.50
47 Travis Wear .60 1.50
48 P.J. Hairston .60 1.50
49 James Ennis .60 1.50
50 Mitch McGary .60 1.50

2014-15 Court Kings Remarkable Rookies Memorabilia

RANDOM INSERTS IN PACKS
1 Aaron Gordon 1.50 4.00
2 Adreian Payne .75 2.00
3 Andrew Wiggins 3.00 8.00
4 Bruno Caboclo .75 2.00
5 C.J. Wilcox .60 1.50
6 Cleanthony Early .60 1.50
7 Cory Jefferson .60 1.50
8 Damien Inglis .60 1.50
9 Dante Exum 1.00 2.50
10 Doug McDermott 1.00 2.50
11 Elfrid Payton 1.00 2.50
12 Gary Harris 1.00 2.50
13 Glenn Robinson III .60 1.50
14 Jabari Parker 1.50 4.00
15 James Ennis .60 1.50
16 James Young .60 1.50
17 Jarnell Stokes .60 1.50
18 Jerami Grant .60 1.50
19 Joe Harris .60 1.50
20 Joel Embiid 3.00 8.00
21 Johnny O'Bryant .60 1.50
22 Jordan Adams .60 1.50
23 Julius Randle 1.50 4.00
24 K.J. McDaniels .75 2.00
25 Kyle Anderson 1.00 2.50
26 Marcus Smart 1.00 2.50
27 Markel Brown .60 1.50
28 Mitch McGary .60 1.50
29 Nik Stauskas .75 2.00
30 Noah Vonleh .75 2.00
31 P.J. Hairston .60 1.50
32 Rodney Hood 1.00 2.50
33 Russ Smith .60 1.50
34 Shabazz Napier .75 2.00
35 Spencer Dinwiddie .75 2.00
36 T.J. Warren 1.00 2.50
37 Tyler Ennis .60 1.50
38 Zach LaVine 1.50 4.00

2014-15 Court Kings Remarkable Rookies Signatures

RANDOM INSERTS IN PACKS
1 Andrew Wiggins 60.00 150.00
2 Jabari Parker 8.00 20.00
3 Joel Embiid 20.00 50.00
4 Aaron Gordon 8.00 20.00
5 Dante Exum 5.00 12.00
6 Marcus Smart 5.00 12.00
7 Julius Randle 20.00 50.00
8 Nik Stauskas 4.00 10.00
9 Noah Vonleh 4.00 10.00
10 Elfrid Payton 5.00 12.00
11 Doug McDermott 5.00 12.00
12 Zach LaVine 8.00 20.00
14 Adreian Payne 4.00 10.00
15 James Young 3.00 8.00
16 Tyler Ennis 3.00 8.00
17 Gary Harris 5.00 12.00
18 Mitch McGary 3.00 8.00
19 Jordan Adams 3.00 8.00
20 Rodney Hood 5.00 12.00
21 Shabazz Napier 4.00 10.00
22 P.J. Hairston 3.00 8.00
23 C.J. Wilcox 3.00 8.00
24 K.J. McDaniels 4.00 10.00
25 Joe Harris 3.00 8.00
26 Jarnell Stokes 3.00 8.00
27 Spencer Dinwiddie 4.00 10.00
28 Glenn Robinson III 3.00 8.00
29 Markel Brown 3.00 8.00
30 Russ Smith 3.00 8.00
31 Cory Jefferson 3.00 8.00
32 Johnny O'Bryant 3.00 8.00
33 Devyn Marble 3.00 8.00
34 Jordan Clarkson 5.00 12.00
35 Cameron Bairstow 3.00 8.00
36 Jusuf Nurkic 8.00 20.00
37 Damjan Rudez 3.00 8.00
38 James Ennis 3.00 8.00
39 Erick Green 3.00 8.00
40 Alex Kirk 3.00 8.00

2014-15 Court Kings Rookie Royalty

RANDOM INSERTS IN PACKS
1 Anthony Davis 2.00 5.00
2 Blake Griffin 1.00 2.50
3 Carmelo Anthony 2.00 5.00
4 Chris Bosh 1.00 2.50
5 Chris Paul 1.25 3.00
6 Derrick Rose 1.25 3.00
7 Dirk Nowitzki 1.25 3.00
8 Dwight Howard .75 2.00
9 Dwyane Wade 1.50 4.00
10 James Harden 1.50 4.00
11 Kevin Durant 2.50 6.00
12 Kevin Garnett 1.50 4.00
13 Kevin Love 1.00 2.50
14 Kobe Bryant 4.00 10.00
15 Kyrie Irving 2.00 5.00
16 LeBron James 4.00 10.00
17 Pau Gasol 1.00 2.50
18 Russell Westbrook 2.50 6.00
19 Steve Nash 1.00 2.50
20 Tim Duncan 1.50 4.00
21 Tony Parker 1.00 2.50
22 Vince Carter 1.25 3.00

2014-15 Court Kings Royal Performances

*SAPPHIRE/25: .6X TO 1.5X BASE HI
1 Tim Duncan 2.50 6.00
2 Shaquille O'Neal 3.00 8.00
3 Jerry West 2.00 5.00
4 Pete Maravich 2.50 6.00
5 Latrell Sprewell 1.25 3.00
6 LeBron James 6.00 15.00
7 Wilt Chamberlain 3.00 8.00
8 Rajon Rondo 1.50 4.00
9 Magic Johnson 4.00 10.00
10 Michael Carter-Williams 1.00 2.50
11 David Thompson 1.25 3.00
12 Clyde Drexler 2.00 5.00
13 Elgin Baylor 1.50 4.00
14 Tracy McGrady 1.50 4.00
15 Carmelo Anthony 2.00 5.00
16 Kevin Durant 4.00 10.00
17 Kobe Bryant 6.00 15.00
18 Timofey Mozgov 1.00 2.50
19 David Robinson 2.50 6.00
20 Anthony Davis 3.00 8.00

2014-15 Court Kings Sketches and Swatches Autographs

RANDOM INSERTS IN PACKS
PRINT RUNS B/WN 25-149 COPIES PER
*PRIME/25: 1X TO 2.5X BASIC
1 Al Horford/35 3.00 8.00
2 Jeff Teague/99 3.00 8.00
3 Kyle Korver/65 8.00 20.00
4 Antoine Walker/149 3.00 8.00
5 Jeff Green/65 3.00 8.00
6 Mason Plumlee/149 3.00 8.00
7 Ben Gordon/35 3.00 8.00
8 Tony Parker/35 20.00 50.00
9 Dwight Howard/25 8.00 20.00
10 Zydrunas Ilgauskas/149 3.00 8.00
11 Josh Smith/35 3.00 8.00
12 Klay Thompson/99 20.00 50.00
13 George Hill/65 3.00 8.00
14 Luis Scola/65 3.00 8.00
15 Hakeem Olajuwon/35 20.00 50.00
16 Carmelo Anthony/25 40.00 100.00
17 Dominique Wilkins/35 5.00 12.00
18 Tony Allen/35 2.50 6.00
19 Ray Allen/25 25.00 60.00
20 Brandon Knight/35 3.00 8.00
21 Tobias Harris/49 3.00 8.00
22 Eric Gordon/35 3.00 8.00
23 Tim Hardaway Jr./149 2.50 6.00
24 Thabo Sefolosha/99 2.50 6.00
25 Alex Len/35 3.00 8.00
26 Isaiah Thomas/149 10.00 25.00
27 Tiago Splitter/49 3.00 8.00
29 Derrick Favors/35 3.00 8.00
30 Trey Burke/35 2.50 6.00
31 Dennis Schroder/149 3.00 8.00
32 Brandon Bass/49 2.50 6.00
33 Kyle Lowry/149 6.00 15.00
34 Kelly Olynyk/149 2.50 6.00
35 Brook Lopez/35 3.00 8.00
36 Joe Johnson/35 3.00 8.00
37 Michael Kidd-Gilchrist/35 3.00 8.00
38 Raymond Felton/35 3.00 8.00
39 Jared Dudley/49 2.50 6.00
40 Chris Bosh/25 6.00 15.00
41 Tayshaun Prince/35 3.00 8.00
42 John Starks/149 5.00 12.00
43 Danny Manning/35 3.00 8.00
44 Xavier McDaniel/149 2.50 6.00
45 Andre Miller/49 3.00 8.00
46 Cody Zeller/35 2.50 6.00
47 J.J. Redick/65 4.00 10.00
48 Kevin Love/35 5.00 12.00
49 LaMarcus Aldridge/35 15.00 40.00
50 M.Carter-Williams/35 8.00 20.00

2014-15 Court Kings Sovereign Signatures

RANDOM INSERTS IN PACKS
PRINT RUNS B/WN 20-149 COPIES PER
*PRIME/25: .6X TO 1.5X BASIC
1 Joakim Noah/49 12.00 30.00
2 Michael Finley/65 6.00 15.00
3 John Wall/20 25.00 60.00
5 Joe Dumars/65 6.00 15.00
6 Stephen Curry/49 50.00 120.00
7 Vince Carter/35 20.00 50.00
8 David Robinson/25 20.00 50.00
9 Manu Ginobili/25 20.00 50.00
10 Gary Payton/25 15.00 40.00
11 Chris Mullin/65 10.00 25.00
12 Bradley Beal/65 6.00 15.00
13 Kevin McHale/25 12.00 30.00
14 Toni Kukoc/149 10.00 25.00
15 Dan Majerle/149 5.00 12.00
16 Sam Perkins/149 4.00 10.00
17 Jason Kidd/25 20.00 50.00
18 Jim Jackson/149 4.00 10.00
19 Andre Iguodala/65 20.00 50.00
20 Dwight Howard/20 15.00 40.00
21 Sleepy Floyd/99 4.00 10.00
22 Yao Ming/20 30.00 80.00
23 Dwyane Wade/20 12.00 30.00
24 Chris Bosh/25 6.00 15.00
25 Robert Horry/149 5.00 12.00

2014-15 Court Kings Studio Signatures

STATED PRINT RUN B/WN 40-99 COPIES PER
*SAPPHIRE: .5X TO 1.2X BASE HI
BTAG Archie Goodwin/99 4.00 10.00
BTAN Andrew Nicholson/99 4.00 10.00
BTBL Brook Lopez/40 5.00 12.00
BTDS Dennis Schroder/99 5.00 12.00
BTEJ Eddie Jones/99 5.00 12.00
BTGA G.Antetokounmpo/99 50.00 120.00
BTGH Gordon Hayward/99 8.00 20.00
BTGM George McGinnis/99 4.00 10.00
BTHB Harrison Barnes/40 5.00 12.00
BTHG Horace Grant/99 6.00 15.00
BTJG Jeff Green/99 5.00 12.00
BTJK Jason Kidd/40 20.00 50.00
BTJS John Salley/99 4.00 10.00
BTJS P.J. Tucker/99 4.00 10.00
BTKO Kelly Olynyk/99 4.00 10.00
BTRK Ryan Kelly/99
BTSA Steven Adams/99 10.00 25.00
BTSC Stephen Curry/40 60.00 150.00

2014-15 Court Kings Vintage Materials

PRINT RUNS B/WN 49-299 COPIES PER
*PRIME/25: .6X TO 1.5X BASE HI
1 Mitch Richmond/49 3.00 8.00
2 Paul Westphal/99 3.00 8.00
3 Walter Davis/299 2.00 5.00
4 Danny Ainge/99 3.00 8.00
5 Doug Collins/199 3.00 8.00
6 Gary Payton/299 3.00 8.00
7 Adrian Dantley/99 2.50 6.00
8 Brad Daugherty/199 2.50 6.00
9 Joe Dumars/199 3.00 8.00
10 Kevin Duckworth/199 2.00 5.00
11 Chris Mullin/99 3.00 8.00
12 Patrick Ewing/299 4.00 10.00
13 Manute Bol/99 3.00 8.00
14 Cedric Maxwell/199 2.00 5.00
15 Scottie Pippen/299 6.00 15.00
16 Glen Rice/199 2.50 6.00
17 Alex English/99 2.50 6.00
18 Kareem Abdul-Jabbar/49 5.00 12.00
19 Kiki Vandeweghe/99 2.50 6.00
20 Byron Scott/199 2.50 6.00
21 Clyde Drexler/299 4.00 10.00
22 Marques Johnson/199 2.50 6.00
23 Moses Malone/49 3.00 8.00
24 Hakeem Olajuwon/199 4.00 10.00
25 Artis Gilmore/49 2.50 6.00

2015-16 Court Kings

167-199 PRINT RUN 299 SER.#'d SETS
200-232 PRINT RUN 149 SER.#'d SETS
233-265 PRINT RUN 75 SER.#'d SETS
266-298 PRINT RUN 10 SER.#'d SETS
NO PRICING AVAILABLE FOR 266-298
1 Al Horford .40 1.00
2 Jimmy Butler .50 1.25
3 Brandon Jennings .30 .75
4 DeAndre Jordan .50 1.25
5 Khris Middleton .40 1.00
6 Serge Ibaka .40 1.00
7 DeMarcus Cousins .50 1.25
8 Dennis Schroder .40 1.00
9 Joakim Noah .40 1.00
10 Kentavious Caldwell-Pope .40 1.00
11 Lance Stephenson .40 1.00
12 Michael Carter-Williams .30 .75
13 Aaron Gordon .40 1.00
14 Rajon Rondo .50 1.25
15 Jeff Teague .40 1.00
16 Nikola Mirotic .40 1.00
17 Reggie Jackson .40 1.00
18 Paul Pierce .50 1.25
19 Andrew Wiggins .75 2.00
20 Elfrid Payton .40 1.00
21 Rudy Gay .50 1.25
22 Paul Millsap .50 1.25
23 Pau Gasol .50 1.25
24 Andre Iguodala .40 1.00
25 Jordan Clarkson .50 1.25
26 Kevin Garnett .75 2.00
27 Tobias Harris .40 1.00
28 Kawhi Leonard .75 2.00
29 Avery Bradley .40 1.00
30 Iman Shumpert .30 .75
31 Draymond Green .60 1.50
32 Julius Randle .50 1.25
33 Ricky Rubio .50 1.25
34 Victor Oladipo .40 1.00
35 LaMarcus Aldridge .50 1.25
36 James Young .30 .75
37 Kevin Love .50 1.25
38 Klay Thompson .60 1.50
39 Kobe Bryant 2.00 5.00
40 Zach LaVine .50 1.25
41 Jerami Grant .30 .75
42 Tim Duncan .75 2.00
43 Jared Sullinger .30 .75
44 Kyrie Irving 1.00 2.50
45 Stephen Curry 2.00 5.00
46 Marc Gasol .50 1.25
47 Anthony Davis 1.00 2.50
48 Nerlens Noel .40 1.00
49 Tony Parker .50 1.25
50 Marcus Smart .40 1.00
51 LeBron James 2.00 5.00
52 Dwight Howard .40 1.00
53 Mike Conley .50 1.25
54 Jrue Holiday .40 1.00
55 Brandon Knight .40 1.00
56 DeMar DeRozan .50 1.25
57 Brook Lopez .40 1.00
58 Chandler Parsons .40 1.00
59 James Harden .75 2.00
60 Zach Randolph .40 1.00
61 Arron Afflalo .30 .75
62 Eric Bledsoe .40 1.00
63 Jonas Valanciunas .40 1.00
64 Joe Johnson .40 1.00
65 Deron Williams .40 1.00
66 Patrick Beverley .30 .75
67 Chris Bosh .50 1.25
68 Carmelo Anthony .60 1.50
69 T.J. Warren .40 1.00
70 Kyle Lowry .40 1.00
71 Shane Larkin .30 .75
72 Dirk Nowitzki .60 1.50
73 Monta Ellis .40 1.00
74 Dwyane Wade .75 2.00
75 Robin Lopez .30 .75
76 Tyson Chandler .40 1.00
77 Gordon Hayward .50 1.25
78 Al Jefferson .40 1.00
79 Gary Harris .40 1.00
80 Paul George .60 1.50
81 Goran Dragic .40 1.00
82 Dion Waiters .40 1.00
83 Al-Farouq Aminu .40 1.00
84 Rudy Gobert .50 1.25
85 Kemba Walker .50 1.25
86 Jusuf Nurkic .30 .75
87 Blake Griffin .50 1.25
88 Giannis Antetokounmpo 1.00 2.50
89 Kevin Durant 1.25 3.00
90 C.J. McCollum .50 1.25
91 Bradley Beal .50 1.25
92 Michael Kidd-Gilchrist .40 1.00
93 Kenneth Faried .40 1.00
94 Chris Paul .60 1.50
95 Jabari Parker .60 1.50
96 Russell Westbrook 1.25 3.00
97 Damian Lillard 1.00 2.50
98 John Wall .60 1.50
99 Derrick Rose .60 1.50
100 Andre Drummond .50 1.25
101 Karl-Anthony Towns RC 4.00 10.00
102 Justise Winslow RC .75 2.00
103 Sam Dekker RC .60 1.50
104 Larry Nance Jr. RC .75 2.00
105 D'Angelo Russell RC 2.00 5.00
106 Myles Turner RC .75 2.00
107 Jerian Grant RC .50 1.25
108 R.J. Hunter RC .50 1.25
109 Jahlil Okafor RC 1.00 2.50
110 Trey Lyles RC .75 2.00
111 Delon Wright RC .60 1.50
112 Montrezl Harrell RC .60 1.50
113 Kristaps Porzingis RC 2.00 5.00
114 Devin Booker RC 2.50 6.00
115 Justin Anderson RC .60 1.50
116 Jordan Mickey RC .50 1.25
117 Mario Hezonja RC .60 1.50
118 Cameron Payne RC .60 1.50
119 Bobby Portis RC .75 2.00
120 Anthony Brown RC .50 1.25
121 Willie Cauley-Stein RC .75 2.00
122 Kelly Oubre Jr. RC .60 1.50
123 Rondae Hollis-Jefferson RC .60 1.50
124 Pat Connaughton RC .50 1.25
125 Emmanuel Mudiay RC .75 2.00
126 Terry Rozier RC .60 1.50
127 Tyus Jones RC .75 2.00
128 Joe Young RC .60 1.50
129 Stanley Johnson RC .60 1.50
130 Rashad Vaughn RC .50 1.25
131 Jarell Martin RC .60 1.50
132 Branden Dawson RC .50 1.25
133 Frank Kaminsky RC .75 2.00
134 Karl-Anthony Towns 4.00 10.00
135 Justise Winslow .75 2.00
136 Sam Dekker .60 1.50
137 Larry Nance Jr. .75 2.00
138 D'Angelo Russell 2.00 5.00
139 Myles Turner .75 2.00
140 Jerian Grant .50 1.25
141 R.J. Hunter .50 1.25
142 Jahlil Okafor 1.00 2.50
143 Trey Lyles .75 2.00
144 Delon Wright .60 1.50
145 Montrezl Harrell .60 1.50
146 Kristaps Porzingis 2.00 5.00
147 Devin Booker 2.50 6.00
148 Justin Anderson .60 1.50
149 Jordan Mickey .50 1.25
150 Mario Hezonja .60 1.50
151 Cameron Payne .60 1.50
152 Bobby Portis .75 2.00
153 Anthony Brown .50 1.25
154 Willie Cauley-Stein .75 2.00
155 Kelly Oubre Jr. .60 1.50
156 Rondae Hollis-Jefferson .60 1.50
157 Pat Connaughton .50 1.25
158 Emmanuel Mudiay .75 2.00
159 Terry Rozier .60 1.50
160 Tyus Jones .75 2.00
161 Joe Young .60 1.50
162 Stanley Johnson .60 1.50
163 Rashad Vaughn .50 1.25
164 Jarell Martin .60 1.50
165 Branden Dawson .50 1.25
166 Frank Kaminsky .75 2.00
167 Karl-Anthony Towns/299 8.00 20.00
168 Justise Winslow/299 1.50 4.00
169 Sam Dekker/299 1.25 3.00
170 Larry Nance Jr./299 1.50 4.00
171 D'Angelo Russell/299 4.00 10.00
172 Myles Turner/299 1.50 4.00
173 Jerian Grant/299 1.00 2.50
174 R.J. Hunter/299 1.00 2.50
175 Jahlil Okafor/299 2.00 5.00
176 Trey Lyles/299 1.50 4.00
177 Delon Wright/299 1.25 3.00
178 Montrezl Harrell/299 1.25 3.00
179 Kristaps Porzingis/299 4.00 10.00
180 Devin Booker/299 5.00 12.00
181 Justin Anderson/299 1.25 3.00
182 Jordan Mickey/299 1.00 2.50
183 Mario Hezonja/299 1.25 3.00
184 Cameron Payne/299 1.25 3.00
185 Bobby Portis/299 1.50 4.00
186 Anthony Brown/299 1.00 2.50
187 Willie Cauley-Stein/299 1.50 4.00
188 Kelly Oubre Jr./299 1.25 3.00
189 Rondae Hollis-Jefferson/299 1.25 3.00
190 Pat Connaughton/299 1.00 2.50
191 Emmanuel Mudiay/299 1.50 4.00
192 Terry Rozier/299 1.25 3.00
193 Tyus Jones/299 1.50 4.00
194 Joe Young/299 1.25 3.00
195 Stanley Johnson/299 1.25 3.00
196 Rashad Vaughn/299 1.00 2.50
197 Jarell Martin/299 1.25 3.00
198 Branden Dawson/299 1.00 2.50
199 Frank Kaminsky/299 1.50 4.00
200 Karl-Anthony Towns/175 10.00 25.00
201 Justise Winslow/175 2.00 5.00
202 Sam Dekker/175 1.50 4.00
203 Larry Nance Jr./175 2.00 5.00
204 D'Angelo Russell/175 5.00 12.00
205 Myles Turner/175 2.00 5.00
206 Jerian Grant/175 1.25 3.00
207 R.J. Hunter/175 1.25 3.00
208 Jahlil Okafor/175 2.50 6.00
209 Trey Lyles/175 2.00 5.00
210 Delon Wright/175 1.50 4.00
211 Montrezl Harrell/175 1.50 4.00
212 Kristaps Porzingis/175 5.00 12.00

213 Devin Booker/175 6.00 15.00
214 Justin Anderson/175 1.50 4.00
215 Jordan Mickey/175 1.25 3.00
216 Mario Hezonja/175 1.50 4.00
217 Cameron Payne/175 1.50 4.00
218 Bobby Portis/175 2.00 5.00
219 Anthony Brown/175 1.25 3.00
220 Willie Cauley-Stein/175 2.00 5.00
221 Kelly Oubre Jr./175 1.50 4.00
222 Rondae Hollis-Jefferson/175 1.50 4.00
223 Pat Connaughton/175 1.25 3.00
224 Emmanuel Mudiay/175 2.00 5.00
225 Terry Rozier/175 1.50 4.00
226 Tyus Jones/175 2.00 5.00
227 Joe Young/175 1.50 4.00
228 Stanley Johnson/175 1.50 4.00
229 Rashad Vaughn/175 1.25 3.00
230 Jarell Martin/175 1.50 4.00
231 Branden Dawson/175 1.25 3.00
232 Frank Kaminsky/175 2.00 5.00
233 Karl-Anthony Towns/75 20.00 50.00
234 Justise Winslow/75 2.50 6.00
235 Sam Dekker/75 2.00 5.00
236 Larry Nance Jr./75 2.50 6.00
237 D'Angelo Russell/75 6.00 15.00
238 Myles Turner/75 2.50 6.00
239 Jerian Grant/75 1.50 4.00
240 R.J. Hunter/75 1.50 4.00
241 Jahlil Okafor/75 3.00 8.00
242 Trey Lyles/75 2.50 6.00
243 Delon Wright/75 2.00 5.00
244 Montrezl Harrell/75 2.00 5.00
245 Kristaps Porzingis/75 6.00 15.00
246 Devin Booker/75 8.00 20.00
247 Justin Anderson/75 2.00 5.00
248 Jordan Mickey/75 1.50 4.00
249 Mario Hezonja/75 2.00 5.00
250 Cameron Payne/75 2.00 5.00
251 Bobby Portis/75 2.50 6.00
252 Anthony Brown/75 1.50 4.00
253 Willie Cauley-Stein/75 2.50 6.00
254 Kelly Oubre Jr./75 2.00 5.00
255 Rondae Hollis-Jefferson/75 2.00 5.00
256 Pat Connaughton/75 1.50 4.00
257 Emmanuel Mudiay/75 2.50 6.00
258 Terry Rozier/75 2.00 5.00
259 Tyus Jones/75 2.50 6.00
260 Joe Young/75 2.00 5.00
261 Stanley Johnson/75 2.00 5.00
262 Rashad Vaughn/75 1.50 4.00
263 Jarell Martin/75 2.00 5.00
264 Branden Dawson/75 1.50 4.00
265 Frank Kaminsky/75 2.50 6.00

2015-16 Court Kings Sapphire

*SAPPHIRE: 2X TO 5X BASIC
RANDOM INSERTS IN PACKS
STATED PRINT RUN 25 SER.#'d SETS

2015-16 Court Kings 2 on 2 Quad Memorabilia

RANDOM INSERTS IN PACKS
PRINT RUNS B/WN 49-99 COPIES PER
*PRIME/25: 1.2X TO 3X BASE HI
1 Wggns/Pytn/Grdn/LVne 8.00 20.00
2 Thmpsn/Jms/Irvng/Crry 30.00 80.00
3 Paul/Hwrd/Hrdn/Grffn 5.00 12.00
4 Prsns/Nwtzki/Dncn/Lnrd 5.00 12.00
5 Beal/Wall/Mddltn/Crtr-Wllms 4.00 10.00
6 Grffn/Jrdn/Gsl/Rndlph 3.00 8.00
7 Grntt/O'Nl/Kobe/Prce 30.00 80.00
8 Stcktn/Kemp/Pytn/Mlne 5.00 12.00
9 Bird/Thms/Dmrs/McHle 8.00 20.00
10 Ervng/Kareem/Magic/Mlne 12.00 30.00
11 Oljwn/Hrdwy/Hrry/O'Nl 8.00 20.00
12 Grtt//Mllsp/Hrfrd 3.00 8.00
13 Hywrd/Knght/Bldse/Brke 3.00 8.00
14 Hrdn/Wstbrk/Drnt/Bvrly 8.00 20.00
15 Wggns/Clrksn/Kobe/Rbo 12.00 30.00
16 Wade/Jhnsn/Deng/Lpz 5.00 12.00

2015-16 Court Kings 5x7 Box Topper Autographs

RANDOMLY INSERTED BOX TOPPER
EXCHANGE DEADLINE 6/9/2017
BTAD Anthony Davis 30.00 120.00
BTDR David Robinson 25.00 60.00
BTDR D'Angelo Russell 40.00 100.00
BTDW Delon Wright 4.00 10.00
BTGP Gary Payton 12.00 30.00
BTJG Jerian Grant 3.00 8.00
BTJO Jahlil Okafor 25.00 60.00
BTKT Karl-Anthony Towns 60.00 150.00
BTRH R.J. Hunter 3.00 8.00
BTRH Robert Horry 10.00 25.00

2015-16 Court Kings 5x7 Box Topper Career Progression

RANDOMLY INSERTED BOX TOPPER
1 Carmelo Anthony 3.00 8.00
2 LeBron James 6.00 15.00
3 Dwight Howard 2.00 5.00
4 Kevin Garnett 4.00 10.00
5 Chris Andersen 2.00 5.00
6 Pau Gasol 2.50 6.00
7 Brandon Knight 2.00 5.00
8 Goran Dragic 2.00 5.00
9 Andre Iguodala 2.00 5.00
10 Kevin Durant 6.00 15.00
11 Chris Paul 3.00 8.00
12 Ray Allen 2.50 6.00
13 Jason Kidd 2.50 6.00
14 Jason Kidd 2.50 6.00
15 Vince Carter 3.00 8.00
16 Vince Carter 3.00 8.00
17 Steve Nash 2.50 6.00
18 Shaquille O'Neal 5.00 12.00
19 Scottie Pippen 5.00 12.00
20 Alonzo Mourning 3.00 8.00
21 Gary Payton 2.50 6.00
22 Anfernee Hardaway 6.00 15.00
23 Dikembe Mutombo 2.50 6.00
24 Dennis Rodman 5.00 12.00
25 Allen Iverson 3.00 8.00

2015-16 Court Kings 5x7 Box Topper Panoramics

RANDOMLY INSERTED BOX TOPPER
1 Kyrie Irving 3.00 8.00
2 Kobe Bryant 6.00 15.00
3 Russell Westbrook 4.00 10.00
4 Blake Griffin 1.50 4.00
5 Dennis Schroder 1.25 3.00
6 LeBron James 6.00 15.00
7 Dwyane Wade 2.50 6.00
8 Damian Lillard 3.00 8.00
9 John Wall 2.00 5.00
10 Jordan Clarkson 1.50 4.00
11 Stephen Curry 6.00 15.00
12 Andrew Wiggins 2.50 6.00
13 Elfrid Payton 1.25 3.00
14 Marcus Smart 1.25 3.00
15 Manu Ginobili 1.50 4.00
16 James Harden 2.50 6.00
17 Anthony Davis 3.00 8.00
18 Kawhi Leonard 2.50 6.00
19 Bradley Beal 1.50 4.00
20 Derrick Rose 2.00 5.00
21 Chris Paul 2.00 5.00
22 Kevin Durant 4.00 10.00
23 DeMar DeRozan 1.50 4.00
24 Dante Exum 1.25 3.00
25 Jimmy Butler 1.50 4.00

2015-16 Court Kings 5x7 Le Cinque Piu Belle Autografo Autographs

RANDOMLY INSERTED BOX TOPPER
PRINT RUNS B/WN 3-35 COPIES PER
NO PRICING ON QTY 3
EXCHANGE DEADLINE 6/9/2017
2 Kobe Bryant/24 400.00 600.00
3 Kevin Durant/35 150.00 250.00
4 Andrew Wiggins/22 EXCH 125.00 250.00
5 Anthony Davis/23

2015-16 Court Kings Art Nouveau Jerseys

RANDOM INSERTS IN PACKS
STATED PRINT RUN 299 SER.#'d SETS
*PRIME/25: 1.2X TO 3X BASIC
1 Karl-Anthony Towns 12.00 30.00
2 D'Angelo Russell 5.00 12.00
3 Jahlil Okafor 5.00 12.00
4 Kristaps Porzingis 6.00 15.00
5 Mario Hezonja 2.00 5.00
6 Willie Cauley-Stein 2.50 6.00
7 Emmanuel Mudiay 2.50 6.00
8 Stanley Johnson 2.00 5.00
9 Frank Kaminsky 2.50 6.00
10 Justise Winslow 2.50 6.00
11 Myles Turner 2.50 6.00
12 Trey Lyles 2.50 6.00
13 Devin Booker 8.00 20.00
14 Cameron Payne 2.00 5.00
15 Kelly Oubre Jr. 2.00 5.00
16 Terry Rozier 2.00 5.00
18 Sam Dekker 2.00 5.00
19 Jerian Grant 1.50 4.00
20 Delon Wright 2.00 5.00
21 Justin Anderson 2.00 5.00
22 Bobby Portis 2.50 6.00
23 Rondae Hollis-Jefferson 2.00 5.00
24 Tyus Jones 2.50 6.00
25 Jarell Martin 2.00 5.00
26 Kevon Looney 2.00 5.00
27 R.J. Hunter 1.50 4.00
28 Chris McCullough 1.50 4.00
29 Montrezl Harrell 2.00 5.00
30 Jordan Mickey 1.50 4.00
31 Anthony Brown 1.50 4.00
32 Rakeem Christmas 1.50 4.00
33 Richaun Holmes 2.00 5.00
34 Pat Connaughton 1.50 4.00
36 Joe Young 2.00 5.00
37 Walter Tavares 1.50 4.00
38 Josh Richardson 2.50 6.00
39 Josh Huestis 1.50 4.00

2015-16 Court Kings Artistic Endeavors Jerseys

RANDOM INSERTS IN PACKS
PRINT RUNS B/WN 185-299 COPIES PER
*PRIME/25: 1X TO 2.5X BASIC
1 Khris Middleton/185 2.00 5.00
2 Michael Carter-Williams/299 1.50 4.00
3 Jared Sullinger/299 1.50 4.00
4 Kelly Olynyk/299 1.50 4.00
5 Patrick Beverley/299 1.50 4.00
6 Chris Andersen/299 2.00 5.00
7 Chris Paul/299 3.00 8.00
8 Noah Vonleh/299 1.50 4.00
9 T.J. Warren/299 2.00 5.00
10 Terrence Jones/299 2.00 5.00
11 Damian Lillard/299 5.00 12.00
12 Aaron Gordon/299 2.00 5.00
13 LaMarcus Aldridge/299 2.50 6.00
14 Avery Bradley/299 2.00 5.00
15 Bojan Bogdanovic/299 1.50 4.00
16 Brook Lopez/299 2.00 5.00
17 Chris Bosh/299 2.50 6.00
18 Dwyane Wade/299 4.00 10.00
19 LeBron James/299 8.00 20.00
20 Kyrie Irving/299 5.00 12.00
21 Ricky Rubio/299 2.50 6.00
22 Danny Green/299 2.00 5.00
23 Kawhi Leonard/299 4.00 10.00
24 Andrew Wiggins/299 4.00 10.00
25 Draymond Green/299 5.00 12.00
26 Klay Thompson/299 3.00 8.00
27 Stephen Curry/299 10.00 25.00
28 Dwight Howard/299 2.00 5.00
29 James Harden/299 4.00 10.00
30 Kobe Bryant/299 10.00 25.00
31 Kevin Durant/299 5.00 12.00
32 Russell Westbrook/299 6.00 15.00
33 Jimmy Butler/299 2.50 6.00
34 Derrick Rose/299 3.00 8.00
35 Nikola Vucevic/299 2.00 5.00

2015-16 Court Kings Aurora

RANDOM INSERTS IN PACKS
1 Derrick Rose 10.00 25.00
2 James Harden 12.00 30.00
3 Zach LaVine 8.00 20.00
4 John Wall 10.00 25.00
5 Bojan Bogdanovic 5.00 12.00
6 Jimmy Butler 8.00 20.00
7 Chris Paul 10.00 25.00
8 Anthony Davis 15.00 40.00
9 Marcus Smart 6.00 15.00
10 Dante Exum 6.00 15.00
11 Kyrie Irving 15.00 40.00
12 Kobe Bryant 40.00 100.00
13 Kevin Durant 20.00 50.00
14 Elfrid Payton 6.00 15.00
15 Dennis Schroder 6.00 15.00
16 LeBron James 40.00 100.00
17 Dwyane Wade 12.00 30.00
18 Russell Westbrook 20.00 50.00
19 Brandon Knight 6.00 15.00
20 Kawhi Leonard 20.00 50.00
21 Stephen Curry 40.00 100.00
22 Andrew Wiggins 12.00 30.00
23 Damian Lillard 15.00 40.00
24 Bradley Beal 8.00 20.00
25 DeMar DeRozan 8.00 20.00

2015-16 Court Kings Autographs

RANDOM INSERTS IN PACKS
PRINT RUNS B/WN 35-199 COPIES PER
EXCHANGE DEADLINE 6/9/2017
*SAPPHIRE/25: .5X TO 1.2X BASIC
CKAD Anthony Davis/35 40.00 100.00
CKBM Ben McLemore/49 2.50 6.00
CKCM C.J. McCollum/99 8.00 20.00
CKDMJ Dan Majerle/99 3.00 8.00
CKDM Doug McDermott/99 3.00 8.00
CKDN Don Nelson/35 12.00 30.00
CKDR David Robinson/35 25.00 60.00
CKDR Dennis Rodman/35 30.00 80.00
CKEJ Eddie Jones/99 3.00 8.00
CKGG Gail Goodrich/35 3.00 8.00
CKGH Grant Hill/35 25.00 60.00
CKGHR Gary Harris/99 3.00 8.00
CKJHK Jeff Hornacek/99 3.00 8.00
CKJH Jrue Holiday/35 5.00 12.00
CKJI Joe Ingles/199 3.00 8.00
CKJN Jusuf Nurkic/99 6.00 15.00
CKJR Julius Randle/35 8.00 20.00
CKJW John Wall/35 25.00 60.00
CKKB Kobe Bryant/35 100.00 250.00
CKKD Kevin Durant/35 125.00 250.00
CKKI Kyrie Irving/35 40.00 100.00
CKKM Khris Middleton/199 3.00 8.00
CKMA Mark Aguirre/99
CKMC Michael Carter-Williams/99 2.50 6.00
CKMD Matthew Dellavedova/199 3.00 8.00
CKMJ Mark Jackson/35 3.00 8.00
CKMP Mason Plumlee/199 3.00 8.00
CKMW Marvin Williams/99 3.00 8.00
CKNC Norris Cole/99 3.00 8.00
CKNM Nikola Mirotic/49 3.00 8.00
CKSS Steve Smith/99 5.00 12.00
CKTM Timofey Mozgov/99 2.50 6.00
CKTP Tony Parker/35 25.00 60.00
CKTP Jordan Clarkson/199 6.00 15.00
CKVD Vlade Divac/99 3.00 8.00
CKZI Zydrunas Ilgauskas/99 3.00 8.00
CKZL Zach LaVine/99 20.00 50.00

2015-16 Court Kings Brush Strokes Autographs

RANDOM INSERTS IN PACKS
PRINT RUNS B/WN 30-199 COPIES PER
EXCHANGE DEADLINE 6/9/2017
*SAPPHIRE/25: .5X TO 1.2X BASIC
BSAE Alex English/99 3.00 8.00
BSAG A.C. Green/99 6.00 15.00
BSAM Antonio McDyess/199 6.00 15.00
BSAW Antoine Walker/199 3.00 8.00
BSBL Bill Laimbeer/199 3.00 8.00
BSBM Bob McAdoo/99 5.00 12.00
BSBS Byron Scott/30 3.00 8.00
BSDI Dan Issel/199 3.00 8.00
BSDR Dennis Rodman/30 40.00 100.00
BSDR Dino Radja/199 8.00 20.00
BSDS Damon Stoudamire/199 3.00 8.00
BSEJ Eddie Jones/199 4.00 10.00
BSFB Fred Brown/199 2.50 6.00
BSGP Gary Payton/30 6.00 15.00
BSGR Glen Rice/30
BSJD Joe Dumars/30 10.00 25.00
BSJS Jerry Stackhouse/99 6.00 15.00
BSJW Jamaal Wilkes/99 4.00 10.00
BSMA Mark Aguirre/99 3.00 8.00
BSNA Nate Archibald/30 3.00 8.00
BSRH Robert Horry/99
BSRS Rik Smits/199 5.00 12.00
BSRS Rony Seikaly/199 2.50 6.00
BSSB Sam Bowie/199 2.50 6.00
BSSE Sean Elliott/199 4.00 10.00
BSTD Tony Delk/199 2.50 6.00
BSVN Vinny Del Negro/30 3.00 8.00

2015-16 Court Kings Calligraphy Autographs

RANDOM INSERTS IN PACKS
PRINT RUNS B/WN 40-199 COPIES PER
EXCHANGE DEADLINE 6/9/2017
*SAPPHIRE/25: .5X TO 1.2X BASIC
CKB Kobe Bryant/40 125.00 300.00
CSM Sidney Moncrief/125 2.50 6.00
CSB Sam Bowie/99 5.00 12.00
CAD Anthony Davis/40
CDI Dan Issel/199 3.00 8.00
CDM Dan Majerle/60 3.00 8.00
CJE James Ennis/199 2.50 6.00
CJG Jeff Green/60 3.00 8.00
CKD Kevin Durant/40 75.00 150.00
CWM Wesley Matthews/60 2.50 6.00
CMH Maurice Harkless/199 2.50 6.00
CMP Mason Plumlee/199 3.00 8.00
CJP Jabari Parker/40 15.00 40.00
CJS Jerry Stackhouse/60 12.00 30.00
CSK Steve Kerr/40 8.00 20.00
CRA Rafer Alston/199 2.50 6.00
CTP Tony Parker/40 25.00 40.00
CMC Michael Carter-Williams/40 2.50 6.00
CMA Mark Aquirre/60 3.00 8.00
CAN Andrew Nicholson/199 2.50 6.00
CBM Bob McAdoo/60 10.00 25.00
CDC DeMarre Carroll/199 2.50 6.00
CGP Gary Payton/40 8.00 20.00
CJW John Wall/40
CJN Jusuf Nurkic/199 2.50 6.00
CTH Tobias Harris/60
CMW Mo Williams/199 3.00 8.00
CLE Len Elmore/199 2.50 6.00
CAA Al-Farouq Aminu/60 3.00 8.00
CBL Bill Laimbeer/199 3.00 8.00
CDS Dennis Schroder/199 6.00 15.00
CEF Evan Fournier/199 3.00 8.00
CJC Jordan Clarkson/199 4.00 10.00
CJR Julius Randle/40 20.00 50.00
CTA Tony Allen/199 2.50 6.00
CNN Nene/60 3.00 8.00
CLG Langston Galloway/199 2.50 6.00
CAE Alex English/60 3.00 8.00
CBML Ben McLemore/40 2.50 6.00
CJI Joe Ingles/199 2.50 6.00
CEK Enes Kanter/60 2.50 6.00
CJH Jrue Holiday/40 3.00 8.00

2015-16 Court Kings Expressionist Memorabilia

RANDOM INSERTS IN PACKS
STATED PRINT RUN 299 SER.#'d SETS
*PRIME/25: 1X TO 2.5X BASIC
1 Kemba Walker 2.50 6.00
2 Reggie Jackson 2.00 5.00
3 Kobe Bryant 10.00 25.00
4 Russell Westbrook 6.00 15.00
5 Draymond Green 5.00 12.00
6 Derrick Rose 3.00 8.00
7 Stephen Curry 15.00 40.00
8 Dwyane Wade 4.00 10.00
9 Damian Lillard 5.00 12.00
10 DeAndre Jordan 2.50 6.00
11 Jimmy Butler 2.50 6.00
12 Dwight Howard 2.00 5.00
13 Andrew Wiggins 4.00 10.00
14 DeMarcus Cousins 2.50 6.00
15 Mike Conley 2.50 6.00
16 Kyrie Irving 5.00 12.00
17 James Harden 4.00 10.00
18 Zach LaVine 2.50 6.00
19 John Wall 3.00 8.00
20 Chris Bosh 2.50 6.00
21 LeBron James 8.00 20.00
22 Blake Griffin 2.50 6.00
23 Anthony Davis 5.00 12.00
24 Isaiah Thomas 2.50 6.00
25 Giannis Antetokounmpo 5.00 12.00
26 Dirk Nowitzki 3.00 8.00
27 Chris Paul 3.00 8.00
28 Carmelo Anthony 3.00 8.00
29 Joakim Noah 2.00 5.00
30 Eric Bledsoe 2.00 5.00
31 Kenneth Faried 2.00 5.00
32 Jordan Clarkson 2.50 6.00
33 Kevin Durant 5.00 12.00
34 Iman Shumpert 1.50 4.00
35 Jason Terry 2.00 5.00

2015-16 Court Kings Expressionists

RANDOM INSERTS IN PACKS
*SAPPHIRE/25: 1.5X TO 4X BASIC
1 Kemba Walker .60 1.50
2 Reggie Jackson .50 1.25
3 Kobe Bryant 2.50 6.00
4 Russell Westbrook 1.50 4.00
5 Draymond Green .75 2.00
6 Derrick Rose .75 2.00
7 Stephen Curry 2.50 6.00
8 Dwyane Wade 1.00 2.50
9 Damian Lillard 1.25 3.00
10 DeAndre Jordan .60 1.50
11 Jimmy Butler .60 1.50
12 Dwight Howard .50 1.25
13 Andrew Wiggins 1.00 2.50
14 DeMarcus Cousins .60 1.50
15 Mike Conley .60 1.50
16 Kyrie Irving 1.25 3.00
17 James Harden 1.00 2.50
18 Zach LaVine .60 1.50
19 John Wall .75 2.00
20 Chris Bosh .60 1.50
21 LeBron James 2.50 6.00
22 Blake Griffin .60 1.50
23 Anthony Davis 1.25 3.00
24 Isaiah Thomas .60 1.50
25 Giannis Antetokounmpo 1.25 3.00
26 Dirk Nowitzki .75 2.00
27 Chris Paul .75 2.00
28 Carmelo Anthony .75 2.00
29 Joakim Noah .50 1.25
30 Eric Bledsoe .50 1.25
31 Kenneth Faried .50 1.25
32 Jordan Clarkson .60 1.50
33 Kevin Durant 1.50 4.00
34 Iman Shumpert .40 1.00
35 Jason Terry .50 1.25

2015-16 Court Kings Fresh Paint Autographs

RANDOM INSERTS IN PACKS
EXCHANGE DEADLINE 6/9/2017
FPAB Anthony Brown 2.50 6.00
FPAH Andrew Harrison 4.00 10.00
FPBP Bobby Portis 4.00 10.00
FPCM Chris McCullough 2.50 6.00
FPCP Cameron Payne 3.00 8.00
FPDB Devin Booker 40.00 100.00
FPDJ Dakari Johnson 2.50 6.00
FPDR D'Angelo Russell 15.00 40.00
FPDW Delon Wright 3.00 8.00
FPEM Emmanuel Mudiay 4.00 10.00
FPFK Frank Kaminsky 6.00 15.00
FPJA Justin Anderson 3.00 8.00
FPJG Jerian Grant 2.50 6.00
FPJM Jordan Mickey 2.50 6.00
FPJO Jahlil Okafor 8.00 20.00
FPJW Justise Winslow 12.00 30.00
FPJY Joe Young 3.00 8.00
FPKA Karl-Anthony Towns 75.00 150.00
FPKO Kelly Oubre Jr. 3.00 8.00
FPKP Kristaps Porzingis 40.00 100.00
FPLN Larry Nance Jr. 8.00 20.00
FPMH Mario Hezonja 3.00 8.00
FPMT Myles Turner 12.00 30.00
FPPC Pat Connaughton 2.50 6.00
FPRH Richaun Holmes 3.00 8.00
FPRJ R.J. Hunter 2.50 6.00
FPRV Rashad Vaughn 2.50 6.00
FPSD Sam Dekker 3.00 8.00
FPSJ Stanley Johnson 3.00 8.00
FPTH Tyler Harvey 2.50 6.00
FPTJ Tyus Jones 4.00 10.00
FPTL Trey Lyles 4.00 10.00
FPTR Terry Rozier 3.00 8.00
FPJMT Jarell Martin 3.00 8.00
FPMHR Montrezl Harrell 3.00 8.00
FPRHJ Rondae Hollis-Jefferson 3.00 8.00
FPWCS Willie Cauley-Stein 12.00 30.00

2015-16 Court Kings Heir Apparent Autographs

RANDOM INSERTS IN PACKS
EXCHANGE DEADLINE 6/9/2017
HAKP Kristaps Porzingis 50.00 120.00
HACAP Cameron Payne 4.00 10.00
HADAR D'Angelo Russell 15.00 40.00
HAEMU Emmanuel Mudiay 12.00 30.00
HAFRK Frank Kaminsky 8.00 20.00
HAJAO Jahlil Okafor 15.00 40.00
HAJEG Jerian Grant 3.00 8.00
HAJUW Justise Winslow 15.00 40.00
HAKAT Karl-Anthony Towns 100.00 200.00
HAMAH Mario Hezonja 4.00 10.00
HASDE Sam Dekker 4.00 10.00
HASJO Stanley Johnson 4.00 10.00

2015-16 Court Kings Impressionist Ink

RANDOM INSERTS IN PACKS
PRINT RUNS B/WN 40-199 COPIES PER
EXCHANGE DEADLINE 6/9/2017
*SAPPHIRE/25: .5X TO 1.2X BASIC
IIAG Aaron Gordon/40 3.00 8.00
IIAL Alex Len/99 2.50 6.00
IIAP Adreian Payne/199 2.50 6.00
IIBB Bojan Bogdanovic/199 2.50 6.00
IIDC DeMarre Carroll/99 2.50 6.00
IIDE Dante Exum/40 10.00 25.00
IIEK Enes Kanter/40
IIGH Gary Harris/99 3.00 8.00
IIJC Jordan Clarkson/199 8.00 20.00
IIJE James Ennis/199 2.50 6.00
IIJP Jabari Parker/40 15.00 40.00
IIJR Julius Randle/40 12.00 30.00
IIJS J.R. Smith/40 6.00 15.00
IIJW John Wall/40 15.00 40.00
IIKB Kobe Bryant/40 EXCH 125.00 250.00
IIKD Kevin Durant/40 60.00 150.00
IIKI Kyrie Irving/40
IIKT Klay Thompson/40 25.00 60.00
IILG Langston Galloway/199 2.50 6.00
IIMD Matthew Dellavedova/199 3.00 8.00
IIMS Marcus Smart/40 3.00 8.00
IINC Norris Cole/40 2.50 6.00
IINM Nikola Mirotic/40 8.00 20.00
IIOP Otto Porter/40
IITB Tarik Black/199 2.50 6.00
IITE Tyler Ennis/40 2.50 6.00
IITH Tobias Harris/40 3.00 8.00
IITM Timofey Mozgov/99 2.50 6.00
IITT Tristan Thompson/40 3.00 8.00
IITW T.J. Warren/60 5.00 12.00
IIZL Zach LaVine/99 15.00 40.00

2015-16 Court Kings Le Cinque Piu Belle Autographs

RANDOM BOX TOPPER INSERT
PRINT RUNS B/WN 1-32 COPIES PER
NO PRICING ON QTY 8 OR LESS
1 Karl-Anthony Towns/32 30.00 80.00
5 Mario Hezonja/23 5.00 12.00

2015-16 Court Kings Performance Art Jerseys

RANDOM INSERTS IN PACKS
STATED PRINT RUN 299 SER.#'d SETS
*PRIME/25: 1.2X TO 3X BASIC
1 Damian Lillard 5.00 12.00
2 Rajon Rondo 2.50 6.00
3 Kawhi Leonard 4.00 10.00
4 Tim Duncan 4.00 10.00
5 Iman Shumpert 1.50 4.00
6 Isaiah Thomas 2.50 6.00
7 Goran Dragic 2.00 5.00
8 Chris Bosh 2.50 6.00
9 DeMarre Carroll 1.50 4.00
10 Khris Middleton 2.00 5.00

2015-16 Court Kings Portraits

RANDOM INSERTS IN PACKS
*RUBY/100: 1X TO 2.5X BASIC
*SAPPHIRE/25: 1.5X TO 4X BASIC
1 Derrick Rose .75 2.00
2 Elfrid Payton .50 1.25
3 Jabari Parker .75 2.00
4 Michael Carter-Williams .40 1.00
5 George Hill .50 1.25
6 Jimmy Butler .60 1.50
7 Blake Griffin .60 1.50
8 Jamal Crawford .60 1.50
9 Robin Lopez .40 1.00
10 Roy Hibbert .50 1.25
11 Kyrie Irving 1.25 3.00
12 John Wall .75 2.00
13 Tyreke Evans .40 1.00
14 Nerlens Noel .50 1.25
15 Jeff Green .50 1.25
16 LeBron James 2.50 6.00
17 Marcus Smart .50 1.25
18 Brandon Knight .50 1.25
19 T.J. Warren .50 1.25
20 Matt Barnes .40 1.00
21 Stephen Curry 2.50 6.00
22 Bradley Beal .60 1.50
23 Bojan Bogdanovic .40 1.00
24 Rajon Rondo .60 1.50
25 Chris Andersen .50 1.25
26 James Harden 1.00 2.50
27 Dante Exum .50 1.25
28 Dirk Nowitzki .75 2.00
29 Tim Duncan 1.00 2.50
30 Shabazz Napier .40 1.00
31 Chris Paul .75 2.00
32 Jordan Clarkson .60 1.50
33 Dwight Howard .50 1.25
34 Jonas Valanciunas .50 1.25
35 Greg Monroe .50 1.25
36 Kobe Bryant 2.50 6.00
37 Manu Ginobili .60 1.50
38 Isaiah Thomas .60 1.50
39 Gordon Hayward .60 1.50
40 Gorgui Dieng .40 1.00
41 Dwyane Wade 1.00 2.50
42 Zach LaVine .60 1.50
43 Joe Johnson .50 1.25
44 Kyle Korver .50 1.25
45 Nikola Vucevic .50 1.25
46 Andrew Wiggins 1.00 2.50
47 Kemba Walker .60 1.50
48 Pau Gasol .60 1.50
49 Thabo Sefolosha .40 1.00
50 Robert Covington .40 1.00
51 Anthony Davis 1.25 3.00
52 Kenneth Faried .50 1.25
53 Kevin Love .60 1.50
54 Nicolas Batum .50 1.25
55 Gerald Henderson .40 1.00
56 Kevin Durant 1.50 4.00
57 Reggie Jackson .50 1.25
58 Brandon Jennings .40 1.00
59 Wesley Matthews .40 1.00
60 Marco Belinelli .40 1.00
61 Russell Westbrook 1.50 4.00
62 Carmelo Anthony .75 2.00
63 Klay Thompson .75 2.00
64 Joffrey Lauvergne .40 1.00
65 DeMarre Carroll .40 1.00
66 Damian Lillard 1.25 3.00
67 DeMarcus Cousins .60 1.50
68 Paul George .75 2.00
69 Harrison Barnes .50 1.25
70 Marcin Gortat .50 1.25

2015-16 Court Kings Rookie Portraits

RANDOM INSERTS IN PACKS
*RUBY/100: .75X TO 2X BASIC
*SAPPHIRE/25: 1.2X TO 3X BASIC
1 D'Angelo Russell 2.50 6.00
2 Mario Hezonja .75 2.00
3 Karl-Anthony Towns 5.00 12.00
4 Willie Cauley-Stein 1.00 2.50
5 Devin Booker 3.00 8.00
6 Jerian Grant .60 1.50
7 Cameron Payne .75 2.00
8 Delon Wright .75 2.00
9 Anthony Brown .60 1.50
10 Pat Connaughton .60 1.50
11 Jahlil Okafor 1.25 3.00
12 Emmanuel Mudiay 1.00 2.50
13 Kristaps Porzingis 2.50 6.00
14 Stanley Johnson .75 2.00
15 Kelly Oubre Jr. .75 2.00
16 Justin Anderson .75 2.00
17 Terry Rozier .75 2.00
18 Bobby Portis 1.00 2.50
19 Joe Young .75 2.00
20 Chris McCullough .60 1.50
21 Myles Turner 1.00 2.50
22 Frank Kaminsky 1.00 2.50
23 Trey Lyles 1.00 2.50
24 Justise Winslow 1.00 2.50
25 Rashad Vaughn .60 1.50
26 Tyus Jones 1.00 2.50
27 Sam Dekker .75 2.00
28 Montrezl Harrell .75 2.00
29 Nemanja Bjelica .75 2.00
30 Nikola Jokic 1.25 3.00

2015-16 Court Kings Studio Signatures

RANDOM INSERTS IN PACKS
PRINT RUNS B/WN 40-99 COPIES PER
EXCHANGE DEADLINE 6/9/2017
*SAPPHIRE/25: .5X TO 1.2X BASIC
SSAD Anthony Davis/40 40.00 100.00
SSAL Alex Len/99 2.50 6.00
SSBB Bojan Bogdanovic/99 2.50 6.00
SSCM C.J. McCollum/99 6.00 15.00
SSDC DeMarre Carroll/99 2.50 6.00
SSDR Damjan Rudez/99 2.50 6.00
SSDS Dennis Schroder/99 3.00 8.00
SSGH Grant Hill/40 12.00 30.00
SSGP Gary Payton/40 8.00 20.00
SSJE Julius Erving/40 30.00 80.00
SSJH Jrue Holiday/40 3.00 8.00
SSJW John Wall/40 15.00 40.00
SSKB Kobe Bryant/40 EXCH 125.00 250.00
SSKD Kevin Durant/40 75.00 150.00
SSKI Kyrie Irving/40 25.00 60.00
SSMC Michael Carter-Williams/99 2.50 6.00
SSMG Marcin Gortat/49
SSMK Michael Kidd-Gilchrist/40
SSNC Norris Cole/99 2.50 6.00
SSNN Nene/49 3.00 8.00
SSNY Nick Young/49 3.00 8.00
SSTH Tim Hardaway Jr./99 2.50 6.00
SSTT Tristan Thompson/40 3.00 8.00
SSWM Wesley Matthews/49 2.50 6.00
SSTBK Tarik Black/99 2.50 6.00

2015-16 Court Kings Swagger

RANDOM INSERTS IN PACKS
*SAPPHIRE/25: 1X TO 2.5X BASIC
1 Dwyane Wade 2.00 5.00
2 Jonas Valanciunas 1.00 2.50
3 Derrick Rose 1.50 4.00
4 DeMarcus Cousins 1.25 3.00
5 Jusuf Nurkic .75 2.00
6 Andrew Wiggins 2.00 5.00
7 DeMar DeRozan 1.25 3.00
8 Jimmy Butler 1.25 3.00
9 DeAndre Jordan 1.25 3.00
10 Zach Randolph 1.00 2.50
11 Ben McLemore .75 2.00
12 Kemba Walker 1.25 3.00
13 Kyrie Irving 2.50 6.00
14 Giannis Antetokounmpo 2.50 6.00
15 Goran Dragic 1.00 2.50
16 Anthony Davis 2.50 6.00
17 Kenneth Faried 1.00 2.50
18 LeBron James 5.00 12.00
19 Eric Bledsoe 1.00 2.50
20 Victor Oladipo 1.00 2.50
21 Kevin Durant 3.00 8.00
22 Reggie Jackson 1.00 2.50
23 Stephen Curry 5.00 12.00
24 Jabari Parker 1.50 4.00
25 Tony Parker 1.25 3.00
26 Russell Westbrook 3.00 8.00
27 Blake Griffin 1.25 3.00
28 James Harden 2.00 5.00
29 Kobe Bryant 5.00 12.00
30 Rudy Gobert 1.25 3.00
31 Damian Lillard 2.50 6.00
32 Carmelo Anthony 1.50 4.00
33 Chris Paul 1.50 4.00
34 Zach LaVine 1.25 3.00
35 Elfrid Payton 1.00 2.50

2015-16 Court Kings Vintage Materials

RANDOM INSERTS IN PACKS
STATED PRINT RUN 199 SER.#'d SETS
*PRIME/25: 1X TO 2.5X BASIC
1 Alonzo Mourning 3.00 8.00
2 Clyde Drexler 3.00 8.00
3 Dan Majerle 2.00 5.00
4 Danny Manning 2.00 5.00
5 David Robinson 5.00 12.00
6 Grant Hill 3.00 8.00
7 Herb Williams 1.50 4.00
8 Kareem Abdul-Jabbar 4.00 10.00
9 Reggie Lewis 2.50 6.00
10 Robert Parish 2.50 6.00
11 Ron Harper 2.50 6.00
12 Scottie Pippen 6.00 15.00
13 Shaquille O'Neal 5.00 12.00
14 Vlade Divac 2.50 6.00
15 Walter Davis 1.50 4.00
16 Xavier McDaniel 1.50 4.00
17 Alex English 2.00 5.00
18 Alvan Adams 1.50 4.00
19 Anfernee Hardaway 5.00 12.00
20 Bernard King 2.00 5.00
21 Bill Laimbeer 2.00 5.00
22 Byron Scott 2.00 5.00
23 Charles Oakley 2.00 5.00
24 Dan Issel 2.00 5.00
25 Detlef Schrempf 2.50 6.00

2016-17 Court Kings

1 Anthony Davis 1.00 2.50
2 Kawhi Leonard .75 2.00
3 James Harden .75 2.00
4 Kyrie Irving 1.00 2.50
5 Vince Carter .60 1.50
6 Marc Gasol .50 1.25
7 Eric Bledsoe .40 1.00
8 Damian Lillard 1.00 2.50
9 Emmanuel Mudiay .40 1.00
10 Aaron Gordon .40 1.00
11 Trevor Ariza .30 .75
12 Brandon Knight .40 1.00
13 Devin Booker .75 2.00
14 Isaiah Thomas .50 1.25
15 Kyle Lowry .40 1.00
16 Avery Bradley .40 1.00
17 Marcus Morris .30 .75
18 Ed Davis .30 .75
19 Kristaps Porzingis 1.00 2.50
20 Bojan Bogdanovic .30 .75
21 DeMarcus Cousins .50 1.25
22 Myles Turner .40 1.00
23 Kevin Love .50 1.25
24 Doug McDermott .40 1.00
25 Carmelo Anthony .60 1.50
26 Jimmy Butler .50 1.25
27 Gordon Hayward .50 1.25
28 Thaddeus Young .30 .75
29 D'Angelo Russell .60 1.50
30 Rudy Gobert .50 1.25
31 Robin Lopez .30 .75
32 LeBron James 2.00 5.00
33 John Wall .60 1.50
34 Kelly Olynyk .30 .75
35 DeAndre Jordan .50 1.25
36 Marco Belinelli .30 .75
37 Tyreke Evans .30 .75
38 Chris Paul .60 1.50
39 Nik Stauskas .30 .75
40 DeMar DeRozan .50 1.25
41 Hassan Whiteside .40 1.00
42 Brook Lopez .40 1.00
43 Jrue Holiday .40 1.00
44 Julius Randle .50 1.25
45 Dennis Schroder .40 1.00
46 Bismack Biyombo .30 .75
47 Nikola Vucevic .40 1.00
48 Ian Mahinmi .30 .75
49 Kemba Walker .50 1.25
50 Reggie Jackson .40 1.00
51 Marcin Gortat .40 1.00
52 Jordan Clarkson .40 1.00
53 Andre Drummond .50 1.25
54 Alex Len .30 .75
55 Cody Zeller .30 .75
56 Paul George .60 1.50
57 Kevin Durant 1.25 3.00
58 Blake Griffin .50 1.25
59 Steven Adams .40 1.00
60 Rajon Rondo .50 1.25
61 Nicolas Batum .40 1.00
62 Zach Randolph .40 1.00
63 Andrew Wiggins .75 2.00
64 Michael Carter-Williams .30 .75
65 J.R. Smith .40 1.00
66 Rodney Hood .40 1.00
67 Stephen Curry 2.00 5.00
68 Giannis Antetokounmpo 1.00 2.50
69 Zach LaVine .50 1.25
70 Jabari Parker .60 1.50
71 Jahlil Okafor .40 1.00
72 Danilo Gallinari .40 1.00
73 Klay Thompson .60 1.50
74 Goran Dragic .40 1.00
75 Wesley Matthews .30 .75
76 Will Barton .30 .75
77 Patrick Beverley .30 .75
78 Serge Ibaka .40 1.00
79 Draymond Green .60 1.50
80 Karl-Anthony Towns 1.25 3.00
81 Dwyane Wade .75 2.00
82 J.J. Barea .40 1.00
83 C.J. McCollum .40 1.00
84 Justise Winslow .40 1.00
85 Festus Ezeli .30 .75
86 Russell Westbrook 1.25 3.00
87 Victor Oladipo .40 1.00
88 Jeff Teague .40 1.00
89 Nikola Mirotic .40 1.00
90 Stanley Johnson .30 .75
91 Tony Parker .50 1.25
92 Elfrid Payton .40 1.00
93 Derrick Rose .60 1.50
94 Bradley Beal .50 1.25
95 DeMarre Carroll .30 .75
96 T.J. McConnell .30 .75
97 LaMarcus Aldridge .50 1.25
98 Dirk Nowitzki .60 1.50
99 Paul Millsap .50 1.25
100 Kenneth Faried .40 1.00
101 Ben Simmons RC 6.00 15.00
102 Brandon Ingram RC 3.00 8.00
103 Jaylen Brown RC 2.00 5.00
104 Dragan Bender RC .60 1.50
105 Kris Dunn RC 1.50 4.00
106 Buddy Hield RC 1.25 3.00
107 Jamal Murray RC 1.50 4.00
108 Marquese Chriss RC 1.25 3.00
109 Jakob Poeltl RC .60 1.50
110 Thon Maker RC 1.50 4.00
111 Isaiah Whitehead RC .50 1.25
112 Taurean Prince RC .75 2.00
113 Denzel Valentine RC .60 1.50
114 Wade Baldwin IV RC .50 1.25
115 Henry Ellenson RC .60 1.50
116 Malik Beasley RC .50 1.25
117 Caris LeVert RC .60 1.50
118 DeAndre' Bembry RC .50 1.25
119 Brice Johnson RC .50 1.25
120 Damian Jones RC .50 1.25
121 Tyler Ulis RC 1.50 4.00
122 Deyonta Davis RC .50 1.25
123 Skal Labissiere RC .75 2.00
124 Dejounte Murray RC 1.00 2.50
125 Pascal Siakam RC .50 1.25
126 Ben Simmons 8.00 20.00
127 Brandon Ingram 4.00 10.00
128 Jaylen Brown 2.50 6.00
129 Dragan Bender .75 2.00
130 Kris Dunn 2.00 5.00
131 Buddy Hield 1.50 4.00
132 Jamal Murray 2.00 5.00
133 Marquese Chriss 1.50 4.00
134 Jakob Poeltl .75 2.00
135 Thon Maker 2.00 5.00
136 Isaiah Whitehead .60 1.50
137 Taurean Prince 1.00 2.50
138 Denzel Valentine .75 2.00
139 Wade Baldwin IV .60 1.50
140 Henry Ellenson .75 2.00
141 Malik Beasley .60 1.50
142 Caris LeVert .75 2.00
143 DeAndre' Bembry .60 1.50
144 Brice Johnson .60 1.50
145 Damian Jones .60 1.50
146 Tyler Ulis 2.00 5.00
147 Deyonta Davis .60 1.50
148 Skal Labissiere 1.00 2.50
149 Dejounte Murray 1.25 3.00
150 Pascal Siakam .60 1.50
151 Ben Simmons 40.00 100.00
152 Brandon Ingram 8.00 20.00
153 Jaylen Brown 5.00 12.00
154 Dragan Bender 1.50 4.00
155 Kris Dunn 4.00 10.00
156 Buddy Hield 3.00 8.00
157 Jamal Murray 4.00 10.00
158 Marquese Chriss 3.00 8.00
159 Jakob Poeltl 1.50 4.00
160 Thon Maker 4.00 10.00
161 Isaiah Whitehead 1.25 3.00
162 Taurean Prince 2.00 5.00
163 Denzel Valentine 1.50 4.00
164 Wade Baldwin IV 1.25 3.00
165 Henry Ellenson 1.50 4.00
166 Malik Beasley 1.25 3.00
167 Caris LeVert 1.50 4.00
168 DeAndre' Bembry 1.25 3.00
169 Brice Johnson 1.25 3.00
170 Damian Jones 1.25 3.00
171 Tyler Ulis 4.00 10.00
172 Deyonta Davis 1.25 3.00
173 Skal Labissiere 2.00 5.00
174 Dejounte Murray 2.50 6.00
175 Pascal Siakam 1.25 3.00
176 Ben Simmons 100.00 250.00
177 Brandon Ingram 20.00 50.00
178 Jaylen Brown 12.00 30.00
179 Dragan Bender 4.00 10.00
180 Kris Dunn 10.00 25.00
181 Buddy Hield 8.00 20.00
182 Jamal Murray 10.00 25.00
183 Marquese Chriss 8.00 20.00
184 Jakob Poeltl 4.00 10.00
185 Thon Maker 10.00 25.00
186 Isaiah Whitehead 3.00 8.00
187 Taurean Prince 5.00 12.00
188 Denzel Valentine 4.00 10.00
189 Wade Baldwin IV 3.00 8.00
190 Henry Ellenson 4.00 10.00
191 Malik Beasley 3.00 8.00
192 Caris LeVert 4.00 10.00
193 DeAndre' Bembry 3.00 8.00
194 Brice Johnson 3.00 8.00
195 Damian Jones 3.00 8.00
196 Tyler Ulis 10.00 25.00

197 Deyonta Davis 3.00 8.00
198 Skal Labissiere 5.00 12.00
199 Dejounte Murray 6.00 15.00
200 Pascal Siakam 3.00 8.00

2016-17 Court Kings Aurora

RANDOM INSERTS IN PACKS
1 Kyrie Irving 15.00 40.00
2 Stephen Curry 40.00 100.00
3 Damian Lillard 12.00 30.00
4 Jimmy Butler 10.00 25.00
5 Draymond Green 10.00 25.00
6 DeMar DeRozan 6.00 15.00
7 Chris Paul 8.00 20.00
8 Russell Westbrook 15.00 40.00
9 LeBron James 40.00 100.00
10 Kyle Lowry 5.00 12.00
11 Klay Thompson 15.00 40.00
12 James Harden 10.00 25.00
13 Paul George 10.00 25.00
14 Kevin Durant 15.00 40.00
15 Andrew Wiggins 10.00 25.00
16 Reggie Jackson 5.00 12.00
17 Dirk Nowitzki 10.00 25.00
18 Isaiah Thomas 6.00 15.00
19 Kristaps Porzingis 12.00 30.00
20 Karl-Anthony Towns 15.00 40.00

2016-17 Court Kings Sapphire

*SAPPHIRE: 1.5X TO 4X BASIC
RANOM INSERTS IN PACKS
STATED PRINT RUN 25 SER.#'d SETS

2016-17 Court Kings 2 on 2 Quad Memorabilia

RANDOM INSERTS IN PACKS
PRINT RUNS B/WN 25-99 COPIES PER
1 Mc/Li/Th/Cu/99 15.00 40.00
2 Th/Du/Mc/Bi/25
3 Jo/Pa/Wo/Bi/25 15.00 40.00
4 Ja/Cu/Gr/Ir/99 10.00 25.00
5 No/Ba/Du/Pa/99
6 Isaiah Thomas 3.00 8.00
Paul Millsap
Dennis Schroder
Jae Crowder/99
7 Pa/Jo/Ha/Ca/99 5.00 12.00
8 Va/El/Lo/Ge/99 4.00 10.00
10 Mu/O'N/Iv/Br/25 20.00 50.00

2016-17 Court Kings 5x7 Box Topper Autographs

RANDOMLY INSERTED BOX TOPPER
EXCHANGE DEADLINE 5/30/2018
2 Anfernee Hardaway 40.00 100.00
3 Jalen Rose 10.00 25.00
4 Damon Stoudamire 10.00 25.00
5 Michael Cooper 5.00 12.00
6 Dell Curry 6.00 15.00
7 Jamal Mashburn 10.00 25.00
8 Nate Archibald
9 A.C. Green 6.00 15.00
11 John Starks 10.00 25.00
12 Toni Kukoc 12.00 30.00
13 Rick Barry 30.00 80.00
14 Spud Webb 6.00 15.00
15 Dominique Wilkins 20.00 50.00
16 Gary Payton 15.00 40.00
17 Julius Erving 30.00 80.00
18 Ray Allen 40.00 100.00
19 George Gervin 10.00 25.00
20 Tim Hardaway 10.00 25.00
21 Larry Bird 60.00 150.00
22 James Worthy
23 Bill Russell 60.00 150.00
24 Latrell Sprewell 20.00 50.00

2016-17 Court Kings 5x7 Box Topper Panoramics

RANDOM INSERTS IN PACKS
1 Carmelo Anthony 2.50 6.00
2 Stephen Curry 8.00 20.00
3 Kyle Lowry 1.50 4.00
4 LeBron James 8.00 20.00
5 Russell Westbrook 5.00 12.00
6 Kyrie Irving 4.00 10.00
7 Andrew Wiggins 3.00 8.00
8 Isaiah Thomas 2.00 5.00
9 Kemba Walker 2.00 5.00
10 Jimmy Butler 2.00 5.00
11 Devin Booker 3.00 8.00
12 Reggie Jackson 1.50 4.00
13 James Harden 3.00 8.00
14 Paul George 2.50 6.00
15 Chris Paul 2.50 6.00
16 D'Angelo Russell 2.50 6.00
17 Karl-Anthony Towns 5.00 12.00
18 Giannis Antetokounmpo 4.00 10.00
19 Anthony Davis 4.00 10.00
20 Kristaps Porzingis 4.00 10.00
21 Blake Griffin 2.00 5.00
22 Klay Thompson 2.50 6.00
23 Damian Lillard 4.00 10.00
24 DeMarcus Cousins 2.00 5.00
25 John Wall 2.50 6.00

2016-17 Court Kings 5x7 Box Topper Rookie Royalty

RANDOM INSERTS IN PACKS
1 Paul Pierce 2.00 5.00
2 Zach Randolph 1.50 4.00
3 Tyreke Evans 1.25 3.00
4 Derrick Rose 2.50 6.00
5 Kevin Durant 5.00 12.00
6 Stephen Curry 8.00 20.00
7 LeBron James 8.00 20.00
8 Russell Westbrook 5.00 12.00
9 Pau Gasol 2.00 5.00
10 John Wall 2.50 6.00
11 Kevin Love 2.00 5.00
12 Dirk Nowitzki 2.50 6.00
13 Carmelo Anthony 2.50 6.00
14 Chris Bosh 2.00 5.00
15 Blake Griffin 2.00 5.00
16 Vince Carter 2.50 6.00
17 Kevin Garnett 3.00 8.00
18 Scottie Pippen 4.00 10.00
19 Chris Webber 2.00 5.00
20 Shaquille O'Neal 5.00 12.00
21 Allen Iverson 2.50 6.00
22 Jason Kidd 2.00 5.00
23 Yao Ming 2.50 6.00
24 Kobe Bryant 8.00 20.00
25 Shawn Kemp 3.00 8.00

2016-17 Court Kings AKA

RANDOM INSERTS IN PACKS
1 Anfernee Hardaway 6.00 15.00
2 DeMarcus Cousins 2.50 6.00
3 LeBron James 10.00 25.00
4 Jimmy Butler 2.50 6.00
5 Rudy Gobert 2.50 6.00
6 Bob Cousy 4.00 10.00
7 Allen Iverson 3.00 8.00
8 Kobe Bryant 10.00 25.00
9 Pete Maravich 4.00 10.00

2016-17 Court Kings Arc-eologists

RANDOM INSERTS IN PACKS
1 Stephen Curry 8.00 20.00
2 James Harden 3.00 8.00
3 Damian Lillard 4.00 10.00
4 J.J. Redick 2.00 5.00
5 J.R. Smith 1.50 4.00
6 Wesley Matthews 1.25 3.00
7 C.J. McCollum 1.50 4.00
8 Evan Fournier 1.50 4.00
9 Kyle Lowry 1.50 4.00
10 Klay Thompson 2.50 6.00

2016-17 Court Kings Art Nouveau Jerseys

RANDOM INSERTS IN PACKS
*SAPPHIRE/25: 1.2X TO 3X BASIC
1 Brandon Ingram 5.00 12.00
2 Jaylen Brown 5.00 12.00
3 Dragan Bender 2.50 6.00
4 Kris Dunn 4.00 10.00
5 Buddy Hield 4.00 10.00
6 Jamal Murray 4.00 10.00
7 Marquese Chriss 5.00 12.00
8 Jakob Poeltl 2.50 6.00
9 Thon Maker 4.00 10.00
10 Georgios Papagiannis 2.00 5.00
11 T. Luwawu-Cabarrot 4.00 10.00
12 Denzel Valentine 2.50 6.00
13 Wade Baldwin IV 2.00 5.00
14 Henry Ellenson 2.50 6.00
15 Malik Beasley 2.00 5.00
16 Caris LeVert 2.50 6.00
17 Ivica Zubac 3.00 8.00
18 Malachi Richardson 2.50 6.00
19 Brice Johnson 2.00 5.00
20 Pascal Siakam 2.00 5.00
21 Skal Labissiere 3.00 8.00
22 Damian Jones 2.00 5.00
23 Deyonta Davis 2.00 5.00
24 Cheick Diallo 2.00 5.00
25 Tyler Ulis 6.00 15.00
26 Chinanu Onuaku 2.00 5.00
27 Patrick McCaw 4.00 10.00
28 Diamond Stone 2.00 5.00
29 Isaiah Whitehead 2.00 5.00
30 Demetrius Jackson 2.00 5.00
31 A.J. Hammons 2.00 5.00
32 Juan Hernangomez 2.50 6.00
33 Stephen Zimmerman 2.00 5.00

2016-17 Court Kings Art Nouveau Jerseys Jumbo

RANDOM INSERTS IN PACKS
STATED PRINT RUN 99 SER.#'d SETS
*SAPPHIRE/25: 1.2X TO 3X BASIC
1 Brandon Ingram 6.00 15.00
2 Jaylen Brown 6.00 15.00
3 Dragan Bender 3.00 8.00
4 Kris Dunn 5.00 12.00
5 Buddy Hield 5.00 12.00
6 Jamal Murray 5.00 12.00
7 Marquese Chriss 6.00 15.00
8 Jakob Poeltl 3.00 8.00
9 Thon Maker 5.00 12.00
10 Georgios Papagiannis 2.50 6.00
11 Taurean Prince 4.00 10.00
12 Denzel Valentine 3.00 8.00
13 Wade Baldwin IV 2.50 6.00
14 Henry Ellenson 3.00 8.00
15 Malik Beasley 2.50 6.00
16 Caris LeVert 3.00 8.00
17 DeAndre' Bembry 2.50 6.00
18 Malachi Richardson 3.00 8.00
19 Brice Johnson 2.50 6.00
20 Pascal Siakam 2.50 6.00
21 Skal Labissiere 4.00 10.00
22 Damian Jones 2.50 6.00
23 Deyonta Davis 2.50 6.00
24 Cheick Diallo 2.50 6.00
25 Tyler Ulis 8.00 20.00
26 Chinanu Onuaku 2.50 6.00
27 Patrick McCaw 5.00 12.00
28 Diamond Stone 2.50 6.00
29 Isaiah Whitehead 2.50 6.00
30 Demetrius Jackson 2.50 6.00
31 A.J. Hammons 2.50 6.00
32 Juan Hernangomez 3.00 8.00
33 Kay Felder 2.50 6.00
34 Malcolm Brogdon 5.00 12.00
35 Stephen Zimmerman 2.50 6.00
36 T. Luwawu-Cabarrot 5.00 12.00
37 Gary Payton II 3.00 8.00
38 Ivica Zubac 4.00 10.00

2016-17 Court Kings Artistic Endeavors Jerseys

RANDOM INSERTS IN PACKS
PRINT RUNS B/WN 49-149 COPIES PER
*PRIME/25: .75X TO 2X BASIC
1 Rudy Gay/149 3.00 8.00
2 Jerian Grant/149 2.00 5.00
3 Danny Green/149 2.50 6.00
4 Karl-Anthony Towns/149 5.00 12.00
5 Kristaps Porzingis/149 4.00 10.00
6 Kemba Walker/149 3.00 8.00
7 Myles Turner/149 2.50 6.00
8 Robert Covington/85 2.00 5.00
9 Carmelo Anthony/149 4.00 10.00
10 Tiago Splitter/149 2.50 6.00
11 Andrew Wiggins/149 4.00 10.00
12 Jonas Valanciunas/149 2.50 6.00
13 Frank Kaminsky/149 2.50 6.00
14 Dwight Howard/149 2.50 6.00
15 Goran Dragic/149 2.50 6.00
16 Gordon Hayward/49 3.00 8.00
17 Klay Thompson/149 4.00 10.00
18 Stephen Curry/149 8.00 20.00
19 LaMarcus Aldridge/149 3.00 8.00
20 Damian Lillard/149 4.00 10.00
21 Tyler Zeller/149 2.50 6.00
22 Bojan Bogdanovic/149 2.00 5.00
23 James Harden/149 4.00 10.00
24 Eric Gordon/149 2.50 6.00
25 Vince Carter/149 4.00 10.00
26 Khris Middleton/149 2.50 6.00
27 Jusuf Nurkic/149 2.00 5.00
28 Kenneth Faried/149 2.50 6.00
29 Dirk Nowitzki/149 4.00 10.00
30 LeBron James/149 12.00 30.00

2016-17 Court Kings Expressionists Memorabilia

RANDOM INSERTS IN PACKS
STATED PRINT RUN 149 COPIES PER
*SAPPHIRE/25: .75X TO 2X BASIC
1 Karl-Anthony Towns 5.00 12.00
2 Carmelo Anthony 4.00 10.00
3 LeBron James 8.00 20.00
4 Zach LaVine 3.00 8.00
5 Damian Lillard 4.00 10.00
6 DeMar DeRozan 3.00 8.00
7 Jimmy Butler 3.00 8.00
8 Russell Westbrook 5.00 12.00
9 J.R. Smith 2.50 6.00
10 D'Angelo Russell 4.00 10.00
11 Kristaps Porzingis 4.00 10.00
12 Anthony Davis 4.00 10.00
13 Paul George 4.00 10.00
14 Dirk Nowitzki 4.00 10.00

2016-17 Court Kings Fresh Paint Autographs

RANDOM INSERTS IN PACKS
EXCHANGE DEADLINE 5/30/2018
*VARIATION/200: .5X TO 1.2X BASIC
FPDS Dario Saric EXCH 12.00 30.00
FPMB Malcolm Brogdon 10.00 25.00
FPPM Patrick McCaw 10.00 25.00
FPTC T. Luwawu-Cabarrot 6.00 15.00
FPAJH A.J. Hammons 2.50 6.00
FPBRI Brandon Ingram 30.00 80.00
FPBRJ Brice Johnson 2.50 6.00
FPBUH Buddy Hield 10.00 25.00
FPCHD Cheick Diallo 2.50 6.00
FPCLE Caris LeVert 3.00 8.00
FPCON Chinanu Onuaku 2.50 6.00
FPDAJ Damian Jones 2.50 6.00
FPDEB DeAndre' Bembry 2.50 6.00
FPDEY Deyonta Davis 2.50 6.00
FPDJA Demetrius Jackson 2.50 6.00
FPDRB Dragan Bender 3.00 8.00
FPDSA Domantas Sabonis 4.00 10.00
FPDST Diamond Stone 2.50 6.00
FPDVA Denzel Valentine 3.00 8.00
FPGP2 Gary Payton II 3.00 8.00
FPGPA Georgios Papagiannis 2.50 6.00
FPHEE Henry Ellenson 3.00 8.00
FPIWH Isaiah Whitehead 2.50 6.00
FPIZU Ivica Zubac 4.00 10.00
FPJAK Jakob Poeltl 3.00 8.00
FPJAM Jamal Murray 15.00 40.00
FPJBR Jaylen Brown 12.00 30.00
FPKFE Kay Felder 2.50 6.00
FPKRD Kris Dunn 8.00 20.00
FPLJC Livio Jean-Charles 2.50 6.00
FPMAC Marquese Chriss 8.00 20.00
FPMAL Malachi Richardson 4.00 10.00
FPMBE Malik Beasley 2.50 6.00
FPPSI Pascal Siakam 2.50 6.00
FPSKL Skal Labissiere 8.00 20.00
FPSZI Stephen Zimmerman 2.50 6.00
FPTMA Thon Maker 15.00 40.00
FPTPR Taurean Prince 4.00 10.00
FPTYU Tyler Ulis 10.00 25.00
FPWB4 Wade Baldwin IV 2.50 6.00

2016-17 Court Kings Fresh Paint Dual Autographs

RANDOM INSERTS IN PACKS
STATED PRINT RUN 50 SER.#'d SETS
EXCHANGE DEADLINE 5/30/2018
1 Ingram/Dunn 125.00 250.00
2 Hield/Murray 30.00 80.00
3 Brown/Ingram 125.00 250.00
4 Davis/Valentine 12.00 30.00
5 Chriss/Bender 30.00 80.00
6 Jackson/Brown 12.00 30.00
7 Baldwin/Dunn 20.00 50.00
8 Johnson/Stone 10.00 25.00
9 Murray/Ulis 30.00 80.00
10 Saric/Luwawu-Cabarrot 30.00 80.00

2016-17 Court Kings Heir Apparent Autographs

RANDOM INSERTS IN PACKS
STATED PRINT RUN 150 SER.#'d SETS
EXCHANGE DEADLINE 5/30/2018
1 Brandon Ingram 60.00 150.00
2 Jaylen Brown 25.00 60.00
3 Dragan Bender 10.00 25.00
4 Kris Dunn 20.00 50.00
5 Buddy Hield 20.00 50.00
6 Jamal Murray 15.00 40.00
7 Marquese Chriss 15.00 40.00
8 Domantas Sabonis 10.00 25.00
9 Wade Baldwin IV 6.00 15.00
10 Henry Ellenson 4.00 10.00

2016-17 Court Kings Le Cinque Piu Belle

RANDOM BOX TOPPER INSERT
PRINT RUNS B/WN 2-41 COPIES PER
NO PRICING ON QTY 10 OR LESS
2 Anthony Davis/23
5 Dirk Nowitzki/41 40.00 100.00

2016-17 Court Kings Maestros

RANDOM INSERTS IN PACKS
1 Ish Smith .60 1.50
2 Giannis Antetokounmpo 2.00 5.00
3 Jimmy Butler 1.00 2.50
4 LeBron James 4.00 10.00
5 Marcus Smart .75 2.00
6 Blake Griffin 1.00 2.50
7 Marc Gasol 1.00 2.50
8 Paul Millsap 1.00 2.50
9 Dwyane Wade 1.50 4.00
10 Jeremy Lin 1.00 2.50
11 Gordon Hayward 1.00 2.50
12 DeMarcus Cousins 1.00 2.50
13 Kristaps Porzingis 2.00 5.00
14 Jordan Clarkson .75 2.00
15 Elfrid Payton .75 2.00
16 Dirk Nowitzki 1.25 3.00
17 Brook Lopez .75 2.00
18 Emmanuel Mudiay .75 2.00
19 Paul George 1.25 3.00
20 Anthony Davis 2.00 5.00
21 Andre Drummond 1.00 2.50
22 Kyle Lowry .75 2.00
23 James Harden 1.50 4.00
24 Kawhi Leonard 1.50 4.00
25 Devin Booker 1.50 4.00
26 Russell Westbrook 2.50 6.00
27 Karl-Anthony Towns 2.50 6.00
28 Damian Lillard 2.00 5.00
29 Klay Thompson 1.25 3.00
30 John Wall 1.25 3.00
31 Jabari Parker 1.25 3.00
32 Derrick Rose 1.25 3.00
33 Kyrie Irving 2.00 5.00
34 Isaiah Thomas 1.00 2.50
35 Chris Paul 1.25 3.00
36 Justise Winslow .75 2.00
37 Kemba Walker 1.00 2.50
38 Rudy Gay 1.00 2.50
39 Carmelo Anthony 1.25 3.00
40 D'Angelo Russell 1.25 3.00
41 Aaron Gordon .75 2.00
42 Myles Turner .75 2.00
43 Kentavious Caldwell-Pope .75 2.00
44 Jonas Valanciunas .75 2.00
45 LaMarcus Aldridge 1.00 2.50
46 Eric Bledsoe .75 2.00
47 Steven Adams .75 2.00
48 Andrew Wiggins 1.50 4.00
49 C.J. McCollum .75 2.00
50 Stephen Curry 4.00 10.00

2016-17 Court Kings Performance Art Jerseys

RANDOM INSERTS IN PACKS
STATED PRINT RUN 249 SER.#'d SETS
*SAPPHIRE/25: .75X TO 2X BASIC
1 Jimmy Butler 3.00 8.00
2 Marcus Smart 2.50 6.00
3 Andre Drummond 3.00 8.00
4 Eric Bledsoe 2.50 6.00
5 Al Horford 2.50 6.00
6 Enes Kanter 2.00 5.00
7 Nicolas Batum 2.50 6.00
8 Tristan Thompson 2.50 6.00
9 Marcin Gortat 2.50 6.00
10 Markieff Morris 2.00 5.00
11 Bobby Portis 2.00 5.00
12 Myles Turner 2.50 6.00
13 Langston Galloway 2.00 5.00
14 Kyle Korver 2.50 6.00
15 Reggie Jackson 2.50 6.00

2016-17 Court Kings Portraits

RANDOM INSERTS IN PACKS
STATED PRINT RUN 175 SER.#'d SETS
*RUBY/75: .75X TO 2X BASIC
*SAPPHIRE/25: 1.5X TO 4X BASIC
1 Stephen Curry 3.00 8.00
2 James Harden 1.25 3.00
3 Russell Westbrook 2.00 5.00
4 Kemba Walker .75 2.00
5 Derrick Rose 1.00 2.50
6 Thaddeus Young .50 1.25
7 Draymond Green 1.00 2.50
8 Clint Capela .50 1.25
9 Kawhi Leonard 1.25 3.00
10 Frank Kaminsky .60 1.50
11 Karl-Anthony Towns 2.00 5.00
12 T.J. McConnell .50 1.25
13 Klay Thompson 1.00 2.50
14 Aaron Gordon .60 1.50
15 Manu Ginobili .75 2.00
16 Reggie Jackson .60 1.50
17 Ricky Rubio .75 2.00
18 Robert Covington .50 1.25
19 LeBron James 3.00 8.00
20 Evan Fournier .60 1.50
21 Dirk Nowitzki 1.00 2.50
22 Kentavious Caldwell-Pope .60 1.50
23 Andrew Wiggins 1.25 3.00
24 Vince Carter 1.00 2.50
25 Kevin Love .75 2.00
26 Lou Williams .60 1.50
27 J.J. Barea .60 1.50
28 Khris Middleton .60 1.50
29 Paul Millsap .75 2.00
30 Zach Randolph .60 1.50
31 Kyrie Irving 1.50 4.00
32 D'Angelo Russell 1.00 2.50
33 J.J. Redick .75 2.00
34 Giannis Antetokounmpo 1.50 4.00
35 Dennis Schroder .60 1.50
36 DeMarcus Cousins .75 2.00
37 Rodney Hood .60 1.50
38 Julius Randle .75 2.00
39 Chris Paul 1.00 2.50
40 Greg Monroe .60 1.50
41 John Wall 1.00 2.50
42 Kosta Koufos .50 1.25
43 Rudy Gobert .75 2.00
44 Kristaps Porzingis 1.50 4.00
45 Paul Pierce .75 2.00
46 DeMar DeRozan .75 2.00
47 Markieff Morris .50 1.25
48 Al Horford .60 1.50
49 Devin Booker 1.25 3.00
50 Carmelo Anthony 1.00 2.50
51 Damian Lillard 1.50 4.00
52 Kyle Lowry .60 1.50
53 Anthony Davis 1.50 4.00
54 Tyson Chandler .60 1.50
55 Isaiah Thomas .75 2.00
56 Allen Crabbe .50 1.25
57 Cory Joseph .50 1.25
58 Eric Gordon .60 1.50
59 Justise Winslow .60 1.50
60 Hassan Whiteside .60 1.50
61 Jared Sullinger .50 1.25
62 Kenneth Faried .60 1.50
63 Jimmy Butler .75 2.00
64 Myles Turner .60 1.50
65 Dwyane Wade 1.25 3.00
66 Enes Kanter .50 1.25
67 Nikola Jokic .75 2.00
68 Doug McDermott .60 1.50
69 Paul George 1.00 2.50
70 Bojan Bogdanovic .50 1.25

2016-17 Court Kings Rookie Portraits

RANDOM INSERTS IN PACKS
STATED PRINT RUN 175 SER.#'d SETS
*RUBY/75: .6X TO 1.5X BASIC
*SAPPHIRE/25: 1.2X TO 3X BASIC
1 Ben Simmons 15.00 40.00
2 Brandon Ingram 4.00 10.00
3 Jaylen Brown 2.50 6.00
4 Dragan Bender .75 2.00
5 Kris Dunn 2.00 5.00
6 Buddy Hield 1.50 4.00
7 Jamal Murray 2.00 5.00
8 Marquese Chriss 1.50 4.00
9 Jakob Poeltl .75 2.00
10 Thon Maker 2.00 5.00
11 Domantas Sabonis 1.00 2.50
12 Taurean Prince 1.00 2.50
13 Denzel Valentine .75 2.00
14 Wade Baldwin IV .60 1.50
15 Henry Ellenson .75 2.00
16 Malik Beasley .60 1.50
17 Isaiah Whitehead .60 1.50
18 Demetrius Jackson .60 1.50
19 Brice Johnson .60 1.50
20 Damian Jones .60 1.50
21 Tyler Ulis 2.00 5.00
22 Deyonta Davis .60 1.50
23 Skal Labissiere 1.00 2.50
24 Dejounte Murray 1.25 3.00
25 Malachi Richardson .75 2.00
26 Ivica Zubac 1.00 2.50
27 A.J. Hammons .60 1.50
28 Diamond Stone .60 1.50
29 Kay Felder .60 1.50
30 Patrick McCaw 1.25 3.00

2016-17 Court Kings Sketches and Swatches

RANDOM INSERTS IN PACKS
PRINT RUNS B/WN 16-199 COPIES PER
NO PRICING ON QTY 16
EXCHANGE DEADLINE 5/30/2018
*PRIME/25: .6X TO 1.5X BASIC
3 Rod Strickland/199 3.00 8.00
4 Karl-Anthony Towns/60 EXCH 40.00 100.00
5 Kyrie Irving/60 20.00 50.00
8 Cedric Maxwell/199 3.00 8.00
9 Christian Laettner/60 4.00 10.00
10 Alvan Adams/149 3.00 8.00
11 Festus Ezeli/149 3.00 8.00
13 Bill Laimbeer/199 4.00 10.00
15 Andrew Wiggins/60 15.00 40.00
16 Glen Rice/125 4.00 10.00
17 Grant Hill/60 10.00 25.00
18 Shabazz Muhammad/75
19 Bernard King/60 4.00 10.00
20 Jusuf Nurkic/65
21 Patrick Ewing/60 50.00 120.00
22 Carmelo Anthony/60 15.00 40.00
25 Dirk Nowitzki/60
26 Draymond Green/26 12.00 30.00
27 Rodney Stuckey/35 3.00 8.00
28 Robert Covington/199 3.00 8.00
29 Zach LaVine/75 12.00 30.00
30 Larry Bird/60 30.00 80.00
31 Kevin Durant/60 EXCH 40.00 100.00
32 Tom Chambers/125 4.00 10.00
33 Kristaps Porzingis/75 20.00 50.00
34 Mark Price/199 5.00 12.00
35 Robert Parish/55 6.00 15.00
36 Paul Millsap/75 5.00 12.00
37 Jordan Adams/199 3.00 8.00
38 Dwight Powell/199 3.00 8.00
39 Matthew Dellavedova/199 4.00 10.00
40 Kobe Bryant/60 75.00 200.00

2016-17 Court Kings Vintage Materials

RANDOM INSERTS IN PACKS
PRINT RUNS B/WN 49-149 COPIES PER
*PRIME/25: .75X TO 2X BASIC
1 Grant Hill/149 4.00 10.00
2 Mark Price/149 3.00 8.00
3 Larry Nance/149 2.50 6.00
4 Danny Manning/75 2.50 6.00
5 Dan Majerle/129 2.50 6.00
6 Rafer Alston/149 2.00 5.00
7 Herb Williams/149 2.00 5.00
8 Kenny Anderson/149 2.50 6.00
9 Tom Chambers/49 2.50 6.00
10 Shane Battier/149 2.50 6.00
11 Kenny Smith/149 2.50 6.00
12 Chauncey Billups/149 2.50 6.00
13 Scottie Pippen/149 5.00 12.00
14 Hakeem Olajuwon/149 4.00 10.00
15 Clyde Drexler/149 4.00 10.00
16 Dan Issel/149 2.50 6.00
17 Chris Mullin/49 3.00 8.00
18 Arvydas Sabonis/149 2.50 6.00
19 Robert Parish/149 3.00 8.00
20 Kobe Bryant/149 8.00 20.00

1991 Cousy Collection Preview

This five-card "preview" standard-size set was issued to honor Bob Cousy, who sparked the Boston Celtics to six world championships during his thirteen year career. The front features vintage black and white photos that highlight Bob Cousy's career. The lettering is in green and white on a black background. The back presents biographical information and is printed in black lettering on gray, with black and green stripes traversing the top of the card. The cards are numbered on the back. The preview cards have a copyright date of 1991 on the card back whereas the regular issue set has a copyright date of 1992.

COMPLETE SET (5) 2.00 5.00
COMMON CARD (1-5) .60 1.50
1 Rookie Card 1.00 2.50

1992 Cousy Collection

Publicist Milton Kahn produced this 25-card set to chronicle the career of former Boston Celtic great and Basketball Hall of Famer Bob Cousy. Production quantities of the standard-size cards were limited to 100,000 sets. The cards were only available in complete set form. The fronts feature black and white photos that capture various moments in Cousy's career. The photos are bordered on the top by a green stripe and by black on the other three sides. The backs have a similar design to the fronts. On a gray background, they have captions for the photos and a card number in the upper left corner. On the back, each card of the set bears a unique serial number. The preview cards have a copyright date of 1991 on the card back whereas the regular issue set has a copyright date of 1992.

COMPLETE SET (25) 2.50 6.00
COMMON CARD (1-25) .20 .50
1 Rookie Card 1.00 2.50
7 Double Trouble .40 1.00
w/Bill Sharman
9 Stan the Man 1955 1.00 2.50
10 Timely Idea 1955 .40 1.00
14 Four Plan 1958-1959 .40 1.00
w/Bill Sharman
16 Victory Watch/1961-1962 .40 1.00
(With Red Auerbach and Tom Heinsohn)
17 Visit with J.F.K./1961-1962 .60 1.50
(With Red Auerbach)
21 Author 1965 .40 1.00
(With Howard Cosell)
22 Podnuhs 1965 .40 1.00

2009-10 Crown Royale

COMP.SET w/o SPs (100) 60.00 120.00
101-140 RC PRINT RUNS LISTED BELOW
1 Kevin Garnett 2.50 6.00
2 Paul Pierce 1.50 4.00
3 Rasheed Wallace 1.50 4.00
4 Ray Allen 1.50 4.00
5 Brook Lopez 1.25 3.00
6 Devin Harris 1.00 2.50
7 Yi Jianlian 1.25 3.00
8 Al Harrington 1.25 3.00
9 Danilo Gallinari 1.25 3.00
10 David Lee 1.00 2.50
11 Nate Robinson 1.00 2.50
12 Allen Iverson 2.00 5.00
13 Andre Iguodala 1.25 3.00
14 Elton Brand 1.50 4.00
15 Louis Williams 1.25 3.00
16 Andrea Bargnani 1.25 3.00
17 Chris Bosh 1.50 4.00
18 Hedo Turkoglu 1.25 3.00
19 Dirk Nowitzki 2.00 5.00
20 J.J. Barea 2.00 5.00
21 Jason Kidd 1.50 4.00
22 Jason Terry 1.25 3.00
23 Aaron Brooks 1.00 2.50
24 Carl Landry 1.00 2.50
25 Trevor Ariza 1.00 2.50
26 O.J. Mayo 1.00 2.50
27 Rudy Gay 1.50 4.00
28 Zach Randolph 1.25 3.00
29 Chris Paul 2.00 5.00
30 David West 1.25 3.00
31 Peja Stojakovic 1.50 4.00
32 Manu Ginobili 1.50 4.00
33 Tim Duncan 2.50 6.00
34 Tony Parker 1.50 4.00
35 Derrick Rose 2.50 6.00
36 John Salmons 1.25 3.00
37 Luol Deng 1.25 3.00
38 LeBron James 6.00 15.00
39 Mo Williams 1.25 3.00
40 Shaquille O'Neal 3.00 8.00
41 Ben Gordon 1.25 3.00
42 Charlie Villanueva 1.00 2.50
43 Richard Hamilton 1.25 3.00
44 Rodney Stuckey 1.00 2.50
45 Dahntay Jones 1.00 2.50
46 Danny Granger 1.25 3.00
47 Troy Murphy 1.00 2.50
48 Andrew Bogut 1.25 3.00
49 Hakim Warrick 1.25 3.00
50 Luke Ridnour 1.25 3.00
51 Carmelo Anthony 2.00 5.00
52 Chauncey Billups 1.50 4.00
53 J.R. Smith 1.25 3.00
54 Nene 1.25 3.00
55 Al Jefferson 1.25 3.00
56 Corey Brewer 1.00 2.50
57 Kevin Love 1.50 4.00
58 Andre Miller 1.25 3.00
59 Brandon Roy 1.50 4.00
60 LaMarcus Aldridge 1.50 4.00
61 Jeff Green 1.25 3.00
62 Kevin Durant 4.00 10.00
63 Russell Westbrook 4.00 10.00
64 Carlos Boozer 1.25 3.00
65 Deron Williams 1.25 3.00
66 Mehmet Okur 1.00 2.50
67 Al Horford 1.50 4.00
68 Jamal Crawford 1.50 4.00
69 Joe Johnson 1.25 3.00
70 Josh Smith 1.25 3.00
71 Gerald Wallace 1.25 3.00
72 Raymond Felton 1.25 3.00
73 Stephen Jackson 1.25 3.00
74 Dwyane Wade 2.50 6.00
75 Jermaine O'Neal 1.25 3.00
76 Michael Beasley 1.00 2.50
77 Dwight Howard 1.25 3.00
78 J.J. Redick 1.50 4.00
79 Rashard Lewis 1.25 3.00
80 Vince Carter 2.00 5.00
81 Antawn Jamison 1.25 3.00
82 Caron Butler 1.25 3.00
83 Randy Foye 1.00 2.50
84 Corey Maggette 1.25 3.00
85 Kelenna Azubuike 1.00 2.50
86 Monta Ellis 1.25 3.00
87 Al Thornton 1.25 3.00
88 Baron Davis 1.25 3.00
89 Chris Kaman 1.25 3.00
90 Eric Gordon 1.25 3.00
91 Andrew Bynum 1.00 2.50
92 Kobe Bryant 6.00 15.00
93 Pau Gasol 1.50 4.00
94 Ron Artest 1.50 4.00
95 Amare Stoudemire 1.25 3.00
96 Jason Richardson 1.50 4.00
97 Steve Nash 1.50 4.00
98 Beno Udrih 1.00 2.50
99 Jason Thompson 1.00 2.50
100 Kevin Martin 1.25 3.00
101 Tyreke Evans AU/399 RC 3.00 8.00
102 Brandon Jennings AU/399 RC 4.00 10.00
103 Stephen Curry AU/399 RC 600.00 900.00
104 James Harden AU/599 RC 150.00 300.00
105 Jonny Flynn AU/149 RC 2.50 6.00
106 Ty Lawson AU/599 RC 6.00 15.00
107 DeJuan Blair AU/699 RC 3.00 8.00
108 Blake Griffin AU/399 RC 40.00 100.00
109 Hasheem Thabeet AU/149 RC 2.50 6.00
110 Omri Casspi AU/650 RC 3.00 8.00
111 Gerald Henderson AU/599 RC 3.00 8.00
112 Taj Gibson AU/599 RC 4.00 10.00
113 Jrue Holiday AU/599 RC 5.00 12.00
114 Rodrigue Beaubois AU/599 RC 2.50 6.00
115 Jeff Teague AU/599 RC 4.00 10.00
116 Earl Clark AU/599 RC 3.00 8.00
117 Chase Budinger AU/699 RC 3.00 8.00
118 Jordan Hill AU/599 RC 3.00 8.00
119 Terrence Williams AU/599 RC 2.50 6.00
120 Tyler Hansbrough AU/612 RC 3.00 8.00
121 Austin Daye AU/599 RC 2.50 6.00
122 Wayne Ellington AU/658 RC 4.00 10.00
123 Darren Collison AU/599 RC 4.00 10.00
124 James Johnson AU/593 RC 3.00 8.00
125 B.J. Mullens AU/699 RC 2.50 6.00
126 Toney Douglas AU/699 RC 2.50 6.00
127 DeMarre Carroll AU/699 RC 3.00 8.00
128 DaJuan Summers AU/699 RC 2.50 6.00
129 Jodie Meeks AU/699 RC 4.00 10.00
130 DeMar DeRozan AU/599 RC 40.00 100.00
131 Jermaine Taylor AU/699 RC 2.50 6.00
132 Jon Brockman AU/699 RC 2.50 6.00
133 Marcus Thornton AU/669 RC 3.00 8.00
134 Jonas Jerebko AU/699 RC 4.00 10.00
135 Sam Young AU/149 RC 2.50 6.00
136 Wesley Matthews AU/699 RC 4.00 10.00
137 Jeff Pendergraph AU/149 RC 2.50 6.00
138 Serge Ibaka AU/699 RC 12.00 30.00
139 David Andersen AU/149 RC 2.50 6.00
140 Dante Cunningham AU/699 RC 2.50 6.00

2009-10 Crown Royale All-Stars

COMPLETE SET (25) 15.00 40.00
RANDOM INSERTS IN PACKS
1 Kobe Bryant 3.00 8.00
2 LeBron James 3.00 8.00
3 Allen Iverson 1.00 2.50
4 Kevin Garnett 1.25 3.00
5 Rajon Rondo .75 2.00
6 Al Horford .75 2.00
7 Brook Lopez .60 1.50
8 Chauncey Billups .75 2.00
9 Danny Granger .60 1.50
10 David Lee .50 1.25
11 Gerald Wallace .60 1.50
12 Pau Gasol .75 2.00
13 Tony Parker .75 2.00
14 Zach Randolph .60 1.50
15 Aaron Brooks .50 1.25
16 Al Jefferson .60 1.50
17 Antawn Jamison .60 1.50
18 Chris Kaman .60 1.50
19 Corey Maggette .60 1.50
20 David West .60 1.50
21 Kevin Martin .60 1.50
22 O.J. Mayo .50 1.25
23 Rashard Lewis .60 1.50
24 Rodney Stuckey .50 1.25
25 Stephen Jackson .60 1.50

2009-10 Crown Royale All-Stars Materials

STATED PRINT RUN 25 TO 599 SER.#'d SETS
1 Kobe Bryant/599 8.00 20.00
2 LeBron James/99 10.00 25.00
3 Allen Iverson/100 5.00 12.00
4 Kevin Garnett/599 4.00 10.00
5 Rajon Rondo/599 2.50 6.00
6 Al Horford/599 2.50 6.00
7 Brook Lopez/599 2.00 5.00
8 Chauncey Billups/100 2.50 6.00
9 Danny Granger/599 2.00 5.00
11 Gerald Wallace/599 2.00 5.00
12 Pau Gasol/299 2.50 6.00
13 Tony Parker/599 2.50 6.00
15 Aaron Brooks/25 3.00 8.00
16 Al Jefferson/599 2.00 5.00
19 Corey Maggette/599 2.00 5.00
20 David West/599 2.00 5.00
21 Kevin Martin/599 2.00 5.00
22 O.J. Mayo/599 1.50 4.00
23 Rashard Lewis/399 2.00 5.00
24 Rodney Stuckey/599 1.50 4.00
25 Stephen Jackson/599 2.00 5.00

2009-10 Crown Royale All-Stars Materials Prime

PRIME: 1.25X TO 3X BASE HI
STATED PRINT RUN ONE TO 25 SER.#'d SETS
SOME UNPRICED DUE TO SCARCITY
3 Allen Iverson/25 20.00 50.00
5 Rajon Rondo/25 12.50 30.00

2009-10 Crown Royale King on the Court

COMPLETE SET (10) 15.00 30.00
RANDOM INSERTS IN PACKS
1 LeBron James 4.00 10.00
2 Joakim Noah .75 2.00
3 Tim Duncan 1.50 4.00
4 Chris Paul 1.25 3.00
5 Kevin Durant 2.50 6.00
6 Dwyane Wade 1.50 4.00
7 Paul Pierce 1.00 2.50
8 Chris Bosh 1.00 2.50
9 Tyreke Evans .75 2.00
10 Kobe Bryant 4.00 10.00

2009-10 Crown Royale King on the Court Materials

STATED PRINT RUN 149 SER.#'d SETS
UNPRICED PRIME PRINT RUN 10 SER.#'d SETS
1 LeBron James 10.00 25.00
2 Joakim Noah 2.50 6.00
3 Tim Duncan 5.00 12.00
4 Chris Paul 4.00 10.00
5 Kevin Durant 8.00 20.00
6 Dwyane Wade 5.00 12.00
7 Paul Pierce 3.00 8.00
8 Chris Bosh 3.00 8.00
9 Tyreke Evans 2.50 6.00
10 Kobe Bryant 10.00 25.00

2009-10 Crown Royale Living Legends

COMPLETE SET (25) 25.00 50.00
RANDOM INSERTS IN PACKS
1 Bob Love 1.50 4.00
2 Brad Daugherty 1.25 3.00
3 Alex English 1.25 3.00
4 Ricky Pierce 1.00 2.50
5 Patrick Ewing 2.00 5.00
6 Chris Webber 1.50 4.00
7 Magic Johnson 4.00 10.00
8 Phil Jackson 2.00 5.00
9 Lafayette Lever 1.50 4.00
10 Larry Bird 4.00 10.00
11 Mark Aguirre 1.25 3.00
12 Mychal Thompson 1.50 4.00
13 Brad Davis 1.50 4.00
14 Oscar Robertson 1.50 4.00
15 M.L. Carr 1.50 4.00
16 Karl Malone 2.00 5.00
17 David Robinson 2.50 6.00
18 Elgin Baylor 1.50 4.00
19 Maurice Lucas 1.50 4.00
20 Scottie Pippen 3.00 8.00
21 Jerry West 2.00 5.00
22 Dan Majerle 1.25 3.00
23 Hakeem Olajuwon 2.00 5.00
24 John Stockton 2.50 6.00
25 George Gervin 1.50 4.00

2009-10 Crown Royale Living Legends Materials

STATED PRINT RUN 25 TO 499 SER.#'d SETS
3 Alex English/499 3.00 8.00
5 Patrick Ewing/299 5.00 12.00
6 Chris Webber/499 4.00 10.00
7 Magic Johnson/99 10.00 25.00
10 Larry Bird/25 10.00 25.00
16 Karl Malone/499 5.00 12.00
19 Maurice Lucas/499 4.00 10.00
20 Scottie Pippen/499 6.00 15.00
21 Jerry West/25 8.00 20.00
23 Hakeem Olajuwon/499 5.00 12.00
24 John Stockton/199 5.00 12.00

2009-10 Crown Royale Living Legends Materials Prime

*PRIME: .75X TO 2X BASE HI
STATED PRINT RUN 5 TO 25 SER.#'d SETS
SOME UNPRICED DUE TO SCARCITY
3 Alex English/25 12.00 30.00
5 Patrick Ewing/25 15.00 30.00
7 Magic Johnson/25 15.00 40.00
20 Scottie Pippen/25 20.00 50.00
24 John Stockton/25 15.00 40.00
25 George Gervin/25 8.00 20.00

2009-10 Crown Royale Majestic Signatures

STATED PRINT RUN 10 TO 99 SER.#'d SETS
AA Alvan Adams/199 6.00 15.00
AB Andrew Bogut/199 10.00 25.00
AI Allen Iverson/25 175.00 350.00
AM Alonzo Mourning/99 20.00 50.00
BD Bob Dandridge/199 6.00 15.00
BJ Bobby Jackson/199 6.00 15.00
BR Bill Russell/49 75.00 150.00
CA Chris Andersen/99 12.00 30.00
CR Cazzie Russell/196 6.00 15.00
CV Charlie Villanueva/196 6.00 15.00
DA D.J. Augustin/199 6.00 15.00
DF Derek Fisher/199 12.00 30.00
DG Danny Granger/99 8.00 20.00
DH Devin Harris/199 6.00 15.00
DL David Lee/199 6.00 15.00
DLM Dan Majerle/199 10.00 25.00
DMW Deron Williams/99 12.00 30.00
DR Doc Rivers/199 10.00 25.00
DS Detlef Schrempf/199 8.00 20.00
DT David Thompson/199 6.00 15.00
EG Eric Gordon/198 8.00 20.00
EO Emeka Okafor/99 8.00 20.00

GM George McGinnis/199 6.00 15.00
GP Gary Payton/99 20.00 50.00
HH Hersey Hawkins/199 8.00 20.00
JB J.J. Barea/199 12.50 30.00
JH John Havlicek/25 25.00 50.00
JK Jason Kidd/49 25.00 60.00
JO Jermaine O'Neal/99 12.00 30.00
JR Jalen Rose/199 6.00 15.00
KB Kobe Bryant/199 100.00 200.00
KL Kevin Love/99 15.00 40.00
LB Larry Bird/25 50.00 120.00
LO Lamar Odom/99 12.00 30.00
MB Michael Beasley/99 8.00 20.00
MJ Magic Johnson/23 60.00 120.00
MW Mo Williams/99 6.00 15.00
OR Oscar Robertson/25 75.00 150.00
PG Pau Gasol/30 30.00 80.00
RA Ray Allen/49 30.00 80.00
RH Robert Horry/99 40.00 80.00
RR Rajon Rondo/199 15.00 40.00
RW Russell Westbrook/99 30.00 80.00
SB Shawn Bradley/199 6.00 15.00
SE Sean Elliott/199 8.00 20.00
SH Spencer Haywood/199 6.00 15.00
SN Steve Nash/96 40.00 80.00
SO Shaquille O'Neal/25 150.00 300.00
SP Scottie Pippen/99 75.00 150.00
TM Tracy McGrady/25 30.00 60.00
TP Tony Parker/99 15.00 40.00
VC Vince Carter/99 20.00 50.00
AI2 Andre Iguodala/199 6.00 15.00

2009-10 Crown Royale Nothing But Net

COMPLETE SET (10) 6.00 15.00
RANDOM INSERTS IN PACKS
1 Danilo Gallinari .75 2.00
2 Channing Frye .75 2.00
3 Aaron Brooks .60 1.50
4 Peja Stojakovic 1.00 2.50
5 Martell Webster .60 1.50
6 Rashard Lewis .75 2.00
7 Mo Williams .75 2.00
8 Jason Kidd 1.00 2.50
9 LeBron James 4.00 10.00
10 Chauncey Billups 1.00 2.50

2009-10 Crown Royale Nothing But Net Materials

STATED PRINT RUN 25 TO 499 SER.#'d SETS
*PRIME: .75X TO 2X HI COLUMN
PRIME PRINT RUN ONE TO 25 SETS
3 Aaron Brooks/25 3.00 8.00
4 Peja Stojakovic/499 3.00 8.00
6 Rashard Lewis/299 2.50 6.00
8 Jason Kidd/399 3.00 8.00
9 LeBron James/99 10.00 25.00
10 Chauncey Billups/100 3.00 8.00

2009-10 Crown Royale Rookie Royalty

COMPLETE SET (10) 8.00 20.00
RANDOM INSERTS IN PACKS
1 Jennings/Curry/Evans 40.00 100.00
2 Collison/Flynn/Lawson 1.00 2.50
3 Griffin/Blair/Gibson 4.00 10.00
4 Budinger/DeRozan/Harden 5.00 12.00
5 Daye/Clark/Casspi .75 2.00
6 Maynor/Teague/Holiday 1.25 3.00
7 Griffin/Thabeet/Harden 5.00 12.00
8 Lawson/Hansbrough/Ellington 1.00 2.50
9 Carroll/Thabeet/Young .75 2.00
10 Johnson/Pendergraph/Hill .75 2.00

2009-10 Crown Royale Rookie Royalty Materials

STATED PRINT RUN 499 SER.#'d SETS
1 Jennings/Curry/Evans 25.00 60.00
2 Collison/Flynn/Lawson 4.00 10.00
3 Griffin/Blair/Gibson 10.00 25.00
4 Budinger/DeRozan/Harden 5.00 12.00
5 Daye/Clark/Casspi 4.00 10.00
6 Maynor/Teague/Holiday 5.00 12.00
7 Griffin/Thabeet/Harden 8.00 20.00
8 Lawson/Hansbrough/Ellington 5.00 12.00
9 Carroll/Thabeet/Young 4.00 10.00
10 Johnson/Pendergraph/Hill 4.00 10.00

2009-10 Crown Royale Rookie Royalty Materials Prime

*PRIME: .75X TO 2X BASE HI
STATED PRINT RUN 25 SER.#'d SETS
1 Jennings/Curry/Evans 40.00 100.00
2 Collison/Flynn/Lawson 20.00 50.00
3 Griffin/Blair/Gibson 25.00 60.00
4 Budinger/DeRozan/Harden 12.50 30.00
6 Maynor/Teague/Holiday 12.50 30.00
7 Griffin/Thabeet/Harden 15.00 40.00
8 Lawson/Hansbrough/Ellington 20.00 50.00

2009-10 Crown Royale Royalty

COMPLETE SET (20) 15.00 30.00
RANDOM INSERTS IN PACKS
1 Kobe Bryant 3.00 8.00
2 LeBron James 3.00 8.00
3 Dwyane Wade 1.25 3.00
4 Carmelo Anthony 1.00 2.50
5 Kevin Durant 2.00 5.00
6 Monta Ellis .60 1.50
7 Dirk Nowitzki 1.00 2.50
8 Chris Bosh .75 2.00
9 Brandon Roy .75 2.00
10 Joe Johnson .60 1.50
11 Dwight Howard .60 1.50
12 Steve Nash .75 2.00
13 Chris Paul 1.00 2.50
14 Tim Duncan 1.25 3.00
15 Paul Pierce .75 2.00
16 Shaquille O'Neal 1.50 4.00
17 Amare Stoudemire .60 1.50
18 Derrick Rose 1.25 3.00
19 Deron Williams .60 1.50
20 Vince Carter 1.00 2.50

2009-10 Crown Royale Royalty Materials

STATED PRINT RUN 99 TO 499 SER.#'d SETS
1 Kobe Bryant/499 8.00 20.00
2 LeBron James/99 10.00 25.00
4 Carmelo Anthony/499 4.00 10.00
5 Kevin Durant/499 6.00 15.00
7 Dirk Nowitzki/499 4.00 10.00
8 Chris Bosh/499 3.00 8.00
9 Brandon Roy/499 3.00 8.00
10 Joe Johnson/499 2.50 6.00
11 Dwight Howard/499 2.50 6.00
13 Chris Paul/499 4.00 10.00
14 Tim Duncan/499 5.00 12.00
15 Paul Pierce/499 3.00 8.00
16 Shaquille O'Neal/499 6.00 15.00
18 Derrick Rose/499 4.00 10.00
19 Deron Williams/499 2.50 6.00
20 Vince Carter/499 4.00 10.00

2009-10 Crown Royale Royalty Materials Prime

PRIME: 1X TO 2.5X BASE HI
STATED PRINT RUN 5 TO 25 SER.#'d SETS
SOME UNPRICED DUE TO SCARCITY
3 Dwyane Wade/25 12.00 30.00

2010 Crown Royale National Convention VIP

MPLETE SET (6) 5.00 12.00
VIP1 Kobe Bryant 2.50 6.00
VIP2 Carmelo Anthony .75 2.00
VIP3 Derrick Rose 2.00 5.00
VIP4 Brandon Jennings .60 1.50
VIP5 Wesley Johnson .60 1.50
VIP6 Evan Turner .60 1.50

2010 Crown Royale National Convention VIP Blue

COMPLETE SET (6) 40.00 80.00
*BLUE: 2X TO 5X BASE HI
ANNOUNCED PRINT RUN 25 SETS

2010 Crown Royale National Convention VIP Green

COMPLETE SET (6) 10.00 25.00
*GREEN: .75X TO 2X BASE HI
ANNOUNCED PRINT RUN 50 SETS

2002-03 Dakota Wizards CBA

Produced by United Digital Printing and Mailing, this 15-card set features color photos and blue borders and was given away at home games as a promotion and also sold by the team.

COMPLETE SET (15) 1.50 4.00
1 Shawn Daniels .15 .40
2 Khalid El-Amin .30 .75
3 Rico Hill .15 .40
4 Courtney James .15 .40
5 Dave Joerger CO .30 .75
6 Ken Johnson .15 .40
7 Mike Johnson .15 .40
8 Casey Owens ACO .15 .40
9 Chris Porter .30 .75
10 Kevin Rice .15 .40
11 Miles Simon .15 .40
12 Marketing Team .15 .40
13 President/Vice President .15 .40
14 Dance Team .15 .40
15 Mascot .15 .40

1991-92 David Robinson Fan Club

Produced by TRG Inc., these two standard-size cards were issued in consecutive years. Card number 1, released in 1991, was designed by David Robinson and features a posed color photo of Robinson with his saxophone. A signed basketball is in the upper left corner and five stars in a circle pattern are in the upper right. Navy blue border stripes at the bottom contain Robinson's nickname "The Admiral," and the words "Inaugural" and "Leisure Series No. 1 '91" in white lettering. The back is beige and displays a close-up photo and player information. Card number 2, released in 1992, features a full-bleed photo of Robinson balancing a basketball on one finger. The words "The Admiral Leisure Series No. 2 '92" are printed in an arch at the top. The back shows a blue tinted photo of Robinson playing golf and includes biography and player information with a facsimile autograph at the bottom. The cards are numbered on the front. These cards were offered directly by The Robinson Group to members of the David Robinson Fan Club, as well as via a mail-in order form included in Strand's "The Story of a Game" video. Reportedly 50,000 complete Leisure Series sets were produced.

COMPLETE SET (2) 4.00 10.00
COMMON CARD (1-2) 2.00 5.00

1977-78 Dell Flipbooks

This set of flipbooks was produced by Pocket Money Basketball Co. and were sold in most retail outlets and toy stores. The retail display featured eight complete sets of six booklets or 48 books individually for sale at a suggested retail price of 50 cents. These flipbooks measure approximately 4" by 3 1/8" and are 24 pages in length. They have color action player photos and career statistics. The booklets are unnumbered and are checklisted below in alphabetical order by subject. The front has a white stripe at the top, and a color head and shoulders shot of the player on a color background. The inside front cover has a table of contents, while the inside back cover has the logos of all 22 NBA teams. Each flipbook features a different play or move by the player; e.g., the Maravich flipbook is titled, "Pete The Pistol Maravich and his Fancy Dribble." When the odd-numbered pages are flipped in a smooth movement from front to back, they form a color "motion picture~ of Maravich crossing over his dribble through his legs. The even-numbered pages present a variety of information on Maravich, his team (New Orleans Jazz), and the 1976-77 NBA season.

COMPLETE SET (6) 40.00 80.00
1 Kareem Abdul-Jabbar 7.50 15.00
2 Dave Cowens 6.00 12.00
3 Julius Erving 7.50 15.00
4 Pete Maravich 20.00 40.00
5 David Thompson 6.00 12.00
6 Bill Walton 6.00 12.00

1970 Detroit Free Press

These color clippings came from the Detroit Free Press News in 1970. The set features six known players (as listed below), but it is assumed that there are more players in the set. We are still looking for additional players to add to the checklist, thus if you know of any, please contact us. The clippings are not numbered and checklisted below in alphabetical order.

COMPLETE SET (6) 30.00 60.00
1 Dave Bing 12.50 25.00
2 Howard Komives 3.00 8.00
3 Eddie Miles 3.00 8.00
4 Ralph Simpson 6.00 12.00
5 Rudy Tomjanovich 10.00 20.00
6 Jimmy Walker 5.00 10.00

2010-11 Donruss

COMPLETE SET (295) 20.00 50.00
EXCHANGE EXP: 6/20/2012
1 Rajon Rondo .30 .75
2 Kevin Garnett .50 1.25
3 Shaquille O'Neal .60 1.50
4 Ray Allen .30 .75
5 Paul Pierce .30 .75
6 Kendrick Perkins .20 .50
7 Nate Robinson .20 .50
8 Jermaine O'Neal .25 .60
9 Jordan Farmar .20 .50
10 Brook Lopez .25 .60
11 Terrence Williams .20 .50
12 Devin Harris .20 .50
13 Troy Murphy .20 .50
14 Anthony Morrow .20 .50
15 Danilo Gallinari .25 .60
16 Amare Stoudemire .25 .60
17 Raymond Felton .25 .60
18 Toney Douglas .20 .50
19 Wilson Chandler .25 .60
20 Anthony Randolph .20 .50
21 Kelenna Azubuike .20 .50
22 Jrue Holiday .30 .75
23 Andres Nocioni .20 .50
24 Elton Brand .30 .75
25 Andre Iguodala .25 .60
26 Spencer Hawes .20 .50
27 Thaddeus Young .20 .50
28 Louis Williams .25 .60
29 Jason Kapono .20 .50
30 Leandro Barbosa .25 .60
31 Andrea Bargnani .25 .60
32 Jose Calderon .20 .50
33 Jarrett Jack .25 .60
34 DeMar DeRozan .30 .75
35 Amir Johnson .20 .50
36 Sonny Weems .20 .50
37 Derrick Rose .40 1.00
38 Taj Gibson .25 .60
39 Joakim Noah .25 .60
40 Luol Deng .25 .60
41 C.J. Watson .20 .50
42 Kyle Korver .25 .60
43 James Johnson .20 .50
44 Carlos Boozer .25 .60
45 Mo Williams .25 .60
46 Antawn Jamison .25 .60
47 Daniel Gibson .25 .60
48 Anderson Varejao .20 .50
49 Ramon Sessions .25 .60
50 Anthony Parker .20 .50
51 Ryan Hollins .20 .50
52 Ben Gordon .25 .60
53 Tracy McGrady .30 .75
54 Jonas Jerebko .20 .50
55 Richard Hamilton .25 .60
56 Ben Wallace .25 .60
57 Charlie Villanueva .20 .50
58 Tayshaun Prince .25 .60
59 Mike Dunleavy .20 .50
60 Dahntay Jones .20 .50
61 T.J. Ford .20 .50
62 Roy Hibbert .25 .60
63 Darren Collison .25 .60
64 Danny Granger .25 .60
65 Tyler Hansbrough .25 .60
66 Brandon Rush .20 .50
67 Andrew Bogut .25 .60
68 Brandon Jennings .20 .50
69 John Salmons .25 .60
70 Corey Maggette .25 .60
71 Carlos Delfino .20 .50
72 Michael Redd .25 .60
73 Drew Gooden .25 .60
74 Rodrigue Beaubois .20 .50
75 Dirk Nowitzki .40 1.00
76 Caron Butler .25 .60
77 Tyson Chandler .25 .60
78 Jason Kidd .30 .75
79 Shawn Marion .25 .60
80 Brendan Haywood .20 .50
81 Jason Terry .25 .60
82 Aaron Brooks .20 .50
83 Yao Ming .40 1.00
84 Jordan Hill .20 .50
85 Courtney Lee .25 .60
86 Kevin Martin .25 .60
87 Shane Battier .25 .60
88 Luis Scola .25 .60
89 Brad Miller .25 .60
90 O.J. Mayo .20 .50
91 Marc Gasol .30 .75
92 Rudy Gay .30 .75
93 Zach Randolph .25 .60
94 Sam Young .20 .50
95 Mike Conley Jr. .30 .75
96 Hasheem Thabeet .20 .50
97 Darrell Arthur .20 .50
98 Chris Paul .40 1.00
99 David West .25 .60
100 Trevor Ariza .20 .50
101 Emeka Okafor .25 .60
102 Marcus Thornton .20 .50
103 Peja Stojakovic .30 .75
104 Marco Belinelli .20 .50
105 DeJuan Blair .20 .50
106 Tim Duncan .50 1.25
107 George Hill .25 .60
108 Antonio McDyess .25 .60
109 Richard Jefferson .25 .60
110 Tony Parker .30 .75
111 Manu Ginobili .30 .75
112 Carmelo Anthony .40 1.00
113 Chris Andersen .25 .60
114 Ty Lawson .20 .50
115 Chauncey Billups .30 .75
116 Al Harrington .25 .60
117 Nene' .25 .60
118 Kenyon Martin .25 .60
119 J.R. Smith .25 .60
120 Michael Beasley .20 .50
121 Jonny Flynn .20 .50
122 Kevin Love .30 .75
123 Luke Ridnour .25 .60
124 Darko Milicic .20 .50
125 Anthony Tolliver .20 .50
126 Corey Brewer .20 .50
127 Marcus Camby .20 .50
128 LaMarcus Aldridge .30 .75
129 Rudy Fernandez .20 .50
130 Brandon Roy .30 .75
131 Andre Miller .25 .60
132 Greg Oden .25 .60
133 Nicolas Batum .25 .60
134 Kevin Durant .75 2.00
135 Jeff Green .25 .60
136 Russell Westbrook .75 2.00
137 Serge Ibaka .25 .60
138 James Harden .50 1.25
139 Nenad Krstic .20 .50
140 Daequan Cook .20 .50
141 Eric Maynor .20 .50
142 Deron Williams .25 .60
143 Al Jefferson .25 .60
144 C.J. Miles .25 .60
145 Raja Bell .25 .60
146 Paul Millsap .25 .60
147 Mehmet Okur .20 .50
148 Andrei Kirilenko .25 .60
149 Joe Johnson .25 .60
150 Jeff Teague .25 .60
151 Mike Bibby .25 .60
152 Josh Smith .25 .60
153 Al Horford .25 .60
154 Marvin Williams .25 .60
155 Jamal Crawford .30 .75
156 Maurice Evans .20 .50
157 Gerald Wallace .25 .60
158 Gerald Henderson .20 .50
159 D.J. Augustin .20 .50
160 Eduardo Najera .20 .50
161 Stephen Jackson .25 .60
162 Tyrus Thomas .20 .50
163 Boris Diaw .25 .60
164 Derrick Brown .20 .50
165 LeBron James 1.50 4.00
166 Dwyane Wade .50 1.25
167 Chris Bosh .30 .75
168 Mike Miller .25 .60
169 Mario Chalmers .25 .60
170 Udonis Haslem .20 .50
171 Juwan Howard .25 .60
172 Carlos Arroyo .20 .50
173 Dwight Howard .25 .60
174 Vince Carter .40 1.00
175 Chris Duhon .20 .50
176 Jason Williams .25 .60
177 J.J. Redick .30 .75
178 Quentin Richardson .25 .60
179 Jameer Nelson .20 .50
180 Rashard Lewis .25 .60
181 Al Thornton .20 .50
182 Kirk Hinrich .25 .60
183 Josh Howard .25 .60
184 Yi Jianlian .25 .60
185 Nick Young .25 .60
186 Gilbert Arenas .25 .60
187 Andray Blatche .20 .50
188 JaVale McGee .25 .60
189 Stephen Curry 1.25 3.00
190 Monta Ellis .25 .60
191 David Lee .20 .50
192 Andris Biedrins .20 .50
193 Reggie Williams RC .60 1.50
194 Charlie Bell .20 .50
195 Vladimir Radmanovic .20 .50
196 Eric Gordon .25 .60
197 Blake Griffin .30 .75
198 Chris Kaman .25 .60
199 Baron Davis .25 .60
200 Craig Smith .20 .50
201 Ryan Gomes .20 .50
202 Rasual Butler .20 .50
203 Kobe Bryant 1.25 3.00
204 Derek Fisher .25 .60
205 Lamar Odom .25 .60
206 Pau Gasol .30 .75
207 Andrew Bynum .20 .50
208 Shannon Brown .20 .50
209 Ron Artest .30 .75
210 Luke Walton .20 .50
211 Sasha Vujacic .20 .50
212 Steve Nash .30 .75
213 Hedo Turkoglu .25 .60
214 Channing Frye .25 .60
215 Robin Lopez .20 .50
216 Earl Clark .20 .50
217 Grant Hill .40 1.00
218 Jared Dudley .20 .50
219 Jason Richardson .30 .75
220 Tyreke Evans .20 .50
221 Carl Landry .20 .50
222 Francisco Garcia .20 .50
223 Omri Casspi .20 .50
224 Jason Thompson .20 .50
225 Samuel Dalembert .20 .50
226 Beno Udrih .20 .50
227 Antoine Wright .20 .50
228 John Wall RC 3.00 8.00
229 Evan Turner RC .50 1.25
230 Derrick Favors RC .75 2.00
231 Wesley Johnson RC .40 1.00
232 DeMarcus Cousins RC 2.00 5.00
233 Ekpe Udoh RC .40 1.00
234 Greg Monroe RC .75 2.00
235 Al-Farouq Aminu RC .60 1.50
236 Gordon Hayward RC 1.00 2.50
237 Paul George RC 2.00 5.00
238 Cole Aldrich RC .50 1.25
239 Xavier Henry RC .40 1.00
240 Ed Davis RC .40 1.00
241 Patrick Patterson RC .50 1.25
242 Larry Sanders RC .40 1.00
243 Luke Babbitt RC .50 1.25
244 Kevin Seraphin RC .40 1.00
245 Eric Bledsoe RC .75 2.00
246 Avery Bradley RC .75 2.00
247 James Anderson RC .40 1.00
248 Craig Brackins RC .40 1.00
249 Elliot Williams RC .40 1.00
250 Trevor Booker RC .50 1.25
251 Damion James RC .40 1.00
252 Dominique Jones RC .40 1.00
253 Quincy Pondexter RC .40 1.00
254 Jordan Crawford RC .50 1.25
255 Greivis Vasquez RC .50 1.25
256 Daniel Orton RC .40 1.00
257 Lazar Hayward RC .40 1.00
258 Dexter Pittman RC .40 1.00
259 Hassan Whiteside RC 1.25 3.00
260 Andy Rautins RC .40 1.00
261 Luke Harangody RC .40 1.00
262 Timofey Mozgov RC .60 1.50
263 Boston Celtics CL .60 1.50
264 New Jersey Nets CL .40 1.00
265 New York Knicks CL .40 1.00
266 Philadelphia 76ers CL .40 1.00
267 Toronto Raptors CL .40 1.00
268 Chicago Bulls CL .40 1.00
269 Cleveland Cavaliers CL .40 1.00
270 Detroit Pistons CL .40 1.00
271 Indiana Pacers CL .40 1.00
272 Milwaukee Bucks CL .40 1.00
273 Atlanta Hawks CL .40 1.00
274 Charlotte Bobcats CL .40 1.00
275 Miami Heat CL .60 1.50
276 Orlando Magic CL .40 1.00
277 Washington Wizards CL .75 2.00
278 Dallas Mavericks CL .40 1.00
279 Houston Rockets CL .40 1.00
280 Memphis Grizzlies CL .40 1.00
281 New Orleans Hornets CL .40 1.00
282 San Antonio Spurs CL .40 1.00
283 Denver Nuggets CL .40 1.00
284 Minnesota Timberwolves CL .40 1.00
285 Portland Trail Blazers CL .40 1.00
286 Oklahoma City Thunder CL .40 1.00
287 Utah Jazz CL .40 1.00
288 Golden State Warriors CL .40 1.00
289 Los Angeles Clippers CL .40 1.00
290 Los Angeles Lakers CL .60 1.50
291 Phoenix Suns CL .40 1.00
292 Sacramento Kings CL .40 1.00
293 Kobe Bryant CL .60 1.50
294 Chris Bosh CL .15 .40
295 Kevin Durant CL .40 1.00

2010-11 Donruss Die Cuts Emerald

*VETS/CL: .75X TO 2X BASE HI
*ROOKIES: .6X TO 1.5X BASE HI
RANDOM INSERTS IN PACKS

2010-11 Donruss Die Cuts Ruby

*VETS/CL: 5X TO 12X BASE HI
*ROOKIES: 2.5X TO 6X BASE HI
*PL CL 293-295: 10X TO 25X BASE HI
STATED PRINT RUN 25 SER.#'d SETS
RANDOMLY INSERTED IN RETAIL PACKS

2010-11 Donruss Die Cuts Sapphire

*VETS/CL: 3X TO 8X BASE HI
*ROOKIES: 2X TO 5X BASE HI
*PL CL 293-295: 6X TO 15X BASE HI
STATED PRINT RUN 49 SER.#'d SETS

2010-11 Donruss Press Proofs

*VETS/CL: 2.5X TO 6X BASE HI
*ROOKIES: 1.5X TO 4X BASE HI
*PL CL 293-295: 5X TO 12X BASE HI
STATED PRINT RUN 100 SER.#'d SETS
237 Paul George 15.00 40.00

2010-11 Donruss Craftsmen

COMPLETE SET (15) 12.50 25.00
STATED PRINT RUN 999 SER.#'d SETS
*DC EMERALD: .5X TO 1.25X HI
DC EMERALD RANDOM INSERTS IN PACKS
*DC RUBY: 1.5X TO 4X HI
DC RUBY PRINT RUN 25 SETS
*DC SAPPHIRE: 1X TO 2.5X HI
DC SAPPHIRE PRINT RUN 49 SETS
*PRESS PROOFS: .75X TO 2X HI
PRESS PROOFS PRINT RUN 100 SETS
1 Kobe Bryant 3.00 8.00
2 Kevin Durant 2.00 5.00
3 LeBron James 4.00 10.00
4 Dwight Howard .60 1.50
5 Carmelo Anthony 1.00 2.50
6 Dwyane Wade 1.25 3.00
7 Dirk Nowitzki 1.00 2.50
8 Amare Stoudemire .60 1.50
9 Steve Nash .75 2.00
10 Deron Williams .60 1.50
11 Andrew Bogut .60 1.50
12 Joe Johnson .60 1.50
13 Brandon Roy .75 2.00
14 Pau Gasol .75 2.00
15 Tim Duncan 1.25 3.00

2010-11 Donruss Craftsmen Materials

STATED PRINT RUN 99 TO 299 SER.#'d SETS
*PRIME: .75X TO 2X HI
PRIME PRINT RUN 5 TO 25 SER.#'d SETS
SOME PRIME UNPRICED DUE TO SCARCITY
1 Kobe Bryant/299 8.00 20.00
2 Kevin Durant/299 6.00 15.00
3 LeBron James/299 10.00 25.00
4 Dwight Howard/299 2.50 6.00
5 Carmelo Anthony/99 4.00 10.00
6 Dwyane Wade/299 5.00 12.00
7 Dirk Nowitzki/299 4.00 10.00
8 Amare Stoudemire/299 2.50 6.00
9 Steve Nash/299 3.00 8.00
10 Deron Williams/299 2.50 6.00
11 Andrew Bogut/99 2.50 6.00
12 Joe Johnson/299 2.50 6.00
13 Brandon Roy/99 3.00 8.00
14 Pau Gasol/299 3.00 8.00
15 Tim Duncan/299 5.00 12.00

2010-11 Donruss Craftsmen Materials Signatures

STATED PRINT RUN ONE TO 25 SER.#'d SETS
SOME UNPRICED DUE TO SCARCITY
UNPRICED SIG.PRIME PRINT RUN 1 TO 5 SETS
1 Kobe Bryant/25 100.00 200.00
8 Amare Stoudemire/25 25.00 60.00
11 Andrew Bogut/25 8.00 20.00
12 Joe Johnson/25 10.00 25.00

2010-11 Donruss Craftsmen Signatures

STATED PRINT RUN ONE TO 49 SER.#'d SETS
SOME UNPRICED DUE TO SCARCITY
1 Kobe Bryant/49 100.00 200.00
8 Amare Stoudemire/25 20.00 50.00
11 Andrew Bogut/25 6.00 15.00
12 Joe Johnson/25 8.00 20.00

2010-11 Donruss Duos

COMPLETE SET (5) 7.50 15.00
RANDOM INSERTS IN PACKS
1 K.Bryant/L.James 3.00 8.00
2 L.Bird/M.Johnson 3.00 8.00
3 A.Stoudemire/D.Howard 1.25 3.00
4 B.Griffin/J.Wall 4.00 10.00
5 D.Wade/K.Durant 2.50 6.00

2010-11 Donruss Gamers

COMPLETE SET (25) 15.00 30.00
STATED PRINT RUN 999 SER.#'d SETS
*DC EMERALD: .5X TO 1.25X HI
DC EMERALD RANDOM INSERTS IN PACKS
*DC RUBY: 1.5X TO 4X HI
DC RUBY PRINT RUN 25 SETS
*DC SAPPHIRE: 1X TO 2.5X HI
DC SAPPHIRE PRINT RUN 49 SETS
*PRESS PROOFS: .75X TO 2X HI
PRESS PROOFS PRINT RUN 100 SETS
1 Derrick Rose 1.00 2.50
2 Kobe Bryant 3.00 8.00
3 LeBron James 4.00 10.00
4 Kevin Garnett 1.25 3.00
5 Dwight Howard .60 1.50
6 Brook Lopez .60 1.50
7 Robin Lopez .50 1.25
8 Eric Gordon .60 1.50
9 David Lee .50 1.25
10 Al Jefferson .60 1.50
11 Russell Westbrook 2.00 5.00
12 Marcus Camby .50 1.25
13 Jonny Flynn .50 1.25
14 Carmelo Anthony 1.00 2.50
15 Manu Ginobili .75 2.00
16 David West .60 1.50
17 Zach Randolph .60 1.50
18 Luis Scola .60 1.50
19 Jason Terry .60 1.50
20 Stephen Jackson .60 1.50
21 Josh Smith .60 1.50
22 Ben Wallace .60 1.50
23 Anderson Varejao .50 1.25
24 Andre Iguodala .60 1.50
25 Amare Stoudemire .60 1.50

2010-11 Donruss Gamers Materials

STATED PRINT RUN 99 TO 299 SER.#'d SETS
*PRIME: .75X TO 2X HI
PRIME PRINT RUN 5 TO 49 SER.#'d SETS
SOME PRIME UNPRICED DUE TO SCARCITY
1 Derrick Rose/299 6.00 15.00
2 Kobe Bryant/299 8.00 20.00
3 LeBron James/299 8.00 20.00
4 Kevin Garnett/299 5.00 12.00
5 Dwight Howard/299 2.50 6.00
6 Brook Lopez/299 2.50 6.00
7 Robin Lopez/299 2.00 5.00
8 Eric Gordon/299 2.50 6.00
9 David Lee/299 2.00 5.00
10 Al Jefferson/299 2.50 6.00
11 Russell Westbrook/299 8.00 20.00
12 Marcus Camby/99 2.00 5.00
13 Jonny Flynn/299 2.00 5.00
14 Carmelo Anthony/99 4.00 10.00
15 Manu Ginobili/299 3.00 8.00
16 David West/299 2.50 6.00
17 Zach Randolph/299 2.50 6.00
18 Luis Scola/199 2.50 6.00
19 Jason Terry/299 2.50 6.00
20 Stephen Jackson/299 2.50 6.00
21 Josh Smith/99 2.50 6.00
24 Andre Iguodala/299 2.50 6.00
25 Amare Stoudemire/299 2.50 6.00

2010-11 Donruss Gamers Materials Signatures

STATED PRINT RUN 5 TO 49 SER.#'d SETS
SOME UNPRICED DUE TO SCARCITY
2 Kobe Bryant/25 100.00 200.00
6 Brook Lopez/25 8.00 20.00
7 Robin Lopez/49 5.00 12.00
9 David Lee/25 8.00 20.00
10 Al Jefferson/25 10.00 25.00
11 Russell Westbrook/25 50.00 120.00
13 Jonny Flynn/25 6.00 15.00
25 Amare Stoudemire/25 10.00 25.00

2010-11 Donruss Gamers Materials Signatures Prime

STATED PRINT RUN 5 TO 25 SER.#'d SETS
SOME UNPRICED DUE TO SCARCITY
7 Robin Lopez/25 6.00 15.00
13 Jonny Flynn/25 8.00 20.00

2010-11 Donruss Gamers Signatures

STATED PRINT RUN 5 TO 99 SER.#'d SETS
SOME UNPRICED DUE TO SCARCITY
2 Kobe Bryant/49 75.00 150.00
6 Brook Lopez/25 5.00 12.00
7 Robin Lopez/99 4.00 10.00
9 David Lee/25 6.00 15.00
10 Al Jefferson/49 4.00 10.00
11 Russell Westbrook/25 50.00 120.00
13 Jonny Flynn/49 4.00 10.00
25 Amare Stoudemire/25 20.00 50.00

2010-11 Donruss Jersey Kings

COMPLETE SET (25) 15.00 40.00
STATED PRINT RUN 999 SER.#'d SETS
*DC EMERALD: .5X TO 1.25X HI
DC EMERALD RANDOM INSERTS IN PACKS
*DC RUBY: 1.5X TO 4X HI
DC RUBY PRINT RUN 25 SETS
*DC SAPPHIRE: 1X TO 2.5X HI
DC SAPPHIRE PRINT RUN 49 SETS
*PRESS PROOFS: .75X TO 2X HI
PRESS PROOFS PRINT RUN 100 SETS
1 Allen Iverson 1.50 4.00
2 Andre Miller 1.00 2.50
3 Ben Gordon 1.00 2.50
4 Xavier McDaniel .75 2.00
5 Vince Carter 1.50 4.00
6 Luis Scola 1.00 2.50
7 J.J. Redick 1.25 3.00
8 Thaddeus Young .75 2.00
9 Baron Davis 1.00 2.50
10 Kevin Love 1.25 3.00
11 Danilo Gallinari 1.00 2.50
12 Joe Dumars 1.25 3.00
13 Maurice Cheeks .75 2.00
14 Dennis Rodman 2.50 6.00
15 Tayshaun Prince 1.00 2.50
16 Andrew Bogut 1.00 2.50
17 Cedric Maxwell 1.25 3.00
18 Jonny Flynn .75 2.00
19 LaMarcus Aldridge 1.25 3.00
20 Mitch Richmond 1.25 3.00
21 Toni Kukoc 1.25 3.00
22 Luol Deng 1.00 2.50
23 Al Horford 1.00 2.50
24 Richard Hamilton 1.00 2.50
25 Dan Majerle 1.00 2.50

2010-11 Donruss Jersey Kings Materials

STATED PRINT RUN 99 TO 299 SER.#'d SETS
*PRIME: .75X TO 2X HI
PRIME PRINT RUN 5 TO 49 SER.#'d SETS
SOME PRIME UNPRICED DUE TO SCARCITY
1 Allen Iverson/99 4.00 10.00
2 Andre Miller/299 2.50 6.00
3 Ben Gordon/299 2.50 6.00
4 Xavier McDaniel/299 2.00 5.00
5 Vince Carter/299 4.00 10.00
6 Luis Scola/199 2.50 6.00
7 J.J. Redick/299 3.00 8.00
8 Thaddeus Young/299 2.00 5.00
9 Baron Davis/99 2.50 6.00
10 Kevin Love/299 3.00 8.00
11 Danilo Gallinari/299 2.50 6.00
12 Joe Dumars/199 3.00 8.00
13 Maurice Cheeks/299 2.00 5.00
14 Dennis Rodman/299 8.00 20.00
15 Tayshaun Prince/299 2.50 6.00
16 Andrew Bogut/99 2.50 6.00
18 Jonny Flynn/299 2.00 5.00
19 LaMarcus Aldridge/299 3.00 8.00
20 Mitch Richmond/299 3.00 8.00
21 Toni Kukoc/299 3.00 8.00
22 Luol Deng/299 2.50 6.00
23 Al Horford/299 2.50 6.00
24 Richard Hamilton/299 2.50 6.00
25 Dan Majerle/299 2.50 6.00

2010-11 Donruss Jersey Kings Materials Signatures

STATED PRINT RUN 10 TO 49 SER.#'d SETS
SOME UNPRICED DUE TO SCARCITY
3 Ben Gordon/25 6.00 15.00
4 Xavier McDaniel/49 8.00 20.00
7 J.J. Redick/25 10.00 25.00
10 Kevin Love/25 12.50 30.00
11 Danilo Gallinari/49 8.00 20.00
12 Joe Dumars/49 15.00 40.00
13 Maurice Cheeks/49 8.00 20.00
14 Dennis Rodman/49 15.00 40.00
16 Andrew Bogut/25 8.00 20.00
18 Jonny Flynn/49 6.00 15.00
21 Toni Kukoc/49 15.00 40.00
24 Richard Hamilton/25 12.50 30.00
25 Dan Majerle/49 12.50 30.00

2010-11 Donruss Jersey Kings Materials Signatures Prime

STATED PRINT RUN 5 TO 25 SER.#'d SETS
SOME UNPRICED DUE TO SCARCITY
4 Xavier McDaniel/25 12.50 30.00
7 J.J. Redick/25 25.00 60.00
10 Kevin Love/25 25.00 60.00
12 Joe Dumars/25 20.00 50.00
13 Maurice Cheeks/25 10.00 25.00
14 Dennis Rodman/25 30.00 80.00
18 Jonny Flynn/25 8.00 20.00
21 Toni Kukoc/25 20.00 50.00
25 Dan Majerle/25 25.00 60.00

2010-11 Donruss Jersey Kings Signatures

STATED PRINT RUN 10 TO 99 SER.#'d SETS
SOME UNPRICED DUE TO SCARCITY
3 Ben Gordon/25 6.00 15.00
4 Xavier McDaniel/75 6.00 15.00
7 J.J. Redick/49 6.00 15.00
10 Kevin Love/25 10.00 25.00
11 Danilo Gallinari/25 6.00 15.00
12 Joe Dumars/25 12.00 30.00
13 Maurice Cheeks/49 5.00 12.00
14 Dennis Rodman/49 20.00 50.00
16 Andrew Bogut/25 4.00 10.00
17 Cedric Maxwell/49 4.00 10.00
18 Jonny Flynn/49 4.00 10.00
21 Toni Kukoc/25 20.00 50.00
24 Richard Hamilton/49 4.00 10.00
25 Dan Majerle/99 10.00 25.00

2010-11 Donruss Magicians

COMPLETE SET (10) 7.50 15.00
STATED PRINT RUN 999 SER.#'d SETS
*DC EMERALD: .5X TO 1.25X HI
DC EMERALD RANDOM INSERTS IN PACKS
*DC RUBY: 1.5X TO 4X HI
DC RUBY PRINT RUN 25 SETS
*DC SAPPHIRE: 1X TO 2.5X HI
DC SAPPHIRE PRINT RUN 49 SETS
*PRESS PROOFS: .75X TO 2X HI
PRESS PROOFS PRINT RUN 100 SETS
1 Steve Nash 1.00 2.50
2 Jason Kidd 1.00 2.50
3 Chris Paul 1.25 3.00
4 Deron Williams .75 2.00
5 Rajon Rondo 1.00 2.50
6 Stephen Curry 4.00 10.00
7 Derrick Rose 1.25 3.00
8 John Stockton 1.50 4.00
9 Pete Maravich 1.50 4.00
10 Isiah Thomas 1.00 2.50

2010-11 Donruss Magicians Materials

STATED PRINT RUN 299 SER.#'d SETS
UNPRICED SIG.MAT.PRINT RUN 5 TO 10 SETS
1 Steve Nash 3.00 8.00
2 Jason Kidd 3.00 8.00
3 Chris Paul 4.00 10.00
4 Deron Williams 2.50 6.00
5 Rajon Rondo 3.00 8.00
6 Stephen Curry 12.00 30.00
7 Derrick Rose 6.00 15.00
8 John Stockton 5.00 12.00

2010-11 Donruss Magicians Materials Prime

STATED PRINT RUN 10 TO 49 SER.#'d SETS
SOME UNPRICED DUE TO SCARCITY
UNPRICED PRIME SIG.MAT.PRINT RUN 5 SETS
1 Steve Nash/25 8.00 20.00
8 John Stockton/49 10.00 25.00
10 Isiah Thomas/49 6.00 15.00

2010-11 Donruss Masters

COMPLETE SET (10) 7.50 15.00
STATED PRINT RUN 999 SER.#'d SETS
*DC EMERALD: .5X TO 1.25X HI
DC EMERALD RANDOM INSERTS IN PACKS
*DC RUBY: 2X TO 5X HI
DC RUBY PRINT RUN 25 SETS
*DC SAPPHIRE: 1X TO 2.5X HI
DC SAPPHIRE PRINT RUN 49 SETS
*PRESS PROOFS: .75X TO 2X HI
PRESS PROOFS PRINT RUN 100 SETS
1 Magic Johnson 2.50 6.00
2 Larry Bird 2.50 6.00
3 Artis Gilmore .75 2.00
4 Chris Mullin 1.00 2.50
5 Clyde Drexler 1.25 3.00
6 Kevin McHale 1.00 2.50
7 Patrick Ewing 1.25 3.00
8 Rolando Blackman .75 2.00
9 Scottie Pippen 2.00 5.00
10 Walt Frazier 1.00 2.50

2010-11 Donruss Masters Materials

STATED PRINT RUN 49 TO 299 SER.#'d SETS
1 Magic Johnson/299 6.00 15.00
2 Larry Bird/299 8.00 20.00
3 Artis Gilmore/49 2.50 6.00
4 Chris Mullin/299 3.00 8.00
5 Clyde Drexler/299 4.00 10.00
6 Kevin McHale/299 3.00 8.00
7 Patrick Ewing/299 4.00 10.00
8 Rolando Blackman/49 2.50 6.00
9 Scottie Pippen/299 6.00 15.00

2010-11 Donruss Masters Materials Prime

*PRIME: .75X TO 2X BASE HI
STATED PRINT RUN 5 TO 49 SER.#'d SETS
SOME UNPRICED DUE TO SCARCITY
7 Patrick Ewing/49 12.50 30.00
9 Scottie Pippen/49 30.00 60.00

2010-11 Donruss Masters Materials Signatures

STATED PRINT RUN ONE TO 49 SER.#'d SETS
SOME UNPRICED DUE TO SCARCITY
3 Artis Gilmore/49 8.00 20.00
4 Chris Mullin/49 8.00 20.00
5 Clyde Drexler/49 15.00 40.00
8 Rolando Blackman/49 8.00 20.00

2010-11 Donruss Masters Materials Signatures Prime

STATED PRINT RUN ONE TO 25 SER.#'d SETS
SOME UNPRICED DUE TO SCARCITY
3 Artis Gilmore/25 15.00 40.00
4 Chris Mullin/25 15.00 40.00
5 Clyde Drexler/25 25.00 60.00
8 Rolando Blackman/25 15.00 40.00

2010-11 Donruss Masters Signatures

STATED PRINT RUN ONE TO 99 SER.#'d SETS
SOME UNPRICED DUE TO SCARCITY
3 Artis Gilmore/49 6.00 15.00
4 Chris Mullin/99 10.00 25.00
5 Clyde Drexler/25 10.00 25.00
8 Rolando Blackman/25 8.00 20.00

2010-11 Donruss Production Line

COMPLETE SET (100) 50.00 100.00
STATED PRINT RUN 999 SER.#'d SETS
*DC EMERALD: .5X TO 1.25X HI
DC EMERALD RANDOM INSERTS IN PACKS
*DC RUBY: 1.5X TO 4X HI
DC RUBY PRINT RUN 25 SETS
*DC SAPPHIRE: 1X TO 2.5X HI
DC SAPPHIRE PRINT RUN 49 SETS

*PRESS PROOFS: .75X TO 2X HI
PRESS PROOFS PRINT RUN 100 SETS
*RACK PACK: .4X TO 1X BASE HI
RACK PACK RANDOM INSERTS IN RACK PACKS

Card	Low	High
1 Kevin Durant	2.00	5.00
2 LeBron James	4.00	10.00
3 Carmelo Anthony	1.00	2.50
4 Kobe Bryant	3.00	8.00
5 Dwyane Wade	1.25	3.00
6 Monta Ellis	.60	1.50
7 Dirk Nowitzki	1.00	2.50
8 Danny Granger	.60	1.50
9 Chris Bosh	.75	2.00
10 Amare Stoudemire	.60	1.50
11 Gilbert Arenas	.60	1.50
12 Brandon Roy	.75	2.00
13 Joe Johnson	.60	1.50
14 Derrick Rose	1.00	2.50
15 Zach Randolph	.60	1.50
16 Stephen Jackson	.60	1.50
17 Kevin Martin	.60	1.50
18 David Lee	.50	1.25
19 Tyreke Evans	.50	1.25
20 Corey Maggette	.60	1.50
21 Dwight Howard	.60	1.50
22 Marcus Camby	.50	1.25
23 Zach Randolph	.60	1.50
24 David Lee	.50	1.25
25 Pau Gasol	.75	2.00
26 Carlos Boozer	.60	1.50
27 Joakim Noah	.60	1.50
28 Kevin Love	.75	2.00
29 Chris Bosh	.75	2.00
30 Troy Murphy	.50	1.25
31 Andrew Bogut	.60	1.50
32 Tim Duncan	1.25	3.00
33 Gerald Wallace	.60	1.50
34 Al Horford	.60	1.50
35 Lamar Odom	.60	1.50
36 Samuel Dalembert	.50	1.25
37 Kenyon Martin	.60	1.50
38 Brendan Haywood	.50	1.25
39 Marc Gasol	.75	2.00
40 Chris Kaman	.60	1.50
41 Steve Nash	.75	2.00
42 Chris Paul	1.00	2.50
43 Deron Williams	.60	1.50
44 Rajon Rondo	.75	2.00
45 Jason Kidd	.75	2.00
46 LeBron James	4.00	10.00
47 Baron Davis	.60	1.50
48 Russell Westbrook	2.00	5.00
49 Gilbert Arenas	.60	1.50
50 Devin Harris	.50	1.25
51 Dwyane Wade	1.25	3.00
52 Derrick Rose	1.00	2.50
53 Jose Calderon	.50	1.25
54 Stephen Curry	3.00	8.00
55 Andre Iguodala	.60	1.50
56 Tyreke Evans	.50	1.25
57 Brandon Jennings	.50	1.25
58 Darren Collison	.60	1.50
59 Tony Parker	.75	2.00
60 Dwight Howard	.60	1.50
61 Andrew Bogut	.60	1.50
62 Greg Oden	.60	1.50
63 Josh Smith	.60	1.50
64 Brendan Haywood	.50	1.25
65 Marcus Camby	.50	1.25
66 Chris Andersen	.60	1.50
67 Samuel Dalembert	.50	1.25
68 Pau Gasol	.75	2.00
69 Brook Lopez	.60	1.50
70 Kendrick Perkins	.50	1.25
71 JaVale McGee	.60	1.50
72 Roy Hibbert	.60	1.50
73 Marc Gasol	.75	2.00
74 Tyrus Thomas	.50	1.25
75 Joakim Noah	.60	1.50
76 Rajon Rondo	.75	2.00
77 Monta Ellis	.60	1.50
78 Chris Paul	1.00	2.50
79 Stephen Curry	3.00	8.00
80 Dwyane Wade	1.25	3.00
81 Jason Kidd	.75	2.00
82 Trevor Ariza	.50	1.25
83 Andre Iguodala	.60	1.50
84 Baron Davis	.60	1.50
85 LeBron James	4.00	10.00
86 Stephen Jackson	.60	1.50
87 Josh Smith	.60	1.50
88 C.J. Watson	.50	1.25
89 Ronnie Brewer	.60	1.50
90 Caron Butler	.60	1.50
91 Aaron Brooks	.50	1.25
92 Danilo Gallinari	.60	1.50
93 Jason Kidd	.75	2.00
94 Channing Frye	.60	1.50
95 Rashard Lewis	.60	1.50
96 Stephen Curry	3.00	8.00
97 Jamal Crawford	.75	2.00
98 Mo Williams	.60	1.50
99 Danny Granger	.60	1.50
100 J.R. Smith	.60	1.50

2010-11 Donruss Production Line Materials

STATED PRINT RUN 49 TO 399 SER.#'d SETS
*STAT DC: .4X TO 1X BASE HI
STAT DC PRINT RUN 49 TO 399 SER.#'d SETS
*PRIME: .75X TO 2X HI
PRIME PRINT RUN 5 TO 49 SER.#'d SETS
*STAT DC PRIME: .75X TO 2X HI
STAT DC PRIME PRINT RUN 5 TO 49 SETS
SOME PRIME UNPRICED DUE TO SCARCITY

Card	Low	High
1 Kevin Durant/399	6.00	15.00
2 LeBron James/399	8.00	20.00
3 Carmelo Anthony/299	4.00	10.00
4 Kobe Bryant/399	8.00	20.00
5 Dwyane Wade/399	5.00	12.00
7 Dirk Nowitzki/399	4.00	10.00
9 Chris Bosh/399	3.00	8.00
10 Amare Stoudemire/399	2.50	6.00
11 Gilbert Arenas/399	2.50	6.00
12 Brandon Roy/99	3.00	8.00
13 Joe Johnson/399	2.50	6.00
14 Derrick Rose/399	4.00	10.00
15 Zach Randolph/399	2.50	6.00
16 Stephen Jackson/399	2.50	6.00
18 David Lee/399	2.00	5.00
19 Tyreke Evans/399	2.00	5.00
20 Corey Maggette/49	2.50	6.00
21 Dwight Howard/399	2.50	6.00
22 Marcus Camby/49	2.00	5.00
23 Zach Randolph/399	2.50	6.00
24 David Lee/399	2.00	5.00
25 Pau Gasol/399	3.00	8.00
26 Carlos Boozer/299	2.50	6.00
27 Joakim Noah/199	2.50	6.00
28 Kevin Love/399	3.00	8.00
29 Chris Bosh/399	3.00	8.00
31 Andrew Bogut/199	2.50	6.00
32 Tim Duncan/399	5.00	12.00
33 Gerald Wallace/399	2.50	6.00
34 Al Horford/299	2.50	6.00
35 Lamar Odom/399	2.50	6.00
36 Samuel Dalembert/299	2.00	5.00
37 Kenyon Martin/399	2.50	6.00
38 Brendan Haywood/199	2.00	5.00
39 Marc Gasol/399	3.00	8.00
40 Chris Kaman/399	2.50	6.00
41 Steve Nash/399	3.00	8.00
42 Chris Paul/399	4.00	10.00
43 Deron Williams/399	2.50	6.00
44 Rajon Rondo/399	3.00	8.00
45 Jason Kidd/399	3.00	8.00
46 LeBron James/399	8.00	20.00
47 Baron Davis/99	2.50	6.00
48 Russell Westbrook/399	8.00	20.00
49 Gilbert Arenas/399	2.50	6.00
51 Dwyane Wade/399	5.00	12.00
52 Derrick Rose/399	8.00	20.00
53 Jose Calderon/399	2.00	5.00
54 Stephen Curry/399	12.00	30.00
55 Andre Iguodala/299	2.50	6.00
56 Tyreke Evans/399	2.00	5.00
57 Brandon Jennings/399	2.00	5.00
58 Darren Collison/199	2.50	6.00
59 Tony Parker/99	3.00	8.00
60 Dwight Howard/199	2.50	6.00
61 Andrew Bogut/199	2.50	6.00
62 Greg Oden/299	2.50	6.00
63 Josh Smith/99	2.50	6.00
64 Brendan Haywood/199	2.00	5.00
65 Marcus Camby/49	2.00	5.00
66 Chris Andersen/399	2.50	6.00
67 Samuel Dalembert/299	2.00	5.00
68 Pau Gasol/399	3.00	8.00
69 Brook Lopez/399	2.50	6.00
73 Marc Gasol/399	3.00	8.00
75 Joakim Noah/199	2.50	6.00
76 Rajon Rondo/399	3.00	8.00
78 Chris Paul/399	4.00	10.00
79 Stephen Curry/399	12.00	30.00
80 Dwyane Wade/399	5.00	12.00
81 Jason Kidd/399	3.00	8.00
83 Andre Iguodala/299	2.50	6.00
84 Baron Davis/99	2.50	6.00
85 LeBron James/399	8.00	20.00
86 Stephen Jackson/399	2.50	6.00
87 Josh Smith/99	2.50	6.00
90 Caron Butler/399	2.50	6.00
92 Danilo Gallinari/399	2.50	6.00
93 Jason Kidd/399	3.00	8.00
94 Channing Frye/74	2.50	6.00
95 Rashard Lewis/399	2.50	6.00
96 Stephen Curry/399	12.00	30.00
100 J.R. Smith/399	2.50	6.00

2010-11 Donruss Production Line Materials Signatures

STATED PRINT RUN ONE TO 25 SER.#'d SETS
SOME UNPRICED DUE TO SCARCITY

Card	Low	High
4 Kobe Bryant/25	100.00	200.00
9 Chris Bosh/25	20.00	50.00
10 Amare Stoudemire/25	25.00	60.00
13 Joe Johnson/25	15.00	40.00
18 David Lee/25	8.00	20.00
19 Tyreke Evans/25	15.00	40.00
24 David Lee/25	8.00	20.00
27 Joakim Noah/25	12.00	30.00
28 Kevin Love/25	12.00	30.00
29 Chris Bosh/25	12.00	30.00
31 Andrew Bogut/25	8.00	20.00
39 Marc Gasol/25	12.00	30.00
48 Russell Westbrook/25	60.00	150.00
56 Tyreke Evans/25	15.00	40.00
59 Tony Parker/25	10.00	25.00
61 Andrew Bogut/25	8.00	20.00
66 Chris Andersen/25	20.00	50.00
69 Brook Lopez/25	8.00	20.00
73 Marc Gasol/25	12.00	30.00
75 Joakim Noah/25	12.00	30.00
90 Caron Butler/15	10.00	25.00
92 Danilo Gallinari/25	8.00	20.00
94 Channing Frye/25	8.00	20.00
100 J.R. Smith/25	8.00	20.00

2010-11 Donruss Production Line Materials Signatures Prime

STATED PRINT RUN ONE TO 49 SER.#'d SETS
SOME UNPRICED DUE TO SCARCITY

Card	Low	High
50 Devin Harris/49	10.00	25.00
90 Caron Butler/15	12.50	30.00
94 Channing Frye/25	10.00	25.00
100 J.R. Smith/25	10.00	25.00

2010-11 Donruss Production Line Signatures

STATED PRINT RUN ONE TO 99 SER.#'d SETS
SOME UNPRICED DUE TO SCARCITY

Card	Low	High
4 Kobe Bryant/49	75.00	150.00
8 Danny Granger/25	6.00	15.00
9 Chris Bosh/25	12.50	30.00
10 Amare Stoudemire/25	20.00	50.00
13 Joe Johnson/25	8.00	20.00
18 David Lee/25	6.00	15.00
19 Tyreke Evans/49	10.00	25.00
24 David Lee/25	6.00	15.00
27 Joakim Noah/25	10.00	25.00
28 Kevin Love/25	10.00	25.00
29 Chris Bosh/25	10.00	25.00
31 Andrew Bogut/25	6.00	15.00
39 Marc Gasol/25	10.00	25.00
48 Russell Westbrook/25	30.00	80.00
50 Devin Harris/25	6.00	15.00
56 Tyreke Evans/49	10.00	25.00
58 Darren Collison/25	6.00	15.00
59 Tony Parker/25	6.00	15.00
61 Andrew Bogut/25	6.00	15.00
66 Chris Andersen/25	12.50	30.00
69 Brook Lopez/25	4.00	10.00
73 Marc Gasol/25	10.00	25.00
75 Joakim Noah/25	10.00	25.00
89 Ronnie Brewer/99	4.00	10.00
90 Caron Butler/15	8.00	20.00
91 Aaron Brooks/99	4.00	10.00
92 Danilo Gallinari/49	4.00	10.00
94 Channing Frye/25	4.00	10.00
98 Mo Williams/25	4.00	10.00
99 Danny Granger/25	6.00	15.00
100 J.R. Smith/49	4.00	10.00

2010-11 Donruss Production Line Stat Die Cuts Materials

STATED PRINT RUN 5 TO 49 SER.#'d SETS
SOME UNPRICED DUE TO SCARCITY

Card	Low	High
1 Kevin Durant/399	6.00	15.00
2 LeBron James/399	8.00	20.00
3 Carmelo Anthony/299	4.00	10.00
4 Kobe Bryant/399	8.00	20.00
5 Dwyane Wade/399	5.00	12.00
7 Dirk Nowitzki/399	4.00	10.00
9 Chris Bosh/399	3.00	8.00
10 Amare Stoudemire/399	2.50	6.00
11 Gilbert Arenas/399	2.50	6.00
12 Brandon Roy/99	3.00	8.00
13 Joe Johnson/399	2.50	6.00
14 Derrick Rose/399	8.00	20.00
15 Zach Randolph/399	2.50	6.00
16 Stephen Jackson/399	2.50	6.00
18 David Lee/399	2.00	5.00
19 Tyreke Evans/399	2.00	5.00
20 Corey Maggette/49	2.50	6.00
21 Dwight Howard/399	2.50	6.00
22 Marcus Camby/49	2.00	5.00
23 Zach Randolph/399	2.50	6.00
24 David Lee/399	2.00	5.00
25 Pau Gasol/399	3.00	8.00
26 Carlos Boozer/299	2.50	6.00
27 Joakim Noah/199	2.50	6.00
28 Kevin Love/399	3.00	8.00
29 Chris Bosh/399	3.00	8.00
31 Andrew Bogut/199	2.50	6.00
32 Tim Duncan/399	5.00	12.00
33 Gerald Wallace/399	2.50	6.00
34 Al Horford/299	2.50	6.00
35 Lamar Odom/399	2.50	6.00
36 Samuel Dalembert/299	2.00	5.00
37 Kenyon Martin/399	2.50	6.00
38 Brendan Haywood/199	2.00	5.00
39 Marc Gasol/399	3.00	8.00
40 Chris Kaman/399	2.50	6.00
41 Steve Nash/399	3.00	8.00
42 Chris Paul/399	4.00	10.00
43 Deron Williams/399	2.50	6.00
44 Rajon Rondo/399	3.00	8.00
45 Jason Kidd/399	3.00	8.00
46 LeBron James/399	8.00	20.00
47 Baron Davis/99	2.50	6.00
48 Russell Westbrook/399	8.00	20.00
49 Gilbert Arenas/399	2.50	6.00
51 Dwyane Wade/399	5.00	12.00
52 Derrick Rose/399	8.00	20.00
53 Jose Calderon/399	2.00	5.00
54 Stephen Curry/399	12.00	30.00
55 Andre Iguodala/299	2.50	6.00
56 Tyreke Evans/399	2.00	5.00
57 Brandon Jennings/399	2.00	5.00
58 Darren Collison/199	2.50	6.00
59 Tony Parker/99	3.00	8.00
60 Dwight Howard/399	2.50	6.00
61 Andrew Bogut/199	2.50	6.00
62 Greg Oden/299	2.50	6.00
63 Josh Smith/99	2.50	6.00
64 Brendan Haywood/199	2.00	5.00
65 Marcus Camby/49	2.00	5.00
66 Chris Andersen/399	2.50	6.00
67 Samuel Dalembert/299	2.00	5.00
68 Pau Gasol/399	3.00	8.00
69 Brook Lopez/399	2.50	6.00
73 Marc Gasol/399	3.00	8.00
75 Joakim Noah/199	2.50	6.00
76 Rajon Rondo/399	3.00	8.00
78 Chris Paul/399	4.00	10.00
79 Stephen Curry/399	12.00	30.00
80 Dwyane Wade/399	5.00	12.00
81 Jason Kidd/399	3.00	8.00
83 Andre Iguodala/299	2.50	6.00
84 Baron Davis/99	2.50	6.00
85 LeBron James/399	8.00	20.00
87 Josh Smith/99	2.50	6.00
90 Caron Butler/399	2.50	6.00
92 Danilo Gallinari/399	2.50	6.00
93 Jason Kidd/399	3.00	8.00
94 Channing Frye/99	2.50	6.00
95 Rashard Lewis/399	2.50	6.00
96 Stephen Curry/399	12.00	30.00
100 J.R. Smith/399	2.50	6.00

2010-11 Donruss Signatures

STATED PRINT RUN ONE TO 599 SER.#'d SETS
SOME UNPRICED DUE TO SCARCITY

Card	Low	High
6 Kendrick Perkins/49	2.50	6.00
10 Brook Lopez/25	6.00	15.00
11 Terrence Williams/199	4.00	10.00
12 Devin Harris/49	4.00	10.00
15 Danilo Gallinari/25	5.00	12.00
18 Toney Douglas/199	4.00	10.00
20 Anthony Randolph/49	4.00	10.00
22 Jrue Holiday/199	5.00	12.00
31 Andrea Bargnani/49	4.00	10.00
34 DeMar DeRozan/99	5.00	12.00
36 Sonny Weems/99	4.00	10.00
39 Joakim Noah/25	12.00	30.00
45 Mo Williams/25	4.00	10.00
52 Ben Gordon/25	6.00	15.00
54 Jonas Jerebko/199	4.00	10.00
55 Richard Hamilton/25	5.00	12.00
57 Charlie Villanueva/49	4.00	10.00
59 Mike Dunleavy/49	4.00	10.00
61 T.J. Ford/49	4.00	10.00
63 Darren Collison/25	5.00	12.00
64 Danny Granger/25	6.00	15.00
65 Tyler Hansbrough/99	4.00	10.00
67 Andrew Bogut/25	6.00	15.00
74 Rodrigue Beaubois/199	2.50	6.00
76 Caron Butler/25	6.00	15.00
82 Aaron Brooks/49	4.00	10.00
84 Jordan Hill/49	4.00	10.00
91 Marc Gasol/49	10.00	25.00
94 Sam Young/299	4.00	10.00
96 Hasheem Thabeet/199	4.00	10.00
101 Emeka Okafor/49	4.00	10.00
102 Marcus Thornton/199	2.50	6.00
105 DeJuan Blair/99	4.00	10.00
110 Tony Parker/25	6.00	15.00
113 Chris Andersen/25	12.00	30.00
114 Ty Lawson/149	5.00	12.00
115 Chauncey Billups/25	5.00	12.00
119 J.R. Smith/49	4.00	10.00
121 Jonny Flynn/99	2.50	6.00
122 Kevin Love/25	10.00	25.00
136 Russell Westbrook/25	50.00	120.00
138 James Harden/49	15.00	40.00
141 Eric Maynor/199	4.00	10.00
143 Al Jefferson/49	4.00	10.00
149 Joe Johnson/25	8.00	20.00
150 Jeff Teague/199	4.00	10.00
151 Mike Bibby/25	6.00	15.00
158 Gerald Henderson/99	4.00	10.00
159 D.J. Augustin/49	4.00	10.00
164 Derrick Brown/399	4.00	10.00
167 Chris Bosh/25	12.00	30.00
177 J.J. Redick/49	10.00	25.00
181 Al Thornton/49	4.00	10.00
183 Josh Howard/49	4.00	10.00
191 David Lee/25	6.00	15.00
197 Blake Griffin/25	30.00	80.00
203 Kobe Bryant/49	100.00	200.00
214 Channing Frye/25	4.00	10.00
215 Robin Lopez/49	4.00	10.00
216 Earl Clark/199	4.00	10.00
220 Tyreke Evans/49	2.50	6.00
221 Carl Landry/49	4.00	10.00
223 Omri Casspi/199	4.00	10.00
228 John Wall/299	30.00	80.00
229 Evan Turner/199	3.00	8.00
230 Derrick Favors/299	5.00	12.00
231 Wesley Johnson/99	2.50	6.00
232 DeMarcus Cousins/299	15.00	40.00
233 Ekpe Udoh/399	2.50	6.00
234 Greg Monroe/399	5.00	12.00
235 Al-Farouq Aminu/399	4.00	10.00
236 Gordon Hayward/299	6.00	15.00
237 Paul George/399	40.00	100.00
238 Cole Aldrich/399	3.00	8.00
239 Xavier Henry/399	2.50	6.00
240 Ed Davis/399	2.50	6.00
241 Patrick Patterson/499	3.00	8.00
242 Larry Sanders/399	2.50	6.00
243 Luke Babbitt/399	3.00	8.00
244 Kevin Seraphin/399	2.50	6.00
245 Eric Bledsoe/399	5.00	12.00
246 Avery Bradley/399	5.00	12.00
247 James Anderson/499	2.50	6.00
248 Craig Brackins/499	2.50	6.00
249 Elliot Williams/499	2.50	6.00
250 Trevor Booker/499	3.00	8.00
251 Damion James/399	2.50	6.00
252 Dominique Jones/399	2.50	6.00
253 Quincy Pondexter/599	2.50	6.00
254 Jordan Crawford/499	3.00	8.00
255 Greivis Vasquez/599	3.00	8.00
256 Daniel Orton/499	2.50	6.00
257 Lazar Hayward/599	2.50	6.00
258 Dexter Pittman/599	2.50	6.00
259 Hassan Whiteside/599	8.00	20.00
260 Andy Rautins/499	2.50	6.00
261 Luke Harangody/499	2.50	6.00
262 Timofey Mozgov/599	4.00	10.00

2014-15 Donruss

Card	Low	High
COMP.SET w/o RCs (200)	12.00	30.00
1 Al Horford	.30	.75
2 Rajon Rondo	.40	1.00
3 Brook Lopez	.30	.75
4 Michael Kidd-Gilchrist	.30	.75
5 Taj Gibson	.30	.75
6 Kyrie Irving	.75	2.00
7 Dirk Nowitzki	.50	1.25
8 JaVale McGee	.30	.75
9 Greg Monroe	.30	.75
10 Klay Thompson	.50	1.25
11 Dwight Howard	.30	.75
12 Roy Hibbert	.30	.75
13 DeAndre Jordan	.40	1.00
14 Steve Nash	.40	1.00
15 Zach Randolph	.30	.75
16 Dwyane Wade	.60	1.50
17 O.J. Mayo	.25	.60
18 Thaddeus Young	.25	.60
19 Tyreke Evans	.25	.60
20 Amar'e Stoudemire	.40	1.00
21 Russell Westbrook	1.00	2.50
22 Brandon Knight	.30	.75
23 Victor Oladipo	.30	.75
24 Luc Mbah a Moute	.25	.60
25 Eric Bledsoe	.30	.75
26 LaMarcus Aldridge	.40	1.00
27 DeMarcus Cousins	.40	1.00
28 Tony Parker	.40	1.00
29 Kyle Lowry	.30	.75
30 Derrick Favors	.30	.75
31 Marcin Gortat	.30	.75
32 Jeff Teague	.30	.75
33 Jeff Green	.30	.75
34 Kevin Garnett	.60	1.50
35 Lance Stephenson	.30	.75
36 Jimmy Butler	.40	1.00
37 Kevin Love	.40	1.00
38 Tyson Chandler	.30	.75
39 Ty Lawson	.25	.60
40 Brandon Jennings	.25	.60
41 Andre Iguodala	.30	.75
42 Trevor Ariza	.25	.60
43 Paul George	.50	1.25
44 Chris Paul	.50	1.25
45 Kobe Bryant	1.50	4.00
46 Marc Gasol	.40	1.00
47 Chris Bosh	.40	1.00
48 Larry Sanders	.25	.60
49 Nikola Pekovic	.25	.60
50 Anthony Davis	.75	2.00
51 Carmelo Anthony	.50	1.25
52 Kevin Durant	1.00	2.50
53 Channing Frye	.30	.75
54 Michael Carter-Williams	.25	.60
55 Marcus Morris	.25	.60
56 Wesley Matthews	.25	.60
57 Rudy Gay	.40	1.00
58 Tim Duncan	.60	1.50
59 Landry Fields	.25	.60
60 Gordon Hayward	.40	1.00
61 Nene	.30	.75
62 Brandon Bass	.25	.60
63 DeMarre Carroll	.25	.60
64 Mirza Teletovic	.25	.60
65 Pau Gasol	.40	1.00
66 Mike-Dunleavy	.25	.60
67 Dion Waiters	.30	.75
68 Raymond Felton	.30	.75
69 J.J. Hickson	.25	.60
70 Stephen Curry	1.50	4.00
71 James Harden	.60	1.50
72 George Hill	.30	.75
73 Jamal Crawford	.40	1.00
74 Nick Young	.30	.75
75 Courtney Lee	.30	.75
76 Norris Cole	.25	.60
77 Anthony Bennett	.25	.60
78 Omer Asik	.30	.75
79 Iman Shumpert	.25	.60
80 Serge Ibaka	.30	.75
81 Nikola Vucevic	.30	.75
82 Nerlens Noel	.30	.75
83 Goran Dragic	.30	.75
84 Isaiah Thomas	.40	1.00
85 C.J. McCollum	.40	1.00
86 Darren Collison	.30	.75
87 Tiago Splitter	.30	.75
88 Jonas Valanciunas	.30	.75
89 Enes Kanter	.25	.60
90 John Wall	.50	1.25
91 Patrick Patterson	.25	.60
92 Danny Green	.30	.75
93 Steve Blake	.25	.60
94 Alexey Shved	.25	.60
95 Nick Collison	.30	.75
96 Jose Calderon	.25	.60
97 Corey Brewer	.25	.60
98 Giannis Antetokounmpo	.75	2.00
99 Luol Deng	.30	.75
100 Tayshaun Prince	.30	.75
101 Jeremy Lin	.40	1.00
102 Rodney Stuckey	.30	.75
103 Jason Terry	.30	.75
104 Andrew Bogut	.30	.75
105 Andre Drummond	.40	1.00
106 Monta Ellis	.30	.75
107 Anderson Varejao	.25	.60
108 Joakim Noah	.30	.75
109 Andrei Kirilenko	.30	.75
110 Tyler Zeller	.30	.75
111 Avery Bradley	.30	.75
112 Paul Millsap	.40	1.00
113 Chandler Parsons	.30	.75
114 Tristan Thompson	.30	.75
115 Arron Afflalo	.25	.60
116 Jonas Jerebko	.25	.60
117 Terrence Jones	.30	.75
118 J.J. Redick	.40	1.00
119 Ed Davis	.25	.60
120 Chris Andersen	.30	.75
121 Ricky Rubio	.40	1.00
122 Samuel Dalembert	.25	.60
123 Tobias Harris	.30	.75
124 Miles Plumlee	.25	.60
125 Ben McLemore	.25	.60
126 Cory Joseph	.25	.60
127 Trey Burke	.25	.60
128 Glen Rice Jr.	.25	.60
129 Damian Lillard	.75	2.00
130 Tony Wroten	.25	.60
131 Tim Hardaway Jr.	.25	.60
132 Eric Gordon	.30	.75
133 Vince Carter	.50	1.25
134 Carlos Boozer	.30	.75
135 Reggie Bullock	.25	.60
136 Isaiah Canaan	.30	.75
137 Draymond Green	.50	1.25
138 Kentavious Caldwell-Pope	.25	.60
139 Jameer Nelson	.25	.60
140 Shawn Marion	.30	.75
141 Kemba Walker	.40	1.00
142 Joe Johnson	.30	.75
143 Dennis Schroder	.30	.75
144 Derrick Rose	.50	1.25
145 Mike Miller	.30	.75
146 Josh Smith	.30	.75
147 David Lee	.25	.60
148 Patrick Beverley	.25	.60
149 Matt Barnes	.25	.60
150 Mike Conley	.30	.75
151 John Henson	.30	.75
152 Ryan Anderson	.25	.60
153 Reggie Jackson	.25	.60
154 Hollis Thompson	.30	.75
155 Nicolas Batum	.30	.75
156 Manu Ginobili	.40	1.00
157 Amir Johnson	.25	.60
158 Paul Pierce	.40	1.00
159 Carl Landry	.25	.60
160 Markieff Morris	.25	.60
161 Maurice Harkless	.25	.60
162 Kendrick Perkins	.25	.60
163 Jrue Holiday	.30	.75
164 Kevin Martin	.30	.75
165 Mario Chalmers	.30	.75
166 Jordan Hill	.25	.60
167 Blake Griffin	.40	1.00
168 Harrison Barnes	.30	.75
169 Devin Harris	.25	.60
170 LeBron James	1.50	4.00
171 Cody Zeller	.25	.60
172 Mason Plumlee	.30	.75
173 Jared Sullinger	.25	.60
174 Kyle Korver	.30	.75
175 Gerald Henderson	.25	.60
176 Kirk Hinrich	.30	.75
177 Kenneth Faried	.30	.75
178 Luis Scola	.30	.75
179 Josh McRoberts	.25	.60
180 Shabazz Muhammad	.30	.75
181 Austin Rivers	.30	.75
182 J.R. Smith	.30	.75
183 Steven Adams	.30	.75
184 Robin Lopez	.25	.60
185 Boris Diaw	.30	.75
186 Terrence Ross	.30	.75
187 Otto Porter	.30	.75
188 Evan Fournier	.25	.60
189 Ersan Ilyasova	.25	.60
190 David West	.30	.75
191 Danilo Gallinari	.25	.60
192 Al Jefferson	.30	.75
193 Deron Williams	.30	.75
194 Kelly Olynyk	.25	.60
195 Derrick Williams	.25	.60
196 Kawhi Leonard	.60	1.50
197 DeMar DeRozan	.40	1.00
198 Rudy Gobert	.40	1.00
199 Bradley Beal	.40	1.00
200 Alec Burks	.25	.60
201 Andrew Wiggins RC	3.00	8.00
202 Jabari Parker RC	1.50	4.00
203 Joel Embiid RC	3.00	8.00
204 Dante Exum RC	1.00	2.50
205 Cory Jefferson RC	.60	1.50
206 Elfrid Payton RC	1.00	2.50
207 Marcus Smart RC	1.00	2.50
208 James Young RC	.60	1.50
209 Aaron Gordon RC	1.50	4.00
210 Jusuf Nurkic RC	1.00	2.50
211 Doug McDermott RC	1.00	2.50
212 Damjan Rudez RC	.60	1.50
213 Kostas Papanikolaou RC	.60	1.50
214 P.J. Hairston RC	.60	1.50
215 Shabazz Napier RC	.75	2.00
216 Rodney Hood RC	1.00	2.50
217 Nik Stauskas RC	.75	2.00
218 Jordan Clarkson RC	1.00	2.50
219 Nikola Mirotic RC	1.25	3.00
220 Cleanthony Early RC	.60	1.50
221 Zach LaVine RC	1.50	4.00
222 James Ennis RC	.60	1.50
223 Kyle Anderson RC	1.00	2.50
224 Julius Randle RC	1.50	4.00
225 T.J. Warren RC	1.00	2.50
226 Noah Vonleh RC	.75	2.00
227 Glenn Robinson III RC	.60	1.50
228 Gary Harris RC	1.00	2.50
229 Spencer Dinwiddie RC	.75	2.00
230 Russ Smith RC	.60	1.50
231 K.J. McDaniels RC	.75	2.00
232 Jarnell Stokes RC	.60	1.50
233 Bruno Caboclo RC	.75	2.00
234 Erick Green RC	.60	1.50
235 Tarik Black RC	.60	1.50
236 Joe Harris RC	.60	1.50
237 Tyler Ennis RC	.60	1.50
238 Langston Galloway RC	1.00	2.50
239 Markel Brown RC	.60	1.50

2014-15 Donruss Press Proofs Blue

*VETS: .8X TO 2X BASE HI
*ROOKIES: .8X TO 2X BASE HI
RANDOM INSERTS IN PACKS
STATED PRINT RUN 99 SER.#'d SETS

Card	Low	High
170 LeBron James	6.00	15.00

2014-15 Donruss Press Proofs Purple

*VETS: .6X TO 1.5X BASE HI
*ROOKIES: .6X TO 1.5X BASE HI
RANDOM INSERTS IN PACKS
STATED PRINT RUN 199 SER.#'d SETS

2014-15 Donruss Press Proofs Silver

*VETS: 1.2X TO 3X BASE HI
*ROOKIES: 1.2X TO 3X BASE HI
RANDOM INSERTS IN PACKS
STATED PRINT RUN 25 SER.#'d SETS

Card	Low	High
170 LeBron James	8.00	20.00
219 Nikola Mirotic	15.00	40.00

2014-15 Donruss Rated Rookies Artists Proofs

*ROOKIES AP: .6X TO 1.5X BASE HI
RANDOM INSERTS IN PACKS
STATED PRINT RUN 99 SER.#'d SETS

Card	Low	High
201 Andrew Wiggins	20.00	50.00
219 Nikola Mirotic	6.00	15.00

2014-15 Donruss Rated Rookies Jersey Numbers

RANDOM INSERTS IN PACKS
STATED PRINT RUN B/WN 1-44 COPIES PER
NO PRICING ON QTY 19 OR LESS

Card	Low	High
201 Andrew Wiggins/22	40.00	100.00

2014-15 Donruss Stat Line Career

*CAREER: 3X TO 8X BASE HI
RANDOM INSERTS IN PACKS
STATED PRINT RUN B/WN 43-440 COPIES PER

2014-15 Donruss Stat Line Season

*SEASON: 2.5X TO 6X BASE HI
RANDOM INSERTS IN PACKS
STATED PRINT RUN B/WN 76-485 COPIES PER

2014-15 Donruss Swirlorama

*VETS: 1.2X TO 3X BASE HI
*ROOKIES: .5X TO 1.2X BASE HI
RANDOM INSERTS IN PACKS

2014-15 Donruss Court Kings

RANDOM INSERTS IN PACKS
*PURPLE: .5X TO 1.2X BASE HI
*BLUE: .8X TO 2X BASE HI
*SILVER: 1X TO 2.5X BASE HI
*CAREER: .8X TO 2X BASE HI
*SEASON: .8X TO 2X BASE HI

Card	Low	High
1 Blake Griffin	.75	2.00
2 Pau Gasol	.75	2.00
3 James Harden	1.25	3.00
4 Zach Randolph	.60	1.50
5 Paul Millsap	.75	2.00
6 Damian Lillard	1.50	4.00
7 LeBron James	3.00	8.00
8 Dwyane Wade	1.25	3.00
9 Greg Monroe	.60	1.50
10 Rajon Rondo	.75	2.00
11 Tim Duncan	1.25	3.00
12 Andre Iguodala	.60	1.50
13 Ricky Rubio	.75	2.00
14 Roy Hibbert	.60	1.50
15 Carmelo Anthony	1.00	2.50
16 Derrick Rose	1.00	2.50
17 Chris Paul	1.00	2.50
18 Goran Dragic	.60	1.50
19 Dirk Nowitzki	1.00	2.50
20 Nikola Vucevic	.60	1.50
21 Ty Lawson	.50	1.25
22 Kobe Bryant	3.00	8.00
23 Tony Parker	.75	2.00
24 Deron Williams	.60	1.50
25 Kevin Durant	2.00	5.00
26 Kevin Love	.75	2.00
27 Marc Gasol	.75	2.00
28 Al Horford	.60	1.50
29 Dwight Howard	.60	1.50
30 Josh Smith	.60	1.50
31 DeMarcus Cousins	.75	2.00
32 Al Jefferson	.60	1.50
33 Iman Shumpert	.50	1.25
34 Jeremy Lin	.75	2.00
35 Tyson Chandler	.60	1.50
36 Chris Bosh	.75	2.00
37 Serge Ibaka	.60	1.50
38 Stephen Curry	3.00	8.00
39 Thaddeus Young	.50	1.25
40 Michael Carter-Williams	.50	1.25
41 Lance Stephenson	.60	1.50
42 DeMar DeRozan	.75	2.00
43 Anthony Davis	1.50	4.00
44 John Wall	1.00	2.50
45 Brandon Knight	.60	1.50
46 Paul Pierce	.75	2.00
47 Nicolas Batum	.60	1.50
48 Gordon Hayward	.75	2.00
49 Eric Bledsoe	.60	1.50
50 Rudy Gay	.75	2.00

2014-15 Donruss Game Threads

RANDOM INSERTS IN PACKS

Card	Low	High
1 Kobe Bryant	6.00	15.00
2 Brook Lopez	1.50	4.00
3 Al Jefferson	1.50	4.00
4 Dirk Nowitzki	2.50	6.00
5 Harrison Barnes	1.50	4.00
6 Paul George	4.00	10.00
7 Zach Randolph	1.50	4.00
8 Larry Sanders	1.25	3.00
9 Eric Gordon	1.50	4.00
10 Victor Oladipo	1.50	4.00
11 Kevin Durant	5.00	12.00
12 Eric Bledsoe	1.50	4.00
13 Michael Kidd-Gilchrist	1.50	4.00
14 Kenneth Faried	1.50	4.00
15 Andrew Bogut	1.50	4.00
16 Roy Hibbert	1.50	4.00
17 Mike Conley	1.50	4.00
18 Nikola Pekovic	1.25	3.00
19 Russell Westbrook	5.00	12.00
20 Damian Lillard	4.00	10.00
21 LeBron James	8.00	20.00
22 Paul Pierce	2.00	5.00
23 Jimmy Butler	2.00	5.00
25 Stephen Curry	3.00	8.00
26 Blake Griffin	4.00	10.00
27 Chris Bosh	2.00	5.00
29 Tobias Harris	1.50	4.00
30 LaMarcus Aldridge	2.00	5.00
31 Kevin Love	2.00	5.00
32 Ben Gordon	1.50	4.00
33 Joakim Noah	1.50	4.00
34 Andre Drummond	2.00	5.00
35 Terrence Jones	1.50	4.00
36 Nick Young	1.50	4.00
38 Austin Rivers	1.50	4.00
40 Tim Duncan	3.00	8.00
41 Kevin Garnett	3.00	8.00
43 Nazr Mohammed	4.00	10.00
44 Josh Smith	1.50	4.00
45 Luis Scola	1.50	4.00

2014-15 Donruss Game Threads Prime

*PRIME: .5X TO 1.2X BASE HI
RANDOM INSERTS IN PACKS
STATED PRINT RUN B/WN 18-20 COPIES PER

Card	Low	High
20 Damian Lillard/20	10.00	25.00
30 LaMarcus Aldridge/20	8.00	20.00

2014-15 Donruss Gamers Jerseys

RANDOM INSERTS IN PACKS
*PRIME/15-20: .75X TO 2X BASE HI

Card	Low	High
1 Tim Duncan	3.00	8.00
2 DeMarcus Cousins	2.00	5.00
3 DeMar DeRozan	2.00	5.00
4 Hakeem Olajuwon	2.50	6.00
5 Chris Kaman	1.50	4.00
6 Dwyane Wade	3.00	8.00
7 Shaquille O'Neal	4.00	10.00
8 Scottie Pippen	4.00	10.00
9 Greg Monroe	1.50	4.00
10 Danny Manning	1.50	4.00
11 Gordon Hayward	2.00	5.00
12 Larry Bird	5.00	12.00
13 Karl Malone	2.50	6.00
14 Ty Lawson	1.25	3.00
15 George Hill	1.50	4.00
16 Derrick Favors	1.50	4.00
17 Kyle Korver	1.50	4.00
18 John Stockton	3.00	8.00
19 Wilson Chandler	1.50	4.00
20 Ben McLemore	1.25	3.00
21 Jimmy Butler	2.00	5.00
22 Serge Ibaka	1.50	4.00
23 Jonas Valanciunas	1.50	4.00
24 Monta Ellis	1.50	4.00
25 Carl Landry	1.25	3.00
26 Kemba Walker	2.00	5.00
27 Kevin Durant	5.00	12.00
28 Gary Payton	2.00	5.00
29 Dirk Nowitzki	2.50	6.00
30 Chris Mullin	2.00	5.00
31 Paul Pierce	2.00	5.00
32 Kobe Bryant	8.00	20.00
33 Kawhi Leonard	3.00	8.00
34 Chris Bosh	2.00	5.00
35 Andre Iguodala	1.50	4.00
36 Robert Parish	2.00	5.00
37 John Wall	2.50	6.00
38 Tony Parker	2.00	5.00
39 LeBron James	8.00	20.00
40 Stephen Curry	10.00	25.00
41 Jeff Green	1.50	4.00
42 Bradley Beal	2.00	5.00
43 Kyle Lowry	1.50	4.00
44 Paul Millsap	2.00	5.00
45 Clyde Drexler	2.50	6.00

2014-15 Donruss Jersey Kings

*PRIME: 1.5X TO 4X BASE HI

Card	Low	High
1 Kobe Bryant	8.00	20.00
2 Kyrie Irving	4.00	10.00
3 Carmelo Anthony	2.50	6.00
4 LeBron James	8.00	20.00
5 Rajon Rondo	2.00	5.00
6 Dirk Nowitzki	2.50	6.00
7 Tim Duncan	3.00	8.00
10 Michael Carter-Williams	1.25	3.00
12 DeMar DeRozan	2.00	5.00
13 LaMarcus Aldridge	2.00	5.00
14 Al Jefferson	1.50	4.00
15 Marc Gasol	2.00	5.00
16 Kevin Garnett	3.00	8.00
18 Damian Lillard	4.00	10.00
19 Stephen Curry	12.00	30.00
21 Blake Griffin	2.00	5.00
22 Eric Bledsoe	1.50	4.00
23 Anthony Davis	4.00	10.00
25 Kenneth Faried	1.50	4.00
26 Kawhi Leonard	3.00	8.00

2014-15 Donruss Production Line Assists

RANDOM INSERTS IN PACKS
*PURPLE: .5X TO 1.2X BASE HI
*BLUE: .6X TO 1.5X BASE HI
*SILVER: .8X TO 2X BASE HI
*CAREER: 1X TO 2.5X BASE HI
*SEASON: 1X TO 2.5X BASE HI
*SWIRLORAMA: 1X TO 2.5X BASE HI

Card	Low	High
1 Chris Paul	1.00	2.50
2 Kendall Marshall	.60	1.50
3 John Wall	1.00	2.50
4 Ty Lawson	.50	1.25
5 Ricky Rubio	.75	2.00
6 Stephen Curry	3.00	8.00
7 Brandon Jennings	.50	1.25
8 Kyle Lowry	.60	1.50
9 Jameer Nelson	.50	1.25
10 Jeff Teague	.60	1.50

2014-15 Donruss Production Line Rebounds

RANDOM INSERTS IN PACKS
*PURPLE: .5X TO 1.2X BASE HI
*BLUE: .6X TO 1.5X BASE HI
*SILVER: .8X TO 2X BASE HI
*CAREER: 1X TO 2.5X BASE HI
*SEASON: 1X TO 2.5X BASE HI
*SWIRLORAMA: .8X TO 2X BASE HI

Card	Low	High
1 DeAndre Jordan	.75	2.00
2 Andre Drummond	.75	2.00
3 Kevin Love	.75	2.00
4 Dwight Howard	.60	1.50
5 DeMarcus Cousins	.75	2.00
6 Joakim Noah	.60	1.50
7 LaMarcus Aldridge	.75	2.00
8 Al Jefferson	.60	1.50
9 Zach Randolph	.60	1.50
10 Anthony Davis	1.50	4.00

2014-15 Donruss Production Line Scoring

RANDOM INSERTS IN PACKS
*PURPLE: .5X TO 1.2X BASE HI
*BLUE: .6X TO 1.5X BASE HI
*SILVER: .8X TO 2X BASE HI
*SWIRLORAMA: .5X TO 1.2X BASE HI

Card	Low	High
1 Kevin Durant	2.00	5.00
2 Carmelo Anthony	1.00	2.50
3 LeBron James	3.00	8.00
4 Kevin Love	.75	2.00
5 James Harden	1.25	3.00
6 Blake Griffin	.75	2.00
7 Stephen Curry	3.00	8.00
8 LaMarcus Aldridge	.75	2.00
9 DeMarcus Cousins	.75	2.00
10 DeMar DeRozan	.75	2.00

2014-15 Donruss Production Line Scoring Stat Line Career

*CAREER: 1X TO 2.5X BASE HI
RANDOM INSERTS IN PACKS
STATED PRINT RUN B/WN 445-528 COPIES PER

Card	Low	High
3 LeBron James/497	4.00	10.00

2014-15 Donruss Production Line Scoring Stat Line Season
*SEASON: 1X TO 2.5X BASE HI
RANDOM INSERTS IN PACKS
STATED PRINT RUN B/WN 227-320 COPIES PER
1 Kevin Durant/320 3.00 8.00

2014-15 Donruss Rated Rookie Signature Patches
RANDOM INSERTS IN PACKS
1 Aaron Gordon 10.00 25.00
2 Adreian Payne 5.00 12.00
3 Andrew Wiggins 60.00 150.00
4 Bruno Caboclo 5.00 12.00
5 C.J. Wilcox 4.00 10.00
6 Cleanthony Early 4.00 10.00
7 Cory Jefferson 4.00 10.00
8 Damien Inglis 6.00 15.00
11 Gary Harris 6.00 15.00
12 Glenn Robinson III 4.00 10.00
13 Jabari Parker 30.00 80.00
14 James Young 4.00 10.00
15 Jarnell Stokes 4.00 10.00
16 Jerami Grant 4.00 10.00
17 Joe Harris 4.00 10.00
18 Joel Embiid 25.00 60.00
19 Johnny O'Bryant 4.00 10.00
20 Jordan Adams 4.00 10.00
21 Julius Randle 10.00 25.00
22 K.J. McDaniels 5.00 12.00
23 Kyle Anderson 6.00 15.00
24 Marcus Smart 6.00 15.00
25 Markel Brown 4.00 10.00
26 Mitch McGary 4.00 10.00
27 Nik Stauskas 5.00 12.00
28 Noah Vonleh 5.00 12.00
29 P.J. Hairston 4.00 10.00
30 Rodney Hood 6.00 15.00
31 Russ Smith 4.00 10.00
32 Shabazz Napier 5.00 12.00
33 Spencer Dinwiddie 5.00 12.00
34 James Ennis 4.00 10.00
35 T.J. Warren 6.00 15.00
36 Tyler Ennis 4.00 10.00
37 Zach LaVine 15.00 40.00

2014-15 Donruss Rookie Autographs
RANDOM INSERTS IN PACKS
STATED PRINT RUN B/WN 99-199 COPIES PER
1 Devyn Marble/199 3.00 8.00
2 Elfrid Payton/149 5.00 12.00
3 Andrew Wiggins/99 75.00 200.00
4 Jabari Parker/99 20.00 50.00
5 Joel Embiid/99 50.00 120.00
6 James Ennis/199 3.00 8.00
7 K.J. McDaniels/199 4.00 10.00
8 Jerami Grant/199 3.00 8.00
9 Kyle Anderson/199 5.00 12.00
10 Glenn Robinson III/149 3.00 8.00
11 Jordan Adams/199 3.00 8.00
12 Erick Green/199 3.00 8.00
13 Dwight Powell/199 3.00 8.00
14 Joe Harris/199 3.00 8.00
15 Marcus Smart/99 5.00 12.00
16 Alex Kirk/199 3.00 8.00
17 James Young/149 3.00 8.00
18 Markel Brown/199 3.00 8.00
19 Lucas Nogueira/199 3.00 8.00
20 Russ Smith/199 3.00 8.00
21 Damjan Rudez/199 3.00 8.00
22 Doug McDermott/149 5.00 12.00
23 T.J. Warren/149 5.00 12.00
24 Aaron Gordon/99 8.00 20.00
25 Spencer Dinwiddie/199 4.00 10.00
26 Jordan Clarkson/199 12.00 30.00
27 P.J. Hairston/199 3.00 8.00
28 Zach LaVine/149 15.00 40.00
29 Jusuf Nurkic/149 6.00 15.00
30 Gary Harris/149 5.00 12.00
31 Shabazz Napier/149 4.00 10.00
32 Mitch McGary/199 3.00 8.00
33 Rodney Hood/199 5.00 12.00

2014-15 Donruss Rookie Autographs Die-Cuts
*DIE CUTS: .6X TO 1.5X BASE HI
RANDOM INSERTS IN PACKS
STATED PRINT RUN 49 SER.#'d SETS

2014-15 Donruss Scoring Kings
*PURPLE: .8X TO 2X BASE HI
*BLUE: 1X TO 2.5X BASE HI
*SILVER: 1.25X TO 3X BASE HI
1 Kevin Durant 1.50 4.00
2 Kobe Bryant 2.50 6.00
3 Dwyane Wade 1.00 2.50
4 Allen Iverson .75 2.00
5 Kevin Garnett 1.00 2.50
6 Paul Pierce .60 1.50
7 James Harden 1.00 2.50
8 Shaquille O'Neal 1.25 3.00
9 David Robinson 1.00 2.50
10 Alex English .50 1.25
11 Adrian Dantley .50 1.25
12 George Gervin .60 1.50
13 Pete Maravich 1.00 2.50
14 Bob McAdoo .50 1.25
15 Kareem Abdul-Jabbar 1.00 2.50
16 Elvin Hayes .60 1.50
17 Rick Barry .50 1.25
18 Karl Malone .75 2.00
19 Tracy McGrady .60 1.50
20 LeBron James 2.50 6.00
21 Vince Carter .75 2.00
22 Dominique Wilkins .75 2.00
23 Dirk Nowitzki .75 2.00
24 Carmelo Anthony .75 2.00
25 Kiki Vandeweghe .50 1.25
26 Hakeem Olajuwon .75 2.00
27 Patrick Ewing .75 2.00
28 Moses Malone .60 1.50
29 Tim Duncan .75 2.00
30 Mitch Richmond .60 1.50
31 Larry Bird 2.00 5.00
32 Julius Erving 1.00 2.50
33 Chris Mullin .60 1.50
34 Bernard King .50 1.25
35 Clyde Drexler .60 1.50
36 World B. Free .50 1.25
37 Dale Ellis .40 1.00
38 Blake Griffin .60 1.50
39 Stephen Curry 2.50 6.00
40 Oscar Robertson .75 2.00
41 Wilt Chamberlain 1.25 3.00
42 Bob Pettit .60 1.50
43 Mark Aguirre .50 1.25
44 Glen Rice .50 1.25
45 Amar'e Stoudemire .60 1.50
46 John Havlicek .75 2.00
47 David Thompson .50 1.25
48 Jerry West .75 2.00
49 Walt Bellamy .50 1.25
50 Gary Payton .60 1.50

2014-15 Donruss Scoring Kings Stat Line Career
*CAREER: 1X TO 2.5X BASE HI
RANDOM INSERTS IN PACKS
STATED PRINT RUN B/WN 157-303 COPIES PER
1 Kevin Durant/274 3.00 8.00
2 Kobe Bryant/254 4.00 10.00
10 Alex English/215 3.00 8.00
20 LeBron James/275 4.00 10.00
31 Larry Bird/243 4.00 10.00

2014-15 Donruss Scoring Kings Stat Line Season
*SEASON: 1X TO 2.5X BASE HI
RANDOM INSERTS IN PACKS
STATED PRINT RUN B/WN 25-302 COPIES PER
8 Shaquille O'Neal/61 5.00 12.00
24 Carmelo Anthony/62 5.00 12.00

2014-15 Donruss Signature Stars
RANDOM INSERTS IN PACKS
STATED PRINT RUN 40 SER.#'d SETS
2 Jabari Parker 25.00 60.00
3 Joel Embiid 30.00 80.00
4 Dante Exum 8.00 20.00
5 Grant Hill 15.00 40.00
6 Allen Iverson 60.00 150.00
7 Chris Webber 60.00 150.00
11 Kevin Durant 60.00 150.00
12 Blake Griffin 8.00 20.00
14 Shaquille O'Neal 75.00 150.00
15 Magic Johnson 20.00 50.00
16 Bill Russell 50.00 120.00
17 Karl Malone 20.00 50.00
18 David Robinson 15.00 40.00
19 Jerry West 20.00 50.00
20 Dwight Howard 6.00 15.00
21 Yao Ming 30.00 80.00
23 Dwyane Wade 20.00 50.00
25 Bradley Beal 8.00 20.00
27 Steve Nash 30.00 80.00
28 Kevin Love 15.00 40.00
31 Chris Bosh 8.00 20.00
33 Elfrid Payton 20.00 50.00

2014-15 Donruss The Rookies
RANDOM INSERTS IN PACKS
*ARTIST PROOFS: 1X TO 2.5X BASE HI
1 Andrew Wiggins 4.00 10.00
2 Jabari Parker 1.00 2.50
3 Joel Embiid 2.00 5.00
4 Dante Exum .60 1.50
5 Marcus Smart .60 1.50
6 Julius Randle 1.00 2.50
7 Zach LaVine 1.00 2.50
8 Aaron Gordon 1.00 2.50
9 Elfrid Payton .60 1.50
10 Doug McDermott .60 1.50
11 James Young .40 1.00
12 Nik Stauskas .50 1.25
13 Shabazz Napier .50 1.25
14 Noah Vonleh .50 1.25
15 T.J. Warren .60 1.50
16 Glenn Robinson III .40 1.00
17 Rodney Hood .60 1.50
18 Gary Harris .60 1.50
19 Cleanthony Early .40 1.00
20 Mitch McGary .40 1.00
21 Kyle Anderson .60 1.50
22 Bruno Caboclo .50 1.25
23 Tyler Ennis .40 1.00
24 Russ Smith .40 1.00
25 Jarnell Stokes .40 1.00
26 Adreian Payne .50 1.25
27 James Ennis .40 1.00
28 Spencer Dinwiddie .50 1.25
29 C.J. Wilcox .40 1.00
30 K.J. McDaniels .50 1.25

2014-15 Donruss The Rookies Press Proofs Blue
*BLUE: .8X TO 2X BASE HI
RANDOM INSERTS IN PACKS
STATED PRINT RUN 99 SER.#'d SETS
1 Andrew Wiggins 15.00 40.00

2014-15 Donruss The Rookies Press Proofs Purple
*PURPLE: .6X TO 1.5X BASE HI
RANDOM INSERTS IN PACKS
STATED PRINT RUN 199 SER.#'d SETS
1 Andrew Wiggins 10.00 25.00

2014-15 Donruss The Rookies Press Proofs Silver
*SILVER: 2X TO 5X BASE HI
RANDOM INSERTS IN PACKS
STATED PRINT RUN 25 SER.#'d SETS
4 Dante Exum 5.00 12.00
27 James Ennis 6.00 15.00

2014-15 Donruss The Rookies Swirlorama
*SWIRLORAMA: 1X TO 2.5X BASE HI
RANDOM INSERTS IN PACKS
1 Andrew Wiggins 15.00 40.00

2014-15 Donruss Timeless Treasures Jersey Autographs
RANDOM INSERTS IN PACKS
STATED PRINT RUN 99 SER.#'d SETS
2 Kevin Durant 50.00 120.00
3 Kyrie Irving 40.00 100.00
5 Stephen Curry 60.00 150.00
6 Andrew Wiggins 150.00 250.00
8 Dante Exum 15.00 40.00
9 Marcus Smart 15.00 40.00
10 Julius Randle 20.00 50.00

2014-15 Donruss Timeless Treasures Jersey Autographs Prime
*PRIME: .6X TO 1.5X BASE HI
RANDOM INSERTS IN PACKS
STATED PRINT RUN B/WN 15-25 COPIES PER
5 Stephen Curry/25 100.00 200.00
7 Jabari Parker/25 75.00 150.00

2015-16 Donruss
COMPLETE SET (250) 50.00 120.00
COMP.SET w/o RCs (200) 12.00 30.00
1 Gorgui Dieng .15 .40
2 Chris Paul .30 .75
3 Wesley Matthews .15 .40
4 Darren Collison .20 .50
5 Vince Carter .30 .75
6 Jodie Meeks .20 .50
7 Tiago Splitter .20 .50
8 David Lee .15 .40
9 Tobias Harris .20 .50
10 Hollis Thompson .15 .40
11 Serge Ibaka .20 .50
12 Paul Pierce .25 .60
13 Devin Harris .15 .40
14 Rajon Rondo .25 .60
15 Anthony Davis .50 1.25
16 Reggie Jackson .20 .50
17 Paul Millsap .25 .60
18 Tyler Zeller .20 .50
19 Nikola Vucevic .20 .50
20 Nik Stauskas .15 .40
21 Dion Waiters .20 .50
22 Lance Stephenson .20 .50
23 Deron Williams .20 .50
24 Ben McLemore .20 .50
25 Ryan Anderson .20 .50
26 Brandon Jennings .15 .40
27 Cody Zeller .15 .40
28 Avery Bradley .20 .50
29 Nene .20 .50
30 Tony Wroten .15 .40
31 Russell Westbrook .60 1.50
32 DeAndre Jordan .25 .60
33 J.J. Barea .20 .50
34 Marco Belinelli .15 .40
35 Omer Asik .20 .50
36 Marcus Morris .15 .40
37 Nicolas Batum .20 .50
38 Marcus Smart .20 .50
39 Bradley Beal .25 .60
40 Isaiah Canaan .20 .50
41 Kevin Durant .60 1.50
42 Brandon Bass .20 .50
43 Chandler Parsons .20 .50
44 Pau Gasol .25 .60
45 Quincy Pondexter .15 .40
46 Andre Drummond .25 .60
47 Jeremy Lamb .15 .40
48 Evan Turner .20 .50
49 John Wall .30 .75
50 Patrick Patterson .15 .40
51 Enes Kanter .15 .40
52 Julius Randle .25 .60
53 Zaza Pachulia .15 .40
54 Taj Gibson .20 .50
55 Tyreke Evans .15 .40
56 Jordan Hill .15 .40
57 Kemba Walker .25 .60
58 Isaiah Thomas .25 .60
59 Otto Porter Jr. .20 .50
60 Luis Scola .20 .50
61 Steven Adams .20 .50
62 Kobe Bryant 1.00 2.50
63 Terrence Jones .20 .50
64 Nikola Mirotic .20 .50
65 Jrue Holiday .20 .50
66 Monta Ellis .20 .50
67 Jeremy Lin .25 .60
68 Jarrett Jack .20 .50
69 Marcin Gortat .20 .50
70 DeMar DeRozan .25 .60
71 Gerald Henderson .15 .40
72 Jordan Clarkson .25 .60
73 James Harden .40 1.00
74 Jimmy Butler .25 .60
75 Eric Gordon .15 .40
76 George Hill .20 .50
77 Michael Kidd-Gilchrist .20 .50
78 Bojan Bogdanovic .15 .40
79 Jared Dudley .15 .40
80 Terrence Ross .20 .50
81 Damian Lillard .50 1.25
82 Nick Young .20 .50
83 Ty Lawson .20 .50
84 Derrick Rose .30 .75
85 Tony Parker .25 .60
86 Rodney Stuckey .15 .40
87 Al Jefferson .20 .50
88 Thaddeus Young .15 .40
89 Kenneth Faried .20 .50
90 Kyle Lowry .30 .75
91 Al-Farouq Aminu .15 .40
92 Roy Hibbert .20 .50
93 Trevor Ariza .15 .40
94 Mike Dunleavy .15 .40
95 Kawhi Leonard .40 1.00
96 Paul George .30 .75
97 Chris Bosh .25 .60
98 Brook Lopez .20 .50
99 Randy Foye .15 .40
100 DeMarre Carroll .15 .40
101 Mason Plumlee .15 .40
102 Markieff Morris .15 .40
103 Corey Brewer .15 .40
104 Joakim Noah .20 .50
105 Tim Duncan .40 1.00
106 Solomon Hill .15 .40
107 Dwyane Wade .40 1.00
108 Joe Johnson .20 .50
109 Gary Harris .20 .50
110 Jonas Valanciunas .20 .50
111 Noah Vonleh .20 .50
112 Mirza Teletovic .15 .40
113 Dwight Howard .25 .60
114 Kevin Love .25 .60
115 LaMarcus Aldridge .25 .60
116 Chase Budinger .15 .40
117 Gerald Green .20 .50
118 Andrea Bargnani .20 .50
119 Jameer Nelson .20 .50
120 Stephen Curry 1.00 2.50
121 Ed Davis .15 .40
122 Eric Bledsoe .20 .50
123 Donatas Motiejunas .15 .40
124 Iman Shumpert .20 .50
125 David West .25 .60
126 Jabari Parker .30 .75
127 Goran Dragic .20 .50
128 Arron Afflalo .15 .40
129 Danilo Gallinari .20 .50
130 Klay Thompson .30 .75
131 Alec Burks .15 .40
132 Brandon Knight .20 .50
133 Mike Conley .20 .50
134 Kyrie Irving .50 1.25
135 Danny Green .20 .50
136 Khris Middleton .20 .50
137 Mario Chalmers .15 .40
138 Jose Calderon .15 .40
139 Wilson Chandler .20 .50
140 Draymond Green .30 .75
141 Trey Burke .15 .40
142 P.J. Tucker .15 .40
143 Tony Allen .20 .50
144 LeBron James 1.00 2.50
145 Manu Ginobili .25 .60
146 O.J. Mayo .15 .40
147 Luol Deng .20 .50
148 Langston Galloway .15 .40
149 Jusuf Nurkic .15 .40
150 Andrew Bogut .20 .50
151 Gordon Hayward .25 .60
152 Tyson Chandler .20 .50
153 Jeff Green .20 .50
154 Timofey Mozgov .15 .40
155 Kyle Korver .20 .50
156 Michael Carter-Williams .15 .40
157 Hassan Whiteside .25 .60
158 Carmelo Anthony .30 .75
159 Kevin Garnett .40 1.00
160 Harrison Barnes .20 .50
161 Rudy Gobert .25 .60
162 Alex Len .15 .40
163 Marc Gasol .25 .60
164 Mo Williams .20 .50
165 Tim Hardaway Jr. .15 .40
166 Greivis Vasquez .20 .50
167 Channing Frye .20 .50
168 Robin Lopez .15 .40
169 Kevin Martin .20 .50
170 Andre Iguodala .20 .50
171 Derrick Favors .20 .50
172 DeMarcus Cousins .25 .60
173 Zach Randolph .20 .50
174 Anderson Varejao .15 .40
175 Jeff Teague .20 .50
176 Giannis Antetokounmpo .50 1.25
177 Aaron Gordon .20 .50
178 Derrick Williams .15 .40
179 Zach LaVine .25 .60
180 Blake Griffin .25 .60
181 Rodney Hood .20 .50
182 Kosta Koufos .15 .40
183 Brandan Wright .15 .40
184 Ersan Ilyasova .15 .40
185 Thabo Sefolosha .15 .40
186 Greg Monroe .20 .50
187 Victor Oladipo .20 .50
188 Nerlens Noel .20 .50
189 Ricky Rubio .25 .60
190 Josh Smith .20 .50
191 Dante Exum .20 .50
192 Rudy Gay .25 .60
193 Courtney Lee .20 .50
194 Kentavious Caldwell-Pope .20 .50
195 Al Horford .20 .50
196 Dirk Nowitzki .30 .75
197 Elfrid Payton .20 .50
198 Robert Covington .15 .40
199 Andrew Wiggins .40 1.00
200 J.J. Redick .25 .60
201 Anthony Brown RC .30 .75
202 Myles Turner RC .50 1.25
203 Joe Young RC .40 1.00
204 Terry Rozier RC .40 1.00
205 Nemanja Bjelica RC .40 1.00
206 Justin Anderson RC .40 1.00
207 Branden Dawson RC .30 .75
208 Karl-Anthony Towns RC 2.50 6.00
209 Larry Nance Jr. RC .50 1.25
210 Willie Cauley-Stein RC .50 1.25
211 Rakeem Christmas RC .30 .75
212 Trey Lyles RC .50 1.25
213 T.J. McConnell RC .40 1.00
214 Rashad Vaughn RC .30 .75
215 Nikola Jokic RC .60 1.50
216 Bobby Portis RC .50 1.25
217 Aaron Harrison RC .40 1.00
218 D'Angelo Russell RC 1.25 3.00
219 R.J. Hunter RC .30 .75
220 Justise Winslow RC .50 1.25
221 Emmanuel Mudiay RC .60 1.50
222 Richaun Holmes RC .40 1.00
223 Devin Booker RC 1.50 4.00
224 Boban Marjanovic RC .40 1.00
225 Sam Dekker RC .40 1.00
226 Raul Neto RC .30 .75
227 Rondae Hollis-Jefferson RC .40 1.00
228 Jonathon Simmons RC .50 1.25
229 Jahlil Okafor RC .60 1.50
230 Chris McCullough RC .30 .75
231 Stanley Johnson RC .40 1.00
232 Pat Connaughton RC .30 .75
233 Cameron Payne RC .40 1.00
234 Walter Tavares RC .30 .75
235 Jerian Grant RC .30 .75
236 Josh Richardson RC .50 1.25
237 Tyus Jones RC .50 1.25
238 Christian Wood RC .30 .75
239 Kristaps Porzingis RC 1.25 3.00
240 Montrezl Harrell RC .40 1.00
241 Frank Kaminsky RC .50 1.25
242 Marcelo Huertas RC .40 1.00
243 Kelly Oubre Jr. RC .40 1.00
244 Kevon Looney RC .40 1.00
245 Delon Wright RC .40 1.00
246 Cliff Alexander RC .30 .75
247 Jarell Martin RC .40 1.00
248 Josh Huestis RC .30 .75
249 Mario Hezonja RC .40 1.00
250 Jordan Mickey RC .30 .75

2015-16 Donruss Assists
*ASSIST p/r 100-102: 1.5X TO 4X BASIC
*ASSIST p/r 51-96: 2X TO 5X BASIC
*ASSIST p/r 26-49: 2.5X TO 6X BASIC
*ASSIST p/r 20-25: 3X TO 8X BASIC
RANDOM INSERTS IN PACKS
PRINT RUNS B/WN 20-102 COPIES PER

2015-16 Donruss Holo
*HOLO: 1.2X TO 3X BASIC
*HOLO RC: .6X TO 1.5X BASIC RC
RANDOM INSERTS IN PACKS
STATED PRINT RUN 199 SER.#'d SETS

2015-16 Donruss Inspirations
*INSP p/r 50-99: 2X TO 5X BASIC
*INSP RC p/r 50-99: 1X TO 2.5X BASIC RC
*INSP p/r 45-46: 2.5X TO 6X BASIC
*INSP RC p/r 45-46: 1.2X TO 3X BASIC RC
RANDOM INSERTS IN PACKS
PRINT RUNS B/WN 12-99 COPIES PER
NO PRICING ON QTY 12
208 Karl-Anthony Towns/68 12.00 3.00

2015-16 Donruss Points
*POINTS p/r 126-281: 1.2X TO 3X BASIC
*POINTS p/r 101-124: 1.5X TO 4X BASIC
*POINTS p/r 52-99: 2X TO 5X BASIC
*POINTS p/r 33-48: 2.5X TO 6X BASIC
RANDOM INSERTS IN PACKS
PRINT RUNS B/WN 33-281 COPIES PER

2015-16 Donruss Rebounds
*RBNDS p/r 127-150: 1.2X TO 3X BASIC
*RBNDS p/r 100-118: 1.5X TO 4X BASIC
*RBNDS p/r 51-98: 2X TO 5X BASIC
*RBNDS p/r 26-49: 2.5X TO 6X BASIC
*RBNDS p/r 20-25: 3X TO 8X BASIC
RANDOM INSERTS IN PACKS
PRINT RUNS B/WN 12-150 COPIES PER
NO PRICING ON QTY 19 OR LESS

2015-16 Donruss Status
*RBNDS p/r 50-88: 2X TO 5X BASIC
*RBNDS RC p/r 50-88: 1X TO 2.5X BASIC RC
*RBNDS p/r 26-44: 2.5X TO 6X BASIC
*RBNDS RC p/r 26-44: 1.2X TO 3X BASIC RC
*RBNDS p/r 20-25: 3X TO 8X BASIC
*RBNDS RC p/r 20-25: 1.5X TO 4X BASIC RC
RANDOM INSERTS IN PACKS
PRINT RUNS B/WN 1-88 COPIES PER
NO PRICING ON QTY 18 OR LESS
62 Kobe Bryant/24 25.00 60.00
105 Tim Duncan/21 10.00 25.00
144 LeBron James/23 25.00 60.00
202 Myles Turner/33 6.00 15.00
208 Karl-Anthony Towns/32 15.00 40.00

2015-16 Donruss Back to the Future Materials
RANDOM INSERTS IN PACKS
PRINT RUNS B/WN 11-99 COPIES PER
NO PRICING ON QTY 11
*PRIME/21-25: 1X TO 2.5X BASIC
1 Aaron Brooks/99 2.00 5.00
2 Al Jefferson/99 2.50 6.00
3 Al-Farouq Aminu/75 2.50 6.00
4 Amar'e Stoudemire/99 2.50 6.00
5 Arron Afflalo/99 2.50 6.00
7 Boris Diaw/99 2.50 6.00
8 Brandon Bass/99 2.00 5.00
10 Caron Butler/99 2.50 6.00
11 Danilo Gallinari/99 2.50 6.00
13 Darren Collison/99 2.50 6.00
14 David West/99 3.00 8.00
15 Metta World Peace/99 3.00 8.00
16 Evan Turner/99 2.50 6.00
18 Isaiah Thomas/99 3.00 8.00
19 J.J. Redick/99 3.00 8.00
20 J.R. Smith/99 3.00 8.00
21 Jameer Nelson/99 2.00 5.00
22 Jason Richardson/99 3.00 8.00
23 Jeremy Lin/99 3.00 8.00
25 Jose Calderon/99 2.00 5.00
26 Jrue Holiday/99 2.00 5.00
27 Kevin Love/99 3.00 8.00
28 Kevin Martin/99 2.50 6.00
29 LeBron James/99 8.00 20.00
30 Luis Scola/99 2.50 6.00
31 Luol Deng/99 2.50 6.00
32 Matt Barnes/99 2.00 5.00
33 Monta Ellis/99 2.50 6.00
35 Nick Young/99 2.50 6.00
36 Nikola Vucevic/99 2.50 6.00
37 Pau Gasol/99 3.00 8.00
39 Paul Pierce/99 3.00 8.00
40 Rajon Rondo/99 3.00 8.00
41 Raymond Felton/99 2.50 6.00
42 Rudy Gay/99 3.00 8.00
43 Ryan Anderson/99 2.00 5.00
44 Spencer Hawes/99 2.00 5.00
45 Thaddeus Young/99 2.00 5.00
46 Tobias Harris/99 2.50 6.00
47 Tyson Chandler/99 2.50 6.00
48 Wilson Chandler/99 2.50 6.00
49 Chandler Parsons/99 2.50 6.00
50 Channing Frye/99 2.50 6.00

2015-16 Donruss Elite Dominator
RANDOM INSERTS IN PACKS
STATED PRINT RUN 999 SER.#'d SETS
1 Pau Gasol .60 1.50
2 James Harden 1.00 2.50
3 Tim Duncan 1.00 2.50
4 Vince Carter .75 2.00
5 Tony Parker .60 1.50
6 Kevin Garnett 1.00 2.50
7 Damian Lillard 1.25 3.00
8 Kobe Bryant 2.50 6.00
9 Chris Bosh .60 1.50
10 Kyrie Irving 1.25 3.00
11 Derrick Rose .75 2.00
12 Stephen Curry 2.50 6.00
13 Dwight Howard .50 1.25
14 Andrew Wiggins 1.00 2.50
15 Russell Westbrook 1.50 4.00
16 Dwyane Wade 1.00 2.50
17 Klay Thompson .75 2.00
18 Kevin Durant 1.50 4.00
19 Dirk Nowitzki .75 2.00
20 Anthony Davis 1.25 3.00
21 Carmelo Anthony .75 2.00
22 LeBron James 2.50 6.00
23 Manu Ginobili .60 1.50
24 Chris Paul .75 2.00
25 Jabari Parker .75 2.00

2015-16 Donruss Elite Dominator Signatures
RANDOM INSERTS IN PACKS
PRINT RUNS B/WN 25-49 COPIES PER
EXCHANGE DEADLINE 8/19/2017
EDSAD Anthony Davis/25 40.00 100.00
EDSAI Allen Iverson/25 50.00 120.00
EDSAW Andrew Wiggins/25 20.00 50.00
EDSBG Blake Griffin/25
EDSCP Chris Paul/25 30.00 80.00
EDSDR D'Angelo Russell/25 25.00 60.00
EDSDR Dennis Rodman/25 20.00 50.00
EDSDW Dwyane Wade/25 40.00 100.00
EDSDW Dominique Wilkins/49 10.00 25.00
EDSEM Emmanuel Mudiay/49 15.00 40.00
EDSGH Grant Hill/49 10.00 25.00
EDSGP Gary Payton/49 8.00 20.00
EDSJO Jahlil Okafor/25 30.00 80.00
EDSJP Jabari Parker/25 15.00 40.00
EDSJW John Wall/25 20.00 50.00
EDSKB Kobe Bryant/25 100.00 200.00
EDSKD Kevin Durant/25 EXCH 50.00 120.00
EDSKI Kyrie Irving/25 EXCH 30.00 80.00
EDSKP Kristaps Porzingis/49 60.00 150.00
EDSKT Karl-Anthony Towns/25 150.00 250.00
EDSLS Latrell Sprewell/25 12.00 30.00
EDSMG Manu Ginobili/25 30.00 80.00
EDSMH Mario Hezonja/49 10.00 25.00
EDSOR Oscar Robertson/25 30.00 80.00
EDSPG Paul George/25 25.00 60.00

2015-16 Donruss Elite Hall Dominator
RANDOM INSERTS IN PACKS
STATED PRINT RUN 999 SER.#'d SETS
1 Pete Maravich 1.00 2.50
2 Wilt Chamberlain 1.25 3.00
3 Larry Bird 1.50 4.00
4 Kareem Abdul-Jabbar 1.00 2.50
5 Hakeem Olajuwon .75 2.00
6 David Robinson .75 2.00
7 Gary Payton .60 1.50
8 Drazen Petrovic .60 1.50
9 Karl Malone .75 2.00
10 Alonzo Mourning .60 1.50
11 Dominique Wilkins .75 2.00
12 Magic Johnson 1.50 4.00
13 Scottie Pippen 1.25 3.00
14 Jerry West .75 2.00
15 Julius Erving 1.00 2.50
16 James Worthy .75 2.00
17 Oscar Robertson .75 2.00
18 Moses Malone .60 1.50
19 George Mikan 1.25 3.00
20 John Stockton 1.00 2.50
21 Elgin Baylor .60 1.50
22 Clyde Drexler .60 1.50
23 Dennis Rodman 1.25 3.00
24 Bill Russell 1.25 3.00
25 Patrick Ewing .75 2.00

2015-16 Donruss Elite Rookie Dominator
RANDOM INSERTS IN PACKS
STATED PRINT RUN 999 SER.#'d SETS
1 Bobby Portis .60 1.50
2 Rondae Hollis-Jefferson .60 1.50
3 Devin Booker 2.50 6.00
4 Emmanuel Mudiay .75 2.00
5 Terry Rozier .60 1.50
6 Justise Winslow .75 2.00
7 Jerian Grant .50 1.25
8 Karl-Anthony Towns 4.00 10.00
9 Jahlil Okafor 1.00 2.50
10 Mario Hezonja .60 1.50
11 Cameron Payne .60 1.50
12 Stanley Johnson .60 1.50
13 Rashad Vaughn .50 1.25
14 Myles Turner .75 2.00
15 Delon Wright .60 1.50
16 D'Angelo Russell 2.00 5.00
17 Kristaps Porzingis 2.00 5.00
18 Willie Cauley-Stein .75 2.00
19 Kelly Oubre Jr. .60 1.50
20 Frank Kaminsky .75 2.00
21 Sam Dekker .60 1.50
22 Tyus Jones .75 2.00
23 Trey Lyles .75 2.00
24 Justin Anderson .60 1.50
25 Larry Nance Jr. .75 2.00

2015-16 Donruss Innovative Ink
RANDOM INSERTS IN PACKS
EXCHANGE DEADLINE 8/19/2017
1 Aaron Gordon 4.00 10.00
2 Adreian Payne 3.00 8.00
3 Andrew Wiggins 15.00 40.00
4 Bruno Caboclo 3.00 8.00
5 C.J. Wilcox 3.00 8.00
6 Cleanthony Early 3.00 8.00
7 Cory Jefferson 3.00 8.00
8 Damien Inglis 3.00 8.00
9 Doug McDermott 4.00 10.00
10 Elfrid Payton 4.00 10.00
11 Gary Harris 4.00 10.00
12 Glenn Robinson III 3.00 8.00
13 Jabari Parker 12.00 30.00
14 James Young 3.00 8.00
15 Jarnell Stokes 3.00 8.00
16 Jerami Grant
17 Joe Harris 3.00 8.00
19 Johnny O'Bryant 3.00 8.00
20 Jordan Adams 3.00 8.00
21 Josh Huestis 3.00 8.00
22 Julius Randle 10.00 25.00
23 K.J. McDaniels 4.00 10.00
24 Kyle Anderson 3.00 8.00
25 Marcus Smart 4.00 10.00
26 Markel Brown
27 Mitch McGary 3.00 8.00
28 Nik Stauskas 3.00 8.00
29 Noah Vonleh 3.00 8.00
30 Rodney Hood 4.00 10.00
31 Russ Smith
32 Shabazz Napier 3.00 8.00
33 Spencer Dinwiddie 3.00 8.00
34 T.J. Warren 4.00 10.00
36 Tyler Ennis
37 Zach LaVine 10.00 25.00

2015-16 Donruss Newly Crowned Rookie Jerseys
RANDOM INSERTS IN PACKS
STATED PRINT RUN 149 SER.#'d SETS
*PRIME/25: .75X TO 2X BASIC
1 Jerian Grant 2.00 5.00
2 Emmanuel Mudiay 3.00 8.00
3 Bobby Portis 3.00 8.00
4 Justise Winslow 3.00 8.00
5 R.J. Hunter 2.00 5.00
6 Devin Booker 4.00 10.00
7 Jordan Mickey 2.00 5.00
8 Karl-Anthony Towns 10.00 25.00
9 Terry Rozier 2.50 6.00
10 Kristaps Porzingis 6.00 15.00
11 Delon Wright 2.50 6.00
12 Stanley Johnson 2.50 6.00
13 Rondae Hollis-Jefferson 2.50 6.00
14 Myles Turner 3.00 8.00
15 Chris McCullough 2.00 5.00
16 Cameron Payne 2.50 6.00
17 Anthony Brown 2.00 5.00
18 D'Angelo Russell 4.00 10.00
19 Joe Young 2.50 6.00
20 Mario Hezonja 2.50 6.00
21 Justin Anderson 2.50 6.00
22 Frank Kaminsky 3.00 8.00
23 Jarell Martin 2.50 6.00
24 Trey Lyles 3.00 8.00
25 Montrezl Harrell 2.50 6.00
26 Kelly Oubre Jr. 2.50 6.00
27 Rakeem Christmas 2.50 6.00
28 Jahlil Okafor 4.00 10.00
29 Sam Dekker 2.50 6.00
30 Willie Cauley-Stein 3.00 8.00

2015-16 Donruss Passing Kings
COMPLETE SET (30) 12.00 30.00
RANDOM INSERTS IN PACKS
*CAR p/r 105-112: 1X TO 2.5X BASIC
*CAR p/r 52-99: 1.2X TO 3X BASIC
1 Oscar Robertson .60 1.50
2 Russell Westbrook 1.25 3.00
3 John Wall .60 1.50
4 Mark Price .50 1.25
5 Rajon Rondo .50 1.25
6 Lenny Wilkens .50 1.25
7 Bob Cousy .75 2.00
8 Damon Stoudamire .40 1.00
9 Magic Johnson 1.25 3.00
10 Tony Parker .50 1.25
11 Isiah Thomas .50 1.25
12 LeBron James 2.00 5.00
13 Deron Williams .40 1.00
14 Gary Payton .50 1.25
15 Tim Hardaway .50 1.25
16 Jerry West .60 1.50
17 Nate Archibald .40 1.00
18 Damian Lillard 1.00 2.50
19 John Stockton .75 2.00
20 Tyreke Evans .30 .75
21 Jason Kidd .50 1.25
22 Stephen Curry 2.00 5.00
23 Steve Nash .50 1.25
24 Maurice Cheeks .30 .75
25 Muggsy Bogues .40 1.00
26 Nick Van Exel .50 1.25
27 Baron Davis .40 1.00
28 Ty Lawson .30 .75
29 Chris Paul .60 1.50
30 Kyle Lowry .40 1.00

2015-16 Donruss Promising Pros Jumbo Swatches
RANDOM INSERTS IN PACKS
STATED PRINT RUN 149 SER.#'d SETS
*PRIME/25: .75X TO 2X BASIC
1 Rakeem Christmas 2.00 5.00
2 Devin Booker 4.00 10.00
3 Kevon Looney 2.50 6.00
4 Karl-Anthony Towns 10.00 25.00
5 Terry Rozier 2.50 6.00
6 Kristaps Porzingis 5.00 12.00
7 Jerian Grant 2.00 5.00
8 Emmanuel Mudiay 3.00 8.00
9 Bobby Portis 3.00 8.00
10 Justise Winslow 3.00 8.00
11 Pat Connaughton 2.00 5.00
12 Cameron Payne 2.50 6.00
13 Josh Richardson 2.50 6.00
14 D'Angelo Russell 6.00 15.00
15 Jordan Mickey 2.00 5.00
16 Mario Hezonja 2.50 6.00
17 Delon Wright 2.50 6.00
18 Stanley Johnson 2.50 6.00
19 Rondae Hollis-Jefferson 2.50 6.00
20 Myles Turner 3.00 8.00
21 Joe Young 2.50 6.00
22 Kelly Oubre Jr. 2.50 6.00
23 Josh Huestis 2.00 5.00
24 Jahlil Okafor 6.00 15.00
25 Sam Dekker 2.50 6.00
26 Willie Cauley-Stein 3.00 8.00
27 Justin Anderson 2.50 6.00
28 Frank Kaminsky 3.00 8.00
29 Jarell Martin 2.50 6.00
30 Trey Lyles 3.00 8.00

2015-16 Donruss Rated Rookie Signature Patches
RANDOM INSERTS IN PACKS
EXCHANGE DEADLINE 8/19/2017
1 Anthony Brown 3.00 8.00
2 Myles Turner 12.00 30.00
3 Joe Young 4.00 10.00
4 Terry Rozier 4.00 10.00
5 Justin Anderson 4.00 10.00
6 Karl-Anthony Towns 60.00 150.00
7 Willie Cauley-Stein 12.00 30.00
8 Rakeem Christmas 3.00 8.00
9 Trey Lyles 5.00 12.00
11 Rashad Vaughn 3.00 8.00
12 Bobby Portis 5.00 12.00
13 D'Angelo Russell 25.00 60.00
14 R.J. Hunter 3.00 8.00
15 Justise Winslow 10.00 25.00
16 Emmanuel Mudiay 5.00 12.00
17 Richaun Holmes 4.00 10.00
18 Devin Booker 25.00 60.00
20 Sam Dekker 4.00 10.00
21 Rondae Hollis-Jefferson 4.00 10.00
22 Jahlil Okafor 20.00 50.00
23 Chris McCullough 3.00 8.00
24 Stanley Johnson 10.00 25.00
25 Pat Connaughton 3.00 8.00
26 Cameron Payne 4.00 10.00
27 Walter Tavares 3.00 8.00
28 Jerian Grant 3.00 8.00
29 Josh Richardson 5.00 12.00
30 Tyus Jones 5.00 12.00
31 Kristaps Porzingis 50.00 120.00
32 Montrezl Harrell 4.00 10.00
33 Frank Kaminsky 6.00 15.00
34 Kelly Oubre Jr. 4.00 10.00
35 Kevon Looney 8.00 20.00
36 Delon Wright 4.00 10.00
37 Jarell Martin 4.00 10.00
38 Josh Huestis 3.00 8.00
39 Jordan Mickey 3.00 8.00
40 Mario Hezonja 10.00 25.00

2015-16 Donruss Rebounding Kings
RANDOM INSERTS IN PACKS
*CAR p/r 127-229: .75X TO 2X BASIC
*CAR p/r 100-123: 1X TO 2.5X BASIC
*CAR p/r 84-98: 1.2X TO 3X BASIC
1 Kevin Love .50 1.25
2 Bill Laimbeer .40 1.00
3 Tim Duncan .75 2.00
4 Shawn Kemp .75 2.00
5 Wilt Chamberlain 1.00 2.50
6 Pau Gasol .50 1.25
7 Wes Unseld .50 1.25
8 Dikembe Mutombo .50 1.25
9 Dennis Rodman 1.00 2.50
10 Larry Bird 1.25 3.00
11 Kareem Abdul-Jabbar .75 2.00
12 Rony Seikaly .30 .75
13 Shaquille O'Neal 1.00 2.50
14 Zach Randolph .40 1.00
15 Bill Russell .75 2.00
16 DeAndre Jordan .50 1.25
17 Dave Cowens .50 1.25
18 Kevin Garnett .75 2.00
19 Dwight Howard .40 1.00
20 Patrick Ewing .60 1.50
21 Hakeem Olajuwon .60 1.50
22 Robert Parish .50 1.25
23 David Robinson .75 2.00
24 Joakim Noah .40 1.00
25 Nate Thurmond .40 1.00
26 DeMarcus Cousins .50 1.25
27 Elgin Baylor .50 1.25
28 Karl Malone .60 1.50
29 Moses Malone .50 1.25
30 Chris Webber .50 1.25

2015-16 Donruss Rookie Material Signatures
RANDOM INSERTS IN PACKS
PRINT RUNS B/WN 149 COPIES PER
EXCHANGE DEADLINE 8/19/2017
*PRIME/25: .6X TO 1.5X BASIC
1 Karl-Anthony Towns 75.00 200.00
2 D'Angelo Russell 30.00 80.00
3 Jahlil Okafor 20.00 50.00
4 Kristaps Porzingis 40.00 100.00
5 Mario Hezonja 8.00 20.00
6 Willie Cauley-Stein 6.00 15.00
7 Emmanuel Mudiay 10.00 25.00
8 Stanley Johnson 10.00 25.00
9 Frank Kaminsky 6.00 15.00
10 Justise Winslow 6.00 15.00
11 Myles Turner 10.00 25.00
12 Trey Lyles 6.00 15.00
13 Devin Booker 25.00 60.00
14 Cameron Payne 5.00 12.00
15 Kelly Oubre Jr. 5.00 12.00
16 Terry Rozier 5.00 12.00
17 Rashad Vaughn 4.00 10.00
18 Sam Dekker 4.00 10.00
19 Jerian Grant 4.00 10.00
20 Delon Wright 4.00 10.00
21 Justin Anderson 5.00 12.00
22 Bobby Portis 6.00 15.00
23 Rondae Hollis-Jefferson 5.00 12.00
24 Jarell Martin 5.00 12.00
25 R.J. Hunter 4.00 10.00
26 Chris McCullough 4.00 10.00
27 Montrezl Harrell 5.00 12.00
28 Jordan Mickey 4.00 10.00
29 Anthony Brown 4.00 10.00
30 Rakeem Christmas 4.00 10.00
31 Pat Connaughton 4.00 10.00
32 Joe Young 5.00 12.00
33 Kevon Looney 5.00 12.00

34 Josh Richardson 6.00 15.00
35 Walter Tavares 4.00 10.00

2015-16 Donruss Scoring Kings

RANDOM INSERTS IN PACKS
*CAR p/r 250-301: .6X TO 1.5X BASIC
*CAR p/r 176-248: .75X TO 2X BASIC
1 Jerry West .60 1.50
2 Hakeem Olajuwon .60 1.50
3 Carmelo Anthony .60 1.50
4 Rick Barry .40 1.00
5 Patrick Ewing .60 1.50
6 Clyde Drexler .60 1.50
7 Julius Erving .75 2.00
8 LaMarcus Aldridge .50 1.25
9 Wilt Chamberlain 1.00 2.50
10 Kyrie Irving 1.00 2.50
11 Allen Iverson .60 1.50
12 Russell Westbrook 1.25 3.00
13 George Gervin .50 1.25
14 John Havlicek .60 1.50
15 Moses Malone .50 1.25
16 Larry Bird 1.25 3.00
17 Dwyane Wade .75 2.00
18 Elgin Baylor .50 1.25
19 Chris Bosh .50 1.25
20 Anthony Davis 1.00 2.50
21 Oscar Robertson .60 1.50
22 David Robinson .75 2.00
23 Karl Malone .60 1.50
24 Paul Pierce .50 1.25
25 Adrian Dantley .40 1.00
26 Tim Duncan .75 2.00
27 Shaquille O'Neal 1.00 2.50
28 Chris Paul .60 1.50
29 LeBron James 2.00 5.00
30 John Wall .60 1.50
31 Kobe Bryant 2.00 5.00
32 Mitch Richmond .50 1.25
33 Dominique Wilkins .60 1.50
34 Chris Webber .50 1.25
35 Pete Maravich .75 2.00
36 Vince Carter .60 1.50
37 Dirk Nowitzki .60 1.50
38 Stephen Curry 2.00 5.00
39 Kevin Durant 1.25 3.00
40 James Harden .75 2.00

2015-16 Donruss Signature Series

RANDOM INSERTS IN PACKS
EXCHANGE DEADLINE 8/19/2017
1 Kobe Bryant 100.00 200.00
2 Dwyane Wade 30.00 80.00
3 Allen Iverson 40.00 100.00
4 Anthony Davis 40.00 100.00
5 Chris Paul
6 Kyrie Irving 20.00 50.00
7 Karl-Anthony Towns 60.00 150.00
8 D'Angelo Russell 20.00 50.00
9 Jahlil Okafor 6.00 15.00
10 Emmanuel Mudiay 4.00 10.00
11 Alex Len 2.50 6.00
12 Kristaps Porzingis 30.00 80.00
13 Mario Hezonja 8.00 20.00
14 Justise Winslow 4.00 10.00
15 Willie Cauley-Stein 4.00 10.00
16 Stanley Johnson 10.00 25.00
17 Frank Kaminsky 6.00 15.00
18 Devin Booker 25.00 60.00
19 Myles Turner 15.00 40.00
20 Trey Lyles 5.00 12.00
21 Scott Wedman 6.00 15.00
22 Sleepy Floyd
23 Mo Williams 3.00 8.00
24 Keith Van Horn 3.00 8.00
25 Michael Cage 2.50 6.00
26 James Jones 2.50 6.00
27 Micheal Ray Richardson 3.00 8.00
28 Jerian Grant
29 Phil Chenier 2.50 6.00
30 Tony Allen 2.50 6.00
31 Hubert Davis 2.50 6.00
32 Cameron Payne 3.00 8.00
33 Rashad Vaughn 2.50 6.00
34 E'Twaun Moore 5.00 12.00
35 Kelly Oubre Jr. 3.00 8.00
36 Terry Rozier 3.00 8.00
37 Sam Dekker 3.00 8.00
38 Damien Inglis 2.50 6.00
39 Donatas Motiejunas 2.50 6.00
40 JaKarr Sampson 2.50 6.00
41 Kyle O'Quinn 2.50 6.00
42 Robert Sacre 2.50 6.00
43 Josh Huestis 2.50 6.00
44 Ray McCallum 4.00 10.00
45 Dwight Powell 2.50 6.00
46 Brian Roberts 2.50 6.00
47 Isaiah Canaan 3.00 8.00
48 Andre Roberson 2.50 6.00
49 Johnny O'Bryant 2.50 6.00
50 Jarnell Stokes 2.50 6.00
51 Solomon Hill 2.50 6.00
52 Lamar Patterson 2.50 6.00
53 Cameron Bairstow 2.50 6.00
54 Mike Muscala 2.50 6.00
55 Boban Marjanovic 3.00 8.00
56 Nikola Jokic 15.00 40.00
57 Robert Covington 2.50 6.00
58 James Ennis
59 Norman Powell 3.00 8.00
60 Ryan Kelly 2.50 6.00
61 James Michael McAdoo 2.50 6.00
62 Hollis Thompson 2.50 6.00
63 Seth Curry 5.00 12.00

2015-16 Donruss Studio Series Rookie Jerseys

RANDOM INSERTS IN PACKS
*PRIME/25: .75X TO 2X BASIC
1 Mario Hezonja 2.50 6.00
2 Myles Turner 3.00 8.00
3 Emmanuel Mudiay 3.00 8.00
4 Devin Booker 5.00 12.00
5 Frank Kaminsky 3.00 8.00
6 Kelly Oubre Jr. 2.50 6.00
7 Karl-Anthony Towns 6.00 15.00
8 Montrezl Harrell 2.50 6.00
9 Jahlil Okafor 5.00 12.00
10 Jerian Grant 2.00 5.00
11 Willie Cauley-Stein 3.00 8.00
12 Trey Lyles 3.00 8.00
13 Stanley Johnson 2.50 6.00
14 Cameron Payne 2.50 6.00
15 Justise Winslow 3.00 8.00
16 Terry Rozier 2.50 6.00
17 D'Angelo Russell 5.00 12.00
18 Sam Dekker 2.50 6.00
19 Kristaps Porzingis 6.00 15.00
20 Justin Anderson 2.50 6.00

2015-16 Donruss Superstar Swatches

RANDOM INSERTS IN PACKS
PRINT RUNS B/WN 49-149 COPIES PER
*PRIME/25: .75X TO 2X BASIC
1 Dwight Howard/149 2.50 6.00
2 Anthony Davis/149 5.00 12.00
3 Blake Griffin/149 3.00 8.00
4 Tony Parker/149 3.00 8.00
5 Dwyane Wade/149 5.00 12.00
6 Kawhi Leonard/149 5.00 12.00
7 Carmelo Anthony/149 4.00 10.00
8 Kobe Bryant/149 10.00 25.00
9 Derrick Rose/149 4.00 10.00
10 Kyrie Irving/149 5.00 12.00
11 Chris Paul/149 4.00 10.00
12 Damian Lillard/149 5.00 12.00
13 Russell Westbrook/149 8.00 20.00
14 Tim Duncan/149 5.00 12.00
15 John Wall/149 4.00 10.00
16 Chris Bosh/149 3.00 8.00
17 Paul George/49 4.00 10.00
18 Kevin Durant/49 6.00 15.00
19 James Harden/149 5.00 12.00
20 Stephen Curry/149 12.00 30.00

2015-16 Donruss Swatch Kings

RANDOM INSERTS IN PACKS
STATED PRINT RUN 149 SER.#'d SETS
*PRIME/25: .75X TO 2X BASIC
1 Kenneth Faried 2.50 6.00
2 Cody Zeller 2.00 5.00
3 Mario Chalmers 2.50 6.00
4 David West 3.00 8.00
5 Reggie Jackson 2.50 6.00
6 Doug McDermott 2.50 6.00
7 Tobias Harris 2.50 6.00
8 Aaron Gordon 2.50 6.00
9 J.J. Hickson 2.00 5.00
10 Bojan Bogdanovic 2.00 5.00
11 Kentavious Caldwell-Pope 2.50 6.00
12 Danilo Gallinari 2.50 6.00
13 Markieff Morris 2.00 5.00
14 DeMar DeRozan 3.00 8.00
15 Robert Sacre 2.00 5.00
16 Eric Bledsoe 2.50 6.00
17 Trey Burke 2.00 5.00
18 Alec Burks 2.00 5.00
19 Jeff Teague 2.50 6.00
20 Boris Diaw 2.50 6.00
21 Kyle Korver 2.50 6.00
22 Danny Green 2.50 6.00
23 Mike Conley 3.00 8.00
24 Dennis Schroder 2.50 6.00
25 Serge Ibaka 2.50 6.00
26 Eric Gordon 2.50 6.00
27 Tristan Thompson 2.50 6.00
28 Alex Len 2.00 5.00
29 Jimmy Butler 3.00 8.00
30 Bradley Beal 3.00 8.00
31 Manu Ginobili 3.00 8.00
32 Dante Exum 2.50 6.00
33 Mo Williams 2.50 6.00
34 Derrick Favors 2.50 6.00
35 Steven Adams 2.50 6.00
36 George Hill 2.50 6.00
37 Victor Oladipo 2.50 6.00
38 Anderson Varejao 2.00 5.00
39 John Henson 2.50 6.00
40 Brandon Jennings 2.00 5.00
41 Marc Gasol 3.00 8.00
42 Darren Collison 2.50 6.00
43 Paul Millsap 3.00 8.00
44 Donatas Motiejunas 2.00 5.00
45 Terrence Ross 2.50 6.00
46 Gordon Hayward 3.00 8.00
47 Zach Randolph 2.50 6.00
48 Andre Drummond 3.00 8.00
49 Jonas Valanciunas 2.50 6.00
50 C.J. McCollum 3.00 8.00

2015-16 Donruss The Rookies

RANDOM INSERTS IN PACKS
*HOLO/199: .75X TO 2X BASIC
*INSP/56-99: 1.2X TO 3X BASIC
*INSP/45: 1.5X TO 4X BASIC
*STATUS/55-88: 1.2X TO 3X BASIC
*STATUS/28-44: 1.5X TO 4X BASIC
*STATUS/20-25: 2X TO 5X BASIC
1 Justin Anderson .40 1.00
2 Josh Richardson .50 1.25
3 Rakeem Christmas .30 .75
4 Frank Kaminsky .50 1.25
5 Bobby Portis .50 1.25
6 Cliff Alexander .30 .75
7 Emmanuel Mudiay .50 1.25
8 Raul Neto .30 .75
9 Anthony Brown .30 .75
10 Stanley Johnson .40 1.00
11 Branden Dawson .30 .75
12 Tyus Jones .50 1.25
13 Trey Lyles .50 1.25
14 T.J. McConnell .40 1.00
15 Aaron Harrison .40 1.00
16 Jarell Martin .40 1.00
17 Richaun Holmes .40 1.00
18 Rondae Hollis-Jefferson .40 1.00
19 Myles Turner .50 1.25
20 Pat Connaughton .30 .75
21 Karl-Anthony Towns 2.50 6.00
22 Boban Marjanovic .40 1.00
23 Christian Wood .30 .75
24 Kelly Oubre Jr. .40 1.00
25 D'Angelo Russell 1.25 3.00
26 Josh Huestis .30 .75
27 Devin Booker 1.50 4.00
28 Jonathon Simmons .50 1.25
29 Joe Young .40 1.00
30 Cameron Payne .40 1.00
31 Larry Nance Jr. .50 1.25
32 Kristaps Porzingis 1.25 3.00
33 Rashad Vaughn .30 .75
34 Kevon Looney .40 1.00
35 R.J. Hunter .30 .75
36 Mario Hezonja .40 1.00
37 Marcelo Huertas .40 1.00
38 Jahlil Okafor .60 1.50
39 Terry Rozier .40 1.00
40 Walter Tavares .30 .75
41 Willie Cauley-Stein .50 1.25
42 Montrezl Harrell .40 1.00
43 Nikola Jokic .60 1.50
44 Delon Wright .40 1.00
45 Justise Winslow .50 1.25
46 Jordan Mickey .30 .75
47 Sam Dekker .40 1.00
48 Chris McCullough .30 .75
49 Nemanja Bjelica .40 1.00
50 Jerian Grant .30 .75

2015-16 Donruss Timeless Treasures Jersey Autographs

RANDOM INSERTS IN PACKS
PRINT RUNS B/WN 49-99 COPIES PER
EXCHANGE DEADLINE 8/19/2017
*PRIME/25: .5X TO 1.2X BASIC
1 Willie Cauley-Stein/75 10.00 25.00
2 Andrew Wiggins/49 30.00 80.00
3 David Thompson/75 5.00 12.00
4 Grant Hill/75 15.00 40.00
5 John Starks/75 5.00 12.00
6 Kobe Bryant/49 75.00 150.00
7 Mario Hezonja/49 5.00 12.00
8 Kyrie Irving/49 30.00 80.00
9 Danny Manning/75 5.00 12.00
10 Karl-Anthony Towns/75 100.00 250.00
11 Stanley Johnson/75 5.00 12.00
12 Jahlil Okafor/75 8.00 20.00
13 Tony Parker/49 12.00 30.00
14 Kristaps Porzingis/75 75.00 150.00
15 Clifford Robinson/75 4.00 10.00
16 Kevin Durant/49 40.00 100.00
17 Justise Winslow/49 15.00 40.00
18 John Wall/49 15.00 40.00
19 Kenny Smith/49 5.00 12.00
20 D'Angelo Russell/75 25.00 60.00
21 Frank Kaminsky/99 6.00 15.00
22 Emmanuel Mudiay/75 6.00 15.00
23 Devin Booker/99 40.00 100.00
24 Steve Kerr/49 10.00 25.00
25 Rik Smits/75 5.00 12.00

2016-17 Donruss

COMPLETE SET (200) 15.00 40.00
1 Joel Embiid .40 1.00
2 Jahlil Okafor .20 .50
3 Nerlens Noel .20 .50
4 T.J. McConnell
5 Giannis Antetokounmpo .50 1.25
6 Jabari Parker .30 .75
7 Khris Middleton .20 .50
8 Matthew Dellavedova .20 .50
9 John Henson .20 .50
10 Jimmy Butler .25 .60
11 Rajon Rondo .25 .60
12 Dwyane Wade .40 1.00
13 Nikola Mirotic .20 .50
14 Bobby Portis .15 .40
15 LeBron James 1.00 2.50
16 Kevin Love .25 .60
17 Kyrie Irving .50 1.25
18 Richard Jefferson .20 .50
19 Tristan Thompson .20 .50
20 Isaiah Thomas .25 .60
21 Avery Bradley .20 .50
22 Al Horford .20 .50
23 Marcus Smart .20 .50
24 Jordan Mickey .15 .40
25 Chris Paul .30 .75
26 DeAndre Jordan .25 .60
27 Blake Griffin .25 .60
28 Jamal Crawford .25 .60
29 J.J. Redick .25 .60
30 Mike Conley .20 .50
31 Chandler Parsons .20 .50
32 Marc Gasol .25 .60
33 Zach Randolph .20 .50
34 Dennis Schroder .20 .50
35 Paul Millsap .25 .60
36 Dwight Howard .20 .50
37 Kent Bazemore .20 .50
38 Kyle Korver .20 .50
39 Justise Winslow .20 .50
40 Josh Richardson .15 .40
41 Goran Dragic .20 .50
42 Chris Bosh .25 .60
43 Hassan Whiteside .20 .50
44 Kemba Walker .25 .60
45 Nicolas Batum .20 .50
46 Frank Kaminsky .20 .50
47 Jeremy Lamb .15 .40
48 Aaron Harrison .15 .40
49 Alec Burks .15 .40
50 Rudy Gobert .25 .60
51 George Hill .20 .50
52 Gordon Hayward .25 .60
53 Rodney Hood .20 .50
54 DeMarcus Cousins .25 .60
55 Ben McLemore .15 .40
56 Willie Cauley-Stein .20 .50
57 Rudy Gay .25 .60
58 Omri Casspi .15 .40
59 Carmelo Anthony .30 .75
60 Kristaps Porzingis .50 1.25
61 Joakim Noah .20 .50
62 Derrick Rose .30 .75
63 Larry Nance Jr. .20 .50
64 D'Angelo Russell .30 .75
65 Julius Randle .25 .60
66 Lou Williams .20 .50
67 Serge Ibaka .20 .50
68 Jeff Green .20 .50
69 Mario Hezonja .15 .40
70 Evan Fournier .20 .50
71 Aaron Gordon .20 .50
72 Bismack Biyombo .15 .40
73 Nikola Vucevic .20 .50
74 Harrison Barnes .20 .50
75 Andrew Bogut .20 .50
76 J.J. Barea .20 .50
77 Dirk Nowitzki .30 .75
78 Deron Williams .20 .50
79 Wesley Matthews .15 .40
80 Brook Lopez .20 .50
81 Rondae Hollis-Jefferson .15 .40
82 Bojan Bogdanovic .15 .40
83 Jeremy Lin .25 .60
84 Chris McCullough .15 .40
85 Emmanuel Mudiay .20 .50
86 Kenneth Faried .20 .50
87 Danilo Gallinari .20 .50
88 Will Barton .15 .40
89 Wilson Chandler .20 .50
90 Nikola Jokic .25 .60
91 Jeff Teague .20 .50
92 Myles Turner .20 .50
93 Paul George .30 .75
94 Monta Ellis .20 .50
95 C.J. Miles .20 .50
96 Thaddeus Young .15 .40
97 Anthony Davis .50 1.25
98 Tyreke Evans .15 .40
99 Jrue Holiday .20 .50
100 Stanley Johnson .15 .40
101 Marcus Morris .15 .40
102 Kentavious Caldwell-Pope .20 .50
103 Reggie Jackson .20 .50
104 Andre Drummond .25 .60
105 DeMar DeRozan .25 .60
106 Kyle Lowry .20 .50
107 Jonas Valanciunas .20 .50
108 DeMarre Carroll .15 .40
109 Norman Powell .15 .40
110 James Harden .40 1.00
111 Trevor Ariza .15 .40
112 Clint Capela .15 .40
113 Sam Dekker .20 .50
114 Patrick Beverley .15 .40
115 LaMarcus Aldridge .25 .60
116 Kawhi Leonard .40 1.00
117 Tony Parker .25 .60
118 Manu Ginobili .25 .60
119 Pau Gasol .25 .60
120 Eric Bledsoe .20 .50
121 Devin Booker .40 1.00
122 Brandon Knight .20 .50
123 Alex Len .15 .40
124 Tyson Chandler .20 .50
125 Andrew Wiggins .40 1.00
126 Zach LaVine .25 .60
127 Ricky Rubio .25 .60
128 Karl-Anthony Towns .60 1.50
129 Kevin Garnett .40 1.00
130 C.J. McCollum .20 .50
131 Damian Lillard .50 1.25
132 Evan Turner .15 .40
133 Al-Farouq Aminu .20 .50
134 Mason Plumlee .20 .50
135 Stephen Curry 1.00 2.50
136 Klay Thompson .30 .75
137 Kevin Durant .60 1.50
138 Draymond Green .30 .75
139 Andre Iguodala .20 .50
140 John Wall .30 .75
141 Markieff Morris .15 .40
142 Marcin Gortat .20 .50
143 Bradley Beal .25 .60
144 Kelly Oubre Jr. .15 .40
145 Russell Westbrook .60 1.50
146 Victor Oladipo .20 .50
147 Steven Adams .20 .50
148 Cameron Payne .15 .40
149 Andre Roberson .15 .40
150 Jordan Clarkson .20 .50
151 Ben Simmons RC 2.00 5.00
152 Brandon Ingram RC 2.00 5.00
153 Jaylen Brown RC 1.25 3.00
154 Dragan Bender RC .40 1.00
155 Kris Dunn RC 1.00 2.50
156 Buddy Hield RC .75 2.00
157 Jamal Murray RC 1.00 2.50
158 Marquese Chriss RC .75 2.00
159 Jakob Poeltl RC .40 1.00
160 Thon Maker RC 1.00 2.50
161 Domantas Sabonis RC .50 1.25
162 Taurean Prince RC .50 1.25
163 Denzel Valentine RC .40 1.00
164 Wade Baldwin IV RC .30 .75
165 Henry Ellenson RC .40 1.00
166 Malik Beasley RC .30 .75
167 Caris LeVert RC .40 1.00
168 DeAndre' Bembry RC .30 .75
169 Malachi Richardson RC .40 1.00
170 Brice Johnson RC .30 .75
171 Pascal Siakam RC .30 .75
172 Skal Labissiere RC .50 1.25
173 Dejounte Murray RC .60 1.50
174 Damian Jones RC .30 .75
175 Deyonta Davis RC .30 .75
176 Ivica Zubac RC .50 1.25
177 Cheick Diallo RC .30 .75
178 Tyler Ulis RC 1.00 2.50
179 Malcolm Brogdon RC .75 2.00
180 Chinanu Onuaku RC .30 .75
181 Patrick McCaw RC .60 1.50
182 Diamond Stone RC .30 .75
183 Stephen Zimmerman RC .30 .75
184 Isaiah Whitehead RC .30 .75
185 Demetrius Jackson RC .30 .75
186 A.J. Hammons RC .30 .75
187 Jake Layman RC .40 1.00
188 Michael Gbinije RC .30 .75
189 Georges Niang RC .30 .75
190 Ben Bentil RC .30 .75
191 Joel Bolomboy RC .30 .75
192 Kay Felder RC .30 .75
193 Marcus Paige RC .30 .75
194 Daniel Hamilton RC .30 .75
195 Georgios Papagiannis RC .30 .75
196 Isaiah Cousins .30 .75
197 Tyrone Wallace RC .30 .75
198 Gary Payton II RC .40 1.00
199 Sheldon McClellan RC .30 .75
200 Ron Baker RC .40 1.00

2016-17 Donruss Holo Blue Laser

*BLUE LASER: 2.5X TO 6X BASIC
*BLUE LASER RC: 1.2X TO 3X BASIC
RANDOM INSERTS IN PACKS
STATED PRINT RUN 49 SER.#'d SETS
151 Ben Simmons 60.00 150.00

2016-17 Donruss Holo Green Laser

*GREEN: 1.5X TO 4X BASIC
*GREEN RC: .75X TO 2X BASIC
RANDOM INSERTS IN PACKS
STATED PRINT RUN 99 SER.#'d SETS
151 Ben Simmons 50.00 120.00

2016-17 Donruss Holo Laser Green and Yellow

*GRN/YLW: 4X TO 10X BASIC
*GRN/YLW RC: 2X TO 5X BASIC
RANDOM INSERTS IN PACKS
151 Ben Simmons 50.00 120.00

2016-17 Donruss Holo Orange Laser

*ORANGE: 3X TO 8X BASIC
*ORANGE RC: 1.5X TO 4X BASIC
RANDOM INSERTS IN PACKS
151 Ben Simmons 20.00 50.00

2016-17 Donruss Holo Red Laser

*RED LASER: 1.5X TO 4X BASIC
*RED LASER RC: .75X TO 2X BASIC
RANDOM INSERTS IN PACKS
STATED PRINT RUN 99 SER.#'d SETS
151 Ben Simmons 50.00 120.00

2016-17 Donruss Holo Yellow Laser

*YELLOW: 4X TO 10X BASIC
*YELLOW RC: 2X TO 5X BASIC
RANDOM INSERTS IN PACKS
STATED PRINT RUN 25 SER.#'d SETS
151 Ben Simmons 75.00 200.00

2016-17 Donruss Press Proofs Blue

*PP BLUE: 4X TO 10X BASIC
*PP BLUE RC: 2X TO 5X BASIC
RANDOM INSERTS IN PACKS
STATED PRINT RUN 25 SER.#'d SETS
151 Ben Simmons 60.00 150.00

2016-17 Donruss Press Proofs Purple

*PP PURPLE: 1.2X TO 3X BASIC
*PP PURPLE RC: .6X TO 1.5X BASIC
RANDOM INSERTS IN PACKS
STATED PRINT RUN 199 SER.#'d SETS
151 Ben Simmons 10.00 25.00

2016-17 Donruss Press Proofs Red

*PP RED: 2X TO 5X BASIC
*PP RED RC: 1X TO 2.5X BASIC
RANDOM INSERTS IN PACKS
STATED PRINT RUN 75 SER.#'d SETS
151 Ben Simmons 30.00 80.00

2016-17 Donruss Press Proofs Silver

*PP SILVER: 1X TO 2.5X BASIC
*PP SILVER RC: .5X TO 1.2X BASIC
RANDOM INSERTS IN PACKS
STATED PRINT RUN 299 SER.#'d SETS
151 Ben Simmons 8.00 20.00

2016-17 Donruss All Stars

RANDOM INSERTS IN PACKS
*PROOF: .6X TO 1.5X BASIC
*PROOF BLUE/99: 1X TO 2.5X BASIC
1 Kobe Bryant 2.00 5.00
2 Larry Bird 1.25 3.00
3 Magic Johnson 1.25 3.00
4 Shaquille O'Neal 1.25 3.00
5 Grant Hill
6 Scottie Pippen 1.00 2.50
7 Isiah Thomas .50 1.25
8 Allen Iverson .60 1.50
9 Wilt Chamberlain 1.00 2.50
10 Steve Nash .50 1.25
11 Dwyane Wade .75 2.00
12 Kyle Lowry .40 1.00
13 LeBron James 2.00 5.00
14 Paul George .60 1.50
15 Carmelo Anthony .60 1.50
16 John Wall .60 1.50
17 Paul Millsap .50 1.25
18 DeMar DeRozan .50 1.25
19 Andre Drummond .50 1.25
20 Isaiah Thomas .50 1.25
21 Stephen Curry 2.00 5.00
22 Russell Westbrook 1.25 3.00
23 Kobe Bryant 2.00 5.00
24 Kevin Durant 1.25 3.00
25 Kawhi Leonard .75 2.00
26 Chris Paul .60 1.50
27 LaMarcus Aldridge .50 1.25
28 James Harden .75 2.00
29 Anthony Davis 1.00 2.50
30 Draymond Green .60 1.50

2016-17 Donruss Back to the Future Materials

RANDOM INSERTS IN PACKS
PRINT RUNS B/WN 150-199 COPIES PER
1 Brandon Jennings/199 1.50 4.00
2 Pau Gasol/199 2.50 6.00
3 Chris Paul/199 3.00 8.00
4 Carmelo Anthony/150 3.00 8.00
5 Markieff Morris/199 1.50 4.00
6 Rajon Rondo/199 2.50 6.00
7 Vince Carter/199 3.00 8.00
8 Kevin Garnett/199 4.00 10.00
9 Reggie Jackson/199 2.00 5.00
10 Wesley Matthews/199 1.50 4.00
11 LaMarcus Aldridge/199 2.50 6.00
12 Monta Ellis/199 2.00 5.00
13 Paul Pierce/199 2.50 6.00
14 Danilo Gallinari/199 2.00 5.00
15 LeBron James/199 8.00 20.00

2016-17 Donruss Court Kings

RANDOM INSERTS IN PACKS
*PROOF: .6X TO 1.5X BASIC
*PROOF ORNG/125: .75X TO 2X BASIC
*PROOF BLUE/99: 1X TO 2.5X BASIC
1 LeBron James 2.00 5.00
2 Stephen Curry 2.00 5.00
3 Dwyane Wade .75 2.00
4 Dirk Nowitzki .60 1.50
5 Chris Paul .60 1.50
6 Anthony Davis 1.00 2.50
7 Kyrie Irving 1.00 2.50
8 Kevin Durant 1.25 3.00
9 James Harden .75 2.00
10 Paul George .60 1.50
11 Jimmy Butler .50 1.25
12 Carmelo Anthony .60 1.50
13 DeMarcus Cousins .50 1.25
14 Blake Griffin .50 1.25
15 Karl-Anthony Towns 1.25 3.00
16 John Wall .60 1.50
17 Derrick Rose .60 1.50
18 Kawhi Leonard .75 2.00
19 Russell Westbrook 1.25 3.00
20 Klay Thompson .60 1.50
21 DeMar DeRozan .50 1.25
22 Damian Lillard 1.00 2.50
23 Kristaps Porzingis 1.00 2.50
24 Giannis Antetokounmpo 1.00 2.50
25 Andrew Wiggins .75 2.00
26 Isaiah Thomas .50 1.25
27 Jeremy Lin .50 1.25
28 Victor Oladipo .40 1.00
29 Eric Bledsoe .40 1.00
30 Kyle Lowry .40 1.00
31 Andre Drummond .50 1.25
32 Kemba Walker .50 1.25
33 Mike Conley .40 1.00
34 Dennis Schroder .40 1.00
35 Justise Winslow .40 1.00
36 Jordan Clarkson .40 1.00
37 Serge Ibaka .40 1.00
38 Gordon Hayward .50 1.25
39 Emmanuel Mudiay .40 1.00
40 Jahlil Okafor .40 1.00

2016-17 Donruss Crashers

RANDOM INSERTS IN PACKS
*PROOF: .6X TO 1.5X BASIC
*PROOF BLUE/99: 1X TO 2.5X BASIC
1 DeAndre Jordan .50 1.25
2 Hassan Whiteside .40 1.00
3 Pau Gasol .50 1.25
4 Andre Drummond .50 1.25
5 Dwight Howard .40 1.00
6 DeMarcus Cousins .50 1.25
7 Rudy Gobert .50 1.25
8 Karl-Anthony Towns 1.25 3.00
9 Anthony Davis 1.00 2.50
10 Julius Randle .50 1.25
11 Kevin Love .50 1.25
12 Marcin Gortat .40 1.00
13 Draymond Green .60 1.50
14 Kenneth Faried .40 1.00
15 LaMarcus Aldridge .50 1.25

2016-17 Donruss Dimes

RANDOM INSERTS IN PACKS
*PROOF: .6X TO 1.5X BASIC
*PROOF BLUE/99: 1X TO 2.5X BASIC
1 Chris Paul .60 1.50
2 John Wall .60 1.50
3 Ricky Rubio .50 1.25
4 James Harden .75 2.00
5 Russell Westbrook 1.25 3.00
6 Damian Lillard 1.00 2.50
7 Goran Dragic .40 1.00
8 Stephen Curry 2.00 5.00
9 Kyle Lowry .40 1.00
10 Isaiah Thomas .50 1.25

2016-17 Donruss Dominator Signatures

RANDOM INSERTS IN PACKS
PRINT RUNS B/WN 25-49 COPIES PER
1 Karl-Anthony Towns/49 30.00 80.00
2 Kristaps Porzingis/49 60.00 150.00
3 Devin Booker/25
4 Justise Winslow/49 4.00 10.00
5 Nikola Jokic/25
6 Jabari Parker/49 15.00 40.00
7 Victor Oladipo/25 4.00 10.00
8 Andrew Wiggins/49
9 Kevin Durant/49 50.00 120.00
10 Kyrie Irving/49 25.00 60.00
11 John Wall/49
12 Bobby Portis/49 3.00 8.00
13 Dwyane Wade/49 30.00 80.00
14 Jordan Clarkson/49 4.00 10.00
15 Eric Bledsoe/25
16 Carmelo Anthony/25 20.00 50.00
17 Giannis Antetokounmpo/25
18 Isaiah Thomas/49 20.00 50.00
19 Kyle Lowry/25 12.00 30.00
20 Klay Thompson/25
21 Draymond Green/25 12.00 30.00
22 Mike Conley/25
23 Marcus Smart/25 20.00 50.00
24 Chris Paul/49
25 Blake Griffin/49
26 Goran Dragic/25 8.00 20.00
27 Allen Iverson/49 30.00 80.00
28 Latrell Sprewell/25 15.00 40.00
29 James Worthy/25 12.00 30.00
30 Nick Van Exel/25 20.00 50.00
31 George Gervin/25
32 Steve Francis/25 10.00 25.00
33 Jalen Rose/25 5.00 12.00
34 John Starks/25 4.00 10.00
35 Bill Russell/49 50.00 120.00
36 Ray Allen/49 15.00 40.00
37 John Stockton/49 15.00 40.00
38 Julius Erving/49 30.00 80.00
39 Jason Kidd/25
40 Anfernee Hardaway/25 30.00 80.00

2016-17 Donruss Elite Series

RANDOM INSERTS IN PACKS
*PROOF: .6X TO 1.5X BASIC
*PROOF BLUE/99: 1X TO 2.5X BASIC
1 Dirk Nowitzki .60 1.50
2 Stephen Curry 2.00 5.00
3 Kevin Durant 1.25 3.00
4 Derrick Rose .60 1.50
5 Dwyane Wade .75 2.00
6 Al Horford .40 1.00
7 Russell Westbrook 1.25 3.00
8 Damian Lillard 1.00 2.50
9 LeBron James 2.00 5.00
10 Anthony Davis 1.00 2.50
11 James Harden .75 2.00
12 Chris Paul .60 1.50
13 Kawhi Leonard .75 2.00
14 LaMarcus Aldridge .50 1.25
15 John Wall .60 1.50
16 Jimmy Butler .50 1.25
17 Kyrie Irving 1.00 2.50
18 Klay Thompson .60 1.50
19 Blake Griffin .50 1.25
20 Kyle Lowry .40 1.00
21 Pau Gasol .50 1.25
22 Marc Gasol .50 1.25
23 Carmelo Anthony .60 1.50
24 Mike Conley .40 1.00
25 Jordan Clarkson .40 1.00

2016-17 Donruss Elite Signatures

PRINT RUNS B/WN 25-99 COPIES PER
1 Kevin Durant/99 40.00 100.00
2 C.J. Miles/25 4.00 10.00
3 T.J. McConnell/99 3.00 8.00
4 Allen Crabbe/25 3.00 8.00
5 Marcelo Huertas/99 3.00 8.00
6 Deron Williams/25 4.00 10.00
7 Jordan McRae/99 3.00 8.00
8 Dennis Schroder/25
9 Carmelo Anthony/25 20.00 50.00
10 Alan Anderson/25 3.00 8.00
11 Kyrie Irving/99 25.00 60.00
12 Aaron Harrison/99 3.00 8.00
13 Mike Muscala/25 10.00 25.00
14 Karl-Anthony Towns/25 40.00 100.00
15 Dirk Nowitzki/49 50.00 120.00
16 Bob Dandridge/49 3.00 8.00
17 Walter Tavares/49 3.00 8.00
18 Draymond Green/25 12.00 30.00
19 Vin Baker/49 3.00 8.00
20 Seth Curry/25 12.00 30.00
21 Mark Price/49 5.00 12.00
22 Luis Montero/99 3.00 8.00
23 Dan Majerle/25 6.00 15.00
24 D'Angelo Russell/25 10.00 25.00
25 Jim Jackson/25 6.00 15.00
26 E'Twaun Moore/49 3.00 8.00
27 Langston Galloway/25 3.00 8.00
28 Glen Rice/25 4.00 10.00
29 C.J. Wilcox/49 3.00 8.00
30 Jamal Mashburn/25 5.00 12.00
31 Rashad Vaughn/25 3.00 8.00
32 Dennis Scott/25 3.00 8.00
33 Noah Vonleh/99 3.00 8.00
34 Dell Curry/25 10.00 25.00
35 Kelly Olynyk/25 3.00 8.00
36 Vinny Del Negro/25 4.00 10.00
37 Anthony Bennett/99 3.00 8.00
38 Glenn Robinson III/25 3.00 8.00
39 Bill Laimbeer/25 4.00 10.00
40 Dikembe Mutombo/25 5.00 12.00
41 James Ennis/99 3.00 8.00
42 Jeff Hornacek/25 8.00 20.00
43 Robert Covington/25 3.00 8.00
45 Jalen Rose/25 5.00 12.00
46 C.J. McCollum/49 4.00 10.00
47 Tim Hardaway/25 12.00 30.00
48 Michael Kidd-Gilchrist/99 4.00 10.00
49 Latrell Sprewell/25 15.00 40.00
50 Dwight Powell/99 3.00 8.00
51 Bobby Portis/25 3.00 8.00
52 Raef LaFrentz/25 3.00 8.00
53 Jonas Valanciunas/25 10.00 25.00
54 Larry Nance/25 4.00 10.00
55 Cody Zeller/99 3.00 8.00
56 Festus Ezeli/25 3.00 8.00
57 Jo Jo White/25 20.00 50.00
58 JaKarr Sampson/99 3.00 8.00
59 P.J. Tucker/25 3.00 8.00
60 Chauncey Billups/25 5.00 12.00
62 Mark Aguirre/25 4.00 10.00
63 Avery Johnson/25 4.00 10.00
64 Reggie Bullock/99 3.00 8.00
65 Marcus Camby/25
66 Antonio McDyess/25 4.00 10.00
67 Steve Novak/49 3.00 8.00
68 Dee Brown/25 3.00 8.00
69 Michael Carter-Williams/49 3.00 8.00
70 Bryon Russell/25
71 Kevon Looney/49 4.00 10.00
72 Rolando Blackman/25 4.00 10.00
73 Steve Smith/25 12.00 30.00
74 Jeff Withey/49 3.00 8.00
75 Scott Skiles/25 4.00 10.00
76 Tyronn Lue/25 15.00 40.00
77 Ian Clark/99 3.00 8.00
78 Jerry Stackhouse/25 4.00 10.00
79 Devin Harris/25 3.00 8.00
80 Mark Jackson/25 4.00 10.00
81 Tristan Thompson/49 4.00 10.00
82 Mike Bibby/25 4.00 10.00
83 Matthew Dellavedova/49 4.00 10.00
84 B.J. Armstrong/25
85 Kyle O'Quinn/99 3.00 8.00
86 Rick Fox/25 4.00 10.00
87 Clifford Robinson/25 3.00 8.00
88 Lamar Patterson/99 3.00 8.00
89 Terry Porter/25 3.00 8.00
90 Kenny Anderson/25 4.00 10.00
92 Tom Gugliotta/25 10.00
93 Tony Delk/25 3.00 8.00
94 Alex Len/99 3.00 8.00
95 Kendall Gill/25 3.00 8.00
97 Sam Bowie/25 3.00 8.00
98 Troy Daniels/99 3.00 8.00
99 Juwan Howard/25 4.00 10.00
100 Josh Huestis/99 3.00 8.00

2016-17 Donruss Hall Dominator Signatues

RANDOM INSERTS IN PACKS
PRINT RUNS B/WN 25-49 COPIES PER
1 Dan Issel/49 4.00 10.00
2 Artis Gilmore/49 4.00 10.00
3 Adrian Dantley/49 4.00 10.00
4 Tom Heinsohn/49 20.00 50.00
5 Elvin Hayes/49 6.00 15.00
6 Jamaal Wilkes/49 5.00 12.00
7 Satch Sanders/49 8.00 20.00
8 David Robinson/49 15.00 40.00
9 Rick Barry/49 4.00 10.00
10 Bob Lanier/25 4.00 10.00
11 Dennis Rodman/49 25.00 60.00
12 David Thompson/49 4.00 10.00
13 John Stockton/49 15.00 40.00
14 Alex English/25 8.00 20.00
15 Bernard King/25 10.00 25.00
16 Oscar Robertson/49 40.00 100.00
17 Hakeem Olajuwon/25 20.00 50.00
18 Kevin McHale/25 12.00 30.00
19 Earl Lloyd/25 40.00 100.00
20 Calvin Murphy/25 6.00 15.00
21 Nate Thurmond/25 4.00 10.00
22 Cliff Hagan/25 10.00 25.00
23 Robert Parish/25 5.00 12.00
24 Wes Unseld/25 8.00 20.00
25 Earl Monroe/25
26 Gary Payton/25 5.00 12.00
27 Gail Goodrich/25 12.00 30.00
28 Willis Reed/25 12.00 30.00
29 Arvydas Sabonis/25 8.00 20.00
30 Dominique Wilkins/25 20.00 50.00

2016-17 Donruss Hall Kings

RANDOM INSERTS IN PACKS
*PROOF: .6X TO 1.5X BASIC
*PROOF ORNG/125: .75X TO 2X BASIC
*PROOF BLUE/99: 1X TO 2.5X BASIC
1 Shaquille O'Neal 1.25 3.00
2 Allen Iverson .60 1.50
3 Yao Ming .60 1.50
4 Alonzo Mourning .60 1.50
5 Gary Payton .50 1.25
6 Bernard King .40 1.00
7 Ralph Sampson .40 1.00
8 Jamaal Wilkes .50 1.25
9 Artis Gilmore .40 1.00
10 Chris Mullin .50 1.25
11 Dennis Rodman 1.00 2.50
12 Karl Malone .60 1.50
13 Scottie Pippen 1.00 2.50
14 David Robinson .75 2.00
15 John Stockton .75 2.00
16 Adrian Dantley .40 1.00
17 Patrick Ewing .60 1.50
18 Hakeem Olajuwon .60 1.50
19 Joe Dumars .50 1.25
20 Dominique Wilkins .60 1.50
21 Clyde Drexler .60 1.50
22 Robert Parish .50 1.25
23 James Worthy .60 1.50
24 Magic Johnson 1.25 3.00
25 Drazen Petrovic .50 1.25
26 Moses Malone .50 1.25
27 Isiah Thomas .50 1.25
28 Bob McAdoo .40 1.00
29 Kevin McHale .50 1.25
30 Larry Bird 1.25 3.00

2016-17 Donruss Jersey Kings

RANDOM INSERTS IN PACKS
1 Jabari Parker 3.00 8.00
2 Jimmy Butler 2.50 6.00
3 LeBron James 8.00 20.00
4 Isaiah Thomas 2.50 6.00
5 DeAndre Jordan 2.50 6.00
6 Marc Gasol 2.50 6.00
7 Paul Millsap 2.50 6.00
8 Kemba Walker 2.50 6.00
9 DeMarcus Cousins 2.50 6.00
10 Carmelo Anthony 3.00 8.00
11 Jordan Clarkson 2.00 5.00
12 Brook Lopez 2.00 5.00
13 Danilo Gallinari 2.00 5.00
14 Paul George 3.00 8.00
15 Jrue Holiday 2.00 5.00
16 Andre Drummond 2.50 6.00
17 DeMar DeRozan 2.50 6.00
18 Karl-Anthony Towns 4.00 10.00
19 Kawhi Leonard 4.00 10.00
20 Gordon Hayward 2.50 6.00
21 Andrew Wiggins 4.00 10.00
22 Damian Lillard 4.00 10.00
23 Stephen Curry 10.00 25.00
24 John Wall 3.00 8.00
25 Russell Westbrook 4.00 10.00

2016-17 Donruss Jersey Series

RANDOM INSERTS IN PACKS
1 Jusuf Nurkic 1.50 4.00
2 Al Horford 2.00 5.00
3 Zach LaVine 2.50 6.00
4 Ben McLemore 1.50 4.00
5 Bojan Bogdanovic 1.50 4.00
6 Bradley Beal 2.50 6.00
7 Brook Lopez 2.00 5.00
8 Carmelo Anthony 3.00 8.00
9 Chandler Parsons 2.00 5.00
10 Chris Bosh 2.50 6.00
11 Cody Zeller 1.50 4.00
12 Danilo Gallinari 2.00 5.00
13 Danny Green 2.00 5.00
14 DeMarcus Cousins 2.50 6.00
15 DeMarre Carroll 1.50 4.00
16 Derrick Rose 3.00 8.00
17 Dirk Nowitzki 3.00 8.00
18 Donatas Motiejunas 1.50 4.00
19 Dwight Howard 2.00 5.00

20 Dwyane Wade 4.00 10.00
21 Eric Gordon 2.00 5.00
22 George Hill 2.00 5.00
23 Gorgui Dieng 1.50 4.00
24 Terrence Ross 2.00 5.00
25 Jabari Parker 3.00 8.00
26 Jared Sullinger 1.50 4.00
27 Jeff Teague 2.00 5.00
28 John Henson 2.00 5.00
29 John Wall 3.00 8.00
30 Jonas Valanciunas 2.00 5.00
31 Jrue Holiday 2.00 5.00
32 Karl-Anthony Towns 4.00 10.00
33 Kemba Walker 2.50 6.00
34 Kenneth Faried 2.00 5.00
35 Kevin Durant 8.00 20.00
36 Kevin Garnett 4.00 10.00
37 Kevin Love 2.50 6.00
38 Kyle Lowry 2.00 5.00
39 Kyrie Irving 4.00 10.00
40 LeBron James 8.00 20.00
41 Marc Gasol 2.50 6.00
42 Marcin Gortat 2.00 5.00
43 Matthew Dellavedova 2.00 5.00
44 Mike Conley 2.00 5.00
45 Nerlens Noel 2.00 5.00
46 Otto Porter 2.00 5.00
47 Patrick Beverley 1.50 4.00
48 Ricky Rubio 2.50 6.00
49 Shabazz Muhammad 2.00 5.00
50 Andrew Bogut 2.00 5.00

2016-17 Donruss Newly Crowned Rookie Jerseys

RANDOM INSERTS IN PACKS
2 Brandon Ingram 5.00 12.00
3 Jaylen Brown 4.00 10.00
4 Dragan Bender 2.00 5.00
5 Kris Dunn 4.00 10.00
6 Buddy Hield 4.00 10.00
7 Jamal Murray 3.00 8.00
8 Marquese Chriss 4.00 10.00
9 Jakob Poeltl 2.00 5.00
10 Thon Maker 3.00 8.00
11 Taurean Prince 2.50 6.00
12 Denzel Valentine 2.00 5.00
13 Wade Baldwin IV 1.50 4.00
14 Henry Ellenson 2.00 5.00
15 Malik Beasley 1.50 4.00
16 Caris LeVert 2.00 5.00
17 DeAndre' Bembry 1.50 4.00
18 Malachi Richardson 2.00 5.00
19 T. Luwawu-Cabarrot 3.00 8.00
20 Brice Johnson 1.50 4.00
21 Pascal Siakam 1.50 4.00
22 Skal Labissiere 2.50 6.00
23 Dejounte Murray 3.00 8.00
24 Damian Jones 1.50 4.00
25 Deyonta Davis 1.50 4.00
26 Ivica Zubac 2.50 6.00
28 Gary Payton II 2.00 5.00
29 Cheick Diallo 1.50 4.00
30 Tyler Ulis 3.00 8.00
31 Malcolm Brogdon 4.00 10.00
32 Patrick McCaw 3.00 8.00
33 Kay Felder 1.50 4.00
34 Diamond Stone 1.50 4.00
35 Isaiah Whitehead 1.50 4.00

2016-17 Donruss Next Day Autographs

RANDOM INSERTS IN PACKS
1 Brandon Ingram 100.00 250.00
2 Jaylen Brown 75.00 200.00
3 Dragan Bender 30.00 80.00
4 Kris Dunn 30.00 80.00
5 Buddy Hield 25.00 60.00
6 Jamal Murray 50.00 120.00
7 Marquese Chriss 30.00 80.00
8 Jakob Poeltl 10.00 25.00
9 Thon Maker 50.00 120.00
10 Taurean Prince 15.00 40.00
11 Georgios Papagiannis 10.00 25.00
12 Denzel Valentine 12.00 30.00
13 Juan Hernangomez 25.00 60.00
14 Wade Baldwin IV 12.00 30.00
15 Henry Ellenson 8.00 20.00
16 Caris LeVert 15.00 40.00
17 DeAndre' Bembry 10.00 25.00
18 Malachi Richardson 15.00 40.00
19 T. Luwawu-Cabarrot 6.00 15.00
20 Brice Johnson 3.00 8.00
21 Pascal Siakam 8.00 20.00
22 Skal Labissiere 30.00 80.00
23 Dejounte Murray 75.00 200.00
24 Damian Jones 8.00 20.00
25 Deyonta Davis 3.00 8.00
26 Cheick Diallo 3.00 8.00
27 Tyler Ulis 40.00 100.00
28 Patrick McCaw 50.00 120.00
29 Malcolm Brogdon 30.00 80.00
30 Isaiah Whitehead 15.00 40.00
31 Demetrius Jackson 10.00 25.00
32 Kay Felder 8.00 20.00
33 Gary Payton II 10.00 25.00
34 Diamond Stone 3.00 8.00
35 Ivica Zubac 40.00 100.00
36 Chinanu Onuaku 6.00 15.00
37 Stephen Zimmerman 3.00 8.00
38 A.J. Hammons 3.00 8.00
39 Malik Beasley 8.00 20.00

2016-17 Donruss Optic Preview

RANDOM INSERTS IN PACKS
1 Ben Simmons 40.00 100.00
2 Nerlens Noel 2.50 6.00
3 Jahlil Okafor 2.50 6.00
4 Damian Lillard 15.00 40.00
5 C.J. McCollum 2.50 6.00
6 Allen Crabbe 2.00 5.00
7 Greg Monroe 2.50 6.00
8 Jabari Parker 10.00 25.00
9 Thon Maker 15.00 40.00
10 Dwyane Wade 15.00 40.00
11 Jimmy Butler 3.00 8.00
12 Rajon Rondo 3.00 8.00
13 LeBron James 40.00 100.00
14 Kyrie Irving 15.00 40.00
15 Kevin Love 10.00 25.00
16 Tristan Thompson 2.50 6.00
17 Isaiah Thomas 3.00 8.00
18 Jared Sullinger 2.00 5.00
19 Jaylen Brown 25.00 60.00
20 Chris Paul 10.00 25.00
21 Blake Griffin 10.00 25.00
22 DeAndre Jordan 3.00 8.00
23 J.J. Redick 3.00 8.00
24 Vince Carter 4.00 10.00
25 Mike Conley 2.50 6.00
26 Zach Randolph 2.50 6.00
27 Marc Gasol 3.00 8.00
28 Chandler Parsons 2.50 6.00
29 Dennis Schroder 2.50 6.00
30 Al Horford 2.50 6.00
31 Paul Millsap 3.00 8.00
32 Chris Bosh 3.00 8.00
33 Joe Johnson 2.50 6.00
34 Hassan Whiteside 2.50 6.00
35 Nicolas Batum 2.50 6.00
36 Al Jefferson 2.50 6.00
37 Michael Kidd-Gilchrist 2.50 6.00
38 Derrick Favors 2.50 6.00
39 Gordon Hayward 3.00 8.00
40 Rudy Gobert 3.00 8.00
41 DeMarcus Cousins 3.00 8.00
42 Willie Cauley-Stein 2.50 6.00
43 Rudy Gay 3.00 8.00
44 Carmelo Anthony 10.00 25.00
45 Kristaps Porzingis 15.00 40.00
46 Derrick Rose 12.00 30.00
47 Jordan Clarkson 2.50 6.00
48 Julius Randle 3.00 8.00
49 D'Angelo Russell 10.00 25.00
50 Brandon Ingram 40.00 100.00
51 Elfrid Payton 2.50 6.00
52 Aaron Gordon 2.50 6.00
53 Serge Ibaka 2.50 6.00
54 Dirk Nowitzki 10.00 25.00
55 Harrison Barnes 2.50 6.00
56 Wesley Matthews 2.00 5.00
57 Jeremy Lin 3.00 8.00
58 Brook Lopez 2.50 6.00
59 Kenneth Faried 2.50 6.00
60 Emmanuel Mudiay 2.50 6.00
61 Jamal Murray 20.00 50.00
62 Paul George 10.00 25.00
63 Jeff Teague 2.50 6.00
64 Myles Turner 2.50 6.00
65 Anthony Davis 15.00 40.00
66 Buddy Hield 15.00 40.00
67 Tyreke Evans 2.00 5.00
68 Andre Drummond 3.00 8.00
69 Stanley Johnson 2.00 5.00
70 Tobias Harris 2.50 6.00
71 DeMar DeRozan 3.00 8.00
72 Kyle Lowry 2.50 6.00
73 Terrence Ross 2.50 6.00
74 Jakob Poeltl 2.50 6.00
75 James Harden 5.00 12.00
76 Dwight Howard 2.50 6.00
77 LaMarcus Aldridge 3.00 8.00
78 Manu Ginobili 3.00 8.00
79 Kawhi Leonard 12.00 30.00
80 Tony Parker 3.00 8.00
81 Eric Bledsoe 2.50 6.00
82 Devin Booker 5.00 12.00
83 Brandon Knight 2.50 6.00
84 Dragan Bender 10.00 25.00
85 Marquese Chriss 10.00 25.00
86 Russell Westbrook 15.00 40.00
87 Enes Kanter 2.00 5.00
88 Victor Oladipo 2.50 6.00
89 Zach LaVine 3.00 8.00
90 Andrew Wiggins 12.00 30.00
91 Ricky Rubio 3.00 8.00
92 Karl-Anthony Towns 20.00 50.00
93 Kris Dunn 25.00 60.00
94 Stephen Curry 40.00 100.00
95 Kevin Durant 20.00 50.00
96 Klay Thompson 10.00 25.00
97 Andre Iguodala 2.50 6.00
98 John Wall 10.00 25.00
99 Bradley Beal 3.00 8.00
100 Marcin Gortat 2.50 6.00

2016-17 Donruss Rookie Dominator Signatures

RANDOM INSERTS IN PACKS
PRINT RUNS B/WN 50-65 COPIES PER
1 Stephen Zimmerman/50 3.00 8.00
2 Marquese Chriss/65 15.00 40.00
3 Buddy Hield/65 15.00 40.00
4 Henry Ellenson/65 4.00 10.00
5 Georges Niang/65 6.00 15.00
6 Demetrius Jackson/65 3.00 8.00
7 Isaiah Whitehead/50 3.00 8.00
8 Thon Maker/65 25.00 60.00
9 Domantas Sabonis/65 12.00 30.00
10 Dragan Bender/65 12.00 30.00
11 T. Luwawu-Cabarrot/65 6.00 15.00
12 Ivica Zubac/65 6.00 15.00
13 Damian Jones/65 3.00 8.00
14 Tyler Ulis/65 6.00 15.00
15 Kris Dunn/50 15.00 40.00
16 Deyonta Davis/65 3.00 8.00
17 Brandon Ingram/50 50.00 120.00
18 Jamal Murray/65 20.00 50.00
19 Denzel Valentine/65 10.00 25.00
20 Jakob Poeltl/65 4.00 10.00
21 Skal Labissiere/50 10.00 25.00
22 Caris LeVert/65 6.00 15.00
23 Diamond Stone/65 3.00 8.00
24 Chinanu Onuaku/65 3.00 8.00
25 Brice Johnson/65 10.00 25.00
26 Malik Beasley/65 3.00 8.00
27 Wade Baldwin IV/65 6.00 15.00
28 Daniel Hamilton/60 3.00 8.00
29 Kay Felder/65 3.00 8.00
30 Michael Gbinije/50 3.00 8.00

2016-17 Donruss Rookie Jerseys

RANDOM INSERTS IN PACKS
*PRIME/25: 1X TO 2.5X BASIC
1 Brandon Ingram 5.00 12.00
2 Jaylen Brown 4.00 10.00
3 Dragan Bender 2.00 5.00
4 Kris Dunn 4.00 10.00
5 Buddy Hield 4.00 10.00
6 Jamal Murray 3.00 8.00
7 Marquese Chriss 4.00 10.00
8 Jakob Poeltl 2.00 5.00
9 Thon Maker 3.00 8.00
10 Taurean Prince 2.50 6.00
11 Denzel Valentine 2.00 5.00
12 Wade Baldwin IV 1.50 4.00
13 Henry Ellenson 2.00 5.00
14 Malik Beasley 1.50 4.00
15 Caris LeVert 2.00 5.00
16 DeAndre' Bembry 1.50 4.00
17 Malachi Richardson 2.00 5.00
18 T. Luwawu-Cabarrot 3.00 8.00
19 Brice Johnson 1.50 4.00
20 Pascal Siakam 1.50 4.00
21 Skal Labissiere 2.50 6.00
22 Dejounte Murray 3.00 8.00
23 Gary Payton II 2.00 5.00
24 Damian Jones 1.50 4.00
25 Deyonta Davis 1.50 4.00
26 Ivica Zubac 2.50 6.00
28 Cheick Diallo 1.50 4.00
29 Tyler Ulis 3.00 8.00
30 Malcolm Brogdon 4.00 10.00
31 Patrick McCaw 3.00 8.00
32 Kay Felder 1.50 4.00
33 Diamond Stone 1.50 4.00
34 Isaiah Whitehead 1.50 4.00
35 Brandon Ingram 5.00 12.00
36 Dragan Bender 2.00 5.00
37 Buddy Hield 4.00 10.00
38 Jamal Murray 3.00 8.00
39 Marquese Chriss 4.00 10.00
40 Jakob Poeltl 2.00 5.00
41 Thon Maker 3.00 8.00
42 Taurean Prince 2.50 6.00
43 Denzel Valentine 2.00 5.00
44 Wade Baldwin IV 1.50 4.00
45 Henry Ellenson 2.00 5.00
46 Malik Beasley 1.50 4.00
47 Caris LeVert 2.00 5.00
48 DeAndre' Bembry 1.50 4.00
49 Malachi Richardson 2.00 5.00
50 T. Luwawu-Cabarrot 3.00 8.00
51 Brice Johnson 1.50 4.00
52 Pascal Siakam 1.50 4.00
53 Skal Labissiere 2.50 6.00
54 Dejounte Murray 3.00 8.00
55 Gary Payton II 2.00 5.00
56 Damian Jones 1.50 4.00
57 Deyonta Davis 1.50 4.00
58 Ivica Zubac 2.50 6.00
60 Cheick Diallo 1.50 4.00
61 Tyler Ulis 3.00 8.00
62 Malcolm Brogdon 4.00 10.00
63 Patrick McCaw 3.00 8.00
64 Kay Felder 1.50 4.00
65 Diamond Stone 1.50 4.00
66 Isaiah Whitehead 1.50 4.00
67 Jaylen Brown 4.00 10.00
68 Brandon Ingram 5.00 12.00
69 Jaylen Brown 4.00 10.00
70 Dragan Bender 2.00 5.00
71 Kris Dunn 4.00 10.00
72 Buddy Hield 4.00 10.00
73 Jamal Murray 3.00 8.00
74 Marquese Chriss 4.00 10.00
75 Jakob Poeltl 2.00 5.00
76 Thon Maker 3.00 8.00
77 Taurean Prince 2.50 6.00
78 Denzel Valentine 2.00 5.00
79 Wade Baldwin IV 1.50 4.00
80 Henry Ellenson 2.00 5.00
81 Malik Beasley 1.50 4.00
82 Caris LeVert 2.00 5.00
83 DeAndre' Bembry 1.50 4.00
84 Malachi Richardson 2.00 5.00
85 T. Luwawu-Cabarrot 3.00 8.00
86 Brice Johnson 1.50 4.00
87 Pascal Siakam 1.50 4.00
88 Skal Labissiere 2.50 6.00
89 Dejounte Murray 3.00 8.00
90 Gary Payton II 2.00 5.00
91 Damian Jones 1.50 4.00
92 Deyonta Davis 1.50 4.00
93 Ivica Zubac 2.50 6.00
95 Cheick Diallo 1.50 4.00
96 Tyler Ulis 3.00 8.00
97 Malcolm Brogdon 4.00 10.00
98 Patrick McCaw 3.00 8.00
99 Diamond Stone 1.50 4.00
100 Kris Dunn 4.00 10.00

2016-17 Donruss Rookie Kings

RANDOM INSERTS IN PACKS
*PROOF: .6X TO 1.5X BASIC
*PROOF ORNG/125: .75X TO 2X BASIC
*PROOF BLUE/99: 1X TO 2.5X BASIC
1 Brandon Ingram 2.50 6.00
2 Ben Simmons 2.50 6.00
3 Jaylen Brown 1.50 4.00
4 Dragan Bender .50 1.25
5 Kris Dunn 1.25 3.00
6 Buddy Hield 1.00 2.50
7 Jamal Murray 1.25 3.00
8 Marquese Chriss 1.00 2.50
9 Jakob Poeltl .50 1.25
10 Thon Maker 1.25 3.00
11 Domantas Sabonis .60 1.50
12 Taurean Prince .60 1.50
13 Denzel Valentine .50 1.25
14 Wade Baldwin IV .40 1.00
15 Henry Ellenson .50 1.25
16 Malik Beasley .40 1.00
17 Caris LeVert .50 1.25
18 DeAndre' Bembry .40 1.00
19 Malachi Richardson .50 1.25
20 T. Luwawu-Cabarrot .75 2.00
21 Brice Johnson .40 1.00
22 Pascal Siakam .40 1.00
23 Skal Labissiere .60 1.50
24 Dejounte Murray .75 2.00
25 Damian Jones .40 1.00
26 Isaiah Whitehead .40 1.00
27 Deyonta Davis .40 1.00
28 Kay Felder .40 1.00
29 A.J. Hammons .40 1.00
30 Dario Saric 1.25 3.00

2016-17 Donruss Rookie Materials Signatures

RANDOM INSERTS IN PACKS
STATED PRINT RUN 75 SER.#'d SETS
1 Brandon Ingram 40.00 100.00
2 Jaylen Brown 25.00 60.00
3 Dragan Bender 5.00 12.00
4 Kris Dunn 12.00 30.00
5 Buddy Hield 15.00 40.00
6 Jamal Murray 25.00 60.00
7 Marquese Chriss 10.00 25.00
8 Jakob Poeltl 5.00 12.00
9 Thon Maker 20.00 50.00
10 Taurean Prince 6.00 15.00
11 Denzel Valentine 5.00 12.00
12 Wade Baldwin IV 4.00 10.00
13 Henry Ellenson 6.00 15.00
14 Malik Beasley 4.00 10.00
15 Caris LeVert 5.00 12.00
16 DeAndre' Bembry 4.00 10.00
17 Malachi Richardson 6.00 15.00
18 T. Luwawu-Cabarrot 8.00 20.00
19 Brice Johnson 4.00 10.00
20 Pascal Siakam 4.00 10.00
21 Skal Labissiere 6.00 15.00
22 Dejounte Murray 8.00 20.00
23 Damian Jones 4.00 10.00
24 Deyonta Davis 4.00 10.00
25 Ivica Zubac 6.00 15.00
26 Cheick Diallo 4.00 10.00
27 Tyler Ulis 20.00 50.00
28 Isaiah Whitehead 4.00 10.00
29 Demetrius Jackson 6.00 15.00
30 Kay Felder 6.00 15.00
31 Gary Payton II 5.00 12.00
32 Diamond Stone 4.00 10.00
33 Malcolm Brogdon 15.00 40.00
34 Chinanu Onuaku 4.00 10.00
35 Patrick McCaw 25.00 60.00

2016-17 Donruss Signature Series

RANDOM INSERTS IN PACKS
1 Cody Zeller 3.00 8.00
2 C.J. McCollum 4.00 10.00
3 Ian Clark 3.00 8.00
4 Dwight Powell 3.00 8.00
5 Josh Huestis 3.00 8.00
6 T.J. McConnell 3.00 8.00
7 James Ennis 3.00 8.00
8 Walter Tavares 3.00 8.00
9 Alex Len 3.00 8.00
10 Allen Crabbe 3.00 8.00
11 Noah Vonleh 3.00 8.00
12 Aaron Harrison 3.00 8.00
13 Kevon Looney 4.00 10.00
14 Tristan Thompson 4.00 10.00
15 C.J. Miles 4.00 10.00
16 Dirk Nowitzki 50.00 120.00
17 Kyle O'Quinn 3.00 8.00
18 Jeff Withey 3.00 8.00
19 Jonas Valanciunas 4.00 10.00
20 Rashad Vaughn 3.00 8.00
21 Seth Curry 12.00 30.00
22 Deron Williams 4.00 10.00
23 D'Angelo Russell 10.00 25.00
24 Kelly Olynyk 3.00 8.00
25 Michael Carter-Williams 3.00 8.00
26 Devin Harris 3.00 8.00
27 Matthew Dellavedova 4.00 10.00
28 Montrezl Harrell 3.00 8.00
29 Draymond Green 15.00 40.00
30 Langston Galloway 3.00 8.00
31 Glenn Robinson III 3.00 8.00
32 Robert Covington 3.00 8.00
33 Bobby Portis 3.00 8.00
34 Festus Ezeli 3.00 8.00
35 Jared Dudley 3.00 8.00
36 Justise Winslow 4.00 10.00
37 Shabazz Muhammad 4.00 10.00
38 Jarell Martin 3.00 8.00
39 Terrence Jones 4.00 10.00
40 Timofey Mozgov 3.00 8.00
41 Al-Farouq Aminu 4.00 10.00
42 Khris Middleton 4.00 10.00
43 Tyus Jones 3.00 8.00
44 Rodney Stuckey 3.00 8.00
45 Luc Mbah a Moute 3.00 8.00
46 Brandon Rush 3.00 8.00
47 James Young 3.00 8.00
48 Avery Bradley 4.00 10.00
49 Kristaps Porzingis 30.00 80.00
50 Anthony Bennett 3.00 8.00

2016-17 Donruss Swatch Kings Jumbo

RANDOM INSERTS IN PACKS
STATED PRINT RUN 99 SER.#'d SETS
1 Nerlens Noel 2.00 5.00
2 Russell Westbrook 6.00 15.00
3 Dwyane Wade 4.00 10.00
4 Kyrie Irving 5.00 12.00
5 Marcus Smart 2.00 5.00
6 J.J. Redick 2.50 6.00
7 Chandler Parsons 2.00 5.00
8 Kent Bazemore 2.00 5.00
9 Goran Dragic 2.00 5.00
10 Nicolas Batum 2.00 5.00
11 Jeremy Lin 2.50 6.00
12 Paul George 3.00 8.00
13 Marcus Morris 1.50 4.00
14 Kyle Lowry 2.00 5.00
15 Derrick Rose 3.00 8.00
16 Patrick Beverley 1.50 4.00
17 Tony Parker 2.50 6.00
18 Damian Lillard 5.00 12.00
19 Kevin Durant 10.00 25.00
20 Karl-Anthony Towns 6.00 15.00
21 Zach LaVine 2.50 6.00
22 Kevin Love 2.50 6.00
23 Jordan Clarkson 2.00 5.00
24 Kentavious Caldwell-Pope 2.00 5.00
25 Nikola Vucevic 2.00 5.00

2016-17 Donruss The Champ Is Here

RANDOM INSERTS IN PACKS
*PROOF: .6X TO 1.5X BASIC
*PROOF BLUE/99: 1X TO 2.5X BASIC
1 LeBron James 2.00 5.00
2 Stephen Curry 2.00 5.00
3 Kyrie Irving 1.00 2.50
4 Klay Thompson .60 1.50
5 Dwyane Wade .75 2.00
6 Shaquille O'Neal 1.25 3.00
7 Kobe Bryant 2.00 5.00
8 Alonzo Mourning .60 1.50
9 Dirk Nowitzki .60 1.50
10 Tony Parker .50 1.25
11 Kevin Garnett .75 2.00
12 Manu Ginobili .50 1.25
13 Scottie Pippen 1.00 2.50
14 Larry Bird 1.25 3.00
15 Magic Johnson 1.25 3.00

2016-17 Donruss The Rookies

RANDOM INSERTS IN PACKS
*PROOF: .6X TO 1.5X BASIC
*PROOF BLUE/99: 1X TO 2.5X BASIC
1 Brandon Ingram 2.50 6.00
2 Ben Simmons 2.50 6.00
3 Kris Dunn 1.25 3.00
4 Buddy Hield 1.00 2.50
5 Marquese Chriss 1.00 2.50

2016-17 Donruss Timeless Treasures Materials Signatures

RANDOM INSERTS IN PACKS
PRINT RUNS B/WN 49-99 COPIES PER
*PRIME/25: .75X TO 2X BASIC
1 Brandon Ingram/99 50.00 120.00
2 Kris Dunn/99 12.00 30.00
3 Buddy Hield/99 15.00 40.00
4 Jaylen Brown/99 15.00 40.00
5 Jamal Murray/99 25.00 60.00
6 Marquese Chriss/99 12.00 30.00
7 Thon Maker/99 15.00 40.00
8 Denzel Valentine/99 5.00 12.00
9 Wade Baldwin IV/99 4.00 10.00
10 Malachi Richardson/99 5.00 12.00
11 Dragan Bender/99 10.00 25.00
12 Kevin Durant/49 60.00 150.00
13 Kyrie Irving/49 25.00 60.00
14 Carmelo Anthony/49 20.00 50.00
15 D'Angelo Russell/49 15.00 40.00
16 Karl-Anthony Towns/49 50.00 120.00
17 Dirk Nowitzki/49 40.00 100.00
18 Mark Price/49 10.00 25.00
19 Dan Issel/49 12.00 30.00
20 Jim Jackson/49 4.00 10.00
21 Glen Rice/49 5.00 12.00
22 Dennis Scott/49 4.00 10.00
23 Bill Laimbeer/49 5.00 12.00
24 Dikembe Mutombo/49 6.00 15.00
25 Jeff Hornacek/49 5.00 12.00

2016-17 Donruss Optic

COMPLETE SET (200) 25.00 60.00
1 Joel Embiid .50 1.25
2 Jahlil Okafor .25 .60
3 Nerlens Noel .25 .60
4 T.J. McConnell .20 .50
5 Giannis Antetokounmpo .60 1.50
6 Jabari Parker .40 1.00
7 Khris Middleton .25 .60
8 Matthew Dellavedova .25 .60
9 John Henson .25 .60
10 Jimmy Butler .30 .75
11 Rajon Rondo .30 .75
12 Dwyane Wade .50 1.25
13 Nikola Mirotic .25 .60
14 Bobby Portis .20 .50
15 LeBron James 1.25 3.00
16 Kevin Love .30 .75
17 Kyrie Irving .60 1.50
18 Richard Jefferson .25 .60
19 Tristan Thompson .25 .60
20 Isaiah Thomas .30 .75
21 Avery Bradley .25 .60
22 Al Horford .25 .60
23 Marcus Smart .25 .60
24 Jordan Mickey .20 .50
25 Chris Paul .40 1.00
26 DeAndre Jordan .30 .75
27 Blake Griffin .30 .75
28 Jamal Crawford .30 .75
29 J.J. Redick .30 .75
30 Mike Conley .25 .60
31 Chandler Parsons .25 .60
32 Marc Gasol .30 .75
33 Zach Randolph .25 .60
34 Dennis Schroder .25 .60
35 Paul Millsap .30 .75
36 Dwight Howard .25 .60
37 Kent Bazemore .25 .60
38 Kyle Korver .25 .60
39 Justise Winslow .25 .60
40 Josh Richardson .20 .50
41 Goran Dragic .25 .60
42 Tyler Johnson .20 .50
43 Hassan Whiteside .25 .60
44 Kemba Walker .30 .75
45 Nicolas Batum .25 .60
46 Frank Kaminsky .25 .60
47 Jeremy Lamb .20 .50
48 Aaron Harrison .20 .50
49 Joe Johnson .25 .60
50 Rudy Gobert .30 .75
51 George Hill .25 .60
52 Gordon Hayward .30 .75
53 Rodney Hood .25 .60
54 DeMarcus Cousins .30 .75
55 Ben McLemore .20 .50
56 Willie Cauley-Stein .25 .60
57 Rudy Gay .30 .75
58 Omri Casspi .20 .50
59 Carmelo Anthony .40 1.00
60 Kristaps Porzingis .60 1.50
61 Joakim Noah .25 .60
62 Derrick Rose .40 1.00
63 Larry Nance Jr. .25 .60
64 D'Angelo Russell .40 1.00
65 Julius Randle .30 .75
66 Lou Williams .25 .60
67 Serge Ibaka .25 .60
68 Jeff Green .25 .60
69 Mario Hezonja .20 .50
70 Evan Fournier .25 .60
71 Aaron Gordon .25 .60
72 Bismack Biyombo .20 .50
73 Nikola Vucevic .25 .60
74 Harrison Barnes .25 .60
75 Andrew Bogut .25 .60
76 J.J. Barea .25 .60
77 Dirk Nowitzki .40 1.00
78 Deron Williams .25 .60
79 Wesley Matthews .20 .50
80 Brook Lopez .25 .60
81 Rondae Hollis-Jefferson .20 .50
82 Bojan Bogdanovic .20 .50
83 Jeremy Lin .30 .75
84 Chris McCullough .20 .50
85 Emmanuel Mudiay .25 .60
86 Kenneth Faried .25 .60
87 Danilo Gallinari .25 .60
88 Will Barton .20 .50
89 Wilson Chandler .25 .60
90 Nikola Jokic .30 .75
91 Jeff Teague .25 .60
92 Myles Turner .25 .60
93 Paul George .40 1.00
94 Monta Ellis .25 .60
95 C.J. Miles .25 .60
96 Thaddeus Young .20 .50
97 Anthony Davis .60 1.50
98 Tyreke Evans .20 .50
99 Jrue Holiday .25 .60
100 Stanley Johnson .20 .50
101 Marcus Morris .20 .50
102 Kentavious Caldwell-Pope .25 .60
103 Reggie Jackson .25 .60
104 Andre Drummond .30 .75
105 DeMar DeRozan .30 .75
106 Kyle Lowry .25 .60
107 Jonas Valanciunas .25 .60
108 DeMarre Carroll .20 .50
109 Norman Powell .20 .50
110 James Harden .50 1.25
111 Trevor Ariza .20 .50
112 Clint Capela .20 .50
113 Sam Dekker .25 .60
114 Patrick Beverley .20 .50
115 LaMarcus Aldridge .30 .75
116 Kawhi Leonard .50 1.25
117 Tony Parker .30 .75
118 Manu Ginobili .30 .75
119 Pau Gasol .30 .75
120 Eric Bledsoe .25 .60
121 Devin Booker .50 1.25
122 Brandon Knight .25 .60
123 Alex Len .20 .50
124 Tyson Chandler .25 .60
125 Andrew Wiggins .50 1.25
126 Zach LaVine .30 .75
127 Ricky Rubio .30 .75
128 Karl-Anthony Towns .75 2.00
129 Gorgui Dieng .20 .50
130 C.J. McCollum .25 .60
131 Damian Lillard .60 1.50
132 Evan Turner .20 .50
133 Al-Farouq Aminu .25 .60
134 Mason Plumlee .25 .60
135 Stephen Curry 1.25 3.00
136 Klay Thompson .40 1.00
137 Kevin Durant .75 2.00
138 Draymond Green .40 1.00
139 Andre Iguodala .25 .60
140 John Wall .40 1.00
141 Markieff Morris .20 .50
142 Marcin Gortat .25 .60
143 Bradley Beal .30 .75
144 Kelly Oubre Jr. .20 .50
145 Russell Westbrook .75 2.00
146 Victor Oladipo .25 .60
147 Steven Adams .25 .60
148 Cameron Payne .20 .50
149 Andre Roberson .20 .50
150 Jordan Clarkson .25 .60
151 Ben Simmons RC 6.00 15.00
152 Brandon Ingram RC 2.50 6.00
153 Jaylen Brown RC 1.50 4.00
154 Dragan Bender RC .50 1.25
155 Kris Dunn RC 1.25 3.00
156 Buddy Hield RC 1.00 2.50
157 Jamal Murray RC 1.25 3.00
158 Marquese Chriss RC 1.00 2.50
159 Jakob Poeltl RC .50 1.25
160 Thon Maker RC 1.25 3.00
161 Domantas Sabonis RC .60 1.50
162 Taurean Prince RC .60 1.50
163 Denzel Valentine RC .50 1.25
164 Wade Baldwin IV RC .40 1.00
165 Henry Ellenson RC .50 1.25
166 Malik Beasley RC .40 1.00
167 Caris LeVert RC .50 1.25
168 DeAndre' Bembry RC .40 1.00
169 Malachi Richardson RC .50 1.25
170 Brice Johnson RC .40 1.00
171 Pascal Siakam RC .40 1.00
172 Skal Labissiere RC .60 1.50
173 Dejounte Murray RC .75 2.00
174 Damian Jones RC .40 1.00
175 Deyonta Davis RC .40 1.00
176 Ivica Zubac RC .60 1.50
177 Cheick Diallo RC .40 1.00
178 Tyler Ulis RC 1.25 3.00
179 Malcolm Brogdon RC 1.00 2.50
180 Chinanu Onuaku RC .40 1.00
181 Patrick McCaw RC .75 2.00
182 Diamond Stone RC .40 1.00
183 Stephen Zimmerman RC .40 1.00
184 Isaiah Whitehead RC .40 1.00
185 Demetrius Jackson RC .40 1.00
186 A.J. Hammons RC .40 1.00
187 Jake Layman RC .50 1.25
188 Michael Gbinije RC .40 1.00
189 Georges Niang RC .40 1.00
190 Tomas Satoransky RC .40 1.00
191 Joel Bolomboy RC .40 1.00
192 Kay Felder RC .40 1.00
193 Paul Zipser RC .60 1.50
194 Mindaugas Kuzminskas RC .50 1.25
195 Georgios Papagiannis RC .40 1.00
196 Alex Abrines RC .60 1.50
197 Willy Hernangomez RC .50 1.25
198 Marshall Plumlee RC .40 1.00
199 Sheldon McClellan RC .40 1.00
200 Ron Baker RC .50 1.25

2016-17 Donruss Optic Aqua

*AQUA: 4X TO 10X BASIC
*AQUA RC: 4X TO 10X BASIC RC
RANDOMLY INSERTED IN PACKS
STATED PRINT RUN 25 SER. #'D SETS
15 LeBron James 30.00 80.00
151 Ben Simmons 400.00 800.00
152 Brandon Ingram 40.00 100.00
157 Jamal Murray 25.00 60.00
158 Marquese Chriss 25.00 60.00
173 Dejounte Murray 30.00 80.00

2016-17 Donruss Optic Blue

*BLUE: 2X TO 5X BASIC
*BLUE RC: 2X TO 5X BASIC RC
RANDOMLY INSERTED IN PACKS
STATED PRINT RUN 49 SER. #'D SETS
15 LeBron James 15.00 40.00
151 Ben Simmons 150.00 400.00
152 Brandon Ingram 20.00 50.00
157 Jamal Murray 10.00 25.00
173 Dejounte Murray 10.00 25.00

2016-17 Donruss Optic Checkerboard

*CHECKER: 4X TO 10X BASIC
*CHECKER RC: 4X TO 10X BASIC RC
RANDOMLY INSERTED IN PACKS
15 LeBron James 75.00 200.00
135 Stephen Curry 25.00 60.00
137 Kevin Durant 20.00 50.00
151 Ben Simmons 300.00 500.00
152 Brandon Ingram 60.00 150.00
153 Jaylen Brown 25.00 60.00
156 Buddy Hield 25.00 60.00
157 Jamal Murray 25.00 60.00
158 Marquese Chriss 25.00 60.00
160 Thon Maker 25.00 60.00
173 Dejounte Murray 15.00 40.00
179 Malcolm Brogdon 25.00 60.00

2016-17 Donruss Optic Holo

*HOLO: .75X TO 2X BASIC
*HOLO RC: .75X TO 2X BASIC RC
RANDOMLY INSERTED IN PACKS
151 Ben Simmons 40.00 100.00
152 Brandon Ingram 12.00 30.00

2016-17 Donruss Optic Orange

*ORANGE: 1.2X TO 3X BASIC
*ORANGE RC: 1.2X TO 3X BASIC RC
RANDOMLY INSERTED IN PACKS
STATED PRINT RUN 199 SER. #'D SETS
151 Ben Simmons 75.00 200.00
152 Brandon Ingram 15.00 40.00
157 Jamal Murray 6.00 15.00
173 Dejounte Murray 6.00 15.00

2016-17 Donruss Optic Pink

*PINK: 4X TO 10X BASIC
*PINK RC: 4X TO 10X BASIC RC
RANDOMLY INSERTED IN PACKS
STATED PRINT RUN 25 SER. #'D SETS
15 LeBron James 30.00 80.00
151 Ben Simmons 400.00 800.00
152 Brandon Ingram 40.00 100.00
157 Jamal Murray 25.00 60.00
158 Marquese Chriss 25.00 60.00
173 Dejounte Murray 30.00 80.00

2016-17 Donruss Optic Purple

*PURPLE: .75X TO 2X BASIC
*PURPLE RC: .75X TO 2X BASIC RC
RANDOMLY INSERTED IN PACKS
151 Ben Simmons 40.00 100.00
152 Brandon Ingram 8.00 20.00

2016-17 Donruss Optic Red

*RED: 1.2X TO 3X BASIC
*RED RC: 1.2X TO 3X BASIC RC
RANDOMLY INSERTED IN PACKS
STATED PRINT RUN 99 SER. #'D SETS
151 Ben Simmons 100.00 250.00
152 Brandon Ingram 15.00 40.00
157 Jamal Murray 6.00 15.00
173 Dejounte Murray 6.00 15.00

2016-17 Donruss Optic White Sparkle

*WHTE SPARKLE: 6X TO 15X BASIC
*WHITE SPARKLE RC: 6X TO 15X BASIC RC
RANDOMLY INSERTED IN PACKS
1 Joel Embiid 12.00 30.00
5 Giannis Antetokounmpo 20.00 50.00
15 LeBron James 300.00 500.00
20 Isaiah Thomas 25.00 60.00
62 Derrick Rose 20.00 50.00
110 James Harden 20.00 50.00
116 Kawhi Leonard 40.00 100.00
121 Devin Booker 40.00 100.00
125 Andrew Wiggins 15.00 4.00
126 Zach LaVine 6.00 15.00
128 Karl-Anthony Towns 60.00 150.00
135 Stephen Curry 40.00 100.00
136 Klay Thompson 20.00 50.00
137 Kevin Durant 40.00 100.00
138 Draymond Green 20.00 50.00
145 Russell Westbrook 40.00 100.00
151 Ben Simmons 1000.00 1500.00
152 Brandon Ingram 250.00 500.00
153 Jaylen Brown 100.00 250.00
154 Dragan Bender 40.00 100.00
155 Kris Dunn 60.00 150.00
156 Buddy Hield 100.00 250.00
157 Jamal Murray 100.00 250.00
158 Marquese Chriss 60.00 150.00
160 Thon Maker 75.00 200.00
161 Domantas Sabonis 15.00 40.00
162 Taurean Prince 20.00 50.00
163 Denzel Valentine 20.00 50.00
164 Wade Baldwin IV 15.00 40.00
165 Henry Ellenson 12.00 30.00
167 Caris LeVert 15.00 40.00
168 DeAndre' Bembry 12.00 30.00
169 Malachi Richardson 30.00 80.00
170 Brice Johnson 20.00 50.00
172 Skal Labissiere 60.00 150.00
173 Dejounte Murray 125.00 300.00
178 Tyler Ulis 60.00 150.00
179 Malcolm Brogdon 75.00 200.00
181 Patrick McCaw 30.00 80.00
197 Willy Hernangomez 12.00 30.00

2016-17 Donruss Optic All-Stars

RANDOM INSERTS IN PACKS
1 Kobe Bryant 2.00 5.00
2 Larry Bird 1.25 3.00
3 Magic Johnson 1.25 3.00
4 Shaquille O'Neal 1.25 3.00
5 Grant Hill .60 1.50
6 Scottie Pippen 1.00 2.50
7 Isiah Thomas .50 1.25
8 Allen Iverson .60 1.50
9 Wilt Chamberlain 1.00 2.50
10 Steve Nash .50 1.25
11 Dwyane Wade .75 2.00
12 Kyle Lowry .40 1.00
13 LeBron James 2.00 5.00
14 Paul George .60 1.50
15 Carmelo Anthony .60 1.50
16 John Wall .60 1.50
17 Paul Millsap .50 1.25
18 DeMar DeRozan .50 1.25
19 Andre Drummond .50 1.25
20 Isaiah Thomas .50 1.25
21 Stephen Curry 2.00 5.00
22 Russell Westbrook 1.25 3.00
23 Kobe Bryant 2.00 5.00
24 Kevin Durant 1.25 3.00
25 Kawhi Leonard .75 2.00
26 Chris Paul .60 1.50
27 LaMarcus Aldridge .50 1.25
28 James Harden .75 2.00
29 Anthony Davis 1.00 2.50
30 Draymond Green .60 1.50

2016-17 Donruss Optic All-Stars Blue

*BLUE: 1.2X TO 3X BASIC
RANDOM INSERTS IN PACKS
STATED PRINT RUN 49 SER. #'D SETS
13 LeBron James 10.00 25.00

2016-17 Donruss Optic All-Stars Holo

*HOLO: .5X TO 1.2X BASIC
RANDOM INSERTS IN PACKS
13 LeBron James 4.00 10.00

2016-17 Donruss Optic All-Stars Red

*RED: .75X TO 2X BASIC
RANDOM INSERTS IN PACKS
STATED PRINT RUN 99 SER. #'D SETS
13 LeBron James 6.00 15.00

2016-17 Donruss Optic Court Kings

RANDOM INSERTS IN PACKS
1 LeBron James 2.00 5.00
2 Stephen Curry 2.00 5.00
3 Dwyane Wade .75 2.00
4 Dirk Nowitzki .60 1.50
5 Chris Paul .60 1.50
6 Anthony Davis 1.00 2.50
7 Kyrie Irving 1.00 2.50
8 Kevin Durant 1.25 3.00
9 James Harden .75 2.00
10 Paul George .60 1.50
11 Jimmy Butler .50 1.25
12 Carmelo Anthony .60 1.50
13 DeMarcus Cousins .50 1.25
14 Blake Griffin .50 1.25
15 Karl-Anthony Towns 1.25 3.00
16 John Wall .60 1.50
17 Derrick Rose .60 1.50
18 Kawhi Leonard .75 2.00
19 Russell Westbrook 1.25 3.00
20 Klay Thompson .60 1.50
21 DeMar DeRozan .50 1.25
22 Damian Lillard 1.00 2.50
23 Kristaps Porzingis 1.00 2.50
24 Giannis Antetokounmpo 1.00 2.50
25 Andrew Wiggins .75 2.00
26 Isaiah Thomas .50 1.25
27 Jeremy Lin .50 1.25
28 Victor Oladipo .40 1.00
29 Eric Bledsoe .40 1.00
30 Kyle Lowry .40 1.00
31 Andre Drummond .50 1.25
32 Kemba Walker .50 1.25
33 Mike Conley .40 1.00
34 Dennis Schroder .40 1.00
35 Justise Winslow .40 1.00
36 Jordan Clarkson .40 1.00
37 Serge Ibaka .40 1.00
38 Gordon Hayward .50 1.25
39 Emmanuel Mudiay .40 1.00
40 Jahlil Okafor .40 1.00

2016-17 Donruss Optic Court Kings Aqua

*AQUA: 2.5X TO 6X BASIC
RANDOM INSERTS IN PACKS
STATED PRINT RUN 25 SER. #'D SETS
1 LeBron James 25.00 60.00
2 Stephen Curry 25.00 60.00

2016-17 Donruss Optic Court Kings Blue

*BLUE: 1.2X TO 3X BASIC
RANDOM INSERTS IN PACKS
STATED PRINT RUN 49 SER. #'D SETS
1 LeBron James 15.00 40.00

2016-17 Donruss Optic Court Kings Holo
*HOLO: .5X TO 1.2X BASIC
RANDOM INSERTS IN PACKS
1 LeBron James 4.00 10.00

2016-17 Donruss Optic Court Kings Orange
*ORANGE: .75X TO 2X BASIC
RANDOM INSERTS IN PACKS
STATED PRINT RUN 199 SER. #'D SETS
1 LeBron James 10.00 25.00

2016-17 Donruss Optic Court Kings Pink
*PINK: 2.5X TO 6X BASIC
RANDOM INSERTS IN PACKS
STATED PRINT RUN 25 SER. #'D SETS
1 LeBron James 25.00 60.00
2 Stephen Curry 25.00 60.00

2016-17 Donruss Optic Court Kings Purple
*PURPLE: .5X TO 1.2X BASIC
RANDOM INSERTS IN PACKS
1 LeBron James 4.00 10.00

2016-17 Donruss Optic Court Kings Red
*RED: .75X TO 2X BASIC
RANDOM INSERTS IN PACKS
STATED PRINT RUN 99 SER. #'D SETS
1 LeBron James 10.00 25.00

2016-17 Donruss Optic Crashers
RANDOM INSERTS IN PACKS
*HOLO: .5X TO 1.2X BASIC
*RED/99: .75X TO 2X BASIC
*BLUE/49: 1.2X TO 3X BASIC
1 DeAndre Jordan .50 1.25
2 Hassan Whiteside .40 1.00
3 Pau Gasol .50 1.25
4 Andre Drummond .50 1.25
5 Dwight Howard .40 1.00
6 DeMarcus Cousins .50 1.25
7 Rudy Gobert .50 1.25
8 Karl-Anthony Towns 1.25 3.00
9 Anthony Davis 1.00 2.50
10 Julius Randle .50 1.25
11 Kevin Love .50 1.25
12 Marcin Gortat .40 1.00
13 Draymond Green .60 1.50
14 Kenneth Faried .40 1.00
15 LaMarcus Aldridge .50 1.25

2016-17 Donruss Optic Dimes
RANDOM INSERTS IN PACKS
*HOLO: .5X TO 1.2X BASIC
1 Chris Paul .60 1.50
2 John Wall .60 1.50
3 Ricky Rubio .50 1.25
4 James Harden .75 2.00
5 Russell Westbrook 1.25 3.00
6 Damian Lillard 1.00 2.50
7 Goran Dragic .40 1.00
8 Stephen Curry 2.00 5.00
9 Kyle Lowry .40 1.00
10 Isaiah Thomas .50 1.25

2016-17 Donruss Optic Dimes Blue
*BLUE: 1.2X TO 3X BASIC
RANDOM INSERTS IN PACKS
STATED PRINT RUN 49 SER. #'D SETS
8 Stephen Curry 10.00 25.00

2016-17 Donruss Optic Dimes Red
*RED: .75X TO 2X BASIC
RANDOM INSERTS IN PACKS
STATED PRINT RUN 99 SER. #'D SETS
8 Stephen Curry 6.00 15.00

2016-17 Donruss Optic Dominator Signatures
RANDOM INSERTS IN PACKS
PRINT RUNS B/WN 25-99 COPIES PER
1 Karl-Anthony Towns/25 50.00 120.00
3 Devin Booker/99 25.00 60.00
4 Justise Winslow/99 4.00 10.00
5 Dirk Nowitzki/25 60.00 150.00
6 Jabari Parker/25 12.00 30.00
7 Victor Oladipo/99 4.00 10.00
8 Andrew Wiggins/25 25.00 60.00
9 Kevin Durant/25 75.00 200.00
10 Kyrie Irving/25 30.00 80.00
11 John Wall/25 25.00 60.00
13 Dwyane Wade/25 30.00 80.00
14 Jordan Clarkson/99 4.00 10.00
15 Eric Bledsoe/99 4.00 10.00
16 Carmelo Anthony/25 12.00 30.00
17 Jeremy Lin/99 20.00 50.00
18 Isaiah Thomas/99 20.00 50.00
19 D'Angelo Russell/25 12.00 30.00
20 Klay Thompson/99 20.00 50.00
22 Paul Millsap/25 8.00 20.00
23 Pau Gasol/25 10.00 25.00
24 Chris Paul/25 20.00 50.00
25 Blake Griffin/99 12.00 30.00
26 Goran Dragic/99 4.00 10.00
27 Allen Iverson/25 50.00 120.00
28 Latrell Sprewell/25 8.00 20.00
29 James Worthy/25 10.00 25.00
30 Vin Baker/25 5.00 12.00
31 George Gervin/25 15.00 40.00
32 Spud Webb/25 6.00 15.00
33 Jalen Rose/50 6.00 15.00
34 John Starks/99 4.00 10.00
35 Bill Russell/25 60.00 150.00
36 Shawn Kemp/25 25.00 60.00
37 Sean Elliott/25 8.00 20.00
38 Kobe Bryant/25 100.00 250.00
39 Jason Kidd/25 12.00 30.00
40 Anfernee Hardaway/25 25.00 60.00

2016-17 Donruss Optic Elite Series
RANDOM INSERTS IN PACKS
1 Dirk Nowitzki .60 1.50
2 Stephen Curry 2.00 5.00
3 Kevin Durant 1.25 3.00
4 Derrick Rose .60 1.50
5 Dwyane Wade .75 2.00
6 Al Horford .40 1.00
7 Russell Westbrook 1.25 3.00
8 Damian Lillard 1.00 2.50
9 LeBron James 2.00 5.00
10 Anthony Davis 1.00 2.50
11 James Harden .75 2.00
12 Chris Paul .60 1.50
13 Kawhi Leonard .75 2.00
14 LaMarcus Aldridge .50 1.25
15 John Wall .60 1.50
16 Jimmy Butler .50 1.25
17 Kyrie Irving 1.00 2.50
18 Klay Thompson .60 1.50
19 Blake Griffin .50 1.25
20 Kyle Lowry .40 1.00
21 Pau Gasol .50 1.25
22 Marc Gasol .50 1.25
23 Carmelo Anthony .60 1.50
24 Mike Conley .40 1.00
25 Jordan Clarkson .40 1.00

2016-17 Donruss Optic Elite Series Blue
*BLUE: 1.2X TO 3X BASIC
RANDOM INSERTS IN PACKS
STATED PRINT RUN 49 SER. #'D SETS
9 LeBron James 12.00 30.00

2016-17 Donruss Optic Elite Series Holo
*HOLO: .5X TO 1.2X BASIC
RANDOM INSERTS IN PACKS
9 LeBron James 4.00 10.00

2016-17 Donruss Optic Elite Series Red
*RED: .75X TO 2X BASIC
RANDOM INSERTS IN PACKS
STATED PRINT RUN 99 SER. #'D SETS
9 LeBron James 8.00 20.00

2016-17 Donruss Optic Hall Dominator Signatures
RANDOM INSERTS IN PACKS
PRINT RUNS B/WN 25-99 COPIES PER
1 Dan Issel/99 4.00 10.00
2 Artis Gilmore/50 5.00 12.00
3 Adrian Dantley/99 4.00 10.00
4 Tom Heinsohn/99 12.00 30.00
5 Elvin Hayes/50 6.00 15.00
6 Jamaal Wilkes/99 5.00 12.00
7 Tom Sanders/99 10.00 25.00
8 David Robinson/25 15.00 40.00
9 Rick Barry/50 5.00 12.00
10 Bob Lanier/99 4.00 10.00
11 Dennis Rodman/50 15.00 40.00
12 Scottie Pippen/25 60.00 150.00
14 Alex English/99 4.00 10.00
15 Bernard King/99 4.00 10.00
16 Alonzo Mourning/25 15.00 40.00
17 Hakeem Olajuwon/50 12.00 30.00
18 Karl Malone/25 25.00 60.00
19 Earl Lloyd/50 12.00 30.00
20 Calvin Murphy/50 5.00 12.00
21 Shaquille O'Neal/50 50.00 120.00
22 Cliff Hagan/50 5.00 12.00
23 James Worthy/25 10.00 25.00
24 Joe Dumars/50 6.00 15.00
25 Nate Archibald/25 6.00 15.00
26 Magic Johnson/25 25.00 60.00
27 Walt Frazier/50 6.00 15.00
28 Oscar Robertson/25 15.00 40.00
29 Louie Dampier/50 6.00 15.00
30 Dominique Wilkins/25 10.00 25.00

2016-17 Donruss Optic Hall Kings
RANDOM INSERTS IN PACKS
*HOLO: .5X TO 1.2X BASIC
*PURPLE: .5X TO 1.2X BASIC
*ORANGE/199: .75X TO 2X BASIC
*RED/99: .75X TO 2X BASIC
*BLUE/49: 1.2X TO 3X BASIC
*AQUA/25: 2.5X TO 6X BASIC
*PINK/25: 2.5X TO 6X BASIC
1 Shaquille O'Neal 1.25 3.00
2 Allen Iverson .60 1.50
3 Yao Ming .60 1.50
4 Alonzo Mourning .60 1.50
5 Gary Payton .50 1.25
6 Bernard King .40 1.00
7 Ralph Sampson .40 1.00
8 Jamaal Wilkes .50 1.25
9 Artis Gilmore .40 1.00
10 Chris Mullin .50 1.25
11 Dennis Rodman 1.00 2.50
12 Karl Malone .60 1.50
13 Scottie Pippen 1.00 2.50
14 David Robinson .75 2.00
15 John Stockton .75 2.00
16 Adrian Dantley .40 1.00
17 Patrick Ewing .60 1.50
18 Hakeem Olajuwon .60 1.50
19 Joe Dumars .50 1.25
20 Dominique Wilkins .60 1.50
21 Clyde Drexler .60 1.50
22 Robert Parish .50 1.25
23 James Worthy .60 1.50
24 Magic Johnson 1.25 3.00
25 Drazen Petrovic .50 1.25
26 Moses Malone .50 1.25
27 Isiah Thomas .50 1.25
28 Bob McAdoo .40 1.00
29 Kevin McHale .50 1.25
30 Larry Bird 1.25 3.00

2016-17 Donruss Optic Rookie Dominator Signatures
RANDOM INSERTS IN PACKS
PRINT RUNS B/WN 25-99 COPIES PER
1 Patrick McCaw/99 10.00 25.00
2 Marquese Chriss/25 20.00 50.00
3 Buddy Hield/25 25.00 60.00
4 Henry Ellenson/99 4.00 10.00
5 Georges Niang/99 3.00 8.00
6 Demetrius Jackson/50 4.00 10.00
7 Dario Saric/25 30.00 80.00
8 Thon Maker/25 30.00 80.00
9 Domantas Sabonis/25 10.00 25.00
10 Dragan Bender/25 12.00 30.00
11 T. Luwawu-Cabarrot/99 6.00 15.00
12 Ivica Zubac/99 6.00 15.00
13 Damian Jones/50 4.00 10.00
15 Kris Dunn/25 15.00 40.00
16 Deyonta Davis/50 4.00 10.00
17 Brandon Ingram/25 50.00 120.00
18 Jamal Murray/25 30.00 80.00
19 Denzel Valentine/50 6.00 15.00
20 Jakob Poeltl/25 6.00 15.00
21 Skal Labissiere/50 12.00 30.00
22 Jake Layman/50 5.00 12.00
23 Diamond Stone/99 3.00 8.00
24 Chinanu Onuaku/99 3.00 8.00
25 Brice Johnson/99 3.00 8.00
26 Malik Beasley/50 4.00 10.00
27 Wade Baldwin IV/25 5.00 12.00
28 Taurean Prince/25 12.00 30.00
29 Kay Felder/99 3.00 8.00
30 Juan Hernangomez/50 8.00 20.00

2016-17 Donruss Optic Rookie Kings
RANDOM INSERTS IN PACKS
1 Brandon Ingram 2.50 6.00
2 Ben Simmons 2.50 6.00
3 Jaylen Brown 1.50 4.00
4 Dragan Bender .50 1.25
5 Kris Dunn 1.25 3.00
6 Buddy Hield 1.00 2.50
7 Jamal Murray 1.25 3.00
8 Marquese Chriss 1.00 2.50
9 Jakob Poeltl .50 1.25
10 Thon Maker 1.25 3.00
11 Domantas Sabonis .60 1.50
12 Taurean Prince .60 1.50
13 Denzel Valentine .50 1.25
14 Wade Baldwin IV .40 1.00
15 Henry Ellenson .50 1.25
16 Malik Beasley .40 1.00
17 Caris LeVert .50 1.25
18 DeAndre' Bembry .40 1.00
19 Malachi Richardson .50 1.25
20 Timothe Luwawu-Cabarrot .75 2.00
21 Brice Johnson .40 1.00
22 Pascal Siakam .40 1.00
23 Skal Labissiere .60 1.50
24 Dejounte Murray .75 2.00
25 Damian Jones .40 1.00
26 Isaiah Whitehead .40 1.00
27 Deyonta Davis .40 1.00
28 Kay Felder .40 1.00
29 A.J. Hammons .40 1.00
30 Dario Saric 1.25 3.00

2016-17 Donruss Optic Rookie Kings Aqua
*AQUA: 2.5X TO 6X BASIC
RANDOM INSERTS IN PACKS
STATED PRINT RUN 25 SER. #'D SETS
1 Brandon Ingram 25.00 60.00
2 Ben Simmons 125.00 300.00
6 Buddy Hield 8.00 20.00
7 Jamal Murray 20.00 50.00
23 Skal Labissiere 10.00 25.00
24 Dejounte Murray 15.00 40.00

2016-17 Donruss Optic Rookie Kings Blue
*BLUE: 1.2X TO 3X BASIC
RANDOM INSERTS IN PACKS
STATED PRINT RUN 49 SER. #'D SETS
2 Ben Simmons 50.00 120.00

2016-17 Donruss Optic Rookie Kings Holo
*HOLO: .5X TO 1.2X BASIC
RANDOM INSERTS IN PACKS
2 Ben Simmons 15.00 40.00

2016-17 Donruss Optic Rookie Kings Orange
*ORANGE: .75X TO 2X BASIC
RANDOM INSERTS IN PACKS
STATED PRINT RUN 199 SER. #'D SETS
2 Ben Simmons 30.00 80.00

2016-17 Donruss Optic Rookie Kings Pink
*PINK: 2.5X TO 6X BASIC
RANDOM INSERTS IN PACKS
STATED PRINT RUN 25 SER. #'D SETS
1 Brandon Ingram 25.00 60.00
2 Ben Simmons 125.00 300.00
6 Buddy Hield 8.00 20.00
7 Jamal Murray 20.00 50.00
23 Skal Labissiere 10.00 25.00
24 Dejounte Murray 15.00 40.00

2016-17 Donruss Optic Rookie Kings Purple
*PURPLE: .5X TO 1.2X BASIC
RANDOM INSERTS IN PACKS
2 Ben Simmons 15.00 40.00

2016-17 Donruss Optic Rookie Kings Red
*RED: .75X TO 2X BASIC
RANDOM INSERTS IN PACKS
STATED PRINT RUN 99 SER. #'D SETS
2 Ben Simmons 30.00 80.00

2016-17 Donruss Optic Rookie Signatures
RANDOM INSERTS IN PACKS
*HOLO: .4X TO 1X BASIC
*BLUE/25: .75X TO 2X BASIC
*PINK/25: .75X TO 2X BASIC
1 Brandon Ingram 25.00 60.00
2 Jaylen Brown 15.00 40.00
3 Kris Dunn 8.00 20.00
4 Buddy Hield 12.00 30.00
5 Jakob Poeltl 3.00 8.00
6 Jamal Murray 15.00 40.00
7 Patrick McCaw 8.00 20.00
8 Malcolm Brogdon 12.00 30.00
9 Wade Baldwin IV 2.50 6.00
10 Deyonta Davis 2.50 6.00
11 Kay Felder 2.50 6.00
12 Dario Saric 15.00 40.00
13 Timothe Luwawu-Cabarrot 5.00 12.00
14 Paul Zipser 4.00 10.00
15 Diamond Stone 2.50 6.00
16 Brice Johnson 2.50 6.00
17 Taurean Prince 6.00 15.00
18 DeAndre' Bembry 2.50 6.00
19 Joel Bolomboy 2.50 6.00
20 Skal Labissiere 8.00 20.00
22 Georgios Papagiannis 2.50 6.00
23 Ron Baker 5.00 12.00
24 Willy Hernangomez 6.00 15.00
25 Mindaugas Kuzminskas 3.00 8.00
26 Ivica Zubac 6.00 15.00
27 Stephen Zimmerman 2.50 6.00
31 Juan Hernangomez 5.00 12.00
32 Malik Beasley 2.50 6.00
33 Cheick Diallo 2.50 6.00
34 Henry Ellenson 3.00 8.00
35 Pascal Siakam 2.50 6.00
36 Chinanu Onuaku 2.50 6.00
37 Yogi Ferrell 3.00 8.00
39 Marquese Chriss 10.00 25.00
40 Dragan Bender 6.00 15.00
41 Domantas Sabonis 5.00 12.00
42 Jake Layman 3.00 8.00
43 Damian Jones 2.50 6.00
44 Sheldon McClellan 2.50 6.00
46 Denzel Valentine 4.00 10.00
47 Demetrius Jackson 2.50 6.00
48 Thon Maker 15.00 40.00
49 Georges Niang 2.50 6.00
50 Fred VanVleet 5.00 12.00

2016-17 Donruss Optic Rookie Signatures Purple
*PURPLE: .4X TO 1X BASIC
RANDOM INSERTS IN PACKS
28 A.J. Hammons 2.50 6.00

2016-17 Donruss Optic Signature Series
RANDOM INSERTS IN PACKS
*HOLO: .4X TO 1X BASIC
*PURPLE: .4X TO 1X BASIC
1 Cody Zeller 2.50 6.00
2 C.J. McCollum 6.00 15.00
3 Ian Clark 2.50 6.00
4 Dwight Powell 2.50 6.00
5 E'Twaun Moore 2.50 6.00
7 James Ennis 2.50 6.00
8 Justin Hamilton 2.50 6.00
9 Alex Len 2.50 6.00
10 Allen Crabbe 2.50 6.00
11 Noah Vonleh 2.50 6.00
12 Spud Webb 3.00 8.00
13 Kevon Looney 3.00 8.00
14 Maurice Harkless 2.50 6.00
15 C.J. Miles 3.00 8.00
16 Dirk Nowitzki 40.00 100.00
17 Kyle O'Quinn 2.50 6.00
18 Jeff Withey 2.50 6.00
19 Mario Hezonja 2.50 6.00
20 Rashad Vaughn 2.50 6.00
21 Jordan McRae 2.50 6.00
22 Deron Williams 3.00 8.00
23 Jason Terry 3.00 8.00
24 Glen Rice 3.00 8.00
25 Michael Carter-Williams 2.50 6.00
26 Jason Smith 2.50 6.00
27 Jeremy Lin 15.00 40.00
28 Vin Baker 5.00 12.00
29 Norman Powell 2.50 6.00
30 Langston Galloway 2.50 6.00
31 Glenn Robinson III 2.50 6.00
32 Will Barton 2.50 6.00
33 Michael Kidd-Gilchrist 3.00 8.00
35 Steve Novak 2.50 6.00
36 James Johnson 2.50 6.00
37 Mike Muscala 2.50 6.00
38 Reggie Bullock 2.50 6.00
39 Troy Daniels 2.50 6.00
40 Alan Anderson 2.50 6.00
41 Rondae Hollis-Jefferson 2.50 6.00
42 Karl-Anthony Towns 25.00 60.00
43 John Wall 12.00 30.00
44 Justise Winslow 3.00 8.00
45 Marc Gasol 6.00 15.00
48 Devin Booker 20.00 50.00
49 Isaiah Canaan 3.00 8.00
50 Justin Anderson 3.00 8.00

2016-17 Donruss Optic Signature Series Blue
*BLUE: .75X TO 2X BASIC
RANDOM INSERTS IN PACKS
STATED PRINT RUN 25 SER. #'D SETS
6 T.J. McConnell 5.00 12.00

2016-17 Donruss Optic Signature Series Pink
*PINK/25: .75X TO 2X BASIC
RANDOM INSERTS IN PACKS
STATED PRINT RUN 25 SER. #'D SETS
6 T.J. McConnell 5.00 12.00

2016-17 Donruss Optic The Champ is Here
RANDOM INSERTS IN PACKS
*HOLO: .5X TO 1.2X BASIC
1 LeBron James 2.00 5.00
2 Stephen Curry 2.00 5.00
3 Kyrie Irving 1.00 2.50
4 Klay Thompson .60 1.50
5 Dwyane Wade .75 2.00
6 Shaquille O'Neal 1.25 3.00
7 Kobe Bryant 2.00 5.00
8 Alonzo Mourning .60 1.50
9 Dirk Nowitzki .60 1.50
10 Tony Parker .50 1.25
11 Kevin Garnett .75 2.00
12 Manu Ginobili .50 1.25
13 Scottie Pippen 1.00 2.50
14 Larry Bird 1.25 3.00
15 Magic Johnson 1.25 3.00

2016-17 Donruss Optic The Champ is Here Blue
*BLUE: 1.2X TO 3X BASIC
RANDOM INSERTS IN PACKS
STATED PRINT RUN 49 SER. #'D SETS
1 LeBron James 15.00 40.00
2 Stephen Curry 10.00 25.00
7 Kobe Bryant 10.00 25.00

2016-17 Donruss Optic The Champ is Here Red
*RED: .75X TO 2X BASIC
RANDOM INSERTS IN PACKS
STATED PRINT RUN 99 SER. #'D SETS
1 LeBron James 10.00 25.00
2 Stephen Curry 6.00 15.00
7 Kobe Bryant 6.00 15.00

2016-17 Donruss Optic The Rookies
RANDOM INSERTS IN PACKS
1 Brandon Ingram 2.00 5.00
2 Ben Simmons 3.00 8.00
3 Kris Dunn 1.00 2.50
4 Buddy Hield .75 2.00
5 Marquese Chriss .75 2.00

2016-17 Donruss Optic The Rookies Blue
*BLUE: 2.5X TO 6X BASIC
RANDOM INSERTS IN PACKS
STATED PRINT RUN 49 SER. #'D SETS
1 Brandon Ingram 20.00 50.00
2 Ben Simmons 75.00 200.00

2016-17 Donruss Optic The Rookies Holo
*HOLO: .75X TO 2X BASIC
RANDOM INSERTS IN PACKS
2 Ben Simmons 25.00 60.00

2016-17 Donruss Optic The Rookies Red
*RED: 2X TO 5X BASIC
RANDOM INSERTS IN PACKS
STATED PRINT RUN 99 SER. #'D SETS
1 Brandon Ingram 15.00 40.00
2 Ben Simmons 60.00 150.00

2009-10 Donruss Elite
COMP.SET w/o SPs (120) 25.00 50.00
121-160 PRINT RUN 499 SER.#'d SETS
161-200 PRINT RUN 499 SER.#'d SETS
UNLESS LISTED IN CHECKLIST
1 Joe Johnson .40 1.00
2 Jamal Crawford .50 1.25
3 Josh Smith .40 1.00
4 Mike Bibby .40 1.00
5 Paul Pierce .50 1.25
6 Kevin Garnett .75 2.00
7 Ray Allen .50 1.25
8 Rajon Rondo .50 1.25
9 Gerald Wallace .40 1.00
10 Boris Diaw .40 1.00
11 Raymond Felton .40 1.00
12 Derrick Rose .75 2.00
13 John Salmons .40 1.00
14 Brad Miller .40 1.00
15 Tyrus Thomas .30 .75
16 LeBron James 2.00 5.00
17 Shaquille O'Neal 1.00 2.50
18 Mo Williams .40 1.00
19 Delonte West .30 .75
20 Dirk Nowitzki .60 1.50
21 Jason Kidd .50 1.25
22 Jason Terry .40 1.00
23 Shawn Marion .40 1.00
24 Carmelo Anthony .60 1.50
25 Chauncey Billups .50 1.25
26 Kenyon Martin .40 1.00
27 Nene .40 1.00
28 Ben Gordon .40 1.00
29 Richard Hamilton .40 1.00
30 Charlie Villanueva .30 .75
31 Tayshaun Prince .40 1.00
32 Stephen Jackson .40 1.00
33 Monta Ellis .40 1.00
34 Corey Maggette .40 1.00
35 Kelenna Azubuike .30 .75
36 Tracy McGrady .50 1.25
37 Shane Battier .50 1.25
38 Luis Scola .40 1.00
39 Trevor Ariza .30 .75
40 Danny Granger .40 1.00
41 Mike Dunleavy .30 .75
42 Troy Murphy .30 .75
43 T.J. Ford .30 .75
44 Eric Gordon .40 1.00
45 Al Thornton .40 1.00
46 Baron Davis .40 1.00
47 Marcus Camby .30 .75
48 Kobe Bryant 2.00 5.00
49 Ron Artest .50 1.25
50 Pau Gasol .50 1.25
51 Andrew Bynum .30 .75
52 Zach Randolph .40 1.00
53 Rudy Gay .50 1.25
54 O.J. Mayo .30 .75
55 Marc Gasol .50 1.25
56 Dwyane Wade .75 2.00
57 Michael Beasley .30 .75
58 Jermaine O'Neal .40 1.00
59 Daequan Cook .30 .75
60 Quentin Richardson .40 1.00
61 Michael Redd .40 1.00
62 Hakim Warrick .40 1.00
63 Andrew Bogut .40 1.00
64 Luke Ridnour .40 1.00
65 Al Jefferson .40 1.00
66 Ryan Gomes .30 .75
67 Kevin Love .50 1.25
68 Devin Harris .30 .75
69 Brook Lopez .40 1.00
70 Yi Jianlian .40 1.00
71 Rafer Alston .30 .75
72 Chris Paul .60 1.50
73 David West .40 1.00
74 Peja Stojakovic .50 1.25
75 James Posey .30 .75
76 Emeka Okafor .40 1.00
77 Nate Robinson .30 .75
78 David Lee .30 .75
79 Al Harrington .40 1.00
80 Larry Hughes .40 1.00
81 Kevin Durant 1.25 3.00
82 Russell Westbrook 1.25 3.00
83 Jeff Green .40 1.00
84 Nenad Krstic .30 .75
85 Dwight Howard .40 1.00
86 Vince Carter .60 1.50
87 Rashard Lewis .40 1.00
88 Jameer Nelson .30 .75
89 Elton Brand .50 1.25
90 Andre Iguodala .40 1.00
91 Thaddeus Young .30 .75
92 Amare Stoudemire .40 1.00
93 Steve Nash .50 1.25
94 Jason Richardson .50 1.25
95 Grant Hill .60 1.50
96 Brandon Roy .50 1.25
97 LaMarcus Aldridge .50 1.25
98 Steve Blake .30 .75
99 Andre Miller .40 1.00
100 Greg Oden .40 1.00
101 Kevin Martin .40 1.00
102 Andres Nocioni .30 .75
103 Francisco Garcia .30 .75
104 Spencer Hawes .30 .75
105 Tony Parker .50 1.25
106 Tim Duncan .75 2.00
107 Manu Ginobili .50 1.25
108 Richard Jefferson .40 1.00
109 Chris Bosh .50 1.25
110 Jose Calderon .30 .75
111 Andrea Bargnani .40 1.00
112 Hedo Turkoglu .40 1.00
113 Deron Williams .40 1.00
114 Mehmet Okur .30 .75
115 Andrei Kirilenko .40 1.00
116 Carlos Boozer .40 1.00
117 Antawn Jamison .40 1.00
118 Caron Butler .40 1.00
119 Gilbert Arenas .40 1.00
120 Randy Foye .30 .75
121 Willis Reed .75 2.00
122 Chris Mullin .75 2.00
123 Kevin Johnson .75 2.00
124 Spencer Haywood .50 1.25
125 David Robinson 1.25 3.00
126 Phil Jackson 1.00 2.50
127 Magic Johnson 2.00 5.00
128 Paul Westphal .75 2.00
129 Alex English .60 1.50
130 Kareem Abdul-Jabbar 1.25 3.00
131 Glen Rice .60 1.50
132 Nate McMillan .75 2.00
133 Bob Cousy 1.25 3.00
134 Mitch Richmond .75 2.00
135 Kelly Tripucka .50 1.25
136 Cedric Maxwell .75 2.00
137 Lenny Wilkens .75 2.00
138 Bill Russell 1.25 3.00
139 Sean Elliott .75 2.00
140 Hersey Hawkins .50 1.25
141 Clyde Drexler 1.00 2.50
142 Larry Bird 2.00 5.00
143 Connie Hawkins .75 2.00
144 Lou Hudson .75 2.00
145 Oscar Robertson .75 2.00
146 Jerry Lucas .75 2.00
147 Kevin McHale .75 2.00
148 Michael Cage .50 1.25
149 Vlade Divac .75 2.00
150 Jerry West 1.00 2.50
151 Bill Walton .75 2.00
152 Rick Barry .60 1.50
153 Artis Gilmore .60 1.50
154 Earl Monroe .75 2.00
155 Xavier McDaniel .50 1.25
156 Jalen Rose .75 2.00
157 Walt Frazier .75 2.00
158 Isiah Thomas .75 2.00
159 James Worthy 1.00 2.50
160 Karl Malone 1.00 2.50
161 Blake Griffin AU RC 30.00 80.00
162 Hasheem Thabeet AU RC 3.00 8.00
163 James Harden/479 AU RC 50.00 120.00
164 Tyreke Evans AU RC 4.00 10.00
165 Jonny Flynn AU RC 3.00 8.00
166 Stephen Curry AU RC 200.00 500.00
167 Jordan Hill AU RC 4.00 10.00
168 Danny Green AU RC 6.00 15.00
169 Brandon Jennings AU RC 8.00 20.00
170 Terrence Williams AU RC 3.00 8.00
171 Gerald Henderson AU RC 4.00 10.00
172 Tyler Hansbrough AU RC 4.00 10.00
173 Earl Clark AU RC 4.00 10.00
174 Austin Daye AU RC 3.00 8.00
175 James Johnson AU RC 4.00 10.00
176 Jrue Holiday AU RC 6.00 15.00
177 Ty Lawson AU RC 5.00 12.00
178 Jeff Teague AU RC 5.00 12.00
179 Eric Maynor/199 AU RC 3.00 8.00
180 Darren Collison/199 AU RC 5.00 12.00
181 Omri Casspi AU RC 4.00 10.00
182 B.J. Mullens AU RC 3.00 8.00
183 Rodrigue Beaubois AU RC 3.00 8.00
184 Taj Gibson/199 AU RC 5.00 12.00
185 DeMarre Carroll AU RC 4.00 10.00
186 Wayne Ellington/199 AU RC 5.00 12.00
187 Toney Douglas AU RC 3.00 8.00
188 Jeff Pendergraph AU RC 3.00 8.00
189 Jermaine Taylor AU RC 3.00 8.00
190 D.Cunningham/199 AU RC 3.00 8.00
191 DaJuan Summers AU RC 3.00 8.00
192 Sam Young/199 AU RC 3.00 8.00
193 DeJuan Blair AU RC 4.00 10.00
194 Jon Brockman AU RC 3.00 8.00
195 A.J. Price AU RC 3.00 8.00
196 Derrick Brown/199 AU RC 3.00 8.00
197 Jodie Meeks AU RC 5.00 12.00
198 Marcus Thornton/199 AU RC 4.00 10.00
199 Chase Budinger AU RC 4.00 10.00
200 Taylor Griffin AU RC 3.00 8.00

2009-10 Donruss Elite Aspirations
*1-120/10-29: 3X TO 8X BASE HI
*1-120/30-55: 2X TO 5X BASE HI
*121-160/10-29: 1.5X TO 4X BASE HI
*121-160/30-55: 1.25X TO 3X BASE HI
PRINT RUNS LISTED IN CHECKLIST
SOME ROOKIES UNPRICED DUE TO SCARCITY
7 Ray Allen/20 5.00 12.00
93 Steve Nash/13 6.00 15.00
95 Grant Hill/33 12.50 30.00
161 Blake Griffin/32 50.00 120.00
162 Hasheem Thabeet/34 1.25 3.00
166 Stephen Curry/30 200.00 400.00
167 Jordan Hill/43 1.50 4.00
169 Brandon Jennings/3
171 Gerald Henderson/15 3.00 8.00
172 Tyler Hansbrough/50 1.50 4.00
173 Earl Clark/55 1.50 4.00
175 James Johnson/16 3.00 8.00
181 Omri Casspi/18 3.00 8.00
182 B.J. Mullens/23 2.50 6.00
184 Taj Gibson/22 4.00 10.00
186 Wayne Ellington/19 4.00 10.00
187 Toney Douglas/23 2.50 6.00
190 Dante Cunningham/33 1.25 3.00
191 DaJuan Summers/35 1.25 3.00
193 DeJuan Blair/45 1.50 4.00
194 Jon Brockman/40 1.25 3.00
195 A.J. Price/22 2.50 6.00
197 Jodie Meeks/23 4.00 10.00
200 Taylor Griffin/32 1.25 3.00

2009-10 Donruss Elite Status
*1-120/45-75: 1.5X TO 4X BASE HI
*1-120/76-99: 1.25X TO 3X BASE HI
*121-160/45-75: 1.25 TO 3X BASE HI
*121-160/76-99: .75X TO 2X BASE HI
PRINT RUNS LISTED IN CHECKLIST
95 Grant Hill/67 6.00 15.00
161 Blake Griffin/68 30.00 80.00
162 Hasheem Thabeet/66 1.25 3.00
163 James Harden/87 12.00 30.00
164 Tyreke Evans/87 1.50 4.00
165 Jonny Flynn/90 1.25 3.00
166 Stephen Curry/70 150.00 300.00
167 Jordan Hill/57 1.50 4.00
168 Danny Green/86 2.50 6.00
169 Brandon Jennings/97 2.00 5.00
170 Terrence Williams/92 1.25 3.00
171 Gerald Henderson/85 1.50 4.00
172 Tyler Hansbrough/50 1.50 4.00
173 Earl Clark/45 1.50 4.00
174 Austin Daye/95 1.25 3.00
175 James Johnson/84 1.50 4.00
176 Jrue Holiday/89 2.50 6.00
177 Ty Lawson/97 2.00 5.00
178 Jeff Teague/99 2.00 5.00
179 Eric Maynor/97 1.25 3.00
180 Darren Collison/98 2.00 5.00
181 Omri Casspi/82 1.50 4.00
182 B.J. Mullens/77 1.25 3.00
183 Rodrigue Beaubois/97 1.25 3.00
184 Taj Gibson/78 2.00 5.00
185 DeMarre Carroll/99 1.50 4.00
186 Wayne Ellington/81 2.00 5.00
187 Toney Douglas/77 1.25 3.00
188 Jeff Pendergraph/96 1.25 3.00
189 Jermaine Taylor/92 1.25 3.00
190 Dante Cunningham/67 1.25 3.00
191 DaJuan Summers/65 1.25 3.00
192 Sam Young/96 1.25 3.00
193 DeJuan Blair/55 1.50 4.00
194 Jon Brockman/60 1.25 3.00
195 A.J. Price/78 1.25 3.00
196 Derrick Brown/96 1.25 3.00
197 Jodie Meeks/77 2.00 5.00
198 Marcus Thornton/95 1.50 4.00
199 Chase Budinger/90 1.50 4.00
200 Taylor Griffin/68 1.25 3.00

2009-10 Donruss Elite Status Gold
*1-120: 4X TO 10X BASE HI
*121-160: 2X TO 5X BASE HI
GOLD PRINT RUN 24 SER.#'d SETS
93 Steve Nash 6.00 15.00
95 Grant Hill 12.00 30.00
125 David Robinson 8.00 20.00
161 Blake Griffin 125.00 250.00
162 Hasheem Thabeet 3.00 8.00
163 James Harden 25.00 60.00
164 Tyreke Evans 4.00 10.00
165 Jonny Flynn 3.00 8.00
166 Stephen Curry 400.00 800.00
167 Jordan Hill 4.00 10.00
168 Danny Green 6.00 15.00
169 Brandon Jennings 5.00 12.00
170 Terrence Williams 3.00 8.00
171 Gerald Henderson 4.00 10.00
172 Tyler Hansbrough 4.00 10.00
173 Earl Clark 4.00 10.00
174 Austin Daye 3.00 8.00
175 James Johnson 4.00 10.00
176 Jrue Holiday 6.00 15.00
177 Ty Lawson 5.00 12.00
178 Jeff Teague 5.00 12.00
179 Eric Maynor 3.00 8.00
180 Darren Collison 5.00 12.00
181 Omri Casspi 4.00 10.00
182 B.J. Mullens 3.00 8.00
183 Rodrigue Beaubois 3.00 8.00
184 Taj Gibson 5.00 12.00
185 DeMarre Carroll 4.00 10.00
186 Wayne Ellington 5.00 12.00
187 Toney Douglas 3.00 8.00
188 Jeff Pendergraph 3.00 8.00
189 Jermaine Taylor 3.00 8.00
190 Dante Cunningham 3.00 8.00
191 DaJuan Summers 3.00 8.00
192 Sam Young 3.00 8.00
193 DeJuan Blair 4.00 10.00
194 Jon Brockman 3.00 8.00
195 A.J. Price 3.00 8.00
196 Derrick Brown 3.00 8.00
197 Jodie Meeks 5.00 12.00
198 Marcus Thornton 4.00 10.00
199 Chase Budinger 4.00 10.00
200 Taylor Griffin 3.00 8.00

2009-10 Donruss Elite Status Gold Autographs
STATED PRINT RUN 5 TO 24 SER.#'d SETS
SOME UNPRICED DUE TO SCARCITY
UNPRICED BLACK PRINT RUN ONE SET
4 Mike Bibby 8.00 20.00
20 Dirk Nowitzki 50.00 125.00
21 Jason Kidd 15.00 40.00
30 Charlie Villanueva 8.00 20.00
37 Shane Battier 8.00 20.00
40 Danny Granger 8.00 20.00
51 Andrew Bynum 10.00 25.00
57 Michael Beasley 12.00 30.00
67 Kevin Love 15.00 40.00
68 Devin Harris 10.00 25.00
90 Andre Iguodala 8.00 20.00
116 Carlos Boozer 8.00 20.00
121 Willis Reed 15.00 40.00
122 Chris Mullin 20.00 50.00
124 Spencer Haywood 8.00 20.00
129 Alex English 8.00 20.00
133 Bob Cousy 12.00 30.00
137 Lenny Wilkens 8.00 20.00
138 Bill Russell 50.00 120.00
139 Sean Elliott 25.00 60.00
143 Connie Hawkins 10.00 25.00
145 Oscar Robertson 30.00 80.00
150 Jerry West 30.00 80.00
151 Bill Walton 10.00 25.00
152 Rick Barry 8.00 20.00
153 Artis Gilmore 10.00 25.00
157 Walt Frazier 12.00 30.00
161 Blake Griffin 175.00 350.00
162 Hasheem Thabeet 6.00 15.00
163 James Harden 100.00 250.00
164 Tyreke Evans 50.00 120.00
165 Jonny Flynn 6.00 15.00
166 Stephen Curry 1000.00 1500.00
167 Jordan Hill 8.00 20.00
168 Danny Green 50.00 125.00
169 Brandon Jennings 25.00 60.00
170 Terrence Williams 6.00 15.00
171 Gerald Henderson 8.00 20.00
172 Tyler Hansbrough 15.00 40.00
173 Earl Clark 8.00 20.00
174 Austin Daye 6.00 15.00
175 James Johnson 8.00 20.00
176 Jrue Holiday 25.00 60.00
177 Ty Lawson 20.00 50.00
178 Jeff Teague 10.00 25.00
179 Eric Maynor 6.00 15.00
180 Darren Collison 10.00 25.00
181 Omri Casspi 8.00 20.00
182 B.J. Mullens 6.00 15.00
183 Rodrigue Beaubois 6.00 15.00
184 Taj Gibson 10.00 25.00
185 DeMarre Carroll 8.00 20.00
186 Wayne Ellington 10.00 25.00
187 Toney Douglas 6.00 15.00
188 Jeff Pendergraph 6.00 15.00
189 Jermaine Taylor 6.00 15.00
190 Dante Cunningham 6.00 15.00
191 DaJuan Summers 6.00 15.00
192 Sam Young 6.00 15.00
193 DeJuan Blair 8.00 20.00
194 Jon Brockman 6.00 15.00
195 A.J. Price 6.00 15.00
196 Derrick Brown 6.00 15.00
197 Jodie Meeks 10.00 25.00
198 Marcus Thornton 8.00 20.00
199 Chase Budinger 8.00 20.00
200 Taylor Griffin 6.00 15.00

2009-10 Donruss Elite ARCeologists
COMPLETE SET (15) 6.00 15.00
*BLACK: 2X TO 5X BASE HI
BLACK PRINT RUN 25 SER.#'d SETS
*GOLD: 1.25X TO 3X BASE HI
GOLD PRINT RUN 100 SER.#'d SETS
*GREEN: .4X TO 1X BASE HI
GREEN RANDOM INSERTS IN RETAIL PACKS
*RED: .6X TO 1.5X BASE HI
RED PRINT RUN 249 SER.#'d SETS
1 Ray Allen .75 2.00
2 Steve Nash .75 2.00
3 Roger Mason .50 1.25
4 Chauncey Billups .75 2.00
5 Rashard Lewis .60 1.50
6 Ben Gordon .60 1.50
7 Kobe Bryant 3.00 8.00
8 Troy Murphy .50 1.25
9 Jason Kidd .75 2.00
10 Mike Bibby .60 1.50
11 Daequan Cook .50 1.25
12 Vince Carter 1.00 2.50
13 Peja Stojakovic .75 2.00
14 Michael Finley .75 2.00
15 O.J. Mayo .50 1.25

2009-10 Donruss Elite ARCeologists Autographs
STATED PRINT RUN 25 TO 50 SER.#'d SETS
7 Kobe Bryant/47 100.00 200.00
9 Jason Kidd/25 15.00 40.00
10 Mike Bibby/50 8.00 20.00

2009-10 Donruss Elite ARCeologists Jerseys
STATED PRINT RUN 99 TO 299 SER.#'d SETS
1 Ray Allen/299 3.00 8.00
5 Rashard Lewis/299 2.50 6.00
7 Kobe Bryant/99 12.50 30.00
9 Jason Kidd/299 3.00 8.00
10 Mike Bibby/299 2.50 6.00
13 Peja Stojakovic/299 3.00 8.00
15 O.J. Mayo/140 2.00 5.00

2009-10 Donruss Elite ARCeologists Jerseys Prime
*PRIME: .75X TO 2X BASE HI
STATED PRINT RUN 24-50 SER.#'d SETS
2 Steve Nash/25 10.00 25.00
7 Kobe Bryant/24 20.00 40.00

2009-10 Donruss Elite Clutch Performers
COMPLETE SET (20) 15.00 30.00
*BLACK: 1.5X TO 4X BASE HI
PRINT RUN 25 SER.#'d SETS
*GOLD: 1X TO 2.5X BASE HI
GOLD PRINT RUN 100 SER.#d SETS

*GREEN: .4X TO 1X BASE HI
GREEN RANDOM INSERTS IN RETAIL PACKS
*RED: .5X TO 1.25X BASE HI
RED PRINT RUN 249 SER.#'d SETS
1 Paul Pierce 1.00 2.50
2 LeBron James 4.00 10.00
3 Jason Terry .75 2.00
4 Manu Ginobili 1.00 2.50
5 Kobe Bryant 4.00 10.00
6 Brandon Roy 1.00 2.50
7 Dwyane Wade 1.50 4.00
8 Deron Williams .75 2.00
9 Andre Iguodala .75 2.00
10 Carmelo Anthony 1.25 3.00
11 Chris Paul 1.25 3.00
12 Tracy McGrady 1.00 2.50
13 Ray Allen 1.00 2.50
14 Stephen Jackson .75 2.00
15 Devin Harris .60 1.50
16 Gilbert Arenas .75 2.00
17 Al Jefferson .75 2.00
18 Richard Hamilton .75 2.00
19 Dirk Nowitzki 1.25 3.00
20 Joe Johnson .75 2.00

2009-10 Donruss Elite Clutch Performers Jerseys

STATED PRINT RUN 35 TO 299 SER.#'d SETS
1 Paul Pierce/299 3.00 8.00
2 LeBron James/199 8.00 20.00
3 Jason Terry/299 2.50 6.00
5 Kobe Bryant/99 10.00 25.00
6 Brandon Roy/125 3.00 8.00
7 Dwyane Wade/199 5.00 12.00
8 Deron Williams/299 2.50 6.00
9 Andre Iguodala/299 2.50 6.00
10 Carmelo Anthony/199 4.00 10.00
11 Chris Paul/199 4.00 10.00
12 Tracy McGrady/299 3.00 8.00
13 Ray Allen/299 3.00 8.00
14 Stephen Jackson/299 2.50 6.00
15 Devin Harris/70 2.00 5.00
17 Al Jefferson/299 2.50 6.00
19 Dirk Nowitzki/35 6.00 15.00
20 Joe Johnson/299 2.50 6.00

2009-10 Donruss Elite Clutch Performers Jerseys Prime

*PRIME: .75X TO 2X BASE HI
STATED PRINT RUN 10 TO 50 SER.#'d SETS
SOME UNPRICED DUE TO SCARCITY
4 Manu Ginobili/50 6.00 15.00
6 Brandon Roy/15 10.00 25.00
7 Dwyane Wade/15 12.00 30.00

2009-10 Donruss Elite In the Zone

MPLETE SET (20) 20.00 40.00
*BLACK: 1.5X TO 4X BASE HI
BLACK PRINT RUN 25 SER.#'d SETS
*GOLD: 1X TO 2.5X BASE HI
GOLD PRINT RUN 100 SER.#'d SETS
*GREEN: .4X TO 1X BASE HI
GREEN RANDOM INSERTS IN RETAIL PACKS
*RED: .5X TO 1.25X BASE HI
RED PRINT RUN 249 SER.#'d SETS
1 Shaquille O'Neal 2.00 5.00
2 Nene .75 2.00
3 Dwight Howard .75 2.00
4 Pau Gasol 1.00 2.50
5 Emeka Okafor .75 2.00
6 David Lee .60 1.50
7 Yao Ming 1.25 3.00
8 Amare Stoudemire .75 2.00
9 Kevin Garnett 1.50 4.00
10 Al Horford 1.00 2.50
11 Tony Parker 1.00 2.50
12 Rajon Rondo 1.00 2.50
13 Tim Duncan 1.50 4.00
14 Steve Nash 1.00 2.50
15 Chris Paul 1.25 3.00
16 Jose Calderon .60 1.50
17 Al Jefferson .75 2.00
18 Dwyane Wade 1.50 4.00
19 LeBron James 4.00 10.00
20 LaMarcus Aldridge 1.00 2.50

2009-10 Donruss Elite In the Zone Jerseys

PRINT RUNS 199 TO 299 SER.#'d SETS
*PRIME: .75X TO 2X BASE HI
PRIME PRINT RUNS 15 TO 50 SER.#'d SETS
3 Dwight Howard 2.50 6.00
4 Pau Gasol/199 3.00 8.00
6 David Lee 2.00 5.00
7 Yao Ming 4.00 10.00
8 Amare Stoudemire 2.50 6.00
9 Kevin Garnett 5.00 12.00
10 Al Horford 3.00 8.00
12 Rajon Rondo 3.00 8.00
13 Tim Duncan 5.00 12.00
15 Chris Paul/199 4.00 10.00
16 Jose Calderon 2.00 5.00
17 Al Jefferson 2.50 6.00
18 Dwyane Wade/199 5.00 12.00
19 LeBron James/199 8.00 20.00
20 LaMarcus Aldridge 3.00 8.00

2009-10 Donruss Elite Jerseys

STATED PRINT RUN 99 SER.#'d SETS
3 Josh Smith 2.50 6.00
4 Mike Bibby 2.50 6.00
5 Paul Pierce 3.00 8.00
6 Kevin Garnett 5.00 12.00
8 Rajon Rondo 3.00 8.00
16 LeBron James 10.00 25.00
21 Jason Kidd 3.00 8.00
22 Jason Terry 2.50 6.00
26 Kenyon Martin 2.50 6.00
31 Tayshaun Prince 2.50 6.00
32 Stephen Jackson 2.50 6.00
36 Tracy McGrady 3.00 8.00
37 Shane Battier 3.00 8.00
38 Luis Scola 2.50 6.00
48 Kobe Bryant 10.00 25.00
50 Pau Gasol 3.00 8.00
51 Andrew Bynum 2.00 5.00
56 Dwyane Wade 5.00 12.00
57 Michael Beasley 2.00 5.00
58 Jermaine O'Neal 2.50 6.00
63 Andrew Bogut 2.50 6.00
65 Al Jefferson 2.50 6.00
67 Kevin Love 3.00 8.00
72 Chris Paul 4.00 10.00
74 Peja Stojakovic 3.00 8.00
77 Nate Robinson 2.00 5.00
78 David Lee 2.00 5.00
85 Dwight Howard 2.50 6.00
87 Rashard Lewis 2.50 6.00
89 Elton Brand 3.00 8.00
91 Thaddeus Young 2.00 5.00
97 LaMarcus Aldridge 3.00 8.00
102 Andres Nocioni 2.00 5.00
106 Tim Duncan 5.00 12.00
109 Chris Bosh 3.00 8.00
110 Jose Calderon 2.00 5.00
111 Andrea Bargnani 2.50 6.00
113 Deron Williams 2.50 6.00
114 Mehmet Okur 2.00 5.00
115 Andrei Kirilenko 2.50 6.00
116 Carlos Boozer 2.50 6.00
122 Chris Mullin 3.00 8.00
123 Kevin Johnson 3.00 8.00
141 Clyde Drexler 4.00 10.00
142 Larry Bird 8.00 20.00
147 Kevin McHale 3.00 8.00
157 Walt Frazier 3.00 8.00
158 Isiah Thomas 3.00 8.00
160 Karl Malone 4.00 10.00

2009-10 Donruss Elite Jerseys Prime

*PRIME: .75X TO 2X BASE HI
STATED PRINT RUN 15 TO 50 SER.#'d SETS
56 Dwyane Wade/15 15.00 40.00
142 Larry Bird/50 20.00 40.00
147 Kevin McHale/50 10.00 25.00
158 Isiah Thomas/50 8.00 20.00

2009-10 Donruss Elite Passing the Torch

COMPLETE SET (15) 20.00 50.00
*BLACK: 1.5X TO 4X BASE HI
BLACK PRINT RUN 25 SER.#'d SETS
*GOLD: .75X TO 2X BASE HI
GOLD PRINT RUN 100 SER.#'d SETS
*GREEN: .4X TO 1X BASE HI
GREEN RANDOM INSERTS IN RETAIL PACKS
*RED: .6X TO 1.5X BASE HI
RED PRINT RUN 249 SER.#'d SETS
1 M.Johnson/K.Bryant 4.00 10.00
2 B.Russell/R.Parish 3.00 8.00
3 L.Bird/R.Allen 3.00 8.00
4 B.Walton/L.Walton 2.00 5.00
5 M.Malone/Y.Ming 2.00 5.00
6 D.Thompson/V.Carter 2.00 5.00
7 D.Rodman/C.Andersen 2.50 6.00
8 M.Malone/S.O'Neal 3.00 8.00
9 D.Robinson/T.Duncan 3.00 8.00
10 D.Curry/S.Curry 10.00 25.00
11 T.Hansbrough/B.Griffin 4.00 10.00
12 D.Majerle/C.Kaman 2.00 5.00
13 G.Gervin/T.Parker 2.50 6.00
14 G.McGinnis/T.Hansbrough 2.50 6.00
15 K.Abdul-Jabbar/K.Bryant 4.00 10.00

2009-10 Donruss Elite Passing the Torch Autographs

STATED PRINT RUN 25 SER.#'d SETS
1 M.Johnson/K.Bryant 200.00 400.00
2 B.Russell/R.Parish 60.00 120.00
3 L.Bird/R.Allen 60.00 120.00
10 D.Curry/S.Curry 150.00 300.00
11 T.Hansbrough/B.Griffin 100.00 200.00
12 D.Majerle/C.Kaman 15.00 40.00
13 G.Gervin/T.Parker 20.00 50.00
14 G.McGinnis/T.Hansbrough 20.00 50.00
15 K.Abdul-Jabbar/K.Bryant 125.00 250.00

2009-10 Donruss Elite Prime Targets

COMPLETE SET (20) 10.00 25.00
*BLACK: 2X TO 5X BASE HI
BLACK PRINT RUN 25 SER.#'d SETS
*GOLD: 1.25X TO 3X BASE HI
GOLD PRINT RUN 100 SER.#'d SETS
*GREEN: .4X TO 1X BASE HI
GREEN RANDOM INSERTS IN RETAIL PACKS
*RED: .6X TO 1.5X BASE HI
RED PRINT RUN 249 SER.#'d SETS
1 Dwyane Wade 1.25 3.00
2 Kobe Bryant 3.00 8.00
2AU Kobe Bryant AU/39
3 Dirk Nowitzki 1.00 2.50
4 LeBron James 3.00 8.00
5 Antawn Jamison .60 1.50
6 Joe Johnson .60 1.50
7 Kevin Durant 2.00 5.00
8 Vince Carter 1.00 2.50
9 Brandon Roy .75 2.00
10 Ben Gordon .60 1.50
11 David West .60 1.50
12 O.J. Mayo .50 1.25
13 Danny Granger .60 1.50
14 Chris Bosh .75 2.00
15 Tony Parker .75 2.00
16 Rudy Gay .75 2.00
17 Chris Paul 1.00 2.50
18 LaMarcus Aldridge .75 2.00
19 Al Harrington .60 1.50
20 Raymond Felton .60 1.50

2009-10 Donruss Elite Prime Targets Jerseys

STATED PRINT RUN 99 TO 299 SER.#'d SETS
1 Dwyane Wade/199 5.00 12.00
2 Kobe Bryant/99 10.00 25.00
4 LeBron James/199 8.00 20.00
6 Joe Johnson/299 2.50 6.00
12 O.J. Mayo/299 2.00 5.00
14 Chris Bosh/299 3.00 8.00
17 Chris Paul/199 4.00 10.00
18 LaMarcus Aldridge/299 3.00 8.00
19 Al Harrington/145 2.50 6.00

2009-10 Donruss Elite Prime Targets Jerseys Prime

*PRIME: .75X TO 2X BASE HI
STATED PRINT RUN 2 TO 50 SER.#'d SETS
SOME UNPRICED DUE TO SCARCITY
7 Kevin Durant/25 15.00 30.00
9 Brandon Roy/50 6.00 15.00
15 Tony Parker/15 10.00 25.00

2009-10 Donruss Elite Series

COMPLETE SET (20) 25.00 50.00
*BLACK: 1.5X TO 4X BASE HI
BLACK PRINT RUN 25 SER.#'d SETS
*GOLD: 1X TO 2.5X BASE HI
GOLD PRINT RUN 100 SER.#'d SETS
*GREEN: .4X TO 1X BASE HI
GREEN RANDOM INSERTS IN RETAIL PACKS
*RED: .6X TO 1.5X BASE HI
RED PRINT RUN 249 SER.#'d SETS
1 Joe Johnson .75 2.00
2 Paul Pierce 1.00 2.50
3 Gerald Wallace .75 2.00
4 Derrick Rose 1.50 4.00
5 LeBron James 4.00 10.00
6 Dirk Nowitzki 1.25 3.00
7 Carmelo Anthony 1.25 3.00
8 Richard Hamilton .75 2.00
9 Stephen Jackson .75 2.00
10 Yao Ming 1.25 3.00
11 Danny Granger .75 2.00
12 Marcus Camby .60 1.50
13 Kobe Bryant 4.00 10.00
14 O.J. Mayo .60 1.50
15 Dwyane Wade 1.50 4.00
16 Michael Redd .75 2.00
17 Al Jefferson .75 2.00
18 Devin Harris .60 1.50
19 Chris Paul 1.25 3.00
20 David Lee .60 1.50
21 Kevin Durant 2.50 6.00
22 Dwight Howard .75 2.00
23 Andre Iguodala .75 2.00
24 Amare Stoudemire .75 2.00
25 Brandon Roy 1.00 2.50
26 Kevin Martin .75 2.00
27 Tim Duncan 1.50 4.00
28 Chris Bosh 1.00 2.50
29 Deron Williams .75 2.00
30 Antawn Jamison .75 2.00

2009-10 Donruss Elite Series Jerseys

ATED PRINT RUN 5 TO 299 SER.#'d SETS
SOME UNPRICED DUE TO SCARCITY
1 Joe Johnson/225 2.50 6.00
2 Paul Pierce/299 3.00 8.00
5 LeBron James/199 8.00 20.00
9 Stephen Jackson/299 2.50 6.00
10 Yao Ming/149 4.00 10.00
13 Kobe Bryant/99 12.50 30.00
14 O.J. Mayo/299 2.00 5.00
15 Dwyane Wade/199 5.00 12.00
16 Michael Redd/249 2.50 6.00
17 Al Jefferson/299 2.50 6.00
19 Chris Paul/199 4.00 10.00
20 David Lee/299 2.00 5.00
22 Dwight Howard/299 2.50 6.00
23 Andre Iguodala/299 2.50 6.00
25 Brandon Roy/299 3.00 8.00
27 Tim Duncan/299 5.00 12.00
28 Chris Bosh/299 3.00 8.00
29 Deron Williams/299 2.50 6.00

2009-10 Donruss Elite Series Jerseys Prime

*PRIME: .75X TO 2X BASE HI
STATED PRINT RUN 10 TO 50 SER.#'d SETS
SOME UNPRICED DUE TO SCARCITY
18 Devin Harris/50 4.00 10.00
19 Chris Paul/15 8.00 20.00
21 Kevin Durant/25 15.00 30.00
24 Amare Stoudemire/50 5.00 12.00
26 Kevin Martin/25 5.00 12.00
27 Tim Duncan/50 10.00 25.00

2009-10 Donruss Elite Teamwork Combos

LACK: 1.5X TO 4X BASE HI
BLACK PRINT RUN 25 SER.#'d SETS
*GOLD: 1X TO 2.5X BASE HI
GOLD PRINT RUN 100 SER.#'d SETS
*GREEN: .4X TO 1X BASE HI
GREEN RANDOM INSERTS IN RETAIL PACKS
*RED: .5X TO 1.25X BASE HI
RED PRINT RUN 249 SER.#'d SETS
1 J.Johnson/M.Bibby .75 2.00
2 K.Garnett/P.Pierce 1.50 4.00
3 G.Henderson/R.Felton .75 2.00
4 D.Rose/J.Salmons 1.50 4.00
5 L.James/S.O'Neal 4.00 10.00
6 D.Nowitzki/J.Kidd 1.25 3.00
7 C.Anthony/C.Billups 1.25 3.00
8 B.Gordon/R.Hamilton .75 2.00
9 M.Ellis/S.Jackson .75 2.00
10 S.Battier/T.McGrady 1.00 2.50
11 D.Granger/M.Dunleavy .75 2.00
12 A.Thornton/E.Gordon .75 2.00
13 K.Bryant/P.Gasol 4.00 10.00
14 O.Mayo/Z.Randolph .75 2.00
15 D.Wade/M.Beasley 1.50 4.00
16 A.Bogut/M.Redd .75 2.00
17 A.Jefferson/R.Gomes .75 2.00
18 B.Lopez/D.Harris .75 2.00
19 C.Paul/D.West 1.25 3.00
20 D.Lee/N.Robinson .60 1.50
21 K.Durant/R.Westbrook 2.50 6.00
22 D.Howard/V.Carter 1.25 3.00
23 A.Iguodala/E.Brand 1.00 2.50
24 A.Stoudemire/S.Nash 1.00 2.50
25 A.Miller/B.Roy 1.00 2.50
26 A.Nocioni/K.Martin .75 2.00
27 T.Duncan/T.Parker 1.50 4.00
28 A.Bargnani/J.Calderon .75 2.00
29 D.Williams/M.Okur .75 2.00
30 A.Jamison/G.Arenas .75 2.00

2009-10 Donruss Elite Teamwork Combos Autographs

STATED PRINT RUN 50 SER.#'d SETS
6 D.Nowitzki/J.Kidd 75.00 150.00
13 K.Bryant/P.Gasol 100.00 200.00
23 A.Iguodala/E.Brand 20.00 40.00

2009-10 Donruss Elite Threads

STATED PRINT RUN 15 TO 99 SER.#'d SESTS
1 Joe Johnson/99 2.50 6.00
2 Mike Bibby/99 2.50 6.00
3 Al Horford/99 3.00 8.00
4 Kevin Garnett/99 5.00 12.00
5 Ray Allen/99 3.00 8.00
6 Gerald Wallace/99 2.50 6.00
7 Derrick Rose/99 5.00 12.00
8 LeBron James/99 10.00 25.00
9 Josh Howard/99 2.50 6.00
10 Dirk Nowitzki/99 4.00 10.00
11 Jason Kidd/99 3.00 8.00
12 Jason Terry/99 2.50 6.00
13 Carmelo Anthony/99 4.00 10.00
14 Kenyon Martin/99 2.50 6.00
15 Austin Daye/99 2.00 5.00
17 Stephen Jackson/99 2.50 6.00
18 Tracy McGrady/99 3.00 8.00
19 Tyler Hansbrough/99 2.50 6.00
20 Blake Griffin/99 15.00 40.00
21 Kobe Bryant/99 10.00 25.00
22 Andrew Bynum/99 2.00 5.00
23 Pau Gasol/99 3.00 8.00
25 O.J. Mayo/99 2.00 5.00
26 Dwyane Wade/99 5.00 12.00
27 Michael Beasley/99 2.00 5.00
28 Michael Redd/99 2.50 6.00
29 Al Jefferson/99 2.50 6.00
31 Chris Paul/99 4.00 10.00
32 David West/99 2.50 6.00
33 Nate Robinson/99 2.00 5.00
35 Dwight Howard/99 2.50 6.00
37 Elton Brand/99 3.00 8.00
38 Andre Iguodala/99 2.50 6.00
39 Amare Stoudemire/99 2.50 6.00
40 Steve Nash/15 8.00 20.00
41 Brandon Roy/99 3.00 8.00
42 Tyreke Evans/99 2.50 6.00
44 Tim Duncan/99 5.00 12.00
45 Manu Ginobili/45 3.00 8.00
46 Chris Bosh/99 3.00 8.00
47 Deron Williams/99 2.50 6.00
48 Carlos Boozer/99 2.50 6.00
49 Andrei Kirilenko/99 2.50 6.00
50 Tayshaun Prince/99 2.50 6.00

2009-10 Donruss Elite Threads Autographs

STATED PRINT RUN 25 SER.#'d SETS
2 Mike Bibby 6.00 15.00
10 Dirk Nowitzki 50.00 120.00
11 Jason Kidd 15.00 40.00
15 Austin Daye 6.00 15.00
19 Tyler Hansbrough 12.50 30.00
20 Blake Griffin 100.00 200.00
21 Kobe Bryant 125.00 225.00
38 Andre Iguodala 6.00 15.00
42 Tyreke Evans 25.00 60.00
48 Carlos Boozer 6.00 15.00

2009-10 Donruss Elite Threads Prime

*PRIME: .75X TO 2X BASE HI
STATED PRINT RUN 10 TO 50 SER.#'d SETS
SOME UNPRICED DUE TO SCARCITY
30 Devin Harris/50 4.00 10.00
34 Kevin Durant/25 15.00 40.00
40 Steve Nash/25 10.00 25.00
43 Tony Parker/50 8.00 20.00

2009-10 Donruss Elite Retail

These cards differ from the hobby version by utilizing a conventional type of cardboard, rather than the traditional metal board. The set is complete at 120 cards and contains no legends or rookies, like the standard Hobby set.
COMPLETE SET (120) 10.00 25.00
*RETAIL: .2X TO .5X HOBBY

2007 Donruss Elite Extra Edition

COMPLETE SET (142)
COMP.SET w/o AU's (92) 8.00 20.00
COMMON CARD (1-92) .20 .50
COMMON AU (92-142) 4.00 10.00
OVERALL AUTO/MEM ODDS 1:5
AU PRINT RUNS B/WN 374-999 COPIES PER
EXCHANGE DEADLINE 07/01/2009
56 Demetris Nichols .20 .50
57 Aaron Gray .20 .50
58 Daequan Cook .20 .50
59 Derrick Byars .20 .50
60 Reyshawn Terry .20 .50
61 Taurean Green .20 .50
62 Don Haskins .20 .50
63 Jerry Tarkanian .20 .50
64 Rick Majerus .20 .50
65 Rollie Massimino .20 .50
67 Dale Brown .20 .50
68 Dean Smith .20 .50
69 Eddie Sutton .20 .50
71 Gene Keady .20 .50
72 Jim Boeheim .20 .50
73 Norm Stewart .20 .50
80 Rebecca Lobo .20 .50
83 Elvin Hayes .20 .50
85 Bill Walton .20 .50
86 Sidney Moncrief .20 .50
87 Dominique Wilkins .20 .50
90 Muggsy Bogues .20 .50
137 Alando Tucker AU/494 4.00 10.00
139 Marc Gasol AU/474 5.00 12.00
140 Stephane Lasme AU/674 4.00 10.00

2007 Donruss Elite Extra Edition Aspirations

*ASP 1-92: 3X TO 8X BASIC
OVERALL INSERT ODDS 1:4
STATED PRINT RUN 100 SER.#'d SETS
136 D. J. Strawberry 2.00 5.00
137 Alando Tucker 1.50 4.00
138 Jared Jordan 1.50 4.00
139 Marc Gasol 2.00 5.00
140 Stephane Lasme 1.50 4.00

2007 Donruss Elite Extra Edition Status

*STATUS 1-92: 4X TO 10X BASIC
OVERALL INSERT ODDS 1:4
STATED PRINT RUN 50 SER.#'d SETS
136 D. J. Strawberry 2.50 6.00
137 Alando Tucker 2.00 5.00
138 Jared Jordan 2.00 5.00
139 Marc Gasol 3.00 8.00
140 Stephane Lasme 2.00 5.00

2007 Donruss Elite Extra Edition College Ties

STATED PRINT RUN 1500 SER.#'d SETS
*GOLD: .6X TO 1.5X BASIC
GOLD PRINT RUN 500 SER.#'d SETS
*RED: 1X TO 2.5X BASIC
RED PRINT RUN 100 SER.#'d SETS
OVERALL INSERT ODDS 1:4
5 T.Green/M.LaPorta 1.25 3.00
7 J.Boeheim/D.Nichols .75 2.00
11 D.Cook/C.Luebke .75 2.00
12 D.Strawberry/B.Cecil .75 2.00

2007 Donruss Elite Extra Edition College Ties Autographs

OVERALL AUTO/MEM ODDS 1:5
PRINT RUNS B/WN 50-100 COPIES PER
EXCHANGE DEADLINE 07/01/2009
5 T.Green/M.LaPorta 10.00 25.00
7 J.Boeheim/D.Nichols EXCH 6.00 15.00
11 D.Cook/C.Luebke 10.00 25.00
12 D.Strawberry/B.Cecil EXCH 6.00 15.00

2007 Donruss Elite Extra Edition Collegiate Patches

OVERALL AUTO/MEM ODDS 1:5
PRINT RUNS B/WN 25-250 COPIES PER
NO PRICING ON QTY 25 OR LESS
5 Dale Brown/250 12.50 30.00
6 Dean Smith/250 30.00 60.00
7 Eddie Sutton/250 10.00 25.00
9 Gene Keady/250 10.00 25.00
11 Jim Boeheim/250 12.50 30.00
12 Sheryl Swoopes/250 12.50 30.00
13 Norm Stewart/250 10.00 25.00
14 Rebecca Lobo/250 10.00 25.00
21 Bill Walton/50 12.00 30.00
22 Sidney Moncrief/250 6.00 15.00
23 Dominique Wilkins/100 10.00 25.00
43 Aaron Gray/250 6.00 15.00
44 Daequan Cook/250 6.00 15.00
46 Rick Majeras/250 EXCH 6.00 15.00
47 Taurean Green/250 6.00 15.00
49 Bobby Hurley/250 EXCH 10.00 25.00
50 Muggsy Bogues/250 10.00 25.00
51 Jerry Tarkanian/250 6.00 15.00
53 Lynette Woodard/249 6.00 15.00

2007 Donruss Elite Extra Edition School Colors

OVERALL INSERT ODDS 1:4
STATED PRINT RUN 1500 SER.#'d SETS
8 Alando Tucker .75 2.00
9 Daequan Cook .75 2.00
10 Eddie Sutton .75 2.00
11 Dean Smith .75 2.00
14 Don Haskins .75 2.00
15 Jerry Tarkanian .75 2.00
16 Rick Majerus .75 2.00
17 Rollie Massimino .75 2.00
19 Dale Brown .75 2.00
21 Gene Keady .75 2.00
22 Jim Boeheim .75 2.00
23 Norm Stewart .75 2.00
25 Bill Walton .75 2.00

2007 Donruss Elite Extra Edition School Colors Autographs

OVERALL AUTO/MEM ODDS 1:5
PRINT RUNS B/WN 10-50 COPIES PER
NO PRICING ON QTY 25 OR LESS
EXCHANGE DEADLINE 07/01/2009
8 Alando Tucker/50 6.00 15.00
9 Daequan Cook/50 6.00 15.00
14 Don Haskins/25 12.50 30.00
21 Gene Keady/25 12.50 30.00
25 Bill Walton/25 10.00 25.00

2007 Donruss Elite Extra Edition Signature Aspirations

OVERALL AU/MEM ODDS 1:5
PRINT RUNS B/WN 5-100 COPIES PER
NO PRICING ON QTY 25 OR LESS
EXCHANGE DEADLINE 07/01/2007
57 Aaron Gray/100 4.00 10.00
58 Daequan Cook/50 10.00 25.00
61 Taurean Green/75 4.00 10.00
62 Don Haskins/100 4.00 10.00
63 Jerry Tarkanian/50 5.00 12.00
64 Rick Majerus/100 4.00 10.00
69 Eddie Sutton/50 5.00 12.00
71 Gene Keady/50 5.00 12.00
72 Jim Boeheim/100 5.00 12.00
80 Rebecca Lobo/100 6.00 15.00
83 Elvin Hayes/100 4.00 10.00
85 Bill Walton/100 6.00 15.00
86 Sidney Moncrief/50 5.00 12.00
87 Dominique Wilkins/50 10.00 25.00
90 Muggsy Bogues/100 4.00 10.00
137 Alando Tucker/50 5.00 12.00
139 Marc Gasol/50 EXCH 10.00 25.00
140 Stephane Lasme/100 4.00 10.00

2007 Donruss Elite Extra Edition Signature Status

OVERALL AU/MEM ODDS 1:5
PRINT RUNS B/WN 1-50 COPIES PER
NO PRICING ON QTY 25 OR LESS
EXCHANGE DEADLINE 07/01/2007
57 Aaron Gray/50 6.00 15.00
61 Taurean Green/29 6.00 15.00
62 Don Haskins/50 6.00 15.00
64 Rick Majerus/50 6.00 15.00
69 Eddie Sutton/25 12.50 30.00
72 Jim Boeheim/50 8.00 20.00
80 Rebecca Lobo/50 10.00 25.00
83 Elvin Hayes/50 6.00 15.00
85 Bill Walton/50 10.00 25.00
86 Sidney Moncrief/25 6.00 15.00
87 Dominique Wilkins/25 20.00 50.00
90 Muggsy Bogues/50 6.00 15.00
140 Stephane Lasme/50 6.00 15.00

2007 Donruss Elite Extra Edition Signature Turn of the Century

OVERALL AU/MEM ODDS 1:5
PRINT RUNS B/WN 10-500 COPIES PER
NO PRICING ON QTY 25 OR LESS
EXCHANGE DEADLINE 07/01/2007
57 Aaron Gray/500 4.00 10.00
58 Daequan Cook/494 4.00 10.00
61 Taurean Green/500 4.00 10.00
62 Don Haskins/194 5.00 12.00
63 Jerry Tarkanian/144 5.00 12.00
64 Rick Majerus/194 5.00 12.00
67 Dale Brown/89 6.00 15.00
69 Eddie Sutton/144 6.00 15.00
71 Gene Keady/144 5.00 12.00
80 Rebecca Lobo/234 6.00 15.00
83 Elvin Hayes/344 4.00 10.00
86 Sidney Moncrief/169 4.00 10.00
90 Muggsy Bogues/94 6.00 15.00
137 Alando Tucker/100 4.00 10.00
140 Stephane Lasme/145 5.00 12.00

2007 Donruss Elite Extra Edition Throwback Threads

OVERALL AUTO/MEM ODDS 1:5
PRINT RUNS B/WN 44-500 COPIES PER
21 Dale Brown/500 3.00 8.00
22 Don Haskins/500 3.00 8.00

2007 Donruss Elite Extra Edition Throwback Threads Prime

*PRIME: .75X TO 2X BASIC
OVERALL AUTO/MEM ODDS 1:5
PRINT RUNS B/WN 3-50 COPIES PER
NO PRICING ON QTY 25 OR LESS

2007 Donruss Elite Extra Edition Throwback Threads Autographs

OVERALL AUTO/MEM ODDS 1:5
PRINT RUNS B/WN 50-100 COPIES PER
EXCHANGE DEADLINE 07/01/2009
21 Dale Brown/50 6.00 15.00
22 Don Haskins/100 12.50 30.00

2008 Donruss Elite Extra Edition

This set was released on November 26, 2008. The base set consists of 199 cards.
COMP.SET w/o AU's (100) 10.00 25.00
COMMON CARD (1-100) .20 .50
COMMON AU (101-200) 3.00 8.00
RANDOM INSERTS IN PACKS
PRINT RUNS B/WN 99-1495
EXCH DEADLINE 5/26/2010
198 Derrick Rose AU/99 15.00 40.00
199 Michael Beasley AU/99 4.00 10.00
200 O.J. Mayo AU/99 4.00 10.00

2008 Donruss Elite Extra Edition Aspirations

*ASP 1-100: 2.5X TO 6X BASIC
RANDOM INSERTS IN PACKS
STATED PRINT RUN 150 SER.#'d SETS
198 Derrick Rose 6.00 15.00
199 Michael Beasley 1.25 3.00
200 O.J. Mayo 3.00 8.00

2008 Donruss Elite Extra Edition Status

*STATUS 1-100: 4X TO 10X BASIC
*STATUS 101-200: .6X TO 1.5X ASP
RANDOM INSERTS IN PACKS
STATED PRINT RUN 50 SER.#'d SETS
198 Derrick Rose 8.00 20.00
199 Michael Beasley 1.50 4.00
200 O.J. Mayo 6.00 15.00

2008 Donruss Elite Extra Edition Collegiate Patches Autographs

OVERALL AUTO/MEM ODDS 1:5
PRINT RUNS B/WN 20-255 COPIES PER
NO PRICING ON QTY 25 OR LESS
EXCH DEADLINE 5/26/2010
4 O.J. Mayo/50 10.00 25.00
7 Michael Beasley/100 8.00 20.00

2008 Donruss Elite Extra Edition School Colors

OVERALL INSERT ODDS 1:2
STATED PRINT RUN 1500 SER.#'d SET
4 O.J. Mayo 1.25 3.00
7 Michael Beasley 1.25 3.00
9 Derrick Rose 2.50 6.00

2008 Donruss Elite Extra Edition School Colors Autographs

OVERALL AUTO/MEM ODDS 1:5
PRINT RUNS B/WN 25-50 COPIES PER
NO PRICING ON QTY 25 OR LESS
EXCH DEADLINE 5/26/2010
4 O.J. Mayo/25 6.00 15.00
7 Michael Beasley/25 6.00 15.00
9 Derrick Rose/25 25.00 60.00

2008 Donruss Elite Extra Edition School Colors Materials

OVERALL AU/MEM ODDS 1:5
STATED PRINT RUN 100 SER.#'d SETS
4 O.J. Mayo 4.00 10.00
7 Michael Beasley 4.00 10.00
9 Derrick Rose 6.00 15.00

2008 Donruss Elite Extra Edition Signature Aspirations

OVERALL AUTO/MEM ODDS 1:5
PRINT RUN B/WN 5-100 COPIES PER
NO PRICING ON QTY 25 OR LESS
EXCH DEADLINE 5/26/2010
200 O.J. Mayo/25 6.00 15.00

2008 Donruss Elite Extra Edition Signature Status

OVERALL AUTO/MEM ODDS 1:5
PRINT RUN B/WN 5-50 COPIES PER
NO PRICING ON QTY 25 OR LESS
EXCH DEADLINE 5/26/2010

2008 Donruss Elite Extra Edition Signature Turn of the Century

OVERALL AUTO/MEM ODDS 1:5
PRINT RUNS B/WN 8-999 COPIES PER
EXCH DEADLINE 5/26/2010
198 Derrick Rose/25 25.00 60.00
199 Michael Beasley/25 6.00 15.00
200 O.J. Mayo/25 6.00 15.00

2008 Donruss Elite Extra Edition Throwback Threads

OVERALL AU/MEM ODDS 1:5
PRINT RUNS B/WN 15-500 COPIES PER
NO PRICING ON QTY 25 OR LESS
10 Derrick Rose/500 4.00 10.00
11 Michael Beasley/500 3.00 8.00
12 O.J. Mayo/400 3.00 8.00

2008 Donruss Elite Extra Edition Throwback Threads Prime

OVERALL AU/MEM ODDS 1:5
PRINT RUNS B/WN 1-50 COPIES PER
NO PRICING ON QTY 10 OR LESS

2008 Donruss Elite Extra Edition Throwback Threads Autographs

OVERALL AUTO/MEM ODDS 1:5
PRINT RUNS B/WN 4-100 COPIES PER
NO PRICING ON QTY 25 OR LESS
EXCH DEADLINE 5/26/2010
10 Derrick Rose/25 40.00 100.00
11 Michael Beasley/25 12.00 30.00
12 O.J. Mayo/25 6.00 15.00

2008 Donruss Elite Extra Edition Throwback Threads Autographs Prime

OVERALL AUTO/MEM ODDS 1:5
PRINT RUNS B/WN 1-25 COPIES PER
NO PRICING DUE TO SCARCITY
EXCH DEADLINE 5/26/2010

2010 Donruss Elite National Convention

ANNOUNCED PRINT RUN 499 SETS
21 Blake Griffin 2.00 5.00
22 Brandon Jennings 1.25 3.00
23 Carmelo Anthony 1.25 3.00
24 Chris Bosh 2.00 5.00
25 DeMarcus Cousins 6.00 15.00
26 Derrick Favors 3.00 8.00
27 Derrick Rose 2.00 5.00
28 Dirk Nowitzki 1.25 3.00
29 Dwight Howard 1.25 3.00
30 Dwyane Wade 2.00 5.00
31 Evan Turner 4.00 10.00
32 John Wall 10.00 25.00
33 Kevin Durant 2.00 5.00
34 Kobe Bryant 3.00 8.00
35 Larry Bird 2.00 5.00
36 LeBron James 8.00 20.00
37 Magic Johnson 1.50 4.00
38 Rajon Rondo 1.25 3.00
39 Tyreke Evans 1.25 3.00
40 Wesley Johnson 3.00 8.00

2010 Donruss Elite National Convention Aspirations

*ASPIRATIONS: .8X TO 2X BASIC CARDS
ANNOUNCED PRINT RUN 50

2010 Donruss Elite National Convention Status

*STATUS: .8X TO 2X BASIC CARDS
ANNOUNCED PRINT RUN 25

2010 Donruss Elite National Convention Autographs

STATED PRINT RUN 1-25
21 Blake Griffin/25 80.00 200.00
22 Brandon Jennings/25 15.00 40.00
25 DeMarcus Cousins/25 40.00 100.00
40 Wesley Johnson/25 20.00 50.00

2011 Donruss Elite National Convention

ANNOUNCED PRINT RUN 500 SETS
*BLUE/10: 2X TO 5X BASIC CARDS
*RED/25: 1.5X TO 4X BASIC CARDS
8 Blake Griffin 1.50 4.00
9 Dirk Nowitzki 1.25 3.00
10 John Wall 1.50 4.00
11 Kevin Durant 1.50 4.00
12 Kobe Bryant 1.50 4.00

1996 Donruss Kazaam Promo

The front of this standard-size card has a white background with a color picture of Shaquille O'Neal as "Kazaam" emanating from an oversized stereo. The kid actor from the movie sits perched on the stereo. The back has a yellow background with another picture of "Kazzam" and a promotional blurb about the forthcoming Donruss Kazaam set. The word "prototype" appears in purple in the top left corner. The card is not numbered.
NNO Shaquille O'Neal (as Kazaam) 1.50 4.00

2008 Donruss Sports Legends

This set was released on December 10, 2008. The base set consists of 144 cards and features cards of players from various sports.
COMPLETE SET (144) 40.00 100.00
3 Larry Bird 1.25 3.00
7 Oscar Robertson .60 1.50
12 John Wooden .75 2.00
14 Clyde Lovellette .50 1.25
19 Dan Issel .50 1.25
22 Elvin Hayes .60 1.50
25 Kevin McHale .60 1.50
26 Sidney Moncrief .50 1.25
32 Walt Frazier .50 1.25
39 Bobby Wanzer .50 1.25
42 Marques Haynes .50 1.25
44 Dolph Schayes .50 1.25
47 Dominique Wilkins .60 1.50
49 Alex English .50 1.25
52 Robert Parish .50 1.25
55 Bailey Howell .40 1.00
57 Don Haskins .40 1.00
61 Dean Smith .50 1.25
62 Rollie Massimino .50 1.25
67 Dick Vitale .50 1.25
72 Rick Majerus .50 1.25
74 Al Cervi .40 1.00
76 Lisa Leslie .60 1.50
77 Jerry West .75 2.00
86 Wes Unseld .50 1.25
87 Bill Walton .60 1.50
89 Arnie Risen .50 1.25
92 Dennis Rodman .60 1.50
97 Jim Boeheim .40 1.00
102 Jerry Tarkanian .50 1.25
107 Lynette Woodard .40 1.00
112 Muggsy Bogues .50 1.25
117 Sheryl Swoopes .60 1.50
121 Nate Thurmond .50 1.25
124 Cliff Hagan .50 1.25
134 George Gervin .50 1.25
146 Bobby Hurley .50 1.25
147 Eddie Sutton .50 1.25
149 David Thompson .60 1.50

2008 Donruss Sports Legends Mirror Blue

*BLUE/100: 2X TO 5X BASIC CARDS
STATED PRINT RUN 100 SER.#'d SETS

2008 Donruss Sports Legends Mirror Gold

*GOLD/25: 3X TO 8X BASIC CARDS
STATED PRINT RUN 25 SER.#'d SETS

2008 Donruss Sports Legends Mirror Red

*RED/250: 1.5X TO 4X BASIC CARDS
STATED PRINT RUN 250 SER.#'d SETS

2008 Donruss Sports Legends Museum Collection

SILVER PRINT RUN 1000 SER.#'d SETS
*GOLD/100: .6X TO 1.5X SILVER/1000
GOLD PRINT RUN 100 SER.#'d SETS
19 Robert Parish 1.25 3.00
23 Dominique Wilkins 1.50 4.00
30 Bill Walton 1.50 4.00

2008 Donruss Sports Legends Museum Collection Materials

STATED PRINT RUN 25-250
*PRIME/25: .6X TO 1.5X BASIC MATERIAL
PRIME PRINT RUN 1-25
SERIAL #'d UNDER 25 NOT PRICED
23 Dominique Wilkins/100 5.00 12.00

2008 Donruss Sports Legends Certified Cuts

STATED PRINT RUN 1-100
SERIAL #'d TO 1 NOT PRICED
1 Jerry West/50 30.00 60.00
4 Nate Thurmond/49 15.00 40.00
6 Larry Bird/50 50.00 100.00
7a Dennis Rodman/40 30.00 60.00
7b Dennis Rodman/20 30.00 60.00
8a Dick Vitale/10 30.00 60.00
8b Dick Vitale/10 30.00 60.00
8c Dick Vitale/10 30.00 60.00
8d Dick Vitale/10 30.00 60.00
8e Dick Vitale/10 30.00 60.00
8f Dick Vitale/10 30.00 60.00
8g Dick Vitale/10 30.00 60.00
8h Dick Vitale/10 30.00 60.00
8i Dick Vitale/10 30.00 60.00
8j Dick Vitale/10 30.00 60.00
8k Dick Vitale/10 30.00 60.00
9a Marques Haynes/20 25.00 50.00
9b Marques Haynes/20 25.00 50.00
10 Oscar Robertson/50 60.00 100.00
11 Robert Parish/100 8.00 20.00
12 John Wooden/20 125.00 250.00
23 George Gervin/50 25.00 50.00

2008 Donruss Sports Legends Champions

SILVER PRINT RUN 1000 SER.#'d SETS
*GOLD/100: .6X TO 1.5X SILVER/1000
GOLD PRINT RUN 100 SER.#'d SETS
1 Jerry West 2.00 5.00
7 Larry Bird 3.00 8.00
10 Dolph Schayes 1.25 3.00
13 Cliff Hagan 1.25 3.00
15 Bill Walton 1.50 4.00
16 Dan Issel 1.25 3.00

2008 Donruss Sports Legends Champions Materials

STATED PRINT RUN 10-250
1 Jerry West Jsy/250 6.00 15.00
16 Dan Issel Jsy/100 4.00 10.00

2008 Donruss Sports Legends Champions Signatures

STATED PRINT RUN 1-100
SERIAL #'d UNDER 25 NOT PRICED
1 Jerry West/50 30.00 50.00
10 Dolph Schayes/100 8.00 20.00
13 Cliff Hagan/100 6.00 15.00
15 Bill Walton/25 25.00 50.00
16 Dan Issel/100 6.00 15.00

2008 Donruss Sports Legends College Heroes

SILVER PRINT RUN 1000 SER.#'d SETS
*GOLD/100: .6X TO 1.5X SILVER/1000
GOLD PRINT RUN 100 SER.#'d SETS
6 Oscar Robertson 1.50 4.00
7 Elvin Hayes 1.50 4.00
9 Dan Issel 1.25 3.00

2008 Donruss Sports Legends College Heroes Materials

STATED PRINT RUN 50-250
6 Oscar Robertson Jsy/250 5.00 12.00

7 Elvin Hayes Jsy/250 5.00 12.00
9 Dan Issel Jsy/250 4.00 10.00

2008 Donruss Sports Legends College Heroes Signatures

STATED PRINT RUN 25-100
6 Oscar Robertson/25 20.00 40.00
7 Elvin Hayes/100 6.00 15.00
9 Dan Issel/100 6.00 15.00

2008 Donruss Sports Legends Collegiate Legends Patch Autographs

STATED PRINT RUN 25-250
4 Lisa Leslie/250 8.00 20.00
5 Oscar Robertson/50 60.00 100.00
6 Jerry West/52 30.00 60.00
10 Arnie Risen/98 8.00 20.00
11 John Wooden/100 60.00 150.00
13 John Wooden/25 75.00 150.00
15 Dan Issel/100 20.00 40.00
16 Elvin Hayes/100 15.00 40.00
17 Clyde Lovellette/100 8.00 20.00
18 Alex English/100 12.00 30.00
19 David Thompson/100 15.00 40.00
20 Cliff Hagan/99 15.00 40.00
23 Wes Unseld/100 10.00 25.00

2008 Donruss Sports Legends Legends of the Game Combos

STATED PRINT RUN 25-100
UNPRICED PRIME PRINT RUN 1-10
6 T.Williams Jsy/L.Bird Jsy/25 30.00 60.00
8 Campbell Jsy/Hayes Jsy 6.00 15.00
9 H.Aaron Bat/D.Wilkins Jsy 8.00 20.00

2008 Donruss Sports Legends Materials Mirror Blue

*MIRROR BLUE: .5X TO 1.2X MIRROR RED
MIRROR BLUE PRINT RUN 5-250
SERIAL #'d UNDER 15 NOT PRICED
3 Larry Bird/25 10.00 25.00
72 Rick Majerus/100 5.00 12.00

2008 Donruss Sports Legends Materials Mirror Gold

*GOLD/25: .8X TO 2X MIRROR RED
GOLD PRINT RUN 1-25 SER.#'d SETS
SERIAL #'d UNDER 20 NOT PRICED
76 Lisa Leslie/20 5.00 12.00

2008 Donruss Sports Legends Materials Mirror Red

MIRROR RED PRINT RUN 10-500
SERIAL #'d UNDER 25 NOT PRICED
*GOLD/25: .8X TO 2X MIRROR RED
UNPRICED MIRROR EMERALD PRINT RUN 1-5
UNPRICED MIRROR BLACK PRINT RUN 1
7 Oscar Robertson Jsy/500 4.00 10.00
19 Dan Issel Jsy/500 4.00 10.00
22 Elvin Hayes Jsy/500 4.00 10.00
26 Sidney Moncrief Jsy/475 4.00 10.00
32 Walt Frazier Jsy/500 3.00 8.00
42 Marques Haynes Jsy/500 3.00 8.00
47 Dominique Wilkins Jsy/300 4.00 10.00
52 Robert Parish Jsy/350 3.00 8.00
55 Bailey Howell Jsy/500 2.50 6.00
57 Don Haskins Shirt/475 2.50 6.00
62 Rollie Massimino Shirt/500 3.00 8.00
72 Rick Majerus Sweater/400 3.00 8.00
77 Jerry West Jsy/500 5.00 12.00
86 Wes Unseld Jsy/500 3.00 8.00
112 Muggsy Bogues Jsy/500 3.00 8.00

2008 Donruss Sports Legends Museum Curator Collection Materials

STATED PRINT RUN 10-100
*PRIME/25: .6X TO 1.5X BASIC MATERIAL
PRIME PRINT RUN 1-25
SERIAL #'d UNDER 25 NOT PRICED
23 Dominique Wilkins/25 8.00 20.00

2008 Donruss Sports Legends Museum Collection Signatures

STATED PRINT RUN 1-250
SERIAL #'d UNDER 25 NOT PRICED
19 Robert Parish/50 10.00 25.00
30 Bill Walton/25 25.00 50.00

2008 Donruss Sports Legends Signature Connection Combos

STATED PRINT RUN 25-100
1 L.Bird/K.McHale/25 90.00 150.00
5 E.Hayes/E.Cmpbll/25 20.00 40.00
6 Sayers/L.Woodard/25 20.00 40.00
8 L.Alworth/Moncrief/10 90.00 150.00
9 B.Walton/Wooden/25 100.00 200.00
12 T.Aikman/B.Walton/25 60.00 100.00

2008 Donruss Sports Legends Signature Connection Triples

STATED PRINT RUN 25-250
1 Bird/Parish/McHale/25 150.00 250.00
3 Wdrd/Hyns/Gbsn/50 30.00 60.00

2008 Donruss Sports Legends Signatures Mirror Blue

MIRROR BLUE PRINT RUN 2-250
SERIAL #'d UNDER 10 NOT PRICED
UNPRICED MIRROR EMERALD PRINT RUN 1-5
UNPRICED MIRROR BLACK PRINT RUN 1
3 Larry Bird/2
7 Oscar Robertson/15 20.00 50.00
12 John Wooden/25 25.00 60.00
14 Clyde Lovellette/150 5.00 12.00
19 Dan Issel/100 6.00 15.00
22 Elvin Hayes/25 10.00 25.00
25 Kevin McHale/100 40.00 80.00
32 Walt Frazier/50 8.00 20.00
39 Bobby Wanzer/250 5.00 12.00
42 Marques Haynes/50 12.00 30.00
44 Dolph Schayes/150 8.00 20.00
52 Robert Parish/50 10.00 25.00
55 Bailey Howell/250 4.00 10.00
62 Rollie Massimino/50 6.00 15.00
67 Dick Vitale/25 8.00 20.00
72 Rick Majerus/15 8.00 20.00
74 Al Cervi/250 4.00 10.00
76 Lisa Leslie/100 8.00 20.00
77 Jerry West/25 30.00 60.00
86 Wes Unseld/50 5.00 12.00
87 Bill Walton/25 20.00 40.00
89 Arnie Risen/250 6.00 15.00
92 Dennis Rodman/50 15.00 40.00
107 Lynette Woodard/50 10.00 25.00
121 Nate Thurmond/100 6.00 15.00
124 Cliff Hagan/150 6.00 15.00
134 George Gervin/50 6.00 15.00
147 Eddie Sutton/27 8.00 20.00
149 David Thompson/250 5.00 12.00

2008 Donruss Sports Legends Signatures Mirror Gold

MIRROR GOLD PRINT RUN 4-25
SERIAL #'d UNDER 10 NOT PRICED
3 Larry Bird/10
7 Oscar Robertson/10 25.00 60.00
12 John Wooden/10 30.00 80.00
14 Clyde Lovellette/25 8.00 20.00
19 Dan Issel/25 8.00 20.00
22 Elvin Hayes/10 12.00 30.00
25 Kevin McHale/25 50.00 100.00
32 Walt Frazier/25 10.00 25.00
39 Bobby Wanzer/25 8.00 20.00
42 Marques Haynes/25 15.00 40.00
44 Dolph Schayes/25 12.00 30.00
52 Robert Parish/25 12.00 30.00
55 Bailey Howell/25 6.00 15.00
62 Rollie Massimino/25 8.00 20.00
67 Dick Vitale/10 10.00 25.00
72 Rick Majerus/10 10.00 25.00
74 Al Cervi/25 6.00 15.00
76 Lisa Leslie/25 10.00 25.00
77 Jerry West/10 30.00 80.00
86 Wes Unseld/25 6.00 15.00
87 Bill Walton/10 20.00 50.00
89 Arnie Risen/25 10.00 25.00
92 Dennis Rodman/25 20.00 50.00
107 Lynette Woodard/25 12.00 30.00
121 Nate Thurmond/25 8.00 20.00
124 Cliff Hagan/25 10.00 25.00
134 George Gervin/25 8.00 20.00
147 Eddie Sutton/10 10.00 25.00
149 David Thompson/25 8.00 20.00

2008 Donruss Sports Legends Signatures Mirror Red

*MIRROR RED: .3X TO .8X MIRROR BLUE
MIRROR RED PRINT RUN 25-1370
7 Oscar Robertson/25 15.00 40.00
12 John Wooden/25 100.00 200.00
14 Clyde Lovellette/659 4.00 10.00
19 Dan Issel/501 5.00 12.00
22 Elvin Hayes/79 8.00 20.00
25 Kevin McHale/369 25.00 60.00
32 Walt Frazier/158 6.00 15.00
39 Bobby Wanzer/658 4.00 10.00
42 Marques Haynes/337 10.00 25.00
44 Dolph Schayes/655 6.00 15.00
52 Robert Parish/211 8.00 20.00
55 Bailey Howell/664 3.00 8.00
62 Rollie Massimino/333 5.00 12.00
67 Dick Vitale/133 6.00 15.00
74 Al Cervi/619 3.00 8.00
76 Lisa Leslie/396 6.00 15.00
77 Jerry West/25 25.00 60.00
86 Wes Unseld/283 4.00 10.00
87 Bill Walton/259 12.00 30.00
89 Arnie Risen/558 5.00 12.00
92 Dennis Rodman/179 12.00 30.00
107 Lynette Woodard/112 8.00 20.00
121 Nate Thurmond/270 5.00 12.00
124 Cliff Hagan/556 5.00 12.00
134 George Gervin/287 5.00 12.00
149 David Thompson/767 4.00 10.00

2008 Donruss Threads Diamond Kings

RANDOM INSERTS IN PACKS
*GOLD: .6X TO 1.5X BASIC
GOLD RANDOMLY INSERTED
GOLD PRINT RUN 100 SER.#'d SETS
FRM.BLK.RANDOMLY INSERTED
FRM.BLK.PRINT RUN 10 SER.#'d SETS
NO FRM.BLK PRINCING AVAILABLE
*FRM.BLUE: .75X TO 2X BASIC
FRM.BLUE RANDOMLY INSERTS
FRM.BLUE PRINT RUN 50 SER.#'d SETS
FRM.GRN.RANDOMLY INSERTED
FRM.GRN.PRINT RUN 25 SER.#'d SETS
NO FRM.GRN PRINCING AVAILABLE
*FRM.RED: .6X TO 1.5X BASIC
FRM.RED RANDOMLY INSERTS
FRM.RED PRINT RUN 100 SER.#'d SETS
PLAT.RANDOMLY INSERTED
PLAT.PRINT RUN 25 SER.#'d SETS
NO PLAT.PRINCING AVAILABLE
*SILVER: .5X TO 1.2X BASIC
SILVER RANDOMLY INSERTS
SILVER PRINT RUN 250 SER.#'d SETS
53 Derrick Rose 1.50 4.00
54 Michael Beasley 1.50 4.00
55 O.J. Mayo 1.50 4.00

2008 Donruss Threads Diamond Kings Signatures

RANDOM INSERTS IN PACKS
PRINT RUNS B/WN 5-500 COPIES PER
NO PRICING ON QTY 25 OR LESS
53 Derrick Rose/60 100.00 200.00

1990 88's Calgary WBL

Measuring roughly 13 1/2" by 20 1/4", this sheet of 24 player cards (and 6 game ticket discount coupons) features the Calgary 88's of the World Basketball League. The sheet was perforated longitudinally, yielding four 6-card strips and a strip of 6 coupons. If the sheet was perforated and the cards cut, they would measure the standard size. On a white card face, the fronts feature posed color player photos or color action shots. The team logo and various sponsor logos overlay the pictures at each corner. In black print on white, the backs carry biography, statistics, or player profile. The coupons entitled the holder to $2.00 off any $5.00 or $7.00 seat at any 1990 regular season home game.

COMPLETE SET (24) 15.00 40.00
1 David Boone .60 1.50
2 Scott Hicks .60 1.50
3 Dwayne McClain 1.25 3.00
4 Chip Engelland 2.00 5.00
Driving to hoop)
5 Perry Young 1.25 3.00
6 Chip Engelland 1.50 4.00
7 Steve Smith .60 1.50
8 Jim Thomas .75 2.00
(Setting up play)
9 George Jackson .60 1.50
(Dunking)
10 George Jackson .60 1.50
11 Perry Young .60 1.50
12 Carlos Clark 1.25 3.00
(Dribbling)
13 Dave Henderson .60 1.50
(Shooting)
14 Carlos Clark 1.25 3.00
15 John Hegwood .60 1.50
16 Perry Young .60 1.50
(Shooting)
17 Chip Engelland 1.50 4.00
(Shooting)
18 Sean Chambers .60 1.50
19 Carlos Clark 1.25 3.00
(Shooting)
20 1989 WBL Playoffs .75 2.00
(Jim Thomas)
21 1989 WBL Playoffs .60 1.50
(Final Standings on back)
22 Jim Thomas .75 2.00
23 Team Photo .60 1.50
24 Perry Young .60 1.50
(Rebounding)

2012-13 Elite

COMPLETE SET (300) 75.00 200.00
COMP.SET w/o RCs (200) 20.00 50.00
RC PRINT RUN 599 SER.#'d SETS
UNPRICED BLACK PRINT RUN ONE SET
1 Kobe Bryant 1.50 4.00
2 Kevin Durant 1.00 2.50
3 Dwyane Wade .60 1.50
4 Dirk Nowitzki .50 1.25
5 Carmelo Anthony .50 1.25
6 LeBron James 1.50 4.00
7 Derrick Rose .50 1.25
8 Kevin Love .40 1.00
9 Blake Griffin .40 1.00
10 Deron Williams .30 .75
11 Dwight Howard .30 .75
12 Tim Duncan .60 1.50
13 Marcin Gortat .30 .75
14 Paul George .50 1.25
15 Chauncey Billups .40 1.00
16 Devin Harris .25 .60
17 John Salmons .30 .75
18 Andrew Bynum .25 .60
19 Toney Douglas .25 .60
20 Charlie Villanueva .25 .60
21 Mike Conley .30 .75
22 Nate Robinson .25 .60
23 Luke Babbitt .25 .60
24 Beno Udrih .25 .60
25 Andrew Bogut .30 .75
26 Raymond Felton .30 .75
27 Hedo Turkoglu .30 .75
28 James Harden .60 1.50
29 Linas Kleiza .25 .60
30 Danilo Gallinari .25 .60
31 Jason Terry .30 .75
32 Elton Brand .40 1.00
33 Pau Gasol .40 1.00
34 Carlos Boozer .30 .75
35 Travis Outlaw .30 .75
36 Rodney Stuckey .30 .75
37 Ray Allen .40 1.00
38 Cory Higgins .25 .60
39 Brook Lopez .30 .75
40 Al Horford .30 .75
41 Jermaine O'Neal .30 .75
42 Danny Granger .30 .75
43 Steve Nash .40 1.00
44 Jason Richardson .40 1.00
45 J.J. Barea .30 .75
46 Darren Collison .30 .75
47 Ed Davis .25 .60
48 Marc Gasol .40 1.00
49 Ekpe Udoh .25 .60
50 Manu Ginobili .40 1.00
51 Rasheed Wallace .40 1.00
52 Stephen Curry 1.50 4.00
53 Tayshaun Prince .30 .75
54 Aaron Brooks .25 .60
55 Joakim Noah .30 .75
56 J.J. Redick .40 1.00
57 Caron Butler .30 .75
58 Brandon Bass .25 .60
59 Hakim Warrick .30 .75
60 Jordan Hill .25 .60
61 Omri Casspi .25 .60
62 Serge Ibaka .30 .75
63 Tyler Hansbrough .30 .75
64 Paul Millsap .40 1.00
65 Chris Bosh .40 1.00
66 Gerald Wallace .30 .75
67 Vince Carter .50 1.25
68 Kyle Korver .30 .75
69 Luis Scola .30 .75
70 Luol Deng .30 .75
71 Andre Iguodala .30 .75
72 Chase Budinger .25 .60
73 Greg Monroe .30 .75
74 Rudy Gay .40 1.00
75 Carl Landry .25 .60
76 Tyson Chandler .30 .75
77 Brandon Jennings .25 .60
78 J.J. Hickson .25 .60
79 Evan Turner .25 .60
80 Tyrus Thomas .25 .60
81 O.J. Mayo .25 .60
82 George Hill .30 .75
83 Al Jefferson .30 .75
84 Kyle Lowry .30 .75
85 Avery Bradley .30 .75
86 Carlos Delfino .25 .60
87 Jameer Nelson .25 .60
88 Jonas Jerebko .25 .60
89 Richard Jefferson .30 .75
90 Josh Smith .30 .75
91 Kendrick Perkins .25 .60
92 Daniel Gibson .30 .75
93 Shane Battier .30 .75
94 Danny Green .30 .75
95 Kirk Hinrich .30 .75
96 Andrei Kirilenko .30 .75
97 Ersan Ilyasova .25 .60
98 Grant Hill .50 1.25
99 Jason Kidd .40 1.00
100 Ty Lawson .25 .60
101 Antawn Jamison .30 .75
102 Kevin Garnett .60 1.50
103 Gordon Hayward .40 1.00
104 Al Harrington .30 .75
105 Jrue Holiday .40 1.00
106 Zach Randolph .30 .75
107 Joe Johnson .30 .75
108 Shawn Marion .30 .75
109 Mario Chalmers .30 .75
110 Robin Lopez .25 .60
111 Roy Hibbert .30 .75
112 Nicolas Batum .30 .75
113 Stephen Jackson .30 .75
114 DeShawn Stevenson .25 .60
115 Brandon Roy .40 1.00
116 DeMar DeRozan .40 1.00
117 Thabo Sefolosha .25 .60
118 Monta Ellis .30 .75
119 Jeremy Lin .40 1.00
120 Francisco Garcia .30 .75
121 Austin Daye .25 .60
122 Metta World Peace .40 1.00
123 Ramon Sessions .30 .75
124 Andre Miller .30 .75
125 David Lee .25 .60
126 Richard Hamilton .30 .75
127 Derrick Favors .30 .75
128 DeAndre Jordan .40 1.00
129 Udonis Haslem .25 .60
130 Goran Dragic .30 .75
131 Amare Stoudemire .30 .75
132 Tony Parker .40 1.00
133 Glen Davis .25 .60
134 Marreese Speights .25 .60
135 C.J. Miles .30 .75
136 Eric Gordon .30 .75
137 Louis Williams .30 .75
138 Chris Kaman .30 .75
139 Thaddeus Young .25 .60
140 Wesley Matthews .25 .60
141 Mike Dunleavy .25 .60
142 Tyreke Evans .25 .60
143 Paul Pierce .40 1.00
144 Timofey Mozgov .25 .60
145 Lamar Odom .30 .75
146 Kris Humphries .25 .60
147 Jose Calderon .25 .60
148 Omer Asik .30 .75
149 Russell Westbrook 1.00 2.50
150 Rashard Lewis .30 .75
151 Michael Beasley .25 .60
152 David West .30 .75
153 Ricky Rubio .40 1.00
154 Brendan Haywood .25 .60
155 Jodie Meeks .30 .75
156 Tiago Splitter .30 .75
157 Will Bynum .25 .60
158 DeMarcus Cousins .40 1.00
159 Brandon Rush .25 .60
160 Samuel Dalembert .25 .60
161 Arron Afflalo .30 .75
162 Chris Paul .50 1.25
163 Taj Gibson .30 .75
164 Tony Allen .25 .60
165 Raja Bell .30 .75
166 Anderson Varejao .25 .60
167 LaMarcus Aldridge .40 1.00
168 Lance Stephenson .30 .75
169 Anthony Randolph .30 .75
170 Jerry Stackhouse .30 .75
171 Ryan Anderson .30 .75
172 Ben Gordon .30 .75
173 Andrea Bargnani .30 .75
174 Kevin Martin .30 .75
175 Rajon Rondo .40 1.00
176 Wilt Chamberlain .75 2.00
177 Bill Russell .60 1.50
178 Oscar Robertson .50 1.25
179 Magic Johnson 1.00 2.50
180 Larry Bird 1.00 2.50
181 Julius Erving .60 1.50
182 Pete Maravich .60 1.50
183 Scottie Pippen .75 2.00
184 Shaquille O'Neal .75 2.00
185 Patrick Ewing .50 1.25
186 Clyde Drexler .50 1.25
187 John Stockton .60 1.50
188 Allen Iverson .50 1.25
189 Dominique Wilkins .50 1.25
190 Kareem Abdul-Jabbar .60 1.50
191 Gary Payton .40 1.00
192 George Gervin .40 1.00
193 Dennis Rodman .75 2.00
194 David Thompson .30 .75
195 Karl Malone .50 1.25
196 Robert Parish .40 1.00
197 Alonzo Mourning .50 1.25
198 Isiah Thomas .40 1.00
199 David Robinson .60 1.50
200 Jerry West .50 1.25
201 Kyrie Irving RC 6.00 15.00
202 Derrick Williams RC .75 2.00
203 Enes Kanter RC 1.00 2.50
204 Tristan Thompson RC 1.25 3.00
205 Jonas Valanciunas RC 1.25 3.00
206 Jan Vesely RC .75 2.00
207 Bismack Biyombo RC .75 2.00
208 Brandon Knight RC 1.25 3.00
209 Kemba Walker RC 2.50 6.00
210 Jimmer Fredette RC .75 2.00
211 Klay Thompson RC 5.00 12.00
212 Alec Burks RC 1.25 3.00
213 Markieff Morris RC 1.25 3.00
214 Marcus Morris RC 1.00 2.50
215 Kawhi Leonard RC 10.00 25.00
216 Nikola Vucevic RC 1.25 3.00
217 Iman Shumpert RC 1.25 3.00
218 Chris Singleton RC .75 2.00
219 Tobias Harris RC 1.25 3.00
220 Nolan Smith RC .75 2.00
221 Kenneth Faried RC 1.25 3.00
222 Reggie Jackson RC 1.25 3.00
223 MarShon Brooks RC 1.00 2.50
224 Pablo Prigioni RC .75 2.00
225 Norris Cole RC .75 2.00
226 Cory Joseph RC .75 2.00
227 Jimmy Butler RC 4.00 10.00
228 Mirza Teletovic RC 1.00 2.50
229 Kyle Singler RC .75 2.00
230 Tornike Shengelia RC .75 2.00
231 Tyler Honeycutt RC .75 2.00
232 Fab Melo RC .75 2.00
233 Trey Thompkins RC .75 2.00
234 Chandler Parsons RC 1.25 3.00
235 Jeremy Tyler RC .75 2.00
236 Jon Leuer RC 1.00 2.50
237 Darius Morris RC .75 2.00
238 Brian Roberts RC .75 2.00
239 Malcolm Lee RC .75 2.00
240 Charles Jenkins RC .75 2.00
241 Josh Harrellson RC .75 2.00
242 Alexey Shved RC .75 2.00
243 Josh Selby RC .75 2.00
244 Lavoy Allen RC .75 2.00
245 DeAndre Liggins RC 1.00 2.50
246 E'Twaun Moore RC .75 2.00
247 Isaiah Thomas RC 2.00 5.00
248 Ivan Johnson RC .75 2.00
249 Greg Stiemsma RC .75 2.00
250 Jeremy Pargo RC .75 2.00
251 Lance Thomas RC .75 2.00
252 Anthony Davis RC 12.00 30.00
253 Michael Kidd-Gilchrist RC 1.25 3.00
254 Bradley Beal RC 2.00 5.00
255 Dion Waiters RC 1.25 3.00
256 Thomas Robinson RC 1.00 2.50
257 Damian Lillard RC 5.00 12.00
258 Harrison Barnes RC 2.00 5.00
259 Terrence Ross RC 1.25 3.00
260 Andre Drummond RC 2.00 5.00
261 Austin Rivers RC 1.25 3.00
262 Meyers Leonard RC 1.00 2.50
263 Jeremy Lamb RC 1.25 3.00
264 Kendall Marshall RC .75 2.00
265 John Henson RC 1.25 3.00
266 Maurice Harkless RC 1.25 3.00
267 Royce White RC .75 2.00
268 Tyler Zeller RC 1.00 2.50
269 Terrence Jones RC 1.00 2.50
270 Andrew Nicholson RC .75 2.00
271 Evan Fournier RC 1.25 3.00
272 Jared Sullinger RC 1.00 2.50
273 Chris Copeland RC .75 2.00
274 John Jenkins RC .75 2.00
275 Jared Cunningham RC .75 2.00
276 Tony Wroten RC 1.00 2.50
277 Miles Plumlee RC .75 2.00
278 Arnett Moultrie RC .75 2.00
279 Perry Jones RC .75 2.00
280 Marquis Teague RC .75 2.00
281 Festus Ezeli RC 1.00 2.50
282 Jeff Taylor RC .75 2.00
283 Luke Zeller RC .75 2.00
284 Bernard James RC .75 2.00
285 Jae Crowder RC 1.00 2.50
286 Draymond Green RC 4.00 10.00
287 Orlando Johnson RC .75 2.00
288 Quincy Acy RC .75 2.00
289 Diante Garrett RC .75 2.00
290 Khris Middleton RC 1.25 3.00
291 Will Barton RC 1.00 2.50
292 Tyshawn Taylor RC .75 2.00
293 Doron Lamb RC .75 2.00
294 Mike Scott RC .75 2.00
295 Kim English RC .75 2.00
296 Darius Miller RC .75 2.00
297 Kevin Murphy RC .75 2.00
298 DeQuan Jones RC .75 2.00
299 Robert Sacre RC .75 2.00
300 Nando De Colo RC .75 2.00

2012-13 Elite Aspirations

*VETS: 3X TO 8X BASE HI
*ROOKIES: 1X TO 2.5X BASE HI
STATED PRINT RUN 6 TO 99 SER.#'d SETS
2 Kevin Durant/65 15.00 40.00
6 LeBron James/94 15.00 40.00
98 Grant Hill/67 8.00 20.00
153 Ricky Rubio/91 12.00 30.00
170 Jerry Stackhouse/58 10.00 25.00
197 Alonzo Mourning/67 8.00 20.00
215 Kawhi Leonard/98 30.00 80.00
247 Isaiah Thomas/78 8.00 20.00
252 Anthony Davis/77 75.00 150.00

2012-13 Elite Status

*VETS P/R 30 AND LESS: 6X TO 15X BASE HI
*VETS P/R 31 AND MORE: 5X TO 12X BASE HI
*ROOKIES P/R 30 AND LESS: 2X TO 5X BASE HI
*ROOKIES P/R 31 AND MORE: 1.5X TO 4X BASE HI
STATED PRINT RUN ONE TO 94 SER.#'d SETS
1 Kobe Bryant/24 30.00 80.00
2 Kevin Durant/35 20.00 50.00
12 Tim Duncan/21 12.00 30.00
37 Ray Allen/34 8.00 20.00
98 Grant Hill/33 10.00 25.00
111 Roy Hibbert/55 3.00 8.00
170 Jerry Stackhouse/42 12.00 30.00
182 Pete Maravich/44 20.00 50.00
183 Scottie Pippen/33 12.00 30.00
185 Patrick Ewing/33 20.00 50.00
221 Kenneth Faried/35 15.00 40.00
234 Chandler Parsons/25 25.00 60.00
241 Josh Harrellson/55 3.00 8.00
244 Lavoy Allen/50 3.00 8.00
246 E'Twaun Moore/55 3.00 8.00
271 Evan Fournier/94 5.00 12.00
297 Kevin Murphy/55 2.50 6.00
299 Robert Sacre/50 3.00 8.00

2012-13 Elite Status Gold

*VETS: 6X TO 15X BASE HI
*ROOKIES: 2X TO 5X BASE HI
STATED PRINT RUN 24 SER.#'d SETS
1 Kobe Bryant 50.00 120.00
2 Kevin Durant 25.00 60.00
6 LeBron James 50.00 120.00
37 Ray Allen 8.00 20.00
98 Grant Hill 12.00 30.00
149 Russell Westbrook 12.00 30.00
153 Ricky Rubio 20.00 50.00
170 Jerry Stackhouse 15.00 40.00
183 Scottie Pippen 15.00 40.00
185 Patrick Ewing 20.00 50.00
187 John Stockton 15.00 40.00
188 Allen Iverson 15.00 40.00
215 Kawhi Leonard 20.00 50.00
221 Kenneth Faried 25.00 60.00
234 Chandler Parsons 25.00 60.00
242 Alexey Shved 25.00 60.00
252 Anthony Davis 30.00 80.00

2012-13 Elite All-Star Salute Materials

RANDOM INSERTS IN PACKS
1 Kobe Bryant 12.00 30.00
2 Dwight Howard 2.50 6.00
3 Al Horford 2.50 6.00
4 Carmelo Anthony 4.00 10.00
5 Chris Paul 4.00 10.00
6 Rajon Rondo 3.00 8.00
7 Paul Pierce 3.00 8.00
8 Dwyane Wade 5.00 12.00
9 Blake Griffin 3.00 8.00
10 Russell Westbrook 8.00 20.00
11 Deron Williams 2.50 6.00
12 Kevin Love 3.00 8.00
13 Kevin Garnett 5.00 12.00
14 Derrick Rose 4.00 10.00
15 Manu Ginobili 3.00 8.00
16 Joe Johnson 2.50 6.00
17 Tim Duncan 5.00 12.00
18 Dirk Nowitzki 4.00 10.00
19 Kevin Durant 8.00 20.00
20 Ray Allen 3.00 8.00
21 Shaquille O'Neal 6.00 15.00
22 Chris Bosh 3.00 8.00
23 LeBron James 12.00 30.00
24 Amare Stoudemire 2.50 6.00
25 Zach Randolph 2.50 6.00

2012-13 Elite All-Star Salute Materials Prime

*PRIME: 1.5X TO 4X BASE HI
STATED PRINT RUN 25 SER.#'d SETS

2012-13 Elite All-Time Greats Signatures

STATED PRINT RUN 25 TO 199 SER.#'d SETS
1 Magic Johnson/49 40.00 100.00
2 Larry Bird/49 40.00 100.00
3 Julius Erving/49 30.00 80.00
4 Alonzo Mourning/49 20.00 50.00
5 Walt Frazier/49 10.00 25.00
6 Bill Walton/49 6.00 15.00
7 Isiah Thomas/49 10.00 25.00
8 Clyde Drexler/49 20.00 50.00
9 Dikembe Mutombo/99 10.00 25.00
10 Rick Barry/49 10.00 25.00
11 Pat Riley/49 12.00 30.00
12 David Robinson/49 15.00 40.00
13 Gail Goodrich/199 6.00 15.00
14 Dominique Wilkins/49 12.00 30.00
15 Jerry West/49 20.00 50.00
16 Larry Johnson/199 6.00 15.00
17 Scottie Pippen/49 40.00 100.00
18 John Stockton/49 30.00 60.00
19 Gary Payton/49 12.00 30.00
20 Robert Parish/49 6.00 15.00
21 Hakeem Olajuwon/49 10.00 25.00
22 Bob Lanier/49 8.00 20.00
23 Dan Majerle/199 6.00 15.00
24 Kobe Bryant/99 75.00 150.00
25 Bill Russell/25 40.00 100.00

2012-13 Elite Back to the Future Materials

RANDOM INSERTS IN PACKS
1 LeBron James 12.00 30.00
2 Grant Hill 8.00 20.00
3 Steve Nash 3.00 8.00
4 Vince Carter 4.00 10.00
5 Kevin Garnett 5.00 12.00
6 Ray Allen 3.00 8.00
7 Amare Stoudemire 2.50 6.00
8 Carmelo Anthony 4.00 10.00
9 Joe Johnson 2.50 6.00
10 David West 2.50 6.00
11 Chris Paul 4.00 10.00
12 Dwight Howard 2.50 6.00
13 Nate Robinson 2.00 5.00
14 Antawn Jamison 2.50 6.00
15 James Harden 5.00 12.00
16 Nene 2.50 6.00
17 Eric Gordon 2.50 6.00
18 Jeff Green 2.50 6.00
19 Shane Battier 2.50 6.00
20 Derek Fisher 2.50 6.00
21 Lamar Odom 2.50 6.00
22 Brandon Roy 3.00 8.00
23 Jermaine O'Neal 2.50 6.00
24 Jason Terry 2.50 6.00
25 Andrei Kirilenko 2.50 6.00

2012-13 Elite Back to the Future Materials Prime

*PRIME: 1X TO 2.5X BASE HI
STATED PRINT RUN 25 SER.#'d SETS

2012-13 Elite Craftsmen

COMPLETE SET (25) 15.00 40.00
RANDOM INSERTS IN PACKS
*GOLD: 2.5X TO 6X HI COLUMN
GOLD STATED PRINT RUN 24 SETS
UNPRICED BLACK PRINT RUN ONE SET
1 Dwight Howard .60 1.50
2 Tyreke Evans .50 1.25
3 Dwyane Wade 1.25 3.00
4 Serge Ibaka .60 1.50
5 Raymond Felton .60 1.50
6 LeBron James 3.00 8.00
7 Darren Collison .60 1.50
8 Steve Novak .50 1.25
9 Kevin Durant 2.00 5.00
10 Grant Hill 1.00 2.50
11 Antawn Jamison .60 1.50
12 Derrick Rose 1.00 2.50
13 Zach Randolph .60 1.50
14 Kevin Garnett 1.25 3.00
15 Blake Griffin .75 2.00
16 Roy Hibbert .60 1.50
17 Jeremy Lin .75 2.00
18 Steve Nash .75 2.00
19 Ty Lawson .50 1.25
20 Brandon Jennings .50 1.25
21 Ricky Rubio .75 2.00
22 Rajon Rondo .75 2.00
23 Brook Lopez .60 1.50
24 Kobe Bryant 3.00 8.00
25 Dirk Nowitzki 1.00 2.50

2012-13 Elite Dominators Materials

RANDOM INSERTS IN PACKS
1 Blake Griffin 3.00 8.00
2 Marc Gasol 3.00 8.00
3 Tim Duncan 5.00 12.00
4 Amare Stoudemire 2.50 6.00
5 Derrick Rose 4.00 10.00
6 LeBron James 12.00 30.00
7 Kevin Durant 8.00 20.00
8 Paul Pierce 3.00 8.00
9 Brook Lopez 2.50 6.00
10 Zach Randolph 2.50 6.00
11 Kevin Garnett 5.00 12.00
12 Al Horford 2.50 6.00
13 Stephen Curry 12.00 30.00
14 Channing Frye 2.50 6.00
15 Tony Parker 3.00 8.00
16 John Wall 4.00 10.00
17 Raymond Felton 2.50 6.00
18 Thaddeus Young 2.00 5.00
19 Al Jefferson 2.50 6.00
20 Metta World Peace 3.00 8.00
21 LaMarcus Aldridge 3.00 8.00
22 Carlos Boozer 2.50 6.00
23 Chris Bosh 3.00 8.00
24 Carmelo Anthony 4.00 10.00
25 Tayshaun Prince 2.50 6.00

2012-13 Elite Dominators Materials Prime

*PRIME: 1X TO 2.5X BASE HI
STATED PRINT RUN 25 SER.#'d SETS

2012-13 Elite Passing the Torch Autographs

STATED PRINT RUN 20 TO 49 SER.#'d SETS
1 K.Bryant/K.Durant/49 400.00 700.00
2 S.Nash/G.Dragic/25 50.00 125.00
3 J.Kidd/D.Collison/25 12.00 30.00
4 J.Harden/J.Starks/49 30.00 80.00
5 D.Majerle/R.Allen/25 20.00 50.00
6 B.Walton/L.Aldridge/49 12.00 30.00
7 J.Erving/B.Griffin/25 60.00 120.00
8 D.Thompson/Iguodala/49 8.00 20.00
9 H.Olajuwon/S.Ibaka/25 30.00
10 Thomas/Paul/25 EXCH 60.00 150.00
11 B.Laimbeer/M.Gortat/49 8.00 20.00
12 D.Rodman/K.Love/25 100.00 200.00
13 G.Gervin/K.Durant/25 75.00 200.00
14 L.Bird/D.Nowitzki/20 150.00 300.00
15 K.Irving/G.Hill/25 60.00 150.00
16 E.Hayes/K.Love/25 15.00 40.00
17 D.Rivers/A.Rivers/49 30.00 60.00
18 S.Curry/D.Curry/49 175.00 350.00
19 Mullin/Lee/49 EXCH 25.00 60.00
20 W.Reed/T.Chandler/25 30.00 60.00
21 R.Sampson/R.Hibbert/49 12.00 30.00
22 W.Free/M.Peace/49 15.00 40.00
23 M.Johnson/S.Nash/25 75.00 200.00
24 K.Irving/A.Davis/25 150.00 400.00
25 S.Pippen/G.Hill/25 300.00 500.00

2012-13 Elite Prime Numbers

COMPLETE SET (25) 20.00 50.00
RANDOM INSERTS IN PACKS
*GOLD: 2X TO 5X HI COLUMN
GOLD STATED PRINT RUN 24 SETS
UNPRICED BLACK PRINT RUN ONE SET
1 Blake Griffin 1.00 2.50
2 Shaquille O'Neal 2.00 5.00
3 John Stockton 1.50 4.00
4 LeBron James 4.00 10.00
5 Gary Payton 1.00 2.50
6 Kareem Abdul-Jabbar 1.50 4.00
7 Ray Allen 1.00 2.50
8 Dennis Rodman 2.00 5.00
9 Kevin Love 1.00 2.50
10 Jason Terry .75 2.00
11 Oscar Robertson 1.25 3.00
12 Elvin Hayes 1.00 2.50
13 Larry Bird 2.50 6.00
14 Jerry West 1.25 3.00
15 Bill Russell 1.50 4.00
16 Adrian Dantley .75 2.00
17 Jason Kidd 1.00 2.50
18 Mark Eaton .60 1.50
19 Magic Johnson 2.50 6.00
20 Robert Parish 1.00 2.50
21 David Robinson 1.50 4.00
22 Hakeem Olajuwon 1.25 3.00
23 Scott Skiles .75 2.00
24 Kobe Bryant 4.00 10.00
25 Dirk Nowitzki 1.25 3.00

2012-13 Elite Rookie Inscriptions

1 Kyrie Irving 50.00 120.00
2 Bismack Biyombo 2.50 6.00
3 Alec Burks 4.00 10.00
4 Iman Shumpert 4.00 10.00
5 MarShon Brooks 3.00 8.00
6 Kyle Singler 2.50 6.00
7 Chandler Parsons 4.00 10.00
8 Malcolm Lee 2.50 6.00
9 E'Twaun Moore 2.50 6.00
10 Anthony Davis 75.00 200.00
11 Harrison Barnes 8.00 20.00
12 Jeremy Lamb EXCH 4.00 10.00
13 Tyler Zeller 3.00 8.00
14 Miles Plumlee EXCH 2.50 6.00
15 Quincy Acy 2.50 6.00
16 Robert Sacre 2.50 6.00
17 Kim English 2.50 6.00
18 Tyshawn Taylor 2.50 6.00
19 Khris Middleton 4.00 10.00
20 Draymond Green 15.00 40.00
21 Bernard James 2.50 6.00
22 Festus Ezeli 3.00 8.00
23 Perry Jones 2.50 6.00
24 Jared Cunningham 2.50 6.00
25 Jared Sullinger 3.00 8.00
26 Andrew Nicholson 2.50 6.00
27 Royce White 2.50 6.00
28 John Henson 4.00 10.00
29 Austin Rivers 4.00 10.00
30 Terrence Ross 4.00 10.00
31 Dion Waiters 4.00 10.00
32 Jeremy Pargo 2.50 6.00
33 Ivan Johnson 2.50 6.00
34 Lavoy Allen 2.50 6.00
35 Josh Harrellson 2.50 6.00
36 Kent Bazemore 4.00 10.00
37 Jon Leuer 3.00 8.00
38 Trey Thompkins 2.50 6.00
39 Jimmy Butler 25.00 60.00
40 Norris Cole 2.50 6.00
41 Reggie Jackson 4.00 10.00
42 Tobias Harris 4.00 10.00
43 Kawhi Leonard 60.00 150.00
44 Markieff Morris EXCH 4.00 10.00
45 Jimmer Fredette 2.50 6.00
46 Brandon Knight 4.00 10.00
47 Jan Vesely 2.50 6.00
48 Derrick Williams 2.50 6.00
49 Tristan Thompson 4.00 10.00
50 Kemba Walker 6.00 15.00
51 Marcus Morris 3.00 8.00
52 Chris Singleton 2.50 6.00
53 Kenneth Faried 4.00 10.00
54 Cory Joseph 2.50 6.00
55 Donatas Motiejunas 3.00 8.00
56 Darius Morris 2.50 6.00
57 Isaiah Thomas 20.00 50.00
58 Michael Kidd-Gilchrist 4.00 10.00
59 Kyle O'Quinn 2.50 6.00
60 Meyers Leonard 3.00 8.00
61 Maurice Harkless 4.00 10.00
62 Evan Fournier 4.00 10.00
63 John Jenkins 2.50 6.00
64 Arnett Moultrie 2.50 6.00
65 Jeff Taylor 2.50 6.00
66 Jae Crowder 3.00 8.00
67 Quincy Miller 2.50 6.00
68 Doron Lamb 2.50 6.00
69 Darius Miller 2.50 6.00
70 Kris Joseph 2.50 6.00
71 Kevin Murphy 2.50 6.00
72 Will Barton 3.00 8.00
73 Tony Wroten 3.00 8.00
74 Terrence Jones 3.00 8.00
75 Andre Drummond 6.00 15.00
76 Lance Thomas 2.50 6.00
77 DeAndre Liggins 3.00 8.00
78 Jeremy Tyler 2.50 6.00
79 Nolan Smith 2.50 6.00
80 Klay Thompson 25.00 60.00
81 Jonas Valanciunas 4.00 10.00
82 Enes Kanter 3.00 8.00
83 Nikola Vucevic 4.00 10.00
84 Tyler Honeycutt 2.50 6.00
85 Charles Jenkins 2.50 6.00
86 Josh Selby 2.50 6.00
87 Greg Stiemsma 2.50 6.00
88 Bradley Beal 12.00 30.00
89 Thomas Robinson EXCH 3.00 8.00
90 Kendall Marshall 2.50 6.00
91 Fab Melo 2.50 6.00
92 Marquis Teague 2.50 6.00
93 Orlando Johnson 2.50 6.00
94 Mike Scott 2.50 6.00
95 Darius Johnson-Odom 2.50 6.00
96 Chris Copeland 2.50 6.00
97 Victor Claver 2.50 6.00
98 Nando De Colo 2.50 6.00
99 DeQuan Jones 2.50 6.00

2012-13 Elite Series Inserts

COMPLETE SET (30) 20.00 50.00
RANDOM INSERTS IN PACKS
*GOLD: 2X TO 5X HI COLUMN
GOLD STATED PRINT RUN 24 SETS
UNPRICED BLACK PRINT RUN ONE SET
1 Blake Griffin 1.00 2.50
2 Kevin Durant 2.50 6.00
3 Carmelo Anthony 1.25 3.00
4 Paul Pierce 1.00 2.50
5 LeBron James 4.00 10.00
6 Chris Paul 1.25 3.00
7 Amare Stoudemire .75 2.00
8 Dirk Nowitzki 1.25 3.00
9 Tim Duncan 1.50 4.00
10 Steve Nash 1.00 2.50
11 Derrick Rose 1.25 3.00
12 Deron Williams .75 2.00
13 Andre Iguodala .75 2.00
14 Danny Granger .75 2.00
15 Russell Westbrook 2.50 6.00
16 LaMarcus Aldridge 1.00 2.50
17 Kevin Love 1.00 2.50

18 Marcin Gortat .75 2.00
19 Joe Johnson .75 2.00
20 Ray Allen 1.00 2.50
21 Ricky Rubio 1.00 2.50
22 Dwyane Wade 1.50 4.00
23 DeMarcus Cousins 1.00 2.50
24 Kobe Bryant 4.00 10.00
25 Tyson Chandler .75 2.00
26 Dwight Howard .75 2.00
27 Tony Parker 1.00 2.50
28 Rajon Rondo 1.00 2.50
29 James Harden 1.50 4.00
30 Marc Gasol 1.00 2.50

2012-13 Elite Rookie Elite Series

COMPLETE SET (20) 25.00 60.00
RANDOM INSERTS IN PACKS
*GOLD: 2X TO 5X HI COLUMN
GOLD STATED PRINT RUN 24 SETS
UNPRICED BLACK PRINT RUN ONE SET
1 Kyrie Irving 8.00 20.00
2 Anthony Davis 5.00 12.00
3 Kawhi Leonard 5.00 12.00
4 Kenneth Faried 1.00 2.50
5 Iman Shumpert 1.00 2.50
6 Michael Kidd-Gilchrist 1.00 2.50
7 Jared Sullinger .75 2.00
8 Isaiah Thomas 1.50 4.00
9 Kemba Walker 2.00 5.00
10 Markieff Morris 1.00 2.50
11 Derrick Williams .60 1.50
12 Bradley Beal 1.50 4.00
13 Chandler Parsons 1.00 2.50
14 Brandon Knight 1.00 2.50
15 Austin Rivers 1.00 2.50
16 Damian Lillard 8.00 20.00
17 MarShon Brooks .75 2.00
18 Thomas Robinson .75 2.00
19 Tristan Thompson 1.00 2.50
20 Lavoy Allen .60 1.50

2012-13 Elite Signatures

STATED PRINT RUN 49 TO 199 SER.#'d SETS
1 Kobe Bryant/197 75.00 150.00
2 Mario Chalmers/49
3 Grant Hill/99 10.00 25.00
4 Kevin Martin/49 4.00 10.00
5 Ryan Anderson/52 4.00 10.00
6 Andrei Kirilenko/99
7 Stephen Curry/199 100.00 250.00
8 Zach Randolph/99 6.00 15.00
9 Ty Lawson/199 4.00 10.00
10 Roy Hibbert/53 4.00 10.00
11 Steve Nash/49 20.00 50.00
12 Jason Kidd/49 12.00 30.00
13 Stephen Jackson/49
14 Taj Gibson/49
15 James Harden/99 15.00 40.00
16 Danny Green/199 6.00 15.00
17 Kevin Love/49 12.00 30.00
18 Jeff Green/49 4.00 10.00
19 Steve Novak/49 4.00 10.00
20 J.J. Hickson/199 4.00 10.00
21 Udonis Haslem/199 4.00 10.00
22 Kevin Durant/49 100.00 200.00
23 Joakim Noah/49 4.00 10.00
24 Luis Scola/49
25 Serge Ibaka/98 4.00 10.00
26 Vince Carter/49 6.00 15.00
27 Hedo Turkoglu/49 4.00 10.00
28 Kris Humphries/49 4.00 10.00
29 Marcin Gortat/199 8.00 20.00
30 LaMarcus Aldridge/99 5.00 12.00
31 Jason Richardson/49 8.00 20.00
32 Devin Harris/49
33 Luc Mbah a Moute/199
34 Rashard Lewis/199 4.00 10.00
35 Tayshaun Prince/49 4.00 10.00
36 Gerald Wallace/49 4.00 10.00
37 Jrue Holiday/199 4.00 10.00
38 Andrew Bynum/49
39 Thabo Sefolosha/49 4.00 10.00
40 Luol Deng/49
41 Blake Griffin/49 12.00 30.00
42 David West/49 6.00 15.00
43 O.J. Mayo/49 4.00 10.00
44 DeAndre Jordan/49
45 Ray Allen/49 20.00 50.00
46 Goran Dragic/199 4.00 10.00
47 Nick Collison/199 4.00 10.00
48 Antawn Jamison/49 8.00 20.00
49 Gordon Hayward/199 6.00 15.00
50 Darren Collison/49

2012-13 Elite Throwback Threads

RANDOM INSERTS IN PACKS
1 Patrick Ewing 5.00 12.00
2 Allen Iverson 8.00 20.00
3 John Stockton 5.00 12.00
4 Shaquille O'Neal 6.00 15.00
5 Dennis Rodman 8.00 20.00
6 Kevin McHale 3.00 8.00
7 Ron Harper 3.00 8.00
8 Alonzo Mourning 6.00 15.00
9 Alex English 2.50 6.00
10 Julius Erving 5.00 12.00
11 Kelly Tripucka 2.00 5.00
12 Earl Monroe 3.00 8.00
13 Glen Rice 2.50 6.00
14 Xavier McDaniel 2.00 5.00
15 Tom Chambers 2.50 6.00
16 Kiki Vandeweghe 2.50 6.00
17 Lou Hudson 3.00 8.00
18 Shawn Kemp 8.00 20.00
19 Zydrunas Ilgauskas 2.50 6.00
20 Chris Webber 3.00 8.00
21 Artis Gilmore 2.50 6.00
22 Rick Mahorn 2.00 5.00
23 Manute Bol 5.00 12.00
24 Kenny Anderson 2.50 6.00
25 Slater Martin 5.00 12.00

2012-13 Elite Throwback Threads Prime

*PRIME: 1.25X TO 3X BASE HI
STATED PRINT RUN 25 SER.#'d SETS
3 John Stockton 20.00 50.00

2012-13 Elite Turn of the Century Autographs

STATED PRINT RUN 25 TO 199 SER.#'d SETS
1 Shane Battier/25
2 Muggsy Bogues/199 6.00 15.00
3 Dwyane Wade/49 25.00 60.00
4 Steve Kerr/49 10.00 25.00
5 Anthony Mason/199 6.00 15.00
6 Anfernee Hardaway/25 75.00 150.00
7 Tim Hardaway/199 6.00 15.00
8 Danny Manning/49 4.00 10.00
9 Mitch Richmond/149 5.00 12.00
10 Trevor Booker/199 2.50 6.00
11 Brook Lopez/25 3.00 8.00
12 Mark Jackson/25
13 George Hill/199 3.00 8.00
14 Greg Monroe/149 3.00 8.00
15 Rodney Stuckey/149 3.00 8.00
16 Marvin Williams/199 3.00 8.00
17 Zaza Pachulia/199 2.50 6.00
18 Andrew Bogut/99 6.00 15.00
19 Stephen Curry/25 125.00 250.00
20 Kevin Durant/49 50.00 120.00
21 Bill Cartwright/149 4.00 10.00
22 Brandon Bass/149 4.00 10.00
23 Andre Iguodala/25
24 Kobe Bryant/199 75.00 150.00
25 Tyson Chandler/25
26 DeMarcus Cousins/25 12.00 30.00
27 Tiago Splitter/199 3.00 8.00
28 Monta Ellis/25 3.00 8.00
29 Tyreke Evans/25 2.50 6.00
30 Brandon Jennings/25
31 Gerald Henderson/149 4.00 10.00
32 Chris Bosh/25 20.00 50.00
33 Eric Gordon/25
34 Marcus Thornton/199 4.00 10.00
35 Michael Finley/25
36 Nick Young/149 4.00 10.00
37 Rick Fox/25 3.00 8.00
38 Steve Novak/99 2.50 6.00
39 Dorell Wright/199
40 Blake Griffin/49 15.00 40.00
41 Ty Lawson/49 2.50 6.00
42 Chase Budinger/199 4.00 10.00
43 Udonis Haslem/199 2.50 6.00
44 Zydrunas Ilgauskas/199 4.00 10.00
45 Wesley Matthews/199 2.50 6.00
46 Tyler Hansbrough/25 3.00 8.00
47 Gordon Hayward/199 5.00 12.00
48 Tayshaun Prince/25
49 Anthony Morrow/199
50 Joe Johnson/25
51 Kyle Lowry/199 4.00 10.00
52 Richard Jefferson/49
53 Danilo Gallinari/25 8.00 20.00
54 Grant Hill/25 30.00 80.00
55 Ronny Turiaf/149 2.50 6.00
56 Richard Hamilton/25
57 Carlos Boozer/25
58 Al-Farouq Aminu/199 3.00 8.00
59 Paul George/149 20.00 50.00
60 Ronnie Price/199 2.50 6.00
61 Rolando Blackman/199 4.00 10.00
62 Mike Conley/49 EXCH 4.00 10.00
63 Marreese Speights/199 4.00 10.00
64 Luol Deng/25
65 Luke Ridnour/149 4.00 10.00
66 Luis Scola/49
67 Louis Williams/199 4.00 10.00
68 Andrew Bynum/25
69 Austin Rivers/25 8.00 20.00
70 Markieff Morris/199 EXCH 4.00 10.00
71 Draymond Green/199 10.00 25.00
72 Kenneth Faried/199 4.00 10.00
73 Kawhi Leonard/199 60.00 150.00
74 Chandler Parsons/199 4.00 10.00
75 Isaiah Thomas/199 25.00 60.00
76 Tyshawn Taylor/199 2.50 6.00
77 Andre Drummond/25
78 Tyler Zeller/199 3.00 8.00
79 Perry Jones/199
80 Jared Sullinger/25
81 Doron Lamb/199 2.50 6.00
82 Jrue Holiday/49 4.00 10.00
83 Meyers Leonard/199 3.00 8.00
84 Jimmer Fredette/199 2.50 6.00
85 Landry Fields/199
86 Andrea Bargnani/25 3.00 8.00
87 JaVale McGee/149 4.00 10.00
88 Jeff Teague/199 4.00 10.00
89 Carlos Delfino/199 4.00 10.00
90 Patrick Patterson/199 4.00 10.00
91 Kevin Love/25
92 Nikola Pekovic/199 2.50 6.00
93 Norris Cole/199 2.50 6.00
94 Sean Elliott/199 6.00 15.00
95 Shannon Brown/199 4.00 10.00
96 Samardo Samuels/199 4.00 10.00
97 Reggie Evans/149 2.50 6.00
98 Rashard Lewis/199 4.00 10.00
99 Marquis Teague/199 2.50 6.00
100 Bradley Beal/25 20.00 50.00

2013-14 Elite

ROOKIE PRINT RUN 999 SER.#'d SETS
RETIRED PRINT RUN 999 SER.#'d SETS
1 Raymond Felton .30 .75
2 Elton Brand .40 1.00
3 Nate Robinson .25 .60
4 Rajon Rondo .40 1.00
5 Josh Smith .30 .75
6 John Wall .50 1.25
7 Ray Allen .40 1.00
8 Louis Williams .30 .75
9 MarShon Brooks .30 .75
10 Tyler Hansbrough .30 .75
11 Taj Gibson .30 .75
12 Josh McRoberts .25 .60
13 Kendrick Perkins .25 .60
14 John Salmons .30 .75
15 Kyle Lowry .30 .75
16 Metta World Peace .40 1.00
17 JaVale McGee .30 .75
18 DeMar DeRozan .40 1.00
19 Andrei Kirilenko .30 .75
20 Klay Thompson .50 1.25
21 Jeff Green .30 .75
22 O.J. Mayo .25 .60
23 Damian Lillard .75 2.00
24 Joakim Noah .30 .75
25 Andre Iguodala .30 .75
26 Al Horford .30 .75
27 Jamal Crawford .40 1.00
28 James Harden .60 1.50
29 Greivis Vasquez .30 .75
30 David West .30 .75
31 Amar'e Stoudemire .30 .75
32 Eric Gordon .30 .75
33 Tony Allen .25 .60
34 Chris Paul .50 1.25
35 Jan Vesely .25 .60
36 Vince Carter .50 1.25
37 Isaiah Thomas .40 1.00
38 Thabo Sefolosha .25 .60
39 Andrew Bynum .25 .60
40 Ryan Anderson .30 .75
41 J.R. Smith .30 .75
42 Kyle Korver .30 .75
43 Tyson Chandler .30 .75
44 Udonis Haslem .25 .60
45 Jason Richardson .40 1.00
46 Danny Granger .30 .75
47 Michael Kidd-Gilchrist .40 1.00
48 Tayshaun Prince .30 .75
49 Gerald Henderson .25 .60
50 J.J. Redick .40 1.00
51 Gerald Wallace .30 .75
52 Kawhi Leonard .60 1.50
53 Deron Williams .30 .75
54 Jordan Hill .25 .60
55 Thaddeus Young .25 .60
56 Tony Parker .40 1.00
57 J.J. Hickson .25 .60
58 Luol Deng .30 .75
59 Kemba Walker .40 1.00
60 Kyrie Irving .75 2.00
61 Nikola Vucevic .30 .75
62 Kevin Garnett .60 1.50
63 Boris Diaw .30 .75
64 Markieff Morris .25 .60
65 Kevin Durant 1.00 2.50
66 Shawn Marion .30 .75
67 Brandon Jennings .25 .60
68 Andrew Bogut .30 .75
69 Marcus Thornton .25 .60
70 Zach Randolph .30 .75
71 Omer Asik .30 .75
72 J.J. Barea .30 .75
73 Matt Barnes .25 .60
74 Dwyane Wade .60 1.50
75 Jason Maxiell .25 .60
76 Manu Ginobili .40 1.00
77 Chris Kaman .30 .75
78 Kirk Hinrich .30 .75
79 George Hill .30 .75
80 Glen Davis .25 .60
81 Marcus Morris .25 .60
82 Robin Lopez .25 .60
83 Jeremy Lin .40 1.00
84 Paul George .50 1.25
85 Michael Beasley .25 .60
86 Serge Ibaka .30 .75
87 Luke Ridnour .30 .75
88 Joe Johnson .30 .75
89 Derrick Williams .25 .60
90 Trevor Ariza .25 .60
91 Andre Miller .30 .75
92 Paul Millsap .40 1.00
93 Kevin Love .40 1.00
94 Mike Conley .30 .75
95 Orlando Johnson .25 .60
96 David Lee .25 .60
97 Jonas Valanciunas .30 .75
98 Steve Nash .40 1.00
99 Wilson Chandler .30 .75
100 Miles Plumlee .25 .60
101 Tiago Splitter .30 .75
102 Brandon Knight .30 .75
103 Wesley Matthews .25 .60
104 Earl Clark .25 .60
105 Stephen Curry 1.50 4.00
106 Dirk Nowitzki .50 1.25
107 Ben Gordon .30 .75
108 Jeff Teague .30 .75
109 Nicolas Batum .30 .75
110 LeBron James 1.50 4.00
111 Bradley Beal .40 1.00
112 Evan Turner .25 .60
113 Russell Westbrook 1.00 2.50
114 Matt Bonner .25 .60
115 Arron Afflalo .25 .60
116 Dwight Howard .30 .75
117 Nikola Pekovic .25 .60
118 Kenneth Faried .30 .75
119 Harrison Barnes .30 .75
120 Greg Monroe .30 .75
121 Dion Waiters .30 .75
122 Spencer Hawes .25 .60
123 Kosta Koufos .25 .60
124 Corey Brewer .25 .60
125 Wayne Ellington .25 .60
126 Andre Drummond .40 1.00
127 Danny Green .30 .75
128 Carlos Boozer .30 .75
129 Roy Hibbert .30 .75
130 Mike Miller .30 .75
131 Nick Young .40 1.00
132 Reggie Evans .25 .60
133 DeAndre Jordan .40 1.00
134 Carmelo Anthony .50 1.25
135 Draymond Green .50 1.25
136 Jimmer Fredette .25 .60
137 Al-Farouq Aminu .30 .75
138 Marcin Gortat .30 .75
139 Thomas Robinson .25 .60
140 Lance Stephenson .30 .75
141 Ricky Rubio .40 1.00
142 Anthony Davis .75 2.00
143 Pau Gasol .40 1.00
144 Alec Burks .25 .60
145 Luis Scola .30 .75
146 Rudy Gay .40 1.00
147 Avery Bradley .30 .75
148 Shane Battier .30 .75
149 LaMarcus Aldridge .40 1.00
150 Paul Pierce .40 1.00
151 Marc Gasol .40 1.00
152 Richard Jefferson .30 .75
153 Iman Shumpert .25 .60
154 Gordon Hayward .40 1.00
155 Nene .30 .75
156 Kevin Martin .30 .75
157 Monta Ellis .30 .75
158 Tony Wroten .25 .60
159 Martell Webster .25 .60
160 Mario Chalmers .30 .75
161 Byron Mullens .25 .60
162 DeMarcus Cousins .40 1.00
163 Amir Johnson .25 .60
164 Danilo Gallinari .25 .60
165 Lavoy Allen .25 .60
166 Chris Andersen .30 .75
167 Tyreke Evans .25 .60
168 Jameer Nelson .25 .60
169 Larry Sanders .25 .60
170 Eric Bledsoe .30 .75
171 Derrick Rose .50 1.25
172 Andray Blatche .25 .60
173 Andrea Bargnani .30 .75
174 Derrick Favors .30 .75
175 Chauncey Billups .40 1.00
176 John Henson .30 .75
177 Blake Griffin .40 1.00
178 Brandon Bass .25 .60
179 Anderson Varejao .25 .60
180 Channing Frye .30 .75
181 Marvin Williams .30 .75
182 Brook Lopez .30 .75
183 Rodney Stuckey .30 .75
184 Goran Dragic .30 .75
185 Derek Fisher .30 .75
186 Chandler Parsons .30 .75
187 C.J. Miles .30 .75
188 Ersan Ilyasova .25 .60
189 Jrue Holiday .40 1.00
190 Aaron Brooks .25 .60
191 Tristan Thompson .30 .75
192 Kris Humphries .25 .60
193 Jimmy Butler .40 1.00
194 Kobe Bryant 1.50 4.00
195 Tim Duncan .60 1.50
196 Jose Calderon .25 .60
197 Al Jefferson .30 .75
198 Ty Lawson .25 .60
199 Chris Bosh .40 1.00
200 Enes Kanter .25 .60
201 Anthony Bennett RC 1.25 3.00
202 Isaiah Canaan RC 1.00 2.50
203 Nate Wolters RC 1.25 3.00
204 Shane Larkin RC 1.00 2.50
205 Vitor Faverani RC 1.00 2.50
206 Tony Snell RC 1.25 3.00
207 Carrick Felix RC 1.00 2.50
208 Pero Antic RC 1.00 2.50
209 Jeff Withey RC 1.00 2.50
210 Gal Mekel RC 1.00 2.50
211 Andre Roberson RC 1.00 2.50
212 Cody Zeller RC 1.25 3.00
213 Kentavious Caldwell-Pope RC 1.50 4.00
214 Reggie Bullock RC 1.25 3.00
215 Tony Mitchell RC 1.00 2.50
216 Dennis Schroder RC 1.50 4.00
217 Ricky Ledo RC 1.00 2.50
218 Sergey Karasev RC 1.00 2.50
219 Luigi Datome RC 1.00 2.50
220 Erik Murphy RC 1.00 2.50
221 Allen Crabbe RC 1.25 3.00
222 Ben McLemore RC 1.25 3.00
223 M.Carter-Williams RC 1.50 4.00
224 Ryan Kelly RC 1.00 2.50
225 Gorgui Dieng RC 1.25 3.00
226 Steven Adams RC 1.50 4.00
227 Peyton Siva RC 1.00 2.50
228 Mason Plumlee RC 1.50 4.00
229 G.Antetokounmpo RC 12.00 30.00
230 Archie Goodwin RC 1.25 3.00
231 Glen Rice Jr. RC 1.00 2.50
232 Kelly Olynyk RC 1.25 3.00
233 Otto Porter RC 1.50 4.00
234 Shabazz Muhammad RC 1.25 3.00
235 Trey Burke RC 1.25 3.00
236 Nemanja Nedovic RC 1.00 2.50
237 Victor Oladipo RC 2.00 5.00
238 Jamaal Franklin RC 1.00 2.50
239 Alex Len RC 1.25 3.00
240 Dwight Buycks RC 1.00 2.50
241 Tim Hardaway Jr. RC 1.50 4.00
242 Solomon Hill RC 1.00 2.50
243 Nerlens Noel RC 2.00 5.00
244 C.J. McCollum RC 2.50 6.00
245 Phil Pressey RC 1.00 2.50
246 Larry Bird 3.00 8.00
247 Drazen Petrovic 1.25 3.00
248 Dikembe Mutombo 1.25 3.00
249 Jack Sikma 1.00 2.50
250 Calvin Murphy 1.00 2.50
251 World B. Free 1.00 2.50
252 Chris Mullin 1.25 3.00
253 Elvin Hayes 1.25 3.00
254 Kareem Abdul-Jabbar 2.00 5.00
255 Bill Russell 2.00 5.00
256 George Gervin 1.25 3.00
257 Gary Payton 1.25 3.00
258 Artis Gilmore 1.00 2.50
259 Bob Cousy 2.00 5.00
260 Willis Reed 1.25 3.00
261 Rick Barry 1.00 2.50
262 Bill Walton 1.25 3.00
263 Hakeem Olajuwon 1.50 4.00
264 Alonzo Mourning 1.50 4.00
265 Magic Johnson 3.00 8.00
266 John Stockton 2.00 5.00
267 Robert Parish 1.25 3.00
268 George Mikan 2.50 6.00
269 Michael Finley 1.25 3.00
270 Fat Lever 1.00 2.50
271 Dennis Rodman 2.50 6.00
272 Kevin McHale 1.25 3.00
273 Oscar Robertson 1.50 4.00
274 David Robinson 2.00 5.00
275 Isiah Thomas 1.25 3.00
276 Yao Ming 1.50 4.00
277 Scottie Pippen 2.50 6.00
278 Maurice Cheeks .75 2.00
279 Shawn Kemp 2.00 5.00
280 Robert Horry 1.00 2.50
281 Kevin Johnson 1.25 3.00
282 James Worthy 1.50 4.00
283 John Havlicek 1.50 4.00
284 Karl Malone 1.50 4.00
285 Shaquille O'Neal 2.50 6.00
286 Julius Erving 2.00 5.00
287 Walt Frazier 1.25 3.00
288 Anfernee Hardaway 3.00 8.00
289 Dolph Schayes 1.25 3.00
290 Moses Malone 1.25 3.00
291 Dave Twardzik .75 2.00
292 Dan Issel 1.00 2.50
293 Grant Hill 1.50 4.00
294 Wilt Chamberlain 2.50 6.00
295 Dominique Wilkins 1.50 4.00
296 Dan Majerle 1.00 2.50
297 Nate Archibald 1.00 2.50
298 Jerry West 1.50 4.00
299 Clyde Drexler 1.50 4.00
300 Bob Pettit 1.25 3.00

2013-14 Elite Status

*STATUS 1-200 p/r 15-25: 5X TO 12X BASE
*STATUS 1-200 p/r 26-49: 4X TO 10X BASE
*STATUS 1-200 p/r 50-99: 3X TO 8X BASE
*STATUS 201-245 p/r 15-25: 1.2X TO 3X BASE
*STATUS 201-245 p/r 26-49: 1X TO 2.5X BASE
*STATUS 246-300 p/r 15-25: 1.5X TO 4X BASE
*STATUS 246-300 p/r 26-49: 1.2X TO 3X BASE
*STATUS 246-300 p/r 50-99: 1X TO 2.5X BASE
PRINT RUNS B/WN 1-99 COPIES PER
NO PRICING ON QTY 14 OR LESS
194 Kobe Bryant/24 40.00 100.00
293 Grant Hill/33 12.00 30.00

2013-14 Elite Status Gold

*STATUS 1-200: 5X TO 12X BASE
*STATUS 201-245: 1.2X TO 3X BASE
*STATUS 246-300: 1.5X TO 4X BASE
STATED PRINT RUN 24 SER.#'d SETS
65 Kevin Durant 30.00 80.00
110 LeBron James 40.00 100.00
194 Kobe Bryant 40.00 100.00
264 Alonzo Mourning 75.00 150.00
288 Anfernee Hardaway 15.00 40.00
293 Grant Hill 15.00 40.00

2013-14 Elite All-Time Greats Autographs

PRINT RUNS B/WN 10-199 COPIES PER
NO PRICING ON QTY 10
EXCHANGE DEADLINE 7/29/2015
1 Gail Goodrich/99
2 Christian Laettner/99 4.00 10.00
4 Scottie Pippen/49 60.00 150.00
5 Magic Johnson/49 30.00 80.00
6 Bob Lanier/49
7 Elgin Baylor/15
8 George McGinnis/149 3.00 8.00
9 Bill Sharman/75
10 Steve Francis/99 4.00 10.00
11 Joe Dumars/75 5.00 12.00
12 Clyde Drexler/25 12.00 30.00
13 Karl Malone/25 20.00 50.00
14 Buck Williams/199 3.00 8.00
15 Ralph Sampson/75
16 Alonzo Mourning/49 20.00 50.00
17 Jerry West/25 20.00 50.00
18 Artis Gilmore/25 4.00 10.00
19 Tom Heinsohn/75 15.00 40.00
20 Sam Cassell/75 4.00 10.00
21 Kelly Tripucka/25 3.00 8.00
23 David Thompson/199 4.00 10.00
24 Elvin Hayes/25
25 Mitch Richmond/75 5.00 12.00

2013-14 Elite Aspirations

*STATUS 1-200 p/r 23: 5X TO 12X BASE
*STATUS 1-200 p/r 26-49: 4X TO 10X BASE
*STATUS 1-200 p/r 50-99: 3X TO 8X BASE
*STATUS 201-245: .75X TO 2X BASE
*STATUS 246-300 p/r 26-49: 1.2X TO 3X BASE
*STATUS 246-300 p/r 50-99: 1X TO 2.5X BASE
PRINT RUNS B/WN 1-99 COPIES PER
NO PRICING ON QTY 12 OR LESS
288 Anfernee Hardaway/99 10.00 25.00
293 Grant Hill/67 10.00 25.00

2013-14 Elite Back to the Future Materials

1 Ray Allen 3.00 8.00
2 Jason Richardson 3.00 8.00
3 Greg Oden 2.50 6.00
4 Rashard Lewis 2.50 6.00
5 John Salmons 2.50 6.00
6 Vince Carter 4.00 10.00
7 Kevin Martin 2.50 6.00
8 Michael Beasley 2.00 5.00
9 Andre Miller 2.50 6.00
10 Danilo Gallinari 2.00 5.00
11 Juwan Howard 2.50 6.00
12 Chris Paul 4.00 10.00
13 Mike Miller 2.50 6.00
14 Ben Gordon 2.50 6.00
15 O.J. Mayo 2.00 5.00
16 Elton Brand 3.00 8.00
17 Andrei Kirilenko 2.50 6.00
18 Darren Collison 2.50 6.00
19 Steve Nash 3.00 8.00
20 Jose Calderon 2.00 5.00
21 Andre Iguodala 2.50 6.00
22 Dwight Howard 2.50 6.00
23 Andrew Bynum 2.00 5.00
24 Jeff Green 2.50 6.00
25 Ryan Anderson 2.50 6.00
26 Kevin Durant 6.00 15.00
27 Chris Andersen 2.50 6.00
28 Chris Bosh 3.00 8.00
29 LeBron James 10.00 25.00
30 Monta Ellis 2.50 6.00

2013-14 Elite Back to the Future Materials Prime

*PRIME: .75X TO 2X BASIC
PRINT RUNS B/WN 5-25 COPIES PER
NO PRICING ON QTY 10 OR LESS

2013-14 Elite Dominators Materials

1 Carmelo Anthony 4.00 10.00
2 Kevin Martin 2.50 6.00
3 Chris Bosh 3.00 8.00
4 Blake Griffin 4.00 10.00
5 Paul Pierce 3.00 8.00
6 Shaquille O'Neal 5.00 12.00
7 Robert Parish 3.00 8.00
8 Kevin Garnett 4.00 10.00
9 Ray Allen 3.00 8.00
10 Kevin Durant 6.00 15.00
11 Kemba Walker 3.00 8.00
12 Tracy McGrady 3.00 8.00
13 Kobe Bryant 6.00 15.00
14 Derrick Rose 4.00 10.00
15 Patrick Ewing 4.00 10.00
16 Kenneth Faried 2.50 6.00
17 Kyrie Irving 5.00 12.00
18 Chris Paul 4.00 10.00
19 Clyde Drexler 4.00 10.00
20 Tim Duncan 5.00 12.00
21 Pau Gasol 3.00 8.00
22 David Robinson 5.00 12.00
23 Dirk Nowitzki 4.00 10.00
24 Dominique Wilkins 4.00 10.00
25 Dwyane Wade 4.00 10.00
26 Tony Parker 3.00 8.00
27 Deron Williams 2.50 6.00
28 Grant Hill 4.00 10.00
29 Joe Dumars 3.00 8.00
30 Ralph Sampson 2.50 6.00

2013-14 Elite Dominators Materials Prime

*PRIME: .75X TO 2X BASIC
PRINT RUNS B/WN 1-25 COPIES PER
NO PRICING ON QTY 10 OR LESS

2013-14 Elite Face 2 Face

1 D.Wade/T.Parker 1.25 3.00
2 K.Bryant/L.James 3.00 8.00
3 C.Bosh/T.Duncan 1.25 3.00
4 M.Gasol/S.Ibaka .75 2.00
5 J.Harden/K.Durant 2.00 5.00
6 B.Griffin/Z.Randolph .75 2.00
7 S.Curry/T.Lawson 3.00 8.00
8 K.Leonard/K.Thompson 1.25 3.00
9 C.Anthony/P.George 1.00 2.50
10 D.Rose/J.Wall 1.00 2.50
11 A.Davis/N.Vucevic 1.50 4.00
12 K.Irving/R.Felton 1.50 4.00
13 C.Paul/D.Williams 1.00 2.50
14 R.Rubio/R.Westbrook 2.00 5.00
15 G.Hill/J.Teague .60 1.50
16 B.Beal/J.Fredette .75 2.00
17 D.DeRozan/D.Waiters .75 2.00
18 D.Lillard/J.Lin 1.50 4.00
19 K.Faried/L.Aldridge .75 2.00
20 A.Drummond/T.Thompson .75 2.00

2013-14 Elite Face 2 Face Gold

*GOLD: 1.5X TO 4X BASIC
STATED PRINT RUN 24 SER.#'d SETS
2 K.Bryant/L.James 40.00 100.00

2013-14 Elite Franchise Future

1 Kyrie Irving 1.50 4.00
2 Andre Drummond .75 2.00
3 Trey Burke .60 1.50
4 Alex Len .60 1.50
5 Victor Oladipo 1.00 2.50
6 Terrence Ross .60 1.50
7 Kawhi Leonard 1.25 3.00
8 Isaiah Thomas .75 2.00
9 Shane Larkin .50 1.25
10 Jimmy Butler .75 2.00
11 Anthony Davis 1.50 4.00
12 Kenneth Faried .60 1.50
13 Cody Zeller .60 1.50
14 Bradley Beal .75 2.00
15 Michael Carter-Williams .75 2.00
16 Larry Sanders .50 1.25
17 Damian Lillard 1.50 4.00
18 Harrison Barnes .60 1.50
19 Chandler Parsons .60 1.50
20 Kelly Olynyk .60 1.50

2013-14 Elite Franchise Future Gold

*GOLD: 2.5X TO 6X BASIC
STATED PRINT RUN 24 SER.#'d SETS

2013-14 Elite New Breed Autograph Jerseys

PRINT RUNS B/WN 149-599 COPIES PER
EXCHANGE DEADLINE 7/29/2015
1 Victor Oladipo/149 6.00 15.00
2 Ricky Ledo/599 3.00 8.00
3 Reggie Bullock/499 4.00 10.00
4 Jeff Withey/599 3.00 8.00
5 Erik Murphy/599 3.00 8.00
6 Peyton Siva/599 3.00 8.00
7 Solomon Hill/499 3.00 8.00
8 Cody Zeller/149 4.00 10.00
9 Tim Hardaway Jr./499 5.00 12.00
10 Dennis Schroder/499 5.00 12.00
11 Nerlens Noel/175 6.00 15.00
12 Trey Burke/199 4.00 10.00
13 Jamaal Franklin/599 3.00 8.00
14 Andre Roberson/599 3.00 8.00
15 Kelly Olynyk/499 4.00 10.00
16 Isaiah Canaan/599 3.00 8.00
17 C.J. McCollum/199 25.00 60.00
18 Glen Rice Jr./499 3.00 8.00
19 G.Antetokounmpo/299 60.00 150.00
20 Otto Porter/149 5.00 12.00
21 Nate Wolters/499 4.00 10.00
22 M.Carter-Williams/175 5.00 12.00
23 Kentavious Caldwell-Pope/175 5.00 12.00
24 Allen Crabbe/499 4.00 10.00
25 Anthony Bennett/149 4.00 10.00
26 Mason Plumlee/199 5.00 12.00
27 Tony Mitchell/599 3.00 8.00
28 Alex Len/149 4.00 10.00
29 Shane Larkin/399 3.00 8.00
30 Steven Adams/199 12.00 30.00
31 Shabazz Muhammad/199 4.00 10.00
32 Ryan Kelly/599 3.00 8.00
33 Archie Goodwin/599 4.00 10.00
34 Tony Snell/499 4.00 10.00
35 Ben McLemore/175 4.00 10.00

2013-14 Elite New Breed Autograph Jerseys Prime

*PRIME: 1X TO 2.5X BASIC
STATED PRINT RUN 25 SER.#'d SETS
EXCHANGE DEADLINE 7/29/2015
10 Dennis Schroder 30.00 60.00

2013-14 Elite Passing The Torch

1 J.Harden/K.Bryant 3.00 8.00
2 G.Gervin/K.Durant 2.00 5.00
3 A.Mourning/A.Davis 1.50 4.00
4 B.Griffin/B.McAdoo .75 2.00
5 J.Stockton/K.Irving 1.50 4.00
6 C.Anthony/W.Frazier 1.00 2.50
7 C.Paul/I.Thomas 1.00 2.50
8 G.Payton/R.Westbrook 2.00 5.00
9 M.Gasol/T.Duncan 1.25 3.00
10 D.Wade/S.Curry 3.00 8.00
11 D.Williams/J.Kidd .75 2.00
12 D.Mutombo/S.Ibaka .75 2.00
13 D.Rodman/K.Faried 1.50 4.00
14 C.Drexler/D.Lillard 1.50 4.00
15 K.Leonard/M.Ginobili 1.25 3.00
16 H.Olajuwon/R.Hibbert 1.00 2.50
17 G.Dragic/S.Nash .75 2.00
18 O.Robertson/R.Rondo 1.00 2.50
19 D.Cousins/V.Divac .75 2.00
20 D.Majerle/K.Thompson 1.00 2.50

2013-14 Elite Passing The Torch Autographs

PRINT RUNS B/WN 10-49 COPIES PER
NO PRICING ON QTY 10
EXCHANGE DEADLINE 7/29/2015
1 J.Harden/K.Bryant/25
2 H.Williams/R.Hibbert/49 20.00 50.00
3 Griffin/Cage/25 EXCH 25.00 60.00
4 K.Walker/T.Ross/25 75.00 150.00
5 D.Green/S.Elliott/49
6 A.Miller/T.Lawson/25
7 G.Rice/G.Rice Jr./49 40.00 80.00
8 C.Laettner/G.Henderson/25 10.00 25.00
9 M.Finley/M.Ellis/25
10 A.Jamison/H.Barnes/49 15.00 40.00
11 A.Horford/K.Willis/49 12.00 30.00
12 I.Thomas/M.Bogues/49 20.00 50.00
13 A.Hardaway/V.Oladipo/49 30.00 80.00
14 D.Howard/H.Olajuwon/49 30.00 80.00
15 A.Gilmore/J.Noah/25
16 A.Iguodala/C.Mullin/49 20.00 50.00
18 A.Bennett/L.Johnson/25
20 Terry/Thompson/25 EXCH 25.00 60.00
21 A.Mason/J.Smith/49 6.00 15.00
22 J.Lucas/J.Lucas III/49
23 A.Davis/W.Unseld/25
24 M.Richardson/M.Conley/49 8.00 20.00
25 Hardaway/Hardaway Jr./49 25.00 60.00

2013-14 Elite Passing The Torch Gold

*GOLD: 1.5X TO 4X BASIC
STATED PRINT RUN 24 SER.#'d SETS

2013-14 Elite Rookie Essentials Autograph Jerseys

PRINT RUNS B/WN 149-599 COPIES PER
EXCHANGE DEADLINE 7/29/2015
1 Ben McLemore/175 4.00 10.00
2 Tony Snell/499 4.00 10.00
3 Archie Goodwin/599 4.00 10.00
4 Ryan Kelly/599 3.00 8.00
5 Shabazz Muhammad/199 4.00 10.00
6 Steven Adams/199 5.00 12.00
7 Shane Larkin/499 3.00 8.00
8 Alex Len/149 4.00 10.00
9 Tony Mitchell/599 3.00 8.00
10 Mason Plumlee/299 5.00 12.00
11 Victor Oladipo/149 6.00 15.00
12 Jeff Withey/599 3.00 8.00
13 Tim Hardaway Jr./499 12.00 30.00
14 Nerlens Noel/175 12.00 30.00
15 Kelly Olynyk/449 4.00 10.00
16 Glen Rice Jr./299 3.00 8.00
17 C.J. McCollum/199 15.00 40.00
18 Otto Porter/149 5.00 12.00
19 Kentavious Caldwell-Pope/175 5.00 12.00
20 Anthony Bennett/149 4.00 10.00
21 Ricky Ledo/599 3.00 8.00
22 Erik Murphy/599 3.00 8.00
23 Cody Zeller/149 4.00 10.00
24 Trey Burke/199 4.00 10.00
25 Isaiah Canaan/599 3.00 8.00
26 Dennis Schroder/499 5.00 12.00
27 G.Antetokounmpo/299 50.00 120.00
28 Nate Wolters/599 4.00 10.00
29 M.Carter-Williams/175 5.00 12.00
30 Allen Crabbe/499 4.00 10.00
31 Reggie Bullock/299 4.00 10.00
32 Peyton Siva/599 3.00 8.00
33 Solomon Hill/599 3.00 8.00
34 Jamaal Franklin/599 3.00 8.00
35 Andre Roberson/599 3.00 8.00

2013-14 Elite Rookie Essentials Autograph Jerseys Prime

*PRIME: 1X TO 2.5X BASIC
STATED PRINT RUN 25 SER.#'d SETS
EXCHANGE DEADLINE 7/29/2015
26 Dennis Schroder 30.00 60.00

2013-14 Elite Series Inserts

1 Kevin Durant 2.00 5.00
2 Dwight Howard .60 1.50
3 Tim Duncan 1.25 3.00
4 Damian Lillard 1.50 4.00
5 Anfernee Hardaway 2.00 5.00
6 Vince Carter 1.00 2.50
7 Kyrie Irving 1.50 4.00
8 Alonzo Mourning 1.00 2.50
9 Rajon Rondo .75 2.00
10 Carmelo Anthony 1.00 2.50
11 Pau Gasol .75 2.00
12 Metta World Peace .75 2.00
13 Isiah Thomas .75 2.00
14 Ricky Rubio .75 2.00
15 Ray Allen .75 2.00
16 Manu Ginobili .75 2.00
17 Magic Johnson 2.00 5.00
18 Tony Parker .75 2.00
19 Paul Pierce .75 2.00
20 Wilt Chamberlain 1.50 4.00
21 Kobe Bryant 3.00 8.00
22 John Wall 1.00 2.50
23 Shaquille O'Neal 1.50 4.00
24 Steve Nash .75 2.00
25 Anthony Davis 1.50 4.00
26 Drazen Petrovic .75 2.00
27 Russell Westbrook 2.00 5.00
28 Dwyane Wade 1.25 3.00
29 Larry Bird 2.00 5.00
30 Dirk Nowitzki 1.00 2.50
31 Chris Paul 1.00 2.50
32 Paul George 1.00 2.50
33 Julius Erving 1.25 3.00
34 Derrick Rose 1.00 2.50
35 LeBron James 3.00 8.00
36 Blake Griffin .75 2.00
37 George Gervin .75 2.00
38 Amar'e Stoudemire .60 1.50
39 Kevin Garnett 1.25 3.00
40 Chris Bosh .75 2.00

2013-14 Elite Series Inserts Gold

*GOLD: 2X TO 5X BASIC
STATED PRINT RUN 24 SER.#'d SETS

2013-14 Elite Signatures

PRINT RUNS B/WN 10-199 COPIES PER
NO PRICING ON QTY 10
EXCHANGE DEADLINE 7/29/2015
1 Kevin Durant/99
2 Monta Ellis/25
3 Nikola Pekovic/125 3.00 8.00
4 Andrei Kirilenko/25
5 Meyers Leonard/49 3.00 8.00
6 Brandon Bass/50 3.00 8.00
7 Rodney Stuckey/49 4.00 10.00
8 MarShon Brooks/75 4.00 10.00
9 Anthony Davis/49 50.00 100.00
12 Greivis Vasquez/149 EXCH 4.00 10.00
13 Klay Thompson/15
15 Isaiah Thomas/199 12.00 30.00
16 Tiago Splitter/199 4.00 10.00
18 D.J. Augustin/199 3.00 8.00
19 Jared Sullinger/100
21 Kyle Korver/149 4.00 10.00
22 Tony Parker/49 12.00 30.00
23 Harrison Barnes/49 4.00 10.00
25 DeAndre Jordan/49
26 Enes Kanter/49
27 Byron Mullens/99
28 Draymond Green/149 10.00 25.00
29 Lavoy Allen/50
30 Stephen Curry/49 100.00 250.00
31 Joe Johnson/25
34 Kobe Bryant/75 75.00 150.00
35 Andre Iguodala/25 12.00 30.00
36 Blake Griffin/49 EXCH 20.00 50.00
37 Luis Scola/150 4.00 10.00
38 J.J. Redick/49 5.00 12.00
39 Josh Smith/99 4.00 10.00
40 Nikola Vucevic/49 4.00 10.00
41 Andre Drummond/25
42 Kyrie Irving/99 EXCH 30.00 80.00
43 Steve Novak/49
45 Jonas Valanciunas/100
46 Raymond Felton/149 4.00 10.00
47 Nando De Colo/99 4.00 10.00
48 John Salmons/99 4.00 10.00
50 Patrick Patterson/99 3.00 8.00

2013-14 Elite Throwback Threads

1 Robert Parish 3.00 8.00
2 Artis Gilmore 2.50 6.00
3 Larry Bird 12.00 30.00
4 Danny Manning 2.50 6.00
5 Kiki Vandeweghe 2.50 6.00
6 Earl Monroe 3.00 8.00
7 Hakeem Olajuwon 4.00 10.00
8 Magic Johnson 8.00 20.00
9 David Robinson 5.00 12.00
10 Larry Nance 2.50 6.00
11 Robert Horry 2.50 6.00
12 Danny Ainge 3.00 8.00
13 Jeff Hornacek 2.50 6.00
14 Jalen Rose 3.00 8.00
15 Jamal Mashburn 3.00 8.00
16 Reggie Lewis 8.00 20.00
17 Clyde Drexler 4.00 10.00
18 Patrick Ewing 4.00 10.00
19 Xavier McDaniel 2.00 5.00
20 Calvin Murphy 2.50 6.00
21 Buck Williams 2.00 5.00
22 Robert Parish 3.00 8.00
23 Alex English 2.50 6.00
24 Kevin McHale 3.00 8.00
25 Shaquille O'Neal 5.00 12.00
26 Larry Johnson 4.00 10.00
27 Joe Dumars 3.00 8.00
28 Jalen Rose 3.00 8.00
29 Anfernee Hardaway 6.00 15.00
30 Dominique Wilkins 4.00 10.00
31 Larry Nance 2.50 6.00
32 Moses Malone 3.00 8.00
33 Ralph Sampson 2.50 6.00
34 Isiah Thomas 3.00 8.00
35 Bernard King 2.50 6.00
36 Alex English 2.50 6.00
37 Karl Malone 4.00 10.00
38 Shaquille O'Neal 5.00 12.00
39 Fat Lever 2.50 6.00
40 Jeff Hornacek 2.50 6.00

2013-14 Elite Throwback Threads Autographs

PRINT RUNS B/WN 25-299 COPIES PER
EXCHANGE DEADLINE 7/29/2015
1 Brent Barry/25
2 Elgin Baylor/25

3 World B. Free/49 4.00 10.00
4 Kelly Tripucka/25
5 Joe Dumars/49 10.00 25.00
6 Magic Johnson/49
7 Karl Malone/25
8 Artis Gilmore/25
9 Scottie Pippen/49 50.00 120.00
10 John Stockton/25
11 Toni Kukoc/149 12.00 30.00
12 Ralph Sampson/25 4.00 10.00
13 Mitch Richmond/75 15.00 40.00
14 Bob Lanier/25
15 Sean Elliott/299 5.00 12.00
16 John Lucas/75
17 Grant Hill/99 20.00 50.00
18 Buck Williams/299 3.00 8.00
19 Jerry West/49 15.00 40.00
20 Alonzo Mourning/25
21 Alex English/99 8.00 20.00
22 Bill Laimbeer/299 5.00 12.00
23 Clyde Drexler/25 20.00 50.00
24 David Robinson/49 20.00 50.00
25 Fat Lever/299 4.00 10.00
26 Robert Parish/25
27 Eddie Johnson/199 3.00 8.00
28 Larry Bird/49 30.00 80.00
29 Nick Anderson/199 5.00 12.00
30 Jamal Mashburn/299 5.00 12.00

2013-14 Elite Throwback Threads Autographs Prime

*PRIME: 1X TO 2.5X BASIC
PRINT RUNS B/WN 3-25 COPIES PER
NO PRICING ON QTY 10 OR LESS
EXCHANGE DEADLINE 7/29/2015

2013-14 Elite Throwback Threads Prime

*PRIME: 1X TO 2.5X BASIC
PRINT RUNS B/WN 3-25 COPIES PER
NO PRICING ON QTY 10 OR LESS

2013-14 Elite Turn of the Century Autographs

PRINT RUNS B/WN 5-100 COPIES PER
NO PRICING ON QTY 10 OR LESS
EXCHANGE DEADLINE 7/29/2015
1 Jason Terry/50 4.00 10.00
2 Donatas Motiejunas/75 4.00 10.00
3 Andray Blatche/100 3.00 8.00
4 Marcus Thornton/75 3.00 8.00
5 Harrison Barnes/75 10.00 25.00
6 Nikola Vucevic/100 4.00 10.00
7 Shane Battier/25
8 Steve Novak/50
9 Brandon Knight/49
10 Eric Gordon/25
11 Kevin Martin/15
12 Austin Rivers/25 4.00 10.00
13 Kawhi Leonard/100 40.00 100.00
14 Marcin Gortat/75 4.00 10.00
15 Anthony Davis/49 30.00 80.00
17 Zaza Pachulia/100 3.00 8.00
18 Lavoy Allen/100 3.00 8.00
19 Draymond Green/75 10.00 15.00
20 Brandon Bass/25
21 Joe Johnson/25
22 Nikola Pekovic/100 3.00 8.00
23 Andrei Kirilenko/100 4.00 10.00
25 Kobe Bryant/100 EXCH 75.00 150.00
26 Gordon Hayward/50 8.00 20.00
27 J.R. Smith/100 4.00 10.00
28 Andrew Bogut/75 4.00 10.00
29 Brandon Rush/50
30 Luc Mbah a Moute/100 EXCH
31 Jeff Green/50
32 Jrue Holiday/50 5.00 12.00
33 Kevin Love/50 8.00 40.00
34 Monta Ellis/50 EXCH 4.00 10.00
35 DeAndre Jordan/25
36 Luis Scola/50 4.00 10.00
37 Raymond Felton/75 4.00 10.00
38 Tristan Thompson/25
39 Tony Allen/25
40 Patrick Patterson/100 3.00 8.00
41 Thomas Robinson/25 3.00 8.00
42 Caron Butler/25 4.00 10.00
43 Danilo Gallinari/25
44 Courtney Lee/100 4.00 10.00
45 Vince Carter/50 15.00 40.00
46 Ben Gordon/25
47 MarShon Brooks/100 4.00 10.00
48 D.J. Augustin/100 3.00 8.00
49 Enes Kanter/75
50 Kyle Korver/50 4.00 10.00
52 DeMarcus Cousins/25
53 Kevin Durant/75 EXCH 75.00 150.00
54 Ramon Sessions/100 4.00 10.00
55 Mario Chalmers/50
56 Alonzo Gee/25
57 Nick Young/25 5.00 12.00
58 Klay Thompson/50 20.00 50.00
59 Byron Mullens/75 3.00 8.00
60 Tayshaun Prince/49 4.00 10.00
61 Jared Sullinger/49
62 Iman Shumpert/50 3.00 8.00
63 Lance Stephenson/75 4.00 10.00
64 Jerryd Bayless/100 EXCH 4.00 10.00
65 Nando De Colo/100 4.00 10.00
66 Stephen Curry/50 125.00 250.00
67 Josh Smith/25 4.00 10.00
68 Steve Blake/100 3.00 8.00
69 Andre Drummond/50 5.00 12.00
70 Taj Gibson/50
71 Randy Foye/50 3.00 8.00
72 Andrea Bargnani/25 4.00 10.00
73 Chase Budinger/50 3.00 8.00
74 Kyle Singler/100 3.00 8.00
75 Blake Griffin/50 EXCH
76 Greivis Vasquez/25 4.00 10.00
77 Tiago Splitter/75 4.00 10.00
78 John Salmons/100 4.00 10.00
79 Michael Kidd-Gilchrist/25
80 Trevor Booker/75 3.00 8.00
81 Dorell Wright/100
82 Kyle Lowry/100 4.00 10.00
83 Joel Anthony/100 3.00 8.00
84 Jan Vesely/100 3.00 8.00
85 Jose Calderon/50 3.00 8.00
86 Kent Bazemore/100 4.00 10.00
87 Darren Collison/50 4.00 10.00
88 Tyreke Evans/50 3.00 8.00
89 Kyrie Irving/100 30.00 80.00
90 Andre Iguodala/25 15.00 40.00
91 Isaiah Thomas/75 20.00 50.00
92 Meyers Leonard/100 3.00 8.00
93 Rodney Stuckey/49
94 J.J. Redick/50 5.00 12.00
95 Ekpe Udoh/100 3.00 8.00
96 J.J. Hickson/100 3.00 8.00
97 Al Horford/25
98 Jonas Valanciunas/50
99 Anthony Morrow/75
100 E'Twaun Moore/100 3.00 8.00

2014-15 Elite

RANDOMLY INSERTED IN 14-15 DONRUSS
1 Derrick Favors .50 1.25
2 Kevin Durant 1.50 4.00
3 Wesley Matthews .40 1.00
4 Russell Westbrook 1.50 4.00
5 Thaddeus Young .40 1.00
6 Kevin Love .60 1.50
7 John Wall .75 2.00
8 Stephen Curry 2.50 6.00
9 Andre Drummond .60 1.50
10 Roy Hibbert .50 1.25
11 James Harden 1.00 2.50
12 Klay Thompson .75 2.00
13 Tony Parker .60 1.50
14 Monta Ellis .50 1.25
15 Goran Dragic .50 1.25
16 Tiago Splitter .50 1.25
17 Joakim Noah .50 1.25
18 Kyle Korver .50 1.25
19 Marc Gasol .60 1.50
20 Deron Williams .50 1.25
21 Paul Millsap .60 1.50
22 Kenneth Faried .50 1.25
23 Kobe Bryant 2.50 6.00
24 Josh Smith .50 1.25
25 Kyrie Irving 1.25 3.00
26 Nicolas Batum .50 1.25
27 Danilo Gallinari .40 1.00
28 Luol Deng .50 1.25
29 Dirk Nowitzki .75 2.00
30 DeMar DeRozan .60 1.50
31 Kawhi Leonard 1.00 2.50
32 Lance Stephenson .50 1.25
33 Blake Griffin .60 1.50
34 Pau Gasol .60 1.50
35 Al Horford .50 1.25
36 Paul Pierce .60 1.50
37 Andrew Bogut .50 1.25
38 Dwight Howard .50 1.25
39 DeAndre Jordan .60 1.50
40 Tyreke Evans .40 1.00
41 Dwyane Wade 1.00 2.50
42 Rajon Rondo .60 1.50
43 Joe Johnson .50 1.25
44 Carmelo Anthony .75 2.00
45 Zach Randolph .50 1.25
46 David Lee .40 1.00
47 Damian Lillard 1.25 3.00
48 Ty Lawson .40 1.00
49 Nene .50 1.25
50 Tim Duncan 1.00 2.50
51 Mike Conley .50 1.25
52 Gordon Hayward .60 1.50
53 Chris Bosh .60 1.50
54 David West .50 1.25
55 Al Jefferson .50 1.25
56 Omer Asik .50 1.25
57 LaMarcus Aldridge .60 1.50
58 Rudy Gay .60 1.50
59 Derrick Rose .75 2.00
60 Brook Lopez .50 1.25
61 Chandler Parsons .50 1.25
62 Anthony Davis 1.25 3.00
63 Bradley Beal .60 1.50
64 Kyle Lowry .50 1.25
65 Nikola Pekovic .40 1.00
66 Serge Ibaka .50 1.25
67 Manu Ginobili .60 1.50
68 Jonas Valanciunas .50 1.25
69 DeMarcus Cousins .60 1.50
70 Jrue Holiday .50 1.25
71 Greg Monroe .50 1.25
72 Chris Paul .75 2.00
73 Tyson Chandler .50 1.25
74 Marcin Gortat .50 1.25
75 Eric Bledsoe .50 1.25
76 Ricky Rubio .60 1.50
77 Andre Iguodala .50 1.25
78 Arron Afflalo .40 1.00
79 Ryan Anderson .40 1.00
80 LeBron James 2.50 6.00
81 Scottie Pippen 1.25 3.00
82 John Stockton 1.00 2.50
83 Julius Erving 1.00 2.50
84 Moses Malone .60 1.50
85 Hakeem Olajuwon .75 2.00
86 Jerry West .75 2.00
87 Oscar Robertson .75 2.00
88 Karl Malone .75 2.00
89 Shaquille O'Neal 1.25 3.00
90 Kevin McHale .60 1.50
91 Bill Russell 1.00 2.50
92 Kareem Abdul-Jabbar 1.00 2.50
93 Allen Iverson .75 2.00
94 Larry Bird 1.50 4.00
95 Patrick Ewing .75 2.00
96 Dennis Rodman 1.25 3.00
97 Magic Johnson 1.50 4.00
98 David Robinson 1.00 2.50
99 Isiah Thomas .60 1.50
100 Wilt Chamberlain 1.25 3.00

2014-15 Elite Blue

*BLUE: .8X TO 2X BASE HI
RANDOM INSERTS IN PACKS
STATED PRINT RUN 99 SER.#'d SETS

2014-15 Elite Purple

*PURPLE: .6X TO 1.5X BASE HI
RANDOM INSERTS IN PACKS
STATED PRINT RUN 199 SER.#'d SETS

2014-15 Elite Red

*RED: 1X TO 2.5X BASE HI
RANDOM INSERTS IN PACKS
STATED PRINT RUN 25 SER.#'d SETS
80 LeBron James 20.00 50.00

2014-15 Elite Status

*STATUS: 2X TO 5X BASE HI
RANDOM INSERTS IN PACKS
STATED PRINT RUN B/WN 9-99 COPIES PER
NO PRICING ON QTY 12 OR LESS

2014-15 Elite Status Signatures

RANDOM INSERTS IN PACKS
STATED PRINT RUN B/WN 125-249 COPIES PER
1 Andrew Wiggins/125 50.00 120.00
2 Jabari Parker/125 15.00 40.00
3 K.J. McDaniels/249 4.00 10.00
4 Johnny O'Bryant/249 3.00 8.00
5 Damien Inglis/249 3.00 8.00
6 Jordan Adams/249 3.00 8.00
7 Lucas Nogueira/249 3.00 8.00
8 Joe Harris/249 3.00 8.00
9 Alex Kirk/249 3.00 8.00
10 James Young/125 3.00 8.00
11 Markel Brown/249 3.00 8.00
12 Russ Smith/249 3.00 8.00
13 Damjan Rudez/249 3.00 8.00
14 T.J. Warren/125 8.00 20.00
15 Devyn Marble/249 3.00 8.00
16 Zach LaVine/199 15.00 40.00
17 Jusuf Nurkic/199 5.00 12.00
18 James Ennis/249 3.00 8.00
19 Cameron Bairstow/249 6.00 15.00
20 Jerami Grant/249 3.00 8.00
21 Nikola Mirotic/125 20.00 50.00
22 Cory Jefferson/249 3.00 8.00
24 Joel Embiid/125 20.00 50.00
25 Aaron Gordon/125 6.00 15.00
26 Nik Stauskas/125 4.00 10.00
27 Bojan Bogdanovic/249 4.00 10.00
28 Zoran Dragic/249 4.00 10.00
30 Doug McDermott/125 15.00 40.00
31 Kyle Anderson/249 5.00 12.00
32 Glenn Robinson III/199 3.00 8.00
33 Jarnell Stokes/249 3.00 8.00
34 Gary Harris/125 5.00 12.00
35 Adreian Payne/249 4.00 10.00
36 Glen Rice/125 4.00 10.00
37 Isiah Thomas/125 5.00 12.00
38 Adrian Dantley/125 4.00 10.00
39 Toni Kukoc/125 5.00 12.00
40 Dikembe Mutombo/125 5.00 12.00
41 Baron Davis/125 4.00 10.00
42 Dee Brown/125 3.00 8.00
43 Fred Brown/199 3.00 8.00
44 Rolando Blackman/125 4.00 10.00
45 Anfernee Hardaway/125 12.00 30.00
46 Jimmy Jones/125 3.00 8.00
47 Freddie Lewis/125 3.00 8.00
48 Rod Strickland/199 3.00 8.00
49 Tracy McGrady/125 10.00 25.00
50 Rudy Tomjanovich/199 4.00 10.00
51 John Starks/125 4.00 10.00
52 Latrell Sprewell/125 20.00 50.00
53 Cedric Maxwell/125 3.00 8.00
54 Brian Grant/199 3.00 8.00
55 Michael Cooper/199 4.00 10.00
56 Rick Fox/125 4.00 10.00
57 Allan Houston/125 4.00 10.00
58 Mark Price/249 5.00 12.00
59 Spud Webb/249 4.00 10.00
60 Vlade Divac/249 5.00 12.00
61 Muggsy Bogues/249 4.00 10.00
62 Eddie Jones/199 4.00 10.00
63 Josh Smith/125 4.00 10.00
64 Caron Butler/125 4.00 10.00
65 Chris Kaman/125 4.00 10.00
66 Andre Iguodala/125 4.00 10.00
67 Brook Lopez/125 4.00 10.00
68 Isaiah Canaan/249 4.00 10.00
69 Andrea Bargnani/125 4.00 10.00
70 Steve Blake/199 3.00 8.00
71 C.J. Watson/125 3.00 8.00
72 Jose Calderon/125 3.00 8.00
73 Gorgui Dieng/249 3.00 8.00
76 Amir Johnson/125 3.00 8.00
77 Gerald Henderson/125 3.00 8.00
78 Alexey Shved/199 3.00 8.00
79 Jason Thompson/125 3.00 8.00
80 Ryan Anderson/125 3.00 8.00
81 Chris Copeland/249 3.00 8.00
82 Timofey Mozgov/199 3.00 8.00
83 Kyle Korver/249 4.00 10.00
84 Greg Smith/125 3.00 8.00
85 Jason Terry/125 4.00 10.00
86 Rasual Butler/199 3.00 8.00
87 Chris Douglas-Roberts/199 3.00 8.00
88 Kevin Martin/125 4.00 10.00
89 Taj Gibson/125 4.00 10.00
90 Dennis Schroder/249 4.00 10.00
91 Troy Daniels/249 3.00 8.00
92 Solomon Hill/249 3.00 8.00
93 Ryan Kelly/249 3.00 8.00
94 Maurice Harkless/199 3.00 8.00
95 Brandon Knight/125 4.00 10.00
96 C.J. Miles/249 4.00 10.00
97 Lance Thomas/249 3.00 8.00
98 Phil Pressey/249 3.00 8.00
99 Matthew Dellavedova/249 4.00 10.00
100 Mike Muscala/249 3.00 8.00

2014-15 Elite Status Signatures Blue

*BLUE: .8X TO 2X BASE HI
RANDOM INSERTS IN PACKS
STATED PRINT RUN 49 SER.#'d SETS
50 Rudy Tomjanovich 8.00 20.00

2014-15 Elite Status Signatures Bronze

*BRONZE: 1X TO 2.5X BASE HI
RANDOM INSERTS IN PACKS
STATED PRINT RUN 25 SER.#'d SETS
LACK OF PRICING DUE TO MARKET INFO
16 Zach LaVine 75.00 150.00
49 Tracy McGrady 25.00 60.00

2014-15 Elite Status Signatures Purple

*PURPLE: .6X TO 1.5X BASE HI
RANDOM INSERTS IN PACKS
STATED PRINT RUN 74 SER.#'d SETS

2014-15 Elite Status Signatures Red

*RED: .5X TO 1.2X BASE HI
RANDOM INSERTS IN PACKS
STATED PRINT RUN 99 SER.#'d SETS

2014-15 Elite Dominators

RANDOM INSERTS IN PACKS
STATED PRINT RUN 999 SER.#'d SETS
1 Kevin Love 1.50 4.00
2 Kevin Durant 4.00 10.00
3 John Wall 2.00 5.00
4 Russell Westbrook 4.00 10.00
5 Stephen Curry 6.00 15.00
6 Andre Drummond 1.50 4.00
7 Roy Hibbert 1.25 3.00
8 James Harden 2.50 6.00
9 Klay Thompson 2.00 5.00
10 Tony Parker 1.50 4.00
11 DeMarcus Cousins 1.50 4.00
12 Anthony Davis 4.00 10.00
13 Al Jefferson 1.25 3.00
14 Kyle Lowry 1.25 3.00
15 Goran Dragic 1.25 3.00
16 Kobe Bryant 4.00 10.00
17 Joakim Noah 1.25 3.00
18 Kyrie Irving 3.00 8.00
19 Marc Gasol 1.50 4.00
20 Serge Ibaka 1.25 3.00
21 Paul Millsap 1.50 4.00
22 Dirk Nowitzki 2.00 5.00
23 DeMar DeRozan 1.50 4.00
24 Kawhi Leonard 2.50 6.00
25 Dwight Howard 1.25 3.00
26 Dwyane Wade 2.50 6.00
27 Rajon Rondo 1.50 4.00
28 Luol Deng 1.25 3.00
29 Blake Griffin 1.50 4.00
30 Pau Gasol 1.50 4.00
31 Carmelo Anthony 2.00 5.00
32 Damian Lillard 3.00 8.00
33 Tim Duncan 2.50 6.00
34 Chris Bosh 1.50 4.00
35 LaMarcus Aldridge 1.50 4.00
36 Chris Paul 2.00 5.00
37 LeBron James 6.00 15.00
38 DeAndre Jordan 1.50 4.00
39 Zach Randolph 1.25 3.00
40 Derrick Rose 2.00 5.00
41 Julius Erving 2.50 6.00
42 John Stockton 2.50 6.00
43 Oscar Robertson 2.00 5.00
44 Karl Malone 2.00 5.00
45 Shaquille O'Neal 3.00 8.00
46 Scottie Pippen 3.00 8.00
47 Bill Russell 2.50 6.00
48 Kareem Abdul-Jabbar 2.50 6.00
49 Allen Iverson 4.00 10.00
50 Magic Johnson 4.00 10.00

2014-15 Elite Dominators Signatures

RANDOM INSERTS IN PACKS
STATED PRINT RUN B/WN 50-149 COPIES PER
1 Alex English/50 4.00 10.00
5 Walt Frazier/50 6.00 15.00
6 George Gervin/50 10.00 25.00
9 Maurice Cheeks/149 4.00 10.00
10 John Starks/99 5.00 12.00
11 Tom Chambers/50 5.00 12.00
12 Bill Cartwright/50 5.00 12.00
13 Norm Nixon/149 4.00 10.00
14 Rod Strickland/149 4.00 10.00
15 Cazzie Russell/149 4.00 10.00
16 Mahmoud Abdul-Rauf/149 6.00 15.00
17 Larry Nance/149 5.00 12.00
21 Fat Lever/149 5.00 12.00
22 Bob Dandridge/149 4.00 10.00
23 Vernon Maxwell/149 4.00 10.00
24 Cedric Ceballos/149 4.00 10.00
25 Dee Brown/149 4.00 10.00
27 Fred Brown/149 4.00 10.00
28 Bo Kimble/149 4.00 10.00
31 Baron Davis/50 5.00 12.00
33 Bill Laimbeer/149 5.00 12.00
34 Bill Walton/50 12.00 30.00
35 Chris Webber/50 100.00 200.00
36 Mark Aguirre/50 5.00 12.00
38 Mitch Richmond/50 75.00 150.00
40 Darryl Dawkins/99 4.00 10.00
41 Rudy Tomjanovich/149 5.00 12.00
42 Jack Sikma/149 5.00 12.00
43 Brad Davis/149 5.00 12.00
45 Mychal Thompson/149 4.00 10.00
46 Spencer Haywood/149 4.00 10.00
47 Dikembe Mutombo/50 6.00 15.00
48 Alonzo Mourning/50 25.00 60.00
49 Tim Hardaway/149 4.00 10.00
50 Tracy McGrady/149 10.00 25.00

2014-15 Elite Jersey Number Die Cuts

*DIE CUTS: 1.5X TO 4X BASE HI
RANDOM INSERTS IN PACKS
STATED PRINT RUN B/WN 1-91 COPIES PER
NO PRICING ON QTY 19 OR LESS
23 Kobe Bryant/24 30.00 80.00
26 Nicolas Batum/88 5.00 12.00
50 Tim Duncan/21 10.00 25.00
62 Anthony Davis/23 20.00 50.00
80 LeBron James/23 40.00 100.00
90 Kevin McHale/32 5.00 12.00

2010-11 Elite Black Box

STATED PRINT RUN 99 SER.#'d SETS
UNPRICED ASPIRATIONS PRINT RUN 5 SETS
1 LeBron James 10.00 25.00
2 Dirk Nowitzki 2.50 6.00
3 Kevin Durant 5.00 12.00
4 Kobe Bryant 8.00 20.00
5 Carmelo Anthony 2.50 6.00
6 LaMarcus Aldridge 2.00 5.00
7 Al Horford 1.50 4.00
8 Kevin Garnett 3.00 8.00
9 Chris Paul 2.50 6.00
10 Dwight Howard 1.50 4.00
11 Dwyane Wade 3.00 8.00
12 Blake Griffin 2.00 5.00
13 Andrea Bargnani 1.50 4.00
14 Kevin Love 2.00 5.00
15 Zach Randolph 1.50 4.00
16 Ray Allen 2.00 5.00
17 Derrick Rose 2.50 6.00
18 Monta Ellis 1.50 4.00
19 Danny Granger 1.50 4.00
20 Ty Lawson 1.25 3.00
21 Tony Parker 2.00 5.00
22 Brook Lopez 1.50 4.00
23 Eric Gordon 1.50 4.00
24 Russell Westbrook 5.00 12.00
25 Tyson Chandler 1.50 4.00
26 Vince Carter 2.50 6.00
27 Amare Stoudemire 1.50 4.00
28 Kevin Martin 1.50 4.00
29 Joe Johnson 1.50 4.00
30 Stephen Jackson 1.50 4.00
31 JaVale McGee 1.50 4.00
32 Chauncey Billups 2.00 5.00
33 Paul Pierce 2.00 5.00
34 Darren Collison 1.50 4.00
35 Serge Ibaka 1.50 4.00
36 J.J. Barea 1.50 4.00
37 Chris Bosh 2.00 5.00
38 Al Jefferson 1.50 4.00
39 Rudy Gay 2.00 5.00
40 Deron Williams 1.50 4.00
41 David West 1.50 4.00
42 Luis Scola 1.50 4.00
43 Antawn Jamison 1.50 4.00
44 Brandon Jennings 1.25 3.00
45 Stephen Curry 8.00 20.00
46 Steve Nash 2.00 5.00
47 Chris Kaman 1.50 4.00
48 Andre Iguodala 1.50 4.00
49 Joakim Noah 1.50 4.00
50 Brandon Roy 2.00 5.00
51 Andrei Kirilenko 1.50 4.00
52 Jameer Nelson 1.25 3.00
53 Jrue Holiday 2.00 5.00
54 Ben Gordon 1.50 4.00
55 Marc Gasol 2.00 5.00
56 Gerald Wallace 1.50 4.00
57 Rajon Rondo 2.00 5.00
58 Tim Duncan 3.00 8.00
59 Pau Gasol 2.00 5.00
60 Michael Beasley 1.25 3.00
61 Tyreke Evans 1.25 3.00
62 David Lee 1.25 3.00
63 DeMar DeRozan 2.00 5.00
64 Wesley Matthews 1.25 3.00
65 Josh Smith 1.50 4.00
66 Juwan Howard 1.50 4.00
67 Nene 1.50 4.00
68 James Harden 3.00 8.00
69 Devin Harris 1.25 3.00
70 Elton Brand 2.00 5.00
71 Emeka Okafor 1.50 4.00
72 Jason Terry 1.50 4.00
73 Luol Deng 1.50 4.00
74 Nick Young 1.50 4.00
75 Danilo Gallinari 1.50 4.00
76 Carlos Boozer 1.50 4.00
77 Andrew Bogut 1.50 4.00
78 Raymond Felton 1.50 4.00
79 Baron Davis 1.50 4.00
80 Manu Ginobili 2.00 5.00
81 Jamal Crawford 2.00 5.00
82 Ben Wallace 1.50 4.00
83 Jason Kidd 2.00 5.00
84 Trevor Ariza 1.25 3.00
85 Kendrick Perkins 1.25 3.00
86 Andrew Bynum 1.25 3.00
87 Aaron Brooks 1.25 3.00
88 Roy Hibbert 1.50 4.00
89 Nick Collison 1.50 4.00
90 J.J. Redick 2.00 5.00
91 J.R. Smith 1.50 4.00
92 Kris Humphries 1.25 3.00
93 Jonny Flynn 1.25 3.00
94 Brandon Bass 1.25 3.00
95 Taj Gibson 1.50 4.00
96 Gerald Henderson 1.25 3.00
97 Glen Davis 1.25 3.00
98 DeJuan Blair 1.25 3.00
99 Tracy McGrady 2.00 5.00
100 Samuel Dalembert 1.25 3.00
101 Wilt Chamberlain 5.00 12.00
102 Karl Malone 2.50 6.00
103 Julius Erving 3.00 8.00
104 Jalen Rose 2.00 5.00
105 Alex English 1.50 4.00
106 Alonzo Mourning 2.50 6.00
107 David Robinson 3.00 8.00
108 Kevin Johnson 2.00 5.00
109 Kevin McHale 2.00 5.00
110 Shaquille O'Neal 4.00 10.00
111 Wes Unseld 2.00 5.00
112 Walt Frazier 2.00 5.00
113 George Gervin 2.00 5.00
114 Gary Payton 2.00 5.00
115 Elgin Baylor 2.00 5.00
116 Bob McAdoo 1.50 4.00
117 Dominique Wilkins 2.50 6.00
118 George Mikan 4.00 10.00
119 Lenny Wilkens 2.00 5.00
120 Jerry West 2.50 6.00
121 Hakeem Olajuwon 2.50 6.00
122 Kenny Smith 1.50 4.00
123 Clyde Drexler 2.50 6.00
124 Nate Thurmond 1.50 4.00
125 John Havlicek 2.50 6.00
126 Darryl Dawkins 1.25 3.00
127 Darrell Griffith 1.25 3.00
128 Danny Manning 1.50 4.00
129 Dan Issel 1.50 4.00
130 Larry Bird 5.00 12.00
131 Sam Perkins 1.25 3.00
132 Bill Laimbeer 1.50 4.00
133 Shawn Bradley 1.25 3.00
134 James Worthy 2.50 6.00
135 Cedric Maxwell 2.00 5.00
136 Bailey Howell 2.00 5.00
137 Magic Johnson 5.00 12.00
138 Kelly Tripucka 1.25 3.00
139 Dikembe Mutombo 2.00 5.00
140 Christian Laettner 1.50 4.00
141 Bob Lanier 1.50 4.00
142 Mark Eaton 1.25 3.00
143 Toni Kukoc 2.00 5.00
144 Earl Monroe 2.00 5.00
145 Glen Rice 1.50 4.00
146 Larry Johnson 2.50 6.00
147 Kiki Vandeweghe 1.50 4.00
148 Chris Webber 2.00 5.00
149 Ron Harper 2.00 5.00
150 Kareem Abdul-Jabbar 3.00 8.00
151 Sam Jones 2.00 5.00
152 Spencer Haywood 2.00 5.00
153 Dennis Scott 1.25 3.00
154 Elvin Hayes 2.00 5.00
155 Robert Horry 2.00 5.00
156 Manute Bol 2.00 5.00
157 Kevin Willis 1.25 3.00
158 Chris Mullin 2.00 5.00
159 Isiah Thomas 2.00 5.00
160 Dave Cowens 1.25 3.00
161 Oscar Robertson 2.50 6.00
162 Rick Barry 1.50 4.00
163 Alvan Adams 1.25 3.00
164 Xavier McDaniel 1.25 3.00
165 Sleepy Floyd 1.25 3.00
166 Mark Aguirre 1.50 4.00
167 Mark Price 2.00 5.00
168 Bernard King 1.50 4.00
169 Joe Dumars 2.00 5.00
170 Reggie Lewis 2.00 5.00
171 Michael Cooper 1.50 4.00
172 Robert Parish 2.00 5.00
173 Danny Ainge 2.00 5.00
174 Maurice Cheeks 1.25 3.00
175 Sidney Moncrief 1.25 3.00
176 Artis Gilmore 1.50 4.00
177 Jeff Hornacek 1.50 4.00
178 Dennis Rodman 8.00 20.00
179 Tom Chambers 1.50 4.00
180 Tim Hardaway 2.00 5.00
181 Mitch Richmond 2.00 5.00
182 Pete Maravich 3.00 8.00
183 Patrick Ewing 2.50 6.00
184 Walt Bellamy 1.50 4.00
185 Vlade Divac 2.00 5.00
186 Steve Smith 1.50 4.00
187 Rolando Blackman 1.50 4.00
188 M.L. Carr 2.00 5.00
189 Kurt Rambis 1.25 3.00
190 Kenny Walker 2.00 5.00
191 Jamal Mashburn 2.00 5.00
192 Connie Hawkins 2.00 5.00
193 Dan Majerle 1.50 4.00
194 Adrian Dantley 1.50 4.00
195 Al Attles 2.00 5.00
196 Ralph Sampson 1.50 4.00
197 Walter Berry 1.25 3.00
198 Bill Russell 3.00 8.00
199 Bill Walton 2.00 5.00
200 World B. Free 1.50 4.00

2010-11 Elite Black Box All-Star Matchups Materials Prime

STATED PRINT RUN 25 SER.#'d SETS
1 Bosh/Wade/KD/Wstbrk 125.00 250.00
2 Duncan/Yao/Howard/KG 40.00 100.00
3 Iverson/Carter/KG/Shaq 75.00 150.00
4 Malone/Kemp/Dmrs/Hard 100.00 200.00
5 English/Magic/Dr.J/Parish 40.00 100.00

2010-11 Elite Black Box All-Star Matchups Signatures

STATED PRINT RUN 5 TO 25 SER.#'d SETS
SOME UNPRICED DUE TO SCARCITY
1 PP/Allen/Kobe/Gasol/25 200.00 400.00
3 VC/Hill/D.Rob/Payton/25 200.00 400.00
4 Mlln/Drxlr/Wilkins/Pytn/25 100.00 200.00
5 Frzr/Unsld/Barry/Hywd/25 50.00 120.00

2010-11 Elite Black Box All-Time Matchups Materials Prime

STATED PRINT RUN 10 TO 25 SER.#'d SETS
SOME UNPRICED DUE TO SCARCITY
2 Erving/M.Johnson/25 40.00 100.00
3 K.Malone/Olajuwon/25 40.00 100.00
4 D.Robinson/Ewing/25 60.00 150.00
5 Abdul-Jabbar/Parish/25 35.00 70.00

2010-11 Elite Black Box All-Time Matchups Signatures

STATED PRINT RUN 10 TO 25 SER.#'d SETS
SOME UNPRICED DUE TO SCARCITY
3 Abdul-Jabbar/Hayes/25 40.00 100.00
4 Drexler/Wilkins/25 40.00 100.00
5 Baylor/Thurmond/25 20.00 50.00

2010-11 Elite Black Box Award Winners Materials Prime

STATED PRINT RUN 15 TO 25 SER.#'d SETS
1 Rose/LJ/Kobe/Dirk/25 150.00 250.00
2 Bird/Moses/Dr.J/KAJ/15 75.00 150.00
3 KM/D.Rob/Olaj/Magic/25 75.00 150.00

2010-11 Elite Black Box Award Winners Signatures

STATED PRINT RUN 5 TO 25 SER.#'d SETS
SOME UNPRICED DUE TO SCARCITY
3 Unsld/Mnr/Brry/Reed/25 75.00 150.00

2010-11 Elite Black Box Black and Blue Signatures

STATED PRINT RUN 10 TO 40 SER.#'d SETS
SOME UNPRICED DUE TO SCARCITY
1 Kobe Bryant/37 100.00 200.00
2 Blake Griffin/25 100.00 200.00
5 Zach Randolph/39 10.00 25.00
6 Monta Ellis/39 10.00 25.00
7 Kevin Martin/49 10.00 25.00
8 LaMarcus Aldridge/39 12.00 30.00
9 Tyreke Evans/25 10.00 25.00
10 Stephen Curry/39 60.00 150.00
11 Kevin Love/40 20.00 50.00
12 Eric Gordon/39 10.00 25.00
13 Paul Pierce/25 EXCH 25.00 60.00
14 Joe Johnson/25 10.00 25.00
15 Andrea Bargnani/39 10.00 25.00
18 Oscar Robertson/25 30.00 80.00

2010-11 Elite Black Box Champions Materials Prime

STATED PRINT RUN ONE TO 25 SER.#'d SETS
SOME UNPRICED DUE TO SCARCITY
1 Los Angeles Lakers/25 125.00 250.00
2 Boston Celtics/25 60.00 150.00
3 San Antonio Spurs/25 100.00 200.00
4 Chicago Bulls/25 200.00 350.00

2010-11 Elite Black Box Champions Signatures

STATED PRINT RUN 10 TO 25 SER.#'d SETS
SOME UNPRICED DUE TO SCARCITY
4 Boston Celtics/25 150.00 300.00
5 Detroit Pistons/25 75.00 150.00

2010-11 Elite Black Box Crusade

STATED PRINT RUN 25 SER.#'d SETS
1 Derrick Rose 5.00 12.00
2 John Wall 20.00 50.00
3 Dwyane Wade 10.00 25.00
4 Chauncey Billups 4.00 10.00
5 Kevin Garnett 10.00 25.00
6 LeBron James 40.00 100.00
7 Carmelo Anthony 5.00 12.00
8 Deron Williams 3.00 8.00
9 Rajon Rondo 4.00 10.00
10 David Lee 2.50 6.00
11 Brook Lopez 3.00 8.00
12 Dwight Howard 3.00 8.00
13 Steve Nash 4.00 10.00
14 Jameer Nelson 2.50 6.00
15 Al Horford 3.00 8.00
16 Pau Gasol 4.00 10.00
17 Anderson Varejao 2.50 6.00
18 Marc Gasol 4.00 10.00
19 Beno Udrih 2.50 6.00
20 Ray Allen 4.00 10.00
21 Tim Duncan 8.00 20.00
22 Rudy Gay 4.00 10.00
23 Jason Richardson 4.00 10.00
24 Kobe Bryant 15.00 40.00
25 Al Jefferson 3.00 8.00
26 Chris Kaman 3.00 8.00
27 Danny Granger 3.00 8.00
28 Elton Brand 4.00 10.00
29 Emeka Okafor 3.00 8.00
30 Stephen Curry 15.00 40.00
31 Jason Terry 3.00 8.00
32 Blake Griffin 4.00 10.00
33 Grant Hill 10.00 25.00
34 Paul Pierce 4.00 10.00
35 Kevin Durant 15.00 40.00
36 Boris Diaw 3.00 8.00
37 Nene 3.00 8.00
38 David West 3.00 8.00
39 Paul Millsap 3.00 8.00
40 Andre Miller 3.00 8.00
41 Dirk Nowitzki 8.00 20.00
42 Kevin Love 4.00 10.00
43 Kris Humphries 2.50 6.00
44 Tayshaun Prince 3.00 8.00
45 J.J. Hickson 2.50 6.00
46 Manu Ginobili 4.00 10.00
47 Raymond Felton 3.00 8.00
48 Andrew Bynum 2.50 6.00
49 John Salmons 3.00 8.00
50 Zach Randolph 3.00 8.00
51 DeMarcus Cousins 12.00 30.00
52 D.J. Augustin 2.50 6.00
53 Tyreke Evans 2.50 6.00
54 James Harden 6.00 15.00
55 Roy Hibbert 3.00 8.00
56 Luke Ridnour 3.00 8.00
57 Joakim Noah 3.00 8.00
58 Kevin Martin 3.00 8.00
59 LaMarcus Aldridge 4.00 10.00
60 Jrue Holiday 4.00 10.00
61 Mike Conley Jr. 4.00 10.00
62 DeMar DeRozan 4.00 10.00
63 Eric Gordon 3.00 8.00
64 Andre Iguodala 3.00 8.00
65 Tony Parker 4.00 10.00
66 Luol Deng 3.00 8.00
67 Michael Beasley 2.50 6.00
68 Monta Ellis 3.00 8.00
69 Jose Calderon 2.50 6.00
70 Danilo Gallinari 3.00 8.00
71 Channing Frye 3.00 8.00
72 Andrea Bargnani 3.00 8.00
73 Lamar Odom 3.00 8.00
74 Kyle Lowry 3.00 8.00
75 Andray Blatche 2.50 6.00
76 Andrew Bogut 3.00 8.00
77 Devin Harris 2.50 6.00
78 Josh Smith 3.00 8.00
79 Carlos Boozer 3.00 8.00
80 Antawn Jamison 3.00 8.00
81 Luis Scola 3.00 8.00
82 Caron Butler 3.00 8.00
83 Gerald Wallace 3.00 8.00
84 Chris Paul 5.00 12.00
85 Baron Davis 3.00 8.00
86 Ramon Sessions 3.00 8.00
87 Brandon Jennings 2.50 6.00
88 Rodney Stuckey 3.00 8.00
89 Wesley Matthews 2.50 6.00
90 Joe Johnson 3.00 8.00
91 Mo Williams 3.00 8.00
92 Darren Collison 3.00 8.00
93 Jason Kidd 4.00 10.00
94 Dorell Wright 2.50 6.00
95 Chris Bosh 4.00 10.00
96 Nick Young 3.00 8.00
97 Amare Stoudemire 3.00 8.00
98 Stephen Jackson 3.00 8.00
99 Shawn Marion 3.00 8.00
100 Russell Westbrook 10.00 25.00

2010-11 Elite Black Box Crusade Materials

STATED PRINT RUN 99 SER.#'d SETS
1 Derrick Rose 5.00 12.00
2 John Wall 12.00 30.00
3 Dwyane Wade 6.00 15.00
4 Chauncey Billups 4.00 10.00
5 Kevin Garnett 6.00 15.00
6 LeBron James 15.00 40.00
7 Carmelo Anthony 5.00 12.00
8 Deron Williams 3.00 8.00
9 Rajon Rondo 4.00 10.00
10 David Lee 2.50 6.00
11 Brook Lopez 3.00 8.00
12 Dwight Howard 3.00 8.00
13 Steve Nash 4.00 10.00
14 Jameer Nelson 2.50 6.00
15 Al Horford 3.00 8.00
16 Pau Gasol 4.00 10.00
17 Anderson Varejao 2.50 6.00
18 Marc Gasol 4.00 10.00
19 Beno Udrih 2.50 6.00
20 Ray Allen 4.00 10.00
21 Tim Duncan 6.00 15.00
22 Rudy Gay 4.00 10.00
23 Jason Richardson 4.00 10.00
24 Kobe Bryant 12.00 30.00
25 Al Jefferson 3.00 8.00
26 Chris Kaman 3.00 8.00
27 Danny Granger 3.00 8.00
28 Elton Brand 4.00 10.00
29 Emeka Okafor 3.00 8.00
30 Stephen Curry 15.00 40.00
31 Jason Terry 3.00 8.00
32 Blake Griffin 4.00 10.00
33 Grant Hill 10.00 25.00
34 Paul Pierce 4.00 10.00
35 Kevin Durant 10.00 25.00
36 Boris Diaw 3.00 8.00
37 Nene 3.00 8.00
38 David West 3.00 8.00
39 Paul Millsap 3.00 8.00
40 Andre Miller 3.00 8.00
41 Dirk Nowitzki 5.00 12.00
42 Kevin Love 4.00 10.00
44 Tayshaun Prince 3.00 8.00
46 Manu Ginobili 4.00 10.00
48 Andrew Bynum 2.50 6.00
49 John Salmons 3.00 8.00
50 Zach Randolph 3.00 8.00
51 DeMarcus Cousins 8.00 20.00
52 D.J. Augustin 2.50 6.00
53 Tyreke Evans 2.50 6.00
54 James Harden 6.00 15.00
55 Roy Hibbert 3.00 8.00
56 Luke Ridnour 3.00 8.00
57 Joakim Noah 3.00 8.00
58 Kevin Martin 3.00 8.00
59 LaMarcus Aldridge 4.00 10.00
60 Jrue Holiday 4.00 10.00
61 Mike Conley Jr. 4.00 10.00
62 DeMar DeRozan 4.00 10.00
63 Eric Gordon 3.00 8.00
64 Andre Iguodala 3.00 8.00
65 Tony Parker 4.00 10.00
66 Luol Deng 3.00 8.00
67 Michael Beasley 2.50 6.00
68 Monta Ellis 3.00 8.00
69 Jose Calderon 2.50 6.00
70 Danilo Gallinari 3.00 8.00
71 Channing Frye 3.00 8.00
72 Andrea Bargnani 3.00 8.00
73 Lamar Odom 3.00 8.00
74 Kyle Lowry 3.00 8.00
76 Andrew Bogut 3.00 8.00
77 Devin Harris 2.50 6.00
78 Josh Smith 3.00 8.00
79 Carlos Boozer 3.00 8.00
80 Antawn Jamison 3.00 8.00
81 Luis Scola 3.00 8.00
82 Caron Butler 3.00 8.00
84 Chris Paul 5.00 12.00
86 Ramon Sessions 3.00 8.00
87 Brandon Jennings 2.50 6.00
89 Wesley Matthews 2.50 6.00
90 Joe Johnson 3.00 8.00
91 Mo Williams 3.00 8.00
92 Darren Collison 3.00 8.00
93 Jason Kidd 4.00 10.00
95 Chris Bosh 4.00 10.00
96 Nick Young 3.00 8.00
97 Amare Stoudemire 3.00 8.00
98 Stephen Jackson 3.00 8.00
99 Shawn Marion 3.00 8.00
100 Russell Westbrook 10.00 25.00

2010-11 Elite Black Box Crusade Materials Signatures

STATED PRINT RUN 5 TO 25 SER.#'d SETS
SOME UNPRICED DUE TO SCARCITY
10 David Lee/25 5.00 12.00
11 Brook Lopez/25 8.00 20.00
14 Jameer Nelson/25 5.00 12.00
15 Al Horford/25 6.00 15.00
17 Anderson Varejao/25 5.00 12.00
19 Beno Udrih/25 5.00 12.00
22 Rudy Gay/25 8.00 20.00
24 Kobe Bryant/25 100.00 200.00
25 Al Jefferson/25 6.00 15.00
26 Chris Kaman/25 5.00 12.00
27 Danny Granger/25 8.00 20.00
29 Emeka Okafor/25 5.00 12.00
30 Stephen Curry/25 60.00 150.00
31 Jason Terry/25 10.00 25.00
33 Grant Hill/25 75.00 150.00
36 Boris Diaw/25 5.00 12.00
39 Paul Millsap/25 10.00 25.00
40 Andre Miller/25 6.00 15.00
50 Zach Randolph/25 12.00 30.00
51 DeMarcus Cousins/25 20.00 50.00
52 D.J. Augustin/25 5.00 12.00
53 Tyreke Evans/25 6.00 15.00
54 James Harden/25 20.00 50.00
55 Roy Hibbert/25 5.00 12.00

56 Luke Ridnour/25 5.00 12.00
57 Joakim Noah/25 EXCH 10.00 25.00
58 Kevin Martin/25 5.00 12.00
59 LaMarcus Aldridge/25 10.00 25.00
60 Jrue Holiday/25 5.00 12.00
61 Mike Conley Jr./25 8.00 20.00
62 DeMar DeRozan/25 12.00 30.00
63 Eric Gordon/25 8.00 20.00
64 Andre Iguodala/25 5.00 12.00
68 Monta Ellis/25 12.00 30.00
69 Jose Calderon/25 10.00 25.00
70 Danilo Gallinari/25 5.00 12.00
71 Channing Frye/20 5.00 12.00
72 Andrea Bargnani/25 6.00 15.00
76 Andrew Bogut/25 12.00 30.00
77 Devin Harris/25 6.00 15.00
78 Josh Smith/25 10.00 25.00
79 Carlos Boozer/25 EXCH 10.00 25.00
80 Antawn Jamison/25 5.00 12.00
81 Luis Scola/25 EXCH 6.00 15.00
82 Caron Butler/25 8.00 20.00
87 Brandon Jennings/25 10.00 25.00
89 Wesley Matthews/25 8.00 20.00
90 Joe Johnson/25 8.00 20.00
91 Mo Williams/25 5.00 12.00
92 Darren Collison/25 5.00 12.00
98 Stephen Jackson/25 5.00 12.00
100 Russell Westbrook/25 50.00 120.00

2010-11 Elite Black Box Crusade Signatures

STATED PRINT RUN 5 TO 149 SER.#'d SETS
SOME UNPRICED DUE TO SCARCITY
10 David Lee/25 10.00 25.00
11 Brook Lopez/25 10.00 25.00
14 Jameer Nelson/25 8.00 20.00
17 Anderson Varejao/49 5.00 12.00
19 Beno Udrih/99 5.00 12.00
22 Rudy Gay/49 6.00 15.00
24 Kobe Bryant/149 75.00 150.00
26 Chris Kaman/49 5.00 12.00
30 Stephen Curry/49 50.00 120.00
31 Jason Terry/25 EXCH 12.00 30.00
36 Boris Diaw/99 5.00 12.00
39 Paul Millsap/99 6.00 15.00
40 Andre Miller/49 5.00 12.00
43 Kris Humphries/99 5.00 12.00
47 Raymond Felton/49 5.00 12.00
50 Zach Randolph/25 12.00 30.00
51 DeMarcus Cousins/25 40.00 100.00
52 D.J. Augustin/25 5.00 12.00
54 James Harden/25 25.00 60.00
55 Roy Hibbert/99 5.00 12.00
56 Luke Ridnour/49 8.00 20.00
58 Kevin Martin/59 5.00 12.00
59 LaMarcus Aldridge/25 8.00 20.00
60 Jrue Holiday/99 8.00 20.00
61 Mike Conley Jr./49 5.00 12.00
62 DeMar DeRozan/25 10.00 25.00
63 Eric Gordon/49 8.00 20.00
64 Andre Iguodala/25 6.00 15.00
68 Monta Ellis/49 10.00 25.00
69 Jose Calderon/49 10.00 25.00
71 Channing Frye/49 5.00 12.00
72 Andrea Bargnani/25 6.00 15.00
77 Devin Harris/25 6.00 15.00
78 Josh Smith/25 12.00 30.00
79 Carlos Boozer/49 12.00 30.00
80 Antawn Jamison/49 6.00 15.00
81 Luis Scola/49 8.00 20.00
82 Caron Butler/25 12.00 30.00
83 Gerald Wallace/25 12.00 30.00
87 Brandon Jennings/25 15.00 40.00
89 Wesley Matthews/99 5.00 12.00
92 Darren Collison/99 6.00 15.00
95 Chris Bosh/20 12.00 30.00
98 Stephen Jackson/99 5.00 12.00
100 Russell Westbrook/25 50.00 120.00

2010-11 Elite Black Box Draft Classes Materials Prime

STATED PRINT RUN 15 TO 99 SER.#'d SETS
1 Magic/Eaton/Laimbeer/99 12.50 30.00
2 Aguirre/Thomas/Ro/15 15.00 40.00
3 Worthy/Wilkins/Floyd/99 10.00 25.00
5 Griffin/Curry/Collison/99 10.00 25.00

2010-11 Elite Black Box Draft Classes Signatures

STATED PRINT RUN 10 TO 49 SER.#'d SETS
SOME UNPRICED DUE TO SCARCITY
2 Aguirre/Thomas/Ro/49 EXCH 20.00 50.00
3 Worthy/Wilkins/Floyd/25 30.00 80.00
4 D.Rob/Smith/Johnson/25 40.00 100.00
5 Griffin/Curry/Collison/25 50.00 120.00

2010-11 Elite Black Box Dream Team Materials Prime

STATED PRINT RUN 99 SER.#'d SETS
UNPRICED AUTO PRINT RUN 10 SETS
1 Drexler/Stockton/Magic 30.00 80.00
2 Mullin/Bird/Robinson 30.00 80.00

2010-11 Elite Black Box Elite Series Materials Prime

STATED PRINT RUN ONE TO 49 SER.#'d SETS
SOME UNPRICED DUE TO SCARCITY
UNPRICED PRIME SIG PRINT RUN 5 SETS
UNPRICED SIG PRINT RUN 5 TO 10 SETS
1 Julius Erving/25 10.00 25.00
2 Magic Johnson/49 15.00 40.00
3 Chris Mullin/49 8.00 20.00
5 Kevin McHale/49 6.00 15.00
6 Nate Thurmond/25 25.00 60.00
10 Mark Price/49 10.00 25.00
11 David Robinson/49 10.00 25.00
12 Michael Cooper/49 5.00 12.00
14 Charles Oakley/49 8.00 20.00
18 Spencer Haywood/49 12.50 30.00
19 Robert Parish/25 6.00 15.00
20 Mark Eaton/49 4.00 10.00
21 Bill Laimbeer/25 5.00 12.00
23 Bernard King/25 5.00 12.00
24 Dennis Rodman/25 20.00 50.00
26 Kareem Abdul-Jabbar/25 10.00 25.00
29 Dominique Wilkins/25 10.00 25.00
30 Gary Payton/25 10.00 25.00
31 Jalen Rose/49 6.00 15.00
34 Alex English/25 5.00 12.00
35 Alonzo Mourning/25 25.00 60.00
37 Dan Issel/25 5.00 12.00
38 Kelly Tripucka/49 4.00 10.00
39 Larry Johnson/49 20.00 50.00
40 Mitch Richmond/49 15.00 40.00
42 Sam Perkins/25 8.00 20.00
44 George Gervin/25 6.00 15.00
46 Hakeem Olajuwon/49 8.00 20.00
48 Maurice Cheeks/25 4.00 10.00
49 Nick Van Exel/49 8.00 20.00
50 Robert Horry/25 6.00 15.00
51 Kobe Bryant/25 30.00 80.00
52 Kevin Durant/25 15.00 40.00
53 Blake Griffin/49 20.00 50.00
55 Kevin Love/25 6.00 15.00
56 Zach Randolph/25 5.00 12.00
57 Derrick Rose/25 30.00 80.00

59 Tony Parker/25 10.00 25.00
60 Paul Pierce/25 6.00 15.00
61 Lamar Odom/25 5.00 12.00
63 Eric Gordon/25 5.00 12.00
64 Carlos Boozer/25 5.00 12.00
65 Danny Granger/25 5.00 12.00
66 Jason Kidd/25 10.00 25.00
67 Kevin Martin/25 5.00 12.00
68 LaMarcus Aldridge/25 6.00 15.00
69 Pau Gasol/15 10.00 25.00
70 Ray Allen/25 8.00 20.00
71 Rudy Gay/25 6.00 15.00
72 Stephen Curry/25 25.00 60.00
73 Ben Gordon/15 5.00 12.00
74 Brandon Jennings/25 4.00 10.00
76 Tyreke Evans/25 4.00 10.00
77 Ty Lawson/25 4.00 10.00
78 Joe Johnson/25 5.00 12.00
79 Andre Miller/25 5.00 12.00
80 Chris Bosh/25 6.00 15.00
81 Chauncey Billups/25 6.00 15.00
84 Jeff Teague/25 5.00 12.00
88 Marc Gasol/25 6.00 15.00
89 Samuel Dalembert/25 4.00 10.00
91 Grant Hill/25 20.00 50.00
93 DeMar DeRozan/25 6.00 15.00
94 Caron Butler/25 5.00 12.00
95 Monta Ellis/25 5.00 12.00
96 Taj Gibson/25 5.00 12.00
97 O.J. Mayo/25 4.00 10.00
98 Trevor Ariza/25 4.00 10.00
99 Jrue Holiday/25 6.00 15.00
100 Steve Nash/25 10.00 25.00

2010-11 Elite Black Box Flag Patches Signatures

STATED PRINT RUN 5 TO 149 SER.#'d SETS
SOME UNPRICED DUE TO SCARCITY
4 Toni Kukoc/99 15.00 40.00
7 Peja Stojakovic/25 25.00 60.00
11 Dikembe Mutombo/99 6.00 15.00
12 Al Horford/25 8.00 20.00
14 Boris Diaw/99 10.00 25.00
15 Shawn Bradley/149 6.00 15.00
16 Chris Kaman/25 10.00 25.00
17 Detlef Schrempf/149 6.00 15.00
19 Andrea Bargnani/25 10.00 25.00
20 Roy Hibbert/149 6.00 15.00
21 Serge Ibaka/99 10.00 25.00
22 Vlade Divac/149 EXCH 8.00 20.00
23 Nenad Krstic/149 6.00 15.00
24 Darko Milicic/149 6.00 15.00
25 Goran Dragic/149 12.00 30.00
26 Jose Calderon/49 8.00 20.00
29 Hedo Turkoglu/49 6.00 15.00
34 Kobe Bryant/99 100.00 200.00
49 Bill Walton/25 12.50 30.00
50 Brook Lopez/25 6.00 15.00
51 Byron Scott/149 6.00 15.00
52 Caron Butler/25 10.00 25.00
56 Dan Majerle/149 8.00 20.00
57 Dave Cowens/25 10.00 25.00
58 David Lee/25 8.00 20.00
59 Dell Curry/149 6.00 15.00
62 Elgin Baylor/25 15.00 40.00
74 Larry Johnson/149 8.00 20.00
75 Lenny Wilkens/25 15.00 40.00
76 Mark Price/149 8.00 20.00
77 Monta Ellis/99 6.00 15.00
83 Robert Horry/99 6.00 15.00
84 Shane Battier/49 6.00 15.00
85 Stephen Curry/99 50.00 120.00
86 Tim Hardaway/149 8.00 20.00
87 Tyson Chandler/25 10.00 25.00
88 A.C. Green/99 8.00 20.00
89 Adrian Dantley/99 6.00 15.00
90 Bernard King/99 8.00 20.00
91 Bill Laimbeer/149 6.00 15.00
92 Cedric Maxwell/149 6.00 15.00
93 Darryl Dawkins/149 6.00 15.00
94 Gail Goodrich/25 12.50 30.00
95 Glen Rice/99 10.00 25.00
96 Jeff Hornacek/149 8.00 20.00
97 Nate Archibald/25 6.00 15.00
98 Nate Thurmond/25 12.00 30.00
99 Sam Perkins/99 6.00 15.00
100 Sean Elliott/149 8.00 20.00

2010-11 Elite Black Box Hall of Fame Materials Prime

STATED PRINT RUN 99 SER.#'d SETS
3 Worthy/English/Wilkins 12.50 30.00
4 Dumars/Drexler/D.Rob 25.00 60.00

2010-11 Elite Black Box Hall of Fame Signatures

STATED PRINT RUN 10 TO 49 SER.#'d SETS
SOME UNPRICED DUE TO SCARCITY
3 Worthy/English/Wilkins/25 25.00 60.00
6 Jones/Thrmnd/Cngham/49 25.00 60.00
7 Gervin/Howell/Risen/49 25.00 60.00
8 Mullin/Gilmore/Rod/25 60.00 150.00

2010-11 Elite Black Box Materials

STATED PRINT RUN 2 TO 99 SER.#'d SETS
SOME UNPRICED DUE TO SCARCITY
1 LeBron James/99 12.00 30.00
2 Dirk Nowitzki/99 5.00 12.00
3 Kevin Durant/99 10.00 25.00
4 Kobe Bryant/99 12.00 30.00
5 Carmelo Anthony/99 5.00 12.00
6 LaMarcus Aldridge/99 4.00 10.00
7 Al Horford/99 3.00 8.00
8 Kevin Garnett/99 6.00 15.00
9 Chris Paul/99 5.00 12.00
10 Dwight Howard/99 3.00 8.00
11 Dwyane Wade/99 6.00 15.00
12 Blake Griffin/99 4.00 10.00
13 Andrea Bargnani/99 3.00 8.00
14 Kevin Love/99 4.00 10.00
15 Zach Randolph/99 3.00 8.00
16 Ray Allen/99 4.00 10.00
17 Derrick Rose/99 5.00 12.00
18 Monta Ellis/99 3.00 8.00
19 Danny Granger/99 3.00 8.00
20 Ty Lawson/99 2.50 6.00
21 Tony Parker/99 4.00 10.00
22 Brook Lopez/99 3.00 8.00
23 Eric Gordon/99 3.00 8.00
24 Russell Westbrook/99 10.00 25.00
25 Tyson Chandler/99 3.00 8.00
26 Vince Carter/99 5.00 12.00
27 Amare Stoudemire/99 3.00 8.00
28 Kevin Martin/99 3.00 8.00
29 Joe Johnson/99 3.00 8.00
30 Stephen Jackson/99 3.00 8.00
31 JaVale McGee/99 3.00 8.00
32 Chauncey Billups/99 4.00 10.00
33 Paul Pierce/99 4.00 10.00
34 Darren Collison/99 3.00 8.00
35 Serge Ibaka/99 3.00 8.00
36 J.J. Barea/99 3.00 8.00
37 Chris Bosh/99 4.00 10.00
38 Al Jefferson/99 3.00 8.00
39 Rudy Gay/99 4.00 10.00
40 Deron Williams/99 3.00 8.00
41 David West/99 3.00 8.00
42 Luis Scola/99 3.00 8.00
43 Antawn Jamison/99 3.00 8.00
44 Brandon Jennings/99 2.50 6.00
45 Stephen Curry/99 15.00 40.00
46 Steve Nash/99 4.00 10.00
47 Chris Kaman/99 3.00 8.00
48 Andre Iguodala/99 3.00 8.00
49 Joakim Noah/99 3.00 8.00
50 Brandon Roy/99 4.00 10.00
51 Andrei Kirilenko/99 3.00 8.00
52 Jameer Nelson/99 2.50 6.00
53 Jrue Holiday/99 4.00 10.00
54 Ben Gordon/99 3.00 8.00
55 Marc Gasol/99 4.00 10.00
56 Gerald Wallace/99 3.00 8.00
57 Rajon Rondo/99 4.00 10.00
58 Tim Duncan/99 6.00 15.00
59 Pau Gasol/99 4.00 10.00
60 Michael Beasley/99 2.50 6.00
61 Tyreke Evans/99 2.50 6.00
62 David Lee/99 2.50 6.00
63 DeMar DeRozan/99 4.00 10.00
64 Wesley Matthews/99 2.50 6.00
65 Josh Smith/99 3.00 8.00
67 Nene/99 3.00 8.00
68 James Harden/99 6.00 15.00
69 Devin Harris/99 2.50 6.00
70 Elton Brand/99 4.00 10.00
71 Emeka Okafor/99 3.00 8.00
72 Jason Terry/99 3.00 8.00
73 Luol Deng/99 3.00 8.00
74 Nick Young/99 3.00 8.00
75 Danilo Gallinari/99 3.00 8.00
76 Carlos Boozer/99 3.00 8.00
77 Andrew Bogut/99 3.00 8.00
80 Manu Ginobili/99 4.00 10.00
82 Ben Wallace/99 3.00 8.00
83 Jason Kidd/99 4.00 10.00
84 Trevor Ariza/99 2.50 6.00
86 Andrew Bynum/99 2.50 6.00
88 Roy Hibbert/99 3.00 8.00
90 J.J. Redick/99 4.00 10.00
91 J.R. Smith/49 3.00 8.00
93 Jonny Flynn/99 2.50 6.00
94 Brandon Bass/99 2.50 6.00
95 Taj Gibson/99 3.00 8.00
97 Glen Davis/99 2.50 6.00
98 DeJuan Blair/99 2.50 6.00
99 Tracy McGrady/99 4.00 10.00
100 Samuel Dalembert/99 2.50 6.00
102 Karl Malone/99 5.00 12.00
103 Julius Erving/49 6.00 15.00
104 Jalen Rose/99 4.00 10.00
105 Alex English/99 3.00 8.00
106 Alonzo Mourning/99 5.00 12.00
107 David Robinson/99 6.00 15.00
108 Kevin Johnson/99 5.00 12.00
109 Kevin McHale/99 4.00 10.00
110 Shaquille O'Neal/99 8.00 20.00
114 Gary Payton/25 8.00 20.00
117 Dominique Wilkins/99 5.00 12.00
118 George Mikan/49 10.00 25.00
120 Jerry West/25 8.00 20.00
121 Hakeem Olajuwon/99 5.00 12.00
123 Clyde Drexler/99 5.00 12.00
124 Nate Thurmond/25 3.00 8.00
127 Darrell Griffith/99 2.50 6.00
128 Danny Manning/99 3.00 8.00
129 Dan Issel/99 3.00 8.00
130 Larry Bird/99 10.00 25.00
132 Bill Laimbeer/99 3.00 8.00
133 Shawn Bradley/99 2.50 6.00
134 James Worthy/99 5.00 12.00
135 Cedric Maxwell/99 4.00 10.00
136 Bailey Howell/25 4.00 10.00
137 Magic Johnson/25 10.00 25.00
138 Kelly Tripucka/99 2.50 6.00
139 Dikembe Mutombo/99 4.00 10.00
142 Mark Eaton/99 2.50 6.00
143 Toni Kukoc/99 4.00 10.00
144 Earl Monroe/99 4.00 10.00
145 Glen Rice/99 3.00 8.00
146 Larry Johnson/99 6.00 15.00
147 Kiki Vandeweghe/99 3.00 8.00
148 Chris Webber/99 4.00 10.00
149 Ron Harper/99 4.00 10.00
150 Kareem Abdul-Jabbar/49 6.00 15.00
151 Sam Jones/49 4.00 10.00
152 Spencer Haywood/49 4.00 10.00
153 Dennis Scott/99 2.50 6.00
155 Robert Horry/49 4.00 10.00
156 Manute Bol/99 4.00 10.00
157 Kevin Willis/99 2.50 6.00
158 Chris Mullin/49 4.00 10.00
159 Isiah Thomas/99 4.00 10.00
163 Alvan Adams/99 2.50 6.00
164 Xavier McDaniel/99 2.50 6.00
165 Sleepy Floyd/99 2.50 6.00
166 Mark Aguirre/99 3.00 8.00
167 Mark Price/25 6.00 15.00
168 Bernard King/25 3.00 8.00
169 Joe Dumars/99 4.00 10.00
170 Reggie Lewis/99 12.50 30.00
171 Michael Cooper/99 3.00 8.00
172 Robert Parish/99 4.00 10.00
173 Danny Ainge/99 4.00 10.00
174 Maurice Cheeks/99 2.50 6.00
177 Jeff Hornacek/25 3.00 8.00
179 Tom Chambers/99 3.00 8.00
181 Mitch Richmond/99 4.00 10.00
183 Patrick Ewing/99 8.00 20.00
186 Steve Smith/99 3.00 8.00
193 Dan Majerle/99 3.00 8.00

2010-11 Elite Black Box Passing the Torch Materials

STATED PRINT RUN 5 TO 99 SER.#'d SETS
SOME UNPRICED DUE TO SCARCITY
1 J.West/K.Bryant/25 30.00 80.00
2 S.Kemp/K.Durant/99 25.00 60.00
5 J.Erving/A.Iguodala/99 12.50 30.00
6 M.Richmond/M.Ellis/99 8.00 20.00
8 C.Drexler/K.Martin/99 10.00 25.00
9 C.Mullin/D.Lee/75 8.00 20.00
10 D.Wilkins/J.Johnson/99 10.00 25.00
13 J.Rose/D.Collison/99 6.00 15.00
15 D.Rodman/K.Love/99 15.00 40.00
16 M.Eaton/A.Bogut/99 6.00 15.00
18 J.Dumars/G.Monroe/99 6.00 15.00
20 A.Mourning/C.Bosh/99 15.00 40.00
22 K.Johnson/S.Nash/99 10.00 25.00
24 R.Parish/M.Camby/99 6.00 15.00
26 R.Allen/S.Curry/99 10.00 25.00
27 G.Payton/E.Gordon/99 10.00 25.00
28 G.Payton/R.Westbrook/99 10.00 25.00
30 D.Robinson/A.Bynum/99 12.00 30.00
31 J.Stockton/J.Barea/99 15.00 40.00
32 G.Gervin/K.Durant/75 15.00 40.00
34 K.Bryant/A.Iguodala/99 12.00 30.00
36 E.Baylor/K.Bryant/25 35.00 70.00
38 T.Kukoc/J.Noah/99 12.00 30.00
39 J.Havlicek/P.Pierce/25 20.00 50.00
41 D.Griffith/D.Harris/99 6.00 15.00
42 I.Thomas/B.Gordon/99 10.00 25.00
45 A.English/J.Smith/25 10.00 25.00
48 D.Mutombo/J.Smith/99 8.00 20.00
49 K.Tripucka/D.Favors/99 6.00 15.00
50 G.Rice/S.Jackson/85 8.00 20.00

2010-11 Elite Black Box Passing the Torch Signatures

STATED PRINT RUN 3 TO 149 SER.#'d SETS
SOME UNPRICED DUE TO SCARCITY
4 W.Frazier/C.Billups/25 15.00 40.00
6 Richmond/M.Ellis/149 EXCH 12.00 30.00
9 C.Mullin/D.Lee/149 15.00 40.00
11 A.Dantley/G.Monroe/149 10.00 25.00
13 J.Rose/Collison/149 10.00 25.00
16 M.Eaton/A.Bogut/149 10.00 25.00
17 S.Perkins/Z.Randolph/99 10.00 25.00
18 J.Dumars/G.Monroe/149 12.00 30.00
19 N.Archibald/B.Jennings/49 10.00 25.00
21 E.Hayes/L.Aldridge/25 15.00 40.00
24 R.Parish/M.Camby/99 12.00 30.00
25 W.Free/M.Ellis/99 10.00 25.00
26 R.Allen/S.Curry/25 75.00 150.00
29 D.Thompson/Crawford/99 10.00 25.00
33 Archibald/Fisher/99 EXCH 10.00 25.00
34 K.Bryant/A.Iguodala/99 100.00 200.00
36 Baylor/K.Bryant/99 EXCH 100.00 200.00
37 S.Perkins/T.Chandler/25 12.00 30.00
38 Kukoc/J.Noah/25 EXCH 30.00 80.00
41 D.Griffith/D.Harris/99 10.00 25.00
43 B.King/L.Fields/149 8.00 20.00
44 Dawkins/B.Lopez/49 EXCH 10.00 25.00
45 A.English/J.Smith/99 10.00 25.00
46 Blackman/J.Terry/49 EXCH 12.00 30.00
48 D.Mutombo/J.Smith/99 15.00 40.00
49 K.Tripucka/D.Favors/99 10.00 25.00
50 G.Rice/S.Jackson/99 10.00 25.00

2010-11 Elite Black Box Private Signings

STATED PRINT RUN 10 TO 199 SER.#'d SETS
SOME UNPRICED DUE TO SCARCITY
2 Artis Gilmore/148 6.00 15.00
3 Dirk Nowitzki/51 125.00 250.00
4 Gail Goodrich/49 5.00 12.00
5 Jack Twyman/99 15.00 40.00
6 Bill Laimbeer/148 5.00 12.00
7 Rolando Blackman/149 8.00 20.00
8 Sean Elliott/199 6.00 15.00
9 Mark Eaton/199 5.00 12.00

2010-11 Elite Black Box Reigning Threes Materials Prime

STATED PRINT RUN 24 TO 49 SER.#'d SETS
1 Kobe Bryant/24 30.00 80.00
2 Kevin Durant/49 15.00 40.00
3 Stephen Curry/49 30.00 80.00
4 Ty Lawson/49 5.00 12.00
5 Ray Allen/49 8.00 20.00
6 Channing Frye/49 6.00 15.00
7 Jason Terry/49 6.00 15.00
8 Danny Granger/49 6.00 15.00
9 Kevin Martin/49 6.00 15.00
10 Toney Douglas/49 5.00 12.00

2010-11 Elite Black Box Reigning Threes Signatures

STATED PRINT RUN 10 TO 99 SER.#'d SETS
SOME UNPRICED DUE TO SCARCITY
1 Kobe Bryant/99 100.00 175.00
3 Stephen Curry/99 60.00 150.00
4 Ty Lawson/99 6.00 15.00
6 Channing Frye/99 5.00 12.00
7 Jason Terry/49 EXCH 6.00 15.00
8 Danny Granger/49 5.00 12.00
9 Kevin Martin/99 5.00 12.00
10 Toney Douglas/49 5.00 12.00

2010-11 Elite Black Box Signatures

STATED PRINT RUN 5 TO 149 SER.#'d SETS
SOME UNPRICED DUE TO SCARCITY
4 Kobe Bryant/99 75.00 150.00
6 LaMarcus Aldridge/24 8.00 20.00
7 Al Horford/24 6.00 15.00
13 Andrea Bargnani/24 4.00 10.00
14 Kevin Love/24 15.00 40.00
15 Zach Randolph/24 8.00 20.00
18 Monta Ellis/149 8.00 20.00
19 Danny Granger/24 6.00 15.00
20 Ty Lawson/149 5.00 12.00
22 Brook Lopez/24 5.00 12.00
23 Eric Gordon/149 6.00 15.00
24 Russell Westbrook/24 30.00 80.00
25 Tyson Chandler/24 6.00 15.00
28 Kevin Martin/149 4.00 10.00
30 Stephen Jackson/49 4.00 10.00
31 JaVale McGee/149 4.00 10.00
34 Darren Collison/149 4.00 10.00
35 Serge Ibaka/149 6.00 15.00
36 J.J. Barea/149 10.00 25.00
39 Rudy Gay/49 EXCH 5.00 12.00
43 Antawn Jamison/49 4.00 10.00
45 Stephen Curry/49 50.00 120.00
47 Chris Kaman/24 4.00 10.00
48 Andre Iguodala/24 5.00 12.00
51 Andrei Kirilenko/24 6.00 15.00
52 Jameer Nelson/24 4.00 10.00
53 Jrue Holiday/49 8.00 20.00
56 Gerald Wallace/24 10.00 25.00
62 David Lee/24 5.00 12.00
63 DeMar DeRozan/24 8.00 20.00
64 Wesley Matthews/99 5.00 12.00
65 Josh Smith/24 8.00 20.00
66 Juwan Howard/99 4.00 10.00
68 James Harden/24 15.00 40.00
69 Devin Harris/24 4.00 10.00
76 Carlos Boozer/24 6.00 15.00
77 Andrew Bogut/149 8.00 20.00
78 Raymond Felton/24 4.00 10.00
79 Baron Davis/24 5.00 12.00
84 Trevor Ariza/24 4.00 10.00
85 Kendrick Perkins/49 6.00 15.00
86 Andrew Bynum/24 8.00 20.00
87 Aaron Brooks/49 4.00 10.00
88 Roy Hibbert/149 6.00 15.00
90 J.J. Redick/99 5.00 12.00
92 Kris Humphries/99 4.00 10.00
93 Jonny Flynn/99 4.00 10.00
95 Taj Gibson/99 5.00 12.00
96 Gerald Henderson/149 4.00 10.00
98 DeJuan Blair/149 4.00 10.00
100 Samuel Dalembert/99 4.00 10.00
105 Alex English/99 4.00 10.00
111 Wes Unseld/24 4.00 10.00
112 Walt Frazier/24 10.00 25.00
113 George Gervin/24 8.00 20.00
115 Elgin Baylor/24 EXCH 10.00 25.00
116 Bob McAdoo/99 8.00 20.00
119 Lenny Wilkens/24 6.00 15.00
122 Kenny Smith/24 4.00 10.00
124 Nate Thurmond/24 6.00 15.00
126 Darryl Dawkins/149 4.00 10.00
127 Darrell Griffith/149 4.00 10.00
128 Danny Manning/24 8.00 20.00
129 Dan Issel/149 6.00 15.00
131 Sam Perkins/99 5.00 12.00
132 Bill Laimbeer/149 4.00 10.00
133 Shawn Bradley/149 4.00 10.00
135 Cedric Maxwell/149 4.00 10.00
136 Bailey Howell/99 8.00 20.00
138 Kelly Tripucka/149 4.00 10.00
139 Dikembe Mutombo/99 10.00 25.00
142 Mark Eaton/149 4.00 10.00
143 Toni Kukoc/99 8.00 20.00
144 Earl Monroe/24 12.00 30.00
145 Glen Rice/49 10.00 25.00
146 Larry Johnson/149 6.00 15.00
147 Kiki Vandeweghe/149 4.00 10.00
149 Ron Harper/149 10.00 25.00
151 Sam Jones/24 10.00 25.00
152 Spencer Haywood/149 4.00 10.00
154 Elvin Hayes/24 5.00 12.00
155 Robert Horry/99 10.00 25.00
156 Manute Bol/49 15.00 40.00
157 Kevin Willis/149 6.00 15.00
158 Chris Mullin/99 8.00 20.00
159 Isiah Thomas/24 EXCH 10.00 25.00
160 Dave Cowens/24 6.00 15.00
162 Rick Barry/24 8.00 20.00
163 Alvan Adams/99 4.00 10.00
164 Xavier McDaniel/149 4.00 10.00
165 Sleepy Floyd/149 5.00 12.00
166 Mark Aguirre/149 6.00 15.00
167 Mark Price/149 6.00 15.00
168 Bernard King/99 4.00 10.00
169 Joe Dumars/24 10.00 25.00
171 Michael Cooper/99 6.00 15.00
172 Robert Parish/24 6.00 15.00
174 Maurice Cheeks/149 4.00 10.00
175 Sidney Moncrief/149 4.00 10.00
176 Artis Gilmore/24 8.00 20.00
177 Jeff Hornacek/149 4.00 10.00
180 Tim Hardaway/99 8.00 20.00
181 Mitch Richmond/99 EXCH 12.50 30.00
184 Walt Bellamy/24 5.00 12.00
185 Vlade Divac/149 8.00 20.00
186 Steve Smith/149 4.00 10.00
187 Rolando Blackman/149 4.00 10.00
188 M.L. Carr/149 6.00 15.00
189 Kurt Rambis/149 10.00 25.00
190 Kenny Walker/99 10.00 25.00
191 Jamal Mashburn/149 10.00 25.00
192 Connie Hawkins/99 8.00 20.00
193 Dan Majerle/149 EXCH 6.00 15.00
194 Adrian Dantley/99 4.00 10.00
195 Al Attles/149 4.00 10.00
196 Ralph Sampson/149 5.00 12.00
197 Walter Berry/149 4.00 10.00
199 Bill Walton/24 6.00 15.00
200 World B. Free/24 6.00 15.00

2010-11 Elite Black Box Teammates Materials Prime

STATED PRINT RUN 49 SER.#'d SETS
1 KD/Westbrook/Ibaka 40.00 100.00
2 Griffin/Gordon/Williams 20.00 50.00
3 Pierce/Allen/Rondo 20.00 50.00
4 James/Wade/Bosh 200.00 400.00
5 Bryant/Gasol/Fisher 50.00 120.00
6 Abdul-Jabbar/Magic/Worthy 30.00 80.00
8 Bird/McHale/Parish 25.00 60.00

2010-11 Elite Black Box Teammates Signatures

STATED PRINT RUN 10 TO 25 SER.#'d SETS
SOME UNPRICED DUE TO SCARCITY
2 Griffin/Gordon/Mo/25 20.00 50.00
5 Bryant/Gasol/Fish/25 EXCH 125.00 225.00
10 Olaj/Drexler/Horry/25 75.00 150.00

2010-11 Elite Black Box The Rookies Materials Dual Prime

STATED PRINT RUN 20 TO 25 SER.#'d SETS
1 J.Wall/D.Cousins/25 20.00 50.00
2 L.Fields/J.Wall/25 15.00 40.00
4 W.Johnson/L.Hayward/20 8.00 20.00
5 D.Cousins/L.Fields/25 10.00 25.00
7 B.Griffin/J.Wall/25 25.00 60.00
9 G.Hayward/D.Favors/25 15.00 40.00
10 W.Johnson/E.Turner/25 10.00 25.00

2010-11 Elite Black Box The Rookies Materials Prime

STATED PRINT RUN 15 TO 99 SER.#'d SETS
1 John Wall/99 12.00 30.00
2 Landry Fields/99 3.00 8.00
3 DeMarcus Cousins/99 12.00 30.00
4 Greg Monroe/99 5.00 12.00
5 Gary Neal/35 4.00 10.00
6 Eric Bledsoe/37 6.00 15.00
7 Paul George/20 25.00 60.00
8 Gordon Hayward/99 6.00 15.00
9 Greivis Vasquez/15 4.00 10.00

2010-11 Elite Black Box The Rookies Materials Triple

STATED PRINT RUN 49 SER.#'d SETS
1 Griffin/Wall/Cousins 20.00 50.00
2 Turner/Favors/Johnson 10.00 25.00
3 Udoh/Monroe/Aminu 8.00 20.00
4 Hayward/George/Davis 6.00 15.00
6 Griffin/Aminu/Warren 12.00 30.00
7 Fields/Neal/Monroe 10.00 25.00
9 Wall/Fields/Monroe 12.50 30.00

2010-11 Elite Black Box The Rookies Signatures

STATED PRINT RUN 10 TO 149 SER.#'d SETS
SOME UNPRICED DUE TO SCARCITY
1 John Wall/25 75.00 150.00
2 Landry Fields/149 4.00 10.00
3 DeMarcus Cousins/49 15.00 40.00
4 Greg Monroe/149 6.00 15.00
5 Gary Neal/149 5.00 12.00
6 Eric Bledsoe/149 6.00 15.00
7 Paul George/149 40.00 100.00
8 Gordon Hayward/149 12.00 30.00
9 Greivis Vasquez/149 4.00 10.00

2010-11 Elite Black Box The Rookies Signatures Dual

STATED PRINT RUN 10 TO 99 SER.#'d SETS
SOME UNPRICED DUE TO SCARCITY
3 E.Bledsoe/A.Aminu/99 6.00 15.00
4 W.Johnson/L.Hayward/25 10.00 25.00
5 D.Cousins/L.Fields/25 20.00 50.00
6 E.Davis/P.George/25 15.00 40.00
9 G.Hayward/D.Favors/49 12.00 30.00

2010-11 Elite Black Box The Rookies Signatures Triple

STATED PRINT RUN 49 SER.#'d SETS
1 Griffin/Wall/Cousins EXCH 200.00 350.00
2 Turner/Favors/Johnson 15.00 40.00
3 Udoh/Monroe/Aminu 15.00 40.00
4 Hayward/George/Davis 30.00 80.00
5 Wall/Cousins/Bldse EXCH 60.00 150.00
6 Griffin/Aminu/Warren 30.00 60.00
7 Fields/Neal/Monroe 15.00 40.00
8 Favors/Hayward/Evans 15.00 40.00
9 Wall/Fields/Monroe EXCH 60.00 150.00
10 Cousins/Neal/Evans 15.00 40.00

2010-11 Elite Black Box Thunderstruck Signatures

COMMON CARD (1-10) 125.00 300.00
STATED PRINT RUN 10 SER.#'d SETS

2010-11 Elite Black Box USA Basketball Materials Prime Signatures

STATED PRINT RUN 25 TO 49 SER.#'d SETS
1 Alonzo Mourning/25 40.00 80.00
2 Carlos Boozer/25 12.50 30.00
3 Christian Laettner/49 30.00 80.00
4 Clyde Drexler/25 50.00 125.00
5 Dan Majerle/49 25.00 60.00
6 Dominique Wilkins/25 40.00 100.00
7 Joe Dumars/49 15.00 40.00
8 Kevin Johnson/49 25.00 60.00
9 Larry Johnson/49 20.00 50.00
10 Steve Smith/49 12.50 30.00

2010-11 Elite Black Box USA Basketball Materials Signatures

STATED PRINT RUN 25 TO 49 SER.#'d SETS
1 Alonzo Mourning/25 40.00 100.00
2 Carlos Boozer/25 12.50 30.00
3 Christian Laettner/49 20.00 50.00
5 Dan Majerle/49 12.50 30.00
6 Dominique Wilkins/25 25.00 60.00
7 Joe Dumars/49 10.00 25.00
9 Larry Johnson/49 20.00 50.00
10 Steve Smith/49 10.00 25.00

2010-11 Elite Black Box USA Basketball Patches Signatures

STATED PRINT RUN 5 TO 49 SER.#'d SETS
SOME UNPRICED DUE TO SCARCITY
2 Chris Mullin/49 20.00 50.00
6 Isiah Thomas/49 EXCH 15.00 40.00
11 Kevin Love/25 15.00 40.00
12 Kobe Bryant/49 100.00 200.00
17 Sean Elliott/49 12.00 30.00
18 Tyson Chandler/25 12.00 30.00
20 Walt Bellamy/25 12.00 30.00

2015-16 Elite Extra Edition

COMPLETE SET (40) 8.00 20.00
*PROD/286: .6X TO 1.5X BASIC
*PROD/127-239: .75X TO 2X BASIC
*PROD/100-120: 1X TO 2.5X BASIC
*PROD/56-99: 1.2X TO 3X BASIC
*PROD/39-42: 1.5X TO 4X BASIC
*PROD/23: 2X TO 5X BASIC
RANDOM INSERTS IN PACKS
1 Derrick Rose .60 1.50
2 Damian Lillard 1.00 2.50
3 Dirk Nowitzki .60 1.50
4 Tony Parker .50 1.25
5 Klay Thompson .60 1.50
6 Dwyane Wade .75 2.00
7 Blake Griffin .50 1.25
8 Anthony Davis 1.00 2.50
9 DeMar DeRozan .50 1.25
10 Elfrid Payton .40 1.00
11 Jimmy Butler .50 1.25
12 DeMarcus Cousins .50 1.25
13 Kenneth Faried .40 1.00
14 Tim Duncan .75 2.00
15 James Harden .75 2.00
16 Chris Bosh .50 1.25
17 Chris Paul .60 1.50
18 Carmelo Anthony .60 1.50
19 Al Horford .40 1.00
20 Nikola Vucevic .40 1.00
21 LeBron James 2.00 5.00
22 John Wall .60 1.50
23 Andre Drummond .50 1.25
24 LaMarcus Aldridge .50 1.25
25 Dwight Howard .40 1.00
26 Jabari Parker .60 1.50
27 Kobe Bryant 2.00 5.00
28 Kevin Durant 1.25 3.00
29 Marcus Smart .40 1.00
30 Nerlens Noel .40 1.00
31 Kyrie Irving 1.00 2.50
32 Bradley Beal .50 1.25
33 Stephen Curry 2.00 5.00
34 Gordon Hayward .50 1.25
35 Paul George .60 1.50
36 Andrew Wiggins .75 2.00
37 Mike Conley .50 1.25
38 Russell Westbrook 1.25 3.00
39 Kemba Walker .50 1.25
40 Eric Bledsoe .40 1.00

2015-16 Elite Franchise Futures

RANDOM INSERTS IN PACKS
*PROD/253: .6X TO 1.5X BASIC
*PROD/173-233: .75X TO 2X BASIC
*PROD/52-97: 1.2X TO 3X BASIC
*PROD/48: 1.5X TO 4X BASIC
1 Karl-Anthony Towns 2.50 6.00
2 D'Angelo Russell 1.25 3.00
3 Jahlil Okafor .60 1.50
4 Kristaps Porzingis 1.25 3.00
5 Mario Hezonja .40 1.00
6 Willie Cauley-Stein .50 1.25
7 Emmanuel Mudiay .50 1.25
8 Stanley Johnson .40 1.00
9 Frank Kaminsky .50 1.25
10 Justise Winslow .50 1.25
11 Myles Turner .50 1.25
12 Trey Lyles .50 1.25
13 Devin Booker 1.50 4.00
14 Cameron Payne .40 1.00
15 Kelly Oubre Jr. .40 1.00
16 Terry Rozier .40 1.00
17 Rashad Vaughn .30 .75
18 Sam Dekker .40 1.00
19 Jerian Grant .30 .75
20 Justin Anderson .40 1.00

2015-16 Elite Series Inserts

COMPLETE SET (40) 8.00 20.00
RANDOM INSERTS IN PACKS
*PROD/258-376: .6X TO 1.5X BASIC
*PROD/139-231: .75X TO 2X BASIC
*PROD/100-121: 1X TO 2.5X BASIC
*PROD/29-41: 1.5X TO 4X BASIC
1 Isiah Thomas .50 1.25
2 Chris Paul .60 1.50
3 Dominique Wilkins .60 1.50
4 Julius Erving .75 2.00
5 Grant Hill .60 1.50
6 Oscar Robertson .60 1.50
7 Chris Webber .50 1.25
8 Kobe Bryant 2.00 5.00
9 Karl Malone .60 1.50
10 Stephen Curry 2.00 5.00
11 Scottie Pippen 1.00 2.50
12 LeBron James 2.00 5.00
13 Gary Payton .50 1.25
14 Wilt Chamberlain 1.00 2.50
15 Shawn Kemp .75 2.00
16 David Robinson .75 2.00
17 Jerry West .60 1.50
18 Kevin Durant 1.25 3.00
19 John Havlicek .60 1.50
20 Russell Westbrook 1.25 3.00
21 Clyde Drexler .60 1.50
22 Magic Johnson 1.25 3.00
23 Tracy McGrady .50 1.25
24 Pete Maravich .75 2.00
25 Anfernee Hardaway 1.25 3.00
26 Bill Russell .75 2.00
27 Alonzo Mourning .60 1.50
28 Kyrie Irving 1.00 2.50
29 Patrick Ewing .60 1.50
30 Blake Griffin .50 1.25
31 Allen Iverson .60 1.50
32 Larry Bird 1.25 3.00
33 Kareem Abdul-Jabbar .75 2.00
34 Hakeem Olajuwon .60 1.50
35 Shaquille O'Neal 1.00 2.50
36 John Stockton .75 2.00
37 George Mikan 1.00 2.50
38 Anthony Davis 1.00 2.50
39 Jason Kidd .50 1.25
40 Tim Duncan .75 2.00

2015-16 Elite Signatures

RANDOM INSERTS IN PACKS
PRINT RUNS B/WN 25-49 COPIES PER
EXCHANGE DEADLINE 8/19/2017
*RED/20-25: .5X TO 1.2X BASIC
ESAFA Al-Farouq Aminu/49 3.00 8.00
ESAD Anthony Davis/49 20.00 50.00
ESAD Andre Drummond/49 4.00 10.00
ESAG Artis Gilmore/49 3.00 8.00
ESAH Allan Houston/49 3.00 8.00
ESAH Anfernee Hardaway/49 12.00 30.00
ESAI Allen Iverson/49 40.00 100.00
ESAJ Amir Johnson/49 2.50 6.00
ESAL Alex Len/49 2.50 6.00
ESAM Antonio McDyess/49 3.00 8.00
ESAR Andre Roberson/49 2.50 6.00
ESAW Andrew Wiggins/49 20.00 50.00
ESBB Bojan Bogdanovic/49 2.50 6.00
ESBB Brandon Bass/49 2.50 6.00
ESBG Blake Griffin/49 6.00 15.00
ESBK Bernard King/49 3.00 8.00
ESBK Brandon Knight/49 3.00 8.00
ESBM Bob McAdoo/49 3.00 8.00
ESCD Clyde Drexler/49 12.00 30.00
ESCH Cliff Hagan/49 3.00 8.00
ESCK Clark Kellogg/49 4.00 10.00
ESCM Calvin Murphy/49 3.00 8.00
ESCM Chris Mullin/49 4.00 10.00
ESDC Dave Cowens/49 2.50 6.00
ESDE Dante Exum/49 6.00 15.00
ESDG Danilo Gallinari/49 3.00 8.00
ESDM Danny Manning/49 3.00 8.00
ESDM Donatas Motiejunas/49 2.50 6.00
ESDM Dikembe Mutombo/49 4.00 10.00
ESDR Dino Radja/49 10.00 25.00
ESDR Dennis Rodman/49 10.00 25.00
ESDS Damon Stoudamire/49 3.00 8.00
ESDW Dwyane Wade/49 12.00 30.00
ESDW Dominique Wilkins/49 10.00 25.00
ESEH Elvin Hayes/49 4.00 10.00
ESGG Gail Goodrich/49 3.00 8.00
ESGG George Gervin/49 8.00 20.00
ESGH Grant Hill/49 20.00 50.00
ESGP Gary Payton/49 8.00 20.00
ESJC Jordan Clarkson/49 6.00 15.00
ESJD Joe Dumars/49 4.00 10.00
ESJL Jerry Lucas/49 4.00 10.00
ESJN Jusuf Nurkic/49 2.50 6.00
ESJR Julius Randle/49 6.00 15.00
ESJS Josh Smith/49 3.00 8.00
ESJS Jerry Stackhouse/49 8.00 20.00
ESJW Jamaal Wilkes/49 4.00 10.00
ESJW James Worthy/49 8.00 20.00
ESKB Kobe Bryant/49 60.00 150.00
ESKD Kevin Durant/49 EXCH 40.00 100.00
ESKI Kyrie Irving/49 EXCH 30.00 80.00
ESKK Kyle Korver/49 3.00 8.00
ESKM K.J. McDaniels/49 3.00 8.00
ESKM Kevin McHale/49 10.00 25.00
ESKR Kurt Rambis/49 2.50 6.00
ESKV Keith Van Horn/49 3.00 8.00
ESKW Kenny Walker/49 2.50 6.00
ESLD Luol Deng/49 3.00 8.00
ESLP Lamar Patterson/49 2.50 6.00
ESLS Latrell Sprewell/49 15.00 40.00
ESLW Lenny Wilkens/49 4.00 10.00
ESMA Mahmoud Abdul-Rauf/49 2.50 6.00
ESMC Michael Carter-Williams/49 2.50 6.00
ESMD Matthew Dellavedova/49 4.00 10.00
ESMG Manu Ginobili/25 20.00 50.00
ESMH Maurice Harkless/49 5.00 12.00
ESMP Mason Plumlee/49 3.00 8.00
ESMR Mitch Richmond/49 5.00 12.00
ESNN Nerlens Noel/25 3.00 8.00
ESNS Nik Stauskas/49 2.50 6.00
ESNV Nick Van Exel/49 4.00 10.00
ESOR Oscar Robertson/49 15.00 40.00
ESPG Pau Gasol/49 6.00 15.00
ESRA Ray Allen/49 12.00 30.00
ESRA Rafer Alston/49 2.50 6.00
ESRA Ryan Anderson/49 3.00 8.00
ESRF Rick Fox/49 3.00 8.00
ESRG Rudy Gobert/49 8.00 20.00
ESRH Roy Hibbert/49 3.00 8.00
ESRH Richard Hamilton/49 3.00 8.00
ESRM Ray McCallum/49 2.50 6.00
ESRP Robert Parish/49 4.00 10.00
ESRS Ralph Sampson/49 3.00 8.00
ESRS Rik Smits/49 3.00 8.00
ESRS Rony Seikaly/49 2.50 6.00
ESSB Sam Bowie/49 2.50 6.00
ESSB Shawn Bradley/39 2.50 6.00
ESSC Seth Curry/49 10.00 25.00
ESSC Stephen Curry/49 100.00 250.00
ESSF Steve Francis/49 3.00 8.00
ESTA Tony Allen/49 2.50 6.00
ESTB Trey Burke/49 2.50 6.00
ESTC Tom Chambers/49 3.00 8.00
ESTD Tony Delk/49 2.50 6.00
ESTM Timofey Mozgov/49 2.50 6.00
ESTM Tracy McGrady/49 12.00 30.00
ESVO Victor Oladipo/49 3.00 8.00

2012-13 Elite Series

200 PRINT RUN 275 SER.#'d SETS
201-275 PRINT RUN 249 SER.#'d SETS
1 Cartier Martin 1.50 4.00
2 Emeka Okafor 1.25 3.00
3 John Wall 2.00 5.00
4 Jordan Crawford 1.00 2.50
5 Trevor Ariza 1.00 2.50
6 Trevor Booker 1.00 2.50
7 Al Jefferson 1.25 3.00
8 Derrick Favors 1.25 3.00
9 Gordon Hayward 1.50 4.00
10 Jamaal Tinsley 1.00 2.50
11 Marvin Williams 1.25 3.00
12 Mo Williams 1.25 3.00
13 Alan Anderson 1.00 2.50
14 Amir Johnson 1.00 2.50
15 Andrea Bargnani 1.25 3.00
16 Ed Davis 1.00 2.50
17 Jose Calderon 1.00 2.50

18 Kyle Lowry 1.25 3.00
19 Landry Fields 1.00 2.50
20 Linas Kleiza 1.00 2.50
21 Boris Diaw 1.25 3.00
22 Danny Green 1.25 3.00
23 DeJuan Blair 1.00 2.50
24 Manu Ginobili 1.50 4.00
25 Stephen Jackson 1.25 3.00
26 Tiago Splitter 1.25 3.00
27 Tim Duncan 2.50 6.00
28 Tony Parker 1.50 4.00
29 DeMarcus Cousins 1.50 4.00
30 Francisco Garcia 1.25 3.00
31 James Johnson 1.00 2.50
32 Jason Thompson 1.00 2.50
33 John Salmons 1.25 3.00
34 Marcus Thornton 1.00 2.50
35 Tyreke Evans 1.00 2.50
36 Elliot Williams 1.00 2.50
37 J.J. Hickson 1.00 2.50
38 Joel Freeland 1.00 2.50
39 LaMarcus Aldridge 1.50 4.00
40 Nicolas Batum 1.25 3.00
41 Goran Dragic 1.25 3.00
42 Marcin Gortat 1.25 3.00
43 Michael Beasley 1.00 2.50
44 Shannon Brown 1.00 2.50
45 Wesley Johnson 1.25 3.00
46 Andrew Bynum 1.00 2.50
47 Evan Turner 1.00 2.50
48 Jason Richardson 1.50 4.00
49 Jrue Holiday 1.50 4.00
50 Kwame Brown 1.00 2.50
51 Nick Young 1.25 3.00
52 Spencer Hawes 1.00 2.50
53 Thaddeus Young 1.00 2.50
54 Al Harrington 1.25 3.00
55 Arron Afflalo 1.25 3.00
56 Glen Davis 1.00 2.50
57 Hedo Turkoglu 1.25 3.00
58 J.J. Redick 1.50 4.00
59 Jameer Nelson 1.00 2.50
60 Hasheem Thabeet 1.00 2.50
61 Kendrick Perkins 1.00 2.50
62 Kevin Durant 4.00 10.00
63 Kevin Martin 1.25 3.00
64 Nick Collison 1.25 3.00
65 Russell Westbrook 4.00 10.00
66 Serge Ibaka 1.25 3.00
67 Thabo Sefolosha 1.00 2.50
68 Amar'e Stoudemire 1.25 3.00
69 Carmelo Anthony 2.00 5.00
70 J.R. Smith 1.25 3.00
71 Jason Kidd 1.50 4.00
72 Marcus Camby 1.25 3.00
73 Rasheed Wallace 1.50 4.00
74 Raymond Felton 1.25 3.00
75 Ronnie Brewer 1.25 3.00
76 Tyson Chandler 1.25 3.00
77 Al-Farouq Aminu 1.25 3.00
78 Greivis Vasquez 1.25 3.00
79 Robin Lopez 1.00 2.50
80 Ryan Anderson 1.25 3.00
81 Andrei Kirilenko 1.25 3.00
82 Chase Budinger 1.00 2.50
83 J.J. Barea 1.25 3.00
84 Kevin Love 1.50 4.00
85 Luke Ridnour 1.25 3.00
86 Nikola Pekovic 1.00 2.50
87 Ricky Rubio 1.50 4.00
88 Brandon Jennings 1.00 2.50
89 Drew Gooden 1.25 3.00
90 Ersan Ilyasova 1.00 2.50
91 Larry Sanders 1.00 2.50
92 Luc Mbah a Moute 1.00 2.50
93 Mike Dunleavy 1.00 2.50
94 Monta Ellis 1.25 3.00
95 Chris Bosh 1.50 4.00
96 Dwyane Wade 2.50 6.00
97 Udonis Haslem 1.00 2.50
98 Joel Anthony 1.00 2.50
99 LeBron James 6.00 15.00
100 Mario Chalmers 1.25 3.00
101 Rashard Lewis 1.25 3.00
102 Ray Allen 1.50 4.00
103 Shane Battier 1.25 3.00
104 Marc Gasol 1.50 4.00
105 Marreese Speights 1.00 2.50
106 Mike Conley 1.25 3.00
107 Rudy Gay 1.50 4.00
108 Tony Allen 1.00 2.50
109 Zach Randolph 1.25 3.00
110 Antawn Jamison 1.25 3.00
111 Devin Ebanks 1.00 2.50
112 Earl Clark 1.00 2.50
113 Kobe Bryant 6.00 15.00
114 Metta World Peace 1.50 4.00
115 Pau Gasol 1.50 4.00
116 Steve Blake 1.00 2.50
117 Steve Nash 1.50 4.00
118 Blake Griffin 1.50 4.00
119 Chauncey Billups 1.50 4.00
120 Chris Paul 2.00 5.00
121 DeAndre Jordan 1.50 4.00
122 Eric Bledsoe 1.25 3.00
123 Grant Hill 2.00 5.00
124 Jamal Crawford 1.50 4.00
125 Lamar Odom 1.25 3.00
126 Matt Barnes 1.00 2.50
127 Ronny Turiaf 1.00 2.50
128 Danny Granger 1.25 3.00
129 David West 1.25 3.00
130 George Hill 1.25 3.00
131 Ian Mahinmi 1.00 2.50
132 Paul George 2.00 5.00
133 Tyler Hansbrough 1.25 3.00
134 Carlos Delfino 1.00 2.50
135 James Harden 2.50 6.00
136 Jeremy Lin 1.50 4.00
137 Omer Asik 1.25 3.00
138 Patrick Patterson 1.00 2.50
139 Andrew Bogut 1.25 3.00
140 Andris Biedrins 1.00 2.50
141 Brandon Rush 1.00 2.50
142 David Lee 1.00 2.50
143 Stephen Curry 6.00 15.00
144 Austin Daye 1.00 2.50
145 Greg Monroe 1.25 3.00
146 Jonas Jerebko 1.00 2.50
147 Rodney Stuckey 1.25 3.00
148 Tayshaun Prince 1.25 3.00
149 Will Bynum 1.00 2.50
150 Andre Iguodala 1.25 3.00
151 Andre Miller 1.25 3.00
152 Corey Brewer 1.00 2.50
153 Danilo Gallinari 1.00 2.50
154 Ty Lawson 1.00 2.50
155 Darren Collison 1.25 3.00
156 Dirk Nowitzki 2.00 5.00
157 Elton Brand 1.50 4.00
158 O.J. Mayo 1.00 2.50
159 Shawn Marion 1.25 3.00
160 Vince Carter 2.00 5.00
161 Alonzo Gee 1.00 2.50
162 Anderson Varejao 1.00 2.50
163 Daniel Gibson 1.25 3.00
164 Carlos Boozer 1.25 3.00
165 Derrick Rose 2.00 5.00
166 Joakim Noah 1.25 3.00
167 Kirk Hinrich 1.25 3.00
168 Luol Deng 1.25 3.00
169 Marco Belinelli 1.00 2.50
170 Richard Hamilton 1.25 3.00
171 Taj Gibson 1.25 3.00
172 Ben Gordon 1.25 3.00
173 Brendan Haywood 1.00 2.50
174 Byron Mullens 1.00 2.50
175 Gerald Henderson 1.00 2.50
176 Ramon Sessions 1.25 3.00
177 Tyrus Thomas 1.00 2.50
178 Andray Blatche 1.00 2.50
179 Brook Lopez 1.25 3.00
180 C.J. Watson 1.00 2.50
181 Deron Williams 1.25 3.00
182 Gerald Wallace 1.25 3.00
183 Jerry Stackhouse 1.25 3.00
184 Joe Johnson 1.25 3.00
185 Kris Humphries 1.00 2.50
186 Reggie Evans 1.00 2.50
187 Avery Bradley 1.25 3.00
188 Brandon Bass 1.00 2.50
189 Courtney Lee 1.25 3.00
190 Jason Terry 1.25 3.00
191 Jeff Green 1.25 3.00
192 Kevin Garnett 2.50 6.00
193 Leandro Barbosa 1.25 3.00
194 Paul Pierce 1.50 4.00
195 Rajon Rondo 1.50 4.00
196 Al Horford 1.25 3.00
197 Devin Harris 1.00 2.50
198 Josh Smith 1.25 3.00
199 Louis Williams 1.25 3.00
200 Zaza Pachulia 1.00 2.50
201 Damian Lillard RC 8.00 20.00
202 MarShon Brooks RC 1.50 4.00
203 Kyrie Irving RC 10.00 25.00
204 Brandon Knight RC 2.00 5.00
205 Orlando Johnson RC 1.25 3.00
206 Anthony Davis RC 10.00 25.00
207 E'Twaun Moore RC 1.25 3.00
208 Will Barton RC 1.50 4.00
209 Terrence Ross RC 2.00 5.00
210 Nando De Colo RC 1.25 3.00
211 Reggie Jackson RC 2.00 5.00
212 Lavoy Allen RC 1.25 3.00
213 Jordan Hamilton RC 1.25 3.00
214 Kent Bazemore RC 2.00 5.00
215 Darius Morris RC 1.25 3.00
216 Tony Wroten RC 1.50 4.00
217 Jimmy Butler RC 6.00 15.00
218 Marquis Teague RC 1.25 3.00
219 Jan Vesely RC 1.25 3.00
220 Quincy Acy RC 1.25 3.00
221 Jared Sullinger RC 1.50 4.00
222 Tristan Thompson RC 2.00 5.00
223 Kyle Singler RC 1.25 3.00
224 Norris Cole RC 1.25 3.00
225 Austin Rivers RC 2.00 5.00
226 Maurice Harkless RC 2.00 5.00
227 Isaiah Thomas RC 6.00 15.00
228 Alec Burks RC 2.00 5.00
229 Marcus Morris RC 1.50 4.00
230 John Jenkins RC 1.25 3.00
231 Tornike Shengelia RC 1.25 3.00
232 Tyler Zeller RC 1.50 4.00
233 Draymond Green RC 6.00 15.00
234 Robert Sacre RC 1.25 3.00
235 Brian Roberts RC 1.25 3.00
236 Nikola Vucevic RC 2.00 5.00
237 Jimmer Fredette RC 1.25 3.00
238 Bradley Beal RC 3.00 8.00
239 Bernard James RC 1.25 3.00
240 Mike Scott RC 1.25 3.00
241 Jeff Taylor RC 1.25 3.00
242 Jae Crowder RC 1.50 4.00
243 Harrison Barnes RC 3.00 8.00
244 John Henson RC 2.00 5.00
245 Lance Thomas RC 1.25 3.00
246 Kendall Marshall RC 1.25 3.00
247 Thomas Robinson RC 1.50 4.00
248 Mirza Teletovic RC 1.50 4.00
249 Pablo Prigioni RC 1.25 3.00
250 Festus Ezeli RC 1.50 4.00
251 Kemba Walker RC 4.00 10.00
252 Evan Fournier RC 2.00 5.00
253 Chandler Parsons RC 2.00 5.00
254 Tobias Harris RC 2.00 5.00
255 Chris Copeland RC 1.25 3.00
256 Greg Stiemsma RC 1.25 3.00
257 Kawhi Leonard RC 15.00 40.00
258 Tyshawn Taylor RC 1.25 3.00
259 Viacheslav Kravtsov RC 1.25 3.00
260 Jeremy Lamb RC 2.00 5.00
261 Michael Kidd-Gilchrist RC 2.00 5.00
262 Kenneth Faried RC 2.00 5.00
263 Terrence Jones RC 1.50 4.00
264 Alexey Shved RC 1.25 3.00
265 Iman Shumpert RC 2.00 5.00
266 Nolan Smith RC 1.25 3.00
267 Jonas Valanciunas RC 2.00 5.00
268 Klay Thompson RC 8.00 20.00
269 Markieff Morris RC 2.00 5.00
270 Perry Jones RC 1.25 3.00
271 Dion Waiters RC 2.00 5.00
272 Andre Drummond RC 3.00 8.00
273 Miles Plumlee RC 1.25 3.00
274 Derrick Williams RC 1.25 3.00
275 Andrew Nicholson RC 1.25 3.00

2012-13 Elite Series Aspirations Autographs

PRINT RUNS B/WN 45-99 COPIES PER
EXCHANGE DEADLINE 02/21/2015
1 Bradley Beal/97 12.00 30.00
2 Alec Burks/90 5.00 12.00
3 Derrick Favors/85 4.00 10.00
4 Gordon Hayward/80 6.00 15.00
5 Jamaal Tinsley/94 3.00 8.00
6 Marvin Williams/98 4.00 10.00
7 Andrea Bargnani/93 4.00 10.00
8 Ed Davis/68 3.00 8.00
9 Jonas Valanciunas/83 5.00 12.00
10 Kyle Lowry/97 4.00 10.00
11 Terrence Ross/69 5.00 12.00
12 George Gervin/56 12.00 30.00
13 Nando De Colo/75 3.00 8.00
14 Tiago Splitter/78 4.00 10.00
15 Isaiah Thomas/78 30.00 80.00
16 Jimmer Fredette/93 3.00 8.00
17 John Salmons/95 4.00 10.00
18 Kyrie Irving/98 75.00 150.00
19 J.J. Hickson/79 EXCH 3.00 8.00
20 Nolan Smith/96
21 Jared Dudley/97 3.00 8.00
22 Nick Young/99 6.00 15.00
23 Kwame Brown/46 3.00 8.00
24 Arron Afflalo/96 EXCH 4.00 10.00
25 E'Twaun Moore/45 3.00 8.00
26 Hedo Turkoglu/85
27 Maurice Harkless/79 5.00 12.00
28 Nikola Vucevic/91 5.00 12.00
29 Kevin Durant/65 EXCH 50.00 120.00
30 Kevin Martin/77 4.00 10.00
31 Reggie Jackson/85 5.00 12.00
32 Thabo Sefolosha/98 3.00 8.00
33 Marcus Camby/77 4.00 10.00
34 Raymond Felton/98 4.00 10.00
35 Ronnie Brewer/92 4.00 10.00
36 Austin Rivers/75
37 Brian Roberts/78
38 Eric Gordon/90
39 Greivis Vasquez/79 4.00 10.00
40 Lance Thomas/58
41 Chase Budinger/90 3.00 8.00
42 Beno Udrih/81 EXCH 3.00 8.00
43 Ekpe Udoh/87 3.00 8.00
44 Ersan Ilyasova/93 3.00 8.00
45 John Henson/69 5.00 12.00
46 Monta Ellis/89 4.00 10.00
47 Mario Chalmers/85 4.00 10.00
48 Rashard Lewis/91 EXCH 4.00 10.00
49 Udonis Haslem/60
50 Antawn Jamison/96 4.00 10.00
51 Bob McAdoo/89 10.00 25.00
52 Kobe Bryant/76 100.00 200.00
53 Michael Cooper/79 4.00 10.00
54 Blake Griffin/68 15.00 40.00
55 Caron Butler/95 4.00 10.00
56 Grant Hill/67 15.00 40.00
57 Danny Granger/67 4.00 10.00
58 Lance Stephenson/99 4.00 10.00
59 Orlando Johnson/89 3.00 8.00
60 Terrence Jones/94 EXCH 4.00 10.00
61 Andrew Bogut/88 4.00 10.00
62 Brandon Rush/96 3.00 8.00
63 Carl Landry/93 3.00 8.00
64 Harrison Barnes/60 12.00 30.00
65 Stephen Curry/70 60.00 150.00
66 Andre Drummond/99 12.00 30.00
67 Austin Daye/95 EXCH 3.00 8.00
68 Brandon Knight/93 5.00 12.00
69 Charlie Villanueva/69 3.00 8.00
70 Isiah Thomas/89 8.00 20.00
71 Rodney Stuckey/97 4.00 10.00
72 Will Bynum/88 3.00 8.00
73 Alex English/98 4.00 10.00
74 Andre Iguodala/91 EXCH 4.00 10.00
75 Danilo Gallinari/92 3.00 8.00
76 David Thompson/67 4.00 10.00
77 Chris Kaman/65 4.00 10.00
78 Jared Cunningham/99 3.00 8.00
79 Anderson Varejao/83 3.00 8.00
80 Jon Leuer/70 3.00 8.00
81 Tristan Thompson/87 5.00 12.00
82 Tyler Zeller/60 4.00 10.00
83 Zydrunas Ilgauskas/89 4.00 10.00
84 Carlos Boozer/95 EXCH 4.00 10.00
85 Joakim Noah/87 4.00 10.00
86 Kirk Hinrich/88 4.00 10.00
87 Marquis Teague/75 3.00 8.00
88 Taj Gibson/78 4.00 10.00
89 Larry Johnson/98 6.00 15.00
90 Michael Kidd-Gilchrist/79 5.00 12.00
91 Jeff Taylor/56 3.00 8.00
92 Kemba Walker/85 20.00 50.00
93 Brook Lopez/89 4.00 10.00
94 Anthony Davis/77 100.00 200.00
95 Tornike Shengelia/80 3.00 8.00
96 Brandon Bass/70 3.00 8.00
97 Courtney Lee/89 4.00 10.00
98 Jared Sullinger/93 4.00 10.00
99 Anthony Morrow/77 EXCH 3.00 8.00
100 Zaza Pachulia/73

2012-13 Elite Series Class Masters

STATED PRINT RUN 99 SER.#'d SETS
1 Yao Ming 3.00 8.00
2 Tim Duncan 4.00 10.00
3 Shawn Marion 2.00 5.00
4 Shaquille O'Neal 5.00 12.00
5 Ray Allen 2.50 6.00
6 Paul Pierce 2.50 6.00
7 Pau Gasol 2.50 6.00
8 LeBron James 10.00 25.00
9 Larry Johnson 3.00 8.00
10 Kobe Bryant 10.00 25.00
11 Kevin Garnett 4.00 10.00
12 Kevin Durant 6.00 15.00
13 John Wall 3.00 8.00
14 Gary Payton 2.50 6.00
15 Elton Brand 2.50 6.00
16 Dwight Howard 2.00 5.00
17 Dirk Nowitzki 3.00 8.00
18 Derrick Rose 3.00 8.00
19 David Robinson 4.00 10.00
20 Carmelo Anthony 3.00 8.00
21 Blake Griffin 2.50 6.00
22 Andrew Bogut 2.00 5.00
23 Andrea Bargnani 2.00 5.00
24 Amar'e Stoudemire 2.00 5.00
25 Allen Iverson 3.00 8.00

2012-13 Elite Series Court Kings Autographs

PRINT RUNS B/WN 25-249 COPIES PER
EXCHANGE DEADLINE 02/21/2015
1 Al Horford/25 15.00 40.00
2 Devin Harris/25 8.00 20.00
3 Dominique Wilkins/99 10.00 25.00
4 Steve Smith/249 4.00 10.00
5 Zaza Pachulia/249 3.00 8.00
6 Jeff Teague/249 EXCH 4.00 10.00
7 Maurice Cheeks/249 3.00 8.00
8 Brook Lopez/25 10.00 25.00
9 Andray Blatche/249 EXCH 3.00 8.00
10 Antoine Walker/249 4.00 10.00
11 Bill Russell/25 75.00 150.00
12 Brandon Bass/99 3.00 8.00
13 Courtney Lee/249 4.00 10.00
14 J.Sullinger/99 8.00 20.00
15 Larry Bird/25
16 Leandro Barbosa/249 4.00 10.00
17 Byron Mullens/249 3.00 8.00
18 K.Walker/99 EXCH 10.00 25.00
19 M.Kidd-Gilchrist/81 5.00 12.00
20 Bob Love/249 5.00 12.00
21 Marco Belinelli/249 EXCH 3.00 8.00
22 Scottie Pippen/25 250.00 350.00
23 Toni Kukoc/99 6.00 15.00
24 Zydrunas Ilgauskas/249 4.00 10.00
25 Alonzo Gee/249 3.00 8.00
26 Jim Jackson/249 3.00 8.00
27 Vince Carter/249 6.00 15.00
28 Corey Brewer/249 3.00 8.00
29 Dikembe Mutombo/99 12.00 30.00
30 Andre Miller/99 4.00 10.00
31 Danilo Gallinari/25 10.00 25.00
32 Fat Lever/249 4.00 10.00
33 Andre Drummond/99 25.00 60.00
34 Isiah Thomas/25
35 Joe Dumars/25 12.00 30.00
36 Greg Monroe/99 4.00 10.00
37 Carl Landry/99 15.00 40.00
38 Stephen Curry/25 125.00 250.00
39 Brandon Rush/249 3.00 8.00
40 Andrew Bogut/99 8.00 20.00
41 Hakeem Olajuwon/25 30.00 60.00
42 George Hill/99 EXCH 4.00 10.00
44 Grant Hill/99 20.00 50.00
45 Caron Butler/25 4.00 10.00
46 Blake Griffin/25 50.00 100.00
47 James Worthy/99 15.00 40.00
48 Antawn Jamison/99 6.00 15.00
49 Kobe Bryant/99 100.00 200.00
50 Magic Johnson/25 60.00 150.00
51 Bob McAdoo/99 4.00 10.00
52 Jerry West/25 40.00 80.00
53 Mike Conley/99 8.00 20.00
55 Alonzo Mourning/99 15.00 40.00
56 Norris Cole/249 EXCH 3.00 8.00
57 Udonis Haslem/249 3.00 8.00
58 Mario Chalmers/99 EXCH 4.00 10.00
59 Larry Sanders/249 3.00 8.00
60 Ersan Ilyasova/249 3.00 8.00
61 Sidney Moncrief/99 3.00 8.00
62 Kevin Love/25 30.00 80.00
63 Chase Budinger/99 3.00 8.00
64 Anthony Davis/25 150.00 250.00
65 Al-Farouq Aminu/249 4.00 10.00
66 Larry Johnson/249 6.00 15.00
67 Ronnie Brewer/249 4.00 10.00
68 Chris Copeland/249 EXCH 3.00 8.00
69 Allan Houston/99 10.00 25.00
70 Mark Jackson/25
71 Kendrick Perkins/99 EXCH 3.00 8.00
72 Kevin Durant/25 75.00 150.00
73 Nick Collison/249 6.00 15.00
74 Kevin Martin/25 10.00 25.00
75 Hedo Turkoglu/99 EXCH 4.00 10.00
76 Nick Anderson/249 5.00 12.00
77 Darryl Dawkins/249 6.00 15.00
78 Jason Richardson/99 EXCH 15.00 40.00
79 Nick Young/99 4.00 10.00
80 Jared Dudley/99 6.00 15.00
81 Kendall Marshall/249 3.00 8.00
82 Bill Walton/25 12.00 30.00
83 LaMarcus Aldridge/25 20.00 50.00
84 Clyde Drexler/25 60.00 120.00
85 J.Crawford/99 EXCH 10.00 25.00
86 Jimmer Fredette/99 3.00 8.00
87 John Salmons/249 4.00 10.00
88 David Robinson/25 75.00 150.00
89 Stephen Jackson/99 4.00 10.00
90 George Gervin/25 10.00 25.00
91 Gary Payton/99 10.00 25.00
92 Sam Perkins/99 3.00 8.00
93 Alan Anderson/249 3.00 8.00
94 Ed Davis/249 EXCH 3.00 8.00
95 Jose Calderon/99 3.00 8.00
96 John Stockton/25 75.00 150.00
97 Gordon Hayward/249 5.00 12.00
98 Marvin Williams/249 4.00 10.00
99 Jordan Crawford/249 EXCH 3.00 8.00
100 Bradley Beal/99 10.00 25.00

2012-13 Elite Series Court Vision

STATED PRINT RUN 49 SER.#'d SETS
1 Andre Miller 3.00 8.00
2 Brandon Jennings 2.50 6.00
3 Brandon Knight 4.00 10.00
4 Chris Paul 5.00 12.00
5 Damian Lillard 15.00 40.00
6 Darren Collison 3.00 8.00
7 Deron Williams 3.00 8.00
8 Derrick Rose 5.00 12.00
9 George Hill 3.00 8.00
10 Goran Dragic 3.00 8.00
11 Jason Kidd 4.00 10.00
12 Jeff Teague 3.00 8.00
13 Jeremy Lin 4.00 10.00
14 Jose Calderon 2.50 6.00
15 Jrue Holiday 4.00 10.00
16 Kobe Bryant 15.00 40.00
17 LeBron James 15.00 40.00
18 Mike Conley 3.00 8.00
19 Rajon Rondo 4.00 10.00
20 Ricky Rubio 4.00 10.00
21 Russell Westbrook 10.00 25.00
22 Stephen Curry 15.00 40.00
23 Steve Nash 4.00 10.00
24 Tony Parker 4.00 10.00
25 Ty Lawson 2.50 6.00

2012-13 Elite Series Electrifying

STATED PRINT RUN 125 SER.#'d SETS
1 Allen Iverson 3.00 8.00
2 Blake Griffin 2.50 6.00
3 Carmelo Anthony 3.00 8.00
4 Chris Bosh 2.50 6.00
5 Chris Paul 3.00 8.00
6 DeMar DeRozan 2.50 6.00
7 Dominique Wilkins 3.00 8.00
8 Harrison Barnes 4.00 10.00
9 James Harden 4.00 10.00
10 John Wall 3.00 8.00
11 Julius Erving 4.00 10.00
12 Kemba Walker 5.00 12.00
13 Kevin Durant 6.00 15.00
14 Kobe Bryant 15.00 40.00
15 LeBron James 25.00 60.00
16 Magic Johnson 6.00 15.00
17 Manu Ginobili 2.50 6.00
18 O.J. Mayo 1.50 4.00
19 Rajon Rondo 2.50 6.00
20 Russell Westbrook 6.00 15.00
21 Stephen Curry 10.00 25.00
22 Steve Nash
23 Tyreke Evans 1.50 4.00
24 Tyson Chandler 2.00 5.00
25 Vince Carter 3.00 8.00

2012-13 Elite Series Elite Glass

1 Kobe Bryant 8.00 20.00
2 Kyrie Irving 10.00 25.00
3 James Harden 3.00 8.00
4 Kevin Durant 5.00 12.00
5 Anthony Davis 10.00 25.00
6 Blake Griffin 2.00 5.00
7 Damian Lillard 8.00 20.00
8 Dwight Howard 1.50 4.00
9 Dirk Nowitzki 2.50 6.00
10 LeBron James 8.00 20.00
11 Kevin Love 2.00 5.00
12 Tim Duncan 3.00 8.00
13 Rajon Rondo 2.00 5.00
14 Derrick Rose 2.50 6.00
15 Carmelo Anthony 2.50 6.00
16 Chris Paul 2.50 6.00
17 Paul Pierce 2.00 5.00
18 Tyson Chandler 1.50 4.00
19 Dwyane Wade 3.00 8.00
20 Russell Westbrook 5.00 12.00
21 Deron Williams 1.50 4.00
22 Joakim Noah 1.50 4.00
23 David Lee 1.25 3.00
24 Kevin Garnett 3.00 8.00
25 Brook Lopez 1.50 4.00

2012-13 Elite Series Elite Glass Gold

*GOLD: .1X TO 2.5X BASIC

2012-13 Elite Series Elite Signings

PRINT RUNS B/WN 25-249 COPIES PER
EXCHANGE DEADLINE 02/21/2015
1 Anderson Varejao/25 3.00 8.00
2 Andre Iguodala/25
3 Antawn Jamison/49
4 Arron Afflalo/25 5.00 12.00
5 Blake Griffin/49 20.00 50.00
6 Bob McAdoo/149 6.00 15.00
7 Brook Lopez/25 4.00 10.00
8 Carlos Boozer/25 6.00 15.00
9 Chase Budinger/149
10 Courtney Lee/249 4.00 10.00
11 Dan Majerle/149 6.00 15.00
12 Derrick Favors/25 4.00 10.00
13 Dikembe Mutombo/149 8.00 20.00
14 Eric Gordon/25
15 George Gervin/25 8.00 20.00
16 George Hill/149 4.00 10.00
17 Grant Hill/49 40.00 80.00
18 Greivis Vasquez/249 4.00 10.00
19 Kevin Love/49 15.00 40.00
20 Hedo Turkoglu/49 EXCH 4.00 10.00
21 Isiah Thomas/25 8.00 20.00
22 Jamaal Tinsley/249 3.00 8.00
23 Jeff Green/49 4.00 10.00
24 Jeff Teague/249 4.00 10.00
25 Joakim Noah/25 4.00 10.00
26 John Henson/25 5.00 12.00
27 Jose Calderon/25 8.00 20.00
28 Kevin Durant/49 60.00 150.00
29 Kirk Hinrich/149 EXCH 4.00 10.00
30 Kyle Lowry/249 4.00 10.00
31 Larry Sanders/249 EXCH 3.00 8.00
32 Leandro Barbosa/249 4.00 10.00
33 Marcus Camby/249 4.00 10.00
34 Mark Aguirre/249 4.00 10.00
35 Marvin Williams/249 4.00 10.00
36 Mitch Richmond/149 10.00 25.00
37 Monta Ellis/25
38 Nick Young/99 4.00 10.00
39 Patrick Patterson/249 3.00 8.00
40 Ralph Sampson/249 4.00 10.00
41 Randy Foye/99 3.00 8.00
42 Raymond Felton/25 4.00 10.00
43 Rolando Blackman/249 4.00 10.00
44 Stephen Curry/25 75.00 200.00
45 Thabo Sefolosha/49 3.00 8.00
46 Tristan Thompson/25 5.00 12.00
47 Tyreke Evans/25 3.00 8.00
48 Wesley Matthews/149 3.00 8.00
49 Zach Randolph/25 12.00 30.00
50 Zaza Pachulia/249 EXCH 3.00 8.00

2012-13 Elite Series Glass Masters

1 Blake Griffin 1.25 3.00
2 Kobe Bryant 5.00 12.00
3 Kevin Durant 3.00 8.00
4 Shaquille O'Neal 2.50 6.00
5 Dwyane Wade 2.00 5.00
6 Grant Hill 1.50 4.00
7 Magic Johnson 3.00 8.00
8 Larry Bird 3.00 8.00
9 David Robinson 2.00 5.00
10 LeBron James 5.00 12.00
11 Anfernee Hardaway 3.00 8.00
12 Steve Nash 1.25 3.00
13 Jeremy Lin 1.25 3.00
14 Ricky Rubio 1.25 3.00
15 John Wall 1.50 4.00
16 Hakeem Olajuwon 1.50 4.00
17 Patrick Ewing 1.50 4.00
18 Yao Ming 1.50 4.00
19 LaMarcus Aldridge 1.25 3.00
20 Amar'e Stoudemire 1.00 2.50
21 Drazen Petrovic 1.25 3.00
22 Kyrie Irving 6.00 15.00
23 Anthony Davis 6.00 15.00
24 Damian Lillard 5.00 12.00

2012-13 Elite Series Glass Masters Gold

*GOLD: 1X TO 2.5X BASIC

2012-13 Elite Series Passing the Torch Autographs

PRINT RUNS B/WN 10-25 COPIES PER
NO PRICING ON SOME DUE TO SCARCITY
EXCHANGE DEADLINE 02/21/2015
1 Durant/Bryant EXCH 400.00 700.00
2 A.Shved/A.Kirilenko 6.00 15.00
3 S.Curry/T.Hardaway 150.00 300.00
4 Drummond/Laimbeer 30.00 60.00
6 Rodman/M.W.Peace 40.00 80.00
7 B.Knight/I.Thomas 12.00 30.00
8 H.Barnes/V.Carter 75.00 150.00
10 Valanciunas/Ilgauskas 8.00 20.00
11 Parsons/Drexler EXCH 30.00 60.00
12 G.Hill/K.Irving 400.00 600.00
13 T.Robinson/R.Sampson 6.00 15.00
14 English/Iguodala EXCH 20.00 50.00
15 A.Mourning/A.Davis 90.00 150.00
16 J.Sullinger/R.Parish 8.00 20.00
17 D.Wilkins/J.Smith 12.00 30.00
18 Hickson/L.Aldridge 8.00 20.00
19 D.Williams/W.Frazier 8.00 20.00
20 I.Shumpert/J.Starks 8.00 20.00
21 A.Bargnani/D.Gallinari 6.00 15.00
22 A.Hardaway/T.Evans 60.00 120.00
23 B.Beal/R.Allen 90.00 150.00
25 M.Jackson/R.Felton 6.00 15.00

2012-13 Elite Series Rookie Elite Series

STATED PRINT RUN 199 SER.#'d SETS
1 Damian Lillard 8.00 20.00
2 Kyrie Irving 10.00 25.00
3 Brandon Knight 2.00 5.00
4 Anthony Davis 10.00 25.00
5 Jared Sullinger 1.50 4.00
6 Tristan Thompson 2.00 5.00
7 Dion Waiters 2.00 5.00
8 Klay Thompson 8.00 20.00
9 Jonas Valanciunas 2.00 5.00
10 Isaiah Thomas 3.00 8.00
11 Thomas Robinson 1.50 4.00
12 Kemba Walker 4.00 10.00
13 Nikola Vucevic 2.00 5.00
14 Jimmer Fredette 1.25 3.00
15 Bradley Beal 12.00 30.00
16 Harrison Barnes 3.00 8.00
17 John Henson 2.00 5.00
18 Chandler Parsons 2.00 5.00
19 Kenneth Faried 2.00 5.00
20 Chris Copeland 1.25 3.00
21 Alexey Shved 1.25 3.00
22 Derrick Williams 1.25 3.00
23 Andre Drummond 3.00 8.00
24 Michael Kidd-Gilchrist 2.00 5.00
25 Kawhi Leonard 10.00 25.00

2012-13 Elite Series Rookie Inscriptions Autographs

EXCHANGE DEADLINE 02/21/2015
1 MarShon Brooks 3.00 8.00
2 Jared Sullinger 3.00 8.00
3 Tornike Shengelia
4 Jeff Taylor 2.50 6.00
5 Kemba Walker EXCH 8.00 20.00
6 Michael Kidd-Gilchrist 4.00 10.00
7 Dion Waiters EXCH 4.00 10.00
8 Kyrie Irving 50.00 120.00
9 Tristan Thompson 4.00 10.00
10 Tyler Zeller 3.00 8.00
11 Jae Crowder 3.00 8.00
12 Evan Fournier 4.00 10.00
13 Kenneth Faried 3.00 8.00
14 Andre Drummond 6.00 15.00
15 Brandon Knight 4.00 10.00
16 Kyle Singler 2.50 6.00
17 Draymond Green 20.00 50.00
18 Harrison Barnes 6.00 15.00
19 Chandler Parsons 4.00 10.00
20 Terrence Jones
22 Orlando Johnson 2.50 6.00
23 Robert Sacre 2.50 6.00
24 Norris Cole EXCH 2.50 6.00
25 John Henson 4.00 10.00
26 Tobias Harris 4.00 10.00
27 Alexey Shved 2.50 6.00
28 Derrick Williams
29 Anthony Davis 100.00 200.00
30 Austin Rivers EXCH 4.00 10.00
31 Brian Roberts 2.50 6.00
33 Chris Copeland
34 Iman Shumpert EXCH 4.00 10.00
35 Andrew Nicholson 2.50 6.00
36 E'Twaun Moore 2.50 6.00
37 Maurice Harkless 4.00 10.00
38 Nikola Vucevic 4.00 10.00
39 Kendall Marshall 2.50 6.00
40 Greg Stiemsma 2.50 6.00
41 Nolan Smith 2.50 6.00
42 Will Barton EXCH 3.00 8.00
43 Isaiah Thomas
44 Jimmer Fredette 2.50 6.00
45 Thomas Robinson EXCH 3.00 8.00
46 Kawhi Leonard 60.00 150.00
47 Jonas Valanciunas 4.00 10.00
48 Terrence Ross EXCH 4.00 10.00
49 Alec Burks 4.00 10.00
50 Bradley Beal 12.00 30.00

2012-13 Elite Series Status Autographs

PRINT RUNS B/WN 1-55 COPIES PER
NO PRICING ON QTY 24 OR LESS
EXCHANGE DEADLINE 02/21/2015
8 Ed Davis/32 4.00 10.00
11 Terrence Ross/31 4.00 10.00
12 George Gervin/44 12.00 30.00
13 Nando De Colo/25 8.00 20.00
14 Tiago Splitter/22 12.00 30.00
15 Isaiah Thomas/22 60.00 150.00
23 Kwame Brown/54 4.00 10.00
25 E'Twaun Moore/55 4.00 10.00
36 Austin Rivers/25 8.00 20.00
40 Lance Thomas/42 4.00 10.00
45 John Henson/31 8.00 20.00
49 Udonis Haslem/40 6.00 15.00
52 Kobe Bryant/24 75.00 150.00
54 Blake Griffin/32 50.00 100.00
56 Grant Hill/33 25.00 60.00
57 Danny Granger/33 10.00 25.00
64 Harrison Barnes/40 40.00 80.00
65 Stephen Curry/30 60.00 150.00
69 Charlie Villanueva/31 4.00 10.00
76 David Thompson/33 4.00 10.00
77 Chris Kaman/35 6.00 15.00
80 Jon Leuer/30 4.00 10.00
82 Tyler Zeller/40 4.00 10.00
87 Marquis Teague/25 6.00 15.00
91 Jeff Taylor/44 4.00 10.00
96 Brandon Bass/30 4.00 10.00
100 Zaza Pachulia/27 4.00 10.00

2012-13 Elite Series Turn of the Century

ATED PRINT RUN 99 SER.#'d SETS
1 Tyson Chandler 2.00 5.00
2 Zach Randolph 1.25 3.00
3 Yao Ming 2.00 5.00
4 Vlade Divac 1.50 4.00
5 Vince Carter 2.00 5.00
6 Steve Nash 1.50 4.00
7 Dirk Nowitzki 2.00 5.00
8 Kevin Garnett 2.50 6.00
9 Ray Allen 1.50 4.00
10 Pau Gasol 1.50 4.00
11 Paul Pierce 1.50 4.00
12 Lamar Odom 1.25 3.00
13 Kobe Bryant 6.00 15.00
14 Andre Miller 1.25 3.00
15 Elton Brand 1.50 4.00
16 Steve Francis 1.25 3.00
17 Shaquille O'Neal 3.00 8.00
18 Alonzo Mourning 2.00 5.00
19 Tim Duncan 2.50 6.00
20 Marcus Camby 1.25 3.00
21 Jerry Stackhouse 1.25 3.00
22 Grant Hill 2.00 5.00
23 Michael Finley 1.50 4.00
24 Antawn Jamison 1.25 3.00
25 Jason Kidd 1.50 4.00

2012-13 Elite Series Veteran Elite Series

STATED PRINT RUN 199 SER.#'d SETS
1 Blake Griffin 2.00 5.00
2 Chris Paul 2.50 6.00
3 Dirk Nowitzki 2.50 6.00
4 Kobe Bryant 8.00 20.00
5 Steve Nash 2.00 5.00
6 Dwight Howard 1.50 4.00
7 James Harden 3.00 8.00
8 David Lee 1.25 3.00
9 Stephen Curry 8.00 20.00
10 Zach Randolph 1.50 4.00
11 Derrick Rose 2.50 6.00
12 Dwyane Wade 3.00 8.00
13 LeBron James 8.00 20.00
14 Kevin Love 2.00 5.00
15 Deron Williams 1.50 4.00
16 Carmelo Anthony 2.50 6.00
17 Kevin Durant 5.00 12.00
18 Russell Westbrook 5.00 12.00
19 LaMarcus Aldridge 2.00 5.00
20 Tim Duncan 3.00 8.00
21 Tony Parker 2.00 5.00
22 John Wall 2.50 6.00
23 Josh Smith
24 Paul Pierce 2.00 5.00
25 Rajon Rondo 2.00 5.00

2012-13 Elite Series Veteran Inscriptions Autographs

PRINT RUNS B/WN 25-249 COPIES PER
EXCHANGE DEADLINE 02/21/2015
1 Anthony Morrow/249 3.00 8.00
3 Jason Terry/25 6.00 15.00
4 Larry Bird/99 50.00 100.00
5 Ben Gordon/25
6 Gerald Henderson/49 3.00 8.00
7 Larry Johnson/249 6.00 15.00
8 Taj Gibson/49 4.00 10.00
9 Horace Grant/25
10 Z.Ilgauskas/249 4.00 10.00
11 Anderson Varejao/25
12 Vince Carter/49 15.00 40.00
13 Rodney Stuckey/49 4.00 10.00
14 Stephen Curry/25 100.00 250.00
15 Chris Mullin/99 10.00 25.00
16 James Harden/25 30.00 80.00
17 S.Francis/49 EXCH 10.00 25.00
18 Hakeem Olajuwon/99 15.00 40.00
19 Sam Cassell/99 4.00 10.00
20 D.Granger/25 EXCH 4.00 10.00
21 George Hill/49 EXCH 4.00 10.00
22 Grant Hill/99 12.00 30.00
23 Blake Griffin/99 15.00 40.00
24 Kobe Bryant/99 75.00 150.00
25 Magic Johnson/99 30.00 60.00
26 R.Horry/49 EXCH 6.00 15.00
27 Antawn Jamison/25 10.00 25.00
28 A.C. Green/49 10.00 25.00
29 Zach Randolph/25 4.00 10.00
30 Shane Battier/25
31 Udonis Haslem/149 3.00 8.00
32 Glen Rice/25 12.00 30.00
33 Kevin Love/99 8.00 20.00
34 Greivis Vasquez/249 4.00 10.00
35 Ryan Anderson/49 4.00 10.00
36 M.Camby/149 EXCH 6.00 15.00
37 Kevin Durant/99 75.00 150.00
38 LaMarcus Aldridge/25 8.00 20.00
39 J.J. Hickson/149 3.00 8.00
40 Isiah Thomas/25
41 David Robinson/99 15.00 40.00
42 Danny Green/249 4.00 10.00
43 Tiago Splitter/149 4.00 10.00
44 Gary Payton/49 15.00 40.00
45 Kyle Lowry/149 4.00 10.00
46 Landry Fields/149 3.00 8.00
47 Andrea Bargnani/25
48 Bill Laimbeer/249 4.00 10.00
49 J.Crawford/249 EXCH 3.00 8.00
50 Trevor Booker/249 3.00 8.00

1994-95 Embossed

Featuring 121 double-sided, standard-size embossed cards, the 1994-95 Embossed set marks the premier of a new product for Topps. Each six-card pack contained five basic cards and one Golden Idols parallel gold foil card, with a suggested retail of 3.00 per pack. The fronts display a color embossed player photo framed by a textured border. The backs carry a second embossed player photo, biography, statistics, and a special "Did You Know" section containing unique information not found on other Topps cards. The cards are grouped alphabetically within teams. The set closes with a silver foil Draft Picks subset (101-120) followed by a Michael Jordan card that was added at the last minute. In addition to the Draft Picks, all of the Houston Rockets cards were given a foil background treatment. Rookie Cards of note in this set include Grant Hill, Juwan Howard, Jason Kidd and Glenn Robinson.

COMPLETE SET (121) 10.00 25.00
1 Stacey Augmon .20 .50
2 Mookie Blaylock .15 .40
3 Ken Norman .15 .40
4 Steve Smith .20 .50
5 Dee Brown .15 .40
6 Blue Edwards .15 .40
7 Dino Radja .15 .40
8 Dominique Wilkins .30 .75
9 Muggsy Bogues .20 .50
10 Dell Curry .15 .40
11 Larry Johnson .25 .60
12 Alonzo Mourning .30 .75
13 B.J. Armstrong .15 .40
14 Ron Harper .20 .50
15 Toni Kukoc .30 .75
16 Scottie Pippen .50 1.25
17 Tyrone Hill .15 .40
18 Mark Price .25 .60
19 John Williams .15 .40
20 Jim Jackson .15 .40
21 Popeye Jones .15 .40
22 Jamal Mashburn .25 .60
23 Mahmoud Abdul-Rauf .15 .40
24 LaPhonso Ellis .15 .40
25 Dikembe Mutombo .25 .60
26 Rodney Rogers .15 .40
27 Joe Dumars .25 .60
28 Lindsey Hunter .15 .40
29 Oliver Miller .15 .40
30 Terry Mills .15 .40
31 Tom Gugliotta .15 .40
32 Tim Hardaway .25 .60
33 Chris Mullin .25 .60
34 Latrell Sprewell .30 .75
35 Sam Cassell FOIL .25 .60
36 Robert Horry FOIL .25 .60
37 Vernon Maxwell FOIL .15 .40
38 Hakeem Olajuwon FOIL .30 .75
39 Otis Thorpe FOIL .15 .40
40 Mark Jackson .20 .50
41 Reggie Miller .30 .75
42 Rik Smits .20 .50
43 Terry Dehere .15 .40
44 Stanley Roberts .15 .40
45 Loy Vaught .15 .40
46 Vlade Divac .25 .60
47 George Lynch .15 .40
48 Nick Van Exel .25 .60
49 Billy Owens .15 .40
50 Glen Rice .25 .60
51 Kevin Willis .15 .40
52 Vin Baker .25 .60
53 Todd Day .15 .40
54 Eric Murdock .15 .40
55 Christian Laettner .20 .50
56 Isaiah Rider .25 .60
57 Micheal Williams .15 .40
58 Kenny Anderson .20 .50
59 P.J. Brown .15 .40
60 Derrick Coleman .20 .50
61 Chris Morris .15 .40
62 Patrick Ewing .30 .75
63 Derek Harper .20 .50
64 Anthony Mason .15 .40
65 Charles Oakley .20 .50
66 John Starks .20 .50
67 Horace Grant .20 .50
68 Anfernee Hardaway .40 1.00
69 Shaquille O'Neal .60 1.50
70 Dennis Scott .15 .40

71 Shawn Bradley .15 .40
72 Jeff Malone .15 .40
73 Clarence Weatherspoon .15 .40
74 Charles Barkley .40 1.00
75 Kevin Johnson .25 .60
76 Dan Majerle .25 .60
77 Danny Manning .20 .50
78 Wayman Tisdale .15 .40
79 Clyde Drexler .30 .75
80 Clifford Robinson .15 .40
81 Rod Strickland .15 .40
82 Bobby Hurley .15 .40
83 Olden Polynice .15 .40
84 Mitch Richmond .25 .60
85 Spud Webb .20 .50
86 Sean Elliott .25 .60
87 Chuck Person .20 .50
88 David Robinson .40 1.00
89 Dennis Rodman .50 1.25
90 Kendall Gill .15 .40
91 Shawn Kemp .25 .60
92 Sarunas Marciulionis .15 .40
93 Gary Payton .25 .60
94 Detlef Schrempf .25 .60
95 Jeff Hornacek .20 .50
96 Karl Malone .30 .75
97 John Stockton .30 .75
98 Don MacLean .15 .40
99 Scott Skiles .15 .40
100 Chris Webber .40 1.00
101 Glenn Robinson FOIL RC .50 1.25
102 Jason Kidd FOIL RC 1.25 3.00
103 Grant Hill FOIL RC 1.25 3.00
104 Donyell Marshall FOIL RC .25 .60
105 Juwan Howard FOIL RC .40 1.00
106 Sharone Wright FOIL RC .20 .50
107 Lamond Murray FOIL RC .25 .60
108 Brian Grant FOIL RC .40 1.00
109 Eric Montross FOIL RC .20 .50
110 Eddie Jones FOIL RC .75 2.00
111 Carlos Rogers FOIL RC .20 .50
112 Khalid Reeves FOIL RC .20 .50
113 Jalen Rose FOIL RC .60 1.50
114 Yinka Dare FOIL RC .15 .40
115 Eric Piatkowski FOIL RC .30 .75
116 Clifford Rozier FOIL RC .15 .40
117 Aaron McKie FOIL RC .25 .60
118 Eric Mobley FOIL RC .15 .40
119 Tony Dumas FOIL RC .25 .60
120 B.J. Tyler FOIL RC .15 .40
121 Michael Jordan 4.00 10.00

1994-95 Embossed Golden Idols

COMPLETE SET (121) 25.00 60.00
*GOLD: .8X TO 2X BASIC CARDS
121 Michael Jordan 10.00 25.00

1994-95 Emotion

The complete 1994-95 Emotion set (produced by SkyBox) consists of 121 standard size cards. The cards were issued in eight-card packs with 36 packs per box. Suggested retail price was $4.99 per pack. The fronts have full-bleed color photos. Predominantly placed in the middle is a one word description of the player. The backs have career statistics and player information against a two photo background. The cards are grouped alphabetically within teams. The set closes with two topical subsets: Rookies (101-110) and Masters (111-120). A Grant Hill SkyMotion card was offered to those who sent in two wrappers and a check or money order for 24.99 before December 31st, 1995. The card shows three seconds of a Hill dunk. Rookie Cards of note in this set include Grant Hill, Juwan Howard, Eddie Jones, Jason Kidd and Glenn Robinson.

COMPLETE SET (121) 12.50 30.00
1 Stacey Augmon .30 .75
2 Mookie Blaylock .25 .60
3 Steve Smith .30 .75
4 Greg Minor RC .40 1.00
5 Eric Montross RC .30 .75
6 Dino Radja .25 .60
7 Dominique Wilkins .50 1.25
8 Muggsy Bogues .30 .75
9 Larry Johnson .40 1.00
10 Alonzo Mourning .50 1.25
11 B.J. Armstrong .25 .60
12 Toni Kukoc .50 1.25
13 Scottie Pippen .75 2.00
14 Dickey Simpkins RC .30 .75
15 Tyrone Hill .25 .60
16 Chris Mills .25 .60
17 Mark Price .40 1.00
18 Tony Dumas RC .40 1.00
19 Jim Jackson .25 .60
20 Jason Kidd RC 2.00 5.00
21 Jamal Mashburn .40 1.00
22 LaPhonso Ellis .25 .60
23 Dikembe Mutombo .40 1.00
24 Rodney Rogers .25 .60
25 Jalen Rose RC 1.00 2.50
26 Bill Curley RC .25 .60
27 Joe Dumars .40 1.00
28 Grant Hill RC 2.00 5.00
29 Tim Hardaway .40 1.00
30 Donyell Marshall RC .40 1.00
31 Chris Mullin .40 1.00
32 Carlos Rogers RC .30 .75
33 Clifford Rozier RC .25 .60
34 Latrell Sprewell .50 1.25
35 Sam Cassell .40 1.00
36 Clyde Drexler .50 1.25
37 Robert Horry .40 1.00
38 Hakeem Olajuwon .50 1.25
39 Mark Jackson .30 .75
40 Reggie Miller .50 1.25
41 Rik Smits .30 .75
42 Lamond Murray RC .40 1.00
43 Eric Piatkowski RC .50 1.25
44 Loy Vaught .25 .60
45 Cedric Ceballos .25 .60
46 Eddie Jones RC 1.25 3.00
47 George Lynch .25 .60
48 Nick Van Exel .40 1.00
49 Harold Miner .25 .60
50 Khalid Reeves RC .30 .75
51 Glen Rice .40 1.00
52 Kevin Willis .25 .60
53 Vin Baker .40 1.00
54 Eric Mobley RC .25 .60
55 Eric Murdock .25 .60
56 Glenn Robinson RC .75 2.00
57 Tom Gugliotta .25 .60
58 Christian Laettner .30 .75
59 Isaiah Rider .40 1.00
60 Kenny Anderson .30 .75
61 Derrick Coleman .30 .75
62 Yinka Dare RC .25 .60
63 Patrick Ewing .50 1.25
64 John Starks .30 .75
65 Charlie Ward RC .40 1.00
66 Monty Williams RC .30 .75
67 Nick Anderson .25 .60
68 Horace Grant .30 .75
69 Anfernee Hardaway .60 1.50
70 Shaquille O'Neal 1.00 2.50
71 Brooks Thompson RC .30 .75
72 Dana Barros .25 .60
73 Shawn Bradley .25 .60
74 B.J. Tyler RC .25 .60
75 Clarence Weatherspoon .25 .60
76 Sharone Wright RC .30 .75
77 Charles Barkley .60 1.50
78 Kevin Johnson .40 1.00
79 Dan Majerle .40 1.00
80 Danny Manning .30 .75
81 Wesley Person RC .40 1.00
82 Aaron McKie RC .40 1.00
83 Clifford Robinson .25 .60
84 Rod Strickland .25 .60
85 Brian Grant RC .60 1.50
86 Bobby Hurley .25 .60
87 Mitch Richmond .40 1.00
88 Sean Elliott .40 1.00
89 David Robinson .60 1.50
90 Dennis Rodman .75 2.00
91 Shawn Kemp .40 1.00
92 Gary Payton .40 1.00
93 Dontonio Wingfield RC .40 1.00
94 Jeff Hornacek .30 .75
95 Karl Malone .50 1.25
96 John Stockton .50 1.25
97 Calbert Cheaney .25 .60
98 Juwan Howard RC .60 1.50
99 Chris Webber .60 1.50
100 Michael Jordan 4.00 10.00
101 Brian Grant ROO .30 .75
102 Grant Hill ROO 1.00 2.50
103 Juwan Howard ROO .30 .75
104 Eddie Jones ROO .60 1.50
105 Jason Kidd ROO 1.00 2.50
106 Eric Montross ROO .15 .40
107 Lamond Murray ROO .20 .50
108 Wesley Person ROO .20 .50
109 Glenn Robinson ROO .40 1.00
110 Sharone Wright ROO .15 .40
111 Anfernee Hardaway MAS .30 .75
112 Shawn Kemp MAS .20 .50
113 Karl Malone MAS .25 .60
114 Alonzo Mourning MAS .25 .60
115 Shaquille O'Neal MAS .50 1.25
116 Hakeem Olajuwon MAS .25 .60
117 Scottie Pippen MAS .40 1.00
118 David Robinson MAS .30 .75
119 Latrell Sprewell MAS .25 .60
120 Chris Webber MAS .30 .75
121 Checklist .25 .60
NNO G.Hill SkyMotion Exch. 20.00 50.00
NNO Grant Hill 1.00 2.50
David Robinson Promo

1994-95 Emotion N-Tense

Cards from this 10-card standard-size set were randomly inserted in Emotion packs at a rate of one in 18. The set contains a selection of some of the top players in the NBA. The fronts have full-bleed color photos and the player's name down the left in a hologram set against a sparkling gold background. The backs have two color action photos with the players name across the middle against a black background. The set is sequenced in alphabetical order.

COMPLETE SET (10) 20.00 50.00
STATED ODDS 1:18
N1 Charles Barkley 2.50 6.00
N2 Patrick Ewing 2.00 5.00
N3 Michael Jordan 15.00 40.00
N4 Shawn Kemp 1.50 4.00
N5 Karl Malone 2.00 5.00
N6 Alonzo Mourning 2.00 5.00
N7 Shaquille O'Neal 4.00 10.00
N8 Hakeem Olajuwon 2.00 5.00
N9 David Robinson 2.50 6.00
N10 Glenn Robinson 1.50 4.00

1994-95 Emotion X-Cited

Cards from this 20-card standard-size set were randomly inserted in Emotion packs at a rate of one in four. The set features a selection of the top guards and small forwards in the NBA. The fronts have full-bleed color photos and the player's last name across the top set against a sparkling background. The backs have two color action photos set against a black background. The set is sequenced in alphabetical order.

COMPLETE SET (20) 10.00 25.00
STATED ODDS 1:4
X1 Kenny Anderson .50 1.25
X2 Anfernee Hardaway 1.00 2.50
X3 Tim Hardaway .60 1.50
X4 Grant Hill 3.00 8.00
X5 Jim Jackson .40 1.00
X6 Eddie Jones 2.00 5.00
X7 Jason Kidd 3.00 8.00
X8 Dan Majerle .60 1.50
X9 Jamal Mashburn .60 1.50
X10 Lamond Murray .60 1.50
X11 Gary Payton .60 1.50
X12 Wesley Person .60 1.50
X13 Scottie Pippen 1.25 3.00
X14 Mark Price .60 1.50
X15 Mitch Richmond .60 1.50
X16 Isaiah Rider .60 1.50
X17 Latrell Sprewell .75 2.00
X18 John Stockton .75 2.00
X19 Rod Strickland .40 1.00
X20 Nick Van Exel .60 1.50

2001 eTopps

eTopps was introduced to the hobby via a special "Topps Trading Floor" on eBay with opening prices of $4.00, $6.50, or $9.50 per card. Six different cards were available each week, and once purchased, the buyer had the option of keeping the cards in his/her portfolio for resale, or delivered in a tamper-proof acrylic case. The eTopps floor was run very similar to the workings of the stock market.

1 Darius Miles/795 1.00 2.50
2 Glenn Robinson/474 3.00 8.00
3 Allen Iverson/4368 1.00 2.50
4 Derek Anderson/635 1.00 2.50
5 David Robinson/931 4.00 10.00
6 Gary Payton/640 2.50 6.00
7 Baron Davis/521 2.50 6.00
8 Antoine Walker/763 1.25 3.00
9 Jerry Stackhouse/400 6.00 15.00
10 Vince Carter/2871 1.00 2.50
11 Shawn Marion/2000 1.00 2.50
12 Grant Hill/542 2.50 6.00
13 Kenyon Martin/646 1.50 4.00
14 Eddie Jones/572 1.00 2.50
15 Kobe Bryant/5000 4.00 10.00
16 Michael Finley/1880 1.00 2.50
17 Andre Miller/688 1.25 3.00
18 Peja Stojakovic/1151 1.00 2.50
19 Richard Hamilton/1237 1.00 2.50
20 Steve Francis/841 1.50 4.00
21 Tracy McGrady/758 1.50 4.00
22 Jason Kidd/722 1.25 3.00
23 Lamar Odom/497 1.50 4.00
24 Antawn Jamison/451 2.50 6.00
25 Paul Pierce/797 1.50 4.00
26 Alonzo Mourning/519 2.50 6.00
27 Marcus Camby/810 1.25 3.00
28 Stephon Marbury/418 15.00 30.00
29 Morris Peterson/642 1.25 3.00
30 Tim Duncan/608 5.00 12.00
31 Jason Terry/605 1.25 3.00
32 Reggie Miller/678 6.00 15.00
33 Patrick Ewing/1497 1.25 3.00
34 Shaquille O'Neal/2270 1.50 4.00
35 Ray Allen/1153 1.25 3.00
36 Allan Houston/459 2.50 6.00
37 Dikembe Mutombo/532 2.00 5.00
38 Mike Bibby/638 1.25 3.00
39 Karl Malone/1015 8.00 20.00
40 Chris Webber/473 2.50 6.00
41 Wang Zhizhi/927 1.50 4.00
42 Elton Brand/648 1.50 4.00
43 Antonio McDyess/424 4.00 10.00
44 Shareef Abdur-Rahim/531 2.50 6.00
45 Jamal Mashburn/490 2.00 5.00
46 Jermaine O'Neal/561 2.50 6.00
47 Latrell Sprewell/1009 1.00 2.50
48 Mike Miller/625 2.50 6.00
49 John Stockton/797 2.50 6.00
50 Kevin Garnett/855 4.00 10.00
51 Hakeem Olajuwon/422 8.00 20.00
52 Dirk Nowitzki/1051 3.00 8.00
53 Rasheed Wallace/664 1.25 3.00
54 Kwame Brown/2640 1.00 2.50
55 Tyson Chandler/953 1.00 2.50
56 Pau Gasol/2262 1.25 3.00
57 Eddy Curry/894 1.00 2.50
58 Jason Richardson/1689 1.00 2.50
59 Shane Battier/1784 1.00 2.50
60 Eddie Griffin/869 15.00 40.00
61 Desagana Diop/649 1.00 2.50
62 Rodney White/491 1.50 4.00
63 Joe Johnson/2005 1.00 2.50
64 Kedrick Brown/573 1.25 3.00
65 Vladimir Radmanovic/711 1.00 2.50
66 Richard Jefferson/1915 1.00 2.50
67 Troy Murphy/545 1.25 3.00
68 Joseph Forte/640 1.25 3.00
69 Gerald Wallace/906 1.25 3.00
70 Tony Parker/2165 1.25 3.00
71 Jamaal Tinsley/2423 1.00 2.50
72 Loren Woods/594 1.00 2.50

2001 eTopps Test Run

This version of eTopps came out three months before regular eTopps IPO's were offered for basketball. Price information is limited so this set remains unpriced.

DD DeSagana Diop
EC Eddy Curry
EG Eddie Griffin
JF Joseph Forte
KB Kwame Brown
LW Loren Woods
RJ Richard Jefferson
RW Rodney White
TM Troy Murphy

2002 eTopps

1 Shaquille O'Neal/2273 2.00 5.00
2 Richard Jefferson/1349 1.00 2.50
3 Tracy McGrady/2090 1.00 2.50
4 Steve Francis/1075 1.00 2.50
5 Dirk Nowitzki/2140 1.25 3.00
6 Paul Pierce/1500 1.00 2.50
7 Ben Wallace/1682 1.00 2.50
8 Ray Allen/1129 1.00 2.50
9 Kevin Garnett/1707 1.00 2.50
10 Jermaine O'Neal/1177 1.00 2.50
11 Vince Carter/1889 1.00 2.50
12 Tim Duncan/1089 1.25 3.00
13 Nikoloz Tskitishvili/1468 1.00 2.50
14 Juan Dixon/3000 1.00 2.50
15 Marcus Haislip/1801 1.00 2.50
16 Mike Dunleavy/2859 1.00 2.50
17 Dan Dickau/2000 1.00 2.50
18 Nene Hilario/3000 1.00 2.50
19 Kareem Rush/2000 1.00 2.50
20 Caron Butler/3000 1.00 2.50
21 Jason Terry/1500 1.00 2.50
22 Elton Brand/801 1.00 2.50
23 Shane Battier/1415 1.00 2.50
24 Kenyon Martin/1087 1.00 2.50
25 Jerry Stackhouse/911 1.00 2.50
26 Eddy Curry/1500 1.00 2.50
27 Allen Iverson/1212 1.00 2.50
28 Chris Webber/1500 1.00 2.50
29 Gary Payton/1089 1.00 2.50
30 Mike Bibby/1280 1.00 2.50
31 Wally Szczerbiak/1072 1.50 4.00
32 Shawn Marion/1906 1.00 2.50
33 Jared Jeffries/1875 1.00 2.50
34 Fred Jones/2000 1.00 2.50
35 Drew Gooden/4000 1.00 2.50
36 Jay Williams/3000 1.00 2.50
37 Frank Williams/1864 1.00 2.50
38 Qyntel Woods/2000 1.00 2.50
39 Chris Wilcox/2000 1.00 2.50
40 Casey Jacobsen/1973 1.00 2.50
41 John Stockton/1500 1.00 2.50
42 Rasheed Wallace/762 1.00 2.50
43 Baron Davis/1000 1.00 2.50
44 Grant Hill/1093 1.00 2.50
45 Kobe Bryant/2000 4.00 10.00
46 Jason Richardson/1370 1.00 2.50
47 Andre Miller/722 1.00 2.50
48 Antoine Walker/1585 1.00 2.50
49 Shareef Abdur-Rahim/700 1.00 2.50
50 Tony Parker/1378 2.00 5.00
51 Jason Kidd/1266 1.00 2.50
52 Darius Miles/1108 1.00 2.50
53 Yao Ming/6000 1.00 2.50
54 Manu Ginobili/2000 1.00 2.50
55 John Salmons/1268 1.00 2.50
56 Melvin Ely/1611 1.00 2.50
57 Dajuan Wagner/4000 1.00 2.50
58 Amare Stoudemire/4000 1.00 2.50
59 Bostjan Nachbar/1851 1.00 2.50
60 Marko Jaric/1533 1.00 2.50
61 Antonio McDyess/951 1.00 2.50
62 Pau Gasol/1097 1.00 2.50
63 Steve Nash/2675 1.00 2.50
64 Karl Malone/1500 1.00 2.50
65 Richard Hamilton/738 1.00 2.50
66 Peja Stojakovic/1507 1.00 2.50
67 Jamal Mashburn/641 2.00 5.00
68 Glenn Robinson/1000 1.25 3.00
69 Jamaal Tinsley/1034 1.25 3.00
70 Tyson Chandler/1500 1.00 2.50
71 Jerome Williams/1219 1.00 2.50
72 Latrell Sprewell/1000 1.00 2.50
73 Scottie Pippen/1050 1.50 4.00
74 Ricky Davis/1145 1.00 2.50
75 Carlos Boozer/2309 1.00 2.50
76 Andrei Kirilenko/1254 1.00 2.50
77 Gordan Giricek/1573 1.00 2.50
78 Gilbert Arenas/2000 1.00 2.50

2002 eTopps Event Series

ES3 Shaquille O'Neal/3000* 2.50 6.00
Lakers Champs

2003 eTopps

1 Tim Duncan/740 1.50 4.00
2 Michael Redd/853 1.00 2.50
3 Antawn Jamison/500 1.00 2.50
4 Allan Houston/532 1.00 2.50
5 Kobe Bryant/1371 4.00 10.00
6 Matt Harpring/635 1.25 3.00
7 Kevin Garnett/664 2.50 6.00
8 Dirk Nowitzki/1000 1.00 2.50
10 Jason Richardson/764 1.00 2.50
11 Amare Stoudemire/554 2.00 5.00
12 Chris Webber/589 2.50 6.00
13 Larry Hughes/717 1.00 2.50
14 Alonzo Mourning/1000 1.00 2.50
15 Yao Ming/1105 1.50 4.00
16 Ron Artest/450 2.50 6.00
17 Kenyon Martin/760 1.00 2.50
19 Stephon Marbury/509 1.25 3.00
20 Shaquille O'Neal/1070 2.00 5.00
21 Jermaine O'Neal/934 1.25 3.00
22 Drew Gooden/392 3.00 8.00
23 Tony Parker/626 3.00 8.00
24 Vince Carter/622 1.25 3.00
25 Jason Kidd/693 1.00 2.50
26 Caron Butler/602 1.50 4.00
27 Paul Pierce/775 1.25 3.00
28 Steve Nash/615 1.00 2.50
29 Al Harrington/642 1.00 2.50
30 Allen Iverson/949 1.25 3.00
31 Troy Hudson/803 1.00 2.50
32 Troy Murphy/607 1.00 2.50
33 Nene/744 1.00 2.50
34 Zydrunas Ilgauskas/558 1.00 2.50
35 Steve Francis/675 1.00 2.50
36 Ray Allen/900 1.00 2.50
37 Bobby Jackson/562 1.00 2.50
38 Ben Wallace/1000 1.00 2.50
39 Quentin Richardson/605 1.00 2.50
40 Tracy McGrady/812 1.00 2.50
41 Shareef Abdur-Rahim/546 6.00 15.00
42 Gary Payton/1000 1.00 2.50
43 LeBron James/10000 30.00 80.00
44 Darko Milicic/1789 1.00 2.50
45 Carmelo Anthony/5000 4.00 10.00
46 Chris Bosh/1571 5.00 12.00
47 Dwyane Wade/1208 15.00 40.00
48 Chris Kaman/641 1.50 4.00
49 Kirk Hinrich/686 1.25 3.00
50 T.J. Ford/1500 1.00 2.50
51 Mike Sweetney/910 1.00 2.50
52 Jarvis Hayes/922 1.00 2.50
53 Mickael Pietrus/902 1.50 4.00
54 Nick Collison/1000 1.00 2.50
55 Marcus Banks/687 1.00 2.50
56 Luke Ridnour/874 1.00 2.50
57 Reece gaines/982 1.00 2.50
58 Troy Bell/821 1.00 2.50
59 Zarko Cabarkapa/641 1.25 3.00
60 David West/876 1.00 2.50
61 Aleksandar Pavlovic/618 1.00 2.50
62 Dahntay Jones/798 1.00 2.50
63 Boris Diaw/701 1.00 2.50
64 Zoran Planinic/573 1.00 2.50
65 Travis Outlaw/798 1.00 2.50
66 Brian Cook/768 1.00 2.50
67 Ndudi Ebi/1000 1.00 2.50
68 Kendrick Perkins/857 1.00 2.50
69 Jason Kapono/547 1.00 2.50
70 Luke Walton/1203 1.00 2.50
71 Leandro Barbosa/1000 1.00 2.50
72 Steve Blake/690 1.00 2.50
73 Josh Howard/1000 1.00 2.50
74 Carlos Arroyo/1000 1.00 2.50
75 Zach Randolph/1250 1.00 2.50
76 Brad Miller/1000 1.00 2.50
77 Desmond Mason/918 1.00 2.50
78 Chauncey Billups/977 1.00 2.50
79 Sam Cassell/1000 1.00 2.50
80 Rashard Lewis/923 1.00 2.50

2004 eTopps

1 Miami Heat/1000 1.00 2.50
2 Detroit Pistons/1000 1.00 2.50
3 Cleveland Cavaliers/1000 6.00 15.00
4 Denver Nuggets/1000 1.00 2.50
5 New York Knicks/605 1.00 2.50
6 Dallas Mavericks/1000 1.00 2.50
7 Minnesota Timberwolves/928 1.00 2.50
8 Phoenix Suns/945 1.00 2.50
9 Toronto Raptors/559 2.00 5.00
10 Seattle Supersonics/925 1.50 4.00
11 Utah Jazz/748 1.50 4.00
12 Boston Celtics/688 1.00 2.50
13 Sacramento Kings/766 1.00 2.50
14 Orlando Magic/770 1.00 2.50
15 Indiana Pacers/745 1.00 2.50
16 San Antonio Spurs/950 1.00 2.50
17 Memphis Grizzlies/640 1.00 2.50
18 Los Angeles Lakers/850 1.00 2.50
19 Charlotte Bobcats/950 1.00 2.50
20 Houston Rockets/511 1.50 4.00
21 Golden State Warriors/531 2.00 5.00
22 Chicago Bulls/750 1.50 4.00
23 Atlanta Hawks/499 8.00 20.00
24 Los Angeles Clippers/719 1.00 2.50
25 Milwaukee Bucks/654 1.00 2.50
26 New Jersey Nets/673 1.00 2.50
27 New Orleans Hornets/688 1.00 2.50
28 Philadelphia 76ers/700 1.00 2.50
29 Portland Trail Blazers/700 1.00 2.50
30 Washington Wizards/700 1.00 2.50
31 Tracy McGrady/1000 1.00 2.50
32 Kenyon Martin/1000 1.00 2.50
33 LeBron James/2000 12.00 30.00
34 Carmelo Anthony/2000 1.00 2.50
35 Dwight Howard/3000 4.00 10.00
36 Emeka Okafor/3000 1.00 2.50
37 Shaquille O'Neal/2000 1.00 2.50
38 Ben Gordon/2000 1.00 2.50
39 Devin Harris/1362 1.00 2.50
40 Kris Humphries/839 1.00 2.50
41 Andre Iguodala/982 1.50 4.00
42 Luke Jackson/1366 1.00 2.50
43 Al Jefferson/1000 1.00 2.50
44 Josh Childress/1220 1.00 2.50
45 Jameer Nelson/1000 2.00 5.00
46 Kobe Bryant/1000 5.00 12.00
47 Kirk Snyder/896 1.00 2.50
48 Sebastian Telfair/1756 1.00 2.50
49 Andris Biedrins/868 1.50 4.00
50 Shaun Livingston/2000 1.00 2.50
51 Robert Swift/813 1.00 2.50
52 Rafael Araujo/877 1.00 2.50
53 Lamar Odom/560 1.00 2.50
54 Luol Deng/1000 1.00 2.50
55 J.R. Smith/1000 1.00 2.50
56 Trevor Ariza/1000 1.00 2.50
57 Dwyane Wade/2000 4.00 10.00
58 Peter John Ramos/626 1.00 2.50
59 Carlos Arroyo/633 1.00 2.50
60 Amare Stoudemire/1000 1.00 2.50
61 Jamal Crawford/739 1.00 2.50
62 Quentin Richardson/548 1.00 2.50
63 Marquis Daniels/688 1.00 2.50
64 Corey Maggette/672 1.00 2.50
65 Yao Ming/1000 1.25 3.00
66 Samuel Dalembert/578 1.50 4.00
67 David Harrison/814 1.00 2.50
68 Chris Duhon/963 1.00 2.50
69 Bonzi Wells/580 1.00 2.50
70 Kevin Garnett/1000 1.00 2.50
71 Dirk Nowitzki/907 1.00 2.50
72 Josh Smith/800 2.00 5.00
73 Allen Iverson/604 1.00 2.50
74 Tim Duncan/1000 1.25 3.00
75 Kyle Korver/800 1.00 2.50
76 Rashard Lewis/800 1.00 2.50
78 Stephon Marbury/800 1.00 2.50

2004 eTopps ECON Cleveland

These cards were given away to VIP attendees to the 2004 edition of The National Sports Collectors Convention in Cleveland. Each card features a famous Cleveland area athlete with The National logo at the top of the card and the eTopps and player names at the bottom.

2 Larry Nance/860* 1.50 4.00

2005 eTopps

1 Al Harrington/463 1.25 3.00
2 Paul Pierce/527 3.00 8.00
3 Emeka Okafor/672 1.00 2.50
4 Kirk Hinrich/690 1.00 2.50
5 Lebron James/1000 6.00 15.00
6 Dirk Nowitzki/577 1.50 4.00
7 Carmelo Anthony/1000 1.00 2.50
8 Ben Wallace/605 1.00 2.50
9 Baron Davis/594 1.00 2.50
10 Yao Ming/695 2.00 5.00
11 Jermaine O'Neal/602 2.00 5.00
12 Elton Brand/620 1.00 2.50
13 Kobe Bryant/1000 5.00 12.00
14 Pau Gasol/551 1.00 2.50
15 Dwyane Wade/1500 1.25 3.00
16 Desmond Mason/461 1.50 4.00
17 Kevin Garnett/1000 1.25 3.00
18 Vince Carter/645 1.00 2.50
19 J.R. Smith/534 10.00 25.00
20 Stephon Marbury/529 1.00 2.50
21 Dwight Howard/937 1.25 3.00
22 Allen Iverson/905 1.00 2.50
23 Steve Nash/641 1.00 2.50
24 Zach Randolph/481 1.25 3.00
25 Mike Bibby/564 1.00 2.50
26 Tim Duncan/983 1.25 3.00
27 Ray Allen/602 1.25 3.00
28 Chris Bosh/525 1.50 4.00
29 Carlos Boozer/490 1.25 3.00
30 Gilbert Arenas/702 1.00 2.50
31 Bobby Simmons/504 1.00 2.50
32 Andres Nocioni/590 1.00 2.50
33 Udonis Haslem/544 1.00 2.50
34 Tayshaun Prince/685 1.00 2.50
35 Primoz Brezec/512 1.00 2.50
36 Nenad Krstic/554 1.00 2.50
37 Rafer Alston/493 1.00 2.50
38 Damon Jones/528 1.00 2.50
39 Brent Barry/525 1.00 2.50
40 Earl Boykins/500 1.50 4.00
41 Gerald Green/1500 1.00 2.50
42 Francisco Garcia/1000 1.00 2.50
43 Joey Graham/579 1.00 2.50
44 Deron Williams/1334 2.00 5.00
45 Andrew Bogut/2000 1.00 2.50
46 Chris Paul/2000 4.00 10.00
47 Hakim Warrick/1000 1.00 2.50
48 Antoine Wright/662 1.00 2.50
49 Rashad McCants/1000 1.00 2.50
50 Sarunas Jasikevicius/847 1.00 2.50
51 Channing Frye/1000 1.00 2.50
52 Ike Diogu/945 1.00 2.50
53 Danny Granger/1000 3.00 8.00
54 Charlie Villanueva/906 1.00 2.50
55 Andrew Bynum/844 4.00 10.00
56 Marvin Williams/2000 1.00 2.50
57 Raymond Felton/1156 1.00 2.50
58 Martell Webster/1000 1.00 2.50
59 Sean May/1000 1.00 2.50
60 Julius Hodge/565 1.00 2.50

2005 eTopps Autographs

AI1 Allen Iverson 50.00 125.00
2001 eTopps/40
AI2 Allen Iverson 50.00 125.00
2002 eTopps/40
AI3 Allen Iverson 50.00 125.00
2003 eTopps/40
DW1 Dwyane Wade 75.00 150.00
2003 eTopps/63
ES1 Steve Nash 200.00 350.00
Dwyane Wade
2005 eTopps Event Series

2005 eTopps Classic

1 Bill Russell/1500 2.50 6.00
2 Elgin Baylor/925 3.00 8.00
4 Oscar Robertson/934 3.00 8.00
5 Willis Reed/672 2.50 6.00
6 Spud Webb/506 3.00 8.00
7 Bill Walton/768 3.00 8.00
8 Chris Mullin/525 3.00 8.00
9 Darryl Dawkins/537 3.00 8.00
10 Earl Monroe/562 3.00 8.00
11 Hal Greer/563 3.00 8.00
12 John Havlicek/759 3.00 8.00
13 Moses Malone/670 2.50 6.00
14 Phil Jackson/589 3.00 8.00
15 Robert Parish/586 2.50 6.00
16 Gail Goodrich/485 5.00 12.00
17 Dolph Schayes/579 2.50 6.00
18 Manute Bol/519 2.50 6.00
19 Bob Pettit/496 4.00 10.00
20 Tom Heinsohn/592 3.00 8.00
21 Magic Johnson/1000 4.00 10.00
22 Dominique Wilkins/635 3.00 8.00
23 Isiah Thomas/941 3.00 8.00
24 Dennis Rodman/849 4.00 10.00

2005 eTopps Playoffs

1 Suns and Heat Sweep/514 1.25 3.00
2 Steve Nash/679 .75 2.00
3 Reggie Miller/1000 2.50 6.00
4 Tony Parker/706 .75 2.00
5 Rasheed Wallace/560 1.00 2.50
6 Robert Horry/609 1.25 3.00
7 Spurs Regain the Throne/1000 .75 2.00
8 Tim Duncan/950 1.25 3.00

2006 eTopps

1 Amare Stoudemire/425 2.50 6.00
1 Dwyane Wade/999 1.50 4.00
2 Chris Paul/999 1.00 2.50
3 Andrea Bargnani/1499 1.00 2.50
4 Randy Foye/999 1.00 2.50
5 Craig Smith/799 1.00 2.50
6 Allen Iverson/655 1.00 2.50
7 Lebron James/999 3.00 8.00
8 Tyrus Thomas/799 1.00 2.50
9 Adam Morrison/999 1.00 2.50
10 Jordan Farmar/799 8.00 20.00
11 Marcus Williams/799 1.00 2.50
12 Brandon Roy/799 2.50 6.00
13 Dirk Nowitzki/499 2.50 6.00
14 Kevin Garnett/799 1.25 3.00
15 Rudy Gay/999 1.25 3.00
16 Rajon Rondo/1025 4.00 10.00
17 Shelden Williams/799 1.00 2.50
19 Kobe Bryant/999 2.00 5.00
20 Lamarcus Aldridge/799 2.50 6.00
21 Allan Ray/799 1.00 2.50
22 J.J. Redick/799 1.00 2.50
23 Rodney Carney/799 1.00 2.50
24 Tim Duncan/405 4.00 10.00
25 Vince Carter/699 1.00 2.50
26 Tracy McGrady/699 1.00 2.50
27 Renaldo Balkman/699 1.00 2.50
28 Josh Boone/699 1.00 2.50
29 Daniel Gibson/699 1.00 2.50
30 Shaquille O'Neal/413 6.00 15.00
31 Carmelo Anthony/699 1.00 2.50
32 Ronnie Brewer/699 1.00 2.50
33 Patrick O'Bryant/699 1.00 2.50
34 Hilton Armstrong/699 1.00 2.50
35 Alexander Johnson/699 1.00 2.50
36 Steve Nash/434 2.00 5.00
37 David Lee/499 1.50 4.00
38 Paul Millsap/699 1.00 2.50
39 Thabo Sefolosha/699 1.00 2.50
40 Kyle Lowry/599 1.50 4.00
41 Jorge Garbajosa/699 1.00 2.50
42 Yao Ming/399 6.00 15.00

2006 eTopps Event Series National VIP Promos

DW Dwyane Wade 2.00 5.00

2006 eTopps Playoffs

9 Dwyane Wade/1161 1.00 2.50

2006 eTopps Autographs

CA1 Carmelo Anthony 2006 eTopps McDonald's/72
25.00 60.00
CP1 Chris Paul 2006 eTopps McDonald's/112 25.00
60.00
DR1 Dennis Rodman 2005 eTopps Classic/50 20.00
50.00

2006 eTopps McDonald's

1 Jermaine O'Neal 2.00 5.00
2 Chris Paul 1.00 2.50
3 Kenny Smith 3.00 8.00
4 Carmelo Anthony 2.50 6.00
5 Shaheen Holloway 3.00 8.00
6 Shaquille O'Neal 1.50 4.00
7 Magic Johnson 1.50 4.00
10 Elton Brand 2.00 5.00
11 Chris Collins 2.00 5.00
12 Tommy Amaker 2.00 5.00
13 Richard Hamilton 1.50 4.00
14 Vince Carter 1.50 4.00
15 Corey Maggette 1.50 4.00
16 Charlie Villanueva 1.50 4.00

2007 eTopps

1 Jermaine O'Neal/699 1.25 3.00
2 Rashard Lewis/699 1.00 2.50
3 Al Horford/999 1.50 4.00
4 Luis Scola/799 1.00 2.50
5 Mike Conley/999 1.00 2.50
6 Kevin Garnett/544 2.00 5.00
7 Chris Paul/699 1.00 2.50
8 Yi Jianlian/999 1.00 2.50
9 Sean Williams/699 1.00 2.50
10 Ray Allen/699 1.00 2.50
11 Greg Oden/1499 1.25 3.00
12 Javaris Crittenton/599 1.00 2.50
13 Dwight Howard/749 1.25 3.00
14 Carmelo Anthony/699 1.25 3.00
15 Glen Davis/749 1.25 3.00
16 Nick Young/749 1.25 3.00
17 Jason Richardson/699 1.00 2.50
18 Kobe Bryant/999 5.00 12.00
19 Kevin Durant/1499 15.00 40.00
20 Zach Randolph/352 8.00 20.00
21 Julian Wright/749 1.00 2.50
22 Joakim Noah/749 1.50 4.00
23 Deron Williams/699 1.25 3.00
24 Chris Bosh/699 1.00 2.50
25 Rodney Stuckey/749 1.00 2.50
26 D.J. Strawberry/749 1.00 2.50
27 Dwyane Wade/899 1.50 4.00
28 Arron Afflalo/699 1.00 2.50
29 Al Thornton/1060 1.00 2.50
30 Tony Parker/499 2.00 5.00
31 Shaquille O'Neal/499 2.00 5.00
32 Brandan Wright/699 1.00 2.50
33 Acie Law/499 1.00 2.50
34 LeBron James/999 6.00 15.00
35 Allen Iverson/649 1.00 2.50
36 Dirk Nowitzki/649 1.00 2.50
37 Corey Brewer/699 1.00 2.50
38 Jeff Green/699 1.25 3.00
39 Jason Kidd/439 2.00 5.00
40 Vince Carter/599 1.00 2.50
41 Thaddeus Young/749 1.00 2.50
42 Jason Smith/709 1.00 2.50
43 Spencer Hawes/499 6.00 15.00
44 Daequan Cook/699 1.00 2.50

2007 eTopps Autographs

BR1 Bill Russell 125.00 250.00
2005 eTopps Classic/50
VC5 Vince Carter 25.00 60.00
2006 eTopps McDonald's/75

2008 eTopps

1 Chris Paul/599 1.50 4.00
2 Eric Gordon/749 3.00 8.00
3 Michael Beasley/999 2.00 5.00
4 Kevin Love/749 8.00 20.00
5 Brook Lopez/749 2.50 6.00
6 Dwight Howard/699 2.00 5.00
7 Marc Gasol/699 3.00 8.00
8 Sun Yue/699 1.00 2.50
9 Joe Johnson/639 2.50 6.00
10 Kevin Garnett/699 2.00 5.00
11 Allen Iverson/670 1.25 3.00
12 Kobe Bryant/484 10.00 25.00
13 O.J. Mayo/899 2.50 6.00
14 Chris Bosh/499 2.00 5.00
15 D.J. Augustin/699 1.25 3.00
16 Danilo Gallinari/561 3.00 8.00
17 Russell Westbrook/699 25.00 60.00
18 Carmelo Anthony/499 2.50 6.00
19 Derrick Rose/999 8.00 20.00
20 Rudy Fernandez/649 1.25 3.00
21 Marreese Speights/599 1.00 2.50
22 Dwyane Wade/499 5.00 12.00
23 Mario Chalmers/599 1.50 4.00
24 Jason Thompson/499 1.50 4.00
25 Shaquille O'Neal/499 2.50 6.00
26 Roy Hibbert/574 2.00 5.00
27 Ray Allen/649 1.50 4.00
28 Deron Williams/649 1.00 2.50
29 Kevin Durant/799 4.00 10.00
30 Anthony Morrow/649 1.50 4.00
31 Luc Mbah A Moute/649 1.00 2.50
32 LeBron James/529 10.00 25.00
44P Barack Obama/999 8.00 20.00

1995-96 E-XL

The 1995-96 Skybox E-XL set was issued in one series totalling 100 cards. Only the top veterans and rookies in the league were selected for inclusion within this premium brand set. The 6-card packs retailed for $4.99 each. Cards are numbered alphabetically within teams. The only subset is Untouchable (91-99). The product picks up where the 1994-95 SkyBox Emotion issue left off. Each player card features silhouetted action photo over a multi-colored background, framed by one of five different shaped die cut window designs. Only the player image and multi-colored backgrounds are UV coated. The rest of the card is non-UV coated, giving the card a unique look and feel. A non-numbered Grant Hill promo card was issued to preview the set.

COMPLETE SET (100) 15.00 40.00
1 Stacey Augmon .30 .75
2 Mookie Blaylock .25 .60
3 Christian Laettner .30 .75
4 Dana Barros .25 .60
5 Dino Radja .25 .60
6 Eric Williams RC .40 1.00
7 Kenny Anderson .30 .75
8 Larry Johnson .40 1.00
9 Glen Rice .40 1.00
10 Michael Jordan 3.00 8.00
11 Toni Kukoc .40 1.00
12 Scottie Pippen .60 1.50
13 Dennis Rodman .75 2.00
14 Terrell Brandon .25 .60
15 Bobby Phills .25 .60
16 Bob Sura RC .30 .75
17 Jim Jackson .25 .60
18 Jason Kidd .60 1.50
19 Jamal Mashburn .40 1.00
20 Mahmoud Abdul-Rauf .25 .60
21 Antonio McDyess RC .50 1.25
22 Dikembe Mutombo .40 1.00
23 Joe Dumars .40 1.00
24 Grant Hill .60 1.50
25 Allan Houston .30 .75
26 Joe Smith RC .50 1.25
27 Latrell Sprewell .40 1.00
28 Kevin Willis .25 .60
29 Sam Cassell .40 1.00
30 Clyde Drexler .50 1.25
31 Robert Horry .30 .75
32 Hakeem Olajuwon .50 1.25
33 Derrick McKey .25 .60
34 Reggie Miller .50 1.25
35 Rik Smits .30 .75
36 Brent Barry RC .60 1.50
37 Loy Vaught .25 .60
38 Brian Williams .25 .60
39 Cedric Ceballos .25 .60
40 Magic Johnson 1.00 2.50
41 Nick Van Exel .40 1.00
42 Tim Hardaway .40 1.00
43 Alonzo Mourning .50 1.25
44 Kurt Thomas RC .40 1.00
45 Walt Williams .25 .60
46 Vin Baker .30 .75
47 Shawn Respert RC .30 .75
48 Glenn Robinson .30 .75
49 Kevin Garnett RC 3.00 8.00
50 Tom Gugliotta .25 .60
51 Isaiah Rider .40 1.00
52 Shawn Bradley .25 .60
53 Chris Childs .25 .60
54 Ed O'Bannon RC .30 .75
55 Patrick Ewing .50 1.25
56 Anthony Mason .25 .60
57 Charles Oakley .30 .75
58 Horace Grant .30 .75
59 Anfernee Hardaway .60 1.50
60 Shaquille O'Neal 1.00 2.50
61 Derrick Coleman .30 .75
62 Jerry Stackhouse RC 1.25 3.00
63 Clarence Weatherspoon .25 .60
64 Charles Barkley .60 1.50
65 Michael Finley RC 1.25 3.00
66 Kevin Johnson .40 1.00
67 Clifford Robinson .25 .60
68 Arvydas Sabonis RC .75 2.00
69 Rod Strickland .25 .60
70 Tyus Edney RC .40 1.00
71 Billy Owens .25 .60
72 Mitch Richmond .40 1.00
73 Sean Elliott .40 1.00
74 Avery Johnson .30 .75
75 David Robinson .60 1.50
76 Shawn Kemp .40 1.00
77 Gary Payton .40 1.00
78 Detlef Schrempf .40 1.00
79 Tracy Murray .25 .60
80 Damon Stoudamire RC 1.00 2.50
81 Sharone Wright .25 .60
82 Jeff Hornacek .30 .75
83 Karl Malone .50 1.25
84 John Stockton .50 1.25
85 Greg Anthony .25 .60
86 Bryant Reeves RC .30 .75
87 Byron Scott .30 .75
88 Juwan Howard .40 1.00
89 Gheorghe Muresan .25 .60
90 Rasheed Wallace RC 1.25 3.00
91 Steve Smith UNT .15 .40
92 Dikembe Mutombo UNT .20 .50
93 Brent Barry UNT .30 .75
94 Glenn Robinson UNT .15 .40
95 Armon Gilliam UNT .12 .30
96 Nick Anderson UNT .12 .30
97 Gary Trent UNT .20 .50
98 Brian Grant UNT .15 .40
99 Bryant Reeves UNT .15 .40
100 Checklist .25 .60
NNO Grant Hill Promo 1.00 2.50

1995-96 E-XL Blue

COMPLETE SET (100) 30.00 80.00
*BLUE: .75X TO 2X BASE CARD HI
ONE OR MORE BLUES PER PACK

1995-96 E-XL A Cut Above

Randomly inserted in hobby and retail packs at a rate of one in 130, this 10-card die-cut insert set features a selection of the NBA's elite stars. Each card front features a unique framing of two different, die-cut photos surrounded by a blue border. Card backs contain an action photo and brief commentary and are numbered as "X of 10".

COMPLETE SET (10) 60.00 120.00
STATED ODDS 1:130
1 Scottie Pippen 8.00 20.00
2 Jason Kidd 8.00 20.00
3 Grant Hill 8.00 20.00
4 Joe Smith 3.00 8.00
5 Hakeem Olajuwon 6.00 15.00
6 Magic Johnson 12.00 30.00
7 Shaquille O'Neal 8.00 20.00
8 Jerry Stackhouse 8.00 20.00
9 Charles Barkley 8.00 20.00
10 David Robinson 8.00 20.00

1995-96 E-XL Natural Born Thrillers

Randomly inserted in hobby and retail packs at a rate of one in 48, this 10-card set highlights a selection of crowd-pleasing players who do incredible things on the court. Each card features a multi-layered die-cut design. Card backs are black and textured with the player's name and a brief commentary in gold foil. The cards are numbered as "X of 10". A non-numbered Jerry Stackhouse card was sent out to preview the set.

COMPLETE SET (10) 125.00 300.00
STATED ODDS 1:48
1 Michael Jordan 100.00 250.00
2 Antonio McDyess 2.00 5.00
3 Grant Hill 5.00 12.00
4 Clyde Drexler 4.00 10.00
5 Kevin Garnett 10.00 25.00
6 Anfernee Hardaway 8.00 20.00
7 Jerry Stackhouse 5.00 12.00
8 Michael Finley 5.00 12.00
9 Shawn Kemp 3.00 8.00
10 Damon Stoudamire 4.00 10.00
NNO Jerry Stackhouse PROMO 2.50 6.00

1995-96 E-XL No Boundaries

Randomly inserted exclusively in hobby packs at a rate of one in 18, this 10-card set features players that can bust open a game on a special die cut designed card. Card fronts have metallic backgrounds with an action shot of the player and the player's name which is written in gold foil. Card backs feature the a head shot of the player in a die-cut circle. The cards are numbered as "X of 10".

COMPLETE SET (10) 25.00 60.00
STATED ODDS 1:18 HOBBY
1 Michael Jordan 12.00 30.00
2 Antonio McDyess 1.25 3.00
3 Hakeem Olajuwon 2.50 6.00
4 Magic Johnson 5.00 12.00
5 Vin Baker 1.50 4.00
6 Patrick Ewing 2.50 6.00
7 Anfernee Hardaway 3.00 8.00
8 Jerry Stackhouse 3.00 8.00
9 Gary Payton 2.00 5.00
10 Damon Stoudamire 2.50 6.00

1995-96 E-XL Unstoppable

Randomly inserted in hobby and retail packs at a rate of one in 6, this 20-card set features 10 players who are "unstoppable" inside the paint and 10 who are "unstoppable" from outside. Card fronts have a large action shot of the player with the player's name written vertically along the border. Card backs have a textured background photo with a brief commentary on the player. The cards are numbered as "X of 20".

COMPLETE SET (20) 20.00 50.00
STATED ODDS 1:6
1 Alan Henderson 1.25 3.00
2 Glen Rice 1.25 3.00
3 Scottie Pippen 2.00 5.00
4 Dennis Rodman 2.50 6.00
5 Terrell Brandon .75 2.00
6 Jason Kidd 2.00 5.00
7 Grant Hill 2.00 5.00
8 Joe Smith 1.50 4.00
9 Sam Cassell 1.25 3.00
10 Reggie Miller 1.50 4.00
11 Alonzo Mourning 1.50 4.00
12 Shaquille O'Neal 3.00 8.00
13 Charles Barkley 2.00 5.00
14 Clifford Robinson .75 2.00
15 Sean Elliott 1.25 3.00
16 David Robinson 2.00 5.00
17 Shawn Kemp 1.25 3.00
18 Karl Malone 1.50 4.00
19 John Stockton 1.50 4.00
20 Juwan Howard 1.25 3.00

1996-97 E-X2000

The SkyBox E-X2000 set was issued in one series totalling 80 cards. Cards were available in 2-card packs with a suggested retail price of $3.99. Card designs are similar to the 1995-96 Hoops SkyView insert with a clear plastic design inside of a frame with a photo of the player overlapped. The cards are designated as Condition Sensitive due to the easy nature of damaging the cards. A Grant Hill Emerald exchange card was also inserted at one in 500 packs. This card was exchangeable for a Grant Hill autographed ball. Reportedly, only 75 balls were signed for the promotion. Also available to dealers who purchased a case was a blow-up Grant Hill E-X2000 card which was serial numbered to 3000. A regular issue-size Grant Hill promo card was also released and is listed below at the end of the set.

COMPLETE SET (82) 60.00 120.00
EMERALD EXCH: STATED ODDS 1:500
1 Christian Laettner .50 1.25
2 Dikembe Mutombo .60 1.50
3 Steve Smith .50 1.25
4 Antoine Walker RC 1.50 4.00
5 David Wesley .40 1.00
6 Tony Delk RC 1.00 2.50
7 Anthony Mason .40 1.00
8 Glen Rice .60 1.50
9 Michael Jordan 8.00 20.00
10 Scottie Pippen 1.00 2.50
11 Dennis Rodman 1.25 3.00
12 Terrell Brandon .40 1.00
13 Chris Mills .40 1.00
14 Shawn Bradley .40 1.00
15 Michael Finley .75 2.00
16 Dale Ellis .40 1.00
17 Antonio McDyess .60 1.50
18 Joe Dumars .60 1.50
19 Grant Hill 1.00 2.50
20 Chris Mullin .60 1.50
21 Joe Smith .50 1.25
22 Latrell Sprewell .60 1.50
23 Charles Barkley 1.00 2.50
24 Clyde Drexler .75 2.00
25 Hakeem Olajuwon .75 2.00
26 Erick Dampier RC 1.00 2.50
27 Reggie Miller .75 2.00
28 Loy Vaught .40 1.00
29 Lorenzen Wright RC .75 2.00
30 Kobe Bryant RC 20.00 50.00
31 Eddie Jones .60 1.50
32 Shaquille O'Neal 1.50 4.00
33 Nick Van Exel .60 1.50
34 Tim Hardaway .60 1.50
35 Jamal Mashburn .50 1.25
36 Alonzo Mourning .75 2.00
37 Ray Allen RC 4.00 10.00
38 Vin Baker .50 1.25
39 Glenn Robinson .50 1.25
40 Kevin Garnett 1.50 4.00
41 Tom Gugliotta .40 1.00
42 Stephon Marbury RC 2.50 6.00
43 Kendall Gill .40 1.00
44 Jim Jackson .40 1.00
45 Kerry Kittles RC 1.00 2.50
46 Patrick Ewing .75 2.00
47 Larry Johnson .60 1.50
48 John Wallace RC 1.00 2.50
49 Nick Anderson .40 1.00
50 Horace Grant .50 1.25
51 Anfernee Hardaway 1.00 2.50
52 Derrick Coleman .50 1.25
53 Allen Iverson RC 6.00 15.00
54 Jerry Stackhouse .75 2.00
55 Cedric Ceballos .40 1.00
56 Kevin Johnson .60 1.50
57 Jason Kidd 1.00 2.50
58 Clifford Robinson .40 1.00
59 Arvydas Sabonis .50 1.25
60 Rasheed Wallace .75 2.00
61 Mahmoud Abdul-Rauf .40 1.00
62 Brian Grant .50 1.25
63 Mitch Richmond .60 1.50
64 Sean Elliott .60 1.50
65 David Robinson 1.00 2.50
66 Dominique Wilkins .75 2.00
67 Shawn Kemp .60 1.50
68 Gary Payton .60 1.50
69 Detlef Schrempf .60 1.50
70 Marcus Camby RC 1.50 4.00
71 Damon Stoudamire .50 1.25
72 Walt Williams .40 1.00
73 Shandon Anderson RC .75 2.00
74 Karl Malone .75 2.00
75 John Stockton .75 2.00
76 Shareef Abdur-Rahim RC 1.50 4.00
77 Bryant Reeves .40 1.00
78 Roy Rogers RC .75 2.00
79 Juwan Howard .50 1.25
80 Chris Webber .75 2.00
81 Checklist .25 .60
82 Checklist .25 .60
NNO Grant Hill Blow-Up/3000 8.00 20.00
NNO Grant Hill AU Ball/75 100.00 200.00
NNO Grant Hill PROMO 1.00 2.50

1996-97 E-X2000 Credentials

*STARS: 8X TO 20X BASE CARD HI
*RCs: 2.5X TO 6X BASE HI
STATED PRINT RUN 499 SERIAL #'d SETS
9 Michael Jordan 500.00 1000.00
10 Scottie Pippen 40.00 100.00
11 Dennis Rodman 60.00 150.00
19 Grant Hill 30.00 80.00
22 Latrell Sprewell 25.00 60.00
23 Charles Barkley 25.00 60.00
27 Reggie Miller 40.00 100.00
30 Kobe Bryant 1000.00 1500.00
32 Shaquille O'Neal 40.00 100.00
37 Ray Allen 60.00 120.00
42 Stephon Marbury 20.00 50.00
46 Patrick Ewing 20.00 50.00
47 Larry Johnson 15.00 40.00
51 Anfernee Hardaway 40.00 100.00
53 Allen Iverson 150.00 400.00
67 Shawn Kemp 25.00 60.00
68 Gary Payton 15.00 40.00
75 John Stockton 20.00 50.00
76 Shareef Abdur-Rahim 15.00 40.00
80 Chris Webber 30.00 80.00

1996-97 E-X2000 A Cut Above

Randomly inserted in packs at a rate of one in 288, this 10-card set features a sawblade die cut at the top of the card.

COMPLETE SET (10) 1700.00 2200.00
STATED ODDS 1:288
1 Kevin Garnett 50.00 120.00
2 Anfernee Hardaway 100.00 175.00
3 Grant Hill 50.00 120.00
4 Allen Iverson 60.00 150.00
5 Michael Jordan 1000.00 1500.00
6 Shawn Kemp 50.00 120.00
7 Hakeem Olajuwon 20.00 50.00
8 Shaquille O'Neal 60.00 150.00
9 Glenn Robinson 12.00 30.00
10 Dennis Rodman 60.00 150.00

1996-97 E-X2000 Net Assets

Randomly inserted in packs at a rate of one in 20, this 20-card set features a precision cut net in the background of the card.

COMPLETE SET (20) 100.00 250.00
STATED ODDS 1:20
1 Ray Allen 4.00 10.00
2 Charles Barkley 3.00 8.00
3 Patrick Ewing 2.50 6.00
4 Kevin Garnett 5.00 12.00
5 Anfernee Hardaway 3.00 8.00
6 Grant Hill 3.00 8.00
7 Allen Iverson 5.00 12.00
8 Michael Jordan 75.00 200.00
9 Jason Kidd 3.00 8.00
10 Kerry Kittles 1.00 2.50
11 Karl Malone 2.50 6.00
12 Alonzo Mourning 2.50 6.00
13 Shaquille O'Neal 5.00 12.00
14 Gary Payton 2.00 5.00
15 Bryant Reeves 1.25 3.00
16 David Robinson 3.00 8.00
17 Dennis Rodman 4.00 10.00
18 Joe Smith 1.50 4.00
19 Damon Stoudamire 1.50 4.00
20 Chris Webber 2.50 6.00

1996-97 E-X2000 Star Date 2000

Randomly inserted in packs at a rate of one in 9, this 15-card set features many of the players from the 1996-97 rookie class on a futuristic outer space background.

COMPLETE SET (15) 20.00 50.00
STATED ODDS 1:9
1 Shareef Abdur-Rahim 1.00 2.50
2 Ray Allen 2.50 6.00
3 Kobe Bryant 12.00 30.00
4 Marcus Camby 1.00 2.50
5 Erick Dampier .60 1.50
6 Juwan Howard .50 1.25
7 Allen Iverson 3.00 8.00
8 Jason Kidd 1.00 2.50
9 Kerry Kittles .60 1.50
10 Stephon Marbury 1.50 4.00
11 Jamal Mashburn .50 1.25
12 Antonio McDyess .60 1.50
13 Joe Smith .50 1.25
14 Damon Stoudamire .50 1.25
15 Antoine Walker 1.00 2.50

1997-98 E-X2001

The 1997-98 SkyBox E-X2001 hobby set only was issued in one series totalling 82 cards - 80 basic and two checklists. Each pack contained two cards that carried a suggested retail price of $3.99. The cards feature a semi-clear plastic background with the player die cut over the top of the card. A Grant Hill sample card was also released and is listed at the end of the base set.

COMPLETE SET (82) 20.00 50.00
1 Grant Hill .75 2.00
2 Kevin Garnett .75 2.00
3 Allen Iverson 1.00 2.50
4 Anfernee Hardaway .75 2.00
5 Dennis Rodman 1.00 2.50
6 Shawn Kemp .50 1.25
7 Shaquille O'Neal 1.25 3.00
8 Kobe Bryant 2.50 6.00
9 Michael Jordan 6.00 15.00
10 Marcus Camby .50 1.25
11 Scottie Pippen .75 2.00
12 Antoine Walker .50 1.25
13 Stephon Marbury .60 1.50
14 Shareef Abdur-Rahim .50 1.25
15 Jerry Stackhouse .50 1.25
16 Eddie Jones .50 1.25
17 Charles Barkley .75 2.00
18 David Robinson .75 2.00
19 Karl Malone .60 1.50
20 Damon Stoudamire .40 1.00
21 Patrick Ewing .60 1.50
22 Kerry Kittles .30 .75
23 Gary Payton .50 1.25
24 Glenn Robinson .40 1.00
25 Hakeem Olajuwon .60 1.50
26 John Starks .40 1.00
27 John Stockton .60 1.50
28 Vin Baker .40 1.00
29 Reggie Miller .60 1.50
30 Clyde Drexler .60 1.50
31 Alonzo Mourning .60 1.50
32 Juwan Howard .40 1.00
33 Ray Allen .60 1.50
34 Christian Laettner .40 1.00
35 Terrell Brandon .30 .75
36 Sean Elliott .50 1.25
37 Rod Strickland .30 .75
38 Rodney Rogers .30 .75
39 Donyell Marshall .30 .75
40 David Wesley .30 .75
41 Sam Cassell .40 1.00
42 Cedric Ceballos .30 .75
43 Mahmoud Abdul-Rauf .30 .75
44 Rik Smits .40 1.00
45 Lindsey Hunter .30 .75
46 Michael Finley .50 1.25
47 Steve Smith .40 1.00
48 Larry Johnson .50 1.25
49 Dikembe Mutombo .50 1.25
50 Tom Gugliotta .30 .75
51 Joe Dumars .50 1.25
52 Glen Rice .50 1.25
53 Bryant Reeves .30 .75
54 Tim Hardaway .50 1.25
55 Isaiah Rider .40 1.00
56 Rasheed Wallace .50 1.25
57 Jason Kidd .75 2.00
58 Joe Smith .40 1.00
59 Chris Webber .50 1.25
60 Mitch Richmond .50 1.25
61 Antonio McDyess .40 1.00
62 Bobby Jackson RC .75 2.00
63 Derek Anderson RC .60 1.50
64 Kelvin Cato RC .50 1.25
65 Jacque Vaughn RC .50 1.25
66 Tariq Abdul-Wahad RC .50 1.25
67 Johnny Taylor RC .50 1.25
68 Chris Anstey RC .40 1.00
69 Maurice Taylor RC .60 1.50
70 Antonio Daniels RC .60 1.50
71 Chauncey Billups RC 2.00 5.00
72 Austin Croshere RC .50 1.25
73 Brevin Knight RC .60 1.50
74 Keith Van Horn RC 1.00 2.50
75 Tim Duncan RC 5.00 12.00
76 Danny Fortson RC .60 1.50
77 Tim Thomas RC .75 2.00
78 Tony Battie RC .60 1.50
79 Tracy McGrady RC 4.00 10.00
80 Ron Mercer RC .75 2.00
81 Checklist (1-82) .30 .75
82 Checklist (inserts) .30 .75
S1 Grant Hill SAMPLE 1.25 3.00

1997-98 E-X2001 Essential Credentials Future

*VETS #'d 41-80: 25X TO 60X BASE HI
*VETS #'d 20-40: 30X TO 80X BASE HI
LOWER PRINT RUNS UNPRICED
1 Grant Hill/80 200.00 400.00
2 Kevin Garnett/79 150.00 400.00
3 Allen Iverson/78 300.00 600.00
4 Anfernee Hardaway/77 250.00 500.00
5 Dennis Rodman/76 300.00 600.00
6 Shawn Kemp/75 40.00 100.00
7 Shaquille O'Neal/74 250.00 500.00
8 Kobe Bryant/73 1000.00 1600.00
9 Michael Jordan/72 1500.00 2300.00
11 Scottie Pippen/70 150.00 300.00
15 Jerry Stackhouse/66 40.00 100.00
17 Charles Barkley/64 150.00 300.00
18 David Robinson/63 125.00 250.00
19 Karl Malone/62 125.00 250.00
21 Patrick Ewing/60 150.00 400.00
23 Gary Payton/58 100.00 200.00
24 Glenn Robinson/57 30.00 80.00
25 Hakeem Olajuwon/56 200.00 500.00
29 Reggie Miller/52 200.00 400.00
30 Clyde Drexler/51 50.00 125.00
31 Alonzo Mourning/50 125.00 250.00
33 Ray Allen/48 200.00 500.00
57 Jason Kidd/24 200.00 400.00
59 Chris Webber/22 250.00 500.00
60 Mitch Richmond/21 200.00 400.00
61 Antonio McDyess/20 80.00 200.00

1997-98 E-X2001 Essential Credentials Now

*VETS #'d 20-30: 30X TO 80X BASE HI
*VETS #'d 31-50: 25X TO 60X BASE HI
*VETS #'d 51-61: 20X TO 50X BASE HI
*RCs #'d 62-80: 10X TO 25X BASE HI
LOWER PRINT RUNS UNPRICED
21 Patrick Ewing/21 100.00 200.00
23 Gary Payton/23 125.00 250.00
25 Hakeem Olajuwon/25 175.00 350.00
27 John Stockton/27 75.00 150.00
29 Reggie Miller/29 150.00 300.00
30 Clyde Drexler/30 75.00 150.00
31 Alonzo Mourning/31 150.00 300.00
33 Ray Allen/33 60.00 120.00
52 Glen Rice/52 30.00 80.00
57 Jason Kidd/57 175.00 350.00
59 Chris Webber/59 100.00 200.00
60 Mitch Richmond/60 50.00 100.00
68 Chris Anstey/68 20.00 50.00
75 Tim Duncan/75 1500.00 2000.00

1997-98 E-X2001 Gravity Denied

Randomly inserted into packs at a rate of one in 24, this 20-card set features two die cut pieces, that form an "aerodynamic" photo of these NBA players in three separate windows.

COMPLETE SET (20) 40.00 100.00
STATED ODDS 1:24
1 Vin Baker 1.25 3.00
2 Charles Barkley 2.50 6.00
3 Tony Battie 1.00 2.50
4 Kobe Bryant 10.00 25.00
5 Patrick Ewing 2.00 5.00
6 Kevin Garnett 2.50 6.00
7 Anfernee Hardaway 2.50 6.00
8 Grant Hill 2.50 6.00
9 Michael Jordan 50.00 120.00
10 Shawn Kemp 1.50 4.00
11 Kerry Kittles 1.00 2.50
12 Karl Malone 2.00 5.00
13 Tracy McGrady 4.00 10.00
14 Hakeem Olajuwon 2.00 5.00
15 Shaquille O'Neal 4.00 10.00
16 Scottie Pippen 2.50 6.00
17 Jerry Stackhouse 1.50 4.00
18 Tim Thomas 1.25 3.00
19 Antoine Walker 1.50 4.00
20 Chris Webber 1.50 4.00

1997-98 E-X2001 Jambalaya

Randomly inserted into packs at a rate of one in 720, this 15-card set features the NBA's best jammers on a die cut background in the shape of an oval.

STATED ODDS 1:720
1 Allen Iverson 300.00 600.00
2 Anfernee Hardaway 200.00 400.00
3 Dennis Rodman 250.00 500.00
4 Grant Hill 200.00 400.00
5 Kevin Garnett 200.00 400.00
6 Michael Jordan 1500.00 3000.00
7 Shaquille O'Neal 250.00 500.00
8 Tim Duncan 400.00 800.00
9 Keith Van Horn 40.00 100.00
10 Stephon Marbury 100.00 175.00
11 Shareef Abdur-Rahim 40.00 100.00
12 Kobe Bryant 800.00 1200.00
13 Damon Stoudamire 50.00 125.00
14 Scottie Pippen 200.00 400.00
15 Eddie Jones 40.00 100.00

1997-98 E-X2001 Star Date 2001

Randomly inserted into packs at a rate of one in 12, this 15-card set features some of the best young stars in the NBA. The cards have a die cut "galaxy" background with silver rainbow holofoil.

COMPLETE SET (15) 12.50 30.00
STATED ODDS 1:12
1 Shareef Abdur-Rahim .75 2.00
2 Tony Battie .50 1.25
3 Kobe Bryant 8.00 20.00
4 Antonio Daniels .50 1.25
5 Tim Duncan 2.50 6.00
6 Adonal Foyle .40 1.00
7 Allen Iverson 1.50 4.00
8 Matt Maloney .50 1.25
9 Stephon Marbury 1.00 2.50
10 Tracy McGrady 2.00 5.00
11 Ron Mercer .60 1.50
12 Tim Thomas .60 1.50
13 Keith Van Horn .75 2.00
14 Jacque Vaughn .40 1.00
15 Antoine Walker .75 2.00

1997-98 E-X2001 Grant Hill Hawaii

This card, virtually identical to the basic Grant Hill SkyBox E-X2001 basic card, was given away to dealers who attended the annual 1998 Kit Young Hawaii Convention. The card is differentiated by a "Hawaii XIII palm tree" in gold foil on the front. The card back is not numbered, but listed as "sample".

S1 Grant Hill 6.00 15.00

1998-99 E-X Century

Continuing with the name change philosophy, this year's Fleer/SkyBox super premium set E-X Century, was released in three-card packs with a suggested retail price of $5.99. This 90 card set features 60 veterans and 30 prospects, which were slightly inserted at one in 1.5.

COMPLETE SET (1-90) 15.00 40.00
RC STATED ODDS 1:1.5
1 Keith Van Horn .40 1.00
2 Scottie Pippen .60 1.50
3 Tim Thomas .40 1.00
4 Stephon Marbury .50 1.25
5 Allen Iverson .75 2.00
6 Grant Hill .60 1.50
7 Tim Duncan .75 2.00
8 Latrell Sprewell .40 1.00
9 Ron Mercer .30 .75
10 Kobe Bryant 1.50 4.00
11 Antoine Walker .40 1.00
12 Reggie Miller .50 1.25
13 Kevin Garnett .60 1.50
14 Shaquille O'Neal 1.00 2.50
15 Karl Malone .50 1.25
16 Dennis Rodman .75 2.00
17 Tracy McGrady .60 1.50
18 Anfernee Hardaway .60 1.50
19 Shareef Abdur-Rahim .40 1.00
20 Marcus Camby .30 .75
21 Eddie Jones .40 1.00
22 Vin Baker .30 .75
23 Charles Barkley .60 1.50
24 Patrick Ewing .50 1.25
25 Jason Kidd .60 1.50
26 Mitch Richmond .40 1.00
27 Tim Hardaway .40 1.00
28 Glen Rice .40 1.00
29 Shawn Kemp .40 1.00
30 John Stockton .50 1.25
31 Ray Allen .50 1.25
32 Brevin Knight .25 .60
33 David Robinson .60 1.50
34 Juwan Howard .30 .75
35 Alonzo Mourning .50 1.25
36 Hakeem Olajuwon .50 1.25
37 Gary Payton .40 1.00
38 Damon Stoudamire .30 .75
39 Steve Smith .30 .75
40 Chris Webber .40 1.00
41 Michael Finley .40 1.00
42 Jayson Williams .25 .60
43 Maurice Taylor .25 .60
44 Jalen Rose .30 .75
45 Sam Cassell .30 .75
46 Jerry Stackhouse .40 1.00
47 Toni Kukoc .40 1.00
48 Charles Oakley .30 .75
49 Jim Jackson .25 .60
50 Dikembe Mutombo .40 1.00
51 Wesley Person .25 .60
52 Antonio Daniels .25 .60
53 Isaiah Rider .30 .75
54 Tom Gugliotta .25 .60
55 Antonio McDyess .30 .75
56 Jeff Hornacek .30 .75
57 Joe Dumars .40 1.00
58 Jamal Mashburn .30 .75
59 Donyell Marshall .25 .60
60 Glenn Robinson .30 .75
61 Jelani McCoy RC 1.00 2.50
62 Peja Stojakovic RC 2.50 6.00
63 Randell Jackson RC 1.00 2.50
64 Brad Miller RC 2.50 6.00
65 Corey Benjamin RC .60 1.50
66 Toby Bailey RC 1.00 2.50
67 Nazr Mohammed RC 1.00 2.50
68 Dirk Nowitzki RC 4.00 10.00
69 Andrae Patterson RC .75 2.00
70 Michael Dickerson RC 1.00 2.50
71 Cory Carr RC .75 2.00
72 Brian Skinner RC 1.00 2.50
73 Pat Garrity RC .75 2.00
74 Ricky Davis RC 1.50 4.00
75 Roshown McLeod RC .60 1.50
76 Matt Harpring RC 1.00 2.50
77 Jason Williams RC 2.50 6.00
78 Keon Clark RC 1.00 2.50
79 Al Harrington RC 1.50 4.00
80 Felipe Lopez RC .60 1.50
81 Michael Doleac RC .75 2.00
82 Paul Pierce RC 4.00 10.00
83 Robert Traylor RC 1.00 2.50
84 Raef LaFrentz RC 1.25 3.00
85 Michael Olowokandi RC 1.25 3.00
86 Mike Bibby RC 1.50 4.00
87 Antawn Jamison RC 1.50 4.00
88 Bonzi Wells RC 1.00 2.50
89 Vince Carter RC 5.00 12.00
90 Larry Hughes RC 2.00 5.00

1998-99 E-X Century Essential Credentials Future

*VETS #'d 71-90: 20X TO 50X BASE HI
*VETS #'d 41-70: 25X TO 60X BASE HI
*VETS #'d 31-40: 30X TO 80X BASE HI
*RCs #'d 15-30: 6X TO 15X BASE HI
LOWER PRINT RUNS UNPRICED
2 Scottie Pippen/89 100.00 250.00
5 Allen Iverson/86 75.00 150.00
6 Grant Hill/85 75.00 150.00
10 Kobe Bryant/81 600.00 1000.00
13 Kevin Garnett/78 100.00 200.00
16 Dennis Rodman/75 125.00 250.00
17 Tracy McGrady/74 40.00 100.00
18 Anfernee Hardaway/73 75.00 150.00
29 Shawn Kemp/62 50.00 100.00
30 John Stockton/61 40.00 100.00
31 Ray Allen/60 40.00 100.00
35 Alonzo Mourning/56 100.00 200.00
36 Hakeem Olajuwon/55 75.00 150.00
37 Gary Payton/54 50.00 100.00
40 Chris Webber/51 50.00 120.00
47 Toni Kukoc/44 100.00 175.00
68 Dirk Nowitzki/23 200.00 400.00

1998-99 E-X Century Essential Credentials Now

*VETS #'d 16-30: 40X TO 100X BASE HI
*VETS #'d 31-40: 30X TO 80X BASE HI
*VETS #'d 41-60: 25X TO 60X BASE HI
*RCs #'d 61-90: 4X TO 10X BASE HI
LOWER PRINT RUNS UNPRICED
16 Dennis Rodman/16 300.00 600.00
17 Tracy McGrady/17 100.00 200.00
18 Anfernee Hardaway/18 150.00 300.00
21 Eddie Jones/21 75.00 150.00
29 Shawn Kemp/29 75.00 150.00
30 John Stockton/30 75.00 150.00
31 Ray Allen/31 50.00 120.00
35 Alonzo Mourning/35 75.00 150.00
36 Hakeem Olajuwon/36 60.00 150.00
37 Gary Payton/37 65.00 125.00
40 Chris Webber/40 60.00 150.00
47 Toni Kukoc/47 100.00 175.00
68 Dirk Nowitzki/68 200.00 400.00
77 Jason Williams/77 40.00 100.00
82 Paul Pierce/82 75.00 200.00
86 Mike Bibby/86 40.00 80.00
89 Vince Carter/89 150.00 300.00

1998-99 E-X Century Authen-Kicks

Randomly inserted in packs, this 12-card set features actual pieces of game worn shoes inserted into the card. The cards are sequentially numbered, with each player having a different serial number due to different shoe sizes.

PRINT RUNS LISTED BELOW
1 Antawn Jamison/225 15.00 40.00
2 Tracy McGrady/225 30.00 80.00
3 Ron Mercer/180 15.00 40.00
4 Antoine Walker/125 20.00 50.00
5 Mike Bibby/165 25.00 50.00
6 Michael Dickerson/230 15.00 40.00
7 Larry Hughes/115 30.00 60.00
8 Raef LaFrentz/160 15.00 40.00
9 Keith Van Horn/125 25.00 60.00
9AU Keith Van Horn AU/44 40.00 100.00
10 Tim Thomas/215 15.00 40.00
11 Allen Iverson/165 50.00 120.00
12 Robert Traylor/215 15.00 40.00

1998-99 E-X Century Dunk 'N Go Nuts

Randomly inserted in packs at one in 36, this 20-card set features players who spend most of their time airborne. The card design is very similar to a "Dunkin' Donuts" box.

COMPLETE SET (20) 250.00 500.00
STATED ODDS 1:36
1 Tim Thomas 6.00 15.00
2 Grant Hill 15.00 40.00
3 Shareef Abdur-Rahim 6.00 15.00
4 Tim Duncan 30.00 80.00
5 Allen Iverson 25.00 60.00
6 Kobe Bryant 75.00 200.00
7 Antoine Walker 8.00 20.00
8 Kevin Garnett 20.00 50.00
9 Shaquille O'Neal 30.00 80.00
10 Tracy McGrady 10.00 25.00
11 Antawn Jamison 10.00 25.00
12 Vince Carter 30.00 80.00
13 Robert Traylor 6.00 15.00
14 Scottie Pippen 12.00 30.00
15 Michael Jordan 500.00 800.00
16 Michael Olowokandi 8.00 20.00
17 Anfernee Hardaway 25.00 60.00
18 Michael Dickerson 6.00 15.00
19 Ron Mercer 5.00 12.00
20 Felipe Lopez 4.00 10.00

1998-99 E-X Century Generation E-X

Randomly inserted in packs at one in 18, this 15-card set focuses on top rookies and young players. The cards feature a black bordered background.

COMPLETE SET (15) 12.50 30.00
STATED ODDS 1:18
1 Larry Hughes 1.00 2.50
2 Michael Olowokandi .60 1.50
3 Tim Duncan 1.50 4.00
4 Vince Carter 2.50 6.00
5 Antawn Jamison .75 2.00
6 Kevin Garnett 1.25 3.00
7 Al Harrington .75 2.00
8 Mike Bibby .75 2.00
9 Raef LaFrentz .60 1.50
10 Ron Mercer .60 1.50
11 Tracy McGrady 1.25 3.00
12 Kobe Bryant 6.00 15.00
13 Keith Van Horn .75 2.00
14 Stephon Marbury 1.00 2.50
15 Allen Iverson 1.50 4.00

1999-00 E-X

The 1999-00 E-X set was released in March,2000 as a 90-card set, with 60 veterans and 30 rookies. Each of the rookies were serial numbered to 3499. Each pack contained 3-cards and carried a suggested retail price of 3.99.

COMPLETE SET (90) 40.00 100.00
COMPLETE SET w/o RC (60) 15.00 30.00
RC PRINT RUN 3499 SERIAL #'d SETS
1 Stephon Marbury .30 .75
2 Antawn Jamison .40 1.00
3 Patrick Ewing .50 1.25
4 Nick Anderson .25 .60
5 Charles Barkley .60 1.50
6 Marcus Camby .30 .75
7 Ron Mercer .30 .75
8 Avery Johnson .30 .75
9 Maurice Taylor .25 .60
10 Isaiah Rider .30 .75
11 Dirk Nowitzki .75 2.00
12 Damon Stoudamire .30 .75
13 Alonzo Mourning .50 1.25
14 Jason Kidd .60 1.50
15 Juwan Howard .30 .75
16 Vince Carter .75 2.00
17 Tim Duncan .75 2.00
18 Paul Pierce .50 1.25
19 Tim Hardaway .40 1.00
20 Grant Hill .50 1.25
21 Keith Van Horn .30 .75
22 Shaquille O'Neal 1.00 2.50
23 Jason Williams .50 1.25
24 Shareef Abdur-Rahim .30 .75
25 Kobe Bryant 1.50 4.00
26 David Robinson .60 1.50
27 Anfernee Hardaway .60 1.50
28 Vin Baker .30 .75
29 Hakeem Olajuwon .50 1.25
30 Michael Olowokandi .25 .60
31 Mike Bibby .40 1.00
32 Tracy McGrady .60 1.50
33 Antoine Walker .40 1.00
34 Larry Hughes .30 .75
35 Chris Webber .40 1.00
36 Ray Allen .40 1.00
37 Danny Fortson .25 .60
38 Shawn Kemp .40 1.00
39 Michael Doleac .25 .60
40 Gary Payton .40 1.00
41 Toni Kukoc .40 1.00
42 Kevin Garnett .60 1.50
43 Steve Smith .30 .75
44 Scottie Pippen .60 1.50
45 Allen Iverson .75 2.00
46 Latrell Sprewell .40 1.00
47 Matt Harpring .25 .60
48 Lindsey Hunter .25 .60
49 Karl Malone .50 1.25
50 Michael Finley .40 1.00
51 Jerry Stackhouse .40 1.00
52 Cedric Ceballos .25 .60
53 Brent Barry .30 .75
54 Elden Campbell .25 .60
55 Glenn Robinson .30 .75
56 Eddie Jones .40 1.00
57 Reggie Miller .40 1.00
58 Mitch Richmond .40 1.00
59 Raef LaFrentz .30 .75
60 John Starks .30 .75
61 Elton Brand RC 2.00 5.00
62 William Avery RC .60 1.50
63 Cal Bowdler RC .50 1.25
64 Dion Glover RC .60 1.50
65 Lamar Odom RC 2.00 5.00
66 Richard Hamilton RC 1.50 4.00
67 Kenny Thomas RC .75 2.00
68 Shawn Marion RC 1.50 4.00
69 Baron Davis RC 2.00 5.00
70 Wally Szczerbiak RC 1.50 4.00
71 Scott Padgett RC .60 1.50
72 Jason Terry RC 1.25 3.00
73 Trajan Langdon RC .75 2.00
74 Andre Miller RC 1.50 4.00
75 Jeff Foster RC .75 2.00
76 Tim James RC .50 1.25
77 A.Radojevic RC .50 1.25
78 Quincy Lewis RC .50 1.25
79 James Posey RC .75 2.00
80 Steve Francis RC 2.00 5.00
81 Jonathan Bender RC .75 2.00
82 Corey Maggette RC 1.25 3.00
83 Obinna Ekezie RC .60 1.50
84 Laron Profit RC .60 1.50
85 Devean George RC .75 2.00
86 Ron Artest RC 1.50 4.00
87 Rafer Alston RC 1.00 2.50
88 Vonteego Cummings RC .50 1.25
89 Evan Eschmeyer RC .60 1.50
90 Jumaine Jones RC .60 1.50
S16 Vince Carter PROMO 1.25 3.00

1999-00 E-X Essential Credentials Future

*VETS #'d 36-60: 20X TO 50X BASE HI
*VETS #'d 21-35: 25X TO 60X BASE HI
*RC #'d 21-30: 8X TO 20X BASE HI
LOWER PRINT RUNS UNPRICED
17 Tim Duncan/44 60.00 150.00
20 Grant Hill/41 40.00 100.00
25 Kobe Bryant/36 300.00 600.00
35 Chris Webber/26 60.00 150.00
36 Ray Allen/25 40.00 100.00
38 Shawn Kemp/23 50.00 120.00

1999-00 E-X Essential Credentials Now

*VETS #'d 36-60: 20X TO 50X BASE HI
*VETS #'d 21-35: 25X TO 60X BASE HI
*RCs #'d 21-30: 8X TO 20X BASE HI
LOWER PRINT RUNS UNPRICED
22 Shaquille O'Neal/22 150.00 300.00
25 Kobe Bryant/25 200.00 400.00
27 Anfernee Hardaway/27 50.00 120.00
29 Hakeem Olajuwon/29 40.00 100.00
35 Chris Webber/35 50.00 120.00
36 Ray Allen/36 30.00 80.00
38 Shawn Kemp/38 40.00 100.00
40 Gary Payton/40 30.00 80.00
44 Scottie Pippen/44 100.00 200.00

1999-00 E-X E-Xceptional Red

Randomly inserted in packs at one in 16, this 15-card set features some of the game's best on die cut, foil-stamped Warp Tech technology. Card backs carry a "XC" prefix.

COMPLETE SET (15) 75.00 150.00
STATED ODDS 1:16
*GREEN: 1X TO 2.5X HI COLUMN
GREEN: PRINT RUN 500 SERIAL #'d SETS
XC1 Jason Williams 4.00 10.00
XC2 Kevin Garnett 5.00 12.00
XC3 Allen Iverson 6.00 15.00
XC4 Paul Pierce 4.00 10.00
XC5 Keith Van Horn 2.50 6.00
XC6 Grant Hill 4.00 10.00
XC7 Scottie Pippen 5.00 12.00
XC8 Stephon Marbury 2.50 6.00
XC9 Tim Duncan 6.00 15.00
XC10 Kobe Bryant 15.00 40.00
XC11 Vince Carter 6.00 15.00
XC12 Shaquille O'Neal 8.00 20.00
XC13 Steve Francis 3.00 8.00
XC14 Elton Brand 3.00 8.00
XC15 Lamar Odom 3.00 8.00

1999-00 E-X E-Xceptional Blue

*BLUE STARS: 2.5X TO 6X HI COLUMN
*BLUE RCs: 2X TO 5X HI COLUMN
STATED PRINT RUN 250 SERIAL #'d SETS

1999-00 E-X E-Xciting

Randomly inserted in packs at one in 24, this 10-card set features jersey-shaped cards on felt stock. Card backs carry a "XCT" prefix.

COMPLETE SET (10) 15.00 40.00
STATED ODDS 1:24
XCT1 Jason Williams 1.50 4.00
XCT2 Vince Carter 2.50 6.00
XCT3 Allen Iverson 2.50 6.00
XCT4 Kevin Garnett 2.00 5.00
XCT5 Shaquille O'Neal 3.00 8.00
XCT6 Larry Hughes 1.00 2.50
XCT7 Tim Duncan 2.50 6.00
XCT8 Kobe Bryant 8.00 20.00
XCT9 Grant Hill 1.50 4.00
XCT10 Paul Pierce 1.50 4.00

1999-00 E-X E-Xplosive

Randomly inserted in packs, this 10-card set features the most explosive players in the NBA on foil-stamped fronts. Each card is serially numbered to 1999. The first 99 cards for each player feature autographs. Card backs carry a "XP" prefix.

STATED PRINT RUN 1999 SERIAL #'d SETS
FIRST 99 ARE AUTOGRAPHED
XP1 William Avery .60 1.50
XP1A William Avery AU 6.00 15.00
XP2 Baron Davis 2.00 5.00
XP2A Baron Davis AU 20.00 50.00
XP3 Richard Hamilton 1.50 4.00
XP3A Richard Hamilton AU 15.00 40.00
XP4 Trajan Langdon .75 2.00
XP4A Trajan Langdon AU 8.00 20.00
XP5 Wally Szczerbiak 1.50 4.00
XP5A Wally Szczerbiak AU 15.00 40.00
XP6 Jason Terry 1.25 3.00
XP6A Jason Terry AU 12.00 30.00
XP7 Shawn Marion 1.50 4.00
XP7A Shawn Marion AU 15.00 40.00
XP8 James Posey .75 2.00
XP8A James Posey AU 8.00 20.00
XP9 Lamar Odom 2.00 5.00
XP9A Lamar Odom AU 20.00 50.00
XP10 Quincy Lewis .50 1.25
XP10A Quincy Lewis AU 5.00 12.00

1999-00 E-X Generation E-X

Randomly inserted in packs at one in eight, this 15-card set focuses on young talent. The cards feature foil-stamped plastic with a holographic metallized background. Card backs carry a "GX" prefix.

COMPLETE SET (15) 8.00 20.00
STATED ODDS 1:8
GX1 Michael Olowokandi .40 1.00
GX2 Kobe Bryant 2.50 6.00
GX3 Allen Iverson 1.25 3.00
GX4 Tim Duncan 1.25 3.00
GX5 Vince Carter 1.25 3.00
GX6 Paul Pierce .75 2.00
GX7 Jason Williams .75 2.00
GX8 Steve Francis 1.50 4.00
GX9 Lamar Odom 1.50 4.00
GX10 Elton Brand 1.50 4.00
GX11 Larry Hughes .50 1.25
GX12 Antawn Jamison .60 1.50
GX13 Mike Bibby .60 1.50
GX14 Keith Van Horn .50 1.25
GX15 Raef LaFrentz .50 1.25

1999-00 E-X Genuine Coverage

Randomly inserted in packs at one in 72, this 20-card set features fan favorites on cards featuring game-worn memorabilia. Card backs carry a "GC" prefix.

STATED ODDS 1:72
GC1 Shaquille O'Neal 6.00 15.00
GC2 Vince Carter 5.00 12.00
GC3 Jason Kidd 4.00 10.00
GC4 Karl Malone 3.00 8.00
GC5 Joe Smith 2.00 5.00
GC6 Terrell Brandon 1.50 4.00
GC7 John Stockton 3.00 8.00
GC8 Lamar Odom 6.00 15.00
GC9 Shareef Abdur-Rahim 2.00 5.00
GC10 David Robinson 4.00 10.00
GC11 Larry Hughes 2.00 5.00
GC12 Michael Olowokandi 1.50 4.00
GC13 Antonio McDyess 2.00 5.00
GC14 Mike Bibby 2.50 6.00
GC15 Stephon Marbury 2.00 5.00
GC16 Michael Finley 2.50 6.00
GC17 Gary Payton 2.50 6.00
GC18 Keith Van Horn 2.00 5.00
GC19 Jamal Mashburn 2.00 5.00
GC20 Grant Hill 3.00 8.00

2000-01 E-X

The 2000-01 E-X product was released in February, 2001 and featured a 130-card base set that was broken into tiers as follows: Base Veterans (1-100), and Rookies (101-130). The rookies were serial numbered as follows: 101-110 were serial numbered to 1000, 111-120 were serial numbered to 1250, and 121-130 were serial numbered to 1500.

COMPLETE SET w/o RC (100) 12.50 30.00
101-110: PRINT RUN 1000 #'d SETS
111-120: PRINT RUN 1250 #'d SETS
121-130: PRINT RUN 1500 #'d SETS

1 Dikembe Mutombo .40 1.00
2 Jim Jackson .25 .60
3 Jason Terry .40 1.00
4 Kenny Anderson .30 .75
5 Antoine Walker .30 .75
6 Paul Pierce .40 1.00
7 Jamal Mashburn .30 .75
8 Baron Davis .40 1.00
9 Derrick Coleman .30 .75
10 Elton Brand .40 1.00
11 Ron Artest .40 1.00
12 Andre Miller .30 .75
13 Brevin Knight .25 .60
14 Trajan Langdon .25 .60
15 Lamond Murray .25 .60
16 Dirk Nowitzki .60 1.50
17 Michael Finley .40 1.00
18 Nick Van Exel .30 .75
19 Antonio McDyess .30 .75
20 Raef LaFrentz .25 .60
21 Tariq Abdul-Wahad .25 .60
22 Cedric Ceballos .25 .60
23 Jerry Stackhouse .30 .75
24 Jerome Williams .25 .60
25 Larry Hughes .30 .75
26 Antawn Jamison .40 1.00
27 Mookie Blaylock .25 .60
28 Steve Francis .30 .75
29 Hakeem Olajuwon .50 1.25
30 Maurice Taylor .25 .60
31 Jonathan Bender .25 .60
32 Reggie Miller .40 1.00
33 Austin Croshere .25 .60
34 Travis Best .25 .60
35 Jalen Rose .30 .75
36 Lamar Odom .30 .75
37 Corey Maggette .30 .75
38 Shaquille O'Neal 1.00 2.50
39 Kobe Bryant 1.50 4.00
40 Horace Grant .30 .75
41 Isaiah Rider .30 .75
42 Brian Grant .25 .60
43 Eddie Jones .40 1.00
44 Tim Hardaway .40 1.00
45 Anthony Mason .25 .60
46 Glenn Robinson .30 .75
47 Ray Allen .40 1.00
48 Sam Cassell .30 .75
49 Tim Thomas .25 .60
50 Kevin Garnett .60 1.50
51 Terrell Brandon .25 .60
52 Joe Smith .30 .75
53 Wally Szczerbiak .30 .75
54 Chauncey Billups .40 1.00
55 Stephon Marbury .30 .75
56 Keith Van Horn .30 .75
57 Kerry Kittles .25 .60
58 Allan Houston .30 .75
59 Latrell Sprewell .30 .75
60 Larry Johnson .40 1.00
61 Glen Rice .30 .75
62 Grant Hill .50 1.25
63 Tracy McGrady .60 1.50
64 Darrell Armstrong .25 .60
65 Allen Iverson .75 2.00
66 Toni Kukoc .40 1.00
67 Theo Ratliff .25 .60
68 Jason Kidd .60 1.50
69 Anfernee Hardaway .60 1.50
70 Tom Gugliotta .25 .60
71 Clifford Robinson .25 .60
72 Shawn Kemp .40 1.00
73 Scottie Pippen .60 1.50
74 Rasheed Wallace .40 1.00
75 Steve Smith .30 .75
76 Chris Webber .40 1.00
77 Jason Williams .40 1.00
78 Peja Stojakovic .40 1.00
79 Tim Duncan .75 2.00
80 David Robinson .60 1.50
81 Sean Elliott .40 1.00
82 Derek Anderson .25 .60
83 Vin Baker .30 .75
84 Rashard Lewis .40 1.00
85 Gary Payton .40 1.00
86 Patrick Ewing .50 1.25
87 Vince Carter .75 2.00
88 Mark Jackson .30 .75
89 Antonio Davis .25 .60
90 Karl Malone .50 1.25
91 John Stockton .50 1.25
92 Bryon Russell .25 .60
93 Donyell Marshall .25 .60
94 Shareef Abdur-Rahim .30 .75
95 Mike Bibby .40 1.00
96 Michael Dickerson .25 .60
97 Mitch Richmond .30 .75
98 Juwan Howard .30 .75
99 Richard Hamilton .30 .75
100 Rod Strickland .25 .60
101 DerMarr Johnson RC 1.25 3.00
102 Kenyon Martin RC 4.00 10.00
103 Marcus Fizer RC 1.50 4.00
104 Courtney Alexander RC 1.25 3.00
105 Stromile Swift RC 1.50 4.00
106 Darius Miles RC 1.50 4.00
107 Mike Miller RC 2.50 6.00
108 Jamal Crawford RC 4.00 10.00
109 Speedy Claxton RC 1.50 4.00
110 Quentin Richardson RC 1.50 4.00
111 Keyon Dooling RC 1.50 4.00
112 Desmond Mason RC 2.00 5.00
113 Mateen Cleaves RC 1.25 3.00
114 Morris Peterson RC 1.50 4.00
115 Hedo Turkoglu RC 2.50 6.00
116 Donnell Harvey RC 1.25 3.00
117 Jerome Moiso RC 1.00 2.50
118 Jason Collier RC 1.50 4.00
119 Jamaal Magloire RC 1.50 4.00
120 Erick Barkley RC 1.00 2.50
121 Etan Thomas RC 1.50 4.00
122 DeShawn Stevenson RC 1.50 4.00
123 Dan Langhi RC 1.00 2.50
124 Mark Madsen RC 1.50 4.00
125 Khalid El-Amin RC 1.00 2.50
126 Lavor Postell RC 1.00 2.50
127 Eddie House RC 1.25 3.00
128 Michael Redd RC 4.00 10.00
129 Chris Porter RC 1.00 2.50
130 Mike Smith RC 1.00 2.50

2000-01 E-X Essential Credentials

*STARS: 8X TO 20X BASE CARD HI
*RCs: 2.5X TO 6X BASE HI
STARS: PRINT RUN 201 SERIAL #'d SETS
RCs: PRINT RUN 21 SERIAL #'d SETS
STATED ODDS 1:42
32 Reggie Miller 12.00 30.00
39 Kobe Bryant 75.00 150.00
69 Anfernee Hardaway 15.00 40.00
72 Shawn Kemp 15.00 40.00
73 Scottie Pippen 15.00 40.00

2000-01 E-X Rookie Memorabilia

STATED PRINT RUN 250 TO 500 SETS
EXCH.DEADLINE 3/01/02
101 DerMarr Johnson JSY/275 2.50 6.00
102 Kenyon Martin JSY/275 8.00 20.00
103 Marcus Fizer BALL/275 3.00 8.00
104 Courtney Alexander AU/500 2.50 6.00
105 Stromile Swift JSY/275 3.00 8.00
106 Darius Miles JSY/275 3.00 8.00
107 Mike Miller JSY/275 5.00 12.00
108 Jamal Crawford AU/250 12.00 30.00
109 Speedy Claxton JSY/275 3.00 8.00
110 Quentin Richardson JSY/275 3.00 8.00
111 Keyon Dooling AU/250 3.00 8.00
112 Desmond Mason AU/500 4.00 10.00
113 Mateen Cleaves AU/500 2.50 6.00
114 Morris Peterson JSY/275 3.00 8.00
115 Hedo Turkoglu AU/250 5.00 12.00
116 Donnell Harvey AU/250 2.50 6.00
117 Jerome Moiso JSY/275 2.00 5.00
118 Jason Collier AU/250 3.00 8.00
120 Erick Barkley AU/250 2.00 5.00
121 Etan Thomas JSY/275 3.00 8.00
122 DeShawn Stevenson JSY/275 3.00 8.00
123 Dan Langhi AU/500 2.00 5.00
125 Khalid El-Amin AU/500 2.00 5.00
126 Lavor Postell AU/500 2.00 5.00
127 Eddie House AU/500 2.50 6.00
128 Michael Redd AU/500 3.00 8.00
129 Chris Porter AU/500 2.00 5.00
130 Mike Smith AU/500 2.00 5.00

2000-01 E-X Vince Carter Rookie Remnants

This three-card insert was randomly inserted into 2000-01 Fleer products. The set includes a Vince Carter floor card (numbered to 100), a Vince Carter floor/jersey card (numbered to 15), and finally an autographed Vince Carter floor/jersey card (numbered 1 of 1).
RANDOM INSERTS IN HOBBY PACKS
NNO Vince Carter FLR JSY/15 20.00 50.00
NNO Vince Carter FLR/100 12.50 30.00

2000-01 E-X Generation E-X

Randomly inserted into packs at one in 24, this 21-card insert set focuses on players that appear to be among the next generation of star athletes in the NBA. Card backs carry a "GE" prefix.
STATED ODDS 1:24
GE1 Vince Carter 2.00 5.00
GE2 Grant Hill 1.25 3.00
GE3 Lamar Odom .75 2.00
GE4 Allen Iverson 2.00 5.00
GE5 Keith Van Horn .75 2.00
GE6 Shareef Abdur-Rahim .75 2.00
GE7 Dirk Nowitzki 1.50 4.00
GE8 Morris Peterson 1.00 2.50
GE9 Mike Miller 1.50 4.00
GE10 Darius Miles 1.00 2.50
GE11 Speedy Claxton 1.00 2.50
GE12 Kenyon Martin 2.50 6.00
GE13 Stromile Swift 1.00 2.50
GE14 Courtney Alexander .75 2.00
GE15 V.Carter/M.Peterson 2.00 5.00
GE16 G.Hill/M.Miller 1.50 4.00
GE17 L.Odom/D.Miles 1.00 2.50
GE18 A.Iverson/S.Claxton 2.00 5.00
GE19 K.Van Horn/K.Martin 2.50 6.00
GE20 S.Abdur-Rahim/S.Swift 1.00 2.50
GE21 D.Nowitzki/C.Alexander 1.50 4.00

2000-01 E-X Generation E-X Game Jerseys

OVERALL STATED ODDS 1:85
SINGLE GJ EXCH: PRINT RUN 600 #'d SETS
DUAL GJ EXCH: PRINT RUN 100 #'d SETS
1 Shareef Abdur-Rahim 2.50 6.00
2 S.Abdur-Rahim/S.Swift 4.00 10.00
3 Vince Carter 6.00 15.00
4 Speedy Claxton 2.50 6.00
5 Grant Hill 4.00 10.00
6 G.Hill/M.Miller 6.00 15.00
7 Allen Iverson 6.00 15.00
8 A.Iverson/S.Claxton 6.00 15.00
9 Kenyon Martin 6.00 15.00
10 Darius Miles 2.50 6.00
11 Mike Miller 4.00 10.00
12 Dirk Nowitzki 5.00 12.00
13 Lamar Odom 2.50 6.00
14 L.Odom/D.Miles 4.00 10.00
15 Morris Peterson
16 Stromile Swift 2.50 6.00
17 Keith Van Horn 2.50 6.00
18 K.Van Horn/K.Martin 6.00 15.00

2000-01 E-X Gravity Denied

Randomly inserted into packs at one in 48, this 10-card insert set focuses on players that defy the laws of gravity. Card backs carry a "GD" prefix.
COMPLETE SET (10) 20.00 50.00
STATED ODDS 1:48
GD1 Vince Carter 3.00 8.00
GD2 Jason Kidd 2.50 6.00
GD3 Eddie Jones 1.50 4.00
GD4 Tracy McGrady 2.50 6.00
GD5 Kobe Bryant 10.00 25.00
GD6 Grant Hill 2.00 5.00
GD7 Lamar Odom 1.25 3.00
GD8 Steve Francis 1.25 3.00
GD9 Kevin Garnett 2.50 6.00
GD10 Allen Iverson 3.00 8.00

2000-01 E-X NBA Debut Postmarks

Randomly inserted into packs at one in 288, this 11-card insert set features U.S. postal marks from the actual day that each of these rookies made their NBA debuts. Card backs carry a "PM" prefix.
STATED ODDS 1:288
PM1 Kenyon Martin 8.00 20.00
PM3 Darius Miles 3.00 8.00
PM4 Marcus Fizer 3.00 8.00
PM5 Mike Miller 5.00 12.00
PM6 Dermarr Johnson 2.50 6.00
PM7 Jamal Crawford 8.00 20.00
PM8 Jerome Moiso 2.00 5.00
PM9 Courtney Alexander 2.50 6.00
PM11 Hedo Turkoglu 5.00 12.00
PM13 Jamaal Magloire 3.00 8.00
PM14 Keyon Dooling 3.00 8.00

2000-01 E-X Net Assets

Randomly inserted into packs at one in 8, this 20-card insert set focuses on players that rip it through the net on a very consistent basis. Card backs carry a "NA" prefix.
COMPLETE SET (20) 15.00 30.00
STATED ODDS 1:8
NA1 Vince Carter 1.50 4.00
NA2 Reggie Miller .75 2.00
NA3 Karl Malone 1.00 2.50
NA4 Ray Allen .75 2.00
NA5 Dirk Nowitzki 1.25 3.00
NA6 Scottie Pippen 1.25 3.00
NA7 Tracy McGrady 1.25 3.00
NA8 Kobe Bryant 3.00 8.00
NA9 Larry Hughes .60 1.50
NA10 Shareef Abdur-Rahim .60 1.50
NA11 Tim Duncan 1.50 4.00
NA12 Gary Payton .75 2.00
NA13 Eddie Jones .75 2.00
NA14 Steve Francis .60 1.50
NA15 Antoine Walker .60 1.50
NA16 Kevin Garnett 1.25 3.00
NA17 Chris Webber .75 2.00
NA18 Shaquille O'Neal 2.00 5.00
NA19 Jason Kidd 1.25 3.00
NA20 Elton Brand .75 2.00

2000-01 E-X No Boundaries

Randomly inserted into packs at one in 12, this 10-card insert set focuses on players that have no boundaries as to where their talent may take them. Card backs carry a "NB" prefix.
COMPLETE SET (10) 10.00 25.00
STATED ODDS 1:12
NB1 Vince Carter 1.50 4.00
NB2 Shareef Abdur-Rahim .60 1.50
NB3 Elton Brand .75 2.00
NB4 Shaquille O'Neal 2.00 5.00
NB5 Kobe Bryant 3.00 8.00
NB6 Allen Iverson 1.50 4.00
NB7 Tim Duncan 1.50 4.00
NB8 Steve Francis .60 1.50
NB9 Kevin Garnett 1.25 3.00
NB10 Grant Hill 1.00 2.50

2001-02 E-X

Released in late February 2002, this 130-card set is comprised of 100 veteran cards (card numbers 1-60 Base, 61-80 Role Players, 81-100 Leading Men) and 30 short printed rookie player cards. Base cards feature full color player action photos with true life backgrounds containing an embossed basketball pattern and a color shift to match the featured player's jersey colors. The upper left and lower right hand corners of the cards are colored in, and the different colors are as follows. Card numbers 1-60 are white, card numbers 61-80 are bronze, card numbers 81-100 are gold, and card numbers 101-130 are purple. The rookies are staggered numbered to 1750, 1250 and 750 in no particular order, so print runs are listed below. E-X was packaged in four card packs with 24 packs per box.
COMPLETE SET (130) 75.00 150.00
COMP.SET w/o SP's (100) 15.00 40.00
1 Shareef Abdur-Rahim .30 .75
2 DerMarr Johnson .25 .60
3 Jason Terry .40 1.00
4 Paul Pierce .40 1.00
5 Antoine Walker .30 .75
6 Baron Davis .40 1.00
7 Jamal Mashburn .30 .75
8 Chris Mihm .25 .60
9 Andre Miller .30 .75
10 Dirk Nowitzki .60 1.50
11 Michael Finley .40 1.00
12 Raef LaFrentz .25 .60
13 Antonio McDyess .30 .75
14 Jerry Stackhouse .30 .75
15 Antawn Jamison .40 1.00
16 Steve Francis .30 .75
17 Jalen Rose .30 .75
18 Elton Brand .40 1.00
19 Darius Miles .25 .60
20 Lamar Odom .30 .75
21 Mitch Richmond .30 .75
22 Michael Dickerson .25 .60
23 Stromile Swift .25 .60
24 Alonzo Mourning .50 1.25
25 Courtney Alexander .25 .60
26 Ray Allen .40 1.00
27 Glenn Robinson .30 .75
28 Terrell Brandon .25 .60
29 Wally Szczerbiak .30 .75
30 Joe Smith .30 .75
31 Jason Kidd .60 1.50
32 Kenyon Martin .40 1.00
33 Keith Van Horn .30 .75
34 Grant Hill .50 1.25
35 Tracy McGrady .60 1.50
36 Mike Miller .30 .75
37 Allen Iverson .75 2.00
38 Speedy Claxton .25 .60
39 Dikembe Mutombo .40 1.00
40 Tom Gugliotta .25 .60
41 Penny Hardaway .60 1.50
42 Stephon Marbury .30 .75
43 Shawn Marion .30 .75
44 Rasheed Wallace .40 1.00
45 Peja Stojakovic .40 1.00
46 Mike Bibby .40 1.00
47 Chris Webber .40 1.00
48 David Robinson .60 1.50
49 Vin Baker .30 .75
50 Rashard Lewis .40 1.00
51 Desmond Mason .30 .75
52 Gary Payton .40 1.00
53 Vince Carter .60 1.50
54 Antonio Davis .25 .60
55 Hakeem Olajuwon .50 1.25
56 Morris Peterson .25 .60
57 Karl Malone .50 1.25
58 DeShawn Stevenson .25 .60
59 John Stockton .50 1.25
60 Richard Hamilton .30 .75
61 Corey Maggette .30 .75
62 Steve Smith .30 .75
63 Tim Thomas .25 .60
64 Lindsey Hunter .25 .60
65 Jermaine O'Neal .30 .75
66 Cuttino Mobley .25 .60
67 Nick Van Exel .30 .75
68 Juwan Howard .30 .75
69 James Posey .25 .60
70 David Wesley .25 .60
71 Marcus Fizer .25 .60
72 Jumaine Jones .25 .60
73 Tim Hardaway .40 1.00
74 Danny Fortson .25 .60
75 Jonathan Bender .25 .60
76 Quentin Richardson .30 .75
77 Eddie House .25 .60
78 Kurt Thomas .25 .60
79 Anthony Mason .25 .60
80 Theo Ratliff .25 .60
81 Allan Houston .30 .75
82 Latrell Sprewell .30 .75
83 Jason Williams .30 .75
84 Eddie Jones .30 .75
85 Damon Stoudamire .30 .75
86 Sam Cassell .30 .75
87 Cliff Robinson .30 .75
88 Patrick Ewing .50 1.25
89 Tim Duncan .75 2.00
90 Marcus Camby .30 .75
91 Brian Grant .25 .60
92 Kobe Bryant 1.50 4.00
93 Ron Mercer .25 .60
94 Reggie Miller .40 1.00
95 Shaquille O'Neal 1.00 2.50
96 Kevin Garnett .60 1.50
97 Scottie Pippen .60 1.50
98 Michael Jordan 6.00 15.00
99 Steve Nash .60 1.50
100 Derek Anderson .25 .60
101 Kedrick Brown/1750 RC .50 1.25
102 Joseph Forte/1750 RC .50 1.25
103 Joe Johnson/1250 RC 1.25 3.00
104 Kirk Haston/1750 RC .50 1.25
105 Tyson Chandler/750 RC 2.50 6.00
106 Eddy Curry/1250 RC 1.00 2.50
107 DeSagana Diop/1750 RC .60 1.50
108 Trenton Hassell/1250 RC .75 2.00
109 Zeljko Rebraca/1250 RC 1.00 2.50
110 Rodney White/1750 RC .50 1.25
111 Troy Murphy/1250 RC 1.00 2.50
112 Jason Richardson/750 RC 2.00 5.00
113 Eddie Griffin/750 RC 1.25 3.00
114 Terence Morris/1750 RC .75 2.00
115 Oscar Torres/1250 RC 1.00 2.50
116 Jamaal Tinsley/750 RC 1.50 4.00
117 Pau Gasol/750 RC 5.00 12.00
118 Shane Battier/750 RC 3.00 8.00
119 Brandon Armstrong/1250 RC .60 1.50
120 Richard Jefferson/750 RC 2.50 6.00
121 Steven Hunter/1250 RC .75 2.00
122 Samuel Dalembert/1750 RC .75 2.00
123 Zach Randolph/1250 RC 1.50 4.00
124 Gerald Wallace/1750 RC 1.00 2.50
125 Tony Parker/750 RC 6.00 15.00
126 V.Radmanovic/1250 RC 1.00 2.50
127 Michael Bradley/1750 RC .50 1.25
128 Jarron Collins/1750 RC .75 2.00
129 Andrei Kirilenko/750 RC 2.50 6.00
130 Kwame Brown/750 RC 1.50 4.00

2001-02 E-X Essential Credentials Future

*STARS #'d 21-40: 10X TO 25X BASE CARD HI
*STARS #'d 41-60: 6X TO 15X BASE CARD HI
*STARS #'d 61-70: 5X TO 12X BASE CARD HI
PRINT RUNS BETWEEN 1 AND 70
LOWER PRINT RUNS NOT PRICED
103 Joe Johnson/28 25.00 60.00
105 Tyson Chandler/26 30.00 80.00
106 Eddy Curry/25 20.00 50.00
108 Trenton Hassell/23 15.00 40.00

2001-02 E-X Essential Credentials Future Memorabilia

*STARS #'d 21-40: 10X TO 25X BASE CARD HI
*STARS #'d 41-60: 12X TO 30X BASE HI
PRINT RUNS BETWEEN 1 AND 60
LOWER PRINT RUNS NOT PRICED
26 Ray Allen/35 15.00 40.00

2001-02 E-X Essential Credentials Now

*STARS #'d 21-40: 10X TO 25X BASE CARD HI
*STARS #'d 41-60: 6X TO 15X BASE CARD HI
PRINT RUNS BETWEEN 1 AND 70
LOWER PRINT RUNS NOT PRICED
103 Joe Johnson/43 15.00 40.00
104 Kirk Haston/44 8.00 20.00
105 Tyson Chandler/45 20.00 50.00
106 Eddy Curry/46 12.00 30.00
107 DeSagana Diop/47 10.00 25.00
108 Trenton Hassell/48 10.00 25.00
109 Zeljko Rebraca/49 12.00 30.00
110 Rodney White/50 8.00 20.00
111 Troy Murphy/51 12.00 30.00
112 Jason Richardson/52 15.00 40.00
113 Eddie Griffin/53 10.00 25.00
114 Terence Morris/54 12.00 30.00
115 Oscar Torres/55 12.00 30.00
116 Jamaal Tinsley/56 12.00 30.00
117 Pau Gasol/57 40.00 100.00
118 Shane Battier/58 25.00 60.00
119 Brandon Armstrong/59 8.00 20.00
120 Richard Jefferson/60 12.00 30.00
121 Steven Hunter/61 10.00 25.00
122 Samuel Dalembert/62 12.00 30.00
123 Zach Randolph/63 20.00 50.00
124 Gerald Wallace/64 15.00 40.00
125 Tony Parker/65 50.00 125.00
126 Vladimir Radmanovic/66 12.00 30.00
127 Michael Bradley/67 8.00 20.00
128 Jarron Collins/68 12.00 30.00
129 Andrei Kirilenko/69 20.00 50.00
130 Kwame Brown/70 12.00 30.00

2001-02 E-X Essential Credentials Now Memorabilia

*STARS #'d 21-40: 12X TO 30X BASE CARD HI
*STARS #'d 41-60: 10X TO 25X BASE HI
PRINT RUNS BETWEEN 1 AND 60
LOWER PRINT RUNS NOT PRICED
26 Ray Allen/26 15.00 40.00
47 Chris Webber/47 12.00 30.00
59 John Stockton/59 15.00 40.00

2001-02 E-X Behind the Numbers

Randomly inserted in packs at the rate of one in 288, this 15-card set is designed horizontally with full color player action photo centered and a portrait style "black and white" photo in the upper left hand corner. The player's number appears on the right side of the card, and background color is set to match the featured player's jersey colors.
STATED ODDS 1:288
1 Larry Bird 15.00 40.00
2 Allen Iverson 12.00 30.00
3 David Robinson 10.00 25.00
4 Karl Malone 8.00 20.00
5 Tracy McGrady 10.00 25.00
6 Steve Francis 5.00 12.00
7 Jason Terry 6.00 15.00
8 Antoine Walker 5.00 12.00
9 Grant Hill 8.00 20.00
10 Michael Finley 6.00 15.00
11 Jason Kidd 10.00 25.00
12 Alonzo Mourning 8.00 20.00
13 Darius Miles 4.00 10.00
14 Ray Allen 6.00 15.00
15A Vince Carter 10.00 25.00
15B Vince Carter AU 15.00 40.00

2001-02 E-X Behind the Numbers Jerseys

Randomly inserted in packs at the rate of one in 24, this 18-card set parallels the design of the base Behind the Numbers set enhanced with a jersey swatch in the shape of the player's number. Gary Payton, Paul Pierce and Michael Finley did not appear in the base set, but have versions in this jersey set.
STATED ODDS 1:24
1 Larry Bird 8.00 20.00
2 Vince Carter 5.00 12.00
3 Baron Davis 3.00 8.00
4 Michael Finley 3.00 8.00
5 Steve Francis 2.50 6.00
6 Grant Hill 4.00 10.00
7 Allen Iverson 6.00 15.00
8 Jason Kidd 5.00 12.00
9 Karl Malone 4.00 10.00
10 Kenyon Martin 3.00 8.00
11 Tracy McGrady 5.00 12.00
12 Darius Miles 2.00 5.00
13 Alonzo Mourning 6.00 15.00
14 Dirk Nowitzki 5.00 12.00
15 Gary Payton 3.00 8.00
16 Paul Pierce 3.00 8.00
17 Jason Terry 3.00 8.00
18 Antoine Walker 2.50 6.00

2001-02 E-X Behind the Numbers Jerseys Autographs

Randomly inserted in packs, this set parallels the design of the Behind the Numbers Jerseys set enhanced with player autographs. Each card is sequentially numbered to the featured player's jersey number.
PRINT RUNS LISTED BELOW
SOME UNPRICED DUE TO SCARCITY
1 Larry Bird/33 125.00 250.00
2 Vince Carter/15 75.00 200.00

2001-02 E-X Box Office Draws

Randomly seeded in packs at the rate of one in 24, this 20-card set is designed to resemble a movie poster. Each card has three photos of the featured player, two in action, and one portrait, and the background color is set to match each player's jersey color.
COMPLETE SET (20) 15.00 40.00
STATED ODDS 1:24
1 Shareef Abdur-Rahim 1.00 2.50
2 John Stockton 1.50 4.00
3 Peja Stojakovic 1.25 3.00
4 Elton Brand 1.25 3.00
5 Stephon Marbury 1.00 2.50
6 Eddie Jones 1.00 2.50
7 Baron Davis 1.25 3.00
8 Keith Van Horn 1.00 2.50
9 Paul Pierce 1.25 3.00
10 Gary Payton 1.25 3.00
11 Grant Hill 1.50 4.00
12 Chris Webber 1.25 3.00
13 Latrell Sprewell 1.00 2.50
14 Jerry Stackhouse 1.00 2.50
15 Vince Carter 2.00 5.00
16 Allen Iverson 2.50 6.00
17 Dirk Nowitzki 2.00 5.00
18 Shawn Marion 1.00 2.50
19 Steve Francis 1.00 2.50
20 Richard Hamilton 1.00 2.50

2001-02 E-X Box Office Draws Memorabilia

Randomly inserted in packs at the rate of one in 33, this 19-card set parallels the base Box Office Draws insert set enhanced with a swatch of either shorts or a warm-up.
STATED ODDS 1:33
1 Shareef Abdur-Rahim Warm 3.00 8.00
2 Elton Brand Warm 4.00 10.00
3 Vince Carter Shorts 6.00 15.00
4 Michael Finley Shorts 4.00 10.00
5 Steve Francis Shorts 3.00 8.00
6 Richard Hamilton Shorts 3.00 8.00
7 Grant Hill Shorts 5.00 12.00
8 Allen Iverson Shorts 8.00 20.00
9 Stephon Marbury Warm 3.00 8.00
10 Shawn Marion Shorts 3.00 8.00
11 Tracy McGrady Shorts 6.00 15.00
12 Dirk Nowitzki Shorts 6.00 15.00
13 Lamar Odom Shorts 3.00 8.00
14 Paul Pierce Warm 4.00 10.00
15 Jerry Stackhouse Warm 3.00 8.00
16 John Stockton Warm 5.00 12.00
17 Peja Stojakovic Warm 4.00 10.00
18 Keith Van Horn Warm 3.00 8.00
19 Chris Webber Warm 4.00 10.00

2001-02 E-X Net Assets

Randomly inserted in packs at the rate of one in 12, this 15-card set features a horizontal card design with player action photos on the right side set against a portrait style photo and a photo of the net from a basketball hoop. Background color is set to match the pictured player's jersey colors.
STATED ODDS 1:12
1 Kobe Bryant 3.00 8.00
2 Kwame Brown .75 2.00
3 Kevin Garnett 1.25 3.00
4 Eddie Griffin .60 1.50
5 Shaquille O'Neal 2.00 5.00
6 Tim Duncan 1.50 4.00
7 Tyson Chandler 1.25 3.00
8 Allen Iverson 1.50 4.00
9 Grant Hill 1.00 2.50
10 Michael Jordan 6.00 15.00
11 Ray Allen .75 2.00
12 Jason Richardson 1.00 2.50
13 Eddy Curry .75 2.00
14 Dirk Nowitzki 1.25 3.00
15 Vince Carter 1.25 3.00

2003-04 E-X

Issued in September of 2003, E-X consisted of a 102-card base set divided up into 72 veteran players and 30 rookies. Cards are printed on acetate plastic and feature a full-color player action photo along with the player's name and number and colored backgrounds to match the player's team colors. E-X was packated in 3-card packs and 20-pack boxes and carried a suggested retail price of $5.99.
COMP.SET w/o SP's (72) 15.00 40.00
1 Shareef Abdur-Rahim .30 .75
2 Ray Allen .40 1.00
3 Gilbert Arenas .30 .75
4 Ron Artest .40 1.00
5 Mike Bibby .40 1.00
6 Chauncey Billups .40 1.00
7 Elton Brand .40 1.00
8 Kwame Brown .25 .60
9 Kobe Bryant 1.50 4.00
10 Caron Butler .30 .75
11 Vince Carter .60 1.50
12 Eddy Curry .25 .60
13 Ricky Davis .30 .75
14 Baron Davis .30 .75
15 Tim Duncan .60 1.50
16 Michael Finley .40 1.00
17 Steve Francis .30 .75
18 Kevin Garnett .60 1.50
19 Pau Gasol .40 1.00
20 Manu Ginobili .50 1.25
21 Drew Gooden .30 .75
22 Nene .30 .75
23 Grant Hill .50 1.25
24 Allan Houston .30 .75
25 Juwan Howard .30 .75
26 Zydrunas Ilgauskas .30 .75
27 Allen Iverson .60 1.50
28 Antawn Jamison .30 .75
29 Richard Jefferson .30 .75
30 Eddie Jones .30 .75
31 Jason Kidd .60 1.50
32 Andrei Kirilenko .40 1.00
33 Rashard Lewis .40 1.00
34 Corey Maggette .30 .75
35 Karl Malone .50 1.25
36 Stephon Marbury .30 .75
37 Shawn Marion .30 .75
38 Kenyon Martin .30 .75
39 Jamal Mashburn .30 .75
40 Tracy McGrady .50 1.25
41 Reggie Miller .40 1.00
42 Mike Miller .30 .75
43 Yao Ming .75 2.00
44 Cuttino Mobley .25 .60
45 Steve Nash .50 1.25
46 Dirk Nowitzki .60 1.50
47 Jermaine O'Neal .30 .75
48 Shaquille O'Neal 1.00 2.50
49 Tony Parker .40 1.00
50 Gary Payton .40 1.00
51 Morris Peterson .25 .60
52 Paul Pierce .40 1.00
53 Scottie Pippen .60 1.50
54 Tayshaun Prince .30 .75
55 Vladimir Radmanovic .25 .60
56 Michael Redd .40 1.00
57 Jason Richardson .40 1.00
58 Glenn Robinson .30 .75
59 Jalen Rose .30 .75
60 Latrell Sprewell .30 .75
61 Jerry Stackhouse .30 .75
62 Peja Stojakovic .40 1.00
63 Amare Stoudemire .50 1.25
64 Wally Szczerbiak .30 .75
65 Jason Terry .30 .75
66 Keith Van Horn .30 .75
67 Dajuan Wagner .25 .60
68 Antoine Walker .40 1.00
69 Ben Wallace .30 .75
70 Rasheed Wallace .40 1.00
71 Chris Webber .40 1.00
72 Bonzi Wells .25 .60
73 Carmelo Anthony RC 10.00 25.00
74 Ndudi Ebi RC 2.00 5.00
75 Luke Ridnour RC 2.50 6.00
76 Josh Howard RC 3.00 8.00
77 Marcus Banks RC 2.00 5.00
78 Zarko Cabarkapa RC 2.00 5.00
79 Kendrick Perkins RC 2.50 6.00
80 Leandro Barbosa RC 3.00 8.00
81 David West RC 3.00 8.00
82 Boris Diaw RC 3.00 8.00
83 Carlos Delfino RC 2.50 6.00
84 Mickael Pietrus RC 2.50 6.00
85 Troy Bell RC 2.00 5.00
86 Reece Gaines RC 2.00 5.00
87 Brian Cook RC 2.00 5.00
88 Kirk Hinrich RC 3.00 8.00
89 Travis Outlaw RC 2.50 6.00
90 Dwyane Wade RC 10.00 25.00
91 Luke Walton RC 3.00 8.00
92 Chris Bosh RC 5.00 12.00
93 Jarvis Hayes RC 2.00 5.00
94 Maciej Lampe RC 2.00 5.00
95 Mike Sweetney RC 2.00 5.00
96 Sofoklis Schortsanitis RC 2.00 5.00
97 Dahntay Jones RC 2.50 6.00
98 Nick Collison RC 2.50 6.00
99 Chris Kaman RC 3.00 8.00
100 Darko Milicic RC 2.50 6.00
101 T.J. Ford RC 2.50 6.00
102 LeBron James RC 75.00 200.00

2003-04 E-X Essential Credentials Future

*SINGLES #'d 25-30: 2.5X TO 6X BASE HI
*SINGLES #'d 31-40: 10X TO 25X BASE HI
*SINGLES #'d 41-60: 8X TO 20X BASE HI
*SINGLES #'d 61-80: 6X TO 15X BASE HI
*SINGLES #'d 81-102: 5X TO 12X BASE HI
STATED ODDS 1:28
SOME NOT PRICED DUE TO SCARCITY
2 Ray Allen/101 8.00 20.00
9 Kobe Bryant/94 75.00 150.00
15 Tim Duncan/88 15.00 40.00
18 Kevin Garnett/85 15.00 40.00
20 Manu Ginobili/83 10.00 25.00
23 Grant Hill/80 12.00 30.00
45 Steve Nash/58 30.00 80.00
73 Carmelo Anthony/30 100.00 200.00

2003-04 E-X Essential Credentials Now

*SINGLES #'d 25-40: 12.5X TO 30X BASE HI
*SINGLES #'d 41-60: 10X TO 25X BASE HI
*SINGLES #'d 61-72: 6X TO 15X BASE HI
*SINGLES #'d 73-102: 1.5X TO 4X BASE HI
STATED ODDS 1:28
SOME NOT PRICED DUE TO SCARCITY
27 Allen Iverson/27 75.00 200.00
35 Karl Malone/35 25.00 60.00
40 Tracy McGrady/40 20.00 50.00
45 Steve Nash/45 40.00 100.00
73 Carmelo Anthony/73 40.00 100.00
102 LeBron James/102 800.00 1200.00

2003-04 E-X Behind the Numbers

Inserted in packs at the rate of one in 80, this 15-card set features a horizontal design with player images on the right and the player's number on the left.
COMPLETE SET (15) 15.00 30.00
STATED ODDS 1:80
1 Dirk Nowitzki 2.00 5.00
2 Antoine Walker 1.25 3.00
3 Tayshaun Prince 1.00 2.50
4 Jason Kidd 2.00 5.00
5 Tracy McGrady 1.50 4.00
6 Allen Iverson 2.00 5.00
7 Pau Gasol 1.25 3.00
8 Eddy Curry .75 2.00
9 Elton Brand 1.25 3.00
10 Amare Stoudemire 1.50 4.00
11 Manu Ginobili 1.50 4.00
12 Andrei Kirilenko 1.25 3.00
13 Kevin Garnett 2.00 5.00
14 Peja Stojakovic 1.25 3.00
15 Kenyon Martin 1.00 2.50

2003-04 E-X Behind the Numbers Game-Used

Seeded at one in 10 packs, this 25-card set parallels the design of the non-jersey version of the Behind the Numbers set. Each card replaces the printed player's number with a swatch of game-worn memorabilia in the shape of the featured player's number.
STATED ODDS 1:10
*GOLD: .5X TO 1.25X BASE HI
GOLD PRINT RUN 150 SER.#'d SETS
1 Dirk Nowitzki 4.00 10.00
2 Antoine Walker 2.50 6.00
3 Tayshaun Prince 2.00 5.00
4 Jason Kidd 4.00 10.00
5 Tracy McGrady 3.00 8.00
6 Allen Iverson 4.00 10.00
7 Pau Gasol 2.50 6.00
8 Eddy Curry 1.50 4.00
9 Elton Brand 2.50 6.00
10 Amare Stoudemire 3.00 8.00
11 Manu Ginobili 3.00 8.00
12 Andrei Kirilenko 2.50 6.00
13 Kevin Garnett 4.00 10.00
14 Peja Stojakovic 2.50 6.00
15 Kenyon Martin 2.00 5.00
16 Tyson Chandler 2.00 5.00
17 Latrell Sprewell 2.00 5.00
18 Caron Butler 2.00 5.00
19 Drew Gooden 2.00 5.00
20 Marcus Haislip 2.00 5.00
21 Kwame Brown 2.00 5.00
22 Vince Carter 4.00 10.00
23 Jermaine O'Neal 2.00 5.00
24 Joe Johnson 2.00 5.00
25 Yao Ming 5.00 12.00

2003-04 E-X Buzzer Beaters

Seeded at the rate of one in 240 packs, this 10-card set is printed horizontally on clear acetate plastic. The backgroud is that of an NBA backboard while full-color player photos appear in the foreground.
COMPLETE SET (10) 40.00 80.00
STATED ODDS 1:240
1 Vince Carter 6.00 15.00
2 Ben Wallace 3.00 8.00
3 Amare Stoudemire 5.00 12.00
4 Tony Parker 4.00 10.00
5 Kenyon Martin 3.00 8.00
6 Tracy McGrady 5.00 12.00
7 Dirk Nowitzki 6.00 15.00
8 Gilbert Arenas 3.00 8.00
9 Kevin Garnett 6.00 15.00
10 Elton Brand 4.00 10.00

2003-04 E-X Buzzer Beaters Autographs

A Parallel of the base Buzzer Beaters set, these 11 cards are enhanced with a foil sticker on which appears the player's autograph.
STATED PRINT RUN 99 TO 299 SETS
1 Ben Wallace/299 15.00 40.00
2 Amare Stoudemire/99 20.00 40.00
5 Tracy McGrady/299 15.00 40.00
6 Gilbert Arenas/99 8.00 20.00
7 Carmelo Anthony/299 25.00 60.00
8 Mike Sweetney/299 8.00 20.00
9 Chris Bosh/299 12.00 30.00
10 Dwyane Wade/299 30.00 80.00

2003-04 E-X Jambalaya

Jambalaya was one of the most popular insert sets upon its release and through the 2003-04 season. Cards are die cut into ovals and appear on an almost 3-D background. Stated odds for the set were one in 480 packs.
STATED ODDS 1:480
1 LeBron James 1500.00 2000.00
2 Carmelo Anthony 60.00 150.00
3 Dwyane Wade 75.00 200.00
4 Darko Milicic 10.00 25.00
5 T.J. Ford 10.00 25.00
6 Chris Bosh 40.00 100.00
7 Mike Sweetney 8.00 20.00
8 Kobe Bryant 400.00 650.00
9 Jermaine O'Neal 20.00 50.00
10 Vince Carter 40.00 100.00
11 Allen Iverson 75.00 200.00
12 Tracy McGrady 40.00 100.00
13 Yao Ming 40.00 100.00
14 Shaquille O'Neal 60.00 150.00
15 Tim Duncan 50.00 120.00

2003-04 E-X Net Assets

Inserted at the rate of one in 32, the 10-card Net Assets insert set places full-color player images against a background that features both the team's colors and a close-up of the net from a basket.
COMPLETE SET (10) 8.00 20.00
STATED ODDS 1:32
1 Kobe Bryant 3.00 8.00
2 Jason Richardson .75 2.00
3 Tim Duncan 1.25 3.00
4 Chris Webber .75 2.00
5 Jason Kidd 1.25 3.00
6 Steve Nash 1.00 2.50
7 Allen Iverson 1.25 3.00
8 Steve Francis .60 1.50
9 Paul Pierce .75 2.00
10 Shaquille O'Neal 2.00 5.00

2003-04 E-X Net Assets Game-Used

Seeded at one in 12, this 15-card set parallels the base Net Assets insert set enhanced with a swatch of game-worn memorabilia.
STATED ODDS 1:12
1 Chris Webber 2.50 6.00
2 Jason Kidd 4.00 10.00
3 Steve Nash 3.00 8.00
4 Allen Iverson 4.00 10.00
5 Steve Francis 2.00 5.00
6 Paul Pierce 2.50 6.00
7 Jerry Stackhouse 2.00 5.00
8 Reggie Miller 2.50 6.00
9 Bonzi Wells 2.00 5.00
10 Shane Battier 2.00 5.00
11 Dajuan Wagner 2.00 5.00
12 Andre Miller 2.00 5.00
13 Nene Hilario 2.00 5.00
14 Tony Parker 2.50 6.00
15 Jamal Mashburn 2.00 5.00

2003-04 E-X Net Assets Patch

*PATCH: 1.25X TO 3X BASE GU HI
STATED PRINT RUN 75 SERIAL #'d SETS
1 Chris Webber 12.00 30.00
4 Allen Iverson 15.00 40.00
8 Reggie Miller 15.00 40.00

2004-05 E-XL

Released in December 2004, E-XL consists of a 107-card based set divided up into 70 veteran players and two tiers of rookies. The first tier, cards 71-94 are sequentially numbered to 399 and the second tier, cards 95-107 are sequentially numbered to 899. Base cards feature player action photos centered by an oval of white with colored backgrouds and bronze foil highlights. E-XL was packaged in both Hobby and Retail formats. Hobby boxes contain 18 packs of five cards each while Retail boxes contain 24 packs of five cards each.
COMP.SET w/o SP's (70) 15.00 40.00
71-94 PRINT RUN 399 SER.#'d SETS
95-110 PRINT RUN 899 SER.#'d SETS
1 Dwyane Wade .60 1.50
2 Kobe Bryant 1.50 4.00
3 Mike Bibby .40 1.00
4 Michael Finley .40 1.00
5 Jamal Mashburn .30 .75
6 Carmelo Anthony .75 2.00

7 Jason Kidd .60 1.50
8 Andrei Kirilenko .30 .75
9 Ron Artest .40 1.00
10 Peja Stojakovic .40 1.00
11 Yao Ming .75 2.00
12 Shawn Marion .30 .75
13 Desmond Mason .30 .75
14 Paul Pierce .40 1.00
15 Pau Gasol .40 1.00
16 Tim Duncan .60 1.50
17 Andre Miller .30 .75
18 Allan Houston .30 .75
19 Ben Wallace .30 .75
20 Stephon Marbury .30 .75
21 Gilbert Arenas .30 .75
22 Luke Walton .25 .60
23 Rashard Lewis .40 1.00
24 Elton Brand .40 1.00
25 Zach Randolph .30 .75
26 Eddy Curry .25 .60
27 Richard Jefferson .30 .75
28 Kirk Hinrich .30 .75
29 Jason Terry .30 .75
30 Ray Allen .40 1.00
31 Mike Dunleavy .30 .75
32 Glenn Robinson .30 .75
33 Darko Milicic .25 .60
34 Steve Francis .30 .75
35 Antawn Jamison .30 .75
36 Jason Williams .30 .75
37 Tracy McGrady .50 1.25
38 Steve Nash .50 1.25
39 Gary Payton .40 1.00
40 Sam Cassell .30 .75
41 Gerald Wallace .30 .75
42 Shaquille O'Neal 1.00 2.50
43 Tony Parker .40 1.00
44 Richard Hamilton .30 .75
45 Kenyon Martin .30 .75
46 Baron Davis .30 .75
47 Jarvis Hayes .25 .60
48 Chris Kaman .30 .75
49 Manu Ginobili .50 1.25
50 Jermaine O'Neal .30 .75
51 Amare Stoudemire .30 .75
52 Latrell Sprewell .30 .75
53 LeBron James 2.50 6.00
54 Michael Redd .30 .75
55 Chris Bosh .40 1.00
56 Juwan Howard .30 .75
57 Jason Richardson .40 1.00
58 Allen Iverson .60 1.50
59 Antoine Walker .40 1.00
60 Eddie Jones .30 .75
61 Carlos Arroyo .25 .60
62 Lamar Odom .30 .75
63 Chris Webber .40 1.00
64 Drew Gooden .25 .60
65 Jamaal Magloire .25 .60
66 Dirk Nowitzki .60 1.50
67 Kevin Garnett .60 1.50
68 Vince Carter .60 1.50
69 Reggie Miller .40 1.00
70 Shareef Abdur-Rahim .30 .75
71 Emeka Okafor RC 2.00 5.00
72 Pavel Podkolzin RC 1.50 4.00
73 Kirk Snyder RC 1.50 4.00
74 Ben Gordon RC 2.50 6.00
75 Devin Harris RC 2.00 5.00
76 Josh Childress RC 2.00 5.00
77 Dorell Wright RC 2.50 6.00
78 Dwight Howard RC 5.00 12.00
79 Andre Iguodala RC 3.00 8.00
80 Viktor Khryapa RC 1.50 4.00
81 Al Jefferson RC 3.00 8.00
82 Kevin Martin RC 3.00 8.00
83 Delonte West RC 2.50 6.00
84 Josh Smith RC 2.50 6.00
85 Luol Deng RC 2.50 6.00
86 Kris Humphries RC 2.50 6.00
87 Sebastian Telfair RC 2.00 5.00
88 Rafael Araujo RC 1.50 4.00
89 Jameer Nelson RC 2.50 6.00
90 Shaun Livingston RC 2.50 6.00
91 Andris Biedrins RC 1.50 4.00
92 Robert Swift RC 1.50 4.00
93 Luke Jackson RC 1.50 4.00
94 J.R. Smith RC 2.50 6.00
95 Tony Allen RC 1.50 4.00
96 Sasha Vujacic RC 1.50 4.00
97 David Harrison RC 1.00 2.50
98 Anderson Varejao RC 1.25 3.00
99 Jackson Vroman RC 1.00 2.50
100 Peter John Ramos RC 1.00 2.50
101 Lionel Chalmers RC 1.50 4.00
102 Donta Smith RC 1.00 2.50
103 Andre Emmett RC 1.00 2.50
104 Trevor Ariza RC 1.50 4.00
105 Tim Pickett RC 1.50 4.00
106 Bernard Robinson RC 1.25 3.00
107 Matt Freije RC 1.25 3.00

2004-05 E-XL Essential Credentials Future

*SINGLES #'d 81-107: 4X TO 10X BASE HI
*SINGLES #'d 61-80: 5X TO 12X BASE HI
*SINGLES #'d 38-60: 6X TO 15X BASE HI
*RCs #'d 26-37: 1.5X TO 4X BASE HI
*RCs #'d 15-25: 2X TO 5X BASE HI
2 Kobe Bryant/106 30.00 80.00
30 Ray Allen/78 6.00 15.00
63 Chris Webber/45 8.00 20.00

2004-05 E-XL Essential Credentials Now

*SINGLES #'d 15-25: 10X TO 25X BASE HI
*SINGLES #'d 26-40: 8X TO 20X BASE HI
*SINGLES #'d 41-60: 6X TO 15X BASE HI
*SINGLES #'d 60-70: 5X TO 12X BASE HI
*RCs #'d 71-94: .6X TO 1.5X BASE HI
*RCs #'d 95-107: .5 TO 1.25 BASE HI
30 Ray Allen/30 10.00 25.00
38 Steve Nash/38 12.00 30.00
63 Chris Webber/63 6.00 15.00

2004-05 E-XL Rookies Die Cuts

*DIE CUTS: .4X TO 1X BASE HI
71-94 STATED PRINT RUN 399 SETS
95-107 STATED PRINT RUN 899 SETS

2004-05 E-XL ConnEXions Autographs

Randomly inserted and limited to varying amounts, this 20-card set is designed horizontally and features player autographs on the left, one on top of the other, and then the corresponding player's photo along the right edge of the card.

PRINT RUNS LISTED IN CHECKLIST
1 J.Howard/M.Daniels/100 8.00 20.00
2 A.Kirilenko/S.Monia 6.00 15.00
4 T.Prince/C.Billups/20 15.00 40.00
5 Z.Randolph/J-Rich/20 20.00 50.00
10 M.Pietrus/T.Parker 12.50 30.00
13 M.Ginobili/C.Arroyo 60.00 120.00
14 V.Carter/A.Jamison/100 20.00 50.00
17 J.Richardson/F.Jones 15.00 40.00
18 J.Smith/J.R.Smith/20 30.00 80.00
19 B.Gordon/J.Nelson 12.50 30.00
20 E.Brand/C.Boozer/50 20.00 50.00

2004-05 E-XL ConnEXions Jerseys

Randomly inserted, this 25-card set places two player pictures on the right and left of each card, two square swatches of memorabilia in the middle and sequential numbering to 22. One of one versions also exist.

PRINT RUN 22 SER.#'d SETS
1 D.Wade/C.Anthony 20.00 50.00
2 A.Jamison/V.Carter 15.00 40.00
3 M.Bibby/P.Stojakovic 15.00 40.00
4 D.Wade/S.O'Neal 25.00 60.00
6 S.Marbury/S.Telfair 10.00 25.00
7 J.Mashburn/J.Magloire 10.00 25.00
8 C.Anthony/K.Martin 10.00 25.00
9 S.O'Neal/T.Duncan 25.00 60.00
11 K.Garnett/A.Stoudemire 12.50 30.00
14 B.Gordon/L.Deng 12.50 30.00
22 Y.Ming/T.McGrady 15.00 40.00
23 B.Wallace/R.Wallace 10.00 25.00
26 T.McGrady/V.Carter 30.00 80.00

2004-05 E-XL Court Authentics

Inserted in packs, this 35-card set places portrait style photos of players on the top of the card and a square swatch of memorabilia in the lower left of the card. Each is highlighted with red foil and is sequentially numbered to 500. Several parallel versions of this set were issued and are as follows: Die Cuts with rounded out corners serially numbered to 75, Namplates that include a swatch of letter from the players nameplate serially numbered to the letters in the player's last name, Patches containing a patch swatch serially numbered to 70, Patches 50 serially numbered to 50, Patches Dual with two patch swatches serially numbered to 50, Patches triple with three patch swatches serially numbered to 13, Patches/Jersey serially numbered to 35, Patches/Warmup serially numbered to 44, Patches/Warmup/Jersey serially numbered to eight.

PRINT RUN 500 SER.#'d SETS
DIE CUTS PRINT RUN 75 SER.#'d SETS
PATCH PRINT RUN 70 SER.#'d SETS
PATCH 50 PRINT RUN 50 SER.#'d SETS
PATCH DUAL PRINT RUN 22 SER.#'d SETS
PATCH/JSY PRINT RUN 35 SER.#'d SETS
PAT/WARM PRINT RUN 44 SER.#'d SETS
AI Allen Iverson 4.00 10.00
AS Amare Stoudemire 2.00 5.00
BD Baron Davis 2.00 5.00
BG Ben Gordon 2.50 6.00
BW Ben Wallace 2.00 5.00
CA Carmelo Anthony 5.00 12.00
CB Chris Bosh 2.50 6.00
CW Chris Webber 3.00 8.00
DH Dwight Howard 5.00 12.00
DH2 Devin Harris 2.00 5.00
DM Darko Milicic 2.00 5.00
DN Dirk Nowitzki 4.00 10.00
DW Dwyane Wade 4.00 10.00
EB Elton Brand 2.50 6.00
JK Jason Kidd 4.00 10.00
JO Jermaine O'Neal 2.00 5.00
JR Jason Richardson 2.50 6.00
KG Kevin Garnett 4.00 10.00
KH Kirk Hinrich 2.00 5.00
KM Kenyon Martin 2.00 5.00
LD Luol Deng 2.50 6.00
MB Mike Bibby 2.50 6.00
PP Paul Pierce 2.50 6.00
RA Ray Allen 2.50 6.00
SF Steve Francis 2.00 5.00
SL Shaun Livingston 2.50 6.00
SM Stephon Marbury 2.00 5.00
SM2 Shawn Marion 2.00 5.00
SN Steve Nash 3.00 8.00
SO Shaquille O'Neal 6.00 15.00
TD Tim Duncan 4.00 10.00
TM Tracy McGrady 3.00 8.00
TP Tony Parker 2.50 6.00
VC Vince Carter 4.00 10.00
YM Yao Ming 5.00 12.00

2004-05 E-XL Court Authentics Signatures

This is the set redeemed from the Autograph Redemptions. The cards look like the Court Authentics set only they feature an autograph instead of a memorabilia swatch and are sequentially numbered from 100 to 200.

COMMON CARD 4.00 10.00
PRINT RUN 100 TO 200 SETS
UNPRICED PARALLEL PRINT RUN 10 SETS
AE Andre Emmett/200 2.50 6.00
AJ Al Jefferson/100 5.00 12.00
CD Carlos Delfino/200 2.50 6.00
JC Josh Childress/100 3.00 8.00
LC Lionel Chalmers/200 4.00 10.00
LD Luol Deng/200 4.00 10.00
NC Nick Collison/100 4.00 10.00

2004-05 E-XL Court Authentics Signatures Jerseys

Randomly inserted in packs, this 40-card set parallels the design of the base Court Authentics set with both a jersey swatch and an autograph and is sequentially numbered from 50 to 70. Several different parallel versions of this set were issued and are as follows: Jersey/Warmup serially numbered to 30, Logos numbered one of one, Patches serially numbered to the player's jersey number and Tags that feature the tags off the jersey and are serially numbered to 5.

PRINT RUN 50 TO 70 SER.#'d SETS
*SIG.JSY/WARM: .5X TO 1.25X BASE HI
SIG.JSY/WARM PRINT RUN 30 SETS
AB Andris Biedrins 3.00 8.00
BD Baron Davis 4.00 10.00
BG Ben Gordon 5.00 12.00
CA Carmelo Anthony 20.00 50.00
CB Chris Bosh 10.00 25.00
DH Devin Harris 8.00 20.00
DW Dwyane Wade 40.00 100.00
JC Josh Childress 4.00 10.00
JK Jason Kidd 15.00 40.00
JN Jameer Nelson 5.00 12.00
JO Jermaine O'Neal/67 10.00 25.00
LD Luol Deng 5.00 12.00
LJ Luke Jackson 3.00 8.00
LO Lamar Odom 12.50 30.00
MB Mike Bibby 10.00 25.00
PP Paul Pierce 12.50 30.00
RA Ray Allen 15.00 40.00
RJ Richard Jefferson 10.00 25.00
SL Shaun Livingston 5.00 12.00
SM Stephon Marbury 12.00 30.00
TF T.J. Ford/50 10.00 25.00
VC Vince Carter 12.00 30.00

2004-05 E-XL E-Xceptional

Inserted in packs at the rate of one in 54, this 10-card set features a foil board card stock with a rainbow holofoil effect, full color player photos and gold foil highlights.

COMPLETE SET (10) 30.00 80.00
STATED ODDS 1:54
*XL PARALLEL: .75X TO 2X BASE
1 Shaquille O'Neal 5.00 12.00
2 LeBron James 12.00 30.00
3 Vince Carter 3.00 8.00
4 Kobe Bryant 8.00 20.00
5 Dwyane Wade 3.00 8.00
6 Kevin Garnett 3.00 8.00
7 Allen Iverson 3.00 8.00
8 Tim Duncan 3.00 8.00
9 Jason Kidd 3.00 8.00
10 Yao Ming 4.00 10.00

2004-05 E-XL Jambalaya

Inserted in packs at the rate of one in 216, this 10-card set features the normal oval-design/split background color for which Jambalaya has come to be known. Cards also have a circular gold logo in the upper right corner. An X-L version of the card was also made. These were inserted at the rate of one in 2160 and are differentiated by holofoil highlights instead of the gold foil.

STATED ODDS 1:216
*XL: .6X TO 1.5X BASE HI
XL STATED ODDS 1:2160
1 Carmelo Anthony 40.00 100.00
2 Shaquille O'Neal 75.00 200.00
3 Kobe Bryant 200.00 400.00
4 Vince Carter 40.00 100.00
5 Tracy McGrady 40.00 100.00
6 Kevin Garnett 40.00 100.00
7 Amare Stoudemire 30.00 80.00
8 Allen Iverson 75.00 200.00
9 LeBron James 400.00 800.00
10 Tim Duncan 75.00 200.00

2004-05 E-XL Signings of the Times

Randomly inserted, this 26-card set features a horizontal design, a black and white picture of the player on the left, a square jersey swatch on the right and an autograph along the bottom. Each card is sequentially numbered to 100. Several different parallels were issued for this set and are sequentially numbered to 50, 25 and one of one.

PRINT RUN 100 SER.#'d SETS
*SIGS 50: .5X TO 1.25X BASE HI
*SIGS 25: .6X TO 1.5X BASE HI
AB Andris Biedrins 4.00 10.00
AJ Al Jefferson 6.00 15.00
AV Anderson Varejao 5.00 12.00
BG Ben Gordon 6.00 15.00
CD Chris Duhon 6.00 15.00
DH Devin Harris 5.00 12.00
DH David Harrison 4.00 10.00
DW Dorell Wright 6.00 15.00
DW Delonte West 6.00 15.00
JC Josh Childress 5.00 12.00
JN Jameer Nelson 6.00 15.00
JS Josh Smith 6.00 15.00
JS2 J.R. Smith 6.00 15.00
KS Kirk Snyder 4.00 10.00
LC Lionel Chalmers 6.00 15.00
LD Luol Deng 6.00 15.00
LJ Luke Jackson 4.00 10.00
PP Pavel Podkolzin 4.00 10.00
RA Rafael Araujo 4.00 10.00
RS Robert Swift 4.00 10.00
SL Shaun Livingston 6.00 15.00
ST Sebastian Telfair 5.00 12.00
TA Tony Allen 6.00 15.00

2006-07 E-X

Released in mid March 2007, E-X boasts an 80-card base set where veteran players are featured on cards 1-40, rookies sequentially numbered to 99 are featured on cards 41-46 and autograph rookies are featured on cards 47-80. Base cards consist of a combination of acetate plastic with foil-board highlights and all rookie autographs are signed directly on the cards (see checklist for print runs). E-X carried an initial suggested retail price of $14.99; boxes contain eight packs of five cards each.

COMP.SET w/o RC's (40) 12.50 30.00
41-46 RC PRINT RUN 99 SER.#'d SETS
47-63 RC PRINT RUN 899 SER.#'d SETS
64-74 RC PRINT RUN 399 SER.#'d SETS
75-80 RC PRINT RUN 199 SER.#'d SETS
1 Joe Johnson .40 1.00
2 Paul Pierce .50 1.25
3 Emeka Okafor .40 1.00
4 Michael Jordan 8.00 20.00
5 Ben Gordon .40 1.00
6 LeBron James 2.00 5.00
7 Dirk Nowitzki .75 2.00
8 Jason Terry .40 1.00
9 Carmelo Anthony 1.25 3.00
10 Chauncey Billups .50 1.25
11 Ben Wallace .40 1.00
12 Baron Davis .40 1.00
13 Jason Richardson .50 1.25
14 Yao Ming .60 1.50
15 Jermaine O'Neal .40 1.00
16 Elton Brand .50 1.25
17 Kobe Bryant 2.00 5.00
18 Pau Gasol .50 1.25
19 Tracy McGrady .60 1.50
20 Shaquille O'Neal 1.00 2.50
21 Dwyane Wade .75 2.00
22 Andrew Bogut .40 1.00
23 Kevin Garnett .75 2.00
24 Vince Carter .60 1.50
25 Jason Kidd .75 2.00
26 Chris Paul .60 1.50
27 Stephon Marbury .40 1.00
28 Dwight Howard .40 1.00
29 Allen Iverson .60 1.50
30 Steve Nash .60 1.50
31 Shawn Marion .40 1.00
32 Martell Webster .40 1.00
33 Mike Bibby .50 1.25
34 Ron Artest .50 1.25
35 Tim Duncan .75 2.00
36 Manu Ginobili .50 1.25
37 Ray Allen .50 1.25
38 Chris Bosh .50 1.25
39 Andrei Kirilenko .40 1.00
40 Gilbert Arenas .40 1.00
41 J.J. Redick/99 RC 8.00 20.00
42 Adam Morrison/99 RC 6.00 15.00
43 Jorge Garbajosa/99 RC 5.00 12.00
44 Saer Sene/99 RC 4.00 10.00
45 Renaldo Balkman/99 RC 5.00 12.00
46 Thabo Sefolosha/99 RC 6.00 15.00
47 Kevin Pittsnogle/899 AU RC 3.00 8.00
48 Daniel Gibson/899 AU RC 3.00 8.00
49 Dee Brown/899 AU RC 2.50 6.00
50 Sergio Rodriguez/899 AU RC 4.00 10.00
51 Bobby Jones/899 AU RC 2.50 6.00
52 Craig Smith/899 AU RC 3.00 8.00
53 David Noel/899 AU RC 2.50 6.00
54 Denham Brown/899 AU RC 2.50 6.00
55 James White/899 AU RC 2.50 6.00
56 Paul Davis/899 AU RC 2.50 6.00
57 P.J. Tucker/899 AU RC 3.00 8.00
58 Solomon Jones/899 AU RC 2.50 6.00
59 Steve Novak/899 AU RC 3.00 8.00
60 Allan Ray/899 AU RC 2.50 6.00
61 Jordan Farmar/899 AU RC 4.00 10.00
62 Josh Boone/899 AU RC 2.50 6.00
63 Mardy Collins/899 AU RC 2.50 6.00
64 Rodney Carney/399 AU RC 4.00 10.00
65 Quincy Douby/399 AU RC 4.00 10.00
66 Shannon Brown/399 AU RC 4.00 10.00
67 Rajon Rondo/399 AU RC 15.00 40.00
68 Maurice Ager/399 AU RC 4.00 10.00
69 Ronnie Brewer/399 AU RC 6.00 15.00
70 Marcus Williams/399 AU RC 4.00 10.00
71 Kyle Lowry/399 AU RC 8.00 20.00
72 Cedric Simmons/399 AU RC 4.00 10.00
73 Patrick O'Bryant/399 AU RC 4.00 10.00
74 Hilton Armstrong/399 AU RC 4.00 10.00
75 Rudy Gay/199 AU RC 8.00 20.00
76 Brandon Roy/199 AU RC 6.00 15.00
77 Shelden Williams/199 AU RC 5.00 12.00
78 Tyrus Thomas/199 AU RC 5.00 12.00
79 LaMarcus Aldridge/199 AU RC 15.00 40.00
80 Andrea Bargnani/199 AU RC 6.00 15.00

2006-07 E-X Behind the Numbers

APPROXIMATE ODDS 1:8
BNAI Andre Iguodala 2.50 6.00
BNBD Baron Davis 2.50 6.00
BNBH Brendan Haywood 2.00 5.00
BNBM Brad Miller 2.50 6.00
BNBW Ben Wallace 2.50 6.00
BNCA Carmelo Anthony 4.00 10.00
BNCB Chauncey Billups 3.00 8.00
BNCM Corey Maggette 2.50 6.00
BNCW Chris Webber 3.00 8.00
BNDW David West 2.50 6.00
BNGA Gilbert Arenas 2.50 6.00
BNJG Joey Graham 2.00 5.00
BNJR Jason Richardson 3.00 8.00
BNJS J.R. Smith 2.50 6.00
BNKB Kobe Bryant 10.00 25.00
BNKH Kirk Hinrich 2.50 6.00
BNKK Kyle Korver 2.50 6.00
BNLJ LeBron James 10.00 25.00
BNLW Luke Walton 2.00 5.00
BNMA Sean May 2.00 5.00
BNPP Paul Pierce 3.00 8.00
BNRI Royal Ivey 2.00 5.00
BNSL Shaun Livingston 2.00 5.00
BNSM Shawn Marion 2.50 6.00
BNSN Steve Nash 4.00 10.00
BNTC Tyson Chandler 2.50 6.00
BNTP Tony Parker 3.00 8.00
BNWS Wally Szczerbiak 2.50 6.00
BNZI Zydrunas Ilgauskas 2.50 6.00

2006-07 E-X Behind the Numbers Autographs

CARDS #'d TO PLAYER JERSEY NUMBER
SOME UNPRICED DUE TO SCARCITY
BNCA Carmelo Anthony/15 30.00 80.00
BNJG Joey Graham/14 8.00 20.00
BNLJ LeBron James/23 200.00 400.00
BNPP Paul Pierce/34 20.00 50.00
BNSN Steve Nash/13 40.00 100.00

2006-07 E-X Clearly Authentics Autographs

APPROXIMATE ODDS 1:8
UNPRICED GOLD PRINT RUN FIVE SETS
UNPRICED JSY/TAG PRINT RUN TEN SETS
CAAAB Andrew Bogut 8.00 20.00
CAAAI Andre Iguodala 4.00 10.00
CAAAJ Al Jefferson 3.00 8.00
CAAAM Amir Johnson 3.00 8.00
CAAAU James Augustine 3.00 8.00
CAABA Brent Barry 5.00 12.00
CAABB Brandon Bass 3.00 8.00
CAABD Baron Davis SP 6.00 15.00
CAABG Ben Gordon SP 12.50 30.00
CAABI Chauncey Billups 8.00 20.00
CAABJ Bobby Jackson 3.00 8.00
CAABO Bruce Bowen 5.00 12.00
CAABS Bobby Simmons 3.00 8.00
CAACA Carmelo Anthony SP 20.00 40.00
CAACB Charlie Bell 3.00 8.00
CAACD Chris Duhon 3.00 8.00
CAACH Chuck Hayes 3.00 8.00
CAACK Chris Kaman 3.00 8.00
CAACM Cedric Maxwell 6.00 15.00
CAACP Chris Paul SP 20.00 50.00
CAADA Damir Markota 3.00 8.00
CAADB Dee Brown 3.00 8.00
CAADD Dan Dickau 3.00 8.00
CAADG Danny Granger 3.00 8.00
CAADH Dwight Howard 12.50 30.00
CAADO Donyell Marshall 3.00 8.00
CAAEC Eddy Curry 3.00 8.00
CAAEI Ersan Ilyasova 3.00 8.00
CAAFG Francisco Garcia 3.00 8.00
CAAGG Gerald Green 3.00 8.00
CAAGW Gerald Wallace 3.00 8.00
CAAHA Hassan Adams 3.00 8.00
CAAIU Ime Udoka 3.00 8.00
CAAJA Antawn Jamison 6.00 15.00
CAAJC Josh Childress 3.00 8.00
CAAJG Joey Graham 3.00 8.00
CAAJK Jason Kapono 3.00 8.00
CAAJR Jalen Rose 4.00 10.00
CAAJS J.R. Smith 4.00 10.00
CAAKD Keyon Dooling 3.00 8.00
CAAKG Kevin Garnett 20.00 50.00
CAAKH Kirk Hinrich 10.00 25.00
CAAKI Jason Kidd SP 15.00 40.00
CAAKK Kyle Korver 5.00 12.00
CAALH Larry Hughes 3.00 8.00
CAALJ LeBron James SP 125.00 250.00
CAALR Lawrence Roberts 3.00 8.00
CAALW Louis Williams 3.00 8.00
CAAMB Mike Bibby 6.00 15.00
CAAMD Marquis Daniels 3.00 8.00
CAAMM Chris Mihm 3.00 8.00
CAAMO Cuttino Mobley 3.00 8.00
CAAMW Martell Webster 3.00 8.00
CAAPO Patrick O'Bryant 3.00 8.00
CAAPP Paul Pierce 10.00 25.00
CAAPS Peja Stojakovic 5.00 12.00
CAAQR Quentin Richardson 3.00 8.00
CAARF Raymond Felton 4.00 10.00
CAARI Luke Ridnour 3.00 8.00
CAARM Rashad McCants 3.00 8.00
CAARW Mile Ilic 3.00 8.00
CAASA Shareef Abdur-Rahim 3.00 8.00
CAASC Speedy Claxton 3.00 8.00
CAASG Stephen Graham 3.00 8.00
CAASI James Singleton 3.00 8.00
CAASL Shaun Livingston 3.00 8.00
CAASN Steve Nash SP 60.00 120.00
CAASS Salim Stoudamire 3.00 8.00
CAAST DeShawn Stevenson 3.00 8.00
CAATA Tony Allen 3.00 8.00
CAATE Sebastian Telfair 3.00 8.00
CAATF T.J. Ford 3.00 8.00
CAATM Tracy McGrady SP 15.00 40.00
CAATP Tayshaun Prince 5.00 12.00
CAAWB Will Blalock 3.00 8.00
CAAWI Marvin Williams 5.00 12.00
CAAWL Damien Wilkins 3.00 8.00
CAAWM Maurice Williams 3.00 8.00
CAAYM Yao Ming SP 20.00 50.00

2006-07 E-X Clearly Authentics Patches

PRINT RUN 75 SER.#'d SETS
CAAB Andrew Bogut 4.00 10.00
CAAI Andre Iguodala 4.00 10.00
CAAJ Al Jefferson 4.00 10.00
CAAL Ray Allen 5.00 12.00
CAAS Amare Stoudemire 4.00 10.00
CABD Baron Davis 4.00 10.00
CABI Chauncey Billups 5.00 12.00
CABM Brad Miller 4.00 10.00
CABO Bruce Bowen 3.00 8.00
CABR Kobe Bryant 20.00 50.00
CABW Ben Wallace 4.00 10.00
CACA Carmelo Anthony 6.00 15.00
CACB Carlos Boozer 4.00 10.00
CACF Channing Frye 4.00 10.00
CACM Corey Maggette 4.00 10.00
CACP Chris Paul 6.00 15.00
CACW Chris Webber 5.00 12.00
CADG Danny Granger 4.00 10.00
CADH Dwight Howard 4.00 10.00
CADM Donyell Marshall 3.00 8.00
CADN Dirk Nowitzki 8.00 20.00
CADW Deron Williams 4.00 10.00
CAEB Elton Brand 5.00 12.00
CAEC Eddy Curry 4.00 10.00
CAEI Ersan Ilyasova 3.00 8.00
CAEO Emeka Okafor 4.00 10.00
CAFG Francisco Garcia 3.00 8.00
CAGG Gerald Green 4.00 10.00
CAGH Grant Hill 20.00 50.00
CAGO Drew Gooden 4.00 10.00
CAHA Devin Harris 3.00 8.00
CAHE Luther Head 4.00 10.00
CAHW Hakim Warrick 4.00 10.00
CAID Ike Diogu 3.00 8.00
CAIV Royal Ivey 3.00 8.00
CAJA Antawn Jamison 4.00 10.00
CAJC Josh Childress 4.00 10.00
CAJG Joey Graham 3.00 8.00
CAJK Jason Kidd 8.00 20.00
CAJM Jamaal Magloire 3.00 8.00
CAJO Jermaine O'Neal 4.00 10.00
CAJR Jalen Rose 4.00 10.00
CAJS J.R. Smith 4.00 10.00
CAJT Jason Terry 4.00 10.00
CAKB Kwame Brown 3.00 8.00
CAKG Kevin Garnett 8.00 20.00
CAKH Kirk Hinrich 4.00 10.00
CAKK Kyle Korver 4.00 10.00
CALB Leandro Barbosa 4.00 10.00
CALD Luol Deng 4.00 10.00
CALH Larry Hughes 4.00 10.00
CALJ LeBron James 20.00 50.00
CALO Lamar Odom 4.00 10.00
CALR Luke Ridnour 4.00 10.00
CAMA Stephon Marbury 4.00 10.00
CAMB Mike Bibby 5.00 12.00
CAMD Marquis Daniels 3.00 8.00
CAMG Manu Ginobili 5.00 12.00
CAMR Michael Redd 4.00 10.00
CAMW Martell Webster 4.00 10.00
CANE Nene 4.00 10.00
CANR Nate Robinson 3.00 8.00
CAPG Pau Gasol 5.00 12.00
CAPP Paul Pierce 5.00 12.00
CAPS Peja Stojakovic 5.00 12.00
CAPT Tayshaun Prince 4.00 10.00
CAQR Quentin Richardson 4.00 10.00
CARA Ron Artest 5.00 12.00
CARF Raymond Felton 4.00 10.00
CARH Richard Hamilton 4.00 10.00
CARI Jason Richardson 5.00 12.00
CARJ Richard Jefferson 4.00 10.00
CARM Rashad McCants 3.00 8.00
CASI Wayne Simien 3.00 8.00
CASJ Sarunas Jasikevicius 4.00 10.00
CASL Shaun Livingston 3.00 8.00
CASM Sean May 3.00 8.00
CASN Steve Nash 6.00 15.00
CASO Shaquille O'Neal 10.00 25.00
CASS Stromile Swift 3.00 8.00
CAST Sebastian Telfair 3.00 8.00
CATC Tyson Chandler 4.00 10.00
CATM Tracy McGrady 6.00 15.00
CATP Tony Parker 5.00 12.00
CAVC Vince Carter 6.00 15.00
CAWE Delonte West 3.00 8.00
CAWS Wally Szczerbiak 4.00 10.00
CAYM Yao Ming 6.00 15.00
CAZI Zydrunas Ilgauskas 4.00 10.00

2006-07 E-X Clearly Authentics Patches Autographs

PRINT RUN 25 SER.#'d SETS
CAAB Andrew Bogut 15.00 40.00
CAAI Andre Iguodala 12.50 30.00
CAAJ Al Jefferson 10.00 25.00
CABD Baron Davis 8.00 20.00
CABI Chauncey Billups 10.00 25.00
CABO Bruce Bowen 8.00 20.00
CACA Carmelo Anthony 40.00 80.00
CACB Carlos Boozer 20.00 50.00
CACF Channing Frye 10.00 25.00
CADG Danny Granger 8.00 20.00
CADH Dwight Howard 30.00 75.00
CADM Donyell Marshall 8.00 20.00
CADW Deron Williams 15.00 40.00
CAEI Ersan Ilyasova 8.00 20.00
CAEO Emeka Okafor 8.00 20.00
CAGG Gerald Green 12.50 30.00
CAHW Hakim Warrick 8.00 20.00
CAJA Antawn Jamison 8.00 20.00
CAJC Josh Childress 8.00 20.00
CAJG Joey Graham 8.00 20.00
CAJK Jason Kidd 12.00 30.00
CAJS J.R. Smith 10.00 25.00
CAKH Kirk Hinrich 15.00 40.00
CAKK Kyle Korver 10.00 25.00
CALB Leandro Barbosa 10.00 25.00
CALJ LeBron James 150.00 300.00
CALR Luke Ridnour 10.00 25.00
CAMB Mike Bibby 10.00 25.00
CAMW Martell Webster 8.00 20.00
CANR Nate Robinson 10.00 25.00
CAPP Paul Pierce 25.00 60.00
CAPS Peja Stojakovic 10.00 25.00
CAPT Tayshaun Prince 10.00 25.00
CARA Ron Artest 8.00 20.00
CARF Raymond Felton 10.00 25.00
CARJ Richard Jefferson 8.00 20.00
CASL Shaun Livingston 8.00 20.00
CASM Sean May 8.00 20.00
CASN Steve Nash 80.00 160.00
CAST Sebastian Telfair 8.00 20.00
CATC Tyson Chandler 8.00 20.00
CATM Tracy McGrady 30.00 80.00
CAVC Vince Carter 60.00 120.00
CAYM Yao Ming 30.00 75.00

2006-07 E-X ConnEXions

PRINT RUN 199 SER.#'d SETS
CNAR R.Allen/L.Ridnour 3.00 8.00
CNBG C.Bosh/J.Graham 3.00 8.00
CNBO L.Odom/K.Brown 3.00 8.00
CNBW C.Boozer/D.Williams 5.00 12.00
CNCK V.Carter/N.Krstic 8.00 20.00
CNDN L.Deng/A.Nocioni 3.00 8.00
CNDP T.Duncan/T.Parker 6.00 15.00
CNGJ D.Granger/S.Jasikevicius 3.00 8.00
CNGM K.Garnett/R.McCants 5.00 12.00
CNHB R.Hamilton/C.Billups 3.00 8.00
CNIJ Z.Ilgauskas/L.James 10.00 25.00
CNJA A.Jamison/G.Arenas 3.00 8.00
CNJW D.Jones/H.Warrick 3.00 8.00
CNMB C.Maggette/E.Brand 3.00 8.00
CNMM T.McGrady/Y.Ming 5.00 12.00
CNNB A.Bogut/D.Noel 3.00 8.00
CNNH D.Nowitzki/D.Harris 4.00 10.00
CNNM S.Nash/S.Marion 5.00 12.00
CNOF E.Okafor/R.Felton 3.00 8.00
CNRF Q.Richardson/C.Frye 3.00 8.00
CNRR Q.Richardson/N.Robinson 3.00 8.00
CNSH S.Swift/H.Warrick 3.00 8.00
CNSI J.Smith/R.Ivey 3.00 8.00
CNSO W.Simien/S.O'Neal 5.00 12.00
CNSW J.Smith/M.Williams 3.00 8.00
CNTH J.Terry/D.Harris 3.00 8.00
CNTW B.Wallace/T.Thomas 4.00 10.00
CNWI C.Webber/A.Iguodala 3.00 8.00
CNWP D.West/C.Paul 4.00 10.00
CNWS W.Szczerbiak/D.West 3.00 8.00

2006-07 E-X ConnEXions Autographs

PRINT RUN 25 SER.#'d SETS
CNBG C.Bosh/J.Graham 20.00 50.00
CNBW C.Boozer/D.Williams 25.00 60.00
CNMM T.McGrady/Y.Ming 40.00 100.00
CNNB D.Noel/A.Bogut 12.00 30.00
CNOF E.Okafor/R.Felton 8.00 20.00
CNRF Q.Richardson/C.Frye 8.00 20.00
CNRR Q.Richardson/N.Robinson 8.00 20.00

2006-07 E-X Essential Credentials Future

SOME UNPRICED DUE TO SCARCITY
1 Joe Johnson/80 6.00 15.00
2 Paul Pierce/79 20.00 50.00
3 Emeka Okafor/78 6.00 15.00
4 Michael Jordan/77 700.00 1000.00
5 Ben Gordon/76 6.00 15.00
6 LeBron James/75 30.00 80.00
7 Dirk Nowitzki/74 12.00 30.00
8 Jason Terry/73 6.00 15.00
9 Carmelo Anthony/72 25.00 60.00
10 Chauncey Billups/71 8.00 20.00
11 Ben Wallace/70 6.00 15.00
12 Baron Davis/69 6.00 15.00
13 Jason Richardson/68 8.00 20.00
14 Yao Ming/67 25.00 60.00
15 Jermaine O'Neal/66 6.00 15.00
16 Elton Brand/65 8.00 20.00
17 Kobe Bryant/64 200.00 400.00
18 Pau Gasol/63 8.00 20.00
19 Tracy McGrady/62 25.00 60.00
20 Shaquille O'Neal/61 40.00 100.00
21 Dwyane Wade/60 50.00 120.00
22 Andrew Bogut/59 6.00 15.00
23 Kevin Garnett/58 30.00 80.00
24 Vince Carter/57 20.00 50.00
25 Jason Kidd/56 15.00 40.00
26 Chris Paul/55 25.00 60.00
27 Stephon Marbury/54 20.00 50.00
28 Dwight Howard/53 20.00 50.00
29 Allen Iverson/52 50.00 120.00
30 Steve Nash/51 20.00 50.00
31 Shawn Marion/50 8.00 20.00
32 Martell Webster/49 8.00 20.00
33 Mike Bibby/48 10.00 25.00
34 Ron Artest/47 10.00 25.00
35 Tim Duncan/46 40.00 100.00
36 Manu Ginobili/45 10.00 25.00
37 Ray Allen/44 30.00 80.00
38 Chris Bosh/43 15.00 40.00
39 Andrei Kirilenko/42 8.00 20.00
40 Gilbert Arenas/41 8.00 20.00
41 J.J. Redick/40 12.00 30.00
42 Adam Morrison/39 10.00 25.00
43 Jorge Garbajosa/38 8.00 20.00
44 Saer Sene/37 6.00 15.00
45 Renaldo Balkman/36 8.00 20.00
46 Thabo Sefolosha/35 10.00 25.00
47 Kevin Pittsnogle AU/34 6.00 15.00
48 Daniel Gibson AU/33 6.00 15.00
49 Dee Brown AU/32 5.00 12.00
50 Sergio Rodriguez AU/31 8.00 20.00
52 Craig Smith AU/29 6.00 15.00
53 David Noel AU/28 5.00 12.00
54 Denham Brown AU/27 5.00 12.00
55 James White AU/26 5.00 12.00
56 Paul Davis AU/25 5.00 12.00
57 P.J. Tucker AU/24 6.00 15.00
58 Solomon Jones AU/23 5.00 12.00
59 Steve Novak AU/22 6.00 15.00
60 Allan Ray AU/21 5.00 12.00
61 Jordan Farmar AU/20 8.00 20.00
62 Josh Boone AU/19 5.00 12.00
63 Mardy Collins AU/18 5.00 12.00
64 Rodney Carney AU/17 5.00 12.00
65 Quincy Douby AU/16 5.00 12.00
66 Shannon Brown AU/15 5.00 12.00

2006-07 E-X Essential Credentials Now

SOME UNPRICED DUE TO SCARCITY
15 Jermaine O'Neal/15 12.00 30.00
16 Elton Brand/16 15.00 40.00
17 Kobe Bryant/17 200.00 400.00
18 Pau Gasol/18 15.00 40.00
19 Tracy McGrady/19 20.00 50.00
20 Shaquille O'Neal/20 150.00 300.00
21 Dwyane Wade/21 100.00 250.00
22 Andrew Bogut/22 12.00 30.00
23 Kevin Garnett/23 25.00 60.00
24 Vince Carter/24 20.00 50.00
25 Jason Kidd/25 25.00 60.00
26 Chris Paul/26 50.00 125.00
27 Stephon Marbury/27 12.00 30.00
28 Dwight Howard/28 12.00 30.00
29 Allen Iverson/29 25.00 60.00
30 Steve Nash/30 25.00 60.00
31 Shawn Marion/31 15.00 40.00
32 Martell Webster/32 8.00 20.00
33 Mike Bibby/33 12.00 30.00
34 Ron Artest/34 10.00 25.00
35 Tim Duncan/35 100.00 200.00
36 Manu Ginobili/36 20.00 50.00
37 Ray Allen/37 75.00 150.00
38 Chris Bosh/38 30.00 80.00
39 Andrei Kirilenko/39 25.00 60.00
40 Gilbert Arenas/40 8.00 20.00
41 J.J. Redick/41 12.00 30.00
42 Adam Morrison/42 10.00 25.00
43 Jorge Garbajosa/43 8.00 20.00
44 Saer Sene/44 6.00 15.00
45 Renaldo Balkman/45 8.00 20.00
46 Thabo Sefolosha/46 10.00 25.00
47 Kevin Pittsnogle AU/47 5.00 12.00
48 Daniel Gibson AU/48 5.00 12.00
49 Dee Brown AU/49 4.00 10.00
50 Sergio Rodriguez AU/50 6.00 15.00
51 Bobby Jones AU/51 4.00 10.00
52 Craig Smith AU/52 5.00 12.00
53 David Noel AU/53 4.00 10.00
54 Denham Brown AU/54 4.00 10.00
55 James White AU/55 4.00 10.00
56 Paul Davis AU/56 4.00 10.00
57 P.J. Tucker AU/57 5.00 12.00
58 Solomon Jones AU/58 4.00 10.00
59 Steve Novak AU/59 5.00 12.00
60 Allan Ray AU/60 4.00 10.00
61 Jordan Farmar AU/61 6.00 15.00
62 Josh Boone AU/62 4.00 10.00
63 Mardy Collins AU/63 4.00 10.00
64 Rodney Carney AU/64 4.00 10.00
65 Quincy Douby AU/65 4.00 10.00
66 Shannon Brown AU/66 4.00 10.00
67 Rajon Rondo AU/67 25.00 60.00
68 Maurice Ager AU/68 4.00 10.00
69 Ronnie Brewer AU/69 6.00 15.00
70 Marcus Williams AU/70 4.00 10.00
71 Kyle Lowry AU/71 10.00 25.00
72 Cedric Simmons AU/72 4.00 10.00
73 Patrick O'Bryant AU/73 4.00 10.00
74 Hilton Armstrong AU/74 4.00 10.00
75 Rudy Gay AU/75 20.00 50.00
76 Brandon Roy AU/76 6.00 15.00
77 Shelden Williams AU/77 5.00 12.00
78 Tyrus Thomas AU/78 5.00 12.00
79 LaMarcus Aldridge AU/79 30.00 60.00
80 Andrea Bargnani AU/80 6.00 15.00

2006-07 E-X Jambalaya

APPROXIMATE ODDS 1:48
JAI Allen Iverson 40.00 100.00
JBR Bill Russell 30.00 80.00
JCD Clyde Drexler 75.00 150.00
JDH Dwight Howard 30.00 80.00
JDR David Robinson 75.00 200.00
JDW Dwyane Wade 125.00 250.00
JHO Hakeem Olajuwon 50.00 125.00
JJE Julius Erving 50.00 125.00
JJK Jason Kidd 40.00 100.00
JJO Magic Johnson 75.00 150.00
JJS John Stockton 60.00 150.00
JLB Larry Bird 60.00 150.00
JLJ LeBron James 125.00 300.00
JMG Manu Ginobili 50.00 125.00
JMJ Michael Jordan 1200.00 2000.00
JPP Paul Pierce 40.00 100.00
JPS Peja Stojakovic 25.00 60.00
JSM Stephon Marbury 25.00 60.00
JTD Tim Duncan 50.00 125.00
JTM Tracy McGrady 30.00 80.00

1967-73 Equitable Sports Hall of Fame

This set consists of copies of art work found over a number of years in many national magazines, especially "Sports Illustrated," honoring sports heroes that Equitable Life Assurance Society selected to be in its very own Sports Hall of Fame. The cards consists of charcoal-type drawings on white backgrounds by artists, George Loh and Robert Riger, and measure approximately 11" by 7 3/4". The unnumbered cards have been assigned numbers below using a sport prefix (BB- baseball, BK- basketball, FB- football, HK- hockey, OT-other).

COMPLETE SET (95) 250.00 500.00
BK1 Elgin Baylor 3.00 6.00
BK2 Wilt Chamberlain 5.00 10.00
BK3 Bob Cousy 3.00 6.00
BK4 Hal Grier 2.00 4.00
BK5 Jerry Lucas 2.00 4.00
BK6 George Mikan 3.00 6.00
BK7 Bob Pettit 3.00 6.00
BK8 Willis Reed 2.00 4.00
BK9 Bill Russell 5.00 10.00
BK10 Dolph Schayes 2.00 4.00

2003-04 Exquisite Collection

Released in early June 2004, UD Exquisite Collection's base set includes 78 cards divided up as follows: 42 base veteran, rookie and retired player cards sequentially numbered to 225; 29 autographed jersey rookie cards, numbers 44-73, sequentially numbered to 225; six autographed jersey rookie cards, number 43 and 74-78, sequentially numbered to 99. Base veteran rookie and retired player cards have white borders on the left and right of the card with full color player photos through the middle and rookie cards place a small action photo on the top of the card below which appears an "R" shaped swatch of memorabilia and an autograph. Exquisite boxes consisted of a single pack in an engraved wooden box and contained five cards with a suggested retail price of $500. Also released were a gold parallel of the veteran cards, a partial jersey parallel of the veteran cards sequentially numbered to 25 and a partial patch parallel sequentially numbered to 10.

1-42 PRINT RUN 225 SER.#'d SETS
44-73 RC PRINT RUN 225 SER.#'d SETS
43, 74-78 RC PRINT RUN 99 SER.#'d SETS
UNPRICED RAINBOW PRINT RUN ONE SET
1 Jason Terry 10.00 25.00
2 Paul Pierce 12.00 30.00
3 Michael Jordan 300.00 600.00
4 Kirk Hinrich RC 12.00 30.00
5 Dajuan Wagner 8.00 20.00
6 Dirk Nowitzki 25.00 60.00
7 Steve Nash 25.00 60.00
8 Andre Miller 10.00 25.00
9 Ben Wallace 15.00 40.00
10 Jason Richardson 12.00 30.00
11 Steve Francis 10.00 25.00
12 Yao Ming 25.00 60.00
13 Jermaine O'Neal 10.00 25.00
14 Elton Brand 12.00 30.00

15 Kobe Bryant 150.00 300.00
16 Gary Payton 12.00 30.00
17 Shaquille O'Neal 40.00 100.00
18 Pau Gasol 12.00 30.00
19 Lamar Odom 10.00 25.00
20 T.J. Ford RC 10.00 25.00
21 Kevin Garnett 30.00 80.00
22 Latrell Sprewell 15.00 40.00
23 Jason Kidd 20.00 50.00
24 Richard Jefferson 10.00 25.00
25 Baron Davis 10.00 25.00
26 Allan Houston 10.00 25.00
27 Stephon Marbury 12.00 30.00
28 Tracy McGrady 25.00 60.00
29 Allen Iverson 50.00 125.00
30 Shawn Marion 10.00 25.00
31 Amare Stoudemire 15.00 40.00
32 Shareef Abdur-Rahim 10.00 25.00
33 Mike Bibby 12.00 30.00
34 Chris Webber 20.00 50.00
35 Tim Duncan 40.00 100.00
36 Manu Ginobili 15.00 40.00
37 Ray Allen 25.00 60.00
38 Nick Collison RC 10.00 25.00
39 Vince Carter 20.00 50.00
40 Andrei Kirilenko 12.00 30.00
41 Gilbert Arenas 10.00 25.00
42 Jerry Stackhouse 20.00 50.00
43 Udonis Haslem JSY AU RC 100.00 225.00
44 Mo Williams JSY AU RC 15.00 40.00
45 Keith Bogans JSY AU RC 5.00 12.00
46 Travis Hansen JSY AU RC 5.00 12.00
47 Jason Kapono JSY AU RC 5.00 12.00
48 Zaza Pachulia JSY AU RC 15.00 40.00
49 Z.Cabarkapa JSY AU RC 5.00 12.00
50 Kyle Korver AU RC 25.00 60.00
51 Luke Walton JSY AU RC 30.00 80.00
52 Maciej Lampe JSY AU RC 25.00 60.00
53 Josh Howard JSY AU RC 8.00 20.00
54 Leandro Barbosa JSY AU RC 20.00 50.00
55 Kendrick Perkins JSY AU RC 20.00 50.00
56 Ndudi Ebi JSY AU RC 12.00 30.00
57 Jerome Beasley JSY AU RC 10.00 25.00
58 Brian Cook JSY AU RC 5.00 12.00
59 Travis Outlaw JSY AU RC 12.00 30.00
60 Zoran Planinic JSY AU RC 5.00 12.00
61 Boris Diaw JSY AU RC 40.00 100.00
62 Steve Blake JSY AU RC 20.00 50.00
63 A.Pavlovic JSY AU RC 6.00 15.00
64 David West JSY AU RC 60.00 120.00
65 Mike Sweetney JSY AU RC 12.00 30.00
66 Troy Bell JSY AU RC 5.00 12.00
67 Reece Gaines JSY AU RC 5.00 12.00
68 Luke Ridnour JSY AU RC 6.00 15.00
69 Marcus Banks JSY AU RC 5.00 12.00
70 Dahntay Jones JSY AU RC 12.00 30.00
71 Mickael Pietrus JSY AU RC 20.00 50.00
72 Chris Kaman JSY AU RC 25.00 60.00
73 Jarvis Hayes JSY AU RC 12.00 30.00
74 Dwyane Wade JSY AU RC 2000.00 4000.00
75 Chris Bosh JSY AU RC 600.00 900.00
76 C.Anthony JSY AU RC 2000.00 3000.00
77 Darko Milicic JSY AU RC 100.00 200.00
78 LeBron James JSY AU RC 10000.00 15000.00

2003-04 Exquisite Collection Gold

*GOLD 1-42: 1X TO 2.5X BASE HI
PRINT RUN 25 SER.#'d SETS
GOLD RCs DO NOT CONTAIN AU OR PATCH
3 Michael Jordan 1500.00 2300.00
7 Steve Nash 75.00 200.00
12 Yao Ming 100.00 250.00
43 Udonis Haslem 30.00 80.00
44 Mo Williams 12.00 30.00
45 Keith Bogans 8.00 20.00
46 Travis Hansen 8.00 20.00
47 Jason Kapono 8.00 20.00
48 Zaur Pachulia 25.00 60.00
49 Zarko Cabarkapa 8.00 20.00
50 Kyle Korver 30.00 80.00
51 Luke Walton 20.00 50.00
52 Maciej Lampe 8.00 20.00
53 Josh Howard 12.00 30.00
54 Leandro Barbosa 50.00 120.00
55 Kendrick Perkins 10.00 25.00
56 Ndudi Ebi 8.00 20.00
57 Jerome Beasley 8.00 20.00
58 Brian Cook 8.00 20.00
59 Travis Outlaw 6.00 15.00
60 Zoran Planinic 8.00 20.00
61 Boris Diaw 12.00 30.00
62 Steve Blake 25.00 60.00
63 Aleksandar Pavlovic 10.00 25.00
64 David West 20.00 50.00
65 Mike Sweetney 8.00 20.00
66 Troy Bell 8.00 20.00
67 Reece Gaines 8.00 20.00
68 Luke Ridnour 25.00 60.00
69 Marcus Banks 8.00 20.00
70 Dahntay Jones 10.00 25.00
71 Mickael Pietrus 20.00 50.00
72 Chris Kaman 25.00 60.00
73 Jarvis Hayes 8.00 20.00
74 Dwyane Wade 600.00 1200.00
75 Chris Bosh 100.00 250.00
76 Carmelo Anthony 450.00 750.00
77 Darko Milicic 30.00 80.00
78 LeBron James 5000.00 8000.00

2003-04 Exquisite Collection Jersey Parallel

*JERSEY: .5X TO 1.2X BASE HI
PRINT RUN 25 SER.#'d SETS
4J, 20J, 38J, 39J NOT RELEASED
UNPRICED AU PATCH PRINT RUN ONE SET
UNPRICED PATCH PRINT RUN 10 SETS
3J Michael Jordan 700.00 1200.00
36J Manu Ginobili 40.00 100.00

2003-04 Exquisite Collection Rookie Patch Parallel

CARD #'d TO PLAYER JERSEY
MOST NOT PRICED DUE TO SCARCITY
43 Udonis Haslem/40 100.00 250.00
44 Mo Williams/25 125.00 250.00
47 Jason Kapono/24 15.00 40.00
48 Zaur Pachulia/27 50.00 120.00
50 Kyle Korver/26 150.00 300.00
55 Kendrick Perkins/43 50.00 120.00
56 Ndudi Ebi/44 15.00 40.00
57 Jerome Beasley/24 15.00 40.00
59 Travis Outlaw/25 20.00 50.00
61 Boris Diaw/32 100.00 200.00
64 David West/30 150.00 300.00
65 Mike Sweetney/50 15.00 40.00
67 Reece Gaines/22 30.00 80.00
70 Dahntay Jones/30 20.00 50.00
72 Chris Kaman/35 75.00 150.00
73 Jarvis Hayes/24 30.00 80.00
76 Carmelo Anthony/15 3000.00 4500.00
77 Darko Milicic/31 100.00 250.00
78 LeBron James/23 10000.00 14000.00

2003-04 Exquisite Collection Emblems of Endorsement

Randomly seeded, this 12-card set has white borders along the top and bottom of the card, a centered black background with a full-color player action photo, two emblem swatches and authentic player autographs. Each card is sequentially numbered to 15.
PRINT RUN 15 SER.#'d SETS
CA Carmelo Anthony 700.00 1200.00
GP Gary Payton 200.00 400.00
KB Kobe Bryant 750.00 1500.00
KG Kevin Garnett 400.00 800.00
LB Larry Bird 300.00 600.00
LJ LeBron James 2500.00 4000.00
MJ Michael Jordan 2500.00 4000.00
RJ Richard Jefferson 100.00 200.00
RM Reggie Miller 175.00 350.00
SM Stephon Marbury 100.00 200.00
TM Tracy McGrady 200.00 400.00
YM Yao Ming 200.00 400.00

2003-04 Exquisite Collection Extra Exquisite

Randomly inserted in packs, this 42-card set places an oversized jersey swatch towards the top of the card and a small head-shot photo on the bottom of the card. Each card is sequentially numbered to 75.
PRINT RUN 75 SER.#'d SETS
*DUAL: .6X TO 1.5X BASE HI
DUAL PRINT RUN 25 SER.#'d SETS
AI Allen Iverson 100.00 250.00
AK Andrei Kirilenko 15.00 40.00
AM Alonzo Mourning 30.00 80.00
AS Amare Stoudemire 30.00 80.00
BD Baron Davis 15.00 40.00
CA Carmelo Anthony 50.00 100.00
CB Chris Bosh 30.00 80.00
CW Chris Webber 25.00 60.00
DN Dirk Nowitzki 30.00 80.00
DR David Robinson 40.00 100.00
DW Dwyane Wade 175.00 350.00
GP Gary Payton 20.00 50.00
IT Isiah Thomas 15.00 40.00
JE Julius Erving 40.00 100.00
JH Jarvis Hayes 15.00 40.00
JK Jason Kidd 25.00 60.00
JO Jermaine O'Neal 15.00 40.00
JR Jason Richardson 15.00 40.00
JS John Stockton 40.00 100.00
KA Kareem Abdul-Jabbar 30.00 80.00
KB Kobe Bryant 200.00 400.00
KB1 Kobe Bryant 200.00 400.00
KG Kevin Garnett 30.00 80.00
LB Larry Bird 50.00 120.00
LJ LeBron James 250.00 500.00
LJ1 LeBron James 250.00 500.00
MA Magic Johnson 40.00 100.00
MJ Michael Jordan 250.00 500.00
MJ1 Michael Jordan 250.00 500.00
PG Pau Gasol 15.00 40.00
PP Paul Pierce 25.00 60.00
RA Ray Allen 40.00 100.00
SF Steve Francis 20.00 50.00
SH Shawn Marion 20.00 50.00
SM Stephon Marbury 15.00 40.00
SN Steve Nash 25.00 60.00
SO Shaquille O'Neal 50.00 120.00
TD Tim Duncan 40.00 100.00
TM Tracy McGrady 30.00 80.00
WA Ben Wallace 15.00 40.00
WC Wilt Chamberlain 100.00 200.00
YM Yao Ming 60.00 150.00

2003-04 Exquisite Collection Limited Logos

This 30-card set is randomly seeded in packs and places a large logo swatch in the middle of the card with a a small head-shot of the featured player on the top and an authentic autograph on the bottom. Each card is sequentially numbered to 75.
PRINT RUN 75 SER.#'d SETS
AJ Antawn Jamison 75.00 150.00
AM Andre Miller 75.00 150.00
AS Amare Stoudemire 100.00 200.00
BD Baron Davis 100.00 200.00
CA1 Carmelo Anthony 600.00 1100.00
CA2 C.Anthony Throwback 600.00 1100.00
CM Corey Maggette 75.00 150.00
DA David Robinson 250.00 500.00
DM Darko Milicic 75.00 150.00
DR Dennis Rodman 400.00 700.00
DY Dwyane Wade 1500.00 2500.00
GA Gilbert Arenas 100.00 200.00
GP Gary Payton 100.00 200.00
JK Jason Kidd 250.00 450.00
JM John Stockton 250.00 500.00
KB Kobe Bryant 3500.00 5200.00
KG Kevin Garnett 350.00 700.00
LB Larry Bird 400.00 800.00
LJ LeBron James 6000.00 8000.00
MA Magic Johnson 400.00 700.00
MJ Michael Jordan 10000.00 15000.00
PE Patrick Ewing 500.00 800.00
PP Paul Pierce 400.00 800.00
PS Peja Stojakovic 125.00 250.00
SA Shareef Abdur-Rahim 75.00 150.00
SC Sam Cassell 75.00 150.00
SM Shawn Marion 100.00 200.00
ST Stephon Marbury 125.00 250.00
TM Tracy McGrady 200.00 350.00
ZO Alonzo Mourning 300.00 600.00

2003-04 Exquisite Collection Noble Nameplates

Randomly inserted, this 30-card set places a full-color action photo on the right side of the card and a swatch of the player's jersey nameplate and autograph on the left. Each card is sequentially numbered to 25.
PRINT RUN 25 SER.#'d SETS
AH Al Harrington 50.00 125.00
AJ Antawn Jamison 40.00 100.00
AK Andrei Kirilenko 100.00 200.00
AS Amare Stoudemire 150.00 300.00
BD Baron Davis 75.00 150.00
CA Carmelo Anthony 600.00 1100.00
CB Chris Bosh 400.00 700.00
CM Corey Maggette 40.00 100.00
DM Darko Milicic 50.00 125.00
DY Dwyane Wade 1700.00 2500.00
GA Gilbert Arenas 100.00 200.00
GP Gary Payton 150.00 300.00
GR Glenn Robinson 40.00 100.00
IT Isiah Thomas 150.00 400.00
JK Jason Kidd 100.00 200.00
KB Kobe Bryant 3000.00 4500.00
KG Kevin Garnett 300.00 600.00
LJ LeBron James 8000.00 12000.00
MJ Michael Jordan 3000.00 6000.00
PE Patrick Ewing 400.00 700.00
PP Paul Pierce 100.00 200.00
PS Peja Stojakovic 60.00 150.00
RJ Richard Jefferson 40.00 100.00
RM Reggie Miller 1000.00 1500.00
SA Shareef Abdur-Rahim 60.00 150.00
SM Shawn Marion 40.00 100.00
ST Stephon Marbury 75.00 150.00
TM Tracy McGrady 200.00 400.00
TP Tony Parker 100.00 200.00
ZO Alonzo Mourning 175.00 350.00

2003-04 Exquisite Collection Number Piece Autographs

Randomly inserted, this 29-card set features full-color player action photos along with a jersey swatch in the shape of the player's jersey number. Each card is numbered to that number and showcases an authentic player autograph.
STATED PRINT RUN ONE TO 91 SETS
SOME UNPRICED DUE TO SCARCITY
AJ Antawn Jamison/33 40.00 100.00
AK Andrei Kirilenko/47 100.00 200.00
AM Alonzo Mourning/33 175.00 350.00
AS Amare Stoudemire/32 125.00 250.00
CA Carmelo Anthony/15 600.00 1100.00
DA David Robinson/50 200.00 350.00
DM Darius Miles/23 40.00 100.00
DR Dennis Rodman/91 150.00 325.00
GP Gary Payton/20 200.00 400.00
KG Kevin Garnett/21 300.00 550.00
LB Larry Bird/33 250.00 500.00
LJ LeBron James/23 3000.00 5000.00
MA Magic Johnson/32 300.00 600.00
MJ Michael Jordan/23 4000.00 6500.00
PE Patrick Ewing/33 300.00 550.00
PP Paul Pierce/34 75.00 150.00
RJ Richard Jefferson/24 40.00 100.00
RM Reggie Miller/31 500.00 800.00
SM Shawn Marion/31 60.00 150.00

2003-04 Exquisite Collection Patches Autographs

Randomly inserted, this 41-card set places a full color player photo on the left, a swatch of jersey patch in the middle and an authentic autograph on the right. Each card is sequentially numbered to 100.
PRINT RUN 100 SER.#'d SETS
AK Andrei Kirilenko 25.00 60.00
AM Antonio McDyess 30.00 80.00
AS Amare Stoudemire 75.00 150.00
BD Baron Davis 30.00 80.00
BR Bill Russell 250.00 450.00
CA Carmelo Anthony 300.00 600.00
CB Chris Bosh 125.00 250.00
CM Corey Maggette 25.00 60.00
DA David Robinson 125.00 250.00
DM Darius Miles 25.00 60.00
DR Dennis Rodman 150.00 300.00
EG Manu Ginobili 300.00 600.00
GA Gilbert Arenas 30.00 80.00
GP Gary Payton 75.00 150.00
GR Glenn Robinson 25.00 60.00
JE Julius Erving 150.00 300.00
JK Jason Kidd 100.00 200.00
JS John Stockton 100.00 250.00
JY Jerry Stackhouse 40.00 100.00
KB Kobe Bryant 2000.00 3000.00
KG Kevin Garnett 150.00 400.00
LB Larry Bird 150.00 400.00
LJ LeBron James 8000.00 12000.00
LO Lamar Odom 30.00 80.00
MA Magic Johnson 150.00 300.00
MB Mike Bibby 30.00 80.00
MJ Michael Jordan 3000.00 5000.00
PE Patrick Ewing 300.00 600.00
PP Paul Pierce 100.00 250.00
PS Peja Stojakovic 100.00 200.00
RH Richard Hamilton 30.00 80.00
RJ Richard Jefferson 20.00 50.00
RM Reggie Miller 300.00 500.00
SA Shareef Abdur-Rahim 25.00 60.00
SC Sam Cassell 30.00 80.00
SH Shawn Marion 20.00 50.00
ST Stephon Marbury 40.00 100.00
TM Tracy McGrady 75.00 150.00
TP Tony Parker 50.00 120.00
YM Yao Ming 60.00 150.00
ZR Zach Randolph 30.00 80.00

2003-04 Exquisite Collection Scripted Swatches

Randomly inserted, this 12-card set utilizes a horizontal design with a small player head-shot along the top and a large swatch of autographed jersey patch in the middle. Each card is sequentially numbered to 25.
PRINT RUN 25 SER.#'d SETS
AS Amare Stoudemire 175.00 350.00
CA Carmelo Anthony 500.00 1000.00
CM Corey Maggette 50.00 120.00
JK Jason Kidd 250.00 500.00
JS John Stockton 300.00 500.00
KG Kevin Garnett 400.00 700.00
LJ LeBron James 2500.00 4000.00
MJ Michael Jordan 2500.00 5000.00
PE Patrick Ewing 500.00 800.00
RM Reggie Miller 300.00 600.00
TM Tracy McGrady 250.00 500.00
YM Yao Ming 300.00 600.00

2004-05 Exquisite Collection

Released in June 2005, the second installation of Exquisite consists of a 90-card set with 42 veteran players and 48 rookie cards, most of which are autograph, memorabilia or both cards. Every card in the set is thick stock and all cards are numbered to either 225 or 99. Exquisite was packaged in one-pack maple wood boxes where packs contained five cards and carried a SRP of $500.
1-84 PRINT RUN 225 SER.#'d SETS
85-90 HAVE BOTH PATCH AND AUTO
UNPRICED BLACK PRINT RUN ONE SET
1 Al Harrington 4.00 10.00
2 Paul Pierce 25.00 60.00
3 Emeka Okafor RC 4.00 10.00
4 Michael Jordan 150.00 400.00
5 LeBron James 100.00 250.00
6 Dirk Nowitzki 20.00 50.00
7 Carmelo Anthony 10.00 25.00
8 Kenyon Martin 4.00 10.00
9 Richard Hamilton 4.00 10.00
10 Ben Wallace 4.00 10.00
11 Jason Richardson 5.00 12.00
12 Yao Ming 10.00 25.00
13 Tracy McGrady 6.00 15.00
14 Reggie Miller 12.00 30.00
15 Corey Maggette 4.00 10.00
16 Kobe Bryant 50.00 120.00
17 Lamar Odom 4.00 10.00
18 Pau Gasol 5.00 12.00
19 Dwyane Wade 8.00 20.00
20 Shaquille O'Neal 12.00 30.00
21 Michael Redd 4.00 10.00
22 Kevin Garnett 8.00 20.00
23 Vince Carter 8.00 20.00
24 Jason Kidd 8.00 20.00
25 Baron Davis 4.00 10.00
26 Jamaal Magloire 3.00 8.00
27 Stephon Marbury 4.00 10.00
28 Steve Francis 4.00 10.00
29 Allen Iverson 8.00 20.00
30 Amare Stoudemire 4.00 10.00
31 Shawn Marion 4.00 10.00
32 Shareef Abdur-Rahim 4.00 10.00
33 Peja Stojakovic 5.00 12.00
34 Mike Bibby 5.00 12.00
35 Tim Duncan 15.00 40.00
36 Tony Parker 6.00 15.00
37 Ray Allen 10.00 25.00
38 Chris Bosh 5.00 12.00
39 Andrei Kirilenko 4.00 10.00
40 Carlos Boozer 4.00 10.00
41 Gilbert Arenas 4.00 10.00
42 Antawn Jamison 4.00 10.00
43 Andre Emmett JSY AU RC 6.00 15.00
44 Jameer Nelson JSY AU RC 10.00 25.00
45 S.Livingston JSY AU RC 15.00 40.00
46 Delonte West JSY AU RC 10.00 25.00
47 Trevor Ariza AU RC 10.00 25.00
48 Tony Allen JSY AU RC 10.00 25.00
49 Luke Jackson JSY AU RC 6.00 15.00
50 Dorell Wright JSY AU RC 30.00 80.00
51 Nenad Krstic JSY AU RC 10.00 25.00
52 Al Jefferson JSY RC 75.00 150.00
53 J.R. Smith JSY AU RC 20.00 50.00
54 Rafael Araujo JSY AU RC 6.00 15.00
55 Andris Biedrins JSY AU RC 3.00 8.00
56 Josh Smith JSY AU RC 20.00 50.00
57 Ha Seung-Jin JSY AU RC 10.00 25.00
58 B.Robinson JSY AU RC 8.00 20.00
59 Kevin Martin JSY AU RC 3.00 8.00
60 David Harrison JSY AU RC 20.00 50.00
61 Kris Humphries JSY AU RC 10.00 25.00
62 A.Varejao JSY AU RC 30.00 80.00
63 Jackson Vroman JSY AU RC 6.00 15.00
64 Sebastian Telfair JSY AU RC 8.00 20.00
65 Chris Duhon JSY AU RC 10.00 25.00
66 Kirk Snyder JSY AU RC 6.00 15.00
67 Andres Nocioni AU RC 8.00 20.00
68 Antonio Burks AU RC 6.00 15.00
69 Beno Udrih AU RC 6.00 15.00
70 D.J. Mbenga AU RC 6.00 15.00
71 Lionel Chalmers JSY AU RC 8.00 20.00
72 Robert Swift AU RC 5.00 12.00
73 Sasha Vujacic JSY AU RC 8.00 20.00
74 Donta Smith AU RC 5.00 12.00
75 Peter John Ramos AU RC 5.00 12.00
76 Justin Reed AU RC 5.00 12.00
77 Pape Sow AU RC 6.00 15.00
78 Pavel Podkolzin AU RC 5.00 12.00
79 Viktor Khryapa AU RC 5.00 12.00
80 John Edwards AU RC 5.00 12.00
81 Royal Ivey AU RC 6.00 15.00
82 Damien Wilkins AU RC 6.00 15.00
83 Erik Daniels AU RC 6.00 15.00
84 Luis Flores AU RC 6.00 15.00
85 Andre Iguodala JSY AU RC 100.00 200.00
86 Josh Childress JSY AU RC 6.00 15.00
87 Devin Harris JSY AU RC 20.00 50.00
88 Ben Gordon JSY AU RC 50.00 120.00
89 Luol Deng JSY AU RC 25.00 60.00
90 Dwight Howard JSY AU RC 400.00 800.00

2004-05 Exquisite Collection Jersey Parallel

*JSY PARALLEL: 1.25X TO 3X BASE HI
PRINT RUN 25 SER.#'d SETS
2 Paul Pierce 30.00 80.00
4 Michael Jordan 400.00 800.00
5 LeBron James 200.00 500.00
7 Carmelo Anthony 40.00 100.00
16 Kobe Bryant 100.00 250.00
20 Shaquille O'Neal 30.00 80.00
38 Chris Bosh 15.00 40.00

2004-05 Exquisite Collection Platinum

*1-42 PLATINUM: 2X TO 5X BASE HI
43-90 DO NOT HAVE JSY OR AU
PRINT RUN 25 SER.#'d SETS
4 Michael Jordan 500.00 1000.00
5 LeBron James 300.00 600.00
16 Kobe Bryant 250.00 600.00
19 Dwyane Wade 100.00 250.00
43 Andre Emmett 10.00 25.00
44 Jameer Nelson 15.00 40.00
45 Shaun Livingston 15.00 40.00
46 Delonte West 15.00 40.00
47 Trevor Ariza 15.00 40.00
48 Tony Allen 15.00 40.00
49 Luke Jackson 10.00 25.00
50 Dorell Wright 15.00 40.00
51 Nenad Krstic 15.00 40.00
52 Al Jefferson 20.00 50.00
53 J.R. Smith 15.00 40.00
54 Rafael Araujo 10.00 25.00
55 Andris Biedrins 10.00 25.00
56 Josh Smith 15.00 40.00
57 Ha Seung-Jin 15.00 40.00
58 Bernard Robinson 12.00 30.00
59 Kevin Martin 10.00 25.00
60 David Harrison 10.00 25.00
61 Kris Humphries 15.00 40.00
62 Anderson Varejao 12.00 30.00
63 Jackson Vroman 10.00 25.00
64 Sebastian Telfair 12.00 30.00
65 Chris Duhon 15.00 40.00
66 Kirk Snyder 10.00 25.00
67 Andres Nocioni 15.00 40.00
68 Antonio Burks 12.00 30.00
69 Beno Udrih 12.00 30.00
70 D.J. Mbenga 12.00 30.00
71 Lionel Chalmers 15.00 40.00
72 Robert Swift 10.00 25.00
73 Sasha Vujacic 15.00 40.00
74 Donta Smith 10.00 25.00
75 Peter John Ramos 10.00 25.00
76 Justin Reed 10.00 25.00
77 Pape Sow 12.00 30.00
78 Pavel Podkolzin 10.00 25.00
79 Viktor Khryapa 10.00 25.00
80 John Edwards 10.00 25.00
81 Royal Ivey 12.00 30.00
82 Damien Wilkins 12.00 30.00
83 Erik Daniels 12.00 30.00
84 Luis Flores 12.00 30.00
85 Andre Iguodala 75.00 200.00
86 Josh Childress 12.00 30.00
87 Devin Harris 12.00 30.00
88 Ben Gordon 15.00 40.00
89 Luol Deng 15.00 40.00
90 Dwight Howard 175.00 350.00

2004-05 Exquisite Collection Rookie Parallel

PRINT RUNS LISTED IN CHECKLIST
SOME NOT PRICED DUE TO SCARCITY
44 Jameer Nelson JSY AU/14 400.00 700.00
45 Shaun Livingston JSY AU/14 50.00 120.00
47 Trevor Ariza AU/21 20.00 50.00
48 Tony Allen JSY AU/42 30.00 80.00
49 Luke Jackson JSY AU/33 12.00 30.00
54 Rafael Araujo JSY AU/55 12.00 30.00
55 Andris Biedrins JSY AU/15 150.00 300.00
58 Bernard Robinson JSY/21 15.00 40.00
59 Kevin Martin JSY AU/23 25.00 60.00
61 Kris Humphries JSY AU/43 20.00 50.00
62 Anderson Varejao JSY AU/17 125.00 300.00
64 Sebastian Telfair JSY AU/31 30.00 80.00
65 Chris Duhon JSY AU/21 40.00 100.00
69 Beno Udrih AU/14 40.00 100.00
70 D.J. Mbenga AU/28 15.00 40.00
72 Robert Swift AU/31 12.00 30.00
73 Sasha Vujacic JSY AU/18 50.00 100.00
74 Donta Smith AU/15 12.00 30.00
75 Peter John Ramos AU/34 12.00 30.00
78 Pavel Podkolzin AU/24 12.00 30.00
79 Viktor Khryapa AU/38 12.00 30.00
80 John Edwards AU/54 12.00 30.00
81 Royal Ivey AU/36 15.00 40.00
83 Erik Daniels AU/15 15.00 40.00
87 Devin Harris JSY AU/34 30.00 80.00

2004-05 Exquisite Collection Dual Signature Shots

Inserted randomly in packs, this seven card set is horizontally designed with two small head shots of the players and an autographed basketball swatch. Each card is sequentially numbered to 25. A version that also contains jersey patch swatches was also inserted and those cards are serially numbered to five.
PRINT RUN 25 SER.#'d SETS
UNPRICED PATCH PRINT RUN FIVE SETS
GD B.Gordon/L.Deng 75.00 150.00
HC D.Harris/J.Childress 30.00 80.00
HN D.Howard/J.Nelson 50.00 120.00
IS A.Iguodala/J.R.Smith 30.00 80.00
KB A.Kirilenko/C.Boozer 40.00 100.00
LT S.Livingston/S.Telfair 15.00 40.00

2004-05 Exquisite Collection Enshrinements Autographs

Randomly seeded in packs, this 42-card set has gold borders on the left and right side of the card, colored borders along the top and bottom of the card to match the player's team colors, a portrait photo, autograph and sequential numbering to 25.
PRINT RUN 25 SER.#'d SETS
ENAS1 A.Stoudemire Purple 40.00 100.00
ENAS2 A.Stoudemire Orange 75.00 150.00
ENBG Ben Gordon 50.00 120.00
ENBR1 Bill Russell Posed 125.00 250.00
ENBR2 Bill Russell Dunk 125.00 250.00
ENBW Ben Wallace 40.00 100.00
ENCA1 C.Anthony Dribble 125.00 250.00
ENCA2 C.Anthony Dunk 125.00 250.00
ENDH Dwight Howard 175.00 350.00
ENDH2 Dwight Howard 175.00 350.00
ENDR David Robinson 125.00 250.00
ENHO Hakeem Olajuwon 75.00 150.00
ENIT Isiah Thomas 40.00 100.00
ENJE1 Julius Erving Red 75.00 150.00
ENJE2 Julius Erving White 75.00 150.00
ENJK Jason Kidd 50.00 120.00
ENJS Josh Smith 40.00 100.00
ENJS1 John Stockton Black 150.00 300.00
ENJS2 John Stockton White 100.00 200.00
ENKB1 Kobe Bryant Yellow 350.00 700.00
ENKB2 Kobe Bryant Purple 350.00 700.00
ENKG Kevin Garnett 100.00 200.00
ENLB1 Larry Bird Green 125.00 250.00
ENLB2 Larry Bird White 100.00 200.00
ENLD Luol Deng 50.00 125.00
ENLJ1 LeBron James Red 800.00 1200.00
ENLJ2 LeBron James White 800.00 1200.00
ENMA1 Magic Johnson 100.00 200.00
ENMA2 Magic Johnson 100.00 200.00
ENMJ1 Michael Jordan Red 1500.00 2000.00
ENMJ2 Michael Jordan White 1500.00 2000.00
ENPP Paul Pierce 50.00 125.00
ENRA Ray Allen 75.00 150.00
ENRO Dennis Rodman 100.00 200.00
ENSN Steve Nash 125.00 225.00
ENSP S.Pippen Straight 50.00 700.00
ENSP2 S.Pippen Head Right 400.00 550.00
ENST Stephon Marbury 50.00 120.00
ENTM1 Tracy McGrady Red 50.00 120.00
ENTM2 Tracy McGrady White 50.00 120.00
ENYM1 Yao Ming Red 50.00 125.00
ENYM2 Yao Ming White 50.00 125.00

2004-05 Exquisite Collection Extra Exquisite Jerseys

Inserted randomly into packs, this 42-card set is horizontally designed, places player photos to the left of a large jersey swatch and is sequentially numbered to 25. An Autographs version sequentially numbered to five and a Dual player version sequentially numbered to 10 were also produced and inserted.
PRINT RUN 25 SER.#'d SETS
UNPRICED DUAL PRINT RUN 10 SETS
UNPRICED AUTO PRINT RUN 5 SETS
AI Allen Iverson 60.00 150.00
AK Andrei Kirilenko 10.00 25.00
AN Andre Iguodala 15.00 40.00
AS Amare Stoudemire 10.00 25.00
BD Baron Davis 10.00 25.00
BG Ben Gordon 12.00 30.00
BW Ben Wallace 10.00 25.00
CA Carmelo Anthony 30.00 80.00
CB Chris Bosh 12.00 30.00
DE Devin Harris 10.00 25.00
DH Dwight Howard 25.00 60.00
DN Dirk Nowitzki 20.00 50.00
DR David Robinson 40.00 80.00
IT Isiah Thomas 12.00 30.00
JE Julius Erving 20.00 50.00
JK Jason Kidd 20.00 50.00
JO Josh Smith 12.00 30.00
JS John Stockton 40.00 80.00
KB1 Kobe Bryant Purple 50.00 125.00
KB2 Kobe Bryant White 50.00 125.00
KG Kevin Garnett 20.00 50.00
LB Larry Bird 30.00 80.00
LD Luol Deng 12.00 30.00
LJ1 LeBron James Red 80.00 200.00
LJ2 LeBron James White 80.00 200.00
MA Magic Johnson 30.00 80.00
MG Manu Ginobili 25.00 60.00
MJ1 Michael Jordan Red 250.00 500.00
MJ2 Michael Jordan White 250.00 500.00
PP Paul Pierce 12.00 30.00
RA Ray Allen 20.00 50.00
RM Reggie Miller 30.00 80.00
RO Dennis Rodman 40.00 100.00
SF Steve Francis 10.00 25.00
SL Shaun Livingston 12.00 30.00
SN Steve Nash 15.00 40.00
SO Shaquille O'Neal 30.00 80.00
SP Scottie Pippen 75.00 150.00
ST Stephon Marbury 10.00 25.00
TD Tim Duncan 20.00 50.00
TM Tracy McGrady 20.00 50.00
YM Yao Ming 50.00 120.00

2004-05 Exquisite Collection Limited Logos

Serially numbered to 50 and inserted randomly, this 42-card set contains an oversized swatch from the player's jersey logos and an autograph.
PRINT RUN 50 SER.#'d SETS
AK Andrei Kirilenko 75.00 150.00
AS Amare Stoudemire 150.00 250.00
BD Baron Davis 75.00 150.00
BG Ben Gordon 50.00 120.00
BW Ben Wallace 150.00 250.00
CA Carmelo Anthony 200.00 400.00
CB Carlos Boozer 50.00 120.00
CM Corey Maggette 50.00 120.00
DH1 Dwight Howard Blue 200.00 400.00
DH2 Dwight Howard White 400.00 750.00
DR David Robinson 200.00 400.00
GA Gilbert Arenas 75.00 150.00
HO Hakeem Olajuwon 150.00 400.00
IT Isiah Thomas 125.00 250.00
JK Jason Kidd 125.00 250.00
JS John Stockton 200.00 400.00
JW Jason Williams 150.00 300.00
KB1 Kobe Bryant Purple 2500.00 4000.00
KB2 Kobe Bryant Yellow 2500.00 4000.00
KG1 Kevin Garnett Black 300.00 600.00
KG2 Kevin Garnett Blue 300.00 600.00
KH Kirk Hinrich 50.00 120.00
LB Larry Bird 200.00 500.00
LD Luol Deng 60.00 150.00
LJ1 LeBron James Red 3000.00 5000.00
LJ2 LeBron James White 3000.00 5000.00
LO Lamar Odom 50.00 120.00
MA Magic Johnson 400.00 800.00
MJ Michael Jordan 4000.00 6000.00
MR Michael Redd 50.00 120.00
PG Pau Gasol 200.00 300.00
PP Paul Pierce 150.00 400.00
PS Peja Stojakovic 100.00 200.00
RA Ray Allen 250.00 500.00
RJ Richard Jefferson 50.00 120.00
RO Dennis Rodman 400.00 800.00
SM Shawn Marion 50.00 120.00
SN Steve Nash 300.00 600.00
ST Stephon Marbury 60.00 150.00
TM Tracy McGrady 300.00 600.00
TP Tony Parker 300.00 600.00
YM Yao Ming 300.00 600.00

2004-05 Exquisite Collection Number Pieces Autographs

Randomly inserted in packs and limited in number to the featured players jersey number, this 42-card set showcases autographs and swatches from the player's jersey number.
PRINT RUNS LISTED IN CHECKLIST
SOME UNPRICED DUE TO SCARCITY
AK Andrei Kirilenko/47 20.00 50.00
AS Amare Stoudemire/32 50.00 125.00
CA Carmelo Anthony/15 250.00 500.00
CM Corey Maggette/50 20.00 50.00
DE Devin Harris/34 25.00 60.00
DR David Robinson/50 100.00 200.00
HO Hakeem Olajuwon/34 60.00 120.00
KG Kevin Garnett/21 125.00 250.00
LB Larry Bird/33 250.00 350.00
LJ LeBron James/23 900.00 1500.00
MA Magic Johnson/34 200.00 400.00
MJ Michael Jordan/23 1200.00 1600.00
PG Pau Gasol/16 75.00 150.00
PP Paul Pierce/34 125.00 250.00
PS Peja Stojakovic/16 60.00 150.00
RA Ray Allen/34 100.00 200.00
RJ Richard Jefferson/24 20.00 50.00
RO Dennis Rodman/91 100.00 200.00
SM Shawn Marion/31 20.00 50.00
SP Scottie Pippen/33 350.00 500.00

2004-05 Exquisite Collection Patches Autographs

This 42-card set was randomly inserted in packs and places a jersey patch swatch in the middle of the card between a player photo and an autograph. Each card is serially numbered to 100.
PRINT RUN 50 TO 100 SER.#'d SETS
AJ Antawn Jamison/100 20.00 50.00
AK Andrei Kirilenko/100 20.00 50.00
AS Amare Stoudemire/100 20.00 50.00
BD Baron Davis/100 25.00 60.00
BG Ben Gordon/100 20.00 50.00
BR Bill Russell/75 200.00 350.00
BW Ben Wallace/100 20.00 50.00
CA Carmelo Anthony/100 75.00 150.00
CB Carlos Boozer/100 20.00 50.00
DE Devin Harris/100 20.00 50.00
DH Dwight Howard/100 60.00 150.00
DR David Robinson/100 60.00 150.00
GP Gary Payton/100 50.00 125.00
HO Hakeem Olajuwon/50 50.00 120.00
IT Isiah Thomas/100 40.00 100.00
JE Julius Erving/50 125.00 250.00
JK Jason Kidd/100 50.00 125.00
JS John Stockton/100 75.00 150.00
KB Kobe Bryant/100 1000.00 1500.00
KG Kevin Garnett/100 75.00 200.00
KH Kirk Hinrich/100 20.00 50.00
LB Larry Bird/100 100.00 200.00
LD Luol Deng/100 20.00 50.00
LJ LeBron James/100 700.00 900.00
MA Magic Johnson/100 125.00 250.00
MB Mike Bibby/100 20.00 50.00
MJ Michael Jordan/100 4000.00 6000.00
MR Michael Redd/100 20.00 50.00
PG Pau Gasol/100 20.00 50.00
PP Paul Pierce/100 50.00 125.00
PS Peja Stojakovic/100 60.00 150.00
RA Ray Allen/100 125.00 225.00
RH Richard Hamilton/100 20.00 50.00
RJ Richard Jefferson/100 20.00 50.00
RO Dennis Rodman/100 100.00 200.00
SA Shareef Abdur-Rahim/100 20.00 50.00
SM Shawn Marion/100 20.00 50.00
SP Scottie Pippen/100 400.00 700.00
ST Stephon Marbury/100 25.00 60.00
TM Tracy McGrady/100 50.00 125.00
TP Tony Parker/100 30.00 80.00
YM Yao Ming/100 75.00 200.00

2004-05 Exquisite Collection Signature Shots Patches

Randomly seeded and serially numbered to 100, this 14-card set is horizontally designed and places a color player photo on the right, and a jersey patch swatch on the left above an autographed swatch of basketball.
PRINT RUN 100 SER.#'d SETS
AI Andre Iguodala 20.00 50.00
AK Andrei Kirilenko 15.00 40.00
BG Ben Gordon 20.00 50.00
BM Brad Miller 12.00 30.00
CB Carlos Boozer 15.00 40.00
DE Devin Harris 12.00 30.00
DH Dwight Howard 50.00 120.00
JC Josh Childress 12.00 30.00
JN Jameer Nelson 12.00 30.00
JR J.R. Smith 20.00 50.00
LD Luol Deng 30.00 80.00
SL Shaun Livingston 15.00 40.00
SM Shawn Marion 12.00 30.00
ST Sebastian Telfair 12.00 30.00

2005-06 Exquisite Collection

Released in July, Exquisite Collection is Upper Deck's most expensive product of the year. The base set pictures veterans on cards 1-42, rookie autograph jerseys serially numbered to 99 on cards 43-48, rookie jersey autographs serially numbered to 225 on cards 49-82 and rookie autographs serially numbered to 225 on cards 85-95. Exquisite was packaged in carved wood boxes that contain five cards and carried a suggested retail price of $500.
1-42 PRINT RUN 225 SER.#'d SETS
43-48 JSY AU RC PRINT RUN 99 SETS
49-82 JSY AU RC PRINT RUN 225 SETS
83-96 AU RC PRINT RUN 225 SER.#'d SETS
UNPRICED RAINBOW PRINT RUN ONE SET
1 Joe Johnson 3.00 8.00
2 Paul Pierce 4.00 10.00
3 Emeka Okafor 3.00 8.00
4 Ben Gordon 3.00 8.00
5 Michael Jordan 125.00 300.00
6 LeBron James 60.00 150.00
7 Dirk Nowitzki 8.00 20.00
8 Carmelo Anthony 8.00 20.00
9 Kenyon Martin 3.00 8.00
10 Chauncey Billups 4.00 10.00
11 Ben Wallace 3.00 8.00
12 Jason Richardson 4.00 10.00
13 Tracy McGrady 5.00 12.00
14 Yao Ming 5.00 12.00
15 Jermaine O'Neal 3.00 8.00
16 Elton Brand 4.00 10.00
17 Kobe Bryant 50.00 125.00
18 Pau Gasol 4.00 10.00
19 Shaquille O'Neal 12.00 30.00
20 Dwyane Wade 6.00 15.00
21 Michael Redd 3.00 8.00
22 Kevin Garnett 6.00 15.00
23 Vince Carter 8.00 20.00
24 Jason Kidd 6.00 15.00
25 J.R. Smith 3.00 8.00
26 Stephon Marbury 3.00 8.00
27 Quentin Richardson 3.00 8.00
28 Steve Francis 3.00 8.00
29 Dwight Howard 3.00 8.00
30 Allen Iverson 10.00 25.00
31 Chris Webber 6.00 15.00
32 Steve Nash 5.00 12.00
33 Amare Stoudemire 3.00 8.00
34 Zach Randolph 3.00 8.00
35 Mike Bibby 3.00 8.00
36 Peja Stojakovic 4.00 10.00
37 Tim Duncan 15.00 40.00
38 Tony Parker 4.00 10.00
39 Ray Allen 4.00 10.00
40 Chris Bosh 4.00 10.00
41 Andrei Kirilenko 3.00 8.00
42 Gilbert Arenas 3.00 8.00
43 Andrew Bogut JSY AU/99 RC 60.00 150.00
44 M.Williams JSY AU/99 RC 15.00 40.00
45 D.Williams JSY AU/99 RC 100.00 250.00
46 Chris Paul JSY AU/99 RC 1200.00 2000.00
47 R.Felton JSY AU RC/99 30.00 80.00
48 C.Frye JSY AU/99 RC 15.00 40.00
49 M.Webster JSY AU RC 12.00 30.00
50 C.Villanueva JSY AU RC 8.00 20.00
51 Ike Diogu JSY AU RC 5.00 12.00
52 Andrew Bynum JSY AU RC 20.00 50.00
53 Sean May JSY AU RC 5.00 12.00
54 Rashad McCants JSY AU RC 20.00 50.00
55 Antoine Wright JSY AU RC 6.00 15.00
56 Joey Graham JSY AU RC 6.00 15.00
57 Danny Granger JSY AU RC 10.00 25.00
58 Gerald Green JSY AU RC 15.00 40.00
59 Hakim Warrick JSY AU RC 6.00 15.00
60 Julius Hodge JSY AU RC 5.00 12.00
61 Nate Robinson JSY AU RC 8.00 20.00
62 Jarrett Jack JSY AU RC 10.00 25.00
63 Francisco Garcia JSY AU RC 6.00 15.00
64 Luther Head JSY AU RC 6.00 15.00
65 Johan Petro JSY AU RC 5.00 12.00
66 Jason Maxiell JSY AU RC 6.00 15.00
67 Linas Kleiza JSY AU RC 5.00 12.00
68 Wayne Simien JSY AU RC 5.00 12.00
69 David Lee JSY AU RC 8.00 20.00
70 Salim Stoudamire JSY AU RC 6.00 15.00
71 Daniel Ewing JSY AU RC 6.00 15.00
72 Brandon Bass JSY AU RC 6.00 15.00
73 C.J. Miles JSY AU RC 8.00 20.00
74 Ersan Ilyasova JSY AU RC 15.00 40.00
75 Travis Diener JSY AU RC 5.00 12.00
76 Monta Ellis JSY AU RC 40.00 100.00
77 Chris Taft JSY AU RC 6.00 15.00
78 M.Andriuskevicius JSY AU RC 5.00 12.00
79 Louis Williams JSY AU RC 15.00 40.00
80 Andray Blatche JSY AU RC 8.00 20.00
81 Ryan Gomes JSY AU RC 6.00 15.00
82 S.Jasikevicius JSY AU RC 8.00 20.00
83 Yaroslav Korolev AU RC 4.00 10.00
85 Von Wafer AU RC 4.00 10.00
86 Orien Greene AU RC 5.00 12.00
87 Robert Whaley AU RC 4.00 10.00
88 Dijon Thompson AU RC 4.00 10.00
89 Bracey Wright AU RC 4.00 10.00
90 Amir Johnson AU RC 6.00 15.00
91 Ronny Turiaf AU RC 6.00 15.00
92 James Singleton AU RC 4.00 10.00
93 Alex Acker AU RC 4.00 10.00
94 Chuck Hayes AU RC 6.00 15.00
95 Lawrence Roberts AU RC 4.00 10.00
96 Stephen Graham AU RC 6.00 15.00

2005-06 Exquisite Collection Gold

*1-42 GOLD: 1.25X TO 3X BASE HI
GOLD PRINT RUN 25 SER.#'d SETS
26 Stephon Marbury 12.00 30.00
43 Andrew Bogut 25.00 60.00
44 Marvin Williams 15.00 40.00
45 Deron Williams 40.00 100.00
46 Chris Paul 250.00 450.00
47 Raymond Felton 15.00 40.00
48 Channing Frye 15.00 40.00
49 Martell Webster 12.00 30.00
50 Charlie Villanueva 15.00 40.00
51 Ike Diogu 10.00 25.00
52 Andrew Bynum 12.00 30.00
53 Sean May 10.00 25.00
54 Rashad McCants 12.00 30.00
55 Antoine Wright 12.00 30.00
56 Joey Graham 12.00 30.00
57 Danny Granger 20.00 50.00
58 Gerald Green 15.00 40.00
59 Hakim Warrick 12.00 30.00
60 Julius Hodge 10.00 25.00
61 Nate Robinson 15.00 40.00
62 Jarrett Jack 15.00 40.00
63 Francisco Garcia 12.00 30.00
64 Luther Head 12.00 30.00
65 Johan Petro 10.00 25.00

66 Jason Maxiell 12.00 30.00
67 Linas Kleiza 10.00 25.00
68 Wayne Simien 10.00 25.00
69 David Lee 15.00 40.00
70 Salim Stoudamire 12.00 30.00
71 Daniel Ewing 12.00 30.00
72 Brandon Bass 12.00 30.00
73 C.J. Miles 15.00 40.00
74 Ersan Ilyasova 15.00 40.00
75 Travis Diener 10.00 25.00
76 Monta Ellis 30.00 80.00
77 Chris Taft 12.00 30.00
78 Martynas Andriuskevicius 10.00 25.00
79 Louis Williams 15.00 40.00
80 Andray Blatche 15.00 40.00
81 Ryan Gomes 12.00 30.00
82 Sarunas Jasikevicius 15.00 40.00
83 Yaroslav Korolev 10.00 25.00
84 Jose Calderon 15.00 40.00
85 Von Wafer 10.00 25.00
86 Orien Greene 12.00 30.00
87 Robert Whaley 10.00 25.00
88 Dijon Thompson 10.00 25.00
89 Bracey Wright 10.00 25.00
90 Amir Johnson 15.00 40.00
91 Ronny Turiaf 15.00 40.00
92 James Singleton 10.00 25.00
93 Alex Acker 10.00 25.00
94 Chuck Hayes 15.00 40.00
95 Lawrence Roberts 10.00 25.00
96 Stephen Graham 15.00 40.00

2005-06 Exquisite Collection Jerseys

*JERSEY: 1.25X TO 3X BASE HI
PRINT RUN 25 SER.#'d SETS
UNPRICED DUAL PRINT RUN 10 SETS
UNPRICED DUAL AUTO PRINT RUN 5 SETS
UNPRICED PATCH PRINT RUN 10 SETS
UNPRICED PATCH QUAD PRINT RUN 3 SETS
UNPRICED PATCH TRIPLE PRINT RUN 10 SETS

2005-06 Exquisite Collection Rookie Parallel

PRINT RUNS LISTED IN CHECKLIST
SOME UNPRICED DUE TO SCARCITY
44AP Marvin Williams JSY AU/24 40.00 100.00
47AP Raymond Felton JSY AU/20 25.00 60.00
50AP Charlie Villanueva JSY AU/31 25.00 60.00
52AP A.Bynum JSY AU/17 600.00 800.00
53AP Sean May JSY AU/42 15.00 40.00
55AP Antoine Wright JSY AU/21 40.00 100.00
56AP Joey Graham JSY AU/14 20.00 50.00
57AP Danny Granger JSY AU/33 30.00 80.00
59AP Hakim Warrick JSY AU/21 150.00 300.00
60AP Julius Hodge JSY AU/32 15.00 40.00
63AP Francisco Garcia JSY AU/32 20.00 50.00
65AP Johan Petro JSY AU/27 15.00 40.00
66AP Jason Maxiell JSY AU/54 30.00 80.00
67AP Linas Kleiza JSY AU/43 15.00 40.00
68AP Wayne Simien JSY AU/25 15.00 40.00
69AP David Lee JSY AU/42 25.00 60.00
70AP Salim Stoudamire JSY AU/20 20.00 50.00
72AP Brandon Bass JSY AU/33 30.00 80.00
73AP C.J. Miles JSY AU/34 60.00 120.00
74AP Ersan Ilyasova JSY AU/23 25.00 60.00
75AP Travis Diener JSY AU/34 15.00 40.00
77AP Chris Taft JSY AU/21 20.00 50.00
78AP Andriuskevicius JSY AU/15 40.00 100.00
79AP Louis Williams JSY AU/23 125.00 250.00
80AP Andray Blatche JSY AU/32 25.00 60.00
85AP Von Wafer AU/23 15.00 40.00
86AP Orien Greene AU/100 20.00 50.00
87AP Robert Whaley AU/21 15.00 40.00
90AP Amir Johnson AU/25 60.00 120.00
91AP Ronny Turiaf AU/21 100.00 200.00
92AP James Singleton AU/15 15.00 40.00
94AP Chuck Hayes AU/44 25.00 60.00
95AP Lawrence Roberts AU/44 15.00 40.00

2005-06 Exquisite Collection Autographs Patches

PRINT RUN 100 SER.#'d SETS
APAB Andrew Bogut 50.00 100.00
APAN Andrew Bynum 40.00 100.00
APAW Antoine Wright 10.00 25.00
APCA Carmelo Anthony 60.00 150.00
APCB Chris Bosh 30.00 80.00
APCF Channing Frye 12.00 30.00
APCH Chauncey Billups 25.00 60.00
APCP Chris Paul 150.00 300.00
APCV Charlie Villanueva 6.00 15.00
APDE Dennis Rodman 50.00 120.00
APDG Danny Granger 25.00 60.00
APDH Dwight Howard 50.00 120.00
APDL David Lee 25.00 60.00
APDR David Robinson 60.00 150.00
APDW Deron Williams 25.00 60.00
APEB Elton Brand 12.00 30.00
APHW Hakim Warrick 10.00 25.00
APID Ike Diogu 10.00 25.00
APJJ Jarrett Jack 12.00 30.00
APJK Jason Kidd 60.00 150.00
APJR J.R. Smith 12.00 30.00
APJS John Stockton 75.00 200.00
APKG Kevin Garnett 125.00 250.00
APLB Larry Bird 100.00 200.00
APLH Larry Hughes 12.00 30.00
APLJ LeBron James 600.00 900.00
APLO Lamar Odom 25.00 60.00
APMA Magic Johnson 175.00 325.00
APMB Mike Bibby 12.00 30.00
APMJ Michael Jordan 500.00 1000.00
APMR Martell Webster 12.00 30.00
APMW Marvin Williams 12.00 30.00
APNR Nate Robinson 15.00 40.00
APPS Peja Stojakovic 20.00 50.00
APRF Raymond Felton 6.00 15.00
APSJ Sarunas Jasikevicius 20.00 50.00
APSM Sean May 10.00 25.00
APSP Scottie Pippen 150.00 300.00
APST Stephon Marbury 15.00 40.00
APTM Tracy McGrady 60.00 150.00
APTP Tayshaun Prince 15.00 40.00
APVC Vince Carter 40.00 100.00

2005-06 Exquisite Collection Emblems of Endorsements

Seeded randomly in packs, this 40-card set is horizontally designed with a player image between two patch swatches from jersey emblems and an autograph along the bottom. Each card is serially numbered to 15.

PRINT RUN 15 SER.#'d SETS
EMAB Andrew Bogut 150.00 300.00
EMAI Andre Iguodala 60.00 150.00
EMAJ Antawn Jamison 30.00 80.00
EMBW Bill Walton 175.00 350.00
EMCA Carmelo Anthony 150.00 300.00
EMCB Chauncey Billups 100.00 250.00
EMCH Chris Bosh 100.00 250.00
EMCM Corey Maggette 30.00 80.00
EMCP Chris Paul 400.00 700.00
EMDH Dwight Howard 150.00 325.00
EMDR David Robinson 175.00 350.00
EMEB Elton Brand 30.00 80.00
EMEO Emeka Okafor 30.00 80.00
EMHO Hakeem Olajuwon 200.00 500.00
EMJE Julius Erving 175.00 350.00
EMJS John Stockton 200.00 350.00
EMKG Kevin Garnett 200.00 400.00
EMKH Kirk Hinrich 30.00 80.00
EMLH Larry Hughes 30.00 80.00
EMLJ LeBron James 2000.00 4000.00
EMLO Lamar Odom 30.00 80.00
EMMJ Michael Jordan 3000.00 6000.00
EMMW Marvin Williams 30.00 80.00
EMPG Pau Gasol 75.00 150.00
EMPP Paul Pierce 150.00 400.00
EMPS Peja Stojakovic 60.00 150.00
EMRA Ron Artest 30.00 80.00
EMRH Richard Hamilton 30.00 80.00
EMRJ Richard Jefferson 30.00 80.00
EMSA Shareef Abdur-Rahim 30.00 80.00
EMSM Stephon Marbury 30.00 80.00
EMSN Steve Nash 200.00 400.00
EMSP Scottie Pippen 300.00 500.00
EMST Sebastian Telfair 30.00 80.00
EMTM Tracy McGrady 150.00 400.00
EMTP Tayshaun Prince 30.00 80.00
EMVC Vince Carter 150.00 400.00
EMYM Yao Ming 200.00 500.00

2005-06 Exquisite Collection Enshrinements

Seeded randomly in packs, this 41-card set places a full color portrait-style photo of players in between a foil design set to appear as a hall of fame plaque with an authentic player autograph. Each card is serially numbered to 25.
PRINT RUN 25 SER.#'d SETS
EEAB Andrew Bogut 20.00 50.00
EEAI Andre Iguodala 12.00 30.00
EEAJ Antawn Jamison 15.00 40.00
EEBD Baron Davis 15.00 40.00
EEBR Bill Russell 100.00 200.00
EECA Carmelo Anthony 40.00 80.00
EECB Chauncey Billups 20.00 50.00
EECF Channing Frye 12.00 30.00
EECH Chris Bosh 50.00 100.00
EECP Chris Paul 250.00 450.00
EEDE Dennis Rodman 100.00 200.00
EEDH Dwight Howard 40.00 100.00
EEDR David Robinson 75.00 150.00
EEDW Deron Williams 50.00 120.00
EEEB Elton Brand 15.00 40.00
EEEO Emeka Okafor 15.00 40.00
EEGG George Gervin 30.00 60.00
EEHO Hakeem Olajuwon 40.00 70.00
EEJE Julius Erving 60.00 120.00
EEJK Jason Kidd 60.00 150.00
EEJS John Stockton 75.00 150.00
EEKA Kareem Abdul-Jabbar 75.00 150.00
EEKG Kevin Garnett 75.00 150.00
EELB Larry Bird 100.00 200.00
EELJ LeBron James 800.00 1200.00
EELO Lamar Odom 20.00 50.00
EEMA Magic Johnson 75.00 150.00
EEMJ Michael Jordan 1800.00 2200.00
EEMW Marvin Williams 25.00 60.00
EEPP Paul Pierce 25.00 50.00
EERA Ron Artest 20.00 50.00
EESA Shareef Abdur-Rahim 15.00 40.00
EESM Stephon Marbury 15.00 40.00
EESN Steve Nash 50.00 120.00
EESP Scottie Pippen 150.00 300.00
EETM Tracy McGrady 40.00 80.00
EEVC Vince Carter 100.00 250.00
EEYM Yao Ming 40.00 80.00
EELJ2 LeBron James 800.00 1200.00
EEMJ2 Michael Jordan 1300.00 1800.00

2005-06 Exquisite Collection Extra Exquisite

Found randomly in packs, this horizontally designed card places a player photo on the left side of the card and a large swatch of jersey that covers roughly 75 percent of the card front. Each is serially numbered to 25.
PRINT RUN 25 SER.#'d SETS
UNPRICED DUAL PRINT RUN 10 SETS
UNPRICED AUTO PRINT RUN 5 SETS
EXAB Andrew Bogut 12.00 30.00
EXBR Bill Russell 50.00 100.00
EXBW Ben Wallace 8.00 20.00
EXCA Carmelo Anthony 20.00 50.00
EXCB Chris Bosh 20.00 40.00
EXCF Channing Frye 10.00 25.00
EXCP Chris Paul 40.00 100.00
EXCV Charlie Villanueva 10.00 25.00
EXDN Dirk Nowitzki 30.00 80.00
EXDR David Robinson 30.00 60.00
EXDW Deron Williams 12.00 30.00
EXEB Elton Brand 10.00 25.00
EXEO Emeka Okafor 8.00 20.00
EXIT Isiah Thomas 10.00 25.00
EXJO Jermaine O'Neal 8.00 20.00
EXJS John Stockton 25.00 50.00
EXKA Kareem Abdul-Jabbar 20.00 50.00
EXKB Kobe Bryant 50.00 100.00
EXKG Kevin Garnett 30.00 60.00
EXLB Larry Bird 40.00 100.00
EXLJ LeBron James 100.00 200.00
EXMA Magic Johnson 25.00 60.00
EXMG Manu Ginobili 15.00 30.00
EXMJ Michael Jordan 200.00 400.00
EXMW Marvin Williams 10.00 25.00
EXPS Peja Stojakovic 10.00 25.00
EXRA Ray Allen 15.00 40.00
EXRF Raymond Felton 10.00 25.00
EXRJ Richard Jefferson 8.00 20.00
EXRO Ron Artest 10.00 25.00
EXSO Shaquille O'Neal 30.00 60.00
EXSP Scottie Pippen 50.00 125.00
EXTD Tim Duncan 25.00 60.00
EXTM Tracy McGrady 12.00 30.00
EXVC Vince Carter 20.00 40.00
EXWC Wilt Chamberlain 75.00 200.00
EXYM Yao Ming 40.00 100.00
EXLJ2 LeBron James 100.00 200.00
EXLJ3 LeBron James 100.00 200.00
EXMJ2 Michael Jordan 200.00 400.00
EXMJ3 Michael Jordan 200.00 400.00
EXMW2 Marvin Williams 10.00 25.00

2005-06 Exquisite Collection Limited Logos

Randomly inserted, this 41-card set places a small head-shot photo on the top, a large patch swatche in the midde, team colored borders and an autograph on the bottom. Cards are limited to 50 serially numbered copies except the Bill Russell, which is numbered to 50.
PRINT RUN 28 TO 50 SER.#'d SETS
LLAB Andrew Bogut 60.00 150.00
LLAJ Antawn Jamison 25.00 60.00
LLAL Al Jefferson 25.00 60.00
LLAN Andrew Bynum 150.00 300.00
LLBG Ben Gordon 40.00 100.00
LLBR Bill Russell/28 350.00 550.00
LLCA Carmelo Anthony 125.00 250.00
LLCB Chauncey Billups 60.00 150.00
LLCF Channing Frye 40.00 100.00
LLCH Chris Bosh 75.00 150.00
LLCP Chris Paul 400.00 700.00
LLCV Charlie Villanueva 25.00 60.00
LLDE Dennis Rodman 250.00 500.00
LLDH Dwight Howard 150.00 300.00
LLDR David Robinson 175.00 350.00
LLDW Deron Williams 200.00 350.00
LLEB Elton Brand 25.00 60.00
LLID Ike Diogu 25.00 60.00
LLJE Julius Erving 200.00 350.00
LLJK Jason Kidd 125.00 250.00
LLKG Kevin Garnett 200.00 400.00
LLLB Larry Bird 175.00 350.00
LLLH Larry Hughes 25.00 60.00
LLLJ LeBron James 1200.00 2000.00
LLMA Magic Johnson 250.00 500.00
LLMJ Michael Jordan 2000.00 3000.00
LLNR Nate Robinson 40.00 100.00
LLPP Paul Pierce 100.00 200.00
LLRA Ron Artest 30.00 80.00
LLRF Raymond Felton 30.00 80.00
LLRM Rashad McCants 25.00 60.00
LLSA Shareef Abdur-Rahim 30.00 80.00
LLSM Sean May 25.00 60.00
LLSN Steve Nash 200.00 400.00
LLSP Scottie Pippen 400.00 700.00
LLTC Tyson Chandler 75.00 200.00
LLTM Tracy McGrady 75.00 150.00
LLTP Tayshaun Prince 25.00 60.00
LLVC Vince Carter 175.00 325.00
LLYM Yao Ming 200.00 300.00
LLMW2 Marvin Williams 30.00 80.00

2005-06 Exquisite Collection Noble Nameplates

Limited to 25 serially numbered copies, this 57-card set places player photos on the right side of the card, a logo swatch and an autograph on the left side of the card.
PRINT RUN 25 SER.#'d SETS
NNAB Andrew Bogut 75.00 150.00
NNAJ Antawn Jamison 20.00 50.00
NNAN Andrew Bynum 200.00 400.00
NNBK Bernard King 20.00 50.00
NNBR Bill Russell 250.00 500.00
NNCA Carmelo Anthony 75.00 150.00
NNCB Carlos Boozer 20.00 50.00
NNCF Channing Frye 40.00 100.00
NNCH Chauncey Billups 20.00 50.00
NNCM Corey Maggette 20.00 50.00
NNCP Chris Paul 400.00 800.00
NNCS Chris Bosh 60.00 150.00
NNCV Charlie Villanueva 30.00 60.00
NNDA David Robinson 80.00 200.00
NNDG Danny Granger 50.00 100.00
NNDH Dwight Howard 125.00 250.00
NNDL David Lee 30.00 60.00
NNDR Dennis Rodman 125.00 250.00
NNEB Elton Brand 20.00 50.00
NNEO Emeka Okafor 20.00 50.00
NNGG Gerald Green 40.00 100.00
NNHO Hakeem Olajuwon 75.00 150.00
NNHW Hakim Warrick 30.00 60.00
NNID Ike Diogu 20.00 50.00
NNJE Julius Erving 125.00 250.00
NNJJ Joe Johnson 20.00 50.00
NNJK Jason Kidd 60.00 120.00
NNJN Jameer Nelson 20.00 50.00
NNJP Johan Petro 20.00 50.00
NNJR J.R. Smith 20.00 50.00
NNJS John Stockton 100.00 200.00
NNKA Kareem Abdul-Jabbar 100.00 200.00
NNLB Larry Bird 150.00 300.00
NNLJ LeBron James 2000.00 3000.00
NNMB Mike Bibby 20.00 50.00
NNMJ Magic Johnson 100.00 200.00
NNMR Michael Redd 20.00 50.00
NNMW Marvin Williams 20.00 50.00
NNNR Nate Robinson 20.00 50.00
NNPP Paul Pierce 30.00 60.00
NNPS Peja Stojakovic 20.00 50.00
NNRA Ron Artest 40.00 100.00
NNRF Raymond Felton 20.00 50.00
NNRH Richard Hamilton 20.00 50.00
NNRJ Richard Jefferson 20.00 50.00
NNRM Rashad McCants 20.00 50.00
NNSA Shareef Abdur-Rahim 20.00 50.00
NNSC Speedy Claxton 20.00 50.00
NNSE Sean May 20.00 50.00
NNSF Stephon Marbury 20.00 50.00
NNSN Steve Nash 125.00 250.00
NNSP Scottie Pippen 250.00 400.00
NNST Sebastian Telfair 20.00 50.00
NNTM Tracy McGrady 80.00 200.00
NNTP Tayshaun Prince 30.00 60.00
NNVC Vince Carter 125.00 250.00
NNWF Walt Frazier 50.00 120.00

2005-06 Exquisite Collection Numbers

Serially numbered to featured player's jersey number, this set places player photos on the left, jersey swatches in the shape of the player's number and an autograph on the right.
STATED PRINT RUN ONE TO 91 SETS
SOME NOT PRICED DUE TO SCARCITY
ENCA Carmelo Anthony/15 250.00 400.00
ENDR Dennis Rodman/91 75.00 200.00
ENEB Elton Brand/42 20.00 50.00
ENEO Emeka Okafor/50 20.00 50.00
ENHO Hakeem Olajuwon/34 100.00 200.00
ENKG Kevin Garnett/21 200.00 400.00
ENLB Larry Bird/33 150.00 400.00
ENLJ LeBron James/23 900.00 1500.00
ENMA Magic Johnson/32 150.00 400.00
ENMJ Michael Jordan/23 1700.00 2500.00
ENMW Marvin Williams/24 40.00 100.00
ENPS Peja Stojakovic/16 50.00 100.00
ENSN Steve Nash/13 200.00 400.00
ENVC Vince Carter/15 200.00 400.00

2005-06 Exquisite Collection Numbers Dual

Serially numbered to featured players' jersey numbers, this set places player photos on each side and centered jersey swatches in the shape of the players' jersey number number along with two autographs.
STATED PRINT RUN 12 TO 50 SETS
DNAB Abdul-Jabbar/Bird/33 200.00 400.00
DNAC C.Anthony/Carter/15 200.00 400.00
DNBM E.Brand/S.May/42 15.00 40.00
DNHS K.Hinrich/Stockton/12 100.00 200.00
DNJH M.Johnson/Hughes/32 150.00 300.00
DNJJ M.Jordan/L.James/23 2000.00 3000.00
DNJW Jefferson/Williams/24 40.00 100.00
DNOR Okafor/D.Robinson/50 50.00 125.00
DNPR T.Prince/M.Redd/22 80.00 160.00
DNSJ J.R.Smith/L.James/23 300.00 600.00
DNWG Warrick/Garnett/21 100.00 200.00

2005-06 Exquisite Collection Scripted Swatches

Randomly seeded in packs, this 29-card set is horizontally designed with player photos on the right side and an autographed jersey patch swatch on the left. Each card is serially numbered to either 3 or 25 copies.
PRINT RUN 3 TO 25 SER.#'d SETS
UNPRICED DUAL PRINT RUN 5 SETS
SSAB Andrew Bogut/25 20.00 50.00
SSCA Carmelo Anthony/25 100.00 200.00
SSCB Chauncey Billups/25 25.00 60.00
SSCF Channing Frye/25 40.00 100.00
SSCH Chris Bosh/25 25.00 60.00
SSCP Chris Paul/25 150.00 300.00
SSCV Charlie Villanueva/25 40.00 100.00
SSDE Dennis Rodman/25 100.00 200.00
SSDH Dwight Howard/25 30.00 80.00
SSDM Desmond Mason/25 25.00 60.00
SSDR David Robinson/25 125.00 250.00
SSDW Deron Williams/25 75.00 150.00
SSEB Elton Brand/25 25.00 60.00
SSJK Jason Kidd/25 75.00 150.00
SSJS John Stockton/25 150.00 300.00
SSKA Kareem Abdul-Jabbar/25 175.00 350.00
SSKG Kevin Garnett/25 150.00 300.00
SSLB Larry Bird/25 200.00 400.00
SSLJ LeBron James/25 500.00 1000.00
SSMA Magic Johnson/25 175.00 350.00
SSMJ Michael Jordan/25 1200.00 1700.00
SSMW Marvin Williams/25 25.00 60.00
SSPP Paul Pierce/25 75.00 200.00
SSPS Peja Stojakovic/25 40.00 80.00
SSSN Steve Nash/25 200.00 350.00
SSTM Tracy McGrady/25 125.00 300.00
SSVC Vince Carter/25 60.00 200.00
SSYM Yao Ming/25 60.00 150.00

2006-07 Exquisite Collection

Released in early August 2007, Exquisite Collection features a 85-card set where cards 1-42 showcase veterans and #4 Adam Morrison's rookie and #31 J.J. Reidick's rookie serially numbered to 225, cards 43-48 showcase rookie autograph patches serially numbered to 99, cards 49-79 showcase rookie autograph patches serially numbered to 225 and cards 80-42 showcase rookie autographs serially numbered to 225. Also inserted in the product were special uncut sheet redemption cards and 24 serially numbered packs autographed by Kobe Bryant. Exquisite Collection originally carried a suggested retail price of $500 for a five-card wooden carved pack.
1-42 PRINT RUN 225 SER.#'d SETS
43-48 PRINT RUN 99 SER.#'d SETS
UNPRICED BLACK PRINT RUN ONE SET
UNPRICED BLACK RNBW PRINT RUN ONE SET
1 Joe Johnson 3.00 8.00
2 Paul Pierce 4.00 10.00
3 Emeka Okafor 3.00 8.00
4 Adam Morrison RC 4.00 10.00
5 Michael Jordan 75.00 200.00
6 Kirk Hinrich 3.00 8.00
7 LeBron James 30.00 80.00
8 Dirk Nowitzki 8.00 20.00
9 Carmelo Anthony 5.00 12.00
10 Allen Iverson 5.00 12.00
11 Chauncey Billups 4.00 10.00
12 Richard Hamilton 3.00 8.00
13 Baron Davis 3.00 8.00
14 Yao Ming 5.00 12.00
15 Tracy McGrady 5.00 12.00
16 Jermaine O'Neal 3.00 8.00
17 Elton Brand 4.00 10.00
18 Kobe Bryant 25.00 60.00
19 Lamar Odom 3.00 8.00
20 Pau Gasol 4.00 10.00
21 Dwyane Wade 6.00 15.00
22 Shaquille O'Neal 8.00 20.00
23 Michael Redd 3.00 8.00
24 Kevin Garnett 6.00 15.00
25 Vince Carter 5.00 12.00
26 Jason Kidd 6.00 15.00
27 Chris Paul 5.00 12.00
28 Peja Stojakovic 4.00 10.00
29 Stephon Marbury 3.00 8.00
30 Dwight Howard 3.00 8.00
31 J.J. Redick RC 10.00 25.00
32 Andre Iguodala 3.00 8.00
33 Steve Nash 5.00 12.00
34 Amare Stoudemire 3.00 8.00
35 Jarrett Jack 3.00 8.00
36 Mike Bibby 4.00 10.00
37 Tim Duncan 6.00 15.00
38 Tony Parker 4.00 10.00
39 Ray Allen 4.00 10.00
40 Chris Bosh 4.00 10.00
41 Deron Williams 3.00 8.00
42 Antawn Jamison 3.00 8.00
43 A.Bargnani JSY AU/99 RC 40.00 100.00
44 L.Aldridge JSY AU/99 RC 200.00 400.00
45 T.Thomas JSY AU/99 RC 6.00 15.00
46 Brandon Roy JSY AU/99 RC 75.00 200.00
47 Rudy Gay JSY AU/99 RC 150.00 250.00
48 S.Williams JSY AU/99 RC 6.00 15.00
49 Randy Foye JSY AU RC 8.00 20.00
50 Patrick O'Bryant JSY AU RC 5.00 12.00
51 Saer Sene JSY AU RC 5.00 12.00
52 H.Armstrong JSY AU RC 5.00 12.00
53 T.Sefolosha JSY AU RC 10.00 25.00
54 Ronnie Brewer JSY AU RC 8.00 20.00
55 Cedric Simmons JSY AU RC 5.00 12.00
56 Rodney Carney JSY AU RC 5.00 12.00
57 Shawne Williams JSY AU RC 5.00 12.00
58 Quincy Douby JSY AU RC 5.00 12.00
59 R.Balkman JSY AU RC 6.00 15.00
60 Rajon Rondo JSY AU RC 100.00 250.00
61 Marcus Williams JSY AU RC 5.00 12.00
62 Josh Boone JSY AU RC 5.00 12.00
63 Allan Ray JSY AU RC 5.00 12.00
64 Shannon Brown JSY AU RC 5.00 12.00
65 Jordan Farmar JSY AU RC 8.00 20.00
66 Dee Brown JSY AU RC 5.00 12.00
67 Maurice Ager JSY AU RC 5.00 12.00
68 Mardy Collins JSY AU RC 5.00 12.00
69 James White JSY AU RC 5.00 12.00
70 Steve Novak JSY AU RC 6.00 15.00
71 Solomon Jones JSY AU RC 5.00 12.00
72 Paul Davis JSY AU RC 5.00 12.00
73 P.J. Tucker JSY AU RC 6.00 15.00
74 Craig Smith JSY AU RC 6.00 15.00
75 Bobby Jones JSY AU RC 5.00 12.00
76 David Noel JSY AU RC 5.00 12.00
77 Jorge Garbajosa JSY AU RC 6.00 15.00
78 Daniel Gibson JSY AU RC 6.00 15.00
79 Sergio Rodriguez AU RC 8.00 20.00
80 Paul Millsap AU RC 20.00 50.00
81 Will Blalock AU RC 5.00 12.00
82 Hassan Adams AU RC 5.00 12.00
83 Kyle Lowry AU RC 20.00 50.00
84 James Augustine AU RC 5.00 12.00

2006-07 Exquisite Collection Gold

*1-42 GOLD: 1.5X TO 4X BASE HI
GOLD PRINT RUN 25 SER.#'d SETS
5 Michael Jordan 300.00 600.00
31 J.J. Redick 30.00 80.00
43 Andrea Bargnani 12.00 30.00
44 LaMarcus Aldridge 40.00 100.00
45 Tyrus Thomas 10.00 25.00
46 Brandon Roy 12.00 30.00
47 Rudy Gay 15.00 40.00
48 Shelden Williams 10.00 25.00
49 Randy Foye 12.00 30.00
50 Patrick O'Bryant 8.00 20.00
51 Saer Sene 8.00 20.00
52 Hilton Armstrong 8.00 20.00
53 Thabo Sefolosha 12.00 30.00
54 Ronnie Brewer 12.00 30.00
55 Cedric Simmons 8.00 20.00
56 Rodney Carney 8.00 20.00
57 Shawne Williams 8.00 20.00
58 Quincy Douby 8.00 20.00
59 Renaldo Balkman 10.00 25.00
60 Rajon Rondo 40.00 100.00
61 Marcus Williams 8.00 20.00
62 Josh Boone 8.00 20.00
63 Allan Ray 8.00 20.00
64 Shannon Brown 8.00 20.00
66 Dee Brown 8.00 20.00
67 Maurice Ager 8.00 20.00
68 Mardy Collins 8.00 20.00
69 James White 8.00 20.00
70 Steve Novak 10.00 25.00
71 Solomon Jones 8.00 20.00
72 Paul Davis 8.00 20.00
73 P.J. Tucker 10.00 25.00
74 Craig Smith 10.00 25.00
75 Bobby Jones 8.00 20.00
76 David Noel 8.00 20.00
77 Jorge Garbajosa 10.00 25.00
79 Sergio Rodriguez 12.00 30.00
80 Paul Millsap 15.00 40.00
81 Will Blalock 8.00 20.00
82 Hassan Adams 8.00 20.00
83 Kyle Lowry 15.00 40.00
84 James Augustine 8.00 20.00

2006-07 Exquisite Collection Jerseys

*JERSEYS: 1.25X TO 3X BASE HI
JSY PRINT RUN 25 SER.#'d SETS
UNPRICED PATCH PRINT RUN 10 SETS
5J Michael Jordan 250.00 500.00
31J J.J. Redick 15.00 40.00
39J Ray Allen 15.00 40.00

2006-07 Exquisite Collection Rookie Parallel

SOME NOT PRICED DUE TO SCARCITY
44 L.Aldridge JSY AU/12 300.00 600.00
45 Tyrus Thomas JSY AU/24 20.00 50.00
47 Rudy Gay JSY AU/22 300.00 600.00
48 Shelden Williams JSY AU/33 20.00 50.00
50 Patrick O'Bryant JSY AU/26 15.00 40.00
51 Saer Sene JSY AU/18 40.00 100.00
52 Hilton Armstrong JSY AU/12 40.00 100.00
55 Cedric Simmons JSY AU/22 15.00 40.00
56 Rodney Carney JSY AU/25 15.00 40.00
59 Renaldo Balkman JSY AU/32 20.00 50.00
66 Dee Brown JSY AU/11 15.00 40.00
67 Maurice Ager JSY AU/13 15.00 40.00
68 Mardy Collins JSY AU/25 15.00 40.00
69 James White JSY AU/33 15.00 40.00
70 Steve Novak JSY AU/20 20.00 50.00
71 Solomon Jones JSY AU/44 15.00 40.00
72 Paul Davis JSY AU/40 15.00 40.00
75 Bobby Jones JSY AU/11 75.00 150.00
76 David Noel JSY AU/34 15.00 40.00
77 Jorge Garbajosa JSY AU/15 125.00 250.00
79 Sergio Rodriguez AU/11 30.00 80.00
80 Paul Millsap AU/24 75.00 150.00
83 Kyle Lowry AU/12 75.00 150.00
84 James Augustine AU/40 15.00 40.00

2006-07 Exquisite Collection Autographs Patches

PRINT RUN 100 SER.#'d SETS
APAB Andrea Bargnani 15.00 40.00
APBG Ben Gordon 15.00 40.00
APBJ Bobby Jones 10.00 25.00
APBO Chris Bosh 30.00 80.00
APBR Brandon Roy 30.00 80.00
APCA Carmelo Anthony 60.00 150.00
APCB Chauncey Billups 20.00 50.00
APCP Chris Paul 75.00 200.00
APCS Craig Smith 10.00 25.00
APDA Baron Davis 15.00 40.00
APDG Daniel Gibson 10.00 25.00
APDN David Noel 10.00 25.00
APDR Dennis Rodman 50.00 125.00
APEO Emeka Okafor 10.00 25.00
APHO Hakeem Olajuwon 50.00 120.00
APJE Julius Erving 125.00 250.00
APJG Jorge Garbajosa 10.00 25.00
APJO Jermaine O'Neal 12.00 30.00
APJS J.R. Smith 15.00 40.00
APKB Kobe Bryant 500.00 1000.00
APLA LaMarcus Aldridge 50.00 125.00
APLB Larry Bird 100.00 200.00
APLJ LeBron James 600.00 1200.00
APMA Magic Johnson 100.00 250.00
APMJ Michael Jordan 1500.00 3000.00
APMW Marcus Williams 10.00 25.00
APPD Paul Davis 10.00 25.00
APRB Renaldo Balkman 10.00 25.00
APRC Rodney Carney 10.00 25.00
APRF Randy Foye 10.00 25.00
APRG Rudy Gay 15.00 40.00
APRJ Richard Jefferson 10.00 25.00
APRO Ronnie Brewer 10.00 25.00
APSB Shannon Brown 10.00 25.00
APSH Shawne Williams 10.00 25.00
APSW Shelden Williams 10.00 25.00
APTF T.J. Ford 10.00 25.00
APTT Tyrus Thomas 10.00 25.00
APVC Vince Carter 75.00 150.00
APWI Marvin Williams 10.00 25.00

2006-07 Exquisite Collection Emblems of Endorsements

PRINT RUN 15 SER.#'d SETS
EMAB Andrea Bargnani 40.00 100.00
EMAI Andre Iguodala 40.00 100.00
EMAJ Antawn Jamison 25.00 60.00
EMAM Alonzo Mourning 125.00 250.00
EMBI Chauncey Billups 40.00 100.00
EMBR Brandon Roy 75.00 200.00
EMCA Carmelo Anthony 100.00 200.00
EMCB Chris Bosh 50.00 120.00
EMCD Clyde Drexler 75.00 150.00
EMCP Chris Paul 125.00 250.00
EMDR Dennis Rodman 75.00 150.00
EMDW Deron Williams 75.00 200.00
EMFE Raymond Felton 25.00 60.00
EMHO Hakeem Olajuwon 50.00 120.00
EMJE Julius Erving 150.00 300.00
EMJH Jeff Hornacek 40.00 100.00
EMJK Jason Kidd 125.00 300.00
EMJO Jermaine O'Neal 25.00 60.00
EMJS John Stockton 150.00 300.00
EMKA Kareem Abdul-Jabbar 75.00 150.00
EMKB Kobe Bryant 900.00 1500.00
EMLA LaMarcus Aldridge 150.00 300.00
EMLB Larry Bird 100.00 250.00
EMLJ LeBron James 900.00 1500.00
EMMA Magic Johnson 100.00 200.00
EMMJ Michael Jordan 2000.00 3000.00
EMMW Marcus Williams 25.00 60.00
EMPP Paul Pierce 75.00 150.00
EMPS Peja Stojakovic 40.00 100.00
EMRC Rodney Carney 25.00 60.00
EMRF Randy Foye 25.00 60.00
EMRG Rudy Gay 60.00 150.00
EMRJ Richard Jefferson 25.00 60.00
EMRO David Robinson 100.00 200.00
EMSL Shaun Livingston 25.00 60.00
EMSN Steve Nash 100.00 250.00
EMTM Tracy McGrady 60.00 150.00
EMTS Thabo Sefolosha 30.00 80.00
EMTT Tyrus Thomas 40.00 100.00
EMVC Vince Carter 75.00 200.00

2006-07 Exquisite Collection Enshrinements

PRINT RUN 25 SER.#'d SETS
UNPRICED DUAL PRINT RUN 10 SETS
EXAB Andrea Bargnani 15.00 40.00
EXBI Chauncey Billups 25.00 60.00
EXBR Bill Russell 80.00 200.00
EXCA Carmelo Anthony 50.00 120.00
EXCB Chris Bosh 30.00 80.00
EXCP Chris Paul 50.00 120.00
EXDA David Robinson 50.00 120.00
EXDR Dennis Rodman 100.00 200.00
EXHO Hakeem Olajuwon 100.00 200.00
EXJE Julius Erving 60.00 120.00
EXJK Jason Kidd 40.00 100.00
EXJO Jermaine O'Neal 15.00 40.00
EXJS John Stockton 60.00 150.00
EXJW James Worthy 40.00 100.00
EXKA Kareem Abdul-Jabbar 60.00 120.00
EXKB Kobe Bryant 300.00 600.00
EXKH Kirk Hinrich 15.00 40.00
EXLA LaMarcus Aldridge 40.00 100.00
EXLB Larry Bird 75.00 200.00
EXLJ LeBron James 600.00 1000.00
EXLJ2 LeBron James 600.00 1000.00
EXMA Magic Johnson 75.00 200.00
EXMJ Michael Jordan 1200.00 1800.00
EXMJ2 Michael Jordan 1200.00 1800.00
EXMW Marcus Williams 15.00 40.00
EXPP Paul Pierce 75.00 200.00
EXPR Tayshaun Prince 15.00 40.00
EXRB Renaldo Balkman 15.00 40.00
EXRC Rodney Carney 15.00 40.00
EXRF Randy Foye 15.00 40.00
EXRG Rudy Gay 30.00 80.00
EXRH Richard Hamilton 15.00 40.00
EXRI Pat Riley 30.00 80.00
EXRO Brandon Roy 20.00 50.00
EXSN Steve Nash 75.00 200.00
EXTF T.J. Ford 15.00 40.00
EXTM Tracy McGrady 100.00 250.00
EXTP Tony Parker 40.00 100.00
EXTT Tyrus Thomas 15.00 40.00
EXVC Vince Carter 50.00 120.00
EXWJ John Wooden 200.00 400.00
EXYM Yao Ming 30.00 80.00

2006-07 Exquisite Collection Extra Exquisite

PRINT RUN 25 SER.#'d SETS
UNPRICED JSY/PATCH PRINT RUN 10 SETS
AUTO PRINT RUN TEN SETS
UNPRICED J/P AUTO PRINT RUN 5 SETS
EEAB Andrea Bargnani 8.00 20.00
EEAI Allen Iverson 20.00 50.00
EEAM Alonzo Mourning 30.00 80.00
EEAR Ron Artest 10.00 25.00
EEAS Amare Stoudemire 6.00 15.00
EEBG Ben Gordon 6.00 15.00
EEBK Bernard King 6.00 15.00
EEBO Carlos Boozer 6.00 15.00
EEBR Brandon Roy 8.00 20.00
EEBW Ben Wallace 6.00 15.00
EECA Carmelo Anthony 15.00 40.00
EECB Chris Bosh 10.00 25.00
EECD Clyde Drexler 15.00 40.00
EECM Chris Mullin 10.00 25.00
EECP Chris Paul 20.00 50.00
EEDH Dwight Howard 6.00 15.00
EEDN Dirk Nowitzki 15.00 40.00
EEDR Dennis Rodman 20.00 50.00
EEEB Elton Brand 8.00 20.00
EEEM Earl Monroe 15.00 40.00
EEEO Emeka Okafor 6.00 15.00
EEGH Grant Hill 30.00 60.00
EEHO Hakeem Olajuwon 15.00 30.00
EEIA Andre Iguodala 6.00 15.00
EEIT Isiah Thomas 10.00 25.00
EEJE Julius Erving 15.00 40.00
EEJG Jorge Garbajosa 6.00 15.00
EEJO Jermaine O'Neal 6.00 15.00
EEJR J.J. Redick 10.00 25.00
EEJS John Stockton 15.00 40.00
EEJT Jason Terry 6.00 15.00
EEJW Jerry West 25.00 50.00
EEKA Kareem Abdul-Jabbar 20.00 40.00
EEKM Karl Malone 10.00 25.00
EELA LaMarcus Aldridge 20.00 50.00
EELJ LeBron James 60.00 150.00
EELJ2 LeBron James 60.00 150.00
EEMA Magic Johnson 20.00 50.00
EEMG Manu Ginobili 15.00 30.00
EEMJ Michael Jordan 150.00 300.00
EEMJ2 Michael Jordan 150.00 300.00
EEOR Oscar Robertson 30.00 80.00
EEPM Pete Maravich 75.00 200.00
EEPP Paul Pierce 8.00 20.00
EEPR Pat Riley 12.50 30.00
EERA Ray Allen 10.00 25.00
EERB Bill Russell 25.00 60.00
EERF Randy Foye 8.00 20.00
EERG Rudy Gay 10.00 25.00
EERI Jason Richardson 8.00 20.00
EERO David Robinson 30.00 80.00
EERR Rajon Rondo 30.00 80.00
EESM Shawn Marion 6.00 15.00
EESO Shaquille O'Neal 30.00 60.00
EETM Tracy McGrady 15.00 40.00
EETP Tony Parker 10.00 25.00
EETT Tyrus Thomas 6.00 15.00
EEVC Vince Carter 15.00 40.00
EEWC Wilt Chamberlain 40.00 80.00
EEYM Yao Ming 20.00 40.00

2006-07 Exquisite Collection Limited Logos

PRINT RUN 50 SER.#'d SETS
LLAB Andrea Bargnani 15.00 40.00
LLBG Ben Gordon 25.00 60.00
LLBI Chauncey Billups 25.00 60.00
LLBR Ronnie Brewer 25.00 60.00
LLCA Carmelo Anthony 100.00 225.00
LLCB Chris Bosh 60.00 150.00
LLCD Clyde Drexler 200.00 400.00
LLCP Chris Paul 200.00 400.00
LLCS Craig Smith 15.00 40.00
LLDA Baron Davis 20.00 50.00
LLDE Dennis Rodman 100.00 225.00
LLDG Daniel Gibson 20.00 50.00
LLDN David Noel 15.00 40.00
LLDR David Robinson 150.00 300.00
LLEO Emeka Okafor 15.00 40.00
LLHO Hakeem Olajuwon 75.00 200.00
LLJE Julius Erving 175.00 350.00
LLJF Jordan Farmar 15.00 40.00
LLJO Jermaine O'Neal 40.00 100.00
LLJS J.R. Smith 25.00 60.00
LLKB Kobe Bryant 1000.00 1600.00
LLLA LaMarcus Aldridge 200.00 400.00
LLLB Larry Bird 125.00 250.00
LLLJ LeBron James 1200.00 2000.00
LLMA Magic Johnson 125.00 250.00
LLMJ Michael Jordan 3000.00 4500.00
LLMW Marcus Williams 15.00 40.00
LLRB Renaldo Balkman 15.00 40.00
LLRC Rodney Carney 15.00 40.00
LLRF Randy Foye 20.00 50.00
LLRG Rudy Gay 100.00 175.00
LLRJ Richard Jefferson 25.00 60.00
LLRO Brandon Roy 100.00 200.00
LLSN Steve Nash 100.00 200.00
LLST John Stockton 150.00 300.00
LLSW Shawne Williams 15.00 40.00
LLTT Tyrus Thomas 15.00 40.00
LLVC Vince Carter 125.00 250.00
LLWI Shelden Williams 15.00 40.00
LLWM Marvin Williams 15.00 40.00

2006-07 Exquisite Collection Noble Nameplates

NT RUN 25 SER.#'d SETS
NNAB Andrea Bargnani 20.00 50.00
NNAJ Al Jefferson 10.00 20.00
NNAM Alonzo Mourning 75.00 200.00
NNBD Baron Davis 40.00 100.00
NNBG Ben Gordon 25.00 60.00
NNBO Chris Bosh 50.00 100.00
NNBR Brandon Roy 10.00 25.00
NNCA Carmelo Anthony 80.00 160.00
NNCB Chauncey Billups 25.00 60.00
NNCD Clyde Drexler 50.00 120.00
NNCP Chris Paul 75.00 150.00
NNCS Craig Smith 10.00 25.00
NNDE Dennis Rodman 75.00 150.00
NNDG Danny Granger 10.00 20.00
NNDI Boris Diaw 20.00 50.00
NNDN David Noel 10.00 20.00
NNDR David Robinson 75.00 150.00
NNEO Emeka Okafor 10.00 20.00
NNFE Raymond Felton 10.00 20.00
NNGD Daniel Gibson 20.00 50.00
NNGG Gerald Green 10.00 20.00
NNHO Hakeem Olajuwon 60.00 120.00
NNHW Hakim Warrick 10.00 20.00
NNJB Josh Boone 10.00 20.00
NNJE Julius Erving 100.00 200.00
NNJG Jorge Garbajosa 10.00 20.00
NNJK Jason Kidd 50.00 120.00
NNJO Jermaine O'Neal 25.00 60.00
NNJS J.R. Smith 25.00 60.00
NNJW Jerry West 150.00 300.00
NNKA Kareem Abdul-Jabbar 75.00 150.00
NNKB Kobe Bryant 400.00 700.00
NNKL Kyle Lowry 40.00 100.00
NNLA LaMarcus Aldridge 50.00 120.00
NNLB Larry Bird 100.00 200.00
NNLJ LeBron James 2000.00 3000.00
NNMA Magic Johnson 75.00 150.00
NNMB Mike Bibby 10.00 20.00
NNMJ Michael Jordan 2000.00 3000.00
NNMW Marcus Williams 10.00 20.00
NNPP Paul Pierce 40.00 100.00
NNPS Peja Stojakovic 30.00 80.00
NNQD Quincy Douby 10.00 20.00
NNRB Renaldo Balkman 10.00 20.00
NNRC Rodney Carney 10.00 20.00
NNRF Randy Foye 10.00 20.00
NNRG Rudy Gay 50.00 120.00
NNRH Richard Hamilton 25.00 60.00
NNRJ Richard Jefferson 10.00 20.00
NNRO Ronnie Brewer 10.00 20.00
NNSB Shannon Brown 25.00 60.00
NNSI Cedric Simmons 10.00 20.00
NNSN Steve Nash 100.00 200.00
NNST John Stockton 80.00 200.00
NNSW Shelden Williams 10.00 20.00
NNTM Tracy McGrady 75.00 200.00
NNTP Tayshaun Prince 10.00 20.00
NNTT Tyrus Thomas 10.00 20.00
NNVC Vince Carter 75.00 200.00
NNYM Yao Ming 60.00 150.00

2006-07 Exquisite Collection Numbers

PRINT RUNS LISTED IN CHECKLIST
SOME NOT PRICED DUE TO SCARCITY
ENAH Al Harrington/32 12.00 30.00
ENAM Alonzo Mourning/33 300.00 500.00
ENCA Carmelo Anthony/15 125.00 250.00
ENCD Clyde Drexler/22 75.00 150.00
ENCM Corey Maggette/50 12.00 30.00
ENDG Danny Granger/33 12.00 30.00
ENDN David Noel/34 12.00 30.00
ENDR David Robinson/50 60.00 150.00
ENEO Emeka Okafor/50 12.00 30.00
ENHO Hakeem Olajuwon/34 100.00 200.00
ENHW Hakim Warrick/21 25.00 60.00
ENKA K.Abdul-Jabbar/33 125.00 250.00
ENKB Kobe Bryant/24 600.00 1000.00
ENLA LaMarcus Aldridge/12 150.00 300.00
ENLB Larry Bird/33 125.00 250.00
ENLH Larry Hughes/32 12.00 30.00
ENLJ LeBron James/23 400.00 800.00
ENMA Magic Johnson/32 125.00 250.00
ENMJ Michael Jordan/23 3000.00 4500.00
ENPO Patrick O'Bryant/26 12.00 30.00
ENPP Paul Pierce/34 50.00 125.00
ENPS Peja Stojakovic/16 50.00 120.00
ENRC Rodney Carney/25 20.00 50.00
ENRE Renaldo Balkman/32 12.00 30.00
ENRG Rudy Gay/22 125.00 250.00
ENRH Richard Hamilton/32 30.00 80.00
ENRJ Richard Jefferson/24 25.00 60.00
ENRO Dennis Rodman/91 100.00 200.00
ENSH Shelden Williams/33 12.00 30.00
ENSI Cedric Simmons/22 12.00 30.00
ENSL Shaun Livingston/14 30.00 60.00
ENTP Tayshaun Prince/22 25.00 60.00
ENTT Tyrus Thomas/24 60.00 150.00
ENVC Vince Carter/15 150.00 300.00
ENWI Marvin Williams/24 15.00 40.00
ENYM Yao Ming/11 125.00 250.00

2006-07 Exquisite Collection Numbers Dual

PRINT RUNS LISTED IN CHECKLIST
SOME NOT PRICED DUE TO SCARCITY
DENAA Aldridge/Armstrong/12 75.00 150.00
DENAC Anthony/V.Carter/15 125.00 250.00
DENAW Kareem/S.Williams/33 60.00 150.00
DENBG L.Bird/D.Granger/33 100.00 225.00
DENBH Balkman/Hughes/32 15.00 40.00
DENBJ Bryant/R.Jefferson/24 300.00 550.00

DENBT Bryant/T.Thomas/24 300.00 600.00
DENCC Carney/M.Collins/25 15.00 40.00
DENDG C.Drexler/R.Gay/22 75.00 150.00
DENJH M.Johnson/Hamilton/32 100.00 200.00
DENJJ Jordan/L.James/23 1500.00 2500.00
DENOP Olajuwon/Pierce/34 60.00 150.00
DENOR Okafor/D.Robinson/50 25.00 60.00
DENPG T.Prince/R.Gay/22 60.00 120.00
DENTW T.Thomas/M.Will/24 50.00 125.00

2006-07 Exquisite Collection Scripted Swatches

PRINT RUN 25 SER.#'d SETS
UNPRICED DUAL PRINT RUN FIVE SETS
SSAB Andrea Bargnani 20.00 50.00
SSAD Adrian Dantley 25.00 60.00
SSAH Al Harrington 10.00 25.00
SSAJ Antawn Jamison 20.00 50.00
SSBD Baron Davis 30.00 80.00
SSBG Ben Gordon 15.00 40.00
SSBO Chris Bosh 40.00 100.00
SSBR Brandon Roy 20.00 50.00
SSCA Carmelo Anthony 125.00 225.00
SSCB Chauncey Billups 20.00 50.00
SSCD Clyde Drexler 60.00 150.00
SSCM Corey Maggette 10.00 25.00
SSCP Chris Paul 100.00 225.00
SSCS Cedric Simmons 10.00 25.00
SSDB Dee Brown 10.00 25.00
SSDE Dennis Rodman 200.00 400.00
SSDG Danny Granger 20.00 50.00
SSDR David Robinson 100.00 200.00
SSDW Deron Williams 40.00 100.00
SSER Julius Erving 125.00 250.00
SSFE Raymond Felton 10.00 25.00
SSGG Gerald Green 10.00 25.00
SSGI Daniel Gibson 10.00 25.00
SSHA Hilton Armstrong 10.00 25.00
SSHO Hakeem Olajuwon 75.00 150.00
SSHW Hakim Warrick 10.00 25.00
SSJB Josh Boone 10.00 25.00
SSJE Richard Jefferson 10.00 25.00
SSJK Jason Kidd 50.00 120.00
SSJM Magic Johnson 60.00 150.00
SSJO Jermaine O'Neal 25.00 60.00
SSJS John Stockton 100.00 200.00
SSJW Jerry West 125.00 250.00
SSKA Kareem Abdul-Jabbar 100.00 200.00
SSKB Kobe Bryant 400.00 700.00
SSKH Kirk Hinrich 40.00 100.00
SSKL Kyle Lowry 25.00 60.00
SSLA LaMarcus Aldridge 75.00 150.00
SSLB Larry Bird 100.00 200.00
SSLJ LeBron James 600.00 900.00
SSLR Luke Ridnour 10.00 25.00
SSMA Marcus Williams 10.00 25.00
SSMB Mike Bibby 10.00 25.00
SSMC Mardy Collins 10.00 25.00
SSMJ Michael Jordan 1000.00 1500.00
SSMP Morris Peterson 10.00 25.00
SSMW Martell Webster 10.00 25.00
SSPS Peja Stojakovic 30.00 80.00
SSPT Tony Parker 50.00 120.00
SSRB Renaldo Balkman 10.00 25.00
SSRC Rodney Carney 10.00 25.00
SSRF Randy Foye 10.00 25.00
SSRG Rudy Gay 100.00 200.00
SSRH Richard Hamilton 20.00 50.00
SSRO Ronnie Brewer 20.00 50.00
SSSB Shannon Brown 10.00 25.00
SSSM Craig Smith 10.00 25.00
SSSN Steve Nash 150.00 300.00
SSST Sebastian Telfair 10.00 25.00
SSSW Shelden Williams 10.00 25.00
SSTM Tracy McGrady 75.00 200.00
SSTP Tayshaun Prince 25.00 60.00
SSTT Tyrus Thomas 40.00 100.00
SSVC Vince Carter 100.00 175.00
SSWI Shawne Williams 10.00 25.00
SSYM Yao Ming 60.00 150.00

2007-08 Exquisite Collection

Released in late July 2008, Exquisite Collection boasts a 112-card set where cards 1-60 feature veterans sequentially numbered to 225, cards 61-93 feature rookie players with both premium patch swatches and autographs sequentially numbered to 225, cards 94-97 feature rookie players with both premium patch swatches and autographs sequentially numbered to 99, cards 98-106 feature rookie players with autographs sequentially numbered to 99 and cards 107-112 feature rookie players sequentially numbered to 99. Every card is printed on an extra-thick card stock, and every autograph in the product is signed directly on card. Exquisite Collection is packaged in five card packs and carried an initial suggested retail price of $600.

PRINT RUN 225 SER.#'d SETS
61-93 RC PRINT RUN 225 SER.#'d SETS
94-112 PRINT RUN 99 SER.#'d SETS
UNPRICED BLACK PRINT RUN ONE SET
1 LeBron James 30.00 80.00
2 Yao Ming 4.00 10.00
3 Kobe Bryant 25.00 60.00
4 Dwyane Wade 12.00 30.00
5 Tracy McGrady 3.00 8.00
6 Allen Iverson 8.00 20.00
7 Shaquille O'Neal 6.00 15.00
8 Kevin Garnett 8.00 20.00
9 Steve Nash 4.00 10.00
10 Dwight Howard 2.50 6.00
11 Gilbert Arenas 2.50 6.00
12 Vince Carter 4.00 10.00
13 Tim Duncan 6.00 15.00
14 Carmelo Anthony 4.00 10.00
15 Dirk Nowitzki 4.00 10.00
16 Amare Stoudemire 2.50 6.00
17 Chris Bosh 3.00 8.00
18 Jermaine O'Neal 2.50 6.00
19 Jason Kidd 3.00 8.00
20 Ben Wallace 2.50 6.00
21 Paul Pierce 3.00 8.00
22 Shawn Marion 2.50 6.00
23 Michael Jordan 75.00 200.00
24 Manu Ginobili 3.00 8.00
25 Tony Parker 3.00 8.00
26 Chauncey Billups 3.00 8.00
27 Chris Paul 4.00 10.00
28 Andre Iguodala 2.50 6.00
29 Stephon Marbury 2.50 6.00
30 Ray Allen 3.00 8.00
31 Lamar Odom 2.50 6.00
32 Jason Terry 2.50 6.00
33 Josh Howard 2.50 6.00
34 Caron Butler 2.50 6.00
35 Emeka Okafor 2.50 6.00
36 Marcus Camby 2.00 5.00
37 Pau Gasol 3.00 8.00
38 Carlos Boozer 2.50 6.00
39 Baron Davis 2.50 6.00
40 Michael Redd 2.50 6.00
41 Ben Gordon 2.50 6.00
42 Richard Hamilton 2.50 6.00
43 Andrew Bogut 2.50 6.00
44 Tyson Chandler 2.50 6.00
45 Eddy Curry 2.00 5.00
46 Larry Hughes 2.50 6.00
47 LaMarcus Aldridge 4.00 10.00
48 Andrea Bargnani 3.00 8.00
49 Mike Bibby 3.00 8.00
50 Elton Brand 3.00 8.00
51 Al Harrington 2.50 6.00
52 Al Jefferson 2.50 6.00
53 Joe Johnson 2.50 6.00
54 Rashard Lewis 2.50 6.00
55 Kevin Martin 2.50 6.00
56 Andre Miller 2.50 6.00
57 Brandon Roy 3.00 8.00
58 Gerald Wallace 2.50 6.00
59 Rasheed Wallace 3.00 8.00
60 Deron Williams 2.50 6.00
61 Arron Afflalo JSY AU RC 8.00 20.00
62 Morris Almond JSY AU RC 5.00 12.00
63 Julian Wright JSY AU RC 5.00 12.00
64 Aaron Brooks JSY AU RC 15.00 40.00
65 Herbert Hill JSY AU RC 5.00 12.00
66 Wilson Chandler JSY AU RC 6.00 15.00
67 Daequan Cook JSY AU RC 6.00 15.00
68 Javaris Crittenton JSY AU RC 5.00 12.00
69 Jermareo Davidson JSY AU RC 5.00 12.00
70 Glen Davis JSY AU RC 6.00 15.00
71 Jared Dudley JSY AU RC 6.00 15.00
72 Corey Brewer JSY AU RC 8.00 20.00
73 Aaron Gray JSY AU RC 5.00 12.00
74 Taurean Green JSY AU RC 5.00 12.00
75 Nick Fazekas JSY AU RC 5.00 12.00
76 Spencer Hawes JSY AU RC 6.00 15.00
77 Al Horford JSY AU RC 30.00 80.00
78 Jeff Green JSY AU RC 8.00 20.00
79 Carl Landry JSY AU RC 5.00 12.00
80 Mike Conley Jr. JSY AU RC 30.00 80.00
81 Acie Law JSY AU RC 5.00 12.00
82 Dominic McGuire JSY AU RC 5.00 12.00
83 Josh McRoberts JSY AU RC 6.00 15.00
84 Demetris Nichols JSY AU RC 5.00 12.00
85 Joakim Noah JSY AU RC 30.00 80.00
86 Gabe Pruitt JSY AU RC 5.00 12.00
87 Chris Richard JSY AU RC 5.00 12.00
88 Jason Smith JSY AU RC 6.00 15.00
89 D.J. Strawberry JSY AU RC 5.00 12.00
90 Rodney Stuckey JSY AU RC 6.00 15.00
91 Sean Williams JSY AU RC 5.00 12.00
92 Al Thornton JSY AU RC 6.00 15.00
93 Alando Tucker JSY AU RC 5.00 12.00
94 K.Durant JSY AU/99 RC 8000.00 12000.00
95 M.Belinelli JSY AU/99 RC 8.00 20.00
96 Luis Scola JSY AU/99 RC 15.00 40.00
97 L.Amundson JSY AU/99 RC 5.00 12.00
98 C.J. Watson AU RC 6.00 15.00
99 Cheikh Samb AU RC 4.00 10.00
100 Juan Navarro AU RC 5.00 12.00
101 JamesOn Curry AU RC 4.00 10.00
102 Ramon Sessions AU RC 6.00 15.00
103 Mario West AU RC 6.00 15.00
104 Coby Karl AU RC 4.00 10.00
105 Oleksiy Pecherov AU RC 6.00 15.00
106 Jamario Moon AU RC 5.00 12.00
107 Kyrylo Fesenko RC 4.00 10.00
108 Yi Jianlian RC 8.00 20.00
109 Brandan Wright RC 6.00 15.00
110 Thaddeus Young RC 6.00 15.00
111 Nick Young RC 8.00 20.00
112 Greg Oden RC 10.00 25.00

2007-08 Exquisite Collection Gold

*1-60 GOLD: 2.5X TO 6X BASE HI
PRINT RUN 25 SER.#'d SETS
2 Yao Ming 30.00 80.00
61 Arron Afflalo 6.00 15.00
62 Morris Almond 4.00 10.00
63 Julian Wright 4.00 10.00
64 Aaron Brooks 40.00 100.00
65 Herbert Hill 4.00 10.00
66 Wilson Chandler 5.00 12.00
67 Daequan Cook 5.00 12.00
68 Javaris Crittenton 4.00 10.00
69 Jermareo Davidson 4.00 10.00
70 Glen Davis 5.00 12.00
71 Jared Dudley 5.00 12.00
72 Corey Brewer 6.00 15.00
73 Aaron Gray 4.00 10.00
74 Taurean Green 4.00 10.00
75 Nick Fazekas 4.00 10.00
76 Spencer Hawes 5.00 12.00
77 Al Horford 20.00 50.00
78 Jeff Green 6.00 15.00
79 Carl Landry 4.00 10.00
80 Mike Conley Jr. 25.00 60.00
81 Acie Law 4.00 10.00
82 Dominic McGuire 4.00 10.00
83 Josh McRoberts 5.00 12.00
84 Demetris Nichols 4.00 10.00
85 Joakim Noah 12.00 30.00
86 Gabe Pruitt 4.00 10.00
87 Chris Richard 4.00 10.00
88 Jason Smith 5.00 12.00
89 D.J. Strawberry 4.00 10.00
90 Rodney Stuckey 5.00 12.00
91 Sean Williams 4.00 10.00
92 Al Thornton 5.00 12.00
93 Alando Tucker 4.00 10.00
94 Kevin Durant 1000.00 1500.00
95 Marco Belinelli 6.00 15.00
96 Luis Scola 8.00 20.00
97 Louis Amundson 4.00 10.00
98 C.J. Watson 6.00 15.00
99 Cheikh Samb 4.00 10.00
100 Juan Navarro 5.00 12.00
101 JamesOn Curry 4.00 10.00
102 Ramon Sessions 6.00 15.00
103 Mario West 6.00 15.00
104 Coby Karl 4.00 10.00
105 Oleksiy Pecherov 6.00 15.00
106 Jamario Moon 5.00 12.00
107 Kyrylo Fesenko 4.00 10.00
108 Yi Jianlian 8.00 20.00
109 Brandan Wright 6.00 15.00
110 Thaddeus Young 6.00 15.00
111 Nick Young 8.00 20.00
112 Greg Oden 8.00 20.00

2007-08 Exquisite Collection Autographs Patches

PRINT RUN 35 SER.#'d SETS
EAAH Al Horford 75.00 150.00
EAAI Andre Iguodala 15.00 40.00
EAAJ Al Jefferson 15.00 40.00
EAAM Alonzo Mourning 100.00 200.00
EABG Ben Gordon 15.00 40.00
EABI Chauncey Billups 30.00 80.00
EABO Carlos Boozer 15.00 40.00
EABR Brandon Roy 30.00 60.00
EACA Carmelo Anthony 75.00 150.00
EACB Corey Brewer 15.00 40.00
EACD Clyde Drexler 60.00 120.00
EACH Chris Bosh 30.00 60.00
EACM Corey Maggette 15.00 40.00
EACP Chris Paul 100.00 200.00
EADG Daniel Gibson 15.00 40.00
EADR David Robinson 100.00 200.00
EAEO Emeka Okafor 15.00 40.00
EAHO Hakeem Olajuwon 40.00 100.00
EAJG Jeff Green 30.00 80.00
EAJK Jason Kidd 40.00 80.00
EAJN Joakim Noah 40.00 100.00
EAJO Magic Johnson 125.00 250.00
EAJS John Stockton 60.00 150.00
EAJW Julian Wright 20.00 50.00
EAKA Kelenna Azubuike 15.00 40.00
EAKD Kevin Durant 1500.00 2000.00
EAKG Kevin Garnett 125.00 250.00
EALB Larry Bird 75.00 150.00
EALH Larry Hughes 20.00 50.00
EALJ LeBron James 300.00 600.00
EAMB Mike Bibby 15.00 40.00
EAMC Mike Conley Jr. 40.00 100.00
EAPP Paul Pierce 40.00 100.00
EARA Ray Allen 100.00 200.00
EARF Raymond Felton 15.00 40.00
EARJ Richard Jefferson 15.00 40.00
EASB Shannon Brown 15.00 40.00
EASL Shaun Livingston 15.00 40.00
EATC Tyson Chandler 15.00 40.00
EATP Tayshaun Prince 20.00 50.00
EAVC Vince Carter 30.00 80.00

2007-08 Exquisite Collection Boxes

VALUES LISTED FOR AUTO EMPTY BOX
AH Al Horford/15 100.00 250.00
JJ M.Jordan/L.James/23 500.00 1000.00
KB Kobe Bryant/24 400.00 600.00
KD Kevin Durant/35 400.00 800.00
LJ LeBron James/23 300.00 550.00
MJ Michael Jordan/23 500.00 700.00
SN Steve Nash/13 125.00 250.00
YM Yao Ming/11 125.00 250.00

2007-08 Exquisite Collection Draft Picks Reservation

A-F PRINT RUN 99 SER.#'d SETS
G-L PRINT RUN 199 SER.#'d SETS
DPA Mayo/Beasley/Rose 125.00 250.00
DPB Mayo/Beasley/Gordon 20.00 50.00
DPC Mayo/Gordon/Bayless 12.00 30.00
DPD Aug/Rose/Westbrk 125.00 250.00
DPE Beasley/Love/Alexander 25.00 60.00
DPF Rose/Gordon/Bayless 75.00 150.00
DPG Lopez/Thmpsn/Alxndr 12.00 30.00
DPH Galli/Love/Westbrk 50.00 120.00
DPI Rush/Gallinari/Westbrk 40.00 100.00
DPJ Augustin/Rush/Bayless 8.00 20.00
DPK Thmpsn/Speights/Alexndr 8.00 20.00
DPL Hibbert/B.Lopez/R.Lopez 20.00 50.00

2007-08 Exquisite Collection Enshrinements

PRINT RUN 25 SER.#'d SETS
ENAE Alex English 20.00 40.00
ENAR Arnie Risen 20.00 40.00
ENBL Bill Laimbeer 20.00 40.00
ENBR Bill Russell 75.00 200.00
ENBS Bill Sharman 20.00 40.00
ENBW Bill Walton 20.00 40.00
ENCD Clyde Drexler 40.00 80.00
ENCH Connie Hawkins 30.00 60.00
ENDR David Robinson 60.00 150.00
ENDT David Thompson 20.00 40.00
ENDW Dominique Wilkins 30.00 60.00
ENEB Elgin Baylor 40.00 80.00
ENGE George Gervin 25.00 60.00
ENGG Gail Goodrich 25.00 50.00
ENHO Hakeem Olajuwon 25.00 50.00
ENJE Julius Erving 75.00 150.00
ENJH John Havlicek 30.00 80.00
ENJK Jason Kidd 30.00 80.00
ENJL Jerry Lucas 25.00 60.00
ENJO Michael Jordan 1000.00 1500.00
ENJS John Stockton 75.00 150.00
ENJW James Worthy 40.00 80.00
ENKA Kareem Abdul-Jabbar 50.00 100.00
ENKB Kobe Bryant 200.00 400.00
ENKG Kevin Garnett 100.00 200.00
ENLA Bob Lanier 20.00 40.00
ENLB Larry Bird 125.00 300.00
ENLJ LeBron James 600.00 1000.00
ENMJ Magic Johnson 125.00 300.00
ENMM Moses Malone 30.00 60.00
ENPP Paul Pierce 100.00 250.00
ENPR Pat Riley 30.00 80.00
ENRB Rick Barry 20.00 40.00
ENRO Dennis Rodman 40.00 80.00
ENRP Robert Parish 20.00 40.00
ENSK Steve Kerr 20.00 40.00
ENSN Steve Nash 40.00 100.00
ENTM Tracy McGrady 30.00 80.00
ENTP Tony Parker 20.00 40.00
ENVC Vince Carter 40.00 100.00
ENWE Jerry West 60.00 120.00
ENWF Walt Frazier 20.00 40.00
ENWU Wes Unseld 20.00 40.00

2007-08 Exquisite Collection Exclusives Autographs

STATED PRINT RUN 5 TO 35 SER.#'d SETS
SOME UNPRICED DUE TO SCARCITY
AH Al Horford/15 25.00 60.00
JG Jeff Green/22 25.00 60.00
JW Julian Wright/32 25.00 60.00
KB Kobe Bryant/24 400.00 800.00
KD Kevin Durant/35 600.00 1200.00
LJ LeBron James/23 250.00 500.00
MJ Michael Jordan/23 400.00 800.00
SN Steve Nash/13 100.00 200.00
YM Yao Ming/11 30.00 80.00

2007-08 Exquisite Collection Exclusives Autographs Patches

STATED PRINT RUN 5 TO 35 SER.#'d SETS
SOME UNPRICED DUE TO SCARCITY
AH Al Horford/15 50.00 120.00
JN Joakim Noah/13 75.00 150.00
KB Kobe Bryant/24 400.00 700.00
KD Kevin Durant/35 600.00 1200.00
LJ LeBron James/23 300.00 600.00
MJ Michael Jordan/23 900.00 1500.00
SN Steve Nash/13 150.00 300.00
YM Yao Ming/11 50.00 120.00

2007-08 Exquisite Collection Exclusives Autographs Dual

STATED PRINT RUN 23 SER.#'d SETS
AMJLJ M.Jordan/L.James 600.00 1000.00

2007-08 Exquisite Collection Exclusives Autographs Patches Dual

STATED PRINT RUN 23 SER.#'d SETS
PMJLJ M.Jordan/L.James 800.00 1200.00

2007-08 Exquisite Collection Exclusives Memorabilia

STATED PRINT RUN 5 TO 35 SER.#'d SETS
SOME UNPRICED DUE TO SCARCITY
MAH Al Horford/15 12.00 30.00
MJG Jeff Green/22
MJN Joakim Noah/13 25.00 60.00
MJW Julian Wright/32 10.00 25.00
MKB Kobe Bryant/24 50.00 120.00
MKD Kevin Durant/35 60.00 150.00
MLJ LeBron James/23 50.00 100.00
MMJ Michael Jordan/23 100.00 200.00
MSN Steve Nash/13 20.00 50.00
MYM Yao Ming/11 15.00 40.00

2007-08 Exquisite Collection Exclusives Memorabilia Dual

STATED PRINT RUN 23 SER.#'d SETS
MMJLJ M.Jordan/L.James 100.00 225.00

2007-08 Exquisite Collection Extra Quad Jerseys

PRINT RUN 25 SER.#'d SETS
UNPRICED AUTO PRINT RUN 10 SETS
UNPRICED PATCH AUTO PRINT RUN 3 SETS
EQAD Adrian Dantley 5.00 12.00
EQAH Al Harrington 5.00 12.00
EQAI Andre Iguodala 5.00 12.00
EQAJ Al Jefferson 5.00 12.00
EQAM Alonzo Mourning 30.00 80.00
EQBD Baron Davis 5.00 12.00
EQBG Ben Gordon 5.00 12.00
EQBK Bernard King 5.00 12.00
EQBL Bill Laimbeer 5.00 12.00
EQBR Brandon Roy 6.00 15.00
EQCA Carmelo Anthony 8.00 20.00
EQCB Chris Bosh 8.00 20.00
EQCD Clyde Drexler 15.00 30.00
EQCM Corey Maggette 5.00 12.00
EQCP Chris Paul 10.00 25.00
EQDH Dwight Howard 10.00 25.00
EQDR David Robinson 15.00 30.00
EQDW Deron Williams 8.00 20.00
EQEO Emeka Okafor 5.00 12.00
EQFE Raymond Felton 5.00 12.00
EQGG George Gervin 8.00 20.00
EQHO Hakeem Olajuwon 10.00 25.00
EQJA Antawn Jamison 5.00 12.00
EQJE Julius Erving 15.00 40.00
EQJK Jason Kidd 6.00 15.00
EQJO Jermaine O'Neal 5.00 12.00
EQJS John Stockton 8.00 20.00
EQJW Jerry West 15.00 40.00
EQKA Kareem Abdul-Jabbar 12.00 30.00
EQKB Kobe Bryant 40.00 100.00
EQKG Kevin Garnett 15.00 40.00
EQKH Kirk Hinrich 5.00 12.00
EQLA LaMarcus Aldridge 5.00 12.00
EQLB Leandro Barbosa 5.00 12.00
EQLH Larry Hughes 5.00 12.00
EQLJ LeBron James 40.00 100.00
EQMA Magic Johnson 15.00 40.00
EQMB Mike Bibby 5.00 12.00
EQME Mark Eaton 6.00 15.00
EQMJ Michael Jordan 75.00 200.00
EQMM Moses Malone 5.00 12.00
EQMR Micheal Ray Richardson 5.00 12.00
EQMU Chris Mullin 5.00 12.00
EQPP Paul Pierce 8.00 20.00
EQPR Tayshaun Prince 5.00 12.00
EQRF Randy Foye 5.00 12.00
EQRG Rudy Gay 5.00 12.00
EQRJ Richard Jefferson 5.00 12.00
EQRO Dennis Rodman 8.00 20.00
EQRT Reggie Theus 5.00 12.00
EQSB Shannon Brown 5.00 12.00
EQSM Shawn Marion 5.00 12.00
EQSN Steve Nash 6.00 15.00
EQTC Tom Chambers 5.00 12.00
EQTM Tracy McGrady 6.00 15.00
EQTP Tony Parker 6.00 15.00
EQTT Tyrus Thomas 5.00 12.00
EQVC Vince Carter 10.00 25.00
EQWO James Worthy 10.00 25.00
EQYM Yao Ming 30.00 80.00

2007-08 Exquisite Collection Finalists Autographs Dual

PRINT RUN 25 SER.#'d SETS
FABG R.Barry/H.Greer 30.00 60.00
FABK K.Bryant/J.Kidd 200.00 350.00
FABS K.Bryant/J.Stockton 250.00 450.00
FACD T.Chambers/C.Drexler 50.00 100.00
FAEJ J.Erving/Abdul-Jabbar 200.00 350.00
FAEW J.Erving/B.Walton 60.00 120.00
FAFJ D.Fisher/R.Jefferson 30.00 60.00
FAGC H.Grant/T.Chambers 30.00 60.00
FAGL H.Grant/B.Laimbeer 30.00 60.00
FAHA Havlicek/Abdul-Jabbar 200.00 400.00
FAJB M.Johnson/L.Bird 250.00 450.00
FAJP T.Parker/L.James 400.00 600.00
FAJR M.Jordan/D.Rodman 800.00 1200.00
FALA Laimbeer/Abdul-Jabbar 75.00 150.00
FANP S.Nash/T.Parker 50.00 120.00
FAOP H.Olajuwon/R.Parish 50.00 120.00
FAOR H.Olajuwon/D.Robinson 75.00 150.00
FAPJ T.Prince/L.James 175.00 350.00
FAPW T.Parker/D.Williams 30.00 60.00
FAWE J.Worthy/J.Erving 50.00 100.00

2007-08 Exquisite Collection Inscriptions

PRINT RUN 25 SER.#'d SETS
IAAB Andrea Bargnani 15.00 40.00
IAAD A.Dantley 2-Time Scoring 40.00 100.00
IAAM Alonzo Mourning ZO 75.00 200.00
IABD Baron Davis BDiddy 40.00 100.00
IABI Larry Bird None 75.00 200.00
IABL Bill Laimbeer Bad Boys 50.00 120.00
IABR Brandon Roy ROY 40.00 100.00
IACP Chris Paul 60.00 150.00
IADA B.Daugherty No 1 Pick 15.00 40.00
IADG Daniel Gibson None 15.00 40.00
IADH D.Howard Superman 100.00 250.00
IADR D.Robinson Admiral 150.00 300.00
IADT D.Thompson Skywalker 20.00 50.00
IADW Dominique Wilkins 50.00 100.00
IAGG George Gervin None 25.00 60.00
IAGO Gail Goodrich None 20.00 50.00
IAHO Hakeem Olajuwon 75.00 200.00
IAJK J.Kidd 6 Time All-NBA 125.00 250.00
IAJW James Worthy 100.00 250.00
IAKA K.Abdul-Jabbar None 60.00 150.00
IAKB Kobe Bryant Mamba 1800.00 3000.00
IAKG K.Garnett Big Ticket 1000.00 2000.00
IALB Leandro Barbosa #10 15.00 40.00
IALJ L.James Chosen One 2000.00 3000.00
IAMC Michael Cooper 25.00 60.00
IAMJ M.Johnson 5 Rings 400.00 800.00
IAMP Morris Peterson MoPete 15.00 40.00
IAPR T.Prince Palace Prince 40.00 100.00
IARO D.Rodman The Worm 200.00 500.00
IARP Robert Parish 60.00 120.00
IASM S.Moncrief Squid 30.00 80.00
IASN Steve Nash None 50.00 125.00
IASP S.Perkins Big Smooth 30.00 80.00
IATM T.McGrady Mac Man 100.00 200.00
IATP Tony Parker 30.00 80.00
IAVC Vince Carter VC 125.00 225.00
IAWA Slick Watts 25.00 50.00
IAWE Jerry West Mr. Clutch 125.00 300.00
IAWF Walt Frazier 60.00 150.00

2007-08 Exquisite Collection Jerseys

PRINT RUN 25 SER.#'d SETS
UNPRICED PATCH PRINT RUN 10 SETS
UNPRICED PATCH AUTO PRINT RUN ONE SET
1 LeBron James 50.00 125.00
2 Yao Ming 15.00 40.00
3 Kobe Bryant 150.00 300.00
4 Dwyane Wade 20.00 50.00
5 Tracy McGrady 12.00 30.00
6 Allen Iverson 20.00 50.00
7 Shaquille O'Neal 25.00 60.00
8 Kevin Garnett 30.00 80.00
9 Steve Nash 15.00 40.00
10 Dwight Howard 10.00 25.00
11 Gilbert Arenas 10.00 25.00
12 Vince Carter 15.00 40.00
13 Tim Duncan 20.00 50.00
14 Carmelo Anthony 15.00 40.00
15 Dirk Nowitzki 15.00 40.00
16 Amare Stoudemire 10.00 25.00
17 Chris Bosh 12.00 30.00
18 Jermaine O'Neal 10.00 25.00
19 Jason Kidd 12.00 30.00
20 Ben Wallace 10.00 25.00
21 Paul Pierce 12.00 30.00
22 Shawn Marion 10.00 25.00
23 Michael Jordan 250.00 500.00
24 Manu Ginobili 12.00 30.00
25 Tony Parker 12.00 30.00
26 Chauncey Billups 12.00 30.00
27 Chris Paul 15.00 40.00
28 Andre Iguodala 10.00 25.00
29 Stephon Marbury 10.00 25.00
30 Ray Allen 30.00 80.00
31 Lamar Odom 10.00 25.00
32 Jason Terry 10.00 25.00
33 Josh Howard 10.00 25.00
34 Caron Butler 10.00 25.00
35 Emeka Okafor 10.00 25.00
36 Marcus Camby 8.00 20.00
37 Pau Gasol 12.00 30.00
38 Carlos Boozer 10.00 25.00
39 Baron Davis 10.00 25.00
40 Michael Redd 10.00 25.00
41 Ben Gordon 10.00 25.00
42 Richard Hamilton 10.00 25.00
43 Andrew Bogut 10.00 25.00
44 Tyson Chandler 10.00 25.00
45 Eddy Curry 8.00 20.00
46 Larry Hughes 10.00 25.00
47 LaMarcus Aldridge 15.00 40.00
48 Andrea Bargnani 12.00 30.00
49 Mike Bibby 12.00 30.00
50 Elton Brand 12.00 30.00
51 Al Harrington 10.00 25.00
52 Al Jefferson 10.00 25.00
53 Joe Johnson 10.00 25.00
54 Rashard Lewis 10.00 25.00
55 Kevin Martin 10.00 25.00
56 Andre Miller 10.00 25.00
57 Brandon Roy 12.00 30.00
58 Gerald Wallace 10.00 25.00
59 Rasheed Wallace 12.00 30.00
60 Deron Williams 10.00 25.00

2007-08 Exquisite Collection Limited Logos

PRINT RUN 50 SER.#'d SETS
LLAB Andrew Bogut 30.00 80.00
LLAI Andre Iguodala 60.00 150.00
LLAJ Al Jefferson 20.00 50.00
LLAL Al Horford 50.00 120.00
LLAM Alonzo Mourning 150.00 300.00
LLBD Baron Davis 30.00 80.00
LLBG Ben Gordon 20.00 50.00
LLBO Chris Bosh 60.00 150.00
LLBR Brandon Roy 50.00 120.00
LLCA Carmelo Anthony 100.00 250.00
LLCB Carlos Boozer 30.00 80.00
LLCP Chris Paul 175.00 350.00
LLDH Dwight Howard 150.00 300.00
LLDW Deron Williams 100.00 200.00
LLGG George Gervin 75.00 200.00
LLHA Al Harrington 20.00 50.00
LLJA Antawn Jamison 20.00 50.00
LLJK Jason Kidd 125.00 250.00
LLKB Kobe Bryant 3000.00 5000.00
LLKD Kevin Durant 6000.00 8000.00
LLKG Kevin Garnett 250.00 500.00
LLKH Kirk Hinrich 20.00 50.00
LLLA LaMarcus Aldridge 40.00 100.00
LLLH Larry Hughes 20.00 50.00
LLLJ LeBron James 3000.00 5000.00
LLMB Mike Bibby 25.00 60.00
LLNA Nate Archibald 50.00 120.00
LLPA Tony Parker 125.00 300.00
LLPP Paul Pierce 100.00 250.00
LLRF Randy Foye 20.00 50.00
LLRG Rudy Gay 40.00 80.00
LLRJ Richard Jefferson 20.00 50.00
LLRL Rashard Lewis 20.00 50.00
LLSB Shannon Brown 20.00 50.00
LLSL Shaun Livingston 20.00 50.00
LLSW Shelden Williams 20.00 50.00
LLTJ T.J. Ford 20.00 50.00
LLTM Tracy McGrady 250.00 500.00
LLTP Tayshaun Prince 20.00 50.00
LLVC Vince Carter 125.00 250.00
LLYM Yao Ming 150.00 300.00

2007-08 Exquisite Collection Noble Nameplates

PRINT RUN 25 SER.#'d SETS
NPAB Andrew Bogut 40.00 80.00
NPAH Al Harrington 15.00 40.00
NPAI Andre Iguodala 20.00 50.00
NPAJ Al Jefferson 15.00 40.00
NPAL Al Horford 30.00 80.00
NPAM Alonzo Mourning 75.00 150.00
NPAS Amare Stoudemire 60.00 120.00
NPBD Baron Davis 20.00 50.00
NPBG Ben Gordon 25.00 50.00
NPBO Chris Bosh 50.00 125.00
NPBR Brandon Roy 30.00 80.00
NPBY Andrew Bynum 50.00 120.00
NPCA Carmelo Anthony 40.00 100.00
NPCB Carlos Boozer 20.00 50.00
NPCO Corey Brewer 15.00 40.00
NPCP Chris Paul 100.00 200.00
NPDG Daniel Gibson 15.00 40.00
NPDH Dwight Howard 150.00 300.00
NPDI Boris Diaw 15.00 40.00
NPDR David Robinson 60.00 120.00
NPDW Deron Williams 50.00 100.00
NPEC Eddy Curry 15.00 40.00
NPEO Emeka Okafor 15.00 40.00
NPGG George Gervin 30.00 60.00
NPGR Darrell Griffith 15.00 40.00
NPJA Antawn Jamison 15.00 40.00
NPJO Jermaine O'Neal 15.00 40.00
NPKB Kobe Bryant 800.00 1200.00
NPKD Kevin Durant 400.00 800.00
NPKG Kevin Garnett 100.00 200.00
NPKH Kirk Hinrich 20.00 50.00
NPKK Jason Kidd 30.00 80.00
NPLA LaMarcus Aldridge 30.00 80.00
NPLH Larry Hughes 15.00 40.00
NPLJ LeBron James 2000.00 3000.00
NPMB Mike Bibby 15.00 40.00
NPMM Moses Malone 100.00 175.00
NPMP Morris Peterson 15.00 40.00
NPPA Tony Parker 25.00 60.00
NPRF Raymond Felton 15.00 40.00
NPRG Rudy Gay 20.00 50.00
NPRJ Richard Jefferson 15.00 40.00
NPRO Dennis Rodman 75.00 150.00
NPSB Shane Battier 15.00 40.00
NPSH Shannon Brown 15.00 40.00
NPSL Shaun Livingston 15.00 40.00
NPSN Steve Nash 200.00 400.00
NPSS Stromile Swift 15.00 40.00
NPSW Shelden Williams 15.00 40.00
NPTJ T.J. Ford 15.00 40.00
NPTM Tracy McGrady 50.00 100.00
NPTP Tayshaun Prince 15.00 40.00
NPTT Tyrus Thomas 15.00 40.00
NPVC Vince Carter 100.00 200.00
NPYM Yao Ming 100.00 200.00

2007-08 Exquisite Collection Numbers

STATED PRINT RUN ONE TO 50 SER.#'d SETS
SOME UNPRICED DUE TO SCARCITY
ENAH Al Horford/15 50.00 120.00
ENAJ Al Jefferson/25 25.00 60.00
ENAM Alonzo Mourning/33 200.00 400.00
ENAT Alando Tucker/29 20.00 50.00
ENCA Carmelo Anthony/15 250.00 500.00
ENCB Corey Brewer/11 30.00 80.00
ENCD Clyde Drexler/22 60.00 120.00
ENCM Corey Maggette/50 20.00 50.00
ENDC Daequan Cook/14 20.00 50.00
ENDG Danny Granger/33 25.00 60.00
ENDH Dwight Howard/12 150.00 300.00
ENDR David Robinson/50 50.00 120.00
ENHO Hakeem Olajuwon/34 60.00 150.00
ENJG Jeff Green/22 50.00 120.00
ENJN Joakim Noah/13 100.00 225.00
ENJO Magic Johnson/32 200.00 400.00
ENJS Jason Smith/14 20.00 50.00
ENJW Jerry West/44 100.00 225.00
ENKA K.Abdul-Jabbar/33 125.00 250.00
ENKB Kobe Bryant/24 500.00 800.00
ENKD Kevin Durant/35 900.00 1500.00
ENKH Kirk Hinrich/12 40.00 100.00
ENLA LaMarcus Aldridge/12 125.00 250.00
ENLB Larry Bird/33 125.00 250.00
ENLJ LeBron James/23 400.00 700.00
ENMA Morris Almond/22 20.00 50.00
ENMB Marco Belinelli/18 30.00 80.00
ENMJ Michael Jordan/23 1000.00 1800.00
ENMM Moses Malone/24 40.00 80.00
ENMR Micheal Ray Richardson/20 20.00 50.00
ENPP Paul Pierce/34 50.00 120.00
ENRA Ray Allen/20 75.00 150.00
ENRF Raymond Felton/20 20.00 50.00
ENRG Rudy Gay/22 25.00 60.00
ENRJ Richard Jefferson/24 20.00 50.00
ENRT Reggie Theus/24 20.00 50.00
ENSH Spencer Hawes/31 25.00 60.00
ENSN Steve Nash/13 125.00 250.00
ENSW Sean Williams/51 20.00 50.00
ENTC Tom Chambers/24 20.00 50.00
ENTH Al Thornton/12 30.00 80.00
ENTP Tayshaun Prince/22 25.00 60.00
ENTT Tyrus Thomas/24 40.00 100.00
ENVC Vince Carter/15 200.00 400.00
ENVD Vlade Divac/13 75.00 200.00
ENWC Wilson Chandler/21 40.00 100.00
ENWO James Worthy/42 100.00 250.00
ENWR Julian Wright/32 20.00 50.00
ENYM Yao Ming/11 125.00 250.00

2007-08 Exquisite Collection Numbers Dual

ATED PRINT RUN ONE TO 44 SER.#'d SETS
SOME UNPRICED DUE TO SCARCITY
AH C.Anthony/A.Horford/15 100.00 200.00
BA L.Bird/K.Abdul-Jabbar/33 150.00 300.00
BM K.Bryant/M.Malone/24 200.00 400.00
CH V.Carter/A.Horford/15 100.00 200.00
DH K.Durant/H.Hill/35 250.00 500.00
FC T.Ford/M.Conley/11 50.00 100.00
GD D.Griffith/K.Durant/35 250.00 500.00
GG R.Gay/J.Green/22 60.00 120.00
HA D.Howard/L.Aldridge/12 150.00 300.00
HS K.Hinrich/J.Stockton/12 100.00 200.00
JJ M.Jordan/L.James/23 1000.00 1500.00
JT R.Jefferson/T.Thomas/24 30.00 80.00
MD Y.Ming/G.Davis/11 100.00 200.00
NN S.Nash/J.Noah/13 100.00 200.00
NP J.Noah/G.Pruitt/13 30.00 80.00
OP H.Olajuwon/P.Pierce/34 50.00 120.00
PD T.Prince/C.Drexler/22 100.00 200.00
RW J.Wright/C.Richard/32 30.00 80.00
SC J.Smith/D.Cook/14 30.00 80.00
TH D.Howard/A.Thornton/12 75.00 150.00
WG J.West/G.Gervin/44 75.00 150.00

2007-08 Exquisite Collection Rookie Parallel

CARD #'d TO PLAYER JSY #
SOME UNPRICED DUE TO SCARCITY
62 Morris Almond JSY AU/22 12.00 30.00
63 Julian Wright JSY AU/32 12.00 30.00
64 Aaron Brooks JSY AU/10 40.00 100.00
66 Wilson Chandler JSY AU 15.00 40.00
67 Daequan Cook JSY AU/14 15.00 40.00
69 Jermareo Davidson JSY AU/23 12.00 30.00
70 Glen Davis JSY AU/11 15.00 40.00
72 Corey Brewer JSY AU/22 20.00 50.00
73 Aaron Gray JSY AU/34 12.00 30.00
74 Taurean Green JSY AU 12.00 30.00
76 Spencer Hawes JSY AU/31 15.00 40.00
77 Al Horford JSY AU/35 75.00 200.00
78 Jeff Green JSY AU/22 20.00 50.00
79 Carl Landry JSY AU/10 12.00 30.00
80 Mike Conley Jr. JSY AU/11 250.00 500.00
81 Acie Law JSY AU 12.00 30.00
82 Dominic McGuire JSY AU 12.00 30.00
84 Demetris Nichols JSY AU/35 12.00 30.00
85 Joakim Noah JSY AU/13 75.00 200.00
86 Gabe Pruitt JSY AU/13 12.00 30.00
87 Chris Richard JSY AU/32 12.00 30.00
88 Jason Smith JSY AU/14 15.00 40.00
91 Sean Williams JSY AU/51 12.00 30.00
92 Al Thornton JSY AU/12 15.00 40.00
93 Alando Tucker JSY AU/29 12.00 30.00
94 Kevin Durant JSY AU/35 10000.00 15000.00
95 Marco Belinelli JSY AU/18 20.00 50.00
96 Luis Scola JSY AU 40.00 100.00
97 Louis Amundson JSY AU/20 12.00 30.00
98 C.J. Watson AU/23 20.00 50.00
99 Cheikh Samb AU/35 12.00 30.00
104 Coby Karl AU/11 12.00 30.00
105 Oleksiy Pecherov AU/14 20.00 50.00
106 Jamario Moon AU/33 15.00 40.00
107 Kyrylo Fesenko/44 12.00 30.00
109 Brandan Wright/32 20.00 50.00
110 Thaddeus Young/21 20.00 50.00
112 Greg Oden/52 30.00 60.00

2007-08 Exquisite Collection Scripted Swatches

PRINT RUN 15 SER.#'d SETS
UNPRICED DUAL PRINT RUN 5 SETS
SSAB Andrew Bogut 25.00 60.00
SSAH Al Harrington 15.00 40.00
SSAI Andre Iguodala 25.00 60.00
SSAJ Al Jefferson 25.00 60.00
SSAM Alonzo Mourning 125.00 250.00
SSBG Ben Gordon 15.00 40.00
SSBI Chauncey Billups 30.00 60.00
SSBO Chris Bosh 40.00 80.00
SSBR Brandon Roy 50.00 100.00
SSCA Carmelo Anthony 80.00 160.00
SSCK Chris Kaman 15.00 40.00
SSCM Chris Mullin 40.00 80.00
SSCO Corey Maggette 25.00 50.00
SSCP Chris Paul 100.00 200.00
SSDG Daniel Gibson 15.00 40.00
SSDH Dwight Howard 60.00 120.00
SSDI Boris Diaw 15.00 40.00
SSDM Desmond Mason 15.00 40.00
SSDR David Robinson 75.00 150.00
SSDW Deron Williams 50.00 120.00
SSEC Eddy Curry 15.00 40.00
SSEO Emeka Okafor 15.00 40.00
SSFE Raymond Felton 15.00 40.00
SSGG George Gervin 40.00 80.00
SSJA Antawn Jamison 20.00 50.00
SSJF Jordan Farmar 15.00 40.00
SSJH John Havlicek 50.00 100.00
SSJK Jason Kidd 60.00 120.00
SSJO Jermaine O'Neal 25.00 50.00
SSJS John Stockton 100.00 175.00
SSKB Kobe Bryant 500.00 900.00
SSKG Kevin Garnett 150.00 300.00
SSKH Kirk Hinrich 25.00 60.00
SSLA LaMarcus Aldridge 30.00 80.00
SSLB Larry Bird 75.00 150.00
SSLH Larry Hughes 15.00 40.00
SSLJ LeBron James 500.00 800.00
SSMA Donyell Marshall 15.00 40.00
SSMB Mike Bibby 15.00 40.00
SSMI Michael Jordan 1000.00 1800.00
SSMJ Magic Johnson 75.00 150.00
SSMM Moses Malone 40.00 80.00
SSMP Morris Peterson 15.00 40.00
SSPA Tony Parker 40.00 80.00
SSPP Paul Pierce 40.00 80.00
SSPR Mark Price 75.00 150.00
SSRC Rodney Carney 15.00 40.00
SSRF Randy Foye 15.00 40.00
SSRG Rudy Gay 40.00 80.00
SSRH Richard Hamilton 20.00 50.00
SSRJ Richard Jefferson 15.00 40.00
SSRL Rashard Lewis 30.00 80.00
SSRO Dennis Rodman 100.00 200.00
SSSB Shane Battier 15.00 40.00
SSSH Shannon Brown 20.00 50.00
SSSL Shaun Livingston 15.00 40.00
SSSN Steve Nash 125.00 250.00
SSSW Shelden Williams 15.00 40.00
SSTJ T.J. Ford 15.00 40.00
SSTM Tracy McGrady 50.00 100.00
SSTP Tayshaun Prince 25.00 60.00
SSTT Tyrus Thomas 15.00 40.00
SSVC Vince Carter 75.00 150.00
SSYM Yao Ming 50.00 100.00

2007-08 Exquisite Collection Uncut Sheet Redemptions

COMMON EXCH (1-22) 200.00 300.00
NO ODDS GIVEN

2008-09 Exquisite Collection

1-60 PRINT RUN 125 SER.#'d SETS
STATED PRINT RUN 55 TO 225 SER.#'d SETS
UNPRICED BLACK PRINT RUN ONE SET
UNPRICED PRESS PLATE PRINT RUN ONE SET
1 Kevin Garnett 8.00 20.00
2 LeBron James 50.00 120.00
3 Dwight Howard 4.00 10.00
4 Kobe Bryant 30.00 80.00
5 Carmelo Anthony 6.00 15.00
6 Tim Duncan 8.00 20.00
7 Yao Ming 6.00 15.00
8 Dwyane Wade 20.00 50.00
9 Dirk Nowitzki 8.00 20.00
10 Jason Kidd 5.00 12.00
11 Allen Iverson 12.00 30.00
12 Tracy McGrady 5.00 12.00
13 Steve Nash 5.00 12.00
14 Ray Allen 5.00 12.00
15 Amare Stoudemire 4.00 10.00
16 Vince Carter 6.00 15.00
17 Shaquille O'Neal 10.00 25.00
18 Chris Bosh 5.00 12.00
19 Gilbert Arenas 4.00 10.00
20 Chauncey Billups 5.00 12.00
21 Paul Pierce 5.00 12.00
22 Chris Paul 6.00 15.00
23 Michael Jordan 100.00 250.00
24 Carlos Boozer 4.00 10.00
25 Manu Ginobili 5.00 12.00
26 Shawn Marion 4.00 10.00
27 Tony Parker 5.00 12.00
28 Baron Davis 4.00 10.00
29 Kevin Durant 40.00 100.00
30 Josh Howard 4.00 10.00
31 Marcus Camby 3.00 8.00
32 Michael Redd 4.00 10.00
33 Caron Butler 4.00 10.00
34 Richard Hamilton 4.00 10.00
35 Andrea Bargnani 4.00 10.00
36 Tyson Chandler 4.00 10.00
37 Andrew Bogut 4.00 10.00
38 Joe Johnson 4.00 10.00
39 T.J. Ford 3.00 8.00
40 Rashard Lewis 4.00 10.00
41 Pau Gasol 5.00 12.00
42 David Lee 3.00 8.00
43 Andre Iguodala 4.00 10.00
44 Greg Oden 4.00 10.00
45 Corey Maggette 4.00 10.00
46 Andrew Bynum 3.00 8.00
47 Mo Williams 4.00 10.00
48 Elton Brand 5.00 12.00
49 Ben Gordon 4.00 10.00
50 Danny Granger 4.00 10.00

51 Richard Jefferson 4.00 10.00
52 Al Horford 5.00 12.00
53 Gerald Wallace 4.00 10.00
54 Rudy Gay 5.00 12.00
55 Deron Williams 4.00 10.00
56 Corey Brewer 4.00 10.00
57 Monta Ellis 4.00 10.00
58 Kevin Martin 4.00 10.00
59 Luol Deng 4.00 10.00
60 Brandon Roy 5.00 12.00
61 Kevin Love JSY AU RC 100.00 250.00
62 Joe Alexander JSY AU RC 6.00 15.00
63 D.J. Augustin JSY AU RC 8.00 20.00
64 Brook Lopez JSY AU RC 30.00 80.00
65 Jason Thompson JSY AU RC 6.00 15.00
66 Brandon Rush JSY AU RC 8.00 20.00
67 A.Randolph JSY AU RC 6.00 15.00
68 Robin Lopez JSY AU RC 10.00 25.00
69 Marreese Speights JSY AU RC 15.00 40.00
70 Roy Hibbert JSY AU RC 10.00 25.00
71 Javale McGee JSY AU RC 12.00 30.00
72 J.J. Hickson JSY AU RC 10.00 25.00
73 Ryan Anderson JSY AU RC 12.00 30.00
74 Courtney Lee JSY AU RC 8.00 20.00
75 Kosta Koufos JSY AU RC 8.00 20.00
76 George Hill JSY AU RC 15.00 40.00
77 Darrell Arthur JSY AU RC 8.00 20.00
78 Donte Greene JSY AU RC 6.00 15.00
79 D.J. White JSY AU/55 RC 8.00 20.00
80 J.R. Giddens JSY AU RC 6.00 15.00
81 Walter Sharpe JSY AU RC 6.00 15.00
82 Joey Dorsey JSY AU RC 6.00 15.00
83 Mario Chalmers JSY AU RC 20.00 50.00
84 DeAndre Jordan JSY AU RC 75.00 150.00
85 Kyle Weaver JSY AU RC 6.00 15.00
86 Sonny Weems JSY AU RC 6.00 15.00
87 C.Douglas-Roberts JSY AU RC 6.00 15.00
88 Rudy Fernandez JSY AU RC 40.00 80.00
89 Marc Gasol JSY AU/150 RC 50.00 120.00
90 O.J. Mayo JSY AU/99 RC 40.00 100.00
91 M.Beasley JSY AU/99 RC 30.00 80.00
92 D.Rose JSY AU/99 RC 400.00 800.00
93 R.Westbrook JSY AU RC 2000.00 3000.00
94 Eric Gordon JSY AU RC 30.00 80.00
95 Nicolas Batum AU/99 RC 80.00 160.00
96 Mike Taylor AU/99 RC 6.00 15.00
97 Alexis Ajinca AU/99 RC 6.00 15.00
98 Luc Mbah A Moute AU/99 RC 8.00 20.00
99 Sean Singletary AU/99 RC 6.00 15.00
100 Danilo Gallinari AU/99 RC 15.00 40.00
NNO Uncut Sheet EXCH 100.00 200.00

2008-09 Exquisite Collection Gold

*1-50 GOLD: .75X TO 2X BASE HI
1-50 PRINT RUN 50 SER.#'d SETS
51-100 PRINT RUN 25 SER.#'d SETS
8 Dwyane Wade 75.00 150.00
14 Ray Allen 15.00 40.00
23 Michael Jordan 350.00 700.00
29 Kevin Durant 125.00 250.00
61 Kevin Love 75.00 150.00
62 Joe Alexander 12.00 30.00
63 D.J. Augustin 15.00 40.00
64 Brook Lopez 40.00 100.00
65 Jason Thompson 12.00 30.00
66 Brandon Rush 15.00 40.00
67 Anthony Randolph 12.00 30.00
68 Robin Lopez 20.00 50.00
69 Marreese Speights 30.00 80.00
70 Roy Hibbert 25.00 60.00
71 JaVale McGee 25.00 60.00
72 J.J. Hickson 15.00 40.00
73 Ryan Anderson 15.00 40.00
74 Courtney Lee 15.00 40.00
75 Kosta Koufos 15.00 40.00
76 George Hill 30.00 80.00
77 Darrell Arthur 15.00 40.00
78 Donte Greene 12.00 30.00
79 D.J. White 15.00 40.00
80 J.R. Giddens 12.00 30.00
81 Walter Sharpe 12.00 30.00
82 Joey Dorsey 12.00 30.00
83 Mario Chalmers 20.00 50.00
84 DeAndre Jordan 25.00 60.00
85 Kyle Weaver 12.00 30.00
86 Sonny Weems 12.00 30.00
87 Chris Douglas-Roberts 12.00 30.00
88 Rudy Fernandez 30.00 80.00
89 Marc Gasol 40.00 100.00
90 O.J. Mayo 40.00 100.00
91 Michael Beasley 20.00 50.00
92 Derrick Rose 400.00 700.00
93 Russell Westbrook 200.00 400.00
94 Eric Gordon 30.00 80.00
95 Nicolas Batum 25.00 60.00
96 Mike Taylor 12.00 30.00
97 Alexis Ajinca 12.00 30.00
98 Luc Mbah A Moute 15.00 40.00
99 Sean Singletary 12.00 30.00
100 Danilo Gallinari 30.00 80.00

2008-09 Exquisite Collection Autographs

STATED PRINT RUN 23 TO 35 SER.#'d SETS
AUTOAD Adrian Dantley/35 10.00 25.00
AUTOAG Artis Gilmore/35 10.00 25.00
AUTOAH Al Horford/35 8.00 20.00
AUTOAM Alonzo Mourning/35 50.00 120.00
AUTOBB Bobby Brown/35 6.00 15.00
AUTOBL Bill Laimbeer/35 10.00 25.00
AUTOBO Bob Lanier/35 10.00 25.00
AUTOBW Bill Walton/35 12.50 30.00
AUTOCB Carlos Boozer/35 10.00 25.00
AUTOCL Clyde Drexler/35 30.00 80.00
AUTODC Daequan Cook/35 10.00 25.00
AUTODE Derrick Rose/35 175.00 350.00
AUTODF Derek Fisher/35 15.00 30.00
AUTODH Dwight Howard/35 40.00 100.00
AUTODO Dominique Wilkins/35 20.00 50.00
AUTODW Deron Williams/35 25.00 50.00
AUTOEG Eric Gordon/35 20.00 50.00
AUTOFE Rudy Fernandez/35 15.00 30.00
AUTOGG George Gervin/35 15.00 40.00
AUTOGW Gerald Wallace/35 6.00 15.00
AUTOJB Jose Barea/35 30.00 80.00
AUTOJH John Havlicek/35 30.00 80.00
AUTOKB Kobe Bryant/24 250.00 500.00
AUTOKD Kevin Durant/35 150.00 300.00
AUTOKG Kevin Garnett/35 50.00 120.00
AUTOLJ LeBron James/23 300.00 600.00
AUTOLO Lamar Odom/35 15.00 40.00
AUTOMB Michael Beasley/35 12.00 30.00
AUTOMC Mike Conley Jr./35 10.00 25.00
AUTOMG Marc Gasol/35 20.00 40.00
AUTOOM O.J. Mayo/35 25.00 60.00
AUTOOR Oscar Robertson/35 100.00 200.00
AUTORD Dennis Rodman/35 40.00 100.00
AUTORF Randy Foye/35 6.00 15.00
AUTORO Brandon Roy/35 25.00 60.00
AUTORP Robert Parish/35 10.00 25.00
AUTORS Rodney Stuckey/35 10.00 25.00
AUTORW Russell Westbrook/35 200.00 400.00
AUTOSI Jack Sikma/35 10.00 25.00
AUTOSM Sidney Moncrief/35 8.00 20.00
AUTOWF Walt Frazier/35 8.00 20.00

2008-09 Exquisite Collection Big Jersey Autographs

STATED PRINT RUN 10 SER.#'d SETS
SOME UNPRICED DUE TO SCARCITY
BIGBD Baron Davis 40.00 100.00
BIGDH Dwight Howard 125.00 250.00
BIGKB Kobe Bryant 800.00 1200.00
BIGKD Kevin Durant 250.00 500.00
BIGKG Kevin Garnett 150.00 300.00
BIGLJ LeBron James 300.00 600.00
BIGRS Rodney Stuckey 40.00 100.00
BIGSN Steve Nash 100.00 200.00

2008-09 Exquisite Collection Emblems of Endorsement

ATED PRINT RUN ONE TO 10 SER.#'d SETS
SOME UNPRICED DUE TO SCARCITY
EEAH Al Horford/10 50.00 100.00
EECP Chris Paul/10 450.00 800.00
EEDE Derrick Rose White/10 1400.00 2100.00
EEDR Derrick Rose Red/10 1400.00 2100.00
EEDW Deron Williams/10 150.00 300.00
EEGH George Hill/10 100.00 200.00
EEJB Jerryd Bayless/10 125.00 250.00
EEJG Jeff Green/10 100.00 200.00
EEJK Jason Kidd/10 150.00 300.00
EEJS John Stockton/10 150.00 300.00
EEJW Jerry West/10 100.00 200.00
EEKB Kobe Bryant/10 4000.00 7000.00
EEKD Kevin Durant/10 250.00 500.00
EEKG Kevin Garnett/10 400.00 750.00
EEMC Mike Conley Jr./10 50.00 100.00
EEMJ Michael Jordan/10 5000.00 8000.00
EEOJ O.J. Mayo/10 150.00 300.00
EEOM O.J. Mayo/10 150.00 300.00
EEPP Paul Pierce/10 125.00 250.00
EERF Rudy Fernandez/10 125.00 250.00
EERO David Robinson/10 125.00 250.00
EERS Rodney Stuckey/10 60.00 120.00
EESW Sonny Weems/10 50.00 100.00
EEVC Vince Carter/10 250.00 500.00

2008-09 Exquisite Collection Enshrinements

PRINT RUN 23 TO 25 SER.#'d SETS
ENBR Bill Russell/25 150.00 300.00
ENCP Chris Paul/25 60.00 150.00
ENDR David Robinson/25 40.00 80.00
ENDW Dominique Wilkins/25 25.00 50.00
ENHO Hakeem Olajuwon/25 25.00 60.00
ENIT Isiah Thomas/25 30.00 60.00
ENJE Julius Erving/25 50.00 125.00
ENJO Magic Johnson/25 50.00 125.00
ENJS John Stockton/25 100.00 200.00
ENJW Jerry West/25 75.00 150.00
ENKA Kareem Abdul-Jabbar/25 50.00 120.00
ENKB Kobe Bryant/24 400.00 800.00
ENKG Kevin Garnett/25 100.00 250.00
ENLB Larry Bird/25 60.00 150.00
ENLJ LeBron James/23 800.00 1200.00
ENMJ Michael Jordan/23 2000.00 2500.00
ENOR Oscar Robertson/25 125.00 225.00
ENRP Robert Parish/25 25.00 50.00
ENVC Vince Carter/25 100.00 200.00
ENWF Walt Frazier/25 20.00 40.00

2008-09 Exquisite Collection Enshrinements Dual

ATED PRINT RUN 23 TO 25 SER.#'d SETS
ENDBA Kareem/McAdoo/25 100.00 200.00
ENDBJ K.Bryant/L.James/25 500.00 800.00
ENDBP K.Bryant/Pierce/25 300.00 500.00
ENDCK Cooper/Kupchak/25 40.00 80.00
ENDCW V.Carter/Wilkins/25 40.00 80.00
ENDGA Gervin/Dantley/25 50.00 120.00
ENDJB Magic/L.Bird/25 250.00 500.00
ENDJJ Jordan/L.James/23 1500.00 2000.00
ENDJR Jordan/Rodman/25 700.00 1200.00
ENDKM Jordan/Bryant/25 1200.00 2000.00
ENDMG Mourning/KG/25 125.00 250.00
ENDMM Yao/McGrady/25 40.00 100.00
ENDNK J.Kidd/S.Nash/25 100.00 200.00
ENDOR Olajuwon/D.Rob/25 75.00 150.00
ENDRH Havlicek/Russell/25 125.00 250.00
ENDRJ O.Rob/L.James/25 250.00 450.00
ENDSH Stdmre/D.Howard/25 50.00 100.00
ENDTP I.Thomas/C.Paul/25 100.00 200.00
ENDWG J.West/Goodrich/25 50.00 125.00
ENDWS Sktn/D.Williams/25 75.00 200.00

2008-09 Exquisite Collection Flawless Autographs

STATED PRINT RUN 23 TO 50 SER.#'d SETS
FLAWAB Andrew Bynum/50 20.00 50.00
FLAWAH Al Horford/50 15.00 40.00
FLAWAM Alonzo Mourning/25 75.00 150.00
FLAWBD Baron Davis/50 25.00 50.00
FLAWBR Bill Russell/25 75.00 150.00
FLAWCD Clyde Drexler/50 40.00 100.00
FLAWCP Chris Paul/25 50.00 120.00
FLAWDF Derek Fisher/47 15.00 40.00
FLAWDW Deron Williams/25 25.00 60.00
FLAWIT Isiah Thomas/25 25.00 60.00
FLAWJE Julius Erving/25 50.00 120.00
FLAWJN Joakim Noah/50 25.00 60.00
FLAWJW Jerry West/25 50.00 125.00
FLAWKA K.Abdul-Jabbar/25 60.00 150.00
FLAWKB Kobe Bryant/24 400.00 800.00
FLAWKD Kevin Durant/50 100.00 200.00
FLAWKG Kevin Garnett/50 50.00 100.00
FLAWLJ LeBron James/23 250.00 500.00
FLAWMC Michael Cooper/50 15.00 40.00
FLAWMJ Michael Jordan/23 1400.00 1800.00
FLAWMK Mitch Kupchak/25 25.00 60.00
FLAWOR Oscar Robertson/25 75.00 150.00
FLAWPP Paul Pierce/50 40.00 100.00
FLAWRO Brandon Roy/50 20.00 50.00
FLAWRP Robert Parish/50 20.00 50.00
FLAWRS Rodney Stuckey/50 15.00 40.00
FLAWTM Tracy McGrady/50 25.00 60.00
FLAWVC Vince Carter/50 30.00 80.00

2008-09 Exquisite Collection Inscriptions

ATED PRINT RUN 20 TO 50 SER.#'d SETS
SCRIPTAD A.Dantley/25 12.00 30.00
SCRIPTAH A.Horford/50 8.00 20.00
SCRIPTAI A.Iguodala/25 15.00 40.00
SCRIPTAM A.Mourning #33/25 75.00 150.00
SCRIPTAS A.Stoudemire #1/25 25.00 60.00
SCRIPTBD Baron Davis/50 12.00 30.00
SCRIPTBL Bill Laimbeer/50 10.00 25.00
SCRIPTBM Bob McAdoo/50 15.00 40.00
SCRIPTBR B.Roy #7/50 20.00 50.00
SCRIPTCB C.Billups/50 20.00 40.00
SCRIPTCP Chris Paul CP3/25 75.00 200.00
SCRIPTDC Daequan Cook/50 8.00 20.00
SCRIPTDG D.Griffith Dr. Dunk/25 15.00 30.00
SCRIPTDH Dwight Howard/50 60.00 150.00
SCRIPTDR Rodman Worm/25 75.00 200.00
SCRIPTDW Dom.Wilkins/25 60.00 150.00
SCRIPTGG George Gervin/50 15.00 40.00
SCRIPTGW Gerald Wallace/50 8.00 20.00
SCRIPTHA H.Armstrong #12/50 8.00 20.00
SCRIPTHO H.Olajuwon #34/25 20.00 40.00
SCRIPTJG Jeff Green/50 20.00 50.00
SCRIPTJK Kidd Mr. TD/50 150.00 400.00
SCRIPTJS J.Sikma 7 AS/50 20.00 50.00
SCRIPTJW Jerry West/25 125.00 250.00
SCRIPTKB Kobe Bryant/24 500.00 800.00
SCRIPTKD Kevin Durant/50 125.00 250.00
SCRIPTKG Kevin Garnett/50 60.00 150.00
SCRIPTMC M.Conley Money Mike/50 40.00 80.00
SCRIPTMW M.Williams #24/50 8.00 20.00
SCRIPTOR O.Robertson/25 100.00 200.00
SCRIPTPA Tony Parker/50 25.00 50.00
SCRIPTPP Pierce The Truth/50 80.00 160.00
SCRIPTRP Robert Parish/50 15.00 40.00
SCRIPTSM Sidney Moncrief/20 8.00 20.00
SCRIPTSN Steve Nash/50 50.00 100.00
SCRIPTTM T.McGrady/50 25.00 50.00
SCRIPTTP T.Prince Palace/25 25.00 60.00
SCRIPTVC V.Carter Sanity/50 60.00 150.00
SCRIPTYM Yao Ming/50 40.00 100.00

2008-09 Exquisite Collection Jerseys

*JERSEY: 1X TO 2.5X BASE HI
STATED PRINT RUN 35 SER.#'d SETS
2 LeBron James 75.00 150.00

2008-09 Exquisite Collection Limited Logos

STATED PRINT RUN 23 TO 25 SER.#'d SETS
LLAH Al Horford/25 25.00 50.00
LLAI Andre Iguodala/25 40.00 100.00
LLBD Baron Davis/25 40.00 100.00
LLCP Chris Paul/25 300.00 500.00
LLDH Dwight Howard/25 250.00 500.00
LLDL David Lee/25 25.00 50.00
LLDR Derrick Rose/25 400.00 800.00
LLDW David West/25 25.00 50.00
LLEG Eric Gordon/25 100.00 200.00
LLGH George Hill/25 50.00 125.00
LLJG Jeff Green/25 40.00 100.00
LLJK Jason Kidd/25 75.00 150.00
LLJR J.R. Giddens/25 20.00 50.00
LLJS John Stockton/25 75.00 150.00
LLKB Kobe Bryant/24 900.00 1500.00
LLKD Kevin Durant/25 1000.00 1500.00
LLKG Kevin Garnett/25 250.00 500.00
LLKL Kevin Love/25 175.00 350.00
LLLJ LeBron James/23 700.00 1300.00
LLMB Michael Beasley/25 30.00 80.00
LLMJ Michael Jordan/23 3000.00 4500.00
LLPP Paul Pierce/25 200.00 400.00
LLRF Rudy Fernandez/25 75.00 150.00
LLRJ Richard Jefferson/25 20.00 50.00
LLRP Robert Parish/25 40.00 70.00
LLRS Rodney Stuckey/25 25.00 60.00
LLSB Shane Battier/25 20.00 50.00
LLSN Steve Nash/24 250.00 500.00
LLTC Tom Chambers/25 30.00 80.00
LLVC Vince Carter/25 200.00 400.00
LLVD Vlade Divac/25 100.00 200.00
LLWI Deron Williams/25 100.00 200.00

2008-09 Exquisite Collection Limited Throwback Logo Autographs

STATED PRINT RUN 22 TO 25 SER.#'d SETS
LTAR Anthony Randolph/25 75.00 150.00
LTBL Brook Lopez/25 50.00 100.00
LTBR Brandon Rush/22 20.00 50.00
LTCD Chris Douglas-Roberts/25 10.00 25.00
LTCL Courtney Lee/25 40.00 100.00
LTDA Darrell Arthur/25 12.00 30.00
LTDG Donte Greene/25 10.00 25.00
LTDJ D.J. Augustin/25 20.00 50.00
LTDR Derrick Rose/25 1000.00 1500.00
LTEG Eric Gordon/25 60.00 120.00
LTGH George Hill/25 60.00 150.00
LTJA Joe Alexander/25 10.00 25.00
LTJB Jerryd Bayless/25 30.00 80.00
LTJD Joey Dorsey/25 10.00 25.00
LTJG J.R. Giddens/25 10.00 25.00
LTJH J.J. Hickson/25 30.00 60.00
LTJM Javale McGee/25 60.00 120.00
LTJT Jason Thompson/25 20.00 50.00
LTKK Kosta Koufos/25 12.00 30.00
LTKL Kevin Love/25 150.00 300.00
LTMB Michael Beasley/25 60.00 150.00
LTMC Mario Chalmers/25 40.00 100.00
LTMS Marreese Speights/25 12.00 30.00
LTOM O.J. Mayo/25 60.00 150.00
LTRA Ryan Anderson/25 12.00 30.00
LTRL Robin Lopez/25 15.00 40.00
LTSW Sonny Weems/25 10.00 25.00
LTWS Walter Sharpe/25 10.00 25.00

2008-09 Exquisite Collection Noble Nameplates

STATED PRINT RUN 5 TO 25 SER.#'d SETS
SOME UNPRICED DUE TO SCARCITY
NAAH Al Horford/25 15.00 40.00
NAAJ Al Jefferson/25 20.00 50.00
NAAL Joe Alexander/25 15.00 40.00
NAAM Alonzo Mourning/25 150.00 300.00
NAAR Anthony Randolph/25 75.00 150.00
NAAT Al Thornton/25 15.00 40.00
NABA Jose Barea/25 75.00 150.00
NABD Baron Davis/25 30.00 80.00
NABG Ben Gordon/25 30.00 80.00
NABI Mike Bibby/25 15.00 40.00
NABR Corey Brewer/25 15.00 40.00
NACB Chauncey Billups/25 40.00 80.00
NACP Chris Paul/25 125.00 250.00
NADA D.J. Augustin/25 30.00 60.00
NADH Dwight Howard/25 50.00 100.00
NADR Derrick Rose/25 300.00 800.00
NADW David West/25 20.00 50.00
NAEG Eric Gordon/25 75.00 150.00
NAFE Raymond Felton/10 15.00 40.00
NAFG Francisco Garcia/25 15.00 40.00
NAGH George Hill/25 40.00 100.00
NAGP Gabe Pruitt/25 15.00 40.00
NAHA Al Harrington/18 15.00 40.00
NAJB Jerryd Bayless/25 40.00 80.00
NAJG Jeff Green/25 30.00 80.00
NAJJ J.J. Hickson/25 25.00 60.00
NAJK Jason Kidd/25 75.00 150.00
NAJM Jamario Moon/25 15.00 40.00
NAJO Jermaine O'Neal/25 15.00 40.00
NAJT Jason Thompson/25 30.00 60.00
NAKB Kobe Bryant/24 2500.00 3500.00
NAKD Kevin Durant/25 200.00 400.00
NAKG Kevin Garnett/25 150.00 300.00
NAKL Kevin Love/25 150.00 300.00
NAKW Kyle Weaver/25 15.00 40.00
NALJ LeBron James/23 2000.00 3000.00
NAMB Michael Beasley/25 60.00 150.00
NAMC Mario Chalmers/14 25.00 60.00
NAMI Mike Conley Jr./25 25.00 60.00
NAMJ Michael Jordan/18 5000.00 8000.00
NAMP Morris Peterson/25 15.00 40.00
NAOM O.J. Mayo/25 60.00 150.00
NAPP Paul Pierce/25 100.00 200.00
NARA Ray Allen/25 150.00 300.00
NARF Rudy Fernandez/25 25.00 60.00
NARJ Richard Jefferson/25 15.00 40.00
NARS Rodney Stuckey/20 25.00 60.00
NARY Ryan Anderson/25 30.00 60.00
NASB Shane Battier/20 15.00 40.00
NASH Spencer Hawes/25 15.00 40.00
NATC Tyson Chandler/25 30.00 80.00
NATM Tracy McGrady/25 500.00 800.00
NATP Tayshaun Prince/25 20.00 50.00
NAWI Deron Williams/25 50.00 100.00

2008-09 Exquisite Collection Patches

*PATCHES: 2X TO 5X BASE HI
PATCH PRINT RUN 10 SER.#'d SETS
UNPRICED AUTO PATCH PRINT RUN ONE SET
2 LeBron James 200.00 500.00
14 Ray Allen 30.00 80.00
22 Chris Paul 60.00 150.00

2008-09 Exquisite Collection Player Box Autographs

STATED PRINT RUN 5 TO 34 SER.#'d SETS
SOME UNPRICED DUE TO SCARCITY
PBAHO Hakeem Olajuwon/34 25.00 60.00
PBAJO Magic Johnson/32 75.00 150.00
PBAJS John Stockton/12 60.00 120.00
PBAKB Kobe Bryant/24 250.00 500.00
PBALB Larry Bird/33 75.00 150.00
PBALJ LeBron James/23 300.00 600.00
PBAMB Michael Beasley/30 30.00 80.00
PBAMJ Michael Jordan/23 1200.00 2000.00
PBAOM O.J. Mayo/32 12.00 30.00

2008-09 Exquisite Collection Player Box Base

STATED PRINT RUN 5 TO 34 SER.#'d SETS
SOME UNPRICED DUE TO SCARCITY
PBHO Hakeem Olajuwon/34 8.00 20.00
PBJO Magic Johnson/32 15.00 40.00
PBJS John Stockton/12 12.00 30.00
PBKB Kobe Bryant/24 40.00 100.00
PBLB Larry Bird/33 15.00 30.00
PBLJ LeBron James/23 30.00 80.00
PBMB Michael Beasley/30 6.00 15.00
PBMJ Michael Jordan/23 100.00 200.00
PBOM O.J. Mayo/32 6.00 15.00

2008-09 Exquisite Collection Player Box Memorabilia

STATED PRINT RUN 5 TO 34 SER.#'d SETS
SOME UNPRICED DUE TO SCARCITY
PBMHO Hakeem Olajuwon/34 10.00 25.00
PBMJO Magic Johnson/32 25.00 60.00
PBMJS John Stockton/12 20.00 40.00
PBMKB Kobe Bryant/24 60.00 120.00
PBMLB Larry Bird/33 20.00 40.00
PBMMB Michael Beasley/30 10.00 25.00
PBMMJ Michael Jordan/23 200.00 400.00
PBMOM O.J. Mayo/32 10.00 25.00

2008-09 Exquisite Collection Player Box Patches Autographs

STATED PRINT RUN 5 TO 50 SER.#'d SETS
SOME UNPRICED DUE TO SCARCITY
PBAMDR Derrick Rose/50 400.00 750.00
PBAMHO Hakeem Olajuwon/34 60.00 120.00
PBAMJO Magic Johnson/32 100.00 200.00
PBAMJS John Stockton/12 100.00 200.00
PBAMKB Kobe Bryant/24 400.00 750.00
PBAMLB Larry Bird/33 100.00 200.00
PBAMLJ LeBron James/23 300.00 600.00
PBAMMB Michael Beasley/30 30.00 80.00
PBAMMJ Michael Jordan/23 1200.00 2000.00
PBAMOM O.J. Mayo/32 60.00 150.00

2008-09 Exquisite Collection Prime

STATED PRINT RUN 35 TO 50 SER.#'d SETS
PRMAB Andrew Bynum 10.00 25.00
PRMAI Allen Iverson 40.00 100.00
PRMAM Adam Morrison 10.00 25.00
PRMAN Andrew Bogut 25.00 50.00
PRMAT Al Thornton 12.00 30.00
PRMBC Carlos Boozer 12.00 30.00
PRMBD Baron Davis 12.00 30.00
PRMBE Marco Belinelli 12.00 30.00
PRMBL Brook Lopez 12.00 30.00
PRMBO Chris Bosh 30.00 80.00
PRMBU Caron Butler 12.00 30.00
PRMBY Michael Beasley 15.00 40.00
PRMCB Chauncey Billups 15.00 40.00
PRMCM Corey Maggette 12.00 30.00
PRMCO Corey Brewer 12.00 30.00
PRMCP Chris Paul 50.00 125.00
PRMDA D.J. Augustin 12.00 30.00
PRMDE Derrick Rose 150.00 300.00
PRMDH Dwight Howard/39 40.00 100.00
PRMDN Dirk Nowitzki 50.00 120.00
PRMDR Derrick Rose 150.00 300.00
PRMEB Elton Brand 15.00 40.00
PRMEG Eric Gordon 40.00 100.00
PRMGH Grant Hill 50.00 100.00
PRMHI George Hill 15.00 40.00
PRMJA Joe Alexander 10.00 25.00
PRMJB Jerryd Bayless 12.00 30.00
PRMJK Jason Kidd 30.00 80.00
PRMJT Jason Thompson 10.00 25.00
PRMKD Kevin Durant 150.00 300.00
PRMKG Kevin Garnett 60.00 150.00
PRMKL Kevin Love 30.00 80.00
PRMKM Kevin Martin 12.00 30.00
PRMLJ LeBron James 300.00 500.00
PRMMA Stephon Marbury 30.00 80.00
PRMMB Mike Bibby 12.00 30.00
PRMMG Manu Ginobili 25.00 60.00
PRMMI Michael Beasley 15.00 40.00
PRMMS Marreese Speights 12.00 30.00
PRMOJ O.J. Mayo 15.00 40.00
PRMOM O.J. Mayo/35 25.00 60.00
PRMPA Tony Parker 25.00 60.00
PRMPG Pau Gasol 20.00 50.00
PRMPP Paul Pierce 25.00 60.00
PRMRF Rudy Fernandez 12.00 30.00
PRMRJ Richard Jefferson 12.00 30.00
PRMRL Rashard Lewis 12.00 30.00
PRMRO Brandon Roy/43 20.00 50.00
PRMRW Rasheed Wallace 15.00 40.00
PRMSB Shane Battier/45 20.00 50.00
PRMSM Shawn Marion 12.00 30.00
PRMSO Shaquille O'Neal 40.00 100.00
PRMTC Tyson Chandler 12.00 30.00
PRMTD Tim Duncan 30.00 80.00
PRMTP Tayshaun Prince 12.00 30.00
PRMTS Thabo Sefolosha 10.00 25.00
PRMWI Deron Williams/40 20.00 50.00
PRMZR Zach Randolph 12.00 30.00

2008-09 Exquisite Collection Rookie Parallel

STATED PRINT RUN ONE TO 44 SER.#'d SETS
SOME UNPRICED DUE TO SCARCITY
61 Kevin Love JSY AU/42 300.00 500.00
62 Joe Alexander JSY AU/11 100.00 200.00
63 D.J. Augustin JSY AU/14 100.00 200.00
64 Brook Lopez JSY AU/11 250.00 400.00
66 Brandon Rush JSY AU/25 30.00 80.00
68 Robin Lopez JSY AU/15 50.00 100.00
69 M.Speights JSY AU/16 75.00 150.00
71 Javale McGee JSY AU/34 100.00 200.00
72 J.J. Hickson JSY AU/21 125.00 250.00
73 Ryan Anderson JSY AU/20 40.00 100.00
74 Courtney Lee JSY AU/11 100.00 200.00
75 Kosta Koufos JSY AU/41 15.00 40.00
78 Donte Greene JSY AU/10 50.00 100.00
81 Walter Sharpe JSY AU/42 12.00 30.00
82 Joey Dorsey JSY AU/15 12.00 30.00
85 Kyle Weaver JSY AU/20 20.00 50.00
86 Sonny Weems JSY AU/13 40.00 100.00
89 Marc Gasol JSY AU/33 60.00 120.00
90 O.J. Mayo JSY AU/32 250.00 500.00
91 Michael Beasley JSY AU/30 30.00 80.00
95 Nicolas Batum AU/12 150.00 300.00
97 Alexis Ajinca AU/21 12.00 30.00
98 Luc Mbah A Moute AU/12 15.00 40.00
99 Sean Singletary AU/44 12.00 30.00
100 Danilo Gallinari AU/44 100.00 200.00

2008-09 Exquisite Collection Scripted Swatches

STATED PRINT RUN 12 TO 25 SER.#'d SETS
SCRPAB Andrew Bynum/25 50.00 125.00
SCRPAD Adrian Dantley/12 40.00 80.00
SCRPAH Al Horford/25 15.00 40.00
SCRPAL Al Jefferson/25 15.00 40.00
SCRPAR Anthony Randolph/25 40.00 100.00
SCRPAS Amare Stoudemire/25 50.00 100.00
SCRPBE Michael Beasley/25 40.00 100.00
SCRPBI Chauncey Billups/25 25.00 60.00
SCRPBL Brook Lopez/25 50.00 100.00
SCRPBR Brandon Roy/25 50.00 120.00
SCRPBY Michael Beasley/25 30.00 80.00
SCRPCL Courtney Lee/25 60.00 120.00
SCRPCM Corey Maggette/25 15.00 40.00
SCRPCP Chris Paul/25 125.00 250.00
SCRPDA Darrell Arthur/25 15.00 40.00
SCRPDE Derrick Rose White/25 300.00 800.00
SCRPDH Dwight Howard/25 125.00 250.00
SCRPDJ D.J. Augustin/25 40.00 80.00
SCRPDL David Lee/25 15.00 40.00
SCRPDO DeAndre Jordan/25 30.00 80.00
SCRPDR Derrick Rose Red/25 300.00 800.00
SCRPEG Eric Gordon Ball Right/25 60.00 150.00
SCRPGG George Gervin/25 15.00 40.00
SCRPGO Eric Gordon Ball Left/25 15.00 40.00
SCRPGR Danny Granger/25 30.00 60.00
SCRPHA Hilton Armstrong/25 15.00 40.00
SCRPHI George Hill/25 40.00 100.00
SCRPHR Al Harrington/25 15.00 40.00
SCRPID Ike Diogu/25 15.00 40.00
SCRPJB Jose Barea/25 75.00 150.00
SCRPJD Joey Dorsey/25 15.00 40.00
SCRPJK Jason Kidd/25 75.00 200.00
SCRPJO Jermaine O'Neal/25 15.00 40.00
SCRPJR J.R. Smith/25 15.00 40.00
SCRPJT Jason Thompson/25 40.00 80.00
SCRPKB Kobe Bryant/24 500.00 850.00
SCRPKD Kevin Durant/25 150.00 300.00
SCRPKG Kevin Garnett/25 175.00 350.00
SCRPKL Kevin Love/25 150.00 300.00
SCRPLB Larry Bird/25 100.00 200.00
SCRPLH Larry Hughes No Auto/25 15.00 40.00
SCRPLJ LeBron James/23 1500.00 3000.00
SCRPMA Desmond Mason/25 15.00 40.00
SCRPMC Mario Chalmers/21 50.00 100.00
SCRPMJ Michael Jordan/16 2000.00 4000.00
SCRPOJ O.J. Mayo Blue/25 20.00 50.00
SCRPOM O.J. Mayo White/25 20.00 50.00
SCRPRA Ryan Anderson/25 20.00 50.00
SCRPRF Rudy Fernandez/25 100.00 200.00
SCRPRJ Richard Jefferson/25 15.00 40.00
SCRPRO David Robinson/25 75.00 150.00
SCRPRS Ramon Sessions/25 20.00 50.00
SCRPRW Russell Westbrook/25 600.00 1200.00
SCRPSB Shane Battier/25 30.00 80.00
SCRPSN Steve Nash/25 100.00 200.00
SCRPST John Stockton/25 125.00 250.00
SCRPVC Vince Carter/25 60.00 150.00
SCRPVD Vlade Divac/25 40.00 80.00

2008-09 Exquisite Collection Triple Patches

STATED PRINT RUN 10 SER.#'d SETS
SOME UNPRICED DUE TO SCARCITY
ETPAI Allen Iverson 75.00 150.00
ETPAS Amare Stoudemire 20.00 50.00
ETPCA Carmelo Anthony 40.00 80.00
ETPDH Dwight Howard 60.00 120.00
ETPDN Dirk Nowitzki 50.00 100.00
ETPDR Derrick Rose 200.00 400.00
ETPGA Gilbert Arenas 20.00 50.00
ETPJK Jason Kidd 20.00 50.00
ETPKB Kobe Bryant 150.00 300.00
ETPKM Kevin Martin 20.00 50.00
ETPLJ LeBron James 125.00 250.00
ETPLW Luke Walton 20.00 50.00
ETPMB Michael Beasley 40.00 100.00
ETPOM O.J. Mayo 40.00 100.00
ETPRA Ray Allen 25.00 60.00
ETPSN Steve Nash 40.00 80.00
ETPTD Tim Duncan 50.00 120.00
ETPVC Vince Carter 40.00 80.00

2009-10 Exquisite Collection

1-42 PRINT RUN 199 SER.#'d SETS
43-79 PRINT RUN 225 SER.#'d SETS
UNPRICED BLACK PRINT RUN ONE SET
1 Dwight Howard 8.00 20.00
2 LeBron James 60.00 150.00
3 Kobe Bryant 80.00 200.00
4 Dwyane Wade 40.00 100.00
5 Yao Ming 12.00 30.00
6 Tim Duncan 15.00 40.00
7 Kevin Garnett 15.00 40.00
8 Allen Iverson 30.00 60.00
9 Yi Jianlian 8.00 20.00
10 Tracy McGrady 12.00 30.00
11 Chris Paul 12.00 30.00
12 Shaquille O'Neal 15.00 40.00
13 Carmelo Anthony 12.00 30.00
14 Vince Carter 8.00 20.00
15 Dirk Nowitzki 12.00 30.00
16 Chris Bosh 10.00 25.00
17 Manu Ginobili 10.00 25.00
18 Pau Gasol 10.00 25.00
19 Ray Allen 12.00 30.00
20 Paul Pierce 10.00 25.00
21 Jamal Crawford 25.00 60.00
22 Steve Nash 10.00 25.00
23 Michael Jordan 150.00 300.00
24 Gilbert Arenas 8.00 20.00
25 Luke Ridnour 8.00 20.00
26 Derrick Rose 40.00 100.00
27 Jose Calderon 6.00 15.00
28 Brandon Roy 10.00 25.00
29 Joe Johnson 8.00 20.00
30 Danny Granger 8.00 20.00
31 Greg Oden 8.00 20.00
32 Al Jefferson 8.00 20.00
33 Kevin Durant 100.00 200.00
34 Andre Iguodala 8.00 20.00
35 David Lee 6.00 15.00
36 Kevin Martin 8.00 20.00
37 O.J. Mayo 6.00 15.00
38 Zach Randolph 8.00 20.00
39 Gerald Wallace 8.00 20.00
40 Russell Westbrook 20.00 50.00
41 Deron Williams 8.00 20.00
42 Mo Williams 8.00 20.00
43 Blake Griffin RC 100.00 250.00
44 Ricky Rubio AU RC 50.00 120.00
45 James Harden AU RC 250.00 500.00
46 Tyreke Evans RC 8.00 20.00
47 Brandon Jennings RC 10.00 25.00
48 James Johnson AU RC 8.00 20.00
49 Earl Clark AU RC 8.00 20.00
50 Chase Budinger AU RC 8.00 20.00
51 DeJuan Blair RC 8.00 20.00
52 B.J. Mullens AU RC 6.00 15.00
53 Darren Collison AU RC 10.00 25.00
54 Tyler Hansbrough RC 8.00 20.00
55 Sam Young AU RC 6.00 15.00
56 Marcus Thornton AU RC 8.00 20.00
57 Jeff Teague AU RC 10.00 25.00
58 Jonny Flynn AU RC 6.00 15.00
59 Terrence Williams RC 6.00 15.00
60 Gerald Henderson AU RC 15.00 40.00
61 Hasheem Thabeet RC 6.00 15.00
62 Ty Lawson AU RC 10.00 25.00
63 Eric Maynor AU RC 6.00 15.00
64 Stephen Curry AU RC 2000.00 3000.00
65 DeMar DeRozan RC 50.00 120.00
66 Patrick Mills RC 12.00 30.00
67 Jordan Hill RC 8.00 20.00
68 Derrick Brown AU RC 6.00 15.00
69 Wayne Ellington AU RC 10.00 25.00
70 DaJuan Summers AU RC 6.00 15.00
71 Eric Maynor AU RC 6.00 15.00
72 Stephen Curry AU 2000.00 3000.00
73 Ricky Rubio AU 50.00 120.00
74 James Harden AU 400.00 800.00
75 James Johnson AU 8.00 20.00
76 Sam Young AU 6.00 15.00
77 Gerald Henderson AU 15.00 40.00
78 B.J. Mullens AU 6.00 15.00
79 Jonny Flynn AU 6.00 15.00

2009-10 Exquisite Collection Rookie Parallel

STATED PRINT RUN ONE TO 50 SETS
SOME UNPRICED DUE TO SCARCITY
43 Blake Griffin/23 1000.00 2000.00
46 Tyreke Evans/12 600.00 1000.00
48 James Johnson AU/23 25.00 60.00
50 Chase Budinger AU/34 25.00 60.00
51 DeJuan Blair/45 25.00 60.00
52 B.J. Mullens AU/32 20.00 50.00
54 Tyler Hansbrough/50 25.00 60.00
55 Sam Young AU/23 20.00 50.00
60 Gerald Henderson AU/15 50.00 125.00
61 Hasheem Thabeet/34 20.00 50.00
64 Stephen Curry AU/30 5000.00 8000.00
66 Patrick Mills/13 60.00 150.00
67 Jordan Hill/43 25.00 60.00
69 Wayne Ellington AU/22 30.00 80.00
72 Stephen Curry AU/31 5000.00 8000.00
75 James Johnson AU/23 25.00 60.00
76 Sam Young AU/23 20.00 50.00
77 Gerald Henderson AU/15 50.00 125.00
78 B.J. Mullens AU/32 20.00 50.00

2009-10 Exquisite Collection Autographs Patches

STATED PRINT RUN 50 SER.#'d SETS
PAA Arron Afflalo 12.00 30.00
PAB Andrew Bynum 50.00 125.00
PAJ Al Jefferson 20.00 50.00
PAM Alonzo Mourning 100.00 175.00
PAS Amare Stoudemire 40.00 100.00
PAZ Kelenna Azubuike 12.00 30.00
PBD Baron Davis 12.00 30.00
PBI Mike Bibby 15.00 40.00
PBL Bill Laimbeer 15.00 40.00
PBM Brad Miller 20.00 40.00
PBR Brandon Roy 40.00 80.00
PCD Clyde Drexler 40.00 100.00
PCH Tyson Chandler 20.00 50.00
PCO Corey Brewer 12.00 30.00
PCP Chris Paul 75.00 200.00
PDG Danny Granger 25.00 60.00
PDH Dwight Howard 125.00 250.00
PDM Desmond Mason 12.00 30.00
PDO Donyell Marshall 12.00 30.00
PDR David Robinson 60.00 150.00
PDW David West 12.00 30.00
PER Julius Erving 75.00 200.00
PGR Darrell Griffith 12.00 30.00
PJB Jerryd Bayless 12.00 30.00
PJE Jeff Green 50.00 100.00
PJF Jordan Farmar 12.00 30.00
PJG J.R. Giddens 12.00 30.00
PJK Jason Kidd 40.00 80.00
PJM Jamario Moon 12.00 30.00
PJN Joakim Noah 40.00 100.00
PJO Jermaine O'Neal 30.00 60.00
PJS J.R. Smith 20.00 50.00
PJW Jerry West 200.00 500.00
PKA Kareem Abdul-Jabbar 125.00 250.00
PKG Kevin Garnett 75.00 150.00
PKL Kevin Love 150.00 300.00
PLA LaMarcus Aldridge 150.00 300.00
PLB Larry Bird 75.00 200.00
PLH Larry Hughes 12.00 30.00
PLJ LeBron James 500.00 800.00
PLO Lamar Odom 35.00 70.00
PLW Luke Walton 20.00 40.00
PMA Magic Johnson 150.00 300.00
PMC Mike Conley Jr. 12.00 30.00
PMJ Michael Jordan 1000.00 2000.00
PMP Mark Price 75.00 150.00
PMW Mo Williams 20.00 40.00
POM O.J. Mayo 40.00 80.00
PPP Paul Pierce 75.00 150.00
PQR Quentin Richardson 12.00 30.00
PRF Randy Foye 15.00 40.00
PRJ Richard Jefferson 12.00 30.00
PRO Derrick Rose 250.00 500.00
PRP Robert Parish 30.00 80.00
PSA Stacey Augmon 12.00 30.00
PSH Spencer Hawes 12.00 30.00
PSN Steve Nash 100.00 200.00
PST John Stockton 60.00 150.00
PTC Tom Chambers 20.00 50.00
PTM Tracy McGrady 60.00 150.00
PTP Tayshaun Prince 15.00 40.00
PVC Vince Carter 50.00 120.00
PVD Vlade Divac 25.00 50.00
PWI Deron Williams 30.00 80.00
PYM Yao Ming 100.00 200.00

2009-10 Exquisite Collection Extra Exquisite Jerseys

PRINT RUN 50 SER.#'d SETS
*GOLD: .6X TO 1.5X BASE HI
GOLD PRINT RUN 25 SER.#'d SETS
XAB Andrew Bynum 5.00 12.00
XAI Allen Iverson 12.50 30.00
XAR Ron Artest 8.00 20.00
XAS Amare Stoudemire 6.00 15.00
XAT Al Thornton 6.00 15.00
XBW Brandan Wright 5.00 12.00
XBY Marcus Camby 5.00 12.00
XCA Carmelo Anthony 15.00 40.00
XCB Chris Bosh 8.00 20.00
XCM Chris Mullin/15 10.00 25.00
XDH Devin Harris 5.00 12.00
XDN Dirk Nowitzki 30.00 80.00
XDR Derrick Rose 50.00 125.00
XEB Elton Brand 8.00 20.00
XEG Eric Gordon 6.00 15.00
XGH Grant Hill 20.00 50.00
XHO Josh Howard 6.00 15.00
XIG Andre Iguodala 6.00 15.00
XJC Jose Calderon 5.00 12.00
XJR Jason Richardson 8.00 20.00
XJS Josh Smith 6.00 15.00
XJT Jason Terry 6.00 15.00
XKB Kobe Bryant 50.00 125.00
XKE Kevin Martin 6.00 15.00
XKG Kevin Garnett 12.00 30.00
XKM Karl Malone 10.00 25.00
XLB Leandro Barbosa 6.00 15.00
XLJ LeBron James 50.00 125.00
XLS Luis Scola 6.00 15.00
XLW Luke Walton 5.00 12.00
XMA Kenyon Martin 6.00 15.00
XME Monta Ellis 6.00 15.00
XMG Manu Ginobili 12.00 30.00
XMJ Michael Jordan 200.00 400.00
XMR Michael Redd 6.00 15.00
XOM O.J. Mayo 5.00 12.00
XPE Patrick Ewing 20.00 50.00
XPG Pau Gasol 15.00 30.00
XPP Paul Pierce 12.00 30.00
XPS Peja Stojakovic 15.00 30.00
XRA Ray Allen 12.00 30.00
XRG Rudy Gay 12.00 30.00
XRH Richard Hamilton 6.00 15.00
XRR Rajon Rondo 20.00 50.00
XRW Rasheed Wallace 8.00 20.00
XSM Shawn Marion 6.00 15.00
XSO Shaquille O'Neal 20.00 50.00
XSP Scottie Pippen 40.00 100.00
XST Sebastian Telfair 5.00 12.00
XSV Sasha Vujacic 5.00 12.00
XTD Tim Duncan 20.00 50.00
XTO Travis Outlaw 6.00 15.00
XTY Thaddeus Young 5.00 12.00
XYI Yi Jianlian 6.00 15.00
XZR Zach Randolph 10.00 25.00

2009-10 Exquisite Collection Extra Exquisite Patches

PRINT RUN 15 SER.#'d SETS
XAI Allen Iverson 100.00 200.00
XAR Ron Artest 40.00 100.00
XAS Amare Stoudemire 30.00 80.00
XAT Al Thornton 30.00 80.00
XBW Brandan Wright 25.00 60.00
XBY Marcus Camby 25.00 60.00
XCA Carmelo Anthony 100.00 200.00
XCB Chris Bosh 60.00 150.00
XCM Chris Mullin 40.00 100.00
XDH Devin Harris 25.00 60.00
XDN Dirk Nowitzki 60.00 150.00
XDR Derrick Rose 60.00 150.00
XEB Elton Brand 40.00 100.00
XEG Eric Gordon 30.00 80.00
XGH Grant Hill 100.00 200.00
XHO Josh Howard 30.00 80.00
XIG Andre Iguodala 30.00 80.00
XJC Jose Calderon 25.00 60.00
XJH Jeff Hornacek 30.00 80.00
XJR Jason Richardson 40.00 100.00
XJS Josh Smith 30.00 80.00
XJT Jason Terry 30.00 80.00
XKB Kobe Bryant 400.00 700.00
XKE Kevin Martin 30.00 80.00
XKG Kevin Garnett 60.00 150.00
XKM Karl Malone 50.00 125.00
XLB Leandro Barbosa 30.00 80.00
XLJ LeBron James 400.00 700.00
XLS Luis Scola 30.00 80.00
XLW Luke Walton 25.00 60.00
XMA Kenyon Martin 30.00 80.00
XMC Kevin McHale 40.00 100.00
XME Monta Ellis 30.00 80.00
XMG Manu Ginobili 40.00 100.00
XMJ Michael Jordan 600.00 1100.00
XMR Michael Redd 30.00 80.00
XNA Nate Archibald 30.00 80.00
XOM O.J. Mayo 25.00 60.00
XOR Oscar Robertson 40.00 100.00
XPE Patrick Ewing 100.00 200.00
XPG Pau Gasol 40.00 100.00
XPP Paul Pierce 40.00 100.00
XPS Peja Stojakovic 40.00 100.00
XRA Ray Allen 50.00 125.00
XRG Rudy Gay 40.00 100.00
XRH Richard Hamilton 30.00 80.00
XRR Rajon Rondo 40.00 100.00
XRW Rasheed Wallace 40.00 100.00
XSM Shawn Marion 50.00 100.00
XSO Shaquille O'Neal 80.00 200.00
XSP Scottie Pippen 125.00 250.00
XST Sebastian Telfair 25.00 60.00
XSV Sasha Vujacic 25.00 60.00
XTD Tim Duncan 125.00 250.00
XTO Travis Outlaw 30.00 80.00
XTY Thaddeus Young 25.00 60.00
XYI Yi Jianlian 30.00 80.00
XZR Zach Randolph 30.00 80.00

2009-10 Exquisite Collection Jerseys

*JERSEYS: .6X TO 1.5X BASE HI
JERSEY PRINT RUN 25 SER.#'d SETS
UNPRICED PATCH PRINT RUN 10 SETS
UNPRICED PATCH AU PRINT RUN ONE SET

- 2 LeBron James 80.00 200.00
- 3 Kobe Bryant 100.00 250.00
- 4 Dwyane Wade 40.00 100.00
- 15 Dirk Nowitzki 30.00 80.00
- 23 Michael Jordan 150.00 400.00
- 26 Derrick Rose 75.00 150.00
- 33 Kevin Durant 80.00 200.00
- 40 Russell Westbrook 50.00 125.00

2009-10 Exquisite Collection Limited Logos

STATED PRINT RUN 7 TO 25 SER.#'d SETS

SOME UNPRICED DUE TO SCARCITY

- LAB Andrew Bynum/13 175.00 350.00
- LAS Amare Stoudemire/15 125.00 250.00
- LDH Dwight Howard/20 200.00 400.00
- LDW David West/17 30.00 80.00
- LJB Jerryd Bayless/20 40.00 100.00
- LJE Julius Erving/20 175.00 350.00
- LJF Jordan Farmar/20 50.00 120.00
- LJG Jeff Green/20 50.00 100.00
- LJK Jason Kidd/12 125.00 250.00
- LJN Joakim Noah/18 60.00 150.00
- LJO Jermaine O'Neal/14 50.00 125.00
- LKL Kevin Love/14 250.00 500.00
- LLB Larry Bird/16 200.00 400.00
- LLJ LeBron James/16 700.00 1200.00
- LLO Lamar Odom/15 75.00 150.00
- LLW Luke Walton/13 50.00 125.00
- LMJ Magic Johnson/16 250.00 500.00
- LMW Mo Williams/18 30.00 80.00
- LQR Quentin Richardson/17 30.00 80.00
- LRA Ray Allen/18 200.00 400.00
- LRO Derrick Rose/16 300.00 600.00
- LSN Steve Nash/19 200.00 400.00
- LTM Tracy McGrady/13 125.00 250.00
- LTP Tayshaun Prince/14 30.00 80.00
- LVC Vince Carter/25 125.00 250.00
- LWI Deron Williams/18 125.00 250.00
- LYM Yao Ming/11 350.00 700.00

2009-10 Exquisite Collection Noble Nameplates

STATED PRINT RUN 3 TO 33 SER.#'d SETS

SOME UNPRICED DUE TO SCARCITY

- NAB Andrew Bynum/15 60.00 120.00
- NBD Baron Davis/19 25.00 60.00
- NBL Bill Laimbeer/15 30.00 80.00
- NBR Brandon Roy/15 75.00 200.00
- NCP Chris Paul/15 125.00 250.00
- NDH Dwight Howard/18 150.00 300.00
- NDM Desmond Mason/25 25.00 60.00
- NDR David Robinson/15 125.00 225.00
- NJB Jerryd Bayless/20 25.00 60.00
- NJE Julius Erving/17 125.00 300.00
- NJF Jordan Farmar/26 25.00 60.00
- NJG Jeff Green/12 25.00 60.00
- NJK Jason Kidd/12 75.00 150.00
- NJO Jermaine O'Neal/15 30.00 80.00
- NJS J.R. Smith/21 30.00 80.00
- NKL Kevin Love/12 100.00 200.00
- NLA LaMarcus Aldridge/15 60.00 150.00
- NLB Larry Bird/12 125.00 250.00
- NLH Larry Hughes/18 25.00 60.00
- NLJ LeBron James/18 600.00 1200.00
- NLO Lamar Odom/16 30.00 80.00
- NMI Michael Jordan/15 1200.00 2000.00
- NMJ Magic Johnson/31 125.00 250.00
- NMW Mo Williams/28 25.00 60.00
- NPP Paul Pierce/15 75.00 150.00
- NQR Quentin Richardson/33 25.00 60.00
- NRA Ray Allen/18 200.00 300.00
- NRO Derrick Rose/20 500.00 800.00
- NRP Robert Parish/15 30.00 80.00
- NSA Stacey Augmon/15 25.00 60.00
- NSN Steve Nash/16 75.00 150.00
- NST John Stockton/15 100.00 200.00
- NTC Tom Chambers/15 25.00 60.00
- NTM Tracy McGrady/20 50.00 100.00
- NTP Tayshaun Prince/12 25.00 60.00
- NVC Vince Carter/19 125.00 250.00
- NWI Deron Williams/26 50.00 120.00

2009-10 Exquisite Collection Numbers

PRINT RUNS B/WN 1-50 COPIES PER

SOME UNPRICED DUE TO SCARCITY

- ADJJ M.Jordan/L.James/23 3000.00 4500.00
- EDMA Mourning/Jabbar/33 175.00 350.00
- EDRS J.Stockton/P.Riley/12 150.00 300.00
- NPAB Andrew Bynum/17 40.00 100.00
- NPAM Alonzo Mourning/33 300.00 600.00
- NPBL Bill Laimbeer/40 30.00 80.00
- NPBW Bill Walton/32 25.00 60.00
- NPCD Clyde Drexler/22 250.00 450.00
- NPDE Dennis Rodman/50 75.00 150.00
- NPDH Dwight Howard/12 200.00 400.00
- NPDR David Robinson/50 75.00 150.00
- NPDW David West/30 25.00 60.00
- NPEO Emeka Okafor/50 25.00 60.00
- NPGG George Gervin/44 125.00 250.00
- NPJG Jeff Green/22 40.00 100.00
- NPJN Joakim Noah/13 60.00 150.00
- NPJW Jerry West/44 100.00 250.00
- NPKA K.Abdul-Jabbar/33 125.00 250.00
- NPKL Kevin Love/42 125.00 300.00
- NPLJ LeBron James/23 500.00 900.00
- NPMJ Michael Jordan/23
- NPMP Mark Price/25 50.00 100.00
- NPOM O.J. Mayo/32 60.00 120.00
- NPPR Pat Riley/12 100.00 200.00
- NPRT Reggie Theus/24 25.00 60.00
- NPSN Steve Nash/13 150.00 300.00
- NPST John Stockton/12 125.00 250.00
- NPTC Tom Chambers/24 100.00 200.00
- NPVC Vince Carter/15 250.00 500.00
- NPVD Vlade Divac/21 25.00 60.00
- NPYM Yao Ming/11 100.00 200.00

2009-10 Exquisite Collection Rookie Patch Flashback

STATED PRINT RUN 25 SER.#'d SETS

- 78A Michael Jordan/23 6000.00 8000.00
- 78C Bill Russell/19 1000.00 1500.00
- 78D Julius Erving/25 400.00 800.00
- 78E Larry Bird/25 400.00 800.00
- 78F Magic Johnson/25 400.00 800.00
- 78G Kareem Abdul-Jabbar/25 300.00 600.00
- 78H Kevin Garnett/25 300.00 550.00
- 78J Peyton Manning/25 400.00 700.00
- 78K John Elway/25 300.00 600.00
- 78L Jerry Rice/25 350.00 650.00
- 78M Barry Sanders/25 400.00 800.00
- 78O Adrian Peterson/25 400.00 800.00
- 78P Wayne Gretzky/25 750.00 1500.00
- 78Q Mario Lemieux/25 400.00 800.00
- 78R Steve Yzerman/25 200.00 400.00
- 78S Sidney Crosby/25 1200.00 2000.00
- 78T Patrick Roy/25 250.00 600.00
- 78U Gordie Howe/25 250.00 500.00

2011-12 Exquisite Collection

1-60 PRINT RUN 99 SER.#'d SETS

AU PRINT RUN 199 SER.#'d SETS

- 1 Michael Jordan 50.00 100.00
- 2 LeBron James 15.00 40.00
- 3 Walt Frazier 4.00 10.00
- 4 Hal Greer 3.00 8.00
- 5 Tim Hardaway 4.00 10.00
- 6 Alonzo Mourning 8.00 20.00
- 7 Larry Johnson 6.00 15.00
- 8 Magic Johnson 10.00 25.00
- 9 Julius Erving 6.00 15.00
- 10 Mark Jackson 3.00 8.00
- 11 Darrell Griffith 2.50 6.00
- 12 Hakeem Olajuwon 5.00 12.00
- 13 Clyde Drexler 6.00 15.00
- 14 David Robinson 6.00 15.00
- 15 Christian Laettner 5.00 12.00
- 16 Bill Sharman 4.00 10.00
- 17 Greg Anthony 2.50 6.00
- 18 Jim Jackson 2.50 6.00
- 19 Adrian Dantley 3.00 8.00
- 20 Jerry West 5.00 12.00
- 21 John Havlicek 5.00 12.00
- 22 Dennis Rodman 8.00 20.00
- 23 Gail Goodrich 3.00 8.00
- 24 Danny Manning 3.00 8.00
- 25 Glen Rice 3.00 8.00
- 26 Anfernee Hardaway 10.00 25.00
- 27 LeBron James 15.00 40.00
- 28 Bob McAdoo 3.00 8.00
- 29 Robert Horry 3.00 8.00
- 30 Michael Jordan 30.00 80.00
- 31 Brad Daugherty 3.00 8.00
- 32 Candace Parker 6.00 15.00
- 33 Jack Sikma 3.00 8.00
- 34 Reggie Theus 3.00 8.00
- 35 Cynthia Cooper 4.00 10.00
- 36 Bill Laimbeer 3.00 8.00
- 37 Grant Hill 12.00 30.00
- 38 Kenny Smith 3.00 8.00
- 39 Toni Kukoc 6.00 15.00
- 40 Don Nelson 4.00 10.00
- 41 Jerry Sloan 4.00 10.00
- 42 B.J. Armstrong 4.00 10.00
- 43 Bill Cartwright 3.00 8.00
- 44 Bobby Hurley 5.00 12.00
- 45 Terry Porter 2.50 6.00
- 46 Rudy Tomjanovich 3.00 8.00
- 47 Lonnie Shelton 2.50 6.00
- 48 Chet Walker 3.00 8.00
- 49 Bill Russell 10.00 25.00
- 50 Micheal Ray Richardson 3.00 8.00
- 51 Cazzie Russell 3.00 8.00
- 52 Sam Cassell 3.00 8.00
- 53 David Thompson 3.00 8.00
- 54 Freddie Lewis 2.50 6.00
- 55 James Worthy 5.00 12.00
- 56 Rick Barry 3.00 8.00
- 57 Larry Bird 10.00 25.00
- 58 George Gervin 4.00 10.00
- 59 Elgin Baylor 4.00 10.00
- 60 Bill Walton 4.00 10.00
- 61 Alec Burks AU 6.00 15.00
- 62 Shelvin Mack AU 4.00 10.00
- 63 JaJuan Johnson AU 4.00 10.00
- 64 Klay Thompson AU 150.00 400.00
- 65 Kawhi Leonard AU 400.00 700.00
- 66 Nikola Vucevic AU 20.00 50.00
- 67 Jimmer Fredette AU 15.00 40.00
- 68 Nolan Smith AU 4.00 10.00
- 69 Malcolm Lee AU 5.00 12.00
- 70 Reggie Jackson AU 15.00 40.00
- 71 Bismack Biyombo AU 6.00 15.00
- 72 Jordan Williams AU 4.00 10.00
- 73 Tobias Harris AU 6.00 15.00
- 74 Marcus Morris AU 5.00 12.00
- 75 MarShon Brooks AU 5.00 12.00
- 76 Tristan Thompson AU 15.00 40.00
- 77 Chris Singleton AU 4.00 10.00
- 78 Markieff Morris AU 6.00 15.00
- 79 J.Valanciunas AU 12.00 30.00
- 80 D.Motiejunas AU 5.00 12.00
- 81 Norris Cole AU 6.00 15.00
- 82 Cory Joseph AU 5.00 12.00
- 83 Tyler Honeycutt AU 5.00 12.00
- 84 Chandler Parsons AU 6.00 15.00
- 85 Josh Selby AU 5.00 12.00

2011-12 Exquisite Collection Holo Parallel

UNPRICED 1-60 PRINT RUN ONE SET

*61-85: 1.2X TO 3X HI COLUMN

61-85 PRINT RUN 25 SER.#'d SETS

- 64 Klay Thompson AU/25 250.00 500.00
- 65 Kawhi Leonard AU/25 1500.00 2000.00
- 70 Reggie Jackson AU/25 50.00 120.00
- 75 MarShon Brooks AU/25 30.00 80.00
- 79 J.Valanciunas AU/25 75.00 150.00

2011-12 Exquisite Collection Championship Bling Autographs

STATED PRINT RUN 50 TO 99 SER.#'d SETS

*GOLD: .4X TO 1X BASE HI

- CBAM Alonzo Mourning/99 12.00 30.00
- CBBD Billy Donovan/50 10.00 25.00
- CBBM Bob McAdoo/99 10.00 25.00
- CBBR Bill Russell/50 30.00 80.00
- CBBW Bill Walton/99 10.00 25.00
- CBCA Vince Carter/99 15.00 40.00
- CBCD Clyde Drexler/50 12.00 30.00
- CBCL Christian Laettner/99 10.00 25.00
- CBCR Cazzie Russell/99 10.00 25.00
- CBDA David Robinson/50 20.00 50.00
- CBDG Darrell Griffith/99 10.00 25.00
- CBDM Danny Manning/99 10.00 25.00
- CBDR David Robinson/50 30.00 80.00
- CBDT David Thompson/99 12.00 30.00
- CBGG Gail Goodrich/99 10.00 25.00
- CBGO Gail Goodrich/99 10.00 25.00
- CBGR Glen Rice/99 10.00 25.00
- CBHO Hakeem Olajuwon/50 20.00 50.00
- CBJA LeBron James/99 150.00 300.00
- CBJB Jim Boeheim/99 50.00 120.00
- CBJH John Havlicek/50 15.00 40.00
- CBJL LeBron James/99 150.00 300.00
- CBJO Michael Jordan/99 250.00 500.00
- CBJW James Worthy/50 10.00 25.00
- CBLA Larry Brown/99 10.00 25.00
- CBLB Larry Bird/50 30.00 80.00
- CBLE LeBron James/99 150.00 300.00
- CBLJ Larry Johnson/99 12.00 30.00
- CBMI Michael Jordan/99 300.00 500.00
- CBMJ Magic Johnson/50 30.00 60.00
- CBOL Hakeem Olajuwon/50 15.00 40.00
- CBRO David Robinson/50 25.00 60.00
- CBRU Bill Russell/50 40.00 100.00
- CBRW Roy Williams/50 15.00 40.00
- CBTI Tom Izzo/99 20.00 50.00
- CBVC Vince Carter/50 20.00 50.00
- CBWA Bill Walton/99 10.00 25.00
- CBWE Jerry West/50 30.00 80.00
- CBWI Roy Williams/50 25.00 60.00
- CBWO James Worthy/50 15.00 40.00

2011-12 Exquisite Collection Dimensions Autographs

RANDOM INSERTS IN PACKS

- DAH Anfernee Hardaway 20.00 50.00
- DAM Alonzo Mourning 15.00 40.00
- DBR Bill Russell 50.00 125.00
- DBW Bill Walton 15.00 40.00
- DCD Clyde Drexler 15.00 40.00
- DCO DeMarcus Cousins 15.00 40.00
- DCR Cazzie Russell 5.00 12.00
- DDA David Robinson 15.00 40.00
- DDC DeMarcus Cousins 15.00 30.00
- DDM Danny Manning 8.00 20.00
- DDR David Robinson 15.00 40.00
- DDT David Thompson 8.00 20.00
- DGG George Gervin 12.00 30.00
- DGH Grant Hill 25.00 60.00
- DGO Gail Goodrich 8.00 20.00
- DGR Glen Rice 8.00 20.00
- DHG Hal Greer 8.00 20.00
- DHO Hakeem Olajuwon 12.00 50.00
- DJA LeBron James 125.00 300.00
- DJE Julius Erving 30.00 80.00
- DJN Michael Jordan 200.00 400.00
- DJO Michael Jordan 200.00 400.00
- DJR Michael Jordan 200.00 400.00
- DJW James Worthy 12.00 30.00
- DKS Kenny Smith 8.00 20.00
- DLA Larry Bird 30.00 80.00
- DLB Larry Bird 30.00 80.00
- DLE LeBron James 125.00 300.00
- DLJ Larry Johnson 8.00 20.00
- DMA Mark Jackson 8.00 20.00
- DMC Magic Johnson 30.00 60.00
- DMG Magic Johnson 30.00 60.00
- DMI Michael Jordan 250.00 500.00
- DMJ Michael Jordan 250.00 500.00
- DML Michael Jordan 200.00 400.00
- DRB Rick Barry 8.00 20.00
- DRO Dennis Rodman 15.00 40.00
- DST John Starks 5.00 30.00
- DWE Jerry West 20.00 50.00
- DWF Walt Frazier 10.00 25.00

2011-12 Exquisite Collection Endorsements

STATED PRINT RUN 10 TO 50 SER.#'d SETS

SOME UNPRICED DUE TO SCARCITY

UNPRICED HOLO PRINT RUN 5 SETS

- EEAH Anfernee Hardaway/50 12.00 30.00
- EEBS Bill Sharman/50 8.00 20.00
- EEBW Bill Walton/50 8.00 20.00
- EEGK George Karl/50 8.00 20.00
- EEHG Hal Greer/50 8.00 20.00
- EEJA LeBron James/50 125.00 250.00
- EEJN Michael Jordan/50 250.00 500.00
- EEJO Michael Jordan/50 350.00 700.00
- EEJS LeBron James/50 175.00 350.00
- EELB Larry Bird/50 40.00 100.00
- EELE LeBron James/50 175.00 350.00
- EEMI Michael Jordan/50 300.00 600.00
- EEMJ Magic Johnson/50 50.00 100.00
- EERB Rick Barry/50 8.00 20.00
- EEST John Starks/50 8.00 20.00
- EEVC Vince Carter/50 25.00 60.00
- EEWF Walt Frazier/50 8.00 20.00

2011-12 Exquisite Collection Endorsements Dual

STATED PRINT RUN 10 TO 20 SER.#'d SETS

SOME UNPRICED DUE TO SCARCITY

UNPRICED HOLO PRINT RUN 5 SETS

- EE2BH L.Bird/J.Havlicek/20 50.00 120.00
- EE2BM D.Manning/L.Brown/20 40.00 80.00
- EE2EJ J.Erving/M.Jordan/20 300.00 550.00
- EE2IB T.Izzo/J.Boeheim/20 30.00 60.00
- EE2JB M.Jordan/L.Bird/20 400.00 700.00
- EE2JE L.James/J.Erving/20 300.00 500.00
- EE2JH A.Hardaway/L.James/20 100.00 200.00
- EE2JJ M.Jordan/M.Johnson/20 300.00 600.00
- EE2JR L.James/P.Riley/20 150.00 300.00
- EE2LA L.James/A.Mourning/20 150.00 300.00
- EE2MJ L.Johnson/Mourning/20 30.00 80.00
- EE2ML L.James/M.Jordan/20 600.00 1000.00
- EE2OD C.Drexler/Olajuwon/20 30.00 80.00
- EE2RO Olajuwon/Robinson/20 75.00 150.00
- EE2WC J.Calhoun/R.Williams/20 30.00 80.00

2011-12 Exquisite Collection Endorsements Triple

STATED PRINT RUN 15 SER.#'d SETS

UNPRICED HOLO PRINT RUN 5 SETS

UNPRICED QUAD PRINT RUN 5 SETS

UNPRICED QUAD HOLO PRINT RUN 3 SETS

- EE3BRH Havlicek/Russell/Bird
- EE3IWC Roy/Izzo/Calhn EXCH 40.00 100.00
- EE3JBJ Bird/LeBron/Jordan
- EE3JJB Jordan/Magic/Bird
- EE3JJE Erving/LeBron/Jordan 500.00 800.00
- EE3JJJ Jordan/Magic/LeBron 800.00 1200.00
- EE3JRM LeBron/Riley/Zo 175.00 350.00
- EE3JWW West/Worthy/Magic 175.00 350.00
- EE3RRO Olaj/Russell/DRob 125.00 250.00
- EE3WEJ Worthy/Erving/LeBron 150.00 300.00
- EE3WIB Izzo/Roy/Boeheim EXCH

2011-12 Exquisite Collection Legacy Autographs

STATED PRINT RUN 10 TO 23 SER.#'d SETS

SOME UNPRICED DUE TO SCARCITY

UNPRICED HOLO PRINT RUN 5 SETS

- ELAD Adrian Dantley/15 20.00 50.00
- ELBR Bill Russell/15 50.00 100.00
- ELCD Clyde Drexler/15 30.00 80.00
- ELDR David Robinson/15 30.00 60.00
- ELHO Hakeem Olajuwon/15
- ELJE Julius Erving/15 40.00 100.00
- ELJH John Havlicek/15 20.00 50.00
- ELJN Michael Jordan/23 300.00 600.00
- ELJO Michael Jordan/23 300.00 600.00
- ELJW James Worthy/15 30.00 80.00
- ELLB Larry Bird/15 50.00 125.00
- ELMI Michael Jordan/23 300.00 600.00
- ELMJ Magic Johnson/15 75.00 150.00
- ELWE Jerry West/15 30.00 80.00

2011-12 Exquisite Collection Personal Touch Car

STATED PRINT RUN 30 SER.#'d SETS

- PTCAH Anfernee Hardaway 12.00 30.00
- PTCAM Alonzo Mourning 12.00 30.00
- PTCBC Bill Cartwright 8.00 20.00
- PTCBM Bob McAdoo 10.00 30.00
- PTCCD Clyde Drexler 15.00 40.00
- PTCDM Danny Manning 8.00 20.00
- PTCDN Don Nelson 8.00 20.00
- PTCDT David Thompson 8.00 20.00
- PTCGR Glen Rice 8.00 20.00
- PTCJA LeBron James 125.00 250.00
- PTCJE Julius Erving 30.00 80.00
- PTCJS Jerry Sloan 8.00 20.00
- PTCJW Jerry West 20.00 50.00
- PTCLJ Larry Johnson 10.00 25.00
- PTCMJ Magic Johnson 30.00 80.00
- PTCRH Robert Horry 8.00 20.00
- PTCRO Dennis Rodman 10.00 25.00
- PTCST John Starks 12.00 30.00
- PTCTP Terry Porter 8.00 20.00
- PTCVC Vince Carter 25.00 60.00
- PTCWF Walt Frazier 8.00 20.00

2011-12 Exquisite Collection Personal Touch Date

STATED PRINT RUN 30 SER.#'d SETS

- PTDAD Adrian Dantley 8.00 20.00
- PTDAH Anfernee Hardaway 20.00 50.00
- PTDAJ Avery Johnson 8.00 20.00
- PTDAM Alonzo Mourning 15.00 40.00
- PTDBC Bill Cartwright 8.00 20.00
- PTDBM Bob McAdoo 25.00 60.00
- PTDBW Bill Walton 8.00 20.00
- PTDCD Clyde Drexler 15.00 40.00
- PTDDM Danny Manning 10.00 25.00
- PTDDN Don Nelson 8.00 20.00
- PTDDT David Thompson 8.00 20.00
- PTDGG George Gervin 8.00 20.00
- PTDGR Glen Rice 15.00 40.00
- PTDHO Hakeem Olajuwon 20.00 50.00
- PTDJA LeBron James 175.00 350.00
- PTDLB Larry Bird 40.00 100.00
- PTDLJ Larry Johnson 12.00 30.00
- PTDRO Dennis Rodman 20.00 50.00
- PTDWF Walt Frazier 12.00 30.00

2011-12 Exquisite Collection Personal Touch Food

STATED PRINT RUN 30 SER.#'d SETS

- PTFAD Adrian Dantley 8.00 20.00
- PTFAH Anfernee Hardaway 30.00 60.00
- PTFAJ Avery Johnson 8.00 20.00
- PTFAM Alonzo Mourning 20.00 50.00
- PTFBW Bill Walton 8.00 20.00
- PTFCD Clyde Drexler 15.00 40.00
- PTFDE Dennis Rodman 12.00 30.00
- PTFDM Danny Manning 8.00 20.00
- PTFDT David Thompson 8.00 20.00
- PTFGG George Gervin 8.00 20.00
- PTFGK George Karl 8.00 20.00
- PTFGR Glen Rice 15.00 40.00
- PTFHG Hal Greer 12.00 30.00
- PTFHO Hakeem Olajuwon 15.00 40.00
- PTFJA LeBron James 175.00 350.00
- PTFJW Jerry West 30.00 80.00
- PTFLB Larry Bird 40.00 100.00
- PTFLJ Larry Johnson 10.00 25.00
- PTFRO David Robinson 20.00 50.00
- PTFST John Starks 12.00 30.00
- PTFWF Walt Frazier 12.00 30.00

2011-12 Exquisite Collection Personal Touch Musician

STATED PRINT RUN 30 SER.#'d SETS

- PTMAH Anfernee Hardaway 40.00 80.00
- PTMAJ Avery Johnson 8.00 20.00
- PTMAM Alonzo Mourning 30.00 80.00
- PTMBM Bob McAdoo 25.00 60.00
- PTMBW Bill Walton 12.00 30.00
- PTMCD Clyde Drexler 12.00 30.00
- PTMCR Cazzie Russell 8.00 20.00
- PTMDM Danny Manning 12.00 30.00
- PTMDN Don Nelson 8.00 20.00
- PTMHG Hal Greer 15.00 40.00
- PTMHO Hakeem Olajuwon 30.00 80.00
- PTMJA LeBron James 175.00 350.00
- PTMJE Julius Erving 30.00 80.00
- PTMKS Kenny Smith 8.00 20.00
- PTMLJ Larry Johnson 20.00 50.00
- PTMRB Rick Barry 8.00 20.00
- PTMRO Dennis Rodman 30.00 80.00
- PTMTP Terry Porter 8.00 20.00
- PTMVC Vince Carter 50.00 125.00

2011-12 Exquisite Collection UD Black Bio-Scripts

STATED PRINT RUN 10 TO 15 SER.#'d SETS

SOME UNPRICED DUE TO SCARCITY

- BSAH Anfernee Hardaway/15 75.00 200.00
- BSAM Alonzo Mourning/15 100.00 200.00
- BSBW Bill Walton/15 30.00 80.00
- BSCP Candace Parker/15 25.00 60.00
- BSCR Cazzie Russell/15 15.00 40.00
- BSDE Dennis Rodman/15 25.00 60.00
- BSDM Danny Manning/15 40.00 100.00
- BSDT David Thompson/15 15.00 40.00
- BSGR Glen Rice/15 25.00 60.00
- BSJA LeBron James/15 200.00 400.00
- BSJJ Jim Jackson/15 30.00 80.00
- BSJO Larry Johnson/15 25.00 60.00
- BSKS Kenny Smith/15 15.00 40.00
- BSLB Larry Brown/15 15.00 40.00
- BSLE LeBron James/15 200.00 400.00
- BSLJ LeBron James/15 200.00 400.00
- BSLS Lonnie Shelton/15 15.00 40.00
- BSRB Rick Barry/15 15.00 40.00
- BSSC Sam Cassell/15 25.00 60.00

2011-12 Exquisite Collection UD Black Blackboard Autographs

STATED PRINT RUN 40 SER.#'d SETS

- BBBD Billy Donovan 20.00 50.00
- BBBH Ben Howland 15.00 40.00
- BBBR Bo Ryan 15.00 40.00
- BBBS Bill Self 20.00 50.00
- BBCA Jim Calhoun 10.00 25.00
- BBGK George Karl 10.00 25.00
- BBGW Gary Williams 15.00 40.00
- BBHU Bob Huggins 12.00 30.00
- BBJB Jim Boeheim 40.00 100.00
- BBJS Jerry Sloan 10.00 25.00
- BBJW Jay Wright 20.00 50.00
- BBLB Larry Brown 20.00 50.00
- BBMF Mark Few 12.00 30.00
- BBMM Mike Montgomery 8.00 20.00
- BBPR Pat Riley 20.00 50.00
- BBRM Rick Majerus 12.00 30.00
- BBRW Roy Williams 30.00 60.00
- BBSF Steve Fisher 8.00 20.00
- BBTI Tom Izzo 30.00 60.00
- BBTS Tubby Smith 10.00 25.00

2011-12 Exquisite Collection UD Black College Logo Autographs

STATED PRINT RUN 40 SER.#'d SETS

- LAM Alonzo Mourning 15.00 40.00
- LBH Bob Huggins 12.00 30.00
- LBR Bill Russell 50.00 120.00
- LBW Bill Walton 10.00 25.00
- LCD Clyde Drexler 15.00 40.00
- LDR David Robinson 20.00 50.00
- LGR Glen Rice 10.00 25.00
- LHO Hakeem Olajuwon 15.00 40.00
- LJB Jim Boeheim 40.00 100.00
- LJE Julius Erving 25.00 60.00
- LJO Michael Jordan 300.00 600.00
- LLB Larry Bird 30.00 80.00
- LLJ LeBron James 175.00 350.00
- LLS Lonnie Shelton 12.50 30.00
- LMJ Magic Johnson 40.00 80.00
- LTI Tom Izzo 30.00 80.00
- LWE Jerry West 30.00 80.00
- LWI Roy Williams 15.00 40.00

2011-12 Exquisite Collection UD Black College Vault Autographs

STATED PRINT RUN 60 SER.#'d SETS

- VAH Anfernee Hardaway 20.00 50.00
- VAM Alonzo Mourning 20.00 50.00
- VBA B.J. Armstrong 20.00 50.00
- VBH Bob Huggins 12.00 30.00
- VBW Bill Walton 12.00 30.00
- VCD Clyde Drexler 12.00 30.00
- VCP Candace Parker 8.00 20.00
- VDA David Robinson 20.00 50.00
- VDC DeMarcus Cousins 12.00 30.00
- VDR Dennis Rodman 20.00 50.00
- VFL Freddie Lewis 8.00 20.00
- VGG Gail Goodrich 8.00 20.00
- VGR Glen Rice 8.00 20.00
- VGW Gary Williams 25.00 60.00
- VHO Hakeem Olajuwon 25.00 60.00
- VJB Jim Boeheim 40.00 100.00
- VJE Julius Erving 50.00 120.00
- VJH John Havlicek 15.00 40.00
- VJJ Jim Jackson 15.00 40.00
- VJO Michael Jordan 300.00 600.00
- VLB Larry Bird 50.00 125.00
- VLJ LeBron James 150.00 300.00
- VLS Lonnie Shelton 8.00 20.00
- VMJ Magic Johnson 40.00 80.00
- VRU Bill Russell 50.00 100.00
- VRW Roy Williams 15.00 40.00
- VSA Steve Alford 12.00 30.00
- VTC Tom Crean 8.00 20.00
- VTH Tim Hardaway 12.00 30.00
- VTI Tom Izzo 25.00 60.00
- VWJ Jerry West 30.00 80.00

2011-12 Exquisite Collection UD Black Dual Patch Autographs

STATED PRINT RUN 23 TO 50 SER.#'d SETS

- LP2BH Boeheim/Howland/25 25.00 60.00
- LP2BJ M.Jordan/L.Bird/25 400.00 600.00
- LP2BW L.Bird/J.West/25 75.00 150.00
- LP2EJ J.Erving/L.James/25 175.00 350.00
- LP2HH Hill/Hardaway/25 EXCH 40.00 100.00
- LP2JE J.Erving/M.Jordan/25 300.00 600.00
- LP2JH L.James/A.Hard/50 175.00 350.00
- LP2JJ L.James/M.Jordan/23 800.00 1200.00
- LP2JM L.James/Mourning/50 150.00 300.00
- LP2JR D.Rodman/M.Jordan/50 200.00 400.00
- LP2JW M.Johnson/J.West/50 60.00 120.00
- LP2MH Mourning/T.Hard/50 20.00 50.00
- LP2ML M.Johnson/L.Bird/25 150.00 300.00
- LP2MM M.Johnson/Jordan/25 500.00 850.00
- LP2OD Drexler/Olajuwon/25 25.00 60.00
- LP2OM Olajuwon/Mourning/50 30.00 80.00
- LP2OR D.Rob/Olajuwon/50 25.00 60.00
- LP2RB B.Russell/L.Bird/25 125.00 250.00
- LP2RR B.Russell/D.Rob/25 100.00 200.00
- LP2SW B.Self/R.Williams/50 60.00 150.00
- LP2TW Walton/Thompson/50 25.00 60.00
- LP2WG B.Walton/Goodrich/50 25.00 60.00

2012-13 Exquisite Collection

1-60 PRINT RUN 99 SER.#'d SETS

61-79 AU PRINT RUN 199 SER.#'d SETS

EXCHANGE DEADLINE 10/23/2015

- 1 Adrian Dantley 2.00 5.00
- 2 Alonzo Mourning 3.00 8.00
- 3 Anfernee Hardaway 6.00 15.00
- 4 Bill Laimbeer 2.00 5.00
- 5 Bill Russell 4.00 10.00
- 6 Bill Walton 2.50 6.00
- 7 Bob McAdoo 2.00 5.00
- 8 Brad Daugherty 2.00 5.00
- 9 Christian Laettner 2.00 5.00
- 10 Clyde Drexler 3.00 8.00
- 11 Danny Manning 2.00 5.00
- 12 David Robinson 4.00 10.00
- 13 David Thompson 2.00 5.00
- 14 Dennis Rodman 5.00 12.00
- 15 Tony Gwynn 2.50 6.00
- 16 Isiah Thomas 2.50 6.00
- 17 Glen Rice 2.00 5.00
- 18 Grant Hill 3.00 8.00
- 19 Hakeem Olajuwon 3.00 8.00
- 20 Hal Greer 2.00 5.00
- 21 Julius Erving 4.00 10.00
- 22 John Havlicek 3.00 8.00
- 23 Larry Bird 6.00 15.00
- 24 Larry Johnson 3.00 8.00
- 25 LeBron James 12.00 30.00
- 26 Magic Johnson 6.00 15.00
- 27 Mark A. Jackson 2.00 5.00
- 28 Michael Jordan 30.00 60.00
- 29 Micheal Ray Richardson 2.00 5.00
- 30 Robert Horry 2.00 5.00
- 31 Tim Hardaway 2.50 6.00
- 32 Toni Kukoc 2.50 6.00
- 33 Walt Frazier 2.50 6.00
- 34 Karl Malone 3.00 8.00
- 35 Jason Kidd 2.50 6.00
- 36 Dominique Wilkins 3.00 8.00
- 37 Sean Elliott 2.50 6.00
- 38 Mookie Blaylock 1.50 4.00
- 39 A.C. Green 2.50 6.00
- 40 Cheryl Miller 2.50 6.00
- 41 Chris Paul 3.00 8.00
- 42 Lou Hudson 2.50 6.00
- 43 Dave Cowens 1.50 4.00
- 44 Derrick Coleman 2.50 6.00
- 45 Nick Van Exel 2.50 6.00
- 46 Vinny Del Negro 1.50 4.00
- 47 Elvin Hayes 2.50 6.00
- 48 Gary Payton 2.50 6.00
- 49 Jamal Mashburn 2.50 6.00
- 50 Jeff Hornacek 2.00 5.00
- 51 Fat Lever 2.00 5.00
- 52 Nate Thurmond 2.00 5.00
- 53 Swen Nater 2.00 5.00
- 54 Antoine Walker 2.00 5.00
- 55 Bernard King 2.00 5.00
- 56 Allen Iverson 3.00 8.00
- 57 Spencer Haywood 1.50 4.00
- 58 Spud Webb 2.00 5.00
- 59 Wilt Chamberlain 5.00 12.00
- 60 Ray Allen 2.50 6.00
- 61 Meyers Leonard AU 4.00 10.00
- 63 Kendall Marshall AU EXCH 10.00 25.00
- 64 Moe Harkless AU 6.00 15.00
- 65 Tyler Zeller AU 5.00 12.00
- 66 Andrew Nicholson AU 3.00 8.00
- 67 Evan Fournier AU 5.00 12.00
- 68 Jared Cunningham AU 3.00 8.00
- 69 Miles Plumlee AU 6.00 15.00
- 70 Arnett Moultrie AU 3.00 8.00
- 71 Bernard James AU 3.00 8.00
- 72 Jae Crowder AU 4.00 10.00
- 73 Draymond Green AU 40.00 100.00
- 74 Quincy Acy AU 3.00 8.00
- 75 Khris Middleton AU 5.00 12.00
- 76 Will Barton AU 4.00 10.00
- 77 Tyshawn Taylor AU 3.00 8.00
- 78 Darius Miller AU 3.00 8.00
- 80 Darius Johnson-Odom AU 3.00 8.00
- 81 Robert Sacre AU 3.00 8.00

2012-13 Exquisite Collection Signatures Silver Spectrum

*SILVER SPECTRUM:.6X TO 1.5X BASIC

STATED PRINT RUN 50 SER.#'d SETS

EXCHANGE DEADLINE 10/23/2015

2012-13 Exquisite Collection 2013-14 Rookies

STATED PRINT RUN 99 SER.#'d SETS

- R1 Skylar Diggins 10.00 25.00
- R2 Giannis Antetokounmpo 100.00 250.00
- R3 Lucas Nogueira 6.00 15.00
- R4 Dennis Schroeder 6.00 15.00
- R5 Shane Larkin 12.00 30.00
- R6 Sergey Karasev 4.00 10.00
- R7 Tony Snell 6.00 15.00
- R8 Mason Plumlee 6.00 15.00
- R9 Solomon Hill 4.00 10.00
- R10 Tim Hardaway Jr. 10.00 25.00
- R11 Reggie Bullock 8.00 20.00
- R12 Andre Roberson 6.00 15.00
- R13 Rudy Gobert 25.00 60.00
- R14 Livio Jean-Charles 4.00 10.00
- R15 Archie Goodwin 6.00 15.00
- R16 Nemanja Nedovic 6.00 15.00

2012-13 Exquisite Collection Autographs

INT RUNS B/WN 30-99 COPIES PER

EXCHANGE DEADLINE 10/23/2015

- AG A.C. Green/99 6.00 15.00
- AH Anfernee Hardaway/99 12.00 30.00
- AI Allen Iverson/30 EXCH 60.00 150.00
- AL Allan Houston/99 5.00 12.00
- AM Alonzo Mourning/30 20.00 50.00
- BO Muggsy Bogues/99 6.00 15.00
- BR Bill Russell/30 40.00 100.00
- CD Clyde Drexler/30 15.00 40.00
- DC Dave Cowens/99 8.00 20.00
- DR David Robinson/30 25.00 60.00
- GH Grant Hill/30 20.00 50.00
- GP Gary Payton/99 8.00 20.00
- HO Hakeem Olajuwon/30 15.00 40.00
- JA LeBron James/30 125.00 250.00
- JE Julius Erving/30 30.00 80.00
- JH Jeff Hornacek/99 6.00 15.00
- JO Michael Jordan/99 250.00 400.00
- KM Karl Malone/30 20.00 50.00
- LB Larry Bird/30 40.00 100.00
- LH Lou Hudson/99 6.00 15.00
- LJ LeBron James/30 125.00 250.00
- MC Michael Cooper/99 5.00 12.00
- MI Michael Jordan/99 250.00 400.00
- MJ Magic Johnson/30 30.00 80.00
- MP Mark Price/99 15.00 40.00
- NT Nate Thurmond/99 4.00 10.00
- RA Ray Allen/99 12.00 30.00
- RO Dennis Rodman/30 15.00 40.00
- SB Shawn Bradley/99 4.00 10.00
- SW Spud Webb/99 8.00 20.00
- TK Toni Kukoc/99 6.00 15.00
- SJN Michael Jordan released in 14-15 SP Authentic

2012-13 Exquisite Collection Collegiate Seal Autographs

PRINT RUNS B/WN 45-99 COPIES PER

EXCHANGE DEADLINE 10/23/2015

- AH Anfernee Hardaway/99 20.00 50.00
- AI Allen Iverson/99 EXCH 40.00 100.00
- AW Antoine Walker/99 6.00 15.00
- BR Bill Russell/45 40.00 100.00
- BW Bill Walton/99 8.00 20.00
- DM Danny Manning/99 6.00 15.00
- DW Dominique Wilkins/45 25.00 60.00
- GH Grant Hill/45 20.00 50.00
- HG Hal Greer/99 6.00 15.00
- HM Harold Miner/99 6.00 15.00
- HO Hakeem Olajuwon/45 20.00 50.00
- JE Julius Erving/45 40.00 100.00
- JH John Havlicek/45 20.00 50.00
- JK Jason Kidd/45 15.00 40.00
- JO Michael Jordan/99 250.00 500.00
- KM Karl Malone/45 25.00 60.00
- LB Larry Bird/45 30.00 80.00
- LH Lou Hudson/99 6.00 15.00
- MA Mark A. Jackson/99 6.00 15.00
- SB Shawn Bradley/99 6.00 15.00
- SE Sean Elliott/99 6.00 15.00
- VE Nick Van Exel/99 12.00 30.00

2012-13 Exquisite Collection Dimensions Autographs

PRINT RUNS B/WN 25-70 COPIES PER

EXCHANGE DEADLINE 10/23/2015

- AH Anfernee Hardaway/70* 15.00 40.00
- AI Allen Iverson/25*
- BR Bill Russell/25* 50.00 120.00
- CM Cheryl Miller/70* 6.00 15.00
- DR David Robinson/70* 20.00 50.00
- DW Dominique Wilkins/25* 12.00 30.00
- GH Grant Hill/70* 15.00 40.00
- GP Gary Payton/70* 12.00 30.00
- HM Harold Miner/70 * 6.00 15.00
- JA LeBron James/25* 125.00 250.00
- JE Julius Erving/70* 30.00 80.00
- JH John Havlicek/70* 12.00 30.00
- JK Jason Kidd/25* 15.00 40.00
- JN Michael Jordan/25* 250.00 400.00
- JO Magic Johnson/25* 40.00 100.00
- KM Karl Malone/25* 25.00 60.00
- LB Larry Bird/25* 40.00 100.00
- LJ LeBron James/25* 125.00 250.00
- MA Mark A. Jackson/70* 6.00 15.00
- MI Michael Jordan/70* 250.00 350.00
- MJ Michael Jordan/70* 250.00 350.00
- OL Hakeem Olajuwon/70* 15.00 40.00
- RO Dennis Rodman/70* 15.00 40.00
- TK Toni Kukoc/70* 10.00 25.00

2012-13 Exquisite Collection Dream Seasons Autographs

PRINT RUNS B/WN 10-70 COPIES PER

NO PRICING ON QTY 10

EXCHANGE DEADLINE 10/23/2015

- AW Antoine Walker/70 10.00 25.00
- BR Bill Russell/35 40.00 100.00
- BW Bill Walton/70 8.00 20.00
- CL Christian Laettner/70 8.00 20.00
- CM Cheryl Miller/70 6.00 15.00
- DM Danny Manning/70 10.00 25.00
- DR David Robinson/35 25.00 60.00
- DT David Thompson/70 6.00 15.00
- GH Grant Hill/70 15.00 40.00
- GR Glen Rice/70 6.00 15.00
- HG Grant Hill/35 25.00 60.00
- HI Grant Hill/35 20.00 50.00
- HO Hakeem Olajuwon/35 12.00 30.00
- IT Isiah Thomas/70 10.00 25.00
- JA LeBron James/10
- JH John Havlicek/35 15.00 40.00
- JM Michael Jordan/70 250.00 400.00
- JO Magic Johnson/35 40.00 100.00
- JS LeBron James/35 150.00 250.00
- KM Karl Malone/35 12.00 30.00
- LA Larry Johnson/70 10.00 25.00
- LB Larry Bird/35 40.00 100.00
- LE LeBron James/10
- LJ LeBron James/10
- MI Michael Jordan/70 250.00 400.00
- MJ Michael Jordan/70 250.00 400.00
- RU Bill Russell/35 40.00 100.00
- SE Sean Elliott/70 6.00 15.00
- SN Swen Nater/70 6.00 15.00
- WA Bill Walton/70 6.00 15.00

2012-13 Exquisite Collection Endorsements

PRINT RUNS B/WN 25-99 COPIES PER

EXCHANGE DEADLINE 10/23/2015

- AI Allen Iverson/25
- AM Alonzo Mourning/99 12.00 30.00
- AW Antoine Walker/99 4.00 10.00
- BR Bill Russell/25 40.00 100.00
- BW Bill Walton/99 10.00 25.00
- CD Clyde Drexler/99 12.00 30.00
- CM Cheryl Miller/99 6.00 15.00
- DR David Robinson/25 20.00 50.00
- DW Dominique Wilkins/25 10.00 25.00
- HA John Havlicek/25 20.00 50.00
- HO Hakeem Olajuwon/99 12.00 30.00
- IT Isiah Thomas/99 12.00 30.00
- JA LeBron James/99 125.00 300.00
- JH Jeff Hornacek/99 4.00 10.00
- JK Jason Kidd/99 12.00 30.00
- JN Michael Jordan/25 300.00 500.00
- JO Magic Johnson/25 30.00 80.00
- JU Julius Erving/25 30.00 80.00
- KM Karl Malone/25 25.00 60.00
- LA Larry Johnson/25 12.00 30.00
- LB Larry Bird/25 40.00 100.00
- LH Lou Hudson/99 4.00 10.00
- LJ LeBron James/25 150.00 400.00
- NT Nate Thurmond/99 4.00 10.00
- RA Ray Allen/99 12.00 30.00
- EEMI Michael Jordan released in 14-15 SP Authentic
- EEMJ Michael Jordan released in 14-15 SP Authentic

2012-13 Exquisite Collection Endorsements Dual

PRINT RUNS B/WN 15-30 COPIES PER

EXCHANGE DEADLINE 10/23/2015

- HH A.Hardaway/G.Hill/15 20.00 50.00
- HL G.Hill/C.Laettner/30 30.00 60.00
- HM G.Hill/J.Mashburn/30 30.00 60.00
- JB Magic/L.Bird/15 EXCH 150.00 300.00
- JE M.Jordan/J.Erving/15 300.00 400.00
- JJ M.Jordan/L.James/30 500.00 800.00
- JM M.Johnson/K.Malone/30 50.00 120.00
- JT M.Johnson/I.Thomas/15 40.00 100.00
- KI J.Kidd/A.Iverson/15 150.00 300.00
- ML M.Jordan/L.Bird/15 300.00 500.00
- MM M.Jordan/M.Johnson/15 300.00 400.00
- MO K.Malone/H.Olajuwon/15 50.00 100.00
- OD H.Olajuwon/C.Drexler/30 30.00 80.00
- RM D.Robinson/K.Malone/15 30.00 80.00
- WM S.Webb/H.Miner/30 10.00 25.00

2012-13 Exquisite Collection Endorsements Triple

PRINT RUNS B/WN 10-35 COPIES PER

NO PRICING ON QTY 10

EXCHANGE DEADLINE 10/23/2015

- HHK Hill/Hardaway/Kidd/35 60.00 120.00
- JHH Jackson/Penny/Hardaway/35 30.00 60.00
- JMR Magic/Malone/Robinson/35 90.00 150.00

2012-13 Exquisite Collection Impressions

PRINT RUNS B/WN 5-20 COPIES PER

NO PRICING ON QTY 5

EXCHANGE DEADLINE 10/23/2015

- AG A.C. Green/20 12.00 30.00
- AH Anfernee Hardaway/20 60.00 120.00
- BL Bill Laimbeer/20 12.00 30.00
- BR Bryant Reeves/20 12.00 30.00
- CD Clyde Drexler/20 40.00 80.00
- DC Dave Cowens/20 12.00 30.00
- DT David Thompson/20 12.00 30.00
- DW Dominique Wilkins20 30.00 80.00
- EH Elvin Hayes/20 12.00 30.00
- GH Grant Hill/14 * 50.00 100.00
- GHB G.Hill G-Money/6 * 75.00 150.00
- HM Harold Miner/20 40.00 80.00
- IT Isiah Thomas/20 30.00 60.00
- JM Jamal Mashburn/20 30.00 80.00
- NT Nate Thurmond/20 15.00 40.00
- RO Dennis Rodman/20 30.00 60.00
- TK Toni Kukoc/20 25.00 60.00

2012-13 Exquisite Collection Impressions Dual

STATED PRINT RUN 15 SER.#'d SETS

EXCHANGE DEADLINE 10/23/2015

- DH Drexler/Hayes 30.00 80.00
- DR Drexler/Robinson
- HC Havlicek/Cowens 50.00 120.00
- HH Hill/Hardaway 60.00 150.00
- HK Hardaway/Kidd
- HM Hardaway/Mashburn 60.00 200.00
- JE James/Erving 350.00 500.00
- JH James/Hardaway 300.00 400.00
- MD Malone/Drexler 90.00 150.00
- MO Malone/Olajuwon 50.00 120.00
- MR Malone/Robinson 50.00 120.00
- OD Olajuwon/Drexler 60.00 120.00
- OH Olajuwon/Hayes 30.00 60.00
- OM Olajuwon/Mourning 30.00 80.00
- RK Rodman/Kukoc 50.00 120.00
- RL Rodman/Laimbeer 30.00 80.00
- RO Robinson/Olajuwon 40.00 100.00
- RT Rodman/Thurmond 40.00 100.00
- TE Thomas/Erving 75.00 150.00
- WO Wilkins/Olajuwon 30.00 80.00

2012-13 Exquisite Collection Limited Logos

PRINT RUNS B/WN 10-25 COPIES PER

EXCHANGE DEADLINE 10/23/2015

ALL VERSIONS EQUALLY PRICE

- TH Tim Hardaway 10.00 25.00
- AD1 Adrian Dantley 15.00 40.00
- AD2 Adrian Dantley 15.00 40.00
- AD3 Adrian Dantley 15.00 40.00
- AD4 Adrian Dantley 15.00 40.00
- AG1 A.C. Green 10.00 25.00
- AG2 A.C. Green 10.00 25.00
- AG3 A.C. Green 10.00 25.00
- AG4 A.C. Green 10.00 25.00
- AH1 Anfernee Hardaway 30.00 80.00
- AH2 Anfernee Hardaway 30.00 80.00
- AH3 Anfernee Hardaway 30.00 80.00
- AH4 Anfernee Hardaway 30.00 80.00
- AI1 Allen Iverson EXCH 60.00 150.00
- AI2 Allen Iverson EXCH 60.00 150.00
- AI3 Allen Iverson EXCH 60.00 150.00
- AI4 Allen Iverson EXCH 60.00 150.00
- AM1 Alonzo Mourning 20.00 50.00
- AM2 Alonzo Mourning 20.00 50.00
- AM3 Alonzo Mourning 20.00 50.00
- AM4 Alonzo Mourning 20.00 50.00
- BR1 Bill Russell 60.00 150.00
- BR2 Bill Russell 60.00 150.00
- BR3 Bill Russell 60.00 150.00
- BR4 Bill Russell 60.00 150.00
- CD1 Clyde Drexler 20.00 50.00

CD2 Clyde Drexler 20.00 50.00
CD3 Clyde Drexler 20.00 50.00
CD4 Clyde Drexler 20.00 50.00
DR1 David Robinson 40.00 100.00
DR2 David Robinson 40.00 100.00
DR3 David Robinson 40.00 100.00
DR4 David Robinson 40.00 100.00
DW1 Dominique Wilkins 30.00 80.00
DW2 Dominique Wilkins 30.00 80.00
DW3 Dominique Wilkins 30.00 80.00
DW4 Dominique Wilkins 30.00 80.00
GP1 Gary Payton 30.00 80.00
GP2 Gary Payton 30.00 80.00
GP3 Gary Payton 30.00 80.00
GP4 Gary Payton 30.00 80.00
GR1 Glen Rice 8.00 20.00
GR2 Glen Rice 8.00 20.00
GR3 Glen Rice 8.00 20.00
GR4 Glen Rice 8.00 20.00
HG1 Hal Greer 15.00 40.00
HG2 Hal Greer 15.00 40.00
HG3 Hal Greer 15.00 40.00
HG4 Hal Greer 15.00 40.00
HI1 Grant Hill 20.00 50.00
HI2 Grant Hill 20.00 50.00
HI3 Grant Hill 20.00 50.00
HI4 Grant Hill 20.00 50.00
HO1 Hakeem Olajuwon 25.00 60.00
HO2 Hakeem Olajuwon 25.00 60.00
HO3 Hakeem Olajuwon 25.00 60.00
HO4 Hakeem Olajuwon 25.00 60.00
JA1 LeBron James 200.00 400.00
JA2 LeBron James 200.00 400.00
JA3 LeBron James 200.00 400.00
JA4 LeBron James 200.00 400.00
JE1 Julius Erving 75.00 150.00
JE2 Julius Erving 75.00 150.00
JE3 Julius Erving 75.00 150.00
JE4 Julius Erving 75.00 150.00
JK1 Jason Kidd 90.00 150.00
JK2 Jason Kidd 90.00 150.00
JK3 Jason Kidd 90.00 150.00
JK4 Jason Kidd 90.00 150.00
JO1 Michael Jordan 300.00 600.00
JO2 Michael Jordan 300.00 600.00
JO3 Michael Jordan 300.00 600.00
JO4 Michael Jordan 300.00 600.00
KM1 Karl Malone 50.00 120.00
KM2 Karl Malone 50.00 120.00
KM3 Karl Malone 50.00 120.00
KM4 Karl Malone 50.00 120.00
LB1 Larry Bird 100.00 200.00
LB2 Larry Bird 100.00 200.00
LB3 Larry Bird 100.00 200.00
LB4 Larry Bird 100.00 200.00
LH1 Lou Hudson 8.00 20.00
LH2 Lou Hudson 8.00 20.00
LH3 Lou Hudson 8.00 20.00
LH4 Lou Hudson 8.00 20.00
LJ1 Larry Johnson 15.00 40.00
LJ2 Larry Johnson 15.00 40.00
LJ3 Larry Johnson 15.00 40.00
LJ4 Larry Johnson 15.00 40.00
MA1 Danny Manning 20.00 50.00
MA2 Danny Manning 20.00 50.00
MA3 Danny Manning 20.00 50.00
MA4 Danny Manning 20.00 50.00
MG1 Magic Johnson 60.00 150.00
MG2 Magic Johnson 60.00 150.00
MG3 Magic Johnson 60.00 150.00
MG4 Magic Johnson 60.00 150.00
MI1 Michael Jordan 400.00 700.00
MI2 Michael Jordan 400.00 700.00
MI3 Michael Jordan 400.00 700.00
MI4 Michael Jordan 400.00 700.00
MJ1 Michael Jordan 400.00 700.00
MJ2 Michael Jordan 400.00 700.00
MJ3 Michael Jordan 400.00 700.00
MJ4 Michael Jordan 400.00 700.00
MP1 Mark Price 10.00 25.00
MP2 Mark Price 10.00 25.00
MP3 Mark Price 10.00 25.00
MP4 Mark Price 10.00 25.00
PG1 Paul George EXCH 75.00 150.00
PG2 Paul George EXCH 75.00 150.00
PG3 Paul George EXCH 75.00 150.00
PG4 Paul George EXCH 75.00 150.00
RO1 Dennis Rodman 25.00 60.00
RO2 Dennis Rodman 25.00 60.00
RO3 Dennis Rodman 25.00 60.00
RO4 Dennis Rodman 25.00 60.00
SB1 Shawn Bradley 10.00 25.00
SB2 Shawn Bradley 10.00 25.00
SB3 Shawn Bradley 10.00 25.00
SB4 Shawn Bradley 10.00 25.00
SE1 Sean Elliott 15.00 40.00
SE2 Sean Elliott 15.00 40.00
SE3 Sean Elliott 15.00 40.00
SE4 Sean Elliott 15.00 40.00

2012-13 Exquisite Collection National Championship Trophy Autographs

PRINT RUNS B/WN 15-50 COPIES PER
EXCHANGE DEADLINE 10/23/2015
BR Bill Russell/15 40.00 100.00
DM Danny Manning/50 12.00 30.00
GH Grant Hill/15 30.00 80.00
GR Glen Rice/50 8.00 20.00
HI Grant Hill/15 30.00 80.00
JH John Havlicek/15 30.00 80.00
JO Michael Jordan/50 250.00 400.00
LA Christian Laettner/50 8.00 20.00
MJ Magic Johnson/15 60.00 150.00
RU Bill Russell/15 40.00 100.00
WA Bill Walton/50 8.00 20.00

2012-13 Exquisite Collection UD Black Autographs

PRINT RUNS B/WN 15-99 COPIES PER
EXCHANGE DEADLINE 10/23/2015
AH Anfernee Hardaway/15 30.00 60.00
BR Bill Russell/15 50.00 100.00
CD Clyde Drexler/15 40.00 80.00
CM Cheryl Miller/15 20.00 50.00
DR David Robinson/15 20.00 50.00
DW Dominique Wilkins/15 12.00 30.00
EJ Eddie Jones/99 10.00 25.00
GP Gary Payton/15 25.00 60.00
HO Hakeem Olajuwon/15 15.00 40.00
JA LeBron James/15
JE Julius Erving/15 60.00 120.00
JK Jason Kidd/15 25.00 60.00
JO Magic Johnson/15 30.00 80.00
KM Karl Malone/15 25.00 60.00
LB Larry Bird/15 40.00 100.00
LJ LeBron James/15 200.00 350.00
MI Michael Jordan/75 250.00 400.00
MJ Michael Jordan/75 250.00 400.00
MR Michael Ray Richardson/99 6.00 15.00
RO Dennis Rodman/15
SB Shawn Bradley/99 6.00 15.00

2012-13 Exquisite Collection UD Black Autographs Dual

PRINT RUNS B/WN 10-35 COPIES PER
NO PRICING ON QTY 10
EXCHANGE DEADLINE 10/23/2015
HH Hardaway/Hardaway/35 15.00 40.00
HL Hill/Laettner/35 40.00 80.00
OD Olajuwon/Drexler/35 40.00 80.00
RK Rodman/Kukoc/35 40.00 80.00
RL Rodman/Laimbeer/35 20.00 50.00
RO Robinson/Olajuwon/35 30.00 80.00

2012-13 Exquisite Collection UD Black Leather Autographs Dual

PRINT RUNS B/WN 20-40 COPIES PER
EXCHANGE DEADLINE 10/23/2015
AJ Walker/Mashburn/40 20.00 50.00
BE Bird/Erving/20 100.00 200.00
BH Bird/John Havlicek/20 100.00 200.00
DR Drexler/Richardson/40 15.00 40.00
EJ LeBron/Erving/20 200.00 300.00
HH Hill/Penny/40 50.00 100.00
HK Penny/Kidd/40 40.00 80.00
HL Hill/Laettner/40 40.00 80.00
JB Jordan/Bird/40 300.00 400.00
JE Jordan/Erving/40 300.00 600.00
JJ Jordan/Magic/40 400.00 500.00
JM Magic/Erving/20 75.00 150.00
KM Kidd/Mashburn/40 20.00 50.00
LJ LeBron/Magic/20 200.00 300.00
MJ Mourning/Johnson/40 30.00 60.00
MM Jordan/Malone/20 300.00 400.00
MO Malone/Olajuwon/20 40.00 80.00
OD Olajuwon/Drexler/40 30.00 60.00
RJ Jordan/Rodman/40 300.00 400.00
RL Laimbeer/Rodman/40 20.00 50.00
WM Wilkins/Malone/20 50.00 100.00
LBJ L.Bird/M.Johnson

2012-13 Exquisite Collection UD Black Legendary Lustrous

STATED PRINT RUN 25 SER.#'d SETS
AI Allen Iverson 75.00 150.00

2012-13 Exquisite Collection UD Black Old School Autographs

PRINT RUNS B/WN 25-75 COPIES PER
EXCHANGE DEADLINE 10/23/2015
BR Bill Russell 50.00 100.00
CW Chet Walker 4.00 10.00
DR Dennis Rodman 20.00 50.00
EH Elvin Hayes
HO Hakeem Olajuwon 20.00 50.00
JE Julius Erving 40.00 80.00
JH John Havlicek 20.00 50.00
JO Magic Johnson 50.00 120.00
LB Larry Bird 40.00 80.00
LH Lou Hudson 8.00 20.00
MJ Michael Jordan 300.00 400.00
RT Reggie Theus 5.00 12.00
SN Swen Nater 4.00 10.00
OSMI Michael Jordan 300.00 400.00
released in 14-15 SP Authentic

2013-14 Exquisite Collection

STATED PRINT RUN 75 SER.#'d SETS
AU PRINT RUN B/WN 60-99 COPIES PER
JSY AU PRINT RUN B/WN 99-199 COPIES PER
EXCHANGE DEADLINE 10/10/2016
1 Michael Jordan 50.00 120.00
2 LeBron James 20.00 50.00
3 Allen Iverson 3.00 8.00
4 Rajon Rondo 2.50 6.00
5 Robert Horry 2.00 5.00
6 Glenn Robinson 2.00 5.00
7 Tony Gwynn 2.50 6.00
8 Dennis Rodman 5.00 12.00
9 Joe Smith 2.00 5.00
10 Elvin Hayes 2.50 6.00
11 Jamal Mashburn 2.50 6.00
12 Alex English 2.00 5.00
13 Antoine Walker 2.00 5.00
14 David Thompson 2.00 5.00
15 Cheryl Miller 2.50 6.00
16 Bill Laimbeer 2.00 5.00
17 Toni Kukoc 2.50 6.00
18 Jerry Stackhouse 2.00 5.00
19 Grant Hill 3.00 8.00
20 Harold Miner 1.50 4.00
21 Allan Houston 2.00 5.00
22 Tim Hardaway 2.50 6.00
23 Alonzo Mourning 3.00 8.00
24 Anfernee Hardaway 6.00 15.00
25 Glen Rice 2.00 5.00
26 Otis Birdsong 2.00 5.00
27 Kenny Anderson 2.00 5.00
28 Micheal Ray Richardson 2.00 5.00
29 Keith Smart 2.50 6.00
30 Christian Laettner 2.00 5.00
31 Isiah Thomas 2.50 6.00
32 Dave Cowens 1.50 4.00
33 Bill Walton 2.50 6.00
34 Danny Manning 2.00 5.00
35 Shawn Bradley 1.50 4.00
36 Paul George 3.00 8.00
37 Bill Russell 4.00 10.00
38 David Robinson 4.00 10.00
39 Derek Harper 2.00 5.00
40 Jerry Lucas 2.50 6.00
41 Hakeem Olajuwon 3.00 8.00
42 Larry Bird 6.00 15.00
43 Jason Kidd 2.50 6.00
44 LaPhonso Ellis 1.50 4.00
45 Jay Williams 1.50 4.00
46 Julius Erving 4.00 10.00
47 Karl Malone 3.00 8.00
48 Larry Johnson 3.00 8.00
49 Dominique Wilkins 3.00 8.00
50 James Harden 4.00 10.00
51 Isaiah Canaan AU/60 4.00 10.00
52 Nemanja Nedovic AU/60 4.00 10.00
54 Mike Muscala AU/60 6.00 15.00
55 Erick Green AU/60 5.00 12.00
56 Ryan Kelly AU/60 4.00 10.00
57 Lorenzo Brown AU/60 4.00 10.00
58 Allen Crabbe JSY AU/199 8.00 20.00
59 Mason Plumlee JSY AU/199 10.00 25.00
60 Rudy Gobert JSY AU/199 20.00 50.00
61 Lucas Nogueira JSY AU/199 6.00 15.00
62 Livio Jean-Charles JSY AU/199 6.00 15.00
63 Reggie Bullock JSY AU/199 8.00 20.00
64 Pierre Jackson JSY AU/199 6.00 15.00
65 Solomon Hill JSY AU/199 6.00 15.00
66 Tony Snell JSY AU/199 8.00 20.00
67 Dennis Schroeder JSY AU/199 10.00 25.00
68 Andre Roberson JSY AU/199 6.00 15.00
69 Sergey Karasev JSY AU/199 6.00 15.00
70 Archie Goodwin JSY AU/199 12.00 30.00
71 Peyton Siva JSY AU/199 6.00 15.00
72 Jamaal Franklin JSY AU/199 6.00 15.00
74 Deshaun Thomas JSY AU/199 6.00 15.00
75 Grant Jerrett JSY AU/199 6.00 15.00
76 G.Antetokounmpo AU/99 75.00 200.00
77 Skylar Diggins JSY AU/99 12.00 30.00
78 Tim Hardaway Jr. JSY AU/99 10.00 25.00
SP1 Paul George JSY AU/99

2013-14 Exquisite Collection Silver

*SILVER: .5X TO 1.2X BASE

2013-14 Exquisite Collection '03-04 Tribute Autographs

RANDOM INSERTS IN PACKS
STATED PRINT RUN 35 SER.#'d SETS
EXCHANGE DEADLINE 10/10/2016
78DR David Robinson 50.00 120.00
78GH Grant Hill 15.00 40.00
78GL Glenn Robinson 10.00 25.00
78GR Glen Rice 10.00 25.00
78JE Julius Erving 50.00 120.00
78JK Jason Kidd 30.00 80.00
78JM Jamal Mashburn 10.00 25.00
78JS Joe Smith
released in 14-15 SP Authentic
78KM Karl Malone 40.00 100.00
78LB Larry Bird 75.00 150.00
78LU Andrew Luck 500.00 1000.00
78MA Magic Johnson 60.00 150.00
78MJ Michael Jordan 500.00 1000.00
78OL Oscar De La Hoya 100.00 200.00
78RO Dennis Rodman 30.00 80.00
78RR Rajon Rondo 15.00 40.00
78TH Tim Hardaway 10.00 25.00

2013-14 Exquisite Collection '03-04 Tribute Patch Autographs

RANDOM INSERTS IN PACKS
STATED PRINT RUN 35 SER.#'d SETS
EXCHANGE DEADLINE 10/10/2016
78AH Anfernee Hardaway 50.00 120.00
78AL Allan Houston 20.00 50.00
78AM Alonzo Mourning 50.00 120.00
78BD Brad Daugherty 10.00 25.00
78BW Bill Walton 30.00 80.00
78CL Christian Laettner 20.00 50.00
78CM Danny Manning 30.00 80.00
78CW Corliss Williamson 10.00 25.00
78DM Donyell Marshall 10.00 25.00
78JH James Harden EXCH 100.00 200.00
78JL Jerry Lucas 25.00 60.00
78JO Larry Johnson 75.00 150.00
78JW Jay Williams 30.00 80.00
78KA Kenny Anderson 10.00 25.00
78LJ LeBron James 2500.00 4000.00
78MR Micheal Ray Richardson 10.00 25.00
78PG Paul George 150.00 250.00
78SP Sam Perkins 30.00 80.00
78ST Jerry Stackhouse 30.00 80.00

2013-14 Exquisite Collection '14-15 Rookie Autographs

RANDOM INSERTS IN PACKS
STATED PRINT RUN 99 SER.#'d SETS
EXCHANGE DEADLINE 10/10/2016
RAG Aaron Gordon 25.00 60.00
RAP Adreian Payne 6.00 15.00
RCW C.J. Wilcox 6.00 15.00
RDM Doug McDermott 50.00 120.00
RDS Dario Saric 75.00 200.00
REP Elfrid Payton 15.00 40.00
RGH Gary Harris 6.00 15.00
RGR Glenn Robinson III 6.00 15.00
RJA Jordan Adams 6.00 15.00
RJN Jusuf Nurkic 15.00 40.00
RJY James Young 6.00 15.00
RMM Mitch McGary 6.00 15.00
RNM Nikola Mirotic 10.00 25.00
RNS Nik Stauskas 6.00 15.00
RRH Rodney Hood 6.00 15.00
RSN Shabazz Napier 6.00 15.00
RTW T.J. Warren 6.00 15.00
RZL Zach LaVine 40.00 100.00

2013-14 Exquisite Collection '14-15 Rookie Autographs Spectrum

*SPECTRUM: .6X TO 1.5X BASE HI
STATED PRINT RUN 25 SER.#'d SETS
EXCHANGE DEADLINE 10/10/2016

2013-14 Exquisite Collection Dimensions Autographs

NDOM INSERTS IN PACKS
EXCHANGE DEADLINE 10/10/2016
DAE Alex English 8.00 20.00
DAH Anfernee Hardaway 25.00 60.00
DAM Alonzo Mourning 12.00 30.00
DBR Bill Russell 40.00 100.00
DBW Bill Walton 8.00 20.00
DCL Christian Laettner 8.00 20.00
DDC Dave Cowens 6.00 15.00
DDM Danny Manning 8.00 20.00
DDR Dennis Rodman 10.00 25.00
DDT David Thompson 8.00 20.00
DEH Elvin Hayes 6.00 15.00
DGL Glenn Robinson 6.00 15.00
DGR Glen Rice 8.00 20.00
DHO Hakeem Olajuwon 12.00 30.00
DJE Julius Erving
DJH James Harden 20.00 50.00
DJK Jason Kidd 10.00 25.00
DJL Jerry Lucas 10.00 25.00
DJN Michael Jordan 250.00 350.00
DJO Larry Johnson 12.00 30.00
DJS Jerry Stackhouse 20.00 50.00
DKA Kenny Anderson 8.00 20.00
DKM Karl Malone 12.00 30.00
DKS Keith Smart
released in 14-15 SP Authentic
DLB Larry Bird 25.00 60.00
DLJ LeBron James 100.00 200.00
DMA Magic Johnson 25.00 60.00
DMI Michael Jordan 250.00 350.00
DMJ Michael Jordan 250.00 350.00
DMR Micheal Ray Richardson 6.00 15.00
DPG Paul George 20.00 50.00
DRO David Robinson 15.00 40.00
DSA Stacey Augmon 6.00 15.00
DSP Sam Perkins 10.00 25.00
DTC Toni Kukoc 10.00 25.00
DTH Tim Hardaway 6.00 15.00

2013-14 Exquisite Collection Enshrinements

RANDOM INSERTS IN PACKS
PRINT RUNS B/WN 23-60 COPIES PER
EXCHANGE DEADLINE 10/10/2016
EEAH Allan Houston/60 8.00 20.00
EEAM Alonzo Mourning/60 12.00 30.00
EEBR Bill Russell/25 50.00 120.00
EECL Christian Laettner/60 10.00 25.00
EEDC Dave Cowens/60 4.00 10.00
EEDM Danny Manning/60 5.00 12.00
EEDR Dennis Rodman/25 12.00 30.00
EEEH Elvin Hayes/60 6.00 15.00
EEGH Grant Hill/25 20.00 50.00
EEHA Anfernee Hardaway/25 25.00 60.00
EEHM Harold Miner/60 4.00 10.00
EEHO Hakeem Olajuwon/25 15.00 40.00
EEJE Julius Erving/25 30.00 80.00
EEJH James Harden/25 20.00 50.00
EEJK Jason Kidd/25 15.00 40.00
EEJL Jerry Lucas/60 8.00 20.00
EEJM Jamal Mashburn/60 12.00 30.00
EEJO Michael Jordan/23 400.00 600.00
EEJS Joe Smith
released in 14-15 SP Authentic
EEJW Jay Williams/60 4.00 10.00
EEKM Karl Malone/25 20.00 50.00
EEKS Keith Smart
released in 14-15 SP Authentic
EELB Larry Bird/25 50.00 120.00
EELJ LeBron James/23 150.00 300.00
EELS Lonnie Shelton/60 4.00 10.00
EEMI Michael Jordan/23 250.00 500.00
EEMJ Magic Johnson/25 30.00 80.00
EEPG Paul George/60 15.00 40.00
EERH Robert Horry/60 6.00 15.00
EERO David Robinson/60 20.00 50.00
EERR Rajon Rondo/60 6.00 15.00
EESP Sam Perkins/60 4.00 10.00
EETH Tim Hardaway/60 6.00 15.00
EETK Toni Kukoc/60 6.00 15.00

2013-14 Exquisite Collection Exquisite Signatures

RANDOM INSERTS IN PACKS
PRINT RUNS B/WN 23-65 COPIES PER
EXCHANGE DEADLINE 10/10/2016
ESAH Allan Houston/65 5.00 12.00
ESAM Alonzo Mourning/65 15.00 40.00
ESBR Bill Russell/25 50.00 120.00
ESBW Buck Williams/65 8.00 20.00
ESCC Calbert Cheaney/65 4.00 10.00
ESDC Dave Cowens/65 4.00 10.00
ESDH Derek Harper/65 5.00 12.00
ESDM Donyell Marshall/65 4.00 10.00
ESDR Dennis Rodman/65 20.00 50.00
ESDT David Thompson/65 5.00 12.00
ESGH Grant Hill/65 20.00 50.00
ESGR Glenn Robinson/65 5.00 12.00
ESHA Anfernee Hardaway/65 15.00 40.00
ESHO Hakeem Olajuwon/65 15.00 40.00
ESJE Julius Erving/25 40.00 100.00
ESJH James Harden/25 25.00 60.00
ESJK Jason Kidd/25 15.00 40.00
ESJL Jerry Lucas/65 10.00 25.00
ESJO Michael Jordan/23 300.00 500.00
ESJS Joe Smith
released in 14-15 SP Authentic
ESJW Jay Williams/65 10.00 25.00
ESKA Kenny Anderson/65 5.00 12.00
ESKM Karl Malone/65 12.00 30.00
ESKS Keith Smart
released in 14-15 SP Authentic
ESLA Larry Johnson/65 8.00 20.00
ESLB Larry Bird/25 40.00 100.00
ESLJ LeBron James/23 200.00 300.00
ESMA Magic Johnson/25 40.00 100.00
ESMI Cheryl Miller/65 6.00 15.00
ESMJ Michael Jordan/23 300.00 500.00
ESMR Micheal Ray Richardson/65 5.00 12.00
ESPG Paul George/65 15.00 40.00
ESRI Glen Rice/65 5.00 12.00
ESRR Rajon Rondo/25 25.00 60.00
ESSA Stacey Augmon/65 8.00 20.00
ESSD Skylar Diggins/65 12.00 30.00
ESTH Tim Hardaway/65 6.00 15.00

2013-14 Exquisite Collection Game Face Autograph Booklets

NDOM INSERTS IN PACKS
EXCHANGE DEADLINE 10/10/2016
GFAH Anfernee Hardaway 10.00 25.00
GFAL Allan Houston 5.00 12.00
GFAM Alonzo Mourning 12.00 30.00
GFAW Antoine Walker 15.00 40.00
GFBR Bill Russell 40.00 100.00
GFBW Bill Walton 10.00 25.00
GFCL Christian Laettner 10.00 25.00
GFDM Danny Manning 10.00 25.00
GFDR David Robinson 15.00 40.00
GFDT David Thompson 5.00 12.00
GFEH Elvin Hayes 6.00 15.00
GFGH Grant Hill 20.00 50.00
GFGL Glenn Robinson 5.00 12.00
GFGR Glen Rice 15.00 40.00
GFHO Hakeem Olajuwon 15.00 40.00
GFJE Julius Erving 30.00 80.00
GFJH James Harden 15.00 40.00
GFJO Larry Johnson 8.00 20.00
GFKA Kenny Anderson 5.00 12.00
GFLB Larry Bird 50.00 100.00
GFLJ LeBron James 200.00 300.00
GFMI Michael Jordan 200.00 350.00
GFMJ Michael Jordan 200.00 350.00
GFPG Paul George 15.00 40.00
GFRR Rajon Rondo 15.00 40.00
GFSA Stacey Augmon 8.00 20.00
GFTH Tim Hardaway 6.00 15.00

2013-14 Exquisite Collection Game Face Autograph Booklets Dual

RANDOM INSERTS IN PACKS
EXCHANGE DEADLINE 10/10/2016
GFDHH G.Hill/A.Hardaway 40.00 100.00
GFDJA S.Augmon/L.Johnson 30.00 80.00
GFDJB L.Bird/M.Johnson 100.00 200.00
GFDJR M.Jordan/D.Rodman 250.00 350.00
GFDLL L.James/M.Jordan
GFDMM Michael Jordan
Michael Jordan
GFDBO D.Robinson/H.Olajuwon 40.00 100.00
GFDRR D.Robinson/B.Russell 75.00 150.00

2013-14 Exquisite Collection Limited Logos

RANDOM INSERTS IN PACKS
STATED PRINT RUN 25 SER.#'d SETS
LLHJ Tim Hardaway Jr. 30.00 80.00
LLMP Mason Plumlee 20.00 50.00
LLSD Skylar Diggins 30.00 80.00

2013-14 Exquisite Collection Rookie Autographs

RANDOM INSERTS IN PACKS
STATED PRINT RUN 75 SER.#'d SETS
EXCHANGE DEADLINE 10/10/2016
R1 Reggie Bullock 6.00 15.00
R2 Andre Roberson 5.00 12.00
R3 Solomon Hill 5.00 12.00
R4 Allen Crabbe 6.00 15.00
R5 Jamaal Franklin 5.00 12.00
R6 Mason Plumlee 8.00 20.00
R7 Shane Larkin 5.00 12.00
R8 Lucas Nogueira 5.00 12.00
R9 Livio Jean-Charles 5.00 12.00
R10 Tim Hardaway Jr. 10.00 25.00
R11 Giannis Antetokounmpo 300.00 600.00
R12 Tony Snell 6.00 15.00
R13 Archie Goodwin 6.00 15.00
R14 Sergey Karasev 5.00 12.00
R15 Skylar Diggins 8.00 20.00
R16 Deshaun Thomas 5.00 12.00
R17 Rudy Gobert 25.00 60.00
R18 Dennis Schroeder 8.00 20.00

2013-14 Exquisite Collection Rookie Autographs Black

*BLACK: .4X TO 1X BASE HI
EXCHANGE DEADLINE 10/10/2016

2013-14 Exquisite Collection Signatures

*VETS: 1.5X TO 4X BASE HI
EXCHANGE DEADLINE 10/10/2016
9 Joe Smith
released in 14-15 SP Authentic
29 Keith Smart
released in 14-15 SP Authentic
37 Bill Russell 30.00 80.00
41 Hakeem Olajuwon 15.00 40.00
46 Julius Erving 20.00 50.00

2013-14 Exquisite Collection Signatures Black

*BLACK: 2X TO 5X BASE HI
EXCHANGE DEADLINE 10/10/2016
1 Michael Jordan 300.00 500.00
2 LeBron James 150.00 300.00
4 Rajon Rondo 12.00 30.00
18 Jerry Stackhouse 25.00 60.00
23 Alonzo Mourning 40.00 100.00
24 Anfernee Hardaway 30.00 80.00
36 Paul George 15.00 40.00
37 Bill Russell 30.00 80.00
38 David Robinson 20.00 50.00
41 Hakeem Olajuwon 15.00 40.00
42 Larry Bird 30.00 80.00
43 Jason Kidd 15.00 40.00
45 Jay Williams 8.00 20.00
46 Julius Erving 20.00 50.00
47 Karl Malone 15.00 40.00
48 Larry Johnson 15.00 40.00
50 James Harden 20.00 50.00

2013-14 Exquisite Collection Signature Kicks Foundations

RANDOM INSERTS IN PACKS
STATED PRINT RUN 35 SER.#'d SETS
*SOLES/35: .4X TO 1X FOUNDATIONS
EXCHANGE DEADLINE 10/10/2016
SFAH Anfernee Hardaway 50.00 120.00
SFBR Bill Russell 50.00 120.00
SFDR David Robinson 25.00 60.00
SFGH Grant Hill 30.00 80.00
SFHA Anfernee Hardaway 50.00 120.00
SFJA LeBron James 200.00 400.00
SFJE Julius Erving 40.00 100.00
SFJH James Harden 30.00 80.00
SFJK Jason Kidd 25.00 60.00
SFJO Michael Jordan 400.00 600.00
SFLA Larry Johnson 15.00 40.00
SFLB Larry Bird 60.00 150.00
SFMA Magic Johnson 40.00 100.00
SFPG Paul George 25.00 60.00
SFRO Dennis Rodman 30.00 80.00
SFTH Tim Hardaway 15.00 40.00

2014 Exquisite Collection

8 Michael Jordan 30.00 80.00

2014 Exquisite Collection Endorsements

STATED PRINT RUN 25-75
EEMJ Michael Jordan/75

2014 Exquisite Collection Signature Masterpieces

GROUP A STATED ODDS 1:37
GROUP B STATED ODDS 1:12
GROUP C STATED ODDS 1:5
GROUP D STATED ODDS 1:2
OVERALL ODDS 1 PER TIN
ESMMJ Michael Jordan A 300.00 400.00

1991 Farley's Fruit Snacks Jordan

This set of four packages of fruit snacks was sponsored by Farley's Candy Co. of Chicago, Illinois. The packages measure 4 1/2" by 2 3/4", and each front features a different three-color (red, orange, and brown) drawing of Jordan and a different set of four answers. The complete list of questions appear on the outside of the box. On the packages, the answers are consecutively numbered (1-4; 5-8; 9-12; 13-16), and the set is checklisted below accordingly.

COMPLETE SET (4) 6.00 15.00
COMMON CARD (1-4) 2.00 5.00

2009-10 Fathead Tradeables

1 LeBron James 4.00 10.00
2 Kobe Bryant 4.00 10.00
3 Dwight Howard .75 2.00
4 Kevin Garnett 1.50 4.00
5 Chauncey Billups 1.00 2.50
6 Al Jefferson .75 2.00
7 Greg Oden .75 2.00
8 Deron Williams .75 2.00
9 Mo Williams .75 2.00
10 Yao Ming 1.25 3.00
11 Chris Paul 1.25 3.00
12 Steve Nash 1.00 2.50
13 Antawn Jamison .75 2.00
14 Manu Ginobili 1.00 2.50
15 Ray Allen 1.00 2.50
16 Baron Davis .75 2.00
17 Elton Brand 1.00 2.50
18 Joe Johnson .75 2.00
19 Kevin Durant 2.50 6.00
20 Tony Parker 1.00 2.50
21 Ben Gordon .75 2.00
22 Gerald Wallace .75 2.00
23 Michael Redd .75 2.00
24 Pau Gasol 1.00 2.50
25 Brandon Roy 1.00 2.50
26 Gilbert Arenas .75 2.00
27 Jason Kidd 1.00 2.50
28 Paul Pierce 1.00 2.50
29 Richard Hamilton .75 2.00
30 Amare Stoudemire .75 2.00
31 Kevin Martin .75 2.00
32 Dwyane Wade 1.50 4.00
33 Vince Carter 1.25 3.00
34 Derrick Rose 1.50 4.00
35 Blake Griffin 4.00 10.00
36 Josh Smith .75 2.00
37 Shaquille O'Neal 2.00 5.00
38 Carmelo Anthony 1.25 3.00
39 David Lee .60 1.50
40 Russell Westbrook 2.50 6.00
41 Tayshaun Prince .75 2.00
42 Andre Iguodala .75 2.00
43 Danny Granger .75 2.00
44 Tracy McGrady 1.00 2.50
45 Monta Ellis .75 2.00
46 O.J. Mayo .60 1.50
47 Dirk Nowitzki 1.25 3.00
48 Devin Harris .60 1.50
49 Chris Bosh 1.00 2.50
50 Tim Duncan 1.50 4.00

2010-11 Fathead Tradeables

1 Kobe Bryant 4.00 10.00
2 Rajon Rondo 1.00 2.50
3 Kevin Durant 2.50 6.00
4 Dwyane Wade 1.50 4.00
5 Dwight Howard .75 2.00
6 Derrick Rose 1.25 3.00
7 Dirk Nowitzki 1.25 3.00
8 Antawn Jamison .75 2.00
9 Andre Iguodala .75 2.00
10 Carmelo Anthony 1.25 3.00
11 Brandon Jennings .60 1.50
12 Chauncey Billups 1.00 2.50
13 Stephen Curry 4.00 10.00
14 Mo Williams .75 2.00
15 Evan Turner .75 2.00
16 Devin Harris .60 1.50
17 Kevin Garnett 1.50 4.00
18 Jason Kidd 1.00 2.50
19 Brandon Roy 1.00 2.50
20 Kevin Martin .75 2.00
21 Chris Paul 1.25 3.00
22 Rudy Gay 1.00 2.50
23 Vince Carter 1.25 3.00
24 Aaron Brooks .60 1.50
25 Jason Richardson 1.00 2.50
26 Danny Granger .75 2.00
27 LaMarcus Aldridge 1.00 2.50
28 Joe Johnson .75 2.00
29 Manu Ginobili 1.00 2.50
30 Deron Williams .75 2.00
31 Ray Allen 1.00 2.50
32 Michael Beasley .60 1.50
33 Eric Gordon .75 2.00
34 Pau Gasol 1.00 2.50
35 Paul Pierce 1.00 2.50
36 Chris Bosh 1.00 2.50
37 Monta Ellis .75 2.00
38 J.J. Hickson .60 1.50
39 Andrea Bargnani .75 2.00
40 Steve Nash 1.00 2.50
41 Joakim Noah .75 2.00
42 Tyreke Evans .60 1.50
43 Tim Duncan 1.50 4.00
44 Shaquille O'Neal 2.00 5.00
45 David West .75 2.00
46 Russell Westbrook 2.50 6.00
47 Amare Stoudemire .75 2.00
48 Richard Hamilton .75 2.00
49 John Wall 5.00 12.00
50 Gerald Wallace .75 2.00

1993 Fax Pax World of Sport

The 1993 Fax Pax World of Sport set was issued in Great Britain and contains 40 standard size cards. This multisport set spotlights notable sports figures from around the world, who are the best in their respective sports. An Olympic subset of seven cards (28-34) is included. The full-bleed fronts feature color action and posed photos with a red-edged white stripe intersecting the photo across the bottom. Within the white stripe is displayed the athlete's name and his country's flag. The horizontal, white backs carry the athlete's name and sport at the top followed by biographical information. Career summary and statistics are printed within a gray box, edged in red.

COMPLETE SET (40) 6.00 15.00
5 Charles Barkley .40 1.00
6 Patrick Ewing .20 .50
7 Michael Jordan 1.50 4.00
8 Shaquille O'Neal .75 2.00
32 Toni Kukoc .10 .30

1993 FCA 50

This 50-card standard-size set was sponsored by Fellowship of Christian Athletes. The color player photos on the fronts are accented on three sides by a thin pink stripe; the card face itself shades from blue to white as one moves toward the bottom. The FCA logo, featuring a cross with two olive branches, is superimposed in the upper left corner, while the player's name is printed beneath the picture and his sport in the pink stripe on the left. On a blue background, the backs carry a close-up photo, biography, and the player's testimony.

COMPLETE SET (50) 10.00 20.00
11 Tanya Crevier BK .20 .50
37 Rob Pelinka BK .20 .50
39 Brent Price BK .20 .50
50 Kay Yow CO BK .20 .50

1993-94 Finest

The premier edition of the 1993-94 Finest basketball set (produced by Topps) contains 220 standard-size cards. The set is comprised of 180 player cards and a 40-card subset of ten of the best players in each of the four divisions. These subset cards are commonly referred to as "brick" cards due to their brick wall background design. The seven-card packs (24 per box) included six player cards plus one subset card and had a suggested retail price of 3.99. Topps also issued a 14-card jumbo pack for 7.99, which included 11 regulars, two subsets, and a jumbo-only Main Attraction chase card. Packs hit the market upon release well above the aforementioned prices. The rainbow colored metallic front features a color action cutout on a metallic marble background. The white bordered back features a color player cutout on the left inset in a marble textured background. Rookie Cards of note include Vin Baker, Anfernee Hardaway, Jamal Mashburn and Chris Webber.

COMPLETE SET (220) 25.00 60.00
1 Michael Jordan 6.00 15.00
2 Larry Bird 1.00 2.50
3 Shaquille O'Neal 2.00 5.00
4 Benoit Benjamin .20 .50
5 Ricky Pierce .20 .50
6 Ken Norman .20 .50
7 Victor Alexander .20 .50
8 Mark Jackson .25 .60
9 Mark West .20 .50
10 Don MacLean .20 .50
11 Reggie Miller .40 1.00
12 Sarunas Marciulionis .20 .50
13 Craig Ehlo .20 .50
14 Toni Kukoc RC 1.50 4.00
15 Glen Rice .30 .75
16 Otis Thorpe .20 .50
17 Reggie Williams .20 .50
18 Charles Smith .20 .50
19 Micheal Williams .20 .50
20 Tom Chambers .25 .60
21 David Robinson .50 1.25
22 Jamal Mashburn RC 1.25 3.00
23 Clifford Robinson .20 .50
24 Acie Earl RC .30 .75
25 Danny Ferry .20 .50
26 Bobby Hurley RC .30 .75
27 Eddie Johnson .20 .50
28 Detlef Schrempf .30 .75
29 Mike Brown .20 .50
30 Latrell Sprewell .75 2.00
31 Derek Harper .25 .60
32 Stacey Augmon .25 .60
33 Pooh Richardson .20 .50
34 Larry Krystkowiak .20 .50
35 Pervis Ellison .20 .50
36 Jeff Malone .20 .50
37 Sean Elliott .30 .75
38 John Paxson .25 .60
39 Robert Parish .30 .75
40 Mark Aguirre .25 .60
41 Danny Ainge .30 .75
42 Brian Shaw .20 .50
43 LaPhonso Ellis .20 .50
44 Carl Herrera .20 .50
45 Terry Cummings .25 .60
46 Chris Dudley .20 .50
47 Anthony Mason .20 .50
48 Chris Morris .20 .50
49 Todd Day .20 .50
50 Nick Van Exel RC 1.50 4.00
51 Larry Nance .25 .60
52 Derrick McKey .20 .50
53 Muggsy Bogues .25 .60
54 Andrew Lang .20 .50
55 Chuck Person .25 .60
56 Michael Adams .20 .50
57 Spud Webb .25 .60
58 Scott Skiles .20 .50
59 A.C. Green .25 .60
60 Terry Mills .20 .50
61 Xavier McDaniel .20 .50
62 B.J. Armstrong .20 .50
63 Donald Hodge .20 .50
64 Gary Grant .20 .50
65 Billy Owens .20 .50
66 Greg Anthony .20 .50
67 Jay Humphries .20 .50
68 Lionel Simmons .20 .50
69 Dana Barros .20 .50
70 Steve Smith .25 .60
71 Ervin Johnson RC .30 .75
72 Sleepy Floyd .20 .50
73 Blue Edwards .20 .50
74 Clyde Drexler .40 1.00
75 Elden Campbell .20 .50
76 Hakeem Olajuwon .40 1.00
77 Clarence Weatherspoon .20 .50
78 Kevin Willis .20 .50
79 Isaiah Rider RC 1.25 3.00
80 Derrick Coleman .25 .60
81 Nick Anderson .20 .50
82 Bryant Stith .20 .50
83 Johnny Newman .20 .50
84 Calbert Cheaney RC .40 1.00
85 Oliver Miller .20 .50
86 Loy Vaught .20 .50
87 Isiah Thomas .30 .75
88 Dee Brown .20 .50
89 Horace Grant .25 .60
90 Patrick Ewing AF .20 .50
91 Clarence Weatherspoon AF .10 .25
92 Rony Seikaly AF .10 .25
93 Dino Radja AF .15 .40
94 Kenny Anderson AF .12 .30
95 John Starks AF .12 .30
96 Tom Gugliotta AF .12 .30
97 Steve Smith AF .12 .30
98 Derrick Coleman AF .12 .30
99 Shaquille O'Neal AF 1.00 2.50
100 Brad Daugherty CF .12 .30
101 Horace Grant CF .12 .30
102 Dominique Wilkins CF .20 .50
103 Joe Dumars CF .15 .40
104 Alonzo Mourning CF .25 .60
105 Scottie Pippen CF .50 1.25
106 Reggie Miller CF .20 .50
107 Mark Price CF .15 .40
108 Ken Norman CF .10 .25
109 Larry Johnson CF .15 .40
110 Jamal Mashburn MF .25 .60
111 Christian Laettner MF .12 .30
112 Karl Malone MF .20 .50
113 Dennis Rodman MF .30 .75
114 Mahmoud Abdul-Rauf MF .10 .25
115 Hakeem Olajuwon MF .20 .50
116 Jim Jackson MF .12 .30
117 John Stockton MF .20 .50
118 David Robinson MF .25 .60
119 Dikembe Mutombo MF .15 .40
120 Vlade Divac PF .15 .40
121 Dan Majerle PF .15 .40
122 Chris Mullin PF .15 .40
123 Shawn Kemp PF .20 .50
124 Danny Manning PF .12 .30
125 Charles Barkley PF .25 .60
126 Mitch Richmond PF .15 .40
127 Tim Hardaway PF .15 .40
128 Detlef Schrempf PF .15 .40
129 Clyde Drexler PF .20 .50
130 Christian Laettner .25 .60
131 Rodney Rogers RC .30 .75
132 Rik Smits .25 .60
133 Chris Mills RC .60 1.50
134 Corie Blount RC .30 .75
135 Mookie Blaylock .20 .50
136 Jim Jackson .25 .60
137 Tom Gugliotta .25 .60
138 Dennis Scott .20 .50
139 Vin Baker RC 1.25 3.00
140 Gary Payton .40 1.00
141 Sedale Threatt .20 .50
142 Orlando Woolridge .20 .50
143 Avery Johnson .25 .60
144 Charles Oakley .25 .60
145 Harvey Grant .20 .50
146 Bimbo Coles .20 .50
147 Vernon Maxwell .20 .50
148 Danny Manning .25 .60
149 Hersey Hawkins .20 .50
150 Kevin Gamble .20 .50
151 Johnny Dawkins .20 .50
152 Olden Polynice .20 .50
153 Kevin Edwards .20 .50
154 Willie Anderson .20 .50
155 Wayman Tisdale .20 .50
156 Popeye Jones RC .30 .75
157 Dan Majerle .30 .75
158 Rex Chapman .20 .50
159 Shawn Kemp UER 136 .40 1.00
160 Eric Murdock .20 .50
161 Randy White .20 .50
162 Larry Johnson .30 .75
163 Dominique Wilkins .40 1.00
164 Dikembe Mutombo .30 .75
165 Patrick Ewing .40 1.00
166 Jerome Kersey .20 .50
167 Dale Davis .20 .50
168 Ron Harper .25 .60
169 Sam Cassell RC 1.50 4.00
170 Bill Cartwright .25 .60
171 John Williams .20 .50
172 Dino Radja RC .30 .75
173 Dennis Rodman .60 1.50
174 Kenny Anderson .25 .60
175 Robert Horry .30 .75
176 Chris Mullin .30 .75
177 John Salley .20 .50
178 Scott Burrell RC .40 1.00
179 Mitch Richmond .30 .75
180 Lee Mayberry .20 .50
181 James Worthy .40 1.00

Card	Low	High
182 Rick Fox	.20	.50
183 Kevin Johnson	.30	.75
184 Lindsey Hunter RC	.60	1.50
185 Marlon Maxey	.20	.50
186 Sam Perkins	.20	.50
187 Kevin Duckworth	.20	.50
188 Jeff Hornacek	.25	.60
189 Anfernee Hardaway RC	4.00	10.00
190 Rex Walters RC	.30	.75
191 Mahmoud Abdul-Rauf	.20	.50
192 Terry Dehere RC	.30	.75
193 Brad Daugherty	.25	.60
194 John Starks	.25	.60
195 Rod Strickland	.20	.50
196 Luther Wright RC	.30	.75
197 Vlade Divac	.30	.75
198 Tim Hardaway	.30	.75
199 Joe Dumars	.30	.75
200 Charles Barkley	.50	1.25
201 Alonzo Mourning	.50	1.25
202 Doug West	.20	.50
203 Anthony Avent	.20	.50
204 Lloyd Daniels	.20	.50
205 Mark Price	.30	.75
206 Rumeal Robinson	.20	.50
207 Kendall Gill	.20	.50
208 Scottie Pippen	1.00	2.50
209 Kenny Smith	.25	.60
210 Walt Williams	.20	.50
211 Hubert Davis	.20	.50
212 Chris Webber RC	4.00	10.00
213 Rony Seikaly	.20	.50
214 Sam Bowie	.20	.50
215 Karl Malone	.40	1.00
216 Malik Sealy	.20	.50
217 Dale Ellis	.20	.50
218 Harold Miner	.20	.50
219 John Stockton	.40	1.00
220 Shawn Bradley RC	.60	1.50

1993-94 Finest Refractors

Card	Low	High
SP (10/35/40/47/49/53)	2.00	5.00
SP (56/190/204/218)	2.00	5.00
SP (33/36/41/91/116/128)	3.00	8.00
SP (147/155/180/211/217)	3.00	8.00
SP (7/12/48/64/66/105/170/182)	10.00	25.00

*VETS: 3X TO 8X BASIC CARDS
*SUBSETS: 6X TO 15X BASIC CARDS
*ROOKIES: 2.5X TO 6X BASIC CARDS
STATED ODDS 1:9 HOBBY, 1:4 JUMBO
SP CARDS: PERCEIVED SCARCITY

Card	Low	High
1 Michael Jordan	300.00	600.00
2 Larry Bird	20.00	50.00
3 Shaquille O'Neal SP !	30.00	80.00
11 Reggie Miller SP	12.00	30.00
12 Sarunas Marciulionis SP	12.00	30.00
21 David Robinson	8.00	20.00
30 Latrell Sprewell	8.00	20.00
50 Nick Van Exel !	10.00	25.00
74 Clyde Drexler SP	4.00	10.00
76 Hakeem Olajuwon	8.00	20.00
78 Kevin Willis SP	20.00	50.00
84 Calbert Cheaney SP	20.00	50.00
87 Isiah Thomas	4.00	10.00
89 Horace Grant SP	4.00	10.00
102 Dominique Wilkins CF	5.00	12.00
104 Alonzo Mourning CF	5.00	12.00
105 Scottie Pippen CF SP	10.00	25.00
106 Reggie Miller CF SP	5.00	12.00
113 Dennis Rodman MF SP !	12.00	30.00
115 Hakeem Olajuwon MF	5.00	12.00
118 David Robinson MF SP	5.00	12.00
123 Shawn Kemp PF	5.00	12.00
125 Charles Barkley PF	5.00	12.00
129 Clyde Drexler PF	4.00	10.00
133 Chris Mills SP	6.00	15.00
140 Gary Payton SP	10.00	25.00
142 Orlando Woolridge SP	5.00	12.00
159 Shawn Kemp UER 136	8.00	20.00
162 Larry Johnson	5.00	12.00
163 Dominique Wilkins	4.00	10.00
164 Dikembe Mutombo	3.00	8.00
165 Patrick Ewing SP	10.00	25.00
170 Bill Cartwright SP	12.00	30.00
173 Dennis Rodman SP	20.00	50.00
176 Chris Mullin	4.00	10.00
181 James Worthy	4.00	10.00
189 Anfernee Hardaway	40.00	100.00
198 Tim Hardaway	4.00	10.00
200 Charles Barkley	8.00	20.00
201 Alonzo Mourning	8.00	20.00
208 Scottie Pippen SP	12.00	30.00
211 Hubert Davis SP	5.00	12.00
212 Chris Webber SP !	60.00	150.00
215 Karl Malone	10.00	25.00
217 Dale Ellis SP	20.00	50.00
219 John Stockton	5.00	12.00

1993-94 Finest Main Attraction

Distributed one per 14-card jumbo pack, a player from each of the 27 NBA teams is represented in this standard size set. The rainbow colored metallic front features a semi-embossed color action cutout on textured metallic background. The brick textured bordered back features a color action shot with a gold border. Player's statistics and profile appear below the photo. The cards are numbered on the back "X of 27."

Card	Low	High
COMPLETE SET (27)	15.00	40.00
ONE PER JUMBO PACK		
1 Dominique Wilkins	.75	2.00
2 Dino Radja	.60	1.50
3 Larry Johnson	.60	1.50
4 Scottie Pippen	2.00	5.00
5 Mark Price	.60	1.50
6 Jamal Mashburn	1.00	2.50
7 Mahmoud Abdul-Rauf	.40	1.00
8 Joe Dumars	.60	1.50
9 Chris Webber	5.00	12.00
10 Hakeem Olajuwon	.75	2.00
11 Reggie Miller	.75	2.00
12 Danny Manning	.50	1.25
13 Doug Christie	.40	1.00
14 Steve Smith	.50	1.25
15 Eric Murdock	.40	1.00
16 Isaiah Rider	1.00	2.50
17 Derrick Coleman	.50	1.25
18 Patrick Ewing	.75	2.00
19 Shaquille O'Neal	3.00	8.00
20 Shawn Bradley	.60	1.50
21 Charles Barkley	1.00	2.50
22 Clyde Drexler	.75	2.00
23 Mitch Richmond	.60	1.50
24 David Robinson	1.00	2.50
25 Shawn Kemp	.75	2.00
26 Karl Malone	.75	2.00
27 Tom Gugliotta	.50	1.25

1994-95 Finest

This 331-card standard size set was issued in two series of 165 and 166 cards each. Cards were distributed in seven-card packs carrying a suggested retail price of $5.00 each. Metallic silver fronts feature a color player photo against a prismatic background. The backs have a small photo, stats, bio and a "Finest Moment '93-94". The backs have blue borders with the player's name and position at the top. Topical subsets featured are City Legend-NYC (1-10), City Legend-Balt/DC (51-55), City Legend-Detroit (101-105), City Legend-Chicago (106-110), City Legend/LA (151-155), Finest's ACC's Best (201-209), Finest's Big East's Best (226-234), Finest's Big Ten's Best (250-259), and Finest's SEC's Best (275-284). Each card features a protective coating on front that was designed to protect the card from problems that may arise from handling. The coating can be removed by carefully peeling it from the card. Values provided below are for unpeeled cards. Peeled cards generally trade for about ten to twenty-five percent less. Rookie Cards of note include Grant Hill, Juwan Howard, Eddie Jones, Jason Kidd and Glenn Robinson.

Card	Low	High
COMPLETE SET (1-331)	40.00	100.00
COMP.SERIES 1 (165)	20.00	50.00
COMP.SERIES 2 (166)	20.00	50.00
1 Chris Mullin CY	.30	.75
2 Anthony Mason CY	.20	.50
3 John Salley CY	.20	.50
4 Jamal Mashburn CY	.30	.75
5 Mark Jackson CY	.25	.60
6 Mario Elie CY	.20	.50
7 Kenny Anderson CY	.25	.60
8 Rod Strickland CY	.20	.50
9 Kenny Smith CY	.25	.60
10 Olden Polynice CY	.20	.50
11 Derek Harper	.50	1.25
12 Danny Ainge	.60	1.50
13 Dino Radja	.40	1.00
14 Eric Murdock	.40	1.00
15 Sean Rooks	.40	1.00
16 Dell Curry	.40	1.00
17 Victor Alexander	.40	1.00
18 Rodney Rogers	.40	1.00
19 John Salley	.40	1.00
20 Brad Daugherty	.50	1.25
21 Elmore Spencer	.40	1.00
22 Mitch Richmond	.60	1.50
23 Rex Walters	.40	1.00
24 Antonio Davis	.40	1.00
25 B.J. Armstrong	.40	1.00
26 Andrew Lang	.40	1.00
27 Carl Herrera	.40	1.00
28 Kevin Edwards	.40	1.00
29 Micheal Williams	.40	1.00
30 Clyde Drexler	.75	2.00
31 Dana Barros	.40	1.00
32 Shaquille O'Neal	1.50	4.00
33 Patrick Ewing	.75	2.00
34 Charles Barkley	1.00	2.50
35 J.R. Reid	.40	1.00
36 Lindsey Hunter	.40	1.00
37 Jeff Malone	.40	1.00
38 Rik Smits	.50	1.25
39 Brian Williams	.40	1.00
40 Shawn Kemp	.60	1.50
41 Terry Porter	.40	1.00
42 James Worthy	.75	2.00
43 Rex Chapman	.40	1.00
44 Stanley Roberts	.40	1.00
45 Chris Smith	.40	1.00
46 Dee Brown	.40	1.00
47 Chris Gatling	.40	1.00
48 Donald Hodge	.40	1.00
49 Bimbo Coles	.40	1.00
50 Derrick Coleman	.50	1.25
51 Muggsy Bogues CY	.25	.60
52 Reggie Williams CY	.20	.50
53 David Wingate CY	.20	.50
54 Sam Cassell CY	.30	.75
55 Sherman Douglas CY	.20	.50
56 Keith Jennings	.40	1.00
57 Kenny Gattison	.40	1.00
58 Brent Price	.40	1.00
59 Luc Longley	.50	1.25
60 Jamal Mashburn	.60	1.50
61 Doug West	.40	1.00
62 Walt Williams	.40	1.00
63 Tracy Murray	.40	1.00
64 Robert Pack	.40	1.00
65 Johnny Dawkins	.40	1.00
66 Vin Baker	.60	1.50
67 Sam Cassell	.60	1.50
68 Dale Davis	.40	1.00
69 Terrell Brandon	.40	1.00
70 Billy Owens	.40	1.00
71 Ervin Johnson	.40	1.00
72 Allan Houston	.60	1.50
73 Craig Ehlo	.40	1.00
74 Loy Vaught	.40	1.00
75 Scottie Pippen	2.00	5.00
76 Sam Bowie	.40	1.00
77 Anthony Mason	.40	1.00
78 Felton Spencer	.40	1.00
79 P.J. Brown	.40	1.00
80 Christian Laettner	.50	1.25
81 Todd Day	.40	1.00
82 Sean Elliott	.60	1.50
83 Grant Long	.40	1.00
84 Xavier McDaniel	.40	1.00
85 David Benoit	.40	1.00
86 Larry Stewart	.40	1.00
87 Donald Royal	.40	1.00
88 Duane Causwell	.40	1.00
89 Vlade Divac	.60	1.50
90 Derrick McKey	.40	1.00
91 Kevin Johnson	.60	1.50
92 LaPhonso Ellis	.40	1.00
93 Jerome Kersey	.40	1.00
94 Muggsy Bogues	.50	1.25
95 Tom Gugliotta	.40	1.00
96 Jeff Hornacek	.50	1.25
97 Kevin Willis	.40	1.00
98 Chris Mills	.40	1.00
99 Sam Perkins	.40	1.00
100 Alonzo Mourning	.75	2.00
101 Derrick Coleman CY	.25	.60
102 Glen Rice CY	.30	.75
103 Kevin Willis CY	.20	.50
104 Chris Webber CY	.75	2.00
105 Terry Mills CY	.20	.50
106 Tim Hardaway CY	.30	.75
107 Nick Anderson CY	.20	.50
108 Terry Cummings CY	.25	.60
109 Hersey Hawkins CY	.20	.50
110 Ken Norman CY	.20	.50
111 Nick Anderson	.40	1.00
112 Tim Perry	.40	1.00
113 Terry Dehere	.40	1.00
114 Chris Morris	.40	1.00
115 John Williams	.40	1.00
116 Jon Barry	.40	1.00
117 Rony Seikaly	.40	1.00
118 Detlef Schrempf	.60	1.50
119 Terry Cummings	.50	1.25
120 Chris Webber	1.50	4.00
121 David Wingate	.40	1.00
122 Popeye Jones	.40	1.00
123 Sherman Douglas	.40	1.00
124 Greg Anthony	.40	1.00
125 Mookie Blaylock	.40	1.00
126 Don MacLean	.40	1.00
127 Lionel Simmons	.40	1.00
128 Scott Brooks	.40	1.00
129 Jeff Turner	.40	1.00
130 Bryant Stith	.40	1.00
131 Shawn Bradley	.40	1.00
132 Byron Scott	.50	1.25
133 Doug Christie	.40	1.00
134 Dennis Rodman	2.00	5.00
135 Dan Majerle	.60	1.50
136 Gary Grant	.40	1.00
137 Bryon Russell	.40	1.00
138 Will Perdue	.40	1.00
139 Gheorghe Muresan	.40	1.00
140 Kendall Gill	.40	1.00
141 Isaiah Rider	.60	1.50
142 Terry Mills	.40	1.00
143 Willie Anderson	.40	1.00
144 Hubert Davis	.40	1.00
145 Lucious Harris	.40	1.00
146 Spud Webb	.50	1.25
147 Glen Rice	.60	1.50
148 Dennis Scott	.40	1.00
149 Robert Horry	.60	1.50
150 John Stockton	.75	2.00
151 Stacey Augmon CY	.25	.60
152 Chris Mills CY	.20	.50
153 Elden Campbell CY	.20	.50
154 Jay Humphries CY	.20	.50
155 Reggie Miller CY	.40	1.00
156 George Lynch	.40	1.00
157 Tyrone Hill	.40	1.00
158 Lee Mayberry	.40	1.00
159 Jon Koncak	.40	1.00
160 Joe Dumars	.60	1.50
161 Vernon Maxwell	.40	1.00
162 Joe Kleine	.40	1.00
163 Acie Earl	.40	1.00
164 Steve Kerr	.50	1.25
165 Rod Strickland	.40	1.00
166 Glenn Robinson RC	1.50	4.00
167 Anfernee Hardaway	1.25	3.00
168 Latrell Sprewell	.60	1.50
169 Sergei Bazarevich RC	.75	2.00
170 Hakeem Olajuwon	.60	1.50
171 Nick Van Exel	.50	1.25
172 Buck Williams	.30	.75
173 Antoine Carr	.30	.75
174 Corie Blount	.30	.75
175 Dominique Wilkins	.60	1.50
176 Yinka Dare RC	.50	1.25
177 Byron Houston	.30	.75
178 LaSalle Thompson	.30	.75
179 Doug Smith	.30	.75
180 David Robinson	.75	2.00
181 Eric Piatkowski RC	1.00	2.50
182 Scott Skiles	.30	.75
183 Scott Burrell	.30	.75
184 Mark West	.30	.75
185 Billy Owens	.30	.75
186 Brian Grant RC	1.25	3.00
187 Scott Williams	.30	.75
188 Gerald Madkins	.30	.75
189 Reggie Williams	.30	.75
190 Danny Manning	.40	1.00
191 Mike Brown	.30	.75
192 Charles Smith	.30	.75
193 Elden Campbell	.30	.75
194 Ricky Pierce	.30	.75
195 Karl Malone	.60	1.50
196 Brooks Thompson RC	.60	1.50
197 Alaa Abdelnaby	.30	.75
198 Tyrone Corbin	.30	.75
199 Johnny Newman	.30	.75
200 Grant Hill CB	2.00	5.00
201 Kenny Anderson CB	.20	.50
202 Olden Polynice CB	.15	.40
203 Horace Grant CB	.20	.50
204 Muggsy Bogues CB	.20	.50
205 Mark Price CB	.25	.60
206 Tom Gugliotta CB	.15	.40
207 Christian Laettner CB	.20	.50
208 Eric Montross CB	.30	.75
209 Sam Cassell CB	.25	.60
210 Charles Oakley	.40	1.00
211 Harold Ellis	.30	.75
212 Nate McMillan	.30	.75
213 Chuck Person	.40	1.00
214 Harold Miner	.30	.75
215 Clarence Weatherspoon	.30	.75
216 Robert Parish	.50	1.25
217 Michael Cage	.30	.75
218 Kenny Smith	.40	1.00
219 Larry Krystkowiak	.30	.75
220 Dikembe Mutombo	.50	1.25
221 Wayman Tisdale	.30	.75
222 Kevin Duckworth	.30	.75
223 Vern Fleming	.30	.75
224 Eric Mobley RC	.50	1.25
225 Patrick Ewing CB	.30	.75
226 Clifford Robinson CB	.15	.40
227 Eric Murdock CB	.15	.40
228 Derrick Coleman CB	.20	.50
229 Otis Thorpe CB	.15	.40
230 Alonzo Mourning CB	.30	.75
231 Donyell Marshall CB	.40	1.00
232 Dikembe Mutombo CB	.25	.60
233 Rony Seikaly CB	.15	.40
234 Chris Mullin CB	.25	.60
235 Reggie Miller	.60	1.50
236 Benoit Benjamin	.30	.75
237 Sean Rooks	.30	.75
238 Terry Davis	.30	.75
239 Anthony Avent	.30	.75
240 Grant Hill RC	6.00	15.00
241 Randy Woods	.30	.75
242 Tom Chambers	.40	1.00
243 Michael Adams	.30	.75
244 Monty Williams RC	.60	1.50
245 Chris Mullin	.50	1.25
246 Bill Wennington	.30	.75
247 Mark Jackson	.40	1.00
248 Blue Edwards	.30	.75
249 Jalen Rose RC	2.50	6.00
250 Glenn Robinson CB	.75	2.00
251 Kevin Willis CB	.15	.40
252 B.J. Armstrong CB	.15	.40
253 Jim Jackson CB	.15	.40
254 Steve Smith CB	.20	.50
255 Chris Webber CB	.60	1.50
256 Glen Rice CB	.25	.60
257 Derek Harper CB	.20	.50
258 Jalen Rose CB	1.00	2.50
259 Juwan Howard CB	.60	1.50
260 Kenny Anderson	.40	1.00
261 Calbert Cheaney	.30	.75
262 Bill Cartwright	.40	1.00
263 Mario Elie	.30	.75
264 Chris Dudley	.30	.75
265 Jim Jackson	.30	.75
266 Antonio Harvey	.30	.75
267 Bill Curley RC	.50	1.25
268 Moses Malone	.50	1.25
269 A.C. Green	.40	1.00
270 Larry Johnson	.50	1.25
271 Marty Conlon	.30	.75
272 Greg Graham	.30	.75
273 Eric Montross RC	.60	1.50
274 Stacey King	.30	.75
275 Charles Barkley CB	.40	1.00
276 Chris Morris CB	.15	.40
277 Robert Horry CB	.25	.60
278 Dominique Wilkins CB	.30	.75
279 Latrell Sprewell CB	.30	.75
280 Shaquille O'Neal CB	1.25	3.00
281 Wesley Person CB	.40	1.00
282 Mahmoud Abdul-Rauf CB	.15	.40
283 Jamal Mashburn CB	.25	.60
284 Dale Ellis CB	.15	.40
285 Gary Payton	.50	1.25
286 Jason Kidd RC	6.00	15.00
287 Ken Norman	.30	.75
288 Juwan Howard RC	1.25	3.00
289 Lamond Murray RC	.75	2.00
290 Clifford Robinson	.30	.75
291 Frank Brickowski	.30	.75
292 Adam Keefe	.30	.75
293 Ron Harper	.40	1.00
294 Tom Hammonds	.30	.75
295 Otis Thorpe	.30	.75
296 Rick Mahorn	.30	.75
297 Alton Lister	.30	.75
298 Vinny Del Negro	.30	.75
299 Danny Ferry	.30	.75
300 John Starks	.40	1.00
301 Duane Ferrell	.30	.75
302 Hersey Hawkins	.30	.75
303 Khalid Reeves RC	.60	1.50
304 Anthony Peeler	.30	.75
305 Tim Hardaway	.50	1.25
306 Rick Fox	.30	.75
307 Jay Humphries	.30	.75
308 Brian Shaw	.30	.75
309 Danny Schayes	.30	.75
310 Stacey Augmon	.40	1.00
311 Oliver Miller	.30	.75
312 Pooh Richardson	.30	.75
313 Donyell Marshall RC	.75	2.00
314 Aaron McKie RC	.75	2.00
315 Mark Price	.50	1.25
316 B.J. Tyler RC	.50	1.25
317 Olden Polynice	.30	.75
318 Avery Johnson	.40	1.00
319 Derek Strong	.30	.75
320 Toni Kukoc	.60	1.50
321 Charlie Ward RC	.75	2.00
322 Wesley Person RC	.75	2.00
323 Eddie Jones RC	3.00	8.00
324 Horace Grant	.40	1.00
325 Mahmoud Abdul-Rauf	.30	.75
326 Sharone Wright RC	.60	1.50
327 Kevin Gamble	.30	.75
328 Sarunas Marciulionis	.30	.75
329 Harvey Grant	.30	.75
330 Bobby Hurley	.30	.75
331 Michael Jordan	8.00	20.00

1994-95 Finest Refractors

*SER.1 STARS: 2.5X TO 6X BASE CARD HI
*SER.2 SUBSETS: 5X TO 12X BASE HI
*SER.2 STARS: 3X TO 8X BASE HI
*SER.2 SUBSETS: 6X TO 15X BASE HI
*RCs: 3X TO 8X BASE HI
SER.1/2 STATED ODDS 1:12
CONDITION SENSITIVE SET
SP CARDS: PERCEIVED SCARCITY

Card	Low	High
22 Mitch Richmond	8.00	20.00
30 Clyde Drexler	8.00	20.00
33 Patrick Ewing	8.00	20.00
34 Charles Barkley	12.00	30.00
40 Shawn Kemp	15.00	40.00
42 James Worthy	15.00	40.00
75 Scottie Pippen	12.00	30.00
100 Alonzo Mourning	10.00	25.00
102 Glen Rice CY SP	30.00	80.00
104 Chris Webber CY SP	20.00	40.00
106 Tim Hardaway CY SP	10.00	20.00
120 Chris Webber SP	40.00	80.00
134 Dennis Rodman	20.00	50.00
150 John Stockton SP	15.00	40.00
155 Reggie Miller CY SP	12.00	30.00
160 Joe Dumars	8.00	20.00
166 Glenn Robinson	25.00	60.00
167 Anfernee Hardaway	15.00	40.00
170 Hakeem Olajuwon	10.00	25.00
171 Nick Van Exel	8.00	20.00
175 Dominique Wilkins	8.00	20.00
180 David Robinson	12.00	30.00
195 Karl Malone	10.00	25.00
200 Grant Hill CB	20.00	50.00
230 Alonzo Mourning CB	10.00	25.00
235 Reggie Miller	8.00	20.00
245 Chris Mullin	8.00	20.00
255 Chris Webber CB	10.00	25.00
275 Charles Barkley CB	10.00	25.00
285 Gary Payton	8.00	20.00
320 Toni Kukoc	12.00	30.00
331 Michael Jordan	125.00	300.00

1994-95 Finest Cornerstone

Randomly inserted in second series packs at a rate of one in every 24, cards from this 15-card standard-size set highlight players who are foundations of their respective teams. The fronts have a color-action photo set against a multi-colored background. The backs have a color-photo and player information. Values provided below are for unpeeled cards. Peeled cards generally trade for ten to twenty-five percent less.

Card	Low	High
COMPLETE SET (15)	15.00	40.00
SER.2 STATED ODDS 1:24		
CS1 Shaquille O'Neal	6.00	15.00
CS2 Alonzo Mourning	3.00	8.00
CS3 Patrick Ewing	3.00	8.00
CS4 Karl Malone	3.00	8.00
CS5 Kenny Anderson	2.00	5.00
CS6 Latrell Sprewell	3.00	8.00
CS7 Dikembe Mutombo	2.50	6.00
CS8 Charles Barkley	4.00	10.00
CS9 John Stockton	3.00	8.00
CS10 Reggie Miller	3.00	8.00
CS11 Jamal Mashburn	2.50	6.00
CS12 Anfernee Hardaway	6.00	15.00
CS13 Jim Jackson	1.50	4.00
CS14 David Robinson	4.00	10.00
CS15 Hakeem Olajuwon	3.00	8.00

1994-95 Finest Cornerstone Refractors Test

This 15-card set is a parallel to the regular Cornerstone insert. The cards feature the "classic" regular refractor technology. These cards are considered test issues since they were never intended to be released to the public. It is unknown how they made their way into the market as these cards were not inserted into packs.

Card	Low	High
CS1 Shaquille O'Neal	125.00	300.00
CS2 Alonzo Mourning	60.00	150.00
CS3 Patrick Ewing	60.00	150.00
CS4 Karl Malone	60.00	150.00
CS5 Kenny Anderson	40.00	100.00
CS6 Latrell Sprewell	60.00	150.00
CS7 Dikembe Mutombo	50.00	125.00
CS8 Charles Barkley	80.00	200.00
CS9 John Stockton	60.00	150.00
CS10 Reggie Miller	60.00	150.00
CS11 Jamal Mashburn	50.00	125.00
CS12 Anfernee Hardaway	80.00	200.00
CS13 Jim Jackson	30.00	80.00
CS14 David Robinson	80.00	200.00
CS15 Hakeem Olajuwon	60.00	150.00

1994-95 Finest Iron Men

Randomly inserted in first series packs at a rate of one in 24, cards from this 10-card standard-size set spotlight players who played at least 3,000 minutes during the 1993-94 NBA season. These transparent cards have a front design much like the basic Finest cards with "Iron Man" at the top. The only design element on back is a small stat box at the bottom. Unlike most other 1994-95 Finest cards, Iron Men inserts have no protective coating.

Card	Low	High
COMPLETE SET (10)	15.00	30.00
SER.1 STATED ODDS 1:24		
1 Shaquille O'Neal	6.00	15.00
2 Kenny Anderson	1.50	4.00
3 Jim Jackson	1.25	3.00
4 Clarence Weatherspoon	1.25	3.00
5 Karl Malone	2.50	6.00
6 Dan Majerle	2.00	5.00
7 Anfernee Hardaway	3.00	8.00
8 David Robinson	3.00	8.00
9 Latrell Sprewell	2.50	6.00
10 Hakeem Olajuwon	2.50	6.00

1994-95 Finest Lottery Prize

Randomly inserted in second series packs at a rate of one in six, cards from this 22-card standard-size set showcase lottery picks who went on to become impact players. The fronts have a color-action photo with background having a large basketball surrounded by a variety of colors and stars. The backs have a color photo and player information with the words "Lottery Prize" set against a basketball. Values provided below are for unpeeled cards. Peeled cards generally trade for ten to twenty-five percent less.

Card	Low	High
COMPLETE SET (22)	12.00	30.00
SER.2 STATED ODDS 1:6		
LP1 Patrick Ewing	1.25	3.00
LP2 Chris Mullin	1.00	2.50
LP3 David Robinson	1.50	4.00
LP4 Scottie Pippen	2.00	5.00
LP5 Kevin Johnson	1.00	2.50
LP6 Danny Manning	.75	2.00
LP7 Mitch Richmond	1.00	2.50
LP8 Derrick Coleman	.75	2.00
LP9 Gary Payton	1.00	2.50
LP10 Mahmoud Abdul-Rauf	.60	1.50
LP11 Larry Johnson	1.00	2.50
LP12 Kenny Anderson	.75	2.00
LP13 Dikembe Mutombo	1.00	2.50
LP14 Stacey Augmon	.75	2.00
LP15 Shaquille O'Neal	2.50	6.00
LP16 Alonzo Mourning	1.25	3.00
LP17 Clarence Weatherspoon	.60	1.50
LP18 Robert Horry	1.00	2.50
LP19 Chris Webber	1.50	4.00
LP20 Anfernee Hardaway	1.50	4.00
LP21 Jamal Mashburn	1.00	2.50
LP22 Vin Baker	1.00	2.50

1994-95 Finest Lottery Prize Refractors Test

This 22-card set is a parallel to the regular Lottery Prize insert. The cards feature the "classic" regular refractor technology. These cards are considered test issues since they were never intended to be released to the public. It is unknown how they made their way into the market as these cards were not inserted into packs.

Card	Low	High
LP1 Patrick Ewing	40.00	100.00
LP2 Chris Mullin	30.00	- 80.00
LP3 David Robinson	50.00	125.00
LP4 Scottie Pippen	60.00	150.00
LP5 Kevin Johnson	30.00	80.00
LP6 Danny Manning	25.00	60.00
LP7 Mitch Richmond	30.00	80.00
LP8 Derrick Coleman	25.00	60.00
LP9 Gary Payton	30.00	80.00
LP10 Mahmoud Abdul-Rauf	20.00	50.00
LP11 Larry Johnson	30.00	80.00
LP12 Kenny Anderson	25.00	60.00
LP13 Dikembe Mutombo	30.00	80.00
LP14 Stacey Augmon	25.00	60.00
LP15 Shaquille O'Neal	80.00	200.00
LP16 Alonzo Mourning	40.00	100.00
LP17 Clarence Weatherspoon	20.00	50.00
LP18 Robert Horry	30.00	80.00
LP19 Chris Webber	50.00	125.00
LP20 Anfernee Hardaway	50.00	125.00
LP21 Jamal Mashburn	30.00	80.00
LP22 Vin Baker	30.00	80.00

1994-95 Finest Marathon Men

Randomly inserted into first series packs at a rate of one in 12, cards from this 12-card standard-size set highlight players who played in all 82 games during the 1993-94 NBA season. These transparent cards have a design on front that is similar to the basic issue with the words "Marathon Man" at the top. The back contains a small stat box at the bottom. Unlike most other 1994-95 Finest cards, Marathon Men inserts have no protective coatings.

Card	Low	High
COMPLETE SET (20)	20.00	50.00
SER.1 STATED ODDS 1:12		
1 Latrell Sprewell	3.00	8.00
2 Gary Payton	2.00	5.00
3 Kenny Anderson	1.50	4.00
4 Jim Jackson	1.25	3.00
5 Lindsey Hunter	1.25	3.00
6 Rod Strickland	1.25	3.00
7 Hersey Hawkins	1.25	3.00
8 Gerald Wilkins	1.25	3.00
9 B.J. Armstrong	1.25	3.00
10 Anfernee Hardaway	5.00	12.00
11 Stacey Augmon	1.50	4.00
12 Eric Murdock	1.25	3.00
13 Clarence Weatherspoon	1.25	3.00
14 Karl Malone	2.50	6.00
15 Charles Oakley	1.50	4.00
16 Rick Fox	1.25	3.00
17 Otis Thorpe	1.25	3.00
18 Dikembe Mutombo	2.00	5.00
19 Mike Brown	1.25	3.00
20 A.C. Green	1.50	4.00

1994-95 Finest Rack Pack

Randomly inserted in second series packs at a rate of one in every 72, cards from this seven-card standard-size set spotlight a selection of top performers from the 1994 NBA draft class. The fronts have a color-action photo with a basketball hoop and lights in the background. The words "Rack Pack" appear at the top in a red-foil. The backs have player information inside of a computer monitor. Like many of the Finest cards, these cards also came with a protective covering. The prices listed below are for peeled cards. Peeled cards generally trade for ten to twenty-five percent less.

Card	Low	High
COMPLETE SET (7)	15.00	40.00
SER.2 STATED ODDS 1:72		
RP1 Grant Hill	8.00	20.00
RP2 Wesley Person	1.50	4.00
RP3 Juwan Howard	2.50	6.00
RP4 Lamond Murray	1.50	4.00
RP5 Glenn Robinson	3.00	8.00
RP6 Donyell Marshall	1.50	4.00
RP7 Jason Kidd	8.00	20.00

1994-95 Finest Rack Pack Refractors Test

This seven-card set is a parallel to the regular Rack Pack insert. The cards feature the "classic" regular refractor technology. These cards are considered test issues since they were never intended to be released to the public. It is unknown how they made their way into the market as these cards were not inserted into packs.

Card	Low	High
RP1 Grant Hill	80.00	200.00
RP2 Wesley Person	15.00	40.00
RP3 Juwan Howard	25.00	60.00
RP4 Lamond Murray	15.00	40.00
RP5 Glenn Robinson	30.00	80.00
RP6 Donyell Marshall	15.00	40.00
RP7 Jason Kidd	80.00	200.00

1995-96 Finest

The 1995-96 Topps Finest set was issued in two separate series of 140 and 111 standard-size cards. Cards for both series were issued in six-card packs (suggested retail price of $5.00). Each pack contained five basic cards and one Mystery insert card. Basic player cards feature blue-bordered metallic fronts and cut-out action shots set against a swirling court background. The Rookie subset cards (111-139) feature orange-bordered cards. Magic Johnson's card (#252) was added very late in the production schedule and unlike other player cards features a red border on front instead of blue. The checklist card (#111) has an uncorrected error - it should have been numbered 140 as the last card in the first series. Also, card #251, originally scheduled to be a checklist for the second series set, was never printed. Each card features an opaque coating that can be carefully peeled off designed to protect the card front from problems that may arise from handling. Values provided below are for unpeeled cards. Peeled cards generally trade for ten to twenty-five percent less. Noteworthy Rookie Cards include Michael Finley, Kevin Garnett, Joe Smith, Jerry Stackhouse and Damon Stoudamire.

Card	Low	High
COMPLETE SET (251)	90.00	180.00
COMP.SERIES 1 (140)	75.00	150.00
COMP.SERIES 2 (111)	15.00	40.00
1 Hakeem Olajuwon	1.00	2.50
2 Stacey Augmon	.60	1.50
3 John Starks	.60	1.50
4 Sharone Wright	.50	1.25
5 Jason Kidd	1.25	3.00
6 Lamond Murray	.50	1.25
7 Kenny Anderson	.60	1.50
8 James Robinson	.50	1.25
9 Wesley Person	.50	1.25
10 Latrell Sprewell	.75	2.00
11 Sean Elliott	.75	2.00
12 Greg Anthony	.50	1.25
13 Kendall Gill	.50	1.25
14 Mark Jackson	.60	1.50
15 John Stockton	1.00	2.50
16 Steve Smith	.60	1.50
17 Bobby Hurley	.50	1.25
18 Ervin Johnson	.50	1.25
19 Elden Campbell	.50	1.25
20 Vin Baker	.60	1.50
21 Micheal Williams	.50	1.25
22 Steve Kerr	.60	1.50
23 Kevin Duckworth	.50	1.25
24 Willie Anderson	.50	1.25
25 Joe Dumars	.75	2.00
26 Dale Ellis	.50	1.25
27 Bimbo Coles	.50	1.25
28 Nick Anderson	.50	1.25
29 Dee Brown	.50	1.25
30 Tyrone Hill	.50	1.25
31 Reggie Miller	1.00	2.50
32 Shaquille O'Neal	2.00	5.00
33 Brian Grant	.60	1.50
34 Charles Barkley	1.25	3.00
35 Cedric Ceballos	.50	1.25
36 Rex Walters	.50	1.25
37 Kenny Smith	.60	1.50
38 Popeye Jones	.50	1.25
39 Harvey Grant	.50	1.25
40 Gary Payton	.75	2.00
41 John Williams	.50	1.25
42 Sherman Douglas	.50	1.25
43 Oliver Miller	.50	1.25
44 Kevin Willis	.50	1.25
45 Isaiah Rider	.75	2.00
46 Gheorghe Muresan	.50	1.25
47 Blue Edwards	.50	1.25
48 Jeff Hornacek	.60	1.50
49 J.R. Reid	.50	1.25
50 Glenn Robinson	.60	1.50
51 Dell Curry	.50	1.25
52 Greg Graham	.50	1.25
53 Ron Harper	.60	1.50
54 Derek Harper	.60	1.50
55 Dikembe Mutombo	.75	-2.00
56 Terry Mills	.50	1.25
57 Victor Alexander	.50	1.25
58 Malik Sealy	.50	1.25
59 Vincent Askew	.50	1.25
60 Mitch Richmond	.75	2.00
61 Duane Ferrell	.50	1.25
62 Dickey Simpkins	.50	1.25
63 Pooh Richardson	.50	1.25
64 Khalid Reeves	.50	1.25
65 Dino Radja	.50	1.25
66 Lee Mayberry	.50	1.25
67 Kenny Gattison	.50	1.25
68 Joe Kleine	.50	1.25
69 Tony Dumas	.50	1.25
70 Nick Van Exel	.75	2.00
71 Armon Gilliam	.50	1.25
72 Craig Ehlo	.50	1.25
73 Adam Keefe	.50	1.25
74 Chris Dudley	.50	1.25
75 Clyde Drexler	1.00	2.50
76 Jeff Turner	.50	1.25
77 Calbert Cheaney	.50	1.25
78 Vinny Del Negro	.50	1.25
79 Tim Perry	.50	1.25
80 Tim Hardaway	.75	2.00
81 B.J. Armstrong	.50	1.25
82 Muggsy Bogues	.60	1.50
83 Mark Macon	.50	1.25
84 Doug West	.50	1.25
85 Jalen Rose	1.00	2.50
86 Chris Mills	.50	1.25
87 Charles Oakley	.60	1.50
88 Andrew Lang	.50	1.25
89 Olden Polynice	.50	1.25
90 Sam Cassell	.75	2.00
91 Todd Day	.50	1.25
92 P.J. Brown	.50	1.25
93 Benoit Benjamin	.50	1.25
94 Sam Perkins	.50	1.25
95 Eddie Jones	.75	2.00
96 Robert Parish	.75	2.00
97 Avery Johnson	.60	1.50
98 Lindsey Hunter	.50	1.25
99 Billy Owens	.50	1.25
100 Shawn Bradley	.50	1.25
101 Dale Davis	.50	1.25
102 Terry Dehere	.50	1.25
103 A.C. Green	.60	1.50
104 Christian Laettner	.60	1.50
105 Horace Grant	.60	1.50
106 Rony Seikaly	.50	1.25
107 Reggie Williams	.50	1.25
108 Toni Kukoc	.75	2.00
109 Terrell Brandon	.50	1.25
110 Clifford Robinson	.50	1.25
111 Joe Smith RC	1.00	2.50
112 Antonio McDyess RC	1.00	2.50
113 Jerry Stackhouse RC	2.50	6.00
114 Rasheed Wallace RC	4.00	10.00
115 Kevin Garnett RC	12.00	30.00
116 Bryant Reeves RC	.60	1.50
117 Damon Stoudamire RC	2.00	5.00
118 Shawn Respert RC	.60	1.50
119 Ed O'Bannon RC	.60	1.50
120 Kurt Thomas RC	.75	2.00
121 Gary Trent RC	.75	2.00
122 Cherokee Parks RC	.60	1.50
123 Corliss Williamson RC	.75	2.00
124 Eric Williams RC	.75	2.00
125 Brent Barry RC	1.25	3.00
126 Alan Henderson RC	.75	2.00
127 Bob Sura RC	.60	1.50
128 Theo Ratliff RC	1.50	4.00
129 Randolph Childress RC	.60	1.50
130 Jason Caffey RC	.75	2.00
131 Michael Finley RC	2.50	6.00
132 George Zidek RC	.60	1.50
133 Travis Best RC	.75	2.00
134 Loren Meyer RC	.50	1.25
135 David Vaughn RC	.75	2.00
136 Sherrell Ford RC	.60	1.50
137 Mario Bennett RC	.60	1.50
138 Greg Ostertag RC	.75	2.00
139 Cory Alexander RC	.75	2.00
140 Checklist UER #111	.50	1.25
141 Chucky Brown	.50	1.25
142 Eric Mobley	.50	1.25
143 Tom Hammonds	.50	1.25
144 Chris Webber	1.00	2.50
145 Carlos Rogers	.50	1.25
146 Chuck Person	.60	1.50
147 Brian Williams	.50	1.25
148 Kevin Gamble	.50	1.25
149 Dennis Rodman	1.50	4.00
150 Pervis Ellison	.50	1.25
151 Jayson Williams	.50	1.25
152 Buck Williams	.50	1.25
153 Allan Houston	.60	1.50
154 Tom Gugliotta	.50	1.25
155 Charles Smith	.50	1.25
156 Chris Gatling	.50	1.25
157 Darrin Hancock	.50	1.25
158 Blue Edwards	.50	1.25
159 Shawn Kemp	.75	2.00
160 Michael Cage	.50	1.25
161 Sedale Threatt	.50	1.25
162 Byron Scott	.60	1.50
163 Elliot Perry	.50	1.25
164 Jim Jackson	.50	1.25
165 Wayman Tisdale	.50	1.25
166 Vernon Maxwell	.50	1.25
167 Brian Shaw	.50	1.25
168 Haywoode Workman	.50	1.25
169 Mookie Blaylock	.50	1.25
170 Donald Royal	.50	1.25
171 Lorenzo Williams	.50	1.25
172 Eric Piatkowski UER	.60	1.50
173 Sarunas Marciulionis	.50	1.25
174 Otis Thorpe	.50	1.25
175 Rex Chapman	.50	1.25
176 Felton Spencer	.50	1.25
177 John Salley	.50	1.25
178 Pete Chilcutt	.50	1.25
179 Scottie Pippen	1.25	3.00
180 Robert Pack	.50	1.25
181 Dana Barros	.50	1.25
182 Mahmoud Abdul-Rauf	.50	1.25
183 Eric Murdock	.50	1.25
184 Anthony Mason	.50	1.25
185 Will Perdue	.50	1.25
186 Jeff Malone	.50	1.25
187 Anthony Peeler	.50	1.25
188 Chris Childs	.50	1.25
189 Glen Rice	.75	2.00
190 Grant Hill	1.25	3.00
191 Michael Smith	.50	1.25
192 Sean Rooks	.50	1.25
193 Clifford Rozier	.50	1.25
194 Rik Smits	.60	1.50
195 Spud Webb	.60	1.50
196 Aaron McKie	.50	1.25
197 Nate McMillan	.50	1.25
198 Bobby Phills	.50	1.25
199 Dennis Scott	.50	1.25
200 Mark West	.50	1.25
201 George McCloud	.50	1.25
202 B.J. Tyler	.50	1.25
203 Lionel Simmons	.50	1.25
204 Loy Vaught	.50	1.25
205 Kevin Edwards	.50	1.25
206 Eric Montross	.50	1.25
207 Kenny Gattison	.50	1.25
208 Mario Elie	.50	1.25
209 Karl Malone	1.00	2.50
210 Ken Norman	.50	1.25
211 Antonio Davis	.50	1.25
212 Doc Rivers	.60	1.50
213 Hubert Davis	.50	1.25
214 Jamal Mashburn	.75	2.00
215 Donyell Marshall	.50	1.25
216 Sasha Danilovic RC	.75	2.00
217 Danny Manning	.60	1.50
218 Scott Burrell	.50	1.25
219 Vlade Divac	.75	2.00
220 Marty Conlon	.50	1.25
221 Clarence Weatherspoon	.50	1.25
222 Terry Porter	.50	1.25
223 Luc Longley	.60	1.50
224 Juwan Howard	.75	2.00

225 Danny Ferry .50 1.25
226 Rod Strickland .50 1.25
227 Bryant Stith .50 1.25
228 Derrick McKey .50 1.25
229 Michael Jordan 6.00 15.00
230 Jamie Watson .50 1.25
231 Rick Fox .50 1.25
232 Scott Williams .50 1.25
233 Larry Johnson .75 2.00
234 Anfernee Hardaway 1.25 3.00
235 Hersey Hawkins .50 1.25
236 Robert Horry .60 1.50
237 Kevin Johnson .75 2.00
238 Rodney Rogers .50 1.25
239 Detlef Schrempf .75 2.00
240 Derrick Coleman .60 1.50
241 Walt Williams .50 1.25
242 LaPhonso Ellis .50 1.25
243 Patrick Ewing 1.00 2.50
244 Grant Long .50 1.25
245 David Robinson 1.25 3.00
246 Chris Mullin .75 2.00
247 Alonzo Mourning 1.00 2.50
248 Dan Majerle .75 2.00
249 Johnny Newman .50 1.25
250 Chris Morris .50 1.25
252 Magic Johnson 2.00 5.00

1995-96 Finest Refractors

*REF: 2.5X TO 6X HI COLUMN
SER.1/2 STATED ODDS: 1:12 HOB, 1:18 RET
229 Michael Jordan 100.00 250.00
252 Magic Johnson 6P 8.00 20.00

1995-96 Finest Dish and Swish

Randomly inserted into first series packs at a rate of one in 24, cards from this dual-sided, 29-card standard-size set feature combinations of two key players from each NBA team. Each side features one of the two players in game action, with the words "Dish" or "Swish" along the bottom. Values provided below are for unpeeled cards. Peeled cards generally trade for ten to twenty-five percent less. The set is sequenced in alphabetical order by team.

COMPLETE SET (29) 30.00 80.00
SER.1 STATED ODDS 1:24
DS1 M.Blaylock/S.Smith 1.25 3.00
DS2 S.Douglas/D.Radja 1.00 2.50
DS3 M.Bogues/L.Johnson 1.50 4.00
DS4 S.Pippen/M.Jordan 12.00 30.00
DS5 M.Price/C.Mills 1.50 4.00
DS6 J.Kidd/J.Mashburn 2.50 6.00
DS7 M.Abdul-Rauf/D.Mutombo 1.50 4.00
DS8 G.Hill/J.Dumars 3.00 8.00
DS9 T.Hardaway/C.Mullin 2.50 6.00
DS10 C.Drexler/H.Olajuwon 3.00 8.00
DS11 M.Jackson/R.Miller 2.50 6.00
DS12 P.Richardson/L.Murray 1.00 2.50
DS13 N.Van Exel/C.Ceballos 1.50 4.00
DS14 G.Rice/K.Reeves 1.50 4.00
DS15 G.Robinson/Murdock 1.25 3.00
DS16 T.Gugliotta/C.Laettner 1.50 4.00
DS17 K.Anderson/D.Coleman 1.25 3.00
DS18 P.Ewing/D.Harper 2.00 5.00
DS19 A.Hardaway/S.O'Neal 5.00 12.00
DS20 D.Barros/C.Weatherspoon 1.00 2.50
DS21 K.Johnson/C.Barkley 2.50 6.00
DS22 R.Strickland/C.Robinson 1.00 2.50
DS23 Richmond/W.Williams 1.50 4.00
DS24 A.Johnson/D.Rob 2.50 6.00
DS25 G.Payton/S.Kemp 2.50 6.00
DS26 B.J.Armstrong/O.Miller 1.00 2.50
DS27 J.Stockton/K.Malone 3.00 8.00
DS28 G.Anthony/B.Scott 1.25 3.00
DS29 J.Howard/C.Webber 3.00 8.00

1995-96 Finest Hot Stuff

Randomly inserted into first series packs at a rate of one in nine, cards from this 15-card standard-size set highlight some of the NBA's top stars in slam-dunk action. Orange-bordered fronts feature game action shots. The words "Hot Stuff" run down the left hand side of the card front. Values provided below are for unpeeled cards. Peeled cards generally trade for ten to twenty-five percent less.

COMPLETE SET (15) 12.50 30.00
SER.1 STATED ODDS 1:9
HS1 Michael Jordan 8.00 20.00
HS2 Grant Hill 1.50 4.00
HS3 Clyde Drexler 1.25 3.00
HS4 Anfernee Hardaway 1.50 4.00
HS5 Sean Elliott 1.00 2.50
HS6 Latrell Sprewell 1.00 2.50
HS7 Larry Johnson 1.00 2.50
HS8 Eddie Jones 1.00 2.50
HS9 Karl Malone 1.25 3.00
HS10 John Starks .75 2.00
HS11 Scottie Pippen 1.50 4.00
HS12 Shawn Kemp 1.00 2.50
HS13 Chris Webber 1.25 3.00
HS14 Isaiah Rider 1.00 2.50
HS15 Robert Horry .75 2.00

1995-96 Finest Mystery

Inserted at a rate of one in every first and second series pack, cards from this 44-piece standard-size set were 1.25 times easier to pull than regular issue cards. The set contains a selection of some of the NBA's top stars and rookies. The first twenty-two cards, issued exclusively in first series packs, were designed in three different parallel styles (Bordered, Borderless and Borderless Refractors). The last twenty-two cards, issued exclusively in second series packs, were also designed in three different parallel styles (Bronze, Silver and Gold). Collectors had to peel off a dark protective coating to find out what version of the card they had obtained. The first series Mystery cards feature a radically different design to the second series. Each first series Bordered card front features a bronze outline, framing a cut-out action shot of the player against a metallic basketball background. The second series Bronze cards feature a mosaic-style, tiled border with bronze-colored features, framing a cut-out action shot of the player. The prices listed below are for the more common Bordered and Bronze cards. Values provided below are for peeled cards.

COMPLETE SET (44) 20.00 45.00
COMP.BORDER.SER.1 (22) 12.50 30.00
COMP.BRONZE SER.2 (22) 7.50 15.00
ONE BORDER PER SER.1 PACK
*BDLS./SILVER: 1.5X TO 4X HI COLUMN
*SILVER RCs: 1.25X TO 3X HI
BDLS: SER.1 STATED ODDS 1:24
SILVER: SER.2 STATED ODDS 1:24
M1 Michael Jordan 6.00 15.00
M2 Grant Hill 1.00 2.50
M3 Anfernee Hardaway 1.00 2.50
M4 Shawn Kemp .60 1.50
M5 Kenny Anderson .50 1.25
M6 Charles Barkley 1.00 2.50
M7 Latrell Sprewell .60 1.50
M8 Chris Webber .75 2.00
M9 Jason Kidd 1.00 2.50
M10 Glenn Robinson .50 1.25
M11 David Robinson 1.00 2.50
M12 Karl Malone .75 2.00
M13 Larry Johnson .60 1.50
M14 Reggie Miller .75 2.00
M15 Scottie Pippen 1.00 2.50
M16 Patrick Ewing .75 2.00
M17 Mitch Richmond .60 1.50
M18 Glen Rice .60 1.50
M19 Jamal Mashburn .60 1.50
M20 Juwan Howard .60 1.50
M21 Hakeem Olajuwon .75 2.00
M22 Shaquille O'Neal 1.50 4.00
M23 Alonzo Mourning .60 1.50
M24 Dennis Rodman 1.00 2.50
M25 Joe Dumars .50 1.25
M26 Tim Hardaway .50 1.25
M27 Clyde Drexler .60 1.50
M28 Jerry Stackhouse 1.50 4.00
M29 John Stockton .60 1.50
M30 Derrick Coleman .40 1.00
M31 Michael Finley 1.50 4.00
M32 Glen Rice .50 1.25
M33 Mahmoud Abdul-Rauf .30 .75
M34 Anthony Mason .30 .75
M35 Nick Van Exel .50 1.25
M36 Vin Baker .40 1.00
M37 Horace Grant .40 1.00
M38 John Starks .40 1.00
M39 Clarence Weatherspoon .30 .75
M40 Kevin Johnson .50 1.25
M41 Joe Smith .60 1.50
M42 Dikembe Mutombo .50 1.25
M43 Damon Stoudamire 1.25 3.00
M44 Antonio McDyess .60 1.50

1995-96 Finest Mystery Borderless Refractors/Gold

*BDLS.REF: 8X TO 20X VALUE
*GOLD STARS: 6X TO 15X VALUE
*GOLD RCs: 4X TO 10X VALUE
BDLS RF: SER.1 STATED ODDS 1:96
GOLD: SER.2 STATED ODDS 1:96

1995-96 Finest Rack Pack

Randomly inserted into packs at a rate of one in 72, cards from this 7-card set features a selection of top rookies from the 1995-96 campaign. Card fronts feature a colorful "swirl-like" background with a player photo and the set name "Rack Pack" underneath the photo. Card backs feature biographical information, a headshot and a brief commentary. Values below are for unpeeled cards. Peeled cards generally trade for ten to twenty-five percent less.

COMPLETE SET (7) 20.00 50.00
SER.2 STATED ODDS 1:72 HOB, 1:96 RET
RP1 Jerry Stackhouse 6.00 15.00
RP2 Brent Barry 3.00 8.00
RP3 Damon Stoudamire 5.00 12.00
RP4 Joe Smith 2.50 6.00
RP5 Michael Finley 6.00 15.00
RP6 Antonio McDyess 2.50 6.00
RP7 Rasheed Wallace 6.00 15.00

1995-96 Finest Rack Pack Refractors Test

This seven-card set is a parallel to the regular Rack Pack insert. The cards feature the "classic" regular refractor technology. These cards are considered test issues since they were never intended to be released to the public. It is unknown how they made their way into the market as these cards were not inserted into packs.

RP1 Jerry Stackhouse 50.00 125.00
RP2 Brent Barry 25.00 60.00
RP3 Damon Stoudamire 40.00 100.00
RP4 Joe Smith 20.00 50.00
RP5 Michael Finley 50.00 125.00
RP6 Antonio McDyess 20.00 50.00
RP7 Rasheed Wallace 50.00 125.00

1995-96 Finest Veteran/Rookie

Randomly inserted in second series packs at a rate of one in 24, this 29-card set features rookie/veteran duos from a selection of NBA teams. The cards are dual-sided with each player getting a full photo on a separate side. Prices provided below are for unpeeled cards. Peeled cards generally trade for about ten to twenty-five percent less.

COMPLETE SET (29) 125.00 250.00
SER.2 STATED ODDS 1:24 HOB, 1:18 RET
RV1 J.Smith/L.Sprewell 4.00 10.00
RV2 A.McDyess/Mutombo 5.00 12.00
RV3 Stackhouse/W'spoon 5.00 12.00
RV4 R.Wallace/C.Webber 8.00 20.00
RV5 K.Garnett/T.Gugliotta 12.00 30.00
RV6 B.Reeves/G.Anthony 3.00 8.00
RV7 Stoudamire/Anderson 4.00 10.00
RV8 S.Respert/V.Baker 2.00 5.00
RV9 E.O'Bannon/A.Gilliam 2.00 5.00
RV10 K.Thomas/Mourning 4.00 10.00
RV11 G.Trent/R.Strickland 2.50 6.00
RV12 C.Parks/J.Mashburn 2.00 5.00
RV13 Williamson/Richmond 3.00 8.00
RV14 E.Williams/D.Radja 2.00 5.00
RV15 B.Barry/L.Vaught 2.50 6.00
RV16 A.Henderson/M.Blaylock 2.50 6.00
RV17 B.Sura/T.Brandon 2.50 6.00
RV18 T.Ratliff/G.Hill 5.00 12.00
RV19 R.Childress/R.Strickland 2.00 5.00
RV20 J.Caffey/M.Jordan 15.00 40.00
RV21 M.Finley/K.Johnson 6.00 15.00
RV22 G.Zidek/L.Johnson 2.50 6.00
RV23 T.Best/R.Miller 4.00 10.00
RV24 L.Meyer/J.Kidd 4.00 10.00
RV25 D.Vaughn/S.O'Neal 10.00 25.00
RV26 S.Ford/S.Kemp 2.50 6.00
RV27 M.Bennett/C.Barkley 4.00 10.00
RV28 G.Ostertag/K.Malone 4.00 10.00
RV29 Alexander/D.Robinson 4.00 10.00

1996-97 Finest

The 1996-97 Finest set was issued in two series totaling 291 cards. The 6-card packs retail for $5.00 each. The series one set is divided into 3-tiers of collectiblity with cards B1-B100 defined as "common" cards, S101-S127 defined as "uncommon" and inserted at a rate of 1:4 packs and G128-G146 defined as "rare" and inserted at a rate of 1:24 packs. Each card is also arranged into individually designed theme sets - Gladiators, Maestros, Apprentices and Sterling. The series two set is also divided into 3-tiers of collectiblity with cards B147-B246 defined as "common", S247-S273 defined as "uncommon" and inserted at a rate of 1:4 packs and G274-G291 defined as "rare" and inserted at a rate of 1:24 packs. Each card is also arranged into individually designed theme sets - Mainstays, Sterling, Heirs and Foundations. Prices below are for unpeeled cards. Peeled cards generally trade for ten to twenty-five percent less. Card numbers 7 and 134 do not exist. The Christian Laettner bronze, Patrick Ewing gold and Jeff Hornacek gold were all numbered 136. Card number 269 (Kobe Bryant gold) is considered part of the gold set, while card number 289 (Shaquille O'Neal silver) is considered part of the silver set, though they are both out of "set" order. The set is condition sensitive.

COMPLETE SET (291) 300.00 600.00
COMPLETE SERIES 1 (146) 150.00 350.00
COMPLETE SERIES 2 (145) 150.00 300.00
COMP.BRONZE SET (200) 70.00 140.00
COMP.BRONZE SER.1 (100) 50.00 100.00
COMP.BRONZE SER.2 (100) 20.00 40.00
SILVER: SER.1/2 STATED ODDS 1:4
GOLD: SER.1/2 STATED ODDS 1:24
CARD NUMBERS 7 AND 134 DO NOT EXIST
LAETTNR B EWING G HORNCEK G #'d 136
NUMBER 269 PART OF GOLD SET
NUMBER 289 PART OF SILVER SET
CONDITION SENSITIVE SET
1 Scottie Pippen B .60 1.50
2 Tim Legler B .25 .60
3 Rex Walters B .25 .60
4 Calbert Cheaney B .25 .60
5 Dennis Rodman B .75 2.00
6 Tyrone Hill B .25 .60
8 Dell Curry B .25 .60
9 Olden Polynice B .25 .60
10 John Wallace B RC .75 2.00
11 Martin Muursepp B RC .50 1.25
12 Chuck Person B .30 .75
13 Grant Hill B .60 1.50
14 Shawn Kemp B .40 1.00
15 B.J. Armstrong B .25 .60
16 Gary Trent B .25 .60
17 Scott Williams B .25 .60
18 Dino Radja B .25 .60
19 Roy Rogers B RC .60 1.50
20 Tony Delk B RC .75 2.00
21 Clifford Robinson B .25 .60
22 Ray Allen B RC 3.00 8.00
23 Clyde Drexler B .50 1.25
24 Elliot Perry B .25 .60
25 Gary Payton B .40 1.00
26 Dale Davis B .25 .60
27 Horace Grant B .30 .75
28 Brian Evans B RC .75 2.00
29 Joe Smith B .30 .75
30 Reggie Miller B .50 1.25
31 Jermaine O'Neal B RC 1.25 3.00
32 Avery Johnson B .30 .75
33 Ed O'Bannon B .25 .60
34 Cedric Ceballos B .25 .60
35 Jamal Mashburn B .30 .75
36 Micheal Williams B .25 .60
37 Detlef Schrempf B .40 1.00
38 Damon Stoudamire B .30 .75
39 Jason Kidd B .60 1.50
40 Tom Gugliotta B .25 .60
41 Arvydas Sabonis B .30 .75
42 Samaki Walker B RC .60 1.50
43 Derek Fisher B RC 1.00 2.50
44 Patrick Ewing B .50 1.25
45 Bryant Reeves B .25 .60
46 Mookie Blaylock B .25 .60
47 George Zidek B .25 .60
48 Jerry Stackhouse B .50 1.25
49 Vin Baker B .30 .75
50 Michael Jordan B 3.00 8.00
51 Terrell Brandon B .25 .60
52 Karl Malone B .50 1.25
53 Lorenzen Wright B RC .60 1.50
54 Shareef Abdur-Rahim B RC 1.25 3.00
55 Kurt Thomas B .25 .60
56 Glen Rice B .40 1.00
57 Shawn Bradley B .25 .60
58 Todd Fuller B RC .50 1.25
59 Dale Ellis B .25 .60
60 David Robinson B .60 1.50
61 Doug Christie B .25 .60
62 Stephon Marbury B RC 2.00 5.00
63 Hakeem Olajuwon B .50 1.25
64 Lindsey Hunter B .25 .60
65 Anfernee Hardaway B .60 1.50
66 Kevin Garnett B 1.00 2.50
67 Kendall Gill B .25 .60
68 Sean Elliott B .40 1.00
69 Allen Iverson B RC 4.00 10.00
70 Erick Dampier B RC .75 2.00
71 Jerome Williams B RC .60 1.50
72 Charles Jones B .25 .60
73 Danny Manning B .30 .75
74 Kobe Bryant B RC 12.00 30.00
75 Steve Nash B RC 4.00 10.00
76 Sam Perkins B .25 .60
77 Horace Grant B .30 .75
78 Alonzo Mourning B .50 1.25
79 Kerry Kittles B RC .75 2.00
80 LaPhonso Ellis B .25 .60
81 Michael Finley B .50 1.25
82 Marcus Camby B RC 1.25 3.00
83 Antonio McDyess B .40 1.00
84 Antoine Walker B RC 1.25 3.00
85 Juwan Howard B .30 .75
86 Bryon Russell B .25 .60
87 Walter McCarty B RC .75 2.00
88 Priest Lauderdale B RC .50 1.25
89 Clarence Weatherspoon B .25 .60
90 John Stockton B .50 1.25
91 Mitch Richmond B .40 1.00
92 Dontae' Jones B RC .75 2.00
93 Michael Smith B .25 .60
94 Brent Barry B .30 .75
95 Chris Mills B .25 .60
96 Dee Brown B .25 .60
97 Terry Dehere B .25 .60
98 Danny Ferry B .25 .60
99 Gheorghe Muresan B .25 .60
100 Checklist B .25 .60
101 Jim Jackson S .60 1.50
102 Cedric Ceballos S .60 1.50
103 Glen Rice S 1.00 2.50
104 Tom Gugliotta S .60 1.50
105 Mario Elie S .60 1.50
106 Nick Anderson S .60 1.50
107 Glenn Robinson S .75 2.00
108 Terrell Brandon S .60 1.50
109 Tim Hardaway S 1.00 2.50
110 John Stockton S 1.25 3.00
111 Brent Barry S .75 2.00
112 Mookie Blaylock S .60 1.50
113 Tyus Edney S .60 1.50
114 Gary Payton S 1.00 2.50
115 Joe Smith S .75 2.00
116 Karl Malone S 1.25 3.00
117 Dino Radja S .60 1.50
118 Alonzo Mourning S 1.25 3.00
119 Bryant Stith S .60 1.50
120 Derrick McKey S .60 1.50
121 Clyde Drexler S 1.25 3.00
122 Michael Finley S 1.25 3.00
123 Sean Elliott S 1.00 2.50
124 Hakeem Olajuwon S 1.25 3.00
125 Joe Dumars S 1.00 2.50
126 Shawn Bradley S .60 1.50
127 Michael Jordan S 8.00 20.00
128 Latrell Sprewell G 3.00 8.00
129 Anfernee Hardaway G 5.00 12.00
130 Grant Hill G 5.00 12.00
131 Damon Stoudamire G 2.50 6.00
132 David Robinson G 5.00 12.00
133 Scottie Pippen G 5.00 12.00
135 Jason Kidd G 5.00 12.00
136A Jeff Hornacek G 2.50 6.00
136B Patrick Ewing G UER 4.00 10.00
136C Christian Laettner B UER .30 .75
137 Jerry Stackhouse G 4.00 10.00
138 Kevin Garnett G 8.00 20.00
139 Mitch Richmond G 3.00 8.00
140 Juwan Howard G 2.50 6.00
141 Reggie Miller G 4.00 10.00
142 Christian Laettner G 2.50 6.00
143 Vin Baker G 2.50 6.00
144 Shawn Kemp G 3.00 8.00
145 Dennis Rodman G 6.00 15.00
146 Shaquille O'Neal G 8.00 20.00
147 Mookie Blaylock B .25 .60
148 Derek Harper B .30 .75
149 Gerald Wilkins B .25 .60
150 Adam Keefe B .25 .60
151 Billy Owens B .25 .60
152 Terrell Brandon B .25 .60
153 Antonio Davis B .25 .60
154 Muggsy Bogues B .30 .75
155 Cherokee Parks B .25 .60
156 Rasheed Wallace B .50 1.25
157 Lee Mayberry B .25 .60
158 Craig Ehlo B .25 .60
159 Todd Fuller B .25 .60
160 Charles Barkley B .60 1.50
161 Glenn Robinson B .30 .75
162 Charles Oakley B .30 .75
163 Chris Webber B .50 1.25
164 Frank Brickowski B .25 .60
165 Mark Jackson B .30 .75
166 Jayson Williams B .25 .60
167 Clarence Weatherspoon B .25 .60
168 Toni Kukoc B .40 1.00
169 Alan Henderson B .25 .60
170 Tony Delk B .40 1.00
171 Jamal Mashburn B .30 .75
172 Vinny Del Negro B .25 .60
173 Greg Ostertag B .25 .60
174 Shawn Bradley B .25 .60
175 Gheorghe Muresan B .25 .60
176 Brent Price B .25 .60
177 Rick Fox B .25 .60
178 Stacey Augmon B .30 .75
179 P.J. Brown B .25 .60
180 Jim Jackson B .25 .60
181 Hersey Hawkins B .25 .60
182 Danny Manning B .30 .75
183 Dennis Scott B .25 .60
184 Tom Gugliotta B .25 .60
185 Tyrone Hill B .25 .60
186 Malik Sealy B .25 .60
187 John Starks B .30 .75
188 Mark Price B .40 1.00
189 Elden Campbell B .25 .60
190 Mahmoud Abdul-Rauf B .25 .60
191 Will Perdue B .25 .60
192 Nate McMillan B .25 .60
193 Robert Horry B .30 .75
194 Dino Radja B .25 .60
195 Loy Vaught B .25 .60
196 Dikembe Mutombo B .40 1.00
197 Eric Montross B .25 .60
198 Sasha Danilovic B .25 .60
199 Kenny Anderson B .30 .75
200 Sean Elliott B .40 1.00
201 Mark West B .25 .60
202 Vlade Divac B .40 1.00
203 Joe Dumars B .40 1.00
204 Allan Houston B .30 .75
205 Kevin Garnett B 1.00 2.50
206 Rod Strickland B .25 .60
207 Robert Parish B .40 1.00
208 Jalen Rose B .30 .75
209 Armon Gilliam B .25 .60
210 Kerry Kittles B .40 1.00
211 Derrick Coleman B .30 .75
212 Greg Anthony B .25 .60
213 Joe Smith B .30 .75
214 Steve Smith B .30 .75
215 Tim Hardaway B .40 1.00
216 Tyus Edney B .25 .60
217 Steve Nash B 2.00 5.00
218 Anthony Mason B .25 .60
219 Otis Thorpe B .25 .60
220 Eddie Jones B .40 1.00
221 Rik Smits B .30 .75
222 Isaiah Rider B .30 .75
223 Bobby Phills B .25 .60
224 Antoine Walker B .60 1.50
225 Rod Strickland B .25 .60
226 Hubert Davis B .25 .60
227 Eric Williams B .25 .60
228 Danny Manning B .30 .75
229 Dominique Wilkins B .50 1.25
230 Brian Shaw B .25 .60
231 Larry Johnson B .40 1.00
232 Kevin Willis B .25 .60
233 Bryant Stith B .25 .60
234 Blue Edwards B .25 .60
235 Robert Pack B .25 .60
236 Brian Grant B .30 .75
237 Latrell Sprewell B .40 1.00
238 Glen Rice B .40 1.00
239 Jerome Williams B .30 .75
240 Allen Iverson B 2.00 5.00
241 Popeye Jones B .25 .60
242 Clifford Robinson B .25 .60
243 Shaquille O'Neal B 1.00 2.50
244 Vitaly Potapenko B RC .60 1.50
245 Ervin Johnson B .25 .60
246 Checklist .25 .60
247 Scottie Pippen S 1.50 4.00
248 Jason Kidd S 1.50 4.00
249 Antonio McDyess S 1.00 2.50
250 Latrell Sprewell S 1.00 2.50
251 Lorenzen Wright S .50 1.25
252 Ray Allen S 2.50 6.00
253 Stephon Marbury S 1.50 4.00
254 Patrick Ewing S 1.25 3.00
255 Anfernee Hardaway S 1.50 4.00
256 Kenny Anderson S .75 2.00
257 David Robinson S 1.50 4.00
258 Marcus Camby S 1.00 2.50
259 Shareef Abdur-Rahim S 1.00 2.50
260 Dennis Rodman S 2.00 5.00
261 Juwan Howard S .75 2.00
262 Damon Stoudamire S .75 2.00
263 Shawn Kemp S 1.00 2.50
264 Mitch Richmond S 1.00 2.50
265 Jerry Stackhouse S 1.25 3.00
266 Horace Grant S .75 2.00
267 Kerry Kittles S .60 1.50
268 Vin Baker S .75 2.00
269 Kobe Bryant G 60.00 150.00
270 Reggie Miller S 1.25 3.00
271 Grant Hill S 1.50 4.00
272 Oliver Miller S .60 1.50
273 Chris Webber S 1.25 3.00
274 Dikembe Mutombo G 3.00 8.00
275 Antonio McDyess G 3.00 8.00
276 Clyde Drexler G 4.00 10.00
277 Brent Barry G 2.50 6.00
278 Tim Hardaway G 3.00 8.00
279 Glenn Robinson G 2.50 6.00
280 Allen Iverson G 10.00 25.00
281 Hakeem Olajuwon G 4.00 10.00
282 Marcus Camby G 3.00 8.00
283 John Stockton G 4.00 10.00
284 Shareef Abdur-Rahim G 3.00 8.00
285 Karl Malone G 4.00 10.00
286 Gary Payton G 3.00 8.00
287 Stephon Marbury G 5.00 12.00
288 Alonzo Mourning G 4.00 10.00
289 Shaquille O'Neal S 2.50 6.00
290 Charles Barkley G 5.00 12.00
291 Michael Jordan G 25.00 60.00

1996-97 Finest Refractors

*BRONZE STARS: 5X TO 12X BASIC CARDS
*BRONZE RCs: 2.5X TO 6X HI
BRONZE: SER.1/2 STATED ODDS 1:12
*SILVER STARS: 2X TO 5X BASIC CARDS
*SILVER RCs: 1.25X TO 3X BASIC CARDS
SILVER: SER.1/2 STATED ODDS 1:48
*GOLD STARS/RCs: 1.25X TO 3X BASIC CARDS
GOLD: SER.1/2 STATED ODDS 1:288
LAETTNR B EWING G HORNCEK G #'d 136
74 Kobe Bryant B 175.00 350.00
127 Michael Jordan S 50.00 120.00
280 Allen Iverson G 50.00 125.00
290 Charles Barkley G 20.00 50.00
291 Michael Jordan G 400.00 800.00

1997-98 Finest Promos

COMPLETE SET (6) 2.50 6.00
27 Chris Webber .60 1.50
45 Vin Baker .50 1.25
57 Allen Iverson 1.25 3.00
67 Eddie Jones .60 1.50
68 Joe Smith .50 1.25
80 Gary Payton .60 1.50

1997-98 Finest

The complete set of Finest contained 326 total cards with the series one set containing 173 cards and the series two set containing 153. Both series were released in six card packs that carried a suggested retail price of $5. Like last year, the set is divided into three tiers: bronze, silver and gold. The bronze, or common, cards are the basic and encompass cards 1-120 and 174-273. The silver, or uncommon, cards were inserted at a rate of one in four packs and encompass cards 121-153 and cards 274-306. The gold, or rare, cards were inserted at a rate of one in 24 and encompass cards 154-173 and cards 307-326. Prices listed below are for unpeeled cards. Peeled cards generally trade for 75% of the listed prices. Please note that card "P68" was given out to dealers and members of the hobby press as a promotional card.

COMPLETE SET (326) 300.00 600.00
COMPLETE SERIES 1 (173) 150.00 300.00
COMPLETE SERIES 2 (153) 150.00 300.00
SILVER: SER.1/2 STATED ODDS 1:4
GOLD: SER.1/2 STATED ODDS 1:24
1 Scottie Pippen B .50 1.25
2 Tim Hardaway B .30 .75
3 Bo Outlaw B .20 .50
4 Rik Smits B .25 .60
5 Dale Ellis B .20 .50
6 Clyde Drexler B .40 1.00
7 Steve Smith B .25 .60
8 Nick Anderson B .20 .50
9 Juwan Howard B .25 .60
10 Cedric Ceballos B .20 .50
11 Shawn Bradley B .20 .50
12 Loy Vaught B .20 .50
13 Todd Day B .20 .50
14 Glen Rice B .30 .75
15 Bryant Stith B .20 .50
16 Bob Sura B .20 .50
17 Derrick McKey B .20 .50
18 Ray Allen B .40 1.00
19 Stephon Marbury B .40 1.00
20 David Robinson B .50 1.25
21 Anthony Peeler B .20 .50
22 Isaiah Rider B .25 .60
23 Mookie Blaylock B .20 .50
24 Damon Stoudamire B .25 .60
25 Rod Strickland B .20 .50
26 Glenn Robinson B .25 .60
27 Chris Webber B .30 .75
28 Christian Laettner B .25 .60
29 Joe Dumars B .30 .75
30 Mark Price B .30 .75
31 Jamal Mashburn B .25 .60
32 Danny Manning B .25 .60
33 John Stockton B .40 1.00
34 Detlef Schrempf B .30 .75
35 Tyus Edney B .20 .50
36 Chris Childs B .20 .50
37 Dana Barros B .20 .50
38 Bobby Phills B .20 .50
39 Michael Jordan B 2.50 6.00
40 Grant Hill B .50 1.25
41 Brent Barry B .25 .60
42 Rony Seikaly B .20 .50
43 Shareef Abdur-Rahim B .30 .75
44 Dominique Wilkins B .40 1.00
45 Vin Baker B .25 .60
46 Kendall Gill B .20 .50
47 Muggsy Bogues B .25 .60
48 Hakeem Olajuwon B .40 1.00
49 Reggie Miller B .40 1.00
50 Shaquille O'Neal B .75 2.00
51 Antonio McDyess B .25 .60
52 Michael Finley B .30 .75
53 Jerry Stackhouse B .30 .75
54 Brian Grant B .20 .50
55 Greg Anthony B .20 .50
56 Patrick Ewing B .40 1.00
57 Allen Iverson B .60 1.50
58 Rasheed Wallace B .30 .75
59 Shawn Kemp B .30 .75
60 Bryant Reeves B .20 .50
61 Kevin Garnett B .50 1.25
62 Allan Houston B .25 .60
63 Stacey Augmon B .25 .60
64 Rick Fox B .20 .50
65 Derek Harper B .25 .60
66 Lindsey Hunter B .20 .50
67 Eddie Jones B .30 .75
68 Joe Smith B .25 .60
69 Alonzo Mourning B .40 1.00
70 LaPhonso Ellis B .20 .50
71 Tyrone Hill B .20 .50
72 Charles Barkley B .50 1.25
73 Malik Sealy B .20 .50
74 Shandon Anderson B .20 .50
75 Arvydas Sabonis B .25 .60
76 Tom Gugliotta B .20 .50
77 Anfernee Hardaway B .50 1.25
78 Sean Elliott B .30 .75
79 Marcus Camby B .30 .75
80 Gary Payton B .30 .75
81 Kerry Kittles B .20 .50
82 Dikembe Mutombo B .30 .75
83 Antoine Walker B .30 .75
84 Terrell Brandon B .20 .50
85 Otis Thorpe B .20 .50
86 Mark Jackson B .25 .60
87 A.C. Green B .25 .60
88 John Starks B .25 .60
89 Kenny Anderson B .25 .60
90 Karl Malone B .40 1.00
91 Mitch Richmond B .30 .75
92 Derrick Coleman B .25 .60
93 Horace Grant B .25 .60
94 John Williams B .20 .50
95 Jason Kidd B .50 1.25
96 Mahmoud Abdul-Rauf B .20 .50
97 Walt Williams B .20 .50
98 Anthony Mason B .20 .50
99 Latrell Sprewell B .30 .75
100 Checklist .20 .50
101 Tim Duncan B RC 2.50 6.00
102 Keith Van Horn B RC .75 2.00
103 Chauncey Billups B RC 1.50 4.00
104 Antonio Daniels B RC .50 1.25
105 Tony Battie B RC .50 1.25
106 Tim Thomas B RC .60 1.50
107 Tracy McGrady B RC 2.00 5.00
108 Adonal Foyle B RC .40 1.00
109 Maurice Taylor B RC .50 1.25
110 Austin Croshere B RC .40 1.00
111 Bobby Jackson B RC .60 1.50
112 Olivier Saint-Jean B RC .40 1.00
113 John Thomas B RC .30 .75
114 Derek Anderson B RC .50 1.25
115 Brevin Knight B RC .50 1.25
116 Charles Smith B RC .40 1.00
117 Johnny Taylor B RC .40 1.00
118 Jacque Vaughn B RC .40 1.00
119 Anthony Parker B RC .50 1.25
120 Paul Grant B RC .30 .75
121 Stephon Marbury S 1.25 3.00
122 Terrell Brandon S .60 1.50
123 Dikembe Mutombo S 1.00 2.50
124 Patrick Ewing S 1.25 3.00
125 Scottie Pippen S 1.50 4.00
126 Antoine Walker S 1.00 2.50
127 Karl Malone S 1.25 3.00
128 Sean Elliott S 1.00 2.50
129 Chris Webber S 1.00 2.50
130 Shawn Kemp S 1.00 2.50
131 Hakeem Olajuwon S 1.25 3.00
132 Tim Hardaway S 1.00 2.50
133 Glen Rice S 1.00 2.50
134 Vin Baker S .75 2.00
135 Jim Jackson S .60 1.50
136 Kevin Garnett S 1.50 4.00
137 Kobe Bryant S 6.00 15.00
138 Damon Stoudamire S .75 2.00
139 Larry Johnson S 1.00 2.50
140 Latrell Sprewell S 1.00 2.50
141 Lorenzen Wright S .60 1.50
142 Toni Kukoc S 1.00 2.50
143 Allen Iverson S 2.00 5.00
144 Elden Campbell S .60 1.50
145 Tom Gugliotta S .60 1.50
146 David Robinson S 1.50 4.00
147 Jayson Williams S .60 1.50
148 Shaquille O'Neal S 2.50 6.00
149 Grant Hill S 1.50 4.00
150 Reggie Miller S 1.25 3.00
151 Clyde Drexler S 1.25 3.00
152 Ray Allen S 1.25 3.00
153 Eddie Jones S 1.00 2.50
154 Michael Jordan G 30.00 80.00
155 Dominique Wilkins G 5.00 12.00
156 Charles Barkley G 6.00 15.00
157 Jerry Stackhouse G 4.00 10.00
158 Juwan Howard G 3.00 8.00
159 Marcus Camby G 4.00 10.00
160 Christian Laettner G 3.00 8.00
161 Anthony Mason G 2.50 6.00
162 Joe Smith G 3.00 8.00
163 Kerry Kittles G 2.50 6.00
164 Mitch Richmond G 4.00 10.00
165 Shareef Abdur-Rahim G 4.00 10.00
166 Alonzo Mourning G 5.00 12.00
167 Dennis Rodman G 8.00 20.00
168 Antonio McDyess G 3.00 8.00
169 Shawn Bradley G 2.50 6.00
170 Anfernee Hardaway G 6.00 15.00
171 Jason Kidd G 6.00 15.00
172 Gary Payton G 4.00 10.00
173 John Stockton G 5.00 12.00
174 Allan Houston B .25 .60
175 Bob Sura B .20 .50
176 Clyde Drexler B .40 1.00
177 Glenn Robinson B .25 .60
178 Joe Smith B .25 .60
179 Larry Johnson B .30 .75
180 Mitch Richmond B .30 .75
181 Rony Seikaly B .20 .50
182 Tyrone Hill B .20 .50
183 Allen Iverson B .60 1.50
184 Brent Barry B .25 .60
185 Damon Stoudamire B .25 .60
186 Grant Hill B .50 1.25
187 John Stockton B .40 1.00
188 Latrell Sprewell B .30 .75
189 Mookie Blaylock B .20 .50
190 Samaki Walker B .20 .50
191 Vin Baker B .25 .60
192 Alonzo Mourning B .40 1.00
193 Brevin Knight B .30 .75
194 Danny Manning B .25 .60
195 Hakeem Olajuwon B .40 1.00
196 Johnny Taylor B .25 .60
197 Lorenzen Wright B .20 .50
198 Olden Polynice B .20 .50
199 Scottie Pippen B .50 1.25
200 Lindsey Hunter B .20 .50
201 Anfernee Hardaway B .50 1.25
202 Greg Anthony B .20 .50
203 David Robinson B .50 1.25
204 Horace Grant B .25 .60
205 Calbert Cheaney B .20 .50
206 Loy Vaught B .20 .50
207 Tariq Abdul-Wahad B .25 .60
208 Sean Elliott B .30 .75
209 Rodney Rogers B .20 .50
210 Anthony Mason B .20 .50
211 Bryant Reeves B .20 .50
212 David Wesley B .20 .50
213 Isaiah Rider B .25 .60
214 Karl Malone B .40 1.00
215 Mahmoud Abdul-Rauf B .20 .50
216 Patrick Ewing B .40 1.00
217 Shaquille O'Neal B .75 2.00
218 Antoine Walker B .30 .75
219 Charles Barkley B .50 1.25
220 Dennis Rodman B .60 1.50
221 Jamal Mashburn B .25 .60
222 Kendall Gill B .20 .50
223 Malik Sealy B .20 .50
224 Rasheed Wallace B .30 .75
225 Shareef Abdur-Rahim B .30 .75
226 Antonio Daniels B .30 .75
227 Charles Oakley B .25 .60
228 Derek Anderson B .30 .75
229 Jason Kidd B .50 1.25
230 Kenny Anderson B .25 .60
231 Marcus Camby B .30 .75
232 Ray Allen B .40 1.00
233 Shawn Bradley B .20 .50
234 Antonio McDyess B .25 .60
235 Chauncey Billups B 1.00 2.50
236 Detlef Schrempf B .30 .75
237 Jayson Williams B .20 .50
238 Kerry Kittles B .20 .50
239 Jalen Rose B .25 .60
240 Reggie Miller B .40 1.00
241 Shawn Kemp B .30 .75
242 Arvydas Sabonis B .25 .60
243 Tom Gugliotta B .20 .50
244 Dikembe Mutombo B .30 .75
245 Jeff Hornacek B .25 .60
246 Kevin Garnett B .50 1.25
247 Matt Maloney B .20 .50
248 Rex Chapman B .20 .50
249 Stephon Marbury B .40 1.00
250 Austin Croshere B .25 .60
251 Chris Childs B .20 .50
252 Eddie Jones B .30 .75
253 Jerry Stackhouse B .30 .75
254 Kevin Johnson B .30 .75
255 Maurice Taylor B .30 .75
256 Chris Mullin B .30 .75
257 Terrell Brandon B .20 .50
258 Avery Johnson B .25 .60
259 Chris Webber B .30 .75
260 Gary Payton B .30 .75
261 Jim Jackson B .20 .50
262 Kobe Bryant B 1.50 4.00
263 Michael Finley B .30 .75
264 Rod Strickland B .20 .50
265 Tim Hardaway B .30 .75
266 B.J. Armstrong B .20 .50
267 Christian Laettner B .25 .60
268 Glen Rice B .30 .75
269 Joe Dumars B .30 .75
270 LaPhonso Ellis B .20 .50
271 Michael Jordan B 2.50 6.00
272 Ron Mercer B RC .60 1.50
273 Checklist B .20 .50
274 Anfernee Hardaway S 1.50 4.00
275 Dennis Rodman S 2.00 5.00
276 Gary Payton S 1.00 2.50
277 Jamal Mashburn S .75 2.00
278 Shareef Abdur-Rahim S 1.00 2.50
279 Steve Smith S .75 2.00
280 Tony Battie S .60 1.50
281 Alonzo Mourning S 1.25 3.00
282 Bobby Jackson S .75 2.00
283 Christian Laettner S .75 2.00
284 Jerry Stackhouse S 1.00 2.50
285 Terrell Brandon S .60 1.50
286 Chauncey Billups S 2.00 5.00
287 Michael Jordan S 10.00 25.00
288 Glenn Robinson S .75 2.00
289 Jason Kidd S 1.50 4.00
290 Joe Smith S .75 2.00
291 Michael Finley S 1.00 2.50
292 Rod Strickland S .60 1.50
293 Ron Mercer S .75 2.00
294 Tracy McGrady S 2.50 6.00
295 Adonal Foyle S .50 1.25
296 Marcus Camby S 1.00 2.50
297 John Stockton S 1.25 3.00
298 Kerry Kittles S .60 1.50
299 Mitch Richmond S 1.00 2.50
300 Shawn Bradley S .60 1.50
301 Anthony Mason S .60 1.50
302 Antonio Daniels S .60 1.50
303 Antonio McDyess S .75 2.00
304 Charles Barkley S 1.50 4.00
305 Keith Van Horn S 1.00 2.50
306 Tim Duncan S 3.00 8.00
307 Dikembe Mutombo G 4.00 10.00
308 Grant Hill G 6.00 15.00
309 Shaquille O'Neal G 10.00 25.00
310 Keith Van Horn G 4.00 10.00
311 Shawn Kemp G 4.00 10.00
312 Antoine Walker G 4.00 10.00
313 Hakeem Olajuwon G 5.00 12.00
314 Vin Baker G 3.00 8.00
315 Patrick Ewing G 5.00 12.00
316 Tracy McGrady G 10.00 25.00
317 Glen Rice G 4.00 10.00
318 Reggie Miller G 5.00 12.00
319 Kevin Garnett G 6.00 15.00
320 Allen Iverson G 8.00 20.00
321 Karl Malone G 5.00 12.00
322 Scottie Pippen G 6.00 15.00
323 Kobe Bryant G 12.00 30.00
324 Stephon Marbury G 5.00 12.00
325 Tim Duncan G 20.00 50.00
326 Chris Webber G 4.00 10.00

1997-98 Finest Embossed

*SILVER: .5X TO 1.25X BASE HI
*SILVER RCs: .4X TO 1X BASE HI
SILVER: SER.1/2 STATED ODDS 1:16
*GOLD STARS: .6X TO 1.5X BASE HI
*GOLD RCs: .5X TO 1.25X BASE HI
GOLD: SER.1/2 STATED ODDS 1:96
154 Michael Jordan G 100.00 250.00

1997-98 Finest Embossed Refractors

*SILVER STARS/RCs: 4X TO 10X BASE HI
SILVER: SER.1/2 STATED ODDS 1:192
STATED PRINT RUN 263 SERIAL #'d SETS
ALL SILVER CARDS ARE NON DIE CUT
*GOLD STARS/RCs: 8X TO 20X BASE HI
GOLD: SER.1/2 STATED ODDS 1:1152
STATED PRINT RUN 74 SERIAL #'d SETS
137 Kobe Bryant S 125.00 250.00
154 Michael Jordan G 5000.00 7000.00
156 Charles Barkley G 250.00 500.00
167 Dennis Rodman G 500.00 1000.00
170 Anfernee Hardaway G 200.00 400.00
287 Michael Jordan S 200.00 400.00
308 Grant Hill G 200.00 400.00
309 Shaquille O'Neal G 300.00 600.00
313 Hakeem Olajuwon G 150.00 300.00
318 Reggie Miller G 175.00 350.00
322 Scottie Pippen G 300.00 600.00
323 Kobe Bryant G 1000.00 2000.00
326 Chris Webber G 150.00 300.00

1997-98 Finest Refractors

*BRONZE STARS: 4X TO 10X BASIC CARDS
BRONZE: SER.1/2 STATED ODDS 1:12
*SILVER: 2X TO 5X BASIC CARDS
SILVER: SER.1/2 STATED ODDS 1:48
STATED PRINT RUN 1090 SERIAL #'d SETS
*GOLD STARS/RCs: 1.2X TO 3X BASIC CARDS
GOLD: SER.1/2 STATED ODDS 1:288
STATED PRINT RUN 289 SERIAL #'d SETS
39 Michael Jordan B 75.00 200.00
101 Tim Duncan B 50.00 120.00
154 Michael Jordan G 300.00 600.00
287 Michael Jordan S 100.00 250.00
323 Kobe Bryant G 150.00 300.00

1998-99 Finest Promos

COMPLETE SET (6) 2.50 6.00
PP1 Dikembe Mutombo .75 2.00
PP2 Antoine Walker .75 2.00
PP3 Reggie Miller 1.00 2.50
PP4 John Stockton 1.00 2.50
PP5 Eddie Jones .75 2.00
PP6 Gary Payton .75 2.00

1998-99 Finest

The 1998-99 Finest set was released in two series with each containing 125 cards for a total of 250. This year's edition featured a thicker 29-point stock and a base set organized by position, with each position identified by a different graphic. Each pack contained six cards with a suggested retail price of $5.

COMPLETE SET (250) 30.00 60.00
COMPLETE SERIES 1 (125) 15.00 30.00
COMPLETE SERIES 2 (125) 15.00 30.00
1 Chris Mills .20 .50
2 Matt Maloney .20 .50
3 Sam Mitchell .20 .50
4 Corliss Williamson .20 .50
5 Bryant Reeves .20 .50
6 Juwan Howard .25 .60
7 Eddie Jones .30 .75
8 Ray Allen .40 1.00
9 Larry Johnson .30 .75
10 Travis Best .20 .50
11 Isaiah Rider .25 .60
12 Hakeem Olajuwon .40 1.00
13 Gary Trent .20 .50
14 Kevin Garnett .50 1.25
15 Dikembe Mutombo .30 .75
16 Brevin Knight .20 .50
17 Keith Van Horn .30 .75
18 Theo Ratliff .25 .60
19 Tim Hardaway .30 .75
20 Blue Edwards .20 .50
21 David Wesley .20 .50
22 Jaren Jackson .20 .50
23 Nick Anderson .20 .50
24 Rodney Rogers .20 .50
25 Antonio Davis .20 .50
26 Clarence Weatherspoon .20 .50
27 Kelvin Cato .20 .50
28 Tracy McGrady .50 1.25
29 Mookie Blaylock .20 .50
30 Ron Harper .25 .60
31 Allan Houston .25 .60
32 Brian Williams .20 .50
33 John Stockton .40 1.00
34 Hersey Hawkins .20 .50
35 Donyell Marshall .20 .50
36 Mark Strickland .20 .50
37 Rod Strickland .20 .50
38 Cedric Ceballos .20 .50
39 Danny Fortson .20 .50
40 Shaquille O'Neal .75 2.00
41 Kendall Gill .20 .50
42 Allen Iverson .60 1.50
43 Travis Knight .20 .50
44 Cedric Henderson .20 .50
45 Steve Kerr .25 .60
46 Antonio McDyess .25 .60
47 Darrick Martin .20 .50
48 Shandon Anderson .20 .50
49 Shareef Abdur-Rahim .30 .75
50 Antoine Carr .20 .50
51 Jason Kidd .50 1.25
52 Calbert Cheaney .20 .50
53 Antoine Walker .30 .75
54 Greg Anthony .20 .50
55 Jeff Hornacek .25 .60
56 Reggie Miller .40 1.00
57 Lawrence Funderburke .20 .50
58 Derek Strong .20 .50
59 Robert Horry .25 .60
60 Shawn Bradley .20 .50
61 Matt Bullard .20 .50
62 Terrell Brandon .20 .50
63 Dan Majerle .30 .75
64 Jim Jackson .20 .50
65 Anthony Peeler .20 .50
66 Bo Outlaw .20 .50
67 Khalid Reeves .20 .50
68 Toni Kukoc .30 .75
69 Mario Elie .20 .50
70 Derek Anderson .20 .50
71 Jalen Rose .25 .60
72 Tyrone Corbin .20 .50
73 Anthony Mason .20 .50
74 Lamond Murray .20 .50
75 Tom Gugliotta .20 .50
76 Arvydas Sabonis .25 .60
77 Brian Shaw .20 .50
78 Rick Fox .20 .50
79 Danny Manning .25 .60
80 Lindsey Hunter .20 .50
81 Michael Jordan 2.50 6.00
82 LaPhonso Ellis .20 .50
83 David Robinson .50 1.25
84 Christian Laettner .25 .60
85 Armon Gilliam .20 .50
86 Sherman Douglas .20 .50
87 Charlie Ward .20 .50
88 Shawn Kemp .30 .75
89 Gary Payton .30 .75
90 Doug Christie .20 .50
91 Voshon Lenard .20 .50
92 Detlef Schrempf .30 .75
93 Walter McCarty .20 .50
94 Sam Cassell .25 .60
95 Jerry Stackhouse .30 .75
96 Billy Owens .20 .50
97 Matt Geiger .20 .50
98 Avery Johnson .25 .60
99 Bobby Jackson .20 .50
100 Rex Chapman .20 .50
101 Andrew DeClercq .20 .50
102 Vlade Divac .30 .75
103 Erick Strickland .20 .50
104 Dean Garrett .20 .50
105 Grant Long .20 .50
106 Adonal Foyle .20 .50
107 Isaac Austin .20 .50
108 Michael Curry .20 .50
109 Darrell Armstrong .20 .50
110 Aaron McKie .20 .50
111 Stacey Augmon .25 .60
112 Anthony Johnson .20 .50
113 Vinny Del Negro .20 .50
114 Reggie Slater .20 .50
115 Lee Mayberry .20 .50
116 Tracy Murray .20 .50
117 Scottie Pippen .50 1.25
118 Sam Perkins .20 .50
119 Derek Fisher .30 .75
120 Mark Bryant .20 .50
121 Dale Davis .20 .50
122 B.J. Armstrong .20 .50
123 Charles Barkley .50 1.25
124 Horace Grant .25 .60
125 Checklist .20 .50
126 Alonzo Mourning .40 1.00
127 Kerry Kittles .20 .50
128 Eldridge Recasner .20 .50
129 Dell Curry .20 .50
130 Jamal Mashburn .25 .60
131 Eric Piatkowski .25 .60
132 Othella Harrington .20 .50
133 Pete Chilcutt .20 .50
134 Dennis Rodman .60 1.50
135 Patrick Ewing .40 1.00
136 Danny Schayes .20 .50
137 John Williams .20 .50
138 Joe Smith .25 .60
139 Tariq Abdul-Wahad .20 .50
140 Vin Baker .25 .60
141 Elden Campbell .20 .50
142 Chris Carr .20 .50
143 John Starks .25 .60
144 Felton Spencer .20 .50
145 Mark Jackson .25 .60
146 Dana Barros .20 .50
147 Eric Williams .20 .50
148 Wesley Person .20 .50
149 Joe Dumars .30 .75
150 Steve Smith .25 .60
151 Randy Brown .20 .50
152 A.C. Green .25 .60
153 Dee Brown .20 .50
154 Brian Grant .20 .50
155 Tim Thomas .30 .75
156 Howard Eisley .20 .50
157 Malik Sealy .20 .50
158 Maurice Taylor .20 .50
159 Tyrone Hill .20 .50
160 Chris Gatling .20 .50
161 Rodrick Rhodes .20 .50
162 Muggsy Bogues .25 .60
163 Kenny Anderson .25 .60
164 Zydrunas Ilgauskas .30 .75
165 Grant Hill .50 1.25
166 Lorenzen Wright .20 .50
167 Tony Battie .25 .60
168 Bobby Phills .20 .50
169 Michael Finley .30 .75
170 Anfernee Hardaway .50 1.25
171 Terry Porter .20 .50
172 P.J. Brown .20 .50
173 Clifford Robinson .20 .50
174 Olden Polynice .20 .50
175 Kobe Bryant 1.25 3.00
176 Sean Elliott .30 .75
177 Latrell Sprewell .30 .75
178 Rik Smits .25 .60
179 Darrell Armstrong .20 .50
180 Stephon Marbury .40 1.00
181 Brent Price .20 .50
182 Danny Fortson .20 .50
183 Vitaly Potapenko .20 .50
184 Anthony Parker .20 .50
185 Glenn Robinson .25 .60
186 Erick Dampier .20 .50
187 George McCloud .20 .50
188 Rasheed Wallace .30 .75
189 Aaron Williams .20 .50
190 Tim Duncan .60 1.50
191 Chauncey Billups .40 1.00
192 Jim McIlvaine .20 .50
193 Chris Mullin .30 .75
194 George Lynch .20 .50
195 Damon Stoudamire .25 .60
196 Bryon Russell .20 .50
197 Luc Longley .25 .60
198 Ron Mercer .25 .60
199 Alan Henderson .20 .50
200 Jayson Williams .20 .50
201 Ben Wallace .25 .60
202 Elliot Perry .20 .50
203 Walt Williams .20 .50
204 Cherokee Parks .20 .50
205 Brent Barry .25 .60
206 Hubert Davis .20 .50
207 Terry Davis .20 .50
208 Loy Vaught .20 .50
209 Adam Keefe .20 .50
210 Karl Malone .40 1.00
211 Chuck Person .25 .60
212 Chris Childs .20 .50
213 Rony Seikaly .20 .50
214 Ervin Johnson .20 .50
215 Derrick McKey .20 .50
216 Jerome Williams .20 .50
217 Glen Rice .30 .75
218 Steve Nash .50 1.25
219 Nick Van Exel .25 .60
220 Chris Webber .30 .75
221 Marcus Camby .25 .60
222 Antonio Daniels .20 .50
223 Mitch Richmond .30 .75
224 Otis Thorpe .20 .50
225 Charles Oakley .25 .60
226 Michael Olowokandi RC .75 2.00
227 Mike Bibby RC 1.00 2.50
228 Raef LaFrentz RC .75 2.00
229 Antawn Jamison RC 1.00 2.50
230 Vince Carter RC 2.50 6.00
231 Robert Traylor RC .60 1.50
232 Jason Williams RC 1.50 4.00
233 Larry Hughes RC 1.25 3.00
234 Dirk Nowitzki RC 4.00 10.00
235 Paul Pierce RC 2.50 6.00
236 Bonzi Wells RC .60 1.50
237 Michael Doleac RC .50 1.25
238 Keon Clark RC .60 1.50
239 Michael Dickerson RC .60 1.50
240 Matt Harpring RC .60 1.50
241 Bryce Drew RC .40 1.00
242 Pat Garrity RC .50 1.25
243 Roshown McLeod RC .40 1.00
244 Ricky Davis RC 1.00 2.50
245 Brian Skinner RC .60 1.50
246 Tyronn Lue RC .60 1.50
247 Felipe Lopez RC .40 1.00
248 Sam Jacobson RC .50 1.25
249 Corey Benjamin RC .40 1.00
250 Nazr Mohammed RC .60 1.50

1998-99 Finest No Protectors

*STARS: 1.5X TO 4X BASE CARD HI
*RCs: .6X TO 1.5X BASE HI
SER.1/2 STATED ODDS 1:4 H/R

1998-99 Finest No Protectors Refractors

*STARS: 6X TO 15X BASE CARD HI
*RCs: 2.5X TO 6X BASE HI
SER.1/2 STATED ODDS 1:24 H/R
81 Michael Jordan 125.00 300.00
230 Vince Carter 25.00 60.00

1998-99 Finest Refractors

*REF.STARS: 3X TO 8X BASE CARD HI
*REF.RCs: 1.5X TO 4X BASE
REF: SER.1/2 STATED ODDS 1:12 H/R
81 Michael Jordan 75.00 200.00
230 Vince Carter 25.00 60.00
234 Dirk Nowitzki 25.00 60.00
235 Paul Pierce 20.00 50.00

1998-99 Finest Arena Stars

Randomly inserted in series two packs at one in 48, this 20-card set features player's who are home crowd favorites. The cards feature a semi-holographic background with stars and basketballs. The card backs are numbered with an "AS" prefix.

COMPLETE SET (20) 75.00 200.00
SER.2 STATED ODDS 1:48 H/R
AS1 Shaquille O'Neal 4.00 10.00
AS2 Stephon Marbury 2.00 5.00
AS3 Allen Iverson 3.00 8.00
AS4 John Stockton 2.00 5.00
AS5 Kobe Bryant 12.00 30.00
AS6 Alonzo Mourning 2.00 5.00
AS7 Damon Stoudamire 1.25 3.00
AS8 Scottie Pippen 2.50 6.00
AS9 Tim Hardaway 1.50 4.00
AS10 Karl Malone 2.00 5.00
AS11 Tim Duncan 3.00 8.00
AS12 Gary Payton 1.50 4.00
AS13 Antoine Walker 1.50 4.00
AS14 Keith Van Horn 1.50 4.00
AS15 Juwan Howard 1.25 3.00
AS16 David Robinson 2.50 6.00
AS17 Michael Finley 1.50 4.00
AS18 Shareef Abdur-Rahim 1.50 4.00
AS19 Michael Jordan 50.00 120.00
AS20 Vin Baker 1.25 3.00

1998-99 Finest Centurions

Randomly inserted into series one packs at a rate of one in 91, this 20-card set features players who will take the game into the year 2000. The cards are serial numbered to 500. Card backs are numbered with a "C" prefix.

SER.1 STATED ODDS 1:91 H/R
STATED PRINT RUN 500 SERIAL #'d SETS
*REF: 3X TO 8X HI COLUMN
REF: PRINT RUN 75 SERIAL #'d SETS
C1 Grant Hill 6.00 15.00
C2 Tim Thomas 4.00 10.00
C3 Eddie Jones 4.00 10.00
C4 Michael Finley 4.00 10.00
C5 Shaquille O'Neal 10.00 25.00
C6 Kobe Bryant 40.00 100.00
C7 Keith Van Horn 4.00 10.00
C8 Tim Duncan 6.00 15.00
C9 Antoine Walker 4.00 10.00
C10 Shareef Abdur-Rahim 4.00 10.00
C11 Stephon Marbury 5.00 12.00
C12 Kevin Garnett 6.00 15.00
C13 Ray Allen 5.00 12.00
C14 Kerry Kittles 2.50 6.00
C15 Allen Iverson 8.00 20.00
C16 Damon Stoudamire 3.00 8.00
C17 Brevin Knight 2.50 6.00
C18 Bryant Reeves 2.50 6.00
C19 Ron Mercer 3.00 8.00
C20 Zydrunas Ilgauskas 4.00 10.00

1998-99 Finest Court Control

Randomly inserted into series two packs at one in 76, this 20-card set features players who control the court baseline, to baseline. The cards are serially numbered to 750. Card backs contain a "CC" prefix.

SER.2 STATED ODDS 1:76 H/R
STATED PRINT RUN 750 SERIAL #'d SETS
*REF: 1.25X TO 3X HI COLUMN
REF: PRINT RUN 150 SERIAL #'d SETS
CC1 Shareef Abdur-Rahim 3.00 8.00
CC2 Keith Van Horn 3.00 8.00
CC3 Tim Duncan 6.00 15.00
CC4 Antoine Walker 3.00 8.00
CC5 Stephon Marbury 4.00 10.00
CC6 Kevin Garnett 5.00 12.00
CC7 Grant Hill 5.00 12.00
CC8 Michael Finley 3.00 8.00
CC9 Ron Mercer 2.50 6.00
CC10 Damon Stoudamire 2.50 6.00
CC11 Michael Olowokandi 2.00 5.00
CC12 Mike Bibby 2.50 6.00
CC13 Antawn Jamison 2.50 6.00
CC14 Vince Carter 8.00 20.00
CC15 Jason Williams 4.00 10.00
CC16 Larry Hughes 3.00 8.00
CC17 Paul Pierce 6.00 15.00
CC18 Michael Dickerson 1.50 4.00
CC19 Bryce Drew 1.00 2.50
CC20 Felipe Lopez 1.00 2.50

1998-99 Finest Hardwood Honors

Randomly inserted in series one packs at a rate of one in 33, this 20-card set features players that captured some of the league's most coveted awards last season with their outstanding play. Card backs feature a "H" prefix.

COMPLETE SET (20) 75.00 150.00
SER.1 STATED ODDS 1:33 H/R
H1 Michael Jordan 40.00 100.00
H2 Shaquille O'Neal 6.00 15.00
H3 Karl Malone 3.00 8.00
H4 Eddie Jones 2.50 6.00
H5 Dikembe Mutombo 2.50 6.00
H6 Wesley Person 1.50 4.00
H7 Glen Rice 2.50 6.00
H8 David Robinson 4.00 10.00
H9 Rik Smits 2.00 5.00
H10 Steve Smith 2.00 5.00
H11 Allen Iverson 5.00 12.00
H12 Jayson Williams 1.50 4.00
H13 Nick Anderson 1.50 4.00
H14 Tim Duncan 5.00 12.00
H15 Jason Kidd 4.00 10.00
H16 Alonzo Mourning 3.00 8.00
H17 Sam Cassell 2.00 5.00
H18 Alan Henderson 1.50 4.00
H19 Gary Payton 2.50 6.00
H20 Scottie Pippen 4.00 10.00

1998-99 Finest Mystery Finest

Randomly inserted in series one packs at a rate of one in 33, and series two packs at 1:36, this 40-card set features superstars of the NBA, each showcased with one of two players on the back. Card backs carry a "M" prefix.

SER.1 STATED ODDS 1:33 H/R
SER.2 STATED ODDS 1:36 H/R
M1 M.Jordan/K.Bryant 15.00 40.00
M2 K.Bryant/S.O'Neal 10.00 25.00
M3 S.O'Neal/D.Robinson 6.00 15.00
M4 D.Robinson/T.Duncan 3.00 8.00
M5 T.Duncan/K.Van Horn 2.00 5.00
M6 K.Van Horn/S.Pippen 2.00 5.00
M7 S.Pippen/S.Abdur-Rahim 4.00 10.00
M8 S.Abdur-Rahim/G.Hill 2.50 6.00
M9 G.Hill/K.Garnett 6.00 15.00
M10 K.Garnett/S.Marbury 4.00 10.00
M11 S.Marbury/G.Payton 1.50 4.00
M12 G.Payton/V.Baker 1.50 4.00
M13 V.Baker/K.Malone 1.50 4.00
M14 K.Malone/S.Kemp 3.00 8.00
M15 S.Kemp/T.Thomas 1.50 4.00
M16 T.Thomas/A.Walker 1.50 4.00
M17 A.Walker/R.Mercer 1.25 3.00
M18 R.Mercer/K.Kittles 1.25 3.00
M19 K.Kittles/E.Jones 1.25 3.00
M20 E.Jones/M.Jordan 12.00 30.00
M21 A.Mourning/S.Pippen 4.00 10.00
M22 S.Pippen/A.Walker 4.00 10.00
M23 A.Walker/S.Abdur-Rahim 2.00 5.00
M24 S.Abdur-Rahim/K.Garnett 4.00 10.00
M25 K.Garnett/K.Van Horn 2.50 6.00
M26 K.Van Horn/T.Thomas 1.25 3.00
M27 T.Thomas/G.Hill 2.00 5.00
M28 G.Hill/A.Hardaway 4.00 10.00
M29 A.Hardaway/K.Kittles 2.50 6.00
M30 K.Kittles/J.Williams 1.25 3.00
M31 J.Williams/K.Malone 1.50 4.00
M32 K.Malone/J.Stockton 2.50 6.00
M33 J.Stockton/G.Payton 2.00 5.00
M34 G.Payton/R.Mercer 1.50 4.00
M35 R.Mercer/S.Marbury 1.50 4.00
M36 S.Marbury/A.Iverson 3.00 8.00
M37 A.Iverson/K.Bryant 6.00 15.00
M38 K.Bryant/T.Duncan 6.00 15.00
M39 T.Duncan/S.O'Neal 5.00 12.00
M40 S.O'Neal/A.Mourning 5.00 12.00

1998-99 Finest Mystery Finest Refractors

*REFRACTORS: .75X TO 2X BASE CARD HI
SER.1 STATED ODDS 1:333 H/R
SER.2 STATED ODDS 1:144 H/R
M1 M.Jordan/K.Bryant 50.00 125.00

1998-99 Finest Oversized

Randomly inserted in series one boxes at one in three, and series two boxes at one per box, this 14-card set features 3 1/2" by 5" oversized Finest cards.

COMPLETE SET (14) 12.50 30.00
COMPLETE SERIES 1 (7) 10.00 20.00
COMPLETE SERIES 2 (7) 5.00 12.00
SER.1 STATED ODDS 1:3 BOXES
SER.2 STATED ODDS ONE PER BOX
*REF: .75X TO 2X HI COLUMN
REF: SER.1/2 STATED ODDS 1:12 BOXES
1 Kevin Garnett 2.00 5.00
2 Keith Van Horn 1.25 3.00
3 Shaquille O'Neal 3.00 8.00
4 Shareef Abdur-Rahim 1.25 3.00
5 Antoine Walker 1.25 3.00
6 Gary Payton 1.25 3.00
7 Scottie Pippen 2.00 5.00
8 Alonzo Mourning .75 2.00
9 Kerry Kittles .40 1.00
10 Kobe Bryant 2.50 6.00
11 Stephon Marbury .75 2.00
12 Tim Duncan 1.25 3.00
13 Ron Mercer .50 1.25
14 Karl Malone .75 2.00

1999-00 Finest Promos

COMPLETE SET (6) 2.50 6.00
PP1 Reggie Miller .60 1.50
PP2 Corliss Williamson .40 1.00
PP3 Tom Gugliotta .40 1.00
PP4 Tracy McGrady 1.00 2.50
PP5 Anfernee Hardaway 1.00 2.50
PP6 Tim Duncan 1.25 3.00

1999-00 Finest

Both series of Finest was released as a 133 card sets, totalling 266 cards. Series one contained 100 veterans and three subsets: Gems, Rookies and Sensations. The subset cards were inserted one per pack. Series two contained 91 veterans and four subsets: Gold Medal Contenders, Catalyts, Edge and Rookies. The series two rookies were serially numbered to 2000 and inserted at one in 14 packs. Each pack contained five cards that carried a suggested retail price of $4.99 per pack.

COMPLETE SET (266) 100.00 210.00
COMPLETE SERIES 1 (133) 25.00 60.00
COMPLETE SERIES 2 (133) 75.00 150.00
COMP.SERIES 2 w/o RC (118) 15.00 40.00
SER.2 RCs STATED ODDS 1:14, 1:6 HTA
SER.2 RCs PRINT RUN 2000 SERIAL #'d SETS
SUBSET CARDS INSERTED ONE PER PACK
1 Shareef Abdur-Rahim .30 .75
2 Kevin Willis .25 .60
3 Sean Elliott .40 1.00
4 Vlade Divac .40 1.00
5 Tom Gugliotta .25 .60
6 Matt Harpring .25 .60
7 Kerry Kittles .25 .60
8 Joe Smith .30 .75
9 Jamal Mashburn .30 .75
10 Tyrone Nesby RC .50 1.25
11 Alan Henderson .25 .60
12 Vitaly Potapenko .25 .60
13 Dickey Simpkins .25 .60
14 Michael Finley .40 1.00
15 Lindsey Hunter .25 .60
16 Antawn Jamison .40 1.00
17 Reggie Miller .40 1.00
18 Maurice Taylor .25 .60
19 Clarence Weatherspoon .25 .60
20 Sam Mitchell .25 .60
21 Latrell Sprewell .40 1.00
22 Michael Doleac .25 .60
23 Rex Chapman .25 .60
24 Peja Stojakovic .40 1.00
25 Vladimir Stepania .25 .60
26 Tracy McGrady .60 1.50
27 Cherokee Parks .25 .60
28 LaPhonso Ellis .25 .60
29 Hakeem Olajuwon .50 1.25
30 Adonal Foyle .25 .60
31 Bryant Stith .25 .60
32 Andrew DeClercq .25 .60
33 Toni Kukoc .40 1.00
34 Kenny Anderson .30 .75
35 Mike Bibby .40 1.00
36 Glen Rice .40 1.00
37 Avery Johnson .30 .75
38 Arvydas Sabonis .30 .75
39 Kornel David RC .50 1.25
40 Hubert Davis .25 .60
41 Grant Hill .50 1.25
42 Donyell Marshall .25 .60
43 Jalen Rose .30 .75
44 Derrick Coleman .30 .75
45 P.J. Brown .25 .60
46 Vin Baker .30 .75
47 Clifford Robinson .25 .60
48 Allan Houston .30 .75
49 Kendall Gill .25 .60
50 Matt Geiger .25 .60
51 Larry Hughes .30 .75
52 Corliss Williamson .25 .60
53 Darrell Armstrong .25 .60
54 Bobby Jackson .25 .60
55 Bryon Russell .25 .60
56 Juwan Howard .30 .75
57 Dikembe Mutombo .40 1.00
58 Eddie Jones .40 1.00
59 Randy Brown .25 .60
60 Dirk Nowitzki .75 2.00
61 Jerome Williams .25 .60
62 Scottie Pippen .60 1.50
63 Dale Davis .25 .60
64 Kobe Bryant 1.50 4.00
65 Robert Traylor .25 .60
66 Tim Hardaway .40 1.00
67 Michael Olowokandi .25 .60
68 Walter McCarty .25 .60
69 Damon Stoudamire .30 .75
70 Othella Harrington .25 .60
71 Chauncey Billups .40 1.00
72 John Starks .30 .75
73 Ricky Davis .40 1.00
74 Glenn Robinson .30 .75
75 Dean Garrett .25 .60
76 Chris Childs .25 .60
77 Shawn Kemp .40 1.00
78 Allen Iverson .75 2.00
79 Brian Grant .25 .60
80 David Robinson .60 1.50
81 Tracy Murray .25 .60
82 Howard Eisley .25 .60
83 Doug Christie .30 .75
84 Gary Payton .40 1.00
85 John Stockton .50 1.25
86 Rod Strickland .25 .60
87 Tyrone Corbin .25 .60
88 Antonio Daniels .25 .60
89 Dee Brown .25 .60
90 Antoine Walker .40 1.00
91 Theo Ratliff .30 .75
92 Larry Johnson .40 1.00
93 Stephon Marbury .30 .75
94 Brevin Knight .25 .60
95 Antonio McDyess .30 .75
96 Bison Dele .25 .60
97 Cuttino Mobley .25 .60
98 Haywoode Workman .25 .60
99 J.R. Reid .25 .60
100 Travis Best .25 .60
101 Chris Webber GEM .60 1.50
102 Grant Hill GEM .75 2.00
103 Kevin Garnett GEM 1.00 2.50
104 Jason Kidd GEM 1.00 2.50
105 Gary Payton GEM .60 1.50
106 Shaquille O'Neal GEM 1.50 4.00
107 Alonzo Mourning GEM .75 2.00
108 Karl Malone GEM .75 2.00
109 John Stockton GEM .75 2.00
110 Elton Brand RC 1.50 4.00
111 Baron Davis RC 1.50 4.00
112 A.Radojevic RC .40 1.00
113 Cal Bowdler RC .40 1.00
114 Jumaine Jones RC .50 1.25
115 Jason Terry RC 1.00 2.50
116 Trajan Langdon RC .60 1.50
117 Dion Glover RC .50 1.25
118 Jeff Foster RC .60 1.50
119 Lamar Odom RC 1.50 4.00
120 Wally Szczerbiak RC 1.25 3.00
121 Shawn Marion RC 1.25 3.00
122 Kenny Thomas RC .60 1.50
123 Devean George RC .60 1.50
124 Scott Padgett RC .50 1.25
125 Tim Duncan SEN 1.25 3.00
126 Jason Williams SEN .75 2.00
127 Paul Pierce SEN .75 2.00
128 Kobe Bryant SEN 2.50 6.00
129 Keith Van Horn SEN .50 1.25
130 Vince Carter SEN 1.25 3.00
131 Matt Harpring SEN .40 1.00
132 Antawn Jamison SEN .60 1.50
133 Tracy McGrady SEN 1.00 2.50
134 Tim Duncan .75 2.00
135 Tariq Abdul-Wahad .25 .60
136 Luc Longley .30 .75
137 Steve Smith .30 .75
138 Alonzo Mourning .50 1.25
139 Kevin Garnett .60 1.50
140 Christian Laettner .30 .75
141 Rik Smits .40 1.00
142 Cedric Henderson .25 .60
143 Jim Jackson .25 .60
144 Dan Majerle .40 1.00
145 Bryant Reeves .25 .60
146 Antonio Davis .25 .60
147 Michael Smith .25 .60
148 Charlie Ward .25 .60
149 Chris Mullin .40 1.00
150 Danny Manning .30 .75
151 Eric Williams .25 .60
152 Hersey Hawkins .25 .60
153 Isaiah Rider .30 .75
154 Shandon Anderson .25 .60
155 Jason Kidd .60 1.50
156 Chris Whitney .25 .60
157 Brent Barry .30 .75
158 Patrick Ewing .50 1.25
159 George Lynch .25 .60
160 Dickey Simpkins .25 .60
161 Derek Anderson .25 .60
162 Ron Mercer .30 .75
163 David Wesley .25 .60
164 Mookie Blaylock .25 .60
165 Terrell Brandon .25 .60
166 Detlef Schrempf .30 .75
167 Olden Polynice .25 .60
168 Jayson Williams .25 .60
169 Eric Piatkowski .30 .75
170 A.C. Green .30 .75
171 Chris Mills .25 .60
172 Chris Webber .40 1.00
173 Jeff Hornacek .30 .75
174 Calbert Cheaney .25 .60
175 Wesley Person .25 .60
176 Corey Benjamin .25 .60
177 Loy Vaught .25 .60
178 Keith Closs .25 .60
179 Bo Outlaw .25 .60
180 Mitch Richmond .40 1.00
181 Charles Oakley .30 .75
182 Felipe Lopez .25 .60
183 Eric Snow .30 .75
184 Paul Pierce .50 1.25
185 Elden Campbell .25 .60
186 Shaquille O'Neal 1.00 2.50
187 Charles Barkley .60 1.50
188 Mark Jackson .30 .75
189 Scott Burrell .25 .60
190 Anfernee Hardaway .60 1.50
191 Samaki Walker .25 .60
192 Karl Malone .50 1.25
193 Jermaine O'Neal .30 .75
194 Mario Elie .25 .60
195 Malik Sealy .25 .60
196 Voshon Lenard .25 .60
197 Chris Gatling .25 .60
198 Walt Williams .25 .60
199 Nick Van Exel .30 .75
200 Bimbo Coles .25 .60
201 John Wallace .25 .60
202 Anthony Mason .25 .60
203 Steve Nash .60 1.50
204 Erick Dampier .25 .60
205 Cedric Ceballos .25 .60
206 Derek Fisher .40 1.00
207 Marcus Camby .30 .75
208 Tyrone Hill .25 .60
209 Nick Anderson .25 .60
210 Sam Cassell .30 .75
211 Raef LaFrentz .30 .75
212 Ruben Patterson .25 .60
213 Rick Fox .25 .60
214 Jason Williams .50 1.25
215 Vince Carter .75 2.00
216 Michael Dickerson .25 .60
217 Steve Kerr .30 .75
218 Rasheed Wallace .40 1.00
219 Keith Van Horn .30 .75
220 Bob Sura .25 .60
221 Ray Allen .40 1.00
222 Jerry Stackhouse .40 1.00
223 Shawn Bradley .25 .60
224 Horace Grant .30 .75
225 Tim Duncan USA 1.25 3.00
226 Kevin Garnett USA 1.00 2.50
227 Jason Kidd USA 1.00 2.50
228 Steve Smith USA .50 1.25
229 Allan Houston USA .50 1.25
230 Tom Gugliotta USA .40 1.00
231 Gary Payton USA .60 1.50
232 Tim Hardaway USA .60 1.50
233 Vin Baker USA .50 1.25
234 Karl Malone CAT .75 2.00
235 Vince Carter CAT 1.25 3.00
236 Jason Williams CAT .75 2.00
237 Alonzo Mourning CAT .75 2.00
238 Anfernee Hardaway CAT 1.00 2.50
239 Mitch Richmond CAT .60 1.50
240 Steve Smith CAT .50 1.25
241 Charles Barkley CAT 1.00 2.50
242 Ron Mercer CAT .50 1.25
243 Shaquille O'Neal EDGE 1.50 4.00
244 Jason Kidd EDGE 1.00 2.50
245 Kevin Garnett EDGE 1.00 2.50
246 Tim Duncan EDGE 1.25 3.00
247 Ray Allen EDGE .60 1.50
248 Chris Webber EDGE .60 1.50
249 Jerry Stackhouse EDGE .60 1.50
250 Keith Van Horn EDGE .50 1.25
251 Patrick Ewing EDGE .75 2.00
252 Steve Francis RC 6.00 15.00
253 Jonathan Bender RC 2.50 6.00
254 Richard Hamilton RC 5.00 12.00
255 Andre Miller RC 5.00 12.00
256 Corey Maggette RC 4.00 10.00
257 William Avery RC 2.00 5.00
258 Ron Artest RC 5.00 12.00
259 James Posey RC 2.50 6.00
260 Quincy Lewis RC 1.50 4.00
261 Tim James RC 1.50 4.00
262 Vonteego Cummings RC 1.50 4.00
263 Anthony Carter RC 2.00 5.00
264 Mirsad Turkcan RC 2.50 6.00
265 Adrian Griffin RC 2.50 6.00
266 Ryan Robertson RC 1.50 4.00

1999-00 Finest Refractors

*STARS: 2.5X TO 6X BASE CARD HI
*SUBSETS: 1.5X TO 4X HI
*SER.1 RCs: 1.25X TO 3X HI
*SER.2 RCs: .5X TO 1.25X HI
SER.2 RCs STATED ODDS 1:138, 1:64 HTA
SER.2 RCs: PRINT RUN 200 SERIAL #'d SETS
SER.1/2 STATED ODDS 1:12, 1:5 HTA
64 Kobe Bryant 15.00 40.00
128 Kobe Bryant SEN 15.00 40.00

1999-00 Finest Refractors Gold

*STARS: 8X TO 20X BASE CARD HI
*SER.1 RCs: 4X TO 10X BASE HI
*SER.2 RCs: 1X TO 2.5X BASE HI
*SUBSETS: 5X TO 12X BASE HI
SER.1 STATED ODDS 1:62, 1:28 HTA
SER.2 STATED ODDS 1:31, 1:14 HTA
STATED PRINT RUN 100 SERIAL #'d SETS
77 Shawn Kemp 10.00 25.00
103 Kevin Garnett GEM 25.00 60.00
134 Tim Duncan 30.00 80.00
226 Kevin Garnett USA 30.00 80.00
241 Charles Barkley CAT 20.00 50.00

1999-00 Finest 24-Karat Touch

Randomly inserted in series two packs at one in 30, this 10-card set focuses on the top shooters in the NBA. The cards feature gold texture on the front. Card backs carry a "KT" prefix.

COMPLETE SET (10) 8.00 20.00
SER.2 STATED ODDS 1:30, 1:15 HTA
*REF: 2X TO 5X HI COLUMN
REF: SER.2 STATED ODDS 1:300, 1:150 HTA
KT1 Reggie Miller 1.50 4.00
KT2 Keith Van Horn 1.25 3.00
KT3 Allan Houston 1.25 3.00
KT4 Patrick Ewing 2.00 5.00
KT5 Anfernee Hardaway 2.50 6.00
KT6 Steve Smith 1.25 3.00
KT7 Glen Rice 1.50 4.00
KT8 Ray Allen 1.50 4.00
KT9 Charles Barkley 2.50 6.00
KT10 Mitch Richmond 1.50 4.00

1999-00 Finest Box Office Draws

Randomly inserted in series two packs at one in 30, this 10-card set features marquee players who are loved by their fans around the world. Card backs carry a "BOD" prefix.

COMPLETE SET (10) 12.00 30.00
SER.2 STATED ODDS 1:30, 1:15 HTA
*REF: 2X TO 5X HI COLUMN
REF: SER.2 STATED ODDS 1:300, 1:150 HTA
BOD1 Shaquille O'Neal 4.00 10.00
BOD2 Patrick Ewing 2.00 5.00
BOD3 Karl Malone 2.00 5.00
BOD4 Jason Williams 2.00 5.00
BOD5 Charles Barkley 2.50 6.00
BOD6 Tim Duncan 3.00 8.00
BOD7 Kevin Garnett 2.50 6.00
BOD8 Alonzo Mourning 2.00 5.00
BOD9 Mitch Richmond 1.50 4.00
BOD10 Elton Brand 4.00 10.00

1999-00 Finest Double Double

Randomly inserted in series two packs at one in 20, this 15-card set features players who are most apt to put up a double-double in any game. Card backs carry a "D" prefix.

COMPLETE SET (15) 20.00 50.00
SER.2 STATED ODDS 1:20, 1:10 HTA
*REF: 2X TO 5X HI COLUMN
REF: SER.2 STATED ODDS 1:200, 1:100 HTA
D1 Jason Kidd 2.50 6.00
D2 Kobe Bryant 6.00 15.00
D3 Antoine Walker 1.50 4.00
D4 Chris Webber 1.50 4.00
D5 Anfernee Hardaway 2.50 6.00
D6 Shawn Kemp 1.50 4.00
D7 Tim Duncan 3.00 8.00
D8 Antonio McDyess 1.25 3.00
D9 Grant Hill 2.00 5.00
D10 Karl Malone 2.00 5.00
D11 Shaquille O'Neal 4.00 10.00
D12 Allen Iverson 3.00 8.00
D13 Jayson Williams 1.00 2.50
D14 Keith Van Horn 1.25 3.00
D15 Gary Payton 1.50 4.00

1999-00 Finest Double Feature Right Refractors

Randomly inserted in series one packs at one in 26, this 14-card set features some of the stars of the NBA paired up using a "split screen". This set is also refered to as Non-Refractor/Refractor. Card backs carry a "DF" prefix:

COMPLETE SET (14) 15.00 30.00
SER.1 STATED ODDS 1:26, 1:12 HTA
RIGHT/LEFT VARIATIONS EQUAL VALUE
*DUAL REF: 1X TO 2.5X BASE HI
DUAL REFRACTOR SER.1 ODDS 1:78, 1:36 HTA
DF1 H.Olajuwon/S.Pippen 1.50 4.00
DF2 P.Pierce/A.Walker 1.25 3.00
DF3 S.Abdur-Rahim/M.Bibby 1.00 2.50
DF4 A.Mourning/T.Hardaway 1.25 3.00
DF5 G.Robinson/R.Allen 1.00 2.50
DF6 K.Garnett/J.Smith 1.50 4.00
DF7 K.Van Horn/S.Marbury .75 2.00
DF8 C.Webber/J.Williams 1.25 3.00
DF9 T.Duncan/D.Robinson 2.00 5.00
DF10 G.Payton/V.Baker 1.00 2.50
DF11 K.Malone/J.Stockton 1.25 3.00
DF12 J.Kidd/T.Gugliotta 1.50 4.00
DF13 M.Richmond/J.Howard 1.00 2.50
DF14 K.Bryant/S.O'Neal 4.00 10.00

1999-00 Finest Dunk Masters

Randomly inserted in series one packs at one in 73, this 15-card set features some of the best dunkers in the league. The cards are serially numbered to 750. Card backs carry a "DM" prefix.

SER.1 STATED ODDS 1:73, 1:34 HTA
STATED PRINT RUN 750 SERIAL #'d SETS
*REFRACTORS: 1.25X TO 3X HI COLUMN
REF: SER.1 ODDS 1:364, 1:168 HTA
REF: PRINT RUN 150 SERIAL #'d SETS
DM1 Kobe Bryant 15.00 40.00
DM2 Shaquille O'Neal 10.00 25.00
DM3 Chris Webber 4.00 10.00
DM4 Antonio McDyess 3.00 8.00
DM5 Michael Finley 4.00 10.00
DM6 Shawn Kemp 4.00 10.00
DM7 Tracy McGrady 6.00 15.00
DM8 Antoine Walker 4.00 10.00
DM9 Alonzo Mourning 5.00 12.00
DM10 Ray Allen 4.00 10.00
DM11 Kevin Garnett 6.00 15.00
DM12 Allen Iverson 8.00 20.00
DM13 Vince Carter 8.00 20.00
DM14 Tim Duncan 8.00 20.00
DM15 Scottie Pippen 6.00 15.00

1999-00 Finest Future's Finest

Randomly inserted in series one packs at one in 73, this 15-card set focuses on rookies from the 1999 draft class. The cards are serially numbered to 750. Card backs carry a "FF" prefix.

SER.1 STATED ODDS 1:73, 1:34 HTA
STATED PRINT RUN 750 SERIAL #'d SETS
REF: 1.25X TO 3X HI COLUMN
REF: SER. ODDS 1:364, 1:168 HTA
REF: PRINT RUN 150 SERIAL #'d SETS
FF1 Elton Brand 3.00 8.00
FF2 Steve Francis 3.00 8.00
FF3 Baron Davis 3.00 8.00
FF4 Lamar Odom 3.00 8.00
FF5 Jonathan Bender 1.25 3.00
FF6 Wally Szczerbiak 2.50 6.00
FF7 Richard Hamilton 2.50 6.00
FF8 Andre Miller 2.50 6.00
FF9 Shawn Marion 2.50 6.00
FF10 Jason Terry 2.00 5.00
FF11 Trajan Langdon 1.25 3.00
FF12 Aleksandar Radojevic .75 2.00
FF13 Corey Maggette 2.00 5.00
FF14 William Avery 1.00 2.50
FF15 Cal Bowdler .75 2.00

1999-00 Finest Heirs to Air

Randomly inserted in series two packs at one in 36, this 10-card set features the top gravity-defiers in the NBA. Card backs carry a "HA" prefix.

COMPLETE SET (10) 15.00 40.00
SER.2 STATED ODDS 1:36, 1:16 HTA
HA1 Michael Finley 2.00 5.00
HA2 Brent Barry 1.50 4.00
HA3 Corey Maggette 3.00 8.00
HA4 Ron Mercer 1.50 4.00
HA5 Eddie Jones 2.00 5.00
HA6 Tracy McGrady 3.00 8.00
HA7 Vince Carter 4.00 10.00
HA8 Jerry Stackhouse 2.00 5.00
HA9 Ray Allen 2.00 5.00
HA10 Kobe Bryant 8.00 20.00

1999-00 Finest Leading Indicators

Randomly inserted in series one packs at one in 30, this 10-card set features the top producing players printed on thermal ink technology. By touching various points on the card, one could reveal each player's statistics from the 98-99 season. Card backs carry a "L" prefix.

COMPLETE SET (10) 10.00 25.00
SER.1 STATED ODDS 1:30, 1:14 HTA
L1 Stephon Marbury 1.00 2.50
L2 Paul Pierce 1.50 4.00
L3 Jason Kidd 2.00 5.00
L4 Gary Payton 1.25 3.00
L5 Keith Van Horn 1.00 2.50
L6 Reggie Miller 1.25 3.00
L7 Jason Williams 1.50 4.00
L8 Vince Carter 2.50 6.00

L9 Ray Allen 1.25 3.00
L10 Kobe Bryant 5.00 12.00

1999-00 Finest New Millennium

Randomly inserted in series one packs at one in 55, this 10-card set focuses on young player who have already proven they can carry the torch into the millennium. The cards are serially numbered to 1500. Card backs carry a "NM" prefix.

SER.1 STATED ODDS 1:55, 1:25 HTA
STATED PRINT RUN 1500 SERIAL #'d SETS
*REF: 1.25X TO 3X HI COLUMN
REF: SER.1 ODDS 1:273, 1:126 HTA
REF: PRINT RUN 300 SERIAL #'d SETS
NM1 Jason Williams 2.00 5.00
NM2 Vince Carter 3.00 8.00
NM3 Paul Pierce 2.00 5.00
NM4 Mike Bibby 1.50 4.00
NM5 Elton Brand 2.50 6.00
NM6 Steve Francis 2.50 6.00
NM7 Baron Davis 2.50 6.00
NM8 Lamar Odom 2.50 6.00
NM9 Jonathan Bender 1.00 2.50
NM10 Wally Szczerbiak 2.00 5.00

1999-00 Finest Next Generation

Randomly inserted in series two packs at one in 20, this 15-card set features young players that will lead the NBA in the next millennium. Card backs carry a "NG" prefix.

SER.2 STATED ODDS 1:20, 1:10 HTA
*REF: 1.5X TO 4X HI COLUMN
REF: SER.2 STATED ODDS 1:200, 1:100 HTA
NG1 Steve Francis 1.25 3.00
NG2 Jonathan Bender .50 1.25
NG3 Richard Hamilton 1.00 2.50
NG4 Andre Miller 1.00 2.50
NG5 Corey Maggette .75 2.00
NG6 William Avery .40 1.00
NG7 Ron Artest 1.00 2.50
NG8 Wally Szczerbiak 1.00 2.50
NG9 Quincy Lewis .30 .75
NG10 Devean George .50 1.25
NG11 Vonteego Cummings .30 .75
NG12 Lamar Odom 1.25 3.00
NG13 Shawn Marion 1.00 2.50
NG14 Elton Brand 1.25 3.00
NG15 Baron Davis 1.25 3.00

1999-00 Finest Producers

Randomly inserted in series one packs at one in 22, this 10-card set features the top producers from the 1998-99 season. Card backs carry a "FP" prefix.

COMPLETE SET (10) 8.00 20.00
SER.1 STATED ODDS 1:22, 1:10 HTA
*REFRACTORS: 1.25X TO 3X HI COLUMN
REF: SER.1 ODDS 1:109, 1:50 HTA
FP1 Shaquille O'Neal 2.50 6.00
FP2 Chris Webber 1.00 2.50
FP3 Karl Malone 1.25 3.00
FP4 Allen Iverson 2.00 5.00
FP5 Kevin Garnett 1.50 4.00
FP6 Jason Kidd 1.50 4.00
FP7 Grant Hill 1.25 3.00
FP8 Shareef Abdur-Rahim .75 2.00
FP9 Gary Payton 1.00 2.50
FP10 Charles Barkley 1.50 4.00

1999-00 Finest Salute

Randomly inserted in series one packs at one in 108 and series two at one in 100, this two card set features Rookie of the Year Vince Carter, NBA Finals MVP Tim Duncan and Scoring leader Allen Iverson on one card and the top six rookies from the Draft on the other. The cards carry a "FS" prefix. In addition to the regular card, a refractor version was inserted at one in 5,305 for series one and one in 4,616 for series two and a gold refractor version at one in 16,992 for series one and one in 8,539 for series two. Both gold refractor versions were serially numbered to 50. The set is considered complete with all six cards.

SER.1 STATED ODDS 1:108, 1:50 HTA
REF: SER.1 ODDS 1:5,305, 1:2,333 HTA
GR: SER.1 ODDS 1:16,992, 1:7,423 HTA
SER.2 STATED ODDS 1:100, 1:50 HTA
REF: SER.2 ODDS 1:4,616, 1:2,194 HTA
GR: SER.2 ODDS 1:8,539, 1:3,790 HTA
GR: PRINT RUN 50 SERIAL #'d SETS
FS1 Carter/Duncn/Iversn 1.50 4.00
FS1 Carter/Duncn/Iversn REF 10.00 25.00
FS1 Carter/Duncn/Iversn GR 50.00 100.00
FS2 Draft Picks 1.50 4.00
FS2 Draft Picks REF 25.00 60.00
FS2 Draft Picks GR 100.00 200.00

1999-00 Finest Team Finest Blue

Randomly inserted in series one packs at one in 55 and series two packs at one in 28, this set focuses on the top stars in the NBA. The cards are serially numbered to 1500. Card backs carry a "TF" prefix.

COMPLETE SET (20) 25.00 65.00
COMPLETE SERIES 1 (10) 10.00 25.00
COMPLETE SERIES 2 (10) 15.00 40.00
SER.1 STATED ODDS 1:55, 1:25 HTA
SER.2 STATED ODDS 1:28, 1:13 HTA
STATED PRINT RUN 1500 SERIAL #'d SETS
*BLUE REF: 1.5X TO 4X BASIC BLUE
BLUE REF: SER.1 ODDS 1:546, 1:252 HTA
BLUE REF: SER.2 ODDS 1:276, 1:127 HTA
BLUE REF: PRINT RUN 150 SERIAL #'d SETS
*RED: .75X TO 2X BASIC BLUE
RED: SER.1 STATED ODDS 1:18 HTA
RED: SER.2 STATED ODDS 1:9 HTA
RED: PRINT RUN 500 SERIAL #'d SETS
*GOLD: 1X TO 2.5X BASIC BLUE
GOLD: SER.1 STATED ODDS 1:35 HTA
GOLD: SER.2 STATED ODDS 1:18 HTA
GOLD: PRINT RUN 250 SERIAL #'d SETS
TF1 Shareef Abdur-Rahim 1.25 3.00
TF2 Stephon Marbury 1.25 3.00
TF3 Shawn Kemp 1.50 4.00
TF4 Allen Iverson 3.00 8.00
TF5 Antoine Walker 1.50 4.00
TF6 Hakeem Olajuwon 2.00 5.00
TF7 Tim Duncan 3.00 8.00
TF8 Karl Malone 2.00 5.00
TF9 Grant Hill 2.00 5.00
TF10 Keith Van Horn 1.25 3.00
TF11 Alonzo Mourning 2.00 5.00
TF12 Jason Kidd 2.50 6.00
TF13 Chris Webber 1.50 4.00
TF14 Shaquille O'Neal 4.00 10.00
TF15 Gary Payton 1.50 4.00
TF16 Kevin Garnett 2.50 6.00
TF17 Antonio McDyess 1.25 3.00
TF18 Kobe Bryant 6.00 15.00
TF19 Scottie Pippen 2.50 6.00
TF20 Vince Carter 3.00 8.00

1999-00 Finest Team Finest Gold Refractors

*REFRACTORS: 5X TO 12X HI COLUMN
STATED PRINT RUN 25 SERIAL #'d SETS
TF7 Tim Duncan 75.00 200.00
TF14 Shaquille O'Neal 60.00 150.00
TF18 Kobe Bryant 200.00 350.00

1999-00 Finest Team Finest Red Refractors

*REFRACTORS: 3X TO 8X HI COLUMN
STATED PRINT RUN 50 SERIAL #'d SETS
TF18 Kobe Bryant 100.00 250.00
TF19 Scottie Pippen 30.00 80.00

2000-01 Finest

The 2000-01 Finest set was released in late November, in just one series. Each pack contained five cards and carried a suggested retail price of $5.00. The series one set was comprised of the following: 125 veterans, 25 rookies (serially numbered to 1599), 13 Off the Meter subset cards (inserted at one in eight) and 10 Gems subset cards (inserted at one in 24 packs).

COMPLETE SET (173) 125.00 250.00
COMPLETE SET w/o SP (125) 15.00 40.00
126-150 STATED ODDS 1:18 H, 1:8 HTA
126-150 PRINT RUN 1599 SERIAL #'d SETS
OTM UNLISTED STARS .50 1.25
OTM: STATED ODDS 1:8 H, 1:3 HTA
GEMS: STATED ODDS 1:24 H, 1:9 HTA
1 Shaquille O'Neal 1.00 2.50
2 P.J. Brown .25 .60
3 Joe Smith .30 .75
4 Kendall Gill .25 .60
5 Corey Maggette .30 .75
6 Marcus Camby .30 .75
7 Toni Kukoc .40 1.00
8 Kobe Bryant 1.50 4.00
9 David Robinson .60 1.50
10 Ruben Patterson .25 .60
11 Allen Iverson .75 2.00
12 Glenn Robinson .30 .75
13 Anthony Carter .25 .60
14 Jonathan Bender .25 .60
15 Vince Carter .75 2.00
16 Jerry Stackhouse .30 .75
17 Raef LaFrentz .25 .60
18 Dikembe Mutombo .40 1.00
19 Baron Davis .40 1.00
20 Kenny Anderson .30 .75
21 Corey Benjamin .25 .60
22 Andre Miller .30 .75
23 Cedric Ceballos .25 .60
24 Christian Laettner .30 .75
25 Shandon Anderson .25 .60
26 Rik Smits .25 .60
27 Michael Olowokandi .25 .60
28 Sam Cassell .30 .75
29 Tom Gugliotta .25 .60
30 Jason Williams .40 1.00
31 Avery Johnson .30 .75
32 Karl Malone .50 1.25
33 Grant Hill .50 1.25
34 Paul Pierce .40 1.00
35 Antonio Davis .25 .60
36 Nick Anderson .25 .60
37 Alan Henderson .25 .60
38 Eddie Jones .40 1.00
39 Ron Artest .40 1.00
40 Brevin Knight .25 .60
41 Keon Clark .25 .60
42 Elton Brand .40 1.00
43 Reggie Miller .40 1.00
44 Steve Francis .30 .75
45 Derek Anderson .25 .60
46 Alonzo Mourning .50 1.25
47 Terrell Brandon .25 .60
48 Larry Johnson .40 1.00
49 Keith Van Horn .30 .75
50 Jason Kidd .60 1.50
51 Scottie Pippen .60 1.50
52 Gary Payton .40 1.00
53 Robert Pack .25 .60
54 Adrian Griffin .25 .60
55 Jim Jackson .25 .60
56 Lamond Murray .25 .60
57 Larry Hughes .30 .75
58 Dirk Nowitzki .60 1.50
59 Vonteego Cummings .25 .60
60 Jalen Rose .30 .75
61 Arvydas Sabonis .30 .75
62 Kerry Kittles .25 .60
63 Kevin Garnett .60 1.50
64 Latrell Sprewell .30 .75
65 Shawn Marion .30 .75
66 Darrell Armstrong .25 .60
67 Ron Mercer .25 .60
68 Damon Stoudamire .30 .75
69 Tracy McGrady .60 1.50
70 Theo Ratliff .25 .60
71 Lamar Odom .30 .75
72 Charlie Ward .25 .60
73 John Amaechi .25 .60
74 Quincy Lewis .25 .60
75 Othella Harrington .25 .60
76 Doug Christie .25 .60
77 Richard Hamilton .30 .75
78 Donyell Marshall .25 .60
79 Vlade Divac .30 .75
80 Clifford Robinson .25 .60
81 Sean Elliott .40 1.00
82 Rashard Lewis .40 1.00
83 Wally Szczerbiak .30 .75
84 Dale Davis .25 .60
85 Kelvin Cato .25 .60
86 Cuttino Mobley .25 .60
87 Travis Best .25 .60
88 Robert Horry .30 .75
89 Maurice Taylor .25 .60
90 Jamal Mashburn .30 .75
91 Tim Thomas .25 .60
92 Stephon Marbury .30 .75
93 Patrick Ewing .50 1.25
94 Eric Snow .25 .60
95 Anfernee Hardaway .60 1.50
96 Steve Smith .30 .75
97 Chris Webber .40 1.00
98 Rodney Rogers .25 .60
99 John Stockton .50 1.25
100 Tim Duncan .75 2.00
101 Ray Allen .40 1.00
102 Glen Rice .30 .75
103 Bryon Russell .25 .60
104 Tim Hardaway .40 1.00
105 Allan Houston .30 .75
106 Rasheed Wallace .40 1.00
107 Vin Baker .30 .75
108 Michael Dickerson .25 .60
109 Juwan Howard .30 .75
110 Hakeem Olajuwon .50 1.25
111 Shareef Abdur-Rahim .30 .75
112 Rod Strickland .25 .60
113 Hersey Hawkins .25 .60
114 Jason Terry .40 1.00
115 Anthony Mason .25 .60
116 Mike Bibby .40 1.00
117 Shawn Kemp .40 1.00
118 Derrick Coleman .30 .75
119 Antoine Walker .30 .75
120 Antawn Jamison .40 1.00
121 Michael Finley .40 1.00
122 Antonio McDyess .30 .75
123 Nick Van Exel .30 .75
124 Mitch Richmond .30 .75
125 Lindsey Hunter .25 .60
126 Kenyon Martin RC 5.00 12.00
127 Stromile Swift RC 2.00 5.00
128 Darius Miles RC 2.00 5.00
129 Marcus Fizer RC 2.00 5.00
130 Mike Miller RC 3.00 8.00
131 DerMarr Johnson RC 1.50 4.00
132 Chris Mihm RC 1.50 4.00
133 Jamal Crawford RC 5.00 12.00
134 Joel Przybilla RC 1.50 4.00
135 Keyon Dooling RC 2.00 5.00
136 Jerome Moiso RC 1.25 3.00
137 Etan Thomas RC 2.00 5.00
138 Courtney Alexander RC 1.50 4.00
139 Mateen Cleaves RC 1.50 4.00
140 Jason Collier RC 2.00 5.00
141 Desmond Mason RC 2.50 6.00
142 Quentin Richardson RC 2.00 5.00
143 Jamaal Magloire RC 2.00 5.00
144 Speedy Claxton RC 2.00 5.00
145 Morris Peterson RC 2.00 5.00
146 Donnell Harvey RC 1.50 4.00
147 DeShawn Stevenson RC 2.00 5.00
148 Mamadou N'Diaye RC 1.25 3.00
149 Erick Barkley RC 1.25 3.00
150 Mark Madsen RC 2.00 5.00
151 A.Iverson/S.Marbury OTM 1.00 2.50
152 V.Carter/K.Bryant OTM 2.00 5.00
153 K.Garnett/Abdur-Rahim OTM .75 2.00
154 T.McGrady/S.Pippen OTM .75 2.00
155 T.Duncan/E.Brand OTM 1.00 2.50
156 S.Francis/G.Payton OTM .50 1.25
157 C.Webber/K.Malone OTM .60 1.50
158 A.Mourning/P.Ewing OTM .60 1.50
159 L.Sprewell/E.Jones OTM .50 1.25
160 J.Kidd/J.Stockton OTM .75 2.00
161 R.Miller/A.Houston OTM .50 1.25
162 R.Wallace/A.Walker OTM .50 1.25
163 J.Stackhouse/J.Rose OTM .40 1.00
164 Shaquille O'Neal GEM 2.50 6.00
165 Kobe Bryant GEM 4.00 10.00
166 Vince Carter GEM 2.00 5.00
167 Kevin Garnett GEM 1.50 4.00
168 Jason Williams GEM 1.00 2.50
169 Tracy McGrady GEM 1.50 4.00
170 Steve Francis GEM .75 2.00
171 Tim Duncan GEM 2.00 5.00
172 Elton Brand GEM 1.00 2.50
173 Grant Hill GEM 1.25 3.00

2000-01 Finest Gold Refractors

*STARS: 10X TO 25X BASE CARD HI
*OTM: 8X TO 20X BASE HI
*GEMS: 4X TO 10X BASE HI
*RCs: 1X TO 2.5X BASE HI
VETS: STATED ODDS 1:67 H, 1:19 HTA
RCs: STATED ODDS 1:336 H, 1:93 HTA
GEM: STATED ODDS 1:840 H, 1:233 HTA
OTM: STATED ODDS 1:323 H, 1:90 HTA
STATED PRINT RUN 100 SERIAL #'d SETS
8 Kobe Bryant 125.00 225.00
33 Grant Hill 15.00 40.00
43 Reggie Miller 12.00 30.00
51 Scottie Pippen 25.00 60.00
64 Latrell Sprewell 10.00 25.00
152 V.Carter/K.Bryant OTM 100.00 225.00
164 Shaquille O'Neal GEM 30.00 80.00
165 Kobe Bryant GEM 125.00 225.00
168 Jason Williams GEM 15.00 40.00
173 Grant Hill GEM 15.00 40.00

2000-01 Finest Man to Man

Randomly inserted in packs at one in 27 (one in 12 for HTA), this 10-card set focuses on comparisons between Tim Duncan and Elton Brand. They are each featured on five variations comparing five elements of the game (Dunking, Rebounding, Shooting, Blocking and Posting Up).

COMPLETE SET (10) 7.50 15.00
STATED ODDS 1:25 H, 1:12 HTA
1A Tim Duncan DUNK 1.50 4.00
1B Elton Brand DUNK .75 2.00
2A Tim Duncan REB 1.50 4.00
2B Elton Brand REB .75 2.00
3A Tim Duncan SH 1.50 4.00
3B Elton Brand SH .75 2.00
4A Tim Duncan BLK 1.50 4.00
4B Elton Brand BLK .75 2.00
5A Tim Duncan PU 1.50 4.00
5B Elton Brand PU .75 2.00

2000-01 Finest Moments

Randomly inserted in packs at one in 14 (one in six HTA), this 21-card set features peak moments from NBA history, as well as from the 1999-2000 season. A special Vince Carter moments card was also produced that was serially numbered to 1000. That card is priced at the end of the set and is not included in the set price. Card backs carry a "FM" prefix.

COMPLETE SET (21) 12.50 25.00
STATED ODDS 1:14 H, 1:6 HTA
*REF: .75X TO 2X HI COLUMN
REF: STATED ODDS 1:24 H, 1:11 HTA
FMAC Anthony Carter .50 1.25
FMAH Allan Houston .60 1.50
FMAI Allen Iverson 1.50 4.00
FMEB Elton Brand .75 2.00
FMGP Gary Payton .75 2.00
FMGR Glen Rice .60 1.50
FMJK Jason Kidd 1.25 3.00
FMJR Jalen Rose .60 1.50
FMJS John Starks .60 1.50
FMKM Karl Malone 1.00 2.50
FMLH Larry Hughes .60 1.50
FMLJ Larry Johnson .75 2.00
FMMC Mateen Cleaves .60 1.50
FMMJ Magic Johnson 1.50 4.00
FMSE Sean Elliott .75 2.00
FMSF Steve Francis .60 1.50
FMSO Shaquille O'Neal 2.00 5.00
FMTD Tim Duncan 1.50 4.00
FMTH Tim Hardaway .75 2.00
FMTK Toni Kukoc .75 2.00
FMTM Tracy McGrady 1.25 3.00
NNO Vince Carter/1000 8.00 20.00

2000-01 Finest Moments Refractors Autographs

Randomly inserted in packs at one in 112 (one in 51 HTA), this 18-card set is a parallel the the Moments insert. Each card features the player's autograph and the Topps "Certified Autograph" logo. Card backs carry a "FM" prefix.

GROUP A ODDS 1:258 H, 1:117 HTA
GROUP B ODDS 1:2026 H, 1:921 HTA
GROUP C ODDS 1:355 H, 1:161 HTA
GROUP D ODDS 1:253 H, 1:115 HTA
OVERALL ODDS 1:90 H, 1:41 HTA
FMAH Allan Houston A 8.00 20.00
FMEB Elton Brand A 10.00 20.00
FMEJ Eddie Jones A 40.00 100.00
FMGP Gary Payton A 10.00 25.00
FMGR Glen Rice A 12.00 30.00
FMJR Jalen Rose A 15.00 30.00
FMJS John Starks D 25.00 60.00
FMLH Larry Hughes A 15.00 30.00
FMLJ Larry Johnson A 150.00 300.00
FMMC Mateen Cleaves D 10.00 25.00
FMMJ Magic Johnson C 50.00 120.00
FMMR Mitch Richmond C 40.00 100.00
FMSE Sean Elliott D 12.00 30.00
FMSF Steve Francis B 12.00 30.00
FMSO Shaquille O'Neal C 150.00 300.00
FMSO2 Shaquille O'Neal 150.00 300.00
FMTD Tim Duncan A 800.00 1200.00
FMTM Tracy McGrady D 12.00 30.00

2000-01 Finest Moments Relics

Randomly inserted in packs at one in 59 (one in 27 for HTA), this 10-card set features swatches of game-worn jerseys from the 2000 USA Mens' Basketball Team. Each card features the Topps "Genuine Issue" sticker. Card backs carry a "FMR" prefix. Special Vince Carter and Kevin Garnett cards were produced also. These are sequentially numbered to 1000.

GROUP A 1:617 H, 1:280 HTA
GROUP B 1:127 H, 1:58 HTA
GROUP C 1:236 H, 1:107 HTA
GROUP D 1:430 H, 1:195 HTA
GROUP E 1:411 H, 1:187 HTA
GROUP F 1:394 H, 1:179 HTA
OVERALL STATED ODDS 1:48 H, 1:22 HTA
FMR1 Vin Baker D 3.00 8.00
FMR2 Antonio McDyess F 3.00 8.00
FMR3 Jason Kidd B 6.00 15.00
FMR4 Tim Hardaway B 4.00 10.00
FMR5 Allan Houston B 3.00 8.00
FMR6 Steve Smith C 3.00 8.00
FMR7 Alonzo Mourning E 5.00 12.00
FMR8 Gary Payton A 4.00 10.00
FMR9 Ray Allen B 4.00 10.00
FMR10 Shareef Abdur-Rahim C 3.00 8.00
FMR11 Vince Carter/1000 20.00 50.00
FMR12 Kevin Garnett/1000 6.00 15.00

2000-01 Finest Showmen

Randomly inserted in packs at one in 18 (one in eight HTA), this 10-card set features some of the flashiest players in the NBA. Card backs carry a "S" prefix.

COMPLETE SET (10) 4.00 10.00
STATED ODDS 1:13 H, 1:8 HTA
S1 Chris Webber .60 1.50
S2 Elton Brand .60 1.50
S3 Tim Duncan 1.25 3.00
S4 Shareef Abdur-Rahim .50 1.25
S5 Jason Williams .60 1.50
S6 Grant Hill .75 2.00
S7 Lamar Odom .50 1.25
S8 Larry Hughes .50 1.25
S9 Michael Finley .60 1.50
S10 Latrell Sprewell .50 1.25

2000-01 Finest Title Quest

Randomly inserted in packs at one in 60 (one in 27 HTA), this 10-card set focuses on players who guided their teams into the playoffs last year. The cards feature Dufex technology. Card backs carry an "APT" prefix.

COMPLETE SET (10) 12.50 30.00
STATED ODDS 1:54 H, 1:27 HTA
APT1 Reggie Miller 1.50 4.00
APT2 Alonzo Mourning 2.00 5.00
APT3 Allen Iverson 3.00 8.00
APT4 Latrell Sprewell 1.25 3.00
APT5 Jalen Rose 1.25 3.00
APT6 Scottie Pippen 2.50 6.00
APT7 Shaquille O'Neal 4.00 10.00
APT8 Kobe Bryant 10.00 25.00
APT9 Chris Webber 1.50 4.00
APT10 Rasheed Wallace 1.50 4.00

2000-01 Finest World's Finest

Randomly inserted in packs at one in 40 (one in 18 HTA), this 15-card set features players who have played for past USA teams. Card backs carry a "WF" prefix.

COMPLETE SET (15) 25.00 60.00
STATED ODDS 1:36 H, 1:18 HTA
WF1 Tim Duncan 4.00 10.00
WF2 Vince Carter 4.00 10.00
WF3 Grant Hill 2.50 6.00
WF4 Kevin Garnett 3.00 8.00
WF5 Scottie Pippen 3.00 8.00
WF6 Karl Malone 2.50 6.00
WF7 Patrick Ewing 2.50 6.00
WF8 Tim Hardaway 2.00 5.00
WF9 Anfernee Hardaway 3.00 8.00
WF10 Reggie Miller 2.00 5.00
WF11 John Stockton 2.50 6.00
WF12 Ray Allen 2.00 5.00
WF13 Hakeem Olajuwon 2.50 6.00
WF14 David Robinson 3.00 8.00
WF15 Steve Smith 1.50 4.00

2002-03 Finest

Released in July 2003, Finest was issued as a 177-card set where base cards fall into several different formats where all cards were printed on foil-board. Card numbers 1-100 compose the base set, card numbers 101-120 feature rookie autographs and are serially numbered to 999, card numbers 121-156 showcase veteran players with a swatch of a jersey and are also sequentially numbered to 999, and card numbers 157-177 utilized the same format as the other rookies-autographed and numbered to 999. Please note that not all RC's had signed cards, and those players are noted with an asterisk. Finest was packaged with three mini-boxes per box. Each mini-box contained six packs of five cards per pack and carried a suggested retail price of $40 per mini box. Ten un-numbered Draft Pick redemption cards were randomly inserted in packs for Draft Pick #1 through Draft Pick #10.

101-120 AU PRINT RUN 999 SER.#'D SETS
121-156 JSY PRINT RUN 999 SER.#'d SETS
157-177 AU PRINT RUN 999 SER.#'d SETS
1 Dirk Nowitzki .60 1.50
2 Jason Terry .30 .75
3 Marcus Camby .30 .75
4 Joe Johnson .30 .75
5 Shawn Marion .30 .75
6 Andrei Kirilenko .40 1.00
7 Jamal Mashburn .30 .75
8 Andre Miller .30 .75
9 Jason Williams .30 .75
10 Tony Delk .25 .60
11 Tyson Chandler .40 1.00
12 Jason Richardson .40 1.00
13 Derek Fisher .30 .75
14 Troy Hudson .25 .60
15 Kerry Kittles .25 .60
16 Peja Stojakovic .40 1.00
17 Kurt Thomas .25 .60
18 Jamaal Tinsley .25 .60
19 Matt Harpring .25 .60
20 Kenny Thomas .25 .60
21 Kwame Brown .25 .60
22 Antonio Davis .25 .60
23 David Robinson .60 1.50
24 Keith Van Horn .30 .75
25 Howard Eisley .25 .60
26 Jalen Rose .30 .75
27 Chauncey Billups .40 1.00
28 Corey Maggette .30 .75
29 Pau Gasol .50 1.25
30 Desmond Mason .30 .75
31 Brian Grant .25 .60
32 Eddie Griffin .25 .60
33 Voshon Lenard .25 .60
34 Al Harrington .30 .75
35 Calbert Cheaney .25 .60
36 Malik Rose .25 .60
37 Bonzi Wells .25 .60
38 Pat Garrity .25 .60
39 P.J. Brown .25 .60
40 Ray Allen .40 1.00
41 Karl Malone .50 1.25
42 Steve Nash .50 1.25
43 Antawn Jamison .40 1.00
44 Ron Artest .40 1.00
45 Shane Battier .40 1.00
46 Gary Payton .40 1.00
47 Kobe Bryant 1.50 4.00
48 Lucious Harris .25 .60
49 Richard Hamilton .30 .75
50 Darius Miles .25 .60
51 Marcus Fizer .25 .60
52 Antoine Walker .30 .75
53 Juwan Howard .30 .75
54 Eddie Jones .30 .75
55 Kenyon Martin .30 .75
56 Derek Anderson .25 .60
57 Stephen Jackson .30 .75
58 Vince Carter .60 1.50
59 Larry Hughes .30 .75
60 Doug Christie .25 .60
61 Derrick Coleman .30 .75
62 Michael Finley .40 1.00
63 Wally Szczerbiak .30 .75
64 David Wesley .25 .60
65 Brad Miller .30 .75
66 Clifford Robinson .25 .60
67 Shandon Anderson .25 .60
68 Stephon Marbury .30 .75
69 Bobby Jackson .25 .60
70 Brent Barry .25 .60
71 Ruben Patterson .25 .60
72 Rashard Lewis .40 1.00
73 Tony Battie .25 .60
74 Ben Wallace .30 .75
75 Theo Ratliff .25 .60
76 Ricky Davis .30 .75
77 Nick Van Exel .30 .75
78 Mike Miller .30 .75
79 Sam Cassell .30 .75
80 Malik Allen .25 .60
81 Mike Bibby .40 1.00
82 Scottie Pippen .60 1.50
83 Dikembe Mutombo .40 1.00
84 Latrell Sprewell .30 .75
85 Predrag Drobnjak .25 .60
86 Joe Smith .30 .75
87 Aaron Mckie .25 .60
88 Jamaal Magloire .25 .60
89 Keon Clark .25 .60
90 Eric Williams .25 .60
91 Raef Lafrentz .25 .60
92 Troy Murphy .30 .75
93 Rick Fox .25 .60
94 Michael Redd .30 .75
95 Radoslav Nesterovic .25 .60
96 Donyell Marshall .25 .60
97 Elton Brand .40 1.00
98 Robert Horry .30 .75
99 Zydrunas Ilgauskas .30 .75
100 Michael Jordan 3.00 8.00
101 Juaquin Hawkins AU RC 2.50 6.00
102 Dan Dickau AU RC 3.00 8.00
104 John Salmons AU RC 4.00 10.00
105 Tamar Slay AU RC 2.50 6.00
106 Melvin Ely AU RC 3.00 8.00
107 Jared Jeffries AU RC 3.00 8.00
108 Junior Harrington AU RC 2.50 6.00
110 Qyntel Woods AU RC 3.00 8.00
111 Ryan Humphrey AU RC 3.00 8.00
112 J.R. Bremer AU RC 2.50 6.00
113 Antoine Rigadeau AU RC 4.00 10.00
114 Jay Williams RC 2.50 6.00
115 Pat Burke AU RC 2.50 6.00
116 Smush Parker AU RC 4.00 10.00
117 Juan Dixon AU RC 4.00 10.00
118 Vincent Yarbrough AU RC 2.50 6.00
120 Rasual Butler AU RC 4.00 10.00
121 Baron Davis JSY 3.00 8.00
122 Shareef Abdur-Rahim JSY 3.00 8.00
123 Gilbert Arenas JSY 4.00 10.00
124 Travis Best JSY 2.50 6.00
125 Vlade Divac JSY 3.00 8.00
126 Tim Duncan JSY 8.00 20.00
127 Jason Kidd JSY 6.00 15.00
128 Kevin Garnett JSY 6.00 15.00
129 Anfernee Hardaway JSY 6.00 15.00
130 Allen Iverson JSY 6.00 15.00
131 Cuttino Mobley JSY 2.50 6.00
132 Steve Francis JSY 3.00 8.00
133 Jermaine O'Neal JSY 3.00 8.00
134 Lamar Odom JSY 3.00 8.00
135 Michael Olowokandi JSY 2.50 6.00
136 Paul Pierce JSY 4.00 10.00
137 Reggie Miller JSY 4.00 10.00
138 Chris Webber JSY 4.00 10.00
139 Richard Jefferson JSY 4.00 10.00
140 Allan Houston JSY 3.00 8.00
141 Glenn Robinson JSY 3.00 8.00
142 Jerome Williams JSY 2.50 6.00
143 John Stockton JSY 5.00 12.00
144 Rasheed Wallace JSY 4.00 10.00
145 Eric Snow JSY 2.50 6.00
146 Tracy McGrady JSY 6.00 15.00
147 Shaquille O'Neal JSY 10.00 25.00
148 Jerry Stackhouse JSY 3.00 8.00
149 Morris Peterson JSY 2.50 6.00
150 Darrell Armstrong JSY 2.50 6.00
151 Tony Parker JSY 5.00 12.00
152 Vladimir Radmanovic JSY 2.50 6.00
153 Anthony Mason JSY 2.50 6.00
154 Charles Oakley JSY 3.00 8.00
155 Grant Hill JSY 5.00 12.00
156 Vin Baker JSY 3.00 8.00
157 Chris Jefferies AU RC 2.50 6.00
158 Drew Gooden AU RC 4.00 10.00
159 Casey Jacobsen AU RC 3.00 8.00
160 Kareem Rush AU RC 3.00 8.00
161 Bostjan Nachbar AU RC 3.00 8.00
162 Tayshaun Prince AU RC 5.00 12.00
163 Manu Ginobili RC 10.00 25.00
164 Gordan Giricek AU RC 4.00 10.00
165 Raul Lopez AU RC 4.00 10.00
166 Dan Gadzuric AU RC 3.00 8.00
167 Marko Jaric AU 4.00 10.00
168 Lonny Baxter AU RC 2.50 6.00
169 Yao Ming AU RC 25.00 60.00
170 Mike Dunleavy AU RC 4.00 10.00
171 Caron Butler AU RC 4.00 10.00
172 Nene Hilario AU RC 4.00 10.00
173 Amare Stoudemire AU RC 5.00 12.00
174 Nikoloz Tskitishvili AU RC 2.50 6.00
175 Fred Jones AU RC 3.00 8.00
176 DaJuan Wagner AU RC 3.00 8.00
177 Carlos Boozer AU RC 4.00 10.00
178 LeBron James XRC 150.00 300.00
179 Darko Milicic XRC 4.00 10.00
180 Carmelo Anthony XRC 6.00 15.00
181 Chris Bosh XRC 8.00 20.00
182 Dwyane Wade XRC 6.00 15.00
183 Chris Kaman XRC 4.00 10.00
184 Kirk Hinrich XRC 5.00 12.00
185 T.J. Ford XRC 4.00 10.00
186 Mike Sweetney XRC 4.00 10.00
187 Jarvis Hayes XRC 4.00 10.00

2002-03 Finest Refractors

*1-100 STARS: 2.5X TO 6X BASE CARD HI
1-100 STATED ODDS 1:24
1-100 PRINT RUN 250 SER.#'d SETS
*101-120 AU RCs: .6X TO 1.5X BASE CARD HI
101-120 AU RC PRINT RUN 250 SER. #'d SETS
*121-156 JSY: .6X TO 1.5X BASE CARD HI
121-156 JSY PRINT RUN 250 SER.#'d SETS
*157-177 AU RCs: .6X TO 1.5X BASE CARD HI
157-177 AU RC PRINT RUN 250 SER.#'d SETS
*XRC: 1X TO 2.5X BASE CARD HI
40 Ray Allen 5.00 12.00
47 Kobe Bryant 30.00 80.00
100 Michael Jordan 125.00 300.00
163 Manu Ginobili 25.00 60.00
169 Yao Ming AU 40.00 100.00
178 LeBron James 700.00 1000.00

2002-03 Finest Refractors Gold

*GOLD 1-100: 20X TO 50X BASE HI
*GOLD AU RC 101-120: 2X TO 5X HI
*GOLD JSY 121-156: 2X TO 5X HI
*GOLD AU RC 157-177: 2X TO 5X HI
*GOLD XRC 178-187: 3X TO 8X HI
STATED PRINT RUN 25 SER.#'d SETS
1 Dirk Nowitzki 50.00 120.00
100 Michael Jordan 200.00 500.00
163 Manu Ginobili 60.00 150.00
178 LeBron James 1500.00 2500.00

2003-04 Finest

Released in late June 2004, Finest features a 185-card base set divided up into 100 veteran base cards, 30 veteran jersey cards numbered to 999, 42 rookie cards numbered to 999 and 13 draft pick redemption cards. All of the cards are printed on holographic foil board and several of the rookie cards implement jerseys, autographs, both or none. The packaging included large boxes that contained three mini-boxes of six packs each. Packs contained five cards and each mini-box carried a suggested retail price of $40.

COMP.SET w/o SP's (100) 15.00 40.00
131-143 PRINT RUN 999 SER.#'d SETS
144-172 AU RC PRINT RUN 999 #'d SETS
XRC EXCH STATED ODDS 1:4
UNPRICED X-FRACTOR PRINT RUN ONE SET
1 Zach Randolph .30 .75
2 Keith Van Horn .30 .75
3 Steve Francis .30 .75
4 Al Harrington .30 .75
5 Jason Kidd .60 1.50
6 Jamaal Tinsley .25 .60
7 Lamar Odom .30 .75
8 Antoine Walker .40 1.00
9 Tony Parker .40 1.00
10 Jamal Mashburn .30 .75
11 Desmond Mason .30 .75
12 Carlos Arroyo .30 .75
13 Chris Andersen .50 1.25
14 Chris Wilcox .25 .60
15 Vince Carter .60 1.50
16 Peja Stojakovic .40 1.00
17 Qyntel Woods .25 .60
18 Mike Dunleavy .30 .75
19 Sam Cassell .30 .75
20 Allan Houston .30 .75
21 Speedy Claxton .25 .60
22 Rafer Alston .25 .60
23 Michael Finley .40 1.00
24 Richard Jefferson .30 .75
25 Larry Hughes .30 .75
26 Pau Gasol .40 1.00
27 Maurice Taylor .25 .60
28 Donyell Marshall .25 .60
29 Darrell Armstrong .25 .60
30 Latrell Sprewell .30 .75
31 Reggie Miller .40 1.00
32 Stephon Marbury .30 .75
33 Antawn Jamison .30 .75
34 DerMarr Johnson .25 .60
35 Shareef Abdur-Rahim .30 .75
36 Tony Battie .25 .60
37 Kwame Brown .25 .60
38 Fred Jones .30 .75
39 Jamal Crawford .40 1.00
40 Kurt Thomas .25 .60
41 Eric Snow .25 .60
42 Andre Miller .30 .75
43 Ray Allen .40 1.00
44 Caron Butler .30 .75
45 Corliss Williamson .25 .60
46 Kenny Thomas .25 .60
47 Jason Terry .30 .75
48 Ronald Murray .25 .60
49 Richard Hamilton .30 .75
50 Elton Brand .40 1.00
51 Ron Artest .40 1.00
52 Jerome Williams .25 .60
53 Ricky Davis .30 .75
54 Brent Barry .25 .60
55 Dikembe Mutombo .40 1.00
56 Earl Boykins .25 .60
57 Brad Miller .30 .75
58 Shane Battier .30 .75
59 Tyson Chandler .30 .75
60 Kelvin Cato .25 .60
61 Shawn Marion .30 .75
62 Bobby Jackson .25 .60
63 Corey Maggette .30 .75
64 Antonio McDyess .30 .75
65 Drew Gooden .30 .75
66 Mike Miller .30 .75
67 Darius Miles .25 .60
68 Stephen Jackson .30 .75
69 Cuttino Mobley .25 .60
70 Gary Payton .40 1.00
71 Toni Kukoc .40 1.00
72 Eddie Jones .30 .75
73 Gilbert Arenas .30 .75
74 Matt Harpring .25 .60
75 Marko Jaric .25 .60
76 Bonzi Wells .25 .60
77 Nick Van Exel .30 .75
78 Quentin Richardson .30 .75
79 Rasho Nesterovic .25 .60
80 Steve Nash .50 1.25
81 Morris Peterson .25 .60
82 Nikoloz Tskitishvili .25 .60
83 Damon Stoudamire .30 .75
84 Bruce Bowen .25 .60
85 Brian Grant .25 .60
86 Jalen Rose .30 .75
87 Jerry Stackhouse .30 .75
88 Kobe Bryant 1.50 4.00
89 Eddy Curry .25 .60
90 Tim Thomas .25 .60
91 Erick Dampier .25 .60
92 Jason Williams .30 .75
93 Troy Murphy .25 .60
94 Kerry Kittles .25 .60
95 Zydrunas Ilgauskas .30 .75
96 Theo Ratliff .25 .60
97 Samuel Dalembert .25 .60
98 Jeff McInnis .25 .60
99 Juwan Howard .30 .75
100 Joe Johnson .30 .75
101 Paul Pierce JSY 2.50 6.00
102 Ben Wallace JSY 2.00 5.00
103 Yao Ming JSY 5.00 12.00
104 Jermaine O'Neal JSY 2.00 5.00
105 Rashard Lewis JSY 2.50 6.00
106 Karl Malone JSY 3.00 8.00
107 Allen Iverson JSY 4.00 10.00
108 Mike Bibby JSY 2.50 6.00
109 Rasheed Wallace JSY 2.50 6.00
110 Nene JSY 2.00 5.00
111 Tracy McGrady JSY 3.00 8.00
112 Andrei Kirilenko JSY 2.50 6.00
113 Manu Ginobili JSY 3.00 8.00
114 Kenyon Martin JSY 2.00 5.00
115 Amare Stoudemire JSY 3.00 8.00
116 Baron Davis JSY 2.00 5.00
117 Michael Olowokandi JSY 2.00 5.00
118 Carlos Boozer JSY 2.00 5.00
119 Jason Richardson JSY 2.50 6.00
120 Dirk Nowitzki JSY 4.00 10.00
121 Chauncey Billups JSY 2.50 6.00
122 Chris Webber JSY 2.50 6.00
123 Glenn Robinson JSY/807 2.00 5.00
124 Kevin Garnett JSY 4.00 10.00
125 Michael Redd JSY 2.50 6.00
126 David Wesley JSY 2.00 5.00
127 Tayshaun Prince JSY 2.00 5.00
128 Jamaal Magloire JSY 2.00 5.00
129 Tim Duncan JSY 4.00 10.00
130 Shaquille O'Neal JSY 8.00 20.00
131 Darko Milicic RC 2.00 5.00
132 Chris Kaman RC 2.50 6.00
133 LeBron James RC 200.00 500.00
134 Richie Frahm RC 2.50 6.00
135 Steve Blake RC 2.00 5.00
136 Zaza Pachulia RC 2.50 6.00
137 Keith Bogans RC 1.50 4.00
138 Kirk Hinrich AU RC 4.00 10.00
139 Jarvis Hayes RC 1.50 4.00
140 Zarko Cabarkapa AU RC 2.50 6.00
141 Zoran Planinic AU RC 2.50 6.00
142 Udonis Haslem RC 2.00 5.00
143 David West RC 2.50 6.00
144 Boris Diaw AU RC 4.00 10.00
146 Brian Cook AU RC 2.50 6.00
147 Ndudi Ebi AU RC 2.50 6.00
148 Josh Howard AU RC 4.00 10.00
149 Jason Kapono AU RC 2.50 6.00
150 Luke Walton AU RC 4.00 10.00
151 Travis Hansen AU RC 2.50 6.00
152 Willie Green AU RC 2.50 6.00
153 Maurice Williams AU RC 4.00 10.00
154 Francisco Elson AU RC 2.50 6.00
155 Kyle Korver AU RC 5.00 12.00
156 Marquis Daniels AU RC 3.00 8.00
157 Chris Bosh AU RC 10.00 25.00
158 Dwyane Wade AU RC 30.00 80.00
159 Aleksandar Pavlovic AU RC 3.00 8.00
160 Mike Sweetney AU RC 2.50 6.00
161 Marcus Banks AU RC 2.50 6.00
162 Luke Ridnour AU RC 3.00 8.00
163 Carmelo Anthony AU RC 25.00 60.00
164 Mickael Pietrus AU RC 3.00 8.00
165 Reece Gaines AU RC 2.50 6.00
166 Kendrick Perkins AU RC 3.00 8.00
167 Troy Bell AU RC 2.50 6.00
168 Leandro Barbosa AU RC 4.00 10.00
169 Dahntay Jones AU RC 3.00 8.00
170 T.J. Ford AU RC 3.00 8.00
171 Nick Collison AU RC 3.00 8.00
172 Theron Smith AU RC 2.50 6.00
173 Dwight Howard XRC 4.00 10.00
174 Emeka Okafor XRC 6.00 15.00
175 Ben Gordon XRC 6.00 15.00
176 Shaun Livingston XRC 5.00 12.00
177 Devin Harris XRC 5.00 12.00
178 Josh Childress XRC 5.00 12.00
179 Luol Deng XRC 8.00 20.00
180 Rafael Araujo XRC 3.00 8.00
181 Andre Iguodala XRC 6.00 15.00
182 Luke Jackson XRC 5.00 12.00
183 Andris Biedrins XRC 3.00 8.00
184 Robert Swift XRC 5.00 12.00
185 Sebastian Telfair XRC 5.00 12.00

2003-04 Finest Refractors

*1-100 REF.SINGLES: 2.5X TO 6X BASE HI
*131-143 REF.SINGLES: .75X TO 2X BASE HI
*XRC: .75X TO 2X BASE HI
5 Jason Kidd JSY 5.00 12.00
101 Paul Pierce JSY 3.00 8.00
103 Yao Ming JSY 6.00 15.00
106 Karl Malone JSY 4.00 10.00
107 Allen Iverson JSY 5.00 12.00
111 Tracy McGrady JSY 4.00 10.00
115 Amare Stoudemire JSY 4.00 10.00
120 Dirk Nowitzki JSY 5.00 12.00
124 Kevin Garnett JSY 5.00 12.00
129 Tim Duncan JSY 5.00 12.00
130 Shaquille O'Neal JSY 10.00 25.00
132 Chris Kaman JSY 3.00 8.00
136 Zaza Pachulia JSY 3.00 8.00
138 Kirk Hinrich JSY AU 6.00 15.00
144 Boris Diaw JSY AU 6.00 15.00
150 Luke Walton AU 5.00 12.00
157 Chris Bosh JSY AU 15.00 40.00
162 Luke Ridnour JSY AU 5.00 12.00
164 Mickael Pietrus JSY AU 5.00 12.00
166 Kendrick Perkins JSY AU 5.00 12.00
168 Leandro Barbosa JSY AU 6.00 15.00
170 T.J. Ford JSY AU 5.00 12.00

2003-04 Finest Refractors Gold

*GOLD 1-100: 12X TO 30X BASE HI
*GOLD JSY 101-130: 1.5X TO 4X BASE HI

*GOLD RC 131-143: 2.5X TO 6X BASE HI
*GOLD AU RC 144-172: 1.5X TO 4X BASE HI
*GOLD XRC 173-185: 1.25X TO 3X BASE HI
PRINT RUN 25 SER.#'d SETS
129 Tim Duncan JSY 25.00 60.00
133 LeBron James 3000.00 5000.00
157 Chris Bosh AU 125.00 250.00
163 Carmelo Anthony AU 125.00 300.00

2004-05 Finest

Released at the end of June, Finest boasts a 220-card set divided up as follows: cards 1-100 feature veteran players, cards 101-130 feature jersey cards sequentially numbered to 299, cards 131-150 features retired players sequentially numbered to 400, cards 151-160 feature rookie player cards sequentially numbered to 400, cards 161-190 feature autographed RC cards sequentially numbered to 299, and cards 191-220 were originally issued as draft pick redemption cards sequentially numbered to 599. The cards are redeemable for the coinciding draft pick where card 191 is the first and picks go on from there. All cards are printed on foil board with a white background, a black strip along the bottom and silver highlights around the player's picture. Finest was released in boxes that contained three mini-boxes and an incased uncirculated refractor blue card. Mini-boxes contained six packs each (18 total per box) and the SRP was $40 per mini-box.

COMP.SET w/o SP's (100) 15.00 40.00
131-160 PRINT RUN 400 SER.#'d SETS
161-190 AU RC PRINT RUN 299 #'d SETS
191-220 XRC PRINT RUN 599 #'d SETS
UNPRICED WHITE PRINT RUN ONE SET
1 Richard Hamilton .30 .75
2 Mike Dunleavy .30 .75
3 Jamaal Tinsley .25 .60
4 Corey Maggette .30 .75
5 Zach Randolph .30 .75
6 Desmond Mason .30 .75
7 Marc Jackson .25 .60
8 Kobe Bryant 1.50 4.00
9 Mike Bibby .40 1.00
10 Vince Carter .60 1.50
11 Bonzi Wells .25 .60
12 Ricky Davis .30 .75
13 Steve Nash .50 1.25
14 Rashard Lewis .40 1.00
15 Eddy Curry .25 .60
16 Carlos Boozer .30 .75
17 Brad Miller .30 .75
18 Kurt Thomas .25 .60
19 Shareef Abdur-Rahim .30 .75
20 Grant Hill .50 1.25
21 Jason Hart .25 .60
22 Larry Hughes .30 .75
23 Lebron James 4.00 10.00
24 Udonis Haslem .25 .60
25 David Wesley .25 .60
26 Kenny Thomas .25 .60
27 Marcus Camby .30 .75
28 Michael Redd .30 .75
29 Rasho Nesterovic .25 .60
30 Keith Van Horn .30 .75
31 Reggie Miller .40 1.00
32 Stephon Marbury .30 .75
33 Donyell Marshall .25 .60
34 Jermaine O'Neal .30 .75
35 Antoine Walker .40 1.00
36 Rasheed Wallace .40 1.00
37 Antonio Daniels .25 .60
38 Damon Jones .25 .60
39 Caron Butler .30 .75
40 Shawn Marion .30 .75
41 Lee Nailon .25 .60
42 Damon Stoudamire .30 .75
43 Bob Sura .25 .60
44 Mehmet Okur .30 .75
45 Shane Battier .30 .75
46 Michael Finley .40 1.00
47 Doug Christie .25 .60
48 Eddie Jones .30 .75
49 Speedy Claxton .25 .60
50 Wally Szczerbiak .30 .75
51 Primoz Brezec .25 .60
52 Marko Jaric .25 .60
53 Antonio McDyess .30 .75
54 Jeff Mcinnis .25 .60
55 Tony Parker .40 1.00
56 Rafer Alston .25 .60
57 Troy Murphy .25 .60
58 Chris Mihm .25 .60
59 Jarvis Hayes .25 .60
60 Marquis Daniels .25 .60
61 Jamal Crawford .40 1.00
62 Morris Peterson .25 .60
63 Luke Ridnour .30 .75
64 Mike Miller .30 .75
65 Carlos Arroyo .25 .60
66 Gary Payton .40 1.00
67 Joe Johnson .30 .75
68 Latrell Sprewell .30 .75
69 Allan Houston .30 .75
70 Earl Boykins .25 .60
71 Brendan Haywood .25 .60
72 Baron Davis .30 .75
73 Fred Jones .25 .60
74 Joe Smith .30 .75
75 Jalen Rose .30 .75
76 Eddie Griffin .25 .60
77 Lamar Odom .30 .75
78 Theo Ratliff .25 .60
79 Gordan Giricek .25 .60
80 Maurice Williams .30 .75
81 Tayshaun Prince .30 .75
82 Kyle Korver .30 .75
83 Andre Miller .30 .75
84 Chris Wilcox .25 .60
85 Alonzo Mourning .50 1.25
86 Gilbert Arenas .30 .75
87 Zydrunas Ilgauskas .30 .75
88 Jamaal Magloire .25 .60
89 Jason Williams .30 .75
90 Chucky Atkins .25 .60
91 Jeff Foster .25 .60
92 Kareem Rush .25 .60
93 Sam Cassell .30 .75
94 Josh Howard .40 1.00
95 Tyronn Lue .25 .60
96 Vladimir Radmanovic .25 .60
97 Chauncey Billups .40 1.00
98 Brent Barry .25 .60
99 Paul Pierce .40 1.00
100 Dwyane Wade .60 1.50
101 Al Harrington JSY 2.00 5.00
102 Antawn Jamison JSY 2.00 5.00
103 Kirk Hinrich JSY 2.00 5.00
104 Tim Duncan JSY 4.00 10.00
105 Gerald Wallace JSY 2.00 5.00
106 Dirk Nowitzki JSY 4.00 10.00
107 Chris Webber JSY 2.50 6.00
108 Jason Kidd JSY 4.00 10.00
109 Carmelo Anthony JSY 5.00 12.00
110 Tracy McGrady JSY 3.00 8.00
111 Elton Brand JSY 2.50 6.00
112 Pau Gasol JSY 2.50 6.00
113 Jason Richardson JSY 2.50 6.00
114 Chris Bosh JSY 2.50 6.00
115 Kevin Garnett JSY 4.00 10.00
116 Steve Francis JSY 2.00 5.00
117 Richard Jefferson JSY 2.00 5.00
118 Baron Davis JSY 2.00 5.00
119 Manu Ginobili JSY 3.00 8.00
120 Shaquille O'Neal JSY 6.00 15.00
121 Amare Stoudemire JSY 2.00 5.00
122 Yao Ming JSY 5.00 12.00
123 Kenyon Martin JSY 2.00 5.00
124 Allen Iverson JSY 4.00 10.00
125 Peja Stojakovic JSY 2.50 6.00
126 Drew Gooden JSY 1.50 4.00
127 Ray Allen JSY 2.50 6.00
128 Ben Wallace JSY 2.00 5.00
129 Andrei Kirilenko JSY 2.00 5.00
130 Quentin Richardson JSY 2.00 5.00
131 Larry Bird 5.00 12.00
132 George Gervin 2.00 5.00
133 Walt Frazier 2.00 5.00
134 Oscar Robertson 2.00 5.00
135 Elgin Baylor 2.00 5.00
136 Moses Malone 2.00 5.00
137 Pete Maravich 3.00 8.00
138 Bob Cousy 3.00 8.00
139 Earl Monroe 2.00 5.00
140 Kareem Abdul-Jabbar 3.00 8.00
141 Isiah Thomas 2.00 5.00
142 Kevin McHale 2.50 6.00
143 Bill Walton 2.00 5.00
144 John Havlicek 2.00 5.00
145 Rick Barry 1.50 4.00
146 Wilt Chamberlain 4.00 10.00
147 Bill Russell 3.00 8.00
148 Willis Reed 2.00 5.00
149 Julius Erving 3.00 8.00
150 Drazen Petrovic 3.00 8.00
151 Andre Iguodala RC 2.50 6.00
152 Luke Jackson RC 1.25 3.00
153 Kirk Snyder RC 1.25 3.00
154 Kevin Martin RC 2.50 6.00
155 Antonio Burks RC 1.50 4.00
156 Robert Swift RC 1.25 3.00
157 Dorell Wright RC 2.00 5.00
158 David Harrison RC 1.25 3.00
159 Dwight Howard RC 4.00 10.00
160 Al Jefferson RC 2.50 6.00
161 Justin Reed AU RC 3.00 8.00
162 Shaun Livingston AU RC 5.00 12.00
163 Luol Deng AU RC 5.00 12.00
164 Josh Smith AU RC 5.00 12.00
165 Jameer Nelson AU RC 5.00 12.00
166 Pavel Podkolzin AU RC 3.00 8.00
167 Emeka Okafor AU RC 4.00 10.00
168 Kris Humphries AU RC 5.00 12.00
169 J.R. Smith AU RC 5.00 12.00
170 Sebastian Telfair AU RC 4.00 10.00
171 Sasha Vujacic AU RC 5.00 12.00
172 Tony Allen AU RC 5.00 12.00
173 Romain Sato AU RC 3.00 8.00
174 Ben Gordon AU RC 5.00 12.00
175 Devin Harris AU RC 4.00 10.00
176 Josh Childress AU RC 4.00 10.00
177 Andre Barrett AU RC 5.00 12.00
178 Jackson Vroman AU RC 3.00 8.00
179 Lionel Chalmers AU RC 5.00 12.00
180 Delonte West AU RC 5.00 12.00
181 Nenad Krstic AU RC 5.00 12.00
182 Donta Smith AU RC 3.00 8.00
183 Chris Duhon AU RC 5.00 12.00
184 Peter John Ramos AU RC 3.00 8.00
185 Bernard Robinson AU RC 4.00 10.00
186 Beno Udrih AU RC 4.00 10.00
187 Andris Biedrins AU RC 3.00 8.00
188 Trevor Ariza AU RC 5.00 12.00
189 Rafael Araujo AU RC 3.00 8.00
190 Andres Nocioni AU RC 5.00 12.00
191 Andrew Bogut XRC 5.00 12.00
192 Marvin Williams XRC 3.00 8.00
193 Deron Williams XRC 4.00 10.00
194 Chris Paul XRC 12.00 30.00
195 Raymond Felton XRC 3.00 8.00
196 Martell Webster XRC 3.00 8.00
197 Charlie Villanueva XRC 4.00 10.00
198 Channing Frye XRC 3.00 8.00
199 Ike Diogu XRC 3.00 8.00
200 Andrew Bynum XRC 2.50 6.00
201 Salim Stoudamire XRC 3.00 8.00
202 Yaroslav Korolev XRC 3.00 8.00
203 Sean May XRC 3.00 8.00
204 Rashad McCants XRC 3.00 8.00
205 Antoine Wright XRC 3.00 8.00
206 Joey Graham XRC 3.00 8.00
207 Danny Granger XRC 4.00 10.00
208 Gerald Green XRC 3.00 8.00
209 Hakim Warrick XRC 3.00 8.00
210 Julius Hodge XRC 3.00 8.00
211 Nate Robinson XRC 3.00 8.00
212 Jarrett Jack XRC 3.00 8.00
213 Francisco Garcia XRC 2.50 6.00
214 Luther Head XRC 3.00 8.00
215 Daniel Ewing XRC 3.00 8.00
216 Jason Maxiell XRC 2.50 6.00
217 Linas Kleiza XRC 3.00 8.00
218 Brandon Bass XRC 2.50 6.00
219 Wayne Simien XRC 3.00 8.00
220 David Lee XRC 4.00 10.00

2004-05 Finest Refractors

*1-100 REFRACTORS: 1.25X TO 3X BASE HI
*101-220 REFRACTORS: .5X TO 1.25X BASE HI
1-100 PRINT RUN 249 SER.#'d SETS
101-130 PRINT RUN 179 SER.#'d SETS
131-160 PRINT RUN 249 SER.#'d SETS
161-190 PRINT RUN 179 SER.#'d SETS
191-220 PRINT RUN 359 SER.#'d SETS
8 Kobe Bryant 15.00 40.00
23 LeBron James 60.00 150.00

2004-05 Finest Refractors Black

*1-100 REF.BLACK: 8X TO 20X BASE HI
*101-220 REF.BLACK: 1.5X TO 4X BASE HI
1-100 PRINT RUN 29 SER.#'d SETS
101-130 JSY PRINT RUN 19 SER.#'d SETS
161-190 PRINT RUN 19 SER.#'d SETS
191-220 PRINT RUN 39 SER.#'d SETS
8 Kobe Bryant 75.00 200.00
20 Grant Hill 12.00 30.00
23 LeBron James 500.00 1000.00
85 Alonzo Mourning 12.00 30.00
120 Shaquille O'Neal JSY 40.00 100.00

2004-05 Finest Refractors Blue

*1-100 REF.BLUE: 4X TO 10X BASE HI
*101-220 REF.BLUE: .75X TO 2X BASE HI
BLUE PRINT RUN 50 SER.#'d SETS
ONE PER BOX AS TOPPER
8 Kobe Bryant 60.00 150.00
20 Grant Hill 6.00 15.00
23 LeBron James 200.00 500.00
85 Alonzo Mourning 8.00 20.00
100 Dwyane Wade 15.00 40.00
159 Dwight Howard 15.00 40.00

2004-05 Finest Refractors Gold

*1-100 REF.GOLD: 10X TO 25X BASE HI
*101-190 REF.GOLD: 2X TO 5X BASE HI
*191-220 REF.GOLD: 2.5X TO 6X BASE HI
1-100 PRINT RUN 15 SER.#'d SETS
101-130 JSY PRINT RUN 12 SER.#'d SETS
131-160 PRINT RUN 15 SER.#'d SETS
161-190 PRINT RUN 12 SER.#'d SETS
191-220 PRINT RUN 25 SER.#'d SETS
8 Kobe Bryant 100.00 250.00
23 LeBron James 600.00 1200.00
85 Alonzo Mourning 15.00 40.00
120 Shaquille O'Neal JSY 40.00 100.00

2004-05 Finest Refractors Green

*1-100 REF.GREEN: 4X TO 10X BASE HI
*101-220 REF.GREEN: .75X TO 2X BASE HI
1-100 PRINT RUN 49 SER.#'d SETS
101-130 JSY PRINT RUN 29 SER.#'d SETS
161-190 PRINT RUN 29 SER.#'d SETS
191-220 PRINT RUN 59 SER.#'d SETS
8 Kobe Bryant 60.00 150.00
23 LeBron James 200.00 500.00
85 Alonzo Mourning 8.00 20.00
159 Dwight Howard 15.00 40.00

2004-05 Finest Refractors Red

*1-100 REF.RED: 1.5X TO 4X BASE HI
*101-220 REF.RED: .6X TO 1.5X BASE HI
1-100 PRINT RUN 149 SER.#'d SETS
101-130 PRINT RUN 79 SER.#'d SETS
161-190 PRINT RUN 79 SER.#'d SETS
191-220 PRINT RUN 159 SER.#'d SETS
8 Kobe Bryant 25.00 60.00
23 LeBron James 75.00 200.00
159 Dwight Howard 12.00 30.00

2004-05 Finest X-Fractors

*1-100 X-FRAC: 1.5X TO 4X BASE HI
*101-220 X-FRAC: .5X TO 1.25X BASE HI
1-100 PRINT RUN 199 SER.#'d SETS
101-130 JSY PRINT RUN 129 SER.#'d SETS
131-160 PRINT RUN 199 SER.#'d SETS
161-190 PRINT RUN 129 SER.#'d SETS
191-220 PRINT RUN 259 SER.#'d SETS
8 Kobe Bryant 20.00 50.00
23 LeBron James 75.00 200.00

2004-05 Finest X-Fractors Black

1-190 PRINT RUN 9 SER.#'d SETS
1-190 NOT PRICED DUE TO SCARCITY
*191-220 X-FRAC.BLACK: 2.5X TO 6X BASE HI

2004-05 Finest X-Fractors Blue

*1-100 X-FRAC BLUE: 10X TO 25X BASE HI
*101-160 X-FRAC.BLUE: 1.5X TO 4X BASE HI
*161-190 X-FRAC BLUE: 1X TO 2.5X BASE HI
*191-220 X-FRAC BLUE: 2.5X TO 6X BASE HI
BLUE PRINT RUN 25 SER.#'d SETS
ONE PER BOX AS TOPPER
8 Kobe Bryant 60.00 150.00
23 LeBron James 300.00 600.00
85 Alonzo Mourning 15.00 40.00

2004-05 Finest X-Fractors Green

*1-100 X-FRAC GREEN: 8X TO 20X BASE HI
*101-130 X-FRAC.GREEN: 2X TO 5X BASE HI
*131-160 X-FRAC.GREEN: 1.5X TO 4X BASE HI
*191-220 X-FRAC.GREEN: 2X TO 5X BASE HI
1-100 PRINT RUN 19 SER.#'d SETS
161-190 PRINT RUN 15 SER.#'d SETS
191-220 PRINT RUN 30 SER.#'d SETS
8 Kobe Bryant 150.00 300.00
23 LeBron James 300.00 600.00
85 Alonzo Mourning 20.00 50.00
120 Shaquille O'Neal JSY 50.00 125.00

2004-05 Finest X-Fractors Red

*1-100 X-FRAC RED: 2.5X TO 6X BASE HI
*101-220 X-FRAC.RED: .6X TO 1.5X BASE HI
8 Kobe Bryant 20.00 50.00
23 LeBron James 125.00 300.00
85 Alonzo Mourning 4.00 10.00
100 Dwyane Wade 10.00 25.00

2004-05 Finest Far East Fabrics

Randomly seeded in packs, this 24-card set is horizontally designed and features a red background along the top and bottom, player photos on the left and a square jersey swatch on the right surrounded by Chinese words. Refractor parallels were issued for this set where base refractors are serially numbered to 50, X-Fractors are serially numbered to 10, and Super Fractors are one of ones.

PRINT RUN 100 SER.#'d SETS
*REFRACTORS: .6X TO 1.5X BASE HI
REF.PRINT RUN 50 SER.#'d SETS
BJ Bobby Jackson 2.50 6.00
BM Brad Miller 3.00 8.00
BN Bostjan Nachbar 2.50 6.00
CW Chris Webber 4.00 10.00
DC Doug Christie 2.50 6.00
DM Dikembe Mutombo 5.00 12.00
DS Darius Songaila 2.50 6.00
ED Erik Daniels 3.00 8.00
GO Greg Ostertag 2.50 6.00
JH Juwan Howard 3.00 8.00
JJ Jim Jackson 2.50 6.00
KM Kevin Martin 5.00 12.00
MB Matt Barnes 2.50 6.00
ME Maurice Evans 4.00 10.00
MT Maurice Taylor 2.50 6.00
PS Peja Stojakovic 4.00 10.00
RB Ryan Bowen 2.50 6.00
RG Reece Gaines 2.50 6.00
SP Scott Padgett 2.50 6.00
TL Tyronn Lue 2.50 6.00
TM Tracy McGrady 5.00 12.00
YM Yao Ming 8.00 20.00
CWA Charlie Ward 2.50 6.00
MBI Mike Bibby 4.00 10.00

2004-05 Finest Moments Autographs

Randomly seeded, this 13-card set is borderless and showcases NBA legends on the top half of the card and a sticker autograph on the bottom half. Each card is sequentially numbered to 50. Several refractor parallels were produced with Topps' rainbow holofoil refractor effect. Refractors are sequentially numbered to 20, X-Fractors are sequentially numbered to seven and Super Fractors are one of ones.

PRINT RUN 50 SER.#'d SETS
*REFRACTORS: .6X TO 1.5X BASE HI
REF.PRINT RUN 20 SER.#'d SETS
BW Bill Walton 15.00 40.00
CD Clyde Drexler 15.00 40.00
DB Dave Bing 40.00 100.00
DC Dave Cowens 12.00 30.00
DS Detlef Schrempf 15.00 40.00
EB Elgin Baylor 15.00 40.00
EM Earl Monroe 15.00 40.00
GG George Gervin 12.00 30.00
ME Mark Eaton 12.00 30.00
MM Moses Malone 12.00 30.00
RB Rick Barry 12.00 30.00
RP Robert Parish 15.00 40.00

2004-05 Finest Perfect Pairs Autographs

Randomly inserted in packs, this 15-card set pairs a two players on each card with their autographed stickers. Some pair a legend and a current player, and others players of the same position. Each card is limited to 50 copies. Refractor parallel versions of this set were issued too: Refractors are serially numbered to 20, X-Fractors are serially numbered to seven and Super Fractors are numbered one of one.

PRINT RUN 50 SER.#'d SETS
*REFRACTORS: .5X TO 1.25X BASE HI
REFRACTOR PRINT RUN 20 SER.#'d SETS
AG C.Anthony/G.Gervin 30.00 60.00
DB L.Deng/E.Baylor 10.00 25.00
DP T.Duncan/R.Parish 60.00 150.00
GB B.Gordon/D.Bing 25.00 60.00
HB R.Hamilton/R.Barry 10.00 25.00
MD T.McGrady/C.Drexler 30.00 60.00
MM S.Marbury/E.Monroe 10.00 25.00
OD S.O'Neal/T.Duncan 150.00 300.00
OH E.Okafor/S.Haywood 10.00 25.00
OL J.O'Neal/B.Lanier 10.00 25.00
SC A.Stoudemire/D.Cowens 40.00 80.00
SS P.Stojakovic/D.Schrempf 25.00 60.00
WE B.Wallace/M.Eaton 10.00 25.00
OHA L.Odom/C.Hawkins 10.00 25.00

2005-06 Finest

Released in June 2005, this 169-card set features veteran players on cards 1-100, celebrities serially numbered to 599 on cards 101-105, rookies serially numbered to 599 on cards 106-125, rookie autographs serially numbered to 349 on cards 126-139 and Draft Pick redemptions for cards 140-169. Finest contains the first live redemption cards for the new 2006-07 rookie class. Base cards are printed on all foil with a basketball-looking background on the top and full color player photos on the bottom. Finest was packaged in a box that contains two six-pack mini boxes. Upon release, mini boxes carried a $40 SRP.

COMP.SET w/o SP's (100) 15.00 40.00
101-125 RC PRINT RUN 599 SER.#'d SETS
126-139 AU RC PRINT RUN 349 SER.#'d SETS
XRC 140-169 ISSUED AS DRAFT EXCH
UNPRICED SUPERFR.PRINT RUN ONE SET
UNPRICED WHITE PRINT RUN ONE SET
UNPRICED WHITE X-FR PRINT RUN ONE SET
1 Shaquille O'Neal .75 2.00
2 Eddy Curry .25 .60
3 Ben Wallace .30 .75
4 Wally Szczerbiak .30 .75
5 Richard Jefferson .30 .75
6 Josh Howard .40 1.00
7 Grant Hill .50 1.25
8 Desmond Mason .25 .60
9 Corey Maggette .30 .75
10 Caron Butler .30 .75
11 Andrei Kirilenko .30 .75
12 Al Harrington .30 .75
13 Tony Parker .40 1.00
14 Stephon Marbury .30 .75
15 Rafer Alston .25 .60
16 Marquis Daniels .25 .60
17 Luke Ridnour .30 .75
18 Kirk Hinrich .30 .75
19 Jason Kidd .60 1.50
20 Morris Peterson .25 .60
21 Yao Ming .50 1.25
22 Nenad Krstic .25 .60
23 Mehmet Okur .25 .60
24 Shareef Abdur-Rahim .30 .75
25 Rashard Lewis .40 1.00
26 Luol Deng .30 .75
27 Elton Brand .40 1.00
28 Dirk Nowitzki .60 1.50
29 Bobby Simmons .25 .60
30 Antawn Jamison .30 .75
31 Tracy McGrady .50 1.25
32 Steve Francis .30 .75
33 Kobe Bryant 1.50 4.00
34 Jason Richardson .40 1.00
35 J.R. Smith .30 .75
36 Tayshaun Prince .30 .75
37 Chauncey Billups .40 1.00
38 Allen Iverson .60 1.50
39 Ricky Davis .30 .75
40 Josh Smith .30 .75
41 Brad Miller .30 .75
42 Zach Randolph .30 .75
43 Troy Murphy .25 .60
44 Shawn Marion .30 .75
45 Pau Gasol .40 1.00
46 Lamar Odom .30 .75
47 Drew Gooden .30 .75
48 Darius Miles .25 .60
49 Chris Bosh .40 1.00
50 Antoine Walker .30 .75
51 Amare Stoudemire .30 .75
52 Rasheed Wallace .40 1.00
53 Emeka Okafor .30 .75
54 Steve Nash .50 1.25
55 Sam Cassell .30 .75
56 Michael Finley .40 1.00
57 Manu Ginobili .40 1.00
58 Mike Dunleavy .30 .75
59 Jason Terry .30 .75
60 Jalen Rose .40 1.00
61 Ron Artest .40 1.00
62 Marcus Camby .30 .75
63 Udonis Haslem .25 .60
64 Kenyon Martin .30 .75
65 Gerald Wallace .30 .75
66 David West .30 .75
67 Samuel Dalembert .25 .60
68 Jermaine O'Neal .30 .75
69 Dwight Howard .30 .75
70 T.J. Ford .25 .60
71 Smush Parker .25 .60
72 Sebastian Telfair .30 .75
73 Ray Allen .40 1.00
74 Michael Redd .30 .75
75 Larry Hughes .30 .75
76 Jamaal Tinsley .25 .60
77 Chris Duhon .25 .60
78 Baron Davis .30 .75
79 Andre Iguodala .30 .75
80 Paul Pierce .40 1.00
81 Zydrunas Ilgauskas .30 .75
82 Tim Duncan .60 1.50
83 Shane Battier .30 .75
84 Peja Stojakovic .40 1.00
85 LeBron James 1.50 4.00
86 Kevin Garnett .60 1.50
87 Chris Webber .40 1.00
88 Carmelo Anthony .75 2.00
89 Vince Carter .60 1.50
90 Stephen Jackson .30 .75
91 Richard Hamilton .30 .75
92 Mike Bibby .40 1.00
93 Marko Jaric .25 .60
94 Jamal Crawford .40 1.00
95 Gilbert Arenas .30 .75
96 Dwyane Wade .60 1.50
97 Delonte West .25 .60
98 Ben Gordon .30 .75
99 Andre Miller .30 .75
100 Joe Johnson .30 .75
101 Jay-Z 2.50 6.00
102 Shannon Elizabeth 2.50 6.00
103 Jenny McCarthy 2.50 6.00
104 Carmen Electra 2.50 6.00
105 Christie Brinkley 2.50 6.00
106 Chris Paul RC 6.00 15.00
107 Channing Frye RC 1.50 4.00
108 Ike Diogu RC 1.00 2.50
109 Marvin Williams RC 1.50 4.00
110 Rashad McCants RC 1.25 3.00
111 Luther Head RC 1.25 3.00
112 Gerald Green RC 1.50 4.00
113 Salim Stoudamire RC 1.25 3.00
114 Jose Calderon RC 1.50 4.00
115 Andrew Bynum RC 1.25 3.00
116 Wayne Simien RC 1.00 2.50
117 Chris Taft RC 1.25 3.00
118 Ryan Gomes RC 1.25 3.00
119 Martell Webster RC 1.25 3.00
120 Johan Petro RC 1.00 2.50
121 Antoine Wright RC 1.25 3.00
122 Jarrett Jack RC 1.50 4.00
123 Daniel Ewing RC 1.25 3.00
124 Joey Graham RC 1.25 3.00
125 Nate Robinson RC 1.50 4.00
126 Andrew Bogut AU RC 6.00 15.00
127 Raymond Felton AU RC 5.00 12.00
128 Francisco Garcia AU RC 4.00 10.00
129 Danny Granger AU RC 6.00 15.00
130 Orien Greene AU RC 4.00 10.00
131 Sarunas Jasikevicius AU RC 5.00 12.00
132 Linas Kleiza AU RC 3.00 8.00
133 David Lee AU RC 5.00 12.00
134 Sean May AU RC 3.00 8.00
135 Fabricio Oberto AU RC 4.00 10.00
136 Charlie Villanueva AU RC 5.00 12.00
137 Hakim Warrick AU RC 4.00 10.00
138 James Singleton AU RC 3.00 8.00
139 Deron Williams AU RC 6.00 15.00
140 Andrea Bargnani XRC 4.00 10.00
141 LaMarcus Aldridge XRC 8.00 20.00
142 Adam Morrison XRC 3.00 8.00
143 Tyrus Thomas XRC 2.50 6.00
144 Shelden Williams XRC 3.00 8.00
145 Brandon Roy XRC 4.00 10.00
146 Randy Foye XRC 3.00 8.00
147 Rudy Gay XRC 5.00 12.00
148 Patrick O'Bryant XRC 2.50 6.00
149 Saer Sene XRC 2.50 6.00
150 J.J. Redick XRC 4.00 10.00
151 Hilton Armstrong XRC 2.50 6.00
152 Thabo Sefolosha XRC 3.00 8.00
153 Ronnie Brewer XRC 3.00 8.00
154 Cedric Simmons XRC 2.50 6.00
155 Rodney Carney XRC 2.50 6.00
156 Shawne Williams XRC 2.50 6.00
157 Craig Smith XRC 3.00 8.00
158 Quincy Douby XRC 2.50 6.00
159 Renaldo Balkman XRC 3.00 8.00
160 Rajon Rondo XRC 6.00 15.00
161 Marcus Williams XRC 2.50 6.00
162 Josh Boone XRC 2.50 6.00
163 Kyle Lowry XRC 4.00 10.00
164 Shannon Brown XRC 3.00 8.00
165 Jordan Farmar XRC 3.00 8.00
166 Sergio Rodriguez XRC 2.00 5.00
167 Maurice Ager XRC 2.00 5.00
168 Mardy Collins XRC 2.50 6.00
169 Paul Millsap XRC 5.00 12.00

2005-06 Finest Refractors

*1-100: 1X TO 2.5X BASE HI
*101-125: .5X TO 1.25X BASE HI
*126-139: SAME VALUE AS BASE
*140-169: .5X TO 1.25X BASE HI
1-100 REF.PRINT RUN 349 SER.#'d SETS
101-125 REF.RC PRINT RUN 249 SER.#'d SETS
126-139 REF.AU RC PRINT RUN 229 SETS
33 Kobe Bryant 8.00 20.00
85 LeBron James 25.00 60.00
106 Chris Paul 10.00 25.00

2005-06 Finest Refractors Black

*1-100: 6X TO 15X BASE HI
*101-125: 3X TO 8X BASE HI
*126-139: 1.25X TO 3X BASE HI
*140-169: 1.5X TO 4X BASE HI
STATED PRINT RUN 19 SER.#'d SETS
33 Kobe Bryant 50.00 125.00
85 LeBron James 125.00 300.00

2005-06 Finest Refractors Gold

*1-100: 5X TO 12X BASE HI
*101-125: 1.5X TO 4X BASE HI
*126-139: 1X TO 2.5X BASE HI
*140-169: 1.25X TO 3X BASE HI
1-125 PRINT RUN 39 SER.#'d SETS
126-139 AU PRINT RUN 59 SER.#'d SETS
33 Kobe Bryant 40.00 100.00
85 LeBron James 100.00 250.00

2005-06 Finest Refractors Green

*1-100: 3X TO 8X BASE HI
*101-125: .75X TO 2X BASE HI
*126-139: .5X TO 1.25X BASE HI
*140-169: .75X TO 2X BASE HI
1-125 PRINT RUN 89 SER.#'d SETS
126-139 AU PRINT RUN 99 SER.#'d SETS
85 LeBron James 60.00 150.00

2005-06 Finest Refractors Red

*1-100: 2.5X TO 6X BASE HI
*101-125: .6X TO 1.5X BASE HI
*126-139: .4X TO 1X BASE HI
*140-169: .6X TO 1.5X BASE HI
1-125 PRINT RUN 169 SER.#'d SETS
126-139 AU PRINT RUN 199 SER.#'d SETS
33 Kobe Bryant 15.00 40.00
85 LeBron James 50.00 120.00

2005-06 Finest X-Fractors

*1-100: 2.5X TO 6X BASE HI
*101-125: .75X TO 2X BASE HI
*126-139: .6X TO 1.5X BASE HI
*140-169: .6X TO 1.5X BASE HI
1-100 PRINT RUN 229 SER.#'d SETS
101-125 PRINT RUN 199 SER.#'d SETS
126-139 PRINT RUN 169 SER.#'d SETS
85 LeBron James 75.00 200.00
106 Chris Paul 15.00 40.00

2005-06 Finest X-Fractors Gold

*1-100: 8X TO 20X BASE HI
*101-125: 2.5X TO 6X BASE HI
*126-139: 1X TO 2.5X BASE HI
*140-169: 1.25X TO 3X BASE HI
1-125 PRINT RUN 29 SER.#'d SETS
126-139 PRINT RUN 39 SER.#'d SETS
85 LeBron James 300.00 600.00

2005-06 Finest X-Fractors Green

*1-100: 4X TO 10X BASE HI
*101-125: 1.25X TO 3X BASE HI
*126-139: .75X TO 2X BASE HI
*140-169: 1X TO 2.5X BASE HI
1-125 PRINT RUN 69 SER.#'d SETS
126-139 PRINT RUN 79 SER.#'d SETS
85 LeBron James 125.00 300.00

2005-06 Finest X-Fractors Red

*1-100: 3X TO 8X BASE HI
*101-125: 1X TO 2.5X BASE HI
*126-139: .6X TO 1.5X BASE HI
*140-169: .75X TO 2X BASE HI
1-125 PRINT RUN 169 SER.#'d SETS
126-169 PRINT RUN 149 SER.#'d SETS
85 LeBron James 100.00 250.00

2005-06 Finest Boxloaders Celebrity Moments

Inserted as box toppers, this five-card set is serially numbered to 399 and features gold foil cards sealed in Topps uncirculated cases.

PRINT RUN 399 SER.#'d SETS
AUTO'S NOT PRICED DUE TO SCARCITY
CB1 Christie Brinkley 2.50 6.00
CE1 Carmen Electra 2.50 6.00
JM1 Jenny McCarthy 2.50 6.00
JZ1 Jay-Z 2.50 6.00
SE1 Shannon Elizabeth 2.50 6.00

2005-06 Finest Boxloaders Iverson Moments

COMMON CARD (AI1-AI20) 2.50 6.00
PRINT RUN 399 SER.#'d SETS
UNPRICED AUTO PRINT RUN 3 SETS

2005-06 Finest Boxloaders Wade Moments

COMMON CARD (DW1-DW20) 4.00 10.00
PRINT RUN 399 SER.#'d SETS
UNPRICED AUTO PRINT RUN 5 SETS

2005-06 Finest Dress for Success Relics

PRINT RUN 99 SER.#'d SETS
*REFRACTORS: .6X TO 1.5X BASE HI
REFRACTOR PRINT RUN 29 SER.#'d SETS
UNPRICED X-FRACTOR PRINT RUN 9 SETS
UNPRICED SUPERFR.PRINT RUN ONE SET
UNPRICED AUTO PRINT RUN 5 SETS
AB Andrew Bogut 5.00 12.00
CV Charlie Villanueva 4.00 10.00
DW Dwyane Wade 6.00 15.00
FO Fabricio Oberto 3.00 8.00
JG Joey Graham 3.00 8.00
OG Orien Greene 3.00 8.00

2005-06 Finest Fact

NT RUN 1899 SER.#'d SETS
*REFRACTORS: .6X TO 1.5X BASE HI
REFRACTOR PRINT RUN 199 SER.#'d SETS
*X-FRACTORS: .75X TO 2X BASE HI
X-FRACTOR PRINT RUN 99 SER.#'d SETS
UNPRICED PLATE PRINT RUN ONE SET
UNPRICED SUPERFR.PRINT RUN ONE SET
FF1 Shawn Marion .75 2.00
FF2 Joey Graham .75 2.00
FF3 Rasheed Wallace 1.00 2.50
FF4 Rashard Lewis 1.00 2.50
FF5 Pau Gasol 1.00 2.50
FF6 Josh Smith .75 2.00
FF7 Josh Howard 1.00 2.50
FF8 Sean May .60 1.50
FF9 Hakim Warrick .75 2.00
FF10 Elton Brand 1.00 2.50
FF11 Antawn Jamison .75 2.00
FF12 Tracy McGrady 1.25 3.00
FF13 Sarunas Jasikevicius 1.00 2.50
FF14 Rashad McCants .75 2.00
FF15 Orien Greene .75 2.00
FF16 Michael Redd .75 2.00
FF17 Gilbert Arenas .75 2.00
FF18 Gerald Green 1.00 2.50
FF19 Dwyane Wade 1.50 4.00
FF20 Allen Iverson 1.50 4.00
FF21 Shaquille O'Neal 2.00 5.00
FF22 Chris Paul 4.00 10.00
FF23 LeBron James 4.00 10.00
FF24 Dirk Nowitzki 1.50 4.00
FF25 Tim Duncan 1.50 4.00

2005-06 Finest Fact Autographs

STATED PRINT RUN 30 TO 65 SETS
*REFRACTORS: .6X TO 1.5X BASE AU HI
REF.PRINT RUN 15 TO 25 SETS
UNPRICED SUPERFR.PRINT RUN ONE SET
UNPRICED X-FR.PRINT RUN 4 TO 9 SETS
AI Allen Iverson 40.00 100.00
CB Christie Brinkley 50.00 100.00
CE Carmen Electra 50.00 100.00
DW Dwyane Wade 60.00 120.00
EO Emeka Okafor 10.00 25.00
JM Jenny McCarthy 50.00 100.00
JZ Jay-Z 50.00 120.00
SE Shannon Elizabeth 20.00 50.00
SO Shaquille O'Neal 40.00 80.00
VC Vince Carter 20.00 40.00

2005-06 Finest Fact Relics

PRINT RUN 1629 SER.#'d SETS
*REFRACTORS: .6X TO 1.5X BASE HI
REFRACTOR PRINT RUN 199 SER.#'d SETS
*X-FRACTORS: .75X TO 2X BASE HI
X-FRAC.PRINT RUN 49 SER.#'d SETS
UNPRICED AUTO PRINT RUN 5 SETS
UNPRICED PLATE PRINT RUN ONE SET
UNPRICED SUPERFR.PRINT RUN ONE SET
AI Allen Iverson 4.00 10.00
AJ Antawn Jamison 2.00 5.00
CP Chris Paul 5.00 12.00
DW Dwyane Wade 4.00 10.00
EB Elton Brand 2.50 6.00
HW Hakim Warrick 2.00 5.00
JG Joey Graham 2.00 5.00
JH Josh Howard 2.50 6.00
JS Josh Smith 2.00 5.00
OG Orien Greene 2.00 5.00
RL Rashard Lewis 2.50 6.00
RM Rashad McCants 2.00 5.00
RW Rasheed Wallace 2.50 6.00
SJ Sarunas Jasikevicius 2.50 6.00
SM Sean May 1.50 4.00
TM Tracy McGrady 3.00 8.00

2005-06 Finest Patchworks

PRINT RUN 99 SER.#'d SETS
*REFRACTORS: .6X TO 1.5X BASE HI
REFRACTOR PRINT RUN 29 SER.#'d SETS
UNPRICED SUPERFR.PRINT RUN ONE SET
UNPRICED X-FRAC PRINT RUN 9 SETS
AI Allen Iverson 10.00 25.00
AS Amare Stoudemire 5.00 12.00
DW Dwyane Wade 12.00 30.00
KB Kobe Bryant 20.00 50.00
KG Kevin Garnett 10.00 25.00
RA Ray Allen 6.00 15.00
SN Steve Nash 8.00 20.00
SO Shaquille O'Neal 12.00 30.00
TD Tim Duncan 10.00 25.00
TM Tracy McGrady 8.00 20.00
VC Vince Carter 10.00 25.00
YM Yao Ming 8.00 20.00

2006-07 Finest

Issued in mid June 2007, Finest is the first 2006-07 product to include redemption cards for the incoming 2007-08 rookie class highlighted by Greg Oden and Kevin Durant. The 131-card set utilizes an all foil-board card stock where cards 1-40 picture veteran players, 41-50 picture retired NBA legends, 51-100 picture rookies and 101-130 are draft pick exchange redemption cards. The base card design features red highlights along the top and bottom of the card for veterans and legends and white highlights for rookies. Draft Exchange cards feature the draft pick number on the front and redemption information on the back. The format for packing includes three mini boxes per box where each mini box contains six packs of five cards each. Finest carried an original suggested retail price of $50.00 per six-pack mini box.

COMP.SET w/o SPs (100) 10.00 25.00
XRC PRINT RUN 539 SER.#'d SETS
UNPRICED SUPERFR.PRINT RUN ONE SET
UNPRICED WHITE X-FRAC.PRINT RUN ONE SET
1 Carmelo Anthony .60 1.50
2 Ben Wallace .40 1.00
3 Baron Davis .40 1.00
4 Jermaine O'Neal .40 1.00
5 Dwyane Wade .75 2.00
6 Vince Carter .60 1.50
7 Dwight Howard .40 1.00
8 Steve Nash .60 1.50
9 Tim Duncan .75 2.00
10 Gilbert Arenas .40 1.00
11 Gerald Wallace .40 1.00
12 Dirk Nowitzki .75 2.00
13 Chauncey Billups .50 1.25
14 Yao Ming .60 1.50
15 Pau Gasol .50 1.25
16 Kevin Garnett .75 2.00
17 Chris Paul .60 1.50
18 Amare Stoudemire .40 1.00
19 Tony Parker .50 1.25
20 Andrei Kirilenko .40 1.00
21 Paul Pierce .50 1.25
22 LeBron James 2.00 5.00
23 Richard Hamilton .40 1.00
24 Tracy McGrady .60 1.50
25 Kobe Bryant 2.00 5.00
26 Michael Redd .40 1.00
27 Stephon Marbury .40 1.00
28 Andre Iguodala .40 1.00
29 Mike Bibby .50 1.25
30 Chris Bosh .50 1.25
31 Joe Johnson .40 1.00
32 Kirk Hinrich .40 1.00
33 Josh Howard .40 1.00
34 Jason Richardson .50 1.25
35 Elton Brand .50 1.25
36 Shaquille O'Neal 1.00 2.50
37 Jason Kidd .75 2.00
38 Allen Iverson .60 1.50
39 Zach Randolph .40 1.00
40 Ray Allen .50 1.25
41 Larry Bird 1.25 3.00
42 Isiah Thomas .50 1.25
43 Dominique Wilkins .60 1.50
44 Willis Reed .50 1.25
45 Robert Parish .50 1.25
46 Chris Mullin .50 1.25
47 Karl Malone .60 1.50
48 Calvin Murphy .40 1.00
49 Xavier McDaniel .30 .75
50 Nate Archibald .40 1.00
51 Steve Novak RC 1.00 2.50
52 Shannon Brown RC .75 2.00
53 Sergio Rodriguez RC 1.25 3.00
54 Saer Sene RC .75 2.00
55 Ryan Hollins RC 1.00 2.50
56 Ronnie Brewer RC 1.25 3.00
57 Mile Ilic RC .75 2.00
58 Kyle Lowry RC 1.50 4.00
59 Hilton Armstrong RC .75 2.00
60 Craig Smith RC 1.00 2.50
61 Will Blalock RC .75 2.00
62 Thabo Sefolosha RC 1.25 3.00
63 Rodney Carney RC .75 2.00
64 Quincy Douby RC .75 2.00
65 P.J. Tucker RC 1.00 2.50
66 Josh Boone RC .75 2.00
67 Jordan Farmar RC 1.25 3.00
68 Damir Markota RC .75 2.00
69 Cedric Simmons RC .75 2.00
70 Allan Ray RC .75 2.00
71 Rudy Gay RC 1.50 4.00
72 Rajon Rondo RC 2.00 5.00
73 Patrick O'Bryant RC .75 2.00
74 Marcus Williams RC .75 2.00
75 Marcus Vinicius RC .75 2.00
76 James White RC .75 2.00
77 Dee Brown RC .75 2.00
78 David Noel RC .75 2.00
79 Daniel Gibson RC 1.00 2.50
80 Bobby Jones RC .75 2.00
81 Tyrus Thomas RC 1.00 2.50
82 Shelden Williams RC 1.00 2.50
83 Pops Mensah-Bonsu RC .75 2.00
84 Paul Davis RC .75 2.00
85 Mardy Collins RC .75 2.00
86 James Augustine RC .75 2.00
87 Hassan Adams RC .75 2.00
88 Chris Quinn RC .75 2.00
89 Brandon Roy RC 1.25 3.00
90 Andrea Bargnani RC 1.25 3.00
91 Solomon Jones RC .75 2.00
92 Shawne Williams RC .75 2.00
93 Renaldo Balkman RC 1.00 2.50
94 Randy Foye RC 1.25 3.00
95 Maurice Ager RC .75 2.00
96 LaMarcus Aldridge RC 3.00 8.00
97 Jorge Garbajosa RC 1.00 2.50
98 J.J. Redick RC 1.50 4.00
99 Alexander Johnson RC .75 2.00
100 Adam Morrison RC 1.25 3.00
101 Greg Oden XRC 4.00 10.00
102 Kevin Durant XRC 40.00 100.00
103 Al Horford XRC 4.00 10.00
104 Mike Conley Jr. XRC 4.00 10.00
105 Jeff Green XRC 3.00 8.00
106 Yi Jianlian XRC 5.00 12.00
107 Corey Brewer XRC 4.00 10.00
108 Brandan Wright XRC 3.00 8.00
109 Joakim Noah XRC 4.00 10.00

110 Spencer Hawes XRC 3.00 8.00
111 Acie Law XRC 3.00 8.00
112 Thaddeus Young XRC 4.00 10.00
113 Julian Wright XRC 3.00 8.00
114 Al Thornton XRC 3.00 8.00
115 Rodney Stuckey XRC 3.00 8.00
116 Nick Young XRC 5.00 12.00
117 Sean Williams XRC 3.00 8.00
118 Marco Belinelli XRC 3.00 8.00
119 Javaris Crittenton XRC 3.00 8.00
120 Jason Smith XRC 3.00 8.00
121 Daequan Cook XRC 3.00 8.00
122 Jared Dudley XRC 2.50 6.00
123 Wilson Chandler XRC 4.00 10.00
124 Carl Landry XRC 3.00 8.00
125 Morris Almond XRC 3.00 8.00
126 Aaron Brooks XRC 3.00 8.00
127 Arron Afflalo XRC 3.00 8.00
128 Gabe Pruitt XRC 3.00 8.00
129 Alando Tucker XRC 3.00 8.00
130 Marcus Williams XRC 3.00 8.00
NNO Rookie Autograph EXCH 75.00 175.00

2006-07 Finest Refractors

*1-50 REF: .75X TO 2X BASE HI
*51-100 REF: .5X TO 1.5X BASE HI
*101-130 XRC REF: .5X TO 1.25X BASE HI
REFRACTOR ODDS 1:6
22 LeBron James 20.00 50.00
102 Kevin Durant 60.00 150.00

2006-07 Finest Refractors Black

*1-50 REF.BLACK: 2.5X TO 6X BASE HI
*51-100 REF.BLACK: 1X TO 2.5X BASE HI
*101-130 REF.BLACK: 1X TO 2.5X BASE HI
PRINT RUN 99 SER.#'d SETS
22 LeBron James 125.00 300.00
72 Rajon Rondo 15.00 40.00
102 Kevin Durant 150.00 300.00

2006-07 Finest Refractors Blue

*1-50 REF.BLUE: 1X TO 2.5X BASE HI
*51-100 REF.BLUE: .75X TO 2X BASE HI
*101-130 REF.BLUE: .6X TO 1.5X BASE HI
REF.BLUE PRINT RUN 299 SER.#'d SETS
22 LeBron James 30.00 80.00
25 Kobe Bryant 8.00 20.00
102 Kevin Durant 100.00 200.00

2006-07 Finest Refractors Gold

*1-50 GOLD.REF: 6X TO 15X BASE HI
*51-100 GOLD.REF: 1.5X TO 4X BASE HI
*101-130 GOLD REF: 1.5X TO 4X BASE HI
PRINT RUN 50 SER.#'d SETS
5 Dwyane Wade 25.00 60.00
22 LeBron James 400.00 800.00
25 Kobe Bryant 50.00 125.00
72 Rajon Rondo 40.00 100.00
98 J.J. Redick 10.00 25.00
101 Greg Oden 20.00 50.00
102 Kevin Durant 400.00 800.00

2006-07 Finest Refractors Green

*1-50 REF.GREEN: 1.25X TO 3X BASE HI
*51-100 REF.GREEN: .75X TO 2X BASE HI
*101-130 REF.GREEN: .75X TO 2X BASE HI
PRINT RUN 199 SER.#'d SETS
22 LeBron James 60.00 150.00
25 Kobe Bryant 12.00 30.00
102 Kevin Durant 125.00 250.00

2006-07 Finest Refractors Silver

*SILVER: .6X TO 1.5X BASE HI
STATED PRINT RUN 319 SER.#'d SETS
102 Kevin Durant 100.00 200.00

2006-07 Finest X-Fractors

*1-50 X-FRAC: 5X TO 12X BASE HI
*51-100 X-FRAC: 2X TO 5X BASE HI
*101-130 X-FRAC: 2X TO 5X BASE HI
X-FRAC.PRINT RUN 25 SER.#'d SETS
22 LeBron James 300.00 600.00
72 Rajon Rondo 30.00 80.00
101 Greg Oden 50.00 120.00
102 Kevin Durant 400.00 800.00

2006-07 Finest Moments

COMPLETE SET (2) 4.00 10.00
ONE PER BOX AS TOPPER
*REFRACTORS: .75X TO 2X BASE HI
REFRACTORS 1:3 BOXES
AM Adam Morrison 1.25 3.00
LB Larry Bird 3.00 8.00

2006-07 Finest Moments Relics Autographs X-Fractors

AM Adam Morrison/50 20.00 40.00
LB Larry Bird/25 60.00 150.00

2006-07 Finest Moments Relics Refractors

AM Adam Morrison/499 5.00 12.00
LB Larry Bird/299 12.00 30.00

2006-07 Finest Rookie Autographs Refractors

GROUP A ODDS 1:456, GROUP B 1:150
GROUP C 1:66, GROUP D 1:48
GROUP E 1:36, GROUP F 1:36
GROUP G 1:144, GROUP H 1:24
*X-FRACTORS: .75X TO 2X BASE HI
X-FRACTOR PRINT RUN 25 SER.#'d SETS
UNPRICED SUPERFR.PRINT RUN ONE SET
51 Steve Novak D 2.00 5.00
52 Shannon Brown C 1.50 4.00
53 Sergio Rodriguez H 2.50 6.00
54 Saer Sene H 1.50 4.00
55 Ryan Hollins E 2.00 5.00
56 Ronnie Brewer D 2.50 6.00
57 Mile Ilic E 1.50 4.00
58 Kyle Lowry F 4.00 10.00
59 Hilton Armstrong D 1.50 4.00
60 Craig Smith F 2.00 5.00
61 Will Blalock H 1.50 4.00
62 Thabo Sefolosha D 6.00 15.00
63 Rodney Carney C 1.50 4.00
64 Quincy Douby C 1.50 4.00
66 Josh Boone D 1.50 4.00
67 Jordan Farmar E 2.50 6.00
68 Damir Markota E 1.50 4.00
69 Cedric Simmons B 1.50 4.00
70 Allan Ray E 1.50 4.00
72 Rajon Rondo E 8.00 20.00
73 Patrick O'Bryant C 1.50 4.00
74 Marcus Williams A 1.50 4.00
75 Marcus Vinicius G 1.50 4.00
76 James White E 1.50 4.00
77 Dee Brown F 1.50 4.00
80 Bobby Jones B 1.50 4.00
82 Shelden Williams C 2.00 5.00
83 Pops Mensah-Bonsu H 1.50 4.00
84 Paul Davis B 1.50 4.00
85 Mardy Collins D 1.50 4.00
87 Hassan Adams D 1.50 4.00
90 Andrea Bargnani A 2.50 6.00
91 Solomon Jones C 1.50 4.00
92 Shawne Williams F 1.50 4.00
93 Renaldo Balkman F 2.00 5.00
94 Randy Foye B 2.50 6.00
95 Maurice Ager C 1.50 4.00
97 Jorge Garbajosa H 2.00 5.00
98 J.J. Redick F 3.00 8.00
100 Adam Morrison H 4.00 10.00

2007-08 Finest

Released in June 2008, Finest boasts a 130-card all-foil base set where cards 1-40 feature base veteran players, cards 41-50 feature retired NBA legends, cards 51-100 feature rookies and cards 101-130 feature draft pick redemption cards for the newly drafted 2008-09 NBA rookie class. These exchange cards are the first ones issued for the 2005-06 class. Finest was packaged in boxes which were broken down into three mini-boxes per containing six packs of five cards each (one autograph card per mini-box). The original suggested retail price of the six-pack mini boxes was $40.

COMP.SET w/o DRAFT (100) 25.00 50.00
UNPRICED SUPERFRACTOR PRINT RUN ONE SET
UNPRICED WHITE X-FR.PRINT RUN ONE SET
1 Gilbert Arenas .40 1.00
2 Ray Allen .50 1.25
3 Dwyane Wade .75 2.00
4 Dirk Nowitzki .60 1.50
5 Manu Ginobili .50 1.25
6 Eddy Curry .30 .75
7 Jermaine O'Neal .40 1.00
8 Carlos Boozer .40 1.00
9 Tony Parker .50 1.25
10 Jason Kidd .50 1.25
11 Chris Bosh .50 1.25
12 Al Jefferson .40 1.00
13 Steve Nash .60 1.50
14 Chris Paul .60 1.50
15 Carmelo Anthony .60 1.50
16 Pau Gasol .50 1.25
17 Joe Johnson .40 1.00
18 Chauncey Billups .50 1.25
19 Andre Iguodala .40 1.00
20 Yao Ming .60 1.50
21 Tim Duncan .75 2.00
22 Michael Redd .40 1.00
23 Allen Iverson .60 1.50
24 Kobe Bryant 2.00 5.00
25 Kevin Garnett .75 2.00
26 Brandon Roy .50 1.25
27 Luol Deng .40 1.00
28 Deron Williams .40 1.00
29 Amare Stoudemire .40 1.00
30 Vince Carter .60 1.50
31 Tracy McGrady .50 1.25
32 Shaquille O'Neal 1.00 2.50
33 Jason Richardson .50 1.25
34 Paul Pierce .50 1.25
35 Baron Davis .40 1.00
36 Dwight Howard .40 1.00
37 Josh Howard .40 1.00
38 Kevin Martin .40 1.00
39 Ben Gordon .40 1.00
40 LeBron James 2.00 5.00
41 Isiah Thomas .50 1.25
42 Dominique Wilkins .60 1.50
43 Magic Johnson 1.25 3.00
44 Bill Russell .75 2.00
45 David Robinson .75 2.00
46 John Stockton .75 2.00
47 Jerry West .60 1.50
48 Moses Malone .50 1.25
49 Dennis Rodman 1.00 2.50
50 Larry Bird 1.25 3.00
51 Al Horford RC 1.25 3.00
52 Ramon Sessions RC 1.00 2.50
53 JamesOn Curry RC .60 1.50
54 Arron Afflalo RC 1.00 2.50
55 Carl Landry RC .60 1.50
56 Glen Davis RC .75 2.00
57 Jermareo Davidson RC .60 1.50
58 Nick Fazekas RC .60 1.50
59 Taurean Green RC .60 1.50
60 Cheikh Samb RC .60 1.50
61 Mike Conley Jr. RC 1.25 3.00
62 Chris Richard RC .60 1.50
63 Josh McRoberts RC .75 2.00
64 Alando Tucker RC .60 1.50
65 Brandan Wright RC 1.00 2.50
66 Jamario Moon RC .75 2.00
67 Jared Dudley RC .75 2.00
68 Dominic McGuire RC .60 1.50
69 Sean Williams RC .60 1.50
70 Mario West RC 1.00 2.50
71 Kevin Durant RC 20.00 50.00
72 Julian Wright RC .60 1.50
73 Yi Jianlian RC 1.25 3.00
74 Coby Karl RC .60 1.50
75 Aaron Brooks RC .75 2.00
76 Kyrylo Fesenko RC .60 1.50
77 Greg Oden RC 1.00 2.50
78 Juan Carlos Navarro RC .75 2.00
79 Nick Young RC 1.25 3.00
80 Thaddeus Young RC 1.00 2.50
81 Joakim Noah RC 1.00 2.50
82 Luis Scola RC 1.25 3.00
83 Aaron Gray RC .60 1.50
84 Herbert Hill RC .60 1.50
85 Al Thornton RC .75 2.00
86 D.J. Strawberry RC .60 1.50
87 Javaris Crittenton RC .60 1.50
88 Morris Almond RC .60 1.50
89 Spencer Hawes RC .75 2.00
90 C.J. Watson RC 1.00 2.50
91 Corey Brewer RC 1.00 2.50
92 Jeff Green RC 1.00 2.50
93 Marco Belinelli RC 1.00 2.50
94 Marcin Gortat RC 1.50 4.00
95 Acie Law RC .60 1.50
96 Daequan Cook RC .75 2.00
97 Gabe Pruitt RC .60 1.50
98 Jason Smith RC .75 2.00
99 Rodney Stuckey RC .75 2.00
100 Wilson Chandler RC .75 2.00
101 Derrick Rose XRC 15.00 40.00
102 Michael Beasley XRC 4.00 10.00
103 O.J. Mayo XRC 4.00 10.00
104 Russell Westbrook XRC 75.00 200.00
105 Kevin Love XRC 10.00 25.00
106 Danilo Gallinari XRC 6.00 15.00
107 Eric Gordon XRC 8.00 20.00
108 Joe Alexander XRC 2.50 6.00
109 D.J. Augustin XRC 3.00 8.00
110 Brook Lopez XRC 6.00 15.00
111 Jerryd Bayless XRC 3.00 8.00
112 Jason Thompson XRC 4.00 10.00
113 Brandon Rush XRC 3.00 8.00
114 Anthony Randolph XRC 4.00 10.00
115 Robin Lopez XRC 4.00 10.00
116 Marreese Speights XRC 4.00 10.00
117 Roy Hibbert XRC 4.00 10.00
118 JaVale McGee XRC 5.00 12.00
119 J.J. Hickson XRC 4.00 10.00
120 Alexis Ajinca XRC 2.50 6.00
121 Ryan Anderson XRC 5.00 12.00
122 Courtney Lee XRC 5.00 12.00
123 Kosta Koufos XRC 4.00 10.00
124 Walter Sharpe XRC 4.00 10.00
125 Nicolas Batum XRC 5.00 12.00
126 George Hill XRC 6.00 15.00
127 Darrell Arthur XRC 4.00 10.00
128 Donte Greene XRC 4.00 10.00
129 D.J. White XRC 4.00 10.00
130 J.R. Giddens XRC 4.00 10.00

2007-08 Finest Refractors

*1-100 REF: .6X TO 1.5X BASE HI
*101-130 REF: .5X TO 1.25X BASE HI
1-100 ODDS APPROX. 1:2
101-130 STATED ODDS 1:5
40 LeBron James 30.00 80.00
71 Kevin Durant 75.00 200.00

2007-08 Finest Refractors Black

*1-50 REF.BLACK: 3X TO 8X BASE HI
*51-100 REF.BLACK: 1.5X TO 4X BASE HI
*101-130 REF.BLACK: 1X TO 2.5X BASE HI
REF.BLACK PRINT RUN 75 SER.#'d SETS
40 LeBron James 100.00 250.00
71 Kevin Durant 400.00 800.00
101 Derrick Rose 100.00 250.00

2007-08 Finest Refractors Blue

*1-50 REF.BLUE: 1.25X TO 3X BASE HI
*51-100 REF.BLUE: .75X TO 2X BASE HI
*101-130 REF.BLUE: .6X TO 1.5X BASE HI
REF.BLUE PRINT RUN 199 SER.#'d SETS
40 LeBron James 60.00 150.00
71 Kevin Durant 200.00 500.00

2007-08 Finest Refractors Gold

*1-50 REF.GOLD: 10X TO 25X BASE HI
*51-100 REF.GOLD: 3X TO 8X BASE HI
*101-130 REF.GOLD: 1.25X TO 3X BASE HI
PRINT RUN 25 SER.#'d SETS
40 LeBron James 300.00 600.00
71 Kevin Durant 800.00 1200.00
101 Derrick Rose 125.00 300.00
104 Russell Westbrook 300.00 600.00

2007-08 Finest Refractors Green

*1-50 REF.GREEN: 2X TO 5X BASE HI
*51-100 REF.GREEN: 1.25X TO 3X BASE HI
*101-130 REF.GREEN: .75X TO 2X BASE HI
REF.GREEN PRINT RUN 149 SER.#'d SETS
40 LeBron James 75.00 200.00
71 Kevin Durant 300.00 600.00

2007-08 Finest Refractors Silver

*SILVER: .5X TO 1.25X BASE HI
STATED PRINT RUN 319 SER.#'d SETS
71 Kevin Durant 75.00 200.00

2007-08 Finest X-Fractors

*1-50 X-FRAC: 8X TO 20X BASE HI
*51-100 X-FRAC: 4X TO 10X BASE HI
*101-130 X-FRAC: 1.5X TO 4X BASE HI
STATED PRINT RUN 15 SER.#'d SETS
24 Kobe Bryant 75.00 200.00
40 LeBron James 300.00 600.00
71 Kevin Durant 1200.00 2000.00
101 Derrick Rose 150.00 400.00
104 Russell Westbrook 400.00 800.00

2007-08 Finest Draft Picks Autographs Refractors

STATED ODDS 1:43
UNPRICED PLATE PRINT RUN ONE SET
UNPRICED SUPERFR.PRINT RUN ONE SET
UNPRICED X-FRACTOR PRINT RUN 10 SETS
102 Michael Beasley 25.00 60.00
103 O.J. Mayo 10.00 25.00
104 Russell Westbrook 75.00 200.00
105 Kevin Love 75.00 200.00
106 Danilo Gallinari 8.00 20.00
107 Eric Gordon 6.00 15.00
108 Joe Alexander 3.00 8.00
109 D.J. Augustin 4.00 10.00
110 Brook Lopez 8.00 20.00
111 Jerryd Bayless 4.00 10.00
112 Jason Thompson 5.00 12.00
113 Brandon Rush 4.00 10.00
114 Anthony Randolph 5.00 12.00
115 Robin Lopez 5.00 12.00
116 Marreese Speights 5.00 12.00
117 Roy Hibbert 5.00 12.00
118 JaVale McGee 6.00 15.00
119 J.J. Hickson 5.00 12.00
120 Alexis Ajinca 3.00 8.00
121 Ryan Anderson 6.00 15.00
122 Courtney Lee 6.00 15.00
123 Kosta Koufos 5.00 12.00
124 Walter Sharpe 5.00 12.00
125 Nicolas Batum 6.00 15.00
126 George Hill 8.00 20.00
127 Darrell Arthur 5.00 12.00
128 Donte Greene 5.00 12.00
129 D.J. White 5.00 12.00
130 J.R. Giddens 5.00 12.00

2007-08 Finest Redemption Autographs

These uniquely designed autographs were distributed via Topps Customer Service for other redemption cards that could not be fulfilled.

BG Ben Gordon 3.00 8.00
BR Brandon Roy 10.00 25.00

2007-08 Finest Rookie Autographs Refractors

GROUP A ODDS 1:31, GROUP B 1:12
GROUP C ODDS 1:4, GROUP D 1:3
GROUP E ODDS 1:3
UNPRICED SUPERFR.PRINT RUN ONE SET
UNPRICED X-FRAC.PRINT RUN 10 SETS
53 JamesOn Curry B 2.50 6.00
54 Arron Afflalo C 4.00 10.00
55 Carl Landry C 2.50 6.00
56 Glen Davis D 3.00 8.00
57 Jermareo Davidson E 2.50 6.00
58 Nick Fazekas D 2.50 6.00
59 Taurean Green B 2.50 6.00
63 Josh McRoberts B 3.00 8.00
64 Alando Tucker D 2.50 6.00
65 Brandan Wright A 4.00 10.00
66 Jamario Moon C 3.00 8.00
67 Jared Dudley D 3.00 8.00
68 Dominic McGuire B 2.50 6.00
69 Sean Williams D 2.50 6.00
70 Mario West E 4.00 10.00
73 Yi Jianlian A 5.00 12.00
74 Coby Karl C 2.50 6.00
75 Aaron Brooks D 3.00 8.00
77 Greg Oden A 4.00 10.00
78 Juan Carlos Navarro C 3.00 8.00
79 Nick Young A 5.00 12.00
80 Thaddeus Young A 4.00 10.00
83 Aaron Gray D 2.50 6.00
84 Herbert Hill E 2.50 6.00
85 Al Thornton C 3.00 8.00
86 D.J. Strawberry E 2.50 6.00
87 Javaris Crittenton B 2.50 6.00
88 Morris Almond C 2.50 6.00
89 Spencer Hawes C 3.00 8.00
93 Marco Belinelli A 4.00 10.00
94 Marcin Gortat C 3.00 8.00
95 Acie Law C 2.50 6.00
96 Daequan Cook B 3.00 8.00
97 Gabe Pruitt C 2.50 6.00
98 Jason Smith D 3.00 8.00
99 Rodney Stuckey C 3.00 8.00
100 Wilson Chandler D 3.00 8.00

2008-09 Finest Redemption Autographs

These uniquely designed autographs were distributed via Topps Customer Service for other redemption cards that could not be fulfilled.

DW Dwyane Wade 20.00 50.00

2001 Fire Fleer WNBA

This nine card perforated set was given out in Portland, Oregon by Fleer at the Fire's game on 7/30/01. It was said to be given to the first 5000 fans.

COMPLETE SET (9) 10.00 25.00
1 Linda Hargrove .40 1.00
2 Sophia Witherspoon .40 1.00
3 Vanessa NyGaard .40 1.00
4 Sylvia Crawley .40 1.00
5 Portland Fire .40 1.00
6 Alisa Burras .40 1.00
7 Jackie Stiles 10.00 25.00
8 Stacey Thomas .40 1.00
9 Spot MASCOT .40 1.00

1991-93 5 Majeur

These French cards measures approximately 3 7/8" by 6" and are printed on thin glossy paper stock. The pictures were perforated and issued in various issues of the French magazine "5 Majeur" between 1991 and 1993. The fronts of most cards feature color action player photos with white borders; however, many other border colors exist. All cards have the same basic format. The player's name is printed in block lettering at the top. The magazine name appears beneath the picture. The backs carry biographical information, statistics, and a player profile in French. The cards are unnumbered and checklisted below in order by magazine. The numbers coincide with the issue number where the cards were released. As you will notice this checklist is not complete, and we will continue to update it as more detailed information is known.

COMPLETE SET 200.00 500.00
1 Kareem Abdul-Jabbar 3.00 8.00
2 Mahmoud Abdul-Rauf .75 2.00
3 Michael Adams .75 2.00
4 Mark Aguirre 1.25 3.00
5 Danny Ainge 1.50 4.00
6 Greg Anderson .75 2.00
7 Nick Anderson 1.00 2.50
8 B.J. Armstrong White 1.00 2.50
9 B.J. Armstrong Red 1.00 2.50
10 Stacey Augmon .75 2.00
11 Charles Barkley 76ers 4.00 10.00
12 Charles Barkley USA 3.00 8.00
13 Dana Barros .75 2.00
14 Larry Bird 6.00 15.00
15 Larry Bird USA 6.00 15.00
16 Mookie Blaylock 1.00 2.50
17 Muggsy Bogues 1.25 3.00
18 Manute Bol .75 2.00
19 Sam Bowie .75 2.00
20 Frank Brickowski .75 2.00
21 Scott Brooks .75 2.00
22 Dee Brown .75 2.00
23 Antoine Carr .75 2.00
24 Bill Cartwright 1.00 2.50
25 Terry Catledge .75 2.00
26 Wilt Chamberlain 5.00 12.00
27 Tom Chambers 1.50 4.00
28 Rex Chapman 1.25 3.00
29 Maurice Cheeks 1.25 3.00
30 Wayne Cooper .75 2.00
31 Tyrone Corbin .75 2.00
32 Terry Cummings 1.25 3.00
33 Lloyd Daniels .75 2.00
34 Brad Daugherty .75 2.00
35 Vinny Del Negro .75 2.00
36 Vlade Divac 1.50 4.00
37 James Donaldson .75 2.00
38 Clyde Drexler USA 4.00 10.00
39 Joe Dumars 2.00 5.00
40 Mark Eaton .75 2.00
41 Craig Ehlo .75 2.00
42 Sean Elliot 1.25 3.00
43 Dale Ellis .75 2.00
44 Patrick Ewing 2.50 6.00
45 Patrick Ewing USA 2.00 5.00
46 Danny Ferry .75 2.00
47 Vern Fleming .75 2.00
48 Kendall Gill .75 2.00
49 Armon Gilliam .75 2.00
50 Horace Grant 1.25 3.00
51 A.C. Green 1.25 3.00
52 Anfernee Hardaway 3.00 8.00
53 Tim Hardaway 1.50 4.00
54 Derek Harper 1.25 3.00
55 Ron Harper 1.25 3.00
56 Hersey Hawkins 1.25 3.00
57 Carl Herrera .75 2.00
58 Bob Hill CO .75 2.00
59 Jeff Hornacek 1.50 4.00
60 Robert Horry 1.50 4.00
61 Phil Jackson CO 1.50 4.00
62 Kevin Johnson 1.50 4.00
63 Magic Johnson USA 5.00 12.00
64 Vinnie Johnson .75. 2.00
65 Michael Jordan White 20.00 40.00
66 Michael Jordan Red 10.00 25.00
67 Michael Jordan USA 15.00 40.00
68 George Karl CO .75 2.00
69 Shawn Kemp 1.50 4.00
70 Jerome Kersey .75 2.00
71 Jon Koncak .75 2.00
72 Christian Laettner USA 1.50 4.00
73 Bill Laimbeer 1.25 3.00
74 Andrew Lang .75 2.00
75 Cliff Levingstone SP .75 2.00
76 Grant Long .75 2.00
77 John Lucas CO .75 2.00
78 Jeff Malone .75 2.00
79 Karl Malone 4.00 10.00
80 Karl Malone USA 3.00 8.00
81 Moses Malone 1.50 4.00
82 Sarunas Marciulionis .75 2.00
83 Vernon Maxwell .75 2.00
84 Rodney McCray .75 2.00
85 Xavier McDaniel .75 2.00
86 Kevin McHale 2.50 6.00
87 Nate McMillan .75 2.00
88 Reggie Miller 3.00 8.00
89 Chris Mullin 1.50 4.00
90 Chris Mullin USA 1.50 4.00
91 Tracy Murray .75 2.00
92 Dikembe Mutombo 1.50 4.00
93 Larry Nance 1.25 3.00
94 Charles Oakley 1.00 2.50
95 Hakeem Olajuwon 3.00 8.00
96 Shaquille O'Neal 6.00 15.00
97 Billy Owens .75 2.00
98 John Paxson White 1.25 3.00
99 John Paxson Red 1.00 2.50
100 Gary Payton 2.50 6.00
101 Will Perdue .75 2.00
102 Sam Perkins 1.25 3.00
103 Drazen Petrovic 3.00 8.00
104 Ricky Pierce .75 2.00
105 Scottie Pippen White 3.00 8.00
106 Scottie Pippen Red 2.50 6.00
107 Scottie Pippen USA 3.00 8.00
108 Olden Polynice .75 2.00
109 Terry Porter 1.00 2.50
110 Paul Pressey .75 2.00
111 Mark Price 1.25 3.00
112 Kurt Rambis 1.25 3.00
113 J.R. Reid .75 2.00
114 Glen Rice 1.25 3.00
115 Pooh Richardson .75 2.00
116 Mitch Richmond 1.50 4.00
117 Fred Roberts .75 2.00
118 David Robinson 4.00 10.00
119 David Robinson USA 3.00 8.00
120 Rumeal Robinson .75 2.00
121 Dennis Rodman 2.00 5.00
122 Donald Royal .75 2.00
123 John Salley 1.00 2.50
124 Detlef Schrempf 1.25 3.00
125 Byron Scott Dribbling 1.25 3.00
126 Byron Scott Shooting 1.25 3.00
127 Dennis Scott .75 2.00
128 Rony Seikaly .75 2.00
129 Scott Skiles 1.25 3.00
130 Kenny Smith 1.25 3.00
131 John Starks 1.25 3.00
132 John Stockton 5.00 12.00
133 John Stockton USA 4.00 10.00
134 Rod Strickland .75 2.00
135 Isiah Thomas 2.50 6.00
136 Otis Thorpe .75 2.00
137 Sedale Threatt .75 2.00
138 Rudy Tomjanovich CO 1.00 2.50
139 Jeff Turner .75 2.00
140 Spud Webb 1.25 3.00
141 Dominique Wilkins White 3.00 8.00
142 Dominique Wilkins Red 1.50 4.00
143 Lenny Wilkens CO 1.25 3.00
144 Herb Williams .75 2.00
145 John Williams .75 2.00
146 Reggie Williams .75 2.00
147 Scott Williams .75 2.00
148 Kevin Willis White .75 2.00
149 Kevin Willis Red .75 2.00
150 David Wingate .75 2.00
151 Orlando Woolridge .75 2.00

1994-95 Flair

This 326-card super-premium standard-size set (made by Fleer) was issued in two series. The first series contains 175 cards while the second has 151 cards (including the late addition of Michael Jordan as card #326). Cards were distributed in 10-card "hardpacks" (featuring a two-piece protective design wrapper), each with a suggested retail price of $4.00. The cards have a polyester laminate protective coating on both sides and are made with extra thick 30 point stock. The front has two color action photos blended. The back has one full color action photo with the player's statistics laid on top. Both sides have the player's name stamped in gold foil along with his team. The cards are numbered on the back and checklisted below alphabetically within teams. The first series includes a "Dream Team II" subset (159-172) commemorating the USA's team victory at the 1994 World Championships in Toronto. Rookie Cards of note in this set include Grant Hill, Juwan Howard, Eddie Jones, Jason Kidd, and Glenn Robinson.

COMPLETE SET (326) 25.00 50.00
COMPLETE SERIES 1 (175) 7.50 15.00
COMPLETE SERIES 2 (151) 15.00 30.00
1 Stacey Augmon .25 .60
2 Mookie Blaylock .20 .50
3 Craig Ehlo .20 .50
4 Jon Koncak .20 .50
5 Andrew Lang .20 .50
6 Dee Brown .20 .50
7 Sherman Douglas .20 .50
8 Acie Earl .20 .50
9 Rick Fox .20 .50
10 Kevin Gamble .20 .50
11 Xavier McDaniel .20 .50
12 Dino Radja .20 .50
13 Tony Bennett .20 .50
14 Dell Curry .20 .50
15 Kenny Gattison .20 .50
16 Hersey Hawkins .20 .50
17 Larry Johnson .30 .75
18 Alonzo Mourning .40 1.00
19 David Wingate .20 .50
20 B.J. Armstrong .20 .50
21 Steve Kerr .25 .60
22 Toni Kukoc .40 1.00
23 Pete Myers .20 .50
24 Scottie Pippen .60 1.50
25 Bill Wennington .20 .50
26 Terrell Brandon .20 .50
27 Brad Daugherty .25 .60
28 Tyrone Hill .20 .50
29 Bobby Phills .20 .50
30 Mark Price .30 .75
31 Gerald Wilkins .20 .50
32 John Williams .20 .50
33 Lucious Harris .20 .50
34 Jim Jackson .20 .50
35 Jamal Mashburn .30 .75
36 Sean Rooks .20 .50
37 Doug Smith .20 .50
38 Mahmoud Abdul-Rauf .20 .50
39 LaPhonso Ellis .20 .50
40 Dikembe Mutombo .30 .75
41 Robert Pack .20 .50
42 Rodney Rogers .20 .50
43 Brian Williams .20 .50
44 Reggie Williams .20 .50
45 Joe Dumars .30 .75
46 Allan Houston .30 .75
47 Lindsey Hunter .20 .50
48 Terry Mills .20 .50
49 Victor Alexander .20 .50
50 Chris Gatling .20 .50
51 Billy Owens .20 .50
52 Latrell Sprewell .40 1.00
53 Chris Webber .50 1.25
54 Sam Cassell .30 .75
55 Carl Herrera .20 .50
56 Robert Horry .30 .75
57 Hakeem Olajuwon .40 1.00
58 Kenny Smith .25 .60
59 Otis Thorpe .20 .50
60 Antonio Davis .20 .50
61 Dale Davis .20 .50
62 Reggie Miller .40 1.00
63 Byron Scott .25 .60
64 Rik Smits .25 .60
65 Haywoode Workman .20 .50
66 Terry Dehere .20 .50
67 Harold Ellis .20 .50
68 Gary Grant .20 .50
69 Elmore Spencer .20 .50
70 Loy Vaught .20 .50
71 Elden Campbell .20 .50
72 Doug Christie .20 .50
73 Vlade Divac .30 .75
74 George Lynch .20 .50
75 Anthony Peeler .20 .50
76 Nick Van Exel .30 .75
77 James Worthy .40 1.00
78 Bimbo Coles .20 .50
79 Harold Miner .20 .50
80 John Salley .20 .50
81 Rony Seikaly .20 .50
82 Steve Smith .25 .60
83 Vin Baker .30 .75
84 Jon Barry .20 .50
85 Todd Day .20 .50
86 Lee Mayberry .20 .50
87 Eric Murdock .20 .50
88 Mike Brown .20 .50
89 Christian Laettner .25 .60
90 Isaiah Rider .30 .75
91 Doug West .20 .50
92 Micheal Williams .20 .50
93 Kenny Anderson .25 .60
94 Benoit Benjamin .20 .50
95 P.J. Brown .20 .50
96 Derrick Coleman .25 .60
97 Kevin Edwards .20 .50
98 Hubert Davis .20 .50
99 Patrick Ewing .40 1.00
100 Derek Harper .25 .60
101 Anthony Mason .20 .50
102 Charles Oakley .25 .60
103 Charles Smith .20 .50
104 John Starks .25 .60
105 Nick Anderson .20 .50
106 Anfernee Hardaway .50 1.25
107 Shaquille O'Neal .75 2.00
108 Dennis Scott .20 .50
109 Jeff Turner .20 .50
110 Dana Barros .20 .50
111 Shawn Bradley .20 .50
112 Jeff Malone .20 .50
113 Tim Perry .20 .50
114 Clarence Weatherspoon .20 .50
115 Danny Ainge .30 .75
116 Charles Barkley .50 1.25
117 A.C. Green .25 .60
118 Kevin Johnson .30 .75
119 Dan Majerle .30 .75
120 Clyde Drexler .40 1.00
121 Harvey Grant .20 .50
122 Jerome Kersey .20 .50
123 Clifford Robinson .20 .50
124 Rod Strickland .20 .50
125 Buck Williams .20 .50
126 Randy Brown .20 .50
127 Olden Polynice .20 .50
128 Mitch Richmond .30 .75
129 Lionel Simmons .20 .50
130 Spud Webb .25 .60
131 Walt Williams .20 .50
132 Willie Anderson .20 .50
133 Vinny Del Negro .20 .50
134 Sean Elliott .30 .75
135 Avery Johnson .25 .60
136 J.R. Reid .20 .50
137 David Robinson .50 1.25
138 Dennis Rodman .60 1.50
139 Kendall Gill .20 .50
140 Ervin Johnson .20 .50
141 Shawn Kemp .30 .75
142 Nate McMillan .20 .50
143 Gary Payton .30 .75
144 Sam Perkins .20 .50
145 David Benoit .20 .50
146 Jeff Hornacek .25 .60
147 Jay Humphries .20 .50
148 Karl Malone .40 1.00
149 Bryon Russell .20 .50
150 Felton Spencer .20 .50
151 John Stockton .40 1.00
152 Rex Chapman .20 .50
153 Calbert Cheaney .20 .50
154 Tom Gugliotta .20 .50
155 Don MacLean .20 .50
156 Gheorghe Muresan .20 .50
157 Doug Overton .20 .50
158 Brent Price .20 .50
159 Derrick Coleman USA .25 .60
160 Joe Dumars USA .30 .75
161 Tim Hardaway USA .30 .75
162 Kevin Johnson USA .30 .75
163 Larry Johnson USA .30 .75
164 Shawn Kemp USA .30 .75
165 Dan Majerle USA .30 .75
166 Reggie Miller USA .40 1.00
167 Alonzo Mourning USA .40 1.00
168 Shaquille O'Neal USA .75 2.00
169 Mark Price USA .30 .75
170 Steve Smith USA .25 .60
171 Isiah Thomas USA .30 .75
172 Dominique Wilkins USA .40 1.00
173 Checklist .20 .50
174 Checklist .20 .50
175 Checklist .20 .50
176 Tyrone Corbin .20 .50
177 Grant Long .20 .50
178 Ken Norman .20 .50
179 Steve Smith .25 .60
180 Blue Edwards .20 .50
181 Pervis Ellison .20 .50
182 Greg Minor RC .30 .75
183 Eric Montross RC .25 .60
184 Derek Strong .20 .50
185 David Wesley .20 .50
186 Dominique Wilkins .40 1.00
187 Michael Adams .20 .50
188 Muggsy Bogues .25 .60
189 Scott Burrell .20 .50
190 Darrin Hancock RC .25 .60
191 Robert Parish .30 .75
192 Jud Buechler .20 .50
193 Ron Harper .25 .60
194 Larry Krystkowiak .20 .50
195 Will Perdue .20 .50
196 Dickey Simpkins RC .25 .60
197 Michael Cage .20 .50
198 Tony Campbell .20 .50
199 Danny Ferry .20 .50
200 Chris Mills .20 .50
201 Popeye Jones .20 .50
202 Jason Kidd RC 1.50 4.00
203 Roy Tarpley .20 .50
204 Lorenzo Williams .20 .50
205 Dale Ellis .20 .50
206 Tom Hammonds .20 .50
207 Jalen Rose RC .75 2.00
208 Reggie Slater .20 .50
209 Bryant Stith .20 .50
210 Rafael Addison .20 .50
211 Bill Curley RC .20 .50
212 Johnny Dawkins .20 .50
213 Grant Hill RC 1.50 4.00
214 Mark Macon .20 .50
215 Oliver Miller .20 .50
216 Ivano Newbill .20 .50
217 Mark West .20 .50
218 Tom Gugliotta .20 .50
219 Tim Hardaway .30 .75
220 Keith Jennings .20 .50
221 Dwayne Morton .20 .50
222 Chris Mullin .30 .75
223 Ricky Pierce .20 .50
224 Carlos Rogers RC .25 .60
225 Clifford Rozier RC .20 .50
226 Rony Seikaly .20 .50
227 Tim Breaux .20 .50
228 Scott Brooks .20 .50
229 Mario Elie .20 .50
230 Vernon Maxwell .20 .50
231 Zan Tabak .20 .50
232 Mark Jackson .25 .60
233 Derrick McKey .20 .50
234 Tony Massenburg .20 .50
235 Lamond Murray RC .30 .75
236 Bo Outlaw .30 .75
237 Eric Piatkowski RC .40 1.00
238 Pooh Richardson .20 .50
239 Malik Sealy .20 .50
240 Cedric Ceballos .20 .50
241 Eddie Jones RC 1.00 2.50
242 Anthony Miller .30 .75
243 Tony Smith .20 .50
244 Sedale Threatt .20 .50
245 Ledell Eackles .20 .50
246 Kevin Gamble .20 .50
247 Matt Geiger .20 .50
248 Brad Lohaus .20 .50
249 Billy Owens .20 .50
250 Khalid Reeves RC .25 .60
251 Glen Rice .30 .75
252 Kevin Willis .20 .50
253 Marty Conlon .20 .50
254 Eric Mobley RC .20 .50
255 Johnny Newman .20 .50
256 Ed Pinckney .20 .50
257 Glenn Robinson RC .60 1.50
258 Pat Durham .20 .50
259 Howard Eisley .30 .75
260 Winston Garland .20 .50
261 Stacey King .20 .50
262 Donyell Marshall RC .30 .75
263 Sean Rooks .20 .50
264 Chris Smith .20 .50
265 Chris Childs RC .25 .60
266 Sleepy Floyd .20 .50
267 Armon Gilliam .20 .50
268 Sean Higgins .20 .50
269 Rex Walters .20 .50
270 Greg Anthony .20 .50
271 Charlie Ward RC .30 .75
272 Herb Williams .20 .50
273 Monty Williams RC .25 .60
274 Anthony Avent .20 .50
275 Anthony Bowie .20 .50
276 Horace Grant .25 .60
277 Donald Royal .20 .50
278 Brian Shaw .20 .50
279 Brooks Thompson RC .25 .60
280 Derrick Alston RC .20 .50
281 Willie Burton .20 .50
282 Greg Graham .20 .50
283 B.J. Tyler RC .20 .50
284 Scott Williams .20 .50
285 Sharone Wright RC .25 .60
286 Joe Kleine .20 .50
287 Danny Manning .25 .60
288 Elliot Perry .20 .50
289 Wesley Person RC .30 .75
290 Trevor Ruffin RC .20 .50
291 Wayman Tisdale .20 .50
292 Mark Bryant .20 .50
293 Chris Dudley .20 .50
294 Aaron McKie RC .30 .75
295 Tracy Murray .20 .50
296 Terry Porter .20 .50
297 James Robinson .20 .50
298 Alaa Abdelnaby .20 .50
299 Duane Causwell .20 .50
300 Brian Grant RC .50 1.25
301 Bobby Hurley .20 .50
302 Michael Smith RC .20 .50
303 Terry Cummings .25 .60
304 Moses Malone .30 .75
305 Julius Nwosu .20 .50
306 Chuck Person .25 .60
307 Doc Rivers .25 .60
308 Vincent Askew .20 .50
309 Sarunas Marciulionis .20 .50
310 Detlef Schrempf .30 .75
311 Dontonio Wingfield .30 .75
312 Antoine Carr .20 .50
313 Tom Chambers .25 .60
314 John Crotty .20 .50
315 Adam Keefe .20 .50
316 Jamie Watson RC .20 .50
317 Mitchell Butler .20 .50
318 Kevin Duckworth .20 .50
319 Juwan Howard RC .50 1.25
320 Jim McIlvaine RC .25 .60
321 Scott Skiles .20 .50
322 Anthony Tucker RC .20 .50
323 Chris Webber .50 1.25
324 Checklist .20 .50
325 Checklist .20 .50
326 Michael Jordan 4.00 10.00

1994-95 Flair Center Spotlight

Randomly inserted at a rate of one in every 25 first series packs, cards from this 6-card set features dominant centers. The fronts have a 100% etched-foil design with a full color action photo with three shadows of him in red, green and blue. The back also has a color photo with the red, green and blue shadowing on a white background along with player information. The cards are numbered on the back as "X of 6" and are sequenced in alphabetical order.

COMPLETE SET (6) 10.00 25.00
SER.1 STATED ODDS 1:25
1 Patrick Ewing 2.00 5.00
2 Alonzo Mourning 2.00 5.00
3 Hakeem Olajuwon 2.00 5.00
4 Shaquille O'Neal 6.00 15.00
5 David Robinson 2.50 6.00
6 Chris Webber 4.00 10.00

1994-95 Flair Hot Numbers

Randomly inserted into first series packs at a rate of one in six, cards from this 20-card standard-size set feature a selection of players who consistently produce big statistics. The player's top statistical numbers are shown on the front of the card without identifying which category. While some numbers are obvious, like the player's points per game, other statistics are not, like steals and blocks, particularly for multi-talented players. The fronts also have full-color action photos

with the team's colors used as the background along with the words "Hot Numbers". The backs also have a color picture with information on what type of player he is. The cards are numbered on the back as "X of 20" and are sequenced in alphabetical order.
COMPLETE SET (20) 15.00 40.00
SER.1 STATED ODDS 1:6
1 Vin Baker 1.00 2.50
2 Sam Cassell 1.00 2.50
3 Patrick Ewing 1.25 3.00
4 Anfernee Hardaway 1.50 4.00
5 Robert Horry 1.00 2.50
6 Shawn Kemp 1.00 2.50
7 Toni Kukoc 1.25 3.00
8 Jamal Mashburn 1.00 2.50
9 Reggie Miller 1.25 3.00
10 Dikembe Mutombo 1.00 2.50
11 Hakeem Olajuwon 1.25 3.00
12 Shaquille O'Neal 2.50 6.00
13 Scottie Pippen 2.00 5.00
14 Isaiah Rider 1.00 2.50
15 David Robinson 1.50 4.00
16 Latrell Sprewell 1.25 3.00
17 John Starks .75 2.00
18 John Stockton 1.25 3.00
19 Nick Van Exel 1.00 2.50
20 Chris Webber 1.50 4.00

1994-95 Flair Playmakers

Randomly inserted into second series packs at a rate of one in four, cards from this 10-card standard-size set feature a selection of the best assist men in the NBA. The fronts have a full color action photo with a hardwood floor in the background. The back also has a color photo with player information set against a hardwood floor. The cards are numbered on the back as "X of 10" and are sequenced in alphabetical order.
COMPLETE SET (10) 3.00 8.00
SER.2 STATED ODDS 1:4
1 Kenny Anderson .40 1.00
2 Mookie Blaylock .30 .75
3 Sam Cassell .50 1.25
4 Anfernee Hardaway .75 2.00
5 Robert Pack .30 .75
6 Scottie Pippen 1.00 2.50
7 Mark Price .50 1.25
8 Mitch Richmond .50 1.25
9 John Stockton .60 1.50
10 Nick Van Exel .50 1.25

1994-95 Flair Rejectors

Randomly inserted into second series packs at a rate of one in 25, cards from this six-card standard-size set feature a selection of top shot blockers in basketball. The fronts are 100% etched foil that have a full color action photo of the player. The background is three hands in red, green and blue seemingly up to reject a shot. The back also has a player photo along with information on him, such as his blocks per game. The background is nearly identical to the background on the front. The cards are numbered on the back as "X of 6" and are sequenced in alphabetical order.
COMPLETE SET (6) 12.00 30.00
SER.2 STATED ODDS 1:25
1 Patrick Ewing 2.50 6.00
2 Alonzo Mourning 2.50 6.00
3 Dikembe Mutombo 2.00 5.00
4 Hakeem Olajuwon 2.50 6.00
5 Shaquille O'Neal 8.00 20.00
6 David Robinson 3.00 8.00

1994-95 Flair Scoring Power

Randomly inserted into first series packs at a rate of one in eight, cards from this 20-card standard-size set feature a selection of perennial NBA scoring leaders. The fronts emphasize the words scoring power as they are the size of the card laid out horizontally against a black background. There is a player photo in front of the words and another inside. The back also says "Scoring Power" across the entire card horizontally. There is also a player photo with information on him, namely about his scoring. The cards are numbered on the back as "X of 10" and are sequenced in alphabetical order.
COMPLETE SET (10) 8.00 20.00
SER.1 STATED ODDS 1:8
1 Charles Barkley 1.50 4.00
2 Patrick Ewing 1.25 3.00
3 Karl Malone 1.25 3.00
4 Hakeem Olajuwon 1.25 3.00
5 Shaquille O'Neal 3.00 8.00
6 Scottie Pippen 2.00 5.00
7 Mitch Richmond 1.00 2.50
8 David Robinson 1.50 4.00
9 Latrell Sprewell 1.25 3.00
10 Dominique Wilkins 1.25 3.00

1994-95 Flair Wave of the Future

Randmly inserted into second series packs at a rate of one in seven, cards from this 10-card standard-size set feature a selection of top rookies from the 1994-95 season. Card fronts are laid out horizontally with three color photos of the player. The one in the middle has yellow glow surrounding it and the picture on the left is the same as the middle. The one on the left is a head shot of the color photo used on the back of the card. The back has player information including some college statistics. Both sides of the card have a wave in the background in the team's colors. The cards are numbered on the back as "X of 10" and are sequenced in alphabetical order.
COMPLETE SET (10) 8.00 20.00
SER.2 STATED ODDS 1:7
1 Brian Grant 1.00 2.50
2 Grant Hill 3.00 8.00
3 Juwan Howard 1.00 2.50
4 Eddie Jones 2.00 5.00
5 Jason Kidd 3.00 8.00
6 Donyell Marshall .60 1.50
7 Eric Montross .50 1.25
8 Lamond Murray .60 1.50
9 Wesley Person .60 1.50
10 Glenn Robinson 1.25 3.00

1995-96 Flair

These 250-standard size cards comprise Fleer's premium1995-96 Flair set which was issued in two separate series of 150 and 100 cards respectively. Cards were issued in 9-card "hardpacks" (featuring a two-piece protective design wrapper) with a suggested retail price of $4.99. Player selection was restricted to recognized starters, top rookies and top players off the bench. Card fronts were upgraded from the previous year, each featuring 100% etched foil designs. Like the previous year, each card was printed on 30-point stock, giving the card twice the thickness of regular issue cards. First and second series cards are numbered alphabetically by team. Two subsets are included in the set: Rookies (199-228) and Style (229-248). Noteworthy Rookie Cards in this set include Michael Finley, Kevin Garnett, Antonio McDyess, Joe Smith, Jerry Stackhouse and Damon Stoudamire.
COMPLETE SET (250) 30.00 80.00
COMPLETE SERIES 1 (150) 15.00 40.00
COMPLETE SERIES 2 (100) 15.00 40.00
1 Stacey Augmon .40 1.00
2 Mookie Blaylock .30 .75
3 Grant Long .30 .75
4 Steve Smith .40 1.00
5 Dee Brown .30 .75
6 Sherman Douglas .30 .75
7 Eric Montross .30 .75
8 Dino Radja .30 .75
9 David Wesley .30 .75
10 Muggsy Bogues .40 1.00
11 Scott Burrell .30 .75
12 Dell Curry .30 .75
13 Larry Johnson .50 1.25
14 Alonzo Mourning .60 1.50
15 Michael Jordan 4.00 10.00
16 Steve Kerr .40 1.00
17 Toni Kukoc .50 1.25
18 Scottie Pippen .75 2.00
19 Terrell Brandon .30 .75
20 Tyrone Hill .30 .75
21 Chris Mills .30 .75
22 Bobby Phills .30 .75
23 Mark Price .50 1.25
24 John Williams .30 .75
25 Jim Jackson .30 .75
26 Popeye Jones .30 .75
27 Jason Kidd .75 2.00
28 Jamal Mashburn .50 1.25
29 Lorenzo Williams .30 .75
30 Mahmoud Abdul-Rauf .30 .75
31 Dikembe Mutombo .50 1.25
32 Robert Pack .30 .75
33 Jalen Rose .60 1.50
34 Bryant Stith .30 .75
35 Reggie Williams .30 .75
36 Joe Dumars .50 1.25
37 Grant Hill .75 2.00
38 Allan Houston .40 1.00
39 Lindsey Hunter .30 .75
40 Terry Mills .30 .75
41 Chris Gatling .30 .75
42 Tim Hardaway .50 1.25
43 Donyell Marshall .30 .75
44 Chris Mullin .50 1.25
45 Carlos Rogers .30 .75
46 Clifford Rozier .30 .75
47 Latrell Sprewell .50 1.25
48 Sam Cassell .50 1.25
49 Clyde Drexler .60 1.50
50 Mario Elie .30 .75
51 Robert Horry .40 1.00
52 Hakeem Olajuwon .60 1.50
53 Kenny Smith .40 1.00
54 Antonio Davis .30 .75
55 Dale Davis .30 .75
56 Mark Jackson .40 1.00
57 Derrick McKey .30 .75
58 Reggie Miller .60 1.50
59 Rik Smits .40 1.00
60 Lamond Murray .30 .75
61 Pooh Richardson .30 .75
62 Malik Sealy .30 .75
63 Loy Vaught .30 .75
64 Elden Campbell .30 .75
65 Cedric Ceballos .30 .75
66 Vlade Divac .50 1.25
67 Eddie Jones .50 1.25
68 Nick Van Exel .50 1.25
69 Bimbo Coles .30 .75
70 Billy Owens .30 .75
71 Khalid Reeves .30 .75
72 Glen Rice .50 1.25
73 Kevin Willis .30 .75
74 Vin Baker .40 1.00
75 Todd Day .30 .75
76 Eric Murdock .30 .75
77 Glenn Robinson .40 1.00
78 Tom Gugliotta .30 .75
79 Christian Laettner .40 1.00
80 Isaiah Rider .50 1.25
81 Doug West .30 .75
82 Kenny Anderson .40 1.00
83 P.J. Brown .30 .75
84 Derrick Coleman .40 1.00
85 Armon Gilliam .30 .75
86 Chris Morris .30 .75
87 Hubert Davis .30 .75
88 Patrick Ewing .60 1.50
89 Derek Harper .40 1.00
90 Anthony Mason .30 .75
91 Charles Oakley .40 1.00
92 Charles Smith .30 .75
93 John Starks .40 1.00
94 Nick Anderson .30 .75
95 Horace Grant .40 1.00
96 Anfernee Hardaway .75 2.00
97 Shaquille O'Neal 1.25 3.00
98 Dennis Scott .30 .75
99 Brian Shaw .30 .75
100 Dana Barros .30 .75
101 Shawn Bradley .30 .75
102 Clarence Weatherspoon .30 .75
103 Sharone Wright .30 .75
104 Charles Barkley .75 2.00
105 A.C. Green .40 1.00
106 Kevin Johnson .50 1.25
107 Dan Majerle .50 1.25
108 Danny Manning .40 1.00
109 Elliot Perry .30 .75
110 Wesley Person .30 .75
111 Terry Porter .30 .75
112 Clifford Robinson .30 .75
113 Rod Strickland .30 .75
114 Otis Thorpe .30 .75
115 Buck Williams .30 .75
116 Brian Grant .40 1.00
117 Bobby Hurley .30 .75
118 Olden Polynice .30 .75
119 Mitch Richmond .50 1.25
120 Walt Williams .30 .75
121 Vinny Del Negro .30 .75
122 Sean Elliott .50 1.25
123 Avery Johnson .40 1.00
124 David Robinson .75 2.00
125 Dennis Rodman 1.00 2.50
126 Shawn Kemp .50 1.25
127 Nate McMillan .30 .75
128 Gary Payton .50 1.25
129 Sam Perkins .30 .75
130 Detlef Schrempf .50 1.25
131 B.J. Armstrong .30 .75
132 Jerome Kersey .30 .75
133 Oliver Miller .30 .75
134 John Salley .30 .75
135 David Benoit .30 .75
136 Antoine Carr .30 .75
137 Jeff Hornacek .40 1.00
138 Karl Malone .60 1.50
139 John Stockton .60 1.50
140 Greg Anthony .30 .75
141 Benoit Benjamin .30 .75
142 Blue Edwards .30 .75
143 Byron Scott .40 1.00
144 Calbert Cheaney .30 .75
145 Juwan Howard .50 1.25
146 Gheorghe Muresan .30 .75
147 Scott Skiles .30 .75
148 Chris Webber .60 1.50
149 Checklist .25 .60
150 Checklist .25 .60
151 Stacey Augmon .40 1.00
152 Mookie Blaylock .30 .75
153 Andrew Lang .30 .75
154 Steve Smith .40 1.00
155 Dana Barros .30 .75
156 Rick Fox .30 .75
157 Kendall Gill .30 .75
158 Khalid Reeves .30 .75
159 Glen Rice .50 1.25
160 Dennis Rodman 1.00 2.50
161 Dan Majerle .50 1.25
162 Tony Dumas .30 .75
163 Dale Ellis .30 .75
164 Otis Thorpe .30 .75
165 Rony Seikaly .30 .75
166 Sam Cassell .50 1.25
167 Clyde Drexler .60 1.50
168 Robert Horry .40 1.00
169 Hakeem Olajuwon .60 1.50
170 Ricky Pierce .30 .75
171 Rodney Rogers .30 .75
172 Brian Williams .30 .75
173 Magic Johnson 1.25 3.00
174 Alonzo Mourning .60 1.50
175 Lee Mayberry .30 .75
176 Terry Porter .30 .75
177 Shawn Bradley .30 .75
178 Jayson Williams .30 .75
179 Gary Grant .30 .75
180 Jon Koncak .30 .75
181 Derrick Coleman .40 1.00
182 Vernon Maxwell .30 .75
183 John Williams .30 .75
184 Aaron McKie .30 .75
185 Michael Smith .30 .75
186 Chuck Person .40 1.00
187 Hersey Hawkins .30 .75
188 Shawn Kemp .50 1.25
189 Gary Payton .50 1.25
190 Detlef Schrempf .50 1.25
191 Chris Morris .30 .75
192 Robert Pack .30 .75
193 Willie Anderson EXP .15 .40
194 Oliver Miller EXP .15 .40
195 Alvin Robertson EXP .15 .40
196 Greg Anthony EXP .15 .40
197 Blue Edwards EXP .15 .40
198 Byron Scott EXP .20 .50
199 Cory Alexander RC .40 1.00
200 Brent Barry RC .60 1.50
201 Travis Best RC .40 1.00
202 Jason Caffey RC .40 1.00
203 Sasha Danilovic RC .40 1.00
204 Tyus Edney RC .40 1.00
205 Michael Finley RC 1.25 3.00
206 Kevin Garnett RC 3.00 8.00
207 Alan Henderson RC .40 1.00
208 Antonio McDyess RC .50 1.25
209 Loren Meyer RC .25 .60
210 Lawrence Moten RC .40 1.00
211 Ed O'Bannon RC .30 .75
212 Greg Ostertag RC .40 1.00
213 Cherokee Parks RC .30 .75
214 Theo Ratliff RC .60 1.50
215 Bryant Reeves RC .30 .75
216 Shawn Respert RC .30 .75
217 Arvydas Sabonis RC .75 2.00
218 Joe Smith RC .50 1.25
219 Jerry Stackhouse RC 1.25 3.00
220 Damon Stoudamire RC 1.00 2.50
221 Bob Sura RC .30 .75
222 Kurt Thomas RC .40 1.00
223 Gary Trent RC .40 1.00
224 David Vaughn RC .40 1.00
225 Rasheed Wallace RC 1.25 3.00
226 Eric Williams RC .40 1.00
227 Corliss Williamson RC .40 1.00
228 George Zidek RC .30 .75
229 Vin Baker STY .20 .50
230 Charles Barkley STY .40 1.00
231 Patrick Ewing STY .30 .75
232 Anfernee Hardaway STY .40 1.00
233 Grant Hill STY .40 1.00
234 Larry Johnson STY .25 .60
235 Michael Jordan STY 2.00 5.00
236 Jason Kidd STY .40 1.00
237 Karl Malone STY .30 .75
238 Jamal Mashburn STY .25 .60
239 Reggie Miller STY .30 .75
240 Shaquille O'Neal STY .60 1.50
241 Scottie Pippen STY .40 1.00
242 Mitch Richmond STY .25 .60
243 Clifford Robinson STY .15 .40
244 David Robinson STY .40 1.00
245 Glenn Robinson STY .20 .50
246 John Stockton STY .30 .75
247 Nick Van Exel STY .25 .60
248 Chris Webber STY .30 .75
249 Checklist .25 .60
250 Checklist .25 .60

1995-96 Flair Anticipation

Randomly inserted in second series packs at a rate of one in 36, cards from this ten card standard-size set feature a collection of fan favorites. Borderless fronts have a full-color action raised cutouts and two ghosted images of the same shot in the player's team colors. Backs have a close-up color shot and a player profile. The set is sequenced in alphabetical order.
COMPLETE SET (10) 40.00 100.00
SER.2 STATED ODDS 1:36
1 Grant Hill 5.00 12.00
2 Michael Jordan 50.00 120.00
3 Shawn Kemp 3.00 8.00
4 Jason Kidd 5.00 12.00
5 Alonzo Mourning 4.00 10.00
6 Hakeem Olajuwon 4.00 10.00
7 Shaquille O'Neal 8.00 20.00
8 Glenn Robinson 2.50 6.00
9 Joe Smith 2.00 5.00
10 Jerry Stackhouse 5.00 12.00

1995-96 Flair Center Spotlight

Randomly inserted in first series packs at a rate of one in 18, cards from this 6-card standard-size set feature a selection of the game's dominant centers. This was the second year in a row Flair included a Center Spotlight insert within their first series product. Each card is printed on clear plastic, with a full color action photo layered on top of a circular designed background. Backs are numbered on the left in gold foil and the player's blue silhouette serves as a background for biography and career highlights which are printed in white. The set is sequenced in alphabetical order.
COMPLETE SET (6) 8.00 20.00
SER.1 STATED ODDS 1:18
1 Vlade Divac 1.50 4.00
2 Patrick Ewing 2.00 5.00
3 Alonzo Mourning 2.00 5.00
4 Hakeem Olajuwon 2.00 5.00
5 Shaquille O'Neal 4.00 10.00
6 David Robinson 2.50 6.00

1995-96 Flair Class of '95

Seeded in first series packs at the same rate as regular issue cards, these 15-cards were added to the first series Flair product just prior to release. Each card features one of the top rookies from the 1995 NBA draft in their new pro uniforms. Full color, cutout player action shots are placed against a glowing orange basketball backdrop. The set is sequenced in alphabetical order.
COMPLETE SET (15) 8.00 20.00
RANDOM INSERTS IN SER.1 PACKS
R1 Brent Barry .60 1.50
R2 Kevin Garnett 3.00 8.00
R3 Antonio McDyess .50 1.25
R4 Ed O'Bannon .30 .75
R5 Cherokee Parks .30 .75
R6 Bryant Reeves .30 .75
R7 Shawn Respert .30 .75
R8 Joe Smith .50 1.25
R9 Jerry Stackhouse 1.25 3.00
R10 Damon Stoudamire 1.00 2.50
R11 Kurt Thomas .40 1.00
R12 Gary Trent .40 1.00
R13 Rasheed Wallace 1.25 3.00
R14 Eric Williams .40 1.00
R15 Corliss Williamson .40 1.00

1995-96 Flair Hot Numbers

Randomly inserted in first series packs at rate of one in 36, cards from this 15-card standard-size set showcase the game's top players. Each card is given a three-dimensional effect by the addition of a special lenticular coating (a ribbed plastic material) on the front. The full color player photos are placed against a swirling background of numbers. The backs continue with the numbers motif that serve as a background for the full-color player cutout. Player's name and short biography are printed in white. The set is sequenced in alphabetical order.
COMPLETE SET (15) 300.00 600.00
SER.1 STATED ODDS 1:36
1 Charles Barkley 20.00 50.00
2 Grant Hill 15.00 40.00
3 Eddie Jones 8.00 20.00
4 Michael Jordan 150.00 400.00
5 Shawn Kemp 15.00 40.00
6 Jason Kidd 15.00 40.00
7 Karl Malone 15.00 40.00
8 Alonzo Mourning 12.00 30.00
9 Dikembe Mutombo 15.00 40.00
10 Hakeem Olajuwon 15.00 40.00
11 Shaquille O'Neal 25.00 60.00
12 Glenn Robinson 6.00 15.00
13 Dennis Rodman 15.00 40.00
14 Latrell Sprewell 15.00 40.00
15 Chris Webber 15.00 40.00

1995-96 Flair New Heights

Randomly inserted in second series hobby packs only at a rate of one in 18, cards from this 10-card standard-size set feature some of the more popular players in the hobby. Borderless fronts have a full-color action cutout with a ghosted image trailing behind. Backs have player profile and biographies. The set is sequenced in alphabetical order.
COMPLETE SET (10) 40.00 100.00
SER.2 STATED ODDS 1:18 HOBBY
1 Anfernee Hardaway 2.50 6.00
2 Grant Hill 2.50 6.00
3 Larry Johnson 1.50 4.00
4 Michael Jordan 30.00 80.00
5 Shawn Kemp 1.50 4.00
6 Karl Malone 2.00 5.00
7 Hakeem Olajuwon 2.00 5.00
8 David Robinson 2.50 6.00
9 Glenn Robinson 1.25 3.00
10 Chris Webber 2.00 5.00

1995-96 Flair Perimeter Power

Randomly inserted in first series packs at a rate of one in 12, cards from this 15-card set feature players that dominate play from the perimeter. Full-bleed team-color backgrounds include a player cutout with silver foil printing on the front. Backs are printed on a white background with another full-color action player shot.
COMPLETE SET (15) 6.00 15.00
SER.1 STATED ODDS 1:12
1 Dana Barros .50 1.25
2 Clyde Drexler 1.00 2.50
3 Anfernee Hardaway 1.25 3.00
4 Tim Hardaway .75 2.00
5 Dan Majerle .75 2.00
6 Jamal Mashburn .75 2.00
7 Reggie Miller 1.00 2.50
8 Gary Payton .75 2.00
9 Scottie Pippen 1.25 3.00
10 Glen Rice .75 2.00
11 Mitch Richmond .75 2.00
12 Steve Smith .60 1.50
13 John Starks .60 1.50
14 John Stockton 1.00 2.50
15 Nick Van Exel .75 2.00

1995-96 Flair Play Makers

Randomly inserted in second series packs at a rate of one in 54 packs, this set of ten standard-size cards features a selection of some of the league's top playmakers. Fronts are printed in a 3-D lenticular format and feature the player in a full-color action shot. The background is a three-color chalkboard diagram. The diagram background continues on the back and a player profile appears in a screened box next to a full-color action player cutout. The set is sequenced in alphabetical order.
COMPLETE SET (10) 50.00 100.00
SER.2 STATED ODDS 1:54
1 Clyde Drexler 8.00 20.00
2 Anfernee Hardaway 10.00 25.00
3 Jamal Mashburn 6.00 15.00
4 Reggie Miller 8.00 20.00
5 Gary Payton 6.00 15.00
6 Scottie Pippen 10.00 25.00
7 Mitch Richmond 6.00 15.00
8 David Robinson 10.00 25.00
9 Jerry Stackhouse 10.00 25.00
10 Nick Van Exel 6.00 15.00

1995-96 Flair Stackhouse's Scrapbook

Randomly inserted into one in every 24 second series packs, these two cards continue the cross-brand set of Fleer spokesperson Jerry Stackhouse. The two Flair cards represent the third of a four series, eight card set. Card fronts feature a a full-color action shot framed by a ghosted white border.
COMPLETE SET (2) 3.00 8.00
COMMON CARD (S5-S6) 2.00 5.00
WRAPPER ODDS 1:24

1995-96 Flair Wave of the Future

The 10 cards in this standard-size set were randomly inserted at a rate of one in 12 second series packs and feature rookie NBA players with potential for greatness. A full-color player action cutout appears on the front with a watercolor backgound painted in a wave pattern. Backs continue with the wave pattern background and have another full-color action cutout. The cards are sequenced in alphabetical order.
COMPLETE SET (10) 8.00 20.00
SER.2 STATED ODDS 1:12
1 Tyus Edney .50 1.25
2 Michael Finley 1.50 4.00
3 Kevin Garnett 4.00 10.00
4 Antonio McDyess .60 1.50
5 Ed O'Bannon .40 1.00
6 Arvydas Sabonis 1.00 2.50
7 Joe Smith .60 1.50
8 Jerry Stackhouse 1.50 4.00
9 Damon Stoudamire 1.25 3.00
10 Rasheed Wallace 1.50 4.00

1996-97 Flair Showcase Row 2

The 1996-97 Flair Showcase set was issued in one series totalling 270 cards and was deemed Hobby only for the first time. Each box contained 24 cards per box, five cards per pack with a suggested retail price of $4.99. The set does contain 270 cards, but is essentially a 90-card set with each player having three different front themes: Row 2 (Style), Row 1 (Grace) and Row 0 (Showcase). Each card also contains the following back themes: Showtime, Show Stoppers and Showpiece. By combining the two different themes, collectors can determine the different scarcity levels. For Row 2, or Style, using Style and Showtime (cards 1-30), the odds are 1.5 to one. Using Style and Showpiece (cards 31-60), the odds are one in 2. Using Style and Show Stoppers (cards 61-90), the odds are one in 1.5. A three-card promo strip of Jerry Stackhouse was released and is priced at the end of the set.
COMPLETE SET (90) 25.00 60.00
1-30 ODDS 1.5:1
31-60 ODDS 1:2
61-90 ODDS 1:1.5
1 Anfernee Hardaway .75 2.00
2 Mitch Richmond .50 1.25
3 Allen Iverson RC 2.50 6.00
4 Charles Barkley .75 2.00
5 Juwan Howard .40 1.00
6 David Robinson .75 2.00
7 Gary Payton .50 1.25
8 Kerry Kittles RC .50 1.25
9 Dennis Rodman 1.00 2.50
10 Shaquille O'Neal 1.25 3.00
11 Stephon Marbury RC 1.25 3.00
12 John Stockton .60 1.50
13 Glenn Robinson .40 1.00
14 Hakeem Olajuwon .60 1.50
15 Jason Kidd .75 2.00
16 Jerry Stackhouse .60 1.50
17 Joe Smith .40 1.00
18 Reggie Miller .60 1.50
19 Grant Hill .75 2.00
20 Damon Stoudamire .40 1.00
21 Kevin Garnett 1.25 3.00
22 Clyde Drexler .60 1.50
23 Michael Jordan 4.00 10.00
24 Antonio McDyess .50 1.25
25 Chris Webber .60 1.50
26 Antoine Walker RC .75 2.00
27 Scottie Pippen .75 2.00
28 Karl Malone .60 1.50
29 Shareef Abdur-Rahim RC .75 2.00
30 Shawn Kemp .50 1.25
31 Kobe Bryant RC 12.00 30.00
32 Derrick Coleman .40 1.00
33 Alonzo Mourning .60 1.50
34 Anthony Mason .30 .75
35 Ray Allen RC 2.00 5.00
36 Arvydas Sabonis .40 1.00
37 Brian Grant .40 1.00
38 Bryant Reeves .30 .75
39 Christian Laettner .40 1.00
40 Tom Gugliotta .30 .75
41 Latrell Sprewell .50 1.25
42 Erick Dampier RC .50 1.25
43 Gheorghe Muresan .30 .75
44 Glen Rice .50 1.25
45 Patrick Ewing .60 1.50
46 Jim Jackson .30 .75
47 Michael Finley .60 1.50
48 Toni Kukoc .50 1.25
49 Marcus Camby RC .75 2.00
50 Kenny Anderson .40 1.00
51 Mark Price .50 1.25
52 Tim Hardaway .50 1.25
53 Mookie Blaylock .30 .75
54 Steve Smith .40 1.00
55 Terrell Brandon .30 .75
56 Lorenzen Wright RC .40 1.00
57 Sasha Danilovic .30 .75
58 Jeff Hornacek .40 1.00
59 Eddie Jones .50 1.25
60 Vin Baker .40 1.00
61 Chris Childs .30 .75
62 Clifford Robinson .30 .75
63 Anthony Peeler .30 .75
64 Dino Radja .30 .75
65 Joe Dumars .50 1.25
66 Loy Vaught .30 .75
67 Rony Seikaly .30 .75
68 Vitaly Potapenko RC .40 1.00
69 Chris Gatling .30 .75
70 Dale Ellis .30 .75
71 Allan Houston .40 1.00
72 Doug Christie .30 .75
73 LaPhonso Ellis .30 .75
74 Kendall Gill .30 .75
75 Rik Smits .40 1.00
76 Bobby Phills .30 .75
77 Malik Sealy .30 .75
78 Sean Elliott .50 1.25
79 Vlade Divac .50 1.25
80 David Wesley .30 .75
81 Dominique Wilkins .50 1.25
82 Danny Manning .40 1.00
83 Detlef Schrempf .50 1.25
84 Hersey Hawkins .30 .75
85 Lindsey Hunter .30 .75
86 Mahmoud Abdul-Rauf .30 .75
87 Shawn Bradley .30 .75
88 Horace Grant .40 1.00
89 Cedric Ceballos .30 .75
90 Jamal Mashburn .40 1.00
NNO Jerry Stackhouse Promo 2.00 5.00
3-card strip

1996-97 Flair Showcase Row 1

*STARS: .75X TO 2X ROW 2
*RCs: .6X TO 1.5X ROW 2
1-30 ODDS 1:2.5
31-60 ODDS 1:2
61-90 ODDS 1:3.5

1996-97 Flair Showcase Row 0

*STARS 1-30: 3X TO 8X ROW 2
*RCs 1-30: 1.5X TO 4X HI
1-30 ODDS 1:24
*STARS 31-60: 2X TO 5X ROW 2
*RCs 31-60: 1X TO 2.5X ROW 2
31-60 ODDS 1:10
*STARS/RCs 61-90: .6X TO 1.5X ROW 2
61-90 ODDS 1:5
3 Allen Iverson 12.00 30.00
23 Michael Jordan 60.00 150.00
31 Kobe Bryant 60.00 150.00

1996-97 Flair Showcase Legacy Collection Row 2

*ROW 1/2 STARS: 15X TO 40X HI COLUMN
*ROW 1/2 RCs: 8X TO 20X HI
STATED ODDS 1:30
STATED PRINT RUN 150 SERIAL #'d SETS
LEGACY: ROW 1 AND 2 SAME VALUE
1 Anfernee Hardaway 100.00 250.00
3 Allen Iverson 100.00 250.00
6 David Robinson 40.00 100.00
9 Dennis Rodman 75.00 200.00
10 Shaquille O'Neal 100.00 250.00
11 Stephon Marbury 30.00 80.00
14 Hakeem Olajuwon 40.00 100.00
15 Jason Kidd 50.00 120.00
18 Reggie Miller 75.00 200.00
19 Grant Hill 60.00 150.00
23 Michael Jordan 1200.00 2000.00
25 Chris Webber 30.00 80.00
27 Scottie Pippen 60.00 150.00
28 Karl Malone 30.00 80.00
30 Shawn Kemp 25.00 60.00
31 Kobe Bryant 1000.00 1800.00
35 Ray Allen 50.00 120.00
41 Latrell Sprewell 30.00 80.00
48 Toni Kukoc 25.00 60.00
81 Dominique Wilkins 15.00 40.00

1996-97 Flair Showcase Legacy Collection Row 0

*STARS: 20X TO 50X HI
*RCs: 10X TO 25X HI
STATED PRINT RUN 150 SER.#'d SETS
1 Anfernee Hardaway 150.00 400.00
3 Allen Iverson 150.00 400.00
4 Charles Barkley 75.00 200.00
6 David Robinson 100.00 250.00
7 Gary Payton 40.00 100.00
9 Dennis Rodman 100.00 250.00
10 Shaquille O'Neal 100.00 250.00
11 Stephon Marbury 40.00 100.00
14 Hakeem Olajuwon 75.00 200.00
15 Jason Kidd 75.00 200.00
18 Reggie Miller 75.00 200.00
19 Grant Hill 75.00 200.00
21 Kevin Garnett 125.00 250.00
23 Michael Jordan 1200.00 2000.00
25 Chris Webber 50.00 120.00
27 Scottie Pippen 150.00 400.00
28 Karl Malone 50.00 120.00
29 Shareef Abdur-Rahim 30.00 80.00
30 Shawn Kemp 50.00 120.00
31 Kobe Bryant 800.00 1200.00
33 Alonzo Mourning 40.00 100.00
35 Ray Allen 75.00 200.00
41 Latrell Sprewell 60.00 150.00
48 Toni Kukoc 30.00 80.00
49 Marcus Camby 40.00 100.00
71 Allan Houston 25.00 60.00
81 Dominique Wilkins 25.00 60.00

1996-97 Flair Showcase Class of '96

Randomly inserted in packs at a rate of one in five, this 20-card set features the top rookies from the class of 1996. Cards feature an embossed design.
COMPLETE SET (20) 15.00 40.00
STATED ODDS 1:5
1 Shareef Abdur-Rahim 1.25 3.00
2 Ray Allen 3.00 8.00
3 Shandon Anderson .60 1.50
4 Kobe Bryant 12.00 30.00
5 Marcus Camby 1.25 3.00
6 Erick Dampier .75 2.00
7 Derek Fisher 1.00 2.50
8 Todd Fuller .50 1.25
9 Othella Harrington .75 2.00
10 Allen Iverson 4.00 10.00
11 Kerry Kittles .75 2.00
12 Travis Knight .75 2.00
13 Matt Maloney .60 1.50
14 Stephon Marbury 2.00 5.00
15 Steve Nash 4.00 10.00
16 Jermaine O'Neal 1.25 3.00
17 Vitaly Potapenko .60 1.50
18 Roy Rogers .60 1.50
19 Antoine Walker 1.25 3.00
20 Lorenzen Wright .60 1.50

1996-97 Flair Showcase Hot Shots

Randomly inserted in packs at a rate of one in 90, this 20-card set features some of the best players in the NBA. Card fronts contain a photo of the player over a basketball surrounded by a die-cut flame. A small percentage of the press run contained errors to the names on the front of the cards.
STATED ODDS 1:90
1 Michael Jordan 600.00 800.00
2 Kevin Garnett 50.00 100.00
3 Damon Stoudamire 10.00 25.00
4 Anfernee Hardaway 50.00 120.00
5 Shaquille O'Neal 60.00 150.00
6 Grant Hill 25.00 60.00
7 Dennis Rodman 60.00 150.00
8 Shawn Kemp 30.00 80.00
9 Scottie Pippen 50.00 120.00
10 Juwan Howard 10.00 25.00
11 Jason Kidd 20.00 50.00
12 Hakeem Olajuwon 20.00 50.00
13 Karl Malone 20.00 50.00
14 Joe Smith 10.00 25.00
15 David Robinson 30.00 80.00
16 Jerry Stackhouse 20.00 50.00
17 Antonio McDyess 12.00 30.00
18 Clyde Drexler 20.00 50.00
19 Gary Payton 20.00 50.00
20 Eddie Jones 15.00 40.00

1997-98 Flair Showcase Row 3

The 1997-98 Flair Showcase set was issued in one series totalling 80 cards. The 5-card packs retailed for $4.99 each. The Row 3 set was broken up into 4 levels with the following odds: Showtime (cards 1-20) at 1:0.9, Showstopper (cards 21-40) at 1:1.1, Showdown (cards 41-60) at 1:1.5 and Showpiece (cards 61-80) at 1:2. A four-card Grant Hill promo strip was also released and is priced at the bottom of the set.
COMPLETE SET (80) 12.00 30.00
1-20 STATED ODDS 1:0.9
21-40 STATED ODDS 1:1.1
41-60 STATED ODDS 1:1.5
61-80 STATED ODDS 1:2
UNPRICED MASTERPIECES SERIAL #'d TO 1
1 Michael Jordan 8.00 20.00
2 Grant Hill .75 2.00
3 Allen Iverson 1.00 2.50
4 Kevin Garnett .75 2.00
5 Tim Duncan RC 3.00 8.00
6 Shawn Kemp .50 1.25
7 Shaquille O'Neal 1.25 3.00
8 Antoine Walker .50 1.25
9 Shareef Abdur-Rahim .50 1.25
10 Damon Stoudamire .40 1.00
11 Anfernee Hardaway .75 2.00
12 Keith Van Horn RC .60 1.50
13 Dennis Rodman 1.00 2.50
14 Ron Mercer RC .50 1.25
15 Stephon Marbury .60 1.50
16 Scottie Pippen 1.00 2.50
17 Kerry Kittles .30 .75
18 Kobe Bryant 2.50 6.00
19 Marcus Camby .50 1.25
20 Chauncey Billups RC 1.25 3.00
21 Tracy McGrady RC 1.50 4.00
22 Joe Smith .40 1.00
23 Brevin Knight RC .40 1.00
24 Danny Fortson RC .40 1.00
25 Tim Thomas RC .50 1.25
26 Gary Payton .50 1.25
27 David Robinson .75 2.00
28 Hakeem Olajuwon .60 1.50
29 Antonio Daniels RC .40 1.00
30 Antonio McDyess .40 1.00
31 Eddie Jones .50 1.25
32 Adonal Foyle RC .30 .75
33 Glenn Robinson .40 1.00
34 Charles Barkley .75 2.00
35 Vin Baker .40 1.00
36 Jerry Stackhouse .50 1.25
37 Ray Allen .60 1.50
38 Derek Anderson RC .40 1.00
39 Isaac Austin .30 .75
40 Tony Battie RC .40 1.00
41 Tariq Abdul-Wahad RC .30 .75
42 Dikembe Mutombo .50 1.25
43 Clyde Drexler .60 1.50
44 Chris Mullin .50 1.25
45 Tim Hardaway .50 1.25
46 Terrell Brandon .30 .75
47 John Stockton .60 1.50
48 Patrick Ewing .60 1.50
49 Horace Grant .40 1.00
50 Tom Gugliotta .30 .75
51 Mookie Blaylock .30 .75
52 Mitch Richmond .50 1.25
53 Anthony Mason .30 .75
54 Michael Finley .50 1.25
55 Jason Kidd .75 2.00
56 Karl Malone .60 1.50
57 Reggie Miller .60 1.50
58 Steve Smith .40 1.00
59 Glen Rice .50 1.25
60 Bryant Stith .30 .75
61 Loy Vaught .30 .75
62 Brian Grant .30 .75
63 Joe Dumars .50 1.25
64 Juwan Howard .40 1.00
65 Rik Smits .40 1.00
66 Alonzo Mourning .60 1.50
67 Allan Houston .40 1.00
68 Chris Webber .50 1.25
69 Kendall Gill .30 .75
70 Rony Seikaly .30 .75
71 Kenny Anderson .40 1.00
72 John Wallace .30 .75
73 Bryant Reeves .30 .75
74 Brian Williams .30 .75
75 Larry Johnson .50 1.25
76 Shawn Bradley .30 .75
77 Kevin Johnson .50 1.25
78 Rod Strickland .30 .75
79 Rodney Rogers .30 .75
80 Rasheed Wallace .50 1.25
NNO Grant Hill PROMO 3.00 8.00

1997-98 Flair Showcase Row 2

COMPLETE SET (80) 25.00 60.00
*STARS/RCs: .5X TO 1.25X ROW 3
1-20 STATED ODDS 1:3
21-40 STATED ODDS 1:2.5
41-60 STATED ODDS 1:4
61-80 STATED ODDS 1:3.5

1997-98 Flair Showcase Row 1

COMPLETE SET (80) 80.00 200.00
*STARS/RCs 1-20: 1.25X TO 3X ROW 3
1-20 STATED ODDS 1:16
*STARS/RCs 21-40: 1.5X TO 4X ROW 3
21-40 STATED ODDS 1:24
*STARS/RCs 41-60: .75X TO 2X ROW 3
41-60 STATED ODDS 1:6
*STARS 61-80: 1X TO 2.5X ROW 3
61-80 STATED ODDS 1:10

1997-98 Flair Showcase Row 0

*STARS 1-20: 8X TO 20X ROW 3
*RCs 1-20: 5X TO 12X ROW 3
STATED PRINT RUN 250 SERIAL #'d SETS
*STARS 21-40: 5X TO 12X ROW 3
*RCs 21-40: 4X TO 10X ROW 3
STATED PRINT RUN 500 SERIAL #'d SETS
*STARS 41-60: 4X TO 10X ROW 3
*RCs 41-60: 3X TO 8X ROW 3
STATED PRINT RUN 1000 SERIAL #'d SETS
*STARS 61-80: 2X TO 5X ROW 3
STATED PRINT RUN 2000 SERIAL #'d SETS
1 Michael Jordan 400.00 800.00
5 Tim Duncan 150.00 300.00
13 Dennis Rodman 30.00 80.00
18 Kobe Bryant 125.00 250.00

1997-98 Flair Showcase Legacy Collection Row 3

*STARS: 15X TO 40X BASE CARD HI
*RCs: 8X TO 20X BASE HI
STATED PRINT RUN 100 SERIAL #'d SETS
LEGACY: ALL ROWS SAME VALUE
1 Michael Jordan 1500.00 2300.00
3 Allen Iverson 150.00 300.00
5 Tim Duncan 300.00 600.00
7 Shaquille O'Neal 100.00 250.00
11 Anfernee Hardaway 40.00 100.00
16 Scottie Pippen 40.00 100.00
18 Kobe Bryant 500.00 1000.00
21 Tracy McGrady 60.00 150.00
26 Gary Payton 25.00 60.00
47 John Stockton 40.00 100.00
57 Reggie Miller 30.00 80.00
66 Alonzo Mourning 40.00 100.00
68 Chris Webber 50.00 120.00

1997-98 Flair Showcase Wave of the Future

Randomly inserted into packs at one in 20, this 12-card set features some of the top rookies not to be included in the basic set. The cards are enclosed in plastic, which contains a liquid to simulate a water background within the card.
COMPLETE SET (12) 10.00 20.00
STATED ODDS 1:20
1 Corey Beck 1.25 3.00
2 Maurice Taylor 1.25 3.00
3 Chris Anstey .75 2.00
4 Keith Booth 1.00 2.50
5 Anthony Parker 1.25 3.00
6 Austin Croshere 1.00 2.50
7 Jacque Vaughn 1.00 2.50
8 God Shammgod 1.25 3.00
9 Bobby Jackson 1.50 4.00
10 Johnny Taylor 1.00 2.50
11 Ed Gray 1.25 3.00
12 Kelvin Cato 1.00 2.50

1998-99 Flair Showcase Row 3

This year's Flair Showcase was changed back to three levels, from four. The 90-card set was released in five-card packs which carried a suggested retail price of $4.99. The base Row 3 set, or Power, had a different insertion ratio for each set of 30 cards. Cards 1-30, or Power/Showtime were inserted one in 0.8; cards 31-60, or Power/Showdown were inserted one per pack and cards 61-90, or Power/Showpiece were inserted one in 1.2.
COMPLETE SET (90) 20.00 50.00
1-30 STATED ODDS 1:0.8
31-60 STATED ODDS 1:1
61-90 STATED ODDS 1:1.2
UNPRICED MASTERPIECES SERIAL #'d TO 1
1 Keith Van Horn .25 .60
1A K.Van Horn PROMO .40 1.00
2 Kobe Bryant 1.00 2.50
3 Tim Duncan .50 1.25
4 Kevin Garnett .40 1.00
5 Grant Hill .40 1.00
6 Allen Iverson .50 1.25
7 Shaquille O'Neal .60 1.50
8 Antoine Walker .25 .60
9 Shareef Abdur-Rahim .25 .60
10 Stephon Marbury .30 .75
11 Ray Allen .30 .75
12 Shawn Kemp .25 .60
13 Tim Thomas .25 .60
14 Scottie Pippen .40 1.00
15 Latrell Sprewell .25 .60
16 Dirk Nowitzki RC 3.00 8.00
17 Antawn Jamison RC .75 2.00
18 Anfernee Hardaway .40 1.00
19 Larry Hughes RC 1.00 2.50
20 Robert Traylor RC .50 1.25
21 Kerry Kittles .15 .40
22 Ron Mercer .20 .50
23 Michael Olowokandi RC .60 1.50
24 Jason Kidd .40 1.00
25 Vince Carter RC 2.50 6.00
26 Charles Barkley .40 1.00
27 Antonio McDyess .20 .50
28 Mike Bibby RC .75 2.00
29 Paul Pierce RC 2.00 5.00
30 Raef LaFrentz RC .60 1.50
31 Reggie Miller .30 .75
32 Michael Finley .25 .60
33 Eddie Jones .25 .60
34 Tim Hardaway .25 .60
35 Glenn Robinson .20 .50
36 Brevin Knight .15 .40
37 Gary Payton .25 .60
38 David Robinson .40 1.00
39 Karl Malone .30 .75
40 Derek Anderson .15 .40
41 Patrick Ewing .30 .75
42 Juwan Howard .20 .50
43 Jayson Williams .15 .40
44 Terrell Brandon .15 .40
45 Hakeem Olajuwon .30 .75
46 Isaac Austin .15 .40
47 Glen Rice .25 .60
48 Maurice Taylor .15 .40
49 Damon Stoudamire .20 .50
50 Brian Skinner RC .50 1.25
51 Nazr Mohammed RC .50 1.25
52 Tom Gugliotta .15 .40
53 Al Harrington RC .75 2.00
54 Pat Garrity RC .40 1.00
55 Jason Williams RC 1.25 3.00
56 Tracy McGrady .40 1.00
57 Keon Clark RC .50 1.25
58 Vin Baker .20 .50
59 Bonzi Wells RC .50 1.25
60 John Stockton .30 .75
61 Isaiah Rider .20 .50
62 Alonzo Mourning .30 .75
63 Allan Houston .20 .50
64 Dennis Rodman .50 1.25
65 Felipe Lopez RC .30 .75
66 Joe Smith .20 .50
67 Chris Webber .25 .60
68 Mitch Richmond .25 .60
69 Brent Barry .20 .50
70 Mookie Blaylock .15 .40
71 Donyell Marshall .15 .40
72 Anthony Mason .15 .40
73 Rod Strickland .15 .40
74 Roshown McLeod RC .30 .75
75 Matt Harpring RC .50 1.25
76 Detlef Schrempf .25 .60
77 Michael Dickerson RC .50 1.25
78 Michael Doleac RC .40 1.00
79 John Starks .20 .50
80 Ricky Davis RC .75 2.00
81 Steve Smith .20 .50
82 Voshon Lenard .15 .40
83 Toni Kukoc .25 .60
84 Steve Nash .40 1.00
85 Vlade Divac .25 .60
86 Rasheed Wallace .25 .60
87 Bryon Russell .15 .40
88 Antonio Daniels .15 .40
89 Rik Smits .20 .50
90 Joe Dumars .25 .60

1998-99 Flair Showcase Row 2

COMPLETE SET (90) 60.00 120.00
*STARS: 1X TO 2.5X ROW 3
*RCs: .5X TO 1.25X ROW 3
1-30: STATED ODDS 1:3
31-60: STATED ODDS 1:1.3
61-90: STATED ODDS 1:2
1A K.Van Horn Promo .75 2.00

1998-99 Flair Showcase Row 1

*1-30 STARS: 3X TO 8X ROW 3
*1-30 RCs: 2X TO 5X ROW 3
1:30: PRINT RUN 1500 SERIAL #'d SETS
*31-60 STARS: 2.5X TO 6X ROW 3
*31-60 RCs: 1.5X TO 4X ROW 3
31-60: PRINT RUN 3000 SERIAL #'d SETS
*61-90 STARS: 1.5X TO 4X ROW 3
*61-90 RCs: .75X TO 2X ROW 3
61-90: STATED ODDS 1:6
61-90: PRINT RUN 6000 SERIAL #'d SETS
1A Keith Van Horn Promo 1.25 3.00

1998-99 Flair Showcase Legacy Collection Row 3

*STARS: 25X TO 60X VALUE
*RCs: 8X TO 20X VALUE
STATED PRINT RUN 99 SERIAL #'d SETS
LEGACY: ALL ROWS EQUAL VALUE
2 Kobe Bryant 350.00 650.00
3 Tim Duncan 100.00 250.00
4 Kevin Garnett 40.00 100.00
5 Grant Hill 30.00 80.00
16 Dirk Nowitzki 100.00 250.00
18 Anfernee Hardaway 40.00 100.00
25 Vince Carter 75.00 200.00
26 Charles Barkley 30.00 80.00
55 Jason Williams 30.00 80.00
64 Dennis Rodman 75.00 150.00

1998-99 Flair Showcase Class of '98

Randomly inserted into packs, this 15-card set features first year stars and sculpture embossing. The cards are serially numbered to 500.
COMPLETE SET (15) 100.00 250.00
STATED PRINT RUN 500 SERIAL #'d SETS
1 Michael Olowokandi 2.00 5.00
2 Mike Bibby 2.50 6.00
3 Raef LaFrentz 2.00 5.00
4 Antawn Jamison 2.50 6.00
5 Vince Carter 20.00 50.00
6 Robert Traylor 1.50 4.00
7 Jason Williams 12.00 30.00
8 Larry Hughes 3.00 8.00
9 Dirk Nowitzki 40.00 100.00
10 Paul Pierce 12.00 30.00
11 Bonzi Wells 1.50 4.00
12 Michael Doleac 1.25 3.00
13 Michael Dickerson 1.50 4.00
14 Pat Garrity 1.25 3.00
15 Al Harrington 2.50 6.00

1998-99 Flair Showcase takeit2.net

Randomly inserted in packs, this 15-card set features computer generated designs of some of the NBA's finest ball players. The cards are serially numbered to 1000.
STATED PRINT RUN 1000 SERIAL #'d SETS
1 Scottie Pippen 15.00 40.00
2 Tim Duncan 25.00 60.00
3 Keith Van Horn 6.00 15.00
4 Grant Hill 15.00 40.00
5 Kobe Bryant 50.00 120.00
6 Antoine Walker 6.00 15.00
7 Kevin Garnett 20.00 50.00
8 Allen Iverson 40.00 100.00
9 Shareef Abdur-Rahim 6.00 15.00
10 Anfernee Hardaway 20.00 50.00
11 Stephon Marbury 8.00 20.00
12 Ron Mercer 10.00 25.00
13 Michael Jordan 350.00 700.00
14 Shaquille O'Neal 20.00 50.00
15 Shawn Kemp 12.00 30.00

1999-00 Flair Showcase

The 1999-00 Fleer Showcase product was released in May, 2000, and features a 130-card base set that is broken into tiers as follows: 100 Base Veterans (1-100), and 30 Rookies (101-130) that are serial numbered to 2000. Each pack contained 5 cards and carried a suggested retail price of $3.99.
COMPLETE SET (130) 75.00 150.00
COMPLETE SET w/o RC (100) 20.00 50.00
101-130 RANDOM INSERTS IN PACKS
101-130 PRINT RUN 2000 SERIAL #'d SETS
UNPRICED MASTERPIECES SERIAL #'d TO 1
1 Vince Carter .75 2.00
2 Anfernee Hardaway .60 1.50
3 Nick Van Exel .30 .75
4 Kerry Kittles .25 .60
5 Michael Doleac .25 .60
6 Sean Elliott .40 1.00
7 Shaquille O'Neal 1.00 2.50
8 Avery Johnson .30 .75
9 Brian Grant .25 .60
10 Jerome Williams .25 .60
11 Larry Hughes .30 .75
12 Jerry Stackhouse .40 1.00
13 Alonzo Mourning .50 1.25
14 Antonio McDyess .30 .75
15 Jason Kidd .60 1.50
16 Bryon Russell .25 .60
17 Hakeem Olajuwon .50 1.25
18 Juwan Howard .30 .75
19 Paul Pierce .50 1.25
20 Vin Baker .30 .75
21 Larry Johnson .40 1.00
22 Gary Trent .25 .60
23 Jayson Williams .25 .60
24 Tim Hardaway .40 1.00
25 Dirk Nowitzki .75 2.00
26 Jamal Mashburn .30 .75
27 Glenn Robinson .30 .75
28 Shawn Bradley .25 .60
29 Tom Gugliotta .25 .60
30 Vlade Divac .40 1.00
31 David Robinson .60 1.50
32 Matt Geiger .25 .60
33 Grant Hill .50 1.25
34 Maurice Taylor .25 .60
35 Toni Kukoc .40 1.00
36 Cedric Ceballos .25 .60
37 Patrick Ewing .50 1.25
38 Ray Allen .40 1.00
39 Michael Finley .40 1.00
40 Robert Traylor .25 .60
41 Brevin Knight .25 .60
42 Marcus Camby .30 .75
43 Sam Cassell .30 .75
44 Antawn Jamison .40 1.00
45 Steve Smith .30 .75
46 Darrell Armstrong .25 .60
47 Mookie Blaylock .25 .60
48 Derek Anderson .25 .60
49 Hersey Hawkins .25 .60
50 Kobe Bryant 1.50 4.00
51 Shawn Kemp .40 1.00
52 Scottie Pippen .60 1.50
53 Chris Webber .40 1.00
54 Damon Stoudamire .30 .75
55 Donyell Marshall .25 .60
56 Isaiah Rider .30 .75
57 Karl Malone .50 1.25
58 Kevin Garnett .60 1.50
59 Mario Elie .25 .60
60 Michael Dickerson .25 .60
61 Jahidi White .25 .60
62 Joe Smith .30 .75
63 Kenny Anderson .30 .75
64 Reggie Miller .40 1.00
65 Ruben Patterson .25 .60
66 Shareef Abdur-Rahim .30 .75
67 Allen Iverson .75 2.00
68 Glen Rice .40 1.00
69 Nick Anderson .25 .60
70 Rex Chapman .25 .60
71 Ron Mercer .30 .75
72 Tim Duncan .75 2.00
73 Al Harrington .40 1.00
74 Brent Barry .30 .75
75 Eddie Jones .40 1.00
76 Mike Bibby .40 1.00
77 Anthony Mason .25 .60
78 Michael Olowokandi .25 .60
79 Matt Harpring .25 .60
80 Stephon Marbury .30 .75
81 Tracy McGrady .60 1.50
82 Allan Houston .30 .75
83 Lindsey Hunter .25 .60
84 Tariq Abdul-Wahad .25 .60
85 Antoine Walker .40 1.00
86 Charles Barkley .60 1.50
87 Gary Payton .40 1.00
88 John Stockton .50 1.25
89 Mitch Richmond .40 1.00
90 Terrell Brandon .25 .60
91 Charles Oakley .30 .75
92 Bryant Reeves .25 .60
93 Dikembe Mutombo .40 1.00
94 Elden Campbell .25 .60
95 Jalen Rose .30 .75
96 Jason Williams .50 1.25
97 Keith Van Horn .30 .75
98 Latrell Sprewell .40 1.00
99 Raef LaFrentz .30 .75
100 Rasheed Wallace .40 1.00
101 Cal Bowdler RC .75 2.00
102 Dion Glover RC 1.00 2.50
103 Jason Terry RC 2.00 5.00
104 Adrian Griffin RC 1.25 3.00
105 Baron Davis RC 3.00 8.00
106 Michael Ruffin RC 1.00 2.50
107 Elton Brand RC 3.00 8.00
108 Ron Artest RC 2.50 6.00
109 Andre Miller RC 2.50 6.00
110 Trajan Langdon RC 1.25 3.00
111 James Posey RC 1.25 3.00
112 Vonteego Cummings RC .75 2.00
113 Kenny Thomas RC 1.25 3.00
114 Steve Francis RC 3.00 8.00
115 Jonathan Bender RC 1.25 3.00
116 Lamar Odom RC 3.00 8.00
117 Devean George RC 1.25 3.00
118 Tim James RC .75 2.00
119 Anthony Carter RC 1.00 2.50
120 Wally Szczerbiak RC 2.50 6.00
121 William Avery RC 1.00 2.50
122 Evan Eschmeyer RC 1.00 2.50
123 Corey Maggette RC 2.00 5.00
124 Jumaine Jones RC 1.00 2.50
125 Shawn Marion RC 2.50 6.00
126 Ryan Robertson RC .75 2.00
127 A.Radojevic RC .75 2.00
128 Quincy Lewis RC .75 2.00
129 Scott Padgett RC 1.00 2.50
130 Richard Hamilton RC 2.50 6.00
P1 Vince Carter PROMO 1.50 4.00

1999-00 Flair Showcase Legacy Collection

*STARS: 30X TO 80X BASE CARD HI
*RCs: 4X TO 10X BASE HI
STATED PRINT RUN 20 SERIAL #'d SETS
33 Grant Hill 75.00 200.00
35 Toni Kukoc 50.00 125.00
51 Shawn Kemp 50.00 125.00
52 Scottie Pippen 100.00 200.00

1999-00 Flair Showcase Ball of Fame

Randomly inserted in packs at one in five, this 15-card set featured rookies against a background of basketballs. Card backs carry a "BF" prefix.
COMPLETE SET (15) 15.00 40.00
STATED ODDS 1:5
BF1 Lamar Odom 2.50 6.00
BF2 Steve Francis 2.50 6.00
BF3 Elton Brand 2.50 6.00
BF4 Wally Szczerbiak 2.00 5.00
BF5 Shawn Marion 2.00 5.00
BF6 Jason Terry 1.50 4.00
BF7 Richard Hamilton 2.00 5.00
BF8 Andre Miller 2.00 5.00
BF9 Corey Maggette 1.50 4.00
BF10 Baron Davis 2.50 6.00
BF11 Vonteego Cummings .60 1.50
BF12 Kenny Thomas 1.00 2.50
BF13 Jumaine Jones .75 2.00
BF14 Trajan Langdon 1.00 2.50
BF15 Jonathan Bender 1.00 2.50

1999-00 Flair Showcase ConVINCEing

Randomly inserted in packs at one in 10, this 10-card set focused on Vince Carter and his on/off the court activities. Card backs carry a "C" prefix.
COMPLETE SET (10) 6.00 15.00
COMMON CARD (C1-C10) 1.25 3.00
STATED ODDS 1:10

1999-00 Flair Showcase Elevators

Randomly inserted in packs at one in 20, this 10-card set featured players who can soar above the others in the NBA. Card backs carry an "E" prefix.
COMPLETE SET (10) 10.00 25.00
STATED ODDS 1:20
E1 Vince Carter 1.50 4.00
E2 Lamar Odom 2.00 5.00
E3 Allen Iverson 1.50 4.00
E4 Kobe Bryant 5.00 12.00
E5 Grant Hill 1.00 2.50
E6 Eddie Jones .75 2.00
E7 Scottie Pippen 1.25 3.00
E8 Kevin Garnett 1.25 3.00
E9 Steve Francis 2.00 5.00
E10 Keith Van Horn .60 1.50

1999-00 Flair Showcase Feel the Game

Randomly inserted in packs at one in 120, this 15-card set featured a swatch of player-worn uniform. The cards are not numbered and listed below in alphabetical order.
STATED ODDS 1:120
1 William Avery 1.50 4.00
2 Vince Carter 10.00 25.00
3 Vonteego Cummings 1.25 3.00
4 Patrick Ewing 6.00 15.00
5 Brian Grant 3.00 8.00
6 Karl Malone 6.00 15.00
7 Shawn Marion 4.00 10.00
8 Alonzo Mourning 6.00 15.00
9 Lamar Odom 5.00 12.00
10 Shaquille O'Neal 12.00 30.00
11 Paul Pierce 6.00 15.00
12 David Robinson 8.00 20.00
13 Damon Stoudamire 4.00 10.00
14 Kenny Thomas 2.00 5.00
15 Antoine Walker 5.00 12.00

1999-00 Flair Showcase Fresh Ink

Randomly inserted in packs at one in 39, this 31-card set featured autographs of top NBA stars and rookies. The cards feature a congratulatory message on the back. The cards are not numbered and listed below in alphabetical order.
STATED ODDS 1:39
1 Tariq Abdul-Wahad 3.00 8.00
2 Ron Artest 6.00 15.00
3 William Avery 2.50 6.00
4 Tony Battie 2.50 6.00
5 Cal Bowdler 2.00 5.00
6 Vince Carter 15.00 40.00
7 Dion Glover 2.50 6.00
8 Chris Herren 2.50 6.00
9 Juwan Howard 4.00 10.00
10 Eddie Jones 5.00 12.00
11 Jumaine Jones 2.50 6.00
12 Brevin Knight 2.00 5.00
13 Toni Kukoc 6.00 15.00
14 Trajan Langdon 3.00 8.00
15 Quincy Lewis 2.00 5.00
16 Corey Maggette 4.00 10.00
17 Stephon Marbury 8.00 20.00
18 Tracy McGrady 15.00 30.00
19 Ron Mercer 2.50 6.00
20 Andre Miller 6.00 15.00
21 Lamar Odom 6.00 15.00
22 Hakeem Olajuwon 12.00 30.00
23 Scott Padgett 2.50 6.00
24 Scottie Pippen 75.00 200.00
25 James Posey 3.00 8.00
26 Aleksandar Radojevic 2.00 5.00
27 Glen Rice 10.00 25.00
28 Wally Szczerbiak 6.00 15.00
29 Jason Terry 4.00 10.00
30 Kenny Thomas 3.00 8.00
31 Jerome Williams 2.00 5.00

1999-00 Flair Showcase Fresh Ink Rock Steady

STATED PRINT RUN 25 SERIAL #'d SETS
1 Vince Carter 80.00 200.00
2 Chris Herren 10.00 25.00
3 Ron Mercer 6.00 15.00
4 Lamar Odom 60.00 150.00
5 Scottie Pippen 200.00 400.00
6 Aleksandar Radojevic 8.00 20.00
7 Kenny Thomas 12.00 30.00

1999-00 Flair Showcase Guaranteed Fresh

Randomly inserted in packs at one in 10, this 10-card set focuses on key players for each NBA team. Card backs carry a "GF" prefix.
COMPLETE SET (10) 6.00 15.00
STATED ODDS 1:10
GF1 Vince Carter 1.00 2.50
GF2 Shaquille O'Neal 1.25 3.00
GF3 Kevin Garnett .75 2.00
GF4 Kobe Bryant 2.00 5.00
GF5 Paul Pierce .60 1.50
GF6 Jason Williams .60 1.50
GF7 Stephon Marbury .40 1.00
GF8 Lamar Odom 1.25 3.00
GF9 Keith Van Horn .40 1.00
GF10 Wally Szczerbiak 1.00 2.50

1999-00 Flair Showcase License to Skill

Randomly inserted in packs at one in 20, this 10-card set featured players who lit-up the scoreboard. The cards are die cut. Card backs carry an "LS" prefix.
COMPLETE SET (10) 8.00 20.00
STATED ODDS 1:20
LS1 Vince Carter 1.50 4.00
LS2 Shaquille O'Neal 2.00 5.00
LS3 Tim Duncan 1.50 4.00
LS4 Keith Van Horn .60 1.50
LS5 Grant Hill 1.00 2.50
LS6 Allen Iverson 1.50 4.00
LS7 Antoine Walker .75 2.00
LS8 Scottie Pippen 1.25 3.00
LS9 Kobe Bryant 4.00 10.00
LS10 Lamar Odom 2.00 5.00

1999-00 Flair Showcase Next

Randomly inserted in packs at one in 2.5, this 20-card set focuses on younger players who will take the NBA into the millennium. Card backs carry an "N" prefix.
COMPLETE SET (20) 6.00 15.00
STATED ODDS 1:2.5
N1 Vince Carter .60 1.50
N2 James Posey .30 .75
N3 Jonathan Bender .30 .75
N4 Corey Maggette .50 1.25
N5 Devean George .30 .75
N6 Trajan Langdon .30 .75
N7 Shawn Marion .60 1.50
N8 William Avery .25 .60
N9 Adrian Griffin .30 .75
N10 Quincy Lewis .20 .50
N11 Kenny Thomas .30 .75
N12 Lamar Odom .75 2.00
N13 Dion Glover .25 .60
N14 Elton Brand .75 2.00
N15 Andre Miller .60 1.50
N16 Jason Terry .50 1.25
N17 Richard Hamilton .60 1.50
N18 Steve Francis .75 2.00
N19 Baron Davis .75 2.00
N20 Wally Szczerbiak .60 1.50

1999-00 Flair Showcase Rookie Showcase Firsts

Randomly inserted into packs, this 30-card insert set features some of the hottest rookies from 1999-00 season. There were only 500 serial-numbered sets of this insert produced.
COMPLETE SET (30) 75.00 150.00
*RC FIRSTS: .75X TO 2X BASE HI
STATED PRINT RUN 500 SERIAL #'d SETS

2001-02 Flair

Released in late October 2001 as a 121 card set, Flair contains 90 regular cards, and 30 rookie cards numbered to 1500. Base cards feature white borders with player acton shots set against player portrait photos. Each box was issed with either a jumbo Sweet Shot memorabilia card or a jumbo Sweet Shot autograph card which is sealed in it's own wrapper. Flair was packaged in 20 pack boxes with each pack containing five cards.
COMP.SET w/o SP's (90) 12.50 30.00
91-120 PRINT RUN 1500 SERIAL #'d SETS
1 Tracy McGrady .60 1.50
2 Derek Fisher .30 .75
3 Allen Iverson .75 2.00
4 Chris Webber .40 1.00
5 Jalen Rose .30 .75
6 Kenyon Martin .40 1.00
7 Jermaine O'Neal .30 .75
8 Kobe Bryant 1.50 4.00
9 Bryon Russell .25 .60
10 Wally Szczerbiak .30 .75
11 Damon Stoudamire .30 .75
12 John Stockton .50 1.25
13 Glenn Robinson .30 .75
14 Steve Francis .30 .75
15 Vince Carter .60 1.50
16 Peja Stojakovic .40 1.00
17 Rick Fox .25 .60
18 Allan Houston .30 .75
19 Danny Fortson .25 .60
20 Gary Payton .40 1.00
21 Darius Miles .25 .60
22 Kevin Garnett .60 1.50
23 Marcus Camby .30 .75
24 Desmond Mason .30 .75
25 Tim Duncan .75 2.00
26 Jamal Mashburn .30 .75
27 Andre Miller .30 .75
28 Antonio McDyess .30 .75
29 Morris Peterson .25 .60
30 Rasheed Wallace .40 1.00
31 Shawn Marion .30 .75
32 Karl Malone .50 1.25
33 Grant Hill .50 1.25
34 Shaquille O'Neal 1.00 2.50
35 Hakeem Olajuwon .50 1.25
36 Corliss Williamson .25 .60
37 Paul Pierce .40 1.00
38 Antonio Davis .25 .60
39 Antonio Daniels .25 .60
40 Ray Allen .40 1.00
41 Dirk Nowitzki .60 1.50
42 Jerry Stackhouse .30 .75
43 Donyell Marshall .25 .60
44 Brian Grant .25 .60
45 Raef LaFrentz .25 .60
46 Corey Maggette .30 .75
47 Mike Miller .30 .75
48 Jason Williams .30 .75
49 Jahidi White .25 .60
50 David Robinson .60 1.50
51 Shareef Abdur-Rahim .30 .75
52 Anfernee Hardaway .60 1.50
53 Baron Davis .40 1.00
54 DerMarr Johnson .25 .60
55 Dikembe Mutombo .40 1.00
56 David Wesley .25 .60
57 Chris Mihm .25 .60
58 Michael Finley .40 1.00
59 Eddie House .25 .60
60 Stromile Swift .25 .60
61 Courtney Alexander .25 .60
62 Ron Mercer .25 .60
63 Cuttino Mobley .25 .60
64 Tim Thomas .25 .60
65 Eddie Jones .30 .75
66 Lamar Odom .30 .75
67 Terrell Brandon .25 .60
68 Rashard Lewis .40 1.00
69 Antoine Walker .30 .75
70 Latrell Sprewell .30 .75
71 Sam Cassell .30 .75
72 Mike Bibby .40 1.00
73 Speedy Claxton .25 .60
74 Steve Nash .60 1.50
75 Mark Jackson .30 .75
76 Ron Artest .40 1.00
77 Matt Harpring .25 .60
78 Wang Zhizhi .30 .75
79 Nazr Mohammed .25 .60
80 Jason Terry .40 1.00
81 Nick Van Exel .30 .75
82 Reggie Miller .40 1.00
83 Joe Smith .30 .75
84 Jason Kidd .60 1.50
85 Richard Hamilton .30 .75
86 Antawn Jamison .40 1.00
87 Alonzo Mourning .50 1.25
88 Stephon Marbury .30 .75
89 Scottie Pippen .60 1.50
90 Elton Brand .40 1.00
91 Kwame Brown RC 1.25 3.00
92 Eddie Griffin RC 1.00 2.50
93 Tyson Chandler RC 2.00 5.00
94 Omar Cook RC 1.25 3.00
95 Loren Woods RC .75 2.00
96 Alton Ford RC 1.25 3.00
97 Shane Battier RC 2.50 6.00
98 Joe Johnson RC 1.50 4.00
99 Rodney White RC .75 2.00
100 Pau Gasol RC 4.00 10.00
101 Zach Randolph RC 2.00 5.00
102 Vladimir Radmanovic RC 1.25 3.00
103 Brendan Haywood RC 1.25 3.00
104 Michael Bradley RC .75 2.00
105 Tony Parker RC 6.00 15.00
106 Jason Richardson RC 1.50 4.00
107 Gerald Wallace RC 1.50 4.00
108 Damone Brown RC .75 2.00
109 Richard Jefferson RC 2.00 5.00
110 Eddy Curry RC 1.25 3.00
111 DeSagana Diop RC 1.00 2.50
112 Brandon Armstrong RC .75 2.00
113 Troy Murphy RC 1.25 3.00
114 Kedrick Brown RC .75 2.00
115 Kirk Haston RC .75 2.00
116 Gilbert Arenas RC 2.00 5.00
117 Jeryl Sasser RC .75 2.00
118 Jamaal Tinsley RC 1.25 3.00
119 Terence Morris RC 1.25 3.00
120 Michael Wright RC 1.25 3.00
121 Michael Jordan 6.00 15.00

2001-02 Flair Courting Greatness

Randomly inserted in packs at the rate of one in 23, this 20-card set features top NBA player photos along with a swatch of a game used court. The cards are set up as a horizontal design, and the colors on the left and right borders match the featured player's team colors.
COMPLETE SET (20) 50.00 120.00
STATED ODDS 1:23 PACKS
1 Vince Carter 5.00 12.00
2 Dirk Nowitzki 5.00 12.00
3 Allen Iverson 6.00 15.00
4 Tracy McGrady 5.00 12.00
5 Karl Malone 4.00 10.00
6 Antawn Jamison 3.00 8.00
7 Peja Stojakovic 3.00 8.00
8 Eddie Jones 2.50 6.00
9 Jason Williams 2.50 6.00
10 Hakeem Olajuwon 4.00 10.00
11 Antoine Walker 2.50 6.00
12 Jerry Stackhouse 2.50 6.00
13 Chris Webber 3.00 8.00
14 Latrell Sprewell 2.50 6.00
15 David Robinson 5.00 12.00
16 Stephon Marbury 2.50 6.00
17 Grant Hill 4.00 10.00
18 Shareef Abdur-Rahim 2.50 6.00
19 Jason Kidd 5.00 12.00
20 Scottie Pippen 5.00 12.00

2001-02 Flair Courting Greatness Ball and Court

Randomly inserted in packs, this 20-card set parallels the base Courting Greatness set enhanced with a swatch of a game used basketball and a piece of game used floor. Each card is serial numbered to 250.
PRINT RUN 250 SERIAL #d SETS
1 Vince Carter 6.00 15.00
2 Dirk Nowitzki 6.00 15.00
3 Allen Iverson 8.00 20.00
4 Tracy McGrady 6.00 15.00
5 Karl Malone 5.00 12.00
6 Antawn Jamison 4.00 10.00
7 Peja Stojakovic 4.00 10.00
8 Eddie Jones 3.00 8.00
9 Jason Williams 3.00 8.00
10 Hakeem Olajuwon 5.00 12.00
11 Antoine Walker 3.00 8.00
12 Jerry Stackhouse 3.00 8.00
13 Chris Webber 4.00 10.00
14 Latrell Sprewell 3.00 8.00
15 David Robinson 6.00 15.00
16 Stephon Marbury 3.00 8.00
17 Grant Hill 5.00 12.00
18 Shareef Abdur-Rahim 3.00 8.00
19 Jason Kidd 6.00 15.00
20 Scottie Pippen 6.00 15.00

2001-02 Flair Hot Numbers

Randomly inserted in packs, this 20-card set features full color player action photos set against a gray and white face portrait. The jersey swatches are cut in the shape of a quarter of a circle, and each card is sequentially numbered to 100.
PRINT RUN 100 SERIAL #'d SETS
1 Darius Miles 5.00 12.00
2 Mike Miller 6.00 15.00
3 Tracy McGrady 12.00 30.00
4 Ray Allen 8.00 20.00
5 Baron Davis 8.00 20.00
6 Dikembe Mutombo 8.00 20.00
7 Kenyon Martin 8.00 20.00
8 Steve Francis 6.00 15.00
9 Patrick Ewing 12.00 30.00
10 Jason Kidd 12.00 30.00
11 Jerome Moiso 5.00 12.00
12 Richard Hamilton 6.00 15.00
13 Vince Carter 12.00 30.00
14 John Stockton 10.00 25.00
15 Mike Bibby 8.00 20.00
16 Reggie Miller 10.00 25.00
17 Jason Terry 8.00 20.00
18 Stephon Marbury 6.00 15.00
19 Chris Webber 8.00 20.00
20 Mitch Richmond 6.00 15.00

2001-02 Flair Jersey Heights

Randomly inserted in packs at the rate of one in 22, this 20-card set features full color player action photos set against a facial portrait of the featured player. Jersey swatches are in the shape of a quarter of a circle.
STATED ODDS 1:22
1 Darius Miles 2.50 6.00
2 Mike Miller 3.00 8.00
3 Tracy McGrady 6.00 15.00
4 Ray Allen 4.00 10.00
5 Baron Davis 4.00 10.00
6 Dikembe Mutombo 4.00 10.00
7 Kenyon Martin 4.00 10.00
8 Steve Francis 3.00 8.00
9 Patrick Ewing 5.00 12.00
10 Jason Kidd 6.00 15.00
11 Jerome Moiso 2.50 6.00
12 Richard Hamilton 3.00 8.00
13 Vince Carter 6.00 15.00
14 John Stockton 5.00 12.00
15 Mike Bibby 4.00 10.00
16 Reggie Miller 4.00 10.00
17 Jason Terry 4.00 10.00
18 Stephon Marbury 3.00 8.00
19 Chris Webber 4.00 10.00
20 Mitch Richmond 3.00 8.00

2001-02 Flair Sweet Shots

Randomly inserted as a jumbo box topper, this 33-card set features either a game used jersey or a player autograph from both veteran and rookie players. Autograph cards are all sequentially numbered-print runs are listed below.
JSY PRINT RUN 250 SERIAL #'d SETS
AU PRINT RUNS LISTED BELOW
STATED ODDS 1 PER BOX
1 Ray Allen JSY 5.00 12.00
2 Vince Carter JSY 8.00 20.00
3 Baron Davis JSY 5.00 12.00
4 Michael Dickerson JSY 3.00 8.00
5 Steve Francis JSY 4.00 10.00
6 Marc Jackson JSY 3.00 8.00
7 Antawn Jamison JSY 5.00 12.00
8 Rashard Lewis JSY 5.00 12.00
9 Karl Malone JSY 6.00 15.00
10 Shawn Marion JSY 4.00 10.00
11 Kenyon Martin JSY 5.00 12.00
12 Antonio McDyess JSY 4.00 10.00
13 Tracy McGrady JSY 8.00 20.00
14 Darius Miles JSY 3.00 8.00
15 Mike Miller JSY 4.00 10.00
16 Lamar Odom JSY 4.00 10.00
17 Gary Payton JSY 5.00 12.00
18 Morris Peterson JSY 3.00 8.00
19 David Robinson JSY 8.00 20.00
20 John Stockton JSY 6.00 15.00
21 Peja Stojakovic JSY 5.00 12.00
22 Jason Terry JSY 5.00 12.00
23 Antoine Walker JSY 4.00 10.00
24 Chris Webber JSY 5.00 12.00
25 Allen Iverson JSY 10.00 25.00
26 Kwame Brown AU/297 4.00 10.00
27 Eddy Curry AU/368 4.00 10.00
28 Michael Bradley AU/433 2.50 6.00
29 Brendan Haywood AU/345 4.00 10.00
30 Jason Collins AU/390 12.00 30.00
31 Richard Jefferson AU/330 6.00 15.00
32 Kedrick Brown AU/342 2.50 6.00
33 Vince Carter AU/245 20.00 50.00

2001-02 Flair Warming Up

Randomly inserted in packs at the rate of one in 27, this 20-card set features photos of players in their warm-up suits on the top half of the card, a black break in the middle of the card with the player's name and team name, and a swatch from a warm-up on the bottom of the card.
STATED ODDS 1:27
1 Jason Terry 3.00 8.00
2 Shareef Abdur-Rahim 2.50 6.00
3 Antoine Walker 2.50 6.00
4 Paul Pierce 3.00 8.00
5 Andre Miller 2.50 6.00
6 Steve Francis 2.50 6.00
7 Lamar Odom 2.50 6.00
8 Corey Maggette 2.50 6.00
9 Kenyon Martin 3.00 8.00
10 Grant Hill 4.00 10.00
11 Allen Iverson 6.00 15.00
12 Dikembe Mutombo 3.00 8.00
13 Stephon Marbury 2.50 6.00
14 Mike Bibby 3.00 8.00
15 Morris Peterson 2.00 5.00
16 Vince Carter 5.00 12.00
17 Karl Malone 4.00 10.00
18 John Stockton 4.00 10.00
19 Keith Van Horn 2.50 6.00
20 DerMarr Johnson 2.00 5.00

2001-02 Flair Warming Up Dual

Randomly inserted in packs at the rate of one in 80, this 10-card set parallels the design of the base Warming Up insert set featuring two players and two warm-up swatches.
STATED ODDS 1:80
1 J.Terry/S.Abdur-Rahim 5.00 12.00
2 A.Walker/P.Pierce 8.00 20.00
3 A.Miller/S.Francis 5.00 12.00
4 L.Odom/C.Maggette 5.00 12.00
5 K.Martin/K.Van Horn 5.00 12.00
6 A.Iverson/D.Mutombo 8.00 20.00
7 S.Marbury/M.Bibby 5.00 12.00
8 M.Peterson/V.Carter 8.00 20.00
9 K.Malone/J.Stockton 15.00 40.00
10 G.Hill/D.Johnson 6.00 15.00

2002-03 Flair

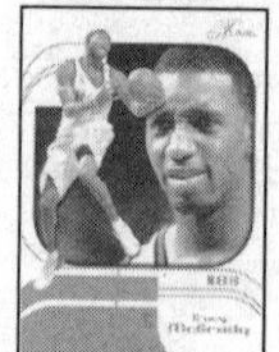

Released in mid-October 2002, this 120-card set features 90 base veteran cards and 30 Class of '02 cards sequentially numbered to 1750. Several of these Class of '02 cards were issued as Rookie Exchange cards. Flair's base design has metallic white ink around the outside, a gray-brown scale picture of the player in the background with a full color action photo superimposed on top. The Class of '02 cards, numbers 91-120, contain those words along the right side of the card and share the design of the base veteran cards. Every card contains bronze foil highlights. Flair was packaged in five card packs at an SRP of $5.99 with boxes containing 20 packs. Each box also contained a special box-topper pack which contained the over-sized sweet swatch cards which feature either a jersey or an autograph.
COMP.SET w/o SP's (90) 25.00 50.00
91-120 PRINT RUN 1750 SER.#'d SETS
1 Tracy McGrady .60 1.50
2 Jamal Mashburn .30 .75
3 Allen Iverson .60 1.50
4 Alonzo Mourning .50 1.25
5 Joe Smith .30 .75
6 Wang Zhizhi .25 .60
7 Karl Malone .50 1.25
8 Keith Van Horn .30 .75
9 Joseph Forte .25 .60
10 Peja Stojakovic .40 1.00
11 Juwan Howard .30 .75
12 Brian Grant .25 .60
13 Glenn Robinson .30 .75
14 Antonio McDyess .30 .75
15 Vince Carter .60 1.50
16 Pau Gasol .50 1.25
17 Bonzi Wells .25 .60
18 Chucky Atkins .25 .60
19 Shane Battier .40 1.00
20 Steve Francis .30 .75
21 Kevin Garnett .60 1.50
22 Antawn Jamison .40 1.00
23 Hedo Turkoglu .30 .75
24 Kenyon Martin .30 .75
25 Cuttino Mobley .25 .60
26 Steve Nash .50 1.25
27 Morris Peterson .25 .60
28 Jason Richardson .40 1.00
29 Antoine Walker .30 .75
30 Rasheed Wallace .40 1.00
31 Tim Duncan .75 2.00
32 Paul Pierce .40 1.00
33 Ben Wallace .30 .75
34 Jason Kidd .60 1.50
35 Gary Payton .40 1.00
36 Mike Miller .30 .75
37 Kobe Bryant 1.50 4.00
38 Baron Davis .30 .75
39 Steve Smith .30 .75
40 Reggie Miller .40 1.00
41 Dirk Nowitzki .60 1.50
42 Rashard Lewis .40 1.00
43 Andre Miller .30 .75
44 David Wesley .25 .60
45 Ray Allen .40 1.00
46 Tyson Chandler .40 1.00
47 Jamaal Tinsley .25 .60
48 Grant Hill .50 1.25
49 Richard Jefferson .40 1.00
50 Latrell Sprewell .30 .75
51 Jason Terry .30 .75
52 Alvin Williams .25 .60
53 Vin Baker .30 .75
54 Robert Horry .30 .75
55 Eddie Jones .30 .75
56 Andrei Kirilenko .40 1.00
57 Darius Miles .25 .60
58 Kedrick Brown .25 .60
59 Jermaine O'Neal .30 .75
60 David Robinson .60 1.50
61 Jason Williams .30 .75
62 Wally Szczerbiak .30 .75
63 Mike Bibby .40 1.00
64 Shawn Marion .30 .75
65 Shaquille O'Neal 1.00 2.50

66 Michael Redd .30 .75
67 Chris Webber .40 1.00
68 Quentin Richardson .30 .75
69 Michael Jordan 3.00 8.00
70 Jamaal Magloire .25 .60
71 Radoslav Nesterovic .25 .60
72 Eddy Curry .25 .60
73 Michael Finley .40 1.00
74 Eddie Griffin .25 .60
75 Aaron McKie .25 .60
76 Tony Parker .50 1.25
77 Shareef Abdur-Rahim .30 .75
78 Jalen Rose .30 .75
79 Jerry Stackhouse .30 .75
80 Jumaine Jones .25 .60
81 Toni Kukoc .40 1.00
82 Vladimir Radmanovic .25 .60
83 Zach Randolph .30 .75
84 John Stockton .50 1.25
85 Mengke Bateer .25 .60
86 Dikembe Mutombo .40 1.00
87 Elton Brand .40 1.00
88 Allan Houston .30 .75
89 Joe Johnson .30 .75
90 Kwame Brown .25 .60
91 Yao Ming RC 4.00 10.00
92 Jay Williams RC 2.00 5.00
93 Mike Dunleavy RC 2.00 5.00
94 Drew Gooden RC 2.00 5.00
95 DaJuan Wagner RC 1.50 4.00
96 Caron Butler RC 2.00 5.00
97 Jared Jeffries RC 1.50 4.00
98 Nene Hilario RC 2.00 5.00
99 Chris Wilcox RC 1.50 4.00
100 Nikoloz Tskitishvili RC 1.25 3.00
101 Kareem Rush RC 1.50 4.00
102 Curtis Borchardt RC 1.25 3.00
103 Qyntel Woods RC 1.50 4.00
104 Melvin Ely RC 1.50 4.00
105 Marcus Haislip RC 1.50 4.00
106 Carlos Boozer RC 2.00 5.00
107 Bostjan Nachbar RC 1.50 4.00
108 Amare Stoudemire RC 2.50 6.00
109 Frank Williams RC 1.25 3.00
110 Jiri Welsch RC 1.50 4.00
111 Fred Jones RC 1.50 4.00
112 Juan Dixon RC 2.00 5.00
113 Ryan Humphrey RC 1.50 4.00
114 Casey Jacobsen RC 1.50 4.00
115 Tayshaun Prince RC 2.50 6.00
116 Dan Dickau RC 1.50 4.00
117 Chris Jefferies RC 1.25 3.00
118 John Salmons RC 2.00 5.00
119 Manu Ginobili RC 5.00 12.00
120 Gordan Giricek RC 2.00 5.00

2002-03 Flair Row 1

*ROW 1 STARS: 4X TO 10X BASE CARD HI
*ROW 1 RCs: .75X TO 2X BASE CARD HI
PRINT RUN 150 SERIAL #'d SETS

2002-03 Flair Row 2

*ROW 2 STARS: 12X TO 30X BASE HI
*ROW 2 RCs: 3X TO 8X BASE HI
PRINT RUN 25 SERIAL #'d SETS
69 Michael Jordan 125.00 300.00

2002-03 Flair Court Kings

Randomly seeded in packs at the rate of one in four, this 25-card set uses a horizontal design with full color player action photos on one side and team logos on the other side. The background is a mix of gray and a wood-colored strip with the key and the three-point line drawn on it. All cards contain bronze foil highlights.

COMPLETE SET (25) 12.00 30.00
STATED ODDS 1:4
1 Kobe Bryant 2.00 5.00
2 Jerry Stackhouse .40 1.00
3 Steve Francis .40 1.00
4 Ray Allen .50 1.25
5 Kevin Garnett .75 2.00
6 Elton Brand .50 1.25
7 Jason Kidd .75 2.00
8 Mike Bibby .50 1.25
9 Allen Iverson .75 2.00
10 Tracy McGrady .75 2.00
11 Baron Davis .40 1.00
12 Tim Duncan 1.00 2.50
13 Latrell Sprewell .40 1.00
14 Paul Pierce .50 1.25
15 Vince Carter .75 2.00
16 Antawn Jamison .50 1.25
17 Eddie Jones .40 1.00
18 Darius Miles .30 .75
19 Dirk Nowitzki .75 2.00
20 Karl Malone .60 1.50
21 Shaquille O'Neal 1.25 3.00
22 Michael Jordan 4.00 10.00
23 Antoine Walker .40 1.00
24 Kenyon Martin .40 1.00
25 Chris Webber .50 1.25

2002-03 Flair Court Kings Ball and Jersey

PRINT RUN 100 SER.#'d SETS
CKAI Allen Iverson 12.00 30.00
CKAJ Antawn Jamison 6.00 15.00
CKAW Antoine Walker 5.00 12.00
CKBD Baron Davis 5.00 12.00
CKCW Chris Webber 8.00 20.00
CKDM Darius Miles 4.00 10.00
CKDN Dirk Nowitzki 10.00 25.00
CKEB Elton Brand 6.00 15.00
CKEJ Eddie Jones 5.00 12.00
CKJK Jason Kidd 10.00 25.00
CKJS Jerry Stackhouse 5.00 12.00
CKKM Karl Malone 8.00 20.00
CKMB Mike Bibby 6.00 15.00
CKPP Paul Pierce 6.00 15.00
CKPS Peja Stojakovic 6.00 15.00
CKRA Ray Allen 6.00 15.00
CKSF Steve Francis 5.00 12.00
CKSM Stephon Marbury 5.00 12.00
CKTM Tracy McGrady 10.00 25.00
CKVC Vince Carter 10.00 25.00

2002-03 Flair Court Kings Game Used

Randomly inserted in packs at the rate of one in 20, this 25-card set parallels the design of the base Court Kings insert. Each card contains a swatch of memorablila. Several players have different versions with different types of memorabilia; these are cataloged below.

STATED ODDS 1:20
CKAI Allen Iverson 5.00 12.00
CKAJ Antawn Jamison 3.00 8.00
CKAW Antoine Walker 2.50 6.00
CKBD Baron Davis 2.50 6.00
CKCW Chris Webber 3.00 8.00
CKDN Dirk Nowitzki 5.00 12.00
CKEB Elton Brand 3.00 8.00
CKEJ Eddie Jones 2.50 6.00
CKJK Jason Kidd 5.00 12.00
CKJS Jerry Stackhouse 2.50 6.00
CKLS Latrell Sprewell 2.50 6.00
CKMB Mike Bibby 3.00 8.00
CKPP Paul Pierce 3.00 8.00
CKRA Ray Allen 3.00 8.00
CKVC Vince Carter 5.00 12.00
CKDM1 Darius Miles WU 2.00 5.00
CKDM2 Darius Miles Shorts 2.00 5.00
CKKM1 Karl Malone WU 4.00 10.00
CKKM2 Karl Malone JSY 4.00 10.00
CKKM1 Kenyon Martin WU 2.50 6.00
CKKM2 Kenyon Martin JSY 2.50 6.00
CKSF1 Steve Francis WU 2.50 6.00
CKSF2 Steve Francis Shorts 2.50 6.00
CKTM1 Tracy McGrady Shorts 5.00 12.00
CKTM2 Tracy McGrady Shirt 5.00 12.00

2002-03 Flair Court Kings Game Used Dual

Randomly inserted in packs, this nine card set parallels the base Court Kings insert design, but features two players on each card and two swatches of jersey. Each card is sequentially numbered to 250.

PRINT RUN 250 SER.#'d SETS
BD/SF B.Davis/S.Francis 8.00 20.00
DN/KM D.Nowitzki/K./Malone 12.50 30.00
EB/DM E.Brand/D.Miles 8.00 20.00
EJ/RA E.Jones/R.Allen 8.00 20.00
JK/KM J.Kidd/K.Martin 8.00 20.00
JS/AI J.Stack/A.Iverson 12.50 30.00
MB/CW M.Bibby/C.Webber 12.50 30.00
PP/AW P.Pierce/A.Walker 8.00 20.00
TM/VC T.McGrady/V.Carter 15.00 40.00

2002-03 Flair Hot Numbers Patches

Randomly seeded in packs, this eight card set parallels the design of the New Heights insert enhanced with a swatch of the number patch off a jersey and the words "Hot Numbers" instead of "New Heights."

PRINT RUN 100 SER.#'d SETS
HNAI Allen Iverson 12.00 30.00
HNDM Darius Miles 5.00 12.00
HNDN Dirk Nowitzki 12.00 30.00
HNJK Jason Kidd 12.00 30.00
HNPG Pau Gasol 10.00 25.00
HNPP Paul Pierce 8.00 20.00
HNTM Tracy McGrady 12.00 30.00
HNVC Vince Carter 12.00 30.00

2002-03 Flair Jersey Heights

Inserted in packs at the rate of one in 16, this eight card set also parallels the design of the New Heights insert set. Each card contains a swatch from a game worn jersey, under which the words, "Jersey Heights" appear.

STATED ODDS 1:16
JHAI Allen Iverson 5.00 12.00
JHDM Darius Miles 2.00 5.00
JHDN Dirk Nowitzki 5.00 12.00
JHJK Jason Kidd 5.00 12.00
JHPG Pau Gasol 4.00 10.00
JHPP Paul Pierce 3.00 8.00
JHTM Tracy McGrady 5.00 12.00
JHVC Vince Carter 5.00 12.00

2002-03 Flair New Heights

Inserted in packs at the rate of one in ten, this 20-card set features a horizontal design with gray along the top and the bottom and a strip of cloudy sky through the middle. Color player photos appear on the right side and team logos appear on the left. Below the team logo, the words, "New Heights" appear. All cards have bronze foil highlights.

COMPLETE SET (20) 15.00 40.00
STATED ODDS 1:10
1 Tracy McGrady 1.25 3.00
2 Vince Carter 1.25 3.00
3 Jason Kidd 1.25 3.00
4 Tim Duncan 1.50 4.00
5 Dirk Nowitzki 1.25 3.00
6 Jamaal Tinsley .50 1.25
7 Kobe Bryant 3.00 8.00
8 Eddy Curry .50 1.25
9 Shane Battier .75 2.00
10 Peja Stojakovic .75 2.00
11 Michael Jordan 6.00 15.00
12 Darius Miles .50 1.25
13 Jason Richardson .75 2.00
14 Pau Gasol 1.00 2.50
15 Jerry Stackhouse .60 1.50
16 Shaquille O'Neal 2.00 5.00
17 Paul Pierce .75 2.00
18 Eddie Griffin .50 1.25
19 Kwame Brown .50 1.25
20 Allen Iverson 1.25 3.00

2002-03 Flair Sweet Swatch Autographs

Inserted in the one-per-box topper pack, these jumbo cards measure 5" X 7 3/4" and feature a large swatch of basketball-type material with bold player signatures. Each card is sequentially numbered-print runs listed below.

SWEET SHOT PACK 1 PER BOX
*GOLD: .75X TO 2X BASE HI
GOLD PRINT RUN 15 SER.#'d SETS
EC Eddy Curry/250 8.00 20.00
GR Glenn Robinson/400 8.00 20.00
JJ Joe Johnson/375 8.00 20.00
KB Kedrick Brown/75 8.00 20.00
MB Michael Bradley/75 8.00 20.00
SA Shareef Abdur-Rahim/500 8.00 20.00
VC Vince Carter/475 15.00 40.00
KBR Kwame Brown/200 8.00 20.00

2002-03 Flair Sweet Swatch Game Used

Inserted in the one-per-box topper pack, these jumbo cards measure 5" X 7 3/4" and feature a large swatch of game-worn memorabilia. Each card is sequentially numbered-print runs listed below.

SWEET SHOT PACK 1 PER BOX
SSAI Allen Iverson/975 8.00 20.00
SSDM Darius Miles/825 3.00 8.00
SSHT Hedo Turkoglu/650 4.00 10.00
SSJK Jason Kidd/800 8.00 20.00
SSJR Jason Richardson/625 5.00 12.00
SSJT Jamaal Tinsley/475 3.00 8.00
SSKM Kenyon Martin/900 4.00 10.00
SSMM Mike Miller/875 4.00 10.00
SSPG Pau Gasol/750 6.00 15.00
SSPP Paul Pierce/625 5.00 12.00
SSPS Peja Stojakovic/725 5.00 12.00
SSRA Ray Allen/850 5.00 12.00
SSSN Steve Nash/625 6.00 15.00
SSTM Tracy McGrady/850 8.00 20.00
SSTP Tony Parker/600 6.00 15.00
SSVC Vince Carter/975 8.00 20.00

2002-03 Flair Sweet Swatch Patches

Randomly inserted in the one-per-box topper packs, this 16-card set parallels the base Sweet Swatch Game Used insert set enhanced with large patch swatches from game-worn memorabilia. Each card is sequentially numbered-print runs listed below.

SWEET SHOT PACK 1 PER BOX
LOWER PRINT RUNS NOT PRICED
SSAI Allen Iverson/33 50.00 125.00
SSDM Darius Miles/26 20.00 50.00
SSJK Jason Kidd/33 40.00 100.00
SSJT Jamaal Tinsley/32 20.00 50.00
SSMM Mike Miller/31 25.00 60.00
SSPG Pau Gasol 40.00 100.00
SSPP Paul Pierce 30.00 80.00
SSRA Ray Allen/49 30.00 80.00
SSTP Tony Parker/32 40.00 100.00
SSVC Vince Carter/35 50.00 125.00

2002-03 Flair Wave of the Future

Randomly seeded in packs at the rate of one in 20, this 11-card set showcases this year's top rookies. Both the left and right side of the card have color strips to match the featured player's jersey colors. Player photos are on the left and team logos and the Draft NY 02 logo appears on the right. All cards contain bronze foil highlights.

COMPLETE SET (11) 15.00 40.00
STATED ODDS 1:20
1 Amare Stoudemire 2.00 5.00
2 Caron Butler 1.50 4.00
3 Chris Wilcox 1.25 3.00
4 DaJuan Wagner 1.25 3.00
5 Drew Gooden 1.50 4.00
6 Jared Jeffries 1.25 3.00
7 Jay Williams 1.50 4.00
8 Melvin Ely 1.25 3.00
9 Mike Dunleavy 1.50 4.00
10 Nene Hilario 1.50 4.00
11 Nikoloz Tskitishvili 1.00 2.50

2002-03 Flair Wave of the Future Jerseys

PRINT RUN 100 SERIAL #'D SETS
*PATCHES: .75X TO 2X HI
PATCH PRINT RUN 50 SER.#'d SETS
AS Amare Stoudemire 5.00 12.00
CB Caron Butler 4.00 10.00
CW Chris Wilcox 3.00 8.00
DG Drew Gooden 4.00 10.00
DW DaJuan Wagner 3.00 8.00
JJ Jared Jeffries 3.00 8.00
NH Nene Hilario 4.00 10.00
NT Nikoloz Tskitishvili 2.50 6.00

2003-04 Flair

Released in November 2003, Flair boasts a 120-card base set divided up into 90 veteran cards and 30 rookie cards sequentially numbered to 500. Base cards combine foreground action photos with background portrait photos and foil highlights. Flair was packaged in 20-pack boxes with packs containing five cards and carried a suggested retail price of $5.99.

COMP.SET w/o SP's (90) 15.00 40.00
91-120 PRINT RUN 500 SER.#'d SETS
UNPRICED ROW 2 PRINT RUN ONE SET
1 Jerry Stackhouse .25 .60
2 Eddie Griffin .20 .50
3 Jermaine O'Neal .25 .60
4 Kobe Bryant 1.25 3.00
5 Juwan Howard .25 .60
6 Alonzo Mourning .40 1.00
7 Kenny Thomas .20 .50
8 Chris Webber .30 .75
9 Radoslav Nesterovic .20 .50
10 Morris Peterson .20 .50
11 DeShawn Stevenson .20 .50
12 Steve Francis .25 .60
13 Andrei Kirilenko .30 .75
14 Kwame Brown .20 .50
15 Tim Duncan .50 1.25
16 Yao Ming .60 1.50
17 Jamaal Tinsley .20 .50
18 Shaquille O'Neal .75 2.00
19 Tracy McGrady .40 1.00
20 Dirk Nowitzki .50 1.25
21 Marcus Camby .25 .60
22 Elton Brand .30 .75
23 Latrell Sprewell .25 .60
24 Grant Hill .40 1.00
25 Shawn Marion .25 .60
26 Rasheed Wallace .30 .75
27 Ray Allen .30 .75
28 Antonio Davis .20 .50
29 Antoine Walker .30 .75
30 Ricky Davis .25 .60
31 Jason Kidd .50 1.25
32 Tony Parker .30 .75
33 Paul Pierce .30 .75
34 Gary Payton .30 .75
35 Kenyon Martin .25 .60
36 Dale Davis .20 .50
37 Vladimir Radmanovic .20 .50
38 Matt Harpring .20 .50
39 Shareef Abdur-Rahim .25 .60
40 Antawn Jamison .25 .60
41 Eddie Jones .25 .60
42 Jamaal Magloire .20 .50
43 Jason Richardson .30 .75
44 Jonathan Bender .20 .50
45 Chris Wilcox .20 .50
46 Manu Ginobili .40 1.00
47 Chauncey Billups .30 .75
48 Jamal Mashburn .25 .60
49 Joe Smith .25 .60
50 Aaron McKie .20 .50
51 Theo Ratliff .20 .50
52 Eddy Curry .20 .50
53 Ron Artest .30 .75
54 Quentin Richardson .25 .60
55 Karl Malone .40 1.00
56 Pau Gasol .30 .75
57 Dan Dickau .20 .50
58 Darius Miles .20 .50
59 Ben Wallace .25 .60
60 Cuttino Mobley .20 .50
61 Lamar Odom .25 .60
62 Shane Battier .25 .60
63 Allan Houston .25 .60
64 Peja Stojakovic .30 .75
65 Dajuan Wagner .20 .50
66 Caron Butler .25 .60
67 Keith Van Horn .25 .60
68 Vincent Yarbrough .20 .50
69 Tim Thomas .20 .50
70 Troy Hudson .20 .50
71 Amare Stoudemire .40 1.00
72 Bobby Jackson .20 .50
73 Bonzi Wells .20 .50
74 Steve Nash .40 1.00
75 Gilbert Arenas .25 .60
76 Glenn Robinson .25 .60
77 Jalen Rose .25 .60
78 Michael Finley .30 .75
79 Nene .25 .60
80 Kevin Garnett .50 1.25
81 Richard Jefferson .25 .60
82 Baron Davis .25 .60
83 Mike Bibby .30 .75
84 Tyson Chandler .25 .60
85 Michael Redd .30 .75
86 Mike Dunleavy .25 .60
87 Drew Gooden .25 .60
88 Allen Iverson .50 1.25
89 Vince Carter .50 1.25
90 Larry Hughes .25 .60
91 Josh Howard RC 1.50 4.00
92 Maciej Lampe RC 1.00 2.50
93 Zarko Cabarkapa RC 1.00 2.50
94 LeBron James RC 100.00 250.00
95 Reece Gaines RC 1.00 2.50
96 Jarvis Hayes RC 1.00 2.50
97 Mickael Pietrus RC 1.25 3.00
98 T.J. Ford RC 1.25 3.00
99 Zoran Planinic RC 1.00 2.50
100 Luke Ridnour RC 1.25 3.00
101 Boris Diaw RC 1.50 4.00
102 Nick Collison RC 1.25 3.00
103 Travis Outlaw RC 1.25 3.00
104 Carmelo Anthony RC 6.00 15.00
105 Chris Kaman RC 1.50 4.00
106 Mike Sweetney RC 1.00 2.50
107 Kendrick Perkins RC 1.25 3.00
108 Jason Kapono RC 1.00 2.50
109 Troy Bell RC 1.00 2.50
110 Chris Bosh RC 2.50 6.00
111 Jerome Beasley RC 1.00 2.50
112 Darko Milicic RC 1.25 3.00
113 Dwyane Wade RC 8.00 20.00
114 David West RC 1.50 4.00
115 Kirk Hinrich RC 1.50 4.00
116 Dahntay Jones RC 1.25 3.00
117 Leandro Barbosa RC 1.50 4.00
118 Marcus Banks RC 1.00 2.50
119 Luke Walton RC 1.50 4.00
120 Ndudi Ebi RC 1.00 2.50

2003-04 Flair Rookie Jumbos

PRINT RUN 400 SER.#'d SETS
1 LeBron James 60.00 150.00
2 Darko Milicic 1.25 3.00
3 Carmelo Anthony 5.00 12.00
4 Chris Bosh 2.50 6.00
5 Dwyane Wade 8.00 20.00
6 Chris Kaman 1.50 4.00
7 Kirk Hinrich 1.50 4.00
8 T.J. Ford 1.25 3.00
9 Mike Sweetney 1.00 2.50
10 Jarvis Hayes 1.00 2.50
11 Mickael Pietrus 1.25 3.00
12 Nick Collison 1.25 3.00
13 Marcus Banks 1.00 2.50
14 Troy Bell 1.00 2.50
15 David West 1.50 4.00

2003-04 Flair Row 1

*1-90 ROW 1 SINGLES: 4X TO 10X BASE HI
*91-120 ROW 1 RCs: 1.25X TO 3X BASE HI
ROW 1 PRINT RUN 100 SER.#'d SETS
4 Kobe Bryant 20.00 50.00
94 LeBron James 400.00 800.00

2003-04 Flair A Cut Above

Randomly inserted in packs, this 20-card set features a full color player image in the foreground, a scale-colored portrait in the background and a swatch of game-worn memorabilia. Each card is sequentially numbered to 500. A Final Cut version was also issued and is sequentially numbered to 50.

PRINT RUN 500 SER.#'d SETS
*FINAL CUT: 1X TO 2.5X BASE HI
FINAL CUT PRINT RUN 50 SER.#'d SETS
AH Allan Houston 2.00 5.00
AJ Antawn Jamison 2.00 5.00
BD Baron Davis 2.00 5.00
BW Bonzi Wells 2.00 5.00
CB Caron Butler 2.00 5.00
CW Chris Webber 2.50 6.00
DW Dajuan Wagner 2.00 5.00
GP Gary Payton 2.50 6.00
JK Jason Kidd 4.00 10.00
JR Jason Richardson 2.50 6.00
MG Manu Ginobili 3.00 8.00
PG Pau Gasol 2.50 6.00
PS Peja Stojakovic 2.50 6.00
RA Ron Artest 2.50 6.00
RD Ricky Davis 2.00 5.00
RM Reggie Miller 2.50 6.00
SA Shareef Abdur-Rahim 2.00 5.00
SN Steve Nash 3.00 8.00
TP Tayshaun Prince 2.00 5.00
VC Vince Carter 4.00 10.00
YM Yao Ming 5.00 12.00

2003-04 Flair Sweet Swatch

With backgrounds set to match the featured player's team color, this 20-card set places a rectangle swatch of game-worn memorabilia centered vertically on the left side of the card. Each card is sequentially numbered to 250. A Patch version sequentially numbered to 50 was also issued.

PRINT RUN 250 SER.#'d SETS
*PATCH: 1.25X TO 3X BASE HI
PATCH PRINT RUN 50 SER.#'d SETS
AH Allan Houston 2.00 5.00
AI Allen Iverson 4.00 10.00
AS Amare Stoudemire 3.00 8.00
CA Carmelo Anthony 8.00 20.00
CB Caron Butler 2.00 5.00
DG Drew Gooden 2.00 5.00
DJ Dahntay Jones 2.00 5.00
DN Dirk Nowitzki 4.00 10.00
DW Dwyane Wade 8.00 20.00
KG Kevin Garnett 4.00 10.00
LW Luke Walton 2.50 6.00
MB Marcus Banks 1.50 4.00
MS Mike Sweetney 1.50 4.00
PP Paul Pierce 2.50 6.00
SF Steve Francis 2.00 5.00
SN Steve Nash 3.00 8.00
TM Tracy McGrady 3.00 8.00
TO Travis Outlaw 2.00 5.00
TP Tony Parker 2.50 6.00
VC Vince Carter 4.00 10.00

2003-04 Flair Sweet Swatch Autographs

Randomly seeded in packs, this 23-card set parallels the design of the Sweet Swatch insert enhanced with authentic player autographs. Each card is sequentially numbered, and print runs are listed below. A Gold version sequentially numbered to 25 and a masterpiece version numbered one of one were also produced.

PRINT RUNS LISTED BELOW
AS Amare Stoudemire/200 8.00 20.00
BC Brian Cook/150 3.00 8.00
CA Carmelo Anthony/271 25.00 60.00
CB Chris Bosh/100 15.00 40.00
DJ Dahntay Jones/200 4.00 10.00
DW Dwyane Wade/145 30.00 60.00
DW David West/200 5.00 12.00
JH Josh Howard 5.00 12.00
JK Jason Kapono/200 3.00 8.00
JO Jermaine O'Neal/20 20.00 50.00
KP Kendrick Perkins/100 4.00 10.00
LR Luke Ridnour/150 4.00 10.00
LW Luke Walton/200 5.00 12.00
MB Marcus Banks/120 3.00 8.00
ML Maciej Lampe/190 3.00 8.00
MP Mickael Pietrus/100 4.00 10.00
MS Mike Sweetney/100 3.00 8.00
PS Peja Stojakovic/15 15.00 40.00
TO Travis Outlaw/200 4.00 10.00
TP Tayshaun Prince/25 20.00 50.00

2003-04 Flair Sweet Swatch Autographs Gold

*GOLD: .75X TO 2X BASE HI
PRINT RUN 25 SER.#'d SETS
CA Carmelo Anthony 100.00 200.00
JO Jermaine O'Neal 12.00 30.00
SF Steve Francis 20.00 50.00
TP Tayshaun Prince 20.00 50.00

2003-04 Flair Sweet Swatch Jumbos Away

Inserted as a box-topper, this 20-card set utilizes the design of the Sweet Swatch insert and places an oversized swatch on the card front. Each card is sequentially numbered and print runs are listed below. A Jersey Home version was also released and these are valued the same as the Away version-Patch versions were also issued and these cards are sequentially numbered to 30.

AMARE DOES NOT HAVE AWAY VERSION
ONE JUMBO TOPPER PER BOX
*HOME VERSION: .4X TO 1X BASE HI
*PATCH: 1.25X TO 3X BASE HI
PATCH PRINT RUN 30 SER.#'d SETS
AH Allan Houston/187 3.00 8.00
AI Allen Iverson/171 6.00 15.00
CA Carmelo Anthony/125 12.00 30.00
CB Caron Butler/201 3.00 8.00
DG Drew Gooden/165 3.00 8.00
DJ Dahntay Jones/144 3.00 8.00
DN Dirk Nowitzki/87 6.00 15.00
DW Dwyane Wade/116 12.00 30.00
KG Kevin Garnett/190 6.00 15.00
LW Luke Walton/199 4.00 10.00
MB Marcus Banks/135 2.50 6.00
MS Mike Sweetney/173 2.50 6.00
PP Paul Pierce/62 6.00 15.00
SF Steve Francis/187 3.00 8.00
SN Steve Nash/116 5.00 12.00
TM Tracy McGrady/183 5.00 12.00
TO Travis Outlaw/165 3.00 8.00
TP Tony Parker/125 4.00 10.00
VC Vince Carter/139 6.00 15.00

2003-04 Flair Sweet Swatch Jumbos Double

Randomly seeded as a box-topper, this 10-card set features the Sweet Swatch design with two players and two swatches of game-worn memorabilia. Each card is sequentially numbered to 50.

PRINT RUN 50 SER.#'d SETS
1 M.Banks/P.Pierce 15.00 40.00
3 T.McGrady/D.Gooden 12.50 30.00
4 D.Wade/C.Butler 15.00 40.00
5 M.Sweetney/A.Houston 10.00 25.00
6 A.Stoudemire/K.Garnett 15.00 40.00
7 A.Iverson/V.Carter 20.00 50.00
8 D.Jones/L.Walton 10.00 25.00
9 C.Anthony/T.Outlaw 15.00 40.00
10 S.Francis/T.Parker 12.50 30.00

2003-04 Flair Sweet Swatch Jumbos Triple

Randomly inserted as a box-topper, this version of the Sweet Swatch Jumbo set showcases three players along with a swatch of game-worn memorabilia from each. Cards are sequentially numbered to 32. An autographed version sequentially numbered to three was also issued.

PRINT RUN 32 SER.#'d SETS
1 Melo/D.Wade/Bosh 30.00 80.00
3 J.O'Neal/Prince/Peja 12.50 30.00
5 Outlaw/West/Cook 12.50 30.00
6 Pietrus/Ridnour/Sweetney 12.50 30.00
7 Howard/Walton/Kapono 12.50 30.00

2003-04 Flair Wave of the Future

Inserted in packs at the rate of one in 20, this 15-card set places rookeis from the 2003 NBA Draft in full-color in front of a water/wave background.

COMPLETE SET (15) 25.00 50.00
STATED ODDS 1:20
1 LeBron James 25.00 60.00
2 Darko Milicic .75 2.00
3 Carmelo Anthony 3.00 8.00
4 Chris Bosh 1.50 4.00
5 Dwyane Wade 3.00 8.00
6 Chris Kaman 1.00 2.50
7 Kirk Hinrich 1.00 2.50
8 T.J. Ford .75 2.00
9 Mike Sweetney .60 1.50
10 Jarvis Hayes .60 1.50
11 Mickael Pietrus .75 2.00
12 Nick Collison .75 2.00
13 Marcus Banks .60 1.50
14 Luke Ridnour .75 2.00
15 Reece Gaines .60 1.50

2003-04 Flair Wave of the Future Game Used

PRINT RUN 250 SER.#'d SETS
*PATCH: .75X TO 2X BASE HI
PATCH PRINT RUN 50 SER.#'d SETS
CA Carmelo Anthony 8.00 20.00
CB Chris Bosh 4.00 10.00
CK Chris Kaman 2.50 6.00
DW Dwyane Wade 8.00 20.00
DW David West 2.50 6.00
JH Jarvis Hayes 1.50 4.00
LR Luke Ridnour 2.00 5.00
MB Marcus Banks 1.50 4.00
MP Mickael Pietrus 2.00 5.00
MS Mike Sweetney 1.50 4.00
RG Reece Gaines 1.50 4.00
TB Troy Bell 1.50 4.00

2003-04 Flair World Leaders

This 20-card horizontally designed set was inserted at the rate of one in 10. Full-color player photos appear on the right of this gold-colored card. A Game Used version was also inserted at the rate of one in 15.

COMPLETE SET (20) 15.00 30.00
STATED ODDS 1:10
1 Paul Pierce .75 2.00
2 Tim Duncan 1.25 3.00
3 Yao Ming 1.50 4.00
4 Shaquille O'Neal 2.00 5.00
5 Tracy McGrady 1.00 2.50
6 Dirk Nowitzki 1.25 3.00
7 Elton Brand .75 2.00
8 Amare Stoudemire 1.00 2.50
9 Kevin Garnett 1.25 3.00
10 Allen Iverson 1.25 3.00
11 Vince Carter 1.25 3.00
12 Steve Francis .60 1.50
13 Tony Parker .75 2.00
14 Pau Gasol .75 2.00
15 Ben Wallace .60 1.50
16 Andrei Kirilenko .75 2.00
17 Gilbert Arenas .60 1.50
18 Jermaine O'Neal .60 1.50
19 Chris Webber .75 2.00
20 Drew Gooden .60 1.50

2003-04 Flair World Leaders Game Used

STATED ODDS 1:15
AI Allen Iverson 4.00 10.00
AK Andrei Kirilenko 2.50 6.00
AS Amare Stoudemire 3.00 8.00
BW Ben Wallace 2.00 5.00
CR Chris Webber 2.50 6.00
DG Drew Gooden 2.00 5.00
DR Dirk Nowitzki 4.00 10.00
EB Elton Brand 2.50 6.00
GA Gilbert Arenas 2.00 5.00
JK Jason Kidd 4.00 10.00
KG Kevin Garnett 4.00 10.00
PG Pau Gasol 2.50 6.00
PP Paul Pierce 2.50 6.00
SF Steve Francis 2.00 5.00
SO Shaquille O'Neal 6.00 15.00
TD Tim Duncan 4.00 10.00
TM Tracy McGrady 3.00 8.00
TP Tony Parker 2.50 6.00
VC Vince Carter 4.00 10.00
YM Yao Ming 5.00 12.00

2004 Flair Significant Cuts

OVERALL AU ODDS 1:1 HOBBY
PRINT RUNS B/WN 1-200 COPIES PER
NO PRICING ON QTY OF 10 OR LESS
VC Vince Carter/200 20.00 40.00

2004-05 Flair

Issued in April 2005, Flair consists of a 90-card base set with 60 veteran players and 30 rookies sequentially numbered to 799. Base cards place full-color player action photography against a white background with a gold strip through the middle for veterans and a silver strip through the middle for rookies. Flair was offered in both Hobby and Retail formats where Hobby boxes contained a single pack of 12 cards and retail boxes contained 24 five-card packs.

COMP.SET w/o SP's (60) 30.00 70.00
61-90 PRINT RUN 799 SER.#'d SETS
UNPRICED ROW 2 PRINT RUN ONE SET
1 Gilbert Arenas .50 1.25
2 Richard Hamilton .50 1.25
3 Stephon Marbury .50 1.25
4 Tony Parker .60 1.50
5 Michael Redd .50 1.25
6 Latrell Sprewell .50 1.25
7 Willie Green .40 1.00
8 Joe Johnson .50 1.25
9 Lamar Odom .50 1.25
10 Tim Duncan 1.00 2.50
11 Ben Wallace .50 1.25
12 Elton Brand .60 1.50
13 Allen Iverson 1.00 2.50
14 Andrei Kirilenko .50 1.25
15 Dirk Nowitzki 1.00 2.50
16 Paul Pierce .60 1.50
17 Mike Dunleavy .50 1.25
18 Zach Randolph .50 1.25
19 David West .50 1.25
20 Corey Maggette .50 1.25
21 Dwyane Wade 1.00 2.50
22 Chris Bosh .60 1.50
23 Michael Finley .60 1.50
24 Kevin Garnett 1.00 2.50
25 Allan Houston .50 1.25
26 Antawn Jamison .50 1.25
27 Jermaine O'Neal .50 1.25
28 Alonzo Mourning .75 2.00
29 Gerald Wallace .50 1.25
30 Jason Williams .50 1.25
31 Tyronn Lue .40 1.00
32 Pau Gasol .60 1.50
33 Jason Kidd 1.00 2.50
34 Shareef Abdur-Rahim .50 1.25
35 LeBron James 4.00 10.00
36 Shaquille O'Neal 1.50 4.00
37 Jason Richardson .60 1.50
38 Rasheed Wallace .60 1.50
39 Nene .50 1.25
40 Tracy McGrady .75 2.00
41 Luke Ridnour .50 1.25
42 Peja Stojakovic .60 1.50
43 Amare Stoudemire .50 1.25
44 Carmelo Anthony 1.25 3.00
45 Steve Francis .50 1.25
46 Antoine Walker .60 1.50
47 Reggie Miller .60 1.50
48 Mike Bibby .60 1.50
49 Sam Cassell .50 1.25
50 Richard Jefferson .50 1.25
51 Jason Kapono .40 1.00
52 Dajuan Wagner .40 1.00
53 Kobe Bryant 2.50 6.00
54 Kenyon Martin .50 1.25
55 T.J. Ford .40 1.00
56 Ray Allen .60 1.50
57 Vince Carter 1.00 2.50
58 Yao Ming 1.25 3.00
59 Baron Davis .50 1.25
60 Joe Smith .50 1.25
61 Luol Deng RC 1.50 4.00
62 J.R. Smith RC 1.50 4.00
63 Josh Childress RC 1.25 3.00
64 Shaun Livingston RC 1.50 4.00
65 Rafael Araujo RC 1.00 2.50
66 Devin Harris RC 1.25 3.00
67 Kevin Martin RC 2.00 5.00
68 Sasha Vujacic RC 1.50 4.00
69 Robert Swift RC 1.00 2.50
70 Andris Biedrins RC 1.00 2.50
71 Kirk Snyder RC 1.00 2.50
72 Jameer Nelson RC 1.50 4.00
73 Tony Allen RC 1.50 4.00
74 Chris Duhon RC 1.50 4.00
75 David Harrison RC 1.00 2.50
76 Andre Iguodala RC 2.00 5.00
77 Josh Smith RC 1.50 4.00
78 Andre Emmett RC 1.00 2.50
79 Luke Jackson RC 1.00 2.50
80 Dorell Wright RC 1.50 4.00
81 Ben Gordon RC 1.50 4.00
82 Dwight Howard RC 3.00 8.00
83 Kris Humphries RC 1.50 4.00
84 Al Jefferson RC 2.00 5.00
85 Jackson Vroman RC 1.00 2.50
86 Beno Udrih RC 1.25 3.00
87 Trevor Ariza RC 1.50 4.00
88 Sebastian Telfair RC 1.25 3.00
89 Emeka Okafor RC 1.25 3.00
90 Peter John Ramos RC 1.00 2.50

2004-05 Flair Row 1

*1-60 ROW 1: 1X TO 2.5X BASE HI
*61-90 ROW 1 RCs: .5X TO 1.25X BASE HI
PRINT RUN 100 SER.#'d SETS

2004-05 Flair Courting Greatness Jerseys

Limited to 150 copies, this 28-card set places two players on each card with one jersey below the featured player on these cards. Patch parallels were also inserted that are sequentially numbered to 50 and logo one of one's exist for each individual player.

PRINT RUN 150 SER.#'d SETS
*PATCHES: .75X TO 2X BASE JSY HI
PATCH PRINT RUN 50 SER.#'d SETS
AI Allen Iverson 5.00 12.00
AJ Antawn Jamison 2.50 6.00
AS Amare Stoudemire 2.50 6.00
BW Ben Wallace 2.50 6.00
CB Chauncey Billups 3.00 8.00
DH Dwight Howard 6.00 15.00
DN Dirk Nowitzki 5.00 12.00
DW Dwyane Wade 5.00 12.00
GA Gilbert Arenas 2.50 6.00
GH Grant Hill 4.00 10.00
GP Gary Payton 3.00 8.00
IG Andre Iguodala 3.00 8.00
JK Jason Kidd 5.00 12.00
JR Jason Richardson 3.00 8.00
KG Kevin Garnett 5.00 12.00
LS Latrell Sprewell 2.50 6.00
MB Mike Bibby 3.00 8.00
MD Mike Dunleavy 2.50 6.00
MG Manu Ginobili 4.00 10.00
PP Paul Pierce 3.00 8.00
PS Peja Stojakovic 3.00 8.00
SN Steve Nash 4.00 10.00
TD Tim Duncan 5.00 12.00
TM Tracy McGrady 4.00 10.00
VC Vince Carter 5.00 12.00
HOW Josh Howard 3.00 8.00
SON Shaquille O'Neal 8.00 20.00
YAO Yao Ming 6.00 15.00

2004-05 Flair Courting Greatness Jerseys Retail

Randomly seeded in Retail packs at the rate of one in 48, this 28-card set parallels the design of the base Courting Greatness Jerseys with no sequential numbering.

2004-05 Flair Courting Greatness Jerseys Dual

Randomly seeded, this 14-card set parallels the design of the base Courting Greatness insert enhanced with two Jerseys and sequential numbering to 99. Dual Patch parallels were also issued and these are serially numbered to 15.

PRINT RUN 99 SER.#'d SETS
*PATCH: 1.25X TO 3X BASE HI
PATCH PRINT RUN 15 SER.#'d SETS
AIAI A.Iguodala/A.Iverson 5.00 12.00
CBBW C.Billups/B.Wallace 3.00 8.00
GAAJ G.Arenas/A.Jamison 2.50 6.00
GHDH G.Hill/D.Howard 6.00 15.00
GPPP G.Payton/P.Pierce 3.00 8.00
JHDN J.Howard/D.Nowitzki 5.00 12.00
JKVC J.Kidd/V.Carter 5.00 12.00
KGLS K.Garnett/L.Sprewell 5.00 12.00
MDJR M.Dunleavy/J.Richardson 3.00 8.00
PSMB P.Stojakovic/M.Bibby 3.00 8.00
SNAS S.Nash/A.Stoudemire 4.00 10.00
SODW S.O'Neal/D.Wade 8.00 20.00
TDMG T.Duncan/M.Ginobili 5.00 12.00
TMYM T.McGrady/Y.Ming 6.00 15.00

2004-05 Flair Cuts and Glory Jerseys

Randomly inserted in packs, this eight card set features a horizontal design with a player photo on the right, a square jersey swatch in the top left and a signature in the middle. Background colors are set to match the player's team colors. All cards are serially numbered, print runs are listed in the checklist.

STATED PRINT RUN 20 TO 100 SETS
JSY/PATCH NOT PRICED DUE TO SCARCITY
BW Ben Wallace/75 20.00 50.00
JC Josh Childress/100 8.00 20.00
JS Jerry Stackhouse/50 8.00 20.00
PG Pau Gasol/100 8.00 20.00
PS Peja Stojakovic/75 15.00 30.00
RH Richard Hamilton/100 10.00 25.00
SM Stephon Marbury/55 12.00 30.00
TM Tracy McGrady/20 30.00 80.00

2004-05 Flair Cuts and Glory Patches

PRINT RUN 50 SER.#'d SETS
BW Ben Wallace 30.00 80.00
JC Josh Childress 15.00 40.00
PG Pau Gasol 20.00 50.00
PS Peja Stojakovic 15.00 40.00
RH Richard Hamilton 15.00 40.00
SM Stephon Marbury 20.00 50.00

2004-05 Flair Dynasty Foundations Jerseys

Randomly inserted in packs, this seven card set parallels the base Dynasty Foundations insert set enhanced with one swatch of game jersey and sequential numbering to 250.

PRINT RUN 250 SER.#'d SETS
*PATCHES: .75X TO 2X BASE HI
PATCH PRINT RUN 99 SER.#'d SETS
4 Nuggets Carmelo JSY 6.00 15.00
9 Hornets Smith JSY 3.00 8.00
10 76ers Iverson JSY 6.00 15.00
12 Trailblazers Randolph JSY 4.00 10.00
13 Spurs Duncan JSY 5.00 12.00
15 Raptors Bosh JSY 4.00 10.00
17 Kings Peja JSY 3.00 8.00

2004-05 Flair Dynasty Foundations Jerseys Dual

Randomly inserted in packs, this six card set parallels the base Dynasty Foundations insert set enhanced with two swatches of game jersey and sequential numbering to 150.

PRINT RUN 150 SER.#'d SETS
PATCH DUAL PRINT RUN 50 SER.#'d SETS
4 Nuggets Melo/K-Mart JSY 6.00 15.00
9 Hornets Davis/Smith JSY 6.00 15.00
10 76ers Barkley/Iverson JSY 20.00 50.00
12 Blazers Randolph/Telfair JSY 6.00 15.00
13 Spurs Admiral/Duncan JSY 10.00 25.00
17 Kings Webber/Peja JSY 8.00 20.00

2004-05 Flair Dynasty Foundations Patches Dual

4 Nuggets Melo/K-Mart JSY 15.00 40.00
9 Hornets Davis/Smith JSY 15.00 40.00
10 76ers Barkley/Iverson JSY 50.00 120.00
12 Blazers Randolph/Telfair JSY 15.00 40.00
13 Spurs Admiral/Duncan JSY 25.00 60.00
17 Kings Webber/Peja JSY 20.00 50.00

2004-05 Flair Dynasty Foundations Jerseys Triple

Randomly inserted in packs, this three card set parallels the base Dynasty Foundations insert set enhanced with three swatches of game jersey and sequential numbering to 99. A Quad Jerseys version numbered to 15 was also inserted along with a Triple Patches version that has patch swatches in the place of jerseys and is sequentially numbered to 25.

PRINT RUN 99 SER.#'d SETS
*PATCH TRIPLE: 1X TO 2.5X BASE HI
PATCH TRIPLE PRINT RUN 25 SER.#'d SETS
9 West/Davis/Smith JSY 10.00 25.00

13 Admiral/Parker/Duncan JSY 20.00 50.00
17 Webber/Bibby/Peja JSY 10.00 25.00

2004-05 Flair Head of the Class Jerseys

Randomly inserted in packs, this 10-card set features a horizontal design and three small black and white head shots of three players from the same year along the top of the card with three jersey swatches below. Each is sequentially numbered to the players' draft year.

STATED PRINT RUN 2 TO 99 SER.#'d SETS
SOME UNPRICED DUE TO SCARCITY
UNPRICED MASTERPIECE PRINT RUN ONE SET
BFD Brand/Francis/B.Davis/99 6.00 15.00
DBM Duncan/Billups/McGrady/97 10.00 25.00
IMA Iverson/Marbury/R.Allen/96 10.00 25.00
NCJ Nowitzki/Carter/Jamison/98 10.00 25.00
OMS Shaq/Mourning/Spree/92 20.00 50.00
RPM Admiral/Pippen/R.Miller/87 30.00 60.00
WHH Webb/Hardway/Houston/93 15.00 40.00

2004-05 Flair Head of the Class Patches

Randomly inserted in packs, this nine-card set parallels the base Head of the Class insert enhanced with patch swatches and sequential numbering to 33. A Masterpiece one of one was also produced.

PRINT RUN 33 SER.#'d SETS
BFD Brand/Francis/B.Davis 25.00 60.00
DBM Duncan/Billups/McGrady 40.00 80.00
IMA Iverson/Marbury/R.Allen 60.00 150.00
NCJ Nowitzki/Carter/Jamison 25.00 60.00
OMS Shaq/Mourning/Spree 75.00 200.00
RPM Admiral/Pippen/R.Miller 100.00 225.00
SMB Amare/Ming/Butler 25.00 60.00
SWG Stack/Wallace/Garnett 30.00 80.00
WHH Webb/Hardway/Houston 75.00 200.00

2004-05 Flair Significant Signings

Randomly seeded in packs, this 21-card set features a tan background, centered player photos and a sticker autograph in the lower left hand corner. Each card is sequentially numbered to various quantities. Parallel version numbered to 50, 35, 25, and masterpiece one of one's were also issued.

PRINT RUN 44 TO 250 SER.#'d SETS
N Nene/200 5.00 12.00
AJ Antawn Jamison/50 6.00 15.00
AS Amare Stoudemire/150 12.00 30.00
BG Ben Gordon/200 10.00 25.00
BM Brad Miller/150 5.00 12.00
CB Chauncey Billups/44 12.00 30.00
DH David Harrison/150 5.00 12.00
DW Dwyane Wade/75 25.00 60.00
DW David West/200 5.00 12.00
EB Elton Brand/75 6.00 15.00
JH Josh Howard/200 5.00 12.00
JS Josh Smith/200 8.00 20.00
JS2 J.R. Smith/250 10.00 25.00
KH Kris Humphries/200 5.00 12.00
KM Kenyon Martin/50 8.00 20.00
LO Lamar Odom/75 8.00 20.00
MB Mike Bibby/50 10.00 25.00
MG Manu Ginobili/75 15.00 40.00
MP Mickael Pietrus/200 5.00 12.00
RA Rafael Araujo/200 5.00 12.00
RJ Richard Jefferson/50 6.00 15.00

2004-05 Flair Significant Signings 50

PRINT RUN 50 SER.#'d SETS
N Nene 6.00 15.00
AS Amare Stoudemire 15.00 40.00
DW Dwyane Wade 50.00 120.00
DW David West 6.00 15.00
JS Josh Smith 6.00 15.00
JS2 J.R. Smith 6.00 15.00
KH Kris Humphries 6.00 15.00

2004-05 Flair Significant Signings 35

PRINT RUN 35 SER.#'d SETS
N Nene 8.00 20.00
BG Ben Gordon 15.00 40.00
BM Brad Miller 8.00 20.00
EB Elton Brand 10.00 25.00
JH Josh Howard 8.00 20.00
KM Kenyon Martin 12.50 30.00
LO Lamar Odom 12.50 30.00
MG Manu Ginobili 25.00 60.00
RA Rafael Araujo 8.00 20.00

2004-05 Flair Significant Signings 25

PRINT RUN 25 SER.#'d SETS
AS Amare Stoudemire 12.00 30.00
DW Dwyane Wade 50.00 120.00
JH Josh Howard 10.00 25.00
MB Mike Bibby 10.00 25.00
MG Manu Ginobili 20.00 50.00
MP Mickael Pietrus 10.00 25.00
RJ Richard Jefferson 10.00 25.00

2004-05 Flair Significant Signings Die Cuts

Randomly inserted in packs, this six card set parallels the base Significant Signings set enhanced with die cut edges and sequential numbering. The print runs are listed in the checklist.

STATED PRINT RUN 18 TO 50 SETS
AJ Al Jefferson/24 15.00 40.00
AS Amare Stoudemire/50 15.00 40.00
DW Dwyane Wade/20 25.00 60.00
DW Dorell Wright/18 10.00 25.00
JS Josh Smith/50 12.50 30.00
KH Kris Humphries/50 6.00 15.00

2004-05 Flair Significant Signings Jerseys

Randomly inserted in packs, this 18-card set parallels the base Significant Signings set enhanced with a jersey swatch and sequential numbering. Print runs for the cards we've found are listed in the checklist. A Jerseys 2 version was also inserted and is serially numbered to two, a Patch version with a patch swatch was inserted and is serially numbered to 10, and Patch one of one's were produced as well.

PRINT RUN 10 TO 25 SER.#'d SETS
N Nene/25 10.00 25.00
AJ Antawn Jamison/15 15.00 40.00
AS Amare Stoudemire/25 25.00 60.00
DH David Harrison/25 10.00 25.00
DW Dwyane Wade/25 80.00 200.00
DW2 David West/25 10.00 25.00
EB Elton Brand/15 12.00 30.00
JH Josh Howard/25 10.00 25.00
JRS J.R. Smith/25 40.00 100.00
JS Josh Smith/25 40.00 100.00
KH Kris Humphries/25 10.00 25.00
KM Kenyon Martin/15 15.00 40.00
LJ Luke Jackson/50 10.00 25.00
LO Lamar Odom/25 15.00 40.00
MG Manu Ginobili/25 25.00 60.00
MP Mickael Pietrus/25 10.00 25.00
RJ Richard Jefferson/15 12.00 30.00

2003-04 Flair Final Edition

Released in late June 2004, Flair Final Edition was Fleer's final product issued for the 2003-04 season. The 90-card set is divided up into 65 base veteran cards and 25 rookie cards sequentially numbered to 799. The base cards show players in full color against a black and white background and have border colors set to match the team colors of the featured player. Flair Final Edition also included redemption cards for draft day materials including the team's logos, player's names and ping pong balls. Flair Final Edition was offered as both a Hobby and a Retail product with two distinctly different packagings. Retail were packed in four-card packs with 24 packs per box and carried a suggested retail price of $2.99; while hobby was packaged as a single-pack box containing 12 cards and no suggested retail price was ever released.

COMP.SET w/o SP's (65) 12.50 30.00
66-90 RC PRINT RUN 799 SER.#'d SETS
UNPRICED ROW 2 PRINT RUN ONE SET
1 Allen Iverson .50 1.25
2 Juwan Howard .25 .60
3 Stephen Jackson .25 .60
4 Manu Ginobili .40 1.00
5 Steve Nash .40 1.00
6 Jason Terry .25 .60
7 Tayshaun Prince .25 .60
8 Stephon Marbury .25 .60
9 Eddie Jones .25 .60
10 Reggie Miller .30 .75
11 Baron Davis .25 .60
12 Donyell Marshall .20 .50
13 Mike Bibby .30 .75
14 Kobe Bryant 1.25 3.00
15 Jason Richardson .30 .75
16 Cuttino Mobley .20 .50
17 Andre Miller .25 .60
18 Corey Maggette .25 .60
19 Michael Finley .30 .75
20 Jason Kidd .50 1.25
21 Lamar Odom .25 .60
22 Tracy McGrady .40 1.00
23 Peja Stojakovic .30 .75
24 Richard Jefferson .25 .60
25 Rasheed Wallace .30 .75
26 Eddy Curry .20 .50
27 Ben Wallace .25 .60
28 Rashard Lewis .30 .75
29 Sam Cassell .25 .60
30 Anfernee Hardaway .50 1.25
31 Carlos Boozer .25 .60
32 Jamal Crawford .30 .75
33 Dirk Nowitzki .50 1.25
34 Steve Francis .25 .60
35 Chris Webber .30 .75
36 Elton Brand .30 .75
37 Michael Redd .30 .75
38 Jason Williams .25 .60
39 Nene .25 .60
40 Nick Van Exel .25 .60
41 Amare Stoudemire .40 1.00
42 Latrell Sprewell .25 .60
43 Tony Parker .30 .75
44 Keith Van Horn .25 .60
45 Pau Gasol .30 .75
46 Andrei Kirilenko .30 .75
47 Shareef Abdur-Rahim .25 .60
48 Tim Thomas .20 .50
49 Jerry Stackhouse .25 .60
50 Jermaine O'Neal .25 .60
51 Jamal Mashburn .25 .60
52 Matt Harpring .20 .50
53 Damon Stoudamire .25 .60
54 Zydrunas Ilgauskas .25 .60
55 Kevin Garnett .50 1.25
56 Tim Duncan .50 1.25
57 Yao Ming .60 1.50
58 Kenyon Martin .25 .60
59 Paul Pierce .30 .75
60 Ron Artest .30 .75
61 Vince Carter .50 1.25
62 Shaquille O'Neal .75 2.00
63 Shawn Marion .25 .60
64 Gilbert Arenas .25 .60
65 Ray Allen .30 .75
66 Chris Bosh RC 3.00 8.00
67 Brian Cook RC 1.25 3.00
68 Luke Ridnour RC 1.50 4.00
69 Willie Green RC 1.25 3.00
70 Zarko Cabarkapa RC 1.25 3.00
71 Maurice Williams RC 2.00 5.00
72 Luke Walton RC 2.00 5.00
73 David West RC 2.00 5.00
74 Mickael Pietrus RC 1.50 4.00
75 LeBron James RC 60.00 150.00
76 Marcus Banks RC 1.25 3.00
77 Keith Bogans RC 1.25 3.00
78 Darko Milicic RC 1.50 4.00
79 Jarvis Hayes RC 1.25 3.00
80 Josh Howard RC 2.00 5.00
81 Chris Kaman RC 2.00 5.00
82 Mike Sweetney RC 1.25 3.00
83 Carmelo Anthony RC 6.00 15.00
84 Travis Outlaw RC 1.50 4.00
85 Kyle Korver RC 2.50 6.00
86 Boris Diaw RC 2.00 5.00
87 Dwyane Wade RC 6.00 15.00
88 Troy Bell RC 1.25 3.00
89 T.J. Ford RC 1.50 4.00
90 Kirk Hinrich RC 2.00 5.00

2003-04 Flair Final Edition Row 1

*1-65 SINGLES: 2.5X TO 6X BASE CARD HI
*66-90 RC SINGLES: .75X TO 2X BASE HI
PRINT RUN 100 SER.#'d SETS
75 LeBron James 200.00 500.00

2003-04 Flair Final Edition Autograph Collection

Randomly seeded in packs, this 35-card set features a black border along the top, a brown-scale photo of the player and a cut signature along the bottom. Each card is sequentially numbered to 200 unless specifically noted below.

PRINT RUN 75 TO 200 SER.#'d SETS
*AUTO 25: .75X TO 2X BASE HI
*AUTO 100: .5X TO 1.25X BASE HI
UNPRICED PARALLEL #'d TO 10 EXISTS
UNPRICED PARALLEL #'d TO ONE EXISTS
N Nene/200 5.00 12.00
AJ Antawn Jamison/200 5.00 12.00
AK Andrei Kirilenko/200 6.00 15.00
AS Amare Stoudemire/200 8.00 20.00
AW Antoine Walker/200 6.00 15.00
BD Baron Davis/200 5.00 12.00
BM Brad Miller/200 5.00 12.00
CM Corey Maggette/200 5.00 12.00
EG Manu Ginobili/200 15.00 40.00
FJ Fred Jones/200 5.00 12.00
GA Gilbert Arenas/200 5.00 12.00
GP Gary Payton/75 12.00 30.00
JD Juan Dixon/200 4.00 10.00
JJ Joe Johnson/200 5.00 12.00
JS Jerry Stackhouse/200 5.00 12.00
JW Jason Williams/200 15.00 40.00
KB Kwame Brown/200 4.00 10.00
LB Leandro Barbosa/200 5.00 12.00
LR Luke Ridnour/200 5.00 12.00
MP Mickael Pietrus/150 5.00 12.00
PP Paul Pierce/200 15.00 40.00
PS Peja Stojakovic/200 6.00 15.00
RH Richard Hamilton/200 5.00 12.00
RJ Richard Jefferson/200 5.00 12.00
RM Ronald Murray/200 4.00 10.00
SB Shane Battier/75 5.00 12.00
TP Tayshaun Prince/200 5.00 12.00
VC Vince Carter/100 12.00 30.00
WG Willie Green/200 4.00 10.00
CAB Carlos Boozer/200 5.00 12.00
CHB Chris Bosh/200 10.00 25.00
DAW Dajuan Wagner/200 5.00 12.00
DAW David West/150 6.00 15.00
DWW Dwyane Wade/200 20.00 50.00

2003-04 Flair Final Edition Courtside Cuts Jerseys 250

Randomly inserted in packs, this 20-card set feature white borders and full color player portrait-style photos with a centered swatch of jersey. Also released were versions sequentially numbered to 175, 125 and 75. Die Cut versions with rounded corners were also produced and versions are sequentially numbered to 25, 18, 13 and eight.

PRINT RUN 250 SER.#'d SETS
*JERSEY 175: .4X TO 1X BASE JSY HI
*JERSEY 125: .5X TO 1.25X BASE JSY HI
*JERSEY 75: .6X TO 1.5X BASE JSY HI
*JERSEY DC: 1X TO 2.5X BASE HI
*JERSEY GREEN: .4X TO 1X BASE HI
JERSEY DIE CUT PRINT RUN 25 SETS
N Nene 2.00 5.00
AI Allen Iverson 4.00 10.00
BD Baron Davis 2.00 5.00
CA Carmelo Anthony 8.00 20.00
CK Chris Kaman 2.50 6.00
CM Cuttino Mobley 1.50 4.00
CW Chris Webber 2.50 6.00
EB Elton Brand 2.50 6.00
GA Gilbert Arenas 2.00 5.00
JS Jerry Stackhouse 2.00 5.00
LO Lamar Odom 2.00 5.00
MF Michael Finley 2.50 6.00
PS Peja Stojakovic 2.50 6.00
RM Reggie Miller 2.50 6.00
SN Steve Francis 2.00 5.00
SN Steve Nash 3.00 8.00
WG Willie Green 1.50 4.00
DAW David West 2.50 6.00
DWW Dwyane Wade 8.00 20.00
JON Jermaine O'Neal 2.00 5.00

2003-04 Flair Final Edition Courtside Cuts Patches

Randomly seeded in packs, this 20-card set parallels the Courtside Cuts set enahanced with premium swatches of patches. Each card is sequentially numbered to 50. A one of one version of this set was also produced along with Die-Cut versions, with rounded corners and versions numbered to five, three and one of one's. Dual versions were also inserted in packs and are sequentially numbered to 10.

*PATCH: 1.25X TO 3X BASE JSY HI
PRINT RUN 50 SER.#'d SETS

2003-04 Flair Final Edition Courtside Cuts Patches Gold

PRINT RUNS LISTED BELOW
SOME NOT PRICED DUE TO SCARCITY
*DIE CUTS: .4X TO 1X BASE HI
N Nene/31 8.00 20.00
CA Carmelo Anthony/15 30.00 80.00
CK Chris Kaman/35 8.00 20.00
DW David West/30 10.00 25.00
EB Elton Brand/42 8.00 20.00
JS Jerry Stackhouse/42 6.00 15.00
RM Reggie Miller/31 12.00 30.00
WG Willie Green/33 5.00 12.00

2003-04 Flair Final Edition Courtside Cuts Patches Platinum

PRINT RUNS LISTED BELOW
*DIE CUTS: .4X TO 1X BASE HI
N Nene/43 6.00 15.00
AI Allen Iverson/33 12.00 30.00
BD Baron Davis/41 6.00 15.00
CA Carmelo Anthony/43 25.00 60.00
CK Chris Kaman/28 8.00 20.00
CM Cuttino Mobley/45 5.00 12.00
CW Chris Webber/55 8.00 20.00
DW Dwyane Wade/42 25.00 60.00
DW David West/51 8.00 20.00
EB Elton Brand/28 8.00 20.00
GA Gilbert Arenas/25 6.00 15.00
JO Jermaine O'Neal/61 6.00 15.00
JS Jerry Stackhouse/25 12.50 30.00
LO Lamar Odom/42 6.00 15.00
MF Michael Finley/52 8.00 20.00
PS Peja Stojakovic/55 8.00 20.00
RM Reggie Miller/61 8.00 20.00
SF Steve Francis/45 6.00 15.00
SN Steve Nash/52 10.00 25.00
WG Willie Green/33 5.00 12.00

2003-04 Flair Final Edition Cuts and Glory Autographs

Inserted in packs randomly, this 17-card set features a full-color portrait style photo, a swatch of game worn memorabilia and a cut signature. Each card is sequentially numbered to 100. Several other versions of this set were issued and are numbered to 50, 15, three and one of one's.

PRINT RUN 100 SER.#'d SETS
*AUTO 50: .5X TO 1.25X BASE AUTO HI
CA Carmelo Anthony 20.00 50.00
CG Mike Bibby 10.00 25.00
DM Darius Miles 8.00 20.00
DR David Robinson 30.00 80.00
EC Eddy Curry 8.00 20.00
JK Jason Kidd 20.00 50.00
JO Jermaine O'Neal 10.00 25.00
KM Kenyon Martin 10.00 25.00
LO Lamar Odom 10.00 25.00
MB Marcus Banks 8.00 20.00
MS Mike Sweetney 8.00 20.00
RG Reece Gaines 8.00 20.00
RM Reggie Miller 40.00 100.00
TM Tracy McGrady 20.00 50.00
TP Tony Parker 10.00 25.00
VC Vince Carter 20.00 40.00
BEN Ben Wallace 20.00 50.00

2003-04 Flair Final Edition Hot Numbers Jerseys 250

Randomly inserted in packs, this 30-card set showcases a horizontal design with a full-color player image on the left, the player's jersey number in the middle and a swatch of jersey on the right. Several other versions were released numbered to 175, 125, 75 with Die Cut version numbered to 25, 18, 13, and eight.

PRINT RUN 250 SER.#'d SETS
*JERSEY 175: .4X TO 1X BASE HI
*JERSEY 125: .5X TO 1.25X BASE HI
*JERSEY 75: .6X TO 1.5X BASE HI
*DIE CUT: 1X TO 2.5X BASE HI
*GREEN: .4X TO 1X BASE HI
DIE CUT PRINT RUN 25 SER.#'d SETS
AI Allen Iverson 4.00 10.00
AS Amare Stoudemire 3.00 8.00
CA Carmelo Anthony 8.00 20.00
CB Chris Bosh 4.00 10.00
CM Corey Maggette 2.00 5.00
DN Dirk Nowitzki 4.00 10.00
DW Dwyane Wade 8.00 20.00
EB Elton Brand 2.50 6.00
JK Jason Kidd 4.00 10.00
JR Jason Richardson 2.50 6.00
KG Kevin Garnett 4.00 10.00
LS Latrell Sprewell 2.00 5.00
MB Mike Bibby 2.50 6.00
MF Michael Finley 2.50 6.00
MG Manu Ginobili 3.00 8.00
MR Michael Redd 2.50 6.00
PG Pau Gasol 2.50 6.00
PP Paul Pierce 2.50 6.00
RA Ray Allen 2.50 6.00
SF Steve Francis 2.00 5.00
TD Tim Duncan 4.00 10.00
TM Tracy McGrady 3.00 8.00
VC Vince Carter 4.00 10.00
JON Jermaine O'Neal 2.00 5.00
KAM Karl Malone 3.00 8.00
KEM Kenyon Martin 2.00 5.00
SHM Shawn Marion 2.00 5.00
SON Shaquille O'Neal 6.00 15.00
STM Stephon Marbury 2.00 5.00
YAO Yao Ming 5.00 12.00

1994 Flair USA

The 120 standard-size cards comprising this set pay tribute to the players of 1994 Team USA. Cards were distributed in 10-card packs (24 per box) with a suggested retail of $3.99. Each player has several cards highlighting various stages in his career. The cards are thicker than traditional basketball cards. The borderless fronts feature two blended color player photos. The player's name appears in gold-foil lettering near the bottom. The borderless backs carry a posed color photo with player information appearing in silver-foil lettering toward the bottom. The set concludes with a USA Basketball Women's Team Legends (113-118) subset and checklists (119-120). A wrapper offer gave collectors the chance to receive an additional 10 Flair USA cards (eight of Kevin Johnson and two team cards) by sending in $4 to Fleer by October 31, 1994.

COMPLETE SET (120) 12.00 30.00
1 Don Chaney CO .15 .40
2 Don Chaney CO .15 .40
3 Pete Gillen CO .15 .40
4 Pete Gillen CO .15 .40
5 Rick Majerus CO .20 .50
6 Rick Majerus CO .20 .50
7 Don Nelson CO .20 .50
8 Don Nelson CO .20 .50
9 Derrick Coleman .15 .40
10 Derrick Coleman .15 .40
11 Derrick Coleman .15 .40
12 Derrick Coleman .15 .40
13 Derrick Coleman .15 .40
14 Derrick Coleman .15 .40
15 Derrick Coleman .15 .40
16 Joe Dumars .20 .50
17 Joe Dumars .20 .50
18 Joe Dumars .20 .50
19 Joe Dumars .20 .50
20 Joe Dumars .20 .50
21 Joe Dumars .20 .50
22 Joe Dumars .20 .50
23 Joe Dumars .20 .50
24 Joe Dumars .20 .50
25 Tim Hardaway .20 .50
26 Tim Hardaway .20 .50
27 Tim Hardaway .20 .50
28 Tim Hardaway .20 .50
29 Tim Hardaway .20 .50
30 Tim Hardaway .20 .50
31 Tim Hardaway .20 .50
32 Tim Hardaway .20 .50
33 Larry Johnson .20 .50
34 Larry Johnson .20 .50
35 Larry Johnson .20 .50
36 Larry Johnson .20 .50
37 Larry Johnson .20 .50
38 Larry Johnson .20 .50
39 Larry Johnson .20 .50
40 Larry Johnson .20 .50
41 Shawn Kemp .20 .50
42 Shawn Kemp .20 .50
43 Shawn Kemp .20 .50
44 Shawn Kemp .20 .50
45 Shawn Kemp .20 .50
46 Shawn Kemp .20 .50
47 Shawn Kemp .20 .50
48 Shawn Kemp .20 .50
49 Dan Majerle .20 .50
50 Dan Majerle .20 .50
51 Dan Majerle .20 .50
52 Dan Majerle .20 .50
53 Dan Majerle .20 .50
54 Dan Majerle .20 .50
55 Dan Majerle .20 .50
56 Dan Majerle .20 .50
57 Reggie Miller .25 .60
58 Reggie Miller .25 .60
59 Reggie Miller .25 .60
60 Reggie Miller .25 .60
61 Reggie Miller .25 .60
62 Reggie Miller .25 .60
63 Reggie Miller .25 .60
64 Reggie Miller .25 .60
65 Alonzo Mourning .25 .60
66 Alonzo Mourning .25 .60
67 Alonzo Mourning .25 .60
68 Alonzo Mourning .25 .60
69 Alonzo Mourning .25 .60
70 Alonzo Mourning .25 .60
71 Alonzo Mourning .25 .60
72 Alonzo Mourning .25 .60
73 Shaquille O'Neal .50 1.25
74 Shaquille O'Neal .50 1.25
75 Shaquille O'Neal .50 1.25
76 Shaquille O'Neal .50 1.25
77 Shaquille O'Neal .50 1.25
78 Shaquille O'Neal .50 1.25
79 Shaquille O'Neal .50 1.25
80 Shaquille O'Neal .50 1.25
81 Mark Price .20 .50
82 Mark Price .20 .50
83 Mark Price .20 .50
84 Mark Price .20 .50
85 Mark Price .20 .50
86 Mark Price .20 .50
87 Mark Price .20 .50
88 Mark Price .20 .50
89 Steve Smith .15 .40
90 Steve Smith .15 .40
91 Steve Smith .15 .40
92 Steve Smith .15 .40
93 Steve Smith .15 .40
94 Steve Smith .15 .40
95 Steve Smith .15 .40
96 Steve Smith .15 .40
97 Isiah Thomas .20 .50
98 Isiah Thomas .20 .50
99 Isiah Thomas .20 .50
100 Isiah Thomas .20 .50
101 Isiah Thomas .20 .50
102 Isiah Thomas .20 .50
103 Isiah Thomas .20 .50
104 Isiah Thomas .20 .50
105 Dominique Wilkins .25 .60
106 Dominique Wilkins .25 .60
107 Dominique Wilkins .25 .60
108 Dominique Wilkins .25 .60
109 Dominique Wilkins .25 .60
110 Dominique Wilkins .25 .60
111 Dominique Wilkins .25 .60
112 Dominique Wilkins .25 .60
113 Carol Blazejowski .40 1.00
114 Teresa Edwards 1.50 4.00
115 Nancy Lieberman-Cline 1.50 4.00
116 Ann Meyers .75 2.00
117 Pat Summitt CO 6.00 15.00
118 Lynette Woodard .75 2.00
119 Checklist .15 .40
120 Checklist .15 .40

1994 Flair USA Kevin Johnson

This 10-card standard-size set was issued as a wrapper redemption offer. The collector sent in $4.00 to Fleer; the offer expired October 31, 1994. The final two cards are team checklist cards that picture on their fronts all the members of the U.S. Olympic basketball team. These reissued checklist cards include Johnson, who was added to the team later, in the team photo.

COMPLETE SET (10) 5.00 12.00
COMMON CARD (M1-M8) .50 1.25
119 Team Checklist 1.00 2.50
120 Team Checklist 1.00 2.50

2003-04 Flair Final Edition Hot Numbers Patches

*50 SINGLES: 1.25X TO 3X BASE JSY HI
PRINT RUN 50 SER.#'d SETS
PATCH ONE OF ONE's EXIST

2003-04 Flair Final Edition Hot Numbers Patches Gold

PRINT RUNS LISTED BELOW
SOME UNPRICED DUE TO SCARCITY
AS Amare Stoudemire/32 10.00 25.00
CA Carmelo Anthony/15 25.00 60.00
CM Corey Maggette/50 6.00 15.00
DN Dirk Nowitzki/41 10.00 25.00
EB Elton Brand/42 6.00 15.00
KG Kevin Garnett/21 12.00 30.00
PG Pau Gasol/16 10.00 25.00
PP Paul Pierce/34 6.00 15.00
RA Ray Allen/34 6.00 15.00
TD Tim Duncan/21 15.00 40.00
SHM Shawn Marion/31 6.00 15.00
SON Shaquille O'Neal/34 15.00 40.00

2003-04 Flair Final Edition Hot Numbers Patches Platinum

PRINT RUNS LISTED BELOW
AI Allen Iverson/33 12.00 30.00
AS Amare Stoudemire/29 10.00 25.00
CA Carmelo Anthony/43 15.00 20.00
CB Chris Bosh/33 12.00 30.00
CM Corey Maggette/28 6.00 15.00
DN Dirk Nowitzki/52 12.00 30.00
DW Dwyane Wade/42 25.00 60.00
EB Elton Brand/28 8.00 20.00
JK Jason Kidd/47 12.00 30.00
JR Jason Richardson/37 8.00 20.00
KG Kevin Garnett/58 12.00 30.00
LS Latrell Sprewell/58 6.00 15.00
MB Mike Bibby/55 8.00 20.00
MF Michael Finley/52 8.00 20.00
MG Manu Ginobili/57 10.00 25.00
MR Michael Redd/41 8.00 20.00
PG Pau Gasol/50 8.00 20.00
PP Paul Pierce/36 8.00 20.00
RA Ray Allen/37 8.00 20.00
SF Steve Francis/45 6.00 15.00
TD Tim Duncan/57 12.00 30.00
TM Tracy McGrady/21 10.00 25.00
VC Vince Carter/33 12.00 30.00
JON Jermaine O'Neal/61 6.00 15.00
KAM Karl Malone/56 10.00 25.00
KEM Kenyon Martin/47 6.00 15.00
SHM Shawn Marion/29 6.00 15.00
SON Shaquille O'Neal/56 20.00 50.00
STM Stephon Marbury/39 6.00 15.00
YAO Yao Ming/45 15.00 40.00

2003-04 Flair Final Edition Hot Numbers Retail

This non-memorabilia version of the Hot Numbers set was inserted in retail packs only. Each card is sequentially numbered to 500

PRINT RUN 500 SER.#'d SETS
RANDOM INSERTS IN RETAIL PACKS
1 Jason Kidd 2.50 6.00
2 Latrell Sprewell 1.25 3.00
3 Tracy McGrady 2.00 5.00
4 Carmelo Anthony 5.00 12.00
5 Manu Ginobili 2.00 5.00
6 Allen Iverson 2.50 6.00
7 Dirk Nowitzki 2.50 6.00
8 Pau Gasol 1.50 4.00
9 Ray Allen 1.50 4.00
10 Yao Ming 3.00 8.00
11 Michael Redd 1.50 4.00
12 Stephon Marbury 1.25 3.00
13 Amare Stoudemire 2.00 5.00
14 Vince Carter 2.50 6.00
15 Kevin Garnett 2.50 6.00
16 Kenyon Martin 1.25 3.00
17 Ben Wallace 1.25 3.00
18 Dwyane Wade 5.00 12.00
19 Zach Randolph 1.25 3.00
20 Paul Pierce 1.50 4.00
21 Jermaine O'Neal 1.25 3.00
22 Elton Brand 1.50 4.00
23 Steve Francis 1.25 3.00
24 Kirk Hinrich 1.50 4.00
25 Shaquille O'Neal 4.00 10.00
26 Mike Bibby 1.50 4.00
27 Shawn Marion 1.25 3.00
28 Michael Finley 1.50 4.00
29 Tim Duncan 2.50 6.00
30 LeBron James 75.00 200.00
31 Karl Malone 2.00 5.00
32 Chris Bosh 2.50 6.00
33 Kobe Bryant 6.00 15.00
34 Jason Richardson 1.50 4.00
35 Corey Maggette 1.25 3.00

2003-04 Flair Final Edition Hot Numbers Retail Gold

CARDS NUMBERED TO PLAYER JERSEY
MOST NOT PRICED DUE TO SCARCITY
8 Pau Gasol/16 10.00 25.00
30 LeBron James/23 700.00 1200.00

2003-04 Flair Final Edition Power Game Jersey and Patch

PRINT RUN 50 TO 75 SER.#'d SETS
N Nene/50 6.00 15.00
AJ Antawn Jamison/50 6.00 15.00
AK Andrei Kirilenko/50 8.00 20.00
CW Chris Webber/75 8.00 20.00
DN Dirk Nowitzki/50 15.00 40.00
JH Jarvis Hayes/75 5.00 12.00
KG Kevin Garnett/50 12.00 30.00
KM Kenyon Martin/50 6.00 15.00
MS Mike Sweetney/50 5.00 12.00
PP Paul Pierce/75 8.00 20.00
RW Ben Wallace/50 6.00 15.00
TD Tim Duncan/50 12.00 30.00
VC Vince Carter/50 12.00 30.00
SON Shaquille O'Neal/50 20.00 50.00
YAO Yao Ming/75 15.00 40.00

2003-04 Flair Final Edition Power Game Jersey and Patch Gold

PRINT RUNS LISTED BELOW
SOME UNPRICED DUE TO SCARCITY
AJ Antawn Jamison/33 8.00 20.00
AK Andrei Kirilenko/47 10.00 25.00
DN Dirk Nowitzki/41 15.00 40.00
JH Jarvis Hayes/24 6.00 15.00
KG Kevin Garnett/21 15.00 40.00
MS Mike Sweetney/50 6.00 15.00
PP Paul Pierce/34 10.00 25.00
TD Tim Duncan/21 15.00 40.00
VC Vince Carter/15 15.00 40.00
SON Shaquille O'Neal/34 25.00 60.00

2003-04 Flair Final Edition Power Game Jersey and Patch Platinum

PRINT RUNS LISTED BELOW
N Nene/43 6.00 15.00
AJ Antawn Jamison/52 6.00 15.00
AK Andrei Kirilenko/42 8.00 20.00
CW Chris Webber/55 8.00 20.00
DN Dirk Nowitzki/52 12.00 30.00
JH Jarvis Hayes/25 5.00 12.00
KG Kevin Garnett/58 12.00 30.00
KM Kenyon Martin/47 6.00 15.00
MS Mike Sweetney/39 5.00 12.00
PP Paul Pierce/36 8.00 20.00
RW Ben Wallace/54 6.00 15.00
TD Tim Duncan/57 12.00 30.00
VC Vince Carter/33 12.00 30.00
SON Shaquille O'Neal/56 20.00 50.00
YAO Yao Ming/45 15.00 40.00

2003-04 Flair Final Edition Power Game Jerseys

Randomly seeded in packs, this 15-card set places a full-color player action photo on the left side of the card and a swatch of game jersey on the right. Each card is sequentially numbered to 250. Several other versions of this card were released including copies numbered to 175 and 125. Die Cut version sequentially numbered to 25, 18, 13 and eight were also produced.

PRINT RUN 250 SER.#'d SETS
*JERSEY 175: .4X TO 1X BASE HI
*JERSEY 125: .5X TO 1.25X BASE HI
*DIE CUT: 1X TO 2.5X BASE HI
DIE CUT PRINT RUN 25 SER.#'d SETS
N Nene 2.00 5.00
AJ Antawn Jamison 2.00 5.00
AK Andrei Kirilenko 2.50 6.00
CW Chris Webber 2.50 6.00
DN Dirk Nowitzki 4.00 10.00
JH Jarvis Hayes 1.50 4.00
KG Kevin Garnett 4.00 10.00
KM Kenyon Martin 2.00 5.00
MS Mike Sweetney 1.50 4.00
PP Paul Pierce 2.50 6.00
RW Ben Wallace 2.00 5.00
TD Tim Duncan 4.00 10.00
VC Vince Carter 4.00 10.00
SON Shaquille O'Neal 6.00 15.00
YAO Yao Ming 5.00 12.00

2003-04 Flair Final Edition Power Game Patches

*75 PATCHES : 1.25X TO 3X BASE JSY HI
PRINT RUN 75 SER.#'d SETS

2003-04 Flair Final Edition SIGnificant Cuts

Randomly seeded, this 15-card set features a horizontal design with a black and white photo on the right side of the card and a cut signature on the left. Each card is sequentially numbered and print runs are listed below.

PRINT RUNS LISTED BELOW
AJ Antawn Jamison/48 8.00 20.00
AK Andrei Kirilenko/76 15.00 40.00
BW Ben Wallace/50 12.00 30.00
CA Carmelo Anthony/50 30.00 80.00
DR David Robinson/50 50.00 120.00
DW Dwyane Wade/60 40.00 100.00
JK Jason Kidd/25 25.00 60.00
KM Kenyon Martin/60 8.00 20.00
MB Mike Bibby/50 8.00 20.00
PP Paul Pierce/60 20.00 50.00
RM Reggie Miller/49 60.00 120.00
SF Steve Francis/60 12.50 30.00
TM Tracy McGrady/50 12.00 30.00
TP Tony Parker/50 12.50 30.00
UH Udonis Haslem/76 8.00 20.00

1961-62 Fleer

The 1961-62 Fleer set was the company's only major basketball issue until the 1986-87 season. The cards were issued in five-cent wax packs with 24 packs in a box. The cards in the set measure the standard 2 1/2" by 3 1/2". Cards numbered 45 to 66 are action shots (designated IA) of players elsewhere in the set. Both the regular cards and the IA cards are numbered alphabetically within that particular subset. No known scarcities exist, although the set is quite popular since it contains the first mainstream basketball cards of many of the game's all-time greats including Elgin Baylor, Wilt Chamberlain, Oscar Robertson and Jerry West. Most cards are frequently found with centering problems

COMPLETE SET (66) 2800.00 4000.00
CONDITION SENSITIVE SET
CARDS PRICED IN NM CONDITION
1 Al Attles RC 30.00 80.00
2 Paul Arizin 25.00 50.00
3 Elgin Baylor RC 100.00 200.00
4 Walt Bellamy RC 30.00 60.00
5 Arlen Bockhorn 12.00 20.00
6 Bob Boozer RC 15.00 25.00
7 Carl Braun 15.00 25.00
8 Wilt Chamberlain RC 400.00 800.00
9 Larry Costello 10.00 15.00
10 Bob Cousy 100.00 200.00
11 Walter Dukes 10.00 15.00
12 Wayne Embry RC 20.00 50.00
13 Dave Gambee 10.00 15.00
14 Tom Gola 12.50 30.00
15 Sihugo Green RC 10.00 25.00
16 Hal Greer RC 40.00 100.00
17 Richie Guerin RC 15.00 40.00
18 Cliff Hagan 20.00 40.00
19 Tom Heinsohn 30.00 80.00
20 Bailey Howell RC 25.00 60.00
21 Rod Hundley 30.00 60.00
22 K.C. Jones RC 40.00 100.00
23 Sam Jones RC 40.00 100.00
24 Phil Jordan 12.00 20.00
25 John Kerr 15.00 40.00
26 Rudy LaRusso RC 15.00 40.00
27 George Lee 10.00 15.00
28 Bob Leonard 8.00 20.00
29 Clyde Lovellette 20.00 40.00
30 John McCarthy 10.00 15.00
31 Tom Meschery RC 15.00 25.00
32 Willie Naulls 15.00 25.00
33 Don Ohl RC 15.00 30.00
34 Bob Pettit 30.00 80.00
35 Frank Ramsey 15.00 30.00
36 Oscar Robertson RC 200.00 400.00
37 Guy Rodgers RC 15.00 25.00
38 Bill Russell ! 175.00 350.00
39 Dolph Schayes 25.00 50.00
40 Frank Selvy 12.00 20.00
41 Gene Shue 12.00 20.00
42 Jack Twyman 15.00 30.00
43 Jerry West RC 300.00 600.00
44 Len Wilkens UER RC 75.00 150.00
45 Paul Arizin IA 10.00 25.00
46 Elgin Baylor IA 50.00 125.00
47 Wilt Chamberlain IA ! 150.00 300.00
48 Larry Costello IA 12.00 20.00
49 Bob Cousy IA 50.00 125.00
50 Walter Dukes IA 10.00 15.00
51 Tom Gola IA 15.00 25.00
52 Richie Guerin IA 12.00 20.00
53 Cliff Hagan IA 15.00 25.00
54 Tom Heinsohn IA 30.00 50.00
55 Bailey Howell IA 15.00 25.00
56 John Kerr IA 15.00 30.00
57 Rudy LaRusso IA 12.00 20.00
58 Clyde Lovellette IA 15.00 30.00
59 Bob Pettit IA 20.00 50.00
60 Frank Ramsey IA 15.00 25.00
61 Oscar Robertson IA ! 90.00 175.00
62 Bill Russell IA ! 100.00 250.00
63 Dolph Schayes IA 15.00 40.00
64 Gene Shue IA 12.00 20.00
65 Jack Twyman IA 15.00 25.00
66 Jerry West IA ! 75.00 200.00

1973-74 Fleer The Shots

This 21-card set was produced by artist R.G. Laughlin for Fleer. The cards measure approximately 2 1/2" by 4". The cards were distributed in packs with one "Shots" card along with two team logo cloth patches and one stick of gum. The fronts feature an illustration of the shot depicted on the card. The illustration is in color, although crudely drawn. The back has a discussion of the shot.

COMPLETE SET (21) 40.00 80.00
COMMON CARD (1-21) 1.50 4.00
21 The Good Shot 2.00 5.00

1974 Fleer Team Patches/Stickers

These cloth patches, each measuring 2 1/2" by 3 3/8", were sold in wax packs. There were two forms of distribution. One entailed packs including one patch, one sticker, one Fleer "The Shots" card, and a stick of gum. The other had two patches instead of a sticker. The team name appears in a color bar across the top of the patch. The team logo is printed inside a round-cut out area in the patch; the words "Property Of" are printed immediately above some of the logos and follow the curve of the logo. The backs are blank. The stickers have the team name across the top and the team logo below. In addition to a NBA logo and sticker, one cloth patch and one sticker were issued for each NBA team. The patches are unnumbered and checklisted below in alphabetical order, with the NBA cloth patches listed first.

COMPLETE SET (38) 40.00 80.00
1 NBA Logo 1.00 2.50
2 Atlanta Hawks .75 2.00
3 Boston Celtics 1.00 2.50
4 Buffalo Braves 1.00 2.50
5 Chicago Bulls .75 2.00
6 Cleveland Cavaliers .75 2.00
7 Detroit Pistons .75 2.00
8 Golden State Warriors 1.00 2.50
9 Houston Rockets .75 2.00
10 Kansas City Kings .75 2.00
11 Los Angeles Lakers 1.00 2.50
12 Milwaukee Bucks .75 2.00
13 New Orleans Jazz 1.00 2.50
14 New York Knicks 1.00 2.50
15 Philadelphia 76ers .75 2.00
16 Phoenix Suns .75 2.00
17 Portland Trail Blazers .75 2.00
18 Seattle Supersonics .75 2.00
19 Washington Bullets .75 2.00
20 NBA Logo 1.25 3.00
21 Atlanta Hawks 1.00 2.50
22 Boston Celtics 1.25 3.00
23 Buffalo Braves 1.25 3.00
24 Chicago Bulls 1.00 2.50
25 Cleveland Cavaliers 1.00 2.50
26 Detroit Pistons 1.00 2.50
27 Golden State Warriors 1.00 2.50
28 Houston Rockets 1.00 2.50
29 Kansas City Kings 1.25 3.00
30 Los Angeles Lakers 1.25 3.00
31 Milwaukee Bucks 1.00 2.50
32 New Orleans Jazz 1.25 3.00
33 New York Knicks 1.25 3.00
34 Philadelphia 76ers 1.00 2.50
35 Phoenix Suns 1.00 2.50
36 Portland Trail Blazers 1.00 2.50
37 Seattle Supersonics 1.00 2.50
38 Washington Bullets 1.00 2.50

1977-78 Fleer Team Stickers

Each measuring 2 1/2" by 3 3/16", this set features one sticker for all twenty-two NBA teams. A color stripe across the top carries the NBA logo and the words "New 'All Pro' Hi-Gloss Stickers." The sticker itself consists of the team name and logo on a white background. Though all 22 NBA teams are represented in this set, there are 71 color variations in the set. The backs are blank. The team stickers are unnumbered and checklisted below in alphabetical order.

COMPLETE SET (22)	7.50	15.00
1 Atlanta Hawks	.30	.75
2 Boston Celtics	.40	1.00
3 Buffalo Braves	.40	1.00
4 Chicago Bulls	.30	.75
5 Cleveland Cavaliers	.30	.75
6 Denver Nuggets	.30	.75
7 Detroit Pistons	.30	.75
8 Golden State Warriors	.30	.75
9 Houston Rockets	.30	.75
10 Indiana Pacers	.30	.75
11 Kansas City Kings	.40	1.00
12 Los Angeles Lakers	.40	1.00
13 Milwaukee Bucks	.30	.75
14 New Jersey Nets	.30	.75
15 New Orleans Jazz	.40	1.00
16 New York Knicks	.40	1.00
17 Philadelphia 76ers	.30	.75
18 Phoenix Suns	.30	.75
19 Portland Trail Blazers	.30	.75
20 San Antonio Spurs	.30	.75
21 Seattle Supersonics	.30	.75
22 Washington Bullets	.30	.75

1986-87 Fleer

This 132-card standard-size set marks Fleer's return to the basketball card industry after a 25-year hiatus. It also marks what is considered to be the beginning of the modern era of basketball cards. The cards were issued in 12-card wax packs (11 cards plus a sticker) that retailed for 50 cents. Wax boxes consisted of 36 packs. A stick of gum was also included in each pack. The set is checklisted alphabetically by the player's last name. Since only the Star Company had been issuing basketball cards nationally since 1983, most of the players in this Fleer set already had cards which are considered Extended Rookie Cards. However, since this Fleer set was the first nationally distributed through wax packs since the 1981-82 Topps issue, most of the players in the set are considered Rookie Cards including Michael Jordan. Other Rookie Cards, of those that had Star Company cards include Charles Barkley, Clyde Drexler, Patrick Ewing, Hakeem Olajuwon, Isiah Thomas and Dominique Wilkins. Rookie Cards of those that did not previously appear in a set include Joe Dumars, Karl Malone, Chris Mullin and Charles Oakley. Red, white and blue borders surround a color photo that contains a Fleer "Premier" logo in an upper corner. The card backs are printed in red and blue on white card stock. Several cards have "Traded" notations on them if the player was traded subsequent to the photo selection process. It's important to note that some of the more expensive cards in this set (especially Michael Jordan) have been counterfeited in the past few years. Checking key detailed printing areas such as the "Fleer Premier" logo on the front and the players' association logo on the back under eight or ten power magnification usually detects the legitimate from the counterfeits. The cards are condition sensitive due to dark borders and centering problems.

COMPLETE w/Stickers (143)	600.00	1100.00
COMP.SET (132)	500.00	900.00
1 Kareem Abdul-Jabbar	8.00	20.00
2 Alvan Adams	.75	2.00
3 Mark Aguirre RC	1.50	4.00
4 Danny Ainge RC	4.00	10.00
5 John Bagley RC	.75	2.00
6 Thurl Bailey RC	2.50	6.00
7 Charles Barkley RC	30.00	80.00
8 Benoit Benjamin RC	1.00	2.50
9 Larry Bird !	12.00	30.00
10 Otis Birdsong	.75	2.00
11 Rolando Blackman RC	1.25	3.00
12 Manute Bol RC	5.00	12.00
13 Sam Bowie RC	.75	2.00
14 Joe Barry Carroll	.75	2.00
15 Tom Chambers RC	2.00	5.00
16 Maurice Cheeks	.75	2.00
17 Michael Cooper	1.00	2.50
18 Wayne Cooper	.75	2.00
19 Pat Cummings	.75	2.00
20 Terry Cummings RC	2.50	6.00
21 Adrian Dantley	1.00	2.50
22 Brad Davis RC	.75	2.00
23 Walter Davis	.75	2.00
24 Darryl Dawkins	1.00	2.50
25 Larry Drew RC	.75	2.00
26 Clyde Drexler RC	15.00	40.00
27 Joe Dumars RC	8.00	20.00
28 Mark Eaton RC	.75	2.00
29 James Edwards	.75	2.00
30 Alex English	1.00	2.50
31 Julius Erving	6.00	15.00
32 Patrick Ewing	15.00	40.00
33 Vern Fleming RC	.75	2.00
34 Sleepy Floyd RC	.75	2.00
35 World B. Free	.75	2.00
36 George Gervin	1.50	4.00
37 Artis Gilmore	1.00	2.50
38 Mike Gminski	.75	2.00
39 Rickey Green	.75	2.00
40 Sidney Green	.75	2.00
41 David Greenwood	.75	2.00
42 Darrell Griffith	.75	2.00
43 Bill Hanzlik	.75	2.00
44 Derek Harper RC	3.00	8.00
45 Gerald Henderson	.75	2.00
46 Roy Hinson	.75	2.00
47 Craig Hodges RC	.75	2.00
48 Phil Hubbard	.75	2.00
49 Jay Humphries RC	.75	2.00
50 Dennis Johnson	2.50	6.00
51 Eddie Johnson RC	1.25	3.00
52 Frank Johnson RC	.75	2.00
53 Magic Johnson	10.00	25.00
54 Marques Johnson	.75	2.00
55 Steve Johnson UER	.75	2.00
56 Vinnie Johnson	.75	2.00
57 Michael Jordan RC	400.00	800.00
58 Clark Kellogg RC	.75	2.00
59 Albert King RC	.75	2.00
60 Bernard King	1.00	2.50
61 Bill Laimbeer	1.00	2.50
62 Allen Leavell	.75	2.00
63 Lafayette Lever RC	.75	2.00
64 Alton Lister	.75	2.00
65 Lewis Lloyd	.75	2.00
66 Maurice Lucas	.75	2.00
67 Jeff Malone RC	2.00	5.00
68 Karl Malone RC	15.00	40.00
69 Moses Malone	1.25	3.00
70 Cedric Maxwell	.75	2.00
71 Rodney McCray RC	.75	2.00
72 Xavier McDaniel RC	2.50	6.00
73 Kevin McHale	1.25	3.00
74 Mike Mitchell	.75	2.00
75 Sidney Moncrief	1.00	2.50
76 Johnny Moore	.75	2.00
77 Chris Mullin RC	12.00	30.00
78 Larry Nance RC	2.50	6.00
79 Calvin Natt	.75	2.00
80 Norm Nixon	.75	2.00
81 Charles Oakley RC	4.00	10.00
82 Hakeem Olajuwon RC	15.00	40.00
83 Louis Orr	.75	2.00
84 Robert Parish UER	1.25	3.00
85 Jim Paxson	.75	2.00
86 Sam Perkins RC	2.50	6.00
87 Ricky Pierce RC	1.00	2.50
88 Paul Pressey RC	.75	2.00
89 Kurt Rambis RC	3.00	8.00
90 Robert Reid	.75	2.00
91 Doc Rivers RC	4.00	10.00
92 Alvin Robertson RC	.75	2.00
93 Cliff Robinson	.75	2.00
94 Tree Rollins	.75	2.00
95 Dan Roundfield	.75	2.00
96 Jeff Ruland	.75	2.00
97 Ralph Sampson RC	3.00	8.00
98 Danny Schayes RC	.75	2.00
99 Byron Scott RC	5.00	12.00
100 Purvis Short	.75	2.00
101 Jerry Sichting	.75	2.00
102 Jack Sikma	.75	2.00
103 Derek Smith	.75	2.00
104 Larry Smith	.75	2.00
105 Rory Sparrow	.75	2.00
106 Steve Stipanovich	.75	2.00
107 Terry Teagle	.75	2.00
108 Reggie Theus	1.00	2.50
109 Isiah Thomas RC	10.00	25.00
110 LaSalle Thompson RC	2.50	6.00
111 Mychal Thompson	.75	2.00
112 Sedale Threatt RC	.75	2.00
113 Wayman Tisdale RC	4.00	10.00
114 Andrew Toney	.75	2.00
115 Kelly Tripucka RC	.75	2.00
116 Mel Turpin	.75	2.00
117 Kiki Vandeweghe RC	1.00	2.50
118 Jay Vincent	.75	2.00
119 Bill Walton	1.50	4.00
120 Spud Webb RC	6.00	15.00
121 Dominique Wilkins RC	15.00	30.00
122 Gerald Wilkins RC	2.00	5.00
123 Buck Williams RC	2.50	6.00
124 Gus Williams	.75	2.00
125 Herb Williams RC	3.00	8.00
126 Kevin Willis RC	2.50	6.00
127 Randy Wittman	.75	2.00
128 Al Wood	.75	2.00
129 Mike Woodson	.75	2.00
130 Orlando Woolridge RC	3.00	8.00
131 James Worthy RC	8.00	20.00
132 Checklist 1-132	6.00	15.00

1986-87 Fleer Stickers

One of these eleven different standard-size stickers was inserted into each 1986-87 Fleer wax pack. The backs of the sticker cards are printed in blue and red on white card stock. The set numbering of the stickers is alphabetical by player's name. Based on the one-to-twelve proportion of stickers to regular cards in the wax packs, there are theoretically an equal number of sticker sets and regular sets. The cards are frequently found off-centered and most card backs are found with wax stains due to packaging.

COMPLETE SET (11)	100.00	200.00
1 Kareem Abdul-Jabbar	12.00	30.00
2 Larry Bird	12.00	30.00
3 Adrian Dantley	2.50	6.00
4 Alex English	2.50	6.00
5 Julius Erving	4.00	10.00
6 Patrick Ewing	4.00	10.00
7 Magic Johnson	5.00	12.00
8 Michael Jordan	75.00	200.00
9 Hakeem Olajuwon	5.00	12.00
10 Isiah Thomas	2.50	6.00
11 Dominique Wilkins	8.00	20.00

1987-88 Fleer

The 1987-88 Fleer basketball set contains 132 standard-size cards. The cards were issued in 12-card wax packs that retailed for 50 cents. A wax box consisted of 36 packs. A sticker card and stick of gum were included. The fronts are white with gray horizontal stripes. The backs are red, white and blue and show each player's complete NBA statistics. The cards are numbered in alphabetical order by last name. Rookie Cards include Brad Daugherty, A.C. Green, Chuck Person, Terry Porter, Detlef Schrempf and Hot Rod Williams. Other key Rookie Cards in this set, who had already had cards in previous Star sets, are Dale Ellis, John Paxson, and Otis Thorpe. The cards are frequently found off-centered.

COMPLETE w/Stickers (143)	100.00	250.00
COMPLETE SET (132)	60.00	150.00
1 Kareem Abdul-Jabbar	3.00	8.00
2 Alvan Adams	.60	1.50
3 Mark Aguirre	.75	2.00
4 Danny Ainge	.75	2.00
5 John Bagley	.60	1.50
6 Thurl Bailey UER	.60	1.50
7 Greg Ballard	.60	1.50
8 Gene Banks	.60	1.50
9 Charles Barkley	6.00	15.00
10 Benoit Benjamin	.60	1.50
11 Larry Bird !	8.00	20.00
12 Rolando Blackman	.60	1.50
13 Manute Bol	.60	1.50
14 Tony Brown	.60	1.50
15 Michael Cage RC	.60	1.50
16 Joe Barry Carroll	.60	1.50
17 Bill Cartwright	.75	2.00
18 Terry Catledge RC	.60	1.50
19 Tom Chambers	.60	1.50
20 Maurice Cheeks	.60	1.50
21 Michael Cooper	.75	2.00
22 Dave Corzine	.60	1.50
23 Terry Cummings	.75	2.00
24 Adrian Dantley	.60	1.50
25 Brad Daugherty RC	1.00	2.50
26 Walter Davis	.60	1.50
27 Johnny Dawkins RC	.60	1.50
28 James Donaldson	.60	1.50
29 Larry Drew	.60	1.50
30 Clyde Drexler	5.00	12.00
31 Joe Dumars	1.50	4.00
32 Mark Eaton	.60	1.50
33 Dale Ellis RC	1.00	2.50
34 Alex English	.75	2.00
35 Julius Erving	5.00	12.00
36 Mike Evans	.60	1.50
37 Patrick Ewing	4.00	10.00
38 Vern Fleming	.60	1.50
39 Sleepy Floyd	.60	1.50
40 Artis Gilmore	.75	2.00
41 Mike Gminski UER	.60	1.50
42 A.C. Green RC	2.50	6.00
43 Rickey Green	.60	1.50
44 Sidney Green	.60	1.50
45 David Greenwood	.60	1.50
46 Darrell Griffith	.60	1.50
47 Bill Hanzlik	.60	1.50
48 Derek Harper	.75	2.00
49 Ron Harper RC	2.50	6.00
50 Gerald Henderson	.60	1.50
51 Roy Hinson	.60	1.50
52 Craig Hodges	.60	1.50
53 Phil Hubbard	.60	1.50
54 Dennis Johnson	.60	1.50
55 Eddie Johnson	.75	2.00
56 Magic Johnson	6.00	15.00
57 Steve Johnson	.60	1.50
58 Vinnie Johnson	.60	1.50
59 Michael Jordan !	50.00	120.00
60 Jerome Kersey RC	.60	1.50
61 Bill Laimbeer	.75	2.00
62 Lafayette Lever UER	.60	1.50
63 Cliff Levingston RC	.60	1.50
64 Alton Lister	.60	1.50
65 John Long	.60	1.50
66 John Lucas	.60	1.50
67 Jeff Malone	.60	1.50
68 Karl Malone	6.00	15.00
69 Moses Malone	1.00	2.50
70 Cedric Maxwell	.60	1.50
71 Tim McCormick	.60	1.50
72 Rodney McCray	.60	1.50
73 Xavier McDaniel	.60	1.50
74 Kevin McHale	1.00	2.50
75 Nate McMillan RC	1.00	2.50
76 Sidney Moncrief	.60	1.50
77 Chris Mullin	1.50	4.00
78 Larry Nance	.75	2.00
79 Charles Oakley	1.00	2.50
80 Hakeem Olajuwon	5.00	12.00
81 Robert Parish UER	1.00	2.50
82 Jim Paxson	.60	1.50
83 John Paxson RC	1.00	2.50
84 Sam Perkins	1.00	2.50
85 Chuck Person RC	1.00	2.50
86 Jim Petersen	.60	1.50
87 Ricky Pierce	.60	1.50
88 Ed Pinckney RC	.60	1.50
89 Terry Porter RC	1.00	2.50
90 Paul Pressey	.60	1.50
91 Robert Reid	.60	1.50
92 Doc Rivers	1.00	2.50
93 Alvin Robertson	.60	1.50
94 Tree Rollins	.60	1.50
95 Ralph Sampson	.60	1.50
96 Mike Sanders RC	.60	1.50
97 Detlef Schrempf RC	4.00	10.00
98 Byron Scott	.75	2.00
99 Jerry Sichting	.60	1.50
100 Jack Sikma	.60	1.50
101 Larry Smith	.60	1.50
102 Rory Sparrow	.60	1.50
103 Steve Stipanovich	.60	1.50
104 Jon Sundvold	.60	1.50
105 Reggie Theus	.75	2.00
106 Isiah Thomas	2.50	6.00
107 LaSalle Thompson	.60	1.50
108 Mychal Thompson	.60	1.50
109 Otis Thorpe RC	2.00	5.00
110 Sedale Threatt	.60	1.50
111 Wayman Tisdale	.60	1.50
112 Kelly Tripucka	.60	1.50
113 Trent Tucker RC	.60	1.50
114 Terry Tyler	.60	1.50
115 Darnell Valentine	.60	1.50
116 Kiki Vandeweghe	.60	1.50
117 Darrell Walker RC	.60	1.50
118 Dominique Wilkins	2.00	5.00
119 Gerald Wilkins	.60	1.50
120 Buck Williams	.75	2.00
121 Herb Williams	.60	1.50
122 John Williams RC	.60	1.50
123 Hot Rod Williams RC	.75	2.00
124 Kevin Willis	.75	2.00
125 David Wingate RC	.60	1.50
126 Randy Wittman	.60	1.50
127 Leon Wood	.60	1.50
128 Mike Woodson	.60	1.50
129 Orlando Woolridge	.60	1.50
130 James Worthy	1.50	4.00
131 Danny Young RC	.60	1.50
132 Checklist 1-132	4.00	10.00

1987-88 Fleer Stickers

The 1987-88 Fleer Stickers is an 11-card standard-size set inserted one per wax pack. The fronts are red, white, blue and yellow. The backs are white and blue and contain career highlights. Based on the one-to-twelve proportion of stickers to regular cards in the wax packs, there are theoretically an equal number of sticker sets and regular sets. Virtually all cards from this set have wax-stained backs as a result of the packaging.

COMPLETE SET (11)	30.00	80.00
1 Magic Johnson	2.50	6.00
2 Michael Jordan	25.00	60.00
3 Hakeem Olajuwon UER	1.50	4.00
4 Larry Bird	2.50	6.00
5 Kevin McHale	1.00	2.50
6 Charles Barkley	2.00	5.00
7 Dominique Wilkins	1.25	3.00
8 Kareem Abdul-Jabbar	1.25	3.00
9 Mark Aguirre	1.00	2.50
10 Chuck Person	1.00	2.50
11 Alex English	1.00	2.50

1988-89 Fleer

The 1988-89 Fleer basketball set contains 132 standard-size cards. There are 119 regular cards, plus 12 All-Star cards and a checklist. This set was issued in wax packs of 12 cards, gum and a sticker. Wax boxes contained 36 wax packs. The outer borders are white and gray, while the inner borders correspond to the team colors. The backs are greenish and show full NBA statistics with limited biographical information. The set is ordered alphabetically by team with a few exceptions due to late trades. The only subset is All-Stars (120-131). Rookie Cards of note include Muggsy Bogues, Dell Curry, Horace Grant, Mark Jackson, Reggie Miller, Derrick McKey, Scottie Pippen, Mark Price and Dennis Rodman. There is also a Rookie Card of John Stockton who had previously only appeared in Star Company sets.

COMPLETE w/Stickers (143)	50.00	120.00
COMPLETE SET (132)	40.00	100.00
1 Antoine Carr RC	.30	.75
2 Cliff Levingston	.20	.50
3 Doc Rivers	.30	.75
4 Spud Webb	.30	.75
5 Dominique Wilkins	.60	1.50
6 Kevin Willis	.30	.75
7 Randy Wittman	.20	.50
8 Danny Ainge	.30	.75
9 Larry Bird	3.00	8.00
10 Dennis Johnson	.20	.50
11 Kevin McHale	.50	1.25
12 Robert Parish	.50	1.25
13 Muggsy Bogues RC	1.00	2.50
14 Dell Curry RC	.60	1.50
15 Dave Corzine	.20	.50
16 Horace Grant RC	2.00	5.00
17 Michael Jordan	20.00	50.00
18 Charles Oakley	.30	.75
19 John Paxson	.30	.75
20 Scottie Pippen UER RC	10.00	25.00
21 Brad Sellers RC	.20	.50
22 Brad Daugherty	.20	.50
23 Ron Harper	.30	.75
24 Larry Nance	.20	.50
25 Mark Price RC	.75	2.00
26 Hot Rod Williams	.20	.50
27 Mark Aguirre	.20	.50
28 Rolando Blackman	.20	.50
29 James Donaldson	.20	.50
30 Derek Harper	.30	.75
31 Sam Perkins	.30	.75
32 Roy Tarpley RC	.20	.50
33 Michael Adams RC	.20	.50
34 Alex English	.30	.75
35 Lafayette Lever	.20	.50
36 Blair Rasmussen RC	.20	.50
37 Danny Schayes	.20	.50
38 Jay Vincent	.20	.50
39 Adrian Dantley	.20	.50
40 Joe Dumars	.60	1.50
41 Vinnie Johnson	.20	.50
42 Bill Laimbeer	.30	.75
43 Dennis Rodman RC	6.00	15.00
44 John Salley RC	.30	.75
45 Isiah Thomas	.60	1.50
46 Winston Garland RC	.20	.50
47 Rod Higgins	.20	.50
48 Chris Mullin	.60	1.50
49 Ralph Sampson	.20	.50
50 Joe Barry Carroll	.20	.50
51 Sleepy Floyd	.20	.50
52 Rodney McCray	.20	.50
53 Hakeem Olajuwon	2.00	5.00
54 Purvis Short	.20	.50
55 Vern Fleming	.20	.50
56 John Long	.20	.50
57 Reggie Miller RC	5.00	12.00
58 Chuck Person	.20	.50
59 Steve Stipanovich	.20	.50
60 Wayman Tisdale	.20	.50
61 Benoit Benjamin	.20	.50
62 Michael Cage	.20	.50
63 Mike Woodson	.20	.50
64 Kareem Abdul-Jabbar	1.50	4.00
65 Michael Cooper	.20	.50
66 A.C. Green	.30	.75
67 Magic Johnson	3.00	8.00
68 Byron Scott	.30	.75
69 Mychal Thompson	.20	.50
70 James Worthy	.60	1.50
71 Duane Washington	.20	.50
72 Kevin Williams	.20	.50
73 Randy Breuer RC	.20	.50
74 Terry Cummings	.30	.75
75 Paul Pressey	.20	.50
76 Jack Sikma	.20	.50
77 John Bagley	.20	.50
78 Roy Hinson	.20	.50
79 Buck Williams	.30	.75
80 Patrick Ewing	1.25	3.00
81 Sidney Green	.20	.50
82 Mark Jackson RC	1.25	3.00
83 Kenny Walker RC	.20	.50
84 Gerald Wilkins	.20	.50
85 Charles Barkley	2.00	5.00
86 Maurice Cheeks	.20	.50
87 Mike Gminski	.20	.50
88 Cliff Robinson	.20	.50
89 Armon Gilliam RC	.60	1.50
90 Eddie Johnson	.20	.50
91 Mark West RC	.20	.50
92 Clyde Drexler	1.25	3.00
93 Kevin Duckworth RC	.20	.50
94 Steve Johnson	.20	.50
95 Jerome Kersey	.20	.50
96 Terry Porter	.20	.50
97 Joe Kleine RC	.20	.50
98 Reggie Theus	.30	.75
99 Otis Thorpe	.30	.75
100 Kenny Smith RC	.60	1.50
101 Greg Anderson RC	.20	.50
102 Walter Berry RC	.20	.50
103 Frank Brickowski RC	.20	.50
104 Johnny Dawkins	.20	.50
105 Alvin Robertson	.20	.50
106 Tom Chambers	.20	.50
107 Dale Ellis	.30	.75
108 Xavier McDaniel	.20	.50
109 Derrick McKey RC	.60	1.50
110 Nate McMillan UER	.20	.50
111 Thurl Bailey	.20	.50
112 Mark Eaton	.20	.50
113 Bobby Hansen RC	.20	.50
114 Karl Malone	2.00	5.00
115 John Stockton RC	6.00	15.00
116 Bernard King	.20	.50
117 Jeff Malone	.20	.50
118 Moses Malone	.60	1.50
119 John Williams	.20	.50
120 Michael Jordan AS	8.00	20.00
121 Mark Jackson AS	.60	1.50
122 Byron Scott AS	.20	.50
123 Magic Johnson AS	1.50	4.00
124 Larry Bird AS	2.00	5.00
125 Dominique Wilkins AS	.30	.75
126 Hakeem Olajuwon AS	.75	2.00
127 John Stockton AS	2.00	5.00
128 Alvin Robertson AS	.20	.50
129 Charles Barkley AS	.75	2.00
130 Patrick Ewing AS	.60	1.50
131 Mark Eaton AS	.20	.50
132 Checklist 1-132	.20	.50

1988-89 Fleer Stickers

The 1988-89 Fleer Stickers is an 11-card standard-size set issued as a one per pack insert along with 12 cards from the regular 132-card set. The fronts are baby blue, red, and white. The backs are blue and pink and contain career highlights. The set is ordered alphabetically. Based on the one-to-twelve proportion of stickers to regular cards in the wax packs, there are theoretically an equal number of sticker sets and regular sets. Virtually all cards from this set have wax-stained backs as a result of the packaging.

COMPLETE SET (11)	12.00	30.00
1 Mark Aguirre	.60	1.50
2 Larry Bird	2.00	5.00
3 Clyde Drexler	1.00	2.50
4 Alex English	.60	1.50
5 Patrick Ewing	1.00	2.50
6 Magic Johnson	2.00	5.00
7 Michael Jordan	8.00	20.00
8 Karl Malone	1.00	2.50
9 Kevin McHale	.75	2.00
10 Isiah Thomas	.75	2.00
11 Dominique Wilkins	1.00	2.50

1989-90 Fleer

The 1989-90 Fleer basketball set consists of 168 standard-size cards. The cards were distributed in 15-card wax packs (and one sticker) and in 36-card rack packs. Wax boxes contained 36 packs. The fronts feature color action player photos, with various color borders between white inner and outer borders. The player's name and position appear in the upper left corner, with the team logo superimposed over the upper right corner of the picture. The horizontally oriented backs have black lettering on red, pink, and white background and present career statistics, biographical information, and a performance index. The set is ordered alphabetically in team subsets (with a few exceptions due to late trades). The only subset is All-Star Game Combos (163-167). Rookie Cards of note in this set include Hersey Hawkins, Jeff Hornacek, Kevin Johnson, Reggie Lewis, Dan Majerle, Danny Manning, Mitch Richmond,, Rik Smits, and Rod Strickland. Cards from this set are frequently found off-center.

COMPLETE w/Stickers (179)	15.00	40.00
COMPLETE SET (168)	12.50	30.00
1 John Battle RC	.08	.20
2 Jon Koncak RC	.08	.20
3 Cliff Levingston	.08	.20
4 Moses Malone	.25	.60
5 Doc Rivers	.10	.30
6 Spud Webb UER	.10	.30
7 Dominique Wilkins	.25	.60
8 Larry Bird	1.25	3.00
9 Dennis Johnson	.08	.20
10 Reggie Lewis RC	.30	.75
11 Kevin McHale	.25	.60
12 Robert Parish	.10	.30
13 Ed Pinckney	.08	.20
14 Brian Shaw RC	.25	.60
15 Rex Chapman RC	.30	.75
16 Kurt Rambis	.08	.20
17 Robert Reid	.08	.20
18 Kelly Tripucka	.08	.20
19 Bill Cartwright UER	.08	.20
20 Horace Grant	.10	.30
21 Michael Jordan	6.00	15.00
22 John Paxson	.08	.20
23 Scottie Pippen	2.00	5.00
24 Brad Sellers	.08	.20
25 Brad Daugherty	.10	.30
26 Craig Ehlo RC	.25	.60
27 Ron Harper	.10	.30
28 Larry Nance	.10	.30
29 Mark Price	.10	.30
30 Mike Sanders	.08	.20
31A Hot Rod Williams ERR	.40	1.00
31B Hot Rod Williams COR	.08	.20
32 Rolando Blackman UER	.08	.20
33 Adrian Dantley	.08	.20
34 James Donaldson	.08	.20
35 Derek Harper	.10	.30
36 Sam Perkins	.10	.30
37 Herb Williams	.08	.20
38 Michael Adams	.08	.20
39 Walter Davis	.08	.20
40 Alex English	.25	.60
41 Lafayette Lever	.10	.30
42 Blair Rasmussen	.08	.20
43 Danny Schayes	.08	.20
44 Mark Aguirre	.08	.20
45 Joe Dumars	.20	.50
46 James Edwards	.08	.20
47 Vinnie Johnson	.10	.30
48 Bill Laimbeer	.10	.30
49 Dennis Rodman	1.25	3.00
50 Isiah Thomas	.25	.60
51 John Salley	.08	.20
52 Manute Bol	.10	.30
53 Winston Garland	.08	.20
54 Rod Higgins	.08	.20
55 Chris Mullin	.25	.60
56 Mitch Richmond RC	1.50	4.00
57 Terry Teagle	.08	.20
58 Derrick Chievous UER	.08	.20
59 Sleepy Floyd	.08	.20
60 Tim McCormick	.08	.20
61 Hakeem Olajuwon	.50	1.25
62 Otis Thorpe	.10	.30
63 Mike Woodson	.08	.20
64 Vern Fleming	.08	.20
65 Reggie Miller	.75	2.00
66 Chuck Person	.10	.30
67 Detlef Schrempf	.10	.30
68 Rik Smits RC	.40	1.00
69 Benoit Benjamin	.08	.20
70 Gary Grant RC	.10	.30
71 Danny Manning RC	.40	1.00
72 Ken Norman RC	.08	.20
73 Charles Smith RC	.25	.60
74 Reggie Williams RC	.08	.20
75 Michael Cooper	.10	.30
76 A.C. Green	.10	.30
77 Magic Johnson	1.00	2.50
78 Byron Scott	.10	.30
79 Mychal Thompson	.08	.20
80 James Worthy	.25	.60
81 Kevin Edwards RC	.08	.20
82 Grant Long RC	.08	.20
83 Rony Seikaly RC	.25	.60
84 Rory Sparrow	.08	.20
85 Greg Anderson UER	.08	.20
86 Jay Humphries	.08	.20
87 Larry Krystkowiak RC	.10	.30
88 Ricky Pierce	.08	.20
89 Paul Pressey	.08	.20
90 Alvin Robertson	.08	.20
91 Jack Sikma	.08	.20
92 Steve Johnson	.08	.20
93 Rick Mahorn	.08	.20
94 David Rivers	.08	.20
95 Joe Barry Carroll	.08	.20
96 Lester Conner UER	.08	.20
97 Roy Hinson	.08	.20
98 Mike McGee	.08	.20
99 Chris Morris RC	.10	.30
100 Patrick Ewing	.30	.75
101 Mark Jackson	.10	.30
102 Johnny Newman RC	.25	.60
103 Charles Oakley	.10	.30
104 Rod Strickland RC	1.00	2.50
105 Trent Tucker	.08	.20
106 Kiki Vandeweghe	.08	.20
107A Gerald Wilkins	.08	.20
107B Gerald Wilkins	.08	.20
108 Terry Catledge	.08	.20
109 Dave Corzine	.08	.20
110 Scott Skiles RC	.25	.60
111 Reggie Theus	.10	.30
112 Ron Anderson RC	.08	.20
113 Charles Barkley	.50	1.25
114 Scott Brooks RC	.25	.60
115 Maurice Cheeks	.08	.20
116 Mike Gminski	.08	.20
117 Hersey Hawkins UER RC	.40	1.00
118 Christian Welp	.08	.20
119 Tom Chambers	.10	.30
120 Armon Gilliam	.08	.20
121 Jeff Hornacek RC	.40	1.00
122 Eddie Johnson	.10	.30
123 Kevin Johnson RC	.60	1.50
124 Dan Majerle RC	.40	1.00
125 Mark West	.08	.20
126 Richard Anderson	.08	.20
127 Mark Bryant RC	.08	.20
128 Clyde Drexler	.30	.75
129 Kevin Duckworth	.08	.20
130 Jerome Kersey	.08	.20
131 Terry Porter	.08	.20
132 Buck Williams	.10	.30
133 Danny Ainge	.10	.30
134 Ricky Berry	.08	.20
135 Rodney McCray	.08	.20
136 Jim Petersen	.08	.20
137 Harold Pressley	.08	.20
138 Kenny Smith	.08	.20
139 Wayman Tisdale	.08	.20
140 Willie Anderson RC	.08	.20
141 Frank Brickowski	.08	.20
142 Terry Cummings	.10	.30
143 Johnny Dawkins	.08	.20
144 Vernon Maxwell RC	.40	1.00
145 Michael Cage	.08	.20
146 Dale Ellis	.10	.30
147 Alton Lister	.08	.20
148 Xavier McDaniel UER	.08	.20
149 Derrick McKey	.08	.20
150 Nate McMillan	.10	.30
151 Thurl Bailey	.08	.20
152 Mark Eaton	.08	.20
153 Darrell Griffith	.08	.20
154 Eric Leckner	.08	.20
155 Karl Malone	.50	1.25
156 John Stockton	.75	2.00
157 Mark Alarie	.08	.20
158 Ledell Eackles RC	.08	.20
159 Bernard King	.10	.30
160 Jeff Malone	.08	.20
161 Darrell Walker	.08	.20
162A John Williams ERR	.20	.50
162B John Williams COR	.08	.20
163 Malone/Stockton/Eaton AS	.40	1.00
164 H.Olajuwon/C.Drexler AS	.25	.60
165 ASG Wilkins/M.Malone	.25	.60
166 ASG Daugh/Price/Nance	.08	.20
167 ASG Ewing/M.Jackson	.25	.60
168 Checklist 1-168	.08	.20

1989-90 Fleer Stickers

This set of 11 insert standard-size stickers features NBA All-Stars. One All-Star sticker was inserted in each 12-card wax pack. The front has a color action player photo. An aqua stripe with dark blue stars traverses the card top, and the same pattern reappears about halfway down the card face. The words "Fleer '89 All-Stars" appear at the top of the picture, with the player's name and position immediately below the picture. The back has a star pattern similar to the front. A career summary is printed in blue on a white background. Most card backs have problems with wax stains as a result of packaging.

COMPLETE SET (11)	5.00	12.00
ONE PER WAX PACK		
1 Karl Malone	.30	.75
2 Hakeem Olajuwon	.30	.75
3 Michael Jordan	5.00	12.00
4 Charles Barkley	.30	.75
5 Magic Johnson	.60	1.50
6 Isiah Thomas	.20	.50
7 Patrick Ewing	.20	.50
8 Dale Ellis	.08	.25
9 Chris Mullin	.20	.50
10 Larry Bird	.75	2.00
11 Tom Chambers	.08	.25

1990-91 Fleer

The 1990-91 Fleer set contains 198 standard-size cards. The cards were available in 15-card wax packs, 23-card cello packs and 36-card rack packs. Wax boxes contained 36 wax packs. There were also 43 card pre-priced packs ($1.49) which containted Rookie Sensation inserts. The fronts feature a color action player photo, with a white inner border and a two-color (red on top and bottom, blue on sides) outer border on a white card face. The team logo is superimposed at the upper left corner of the picture, with the player's name and position appearing below the picture. The backs are printed in black, gray, and yellow, and present biographical and statistical information. The set is ordered alphabetically in team subsets (with a few exceptions due to late trades). The description, All-American, is properly capitalized on the back of cards 134 and 144, but is not capitalized on cards 20, 29, 51, 53, 59, 70, 119, 130, 178, and 192. Rookie Cards of note in the set include Nick Anderson, Mookie Blaylock, Vlade Divac, Sean Elliott, Tim Hardaway, Shawn Kemp, Glen Rice, and Clifford Robinson.

COMPLETE SET (198)	4.00	10.00
1 John Battle UER	.02	.10
2 Cliff Levingston	.02	.10
3 Moses Malone	.05	.15
4 Kenny Smith	.02	.10
5 Spud Webb	.02	.10
6 Dominique Wilkins	.05	.15
7 Kevin Willis	.02	.10
8 Larry Bird	.25	.60
9 Dennis Johnson	.02	.10
10 Joe Kleine	.02	.10
11 Reggie Lewis	.02	.10
12 Kevin McHale	.02	.10
13 Robert Parish	.02	.10
14 Jim Paxson	.02	.10
15 Ed Pinckney	.02	.10
16 Muggsy Bogues	.02	.10
17 Rex Chapman	.05	.15
18 Dell Curry	.02	.10
19 Armon Gilliam	.02	.10
20 J.R. Reid RC	.02	.10
21 Kelly Tripucka	.02	.10
22 B.J. Armstrong RC	.02	.10
23A Bill Cartwright ERR	.15	.40
23B Bill Cartwright COR	.02	.10
24 Horace Grant	.02	.10
25 Craig Hodges	.02	.10
26 Michael Jordan UER	1.50	4.00
27 Stacey King UER RC	.02	.10
28 John Paxson	.02	.10
29 Will Perdue	.02	.10
30 Scottie Pippen UER	.25	.60
31 Brad Daugherty	.02	.10
32 Craig Ehlo	.02	.10
33 Danny Ferry RC	.02	.10
34 Steve Kerr	.05	.15
35 Larry Nance	.02	.10
36 Mark Price UER	.02	.10
37 Hot Rod Williams	.02	.10
38 Rolando Blackman	.02	.10
39A Adrian Dantley ERR	.15	.40
39B Adrian Dantley COR	.02	.10
40 Brad Davis	.02	.10
41 James Donaldson UER	.02	.10
42 Derek Harper	.02	.10
43 Sam Perkins UER	.02	.10
44 Bill Wennington	.02	.10
45 Herb Williams	.02	.10
46 Michael Adams	.02	.10
47 Walter Davis	.02	.10
48 Alex English UER	.02	.10
49 Bill Hanzlik	.02	.10
50 Lafayette Lever UER	.02	.10
51 Todd Lichti RC	.02	.10
52 Blair Rasmussen	.02	.10
53 Danny Schayes	.02	.10
54 Mark Aguirre	.02	.10
55 Joe Dumars	.05	.15
56 James Edwards	.02	.10
57 Vinnie Johnson	.02	.10
58 Bill Laimbeer	.02	.10
59 Dennis Rodman UER	.15	.40
60 John Salley	.02	.10
61 Isiah Thomas	.05	.15
62 Manute Bol	.02	.10
63 Tim Hardaway RC	.40	1.00
64 Rod Higgins	.02	.10
65 Sarunas Marciulionis RC	.02	.10
66 Chris Mullin	.05	.15
67 Mitch Richmond	.07	.20
68 Terry Teagle	.02	.10
69 Anthony Bowie UER RC	.02	.10
70 Sleepy Floyd	.02	.10
71 Buck Johnson	.02	.10
72 Vernon Maxwell	.02	.10
73 Hakeem Olajuwon	.08	.25
74 Otis Thorpe	.02	.10
75 Mitchell Wiggins	.02	.10
76 Vern Fleming	.02	.10
77 George McCloud RC	.05	.15
78 Reggie Miller	.07	.20
79 Chuck Person	.02	.10
80 Mike Sanders	.02	.10
81 Detlef Schrempf	.02	.10
82 Rik Smits	.05	.15
83 LaSalle Thompson	.02	.10
84 Benoit Benjamin	.02	.10
85 Winston Garland	.02	.10
86 Ron Harper	.02	.10
87 Danny Manning	.02	.10
88 Ken Norman	.02	.10
89 Charles Smith	.02	.10
90 Michael Cooper	.02	.10
91 Vlade Divac RC	.15	.40
92 A.C. Green	.02	.10
93 Magic Johnson	.20	.50
94 Byron Scott	.02	.10
95 Mychal Thompson UER	.02	.10
96 Orlando Woolridge	.02	.10
97 James Worthy	.05	.15
98 Sherman Douglas RC	.05	.15
99 Kevin Edwards	.02	.10
100 Grant Long	.02	.10
101 Glen Rice RC	.25	.60
102 R.Seikaly/M.Jordan UER	.50	1.25
103 Billy Thompson	.02	.10
104 Jeff Grayer RC	.02	.10
105 Jay Humphries	.02	.10
106 Ricky Pierce	.02	.10
107 Paul Pressey	.02	.10
108 Fred Roberts	.02	.10
109 Alvin Robertson	.02	.10
110 Jack Sikma	.02	.10
111 Randy Breuer	.02	.10
112 Tony Campbell	.02	.10
113 Tyrone Corbin	.02	.10
114 Sam Mitchell UER RC	.02	.10
115 Tod Murphy UER	.02	.10
116 Pooh Richardson RC	.02	.10
117 Mookie Blaylock RC	.08	.25
118 Sam Bowie	.02	.10
119 Lester Conner	.02	.10
120 Dennis Hopson	.02	.10
121 Chris Morris	.02	.10
122 Charles Shackleford	.02	.10
123 Purvis Short	.02	.10
124 Maurice Cheeks	.02	.10
125 Patrick Ewing	.05	.15
126 Mark Jackson	.02	.10
127A Johnny Newman ERR	.15	.40
127B Johnny Newman COR	.02	.10
128 Charles Oakley	.02	.10
129 Trent Tucker	.02	.10
130 Kenny Walker	.02	.10
131 Gerald Wilkins	.02	.10
132 Nick Anderson RC	.08	.25
133 Terry Catledge	.02	.10
134 Sidney Green	.02	.10
135 Otis Smith	.02	.10
136 Reggie Theus	.02	.10
137 Sam Vincent	.02	.10
138 Ron Anderson	.02	.10
139 Charles Barkley UER	.08	.25
140 Scott Brooks UER	.02	.10
141 Johnny Dawkins	.02	.10
142 Mike Gminski	.02	.10
143 Hersey Hawkins	.02	.10
144 Rick Mahorn	.02	.10
145 Derek Smith	.02	.10
146 Tom Chambers	.02	.10
147 Jeff Hornacek	.02	.10
148 Eddie Johnson	.02	.10
149 Kevin Johnson	.05	.15
150A Dan Majerle ERR 1988	.30	.75
150B Dan Majerle COR 1989	.05	.15
151 Tim Perry	.02	.10
152 Kurt Rambis	.02	.10
153 Mark West	.02	.10
154 Clyde Drexler	.05	.15
155 Kevin Duckworth	.02	.10
156 Byron Irvin	.02	.10
157 Jerome Kersey	.02	.10
158 Terry Porter	.02	.10
159 Clifford Robinson RC	.08	.25
160 Buck Williams	.02	.10
161 Danny Young	.02	.10
162 Danny Ainge	.02	.10
163 Antoine Carr	.02	.10
164 Pervis Ellison RC	.02	.10
165 Rodney McCray	.02	.10
166 Harold Pressley	.02	.10
167 Wayman Tisdale	.02	.10
168 Willie Anderson	.02	.10
169 Frank Brickowski	.02	.10
170 Terry Cummings	.02	.10
171 Sean Elliott RC	.10	.30
172 David Robinson	.20	.50
173 Rod Strickland	.05	.15
174 David Wingate	.02	.10
175 Dana Barros RC	.05	.15
176 Michael Cage UER	.02	.10
177 Dale Ellis	.02	.10
178 Shawn Kemp RC	.60	1.50
179 Xavier McDaniel	.02	.10
180 Derrick McKey	.02	.10
181 Nate McMillan	.02	.10
182 Thurl Bailey	.02	.10
183 Mike Brown	.02	.10
184 Mark Eaton	.02	.10
185 Blue Edwards RC	.02	.10
186 Bobby Hansen	.02	.10
187 Eric Leckner	.02	.10
188 Karl Malone	.08	.25
189 John Stockton	.07	.20
190 Mark Alarie	.02	.10
191 Ledell Eackles	.02	.10
192A Harvey Grant FFC Black	.30	.75

192B Harvey Grant FFC White	.02	.10
193 Tom Hammonds RC	.02	.10
194 Bernard King	.02	.10
195 Jeff Malone	.02	.10
196 Darrell Walker	.02	.10
197 Checklist 1-99	.02	.10
198 Checklist 100-198	.02	.10

1990-91 Fleer All-Stars

The 12-card All-Star insert standard-size set was randomly inserted in 1990-91 Fleer 12-card packs at a rate of one in five. The fronts feature a color action photo, framed by a basketball hoop and net on an aqua background. An orange stripe at the top represents the bottom of the backboard and has the words "Fleer '90 All-Stars." The player's name and position are given at the bottom between stars. The backs are printed in blue and pink with white borders and have career summaries.

COMPLETE SET (12)	4.00	10.00
RANDOM INSERTS IN WAX PACKS		
1 Charles Barkley	.25	.60
2 Larry Bird	.60	1.50
3 Hakeem Olajuwon	.25	.60
4 Magic Johnson	.50	1.25
5 Michael Jordan	3.00	8.00
6 Isiah Thomas	.20	.50
7 Karl Malone	.25	.60
8 Tom Chambers	.08	.25
9 John Stockton	.25	.60
10 David Robinson	.50	1.25
11 Clyde Drexler	.20	.50
12 Patrick Ewing	.20	.50

1990-91 Fleer Rookie Sensations

Randomly inserted in 23-card cello packs, the 1990-91 Fleer Rookie Sensations set consists of 10 standard-size cards. Cards were inserted at a rate of approximately one in five packs. The fronts feature color action player photos, with white and red borders on an aqua background. A basketball overlays the lower left corner of the picture, with the words "Rookie Sensation" in yellow lettering, and the player's name appearing in white lettering in the bottom red border. The backs are printed in black and red on gray background (with white borders) and present summaries of their college careers and rookie seasons. The key card is David Robinson's first insert.

COMPLETE SET (10)	6.00	15.00
RANDOM INSERTS IN CELLO PACKS		
1 David Robinson UER	3.00	8.00
2 Sean Elliott UER	.75	2.00
3 Glen Rice	1.50	4.00
4 J.R. Reid	.20	.50
5 Stacey King	.10	.30
6 Pooh Richardson	.20	.50
7 Nick Anderson	.60	1.50
8 Tim Hardaway	2.50	6.00
9 Vlade Divac	1.00	2.50
10 Sherman Douglas	.20	.50

1990-91 Fleer Update

These cards are the same size and design as the regular issue yet were issued only in complete set form. Factory sets were distributed exclusively through hobby dealers. The set numbering is arranged alphabetically by team. The card numbers have a "U" prefix. Rookie Cards of note include Dee Brown, Elden Campbell, Cedric Ceballos, Derrick Coleman, Kendall Gill, Chris Jackson, Gary Payton, Drazen Petrovic, Dennis Scott and Loy Vaught. It's interesting to note that this is one of the first sets to actually get current year rookies pictured on trading cards.

COMPLETE SET (100)	3.00	8.00
U1 Jon Koncak	.01	.05
U2 Tim McCormick	.01	.05
U3 Doc Rivers	.05	.15
U4 Rumeal Robinson RC	.01	.05
U5 Trevor Wilson	.01	.05
U6 Dee Brown RC	.10	.30
U7 Dave Popson	.01	.05
U8 Kevin Gamble	.01	.05
U9 Brian Shaw	.10	.30
U10 Michael Smith	.01	.05
U11 Kendall Gill RC	.25	.60
U12 Johnny Newman	.01	.05
U13 Steve Scheffler RC	.01	.05
U14 Dennis Hopson	.01	.05
U15 Cliff Levingston	.01	.05
U16 Chucky Brown RC	.01	.05
U17 John Morton RC	.01	.05
U18 Gerald Paddio RC	.01	.05
U19 Alex English	.01	.05
U20 Fat Lever	.01	.05
U21 Rodney McCray	.01	.05
U22 Roy Tarpley	.01	.05
U23 Randy White RC	.01	.05
U24 Anthony Cook RC	.01	.05
U25 Chris Jackson RC	.10	.30
U26 Marcus Liberty RC	.01	.05
U27 Orlando Woolridge	.01	.05
U28 William Bedford RC	.01	.05
U29 Lance Blanks RC	.01	.05
U30 Scott Hastings	.01	.05
U31 Tyrone Hill RC	.05	.15
U32 Les Jepsen	.01	.05
U33 Steve Johnson	.01	.05
U34 Kevin Pritchard RC	.01	.05
U35 Dave Jamerson RC	.01	.05
U36 Kenny Smith	.01	.05
U37 Greg Dreiling RC	.01	.05
U38 Kenny Williams RC	.01	.05
U39 Micheal Williams UER	.05	.15
U40 Gary Grant	.01	.05
U41 Bo Kimble RC	.01	.05
U42 Loy Vaught RC	.20	.50
U43 Elden Campbell RC	.25	.60
U44 Sam Perkins	.05	.15
U45 Tony Smith RC	.01	.05
U46 Terry Teagle	.01	.05
U47 Willie Burton RC	.01	.05
U48 Bimbo Coles RC	.10	.30
U49 Terry Davis RC	.01	.05
U50 Alec Kessler RC	.01	.05
U51 Greg Anderson	.01	.05
U52 Frank Brickowski	.01	.05
U53 Steve Henson RC	.01	.05
U54 Brad Lohaus	.01	.05
U55 Danny Schayes	.01	.05
U56 Gerald Glass RC	.01	.05
U57 Felton Spencer RC	.05	.15
U58 Doug West RC	.10	.30
U59 Jud Buechler RC	.05	.15
U60 Derrick Coleman RC	.25	.60
U61 Tate George RC	.01	.05
U62 Reggie Theus	.05	.15
U63 Greg Grant RC	.01	.05
U64 Jerrod Mustaf RC	.01	.05
U65 Eddie Lee Wilkins RC	.01	.05
U66 Michael Ansley	.01	.05
U67 Jerry Reynolds	.01	.05
U68 Dennis Scott RC	.15	.40
U69 Manute Bol	.01	.05
U70 Armon Gilliam	.01	.05
U71 Brian Oliver	.01	.05
U72 Kenny Payne RC	.01	.05
U73 Jayson Williams RC	.40	1.00
U74 Kenny Battle RC	.01	.05
U75 Cedric Ceballos RC	.20	.50
U76 Negele Knight RC	.01	.05
U77 Xavier McDaniel	.01	.05
U78 Alaa Abdelnaby RC	.01	.05
U79 Danny Ainge	.05	.15
U80 Mark Bryant	.01	.05
U81 Drazen Petrovic RC	.10	.30
U82 Anthony Bonner RC	.01	.05
U83 Duane Causwell RC	.01	.05
U84 Bobby Hansen	.01	.05
U85 Eric Leckner	.01	.05
U86 Travis Mays RC	.01	.05
U87 Lionel Simmons RC	.05	.15
U88 Sidney Green	.01	.05
U89 Tony Massenburg	.01	.05
U90 Paul Pressey	.01	.05
U91 Dwayne Schintzius RC	.01	.05
U92 Gary Payton RC	2.50	6.00
U93 Olden Polynice	.01	.05
U94 Jeff Malone	.01	.05
U95 Walter Palmer	.01	.05
U96 Delaney Rudd	.01	.05
U97 Pervis Ellison	.05	.15
U98 A.J. English RC	.01	.05
U99 Greg Foster RC	.05	.15
U100 Checklist 1-100	.01	.05

1991-92 Fleer

The complete 1991-92 Fleer basketball card set contains 400 standard-size cards. The set was distributed in two series of 240 and 160 cards, respectively. The cards were distributed in 12-card wax packs, 23-card cello packs and 36-card rack packs. Wax boxes contained 36 packs. The fronts feature color action player photos, bordered by a red stripe on the bottom, and gray and red stripes on the top. A 3/4" blue stripe checkered with black NBA logos runs the length of the card and serves as the left border of the picture. The team logo, player's name, and position are printed in white lettering in this stripe. The picture is bordered on the right side by a thin gray stripe and a thicker blue one. The backs present career summaries and are printed with black lettering on various pastel colors, superimposed over a wooden basketball floor background. The cards are numbered and checklisted below alphabetically according to teams within each series. Subsets include All-Stars (210-219), League Leaders (220-226), Slam Dunk (227-232), All Star Game Highlights (233-238) and Team Leaders (372-398). Rookie Cards of note include Kenny Anderson, Stacey Augmon, Terrell Brandon, Larry Johnson, Anthony Mason, Dikembe Mutombo, Steve Smith, and John Starks.

COMPLETE SET (400)	5.00	10.00
COMPLETE SERIES 1 (240)	2.50	5.00
COMPLETE SERIES 2 (160)	2.50	5.00
1 John Battle	.02	.10
2 Jon Koncak	.02	.10
3 Rumeal Robinson	.02	.10
4 Spud Webb	.02	.10
5 Bob Weiss CO	.02	.10
6 Dominique Wilkins	.05	.15
7 Kevin Willis	.02	.10
8 Larry Bird	.25	.60
9 Dee Brown	.02	.10
10 Chris Ford CO	.02	.10
11 Kevin Gamble	.02	.10
12 Reggie Lewis	.02	.10
13 Kevin McHale	.02	.10
14 Robert Parish	.02	.10
15 Ed Pinckney	.02	.10
16 Brian Shaw	.02	.10
17 Muggsy Bogues	.02	.10
18 Rex Chapman	.02	.10
19 Dell Curry	.02	.10
20 Kendall Gill	.02	.10
21 Eric Leckner	.02	.10
22 Gene Littles CO	.02	.10
23 Johnny Newman	.02	.10
24 J.R. Reid	.02	.10
25 B.J. Armstrong	.02	.10
26 Bill Cartwright	.02	.10
27 Horace Grant	.02	.10
28 Phil Jackson CO	.08	.25
29 Michael Jordan	.75	2.00
30 Cliff Levingston	.02	.10
31 John Paxson	.02	.10
32 Will Perdue	.02	.10
33 Scottie Pippen	.20	.50
34 Brad Daugherty	.02	.10
35 Craig Ehlo	.02	.10
36 Danny Ferry	.02	.10
37 Larry Nance	.02	.10
38 Mark Price	.02	.10
39 Darnell Valentine	.02	.10
40 Hot Rod Williams	.02	.10
41 Lenny Wilkens CO	.02	.10
42 Richie Adubato CO	.02	.10
43 Rolando Blackman	.02	.10
44 James Donaldson	.02	.10
45 Derek Harper	.02	.10
46 Rodney McCray	.02	.10
47 Randy White	.02	.10
48 Herb Williams	.02	.10
49 Chris Jackson	.02	.10
50 Marcus Liberty	.02	.10
51 Todd Lichti	.02	.10
52 Blair Rasmussen	.02	.10
53 Paul Westhead CO	.02	.10
54 Reggie Williams	.02	.10
55 Joe Wolf	.02	.10
56 Orlando Woolridge	.02	.10
57 Mark Aguirre	.02	.10
58 Chuck Daly CO	.02	.10
59 Joe Dumars	.05	.15
60 James Edwards	.02	.10
61 Vinnie Johnson	.02	.10
62 Bill Laimbeer	.02	.10
63 Dennis Rodman	.10	.30
64 Isiah Thomas	.05	.15
65 Tim Hardaway	.08	.25
66 Rod Higgins	.02	.10
67 Tyrone Hill	.02	.10
68 Sarunas Marciulionis	.02	.10
69 Chris Mullin	.05	.15
70 Don Nelson CO	.02	.10
71 Mitch Richmond	.05	.15
72 Tom Tolbert	.02	.10
73 Don Chaney CO	.02	.10
74 Eric (Sleepy) Floyd	.02	.10
75 Buck Johnson	.02	.10
76 Vernon Maxwell	.02	.10
77 Hakeem Olajuwon	.08	.25
78 Kenny Smith	.02	.10
79 Larry Smith	.02	.10
80 Otis Thorpe	.02	.10
81 Vern Fleming	.02	.10
82 Bob Hill CO RC	.02	.10
83 Reggie Miller	.05	.15
84 Chuck Person	.02	.10
85 Detlef Schrempf	.02	.10
86 Rik Smits	.02	.10
87 LaSalle Thompson	.02	.10
88 Micheal Williams	.02	.10
89 Gary Grant	.02	.10
90 Ron Harper	.02	.10
91 Bo Kimble	.02	.10
92 Danny Manning	.02	.10
93 Ken Norman	.02	.10
94 Olden Polynice	.02	.10
95 Mike Schuler CO	.02	.10
96 Charles Smith	.02	.10
97 Vlade Divac	.02	.10
98 Mike Dunleavy CO	.02	.10
99 A.C. Green	.02	.10
100 Magic Johnson	.20	.50
101 Sam Perkins	.02	.10
102 Byron Scott	.02	.10
103 Terry Teagle	.02	.10
104 James Worthy	.05	.15
105 Willie Burton	.02	.10
106 Bimbo Coles	.02	.10
107 Sherman Douglas	.02	.10
108 Kevin Edwards	.02	.10
109 Grant Long	.02	.10
110 Kevin Loughery CO	.02	.10
111 Glen Rice	.05	.15
112 Rony Seikaly	.02	.10
113 Frank Brickowski	.02	.10
114 Dale Ellis	.02	.10
115 Del Harris CO	.02	.10
116 Jay Humphries	.02	.10
117 Fred Roberts	.02	.10
118 Alvin Robertson	.02	.10
119 Danny Schayes	.02	.10
120 Jack Sikma	.02	.10
121 Tony Campbell	.02	.10
122 Tyrone Corbin	.02	.10
123 Sam Mitchell	.02	.10
124 Tod Murphy	.02	.10
125 Pooh Richardson	.02	.10
126 Jimmy Rodgers CO	.02	.10
127 Felton Spencer	.02	.10
128 Mookie Blaylock	.02	.10
129 Sam Bowie	.02	.10
130 Derrick Coleman	.02	.10
131 Chris Dudley	.02	.10
132 Bill Fitch CO	.02	.10
133 Chris Morris	.02	.10
134 Drazen Petrovic	.02	.10
135 Maurice Cheeks	.02	.10
136 Patrick Ewing	.05	.15
137 Mark Jackson	.02	.10
138 Charles Oakley	.02	.10
139 Pat Riley CO	.02	.10
140 Trent Tucker	.02	.10
141 Kiki Vandeweghe	.02	.10
142 Gerald Wilkins	.02	.10
143 Nick Anderson	.02	.10
144 Terry Catledge	.02	.10
145 Matt Guokas CO	.02	.10
146 Jerry Reynolds	.02	.10
147 Dennis Scott	.02	.10
148 Scott Skiles	.02	.10
149 Otis Smith	.02	.10
150 Ron Anderson	.02	.10
151 Charles Barkley	.08	.25
152 Johnny Dawkins	.02	.10
153 Armon Gilliam	.02	.10
154 Hersey Hawkins	.02	.10
155 Jim Lynam CO	.02	.10
156 Rick Mahorn	.02	.10
157 Brian Oliver	.02	.10
158 Tom Chambers	.02	.10
159 Cotton Fitzsimmons CO	.02	.10
160 Jeff Hornacek	.02	.10
161 Kevin Johnson	.05	.15
162 Negele Knight	.02	.10
163 Dan Majerle	.02	.10
164 Xavier McDaniel	.02	.10
165 Mark West	.02	.10
166 Rick Adelman CO	.02	.10
167 Danny Ainge	.02	.10
168 Clyde Drexler	.05	.15
169 Kevin Duckworth	.02	.10
170 Jerome Kersey	.02	.10
171 Terry Porter	.02	.10
172 Clifford Robinson	.02	.10
173 Buck Williams	.02	.10
174 Antoine Carr	.02	.10
175 Duane Causwell	.02	.10
176 Jim Les RC	.02	.10
177 Travis Mays	.02	.10
178 Dick Motta CO	.02	.10
179 Lionel Simmons	.02	.10
180 Rory Sparrow	.02	.10
181 Wayman Tisdale	.02	.10
182 Willie Anderson	.02	.10
183 Larry Brown CO	.02	.10
184 Terry Cummings	.02	.10
185 Sean Elliott	.02	.10
186 Paul Pressey	.02	.10
187 David Robinson	.10	.30
188 Rod Strickland	.05	.15
189 Benoit Benjamin	.02	.10
190 Eddie Johnson	.02	.10
191 K.C. Jones CO	.02	.10
192 Shawn Kemp	.15	.40
193 Derrick McKey	.02	.10
194 Gary Payton	.15	.40
195 Ricky Pierce	.02	.10
196 Sedale Threatt	.02	.10
197 Thurl Bailey	.02	.10
198 Mark Eaton	.02	.10
199 Blue Edwards	.02	.10
200 Jeff Malone	.02	.10
201 Karl Malone	.08	.25
202 Jerry Sloan CO	.02	.10
203 John Stockton	.05	.15
204 Ledell Eackles	.02	.10
205 Pervis Ellison	.02	.10
206 A.J. English	.02	.10
207 Harvey Grant	.02	.10
208 Bernard King	.02	.10
209 Wes Unseld CO	.02	.10
210 Kevin Johnson AS	.02	.10
211 Michael Jordan AS	.40	1.00
212 Dominique Wilkins AS	.02	.10
213 Charles Barkley AS	.05	.15
214 Hakeem Olajuwon AS	.05	.15
215 Patrick Ewing AS	.02	.10
216 Tim Hardaway AS	.05	.15
217 John Stockton AS	.02	.10
218 Chris Mullin AS	.02	.10
219 Karl Malone AS	.05	.15
220 Michael Jordan LL	.40	1.00
221 John Stockton LL	.02	.10
222 Alvin Robertson LL	.02	.10
223 Hakeem Olajuwon LL	.05	.15
224 Buck Williams LL	.02	.10
225 David Robinson LL	.05	.15
226 Reggie Miller LL	.02	.10
227 Blue Edwards SD	.02	.10
228 Dee Brown SD	.02	.10
229 Rex Chapman SD	.02	.10
230 Kenny Smith SD	.02	.10
231 Shawn Kemp SD	.05	.15
232 Kendall Gill SD	.02	.10
233 M.Jordan/Group ASG	.25	.60
234 C.Drexler/K.McHale ASG	.05	.15
235 Alvin Robertson ASG	.02	.10
236 P.Ewing/K.Malone ASG	.02	.10
237 Superstars/Group ASG	.25	.60
238 Michael Jordan ASG	.40	1.00
239 Checklist 1-120	.02	.10
240 Checklist 121-240	.02	.10
241 Stacey Augmon RC	.05	.15
242 Maurice Cheeks	.02	.10
243 Paul Graham RC	.02	.10
244 Rodney Monroe RC	.02	.10
245 Blair Rasmussen	.02	.10
246 Alexander Volkov	.02	.10
247 John Bagley	.02	.10
248 Rick Fox RC	.05	.15
249 Rickey Green	.02	.10
250 Joe Kleine	.02	.10
251 Stojko Vrankovic	.02	.10
252 Allan Bristow CO	.02	.10
253 Kenny Gattison	.02	.10
254 Mike Gminski	.02	.10
255 Larry Johnson RC	.25	.60
256 Bobby Hansen	.02	.10
257 Craig Hodges	.02	.10
258 Stacey King	.02	.10
259 Scott Williams RC	.02	.10
260 John Battle	.02	.10
261 Winston Bennett	.02	.10
262 Terrell Brandon RC	.20	.50
263 Henry James	.02	.10
264 Steve Kerr	.02	.10
265 Jimmy Oliver RC	.02	.10
266 Brad Davis	.02	.10
267 Terry Davis	.02	.10
268 Donald Hodge RC	.02	.10
269 Mike Iuzzolino RC	.02	.10
270 Fat Lever	.02	.10
271 Doug Smith RC	.02	.10
272 Greg Anderson	.02	.10
273 Kevin Brooks RC	.02	.10
274 Walter Davis	.02	.10
275 Winston Garland	.02	.10
276 Mark Macon RC	.02	.10
277 Dikembe Mutombo RC	.25	.60
277B D.Mutombo 91-92 RC	.25	.60
278 William Bedford	.02	.10
279 Lance Blanks	.02	.10
280 John Salley	.02	.10
281 Charles Thomas RC	.02	.10
282 Darrell Walker	.02	.10
283 Orlando Woolridge	.02	.10
284 Victor Alexander RC	.02	.10
285 Vincent Askew RC	.02	.10
286 Mario Elie RC	.05	.15
287 Alton Lister	.02	.10
288 Billy Owens RC	.05	.15
289 Matt Bullard RC	.02	.10
290 Carl Herrera RC	.02	.10
291 Tree Rollins	.02	.10
292 John Turner	.02	.10
293 Dale Davis UER RC	.05	.15
294 Sean Green RC	.02	.10
295 Kenny Williams	.02	.10
296 James Edwards	.02	.10
297 LeRon Ellis RC	.02	.10
298 Doc Rivers	.02	.10
299 Loy Vaught	.02	.10
300 Elden Campbell	.02	.10
301 Jack Haley	.02	.10
302 Keith Owens	.02	.10
303 Tony Smith	.02	.10
304 Sedale Threatt	.02	.10
305 Keith Askins RC	.02	.10
306 Alec Kessler	.02	.10
307 John Morton	.02	.10
308 Alan Ogg	.02	.10
309 Steve Smith RC	.25	.60
310 Lester Conner	.02	.10
311 Jeff Grayer	.02	.10
312 Frank Hamblen CO	.02	.10
313 Steve Henson	.02	.10
314 Larry Krystkowiak	.02	.10
315 Moses Malone	.05	.15
316 Thurl Bailey	.02	.10
317 Randy Breuer	.02	.10
318 Scott Brooks	.02	.10
319 Gerald Glass	.02	.10
320 Luc Longley RC	.05	.15
321 Doug West	.02	.10
322 Kenny Anderson RC	.10	.30
323 Tate George	.02	.10
324 Terry Mills RC	.05	.15
325 Greg Anthony RC	.05	.15
326 Anthony Mason RC	.10	.30
327 Tim McCormick	.02	.10
328 Xavier McDaniel	.02	.10
329 Brian Quinnett	.02	.10
330 John Starks RC	.05	.15
331 Stanley Roberts RC	.02	.10
332 Jeff Turner	.02	.10
333 Sam Vincent	.02	.10
334 Brian Williams RC	.05	.15
335 Manute Bol	.02	.10
336 Kenny Payne	.02	.10
337 Charles Shackleford	.02	.10
338 Jayson Williams	.05	.15
339 Cedric Ceballos	.02	.10
340 Andrew Lang	.02	.10
341 Jerrod Mustaf	.02	.10
342 Tim Perry	.02	.10
343 Kurt Rambis	.02	.10
344 Alaa Abdelnaby	.02	.10
345 Robert Pack RC	.02	.10
346 Danny Young	.02	.10
347 Anthony Bonner	.02	.10
348 Pete Chilcutt RC	.02	.10
349 Rex Hughes CO	.02	.10
350 Mitch Richmond	.05	.15
351 Dwayne Schintzius	.02	.10
352 Spud Webb	.02	.10
353 Antoine Carr	.02	.10
354 Sidney Green	.02	.10
355 Vinnie Johnson	.02	.10
356 Greg Sutton RC	.02	.10
357 Dana Barros	.02	.10
358 Michael Cage	.02	.10
359 Marty Conlon RC	.02	.10
360 Rich King RC	.02	.10
361 Nate McMillan	.02	.10
362 David Benoit RC	.02	.10
363 Mike Brown	.02	.10
364 Tyrone Corbin	.02	.10
365 Eric Murdock RC	.02	.10
366 Delaney Rudd	.02	.10
367 Michael Adams	.02	.10
368 Tom Hammonds	.02	.10
369 Larry Stewart RC	.02	.10
370 Andre Turner	.02	.10
371 David Wingate	.02	.10
372 Dominique Wilkins TL	.02	.10
373 Larry Bird TL	.10	.30
374 Rex Chapman TL	.02	.10
375 Michael Jordan TL	.40	1.00
376 Brad Daugherty TL	.02	.10
377 Derek Harper TL	.02	.10
378 Dikembe Mutombo TL	.05	.15
379 Joe Dumars TL	.02	.10
380 Chris Mullin TL	.02	.10
381 Hakeem Olajuwon TL	.05	.15
382 Chuck Person TL	.02	.10
383 Charles Smith TL	.02	.10
384 James Worthy TL	.02	.10
385 Glen Rice TL	.02	.10
386 Alvin Robertson TL	.02	.10
387 Tony Campbell TL	.02	.10
388 Derrick Coleman TL	.02	.10
389 Patrick Ewing TL	.02	.10
390 Scott Skiles TL	.02	.10
391 Charles Barkley TL	.05	.15
392 Kevin Johnson TL	.02	.10
393 Clyde Drexler TL	.02	.10
394 Lionel Simmons TL	.02	.10
395 David Robinson TL	.05	.15
396 Ricky Pierce TL	.02	.10
397 John Stockton TL	.02	.10
398 Michael Adams TL	.02	.10
399 Checklist	.02	.10
400 Checklist	.02	.10
29-3D Michael Jordan 3-D	400.00	800.00

1991-92 Fleer 3D

NO PRICING DUE TO SCARCITY

1991-92 Fleer Dikembe Mutombo

This 12-card standard-size set was randomly inserted in 1991-92 Fleer second series 12-card wax packs at a rate of approximately one in six. The set highlights the accomplishments of then Denver Nuggets' rookie Dikembe Mutombo. The front borders are dark red and checkered with miniature black NBA logos. The background of the color action photo is ghosted so that the featured player stands out, and the color of the lettering on the front is mustard. On a pink background, the back has a color close-up photo and a summary of the player's performance. Mutombo autographed over 2,000 of these cards which were also randomly inserted into packs. Those cards inserted in packs feature embossed Fleer logos for authenticity.

COMPLETE SET (12)	2.00	5.00
COMMON MUTOMBO (1-12)	.20	.50
COMMON AUTOGRAPH (AU)	12.00	30.00
RANDOM INSERTS IN ALL SER.2 PACKS		

1991-92 Fleer Pro-Visions

This six-card standard-size set showcases outstanding NBA players. The set was distributed as a random insert in 1991-92 Fleer first series 12-card plastic-wrap packs at a rate of approximately one per six packs. The fronts feature a color player portrait by sports artist Terry Smith. The portrait is bordered on all sides by white, with the player's name in red lettering below the picture. The backs present biographical information and career summary in black lettering on a color background (with white borders).

COMPLETE SET (6)	1.50	4.00
RANDOM INSERTS IN ALL SER.1 PACKS		
1 David Robinson	.20	.50
2 Michael Jordan	1.25	3.00
3 Charles Barkley	.15	.40
4 Patrick Ewing	.08	.25
5 Karl Malone	.15	.40
6 Magic Johnson	.30	.75

1991-92 Fleer Rookie Sensations

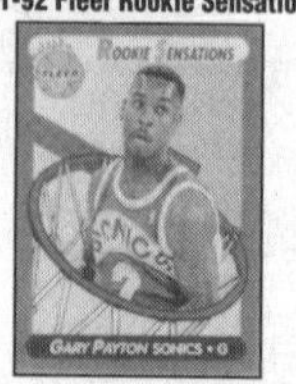

This 10-card standard-size set showcases outstanding rookies from the 1990-91 season. The set was distributed as a random insert in 1991-92 Fleer 23-card cello packs at a rate of approximately two in every three packs. The card fronts feature a color player photo inside a basketball rim and net. The picture is bordered in magenta on all sides. The words "Rookie Sensations" appear above the picture, and player information is given below the picture. An orange basketball with the words "Fleer '91" appears in the upper left corner on both sides of the card. The back has a magenta border and includes highlights of the player's rookie season.

COMPLETE SET (10)	3.00	8.00
RANDOM INSERTS IN SER.1 CELLO PACKS		
1 Lionel Simmons	.20	.50
2 Dennis Scott	.30	.75
3 Derrick Coleman	.60	1.50
4 Kendall Gill	.60	1.50
5 Travis Mays	.20	.50
6 Felton Spencer	.20	.50
7 Willie Burton	.20	.50
8 Chris Jackson	.20	.50
9 Gary Payton	2.50	6.00
10 Dee Brown	.20	.50

1991-92 Fleer Schoolyard

This six-card standard-size set of "Schoolyard Stars" was inserted one per 1991-92 Fleer 36-card rack packs. The card front features color action player photos. The photos are bordered on the left and bottom by a black stripe and a broken pink stripe. Yellow stripes traverse the card top and bottom, and the background is a gray cement-colored design. The back has a similar layout and presents a basketball tip in black lettering on white.

COMPLETE SET (6)	4.00	8.00
1 Chris Mullin	.60	1.50
2 Isiah Thomas	.60	1.50
3 Kevin McHale	.60	1.50
4 Kevin Johnson	.60	1.50
5 Karl Malone	2.50	6.00
6 Alvin Robertson	.30	.75

1991-92 Fleer Dominique Wilkins

Cards from this 12-card insert standard-size set were randomly inserted in 1991-92 Fleer second series 12-card wax packs at a rate of approximately one per six. The set highlights the career of superstar Dominique Wilkins. The front borders are dark red and checkered with miniature black NBA logos. The background of the color action photo is ghosted so that the featured player stands out, and the color of the lettering on the front is mustard. On a pink background, the back has a color close-up photo and a summary of the player's performance. Wilkins personally autographed over 2,000 of these cards which were also randomly inserted in packs. Those cards inserted in packs feature embossed Fleer logos for authenticity.

COMPLETE SET (12)	1.50	4.00
COMMON WILKINS (1-12)	.20	.50
COMMON AUTOGRAPH (AU)	30.00	60.00
RANDOM INSERTS IN ALL SER.2 PACKS		

1991-92 Fleer Mutombo/Wilkins Promo

The Dikembe Mutombo/Dominique Wilkins Commemorative Card was issued to announce the introduction of the 1991-92 Fleer NBA set featuring Dikembe Mutombo and Dominique Wilkins. The card measures the standard size and displays a posed color photo of Dikembe Mutombo and Dominique Wilkins with Jeff Massien, Vice President of Fleercorp. The card is unnumbered. The card was issued to the Fleer dealer network and to various media.

1 Dikembe Mutombo Dominique Wilkins With Jeff Massien Fleer VP	5.00	12.00

1991-92 Fleer Tony's Pizza

These standard-size cards were issued in three-card plastic packs in specially marked boxes of Tony's Frozen Pizza during March and April. Reportedly the promotion went so well that regular cards were inserted when the special S-prefix numbered cards ran out. The cards feature glossy color player action shots with red, gray, and blue borders on their fronts. The player's name, position, and team logo appear in white lettering in the broad blue left margin, which has a pattern of small black NBA logos within it. The back of each card displays a head shot and another action photo at the top, with a brief player biography beneath, and a blue- and white-banded stat panel toward the bottom, all superimposed upon a wooden basketball floor pattern. These 120 cards are the same as the regular-issue cards and are numbered on the back with an "S- prefix.

COMPLETE SET (120)	120.00	300.00
1 Terry Teagle	.75	2.00
2 Karl Malone	5.00	12.00
3 Patrick Ewing	3.00	8.00
4 Alvin Robertson	.60	1.50
5 Scott Skiles	.75	2.00
6 Frank Brickowski	.60	1.50
7 Mookie Blaylock	.75	2.00
8 Ricky Pierce	.60	1.50
9 Gary Payton	3.00	8.00
10 Dennis Scott	.75	2.00
11 Derrick McKey	.60	1.50
12 Mark West	.60	1.50
13 Mark Jackson	1.50	4.00
14 Glen Rice	2.00	5.00
15 Charles Barkley	5.00	12.00
16 David Robinson	4.00	10.00
17 Sam Bowie	.75	2.00
18 Ron Harper	1.25	3.00
19 Reggie Miller	4.00	10.00
20 Lionel Simmons	.60	1.50
21 Jerome Kersey	.75	2.00
22 Rod Strickland	.60	1.50
23 Charles Oakley	.60	1.50
24 Rony Seikaly	.60	1.50
25 Johnny Dawkins	.60	1.50
26 Fred Roberts	.60	1.50
27 Derrick Coleman	.75	2.00
28 Bo Kimble	.60	1.50
29 Chuck Person	.60	1.50
30 Kiki Vandeweghe	1.25	3.00
31 Jeff Malone	.60	1.50
32 Vlade Divac	1.25	3.00
33 Michael Jordan	12.00	30.00
34 Gerald Wilkins	.75	2.00
35 Sarunas Marciulionis	.75	2.00
36 Pooh Richardson	.60	1.50
37 Hakeem Olajuwon	4.00	9.00
38 Rodney McCray	.60	1.50
39 Larry Nance	.75	2.00
40 Wayman Tisdale	.75	2.00
41 Tom Chambers	1.00	2.50
42 A.C. Green	1.00	2.50
43 Bernard King	1.00	2.50
44 Reggie Williams	.60	1.50
45 Chris Mullin	1.50	4.00
46 Bill Laimbeer	1.25	3.00
47 Kenny Smith	.75	2.00
48 Harvey Grant	.60	1.50
49 Mark Price	1.00	2.50
50 Olden Polynice	.60	1.50
51 Isiah Thomas	3.00	8.00
52 Magic Johnson	6.00	15.00
53 John Paxson	.75	2.00
54 Muggsy Bogues	1.25	3.00
55 Mitch Richmond	3.00	8.00
56 Dennis Rodman	4.00	10.00
57 Otis Thorpe	.75	2.00
58 Larry Bird	8.00	20.00
59 Hot Rod Williams	.60	1.50
60 Hersey Hawkins	.75	2.00
61 Brian Shaw	.75	2.00
62 Detlef Schrempf	.75	2.00
63 Danny Manning	1.00	2.50
64 Thurl Bailey	.60	1.50
65 Benoit Benjamin	.60	1.50
66 Nick Anderson	.75	2.00
67 Rex Chapman	.75	2.00
68 Danny Ainge	1.25	3.00
69 Dee Brown	.60	1.50
70 Chris Dudley	.60	1.50
71 Kevin McHale	2.00	5.00
72 Dell Curry	1.00	2.50
73 Ken Norman	.60	1.50
74 Mark Eaton	.60	1.50
75 Shawn Kemp	2.50	6.00
76 Bill Cartwright	.75	2.00
77 Terry Cummings	.75	2.00
78 Clyde Drexler	4.00	10.00
79 Kevin Johnson	1.25	3.00
80 Dale Ellis	.75	2.00
81 Tod Murphy	.60	1.50
82 Brad Daugherty	.60	1.50
83 Charles Smith	.60	1.50
84 Horace Grant	1.25	3.00
85 Vernon Maxwell	.60	1.50
86 Todd Lichti	.60	1.50
87 Sean Elliott	1.25	3.00
88 Kevin Duckworth	.60	1.50
89 Dan Majerle	1.25	3.00
90 James Worthy	1.50	4.00
91 Mark Aguirre	.75	2.00
92 Kevin Willis	.75	2.00
93 Reggie Lewis	1.25	3.00
94 Rumeal Robinson	.60	1.50
95 Terry Porter	.75	2.00
96 Rolando Blackman	.75	2.00
97 Tony Campbell	.60	1.50
98 Sam Perkins	1.25	3.00
99 Willie Burton	.60	1.50
100 Joe Dumars	1.50	4.00
101 Felton Spencer	.60	1.50
102 Danny Ferry	.60	1.50
103 James Donaldson	.60	1.50
104 Craig Ehlo	.75	2.00
105 Clifford Robinson	1.00	2.50
106 Pervis Ellison	.60	1.50
107 Tyrone Corbin	.60	1.50
108 Byron Scott	1.25	3.00
109 Sherman Douglas	.60	1.50
110 Tim Hardaway	2.00	5.00
111 Kendall Gill	.75	2.00
112 J.R. Reid	.60	1.50
113 Robert Parish	1.25	3.00
114 Dominique Wilkins	3.00	8.00
115 Buck Williams	.75	2.00
116 Scottie Pippen	5.00	12.00
117 Sam Mitchell	.60	1.50
118 John Stockton	8.00	20.00
119 Derek Harper	.75	2.00
120 Chris Jackson	.60	1.50

1991-92 Fleer Wheaties Sheets

These Fleer regular issue (gray back) cards were issued nine cards per collector sheet on the back of Wheaties cereal boxes. Eight different collector sheets were produced, and we have checklisted the cards below by boxes. These eight different nine-card gray-back sample sheets were offered on the back of more than four million Wheaties cereal boxes from February to April, 1992. The sheets included regular cards as well as insert and special cards; the non-regular cards are indicated below, e.g., All-Stars (AS), League Leaders (LL), Pro Visions (PV), Rookie Sensations (RS), Schoolyard (SY), and Slam Dunk (SD).

COMPLETE SET (8)	40.00	100.00
1 Wheaties Box 1	6.00	15.00
2 Wheaties Box 2	4.00	10.00
3 Wheaties Box 3	3.00	8.00
4 Wheaties Box 4	3.00	8.00
5 Wheaties Box 5	3.00	8.00
6 Wheaties Box 6	15.00	40.00
7 Wheaties Box 7	8.00	20.00
8 Wheaties Box 8	8.00	20.00

1992-93 Fleer

The complete 1992-93 Fleer basketball set contains 444 standard-size cards. The set was distributed in two series of 264 and 180 cards, respectively. First series cards were distributed in 17-card plastic-wrap packs, 32-card cello packs, and 42-card rack packs. Second series cards were distributed in 15-card plastic-wrap packs and 32-card cello packs. The fronts display color action player photos, enclosed by metallic bronze borders and accented on the right by two pebble-grain colored stripes. On a tan pebble-grain background, the horizontally oriented backs have a color close-up photo in the shape of the lane under the basket. Biography, career statistics, and player profile are included on the backs. The cards are numbered on the back and checklisted below alphabetically according to teams. Subsets include League Leaders (238-245), Award Winners (246-249), Pro-Visions (250-255), Schoolyard Stars (256-264) and Slam Dunk (265-300). The Slam Dunk subset is divided into five categories: Power, Grace, Champions, Little Big Men, and Great Defenders. Randomly inserted throughout the packs were more than 3,000 (Slam Dunk subset) cards signed by former NBA players Darryl Dawkins and Kenny Walker as well as by current NBA star Shawn Kemp. According to Fleer's advertising material, odds of finding a signed Slam Dunk card are one in 5,000 packs. Rookie Cards of note include Tom Gugliotta, Robert Horry, Christian Laettner, Alonzo Mourning, Shaquille O'Neal, Latrell Sprewell and Clarence Weatherspoon. A second series mail-in offer featuring an "All-Star Slam Dunk Team" card and an issue of Inside Stuff was available (expiring 6/30/93) in return for ten second series wrappers plus a dollar.

COMPLETE SET (444)	12.00	30.00
COMPLETE SERIES 1 (264)	6.00	15.00
COMPLETE SERIES 2 (180)	6.00	15.00
SLM DNK AUs: SER.2 STATED ODDS 1:5,000		
1 Stacey Augmon	.02	.10
2 Duane Ferrell	.02	.10
3 Paul Graham	.02	.10
4A Jon Koncak#(Shooting pose on back	.02	.10
4B Jon Koncak Playing defense on back	.02	.10
5 Blair Rasmussen	.02	.10
6 Rumeal Robinson	.02	.10
7 Bob Weiss CO	.02	.10
8 Dominique Wilkins	.08	.25
9 Kevin Willis	.02	.10
10 John Bagley	.02	.10
11 Larry Bird	.40	1.00
12 Dee Brown	.02	.10
13 Chris Ford CO	.02	.10
14 Rick Fox	.02	.10
15 Kevin Gamble	.02	.10
16 Reggie Lewis	.02	.10
17 Kevin McHale	.08	.25
18 Robert Parish	.02	.10
19 Ed Pinckney	.02	.10
20 Muggsy Bogues	.02	.10
21 Allan Bristow CO	.02	.10
22 Dell Curry	.02	.10
23 Kenny Gattison	.02	.10
24 Kendall Gill	.02	.10
25 Larry Johnson	.10	.30
26 Johnny Newman	.02	.10
27 J.R. Reid	.02	.10
28 B.J. Armstrong	.02	.10
29 Bill Cartwright	.02	.10
30 Horace Grant	.02	.10
31 Phil Jackson CO	.02	.10
32 Michael Jordan	1.25	3.00
33 Stacey King	.02	.10
34 Cliff Levingston	.02	.10
35 John Paxson	.02	.10
36 Scottie Pippen	.30	.75
37 Scott Williams	.02	.10
38 John Battle	.02	.10
39 Terrell Brandon	.08	.25
40 Brad Daugherty	.02	.10
41 Craig Ehlo	.02	.10
42 Larry Nance	.02	.10
43 Mark Price	.02	.10
44 Mike Sanders	.02	.10
45 Lenny Wilkens CO	.02	.10
46 John Hot Rod Williams	.02	.10
47 Richie Adubato CO	.02	.10
48 Terry Davis	.02	.10
49 Derek Harper	.02	.10
50 Donald Hodge	.02	.10
51 Mike Iuzzolino	.02	.10
52 Rodney McCray	.02	.10

53 Doug Smith .02 .10
54 Greg Anderson .02 .10
55 Winston Garland .02 .10
56 Dan Issel CO .02 .10
57 Chris Jackson .02 .10
58 Marcus Liberty .02 .10
59 Mark Macon .02 .10
60 Dikembe Mutombo .10 .30
61 Reggie Williams .02 .10
62 Mark Aguirre .02 .10
63 Joe Dumars .08 .25
64 Bill Laimbeer .02 .10
65 Olden Polynice .02 .10
66 Dennis Rodman .20 .50
67 Ron Rothstein CO .02 .10
68 John Salley .02 .10
69 Isiah Thomas .08 .25
70 Darrell Walker .02 .10
71 Orlando Woolridge .02 .10
72 Victor Alexander .02 .10
73 Mario Elie .02 .10
74 Tim Hardaway .10 .30
75 Tyrone Hill .02 .10
76 Sarunas Marciulionis .02 .10
77 Chris Mullin .08 .25
78 Don Nelson CO .02 .10
79 Billy Owens .02 .10
80 Sleepy Floyd UER .02 .10
81 Avery Johnson .02 .10
82 Buck Johnson .02 .10
83 Vernon Maxwell .02 .10
84 Hakeem Olajuwon .15 .40
85 Kenny Smith .02 .10
86 Otis Thorpe .02 .10
87 Rudy Tomjanovich CO .02 .10
88 Dale Davis .02 .10
89 Vern Fleming .02 .10
90 Bob Hill CO .02 .10
91 Reggie Miller .08 .25
92 Chuck Person .02 .10
93 Detlef Schrempf .02 .10
94 Rik Smits .02 .10
95 LaSalle Thompson .02 .10
96 Micheal Williams .02 .10
97 Larry Brown CO .02 .10
98 James Edwards .02 .10
99 Gary Grant .02 .10
100 Ron Harper .02 .10
101 Danny Manning .02 .10
102 Ken Norman .02 .10
103 Doc Rivers .02 .10
104 Charles Smith .02 .10
105 Loy Vaught .02 .10
106 Elden Campbell .02 .10
107 Vlade Divac .02 .10
108 A.C. Green .02 .10
109 Sam Perkins .02 .10
110 Randy Pfund CO RC .02 .10
111 Byron Scott .02 .10
112 Terry Teagle .02 .10
113 Sedale Threatt .02 .10
114 James Worthy .08 .25
115 Willie Burton .02 .10
116 Bimbo Coles .02 .10
117 Kevin Edwards .02 .10
118 Grant Long .02 .10
119 Kevin Loughery CO .02 .10
120 Glen Rice .08 .25
121 Rony Seikaly .02 .10
122 Brian Shaw .02 .10
123 Steve Smith .10 .30
124 Frank Brickowski .02 .10
125 Mike Dunleavy CO .02 .10
126 Blue Edwards .02 .10
127 Moses Malone .08 .25
128 Eric Murdock .02 .10
129 Fred Roberts .02 .10
130 Alvin Robertson .02 .10
131 Thurl Bailey .02 .10
132 Tony Campbell .02 .10
133 Gerald Glass .02 .10
134 Luc Longley .02 .10
135 Sam Mitchell .02 .10
136 Pooh Richardson .02 .10
137 Jimmy Rodgers CO .02 .10
138 Felton Spencer .02 .10
139 Doug West .02 .10
140 Kenny Anderson .08 .25
141 Mookie Blaylock .02 .10
142 Sam Bowie .02 .10
143 Derrick Coleman .02 .10
144 Chuck Daly CO .02 .10
145 Terry Mills .02 .10
146 Chris Morris .02 .10
147 Drazen Petrovic .02 .10
148 Greg Anthony .02 .10
149 Rolando Blackman .02 .10
150 Patrick Ewing .08 .25
151 Mark Jackson .02 .10
152 Anthony Mason .08 .25
153 Xavier McDaniel .02 .10
154 Charles Oakley .02 .10
155 Pat Riley CO .02 .10
156 John Starks .02 .10
157 Gerald Wilkins .02 .10
158 Nick Anderson .02 .10
159 Anthony Bowie .02 .10
160 Terry Catledge .02 .10
161 Matt Guokas CO .02 .10
162 Stanley Roberts .02 .10
163 Dennis Scott .02 .10
164 Scott Skiles .02 .10
165 Brian Williams .02 .10
166 Ron Anderson .02 .10
167 Manute Bol .02 .10
168 Johnny Dawkins .02 .10
169 Armon Gilliam .02 .10
170 Hersey Hawkins .02 .10
171 Jeff Hornacek .02 .10
172 Andrew Lang .02 .10
173 Doug Moe CO .02 .10
174 Tim Perry .02 .10
175 Jeff Ruland .02 .10
176 Charles Shackleford .02 .10
177 Danny Ainge .02 .10
178 Charles Barkley .15 .40
179 Cedric Ceballos .02 .10
180 Tom Chambers .02 .10
181 Kevin Johnson .08 .25
182 Dan Majerle .02 .10
183 Mark West UER .02 .10
184 Paul Westphal CO .02 .10
185 Rick Adelman CO .02 .10
186 Clyde Drexler .08 .25
187 Kevin Duckworth .02 .10
188 Jerome Kersey .02 .10
189 Robert Pack .02 .10
190 Terry Porter .02 .10
191 Clifford Robinson .02 .10
192 Rod Strickland .08 .25
193 Buck Williams .02 .10
194 Anthony Bonner .02 .10
195 Duane Causwell .02 .10
196 Mitch Richmond .08 .25
197 Garry St. Jean CO RC .02 .10
198 Lionel Simmons .02 .10
199 Wayman Tisdale .02 .10
200 Spud Webb .02 .10
201 Willie Anderson .02 .10
202 Antoine Carr .02 .10
203 Terry Cummings .02 .10
204 Sean Elliott .02 .10
205 Dale Ellis .02 .10
206 Vinnie Johnson .02 .10
207 David Robinson .15 .40
208 Jerry Tarkanian CO RC .08 .25
209 Benoit Benjamin .02 .10
210 Michael Cage .02 .10
211 Eddie Johnson .02 .10
212 George Karl CO .02 .10
213 Shawn Kemp .20 .50
214 Derrick McKey .02 .10
215 Nate McMillan .02 .10
216 Gary Payton .20 .50
217 Ricky Pierce .02 .10
218 David Benoit .02 .10
219 Mike Brown .02 .10
220 Tyrone Corbin .02 .10
221 Mark Eaton .02 .10
222 Jay Humphries .02 .10
223 Larry Krystkowiak .02 .10
224 Jeff Malone .02 .10
225 Karl Malone .15 .40
226 Jerry Sloan CO .02 .10
227 John Stockton .08 .25
228 Michael Adams .02 .10
229 Rex Chapman .02 .10
230 Ledell Eackles .02 .10
231 Pervis Ellison .02 .10
232 A.J. English .02 .10
233 Harvey Grant .02 .10
234 LaBradford Smith .02 .10
235 Larry Stewart .02 .10
236 Wes Unseld CO .02 .10
237 David Wingate .02 .10
238 Michael Jordan LL .60 1.50
239 Dennis Rodman LL .08 .25
240 John Stockton LL .02 .10
241 Buck Williams LL .02 .10
242 Mark Price LL .02 .10
243 Dana Barros LL .02 .10
244 David Robinson LL .08 .25
245 Chris Mullin LL .02 .10
246 Michael Jordan MVP .60 1.50
247 Larry Johnson ROY UER .08 .25
248 David Robinson POY .08 .25
249 Detlef Schrempf SM .02 .10
250 Clyde Drexler PV .02 .10
251 Tim Hardaway PV .08 .25
252 Kevin Johnson PV .02 .10
253 Larry Johnson PV UER .08 .25
254 Scottie Pippen PV .15 .40
255 Isiah Thomas PV .02 .10
256 Larry Bird SY .20 .50
257 Brad Daugherty SY .02 .10
258 Kevin Johnson SY .02 .10
259 Larry Johnson SY .08 .25
260 Scottie Pippen SY .15 .40
261 Dennis Rodman SY .08 .25
262 Checklist 1 .02 .10
263 Checklist 2 .02 .10
264 Checklist 3 .02 .10
265 Charles Barkley SD .08 .25
266 Shawn Kemp SD .08 .25
267 Dan Majerle SD .02 .10
268 Karl Malone SD .08 .25
269 Buck Williams SD .02 .10
270 Clyde Drexler SD .02 .10
271 Sean Elliott SD .02 .10
272 Ron Harper SD .02 .10
273 Michael Jordan SD .60 1.50
274 James Worthy SD .02 .10
275 Cedric Ceballos SD .02 .10
276 Larry Nance SD .02 .10
277 Kenny Walker SD .02 .10
278 Spud Webb SD .02 .10
279 Dominique Wilkins SD .02 .10
280 Terrell Brandon SD .02 .10
281 Dee Brown SD .02 .10
282 Kevin Johnson SD .02 .10
283 Doc Rivers SD .02 .10
284 Byron Scott SD .02 .10
285 Manute Bol SD .02 .10
286 Dikembe Mutombo SD .08 .25
287 Robert Parish SD .02 .10
288 David Robinson SD .08 .25
289 Dennis Rodman SD .08 .25
290 Blue Edwards SD .02 .10
291 Patrick Ewing SD .02 .10
292 Larry Johnson SD .08 .25
293 Jerome Kersey SD .02 .10
294 Hakeem Olajuwon SD .08 .25
295 Stacey Augmon SD .02 .10
296 Derrick Coleman SD .02 .10
297 Kendall Gill SD .02 .10
298 Shaquille O'Neal SD 1.25 3.00
299 Scottie Pippen SD .15 .40
300 Darryl Dawkins SD .02 .10
301 Mookie Blaylock .02 .10
302 Adam Keefe RC .02 .10
303 Travis Mays .02 .10
304 Morlon Wiley .02 .10
305 Sherman Douglas .02 .10
306 Joe Kleine .02 .10
307 Xavier McDaniel .02 .10
308 Tony Bennett RC .02 .10
309 Tom Hammonds .02 .10
310 Kevin Lynch .02 .10
311 Alonzo Mourning RC .60 1.50
312 David Wingate .02 .10
313 Rodney McCray .02 .10
314 Will Perdue .02 .10
315 Trent Tucker .02 .10
316 Corey Williams RC .02 .10
317 Danny Ferry .02 .10
318 Jay Guidinger RC .02 .10
319 Jerome Lane .02 .10
320 Gerald Wilkins .02 .10
321 Steve Bardo RC .02 .10
322 Walter Bond RC .02 .10
323 Brian Howard RC .02 .10
324 Tracy Moore RC .02 .10
325 Sean Rooks RC .02 .10
326 Randy White .02 .10
327 Kevin Brooks .02 .10
328 LaPhonso Ellis RC .08 .25
329 Scott Hastings .02 .10
330 Todd Lichti .02 .10
331 Robert Pack .02 .10
332 Bryant Stith RC .02 .10
333 Gerald Glass .02 .10
334 Terry Mills .02 .10
335 Isaiah Morris RC .02 .10
336 Mark Randall .02 .10
337 Danny Young .02 .10
338 Chris Gatling .02 .10
339 Jeff Grayer .02 .10
340 Byron Houston RC .02 .10
341 Keith Jennings RC .02 .10
342 Alton Lister .02 .10
343 Latrell Sprewell RC .75 2.00
344 Scott Brooks .02 .10
345 Matt Bullard .02 .10
346 Carl Herrera .02 .10
347 Robert Horry RC .08 .25
348 Tree Rollins .02 .10
349 Greg Dreiling .02 .10
350 George McCloud .02 .10
351 Sam Mitchell .02 .10
352 Pooh Richardson .02 .10
353 Malik Sealy RC .02 .10
354 Kenny Williams .02 .10
355 Jaren Jackson RC .02 .10
356 Mark Jackson .02 .10
357 Stanley Roberts .02 .10
358 Elmore Spencer RC .02 .10
359 Kiki Vandeweghe .02 .10
360 John S. Williams .02 .10
361 Randy Woods RC .02 .10
362 Duane Cooper RC .02 .10
363 James Edwards .02 .10
364 Anthony Peeler RC .02 .10
365 Tony Smith .02 .10
366 Keith Askins .02 .10
367 Matt Geiger RC .02 .10
368 Alec Kessler .02 .10
369 Harold Miner RC .02 .10
370 John Salley .02 .10
371 Anthony Avent RC .02 .10
372 Todd Day RC .02 .10
373 Blue Edwards .02 .10
374 Brad Lohaus .02 .10
375 Lee Mayberry RC .02 .10
376 Eric Murdock .02 .10
377 Danny Schayes .02 .10
378 Lance Blanks .02 .10
379 Christian Laettner RC .20 .50
380 Bob McCann RC .02 .10
381 Chuck Person .02 .10
382 Brad Sellers .02 .10
383 Chris Smith RC .02 .10
384 Micheal Williams .02 .10
385 Rafael Addison .02 .10
386 Chucky Brown .02 .10
387 Chris Dudley .02 .10
388 Tate George .02 .10
389 Rick Mahorn .02 .10
390 Rumeal Robinson .02 .10
391 Jayson Williams .02 .10
392 Eric Anderson RC .02 .10
393 Rolando Blackman .02 .10
394 Tony Campbell .02 .10
395 Hubert Davis RC .02 .10
396 Doc Rivers .02 .10
397 Charles Smith .02 .10
398 Herb Williams .02 .10
399 Litterial Green RC .02 .10
400 Greg Kite .02 .10
401 Shaquille O'Neal RC 2.50 6.00
402 Jerry Reynolds .02 .10
403 Jeff Turner .02 .10
404 Greg Grant .02 .10
405 Jeff Hornacek .02 .10
406 Andrew Lang .02 .10
407 Kenny Payne .02 .10
408 Tim Perry .02 .10
409 C.Weatherspoon RC .08 .25
410 Danny Ainge .02 .10
411 Charles Barkley .15 .40
412 Negele Knight .02 .10
413 Oliver Miller RC .02 .10
414 Jerrod Mustaf .02 .10
415 Mark Bryant .02 .10
416 Mario Elie .02 .10
417 Dave Johnson RC .02 .10
418 Tracy Murray RC .02 .10
419 Reggie Smith RC .02 .10
420 Rod Strickland .08 .25
421 Randy Brown .02 .10
422 Pete Chilcutt .02 .10
423 Jim Les .02 .10
424 Walt Williams RC .08 .25
425 Lloyd Daniels RC .02 .10
426 Vinny Del Negro .02 .10
427 Dale Ellis .02 .10
428 Sidney Green .02 .10
429 Avery Johnson .02 .10
430 Dana Barros .02 .10
431 Rich King .02 .10
432 Isaac Austin RC .02 .10
433 John Crotty RC .02 .10
434 Stephen Howard RC .02 .10
435 Jay Humphries .02 .10
436 Larry Krystkowiak .02 .10
437 Tom Gugliotta RC .30 .75
438 Buck Johnson .02 .10
439 Charles Jones .02 .10
440 Don MacLean RC .02 .10
441 Doug Overton .02 .10
442 Brent Price RC .02 .10
443 Checklist 1 .02 .10
444 Checklist 2 .02 .10
SD266 Shawn Kemp AU 30.00 80.00
SD277 Kenny Walker AU 15.00 40.00
SD300 Darryl Dawkins AU 15.00 40.00
NNO Slam Dunk Wrapper Exch. 1.25 3.00

1992-93 Fleer All-Stars

%This 24-card standard-size set was randomly inserted in first series 17-card packs and features outstanding players from the Eastern (1-12) and Western (13-24) Conference. According to Fleer's advertising materials, the odds of pulling an All-Star insert are approximately one per nine packs. The horizontal fronts display two color images of the featured player against a gradated silver-blue background. The cards are bordered by a darker silver-blue, and the player's name is gold-foil stamped at the lower right corner. The Orlando All-Star Weekend logo is in the upper right and the team logo in the lower left corner. The backs are white with silver-blue borders and present career highlights, the player's name, and the Orlando All-Star Weekend logo. The cards are numbered on the back in alphabetical order.

COMPLETE SET (24) 25.00 60.00
SER.1 STATED ODDS 1:9
1 Michael Adams .40 1.00
2 Charles Barkley 2.50 6.00
3 Brad Daugherty .40 1.00
4 Joe Dumars 1.50 4.00
5 Patrick Ewing 1.50 4.00
6 Michael Jordan ! 15.00 40.00
7 Reggie Lewis 1.00 2.50
8 Scottie Pippen 5.00 12.00
9 Mark Price .40 1.00
10 Dennis Rodman 3.00 8.00
11 Isiah Thomas 1.50 4.00
12 Kevin Willis .40 1.00
13 Clyde Drexler 1.50 4.00
14 Tim Hardaway 2.00 5.00
15 Jeff Hornacek 1.00 2.50
16 Dan Majerle 1.00 2.50
17 Karl Malone 2.50 6.00
18 Chris Mullin 1.50 4.00
19 Dikembe Mutombo 1.50 4.00
20 Hakeem Olajuwon 2.50 6.00
21 David Robinson 2.50 6.00
22 John Stockton 1.50 4.00
23 Otis Thorpe 1.00 2.50
24 James Worthy 1.50 4.00

1992-93 Fleer Larry Johnson Promo

This Larry Johnson Commemorative Card was issued to announce the introduction of the 1992-93 Fleer NBA set featuring Larry Johnson. The standard-size card features a posed color photo of Larry Johnson with Paul Mullan, chairman and CEO of Fleercorp. The card has a gold metallic border and Larry Johnson's name is printed vertically in white lettering on blue and blue-green wedge-shaped stripes that have a pebble-grain texture. Paul Mullan's name is superimposed on the picture. A '92 Commemorative Card logo is in the lower right corner. The back has a beige pebble-grain background and displays information about the 1992-93 Fleer NBA set and the 1992-93 Fleer Larry Johnson NBA Rookie of the Year 12-card subset. The card is unnumbered.

NNO Larry Johnson 4.00 10.00
(With Paul Mullan, CEO of Fleer)

1992-93 Fleer Larry Johnson

Larry Johnson, the 1991-92 NBA Rookie of the Year, is featured in this 15-card signature series. The first 12 cards were available as random inserts in all forms of Fleer's first series packaging. The odds of pulling a Larry Johnson insert from a 17-card pack were one in 18, from a 32-card cello pack were one in 13 and from a 42-card rack pack were one in six. In addition, Larry personally autographed more than 2,000 of these cards, which were randomly inserted in the wax packs. These cards feature embossed Fleer logos on front for authenticity. According to Fleer's advertising materials, the odds of finding a signed Larry Johnson were approximately one in 15,000 packs. Collectors were also able to receive three additional Johnson cards and the premiere edition of NBA Inside Stuff magazine by sending in ten wrappers and 1.00 in a mail-in offer expiring 6/30/93. These standard-size cards feature color player photos framed by thin orange and blue borders on a silver-blue card face. The player's name and the words "NBA Rookie of the Year" are gold foil-stamped at the top. The backs feature an orange panel that summarizes Johnson's game and demeanor. His name and "NBA Rookie of the Year" appear at the top in a lighter orange.

COMMON L.JOHNSON (1-12) .50 1.25
SER.1 STATED ODDS 1:18
COMMON AUTOGRAPH (AU) 10.00 25.00
COMMON SEND-OFF (13-15) 1.50 4.00
THREE CARDS PER 10 SER.1 WRAPPERS
LJ WRAPPER EXPIRATION: 6/30/93

1992-93 Fleer Rookie Sensations

Randomly inserted in first series 32-card cello packs, this set features 12 of the top rookies from the 1991-92 season. According to information released by Fleer, the odds of pulling a Rookie Sensation is approximately one per five packs. Measuring the standard size, the cards feature the player in action against a computer generated team emblem on a gradated purple background. The words "Rookie Sensations" and the player's name are gold foil-stamped at the bottom. The backs display career highlights on a mint-green face with a purple border. The cards are numbered on the back in alphabetical order.

COMPLETE SET (12) 8.00 20.00
SER.1 STATED ODDS 1:5 CELLO
1 Greg Anthony .40 1.00
2 Stacey Augmon .75 2.00
3 Terrell Brandon 2.00 5.00
4 Rick Fox .75 2.00
5 Larry Johnson 2.50 6.00
6 Mark Macon .40 1.00
7 Dikembe Mutombo 2.50 6.00
8 Billy Owens .75 2.00
9 Stanley Roberts .40 1.00
10 Doug Smith .40 1.00
11 Steve Smith 2.50 6.00
12 Larry Stewart .40 1.00

1992-93 Fleer Sharpshooters

Randomly inserted in second series 15-card plastic-wrap packs, these 18 standard-size cards feature some of the NBA's best shooters. According to Fleer's advertising materials, the odds of finding a Sharpshooter card are approximately one in three packs. The color action photos on the fronts are odd-shaped, overlaying a purple geometric shape and resting on a silver card face. The "Sharp Shooter" logo is gold-foil stamped at the upper left corner, while the player's name is gold-foil stamped below the picture. On a wheat-colored panel inside blue borders, the backs present a player profile.

COMPLETE SET (18) 10.00 20.00
SER.2 STATED ODDS 1:3
1 Reggie Miller 1.50 4.00
2 Dana Barros .30 .75
3 Jeff Hornacek .60 1.50
4 Drazen Petrovic .30 .75
5 Glen Rice 1.50 4.00
6 Terry Porter .30 .75
7 Mark Price .30 .75
8 Michael Adams .30 .75
9 Hersey Hawkins .60 1.50
10 Chuck Person .30 .75
11 John Stockton 1.50 4.00
12 Dale Ellis .30 .75
13 Clyde Drexler 1.50 4.00
14 Mitch Richmond 1.50 4.00
15 Craig Ehlo .30 .75
16 Dell Curry .30 .75
17 Chris Mullin 1.50 4.00
18 Rolando Blackman .30 .75

1992-93 Fleer Team Leaders

The 1992-93 Fleer Team Leaders were inserted into five of every six first series 42-card rack packs. A Larry Johnson Signature Series insert card replaced a Team Leader in every sixth rack pack. These 27 standard size cards feature a key member of each NBA team. The color action photos on the front are surrounded by thick dark blue borders, covered by a slick UV coating and stamped with gold foil printing. Because of the dark borders, these cards are condition sensitive. The full-color card backs include a player head shot accompanied by written text summarizing the player's career. The cards are numbered on the back in alphabetical order by team. A low production run of rack packs has contributed largely to the popularity of this set.

COMPLETE SET (27) 125.00 225.00
ONE TL OR JOHNSON PER SER.1 RACK PACK
1 Dominique Wilkins 5.00 12.00
2 Reggie Lewis 5.00 12.00
3 Larry Johnson 5.00 12.00
4 Michael Jordan ! 50.00 120.00
5 Mark Price 2.50 6.00
6 Terry Davis 2.50 6.00
7 Dikembe Mutombo 5.00 12.00
8 Isiah Thomas 5.00 12.00
9 Chris Mullin 5.00 12.00
10 Hakeem Olajuwon 8.00 20.00
11 Reggie Miller 5.00 12.00
12 Danny Manning 2.50 6.00
13 James Worthy 5.00 12.00
14 Glen Rice 5.00 12.00
15 Alvin Robertson 2.50 6.00
16 Tony Campbell 1.50 4.00
17 Derrick Coleman 2.50 6.00
18 Patrick Ewing 5.00 12.00
19 Scott Skiles 2.50 6.00
20 Hersey Hawkins 2.50 6.00
21 Kevin Johnson 5.00 12.00
22 Clyde Drexler 5.00 12.00
23 Mitch Richmond 5.00 12.00
24 David Robinson 6.00 15.00
25 Ricky Pierce 2.50 6.00
26 Karl Malone 8.00 20.00
27 Pervis Ellison 2.50 6.00

1992-93 Fleer Total D

The 1992-93 Fleer Total D cards were randomly inserted into second series 32-card cello packs. According to Fleer's advertising materials, the odds of pulling a Total D card were approximately one per five packs. These 15 standard size cards feature some of the NBA's top defensive players. Card fronts feature colorized players against a black border, covered with a slick UV coating and gold stamped lettering. Because of these black borders, the cards are condition sensitive. The full-color card backs feature small player head shots accompanied by text describing the player's defensive abilities.

COMPLETE SET (15) 40.00 80.00
SER.2 STATED ODDS 1:5 CELLO
1 David Robinson 2.00 5.00
2 Dennis Rodman 3.00 8.00
3 Scottie Pippen 6.00 15.00
4 Joe Dumars 1.25 3.00
5 Michael Jordan ! 40.00 100.00
6 John Stockton 1.25 3.00
7 Patrick Ewing 1.25 3.00
8 Micheal Williams .60 1.50
9 Larry Nance .60 1.50
10 Buck Williams .75 2.00
11 Alvin Robertson .60 1.50
12 Dikembe Mutombo 1.25 3.00
13 Mookie Blaylock .75 2.00
14 Hakeem Olajuwon 2.00 5.00
15 Rony Seikaly .60 1.50

1992-93 Fleer Drake's

Sponsored by Drake's Bakery, four cards protected by a cello pack were inserted in selected Drake bakery products. The 54 cards in this set measure the standard size. The card design is identical to the 1992-93 Fleer regular issue, with color action player photos bordered in bronze; the only difference is in the card number. A basketball textured design in team colors runs down the right edge of the picture and carries the player's name. The horizontal backs display a player photo in an arch-shaped design that is team colored. Biographical information, statistics, and career highlights round out the back. The background has the texture and color of a basketball. The cards are numbered on the back and checklisted below alphabetically according to teams.

COMPLETE SET (55) 30.00 80.00
1 Dominique Wilkins 1.00 2.50
2 Mookie Blaylock .20 .50
3 Reggie Lewis .60 1.50
4 Dee Brown .25 .60
5 Alonzo Mourning 2.50 6.00
6 Larry Johnson .75 2.00
7 Michael Jordan 12.00 30.00
8 Scottie Pippen 2.50 6.00
9 Mark Price .40 1.00
10 Brad Daugherty .20 .50
11 Derek Harper .40 1.00
12 Sean Rooks .08 .25
13 Dikembe Mutombo .75 2.00
14 Chris Jackson .08 .25
15 Isiah Thomas 1.00 2.50
16 Joe Dumars .75 2.00
17 Chris Mullin .75 2.00
18 Tim Hardaway .60 1.50
19 Hakeem Olajuwon 1.25 3.00
20 Kenny Smith .20 .50
21 Reggie Miller 1.25 3.00
22 Detlef Schrempf .25 .60
23 Danny Manning .30 .75
24 Mark Jackson .40 1.00
25 Sedale Threatt .08 .25
26 James Worthy .75 2.00
27 Glen Rice .40 1.00
28 Rony Seikaly .08 .25
29 Blue Edwards .08 .25
30 Eric Murdock .08 .25
31 Christian Laettner 2.00 5.00
32 Micheal Williams .08 .25
33 Drazen Petrovic 2.00 5.00
34 Derrick Coleman .20 .50
35 Patrick Ewing 1.25 3.00
36 John Starks .40 1.00
37 Shaquille O'Neal 5.00 12.00
38 Scott Skiles .30 .75
39 Jeff Hornacek .40 1.00
40 Clarence Weatherspoon .40 1.00
41 Charles Barkley 1.50 4.00
42 Dan Majerle .50 1.25
43 Clyde Drexler 1.25 3.00
44 Terry Porter .20 .50
45 Mitch Richmond .75 2.00
46 Lionel Simmons .08 .25
47 David Robinson 1.50 4.00
48 Sean Elliott .50 1.25
49 Shawn Kemp 1.00 2.50
50 Gary Payton 1.50 4.00
51 John Stockton 2.00 5.00
52 Karl Malone 1.50 4.00
53 Pervis Ellison .08 .25
54 Tom Gugliotta 1.00 2.50
NNO Checklist Card .08 .25

1992-93 Fleer NBA Rising Stars Magazine Sheet

Inserted as a sheet in the NBA's Rising Stars Magazine, this 8-card sheet features perforated cards utilizing the same design as the 1992-93 base Fleer product. The cards are not numbered and are listed in order from top left to bottom right.

NNO Shaquille O'Neal 3.00 8.00
NNO Lionel Simmons .30 .75
NNO Blue Edwards .30 .75
NNO Gary Payton .50 1.25
NNO Clarence Weatherspoon .30 .75
NNO Cliff Robinson .30 .75
NNO Kenny Anderson .30 .75
NNO Kendall Gill .30 .75
NNO Complete Sheet 5.00 12.00

1992-93 Fleer Spalding Schoolyard Stars

These five standard-size promo cards were produced by Fleer for Spalding, and they were packaged in a cello pack and distributed with the purchase of a specially marked Spalding basketball. The packs are marked "For promotional use only, not for resale." The fronts feature color action player photos with black shadow borders on a gold card face. The player's name is in the upper left corner. The words "NBA Schoolyard Stars" are printed in white and yellow along the left edge of the picture. The backs have a basketball color and texture design with a pale blue shadow-bordered panel. The panel discusses an aspect of the player's game and concludes with several schoolyard tips. The cards are unnumbered and checklisted below in alphabetical order.

COMPLETE SET (5) 1.00 2.50
1 Larry Bird .60 1.50
2 Kevin Johnson .15 .40
3 Larry Johnson .25 .60
4 Scottie Pippen .40 1.00
5 Title Card .02 .10

1992-93 Fleer Team Night Sheets

Each of these 1992-93 Fleer Sheets is perforated and features slots for 12 standard-size player cards. Though some of the sheets show 12 players, others show 10 or 11, with the other slots filled by advertisement cards. We have cataloged the single cards in alphabetical order, followed by the unperforated team sheets. Each sheet was given away in connection with a promotion. The Bulls sheet was available at Shell gas stations in the Chicago area, sold for 99 cents with an eight-gallon minimum purchase. The Mavs sheet was handed out to all attendees of a late season Mavericks-Timberwolves game. The sheet featured one of the first Jim Jackson pro cards due to his late signing. The Magic sheet was promoted by Gooding's, a supermarket chain in central Florida. Its owner, a season ticket holder, sponsored the giveaway of these sheets to the first 15,000 individuals at the Fan Appeal game (the last game of the year). The fronts feature color action player photos, enclosed by metallic bronze borders and accented on the right by two team color-coded pebble-grain stripes. On a tan pebble-grain background, the horizontal back carries on its left side a color close-up framed by an arch. On the right side are the player's name and position on two team color-coded stripes, followed below by biography, statistics, and career highlights. The cards differ from their regular issue counterparts in that they are unnumbered.

1 Nick Anderson .15 .40
2 B.J. Armstrong .15 .40
3 Keith Askins .15 .40
4 Anthony Avent .15 .40
5 John Bagley .15 .40
6 Belk .15 .40
Ad Card
7 Tony Bennett .15 .40
8 Muggsy Bogues .20 .50
9 Walter Bond .15 .40
10 Anthony Bowie .15 .40
11 Frank Brickowski .15 .40
12 Dee Brown .15 .40
13 Willie Burton .15 .40
14 Dexter Cambridge .15 .40
15 Elden Campbell .15 .40
16 Bill Cartwright .20 .50
17 Terry Catledge .15 .40
18 Bimbo Coles .15 .40
19 Duane Cooper .15 .40
20 Dell Curry .15 .40
21 Dale Davis .15 .40
22 Terry Davis .15 .40
23 Todd Day .15 .40
24 Vlade Divac .25 .60
25 Sherman Douglas .15 .40
26 Mike Dunleavy CO .15 .40
27 Blue Edwards .15 .40
28 James Edwards .15 .40
29 Kevin Edwards .15 .40
30 Vern Fleming .15 .40
31 Rick Fox .15 .40
32 Kevin Gamble .15 .40
33 Kenny Gattison .15 .40
34 Kendall Gill .15 .40
35 Mike Gminski .15 .40
36 Gooding's .15 .40
Ad Card
37 Horace Grant .20 .50
38 A.C. Green .20 .50
39 Derek Harper .20 .50
40 Bob Hill CO .15 .40
41 Donald Hodge .15 .40
42 Hugo (Mascot) .15 .40
43 Mike Iuzzolino .15 .40
44 Jim Jackson .20 .50
45 Larry Johnson .25 .60
46 Michael Jordan 2.00 5.00
47 Steve Kerr .20 .50
48 Alec Kessler .15 .40
49 Stacey King .15 .40
50 Greg Kite .15 .40
51 Joe Kleine .15 .40
52 Reggie Lewis .25 .60
53 Brad Lohaus .15 .40
54 Grant Long .15 .40
55 Moses Malone .25 .60
56 Lee Mayberry .15 .40
57 Lay's Potato Chips .15 .40
Ad Card
58 George McCloud .15 .40
59 Rodney McCray .15 .40
60 Xavier McDaniel .15 .40
61 Kevin McHale .30 .75
62 Reggie Miller .30 .75
63 Harold Miner .15 .40
64 Sam Mitchell .15 .40
65 Alonzo Mourning .40 1.00
66 Eric Murdock .15 .40
67 Johnny Newman .15 .40
68 Shaquille O'Neal 1.00 2.50
69 Pacers Gift Shop .15 .40
Ad Card
70 Robert Parish .25 .60
71 John Paxson .20 .50
72 Anthony Peeler .15 .40
73 Will Perdue .15 .40
74 Sam Perkins .15 .40
75 Ed Pinckney .15 .40
76 Scottie Pippen .50 1.25
77 Jerry Reynolds .15 .40
78 Glen Rice .25 .60
79 Pooh Richardson .15 .40
80 Fred Roberts .15 .40
81 Alvin Robertson .15 .40
82 Sean Rooks .15 .40
83 John Salley .15 .40
84 Dan Schayes .15 .40
85 Detlef Schrempf .25 .60
86 Byron Scott .25 .60
87 Dennis Scott .15 .40
88 Malik Sealy .15 .40
89 Rony Seikaly .15 .40
90 Brian Shaw .15 .40
91 Scott Skiles .15 .40
92 Doug Smith .15 .40
93 Steve Smith .20 .50
94 Rik Smits .20 .50
95 LaSalle Thompson .15 .40
96 Sedale Threatt .15 .40
97 Trent Tucker .15 .40
98 Jeff Turner .15 .40
99 Toyota .15 .40
Ad Card
100 UNO Pizzeria .15 .40
Ad Card
101 Randy White .15 .40
102 Morlon Wiley .15 .40
103 Brian Williams .15 .40
104 Corey Williams .15 .40
105 Scott Williams .15 .40
106 David Wingate .15 .40
107 James Worthy .30 .75
108 John Bagley 2.50 6.00
Dee Brown
Sherman Douglas
Rick Fox
Kevin Gamble
Joe Kleine
Reggie Lewis
Xavier McDaniel
Kevin McHale
Robert Parish
Ed Pinckney
UNO Pizzeria (Ad card)
109 Tony Bennett 2.50 6.00
Muggsy Bogues
Dell Curry
Kenny Gattison
Kendall Gill
Mike Gminski
Hugo (Mascot)
Larry Johnson
Alonzo Mourning
Johnny Newman
David Wingate
Belk (Ad Card)
110 B.J. Armstrong 5.00 12.00
Bill Cartwright
Horace Grant
Michael Jordan
Stacey King
Rodney McCray
John Paxson
Will Perdue
Scottie Pippen
Trent Tucker
Corey Williams
Scott Williams
111 Walter Bond 2.50 6.00
Dexter Cambridge
Terry Davis
Derek Harper
Donald Hodge
Mike Iuzzolino
Jim Jackson
Sean Rooks
Doug Smith
Randy White
Morlon Wiley
Lay's Potato Chips/(Ad card)
112 Dale Davis 2.50 6.00
Vern Fleming
Bob Hill CO
George McCloud
Reggie Miller
Sam Mitchell
Pooh Richardson
Detlef Schrempf
Malik Sealy
Rik Smits
LaSalle Thompson
Pacers Gift Shop/(Ad card)
113 Elden Campbell 2.50 6.00
Duane Cooper
Vlade Divac
James Edwards
A.C. Green
Anthony Peeler
Sam Perkins
Byron Scott
Sedale Threatt
James Worthy
Toyota (Two ad cards)
114 Keith Askins 2.50 6.00
Willie Burton
Bimbo Coles
Kevin Edwards
Alec Kessler
Grant Long
Harold Miner
Glen Rice
John Salley
Rony Seikaly
Brian Shaw
Steve Smith
115 Anthony Avent 2.50 6.00
Frank Brickowski
Todd Day
Mike Dunleavy CO
Blue Edwards
Brad Lohaus
Moses Malone
Lee Mayberry
Eric Murdock
Fred Roberts
Alvin Robertson
Dan Schayes
116 Nick Anderson 3.00 8.00
Anthony Bowie
Terry Catledge
Steve Kerr
Greg Kite
Shaquille O'Neal
Jerry Reynolds
Dennis Scott
Scott Skiles
Jeff Turner
Brian Williams
Gooding's (Ad card)

1992-93 Fleer Tony's Pizza

These 108 standard-size cards came three to each pack

(or two cards along with a coupon card) inserted into packages of Tony's frozen pizza. In design, all these cards are identical to 1992-93 Fleer regular issue cards; 72 of them derive from the first series and the 36 Slam Dunk cards derive from the second series. The Slam Dunk cards are harder to find as they were not inserted into the two-card packs that contained the coupon card. The fronts feature gold-bordered color player action photos, with the player's name and position displayed in team color-coded strips along the right edge that have the dimpled look of a basketball. The team logo appears at the bottom right. The simulated basketball texture continues on the horizontal reverse, but in tan. A color player action picture graces the left side, and a stat table is shown on the right. The player's name and position appear in team color-coded bars at the top. A brief biography and the team logo appear beneath and to the right, respectively, of the bars. Unlike the regular issue cards, these cards are unnumbered and thus checklisted below in alphabetical order.

COMPLETE SET (110) 12.50 30.00
1 Chris Jackson .08 .25
2 Michael Adams .08 .25
3 Kenny Anderson .20 .50
4 Willie Anderson .08 .25
5 Greg Anthony .08 .25
6 B.J. Armstrong .08 .25
7 Stacey Augmon SD .40 1.00
8 Thurl Bailey .08 .25
9 Charles Barkley SD 2.00 5.00
10 Benoit Benjamin .08 .25
11 Muggsy Bogues .30 .75
12 Manute Bol SD .50 1.25
13 Sam Bowie .08 .25
14 Terrell Brandon SD .40 1.00
15 Frank Brickowski .08 .25
16 Dee Brown SD .40 1.00
17 Terry Davis .08 .25
17 Michael Cage .08 .25
18 Antoine Carr .08 .25
19 Duane Causwell .08 .25
20 Cedric Ceballos SD .40 1.00
21 Rex Chapman .20 .50
22 Derrick Coleman SD .40 1.00
23 Tyrone Corbin .08 .25
24 Brad Daugherty .08 .25
26 Darryl Dawkins SD .40 1.00
27 Johnny Dawkins .08 .25
28 Brian Williams .08 .25
29 Vlade Divac .20 .50
30 Clyde Drexler SD 1.50 4.00
31 Joe Dumars .60 1.50
32 Blue Edwards SD .40 1.00
33 Craig Ehlo .08 .25
34 Sean Elliott SD .60 1.50
35 Pervis Ellison .08 .25
36 Patrick Ewing SD 1.25 3.00
37 Duane Ferrell .08 .25
37 Kevin McHale .75 2.00
38 Vern Fleming .08 .25
39 Winston Garland .08 .25
40 Kendall Gill SD .50 1.25
41 Horace Grant .40 1.00
42 Tim Hardaway .60 1.50
43 Derek Harper .20 .50
44 Ron Harper SD .60 1.50
45 Hersey Hawkins .20 .50
46 Kevin Johnson SD .50 1.25
47 Larry Johnson SD .60 1.50
48 Michael Jordan SD 6.00 15.00
49 Shawn Kemp SD .75 2.00
50 Jerome Kersey SD .40 1.00
51 Stacey King .20 .50
52 Reggie Lewis .30 .75
53 Dan Majerle SD .50 1.25
54 Jeff Malone .08 .25
55 Karl Malone SD 1.50 4.00
56 Moses Malone .40 1.00
57 Danny Manning .20 .50
58 Sarunas Marciulionis .08 .25
59 Vernon Maxwell .08 .25
61 Reggie Miller 1.25 3.00
62 Chris Mullin .60 1.50
63 Dikembe Mutombo SD .60 1.50
64 Larry Nance SD .50 1.25
65 Ken Norman .08 .25
66 Charles Oakley .20 .50
67 Hakeem Olajuwon SD 1.00 2.50
68 Shaquille O'Neal SD 6.00 15.00
69 Billy Owens .08 .25
70 Robert Parish SD .50 1.25
71 Drazen Petrovic 1.00 2.50
72 Ricky Pierce .08 .25
73 Scottie Pippen SD 1.50 4.00
74 J.R. Reid .08 .25
75 Glen Rice .40 1.00
76 Mitch Richmond .50 1.25
77 Doc Rivers SD .50 1.25
78 Alvin Robertson .08 .25
79 Clifford Robinson .20 .50
80 David Robinson SD 1.50 4.00
81 Rumeal Robinson .08 .25
82 Dennis Rodman SD 1.00 2.50
83 Detlef Schrempf .20 .50
84 Byron Scott SD .50 1.25
85 Dennis Scott .08 .25
86 Rony Seikaly .08 .25
87 Charles Shackleford .08 .25
88 Brian Shaw .08 .25
89 Scott Skiles .20 .50
90 Doug Smith .08 .25
91 Kenny Smith .20 .50
92 Steve Smith .40 1.00
93 Felton Spencer .08 .25
94 John Stockton 1.25 3.00
95 Isiah Thomas .75 2.00
96 Otis Thorpe .20 .50
97 Sedale Threatt .08 .25
98 Wayman Tisdale .08 .25
99 Loy Vaught .08 .25
100 Kenny Walker SD .40 1.00
101 Spud Webb SD .50 1.25
102 Doug West .08 .25
103 Dominique Wilkins SD 1.25 3.00
104 Buck Williams SD .50 1.25
105 Micheal Williams .08 .25
106 Reggie Williams .08 .25
107 Scott Williams .08 .25
108 Orlando Woolridge .08 .25
109 James Worthy SD .60 1.50
XX Coupon Card .20 .50

1993-94 Fleer

The 1993-94 Fleer basketball card set contains 400 standard-size cards. The set was issued in two series consisting of 240 and 160 cards. Cards were primarily distributed in 15-card wax packs (1.29 suggested retail) and 21-card cello packs (1.99). Unlike the first series packs, all second series packs contained an insert card. There are 36 packs per wax box. The fronts are UV-coated and feature color action player photos and are enclosed by white borders. The player's name appears in the lower left and is superimposed over a colorful florescent background. The backs feature full-color printing and bold graphics combining the player's picture, name, and complete statistics. With the exception of card numbers 131, 174, and 216, the cards are numbered and checklisted below alphabetically in team order. Subsets are NBA League Leaders (221-228), NBA Award Winners (229-232), Pro-Visions (223-237), and checklists (238-240). Players traded since the first series are pictured with their new team in a 160-card second series (241-400) offering. Rookie Cards of note include Vin Baker, Anfernee Hardaway, Jamal Mashburn, Nick Van Exel and Chris Webber.

COMPLETE SET (400) 10.00 20.00
COMPLETE SERIES 1 (240) 5.00 10.00
COMPLETE SERIES 2 (160) 5.00 10.00
1 Stacey Augmon .07 .20
2 Mookie Blaylock .05 .15
3 Duane Ferrell .05 .15
4 Paul Graham .05 .15
5 Adam Keefe .05 .15
6 Jon Koncak .05 .15
7 Dominique Wilkins .12 .30
8 Kevin Willis .05 .15
9 Alaa Abdelnaby .05 .15
10 Dee Brown .05 .15
11 Sherman Douglas .05 .15
12 Rick Fox .05 .15
13 Kevin Gamble .05 .15
14 Reggie Lewis .10 .25
15 Xavier McDaniel .05 .15
16 Robert Parish .10 .25
17 Muggsy Bogues .07 .20
18 Dell Curry .05 .15
19 Kenny Gattison .05 .15
20 Kendall Gill .05 .15
21 Larry Johnson .10 .25
22 Alonzo Mourning .15 .40
23 Johnny Newman .05 .15
24 David Wingate .05 .15
25 B.J. Armstrong .05 .15
26 Bill Cartwright .07 .20
27 Horace Grant .07 .20
28 Michael Jordan .75 2.00
29 Stacey King .05 .15
30 John Paxson .07 .20
31 Will Perdue .05 .15
32 Scottie Pippen .20 .50
33 Scott Williams .05 .15
34 Terrell Brandon .07 .20
35 Brad Daugherty .07 .20
36 Craig Ehlo .05 .15
37 Danny Ferry .05 .15
38 Larry Nance .07 .20
39 Mark Price .10 .25
40 Mike Sanders .05 .15
41 Gerald Wilkins .05 .15
42 John Williams .05 .15
43 Terry Davis .05 .15
44 Derek Harper .07 .20
45 Mike Iuzzolino .05 .15
46 Jim Jackson .07 .20
47 Sean Rooks .05 .15
48 Doug Smith .05 .15
49 Randy White .05 .15
50 Mahmoud Abdul-Rauf .05 .15
51 LaPhonso Ellis .05 .15
52 Marcus Liberty .05 .15
53 Mark Macon .05 .15
54 Dikembe Mutombo .10 .25
55 Robert Pack .05 .15
56 Bryant Stith .05 .15
57 Reggie Williams .05 .15
58 Mark Aguirre .07 .20
59 Joe Dumars .10 .25
60 Bill Laimbeer .07 .20
61 Terry Mills .05 .15
62 Olden Polynice .05 .15
63 Alvin Robertson .05 .15
64 Dennis Rodman .20 .50
65 Isiah Thomas .10 .25
66 Victor Alexander .05 .15
67 Tim Hardaway .10 .25
68 Tyrone Hill .05 .15
69 Byron Houston .05 .15
70 Sarunas Marciulionis .05 .15
71 Chris Mullin .10 .25
72 Billy Owens .05 .15
73 Latrell Sprewell .15 .40
74 Scott Brooks .05 .15
75 Matt Bullard .05 .15
76 Carl Herrera .05 .15
77 Robert Horry .10 .25
78 Vernon Maxwell .05 .15
79 Hakeem Olajuwon .12 .30
80 Kenny Smith .07 .20
81 Otis Thorpe .05 .15
82 Dale Davis .05 .15
83 Vern Fleming .05 .15
84 George McCloud .05 .15
85 Reggie Miller .12 .30
86 Sam Mitchell .05 .15
87 Pooh Richardson .05 .15
88 Detlef Schrempf .10 .25
89 Rik Smits .07 .20
90 Gary Grant .05 .15
91 Ron Harper .07 .20
92 Mark Jackson .07 .20
93 Danny Manning .07 .20
94 Ken Norman .05 .15
95 Stanley Roberts .05 .15
96 Loy Vaught .05 .15
97 John Williams .05 .15
98 Elden Campbell .05 .15
99 Doug Christie .05 .15
100 Duane Cooper .05 .15
101 Vlade Divac .10 .25
102 A.C. Green .07 .20
103 Anthony Peeler .05 .15
104 Sedale Threatt .05 .15
105 James Worthy .12 .30
106 Bimbo Coles .05 .15
107 Grant Long .05 .15
108 Harold Miner .05 .15
109 Glen Rice .10 .25
110 John Salley .05 .15
111 Rony Seikaly .05 .15
112 Brian Shaw .05 .15
113 Steve Smith .07 .20
114 Anthony Avent .05 .15
115 Jon Barry .05 .15
116 Frank Brickowski .05 .15
117 Todd Day .05 .15
118 Blue Edwards .05 .15
119 Brad Lohaus .05 .15
120 Lee Mayberry .05 .15
121 Eric Murdock .05 .15
122 Thurl Bailey .05 .15
123 Christian Laettner .07 .20
124 Luc Longley .07 .20
125 Chuck Person .07 .20
126 Felton Spencer .05 .15
127 Doug West .05 .15
128 Micheal Williams .05 .15
129 Rafael Addison .05 .15
130 Kenny Anderson .07 .20
131 Sam Bowie .05 .15
132 Chucky Brown .05 .15
133 Derrick Coleman .07 .20
134 Chris Dudley .05 .15
135 Chris Morris .05 .15
136 Rumeal Robinson .05 .15
137 Greg Anthony .05 .15
138 Rolando Blackman .07 .20
139 Tony Campbell .05 .15
140 Hubert Davis .05 .15
141 Patrick Ewing .12 .30
142 Anthony Mason .05 .15
143 Charles Oakley .07 .20
144 Doc Rivers .07 .20
145 Charles Smith .05 .15
146 John Starks .07 .20
147 Nick Anderson .05 .15
148 Anthony Bowie .05 .15
149 Shaquille O'Neal .40 1.00
150 Donald Royal .05 .15
151 Dennis Scott .05 .15
152 Scott Skiles .05 .15
153 Tom Tolbert .05 .15
154 Jeff Turner .05 .15
155 Ron Anderson .05 .15
156 Johnny Dawkins .05 .15
157 Hersey Hawkins .05 .15
158 Jeff Hornacek .07 .20
159 Andrew Lang .05 .15
160 Tim Perry .05 .15
161 Clarence Weatherspoon .05 .15
162 Danny Ainge .10 .25
163 Charles Barkley .15 .40
164 Cedric Ceballos .07 .20
165 Tom Chambers .07 .20
166 Richard Dumas .05 .15
167 Kevin Johnson .10 .25
168 Negele Knight .05 .15
169 Dan Majerle .10 .25
170 Oliver Miller .05 .15
171 Mark West .05 .15
172 Mark Bryant .05 .15
173 Clyde Drexler .12 .30
174 Kevin Duckworth .05 .15
175 Mario Elie .05 .15
176 Jerome Kersey .05 .15
177 Terry Porter .05 .15
178 Clifford Robinson .05 .15
179 Rod Strickland .05 .15
180 Buck Williams .05 .15
181 Anthony Bonner .05 .15
182 Duane Causwell .05 .15
183 Mitch Richmond .10 .25
184 Lionel Simmons .05 .15
185 Wayman Tisdale .05 .15
186 Spud Webb .07 .20
187 Walt Williams .05 .15
188 Antoine Carr .05 .15
189 Terry Cummings .07 .20
190 Lloyd Daniels .05 .15
191 Vinny Del Negro .05 .15
192 Sean Elliott .10 .25
193 Dale Ellis .05 .15
194 Avery Johnson .07 .20
195 J.R. Reid .05 .15
196 David Robinson .15 .40
197 Michael Cage .05 .15
198 Eddie Johnson .05 .15
199 Shawn Kemp .12 .30
200 Derrick McKey .05 .15
201 Nate McMillan .05 .15
202 Gary Payton .12 .30
203 Sam Perkins .05 .15
204 Ricky Pierce .05 .15
205 David Benoit .05 .15
206 Tyrone Corbin .05 .15
207 Mark Eaton .05 .15
208 Jay Humphries .05 .15
209 Larry Krystkowiak .05 .15
210 Jeff Malone .05 .15
211 Karl Malone .12 .30
212 John Stockton .12 .30
213 Michael Adams .05 .15
214 Rex Chapman .05 .15
215 Pervis Ellison .05 .15
216 Harvey Grant .05 .15
217 Tom Gugliotta .07 .20
218 Buck Johnson .05 .15
219 LaBradford Smith .05 .15
220 Larry Stewart .05 .15
221 B.J. Armstrong LL .05 .15
222 Cedric Ceballos LL .07 .20
223 Larry Johnson LL .10 .25
224 Michael Jordan LL .75 2.00
225 Hakeem Olajuwon LL .12 .30
226 Mark Price LL .10 .25
227 Dennis Rodman LL .20 .50
228 John Stockton LL .12 .30
229 Charles Barkley AW .15 .40
230 Hakeem Olajuwon AW .12 .30
231 Shaquille O'Neal AW .40 1.00
232 Clifford Robinson AW .05 .15
233 Shawn Kemp PV .12 .30
234 Alonzo Mourning PV .15 .40
235 Hakeem Olajuwon PV .12 .30
236 John Stockton PV .12 .30
237 Dominique Wilkins PV .12 .30
238 Checklist 1-85 .05 .15
239 Checklist 86-165 .05 .15
240 Checklist 166-240 UER .05 .15
241 Doug Edwards RC .15 .40
242 Craig Ehlo .05 .15
243 Andrew Lang .05 .15
244 Ennis Whatley .05 .15
245 Chris Corchiani .05 .15
246 Acie Earl RC .15 .40
247 Jimmy Oliver .05 .15
248 Ed Pinckney .05 .15
249 Dino Radja RC .15 .40
250 Matt Wenstrom RC .15 .40
251 Tony Bennett .05 .15
252 Scott Burrell RC .15 .40
253 LeRon Ellis .05 .15
254 Hersey Hawkins .05 .15
255 Eddie Johnson .05 .15
256 Corie Blount RC .15 .40
257 Jo Jo English RC .15 .40
258 Dave Johnson .05 .15
259 Steve Kerr .07 .20
260 Toni Kukoc RC .40 1.00
261 Pete Myers .05 .15
262 Bill Wennington .05 .15
263 John Battle .05 .15
264 Tyrone Hill .05 .15
265 Gerald Madkins RC .15 .40
266 Chris Mills RC .15 .40
267 Bobby Phills .05 .15
268 Greg Dreiling .05 .15
269 Lucious Harris RC .15 .40
270 Donald Hodge .05 .15
271 Popeye Jones RC .15 .40
272 Tim Legler RC .15 .40
273 Fat Lever .07 .20
274 Jamal Mashburn RC .25 .60
275 Darren Morningstar RC .15 .40
276 Tom Hammonds .05 .15
277 Darnell Mee RC .15 .40
278 Rodney Rogers RC .15 .40
279 Brian Williams .05 .15
280 Greg Anderson .05 .15
281 Sean Elliott .10 .25
282 Allan Houston RC .30 .75
283 Lindsey Hunter RC .15 .40
284 Marcus Liberty .05 .15
285 Mark Macon .05 .15
286 David Wood .05 .15
287 Jud Buechler .05 .15
288 Chris Gatling .05 .15
289 Josh Grant RC .15 .40
290 Jeff Grayer .05 .15
291 Avery Johnson .07 .20
292 Chris Webber RC .75 2.00
293 Sam Cassell RC .30 .75
294 Mario Elie .05 .15
295 Richard Petruska RC .15 .40
296 Eric Riley RC .15 .40
297 Antonio Davis RC .20 .50
298 Scott Haskin RC .15 .40
299 Derrick McKey .05 .15
300 Byron Scott .10 .25
301 Malik Sealy .05 .15
302 LaSalle Thompson .05 .15
303 Kenny Williams .05 .15
304 Haywoode Workman .05 .15
305 Mark Aguirre .07 .20
306 Terry Dehere RC .15 .40
307 Bob Martin RC .15 .40
308 Elmore Spencer .05 .15
309 Tom Tolbert .05 .15
310 Randy Woods .05 .15
311 Sam Bowie .05 .15
312 James Edwards .05 .15
313 Antonio Harvey RC .15 .40
314 George Lynch RC .15 .40
315 Tony Smith .05 .15
316 Nick Van Exel RC .30 .75
317 Manute Bol .05 .15
318 Willie Burton .05 .15
319 Matt Geiger .05 .15
320 Alec Kessler .05 .15
321 Vin Baker RC .25 .60
322 Ken Norman .05 .15
323 Danny Schayes .05 .15
324 Derek Strong RC .15 .40
325 Mike Brown .05 .15
326 Brian Davis RC .15 .40
327 Tellis Frank .05 .15
328 Marlon Maxey .05 .15
329 Isaiah Rider RC .25 .60
330 Chris Smith .05 .15
331 Benoit Benjamin .05 .15
332 P.J. Brown RC .15 .40
333 Kevin Edwards .05 .15
334 Armon Gilliam .05 .15
335 Rick Mahorn .05 .15
336 Dwayne Schintzius .05 .15
337 Rex Walters RC .15 .40
338 David Wesley RC .15 .40
339 Jayson Williams .05 .15
340 Anthony Bonner .05 .15
341 Herb Williams .05 .15
342 Litterial Green .05 .15
343 Anfernee Hardaway RC .75 2.00
344 Greg Kite .05 .15
345 Larry Krystkowiak .05 .15
346 Todd Lichti .05 .15
347 Keith Tower RC .15 .40
348 Dana Barros .05 .15
349 Shawn Bradley RC .15 .40
350 Michael Curry RC .15 .40
351 Greg Graham RC .15 .40
352 Warren Kidd RC .15 .40
353 Moses Malone .10 .25
354 Orlando Woolridge .05 .15
355 Duane Cooper .05 .15
356 Joe Courtney RC .15 .40
357 A.C. Green .07 .20
358 Frank Johnson .05 .15
359 Joe Kleine .05 .15
360 Malcolm Mackey RC .15 .40
361 Jerrod Mustaf .05 .15
362 Chris Dudley .05 .15
363 Harvey Grant .05 .15
364 Tracy Murray .05 .15
365 James Robinson RC .15 .40
366 Reggie Smith .05 .15
367 Kevin Thompson RC .15 .40
368 Randy Breuer .05 .15
369 Randy Brown .05 .15
370 Evers Burns RC .15 .40
371 Pete Chilcutt .05 .15
372 Bobby Hurley RC .15 .40
373 Jim Les .05 .15
374 Mike Peplowski RC .15 .40
375 Willie Anderson .05 .15
376 Sleepy Floyd .05 .15
377 Negele Knight .05 .15
378 Dennis Rodman .20 .50
379 Chris Whitney RC .15 .40
380 Vincent Askew .05 .15
381 Kendall Gill .05 .15
382 Ervin Johnson RC .15 .40
383 Chris King RC .15 .40
384 Rich King .05 .15
385 Steve Scheffler .05 .15
386 Detlef Schrempf .10 .25
387 Tom Chambers .07 .20
388 John Crotty .05 .15
389 Bryon Russell RC .15 .40
390 Felton Spencer .05 .15
391 Luther Wright RC .15 .40
392 Mitchell Butler RC .15 .40
393 Calbert Cheaney RC .15 .40
394 Kevin Duckworth .05 .15
395 Don MacLean .05 .15
396 Gheorghe Muresan RC .15 .40
397 Doug Overton .05 .15
398 Brent Price .05 .15
399 Checklist .05 .15
400 Checklist .05 .15

1993-94 Fleer All-Stars

Randomly inserted in 1993-94 Fleer first series 15-card packs, this 24-card standard-size set features 12 players from the Eastern Conference (1-12) and the Western Conference (13-24) that participated in the 1992-93 All-Star Game in Salt Lake City. According to wrapper information, All-Stars are randomly inserted into one of every 10 packs. The fronts are UV-coated and feature color action player photos enclosed by purple borders. The NBA All-Star logo appears in the lower left or right corner. The player's name is stamped in gold foil and appears at the bottom. The backs are also UV-coated and feature a full-color shot of the player along with a statistical performance sketch from the previous year. Each division's All-Stars are in alphabetical order.

COMPLETE SET (24) 10.00 25.00
SER.1 STATED ODDS 1:10 HOBBY
1 Brad Daugherty .50 1.25
2 Joe Dumars .60 1.50
3 Patrick Ewing .75 2.00
4 Larry Johnson .60 1.50
5 Michael Jordan 5.00 12.00
6 Larry Nance .50 1.25
7 Shaquille O'Neal 2.50 6.00
8 Scottie Pippen UER 2.50 6.00
9 Mark Price .60 1.50
10 Detlef Schrempf .60 1.50
11 Isiah Thomas .60 1.50
12 Dominique Wilkins .75 2.00
13 Charles Barkley 1.00 2.50
14 Clyde Drexler .75 2.00
15 Sean Elliott .60 1.50
16 Tim Hardaway .60 1.50
17 Shawn Kemp .75 2.00
18 Dan Majerle .60 1.50
19 Karl Malone .75 2.00
20 Danny Manning .50 1.25
21 Hakeem Olajuwon .75 2.00
22 Terry Porter .40 1.00
23 David Robinson 1.00 2.50
24 John Stockton .75 2.00

1993-94 Fleer Clyde Drexler

Randomly inserted in all 1993-94 Fleer first series packs at an approximate rate of one in six, this 12-card standard-size set captures the greatest moments in Drexler's career. Drexler autographed more than 2,000 of his cards. These cards are embossed with Fleer logos for authenticity. Odds of getting a signed card were approximately 1 in 7,000 packs. The collector could acquire three additional cards and an issue of NBA Inside Stuff magazine through a mail-in for ten wrappers plus 1.50. The offer expired June 10, 1994. An additional card (No. 16) was offered free to collectors who subscribed to NBA Inside Stuff magazine. Since 12 cards were issued through packs, a 12-card set is considered complete. All 16 cards have the same basic design with the front featuring a unique two photo design, one color, and the other red-screened, serving as the background. The player's name as well as the Fleer logo appear at the top of the card in gold foil. The bottom of the card carries the words "Career Highlights," also stamped in gold foil. The back of the cards carry information about Drexler, with another red-screened photo again as the background. The cards are numbered on the back.The first twelve cards are numbered "X of 12" and the last four cards are simply numbered 13, 14, 15 and 16.

COMPLETE SET (12) 2.50 5.00
COMMON DREXLER (1-12) .20 .50
SER.1 STATED ODDS 1:6
COMMON AUTOGRAPH (AU) 25.00 60.00
DREXLER AU: SER.1 STATED ODDS 1:7,000
COMMON SEND-OFF (13-15) .75 2.00

1993-94 Fleer First Year Phenoms

These 10 standard-size cards feature top rookies from the 1993-94 season. Cards were randomly inserted in 1993-94 Fleer second-series 15-card wax and 21-card jumbo packs. The insertion rate was approximately one in four wax packs and one in three cello packs. The yellow-bordered fronts feature color player action cutouts superposed upon purple, yellow, and black florescent basketball court designs. The player's name appears vertically in gold foil near one corner, and the gold-foil set logo appears at the bottom left. The horizontal back sports a similar florescent design. A color player close-up cutout appears on one side; his name, team, and career highlights appear on the other. The cards are numbered on the back as "X of 10" and sequenced in alphabetical order.

COMPLETE SET (10) 1.50 4.00
SER.2 STATED ODDS 1:4 HOBBY, 1:3 CELLO
1 Shawn Bradley .15 .40
2 Anfernee Hardaway .75 2.00
3 Lindsey Hunter .15 .40
4 Bobby Hurley .15 .40
5 Toni Kukoc .40 1.00
6 Jamal Mashburn .25 .60
7 Dino Radja .15 .40
8 Isaiah Rider .25 .60
9 Nick Van Exel .30 .75
10 Chris Webber .75 2.00

1993-94 Fleer Internationals

This 12-card insert standard-size set features NBA players born outside the United States. The cards were randomly inserted in first series 15-card packs at a rate of one in 10. The fronts are UV-coated and feature a color player photo superimposed over a map of his country of origin. The player's name appears at the top of the card and is gold foil stamped. The backs are also UV-coated and feature a color shot of the player along with a brief biographical sketch. The set is sequenced in alphabetical order.

COMPLETE SET (12) 1.25 3.00
SER.1 STATED ODDS 1:10
1 Alaa Abdelnaby .12 .30
2 Vlade Divac .20 .50
3 Patrick Ewing .25 .60
4 Carl Herrera .12 .30
5 Luc Longley .15 .40
6 Sarunas Marciulionis .12 .30
7 Dikembe Mutombo .20 .50
8 Rumeal Robinson .12 .30
9 Detlef Schrempf .20 .50
10 Rony Seikaly .12 .30
11 Rik Smits .15 .40
12 Dominique Wilkins .25 .60

1993-94 Fleer Living Legends

These six standard-size cards honoring veteran superstars were randomly inserted in 1993-94 Fleer second series 15-card (ratio of one in 37) and 21-card (one in 24) packs. The horizontal fronts feature color player action cutouts superimposed upon a borderless metallic motion-streaked background. The player's name and the set's logo appear at the bottom in gold foil. The horizontal back carries a color player close-up cutout on one side; his name, team, and career highlights appear on the other. The cards are numbered on the back as "X of 6" and are sequenced in alphabetical order

COMPLETE SET (6) 8.00 20.00
SER.2 STATED ODDS 1:37 HOB, 1:24 JUM
1 Charles Barkley 1.25 3.00
2 Larry Bird 2.50 6.00
3 Patrick Ewing 1.00 2.50
4 Michael Jordan 12.00 30.00
5 Hakeem Olajuwon 1.00 2.50
6 Dominique Wilkins 1.00 2.50

1993-94 Fleer Lottery Exchange

This 11-card standard-size set features the top players from the 1993 NBA Draft. Card fronts resemble that of the basic Fleer issue with the exception of a notation of what number pick the player was. Backs have a photo and statistics. The set could be obtained in exchange for the Draft Exchange card that was randomly inserted (one in 180) in first series packs. The expiration date was April 1, 1994. The cards are numbered on the back in draft order.

COMPLETE SET (11) 6.00 15.00
EXCH.CARD: SER.1 STATED ODDS 1:180
1 Chris Webber 3.00 8.00
2 Shawn Bradley .40 1.00
3 Anfernee Hardaway 2.00 5.00
4 Jamal Mashburn .60 1.50
5 Isaiah Rider .60 1.50
6 Calbert Cheaney .40 1.00
7 Bobby Hurley .40 1.00
8 Vin Baker .60 1.50
9 Rodney Rogers .40 1.00
10 Lindsey Hunter .40 1.00
11 Allan Houston .75 2.00
NNO Expired Exchange Card .20 .50

1993-94 Fleer NBA Superstars

These 20 standard-size cards featuring NBA stars were randomly inserted in 1993-94 Fleer second-series 15-card packs. The fronts feature color player action cutouts superimposed upon multiple color action shots on the right side and the player's name in team color-coded vertical block lettering on the left. The set's title appears vertically along the left edge in gold foil. The horizontal back carries a color player close-up cutout on one side; his name, team, and career highlights appear on the other. The cards are numbered on the back as "X of 20" and are sequenced in alphabetical order.

COMPLETE SET (20) 8.00 20.00
RANDOM INSERTS IN SER.2 HOBBY PACKS
1 Mahmoud Abdul-Rauf .20 .50
2 Charles Barkley .50 1.25
3 Derrick Coleman .25 .60
4 Clyde Drexler .40 1.00
5 Joe Dumars .30 .75
6 Patrick Ewing .40 1.00
7 Michael Jordan 2.50 6.00
8 Shawn Kemp .40 1.00
9 Christian Laettner .25 .60
10 Karl Malone .40 1.00
11 Danny Manning .25 .60
12 Reggie Miller .40 1.00
13 Alonzo Mourning .50 1.25
14 Chris Mullin .30 .75
15 Hakeem Olajuwon .40 1.00
16 Shaquille O'Neal 1.25 3.00
17 Mark Price .30 .75
18 Mitch Richmond .30 .75
19 David Robinson .50 1.25
20 Dominique Wilkins .40 1.00

1993-94 Fleer Rookie Sensations

Randomly inserted in 29-card series one jumbo packs, these 24 standard-size UV-coated cards feature top rookies from the 1992-93 season. Odds of finding a Rookie Sensations card are approximately one in every five packs. The cards feature color player action photos on the fronts within silver-colored borders. Each player photo is superimposed upon a card design that has a basketball "earth" at the card bottom radiating "spotlight" beams that shade from yellow to magenta on a sky blue background. The player's name and the Rookie Sensations logo, both stamped in gold foil, appear in the lower left. Bordered in silver, the backs feature color close-ups of the players in the lower right or left. Blue "sky" and two intersecting yellow-to-magenta "spotlight" beams form the background. The player's name appears in silver-colored lettering at the top of the card above the player's NBA rookie-year highlights. The set is sequenced in alphabetical order.

COMPLETE SET (24) 15.00 40.00
SER.1 STATED ODDS 1:5 CELLO
1 Anthony Avent .40 1.00
2 Doug Christie .40 1.00
3 Lloyd Daniels .40 1.00
4 Hubert Davis .40 1.00
5 Todd Day .40 1.00
6 Richard Dumas .40 1.00
7 LaPhonso Ellis .40 1.00
8 Tom Gugliotta .50 1.25
9 Robert Horry .60 1.50
10 Byron Houston .40 1.00
11 Jim Jackson UER .50 1.25
12 Adam Keefe .40 1.00
13 Christian Laettner .50 1.25
14 Lee Mayberry .40 1.00
15 Oliver Miller .40 1.00
16 Harold Miner .40 1.00
17 Alonzo Mourning 2.50 6.00
18 Shaquille O'Neal 6.00 15.00
19 Anthony Peeler .40 1.00
20 Sean Rooks .40 1.00
21 Latrell Sprewell 2.50 6.00
22 Bryant Stith .40 1.00
23 Clarence Weatherspoon .40 1.00
24 Walt Williams .40 1.00

1993-94 Fleer Sharpshooters

These 10 standard-size cards were randomly inserted in 1993-94 Fleer second-series 15-card packs. The fronts feature color player action cutouts superposed upon color-screened action shots. The player's name appears at the upper right in gold foil. The set's logo appears at the bottom left. The black horizontal back carries a color player close-up cutout on one side; his name, card title, and career highlights appear on the other. The cards are numbered on the back as "X of 10" and are sequenced in alphabetical order.

COMPLETE SET (10) 10.00 25.00
RANDOM INSERTS IN SER.2 HOBBY PACKS
1 Tom Gugliotta .40 1.00
2 Jim Jackson .40 1.00
3 Michael Jordan 6.00 15.00
4 Dan Majerle .50 1.25
5 Mark Price .50 1.25
6 Glen Rice .50 1.25
7 Mitch Richmond .50 1.25
8 Latrell Sprewell .75 2.00
9 John Starks .40 1.00
10 Dominique Wilkins .60 1.50

1993-94 Fleer Towers of Power

These 30 standard-size cards were randomly inserted in 1993-94 Fleer second series 21-card jumbo packs at an approximate rate of two in every three packs. The fronts feature color player action cutouts superposed upon borderless backgrounds of city skylines. The player's name appears in gold foil in a lower corner. The gold-foil set logo appears in an upper corner. The back has the same borderless skyline background photo as the front and carries a color player cutout on one side, and his career highlights on the other. The cards are numbered on the back as "X of 30" and sequenced in alphabetical order.

COMPLETE SET (30) 10.00 25.00
SER.2 STATED ODDS 2:3 CELLO
1 Charles Barkley 1.50 4.00
2 Shawn Bradley .60 1.50
3 Derrick Coleman .50 1.25
4 Brad Daugherty .50 1.25
5 Dale Davis .40 1.00
6 Vlade Divac .60 1.50
7 Patrick Ewing .75 2.00
8 Horace Grant .50 1.25
9 Tom Gugliotta .50 1.25
10 Larry Johnson .60 1.50
11 Shawn Kemp 1.25 3.00
12 Christian Laettner .50 1.25
13 Karl Malone 1.50 4.00
14 Danny Manning .50 1.25
15 Jamal Mashburn 1.00 2.50
16 Oliver Miller .40 1.00
17 Alonzo Mourning 1.50 4.00
18 Dikembe Mutombo 1.25 3.00
19 Ken Norman .40 1.00
20 Hakeem Olajuwon 1.50 4.00
21 Shaquille O'Neal 5.00 12.00
22 Robert Parish .60 1.50
23 Olden Polynice .40 1.00
24 Clifford Robinson .40 1.00
25 David Robinson 1.50 4.00
26 Dennis Rodman 2.50 6.00
27 Rony Seikaly .40 1.00
28 Wayman Tisdale .40 1.00
29 Chris Webber 6.00 15.00
30 Dominique Wilkins .75 2.00

1994-95 Fleer

The 390 cards comprising Fleer's '94-95 base-brand standard-size set were distributed in two separate series of 240 and 150 cards each. Cards were distributed in 15-card packs (SRP $1.29), 21-card magazine cello packs (SRP $1.99) and 23-card retail jumbo packs (SRP $2.27). The cards feature color player action shots on their white-bordered fronts. The player's name, team, and position appear in team-colored lettering set on an irregular team-colored foil patch at the lower left. The black-bordered back carries a color player action shot on the left side, with the player's name, biography, team logo, and statistics displayed on a team-colored background on the right. The cards are numbered on the back and grouped alphabetically within teams. Unlike previous years, there were no subset cards featured in this set. Each pack contained at least one insert card. One in every 72 packs (Hot Packs) contained only inserts. Rookie Cards of note in this set include Grant Hill, Juwan Howard, Eddie Jones, Jason Kidd and Glenn Robinson.

COMPLETE SET (390) 12.00 24.00
COMPLETE SERIES 1 (240) 6.00 12.00
COMPLETE SERIES 2 (150) 6.00 12.00
1 Stacey Augmon .12 .30
2 Mookie Blaylock .10 .25
3 Craig Ehlo .10 .25
4 Duane Ferrell .10 .25
5 Adam Keefe .10 .25
6 Jon Koncak .10 .25
7 Andrew Lang .10 .25
8 Danny Manning .12 .30
9 Kevin Willis .10 .25
10 Dee Brown .10 .25
11 Sherman Douglas .10 .25
12 Acie Earl .10 .25
13 Rick Fox .10 .25
14 Kevin Gamble .10 .25
15 Xavier McDaniel .10 .25
16 Robert Parish .15 .40
17 Ed Pinckney .10 .25
18 Dino Radja .10 .25
19 Muggsy Bogues .12 .30
20 Frank Brickowski .10 .25
21 Scott Burrell .10 .25
22 Dell Curry .10 .25
23 Kenny Gattison .10 .25
24 Hersey Hawkins .10 .25
25 Eddie Johnson .10 .25
26 Larry Johnson .15 .40
27 Alonzo Mourning .20 .50
28 David Wingate .10 .25
29 B.J. Armstrong .10 .25
30 Horace Grant .12 .30
31 Steve Kerr .12 .30
32 Toni Kukoc .20 .50
33 Luc Longley .12 .30
34 Pete Myers .10 .25
35 Scottie Pippen .30 .75
36 Bill Wennington .10 .25
37 Scott Williams .10 .25
38 Terrell Brandon .10 .25
39 Brad Daugherty .12 .30
40 Tyrone Hill .10 .25
41 Chris Mills .10 .25
42 Larry Nance .12 .30
43 Bobby Phills .10 .25
44 Mark Price .15 .40
45 Gerald Wilkins .10 .25
46 John Williams .10 .25
47 Lucious Harris .10 .25
48 Donald Hodge .10 .25
49 Jim Jackson .10 .25
50 Popeye Jones .10 .25
51 Tim Legler .10 .25
52 Fat Lever .15 .40
53 Jamal Mashburn .15 .40
54 Sean Rooks .10 .25
55 Doug Smith .10 .25
56 Mahmoud Abdul-Rauf .10 .25
57 LaPhonso Ellis .10 .25
58 Dikembe Mutombo .15 .40
59 Robert Pack .10 .25
60 Rodney Rogers .10 .25
61 Bryant Stith .10 .25
62 Brian Williams .10 .25
63 Reggie Williams .10 .25
64 Greg Anderson .10 .25
65 Joe Dumars .15 .40
66 Sean Elliott .15 .40
67 Allan Houston .15 .40
68 Lindsey Hunter .10 .25
69 Terry Mills .10 .25
70 Victor Alexander .10 .25
71 Chris Gatling .10 .25
72 Tim Hardaway .15 .40
73 Keith Jennings .10 .25
74 Avery Johnson .12 .30
75 Chris Mullin .15 .40
76 Billy Owens .10 .25
77 Latrell Sprewell .20 .50
78 Chris Webber .25 .60
79 Scott Brooks .10 .25
80 Sam Cassell .15 .40
81 Mario Elie .10 .25
82 Carl Herrera .10 .25
83 Robert Horry .15 .40
84 Vernon Maxwell .10 .25
85 Hakeem Olajuwon .20 .50
86 Kenny Smith .12 .30
87 Otis Thorpe .10 .25
88 Antonio Davis .10 .25
89 Dale Davis .10 .25
90 Vern Fleming .10 .25
91 Derrick McKey .10 .25
92 Reggie Miller .20 .50
93 Pooh Richardson .10 .25
94 Byron Scott .12 .30
95 Rik Smits .12 .30
96 Haywoode Workman .10 .25
97 Terry Dehere .10 .25

98 Harold Ellis .10 .25
99 Gary Grant .10 .25
100 Ron Harper .12 .30
101 Mark Jackson .12 .30
102 Stanley Roberts .10 .25
103 Elmore Spencer .10 .25
104 Loy Vaught .10 .25
105 Dominique Wilkins .20 .50
106 Elden Campbell .10 .25
107 Doug Christie .10 .25
108 Vlade Divac .15 .40
109 George Lynch .10 .25
110 Anthony Peeler .10 .25
111 Tony Smith .10 .25
112 Sedale Threatt .10 .25
113 Nick Van Exel .15 .40
114 James Worthy .20 .50
115 Bimbo Coles .10 .25
116 Grant Long .10 .25
117 Harold Miner .10 .25
118 Glen Rice .15 .40
119 John Salley .10 .25
120 Rony Seikaly .10 .25
121 Brian Shaw .10 .25
122 Steve Smith .12 .30
123 Vin Baker .15 .40
124 Jon Barry .10 .25
125 Todd Day .10 .25
126 Blue Edwards .10 .25
127 Lee Mayberry .10 .25
128 Eric Murdock .10 .25
129 Ken Norman .10 .25
130 Derek Strong .10 .25
131 Thurl Bailey .10 .25
132 Stacey King .10 .25
133 Christian Laettner .12 .30
134 Chuck Person .12 .30
135 Isaiah Rider .15 .40
136 Chris Smith .10 .25
137 Doug West .10 .25
138 Micheal Williams .10 .25
139 Kenny Anderson .12 .30
140 Benoit Benjamin .10 .25
141 P.J. Brown .10 .25
142 Derrick Coleman .12 .30
143 Kevin Edwards .10 .25
144 Armon Gilliam .10 .25
145 Chris Morris .10 .25
146 Johnny Newman .10 .25
147 Greg Anthony .10 .25
148 Anthony Bonner .10 .25
149 Hubert Davis .10 .25
150 Patrick Ewing .20 .50
151 Derek Harper .12 .30
152 Anthony Mason .10 .25
153 Charles Oakley .12 .30
154 Doc Rivers .12 .30
155 Charles Smith .10 .25
156 John Starks .12 .30
157 Nick Anderson .10 .25
158 Anthony Avent .10 .25
159 Anfernee Hardaway .25 .60
160 Shaquille O'Neal .40 1.00
161 Donald Royal .10 .25
162 Dennis Scott .10 .25
163 Scott Skiles .10 .25
164 Jeff Turner .10 .25
165 Dana Barros .10 .25
166 Shawn Bradley .10 .25
167 Greg Graham .10 .25
168 Eric Leckner .10 .25
169 Jeff Malone .10 .25
170 Moses Malone .15 .40
171 Tim Perry .10 .25
172 Clarence Weatherspoon .10 .25
173 Orlando Woolridge .10 .25
174 Danny Ainge .15 .40
175 Charles Barkley .25 .60
176 Cedric Ceballos .10 .25
177 A.C. Green .12 .30
178 Kevin Johnson .15 .40
179 Joe Kleine .10 .25
180 Dan Majerle .15 .40
181 Oliver Miller .10 .25
182 Mark West .10 .25
183 Clyde Drexler .20 .50
184 Harvey Grant .10 .25
185 Jerome Kersey .10 .25
186 Tracy Murray .10 .25
187 Terry Porter .10 .25
188 Clifford Robinson .10 .25
189 James Robinson .10 .25
190 Rod Strickland .10 .25
191 Buck Williams .10 .25
192 Duane Causwell .10 .25
193 Bobby Hurley .10 .25
194 Olden Polynice .10 .25
195 Mitch Richmond .15 .40
196 Lionel Simmons .10 .25
197 Wayman Tisdale .10 .25
198 Spud Webb .12 .30
199 Walt Williams .10 .25
200 Trevor Wilson .10 .25
201 Willie Anderson .10 .25
202 Antoine Carr .10 .25
203 Terry Cummings .12 .30
204 Vinny Del Negro .10 .25
205 Dale Ellis .10 .25
206 Negele Knight .10 .25
207 J.R. Reid .10 .25
208 David Robinson .25 .60
209 Dennis Rodman .30 .75
210 Vincent Askew .10 .25
211 Michael Cage .10 .25
212 Kendall Gill .10 .25
213 Shawn Kemp .15 .40
214 Nate McMillan .10 .25
215 Gary Payton .15 .40
216 Sam Perkins .10 .25
217 Ricky Pierce .10 .25
218 Detlef Schrempf .15 .40
219 David Benoit .10 .25
220 Tom Chambers .12 .30
221 Tyrone Corbin .10 .25
222 Jeff Hornacek .12 .30
223 Jay Humphries .10 .25
224 Karl Malone .20 .50
225 Bryon Russell .10 .25
226 Felton Spencer .10 .25
227 John Stockton .20 .50
228 Michael Adams .10 .25
229 Rex Chapman .10 .25
230 Calbert Cheaney .10 .25
231 Kevin Duckworth .10 .25
232 Pervis Ellison .10 .25
233 Tom Gugliotta .10 .25
234 Don MacLean .10 .25
235 Gheorghe Muresan .10 .25
236 Brent Price .10 .25
237 Toronto Raptors Logo .10 .25
238 Checklist .10 .25
239 Checklist .10 .25
240 Checklist .10 .25
241 Sergei Bazarevich RC .15 .40
242 Tyrone Corbin .10 .25
243 Grant Long .10 .25
244 Ken Norman .10 .25
245 Steve Smith .12 .30
246 Fred Vinson .10 .25
247 Blue Edwards .10 .25
248 Greg Minor RC .15 .40
249 Eric Montross RC .12 .30
250 Derek Strong .10 .25
251 David Wesley .10 .25
252 Dominique Wilkins .20 .50
253 Michael Adams .10 .25
254 Tony Bennett .10 .25
255 Darrin Hancock RC .12 .30
256 Robert Parish .15 .40
257 Corie Blount .10 .25
258 Jud Buechler .10 .25
259 Greg Foster .10 .25
260 Ron Harper .12 .30
261 Larry Krystkowiak .10 .25
262 Will Perdue .10 .25
263 Dickey Simpkins RC .12 .30
264 Michael Cage .10 .25
265 Tony Campbell .10 .25
266 Terry Davis .10 .25
267 Tony Dumas RC .15 .40
268 Jason Kidd RC .75 2.00
269 Roy Tarpley .10 .25
270 Morlon Wiley .10 .25
271 Lorenzo Williams .10 .25
272 Dale Ellis .10 .25
273 Tom Hammonds .10 .25
274 Cliff Levingston .10 .25
275 Darnell Mee .10 .25
276 Jalen Rose RC .40 1.00
277 Reggie Slater .10 .25
278 Bill Curley RC .10 .25
279 Johnny Dawkins .10 .25
280 Grant Hill RC .75 2.00
281 Eric Leckner .10 .25
282 Mark Macon .10 .25
283 Oliver Miller .10 .25
284 Mark West .10 .25
285 Manute Bol .10 .25
286 Tom Gugliotta .10 .25
287 Ricky Pierce .10 .25
288 Carlos Rogers RC .12 .30
289 Clifford Rozier RC .10 .25
290 Rony Seikaly .10 .25
291 Tim Breaux .10 .25
292 Chris Jent .10 .25
293 Eric Riley .10 .25
294 Zan Tabak .10 .25
295 Duane Ferrell .10 .25
296 Mark Jackson .12 .30
297 John Williams .10 .25
298 Matt Fish .10 .25
299 Tony Massenburg .10 .25
300 Lamond Murray RC .15 .40
301 Bo Outlaw RC .15 .40
302 Eric Piatkowski RC .20 .50
303 Pooh Richardson .10 .25
304 Randy Woods .10 .25
305 Sam Bowie .10 .25
306 Cedric Ceballos .10 .25
307 Antonio Harvey .10 .25
308 Eddie Jones RC .50 1.25
309 Anthony Miller RC .15 .40
310 Ledell Eackles .10 .25
311 Kevin Gamble .10 .25
312 Brad Lohaus .10 .25
313 Billy Owens .10 .25
314 Khalid Reeves RC .12 .30
315 Kevin Willis .10 .25
316 Marty Conlon .10 .25
317 Eric Mobley RC .10 .25
318 Johnny Newman .10 .25
319 Ed Pinckney .10 .25
320 Glenn Robinson RC .30 .75
321 Mike Brown .10 .25
322 Pat Durham .10 .25
323 Howard Eisley RC .15 .40
324 Andres Guibert .10 .25
325 Donyell Marshall RC .15 .40
326 Sean Rooks .10 .25
327 Yinka Dare RC .10 .25
328 Sleepy Floyd .10 .25
329 Sean Higgins .10 .25
330 Rick Mahorn .10 .25
331 Rex Walters .10 .25
332 Jayson Williams .10 .25
333 Charlie Ward RC .15 .40
334 Herb Williams .10 .25
335 Monty Williams RC .12 .30
336 Anthony Bowie .10 .25
337 Horace Grant .12 .30
338 Geert Hammink .10 .25
339 Tree Rollins .10 .25
340 Brian Shaw .10 .25
341 Brooks Thompson RC .12 .30
342 Derrick Alston RC .10 .25
343 Willie Burton .10 .25
344 Jaren Jackson .10 .25
345 B.J. Tyler RC .10 .25
346 Scott Williams .10 .25
347 Sharone Wright RC .12 .30
348 Antonio Lang RC .15 .40
349 Danny Manning .12 .30
350 Elliot Perry .10 .25
351 Wesley Person RC .15 .40
352 Trevor Ruffin .10 .25
353 Danny Schayes .10 .25
354 Aaron Swinson RC .15 .40
355 Wayman Tisdale .10 .25
356 Mark Bryant .10 .25
357 Chris Dudley .10 .25
358 James Edwards .10 .25
359 Aaron McKie RC .15 .40
360 Alaa Abdelnaby .10 .25
361 Frank Brickowski .10 .25
362 Randy Brown .10 .25
363 Brian Grant RC .25 .60
364 Michael Smith RC .10 .25
365 Henry Turner .10 .25
366 Sean Elliott .15 .40
367 Avery Johnson .12 .30
368 Moses Malone .15 .40
369 Julius Nwosu .10 .25
370 Chuck Person .12 .30
371 Chris Whitney .10 .25
372 Bill Cartwright .12 .30
373 Byron Houston .10 .25
374 Ervin Johnson .10 .25
375 Sarunas Marciulionis .10 .25
376 Antoine Carr .10 .25
377 John Crotty .10 .25
378 Adam Keefe .10 .25
379 Jamie Watson RC .10 .25
380 Mitchell Butler .10 .25
381 Juwan Howard RC .25 .60
382 Jim McIlvaine RC .12 .30
383 Doug Overton .10 .25
384 Scott Skiles .10 .25
385 Larry Stewart .10 .25
386 Kenny Walker .10 .25
387 Chris Webber .25 .60
388 Vancouver Grizzlies .10 .25
389 Checklist .10 .25
390 Checklist .10 .25

1994-95 Fleer All-Defensive

Randomly inserted in all first-series packs at a rate of one in nine, these 10 standard-size cards feature first and second All-NBA Defensive teams. Card fronts are borderless with color player action shots that have been faded to black-and-white. The player's name and first or second team designation appear in silver-foil lettering near the bottom. On a color-screened background, the back carries a color player cutout on one side and career highlights on the other. The cards are numbered on the back as "X of 10" and are sequenced in alphabetical order.

COMPLETE SET (10) 2.50 6.00
SER.1 STATED ODDS 1:9 HOBBY/RETAIL
1 Mookie Blaylock .25 .60
2 Charles Oakley .30 .75
3 Hakeem Olajuwon .50 1.25
4 Gary Payton .40 1.00
5 Scottie Pippen .75 2.00
6 Horace Grant .30 .75
7 Nate McMillan .25 .60
8 David Robinson .60 1.50
9 Dennis Rodman .75 2.00
10 Latrell Sprewell .50 1.25

1994-95 Fleer All-Stars

Randomly inserted in 15-card first-series packs at a rate of one in two, these 26 standard-size cards feature borderless fronts with color player action shots and backgrounds that fade to black-and-white. The player's name and first or second team designation appear in silver-foil lettering near the bottom. On a color-screened background, the back carries a color player cutout on one side and career highlights on the other.

COMPLETE SET (26) 10.00 25.00
SER.1 STATED ODDS 1:2 HOBBY
1 Kenny Anderson .50 1.25
2 B.J. Armstrong .40 1.00
3 Mookie Blaylock .40 1.00
4 Derrick Coleman .50 1.25
5 Patrick Ewing .75 2.00
6 Horace Grant .50 1.25
7 Alonzo Mourning .75 2.00
8 Charles Oakley .50 1.25
9 Shaquille O'Neal 1.50 4.00
10 Scottie Pippen 1.25 3.00
11 Mark Price .60 1.50
12 John Starks .50 1.25
13 Dominique Wilkins .75 2.00
14 Charles Barkley 1.00 2.50
15 Clyde Drexler .75 2.00
16 Kevin Johnson .60 1.50
17 Shawn Kemp .60 1.50
18 Karl Malone .75 2.00
19 Danny Manning .50 1.25
20 Hakeem Olajuwon .75 2.00
21 Gary Payton .60 1.50
22 Mitch Richmond .60 1.50
23 Clifford Robinson .40 1.00
24 David Robinson 1.00 2.50
25 Latrell Sprewell .75 2.00
26 John Stockton .75 2.00

1994-95 Fleer Award Winners

These four standard-size cards were random inserts in all first series packs at an approximate rate of one in 22. The set highlights four NBA award winners from the 1993-94 season. The horizontal fronts feature multiple player images. The player's name and his award appear at the bottom in gold-foil lettering. The horizontal back carries a color player close-up on one side and career highlights on the other. The cards are numbered "X of 4" and are sequenced in alphabetical order.

COMPLETE SET (4) 1.25 3.00
SER.1 STATED ODDS 1:22 HOBBY/RETAIL
1 Dell Curry .30 .75
2 Don MacLean .30 .75
3 Hakeem Olajuwon .60 1.50
4 Chris Webber .75 2.00

1994-95 Fleer Career Achievement

Randomly inserted in all first series packs at rate of one in 37, these six standard-size cards feature veteran NBA superstars. The fronts feature color player cutouts on their borderless metallic fronts. The player's name appears in gold-foil lettering in a lower corner. The back carries a color player close-up in a lower corner, with career highlights appearing above and alongside. The cards are numbered on the back as "X of 6" and are sequenced in alphabetical order.

COMPLETE SET (6) 5.00 12.00
SER.1 STATED ODDS 1:37 HOBBY/RETAIL
1 Patrick Ewing 1.50 4.00
2 Karl Malone 1.50 4.00
3 Hakeem Olajuwon 1.50 4.00
4 Robert Parish 1.25 3.00
5 Scottie Pippen 2.50 6.00
6 Dominique Wilkins 1.50 4.00

1994-95 Fleer First Year Phenoms

Randomly inserted into all second series packs at a rate of one in five, cards from this 10-card standard-size set feature a selection of the top rookies from 1994. These borderless cards feature a full color, cut-out player photo bursting forth from the center of the card, against a multi-imaged, shaded photo background. Card backs feature brief text on each player. The set is sequenced in alphabetical order.

COMPLETE SET (10) 4.00 10.00
SER.2 STATED ODDS 1:5 HOBBY/RETAIL
1 Grant Hill 1.50 4.00
2 Jason Kidd 1.50 4.00
3 Donyell Marshall .30 .75
4 Eric Montross .25 .60
5 Lamond Murray .30 .75
6 Wesley Person .30 .75
7 Khalid Reeves .25 .60
8 Glenn Robinson .60 1.50
9 Jalen Rose .75 2.00
10 Sharone Wright .25 .60

1994-95 Fleer League Leaders

Randomly inserted in all first series Fleer packs at an approximate rate of one in 11, these eight standard-size cards showcase league statistical leaders from the 1993-94 season. Card fronts feature a horizontal design with color player cutouts set on hardwood backgrounds. The player's name and the category in which he led the NBA appear in gold-foil lettering at the bottom. On a hardwood background, the horizontal back carries a color player close-up on one side and career highlights on the other. The cards are numbered on the back as "X of 8" and are sequenced in alphabetical order.

COMPLETE SET (8) 1.50 4.00
SER.1 STATED ODDS 1:11 HOBBY/RETAIL
1 Mahmoud Abdul-Rauf .20 .50
2 Nate McMillan .20 .50
3 Tracy Murray .20 .50
4 Dikembe Mutombo .30 .75
5 Shaquille O'Neal .75 2.00
6 David Robinson .50 1.25
7 Dennis Rodman .60 1.50
8 John Stockton .40 1.00

1994-95 Fleer Lottery Exchange

This 11-card standard-size set was available exclusively by redeeming the Fleer Lottery Exchange card, which was randomly inserted into all first series packs at a rate of one in 175. The expiration date for the redemption was April 1st, 1995. Card design is very similar to the basic issue Fleer cards except for the Lottery Pick logo on front.

COMPLETE SET (11) 6.00 15.00
EXCH.CARD: SER.1 STATED ODDS 1:175
1 Glenn Robinson .75 2.00
2 Jason Kidd 2.00 5.00
3 Grant Hill 2.00 5.00
4 Donyell Marshall .40 1.00
5 Juwan Howard .60 1.50
6 Sharone Wright .30 .75
7 Lamond Murray .40 1.00
8 Brian Grant .60 1.50
9 Eric Montross .30 .75
10 Eddie Jones 1.25 3.00
11 Carlos Rogers .30 .75
NNO Expired Exch.Card .40 1.00

1994-95 Fleer Pro-Visions

Randomly inserted in all first-series packs at a rate of one in five, these nine standard-size cards highlight some top NBA stars. Borderless fronts feature color paintings of the players on fanciful backgrounds. The player's name appears in gold-foil lettering in a lower corner. The back carries career highlights on a colorful ghosted abstract background.

COMPLETE SET (9) 1.25 3.00
SER.1 STATED ODDS 1:5 HOBBY/RETAIL
1 Jamal Mashburn .25 .60
2 John Starks .20 .50
3 Toni Kukoc .30 .75
4 Derrick Coleman .20 .50
5 Chris Webber .40 1.00
6 Dennis Rodman .50 1.25
7 Gary Payton .25 .60
8 Anfernee Hardaway .40 1.00
9 Dan Majerle .25 .60

1994-95 Fleer Rookie Sensations

Randomly inserted at a rate of one in three first-series 21-card cello packs, these 25 standard-size cards feature a selection of the top rookies from the 1993-94 season. Card fronts feature color player action cutouts "breaking out" of borderless multicolored backgrounds. The player's name appears in gold-foil lettering in a lower corner. The back carries another color player action cutout on one side, and career highlights within a colored panel on the other. The cards are numbered on the back as "X of 25" and are sequenced in alphabetical order.

COMPLETE SET (25) 10.00 25.00
SER.1 STATED ODDS 1:3 CELLO
1 Vin Baker 1.00 2.50
2 Shawn Bradley .60 1.50
3 P.J. Brown .60 1.50
4 Sam Cassell 1.00 2.50
5 Calbert Cheaney .60 1.50
6 Antonio Davis .60 1.50
7 Acie Earl .60 1.50
8 Harold Ellis .60 1.50
9 Anfernee Hardaway 1.50 4.00
10 Allan Houston 1.00 2.50
11 Lindsey Hunter .60 1.50
12 Bobby Hurley .60 1.50
13 Popeye Jones .60 1.50
14 Toni Kukoc 1.25 3.00
15 George Lynch .60 1.50
16 Jamal Mashburn 1.00 2.50
17 Chris Mills .60 1.50
18 Gheorghe Muresan .60 1.50
19 Dino Radja .60 1.50
20 Isaiah Rider 1.00 2.50
21 James Robinson .60 1.50
22 Rodney Rogers .60 1.50
23 Bryon Russell .60 1.50
24 Nick Van Exel 1.00 2.50
25 Chris Webber 1.50 4.00

1994-95 Fleer Sharpshooters

Randomly inserted exclusively into second series retail packs at a rate of one in seven, cards from this 10-card standard-size set feature a selection of the NBA's best long-distance shooters. Card fronts feature color player photos cut out against a neon basketball background overlapped by a basketball net. The set is sequenced in alphabetical order.

COMPLETE SET (10) 5.00 12.00
SER.2 STATED ODDS 1:7 RETAIL
1 Dell Curry .60 1.50
2 Joe Dumars 1.00 2.50
3 Dale Ellis .60 1.50
4 Dan Majerle 1.00 2.50
5 Reggie Miller 1.25 3.00
6 Mark Price 1.00 2.50
7 Glen Rice 1.00 2.50
8 Mitch Richmond 1.00 2.50
9 Dennis Scott .60 1.50
10 Latrell Sprewell 1.25 3.00

1994-95 Fleer Superstars

Randomly inserted into all second series packs at a rate of one in 37, cards from this six-card set feature a selection of veteran NBA stars with true Hall of Fame potential. Card fronts feature psychedelic, etched-foil backgrounds against a full color, cut out player photo. The set is sequenced in alphabetical order.

COMPLETE SET (6) 6.00 15.00
SER.2 STATED ODDS 1:37 HOBBY/RETAIL
1 Charles Barkley 2.50 6.00
2 Patrick Ewing 2.00 5.00
3 Hakeem Olajuwon 2.00 5.00
4 Robert Parish 1.50 4.00
5 Scottie Pippen 3.00 8.00
6 Dominique Wilkins 2.00 5.00

1994-95 Fleer Team Leaders

Randomly inserted into all second series packs at a rate of one in three, cards from this nine-card standard-size set each feature three key players from an NBA team. Horizontal card fronts feature three full color, cut out player photos against a computer-enhanced graphic background. The backs have a head shot of all three players and infomation on them. The cards are numbered "X of 9." There are two variations of card #3. The error version lists Joe Dumars as a Houston Rocket. The corrected version lists him as a Detroit Piston. It appears that equal quantities of both versions exist.

COMPLETE SET (9) 1.25 3.00
SER.2 STATED ODDS 1:3 HOBBY/RETAIL
1 Blaylock/Wilkins/Mourning .25 .60
2 Pippen/Price/Mashburn .40 1.00
3 Mutom/Dumars/Spree ERR .25 .60
3A Mutom/Dumars/Spree COR .25 .60
4 Olajuwon/R.Miller/Vaught .25 .60
5 Divac/Rice/Baker .20 .50
6 Rider/Anderson/Ewing .25 .60
7 O'Neal/Weather/Barkley .50 1.25
8 Strick/Richmond/D.Rob .30 .75
9 Kemp/Stockton/Chapman .25 .60

1994-95 Fleer Total D

Randomly inserted exclusively into second series hobby packs at a rate of one in seven, cards from this 10-card standard-size set feature a selection of the NBA's top defensive players. The fronts are laid out horizontally with a color photo and the player's name and team is in gold-foil at the bottom. "Total D" is in the background many times with a variety of colors set behind that. The backs have a head shot and information and why the player is so good defensively with a similar background to the front. The cards are numbered "X of 10" and are sequenced in alphabetical order.

COMPLETE SET (10) 3.00 8.00
SER.2 STATED ODDS 1:7 HOBBY
1 Mookie Blaylock .40 1.00
2 Nate McMillan .40 1.00
3 Dikembe Mutombo .60 1.50
4 Charles Oakley .50 1.25
5 Hakeem Olajuwon .75 2.00
6 Gary Payton .60 1.50
7 Scottie Pippen 1.25 3.00
8 David Robinson 1.00 2.50
9 Latrell Sprewell .75 2.00
10 John Stockton .75 2.00

1994-95 Fleer Towers of Power

Randomly inserted exclusively into second series 21-card retail packs at a rate of one in five, cards from this 10-card standard-size set feature a selection of the top centers and power forwards in the NBA. The fronts have a color-action photo surrounded by a yellow glow with a tower in the background. The words "Tower of Power" are at the bottom in gold-foil. The backs are the same except for a different photo and player information at the bottom. The cards are numbered "X of 10" and are sequenced in alphabetical order.

COMPLETE SET (10) 8.00 20.00
SER.2 STATED ODDS 1:5 CELLO
1 Charles Barkley 1.50 4.00
2 Patrick Ewing 1.25 3.00
3 Shawn Kemp 1.00 2.50
4 Karl Malone 1.25 3.00
5 Alonzo Mourning 1.25 3.00
6 Dikembe Mutombo 1.00 2.50
7 Hakeem Olajuwon 1.25 3.00
8 Shaquille O'Neal 4.00 10.00
9 David Robinson 1.50 4.00
10 Chris Webber 1.50 4.00

1994-95 Fleer Triple Threats

Randomly inserted in all first-series packs at an approximate rate of one in nine, these 10 standard-size cards spotlight some top NBA stars. Card fronts feature borderless fronts with multiple color player action cutouts on black backgrounds highlighted by colorful basketball court designs. The player's name appears in gold-foil lettering in a lower corner. This background design continues on the back, which carries a color player cutout on one side and career highlights in a ghosted strip on the other. The cards are numbered on the back as "X of 10" and are sequenced in alphabetical order.

COMPLETE SET (10) 2.00 5.00
SER.1 STATED ODDS 1:9 HOBBY/RETAIL
1 Mookie Blaylock .20 .50
2 Patrick Ewing .40 1.00
3 Shawn Kemp .30 .75
4 Karl Malone .40 1.00
5 Reggie Miller .40 1.00
6 Hakeem Olajuwon .40 1.00
7 Shaquille O'Neal .75 2.00
8 Scottie Pippen .60 1.50
9 David Robinson .50 1.25
10 Latrell Sprewell .40 1.00

1994-95 Fleer Young Lions

Randomly inserted into all second series packs at a rate of one in five, cards from this 6-card standard-size set feature a selection of popular players with three years or less of NBA experience. Fronts feature a player photo on the left and a lion photo on the right. In the bottom right corner there is gold-foil stamping of a lion, the term "Young Lion" and the player's name. The back has a brief biography and another player photo. The card is numbered in the lower right as "X" of 6. The set is sequenced in alphabetical order.

COMPLETE SET (6) 1.50 4.00
SER.2 STATED ODDS 1:5 HOBBY/RETAIL
1 Vin Baker .30 .75
2 Anfernee Hardaway .50 1.25
3 Larry Johnson .30 .75
4 Alonzo Mourning .40 1.00
5 Shaquille O'Neal .75 2.00
6 Chris Webber .50 1.25

1995-96 Fleer

The 1995-96 Fleer set was issued in two separate series of 200 and 150 cards, respectively, for a total of 350. Cards were distributed in 11-card hobby and retail packs (SRP $1.49) and 17-card retail pre-priced packs (SRP $2.29). Each pack contains at least two insert cards. Special Hot Packs, containing a selection of only insert cards, were randomly seeded into one in every 72 packs. The borderless fronts feature four different background designs (one for each division) against a cut-out color player action shot. The backs have a color-action photo and the same picture set against a pixeled background, along with statistics. The cards are grouped alphabetically within teams. The set concludes with the following topical subsets: Rookies (280-319) and Firm Foundations (320-348). Rookie Cards of note in this set include Michael Finley, Kevin Garnett, Antonio McDyess, Joe Smith, Jerry Stackhouse and Damon Stoudamire.

COMPLETE SET (350) 15.00 40.00
COMPLETE SERIES 1 (200) 8.00 20.00
COMPLETE SERIES 2 (150) 8.00 20.00
1 Stacey Augmon .12 .30
2 Mookie Blaylock .10 .25
3 Craig Ehlo .10 .25
4 Andrew Lang .10 .25
5 Grant Long .10 .25
6 Ken Norman .10 .25
7 Steve Smith .12 .30
8 Dee Brown .10 .25
9 Sherman Douglas .10 .25
10 Eric Montross .10 .25
11 Dino Radja .10 .25
12 David Wesley .10 .25
13 Dominique Wilkins .20 .50
14 Muggsy Bogues .12 .30
15 Scott Burrell .10 .25
16 Dell Curry .10 .25
17 Hersey Hawkins .10 .25
18 Larry Johnson .15 .40
19 Alonzo Mourning .20 .50
20 Robert Parish .15 .40
21 B.J. Armstrong .10 .25
22 Michael Jordan 1.25 3.00
23 Steve Kerr .12 .30
24 Toni Kukoc .15 .40
25 Will Perdue .10 .25
26 Scottie Pippen .25 .60
27 Terrell Brandon .10 .25
28 Tyrone Hill .10 .25
29 Chris Mills .10 .25
30 Bobby Phills .10 .25
31 Mark Price .15 .40
32 John Williams .10 .25
33 Lucious Harris .10 .25
34 Jim Jackson .10 .25
35 Popeye Jones .10 .25
36 Jason Kidd .25 .60
37 Jamal Mashburn .15 .40
38 George McCloud .10 .25
39 Roy Tarpley .10 .25
40 Lorenzo Williams .10 .25
41 Mahmoud Abdul-Rauf .10 .25
42 Dale Ellis .10 .25
43 LaPhonso Ellis .10 .25
44 Dikembe Mutombo .15 .40
45 Robert Pack .10 .25
46 Rodney Rogers .10 .25
47 Jalen Rose .20 .50
48 Bryant Stith .10 .25
49 Reggie Williams .10 .25
50 Joe Dumars .15 .40
51 Grant Hill .25 .60
52 Allan Houston .12 .30
53 Lindsey Hunter .10 .25
54 Oliver Miller .10 .25
55 Terry Mills .10 .25
56 Mark West .10 .25
57 Chris Gatling .10 .25
58 Tim Hardaway .15 .40
59 Donyell Marshall .10 .25
60 Chris Mullin .15 .40
61 Carlos Rogers .10 .25
62 Clifford Rozier .10 .25
63 Rony Seikaly .10 .25
64 Latrell Sprewell .15 .40
65 Sam Cassell .15 .40
66 Clyde Drexler .20 .50
67 Mario Elie .10 .25
68 Carl Herrera .10 .25
69 Robert Horry .12 .30
70 Vernon Maxwell .10 .25
71 Hakeem Olajuwon .20 .50
72 Kenny Smith .12 .30
73 Dale Davis .10 .25
74 Mark Jackson .12 .30
75 Derrick McKey .10 .25
76 Reggie Miller .20 .50
77 Sam Mitchell .10 .25
78 Byron Scott .12 .30
79 Rik Smits .12 .30
80 Terry Dehere .10 .25
81 Tony Massenburg .10 .25
82 Lamond Murray .10 .25
83 Pooh Richardson .10 .25
84 Malik Sealy .10 .25
85 Loy Vaught .10 .25
86 Elden Campbell .10 .25
87 Cedric Ceballos .10 .25
88 Vlade Divac .15 .40
89 Eddie Jones .15 .40
90 Anthony Peeler .10 .25
91 Sedale Threatt .10 .25
92 Nick Van Exel .15 .40
93 Bimbo Coles .10 .25
94 Matt Geiger .10 .25
95 Billy Owens .10 .25
96 Khalid Reeves .10 .25
97 Glen Rice .15 .40
98 John Salley .10 .25
99 Kevin Willis .10 .25
100 Vin Baker .12 .30
101 Marty Conlon .10 .25
102 Todd Day .10 .25
103 Lee Mayberry .10 .25
104 Eric Murdock .10 .25
105 Glenn Robinson .12 .30
106 Winston Garland .10 .25
107 Tom Gugliotta .10 .25
108 Christian Laettner .12 .30
109 Isaiah Rider .15 .40
110 Sean Rooks .10 .25
111 Doug West .10 .25
112 Kenny Anderson .12 .30
113 Benoit Benjamin .10 .25
114 P.J. Brown .10 .25
115 Derrick Coleman .12 .30
116 Armon Gilliam .10 .25
117 Chris Morris .10 .25
118 Rex Walters .10 .25
119 Hubert Davis .10 .25
120 Patrick Ewing .20 .50
121 Derek Harper .12 .30
122 Anthony Mason .10 .25
123 Charles Oakley .12 .30
124 Charles Smith .10 .25
125 John Starks .12 .30
126 Nick Anderson .10 .25
127 Anthony Bowie .10 .25
128 Horace Grant .12 .30
129 Anfernee Hardaway .25 .60
130 Shaquille O'Neal .40 1.00
131 Donald Royal .10 .25
132 Dennis Scott .10 .25
133 Brian Shaw .10 .25
134 Derrick Alston .10 .25
135 Dana Barros .10 .25
136 Shawn Bradley .10 .25
137 Willie Burton .10 .25
138 Clarence Weatherspoon .10 .25
139 Scott Williams .10 .25
140 Sharone Wright .10 .25
141 Danny Ainge .15 .40
142 Charles Barkley .25 .60
143 A.C. Green .12 .30
144 Kevin Johnson .15 .40
145 Dan Majerle .15 .40
146 Danny Manning .12 .30
147 Elliot Perry .10 .25
148 Wesley Person .10 .25
149 Wayman Tisdale .10 .25
150 Chris Dudley .10 .25
151 Jerome Kersey .10 .25
152 Aaron McKie .10 .25
153 Terry Porter .10 .25
154 Clifford Robinson .10 .25
155 James Robinson .10 .25
156 Rod Strickland .10 .25
157 Otis Thorpe .10 .25
158 Buck Williams .10 .25
159 Brian Grant .12 .30
160 Bobby Hurley .10 .25
161 Olden Polynice .10 .25
162 Mitch Richmond .15 .40
163 Michael Smith .10 .25
164 Spud Webb .12 .30
165 Walt Williams .10 .25
166 Terry Cummings .12 .30
167 Vinny Del Negro .10 .25
168 Sean Elliott .15 .40
169 Avery Johnson .12 .30
170 Chuck Person .12 .30
171 J.R. Reid .10 .25
172 Doc Rivers .12 .30
173 David Robinson .25 .60
174 Dennis Rodman .30 .75
175 Vincent Askew .10 .25
176 Kendall Gill .10 .25
177 Shawn Kemp .15 .40
178 Sarunas Marciulionis .10 .25
179 Nate McMillan .10 .25
180 Gary Payton .15 .40
181 Sam Perkins .10 .25
182 Detlef Schrempf .15 .40
183 David Benoit .10 .25
184 Antoine Carr .10 .25
185 Blue Edwards .10 .25
186 Jeff Hornacek .12 .30
187 Adam Keefe .10 .25
188 Karl Malone .20 .50
189 Felton Spencer .10 .25
190 John Stockton .20 .50
191 Rex Chapman .10 .25
192 Calbert Cheaney .10 .25
193 Juwan Howard .15 .40
194 Don MacLean .10 .25
195 Gheorghe Muresan .10 .25
196 Scott Skiles .10 .25
197 Chris Webber .20 .50
198 Checklist .10 .25
199 Checklist .10 .25
200 Checklist .10 .25
201 Stacey Augmon .12 .30
202 Mookie Blaylock .10 .25
203 Grant Long .10 .25
204 Ken Norman .10 .25
205 Steve Smith .12 .30
206 Spud Webb .12 .30
207 Dana Barros .10 .25
208 Rick Fox .10 .25
209 Kendall Gill .10 .25
210 Khalid Reeves .10 .25
211 Glen Rice .15 .40
212 Luc Longley .12 .30
213 Dennis Rodman .30 .75
214 Dan Majerle .15 .40
215 Tony Dumas .10 .25
216 Tom Hammonds .10 .25
217 Elmore Spencer .10 .25
218 Otis Thorpe .10 .25
219 B.J. Armstrong .10 .25
220 Sam Cassell .15 .40
221 Clyde Drexler .20 .50
222 Mario Elie .10 .25
223 Robert Horry .12 .30
224 Hakeem Olajuwon .20 .50
225 Kenny Smith .12 .30
226 Antonio Davis .10 .25
227 Eddie Johnson .10 .25
228 Ricky Pierce .10 .25
229 Eric Piatkowski .12 .30
230 Rodney Rogers .10 .25
231 Brian Williams .10 .25
232 Corie Blount .10 .25
233 George Lynch .10 .25
234 Kevin Gamble .10 .25
235 Alonzo Mourning .20 .50
236 Eric Mobley .10 .25
237 Terry Porter .10 .25
238 Micheal Williams .10 .25
239 Kevin Edwards .10 .25
240 Vern Fleming .10 .25
241 Charlie Ward .10 .25
242 Jon Koncak .10 .25
243 Richard Dumas .10 .25
244 Jeff Malone .10 .25
245 Vernon Maxwell .10 .25
246 John Williams .10 .25
247 Harvey Grant .10 .25
248 Dontonio Wingfield .10 .25
249 Tyrone Corbin .10 .25
250 Sarunas Marciulionis .10 .25
251 Will Perdue .10 .25
252 Hersey Hawkins .10 .25
253 Ervin Johnson .10 .25
254 Shawn Kemp .15 .40
255 Gary Payton .15 .40
256 Sam Perkins .10 .25
257 Detlef Schrempf .15 .40
258 Chris Morris .10 .25
259 Robert Pack .10 .25
260 Willie Anderson ET .10 .25
261 Jimmy King ET .10 .25
262 Oliver Miller ET .10 .25
263 Tracy Murray ET .10 .25
264 Ed Pinckney ET .10 .25
265 Alvin Robertson ET .10 .25
266 Carlos Rogers ET .10 .25
267 John Salley ET .10 .25
268 Damon Stoudamire ET .25 .60
269 Zan Tabak ET .10 .25
270 Ashraf Amaya ET .10 .25
271 Greg Anthony ET .10 .25
272 Benoit Benjamin ET .10 .25
273 Blue Edwards ET .10 .25
274 Kenny Gattison ET .10 .25
275 Antonio Harvey ET .10 .25
276 Chris King ET .10 .25
277 Lawrence Moten ET .10 .25
278 Bryant Reeves ET .07 .20
279 Byron Scott ET .12 .30
280 Cory Alexander RC .15 .40
281 Jerome Allen RC .15 .40
282 Brent Barry RC .25 .60
283 Mario Bennett RC .12 .30
284 Travis Best RC .15 .40
285 Junior Burrough RC .15 .40
286 Jason Caffey RC .15 .40
287 Randolph Childress RC .12 .30
288 Sasha Danilovic RC .15 .40
289 Mark Davis RC .15 .40
290 Tyus Edney RC .15 .40
291 Michael Finley RC .50 1.25
292 Sherrell Ford RC .12 .30
293 Kevin Garnett RC 1.25 3.00
294 Alan Henderson RC .15 .40
295 Frankie King RC .15 .40
296 Jimmy King RC .15 .40
297 Donny Marshall RC .15 .40
298 Antonio McDyess RC .20 .50

299 Loren Meyer RC .10 .25
300 Lawrence Moten RC .15 .40
301 Ed O'Bannon RC .12 .30
302 Greg Ostertag RC .15 .40
303 Cherokee Parks RC .12 .30
304 Theo Ratliff RC .25 .60
305 Bryant Reeves RC .12 .30
306 Shawn Respert RC .12 .30
307 Lou Roe RC .15 .40
308 Arvydas Sabonis RC .30 .75
309 Joe Smith RC .20 .50
310 Jerry Stackhouse RC .50 1.25
311 Damon Stoudamire RC .40 1.00
312 Bob Sura RC .12 .30
313 Kurt Thomas RC .15 .40
314 Gary Trent RC .15 .40
315 David Vaughn RC .15 .40
316 Rasheed Wallace RC .50 1.25
317 Eric Williams RC .15 .40
318 Corliss Williamson RC .15 .40
319 George Zidek RC .12 .30
320 Mookie Blaylock FF .10 .25
321 Dino Radja FF .10 .25
322 Larry Johnson FF .15 .40
323 Michael Jordan FF 1.25 3.00
324 Tyrone Hill FF .10 .25
325 Jason Kidd FF .25 .60
326 Dikembe Mutombo FF .15 .40
327 Grant Hill FF .25 .60
328 Joe Smith FF .12 .30
329 Hakeem Olajuwon FF .20 .50
330 Reggie Miller FF .20 .50
331 Loy Vaught FF .10 .25
332 Nick Van Exel FF .15 .40
333 Alonzo Mourning FF .20 .50
334 Glenn Robinson FF .12 .30
335 Kevin Garnett FF .75 2.00
336 Kenny Anderson FF .12 .30
337 Patrick Ewing FF .20 .50
338 Shaquille O'Neal FF .40 1.00
339 Jerry Stackhouse FF .30 .75
340 Charles Barkley FF .25 .60
341 Clifford Robinson FF .10 .25
342 Mitch Richmond FF .15 .40
343 David Robinson FF .25 .60
344 Shawn Kemp FF .15 .40
345 Damon Stoudamire FF .25 .60
346 Karl Malone FF .20 .50
347 Bryant Reeves FF .07 .20
348 Chris Webber FF .20 .50
349 Checklist (201-319) .10 .25
350 Checklist (320-350/ins.) .10 .25

1995-96 Fleer All-Stars

Randomly inserted in all first series packs at an approximate rate of one in three, these thirteen dual-player, double-sided standard-size cards feature members of the 1994-95 Eastern and Western Conference All-Star squads. Only All-Star MVP Mitch Richmond is given his own card. Both sides have a full-color action photo taken at the All-Star game with the West having a purple background and the East a green background. The bottoms have the Phoenix All-Star Weekend insignia with the player's name and conference in gold-foil. The cards are numbered "X of 13."

COMPLETE SET (13) 2.00 5.00
SER.1 STATED ODDS 1:3 HOBBY/RETAIL
1 G.Hill/C.Barkley .40 1.00
2 S.Pippen/S.Kemp .40 1.00
3 S.O'Neal/H.Olajuwon .60 1.50
4 A.Hardaway/D.Majerle .40 1.00
5 R.Miller/L.Sprewell .30 .75
6 V.Baker/C.Ceballos .20 .50
7 T.Hill/K.Malone .30 .75
8 L.Johnson/D.Schrempf .25 .60
9 P.Ewing/D.Robinson .40 1.00
10 A.Mourning/D.Mutombo .30 .75
11 D.Barros/G.Payton .25 .60
12 J.Dumars/J.Stockton .30 .75
13 Mitch Richmond .25 .60

1995-96 Fleer Class Encounters

Randomly inserted in all second series packs at a rate of one in two, this 40-card standard-size set highlights the first 20 players of the 1995 draft and 20 of the most sucessful players from the 1994 draft. Full-bleed fronts have gold foil printing and one full-color action shot as the main background. Three head shots of the original appear in increasing size on the right side. Horizontal backs have a white-bordered, off-center head shot with a player profile printed in black type on a red background. Each group of cards is sequenced in alphabetical order.

COMPLETE SET (40) 8.00 20.00
SER.2 STATED ODDS 1:2 HOBBY/RETAIL
1 Derrick Alston .25 .60
2 Brian Grant .30 .75
3 Grant Hill .60 1.50
4 Juwan Howard .40 1.00
5 Eddie Jones .40 1.00
6 Jason Kidd .60 1.50
7 Donyell Marshall .25 .60
8 Anthony Miller .25 .60
9 Eric Mobley .25 .60
10 Eric Montross .25 .60
11 Lamond Murray .25 .60
12 Wesley Person .25 .60
13 Eric Piatkowski .30 .75
14 Khalid Reeves .25 .60
15 Glenn Robinson .30 .75
16 Carlos Rogers .25 .60
17 Jalen Rose .50 1.25
18 Clifford Rozier .25 .60
19 Michael Smith .25 .60
20 Sharone Wright .25 .60
21 Brent Barry .50 1.25
22 Jason Caffey .30 .75
23 Randolph Childress .25 .60
24 Kevin Garnett 2.50 6.00
25 Alan Henderson .30 .75
26 Antonio McDyess .40 1.00
27 Ed O'Bannon .25 .60
28 Cherokee Parks .25 .60
29 Theo Ratliff .50 1.25
30 Bryant Reeves .25 .60
31 Shawn Respert .25 .60
32 Joe Smith .40 1.00
33 Jerry Stackhouse 1.00 2.50
34 Damon Stoudamire .75 2.00
35 Bob Sura .25 .60
36 Kurt Thomas .30 .75
37 Gary Trent .30 .75
38 Rasheed Wallace 1.00 2.50
39 Eric Williams .30 .75
40 Corliss Williamson .30 .75

1995-96 Fleer Double Doubles

Randomly inserted in all first series packs at an approximate rate of one in three, these 12 cards feature players who averaged double figures per game in two statistical categories during the 1994-95 season. Full-bleed fronts features the player in two, split-shot color action photos separated by the words "Double Double" which are printed in the player's team colors. The player is again featured in full-color on the back with a career synopsis and '94-95 stats printed in black type. The set is sequenced in alphabetical order.

COMPLETE SET (12) 1.50 4.00
SER.1 STATED ODDS 1:3 HOBBY/RETAIL
1 Vin Baker .25 .60
2 Vlade Divac .30 .75
3 Patrick Ewing .40 1.00
4 Tyrone Hill .20 .50
5 Popeye Jones .20 .50
6 Shawn Kemp .30 .75
7 Karl Malone .40 1.00
8 Dikembe Mutombo .30 .75
9 Hakeem Olajuwon .40 1.00
10 Shaquille O'Neal .75 2.00
11 David Robinson .50 1.25
12 John Stockton .40 1.00

1995-96 Fleer End to End

Randomly inserted in all second series packs at a rate of one in four, cards from this 20-card set focus on the NBA's leaders at both ends of the court. Borderless, horizontal fronts are split between two panels, one having a blue background with "End to End" in repeating print, and the other with a full-color action player shot. A player cutout is placed in the middle of the two panels. Horizontal backs have a full-color action cutout and a player profile.

COMPLETE SET (20) 6.00 15.00
SER.2 STATED ODDS 1:4 HOBBY/RETAIL
1 Mookie Blaylock .25 .60
2 Vlade Divac .40 1.00
3 Clyde Drexler .50 1.25
4 Patrick Ewing .50 1.25
5 Horace Grant .30 .75
6 Anfernee Hardaway .60 1.50
7 Grant Hill .60 1.50
8 Eddie Jones .40 1.00
9 Michael Jordan 3.00 8.00
10 Jason Kidd .60 1.50
11 Alonzo Mourning .50 1.25
12 Dikembe Mutombo .40 1.00
13 Hakeem Olajuwon .50 1.25
14 Shaquille O'Neal 1.00 2.50
15 Gary Payton .40 1.00
16 Scottie Pippen .60 1.50
17 David Robinson .60 1.50
18 Latrell Sprewell .40 1.00
19 John Stockton .50 1.25
20 Rod Strickland .25 .60

1995-96 Fleer Flair Hardwood Leaders

Issued one per pack in all first series packs, these 27 super-premium, double-thick Flair style standard-size cards feature each team's statistical leader or award winner from the 1994-95 season. The fronts have a color action photo with the key as the background. The backs have a color photo with a hardwood background and player information. The entire 27-card set was also issued as a commemorative sheet most notably distributed as a wrapper redemption at the San Antonio All-Star Jam Session show. The set is sequenced in alphabetical order by team.

COMPLETE SET (27) 7.50 15.00
ONE PER SER.1 PACK
1 Mookie Blaylock .25 .60
2 Dominique Wilkins .50 1.25
3 Alonzo Mourning .50 1.25
4 Michael Jordan 5.00 12.00
5 Mark Price .40 1.00
6 Jim Jackson .25 .60
7 Dikembe Mutombo .40 1.00
8 Grant Hill .60 1.50
9 Tim Hardaway .40 1.00
10 Hakeem Olajuwon .50 1.25
11 Reggie Miller .50 1.25
12 Loy Vaught .25 .60
13 Cedric Ceballos .25 .60
14 Glen Rice .40 1.00
15 Glenn Robinson .30 .75
16 Christian Laettner .30 .75
17 Derrick Coleman .30 .75
18 Patrick Ewing .50 1.25
19 Shaquille O'Neal 1.00 2.50
20 Dana Barros .25 .60
21 Charles Barkley .60 1.50
22 Clifford Robinson .25 .60
23 Mitch Richmond .40 1.00
24 David Robinson .60 1.50
25 Gary Payton .40 1.00
26 Karl Malone .50 1.25
27 Chris Webber .50 1.25
NNO Uncut Sheet 8.00 20.00

1995-96 Fleer Franchise Futures

Randomly inserted into all first series packs at an approximate rate of one in 37, these nine etched-foil standard-size cards feature a selection of the game's hottest young stars. The fronts have a full-color action photo with a huge basketball and fire underneath it in the background. The backs have a color photo with a similar yet less snazzy version of the front background. The set is sequenced in alphabetical order.

COMPLETE SET (9) 12.50 30.00
SER.1 STATED ODDS 1:37 HOBBY/RETAIL
1 Vin Baker 1.50 4.00
2 Anfernee Hardaway 3.00 8.00
3 Jim Jackson 1.25 3.00
4 Jamal Mashburn 2.00 5.00
5 Alonzo Mourning 2.50 6.00
6 Dikembe Mutombo 2.00 5.00
7 Shaquille O'Neal 5.00 12.00
8 Nick Van Exel 2.00 5.00
9 Chris Webber 2.50 6.00

1995-96 Fleer Rookie Phenoms

The 10 cards in this set were randomly inserted in second series hobby packs only at a rate of one in 24 and highlight the play of the NBA's best rookies. Borderless fronts are gold and silver foil finished with a full-color action cutout. Backs carry an extreme vertical color shot on the left and a player profile on the right.

COMPLETE SET (10) 12.00 30.00
SER.2 STATED ODDS 1:24 HOBBY
HP CARDS: .1X TO .3X HI COLUMN
HP: SER.2 STATED ODDS 1:72 HOBBY
1 Kevin Garnett 6.00 15.00
2 Antonio McDyess 1.00 2.50
3 Ed O'Bannon .60 1.50
4 Bryant Reeves .60 1.50
5 Shawn Respert .60 1.50
6 Joe Smith 1.00 2.50
7 Jerry Stackhouse 2.50 6.00
8 Damon Stoudamire 2.00 5.00
9 Gary Trent .75 2.00
10 Rasheed Wallace 2.50 6.00

1995-96 Fleer Rookie Sensations

Randomly inserted exclusively into first series 17-card retail pre-priced packs at an approximate rate of one in five, these 15 cards spotlight the top rookies from the 1994-95 season. The fronts have a full-color action photo with the words "Rookie Sensation" in gold-foil around a basketball. The backs have a full-color photo with player information at the bottom in a yellow haze.

COMPLETE SET (15) 10.00 25.00
SER.1 STATED ODDS 1:5 CELLO
1 Brian Grant 1.25 3.00
2 Grant Hill 2.50 6.00
3 Juwan Howard 1.50 4.00
4 Eddie Jones 1.50 4.00
5 Jason Kidd 2.50 6.00
6 Donyell Marshall 1.00 2.50
7 Eric Montross 1.00 2.50
8 Lamond Murray 1.00 2.50
9 Wesley Person 1.00 2.50
10 Khalid Reeves 1.00 2.50
11 Glenn Robinson 1.25 3.00
12 Jalen Rose 2.00 5.00
13 Clifford Rozier 1.00 2.50
14 Michael Smith 1.00 2.50
15 Sharone Wright 1.00 2.50

1995-96 Fleer Stackhouse's Scrapbook

Randomly inserted into all second series packs at a rate one in every 24, these two cards represent the first part of a multi-series, eight-card, cross-brand set devoted to Fleer spokesperson Jerry Stackhouse.

COMPLETE SET (2) 1.50 4.00
COMMON CARD (S1-S2) 1.00 2.50
SER.2 STATED ODDS 1:24 PACKS

1995-96 Fleer Total D

Randomly inserted into first series 11-card hobby and retail packs at an approximate rate of one in five, these 12 standard-size cards feature a selection of the NBA's top defenders. The fronts have a color-action photo with the player's name and "Total D" on the side in gold-foil. The horizontal backs are split between a color action player photo on the left and a player profile printed in white and set against a gradated color background on the right. The set is sequenced in alphabetical order.

COMPLETE SET (12) 5.00 12.00
SER.1 STATED ODDS 1:5 HOBBY/RETAIL
1 Mookie Blaylock .25 .60
2 Patrick Ewing .50 1.25
3 Michael Jordan 3.00 8.00
4 Alonzo Mourning .50 1.25
5 Dikembe Mutombo .40 1.00
6 Hakeem Olajuwon .50 1.25
7 Shaquille O'Neal 1.00 2.50
8 Gary Payton .40 1.00
9 Scottie Pippen .60 1.50
10 David Robinson .60 1.50
11 Dennis Rodman .75 2.00
12 John Stockton .50 1.25

1995-96 Fleer Total O

Randomly inserted in second series retail packs only at a rate of one in 12, cards from this 10-card standard-size set spotlight the NBA's offensive talent. Borderless fronts capture the player in a full-color action cutout with two red foil rings surrounding the image. All are on a backdrop of a basketball in the hands of a shooter and "Total O" is printed in silver foil on the ball. Backs are split between a full-color action player shot and a colored rock background containing a player profile printed in white type.

COMPLETE SET (10) 10.00 25.00
SER.2 STATED ODDS 1:12 RETAIL
HP CARDS: .25X TO .6X HI COLUMN
HP: SER.2 STATED ODDS 1:72 RETAIL
1 Grant Hill 1.25 3.00
2 Michael Jordan 6.00 15.00
3 Jamal Mashburn .75 2.00
4 Reggie Miller 1.00 2.50
5 Hakeem Olajuwon 1.00 2.50
6 Shaquille O'Neal 2.00 5.00
7 Mitch Richmond .75 2.00
8 David Robinson 1.25 3.00
9 Glenn Robinson .60 1.50
10 Jerry Stackhouse 1.25 3.00

1995-96 Fleer Towers of Power

The big "Earth Shakers" of the NBA are represented in this 10-card set. Cards were randomly inserted into one in every 54 second series packs. Borderless fronts have etched copper foil designs and a full-color action player cutout. Backs are a three-tone color screen with a one-color action shot near the top right. A player profile appears in black type on the bottom half.

COMPLETE SET (10) 40.00 75.00
SER.2 STATED ODDS 1:54 HOBBY/RETAIL
1 Shawn Kemp 3.00 8.00
2 Karl Malone 4.00 10.00
3 Antonio McDyess 2.50 6.00
4 Alonzo Mourning 4.00 10.00
5 Hakeem Olajuwon 4.00 10.00
6 Shaquille O'Neal 8.00 20.00
7 David Robinson 5.00 12.00
8 Glenn Robinson 2.50 6.00
9 Joe Smith 3.00 8.00
10 Chris Webber 4.00 10.00

1996 Fleer French Kellogg's Frosties

Produced by Fleer, these 30-cards are very similar to the Pop-Up cards that were produced for the 1995-96 Jam Session American issue, except these are mini versions. These cards were inserted into boxes of Kellogg's Frosties in France. The cards are not numbered and are checklisted below in alphabetical order.

COMPLETE SET (30) 30.00 80.00
1 Kenny Anderson 2.00 5.00
2 Mookie Blaylock 1.50 4.00
3 Muggsy Bogues 2.00 5.00
4 Sam Cassell 2.00 5.00
5 Clyde Drexler 3.00 8.00
6 Brian Grant 2.00 5.00
7 Horace Grant 2.00 5.00
8 Tim Hardaway 2.50 6.00
9 Grant Hill 4.00 10.00
10 Kevin Johnson 2.50 6.00
11 Jim Jackson 1.50 4.00
12 Jason Kidd 4.00 10.00
13 Christian Laettner 2.00 5.00
14 Dan Majerle 2.50 6.00
15 Vernon Maxwell 1.50 4.00
16 Oliver Miller 1.50 4.00
17 Eric Montross 1.50 4.00
18 Gheorghe Muresan 1.50 4.00
19 Lamond Murray 1.50 4.00
20 Dikembe Mutombo 2.50 6.00
21 Charles Oakley 2.00 5.00
22 Hakeem Olajuwon 3.00 8.00
23 Scottie Pippen 4.00 10.00
24 Glen Rice 2.50 6.00
25 Clifford Robinson 1.50 4.00
26 Glenn Robinson 2.00 5.00
27 Byron Scott 2.00 5.00
28 Rik Smits 2.00 5.00
29 John Stockton 3.00 8.00
30 Tony the Tiger .75 2.00

1996 Fleer/Mountain Dew Stackhouse

This five-card standard-sized set was inserted in the Philadelphia area as a premium for purchasing Mountain Dew soda. The cards have the same design as the regular issues, but have a Moutain Dew logo on the back of each card.

COMPLETE SET (5) 3.00 8.00
COMMON CARD (1-5) .75 2.00

1996-97 Fleer

The 1996-97 Fleer set was issued in two series totalling 300 cards. Both series had 150 cards issued in 11-card packs carrying a suggested retail price of $1.49 each. Card fronts contain a full-bleed photo with the player's last name in ghosted white letters and their first name in gold foil laid over it. The player's team name is also in gold foil under the player's first name. Card backs are horizontal with the team colors setting the background along with a basketball and the team logo. A photo of the player is provided along with statistical and biographical information. Cards are sequenced alphabetically within team order. The only subset is Hardwood Leaders (120-148). No Rookie Cards are featured in the first series. Card #83 (Jerry Stackhouse) was also used for promotional purposes.

COMPLETE SET (300) 17.50 35.00
COMPLETE SERIES 1 (150) 7.50 15.00
COMPLETE SERIES 2 (150) 10.00 20.00
1 Stacey Augmon .12 .30
2 Mookie Blaylock .10 .25
3 Christian Laettner .12 .30
4 Grant Long .10 .25
5 Steve Smith .12 .30
6 Rick Fox .10 .25
7 Dino Radja .10 .25
8 Eric Williams .10 .25
9 Kenny Anderson .12 .30
10 Dell Curry .10 .25
11 Larry Johnson .15 .40
12 Glen Rice .15 .40
13 Michael Jordan 1.25 3.00
14 Toni Kukoc .15 .40
15 Scottie Pippen .25 .60
16 Dennis Rodman .30 .75
17 Terrell Brandon .10 .25
18 Chris Mills .10 .25
19 Bobby Phills .10 .25
20 Bob Sura .10 .25
21 Jim Jackson .10 .25
22 Jason Kidd .25 .60
23 Jamal Mashburn .12 .30
24 George McCloud .10 .25
25 Mahmoud Abdul-Rauf .10 .25
26 Antonio McDyess .15 .40
27 Dikembe Mutombo .15 .40
28 Jalen Rose .12 .30
29 Bryant Stith .10 .25
30 Joe Dumars .15 .40
31 Grant Hill .25 .60
32 Allan Houston .12 .30
33 Theo Ratliff .10 .25
34 Otis Thorpe .10 .25
35 Chris Mullin .15 .40
36 Joe Smith .12 .30
37 Latrell Sprewell .15 .40
38 Kevin Willis .10 .25
39 Sam Cassell .12 .30
40 Clyde Drexler .20 .50
41 Robert Horry .12 .30
42 Hakeem Olajuwon .20 .50
43 Dale Davis .10 .25
44 Mark Jackson .12 .30
45 Derrick McKey .10 .25
46 Reggie Miller .20 .50
47 Rik Smits .12 .30
48 Brent Barry .12 .30
49 Malik Sealy .10 .25
50 Loy Vaught .10 .25
51 Brian Williams .10 .25
52 Elden Campbell .10 .25
53 Cedric Ceballos .10 .25
54 Vlade Divac .15 .40
55 Eddie Jones .15 .40
56 Nick Van Exel .15 .40
57 Tim Hardaway .15 .40
58 Alonzo Mourning .20 .50
59 Kurt Thomas .10 .25
60 Walt Williams .10 .25
61 Vin Baker .12 .30
62 Sherman Douglas .10 .25
63 Glenn Robinson .12 .30
64 Kevin Garnett .40 1.00
65 Tom Gugliotta .10 .25
66 Isaiah Rider .12 .30
67 Shawn Bradley .10 .25
68 Chris Childs .10 .25
69 Armon Gilliam .10 .25
70 Ed O'Bannon .10 .25
71 Patrick Ewing .20 .50
72 Derek Harper .12 .30
73 Anthony Mason .10 .25
74 Charles Oakley .12 .30
75 John Starks .12 .30
76 Nick Anderson .10 .25
77 Horace Grant .12 .30
78 Anfernee Hardaway .25 .60
79 Shaquille O'Neal .40 1.00
80 Dennis Scott .10 .25
81 Derrick Coleman .12 .30
82 Vernon Maxwell .10 .25
83 Jerry Stackhouse .20 .50
84 Clarence Weatherspoon .10 .25
85 Charles Barkley .25 .60
86 Michael Finley .20 .50
87 Kevin Johnson .15 .40
88 Wesley Person .10 .25
89 Clifford Robinson .10 .25
90 Arvydas Sabonis .12 .30
91 Rod Strickland .10 .25
92 Gary Trent .10 .25
93 Tyus Edney .10 .25
94 Brian Grant .12 .30
95 Billy Owens .10 .25
96 Mitch Richmond .15 .40
97 Vinny Del Negro .10 .25
98 Sean Elliott .15 .40
99 Avery Johnson .12 .30
100 David Robinson .25 .60
101 Hersey Hawkins .10 .25
102 Shawn Kemp .15 .40
103 Gary Payton .15 .40
104 Detlef Schrempf .15 .40
105 Oliver Miller .10 .25
106 Tracy Murray .10 .25
107 Damon Stoudamire .12 .30
108 Sharone Wright .10 .25
109 Jeff Hornacek .12 .30
110 Karl Malone .20 .50
111 John Stockton .20 .50
112 Greg Anthony .10 .25
113 Bryant Reeves .10 .25
114 Byron Scott .12 .30
115 Calbert Cheaney .10 .25
116 Juwan Howard .12 .30
117 Gheorghe Muresan .10 .25
118 Rasheed Wallace .20 .50
119 Chris Webber .20 .50
120 Mookie Blaylock HL .10 .25
121 Dino Radja HL .10 .25
122 Larry Johnson HL .15 .40
123 Michael Jordan HL 1.25 3.00
124 Terrell Brandon HL .10 .25
125 Jason Kidd HL .25 .60
126 Antonio McDyess HL .15 .40
127 Grant Hill HL .25 .60
128 Latrell Sprewell HL .15 .40
129 Hakeem Olajuwon HL .20 .50
130 Reggie Miller HL .20 .50
131 Loy Vaught HL .10 .25
132 Cedric Ceballos HL .10 .25
133 Alonzo Mourning HL .20 .50
134 Vin Baker HL .12 .30
135 Isaiah Rider HL .12 .30
136 Armon Gilliam HL .10 .25
137 Patrick Ewing HL .20 .50
138 Shaquille O'Neal HL .40 1.00
139 Jerry Stackhouse HL .20 .50
140 Charles Barkley HL .25 .60
141 Clifford Robinson HL .10 .25
142 Mitch Richmond HL .15 .40
143 David Robinson HL .25 .60
144 Shawn Kemp HL .15 .40
145 Damon Stoudamire HL .12 .30
146 Karl Malone HL .20 .50
147 Bryant Reeves HL .10 .25
148 Juwan Howard HL .12 .30
149 Checklist .10 .25
150 Checklist .10 .25
151 Alan Henderson .10 .25
152 Priest Lauderdale RC .10 .25
153 Dikembe Mutombo .15 .40
154 Dana Barros .10 .25
155 Todd Day .10 .25
156 Brett Szabo RC .15 .40
157 Antoine Walker RC .25 .60
158 Scott Burrell .10 .25
159 Tony Delk RC .15 .40
160 Vlade Divac .15 .40
161 Matt Geiger .10 .25
162 Anthony Mason .10 .25
163 Malik Rose RC .20 .50
164 Ron Harper .12 .30
165 Steve Kerr .12 .30
166 Luc Longley .12 .30
167 Danny Ferry .10 .25
168 Tyrone Hill .10 .25
169 Vitaly Potapenko RC .12 .30
170 Tony Dumas .10 .25
171 Chris Gatling .10 .25
172 Oliver Miller .10 .25
173 Eric Montross .10 .25
174 Samaki Walker RC .12 .30
175 Darvin Ham RC .15 .40
176 Mark Jackson .12 .30
177 Ervin Johnson .10 .25
178 Stacey Augmon .12 .30
179 Joe Dumars .15 .40
180 Grant Hill .25 .60
181 Grant Long .10 .25
182 Terry Mills .10 .25
183 Otis Thorpe .10 .25
184 Jerome Williams RC .12 .30
185 B.J. Armstrong .10 .25
186 Todd Fuller RC .10 .25
187 Ray Owes RC .15 .40
188 Mark Price .15 .40
189 Felton Spencer .10 .25
190 Charles Barkley .25 .60
191 Mario Elie .10 .25
192 Othella Harrington RC .15 .40
193 Matt Maloney RC .12 .30
194 Brent Price .10 .25
195 Kevin Willis .10 .25
196 Travis Best .10 .25
197 Erick Dampier RC .15 .40
198 Antonio Davis .10 .25
199 Jalen Rose .12 .30
200 Pooh Richardson .10 .25
201 Rodney Rogers .10 .25
202 Lorenzen Wright RC .12 .30
203 Kobe Bryant RC 3.00 8.00
204 Derek Fisher RC .20 .50
205 Travis Knight RC .15 .40
206 Shaquille O'Neal .40 1.00
207 Byron Scott .12 .30
208 P.J. Brown .10 .25
209 Sasha Danilovic .10 .25
210 Dan Majerle .15 .40
211 Martin Muursepp RC .10 .25
212 Ray Allen RC .60 1.50
213 Armon Gilliam .10 .25
214 Andrew Lang .10 .25
215 Moochie Norris RC .15 .40
216 Kevin Garnett .40 1.00
217 Tom Gugliotta .10 .25
218 Shane Heal RC .15 .40
219 Stephon Marbury RC .40 1.00
220 Stojko Vrankovic .10 .25
221 Kerry Kittles RC .15 .40
222 Robert Pack .10 .25
223 Jayson Williams .10 .25
224 Allan Houston .12 .30
225 Larry Johnson .15 .40
226 Dontae' Jones RC .15 .40
227 Walter McCarty RC .15 .40
228 John Wallace RC .15 .40
229 Charlie Ward .10 .25
230 Brian Evans RC .15 .40
231 Amal McCaskill RC .15 .40
232 Brian Shaw .10 .25
233 Mark Davis .10 .25
234 Lucious Harris .10 .25
235 Allen Iverson RC .75 2.00
236 Sam Cassell .12 .30
237 Robert Horry .12 .30
238 Danny Manning .12 .30
239 Steve Nash RC .75 2.00
240 Kenny Anderson .12 .30
241 Aleksandar Djordjevic RC .15 .40
242 Jermaine O'Neal RC .25 .60
243 Isaiah Rider .12 .30
244 Rasheed Wallace .20 .50
245 Mahmoud Abdul-Rauf .10 .25
246 Michael Smith .10 .25
247 Corliss Williamson .10 .25
248 Vernon Maxwell .10 .25
249 Charles Smith .10 .25
250 Dominique Wilkins .20 .50
251 Craig Ehlo .10 .25
252 Jim McIlvaine .10 .25
253 Sam Perkins .10 .25
254 Marcus Camby RC .25 .60
255 Popeye Jones .10 .25
256 Donald Whiteside RC .15 .40
257 Walt Williams .10 .25
258 Jeff Hornacek .12 .30
259 Karl Malone .20 .50
260 Bryon Russell .10 .25
261 John Stockton .20 .50
262 Shareef Abdur-Rahim RC .25 .60
263 Anthony Peeler .10 .25
264 Roy Rogers RC .12 .30
265 Tim Legler .10 .25
266 Tracy Murray .10 .25
267 Rod Strickland .10 .25
268 Ben Wallace RC .75 2.00
269 Kevin Garnett CB .40 1.00
270 Allan Houston CB .12 .30
271 Eddie Jones CB .15 .40
272 Jamal Mashburn CB .12 .30
273 Antonio McDyess CB .15 .40
274 Glenn Robinson CB .12 .30
275 Joe Smith CB .12 .30
276 Steve Smith CB .12 .30
277 Jerry Stackhouse CB .20 .50
278 Damon Stoudamire CB .12 .30
279 Hakeem Olajuwon AS .20 .50
280 Charles Barkley AS .25 .60
281 Patrick Ewing AS .20 .50
282 Michael Jordan AS 1.25 3.00
283 Clyde Drexler AS .20 .50
284 Karl Malone AS .20 .50
285 John Stockton AS .20 .50
286 David Robinson AS .25 .60
287 Scottie Pippen AS .25 .60
288 Shawn Kemp AS .15 .40
289 Shaquille O'Neal AS .40 1.00
290 Mitch Richmond AS .15 .40
291 Reggie Miller AS .20 .50
292 Alonzo Mourning AS .20 .50
293 Gary Payton AS .15 .40
294 Anfernee Hardaway AS .25 .60
295 Grant Hill AS .25 .60
296 Dennis Rodman AS .30 .75
297 Juwan Howard AS .12 .30
298 Jason Kidd AS .25 .60
299 Checklist .10 .25
300 Checklist .10 .25

1996-97 Fleer Decade of Excellence

Randomly inserted exclusively into both series hobby packs at a rate of one in 72, this 20-card set features reprints from the popular 1986-87 debut Fleer set. Card fronts are designated with the card name "Fleer Decade of Excellence 1986-1996" in gold foil to distinguish the card from the original issue. Card backs are identical to the 1986-87 release, but with a "1996" copyright.

COMPLETE SET (20) 50.00 110.00
COMPLETE SERIES 1 (10) 25.00 60.00
COMPLETE SERIES 2 (10) 25.00 50.00
SER.1/2 STATED ODDS 1:72 HOBBY
1 Clyde Drexler 4.00 10.00
2 Joe Dumars 3.00 8.00
3 Derek Harper 2.50 6.00
4 Michael Jordan 10.00 25.00
5 Karl Malone 6.00 15.00
6 Chris Mullin 3.00 8.00
7 Charles Oakley 2.50 6.00
8 Sam Perkins 2.00 5.00
9 Ricky Pierce 2.00 5.00
10 Buck Williams 2.00 5.00
11 Charles Barkley 8.00 20.00
12 Patrick Ewing 4.00 10.00
13 Eddie Johnson 2.00 5.00
14 Hakeem Olajuwon 6.00 15.00
15 Robert Parish 3.00 8.00
16 Byron Scott 2.50 6.00
17 Wayman Tisdale 2.00 5.00
18 Gerald Wilkins 2.00 5.00
19 Herb Williams 2.00 5.00
20 Kevin Willis 2.00 5.00

1996-97 Fleer Franchise Futures

Randomly inserted exclusively into first series hobby packs at a rate of one in 54, this 10-card set features young stars that may be the future of their respecive teams. Card fronts feature an embossed photo with the card name "Franchise Future" running along the left side of the card in silver foil. The player's name is also treated with silver foil at the bottom of the card. Card backs feature a brief commentary on the player and are numbered "X of 10".

COMPLETE SET (10) 6.00 15.00
SER.1 STATED ODDS 1:54 HOBBY
1 Kevin Garnett 2.50 6.00
2 Anfernee Hardaway 1.50 4.00
3 Grant Hill 1.50 4.00
4 Juwan Howard .75 2.00
5 Jason Kidd 1.50 4.00
6 Antonio McDyess 1.00 2.50
7 Glenn Robinson .75 2.00
8 Joe Smith .75 2.00
9 Jerry Stackhouse 1.25 3.00
10 Damon Stoudamire .75 2.00

1996-97 Fleer Game Breakers

Randomly inserted exclusively into first series retail packs at a rate of one in 48, this 15-card set features some of the top duos from the NBA. The card fronts are made of plastic and feature color action shots of both players represented. Both player's last names are in gold foil at the bottom under the Game Breakers card name. Card backs feature a background of the team's colors with a brief commentary on each individual player and are numbered "X of 15".

COMPLETE SET (15) 60.00 150.00
SER.1 STATED ODDS 1:48 RETAIL
1 M.Jordan/S.Pippen 30.00 80.00
2 J.Jackson/J.Kidd 5.00 12.00
3 G.Hill/A.Houston 5.00 12.00
4 J.Smith/L.Sprewell 3.00 8.00
5 C.Drexler/H.Olajuwon 4.00 10.00
6 C.Ceballos/N.Van Exel 3.00 8.00
7 T.Hardaway/A.Mourning 4.00 10.00
8 V.Baker/G.Robinson 2.50 6.00
9 K.Garnett/I.Rider 8.00 20.00
10 A.Hardaway/S.O'Neal 12.00 30.00
11 J.Stackhouse/C.Weatherspoon 4.00 10.00
12 C.Barkley/M.Finley 5.00 12.00
13 S.Elliott/D.Robinson 5.00 12.00
14 S.Kemp/G.Payton 8.00 20.00
15 K.Malone/J.Stockton 4.00 10.00

1996-97 Fleer Lucky 13

Randomly inserted into all first series packs at a rate of one in 30, this 13-card set features cards that are redeemable for the top 13 player's selected in the 1996 NBA Draft. Card fronts contain a colorful background with a number from 1-13. Whatever card number is on the front corresponds to the rookie selected at that spot in the 1996 NBA draft and can be redeemed for a special card featuring that player. The expiration date for this redemption is April 1, 1997. Cards are numbered on the back as "X of 13".

COMPLETE SET (13) 25.00 60.00
EXCH.CARDS: SER.1 STATED ODDS 1:30
1 Allen Iverson 5.00 12.00
2 Marcus Camby 1.50 4.00
3 Shareef Abdur-Rahim 1.50 4.00
4 Stephon Marbury 2.50 6.00
5 Ray Allen 4.00 10.00
6 Antoine Walker 1.50 4.00
7 Lorenzen Wright .75 2.00
8 Kerry Kittles 1.00 2.50
9 Samaki Walker .75 2.00
10 Erick Dampier 1.00 2.50
11 Todd Fuller .60 1.50
12 Vitaly Potapenko .75 2.00
13 Kobe Bryant 10.00 25.00
NNO Expired Trade Cards .10 .30

1996-97 Fleer Rookie Rewind

Randomly inserted in all first series packs at a rate of one in 24, this 15-card set takes a look back at the top rookies from the 1995-96 class. Card fronts contain team colors in the background with both the card name "Rookie Rewind" and the player's last name treated in gold foil. Card backs contain another player shot and a brief commentary. Card backs are numbered as "X of 15".

COMPLETE SET (15) 10.00 25.00
SER.1 STATED ODDS 1:24 HOBBY/RETAIL
1 Brent Barry 1.00 2.50
2 Tyus Edney .75 2.00
3 Michael Finley 1.50 4.00
4 Kevin Garnett 3.00 8.00
5 Antonio McDyess 1.25 3.00
6 Bryant Reeves .75 2.00
7 Arvydas Sabonis 1.00 2.50
8 Joe Smith 1.00 2.50
9 Jerry Stackhouse 1.50 4.00
10 Damon Stoudamire 1.00 2.50
11 Bob Sura .75 2.00
12 Kurt Thomas .75 2.00
13 Gary Trent .75 2.00
14 Rasheed Wallace 1.50 4.00
15 Eric Williams .75 2.00

1996-97 Fleer Rookie Sensations

Randomly inserted into all second series packs at a rate of one in 90, this 15-card set features etched-foil and embossing and focuses on the top rookies from the 1996-97 season.

COMPLETE SET (15) 75.00 150.00
SER.2 STATED ODDS 1:90 HOBBY/RETAIL
1 Shareef Abdur-Rahim 3.00 8.00
2 Ray Allen 8.00 20.00
3 Kobe Bryant 25.00 60.00
4 Marcus Camby 3.00 8.00
5 Erick Dampier 2.00 5.00
6 Tony Delk 2.00 5.00
7 Allen Iverson 10.00 25.00
8 Kerry Kittles 2.00 5.00
9 Stephon Marbury 5.00 12.00
10 Steve Nash 8.00 20.00
11 Roy Rogers 1.50 4.00
12 Antoine Walker 3.00 8.00
13 Samaki Walker 1.50 4.00
14 John Wallace 2.00 5.00
15 Lorenzen Wright 1.50 4.00

1996-97 Fleer Stackhouse's All-Fleer

Randomly inserted in first series nine-card packs at a rate of one in 12 and one per special first series retail pack, this 12-card set features some of the top player's in the NBA as seen through Fleer Spokesman Jerry Stackhouse's eyes. Card fronts contain team colors in the background and have both the card name and the player's name running vertical in gold foil. Card backs contain a brief statistical summary and are numbered as "X of 12".

COMPLETE SET (12) 6.00 15.00
SER.1 STATED ODDS 1:12 HOBBY/RETAIL
ONE PER SPECIAL SER.1 RETAIL PACK
1 Charles Barkley .60 1.50
2 Anfernee Hardaway .60 1.50
3 Grant Hill .60 1.50
4 Michael Jordan 3.00 8.00
5 Shawn Kemp .40 1.00
6 Jason Kidd .60 1.50
7 Karl Malone .50 1.25
8 Hakeem Olajuwon .50 1.25
9 Shaquille O'Neal 1.00 2.50
10 Gary Payton .40 1.00
11 Scottie Pippen .60 1.50
12 David Robinson .60 1.50

1996-97 Fleer Stackhouse's Scrapbook

Randomly inserted into all first series packs at a rate of one in 24, cards from this two-card set highlight moments from Stackhouse's rookie year. In addition, they are the last installment to the cross-brand insert from all of the 1995-96 Fleer products.

COMPLETE SET (2) 1.50 4.00
COMMON STACK. (S9-S10) 1.00 2.50
SER.1 STATED ODDS 1:24 HOB/RET

1996-97 Fleer Swing Shift

Randomly inserted into all second series packs at a rate of one in 6, this 15-card set focuses on players who can not only play well from the outside, but who can also post up down low. Card fronts feature a "shattered" glass colored background.

COMPLETE SET (15) 5.00 12.00
SER.2 STATED ODDS 1:6 HOBBY/RETAIL
1 Ray Allen 1.00 2.50
2 Charles Barkley .75 2.00
3 Michael Finley .60 1.50
4 Anfernee Hardaway .75 2.00
5 Grant Hill .75 2.00
6 Jim Jackson .30 .75
7 Eddie Jones .50 1.25
8 Kerry Kittles .25 .60
9 Reggie Miller .60 1.50
10 Gary Payton .50 1.25
11 Scottie Pippen .75 2.00
12 Mitch Richmond .50 1.25
13 Steve Smith .40 1.00
14 Latrell Sprewell .50 1.25
15 Jerry Stackhouse .60 1.50

1996-97 Fleer Thrill Seekers

Randomly inserted into second series hobby packs only at a rate of one in 240, this 15-card set uses

Lenticular technology and showcases NBA players who know how to "thrill" NBA fans.
SER.2 STATED ODDS 1:240 HOBBY
1 Shareef Abdur-Rahim 25.00 60.00
2 Charles Barkley 60.00 150.00
3 Anfernee Hardaway 50.00 120.00
4 Grant Hill 60.00 150.00
5 Allen Iverson 100.00 250.00
6 Michael Jordan 1000.00 1500.00
7 Shawn Kemp 60.00 150.00
8 Jason Kidd 60.00 150.00
9 Stephon Marbury 30.00 80.00
10 Antonio McDyess 30.00 80.00
11 Reggie Miller 100.00 250.00
12 Alonzo Mourning 75.00 200.00
13 Shaquille O'Neal 75.00 200.00
14 David Robinson 75.00 200.00
15 Damon Stoudamire 30.00 80.00

1996-97 Fleer Total O

Randomly inserted into second series retail packs only at a rate of one in 44, this 10-card set features NBA players known for their offensive ability. Cards are printed on clear plastic stock and card fronts feature half of a colorful basketball in the background.

COMPLETE SET (10) 60.00 150.00
SER.2 STATED ODDS 1:44 RETAIL
1 Anfernee Hardaway 6.00 15.00
2 Grant Hill 5.00 12.00
3 Juwan Howard 2.50 6.00
4 Michael Jordan 50.00 120.00
5 Shawn Kemp 3.00 8.00
6 Karl Malone 4.00 10.00
7 Alonzo Mourning 4.00 10.00
8 Hakeem Olajuwon 4.00 10.00
9 Shaquille O'Neal 8.00 20.00
10 Jerry Stackhouse 4.00 10.00

1996-97 Fleer Towers of Power

Randomly inserted into all second series packs at a rate of one in 30, this 10-card set focuses on the dominent men of the NBA. Card fronts feature etched foil.

COMPLETE SET (10) 15.00 30.00
SER.2 STATED ODDS 1:30 HOBBY/RETAIL
1 Shareef Abdur-Rahim 1.25 3.00
2 Marcus Camby 1.25 3.00
3 Patrick Ewing 2.00 5.00
4 Kevin Garnett 4.00 10.00
5 Shawn Kemp 1.50 4.00
6 Hakeem Olajuwon 2.00 5.00
7 Shaquille O'Neal 4.00 10.00
8 David Robinson 2.50 6.00
9 Dennis Rodman 3.00 8.00
10 Joe Smith 1.25 3.00

1997-98 Fleer

This 350-card set was released in two series with 10-card packs that carried a suggested retail price of $1.49 and $1.59. The cards carry a Textured Legend matte finish that makes the cards idea for autographs. The cards feature full-bleed action photos with the player's name appearing in gold foil block type at the bottom. The player's team and position are in gold foil script below the name. The backs carry career statistics.

COMPLETE SET (350) 20.00 40.00
COMPLETE SERIES 1 (200) 10.00 20.00
COMPLETE SERIES 2 (150) 10.00 20.00
1 Anfernee Hardaway .25 .60
2 Mitch Richmond .15 .40
3 Allen Iverson .30 .75
4 Chris Webber .15 .40
5 Sasha Danilovic .10 .25
6 Avery Johnson .12 .30
7 Kenny Anderson .12 .30
8 Antoine Walker .15 .40
9 Nick Van Exel .12 .30
10 Mookie Blaylock .10 .25
11 Wesley Person .10 .25
12 Vlade Divac .15 .40
13 Glenn Robinson .12 .30
14 Chris Mills .10 .25
15 Latrell Sprewell .15 .40
16 Jayson Williams .10 .25
17 Travis Best .10 .25
18 Charlie Ward .10 .25
19 Theo Ratliff .12 .30
20 Gary Payton .15 .40
21 Marcus Camby .15 .40
22 Clyde Drexler .20 .50
23 Michael Jordan 1.25 3.00
24 Antonio McDyess .12 .30
25 Stephon Marbury .20 .50
26 Isaac Austin .10 .25
27 Shareef Abdur-Rahim .15 .40
28 Malik Sealy .10 .25
29 Arvydas Sabonis .12 .30
30 Kerry Kittles .10 .25
31 Reggie Miller .20 .50
32 Karl Malone .20 .50
33 Grant Hill .25 .60
34 Hakeem Olajuwon .20 .50
35 Danny Ferry .10 .25
36 Dominique Wilkins .20 .50
37 Armon Gilliam .10 .25
38 Danny Manning .12 .30
39 Larry Johnson .15 .40
40 Dino Radja .10 .25
41 Jason Caffey .10 .25
42 Jerry Stackhouse .15 .40
43 Alonzo Mourning .20 .50
44 Shawn Bradley .10 .25
45 Bo Outlaw .10 .25
46 Bryon Russell .10 .25
47 Doug West .10 .25
48 Lawrence Moten .10 .25
49 Dale Ellis .10 .25
50 Kobe Bryant .75 2.00
51 Carlos Rogers .10 .25
52 Todd Fuller .10 .25
53 Tyus Edney .10 .25
54 Horace Grant .12 .30
55 Dikembe Mutombo .15 .40
56 Jim McIlvaine .10 .25
57 Harvey Grant .10 .25
58 Dean Garrett .10 .25
59 Samaki Walker .10 .25
60 Johnny Newman .10 .25
61 Antonio Davis .10 .25
62 Jamal Mashburn .12 .30
63 Muggsy Bogues .12 .30
64 Rod Strickland .10 .25
65 Craig Ehlo .10 .25
66 Rex Walters .10 .25
67 Bob Sura .10 .25
68 Travis Knight .10 .25
69 Toni Kukoc .15 .40
70 Antoine Carr .10 .25
71 Mario Elie .10 .25
72 Popeye Jones .10 .25
73 David Wesley .10 .25
74 John Wallace .10 .25
75 Calbert Cheaney .10 .25
76 Grant Long .10 .25
77 Will Perdue .10 .25
78 Rasheed Wallace .15 .40
79 Chris Gatling .10 .25
80 Corliss Williamson .10 .25
81 B.J. Armstrong .10 .25
82 Brian Shaw .10 .25
83 Darrick Martin .10 .25
84 Vinny Del Negro .10 .25
85 Tony Delk .10 .25
86 Greg Anthony .10 .25
87 Mark Davis .10 .25
88 Anthony Goldwire .10 .25
89 Rex Chapman .10 .25
90 Stojko Vrankovic .10 .25
91 Dennis Rodman .30 .75
92 Detlef Schrempf .15 .40
93 Henry James .10 .25
94 Tracy Murray .10 .25
95 Voshon Lenard .10 .25
96 Sharone Wright .10 .25
97 Ed O'Bannon .10 .25
98 Gerald Wilkins .10 .25
99 Kevin Willis .10 .25
100 Shaquille O'Neal .40 1.00
101 Jim Jackson .10 .25
102 Mark Price .15 .40
103 Patrick Ewing .20 .50
104 Lorenzen Wright .10 .25
105 Tyrone Hill .10 .25
106 Ray Allen .20 .50
107 Jermaine O'Neal .12 .30
108 Anthony Mason .12 .30
109 Mahmoud Abdul-Rauf .10 .25
110 Terry Mills .10 .25
111 Gheorghe Muresan .10 .25
112 Mark Jackson .12 .30
113 Greg Ostertag .10 .25
114 Kevin Johnson .15 .40
115 Anthony Peeler .10 .25
116 Rony Seikaly .10 .25
117 Keith Askins .10 .25
118 Todd Day .10 .25
119 Chris Childs .10 .25
120 Chris Carr .10 .25
121 Erick Strickland RC .12 .30
122 Elden Campbell .10 .25
123 Elliot Perry .10 .25
124 Pooh Richardson .10 .25
125 Juwan Howard .12 .30
126 Ervin Johnson .10 .25
127 Eric Montross .10 .25
128 Otis Thorpe .10 .25
129 Hersey Hawkins .10 .25
130 Bimbo Coles .10 .25
131 Olden Polynice .10 .25
132 Christian Laettner .12 .30
133 Sean Elliott .15 .40
134 Othella Harrington .10 .25
135 Erick Dampier .10 .25
136 Vitaly Potapenko .10 .25
137 Doug Christie .10 .25
138 Luc Longley .10 .25
139 Clarence Weatherspoon .10 .25
140 Gary Trent .10 .25
141 Shandon Anderson .10 .25
142 Sam Perkins .10 .25
143 Derek Harper .12 .30
144 Robert Horry .12 .30
145 Roy Rogers .10 .25
146 John Starks .12 .30
147 Tyrone Corbin .10 .25
148 Andrew Lang .10 .25
149 Derek Strong .10 .25
150 Joe Smith .12 .30
151 Ron Harper .12 .30
152 Sam Cassell .12 .30
153 Brent Barry .10 .25
154 LaPhonso Ellis .10 .25
155 Matt Geiger .10 .25
156 Steve Nash .30 .75
157 Michael Smith .10 .25
158 Eric Williams .10 .25
159 Tom Gugliotta .10 .25
160 Monty Williams .10 .25
161 Lindsey Hunter .10 .25
162 Oliver Miller .10 .25
163 Brent Price .10 .25
164 Derrick McKey .10 .25
165 Robert Pack .10 .25
166 Derrick Coleman .12 .30
167 Isaiah Rider .12 .30
168 Dan Majerle .15 .40
169 Jeff Hornacek .12 .30
170 Terrell Brandon .12 .30
171 Nate McMillan .10 .25
172 Cedric Ceballos .10 .25
173 Derek Fisher .15 .40
174 Rodney Rogers .10 .25
175 Blue Edwards .10 .25
176 Brooks Thompson .10 .25
177 Sherman Douglas .10 .25
178 Sam Mitchell .10 .25
179 Charles Oakley .12 .30
180 Greg Minor .10 .25
181 Chris Mullin .20 .50
182 P.J. Brown .10 .25
183 Stacey Augmon .12 .30
184 Don MacLean .10 .25
185 Aaron McKie .10 .25
186 Dale Davis .10 .25
187 Vernon Maxwell .10 .25
188 Dell Curry .10 .25
189 Kendall Gill .10 .25
190 Billy Owens .10 .25
191 Steve Kerr .12 .30
192 Matt Maloney .10 .25
193 Dennis Scott .10 .25
194 A.C. Green .12 .30
195 George McCloud .10 .25
196 Walt Williams .10 .25
197 Eldridge Recasner .10 .25
198 Checklist (Hawks/Bucks) .10 .25
199 Checklist (T'wolves/Wizards) .10 .25
200 Checklist (inserts) .10 .25
201 Tim Duncan RC .75 2.00
202 Tim Thomas RC .20 .50
203 Clifford Rozier .10 .25
204 Bryant Reeves .10 .25
205 Glen Rice .15 .40
206 Darrell Armstrong .15 .40
207 Juwan Howard .12 .30
208 John Stockton .20 .50
209 Antonio McDyess .12 .30
210 James Cotton RC .10 .25
211 Brian Grant .12 .30
212 Chris Whitney .10 .25
213 Antonio Davis .10 .25
214 Kendall Gill .10 .25
215 Adonal Foyle RC .12 .30
216 Dean Garrett .10 .25
217 Dennis Scott .10 .25
218 Zydrunas Ilgauskas .12 .30
219 Antonio Daniels RC .15 .40
220 Derek Harper .12 .30
221 Travis Knight .10 .25
222 Bobby Hurley .10 .25
223 Greg Anderson .10 .25
224 Rod Strickland .10 .25
225 David Benoit .10 .25
226 Tracy McGrady RC .60 1.50
227 Brian Williams .10 .25
228 James Robinson .10 .25
229 Randy Brown .10 .25
230 Greg Foster .10 .25
231 Reggie Miller .20 .50
232 Eric Montross .10 .25
233 Malik Rose .10 .25
234 Charles Barkley .25 .60
235 Tony Battie RC .15 .40
236 Terry Mills .10 .25
237 Jerald Honeycutt RC .15 .40
238 Bubba Wells RC .15 .40
239 John Wallace .10 .25
240 Jason Kidd .25 .60
241 Mark Price .15 .40
242 Ron Mercer RC .20 .50
243 Derrick Coleman .12 .30
244 Fred Hoiberg .10 .25
245 Wesley Person .10 .25
246 Eddie Jones .15 .40
247 Allan Houston .12 .30
248 Keith Van Horn RC .25 .60
249 Johnny Newman .10 .25
250 Kevin Garnett .25 .60
251 Latrell Sprewell .15 .40
252 Tracy Murray .10 .25
253 Charles O'Bannon RC .15 .40
254 Lamond Murray .10 .25
255 Jerry Stackhouse .15 .40
256 Rik Smits .12 .30
257 Alan Henderson .10 .25
258 Tariq Abdul-Wahad RC .12 .30
259 Nick Anderson .10 .25
260 Calbert Cheaney .10 .25
261 Scottie Pippen .25 .60
262 Rodrick Rhodes RC .10 .25
263 Derek Anderson RC .15 .40
264 Dana Barros .10 .25
265 Todd Day .10 .25
266 Michael Finley .15 .40
267 Kevin Edwards .10 .25
268 Terrell Brandon .12 .30
269 Bobby Phills .10 .25
270 Kelvin Cato RC .12 .30
271 Vin Baker .12 .30
272 Eric Washington RC .15 .40
273 Jim Jackson .10 .25
274 Joe Dumars .15 .40
275 David Robinson .25 .60
276 Jayson Williams .10 .25
277 Travis Best .10 .25
278 Kurt Thomas .10 .25
279 Otis Thorpe .10 .25
280 Damon Stoudamire .12 .30
281 John Williams .10 .25
282 Loy Vaught .10 .25
283 Bo Outlaw .10 .25
284 Todd Fuller .10 .25
285 Terry Davis .10 .25
286 Clarence Weatherspoon .10 .25
287 Danny Fortson RC .15 .40
288 Howard Eisley .10 .25
289 Steve Smith .12 .30
290 Chris Webber .15 .40
291 Shawn Kemp .15 .40
292 Sam Cassell .12 .30
293 Rick Fox .10 .25
294 Walter McCarty .10 .25
295 Mark Jackson .12 .30
296 Chris Mills .10 .25
297 Jacque Vaughn RC .12 .30
298 Shawn Respert .10 .25
299 Scott Burrell .10 .25
300 Allen Iverson .30 .75
301 Charles Smith RC .12 .30
302 Ervin Johnson .10 .25
303 Hubert Davis .10 .25
304 Eddie Johnson .10 .25
305 Erick Dampier .10 .25
306 Eric Williams .10 .25
307 Anthony Johnson RC .15 .40
308 David Wesley .10 .25
309 Eric Piatkowski .10 .25
310 Austin Croshere RC .20 .50
311 Malik Sealy .10 .25
312 George McCloud .10 .25
313 Anthony Parker RC .15 .40
314 Cedric Henderson RC .15 .40
315 John Thomas RC .10 .25
316 Cory Alexander .10 .25
317 Johnny Taylor RC .12 .30
318 Chris Mullin .20 .50
319 J.R. Reid .10 .25
320 George Lynch .10 .25
321 Lawrence Funderburke RC .15 .40
322 God Shammgod RC .15 .40
323 Bobby Jackson RC .20 .50
324 Khalid Reeves .10 .25
325 Zan Tabak .10 .25
326 Chris Gatling .10 .25
327 Alvin Williams RC .15 .40
328 Scot Pollard RC .15 .40
329 Kerry Kittles .10 .25
330 Tim Hardaway .15 .40
331 Maurice Taylor RC .15 .40
332 Keith Booth RC .10 .25
333 Chris Morris .10 .25
334 Bryant Stith .10 .25
335 Terry Cummings .10 .25
336 Ed Gray RC .15 .40
337 Eric Snow .12 .30
338 Clifford Robinson .10 .25
339 Chris Dudley .10 .25
340 Chauncey Billups RC .50 1.25
341 Paul Grant RC .10 .25
342 Tyrone Hill .10 .25
343 Joe Smith .12 .30
344 Sean Rooks .10 .25
345 Harvey Grant .10 .25
346 Dale Davis .10 .25
347 Brevin Knight RC .15 .40
348 Serge Zwikker RC .10 .25
349 Checklist (Hawks/Kings) .10 .25
350 Checklist (Spurs/Wizards/Inserts) .10 .25

1997-98 Fleer Crystal Collection

*STARS: 1.5X TO 4X BASE CARD HI
*RCs: 1.25X TO 3X BASE HI
BOTH SERIES STATED ODDS 1:2 HOBBY
23 Michael Jordan 6.00 15.00
201 Tim Duncan 5.00 12.00

1997-98 Fleer Tiffany Collection

*STARS: 10X TO 25X BASE CARD HI
*RCs: 5X TO 12X BASE HI
SER.1/2 STATED ODDS 1:20 HOBBY
23 Michael Jordan 50.00 120.00
201 Tim Duncan 40.00 100.00

1997-98 Fleer Decade of Excellence

Randomly inserted in series one hobby packs only at a rate of one in 36, this 12-card set showcases players that have been in the NBA for 10 or more years using photos from the 1987-88 season and graphic design showcasing the 1987-88 Fleer basketball design.

SER.1 STATED ODDS 1:36 HOBBY
*RARE TRAD: 1.5X TO 4X HI COLUMN
RARE TRAD: SER.1 STATED ODDS 1:360 HOB
1 Charles Barkley 2.50 6.00
2 Clyde Drexler 2.00 5.00
3 Patrick Ewing 2.00 5.00
4 Kevin Johnson 1.50 4.00
5 Michael Jordan 12.00 30.00
6 Karl Malone 2.00 5.00
7 Reggie Miller 2.00 5.00
8 Hakeem Olajuwon 2.00 5.00
9 Scottie Pippen 2.50 6.00
10 Dennis Rodman 3.00 8.00
11 John Stockton 2.00 5.00
12 Dominique Wilkins 2.00 5.00

1997-98 Fleer Flair Hardwood Leaders

Randomly inserted in all series one packs at a rate of one in six, this 29-card set features the heavier stock associated with the Flair brand. One player or "leader" from each team is depicted in the set.

COMPLETE SET (29) 15.00 40.00
SER.1 STATED ODDS 1:6 HOBBY/RETAIL
1 Christian Laettner .50 1.25
2 Antoine Walker .60 1.50
3 Glen Rice .60 1.50
4 Michael Jordan 5.00 12.00
5 Terrell Brandon .40 1.00
6 Michael Finley .60 1.50
7 Antonio McDyess .50 1.25
8 Grant Hill 1.00 2.50
9 Latrell Sprewell .60 1.50
10 Hakeem Olajuwon .75 2.00
11 Reggie Miller .75 2.00
12 Loy Vaught .40 1.00
13 Shaquille O'Neal 1.50 4.00
14 Alonzo Mourning .75 2.00
15 Vin Baker .50 1.25
16 Kevin Garnett 1.00 2.50
17 Kerry Kittles .40 1.00
18 Patrick Ewing .75 2.00
19 Anfernee Hardaway 1.00 2.50
20 Jerry Stackhouse .60 1.50
21 Jason Kidd 1.00 2.50
22 Kenny Anderson .50 1.25
23 Mitch Richmond .60 1.50
24 David Robinson 1.00 2.50
25 Shawn Kemp .60 1.50
26 Damon Stoudamire .50 1.25
27 Karl Malone .75 2.00
28 Shareef Abdur-Rahim .60 1.50
29 Chris Webber .60 1.50

1997-98 Fleer Franchise Futures

Randomly inserted in series one retail packs only at a rate of one in 36, this 10-card set focuses on players with up to three years experience who are their team's future. The cards feature a die cut design with a full etched foil front.

COMPLETE SET (10) 8.00 20.00
SER.1 STATED ODDS 1:36 RETAIL
1 Shareef Abdur-Rahim 1.00 2.50
2 Ray Allen 1.25 3.00
3 Kobe Bryant 6.00 15.00
4 Kevin Garnett 1.50 4.00
5 Grant Hill 1.50 4.00
6 Juwan Howard .75 2.00
7 Allen Iverson 2.00 5.00
8 Kerry Kittles .60 1.50
9 Joe Smith .75 2.00
10 Damon Stoudamire .75 2.00

1997-98 Fleer Game Breakers

Randomly inserted in all series one packs at a rate of one in 288, this 12-card dual player set features some of the NBA's best duos. Card fronts carry etched-foil.

SER.1 STATED ODDS 1:288 HOBBY/RETAIL
1 M.Jordan/D.Rodman 60.00 150.00
2 J.Dumars/G.Hill 10.00 25.00
3 J.Smith/L.Sprewell 6.00 15.00
4 C.Barkley/H.Olajuwon 8.00 20.00
5 E.Jones/S.O'Neal 12.00 30.00
6 K.Garnett/S.Marbury 12.00 30.00
7 N.Anderson/A.Hardaway 8.00 20.00
8 A.Iverson/J.Stackhouse 10.00 25.00
9 S.Kemp/G.Payton 10.00 25.00
10 M.Camby/D.Stoudamire 6.00 15.00
11 K.Malone/J.Stockton 8.00 20.00
12 J.Howard/C.Webber 8.00 20.00

1997-98 Fleer Goudey Greats

Randomly inserted into series two packs at a rate of one in four, this 15-card set features some of today's players in the Goudey card style from yesteryear complete with commentary from NBA Hall of Famer Nate "Tiny" Archibald.

COMPLETE SET (15) 4.00 10.00
SER.2 STATED ODDS 1:4 HOBBY/RETAIL
1 Ray Allen .50 1.25
2 Clyde Drexler .50 1.25
3 Patrick Ewing .50 1.25
4 Anfernee Hardaway .60 1.50
5 Grant Hill .60 1.50
6 Stephon Marbury .50 1.25
7 Alonzo Mourning .50 1.25
8 Shaquille O'Neal 1.00 2.50
9 Gary Payton .60 1.50
10 Scottie Pippen .60 1.50
11 David Robinson .60 1.50
12 Joe Smith .30 .75
13 John Stockton .50 1.25
14 Damon Stoudamire .30 .75
15 Antoine Walker .30 .75

1997-98 Fleer Key Ingredient

Randomly inserted in series one retail packs only at a rate of one in two, this 15-card set features players who are the "key" to their teams' success.

COMPLETE SET (15) 2.00 5.00
SER.1 STATED ODDS 1:2 RETAIL
*GOLD: 2.5X TO 6X KEY INGRED. HI
GOLD: SER.1 STATED ODDS 1:18 HOB/RET
1 Charles Barkley .30 .75
2 Marcus Camby .20 .50
3 Anfernee Hardaway .30 .75
4 Juwan Howard .15 .40
5 Shawn Kemp .20 .50
6 Karl Malone .25 .60
7 Stephon Marbury .25 .60
8 Alonzo Mourning .25 .60
9 Shaquille O'Neal .50 1.25
10 Scottie Pippen .30 .75
11 Mitch Richmond .20 .50
12 David Robinson .30 .75
13 Joe Smith .15 .40
14 Jerry Stackhouse .20 .50
15 Antoine Walker .20 .50

1997-98 Fleer Million Dollar Moments

These cards were inserted one per pack in all 1997-98 Fleer basketball products. The set contains 50 cards. If a collector put together the complete set, they could win the Grand Prize of $1,000,000. The game ended on August 31, 1998. Cards numbered 46-50 originally were the tougher cards to pull, but were available at the more common level after the game ended.

COMPLETE SET (50) 2.50 6.00
1 Checklist (1-50) .05 .15
2 Mark Jackson .07 .20
3 Charles Barkley .15 .40
4 Terrell Brandon .05 .15
5 Wayman Tisdale .05 .15
6 Clyde Drexler .12 .30
7 Patrick Ewing .12 .30
8 Kevin Garnett .15 .40
9 Tom Gugliotta .05 .15
10 Anfernee Hardaway .15 .40
11 Tim Hardaway .10 .25
12 Grant Hill .15 .40
13 Allen Iverson .20 .50
14 Shawn Kemp .10 .25
15 Jason Kidd .15 .40
16 Charles Oakley .07 .20
17 Karl Malone .12 .30
18 Alonzo Mourning .12 .30
19 Shaquille O'Neal .25 .60
20 Hakeem Olajuwon .12 .30
21 Chris Webber .10 .25
22 Scottie Pippen .15 .40
23 Glen Rice .07 .20
24 Mitch Richmond .07 .20
25 David Robinson .15 .40
26 Dennis Rodman .20 .50
27 Jerry Stackhouse .10 .25
28 John Stockton .12 .30
29 Mookie Blaylock .05 .15
30 Muggsy Bogues .07 .20
31 Kobe Bryant .50 1.25
32 Rex Chapman .05 .15
33 Joe Dumars .10 .25
34 Dale Ellis .05 .15
35 Horace Grant .07 .20
36 Jeff Hornacek .07 .20
37 Damon Stoudamire .07 .20
38 Kevin Johnson .10 .25
39 Larry Johnson .10 .25
40 Toni Kukoc .10 .25
41 Danny Manning .07 .20
42 Stephon Marbury .12 .30
43 Reggie Miller .12 .30
44 Chris Mullin .10 .25
45 Dikembe Mutombo .10 .25
46 Gary Payton .10 .25
47 Christian Laettner .07 .20
48 Glenn Robinson .07 .20
49 Nick Van Exel .07 .20
50 Marcus Camby .10 .25

1997-98 Fleer Rookie Rewind

Randomly inserted in all series one packs at a rate of one in four, this 10-card set takes a look back at some of the best rookies from the 1996-97 season.

COMPLETE SET (10) 5.00 12.00
SER.1 STATED ODDS 1:4 HOBBY/RETAIL
1 Shareef Abdur-Rahim .60 1.50
2 Ray Allen .75 2.00
3 Kobe Bryant 3.00 8.00
4 Marcus Camby .60 1.50
5 Allen Iverson 1.25 3.00
6 Kerry Kittles .40 1.00
7 Matt Maloney .40 1.00
8 Stephon Marbury .75 2.00
9 Roy Rogers .40 1.00
10 Antoine Walker .60 1.50

1997-98 Fleer Rookie Sensations

Randomly inserted into series two packs at a rate of one in eight, this 10-card set features color photos of some of the top rookies from the 1997 class.

COMPLETE SET (10) 4.00 10.00
SER.2 STATED ODDS 1:8 HOBBY/RETAIL
1 Derek Anderson .30 .75
2 Tony Battie .30 .75
3 Chauncey Billups 1.00 2.50
4 Austin Croshere .25 .60
5 Antonio Daniels .30 .75
6 Tim Duncan 1.50 4.00
7 Tracy McGrady 1.25 3.00
8 Ron Mercer .40 1.00
9 Tim Thomas .40 1.00
10 Keith Van Horn .40 1.00

1997-98 Fleer Soaring Stars

Randomly inserted into series two retail packs at a rate of 1:2, this 20-card set showcases players who make headlines for their teams.

COMPLETE SET (20) 6.00 15.00
SER.2 STATED ODDS 1:2 RETAIL
*HIGH STARS: 1.5X TO 4X SOARING HI
HIGH FLY: SER.2 STATED ODDS 1:24 H/R
1 Shareef Abdur-Rahim .40 1.00
2 Ray Allen .50 1.25
3 Charles Barkley .60 1.50
4 Kobe Bryant 2.00 5.00
5 Marcus Camby .40 1.00
6 Kevin Garnett .60 1.50
7 Tim Hardaway .40 1.00
8 Eddie Jones .40 1.00
9 Michael Jordan 5.00 12.00
10 Shawn Kemp .40 1.00
11 Jason Kidd .60 1.50
12 Kerry Kittles .25 .60
13 Karl Malone .50 1.25
14 Antonio McDyess .30 .75
15 Glen Rice .40 1.00
16 Mitch Richmond .40 1.00
17 Latrell Sprewell .40 1.00
18 Jerry Stackhouse .40 1.00
19 Antoine Walker .40 1.00
20 Chris Webber .40 1.00

1997-98 Fleer Thrill Seekers

Randomly inserted into series two packs at a rate of one in 288, this 10-card set highlights some of the NBA's ultimate crowd pleasers. The cards feature matte finish frames and 100% etched silver holofoil background and spot UV coating.

SER.2 STATED ODDS 1:288 HOBBY/RETAIL
1 Shareef Abdur-Rahim 8.00 20.00
2 Kobe Bryant 50.00 120.00
3 Tim Duncan 30.00 80.00
4 Anfernee Hardaway 20.00 50.00
5 Grant Hill 12.00 30.00
6 Allen Iverson 15.00 40.00
7 Michael Jordan 150.00 400.00
8 Stephon Marbury 10.00 25.00
9 Dennis Rodman 25.00 60.00
10 Joe Smith 6.00 15.00

1997-98 Fleer Total O

Randomly inserted into series two retail packs only at a rate of one in 18, this 10-card set focuses on key offensive players.

COMPLETE SET (10) 25.00 60.00
SER.2 STATED ODDS 1:18 RETAIL
1 Anfernee Hardaway 4.00 10.00
2 Grant Hill 1.50 4.00
3 Juwan Howard .75 2.00
4 Allen Iverson 4.00 10.00
5 Michael Jordan 20.00 50.00
6 Karl Malone 1.25 3.00
7 Stephon Marbury 1.25 3.00
8 Hakeem Olajuwon 1.25 3.00
9 Shaquille O'Neal 2.50 6.00
10 Damon Stoudamire .75 2.00

1997-98 Fleer Towers of Power

Randomly inserted into series two packs at a rate of one in 18, this 12-card set features some of the NBA's most dominate big men. Cards feature a die cut design.

COMPLETE SET (12) 12.00 30.00
SER.2 STATED ODDS 1:18 HOBBY/RETAIL
1 Shareef Abdur-Rahim 1.25 3.00
2 Marcus Camby 1.25 3.00
3 Patrick Ewing 1.50 4.00
4 Kevin Garnett 2.00 5.00
5 Shawn Kemp 1.25 3.00
6 Karl Malone 1.50 4.00
7 Hakeem Olajuwon 1.50 4.00
8 Shaquille O'Neal 3.00 8.00
9 Dennis Rodman 2.50 6.00
10 Joe Smith 1.00 2.50
11 Antoine Walker 1.25 3.00
12 Chris Webber 1.25 3.00

1997-98 Fleer Zone

Randomly inserted into series two hobby packs only at a rate of one in 36, this 15-card set focuses on players known for getting into a "zone" during a game. Card design includes silver rainbow holofoil and a 100% etched foil background.

SER.2 STATED ODDS 1:36 HOBBY
1 Shareef Abdur-Rahim 2.00 5.00
2 Kobe Bryant 10.00 25.00
3 Marcus Camby 2.00 5.00
4 Tim Duncan 6.00 15.00
5 Kevin Garnett 3.00 8.00
6 Anfernee Hardaway 3.00 8.00
7 Grant Hill 3.00 8.00
8 Juwan Howard 1.50 4.00
9 Allen Iverson 4.00 10.00
10 Michael Jordan 40.00 100.00
11 Hakeem Olajuwon 2.50 6.00
12 Gary Payton 2.50 6.00
13 Scottie Pippen 3.00 8.00
14 Glen Rice 2.00 5.00
15 Keith Van Horn 3.00 8.00

1998-99 Fleer

The 1998-99 Fleer set, which is also known as Fleer Tradition, was issued in one series with a total of 150 cards. The packs were issued with 10 cards per pack carrying a suggested retail price of $1.59. The set contains the topical subset: Plus Factor (133-147).

COMPLETE SET (150) 10.00 20.00
1 Kobe Bryant .60 1.50
2 Corliss Williamson .10 .25
3 Allen Iverson .30 .75
4 Michael Finley .15 .40
5 Juwan Howard .12 .30
6 Marcus Camby .12 .30
7 Toni Kukoc .15 .40
8 Antoine Walker .15 .40
9 Stephon Marbury .20 .50
10 Tim Hardaway .15 .40
11 Zydrunas Ilgauskas .12 .30
12 John Stockton .20 .50
13 Glenn Robinson .12 .30
14 Isaiah Rider .12 .30
15 Danny Fortson .10 .25
16 Donyell Marshall .10 .25
17 Chris Mullin .20 .50
18 Shareef Abdur-Rahim .15 .40
19 Bobby Phills .10 .25
20 Gary Payton .15 .40
21 Derrick Coleman .12 .30
22 Larry Johnson .12 .30
23 Michael Jordan 1.25 3.00
24 Danny Manning .12 .30
25 Nick Anderson .10 .25
26 Chris Gatling .10 .25
27 Steve Smith .12 .30
28 Chris Whitney .10 .25
29 Terrell Brandon .12 .30
30 Rasheed Wallace .15 .40
31 Reggie Miller .20 .50
32 Karl Malone .20 .50
33 Grant Hill .25 .60
34 Hakeem Olajuwon .20 .50
35 Erick Dampier .12 .30
36 Vin Baker .12 .30
37 Tim Thomas .15 .40
38 Mark Price .15 .40
39 Shawn Bradley .10 .25
40 Calbert Cheaney .10 .25
41 Glen Rice .15 .40
42 Kevin Willis .10 .25
43 Chris Carr .10 .25
44 Keith Van Horn .15 .40
45 Jamal Mashburn .12 .30
46 Eddie Jones .15 .40
47 Brevin Knight .10 .25
48 Olden Polynice .10 .25
49 Bobby Jackson .10 .25
50 David Robinson .20 .50
51 Patrick Ewing .20 .50
52 Samaki Walker .10 .25
53 Antonio Daniels .10 .25
54 Rodney Rogers .10 .25
55 Dikembe Mutombo .15 .40
56 Tracy McGrady .50 1.25
57 Walt Williams .10 .25
58 Walter McCarty .10 .25
59 Detlef Schrempf .12 .30
60 Ervin Johnson .10 .25
61 Michael Smith .10 .25
62 Clifford Robinson .10 .25
63 Brian Williams .10 .25
64 Shandon Anderson .10 .25
65 P.J. Brown .10 .25
66 Scottie Pippen .25 .60
67 Anthony Peeler .10 .25
68 Tony Delk .10 .25
69 David Wesley .10 .25
70 John Starks .12 .30
71 Nick Van Exel .15 .40
72 Kerry Kittles .10 .25
73 Tony Battie .10 .25
74 Lamond Murray .10 .25
75 Anfernee Hardaway .25 .60
76 Jalen Rose .20 .50
77 Derek Anderson .20 .50
78 Avery Johnson .10 .25
79 Michael Stewart .10 .25
80 Brian Shaw .10 .25
81 Dean Garrett .10 .25
82 Kenny Anderson .12 .30
83 Bryon Russell .10 .25
84 Jason Kidd .25 .60
85 Tyrone Hill .10 .25
86 Jim McIlvaine .10 .25
87 Brian Grant .10 .25
88 Bryant Stith .10 .25
89 Brent Price .10 .25
90 John Wallace .10 .25
91 Dennis Rodman .30 .75
92 Alonzo Mourning .20 .50
93 Bimbo Coles .10 .25
94 Chris Anstey .10 .25
95 Lindsey Hunter .10 .25
96 Ed Gray .10 .25
97 Chris Mills .10 .25
98 Rick Fox .10 .25
99 Lorenzen Wright .10 .25
100 Kevin Garnett .25 .60
101 Shawn Kemp .15 .40
102 Mark Jackson .12 .30
103 Sam Cassell .12 .30
104 Monty Williams .10 .25
105 Ron Mercer .12 .30
106 Bryant Reeves .10 .25
107 Tracy Murray .10 .25
108 Ray Allen .20 .50
109 Maurice Taylor .10 .25
110 Jerome Williams .10 .25
111 Horace Grant .12 .30
112 Tariq Abdul-Wahad .10 .25
113 Travis Knight .10 .25
114 Kendall Gill .10 .25
115 Aaron McKie .10 .25
116 Dean Garrett .10 .25
117 Jeff Hornacek .12 .30
118 Todd Fuller .10 .25
119 Arvydas Sabonis .12 .30
120 Voshon Lenard .10 .25
121 Steve Nash .25 .60
122 Cedric Henderson .10 .25
123 Rodrick Rhodes .10 .25
124 Mookie Blaylock .10 .25
125 Hersey Hawkins .10 .25
126 Doug Christie .10 .25
127 Eric Piatkowski .12 .30
128 Sean Elliott .15 .40
129 Anthony Mason .12 .30
130 Allan Houston .12 .30
131 Antonio Davis .10 .25
132 Hubert Davis .10 .25
133 Rod Strickland PF .10 .25
134 Jason Kidd PF .25 .60
135 Mark Jackson PF .12 .30
136 Marcus Camby PF .12 .30
137 Dikembe Mutombo PF .15 .40
138 Shawn Bradley PF .10 .25
139 Dennis Rodman PF .30 .75
140 Jayson Williams PF .10 .25
141 Tim Duncan PF .30 .75
142 Michael Jordan PF 1.25 3.00
143 Shaquille O'Neal PF .40 1.00
144 Karl Malone PF .20 .50
145 Mookie Blaylock PF .10 .25
146 Brevin Knight PF .10 .25
147 Doug Christie PF .10 .25
148 Checklist .10 .25
149 Checklist .10 .25
150 Checklist .10 .25
S44 Keith Van Horn SAMPLE .75 2.00

1998-99 Fleer Vintage '61

COMPLETE SET (147) 40.00 70.00
*STARS: 1.5X TO 4X BASE CARD HI
ONE PER HOBBY PACK

1998-99 Fleer Classic '61

*STARS: 80X TO 200X BASE CARD HI
STATED PRINT RUN 61 SERIAL #'d SETS
1 Kobe Bryant 300.00 600.00
12 John Stockton 50.00 120.00
23 Michael Jordan 2000.00 3000.00
66 Scottie Pippen 60.00 150.00
142 Michael Jordan PF 1000.00 1500.00

1998-99 Fleer Electrifying

Randomly inserted in packs at a rate of one in 72, this 10-card set features player's who consistently have electrifying performances. The card fronts feature a gold patterened full-foil background with embossed "electricity".

COMPLETE SET (10) 150.00 400.00
STATED ODDS 1:72 HOB/RET
1 Kobe Bryant 20.00 50.00
2 Kevin Garnett 12.00 30.00
3 Anfernee Hardaway 10.00 25.00
4 Grant Hill 8.00 20.00
5 Allen Iverson 15.00 40.00
6 Michael Jordan 100.00 250.00
7 Shawn Kemp 5.00 12.00
8 Stephon Marbury 6.00 15.00
9 Gary Payton 6.00 15.00
10 Dennis Rodman 10.00 25.00

1998-99 Fleer Great Expectations

Randomly inserted in packs at a rate of one in 20, this 10-card set features players that represent the future of the NBA. The card fronts are bordered in gold holofoil with a matte finish background.

COMPLETE SET (10) 8.00 20.00
STATED ODDS 1:20 HOB/RET
1 Shareef Abdur-Rahim .75 2.00
2 Ray Allen 1.00 2.50
3 Kobe Bryant 3.00 8.00
4 Tim Duncan 1.50 4.00
5 Kevin Garnett 1.25 3.00
6 Grant Hill 1.25 3.00
7 Allen Iverson 1.50 4.00
8 Stephon Marbury 1.00 2.50
9 Keith Van Horn .75 2.00
10 Antoine Walker .75 2.00

1998-99 Fleer Lucky 13

Randomly inserted in packs at a rate of 1:96, this 13-card set features cards that were redeemable for corresponding draft picks. The expiration was June 1, 1999.

STATED ODDS 1:96 HOB/RET
1 Michael Olowokandi 3.00 8.00
2 Mike Bibby 4.00 10.00
3 Raef LaFrentz 3.00 8.00
4 Antawn Jamison 4.00 10.00
5 Vince Carter 20.00 50.00
6 Robert Traylor 2.50 6.00

7 Jason Williams 6.00 15.00
8 Larry Hughes 5.00 12.00
9 Dirk Nowitzki 50.00 120.00
10 Paul Pierce 15.00 40.00
11 Bonzi Wells 2.50 6.00
12 Michael Doleac 2.00 5.00
13 Keon Clark 2.50 6.00
NNO Expired Trade Cards .20 .50

1998-99 Fleer Playmakers Theatre

Randomly inserted into packs, this 15-card set features players that have a great impact on the game. The cards feature die cut, sculptured curtains against gold holofoil. The card backs feature commentary that recaps some of the player's greatest moments and sequential numbering to 100.

STATED PRINT RUN 100 SERIAL #'d SETS
1 Shareef Abdur-Rahim 100.00 250.00
2 Ray Allen 125.00 300.00
3 Kobe Bryant 400.00 800.00
4 Tim Duncan 400.00 800.00
5 Kevin Garnett 300.00 600.00
6 Anfernee Hardaway 250.00 500.00
7 Grant Hill 250.00 500.00
8 Allen Iverson 250.00 600.00
9 Michael Jordan 3500.00 5000.00
10 Karl Malone 150.00 400.00
11 Stephon Marbury 150.00 400.00
12 Shaquille O'Neal 350.00 700.00
13 Scottie Pippen 200.00 500.00
14 Keith Van Horn 100.00 250.00
15 Antoine Walker 60.00 150.00

1998-99 Fleer Rookie Rewind

Randomly inserted in packs at one in 36, this 10-card set featues the players named by the NBA to the 1997-98 NBA All-Rookie Team. The card fronts feature silver hologoil accents and embossing.

COMPLETE SET (10) 6.00 15.00
STATED ODDS 1:36 HOB/RET
1 Derek Anderson .75 2.00
2 Tim Duncan 2.50 6.00
3 Cedric Henderson .75 2.00
4 Zydrunas Ilgauskas 1.25 3.00
5 Bobby Jackson .75 2.00
6 Brevin Knight .75 2.00
7 Ron Mercer 1.00 2.50
8 Maurice Taylor .75 2.00
9 Tim Thomas 1.25 3.00
10 Keith Van Horn 1.25 3.00

1998-99 Fleer Timeless Memories

Randomly inserted into packs at a rate of one in 12, this 10-card set features players that make the moments great. Card fronts feature the player's face in a watch face with clouds swirling below.

COMPLETE SET (10) 4.00 10.00
STATED ODDS 1:12 HOB/RET
1 Shareef Abdur-Rahim .60 1.50
2 Ray Allen .75 2.00
3 Vin Baker .50 1.25
4 Anfernee Hardaway 1.00 2.50
5 Tim Hardaway .60 1.50
6 Shaquille O'Neal 1.50 4.00
7 Scottie Pippen 1.00 2.50
8 David Robinson 1.00 2.50
9 Dennis Rodman 1.25 3.00
10 Antoine Walker .60 1.50

1999-00 Fleer

This product, also known as Fleer Tradition, was released as a 220-card set. The 10-card packs carried a suggested retail price of $1.59. Each card contains full UV coating, foil stamping and complete statistics. Cards feature one of three foil colors: blue for Eastern Conference players, red for Western Conference players and gold for rookies. Three numbereless checklist cards were also available and inserted one in six packs.

COMPLETE SET (220) 20.00 40.00
NNO CL STATED ODDS 1:6
1 Vince Carter .40 1.00
2 Kobe Bryant .75 2.00
3 Keith Van Horn .15 .40
4 Tim Duncan .40 1.00
5 Grant Hill .25 .60
6 Kevin Garnett .30 .75
7 Anfernee Hardaway .30 .75
8 Jason Williams .25 .60
9 Paul Pierce .25 .60
10 Mookie Blaylock .12 .30
11 Shawn Bradley .12 .30
12 Kenny Anderson .15 .40
13 Chauncey Billups .20 .50
14 Elden Campbell .12 .30
15 Jason Caffey .12 .30
16 Brent Barry .15 .40
17 Charles Barkley .30 .75
18 Derek Anderson .12 .30
19 Darrick Martin .12 .30
20 Bison Dele .12 .30
21 Rick Fox .12 .30
22 Antonio Davis .12 .30
23 Terrell Brandon .12 .30
24 P.J. Brown .12 .30
25 Toby Bailey .12 .30
26 Ray Allen .20 .50
27 Brian Grant .12 .30
28 Scott Burrell .12 .30
29 Tariq Abdul-Wahad .12 .30
30 Marcus Camby .15 .40
31 John Stockton .25 .60
32 Nick Anderson .12 .30
33 Antonio Daniels .12 .30
34 Matt Geiger .12 .30
35 Vin Baker .15 .40
36 Dee Brown .12 .30
37 Shandon Anderson .12 .30
38 Calbert Cheaney .12 .30
39 Shareef Abdur-Rahim .15 .40
40 LaPhonso Ellis .12 .30
41 Cedric Ceballos .12 .30
42 Tony Battie .15 .40
43 Keon Clark .12 .30
44 Derrick Coleman .15 .40
45 Erick Dampier .12 .30
46 Corey Benjamin .12 .30
47 Michael Dickerson .12 .30
48 Cedric Henderson .12 .30
49 Lamond Murray .12 .30
50 Horace Grant .15 .40
51 Shaquille O'Neal .50 1.25
52 Dale Davis .12 .30
53 Dean Garrett .12 .30
54 Tim Hardaway .20 .50
55 Gerald Brown RC .20 .50
56 Sam Cassell .15 .40
57 Jim Jackson .12 .30
58 Kendall Gill .12 .30
59 Eric Williams .12 .30
60 Chris Childs .12 .30
61 Vlade Divac .20 .50
62 Darrell Armstrong .12 .30
63 Mario Elie .12 .30
64 Tyrone Hill .12 .30
65 Dale Ellis .12 .30
66 Doug Christie .15 .40
67 Howard Eisley .12 .30
68 Juwan Howard .15 .40
69 Mike Bibby .20 .50
70 Alan Henderson .12 .30
71 Michael Finley .20 .50
72 Dana Barros .12 .30
73 Danny Fortson .12 .30
74 Ricky Davis .20 .50
75 Adonal Foyle .12 .30
76 Cory Carr .12 .30
77 Bryce Drew .12 .30
78 Shawn Kemp .20 .50
79 Tyrone Nesby RC .15 .40
80 Lindsey Hunter .12 .30
81 Ruben Patterson .12 .30
82 Al Harrington .20 .50
83 Bobby Jackson .12 .30
84 Dan Majerle .20 .50
85 Rex Chapman .12 .30
86 Dell Curry .12 .30
87 Walt Williams .12 .30
88 Kerry Kittles .12 .30
89 Isaiah Rider .15 .40
90 Patrick Ewing .25 .60
91 Lawrence Funderburke .12 .30
92 Isaac Austin .12 .30
93 Sean Elliott .20 .50
94 Larry Hughes .15 .40
95 Hersey Hawkins .12 .30
96 Tracy McGrady .30 .75
97 Jeff Hornacek .15 .40
98 Randell Jackson .12 .30
99 J.R. Henderson .12 .30
100 Roshown McLeod .12 .30
101 Steve Nash .30 .75
102 Ron Mercer .15 .40
103 Raef LaFrentz .15 .40
104 Eddie Jones .20 .50
105 Antawn Jamison .20 .50
106 Kornel David RC .15 .40
107 Othella Harrington .12 .30
108 Brevin Knight .12 .30
109 Michael Olowokandi .12 .30
110 Christian Laettner .15 .40
111 J.R. Reid .12 .30
112 Reggie Miller .20 .50
113 Andrae Patterson .12 .30
114 Jamal Mashburn .15 .40
115 Glenn Robinson .15 .40
116 Pat Garrity .12 .30
117 Stephon Marbury .15 .40
118 Arvydas Sabonis .15 .40
119 Allan Houston .15 .40
120 Peja Stojakovic .20 .50
121 Michael Doleac .12 .30
122 Avery Johnson .15 .40
123 Allen Iverson .40 1.00
124 Rashard Lewis .20 .50
125 Charles Oakley .15 .40
126 Karl Malone .25 .60
127 Tracy Murray .12 .30
128 Felipe Lopez .12 .30
129 Dikembe Mutombo .20 .50
130 Dirk Nowitzki .40 1.00
131 Vitaly Potapenko .12 .30
132 Antonio McDyess .15 .40
133 Anthony Mason .12 .30
134 Donyell Marshall .12 .30
135 Ron Harper .12 .30
136 Cuttino Mobley .12 .30
137 Wesley Person .12 .30
138 Rodney Rogers .12 .30
139 Jerry Stackhouse .20 .50
140 Glen Rice .20 .50
141 Chris Mullin .20 .50
142 Anthony Peeler .12 .30
143 Alonzo Mourning .25 .60
144 Tom Gugliotta .12 .30
145 Tim Thomas .15 .40
146 Damon Stoudamire .15 .40
147 Jayson Williams .12 .30
148 Larry Johnson .20 .50
149 Chris Webber .20 .50
150 Matt Harpring .12 .30
151 David Robinson .30 .75
152 George Lynch .12 .30
153 Gary Payton .20 .50
154 John Wallace .12 .30
155 Greg Ostertag .12 .30
156 Mitch Richmond .20 .50
157 Cherokee Parks .12 .30
158 Steve Smith .15 .40
159 Gary Trent .12 .30
160 Antoine Walker .20 .50
161 Johnny Taylor .12 .30
162 Brad Miller .15 .40
163 Chris Mills .12 .30
164 Charles Jones RC .12 .30
165 Hakeem Olajuwon .25 .60
166 Bob Sura .12 .30
167 Brian Skinner .12 .30
168 Korleone Young .12 .30
169 Tyronn Lue .12 .30
170 Jalen Rose .15 .40
171 Joe Smith .15 .40
172 Clarence Weatherspoon .12 .30
173 Jason Kidd .30 .75
174 Robert Traylor .12 .30
175 Rasheed Wallace .20 .50
176 Latrell Sprewell .20 .50
177 Corliss Williamson .12 .30
178 Bo Outlaw .12 .30
179 Malik Rose .12 .30
180 Nazr Mohammed .12 .30
181 Olden Polynice .12 .30
182 Kevin Willis .12 .30
183 Bryon Russell .12 .30
184 Bryant Reeves .12 .30
185 Rod Strickland .12 .30
186 Samaki Walker .12 .30
187 Nick Van Exel .15 .40
188 David Wesley .12 .30
189 John Starks .15 .40
190 Toni Kukoc .20 .50
191 Scottie Pippen .30 .75
192 Zydrunas Ilgauskas .15 .40
193 Maurice Taylor .12 .30
194 Rik Smits .20 .50
195 Clifford Robinson .12 .30
196 Bonzi Wells .12 .30
197 Charlie Ward .12 .30
198 Detlef Schrempf .15 .40
199 Theo Ratliff .15 .40
200 Rodrick Rhodes .12 .30
201 Ron Artest RC .40 1.00
202 William Avery RC .15 .40
203 Elton Brand RC .50 1.25
204 Baron Davis RC .50 1.25
205 Jumaine Jones RC .15 .40
206 Andre Miller RC .40 1.00
207 Lee Nailon RC .20 .50
208 James Posey RC .20 .50
209 Jason Terry RC .30 .75
210 Kenny Thomas RC .20 .50
211 Steve Francis RC .50 1.25
212 Wally Szczerbiak RC .40 1.00
213 Richard Hamilton RC .40 1.00
214 Jonathan Bender RC .20 .50
215 Shawn Marion RC .40 1.00
216 A.Radojevic RC .12 .30
217 Tim James RC .12 .30
218 Trajan Langdon RC .20 .50
219 Lamar Odom RC .50 1.25
220 Corey Maggette RC .60 1.50
NNO Checklist #3 .12 .30
NNO Checklist #2 .12 .30
NNO Checklist #1 .12 .30

1999-00 Fleer Roundball Collection

*ROUND: 1X TO 2.5X BASE CARD HI
ONE PER RETAIL PACK

1999-00 Fleer Supreme Court Collection

*STARS: 50X TO 125X BASE CARD HI
*RCs: 20X TO 50X BASE HI
STATED PRINT RUN 20 SERIAL #'d SETS
4 Tim Duncan 75.00 200.00
5 Grant Hill 100.00 250.00
7 Anfernee Hardaway 75.00 200.00
51 Shaquille O'Neal 125.00 300.00

1999-00 Fleer Fresh Ink

Randomly inserted in Fleer packs, this set features autographs from NBA players. The cards feature a congratulatory message on the back. Each card was serially numbered to 400. The cards are not numbered and listed below in alphabetical order.

STATED PRINT RUN 400 SERIAL #'d SETS
1 Corey Benjamin 4.00 10.00
2 Mike Bibby 6.00 15.00
3 Michael Dickerson 4.00 10.00
4 Michael Doleac 4.00 10.00
5 Bryce Drew 4.00 10.00
6 Pat Garrity 4.00 10.00
7 Matt Harpring 4.00 10.00
8 Larry Hughes 6.00 15.00
9 Antawn Jamison 6.00 15.00
10 Raef LaFrentz 4.00 10.00
11 Felipe Lopez 4.00 10.00
12 Jelani McCoy 4.00 10.00
13 Brad Miller 6.00 15.00
14 Michael Olowokandi 4.00 10.00
15 Robert Traylor 4.00 10.00

1999-00 Fleer Game Breakers

Randomly inserted in series one packs, this 15-card set features NBA stars who can break a game wide open. The cards are die cut and serially numbered to 100.

PRINT RUN 100 SERIAL #'d SETS
1 Shareef Abdur-Rahim 40.00 100.00
2 Kobe Bryant 300.00 600.00
3 Vince Carter 100.00 250.00
4 Tim Duncan 75.00 200.00
5 Kevin Garnett 60.00 150.00
6 Anfernee Hardaway 60.00 150.00
7 Grant Hill 60.00 150.00
8 Allen Iverson 60.00 150.00
9 Shawn Kemp 40.00 100.00
10 Stephon Marbury 12.00 30.00
11 Ron Mercer 12.00 30.00
12 Shaquille O'Neal 150.00 400.00
13 Keith Van Horn 12.00 30.00
14 Antoine Walker 15.00 40.00
15 Jason Williams 40.00 100.00

1999-00 Fleer Masters of the Hardwood

Randomly inserted in series one packs at one in 18, this 15-card set showcases highly skilled player's who have mastered their position. Card fronts feature a silhouetted player against a simulated wood background.

COMPLETE SET (15) 15.00 30.00
STATED ODDS 1:18
1 Shareef Abdur-Rahim .75 2.00
2 Mike Bibby 1.00 2.50
3 Kobe Bryant 4.00 10.00
4 Tim Duncan 2.00 5.00
5 Kevin Garnett 1.50 4.00
6 Anfernee Hardaway 1.50 4.00
7 Grant Hill 1.25 3.00
8 Allen Iverson 2.00 5.00
9 Karl Malone 1.25 3.00
10 Stephon Marbury .75 2.00
11 Tracy McGrady 1.50 4.00
12 Ron Mercer .75 2.00
13 Scottie Pippen 1.50 4.00
14 Antoine Walker 1.00 2.50
15 Jason Williams 1.25 3.00

1999-00 Fleer Net Effect

Randomly inserted in series one packs at one in 96, this 10-card set features players who have a great effect on the game. The die cut cards are printed on opaque plastic stock and silhouettes the player's image against his team's primary color.

COMPLETE SET (10) 12.00 30.00
STATED ODDS 1:96
1 Kobe Bryant 4.00 10.00
2 Vince Carter 2.00 5.00
3 Tim Duncan 2.00 5.00
4 Kevin Garnett 1.50 4.00
5 Grant Hill 1.25 3.00
6 Allen Iverson 2.00 5.00
7 Shaquille O'Neal 2.50 6.00
8 Paul Pierce 1.25 3.00
9 Scottie Pippen 1.50 4.00
10 Keith Van Horn .75 2.00

1999-00 Fleer Rookie Sensations

Randomly inserted in series one packs at one in six, this 20-card set profiles players from the 98-99 rookie class. The player's image appears on a full gold foil stamped card.

COMPLETE SET (20) 6.00 15.00
STATED ODDS 1:6
1 Mike Bibby .60 1.50
2 Vince Carter 1.25 3.00
3 Ricky Davis .60 1.50
4 Michael Dickerson .40 1.00
5 Michael Doleac .40 1.00
6 Matt Harpring .40 1.00
7 Larry Hughes .50 1.25
8 Randell Jackson .40 1.00
9 Antawn Jamison .60 1.50
10 Raef LaFrentz .50 1.25
11 Felipe Lopez .40 1.00
12 Roshown McLeod .40 1.00
13 Brad Miller .50 1.25
14 Cuttino Mobley .40 1.00
15 Dirk Nowitzki 1.25 3.00
16 Michael Olowokandi .40 1.00
17 Paul Pierce .75 2.00
18 Peja Stojakovic .60 1.50
19 Robert Traylor .40 1.00
20 Jason Williams .75 2.00

2000-01 Fleer

The 2000-01 Fleer product, which is also known as Fleer Tradition, was released in January 2001, and featured a 300-card base set that was broken into tiers as follows: Base Veterans (1-226) Rookies (227-271) and Team Checklists (272-300). Each pack contained 10 cards and carried a suggested retail price of $2.99. Four versions were available of the NNO Vince Carter Old School Raptor card. Retail versions were not serial numbered, and the other versions include a sticker, one serial numbered to 1986, and an autograph numbered out of 15.

CARTER OSR: RANDOM INS.IN PACKS
CARTER OSR AU: RANDOM INS.IN PACKS
CARTER OSR STCKR: STATED ODDS 1:36
1 Lamar Odom .15 .40
2 Christian Laettner .15 .40
3 Michael Olowokandi .12 .30
4 Anthony Carter .12 .30
5 Steve Francis .15 .40
6 Darvin Ham .12 .30
7 Mitch Richmond .15 .40
8 Corliss Williamson .12 .30
9 Jason Terry .20 .50
10 Brian Grant .12 .30
11 Peja Stojakovic .20 .50
12 Rick Fox .12 .30
13 Tyrone Hill .12 .30
14 Chauncey Billups .20 .50
15 Otis Thorpe .15 .40
16 Richard Hamilton .15 .40
17 Ervin Johnson .12 .30
18 Jim Jackson .12 .30
19 Theo Ratliff .12 .30
20 Doug Christie .12 .30
21 Jalen Rose .15 .40
22 John Wallace .12 .30
23 Ruben Patterson .12 .30
24 Steve Nash .30 .75
25 Toni Kukoc .20 .50
26 Anthony Peeler .12 .30
27 Ray Allen .20 .50
28 Adonal Foyle .12 .30
29 Chris Whitney .12 .30
30 Nick Van Exel .15 .40
31 Sean Elliott .20 .50
32 Erick Strickland .12 .30
33 Jerry Stackhouse .15 .40
34 Antawn Jamison .20 .50
35 Grant Hill .25 .60
36 Antonio Daniels .12 .30
37 Karl Malone .25 .60
38 Keith Van Horn .15 .40
39 Ron Harper .15 .40
40 Stephon Marbury .15 .40
41 Bryon Russell .12 .30
42 Corey Maggette .15 .40
43 Hersey Hawkins .12 .30
44 Vince Carter .40 1.00
45 Paul Pierce .20 .50
46 Mikki Moore RC .20 .50
47 Othella Harrington .12 .30
48 Erick Dampier .12 .30
49 Jerome Williams .12 .30
50 Nick Anderson .12 .30
51 Tim Hardaway .20 .50
52 Allan Houston .15 .40
53 Tyrone Nesby .20 .50
54 Brevin Knight .12 .30
55 Chris Mills .12 .30
56 Ron Artest .20 .50
57 Walt Williams .12 .30
58 Duane Causwell .12 .30
59 Bonzi Wells .12 .30
60 Rasheed Wallace .20 .50
61 Dikembe Mutombo .20 .50
62 Jahidi White .12 .30
63 Chris Webber .20 .50
64 Tony Battie .12 .30
65 Mahmoud Abdul-Rauf .12 .30
66 Monty Williams .12 .30
67 Charlie Ward .12 .30
68 David Robinson .30 .75
69 Eric Snow .12 .30
70 Jermaine O'Neal .15 .40
71 Kurt Thomas .12 .30
72 James Posey .12 .30
73 Travis Best .12 .30
74 Jonathan Bender .12 .30
75 John Stockton .25 .60
76 Jacque Vaughn .12 .30
77 Ron Mercer .12 .30
78 Shawn Marion .15 .40
79 Larry Johnson .20 .50
80 Maurice Taylor .12 .30
81 Clifford Robinson .12 .30
82 Scot Pollard .12 .30
83 Patrick Ewing .25 .60
84 Terrell Brandon .12 .30
85 Horace Grant .15 .40
86 Vin Baker .15 .40
87 Al Harrington .15 .40
88 Larry Hughes .15 .40
89 David Wesley .12 .30
90 Wally Szczerbiak .15 .40
91 Charles Oakley .15 .40
92 Tim Thomas .12 .30
93 Mookie Blaylock .12 .30
94 Jamal Mashburn .15 .40
95 Roshown McLeod .12 .30
96 John Starks .15 .40
97 Rodney Rogers .12 .30
98 Juwan Howard .15 .40
99 Isaiah Rider .15 .40
100 Rashard Lewis .20 .50
101 Dion Glover .12 .30
102 Johnny Newman .12 .30
103 Avery Johnson .15 .40
104 Darrell Armstrong .12 .30
105 Eric Williams .12 .30
106 Gary Payton .20 .50
107 Antonio Davis .12 .30
108 Dirk Nowitzki .30 .75
109 Trajan Langdon .12 .30
110 Michael Dickerson .12 .30
111 Joe Smith .15 .40
112 Rod Strickland .12 .30
113 Shawn Kemp .20 .50
114 Voshon Lenard .12 .30
115 Marcus Camby .15 .40
116 Matt Harpring .12 .30
117 Isaac Austin .12 .30
118 Malik Rose .12 .30
119 Pat Garrity .12 .30
120 Kenny Thomas .12 .30
121 LaPhonso Ellis .15 .40
122 Danny Fortson .12 .30
123 Elton Brand .20 .50
124 Jason Williams .20 .50
125 Kobe Bryant .75 2.00
126 Tariq Abdul-Wahad .12 .30
127 Tracy McGrady .30 .75
128 Matt Geiger .12 .30
129 Antoine Walker .15 .40
130 Michael Finley .20 .50
131 Andre Miller .15 .40
132 Robert Horry .15 .40
133 Donyell Marshall .12 .30
134 Shareef Abdur-Rahim .15 .40
135 Vonteego Cummings .12 .30
136 Anthony Mason .12 .30
137 Mike Bibby .20 .50
138 Raef LaFrentz .12 .30
139 Glen Rice .15 .40
140 Chris Gatling .12 .30
141 Latrell Sprewell .15 .40
142 Austin Croshere .12 .30
143 Kenny Anderson .15 .40
144 Elden Campbell .12 .30
145 Jason Kidd .30 .75
146 Michael Doleac .12 .30
147 Muggsy Bogues .15 .40
148 Tim Duncan .40 1.00
149 Samaki Walker .12 .30
150 Gary Trent .12 .30
151 Kevin Garnett .30 .75
152 Allen Iverson .40 1.00
153 Anfernee Hardaway .30 .75
154 Robert Traylor .12 .30
155 Scottie Pippen .30 .75
156 Shaquille O'Neal .50 1.25
157 Vlade Divac .15 .40
158 Lucious Harris .12 .30
159 Keon Clark .12 .30
160 Bo Outlaw .12 .30
161 P.J. Brown .12 .30
162 Derrick Coleman .15 .40
163 Mark Jackson .15 .40
164 Lamond Murray .12 .30
165 Dan Majerle .20 .50
166 Eddie Jones .20 .50
167 Cedric Ceballos .12 .30
168 Kendall Gill .12 .30
169 Tom Gugliotta .12 .30
170 Jeff McInnis .12 .30
171 Steve Smith .15 .40
172 Kevin Willis .12 .30
173 Lindsey Hunter .12 .30
174 Derek Anderson .12 .30
175 Shandon Anderson .12 .30
176 Adrian Griffin .12 .30
177 Baron Davis .20 .50
178 Radoslav Nesterovic .12 .30
179 Glenn Robinson .15 .40
180 Sam Cassell .15 .40
181 Chucky Atkins .12 .30
182 Arvydas Sabonis .15 .40
183 Damon Stoudamire .15 .40
184 Antonio McDyess .15 .40
185 Derek Fisher .20 .50
186 Bryant Reeves .12 .30
187 Hakeem Olajuwon .25 .60
188 Kerry Kittles .12 .30
189 Alan Henderson .12 .30
190 Sam Perkins .12 .30
191 Felipe Lopez .12 .30
192 Tracy Murray .12 .30
193 Shammond Williams .12 .30
194 Vitaly Potapenko .12 .30
195 John Amaechi .12 .30
196 Quincy Lewis .12 .30
197 Reggie Miller .20 .50
198 Cuttino Mobley .12 .30
199 Rex Chapman .12 .30
200 Dale Davis .12 .30
201 Andrew DeClercq .12 .30
202 Kelvin Cato .12 .30
203 Jon Barry .12 .30
204 Greg Anthony .12 .30
205 Brent Barry .12 .30
206 Derrick McKey .12 .30
207 Vince Carter UH .40 1.00
208 David Robinson UH .30 .75
209 Eric Snow UH .12 .30
210 Ray Allen UH .20 .50
211 Lamar Odom UH .15 .40
212 Dikembe Mutombo UH .20 .50
213 Brevin Knight UH .12 .30
214 Vin Baker UH .15 .40
215 Antoine Walker UH .15 .40
216 Mitch Richmond UH .15 .40
217 Elton Brand UH .20 .50
218 Jerome Williams UH .12 .30
219 Keith Van Horn UH .15 .40
220 Nick Van Exel UH .15 .40
221 Shaquille O'Neal UH .25 .60
222 Allan Houston UH .15 .40
223 Shareef Abdur-Rahim UH .15 .40
224 Karl Malone UH .25 .60
225 Terrell Brandon UH .12 .30
226 Eddie Jones UH .20 .50
227 Stromile Swift RC .25 .60
228 Dalibor Bagaric RC .20 .50
229 Erick Barkley RC .15 .40
230 Mike Miller RC .40 1.00
231 Kenyon Martin RC .60 1.50
232 Michael Redd RC .60 1.50
233 Darius Miles RC .25 .60
234 Chris Mihm RC .20 .50
235 Brian Cardinal RC .20 .50
236 Khalid El-Amin RC .15 .40
237 Hanno Mottola RC .15 .40
238 Jamaal Magloire RC .25 .60
239 Courtney Alexander RC .20 .50
240 Mamadou N'Diaye RC .15 .40
241 Chris Porter RC .15 .40
242 Quentin Richardson RC .25 .60
243 Eddie House RC .20 .50
244 Joel Przybilla RC .20 .50
245 Soumaila Samake RC .15 .40
246 Speedy Claxton RC .25 .60
247 Desmond Mason RC .30 .75
248 Mike Smith RC .15 .40
249 Lavor Postell RC .15 .40
250 Ruben Garces RC .25 .60
251 DeShawn Stevenson RC .25 .60
252 Hedo Turkoglu RC .40 1.00
253 Keyon Dooling RC .25 .60
254 Dan Langhi RC .15 .40
255 Mateen Cleaves RC .20 .50
256 Donnell Harvey RC .20 .50
257 DerMarr Johnson RC .20 .50
258 Jason Collier RC .25 .60
259 Jake Voskuhl RC .15 .40
260 Mark Madsen RC .25 .60
261 Pepe Sanchez RC .25 .60
262 Morris Peterson RC .25 .60
263 Daniel Santiago RC .25 .60
264 Etan Thomas RC .25 .60
265 A.J. Guyton RC .15 .40
266 Marcus Fizer RC .25 .60
267 Jamal Crawford RC .60 1.50
268 Jerome Moiso RC .15 .40
269 Olumide Oyedeji RC .15 .40
270 Paul McPherson RC .15 .40
271 Eduardo Najera RC .25 .60
272 Dallas Mavericks CL .05 .15
273 Denver Nuggets CL .05 .15
274 Houston Rockets CL .10 .30
275 Minnesota Timberwolves CL .10 .30
276 San Antonio Spurs CL .10 .30
277 Utah Jazz CL .10 .30
278 Vancouver Grizzlies CL .10 .30
279 Golden State Warriors CL .10 .30
280 Los Angeles Clippers CL .10 .30
281 Los Angeles Lakers CL .20 .50
282 Phoenix Suns CL .10 .30
283 Portland Trail Blazers CL .10 .30
284 Sacramento Kings CL .10 .30
285 Seattle Supersonics CL .10 .30
286 Boston Celtics CL .05 .15
287 Miami Heat CL .05 .15
288 New Jersey Nets CL .10 .30
289 New York Knicks CL .10 .30
290 Orlando Magic CL .20 .50
291 Philadelphia 76ers CL .10 .30
292 Washington Wizards CL .05 .15
293 Atlanta Hawks CL .05 .15
294 Charlotte Hornets CL .05 .15
295 Chicago Bulls CL .10 .30
296 Cleveland Cavaliers CL .05 .15
297 Detroit Pistons CL .05 .15
298 Indiana Pacers CL .10 .30
299 Milwaukee Bucks CL .05 .15
300 Toronto Raptors CL .20 .50
NNO Vince Carter OSR Sticker 2.00 5.00
NNO Vince Carter OSR/1986 8.00 20.00
NNO Vince Carter OSR AU/15 20.00 50.00

2000-01 Fleer Stickers

*STARS: 3X TO 8X BASE HI
*RCs: 2X TO 5X BASE HI
*CL: 8X TO 20X BASE HI
STATED ODDS 1:36

2000-01 Fleer Autographics

Randomly inserted in 2000-01 Fleer products, this insert features autographed cards from some of the hottest players in the NBA. Please note that the cards are listed below in alphabetical order. Gold and silver versions were also issued and numbered to 50 and 250 respectively.

FOCUS STATED ODDS 1:48
GAME TIME STATED ODDS 1:287
GENUINE STATED ODDS 1:23
GLOSSY: AUTO OR GAME WORN 1:48
GLOSSY STATED ODDS 1:96 RETAIL
HOOPS STATED ODDS 1:72
MYSTIQUE STATED ODDS 1:48
PREMIUM STATED ODDS 1:288
ULTRA STATED ODDS 1:48
NNO CARDS LISTED BELOW ALPHABETICALLY
*GOLD: 1.25X TO 3X BASE AUTO HI
GOLD PRINT RUN 50 SER.#'d SETS
*SILVER: .5X TO 1.25X BASE AUTO HI
SILVER PRINT RUN 250 SER.#'d SETS
1 Darrell Armstrong 3.00 8.00
2 Ron Artest 6.00 15.00
3 Chucky Atkins 3.00 8.00
4 Travis Best 3.00 8.00
5 Mike Bibby 5.00 12.00
6 Muggsy Bogues 5.00 12.00
7 P.J. Brown 3.00 8.00
8 Elden Campbell 3.00 8.00
9 Vince Carter 12.00 30.00
10 Jason Collier 3.00 8.00
11 Baron Davis 4.00 10.00
12 Andrew DeClercq 3.00 8.00
13 Michael Dickerson 3.00 8.00
14 Vlade Divac 4.00 10.00
15 Michael Doleac 3.00 8.00
16 Dion Glover 3.00 8.00
17 Brian Grant 4.00 10.00
18 Adrian Griffin 3.00 8.00
19 Tom Gugliotta 3.00 8.00
20 Richard Hamilton 5.00 12.00
21 Al Harrington 3.00 8.00
22 Othella Harrington 3.00 8.00
23 Jason Hart 3.00 8.00
24 Allen Iverson 75.00 200.00
25 Antawn Jamison 3.00 8.00
26 Brevin Knight 3.00 8.00
27 Toni Kukoc 8.00 20.00
28 Raef LaFrentz 3.00 8.00
29 Dan Langhi 3.00 8.00
30 Voshon Lenard 3.00 8.00
31 Quincy Lewis 3.00 8.00
32 George Lynch 3.00 8.00
33 Corey Maggette 3.00 8.00
34 Stephon Marbury 6.00 15.00
35 Shawn Marion 3.00 8.00
36 Donyell Marshall 3.00 8.00
37 Jamal Mashburn 5.00 12.00
38 Tracy McGrady 15.00 40.00
39 Ron Mercer 6.00 15.00
40 Andre Miller 5.00 12.00
41 Reggie Miller 75.00 150.00
42 Alonzo Mourning 12.00 30.00
43 Dirk Nowitzki 50.00 120.00
44 Lamar Odom 3.00 8.00
45 Hakeem Olajuwon 8.00 60.00
46 Jermaine O'Neal 5.00 12.00
47 Ruben Patterson 3.00 8.00
48 Scot Pollard 3.00 8.00
49 Theo Ratliff 3.00 8.00
50 Michael Redd 3.00 8.00
51 Eddie Robinson 3.00 8.00
52 Glenn Robinson 5.00 12.00
53 Steve Smith 5.00 12.00
54 Jerry Stackhouse 5.00 12.00
55 Jason Terry 4.00 10.00
56 Kenny Thomas 3.00 8.00
57 Keith Van Horn 6.00 15.00
58 Antoine Walker 3.00 8.00
59 Shareef Abdur-Rahim 4.00 10.00
60 Howard Eisley 3.00 8.00
61 Austin Croshere 3.00 8.00
62 Kurt Thomas 6.00 15.00
63 Pat Garrity 3.00 8.00

2000-01 Fleer Vince Carter Rookie Remnants

This three-card insert was randomly inserted into 2000-01 Fleer products. The set includes a Vince Carter floor card (numbered to 100), a Vince Carter floor/jersey card (numbered to 15), and finally an autographed Vince Carter floor/jersey card (numbered 1/1).

RANDOM INSERTS IN HOBBY PACKS
NNO Vince Carter FLR/100 12.50 30.00
NNO Vince Carter FLR JSY/15 20.00 50.00

2000-01 Fleer Courting History

Randomly inserted into packs at one in 18, this 10-card insert set features players that look to put themselves into the record books in the very near future. Card backs carry a "CH" prefix.

COMPLETE SET (10) 6.00 15.00
STATED ODDS 1:18
CH1 Vince Carter 1.00 2.50
CH2 Shaquille O'Neal 1.25 3.00
CH3 Grant Hill .60 1.50
CH4 Kobe Bryant 2.00 5.00
CH5 Tim Duncan 1.00 2.50
CH6 Jason Kidd .75 2.00
CH7 Kevin Garnett .75 2.00
CH8 Allen Iverson 1.00 2.50
CH9 Steve Francis .40 1.00
CH10 Elton Brand .50 1.25

2000-01 Fleer Feel the Game

Randomly inserted in multiple releases, this set features swatches of game-used jerseys from top veterans and rookies in the NBA. The cards are not numbered on the back and listed in alphabetical order. Gold and silver versions were also issued and numbered to 50 and 250 respectively. The descriptions of the cards refer to what the player is pictured wearing, not the actual color or swatch material.

EX STATED ODDS 1:72
FOCUS STATED ODDS 1:48
FUTURES STATED ODDS 1:331
MYSTIQUE STATED ODDS 1:72
PREMIUM STATED ODDS 1:56
SHOWCASE STATED ODDS 1:72
ULTRA STATED ODDS 1:48
NNO CARDS LISTED BELOW ALPHABETICALLY
*GOLD: 1.25X TO 3X BASE HI
GOLD PRINT RUN 50 SER.#'d SETS
*SILVER: .5X TO 1.25X BASE HI
SILVER PRINT RUN 250 SER.#'d SETS
ALL PICTURE VARIATIONS SAME VALUE
1A Shareef Abdur-Rahim White 2.50 6.00
1B Shareef Abdur-Rahim Blue 2.50 6.00
2 Mike Bibby 3.00 8.00
3 Terrell Brandon 2.00 5.00
4 Vince Carter 6.00 15.00
5 Sam Cassell 2.50 6.00
6 Baron Davis 3.00 8.00
7 Michael Finley 3.00 8.00
8 Steve Francis 2.50 6.00
9 Robert Horry 2.50 6.00
10 Allan Houston 2.50 6.00
11A Allen Iverson Black 6.00 15.00
11B Allen Iverson White 6.00 15.00
12 Eddie Jones 3.00 8.00
13 Jason Kidd 5.00 12.00
14 Quincy Lewis 2.00 5.00
15 Tyronn Lue 2.00 5.00
16 George Lynch 2.00 5.00
17 Corey Maggette 2.50 6.00
18A Karl Malone Black 4.00 10.00
18B Karl Malone Purple 4.00 10.00
19A Stephon Marbury Gray 2.50 6.00
19B Stephon Marbury White 2.50 6.00
20 Shawn Marion 2.50 6.00
21 Tracy McGrady 5.00 12.00
22 Reggie Miller 3.00 8.00
23 Alonzo Mourning 4.00 10.00
24A Lamar Odom White 2.50 6.00
24B Lamar Odom Red 2.50 6.00
25 Hakeem Olajuwon 4.00 10.00
26 Michael Olowokandi 2.00 5.00
27A Shaquille O'Neal Purple 8.00 20.00
27B Shaquille O'Neal Yellow 8.00 20.00
27C Shaquille O'Neal Warm-Up 8.00 20.00
28 Scott Padgett 2.00 5.00
29 Gary Payton 3.00 8.00
30 Glenn Robinson 2.50 6.00
31 Joe Smith 2.50 6.00
32 John Stockton 4.00 10.00
33A Jason Terry Red 3.00 8.00
33B Jason Terry Warm-Up 3.00 8.00
34 Keith Van Horn 2.50 6.00
35 Antoine Walker 2.50 6.00
36 Chris Webber 3.00 8.00
37 Jason Williams 3.00 8.00
38 David Robinson SP 5.00 12.00
39 Richard Hamilton

2000-01 Fleer Genuine Coverage Nostalgic

Randomly inserted into packs at 1:144 Hobby, and 1:240 Retail, this 16-card insert features game-jersey swatches from up and coming prospects. Card backs are not numbered and are listed below in alphabetical order for convenience.

STATED ODDS 1:144 HOB, 1:240 RET
1 Courtney Alexander 1.50 4.00
2 Erick Barkley 1.25 3.00
3 Speedy Claxton 2.00 5.00
4 Mateen Cleaves 1.50 4.00
5 Donnell Harvey 1.50 4.00
6 DerMarr Johnson 1.50 4.00
7 Mark Madsen 2.00 5.00
8 Kenyon Martin 5.00 12.00
9 Desmond Mason 2.50 6.00
10 Mike Miller 3.00 8.00
11 Jerome Moiso 1.25 3.00
12 Joel Przybilla 1.50 4.00
13 DeShawn Stevenson 2.00 5.00
14 Stromile Swift 2.00 5.00
15 Etan Thomas 2.00 5.00
16 Hedo Turkoglu 3.00 8.00

2000-01 Fleer Hardcourt Classics

Randomly inserted into packs at one in 9, this 15-card insert set features players that will go down in history as some of the best to ever play the game. Card backs carry a "HC" prefix.

COMPLETE SET (15) 7.50 15.00
STATED ODDS 1:9
HC1 Vince Carter .75 2.00
HC2 Karl Malone .50 1.25
HC3 Kobe Bryant 1.50 4.00
HC4 Tim Duncan .75 2.00
HC5 Lamar Odom .30 .75
HC6 Jason Williams .40 1.00
HC7 Kevin Garnett .60 1.50
HC8 Jason Kidd .60 1.50
HC9 Shaquille O'Neal 1.00 2.50
HC10 Chris Webber .40 1.00
HC11 Allen Iverson .75 2.00
HC12 Scottie Pippen .60 1.50
HC13 Grant Hill .50 1.25
HC14 Elton Brand .40 1.00
HC15 Tracy McGrady .60 1.50

2000-01 Fleer Rookie Retro

Randomly inserted into packs at one in 36, this 20-card insert set features rookies on a retro designed card. Card backs carry a "RR" prefix.

COMPLETE SET (20) 8.00 20.00
STATED ODDS 1:36
RR1 Morris Peterson .50 1.25
RR2 DerMarr Johnson .40 1.00
RR3 Jerome Moiso .30 .75
RR4 Darius Miles .50 1.25
RR5 Marcus Fizer .50 1.25
RR6 Hedo Turkoglu .75 2.00
RR7 Mateen Cleaves .40 1.00
RR8 Kenyon Martin 1.25 3.00
RR9 Jamaal Magloire .50 1.25
RR10 Keyon Dooling .50 1.25
RR11 DeShawn Stevenson .50 1.25
RR12 Quentin Richardson .50 1.25
RR13 Courtney Alexander .40 1.00
RR14 Mark Madsen .50 1.25
RR15 Mike Miller .75 2.00
RR16 Desmond Mason .60 1.50
RR17 Stromile Swift .50 1.25
RR18 Speedy Claxton .50 1.25
RR19 Etan Thomas .50 1.25
RR20 Chris Mihm .40 1.00

2000-01 Fleer Season Pass

This insert set was issued in a variety of Fleer products throughtout the 2000-01 season. Individuals that pulled one of these cards were able to redeem the card for every 2000-01 Fleer card of the depicted player (with exception of one of one masterpiece cards). Please note that the exchange deadline for these cards was 12/01/01.

2000-01 Fleer Sharpshooters

Randomly inserted into packs at one in 6, this 20-card insert set features players that can flat out shoot the basketball. Card backs carry a "SS" prefix.

COMPLETE SET (20) 7.50 15.00
STATED ODDS 1:6
SS1 Vince Carter .75 2.00
SS2 Wally Szczerbiak .30 .75
SS3 Kobe Bryant 1.50 4.00
SS4 Eddie Jones .40 1.00
SS5 John Stockton .50 1.25
SS6 Ray Allen .40 1.00
SS7 Tracy McGrady .60 1.50
SS8 Shareef Abdur-Rahim .30 .75
SS9 Antoine Walker .30 .75
SS10 Tim Duncan .75 2.00
SS11 Larry Hughes .30 .75
SS12 Gary Payton .40 1.00
SS13 Dirk Nowitzki .60 1.50
SS14 Grant Hill .50 1.25
SS15 Scottie Pippen .60 1.50
SS16 Chris Webber .40 1.00
SS17 Stephon Marbury .30 .75
SS18 Anfernee Hardaway .60 1.50
SS19 Reggie Miller .40 1.00
SS20 Steve Francis .30 .75

2006-07 Fleer

Released in early February 2007, Fleer boasts a 251-card base set with veteran players pictured on cards 1-200 and rookies pictured on cards 201-251. Veteran cards showcase full-color player images on a basic white-bordered card design while rookie cards feature a slighly different design that includes a silver border. Also found in boxes are redemption cards for buyback autographs signed on an original Fleer card from 1986-87, 1987-88 or 1988-89. Though no odds were released for these buyback autographs, each box does contain an original Fleer card from one of the aforementioned years. Packaging for Fleer includes both Hobby and Retail formats where each contains 36 ten-card packs. The original suggested retail price for Fleer was $1.59 per pack.

COMPLETE SET (250) 30.00 70.00
COMP.SET w/o RC's (200) 10.00 25.00
RC ODDS APPROXIMATELY ONE PER PACK
ONE ORIGINAL FLEER CARD PER BOX
1 Josh Childress .20 .50
2 Al Harrington .20 .50
3 Joe Johnson .20 .50
4 Tyronn Lue .15 .40
5 Josh Smith .20 .50
6 Salim Stoudamire .15 .40
7 Marvin Williams .20 .50
8 Tony Allen .15 .40
9 Dan Dickau .15 .40
10 Al Jefferson .20 .50
11 Michael Olowokandi .15 .40
12 Paul Pierce .25 .60
13 Wally Szczerbiak .20 .50
14 Gerald Green .20 .50
15 Raymond Felton .20 .50
16 Brevin Knight .15 .40
17 Sean May .15 .40
18 Emeka Okafor .20 .50
19 Othella Harrington .15 .40
20 Gerald Wallace .20 .50
21 Tyson Chandler .20 .50
22 Luol Deng .20 .50
23 Chris Duhon .15 .40
24 Ben Gordon .20 .50
25 Kirk Hinrich .20 .50
26 Mike Sweetney .15 .40
27 Michael Jordan 2.00 5.00
28 Drew Gooden .20 .50
29 Larry Hughes .20 .50
30 Zydrunas Ilgauskas .20 .50
31 Damon Jones .15 .40
32 LeBron James 1.00 2.50
33 Donyell Marshall .15 .40
34 Anderson Varejao .15 .40
35 Erick Dampier .15 .40
36 Marquis Daniels .15 .40
37 Devin Harris .15 .40
38 Josh Howard .20 .50
39 Dirk Nowitzki .40 1.00
40 Jerry Stackhouse .20 .50
41 Jason Terry .20 .50
42 Carmelo Anthony .30 .75
43 Marcus Camby .20 .50
44 Reggie Evans .15 .40
45 Kenyon Martin .20 .50
46 Andre Miller .20 .50
47 Eduardo Najera .15 .40
48 Nene .20 .50
49 Chauncey Billups .25 .60
50 Richard Hamilton .20 .50
51 Jason Maxiell .15 .40
52 Antonio McDyess .20 .50
53 Tayshaun Prince .20 .50
54 Ben Wallace .20 .50
55 Rasheed Wallace .25 .60
56 Baron Davis .20 .50
57 Ike Diogu .15 .40
58 Mike Dunleavy .20 .50
59 Derek Fisher .20 .50
60 Adonal Foyle .15 .40
61 Troy Murphy .15 .40
62 Jason Richardson .25 .60
63 Rafer Alston .15 .40
64 Chuck Hayes .15 .40
65 Luther Head .20 .50
66 Juwan Howard .20 .50
67 Tracy McGrady .30 .75
68 Stromile Swift .15 .40
69 Yao Ming .30 .75
70 Austin Croshere .15 .40
71 Danny Granger .20 .50
72 Sarunas Jasikevicius .20 .50
73 Stephen Jackson .20 .50
74 Jermaine O'Neal .20 .50
75 Peja Stojakovic .25 .60
76 Jamaal Tinsley .15 .40
77 Elton Brand .25 .60
78 Sam Cassell .20 .50
79 Chris Kaman .20 .50
80 Yaroslav Korolev .15 .40
81 Shaun Livingston .15 .40
82 Corey Maggette .20 .50
83 Cuttino Mobley .15 .40
84 Kwame Brown .15 .40
85 Kobe Bryant 1.00 2.50
86 Andrew Bynum .15 .40
87 Devean George .15 .40
88 Lamar Odom .20 .50
89 Ronny Turiaf .20 .50
90 Luke Walton .15 .40
91 Shane Battier .20 .50
92 Pau Gasol .25 .60
93 Bobby Jackson .15 .40
94 Mike Miller .20 .50
95 Lawrence Roberts .15 .40
96 Damon Stoudamire .20 .50
97 Hakim Warrick .20 .50
98 Alonzo Mourning .30 .75
99 Shaquille O'Neal .50 1.25
100 Gary Payton .25 .60
101 Wayne Simien .15 .40
102 Dwyane Wade .40 1.00
103 Antoine Walker .20 .50
104 Jason Williams .20 .50
105 Andrew Bogut .20 .50
106 T.J. Ford .15 .40
107 Jamaal Magloire .15 .40
108 Michael Redd .20 .50
109 Bobby Simmons .15 .40
110 Maurice Williams .20 .50
111 Mark Blount .15 .40
112 Ricky Davis .20 .50
113 Kevin Garnett .40 1.00
114 Eddie Griffin .15 .40
115 Troy Hudson .15 .40
116 Rashad McCants .15 .40
117 Vince Carter .30 .75
118 Jason Collins .15 .40
119 Richard Jefferson .20 .50
120 Jason Kidd .40 1.00
121 Nenad Krstic .15 .40
122 Jeff McInnis .15 .40
123 Antoine Wright .15 .40
124 Brandon Bass .20 .50
125 David West .20 .50
126 Desmond Mason .15 .40
127 Chris Paul .30 .75
128 J.R. Smith .20 .50
129 Kirk Snyder .15 .40
130 Jamal Crawford .25 .60
131 Steve Francis .20 .50
132 Channing Frye .20 .50
133 Stephon Marbury .20 .50
134 Quentin Richardson .20 .50
135 Nate Robinson .15 .40
136 Jalen Rose .20 .50
137 Carlos Arroyo .15 .40
138 Keyon Dooling .15 .40
139 Grant Hill .30 .75
140 Dwight Howard .20 .50
141 Darko Milicic .15 .40
142 Jameer Nelson .15 .40
143 DeShawn Stevenson .15 .40
144 Samuel Dalembert .15 .40
145 Steven Hunter .15 .40
146 Andre Iguodala .20 .50
147 Allen Iverson .30 .75
148 Kyle Korver .20 .50
149 Chris Webber .25 .60
150 Leandro Barbosa .20 .50
151 Raja Bell .20 .50
152 Boris Diaw .20 .50
153 Shawn Marion .20 .50
154 Steve Nash .30 .75
155 Amare Stoudemire .20 .50
156 Kurt Thomas .15 .40
157 Steve Blake .15 .40
158 Juan Dixon .15 .40
159 Joel Przybilla .15 .40
160 Zach Randolph .20 .50
161 Travis Outlaw .20 .50
162 Sebastian Telfair .15 .40
163 Martell Webster .20 .50
164 Shareef Abdur-Rahim .20 .50
165 Ron Artest .25 .60
166 Mike Bibby .25 .60
167 Francisco Garcia .15 .40
168 Brad Miller .20 .50
169 Kenny Thomas .15 .40
170 Bonzi Wells .15 .40
171 Bruce Bowen .15 .40
172 Tim Duncan .40 1.00
173 Michael Finley .25 .60
174 Manu Ginobili .25 .60
175 Tony Parker .25 .60
176 Ray Allen .25 .60
177 Danny Fortson .15 .40
178 Rashard Lewis .25 .60
179 Luke Ridnour .20 .50
180 Robert Swift .15 .40
181 Chris Wilcox .15 .40
182 Chris Bosh .25 .60
183 Jose Calderon .15 .40
184 Joey Graham .15 .40
185 Pape Sow .15 .40
186 Charlie Villanueva .15 .40
187 Morris Peterson .15 .40
188 Carlos Boozer .20 .50
189 Gordan Giricek .15 .40
190 Kris Humphries .15 .40
191 Andrei Kirilenko .20 .50
192 Mehmet Okur .15 .40
193 Deron Williams .20 .50
194 Gilbert Arenas .20 .50
195 Andray Blatche .15 .40
196 Caron Butler .20 .50
197 Brendan Haywood .15 .40
198 Antawn Jamison .20 .50
199 Etan Thomas .15 .40
200 Antonio Daniels .15 .40
201 Tyrus Thomas RC .50 1.25
202 Adam Morrison RC .60 1.50
203 LaMarcus Aldridge RC 1.50 4.00
204 Rudy Gay RC .75 2.00
205 Andrea Bargnani RC .60 1.50
206 Rodney Carney RC RC .40 1.00
207 Alexander Johnson RC .40 1.00
208 Brandon Roy RC .60 1.50
209 Patrick O'Bryant RC .40 1.00
210 Randy Foye RC .60 1.50
211 Ronnie Brewer RC .60 1.50
212 Mardy Collins RC .40 1.00
213 Shelden Williams RC .50 1.25
214 J.J. Redick RC .75 2.00
215 Hilton Armstrong RC .40 1.00
216 Marcus Williams RC .40 1.00
217 Rajon Rondo RC 1.00 2.50
218 Cedric Simmons RC .40 1.00
219 Bobby Jones RC .40 1.00
220 Jordan Farmar RC .60 1.50
221 Maurice Ager RC .40 1.00
222 David Noel RC .40 1.00
223 James White RC .40 1.00
224 Leon Powe RC .50 1.25
225 Paul Millsap RC .75 2.00
226 Josh Boone RC .40 1.00
227 Kevin Pittsnogle RC .50 1.25
228 Daniel Gibson RC .50 1.25
229 Hassan Adams RC .40 1.00
230 Kyle Lowry RC .75 2.00
231 Renaldo Balkman RC .50 1.25
232 Dee Brown RC .40 1.00
233 Shawne Williams RC .40 1.00
234 P.J. Tucker RC .50 1.25
235 Craig Smith RC .50 1.25
236 Paul Davis RC .40 1.00
237 Pops Mensah-Bonsu RC .40 1.00
238 Denham Brown RC .40 1.00
239 Ryan Hollins RC .50 1.25
240 Allan Ray RC .40 1.00
241 Saer Sene RC .40 1.00
242 Shannon Brown RC .40 1.00
243 Thabo Sefolosha RC .60 1.50
244 Quincy Douby RC .40 1.00
245 Solomon Jones RC .40 1.00
246 Damir Markota RC. .40 1.00
247 Steve Novak RC .50 1.25
248 Will Blalock RC .40 1.00
249 Tarence Kinsey RC .40 1.00
250 Vassilis Spanoulis RC .40 1.00
NNO Michael Jordan .40 1.00

2006-07 Fleer Glossy Parallel

*GLOSSY: .75X TO 2X BASE HI
GLOSSY RANDOM INSERTS IN PACKS
27 Michael Jordan 5.00 12.00

2006-07 Fleer 1986-87 20th Anniversary

APPROXIMATE ODDS 1:2
1 Nene 1.00 2.50
2 Andrea Bargnani 1.25 3.00
3 Maurice Ager .75 2.00
4 Allen Iverson 1.50 4.00
5 Antawn Jamison 1.00 2.50
6 Andrei Kirilenko 1.00 2.50
7 Adam Morrison 1.25 3.00
8 Amare Stoudemire 1.00 2.50
9 Shane Battier 1.00 2.50
10 Baron Davis 1.00 2.50
11 Ben Gordon 1.00 2.50
12 Chauncey Billups 1.25 3.00
13 Steve Blake .75 2.00
14 Brad Miller 1.00 2.50
15 Andrew Bogut 1.00 2.50
16 Brandon Roy 1.25 3.00
17 Bobby Simmons .75 2.00
18 Ben Wallace 1.00 2.50
19 Andrew Bynum .75 2.00
20 Carmelo Anthony 1.50 4.00
21 Chris Bosh 1.25 3.00
22 Channing Frye 1.00 2.50
23 Josh Childress 1.00 2.50
24 Chris Kaman 1.00 2.50
25 Cuttino Mobley .75 2.00
26 Chris Paul 1.50 4.00
27 Cedric Simmons .75 2.00
28 Charlie Villanueva .75 2.00
29 Dwight Howard 1.00 2.50
30 Boris Diaw 1.00 2.50
31 Dirk Nowitzki 2.00 5.00
32 Mike Dunleavy 1.00 2.50
33 Dwyane Wade 2.00 5.00
34 Elton Brand 1.25 3.00
35 Eddy Curry 1.00 2.50
36 Fred Jones .75 2.00
37 Randy Foye 1.25 3.00
38 Gilbert Arenas 1.00 2.50
39 Gerald Green 1.00 2.50
40 Grant Hill 1.50 4.00
41 Hilton Armstrong .75 2.00
42 Hedo Turkoglu 1.25 3.00
43 Larry Hughes 1.00 2.50
44 Hakim Warrick 1.00 2.50
45 Andre Iguodala 1.00 2.50
46 Josh Boone .75 2.00
47 Jamal Crawford 1.25 3.00
48 Al Jefferson 1.00 2.50
49 Jordan Farmar 1.25 3.00
50 Josh Howard 1.00 2.50
51 Joe Johnson 1.00 2.50
52 Jason Kidd 2.00 5.00
53 Jermaine O'Neal 1.00 2.50
54 Jason Richardson 1.25 3.00
55 Jerry Stackhouse 1.00 2.50
56 Jason Terry 1.00 2.50
57 Michael Jordan 30.00 80.00
58 Kobe Bryant 5.00 12.00
59 Kevin Garnett 2.00 5.00
60 Kirk Hinrich 1.00 2.50
61 Kyle Korver 1.00 2.50
62 Kyle Lowry 1.50 4.00
63 Kenyon Martin 1.00 2.50
64 Kevin Pittsnogle 1.00 2.50
65 Kirk Snyder .75 2.00
66 Kurt Thomas .75 2.00
67 LaMarcus Aldridge 3.00 8.00
68 Luol Deng 1.00 2.50
69 Rashard Lewis 1.25 3.00
70 Luther Head 1.00 2.50
71 LeBron James 15.00 40.00
72 Lamar Odom 1.00 2.50
73 Luke Ridnour 1.00 2.50
74 Luke Walton .75 2.00
75 Shawn Marion 1.00 2.50
76 Mike Bibby 1.25 3.00
77 Mardy Collins .75 2.00
78 Marquis Daniels .75 2.00
79 Manu Ginobili 1.25 3.00
80 Andre Miller 1.00 2.50
81 Jason Williams 1.00 2.50
82 Mehmet Okur .75 2.00
83 Morris Peterson .75 2.00
84 Michael Redd 1.00 2.50
85 Troy Murphy .75 2.00
86 Marcus Williams .75 2.00
87 Nate Robinson .75 2.00
88 Tony Parker 1.25 3.00
89 Pau Gasol 1.25 3.00
90 Patrick O'Bryant .75 2.00
91 Paul Pierce 1.25 3.00
92 Peja Stojakovic 1.25 3.00
93 P.J. Tucker 1.00 2.50
94 Quincy Douby .75 2.00
95 Ray Allen 1.25 3.00
96 Ronnie Brewer 1.25 3.00
97 Rodney Carney .75 2.00
98 Ricky Davis 1.00 2.50
99 J.J. Redick 1.50 4.00
100 Raymond Felton 1.00 2.50
101 Rudy Gay 1.50 4.00
102 Richard Hamilton 1.00 2.50
103 Richard Jefferson 1.00 2.50
104 Raef LaFrentz .75 2.00
105 Rashad McCants .75 2.00
106 Jalen Rose 1.00 2.50
107 Rajon Rondo 2.00 5.00
108 Rasheed Wallace 1.25 3.00
109 Shannon Brown .75 2.00
110 Sam Cassell 1.00 2.50
111 Samuel Dalembert .75 2.00
112 Steve Francis 1.00 2.50
113 Sean May .75 2.00
114 Steve Nash 1.50 4.00
115 Shaquille O'Neal 2.50 6.00
116 Saer Sene .75 2.00
117 Stephon Marbury 1.00 2.50
118 Shelden Williams 1.00 2.50
119 Tyson Chandler 1.00 2.50
120 Tim Duncan 2.00 5.00
121 Tracy McGrady 1.50 4.00
122 Tayshaun Prince 1.00 2.50
123 Thabo Sefolosha 1.25 3.00
124 Tyrus Thomas 1.00 2.50
125 Udonis Haslem .75 2.00
126 Vince Carter 1.50 4.00
127 Bonzi Wells .75 2.00
128 Deron Williams 1.00 2.50
129 Marvin Williams 1.00 2.50
130 Wally Szczerbiak 1.00 2.50
131 Yao Ming 1.50 4.00
132 Zach Randolph 1.00 2.50

2006-07 Fleer Michael Jordan Buyback Autographs

5 Michael Jordan
1990 Fleer All-Stars
57 Michael Jordan/23 6000.00 10000.00

2006-07 Fleer Autographics

RANDOM INSERTS IN PACKS
AA Alex Acker 5.00 12.00
AB Andrea Bargnani 12.00 30.00
AI Andre Iguodala 8.00 20.00
BB Brent Barry 6.00 15.00
BJ Bobby Jones 5.00 12.00
BO Andrew Bogut SP 6.00 15.00
BS Bobby Simmons 5.00 12.00
CK Chris Kaman SP 6.00 15.00
CP Chris Paul SP 30.00 80.00
CS Cedric Simmons 5.00 12.00
CT Chris Taft 5.00 12.00
DH Dwight Howard SP 15.00 40.00
DN David Noel 5.00 12.00
DW Deron Williams 10.00 25.00
HA Hilton Armstrong 5.00 12.00
JF Jordan Farmar 8.00 20.00
KA Kareem Abdul-Jabbar SP 40.00 100.00
KL Kyle Lowry 6.00 15.00
LA LaMarcus Aldridge 12.00 30.00
LJ LeBron James SP 150.00 300.00
MA Maurice Ager 5.00 12.00
MC Mardy Collins 5.00 12.00
MW Marcus Williams 5.00 12.00
PM Paul Millsap 8.00 20.00
PS Peja Stojakovic 5.00 12.00
RB Ronnie Brewer 6.00 15.00
RG Rudy Gay 6.00 15.00
RO Brandon Roy 15.00 40.00
RR Rajon Rondo 25.00 60.00
SS Saer Sene 5.00 12.00
TT Tyrus Thomas 10.00 25.00

2006-07 Fleer Autographics Michael Jordan Autographics

COMMON CARD 350.00 650.00
RANDOM INSERTS IN PACKS

2006-07 Fleer Jordan's Greatest Moments

COMPLETE SET (10) 20.00 50.00
COMMON CARD 4.00 10.00
RANDOM INSERTS IN PACKS
UNPRICED AUTO PRINT RUN ONE SET

2006-07 Fleer Jordan's Platinum Influence

COMPLETE SET (20) 8.00 20.00
APPROXIMATE ODDS 1:3
AH A.J. Hawk 1.00 2.50
BA Renaldo Balkman .75 2.00
BU Reggie Bush 2.50 6.00
HA Hilton Armstrong .60 1.50
JR J.J. Redick 1.25 3.00
LA LaMarcus Aldridge 2.50 6.00
ML Matt Leinart 1.00 2.50
MW Marcus Williams .60 1.50
PO Patrick O'Bryant .60 1.50
QD Quincy Douby .60 1.50
RB Ronnie Brewer 1.00 2.50
RC Rodney Carney .60 1.50
RF Randy Foye 1.00 2.50
RG Rudy Gay 1.25 3.00
SH Santonio Holmes 1.00 2.50
SW Shelden Williams .75 2.00
TT Tyrus Thomas .75 2.00
VD Vernon Davis 1.00 2.50
VY Vince Young 2.00 5.00
WI Mario Williams 1.00 2.50

2006-07 Fleer Michael Jordan Missing Links

COMMON CARD 25.00 60.00
RANDOM INSERTS IN PACKS

2006-07 Fleer Rookie Sensations

COMPLETE SET (10) 6.00 15.00
APPROXIMATE ODDS 1:5
AB Andrea Bargnani .60 1.50
AM Adam Morrison .60 1.50
BR Brandon Roy .60 1.50
JM Shelden Williams .50 1.25
LA LaMarcus Aldridge 1.50 4.00
PO Patrick O'Bryant .40 1.00
RC Rodney Carney .40 1.00
RF Randy Foye .60 1.50
RG Rudy Gay .75 2.00
TT Tyrus Thomas .50 1.25

2006-07 Fleer Team Leaders

COMPLETE SET (20) 5.00 12.00
APPROXIMATE ODDS 1:2
AI Allen Iverson .50 1.25
BD Baron Davis .30 .75
CB Chauncey Billups .40 1.00
DN Dirk Nowitzki .60 1.50
DW Dwyane Wade .60 1.50
EO Emeka Okafor .30 .75
GA Gilbert Arenas .30 .75
JK Jason Kidd .60 1.50
KB Kobe Bryant 1.50 4.00
KG Kevin Garnett .60 1.50
LJ LeBron James 1.50 4.00
MB Mike Bibby .40 1.00
MJ Michael Jordan 3.00 8.00
PP Paul Pierce .40 1.00
RA Ray Allen .40 1.00
SC Sam Cassell .30 .75
SN Steve Nash .50 1.25
SO Shaquille O'Neal .75 2.00
TD Tim Duncan .60 1.50
TM Tracy McGrady .50 1.25

2006-07 Fleer Throwbacks

APPROXIMATE ODDS ONE PER BOX
BA Renaldo Balkman 2.00 5.00
BJ Bobby Jones 1.50 4.00
CS Craig Smith 2.00 5.00
DB Dee Brown 1.50 4.00
HA Hilton Armstrong 1.50 4.00
JB Josh Boone 1.50 4.00
JF Jordan Farmar 2.50 6.00
JR J.J. Redick 3.00 8.00
JW James White 1.50 4.00
KL Kyle Lowry 3.00 8.00
KP Kevin Pittsnogle 2.00 5.00
LA LaMarcus Aldridge 6.00 15.00
MA Maurice Ager 1.50 4.00
MC Mardy Collins 1.50 4.00
MW Marcus Williams 1.50 4.00
PD Paul Davis 1.50 4.00
PO Patrick O'Bryant 1.50 4.00
PT P.J. Tucker 2.00 5.00
RB Ronnie Brewer 2.50 6.00
RC Rodney Carney 1.50 4.00
RF Randy Foye 2.50 6.00
RG Rudy Gay 3.00 8.00
RR Rajon Rondo 6.00 15.00
SB Shannon Brown 1.50 4.00
SI Cedric Simmons 1.50 4.00
SJ Solomon Jones 1.50 4.00
SN Steve Novak 2.00 5.00
SW Shelden Williams 2.00 5.00
TT Tyrus Thomas 2.00 5.00
WI Shawne Williams 1.50 4.00

2006-07 Fleer Wal-Mart Rookie Exclusive

*WALMART: .6X TO 1.5X BASE HI
UNPRICED AUTO PRINT RUN ONE SET

2007-08 Fleer

This 235-card set was released in January, 2008. The set was issued into the hobby in 15 card packs, which came 16 packs to a box and 12 boxes to a case where packs carried an intial suggested retail price of $3.99. Cards numbered 1-200 feature veterans while cards numbered 201-235 feature NBA rookies.

COMPLETE SET (235) 30.00 60.00
ONE ROOKIE PER PACK
ONE JORDAN RELIC PER RETAIL SET
1 Chauncey Billups .20 .50
2 Amir Johnson .12 .30
3 Richard Hamilton .15 .40
4 Jason Maxiell .12 .30
5 Tayshaun Prince .15 .40
6 Rasheed Wallace .20 .50
7 Antonio McDyess .15 .40
8 Daniel Gibson .15 .40
9 Larry Hughes .15 .40
10 Zydrunas Ilgauskas .15 .40
11 Devin Brown .12 .30
12 LeBron James .75 2.00
13 Donyell Marshall .12 .30
14 Eric Snow .12 .30
15 Andrea Bargnani .20 .50
16 Chris Bosh .20 .50
17 T.J. Ford .12 .30
18 Jorge Garbajosa .15 .40
19 Radoslav Nesterovic .12 .30
20 Jose Calderon .12 .30
21 James Posey .12 .30
22 Alonzo Mourning .25 .60
23 Shaquille O'Neal .40 1.00
24 Dwyane Wade .30 .75
25 Antoine Walker .15 .40
26 Jason Williams .15 .40
27 Udonis Haslem .12 .30
28 Luol Deng .15 .40
29 Ben Gordon .15 .40
30 Kirk Hinrich .15 .40
31 Ben Wallace .15 .40
32 Tyrus Thomas .12 .30
33 Thabo Sefolosha .12 .30
34 Chris Duhon .12 .30
35 Vince Carter .25 .60
36 Jason Collins .12 .30
37 Richard Jefferson .15 .40
38 Jason Kidd .20 .50
39 Nenad Krstic .12 .30
40 Marcus Williams .12 .30
41 Josh Boone .12 .30
42 Gilbert Arenas .15 .40
43 Caron Butler .15 .40
44 Antawn Jamison .15 .40
45 Brendan Haywood .12 .30
46 Antonio Daniels .12 .30
47 Etan Thomas .12 .30
48 Trevor Ariza .12 .30
49 Dwight Howard .15 .40
50 Rashard Lewis .15 .40
51 Jameer Nelson .12 .30
52 J.J. Redick .20 .50
53 Hedo Turkoglu .15 .40
54 Carlos Arroyo .12 .30
55 Ike Diogu .12 .30
56 Mike Dunleavy .15 .40
57 Jeff Foster .12 .30
58 Jermaine O'Neal .15 .40
59 Jamaal Tinsley .12 .30
60 Shawne Williams .12 .30
61 Rodney Carney .12 .30
62 Andre Iguodala .15 .40
63 Kyle Korver .15 .40
64 Andre Miller .15 .40
65 Willie Green .12 .30
66 Samuel Dalembert .12 .30
67 Raymond Felton .20 .50
68 Sean May .12 .30
69 Adam Morrison .12 .30
70 Emeka Okafor .15 .40
71 Jason Richardson .20 .50
72 Gerald Wallace .15 .40
73 Ryan Hollins .12 .30
74 David Lee .12 .30
75 Jamal Crawford UER .20 .50
76 Eddy Curry .12 .30
77 Stephon Marbury .15 .40
78 Zach Randolph .15 .40
79 Nate Robinson .12 .30
80 Quentin Richardson .15 .40
81 Josh Childress .15 .40
82 Joe Johnson .15 .40
83 Tyronn Lue .12 .30
84 Josh Smith .15 .40
85 Marvin Williams .15 .40
86 Shelden Williams .12 .30
87 Salim Stoudamire .12 .30
88 Andrew Bogut .15 .40
89 Bobby Simmons .12 .30
90 David Noel .12 .30
91 Michael Redd .15 .40
92 Charlie Villanueva .12 .30
93 Desmond Mason .12 .30
94 Ray Allen .20 .50
95 Rajon Rondo .20 .50
96 Al Jefferson .15 .40
97 Paul Pierce .20 .50
98 Leon Powe .12 .30
99 Tony Allen .12 .30
100 Pau Gasol .20 .50
101 Rudy Gay .20 .50
102 Darko Milicic .12 .30
103 Damon Stoudamire .15 .40
104 Hakim Warrick .15 .40
105 Mike Miller .15 .40
106 Johan Petro .12 .30
107 Wally Szczerbiak .15 .40
108 Delonte West .12 .30
109 Luke Ridnour .15 .40
110 Chris Wilcox .12 .30
111 Nick Collison .15 .40
112 LaMarcus Aldridge .25 .60
113 Channing Frye .15 .40
114 Jarrett Jack .15 .40
115 Brandon Roy .20 .50
116 Martell Webster .15 .40
117 Sergio Rodriguez .12 .30
118 James Jones .12 .30
119 Shareef Abdur-Rahim .15 .40
120 Ron Artest .20 .50
121 Mike Bibby .20 .50
122 Francisco Garcia .12 .30
123 Kevin Martin .15 .40
124 Brad Miller .15 .40
125 Mikki Moore .12 .30
126 Ricky Davis .15 .40
127 Randy Foye .20 .50
128 Kevin Garnett .30 .75
129 Juwan Howard .15 .40
130 Marko Jaric .12 .30
131 Rashad McCants .12 .30
132 Craig Smith .12 .30
133 Hilton Armstrong .12 .30
134 Tyson Chandler .15 .40
135 Bobby Jackson .12 .30
136 Chris Paul .25 .60
137 Rasual Butler .12 .30
138 Peja Stojakovic .20 .50
139 Morris Peterson .12 .30
140 Elton Brand .20 .50
141 Sam Cassell .15 .40
142 Paul Davis .12 .30
143 Corey Maggette .15 .40
144 Cuttino Mobley .15 .40
145 Chris Kaman .15 .40
146 Baron Davis .15 .40
147 Monta Ellis .15 .40
148 Al Harrington .15 .40
149 Stephen Jackson .15 .40
150 Matt Barnes .12 .30
151 Andris Biedrins .12 .30
152 Kwame Brown .12 .30
153 Kobe Bryant .75 2.00
154 Andrew Bynum .12 .30
155 Jordan Farmar .12 .30
156 Lamar Odom .15 .40
157 Luke Walton .12 .30
158 Maurice Evans .12 .30
159 Carmelo Anthony .25 .60
160 Marcus Camby .12 .30
161 Allen Iverson .25 .60
162 Kenyon Martin .15 .40
163 Nene .15 .40
164 J.R. Smith .15 .40
165 Yakhouba Diawara .12 .30
166 Shane Battier .15 .40
167 Luther Head .15 .40
168 Tracy McGrady .20 .50
169 Yao Ming .25 .60
170 Rafer Alston .12 .30
171 Bonzi Wells .12 .30
172 Steve Novak .12 .30
173 Carlos Boozer .15 .40
174 Ronnie Brewer .15 .40
175 Andrei Kirilenko .15 .40
176 Paul Millsap .15 .40
177 Mehmet Okur .12 .30
178 Deron Williams .15 .40
179 Jarron Collins .12 .30
180 Tim Duncan .30 .75
181 Tony Parker .20 .50
182 Manu Ginobili .20 .50
183 Bruce Bowen .12 .30
184 Brent Barry .12 .30
185 Robert Horry .15 .40
186 Michael Finley .20 .50
187 Leandro Barbosa .15 .40
188 Grant Hill .25 .60
189 Shawn Marion .15 .40
190 Steve Nash .25 .60
191 Amare Stoudemire .15 .40
192 Boris Diaw .15 .40
193 Raja Bell .15 .40
194 Maurice Ager .12 .30
195 Devean George .12 .30
196 Devin Harris .12 .30
197 Josh Howard .15 .40
198 Dirk Nowitzki .25 .60
199 Jerry Stackhouse .15 .40
200 Jason Terry .15 .40
201 Arron Afflalo RC .50 1.25
202 Morris Almond RC .30 .75
203 Marco Belinelli RC .50 1.25
204 Corey Brewer RC .50 1.25
205 Wilson Chandler RC .40 1.00
206 Mike Conley Jr. RC .60 1.50
207 Daequan Cook RC .40 1.00
208 Javaris Crittenton RC .30 .75
209 Jermareo Davidson RC .30 .75
210 Glen Davis RC .40 1.00
211 Jared Dudley RC .40 1.00
212 Kevin Durant RC 5.00 12.00
213 Nick Fazekas RC .30 .75
214 Jeff Green RC .50 1.25
215 Taurean Green RC .30 .75
216 Spencer Hawes RC .40 1.00
217 Al Horford RC .60 1.50
218 Aaron Brooks RC .40 1.00
219 Carl Landry RC .30 .75
220 Acie Law RC .30 .75
221 Josh McRoberts RC .40 1.00
222 Joakim Noah RC .50 1.25
223 Greg Oden RC .50 1.25
224 Gabe Pruitt RC .30 .75
225 Jason Smith RC .40 1.00
226 Rodney Stuckey RC .40 1.00
227 Al Thornton RC .40 1.00
228 Alando Tucker RC .30 .75
229 Sean Williams RC .30 .75
230 Yi Jianlian RC .60 1.50
231 Brandan Wright RC .50 1.25
232 Julian Wright RC .30 .75
233 Nick Young RC .60 1.50
234 Thaddeus Young RC .50 1.25
235 Chris Richard RC .30 .75
RCF Michael Jordan Floor 12.00 30.00
COAF M.Jordan Floor AU/23 1000.00 2000.00
COFJ M.Jordan JSY Flr/230 60.00 120.00
RCPJ M.Jordan JSY White 30.00 80.00
RCWU M.Jordan JSY Black/250 60.00 120.00

2007-08 Fleer Glossy

*GLOSSY: .75X TO 2X BASE HI
RANDOM INSERTS IN PACKS

2007-08 Fleer 1961-62

*1961-62 SINGLES: 1X TO 2.5X BASE HI
RANDOM INSERTS IN PACKS

2007-08 Fleer 1986-87 Rookies

*1986-87 RCs: .6X TO 1.5X BASE HI
APPROXIMATELY ONE PER PACK
*1986-87 RC GLOSSY: .75X TO 2X BASE HI
GLOSSY RANDOM INSERTS IN PACKS

2007-08 Fleer 1987-88

*1987-88: .6X TO 1.5X BASE HI
APPROXIMATELY ONE PER PACK
R71 Michael Jordan 10.00 25.00

2007-08 Fleer Decades of Excellence

COMPLETE SET (20) 25.00 50.00
RANDOM INSERTS IN PACKS
*GLOSSY: .6X TO 1.5X BASE HI
GLOSSY RANDOM INSERTS IN PACKS
1 Larry Bird 2.50 6.00
2 Magic Johnson 2.50 6.00
3 Michael Jordan 8.00 20.00
4 Bill Laimbeer .75 2.00
5 David Robinson 1.50 4.00
6 Grant Hill 1.25 3.00
7 Hakeem Olajuwon 1.25 3.00
8 Robert Parish 1.00 2.50
9 John Stockton 1.50 4.00
10 Michael Jordan 8.00 20.00
11 Dennis Rodman 2.00 5.00
12 Shaquille O'Neal 2.00 5.00
13 LeBron James 4.00 10.00
14 Chauncey Billups 1.00 2.50
15 Kobe Bryant 4.00 10.00
16 Steve Nash 1.25 3.00
17 Dwyane Wade 1.50 4.00
18 Allen Iverson 1.25 3.00
19 Baron Davis .75 2.00
20 Tim Duncan 1.50 4.00

2007-08 Fleer Feel The Game

APPROXIMATE ODDS ONE PER BOX
FGAB Andrea Bargnani 2.50 6.00
FGAI Allen Iverson 3.00 8.00
FGAJ Antawn Jamison 2.00 5.00
FGAM Alonzo Mourning 3.00 8.00
FGAS Amare Stoudemire 2.00 5.00
FGBO Carlos Boozer 2.00 5.00
FGBW Ben Wallace 2.00 5.00
FGCA Carmelo Anthony 3.00 8.00
FGCB Chauncey Billups 2.50 6.00
FGCH Chris Bosh 2.50 6.00
FGDH Dwight Howard 2.00 5.00
FGDN Dirk Nowitzki 3.00 8.00
FGDR David Robinson 4.00 10.00
FGEB Elton Brand 2.50 6.00
FGGH Grant Hill 4.00 10.00
FGHO Hakeem Olajuwon 3.00 8.00
FGJJ Joe Johnson 2.00 5.00
FGJK Jason Kidd 2.50 6.00
FGJO Michael Jordan 20.00 50.00
FGKB Kobe Bryant 6.00 15.00
FGKG Kevin Garnett 4.00 10.00
FGLB Larry Bird 6.00 15.00
FGLJ LeBron James 10.00 25.00
FGMJ Magic Johnson 6.00 15.00
FGMR Michael Redd 2.00 5.00
FGO' Jermaine O'Neal 2.00 5.00
FGPG Pau Gasol 2.50 6.00
FGPP Paul Pierce 2.50 6.00
FGPS Peja Stojakovic 2.50 6.00
FGRA Ray Allen 2.50 6.00
FGRH Richard Hamilton 2.00 5.00
FGRO Dennis Rodman 5.00 12.00
FGRW Rasheed Wallace 2.50 6.00
FGSM Stephon Marbury 2.00 5.00
FGSO Shaquille O'Neal 5.00 12.00
FGTD Tim Duncan 4.00 10.00
FGTM Tracy McGrady 2.50 6.00
FGTP Tony Parker 2.50 6.00
FGVC Vince Carter 3.00 8.00
FGYM Yao Ming 3.00 8.00

2007-08 Fleer Michael Jordan Missing Links

COMMON CARD 25.00 60.00
RANDOM INSERTS IN PACKS

2007-08 Fleer NBA Classics

APPROXIMATELY ONE PER BOX
TTAA Arron Afflalo 2.50 6.00
TTAB Aaron Brooks 2.00 5.00
TTAG Aaron Gray 1.50 4.00
TTAH Al Horford 3.00 8.00
TTAL Acie Law 1.50 4.00
TTAT Al Thornton 2.00 5.00
TTCB Corey Brewer 2.50 6.00
TTCL Carl Landry 1.50 4.00
TTCR Chris Richard 1.50 4.00
TTDM Dominic McGuire 1.50 4.00
TTDU Jared Dudley 2.00 5.00
TTGD Glen Davis 2.00 5.00
TTGP Gabe Pruitt 1.50 4.00
TTHA Adam Haluska 1.50 4.00
TTHH Herbert Hill 1.50 4.00
TTJC Javaris Crittenton 1.50 4.00
TTJD Jermareo Davidson 1.50 4.00
TTJG Jeff Green 2.50 6.00
TTJN Joakim Noah 2.50 6.00
TTJS Jason Smith 2.00 5.00
TTJW Julian Wright 1.50 4.00
TTKD Kevin Durant 10.00 25.00
TTMA Morris Almond 1.50 4.00
TTMC Mike Conley Jr. 3.00 8.00

TTNF Nick Fazekas 1.50 4.00
TTNY Nick Young 3.00 8.00
TTRS Rodney Stuckey 2.00 5.00
TTSH Spencer Hawes 2.00 5.00
TTSW Sean Williams 1.50 4.00
TTTG Taurean Green 1.50 4.00
TTTU Alando Tucker 1.50 4.00
TTTY Thaddeus Young 2.50 6.00
TTWC Wilson Chandler 2.00 5.00

2007-08 Fleer Rookie Sensations

COMPLETE SET (15) 10.00 25.00
RANDOM INSERTS IN PACKS
*GLOSSY: .6X TO 1.5X BASE HI
GLOSSY RANDOM INSERTS IN PACKS
RS1 Greg Oden .75 2.00
RS2 Kevin Durant 8.00 20.00
RS3 Al Horford 1.00 2.50
RS4 Mike Conley Jr. 1.00 2.50
RS5 Jeff Green .75 2.00
RS6 Thaddeus Young .75 2.00
RS7 Corey Brewer .75 2.00
RS8 Brandan Wright .75 2.00
RS9 Joakim Noah .75 2.00
RS10 Spencer Hawes .60 1.50
RS11 Acie Law .50 1.25
RS12 Julian Wright .50 1.25
RS13 Al Thornton .60 1.50
RS14 Rodney Stuckey .60 1.50
RS15 Nick Young 1.00 2.50

2008-09 Fleer

This set was released on January 6, 2009. The base set consists of 247 cards. Cards 1-200 feature veterans, and cards 201-247 feature rookie players.

COMPLETE SET (247) 20.00 50.00
ROOKIE STATED ODDS 1:1
TRI-CARD STATED ODDS 1:3
1 Ray Allen .20 .50
2 Kevin Garnett .30 .75
3 Paul Pierce .20 .50
4 Glen Davis .12 .30
5 Rajon Rondo .20 .50
6 Leon Powe .12 .30
7 James Posey .12 .30
8 Chauncey Billups .20 .50
9 Richard Hamilton .15 .40
10 Jason Maxiell .12 .30
11 Tayshaun Prince .15 .40
12 Rasheed Wallace .20 .50
13 Rodney Stuckey .15 .40
14 Antonio McDyess .15 .40
15 Keith Bogans .12 .30
16 Maurice Evans .12 .30
17 Dwight Howard .15 .40
18 Rashard Lewis .15 .40
19 Jameer Nelson .12 .30
20 Hedo Turkoglu .15 .40
21 Anthony Johnson .12 .30
22 Ben Wallace .15 .40
23 LeBron James .75 2.00
24 Zydrunas Ilgauskas .15 .40
25 Delonte West .12 .30
26 Anderson Varejao .12 .30
27 Daniel Gibson .15 .40
28 Mo Williams .15 .40
29 Gilbert Arenas .15 .40
30 Caron Butler .15 .40
31 Brendan Haywood .12 .30
32 Antawn Jamison .15 .40
33 DeShawn Stevenson .12 .30
34 Nick Young .15 .40
35 Antonio Daniels .12 .30
36 Andrea Bargnani .15 .40
37 Chris Bosh .20 .50
38 Jose Calderon .12 .30
39 Jermaine O'Neal .15 .40
40 Anthony Parker .12 .30
41 Jamario Moon .12 .30
42 Elton Brand .20 .50
43 Samuel Dalembert .12 .30
44 Willie Green .12 .30
45 Andre Iguodala .15 .40
46 Andre Miller .15 .40
47 Louis Williams .15 .40
48 Thaddeus Young .15 .40
49 Mike Bibby .15 .40
50 Zaza Pachulia .12 .30
51 Al Horford .20 .50
52 Joe Johnson .15 .40
53 Josh Smith .15 .40
54 Marvin Williams .15 .40
55 Acie Law .15 .40
56 Danny Granger .15 .40
57 T.J. Ford .12 .30
58 Mike Dunleavy .15 .40
59 Jamaal Tinsley .12 .30
60 Troy Murphy .12 .30
61 Jeff Foster .12 .30
62 Vince Carter .25 .60
63 Yi Jianlian .20 .50
64 Sean Williams .15 .40
65 Devin Harris .12 .30
66 Keyon Dooling .12 .30
67 Josh Boone .12 .30
68 Michael Jordan 1.50 4.00
69 Luol Deng .15 .40
70 Ben Gordon .15 .40
71 Joakim Noah .15 .40
72 Kirk Hinrich .15 .40
73 Andres Nocioni .12 .30
74 Larry Hughes .15 .40
75 Gerald Wallace .15 .40
76 Emeka Okafor .15 .40
77 Jason Richardson .20 .50
78 Raymond Felton .15 .40
79 Adam Morrison .12 .30
80 Jared Dudley .15 .40
81 Nazr Mohammed .12 .30
82 Andrew Bogut .15 .40
83 Charlie Villanueva .12 .30
84 Michael Redd .15 .40
85 Ramon Sessions .15 .40
86 Richard Jefferson .15 .40
87 Charlie Bell .12 .30
88 Jamal Crawford .20 .50
89 Eddy Curry .12 .30
90 Stephon Marbury .15 .40
91 Zach Randolph .15 .40
92 Quentin Richardson .15 .40
93 Nate Robinson .12 .30
94 David Lee .12 .30
95 Dwyane Wade .30 .75
96 Daequan Cook .12 .30
97 Shawn Marion .15 .40
98 Alonzo Mourning .25 .60
99 Udonis Haslem .12 .30
100 Dorell Wright .12 .30
101 Kobe Bryant .75 2.00
102 Andrew Bynum .12 .30
103 Jordan Farmar .12 .30
104 Pau Gasol .20 .50
105 Lamar Odom .15 .40
106 Luke Walton .12 .30
107 Sasha Vujacic .12 .30
108 Tyson Chandler .15 .40
109 Chris Paul .25 .60
110 Hilton Armstrong .12 .30
111 Peja Stojakovic .20 .50
112 Rasual Butler .12 .30
113 Julian Wright .15 .40
114 Morris Peterson .12 .30
115 Tony Parker .20 .50
116 Tim Duncan .30 .75
117 Manu Ginobili .20 .50
118 Michael Finley .20 .50
119 Kurt Thomas .12 .30
120 Bruce Bowen .12 .30
121 Fabricio Oberto .12 .30
122 Mehmet Okur .12 .30
123 Deron Williams .15 .40
124 Carlos Boozer .15 .40
125 Kyle Korver .15 .40
126 Andrei Kirilenko .15 .40
127 Paul Millsap .15 .40
128 Ronnie Brewer .15 .40
129 Shane Battier .15 .40
130 Tracy McGrady .20 .50
131 Yao Ming .25 .60
132 Luis Scola .15 .40
133 Luther Head .12 .30
134 Carl Landry .12 .30
135 Ron Artest .20 .50
136 Grant Hill .25 .60
137 Amare Stoudemire .15 .40
138 Steve Nash .20 .50
139 Shaquille O'Neal .40 1.00
140 Leandro Barbosa .15 .40
141 Boris Diaw .15 .40
142 Raja Bell .15 .40
143 Dirk Nowitzki .25 .60
144 Jason Kidd .20 .50
145 Josh Howard .15 .40
146 Jerry Stackhouse .15 .40
147 Jason Terry .15 .40
148 Brandon Bass .12 .30
149 Erick Dampier .12 .30
150 Carmelo Anthony .25 .60
151 Nene .15 .40
152 Allen Iverson .25 .60
153 Kenyon Martin .15 .40
154 J.R. Smith .15 .40
155 Linas Kleiza .12 .30
156 Corey Maggette .15 .40
157 Monta Ellis .15 .40
158 Stephen Jackson .15 .40
159 Al Harrington .15 .40
160 Andris Biedrins .12 .30
161 Kelenna Azubuike .12 .30
162 C.J. Watson .12 .30
163 LaMarcus Aldridge .20 .50
164 Travis Outlaw .15 .40
165 Greg Oden .15 .40
166 Brandon Roy .20 .50
167 Martell Webster .15 .40
168 Steve Blake .12 .30
169 Bobby Brown .12 .30
170 Beno Udrih .12 .30
171 Kevin Martin .15 .40
172 Francisco Garcia .12 .30
173 Brad Miller .15 .40
174 John Salmons .12 .30
175 Mikki Moore .12 .30
176 Baron Davis .15 .40
177 Chris Kaman .15 .40
178 Shaun Livingston .12 .30
179 Marcus Camby .12 .30
180 Al Thornton .15 .40
181 Cuttino Mobley .12 .30
182 Ricky Davis .15 .40
183 Corey Brewer .15 .40
184 Randy Foye .20 .50
185 Al Jefferson .15 .40
186 Rashad McCants .12 .30
187 Mike Miller .15 .40
188 Sebastian Telfair .12 .30
189 Mike Conley Jr. .15 .40
190 Rudy Gay .20 .50
191 Kyle Lowry .20 .50
192 Hakim Warrick .15 .40
193 Marko Jaric .12 .30
194 Javaris Crittenton .12 .30
195 Kevin Durant .50 1.25
196 Jeff Green .15 .40
197 Chris Wilcox .12 .30
198 Damien Wilkins .12 .30
199 Earl Watson .12 .30
200 Desmond Mason .12 .30
201 Derrick Rose RC 2.00 5.00
202 Michael Beasley RC .50 1.25
203 O.J. Mayo RC .50 1.25
204 Russell Westbrook RC 3.00 8.00
205 Kevin Love RC 1.50 4.00
206 Danilo Gallinari RC .75 2.00
207 Eric Gordon RC .75 2.00
208 Joe Alexander RC .30 .75
209 D.J. Augustin RC .40 1.00
210 Brook Lopez RC .60 1.50
211 Jerryd Bayless RC .40 1.00
212 Jason Thompson RC .30 .75
213 Brandon Rush RC .40 1.00
214 Anthony Randolph RC .30 .75
215 Robin Lopez RC .50 1.25
216 Marreese Speights RC .40 1.00
217 Roy Hibbert RC .50 1.25
218 Javale McGee RC .60 1.50
219 J.J. Hickson RC .40 1.00
220 Alexis Ajinca RC .30 .75
221 Ryan Anderson RC .40 1.00
222 Courtney Lee RC .40 1.00
223 Kosta Koufos RC .40 1.00
224 George Hill RC .50 1.25
225 Darrell Arthur RC .40 1.00
226 Donte Greene RC .30 .75
227 D.J. White RC .40 1.00
228 J.R. Giddens RC .30 .75
229 Walter Sharpe RC .30 .75
230 Joey Dorsey RC .30 .75
231 Mario Chalmers RC .50 1.25
232 Kyle Weaver RC .30 .75
233 Sonny Weems RC .30 .75
234 Chris Douglas-Roberts RC .30 .75
235 Rudy Fernandez RC .40 1.00
236 Rose/Beasley/Mayo 2.00 5.00
237 Westbrook/Love/Gallinari 2.50 6.00
238 Gordon/Alexander/Augustin 1.50 4.00
239 Lopez/Bayless/Thompson 1.50 4.00
240 Rush/Randolph/Lopez 1.50 4.00
241 Speights/Hibbert/McGee 1.50 4.00
242 Hickson/Ajinca/Anderson 1.50 4.00
243 Lee/Koufos/Hill 1.50 4.00
244 Arthur/Greene/White 1.50 4.00
245 Giddens/Sharpe/Dorsey 1.50 4.00
246 Chalmers/Jordan/Weaver 2.00 5.00
247 Weems/Douglas-Roberts/Fernandez 1.50 4.00

2008-09 Fleer Glossy

*GLOSSY: .6X TO 1.5X BASE HI
RANDOM INSERTS IN PACKS

2008-09 Fleer 1986-87 Rookies

COMPLETE SET (30) 15.00 40.00
STATED ODDS 1:2
*GLOSSY: .6X TO 1.5X BASE HI
GLOSSY: RANDOM INSERTS IN PACKS
86R163 Derrick Rose 3.00 8.00
86R164 Michael Beasley .75 2.00
86R165 O.J. Mayo .75 2.00
86R166 Russell Westbrook 6.00 15.00
86R167 Kevin Love 2.50 6.00
86R168 Eric Gordon 1.25 3.00
86R169 Joe Alexander .50 1.25
86R170 D.J. Augustin .60 1.50
86R171 Brook Lopez 1.00 2.50
86R172 Jerryd Bayless .60 1.50
86R173 Jason Thompson .50 1.25
86R174 Brandon Rush .60 1.50
86R175 Anthony Randolph .50 1.25
86R176 Robin Lopez .75 2.00
86R177 Marreese Speights .60 1.50
86R178 Roy Hibbert .75 2.00
86R179 Javale McGee 1.00 2.50
86R180 J.J. Hickson .60 1.50
86R181 Ryan Anderson .60 1.50
86R182 Courtney Lee .60 1.50
86R183 Kosta Koufos .60 1.50
86R184 George Hill .75 2.00
86R185 Darrell Arthur .60 1.50
86R186 Donte Greene .50 1.25
86R187 D.J. White .60 1.50
86R188 J.R. Giddens .50 1.25
86R189 Joey Dorsey .50 1.25
86R190 Sonny Weems .50 1.25
86R191 Chris Douglas-Roberts .50 1.25
86R192 Rudy Fernandez .60 1.50

2008-09 Fleer 1988-89

COMPLETE SET (132) 30.00 60.00
*88-89: .75X TO 2X BASE HI
APPROXIMATE ODDS 1:3

2008-09 Fleer All-Star Sensations

COMPLETE SET (26) 15.00 30.00
AS1 Allen Iverson .60 1.50
AS2 David Robinson .75 2.00
AS3 Dirk Nowitzki .60 1.50
AS4 Dominique Wilkins .60 1.50
AS5 Dwight Howard .40 1.00
AS6 Grant Hill .60 1.50
AS7 Jason Kidd .50 1.25
AS8 Jason Richardson .50 1.25
AS9 John Stockton .75 2.00
AS10 Josh Smith .40 1.00
AS11 Julius Erving .75 2.00
AS12 Kevin Garnett .75 2.00
AS13 Kobe Bryant 2.00 5.00
AS14 Larry Bird 1.25 3.00
AS15 LeBron James 2.00 5.00
AS16 Magic Johnson 1.25 3.00
AS17 Michael Jordan 4.00 10.00
AS18 Ray Allen .50 1.25
AS19 Rolando Blackman .40 1.00
AS20 Shaquille O'Neal 1.00 2.50
AS21 Spud Webb .40 1.00
AS22 Tim Duncan .75 2.00
AS23 Tom Chambers .40 1.00
AS24 Tracy McGrady .50 1.25
AS25 Vince Carter .60 1.50
AS26 Yao Ming .60 1.50

2008-09 Fleer Feel the Game

RANDOM INSERTS IN PACKS
FGCA Carmelo Anthony 3.00 8.00
FGDH Dwight Howard 2.00 5.00
FGGA Gilbert Arenas 2.00 5.00
FGKB Kobe Bryant 8.00 20.00
FGKG Kevin Garnett 4.00 10.00
FGLJ LeBron James 8.00 20.00
FGMJ Michael Jordan 20.00 50.00
FGSN Steve Nash 2.50 6.00
FGSO Shaquille O'Neal 5.00 12.00
FGYM Yao Ming 3.00 8.00

2008-09 Fleer First Year Phenoms

COMPLETE SET (10) 10.00 25.00
PH1 Derrick Rose 4.00 10.00
PH2 Michael Beasley 1.00 2.50
PH3 O.J. Mayo 1.00 2.50
PH4 Russell Westbrook 8.00 20.00
PH5 Kevin Love 3.00 8.00
PH6 Danilo Gallinari 1.50 4.00
PH7 Eric Gordon 1.50 4.00
PH8 Joe Alexander .60 1.50
PH9 D.J. Augustin .75 2.00
PH10 Brook Lopez 1.25 3.00

2008-09 Fleer Genuine Coverage

APPROXIMATE ODDS 1:10
GCAI Andre Iguodala 2.00 5.00
GCAK Andrei Kirilenko 2.00 5.00
GCAS Amare Stoudemire 2.00 5.00
GCBO Chris Bosh 2.50 6.00
GCCA Carmelo Anthony 3.00 8.00
GCCB Chauncey Billups 2.50 6.00
GCCM Corey Maggette 2.00 5.00
GCDH Dwight Howard 2.00 5.00
GCDN Dirk Nowitzki 3.00 8.00
GCEB Elton Brand 2.50 6.00
GCGA Gilbert Arenas 2.00 5.00
GCJK Jason Kidd 2.50 6.00
GCJO Jermaine O'Neal 2.00 5.00
GCKB Kobe Bryant 10.00 25.00
GCKG Kevin Garnett 4.00 10.00
GCLJ LeBron James 10.00 25.00
GCRA Ray Allen 2.50 6.00
GCRH Richard Hamilton 2.00 5.00
GCRW Rasheed Wallace 2.50 6.00
GCSM Shawn Marion 2.00 5.00
GCSO Shaquille O'Neal 5.00 12.00
GCTD Tim Duncan 4.00 10.00
GCTM Tracy McGrady 2.50 6.00
GCVC Vince Carter 3.00 8.00
GCYM Yao Ming 3.00 8.00

2008-09 Fleer Living Legacies

COMPLETE SET (12) 15.00 30.00
LL1 Bill Russell 1.50 4.00
LL2 Bill Walton 1.00 2.50
LL3 Clyde Drexler 1.25 3.00
LL4 Dominique Wilkins 1.25 3.00
LL5 Hakeem Olajuwon 1.25 3.00
LL6 James Worthy 1.00 2.50
LL7 Julius Erving 1.50 4.00
LL8 Larry Bird 2.50 6.00
LL9 Magic Johnson 2.50 6.00
LL10 Michael Jordan 8.00 20.00
LL11 Oscar Robertson 1.00 2.50
LL12 Robert Parish 1.00 2.50

2008-09 Fleer Michael Jordan Retrospective

COMPLETE SET (23) 15.00 40.00
*GLOSSY: .6X TO 1.5X BASE HI
RANDOM INSERTS IN PACKS

2008-09 Fleer NBA Classics

APPROXIMATE ODDS 1:10
NBAAR Anthony Randolph 1.25 3.00
NBABL Brook Lopez 2.50 6.00
NBABR Brandon Rush 1.50 4.00
NBACD Chris Douglas-Roberts 1.25 3.00
NBACL Courtney Lee 1.50 4.00
NBADA D.J. Augustin 1.50 4.00
NBADG Donte Greene 1.25 3.00
NBADJ DeAndre Jordan 2.50 6.00
NBADR Derrick Rose 8.00 20.00
NBAEG Eric Gordon 3.00 8.00
NBAGH George Hill 2.00 5.00
NBAJA Joe Alexander 1.25 3.00
NBAJB Jerryd Bayless 1.50 4.00
NBAJH J.J. Hickson 1.50 4.00
NBAJM Javale McGee 2.50 6.00
NBAJT Jason Thompson 1.25 3.00
NBAKK Kosta Koufos 1.50 4.00
NBAKL Kevin Love 6.00 15.00
NBAKW Kyle Weaver 1.25 3.00
NBAMB Michael Beasley 2.00 5.00
NBAMC Mario Chalmers 2.00 5.00
NBAMS Marreese Speights 1.50 4.00
NBAOM O.J. Mayo 2.00 5.00
NBAPE Patrick Ewing Jr 1.25 3.00
NBARA Ryan Anderson 1.50 4.00
NBARH Roy Hibbert 2.00 5.00
NBARL Robin Lopez 2.00 5.00
NBASW Sonny Weems 1.25 3.00
NBAWS Walter Sharpe 1.25 3.00

2008-09 Fleer Sharp Shooters

COMPLETE SET (20) 20.00 40.00
SS1 Anthony Parker .75 2.00
SS2 B.J. Armstrong 1.25 3.00
SS3 Ben Gordon 1.00 2.50
SS4 Chauncey Billups 1.25 3.00
SS5 Daniel Gibson 1.00 2.50
SS6 Jason Kapono .75 2.00
SS7 John Stockton 2.00 5.00
SS8 Kenny Smith 1.00 2.50
SS9 Kevin Martin 1.00 2.50
SS10 Larry Bird 3.00 8.00
SS11 Leandro Barbosa 1.00 2.50
SS12 Manu Ginobili 1.25 3.00
SS13 Mark Price 2.00 5.00
SS14 Michael Redd 1.00 2.50
SS15 Mike Miller 1.00 2.50
SS16 Peja Stojakovic 1.25 3.00
SS17 Rashard Lewis 1.00 2.50
SS18 Ray Allen 1.25 3.00
SS19 Steve Kerr 1.25 3.00
SS20 Steve Nash 1.25 3.00

2008-09 Fleer Signature Approval

APPROXIMATE ODDS 1:15
SAAA Alexis Ajinca 5.00 12.00
SAAB Aaron Brooks 3.00 8.00
SAAM Alonzo Mourning 40.00 70.00
SAAN Carmelo Anthony 12.00 30.00
SAAT Al Thornton 3.00 8.00
SABB Bobby Brown 3.00 8.00
SABE Marco Belinelli 3.00 8.00
SABI Mike Bibby 5.00 12.00
SACA ML Carr 6.00 15.00
SACB Corey Brewer 3.00 8.00
SACH Maurice Cheeks 5.00 12.00
SACL Carl Landry 3.00 8.00
SACR Chris Richard 3.00 8.00
SACS Cheikh Samb 3.00 8.00
SADA D.J. Augustin 3.00 8.00
SADG Danilo Gallinari 8.00 20.00
SADH Dwight Howard 8.00 20.00
SADI Boris Diaw 4.00 10.00
SADJ Darnell Jackson 3.00 8.00
SADR Derrick Rose 30.00 80.00
SADS D.J. Strawberry 3.00 8.00
SAGD Glen Davis 3.00 8.00
SAJA Antawn Jamison 6.00 15.00
SAJG Jeff Green 3.00 8.00
SAJN Joakim Noah 6.00 15.00
SAKB Kobe Bryant 100.00 200.00
SAKD Kevin Durant 75.00 150.00
SAKG Kevin Garnett 40.00 80.00
SALM Luc Richard Mbah A Moute 3.00 8.00
SALO Lamar Odom 6.00 15.00
SALS Luis Scola 3.00 8.00
SAMA Morris Almond 3.00 8.00
SAMB Michael Beasley 6.00 15.00
SAMC Mike Conley Jr. 8.00 20.00
SAMJ Michael Jordan 300.00 500.00
SAOM O.J. Mayo 3.00 8.00
SAPO Patrick O'Bryant 3.00 8.00
SAPR Pat Riley 20.00 50.00
SARH Richard Hendrix 3.00 8.00
SARM Rick Mahorn 8.00 20.00
SARS Ramon Sessions 3.00 8.00
SARW Russell Westbrook 60.00 150.00
SAST Rodney Stuckey 3.00 8.00
SASW Sean Williams 3.00 8.00
SAVC Vince Carter 15.00 30.00
SAWC Wilson Chandler 3.00 8.00
SAWH Walter Herrmann 3.00 8.00

2002 Fleer All-Star NBA Jam Session

Distributed by Fleer at the 2002 NBA All-Star Jam Session show in Philadelphia, this card was available at the Fleer show booth. Cards feature a full color photo of Eric Snow set against a background with the American flag along the top, the NBA Jam-Session Logo in the lower right-hand corner and the words, "2002 NBA All-Star Jam Session Presented by Fleer-Spokesman" along the bottom

1 Eric Snow .60 1.50

2004 Fleer Authentic Player Autographs

ISSUED FOR UNFUFILLED EXCH
CARDS FROM 2002-2004
BG1 Ben Gordon JSY/100 15.00 40.00
BG2 Ben Gordon/100 12.50 30.00
BG3 Ben Gordon/75 15.00 40.00
BG4 Ben Gordon/50 20.00 50.00
BW Ben Wallace/100 10.00 25.00
DW David West/59 6.00 15.00
DW1 Dwyane Wade JSY/100 30.00 60.00
DW2 Dwyane Wade JSY/25 50.00 100.00
JK Jason Kidd/300 15.00 40.00
JS1 Jerry Stackhouse/126 5.00 12.00
JS2 Jerry Stackhouse/100 6.00 15.00
JS3 Jerry Stackhouse/50 10.00 25.00
MB Marcus Banks/75 10.00 25.00
ST1 Sebastian Telfair/250 6.00 15.00
ST2 Sebastian Telfair/75 8.00 20.00
ST3 Sebastian Telfair/50 10.00 25.00
VC1 Vince Carter/300 15.00 40.00
VC2 Vince Carter/150 20.00 40.00

2005 Fleer Authentic Player Autographs

BG1 Ben Gordon/300 6.00 15.00
BG2 Ben Gordon/150 8.00 20.00
BG3 Ben Gordon/100 10.00 25.00
BG4 Ben Gordon/75 12.50 30.00
DG1 Drew Gooden/300 5.00 12.00
DG2 Drew Gooden/150 6.00 15.00
DW Dwyane Wade/50 25.00 60.00
JK Jason Kidd/225 12.50 30.00
TP Tayshaun Prince/50 8.00 20.00
TP1 Tayshaun Prince/300 5.00 12.00
BGJ1 Ben Gordon JSY/100 8.00 20.00
TPJ Tayshaun Prince JSY/25 10.00 25.00

2001-02 Fleer Authentix

Released in mid December 2001, this 135-card base set contains standard size cards. The cards have a white borders and a ticket style themed background. Player action photos are set where poses are facing the camera either in a jump shot pose or an "attacking the rim" pose. Authentix set contains 100 veteran players and 35 rookie players. The rookie cards feature an embedded team replica ticket numbered to 1,250. Authentix was packaged in 24 pack boxes where packs contained five cards.

COMP.SET w/o SP'S 12.50 30.00
101-135 PRINT RUN 1250 SER.#'d SETS
1 Vince Carter .50 1.25
2 Terrell Brandon .20 .50
3 Raef LaFrentz .20 .50
4 Iakovos Tsakalidis .20 .50
5 Elton Brand .30 .75
6 David Robinson .50 1.25
7 Lamar Odom .25 .60
8 Larry Hughes .25 .60
9 Gary Payton .30 .75
10 Rick Fox .20 .50
11 Jamal Mashburn .25 .60
12 Brian Grant .20 .50
13 David Wesley .20 .50
14 Steve Smith .25 .60
15 Corey Maggette .25 .60
16 Michael Jordan 3.00 8.00
17 Wally Szczerbiak .25 .60
18 Antoine Walker .25 .60
19 Marcus Camby .25 .60
20 Rasheed Wallace .30 .75
21 Travis Best .20 .50
22 Theo Ratliff .20 .50
23 LaPhonso Ellis .25 .60
24 Dirk Nowitzki .50 1.25
25 Kurt Thomas .20 .50
26 Steve Francis .25 .60
27 Tim Duncan .60 1.50
28 Eddie House .20 .50
29 Ron Mercer .20 .50
30 Allan Houston .25 .60
31 Trajan Langdon .20 .50
32 Karl Malone .40 1.00
33 Glenn Robinson .25 .60
34 Wang Zhizhi .25 .60
35 Jason Kidd .50 1.25
36 Maurice Taylor .20 .50
37 Chris Webber .30 .75
38 Michael Dickerson .20 .50
39 Paul Pierce .30 .75
40 Bonzi Wells .20 .50
41 Antawn Jamison .30 .75
42 Rashard Lewis .30 .75
43 Reggie Miller .30 .75
44 Patrick Ewing .40 1.00
45 Marcus Fizer .20 .50
46 Aaron McKie .20 .50
47 Marc Jackson .20 .50
48 Desmond Mason .25 .60
49 Jermaine O'Neal .25 .60
50 DeShawn Stevenson .20 .50
51 John Stockton .40 1.00
52 Tim Thomas .20 .50
53 Andre Miller .25 .60
54 Jumaine Jones .20 .50
55 Nick Van Exel .25 .60
56 Damon Stoudamire .25 .60
57 Stephon Marbury .25 .60
58 Clifford Robinson .20 .50
59 Hedo Turkoglu .25 .60
60 Kobe Bryant 1.25 3.00
61 Richard Hamilton .25 .60
62 Stromile Swift .20 .50
63 Chris Mihm .20 .50
64 Tracy McGrady .50 1.25
65 Jalen Rose .25 .60
66 Morris Peterson .20 .50
67 Alonzo Mourning .40 1.00
68 Courtney Alexander .20 .50
69 Michael Finley .30 .75
70 Shawn Marion .25 .60
71 Darius Miles .20 .50
72 Antonio Davis .20 .50
73 Ray Allen .30 .75
74 Shareef Abdur-Rahim .25 .60
75 Kevin Garnett .50 1.25
76 Latrell Sprewell .25 .60
77 Antonio McDyess .25 .60
78 Derek Anderson .20 .50
79 Derek Fisher .25 .60
80 Jason Terry .30 .75
81 Eddie Jones .25 .60
82 Hakeem Olajuwon .40 1.00
83 Toni Kukoc .30 .75
84 Sam Cassell .25 .60
85 Jamal Crawford .30 .75
86 Allen Iverson .60 1.50
87 Steve Nash .50 1.25
88 Dikembe Mutombo .30 .75
89 Shaquille O'Neal .75 2.00
90 Jerome Moiso .20 .50
91 Kenyon Martin .30 .75
92 Chucky Atkins .20 .50
93 Grant Hill .40 1.00
94 Jerry Stackhouse .25 .60
95 Jason Williams .25 .60
96 Baron Davis .30 .75
97 Mike Miller .25 .60
98 Joe Smith .25 .60
99 Peja Stojakovic .30 .75
100 Cuttino Mobley .20 .50
101 Kwame Brown RC 1.25 3.00
102 Jason Collins RC 1.00 2.50
103 Willie Solomon RC 1.25 3.00
104 Brendan Haywood RC 1.25 3.00
105 Jeff Trepagnier RC .75 2.00
106 Eddie Griffin RC 1.00 2.50
107 Joseph Forte RC .75 2.00
108 Rodney White RC .75 2.00
109 Jeryl Sasser RC .75 2.00
110 Samuel Dalembert RC 1.25 3.00
111 Shane Battier RC 2.50 6.00
112 Tony Parker RC 5.00 12.00
113 DeSagana Diop RC 1.00 2.50
114 Steven Hunter RC 1.00 2.50
115 Trenton Hassell RC 1.00 2.50
116 Michael Bradley RC .75 2.00
117 Brian Scalabrine RC 1.25 3.00
118 Troy Murphy RC 1.25 3.00
119 Brandon Armstrong RC .75 2.00
120 Pau Gasol RC 4.00 10.00
121 Gerald Wallace RC 1.50 4.00
122 Jason Richardson RC 1.50 4.00
123 Joe Johnson RC 1.50 4.00
124 Loren Woods RC .75 2.00
125 Vladimir Radmanovic RC 1.25 3.00
126 Jamaal Tinsley RC 1.25 3.00
127 Omar Cook RC 1.25 3.00
128 Kedrick Brown RC .75 2.00
129 Terence Morris RC 1.25 3.00
130 Richard Jefferson RC 2.00 5.00
131 Gilbert Arenas RC 2.00 5.00
132 Tyson Chandler RC 2.00 5.00
133 Kirk Haston RC .75 2.00
134 Eddy Curry RC 1.25 3.00
135 Zach Randolph RC 2.00 5.00

2001-02 Fleer Authentix Front Row Parallel

*STARS: 4X TO 10X BASE CARD HI
*RCs: 1.5X TO 4X BASE CARD HI
STATED PRINT RUN 100 SERIAL #'d SETS

2001-02 Fleer Authentix Second Row Parallel

*STARS: 2.5X TO 6X BASE CARD HI
*RCs: 1X TO 2.5X BASE CARD HI
STATED PRINT RUN 200 SERIAL #'d SETS

2001-02 Fleer Authentix Autograph Authentix

Randomly inserted in packs at a rate of one in 639, this insert set was horizontally designed with full colo player action photos. The player's team number is found in the upper left-hand corner, and basketball design is found in the lower left-hand corner. The center of the card features a ticket stub design with the player's autograph written across it. The right-hand side of the card has a perforated edge indicating it is the "ripped version".

STATED ODDS 1:639
1 Kwame Brown 10.00 25.00
2 Eddy Curry 12.00 30.00
3 Vince Carter 15.00 40.00

2001-02 Fleer Authentix Autograph Authentix UnRipped

STATED PRINT RUN 25 SER. #'d SETS
1 Kwame Brown 15.00 40.00
2 Eddy Curry 25.00 60.00
3 Vince Carter 30.00 80.00

2001-02 Fleer Authentix Autographed Jersey Authentix

This one of one set features Vince Carter along with a swatch of his jersey and a his autograph. Originally issued as a redemption card, this is also the ripped verson with a perforated right edge.

STATED ODDS 1:4971
UNRIPPED SER.#'d TO 1 EXISTS
1 Vince Carter 40.00 100.00

2001-02 Fleer Authentix Courtside Classics

Inserted one in every 22 packs, this 15-card set features some of the great players of the NBA. The standard size cards are horizontally designed with a black & white player photo in the foreground and fans sitting courtside in the background.

COMPLETE SET (15) 25.00 50.00
STATED ODDS 1:22
1 Steve Francis .75 2.00
2 Mike Miller .75 2.00
3 Kenyon Martin 1.00 2.50
4 Vince Carter 1.50 4.00
5 Alonzo Mourning 1.25 3.00
6 Anfernee Hardaway 1.50 4.00
7 Dikembe Mutombo 1.00 2.50
8 Chris Webber 1.00 2.50
9 Glenn Robinson .75 2.00
10 Jerry Stackhouse .75 2.00
11 Kobe Bryant 4.00 10.00
12 Kevin Garnett 1.50 4.00
13 Tim Duncan 2.00 5.00
14 Shaquille O'Neal 2.50 6.00
15 Michael Jordan 8.00 20.00

2001-02 Fleer Authentix Courtside Classics Memorabilia

STATED ODDS 1:74
*MULT PAR: 1X TO 2.5X BASE HI
MULT PAR PRINT RUN 150 SER.#'d SETS
AH Anfernee Hardaway 8.00 20.00
AM Alonzo Mourning 8.00 20.00
CW Chris Webber 5.00 12.00
DM Dikembe Mutombo 5.00 12.00
GR Glenn Robinson 4.00 10.00
JS Jerry Stackhouse 4.00 10.00
KM Kenyon Martin 5.00 12.00
MM Mike Miller 4.00 10.00
SF Steve Francis 4.00 10.00
VC Vince Carter 8.00 20.00

2001-02 Fleer Authentix Jersey Authentix Ripped

Inserted one in every 33 packs, this 15-card set features a replica team ticket and a piece of a game used jersey. The "ripped" version has a perforated right-hand side. An Unripped verions numbered to 50 was also issued.

STATED ODDS 1:33
*UNRIPPED: 1.5X TO 3X RIPPED JSY
UNRIPPED PRINT RUN 50 SER.#'d SETS
1 Allen Iverson 8.00 20.00
2 Darius Miles 2.50 6.00
3 Tracy McGrady 6.00 15.00
4 Glenn Robinson 3.00 8.00
5 Rashard Lewis 4.00 10.00
6 Elton Brand 4.00 10.00
7 Andre Miller 3.00 8.00
8 Jason Terry 4.00 10.00
9 Vince Carter 6.00 15.00
10 Karl Malone 5.00 12.00
11 David Robinson 6.00 15.00
12 Lamar Odom 3.00 8.00
13 Antoine Walker 3.00 8.00
14 Shareef Abdur-Rahim 3.00 8.00
15 Jamal Mashburn 3.00 8.00

2001-02 Fleer Authentix Sweet Selections

Inserted one in every eleven packs, this 15-card set features 15 rookies where the words "Sweet Selections" appear vertically along the left hand side of the card. The background is white, and full color player photos are set against a gray scale portrait photo of the featured player.

COMPLETE SET (15) 12.50 30.00
STATED ODDS 1:11
1 Kwame Brown .75 2.00
2 Tyson Chandler 1.25 3.00
3 Pau Gasol 2.50 6.00
4 Eddy Curry .75 2.00
5 Jason Richardson 1.00 2.50
6 Shane Battier 1.50 4.00
7 Eddie Griffin .60 1.50
8 DeSagana Diop .60 1.50
9 Rodney White .50 1.25
10 Joe Johnson 1.00 2.50
11 Kedrick Brown .50 1.25
12 Vladimir Radmanovic .75 2.00
13 Richard Jefferson 1.25 3.00
14 Troy Murphy .75 2.00
15 Steven Hunter .60 1.50

2002-03 Fleer Authentix

Issued in late October 2002, Fleer Authentix boasts a 135-card base set divided up into 100 veteran cards and 35 Rookie Authentix cards sequentially numbered to 1250. Base cards feature a full-color player action photo and an embedded mini-ticket. Authentix was released in five card packs that carried a suggested retail price of $3.99 with 24 packs per box.

COMPLETE SET (135) 25.00 60.00
COMP.SET w/o SP's (100) 6.00 15.00
101-135 PRINT RUN 1250 SER.#'d SETS
1 Vince Carter .50 1.25
2 Bobby Jackson .20 .50
3 Cuttino Mobley .20 .50
4 John Stockton .40 1.00
5 Jamal Mashburn .25 .60
6 Ben Wallace .25 .60
7 Tim Duncan .60 1.50
8 Richard Jefferson .30 .75
9 Clifford Robinson .20 .50
10 Gary Payton .30 .75
11 Terrell Brandon .20 .50
12 Michael Finley .30 .75
13 Rasheed Wallace .30 .75
14 Jason Williams .25 .60
15 Andre Miller .25 .60
16 Shawn Marion .25 .60
17 Kobe Bryant 1.25 3.00
18 Jason Terry .25 .60
19 Latrell Sprewell .25 .60
20 Jerry Stackhouse .25 .60
21 Tony Parker .40 1.00
22 Ray Allen .30 .75
23 Dirk Nowitzki .50 1.25
24 Chris Webber .30 .75
25 Rick Fox .20 .50
26 Jermaine O'Neal .25 .60
27 Karl Malone .40 1.00
28 Allan Houston .25 .60
29 Jason Richardson .30 .75
30 Morris Peterson .20 .50
31 Kevin Garnett .50 1.25
32 Antawn Jamison .30 .75
33 Rashard Lewis .30 .75
34 Jason Kidd .50 1.25
35 Joe Smith .25 .60
36 David Robinson .50 1.25
37 Brian Grant .20 .50
38 Lamond Murray .20 .50
39 Damon Stoudamire .25 .60
40 Shane Battier .30 .75
41 Eddy Curry .20 .50
42 Dikembe Mutombo .30 .75
43 Jamaal Tinsley .20 .50
44 Courtney Alexander .20 .50
45 Wally Szczerbiak .25 .60
46 Antonio McDyess .25 .60
47 Mike Bibby .30 .75
48 Alonzo Mourning .40 1.00
49 Tyson Chandler .30 .75
50 Stephon Marbury .25 .60
51 Sam Cassell .25 .60
52 Steve Nash .40 1.00
53 Bonzi Wells .20 .50
54 Pau Gasol .40 1.00
55 Rodney Rogers .20 .50
56 Allen Iverson .50 1.25
57 Derek Fisher .25 .60
58 Travis Best .20 .50
59 Aaron McKie .20 .50
60 Darius Miles .20 .50
61 Richard Hamilton .25 .60
62 Marcus Camby .25 .60
63 Eddie Griffin .20 .50
64 Antonio Davis .20 .50
65 David Wesley .20 .50
66 Stromile Swift .20 .50
67 Brent Barry .20 .50
68 Glenn Robinson .25 .60
69 Antoine Walker .25 .60
70 Tracy McGrady .50 1.25
71 Steve Smith .25 .60
72 Michael Jordan 2.50 6.00
73 Mike Miller .25 .60
74 DeShawn Stevenson .20 .50
75 Raef LaFrentz .20 .50
76 Al Harrington .25 .60
77 Vlade Divac .25 .60
78 Eddie Jones .25 .60
79 Wesley Person .20 .50
80 Kenny Anderson .25 .60
81 Elton Brand .30 .75
82 Jalen Rose .25 .60
83 Joe Johnson .25 .60
84 Shaquille O'Neal .75 2.00
85 Paul Pierce .30 .75
86 Grant Hill .40 1.00
87 Steve Francis .25 .60
88 Keon Clark .20 .50
89 Baron Davis .25 .60
90 Tim Thomas .20 .50
91 Shareef Abdur-Rahim .25 .60
92 Kenyon Martin .25 .60
93 Juwan Howard .25 .60
94 Peja Stojakovic .30 .75
95 Lamar Odom .25 .60
96 Toni Kukoc .30 .75
97 Darrell Armstrong .20 .50
98 Reggie Miller .30 .75
99 Andrei Kirilenko .30 .75
100 Keith Van Horn .25 .60
101 Yao Ming RC 4.00 10.00
102 Jay Williams RC 2.00 5.00
103 Mike Dunleavy RC 2.00 5.00
104 Drew Gooden RC 2.00 5.00
105 Nikoloz Tskitishvili RC 1.25 3.00
106 Caron Butler RC 2.00 5.00
107 Chris Wilcox RC 1.50 4.00
108 DaJuan Wagner RC 1.50 4.00
109 Nene Hilario RC 2.00 5.00
110 Qyntel Woods RC 1.50 4.00
111 Jared Jeffries RC 1.50 4.00
112 Tamar Slay RC 1.25 3.00
113 Marcus Haislip RC 1.50 4.00
114 Kareem Rush RC 1.50 4.00
115 Bostjan Nachbar RC 1.50 4.00

116 Melvin Ely RC 1.50 4.00
117 Jiri Welsch RC 1.50 4.00
118 Amare Stoudemire RC 2.50 6.00
119 Frank Williams RC 1.25 3.00
120 Rasual Butler RC 2.00 5.00
121 Dan Dickau RC 1.50 4.00
122 Carlos Boozer RC 2.00 5.00
123 Roger Mason RC 1.50 4.00
124 Corsley Edwards RC 1.50 4.00
125 Robert Archibald RC 1.25 3.00
126 John Salmons RC 2.00 5.00
127 Rod Grizzard RC 1.25 3.00
128 Dan Gadzuric RC 1.50 4.00
129 Sam Clancy RC 1.50 4.00
130 Fred Jones RC 1.50 4.00
131 Casey Jacobsen RC 1.50 4.00
132 Ryan Humphrey RC 1.50 4.00
133 Vincent Yarbrough RC 1.25 3.00
134 Juan Dixon RC 2.00 5.00
135 Tayshaun Prince RC 2.50 6.00

2002-03 Fleer Authentix Balcony

*BALCONY STARS: 2.5X TO 6X BASE CARD HI
*BALCONY RCs: .5X TO 1.25X BASE CARD HI
PRINT RUN 250 SER.#'d SETS

2002-03 Fleer Authentix Club

*CLUB STARS: 4X TO 10X BASE CARD HI
*CLUB RCs: 1X TO 2.5X BASE CARD HI
PRINT RUN 100 SER.#'d SETS

2002-03 Fleer Authentix Standing Room Only

*SRO STARS: 15X TO 40X BASE HI
*SRO RCs: 3X TO 8X BASE HI
PRINT RUN 25 SER.#'d SETS

2002-03 Fleer Authentix Autographed Authentix

Randomly inserted in packs at the rate of one in 586, this four card set looks very similar to the base cards and contains an authentic player autograph.
STATED ODDS 1:586
1 Vince Carter 15.00 40.00

2002-03 Fleer Authentix Courtside Classics Silver

Randomly inserted in packs, this 15-card set features an oval die cut design with four corners protruding out of the oval as if it was overlayed with a rectangle. Full color player action photos appear on top of a wood grain and gray scale photo background.
COMPLETE SET (15) 25.00 60.00
PRINT RUN 750 SERIAL #'D SETS
*GOLD: .4X TO 1X BASE HI
GOLD RANDOM INSERTS IN RETAIL PACKS
1 Vince Carter 2.00 5.00
2 Tim Duncan 2.50 6.00
3 Ray Allen 1.25 3.00
4 Tony Parker 1.50 4.00
5 Michael Jordan 10.00 25.00
6 Chris Webber 1.25 3.00
7 Shaquille O'Neal 3.00 8.00
8 Kobe Bryant 5.00 12.00
9 Jason Kidd 2.00 5.00
10 Dirk Nowitzki 2.00 5.00
11 Shane Battier 1.25 3.00
12 Kevin Garnett 2.00 5.00
13 Jason Richardson 1.25 3.00
14 Karl Malone 1.50 4.00
15 Pau Gasol 1.50 4.00

2002-03 Fleer Authentix Draft Day Ticket

Randomly inserted in packs, this 10-card set features a horizontal design with player photos on the top and an embedded ticket from the 2002 NBA draft. Yao Ming is the only one in the set sequentially numbered to 100.
RANDOM INSERTS IN PACKS
1 Yao Ming/100 15.00 40.00
2 Drew Gooden 4.00 10.00
3 Amare Stoudemire 5.00 12.00
4 Caron Butler 4.00 10.00
5 Chris Wilcox 3.00 8.00
6 DaJuan Wagner 3.00 8.00
7 Dan Dickau 3.00 8.00
8 Qyntel Woods 3.00 8.00

2002-03 Fleer Authentix Hometown Heroes Silver

Randomly inserted in packs, this 20-card set showcases a horizontal design with full color player action photos set against the back-drop of their team's home city. Each card is sequentially numbered to 500.
COMPLETE SET (20) 25.00 60.00
PRINT RUN 500 SERIAL #'D SETS
*GOLD: .25X TO .6X BASE HI
GOLD RANDOM INSERTS IN RETAIL PACKS
1 Vince Carter 2.50 6.00
2 Tim Duncan 3.00 8.00
3 Kobe Bryant 6.00 15.00
4 Chris Wilcox 1.25 3.00
5 Jay Williams 1.50 4.00
6 Dirk Nowitzki 2.50 6.00
7 Jared Jeffries 1.25 3.00
8 Kevin Garnett 2.50 6.00
9 Drew Gooden 1.50 4.00
10 Shane Battier 1.50 4.00
11 Juan Dixon 1.50 4.00
12 Allen Iverson 2.50 6.00
13 Jason Richardson 1.50 4.00
14 Mike Dunleavy 1.50 4.00
15 Tracy McGrady 2.50 6.00
16 Michael Jordan 12.00 30.00
17 Shaquille O'Neal 4.00 10.00
18 Paul Pierce 1.50 4.00
19 Steve Francis 1.25 3.00
20 Baron Davis 1.25 3.00

2002-03 Fleer Authentix Jersey Authentix

Randomly seeded in packs at the rate of one in 17, this 30-card set features a full color player photo at the top right and a jersey swatch at the top left. The bottom of the card has an embedded ticket below which the edge is jagged as if a stub has been torn off. All cards have red foil highlights. An Unripped version was also issued and is sequentially numbered to 50.
STATED ODDS 1:17
*UNRIPPED: .75X TO 2X BASE HI
UNRIPPED PRINT RUN 50 SER.#'d SETS
1 Shareef Abdur-Rahim 2.50 6.00
2 Antoine Walker 2.50 6.00
3 Paul Pierce 3.00 8.00
4 Eddy Curry SP 2.00 5.00
5 Glenn Robinson 2.50 6.00
6 Vince Carter SP 5.00 12.00
7 Steve Francis 2.50 6.00
8 Reggie Miller 3.00 8.00
9 Darius Miles 2.00 5.00
10 Elton Brand 3.00 8.00
11 Lamar Odom 2.50 6.00
12 Stromile Swift 2.00 5.00
13 Ray Allen SP 3.00 8.00
14 Jason Kidd 5.00 12.00
15 Richard Jefferson 3.00 8.00
16 Kenyon Martin 2.50 6.00
17 Keith Van Horn 2.50 6.00
18 Baron Davis 2.50 6.00
19 Mike Miller 2.50 6.00
20 Grant Hill 5.00 12.00
21 Tracy McGrady 5.00 12.00
22 Allen Iverson 5.00 12.00
23 Dikembe Mutombo 3.00 8.00
24 Shawn Marion 2.50 6.00
25 Stephon Marbury 2.50 6.00
26 Chris Webber 3.00 8.00
27 Gary Payton 3.00 8.00
28 John Stockton 4.00 10.00
29 Karl Malone 4.00 10.00
30 Richard Hamilton 2.50 6.00

2002-03 Fleer Authentix Jersey Authentix All Star Tickets

DM Dikembe Mutombo 6.00 15.00

2002-03 Fleer Authentix Jersey Authentix Game of the Week

Randomly inserted in packs at the rate of one in 53, this 15-card set utilizes the set design from the base Jersey Authentix insert with two swatches of jersey along the top. The two featured players appear behind the jersey swatch. Card bottoms are jagged as if a ticket stub had been torn off.
STATED ODDS 1:53
1 J.Kidd/A.Iverson 6.00 15.00
2 S.Marbury/J.Stockton 5.00 12.00
3 S.Abdur-Rahim/D.Miles 3.00 8.00
4 B.Davis/R.Miller 4.00 10.00
5 R.Hamilton/R.Jefferson 4.00 10.00
6 K.Malone/E.Brand 5.00 12.00
7 V.Carter/P.Pierce 6.00 15.00
8 R.Allen/S.Francis 4.00 10.00
9 K.Martin/L.Odom 3.00 8.00
10 A.Walker/C.Webber 4.00 10.00
11 E.Curry/G.Robinson 3.00 8.00
12 G.Hill/G.Payton 5.00 12.00
13 T.McGrady/S.Marion 6.00 15.00
14 M.Miller/K.Van Horn 3.00 8.00
15 S.Swift/D.Mutombo 3.00 8.00

2002-03 Fleer Authentix Ticket for Four

Randomly inserted in packs, this 10-card set features a dual-sided design with two players and their jerseys on each side. Cards have white borders with a line right down the middle of each side and two separate colors-one for each of the players. Sequential numbering to 200 appears on the card back right in the middle.
PRINT RUN 200 SERIAL #'D SETS
1 Carter/Davis/Francis/Iverson 15.00 40.00
2 Carter/Jeffrsn/T-Mac/Miles 12.00 30.00
3 Carter/Garnett/Malone/Dirk 12.00 30.00
4 Cartr/Chndlr/Pierce/C-Webb 15.00 40.00
5 Battier/Marion/Bibby/Carter 12.00 30.00
6 Carter/Kidd/Tinsley/Walker 12.00 30.00
7 Allen/Carter/Marbury/Mobley 20.00 50.00
8 Carter/Miller/Richrdsn/Swift 12.00 30.00
9 Brand/Carter/Martin/MoPete 12.00 30.00
10 Rahim/Cartr/Stock/Vn Horn 12.00 30.00

2002-03 Fleer Authentix Tip-Off Ticket

Randomly seeded, this five card set parallels the design of the base Draft Day Tickets where each card is sequentially numbered to 15.
PRINT RUN 15 SER.#'d SETS
1 Yao Ming 25.00 60.00
2 Amare Stoudemire 15.00 40.00
3 Caron Butler 12.00 30.00
4 Chris Wilcox 10.00 25.00
5 Qyntel Woods 10.00 25.00

2003-04 Fleer Authentix

Issued in October 2003, Authentix boasts a 130-card set divided up into 100 veteran players and 30 rookies sequentially numbered to 1250. Authentix base cards place players in action on a background set to look like a ticket. Authentix was packaged in 24-pack boxes where packs contained five cards and carried a suggested retail price of $3.99.
COMP.SET w/o SP's (1-100) 15.00 40.00
1 Vince Carter .50 1.25
2 David Wesley .20 .50
3 Eddie Griffin .20 .50
4 Andrei Kirilenko .30 .75
5 Kerry Kittles .20 .50
6 Tayshaun Prince .25 .60
7 Tim Duncan .50 1.25
8 Troy Hudson .20 .50
9 Ben Wallace .25 .60
10 Manu Ginobili .40 1.00
11 Gary Payton .30 .75
12 Dajuan Wagner .20 .50
13 Stephon Marbury .25 .60
14 Shane Battier .25 .60
15 Zydrunas Ilgauskas .25 .60
16 Eric Snow .20 .50
17 Andre Miller .25 .60
18 Shareef Abdur-Rahim .25 .60
19 Kurt Thomas .20 .50
20 Vincent Yarbrough .20 .50
21 Mike Bibby .30 .75
22 Desmond Mason .25 .60
23 Steve Nash .40 1.00
24 Rasheed Wallace .30 .75
25 Kobe Bryant 1.25 3.00
26 Cuttino Mobley .20 .50
27 Matt Harpring .20 .50
28 Jamal Mashburn .25 .60
29 Mike Dunleavy .25 .60
30 Antonio Davis .20 .50
31 Michael Redd .30 .75
32 Richard Hamilton .25 .60
33 Predrag Drobnjak .20 .50
34 Kevin Garnett .50 1.25
35 Nene .25 .60
36 Bobby Jackson .20 .50
37 Jason Williams .25 .60
38 Ricky Davis .25 .60
39 Shawn Marion .25 .60
40 Kareem Rush .20 .50
41 Eddy Curry .20 .50
42 Gordan Giricek .20 .50
43 Brad Miller .25 .60
44 Kwame Brown .20 .50
45 Sam Cassell .25 .60
46 Juwan Howard .25 .60
47 Peja Stojakovic .30 .75
48 Brian Grant .20 .50
49 Al Harrington .25 .60
50 Allen Iverson .50 1.25
51 Caron Butler .25 .60
52 Dirk Nowitzki .50 1.25
53 Zach Randolph .25 .60
54 Pau Gasol .30 .75
55 Tony Delk .20 .50
56 Grant Hill .40 1.00
57 Shaquille O'Neal .75 2.00
58 Tyson Chandler .25 .60
59 Tracy McGrady .40 1.00
60 Ron Artest .30 .75
61 Jerry Stackhouse .25 .60
62 Jamaal Magloire .20 .50
63 Jason Richardson .30 .75
64 Morris Peterson .20 .50
65 Richard Jefferson .25 .60
66 Kenny Thomas .20 .50
67 Tony Parker .30 .75
68 Eddie Jones .25 .60
69 Paul Pierce .30 .75
70 Drew Gooden .25 .60
71 Jermaine O'Neal .25 .60
72 Juan Dixon .20 .50
73 Baron Davis .25 .60
74 Antawn Jamison .25 .60
75 Rashard Lewis .30 .75
76 Nick Van Exel .25 .60
77 Bonzi Wells .20 .50
78 Speedy Claxton .20 .50
79 Carlos Boozer .25 .60
80 Amare Stoudemire .40 1.00
81 Elton Brand .30 .75
82 Jalen Rose .25 .60
83 Keith Van Horn .25 .60
84 Corey Maggette .25 .60
85 Antoine Walker .30 .75
86 Latrell Sprewell .25 .60
87 Yao Ming .60 1.50
88 Glenn Robinson .25 .60
89 Jason Kidd .50 1.25
90 Gilbert Arenas .25 .60
91 Ray Allen .30 .75
92 Wally Szczerbiak .25 .60
93 Michael Finley .30 .75
94 Chris Webber .30 .75
95 Reggie Miller .30 .75
96 Jason Terry .25 .60
97 Allan Houston .25 .60
98 Steve Francis .25 .60
99 Karl Malone .40 1.00
100 Kenyon Martin .25 .60
101 Carmelo Anthony RC 5.00 12.00
102 Troy Bell RC 1.00 2.50
103 T.J. Ford RC 1.25 3.00
104 LeBron James RC 40.00 100.00
105 Travis Outlaw RC 1.25 3.00
106 Mike Sweetney RC 1.00 2.50
107 Aleksandar Pavlovic RC 1.25 3.00
108 Dahntay Jones RC 1.25 3.00
109 Chris Bosh RC 2.50 6.00
110 Boris Diaw RC 1.50 4.00
111 Jarvis Hayes RC 1.00 2.50
112 Brian Cook RC 1.00 2.50
113 Luke Ridnour RC 1.25 3.00
114 David West RC 1.50 4.00
115 Zoran Planinic RC 1.00 2.50
116 Zarko Cabarkapa RC 1.00 2.50
117 Marcus Banks RC 1.00 2.50
118 Kirk Hinrich RC 1.50 4.00
119 Darko Milicic RC 1.25 3.00
120 Sofoklis Schortsanitis RC 1.00 2.50
121 Ndudi Ebi RC 1.00 2.50
122 Kendrick Perkins RC 1.25 3.00
123 Leandro Barbosa RC 1.50 4.00
124 Nick Collison RC 1.25 3.00
125 Reece Gaines RC 1.00 2.50
126 Chris Kaman RC 1.50 4.00
127 Mickael Pietrus RC 1.25 3.00
128 Dwyane Wade RC 5.00 12.00
129 Josh Howard RC 1.50 4.00
130 Carlos Delfino RC 1.25 3.00

2003-04 Fleer Authentix Balcony

*1-100 STARS: 2.5X TO 6X BASE HI
*101-130 RC's: .75X TO 2X BASE HI
PRINT RUN 250 SER.#'d SETS
104 LeBron James 50.00 120.00

2003-04 Fleer Authentix Club Box

*1-100 STARS: 4X TO 10X BASE HI
*101-130 RC's: 1.25X TO 3X BASE HI
PRINT RUN 100 SER.#'d SETS
25 Kobe Bryant 20.00 50.00

2003-04 Fleer Authentix Rookie Tickets

*TICKETS: .4X TO 1X BASE HI
ANNOUNCED PRINT RUN 250 SETS
104 LeBron James 25.00 60.00

2003-04 Fleer Authentix Standing Room Only

*1-100 STARS: 8X TO 20X BASE HI
*101-130 RCs: 3X TO 8X BASE HI
PRINT RUN 25 SER.#'d SETS

2003-04 Fleer Authentix Autographs

Randomly inserted, this 12-card set incorporates a horizontal design with a color player photo on the top and a cut signature on the bottom. The background is similar to that of the base cards, set to look like a ticket. Print runs are listed below.
PRINT RUNS LISTED BELOW
AAAS Amare Stoudemire/225 12.50 30.00
AABW Ben Wallace/225 10.00 25.00
AACA Carmelo Anthony/225 25.00 60.00
AACB Chris Bosh/325 8.00 20.00
AADW Dwyane Wade/325 25.00 60.00
AAJH Josh Howard/225 5.00 12.00
AAKM Kenyon Martin/225 5.00 12.00
AAMS Mike Sweetney/325 5.00 12.00
AATB Troy Bell/225 5.00 12.00
AATP2 Tayshaun Prince/225 5.00 12.00

2003-04 Fleer Authentix Autographs All-Star

PRINT RUN 150 SER.#'d SETS
*PLAYOFF: .5X TO 1.25X ALL STAR HI
PLAYOFF PRINT RUN 50 SER.#'d SETS
AAAM Alonzo Mourning 12.00 30.00
AAAS Amare Stoudemire 15.00 40.00
AABW Ben Wallace 12.00 30.00
AACA Carmelo Anthony 20.00 50.00
AACB Chris Bosh 10.00 25.00
AADW Dwyane Wade 25.00 60.00
AAJH Josh Howard 6.00 15.00
AAKM Kenyon Martin 6.00 15.00
AAMG Manu Ginobili 10.00 25.00
AAMS Mike Sweetney 6.00 15.00
AATB Troy Bell 6.00 15.00
AATP Tony Parker 8.00 20.00
AATP2 Tayshaun Prince 6.00 15.00

2003-04 Fleer Authentix Courtside Classics

Seeded in packs at the rate of one in 12, this 10-card set features a die-cut design with a frame around the edges. Full color player action photos are set against a colored background.
COMPLETE SET (10) 8.00 20.00
STATED ODDS 1:12
1 Kevin Garnett 1.25 3.00
2 Vince Carter 1.25 3.00
3 Allen Iverson 1.25 3.00
4 Yao Ming 1.50 4.00
5 Tracy McGrady 1.00 2.50
6 Amare Stoudemire 1.00 2.50
7 Jason Richardson .75 2.00
8 Dirk Nowitzki 1.25 3.00
9 Jason Kidd 1.25 3.00
10 Tony Parker .75 2.00

2003-04 Fleer Authentix Courtside Classics Game-Used

STATED ODDS 1:37
1 Kevin Garnett 4.00 10.00
2 Vince Carter 4.00 10.00
3 Allen Iverson 4.00 10.00
4 Yao Ming 5.00 12.00
5 Tracy McGrady 3.00 8.00
6 Amare Stoudemire 3.00 8.00
7 Jason Richardson 2.50 6.00
8 Dirk Nowitzki 4.00 10.00
9 Jason Kidd 4.00 10.00
10 Tony Parker 2.50 6.00

2003-04 Fleer Authentix Draft Day Ticket

This 10-card set is sequentially numbered to 400 and randomly seeded in packs. Each card features player photo and a swatch of a ticket from the 2003 NBA draft. A Gold version sequentially numbered to 10 was also issued.
PRINT RUN 400 SER.#'d SETS
1 Carmelo Anthony 8.00 20.00
2 Mike Sweetney 1.50 4.00
3 Chris Bosh 4.00 10.00
4 Dwyane Wade 8.00 20.00
5 Chris Kaman 2.50 6.00
6 Kirk Hinrich 2.50 6.00
7 T.J. Ford 2.00 5.00
8 Darko Milicic 2.00 5.00
9 Jarvis Hayes 1.50 4.00
10 Nick Collison 2.00 5.00

2003-04 Fleer Authentix Jersey Authentix

Inserted at the rate of one in 37, this 25-card set places a ticket replica towards the bottom of the horizontal design and a swatch of game-worn jersey and player photo towards the top. An All-Star version sequentially numbered to 80, and All-Star Unripped one of one and an Unripped version sequentially numbered to 50 were also produced.
STATED ODDS 1:37
*AS SINGLES: .75X TO 2X BASE JSY HI
ALL STAR PRINT RUN 80 SER.#'d SETS
*RIPPED: 1X TO 2.5X BASE JSY HI
RIPPED PRINT RUN 50 SER.#'d SETS
JAN Nene 2.50 6.00
JAAI Allen Iverson 4.00 10.00
JAAS Amare Stoudemire 3.00 8.00
JABW Bonzi Wells 2.00 5.00
JABW Ben Wallace 2.00 5.00
JACB Carlos Boozer 2.00 5.00
JADN Dirk Nowitzki 4.00 10.00
JADW DaJuan Wagner 2.00 5.00
JAEC Eddy Curry 1.50 4.00
JAJK Jason Kidd 4.00 10.00
JAJO Jermaine O'Neal 2.00 5.00
JAJR Jason Richardson 2.50 6.00
JAKG Kevin Garnett 4.00 10.00
JAKM Kenyon Martin 2.00 5.00
JAKM Karl Malone 3.00 8.00
JALS Latrell Sprewell 2.00 5.00
JAPG Pau Gasol 2.50 6.00
JAPP Paul Pierce 2.50 6.00
JARM Reggie Miller 2.50 6.00
JASF Steve Francis 2.00 5.00
JASN Steve Nash 3.00 8.00
JATM Tracy McGrady 3.00 8.00
JATP Tayshaun Prince 2.00 5.00
JAVC Vince Carter 4.00 10.00
JAYM Yao Ming 5.00 12.00

2003-04 Fleer Authentix Jersey Authentix Autographs

Randomly inserted in packs, this 11-card set parallels the design from the Jersey Authentix set and is enhanced by a cut signature embedded towards the bottom of the horizontal design where the base version has the ticket replica. An All-Star version sequentially numbered to 50 was also produced along with a Playoff version sequentially numbered to 25.
PRINT RUN 100 SER.#'d SETS
*AS AUTO: .5X TO 1.25X BASE HI
ALL STAR AU PRINT RUN 50 SER.#'d SETS
*PLAYOFF AUTO: .75X TO 2X BASE HI
PLAYOFF AU PRINT RUN 25 SER.#'d SETS
AJAAM Alonzo Mourning 25.00 60.00
AJAAS Amare Stoudemire 12.00 30.00
AJABW Ben Wallace 20.00 50.00
AJACA Carmelo Anthony 15.00 40.00
AJACB Chris Bosh 8.00 20.00
AJADW Dwyane Wade 25.00 60.00
AJAKM Kenyon Martin 8.00 20.00
AJAMS Mike Sweetney 8.00 20.00
AJATP2 Tayshaun Prince 8.00 20.00

2003-04 Fleer Authentix Jersey Authentix Game of the Week

Inserted at the rate of one in 20, this 10-card set pairs two players along with two jersey swatches, one from each player, and a mini replica ticket towards the bottom of the card. An Ripped version sequentially numbered to 50 was also issued in packs.
STATED ODDS 1:20
*RIPPED: 1X TO 2.5X BASE JSY HI
RIPPED PRINT RUN 50 SER.#'d SETS
1 T.McGrady/B.Wallace 6.00 15.00
2 Y.Ming/A.Stoudemire 8.00 20.00
3 K.Garnett/J.Kidd 8.00 20.00
4 K.Martin/V.Carter 8.00 20.00
5 D.Nowitzki/P.Gasol 6.00 15.00
6 S.Francis/A.Iverson 6.00 15.00
7 S.Nash/J.Richardson 5.00 12.00
8 Nene/K.Malone 5.00 12.00
9 T.Prince/P.Pierce 5.00 12.00
10 C.Boozer/E.Curry 5.00 12.00

2003-04 Fleer Authentix Ticket for Four

Inserted in packs randomly, this 10-card set places four players and four jerseys on each card; two on the front and two on the back. Cards are sequentially numbered to 100.
PRINT RUN 100 SERIAL #'d SETS
BGMM Booz/Manu/Marb/Miller 15.00 40.00
BHMB Biby/Hamltn/Marion/Brow 15.00 40.00
JGDR Jeffr/Gdn/Baron/GRob 15.00 40.00
KPCW Kidd/Parker/Vince/Web 20.00 50.00
MFIW T-Mac/Frncis/Al/Web 25.00 50.00
NGMN Nene/Gasol/Miller/Nash 15.00 40.00
OPMW J.O'Neal/Princ/Mlne/Wallce 15.00 40.00
PRGW Pierce/J-Rich/KG/Wells 25.00 50.00
SBCS Peja/Butler/Chand/Stack 15.00 40.00
WMSC Wagner/Yao/Spree/Curry 15.00 40.00

2003-04 Fleer Authentix Ticket Studs

Inserted at one in six, this 15-card set is designed as a ticket to a game. Each has a full-color player action photo along with a section number, row number and seat number.
COMPLETE SET (15) 15.00 40.00
STATED ODDS 1:6
1 LeBron James 8.00 20.00
2 Vince Carter 1.00 2.50
3 Mike Sweetney .40 1.00
4 Chris Webber .60 1.50
5 Chris Bosh 1.00 2.50
6 Kobe Bryant 2.50 6.00
7 Dwyane Wade 2.00 5.00
8 Shaquille O'Neal 1.50 4.00
9 T.J. Ford .50 1.25
10 Kenyon Martin .50 1.25
11 Paul Pierce .60 1.50
12 Carmelo Anthony 2.00 5.00
13 Tim Duncan 1.00 2.50
14 Pau Gasol .60 1.50
15 Steve Francis .50 1.25

2004-05 Fleer Authentix

Releassed in November 2004, Fleer Authentix is a 138-card set consisting of 99 veterans (cards 1-100, card 55 not released) and 39 rookies (card 101 not released). Two tiers of rookies were issued: cards 101-129 are sequentially numbered to 750 and cards 130-140 feature a rookie player along with a cut signature of a member of the organization that drafted him. Cards 130-140 are sequentially numbered to 200. All cards feature tan borders, a full-color player action photo along the top and a ticket-themed bottom containing the player's name, position and team. Authentix was issued for both Hobby and Retail, with boxes containing 24 packs of five cards each.
COMPLETE SET (137)
COMP.SET w/o SP's (100) 15.00 40.00
130-140 RC PRINT RUN 200 SER.#'d SETS
UNPRICED PARALLEL PRINT RUN 10 SETS
1 Allen Iverson .50 1.25
2 Allan Houston .25 .60
3 Jermaine O'Neal .25 .60
4 Andrei Kirilenko .25 .60
5 Baron Davis .25 .60
6 Rasheed Wallace .30 .75
7 Manu Ginobili .40 1.00
8 Kenyon Martin .25 .60
9 Richard Hamilton .25 .60
10 Tony Parker .30 .75
11 Keith Van Horn .25 .60
12 Steve Nash .40 1.00
13 Darius Miles .20 .50
14 Jason Williams .25 .60
15 Carlos Boozer .25 .60
16 Amare Stoudemire .25 .60
17 Kobe Bryant 1.25 3.00
18 Jason Terry .25 .60
19 Stephon Marbury .25 .60
20 Ben Wallace .25 .60
21 Tim Duncan .50 1.25
22 Michael Redd .25 .60
23 Antoine Walker .30 .75
24 Shareef Abdur-Rahim .25 .60
25 Luke Walton .20 .50
26 Reggie Miller .30 .75
27 Antawn Jamison .25 .60
28 Anfernee Hardaway .75 2.00
29 Yao Ming .60 1.50
30 Chris Bosh .30 .75
31 Latrell Sprewell .25 .60
32 Mike Dunleavy .25 .60
33 Luke Ridnour .25 .60
34 Kevin Garnett .50 1.25
35 Darko Milicic .20 .50
36 Bobby Jackson .20 .50
37 Caron Butler .25 .60
38 Dirk Nowitzki .50 1.25
39 Joe Johnson .25 .60
40 Pau Gasol .30 .75
41 Kirk Hinrich .25 .60
42 Willie.Green .20 .50
43 Jamaal Tinsley .20 .50
44 Jarvis Hayes .20 .50
45 Sam Cassell .25 .60
46 Nene .25 .60
47 Mike Bibby .30 .75
48 Lamar Odom .25 .60
49 LeBron James 2.00 5.00
50 Marquis Daniels .20 .50
51 T.J. Ford .20 .50
52 Michael Finley .30 .75
53 Zach Randolph .25 .60
54 Bonzi Wells .20 .50
56 Stephen Jackson .25 .60
57 Gary Payton .30 .75
58 Jason Kapono .20 .50
59 Glenn Robinson .25 .60
60 Elton Brand .30 .75
61 Jerry Stackhouse .25 .60
62 Jamaal Magloire .20 .50
63 Tracy McGrady .40 1.00
64 Jalen Rose .25 .60
65 Kerry Kittles .20 .50
66 Nick Van Exel .25 .60
67 Rashard Lewis .30 .75
68 Desmond Mason .25 .60
69 Gerald Wallace .25 .60
70 Drew Gooden .20 .50
71 Corey Maggette .25 .60
72 Gilbert Arenas .25 .60
73 Tim Thomas .20 .50
74 Jason Richardson .30 .75
75 Ray Allen .30 .75
76 Carmelo Anthony .60 1.50
77 Peja Stojakovic .30 .75
78 Dwyane Wade .50 1.25
79 Dajuan Wagner .20 .50
80 Shawn Marion .25 .60
81 Shaquille O'Neal .75 2.00
82 Eddy Curry .20 .50
83 Samuel Dalembert .20 .50
84 Karl Malone .40 1.00
85 Ricky Davis .25 .60
86 Steve Francis .25 .60
87 Juwan Howard .25 .60
88 Carlos Arroyo .20 .50
89 Jamal Mashburn .25 .60
90 Mickael Pietrus .25 .60
91 Vince Carter .50 1.25
92 Jason Kidd .50 1.25
93 Andre Miller .25 .60
94 Chris Webber .30 .75
95 Chris Kaman .25 .60
96 Paul Pierce .30 .75
97 Cuttino Mobley .20 .50
98 Ron Artest .30 .75
99 Matt Harpring .20 .50
100 Richard Jefferson .25 .60
102 Albert Miralles RC 1.50 4.00
103 Chris Duhon RC 1.50 4.00
104 Ha Seung-Jin RC 1.50 4.00
105 Antonio Burks RC 1.25 3.00
106 Andre Emmett RC 1.00 2.50
107 Donta Smith RC 1.00 2.50
108 Lionel Chalmers RC 1.50 4.00
109 Rickey Paulding RC 1.00 2.50
110 Jackson Vroman RC 1.00 2.50
111 Anderson Varejao RC 1.25 3.00
112 Beno Udrih RC 1.25 3.00
113 Sasha Vujacic RC 1.50 4.00
114 Kevin Martin RC 2.00 5.00
115 Tony Allen RC 1.50 4.00
116 Delonte West RC 1.50 4.00
117 Sergei Monia RC 1.00 2.50
118 Romain Sato RC 1.00 2.50
119 Jameer Nelson RC 1.50 4.00
120 Josh Smith RC 1.50 4.00
121 Kirk Snyder RC 1.00 2.50
122 Robert Swift RC 1.00 2.50
123 Andre Iguodala RC 2.00 5.00
124 Rafael Araujo RC 1.00 2.50
125 Luol Deng RC 1.50 4.00
126 Josh Childress RC 1.25 3.00
127 Ben Gordon RC 1.50 4.00
128 Emeka Okafor RC 1.25 3.00
129 Dwight Howard RC 3.00 8.00
130 D.Harrison RC/L.Bird AU 30.00 75.00
131 Livingston RC/E.Baylor AU 10.00 25.00
132 D.Harris RC/D.Nelson AU 10.00 25.00
133 L.Jackson RC/P.Silas AU 6.00 15.00
134 A.Biedrins RC/C.Mullin AU 6.00 15.00
135 S.Telfair RC/M.Cheeks AU 6.00 15.00
136 K.Humphries RC/J.Sloan AU 12.00 30.00
137 A.Jefferson RC/D.Ainge AU 12.00 30.00
138 J.R.Smith RC/B.Scott AU 15.00 40.00
139 D.Wright RC/P.Riley AU 10.00 25.00
140 T.Ariza RC/I.Thomas AU 8.00 20.00

2004-05 Fleer Authentix Parallel 100

*1-100: 2.5X TO 6X BASE CARD HI
*101-129: 1X TO 2.5X BASE CARD HI
STATED PRINT RUN 100 SER.#'d SETS
CARDS 55 & 101 NOT ISSUED
132 Devin Harris 3.00 8.00
134 Andris Biedrins 2.50 6.00
137 Al Jefferson 5.00 12.00
138 J.R. Smith 4.00 10.00
139 Dorell Wright 4.00 10.00
140 Trevor Ariza 4.00 10.00

2004-05 Fleer Authentix Parallel 75

*1-100: 3X TO 8X BASE CARD HI
*101-129: 1.25X TO 3X BASE CARD HI
CARDS 55 & 101 NOT ISSUED
132 Devin Harris 4.00 10.00
134 Andris Biedrins 3.00 8.00
137 Al Jefferson 6.00 15.00
138 J.R. Smith 5.00 12.00
139 Dorell Wright 5.00 12.00
140 Trevor Ariza 5.00 12.00

2004-05 Fleer Authentix Parallel 50

*1-100: 4X TO 10X BASE CARD HI
*101-129: 1.5X TO 4X BASE CARD HI
STATED PRINT RUN 50 SER.#'d SETS
CARDS 55 & 101 NOT ISSUED
132 Devin Harris 5.00 12.00
134 Andris Biedrins 4.00 10.00
137 Al Jefferson 8.00 20.00
138 J.R. Smith 6.00 15.00
139 Dorell Wright 6.00 15.00
140 Trevor Ariza 6.00 15.00

2004-05 Fleer Authentix Parallel 25

*1-100: 6X TO 15X BASE HI
*101-129: 2X TO 5X BASE HI
STATED PRINT RUN 25 SER.#'d SETS
CARDS 55 & 101 NOT ISSUED
26 Reggie Miller 10.00 25.00
132 Devin Harris 6.00 15.00
134 Andris Biedrins 5.00 12.00
137 Al Jefferson 10.00 25.00
138 J.R. Smith 8.00 20.00
139 Dorell Wright 8.00 20.00
140 Trevor Ariza 8.00 20.00

2004-05 Fleer Authentix Autographs

Limited to 50 serially numbered copies, this 28-card set features a ticket-style theme along the top of the card with a player photo and a cut signature along the bottom. Several parallel versions were issued for this set and are serially numbered to 25, 15, five and one of one.
PRINT RUN 50 SER.#'d SETS
*AUTO 25: .6X TO 1.5X BASE HI
BG Ben Gordon 6.00 15.00
CD Carlos Delfino 6.00 15.00
DH Devin Harris 5.00 12.00
DW Delonte West 6.00 15.00
GA Gilbert Arenas 6.00 15.00
HS Ha Seung-Jin 6.00 15.00
JC Josh Childress 5.00 12.00
JH Josh Howard 6.00 15.00
JS Josh Smith 6.00 15.00
KB Kwame Brown 6.00 15.00
KH Kris Humphries 6.00 15.00
KS Kirk Snyder 4.00 10.00
LD Luol Deng 6.00 15.00
LJ Luke Jackson 4.00 10.00
LO Lamar Odom 10.00 25.00
MB Marcus Banks 6.00 15.00
PP Paul Pierce 10.00 25.00
PS Peja Stojakovic 10.00 25.00
RH Richard Hamilton 10.00 25.00
RS Robert Swift 4.00 10.00
SL Shaun Livingston 6.00 15.00
SM Shawn Marion 8.00 20.00
ST Sebastian Telfair 5.00 12.00
VC Vince Carter 15.00 40.00
YT Yuta Tabuse 6.00 15.00

2004-05 Fleer Authentix Autographs Jerseys

Randomly inserted, this 25-card set parallels the design of the Autographs enahnced with a square swatch of game worn jersey centered towards the top of the cards and sequential numbering to 50. Several different parallel sets numbered to 25, 15, five and one of one.
PRINT RUN 50 SER.#'d SETS
*AUTO 25: .6X TO 1.5X BASE HI
AS Amare Stoudemire 15.00 40.00
BD Baron Davis 10.00 25.00
CA Carmelo Anthony 25.00 60.00
CB Chris Bosh 12.50 30.00
CW Dwyane Wade 40.00 100.00
GA Gilbert Arenas 10.00 25.00
HS Ha Seung-Jin 8.00 20.00
JC Josh Childress 6.00 15.00
JK Jason Kidd 15.00 40.00
JO Jermaine O'Neal 10.00 25.00
KB Kwame Brown 8.00 20.00
KM Kenyon Martin 10.00 25.00
LO Lamar Odom 12.50 30.00
PP Paul Pierce 12.50 30.00
PS Peja Stojakovic 15.00 30.00
RG Reece Gaines 8.00 20.00
RH Richard Hamilton 12.50 30.00
SA Shareef Abdur-Rahim 8.00 20.00
SF Steve Francis 8.00 20.00
SM Shawn Marion 10.00 25.00
TO Travis Outlaw 8.00 20.00
VC Vince Carter 15.00 40.00
YT Yuta Tabuse 8.00 20.00
ZR Zach Randolph 8.00 20.00

2004-05 Fleer Authentix Autographs Patches

Randomly inserted, this 24-card set parallels the base Autographs set enhanced with a swatch of patch along the top of the card and sequential numbering to 25. Four parallel versions of this set were also released sequentially numbered to 15, 10, five and one of one.
PRINT RUN 25 SER.#'d SETS
AS Amare Stoudemire 30.00 80.00
BD Baron Davis 20.00 50.00
CA Carmelo Anthony 40.00 100.00
DW Dwyane Wade 80.00 200.00
GA Gilbert Arenas 15.00 40.00
JK Jason Kidd 30.00 80.00
JO Jermaine O'Neal 20.00 50.00
KB Kwame Brown 15.00 40.00
KM Kenyon Martin 20.00 50.00
LO Lamar Odom 25.00 60.00
RG Reece Gaines 15.00 40.00
SA Shareef Abdur-Rahim 15.00 40.00
SF Steve Francis 15.00 40.00
SM Shawn Marion 20.00 50.00
SN Steve Nash 75.00 150.00
TO Travis Outlaw 15.00 40.00
VC Vince Carter 25.00 60.00
ZR Zach Randolph 15.00 40.00

2004-05 Fleer Authentix Draft Night Flashbacks

Inseted in packs at one in 248 Hobby and one in 480 Retail, this six cards set features players from the 2003-04 NBA Draft. The cards are horizontally designed with black borders along the left and bottom edges, and have a white background where player photos are on the right and a mock-ticket from the draft is on the left.
COMPLETE SET (6) 12.00 30.00
STATED ODDS 1:248 H, 1:480 R
CA Carmelo Anthony 3.00 8.00
CB Chris Bosh 1.50 4.00
DM Darko Milicic 1.00 2.50
DW Dwyane Wade 2.50 6.00
KH Kirk Hinrich 1.25 3.00
LJ LeBron James 10.00 25.00

2004-05 Fleer Authentix Draft Night Tickets

Inserted in packs at the rate of one in 240 Hobby and one in 480 Retail, this 10-card set features the 2004-05 Draft Class. The design is almost identical to the Draft Night Flashbacks set mentioned above, but contains an actual swatch of ticket from the draft event on the left.
COMPLETE SET (10) 25.00 60.00
STATED ODDS 1:240 H, 1:480 R
AJ Al Jefferson 3.00 8.00
BG Ben Gordon 2.50 6.00
DH Devin Harris 2.00 5.00
DH Dwight Howard 5.00 12.00
EO Emeka Okafor 2.00 5.00
JC Josh Childress 2.00 5.00
LD Luol Deng 2.50 6.00
LJ Luke Jackson 1.50 4.00
SL Shaun Livingston 2.50 6.00
ST Sebastian Telfair 2.00 5.00

2004-05 Fleer Authentix Game of the Week Jerseys

Randomly seeded in packs, this 20-card set parallels the design utilized by all of the aformentioned autograph and memorabilia insert sets, but features two players along the top and two swatches of jersey along the bottom. Each card is sequentially numbered, see checklist for print runs. A Patch version enhanced with two game worn patches and sequentially numbered to 10 was also inserted.
STATED PRINT RUN 10 TO 200 SER.#'d SETS
AM C.Anthony/T.McGrady/120 5.00 12.00
AW C.Anthony/D.Wade/60 5.00 12.00
CM V.Carter/T.McGrady/100 4.00 10.00
CM V.Carter/K.Martin/180 4.00 10.00
DG T.Duncan/K.Garnett/110 4.00 10.00
GS K.Garnett/A.Stoudemire/140 4.00 10.00
IF A.Iverson/S.Francis/90 4.00 10.00
MK S.Marbury/J.Kidd/80 4.00 10.00
MS K.Martin/A.Stoudemire/50 2.00 5.00
NF S.Nash/M.Finley/170 3.00 8.00
OD S.O'Neal/T.Duncan/130 6.00 15.00
PR P.Pierce/J.Richardson/190 2.50 6.00
RA M.Redd/R.Allen/150 2.50 6.00
RW Z.Randolph/B.Wallace/200 2.00 5.00
SN P.Stojakovic/D.Nowitzki/40 4.00 10.00
WH D.Wade/K.Hinrich/160 4.00 10.00
WO B.Wallace/J.O'Neal/30 2.00 5.00
WW C.Webber/R.Wallace/70 2.50 6.00

2004-05 Fleer Authentix Hot Tickets

Inserted in packs at the rate of one in 24 Hobby and one in 48 Retail, this 10-card set has tan backgrounds where the outside of the card is framed and the inside features a lighter-colored oval. Inside the oval is a color portrait-style shot of the player along the top, set name and player name in foil to match the player's team color in the middle and team logo on the bottom.
COMPLETE SET (10) 8.00 20.00
STATED ODDS 1:24 H, 1:48 R
AI Allen Iverson .75 2.00
CA Carmelo Anthony 1.00 2.50
KB Kobe Bryant 2.00 5.00
KG Kevin Garnett .75 2.00
LJ LeBron James 3.00 8.00
SO Shaquille O'Neal 1.25 3.00
TD Tim Duncan .75 2.00
TM Tracy McGrady .60 1.50
VC Vince Carter .75 2.00
YM Yao Ming 1.00 2.50

2004-05 Fleer Authentix Hot Tickets Jerseys

PRINT RUN 450 SER.#'d SETS
AI Allen Iverson 4.00 10.00
CA Carmelo Anthony 5.00 12.00
KG Kevin Garnett 4.00 10.00
SO Shaquille O'Neal 6.00 15.00
TD Tim Duncan 4.00 10.00
TM Tracy McGrady 3.00 8.00
VC Vince Carter 4.00 10.00
YM Yao Ming 5.00 12.00

2004-05 Fleer Authentix Jerseys

Randomly inserted in packs, this 35-card set parallels the design of all previously described autographed an memorabilia sets, but places a square swatch of jersey in the bottom center of the card--each is serially numbered to 175. Four parallel versions of the Jerseys set were issued and fie Patch parallels were issued. The Jerseys parallels are sequentially numbered to 150, 75, 25 and 10. Patch parallels are sequentially numbered to 50, 25, 15 and five.
PRINT RUN 175 SER.#'d SETS
*JERSEY 150: .4X TO 1X BASE HI
*JERSEY 75: .5X TO 1.25X BASE HI

*JERSEY 25: .75X TO 2X BASE HI
*PATCH: .75X TO 2X BASE JSY HI
PATCH PRINT RUN 50 SER.#'d SETS
*PATCH 25: 1.25X TO 3X BASE HI
1 Allen Iverson 4.00 10.00
2 Tim Duncan 4.00 10.00
3 Carmelo Anthony 5.00 12.00
4 Kevin Garnett 4.00 10.00
5 Vince Carter 4.00 10.00
6 Paul Pierce 2.50 6.00
7 Dwyane Wade 4.00 10.00
8 Yao Ming 5.00 12.00
9 Shaquille O'Neal 6.00 15.00
10 Jason Kidd 4.00 10.00
11 Dirk Nowitzki 4.00 10.00
12 Steve Francis 2.00 5.00
13 Tracy McGrady 3.00 8.00
14 Amare Stoudemire 2.00 5.00
15 Stephon Marbury 2.00 5.00
16 Kenyon Martin 2.00 5.00
17 Michael Finley 2.50 6.00
18 Steve Nash 3.00 8.00
19 Jason Richardson 2.50 6.00
20 Chris Webber 2.50 6.00
21 Karl Malone 3.00 8.00
22 Jermaine O'Neal 2.00 5.00
23 Tony Parker 2.50 6.00
24 Peja Stojakovic 2.50 6.00
25 Reggie Miller 2.50 6.00
26 Michael Redd 2.00 5.00
27 Rasheed Wallace 2.50 6.00
28 Ray Allen 2.50 6.00
29 Kirk Hinrich 2.00 5.00
30 Latrell Sprewell 2.00 5.00
31 Baron Davis 2.00 5.00
32 Ben Wallace 2.00 5.00
33 Shawn Marion 2.00 5.00
34 Lamar Odom 2.00 5.00
35 Zach Randolph 2.00 5.00

2004-05 Fleer Authentix Showstoppers

Inserted in packs at the rate of one in eight Hobby and one in 12 Retail, this 15-card set is horizontally designed with a green and black background, yellow lettering, a lighted sign that relembles the "Welcome to Las Vegas Sign" and places a player image on the right side of the card.

COMPLETE SET (15) 6.00 15.00
STATED ODDS 1:8 H, 1:12 R
1 Shaquille O'Neal .75 2.00
2 Kobe Bryant 1.25 3.00
3 Jason Kidd .50 1.25
4 LeBron James 2.00 5.00
5 Carmelo Anthony .60 1.50
6 Mike Bibby .30 .75
7 Amare Stoudemire .25 .60
8 Dwyane Wade .50 1.25
9 Kevin Garnett .50 1.25
10 Allen Iverson .50 1.25
11 Tim Duncan .50 1.25
12 Paul Pierce .30 .75
13 Vince Carter .50 1.25
14 Yao Ming .60 1.50
15 Dirk Nowitzki .50 1.25

2004-05 Fleer Authentix Tip-Off Trios

Randomly inserted in packs, this 15-card set features three player head shots on the left, top to bottom and three swatches of jersey to the right. Each card is sequentially numbered to 75. Two parallel versions were printed for this set and are numbered to 25 and five.

PRINT RUN 75 SER.#'d SETS
*TRIO 25: 1X TO 2.5X BASE HI
DM Nowitzki/Finley/Terry 10.00 25.00
DN Melo/Nene/A.Miller 10.00 25.00
DP B.Wallace/R.Wallace/Rip 10.00 25.00
HR T-Mac/Yao/J.Howard 10.00 25.00
IP Miller/J.O'Neal/Artest 10.00 25.00
LL Odom/Malone/Walton 10.00 25.00
MB Ford/Mason/Redd 10.00 25.00
MH Jones/Shaq/Wade 25.00 60.00
MT Garnett/Cassell/Spree 12.50 30.00
NH B.Davis/Mash/Magloire 10.00 25.00
NK Houston/Marbury/Crawford 10.00 25.00
OM Hill/Francis/D.Howard 12.50 30.00
PS Nash/Marion/Amare 10.00 25.00
SK Webber/Bibby/Peja 10.00 25.00
SS Duncan/Manu/Parker 12.00 30.00

2002 Fleer Authentix WNBA

Released in the summer of 2002, this 120-card set is divided up into 100 veteran players and 20 rookie cards. Veteran cards place players on a ticket backdrop with an embedded ticket swatch in the card. Rookie cards are sequentially numbered to 2002.

COMPLETE SET (120) 30.00 80.00
COMPLETE SET w/o RC's (100) 6.00 15.00
101-120 PRINT RUN 2002 SER.#'d SETS
1 Jackie Stiles .75 2.00
2 Taj McWilliams-Franklin .20 .50
3 Allison Feaster .25 .60
4 Sheryl Swoopes 1.25 3.00
5 Edwina Brown .25 .60
6 DeLisha Milton .25 .60
7 Tonya Edwards .20 .50
8 Svetlana Abrosimova .20 .50
9 Alicia Thompson .20 .50
10 Kristen Rasmussen .20 .50
11 Marie Ferdinand .20 .50
12 Coco Miller .20 .50
13 Tari Phillips .20 .50
14 Kristin Folkl .30 .75
15 Annie Burgess RC .20 .50
16 Elaine Powell .20 .50
17 Jamie Redd .20 .50
18 Sophia Witherspoon .30 .75
19 Shannon Johnson .20 .50
20 Amanda Lassiter .20 .50
21 Dawn Staley .50 1.25
22 Dominique Canty .30 .75
23 Jessie Hicks .20 .50
24 Mwadi Mabika .20 .50
25 Georgia Schweitzer .20 .50
26 Lauren Jackson 1.00 2.50
27 Natalie Williams .20 .50
28 Tynesha Lewis .20 .50
29 Rushia Brown .20 .50
30 Tamicha Jackson .20 .50
31 Chasity Melvin .20 .50
32 Chamique Holdsclaw 1.25 3.00
33 Michelle Marciniak .30 .75
34 Lynn Pride .20 .50
35 Tammy Sutton-Brown .20 .50
36 Sandy Brondello .50 1.25
37 Semeka Randall .20 .50
38 Tammy Jackson .20 .50
39 Ukari Figgs .20 .50
40 Ruthie Bolton .60 1.50
41 Lisa Harrison .30 .75
42 Kate Starbird .30 .75
43 Katie Douglas .30 .75
44 Coquese Washington .20 .50
45 Sheri Sam .20 .50
46 Vickie Johnson .30 .75
47 Latasha Byears .30 .75
48 Erin Buescher .20 .50
49 Ann Wauters .25 .60
50 Kedra Holland-Corn .20 .50
51 Astou Ndiaye-Diatta .30 .75
52 Kara Wolters .25 .60
53 Tully Bevilaqua .20 .50
54 Simone Edwards RC .20 .50
55 Vicky Bullett .30 .75
56 Nykesha Sales .30 .75
57 Crystal Robinson .20 .50
58 Tina Thompson .60 1.50
59 Lisa Leslie 1.00 2.50
60 Deanna Nolan .20 .50
61 Jennifer Gillom .50 1.25
62 Nadine Malcolm RC .20 .50
63 Merlakia Jones .30 .75
64 Rebecca Lobo .60 1.50
65 Tamecka Dixon .30 .75
66 Yolanda Griffith .60 1.50
67 Teresa Weatherspoon .75 2.00
68 Penny Taylor .30 .75
69 Brooke Wyckoff .40 1.00
70 Murriel Page .25 .60
71 Adrienne Goodson .20 .50
72 Camille Cooper .20 .50
73 Kamila Vodichkova .20 .50
74 Jennifer Azzi .60 1.50
75 Katie Smith .60 1.50
76 Kristen Veal .20 .50
77 Tamika Catchings .30 .75
78 Clarisse Machanguana .20 .50
79 Wendy Palmer .50 1.25
80 Ticha Penicheiro .50 1.25
81 Becky Hammon 1.25 3.00
82 Jennifer Rizzotti .50 1.25
83 Helen Luz .20 .50
84 Adrain Williams .20 .50
85 Tamika Whitmore .20 .50
86 Sylvia Crawley .20 .50
87 Edna Campbell .25 .60
88 Sonja Henning .20 .50
89 Vedrana Grgin .20 .50
90 Tracy Reid .30 .75
91 Betty Lennox .50 1.25
92 Andrea Stinson .40 1.00
93 Tangela Smith .20 .50
94 Margo Dydek .30 .75
95 Nikki McCray .50 1.25
96 Sue Wicks .30 .75
97 Olympia Scott-Richardson .20 .50
98 Ruth Riley .30 .75
99 Janeth Arcain .20 .50
100 Rita Williams .25 .60
101 Sue Bird RC 12.00 30.00
102 Swin Cash RC 4.00 10.00
103 S.Dales-Schuman RC 4.00 10.00
104 Asjha Jones RC 4.00 10.00
105 Nikki Teasley RC 2.50 6.00
106 Tamika Williams RC 4.00 10.00
107 Sheila Lambert RC 2.50 6.00
108 Lindsey Yamasaki RC 2.50 6.00
109 Shaunzinski Gortman RC 2.50 6.00
110 Michelle Snow RC 4.00 10.00
111 Danielle Crockrom RC 3.00 8.00
112 Hamchetou Maiga RC 2.50 6.00
113 Tawana McDonald RC 2.50 6.00
114 LaNeishea Caufield RC 2.50 6.00
115 Tamara Moore RC 2.50 6.00
116 Rosalind Ross RC 2.50 6.00
117 Zuzi Klimesova RC 2.50 6.00
118 Lenae Williams RC 2.50 6.00
119 Iziane Castro-Marques RC 2.50 6.00
120 Ayana Walker RC 3.00 8.00

2002 Fleer Authentix WNBA Front Row

*STARS 1-100: 5X TO 12X BASE CARD HI
*RCs 101-120: .75X TO 2X BASE HI
PRINT RUN 100 SERIAL #'d SETS

2002 Fleer Authentix WNBA Autographed Authentix

Randomly inserted in packs, this set features three different Jackie Stiles autograph cards. The cards are sequentially numbered to 90, 49, and one.

PRINT RUNS LISTED BELOW
1A Jackie Stiles AU/90 75.00 150.00
1B Jackie Stiles JSY AU/49 100.00 200.00

2002 Fleer Authentix WNBA Courtside Classics

Randomly inserted in packs at the rate of one in 22, this 10-card set features the WNBA's brightest stars.

COMPLETE SET (10) 10.00 25.00
1 Jackie Stiles 2.50 6.00
2 Sheri Sam .60 1.50
3 Betty Lennox 1.50 4.00
4 Teresa Weatherspoon 2.50 6.00
5 Katie Douglas 1.00 2.50
6 DeLisha Milton .60 1.50
7 Lauren Jackson 3.00 8.00
8 Murriel Page .75 2.00
9 Kedra Holland-Corn .60 1.50
10 Tina Thompson 2.00 5.00

2002 Fleer Authentix WNBA Memorabilia Authentix Ripped

Inserted in packs at the rate of one in eight, this 13-card set places a swatch of game worn memorabilia in the middle and the bottom edge of the card is jagged is if it has been ripped like a ticket stub.

STATED ODDS 1:8
*UNRIPPED: 3X TO 8X HI
UNRIPPED PRINT RUN 50 SER.#'d SETS
1 Jackie Stiles 5.00 12.00
2 Jennifer Gillom 3.00 8.00
3 Dawn Staley 3.00 8.00
4 Nikki McCray 3.00 8.00
5 Nykesha Sales 2.00 5.00
6 Becky Hammon 8.00 20.00
7 Sheryl Swoopes 6.00 15.00
8 Yolanda Griffith 4.00 10.00
9 Sue Bird 5.00 12.00
10 Lisa Leslie 6.00 15.00
11 Ruthie Bolton 4.00 10.00
12 Natalie Williams 2.50 6.00
13 Chamique Holdsclaw 6.00 15.00

2002 Fleer Authentix WNBA The Ticket

Inserted in packs, this 16-card set places a swatch of a ticket to a WBNA game next to the featured player. Each card is sequentially numbered.

PRINT RUNS LISTED BELOW
1 Jackie Stiles/500 4.00 10.00
2 Lauren Jackson/575 5.00 12.00
3 Andrea Stinson/320 2.00 5.00
4 Jennifer Rizzotti/500 2.50 6.00
5 Ruth Riley/565 1.50 4.00
6 Deanna Nolan/310 1.00 2.50
7 Tamika Catchings/330 1.50 4.00
8 Sheryl Swoopes/600 6.00 15.00
9 Katie Smith/475 3.00 8.00
10 Becky Hammon/390 6.00 15.00
11 Nykesha Sales/375 1.50 4.00
12 Lisa Harrison/475 1.50 4.00
13 Yolanda Griffith/160 3.00 8.00
14 Natalie Williams/495 2.00 5.00
15 Chamique Holdsclaw/410 5.00 12.00
16 Lisa Leslie/450 5.00 12.00

2000-01 Fleer Authority

The 2000-01 Fleer Authority product was released in late February, 2001 and featured a 141-card base set that was broken into tiers as follows: Base Veterans (1-110), and Rookies (111-141) that were serial numbered to 650 and inserted at 1:16 packs.

COMPLETE SET (141) 80.00 160.00
COMP.SET w/o SP's (110) 10.00 25.00
111-141 PRINT RUN 650 SERIAL #'d SETS
FLEER/BGS REDEMPTION CARD ODDS 1:16
1 Dikembe Mutombo .30 .75
2 Cuttino Mobley .20 .50
3 Brian Grant .20 .50
4 Grant Hill .40 1.00
5 Jim Jackson .20 .50
6 Derek Anderson .20 .50
7 Jerry Stackhouse .25 .60
8 Eddie Jones .30 .75
9 Tracy McGrady .50 1.25
10 Vin Baker .25 .60
11 Jason Terry .30 .75
12 Jerome Williams .20 .50
13 Tim Hardaway .30 .75
14 Darrell Armstrong .20 .50
15 Rashard Lewis .30 .75
16 Kenny Anderson .25 .60
17 Larry Hughes .25 .60
18 Anthony Mason .25 .60
19 Allen Iverson .60 1.50
20 Gary Payton .30 .75
21 Antoine Walker .25 .60
22 Antawn Jamison .25 .60
23 Glenn Robinson .25 .60
24 Toni Kukoc .30 .75
25 Ruben Patterson .20 .50
26 Paul Pierce .30 .75
27 Mookie Blaylock .20 .50
28 Ray Allen .25 .60
29 Theo Ratliff .20 .50
30 Vince Carter .60 1.50
31 Jamal Mashburn .25 .60
32 Steve Francis .25 .60
33 Sam Cassell .25 .60
34 Jason Kidd .50 1.25
35 Mark Jackson .25 .60
36 Baron Davis .30 .75
37 Hakeem Olajuwon .40 1.00
38 Darvin Ham .20 .50
39 Shawn Marion .25 .60
40 Antonio Davis .20 .50
41 Derrick Coleman .20 .50
42 Maurice Taylor .20 .50
43 Kevin Garnett .50 1.25
44 Tom Gugliotta .20 .50
45 Karl Malone .40 1.00
46 Elton Brand .30 .75
47 Jonathan Bender .25 .60
48 Terrell Brandon .25 .60
49 Clifford Robinson .20 .50
50 John Stockton .40 1.00
51 Ron Artest .30 .75
52 Reggie Miller .30 .75
53 Joe Smith .25 .60
54 Shawn Kemp .25 .60
55 Bryon Russell .20 .50
56 Andre Miller .25 .60
57 Austin Croshere .25 .60
58 Wally Szczerbiak .25 .60
59 Scottie Pippen .50 1.25
60 Donyell Marshall .25 .60
61 Brevin Knight .20 .50
62 Travis Best .20 .50
63 Chauncey Billups .30 .75
64 Rasheed Wallace .30 .75
65 Shareef Abdur-Rahim .30 .75
66 Trajan Langdon .20 .50
67 Jalen Rose .25 .60
68 Stephon Marbury .25 .60
69 Steve Smith .25 .60
70 Mike Bibby .30 .75
71 Lamond Murray .20 .50
72 Lamar Odom .30 .75
73 Keith Van Horn .25 .60
74 Chris Webber .30 .75
75 Michael Dickerson .20 .50
76 Dirk Nowitzki .50 1.25
77 Corey Maggette .25 .60
78 Kerry Kittles .20 .50
79 Jason Williams .25 .60
80 Mitch Richmond .25 .60
81 Michael Finley .25 .60
82 Shaquille O'Neal .75 2.00
83 Allan Houston .25 .60
84 Peja Stojakovic .30 .75
85 Juwan Howard .25 .60
86 Nick Van Exel .25 .60
87 Kobe Bryant 1.25 3.00
88 Latrell Sprewell .25 .60
89 Tim Duncan .60 1.50
90 Richard Hamilton .25 .60
91 Antonio McDyess .25 .60
92 Glen Rice .25 .60
93 Larry Johnson .25 .60
94 David Robinson .30 .75
95 Rod Strickland .20 .50
96 Raef LaFrentz .25 .60
97 Ron Harper .25 .60
98 Patrick Ewing .40 1.00
99 Sean Elliott .30 .75
100 Tariq Abdul-Wahad .20 .50
101 Chucky Atkins .20 .50
102 Marcus Camby .25 .60
103 Corliss Williamson .20 .50
104 Rodney Rogers .20 .50
105 Othella Harrington .20 .50
106 Alan Henderson .20 .50
107 David Wesley .20 .50
108 Michael Doleac .20 .50
109 Doug Christie .25 .60
110 Vitaly Potapenko .20 .50
111 DerMarr Johnson RC 1.25 3.00
112 Jamal Crawford RC 4.00 10.00
113 Morris Peterson RC 1.50 4.00
114 Erick Barkley RC 1.00 2.50
115 Kenyon Martin RC 4.00 10.00
116 Joel Przybilla RC 1.25 3.00
117 Speedy Claxton RC 1.50 4.00
118 Hedo Turkoglu RC 2.50 6.00
119 Etan Thomas RC 1.50 4.00
120 Eddie House RC 1.25 3.00
121 Marcus Fizer RC 1.50 4.00
122 Quentin Richardson RC 1.50 4.00
123 Donnell Harvey RC 1.25 3.00
124 DeShawn Stevenson RC 1.50 4.00
125 Chris Mihm RC 1.25 3.00
126 Courtney Alexander RC 1.25 3.00
127 Keyon Dooling RC 1.50 4.00
128 Jerome Moiso RC 1.00 2.50
129 Stephen Jackson RC 2.50 6.00
130 Chris Porter RC 1.00 2.50
131 Stromile Swift RC 1.50 4.00
132 Desmond Mason RC 2.00 5.00
133 Jason Collier RC 1.50 4.00
134 Mark Madsen RC 1.50 4.00
135 Mamadou N'Diaye RC 1.00 2.50
136 Darius Miles RC 1.50 4.00
137 Mateen Cleaves RC 1.25 3.00
138 Jamaal Magloire RC 1.50 4.00
139 Khalid El-Amin RC 1.00 2.50
140 Mike Miller RC 2.50 6.00
141 Marc Jackson RC 1.25 3.00

2000-01 Fleer Authority Rookies 1250

*RC 1250: .2X TO .5X BASE RC
STATED ODDS 1:2 GRADED PACKS
STATED PRINT RUN 1250 SETS

2000-01 Fleer Authority Prominence 125/75

*STARS 1-110: 8X TO 20X BASE HI
1-110 PRINT RUN 125 SERIAL #'d SETS
*ROOKIES 111-141: .6X TO 1.5X BASE HI
111-141 PRINT RUN 75 SERIAL #'d SETS

2000-01 Fleer Authority Prominence 75/25

*STARS 1-110: 10X TO 25X BASE HI
*ROOKIES 111-141: 1.25X TO 3X BASE HI
111-141 PRINT RUN 25 SERIAL #'d SETS

2000-01 Fleer Authority Autographics SSD

The Fleer Authority Autographics SSD set is comprised of regular 2000-01 Fleer Autographics cards, but are enhanced with an embossed Fleer stamp of authority. Upon release, these cards were available in graded form only. Since that time, a limited number of cards have found their way outside of their BGS slab cases.

RANDOM INSERTS IN GRADED PACKS
SEE 2000-01 FLEER AUTOS FOR PRICES

2000-01 Fleer Authority Autographics SSD Gold

SEE 2000-01 FLEER AUTO GOLD FOR PRICES

2000-01 Fleer Authority Autographics SSD Silver

SEE 2000-01 FLEER AUTO SILVER FOR PRICES

2000-01 Fleer Authority Vince Carter Rookie Remnants

This three-card insert was randomly inserted into 2000-01 Fleer products. The set includes a Vince Carter floor card (numbered to 100), a Vince Carter floor/jersey card (numbered to 15), and finally an autographed Vince Carter floor/jersey card (numbered 1 of 1).

RANDOM INSERTS IN HOBBY PACKS
VCRR1 Vince Carter FLR/100 12.50 30.00
VCRR2 Vince Carter FLR JSY/15 20.00 50.00

2000-01 Fleer Authority Feel the Game

Randomly inserted in multiple releases, this set features swatches of game-used jerseys from top veterans and rookies in the NBA. The cards were inserted at one in 56 for Fleer Premium, 1:72 for Fleer Mystique, 1:48 Fleer Focus, and 1:48 for Ultra. The cards are not numbered on the back and listed in alphabetical order.

FEEL GAME OR REFLECTION ODDS 1:16
SEE 2000-01 FLEER FEEL GAME FOR PRICES

2000-01 Fleer Authority Figures

Randomly inserted in packs at the rate of one in 16, this 15-card set features a veteran player portrait style photo on the top half of the card, and a young star in action on the lower right hand side. Each card is sequentially numbered to 1250.

COMPLETE SET (15) 10.00 25.00
STATED ODDS 1:16
STATED PRINT RUN 1250 SERIAL #'d SETS
*FIGURES 499: .6X TO 1.5X HI
AF1 C.Alexander/M.Finley .60 1.50
AF2 M.Madsen/K.Bryant 2.50 6.00
AF3 D.Johnson/D.Mutombo .60 1.50
AF4 M.Cleaves/J.Stackhouse .50 1.25
AF5 K.Martin/K.Van Horn 1.50 4.00
AF6 M.Peterson/V.Carter 1.25 3.00
AF7 D.Miles/L.Odom .60 1.50
AF8 D.Mason/G.Payton .75 2.00
AF9 S.Swift/S.Abdur-Rahim .60 1.50
AF10 S.Claxton/A.Iverson 1.25 3.00
AF11 D.Stevenson/K.Malone .75 2.00
AF12 M.Fizer/E.Brand .60 1.50
AF13 H.Turkoglu/C.Webber 1.00 2.50
AF14 J.Collier/S.Francis .60 1.50
AF15 M.Miller/G.Hill 1.00 2.50

2000-01 Fleer Authority Rookie Reflections

Authority Rookie Reflections and Fleer Feel the Game were inserted in packs at the combined ration of one in 16. This 22-card set features a horizontal card design with player action photos on the left side of the card, a swatch of game worn memorabilia in the center, and a portrait style photograph on the right.

FEEL GAME OR REFLECTION ODDS 1:16
RR1 Vince Carter 6.00 15.00
RR2 Grant Hill 4.00 10.00
RR3 Keyon Dooling 3.00 8.00
RR4 Jason Kidd 5.00 12.00
RR5 Chris Mihm 2.50 6.00
RR6 Darius Miles 3.00 8.00
RR7 Mike Miller 5.00 12.00
RR8 Quentin Richardson 3.00 8.00
RR9 Hanno Mottola 2.00 5.00
RR10 Allen Iverson 6.00 15.00
RR11 Desmond Mason 4.00 10.00
RR12 Andre Miller 2.50 6.00
RR13 Tracy McGrady 5.00 12.00
RR14 Shawn Marion 2.50 6.00
RR15 John Stockton 4.00 10.00
RR16 Lamar Odom 2.50 6.00
RR17 V.Carter/D.Miles 8.00 20.00
RR18 G.Hill/D.Mason 4.00 10.00
RR19 J.Kidd/Q.Richardson 5.00 12.00
RR20 A.Iverson/K.Dooling 6.00 15.00
RR21 T.McGrady/M.Miller 6.00 15.00
RR22 A.Miller/C.Mihm 3.00 8.00

2000-01 Fleer Authority Seal of Approval

Upon release, these cards were available in graded form only. Since that time, a limited number of cards have found their way outside of their BGS slab cases.

COMPLETE SET (15) 30.00 60.00
STATED PRINT RUN 250 SERIAL #'d SETS
SA1 Kobe Bryant 12.00 30.00
SA2 Tim Duncan 4.00 10.00
SA3 Jason Kidd 3.00 8.00
SA4 Lamar Odom 1.50 4.00
SA5 Kevin Garnett 3.00 8.00
SA6 Elton Brand 2.00 5.00
SA7 Steve Francis 1.50 4.00
SA8 Stromile Swift 2.00 5.00
SA9 Kenyon Martin 5.00 12.00
SA10 Tracy McGrady 3.00 8.00
SA11 Allen Iverson 4.00 10.00
SA12 Grant Hill 2.50 6.00
SA13 Marcus Fizer 2.00 5.00
SA14 Shaquille O'Neal 5.00 12.00
SA15 Vince Carter 4.00 10.00

2000-01 Fleer Authority With Authority

Randomly seeded in packs at the rate of one in 16, this 20-card set features the game's most dominating names set against a background that fades to white along the edges. The upper left hand corner of the card is cut and rounded. Each card is sequentially numbered to 999.

STATED ODDS 1:16
STATED PRINT RUN 999 SERIAL #'d SETS
*WA 299: .5X TO 1.25X HI
WA1 Dirk Nowitzki 1.50 4.00
WA2 Larry Hughes .75 2.00
WA3 Eddie Jones 1.00 2.50
WA4 Chris Webber 1.00 2.50
WA5 Grant Hill 1.25 3.00
WA6 Scottie Pippen 1.50 4.00
WA7 Shareef Abdur-Rahim .75 2.00
WA8 Kevin Garnett 1.50 4.00
WA9 Allen Iverson 2.00 5.00
WA10 Karl Malone 1.25 3.00
WA11 Kobe Bryant 4.00 10.00
WA12 Tim Duncan 2.00 5.00
WA13 Stephon Marbury .75 2.00
WA14 Shaquille O'Neal 2.50 6.00
WA15 Vince Carter 2.00 5.00
WA16 Tracy McGrady 1.50 4.00
WA17 Gary Payton 1.00 2.50
WA18 Steve Francis .75 2.00
WA19 Elton Brand 1.00 2.50
WA20 Ray Allen 1.00 2.50

2003-04 Fleer Avant

Released in late January 2004, this 90-card set is divided up into 56 veteran player cards, eight team USA cards sequentially numbered to 699 (cards 57-64) and 25 rookie players sequentially numbered to 699. Base cards are framed with a textured border and have painting-like pictures for the cards themselves. Avant was packaged in 18-pack boxes where packs contained four cards and carried a suggested retail price of $7.99.

COMP.SET w/o SP's 15.00 40.00
57-64 PRINT RUN 699 SER.#'d SETS
65-90 PRINT RUN 699 SER.#'d SETS
1 Ben Wallace .50 1.25
2 Glenn Robinson .50 1.25
3 Pau Gasol .60 1.50
4 Keon Clark .40 1.00
5 Kobe Bryant 2.50 6.00
6 Morris Peterson .40 1.00
7 Steve Francis .50 1.25
8 Amare Stoudemire .75 2.00
9 Mike Dunleavy Jr. .50 1.25
10 Kevin Garnett 1.00 2.50
11 Yao Ming 1.25 3.00
12 Stephon Marbury .60 1.50
13 Jason Richardson .60 1.50
14 Rasheed Wallace .60 1.50
15 Tayshaun Prince .50 1.25
16 Steve Nash .75 2.00
17 Jamal Mashburn .50 1.25
18 Reggie Miller .60 1.50
19 Chris Webber .60 1.50
20 Andre Miller .50 1.25
21 Peja Stojakovic .60 1.50
22 Nene .50 1.25
23 Manu Ginobili .75 2.00
24 Bonzi Wells .40 1.00
25 Lamar Odom .60 1.50
26 Kwame Brown .40 1.00
27 Caron Butler .50 1.25
28 Gilbert Arenas .50 1.25
29 Dirk Nowitzki 1.00 2.50
30 Allan Houston .50 1.25
31 Michael Finley .60 1.50
32 Drew Gooden .50 1.25
33 Shareef Abdur-Rahim .50 1.25
34 Michael Redd .60 1.50
35 Jerry Stackhouse .60 1.50
36 Scottie Pippen 1.00 2.50
37 Latrell Sprewell .60 1.50
38 Ron Artest .60 1.50
39 Derrick Coleman .50 1.25
40 Eddy Curry .40 1.00
41 Wally Szczerbiak .50 1.25
42 Dajuan Wagner .40 1.00
43 Baron Davis .60 1.50
44 Karl Malone .75 2.00
45 Andrei Kirilenko .60 1.50
46 Paul Pierce .60 1.50
47 Desmond Mason .60 1.50
48 Shaquille O'Neal 1.50 4.00
49 Rashard Lewis .60 1.50
50 Ricky Davis .50 1.25
51 Kerry Kittles .40 1.00
52 Quentin Richardson .50 1.25
53 Tony Parker .60 1.50
54 Elton Brand .60 1.50
55 Richard Jefferson .50 1.25
56 Kenyon Martin .60 1.50
57 Ray Allen 1.50 4.00
58 Mike Bibby 1.50 4.00
59 Tim Duncan 2.50 6.00
60 Allen Iverson 2.50 6.00
61 Jason Kidd 2.50 6.00
62 Tracy McGrady 2.50 6.00
63 Jermaine O'Neal 1.25 3.00
64 Larry Brown 1.50 4.00
65 LeBron James RC 75.00 200.00
66 Darko Milicic RC 4.00 10.00
67 Carmelo Anthony RC 6.00 15.00
68 Chris Bosh RC 3.00 8.00
69 Dwyane Wade RC 6.00 15.00
70 Chris Kaman RC 2.00 5.00
71 Kirk Hinrich RC 2.00 5.00
72 T.J. Ford RC 1.50 4.00
73 Mike Sweetney RC 1.25 3.00
74 Jarvis Hayes RC 1.25 3.00
75 Mickael Pietrus RC 1.50 4.00
76 Travis Hansen RC 1.25 3.00
77 Marcus Banks RC 1.25 3.00
78 Luke Ridnour RC 1.50 4.00
79 Reece Gaines RC 1.25 3.00
80 Troy Bell RC 1.25 3.00
81 Zarko Cabarkapa RC 1.25 3.00
82 David West RC 2.00 5.00
83 Aleksandar Pavlovic RC 1.50 4.00
84 Dahntay Jones RC 1.50 4.00
85 Boris Diaw RC 2.50 6.00
86 Zoran Planinic RC 1.25 3.00
87 Travis Outlaw RC 1.50 4.00
88 Brian Cook RC 1.25 3.00
89 Maciej Lampe RC 1.25 3.00
90 Nick Collison RC 1.50 4.00

2003-04 Fleer Avant Black and White

*1-56 SINGLES: 1.25X TO 3X BASE HI
*57-64 USA SINGLES: .6X TO 1.5X BASE HI
*65-90 RC SINGLES: .6X TO 1.5X BASE HI
B&W PRINT RUN 199 SER.#'d SETS
5 Kobe Bryant 12.00 30.00
65 LeBron James 200.00 500.00

2003-04 Fleer Avant Candid Collection

Randomly seeded, this 20-card set utilizes a horizontal format with close-up portrait style photos of players striking familiar non-playing court poses and white borders. Each card is sequentially numbered to 199.

PRINT RUN 199 SERIAL #'d SETS
1 Allen Iverson 2.50 6.00
2 Steve Francis 1.25 3.00
3 Amare Stoudemire 2.00 5.00
4 Chris Webber 1.50 4.00
5 Paul Pierce 1.50 4.00
6 Caron Butler 1.25 3.00
7 Yao Ming 3.00 8.00
8 Ben Wallace 1.25 3.00
9 Kevin Garnett 2.50 6.00
10 Tim Duncan 2.50 6.00
11 Dirk Nowitzki 2.50 6.00
12 Carmelo Anthony 5.00 12.00
13 Jason Kidd 2.50 6.00
14 Vince Carter 2.50 6.00
15 Tracy McGrady 2.00 5.00
16 Jermaine O'Neal 1.25 3.00
17 Ray Allen 1.50 4.00
18 Shaquille O'Neal 4.00 10.00
19 Kobe Bryant 6.00 15.00
20 LeBron James 50.00 120.00

2003-04 Fleer Avant Candid Collection Memorabilia

Randomly inserted, this 10-card set parallels the design of the base Candid Collection insert enhanced with a swatch of game worn memorabilia. Each card is sequentially numbered to 250.

PRINT RUN 250 SERIAL #'d SETS
AI Allen Iverson 4.00 10.00
AS Amare Stoudemire 3.00 8.00
BW Ben Wallace 2.00 5.00
DN Dirk Nowitzki 4.00 10.00
JK Jason Kidd 4.00 10.00
KG Kevin Garnett 4.00 10.00
SF Steve Francis 2.00 5.00
TD Tim Duncan 4.00 10.00
TM Tracy McGrady 3.00 8.00
YM Yao Ming 5.00 12.00

2003-04 Fleer Avant Materials

Inserted in packs at the overall ratio of one in six packs for all memorabilia cards, this 45-card set parallels the look of the base Avant cards enhanced with a square swatch of game worn memorabilia. Several different versions of this set were issued, a Blue foil version numbered to 400, a Gold foil version numbered to 75 and a Patch version sequentially numbered to 25.

OVERALL MEMORABILIA ODDS 1:6
*BLUE: .4X TO 1X BASE HI
BLUE PRINT RUN 400 SER.#'d SETS
*GOLD: .6X TO 1.5X BASE HI
GOLD PRINT RUN 75 SER.#'d SETS
*PATCH: 1.5X TO 4X BASE HI
PATCH PRINT RUN 25 SER.#'d SETS
BC Brian Cook 1.50 4.00
BD Baron Davis 2.00 5.00
BW Ben Wallace 2.00 5.00
CA Carmelo Anthony 8.00 20.00
CB Chris Bosh 4.00 10.00
CK Chris Kaman 2.50 6.00
DG Drew Gooden 2.00 5.00
DJ Dahntay Jones 2.00 5.00
DW1 Dajuan Wagner 2.00 5.00
DW2 David West 2.50 6.00
DW3 Dwyane Wade 8.00 20.00
JH Jarvis Hayes 1.50 4.00
JK Jason Kidd 4.00 10.00
JO Jermaine O'Neal 2.00 5.00
JR Jason Richardson 2.00 5.00
KG Kevin Garnett 4.00 10.00
LR Luke Ridnour 2.00 5.00
MB1 Marcus Banks 1.50 4.00
MB2 Mike Bibby 2.50 6.00
MD Mike Dunleavy 2.00 5.00
MS Mike Sweetney 1.50 4.00
PG Pau Gasol 2.50 6.00
RA Ray Allen 2.50 6.00
RG Reece Gaines 1.50 4.00
SA Shareef Abdur-Rahim 2.00 5.00
SF Steve Francis 2.00 5.00
SM Stephon Marbury 2.00 5.00
SO Shaquille O'Neal 6.00 15.00
TB Troy Bell 1.50 4.00
TH Travis Hansen 1.50 4.00
TM Tracy McGrady 3.00 8.00
TO Travis Outlaw 2.00 5.00
TP1 Tayshaun Prince 2.00 5.00
WS Wally Szczerbiak 2.00 5.00
YM Yao Ming 5.00 12.00

2003-04 Fleer Avant Stars and Stripes

Randomly seeded in packs, this eight-card set features players on the original 2004 USA Dream Team roster. The cards are set to look like the American flag with a player photo on the left and the player's Dream Team jersey number in a red star on the right. Each card is sequentially numbered to 204.

PRINT RUN 204 SERIAL #'d SETS
1 Ray Allen 4.00 10.00
2 Mike Bibby 4.00 10.00
3 Larry Brown 4.00 10.00
4 Tim Duncan 6.00 15.00
5 Allen Iverson 6.00 15.00
6 Jason Kidd 6.00 15.00
7 Tracy McGrady 5.00 12.00
8 Jermaine O'Neal 3.00 8.00

2003-04 Fleer Avant Stars and Stripes Jerseys

PRINT RUN 500 SER.#'d SETS
*RED SINGLES: .5X TO 1.25X BASE JSY HI
RED PRINT RUN 100 SER.#'d SETS
UNPRICED PATCH PRINT RUN TO USA JSY #
AI Allen Iverson 8.00 20.00
JK Jason Kidd 8.00 20.00
JO Jermaine O'Neal 4.00 10.00
MB Mike Bibby 5.00 12.00
RA Ray Allen 5.00 12.00
TD Tim Duncan 8.00 20.00
TM Tracy McGrady 6.00 15.00

2003-04 Fleer Avant Work of Heart

Inserted randomly, this 15-card set places two-tone brown-scale photos on a card with white borders. Each card is sequentially numbered to 299.

PRINT RUN 299 SERIAL #'d SETS
1 Yao Ming 3.00 8.00
2 Allen Iverson 2.50 6.00
3 Jason Kidd 2.50 6.00
4 Tim Duncan 2.50 6.00
5 Vince Carter 2.50 6.00
6 Ben Wallace 1.25 3.00
7 Dirk Nowitzki 2.50 6.00
8 Carmelo Anthony 5.00 12.00
9 Tracy McGrady 2.50 6.00
10 Kevin Garnett 2.50 6.00
11 Shaquille O'Neal 4.00 10.00
12 LeBron James 100.00 250.00
13 Kobe Bryant 6.00 15.00
14 Paul Pierce 1.50 4.00
15 Chris Webber 1.50 4.00

2003-04 Fleer Avant Work of Heart Jerseys

Sequentially numbered to 300, this 10-card set parallels the base Work of Heart set enhanced with jersey swatches.

PRINT RUN 300 SERIAL #'d SETS
AI Allen Iverson 4.00 10.00
BW Ben Wallace 2.00 5.00
CA Carmelo Anthony 8.00 20.00
DN Dirk Nowitzki 4.00 10.00
JK Jason Kidd 4.00 10.00
KG Kevin Garnett 4.00 10.00
TD Tim Duncan 4.00 10.00
TM Tracy McGrady 3.00 8.00
VC Vince Carter 4.00 10.00
YM Yao Ming 5.00 12.00

2002-03 Fleer Box Score

Released in early February 2003, this 240-card set features 135 base cards, 15 Rookie cards sequentially numbered to 1999, 30 Rising Star rookie cards, 30 All-Star cards, and 30 Around the World cards. Base cards feature full-color player action photography set against a white and silver background with white and silver borders. Rookie card numbers 136-150 utilize the same base card design enhanced with gold backgrounds and borders in place of the silver and Rising Star rookie cards, numbers 151-180, do the same with a shift to bronze. All-Star cards, numbers 181-210, place full color action photography on a yellow star with solid pastel colored backgrounds, and Around the World cards, numbers 211-240, place players on a globe with the Around the World logo along the top of the card which utilizes different nation's flags. Fleer Box Score was packaged in 18-pack boxes where packs contained seven cards and carried an SRP of $4.99. Each box also included a smaller supplemental box which contained a complete set of one of the subsets-Rising Stars, All-Stars, Around the World or Classic Miniatures (parallel base set design-30 cards). Supplemental boxes were all included one memorabilia card. Gold supplemental boxes were available as well containing a seal with a serial number out of 100.

COMP.SET w/o SP's (135) 12.00 30.00
136-150 PRINT RUN 1999 SER.#'d SETS
1 Kwame Brown .25 .60
2 Eddy Curry .30 .75
3 Allen Iverson .60 1.50
4 Elton Brand .40 1.00
5 Jason Kidd .60 1.50
6 Kedrick Brown .25 .60
7 Elden Campbell .25 .60
8 Jason Richardson .40 1.00
9 Shawn Marion .30 .75
10 John Stockton .50 1.25
11 Theo Ratliff .25 .60
12 Marcus Fizer .25 .60
13 Tony Parker .50 1.25
14 Michael Redd .30 .75
15 Vince Carter .60 1.50
16 Aaron McKie .25 .60
17 Michael Finley .40 1.00
18 Rashard Lewis .40 1.00
19 Steve Nash .50 1.25
20 Reggie Miller .40 1.00
21 Tim Duncan .75 2.00
22 Marcus Camby .25 .60
23 Michael Jordan 3.00 8.00
24 Donnell Harvey .25 .60
25 Michael Dickerson .25 .60
26 James Posey .25 .60
27 Vin Baker .30 .75
28 Antonio McDyess .30 .75
29 Mike Miller .30 .75
30 Karl Malone .50 1.25
31 Corliss Williamson .25 .60
32 Derek Anderson .25 .60
33 Scottie Pippen .60 1.50
34 Paul Pierce .40 1.00
35 Steve Francis .30 .75
36 Terrell Brandon .25 .60
37 Cuttino Mobley .25 .60
38 Ron Artest .40 1.00
39 Jonathan Bender .25 .60
40 Ron Mercer .25 .60
41 Dirk Nowitzki .60 1.50
42 Jermaine O'Neal .30 .75
43 Ray Allen .40 1.00
44 Jason Terry .30 .75
45 Pau Gasol .50 1.25
46 Lamar Odom .30 .75
47 P.J. Brown .25 .60
48 Kurt Thomas .25 .60
49 Grant Hill .50 1.25
50 David Robinson .60 1.50
51 Rasheed Wallace .40 1.00
52 Antawn Jamison .40 1.00
53 Juwan Howard .30 .75
54 Andre Miller .30 .75
55 Kenyon Martin .30 .75
56 Jason Williams .30 .75
57 Travis Best .25 .60
58 Brian Grant .25 .60
59 Keith Van Horn .25 .60
60 Alonzo Mourning .50 1.25
61 Rod Strickland .25 .60
62 Jamal Tinsley .25 .60

63 Sam Cassell .30 .75
64 Jalen Rose .30 .75
65 Tim Thomas .25 .60
66 Eddie Griffin .25 .60
67 Kevin Garnett .60 1.50
68 Darrell Armstrong .25 .60
69 Joe Smith .30 .75
70 Wally Szczerbiak .30 .75
71 Richard Jefferson .40 1.00
72 Chauncey Billups .40 1.00
73 Kerry Kittles .25 .60
74 Stromile Swift .25 .60
75 Dikembe Mutombo .40 1.00
76 Courtney Alexander .25 .60
77 Tony Delk .25 .60
78 Baron Davis .30 .75
79 Ricky Davis .30 .75
80 Vlade Divac .30 .75
81 Allan Houston .30 .75
82 Richard Hamilton .30 .75
83 Moochie Norris .25 .60
84 Quentin Richardson .30 .75
85 Charlie Ward .25 .60
86 Troy Hudson .25 .60
87 Pat Garrity .25 .60
88 Kobe Bryant 1.50 4.00
89 Tracy McGrady .60 1.50
90 Clifford Robinson .25 .60
91 Glenn Robinson .30 .75
92 Todd MacCulloch .25 .60
93 Lamond Murray .25 .60
94 Eric Snow .25 .60
95 Eddie Jones .30 .75
96 Tom Gugliotta .25 .60
97 Anfernee Hardaway .60 1.50
98 Stephon Marbury .30 .75
99 Antoine Walker .30 .75
100 Gilbert Arenas .40 1.00
101 Ruben Patterson .25 .60
102 Shane Battier .40 1.00
103 David Wesley .25 .60
104 Damon Stoudamire .30 .75
105 Shaquille O'Neal 1.00 2.50
106 Bonzi Wells .25 .60
107 Mike Bibby .40 1.00
108 Jamal Mashburn .30 .75
109 Peja Stojakovic .40 1.00
110 Latrell Sprewell .30 .75
111 Chris Webber .40 1.00
112 Alvin Williams .25 .60
113 Trenton Hassell .25 .60
114 Derek Fisher .30 .75
115 Malik Rose .25 .60
116 Kenny Anderson .30 .75
117 Zydrunas Ilgauskas .30 .75
118 Raef LaFrentz .25 .60
119 Gary Payton .40 1.00
120 Vladimir Radmanovic .25 .60
121 Darius Miles .25 .60
122 Antonio Davis .25 .60
123 Larry Hughes .30 .75
124 Maurice Taylor .25 .60
125 Morris Peterson .25 .60
126 Nick Van Exel .30 .75
127 Ira Newble .25 .60
128 Eric Williams .25 .60
129 Andrei Kirilenko .40 1.00
130 Ben Wallace .30 .75
131 Tyson Chandler .40 1.00
132 Desmond Mason .30 .75
133 Shareef Abdur-Rahim .30 .75
134 Danny Fortson .25 .60
135 Jerry Stackhouse .30 .75
136 Yao Ming RC 3.00 8.00
137 Juan Dixon RC 1.50 4.00
138 Caron Butler RC 1.50 4.00
139 Drew Gooden RC 1.50 4.00
140 DaJuan Wagner RC 1.25 3.00
141 Jared Jeffries RC 1.25 3.00
142 Pat Burke RC 1.00 2.50
143 Kareem Rush RC 1.25 3.00
144 Ryan Humphrey RC 1.25 3.00
145 Manu Ginobili RC 4.00 10.00
146 Predrag Savovic RC 1.25 3.00
147 Marcus Haislip RC 1.25 3.00
148 John Salmons RC 1.50 4.00
149 Fred Jones RC 1.25 3.00
150 Roger Mason RC 1.25 3.00
151 Jay Williams RS RC 1.00 2.50
152 Mike Dunleavy RS RC 1.00 2.50
153 Carlos Boozer RS RC 1.00 2.50
154 Dan Dickau RS RC .75 2.00
155 Tayshaun Prince RS RC 1.25 3.00
156 Nene Hilario RS RC 1.00 2.50
157 Amare Stoudemire RS RC 1.25 3.00
158 Frank Williams RS RC .60 1.50
159 Chris Wilcox RS RC .75 2.00
160 Robert Archibald RS RC .60 1.50
161 Lonny Baxter RS RC .60 1.50
162 Curtis Borchardt RS RC .60 1.50
163 Sam Clancy RS RC .75 2.00
164 Melvin Ely RS RC .75 2.00
165 Dan Gadzuric RS RC .75 2.00
166 Smush Parker RS RC 1.00 2.50
167 Chris Jefferies RS RC .60 1.50
168 Nikoloz Tskitishvili RS RC .60 1.50
169 Casey Jacobsen RS RC .75 2.00
170 Ronald Murray RS RC 1.00 2.50
171 Gordan Giricek RS RC 1.00 2.50
172 Rasual Butler RS RC 1.00 2.50
173 Jannero Pargo RS RC .60 1.50
174 Bostjan Nachbar RS RC .75 2.00
175 Jiri Welsch RS RC .75 2.00
176 Qyntel Woods RS RC .75 2.00
177 Vincent Yarbrough RS RC .60 1.50
178 Raul Lopez RS RC 1.00 2.50
179 Mehmet Okur RS RC 1.00 2.50
180 Reggie Evans RS RC 1.00 2.50
181 Karl Malone AS .50 1.25
182 Michael Jordan AS 3.00 8.00
183 Glen Rice AS .30 .75
184 John Stockton AS .50 1.25
185 David Robinson AS .60 1.50
186 Shaquille O'Neal AS 1.00 2.50
187 Dikembe Mutombo AS .40 1.00
188 Gary Payton AS .40 1.00
189 Alonzo Mourning AS .50 1.25
190 Scottie Pippen AS .60 1.50
191 Grant Hill AS .50 1.25
192 Vin Baker AS .30 .75
193 Kevin Garnett AS .60 1.50
194 Jason Kidd AS .60 1.50
195 Reggie Miller AS .40 1.00
196 Ray Allen AS .40 1.00
197 Kobe Bryant AS 1.50 4.00
198 Tim Duncan AS .75 2.00
199 Chris Webber AS .40 1.00
200 Anfernee Hardaway AS .60 1.50
201 Latrell Sprewell AS .30 .75
202 Vince Carter AS .60 1.50
203 Allen Iverson AS .60 1.50
204 Eddie Jones AS .30 .75
205 Antoine Walker AS .30 .75
206 Michael Finley AS .40 1.00
207 Tracy McGrady AS .60 1.50
208 Jerry Stackhouse AS .30 .75
209 Glenn Robinson AS .30 .75
210 Allan Houston AS .30 .75
211 Baron Davis AW .30 .75
212 Tony Parker AW .50 1.25
213 Rick Fox AW .25 .60
214 Steve Nash AW .50 1.25
215 Jamaal Magloire AW .25 .60
216 Wang Zhizhi AW .25 .60
217 Mengke Bateer AW .25 .60
218 Dirk Nowitzki AW .60 1.50
219 Jake Tsakalidis AW .25 .60
220 Adonal Foyle AW .25 .60
221 Marko Jaric AW .40 1.00
222 Arvydas Sabonis AW .30 .75
223 Eduardo Najera AW .25 .60
224 Michael Olowokandi AW .25 .60
225 Darius Miles AW .25 .60
226 Andrei Kirilenko AW .40 1.00
227 Mamadou N'Diaye AW .25 .60
228 DeSagana Diop AW .25 .60
229 Rasho Nesterovic AW .25 .60
230 Pau Gasol AW .50 1.25
231 Vladimir Radmanovic AW .25 .60
232 Hedo Turkoglu AW .30 .75
233 Tim Duncan AW .75 2.00
234 Peja Stojakovic AW .40 1.00
235 Toni Kukoc AW .40 1.00
236 Zeljko Rebraca AW .25 .60
237 Vlade Divac AW .30 .75
238 Dikembe Mutombo AW .40 1.00
239 Shareef Abdur-Rahim AW .30 .75
240 Jason Richardson AW .40 1.00

2002-03 Fleer Box Score First Edition

*STARS 1-135: 3X TO 8X BASE CARD HI
*RCs 136-150: 1.25X TO 3X BASE CARD HI
*RCs 151-180: 2X TO 5X BASE HI
*AS 181-210: 3X TO 8X BASE HI
*AW 211-240: 3X TO 8X BASE HI
STATED PRINT RUN 100 SER.#'d SETS

2002-03 Fleer Box Score All-Stars Roster Game-Used

Randomly inserted at the rate of one per All-Stars supplemental box, this 10-card set utilizes the same design as the All-Stars subset cards enhanced with a swatch of game-used memorabilia.

ONE PER ALL-STAR EDITION SEALED SET
ASR1 Malone WU/Duncn/C-Web 4.00 10.00
ASR2 Payton Jsy/Kidd/Stockton 4.00 10.00
ASR3 Hill Jsy/Finley/Allen 4.00 10.00
ASR4 Garnett Jsy/Shaq/Duncan 6.00 15.00
ASR5 Kidd Jsy/Iverson/T-Mac 5.00 12.00
ASR6 Carter Jsy/MJ/Kobe 8.00 20.00
ASR7 Iverson Jsy/MJ/Kobe 6.00 15.00
ASR8 McGrady Jsy/Kobe/Iverson 5.00 12.00
ASR9 Stackhouse Jsy/MJ/Carter 4.00 10.00
ASR10 E.Jones Jsy/Walker/Sprwll 4.00 10.00

2002-03 Fleer Box Score Around the World Memorabilia

Randomly inserted at the rate of one per Around the World supplemental box, this 10-card set utilizes the same design as the Around the World subset cards enhanced with a swatch of game-used memorabilia.

ONE PER AROUND THE WORLD SEALED SET
ATWM1 Tony Parker 4.00 10.00
ATWM2 Steve Nash JSY 4.00 10.00
ATWM3 Wang Zhizhi JSY 2.00 5.00
ATWM4 Dirk Nowitzki JSY 5.00 12.00
ATWM5 Michael Olowokandi JSY 2.00 5.00
ATWM6 Andrei Kirilenko Shirt 3.00 8.00
ATWM7 Pau Gasol Jacket 4.00 10.00
ATWM8 Hedo Turkoglu Pants 2.50 6.00
ATWM9 Peja Stojakovic Pants 3.00 8.00
ATWM10 Dikembe Mutombo Jacket 3.00 8.00

2002-03 Fleer Box Score Box Score Debuts

Randomly seeded in packs, this 15-card set includes a small photo of the featured player along the top, and placed in the middle of the cut-out borders is a piece of newsprint containing the player's debut game statistics. Each card is sequentially numbered to 2002.

STATED PRINT RUN 2002 SERIAL #'d SETS
BSD1 Yao Ming 2.50 6.00
BSD2 Juan Dixon 1.25 3.00
BSD3 Caron Butler 1.25 3.00
BSD4 Drew Gooden 1.25 3.00
BSD5 DaJuan Wagner 1.00 2.50
BSD6 Jared Jeffries 1.00 2.50
BSD7 Manu Ginobili 3.00 8.00
BSD8 Kareem Rush 1.00 2.50
BSD9 Jay Williams 1.25 3.00
BSD10 Mike Dunleavy 1.25 3.00
BSD11 Chris Wilcox 1.00 2.50
BSD12 Dan Dickau 1.00 2.50
BSD13 Tayshaun Prince 1.50 4.00
BSD14 Nene Hilario 1.25 3.00
BSD15 Amare Stoudemire 1.50 4.00

2002-03 Fleer Box Score Classic Miniatures

Randomly inserted in boxes as a Supplemental box, this 30-card set uses the base design on card that measure 2 1/2" X 3 1/4".

COMP.SEALED SET (31) 15.00 40.00
SET: RANDOMLY INSERTED INTO BOXES
*1ST EDITION: 1.5X TO 4X MINIATURE HI
1ST EDITION PRINT RUN 100 SETS
CM1 Glenn Robinson .50 1.25
CM2 Paul Pierce .60 1.50
CM3 Jalen Rose .50 1.25
CM4 Darius Miles .40 1.00
CM5 Dirk Nowitzki 1.00 2.50
CM6 Jason Richardson .60 1.50
CM7 Antawn Jamison .60 1.50
CM8 Steve Francis .50 1.25
CM9 Reggie Miller .60 1.50
CM10 Jermaine O'Neal .50 1.25
CM11 Elton Brand .60 1.50
CM12 Kobe Bryant 2.50 6.00
CM13 Shaquille O'Neal 1.50 4.00
CM14 Pau Gasol .75 2.00
CM15 Ray Allen .60 1.50
CM16 Kevin Garnett 1.00 2.50
CM17 Jason Kidd 1.00 2.50
CM18 Baron Davis .50 1.25
CM19 Grant Hill .75 2.00
CM20 Tracy McGrady 1.00 2.50
CM21 Allen Iverson 1.00 2.50
CM22 Shawn Marion .50 1.25
CM23 Mike Bibby .60 1.50
CM24 Chris Webber .60 1.50
CM25 Tim Duncan 1.25 3.00
CM26 David Robinson 1.00 2.50
CM27 Gary Payton .60 1.50
CM28 Vince Carter 1.00 2.50
CM29 John Stockton .75 2.00
CM30 Michael Jordan 5.00 12.00

2002-03 Fleer Box Score Classic Miniatures Game-Used

Randomly inserted at the rate of one per Classic Miniatures supplemental box, this 10-card set utilizes the same design as the Classic Miniatures subset cards enhanced with a swatch of game-used memorabilia.

ONE PER SEALED MINI SET
CMGU1 Elton Brand JSY 3.00 8.00
CMGU2 Steve Francis JSY 2.50 6.00
CMGU3 Jason Kidd JSY 5.00 12.00
CMGU4 Jermaine O'Neal JSY 2.50 6.00
CMGU5 Antawn Jamison Jacket 3.00 8.00
CMGU6 Mike Bibby JSY 3.00 8.00
CMGU7 Grant Hill JSY 4.00 10.00
CMGU8 Dirk Nowitzki JSY 5.00 12.00
CMGU9 Paul Pierce JSY 3.00 8.00
CMGU10 Allen Iverson JSY 5.00 12.00

2002-03 Fleer Box Score Dish and Swish

Randomly inserted in packs at the rate of one in nine, this 20-card set showcases full-color player action photography set against a blacked-out true live background with the word"DISH" or "SWISH" in large letters along the top and red foil highlights.

COMPLETE SET (20) 10.00 25.00
STATED ODDS 1:9
DS1 Jason Terry .60 1.50
DS2 Shareef Abdur-Rahim .60 1.50
DS3 Andre Miller .60 1.50
DS4 Elton Brand .75 2.00
DS5 Tracy McGrady 1.25 3.00
DS6 Grant Hill 1.00 2.50
DS7 Allen Iverson 1.25 3.00
DS8 Keith Van Horn .60 1.50
DS9 Mike Bibby .75 2.00
DS10 Chris Webber .75 2.00
DS11 Jason Kidd 1.25 3.00
DS12 Kenyon Martin .60 1.50
DS13 Steve Nash 1.00 2.50
DS14 Dirk Nowitzki 1.25 3.00
DS15 John Stockton 1.00 2.50
DS16 Karl Malone 1.00 2.50
DS17 Paul Pierce .75 2.00
DS18 Antoine Walker .60 1.50
DS19 Shane Battier .75 2.00
DS20 Pau Gasol 1.00 2.50

2002-03 Fleer Box Score Dish and Swish Dual

Randomly seeded in packs at the rate of one in 108, this 10-card set utilizes the same design as the base Dish and Swish cards in a two-sided format where the "dish" player appears on one side and the "swish" player on the other.

COMPLETE SET (10) 20.00 50.00
STATED ODDS 1:108
DSD1 J.Terry/S.Abdur-Rahim 2.00 5.00
DSD2 A.Miller/E.Brand 2.50 6.00
DSD3 T.McGrady/G.Hill 4.00 10.00
DSD4 A.Iverson/K.Van Horn 4.00 10.00
DSD5 M.Bibby/C.Webber 2.50 6.00
DSD6 J.Kidd/K.Martin 4.00 10.00
DSD7 S.Nash/D.Nowitzki 4.00 10.00
DSD8 J.Stockton/K.Malone 3.00 8.00
DSD9 P.Pierce/A.Walker 2.50 6.00
DSD10 S.Battier/P.Gasol 3.00 8.00

2002-03 Fleer Box Score Dish and Swish Memorabilia

Randomly inserted in packs at the rate of one in 12, this 20-card set parallels the design on the base Dish and Swish set enahnced with a swatch of game used memorabilia. Several different materials were used and are cataloged below.

STATED ODDS 1:12
DSM1 Jason Terry JSY 2.50 6.00
DSM2 Shareef Abdur-Rahim Jacket 2.50 6.00
DSM3 Andre Miller Shorts 2.50 6.00
DSM4 Elton Brand Shorts 3.00 8.00
DSM5 Tracy McGrady Jacket 5.00 12.00
DSM6 Grant Hill Pants 4.00 10.00
DSM7 Allen Iverson Shorts 5.00 12.00
DSM8 Keith Van Horn Pants 2.50 6.00
DSM9 Mike Bibby Jacket 3.00 8.00
DSM10 Chris Webber Pants 3.00 8.00
DSM11 Jason Kidd JSY 5.00 12.00
DSM12 Kenyon Martin Shorts 2.50 6.00
DSM13 Steve Nash JSY 4.00 10.00
DSM14 Dirk Nowitzki JSY 5.00 12.00
DSM15 John Stockton Pants 4.00 10.00
DSM16 Karl Malone Jacket 4.00 10.00
DSM17 Paul Pierce JSY 3.00 8.00
DSM18 Antoine Walker JSY 2.50 6.00
DSM19 Shane Battier JSY 3.00 8.00
DSM20 Pau Gasol JSY 4.00 10.00

2002-03 Fleer Box Score Freshman Orientation

Randomly inserted at one per Rising Stars supplemental box, this 10-card set has a horizontal design with a full color player action photo on the right and a swatch of game used memorabilia on the left against a white background.

ONE PER RISING STARS SEALED SET
FO1 Amare Stoudemire Shirt 4.00 10.00
FO2 Lonny Baxter Shirt 2.00 5.00
FO5 Yao Ming JSY 6.00 15.00
FO6 Gordan Giricek Shirt 3.00 8.00
FO7 Caron Butler Shorts 3.00 8.00
FO8 Drew Gooden Shirt 3.00 8.00
FO9 DaJuan Wagner Shirt 2.50 6.00
FO10 Jared Jeffries Shirt 2.50 6.00

2002-03 Fleer Box Score Press Clippings

Randomly inserted at the rate of one in 18, this 15-card set features a horizontal design with a full color player action photo on one side and a montage of newspaper articles on the other. There are no true borders on these cards, however, outside coloring matches the featured player's team colors. Each card is enhanced with silver foil highlights.

COMPLETE SET (15) 12.50 30.00
STATED ODDS 1:18
PC1 Vince Carter 1.25 3.00
PC2 Jason Richardson .75 2.00
PC3 Stephon Marbury .60 1.50
PC4 Steve Francis .60 1.50
PC5 Ray Allen .75 2.00
PC6 Peja Stojakovic .75 2.00
PC7 Baron Davis .60 1.50
PC8 Reggie Miller .75 2.00
PC9 Darius Miles .50 1.25
PC10 Kevin Garnett 1.25 3.00
PC11 Tim Duncan 1.50 4.00
PC12 Michael Jordan 8.00 20.00
PC13 Shaquille O'Neal 2.00 5.00
PC14 Latrell Sprewell .60 1.50
PC15 Kobe Bryant 3.00 8.00

2002-03 Fleer Box Score Press Clippings Memorabilia

Randomly seeded in packs at the rate of one in 12, this 10-card set paralells the base Press Clippings insert enahanced with a swatch of game used memorabilia. Patch versions were also issued and cards are sequentially numbered to 50.

STATED ODDS 1:12
*PATCH: 1.5X TO 4X BASE HI
PATCH PRINT RUN 50 SER.#'d SETS
PCM1 Vince Carter JSY 5.00 12.00
PCM2 Jason Richardson Jacket 3.00 8.00
PCM3 Stephon Marbury JSY 2.50 6.00
PCM4 Steve Francis JSY 2.50 6.00
PCM6 Peja Stojakovic JSY 3.00 8.00
PCM7 Baron Davis Shirt 2.50 6.00
PCM8 Reggie Miller Shorts 3.00 8.00
PCM9 Darius Miles JSY 2.00 5.00
PCM10 Kevin Garnett JSY 5.00 12.00

1998-99 Fleer Brilliants

The debut 125-card set of Fleer Brilliants was released as a single series in five-card packs with a suggested retail price of $4.99. Card fronts feature a silver mirrored styrene card with a background swirl pattern. Card backs are horizontal with vitals and last year's statistics. The rookie cards were slightly shortprinted, inserted at a rate of one in two packs.

COMPLETE SET (125) 25.00 60.00
COMPLETE SET w/o SP (100) 15.00 30.00
RC: STATED ODDS 1:2
1 Tim Duncan .60 1.50
2 Dikembe Mutombo .30 .75
3 Steve Nash .50 1.25
4 Charles Barkley .50 1.25
5 Eddie Jones .30 .75
6 Ray Allen .40 1.00
7 Stephon Marbury .40 1.00
8 Anfernee Hardaway .50 1.25
9 Gary Payton .30 .75
10 Ron Mercer .25 .60
11 Nick Van Exel .25 .60
12 Brent Barry .25 .60
13 Allan Houston .25 .60
14 Avery Johnson .25 .60
15 Shareef Abdur-Rahim .30 .75
16 Rod Strickland .20 .50
17 Vin Baker .25 .60
18 Patrick Ewing .40 1.00
19 Maurice Taylor .20 .50
20 Shawn Kemp .30 .75
21 Michael Finley .30 .75
22 Reggie Miller .40 1.00
23 Joe Smith .25 .60
24 Toni Kukoc .30 .75
25 Blue Edwards .20 .50
26 Joe Dumars .30 .75
27 Tom Gugliotta .20 .50
28 Terrell Brandon .20 .50
29 Erick Dampier .20 .50
30 Antonio McDyess .25 .60
31 Donyell Marshall .20 .50
32 Jeff Hornacek .25 .60
33 David Wesley .20 .50
34 Derek Anderson .20 .50
35 Ron Harper .25 .60
36 John Starks .25 .60
37 Kenny Anderson .25 .60
38 Anthony Mason .20 .50
39 Brevin Knight .20 .50
40 Antoine Walker .30 .75
41 Mookie Blaylock .20 .50
42 LaPhonso Ellis .20 .50
43 Tim Hardaway .30 .75
44 Jim Jackson .20 .50
45 Matt Maloney .20 .50
46 Lamond Murray .20 .50
47 Voshon Lenard .20 .50
48 Isaiah Rider .25 .60
49 Tracy Murray .20 .50
50 Grant Hill .50 1.25
51 Vlade Divac .30 .75
52 Glenn Robinson .25 .60
53 Tony Battie .25 .60
54 Bobby Jackson .20 .50
55 Jayson Williams .20 .50
56 Doug Christie .20 .50
57 Glen Rice .30 .75
58 Tim Thomas .30 .75
59 Lindsey Hunter .20 .50
60 Scottie Pippen .50 1.25
61 Marcus Camby .25 .60
61B Keith Van Horn Promo .60 1.50
62 Clifford Robinson .20 .50
63 John Wallace .20 .50
64 Larry Johnson .30 .75
65 Bryon Russell .20 .50
66 Isaac Austin .20 .50
67 Sam Cassell .25 .60
68 Allen Iverson .60 1.50
69 Chauncey Billups .40 1.00
70 Kobe Bryant 1.25 3.00
71 Kevin Willis .20 .50
72 Jason Kidd .50 1.25
73 Chris Webber .30 .75
74 Rasheed Wallace .30 .75
75 Karl Malone .40 1.00
76 Shawn Bradley .20 .50
77 Kerry Kittles .20 .50
78 Mitch Richmond .30 .75
79 Antonio Daniels .20 .50
80 Kevin Garnett .50 1.25
81 Nick Anderson .20 .50
82 David Robinson .50 1.25
83 Jamal Mashburn .25 .60
84 Rodney Rogers .20 .50
85 Michael Stewart .20 .50
86 Rik Smits .25 .60
87 Billy Owens .20 .50
88 Damon Stoudamire .25 .60
89 Theo Ratliff .25 .60
90 Keith Van Horn .30 .75
91 Hakeem Olajuwon .40 1.00
92 Alonzo Mourning .40 1.00
93 Steve Smith .25 .60
94 Mark Jackson .25 .60
95 Cedric Ceballos .20 .50
96 Bryant Reeves .20 .50
97 Juwan Howard .25 .60
98 Detlef Schrempf .30 .75
99 John Stockton .40 1.00
100 Shaquille O'Neal .75 2.00
101 Michael Olowokandi RC .75 2.00
102 Mike Bibby RC 1.00 2.50
103 Raef LaFrentz RC .75 2.00
104 Antawn Jamison RC 1.00 2.50
105 Vince Carter RC 3.00 8.00
106 Robert Traylor RC .60 1.50
107 Jason Williams RC 1.50 4.00
108 Larry Hughes RC 1.25 3.00
109 Dirk Nowitzki RC 4.00 10.00
110 Paul Pierce RC 2.50 6.00
111 Bonzi Wells RC .60 1.50
112 Michael Doleac RC .50 1.25
113 Keon Clark RC .60 1.50
114 Michael Dickerson RC .60 1.50
115 Matt Harpring RC .60 1.50
116 Bryce Drew RC .40 1.00
117 Pat Garrity RC .50 1.25
118 Roshown McLeod RC .40 1.00
119 Ricky Davis RC 1.00 2.50
120 Rashard Lewis RC 1.50 4.00
121 Tyronn Lue RC .60 1.50
122 Al Harrington RC 1.00 2.50
123 Corey Benjamin RC .40 1.00
124 Felipe Lopez RC .40 1.00
125 Korleone Young RC .60 1.50

1998-99 Fleer Brilliants 24-Karat Gold

*STARS: 40X TO 100X BASE CARD HI
*RCs: 10X TO 25X BASE HI
STATED PRINT RUN 24 SERIAL #'d SETS
1 Tim Duncan 200.00 500.00
4 Charles Barkley 200.00 500.00
8 Anfernee Hardaway 150.00 400.00
20 Shawn Kemp 100.00 250.00
36 John Starks 60.00 150.00
40 Antoine Walker 100.00 250.00
50 Grant Hill 200.00 500.00
60 Scottie Pippen 200.00 500.00
70 Kobe Bryant 400.00 800.00
74 Rasheed Wallace 150.00 400.00
80 Kevin Garnett 125.00 300.00
92 Alonzo Mourning 75.00 150.00
100 Shaquille O'Neal 100.00 250.00
104 Antawn Jamison 60.00 150.00
105 Vince Carter 150.00 300.00
109 Dirk Nowitzki 400.00 800.00

1998-99 Fleer Brilliants Blue

COMPLETE SET (125) 40.00 100.00
*STARS: .75X TO 2X BASE CARD HI
*RCs: .5X TO 1.25X BASE
STARS: STATED ODDS 1:3
RCs: STATED ODDS 1:6

1998-99 Fleer Brilliants Gold

*STARS: 15X TO 40X BASE CARD HI
*RCs: 5X TO 12X BASE HI
STATED PRINT RUN 99 SERIAL #'d SETS
105 Vince Carter 60.00 150.00
109 Dirk Nowitzki 100.00 250.00
110 Paul Pierce 40.00 100.00

1998-99 Fleer Brilliants Illuminators

Randomly inserted in packs at one in ten, this 15-card set features young superstars who light up the scoreboard. The cards are printed on thick styrene with highly reflective mirrored foil.

COMPLETE SET (15) 15.00 40.00
STATED ODDS 1:10
1 Michael Olowokandi 1.00 2.50
2 Mike Bibby 1.25 3.00
3 Antawn Jamison 1.25 3.00
4 Vince Carter 4.00 10.00
5 Robert Traylor .75 2.00
6 Larry Hughes 1.50 4.00
7 Paul Pierce 3.00 8.00
8 Raef LaFrentz 1.00 2.50
9 Dirk Nowitzki 5.00 12.00
10 Corey Benjamin .50 1.25
11 Michael Dickerson .75 2.00
12 Roshown McLeod .50 1.25
13 Ricky Davis 1.25 3.00
14 Tyronn Lue .75 2.00
15 Al Harrington 1.25 3.00

1998-99 Fleer Brilliants Shining Stars

Randomly inserted in packs at one in 20, this 15-card set features some of the NBA's top veterans. The cards are printed on two-sided mirrored foil.

COMPLETE SET (15) 12.00 30.00
STATED ODDS 1:20
*PULSARS: 4X TO 10X HI COLUMN
PULSARS: STATED ODDS 1:400
1 Tim Thomas 1.25 3.00
2 Antoine Walker 1.25 3.00
3 Tim Duncan 2.50 6.00
4 Keith Van Horn 1.25 3.00
5 Grant Hill 2.00 5.00
6 Shaquille O'Neal 3.00 8.00
7 Kevin Garnett 2.00 5.00
8 Allen Iverson 2.50 6.00
9 Shareef Abdur-Rahim 1.25 3.00
10 Shawn Kemp 1.25 3.00
11 Anfernee Hardaway 2.00 5.00
12 Scottie Pippen 2.00 5.00
13 Stephon Marbury 1.50 4.00
14 Kobe Bryant 5.00 12.00
15 Ron Mercer 1.00 2.50

1994-95 Fleer European

This 270-card standard-size set was issued by Fleer for the French, Italian, German and Spanish markets. The cards were distributed in 8-card packs (30 packs per box). The set closely parallels the American 1994-95 Fleer issue. Unlike other U.S.-based foreign issues, these cards contain no foreign text but the wrapper and box are multi-lingual. A selection of cards share common numbers with the American versions, making them almost impossible to separately identify (for example card #1 Stacey Augmon). In these cases, the only difference can be found in the tiny trademark print on the card backs. European cards all say "1995 Fleer Corp." and American versions all say "1994 Fleer Corp.". The card fronts feature color player action shots surrounded by white borders. The player's name, team and position appear in team color-coded lettering set on an irregular team color-coded foil patch at the lower left. The black-bordered back carries a color player action shot on the left side, with the player's name, biography, team logo, and statistics displayed on the right. The cards are numbered on the back and grouped alphabetically according to teams.

COMPLETE SET (270) 15.00 40.00
1 Stacey Augmon .15 .40
2 Sergei Bazarevich .20 .50
3 Mookie Blaylock .12 .30
4 Tyrone Corbin .12 .30
5 Craig Ehlo .12 .30
6 Andrew Lang .12 .30
7 Grant Long .12 .30
8 Ken Norman .12 .30
9 Steve Smith .15 .40
10 Dee Brown .12 .30
11 Sherman Douglas .12 .30
12 Acie Earl .12 .30
13 Blue Edwards .12 .30
14 Rick Fox .12 .30
15 Xavier McDaniel .12 .30
16 Greg Minor .20 .50
17 Eric Montross .15 .40
18 Dino Radja .12 .30
19 Dominique Wilkins .25 .60
20 Michael Adams .12 .30
21 Muggsy Bogues .15 .40
22 Scott Burrell .12 .30
23 Dell Curry .12 .30
24 Kenny Gattison .12 .30
25 Hersey Hawkins .12 .30
26 Larry Johnson .20 .50
27 Alonzo Mourning .25 .60
28 Robert Parish .20 .50
29 David Wingate .12 .30
30 B.J. Armstrong .12 .30
31 Corie Blount .12 .30
32 Steve Kerr .15 .40
33 Larry Krystkowiak .12 .30
34 Toni Kukoc .25 .60
35 Luc Longley .15 .40
36 Will Perdue .12 .30
37 Scottie Pippen .40 1.00
38 Dickey Simpkins .15 .40
39 Terrell Brandon .12 .30
40 Brad Daugherty .15 .40
41 Tyrone Hill .12 .30
42 Chris Mills .12 .30
43 Bobby Phills .12 .30
44 Mark Price .20 .50
45 Gerald Wilkins .12 .30
46 John Williams .12 .30
47 Tony Dumas .20 .50
48 Jim Jackson .12 .30
49 Popeye Jones .12 .30
50 Jason Kidd 1.00 2.50
51 Jamal Mashburn .20 .50
52 Doug Smith .12 .30
53 Roy Tarpley .12 .30
54 Mahmoud Abdul-Rauf .12 .30
55 Dale Ellis .12 .30
56 LaPhonso Ellis .12 .30
57 Dikembe Mutombo .20 .50
58 Robert Pack .12 .30
59 Rodney Rogers .12 .30
60 Jalen Rose .50 1.25
61 Bryant Stith .12 .30
62 Brian Williams .12 .30
63 Reggie Williams .12 .30
64 Bill Curley .12 .30
65 Johnny Dawkins .12 .30
66 Joe Dumars .20 .50
67 Grant Hill 1.00 2.50
68 Allan Houston .20 .50
69 Lindsey Hunter .12 .30
70 Oliver Miller .12 .30
71 Terry Mills .12 .30
72 Mark West .12 .30
73 Victor Alexander .12 .30
74 Manute Bol .12 .30
75 Chris Gatling .12 .30
76 Tim Hardaway .20 .50
77 Chris Mullin .20 .50
78 Ricky Pierce .12 .30
79 Clifford Rozier .12 .30
80 Rony Seikaly .12 .30
81 Latrell Sprewell .25 .60
82 Chris Webber .30 .75
83 Scott Brooks .12 .30
84 Sam Cassell .20 .50
85 Mario Elie .12 .30
86 Carl Herrera .12 .30
87 Robert Horry .20 .50
88 Vernon Maxwell .12 .30
89 Hakeem Olajuwon .25 .60
90 Kenny Smith .15 .40
91 Otis Thorpe .12 .30
92 Antonio Davis .12 .30
93 Dale Davis .12 .30
94 Vern Fleming .12 .30
95 Mark Jackson .15 .40
96 Derrick McKey .12 .30
97 Reggie Miller .25 .60
98 Byron Scott .15 .40
99 Rik Smits .15 .40
100 John Williams .12 .30
101 Haywoode Workman .12 .30
102 Terry Dehere .12 .30
103 Gary Grant .12 .30
104 Lamond Murray .20 .50
105 Eric Piatkowski .25 .60
106 Pooh Richardson .12 .30
107 Malik Sealy .12 .30
108 Elmore Spencer .12 .30
109 Loy Vaught .12 .30
110 Elden Campbell .12 .30
111 Cedric Ceballos .12 .30
112 Vlade Divac .20 .50
113 Eddie Jones .60 1.50
114 George Lynch .12 .30
115 Anthony Peeler .12 .30
116 Tony Smith .12 .30
117 Sedale Threatt .12 .30
118 Nick Van Exel .20 .50
119 Bimbo Coles .12 .30
120 Kevin Gamble .12 .30
121 Harold Miner .12 .30
122 Billy Owens .12 .30
123 Khalid Reeves .15 .40
124 Glen Rice .20 .50
125 John Salley .12 .30
126 Kevin Willis .12 .30
127 Vin Baker .20 .50
128 Jon Barry .12 .30
129 Todd Day .12 .30
130 Lee Mayberry .12 .30
131 Eric Mobley .12 .30
132 Eric Murdock .12 .30
133 Johnny Newman .12 .30
134 Glenn Robinson .40 1.00
135 Mike Brown .12 .30
136 Stacey King .12 .30
137 Christian Laettner .15 .40
138 Donyell Marshall .20 .50
139 Isaiah Rider .20 .50
140 Sean Rooks .12 .30
141 Doug West .12 .30
142 Micheal Williams .12 .30
143 Kenny Anderson .15 .40
144 Benoit Benjamin .12 .30
145 P.J. Brown .12 .30
146 Derrick Coleman .15 .40
147 Yinka Dare .12 .30
148 Kevin Edwards .12 .30
149 Sleepy Floyd .12 .30
150 Armon Gilliam .12 .30
151 Chris Morris .12 .30
152 Greg Anthony .12 .30
153 Hubert Davis .12 .30
154 Patrick Ewing .25 .60
155 Derek Harper .15 .40
156 Anthony Mason .12 .30
157 Charles Oakley .15 .40
158 Doc Rivers .15 .40
159 Charles Smith .12 .30
160 John Starks .15 .40
161 Charlie Ward .20 .50
162 Monty Williams .15 .40
163 Nick Anderson .12 .30
164 Anthony Avent .12 .30
165 Horace Grant .15 .40
166 Anfernee Hardaway .30 .75
167 Shaquille O'Neal .50 1.25
168 Donald Royal .12 .30
169 Dennis Scott .12 .30
170 Brooks Thompson .15 .40
171 Jeff Turner .12 .30
172 Dana Barros .12 .30
173 Shawn Bradley .12 .30
174 Jeff Malone .12 .30
175 Tim Perry .12 .30
176 B.J. Tyler .12 .30
177 Clarence Weatherspoon .12 .30
178 Sharone Wright .15 .40
179 Danny Ainge .20 .50
180 Charles Barkley .30 .75
181 A.C. Green .15 .40
182 Kevin Johnson .20 .50
183 Joe Kleine .12 .30
184 Dan Majerle .20 .50
185 Danny Manning .15 .40
186 Wesley Person .20 .50
187 Wayman Tisdale .12 .30
188 Clyde Drexler .25 .60
189 Harvey Grant .12 .30
190 Jerome Kersey .12 .30
191 Aaron McKie .20 .50
192 Tracy Murray .12 .30
193 Terry Porter .12 .30
194 Clifford Robinson .12 .30
195 Rod Strickland .12 .30
196 Buck Williams .12 .30
197 Brian Grant .30 .75
198 Bobby Hurley .12 .30
199 Olden Polynice .12 .30
200 Mitch Richmond .20 .50
201 Lionel Simmons .12 .30
202 Spud Webb .15 .40
203 Walt Williams .12 .30
204 Trevor Wilson .12 .30
205 Willie Anderson .12 .30
206 Terry Cummings .15 .40
207 Vinny Del Negro .12 .30
208 Sean Elliott .20 .50
209 Avery Johnson .15 .40
210 Moses Malone .20 .50
211 J.R. Reid .12 .30
212 David Robinson .30 .75
213 Dennis Rodman .40 1.00
214 Bill Cartwright .15 .40
215 Kendall Gill .12 .30
216 Ervin Johnson .12 .30
217 Shawn Kemp .20 .50
218 Sarunas Marciulionis .12 .30
219 Nate McMillan .12 .30
220 Gary Payton .20 .50
221 Sam Perkins .12 .30
222 Detlef Schrempf .20 .50
223 David Benoit .12 .30
224 Jeff Hornacek .15 .40
225 Jay Humphries .12 .30
226 Karl Malone .25 .60
227 Bryon Russell .12 .30
228 Felton Spencer .12 .30
229 John Stockton .25 .60
230 Mitchell Butler .12 .30
231 Rex Chapman .12 .30
232 Calbert Cheaney .12 .30
233 Kevin Duckworth .12 .30
234 Tom Gugliotta .12 .30
235 Don MacLean .12 .30
236 Gheorghe Muresan .12 .30
237 Scott Skiles .12 .30
238 Atlanta Hawks .12 .30
239 Boston Celtics .12 .30
240 Charlotte Hornets .12 .30
241 Chicago Bulls .12 .30
242 Cleveland Cavaliers .12 .30
243 Dallas Mavericks .12 .30
244 Denver Nuggets .12 .30
245 Detroit Pistons .12 .30
246 Golden State Warriors .12 .30
247 Houston Rockets .12 .30
248 Indiana Pacers .12 .30
249 Los Angeles Clippers .12 .30
250 Los Angeles Lakers .12 .30
251 Miami Heat .12 .30
252 Milwaukee Bucks .12 .30
253 Minnesota Timberwolves .12 .30
254 New Jersey Nets .12 .30
255 New York Knicks .12 .30
256 Orlando Magic .12 .30
257 Philadelphia 76ers .12 .30
258 Phoenix Suns .12 .30
259 Portland Trail Blazers .12 .30
260 Sacramento Kings .12 .30
261 San Antonio Spurs .12 .30
262 Seattle Supersonics .12 .30
263 Utah Jazz .12 .30
264 Washington Bullets .12 .30
265 Toronto Raptors .12 .30
266 Vancouver Grizzlies .12 .30
267 NBA Logo .12 .30
268 Checklist 1-103 .12 .30
269 Checklist 104-204 .12 .30
270 Checklist 205-270 .12 .30
(Checklist Insert Sets)

1994-95 Fleer European All-Defensive

Randomly inserted in Fleer European packs at an approximate rate of one in six, these five standard-size, double-sided cards feature first and second team All-NBA Defensive teams. The cards are borderless with color player action shots that have been faded to black and white. The player's name and first or second team designation appear in silver foil lettering near the bottom. The cards are unnumbered and checklisted below in alphabetical order.

COMPLETE SET (5) 1.25 3.00
1 Mookie Blaylock .60 1.50
Scottie Pippen
2 Horace Grant .30 .75
Gary Payton
3 Nate McMillan .60 1.50
Dennis Rodman
4 Charles Oakley .50 1.25
David Robinson
5 Hakeem Olajuwon .40 1.00
Latrell Sprewell

1994-95 Fleer European Award Winners

Randomly inserted in Fleer European packs at an approximate rate of one in twelve, these two standard-size, double-sided cards highlight four NBA award winners from the 1993-94 season. The cards feature multiple player images. The player's name and his award appear at the bottom in gold- foil lettering. The cards are unnumbered and checklisted below in alphabetical order.

COMPLETE SET (2) .60 1.50

Card	Low	High
1 Dell Curry	.60	1.50
Chris Webber		
2 Don MacLean	.50	1.25
Hakeem Olajuwon		

1994-95 Fleer European Career Achievement Awards

Randomly inserted in Fleer European packs at an approximate rate of one in twelve, these two standard-size, double-sided cards highlight four NBA veteran superstars. The borderless cards feature color player action cutouts against a larger facial background shot. Unlike their American counterparts, the backgrounds of these cards are not foil-coated. The player's name appears in gold-foil lettering in a lower corner. The cards are unnumbered and checklisted below in alphabetical order.

Card	Low	High
COMPLETE SET (2)	1.50	4.00
1 Patrick Ewing	1.00	2.50
Karl Malone		
2 Hakeem Olajuwon	1.50	4.00
Scottie Pippen		

1994-95 Fleer European League Leaders

Randomly inserted in Fleer European packs at an approximate rate of one in five, these four standard-size, double-sided cards showcase eight NBA statistical leaders from the 1993-94 season. The cards feature a horizontal design with color player cutouts set on hardwood backgrounds. The player's name and the category in which he led the NBA appear in gold-foil lettering at the bottom. The cards are unnumbered and checklisted below in alphabetical order.

Card	Low	High
COMPLETE SET (4)	1.25	3.00
1 Mahmoud Abdul-Rauf	.60	1.50
Dennis Rodman		
2 Tracy Murray	.30	.75
Dikembe Mutombo		
3 Shaquille O'Neal	.75	2.00
David Robinson		
4 John Stockton	.40	1.00
Nate McMillan		

1994-95 Fleer European Triple Threats

Randomly inserted in Fleer European packs at an approximate rate of one in five, these five standard-size, double-sided cards highlight ten multi-dimensional NBA stars. The cards are borderless with multiple color player action cutouts on black backgrounds highlighted by colorful basketball court designs. The player's name appears in gold- foil lettering in a lower corner. The cards are unnumbered and checklisted below in alphabetical order.

Card	Low	High
COMPLETE SET (5)	2.00	5.00
1 Mookie Blaylock	.60	1.50
Reggie Miller		
2 Patrick Ewing	1.25	3.00
Shaquille O'Neal		
3 Shawn Kemp	.75	2.00
David Robinson		
4 Karl Malone	.60	1.50
Latrell Sprewell		
5 Hakeem Olajuwon	1.00	2.50
Scottie Pippen		

1995-96 Fleer European

Card	Low	High
COMPLETE SET (499)	20.00	50.00
1 Stacey Augmon	.12	.30
2 Mookie Blaylock	.10	.25
3 Craig Ehlo	.10	.25
4 Andrew Lang	.10	.25
5 Grant Long	.10	.25
6 Ken Norman	.10	.25
7 Steve Smith	.12	.30
8 Dee Brown	.10	.25
9 Sherman Douglas	.10	.25
10 Eric Montross	.10	.25
11 Dino Radja	.10	.25
12 David Wesley	.10	.25
13 Dominique Wilkins	.20	.50
14 Muggsy Bogues	.12	.30
15 Scott Burrell	.10	.25
16 Dell Curry	.10	.25
17 Hersey Hawkins	.10	.25
18 Larry Johnson	.15	.40
19 Alonzo Mourning	.20	.50
20 Robert Parish	.15	.40
21 B.J. Armstrong	.10	.25
22 Michael Jordan	1.25	3.00
23 Steve Kerr	.12	.30
24 Toni Kukoc	.15	.40
25 Will Perdue	.10	.25
26 Scottie Pippen	.25	.60
27 Terrell Brandon	.10	.25
28 Tyrone Hill	.10	.25
29 Chris Mills	.10	.25
30 Bobby Phills	.10	.25
31 Mark Price	.15	.40
32 John Williams	.10	.25
33 Lucious Harris	.10	.25
34 Jim Jackson	.10	.25
35 Popeye Jones	.10	.25
36 Jason Kidd	.25	.60
37 Jamal Mashburn	.15	.40
38 George McCloud	.10	.25
39 Roy Tarpley	.10	.25
40 Lorenzo Williams	.10	.25
41 Mahmoud Abdul-Rauf	.10	.25
42 Dale Ellis	.10	.25
43 LaPhonso Ellis	.10	.25
44 Dikembe Mutombo	.15	.40
45 Robert Pack	.10	.25
46 Rodney Rogers	.10	.25
47 Jalen Rose	.20	.50
48 Bryant Stith	.10	.25
49 Reggie Williams	.10	.25
50 Joe Dumars	.15	.40
51 Grant Hill	.25	.60
52 Allan Houston	.12	.30
53 Lindsey Hunter	.10	.25
54 Oliver Miller	.10	.25
55 Terry Mills	.10	.25
56 Mark West	.10	.25
57 Chris Gatling	.10	.25
58 Tim Hardaway	.15	.40
59 Donyell Marshall	.10	.25
60 Chris Mullin	.15	.40
61 Carlos Rogers	.10	.25
62 Clifford Rozier	.10	.25
63 Rony Seikaly	.10	.25
64 Latrell Sprewell	.15	.40
65 Sam Cassell	.15	.40
66 Clyde Drexler	.20	.50
67 Mario Elie	.10	.25
68 Carl Herrera	.10	.25
69 Robert Horry	.12	.30
70 Vernon Maxwell	.10	.25
71 Hakeem Olajuwon	.20	.50
72 Kenny Smith	.12	.30
73 Dale Davis	.10	.25
74 Mark Jackson	.12	.30
75 Derrick McKey	.10	.25
76 Reggie Miller	.20	.50
77 Sam Mitchell	.10	.25
78 Byron Scott	.12	.30
79 Rik Smits	.12	.30
80 Terry Dehere	.10	.25
81 Tony Massenburg	.10	.25
82 Lamond Murray	.10	.25
83 Pooh Richardson	.10	.25
84 Malik Sealy	.10	.25
85 Loy Vaught	.10	.25
86 Elden Campbell	.10	.25
87 Cedric Ceballos	.10	.25
88 Vlade Divac	.15	.40
89 Eddie Jones	.15	.40
90 Anthony Peeler	.10	.25
91 Sedale Threatt	.10	.25
92 Nick Van Exel	.15	.40
93 Bimbo Coles	.10	.25
94 Matt Geiger	.10	.25
95 Billy Owens	.10	.25
96 Khalid Reeves	.10	.25
97 Glen Rice	.15	.40
98 John Salley	.10	.25
99 Kevin Willis	.10	.25
100 Vin Baker	.12	.30
101 Marty Conlon	.10	.25
102 Todd Day	.10	.25
103 Lee Mayberry	.10	.25
104 Eric Murdock	.10	.25
105 Glenn Robinson	.12	.30
106 Winston Garland	.10	.25
107 Tom Gugliotta	.10	.25
108 Christian Laettner	.12	.30
109 Isaiah Rider	.15	.40
110 Sean Rooks	.10	.25
111 Doug West	.10	.25
112 Kenny Anderson	.12	.30
113 Benoit Benjamin	.10	.25
114 P.J. Brown	.10	.25
115 Derrick Coleman	.12	.30
116 Armon Gilliam	.10	.25
117 Chris Morris	.10	.25
118 Rex Walters	.10	.25
119 Hubert Davis	.10	.25
120 Patrick Ewing	.20	.50
121 Derek Harper	.12	.30
122 Anthony Mason	.10	.25
123 Charles Oakley	.12	.30
124 Charles Smith	.10	.25
125 John Starks	.12	.30
126 Nick Anderson	.10	.25
127 Anthony Bowie	.10	.25
128 Horace Grant	.12	.30
129 Anfernee Hardaway	.25	.60
130 Shaquille O'Neal	.40	1.00
131 Donald Royal	.10	.25
132 Dennis Scott	.10	.25
133 Brian Shaw	.10	.25
134 Derrick Alston	.10	.25
135 Dana Barros	.10	.25
136 Shawn Bradley	.10	.25
137 Willie Burton	.10	.25
138 Clarence Weatherspoon	.10	.25
139 Scott Williams	.10	.25
140 Sharone Wright	.10	.25
141 Danny Ainge	.15	.40
142 Charles Barkley	.25	.60
143 A.C. Green	.12	.30
144 Kevin Johnson	.15	.40
145 Dan Majerle	.15	.40
146 Danny Manning	.12	.30
147 Elliot Perry	.10	.25
148 Wesley Person	.10	.25
149 Wayman Tisdale	.10	.25
150 Chris Dudley	.10	.25
151 Jerome Kersey	.10	.25
152 Aaron McKie	.10	.25
153 Terry Porter	.10	.25
154 Clifford Robinson	.10	.25
155 James Robinson	.10	.25
156 Rod Strickland	.10	.25
157 Otis Thorpe	.10	.25
158 Buck Williams	.10	.25
159 Brian Grant	.12	.30
160 Bobby Hurley	.10	.25
161 Olden Polynice	.10	.25
162 Mitch Richmond	.15	.40
163 Michael Smith	.10	.25
164 Spud Webb	.12	.30
165 Walt Williams	.10	.25
166 Terry Cummings	.12	.30
167 Vinny Del Negro	.10	.25
168 Sean Elliott	.15	.40
169 Avery Johnson	.12	.30
170 Chuck Person	.12	.30
171 J.R. Reid	.10	.25
172 Doc Rivers	.12	.30
173 David Robinson	.25	.60
174 Dennis Rodman	.30	.75
175 Vincent Askew	.10	.25
176 Kendall Gill	.10	.25
177 Shawn Kemp	.15	.40
178 Sarunas Marciulionis	.10	.25
179 Nate McMillan	.10	.25
180 Gary Payton	.15	.40
181 Sam Perkins	.10	.25
182 Detlef Schrempf	.15	.40
183 David Benoit	.10	.25
184 Antoine Carr	.10	.25
185 Blue Edwards	.10	.25
186 Jeff Hornacek	.12	.30
187 Adam Keefe	.10	.25
188 Karl Malone	.20	.50
189 Felton Spencer	.10	.25
190 John Stockton	.20	.50
191 Rex Chapman	.10	.25
192 Calbert Cheaney	.10	.25
193 Juwan Howard	.15	.40
194 Don MacLean	.10	.25
195 Gheorghe Muresan	.10	.25
196 Scott Skiles	.10	.25
197 Chris Webber	.20	.50
198 Mookie Blaylock TD	.10	.25
199 Patrick Ewing TD	.20	.50
200 Michael Jordan TD	1.25	3.00
201 Alonzo Mourning TD	.20	.50
202 Dikembe Mutombo TD	.15	.40
203 Hakeem Olajuwon TD	.20	.50
204 Shaquille O'Neal TD	.40	1.00
205 Gary Payton TD	.15	.40
206 Scottie Pippen TD	.25	.60
207 David Robinson TD	.25	.60
208 Dennis Rodman TD	.30	.75
209 John Stockton TD	.20	.50
210 Brian Grant RS	.12	.30
211 Grant Hill RS	.25	.60
212 Juwan Howard RS	.15	.40
213 Eddie Jones RS	.15	.40
214 Jason Kidd RS	.25	.60
215 Donyell Marshall RS	.10	.25
216 Eric Montross RS	.10	.25
217 Lamond Murray RS	.10	.25
218 Wesley Person RS	.10	.25
219 Khalid Reeves RS	.10	.25
220 Glenn Robinson RS	.12	.30
221 Jalen Rose RS	.20	.50
222 Clifford Rozier RS	.10	.25
223 Michael Smith RS	.10	.25
224 Sharone Wright RS	.10	.25
225 Grant Hill	.25	.60
Charles Barkley AS		
226 Scottie Pippen	.25	.60
Shawn Kemp AS		
227 Shaquille O'Neal	.40	1.00
Hakeem Olajuwon AS		
228 Anfernee Hardaway	.25	.60
Dan Majerle AS		
229 Reggie Miller	.20	.50
Latrell Sprewell AS		
230 Vin Baker	.12	.30
Cedric Ceballos AS		
231 Tyrone Hill	.20	.50
Karl Malone AS		
232 Larry Johnson	.15	.40
Detlef Schrempf AS		
233 Patrick Ewing	.25	.60
David Robinson AS		
234 Alonzo Mourning	.20	.50
Dikembe Mutombo AS		
235 Dana Barros	.15	.40
Gary Payton AS		
236 Joe Dumars	.20	.50
John Stockton AS		
237 Mitch Richmond MVP	.15	.40
238 Atlanta Hawks Logo	.10	.25
239 Boston Celtics Logo	.10	.25
240 Charlotte Hornets Logo	.10	.25
241 Chicago Bulls Logo	.10	.25
242 Cleveland Cavaliers Logo	.10	.25
243 Dallas Mavericks Logo	.10	.25
244 Denver Nuggets Logo	.10	.25
245 Detroit Pistons Logo	.10	.25
246 Golden State Warriors Logo	.10	.25
247 Houston Rockets Logo	.10	.25
248 Indiana Pacers Logo	.10	.25
249 Los Angeles Clippers Logo	.10	.25
250 Los Angeles Lakers Logo	.10	.25
251 Miami Heat Logo	.10	.25
252 Milwaukee Bucks Logo	.10	.25
253 Minnesota Timberwolves Logo	.10	.25
254 New Jersey Nets Logo	.10	.25
255 New York Knicks Logo	.10	.25
256 Orlando Magic Logo	.10	.25
257 Philadelphia 76ers Logo	.10	.25
258 Phoenix Suns Logo	.10	.25
259 Portland Trail Blazers Logo	.10	.25
260 Sacramento Kings Logo	.10	.25
261 San Antonio Spurs Logo	.10	.25
262 Seattle Supersonics Logo	.10	.25
263 Toronto Raptors Logo	.10	.25
264 Utah Jazz Logo	.10	.25
265 Vancouver Grizzlies Logo	.10	.25
266 Washington Bullets Logo	.10	.25
267 NBA Logo	.10	.25
268 Checklist #1	.10	.25
269 Checklist #2	.10	.25
270 Checklist #3	.10	.25
271 Stacey Augmon	.12	.30
272 Mookie Blaylock	.10	.25
273 Grant Long	.10	.25
274 Ken Norman	.10	.25
275 Steve Smith	.12	.30
276 Spud Webb	.12	.30
277 Dana Barros	.10	.25
278 Rick Fox	.10	.25
279 Kendall Gill	.10	.25
280 Khalid Reeves	.10	.25
281 Glen Rice	.15	.40
282 Luc Longley	.12	.30
283 Dennis Rodman	.30	.75
284 Dan Majerle	.15	.40
285 Tony Dumas	.10	.25
286 Elmore Spencer	.10	.25
287 Otis Thorpe	.10	.25
288 B.J. Armstrong	.10	.25
289 Sam Cassell	.15	.40
290 Clyde Drexler	.20	.50
291 Mario Elie	.10	.25
292 Robert Horry	.12	.30
293 Hakeem Olajuwon	.20	.50
294 Kenny Smith	.12	.30
295 Antonio Davis	.10	.25
296 Eddie Johnson	.10	.25
297 Ricky Pierce	.10	.25
298 Eric Piatkowski	.12	.30
299 Rodney Rogers	.10	.25
300 Brian Williams	.10	.25
301 Corie Blount	.10	.25
302 George Lynch	.10	.25
303 Kevin Gamble	.10	.25
304 Alonzo Mourning	.20	.50
305 Eric Mobley	.10	.25
306 Terry Porter	.10	.25
307 Micheal Williams	.10	.25
308 Kevin Edwards	.10	.25
309 Vern Fleming	.10	.25
310 Charlie Ward	.10	.25
311 Jon Koncak	.10	.25
312 Richard Dumas	.10	.25
313 Jeff Malone	.10	.25
314 Vernon Maxwell	.10	.25
315 John Williams	.10	.25
316 Harvey Grant	.10	.25
317 Dontonio Wingfield	.10	.25
318 Tyrone Corbin	.10	.25
319 Sarunas Marciulionis	.10	.25
320 Will Perdue	.10	.25
321 Hersey Hawkins	.10	.25
322 Ervin Johnson	.10	.25
323 Shawn Kemp	.15	.40
324 Gary Payton	.15	.40
325 Sam Perkins	.10	.25
326 Detlef Schrempf	.15	.40
327 Chris Morris	.10	.25
328 Robert Pack	.10	.25
329 Willie Anderson ET	.10	.25
330 Jimmy King ET	.10	.25
331 Oliver Miller ET	.10	.25
332 Tracy Murray ET	.10	.25
333 Ed Pinckney ET	.10	.25
334 Alvin Robertson ET	.10	.25
335 Carlos Rogers ET	.10	.25
336 John Salley ET	.10	.25
337 Damon Stoudamire ET	.25	.60
338 Zan Tabak ET	.10	.25
339 Ashraf Amaya ET	.10	.25
340 Greg Anthony ET	.10	.25
341 Benoit Benjamin ET	.10	.25
342 Blue Edwards ET	.10	.25
343 Kenny Gattison ET	.10	.25
344 Antonio Harvey ET	.10	.25
345 Chris King ET	.10	.25
346 Lawrence Moten ET	.10	.25
347 Bryant Reeves ET	.07	.20
348 Byron Scott ET	.12	.30
349 Cory Alexander	.15	.40
350 Jerome Allen	.15	.40
351 Brent Barry	.25	.60
352 Mario Bennett	.12	.30
353 Travis Best	.15	.40
354 Junior Burrough	.15	.40
355 Jason Caffey	.15	.40
356 Randolph Childress	.12	.30
357 Sasha Danilovic	.15	.40
358 Mark Davis	.15	.40
359 Tyus Edney	.15	.40
360 Michael Finley	.50	1.25
361 Sherrell Ford	.12	.30
362 Kevin Garnett	1.25	3.00
363 Alan Henderson	.15	.40
364 Frankie King	.15	.40
365 Jimmy King	.15	.40
366 Donny Marshall	.15	.40
367 Antonio McDyess	.20	.50
368 Loren Meyer	.10	.25
369 Lawrence Moten	.15	.40
370 Ed O'Bannon	.12	.30
371 Greg Ostertag	.15	.40
372 Cherokee Parks	.12	.30
373 Theo Ratliff	.25	.60
374 Bryant Reeves	.12	.30
375 Shawn Respert	.12	.30
376 Lou Roe	.15	.40
377 Arvydas Sabonis	.30	.75
378 Joe Smith	.20	.50
379 Jerry Stackhouse	.50	1.25
380 Damon Stoudamire	.40	1.00
381 Bob Sura	.12	.30
382 Kurt Thomas	.15	.40
383 Gary Trent	.15	.40
384 David Vaughn	.15	.40
385 Rasheed Wallace	.50	1.25
386 Eric Williams	.15	.40
387 Corliss Williamson	.15	.40
388 George Zidek	.12	.30
389 Checklist	.10	.25
390 Checklist	.10	.25
391 Mookie Blaylock FF	.10	.25
392 Dino Radja FF	.10	.25
393 Larry Johnson FF	.15	.40
394 Michael Jordan FF	1.25	3.00
395 Tyrone Hill FF	.10	.25
396 Jason Kidd FF	.25	.60
397 Dikembe Mutombo FF	.15	.40
398 Grant Hill FF	.25	.60
399 Joe Smith FF	.20	.50
400 Hakeem Olajuwon FF	.20	.50
401 Reggie Miller FF	.20	.50
402 Loy Vaught FF	.10	.25
403 Nick Van Exel FF	.15	.40
404 Alonzo Mourning FF	.20	.50
405 Glenn Robinson FF	.12	.30
406 Kevin Garnett FF	1.25	3.00
407 Kenny Anderson FF	.12	.30
408 Patrick Ewing FF	.20	.50
409 Shaquille O'Neal FF	.40	1.00
410 Jerry Stackhouse FF	.50	1.25
411 Charles Barkley FF	.25	.60
412 Clifford Robinson FF	.10	.25
413 Mitch Richmond FF	.15	.40
414 David Robinson FF	.25	.60
415 Shawn Kemp FF	.15	.40
416 Damon Stoudamire FF	.40	1.00
417 Karl Malone FF	.20	.50
418 Bryant Reeves FF	.12	.30
419 Chris Webber FF	.20	.50
420 Shawn Kemp TP	.15	.40
421 Karl Malone TP	.20	.50
422 Antonio McDyess TP	.20	.50
423 Alonzo Mourning TP	.20	.50
424 Hakeem Olajuwon TP	.20	.50
425 Shaquille O'Neal TP	.40	1.00
426 David Robinson TP	.25	.60
427 Glenn Robinson TP	.12	.30
428 Joe Smith TP	.20	.50
429 Chris Webber TP	.20	.50
430 Derrick Alston CE	.10	.25
431 Brian Grant CE	.12	.30
432 Grant Hill CE	.25	.60
433 Juwan Howard CE	.15	.40
434 Eddie Jones CE	.15	.40
435 Jason Kidd CE	.25	.60
436 Donyell Marshall CE	.10	.25
437 Anthony Miller CE	.10	.25
438 Eric Mobley CE	.10	.25
439 Eric Montross CE	.10	.25
440 Lamond Murray CE	.10	.25
441 Wesley Person CE	.10	.25
442 Eric Piatkowski CE	.12	.30
443 Khalid Reeves CE	.10	.25
444 Glenn Robinson CE	.12	.30
445 Carlos Rogers CE	.10	.25
446 Jalen Rose CE	.20	.50
447 Clifford Rozier CE	.10	.25
448 Michael Smith CE	.10	.25
449 Sharone Wright CE	.10	.25
450 Brent Barry CE	.25	.60
451 Jason Caffey CE	.15	.40
452 Randolph Childress CE	.12	.30
453 Kevin Garnett CE	1.25	3.00
454 Alan Henderson CE	.15	.40
455 Antonio McDyess CE	.20	.50
456 Ed O'Bannon CE	.12	.30
457 Cherokee Parks CE	.12	.30
458 Theo Ratliff CE	.25	.60
459 Bryant Reeves CE	.12	.30
460 Shawn Respert CE	.12	.30
461 Joe Smith CE	.20	.50
462 Jerry Stackhouse CE	.50	1.25
463 Damon Stoudamire CE	.40	1.00
464 Bob Sura CE	.12	.30
465 Kurt Thomas CE	.15	.40
466 Gary Trent CE	.15	.40
467 Rasheed Wallace CE	.50	1.25
468 Eric Williams CE	.15	.40
469 Corliss Williamson CE	.15	.40
470 Mookie Blaylock EE	.10	.25
471 Vlade Divac EE	.15	.40
472 Clyde Drexler EE	.20	.50
473 Patrick Ewing EE	.20	.50
474 Horace Grant EE	.12	.30
475 Anfernee Hardaway EE	.25	.60
476 Grant Hill EE	.25	.60
477 Eddie Jones EE	.15	.40
478 Michael Jordan EE	1.25	3.00
479 Jason Kidd EE	.25	.60
480 Alonzo Mourning EE	.20	.50
481 Dikembe Mutombo EE	.15	.40
482 Hakeem Olajuwon EE	.20	.50
483 Shaquille O'Neal EE	.40	1.00
484 Gary Payton EE	.15	.40
485 Scottie Pippen EE	.25	.60
486 David Robinson EE	.25	.60
487 Latrell Sprewell EE	.15	.40
488 John Stockton EE	.20	.50
489 Rod Strickland EE	.10	.25
490 Kevin Garnett RP	1.25	3.00
491 Antonio McDyess RP	.20	.50
492 Ed O'Bannon RP	.12	.30
493 Bryant Reeves RP	.12	.30
494 Shawn Respert RP	.12	.30
495 Joe Smith RP	.20	.50
496 Jerry Stackhouse RP	.50	1.25
497 Damon Stoudamire RP	.40	1.00
498 Gary Trent RP	.15	.40
499 Rasheed Wallace RP	.50	1.25

1996-97 Fleer European

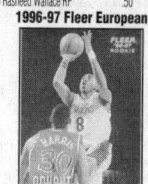

This 330-card standard-size set was issued by Fleer for the French, Spanish, Italian, Portugese, German, Japanese and Chinese markets. The cards were distributed in 8-card packs, in two series, with 36 packs per box. The set closely parallels the American 1996-97 Fleer issue. The series one set contains 150 cards, as does the series two. But, a 30-card translation set, featuring team logos, was inserted in both series one and series two packs. Thus, a separate set line has been established for that set and each series has 150 cards. Unlike other U.S.-based foreign issues, these cards contain no foreign text, but the wrapper and box are multilingual. A selection of cards share common numbers with the American version, making them almost impossible to separately identify. Everything is identical, even the trademark lines. Most of those cards are from series one. Series two, for the most part, contains different card numbers. The main difference in the sets is the European also contains a Team Logo Translation subset, which the American version does not have. The backs of these cards have the basic American descriptions translated into the various languages. The following inserts were also available: Rookie Rewind and Stackhouse's All-Fleer in series one and Swing Shift in series two. Because these inserts are identical to the regular American inserts, they are priced the same. Please refer to those American inserts for values. The cards were distributed by Panini.

Card	Low	High
COMPLETE SET (330)	40.00	100.00
COMPLETE SERIES 1 (150)	12.50	30.00
COMPLETE SERIES 2 (150)	25.00	60.00
COMP.TRANSLATION SET (30)	2.50	6.00
1 Stacey Augmon	.20	.50
2 Mookie Blaylock	.15	.40
3 Christian Laettner	.20	.50
4 Grant Long	.15	.40
5 Steve Smith	.20	.50
6 Rick Fox	.15	.40
7 Dino Radja	.15	.40
8 Eric Williams	.15	.40
9 Kenny Anderson	.20	.50
10 Dell Curry	.15	.40
11 Larry Johnson	.25	.60
12 Glen Rice	.25	.60
13 Michael Jordan	2.00	5.00
14 Toni Kukoc	.25	.60
15 Scottie Pippen	.40	1.00
16 Dennis Rodman	.50	1.25
17 Terrell Brandon	.15	.40
18 Chris Mills	.15	.40
19 Bobby Phills	.15	.40
20 Bob Sura	.15	.40
21 Jim Jackson	.15	.40
22 Jason Kidd	.40	1.00
23 Jamal Mashburn	.20	.50
24 George McCloud	.15	.40
25 Mahmoud Abdul-Rauf	.15	.40
26 Antonio McDyess	.25	.60
27 Dikembe Mutombo	.25	.60
28 Jalen Rose	.20	.50
29 Bryant Stith	.15	.40
30 Joe Dumars	.25	.60
31 Grant Hill	.40	1.00
32 Allan Houston	.20	.50
33 Theo Ratliff	.15	.40
34 Otis Thorpe	.15	.40
35 Chris Mullin	.25	.60
36 Joe Smith	.20	.50
37 Latrell Sprewell	.25	.60
38 Kevin Willis	.15	.40
39 Sam Cassell	.20	.50
40 Clyde Drexler	.30	.75
41 Robert Horry	.20	.50
42 Hakeem Olajuwon	.30	.75
43 Dale Davis	.15	.40
44 Mark Jackson	.20	.50
45 Derrick McKey	.15	.40
46 Reggie Miller	.30	.75
47 Rik Smits	.20	.50
48 Brent Barry	.20	.50
49 Malik Sealy	.15	.40
50 Loy Vaught	.15	.40
51 Brian Williams	.15	.40
52 Elden Campbell	.15	.40
53 Cedric Ceballos	.15	.40
54 Vlade Divac	.25	.60
55 Eddie Jones	.25	.60
56 Nick Van Exel	.25	.60
57 Tim Hardaway	.25	.60
58 Alonzo Mourning	.30	.75
59 Kurt Thomas	.15	.40
60 Walt Williams	.15	.40
61 Vin Baker	.20	.50
62 Sherman Douglas	.15	.40
63 Glenn Robinson	.20	.50
64 Kevin Garnett	.60	1.50
65 Tom Gugliotta	.15	.40
66 Isaiah Rider	.20	.50
67 Shawn Bradley	.15	.40
68 Chris Childs	.15	.40
69 Armon Gilliam	.15	.40
70 Ed O'Bannon	.15	.40
71 Patrick Ewing	.30	.75
72 Derek Harper	.20	.50
73 Anthony Mason	.15	.40
74 Charles Oakley	.20	.50
75 John Starks	.20	.50
76 Nick Anderson	.15	.40
77 Horace Grant	.20	.50
78 Anfernee Hardaway	.40	1.00
79 Shaquille O'Neal	.60	1.50
80 Dennis Scott	.15	.40
81 Derrick Coleman	.20	.50
82 Vernon Maxwell	.15	.40
83 Jerry Stackhouse	.30	.75
84 Clarence Weatherspoon	.15	.40
85 Charles Barkley	.40	1.00
86 Michael Finley	.30	.75
87 Kevin Johnson	.25	.60
88 Wesley Person	.15	.40
89 Clifford Robinson	.15	.40
90 Arvydas Sabonis	.20	.50
91 Rod Strickland	.15	.40
92 Gary Trent	.15	.40
93 Tyus Edney	.15	.40
94 Brian Grant	.20	.50
95 Billy Owens	.15	.40
96 Mitch Richmond	.25	.60
97 Vinny Del Negro	.15	.40
98 Sean Elliott	.25	.60
99 Avery Johnson	.20	.50
100 David Robinson	.40	1.00
101 Hersey Hawkins	.15	.40
102 Shawn Kemp	.25	.60
103 Gary Payton	.25	.60
104 Detlef Schrempf	.25	.60
105 Oliver Miller	.15	.40
106 Tracy Murray	.15	.40
107 Damon Stoudamire	.20	.50
108 Sharone Wright	.15	.40
109 Jeff Hornacek	.20	.50
110 Karl Malone	.30	.75
111 John Stockton	.30	.75
112 Greg Anthony	.15	.40
113 Bryant Reeves	.15	.40
114 Byron Scott	.20	.50
115 Calbert Cheaney	.15	.40
116 Juwan Howard	.20	.50
117 Gheorghe Muresan	.15	.40
118 Rasheed Wallace	.30	.75
119 Chris Webber	.30	.75
120 Mookie Blaylock HL	.15	.40
121 Dino Radja HL	.15	.40
122 Larry Johnson HL	.25	.60
123 Michael Jordan HL	2.00	5.00
124 Terrell Brandon HL	.15	.40
125 Jason Kidd HL	.40	1.00
126 Antonio McDyess HL	.25	.60
127 Grant Hill HL	.40	1.00
128 Latrell Sprewell HL	.25	.60
129 Hakeem Olajuwon HL	.30	.75
130 Reggie Miller HL	.30	.75
131 Loy Vaught HL	.15	.40
132 Cedric Ceballos HL	.15	.40
133 Alonzo Mourning HL	.30	.75
134 Vin Baker HL	.20	.50
135 Isaiah Rider HL	.20	.50
136 Armon Gilliam HL	.15	.40
137 Patrick Ewing HL	.30	.75
138 Shaquille O'Neal HL	.60	1.50
139 Jerry Stackhouse HL	.30	.75
140 Charles Barkley HL	.40	1.00
141 Clifford Robinson HL	.15	.40
142 Mitch Richmond HL	.25	.60
143 David Robinson HL	.40	1.00
144 Shawn Kemp HL	.25	.60
145 Damon Stoudamire HL	.20	.50
146 Karl Malone HL	.30	.75
147 Bryant Reeves HL	.15	.40
148 Juwan Howard HL	.20	.50
149 Checklist	.15	.40
150 Checklist	.15	.40
151 Atlanta Hawks	.20	.50
152 Boston Celtics	.20	.50
153 Charlotte Hornets	.20	.50
154 Chicago Bulls	.20	.50
155 Cleveland Cavaliers	.20	.50
156 Dallas Mavericks	.20	.50
157 Denver Nuggets	.20	.50
158 Detroit Pistons	.20	.50
159 Golden State Warriors	.20	.50
160 Houston Rockets	.20	.50
161 Indiana Pacers	.20	.50
162 Los Angeles Clippers	.20	.50
163 Los Angeles Lakers	.20	.50
164 Miami Heat	.20	.50
165 Milwaukee Bucks	.20	.50
166 Minnesota Timberwolves	.20	.50
167 New Jersey Nets	.20	.50
168 New York Knicks	.20	.50
169 Orlando Magic	.20	.50
170 Philadelphia 76ers	.20	.50
171 Phoenix Suns	.20	.50
172 Portland Trailblazers	.20	.50
173 Sacramento Kings	.20	.50
174 San Antonio Spurs	.20	.50
175 Seattle Supersonics	.20	.50
176 Toronto Raptors	.20	.50
177 Utah Jazz	.20	.50
178 Vancouver Grizzlies	.20	.50
179 Washington Bullets	.20	.50
180 NBA Logo	.20	.50
181 Alan Henderson	.15	.40
182 Priest Lauderdale	.30	.75
183 Dikembe Mutombo	.25	.60
184 Dana Barros	.15	.40
185 Todd Day	.15	.40
186 Brett Szabo	.50	1.25
187 Antoine Walker	.75	2.00
188 Scott Burrell	.15	.40
189 Tony Delk	.50	1.25
190 Vlade Divac	.25	.60
191 Matt Geiger	.15	.40
192 Anthony Mason	.15	.40
193 Malik Rose	.60	1.50
194 Ron Harper	.20	.50
195 Steve Kerr	.20	.50
196 Luc Longley	.20	.50
197 Danny Ferry	.15	.40
198 Tyrone Hill	.15	.40
199 Vitaly Potapenko	.40	1.00
200 Tony Dumas	.15	.40
201 Chris Gatling	.15	.40
202 Oliver Miller	.15	.40
203 Eric Montross	.15	.40
204 Samaki Walker	.40	1.00
205 Darvin Ham	.50	1.25
206 Mark Jackson	.20	.50
207 Ervin Johnson	.15	.40
208 Stacey Augmon	.20	.50
209 Joe Dumars	.25	.60
210 Grant Hill	.40	1.00
211 Grant Long	.15	.40
212 Terry Mills	.15	.40
213 Otis Thorpe	.15	.40
214 Jerome Williams	.40	1.00
215 B.J. Armstrong	.15	.40
216 Todd Fuller	.30	.75
217 Ray Owes	.50	1.25
218 Mark Price	.25	.60
219 Felton Spencer	.15	.40
220 Charles Barkley	.40	1.00
221 Mario Elie	.15	.40
222 Othella Harrington	.50	1.25
223 Matt Maloney	.40	1.00
224 Brent Price	.15	.40
225 Kevin Willis	.15	.40
226 Travis Best	.15	.40
227 Erick Dampier	.50	1.25
228 Antonio Davis	.15	.40
229 Jalen Rose	.20	.50
230 Pooh Richardson	.15	.40
231 Rodney Rogers	.15	.40
232 Lorenzen Wright	.40	1.00
233 Kobe Bryant	10.00	25.00
234 Derek Fisher	.60	1.50
235 Travis Knight	.50	1.25
236 Shaquille O'Neal	.60	1.50
237 Byron Scott	.20	.50
238 P.J. Brown	.15	.40
239 Sasha Danilovic	.15	.40
240 Dan Majerle	.25	.60
241 Martin Muursepp	.30	.75
242 Ray Allen	2.00	5.00
243 Armon Gilliam	.15	.40
244 Andrew Lang	.15	.40
245 Moochie Norris	.50	1.25
246 Kevin Garnett	.60	1.50
247 Tom Gugliotta	.15	.40
248 Shane Heal	.50	1.25
249 Stephon Marbury	1.25	3.00
250 Stojko Vrankovic	.15	.40
251 Kerry Kittles	.50	1.25
252 Robert Pack	.15	.40
253 Jayson Williams	.15	.40
254 Allan Houston	.20	.50
255 Larry Johnson	.25	.60
256 Dontae Jones	.50	1.25
257 Walter McCarty	.50	1.25
258 John Wallace	.50	1.25
259 Charlie Ward	.15	.40
260 Brian Evans	.50	1.25
261 Amal McCaskill	.50	1.25
262 Brian Shaw	.15	.40
263 Mark Davis	.15	.40
264 Lucious Harris	.15	.40
265 Allen Iverson	2.50	6.00
266 Sam Cassell	.20	.50
267 Robert Horry	.20	.50
268 Danny Manning	.20	.50
269 Steve Nash	2.50	6.00
270 Kenny Anderson	.20	.50
271 Aleksandar Djordjevic	.50	1.25
272 Jermaine O'Neal	.75	2.00
273 Isaiah Rider	.20	.50
274 Rasheed Wallace	.30	.75
275 Mahmoud Abdul-Rauf	.15	.40
276 Michael Smith	.15	.40
277 Corliss Williamson	.15	.40
278 Vernon Maxwell	.15	.40
279 Charles Smith	.15	.40
280 Dominique Wilkins	.30	.75
281 Craig Ehlo	.15	.40
282 Jim McIlvaine	.15	.40
283 Sam Perkins	.15	.40
284 Marcus Camby	.75	2.00
285 Popeye Jones	.15	.40
286 Donald Whiteside	.50	1.25
287 Walt Williams	.15	.40
288 Jeff Hornacek	.20	.50
289 Karl Malone	.30	.75
290 Bryon Russell	.15	.40
291 John Stockton	.30	.75
292 Shareef Abdur-Rahim	.75	2.00
293 Anthony Peeler	.15	.40
294 Roy Rogers	.40	1.00
295 Tim Legler	.15	.40
296 Tracy Murray	.15	.40
297 Rod Strickland	.15	.40
298 Ben Wallace	2.50	6.00
299 Kevin Garnett CB	.60	1.50
300 Allan Houston CB	.20	.50
301 Eddie Jones CB	.25	.60
302 Jamal Mashburn CB	.20	.50
303 Antonio McDyess CB	.25	.60
304 Glenn Robinson CB	.20	.50
305 Joe Smith CB	.20	.50
306 Steve Smith CB	.20	.50
307 Jerry Stackhouse CB	.30	.75
308 Damon Stoudamire CB	.20	.50
309 Hakeem Olajuwon AS	.30	.75
310 Charles Barkley AS	.40	1.00
311 Patrick Ewing AS	.30	.75
312 Michael Jordan AS	2.00	5.00
313 Clyde Drexler AS	.30	.75
314 Karl Malone AS	.30	.75
315 John Stockton AS	.30	.75
316 David Robinson AS	.40	1.00
317 Scottie Pippen AS	.40	1.00
318 Shawn Kemp AS	.25	.60
319 Shaquille O'Neal AS	.60	1.50
320 Mitch Richmond AS	.25	.60
321 Reggie Miller AS	.30	.75
322 Alonzo Mourning AS	.30	.75
323 Gary Payton AS	.25	.60
324 Anfernee Hardaway AS	.40	1.00
325 Grant Hill AS	.40	1.00
326 Dennis Rodman AS	.50	1.25
327 Juwan Howard AS	.20	.50
328 Jason Kidd AS	.40	1.00
329 Checklist	.15	.40
330 Checklist	.15	.40

2001-02 Fleer Exclusive

Released in early January of 2002, this 149-card set features 120 veteran players on colorful card stock where the backgrounds match the pictured player's team colors, and each card front showcases two photos of the player. 29 rookie players were also included, and these cards have a gray background and, a photo of the rookie, and a swatch of a player worn jersey patch. The vast majority of rookie cards are multi-colored. These RC cards are not sequentially numbered, but print runs, provided by Fleer, are listed below. Exclusive was packed out in 24 pack boxes where each pack contained five cards.

Card	Low	High
COMPLETE SET (149)	150.00	300.00
COMP.SET w/o SP's (120)	15.00	40.00
121-149 STATED ODDS 1:24		
121-149 HAVE JERSEY PATCH		
PRINT RUNS PROVIDED BY FLEER		
1 Vince Carter	.60	1.50
2 Tracy McGrady	.60	1.50
3 Dikembe Mutombo	.40	1.00
4 Kobe Bryant	1.50	4.00
5 Baron Davis	.40	1.00
6 Alonzo Mourning	.50	1.25
7 Allan Houston	.30	.75
8 Paul Pierce	.40	1.00
9 Jason Williams	.30	.75
10 Marcus Camby	.30	.75
11 Jason Terry	.40	1.00
12 Anfernee Hardaway	.60	1.50
13 Cuttino Mobley	.25	.60
14 Kenyon Martin	.40	1.00
15 Rashard Lewis	.40	1.00
16 Darius Miles	.25	.60
17 Jamal Mashburn	.30	.75
18 Derek Fisher	.30	.75
19 Sam Cassell	.30	.75
20 Antonio McDyess	.30	.75
21 John Stockton	.50	1.25
22 Andre Miller	.30	.75
23 Shawn Marion	.30	.75
24 Steve Nash	.60	1.50
25 Kevin Garnett	.60	1.50
26 Peja Stojakovic	.40	1.00
27 Dirk Nowitzki	.60	1.50
28 Chris Webber	.40	1.00
29 Shaquille O'Neal	1.00	2.50
30 Stephon Marbury	.30	.75
31 Eddie Jones	.30	.75
32 Raef LaFrentz	.25	.60

33 Wally Szczerbiak .30 .75
34 Richard Hamilton .30 .75
35 Michael Finley .40 1.00
36 Jason Kidd .60 1.50
37 Courtney Alexander .25 .60
38 Glenn Robinson .30 .75
39 Tim Duncan .75 2.00
40 Steve Francis .30 .75
41 Stromile Swift .25 .60
42 Desmond Mason .30 .75
43 Shareef Abdur-Rahim .30 .75
44 Terrell Brandon .25 .60
45 Antawn Jamison .40 1.00
46 Latrell Sprewell .30 .75
47 Mateen Cleaves .25 .60
48 Karl Malone .50 1.25
49 Lamar Odom .30 .75
50 Grant Hill .50 1.25
51 Reggie Miller .40 1.00
52 Ray Allen .40 1.00
53 David Robinson .60 1.50
54 Elton Brand .40 1.00
55 Jerry Stackhouse .30 .75
56 Brian Grant .25 .60
57 Hakeem Olajuwon .50 1.25
58 Jalen Rose .30 .75
59 Allen Iverson .75 2.00
60 Darrell Armstrong .25 .60
61 Joe Smith .30 .75
62 Anthony Mason .25 .60
63 Mike Bibby .40 1.00
64 Gary Payton .40 1.00
65 Glen Rice .30 .75
66 Shandon Anderson .25 .60
67 Antoine Walker .30 .75
68 Tim Thomas .25 .60
69 Patrick Ewing .50 1.25
70 Ben Wallace .30 .75
71 Corey Maggette .30 .75
72 Larry Hughes .30 .75
73 Scottie Pippen .60 1.50
74 Michael Doleac .25 .60
75 Clifford Robinson .25 .60
76 Aaron McKie .25 .60
77 Marc Jackson .25 .60
78 Tom Gugliotta .25 .60
79 James Posey .25 .60
80 Moochie Norris .25 .60
81 Speedy Claxton .25 .60
82 Michael Redd .40 1.00
83 Rasheed Wallace .40 1.00
84 Juwan Howard .30 .75
85 Nick Van Exel .30 .75
86 Toni Kukoc .40 1.00
87 Jamaal Magloire .25 .60
88 Jermaine O'Neal .30 .75
89 Anthony Peeler .25 .60
90 Marcus Fizer .25 .60
91 Jumaine Jones .25 .60
92 Kendall Gill .25 .60
93 Antonio Daniels .25 .60
94 DerMarr Johnson .25 .60
95 Mitch Richmond .30 .75
96 Antonio Davis .25 .60
97 Ron Mercer .25 .60
98 Keyon Dooling .25 .60
99 Morris Peterson .25 .60
100 Derek Anderson .25 .60
101 Allen Iverson MO .75 2.00
102 Glenn Robinson MO .30 .75
103 Tim Duncan MO .75 2.00
104 Shaquille O'Neal MO 1.00 2.50
105 Vince Carter MO .60 1.50
106 Tracy McGrady MO .60 1.50
107 Jason Kidd MO .60 1.50
108 Karl Malone MO .50 1.25
109 Michael Jordan MO 6.00 15.00
110 Shareef Abdur-Rahim MO .30 .75
111 Grant Hill MO .50 1.25
112 Stephon Marbury MO .30 .75
113 Michael Finley MO .40 1.00
114 Antoine Walker MO .30 .75
115 Kobe Bryant MO 1.50 4.00
116 Dirk Nowitzki MO .60 1.50
117 Alonzo Mourning MO .50 1.25
118 John Stockton MO .50 1.25
119 Kevin Garnett MO .60 1.50
120 Eddie Jones MO .30 .75
121 Steven Hunter/500 RC 2.50 6.00
122 Tony Parker/500 RC 12.00 30.00
123 Zach Randolph/478 RC 5.00 12.00
124 Richard Jefferson/500 RC 5.00 12.00
125 Kedrick Brown/433 RC 2.00 5.00
126 Kwame Brown/472 RC 3.00 8.00
127 Brandon Armstrong/500 RC 2.00 5.00
128 Pau Gasol/474 RC 10.00 25.00
129 Troy Murphy/500 RC 3.00 8.00
130 Rodney White/500 RC 2.00 5.00
131 Jamaal Tinsley/500 RC 3.00 8.00
132 Jeryl Sasser/500 RC 2.00 5.00
133 Eddie Griffin/500 RC 2.50 6.00
134 Michael Bradley/476 RC 2.00 5.00
135 V.Radmanovic/500 RC 3.00 8.00
136 Jason Richardson/388 RC 4.00 10.00
137 Shane Battier/500 RC 6.00 15.00
138 Joe Johnson/300 RC 4.00 10.00
139 Andrei Kirilenko/500 RC 5.00 12.00
140 Kirk Haston/500 RC 2.00 5.00
141 Jason Collins/500 RC 2.50 6.00
142 Tyson Chandler/500 RC 5.00 12.00
143 DeSagana Diop/499 RC 2.50 6.00
144 Gerald Wallace/467 RC 4.00 10.00
145 Joseph Forte/450 RC 2.00 5.00
146 Brendan Haywood/500 RC 3.00 8.00
147 Samuel Dalembert/360 RC 3.00 8.00
148 Eddy Curry/500 RC 3.00 8.00
149 Primoz Brezec/500 RC 3.00 8.00

2001-02 Fleer Exclusive Game Exclusives

Randomly inserted in packs, this 19-card set includes full color player action photos set against a white and gray backdrop and a swatch of a jersey in the lower left hand corner of the card front. Each card is sequentially numbered to 100.

STATED PRINT RUN 100 SER.#'d SETS
*PATCH: 1.25X TO 3X HI
PATCH PRINT RUN 25 SER.#'d SETS
1 Vince Carter 8.00 20.00
2 Allen Iverson 10.00 25.00
3 Alonzo Mourning 8.00 20.00
4 Karl Malone 6.00 15.00
5 Darius Miles 3.00 8.00
6 Antonio McDyess 4.00 10.00
7 Ray Allen 5.00 12.00
8 Steve Francis 4.00 10.00
9 Lamar Odom 4.00 10.00
10 Kenyon Martin 5.00 12.00
11 Andre Miller 4.00 10.00
12 Rashard Lewis 5.00 12.00
13 Stromile Swift 3.00 8.00
14 Antonio Davis 3.00 8.00
15 Latrell Sprewell 4.00 10.00
16 Tracy McGrady 8.00 20.00
17 Jamal Mashburn 4.00 10.00
18 Dikembe Mutombo 5.00 12.00
19 Morris Peterson 3.00 8.00

2001-02 Fleer Exclusive Letter Perfect

Randomly inserted in packs at the rate of one in 8, this 25-card set has player action photos set against a colored background to match the featured players jersey colors. This horizontal card design places players on the left side of the card in action, and his initials on the right side. The right edge of the card is done in a different color and is slightly embossed.

COMPLETE SET (25) 10.00 25.00
STATED ODDS 1:8
1 Vince Carter 1.00 2.50
2 Allen Iverson 1.25 3.00
3 Alonzo Mourning .75 2.00
4 Karl Malone .75 2.00
5 Darius Miles .40 1.00
7 Antonio McDyess .50 1.25
8 Ray Allen .60 1.50
9 Steve Francis .50 1.25
10 Lamar Odom .50 1.25
11 Kenyon Martin .60 1.50
12 Andre Miller .50 1.25
13 Rashard Lewis .60 1.50
14 Stromile Swift .40 1.00
15 Antonio Davis .40 1.00
16 Latrell Sprewell .50 1.25
17 Keith Van Horn .50 1.25
18 Tracy McGrady 1.00 2.50
19 Desmond Mason .50 1.25
20 Jason Terry .60 1.50
21 Jamal Mashburn .50 1.25
22 Paul Pierce .60 1.50
23 Morris Peterson .40 1.00
24 Baron Davis .60 1.50
25 Antoine Walker .50 1.25
6 Mike Miller .50 1.25

2001-02 Fleer Exclusive Letter Perfect JV

STATED PRINT RUN 100 SER.#'d SETS
*VARSITY: 1.25X TO 3X BASE HI
VARSITY PRINT RUN 25 SER.#'d SETS
1 Vince Carter 8.00 20.00
2 Allen Iverson 10.00 25.00
3 Alonzo Mourning 8.00 20.00
4 Karl Malone 6.00 15.00
5 Darius Miles 3.00 8.00
6 Antonio McDyess 4.00 10.00
7 Ray Allen 5.00 12.00
8 Steve Francis 4.00 10.00
9 Lamar Odom 4.00 10.00
10 Kenyon Martin 5.00 12.00
11 Andre Miller 4.00 10.00
12 Rashard Lewis 5.00 12.00
13 Stromile Swift 3.00 8.00
14 Antonio Davis 3.00 8.00
15 Latrell Sprewell 4.00 10.00
16 Keith Van Horn 4.00 10.00
17 Tracy McGrady 8.00 20.00
18 Desmond Mason 4.00 10.00
19 Jason Terry 5.00 12.00
20 Jamal Mashburn 4.00 10.00
21 Paul Pierce 5.00 12.00
22 Morris Peterson 3.00 8.00
23 Baron Davis 5.00 12.00
24 Antoine Walker 4.00 10.00

2001-02 Fleer Exclusive Team Fleer

This eight card set features an array of jerseys, patches and autographs. Abbreviations have been added below to denote which card contains the above mentioned elements. The odds on pulling card number one are stated at 96, and print runs have been added for the rest of the set. The cards are set up horizontally with color player action photos set above a crown or crowns (depending on how many players are on each card), and on the jersey versions, the crown is where the jersey swatch is placed.

CARD #1 STATED ODDS 1:96
2-8 PRINT RUNS LISTED BELOW
1 V.Carter/L.Bird 6.00 15.00
2 V.Carter/L.Bird JSY/500 10.00 25.00
3 Vince Carter JSY/98 10.00 25.00
4 V.Carter JSY Patch/15 20.00 50.00
5 V.Carter JSY AU/100 20.00 50.00
6 Larry Bird JSY/79 25.00 60.00
7 L.Bird JSY Patch/33 50.00 100.00
8 L.Bird JSY AU/100 100.00 200.00

2001-02 Fleer Exclusive Vinsanity Collection

Randomly inserted in packs at the rate of one in 70, this five card set follows the career of Vince Carter. Each card contains a swatch of some type of game-used memorabilia where abbreviations of each item appear below. The cards are full color and have circular memorabilia swatches. The #5, USA card, was initially issued as a redemption.

STATED ODDS 1:70
1 Vince Carter UNC Shirt 8.00 20.00
2 Vince Carter Shirt 8.00 20.00
3 Vince Carter Warm 8.00 20.00
4 Vince Carter JSY 10.00 25.00
5 Vince Carter USA 10.00 25.00

2001-02 Fleer Exclusive Vinsanity Collection Autographs

STATED PRINT RUN 30 SER.#'d SETS
1 Vince Carter UNC Shirt 50.00 120.00
2 Vince Carter Shirt 50.00 120.00
3 Vince Carter Warm 50.00 120.00
4 Vince Carter JSY 60.00 150.00
5 Vince Carter USA JSY 60.00 150.00

1999-00 Fleer Focus

The Fleer Focus set was released in one series, containing 150 cards. Each pack contained 10-cards with a suggested retail price of $2.99. The base set is broken up into 100 veterans and 50 rookies, with the rookies serially numbered to 3999. The first 999 cards contain a portrait photo, while the remaining 3000 cards have an action photo.

COMPLETE SET (150) 75.00 150.00
COMPLETE SET w/o RC (100) 10.00 20.00
101-150 FIRST 999 ARE PORTRAIT PHOTO
101-150 REMAINING 3000 ARE ACTION PHOTO
101-150 PORTRAIT PHOTO LISTED AS SP's
UNPRICED MASTERPIECES SERIAL #'d TO 1
1 Anfernee Hardaway .50 1.25
2 Derek Anderson .20 .50
3 Jayson Williams .20 .50
4 Ron Mercer .25 .60
5 Jerry Stackhouse .30 .75
6 Tariq Abdul-Wahad .20 .50
7 Sean Elliott .30 .75
8 Lindsey Hunter .20 .50
9 Larry Johnson .30 .75
10 Steve Smith .25 .60
11 Raef LaFrentz .25 .60
12 Jalen Rose .25 .60
13 Stephon Marbury .25 .60
14 Detlef Schrempf .25 .60
15 Rod Strickland .20 .50
16 Paul Pierce .40 1.00
17 Maurice Taylor .20 .50
18 Allen Iverson .60 1.50
19 Mitch Richmond .30 .75
20 Gary Trent .20 .50
21 Reggie Miller .30 .75
22 Kerry Kittles .20 .50
23 Rasheed Wallace .30 .75
24 Steve Nash .50 1.25
25 Scottie Pippen .50 1.25
26 Joe Smith .25 .60
27 Jason Williams .40 1.00
28 Michael Finley .30 .75
29 Hakeem Olajuwon .40 1.00
30 Kevin Garnett .50 1.25
31 Darrell Armstrong .20 .50
32 David Robinson .50 1.25
33 Anthony Mason .20 .50
34 Jamal Mashburn .25 .60
35 Gary Payton .30 .75
36 Bryon Russell .20 .50
37 Cedric Ceballos .20 .50
38 Michael Dickerson .20 .50
39 Robert Traylor .20 .50
40 Vin Baker .25 .60
41 Shawn Kemp .30 .75
42 Charles Barkley .50 1.25
43 Glenn Robinson .25 .60
44 Vince Carter .60 1.50
45 Zydrunas Ilgauskas .25 .60
46 Sam Cassell .25 .60
47 Tracy McGrady .50 1.25
48 Chris Mills .20 .50
49 Antawn Jamison .30 .75
50 Nick Anderson .20 .50
51 Avery Johnson .25 .60
52 Brent Barry .25 .60
53 Alonzo Mourning .40 1.00
54 Karl Malone .40 1.00
55 Toni Kukoc .30 .75
56 Ray Allen .30 .75
57 Charles Oakley .25 .60
58 Cuttino Mobley .20 .50
59 Kenny Anderson .25 .60
60 Tom Gugliotta .20 .50
61 Antoine Walker .30 .75
62 Kobe Bryant 1.25 3.00
63 Larry Hughes .25 .60
64 Vlade Divac .30 .75
65 Juwan Howard .25 .60
66 Isaiah Rider .25 .60
67 Antonio McDyess .25 .60
68 Rik Smits .30 .75
69 Keith Van Horn .25 .60
70 Doug Christie .25 .60
71 Elden Campbell .20 .50
72 Shaquille O'Neal .75 2.00
73 Matt Geiger .20 .50
74 Chris Webber .30 .75
75 Troy Hudson .30 .75
76 Eddie Jones .30 .75
77 Tim Hardaway .30 .75
78 Hersey Hawkins .20 .50
79 Shareef Abdur-Rahim .25 .60
80 Christian Laettner .25 .60
81 Latrell Sprewell .30 .75
82 Damon Stoudamire .25 .60
83 Jason Caffey .20 .50
84 Michael Olowokandi .20 .50
85 Horace Grant .25 .60
86 Grant Hill .40 1.00
87 Patrick Ewing .40 1.00
88 Clifford Robinson .20 .50
89 Ricky Davis .30 .75
90 Glen Rice .30 .75
91 Matt Harpring .20 .50
92 Mike Bibby .30 .75
93 Dikembe Mutombo .30 .75
94 Chris Mullin .30 .75
95 Marcus Camby .25 .60
96 Jason Kidd .50 1.25
97 John Starks .25 .60
98 Terrell Brandon .20 .50
99 Tim Duncan .60 1.50
100 John Stockton .40 1.00
101 Ron Artest RC 2.00 5.00
101A Ron Artest SP 3.00 8.00
102 William Avery RC .75 2.00
102A William Avery SP 1.25 3.00
103 Jonathan Bender RC 1.00 2.50
103A Jonathan Bender SP 1.50 4.00
104 Cal Bowdler RC .60 1.50
104A Cal Bowdler SP 1.00 2.50
105 Elton Brand RC 2.50 6.00
105A Elton Brand SP 4.00 10.00
106 Vonteego Cummings RC .60 1.50
106A Vonteego Cummings SP 1.00 2.50
107 Baron Davis RC 2.50 6.00
107A Baron Davis SP 4.00 10.00
108 Jeff Foster RC 1.00 2.50
108A Jeff Foster SP 1.50 4.00
109 Steve Francis RC 2.50 6.00
109A Steve Francis SP 4.00 10.00
110 Devean George RC 1.00 2.50
110A Devean George SP 1.50 4.00
111 Dion Glover RC .75 2.00
111A Dion Glover SP 1.25 3.00
112 Richard Hamilton RC 2.00 5.00
112A Richard Hamilton SP 3.00 8.00
113 Tim James RC .60 1.50
113A Tim James SP 1.00 2.50
114 Trajan Langdon RC 1.00 2.50
114A Trajan Langdon SP 1.50 4.00
115 Quincy Lewis RC .60 1.50
115A Quincy Lewis SP 1.00 2.50
116 Corey Maggette RC 1.50 4.00
116A Corey Maggette SP 2.50 6.00
117 Shawn Marion RC 2.00 5.00
117A Shawn Marion SP 3.00 8.00
118 Andre Miller RC 2.00 5.00
118A Andre Miller SP 3.00 8.00
119 Lamar Odom RC 2.50 6.00
119A Lamar Odom SP 4.00 10.00
120 Scott Padgett RC .75 2.00
120A Scott Padgett SP 1.25 3.00
121 James Posey RC 1.00 2.50
121A James Posey SP 1.50 4.00
122 A.Radojevic RC .60 1.50
122A A.Radojevic SP 1.00 2.50
123 Wally Szczerbiak RC 2.00 5.00
123A Wally Szczerbiak SP 3.00 8.00
124 Jason Terry RC 1.50 4.00
124A Jason Terry SP 2.50 6.00
125 Kenny Thomas RC 1.00 2.50
125A Kenny Thomas SP 1.50 4.00
126 Jumaine Jones RC .75 2.00
126A Jumaine Jones SP 1.25 3.00
127 Rick Hughes RC 1.00 2.50
127A Rick Hughes SP 1.50 4.00
128 John Celestand RC .60 1.50
128A John Celestand SP 1.00 2.50
129 Adrian Griffin RC 1.00 2.50
129A Adrian Griffin SP 1.50 4.00
130 Michael Ruffin RC .75 2.00
130A Michael Ruffin SP 1.25 3.00
131 Chris Herren RC .75 2.00
131A Chris Herren SP 1.25 3.00
132 Evan Eschmeyer RC .75 2.00
132A Evan Eschmeyer SP 1.25 3.00
133 Tim Young RC 1.00 2.50
133A Tim Young SP 1.50 4.00
134 Obinna Ekezie RC .75 2.00
134A Obinna Ekezie SP 1.25 3.00
135 Laron Profit RC .75 2.00
135A Laron Profit SP 1.25 3.00
136 A.J. Bramlett RC 1.00 2.50
136A A.J. Bramlett SP 1.50 4.00
137 Eddie Robinson RC 1.00 2.50
137A Eddie Robinson SP 1.50 4.00
138 Ryan Bowen RC 1.00 2.50
138A Ryan Bowen SP 1.50 4.00
139 Chucky Atkins RC 1.00 2.50
139A Chucky Atkins SP 1.50 4.00
140 Ryan Robertson RC .60 1.50
140A Ryan Robertson SP 1.00 2.50
141 Derrick Dial RC 1.00 2.50
141A Derrick Dial SP 1.50 4.00
142 Todd MacCulloch RC 1.00 2.50
142A Todd MacCulloch SP 1.50 4.00
143 DeMarco Johnson RC 1.00 2.50
143A DeMarco Johnson SP 1.50 4.00
144 Anthony Carter RC .75 2.00
144A Anthony Carter SP 1.25 3.00
145 Lazaro Borrell RC 1.00 2.50
145A Lazaro Borrell SP 1.50 4.00
146 Rafer Alston RC 1.25 3.00
146A Rafer Alston SP 2.00 5.00
147 Nikita Morgunov RC 1.00 2.50
147A Nikita Morgunov SP 1.50 4.00
148 Rodney Buford RC 1.00 2.50
148A Rodney Buford SP 1.50 4.00
149 Milt Palacio RC 1.00 2.50
149A Milt Palacio SP 1.50 4.00
150 Jermaine Jackson RC 1.00 2.50
150A Jermaine Jackson SP 1.50 4.00

1999-00 Fleer Focus Masterpiece Mania

*STARS: 4X TO 10X BASE CARD HI
*RCs: .6X TO 1.5X BASE HI
STATED PRINT RUN 300 SERIAL #'d SETS

1999-00 Fleer Focus Feel the Game

Randomly inserted in packs at one in 288, this 10-card set features pieces of player-worn jerseys.

STATED ODDS 1:288
1 Vince Carter 10.00 25.00
2 Kevin Garnett 8.00 20.00
3 Paul Pierce 6.00 15.00
4 Grant Hill 8.00 20.00
5 Tim Hardaway 5.00 12.00
6 Jayson Williams 3.00 8.00
7 Bryon Russell 3.00 8.00
8 Bryant Reeves 3.00 8.00
9 Keith Van Horn 4.00 10.00
10 Vin Baker 4.00 10.00

1999-00 Fleer Focus Focus Pocus

Randomly inserted in packs at one in 20, this 10-card set features players who are "magic" on the court. The cards feature silver and patterned holo-foil. Card backs carry a "FP" prefix.

STATED ODDS 1:20
FP1 Vince Carter 2.00 5.00
FP2 Tim Duncan 2.00 5.00
FP3 Shaquille O'Neal 2.50 6.00
FP4 Paul Pierce 1.25 3.00
FP5 Kobe Bryant 4.00 10.00
FP6 Kevin Garnett 1.50 4.00
FP7 Keith Van Horn .75 2.00
FP8 Jason Williams 1.25 3.00
FP9 Grant Hill 1.25 3.00
FP10 Allen Iverson 2.00 5.00

1999-00 Fleer Focus Fresh Ink

Randomly inserted in packs at one in 96, this 27-card set features autographs of top NBA stars and rookies. The cards are not numbered on the back and listed below in alphabetical order.

STATED ODDS 1:96
1 Charles Barkley 500.00 1000.00
2 Vince Carter 15.00 40.00
3 Obinna Ekezie 2.50 6.00
4 Jeff Foster 3.00 8.00
5 Devean George 3.00 8.00
6 Tim Hardaway 8.00 20.00
7 Matt Harpring 3.00 8.00
8 Al Harrington 3.00 8.00
9 Juwan Howard 5.00 12.00
10 Eddie Jones 6.00 15.00
11 Shawn Kemp 30.00 80.00
12 Brevin Knight 3.00 8.00
13 Trajan Langdon 3.00 8.00
14 Stephon Marbury 8.00 20.00
15 Shawn Marion 6.00 15.00
16 Tracy McGrady 12.00 30.00
17 Roshown McLeod 3.00 8.00
18 Brad Miller 6.00 15.00
19 Alonzo Mourning 35.00 70.00
20 Shaquille O'Neal 50.00 120.00
21 Scott Padgett 2.50 6.00
22 Michael Ruffin 2.50 6.00
23 Damon Stoudamire 3.00 8.00
24 Wally Szczerbiak 6.00 15.00
25 Jason Terry 3.00 8.00
26 Keith Van Horn 5.00 12.00
27 Chris Webber 100.00 225.00

1999-00 Fleer Focus Ray of Light

Randomly inserted in packs at one in 20, this 15-card set features the top rookies from the 1999 NBA Draft Class. Each card features "light pen" signature art. Card backs carry a "RL" prefix.

COMPLETE SET (15) 8.00 20.00
STATED ODDS 1:20
RL1 Andre Miller 1.00 2.50
RL2 Baron Davis 1.25 3.00
RL3 Corey Maggette .75 2.00
RL4 Dion Glover .40 1.00
RL5 Elton Brand 1.25 3.00
RL6 Jason Terry .75 2.00
RL7 Jonathan Bender .50 1.25
RL8 Lamar Odom 1.25 3.00
RL9 Richard Hamilton 1.00 2.50
RL10 Shawn Marion 1.00 2.50
RL11 Steve Francis 1.25 3.00
RL12 Tim James .30 .75
RL13 Trajan Langdon .50 1.25
RL14 Wally Szczerbiak 1.00 2.50
RL15 William Avery .40 1.00

1999-00 Fleer Focus Sean Elliott Night

This card was released by Fleer and given out to fans on the night of April 17, 2000 to help welcome Sean Elliott back into the lineup. The card is sequentially numbered to 30,000.

1 Sean Elliott .75 2.00

1999-00 Fleer Focus Soar Subjects

Randomly inserted in packs at one in six, this 15-card set highlights NBA stars who play with style and grace. Card backs carry a "SS" prefix.

COMPLETE SET (15) 6.00 15.00
STATED ODDS 1:6
*VIVID: 40X TO 100X HI COLUMN
VIVID: PRINT RUN 50 SERIAL #'d SETS
SS1 Allen Iverson .75 2.00
SS2 Anfernee Hardaway .60 1.50
SS3 Paul Pierce .50 1.25
SS4 Antoine Walker .40 1.00
SS5 Grant Hill .50 1.25
SS6 Keith Van Horn .30 .75
SS7 Kevin Garnett .60 1.50
SS8 Kobe Bryant 1.50 4.00
SS9 Larry Hughes .30 .75
SS10 Jason Williams .50 1.25
SS11 Scottie Pippen .60 1.50
SS12 Shaquille O'Neal 1.00 2.50
SS13 Vince Carter .75 2.00
SS14 Stephon Marbury .30 .75
SS15 Tim Duncan .75 2.00

1999-00 Fleer Focus Toni Kukoc Night

This card was released by Fleer, and given to fans to welcome Toni Kukoc to his new team. The card is sequentially numbered to 30,000.

1 Toni Kukoc 2.00 5.00

2000-01 Fleer Focus

The 2000-01 Fleer Focus product was released in mid-December, 2001 and features a 236-card base set. The base set is broken into tiers as follows: 180 Veterans (1-180), 36 Rookies (181-216), and (20) 20/20 Subset cards. Each pack contained 10-card, and carried a $1.99 SRP.

COMPLETE SET w/o RC (200) 15.00 40.00
RCs A: PRINT RUN 4999 SERIAL #'d SETS
RCs B: PRINT RUN 3499 SERIAL #'d SETS
RCs C: PRINT RUN 2999 SERIAL #'d SETS
RCs D: PRINT RUN 3999 SERIAL #'d SETS
RCs E: PRINT RUN 2499 SERIAL #'d SETS
RCs F: PRINT RUN 1999 SERIAL #'d SETS
SUBSET CARDS HALF VALUE OF BASE CARDS
1 Vince Carter .60 1.50
2 Shawn Marion .25 .60
3 Muggsy Bogues .25 .60
4 Dikembe Mutombo .30 .75
5 Stephon Marbury .25 .60
6 Michael Dickerson .20 .50
7 Andre Miller .25 .60
8 Toni Kukoc .30 .75
9 Nick Van Exel .25 .60
10 Aaron Williams .20 .50
11 Derrick Coleman .25 .60
12 Wally Szczerbiak .25 .60
13 Rodney Rogers .20 .50
14 Tom Gugliotta .20 .50
15 Vonteego Cummings .20 .50
16 Cedric Ceballos .20 .50
17 Malik Rose .20 .50
18 Shawn Bradley .20 .50
19 Shandon Anderson .20 .50
20 Jacque Vaughn .20 .50
21 Jamie Feick .20 .50
22 Shawn Kemp .30 .75
23 Monty Williams .20 .50
24 Allan Houston .25 .60
25 Chauncey Billups .30 .75
26 Vlade Divac .25 .60
27 Othella Harrington .20 .50
28 Dale Davis .20 .50
29 Charlie Ward .20 .50
30 Hakeem Olajuwon .40 1.00
31 Ray Allen .30 .75
32 Lamar Odom .25 .60
33 Shaquille O'Neal .75 2.00
34 Chris Childs .20 .50
35 Nick Anderson .20 .50
36 Keon Clark .20 .50
37 Danny Fortson .20 .50
38 Sam Mitchell .20 .50
39 Travis Best .20 .50
40 Chris Webber .30 .75
41 Brent Barry .20 .50
42 Scottie Pippen .50 1.25
43 Reggie Miller .30 .75
44 Bryant Reeves .20 .50
45 Bobby Jackson .20 .50
46 Antonio McDyess .25 .60
47 Elden Campbell .20 .50
48 Kenny Anderson .25 .60
49 Christian Laettner .25 .60
50 Darrell Armstrong .20 .50
51 Vinny Del Negro .20 .50
52 Quincy Lewis .20 .50
53 Peja Stojakovic .30 .75
54 Matt Geiger .20 .50
55 Larry Hughes .25 .60
56 Tracy McGrady .50 1.25
57 Tim Hardaway .30 .75
58 Brevin Knight .20 .50
59 Michael Finley .30 .75
60 Jason Kidd .50 1.25
61 Matt Harpring .20 .50
62 Antawn Jamison .30 .75
63 Wesley Person .20 .50
64 Antonio Davis .20 .50
65 Roshown McLeod .20 .50
66 Anthony Peeler .20 .50
67 Grant Hill .40 1.00
68 Michael Olowokandi .20 .50
69 Kerry Kittles .20 .50
70 Elton Brand .30 .75
71 Tariq Abdul-Wahad .20 .50
72 Aaron McKie .20 .50
73 Andrew DeClercq .20 .50
74 Anfernee Hardaway .50 1.25
75 Bimbo Coles .20 .50
76 Terrell Brandon .20 .50
77 Jalen Rose .25 .60
78 Radoslav Nesterovic .20 .50
79 Howard Eisley .20 .50
80 Steve Smith .25 .60
81 Arvydas Sabonis .25 .60
82 Jim Jackson .20 .50
83 Corey Maggette .25 .60
84 James Posey .20 .50
85 LaPhonso Ellis .25 .60
86 Eric Snow .20 .50
87 Mikki Moore RC .30 .75
88 Baron Davis .30 .75
89 Jason Williams .30 .75
90 Mike Bibby .30 .75
91 Marcus Camby .25 .60
92 Bryon Russell .20 .50
93 Steve Francis .25 .60
94 Sam Cassell .25 .60
95 Rasheed Wallace .30 .75
96 Keith Van Horn .25 .60
97 Eddie Jones .30 .75
98 Corliss Williamson .20 .50
99 Ron Mercer .20 .50
100 Sean Elliott .30 .75
101 Shareef Abdur-Rahim .25 .60
102 Glen Rice .25 .60
103 Patrick Ewing .40 1.00
104 Adrian Griffin .20 .50
105 David Robinson .50 1.25
106 Isaac Austin .20 .50
107 Anthony Mason .20 .50
108 P.J. Brown .20 .50
109 Kendall Gill .20 .50
110 Tyrone Nesby .30 .75
111 Damon Stoudamire .25 .60
112 Latrell Sprewell .25 .60
113 Tim Duncan .60 1.50
114 Glenn Robinson .25 .60
115 John Wallace .20 .50
116 Erick Strickland .20 .50
117 Doug Christie .20 .50
118 Juwan Howard .25 .60
119 Tim Thomas .20 .50
120 Tyrone Hill .20 .50
121 Avery Johnson .25 .60
122 Jerome Williams .20 .50
123 Mitch Richmond .25 .60
124 Hersey Hawkins .20 .50
125 Donyell Marshall .20 .50
126 Derek Anderson .20 .50
127 Jamal Mashburn .25 .60
128 Richard Hamilton .25 .60
129 Alonzo Mourning .40 1.00
130 Kelvin Cato .20 .50
131 Lamond Murray .20 .50
132 Bo Outlaw .20 .50
133 Chris Carr .20 .50
134 Jonathan Bender .20 .50
135 Paul Pierce .30 .75
136 Dan Majerle .30 .75
137 Ron Artest .30 .75
138 Jermaine O'Neal .25 .60
139 Chris Whitney .20 .50
140 Anthony Carter .20 .50
141 Gary Payton .30 .75
142 Kevin Garnett .50 1.25
143 Kevin Willis .20 .50
144 Charles Oakley .25 .60
145 Larry Johnson .30 .75
146 Bonzi Wells .20 .50
147 Clifford Robinson .20 .50
148 Chucky Atkins .20 .50
149 Brian Grant .20 .50
150 Voshon Lenard .20 .50
151 Antoine Walker .25 .60
152 Cuttino Mobley .20 .50
153 Robert Horry .25 .60
154 Tracy Murray .20 .50
155 Kobe Bryant 1.25 3.00
156 Joe Smith .25 .60
157 Jaren Jackson .20 .50
158 Scott Williams .20 .50
159 Allen Iverson .60 1.50
160 Rashard Lewis .30 .75
161 Chris Mills .20 .50
162 Karl Malone .40 1.00
163 John Amaechi .20 .50
164 Jason Terry .30 .75
165 Ruben Patterson .20 .50
166 Austin Croshere .20 .50
167 Maurice Taylor .20 .50
168 Rod Strickland .20 .50
169 Clarence Weatherspoon .20 .50
170 Lindsey Hunter .20 .50
171 David Wesley .20 .50
172 Jerry Stackhouse .25 .60
173 Scott Burrell .20 .50
174 John Stockton .40 1.00
175 Vitaly Potapenko .20 .50
176 Dirk Nowitzki .50 1.25
177 Vin Baker .25 .60
178 Rick Fox .20 .50
179 Mookie Blaylock .20 .50
180 Felipe Lopez .20 .50
181 Chris Mihm A RC .30 .75
182 Mamadou N'Diaye A RC .25 .60
183 Joel Przybilla A RC .30 .75
184 Jamaal Magloire A RC .40 1.00
185 Iakovos Tsakalidis A RC .25 .60
186 Etan Thomas A RC .40 1.00
187 Mark Madsen B RC .40 1.00
188 Hanno Mottola B RC .25 .60
189 Donnell Harvey B RC .30 .75
190 Jason Collier B RC .40 1.00
191 Eduardo Najera B RC .40 1.00
192 Jerome Moiso B RC .25 .60
193 Mateen Cleaves C RC .50 1.25
194 Keyon Dooling C RC .60 1.50
195 Speedy Claxton C RC .60 1.50
196 Erick Barkley C RC .40 1.00
197 A.J. Guyton C RC .40 1.00
198 Jamal Crawford C RC 1.50 4.00
199 Dan Langhi D RC .25 .60
200 Desmond Mason D RC .50 1.25
201 Chris Porter D RC .25 .60
202 Corey Hightower D RC .40 1.00
203 Morris Peterson D RC .40 1.00
204 Hedo Turkoglu D RC .60 1.50
205 Courtney Alexander E RC .60 1.50
206 Quentin Richardson E RC .75 2.00
207 D.Stevenson E RC .75 2.00
208 Michael Redd E RC 2.00 5.00
209 Chris Carrawell E RC .75 2.00
210 Mark Karcher E RC .50 1.25
211 Kenyon Martin F RC 3.00 8.00
212 Marcus Fizer F RC 1.25 3.00
213 Darius Miles F RC 1.25 3.00
214 Mike Miller F RC 2.00 5.00
215 DerMarr Johnson F RC 1.00 2.50
216 Stromile Swift F RC 1.25 3.00
217 Shaquille O'Neal 20 .50 1.25
218 Allen Iverson 20 .40 1.00
219 Grant Hill 20 .25 .60
220 Vince Carter 20 .40 1.00
221 Karl Malone 20 .25 .60
222 Chris Webber 20 .20 .50
223 Gary Payton 20 .20 .50
224 Jerry Stackhouse 20 .15 .40
225 Tim Duncan 20 .40 1.00
226 Kevin Garnett 20 .30 .75
227 Michael Finley 20 .20 .50
228 Kobe Bryant 20 .75 2.00
229 Stephon Marbury 20 .15 .40
230 Ray Allen 20 .20 .50
231 Alonzo Mourning 20 .25 .60
232 Glenn Robinson 20 .15 .40
233 Antoine Walker 20 .15 .40
234 Shareef Abdur-Rahim 20 .15 .40
235 Elton Brand 20 .20 .50
236 Eddie Jones 20 .20 .50

2000-01 Fleer Focus Draft Position

*100 STARS: 8X TO 20X BASE CARD HI
*200 STARS: 5X TO 12X BASE HI
*300 STARS: 4X TO 10X BASE HI
PRINT RUN 100, 200 OR 300 #'d SETS
155 Kobe Bryant/100 25.00 60.00
181 Chris Mihm/100 3.00 8.00
182 Mamadou N'Diaye/100 2.50 6.00
183 Joel Przybilla/100 3.00 8.00
184 Jamaal Magloire/100 4.00 10.00
185 Iakovos Tsakalidis/100 2.50 6.00
186 Etan Thomas/100 4.00 10.00
187 Mark Madsen/100 4.00 10.00
188 Hanno Mottola/200 1.50 4.00
189 Donnell Harvey/100 3.00 8.00
190 Jason Collier/100 4.00 10.00
191 Eduardo Najera/200 2.50 6.00
192 Jerome Moiso/100 2.50 6.00
193 Mateen Cleaves/100 3.00 8.00
194 Keyon Dooling/100 4.00 10.00
195 Speedy Claxton/100 4.00 10.00
196 Erick Barkley/100 2.50 6.00
197 A.J. Guyton/200 1.50 4.00
198 Jamal Crawford/100 10.00 25.00
199 Dan Langhi/200 1.50 4.00
200 Desmond Mason/100 5.00 12.00
201 Chris Porter/200 1.50 4.00
202 Corey Hightower/200 2.50 6.00
203 Morris Peterson/100 4.00 10.00
204 Hedo Turkoglu/100 6.00 15.00
205 Courtney Alexander/100 3.00 8.00
206 Quentin Richardson/100 4.00 10.00
207 DeShawn Stevenson/100 4.00 10.00
208 Michael Redd/200 6.00 15.00
209 Chris Carrawell/200 2.50 6.00
210 Mark Karcher/200 1.50 4.00
211 Kenyon Martin/100 10.00 25.00
212 Marcus Fizer/100 4.00 10.00
213 Darius Miles/100 4.00 10.00
214 Mike Miller/100 6.00 15.00
215 DerMarr Johnson/100 3.00 8.00
216 Stromile Swift/100 4.00 10.00

2000-01 Fleer Focus Arena Vision

Randomly inserted in packs at one in 12, this 15-card set showcases the NBA's top players. Card backs carry a "AV" prefix.

COMPLETE SET (15) 8.00 20.00
STATED ODDS 1:12
VIP: PRINT RUN 50 SERIAL #'d SETS
AV1 Vince Carter 1.00 2.50
AV2 Eddie Jones .50 1.25
AV3 Tim Duncan 1.00 2.50
AV4 Kevin Garnett .75 2.00
AV5 Steve Francis .40 1.00
AV6 Jason Williams .50 1.25
AV7 Grant Hill .60 1.50
AV8 Elton Brand .50 1.25
AV9 Allen Iverson 1.00 2.50
AV10 Lamar Odom .40 1.00
AV11 Kobe Bryant 2.00 5.00
AV12 Jalen Rose .40 1.00
AV13 Paul Pierce .50 1.25
AV14 Shaquille O'Neal 1.25 3.00
AV15 Stephon Marbury .40 1.00

2000-01 Fleer Focus Vince Carter Rookie Remnants

This three-card insert was randomly inserted into 2000-01 Fleer products. The set includes a Vince Carter floor card (numbered to 100), a Vince Carter floor/jersey card (numbered to 15), and finally an autographed Vince Carter floor/jersey card (numbered 1 of 1).

RANDOM INSERTS IN HOBBY PACKS
NNO Vince Carter FLR/100 12.50 30.00
NNO Vince Carter FLR JSY/15 20.00 50.00

2000-01 Fleer Focus Planet Hardwood

Randomly inserted in packs at one in 24, this 10-card set showcases some of the best players to have every stepped onto the hardwood court. Card backs carry a "PH" prefix.

COMPLETE SET (10) 12.50 25.00
STATED ODDS 1:24
*VIP: 2.5X TO 6X VALUE
VIP: PRINT RUN 50 SERIAL #'d SETS
PH1 Vince Carter 1.50 4.00
PH2 Tim Duncan 1.50 4.00
PH3 Kevin Garnett 1.25 3.00
PH4 Kobe Bryant 3.00 8.00
PH5 Lamar Odom .60 1.50
PH6 Steve Francis .60 1.50
PH7 Shaquille O'Neal 2.00 5.00
PH8 Tracy McGrady 1.25 3.00
PH9 Grant Hill 1.00 2.50
PH10 Allen Iverson 1.50 4.00

2000-01 Fleer Focus Welcome to the NBA

Randomly inserted in packs at one in six, this 15-card set showcases the top rookies from the 1999-2000 season. Card backs carry a "WN" prefix.

COMPLETE SET (15) 3.00 8.00
STATED ODDS 1:6
*VIP: 5X TO 12X VALUE
VIP: PRINT RUN 50 SERIAL #'d SETS
WN1 Kenyon Martin .75 2.00
WN2 Stromile Swift .30 .75
WN3 Darius Miles .30 .75
WN4 Marcus Fizer .30 .75
WN5 Mike Miller .50 1.25
WN6 DerMarr Johnson .25 .60
WN7 Chris Mihm .25 .60
WN8 Jamal Crawford .75 2.00
WN9 Keyon Dooling .30 .75
WN10 Jerome Moiso .20 .50
WN11 Etan Thomas .30 .75
WN12 Courtney Alexander .25 .60
WN13 Mateen Cleaves .25 .60
WN14 Jason Collier .30 .75
WN15 Desmond Mason .40 1.00

2001-02 Fleer Focus

Released in March of 2002, Fleer Focus was a 130-card set broken down into 100 veteran player cards and 30 rookie cards sequentially numbered to 1850. Base cards showcase full colore player action photos with a white and gold border and the Fleer Focus logo in the upper left hand corner. A colored box, set to match team colors contains the player's name in gold ink. The rookie cards have the same design with a color shift from gold to silver on both the borders and the player names. A number box appears on the back of the card where RC's are sequentially numbered to 1850. Five Ultra Update cards were also included in the pack-out, and these cards are listed under the base 2001-02 Ultra set. Fleer Focus was issued in 24 pack boxes where packs contained seven cards each.

COMP.SET w/o SP's (100) 10.00 25.00
101-130 PRINT RUN 1850 SER.#'d SETS
1 Vince Carter .50 1.25
2 Steve Nash .50 1.25
3 Anthony Mason .20 .50
4 Avery Johnson .25 .60
5 Peja Stojakovic .30 .75
6 Shaquille O'Neal .75 2.00
7 Jason Kidd .50 1.25
8 Steve Smith .25 .60
9 Kobe Bryant 1.25 3.00
10 Eddie Robinson .20 .50
11 Allan Houston .25 .60
12 Larry Hughes .25 .60
13 Gary Payton .30 .75
14 Alonzo Mourning .40 1.00
15 Baron Davis .30 .75
16 Speedy Claxton .20 .50
17 Hakeem Olajuwon .40 1.00
18 Anthony Carter .20 .50
19 Raef LaFrentz .20 .50
20 Dikembe Mutombo .30 .75
21 Moochie Norris .20 .50
22 Karl Malone .40 1.00
23 Darrell Armstrong .20 .50
24 Allen Iverson .60 1.50
25 Danny Fortson .20 .50
26 Antonio Davis .20 .50
27 Eddie Jones .25 .60
28 Patrick Ewing .40 1.00
29 Stephon Marbury .25 .60
30 Cuttino Mobley .20 .50
31 Morris Peterson .20 .50
32 Glenn Robinson .25 .60
33 Paul Pierce .30 .75
34 Shawn Marion .25 .60
35 Jermaine O'Neal .25 .60
36 Donyell Marshall .20 .50
37 Chauncey Billups .30 .75
38 Tracy McGrady .50 1.25
39 Vlade Divac .25 .60
40 Lamar Odom .25 .60
41 Chris Mihm .20 .50
42 Kenyon Martin .30 .75
43 Antonio McDyess .25 .60
44 Mike Bibby .30 .75
45 Darius Miles .20 .50
46 Wesley Person .20 .50
47 Mark Jackson .25 .60
48 Nick Van Exel .25 .60
49 Tim Duncan .60 1.50
50 Sam Cassell .25 .60
51 Jason Terry .30 .75
52 Bonzi Wells .20 .50
53 Al Harrington .25 .60
54 Richard Hamilton .25 .60
55 Wally Szczerbiak .25 .60
56 Toni Kukoc .30 .75
57 Rasheed Wallace .30 .75
58 Reggie Miller .30 .75
59 Courtney Alexander .20 .50
60 Terrell Brandon .20 .50
61 Dirk Nowitzki .50 1.25
62 Chris Webber .30 .75
63 Lindsey Hunter .20 .50
64 Andre Miller .25 .60
65 Clifford Robinson .20 .50
66 David Robinson .50 1.25
67 Stromile Swift .20 .50
68 Nazr Mohammed .20 .50
69 Kurt Thomas .20 .50
70 Corliss Williamson .20 .50
71 Rashard Lewis .30 .75
72 Lorenzen Wright .20 .50
73 David Wesley .20 .50
74 Derrick Coleman .25 .60
75 Jerry Stackhouse .25 .60
76 Antonio Daniels .20 .50
77 Mitch Richmond .25 .60
78 Ron Mercer .20 .50
79 Latrell Sprewell .25 .60
80 Antawn Jamison .30 .75
81 Desmond Mason .25 .60
82 Jason Williams .25 .60
83 Jamal Mashburn .25 .60
84 Grant Hill .40 1.00
85 Elton Brand .30 .75
86 Brian Grant .20 .50
87 Antoine Walker .25 .60
88 Anfernee Hardaway .50 1.25
89 Steve Francis .25 .60
90 John Stockton .40 1.00
91 Ray Allen .30 .75
92 Tim Hardaway .30 .75
93 Derek Anderson .20 .50
94 Jalen Rose .25 .60
95 Michael Jordan 5.00 12.00
96 Kevin Garnett .50 1.25
97 Shareef Abdur-Rahim .25 .60
98 Tony Delk .20 .50
99 Quentin Richardson .25 .60
100 Michael Finley .30 .75
101 Jamaal Tinsley RC .75 2.00
102 Zach Randolph RC 1.25 3.00
103 Kedrick Brown RC .50 1.25
104 Kirk Haston RC .50 1.25
105 Tyson Chandler RC 1.25 3.00
106 Shane Battier RC 1.50 4.00
107 Richard Jefferson RC 1.25 3.00
108 Gerald Wallace RC 1.00 2.50
109 DeSagana Diop RC .60 1.50
110 Ruben Boumtje-Boumtje RC .75 2.00
111 Rodney White RC .50 1.25
112 Eddie Griffin RC .60 1.50
113 Pau Gasol RC 2.50 6.00
114 Tony Parker RC 3.00 8.00
115 Kwame Brown RC .75 2.00
116 Vladimir Radmanovic RC .75 2.00
117 Troy Murphy RC .75 2.00
118 Loren Woods RC .50 1.25
119 Joe Johnson RC 1.00 2.50
120 Brandon Armstrong RC .50 1.25
121 Trenton Hassell RC .60 1.50
122 Andrei Kirilenko RC 1.25 3.00
123 Jason Richardson RC 1.00 2.50
124 Jason Collins RC .60 1.50
125 Jeryl Sasser RC .50 1.25
126 Michael Bradley RC .50 1.25
127 Eddy Curry RC .75 2.00
128 Joseph Forte RC .50 1.25
129 Brendan Haywood RC .75 2.00
130 Zeljko Rebraca RC .75 2.00

2001-02 Fleer Focus Numbers

*STARS/20: 15X TO 40X BASE CARD HI
*RCs/20: 6X TO 15X BASE CARD HI
*STARS/30:10X TO 25X BASE CARD HI
*RCs/30: 4X TO 10X BASE CARD HI
*STARS/40: 8X TO 20X BASE CARD HI
*RCs/40: 3X TO 8X BASE CARD HI
*STARS/50: 8X TO 20X BASE CARD HI
*RCs/50: 2.5X TO 6X BASE CARD HI
PRINT RUNS BETWEEN 10 AND 50
SOME NOT PRICED DUE TO SCARCITY

2001-02 Fleer Focus Materialistic Away

Randomly inserted in packs at the rate of one in 26, this 21-card set is a unique insert in which the center of the card is made of jersey material with a player likeness printed on it. Two images of the player appear on the felt, the left one is clearer while the second is blurry and appears to be a shadow. These cards have cardboard borders with the Fleer Focus logo appearing along the right side of the card, and the word "Away" and the player's name and team name centered along the bottom. A Home version was also issued and features a foil shift from silver to gold and is sequentially numbered to 50.

STATED ODDS 1:26
*HOME: 2X TO 5X AWAY HI
HOME PRINT RUN 50 SER.#'d SETS
1 Kobe Bryant 10.00 25.00
2 Shaquille O'Neal 6.00 15.00
3 Kevin Garnett 4.00 10.00
4 Tim Duncan 5.00 12.00
5 Michael Jordan 30.00 80.00
6 Allen Iverson 5.00 12.00
7 Dirk Nowitzki 4.00 10.00
8 Kwame Brown 2.50 6.00
9 Tyson Chandler 4.00 10.00
10 Eddie Griffin 2.00 5.00
11 Shane Battier 5.00 12.00
12 Tracy McGrady 4.00 10.00
13 Steve Francis 2.00 5.00
14 Chris Webber 2.50 6.00
15 Vince Carter 4.00 10.00
15A Vince Carter AU 25.00 60.00
16 Jamaal Tinsley 2.50 6.00
17 Grant Hill 3.00 8.00
18 Jason Kidd 4.00 10.00
19 Karl Malone 3.00 8.00
20 Ray Allen 2.50 6.00
21 Pau Gasol 8.00 20.00

2001-02 Fleer Focus ROY Collection

Randomly seeded in packs at the rate of one in 22, this 15-card set revolves around NBA rookies of the year. The top of the card reveals what year the featured player won this honor in gold foil. A player action photo appear on the left side of this horizontal card design and a portrait photo on the right. Centered between these photos are the letters "ROY."

COMPLETE SET (15) 20.00 50.00
STATED ODDS 1:22
1 Vince Carter 2.00 5.00
2 Allen Iverson 2.50 6.00
3 Chris Webber 1.25 3.00
4 David Robinson 2.00 5.00
5 Steve Francis 1.00 2.50
6 Patrick Ewing 1.50 4.00
7 Damon Stoudamire 1.00 2.50
8 Jason Kidd 2.00 5.00
9 Mike Miller 1.00 2.50
10 Larry Bird 3.00 8.00
11 Grant Hill 1.50 4.00
12 Michael Jordan 10.00 25.00
13 Shaquille O'Neal 3.00 8.00
14 Elton Brand 1.25 3.00
15 Tim Duncan 2.50 6.00

2001-02 Fleer Focus ROY Collection Jerseys

OMPLETE SET (9) 40.00 100.00
STATED ODDS 1:55
*PATCHES: 1.25X TO 3X JERSEY HI
PATCH PRINT RUN 99 SER.#'d SETS
1 Vince Carter 6.00 15.00
1A Vince Carter AU/15 60.00 150.00
1B Vince Carter AU/99 30.00 80.00
2 Allen Iverson 8.00 20.00
3 Chris Webber 4.00 10.00
4 David Robinson 6.00 15.00
6 Patrick Ewing 6.00 15.00
8 Jason Kidd 6.00 15.00
9 Mike Miller 3.00 8.00
10 Larry Bird 10.00 25.00
11 Grant Hill 5.00 12.00

2001-02 Fleer Focus Trading Places

Randomly inserted in packs at the rate of one in 12, this 15-card set showcases two photos of a player that was either traded sometime durning the last season or during the off-season, or players in their college jerseys and their professional jerseys. The photo on the left is set against a black background, and the photo on the right against a white background. The player's name is centered between these two photos in silver ink.

COMPLETE SET (15) 15.00 30.00
STATED ODDS 1:12
1 Vince Carter 1.25 3.00
2 Patrick Ewing 1.00 2.50
3 Mike Bibby .75 2.00
4 Jason Kidd 1.25 3.00
5 Stephon Marbury .60 1.50
6 Corey Maggette .60 1.50
7 Elton Brand .75 2.00
8 Hakeem Olajuwon 1.00 2.50
9 Dikembe Mutombo .75 2.00
10 Eddie Jones .60 1.50
11 Michael Jordan 6.00 15.00
12 Grant Hill 1.00 2.50
13 Chris Webber .75 2.00
14 Shaquille O'Neal 2.00 5.00
15 Tracy McGrady 1.25 3.00

2001-02 Fleer Focus Trading Places Jerseys

S.ABDUR-RAHIM HAS JSY VERSIONS ONLY
STATED ODDS 1:51
*PATCHES: 1.5X TO 4X JERSEYS HI
PATCH PRINT RUN 50 SER.#'d SETS
1 Vince Carter 6.00 15.00
2 Patrick Ewing 5.00 12.00
4 Jason Kidd 6.00 15.00
5 Stephon Marbury 3.00 8.00
6 Corey Maggette 3.00 8.00
7 Elton Brand 4.00 10.00
9 Dikembe Mutombo 4.00 10.00
10 Eddie Jones 3.00 8.00
13 Chris Webber 4.00 10.00
TPSA Shareef Abdur-Rahim 3.00 8.00

2003-04 Fleer Focus

Released in October 2003, Focus boasts a 160-card set divided up into 120 veteran players and 40 rookies sequentially numbered to 499. The design places players in full color against assorted single-color backgrounds which fade into white around the borders. Focus was packaged in 24-pack boxes where packs contained five cards and carried a suggested retail price of $2.99.

COMP.SET w/o SP's 12.50 30.00
1 Allan Houston .25 .60
2 Manu Ginobili .40 1.00
3 Allen Iverson .50 1.25
4 Kenyon Martin .25 .60
5 Rasho Nesterovic .20 .50
6 Tracy McGrady .40 1.00
7 Drew Gooden .25 .60
8 Tony Parker .30 .75
9 Troy Murphy .20 .50
10 Alonzo Mourning .40 1.00
11 Rasual Butler .20 .50
12 Alvin Williams .20 .50
13 Troy Hudson .20 .50
14 Gary Payton .30 .75
15 Tyson Chandler .25 .60
16 Ray Allen .30 .75
17 Amare Stoudemire .40 1.00
18 Chauncey Billups .30 .75
19 Gilbert Arenas .25 .60
20 Eddie Jones .25 .60
21 Vince Carter .50 1.25
22 Kobe Bryant 1.25 3.00
23 Reggie Miller .30 .75
24 Vincent Yarbrough .20 .50
25 Kevin Garnett .50 1.25
26 Andre Miller .25 .60
27 Glenn Robinson .25 .60
28 Kurt Thomas .20 .50
29 Vladimir Radmanovic .20 .50
30 Richard Jefferson .25 .60
31 Andrei Kirilenko .30 .75
32 Wally Szczerbiak .25 .60
33 Gordan Giricek .20 .50
34 Kwame Brown .20 .50
35 Yao Ming .60 1.50
36 Devean George .20 .50
37 Richard Hamilton .25 .60
38 Anfernee Hardaway .50 1.25
39 Grant Hill .40 1.00
40 Zach Randolph .25 .60
41 Dirk Nowitzki .50 1.25
42 Zydrunas Ilgauskas .25 .60
43 Antawn Jamison .25 .60
44 J.R. Bremer .20 .50
45 Latrell Sprewell .25 .60
46 Ron Artest .30 .75
47 Antoine Walker .30 .75
48 Eddy Curry .20 .50
49 Larry Hughes .25 .60
50 Jalen Rose .25 .60
51 Matt Harpring .20 .50
52 Sam Cassell .25 .60
53 Antonio McDyess .25 .60
54 Jamaal Tinsley .20 .50
55 Mehmet Okur .25 .60
56 Scottie Pippen .50 1.25
57 Antonio Davis .20 .50
58 Jamaal Magloire .20 .50
59 Michael Olowokandi .20 .50
60 Shane Battier .25 .60
61 Desmond Mason .25 .60
62 Baron Davis .25 .60
63 Jamal Mashburn .25 .60
64 Michael Redd .30 .75
65 Shaquille O'Neal .75 2.00
66 Ben Wallace .25 .60
67 Jason Terry .25 .60
68 Michael Finley .30 .75
69 Shareef Abdur-Rahim .25 .60
70 Bobby Jackson .20 .50
71 Jason Williams .25 .60
72 Mike Bibby .30 .75
73 Shawn Marion .25 .60
74 Ricky Davis .25 .60
75 Bonzi Wells .20 .50
76 Jason Kidd .50 1.25
77 Mike Miller .25 .60
78 Stephen Jackson .25 .60
79 Brad Miller .25 .60
80 Jason Richardson .30 .75
81 Mike Dunleavy Jr. .25 .60
82 Stephon Marbury .25 .60
83 Brian Grant .20 .50
84 Jay Williams .20 .50
85 Morris Peterson .20 .50
86 Steve Nash .40 1.00
87 Carlos Boozer .25 .60
88 Jermaine O'Neal .25 .60
89 Nene .25 .60
90 Eric Snow .20 .50
91 Steve Francis .25 .60
92 Caron Butler .25 .60
93 Jerry Stackhouse .25 .60
94 Nick Van Exel .25 .60
95 Tayshaun Prince .25 .60
96 Calbert Cheaney .20 .50
97 Pau Gasol .30 .75
98 Theo Ratliff .20 .50
99 Chris Webber .30 .75
100 Juan Dixon .20 .50
101 Paul Pierce .30 .75
102 Tim Thomas .20 .50
103 Eddie Griffin .20 .50
104 Corey Maggette .25 .60
105 Juwan Howard .25 .60
106 Peja Stojakovic .30 .75
107 Tim Duncan .50 1.25
108 Keith Van Horn .25 .60
109 Cuttino Mobley .20 .50
110 Kareem Rush .20 .50
111 Predrag Drobnjak .20 .50
112 Tony Delk .20 .50
113 Dajuan Wagner .20 .50
114 Karl Malone .40 1.00
115 Rashard Lewis .30 .75
116 David Wesley .20 .50
117 Rasheed Wallace .30 .75
118 Derrick Coleman .25 .60
119 Donnell Harvey .20 .50
120 Elton Brand .30 .75
121 Carmelo Anthony RC 8.00 20.00
122 Keith Bogans RC 1.50 4.00
123 Leandro Barbosa RC 2.50 6.00
124 Troy Bell RC 1.50 4.00
125 Chris Bosh RC 4.00 10.00
126 Zarko Cabarkapa RC 1.50 4.00
127 Jason Kapono RC 1.50 4.00
128 Nick Collison RC 2.00 5.00
129 Boris Diaw-Riffiod RC 2.50 6.00
130 Marcus Banks RC 1.50 4.00
131 T.J. Ford RC 2.00 5.00
132 Reece Gaines RC 1.50 4.00
133 Travis Hansen RC 1.50 4.00
134 Jarvis Hayes RC 1.50 4.00
135 Kirk Hinrich RC 2.50 6.00
136 Josh Howard RC 2.50 6.00
137 LeBron James RC 60.00 150.00
138 Dahntay Jones RC 2.00 5.00
139 Chris Kaman RC 2.50 6.00
140 Maciej Lampe RC 1.50 4.00
141 Darko Milicic RC 2.00 5.00
142 Travis Outlaw RC 2.00 5.00
143 Mickael Pietrus RC 2.00 5.00
144 Rick Rickert RC 1.50 4.00
145 Luke Ridnour RC 2.00 5.00
146 Sofoklis Schortsanitis RC 1.50 4.00
147 Mike Sweetney RC 1.50 4.00
148 Dwyane Wade RC 8.00 20.00
149 Luke Walton RC 2.50 6.00
150 David West RC 2.50 6.00
151 Zoran Planinic RC 1.50 4.00
152 Ndudi Ebi RC 1.50 4.00
153 Aleksandar Pavlovic RC 2.00 5.00
154 Kendrick Perkins RC 2.00 5.00
155 Maurice Williams RC 2.50 6.00
156 Jerome Beasley RC 1.50 4.00
157 Slavko Vranes RC 1.50 4.00
158 Zaur Pachulia RC 2.50 6.00
159 Carlos Delfino RC 2.00 5.00
160 Brian Cook RC 1.50 4.00

2003-04 Fleer Focus Gold

*GOLD SINGLES: 5X TO 12X BASE HI
*GOLD RCs: 1.25X TO 3X BASE HI
PRINT RUN 50 SERIAL #'d SETS
148 Dwyane Wade 25.00 60.00

2003-04 Fleer Focus Numbers Century

*SINGLES: 4X TO 10X BASE CARD HI
*RCs .6X TO 1.5X BASE CARD HI
PRINT RUN 100 SERIAL #'d SETS
137 LeBron James 100.00 250.00
148 Dwyane Wade 12.00 30.00

2003-04 Fleer Focus Silver

*1-120 SILVER: 8X TO 20X BASE HI
*121-160 SILVER RCs: 1.5X TO 4X BASE HI
PRINT RUN 25 SER.#'d SETS
148 Dwyane Wade 30.00 80.00

2003-04 Fleer Focus Auto Focus

Inserted in packs, this 24-card set places player photos on the right side of the card where background colors are set to match the featured player's team colors and cards are sequentially numbered to 250.

PRINT RUN 250 SERIAL #'d SETS
1 Manu Ginobili 2.00 5.00
2 Eddy Curry 1.00 2.50
3 Tracy McGrady 2.00 5.00
4 Drew Gooden 1.25 3.00
5 Caron Butler 1.25 3.00
6 Amare Stoudemire 2.00 5.00
7 Tayshaun Prince 1.25 3.00
8 Vince Carter 2.50 6.00
9 Kevin Garnett 2.50 6.00
10 Dirk Nowitzki 2.50 6.00
11 Ben Wallace 1.25 3.00
12 Tony Parker 1.50 4.00
13 Steve Francis 1.25 3.00
14 Mike Bibby 1.50 4.00
15 Alonzo Mourning 2.00 5.00
16 Carmelo Anthony 5.00 12.00
17 Marcus Banks 1.00 2.50
18 Maciej Lampe 1.00 2.50
19 Mickael Pietrus 1.25 3.00
20 Luke Ridnour 1.25 3.00
21 Dwyane Wade 5.00 12.00
22 David West 1.50 4.00
23 Chris Bosh 2.50 6.00
24 Mike Sweetney 1.00 2.50
25 Troy Bell 1.00 2.50

2003-04 Fleer Focus Auto Focus Autographs

This 24-card set parallels the design of the base Auto Focus insert set enhanced with a vertial cut-signature on the left side of the card and sequential numbering to 100. Versions sequentially numbered to 50 and 25 were also issued.

PRINT RUN 100 SERIAL #'d SETS
*AUTO 50: .5X TO 1.25X BASE HI
1 Manu Ginobili 12.50 30.00
2 Eddy Curry 6.00 15.00
3 Steve Francis 6.00 15.00
4 Mike Bibby 12.50 30.00
5 Amare Stoudemire 10.00 25.00
6 Tayshaun Prince 8.00 20.00
7 Tracy McGrady 20.00 50.00
8 Alonzo Mourning 30.00 80.00
9 Ben Wallace 15.00 40.00
11 Carmelo Anthony 30.00 80.00
12 Marcus Banks 6.00 15.00
14 Mickael Pietrus 8.00 20.00
15 Luke Ridnour 8.00 20.00
16 Dwyane Wade 40.00 100.00
17 David West 8.00 20.00
18 Chris Bosh 20.00 50.00
19 Michael Sweetney 6.00 15.00
20 Troy Bell 6.00 15.00
22 Josh Howard 6.00 15.00
23 Leandro Barbosa 8.00 20.00

2003-04 Fleer Focus Autographs

This 24-card set parallels the design of the base Focus set enhanced with embedded cut signatures and sequential numbering to 100. Versions sequentially numbered to 50 and 25 were also produced.

PRINT RUN 100 SERIAL #'d SETS
*AUTO 50: .5X TO 1.25X BASE HI
*AUTO 25: .6X TO 1.5X BASE HI
4 Eddy Curry 6.00 15.00
10 Alonzo Mourning 30.00 80.00
17 Amare Stoudemire 12.00 30.00
91 Steve Francis 12.50 30.00
121 Carmelo Anthony 25.00 60.00
123 Leandro Barbosa 8.00 20.00
124 Troy Bell 6.00 15.00
125 Chris Bosh 12.00 30.00
130 Marcus Banks 6.00 15.00
143 Mickael Pietrus 8.00 20.00
145 Luke Ridnour 8.00 20.00
148 Dwyane Wade 40.00 100.00
150 David West 6.00 15.00
155 Mo Williams 8.00 20.00

2003-04 Fleer Focus Home and Aways

Randomly seeded and sequentially numbered to 500, this 15-card set features players with both home and away jerseys.

COMPLETE SET (15) 15.00 30.00
PRINT RUN 500 SERIAL #'d SETS
1 Kevin Garnett 2.00 5.00
2 Chris Webber 1.25 3.00
3 Allen Iverson 2.00 5.00
4 Scottie Pippen 2.00 5.00
5 Paul Pierce 1.25 3.00
6 Jason Kidd 2.00 5.00
7 Baron Davis 1.00 2.50
8 Steve Francis 1.00 2.50
9 Stephon Marbury 1.00 2.50
10 Antoine Walker 1.25 3.00
11 Vince Carter 2.00 5.00
12 Latrell Sprewell 1.00 2.50
13 Manu Ginobili 1.50 4.00
14 Caron Butler 1.00 2.50
15 Jason Richardson 1.25 3.00

2003-04 Fleer Focus Home and Aways Dual Jerseys

Inserted and sequentially numbered to 199, this 15-card set features swatches of players home and away jerseys with the home jersey in the shape of an "H" on one side and an away jersey in the shape of an "A" on the other.

PRINT RUN 199 SERIAL #'d SETS
HAAI Allen Iverson 8.00 20.00
HAAW Antoine Walker 5.00 12.00
HABD Baron Davis 4.00 10.00
HACB Caron Butler 4.00 10.00
HACW Chris Webber 5.00 12.00
HAJK Jason Kidd 8.00 20.00
HAJR Jason Richardson 5.00 12.00
HAKG Kevin Garnett 8.00 20.00
HALS Latrell Sprewell 4.00 10.00
HAMG Manu Ginobili 6.00 15.00
HAPP Paul Pierce 5.00 12.00
HASF Steve Francis 4.00 10.00
HASP Scottie Pippen 10.00 25.00
HAVC Vince Carter 8.00 20.00

2003-04 Fleer Focus NBA Shirtified

Randomly inserted in packs, this 25-card set places full-color player action photography on a solid colored background with his team logo in the lower left hand corner of the card. Each card is sequentially numbered to 750.

COMPLETE SET (25) 30.00 60.00
PRINT RUN 750 SERIAL #'d SETS
1 Tracy McGrady 1.50 4.00
2 Mike Bibby 1.25 3.00
3 Allen Iverson 2.00 5.00
4 Dirk Nowitzki 2.00 5.00
5 Paul Pierce 1.25 3.00
6 Antawn Jamison 1.00 2.50
7 Kenyon Martin 1.00 2.50
8 Shawn Marion 1.00 2.50
9 Rasheed Wallace 1.25 3.00
10 Caron Butler 1.00 2.50
11 Elton Brand 1.25 3.00
12 Eddy Curry .75 2.00
13 Michael Finley 1.25 3.00
14 Yao Ming 2.50 6.00
15 Vince Carter 2.00 5.00
16 Amare Stoudemire 1.50 4.00
17 Jermaine O'Neal 1.00 2.50
18 Peja Stojakovic 1.25 3.00
19 Karl Malone 1.50 4.00
20 Ben Wallace 1.00 2.50
21 Steve Francis 1.00 2.50
22 Baron Davis 1.00 2.50
23 Kobe Bryant 5.00 12.00
24 Shaquille O'Neal 3.00 8.00
25 Tim Duncan 2.00 5.00

2003-04 Fleer Focus NBA Shirtified Jerseys 250

Randomly seeded in packs, this 20-card set parallels the design of the base NBA Shirtified insert set enhanced with a swatch of jersey and sequential numbering to 250. Versions numbered to 150, 75, Numbers with swatches from the jersey number serially numbered to 99, Nameplates with swatches from the player's name numbered to 50 and NBA Logos numbered one of one.

PRINT RUN 250 SERIAL #'d SETS
*150 SINGLES: .5X TO 1.25X BASE HI
*75 SINGLES: .6X TO 1.5X BASE HI
*NAMEPLATES: 1.25X TO 3X BASE HI
NAMPLATES PRINT RUN 50 SER.#'d SETS
*NUMBERS SINGLES: 1X TO 2.5X BASE HI
NUMBERS PRINT RUN 99 SER.#'d SETS
NSAI Allen Iverson 4.00 10.00
NSAJ Antawn Jamison 2.00 5.00
NSAS Amare Stoudemire 3.00 8.00
NSBW Ben Wallace 2.00 5.00
NSDN Dirk Nowitzki 4.00 10.00
NSEB Elton Brand 2.50 6.00
NSEC Eddy Curry 1.50 4.00
NSJO Jermaine O'Neal 2.00 5.00
NSKM Karl Malone 3.00 8.00
NSKM Kenyon Martin 2.00 5.00
NSLS Caron Butler 2.00 5.00
NSMB Mike Bibby 2.50 6.00
NSMF Michael Finley 2.50 6.00
NSPP Paul Pierce 2.50 6.00
NSPS Peja Stojakovic 2.50 6.00
NSRW Rasheed Wallace 2.50 6.00
NSSM Shawn Marion 2.00 5.00
NSTM Tracy McGrady 3.00 8.00
NSVC Vince Carter 4.00 10.00
NSYM Yao Ming 5.00 12.00

2003-04 Fleer Focus Tag Team

Randomly inserted in packs, this 15-card set pairs players with something in common. Ie: same team, same rookie crop etc. One player appears on the top of the other and both are set against a marble background set to match the team color schemes of the players. Each card is sequentially numbered to 350.

PRINT RUN 350 SERIAL #'d SETS
1 J.Kidd/K.Martin 1.50 4.00
2 M.Bibby/P.Stojakovic 1.00 2.50
3 T.Prince/B.Wallace .75 2.00
4 A.Houston/L.Sprewell .75 2.00
5 K.Garnett/T.Hudson 1.50 4.00
6 S.Francis/Y.Ming 2.00 5.00
7 S.Nash/D.Nowitzki 1.50 4.00
8 P.Pierce/A.Walker 1.00 2.50
9 T.McGrady/D.Gooden 1.25 3.00
10 S.Marbury/A.Stoudemire 1.25 3.00
11 D.Milicic/C.Bosh 1.50 4.00
12 T.Ford/D.Wade 3.00 8.00
13 L.James/C.Anthony 15.00 40.00
14 T.Duncan/T.Parker 1.50 4.00
15 K.Bryant/S.O'Neal 4.00 10.00

2003-04 Fleer Focus Tag Team Jerseys

Randomly inserted, this 10-card set parallels the design of the base Tag Team set enhanced with two swatches, one from each player, of game worn jersey. Each card is sequentially numbered to 250. A Tag version numbered one of one was also inserted.

PRINT RUN 250 SERIAL #'d SETS
1 J.Kidd/K.Martin 6.00 15.00
2 M.Bibby/P.Stojakovic 5.00 12.00
3 T.Prince/B.Wallace 5.00 12.00
4 A.Houston/L.Sprewell 6.00 15.00
5 K.Garnett/T.Hudson 8.00 20.00
6 S.Francis/Y.Ming 10.00 25.00
7 S.Nash/D.Nowitzki 8.00 20.00
9 T.McGrady/D.Gooden 6.00 15.00
10 S.Marbury/A.Stoudemire 6.00 15.00

1999-00 Fleer Force

Debuting in 1999-00, the Fleer Force set contained 235-cards with 200 veterans and 35 rookies. The rookies were serially numbered to 1600. The cards base design is similar to the 99-00 Fleer Tradition set, but the front carries a metallic look. Two special Vince Carter cards were also randomly inserted called Sgt. Carter. The first card features a swatch of "GI gear" worn by Carter. Those cards were inserted at one in 300. The second is an autographed version of the same card, numbered to 15. Those cards are listed at the end of the base set.

COMPLETE SET (235) 75.00 150.00
COMPLETE SET w/o RC (200) 15.00 30.00
201-235 PRINT RUN 1600 SERIAL #'d SETS
SGT.CARTER CARD: STATED ODDS 1:300
CARTER AU: PRINT RUN 300 SETS
1 Vince Carter .60 1.50
2 Kobe Bryant 1.25 3.00
3 Keith Van Horn .25 .60
4 Tim Duncan .60 1.50
5 Grant Hill .40 1.00
6 Kevin Garnett .50 1.25
7 Anfernee Hardaway .50 1.25
8 Jason Williams .40 1.00
9 Paul Pierce .40 1.00
10 Mookie Blaylock .20 .50
11 Shawn Bradley .20 .50
12 Kenny Anderson .25 .60
13 Chauncey Billups .30 .75
14 Elden Campbell .20 .50
15 Jason Caffey .20 .50
16 Brent Barry .25 .60
17 Charles Barkley .50 1.25
18 Derek Anderson .20 .50
19 Darrick Martin .20 .50
20 Michael Curry .20 .50
21 Rick Fox .20 .50
22 Antonio Davis .20 .50
23 Terrell Brandon .20 .50
24 P.J. Brown .20 .50
25 Toby Bailey .20 .50
26 Ray Allen .30 .75
27 Brian Grant .20 .50
28 Scott Burrell .20 .50
29 Tariq Abdul-Wahad .20 .50
30 Marcus Camby .25 .60
31 John Stockton .40 1.00
32 Nick Anderson .20 .50
33 Jamie Feick RC .25 .60
34 Matt Geiger .20 .50
35 Vin Baker .25 .60
36 Dee Brown .20 .50
37 Shandon Anderson .20 .50
38 Vernon Maxwell .20 .50
39 Shareef Abdur-Rahim .25 .60
40 LaPhonso Ellis .20 .50
41 Cedric Ceballos .20 .50
42 Tony Battie .25 .60
43 Keon Clark .20 .50
44 Derrick Coleman .25 .60
45 Erick Dampier .20 .50
46 Corey Benjamin .20 .50
47 Michael Dickerson .20 .50
48 Cedric Henderson .20 .50
49 Lamond Murray .20 .50
50 Jerome Williams .20 .50
51 Shaquille O'Neal .75 2.00
52 Dale Davis .20 .50
53 Dean Garrett .20 .50
54 Tim Hardaway .30 .75
55 Dennis Rodman .60 1.50
56 Sam Cassell .25 .60
57 Jim Jackson .20 .50
58 Kendall Gill .20 .50
59 Eric Williams .20 .50
60 Chris Childs .20 .50
61 Vlade Divac .30 .75
62 Darrell Armstrong .20 .50
63 Mario Elie .20 .50
64 Jaren Jackson .20 .50
65 Dale Ellis .20 .50
66 Doug Christie .25 .60
67 Howard Eisley .20 .50
68 Juwan Howard .25 .60
69 Mike Bibby .30 .75
70 Alan Henderson .20 .50
71 Michael Finley .30 .75
72 Dana Barros .20 .50
73 Troy Hudson .30 .75
74 Ricky Davis .30 .75
75 John Amaechi RC .30 .75
76 Erick Strickland .20 .50
77 Bryce Drew .20 .50
78 Shawn Kemp .30 .75
79 Tyrone Nesby RC .25 .60
80 Lindsey Hunter .20 .50
81 Ruben Patterson .20 .50
82 Al Harrington .30 .75
83 Bobby Jackson .20 .50
84 Dan Majerle .30 .75
85 Rex Chapman .20 .50
86 Dell Curry .20 .50
87 Robert Pack .20 .50
88 Kerry Kittles .20 .50
89 Isaiah Rider .25 .60
90 Patrick Ewing .40 1.00
91 Lawrence Funderburke .20 .50
92 Isaac Austin .20 .50
93 Sean Elliott .30 .75
94 Larry Hughes .25 .60
95 Jelani McCoy .20 .50
96 Tracy McGrady .50 1.25
97 Jeff Hornacek .25 .60
98 Jahidi White .20 .50
99 Danny Manning .25 .60
100 Roshown McLeod .20 .50
101 Steve Nash .50 1.25
102 Ron Mercer .25 .60
103 Raef LaFrentz .25 .60
104 Eddie Jones .30 .75
105 Antawn Jamison .30 .75
106 Chucky Atkins RC .30 .75
107 Othella Harrington .20 .50
108 Brevin Knight .20 .50
109 Michael Olowokandi .20 .50
110 Christian Laettner .25 .60
111 J.R. Reid .20 .50
112 Reggie Miller .30 .75
113 Lazaro Borrell RC .30 .75
114 Jamal Mashburn .25 .60
115 Glenn Robinson .25 .60
116 Pat Garrity .20 .50
117 Stephon Marbury .25 .60
118 Arvydas Sabonis .25 .60
119 Allan Houston .25 .60
120 Peja Stojakovic .30 .75
121 Michael Doleac .20 .50
122 Avery Johnson .25 .60
123 Allen Iverson .60 1.50
124 Rashard Lewis .30 .75
125 Charles Oakley .25 .60
126 Karl Malone .40 1.00
127 Tracy Murray .20 .50
128 Felipe Lopez .20 .50
129 Dikembe Mutombo .30 .75
130 Dirk Nowitzki .60 1.50
131 Vitaly Potapenko .20 .50
132 Antonio McDyess .25 .60
133 Anthony Mason .20 .50
134 Donyell Marshall .20 .50
135 Dickey Simpkins .20 .50
136 Cuttino Mobley .20 .50
137 Wesley Person .20 .50
138 Rodney Rogers .20 .50
139 Jerry Stackhouse .30 .75
140 Glen Rice .30 .75
141 Chris Mullin .30 .75
142 Anthony Peeler .20 .50
143 Alonzo Mourning .40 1.00
144 Tom Gugliotta .20 .50
145 Tim Thomas .25 .60
146 Damon Stoudamire .25 .60
147 Jayson Williams .20 .50
148 Larry Johnson .30 .75
149 Chris Webber .30 .75
150 Matt Harpring .20 .50
151 David Robinson .50 1.25
152 George Lynch .20 .50
153 Gary Payton .30 .75
154 John Wallace .20 .50
155 Greg Ostertag .20 .50
156 Mitch Richmond .30 .75
157 Cherokee Parks .20 .50
158 Steve Smith .25 .60
159 Gary Trent .20 .50
160 Antoine Walker .30 .75
161 Chris Herren RC .25 .60
162 Ron Harper .20 .50
163 Chris Mills .20 .50
164 Fred Hoiberg .20 .50
165 Hakeem Olajuwon .40 1.00
166 Bob Sura .20 .50
167 Brian Skinner .20 .50
168 Loy Vaught .20 .50
169 A.C. Green .25 .60
170 Jalen Rose .25 .60
171 Joe Smith .25 .60
172 Clarence Weatherspoon .20 .50
173 Jason Kidd .50 1.25
174 Robert Traylor .20 .50
175 Rasheed Wallace .30 .75
176 Latrell Sprewell .30 .75
177 Corliss Williamson .20 .50
178 Bo Outlaw .20 .50
179 Malik Rose .20 .50
180 Nazr Mohammed .20 .50
181 Eric Murdock .20 .50
182 Kevin Willis .20 .50
183 Bryon Russell .20 .50
184 Bryant Reeves .20 .50
185 Rod Strickland .20 .50
186 Samaki Walker .20 .50
187 Nick Van Exel .25 .60
188 David Wesley .20 .50
189 John Starks .25 .60
190 Toni Kukoc .30 .75
191 Scottie Pippen .50 1.25
192 Johnny Newman .20 .50
193 Maurice Taylor .20 .50
194 Rik Smits .30 .75
195 Clifford Robinson .20 .50
196 Bonzi Wells .20 .50
197 Charlie Ward .20 .50
198 Detlef Schrempf .25 .60
199 Theo Ratliff .25 .60
200 Kelvin Cato .20 .50
201 Ron Artest RC 3.00 8.00
202 William Avery RC 1.25 3.00
203 Elton Brand RC 4.00 10.00
204 Baron Davis RC 4.00 10.00
205 Jumaine Jones RC 1.25 3.00
206 Andre Miller RC 3.00 8.00
207 Eddie Robinson RC 1.50 4.00
208 James Posey RC 1.50 4.00
209 Jason Terry RC 2.50 6.00
210 Kenny Thomas RC 1.50 4.00
211 Steve Francis RC 4.00 10.00
212 Wally Szczerbiak RC 3.00 8.00
213 Richard Hamilton RC 3.00 8.00
214 Jonathan Bender RC 1.50 4.00
215 Shawn Marion RC 3.00 8.00
216 A.Radojevic RC 1.00 2.50
217 Tim James RC 1.00 2.50
218 Trajan Langdon RC 1.50 4.00
219 Lamar Odom RC 4.00 10.00
220 Corey Maggette RC 2.50 6.00
221 Dion Glover RC 1.25 3.00
222 Cal Bowdler RC 1.00 2.50
223 Vonteego Cummings RC 1.00 2.50
224 Devean George RC 1.50 4.00
225 Anthony Carter RC 1.25 3.00
226 Laron Profit RC 1.25 3.00
227 Quincy Lewis RC 1.00 2.50
228 John Celestand RC 1.00 2.50
229 Obinna Ekezie RC 1.25 3.00
230 Scott Padgett RC 1.25 3.00
231 Michael Ruffin RC 1.25 3.00
232 Jeff Foster RC 1.50 4.00
233 Jermaine Jackson RC 1.50 4.00
234 Adrian Griffin RC 1.50 4.00
235 Todd MacCulloch RC 1.50 4.00
NNO V.Carter Sgt. JSY 8.00 20.00
NNO V.Carter Sgt. AU/300 25.00 60.00

1999-00 Fleer Force Forcefield

*STARS: 1.25X TO 3X BASE CARD HI
*RCs: .75X TO 2X BASE HI
STARS: STATED ODDS 1:12
RCs: PRINT RUN 100 SERIAL #'d SETS

1999-00 Fleer Force Air Force One Five

Randomly inserted into packs at one in 24, this 15-card set highlights Vince Carter. Card backs carry an "AF" prefix.

COMPLETE SET (15) 12.00 30.00
COMMON CARD (AF1-AF15) 1.50 4.00
STATED ODDS 1:24
*FORCEFIELD: 2.5X TO 6X BASE HI
FF: PRINT RUN 150 SERIAL #'d SETS

1999-00 Fleer Force Attack Force

Randomly inserted in packs at one in six, this 20-card set focused on younger players in the league who will lead the attack in the next century. Card backs carry an "A" prefix.

COMPLETE SET (20) 8.00 20.00
STATED ODDS 1:6
*FF: .75X TO 2X BASE CARD HI
FF: STATED ODDS 1:24
A1 Vince Carter 1.00 2.50
A2 Lamar Odom 1.25 3.00
A3 Stephon Marbury .40 1.00
A4 Jason Terry .75 2.00
A5 Richard Hamilton 1.00 2.50
A6 Steve Francis 1.25 3.00
A7 Wally Szczerbiak 1.00 2.50
A8 Tracy McGrady .75 2.00
A9 Michael Finley .50 1.25
A10 Baron Davis 1.25 3.00
A11 Shawn Marion 1.00 2.50
A12 Jonathan Bender .50 1.25
A13 Elton Brand 1.25 3.00
A14 Shareef Abdur-Rahim .40 1.00
A15 Keith Van Horn .40 1.00
A16 Jerry Stackhouse .50 1.25
A17 Antonio McDyess .40 1.00
A18 Antoine Walker .50 1.25
A19 Steve Smith .40 1.00
A20 Ron Artest 1.00 2.50

1999-00 Fleer Force Forceful

Randomly inserted in packs at one in 36, this 15-card set features impact players in the NBA. Card backs carry a "F" prefix.

COMPLETE SET (15) 20.00 50.00
STATED ODDS 1:36
*FF: .75X TO 2X BASE CARD HI
FF: STATED ODDS 1:144
F1 Vince Carter 2.50 6.00
F2 Lamar Odom 3.00 8.00
F3 Shaquille O'Neal 3.00 8.00
F4 Alonzo Mourning 1.50 4.00
F5 Kevin Garnett 2.00 5.00
F6 Tim Duncan 2.50 6.00
F7 Kobe Bryant 5.00 12.00
F8 Allen Iverson 2.50 6.00
F9 Jason Williams 1.50 4.00
F10 Paul Pierce 1.50 4.00
F11 Shareef Abdur-Rahim 1.00 2.50
F12 Stephon Marbury 1.00 2.50
F13 Grant Hill 1.50 4.00
F14 Keith Van Horn 1.00 2.50
F15 Karl Malone 1.50 4.00

1999-00 Fleer Force Mission Accomplished

Randomly inserted in packs at one in 12, this 15-card set features players who carry out the game plan night-in and night-out. Card backs carry a "MA" prefix.

COMPLETE SET (15) 10.00 25.00
STATED ODDS 1:12
*FF: .75X TO 2X BASE CARD HI
FF: STATED ODDS 1:48
MA1 Vince Carter 1.25 3.00
MA2 Lamar Odom 1.50 4.00
MA3 Allen Iverson 1.25 3.00
MA4 Tim Duncan 1.25 3.00
MA5 Charles Barkley 1.00 2.50
MA6 Jason Kidd 1.00 2.50
MA7 Steve Francis 1.50 4.00
MA8 Elton Brand 1.50 4.00
MA9 Kevin Garnett 1.00 2.50
MA10 Baron Davis 1.50 4.00
MA11 Paul Pierce .75 2.00
MA12 Scottie Pippen 1.00 2.50
MA13 Chris Webber .60 1.50
MA14 Anfernee Hardaway 1.00 2.50
MA15 David Robinson 1.00 2.50

1999-00 Fleer Force Operation Invasion

Randomly inserted in packs at one in 24, this 15-card set features the top players in the NBA that lead their team into battle. The cards feature on oval die cut design on the top and bottom. Card backs carry an "OI" prefix.

COMPLETE SET (15) 12.50 30.00
STATED ODDS 1:24
*FF: .75X TO 2X BASE CARD HI
FF: STATED ODDS 1:96
OI1 Vince Carter 2.00 5.00
OI2 Lamar Odom 2.50 6.00
OI3 Kobe Bryant 4.00 10.00
OI4 Tim Duncan 2.00 5.00
OI5 Paul Pierce 1.25 3.00
OI6 Kevin Garnett 1.50 4.00
OI7 Grant Hill 1.25 3.00
OI8 Allen Iverson 2.00 5.00
OI9 Jason Williams 1.25 3.00
OI10 Ron Mercer .75 2.00
OI11 Shaquille O'Neal 2.50 6.00
OI12 Keith Van Horn .75 2.00
OI13 Shareef Abdur-Rahim .75 2.00
OI14 Alonzo Mourning 1.25 3.00
OI15 Stephon Marbury .75 2.00

1999-00 Fleer Force Special Forces

Randomly inserted in packs at one in 12, this 15-card set features players who bring a special quality to the NBA. Card backs carry a "SF" prefix.

COMPLETE SET (15) 8.00 20.00
STATED ODDS 1:12
*FF: .75X TO 2X BASE CARD HI
FF: STATED ODDS 1:48
SF1 Vince Carter 1.25 3.00
SF2 Lamar Odom 1.50 4.00
SF3 Keith Van Horn .50 1.25
SF4 Stephon Marbury .50 1.25
SF5 Scottie Pippen 1.00 2.50
SF6 Ray Allen .60 1.50
SF7 Chris Webber .60 1.50
SF8 Jason Williams .75 2.00
SF9 Karl Malone .75 2.00
SF10 Patrick Ewing .75 2.00
SF11 Elton Brand 1.50 4.00
SF12 Grant Hill .75 2.00
SF13 Eddie Jones .60 1.50
SF14 Shaquille O'Neal 1.50 4.00
SF15 Kobe Bryant 2.50 6.00

2001-02 Fleer Force

Released in early February 2002, Fleer Force was a 180-card set divided up into 150 veteran player cards, which feature a white backdrop with player action photos set against an artist drawn portrait close-up of the player's face, and 30 rookie cards set up in a horizontal design with player portrait photos and gold foil stamping set against a basketball court style backdrop. The player photos appear along the left side of the card, and the player's number and the word "Rookie" appears on the right side. All of the cards in the set hava a colored strip set above the bottom border of the card containing the player's name, team, and position. The rookie cards have a number box in this strip on the right side of the card and are sequentially numbered to 999. The first 300 serially numbered rookie cards contain a postage stamp and a post office stamp of the city and date that the player made his league debut in. Force was packaged in 24 pack boxes where packs contained seven cards.

COMPLETE SET (180) 75.00 150.00
COMPLETE SET w/o SP's (150) 12.50 30.00
101-130 PRINT RUN 999 SER.#'d SETS
FIRST 300 SER.#'d SETS RC POSTMARKS
1 Vince Carter .50 1.25
2 Allan Houston .25 .60
3 Steve Francis .25 .60
4 Karl Malone .40 1.00
5 Joe Smith .25 .60
6 Raef LaFrentz .20 .50
7 David Robinson .50 1.25
8 Tim Thomas .20 .50
9 Antonio McDyess .25 .60
10 Steve Smith .25 .60
11 Eddie Jones .25 .60
12 Jumaine Jones .20 .50
13 Derek Anderson .20 .50
14 Shaquille O'Neal .75 2.00
15 Eddie Robinson .20 .50
16 Stephon Marbury .25 .60
17 Darius Miles .20 .50
18 Toni Kukoc .30 .75
19 Latrell Sprewell .25 .60
20 Wang Zhizhi .25 .60
21 Tim Duncan .60 1.50
22 Eddie House .20 .50
23 Chris Mihm .20 .50
24 Rasheed Wallace .30 .75
25 Kobe Bryant 1.25 3.00
26 Kenny Thomas .20 .50
27 John Stockton .40 1.00
28 Mike Bibby .30 .75
29 Larry Hughes .25 .60
30 Antonio Davis .20 .50
31 Ray Allen .30 .75
32 Corliss Williamson .20 .50
33 Desmond Mason .25 .60
34 Sam Cassell .25 .60
35 Dirk Nowitzki .50 1.25
36 Chris Webber .30 .75
37 Michael Dickerson .20 .50
38 Ron Mercer .20 .50
39 Iakovos Tsakalidis .20 .50
40 Derek Fisher .25 .60
41 Baron Davis .30 .75
42 Allen Iverson .60 1.50
43 Avery Johnson .25 .60
44 Courtney Alexander .20 .50
45 Alonzo Mourning .40 1.00
46 Steve Nash .50 1.25
47 Hedo Turkoglu .25 .60
48 Jason Williams .25 .60
49 David Wesley .20 .50
50 Dikembe Mutombo .30 .75
51 LaPhonso Ellis .25 .60
52 Trajan Langdon .20 .50
53 Damon Stoudamire .25 .60
54 Rick Fox .20 .50
55 Paul Pierce .30 .75
56 Tracy McGrady .50 1.25
57 Lamar Odom .25 .60
58 Antoine Walker .25 .60
59 Mike Miller .25 .60
60 Jermaine O'Neal .25 .60
61 Michael Jordan 4.00 10.00
62 Jason Kidd .50 1.25
63 Marc Jackson .20 .50
64 Hakeem Olajuwon .40 1.00
65 Kevin Garnett .50 1.25
66 Nick Van Exel .25 .60
67 Rashard Lewis .30 .75
68 Brian Grant .20 .50
69 Keith Van Horn .25 .60
70 Grant Hill .40 1.00
71 Reggie Miller .30 .75
72 Richard Hamilton .25 .60
73 Marcus Camby .25 .60
74 Clifford Robinson .20 .50
75 Gary Payton .30 .75
76 Andre Miller .25 .60
77 Bonzi Wells .20 .50
78 Stromile Swift .20 .50
79 Marcus Fizer .20 .50
80 Shawn Marion .25 .60
81 Elton Brand .30 .75
82 Jamal Mashburn .25 .60
83 Aaron McKie .20 .50
84 Corey Maggette .25 .60
85 Jason Terry .30 .75
86 Anfernee Hardaway .50 1.25
87 Antawn Jamison .30 .75
88 Morris Peterson .20 .50
89 Wally Szczerbiak .25 .60
90 Jerry Stackhouse .25 .60
91 Shareef Abdur-Rahim .25 .60
92 Glenn Robinson .25 .60
93 Michael Finley .30 .75
94 Peja Stojakovic .30 .75
95 Jalen Rose .25 .60
96 Theo Ratliff .20 .50
97 Kurt Thomas .20 .50
98 Cuttino Mobley .20 .50
99 DeShawn Stevenson .20 .50
100 Terrell Brandon .20 .50
101 Kwame Brown RC 1.00 2.50
102 Tyson Chandler RC 1.50 4.00
103 Pau Gasol RC 3.00 8.00
104 Eddy Curry RC 1.00 2.50
105 Jason Richardson RC 1.25 3.00
106 Shane Battier RC 2.00 5.00
107 Eddie Griffin RC .75 2.00
108 DeSagana Diop RC .75 2.00
109 Rodney White RC .60 1.50
110 Joe Johnson RC 1.25 3.00
111 Kedrick Brown RC .60 1.50
112 Vladimir Radmanovic RC 1.00 2.50
113 Richard Jefferson RC 1.50 4.00
114 Troy Murphy RC 1.00 2.50
115 Steven Hunter RC .75 2.00
116 Kirk Haston RC .60 1.50
117 Michael Bradley RC .60 1.50
118 Jason Collins RC .75 2.00
119 Zach Randolph RC 1.50 4.00
120 Brendan Haywood RC 1.00 2.50
121 Joseph Forte RC .60 1.50
122 Jeryl Sasser RC .60 1.50
123 Brandon Armstrong RC .60 1.50
124 Andrei Kirilenko RC 1.50 4.00
125 Gerald Wallace RC 1.25 3.00
126 Samuel Dalembert RC 1.00 2.50
127 Jamaal Tinsley RC 1.00 2.50
128 Tony Parker RC 4.00 10.00
129 Loren Woods RC .60 1.50
130 Primoz Brezec RC 1.00 2.50
131 Dion Glover .20 .50
132 Moochie Norris .20 .50
133 Mark Jackson .25 .60
134 Bryon Russell .20 .50
135 Danny Fortson .20 .50
136 Kenyon Martin .30 .75
137 Alvin Williams .20 .50
138 Erick Dampier .20 .50
139 Clarence Weatherspoon .20 .50
140 Brent Barry .20 .50
141 Lamond Murray .20 .50
142 Lindsey Hunter .20 .50
143 Speedy Claxton .20 .50
144 James Posey .20 .50
145 Anthony Mason .20 .50
146 Mateen Cleaves .20 .50
147 Kenny Anderson .25 .60
148 Travis Best .20 .50
149 Patrick Ewing .40 1.00
150 Dana Barros .20 .50
151 Lorenzen Wright .20 .50
152 Rodney Rogers .20 .50
153 Brad Miller .30 .75
154 Anthony Peeler .20 .50
155 Antonio Daniels .20 .50
156 Tim Hardaway .30 .75
157 Quentin Richardson .25 .60
158 Darrell Armstrong .20 .50
159 Nazr Mohammad .20 .50
160 Todd MacCulloch .20 .50
161 Ruben Patterson .20 .50
162 Wesley Person .20 .50
163 Jeff McInnis .20 .50
164 Vin Baker .25 .60
165 George McCloud .20 .50
166 Chris Gatling .20 .50
167 Derrick Coleman .25 .60
168 Elden Campbell .20 .50
169 Glen Rice .25 .60
170 Donyell Marshall .20 .50
171 Juwan Howard .25 .60
172 Mitch Richmond .25 .60
173 Tom Gugliotta .20 .50
174 Chucky Atkins .20 .50
175 Michael Redd .30 .75
176 Malik Rose .20 .50
177 Lee Nailon .20 .50
178 Al Harrington .25 .60
179 Matt Harpring .20 .50
180 Tyronn Lue .20 .50

2001-02 Fleer Force Rookie Postmarks

*RC POSTMARKS: .75X TO 2X BASE RC HI
PRINT RUN FIRST 300 SER.#'d SETS

2001-02 Fleer Force Special Forces

*SF STARS: 4X TO 10X BASE CARD HI
1-100, 131-180 PRINT RUN 250 SER.#'d SETS
*SF ROOKIES: 2.5X TO 6X BASE CARD HI
101-130 PRINT RUN 50 SER.#'d SETS
61 Michael Jordan 20.00 50.00

2001-02 Fleer Force Emblematic

Randomly seeded in packs, this 25-card die-cut horizontal set design contains two color photos of the featured player. The photo on the left is a full color action photo, and the photo on the right is a framed, in colors that match the player's team, portrait style photo. Card background have the team logo of the pictured player centered on a basketball court print, and the word "Emblem@tic" appears along the bottom third of the card and is enhanced with silver foil highlights. The bottom of the card is solid colored, again to match team colors, and the players name and team appears in silver foil. Each card is sequentailly numbered to 399.

STATED PRINT RUN 399 SER.#'d SETS
1 Vince Carter 2.00 5.00
2 Dikembe Mutombo 1.25 3.00
3 Tracy McGrady 2.00 5.00
4 Lamar Odom 1.00 2.50
5 Jason Kidd 2.00 5.00
6 Ray Allen 1.25 3.00
7 John Stockton 1.50 4.00
8 Paul Pierce 1.25 3.00
9 Baron Davis 1.25 3.00
10 Kenyon Martin 1.25 3.00
11 Richard Hamilton 1.00 2.50
12 Grant Hill 1.50 4.00
13 Morris Peterson .75 2.00
14 Shareef Abdur-Rahim 1.00 2.50
15 Peja Stojakovic 1.25 3.00
16 Gary Payton 1.25 3.00
17 Karl Malone 1.50 4.00
18 Keith Van Horn 1.00 2.50
19 Darius Miles .75 2.00
20 Allen Iverson 2.50 6.00
21 Michael Jordan 12.00 30.00
22 Kobe Bryant 5.00 12.00
23 Kevin Garnett 2.00 5.00
24 Shaquille O'Neal 3.00 8.00
25 Tim Duncan 2.50 6.00

2001-02 Fleer Force Emblematic Jerseys

Randomly seeded in packs, this 25-card set parallels the base Emblematic insert set enhanced with a swatch of a game-worn jersey. Each card is sequentially numbered to 50.

STATED PRINT RUN 50 SER.#'d SETS
1 Vince Carter 15.00 40.00
2 Dikembe Mutombo 10.00 25.00
3 Tracy McGrady 15.00 40.00
4 Lamar Odom 8.00 20.00
5 Jason Kidd 15.00 40.00
6 Ray Allen 10.00 25.00
7 John Stockton 12.00 30.00
8 Paul Pierce 10.00 25.00
9 Baron Davis 10.00 25.00
10 Kenyon Martin 10.00 25.00
11 Richard Hamilton 8.00 20.00
12 Grant Hill 12.00 30.00
13 Morris Peterson 6.00 15.00
14 Shareef Abdur-Rahim 8.00 20.00
15 Peja Stojakovic 10.00 25.00
16 Gary Payton 10.00 25.00
17 Karl Malone 12.00 30.00
18 Keith Van Horn 8.00 20.00
19 Darius Miles 6.00 15.00
20 Allen Iverson 20.00 50.00

2001-02 Fleer Force Inside the Game

Randomly inserted in packs, this 20-card set features full color player action photos set against a basketball court background. The bottom third of the card is separated and the player's name, the words "inside the game," and the player's team name appear in silver foil. Each card is sequentially numbered to 699.

STATED PRINT RUN 699 SER.#'d SETS
1 Karl Malone 2.00 5.00
2 Keith Van Horn 1.25 3.00
3 Darius Miles 1.00 2.50
4 John Stockton 2.00 5.00
5 Allen Iverson 3.00 8.00
6 Alonzo Mourning 2.00 5.00
7 Dikembe Mutombo 1.50 4.00
8 Tracy McGrady 2.50 6.00
9 Lamar Odom 1.25 3.00
10 Baron Davis 1.50 4.00
11 Michael Jordan 12.00 30.00
12 Kobe Bryant 6.00 15.00
13 Kevin Garnett 2.50 6.00
14 Shaquille O'Neal 4.00 10.00
15 Tim Duncan 3.00 8.00
16 Vince Carter 2.50 6.00
17 Steve Francis 1.25 3.00
18 Dirk Nowitzki 2.50 6.00
19 Chris Webber 1.50 4.00
20 Peja Stojakovic 1.50 4.00
NNO Vince Carter AU/275 15.00 40.00

2001-02 Fleer Force Inside the Game Jerseys

PRINT RUN 399 SER.#'d SETS
*NUMBERS: 1.5X TO 4X JSY HI
NUMBERS PRINT RUN 99 SER.#'d SETS
1 Karl Malone 4.00 10.00
2 Keith Van Horn 2.50 6.00
3 Darius Miles 2.00 5.00
4 John Stockton 4.00 10.00
5 Allen Iverson 6.00 15.00
6 Alonzo Mourning 4.00 10.00
7 Dikembe Mutombo 3.00 8.00
8 Tracy McGrady 5.00 12.00
9 Lamar Odom 2.50 6.00
10 Baron Davis 3.00 8.00
11 Vince Carter 5.00 12.00
12 Steve Francis 2.50 6.00
13 Dirk Nowitzki 5.00 12.00
14 Chris Webber 3.00 8.00
15 Peja Stojakovic 3.00 8.00

2001-02 Fleer Force True Colors Jerseys

Randomly inserted in packs, this 30-card set features full color player portrait photos set against their team's logo. The words "True Colors Game Worn Jersey" appear along the center of the card in silver foil, and the bottom of the card is white with a centered piece of a game worn jersey. The bottom of the card contains the words "1st Color" and the player's team in silver ink. Each card is sequentially numbered to 400. Versions with multiple colors were also issued. Four color cards are sequentially numbered to 50, three color cards are sequentially numbered to 100 and two color cards are sequentially numbered to 200.

PRINT RUN 400 SER.#'d SETS
*FOUR COLOR: 2X TO 5X ONE COLOR HI
FOUR COLOR PRINT RUN 50 SER.#'d SETS
*THREE COLOR: 1.25X TO 3X ONE COLOR HI
THREE COLOR PRINT RUN 100 SER.#'d SETS
*TWO COLOR: .75X TO 2X ONE COLOR HI
TWO COLOR PRINT RUN 200 SER.#'d SETS
1 Vince Carter 5.00 12.00
2 Kenyon Martin 3.00 8.00
3 Baron Davis 3.00 8.00
4 Tracy McGrady 5.00 12.00
5 Mike Miller 2.50 6.00
6 Aaron McKie 2.00 5.00
7 Darius Miles 2.00 5.00
8 Lamar Odom 2.50 6.00
9 Glenn Robinson 2.50 6.00
10 Karl Malone 4.00 10.00
11 John Stockton 4.00 10.00
12 Paul Pierce 3.00 8.00
13 Alonzo Mourning 4.00 10.00
14 Gary Payton 3.00 8.00
15 Stephon Marbury 2.50 6.00
16 Dikembe Mutombo 3.00 8.00
17 Shawn Marion 2.50 6.00
18 Richard Hamilton 2.50 6.00
19 Stromile Swift 2.00 5.00
20 Reggie Miller 3.00 8.00
21 Keith Van Horn 2.50 6.00
22 Steve Francis 2.50 6.00
23 Morris Peterson 2.00 5.00
24 Andre Miller 2.50 6.00
25 Quentin Richardson 2.50 6.00
26 Antonio McDyess 2.50 6.00
27 Anfernee Hardaway 5.00 12.00
28 Jason Williams 2.50 6.00
29 Grant Hill 4.00 10.00
30 Jason Terry 3.00 8.00

2000-01 Fleer Futures

The 2000-01 Fleer Futures product was released in Feb. 2001 and featured a 250-card base set broken into tiers as follows: Base Veterans (1-200), and Rookies (201-250) (Please note that the even numbered rookies were inserted at 1:2, while the odd numbered rookies were inserted at 1:7). Card packs carried eight cards at the suggested retail price of $2.99.

COMPLETE SET (250) 40.00 80.00
COMPLETE SET w/o RCs (200) 10.00 25.00
RCs: STATED ODDS 1:2 FOR EVEN #'s
RCs: STATED ODDS 1:7 FOR ODD #'s
1 Vince Carter .50 1.25
2 Dan Majerle .25 .60
3 George McCloud .15 .40
4 Radoslav Nesterovic .15 .40
5 Corey Maggette .20 .50
6 Derek Anderson .15 .40
7 Ray Allen .25 .60
8 Greg Ostertag .15 .40
9 Cedric Ceballos .15 .40
10 Danny Fortson .15 .40
11 Roshown McLeod .15 .40
12 Christian Laettner .20 .50
13 Avery Johnson .20 .50
14 Clarence Weatherspoon .15 .40
15 Michael Curry .15 .40
16 Chris Whitney .15 .40
17 Anthony Mason .15 .40
18 Antonio McDyess .20 .50
19 Vitaly Potapenko .15 .40
20 Shaquille O'Neal .60 1.50
21 David Robinson .40 1.00
22 Tyrone Hill .15 .40
23 Otis Thorpe .20 .50
24 Reggie Miller .25 .60
25 Kevin Garnett .40 1.00
26 Michael Dickerson .15 .40
27 John Amaechi .15 .40
28 Jason Kidd .40 1.00
29 Ron Artest .25 .60
30 Muggsy Bogues .20 .50
31 Antawn Jamison .25 .60
32 Brian Grant .15 .40
33 Stephon Marbury .20 .50
34 William Avery .15 .40
35 Paul Pierce .25 .60
36 Marcus Camby .20 .50
37 Kevin Willis .15 .40
38 Dikembe Mutombo .25 .60
39 Rashard Lewis .25 .60
40 Allan Houston .20 .50
41 Hakeem Olajuwon .30 .75
42 Rod Strickland .15 .40
43 Derrick Coleman .20 .50
44 Tariq Abdul-Wahad .15 .40
45 Terrell Brandon .15 .40
46 Michael Olowokandi .15 .40
47 Robert Horry .20 .50
48 Kelvin Cato .15 .40
49 Eric Williams .15 .40
50 Glen Rice .20 .50
51 Carlos Rogers .15 .40
52 Allen Iverson .50 1.25
53 P.J. Brown .15 .40
54 Jalen Rose .20 .50
55 Damon Stoudamire .20 .50
56 Damon Jones RC .25 .60
57 Darrell Armstrong .15 .40
58 Samaki Walker .15 .40
59 John Stockton .30 .75
60 Chucky Atkins .15 .40
61 Rasheed Wallace .25 .60
62 Jason Terry .25 .60
63 Aaron Williams .15 .40
64 Steve Nash .40 1.00
65 Antoine Walker .20 .50
66 Patrick Ewing .30 .75
67 Cuttino Mobley .15 .40
68 Aaron McKie .15 .40
69 Jamal Mashburn .20 .50
70 Scottie Pippen .40 1.00
71 Bryant Reeves .15 .40
72 Isaiah Rider .20 .50
73 Jaren Jackson .15 .40
74 Lindsey Hunter .15 .40
75 Jacque Vaughn .15 .40
76 Travis Best .15 .40
77 Vinny Del Negro .15 .40
78 Othella Harrington .15 .40
79 Michael Finley .25 .60
80 Brent Barry .15 .40
81 Brevin Knight .15 .40
82 Kurt Thomas .15 .40
83 Mark Jackson .20 .50
84 Richard Hamilton .20 .50
85 Anthony Carter .15 .40
86 Matt Harpring .15 .40
87 Bobby Jackson .15 .40
88 Jerome Williams .15 .40
89 Jahidi White .15 .40
90 Lorenzen Wright .15 .40
91 Kerry Kittles .15 .40
92 Anthony Peeler .15 .40
93 Kenny Anderson .20 .50
94 Latrell Sprewell .20 .50
95 Maurice Taylor .15 .40
96 Toni Kukoc .25 .60
97 Eddie Robinson .15 .40
98 Voshon Lenard .15 .40
99 Sam Mitchell .15 .40
100 Isaac Austin .15 .40
101 Michael Doleac .15 .40
102 Andre Miller .20 .50
103 Jason Williams .25 .60
104 Charles Oakley .20 .50
105 Mitch Richmond .20 .50
106 Bruce Bowen .15 .40
107 Keith Van Horn .20 .50
108 Wally Szczerbiak .20 .50
109 Tony Battie .15 .40
110 Larry Johnson .25 .60
111 Shandon Anderson .15 .40
112 Sam Cassell .20 .50
113 David Wesley .15 .40
114 James Posey .15 .40
115 Bonzi Wells .15 .40
116 Mike Bibby .25 .60
117 Andrew DeClercq .15 .40
118 Clifford Robinson .15 .40
119 Corliss Williamson .15 .40
120 Antonio Davis .15 .40
121 Eddie Jones .25 .60
122 Jamie Feick .15 .40
123 Anfernee Hardaway .40 1.00
124 Adrian Griffin .15 .40
125 Erick Strickland .15 .40
126 Doug Christie .15 .40
127 Scot Pollard .15 .40
128 Sam Perkins .15 .40
129 Raef LaFrentz .15 .40
130 Dale Davis .15 .40
131 Tyrone Nesby .25 .60
132 Rick Fox .15 .40
133 Tom Gugliotta .15 .40
134 Glenn Robinson .20 .50
135 Quincy Lewis .15 .40
136 Austin Croshere .15 .40
137 Shawn Kemp .25 .60
138 Lamar Odom .20 .50
139 Tim Duncan .50 1.25
140 Tim Thomas .15 .40
141 Bryon Russell .15 .40
142 Jermaine O'Neal .20 .50
143 Erick Dampier .15 .40
144 Shareef Abdur-Rahim .20 .50
145 Bo Outlaw .15 .40
146 Gary Payton .25 .60
147 Chris Gatling .15 .40
148 Vlade Divac .20 .50
149 Ben Wallace .20 .50
150 Larry Hughes .20 .50
151 Ron Mercer .15 .40
152 Karl Malone .30 .75
153 Jonathan Bender .15 .40
154 Mookie Blaylock .15 .40
155 Jim Jackson .15 .40
156 Chris Crawford .15 .40
157 Vin Baker .20 .50
158 Lamond Murray .15 .40
159 Charlie Ward .15 .40
160 Steve Francis .20 .50
161 Cherokee Parks .15 .40
162 Baron Davis .25 .60
163 Keon Clark .15 .40
164 Ruben Patterson .15 .40
165 Tracy McGrady .40 1.00
166 Antonio Daniels .15 .40
167 Scott Williams .15 .40
168 John Starks .20 .50
169 Jerry Stackhouse .20 .50
170 Vonteego Cummings .15 .40
171 LaPhonso Ellis .20 .50
172 Dirk Nowitzki .40 1.00
173 Horace Grant .20 .50
174 Wesley Person .15 .40
175 Peja Stojakovic .25 .60
176 Eric Snow .15 .40
177 Juwan Howard .20 .50
178 Tim Hardaway .25 .60
179 Kendall Gill .15 .40
180 Chauncey Billups .25 .60
181 Kobe Bryant 1.00 2.50
182 Sean Elliott .25 .60
183 Donyell Marshall .15 .40
184 Al Harrington .20 .50
185 Arvydas Sabonis .20 .50
186 Grant Hill .30 .75
187 Malik Rose .15 .40
188 Nazr Mohammed .15 .40
189 Elden Campbell .15 .40
190 Nick Van Exel .20 .50
191 Steve Smith .20 .50
192 Sean Rooks .15 .40
193 Monty Williams .15 .40
194 Elton Brand .25 .60
195 Chris Webber .25 .60
196 Mikki Moore RC .25 .60
197 Chris Mills .15 .40
198 Alan Henderson .15 .40
199 Shawn Bradley .15 .40
200 Shawn Marion .20 .50
201 Hedo Turkoglu RC 1.00 2.50
202 Iakovos Tsakalidis RC .15 .40
203 Kenyon Martin RC 1.50 4.00
204 Mamadou N'Diaye RC .15 .40
205 Stromile Swift RC .60 1.50
206 Pepe Sanchez RC .25 .60
207 Chris Mihm RC .50 1.25
208 Lavor Postell RC .15 .40
209 Marcus Fizer RC .60 1.50
210 Ruben Garces RC .25 .60
211 Courtney Alexander RC .50 1.25
212 A.J. Guyton RC .15 .40
213 Darius Miles RC .60 1.50
214 Ademola Okulaja RC .25 .60
215 Jerome Moiso RC .40 1.00
216 Khalid El-Amin RC .15 .40
217 Joel Przybilla RC .50 1.25
218 Mike Smith RC .15 .40
219 DerMarr Johnson RC .50 1.25
220 Soumaila Samake RC .15 .40
221 Mike Miller RC 1.00 2.50
222 Eddie House RC .20 .50
223 Quentin Richardson RC .60 1.50
224 Eduardo Najera RC .25 .60
225 Morris Peterson RC .60 1.50
226 Hanno Mottola RC .15 .40
227 Speedy Claxton RC .60 1.50
228 Ruben Wolkowyski RC .15 .40
229 Keyon Dooling RC .60 1.50
230 Olumide Oyedeji RC .15 .40
231 Mark Madsen RC .60 1.50
232 Mike Penberthy RC .25 .60
233 Mateen Cleaves RC .50 1.25
234 Brian Cardinal RC .20 .50
235 Etan Thomas RC .60 1.50
236 Garth Joseph RC .25 .60
237 Jason Collier RC .60 1.50
238 Paul McPherson RC .15 .40
239 Erick Barkley RC .40 1.00
240 Stephen Jackson RC .40 1.00
241 Desmond Mason RC .75 2.00
242 Jason Hart RC .25 .60
243 Jamal Crawford RC 1.50 4.00
244 Daniel Santiago RC .25 .60
245 DeShawn Stevenson RC .60 1.50
246 S.Medvedenko RC .25 .60
247 Donnell Harvey RC .50 1.25
248 Chris Porter RC .15 .40
249 Jamaal Magloire RC .60 1.50
250 Dalibor Bagaric RC .20 .50

2000-01 Fleer Futures Black Gold

*EVEN RCs: 2.5X TO 6X BASE CARD HI
*ODD RCs: 1X TO 2.5X BASE HI
STATED PRINT RUN 500 SERIAL #'d SETS

2000-01 Fleer Futures Copper

*STARS: 2.5X TO 6X BASE CARD HI
STATED PRINT RUN 750 SERIAL #'d SETS

2000-01 Fleer Futures Gold

*EVEN RCs: 2.5X TO 6X BASE CARD HI
*ODD RCs: 1X TO 2.5X BASE HI
STATED PRINT RUN 500 SERIAL #'d SETS

2000-01 Fleer Futures Autographics On Location

Randomly inserted into packs at one in 403, this 12-card insert features some of the hottest players in the league. Card backs carry a "AOL" prefix. Please note that there were only 240 produced for Vince Carter, Austin Croshere and Rashard Lewis. Lamar Odom and Jerry Stackhouse were redemptions that were not produced.

STATED ODDS 1:403
AOL1 Shareef Abdur-Rahim 10.00 25.00
AOL2 Travis Best 12.50 30.00
AOL3 Vince Carter/240 25.00 60.00
AOL4 Austin Croshere/240 10.00 25.00
AOL5 Baron Davis 20.00 50.00
AOL6 Rashard Lewis/240 20.00 50.00
AOL7 Dan Majerle 60.00 120.00
AOL8 Dirk Nowitzki 300.00 600.00
AOL10 Mitch Richmond 20.00 50.00
AOL11 Jalen Rose 10.00 25.00

2000-01 Fleer Futures Vince Carter Rookie Remnants

This three-card insert was randomly inserted into 2000-01 Fleer products. The set includes a Vince Carter floor card (numbered to 100), a Vince Carter floor/jersey card (numbered to 15), and finally an autographed Vince Carter floor/jersey card (numbered 1/1).

RANDOM INSERTS IN HOBBY PACKS
NNO Vince Carter FLR/100 12.50 30.00
NNO Vince Carter FLR JSY/15 20.00 50.00

2000-01 Fleer Futures Characteristics

Randomly inserted into packs at one in 28, this 10-card insert features some of the real "characters" in the NBA. Card backs carry a "C" prefix.

COMPLETE SET (10) 12.50 25.00
STATED ODDS 1:28
C1 Vince Carter 2.00 5.00
C2 Kobe Bryant 4.00 10.00
C3 Lamar Odom .75 2.00
C4 Kevin Garnett 1.50 4.00
C5 Allen Iverson 2.00 5.00
C6 Grant Hill 1.25 3.00
C7 Tim Duncan 2.00 5.00
C8 Steve Francis .75 2.00
C9 Jason Williams 1.00 2.50
C10 Shaquille O'Neal 2.50 6.00

2000-01 Fleer Futures Hot Commodities

Randomly inserted into packs at one in 28, this 10-card insert features some of the hottest players in the league. Card backs carry a "HC" prefix.

COMPLETE SET (10) 10.00 25.00
STATED ODDS 1:28
HC1 Vince Carter 1.50 4.00
HC2 Kobe Bryant 3.00 8.00
HC3 Kevin Garnett 1.25 3.00
HC4 Allen Iverson 1.50 4.00
HC5 Shaquille O'Neal 2.00 5.00
HC6 Steve Francis .60 1.50
HC7 Grant Hill 1.00 2.50
HC8 Tim Duncan 1.50 4.00
HC9 Lamar Odom .60 1.50
HC10 Tracy McGrady 1.25 3.00

2000-01 Fleer Futures Question Air

Randomly inserted into packs at one in 14, this 15-card insert features rookies that that hope to contribute in the NBA. Card backs carry a "QA" prefix.

COMPLETE SET (15) 3.00 8.00
STATED ODDS 1:14
QA1 Kenyon Martin .75 2.00
QA2 Stromile Swift .30 .75
QA3 Chris Mihm .25 .60
QA4 Marcus Fizer .30 .75
QA5 Courtney Alexander .25 .60
QA6 Darius Miles .30 .75
QA7 Jerome Moiso .20 .50
QA8 Desmond Mason .40 1.00
QA9 DerMarr Johnson .25 .60
QA10 Mike Miller .50 1.25
QA11 Quentin Richardson .30 .75
QA12 Morris Peterson .30 .75
QA13 Etan Thomas .30 .75
QA14 Keyon Dooling .30 .75
QA15 Mateen Cleaves .25 .60

2000-01 Fleer Futures Rookie Game Jerseys

*GJ: 1.5X TO 4X BASE HI 2.50 6.00
STATED PRINT RUN 300 SERIAL #'d SETS

2000-01 Fleer Game Time

The 2000-01 Fleer Game Time product was released in late December 2001, and features a 120-card base set. The set is broken into tiers as follows: 90 Base Veterans (1-90), and 30 Rookies (91-120) (each rookie card is individually serial numbered to 2500). Each pack contained 5 cards, and carried a suggested retail price of $3.99.

COMPLETE SET w/o RC (90) 12.50 25.00
RCs: PRINT RUN 2500 SERIAL #'d SETS
CARTER REMNANTS LISTED UNDER FLE.PREM.
1 Vince Carter .60 1.50
2 Raef LaFrentz .20 .50
3 Kobe Bryant 1.25 3.00
4 Toni Kukoc .30 .75
5 Bonzi Wells .20 .50
6 Rashard Lewis .30 .75
7 Karl Malone .40 1.00
8 Juwan Howard .25 .60
9 Lindsey Hunter .20 .50
10 Alonzo Mourning .40 1.00
11 Larry Hughes .25 .60
12 Austin Croshere .20 .50
13 Charles Oakley .25 .60
14 Patrick Ewing .40 1.00
15 Vlade Divac .25 .60
16 Michael Finley .30 .75
17 Tim Hardaway .30 .75
18 Jason Kidd .50 1.25
19 Cal Bowdler .20 .50
20 Dirk Nowitzki .50 1.25
21 Terrell Brandon .20 .50
22 Allan Houston .25 .60
23 Theo Ratliff .20 .50
24 Chris Webber .30 .75
25 Shawn Kemp .30 .75
26 Jalen Rose .25 .60
27 Bryon Russell .20 .50
28 Jahidi White .20 .50
29 Trajan Langdon .20 .50
30 Baron Davis .30 .75
31 Cuttino Mobley .20 .50
32 Wally Szczerbiak .25 .60
33 Michael Dickerson .20 .50
34 Andre Miller .25 .60
35 Michael Olowokandi .20 .50
36 Ray Allen .30 .75
37 Latrell Sprewell .25 .60
38 Jason Williams .30 .75
39 Mikki Moore RC .30 .75
40 Shawn Marion .25 .60
41 Radoslav Nesterovic .20 .50
42 Ron Artest .30 .75
43 Vonteego Cummings .20 .50
44 Anfernee Hardaway .50 1.25
45 Jerome Williams .20 .50
46 John Stockton .40 1.00
47 Antawn Jamison .30 .75
48 Grant Hill .40 1.00
49 Elden Campbell .20 .50
50 Steve Francis .25 .60
51 Jamie Feick .20 .50
52 Gary Payton .30 .75
53 Elton Brand .30 .75
54 Eddie Jones .30 .75
55 Tom Gugliotta .20 .50
56 Richard Hamilton .25 .60
57 Dion Glover .20 .50
58 Shaquille O'Neal .75 2.00
59 Kevin Garnett .50 1.25
60 Paul Pierce .30 .75
61 Brian Grant .20 .50
62 Tim Thomas .20 .50
63 Tracy McGrady .50 1.25
64 Jonathan Bender .20 .50
65 Adrian Griffin .20 .50
66 Lamar Odom .25 .60
67 Rasheed Wallace .30 .75
68 Mike Bibby .30 .75
69 Glenn Robinson .25 .60
70 Eddie Robinson .20 .50
71 Robert Horry .25 .60
72 Jerry Stackhouse .25 .60
73 Stephon Marbury .25 .60
74 Marcus Camby .25 .60
75 Scottie Pippen .50 1.25
76 David Robinson .50 1.25
77 Jason Terry .30 .75
78 Reggie Miller .30 .75
79 Larry Johnson .30 .75
80 Antonio Daniels .20 .50
81 Shareef Abdur-Rahim .25 .60
82 Ruben Patterson .20 .50
83 Nick Van Exel .25 .60
84 Keith Van Horn .25 .60
85 Antonio Davis .20 .50
86 Antoine Walker .25 .60
87 Allen Iverson .60 1.50
88 Antonio McDyess .25 .60
89 Tim Duncan .60 1.50
90 Hakeem Olajuwon .40 1.00
91 Jamaal Magloire RC .60 1.50
92 DerMarr Johnson RC .50 1.25
93 Jerome Moiso RC .40 1.00
94 Marcus Fizer RC .60 1.50
95 Jamal Crawford RC 1.50 4.00
96 Chris Mihm RC .50 1.25
97 Donnell Harvey RC .50 1.25
98 Courtney Alexander RC .50 1.25
99 Etan Thomas RC .60 1.50
100 Mamadou N'Diaye RC .40 1.00
101 Mateen Cleaves RC .50 1.25
102 Chris Porter RC .40 1.00
103 Jason Collier RC .60 1.50
104 Keyon Dooling RC .60 1.50
105 Darius Miles RC .60 1.50
106 Mark Madsen RC .60 1.50
107 Eddie House RC .50 1.25
108 Joel Przybilla RC .50 1.25

109 Kenyon Martin RC 1.50 4.00
110 Mike Miller RC 1.00 2.50
111 Speedy Claxton RC .60 1.50
112 Iakovos Tsakalidis RC .40 1.00
113 Erick Barkley RC .40 1.00
114 Hedo Turkoglu RC 1.00 2.50
115 Eduardo Najera RC .60 1.50
116 Desmond Mason RC .75 2.00
117 Morris Peterson RC .60 1.50
118 DeShawn Stevenson RC .60 1.50
119 Stromile Swift RC .60 1.50
120 Mike Smith RC .40 1.00

2000-01 Fleer Game Time Extra

*STARS: 1.5X TO 4X BASE CARD HI
*RCs: 1X TO 2.5X BASE HI
STARS: STATED ODDS 1:8
RCs: PRINT RUN 250 SERIAL #'d SETS

2000-01 Fleer Game Time Attack the Rack

Randomly inserted into packs at one in four, this 20-card insert features players that are not afraid to attack the rack. Card backs carry an "AR" prefix.

COMPLETE SET (20) 7.50 15.00
STATED ODDS 1:4
AR1 Vince Carter .75 2.00
AR2 Lamar Odom .30 .75
AR3 Kobe Bryant 1.50 4.00
AR4 Shareef Abdur-Rahim .30 .75
AR5 Allen Iverson .75 2.00
AR6 Jason Williams .40 1.00
AR7 Kevin Garnett .60 1.50
AR8 Tim Duncan .75 2.00
AR9 Latrell Sprewell .30 .75
AR10 Shaquille O'Neal 1.00 2.50
AR11 Jalen Rose .30 .75
AR12 Antawn Jamison .40 1.00
AR13 Paul Pierce .40 1.00
AR14 Grant Hill .50 1.25
AR15 Eddie Jones .40 1.00
AR16 Karl Malone .50 1.25
AR17 Elton Brand .40 1.00
AR18 Tracy McGrady .60 1.50
AR19 Michael Finley .40 1.00
AR20 Steve Francis .30 .75

2000-01 Fleer Game Time Vince Carter Rookie Remnants

This three-card insert was randomly inserted into 2000-01 Fleer products. The set includes a Vince Carter floor card (numbered to 100), a Vince Carter floor/jersey card (numbered to 15), and finally an autographed Vince Carter floor/jersey card (numbered 1/1).

RANDOM INSERTS IN HOBBY PACKS
NNO Vince Carter FLR/100 12.50 30.00
NNO Vince Carter FLR JSY/15 20.00 50.00

2000-01 Fleer Game Time Change the Game

Randomly inserted into packs at one in 24, this 15-card insert features players that are changing the way people view the NBA. Card backs carry an "CG" prefix.

STATED ODDS 1:24
CG1 Vince Carter 2.00 5.00
CG2 Lamar Odom .75 2.00
CG3 Kobe Bryant 4.00 10.00
CG4 Allen Iverson 2.00 5.00
CG5 Jason Kidd 1.50 4.00
CG6 Grant Hill 1.25 3.00
CG7 Tim Duncan 2.00 5.00
CG8 Shaquille O'Neal 2.50 6.00
CG9 Kevin Garnett 1.50 4.00
CG10 Elton Brand 1.00 2.50
CG11 Stephon Marbury .75 2.00
CG12 Jason Williams 1.00 2.50
CG13 Keith Van Horn .75 2.00
CG14 Steve Francis .75 2.00
CG15 Gary Payton 1.00 2.50

2000-01 Fleer Game Time Uniformity

Randomly inserted into packs at one in 24, this 23-card insert features actual swatches from game-used jerseys. Please note that we have catalogued these cards below in alphabetical order for convenience. A special Vince Carter autographed jersey card was also released in this product, and are individually serial numbered to 150.

STATED ODDS 1:24
1 Shareef Abdur-Rahim 2.00 5.00
2 Mike Bibby 2.50 6.00
3 Vince Carter 5.00 12.00
4 Baron Davis 2.50 6.00
5 Sean Elliott 2.50 6.00
6 Allen Iverson 5.00 12.00
7 Toni Kukoc 2.50 6.00
8 Karl Malone 3.00 8.00
9 Stephon Marbury 2.00 5.00
10 Shawn Marion 2.00 5.00
11 Alonzo Mourning 3.00 8.00
12 Lamar Odom 2.00 5.00
13 Shaquille O'Neal Gold 6.00 15.00
14 Shaquille O'Neal Purple 6.00 15.00
15 Gary Payton 2.50 6.00
16 Scot Pollard 2.00 5.00
17 Jalen Rose 2.00 5.00
18 John Stockton 3.00 8.00
19 Wally Szczerbiak 2.00 5.00
20 Jason Terry 2.50 6.00
21 Keith Van Horn 2.00 5.00
22 Antoine Walker 2.00 5.00
23 David Wesley 1.50 4.00
GUVI Vince Carter AU/150 25.00 60.00

2000-01 Fleer Game Time Vince and the Revolution

Randomly inserted into packs, this 15-card insert features one of the NBA's most fascinating stars Vince Carter. Cards 1-5 were inserted into packs at one in nine, cards 6-10 were inserted at one in 24, and 11-15 were inserted at one in 144.

COMPLETE SET (15) 30.00 60.00
COMMON CARD (1-5) 1.00 2.50
1-5 STATED ODDS 1:9
COMMON CARD (6-10) 2.00 5.00
6-10 STATED ODDS 1:24
COMMON CARD (11-15) 5.00 12.00
11-15 STATED ODDS 1:144

2000-01 Fleer Genuine

The 2000-01 Fleer Genuine product was released in late December,2000 and features a 130-card base set. The base set consists of 100 Veterans (1-100), and 30 Rookies (101-130) that are individually serial numbered to 1500. Each pack contained 5 cards, and had a suggested retail price of $2.99.

COMPLETE SET w/o RC (100) 20.00 40.00
RCs: PRINT RUN 1500 SERIAL #'d SETS
1 Vince Carter .75 2.00
2 Glenn Robinson .30 .75
3 Rasheed Wallace .40 1.00
4 Michael Dickerson .25 .60
5 Mikki Moore RC .40 1.00
6 Wally Szczerbiak .30 .75
7 Shawn Marion .30 .75
8 Dan Majerle .40 1.00
9 Trajan Langdon .25 .60
10 Chauncey Billups .40 1.00
11 Jason Kidd .60 1.50
12 Derrick Coleman .30 .75
13 Jason Terry .40 1.00
14 Eddie Jones .40 1.00
15 Scottie Pippen .60 1.50
16 Mike Bibby .40 1.00
17 Ron Mercer .25 .60
18 Hakeem Olajuwon .50 1.25
19 Patrick Ewing .50 1.25
20 Ruben Patterson .25 .60
21 Kenny Anderson .30 .75
22 Alonzo Mourning .50 1.25
23 Steve Smith .30 .75
24 Juwan Howard .30 .75
25 Antoine Walker .30 .75
26 Kobe Bryant 1.50 4.00
27 Chris Webber .40 1.00
28 Mitch Richmond .30 .75
29 Paul Pierce .40 1.00
30 Shaquille O'Neal 1.00 2.50
31 Jason Williams .40 1.00
32 Richard Hamilton .30 .75
33 Michael Finley .40 1.00
34 Jalen Rose .30 .75
35 Grant Hill .50 1.25
36 John Stockton .50 1.25
37 Vitaly Potapenko .25 .60
38 Glen Rice .30 .75
39 Vlade Divac .30 .75
40 Jahidi White .25 .60
41 Baron Davis .40 1.00
42 Michael Olowokandi .25 .60
43 Tim Duncan .75 2.00
44 Rod Strickland .25 .60
45 Jamal Mashburn .30 .75
46 Lamar Odom .30 .75
47 David Robinson .60 1.50
48 Travis Best .25 .60
49 Raef LaFrentz .25 .60
50 Keith Van Horn .30 .75
51 Vonteego Cummings .25 .60
52 Jerome Williams .25 .60
53 Kevin Garnett .60 1.50
54 Anfernee Hardaway .60 1.50
55 Antonio McDyess .30 .75
56 Reggie Miller .40 1.00
57 Tracy McGrady .60 1.50
58 Bryon Russell .25 .60
59 Nick Van Exel .30 .75
60 Allen Iverson .75 2.00
61 Karl Malone .50 1.25
62 David Wesley .25 .60
63 Bob Sura .25 .60
64 Stephon Marbury .30 .75
65 Antonio Daniels .25 .60
66 Shawn Kemp .40 1.00
67 Cuttino Mobley .25 .60
68 Marcus Camby .30 .75
69 Gary Payton .40 1.00
70 Dikembe Mutombo .40 1.00
71 Tim Hardaway .40 1.00
72 Bonzi Wells .25 .60
73 Shareef Abdur-Rahim .30 .75
74 Brevin Knight .25 .60
75 Steve Francis .30 .75
76 Allan Houston .30 .75
77 Dion Glover .25 .60
78 Dirk Nowitzki .60 1.50
79 Jonathan Bender .25 .60
80 Darrell Armstrong .25 .60
81 Antonio Davis .25 .60
82 Jerry Stackhouse .30 .75
83 Terrell Brandon .25 .60
84 Tom Gugliotta .25 .60
85 Sean Elliott .40 1.00
86 Elton Brand .40 1.00
87 Larry Hughes .30 .75
88 Kerry Kittles .25 .60
89 Vin Baker .30 .75
90 Donyell Marshall .25 .60
91 Tim Thomas .25 .60
92 Toni Kukoc .40 1.00
93 Charles Oakley .30 .75
94 Andre Miller .30 .75
95 Austin Croshere .25 .60
96 Latrell Sprewell .30 .75
97 Mark Jackson .30 .75
98 Antawn Jamison .40 1.00
99 Ray Allen .40 1.00
100 Theo Ratliff .25 .60
101 Chris Mihm RC 1.25 3.00
102 Mateen Cleaves RC 1.25 3.00
103 Etan Thomas RC 1.50 4.00
104 Morris Peterson RC 1.50 4.00
105 Jamal Crawford RC 4.00 10.00
106 Darius Miles RC 1.50 4.00
107 Desmond Mason RC 2.00 5.00
108 Joel Przybilla RC 1.25 3.00
109 Mike Miller RC 2.50 6.00
110 Quentin Richardson RC 1.50 4.00
111 Jason Collier RC 1.50 4.00
112 Keyon Dooling RC 1.50 4.00
113 Courtney Alexander RC 1.25 3.00
114 Eddie House RC 1.25 3.00
115 DerMarr Johnson RC 1.25 3.00
116 Michael Redd RC 4.00 10.00
117 Mark Madsen RC 1.50 4.00
118 Stromile Swift RC 1.50 4.00
119 Mamadou N'Diaye RC 1.00 2.50
120 DeShawn Stevenson RC 1.50 4.00
121 Hedo Turkoglu RC 2.50 6.00
122 Stephen Jackson RC 2.50 6.00
123 Marcus Fizer RC 1.50 4.00
124 Khalid El-Amin RC 1.00 2.50
125 Speedy Claxton RC 1.50 4.00
126 Hanno Mottola RC 1.00 2.50
127 Jerome Moiso RC 1.00 2.50
128 Jamaal Magloire RC 1.50 4.00
129 Donnell Harvey RC 1.25 3.00
130 Kenyon Martin RC 4.00 10.00
NNO Vince Carter MM/1500 15.00 40.00
NNO Vince Carter MM AU/15 200.00 400.00

2000-01 Fleer Genuine Formidable

Randomly inserted into packs at one in 23, this 15-card insert features some of the hottest players in the league. Card backs carry a "F" prefix.

COMPLETE SET (15) 20.00 40.00
STATED ODDS 1:23
F1 Vince Carter 2.00 5.00
F2 Lamar Odom .75 2.00
F3 Tracy McGrady 1.50 4.00
F4 Jason Williams 1.00 2.50
F5 Jason Kidd 1.50 4.00
F6 Chris Webber 1.00 2.50
F7 Elton Brand 1.00 2.50
F8 Steve Francis .75 2.00
F9 Grant Hill 1.25 3.00
F10 Shaquille O'Neal 2.50 6.00
F11 Allen Iverson 2.00 5.00
F12 Kobe Bryant 4.00 10.00
F13 Tim Duncan 2.00 5.00
F14 Kevin Garnett 1.50 4.00
F15 Latrell Sprewell .75 2.00

2000-01 Fleer Genuine Genuine Coverage Plus

Randomly inserted into packs, this 9-card set features swatches from actual game-worn jerseys. Card backs are not numbered, but are listed below in alphabetical order for convenience.

STATED PRINT RUN 150 SERIAL #'d SETS
1 Vince Carter 10.00 25.00
2 Karl Malone 6.00 15.00
3 Shawn Marion 4.00 10.00
4 Lamar Odom 4.00 10.00
5 Shaquille O'Neal 12.00 30.00
6 Paul Pierce 5.00 12.00
7 David Robinson 8.00 20.00
8 Antoine Walker 4.00 10.00

2000-01 Fleer Genuine Northern Flights

Randomly inserted into packs at one in 22, this six-card insert features cards of high-flying Vince Carter. Card backs carry a "NF" prefix. Please note that there is also an autographed Vince Carter card in this set that is unnumbered but serial numbered to 150.

COMPLETE SET (5) 25.00 60.00
COMMON CARD (NF1-NF5) 6.00 15.00
STATED ODDS 1:22
NNO Vince Carter AU/150 25.00 60.00

2000-01 Fleer Genuine Smooth Operators

Randomly inserted into packs at one in 23, this 15-card insert features players that are as smooth as ice on the court. Card backs carry a "SO" prefix.

COMPLETE SET (15) 15.00 30.00
STATED ODDS 1:23
SO1 Vince Carter 2.00 5.00
SO2 Lamar Odom .75 2.00
SO3 Allen Iverson 2.00 5.00
SO4 Kobe Bryant 4.00 10.00
SO5 Kevin Garnett 1.50 4.00
SO6 Tim Duncan 2.00 5.00
SO7 Antawn Jamison 1.00 2.50
SO8 Michael Finley 1.00 2.50
SO9 Ray Allen 1.00 2.50
SO10 Paul Pierce 1.00 2.50
SO11 Karl Malone 1.25 3.00
SO12 Shaquille O'Neal 2.50 6.00
SO13 Elton Brand 1.00 2.50
SO14 Jason Williams 1.00 2.50
SO15 Jalen Rose .75 2.00

2000-01 Fleer Genuine Yes Men

Randomly inserted into packs at one in 23, this 10-card insert features players that do what it takes to win. Card backs carry a "Y" prefix.

COMPLETE SET (10) 8.00 20.00
STATED ODDS 1:23
Y1 Vince Carter 1.50 4.00
Y2 Lamar Odom .60 1.50
Y3 Kobe Bryant 3.00 8.00
Y4 Kevin Garnett 1.25 3.00
Y5 Tim Duncan 1.50 4.00
Y6 Eddie Jones .75 2.00
Y7 Allan Houston .60 1.50
Y8 Grant Hill 1.00 2.50
Y9 Elton Brand .75 2.00
Y10 Steve Francis .60 1.50

2001-02 Fleer Genuine

Released in mid October 2001, this 150-card base set is made up of holofoil card stock on standard size cards. Each card is borderless, but has a drawn box outlining a color action shot of the featured player. The player's team name runs down the left-side of the card and the player's name runs horizontal across the bottom of the card. The set contains 120 veteran players and 30 rookies sequentially numbered to 1000 on the card back. Genuine was packaged in 24 pack boxes with each pack conatining five cards.

COMPLETE SET (150) 75.00 150.00
COMP.SET w/o SP's (120) 12.50 30.00
ROOKIE STATED PRINT RUN 1000 SETS
1 Larry Hughes .30 .75
2 Wally Szczerbiak .30 .75
3 Jahidi White .25 .60
4 Aaron McKie .25 .60
5 Antonio McDyess .30 .75
6 Tom Gugliotta .25 .60
7 Elton Brand .40 1.00
8 Lamar Odom .30 .75
9 Chris Webber .40 1.00
10 Ron Artest .40 1.00
11 Gary Payton .40 1.00
12 Brian Grant .25 .60
13 Steve Nash .60 1.50
14 DerMarr Johnson .25 .60
15 Vince Carter .60 1.50
16 Kurt Thomas .25 .60
17 Cuttino Mobley .25 .60
18 Marc Jackson .25 .60
19 Stromile Swift .25 .60
20 Grant Hill .50 1.25
21 Raef LaFrentz .25 .60
22 Marcus Fizer .25 .60
23 Antonio Davis .25 .60
24 John Starks .25 .60
25 Trajan Langdon .25 .60
26 Jason Williams .30 .75
27 Toni Kukoc .40 1.00
28 Morris Peterson .25 .60
29 Allen Iverson .75 2.00
30 Andre Miller .30 .75
31 Larry Johnson .40 1.00
32 Vitaly Potapenko .25 .60
33 Tim Thomas .25 .60
34 Eddie House .25 .60
35 Juwan Howard .30 .75
36 Joel Przybilla .25 .60
37 John Stockton .50 1.25
38 Michael Finley .40 1.00
39 Hedo Turkoglu .30 .75
40 Keith Van Horn .30 .75
41 Shawn Marion .30 .75
42 Derek Fisher .30 .75
43 Terrell Brandon .25 .60
44 Jamal Mashburn .30 .75
45 Shareef Abdur-Rahim .30 .75
46 Brevin Knight .25 .60
47 Antoine Walker .30 .75
48 Mateen Cleaves .25 .60
49 Alonzo Mourning .50 1.25
50 Jermaine O'Neal .30 .75
51 Kenyon Martin .40 1.00
52 Steve Smith .30 .75
53 Jerry Stackhouse .30 .75
54 Mike Bibby .40 1.00
55 Latrell Sprewell .30 .75
56 Iakovos Tsakalidis .25 .60
57 Sam Cassell .30 .75
58 Michael Dickerson .25 .60
59 Alan Henderson .25 .60
60 Allan Houston .30 .75
61 Patrick Ewing .50 1.25
62 Joe Smith .30 .75
63 Rick Fox .25 .60
64 Tracy McGrady .60 1.50
65 Scottie Pippen .60 1.50
66 Chauncey Billups .40 1.00
67 Voshon Lenard .25 .60
68 Jalen Rose .30 .75
69 Derrick Coleman .30 .75
70 Shaquille O'Neal 1.00 2.50
71 Anfernee Hardaway .60 1.50
72 Derek Anderson .25 .60
73 Travis Best .25 .60
74 Darius Miles .25 .60
75 Glenn Robinson .30 .75
76 Darrell Armstrong .25 .60
77 Dirk Nowitzki .60 1.50
78 Stephon Marbury .30 .75
79 Tyronn Lue .25 .60
80 Bonzi Wells .25 .60
81 Mike Miller .30 .75
82 Tim Duncan .75 2.00
83 Tim Hardaway .40 1.00
84 Desmond Mason .30 .75
85 Ray Allen .40 1.00
86 Sean Elliott .40 1.00
87 David Wesley .25 .60
88 Rasheed Wallace .40 1.00
89 Kevin Garnett .60 1.50
90 Dikembe Mutombo .40 1.00
91 Baron Davis .40 1.00
92 Donyell Marshall .25 .60
93 Eddie Jones .30 .75
94 Vin Baker .30 .75
95 Peja Stojakovic .40 1.00
96 Antawn Jamison .40 1.00
97 Maurice Taylor .25 .60
98 Courtney Alexander .25 .60
99 Steve Francis .30 .75
100 Chris Mihm .25 .60
101 Kobe Bryant 1.50 4.00
102 Hakeem Olajuwon .50 1.25
103 Richard Hamilton .30 .75
104 Karl Malone .50 1.25
105 Chucky Atkins .25 .60
106 Eric Snow .25 .60
107 Ruben Patterson .25 .60
108 David Robinson .60 1.50
109 Bryon Russell .25 .60
110 Jason Terry .40 1.00
111 Jason Kidd .60 1.50
112 Charles Oakley .30 .75
113 Wang Zhizhi .30 .75
114 Quentin Richardson .30 .75
115 Clarence Weatherspoon .25 .60
116 Nick Van Exel .30 .75
117 Reggie Miller .40 1.00
118 Marcus Camby .30 .75
119 Corey Maggette .30 .75
120 Paul Pierce .40 1.00
121 Kwame Brown RC 1.25 3.00
122 Eddie Griffin RC 1.00 2.50
123 Eddy Curry RC 1.25 3.00
124 Jamaal Tinsley RC 1.25 3.00
125 Jason Richardson RC 1.50 4.00
126 Shane Battier RC 2.50 6.00
127 Troy Murphy RC 1.25 3.00
128 Richard Jefferson RC 2.00 5.00
129 DeSagana Diop RC 1.00 2.50
130 Tyson Chandler RC 2.00 5.00
131 Joe Johnson RC 1.50 4.00
132 Zach Randolph RC 2.00 5.00
133 Gerald Wallace RC 1.50 4.00
134 Loren Woods RC .75 2.00
135 Jason Collins RC 1.00 2.50
136 Rodney White RC .75 2.00
137 Jeryl Sasser RC .75 2.00
138 Kirk Haston RC .75 2.00
139 Pau Gasol RC 4.00 10.00
140 Kedrick Brown RC .75 2.00
141 Steven Hunter RC 1.00 2.50
142 Michael Bradley RC .75 2.00
143 Joseph Forte RC .75 2.00
144 Brandon Armstrong RC .75 2.00
145 Samuel Dalembert RC 1.25 3.00
146 Trenton Hassell RC 1.00 2.50
147 Gilbert Arenas RC 2.00 5.00
148 Omar Cook RC 1.25 3.00
149 Tony Parker RC 5.00 12.00
150 Terence Morris RC 1.25 3.00

2001-02 Fleer Genuine At Large

Randomly inserted in packs at a rate of one in 23, this 15-card insert set was designed horizontally on standard size cards. Each card background features a glowing city skyline of the player's corresponding team. The player stands in the forefront of the card outsizing the skyline.

COMPLETE SET (15) 20.00 40.00
STATED ODDS 1:23
AL1 Vince Carter 1.50 4.00
AL2 Dirk Nowitzki 1.50 4.00
AL3 Courtney Alexander .60 1.50
AL4 Jason Williams .75 2.00
AL5 Reggie Miller 1.00 2.50
AL6 Chris Webber 1.00 2.50
AL7 Elton Brand 1.00 2.50
AL8 Peja Stojakovic 1.00 2.50
AL9 Ray Allen 1.00 2.50
AL10 Shaquille O'Neal 2.50 6.00
AL11 Kevin Garnett 1.50 4.00
AL12 Kobe Bryant 4.00 10.00
AL13 Tim Duncan 2.00 5.00
AL14 Antawn Jamison 1.00 2.50
AL15 Latrell Sprewell .75 2.00

2001-02 Fleer Genuine Coverage Plus

Randomly inserted in packs at a rate of one in 24, this "Plus" insert set offers pieces of the featured player's game-worn jerseys. The cards have a horizontal design on standard size cards. White borders are present with an inside colored box highlighting the featured player. The player's name and team name run horizontal along the bottom edge and a circular swatch of a game worn unifom is placed in the lower left hand corner.

STATED ODDS 1:24
1 Shareef Abdur-Rahim 2.50 6.00
2 Darrell Armstrong 2.00 5.00
3 Mike Bibby 3.00 8.00
4 Vince Carter 5.00 12.00
5 Vince Carter WU 5.00 12.00
6 Michael Dickerson 2.00 5.00
7 Patrick Ewing 4.00 10.00
8 Steve Francis 2.50 6.00
9 Richard Hamilton 2.50 6.00
10 Anfernee Hardaway 5.00 12.00
11 Grant Hill 4.00 10.00
12 DerMarr Johnson 2.00 5.00
13 Jason Kidd 5.00 12.00
14 Rashard Lewis 3.00 8.00
15 Corey Maggette 2.50 6.00
16 Stephon Marbury 2.50 6.00
17 Shawn Marion 2.50 6.00
18 Kenyon Martin 3.00 8.00
19 Tracy McGrady 5.00 12.00
20 Mike Miller 2.50 6.00
21 Lamar Odom 2.50 6.00
22 Quentin Richardson 2.50 6.00
23 Jerry Stackhouse 2.50 6.00
24 Keith Van Horn 2.50 6.00

2001-02 Fleer Genuine Final Cut

Randomly inserted in packs at a rate of one in 24, this 35-card insert set features square swatches of game-worn jerseys from the featured player. Full color player photos appear on the left while the top and bottom edge of this horizontal set design are black and contain the player's name and team. A black and white photo of a basketball arena appears in the background.

STATED ODDS 1:24
1 Shareef Abdur-Rahim 2.50 6.00
2 Vince Carter 5.00 12.00
3 Baron Davis 3.00 8.00
4 Sean Elliott 3.00 8.00
5 Patrick Ewing 4.00 10.00
6 Michael Finley 3.00 8.00
7 Anfernee Hardaway 5.00 12.00
8 Grant Hill 4.00 10.00
9 Allan Houston 2.50 6.00
10 Allen Iverson 6.00 15.00
11 Jason Kidd 5.00 12.00
12 Tyronn Lue 2.00 5.00
13 Karl Malone 4.00 10.00
14 Stephon Marbury 2.50 6.00
15 Shawn Marion 2.50 6.00
16 Kenyon Martin 3.00 8.00
17 Desmond Mason 2.50 6.00
18 Tracy McGrady 5.00 12.00
19 Mike Miller 2.50 6.00
20 Andre Miller 2.50 6.00
21 Alonzo Mourning 6.00 15.00
22 Lamar Odom 2.50 6.00
23 Gary Payton 3.00 8.00
24 Paul Pierce 3.00 8.00
25 Quentin Richardson 2.50 6.00
26 David Robinson 5.00 12.00
27 Glenn Robinson 2.50 6.00
28 John Stockton 4.00 10.00
29 Stromile Swift 2.00 5.00
30 Wally Szczerbiak 2.50 6.00
31 Jason Terry 3.00 8.00
32 Keith Van Horn 2.50 6.00
33 Antoine Walker 2.50 6.00
34 David Wesley 2.00 5.00
35 Jason Williams 2.50 6.00

2001-02 Fleer Genuine Names of the Game

Randomly inserted in packs at a rate of one in 26, this 15-card insert set pays homage to the various nicknames of NBA players and includes swatches of their game-worn jerseys. The standard size cards are horizontally designed with top and bottom borders. The player's name and team name are found in the center of the card with a color player photo on the left and the player's team logo on the right.

STATED ODDS 1:24
1 Shareef Abdur-Rahim 2.50 6.00
2 Vince Carter 5.00 12.00
3 Steve Francis 2.50 6.00
4 Anfernee Hardaway 5.00 12.00
5 Allen Iverson 6.00 15.00
6 Jason Kidd 5.00 12.00
7 Karl Malone 4.00 10.00
8 Tracy McGrady 5.00 12.00
9 Dikembe Mutombo 3.00 8.00
10 Hakeem Olajuwon 4.00 10.00
11 Gary Payton 3.00 8.00
12 Morris Peterson 2.00 5.00
13 David Robinson 5.00 12.00
14 Glenn Robinson 2.50 6.00
15 Chris Webber 3.00 8.00

2001-02 Fleer Genuine Names of the Game Autographs

Randomly inserted in packs, this five card set parallels the base Names of the Game insert enhanced with authentic player autographs. Each card is sequentially numbered to 100, and upon release, Shareef Abdur-Rahim was the only card not issued as an exchange

STATED PRINT RUN 100 SERIAL #'d SETS
1 Dikembe Mutombo 12.00 30.00
2 Hakeem Olajuwon 25.00 60.00
3 Shareef Abdur-Rahim 8.00 20.00
4 Vince Carter 30.00 80.00

2001-02 Fleer Genuine Skywalkers

Randomly inserted in packs at a rate of one in 23, this 15-card set has silver backgrounds with both a player action photo on the right and a portrait gray-scale photo on the left. The player's name and team name appear along the bottom in foil, and the word "Skywalkers" appears in blue.

COMPLETE SET (15) 15.00 30.00
STATED ODDS 1:23
SW1 Vince Carter 1.50 4.00
SW2 Lamar Odom .75 2.00
SW3 Shawn Marion .75 2.00
SW4 Kobe Bryant 4.00 10.00
SW5 Kevin Garnett 1.50 4.00
SW6 Tim Duncan 2.00 5.00
SW7 Antawn Jamison 1.00 2.50
SW8 Michael Finley 1.00 2.50
SW9 Ray Allen 1.00 2.50
SW10 Paul Pierce 1.00 2.50
SW11 Baron Davis 1.00 2.50
SW12 Antoine Walker .75 2.00
SW13 Desmond Mason .75 2.00
SW14 Jason Williams .75 2.00
SW15 Darius Miles .60 1.50

2001-02 Fleer Genuine Unstoppable

Randomly inserted in packs at the rate of one in 23, this 10-card die cut set appers as a "stretched" stopsign. The backgrounds are red and feature a full color player action photo as well as a gray scale "shadow" of the same picture in the background.

STATED ODDS 1:23
US1 Vince Carter 1.25 3.00
US2 Darius Miles .50 1.25
US3 Shaquille O'Neal 2.00 5.00
US4 Jerry Stackhouse .60 1.50
US5 Tim Duncan 1.50 4.00
US6 Eddie Jones .60 1.50
US7 Jason Kidd 1.25 3.00
US8 Glenn Robinson .60 1.50
US9 Elton Brand .75 2.00
US10 Dirk Nowitzki 1.25 3.00

2002-03 Fleer Genuine

Released in late August 2002, Fleer Genuine boasts a 135-card set comprised of 100 veteran players and 35 rookies sequentially numbered to 2002. The base cards have have "wooded" printed borders with a player photo set in the middle. The bottom edge of the card is solid colored and contains the player's name and team in foil. Upon initial release several of the rookies were available via redemption only. Fleer Genuine was packaged in 24-pack boxes where packs contained five cards and carried a suggested retail price of $2.99.

COMPLETE SET (135) 100.00 200.00
COMP.SET w/o SP's (100) 20.00 40.00
101-135 PRINT RUN 2002 SER.#'d SETS
1 Shaquille O'Neal .75 2.00
2 Allen Iverson .50 1.25
3 Jerry Stackhouse .25 .60
4 Kobe Bryant 1.25 3.00
5 Jason Kidd .50 1.25
6 Andre Miller .25 .60
7 David Robinson .50 1.25
8 John Stockton .40 1.00
9 Glenn Robinson .25 .60
10 Chauncey Billups .30 .75
11 Chris Webber .30 .75
12 Antawn Jamison .30 .75
13 Sam Cassell .25 .60
14 Vlade Divac .25 .60
15 P.J. Brown .20 .50
16 Robert Horry .25 .60
17 Eric Snow .20 .50
18 Popeye Jones .20 .50
19 Paul Pierce .30 .75
20 Eddie Griffin .20 .50
21 Marcus Camby .25 .60
22 Gary Payton .30 .75
23 Michael Jordan 2.50 6.00
24 Shareef Abdur-Rahim .25 .60
25 Anfernee Hardaway .50 1.25
26 Michael Finley .30 .75
27 Steve Nash .40 1.00
28 Shane Battier .30 .75
29 Stephon Marbury .25 .60
30 Dirk Nowitzki .50 1.25
31 Pau Gasol .40 1.00
32 Shawn Marion .25 .60
33 Rodney Rogers .20 .50
34 Steve Smith .25 .60
35 Darrell Armstrong .20 .50
36 Alvin Williams .20 .50
37 Nick Van Exel .25 .60
38 Jason Williams .25 .60
39 Ruben Patterson .20 .50
40 Juwan Howard .25 .60
41 Brian Grant .20 .50
42 Damon Stoudamire .25 .60
43 Antonio McDyess .25 .60
44 Eddie Jones .25 .60
45 Rasheed Wallace .30 .75
46 Larry Hughes .25 .60
47 Wally Szczerbiak .25 .60
48 Tony Parker .40 1.00
49 Ron Artest .30 .75
50 Kevin Garnett .50 1.25
51 Tim Duncan .60 1.50
52 Marcus Fizer .20 .50
53 Darius Miles .20 .50
54 Grant Hill .40 1.00
55 Andrei Kirilenko .30 .75
56 Jalen Rose .25 .60
57 Lamar Odom .25 .60
58 Tracy McGrady .50 1.25
59 Karl Malone .40 1.00
60 Jason Terry .25 .60
61 Steve Francis .25 .60
62 Kenyon Martin .25 .60
63 Brent Barry .20 .50
64 Antoine Walker .25 .60
65 Reggie Miller .30 .75
66 Allan Houston .25 .60
67 Vince Carter .50 1.25
68 Toni Kukoc .30 .75
69 Lamond Murray .20 .50
70 Jason Richardson .30 .75
71 Rick Fox .20 .50
72 Kerry Kittles .20 .50
73 Dikembe Mutombo .30 .75
74 Tyson Chandler .30 .75
75 Richard Hamilton .25 .60
76 Elden Campbell .20 .50
77 Jermaine O'Neal .25 .60
78 Mike Miller .25 .60
79 Morris Peterson .20 .50
80 Jamal Mashburn .25 .60
81 Elton Brand .30 .75
82 Kurt Thomas .20 .50
83 Antonio Davis .20 .50
84 Ben Wallace .25 .60
85 Anthony Mason .20 .50
86 Peja Stojakovic .30 .75
87 Kenny Anderson .25 .60
88 Cuttino Mobley .20 .50
89 Keith Van Horn .25 .60
90 Rashard Lewis .30 .75
91 Clifford Robinson .20 .50
92 Ray Allen .30 .75
93 Mike Bibby .30 .75
94 Baron Davis .25 .60
95 Jamaal Tinsley .20 .50
96 Latrell Sprewell .25 .60
97 Jon Barry .20 .50
98 Desmond Mason .25 .60
99 Alonzo Mourning .40 1.00
100 Bonzi Wells .20 .50
101 Jay Williams RC 1.50 4.00
102 Mike Dunleavy RC 1.50 4.00
103 Amare Stoudemire RC 2.00 5.00
104 Caron Butler RC 1.50 4.00
105 Jared Jeffries RC 1.25 3.00
106 Fred Jones RC 1.25 3.00
107 Bostjan Nachbar RC 1.25 3.00
108 Jiri Welsch RC 1.25 3.00
109 Juan Dixon RC 1.50 4.00
110 Curtis Borchardt RC 1.00 2.50
111 Kareem Rush RC 1.25 3.00
112 Qyntel Woods RC 1.25 3.00
113 Casey Jacobsen RC 1.25 3.00
114 Frank Williams RC 1.00 2.50
115 John Salmons RC 1.50 4.00
116 Dan Dickau RC 1.25 3.00
117 DaJuan Wagner RC 1.25 3.00
118 Drew Gooden RC 1.50 4.00
119 Nikoloz Tskitishvili RC 1.00 2.50
120 Yao Ming RC 3.00 8.00
121 Nene Hilario RC 1.50 4.00
122 Chris Wilcox RC 1.25 3.00
123 Melvin Ely RC 1.25 3.00
124 Marcus Haislip RC 1.25 3.00
125 Ryan Humphrey RC 1.25 3.00
126 Tayshaun Prince RC 2.00 5.00
127 Tito Maddox RC 1.00 2.50
128 Chris Jefferies RC 1.00 2.50
129 Manu Ginobili RC 4.00 10.00
130 Roger Mason RC 1.25 3.00
131 Robert Archibald RC 1.00 2.50
132 Vincent Yarbrough RC 1.00 2.50
133 Dan Gadzuric RC 1.25 3.00
134 Carlos Boozer RC 1.50 4.00
135 Rasual Butler RC 1.50 4.00

2002-03 Fleer Genuine Coverage

Randomly seeded in packs at the rate of one in 24, this 15-card set features a horizontal card design with printed "wood" borders along the top and bottom and a gray strip through the center. On this strip appears a player photo on the right and a rectangular swatch of memorabilia. Each card is enhanced with silver foil highlights. A gold version also packed out with the product where each card is sequentially numbered to 100.

STATED ODDS 1:24
*GOLD: .6X TO 1.5X HI
GOLD PRINT RUN 100 SER.#'d SETS
1 Vince Carter 5.00 12.00
2 Michael Dickerson 2.00 5.00
3 Keyon Dooling 2.00 5.00
4 Michael Finley 3.00 8.00
5 Tom Gugliotta 2.00 5.00
6 Richard Hamilton 2.50 6.00
7 Anfernee Hardaway 5.00 12.00
8 Grant Hill 4.00 10.00
9 DerMarr Johnson 2.00 5.00
10 Rashard Lewis 3.00 8.00
11 Antonio McDyess 2.50 6.00
12 Desmond Mason 2.50 6.00
13 Lamar Odom 2.50 6.00
14 Keith Van Horn 2.50 6.00
15 Antoine Walker 2.50 6.00

2002-03 Fleer Genuine Global Warning

Randomly inserted in pack at the rate of one in 12, this 10-card set showcases the top foreign players of the NBA. The bottom of the card background is a globe, the middle of the card contains silver foil higlights with the set name and player's name, above this appears the player's photo, and the top of the card fades to black.

COMPLETE SET (10) 5.00 12.00
STATED ODDS 1:12
1 Tim Duncan 1.25 3.00
2 Pau Gasol .75 2.00
3 Andrei Kirilenko .60 1.50
4 Patrick Ewing .75 2.00
5 Dikembe Mutombo .60 1.50
6 Steve Nash .75 2.00
7 Hakeem Olajuwon .75 2.00
8 Tony Parker .75 2.00
9 Dirk Nowitzki 1.00 2.50
10 Peja Stojakovic .60 1.50

2002-03 Fleer Genuine Global Warning Jersey

STATED ODDS 1:30
1 Pau Gasol 4.00 10.00
2 Andrei Kirilenko 3.00 8.00
3 Patrick Ewing 4.00 10.00
4 Dikembe Mutombo 3.00 8.00
5 Tony Parker 4.00 10.00
6 Peja Stojakovic 3.00 8.00

2002-03 Fleer Genuine Leaders

Randomly inserted in packs at the rate of one in 24, this 15-card set features a horizontal card design with an in-action player photo along the right of the card and an open space on the left. The background colors of the card are set to match the featured player's team colors.

COMPLETE SET (15) 15.00 40.00
STATED ODDS 1:24
1 Allen Iverson 1.50 4.00
2 Shaquille O'Neal 2.50 6.00
3 Paul Pierce 1.00 2.50
4 Tracy McGrady 1.50 4.00
5 Tim Duncan 2.00 5.00
6 Kobe Bryant 4.00 10.00
7 Vince Carter 1.50 4.00
8 Dirk Nowitzki 1.50 4.00
9 Michael Jordan 8.00 20.00
10 Steve Francis .75 2.00
11 Karl Malone 1.25 3.00
12 Elton Brand 1.00 2.50
13 Andre Miller .75 2.00
14 Jason Kidd 1.50 4.00
15 Baron Davis .75 2.00

2002-03 Fleer Genuine Leaders Jerseys

Randomly inserted in packs at the rate of one in 40, this 15-card set features a horizontal card design with an in-action player photo along the right of the card and a jersey swatch on the left. The top border of the card is in dark colors and the player's face appears just below. A Gold version sequentially numbered to 25 was inserted into packs as well.

STATED ODDS 1:40
*GOLD: 1.25X TO 3X HI
GOLD PRINT RUN 25 SER.#'d SETS
1 Allen Iverson 5.00 12.00
2 Paul Pierce 3.00 8.00
3 Tracy McGrady 5.00 12.00
4 Vince Carter 5.00 12.00
5 Steve Francis 2.50 6.00
6 Karl Malone 4.00 10.00
7 Elton Brand 3.00 8.00
8 Andre Miller 2.50 6.00
9 Jason Kidd 5.00 12.00
10 Baron Davis 2.50 6.00

2002-03 Fleer Genuine Names of the Game

Randomly inserted in packs at the rate of one in 12, this 15-card set features all white borders, a color player photo and silver foil highlights through the center of the card containing the set name and player's name.

COMPLETE SET (15) 10.00 25.00
STATED ODDS 1:12
1 Kobe Bryant 2.50 6.00
2 Ray Allen .60 1.50
3 Tracy McGrady 1.00 2.50
4 John Stockton .75 2.00
5 Paul Pierce .60 1.50
6 Allen Iverson 1.00 2.50
7 Michael Jordan 5.00 12.00
8 Vince Carter 1.00 2.50
9 Shaquille O'Neal 1.50 4.00
10 David Robinson 1.00 2.50
11 Kevin Garnett 1.00 2.50
12 Jason Kidd 1.00 2.50
13 Chris Webber .60 1.50
14 Ben Wallace .50 1.25
15 Shawn Marion .50 1.25

2002-03 Fleer Genuine Names of the Game Jerseys

Randomly inserted in packs at the rate of one in 30,

this 10-card set parallels the design of the base Names of the Game insert set enhanced with a centered rectangular swatch of game worn memorabilia.
STATED ODDS 1:30
*GOLD: 1X TO 2.5X HI
GOLD: STATED PRINT RUN 50 SER.#'d SETS

1 Ray Allen	2.50	6.00
2 Tracy McGrady	4.00	10.00
3 John Stockton	3.00	8.00
4 Paul Pierce	2.50	6.00
5 Allen Iverson	4.00	10.00
6 Vince Carter	4.00	10.00
7 David Robinson	4.00	10.00
8 Jason Kidd	4.00	10.00
9 Chris Webber	2.50	6.00
10 Shawn Marion	2.00	5.00

2002-03 Fleer Genuine On the Up

Randomly inserted in packs at the rate of one in 12, this 15-card set features a die cut design in the shape of an arrow. The borders of the card are black, and the bottom contains silver foil highlights and the words, "On the Up" in white. Full color player action photos appear towards the top of the card in the middle of the arrow.

COMPLETE SET (15)	5.00	12.00
STATED ODDS 1:12		
1 Pau Gasol	.75	2.00
2 Jamaal Tinsley	.40	1.00
3 Jason Richardson	.60	1.50
4 Tony Parker	.75	2.00
5 Shane Battier	.60	1.50
6 Andrei Kirilenko	.60	1.50
7 Kenyon Martin	.50	1.25
8 Gilbert Arenas	.60	1.50
9 Mike Miller	.50	1.25
10 Darius Miles	.40	1.00
11 Stromile Swift	.40	1.00
12 Marcus Fizer	.40	1.00
13 Iakovos Tsakalidis	.40	1.00
14 Richard Jefferson	.60	1.50
15 Speedy Claxton	.40	1.00

2002-03 Fleer Genuine On the Up Jerseys

Randomly seeded in packs at the rate of one in 36, this eight card set parallels the base design of the On the Up insert set enhanced with a square swatch of game worn memorabilia.
STATED ODDS 1:36

1 Jason Richardson	3.00	8.00
2 Shane Battier	3.00	8.00
3 Kenyon Martin	2.50	6.00
4 Mike Miller	2.50	6.00
5 Darius Miles	2.00	5.00
6 Stromile Swift	2.00	5.00
7 Richard Jefferson	3.00	8.00
8 Speedy Claxton	2.00	5.00

2002-03 Fleer Genuine Prime Time Players

Randomly inserted in packs at the rate of one in 288, this 10-card set features a horizontal design with a light background. Player action photos appear on the left side of the card, and right below this photo, the player's number appears. The top right side of the card contains the words "Prime Time Players" in gold and the player's name and team name in the lower right hand corner.

COMPLETE SET (10)	40.00	100.00
STATED ODDS 1:288		
1 Shaquille O'Neal	6.00	15.00
2 Allen Iverson	4.00	10.00
3 Vince Carter	4.00	10.00
4 Michael Jordan	20.00	50.00
5 Tracy McGrady	4.00	10.00
6 Tim Duncan	5.00	12.00
7 Kevin Garnett	4.00	10.00
8 Dirk Nowitzki	4.00	10.00
9 Paul Pierce	2.50	6.00
10 Kobe Bryant	10.00	25.00

2002-03 Fleer Genuine Prime Time Players Jerseys

Randomly seeded in packs at the rate of one in 300, this five card set parallels the design of the base Prime Time Players set enhanced with a square swatch of game used memorabilia.
STATED ODDS 1:300

1 Allen Iverson	6.00	15.00
2 Vince Carter	6.00	15.00
3 Tracy McGrady	6.00	15.00
4 Dirk Nowitzki	6.00	15.00
5 Paul Pierce	4.00	10.00

2003-04 Fleer Genuine Insider

Released in February 2004, Genuine Insider features a 140-card set divided up into 100 veteran player cards, 10 rookie cards sequentially numbered to 499 (cards 101-110), 20 rookie cards sequentially numbered to 799 (cards 111-130), and 10 mini rookie cards sequentially numbered to 350 (cards 131-140). The mini cards are found as inserts inside cards 101-110, hence the product name, Insider. Base cards feature colored background with the main focus being color to match the player's team colors. Genuine Insider was packaged in 24-pack boxes where packs contained five cards and carried a suggested retail price of $4.99.

COMP.SET w/o SP's (100)	12.50	30.00
111-130 RC PRINT RUN 799 SER.#'d SETS		
131-140 MINIS FOUND INSIDE 101-110 RC's		
MINI PRINT RUN 350 SER.#'d SETS		
1 Shareef Abdur-Rahim	.25	.60
2 Andre Miller	.25	.60
3 Reggie Miller	.30	.75
4 Michael Redd	.30	.75
5 Allan Houston	.25	.60
6 Mike Bibby	.30	.75
7 Kwame Brown	.20	.50
8 Earl Boykins	.20	.50
9 Ron Artest	.30	.75
10 Eddie Jones	.25	.60
11 Zach Randolph	.25	.60
12 Derek Anderson	.20	.50
13 Andrei Kirilenko	.30	.75
14 Carlos Boozer	.25	.60
15 Yao Ming	.60	1.50
16 Pau Gasol	.30	.75
17 Jamal Mashburn	.25	.60
18 Shawn Marion	.25	.60
19 Vince Carter	.50	1.25
20 Eddy Curry	.20	.50
21 Mike Dunleavy Jr.	.25	.60
22 Kobe Bryant	1.25	3.00
23 Tim Thomas	.20	.50
24 Drew Gooden	.25	.60
25 Tim Duncan	.50	1.25
26 Dajuan Wagner	.20	.50
27 Speedy Claxton	.20	.50
28 Karl Malone	.40	1.00
29 Jason Kidd	.50	1.25
30 Kenny Thomas	.20	.50
31 Vladimir Radmanovic	.20	.50
32 Tyson Chandler	.25	.60
33 Jason Richardson	.30	.75
34 Quentin Richardson	.25	.60
35 Kerry Kittles	.20	.50
36 Derrick Coleman	.25	.60
37 Manu Ginobili	.40	1.00
38 Paul Pierce	.30	.75
39 Ben Wallace	.25	.60
40 Corey Maggette	.25	.60
41 Sam Cassell	.25	.60
42 Hedo Turkoglu	.25	.60
43 Peja Stojakovic	.30	.75
44 Gilbert Arenas	.25	.60
45 Dirk Nowitzki	.50	1.25
46 Al Harrington	.25	.60
47 Caron Butler	.25	.60
48 Baron Davis	.25	.60
49 Rasheed Wallace	.30	.75
50 Morris Peterson	.20	.50
51 Steve Nash	.40	1.00
52 Steve Francis	.25	.60
53 Lamar Odom	.25	.60
54 Jamaal Magloire	.20	.50
55 Amare Stoudemire	.40	1.00
56 Antonio Davis	.20	.50
57 Dan Dickau	.20	.50
58 Cuttino Mobley	.20	.50
59 Jason Williams	.25	.60
60 David Wesley	.20	.50
61 Stephon Marbury	.25	.60
62 Ray Allen	.30	.75
63 Scottie Pippen	.50	1.25
64 Nick Van Exel	.25	.60
65 Shaquille O'Neal	.75	2.00
66 Richard Jefferson	.25	.60
67 Allen Iverson	.50	1.25
68 Tony Parker	.30	.75
69 Jason Terry	.25	.60
70 NenÃª	.25	.60
71 Marko Jaric	.20	.50
72 Troy Hudson	.20	.50
73 Malik Rose	.20	.50
74 Bobby Jackson	.20	.50
75 Jerry Stackhouse	.25	.60
76 Voshon Lenard	.20	.50
77 Richard Hamilton	.25	.60
78 Scot Pollard	.20	.50
79 Latrell Sprewell	.25	.60
80 Tracy McGrady	.40	1.00
81 Chris Webber	.30	.75
82 Raef LaFrentz	.20	.50
83 Tayshaun Prince	.25	.60
84 Elton Brand	.30	.75
85 Kevin Garnett	.50	1.25
86 Keon Clark	.20	.50
87 Brad Miller	.25	.60
88 Alvin Williams	.20	.50
89 Michael Finley	.30	.75
90 Jermaine O'Neal	.25	.60
91 Desmond Mason	.25	.60
92 Keith Van Horn	.25	.60
93 Bonzi Wells	.20	.50
94 Matt Harpring	.20	.50
95 Darius Miles	.20	.50
96 Eddie Griffin	.20	.50
97 Shane Battier	.25	.60
98 Kenyon Martin	.25	.60
99 Glenn Robinson	.25	.60
100 Rashard Lewis	.30	.75
101 Carmelo Anthony RC	8.00	20.00
102 Troy Bell RC	1.50	4.00
103 T.J. Ford RC	2.00	5.00
104 LeBron James RC	50.00	120.00
105 Mike Sweetney RC	1.50	4.00
106 Chris Bosh RC	4.00	10.00
107 Jarvis Hayes RC	1.50	4.00
108 Darko Milicic RC	2.00	5.00
109 Chris Kaman RC	2.50	6.00
110 Dwyane Wade RC	8.00	20.00
111 Udonis Haslem RC	1.50	4.00
112 Josh Howard RC	2.00	5.00
113 Mickael Pietrus RC	1.50	4.00
114 Reece Gaines RC	1.25	3.00
115 Nick Collison RC	1.50	4.00
116 Leandrinho Barbosa RC	2.00	5.00
117 Kendrick Perkins RC	1.50	4.00
118 Ndudi Ebi RC	1.25	3.00
119 Willie Green RC	1.25	3.00
120 Kirk Hinrich RC	2.00	5.00
121 Marcus Banks RC	1.25	3.00
122 Zarko Cabarkapa RC	1.25	3.00
123 Zoran Planinic RC	1.25	3.00
124 David West RC	2.00	5.00
125 Luke Ridnour RC	1.50	4.00
126 Brian Cook RC	1.25	3.00
127 Boris Diaw RC	2.00	5.00
128 Dahntay Jones RC	1.50	4.00
129 Maciej Lampe RC	1.25	3.00
130 Travis Outlaw RC	1.50	4.00
131 Ben Handlogten MM RC	1.25	3.00
132 Jerome Beasley MM RC	1.25	3.00
133 Marquis Daniels MM RC	1.50	4.00
134 Luke Walton MM RC	2.00	5.00
135 Aleksandar Pavlovic MM RC	1.50	4.00
136 Matt Carroll MM RC	1.25	3.00
137 Curtis Borchardt MM	2.00	5.00
138 Jason Kapono MM RC	1.25	3.00
139 Steve Blake MM RC	1.50	4.00
140 Keith Bogans MM RC	1.25	3.00

2003-04 Fleer Genuine Insider Reflections

*1-100 REF: 4X TO 10X BASE HI
*101-110 RC REF: .6X TO 1.5X BASE HI
*111-130 RC REF: .75X TO 2X BASE HI
*131-140 RC REF: .75X TO 2X BASE HI
131-140 PRINT RUN 148 SER.#'d SETS

2003-04 Fleer Genuine Insider Genuine Article Insider

Inserted in packs, this 19-card set utilizes a horizontal design with full color player photos on the left and a swatch of game worn memorabilia on the right. Each card is sequentially numbered to 400.
PRINT RUN 400 SER.#'d SETS
*PATCH: 1.25X TO 3X BASE HI
PATCH PRINT RUN 50 SER.#'d SETS

1 Baron Davis	2.00	5.00
2 Nene	2.00	5.00
3 Mike Dunleavy	2.00	5.00
4 Tracy McGrady	3.00	8.00
5 Vince Carter	4.00	10.00
6 Allen Iverson	4.00	10.00
7 Jason Kidd	4.00	10.00
8 Shaquille O'Neal	6.00	15.00
9 Yao Ming	5.00	12.00
10 Steve Francis	2.00	5.00
11 Tyson Chandler	2.00	5.00
12 Amare Stoudemire	3.00	8.00
13 Kevin Garnett	4.00	10.00
14 Tim Duncan	4.00	10.00
15 Ben Wallace	2.00	5.00
16 Kenyon Martin	2.00	5.00
17 Peja Stojakovic	2.50	6.00
18 Mike Sweetney	1.50	4.00
19 Carmelo Anthony	8.00	20.00

2003-04 Fleer Genuine Insider Genuine Autograph Insider

Inserted at one in 24, this 15-card set places full-color player photos in the middle of the horizontal design, team logo in the upper left hand corner and a centered cut signature below the player photo.
STATED ODDS 1:24

2 Carmelo Anthony	15.00	40.00
3 Dwyane Wade	30.00	80.00
5 Amare Stoudemire	10.00	25.00
6 Gilbert Arenas	8.00	20.00
7 Luke Ridnour	3.00	8.00
8 Dajuan Wagner	2.50	6.00
9 Tayshaun Prince	5.00	12.00
10 Earl Boykins	4.00	10.00
12 Maurice Williams	4.00	10.00
13 Travis Outlaw	3.00	8.00
14 Zarko Cabarkapa	2.50	6.00
15 Vince Carter	15.00	40.00

2003-04 Fleer Genuine Insider Scoring Threats

Seeded in packs at the rate of one in 20, this 10-card set places two player portrait photos, one on the top and one on the bottom in a one-color scale to match the player's team color.

COMPLETE SET (10)	8.00	20.00
STATED ODDS 1:20		
1 T.McGrady/V.Carter	1.25	3.00
2 A.Iverson/J.Kidd	1.25	3.00
3 S.O'Neal/Y.Ming	2.00	5.00
4 S.Francis/J.Richardson	.75	2.00
5 A.Stoudemire/K.Garnett	1.25	3.00
6 P.Pierce/A.Walker	.75	2.00
7 D.Nowitzki/P.Gasol	1.25	3.00
8 R.Allen/M.Bibby	.75	2.00
9 R.Jefferson/K.Martin	.60	1.50
10 T.Duncan/J.O'Neal	1.25	3.00

2003-04 Fleer Genuine Insider Scoring Threats Game Used

Inserted in packs at the rate of one in 48, this 10-card set parallels the design of the base Scoring Threats insert set enhanced with a swatch of memorabilia from one of the two players.
STATED ODDS 1:48

1 McGrady/Carter JSY	4.00	10.00
2 Iverson JSY/Kidd	4.00	10.00
3 S.O'Neal JSY/Ming	6.00	15.00
4 Francis JSY/ J.Richardson	2.50	6.00
5 Stoudemire/Garnett JSY	5.00	12.00
6 Pierce JSY/Walker	3.00	8.00
7 Nowitzki JSY/Gasol	4.00	10.00
8 Allen/Bibby JSY	2.50	6.00
9 Jefferson/K.Martin JSY	2.50	6.00
10 Duncan JSY/J.O'Neal	4.00	10.00

2003-04 Fleer Genuine Insider Scoring Threats Game Used Dual

Sequentially numbered to 100, this seven cards set parallels the design of the Scoring Threats insert set enhanced with a swatch of jersey from each of the two players appearing on the card.
PRINT RUN 100 SER.#'d SETS

1 T.McGrady/V.Carter	10.00	25.00
2 A.Iverson/J.Kidd	8.00	20.00
4 A.Stoudemire/K.Garnett	8.00	20.00
5 D.Nowitzki/P.Gasol	8.00	20.00
6 T.Duncan/J.O'Neal	10.00	25.00

2003-04 Fleer Genuine Insider Team USA Insider

This set is horizontally designed and sequentially numbered to 325. The motif of the design is American flags with a player action photo in the middle, the Team USA and Genuine Insider logos to the left and a swatch of Team USA memorabilia on the right. Larry Brown's card does not include a swatch of memorabilia.
PRINT RUN 325 SER.#'d SETS
NO JSY FOR LARRY BROWN

1 Ray Allen	5.00	12.00
2 Mike Bibby	5.00	12.00
3 Tim Duncan	8.00	20.00
4 Allen Iverson	8.00	20.00
5 Jason Kidd	8.00	20.00
6 Tracy McGrady	6.00	15.00
7 Jermaine O'Neal	4.00	10.00
8 Larry Brown	1.50	4.00

2003-04 Fleer Genuine Insider Tools of the Game

Inserted at one in eight, this 15-card set is horizontally designed and places a full-color player action photo in the middle and three small squares on the right side, stacked on top of eachother, with photos of the game's tool's such as ball, jerseys and warmups.

COMPLETE SET (15)	5.00	12.00
STATED ODDS 1:8		
1 Amare Stoudemire	.50	1.25
2 Shaquille O'Neal	1.00	2.50
3 Kevin Garnett	.60	1.50
4 Vince Carter	.60	1.50
5 Paul Pierce	.40	1.00
6 Yao Ming	.75	2.00
7 Jason Richardson	.40	1.00
8 Chris Webber	.40	1.00
9 Antoine Walker	.40	1.00
10 Scottie Pippen	.60	1.50
11 Elton Brand	.40	1.00
12 Richard Jefferson	.30	.75
13 Steve Francis	.30	.75
14 Pau Gasol	.40	1.00
15 Stephon Marbury	.30	.75

2003-04 Fleer Genuine Insider Tools of the Game Game Used

Sequentially numbered to 199, this 15-card set parallels the design of the Tools of the Game set enhanced with a single swatch of memorabilia. Versions with Dual swatches (of which include, jerseys, balls, warmups etc.) are sequentially numbered to 99 and Triple swatch versions are sequentially numbered to 25.
PRINT RUN 199 SER.#'d SETS
*DUAL: .6X TO 1.5X BASE HI
DUAL PRINT RUN 99 SER.#'d SETS
*TRIPLE: 1.25X TO 3X BASE HI
TRIPLE PRINT RUN 25 SER.#'d SETS

1 Amare Stoudemire	3.00	8.00
2 Shaquille O'Neal	6.00	15.00
3 Kevin Garnett	4.00	10.00
4 Vince Carter	4.00	10.00
5 Paul Pierce	2.50	6.00
6 Yao Ming	5.00	12.00
7 Jason Richardson	2.50	6.00
8 Chris Webber	2.50	6.00
9 Antoine Walker	2.50	6.00
10 Scottie Pippen	6.00	15.00
11 Elton Brand	2.50	6.00
12 Richard Jefferson	2.00	5.00
13 Steve Francis	2.00	5.00
14 Pau Gasol	2.50	6.00
15 Stephon Marbury	2.00	5.00

2004-05 Fleer Genuine

Released in June, Genuine boasts a 135-card set divided up into 100 veteran players (cards 1-100) 10 retired players serially numbered to 500 (cards 101-110) and 25 rookies serially numbered to 500 (cards 111-135). Base cards have white borders with an oval-shaped area showcasing the player in action and is highlighted with the player's team colors. The cards also have embossed "dots" in on each of the sides. Buybacks were also inserted of original Fleer cards and are checklisted on our website at www.beckett.com. Genuine was released for both Hobby and Retail where Hobby boxes contained two mini-boxes of nine packs and Retal contained 24 packs. All packs contained five cards.

COMP.SET w/o SP's (100)	15.00	40.00
111-135 RC PRINT RUN 500 SER.#'d SETS		
UNPRICED PARALLEL PRINT RUN 10 SETS		
1 Rasheed Wallace	.30	.75
2 Larry Hughes	.25	.60
3 Allen Iverson	.50	1.25
4 Josh Howard	.30	.75
5 Bonzi Wells	.20	.50
6 Jamaal Magloire	.20	.50
7 Luke Ridnour	.25	.60
8 Chauncey Billups	.30	.75
9 Dwyane Wade	.50	1.25
10 Amare Stoudemire	.25	.60
11 Earl Boykins	.20	.50
12 Damon Jones	.20	.50
13 Marquis Daniels	.20	.50
14 Luke Walton	.20	.50
15 Jamal Crawford	.30	.75
16 Corliss Williamson	.20	.50
17 Vince Carter	.50	1.25
18 Antoine Walker	.30	.75
19 Jason Richardson	.30	.75
20 Jason Kidd	.50	1.25
21 Peja Stojakovic	.30	.75
22 Jeff McInnis	.20	.50
23 Lamar Odom	.25	.60
24 Allan Houston	.25	.60
25 Jalen Rose	.25	.60
26 LeBron James	2.00	5.00
27 Caron Butler	.25	.60
28 Stephon Marbury	.25	.60
29 Carlos Arroyo	.20	.50
30 Zydrunas Ilgauskas	.25	.60
31 Kobe Bryant	1.25	3.00
32 Steve Francis	.25	.60
33 Carlos Boozer	.25	.60
34 Primoz Brezec	.20	.50
35 Reggie Miller	.30	.75
36 Sam Cassell	.25	.60
37 Ray Allen	.30	.75
38 Drew Gooden	.20	.50
39 Chris Wilcox	.20	.50
40 Grant Hill	.40	1.00
41 Andrei Kirilenko	.25	.60
42 Kirk Hinrich	.25	.60
43 Corey Maggette	.25	.60
44 Cuttino Mobley	.20	.50
45 Gilbert Arenas	.25	.60
46 Tyson Chandler	.25	.60
47 Elton Brand	.30	.75
48 Samuel Dalembert	.20	.50
49 Jarvis Hayes	.20	.50
50 Ben Wallace	.25	.60
51 Shawn Marion	.25	.60
52 Michael Redd	.25	.60
53 Richard Hamilton	.25	.60
54 Desmond Mason	.25	.60
55 Steve Nash	.40	1.00
56 Antawn Jamison	.25	.60
57 Kareem Rush	.20	.50
58 Jermaine O'Neal	.25	.60
59 Keith Van Horn	.25	.60
60 Rashard Lewis	.30	.75
61 Gerald Wallace	.25	.60
62 Jamaal Tinsley	.20	.50
63 Vladimir Radmanovic	.20	.50
64 Predrag Drobnjak	.20	.50
65 Mike Dunleavy	.25	.60
66 Baron Davis	.25	.60
67 Mike Bibby	.30	.75
68 Ricky Davis	.25	.60
69 Tracy McGrady	.40	1.00
70 Richard Jefferson	.25	.60
71 Chris Webber	.30	.75
72 Michael Finley	.30	.75
73 Pau Gasol	.30	.75
74 David West	.25	.60
75 Chris Bosh	.30	.75
76 Gary Payton	.30	.75
77 Yao Ming	.60	1.50
78 Wally Szczerbiak	.25	.60
79 Tim Duncan	.50	1.25
80 Keith Bogans	.20	.50
81 Stephen Jackson	.25	.60
82 Kevin Garnett	.50	1.25
83 Tony Parker	.30	.75
84 Kenyon Martin	.25	.60
85 Shaquille O'Neal	.75	2.00
86 Shareef Abdur-Rahim	.25	.60
87 Al Harrington	.25	.60
88 Adonal Foyle	.20	.50
89 Brian Scalabrine	.20	.50
90 Brad Miller	.25	.60
91 Carmelo Anthony	.60	1.50
92 Udonis Haslem	.20	.50
93 Zach Randolph	.25	.60
94 Paul Pierce	.30	.75
95 Maurice Taylor	.20	.50
96 Latrell Sprewell	.25	.60
97 Manu Ginobili	.40	1.00
98 Dirk Nowitzki	.50	1.25
99 Jason Williams	.25	.60
100 Nick Van Exel	.25	.60
101 Charles Barkley	3.00	8.00
102 Jerry West	2.50	6.00
103 Magic Johnson	5.00	12.00
104 Kareem Abdul-Jabbar	3.00	8.00
105 Pete Maravich	3.00	8.00
106 Maurice Cheeks	1.25	3.00
107 Alex English	1.50	4.00
108 George Mikan	4.00	10.00
109 Wilt Chamberlain	4.00	10.00
110 Dominique Wilkins	2.50	6.00
111 Josh Childress RC	1.25	3.00
112 Josh Smith RC	1.50	4.00
113 Al Jefferson RC	2.00	5.00
114 Delonte West RC	1.50	4.00
115 Tony Allen RC	1.50	4.00
116 Emeka Okafor RC	1.25	3.00
117 Chris Duhon RC	1.50	4.00
118 Ben Gordon RC	1.50	4.00
119 Luol Deng RC	1.50	4.00
120 Andres Nocioni RC	1.50	4.00
121 David Harrison RC	1.00	2.50
122 Devin Harris RC	1.25	3.00
123 Shaun Livingston RC	1.50	4.00
124 Dorell Wright RC	1.50	4.00
125 J.R. Smith RC	1.50	4.00
126 Trevor Ariza RC	1.50	4.00
127 Dwight Howard RC	3.00	8.00
128 Jameer Nelson RC	1.50	4.00
129 Andre Iguodala RC	2.00	5.00
130 Sebastian Telfair RC	1.25	3.00
131 Kevin Martin RC	2.00	5.00
132 Ha Seung-Jin RC	1.50	4.00
133 Rafael Araujo RC	1.00	2.50
134 Kirk Snyder RC	1.00	2.50
135 Beno Udrih RC	1.25	3.00

2004-05 Fleer Genuine 100

Randomly inserted in packs, this 135-card set parallels the base set enhanced with silver highlights and sequential numbering to 100. A parallel version serially numbered to 10 was also issued with cards that contain bronze highlights.
*1-100: 2.5X TO 6X BASE HI
*101-110: 1.25X TO 3X BASE HI
*111-135: .5X TO 1.25X BASE HI
PRINT RUN 100 SER.#'d SETS

105 Pete Maravich	30.00	80.00

2004-05 Fleer Genuine Article

Inserted in Hobby packs at the rate of one in 12 and Retail at the rate of one in 15, this set is designed to look like a newspaper with a player photo on the left, text on the right and the set name along the top in silver foil.

COMPLETE SET (15)	10.00	25.00
STATED ODDS 1:12 H, 1:15 R		
1 Amare Stoudemire	.50	1.25
2 LeBron James	4.00	10.00
3 Carmelo Anthony	1.25	3.00
4 Tracy McGrady	.75	2.00
5 Jermaine O'Neal	.50	1.25
6 Kobe Bryant	2.50	6.00
7 Pau Gasol	.60	1.50
8 Shaquille O'Neal	1.50	4.00
9 Dwyane Wade	1.00	2.50
10 Michael Redd	.50	1.25
11 Allen Iverson	1.00	2.50
12 Vince Carter	1.00	2.50
13 Chris Webber	.60	1.50
14 Tony Parker	.60	1.50
15 Andrei Kirilenko	.50	1.25

2004-05 Fleer Genuine Article Autographs

Randomly seeded in packs, this eight card set features a similar, but horizontal design to the base Genuine Article set enhanced with sequential numbering, and autograph and silver foil highlights. Print runs range from 50 to 125.
STATED PRINT RUN 50 TO 125 SETS

AK Andrei Kirilenko/50	6.00	15.00
CA Carmelo Anthony/50	20.00	50.00
DW Dwyane Wade/50	20.00	50.00
JH Josh Howard/125	5.00	12.00
LJ Luke Jackson/125	5.00	12.00
LR Luke Ridnour/50	5.00	12.00
PG Pau Gasol/50	8.00	20.00
DWE David West	5.00	12.00

2004-05 Fleer Genuine Article Autographs Gold

*GOLD: .5X TO 1.25X BASE HI
STATED PRINT RUN 20 TO 40 SER.#'d SETS

DW Dwyane Wade/20	30.00	80.00

2004-05 Fleer Genuine Article Autographs Patches

Randomly seeded, this eight card set parallels the base Genuine Article Autographs insert enhanced with a swatch of game worn patch and sequential numbering ranging from 10 to 40.
STATED PRINT RUN 10 TO 30 SETS

AK Andrei Kirilenko/30	12.50	30.00
CA Carmelo Anthony/20	50.00	125.00
JH Josh Howard/20	12.50	30.00
JO Jermaine O'Neal/20	15.00	40.00
LR Luke Ridnour/20	12.50	30.00
PG Pau Gasol/20	20.00	50.00
DWE David West/30	12.50	30.00
DWE1 David West/20	12.50	30.00

2004-05 Fleer Genuine Article Game Used

Randomly seeded in Hobby packs at the rate of one in 50 and Retail packs at the rate of one in 270, this 10-card set parallels the design of the base Genuine Article set enhanced with a swatch of memorabilia in the lower right hand corner and green foil highlights. Two parallel versions of the set were issued, one featuring red foil and sequential numbering to 149, and another featuring a patch swatch and sequential numbering to 15.
STATED ODDS 1:50 H, 1:270 R
*GAME USED 149: .5X TO 1.25X BASE GU HI
PRINT RUN 149 SER.#'d SETS

AI Allen Iverson	4.00	10.00
AK Andrei Kirilenko	2.00	5.00
AS Amare Stoudemire	2.00	5.00
CA Carmelo Anthony	5.00	12.00
DW Dwyane Wade	6.00	15.00
JO Jermaine O'Neal	2.00	5.00
PG Pau Gasol	2.50	6.00
SO Shaquille O'Neal	6.00	15.00
TM Tracy McGrady	3.00	8.00
VC Vince Carter	4.00	10.00

2004-05 Fleer Genuine At Large

Inserted in Hobby packs at the rate of one in six and Retail at the rate of one in eight, this 20-card set features cards with white borders along the top and bottom and a starburst background colored to match the featured player's jersey. In the spelling of the word, large on the card, the @ symbol is used instead of an a.

COMPLETE SET (20)	10.00	25.00
STATED ODDS 1:6 H, 1:8 R		
1 Corey Maggette	.40	1.00
2 Steve Francis	.40	1.00
3 Jason Richardson	.50	1.25
4 Dwyane Wade	.75	2.00
5 Richard Jefferson	.40	1.00
6 Ben Wallace	.40	1.00
7 Carmelo Anthony	1.00	2.50
8 Kevin Garnett	.75	2.00
9 Tim Duncan	.75	2.00
10 Yao Ming	1.00	2.50
11 Vince Carter	.75	2.00
12 Kobe Bryant	2.00	5.00
13 Ray Allen	.50	1.25
14 Dirk Nowitzki	.75	2.00
15 Shaquille O'Neal	1.25	3.00
16 Baron Davis	.40	1.00
17 Jermaine O'Neal	.40	1.00
18 Paul Pierce	.50	1.25
19 LeBron James	3.00	8.00
20 Allen Iverson	.75	2.00

2004-05 Fleer Genuine At Large Autographs

Randomly inserted, this nine-card set features a similar design to the base At Large set but with a horizontal design that utilizes a large blank white area towards the right side. Each card is serially numbered between 50 and 150.
STATED PRINT RUN 50 TO 150 SETS

AJ Al Jefferson/150	10.00	25.00
BD Baron Davis	6.00	15.00
BW Ben Wallace/50	10.00	25.00
DW Dwyane Wade/50	50.00	100.00
JR Jason Richardson	6.00	15.00
JS J.R. Smith/150	8.00	20.00
RA Rafael Araujo/150	6.00	15.00
RJ Richard Jefferson/50	6.00	15.00
VC Vince Carter	15.00	40.00

2004-05 Fleer Genuine At Large Autographs Gold

*GOLD: .5X TO 1.25X BASE HI
STATED PRINT RUN 20 TO 40 SETS

2004-05 Fleer Genuine At Large Autographs Patches

Randomly inserted, this nine card set parallels the base At Large Autographs insert enhanced with a patch swatch and serial numbering between 10 and 30.
STATED PRINT RUN 10 TO 30 SETS

AJ Al Jefferson/30	25.00	60.00
BG Ben Gordon/30	15.00	40.00
BW Ben Wallace/30	20.00	50.00
DW Dwyane Wade/20	40.00	100.00
JR Jason Richardson/20	12.50	30.00
JS J.R. Smith/30	15.00	40.00

2004-05 Fleer Genuine At Large Game Used

Randomly seeded in Hobby packs at the rate of one in 40 and Retail packs at the rate of one in 72, this 10-card set parallels the design of the base Genuine Article set enhanced with a centered swatch of memorabilia and green foil highlights. Two parallel versions of the set were issued, one featuring red foil and sequential numbering to 199, and another featuring a patch swatch and sequential numbering to 25.
STATED ODDS 1:40 H, 1:72 R
*GAME USED 199: .5X TO 1.25X BASE GU HI
PRINT RUN 199 SER.#'d SETS
*PATCH: 1.25X TO 3X BASE HI
PATCH PRINT RUN 25 SER.#'d SETS

AI Allen Iverson	4.00	10.00
BD Baron Davis	2.00	5.00
BW Ben Wallace	2.00	5.00
CA Carmelo Anthony	5.00	12.00
DW Dwyane Wade	4.00	10.00
JO Jermaine O'Neal	2.00	5.00
KG Kevin Garnett	4.00	10.00
PP Paul Pierce	2.50	6.00
RA Ray Allen	2.50	6.00
RJ Richard Jefferson	2.00	5.00
SF Steve Francis	2.00	5.00
SO Shaquille O'Neal	6.00	15.00
TD Tim Duncan	4.00	10.00
VC Vince Carter	4.00	10.00
YM Yao Ming	5.00	12.00

2004-05 Fleer Genuine Big Time

Inserted in Hobby packs at the rate of one in 99 and Retail at the rate of one in 125, this 15-card set places a color photo centered between silver and white borders on the top of the card and a white bottom half with the insert name, team logo and Fleer logo.

COMPLETE SET (15)	25.00	60.00
STATED ODDS 1:99 H, 1:125 R		
1 Dwyane Wade	2.50	6.00
2 LeBron James	10.00	25.00
3 Kobe Bryant	6.00	15.00
4 Shaquille O'Neal	4.00	10.00
5 Tim Duncan	2.50	6.00
6 Tracy McGrady	2.00	5.00
7 Richard Hamilton	1.25	3.00
8 Kevin Garnett	2.50	6.00
9 Allen Iverson	2.50	6.00
10 Chris Webber	1.50	4.00
11 Paul Pierce	1.50	4.00
12 Yao Ming	3.00	8.00
13 Pau Gasol	1.50	4.00
14 Carmelo Anthony	3.00	8.00
15 Andrei Kirilenko	1.25	3.00

2004-05 Fleer Genuine Big Time Autographs

Randomly inserted, this 11-card set features a similar design to the base Big Time set but with a horizontal design that utilizes a large blank white area towards the right side. No odds were given. Gold versions sequentially numbered between 25 and 50 were also inserted.
RANDOM INSERTS IN PACKS
*GOLD: .6X TO 1.5X BASE AU HI
GOLD PRINT RUN 25 TO 50 SER.#'d SETS

AB Andris Biedrins	5.00	12.00
AK Andrei Kirilenko	4.00	10.00
AV Anderson Varejao	4.00	10.00
BW Ben Wallace	10.00	25.00
CD Carlos Delfino	4.00	10.00
DW Dorell Wright	8.00	20.00
KS Kirk Snyder	4.00	10.00
LC Lionel Chalmers	4.00	10.00
MP Mickael Pietrus	4.00	10.00
TA Tony Allen	5.00	12.00

2004-05 Fleer Genuine Big Time Autographs Patches

Randomly inserted, this nine card set parallels the base At Large Autographs insert enhanced with a patch swatch and serial numbering between 10 and 40.
STATED PRINT RUN 10 TO 40 SETS
SOME UNPRICED DUE TO SCARCITY

AB Andris Biedrins/40	10.00	25.00
AK Andrei Kirilenko/20	10.00	25.00
AV Anderson Varejao/40	12.50	30.00
CD Carlos Delfino/40	10.00	25.00
CD1 Carlos Delfino/20	12.50	30.00
DH David Harrison/40	10.00	25.00
DH1 David Harrison/20	12.50	30.00
KS Kirk Snyder/40	10.00	25.00
MP Mickael Pietrus/40	10.00	25.00
TA Tony Allen/20	8.00	20.00

2004-05 Fleer Genuine Big Time Game Used

Randomly seeded in Hobby packs at the rate of one in 60 and Retail packs at the rate of one in 308, this 10-card set parallels the design of the base Genuine Article set enhanced with a centered swatch of memorabilia and green foil highlights. Two parallel versions of the set were issued, one featuring red foil and sequential numbering to 49, and another featuring a patch swatch and sequential numbering to 10.
STATED ODDS 1:60 H, 1:308 R
*GAME USED 49: .6X TO 1.5X BASE HI
PRINT RUN 49 SER.#'d SETS

AI Allen Iverson	4.00	10.00
AK Andrei Kirilenko	2.00	5.00
CA Carmelo Anthony	5.00	12.00
CW Chris Webber	2.50	6.00
DW Dwyane Wade	4.00	10.00
JO Jermaine O'Neal	2.00	5.00
KG Kevin Garnett	4.00	10.00
PG Pau Gasol	2.50	6.00
PP Paul Pierce	2.50	6.00
SO Shaquille O'Neal	6.00	15.00
TD Tim Duncan	4.00	10.00
TM Tracy McGrady	3.00	8.00
TP Tony Parker	2.50	6.00
YM Yao Ming	5.00	12.00
ZR Zach Randolph	2.00	5.00

2004-05 Fleer Genuine Buyback Autographs

Inserted in packs at the rate of one in 218, this set consists of the original cards.
STATED ODDS 1:218
SOME UNPRICED DUE TO SCARCITY

3B C.Drexler 88-9Fleer	25.00	60.00
7B M.Johnson 86-7Fleer	50.00	120.00
8 D.Ainge 88-9Fleer	20.00	50.00
26 C.Drexler 86-7Fleer	75.00	150.00
30 C.Drexler 87-8Fleer	30.00	80.00
36 G.Gervin 86-7Fleer	12.50	30.00
68 R.Smits 89-0Fleer	15.00	40.00
119 B.Walton 86-7Fleer	15.00	40.00
133 D.Ainge 89-0Fleer	15.00	40.00
138 D.Robinson 89-0Hoops	40.00	100.00

2000-01 Fleer Glossy

The 2000-01 Fleer Glossy product was released in March, 2001 and featured a 245-card base set that was broken into tiers as follows: Base Veterans (1-200), and Rookies (201-245). Please note that the rookies were shortprinted as follows: Tier 1 201-210 serial numbered to 1000, Tier 2 211-235 serial numbered to 1500, and Tier 3 236-245 serial numbered to 1250. Also note that this was the first time that Fleer had ever released their "Glossy" brand in pack form. Card packs contained eight cards, and carried a suggested retail price of $2.99.

COMP.SET w/o SP's (200)	12.50	30.00
201-210 PRINT RUN 1000 SERIAL #'d SETS		
211-235 PRINT RUN 1500 SERIAL #'d SETS		
236-245 PRINT RUN 1250 SERIAL #'d SETS		
246-251 PRINT RUN 500 SER.#'d SETS		
201-251 STATED ODDS AT LEAST 2 PER BOX		
1 Lamar Odom	.25	.60
2 Christian Laettner	.25	.60
3 Michael Olowokandi	.20	.50
4 Anthony Carter	.20	.50
5 Steve Francis	.25	.60
6 Darvin Ham	.20	.50
7 Mitch Richmond	.25	.60
8 Corliss Williamson	.20	.50
9 Jason Terry	.30	.75
10 Brian Grant	.20	.50
11 Peja Stojakovic	.30	.75
12 Rick Fox	.20	.50
13 Tyrone Hill	.20	.50
14 Chauncey Billups	.30	.75
15 Otis Thorpe	.25	.60
16 Richard Hamilton	.25	.60
17 Ervin Johnson	.20	.50
18 Jim Jackson	.20	.50
19 Theo Ratliff	.20	.50
20 Doug Christie	.20	.50
21 Jalen Rose	.25	.60
22 John Wallace	.20	.50
23 Ruben Patterson	.20	.50
24 Steve Nash	.50	1.25
25 Toni Kukoc	.30	.75
26 Anthony Peeler	.20	.50
27 Ray Allen	.30	.75
28 Adonal Foyle	.20	.50
29 Chris Whitney	.20	.50
30 Nick Van Exel	.25	.60
31 Sean Elliott	.30	.75
32 Erick Strickland	.20	.50
33 Jerry Stackhouse	.25	.60
34 Antawn Jamison	.30	.75
35 Grant Hill	.40	1.00
36 Antonio Daniels	.20	.50
37 Karl Malone	.40	1.00
38 Keith Van Horn	.25	.60
39 Ron Harper	.25	.60
40 Stephon Marbury	.25	.60
41 Bryon Russell	.20	.50
42 Corey Maggette	.25	.60
43 Hersey Hawkins	.20	.50
44 Vince Carter	.60	1.50
45 Paul Pierce	.30	.75
46 Mikki Moore RC	.30	.75
47 Othella Harrington	.20	.50
48 Erick Dampier	.20	.50
49 Jerome Williams	.20	.50
50 Nick Anderson	.20	.50
51 Tim Hardaway	.30	.75
52 Allan Houston	.25	.60
53 Tyrone Nesby	.30	.75
54 Brevin Knight	.20	.50
55 Chris Mills	.20	.50
56 Ron Artest	.30	.75
57 Walt Williams	.20	.50
58 Duane Causwell	.20	.50
59 Bonzi Wells	.20	.50
60 Rasheed Wallace	.30	.75
61 Dikembe Mutombo	.30	.75
62 Jahidi White	.20	.50
63 Chris Webber	.30	.75
64 Tony Battie	.20	.50
65 Mahmoud Abdul-Rauf	.20	.50
66 Monty Williams	.20	.50
67 Charlie Ward	.20	.50
68 David Robinson	.50	1.25
69 Eric Snow	.20	.50
70 Jermaine O'Neal	.25	.60
71 Kurt Thomas	.20	.50
72 James Posey	.20	.50
73 Travis Best	.20	.50
74 Jonathan Bender	.20	.50
75 John Stockton	.40	1.00
76 Jacque Vaughn	.20	.50
77 Ron Mercer	.20	.50
78 Shawn Marion	.25	.60
79 Larry Johnson	.30	.75
80 Maurice Taylor	.20	.50
81 Clifford Robinson	.20	.50
82 Scot Pollard	.20	.50
83 Patrick Ewing	.40	1.00
84 Terrell Brandon	.20	.50
85 Horace Grant	.25	.60
86 Vin Baker	.25	.60
87 Al Harrington	.25	.60
88 Larry Hughes	.25	.60
89 David Wesley	.20	.50
90 Wally Szczerbiak	.25	.60
91 Charles Oakley	.25	.60
92 Tim Thomas	.20	.50
93 Mookie Blaylock	.20	.50
94 Jamal Mashburn	.25	.60
95 Roshown McLeod	.20	.50
96 John Starks	.25	.60

Card	Low	High
97 Rodney Rogers	.20	.50
98 Juwan Howard	.25	.60
99 Isaiah Rider	.25	.60
100 Rashard Lewis	.30	.75
101 Dion Glover	.20	.50
102 Johnny Newman	.20	.50
103 Avery Johnson	.25	.60
104 Darrell Armstrong	.20	.50
105 Eric Williams	.20	.50
106 Gary Payton	.30	.75
107 Antonio Davis	.20	.50
108 Dirk Nowitzki	.50	1.25
109 Trajan Langdon	.20	.50
110 Michael Dickerson	.20	.50
111 Joe Smith	.25	.60
112 Rod Strickland	.20	.50
113 Shawn Kemp	.30	.75
114 Voshon Lenard	.20	.50
115 Marcus Camby	.25	.60
116 Matt Harpring	.20	.50
117 Isaac Austin	.20	.50
118 Malik Rose	.20	.50
119 Pat Garrity	.20	.50
120 Kenny Thomas	.20	.50
121 LaPhonso Ellis	.25	.60
122 Danny Fortson	.20	.50
123 Elton Brand	.30	.75
124 Jason Williams	.30	.75
125 Kobe Bryant	1.25	3.00
126 Tariq Abdul-Wahad	.20	.50
127 Tracy McGrady	.50	1.25
128 Matt Geiger	.20	.50
129 Antoine Walker	.25	.60
130 Michael Finley	.30	.75
131 Andre Miller	.25	.60
132 Robert Horry	.25	.60
133 Donyell Marshall	.20	.50
134 Shareef Abdur-Rahim	.25	.60
135 Vonteego Cummings	.20	.50
136 Anthony Mason	.20	.50
137 Mike Bibby	.30	.75
138 Raef LaFrentz	.20	.50
139 Glen Rice	.25	.60
140 Chris Gatling	.20	.50
141 Latrell Sprewell	.25	.60
142 Austin Croshere	.20	.50
143 Kenny Anderson	.25	.60
144 Elden Campbell	.20	.50
145 Jason Kidd	.50	1.25
146 Michael Doleac	.20	.50
147 Muggsy Bogues	.25	.60
148 Tim Duncan	.60	1.50
149 Samaki Walker	.20	.50
150 Gary Trent	.20	.50
151 Kevin Garnett	.50	1.25
152 Allen Iverson	.60	1.50
153 Anfernee Hardaway	.50	1.25
154 Robert Traylor	.20	.50
155 Scottie Pippen	.50	1.25
156 Shaquille O'Neal	.75	2.00
157 Vlade Divac	.25	.60
158 Lucious Harris	.20	.50
159 Keon Clark	.20	.50
160 Bo Outlaw	.20	.50
161 P.J. Brown	.20	.50
162 Derrick Coleman	.25	.60
163 Mark Jackson	.25	.60
164 Lamond Murray	.20	.50
165 Dan Majerle	.30	.75
166 Eddie Jones	.30	.75
167 Cedric Ceballos	.20	.50
168 Kendall Gill	.20	.50
169 Tom Gugliotta	.20	.50
170 Jeff McInnis	.20	.50
171 Steve Smith	.25	.60
172 Kevin Willis	.20	.50
173 Lindsey Hunter	.20	.50
174 Derek Anderson	.20	.50
175 Shandon Anderson	.20	.50
176 Adrian Griffin	.20	.50
177 Baron Davis	.30	.75
178 Radoslav Nesterovic	.20	.50
179 Glenn Robinson	.25	.60
180 Sam Cassell	.25	.60
181 Chucky Atkins	.20	.50
182 Arvydas Sabonis	.25	.60
183 Damon Stoudamire	.25	.60
184 Antonio McDyess	.25	.60
185 Derek Fisher	.30	.75
186 Bryant Reeves	.20	.50
187 Hakeem Olajuwon	.40	1.00
188 Kerry Kittles	.20	.50
189 Alan Henderson	.20	.50
190 Sam Perkins	.20	.50
191 Felipe Lopez	.20	.50
192 Tracy Murray	.20	.50
193 Shammond Williams	.20	.50
194 Vitaly Potapenko	.20	.50
195 John Amaechi	.20	.50
196 Quincy Lewis	.20	.50
197 Reggie Miller	.30	.75
198 Cuttino Mobley	.20	.50
199 Rex Chapman	.20	.50
200 Dale Davis	.20	.50
201 Stromile Swift RC	1.50	4.00
202 Stephen Jackson RC	2.50	6.00
203 Erick Barkley RC	1.00	2.50
204 Mike Miller RC	2.50	6.00
205 Kenyon Martin RC	4.00	10.00
206 Michael Redd RC	4.00	10.00
207 Darius Miles RC	1.50	4.00
208 Chris Mihm RC	1.25	3.00
209 Brian Cardinal RC	1.25	3.00
210 Khalid El-Amin RC	1.00	2.50
211 Hanno Mottola RC	.75	2.00
212 Jamaal Magloire RC	1.25	3.00
213 Courtney Alexander RC	1.00	2.50
214 Mamadou N'Diaye RC	.75	2.00
215 Chris Porter RC	.75	2.00
216 Quentin Richardson RC	1.25	3.00
217 Eddie House RC	1.00	2.50
218 Joel Przybilla RC	1.00	2.50
219 Soumaila Samake RC	.75	2.00
220 Speedy Claxton RC	1.25	3.00
221 Desmond Mason RC	1.50	4.00
222 Mike Smith RC	.75	2.00
223 Lavor Postell RC	.75	2.00
224 Pepe Sanchez RC	1.25	3.00
225 DeShawn Stevenson RC	1.25	3.00
226 Hedo Turkoglu RC	2.00	5.00
227 Keyon Dooling RC	1.25	3.00
228 Dan Langhi RC	.75	2.00
229 Mateen Cleaves RC	1.00	2.50
230 Donnell Harvey RC	1.00	2.50
231 DerMarr Johnson RC	1.00	2.50
232 Jason Collier RC	1.25	3.00
233 Jake Voskuhl RC	.75	2.00
234 Mark Madsen RC	1.25	3.00
235 Jabari Smith RC	.75	2.00
236 Morris Peterson RC	1.25	3.00
237 Daniel Santiago RC	1.25	3.00
238 Etan Thomas RC	1.25	3.00
239 A.J. Guyton RC	.75	2.00
240 Marcus Fizer RC	1.25	3.00
241 Jamal Crawford RC	3.00	8.00
242 Jerome Moiso RC	.75	2.00
243 Olumide Oyedeji RC	.75	2.00
244 Paul McPherson RC	.75	2.00
245 Eduardo Najera RC	1.25	3.00
246 Marc Jackson AU RC	2.50	6.00
247 Mike Penberthy AU RC	3.00	8.00
248 Dragan Tarlac AU RC	2.00	5.00
249 Ruben Wolkowyski AU RC	2.00	5.00
250 Iakovos Tsakalidis AU RC	2.00	5.00
251 Ruben Garces AU RC	3.00	8.00

2000-01 Fleer Glossy Vince Carter Rookie Remnants

This three-card insert was randomly inserted into 2000-01 Fleer products. The set includes a Vince Carter floor card (numbered to 100), a Vince Carter floor/jersey card (numbered to 15), and finally an autographed Vince Carter floor/jersey card (numbered 1/1).

RANDOM INSERTS IN HOBBY PACKS
STATED PRINT RUNS LISTED BELOW

Card	Low	High
NNO Vince Carter FLR JSY/15	20.00	50.00
NNO Vince Carter FLR/100	12.50	30.00

2000-01 Fleer Glossy Class Acts

Randomly inserted into packs at one in 72, this 25-card insert features players that are class acts on and off the court. Card backs carry a "CA" prefix.

Card	Low	High
COMPLETE SET (25)	50.00	100.00
STATED ODDS 1:72		
CA1 Hakeem Olajuwon	2.00	5.00
CA2 Karl Malone	2.00	5.00
CA3 Patrick Ewing	2.00	5.00
CA4 Ron Harper	1.25	3.00
CA5 David Robinson	2.50	6.00
CA6 Scottie Pippen	2.50	6.00
CA7 Mitch Richmond	1.25	3.00
CA8 Tim Hardaway	1.50	4.00
CA9 Gary Payton	1.50	4.00
CA10 Larry Johnson	1.50	4.00
CA11 Shaquille O'Neal	4.00	10.00
CA12 Allan Houston	1.25	3.00
CA13 Chris Webber	1.50	4.00
CA14 Jason Kidd	2.50	6.00
CA15 Grant Hill	2.00	5.00
CA16 Kevin Garnett	2.50	6.00
CA17 Allen Iverson	3.00	8.00
CA18 Kobe Bryant	6.00	15.00
CA19 Tracy McGrady	2.50	6.00
CA20 Tim Duncan	3.00	8.00
CA21 Dirk Nowitzki	2.50	6.00
CA22 Larry Hughes	1.25	3.00
CA23 Vince Carter	3.00	8.00
CA24 Elton Brand	1.50	4.00
CA25 Steve Francis	1.25	3.00

2000-01 Fleer Glossy Coach's Corner

Randomly inserted into packs at one in 108, this 7-card insert features autographed cards from some of the greatest modern-day coaches. The cards are listed below in alphabetical order for convenience.

Card	Low	High
STATED ODDS 1:108		
1 Pat Riley	15.00	40.00
2 Doc Rivers	6.00	15.00
3 Paul Silas	6.00	15.00
4 Isiah Thomas	6.00	15.00
5 Rudy Tomjanovich	8.00	20.00
6 Jeff Van Gundy	10.00	25.00
7 Lenny Wilkens	10.00	25.00

2000-01 Fleer Glossy Game Breakers

Randomly inserted into packs at one in 24, this 10-card insert features players that are capable of breaking the game wide open. Card backs carry an "X of 10 GB" card number.

Card	Low	High
COMPLETE SET (10)	10.00	25.00
STATED ODDS 1:24		
1 Allen Iverson	1.50	4.00
2 Elton Brand	.75	2.00
3 Grant Hill	1.00	2.50
4 Jason Kidd	1.25	3.00
5 Kevin Garnett	1.25	3.00
6 Kobe Bryant	3.00	8.00
7 Shaquille O'Neal	2.00	5.00
8 Steve Francis	.60	1.50
9 Tim Duncan	1.50	4.00
10 Vince Carter	1.50	4.00

2000-01 Fleer Glossy Hardwood Leaders

Randomly inserted into packs at one in 12, this 15-card insert features players that are the predominant leaders on the court. Card backs carry a "HL" prefix.

Card	Low	High
COMPLETE SET (15)	8.00	20.00
STATED ODDS 1:12		
HL1 Allen Iverson	1.00	2.50
HL2 Jason Williams	.50	1.25
HL3 Vince Carter	1.00	2.50
HL4 Scottie Pippen	.75	2.00
HL5 Kevin Garnett	.75	2.00
HL6 Karl Malone	.60	1.50
HL7 Grant Hill	.60	1.50
HL8 Jason Kidd	.75	2.00
HL9 Kobe Bryant	2.00	5.00
HL10 Elton Brand	.50	1.25
HL11 Shaquille O'Neal	1.25	3.00
HL12 Tim Duncan	1.00	2.50
HL13 Tracy McGrady	.75	2.00
HL14 Chris Webber	.50	1.25
HL15 Lamar Odom	.40	1.00

2000-01 Fleer Glossy Rookie Sensations

Randomly inserted into packs at one in 6, this 25-card insert features rookies that look to make a difference for their teams in years to come. Card backs carry a "RS" prefix.

Card	Low	High
COMPLETE SET (25)	6.00	15.00
STATED ODDS 1:6		
RS1 Jamaal Magloire	.40	1.00
RS2 Etan Thomas	.40	1.00
RS3 Chris Mihm	.30	.75
RS4 Joel Przybilla	.30	.75
RS5 Mamadou N'Diaye	.25	.60
RS6 Jason Collier	.40	1.00
RS7 DerMarr Johnson	.30	.75
RS8 Jerome Moiso	.25	.60
RS9 Darius Miles	.40	1.00
RS10 Marcus Fizer	.40	1.00
RS11 Kenyon Martin	1.00	2.50
RS12 Mark Madsen	.40	1.00
RS13 Mike Miller	.60	1.50
RS14 Desmond Mason	.50	1.25
RS15 Morris Peterson	.40	1.00
RS16 Hedo Turkoglu	.60	1.50
RS17 Mateen Cleaves	.30	.75
RS18 Keyon Dooling	.40	1.00
RS19 DeShawn Stevenson	.40	1.00
RS20 Quentin Richardson	.40	1.00
RS21 Courtney Alexander	.30	.75
RS22 Stromile Swift	.40	1.00
RS23 Stephen Jackson	.60	1.50
RS24 Erick Barkley	.25	.60
RS25 Khalid El-Amin	.25	.60

2000-01 Fleer Glossy Traditional Threads

Randomly inserted into packs at one in 63, this 29-card insert features swatches from actual game-used jerseys. Please note that the cards have been listed below in alphabetical order for convenience.

Card	Low	High
STATED ODDS 1:63		
1 Vince Carter	6.00	15.00
2 Baron Davis	3.00	8.00
3 Trajan Langdon	2.00	5.00
4 Grant Hill	4.00	10.00
5 Allen Iverson	6.00	15.00
6 Jason Kidd	5.00	12.00
7 Karl Malone	4.00	10.00
8 Stephon Marbury	2.50	6.00
9 Shawn Marion	2.50	6.00
10 Tracy McGrady	5.00	12.00
11 Andre Miller	2.50	6.00
12 Dikembe Mutombo	3.00	8.00
13 Lamar Odom	2.50	6.00
14 Shaquille O'Neal	10.00	25.00
15 Gary Payton	3.00	8.00
16 Jason Terry	3.00	8.00
17 John Stockton	4.00	10.00
18 Anfernee Hardaway	5.00	12.00
19 Jason Williams	3.00	8.00
20 Darius Miles	3.00	8.00
21 Chris Mihm	2.50	6.00
22 Desmond Mason	4.00	10.00
23 Keyon Dooling	3.00	8.00
24 DerMarr Johnson	2.50	6.00
25 Speedy Claxton	3.00	8.00
26 Kenyon Martin	8.00	20.00
27 Hanno Mottola	2.00	5.00
28 Mike Miller	5.00	12.00
29 Quentin Richardson	3.00	8.00

2000-01 Fleer Glossy Mutombo Arena

Limited to 25,000 copies, this special Dikembe Mutombo was given away in Philadelphia at a 76ers game sometime early in the 2000-01 NBA season.

Card	Low	High
1 Dikembe Mutombo	.50	1.25

2001 Fleer Hawaii Bobby Knight

Given away to participants by Fleer at the 2001 Kit Young Hawaii conference, this card features Bobby Knight, some information about him on the back, and a circular swatch of a game-worn coaching sweater.

Card	Low	High
NNO Bobby Knight	15.00	40.00

2006-07 Fleer Hot Prospects

Released in mid November 2006, Fleer Hot Prospects boasts a 112-card set which pictures veteran players on cards 1-60, rookie jersey sticker-autographs serially numbered to 150 on cards 61-70, rookie jersey sticker-autgraphs serially numbered to 250 on cards 71-89, rookie sticker-autographs on cards 90-103 serially numbered to either 500 or 150 (150 cards noted in checklist) and rookie cards serially numbered to 150 on cards 104-112. Base cards place full-color player auction photos on the middle with silver borders on the left and right and silver foil highlights. Hot Prospects boxes contain 15 pack of five cards each and carried an original per-pack suggested retail price of $9.99.

61-70 RC PRINT RUN 150 SER.#'d SETS
71-90 RC PRINT RUN 250 SER.#'d SETS
91-104 PRINT RUN 500 SER.#'d SETS
UNLESS LISTED IN CHECKLIST
105-113 RC PRINT RUN 150 SER.#'d SETS
UNPRICED WHITE PRINT RUN 15 SETS

Card	Low	High
1 Joe Johnson	.30	.75
2 Marvin Williams	.30	.75
3 Tony Allen	.25	.60
4 Paul Pierce	.40	1.00
5 Raymond Felton	.30	.75
6 Emeka Okafor	.30	.75
7 Ben Gordon	.30	.75
8 Michael Jordan	3.00	8.00
9 Zydrunas Ilgauskas	.30	.75
10 LeBron James	1.50	4.00
11 Devin Harris	.25	.60
12 Dirk Nowitzki	.60	1.50
13 Carmelo Anthony	.50	1.25
14 Nene	.30	.75
15 Chauncey Billups	.40	1.00
16 Ben Wallace	.30	.75
17 Baron Davis	.30	.75
18 Troy Murphy	.25	.60
19 Tracy McGrady	.50	1.25
20 Yao Ming	.50	1.25
21 Jermaine O'Neal	.30	.75
22 Peja Stojakovic	.40	1.00
23 Corey Maggette	.30	.75
24 Sam Cassell	.30	.75
25 Kobe Bryant	1.50	4.00
26 Lamar Odom	.30	.75
27 Pau Gasol	.40	1.00
28 Hakim Warrick	.30	.75
29 Shaquille O'Neal	.75	2.00
30 Dwyane Wade	.60	1.50
31 T.J. Ford	.25	.60
32 Michael Redd	.30	.75
33 Kevin Garnett	.60	1.50
34 Troy Hudson	.25	.60
35 Vince Carter	.50	1.25
36 Jason Kidd	.60	1.50
37 Desmond Mason	.25	.60
38 Chris Paul	.50	1.25
39 Stephon Marbury	.30	.75
40 Nate Robinson	.25	.60
41 Grant Hill	.50	1.25
42 Darko Milicic	.25	.60
43 Andre Iguodala	.30	.75
44 Allen Iverson	.50	1.25
45 Steve Nash	.50	1.25
46 Amare Stoudemire	.30	.75
47 Zach Randolph	.30	.75
48 Sebastian Telfair	.25	.60
49 Ron Artest	.40	1.00
50 Mike Bibby	.40	1.00
51 Tim Duncan	.60	1.50
52 Manu Ginobili	.40	1.00
53 Ray Allen	.40	1.00
54 Rashard Lewis	.40	1.00
55 Chris Bosh	.40	1.00
56 Charlie Villanueva	.25	.60
57 Andrei Kirilenko	.30	.75
58 Deron Williams	.30	.75
59 Gilbert Arenas	.30	.75
60 Antawn Jamison	.30	.75
61 Ronnie Brewer JSY AU RC	8.00	20.00
62 L.Aldridge JSY AU RC	30.00	80.00
63 Tyrus Thomas JSY AU RC	6.00	15.00
64 She.Williams JSY AU RC	6.00	15.00
65 Cedric Simmons JSY AU RC	5.00	12.00
66 Randy Foye JSY AU RC	8.00	20.00
67 Rudy Gay JSY AU RC	10.00	25.00
68 Patrick O'Bryant JSY AU RC	5.00	12.00
69 Rodney Carney JSY AU RC	5.00	12.00
70 Hilton Armstrong JSY AU RC	5.00	12.00
71 Denham Brown JSY AU RC	4.00	10.00
72 Dee Brown JSY AU RC	4.00	10.00
73 Allan Ray JSY AU RC	4.00	10.00
74 Shawne Williams JSY AU RC	4.00	10.00
75 Quincy Douby JSY AU RC	4.00	10.00
76 Renaldo Balkman JSY AU RC	5.00	12.00
77 Rajon Rondo JSY AU RC	10.00	25.00
78 Ma.Williams JSY AU RC	4.00	10.00
79 Josh Boone JSY AU RC	4.00	10.00
80 Kyle Lowry JSY AU RC	8.00	20.00
82 Jordan Farmar JSY AU RC	6.00	15.00
83 Maurice Ager JSY AU RC	4.00	10.00
84 Mardy Collins JSY AU RC	4.00	10.00
85 Shannon Brown JSY AU RC	4.00	10.00
86 James White JSY AU RC	4.00	10.00
87 Steve Novak JSY AU RC	5.00	12.00
88 Solomon Jones JSY AU RC	4.00	10.00
89 Paul Davis JSY AU RC	4.00	10.00
90 P.J. Tucker JSY AU RC	5.00	12.00
91 Craig Smith AU RC	4.00	10.00
92 Bobby Jones AU RC	3.00	8.00
93 David Noel AU RC	3.00	8.00
94 A.Bargnani AU/150 RC	5.00	12.00
95 James Augustine AU RC	3.00	8.00
96 Daniel Gibson AU RC	4.00	10.00
97 Brandon Roy AU/150 RC	5.00	12.00
98 Ryan Hollins AU RC	4.00	10.00
99 Hassan Adams AU RC	3.00	8.00
100 Pops Mensah-Bonsu AU RC	3.00	8.00
101 Will Blalock AU RC	3.00	8.00
102 Damir Markota AU RC	3.00	8.00
103 Saer Sene AU RC	3.00	8.00
104 Thabo Sefolosha AU RC	5.00	12.00
105 Leon Powe RC	2.00	5.00
106 J.J. Redick RC	3.00	8.00
107 Adam Morrison RC	2.50	6.00
108 Paul Millsap RC	3.00	8.00
109 J.R. Pinnock RC	1.50	4.00
110 Jorge Garbajosa RC	2.00	5.00
111 Vassilis Spanoulis RC	1.50	4.00
112 Yakhouba Diawara RC	1.50	4.00
113 Alexander Johnson RC	1.50	4.00

2006-07 Fleer Hot Prospects Red Hot

*1-60 RED: 2X TO 5X BASE HI
*61-70/94/97 RC RED: .6X TO 1.5X BASE HI
*71-113 RC RED: .75X TO 2X BASE HI
RED HOT PRINT RUN 50 SER.#'d SETS

Card	Low	High
10 LeBron James	25.00	60.00

2006-07 Fleer Hot Prospects Alumni Ink

PRINT RUN 10 TO 25 SER.#'d SETS
UNPRICED RED PRINT RUN 10 SETS

Card	Low	High
AF C.Frye/H.Adams/25	6.00	15.00
AW C.Anthony/Warrick/25	20.00	50.00
BA D.Brown/Augustine/25	6.00	15.00
BB C.Boozer/E.Brand/25	6.00	15.00
CJ V.Carter/Jamison/25	25.00	60.00
DW Walton/B.Davis/25	12.00	30.00
EW Shd.Williams/D.Ewing/25	6.00	15.00
FH R.Hollins/Farmar/25	6.00	15.00
FL K.Lowry/R.Foye/25	8.00	20.00
MG D.Marshall/R.Gay/25	6.00	15.00
OD Drexler/Olajuwon/10	100.00	200.00
OG E.Okafor/R.Gay/25	6.00	15.00
PH K.Hinrich/Pierce/25	25.00	60.00
PR R.Rondo/Prince/25	10.00	25.00

2006-07 Fleer Hot Prospects Double Team Memorabilia

PRINT RUN 50 SER.#'d SETS
*RED HOT: .75X TO 2X BASE HI
RED HOT PRINT RUN 25 SER.#'d SETS
UNPRICED PATCH PRINT RUN 10 SETS

Card	Low	High
AB G.Arenas/C.Butler	4.00	10.00
AI A.Iverson/A.Iguodala	6.00	15.00
AK A.Kirilenko/R.Araujo	4.00	10.00
AL R.Allen/R.Lewis	4.00	10.00
BB K.Bryant/K.Brown	8.00	20.00
BC C.Bosh/J.Calderon	4.00	10.00
BK B.Wallace/K.Hinrich	4.00	10.00
BW A.Bogut/Mv.Williams	4.00	10.00
CB T.Chandler/Kw.Brown	4.00	10.00
CF E.Curry/C.Frye	4.00	10.00
CJ V.Carter/A.Jamison	5.00	12.00
CS T.Chandler/P.Stojakovic	4.00	10.00
CW B.Cook/L.Walton	4.00	10.00
DG T.Duncan/M.Ginobili	6.00	15.00
DI S.Dalembert/A.Iguodala	4.00	10.00
DJ J.Howard/D.Harris	4.00	10.00
DK S.Dalembert/K.Korver	4.00	10.00
FB M.Finley/B.Bowen	5.00	12.00
FM R.Felton/S.May	4.00	10.00
FR S.Francis/Q.Richardson	4.00	10.00
GD L.Deng/B.Gordon	4.00	10.00
HH G.Hill/D.Howard	6.00	15.00
HP R.Hamilton/T.Prince	5.00	12.00
IG Z.Ilgauskas/D.Gooden	4.00	10.00
JD M.Daniels/S.Jasikevicius	4.00	10.00
JH A.Jamison/B.Haywood	4.00	10.00
JI A.Iverson/L.James	12.50	30.00
KC J.Kidd/V.Carter	6.00	15.00
KR K.Garnett/R.Davis	4.00	10.00
KW A.Kirilenko/D.Williams	4.00	10.00
MD J.Magloire/J.Dixon	4.00	10.00
MF R.McCants/R.Felton	4.00	10.00
ML C.Maggette/S.Livingston	4.00	10.00
MM T.McGrady/Y.Ming	5.00	12.00
MP D.Mason/C.Paul	6.00	15.00
MR S.Marbury/N.Robinson	4.00	10.00
MS K.Martin/S.Swift	4.00	10.00
NM S.Nash/S.Marion	5.00	12.00
OH E.Okafor/D.Howard	5.00	12.00
PG T.Parker/M.Ginobili	4.00	10.00
PS P.Pierce/W.Szczerbiak	4.00	10.00
RJ Z.Randolph/J.Jack	4.00	10.00
RV M.Redd/C.Villanueva	4.00	10.00
TS K.Thomas/A.Stoudemire	4.00	10.00
WH D.Williams/L.Head	5.00	12.00
WK N.Krstic/A.Wright	4.00	10.00
WR C.Wilcox/L.Ridnour	4.00	10.00
WS A.Walker/W.Simien	4.00	10.00

2006-07 Fleer Hot Prospects Draft Day Postmarks Autographs

PRINT RUN 100 SER.#'d SETS

Card	Low	High
AB Andrea Bargnani	6.00	15.00
AD Hassan Adams	4.00	10.00
BA Renaldo Balkman	5.00	12.00
BJ Bobby Jones	4.00	10.00
BR Brandon Roy	15.00	40.00
CS Cedric Simmons	4.00	10.00
DB Denham Brown	4.00	10.00
DE Dee Brown	4.00	10.00
DN David Noel	4.00	10.00
HA Hilton Armstrong	4.00	10.00
JA James Augustine	4.00	10.00
JB Josh Boone	4.00	10.00
JF Jordan Farmar	6.00	15.00
JW James White	4.00	10.00
KL Kyle Lowry	8.00	20.00
LA LaMarcus Aldridge	25.00	60.00
MA Maurice Ager	4.00	10.00
MC Mardy Collins	4.00	10.00
MW Marcus Williams	4.00	10.00
PD Paul Davis	4.00	10.00
PO Patrick O'Bryant	4.00	10.00
PT P.J. Tucker	5.00	12.00
QD Quincy Douby	4.00	10.00
RB Ronnie Brewer	6.00	15.00
RC Rodney Carney	4.00	10.00
RF Randy Foye	6.00	15.00
RG Rudy Gay	8.00	20.00
RH Ryan Hollins	5.00	12.00
RR Rajon Rondo	40.00	80.00
SB Shannon Brown	4.00	10.00
SJ Solomon Jones	4.00	10.00
SM Craig Smith	5.00	12.00
SN Steve Novak	5.00	12.00
SS Saer Sene	4.00	10.00
SW Shelden Williams	5.00	12.00
TS Thabo Sefolosha	6.00	15.00
TT Tyrus Thomas	5.00	12.00
WI Shawne Williams	4.00	10.00

2006-07 Fleer Hot Prospects Draft Rewind

Card	Low	High
COMPLETE SET (60)	25.00	60.00
APPROXIMATE ODDS TWO PER BOX		
AB Andrew Bogut	.75	2.00
AI Andre Iguodala	.75	2.00
AJ Al Jefferson	.75	2.00
AS Amare Stoudemire	.75	2.00
BD Baron Davis	.75	2.00
BG Ben Gordon	.75	2.00
BM Brad Miller	.75	2.00
BR Kobe Bryant	4.00	10.00
CA Carmelo Anthony	1.25	3.00
CB Chauncey Billups	1.00	2.50
CP Chris Paul	1.25	3.00
DG Drew Gooden	.75	2.00
DM Darko Milicic	.60	1.50
DN Dirk Nowitzki	1.50	4.00
DW Delonte West	.60	1.50
EB Elton Brand	1.00	2.50
EC Eddy Curry	.75	2.00
GA Gilbert Arenas	.75	2.00
GD Devean George	.60	1.50
IV Allen Iverson	1.25	3.00
JA LeBron James	4.00	10.00
JC Jamal Crawford	1.00	2.50
JD Juan Dixon	.60	1.50
JK Jason Kidd	1.50	4.00
JM Jamaal Magloire	.60	1.50
JO Jermaine O'Neal	.75	2.00
JR Jason Richardson	1.00	2.50
JT Jason Terry	.75	2.00
KB Kwame Brown	.60	1.50
KG Kevin Garnett	1.50	4.00
KK Kyle Korver	.75	2.00
KM Kenyon Martin	.75	2.00
LJ Luke Jackson	.60	1.50
LO Lamar Odom	.75	2.00
LW Luke Walton	.60	1.50
MA Shawn Marion	.75	2.00
MB Mike Bibby	1.00	2.50
MJ Michael Jordan	8.00	20.00
MM Mike Miller	.75	2.00
MP Mickael Pietrus	.75	2.00
MS Mike Sweetney	.60	1.50
PG Pau Gasol	1.00	2.50
PS Peja Stojakovic	1.00	2.50
RA Ron Artest	1.00	2.50
RH Richard Hamilton	.75	2.00
SD Samuel Dalembert	.60	1.50
SF Steve Francis	.75	2.00
SL Shaun Livingston	.60	1.50
SM Stephon Marbury	.75	2.00
SN Steve Nash	1.25	3.00
SO Shaquille O'Neal	2.00	5.00
TC Tyson Chandler	.75	2.00
TD Tim Duncan	1.50	4.00
TI Jamaal Tinsley	.60	1.50
TM Tracy McGrady	1.25	3.00
TP Tony Parker	1.00	2.50
VC Vince Carter	1.25	3.00
WA Dwyane Wade	1.50	4.00
WS Wally Szczerbiak	.75	2.00
YM Yao Ming	1.25	3.00
ZI Zydrunas Ilgauskas	.75	2.00

2006-07 Fleer Hot Prospects Draft Rewind Memorabilia

PRINT RUN 50 SER.#'d SETS
*RED HOT: .75X TO 2X BASE HI
RED HOT PRINT RUN 25 SER.#'d SETS
UNPRICED PATCH PRINT RUN 10 SETS

Card	Low	High
AI Andre Iguodala	2.50	6.00
AS Amare Stoudemire	2.50	6.00
BD Baron Davis	2.50	6.00
BG Ben Gordon	2.50	6.00
BR Kobe Bryant	10.00	25.00
CA Carmelo Anthony	4.00	10.00
DG Drew Gooden	2.50	6.00
DN Dirk Nowitzki	5.00	12.00
DW Delonte West	2.00	5.00
EB Elton Brand	3.00	8.00
EC Eddy Curry	2.50	6.00
GA Gilbert Arenas	2.50	6.00
GD Devean George	2.00	5.00
JA LeBron James	15.00	40.00
JC Jamal Crawford	3.00	8.00
JD Juan Dixon	2.50	6.00
JK Jason Kidd	5.00	12.00
JM Jamaal Magloire	2.00	5.00
JO Jermaine O'Neal	2.50	6.00
JR Jason Richardson	3.00	8.00
KB Kwame Brown	2.50	6.00
KG Kevin Garnett	5.00	12.00
KK Kyle Korver	2.50	6.00
KM Kenyon Martin	2.50	6.00
LJ Luke Jackson	2.50	6.00
LO Lamar Odom	2.50	6.00
LW Luke Walton	2.00	5.00
MA Shawn Marion	2.50	6.00
MB Mike Bibby	3.00	8.00
MP Mickael Pietrus	2.50	6.00
MS Mike Sweetney	2.50	6.00
PS Peja Stojakovic	3.00	8.00
RH Richard Hamilton	2.50	6.00
SD Samuel Dalembert	2.00	5.00
SF Steve Francis	2.50	6.00
SL Shaun Livingston	2.50	6.00
SM Stephon Marbury	2.50	6.00
SN Steve Nash	4.00	10.00
SO Shaquille O'Neal	6.00	15.00
TC Tyson Chandler	2.50	6.00
TD Tim Duncan	5.00	12.00
TI Jamaal Tinsley	2.00	5.00
TM Tracy McGrady	4.00	10.00
TP Tony Parker	3.00	8.00
VC Vince Carter	4.00	10.00
WS Wally Szczerbiak	2.50	6.00
YM Yao Ming	4.00	10.00
ZI Zydrunas Ilgauskas	2.50	6.00

2006-07 Fleer Hot Prospects Hot Materials Jerseys

Card	Low	High
COMMON CARD	2.50	6.00
PRINT RUN 50 SER.#'d SETS		
*RED HOT: .75X TO 2X BASE HI		
RED HOT PRINT RUN 25 SER.#'d SETS		
UNPRICED PATCH PRINT RUN 10 SETS		
AB Andrew Bogut	2.50	6.00
AI Andre Iguodala	2.50	6.00
AS Amare Stoudemire	2.50	6.00
BA Andrea Bargnani	3.00	8.00
BD Baron Davis	2.50	6.00
BG Ben Gordon	2.50	6.00
BM Brad Miller	2.50	6.00
BR Brandon Roy	3.00	8.00
CB Chauncey Billups	3.00	8.00
CP Chris Paul	4.00	10.00
CW Chris Webber	3.00	8.00
DH Dwight Howard	2.50	6.00
DN Dirk Nowitzki	5.00	12.00
EB Elton Brand	3.00	8.00
EO Emeka Okafor	2.50	6.00
JK Jason Kidd	5.00	12.00
KB Kobe Bryant	10.00	25.00
KG Kevin Garnett	5.00	12.00
LA LaMarcus Aldridge	8.00	20.00
LJ LeBron James	10.00	25.00
LO Lamar Odom	2.50	6.00
MG Manu Ginobili	3.00	8.00
MW Marvin Williams	2.50	6.00
PG Pau Gasol	3.00	8.00
PP Paul Pierce	3.00	8.00
PS Peja Stojakovic	3.00	8.00
RB Ronnie Brewer	3.00	8.00
RF Randy Foye	3.00	8.00
RG Rudy Gay	4.00	10.00
RR Rajon Rondo	8.00	20.00
SF Steve Francis	2.50	6.00
SM Shawn Marion	2.50	6.00
SW Shelden Williams	2.50	6.00
TC Tyson Chandler	2.50	6.00
TT Tyrus Thomas	2.50	6.00
WI Chris Wilcox	2.50	6.00
WM Marcus Williams	2.00	5.00
WS Wally Szczerbiak	2.50	6.00
ZI Zydrunas Ilgauskas	2.50	6.00

2006-07 Fleer Hot Prospects Notable Newcomers

Card	Low	High
COMPLETE SET (20)	12.50	30.00
APPROXIMATE ODDS TWO PER BOX		
AB Andrea Bargnani	1.00	2.50
AD Hassan Adams	.60	1.50
BJ Bobby Jones	.60	1.50
BR Brandon Roy	1.00	2.50
CS Craig Smith	.75	2.00
DN David Noel	.60	1.50
HA Hilton Armstrong	.60	1.50
JF Jordan Farmar	1.00	2.50
LA LaMarcus Aldridge	2.50	6.00
MC Mardy Collins	.60	1.50
MW Marcus Williams	.60	1.50
PO Patrick O'Bryant	.60	1.50
QD Quincy Douby	.60	1.50
RF Randy Foye	1.00	2.50
RG Rudy Gay	1.25	3.00
RH Ryan Hollins	.75	2.00
RR Rajon Rondo	1.50	4.00
SN Steve Novak	.75	2.00
SW Shelden Williams	.75	2.00
TT Tyrus Thomas	.75	2.00

2006-07 Fleer Hot Prospects Notable Notations

PRINT RUN 50 SER.#'d SETS
UNPRICED RED HOT PRINT RUN 10 SETS

Card	Low	High
AB Andrea Bargnani	5.00	12.00
BA Renaldo Balkman	4.00	10.00
BR Brandon Roy	5.00	12.00
CS Cedric Simmons	3.00	8.00
DB Denham Brown	3.00	8.00
DE Dee Brown	3.00	8.00
DN David Noel	3.00	8.00
JB Josh Boone	3.00	8.00
KP Kevin Pittsnogle	4.00	10.00
LA LaMarcus Aldridge	12.00	30.00
MA Maurice Ager	3.00	8.00
PD Paul Davis	3.00	8.00
QD Quincy Douby	3.00	8.00
RF Randy Foye	8.00	20.00
RG Rudy Gay	12.50	30.00
SB Shannon Brown	3.00	8.00
SC Craig Smith	4.00	10.00
TT Tyrus Thomas	4.00	10.00
WI Shawne Williams	3.00	8.00

2006-07 Fleer Hot Prospects Rookie Materials Letter Autographs

RANDOM INSERTS IN PACKS

Card	Low	High
AB Andrea Bargnani	25.00	50.00
BR Brandon Roy	25.00	60.00
CS Cedric Simmons	5.00	12.00
HA Hilton Armstrong	5.00	12.00
JB Josh Boone	5.00	12.00
JF Jordan Farmar	8.00	20.00
LA LaMarcus Aldridge	25.00	50.00
MC Mardy Collins	5.00	12.00
MW Marcus Williams	5.00	12.00
PO Patrick O'Bryant	5.00	12.00
QD Quincy Douby	5.00	12.00
RB Ronnie Brewer	8.00	20.00
RC Rodney Carney	5.00	12.00
RF Randy Foye	10.00	25.00
RG Rudy Gay	25.00	50.00
RR Rajon Rondo	40.00	100.00
SW Shelden Williams	6.00	15.00
TS Thabo Sefolosha	12.50	30.00
TT Tyrus Thomas	10.00	25.00
WI Shawne Williams	5.00	12.00

2006-07 Fleer Hot Prospects Sweet Selections Autographs

PRINT RUN 50 SER.#'d SETS

Card	Low	High
BR Brandon Roy	12.00	30.00
CA Carmelo Anthony	15.00	40.00
CB Carlos Boozer	5.00	12.00
CM Cuttino Mobley	5.00	12.00
CP Chris Paul	30.00	80.00
CS Cedric Simmons	5.00	12.00
DB Dee Brown	5.00	12.00
DE Denham Brown	5.00	12.00
DM Donyell Marshall	5.00	12.00
FR Randy Foye	5.00	12.00
HW Hakim Warrick	5.00	12.00
ID Ike Diogu	5.00	12.00
JA Antawn Jamison	5.00	12.00
JB Josh Boone	5.00	12.00
JC Josh Childress	5.00	12.00
JJ Joe Johnson	5.00	12.00
JR Jalen Rose	5.00	12.00
KA Kareem Abdul-Jabbar	40.00	80.00
KB Kwame Brown	5.00	12.00
KH Kirk Hinrich	5.00	12.00
KP Kevin Pittsnogle	5.00	12.00
LJ LeBron James	200.00	500.00
LR Luke Ridnour	5.00	12.00
MA Maurice Ager	5.00	12.00
MW Martell Webster	5.00	12.00
NR Nate Robinson	5.00	12.00
PO Patrick O'Bryant	5.00	12.00
PP Paul Pierce	15.00	40.00
RC Rodney Carney	5.00	12.00
RF Raymond Felton	5.00	12.00
RG Rudy Gay	8.00	20.00
RJ Richard Jefferson	5.00	12.00
RM Rashad McCants	5.00	12.00
SC Craig Smith	5.00	12.00
SN Steve Novak	5.00	12.00
SS Saer Sene	5.00	12.00
TF T.J. Ford	5.00	12.00
TP Tayshaun Prince	6.00	15.00
WS Shelden Williams	5.00	12.00
YM Yao Ming	15.00	40.00

2006-07 Fleer Hot Prospects Sweet Selections Autographs Jerseys

PRINT RUN 25 SER.#'d SETS
UNPRICED LOGO PRINT RUN ONE SET

Card	Low	High
CB Carlos Boozer	8.00	20.00
CP Chris Paul	30.00	80.00
CS Cedric Simmons	5.00	12.00
DE Denham Brown	5.00	12.00
DM Donyell Marshall	8.00	20.00
FR Randy Foye	8.00	20.00
HW Hakim Warrick	8.00	20.00
ID Ike Diogu	8.00	20.00
JA Antawn Jamison	10.00	25.00
JB Josh Boone	5.00	12.00
JC Josh Childress	8.00	20.00
JJ Joe Johnson	10.00	25.00
JR Jalen Rose	10.00	25.00
KA Kareem Abdul-Jabbar	75.00	150.00
KB Kwame Brown	8.00	20.00
KH Kirk Hinrich	8.00	20.00
LA LaMarcus Aldridge	20.00	50.00
LJ LeBron James	300.00	600.00
MA Maurice Ager	5.00	12.00
NR Nate Robinson	10.00	25.00
PP Paul Pierce	12.50	30.00
RC Rodney Carney	5.00	12.00
RF Raymond Felton	10.00	25.00
RG Rudy Gay	10.00	25.00
RJ Richard Jefferson	8.00	20.00
RM Rashad McCants	8.00	20.00
SC Craig Smith	6.00	15.00
SS Saer Sene	5.00	12.00
TP Tayshaun Prince	8.00	20.00
WS Shelden Williams	6.00	15.00
YM Yao Ming	25.00	60.00

2006-07 Fleer Hot Prospects We're #1

Card	Low	High
COMPLETE SET	6.00	15.00
APPROXIMATE ODDS ONE PER BOX		
AB Andrew Bogut	.75	2.00
CW Chris Webber	1.00	2.50
DH Dwight Howard	.75	2.00
EB Elton Brand	1.00	2.50
KB Kwame Brown	.60	1.50
KM Kenyon Martin	.75	2.00
LJ LeBron James	4.00	10.00
SO Shaquille O'Neal	2.00	5.00
TD Tim Duncan	1.50	4.00
YM Yao Ming	1.25	3.00
AB2 Andrea Bargnani	1.00	2.50

2006-07 Fleer Hot Prospects We're #1 Memorabilia

PRINT RUN 50 SER.#'d SETS
*RED HOT: .75X TO 2X BASE HI
RED PRINT RUN 25 SER.#'d SETS
UNPRICED PATCH PRINT RUN 10 SETS

Card	Low	High
AB Andrew Bogut	2.50	6.00
CW Chris Webber	3.00	8.00
DH Dwight Howard	2.50	6.00
KB Kwame Brown	2.50	6.00
KM Kenyon Martin	2.50	6.00
LJ LeBron James	12.00	30.00
SO Shaquille O'Neal	6.00	15.00
TD Tim Duncan	5.00	12.00
YM Yao Ming	4.00	10.00

2007-08 Fleer Hot Prospects

This 133-card set was released in November, 2008. The set was issued into the hobby in five-card packs which came 18 packs to a box and packs carried an initial SRP of $6.99. Cards numbered 1-66 feature veterans while cards numbered 67-78 feature retired greats. All cards numbered 61-78 were issued to a stated print run of 399 serial numbered sets. Cards numbered 81-133 all feature 2007-08 NBA rookies and in that grouping cards numbered 85-93 were signed by the player and cards numbered 94-133 have both player-worn swatches as well as a signature. Cards numbered 79-84 were issued to a stated print run of 199 serial numbered sets, Cards numbered 85-93 were issued to a stated print run of 899 serial numbered sets while cards 94-121 were issued to a stated print run of 599 serial numbered sets and the set concludes with cards numbered 122-133 which were issued to a stated print run of 399 serial numbered sets.

Card	Low	High
COMP.SET w/o SP's (60)	10.00	25.00
61-78 PRINT RUN 399 SER.#'d SETS		
COMMON CARD (79-84)	3.00	8.00
85-93 RC PRINT RUN 899 SER.#'d SETS		
94-121 RC PRINT RUN 599 SER.#'d SETS		
122-133 RC PRINT RUN 399 SER.#'d SETS		
UNPRICED BLUE PRINT RUN 10 SER.#'d SETS		
1 Kobe Bryant	1.25	3.00
2 Carmelo Anthony	.40	1.00
3 Gilbert Arenas	.25	.60
4 Dwyane Wade	.50	1.25
5 LeBron James	1.25	3.00
6 Michael Redd	.25	.60
7 Ray Allen	.30	.75
8 Allen Iverson	.40	1.00
9 Vince Carter	.40	1.00
10 Yao Ming	.40	1.00

11 Joe Johnson .25 .60
12 Paul Pierce .30 .75
13 Tracy McGrady .30 .75
14 Dirk Nowitzki .40 1.00
15 Zach Randolph .25 .60
16 Chris Bosh .30 .75
17 Kevin Garnett .50 1.25
18 Rashard Lewis .25 .60
19 Ben Gordon .25 .60
20 Carlos Boozer .25 .60
21 Pau Gasol .30 .75
22 Elton Brand .30 .75
23 Michael Jordan 2.50 6.00
24 Amare Stoudemire .25 .60
25 Kevin Martin .25 .60
26 Baron Davis .25 .60
27 Tim Duncan .50 1.25
28 Richard Hamilton .25 .60
29 Eddy Curry .20 .50
30 Jermaine O'Neal .25 .60
31 Caron Butler .25 .60
32 Josh Howard .25 .60
33 Ron Artest .30 .75
34 Luol Deng .25 .60
35 Steve Nash .40 1.00
36 Tony Parker .30 .75
37 David West .25 .60
38 Andre Iguodala .25 .60
39 Gerald Wallace .25 .60
40 Jamal Crawford .30 .75
41 Dwight Howard .25 .60
42 Mehmet Okur .20 .50
43 Shawn Marion .25 .60
44 Maurice Williams .25 .60
45 Shaquille O'Neal .60 1.50
46 Chris Paul .40 1.00
47 Chauncey Billups .30 .75
48 Brandon Roy .30 .75
49 Josh Smith .25 .60
50 Deron Williams .25 .60
51 Jason Richardson .30 .75
52 Al Jefferson .25 .60
53 Lamar Odom .25 .60
54 Raymond Felton .30 .75
55 Andre Miller .25 .60
56 Jason Kidd .30 .75
57 Zydrunas Ilgauskas .25 .60
58 Andrea Bargnani .30 .75
59 Marcus Camby .20 .50
60 Rudy Gay .30 .75
61 LeBron James 3.00 8.00
62 Amare Stoudemire .60 1.50
63 Vince Carter 1.00 2.50
64 Tim Duncan 1.25 3.00
65 Allen Iverson 1.00 2.50
66 Shaquille O'Neal 1.50 4.00
67 David Robinson 1.25 3.00
68 Michael Jordan 6.00 15.00
69 Darrell Griffith .50 1.25
70 Larry Bird 2.00 5.00
71 Adrian Dantley .60 1.50
72 Bob McAdoo .60 1.50
73 Kareem Abdul-Jabbar 1.25 3.00
74 Wes Unseld .75 2.00
75 Dave Bing .75 2.00
76 Willis Reed .75 2.00
77 Oscar Robertson .75 2.00
78 Wilt Chamberlain 1.50 4.00
79 Greg Oden RC 3.00 8.00
80 Brandan Wright RC 3.00 8.00
81 Yi Jianlian RC 4.00 10.00
82 Nick Young RC 4.00 10.00
83 Thaddeus Young RC 3.00 8.00
84 Kyrylo Fesenko RC 2.00 5.00
85 Sun Yue AU RC 3.00 8.00
86 Brad Newley AU RC 3.00 8.00
87 Ramon Sessions AU RC 3.00 8.00
88 Sammy Mejia AU RC 2.00 5.00
89 JamesOn Curry AU RC 2.00 5.00
90 Renaldas Seibutis AU RC 3.00 8.00
91 Milovan Rakovic AU RC 3.00 8.00
92 Marco Belinelli AU RC 3.00 8.00
93 Darryl Watkins AU RC 2.00 5.00
94 Demetris Nichols JSY AU RC 4.00 10.00
95 Javaris Crittenton JSY AU RC 4.00 10.00
96 Jason Smith JSY AU RC 5.00 12.00
97 Daequan Cook JSY AU RC 5.00 12.00
98 Jared Dudley JSY AU RC 5.00 12.00
99 Wilson Chandler JSY AU RC 5.00 12.00
100 Morris Almond JSY AU RC 4.00 10.00
101 Aaron Brooks JSY AU RC 5.00 12.00
102 Arron Afflalo JSY AU RC 6.00 15.00
103 Alando Tucker JSY AU RC 4.00 10.00
104 Carl Landry JSY AU RC 4.00 10.00
105 Gabe Pruitt JSY AU RC 4.00 10.00
106 Marcus Williams JSY AU RC 4.00 10.00
107 Nick Fazekas JSY AU RC 4.00 10.00
108 Glen Davis JSY AU RC 5.00 12.00
109 Jermareo Davidson JSY AU RC 4.00 10.00
110 Josh McRoberts JSY AU RC 5.00 12.00
111 Herbert Hill JSY AU RC 4.00 10.00
112 Derrick Byars JSY AU RC 4.00 10.00
113 Adam Haluska JSY AU RC 4.00 10.00
114 Reyshawn Terry JSY AU RC 4.00 10.00
115 Jared Jordan JSY AU RC 4.00 10.00
116 Stephane Lasme JSY AU RC 4.00 10.00
117 Dominic McGuire JSY AU RC 4.00 10.00
118 Aaron Gray JSY AU RC 4.00 10.00
119 Taurean Green JSY AU RC 4.00 10.00
120 D.J. Strawberry JSY AU RC 4.00 10.00
121 Chris Richard JSY AU RC 4.00 10.00
122 Rodney Stuckey JSY AU RC 5.00 12.00
123 Kevin Durant JSY AU RC 200.00 400.00
124 Al Thornton JSY AU RC 5.00 12.00
125 Julian Wright JSY AU RC 4.00 10.00
126 Sean Williams JSY AU RC 4.00 10.00
127 Al Horford JSY AU RC 8.00 20.00
128 Mike Conley Jr. JSY AU RC 10.00 25.00
129 Jeff Green JSY AU RC 6.00 15.00
130 Corey Brewer JSY AU RC 6.00 15.00
131 Joakim Noah JSY AU RC 6.00 15.00
132 Spencer Hawes JSY AU RC 5.00 12.00
133 Acie Law JSY AU RC 4.00 10.00

2007-08 Fleer Hot Prospects Red

*1-60 RED: 5X TO 12X BASE HI
*61-78 RED: 1.5X TO 4X BASE HI
*79-93 RC RED: 1X TO 2.5X BASE HI
*94-133 RC RED: .6X TO 1.5X BASE HI
PRINT RUN 25 SER.#'d SETS
68 Michael Jordan 40.00 100.00

2007-08 Fleer Hot Prospects Autographics

APPROXIMATE ODDS ONE PER BOX
CARDS WITH F INSERTED IN FLEER
AA Arron Afflalo 4.00 10.00
AB Aaron Brooks F 3.00 8.00
AG Aaron Gray 2.50 6.00
AH Adam Haluska 2.50 6.00
AH2 Adam Haluska Blue 2.50 6.00
AH3 Al Horford Blue 6.00 15.00
AH4 Al Horford 6.00 15.00
AL Acie Law F 2.50 6.00
AT Al Thornton 3.00 8.00
AT2 Al Thornton Blue 3.00 8.00
AT3 Alando Tucker F 2.50 6.00
CA Carmelo Anthony Blue 15.00 40.00
CB Corey Brewer 4.00 10.00
CB2 Corey Brewer Blue 4.00 10.00
CL Carl Landry 2.50 6.00
CL2 Carl Landry Blue 2.50 6.00
CR Chris Richard 2.50 6.00
CR2 Chris Richard Blue 2.50 6.00
DB Derrick Byars 2.50 6.00
DB2 Derrick Byars Blue 2.50 6.00
DC Daequan Cook 3.00 8.00
DS D.J. Strawberry F 2.50 6.00
DS2 D.J. Strawberry Blue F 2.50 6.00
GD Glen Davis 3.00 8.00
GP Gabe Pruitt F 2.50 6.00
HH Herbert Hill F 2.50 6.00
JC Javaris Crittenton 2.50 6.00
JC2 Javaris Crittenton Blue 2.50 6.00
JD Jared Dudley 3.00 8.00
JD2 Jared Dudley Blue 3.00 8.00
JD3 Jermareo Davidson 2.50 6.00
JG Jeff Green 4.00 10.00
JG2 Jeff Green Blue 10.00 25.00
JM Josh McRoberts 3.00 8.00
JM2 Josh McRoberts Blue 3.00 8.00
JN Joakim Noah 4.00 10.00
JN2 Joakim Noah Blue 6.00 15.00
JS Jason Smith F 3.00 8.00
JW Julian Wright 2.50 6.00
KD Kevin Durant 125.00 250.00
KD2 Kevin Durant Blue 150.00 300.00
MA Morris Almond F 2.50 6.00
MB Marco Belinelli Blue F 4.00 10.00
MC Mike Conley Jr. F 5.00 12.00
MC2 Mike Conley Jr. Blue F 5.00 12.00
MW Marcus Williams 2.50 6.00
RS Rodney Stuckey 3.00 8.00
RS2 Rodney Stuckey Green 3.00 8.00
RT Reyshawn Terry 2.50 6.00
RT2 Reyshawn Terry Blue 2.50 6.00
SH Spencer Hawes 3.00 8.00
SH2 Spencer Hawes Blue F 3.00 8.00
SH3 Spencer Hawes Red F 3.00 8.00
SL Stephane Lasme 2.50 6.00
SM Craig Smith F 2.50 6.00
TG Taurean Green 2.50 6.00
TG2 Taurean Green Blue 2.50 6.00
WC Wilson Chandler 3.00 8.00

2007-08 Fleer Hot Prospects Class of

COMPLETE SET (15) 25.00 60.00
PRINT RUNS SAME AS CARD #
1960 Robertson/West/Wilkens 2.50 6.00
1962 DeBusschere/Lucas/Havlicek 2.50 6.00
1967 Frazier/Riley/Jackson 3.00 8.00
1970 Lanier/Maravich/Archibald 5.00 12.00
1972 McAdoo/Westphal/Erving 2.50 6.00
1979 Johnson/Cartwright/Laimbeer 3.00 8.00
1984 Olajuwon/Jordan/Stockton 6.00 15.00
1992 O'Neal/Mourning/Horry 3.00 8.00
1996 Iverson/Bryant/Nash 4.00 10.00
1997 Duncan/Billups/McGrady 3.00 8.00
1998 Carter/Nowitzki/Pierce 3.00 8.00
2001 Gasol/Parker/Arenas 2.50 6.00
2003 James/Anthony/Wade 4.00 10.00
2007A Oden/Durant/Conley 5.00 12.00
2007B Noah/Horford/Brewer 4.00 10.00

2007-08 Fleer Hot Prospects Double Scribble

PRINT RUN 25 SER.#'d SETS
UNPRICED BLUE PRINT RUN ONE SET
UNPRICED RED PRINT RUN 10 SER.#'d SETS
AR L.Aldridge/B.Roy 30.00 60.00
BN S.Nash/K.Bryant 125.00 250.00
FG T.Ford/D.Gibson 10.00 25.00
FL K.Lowry/R.Foye 12.00 30.00
GB D.Gibson/S.Brown 10.00 25.00
GR B.Gordon/R.Rondo 20.00 50.00
GT T.Thomas/H.Grant 50.00 100.00
HA D.Howard/J.Augustine 15.00 40.00
JJ L.James/M.Jordan 600.00 1000.00
JP J.Jack/M.Price 12.00 30.00
PD T.Prince/A.Dantley 12.50 30.00
RC M.Collins/Q.Richardson 10.00 25.00
WB D.Brown/D.Williams 12.50 30.00

2007-08 Fleer Hot Prospects Draft Day Postmarks

PRINT RUN 50 SER.#'d SETS
UNPRICED RED PRINT RUN 10 SER.#'d SETS
AA Arron Afflalo 6.00 15.00
AB Aaron Brooks 5.00 12.00
AG Aaron Gray 4.00 10.00
AH Al Horford 15.00 40.00
AL Acie Law 4.00 10.00
AT Al Thornton 5.00 12.00
CB Corey Brewer 6.00 15.00
CL Carl Landry 4.00 10.00
CR Chris Richard 4.00 10.00
DA Jermareo Davidson 4.00 10.00
DB Derrick Byars 4.00 10.00
DC Daequan Cook 8.00 20.00
DN Demetris Nichols 4.00 10.00
DS D.J. Strawberry 4.00 10.00
GD Glen Davis 5.00 12.00
GP Gabe Pruitt 4.00 10.00
HA Adam Haluska 4.00 10.00
JC Javaris Crittenton 4.00 10.00
JC JamesOn Curry 4.00 10.00
JD Jared Dudley 5.00 12.00
JG Jeff Green 12.50 30.00
JM Josh McRoberts 5.00 12.00
JN Joakim Noah 30.00 80.00
JW Julian Wright 8.00 20.00
KD Kevin Durant 250.00 500.00
MA Morris Almond 4.00 10.00
MC Mike Conley Jr. 12.50 30.00
MW Marcus Williams 4.00 10.00
NF Nick Fazekas 4.00 10.00
RS Ramon Sessions 6.00 15.00
SH Spencer Hawes 5.00 12.00
SL Stephane Lasme 4.00 10.00
SM Sammy Mejia 4.00 10.00
SW Sean Williams 4.00 10.00
TG Taurean Green 4.00 10.00
TU Alando Tucker 4.00 10.00
WC Wilson Chandler 5.00 12.00
KDP Kevin Durant PROMO 15.00 40.00

2007-08 Fleer Hot Prospects Hot Materials

APPROXIMATE ODDS ONE PER RETAIL BOX
*RED: .75X TO 2X BASE HI
RED PRINT RUN 25 SER.#'d SETS
AH Al Horford 3.00 8.00
AS Amare Stoudemire 2.00 5.00
BL Bill Laimbeer 2.00 5.00
BR Bill Russell 20.00 50.00
CB Corey Brewer 2.50 6.00
CD Clyde Drexler 3.00 8.00
CM Corey Maggette 2.00 5.00
DM Donyell Marshall 2.00 5.00
DN Dirk Nowitzki 3.00 8.00
EB Elton Brand 2.50 6.00
GH Grant Hill 5.00 12.00
HG Horace Grant 2.50 6.00
JE Julius Erving 4.00 10.00
JK Jason Kidd 2.50 6.00
JN Joakim Noah 2.50 6.00
JO Jermaine O'Neal 2.00 5.00
JR Jason Richardson 2.50 6.00
JS John Stockton 4.00 10.00
JT Jamaal Tinsley 2.00 5.00
JW Julian Wright 1.50 4.00
KB Kobe Bryant 6.00 15.00
KD Kevin Durant 25.00 60.00
KG Kevin Garnett 4.00 10.00
LH Larry Hughes 2.00 5.00
LJ LeBron James 6.00 15.00
MC Mike Conley Jr. 3.00 8.00
MP Morris Peterson 1.50 4.00
N Nene 2.00 5.00
RA Ray Allen 2.50 6.00
RL Rashard Lewis 2.00 5.00
RW Rasheed Wallace 2.50 6.00
SM Shawn Marion 2.00 5.00
TC Tyson Chandler 2.00 5.00
TD Tim Duncan 4.00 10.00
TP Tony Parker 2.50 6.00
ZI Zydrunas Ilgauskas 2.00 5.00

2007-08 Fleer Hot Prospects NBA Game Issue

PRINT RUN 99 SER.#'d SETS
UNPRICED BLUE PRINT RUN ONE SET
*RED: .75X TO 2X BASE HI
RED PRINT RUN 25 SER.#'d SETS
AI Allen Iverson 5.00 12.00
BH Brendan Haywood 3.00 8.00
BL Bill Laimbeer 4.00 10.00
CA Carmelo Anthony 4.00 10.00
CD Clyde Drexler 5.00 12.00
DR David Robinson 8.00 20.00
EB Elton Brand 3.00 8.00
GH Grant Hill 8.00 20.00
HG Horace Grant 3.00 8.00
JE Julius Erving 5.00 12.00
JK Jason Kidd 3.00 8.00
JO Jermaine O'Neal 3.00 8.00
JS John Stockton 5.00 12.00
KB Kobe Bryant 12.00 30.00
KG Kevin Garnett 5.00 12.00
LJ LeBron James 10.00 25.00
MJ Michael Jordan 30.00 80.00
RA Ray Allen 3.00 8.00
RH Richard Hamilton 3.00 8.00
TD Tim Duncan 4.00 10.00

2007-08 Fleer Hot Prospects Notable Newcomers

COMPLETE SET (20) 15.00 40.00
APPROXIMATELY TWO PER BOX
1 Kevin Durant 10.00 25.00
2 Joakim Noah 1.00 2.50
3 Al Horford 1.25 3.00
4 Corey Brewer 1.00 2.50
5 Julian Wright .60 1.50
6 Mike Conley Jr. 1.25 3.00
7 Jeff Green 1.00 2.50
8 Rodney Stuckey .75 2.00
9 Spencer Hawes .75 2.00
10 Acie Law .60 1.50
11 Al Thornton .75 2.00
12 Arron Afflalo 1.00 2.50
13 Marco Belinelli 1.00 2.50
14 Alando Tucker .60 1.50
15 Aaron Brooks .75 2.00
16 Javaris Crittenton .60 1.50
17 Wilson Chandler .75 2.00
18 Sun Yue 1.00 2.50
19 Taurean Green .60 1.50
20 D.J. Strawberry .60 1.50

2007-08 Fleer Hot Prospects Notable Notations

PRINT RUN 24 TO 50 SER.#'d SETS
UNPRICED BLUE PRINT RUN ONE SET
*RED: .5X TO 1.25X BASE HI
RED PRINT RUN 25 SER.#'d SETS
AM Alonzo Mourning/50 20.00 50.00
BD Baron Davis/50 6.00 15.00
BL Bill Laimbeer/50 10.00 25.00
DM Dan Majerle/50 15.00 40.00
DR Dennis Rodman/50 25.00 50.00
DT David Thompson/50 6.00 15.00
DW Slick Watts/50 6.00 15.00
HO Hakeem Olajuwon/50 15.00 40.00
JW Jamaal Wilkes/50 6.00 15.00
KB Kobe Bryant/24 100.00 175.00
LB Leandro Barbosa/50 6.00 15.00
LJ LeBron James/50 100.00 200.00
MP Morris Peterson/25 6.00 15.00
SM Sidney Moncrief/50 10.00 25.00
SP Sam Perkins/50 6.00 15.00
VC Vince Carter/48 15.00 40.00

2007-08 Fleer Hot Prospects Property of

STATED PRINT RUN 149 SER.#'d SETS
UNPRICED BLUE PRINT RUN ONE SET
*RED: .75X TO 2X BASE HI
RED PRINT RUN 25 SER.#'d SETS
AB Andrew Bogut 2.50 6.00
AK Andrei Kirilenko 2.50 6.00
AS Amare Stoudemire 2.50 6.00
BB Bruce Bowen 2.00 5.00
BR Elton Brand 3.00 8.00
CB Chauncey Billups 3.00 8.00
CF Channing Frye 2.50 6.00
CW Chris Wilcox 2.00 5.00
DB Devin Harris 2.00 5.00
DG Danny Granger 2.50 6.00
DH Dwight Howard 2.50 6.00
DM Desmond Mason 2.00 5.00
DN Dirk Nowitzki 4.00 10.00
DR David Robinson 5.00 12.00
DW Delonte West 2.00 5.00
EJ Eddie Jones 2.50 6.00
GW Gerald Wallace 2.50 6.00
JF Jordan Farmar 2.00 5.00
JM Jamaal Magloire 2.00 5.00
JR Jalen Rose 2.50 6.00
JT Jason Terry 2.50 6.00
KG Kevin Garnett 5.00 12.00
KH Kirk Hinrich 2.50 6.00
LD Luol Deng 2.50 6.00
LJ LeBron James 8.00 20.00
MD Mike Dunleavy 2.50 6.00
MG Manu Ginobili 3.00 8.00
MR Michael Redd 2.50 6.00
PG Pau Gasol 3.00 8.00
PP Paul Pierce 3.00 8.00
PS Peja Stojakovic 3.00 8.00
RA Ron Artest 3.00 8.00
RH Richard Hamilton 2.50 6.00
RJ Richard Jefferson 2.50 6.00
RL Rashard Lewis 2.50 6.00
SB Shane Battier 2.50 6.00
SF Steve Francis 2.50 6.00
SL Shaun Livingston 2.00 5.00
SM Shawn Marion 2.50 6.00
ZI Zydrunas Ilgauskas 2.50 6.00

2007-08 Fleer Hot Prospects Rookie Materials Autographs

RANDOM INSERTS IN PACKS
AA Arron Afflalo 8.00 20.00
AB Aaron Brooks 6.00 15.00
AG Aaron Gray 5.00 12.00
AH Adam Haluska 5.00 12.00
AL Acie Law 5.00 12.00
AT Al Thornton 6.00 15.00
CB Corey Brewer 8.00 20.00
CL Carl Landry 5.00 12.00
CR Chris Richard 5.00 12.00
DA Jermareo Davidson 5.00 12.00
DB Derrick Byars 5.00 12.00
DM Dominic McGuire 5.00 12.00
GD Glen Davis 6.00 15.00
GP Gabe Pruitt 5.00 12.00
HO Al Horford 10.00 25.00
JA Javaris Crittenton 5.00 12.00
JD Jared Dudley 6.00 15.00
JG Jeff Green 6.00 15.00
JJ Jared Jordan 5.00 12.00
JM Josh McRoberts 6.00 15.00
JN Joakim Noah 8.00 20.00
JS Jason Smith 6.00 15.00
JW Julian Wright 5.00 12.00
KD Kevin Durant 100.00 200.00
MA Morris Almond 5.00 12.00
MB Marco Belinelli 8.00 20.00
MC Mike Conley Jr. 10.00 25.00
MW Marcus Williams 5.00 12.00
NF Nick Fazekas 5.00 12.00
RS Rodney Stuckey 6.00 15.00
RT Reyshawn Terry 5.00 12.00
SH Spencer Hawes 6.00 15.00
SL Stephane Lasme 5.00 12.00
SW Sean Williams 5.00 12.00
TU Alando Tucker 5.00 12.00
WC Wilson Chandler 6.00 15.00

2007-08 Fleer Hot Prospects Rookie Photo Shoot Postmarks

STATED PRINT RUN 50 SER.#'d SETS
UNPRICED RED PRINT RUN 10 SETS
AA Arron Afflalo 6.00 15.00
AB Aaron Brooks 5.00 12.00
AG Aaron Gray 4.00 10.00
AH Al Horford 15.00 40.00
AL Acie Law 4.00 10.00
AT Al Thornton 5.00 12.00
CB Corey Brewer 6.00 15.00
CL Carl Landry 4.00 10.00
CR Chris Richard 4.00 10.00
DA Jermareo Davidson 4.00 10.00
DB Derrick Byars 4.00 10.00
DC Daequan Cook 5.00 12.00
DN Demetris Nichols 4.00 10.00
DS D.J. Strawberry 4.00 10.00
GD Glen Davis 5.00 12.00
GP Gabe Pruitt 4.00 10.00
HA Adam Haluska 4.00 10.00
JC Javaris Crittenton 4.00 10.00
JC JamesOn Curry 4.00 10.00
JD Jared Dudley 5.00 12.00
JG Jeff Green 12.50 30.00
JM Josh McRoberts 5.00 12.00
JN Joakim Noah 30.00 80.00
JW Julian Wright 8.00 20.00
KD Kevin Durant 175.00 350.00
MA Morris Almond 4.00 10.00
MC Mike Conley Jr. 12.50 30.00
MW Marcus Williams 4.00 10.00
NF Nick Fazekas 4.00 10.00
RS Ramon Sessions 15.00 40.00
SH Spencer Hawes 5.00 12.00
SL Stephane Lasme 4.00 10.00
SM Sammy Mejia 4.00 10.00
SW Sean Williams 4.00 10.00
TG Taurean Green 4.00 10.00
TU Alando Tucker 4.00 10.00
WC Wilson Chandler 5.00 12.00

2007-08 Fleer Hot Prospects Stat Tracker

COMPLETE SET (35) 20.00 40.00
APPROXIMATELY TWO PER BOX
1 A.C. Green .75 2.00
2 Adrian Dantley .60 1.50
3 Andre Miller .60 1.50
4 Andrea Bargnani .75 2.00
5 Antawn Jamison .60 1.50
6 Artis Gilmore .60 1.50
7 B.J. Armstrong .75 2.00
8 Baron Davis .60 1.50
9 Bill Laimbeer .60 1.50
10 Bill Russell 1.25 3.00
11 Bill Walton .75 2.00
12 Brandon Roy .75 2.00
13 Daniel Gibson .60 1.50
14 Dennis Rodman 1.50 4.00
15 Deron Williams .60 1.50
16 Donyell Marshall .50 1.25
17 Emeka Okafor .60 1.50
18 Hakeem Olajuwon 1.00 2.50
19 Jason Kidd .75 2.00
20 John Stockton 1.25 3.00
21 Kobe Bryant 3.00 8.00
22 Kobe Bryant 3.00 8.00
23 LeBron James 3.00 8.00
24 Magic Johnson 2.00 5.00
25 Mark Price .75 2.00
26 Michael Jordan 6.00 15.00
27 Michael Jordan 6.00 15.00
28 Paul Pierce .75 2.00
29 Robert Parish .75 2.00
30 Slick Watts .50 1.25
31 Steve Kerr .75 2.00
32 Steve Nash 1.00 2.50
33 Tom Chambers .60 1.50
34 Tyson Chandler .60 1.50
35 Vince Carter 1.00 2.50

2007-08 Fleer Hot Prospects Stat Tracker Jersey Autographs

PRINT RUN 23 TO 50 SER.#'d SETS
UNPRICED BLUE PRINT RUN ONE SET
*RED: .5X TO 1.25X BASE HI
RED PRINT RUN 25 SER.#'d SETS
2 Adrian Dantley/50 6.00 15.00
4 Andrea Bargnani/37 6.00 15.00
5 Antawn Jamison/50 6.00 15.00
8 Baron Davis/50 6.00 15.00
10 Bill Russell/50 75.00 150.00
11 Bill Walton/50 10.00 25.00
12 Brandon Roy/50 12.00 30.00
13 Daniel Gibson/50 6.00 15.00
14 Dennis Rodman/50 30.00 60.00
15 Deron Williams/50 15.00 30.00
16 Donyell Marshall/50 6.00 15.00
17 Emeka Okafor/50 6.00 15.00
18 Hakeem Olajuwon/50 20.00 50.00
19 Jason Kidd/50 15.00 30.00
20 John Stockton/50 30.00 60.00
22 Kobe Bryant/24 125.00 250.00
23 LeBron James/50 150.00 300.00
24 Magic Johnson/50 40.00 80.00
26 Michael Jordan/23 500.00 1000.00
27 Michael Jordan/23 500.00 1000.00
28 Paul Pierce/50 15.00 30.00
31 Steve Kerr/50 15.00 30.00
32 Steve Nash/50 15.00 40.00
33 Tom Chambers/50 10.00 25.00
34 Tyson Chandler/50 6.00 15.00
35 Vince Carter/50 20.00 40.00

2007-08 Fleer Hot Prospects Supreme Court

COMPLETE SET (30) 15.00 30.00
APPROXIMATELY TWO PER BOX
1 Shareef Abdur-Rahim .60 1.50
2 Leandro Barbosa .60 1.50
3 Rick Barry .60 1.50
4 Mike Bibby .75 2.00
5 Tom Chambers .60 1.50
6 Michael Cooper .60 1.50
7 Chuck Daly .75 2.00
8 Adrian Dantley .60 1.50
9 Brad Daugherty .60 1.50
10 Sean Elliott .75 2.00
11 Walt Frazier .75 2.00
12 A.C. Green .75 2.00
13 Connie Hawkins .75 2.00
14 Bobby Jackson .50 1.25
15 Antawn Jamison .60 1.50
16 Michael Jordan 6.00 15.00
17 Steve Kerr .75 2.00
18 Jason Kidd .75 2.00
19 Dan Majerle .60 1.50
20 Donyell Marshall .50 1.25
21 Chris Mihm .50 1.25
22 Andre Miller .60 1.50
23 Don Nelson .75 2.00
24 Robert Parish .75 2.00
25 Tony Parker .75 2.00
26 Mark Price .75 2.00
27 Tayshaun Prince .60 1.50
28 Glen Rice .60 1.50
29 Dennis Scott .50 1.25
30 Jerry Sloan .75 2.00

2007-08 Fleer Hot Prospects Supreme Court Autographs

PRINT RUN 15 TO 25 SER.#'d SETS
UNPRICED RED PRINT RUN 10 SER.#'d SETS
UNPRICED BLUE PRINT RUN ONE SET
AJ Antawn Jamison/25 6.00 15.00
AM Andre Miller/25 6.00 15.00
BJ Bobby Jackson/25 6.00 15.00
CH Connie Hawkins/25 15.00 30.00
JK Jason Kidd/25 15.00 30.00
LB Leandro Barbosa/25 6.00 15.00
MJ Michael Jordan/25 300.00 550.00
MP Mark Price/25 25.00 50.00
PR Tayshaun Prince/25 6.00 15.00
SA Shareef Abdur-Rahim/25 6.00 15.00
SK Steve Kerr/25 15.00 30.00
TC Tom Chambers/25 6.00 15.00
WF Walt Frazier/15 8.00 20.00

2002-03 Fleer Hot Shots

Issued in late January 2003, the 207-card Fleer Hot Shots set consisted of 100 base cards, 29 dual player give and go cards featuring a scorer and passer from each of the NBA's teams, 39 All-Star cards and 39 rookie cards. Base cards picture full color action player shots centered with a zoom-in portrait style photo on the right side. Rookie cards were designed horizontally and were available in several different formats: Shirt swatch RC cards were sequentially numbered to 200 while other versions are denoted with a material and a print run below. Several players that fall between numbers 169 and 207 do not have any material on the card, and card numbers 196-201 feature rookie players coupled with Vince Carter and a swatch of a VC jersey. Fleer Hot Shots was packaged in 20-pack boxes were packs contained eight cards and carried an SRP of $3.99.

COMP.SET w/o SP's (168) 15.00 40.00
RC PRINT RUN 200 SETS UNLESS NOTED
RC CONTAIN SHOOTING SHIRT UNLESS NOTED
1 Shareef Abdur-Rahim .25 .60
2 Kedrick Brown .20 .50
3 Trenton Hassell .20 .50
4 Raef LaFrentz .20 .50
5 Donnell Harvey .20 .50
6 Danny Fortson .20 .50
7 Maurice Taylor .20 .50
8 Wang Zhizhi .20 .50
9 Malik Allen .20 .50
10 Tim Thomas .20 .50
11 Jason Kidd .50 1.25
12 Jamaal Magloire .20 .50
13 Grant Hill .40 1.00
14 Anfernee Hardaway .50 1.25
15 Bonzi Wells .20 .50
16 Malik Rose .20 .50
17 Antonio Davis .20 .50
18 John Stockton .40 1.00
19 Theo Ratliff .20 .50
20 Paul Pierce .30 .75
21 Jalen Rose .25 .60
22 Eduardo Najera .20 .50
23 Chauncey Billups .30 .75
24 Antawn Jamison .30 .75
25 Jonathan Bender .20 .50
26 Rick Fox .20 .50
27 Brian Grant .20 .50
28 Kevin Garnett .50 1.25
29 Kenyon Martin .25 .60
30 Allan Houston .25 .60
31 Tracy McGrady .50 1.25
32 Stephon Marbury .25 .60
33 Mike Bibby .30 .75
34 Predrag Drobnjak .20 .50
35 Lamond Murray .20 .50
36 Kwame Brown .20 .50
37 Glenn Robinson .25 .60
38 Antoine Walker .25 .60
39 Zydrunas Ilgauskas .25 .60
40 Clifford Robinson .20 .50
41 Dirk Nowitzki .50 1.25
42 Troy Murphy .25 .60
43 Al Harrington .25 .60
44 Shaquille O'Neal .75 2.00
45 Eddie House .20 .50
46 Troy Hudson .20 .50
47 Rodney Rogers .20 .50
48 Latrell Sprewell .25 .60
49 Allen Iverson .50 1.25
50 Derek Anderson .20 .50
51 Vlade Divac .25 .60
52 Rashard Lewis .30 .75
53 Morris Peterson .20 .50
54 Jerry Stackhouse .25 .60
55 Jason Terry .25 .60
56 Tyson Chandler .30 .75
57 Jumaine Jones .20 .50
58 Nick Van Exel .25 .60
59 Ben Wallace .25 .60
60 Jason Richardson .30 .75
61 Ron Mercer .20 .50
62 Shane Battier .30 .75
63 Eddie Jones .25 .60
64 Joe Smith .25 .60
65 Courtney Alexander .20 .50
66 Kurt Thomas .20 .50
67 Todd MacCulloch .20 .50
68 Ruben Patterson .20 .50
69 Tim Duncan .60 1.50
70 Gary Payton .30 .75
71 Jarron Collins .20 .50
72 Vin Baker .25 .60
73 Eddy Curry .20 .50
74 Michael Finley .30 .75
75 Marcus Camby .25 .60
76 Corliss Williamson .20 .50
77 Steve Francis .25 .60
78 Jermaine O'Neal .25 .60
79 Michael Dickerson .20 .50
80 Alonzo Mourning .40 1.00
81 Rod Strickland .20 .50
82 Elden Campbell .20 .50
83 Charlie Ward .20 .50
84 Aaron McKie .20 .50
85 Scottie Pippen .50 1.25
86 Tony Parker .40 1.00
87 Vladimir Radmanovic .20 .50
88 Matt Harpring .20 .50
89 Eddie Griffin .20 .50
90 Michael Olowokandi .20 .50
91 Stromile Swift .20 .50
92 Michael Redd .25 .60
93 Richard Jefferson .30 .75
94 Baron Davis .25 .60
95 Pat Garrity .20 .50
96 Tom Gugliotta .20 .50
97 Arvydas Sabonis .25 .60
98 David Robinson .50 1.25
99 Michael Bradley .20 .50
100 Karl Malone .40 1.00
101 J.Terry/G.Robinson .25 .60
102 T.Delk/P.Pierce .30 .75
103 J.Rose/M. Fizer .25 .60
104 D.Miles/R.Davis .25 .60
105 S.Nash/D.Nowitzki .50 1.25
106 K.Satterfield/J.Howard .25 .60
107 R.Hamilton/B.Wallace .25 .60
108 G.Arenas/A.Jamison .30 .75
109 M.Norris/C.Mobley .20 .50
110 J.Tinsley/R.Miller .30 .75
111 A.Miller/L.Odom .25 .60
112 D.Fisher/K.Bryant 1.25 3.00
113 J.Williams/S.Battier .30 .75
114 T.Best/E.Jones .25 .60
115 S.Cassell/R.Allen .30 .75
116 T.Brandon/W.Szczerbiak .25 .60
117 K.Kittles/R.Jefferson .30 .75
118 D.Wesley/J.Mashburn .25 .60
119 L.Sprewell/A.McDyess .25 .60
120 D.Armstrong/M.Miller .25 .60
121 E.Snow/K.Van Horn .20 .50
122 S.Marbury/S.Marion .25 .60
123 D.Stoudamire/R.Wallace .30 .75
124 M.Bibby/C.Webber .30 .75
125 T.Parker/D.Robinson .50 1.25
126 K.Anderson/R.Lewis .30 .75
127 A.Williams/V.Carter .50 1.25
128 J.Stockton/K.Malone .40 1.00
129 L.Hughes/M.Jordan 2.50 6.00
130 Joe Johnson AS .25 .60
131 Andrei Kirilenko AS .30 .75
132 Brendan Haywood AS .20 .50
133 Zeljko Rebraca AS .20 .50
134 Quentin Richardson AS .25 .60
135 Chris Mihm AS .20 .50
136 Darius Miles AS .20 .50
137 Desmond Mason AS .25 .60
138 Hedo Turkoglu AS .25 .60
139 Jason Richardson AS .30 .75
140 Gerald Wallace AS .25 .60
141 Steve Francis AS .25 .60
142 Steve Nash AS .40 1.00
143 Peja Stojakovic AS .30 .75
144 Ray Allen AS .30 .75
145 Mike Miller AS .25 .60
146 Pau Gasol AS .40 1.00
147 Steve Smith AS .25 .60
148 Paul Pierce AS .30 .75
149 Derek Fisher AS .25 .60
150 Cuttino Mobley AS .20 .50
151 Dikembe Mutombo AS .30 .75
152 Vince Carter AS .50 1.25
153 Antoine Walker AS .25 .60
154 Allen Iverson AS .50 1.25
155 Michael Jordan AS 2.50 6.00
156 Shaquille O'Neal AS .75 2.00
157 Tim Duncan AS .60 1.50
158 Kevin Garnett AS .50 1.25
159 Kobe Bryant AS 1.25 3.00
160 Shareef Abdur-Rahim AS .25 .60
161 Baron Davis AS .25 .60
162 Jason Kidd AS .50 1.25
163 Tracy McGrady AS .50 1.25
164 Jermaine O'Neal AS .25 .60
165 Elton Brand AS .30 .75
166 Gary Payton AS .30 .75
167 Wally Szczerbiak AS .25 .60
168 Chris Webber AS .30 .75
169 Yao Ming JSY/350 RC 8.00 20.00
170 Fred Jones/350 RC 3.00 8.00
171 Ryan Humphrey RC 3.00 8.00
172 Drew Gooden Hat/300 RC 4.00 10.00
173 Nikoloz Tskitishvili RC 2.50 6.00
174 Caron Butler Shorts/350 RC 4.00 10.00
175 Vincent Yarbrough RC 2.50 6.00
176 DaJuan Wagner RC 3.00 8.00
177 Nene Hilario RC 4.00 10.00
178 Qyntel Woods/350 RC 3.00 8.00
179 Jared Jeffries RC 3.00 8.00
180 Casey Jacobsen RC 3.00 8.00
181 Marcus Haislip Hat/300 RC 3.00 8.00
182 Kareem Rush/350 RC 3.00 8.00
183 Predrag Savovic RC 3.00 8.00
184 Melvin Ely RC 3.00 8.00
185 Amare Stoudemire RC 5.00 12.00
186 John Salmons RC 4.00 10.00
187 Chris Jefferies RC 2.50 6.00
188 Juan Dixon RC 4.00 10.00
189 Carlos Boozer RC 4.00 10.00
190 Roger Mason/350 RC 3.00 8.00
191 Ronald Murray/350 RC 4.00 10.00
192 Tayshaun Prince RC 5.00 12.00
193 Chris Wilcox/350 RC 3.00 8.00
194 Sam Clancy RC 3.00 8.00
195 Dan Gadzuric RC 3.00 8.00
196 D.Dickau RC/Carter JSY 4.00 10.00
197 F.Williams RC/Carter JSY 4.00 10.00
198 Dunleavy RC/VC JSY/350 5.00 12.00
199 J.Will RC/Carter JSY/350 5.00 12.00
200 Borchardt RC/VC JSY/350 4.00 10.00
201 Giricek RC/Carter JSY/350 4.00 10.00
202 Pat Burke RC 1.50 4.00
203 Reggie Evans RC 2.50 6.00
204 Rasual Butler RC 2.50 6.00
205 Jiri Welsch RC 2.00 5.00
206 Mehmet Okur RC 2.50 6.00
207 Jannero Pargo RC 1.50 4.00

2002-03 Fleer Hot Shots Hot Hands

*STARS: 3X TO 8X BASE CARD HI
PRINT RUN 199 SERIAL #'d SETS
*RCs 168-201: .5X TO 1.25X BASE CARD HI
*RCs 202-207: .75X TO 2X BASE HI
169-207 PRINT RUN 99 SER.#'d SETS
CARDS DO NOT CONTAIN MEMORABILIA

2002-03 Fleer Hot Shots Rookie Hats Off

*HATS OFF: .4X TO 1X BASE RC HI
CARDS CONTAIN HAT UNLESS NOTED
SKIP NUMBERED SET
PRINT RUN 150 SETS UNLESS NOTED

2002-03 Fleer Hot Shots All-Stars Triple Game-Used

Randomly seeded in packs, this 10-card set features three players on each card front. A small head shot is present on the right side of the card while square swatches of game used memorabilia appear on the left. Each card is sequentially numbered to 25.

STATED PRINT RUN 25 SER.#'d SETS
1 Carter/T-Mac/Iverson 50.00 120.00
2 Kidd/Pierce/Davis 50.00 100.00
3 Pierce/Stojakovic/Allen 20.00 50.00
4 Gasol/J-Rich/Turkoglu 20.00 50.00
5 J.O'Neal/Mtmbo/A-Rahim 20.00 50.00
6 Szczb/Miller/Gasol 20.00 50.00
7 Brand/Garnett/Webber 75.00 150.00
8 Miles/Johnson/Kirilenko 20.00 50.00
9 Payton/Kidd/Nash 40.00 100.00
10 J-Rich/Mason/Francis 20.00 50.00

2002-03 Fleer Hot Shots En Fuego

Seeded in packs at the rate of one in 12, this 12-card set showcases a horizontal design with player photos set against a fire background. All cards are highlighted with silver foil.

COMPLETE SET (12) 6.00 15.00
STATED ODDS 1:12
EF1 Elton Brand .60 1.50
EF2 Allen Iverson 1.00 2.50
EF3 Tracy McGrady 1.00 2.50
EF4 Jason Richardson .60 1.50
EF5 Vince Carter 1.00 2.50
EF6 Karl Malone .75 2.00
EF7 Stephon Marbury .50 1.25
EF8 Shareef Abdur-Rahim .50 1.25
EF9 Steve Francis .50 1.25
EF10 Kenyon Martin .50 1.25
EF11 Shaquille O'Neal 1.50 4.00
EF12 Tim Duncan 1.25 3.00

2002-03 Fleer Hot Shots En Fuego Game-Used

Randomly seeded in packs, this 10-card set parallels the base En Fuego insert set enhanced with bronze foil highlights and a square swatch of game used memorabilia. A Gold version was issued as well and is sequentially numbered to 50.

RANDOM INSERTS IN PACKS
*GOLD: .5X TO 1.25X GAME USED HI
GOLD PRINT RUN 150 SER.#'d SETS
AI Allen Iverson 5.00 12.00
EB Elton Brand Shorts 3.00 8.00
JR Jason Richardson 3.00 8.00
KM Karl Malone 4.00 10.00
KM Kenyon Martin Shorts 2.50 6.00
SA Shareef Abdur-Rahim 2.50 6.00
SF Steve Francis 2.50 6.00
SM Stephon Marbury 2.50 6.00
TM Tracy McGrady 5.00 12.00
VC Vince Carter 5.00 12.00

2002-03 Fleer Hot Shots Give and Go Game-Used

STATED PRINT RUN 50 SER.#'d SETS
101 Terry Jkt/G.Robinson Jkt 8.00 20.00
102 Delk Jsy/Pierce Jsy 10.00 25.00
103 Rose Jsy/Fizer Pants 8.00 20.00
104 Miles Jsy/R.Davis Jsy 8.00 20.00
105 Nash Jsy/Nowitzki Jsy 12.50 30.00
106 Satterfield Jsy/Howard Jsy 8.00 20.00
107 Hamilton Shirt/Wallace Jsy 8.00 20.00
108 Arenas Jkt/Jamison Pants 8.00 20.00
109 Norris Jsy/Mobley Jkt 8.00 20.00
110 Tinsley Jsy/R.Miller Jsy 10.00 25.00
111 A.Miller Jsy/Odom Jacket 8.00 20.00
113 J.Williams Jsy/Battier Jsy 8.00 20.00
114 Best Jsy/E.Jones Jsy 8.00 20.00
115 Cassell Shirt/R.Allen Shirt 10.00 25.00
116 T.Brandn Jsy/Szczerb Jsy 8.00 20.00
117 Kittles Jkt/R.Jeffrsn Shrts 8.00 20.00
118 Wesley Jsy/Mashburn Jsy 8.00 20.00
119 Spree Shrts/McDyes Jsy 8.00 20.00
120 Armstrong Jsy/M.Miller Jsy 8.00 20.00
121 Snow Jkt/Van Horn Pants 8.00 20.00
122 Marbury Jsy/Marion Jsy 8.00 20.00
123 D-Stoud Jkt/R.Wallce Shrt 8.00 20.00
124 Bibby Jsy/Webber Jsy 10.00 25.00
125 Parker Jsy/D.Robinson Jsy 12.50 30.00
126 K.Andersn Jsy/R.Lewis Jsy 8.00 20.00
127 A.Williams Shirt/V.Carter Jsy 8.00 20.00
128 Stockton Jsy/Malone Jkt 12.50 30.00

2002-03 Fleer Hot Shots Hot Numbers

Randomly inserted in packs at the rate of one in 20, this 20-card set utilizes a horizontal card design with a small player photo centered and a number statistic on the right side of the card. Each card is highlighted with silver foil.

COMPLETE SET (20) 15.00 40.00
STATED ODDS 1:20
STATED PRINT RUN 350 SER.#'d SETS
HN1 Vince Carter 1.25 3.00
HN2 Gary Payton .75 2.00
HN3 Jason Kidd 1.25 3.00
HN4 Kevin Garnett 1.25 3.00
HN5 Pau Gasol 1.00 2.50
HN6 Darius Miles .50 1.25
HN7 Richard Jefferson .75 2.00
HN8 Corey Maggette .60 1.50
HN9 Kwame Brown .50 1.25

HN10 Antoine Walker .60 1.50
HN11 Shane Battier .75 2.00
HN12 Eddie Jones .60 1.50
HN13 Shawn Marion .60 1.50
HN14 Mike Bibby .75 2.00
HN15 Grant Hill 1.00 2.50
HN16 John Stockton 1.00 2.50
HN17 Lamar Odom .60 1.50
HN18 Keith Van Horn .60 1.50
HN19 Kobe Bryant 3.00 8.00
HN20 Michael Jordan 8.00 20.00

2002-03 Fleer Hot Shots Hot Numbers Game-Used

Randomly inserted in packs, this five card set parallels the base Hot Numbers set enhanced with a swatch of game used memorabilia and sequential numbering to 50.

STATED PRINT RUN 50 SER.#'d SETS
DM Darius Miles 3.00 8.00
JK Jason Kidd 8.00 20.00
KB Kwame Brown 3.00 8.00
KG Kevin Garnett 8.00 20.00
VC Vince Carter 12.00 30.00

2002-03 Fleer Hot Shots Hot Shots Inserts

Randomly inserted in packs at the rate of one in eight, this 12-card set features top draft picks on a vertical card design with the words "Hot Shots" along the top where the word "hot" is printed in gold. Player portrait shots are placed in front of a red background where the top and bottom of the card are white.

COMPLETE SET (12) 10.00 25.00
STATED ODDS 1:8
1 Juan Dixon .75 2.00
2 Yao Ming 1.50 4.00
3 Caron Butler .75 2.00
4 Kareem Rush .60 1.50
5 Nene Hilario .75 2.00
6 Jay Williams .75 2.00
7 Jared Jeffries .60 1.50
8 Amare Stoudemire 1.00 2.50
9 Carlos Boozer .75 2.00
10 Drew Gooden .75 2.00
11 DaJuan Wagner .60 1.50
12 Mike Dunleavy .75 2.00

2002-03 Fleer Hot Shots Hot Shots Inserts Game-Used

Randomly seeded in packs, this 10-card set parallels the base Hot Shots insert card enhanced with a swatch of game used memorabilia. A Gold version sequentially numbered to 150 was also inserted in packs.

SWATCHES ARE SHIRT UNLESS NOTED
RANDOM INSERTS IN PACKS
*GOLD: .75X TO 2X GAME USED HI
GOLD PRINT RUN 150 SER.#'d SETS
AS Amare Stoudemire 3.00 8.00
CB Caron Butler 2.50 6.00
CB Carlos Boozer 2.50 6.00
DG Drew Gooden 2.50 6.00
DW Dajuan Wagner 2.00 5.00
JD Juan Dixon 2.50 6.00
JJ Jared Jeffries 2.00 5.00
KR Kareem Rush 2.00 5.00
NH Nene Hilario 2.50 6.00
YM Yao Ming Jsy 5.00 12.00

2002-03 Fleer Hot Shots Net Burners

Randomly inserted in packs at the rate of one in 24, this 10-card set features a black border along the bottom and a white border along the top. Full color player photos are set against a burned net background, and cards are highlighted with silver foil.

COMPLETE SET (10) 8.00 20.00
STATED ODDS 1:24
NB1 Ray Allen 1.00 2.50
NB2 Peja Stojakovic 1.00 2.50
NB3 Reggie Miller 1.00 2.50
NB4 Dirk Nowitzki 1.50 4.00
NB5 Paul Pierce 1.00 2.50
NB6 Baron Davis .75 2.00
NB7 Steve Nash 1.25 3.00
NB8 Latrell Sprewell .75 2.00
NB9 Jermaine O'Neal .75 2.00
NB10 David Robinson 1.50 4.00

2002-03 Fleer Hot Shots Net Burners Game-Used

Seeded in packs, this five card set parallels the design of the base Net Burners insert enhanced with a swatch of game used memorabilia and sequential numbering to 100.

STATED PRINT RUN 100 SER.#'d SETS
BW Ben Wallace JSY 4.00 10.00
CB Caron Butler Shorts 5.00 12.00
DN Dirk Nowitzki JSY 8.00 20.00
JS Jerry Stackhouse JSY 4.00 10.00
PP Paul Pierce JSY 5.00 12.00

2002-03 Fleer Hot Shots Net Burners Gold

STATED PRINT RUN 105 SER.#'d SETS
1 Michael Finley 3.00 8.00
2 Ben Wallace 2.50 6.00
3 Jerry Stackhouse 2.50 6.00
4 Antawn Jamison 3.00 8.00
5 Jay Williams 3.00 8.00
6 Yao Ming 6.00 15.00
7 Drew Gooden 3.00 8.00
8 Amare Stoudemire 4.00 10.00
9 Caron Butler 3.00 8.00
10 Mike Dunleavy 3.00 8.00

2000-01 Fleer Legacy

The 2000-01 Fleer Legacy product released in June, 2001 and featured a 115-card base set that was broken into tiers as follows: 90 Base Veterans (1-90), and 25 Rookies; 12 of which include swatches of game-used jersey. Please note that each rookie card is serial numbered to 799. Each pack contained 5 cards, and a suggested retail price of $175 per box. Also note that this hobby exclusive product contained one Autographed Replica Jersey per box.

COMP.SET w/o SP's (90) 20.00 50.00
91-115 PRINT RUN 799 SERIAL #'d SETS
1 Vince Carter .75 2.00
2 Tim Duncan .75 2.00
3 Darrell Armstrong .25 .60
4 Chauncey Billups .40 1.00
5 Shawn Kemp .40 1.00
6 Stephon Marbury .30 .75
7 Dan Majerle .40 1.00
8 Antawn Jamison .40 1.00
9 Hakeem Olajuwon .50 1.25
10 Kobe Bryant 1.50 4.00
11 Paul Pierce .40 1.00
12 Patrick Ewing .50 1.25
13 Steve Francis .30 .75
14 Latrell Sprewell .30 .75
15 Andre Miller .30 .75
16 Gary Payton .40 1.00
17 Michael Finley .40 1.00
18 Brian Grant .25 .60
19 Scottie Pippen .60 1.50
20 Antonio Davis .25 .60
21 Jason Williams .40 1.00
22 Chris Gatling .25 .60
23 David Robinson .60 1.50
24 John Stockton .50 1.25
25 Matt Harpring .25 .60
26 Rashard Lewis .40 1.00
27 Dirk Nowitzki .60 1.50
28 Alan Henderson .25 .60
29 Rasheed Wallace .40 1.00
30 Ben Wallace .30 .75
31 Chris Webber .40 1.00
32 Elton Brand .40 1.00
33 Anfernee Hardaway .60 1.50
34 Isaiah Rider .30 .75
35 Baron Davis .40 1.00
36 Eric Snow .25 .60
37 Tom Gugliotta .25 .60
38 Grant Hill .50 1.25
39 Lamar Odom .30 .75
40 Kevin Garnett .60 1.50
41 Reggie Miller .40 1.00
42 Karl Malone .50 1.25
43 Ray Allen .40 1.00
44 Derek Anderson .25 .60
45 Glen Rice .30 .75
46 Antonio McDyess .30 .75
47 Eddie Jones .40 1.00
48 Mitch Richmond .30 .75
49 Mark Jackson .30 .75
50 Larry Johnson .40 1.00
51 Ron Mercer .25 .60
52 Jason Kidd .60 1.50
53 Voshon Lenard .25 .60
54 Rick Fox .25 .60
55 Rod Strickland .25 .60
56 Jalen Rose .30 .75
57 Tracy McGrady .60 1.50
58 Dikembe Mutombo .40 1.00
59 Richard Hamilton .30 .75
60 Jerry Stackhouse .30 .75
61 Peja Stojakovic .40 1.00
62 Sam Cassell .30 .75
63 Sean Elliott .40 1.00
64 Keith Van Horn .30 .75
65 Mike Bibby .40 1.00
66 Larry Hughes .30 .75
67 Nick Van Exel .30 .75
68 Michael Dickerson .25 .60
69 Terrell Brandon .25 .60
70 Chucky Atkins .25 .60
71 John Starks .30 .75
72 Glenn Robinson .30 .75
73 Cuttino Mobley .25 .60
74 Shaquille O'Neal 1.00 2.50
75 Shareef Abdur-Rahim .30 .75
76 Danny Fortson .25 .60
77 Austin Croshere .25 .60
78 Jamal Mashburn .30 .75
79 Kenny Anderson .30 .75
80 Shawn Marion .30 .75
81 Travis Best .25 .60
82 Derrick Coleman .30 .75
83 Toni Kukoc .40 1.00
84 Allen Iverson .75 2.00
85 Allan Houston .30 .75
86 Antoine Walker .30 .75
87 Wally Szczerbiak .30 .75
88 Raef LaFrentz .25 .60
89 Tim Hardaway .40 1.00
90 Juwan Howard .30 .75
91 Kenyon Martin JSY RC 8.00 20.00
92 Stromile Swift RC 2.00 5.00
93 Darius Miles JSY RC 3.00 8.00
94 Mike Miller JSY RC 5.00 12.00
95 Marcus Fizer RC 2.00 5.00
96 Jerome Moiso JSY RC 2.00 5.00
97 DerMarr Johnson JSY RC 2.50 6.00
98 Q.Richardson JSY RC 3.00 8.00
99 Morris Peterson JSY RC 3.00 8.00
100 Jamaal Magloire RC 2.00 5.00
101 Mateen Cleaves RC 1.50 4.00
102 Hedo Turkoglu RC 3.00 8.00
103 Chris Mihm JSY RC 2.50 6.00
104 Courtney Alexander RC 1.50 4.00
105 Joel Przybilla RC 1.50 4.00
106 Speedy Claxton JSY RC 3.00 8.00
107 Keyon Dooling JSY RC 3.00 8.00
108 Desmond Mason JSY RC 4.00 10.00
109 Jamal Crawford RC 5.00 12.00
110 DeShawn Stevenson RC 2.00 5.00
111 Stephen Jackson RC 3.00 8.00
112 Marc Jackson RC 1.50 4.00
113 Hanno Mottola JSY RC 2.00 5.00
114 Eduardo Najera RC 2.00 5.00
115 Wang Zhizhi RC 4.00 10.00
WUSA1 Vince Carter/600 30.00 80.00

2000-01 Fleer Legacy Ultimate Legacy

*STARS: 2.5X TO 6X BASE
*RCs: .6X TO 1.5X BASE
*JSY RCs: .4X TO 1X BASE
STATED PRINT RUN 175 SERIAL #'d SETS

2000-01 Fleer Legacy Ball Of Fame

Randomly inserted into packs at one in 40, this 20-card set features a swatch of actual game-used basketball. Card backs carry a "BF" prefix.

STATED ODDS 1:40
BF1 Vince Carter 6.00 15.00
BF2 Kenyon Martin 8.00 20.00
BF3 Jason Williams 3.00 8.00
BF4 Ray Allen 3.00 8.00
BF5 Lamar Odom 2.50 6.00
BF6 Allen Iverson 6.00 15.00
BF7 Stephon Marbury 2.50 6.00
BF8 Tracy McGrady 5.00 12.00
BF9 Darius Miles 3.00 8.00
BF10 Steve Francis 2.50 6.00
BF11 Stromile Swift 3.00 8.00
BF12 Shawn Marion 2.50 6.00
BF13 Shawn Kemp 3.00 8.00
BF14 Larry Hughes 2.50 6.00
BF15 Baron Davis 3.00 8.00
BF16 Jalen Rose 2.50 6.00
BF17 Patrick Ewing 4.00 10.00
BF18 Karl Malone 4.00 10.00
BF19 Marcus Fizer 3.00 8.00
BF20 Wally Szczerbiak 2.50 6.00

2000-01 Fleer Legacy Floor Generals

Randomly inserted into packs at one in 18, this 20-card set features a swatch of actual game-used floor. Card backs carry an "FG" prefix.

STATED ODDS 1:18
FG1 Vince Carter 5.00 12.00
FG2 Allen Iverson 6.00 15.00
FG3 Chris Webber 2.50 6.00
FG4 Shaquille O'Neal 6.00 15.00
FG5 Reggie Miller 2.50 6.00
FG6 Tracy McGrady 4.00 10.00
FG7 David Robinson 4.00 10.00
FG8 Jason Kidd 4.00 10.00
FG9 Latrell Sprewell 2.00 5.00
FG10 Eddie Jones 2.50 6.00
FG11 Michael Finley 2.50 6.00
FG12 Jerry Stackhouse 2.00 5.00
FG13 Karl Malone 3.00 8.00
FG14 Anfernee Hardaway 4.00 10.00
FG15 Gary Payton 2.50 6.00
FG16 Shareef Abdur-Rahim 2.00 5.00
FG17 Tim Hardaway 2.50 6.00
FG18 Ray Allen 2.50 6.00
FG19 Stephon Marbury 2.00 5.00
FG20 John Stockton 3.00 8.00

2000-01 Fleer Legacy NBA Game Issue

Randomly inserted into packs at one in 15, this 30-card set features a swatch of actual game-used jersey. Card backs carry a "GI" prefix.

STATED ODDS 1:15
GI1 Vince Carter 5.00 12.00
GI2 Baron Davis 2.50 6.00
GI3 Trajan Langdon 2.00 5.00
GI4 Grant Hill 3.00 8.00
GI5 Allen Iverson 5.00 12.00
GI6 Jason Kidd 4.00 10.00
GI7 Karl Malone 3.00 8.00
GI8 Stephon Marbury 2.00 5.00
GI9 Shawn Marion 2.00 5.00
GI10 Tracy McGrady 4.00 10.00
GI11 Andre Miller 2.00 5.00
GI12 Dikembe Mutombo 2.50 6.00
GI13 Lamar Odom 2.00 5.00
GI14 Shaquille O'Neal 6.00 15.00
GI15 Gary Payton 2.50 6.00
GI16 Jason Terry 2.50 6.00
GI17 John Stockton 3.00 8.00
GI18 Patrick Ewing 3.00 8.00
GI19 Anfernee Hardaway 4.00 10.00
GI20 Jason Williams 2.50 6.00
GI21 Darius Miles 2.50 6.00
GI22 Chris Mihm 2.00 5.00
GI23 Desmond Mason 3.00 8.00
GI24 Keyon Dooling 2.50 6.00
GI25 DerMarr Johnson 2.00 5.00
GI26 Speedy Claxton 2.50 6.00
GI27 Kenyon Martin 6.00 15.00
GI28 Hanno Mottola 1.50 4.00
GI29 Mike Miller 4.00 10.00
GI30 Quentin Richardson 2.50 6.00

2000-01 Fleer Legacy Replica Jersey Autographs

Randomly inserted at one per box (box-topper), this 32-jersey set features autographed replica jerseys of some of the hottest players in the NBA. Please note that a few of the jerseys packed out as exchange cards, and must be redeemed to Fleer no longer than 6/01/02.

STATED ODDS ONE PER BOX
JERSEY ARJ29 DOES NOT EXIST
ARJ1 A.Mourning Black/250 75.00 150.00
ARJ2 A.Walker Green/250 25.00 60.00
ARJ3 C.Alexander Blue/375 20.00 50.00
ARJ4 D.Miles Red/300 20.00 50.00
ARJ5 D.Johnson Red/400 20.00 50.00
ARJ6 D.Mason Red/350 20.00 50.00
ARJ7 D.Mutombo Black/150 50.00 120.00
ARJ8 E.House Black/325 20.00 50.00
ARJ9 E.Jones Black/150 30.00 80.00
ARJ11 J.Crawford Black/400 25.00 60.00
ARJ12 J.Terry Red/500 20.00 50.00
ARJ13 K.Van Horn Black/100 25.00 60.00
ARJ14 K.Martin Blue/300 25.00 60.00
ARJ14A K.Martin Black/250 30.00 80.00
ARJ16 L.Hughes Black/250 20.00 50.00
ARJ17 M.Jackson Black/500 20.00 50.00
ARJ18 M.Camby Blue/400 25.00 60.00
ARJ19 M.Fizer Red/300 20.00 50.00
ARJ19A M.Fizer Black/100 25.00 60.00
ARJ20 M.Cleaves Blue/400 20.00 50.00
ARJ20A M.Cleaves Red/350 20.00 50.00
ARJ21 M.Bibby Black/250 20.00 50.00
ARJ22 P.Pierce Green/500 30.00 80.00
ARJ23 P.Stojakovic Black/150 30.00 80.00
ARJ23A P.Stojakovic Purple/150 30.00 80.00
ARJ24 R.LaFrentz Black/400 20.00 50.00
ARJ25 R.Artest Red/200 30.00 80.00
ARJ26 S.Marion Purple/400 25.00 60.00
ARJ28 S.Francis Blue/400 20.00 50.00
ARJ30 T.Gugliotta Purple/400 20.00 50.00
ARJ31 V.Carter Black/750 50.00 120.00
ARJ31A V.Carter White/250 75.00 150.00
ARJ32 W.Szczerbiak Blue/400 20.00 50.00
ARJ32A W.Szczerbiak Black/200 20.00 50.00

2001-02 Fleer Marquee

Released in early April 2002, Fleer Marquee breaks down into a 126-card set with 100 veteran player cards and 26 rookie cards. Card number 126, Mengke Bateer was a last minute addition to the set, so on press material, boxes and packs, Marquee is referred to as a 125-card set. The rookie breakdown is as follows: Card numbers 101-115 are sequentially numbered to 1500, card number 116-125 are sequentially numbered to 2500, and number 126 is sequentially numbered to 1500. Also included in packs was a limited Vince Carter NNO autographed card sequentially numbered to 113. Base cards feature an embossed gray-scale basketball texture along the bottom of the card with a silver foil Marquee logo in the left hand corner, and the player's name in the right. Full color action photos are centered with a solid white border and a fade to white edges on the left and right. Rookie cards are white on both the top and the bottom fading into the same embossed silver basketball texturing found on the veteran cards. Player action photos are set against an oval with runs directly through the center of the card. Each Hobby box contained a jumbo box-topper pack of one Feature Presentation card. See those sets for descriptions.

COMPLETE SET w/o SPs 12.50 30.00
101-115 PRINT RUN 1500 SER.#'d SETS
116-125 PRINT RUN 2500 SER.#'d SETS
1 DerMarr Johnson .20 .50
2 Darius Miles .20 .50
3 Michael Jordan 5.00 12.00
4 Speedy Claxton .20 .50
5 Stromile Swift .20 .50
6 Michael Finley .30 .75
7 Kurt Thomas .20 .50
8 Tim Duncan .60 1.50
9 Kenyon Martin .30 .75
10 Jermaine O'Neal .25 .60
11 Elton Brand .30 .75
12 Jamal Mashburn .25 .60
13 Jumaine Jones .20 .50
14 Stephon Marbury .25 .60
15 Eddie Jones .25 .60
16 Antonio McDyess .25 .60
17 Tim Thomas .20 .50
18 Gary Payton .30 .75
19 Latrell Sprewell .25 .60
20 Grant Hill .40 1.00
21 Jason Terry .30 .75
22 Marcus Fizer .20 .50
23 Anthony Mason .20 .50
24 Bonzi Wells .20 .50
25 Sam Cassell .25 .60
26 Jerry Stackhouse .25 .60
27 Hedo Turkoglu .25 .60
28 Morris Peterson .20 .50
29 John Stockton .40 1.00
30 Dikembe Mutombo .30 .75
31 Mitch Richmond .25 .60
32 Andre Miller .25 .60
33 Joe Smith .25 .60
34 Mike Bibby .30 .75
35 Wally Szczerbiak .25 .60
36 Steve Francis .25 .60
37 Nazr Mohammed .20 .50
38 Antoine Walker .25 .60
39 Courtney Alexander .20 .50
40 Shawn Marion .25 .60
41 Jason Williams .25 .60
42 Steve Nash .50 1.25
43 Antonio Davis .20 .50
44 Steve Smith .25 .60
45 Jason Kidd .50 1.25
46 Reggie Miller .30 .75
47 Quentin Richardson .25 .60
48 Baron Davis .30 .75
49 Juwan Howard .25 .60
50 Rasheed Wallace .30 .75
51 Brian Grant .20 .50
52 Nick Van Exel .25 .60
53 Donyell Marshall .20 .50
54 Vin Baker .25 .60
55 Allan Houston .25 .60
56 Mike Miller .25 .60
57 Shaquille O'Neal .75 2.00
58 Ron Mercer .20 .50
59 Lindsey Hunter .20 .50
60 Peja Stojakovic .30 .75
61 Ray Allen .30 .75
62 Antawn Jamison .30 .75
63 Theo Ratliff .20 .50
64 Vince Carter .50 1.25
65 DeShawn Stevenson .20 .50
66 Allen Iverson .60 1.50
67 Derek Fisher .25 .60
68 Dirk Nowitzki .50 1.25
69 Keith Van Horn .25 .60
70 David Robinson .50 1.25
71 Terrell Brandon .20 .50
72 Cuttino Mobley .20 .50
73 Shareef Abdur-Rahim .25 .60
74 Paul Pierce .30 .75
75 Elden Campbell .20 .50
76 Anfernee Hardaway .50 1.25
77 Alonzo Mourning .40 1.00
78 Raef LaFrentz .20 .50
79 Richard Hamilton .25 .60
80 Rashard Lewis .30 .75
81 Marcus Camby .25 .60
82 Jalen Rose .25 .60
83 Lamar Odom .25 .60
84 David Wesley .20 .50
85 James Posey .20 .50
86 Derek Anderson .20 .50
87 Glenn Robinson .25 .60
88 Clifford Robinson .20 .50
89 Kerry Kittles .20 .50
90 Hakeem Olajuwon .40 1.00
91 Patrick Ewing .40 1.00
92 Tracy McGrady .50 1.25
93 Kobe Bryant 1.25 3.00
94 Chris Mihm .20 .50
95 Lorenzen Wright .20 .50
96 Chris Webber .30 .75
97 Kevin Garnett .50 1.25
98 Larry Hughes .25 .60
99 Keyon Dooling .20 .50
100 Karl Malone .40 1.00
101 Joe Johnson RC 1.00 2.50
102 Tyson Chandler RC 1.25 3.00
103 Eddy Curry RC .75 2.00
104 Jason Richardson RC 1.00 2.50
105 Troy Murphy RC .75 2.00
106 Eddie Griffin RC .60 1.50
107 Jamaal Tinsley RC .75 2.00
108 Pau Gasol RC 2.50 6.00
109 Shane Battier RC 1.50 4.00
110 Richard Jefferson RC 1.25 3.00
111 Steven Hunter RC .60 1.50
112 Tony Parker RC 3.00 8.00
113 Vladimir Radmanovic RC .75 2.00
114 Andrei Kirilenko RC 1.25 3.00
115 Kwame Brown RC .75 2.00
116 S.Dalembrt RC/D.Brown RC .75 2.00
117 J.Forte RC/Ke.Brown RC .50 1.25
118 Randolph RC/R.Boumtje RC 1.25 3.00
119 O.Torres RC/T.Morris RC .75 2.00
120 A.Ford RC/K.Satterfield RC .75 2.00
121 R.White RC/Z.Rebraca RC .75 2.00
122 T.Hassell RC/E.Watson RC .75 2.00
123 D.Diop RC/P.Brezec RC .75 2.00
124 E.Brown RC/G.Wallace RC 1.00 2.50
125 L.Woods RC/B.Haywood RC .75 2.00
126 Mengke Bateer RC .75 2.00
NNO Vince Carter AU/113 25.00 60.00

2001-02 Fleer Marquee Banner Season

Randomly inserted in packs at the rate of one in 20, this 20-card set places full color player photos against an American flag and a fade to solid color bottom of the card where the color is set to match the featured player's unifor colors. The player's name and "Banner Season" appear in silver foil with the player's team name across the bottom in white.

COMPLETE SET (20) 30.00 80.00
STATED ODDS 1:20
1 Vince Carter 2.00 5.00
2 Shaquille O'Neal 3.00 8.00
3 Allen Iverson 2.50 6.00
4 Kevin Garnett 2.00 5.00
5 Dirk Nowitzki 2.00 5.00
6 Tim Duncan 2.50 6.00
7 Michael Jordan 10.00 25.00
8 Steve Francis 1.00 2.50
9 Grant Hill 1.50 4.00
10 Kobe Bryant 5.00 12.00
11 Kenyon Martin 1.25 3.00
12 Shareef Abdur-Rahim 1.00 2.50
13 Ray Allen 1.25 3.00
14 Tracy McGrady 2.00 5.00
15 Baron Davis 1.25 3.00
16 Chris Webber 1.25 3.00
17 Jason Kidd 2.00 5.00
18 Darius Miles .75 2.00
19 Paul Pierce 1.25 3.00
20 Karl Malone 1.50 4.00

2001-02 Fleer Marquee Banner Season Memorabilia

STATED ODDS 1:15
AI Allen Iverson 6.00 15.00
BD Baron Davis 3.00 8.00
CW Chris Webber 3.00 8.00
DM Darius Miles 2.00 5.00
DN Dirk Nowitzki 5.00 12.00
GH Grant Hill 4.00 10.00
JK Jason Kidd 5.00 12.00
KM Kenyon Martin 3.00 8.00
MM Karl Malone 4.00 10.00
PP Paul Pierce 3.00 8.00
RA Ray Allen 3.00 8.00
SF Steve Francis 2.50 6.00
SR Shareef Abdur-Rahim 2.50 6.00
TM Tracy McGrady 5.00 12.00
VC Vince Carter 5.00 12.00

2001-02 Fleer Marquee Co-Stars

Randomly seeded in packs at the rate of one in 10, this 10-card set features a die cut design where the upper right hand corner and the lower left hand corner are rounded. Veteran player portraits appear on the right side of the card, and a rookie teammate action photo appears on the left. These two photos are split apart by a strip down the middle that contains both player names and the words, "Co-Stars" in silver foil.

STATED ODDS 1:10
1 M.Jordan/K.Brown 3.00 8.00
2 S.Francis/E.Griffin 1.00 2.50
3 T.McGrady/S.Hunter 1.25 3.00
4 K.Malone/A.Kirilenko 1.25 3.00
5 R.Miller/J.Tinsley 1.00 2.50
6 T.Parker/D.Robinson 2.50 6.00
7 S.Battier/P.Gasol 2.00 5.00
8 J.Kidd/R.Jefferson 1.25 3.00
9 A.Jamison/J.Richardson 1.00 2.50
10 R.Mercer/E.Curry 1.00 2.50

2001-02 Fleer Marquee Feature Presentation Film

Randomly inserted as a box-topper, this jumbo card features a player photo along the top, silver highlights and a single-slide from an actual game film. Each card is sequentially numbered to 350. A Vince Carter autographed version was also inserted with this set, and is sequentially numbered to 208.

PRINT RUN 350 SER.#'d SETS
1 Vince Carter 4.00 10.00
1A Vince Carter AU/208 25.00 50.00
2 Darius Miles 1.50 4.00
3 Jason Kidd 4.00 10.00
4 Grant Hill 3.00 8.00
5 Chris Webber 2.50 6.00
6 Dirk Nowitzki 4.00 10.00
7 Allen Iverson 5.00 12.00
8 Tracy McGrady 4.00 10.00
9 Steve Francis 2.00 5.00
10 Karl Malone 3.00 8.00
12 Kevin Garnett 4.00 10.00
13 Kobe Bryant 10.00 25.00
14 Tim Duncan 5.00 12.00
15 Shaquille O'Neal 6.00 15.00

2001-02 Fleer Marquee Feature Presentation Film/Jerseys

Randomly seeded as a box-topper, this 10-card set parallels the design of the base Feature Presentation Film set enhanced with a large swatch of game used memorabilia. Each card is sequentailly numbered to 250.

*FILM/JSY: 1X TO 2.5X BASE HI 4.00 10.00
PRINT RUN 250 SER.#'d SETS

2001-02 Fleer Marquee Feature Presentation Triples

Randomly seeded as a box-topper, this 10-card set parallels the design of the base Feature Presentation Film set enhanced with three different game film slides. Each card is sequentailly numbered to 100.

PRINT RUN 100 SER.#'d SETS
4 Grant Hill 8.00 20.00
5 Chris Webber 12.00 30.00

2001-02 Fleer Marquee We're Number One

Randomly seeded in packs at the rate of one in 240, this 11-card set features die-cut cards in the shape of the number one. The outside of the card is highlighted with silver ink, player photos are centered on top of a strip printed to look like a basketball, and the set name, Marquee logo, and player's name appears centered on the bottom in silver hologfoil.

STATED ODDS 1:240
1 Hakeem Olajuwon 3.00 8.00
2 David Robinson 5.00 12.00
3 Shaquille O'Neal 6.00 15.00
4 Chris Webber 2.50 6.00
5 Allen Iverson 6.00 15.00
6 Tim Duncan 5.00 12.00
7 Elton Brand 2.50 6.00
8 Kenyon Martin 2.50 6.00
9 Kwame Brown 2.50 6.00
10 Vince Carter 4.00 10.00
11 Larry Bird 6.00 15.00

2001-02 Fleer Marquee We're Number One Memorabilia

Randomly inserted in packs at the rate of one in 32, this eight card set parallels the design of the We're Number One set enhanced with a swatch of game-used memorabilia.

STATED ODDS 1:32
1 Hakeem Olajuwon 6.00 15.00
2 David Robinson 8.00 20.00
3 Allen Iverson 10.00 25.00
4 Elton Brand 5.00 12.00
5 Kenyon Martin 5.00 12.00
6 Kwame Brown 5.00 12.00
6A Kwame Brown AU/101 10.00 25.00
7 Vince Carter 8.00 20.00
7A Vince Carter AU/4 25.00 60.00
8 Larry Bird 12.00 30.00
8A Larry Bird AU/78 60.00 150.00

2001-02 Fleer Maximum

This 220 card set was issued in 15 card packs and released in March, 2002. The first 180 cards of the set featured veteran players while the final 40 cards of the set honored the leading NBA rookies. Those Rookie Cards had a stated print run of 1000 cards. A Vince Carter autograph card with a stated print run of 375 is noted at the end of these listings but is not considered part of the complete set.

COMPLETE SET (220) 75.00 150.00
COMP.SET w/o SP's (180) 12.50 30.00
181-220 PRINT RUN 1000 SERIAL #'d SETS
1 Ray Allen .25 .60
2 Elton Brand .25 .60
3 Grant Hill .30 .75
4 Tracy McGrady .40 1.00
5 Chris Webber .25 .60
6 Latrell Sprewell .20 .50
7 Paul Pierce .25 .60
8 Jason Kidd .40 1.00
9 Shaquille O'Neal .60 1.50
10 Stephon Marbury .20 .50
11 Steve Francis .20 .50
12 Vince Carter .40 1.00
13 Allen Iverson .50 1.25
14 Kevin Garnett .40 1.00
15 Eddie Jones .20 .50
16 Antoine Walker .20 .50
17 Kobe Bryant 1.00 2.50
18 Avery Johnson .20 .50
19 Damon Stoudamire .20 .50
20 Kurt Thomas .15 .40
21 Aaron McKie .15 .40
22 Chris Whitney .15 .40
23 David Robinson .40 1.00
24 Erick Dampier .15 .40
25 Jumaine Jones .15 .40
26 Radoslav Nesterovic .15 .40
27 Robert Horry .20 .50
28 Ben Wallace .20 .50
29 Christian Laettner .20 .50
30 Eddie Robinson .15 .40
31 Alvin Williams .15 .40
32 Matt Harpring .15 .40
33 Terrell Brandon .15 .40
34 Tim Duncan .50 1.25
35 Bonzi Wells .15 .40
36 Clarence Weatherspoon .15 .40
37 George McCloud .15 .40
38 Jermaine O'Neal .20 .50
39 Al Harrington .20 .50
40 Antawn Jamison .25 .60
41 John Amaechi .15 .40
42 Rod Strickland .15 .40
43 Stacey Augmon .15 .40
44 Dion Glover .15 .40
45 Michael Dickerson .15 .40
46 Anfernee Hardaway .40 1.00
47 Rashard Lewis .25 .60
48 Shawn Bradley .15 .40
49 Todd MacCulloch .15 .40
50 Antonio McDyess .20 .50
51 Darrell Armstrong .15 .40
52 Jalen Rose .20 .50
53 Mike Bibby .25 .60
54 P.J. Brown .15 .40
55 Quincy Lewis .15 .40
56 Doug Christie .15 .40
57 Elden Campbell .15 .40
58 James Posey .15 .40
59 Karl Malone .30 .75
60 Patrick Ewing .30 .75
61 Sam Cassell .20 .50
62 Baron Davis .25 .60
63 Corey Maggette .20 .50
64 Donyell Marshall .15 .40
65 Ervin Johnson .15 .40
66 Horace Grant .20 .50
67 Nick Van Exel .20 .50
68 Vlade Divac .20 .50
69 Allan Houston .20 .50
70 Antonio Davis .15 .40
71 Dale Davis .15 .40
72 Eduardo Najera .15 .40
73 Kenny Anderson .20 .50
74 Kevin Willis .15 .40
75 LaPhonso Ellis .20 .50
76 Anthony Mason .15 .40
77 Greg Ostertag .15 .40
78 Jamal Mashburn .20 .50
79 Jeff McInnis .15 .40
80 Peja Stojakovic .25 .60
81 Scott Williams .15 .40
82 Bryon Russell .15 .40
83 Chucky Atkins .15 .40
84 Darius Miles .15 .40
85 David Wesley .15 .40
86 Hedo Turkoglu .20 .50
87 Mark Pope .15 .40
88 Dana Barros .15 .40
89 Glenn Robinson .20 .50
90 John Stockton .30 .75
91 Lamar Odom .20 .50
92 Mike Miller .20 .50
93 Ron Artest .25 .60
94 Adonal Foyle .15 .40
95 Andre Miller .20 .50
96 Eric Snow .15 .40
97 Stanislav Medvedenko .15 .40
98 Steve Smith .20 .50
99 Wally Szczerbiak .20 .50
100 Chris Mihm .15 .40
101 Danny Fortson .15 .40
102 Dikembe Mutombo .25 .60
103 Joe Smith .20 .50
104 Lindsey Hunter .15 .40
105 Malik Rose .15 .40
106 Austin Croshere .15 .40
107 Chris Gatling .15 .40
108 Hakeem Olajuwon .30 .75
109 Mark Jackson .20 .50
110 Milt Palacio .15 .40
111 Ruben Patterson .15 .40
112 Steve Nash .40 1.00
113 Brian Grant .15 .40
114 Dirk Nowitzki .40 1.00
115 Jeff Foster .15 .40
116 Morris Peterson .15 .40
117 Scottie Pippen .40 1.00
118 Lamond Murray .15 .40
119 Larry Hughes .20 .50
120 Shareef Abdur-Rahim .20 .50
121 Tony Delk .15 .40
122 Vin Baker .20 .50
123 Art Long .15 .40
124 Kenyon Martin .25 .60
125 Michael Finley .25 .60
126 Stromile Swift .15 .40
127 Toni Kukoc .25 .60
128 Alonzo Mourning .30 .75
129 Charlie Ward .15 .40
130 Eric Williams .15 .40
131 Jerome Williams .15 .40
132 Raef LaFrentz .15 .40
133 Rasheed Wallace .25 .60
134 Reggie Miller .25 .60
135 Cuttino Mobley .15 .40
136 Desmond Mason .20 .50
137 Jason Williams .20 .50
138 Keith Van Horn .20 .50
139 Nazr Mohammed .15 .40
140 Shawn Marion .20 .50
141 Tim Hardaway .25 .60
142 Anthony Carter .15 .40
143 Danny Manning .20 .50
144 Derek Anderson .15 .40
145 Jason Terry .25 .60
146 Kenny Thomas .15 .40
147 Othella Harrington .15 .40
148 Corliss Williamson .15 .40
149 Derek Fisher .20 .50
150 Ricky Davis .20 .50
151 Stephen Jackson .20 .50
152 Tryone Nesby .15 .40
153 Calvin Booth .15 .40
154 Emanual Davis .15 .40
155 Kerry Kittles .15 .40
156 Marc Jackson .15 .40
157 Samaki Walker .15 .40
158 Tom Gugliotta .15 .40
159 Wesley Person .15 .40
160 Antonio Daniels .15 .40
161 Charles Oakley .20 .50
162 Chauncey Billups .25 .60
163 Derrick Coleman .20 .50
164 Jerry Stackhouse .20 .50
165 Michael Jordan 4.00 10.00
166 Quentin Richardson .20 .50
167 Gary Payton .25 .60
168 Iakovos Tsakalidis .15 .40
169 Juwan Howard .20 .50
170 Lorenzen Wright .15 .40
171 Marcus Camby .20 .50
172 Maurice Taylor .15 .40
173 Jacque Vaughn .15 .40
174 Bruce Bowen .15 .40
175 Clifford Robinson .15 .40
176 Michael Olowokandi .15 .40
177 Richard Hamilton .20 .50
178 Ron Mercer .15 .40
179 Speedy Claxton .15 .40
180 Tim Thomas .15 .40
181 Joe Johnson HW RC 1.25 3.00
182 Pau Gasol HW RC 3.00 8.00
183 Kwame Brown HW RC 1.00 2.50
184 Zach Randolph HW RC 1.50 4.00
185 Jason Richardson HW RC 1.25 3.00
186 Jamaal Tinsley HW RC 1.00 2.50
187 Oscar Torres HW RC 1.00 2.50
188 Rodney White HW RC .60 1.50
189 Kedrick Brown HW RC .60 1.50
190 Tony Parker HW RC 4.00 10.00
191 Samuel Dalembert HW RC 1.00 2.50
192 Shane Battier HW RC 2.00 5.00
193 Loren Woods HW RC .60 1.50
194 Richard Jefferson HW RC 1.50 4.00
195 Jeff Trepagnier HW RC .60 1.50
196 Terence Morris HW RC 1.00 2.50
197 Eddie Griffin TC RC .75 2.00
198 Primoz Brezec TC RC 1.00 2.50
199 V.Radmanovic TC RC 1.00 2.50
200 Gerald Wallace TC RC 1.25 3.00
201 Alton Ford TC RC 1.00 2.50
202 Steven Hunter TC RC .75 2.00
203 Michael Bradley TC RC .60 1.50
204 Brandon Armstrong TC RC .60 1.50
205 Jamaal Tinsley TC RC 1.00 2.50
206 Bobby Simmons TC RC 1.00 2.50
207 Zeljko Rebraca TC RC 1.00 2.50
208 Tony Parker TC RC 4.00 10.00
209 Troy Murphy TC RC 1.00 2.50
210 Kwame Brown TC RC 1.00 2.50
211 Andrei Kirilenko TC RC 1.50 4.00
212 Trenton Hassell TC RC .75 2.00
213 Pau Gasol TC RC 3.00 8.00
214 Tang Hamilton TC RC 1.00 2.50
215 Joseph Forte TC RC .60 1.50
216 Eddy Curry TC RC 1.00 2.50
217 DeSagana Diop TC RC .75 2.00
218 Joe Johnson TC RC 1.25 3.00
219 Tyson Chandler TC RC 1.50 4.00
220 Jason Collins TC RC .75 2.00
NNO Vince Carter AU/375 10.00 25.00

2001-02 Fleer Maximum Big Shots

Issued in packs at stated odds of one in eight, this 15 card set honors players who are known for not being afraid to take the final shot in a game.

COMPLETE SET (15) 8.00 20.00
STATED ODDS 1:8
1 Grant Hill .75 2.00
2 Ray Allen .60 1.50
3 Allen Iverson 1.25 3.00
4 Elton Brand .60 1.50
5 Baron Davis .60 1.50
6 Jason Terry .60 1.50
7 Mike Bibby .60 1.50
8 David Robinson 1.00 2.50
9 Paul Pierce .60 1.50
10 Dirk Nowitzki 1.00 2.50
11 Jerry Stackhouse .50 1.25
12 Shawn Marion .50 1.25
13 Tracy McGrady 1.00 2.50
14 Anfernee Hardaway 1.00 2.50
15 Vince Carter 1.00 2.50

2001-02 Fleer Maximum Big Shots Jerseys

STATED ODDS 1:20
1 Grant Hill 4.00 10.00
2 Allen Iverson 6.00 15.00
3 Elton Brand 3.00 8.00
4 Jason Terry 3.00 8.00
5 Mike Bibby 3.00 8.00
6 David Robinson 5.00 12.00
7 Paul Pierce 3.00 8.00
8 Shawn Marion 2.50 6.00
9 Tracy McGrady 5.00 12.00
10 Anfernee Hardaway 5.00 12.00
11 Vince Carter 5.00 12.00

2001-02 Fleer Maximum Floor Score

Issued at stated odds of one in eight, this 15-card set honors some of the NBA's leading scorers.

COMPLETE SET (15) 12.50 30.00
STATED ODDS 1:8
1 Jason Kidd 1.00 2.50
2 Lamar Odom .50 1.25
3 Baron Davis .60 1.50
4 Dirk Nowitzki 1.00 2.50
5 Ray Allen .60 1.50
6 Anfernee Hardaway 1.00 2.50
7 Latrell Sprewell .50 1.25
8 Chris Webber .60 1.50
9 Grant Hill .75 2.00
10 Vince Carter 1.00 2.50
11 Shaquille O'Neal 1.50 4.00
12 Michael Jordan 5.00 12.00
13 Kobe Bryant 2.50 6.00
14 Kevin Garnett 1.00 2.50
15 Tim Duncan 1.25 3.00

2001-02 Fleer Maximum Floor Score Court

STATED ODDS 1:40
1 Jason Kidd 5.00 12.00
2 Lamar Odom 2.50 6.00
3 Baron Davis 3.00 8.00
4 Dirk Nowitzki 5.00 12.00
5 Ray Allen 3.00 8.00
6 Anfernee Hardaway 5.00 12.00
7 Latrell Sprewell 2.50 6.00

8 Chris Webber 3.00 8.00
9 Grant Hill 4.00 10.00
10 Vince Carter 5.00 12.00

2001-02 Fleer Maximum Performance

Randomly inserted into packs, these 10 cards feature players known for the full effort each night on the court. These cards were printed to a stated print run of 100 serial numbered sets.

STATED PRINT RUN 100 SER.#'d SETS
1 Vince Carter 8.00 20.00
2 Tracy McGrady 8.00 20.00
3 Kobe Bryant 20.00 50.00
4 Michael Jordan 40.00 100.00
5 Shaquille O'Neal 12.00 30.00
6 Allen Iverson 10.00 25.00
7 Grant Hill 6.00 15.00
8 Kevin Garnett 8.00 20.00
9 Steve Francis 4.00 10.00
10 Tim Duncan 10.00 25.00

2001-02 Fleer Maximum Power

Issued at stated odds of one in 16, these 15 cards feature players known for their powerful perfomances on the court.

COMPLETE SET (15) 15.00 40.00
STATED ODDS 1:16
1 Kobe Bryant 4.00 10.00
2 Michael Jordan 8.00 20.00
3 Shaquille O'Neal 2.50 6.00
4 Kevin Garnett 1.50 4.00
5 Tim Duncan 2.00 5.00
6 Jason Kidd 1.50 4.00
7 Richard Hamilton .75 2.00
8 Vince Carter 1.50 4.00
9 Alonzo Mourning 1.25 3.00
10 John Stockton 1.25 3.00
11 Elton Brand 1.00 2.50
12 Steve Francis .75 2.00
13 Keith Van Horn .75 2.00
14 Stephon Marbury .75 2.00
15 Darius Miles .60 1.50

2001-02 Fleer Maximum Power Warm-Ups

Inserted at stated odds of one in 20, these 10 cards are a partial parallel to the Power insert set. These cards feature a swatch of the warm up uniforms worn by the featured player. A gold version was also produced with cards sequentially numbered to 25.

STATED ODDS 1:20
*GOLD: 2X TO 5X BASE HI
GOLD PRINT RUN 25 SER.#'d SETS
1 Jason Kidd 5.00 12.00
2 Richard Hamilton 2.50 6.00
3 Vince Carter 5.00 12.00
4 Alonzo Mourning 4.00 10.00
5 John Stockton 4.00 10.00
6 Elton Brand 3.00 8.00
7 Steve Francis 2.50 6.00
8 Keith Van Horn 2.50 6.00
9 Stephon Marbury 2.50 6.00
10 Darius Miles 2.00 5.00

2001-02 Fleer Maximum Two Point Shot Jersey/Floor

Randomly inserted into packs, these eight cards feature both a game-worn uniform swatch and a piece of a game-used floor. These cards have a stated print run of 25 serial numbered sets and are not priced due to market scarcity.

STATED PRINT RUN 25 SERIAL #'d SETS
1 Vince Carter 30.00 80.00
2 Elton Brand 20.00 50.00
3 Steve Francis 15.00 40.00
4 Jason Kidd 30.00 80.00
5 Allen Iverson 40.00 100.00
6 Tracy McGrady 30.00 80.00
7 Darius Miles 12.00 30.00
8 Paul Pierce 20.00 50.00

2007 Fleer Michael Jordan

COMPLETE SET (100) 25.00 60.00
COMMON CARD (1-100) .40 1.00

2007 Fleer Michael Jordan Award Winners

COMPLETE SET (20) 3.00 8.00
COMMON CARD .40 1.00

2007 Fleer Michael Jordan Playoff Highlights

COMPLETE SET (30) 6.00 15.00
COMMON CARD .40 1.00

2007 Fleer Michael Jordan Season Achievements

COMPLETE SET (50) 12.50 30.00
COMMON CARD .40 1.00

1999-00 Fleer Mystique

The 1999-00 Fleer Mystique product was released in April,2000 as a 150-card set. The set features 100 player cards, 40 rookie cards, and 10 superstar cards. The 40-card rookie subset is serial numbered to 2999, while the superstar subset is serial numbered to 2500. Each pack contained 5-cards and carried a suggested retail price of 4.99.

COMPLETE SET (150) 75.00 150.00
COMPLETE SET w/o SP (100) 15.00 30.00
101-140 PRINT RUN 2999 SERIAL #'d SETS
141-150 PRINT RUN 2500 SERIAL #'d SETS
UNPRICED MASTER PRINT RUN ONE SET
1 Allen Iverson .75 2.00
2 Grant Hill .50 1.25
3 Antawn Jamison .40 1.00
4 Glenn Robinson .30 .75
5 Kenny Anderson .30 .75
6 Dikembe Mutombo .40 1.00
7 Gary Trent .25 .60
8 Brevin Knight .25 .60
9 Chucky Brown .25 .60
10 Derek Anderson .25 .60
11 Ricky Davis .40 1.00
12 Chris Webber .40 1.00
13 Jalen Rose .30 .75
14 Antoine Walker .40 1.00
15 Michael Dickerson .25 .60
16 Tim Hardaway .40 1.00
17 Toni Kukoc .40 1.00
18 Raef LaFrentz .30 .75
19 Anthony Mason .25 .60
20 John Stockton .50 1.25
21 Hakeem Olajuwon .50 1.25
22 Shaquille O'Neal 1.00 2.50
23 Scottie Pippen .60 1.50
24 Maurice Taylor .25 .60
25 Tariq Abdul-Wahad .25 .60
26 Tracy McGrady .60 1.50
27 Joe Smith .30 .75
28 Rod Strickland .25 .60
29 Ruben Patterson .25 .60
30 Tom Gugliotta .25 .60
31 Ray Allen .40 1.00
32 Elden Campbell .25 .60
33 Lindsey Hunter .25 .60
34 Larry Johnson .40 1.00
35 Michael Olowokandi .25 .60
36 Mario Elie .25 .60
37 Anfernee Hardaway .60 1.50
38 Juwan Howard .30 .75
39 Karl Malone .50 1.25
40 Alonzo Mourning .50 1.25
41 Billy Owens .25 .60
42 Mitch Richmond .40 1.00
43 Darrell Armstrong .25 .60
44 Jason Williams .50 1.25
45 Mookie Blaylock .25 .60
46 Gary Payton .40 1.00
47 Brian Grant .25 .60
48 Paul Pierce .50 1.25
49 Michael Finley .40 1.00
50 Reggie Miller .40 1.00
51 Corliss Williamson .25 .60
52 Shandon Anderson .25 .60
53 Stephon Marbury .30 .75
54 Sam Cassell .30 .75
55 Bryon Russell .25 .60
56 Rasheed Wallace .40 1.00
57 Jayson Williams .25 .60
58 Damon Stoudamire .30 .75
59 Terrell Brandon .25 .60
60 Loy Vaught .25 .60
61 Kobe Bryant 1.50 4.00
62 Vlade Divac .40 1.00
63 Derek Fisher .40 1.00
64 Isaiah Rider .30 .75
65 Eddie Jones .40 1.00
66 Kevin Garnett .60 1.50
67 David Robinson .60 1.50
68 Marcus Camby .30 .75
69 Glen Rice .40 1.00
70 Mike Bibby .40 1.00
71 Patrick Ewing .50 1.25
72 Robert Traylor .25 .60
73 Tim Duncan .75 2.00
74 Michael Doleac .25 .60
75 Steve Smith .30 .75
76 Allan Houston .30 .75
77 Jamal Mashburn .30 .75
78 Brent Barry .30 .75
79 Charles Barkley .60 1.50
80 Ron Mercer .30 .75
81 Jerry Stackhouse .40 1.00
82 Keith Van Horn .30 .75
83 Hersey Hawkins .25 .60
84 Avery Johnson .30 .75
85 Cedric Ceballos .25 .60
86 P.J. Brown .25 .60
87 Doug Christie .30 .75
88 Shawn Kemp .40 1.00
89 Dirk Nowitzki .75 2.00
90 Erick Dampier .25 .60
91 Antonio McDyess .30 .75
92 Mark Jackson .30 .75
93 Clifford Robinson .25 .60
94 Vince Carter .75 2.00
95 Shareef Abdur-Rahim .30 .75
96 Vin Baker .30 .75
97 Larry Hughes .30 .75
98 Jason Kidd .60 1.50
99 Kerry Kittles .25 .60
100 Latrell Sprewell .40 1.00
101 Lamar Odom RC 2.00 5.00
102 Elton Brand RC 2.00 5.00
103 Baron Davis RC 2.00 5.00
104 Jason Terry RC 1.25 3.00
105 Corey Maggette RC 1.25 3.00
106 Wally Szczerbiak RC 1.50 4.00
107 Richard Hamilton RC 1.50 4.00
108 Milt Palacio RC .75 2.00
109 Ron Artest RC 1.50 4.00
110 Eddie Robinson RC .75 2.00
111 Jumaine Jones RC .60 1.50
112 Andre Miller RC 1.50 4.00
113 Chucky Atkins RC .75 2.00
114 Kenny Thomas RC .75 2.00
115 Scott Padgett RC .60 1.50
116 Devean George RC .75 2.00
117 Tim Young RC .75 2.00
118 Tim James RC .50 1.25
119 Quincy Lewis RC .50 1.25
120 James Posey RC .75 2.00
121 Shawn Marion RC 1.50 4.00
122 A.Radojevic RC .50 1.25
123 Trajan Langdon RC .75 2.00
124 Laron Profit RC .60 1.50
125 Jonathan Bender RC .75 2.00
126 William Avery RC .60 1.50
127 Cal Bowdler RC .50 1.25
128 Dion Glover RC .60 1.50
129 Jeff Foster RC .75 2.00
130 Steve Francis RC 2.00 5.00
131 Adrian Griffin RC .75 2.00
132 Vonteego Cummings RC .50 1.25
133 Rafer Alston RC 1.00 2.50
134 Michael Ruffin RC .60 1.50
135 Chris Herren RC .60 1.50
136 Jermaine Jackson RC .75 2.00
137 Lazaro Borrell RC .75 2.00
138 Obinna Ekezie RC .60 1.50
139 Rick Hughes RC .75 2.00
140 Todd MacCulloch RC .75 2.00
141 Kobe Bryant STAR 5.00 12.00
142 Vince Carter STAR 2.50 6.00
143 Tim Duncan STAR 2.50 6.00
144 Kevin Garnett STAR 2.00 5.00
145 Allen Iverson STAR 2.50 6.00
146 Keith Van Horn STAR 1.00 2.50
147 Grant Hill STAR 1.50 4.00
148 Stephon Marbury STAR 1.00 2.50
149 Antoine Walker STAR 1.25 3.00
150 Shaquille O'Neal STAR 3.00 8.00

1999-00 Fleer Mystique Gold

*GOLD: 1.25X TO 3X BASE CARD HI
GOLD: STATED ODDS 1:4

1999-00 Fleer Mystique Feel the Game

Randomly inserted in packs at one in 120, this insert set features 11 superstars with swatches of their game-used jerseys. Card backs are not numbered, thus the cards are listed below alphabetically.

STATED ODDS 1:120
1 Vince Carter 10.00 25.00
2 Brian Grant 3.00 8.00
3 Raef LaFrentz 4.00 10.00
4 Karl Malone 6.00 15.00
5 Alonzo Mourning 6.00 15.00
6 Shaquille O'Neal 10.00 25.00
7 Gary Payton 5.00 12.00
8 David Robinson 8.00 20.00
9 Glenn Robinson 4.00 10.00
10 Joe Smith 4.00 10.00
11 John Stockton 6.00 15.00

1999-00 Fleer Mystique Fresh Ink

Randomly inserted in packs at one in 40, this insert set features autographed cards of 43 NBA players. The cards are not numbered and listed below alphabetically.

STATED ODDS 1:40
1 Ray Allen 10.00 25.00
2 Ron Artest 6.00 15.00
3 William Avery 2.50 6.00
4 Jonathan Bender 3.00 8.00
5 Mike Bibby 5.00 12.00
6 Cal Bowdler 2.00 5.00
7 Vince Carter 12.00 30.00
8 John Celestand 2.00 5.00
9 Vonteego Cummings 2.00 5.00
10 Baron Davis 6.00 15.00
11 Michael Dickerson 3.00 8.00
12 Michael Doleac 3.00 8.00
13 Evan Eschmeyer 2.50 6.00
14 Michael Finley 6.00 15.00
15 Steve Francis 8.00 20.00
16 Pat Garrity 3.00 8.00
17 Dion Glover 2.50 6.00
18 Brian Grant 3.00 8.00
19 Richard Hamilton 6.00 15.00
20 Tim Hardaway 8.00 20.00
21 Jumaine Jones 2.50 6.00
22 Shawn Kemp 25.00 60.00
23 Raef LaFrentz 3.00 8.00
24 Quincy Lewis 2.00 5.00
25 Stephon Marbury 5.00 12.00
26 Antonio McDyess 3.00 8.00
27 Andre Miller 4.00 10.00
28 Cuttino Mobley 3.00 8.00
29 Alonzo Mourning 25.00 60.00
30 Shaquille O'Neal 50.00 125.00
31 Lamar Odom 10.00 25.00
32 Hakeem Olajuwon 15.00 40.00
33 Michael Olowokandi 3.00 8.00
34 James Posey 3.00 8.00
35 Aleksandar Radojevic 2.00 5.00
36 Kenny Thomas 3.00 8.00
37 Robert Traylor 3.00 8.00
38 Keith Van Horn 5.00 12.00

1999-00 Fleer Mystique Point Perfect

Randomly inserted in packs, this 10-card insert features some of the NBA's top point guards. Each card was serial numbered to 1999. Card backs carry a "PP" prefix.

COMPLETE SET (10) 10.00 25.00
STATED PRINT RUN 1999 SERIAL #'d SETS
PP1 Mike Bibby 1.00 2.50
PP2 Stephon Marbury .75 2.00
PP3 Jason Williams 1.25 3.00
PP4 Jason Kidd 1.50 4.00
PP5 William Avery .75 2.00
PP6 Allen Iverson 2.00 5.00
PP7 Andre Miller 2.00 5.00
PP8 Baron Davis 2.50 6.00
PP9 Steve Francis 2.50 6.00
PP10 Jason Terry 1.50 4.00

1999-00 Fleer Mystique Raise the Roof

Randomly inserted in packs, this 10-card insert features some of the most electrifying players in the NBA. Each card was serial numbered to 100. Card backs carry an "RR" prefix.

STATED PRINT RUN 100 SERIAL #'d SETS
RR1 Grant Hill 100.00 250.00
RR2 Keith Van Horn 25.00 60.00
RR3 Tim Duncan 200.00 500.00
RR4 Kobe Bryant 500.00 1000.00
RR5 Vince Carter 200.00 500.00
RR6 Allen Iverson 125.00 300.00
RR7 Kevin Garnett 200.00 500.00
RR8 Shaquille O'Neal 200.00 500.00
RR9 Paul Pierce 100.00 250.00
RR10 Anfernee Hardaway 125.00 300.00

1999-00 Fleer Mystique Slamboree

Randomly inserted in packs, this insert set showcases 10-players that have turned slam dunks into an art form. Each card was serial numbered to 999. Card backs carry a "S" prefix.

COMPLETE SET (10) 12.00 30.00
STATED PRINT RUN 999 SERIAL #'d SETS
S1 Antoine Walker 1.50 4.00
S2 Shareef Abdur-Rahim 1.25 3.00
S3 Antawn Jamison 1.50 4.00
S4 Tracy McGrady 4.00 10.00
S5 Larry Hughes 1.25 3.00
S6 Wally Szczerbiak 3.00 8.00
S7 Corey Maggette 2.50 6.00
S8 Lamar Odom 3.00 8.00
S9 Elton Brand 3.00 8.00
S10 Stephon Marbury 1.25 3.00

2000-01 Fleer Mystique

The 2000-01 Fleer Mystique product was released in October, 2000 and featured a 136-card base set that was broken into tiers as follows: Base Veterans (1-100), and Rookies (101-136) that were serial numbered as follows: 101-106 (numbered to 750), 107-112 (numbered to 1000), 113-118 (numbered to 2000), 119-124 (numbered to 3000), 125-130 (numbered to 4000), and 131-136 (numbered to 5000). Each pack contained five-cards and carried a suggested retail price of $4.99.

COMPLETE SET w/o RC (100) 15.00 30.00
101-106 A: PRINT RUN 750 SERIAL #'d SETS
107-112 B: PRINT RUN 1000 SERIAL #'d SETS
113-117 C: PRINT RUN 2000 SERIAL #'d SETS
118-124 D: PRINT RUN 3000 SERIAL #'d SETS
125-130 E: PRINT RUN 4000 SERIAL #'d SETS
131-136 F: PRINT RUN 5000 SERIAL #'d SETS
1 Shaquille O'Neal .75 2.00
2 Gary Payton .30 .75
3 Nick Van Exel .25 .60
4 Alonzo Mourning .40 1.00
5 Shawn Marion .25 .60
6 Rod Strickland .20 .50
7 Mookie Blaylock .20 .50
8 Terrell Brandon .20 .50
9 Bryon Russell .20 .50
10 Jerry Stackhouse .25 .60
11 Glenn Robinson .25 .60
12 Rasheed Wallace .30 .75
13 Tracy McGrady .50 1.25
14 Raef LaFrentz .20 .50
15 P.J. Brown .20 .50
16 Anfernee Hardaway .50 1.25
17 Mike Bibby .30 .75
18 Elden Campbell .20 .50
19 Steve Francis .25 .60
20 Keith Van Horn .25 .60
21 Karl Malone .40 1.00
22 Dirk Nowitzki .50 1.25
23 Glen Rice .25 .60
24 Tom Gugliotta .20 .50
25 Avery Johnson .25 .60
26 Michael Finley .30 .75
27 Theo Ratliff .20 .50
28 Juwan Howard .25 .60
29 Anthony Carter .20 .50
30 Kobe Bryant 1.25 3.00
31 Toni Kukoc .30 .75
32 Jason Terry .30 .75
33 Elton Brand .30 .75
34 Reggie Miller .30 .75
35 Latrell Sprewell .25 .60
36 Adrian Griffin .20 .50
37 Cuttino Mobley .20 .50
38 Maurice Taylor .20 .50
39 Allen Iverson .60 1.50
40 Tim Duncan .60 1.50
41 Andre Miller .25 .60
42 Antonio Davis .20 .50
43 Howard Eisley .20 .50
44 Vlade Divac .25 .60
45 Brevin Knight .20 .50
46 Lamar Odom .25 .60
47 Ron Mercer .20 .50
48 Jason Williams .30 .75
49 Antawn Jamison .30 .75
50 Wally Szczerbiak .25 .60
51 Chris Webber .30 .75
52 Larry Hughes .25 .60
53 Kevin Garnett .50 1.25
54 Michael Dickerson .20 .50
55 Chucky Atkins .20 .50
56 Jalen Rose .25 .60
57 John Amaechi .20 .50
58 Shareef Abdur-Rahim .25 .60
59 Shawn Kemp .30 .75
60 Derek Anderson .20 .50
61 Darrell Armstrong .20 .50
62 Vin Baker .25 .60
63 Paul Pierce .30 .75
64 Donyell Marshall .20 .50
65 Jamie Feick .20 .50
66 Travis Best .20 .50
67 Baron Davis .30 .75
68 Hakeem Olajuwon .40 1.00
69 Joe Smith .25 .60
70 Ruben Patterson .20 .50
71 Antonio McDyess .25 .60
72 Jamal Mashburn .25 .60
73 Jason Kidd .50 1.25
74 Eddie Jones .30 .75
75 Kenny Thomas .20 .50
76 Marcus Camby .25 .60
77 Doug Christie .20 .50
78 Ron Artest .30 .75
79 Mark Jackson .25 .60
80 Allan Houston .25 .60
81 John Stockton .40 1.00
82 Jerome Williams .20 .50
83 Tim Thomas .20 .50
84 Alan Henderson .20 .50
85 Antoine Walker .25 .60
86 Robert Horry .25 .60
87 Stephon Marbury .25 .60
88 David Robinson .50 1.25
89 Lindsey Hunter .20 .50
90 Richard Hamilton .25 .60
91 Damon Stoudamire .25 .60
92 Dikembe Mutombo .30 .75
93 Anthony Mason .20 .50
94 Austin Croshere .20 .50
95 Patrick Ewing .40 1.00
96 Mitch Richmond .25 .60
97 Grant Hill .40 1.00
98 Ray Allen .30 .75
99 Scottie Pippen .50 1.25
100 Vince Carter .60 1.50
101 Kenyon Martin A RC 6.00 15.00
102 Stromile Swift A RC 2.50 6.00
103 Darius Miles A RC 2.50 6.00
104 Marcus Fizer A RC 2.50 6.00
105 Mike Miller A RC 4.00 10.00
106 DerMarr Johnson A RC 2.00 5.00
107 Chris Mihm B RC 1.50 4.00
108 Jamal Crawford B RC 5.00 12.00
109 Joel Przybilla B RC 1.50 4.00
110 Keyon Dooling B RC 2.00 5.00
111 Jerome Moiso B RC 1.25 3.00
112 Etan Thomas B RC 2.00 5.00
113 Courtney Alexander C RC 1.25 3.00
114 Mateen Cleaves C RC 1.25 3.00
115 Jason Collier C RC 1.50 4.00
116 Hedo Turkoglu C RC 2.50 6.00
117 Desmond Mason C RC 2.00 5.00
118 Quentin Richardson C RC 1.50 4.00
119 Jamaal Magloire D RC 1.00 2.50
120 Speedy Claxton D RC 1.00 2.50
121 Morris Peterson D RC 1.00 2.50
122 Donnell Harvey D RC .75 2.00
123 D.Stevenson D RC 1.00 2.50
124 Mark Karcher D RC .60 1.50
125 Mamadou N'Diaye E RC .40 1.00
126 Erick Barkley E RC .40 1.00
127 Mark Madsen E RC .60 1.50
128 Corey Hightower E RC .60 1.50
129 Dan McClintock E RC .60 1.50
130 Soumaila Samake E RC .40 1.00
131 Hanno Mottola F RC .30 .75
132 Chris Carrawell F RC .50 1.25
133 Olumide Oyedeji F RC .30 .75
134 Michael Redd F RC 1.25 3.00
135 Chris Porter F RC .30 .75
136 Jabari Smith F RC .30 .75

2000-01 Fleer Mystique Gold

COMPLETE SET (136) 125.00 250.00
*STARS: 1.5X TO 4X BASE CARD HI
*RCs: .2X TO .5X BASE HI
STATED ODDS 1:20

2000-01 Fleer Mystique Vince Carter Rookie Remnants

This three-card insert was randomly inserted into 2000-01 Fleer products. The set includes a Vince Carter floor card (numbered to 100), a Vince Carter floor/jersey card (numbered to 15), and finally an autographed Vince Carter floor/jersey card (numbered 1 of 1).

RANDOM INSERTS IN HOBBY PACKS
NNO Vince Carter FLR/100 12.50 30.00
NNO Vince Carter FLR JSY/15 20.00 50.00

2000-01 Fleer Mystique Dial 1

Randomly inserted in packs at one in 10, this 10-card set featurs players who can hit the long shots. Card backs carry a "DO" prefix.

COMPLETE SET (10) 3.00 8.00
STATED ODDS 1:10
DO1 Jason Kidd .75 2.00
DO2 Stephon Marbury .40 1.00
DO3 Allen Iverson 1.00 2.50
DO4 Jason Williams .50 1.25
DO5 Allan Houston .40 1.00
DO6 Eddie Jones .50 1.25
DO7 Ray Allen .50 1.25
DO8 Jalen Rose .40 1.00
DO9 Anfernee Hardaway .75 2.00
DO10 Vince Carter 1.00 2.50

2000-01 Fleer Mystique Film at Eleven

Randomly inserted in packs at one in 40, this 10-card set focuses on players who dominate the late night highlight reels. Card backs carry a "FE" prefix.

COMPLETE SET (10) 25.00 50.00
STATED ODDS 1:40
UNPRICED PARALLEL SERIAL #'d TO 11
FE1 Vince Carter 3.00 8.00
FE2 Kobe Bryant 6.00 15.00
FE3 Allen Iverson 3.00 8.00
FE4 Kevin Garnett 2.50 6.00
FE5 Tim Duncan 3.00 8.00
FE6 Steve Francis 1.25 3.00
FE7 Lamar Odom 1.25 3.00
FE8 Elton Brand 1.50 4.00
FE9 Tracy McGrady 2.50 6.00
FE10 Jason Williams 1.50 4.00

2000-01 Fleer Mystique Middle Men

Randomly inserted in packs at one in 10, this 10-card set focuses on players who are always in the "middle of the action" on the court. Card backs carry a "MM" prefix.

COMPLETE SET (10) 4.00 10.00
STATED ODDS 1:10
MM1 Shaquille O'Neal 1.25 3.00
MM2 Vince Carter 1.00 2.50
MM3 Paul Pierce .50 1.25
MM4 Tim Duncan 1.00 2.50
MM5 Grant Hill .60 1.50
MM6 David Robinson .75 2.00
MM7 Tracy McGrady .75 2.00
MM8 Jason Williams .50 1.25
MM9 Elton Brand .50 1.25
MM10 Lamar Odom .40 1.00

2000-01 Fleer Mystique NBAwesome

Randomly inserted in packs at one in 20, this 10-card set focuses on players who bring the fans out of their seats. Card backs carry a "NA" prefix.

COMPLETE SET (10) 12.50 25.00
STATED ODDS 1:20
NA1 Grant Hill 1.50 4.00
NA2 Steve Francis 1.00 2.50
NA3 Kobe Bryant 5.00 12.00
NA4 Elton Brand 1.25 3.00
NA5 Vince Carter 2.50 6.00
NA6 Lamar Odom 1.00 2.50
NA7 Kevin Garnett 2.00 5.00
NA8 Allen Iverson 2.50 6.00
NA9 Shareef Abdur-Rahim 1.00 2.50
NA10 Shaquille O'Neal 3.00 8.00

2000-01 Fleer Mystique Player of the Week

Randomly inserted in packs at one in five, this 15-card set features players who were voted as Player of the Week during the 1999-00 season. Card backs carry a "PW" prefix.

COMPLETE SET (15) 7.50 15.00
STATED ODDS 1:5
PW1 Sam Cassell .30 .75
PW2 Kevin Garnett .60 1.50
PW3 Vince Carter .75 2.00
PW4 Tim Duncan .75 2.00
PW5 Shaquille O'Neal 1.00 2.50
PW6 Alonzo Mourning .50 1.25
PW7 Jason Kidd .60 1.50
PW8 Chris Webber .40 1.00
PW9 Grant Hill .50 1.25
PW10 Steve Francis .30 .75
PW11 Dikembe Mutombo .40 1.00
PW12 Michael Finley .40 1.00
PW13 Karl Malone .50 1.25
PW14 Jalen Rose .30 .75
PW15 Kobe Bryant 1.50 4.00

2003-04 Fleer Mystique

Released in January 2004, Mystique boasts a 120-card set comprised of 80 veteran player cards and 40 rookie cards sequentially numbered to 999. Base cards have a white and gray background that draws attention to the full-color player action photos and gold foil highlights. Mystique was packaged in 20-pack boxes where packs contained four cards and carried a suggested retail price of $5.99.

COMP.SET w/o SP's (80) 15.00 40.00
81-120 PRINT RUN 999 SER.#'d SETS
1 Eric Williams .20 .50
2 Dirk Nowitzki .50 1.25
3 Jason Richardson .30 .75
4 Corey Maggette .25 .60
5 Troy Hudson .20 .50
6 Tracy McGrady .40 1.00
7 Zach Randolph .25 .60
8 Bobby Jackson .20 .50
9 Dan Gadzuric .20 .50
10 Kevin Garnett .50 1.25
11 Manu Ginobili .40 1.00
12 Andrei Kirilenko .30 .75
13 Richard Hamilton .25 .60
14 Mike Bibby .30 .75
15 Vince Carter .50 1.25
16 Jermaine O'Neal .25 .60
17 Antoine Walker .30 .75
18 Jalen Rose .25 .60
19 Dajuan Wagner .20 .50
20 Nene .25 .60
21 Jamaal Tinsley .20 .50
22 Kobe Bryant 1.25 3.00
23 Shane Battier .25 .60
24 Allan Houston .25 .60
25 Jerry Stackhouse .25 .60
26 Eddie Jones .25 .60
27 Morris Peterson .20 .50
28 Richard Jefferson .25 .60
29 Tony Parker .30 .75
30 Glenn Robinson .25 .60
31 Ron Artest .30 .75
32 Marcus Haislip .20 .50
33 Drew Gooden .25 .60
34 Keith Van Horn .25 .60
35 Shareef Abdur-Rahim .25 .60
36 Michael Redd .30 .75
37 Stephon Marbury .25 .60
38 Tim Duncan .50 1.25
39 Eddie Griffin .20 .50
40 Kwame Brown .20 .50
41 Steve Francis .25 .60
42 Vladimir Radmanovic .20 .50
43 Kenyon Martin .25 .60
44 Eddy Curry .20 .50
45 Nikoloz Tskitishvili .20 .50
46 Shaquille O'Neal .75 2.00
47 Allen Iverson .50 1.25
48 Jason Kidd .50 1.25
49 Ben Wallace .25 .60
50 Caron Butler .25 .60
51 Dan Dickau .20 .50
52 Baron Davis .25 .60
53 Bruce Bowen .20 .50
54 Amare Stoudemire .40 1.00
55 Michael Finley .30 .75
56 Jamal Mashburn .25 .60
57 Pau Gasol .30 .75
58 Shawn Marion .25 .60
59 Rasheed Wallace .30 .75
60 Chris Webber .30 .75
61 Rodney White .20 .50
62 Tayshaun Prince .25 .60
63 Yao Ming .60 1.50
64 Latrell Sprewell .25 .60
65 Aaron McKie .20 .50
66 Bonzi Wells .20 .50
67 HedoTurkoglu .25 .60
68 Ray Allen .30 .75
69 Matt Harpring .20 .50
70 Paul Pierce .30 .75
71 Darius Miles .20 .50
72 Chris Wilcox .20 .50
73 Steve Nash .40 1.00
74 Antawn Jamison .25 .60
75 Juan Dixon .20 .50
76 Peja Stojakovic .30 .75
77 Antonio Davis .20 .50
78 Kenny Thomas .20 .50
79 Elton Brand .30 .75
80 Gilbert Arenas .25 .60
81 Mickael Pietrus RC 1.50 4.00
82 Keith Bogans RC 1.25 3.00
83 Dahntay Jones RC 1.50 4.00
84 Darko Milicic RC 1.50 4.00
85 Torraye Braggs RC 1.25 3.00
86 Troy Bell RC 1.25 3.00
87 Maciej Lampe RC 1.25 3.00
88 Kendrick Perkins RC 1.50 4.00
89 Kirk Hinrich RC 2.00 5.00
90 Jason Kapono RC 1.25 3.00
91 Udonis Haslem RC 1.50 4.00
92 James Lang RC 1.25 3.00
93 Willie Green RC 1.25 3.00
94 Travis Outlaw RC 1.50 4.00
95 Nick Collison RC 1.50 4.00
96 Jarvis Hayes RC 1.25 3.00
97 Boris Diaw RC 2.00 5.00
98 Chris Bosh RC 3.00 8.00
99 LeBron James RC 60.00 150.00
100 Zarko Cabarkapa RC 1.25 3.00
101 Travis Hansen RC 1.25 3.00
102 James Jones RC 1.25 3.00
103 Aleksandar Pavlovic RC 1.50 4.00
104 Luke Walton RC 2.00 5.00
105 Maurice Williams RC 2.00 5.00
106 Linton Johnson RC 1.25 3.00
107 David West RC 2.00 5.00
108 Carmelo Anthony RC 6.00 15.00
109 T.J. Ford RC 1.50 4.00
110 Ndudi Ebi RC 1.25 3.00
111 Reece Gaines RC 1.25 3.00
112 Leandro Barbosa RC 2.00 5.00
113 Luke Ridnour RC 1.50 4.00
114 Brian Cook RC 1.25 3.00
115 Marcus Banks RC 1.25 3.00
116 Josh Howard RC 2.00 5.00
117 Chris Kaman RC 2.00 5.00
118 Zoran Planinic RC 1.25 3.00
119 Dwyane Wade RC 6.00 15.00
120 Mike Sweetney RC 1.25 3.00

2003-04 Fleer Mystique Die Cut

*81-120 DC SINGLES: .5X TO 1.25X BASE HI
DIE CUT PRINT RUN 600 SER.#'d SETS

2003-04 Fleer Mystique Gold

*1-80 SINGLES: 2.5X TO 6X BASE HI
1-80 PRINT RUN 150 SER.#'d SETS
*81-120 RCs: 1X TO 2.5X BASE HI
81-120 RC PRINT RUN 50 SER.#'d SETS
99 LeBron James 125.00 250.00

2003-04 Fleer Mystique Awe Pairs

Inserted in packs, this 20-card set pairs players from the same team on a horizontal card design that includes full color player portrait photos. Each card is squentially numbered to 500. Gold versions were also issued and are sequentially numbered to the total number of victories the featured players' total wins from the 2002-03 season..

PRINT RUN 500 SER.#'d SETS
*GOLD SINGLES/25-40: 1.5X TO 4X BASE HI
*GOLD SINGLES/40-60: 1.25X TO 3X HI COL.
GOLD #'d TO TEAM VICTORIES IN 2002-03
1 S.Battier/P.Gasol 1.00 2.50
2 S.Marion/A.Stoudemire 1.25 3.00
3 P.Pierce/M.Banks 1.00 2.50
4 J.Rose/E.Curry .75 2.00
5 D.Wagner/L.James 25.00 60.00
6 K.Garnett/T.Hudson 1.50 4.00
7 T.Prince/B.Wallace .75 2.00
8 Nene/C.Anthony 3.00 8.00
9 K.Bryant/S.O'Neal 4.00 10.00
10 D.Gooden/T.McGrady 1.25 3.00
11 A.Iverson/A.McKie 1.50 4.00
12 C.Butler/D.Wade 3.00 8.00
13 Y.Ming/S.Francis 2.00 5.00
14 E.Brand/C.Kaman 1.00 2.50
15 A.Houston/M.Sweetney .75 2.00
16 P.Stojakovic/C.Webber 1.00 2.50
17 J.O'Neal/R.Artest 1.00 2.50
18 T.Duncan/T.Parker 1.50 4.00
19 V.Carter/C.Bosh 1.50 4.00
20 M.Dunleavy/J.Richardson 1.00 2.50

2003-04 Fleer Mystique Awe Pairs Dual Jerseys

Randomly inserted in packs, this 17-card set parallels the design of the Awe Pairs set enhanced with a jersey swatch from each player and sequential numbering to 350. Several of the rookie players have Event Worn memorabilia on their cards rather than game worn memorabilia. Versions sequentially numbered to 250 and 35 were also produced.

PRINT RUN 350 SER.#'d SETS
*JSY/250 SINGLES: .5X TO 1.25X HI COL.
*JSY/35 SINGLES: 2X TO 5X HI COL.
JSY 35 PRINT RUN 35 SER.#'d SETS
AHMS Houston/Sweetney 4.00 10.00
AIAM A.Iverson/A.McKie 5.00 12.00
CBDW C.Butler/D.Wade 8.00 20.00
DGTM D.Gooden/T.McGrady 4.00 10.00
EBCK E.Brand/C.Kaman 4.00 10.00
JONRA J.O'Neal/R.Artest 4.00 10.00
JREC J.Rose/E.Curry 4.00 10.00
KGTH K.Garnett/T.Hudson 5.00 12.00
MDJR M.Dunleavy/J-Rich 4.00 10.00
PPMB P.Pierce/M.Banks 4.00 10.00
PSCW P.Stojakovic/C.Webber 5.00 12.00
SBPG S.Battier/P.Gasol 4.00 10.00
SMAS S.Marion/Amare 5.00 12.00
TDTP T.Duncan/T.Parker 6.00 15.00
TPBW T.Prince/B.Wallace 4.00 10.00
VCCB V.Carter/C.Bosh 6.00 15.00
YMSF Y.Ming/S.Francis 6.00 15.00

2003-04 Fleer Mystique Ink Appeal

Randomly seeded in packs, this 10-card set utilizes a horizontal design with a player portrait centered towards the top of the card and a cut signature embedded in the bottom. Each card has red foil highlights and is sequentially numbered. Print runs are listed below. A sequentially numbered gold version was also issued, and these cards are not priced due to scarcity.

PRINT RUNS LISTED BELOW
CA Carmelo Anthony/225 25.00 60.00
DW Dwyane Wade/150 20.00 50.00
JH Josh Howard/100 6.00 15.00
JK Jason Kapono/200 6.00 15.00
LR Luke Ridnour/100 6.00 15.00
MP Mickael Pietrus/150 6.00 15.00
VC Vince Carter/250 12.50 30.00
DWG Dajuan Wagner/125 6.00 15.00

2003-04 Fleer Mystique Ink Appeal Gold

PRINT RUNS LISTED BELOW
MOST NOT PRICED DUE TO SCARCITY
CA Carmelo Anthony/15 50.00 125.00
VC Vince Carter/15 20.00 50.00

2003-04 Fleer Mystique Rare Finds

Randomly inserted in packs, this 10-card set is horizontally designed, places three players across the card left to right and is sequentially numbered to 500.

COMPLETE SET (10) 12.50 30.00
PRINT RUN 500 SER.#'d SETS
1 Bryant/Garnett/Amare 3.00 8.00
2 Ginobili/Peja/Kirilenko 2.00 5.00
3 Parker/Francis/Payton 2.00 5.00
4 K-Mart/Kidd/Jefferson 2.00 5.00
5 Nowitzki/Nash/Finley 2.00 5.00
6 McGrady/Iverson/Pierce 2.00 5.00
7 Duncan/Ming/Shaq 5.00 12.00
8 Vince/Stack/Jamison 2.00 5.00
9 Rose/Webber/Howard 2.00 5.00
10 Hamilton/Butler/Allen 2.00 5.00

2003-04 Fleer Mystique Rare Finds 50

This five-card set uses a similar design to the base rare finds set and cards are sequentially numbered to 50. A version numbered to 10 was also inserted in packs.

PRINT RUN 50 SER.#'d SETS
RARE/10 NOT PRICED DUE TO SCARCITY
AS Amare Stoudemire 12.50 30.00
CA Carmelo Anthony 25.00 60.00
DG Drew Gooden 5.00 12.00
TP Tayshaun Prince 5.00 12.00
VC Vince Carter 20.00 40.00

2003-04 Fleer Mystique Rare Finds Jerseys

Randomly seeded in packs, this 20-card set utilizes the same design as the Rare Finds 50 set enhanced with game worn jersey swatches and sequential numbering to 300. A version numbered to 30 was also inserted in packs.

PRINT RUN 300 SER.#'d SETS
*JERSEY 30: 1X TO 2.5X HI COL.
RFAI Allen Iverson 4.00 10.00
RFAS Amare Stoudemire 3.00 8.00
RFCB Caron Butler 2.00 5.00
RFCW Chris Webber 2.50 6.00
RFDN Dirk Nowitzki 4.00 10.00
RFJK Jason Kidd 4.00 10.00
RFJS Jerry Stackhouse 2.00 5.00
RFKG Kevin Garnett 4.00 10.00
RFMF Michael Finley 2.50 6.00
RFPP Paul Pierce 2.50 6.00
RFPS Peja Stojakovic 2.50 6.00
RFSN Steve Nash 3.00 8.00
RFSO Shaquille O'Neal 6.00 15.00
RFST Steve Francis 2.00 5.00
RFTD Tim Duncan 4.00 10.00
RFTM Tracy McGrady 3.00 8.00
RFTP Tony Parker 2.50 6.00
RFVC Vince Carter 4.00 10.00
RTKM Kenyon Martin 2.00 5.00
RTYM Yao Ming 5.00 12.00

2003-04 Fleer Mystique Rare Finds Jerseys Dual

Inserted in packs, this 15-card set parallels the design of the base Rare Finds insert set with two players enhanced with a jersey swatch from each player and sequential numbering to 250. A version numbered to 25 was issued as well.

PRINT RUN 250 SER.#'d SETS
*DUAL 25: 1.25X TO 3X BASE HI
CWJH C.Webber/J.Howard 6.00 15.00
DNMF D.Nowitzki/M.Finley 6.00 15.00
DNSN D.Nowitzki/S.Nash 6.00 15.00
KGAS K.Garnett/Amare 6.00 15.00
KMJK K-Mart/J.Kidd 6.00 15.00
PSAK Stojakovic/Kirilenko 6.00 15.00
SFGP S.Francis/G.Payton 6.00 15.00
TDSO T.Duncan/S.O'Neal 8.00 20.00
TDYM T.Duncan/Y.Ming 8.00 20.00
TMAI T.McGrady/A.Iverson 8.00 20.00
TMPP T.McGrady/P.Pierce 8.00 20.00
TPSF T.Parker/S.Francis 6.00 15.00
VCAJ V.Carter/A.Jamison 6.00 15.00
VCJS V.Carter/J.Stackhouse 6.00 15.00
YMSO Y.Ming/S.O'Neal 10.00 25.00

2003-04 Fleer Mystique Rare Finds Jerseys Triple

Randomly inserted in packs, this nine cards set parallels the design of the Rare Finds insert set enhanced with three players, three jersey swatches and sequential numbering to 150. A version sequentially numbered to 15 was also produced and inserted into packs.

PRINT RUN 150 SER.#'d SETS
TRIPLE/15 NOT PRICED DUE TO SCARCITY
DSM Nowitzki/Nash/Finley 12.50 30.00
JCJ Rose/Webber/JuHoward 10.00 25.00
KJR K-Mart/Kidd/Jefferson 8.00 20.00
MPA Manu/Peja/Kirilenko 8.00 20.00
RCR Hamilton/Butler/Allen 8.00 20.00
TAP T-Mac/Iverson/Pierce 8.00 20.00
TSG Parker/Francis/Payton 8.00 20.00
TYS Duncan/Yao/Shaq 12.50 30.00
VJA Vince/Stack/Jamison 8.00 20.00

2003-04 Fleer Mystique Secret Weapons

Randomly seeded and sequentially numbered to 500, this 15-card set places a line of color along the left side of the card and a full-color player action photo set on a gray block background. Each card is sequentially numbered to 500. A Gold version sequentially numbered to the player's jersey number was also inserted.

COMPLETE SET (15) 30.00 75.00
PRINT RUN 500 SER.#'d SETS

*GOLD/30-50 SNGLS: .75X TO 2X HI COL.
1 LeBron James 60.00 150.00
2 Carmelo Anthony 5.00 12.00
3 Darko Milicic 1.25 3.00
4 Chris Kaman 1.50 4.00
5 Dwyane Wade 5.00 12.00
6 T.J. Ford 1.25 3.00
7 Chris Bosh 2.50 6.00
8 Kirk Hinrich 1.50 4.00
9 Mike Sweetney 1.00 2.50
10 Jarvis Hayes 1.00 2.50
11 Marcus Banks 1.00 2.50
12 Mickael Pietrus 1.25 3.00
13 Nick Collison 1.25 3.00
14 David West 1.50 4.00
15 Maciej Lampe 1.00 2.50

2003-04 Fleer Mystique Shining Stars

Seeded in packs randomly, this 15-card set places full color player action photos on a card with stars appearing in the background and a line of color along the left side to match the player's team color. Each card is sequentially numbered to 500. A Gold version sequentially numbered to 75 was also inserted in packs.

PRINT RUN 500 SER.#'d SETS
*GOLD SINGLES: .75X TO 2X HI COL.
GOLD PRINT RUN 75 SER.#'d SETS
1 Antoine Walker 1.50 4.00
2 Dirk Nowitzki 2.50 6.00
3 Baron Davis 1.25 3.00
4 Peja Stojakovic 1.50 4.00
5 Ray Allen 1.50 4.00
6 Jason Kidd 2.50 6.00
7 Gilbert Arenas 1.25 3.00
8 Jason Richardson 1.50 4.00
9 Tim Duncan 2.50 6.00
10 Vince Carter 2.50 6.00
11 Shaquille O'Neal 4.00 10.00
12 Drew Gooden 1.25 3.00
13 Pau Gasol 1.50 4.00
14 Caron Butler 1.25 3.00
15 Manu Ginobili 2.00 5.00

2003-04 Fleer Mystique Shining Stars Jerseys

Randomly seeded, this 14-card set parallels the design of the base Shining Stars insert set and is enhanced with a star-shaped jersey swatch in the lower right hand corner of the card. Each card is sequentially numbered to 350. Other Jersey versions of this set numbered to 250 and 75 were produced along with a warm up version numbered to 100. The warm-up versons were only available in Hobby and Retail blaster boxes.

PRINT RUN 350 SER.#'d SETS
*JERSEY/250: .4X TO 1X HI COL.
*JERSEY/75: .75X TO 2X HI COL.
*WARM-UPS: .4X TO 1X HI COL.
WARM-UPS PRINT RUN 250 SETS
SSAW Antoine Walker 2.50 6.00
SSBD Baron Davis 2.00 5.00
SSCB Caron Butler 2.00 5.00
SSDG Drew Gooden 2.00 5.00
SSDN Dirk Nowitzki 4.00 10.00
SSJK Jason Kidd 4.00 10.00
SSJR Jason Richardson 2.50 6.00
SSMG Manu Ginobili 3.00 8.00
SSPG Pau Gasol 2.50 6.00
SSPS Peja Stojakovic 2.50 6.00
SSRA Ray Allen 2.50 6.00
SSSO Shaquille O'Neal 6.00 15.00
SSTD Tim Duncan 4.00 10.00
SSVC Vince Carter 4.00 10.00

2003-04 Fleer Mystique Skyview

Randomly inserted in packs, this ten-card set is designed like the 1996-97 E-X basketball set with a border around the outside and full-color player photos against a cloudy sky background. Each card is sequentially numbered to 100. A Gold version where cards are sequentially numbered to between 30 and 58 was also issued.

COMPLETE SET (10) 40.00 80.00
PRINT RUN 100 SER.#'d SETS
*GOLD/30-50: 1X TO 2.5X HI COL.
*GOLD/50-60: .75X TO 2X HI COL.
1 Dirk Nowitzki 5.00 12.00
2 Yao Ming 6.00 15.00
3 Kevin Garnett 5.00 12.00
4 Tracy McGrady 4.00 10.00
5 Allen Iverson 5.00 12.00
6 Steve Francis 2.50 6.00
7 Kobe Bryant 90.00 150.00
8 Amare Stoudemire 4.00 10.00
9 Chris Webber 3.00 8.00
10 Vince Carter 5.00 12.00

2003-04 Fleer Mystique Skyview Jerseys

Inserted in packs, this nine-card set parallels the look of the base Skyview insert enhanced with a square swatch of game worn jersey at the bottom of the card. Each card is sequentially numbered to 250. Two other versions of this card were also issued, one sequentially numbered to 150 and another to 25.

PRINT RUN 250 SER.#'d SETS
*JERSEY/150: .5X TO 1.25X BASE HI
*JERSEY/25: 2X TO 5X BASE HI
SVAI Allen Iverson 5.00 12.00
SVAS Amare Stoudemire 4.00 10.00
SVCW Chris Webber 3.00 8.00
SVDN Dirk Nowitzki 5.00 12.00
SVKG Kevin Garnett 5.00 12.00
SVSM Steve Francis 2.50 6.00
SVTM Tracy McGrady 4.00 10.00
SVVC Vince Carter 5.00 12.00
SVYM Yao Ming 6.00 15.00

2001-02 Fleer NBA All-Star Jam Session

Given away at the NBA All-Star Game Show from February 8th-10th, this single card set features Philadelphia home town hero, Eric Snow, the spokseman. The card features both the Fleer and the Jam Session logo and placed Eric Snow against an American flag background.

NNO Eric Snow .40 1.00

1997 Fleer NBA Jam Session Commemorative Sheet

Issued at the 1997 NBA Jam Session in Cleveland, this Design a Card Commemorative Sheet was available through a wrapper exchange program at the Fleer booth. The sheet features six of the cards from the Fresh Faces insert in 1996-97 Fleer series one as designed by Shinto Imai and six of the cards from the All-Star subset in 1996-97 Fleer series two as designed by Krystin Penrod. Unfortunately, these cards were not renumbered and could be cut and sold as legitimate inserts/cards from packs.

1 Shareef Abdur-Rahim FF 3.00 8.00
Ray Allen FF
Kobe Bryant FF
Marcus Camby FF
Kerry Kittles FF
Stephon Marbury FF
Charles Barkley AS
Patrick Ewing AS
John Stockton AS
Alonzo Mourning AS
Grant Hill AS
Jason Kidd AS

2000 Fleer NBA Jam Session Commemorative Sheet

This sheet, featuring cards from the Fleer Focus set, was available at the 2000 NBA Jam Session in Oakland. The sheets were available via a wrapper exchange program at the Fleer/SkyBox booth.

NNO Vince Carter 4.00 10.00
Lamar Odom
Stephon Marbury
Keith Van Horn
Antawn Jamison
Allen Iverson
Grant Hill
Jason Williams

2003-04 Fleer Patchworks

Released in late March/early April 2004, this 120-card set is divided up into 90 veteran player cards and 30 rookie cards sequentially numbered to 799. Base cards feature a horizontal design with a black left side and a full color action photo right side. The player's team logo appears in the black on the left side. Fleer Patchworks was packaged in 18-pack boxes where packs contained five cards and carried a suggested retail price of $120 per box.

COMP.SET w/o SP's (90) 12.00 30.00
91-120 PRINT RUN 799 SER.#'d SETS
1 Shareef Abdur-Rahim .25 .60
2 Theo Ratliff .20 .50
3 Jason Terry .25 .60
4 Carlos Boozer .25 .60
5 Paul Pierce .30 .75
6 Ricky Davis .25 .60
7 Tyson Chandler .25 .60
8 Jamal Crawford .30 .75
9 Eddy Curry .20 .50
10 Darius Miles .20 .50
11 Dajuan Wagner .20 .50
12 Michael Finley .30 .75
13 Steve Nash .40 1.00
14 Dirk Nowitzki .50 1.25
15 Earl Boykins .20 .50
16 Andre Miller .25 .60
17 Nene .25 .60
18 Richard Hamilton .25 .60
19 Tayshaun Prince .25 .60
20 Ben Wallace .25 .60
21 Mike Dunleavy .25 .60
22 Troy Murphy .20 .50
23 Jason Richardson .30 .75
24 Steve Francis .25 .60
25 Yao Ming .60 1.50
26 Cuttino Mobley .20 .50
27 Maurice Taylor .20 .50
28 Ron Artest .30 .75
29 Reggie Miller .30 .75
30 Jermaine O'Neal .25 .60
31 Jamaal Tinsley .20 .50
32 Elton Brand .30 .75
33 Marko Jaric .20 .50
34 Corey Maggette .25 .60
35 Kobe Bryant 1.25 3.00
36 Karl Malone .40 1.00
37 Shaquille O'Neal .75 2.00
38 Shane Battier .25 .60
39 Pau Gasol .30 .75
40 Jason Williams .25 .60
41 Caron Butler .25 .60
42 Lamar Odom .25 .60
43 Desmond Mason .25 .60
44 Michael Redd .30 .75
45 Tim Thomas .20 .50
46 Sam Cassell .25 .60
47 Kevin Garnett .50 1.25
48 Latrell Sprewell .25 .60
49 Wally Szczerbiak .25 .60
50 Richard Jefferson .25 .60
51 Jason Kidd .50 1.25
52 Kenyon Martin .25 .60
53 Baron Davis .25 .60
54 Jamal Mashburn .25 .60
55 Jamaal Magloire .20 .50
56 Allan Houston .25 .60
57 Stephon Marbury .25 .60
58 Kurt Thomas .20 .50
59 Drew Gooden .25 .60
60 Juwan Howard .25 .60
61 Tracy McGrady .40 1.00
62 Allen Iverson .50 1.25
63 Aaron McKie .20 .50
64 Glenn Robinson .25 .60
65 Kenny Thomas .20 .50
66 Shawn Marion .25 .60
67 Antonio McDyess .25 .60
68 Amare Stoudemire .40 1.00
69 Zach Randolph .25 .60
70 Damon Stoudamire .25 .60
71 Rasheed Wallace .30 .75
72 Qyntel Woods .20 .50
73 Mike Bibby .30 .75
74 Peja Stojakovic .30 .75
75 Chris Webber .30 .75
76 Tim Duncan .50 1.25
77 Manu Ginobili .40 1.00
78 Tony Parker .30 .75
79 Malik Rose .20 .50
80 Ray Allen .30 .75
81 Rashard Lewis .30 .75
82 Vladimir Radmanovic .20 .50
83 Vince Carter .50 1.25
84 Donyell Marshall .20 .50
85 Jalen Rose .25 .60
86 Matt Harpring .20 .50
87 Andrei Kirilenko .30 .75
88 Gilbert Arenas .25 .60
89 Larry Hughes .25 .60
90 Jerry Stackhouse .25 .60
91 Carmelo Anthony RC 4.00 10.00
92 Marcus Banks RC .75 2.00
93 Troy Bell RC .75 2.00
94 Chris Bosh RC 2.00 5.00
95 Zarko Cabarkapa RC .75 2.00
96 Nick Collison RC 1.00 2.50
97 Boris Diaw RC 1.25 3.00
98 Francisco Elson RC .75 2.00
99 T.J. Ford RC 1.00 2.50
100 Reece Gaines RC .75 2.00
101 Udonis Haslem RC 1.00 2.50
102 Jarvis Hayes RC .75 2.00
103 Kirk Hinrich RC 1.25 3.00
104 Josh Howard RC 1.25 3.00
105 LeBron James RC 75.00 200.00
106 Dahntay Jones RC 1.00 2.50
107 Chris Kaman RC 1.25 3.00
108 Jason Kapono RC .75 2.00
109 Raul Lopez 1.25 3.00
110 Darko Milicic RC 1.00 2.50
111 Zaur Pachulia RC 1.25 3.00
112 Mickael Pietrus RC 1.00 2.50
113 Zoran Planinic RC .75 2.00
114 Luke Ridnour RC 1.00 2.50
115 Darius Songaila .75 2.00
116 Mike Sweetney RC .75 2.00
117 Dwyane Wade RC 4.00 10.00
118 Luke Walton RC 1.25 3.00
119 David West RC 1.25 3.00
120 Maurice Williams RC 1.25 3.00

2003-04 Fleer Patchworks Ruby

*1-90 RUBY SINGLES: 5X TO 12X BASE HI
*91-120 RUBY RCs: 1.5X TO 4X BASE HI
RUBY PRINT RUN 50 SER.#'d SETS
105 LeBron James 700.00 1000.00

2003-04 Fleer Patchworks By The Numbers

Inserted in Hobby packs at the rate of one in 24, Retail at one in 12 and Blasters at one in 24, this 15-card set is horizontally designed with a hardwood floor background. Player photos appear on the left while the player's jersey number appears on the right.

COMPLETE SET (15) 20.00 40.00
STATED ODDS 1:24 H, 1:12 R, 1:24 BLAST
1 Carmelo Anthony 2.50 6.00
2 Steve Francis .60 1.50
3 Shaquille O'Neal 2.00 5.00
4 Kevin Garnett 1.25 3.00
5 Dwyane Wade 2.50 6.00
6 Tracy McGrady 1.00 2.50
7 Allen Iverson 1.25 3.00
8 Chris Webber .75 2.00
9 Tim Duncan 1.25 3.00
10 Dirk Nowitzki 1.25 3.00
11 Paul Pierce .75 2.00
12 LeBron James 8.00 20.00
13 Kobe Bryant 3.00 8.00
14 Jason Kidd 1.25 3.00
15 Vince Carter 1.25 3.00

2003-04 Fleer Patchworks By The Numbers Jerseys

Randomly inserted at the rate of one in 300 Hobby and one in 77 Retail, this 12-card set parallels the design of the base By the Numbers insert set enhanced with jersey swatches in the shape of the featured player's jersey number. A patch version sequentially numbered to 100 was also inserted.

STATED ODDS 1:300 H, 1:77 R
*PATCHES: .75X TO 2X BASE JSY HI
PATCH PRINT RUN 100 SER.#'d SETS
CA Carmelo Anthony 8.00 20.00
CW Chris Webber 2.50 6.00
DN Dirk Nowitzki 4.00 10.00
DW Dwyane Wade 8.00 20.00
JK Jason Kidd 4.00 10.00
KG Kevin Garnett 4.00 10.00
PP Paul Pierce 2.50 6.00
SF Steve Francis 2.00 5.00
TD Tim Duncan 4.00 10.00
TM Tracy McGrady 3.00 8.00
VC Vince Carter 4.00 10.00
SON Shaquille O'Neal 6.00 15.00

2003-04 Fleer Patchworks Courting Greatness

Randomly inserted in Hobby packs at the rate of one in 12, Retail at the rate of one in six and Blasters at the rate of one in 12, this 25-card set is also horizontally designed and the top and bottom of the card are framed by a basketball with the background designed to look like hard wood. Full color player photos appear to the left.

COMPLETE SET (24) 20.00 40.00
STATED ODDS 1:12 H, 1:6 R, 1:12 BLASTER
1 Dirk Nowitzki 1.00 2.50
2 Jarvis Hayes .40 1.00
3 Tony Parker .60 1.50
4 Drew Gooden .50 1.25
5 Yao Ming 1.25 3.00
6 Udonis Haslem .50 1.25
7 Zach Randolph .50 1.25
8 Carmelo Anthony 2.00 5.00
9 Kobe Bryant 2.50 6.00
10 Chris Bosh 1.00 2.50
11 Antawn Jamison .50 1.25
12 Ben Wallace .50 1.25
13 Manu Ginobili .75 2.00
14 Baron Davis .50 1.25
15 Vince Carter 1.00 2.50
16 Tayshaun Prince .50 1.25
17 Jermaine O'Neal .50 1.25
18 T.J. Ford .50 1.25
19 Josh Howard .60 1.50
20 Amare Stoudemire .75 2.00
21 Dwyane Wade 2.00 5.00
22 Michael Redd .60 1.50
23 LeBron James 12.00 30.00
24 Jason Richardson .60 1.50
25 Darko Milicic .50 1.25

2003-04 Fleer Patchworks Courting Greatness Jerseys

Randomly seeded, this 20-card set parallels the design of the base Courting Greatness insert set enhanced with a swatch of jersey on the left and sequential numbering to 350. A Patch version sequentially numbered to 150 was also inserted.

PRINT RUN 350 SER.#'d SETS
*PATCH: .75X TO 2X BASE JSY HI
PATCH PRINT RUN 150 SER.#'d SETS
AJ Antawn Jamison 2.00 5.00
AS Amare Stoudemire 3.00 8.00
BD Baron Davis 2.00 5.00
BW Ben Wallace 2.00 5.00
CA Carmelo Anthony 8.00 20.00
CB Chris Bosh 4.00 10.00
DG Drew Gooden 2.00 5.00
DN Dirk Nowitzki 4.00 10.00
DW Dwyane Wade 8.00 20.00
JH Jarvis Hayes 1.50 4.00
JH Josh Howard 2.50 6.00
JR Jason Richardson 2.50 6.00
MG Manu Ginobili 3.00 8.00
MR Michael Redd 2.50 6.00
TP Tayshaun Prince 2.00 5.00
TP Tony Parker 2.50 6.00
VC Vince Carter 4.00 10.00
YM Yao Ming 5.00 12.00
ZR Zach Randolph 2.00 5.00
JON Jermaine O'Neal 2.00 5.00

2003-04 Fleer Patchworks Jerseys

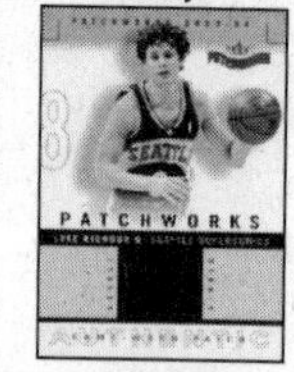

Randomly inserted in packs, this 20-card set features a split design with full color player action photos across the top and a tan bar on the bottom quarter of the card with a square swatch of jersey. Several multi-color versions were also inserted into packs: Dual color cards are sequentially numbered to 100 and Multicolor cards are sequentially numbered to 50.

PRINT RUN 200 SER.#'d SETS
*DUAL COLOR: .75X TO 2X BASE JSY HI
DUAL PRINT RUN 100 SER.#'d SETS
*MULITICOLOR: 1X TO 2.5X BASE JSY HI
MULTI PRINT RUN 50 SER.#'d SETS
N Nene 2.00 5.00
AI Allen Iverson 4.00 10.00
AK Andrei Kirilenko 2.50 6.00
AS Amare Stoudemire 3.00 8.00
DW Dajuan Wagner 2.00 5.00
GA Gilbert Arenas 2.00 5.00
GR Glenn Robinson 2.00 5.00
KG Kevin Garnett 4.00 10.00
KM Kenyon Martin 2.00 5.00
LR Luke Ridnour 2.00 5.00
MB Marcus Banks 1.50 4.00
MF Michael Finley 2.50 6.00
PS Peja Stojakovic 2.50 6.00
RH Richard Hamilton 2.00 5.00
RM Reggie Miller 2.50 6.00
SB Shane Battier 2.00 5.00
SN Steve Nash 3.00 8.00
TP Tony Parker 2.50 6.00
VC Vince Carter 4.00 10.00
YAO Yao Ming 5.00 12.00

2003-04 Fleer Patchworks Licensed Apparel

Randomly inserted in packs, this 20-card set features a horizontal design with a white background and the words "Licensed Apparel" appearing in purple. Each card has a jersey swatch and is sequentially numbered to 300. Several other versions of this set were issued: A Name version with swatches from the team's name is sequentially numbered to 150, a Number versions with swatches from jersey numbers is sequentially numbered to 100, a Name version with swatches from the player's name on the back of the jersey numbered to 50, a Tag version with swatches from the jersey tags sequentially numbered to 10 and an NBA logo from a jersey version is numbered one of one.

PRINT RUN 300 SER.#'d SETS
*NAME: 1.25X TO 3X BASE LIC.APP. HI
NAME PRINT RUN 50 SER.#'d SETS
*NUMBER: .6X TO 1.5X BASE LIC.APP. HI
NUMBER PRINT RUN 100 SER.#'d SETS
*TEAM NAME: .75X TO 2X BASE LIC.APP. HI
TEAM NAME PRINT RUN 150 SER.#'d SETS
AH Allan Houston 2.00 5.00
BD Baron Davis 2.00 5.00
CW Chris Webber 2.50 6.00
EB Elton Brand 2.50 6.00
JR Jason Richardson 2.50 6.00
JS Jerry Stackhouse 2.00 5.00
KM Kenyon Martin 2.00 5.00
KM Karl Malone 3.00 8.00
LS Latrell Sprewell 2.00 5.00
MB Mike Bibby 2.50 6.00
MD Mike Dunleavy 2.00 5.00
MF Michael Finley 2.50 6.00
PG Pau Gasol 2.50 6.00
PP Paul Pierce 2.50 6.00
RA Ray Allen 3.00 8.00
SF Steve Francis 2.00 5.00
SM Stephon Marbury 2.00 5.00
TM Tracy McGrady 3.00 8.00
SAR Shareef Abdur-Rahim 2.00 5.00
SON Shaquille O'Neal 6.00 15.00

2003-04 Fleer Patchworks National Pastime

Randomly inserted in packs, this eight card set features players from the USA Olympic team. Cards are framed with gold borders and an arch towards the top of the card and are sequentially numbered to 250.

COMPLETE SET (8) 15.00 30.00
PRINT RUN 250 SER.#'d SETS
1 Jermaine O'Neal 1.25 3.00
2 Jason Kidd 2.50 6.00
3 Tracy McGrady 2.00 5.00
4 Allen Iverson 2.50 6.00
5 Mike Bibby 1.50 4.00
6 Tim Duncan 2.50 6.00
7 Ray Allen 1.50 4.00
8 Larry Brown 1.50 4.00

2003-04 Fleer Patchworks National Patchtime Jerseys NBA

Randomly seeded, this seven-card set parallels the design of the base National Patchtime set enhanced with a swatch of an NBA game jersey. Each card is sequentially numbered to 350. Several other versions of this set were issued: an NBA Patch version with premium swatches and sequential numbering to 100, a USA jersey version sequentially numbered to 200, a USA Patch version sequentially numbered to 75 and a USA/NBA Patch, which has two jersey swatches, sequentially numbered to 25.

PRINT RUN 350 SER.#'d SETS
*NBA PATCHES: 1.25X TO 3X BASE JSY HI
NBA PATCH PRINT RUN 100 SER.#'d SETS
*USA JERSEY: .6X TO 1.5X BASE JSY HI
*USA PATCHES: 2X TO 5X BASE JSY HI
USA PATCH PRINT RUN 75 SER.#'d SETS
*USA/NBA PATCH: 3X TO 8X BASE HI
USA/NBA PATCH PRINT RUN 25 SETS
AI Allen Iverson 4.00 10.00
JK Jason Kidd 4.00 10.00
MB Mike Bibby 2.50 6.00
RA Ray Allen 2.50 6.00
TD Tim Duncan 4.00 10.00
TM Tracy McGrady 3.00 8.00
JON Jermaine O'Neal 2.00 5.00

2003-04 Fleer Patchworks Vince Carter Autographs

Inserted in packs at the overall odds of one in 216, this nine-card set features various combinations of Vince Carter jerseys, jersey colors and autographs. Each checklist description contains the color of the jersey Vince Carter is wearing in the picture, not the color of the jersey swatch on the card. Print runs are as follows: Jersey Autograph combos are sequentially numbered to 100, Jersey Patch Autographs are sequentially numbered to 150, Team Name Patch Autographs are sequentially numbered to 15 and NBA Logo Autographs are numbered one of one.

JSY AU PRINT RUN 100 SER.#'d SETS
PATCH AU PRINT RUN 150 SER.#'d SETS
WHITE, PURPLE, RED VERSIONS EXIST
COLORS REFER TO JERSEY IN PICTURE
OVERALL AU STATED ODDS 1:216
VC4 V.Carter JSY AU White 15.00 40.00
VC5 V.Carter JSY AU Purple 15.00 40.00
VC6 V.Carter JSY AU Red 15.00 40.00
VC7 V.Carter Patch AU White 20.00 50.00
VC8 V.Carter Patch AU Purple 20.00 50.00
VC9 V.Carter Patch AU Red 20.00 50.00

2001-02 Fleer Platinum

Released as a 250 card set, Fleer Platinum contains 200 regular cards, 30 rookies inserted at the rate of one in six hobby, one in three jumbo, and one in three rack pack, and 20 Highlight Film cards inserted at the same rate as the rookies. The base cards utilize the 1961-62 Fleer design where the top half of the card is in one bold color that contains the player's name, and the bottom half has a bold colored background which is overlayed by a black and white player photo. The rookie cards designed in the 1986-87 Fleer red, white and blue card stock. Highlight Film cards also use the base card stock except the bottom half has actual backgrounds behind the player action photos. Fleer Platinum was issued in late October of 2001, and was packed out in three different versions: hobby, jumbo and rack packs.

COMPLETE SET (250) 100.00 200.00
COMP.SET w/o SP's (200) 8.00 20.00
201-220 ODDS 1:6, 1:3 JUMBO, 1:2 RACK
221-250 ODDS 1:6, 1:3 JUMBO, 1:2 RACK
1 Tyrone Hill .15 .40
2 Sam Cassell .20 .50
3 Elton Brand .25 .60
4 Andre Miller .20 .50
5 Vitaly Potapenko .15 .40
6 Lamar Odom .20 .50
7 Mike Bibby .25 .60
8 Alan Henderson .15 .40
9 Dan Majerle .25 .60
10 Donyell Marshall .15 .40
11 Jason Williams .20 .50
12 Glen Rice .20 .50
13 Kobe Bryant 1.00 2.50
14 Pat Garrity .15 .40
15 Shawn Bradley .15 .40
16 Aaron Williams .15 .40
17 Antonio McDyess .20 .50
18 Jonathan Bender .15 .40
19 Ben Wallace .20 .50
20 Vince Carter .40 1.00
21 Maurice Taylor .15 .40
22 Antonio Daniels .15 .40
23 Rodney Rogers .15 .40
24 Patrick Ewing .30 .75
25 Chauncey Billups .25 .60
26 Steve Smith .20 .50
27 Antawn Jamison .25 .60
28 Mitch Richmond .20 .50
29 Jumaine Jones .15 .40
30 Glenn Robinson .20 .50
31 Ron Mercer .15 .40
32 Jelani McCoy .15 .40
33 Paul Pierce .25 .60
34 Jeff McInnis .15 .40
35 Michael Dickerson .15 .40
36 Toni Kukoc .25 .60
37 Anthony Mason .15 .40
38 Jamal Mashburn .20 .50
39 John Stockton .30 .75
40 Peja Stojakovic .25 .60
41 Charlie Ward .15 .40
42 Donnell Harvey .15 .40
43 Darrell Armstrong .15 .40
44 Michael Finley .25 .60
45 Kerry Kittles .15 .40
46 Voshon Lenard .15 .40
47 Reggie Miller .25 .60
48 Joe Smith .20 .50
49 Antonio Davis .15 .40
50 Hakeem Olajuwon .30 .75
51 David Robinson .40 1.00
52 Tony Delk .15 .40
53 Gary Payton .25 .60
54 Kevin Garnett .40 1.00
55 Arvydas Sabonis .20 .50
56 Larry Hughes .20 .50
57 Richard Hamilton .20 .50
58 Aaron McKie .15 .40
59 Tim Thomas .15 .40
60 Ron Artest .25 .60
61 Matt Harpring .15 .40
62 Kenny Anderson .20 .50
63 Quentin Richardson .20 .50
64 Damon Jones .15 .40
65 Theo Ratliff .15 .40
66 Brian Grant .15 .40
67 Eddie Robinson .15 .40
68 Karl Malone .30 .75
69 Bobby Jackson .15 .40
70 Larry Johnson .25 .60
71 Shareef Abdur-Rahim .20 .50
72 Grant Hill .30 .75
73 Eduardo Najera .15 .40
74 Keith Van Horn .20 .50
75 Nick Van Exel .20 .50
76 Jalen Rose .20 .50
77 Jerry Stackhouse .20 .50
78 Jerome Williams .15 .40
79 Cuttino Mobley .15 .40
80 Derek Anderson .15 .40
81 Anfernee Hardaway .40 1.00
82 Rashard Lewis .25 .60
83 Terrell Brandon .15 .40
84 Scottie Pippen .40 1.00
85 Danny Fortson .15 .40
86 Jahidi White .15 .40
87 Eric Snow .15 .40
88 Ervin Johnson .15 .40
89 Marcus Fizer .15 .40
90 Lamond Murray .15 .40
91 Antoine Walker .20 .50
92 Keyon Dooling .15 .40
93 Bryant Reeves .15 .40
94 Hanno Mottola .15 .40
95 Tim Hardaway .25 .60
96 David Wesley .15 .40
97 John Starks .15 .40
98 Hedo Turkoglu .20 .50
99 Allan Houston .20 .50
100 Rick Fox .15 .40
101 Bo Outlaw .15 .40
102 Juwan Howard .20 .50
103 Kendall Gill .15 .40
104 Raef LaFrentz .15 .40
105 Austin Croshere .15 .40
106 Chucky Atkins .15 .40
107 Morris Peterson .15 .40
108 Shandon Anderson .15 .40
109 Sean Elliott .25 .60
110 Tom Gugliotta .15 .40
111 Vin Baker .20 .50
112 Wally Szczerbiak .20 .50
113 Rasheed Wallace .25 .60
114 Vonteego Cummings .15 .40
115 Christian Laettner .20 .50
116 Dikembe Mutombo .25 .60
117 Lindsey Hunter .15 .40
118 Jamal Crawford .25 .60
119 Jim Jackson .15 .40
120 Bryant Stith .15 .40
121 Corey Maggette .20 .50
122 Mahmoud Abdul-Rauf .15 .40
123 Lorenzen Wright .15 .40
124 Alonzo Mourning .30 .75
125 Jamaal Magloire .15 .40
126 Bryon Russell .15 .40
127 Vlade Divac .20 .50
128 Marcus Camby .20 .50
129 Derek Fisher .20 .50
130 Mike Miller .20 .50
131 Steve Nash .40 1.00
132 Kenyon Martin .25 .60
133 James Posey .15 .40
134 Travis Best .15 .40
135 Corliss Williamson .15 .40
136 Alvin Williams .15 .40
137 Walt Williams .15 .40
138 Malik Rose .15 .40
139 Clifford Robinson .15 .40
140 Ruben Patterson .15 .40
141 LaPhonso Ellis .20 .50
142 Rod Strickland .15 .40
143 Marc Jackson .15 .40
144 Hubert Davis .15 .40
145 Speedy Claxton .15 .40
146 Scott Williams .15 .40
147 Tyronn Lue .15 .40
148 Chris Mihm .15 .40
149 George Lynch .15 .40
150 Michael Olowokandi .15 .40
151 Nazr Mohammed .15 .40
152 Eddie House .15 .40
153 Elden Campbell .15 .40
154 DeShawn Stevenson .15 .40
155 Doug Christie .15 .40
156 Kurt Thomas .15 .40
157 Robert Horry .20 .50
158 Radoslav Nesterovic .15 .40
159 Wang Zhizhi .20 .50
160 Stephen Jackson .20 .50
161 George McCloud .15 .40
162 Jermaine O'Neal .20 .50
163 Mateen Cleaves .15 .40
164 Charles Oakley .20 .50
165 Kenny Thomas .15 .40
166 Terry Porter .15 .40
167 Iakovos Tsakalidis .15 .40
168 Shammond Williams .15 .40
169 Anthony Peeler .15 .40
170 Damon Stoudamire .20 .50
171 Chris Porter .15 .40
172 Chris Whitney .15 .40
173 Raja Bell RC .30 .75
174 Darvin Ham .15 .40
175 A.J. Guyton .15 .40
176 Trajan Langdon .15 .40
177 Jerome Moiso .15 .40
178 Anthony Carter .15 .40
179 P.J. Brown .15 .40
180 Danny Manning .20 .50
181 Scot Pollard .15 .40
182 Mark Jackson .20 .50
183 Mark Madsen .15 .40
184 Michael Doleac .15 .40
185 Calvin Booth .15 .40
186 Kevin Willis .15 .40
187 Al Harrington .20 .50
188 Mikki Moore .15 .40
189 Keon Clark .15 .40
190 Moochie Norris .15 .40
191 Ron Harper .20 .50
192 Danny Ferry .15 .40
193 Jacque Vaughn .15 .40
194 Derrick Coleman .20 .50
195 Brent Barry .15 .40
196 Dion Glover .15 .40
197 Felipe Lopez .15 .40
198 Shawn Kemp .25 .60
199 Mookie Blaylock .15 .40
200 Bonzi Wells .15 .40
201 Vince Carter HL 1.50 4.00
202 Ray Allen HL 1.00 2.50
203 Darius Miles HL .60 1.50
204 Shaquille O'Neal HL 2.50 6.00
205 Stromile Swift HL .60 1.50
206 DerMarr Johnson HL .60 1.50
207 Eddie Jones HL .75 2.00
208 Chris Webber HL 1.00 2.50
209 Latrell Sprewell HL .75 2.00
210 Tracy McGrady HL 1.50 4.00
211 Dirk Nowitzki HL 1.50 4.00
212 Stephon Marbury HL .75 2.00
213 Steve Francis HL .75 2.00
214 Tim Duncan HL 2.00 5.00
215 Jason Kidd HL 1.50 4.00
216 Shawn Marion HL .75 2.00
217 Desmond Mason HL .75 2.00
218 Courtney Alexander HL .60 1.50
219 Baron Davis HL 1.00 2.50
220 Allen Iverson HL 2.00 5.00
221 Joe Johnson RC 1.25 3.00
222 Kedrick Brown RC .60 1.50
223 Joseph Forte RC .60 1.50
224 Kirk Haston RC .60 1.50
225 Tyson Chandler RC 1.50 4.00
226 Eddy Curry RC 1.00 2.50
227 DeSagana Diop RC .75 2.00
228 Jeff Trepagnier RC .60 1.50
229 Oscar Torres RC 1.00 2.50
230 Rodney White RC .60 1.50
231 Jason Richardson RC 1.25 3.00
232 Troy Murphy RC 1.00 2.50
233 Eddie Griffin RC .75 2.00
234 Jamaal Tinsley RC 1.00 2.50
235 Pau Gasol RC 3.00 8.00
236 Shane Battier RC 2.00 5.00
237 Richard Jefferson RC 1.50 4.00
238 Jason Collins RC .75 2.00
239 Brendan Haywood RC 1.00 2.50
240 Steven Hunter RC .75 2.00
241 Zach Randolph RC 1.50 4.00
242 Gerald Wallace RC 1.25 3.00
243 Tony Parker RC 4.00 10.00
244 Vladimir Radmanovic RC 1.00 2.50
245 Michael Bradley RC .60 1.50
246 Andrei Kirilenko RC 1.50 4.00
247 Kwame Brown RC 1.00 2.50
248 Alton Ford RC 1.00 2.50
249 Zeljko Rebraca RC 1.00 2.50
250 Trenton Hassell RC .75 2.00

2001-02 Fleer Platinum 15th Anniversary Reprints

Randomly inserted in hobby packs at the rate of one in 12, one six jumbo, and one in three in rack packs, this 25 card set reprints some of Fleer's most famous rookie cards in original Fleer card stock. Each card contains a Fleer Platinum logo stamp in one of the card's corners.

COMPLETE SET (25) 60.00 120.00
STATED ODDS 1:12, 1:6 JUMBO, 1:3 RACK
1 Michael Jordan 15.00 40.00
2 Karl Malone 2.50 6.00
3 Hakeem Olajuwon 2.50 6.00
4 Patrick Ewing 2.50 6.00
5 Reggie Miller 2.00 5.00
6 John Stockton 2.50 6.00
7 Scottie Pippen 3.00 8.00
8 David Robinson 3.00 8.00
9 Shaquille O'Neal 5.00 12.00
10 Alonzo Mourning 2.50 6.00
11 Chris Webber 2.00 5.00
12 Grant Hill 2.50 6.00
13 Jason Kidd 3.00 8.00
14 Eddie Jones 1.50 4.00
15 Kevin Garnett 3.00 8.00
16 Kobe Bryant 10.00 25.00
17 Allen Iverson 4.00 10.00
18 Shareef Abdur-Rahim 1.50 4.00
19 Tim Duncan 4.00 10.00
20 Tracy McGrady 3.00 8.00
21 Vince Carter 3.00 8.00
22 Dirk Nowitzki 3.00 8.00
23 Steve Francis 1.50 4.00
24 Darius Miles 1.25 3.00
25 Mike Miller 1.50 4.00

2001-02 Fleer Platinum Anniversary Edition

*ANNIV 1-200: 5X TO 12X BASE CARD HI
*ANNIV 201-250: 6X TO 15X HI
1-200 PRINT RUN 201 SERIAL #'d SETS
201-250 PRINT RUN 21 SERIAL #'d SETS
13 Kobe Bryant 20.00 50.00

2001-02 Fleer Platinum Classic Combinations

Randomly inserted in packs, this 15-card set features dual player cards sequentially numbered between 500 and 2000. Additionally, twelve cards contain dual game worn jersey swatches and are sequentially numbered to 100.

1-5 PRINT RUN 1000 SERIAL #'d SETS
6-10 PRINT RUN 500 SERIAL #'d SETS
11-15 PRINT RUN 2000 SERIAL #'d SETS
1 Stocktn/Malone/1000 3.00 8.00
2 Iverson/Mutmbo/1000 3.00 8.00
3 J.Kidd/G.Hill/1000 3.00 8.00
4 Francis/Brand/1000 3.00 8.00
5 Carter/Jamison/1000 3.00 8.00
6 Olajuwon/Ewing/500 3.00 8.00
7 Carter/McGrady/500 6.00 15.00
8 K.Bryant/S.O'Neal/500 6.00 15.00
9 Duncan/Robinsn/500 4.00 10.00
10 K.Garnett/D.Miles/500 3.00 8.00
11 Nowitzki/Finley/2000 3.00 8.00
12 Walker/Pierce/2000 3.00 8.00
13 Allen/Robinson/2000 3.00 8.00
14 Sprwell/Houston/2000 3.00 8.00
15 Ewing/Mrning/2000 3.00 8.00

2001-02 Fleer Platinum Classic Combinations Jerseys

PRINT RUN 100 SERIAL #'d SETS
1 J.Stockton/K.Malone 12.00 30.00
2 A.Iverson/D.Mutombo 10.00 25.00
3 J.Kidd/G.Hill 10.00 25.00
4 S.Francis/E.Brand 8.00 20.00
5 V.Carter/A.Jamison 10.00 25.00
6 H.Olajuwon/P.Ewing 10.00 25.00
7 V.Carter/T.McGrady 15.00 40.00
11 D.Nowitzki/M.Finley 8.00 20.00
12 A.Walker/P.Pierce 8.00 20.00
13 R.Allen/G.Robinson 8.00 20.00
15 P.Ewing/A.Mourning 15.00 40.00

2001-02 Fleer Platinum Lucky 13

Randomly inserted in packs, these cards were issued as redemptions for the 13 "lottery" picks in the 2002 NBA draft. Upon redemption, a collector received a card of the player which had a stated print run of 500 serial numbered sets.

COMPLETE SET (13) 75.00 150.00
PRINT RUN 500 SERIAL #'d SETS
1 Kwame Brown 4.00 10.00
2 Tyson Chandler 6.00 15.00
3 Pau Gasol 12.00 30.00
4 Eddy Curry 4.00 10.00
5 Jason Richardson 5.00 12.00
6 Shane Battier 8.00 20.00
7 Eddie Griffin 3.00 8.00
8 DeSagana Diop 3.00 8.00
9 Rodney White 2.50 6.00
10 Joe Johnson 5.00 12.00
11 Kedrick Brown 2.50 6.00
12 Vladimir Radmanovic 4.00 10.00
13 Richard Jefferson 6.00 15.00

2001-02 Fleer Platinum Nameplates

Randomly inserted in Jumbo packs at the rate of one in 12, this 13-card set features top players on a license plate card stock of their respective team's home state. Each card contains both color action player photos and a swatch of a game worn jersey.

STATED ODDS 1:12 JUMBO
1 Alonzo Mourning/175 15.00 40.00
2 Hakeem Olajuwon/175 12.00 30.00
3 Allen Iverson/150 20.00 50.00
4 Stephon Marbury/100 8.00 20.00
5 Gary Payton/100 10.00 25.00
6 Glenn Robinson/50 8.00 20.00
7 Shareef Abdur-Rahim/250 8.00 20.00
8 Keith Van Horn/225 8.00 20.00
9 John Stockton/100 20.00 50.00
10 Antoine Walker/100 8.00 20.00
11 David Robinson/125 20.00 50.00
12 Michael Finley/175 10.00 25.00
13 Vince Carter/75 15.00 40.00

2001-02 Fleer Platinum National Patch Time

Inserted one in 24 packs, this 26-card set features cards with swatches of game-used pants and jersey. Each card has a color action player photo on the right, and a silver logo on the top left above a game used uniform swatch.

STATED ODDS 1:24 HOBBY
1 Tom Gugliotta 2.00 5.00
2 Shawn Marion 2.50 6.00
3 Darius Miles 2.00 5.00
4 Mike Miller 2.50 6.00
5 Jason Terry 3.00 8.00
6 Stromile Swift 2.00 5.00
7 Keith Van Horn 2.50 6.00
8 Ray Allen 3.00 8.00
9 Baron Davis 3.00 8.00
10 Shareef Abdur-Rahim 2.50 6.00

11 Stephon Marbury 2.50 6.00
12 Jason Kidd 5.00 12.00
13 Mike Bibby 3.00 8.00
14 Jerome Moiso 2.00 5.00
15 Richard Hamilton 2.50 6.00
16 Paul Pierce 3.00 8.00
17 Dikembe Mutombo 3.00 8.00
18 Gary Payton 3.00 8.00
19 Patrick Ewing 4.00 10.00
20 Vince Carter 5.00 12.00
21 Corey Maggette 2.50 6.00
22 Jacque Vaughn 2.00 5.00
23 Darrell Armstrong 2.00 5.00
24 Mitch Richmond 2.50 6.00
25 Allen Iverson 6.00 15.00
26 Desmond Mason 2.50 6.00

2001-02 Fleer Platinum Stadium Standouts

Randomly inserted at the rate of one in 18 hobby, one in six jumbo, and one in three rack pack, this set features 15 NBA player photos set in front of their home stadiums.

COMPLETE SET (15) 20.00 50.00
STATED ODDS 1:18, 1:6 JUMBO, 1:3 RACK
1 Vince Carter 2.00 5.00
2 Grant Hill 1.50 4.00
3 Kobe Bryant 5.00 12.00
4 Steve Francis 1.00 2.50
5 Tracy McGrady 2.00 5.00
6 Elton Brand 1.25 3.00
7 Kevin Garnett 2.00 5.00
8 Allen Iverson 2.50 6.00
9 Dirk Nowitzki 2.00 5.00
10 Shaquille O'Neal 3.00 8.00
11 Tim Duncan 2.50 6.00
12 Jason Kidd 2.00 5.00
13 Darius Miles .75 2.00
14 Chris Webber 1.25 3.00
15 Ray Allen 1.25 3.00

2002-03 Fleer Platinum

Released in late April 2003, Fleer Platinum boasts a 200-card set divided up into 160 base veteran cards and 40 rookie cards. Base cards feature a throw-back style base card with white borders, full color player action photography and the player's team logo in a circle in the lower right corner of the card. Platinum was packed in 19-pack boxes where the packs were divided up as follows: 14 wax packs with seven cards per pack, four jumbo packs with 20 cards per pack and one tri-pouch rack pack with 30 cards per pack. Each different pack set up had 10 rookies that were exclusive to that pack format and 10 rookies dispersed between all formats, card numbers 161-170. Cards 171-180 were only inseted in wax packs and were sequentially numbered to 750. Cards 181-190 were only inserted in jumbo packs and were sequentially numbered to 350, and cards 191-200 were only inserted in rack packs and were sequentially numbered to 250. Fleer Platinum Wax packs carried an SRP of $2.99.

COMP.SET w/o SP's (160) 15.00 40.00
ODDS 1:1 RACK, 1:2 JUMBO, 1:4 WAX
171-180 PRINT RUN 750 SERIAL #'d SETS
181-190 PRINT RUN 350 SERIAL #'d SETS
181-190 INSERTED ONLY IN JUMBO PACKS
191-200 PRINT RUN 250 SERIAL #'d SETS
191-200 INSERTED ONLY IN RACK PACKS
1 Vince Carter .50 1.25
2 Lamar Odom .25 .60
3 Darrell Armstrong .20 .50
4 Kwame Brown .20 .50
5 Ron Artest .30 .75
6 Kurt Thomas .20 .50
7 Jerry Stackhouse .25 .60
8 Eddie Griffin .20 .50
9 David Wesley .20 .50
10 Morris Peterson .20 .50
11 Jon Barry .20 .50
12 Troy Hudson .20 .50
13 Kenny Anderson .25 .60
14 Corliss Williamson .20 .50
15 Kevin Garnett .50 1.25
16 Desmond Mason .25 .60
17 Lucious Harris .20 .50
18 Steve Smith .25 .60
19 Nick Van Exel .25 .60
20 Tyson Chandler .30 .75
21 Shane Battier .30 .75
22 Rasheed Wallace .30 .75
23 Donyell Marshall .20 .50
24 Anfernee Hardaway .50 1.25
25 Antoine Walker .25 .60
26 Kobe Bryant 1.25 3.00
27 Keith Van Horn .25 .60
28 Elton Brand .30 .75
29 Grant Hill .40 1.00
30 Elden Campbell .20 .50
31 John Stockton .40 1.00
32 Wally Szczerbiak .25 .60
33 Speedy Claxton .20 .50
34 Voshon Lenard .20 .50
35 Eddie Jones .25 .60
36 Bonzi Wells .20 .50
37 Jalen Rose .25 .60
38 Jason Williams .25 .60
39 Tom Gugliotta .20 .50
40 Juwan Howard .25 .60
41 Michael Redd .25 .60
42 David Robinson .50 1.25
43 Steve Nash .40 1.00
44 Vlade Divac .25 .60
45 Avery Johnson .25 .60
46 Scottie Pippen .50 1.25
47 Eric Williams .20 .50
48 Derek Fisher .25 .60
49 Tony Battie .20 .50
50 Rick Fox .20 .50
51 Theo Ratliff .20 .50
52 Corey Maggette .25 .60
53 Jermaine O'Neal .25 .60
54 Bryon Russell .20 .50
55 Steve Francis .25 .60
56 Jamal Mashburn .25 .60
57 Jerome Williams .20 .50
58 Gilbert Arenas .30 .75
59 Joe Smith .25 .60
60 Brent Barry .20 .50
61 Marcus Camby .25 .60
62 Toni Kukoc .30 .75
63 Tim Duncan .60 1.50
64 Ira Newble .20 .50
65 Brian Grant .20 .50
66 Jason Terry .25 .60
67 Andre Miller .25 .60
68 Mike Miller .25 .60
69 Troy Murphy .25 .60
70 P.J. Brown .20 .50
71 Jason Richardson .30 .75
72 Glenn Robinson .25 .60
73 Richard Jefferson .30 .75
74 Richard Hamilton .25 .60
75 Jason Kidd .50 1.25
76 Rashard Lewis .30 .75
77 Kenny Satterfield .20 .50
78 Terrell Brandon .20 .50
79 Dirk Nowitzki .50 1.25
80 Chris Webber .30 .75
81 Michael Finley .30 .75
82 Malik Allen .20 .50
83 Bobby Jackson .20 .50
84 Darius Miles .20 .50
85 Kendall Gill .20 .50
86 Damon Stoudamire .25 .60
87 Shammond Williams .20 .50
88 Stephon Marbury .25 .60
89 Shareef Abdur-Rahim .25 .60
90 Charlie Ward .20 .50
91 Michael Jordan 2.50 6.00
92 Jamaal Magloire .20 .50
93 Karl Malone .40 1.00
94 Kerry Kittles .20 .50
95 Lindsey Hunter .20 .50
96 Gary Payton .30 .75
97 Travis Best .20 .50
98 Derek Anderson .20 .50
99 Stromile Swift .20 .50
100 Shaquille O'Neal .75 2.00
101 Derrick Coleman .25 .60
102 DeShawn Stevenson .20 .50
103 Jamaal Tinsley .20 .50
104 Latrell Sprewell .25 .60
105 Larry Hughes .25 .60
106 Eddy Curry .20 .50
107 Shawn Marion .25 .60
108 Paul Pierce .30 .75
109 Samaki Walker .20 .50
110 Allen Iverson .50 1.25
111 Michael Olowokandi .20 .50
112 Tracy McGrady .50 1.25
113 Shawn Bradley .20 .50
114 Reggie Miller .30 .75
115 Antonio McDyess .25 .60
116 Calbert Chaney .20 .50
117 Al Harrington .25 .60
118 Allan Houston .25 .60
119 Andrei Kirilenko .30 .75
120 Courtney Alexander .20 .50
121 Alvin Williams .20 .50
122 Antawn Jamison .30 .75
123 Dikembe Mutombo .30 .75
124 Tony Parker .40 1.00
125 Raef LaFrentz .20 .50
126 Ray Allen .30 .75
127 Peja Stojakovic .30 .75
128 Zydrunas Ilgauskas .25 .60
129 Gerald Wallace .25 .60
130 Ruben Patterson .20 .50
131 Pau Gasol .40 1.00
132 Joe Johnson .25 .60
133 Aaron McKie .20 .50
134 Walter McCarty .20 .50
135 Baron Davis .25 .60
136 Kenyon Martin .25 .60
137 Antonio Davis .20 .50
138 Ben Wallace .25 .60
139 Sam Cassell .25 .60
140 Mike Bibby .30 .75
141 Cuttino Mobley .20 .50
142 LaPhonso Ellis .25 .60
143 Shandon Anderson .20 .50
144 Hedo Turkoglu .25 .60
145 Matt Harpring .20 .50
146 Dion Glover .20 .50
147 Tony Delk .20 .50
148 Ricky Davis .25 .60
149 James Posey .20 .50
150 Chucky Atkins .20 .50
151 Danny Fortson .20 .50
152 Robert Horry .25 .60
153 Radoslav Nesterovic .20 .50
154 Pat Garrity .20 .50
155 Todd MacCulloch .20 .50
156 Eric Snow .20 .50
157 Malik Rose .20 .50
158 Vladimir Radmanovic .20 .50
159 Trenton Hassell .20 .50
160 Brad Miller .25 .60
161 Kareem Rush RC 1.00 2.50
162 Nikoloz Tskitishvili RC .75 2.00
163 Nene Hilario RC 1.25 3.00
164 Marcus Haislip RC 1.00 2.50
165 Jiri Welsch RC 1.00 2.50
166 Dan Dickau RC 1.00 2.50
167 Vincent Yarbrough RC .75 2.00
168 Tito Maddox RC .75 2.00
169 Mike Dunleavy RC 1.25 3.00
170 Chris Wilcox RC 1.00 2.50
171 Jared Jeffries RC 1.50 4.00
172 Bostjan Nachbar RC 1.50 4.00
173 Frank Williams RC 1.25 3.00
174 Reggie Evans RC 2.00 5.00
175 Casey Jacobsen RC 1.50 4.00
176 Tayshaun Prince RC 2.50 6.00
177 Mike Batiste RC 1.25 3.00
178 Drew Gooden RC 2.00 5.00
179 DaJuan Wagner RC 1.50 4.00
180 Tamar Slay RC 1.25 3.00
181 Melvin Ely RC 2.00 5.00
182 Rasual Butler RC 2.50 6.00
183 Dan Gadzuric RC 2.00 5.00
184 Ryan Humphrey RC 2.00 5.00
185 Gordan Giricek RC 2.50 6.00
186 Mehmet Okur RC 2.50 6.00
187 Jay Williams RC 2.50 6.00
188 Caron Butler RC 2.50 6.00
189 Qyntel Woods RC 2.00 5.00
190 Amare Stoudemire RC 3.00 8.00
191 Yao Ming RC 6.00 15.00
192 Carlos Boozer RC 3.00 8.00
193 John Salmons RC 3.00 8.00
194 Fred Jones RC 2.50 6.00
195 Juan Dixon RC 3.00 8.00
196 Manu Ginobili RC 8.00 20.00
197 Pat Burke RC 2.00 5.00
198 Smush Parker RC 3.00 8.00
199 Lonny Baxter RC 2.00 5.00
200 Ronald Murray RC 3.00 8.00

2002-03 Fleer Platinum Finish

*STARS: 4X TO 10X BASE CARD HI
*161-170 RCs: 1.5X TO 4X BASE CARD HI
*171-180 RCs: 1X TO 2.5X BASE CARD HI
*181-190 RCs: .75X TO 2X BASE CARD HI
*191-200 RCs: .6X TO 1.5X BASE CARD HI
PRINT RUN 100 SERIAL #'d SETS

2002-03 Fleer Platinum Freshman Fabric

Randomly seeded in Rack packs at the rate of one in two, this 15-card set is designed horizontally with a close-up portrait photo of the player along the left side and a rather generous swatch of game used memorabilia on the right side.

STATED ODDS 1:2 RACK PACKS
AS Amare Stoudemire 3.00 8.00
CB Caron Butler 2.50 6.00
CB2 Carlos Boozer 2.50 6.00
CW Chris Wilcox 2.00 5.00
DD Dan Dickau 2.00 5.00
DG Drew Gooden 2.50 6.00
DW DaJuan Wagner 2.00 5.00
EG Manu Ginobili 6.00 15.00
JD Juan Dixon 2.50 6.00
KR Kareem Rush 2.00 5.00
NH Nene Hilario 2.50 6.00
NT Nikoloz Tskitishvili 1.50 4.00
QW Qyntel Woods 2.00 5.00
TP Tayshaun Prince 3.00 8.00
YM Yao Ming 5.00 12.00

2002-03 Fleer Platinum Guts and Glory

Randomly inserted in Rack packs at the rate of one in one, Jumbo packs at the rate of one in two, and Wax packs at the rate of one in four, this 10-card set places full-color player action photos on a green back-drop with white borders.

COMPLETE SET (10) 6.00 15.00
ODDS: 1:1 RACK, 1:2 JUMBO, 1:4 WAX
1GG Steve Nash 1.25 3.00
2GG Ben Wallace .75 2.00
3GG Antawn Jamison 1.00 2.50
4GG Elton Brand 1.00 2.50
5GG Kenyon Martin .75 2.00
6GG Rasheed Wallace 1.00 2.50
7GG Reggie Miller 1.00 2.50
8GG Andre Miller .75 2.00
9GG Vince Carter 1.50 4.00
10GG Richard Jefferson 1.00 2.50

2002-03 Fleer Platinum Inside the Playbook

Randomly seeded in packs, this 15-card set is die-cut in the shape of a note book with an embossed card front and small pictures of the featured player. Each card is sequentially numbered to 400.

STATED PRINT RUN 400 SERIAL #'d SETS
1PB Paul Pierce 1.25 3.00
2PB Kobe Bryant 5.00 12.00
3PB Caron Butler 1.25 3.00
4PB Tracy McGrady 2.00 5.00
5PB Allen Iverson 2.00 5.00
6PB Tim Duncan 2.50 6.00
7PB Vince Carter 2.00 5.00
8PB Jay Williams 1.25 3.00
9PB Michael Jordan 10.00 25.00
10PB DaJuan Wagner 1.00 2.50
11PB Steve Nash 1.50 4.00
12PB Nene Hilario 1.25 3.00
13PB Ben Wallace 1.00 2.50
14PB Mike Dunleavy 1.25 3.00
15PB Yao Ming 2.50 6.00

2002-03 Fleer Platinum Inside the Playbook Game Used

TED PRINT RUN 250 SERIAL #'d SETS
INSERTED ONLY IN WAX PACKS
AI Allen Iverson 5.00 12.00
BW Ben Wallace 2.50 6.00
CB Caron Butler 3.00 8.00
DW DaJuan Wagner 2.50 6.00
NH Nene Hilario 3.00 8.00
PP Paul Pierce 3.00 8.00
SN Steve Nash 4.00 10.00
TM Tracy McGrady 5.00 12.00
VC Vince Carter 5.00 12.00
YM Yao Ming 6.00 15.00

2002-03 Fleer Platinum Nameplates

Inserted randomly in Jumbo packs, this 30-card set showcases a horizontal design with a white background, a player photo on the right, a swatch of the name patch from the player's jersey and colored highlights to match the team colors. Each card has rounded corners and is sequentially numbered with print runs listed below.

INSERTED ONLY IN JUMBO PACKS
AI Allen Iverson/485 12.50 30.00
AM Andre Miller/260 6.00 15.00
AS Amare Stoudemire/315 6.00 15.00
BD Baron Davis/110 15.00 40.00
BW Ben Wallace/145 12.00 30.00
CB Caron Butler/280 10.00 25.00
DG Drew Gooden/220 10.00 25.00
DM Darius Miles/115 10.00 25.00
DN Dirk Nowitzki/255 15.00 40.00
DR David Robinson/210 15.00 40.00
EB Elton Brand/225 6.00 15.00
JK Jason Kidd/300 12.00 30.00
JO Jermaine O'Neal/135 15.00 40.00
JS John Stockton/230 15.00 40.00
KB Kwame Brown/355 6.00 15.00
KG Kevin Garnett/400 15.00 40.00
KM Kenyon Martin/170 6.00 15.00
LS Latrell Sprewell/190 15.00 40.00
PG Pau Gasol/350 10.00 25.00
PP Paul Pierce/200 15.00 40.00
QW Qyntel Woods/325 6.00 15.00
RA Ray Allen/400 10.00 25.00
SF Steve Francis/385 8.00 20.00
SN Steve Nash/110 20.00 50.00
TC Tyson Chandler/355 6.00 15.00
TM Tracy McGrady/175 10.00 25.00
TP Tony Parker/115 15.00 40.00
VC Vince Carter/545 10.00 25.00
YM Yao Ming/290 12.00 30.00

2002-03 Fleer Platinum Portraits

Inserted randomly in Rack packs at one in four, Jumbo packs at one in eight and Wax packs at one in 14, this 15-card set features a close-up shot of the player with a dark colored border that matches team colors. All cards contain silver foil highlights.

COMPLETE SET (15) 15.00 40.00
ODDS: 1:4 RACK, 1:8 JUMBO, 1:14 WAX
1PP Vince Carter 1.50 4.00
2PP Jason Kidd 1.50 4.00
3PP Shane Battier 1.00 2.50
4PP Steve Francis .75 2.00
5PP Chris Webber 1.00 2.50
6PP Jason Richardson 1.00 2.50
7PP Richard Jefferson 1.00 2.50
8PP Dirk Nowitzki 1.50 4.00
9PP Kevin Garnett 1.50 4.00
10PP Baron Davis .75 2.00
11PP Darius Miles .60 1.50
12PP Tim Duncan 2.00 5.00
13PP Kobe Bryant 4.00 10.00
14PP Shaquille O'Neal 2.50 6.00
15PP Michael Jordan 8.00 20.00

2002-03 Fleer Platinum Portraits Game Worn Jerseys

STATED ODDS 1:21 WAX PACKS
*PATCH: 1X TO 2.5X BASE HI
PATCH STATED PRINT RUN 100 SETS
BD Baron Davis 2.00 5.00
DN Dirk Nowitzki 4.00 10.00
JK Jason Kidd 4.00 10.00
JR Jason Richardson 2.50 6.00
KG Kevin Garnett 4.00 10.00
RJ Richard Jefferson 2.50 6.00
SB Shane Battier 2.50 6.00
SF Steve Francis 2.00 5.00
VC Vince Carter 4.00 10.00

2002-03 Fleer Platinum Vince Carter's All-Stars Game Used

Inserted randomly in Wax packs, this six card set pairs up Vince Carter with some of the NBA's top All-Stars on a throwback style card with a close up of Vince's face and a smaller full-body shot of the All-Star player. A swatch from each player is cut in the shap of a star and both are centered on the card horizontally. Each card is sequentially numbered to 250.

PRINT RUN 250 SERIAL #'d SETS
INSERTED ONLY IN WAX PACKS
AI V.Carter/A.Iverson 10.00 25.00
BW V.Carter/B.Wallace 10.00 25.00
DN V.Carter/D.Nowitzki 10.00 25.00
JK V.Carter/J.Kidd 10.00 25.00
KG V.Carter/K.Garnett 12.50 30.00
TM V.Carter/T.McGrady 10.00 25.00

2003-04 Fleer Platinum

Issued in March 2004, Platinum boasts a 200-card base set divided up as follows: 170 base veteran cards, where 1-141 share the same throwback design with a single color background and a sold color bar along the bottom, and cards 142-170 share an unsung heroes design that includes a close-up player portrait style shot and white borders. Cards 171-200 are rookies and utilize a design that resembles that of 1984 Fleer Baseball. Cards 171-180 are seeded at one in three for Wax, and one in two for Jumbo packs. Cards 181-190 were inserted in Wax packs only and are sequentially numbered to 750, and cards 191-200 were inserted in Jumbo packs only and are sequentially numbered to 500. Fleer Platinum was packaged in 20-pack boxes where 16 packs were Wax with seven cards per pack and a suggested retail price of $2.99 and four packs were Jumbo with 20 cards per pack and a suggested retail price of $4.99. Also included was one 2004 Ultra Hummer which sealed both a card and a die-cast GM Hummer with team logos to match the player on the card.

COMPLETE SET (200) 75.00 150.00
COMP.SET w/o SP's (170) 15.00 30.00
STATED ODDS 1:3 WAX, 1:2 JUMBO
181-190 PRINT RUN 750 SER.#'d SETS
181-190 INSERTED IN WAX ONLY
191-200 PRINT RUN 500 SER.#'d SETS
191-200 INSERTED IN JUMBO PACKS ONLY
1 Shane Battier .20 .50
2 Brad Miller .20 .50
3 Jason Kidd .40 1.00
4 Nick Van Exel .20 .50
5 David Wesley .15 .40
6 Corey Maggette .20 .50
7 Juan Dixon .15 .40
8 Jamaal Tinsley .15 .40
9 Stromile Swift .15 .40
10 Dajuan Wagner .15 .40
11 Joe Smith .20 .50
12 Jermaine O'Neal .20 .50
13 Steve Nash .30 .75
14 Karl Malone .30 .75
15 Vince Carter .40 1.00
16 Antonio McDyess .20 .50
17 Tim Thomas .15 .40
18 Vladimir Radmanovic .15 .40
19 Scottie Pippen .40 1.00
20 Tracy McGrady .30 .75
21 Darius Miles .15 .40
22 Toni Kukoc .25 .60
23 Antonio Davis .15 .40
24 Jamal Crawford .25 .60
25 Rasho Nesterovic .15 .40
26 Carlos Boozer .20 .50
27 Cuttino Mobley .15 .40
28 Larry Hughes .20 .50
29 Alvin Williams .15 .40
30 Andre Miller .20 .50
31 Amare Stoudemire .30 .75
32 Eric Williams .15 .40
33 Pau Gasol .25 .60
34 Kenyon Martin .20 .50
35 Elton Brand .25 .60
36 Charlie Ward .15 .40
37 Andrei Kirilenko .25 .60
38 Aaron McKie .15 .40
39 Maurice Taylor .15 .40
40 Baron Davis .20 .50
41 Dirk Nowitzki .40 1.00
42 Gary Payton .25 .60
43 Grant Hill .30 .75
44 Jalen Rose .20 .50
45 Allan Houston .20 .50
46 Erick Dampier .15 .40
47 Brian Grant .15 .40
48 Wally Szczerbiak .20 .50
49 Greg Ostertag .15 .40
50 Gilbert Arenas .20 .50
51 Kenny Anderson .20 .50
52 Juwan Howard .20 .50
53 Jason Terry .20 .50
54 Raef LaFrentz .15 .40
55 Ricky Davis .20 .50
56 Kobe Bryant 1.00 2.50
57 Chris Webber .25 .60
58 P.J. Brown .15 .40
59 Nene .20 .50
60 Kenny Thomas .15 .40
61 Mike Bibby .25 .60
62 Chris Wilcox .15 .40
63 Anfernee Hardaway .40 1.00
64 Drew Gooden .20 .50
65 Rodney White .15 .40
66 Shareef Abdur-Rahim .20 .50
67 Quentin Richardson .20 .50
68 Ben Wallace .20 .50
69 Latrell Sprewell .20 .50
70 Shaquille O'Neal .60 1.50
71 Vin Baker .15 .40
72 Tony Parker .25 .60
73 Stephen Jackson .20 .50
74 Ray Allen .25 .60
75 Eric Snow .15 .40
76 Jason Richardson .25 .60
77 Shammond Williams .15 .40
78 Tayshaun Prince .20 .50
79 Antawn Jamison .20 .50
80 Derek Fisher .20 .50
81 Jeff Foster .15 .40
82 Kwame Brown .15 .40
83 Yao Ming .50 1.25
84 Rasheed Wallace .25 .60
85 Tyson Chandler .20 .50
86 Mike Dunleavy .20 .50
87 Alan Henderson .15 .40
88 Rashard Lewis .25 .60
89 Jamaal Magloire .15 .40
90 Stephon Marbury .20 .50
91 DeShawn Stevenson .15 .40
92 Damon Stoudamire .20 .50
93 Eddy Curry .15 .40
94 Peja Stojakovic .25 .60
95 Glenn Robinson .20 .50
96 Mike Miller .20 .50
97 Richard Hamilton .20 .50
98 Kevin Garnett .40 1.00
99 Zach Randolph .20 .50
100 Tony Delk .15 .40
101 Clifford Robinson .15 .40
102 Steve Francis .20 .50
103 Curtis Borchardt .25 .60
104 Jerry Stackhouse .20 .50
105 Desmond Mason .20 .50
106 Chauncey Billups .25 .60
107 Sam Cassell .20 .50
108 Michael Finley .25 .60
109 Hedo Turkoglu .20 .50
110 Ronald Murray .15 .40
111 Allen Iverson .40 1.00
112 Richard Jefferson .20 .50
113 Theo Ratliff .15 .40
114 Ron Artest .25 .60
115 Doug Christie .15 .40
116 Lamar Odom .20 .50
117 Lamond Murray .15 .40
118 Bonzi Wells .15 .40
119 Caron Butler .20 .50
120 Marcus Camby .20 .50
121 Manu Ginobili .30 .75
122 Paul Pierce .25 .60
123 Troy Hudson .15 .40
124 Jim Jackson .15 .40
125 Keith Van Horn .20 .50
126 Reggie Miller .25 .60
127 Tim Duncan .40 1.00
128 Shawn Marion .20 .50
129 Eddie Jones .20 .50
130 Matt Harpring .15 .40
131 Elden Campbell .15 .40
132 Marko Jaric .15 .40
133 John Wallace .15 .40
134 Erick Strickland .15 .40
135 Voshon Lenard .15 .40
136 Aaron Williams .15 .40
137 Qyntel Woods .15 .40
138 Kelvin Cato .15 .40
139 Michael Curry .15 .40
140 Vlade Divac .20 .50
141 Jason Hart .15 .40
142 Nazr Mohammed UH .15 .40
143 Mike James UH .15 .40
144 Jerome Williams UH .15 .40
145 Zydrunas Ilgauskas UH .20 .50
146 Antoine Walker UH .25 .60
147 Earl Boykins UH .15 .40
148 Mehmet Okur UH .20 .50
149 Brian Cardinal UH .15 .40
150 Bostjan Nachbar UH .15 .40
151 Al Harrington UH .20 .50
152 Eddie House UH .15 .40
153 Devean George UH .15 .40
154 Jason Williams UH .20 .50
155 Rafer Alston UH .15 .40
156 Michael Redd UH .25 .60
157 Gary Trent UH .15 .40
158 Kerry Kittles UH .15 .40
159 Jamal Mashburn UH .20 .50
160 Kurt Thomas UH .15 .40
161 Tyronn Lue UH .15 .40
162 Derrick Coleman UH .20 .50
163 Joe Johnson UH .20 .50
164 Dale Davis UH .15 .40
165 Bobby Jackson UH .15 .40
166 Malik Rose UH .15 .40
167 Brent Barry UH .15 .40
168 Donyell Marshall UH .15 .40
169 Carlos Arroyo UH .20 .50
170 Etan Thomas UH .15 .40
171 Zoran Planinic RC .60 1.50
172 Jason Kapono RC .60 1.50
173 Zarko Cabarkapa RC .60 1.50
174 Darko Milicic RC .75 2.00
175 Aleksandar Pavlovic RC .75 2.00
176 Marcus Banks RC .60 1.50
177 Willie Green RC .60 1.50
178 Udonis Haslem RC .75 2.00
179 Nick Collison RC .75 2.00
180 Chris Kaman RC 1.00 2.50
181 T.J. Ford RC 1.25 3.00
182 Travis Outlaw RC 1.25 3.00
183 LeBron James RC 40.00 100.00
184 Troy Bell RC 1.00 2.50
185 Reece Gaines RC 1.00 2.50
186 David West RC 1.50 4.00
187 Kirk Hinrich RC 1.50 4.00
188 Chris Bosh RC 2.50 6.00
189 Leandro Barbosa RC 1.50 4.00
190 Dwyane Wade RC 5.00 12.00
191 Mike Sweetney RC 1.25 3.00
192 Darius Songaila 1.25 3.00
193 Luke Ridnour RC 1.50 4.00
194 Carmelo Anthony RC 6.00 15.00
195 Jarvis Hayes RC 1.25 3.00
196 Mickael Pietrus RC 1.50 4.00
197 Dahntay Jones RC 1.50 4.00
198 Josh Howard RC 2.00 5.00
199 Maciej Lampe RC 1.25 3.00
200 Luke Walton RC 2.00 5.00

2003-04 Fleer Platinum Finish

*1-170 SINGLES: 3X TO 8X BASE HI
*171-180 RCs: 1.25X TO 3X BASE HI
*181-190 RCs: 1X TO 2.5X BASE HI
*191-200 RCs: .75X TO 2X BASE HI
PRINT RUN 100 SER.#'d SETS
56 Kobe Bryant 15.00 40.00
183 LeBron James 100.00 250.00

2003-04 Fleer Platinum Big Signs

Randomly inserted in Wax at the rate of one in nine and Jumbo at the rate of one in eight, this 15-card set features a fold-out jumbo design with the player's photo in the middle of the opened card.

COMPLETE SET (15) 12.50 30.00
STATED ODDS 1:9 H WAX, 1:2 JUMBO 1:8 R
1 Kevin Garnett 1.00 2.50
2 Allen Iverson 1.00 2.50
3 Shaquille O'Neal 1.50 4.00
4 Darko Milicic .50 1.25
5 Kobe Bryant 2.50 6.00
6 Ben Wallace .50 1.25
7 LeBron James 6.00 15.00
8 Dwyane Wade 2.00 5.00
9 Dirk Nowitzki 1.00 2.50
10 Baron Davis .50 1.25
11 Yao Ming 1.25 3.00
12 Carmelo Anthony 2.00 5.00
13 Peja Stojakovic .60 1.50
14 Jermaine O'Neal .50 1.25
15 Vince Carter 1.00 2.50

2003-04 Fleer Platinum Big Signs Autographs

Randomly seeded in packs, this four card set is an autographed parallel of the big signs set where each card is sequentially numbered to 50.

PRINT RUN 50 SER.#'d SETS
BW Ben Wallace 12.50 30.00
DW Dwyane Wade 75.00 200.00
VC Vince Carter 15.00 40.00

2003-04 Fleer Platinum Inscribed

Randomly seeded, all of these cards are sequentially numbered and feature a horizontal design with full-color player portrait photos on the right and an embedded cut signature on the left.

PRINT RUNS LISTED IN CHECKLIST
N Nene/188 4.00 10.00
AK Andrei Kirilenko/193 10.00 25.00
BW Ben Wallace/35 15.00 40.00
CA1 Carmelo Anthony/282 15.00 40.00
CA2 Carmelo Anthony 25.00 60.00
CB Chris Bosh/250 6.00 15.00
DG Drew Gooden/66 6.00 15.00
DR David Robinson/195 30.00 80.00
DW David West/250 4.00 10.00
GA1 Gilbert Arenas/315 8.00 20.00
GA2 Gilbert Arenas/32 15.00 40.00
KK Kyle Korver/87 15.00 30.00
KR Kareem Rush/248 4.00 10.00
LB Leandro Barbosa/196 4.00 10.00
LR Luke Ridnour/197 3.00 8.00
LW Luke Walton/132 4.00 10.00
MB1 Marcus Banks/350 2.50 6.00
MG Manu Ginobili/198 12.50 30.00
ML Maciej Lampe/185 2.50 6.00
MP Mickael Pietrus/249 3.00 8.00
MS Mike Sweetney/264 2.50 6.00
TC Tyson Chandler/195 4.00 10.00
TM Tracy McGrady/99 20.00 50.00
TO Travis Outlaw/276 3.00 8.00
TP Tayshaun Prince/185 6.00 15.00
UH Udonis Haslem/195 3.00 8.00
VC1 Vince Carter/280 10.00 25.00
ZC1 Zarko Cabarkapa/235 2.50 6.00
ZC2 Zarko Cabarkapa/37 8.00 20.00
CAR1 Caron Butler/365 5.00 12.00
CAR2 Caron Butler/28 20.00 50.00
JHO Josh Howard/250 4.00 10.00
SHM Shawn Marion/101 8.00 20.00

2003-04 Fleer Platinum Locker Room Memorabilia

Randomly inserted in Hobby Wax packs at the rate of one in 24 and Retail at one in 96, this 25-card set features a horizontal design with player photos on the left and swatches of memorabilia on the right. A dual memorabilia version, where swatches are stacked on top of eachother was also inserted and is sequentially numbered to 50.

STATED ODDS 1:24 H, 1:96 R
*DUAL SINGLES: 1.25X TO 3X BASE MEM.HI
DUAL PRINT RUN 50 SER.#'d SETS
N Nene 2.00 5.00
AK Andrei Kirilenko 2.50 6.00
BD Baron Davis 2.00 5.00
BW Ben Wallace 2.00 5.00
CB Caron Butler 2.00 5.00
EB Elton Brand 2.50 6.00
GR Glenn Robinson 2.00 5.00
JH Jarvis Hayes 1.50 4.00
JK Jason Kidd 4.00 10.00
JR Jason Richardson 2.50 6.00
KM Karl Malone 4.00 10.00
MD Mike Dunleavy 2.00 5.00
MF Michael Finley 2.50 6.00
MG Manu Ginobili 3.00 8.00
MR Michael Redd 2.50 6.00
PP Paul Pierce 2.50 6.00
PS Peja Stojakovic 2.50 6.00
RM Reggie Miller 2.50 6.00
SF Steve Francis 2.00 5.00
SM Stephon Marbury 2.00 5.00
SN Steve Nash 3.00 8.00
JON Jermaine O'Neal 2.00 5.00
SHM Shawn Marion 2.00 5.00
YAO Yao Ming 5.00 12.00
KMAR Kenyon Martin 2.00 5.00

2003-04 Fleer Platinum Nameplates

Randomly insertred in packs, this 30-card set is sequentially numbered and is set to look like a license plate with both a full-color player image and a premium swatch of memorabilia. A Dual player version was also produced and inserted and those cards are sequentially numbered to 25.

PRINT RUNS LISTED BELOW
AH Allan Houston/450 5.00 12.00
AJ Antawn Jamison/145 5.00 12.00
BW Ben Wallace/90 8.00 20.00
CA Carmelo Anthony/380 15.00 40.00
CK Chris Kaman/465 5.00 12.00
CW Chris Webber/695 12.00 30.00
DW Dwyane Wade/465 15.00 40.00
DW Dajuan Wagner/585 4.00 10.00
GA Gilbert Arenas/235 5.00 12.00
JC Jamal Crawford/323 8.00 20.00
JH Jarvis Hayes/375 3.00 8.00
LR Luke Ridnour/710 4.00 10.00
LW Luke Walton/215 5.00 12.00
MB Mike Bibby/365 6.00 15.00
MD Mike Dunleavy/250 5.00 12.00
MG Manu Ginobili/195 8.00 20.00
MM Mike Miller/590 5.00 12.00
MP Mickael Pietrus/253 4.00 10.00
MR Michael Redd/725 6.00 15.00
RH Richard Hamilton/170 5.00 12.00
SB Shane Battier/715 5.00 12.00
SP Scottie Pippen/390 15.00 40.00
TD Tim Duncan/725 10.00 25.00
TO Travis Outlaw/590 4.00 10.00
TP Tayshaun Prince/455 5.00 12.00
VC Vince Carter/725 10.00 25.00
ZR Zach Randolph/210 5.00 12.00
SAR Shareef Abdur-Rahim/600 5.00 12.00

2003-04 Fleer Platinum Nameplates Dual

This set parallels the design of the Nameplates set but features two players and two swatches of memorabilia. Each card is sequentially numbered to 25.

PRINT RUN 25 SER.#'d SETS
GAJH G.Arenas/J.Hayes 25.00 60.00
GPLW G.Payton/L.Walton 25.00 60.00
MBCW M.Bibby/C.Webber 15.00 40.00
MDMP M.Dunleavy/M.Pietrus 20.00 50.00
SBMM S.Battier/M.Miller 15.00 40.00
TDMG T.Duncan/M.Ginobili 30.00 80.00
TOZR T.Outlaw/Z.Randolph 15.00 40.00

2003-04 Fleer Platinum NBA Scouting Report

Randomly seeded in packs, this 15-card set was designed to look like an open notebook where the outside is the texture of a basketball and the inside shows statistics and a small picture of the featured player. Each card is sequentially numbered to 400.

COMPLETE SET (15) 20.00 40.00
PRINT RUN 400 SER.#'d SETS
1 Shaquille O'Neal 2.50 6.00
2 Tracy McGrady 1.25 3.00
3 Tim Duncan 1.50 4.00
4 Jason Kidd 1.50 4.00
5 Amare Stoudemire 1.25 3.00
6 Kobe Bryant 4.00 10.00
7 Steve Francis .75 2.00
8 Kevin Garnett 1.50 4.00
9 Dirk Nowitzki 1.50 4.00
10 Jason Richardson 1.00 2.50
11 Darko Milicic .75 2.00
12 Jarvis Hayes .60 1.50
13 LeBron James 40.00 100.00
14 Chris Webber 1.00 2.50
15 Chris Bosh 1.50 4.00

2003-04 Fleer Platinum NBA Scouting Report Jerseys

Randomly inserted, this set parallels the design of the Scouting Report insert set enhanced with a jersey swatch and sequential numbering to 250.

PRINT RUN 250 SER.#'d SETS
INSERTED IN HOBBY WAX AND RETAIL
AS Amare Stoudemire 3.00 8.00
CB Chris Bosh 4.00 10.00
DN Dirk Nowitzki 4.00 10.00
JH Jarvis Hayes 1.50 4.00
JK Jason Kidd 4.00 10.00
KG Kevin Garnett 4.00 10.00
SF Steve Francis 2.00 5.00
SO Shaquille O'Neal 6.00 15.00
TD Tim Duncan 4.00 10.00
TM Tracy McGrady 3.00 8.00

2003-04 Fleer Platinum Portraits

Randomly inserted in Hobby Wax packs at the rate of one in 18, Jumbo at one in four, and Retail at one in 14, this 15-card set features a bordered all-foil design with close-up player portrait style photos.

COMPLETE SET (15) 15.00 30.00
STAT.ODDS 1:18 H WAX, 1:4 JUMBO 1:14 R
1 Pau Gasol 1.25 3.00
2 Yao Ming 2.50 6.00
3 Michael Finley 1.25 3.00
4 Tony Parker 1.25 3.00
5 Dwyane Wade 4.00 10.00
6 Darko Milicic 1.00 2.50
7 Tracy McGrady 1.50 4.00
8 Allen Iverson 2.00 5.00
9 Reggie Miller 1.25 3.00
10 Paul Pierce 1.25 3.00
11 Amare Stoudemire 1.50 4.00
12 Steve Nash 1.50 4.00
13 Caron Butler 1.00 2.50
14 Drew Gooden 1.00 2.50
15 Vince Carter 2.00 5.00

2003-04 Fleer Platinum Portraits Jerseys

Randomly seeded in Hobby Wax at the rate of one in 40 and Retail at one in 120, this 10-card set parallels the design of the base Portraits insert set enhanced with a square jersey swatch. A Patch version was also produced and is sequentially numbered to 100.

STATED ODDS 1:40 H WAX, 1:120 R
*PATCHES: 1X TO 2.5X BASE JSY HI
PATCH PRINT RUN 100 SER.#'d SETS
AI Allen Iverson 4.00 10.00
AS Amare Stoudemire 3.00 8.00
DW Dwyane Wade 8.00 20.00
MF Michael Finley 2.50 6.00
PG Pau Gasol 2.50 6.00
RM Reggie Miller 2.50 6.00
TM Tracy McGrady 3.00 8.00
TP Tony Parker 2.50 6.00
VC Vince Carter 4.00 10.00
YAO Yao Ming 5.00 12.00

2003-04 Fleer Platinum Showdown Series

Inserted in Hobby Wax packs at the rate of one in 288 and Retail at one in 480, this 10-card set is designed in the format of a faded old boxing match poster with one player on the left and the other on the right.

STATED ODDS 1:288 H WAX, 1:480 R
1 A.Iverson/K.Bryant 5.00 12.00
2 J.Kidd/T.Parker 4.00 10.00
3 S.O'Neal/T.Duncan 6.00 15.00
4 P.Pierce/A.Walker 4.00 10.00
5 L.James/C.Anthony 20.00 50.00
6 J.O'Neal/B.Wallace 4.00 10.00
7 V.Carter/T.McGrady 4.00 10.00
8 D.Nowitzki/C.Webber 5.00 12.00
9 K.Garnett/Stoudemire 4.00 10.00
10 N.Collison/K.Hinrich 4.00 10.00

2000-01 Fleer Premium

The 2000-01 Fleer Premium set was released in November, 2000. The 241-card base set features 200 veterans, and 41 Rookie cards. Please note that all rookies are serial numbered to 1999, and that the first 250 of cards 217-241 contain a ball swatch. Each pack contained eight cards, and carried a suggested retail price of $2.99.

COMPLETE SET w/o RC (200) 12.50 30.00
RCs: STATED PRINT RUN 1999 SERIAL #'d SETS
217-241: FIRST 250 CONTAIN BALL SWATCH
1 Vince Carter .60 1.50
2 Kobe Bryant 1.25 3.00
3 Jermaine Jackson .20 .50
4 Lamar Odom .25 .60
5 Robert Traylor .20 .50
6 Jason Kidd .50 1.25
7 Rashard Lewis .30 .75
8 Ron Artest .30 .75
9 Grant Hill .40 1.00
10 Kenny Thomas .20 .50
11 Anthony Carter .20 .50
12 Kerry Kittles .20 .50
13 Pat Garrity .20 .50
14 David Robinson .50 1.25
15 Bryant Reeves .20 .50
16 Fred Hoiberg .20 .50
17 Jerry Stackhouse .25 .60
18 Donyell Marshall .20 .50
19 Ron Harper .25 .60
20 Scott Burrell .20 .50
21 Ron Mercer .20 .50
22 Avery Johnson .25 .60
23 Jacque Vaughn .20 .50
24 Adrian Griffin .20 .50
25 Antonio McDyess .25 .60
26 Adonal Foyle .20 .50
27 Derek Fisher .30 .75
28 Terrell Brandon .20 .50
29 Matt Harpring .20 .50
30 Nazr Mohammed .20 .50
31 Tom Gugliotta .20 .50
32 Scott Padgett .20 .50
33 Detlef Schrempf .25 .60
34 Dirk Nowitzki .50 1.25
35 Mookie Blaylock .20 .50
36 James Posey .20 .50
37 Latrell Sprewell .25 .60
38 Michael Doleac .20 .50
39 Damon Stoudamire .25 .60
40 Tim Duncan .60 1.50
41 John Stockton .40 1.00
42 Danny Fortson .20 .50
43 Raef LaFrentz .20 .50
44 Steve Francis .25 .60
45 Travis Knight .20 .50

46 Kevin Garnett .50 1.25
47 Mitch Richmond .25 .60
48 Olden Polynice .20 .50
49 Derrick Coleman .25 .60
50 Ervin Johnson .20 .50
51 Shandon Anderson .20 .50
52 Jamal Mashburn .25 .60
53 Joe Smith .25 .60
54 Bo Outlaw .20 .50
55 Clifford Robinson .20 .50
56 Scottie Pippen .50 1.25
57 Chris Webber .30 .75
58 Doug Christie .20 .50
59 Michael Dickerson .20 .50
60 Anthony Mason .20 .50
61 Shawn Bradley .20 .50
62 Reggie Miller .30 .75
63 P.J. Brown .20 .50
64 Wally Szczerbiak .25 .60
65 Keon Clark .20 .50
66 Anthony Peeler .20 .50
67 Doug West .20 .50
68 Antoine Walker .25 .60
69 Trajan Langdon .20 .50
70 Mark Jackson .25 .60
71 Sam Cassell .25 .60
72 Kurt Thomas .20 .50
73 Ruben Patterson .20 .50
74 Alvin Williams .20 .50
75 Juwan Howard .25 .60
76 Baron Davis .30 .75
77 Otis Thorpe .25 .60
78 Austin Croshere .20 .50
79 Tony Delk .20 .50
80 William Avery .20 .50
81 Matt Geiger .20 .50
82 Richard Hamilton .25 .60
83 Ricky Davis .25 .60
84 Hubert Davis .20 .50
85 Jalen Rose .25 .60
86 Theo Ratliff .20 .50
87 Bobby Jackson .20 .50
88 Glenn Robinson .25 .60
89 Kendall Gill .20 .50
90 Laron Profit .20 .50
91 Brad Miller .25 .60
92 Cedric Ceballos .20 .50
93 Arvydas Sabonis .25 .60
94 Vitaly Potapenko .20 .50
95 Rod Strickland .20 .50
96 Erick Dampier .20 .50
97 Ryan Bowen .20 .50
98 Dale Davis .20 .50
99 Larry Johnson .30 .75
100 John Thomas .20 .50
101 Rodney Rogers .20 .50
102 Ray Allen .30 .75
103 Isaac Austin .20 .50
104 Radoslav Nesterovic .20 .50
105 Tariq Abdul-Wahad .20 .50
106 Jonathan Bender .20 .50
107 Tim Hardaway .30 .75
108 Jamie Feick .20 .50
109 Toni Kukoc .30 .75
110 Tyrone Corbin .20 .50
111 Aleksandar Radojevic .20 .50
112 Tony Battie .20 .50
113 Andre Miller .25 .60
114 Derek Anderson .20 .50
115 Tim Thomas .20 .50
116 Corey Maggette .25 .60
117 Rasheed Wallace .30 .75
118 Shammond Williams .20 .50
119 Charlie Ward .20 .50
120 Paul Pierce .30 .75
121 Shawn Kemp .30 .75
122 Darrell Armstrong .20 .50
123 Fred Vinson .20 .50
124 Jim Jackson .20 .50
125 Steve Nash .50 1.25
126 Michael Stewart .20 .50
127 Maurice Taylor .20 .50
128 Michael Ruffin .20 .50
129 Vlade Divac .25 .60
130 LaPhonso Ellis .25 .60
131 Eddie Jones .30 .75
132 Hakeem Olajuwon .40 1.00
133 Rick Fox .20 .50
134 Patrick Ewing .40 1.00
135 Brian Grant .20 .50
136 Jaren Jackson .20 .50
137 Christian Laettner .25 .60
138 Greg Ostertag .20 .50
139 Anfernee Hardaway .50 1.25
140 Nick Van Exel .25 .60
141 Jason Caffey .20 .50
142 Michael Olowokandi .20 .50
143 Darvin Ham .20 .50
144 Calbert Cheaney .20 .50
145 Steve Smith .25 .60
146 Jason Williams .30 .75
147 Jelani McCoy .20 .50
148 Karl Malone .40 1.00
149 Dikembe Mutombo .30 .75
150 Wesley Person .20 .50
151 Kelvin Cato .20 .50
152 Alonzo Mourning .40 1.00
153 Terry Mills .20 .50
154 Allen Iverson .60 1.50
155 Bonzi Wells .20 .50
156 Antonio Daniels .20 .50
157 Shareef Abdur-Rahim .25 .60
158 Randy Brown .20 .50
159 Mike Bibby .30 .75
160 Travis Best .20 .50
161 Dan Majerle .30 .75
162 Aaron McKie .20 .50
163 Jason Terry .30 .75
164 Michael Finley .30 .75
165 Antonio Davis .20 .50
166 Lindsey Hunter .20 .50
167 Cuttino Mobley .20 .50
168 Glen Rice .25 .60
169 Stephon Marbury .25 .60
170 Sean Elliott .30 .75
171 Cedric Henderson .20 .50
172 Eric Snow .20 .50
173 Othella Harrington .20 .50
174 Vonteego Cummings .20 .50
175 John Amaechi .20 .50
176 Allan Houston .25 .60
177 Shawn Marion .25 .60
178 Scot Pollard .20 .50
179 Elton Brand .30 .75
180 Loy Vaught .20 .50
181 Larry Hughes .25 .60
182 Shaquille O'Neal .75 2.00
183 Keith Van Horn .25 .60
184 Terry Porter .20 .50
185 Quincy Lewis .20 .50
186 Alan Henderson .20 .50
187 Brevin Knight .20 .50
188 Walt Williams .20 .50
189 Clarence Weatherspoon .20 .50
190 Marcus Camby .25 .60
191 Corliss Williamson .20 .50
192 Gary Payton .30 .75
193 Felipe Lopez .20 .50
194 Elden Campbell .20 .50
195 Jerome Williams .20 .50
196 Antawn Jamison .30 .75
197 Gerard King .20 .50
198 Andrae Patterson .20 .50
199 Vin Baker .25 .60
200 Tracy McGrady .50 1.25
201 Chris Carrawell RC 1.25 3.00
202 Eduardo Najera RC 1.25 3.00
203 Olumide Oyedeji RC .75 2.00
204 Hanno Mottola RC .75 2.00
205 Dan McClintock RC 1.25 3.00
206 Jacquay Walls RC 1.25 3.00
207 Corey Hightower RC 1.25 3.00
208 Jamal Crawford RC 3.00 8.00
209 Soumaila Samake RC .75 2.00
210 Michael Redd RC 3.00 8.00
211 Jason Hart RC 1.25 3.00
212 Mark Karcher RC .75 2.00
213 Chris Porter RC .75 2.00
214 Eddie House RC 1.00 2.50
215 Jabari Smith RC .75 2.00
216 Dan Langhi RC .75 2.00
217 Desmond Mason RC 1.50 4.00
218 Darius Miles RC 1.25 3.00
219 Donnell Harvey RC 1.00 2.50
220 DeShawn Stevenson RC 1.25 3.00
221 Kenyon Martin RC 3.00 8.00
222 Joel Przybilla RC 1.00 2.50
223 Keyon Dooling RC 1.25 3.00
224 Speedy Claxton RC 1.25 3.00
225 Jerome Moiso RC .75 2.00
226 Hedo Turkoglu RC 2.00 5.00
227 Mark Madsen RC 1.25 3.00
228 Morris Peterson RC 1.25 3.00
229 Courtney Alexander RC 1.00 2.50
230 Etan Thomas RC 1.25 3.00
231 Mateen Cleaves RC 1.00 2.50
232 Stromile Swift RC 1.25 3.00
233 Marcus Fizer RC 1.25 3.00
234 Quentin Richardson RC 1.25 3.00
235 Jason Collier RC 1.25 3.00
236 Jamaal Magloire RC 1.25 3.00
237 Erick Barkley RC .75 2.00
238 DerMarr Johnson RC 1.00 2.50
239 Chris Mihm RC 1.00 2.50
240 Mamadou N'Diaye RC .75 2.00
241 Mike Miller RC 2.00 5.00

2000-01 Fleer Premium Rookie Game Balls

*GAME BALL: .6X TO 1.5X HI COLUMN

2000-01 Fleer Premium 10th Anni-VINCE-ry

Randomly inserted in packs at one in 24, this 10-card set celebrates the ten year anniversary of the Fleer/SkyBox Premium line. Each card features Vince Carter in the design for that particular year. Card backs carry an "AV" prefix.
COMPLETE SET (10) 20.00 40.00
COMMON CARD (AV1-AV10) 2.50 6.00
STATED ODDS 1:24 HOB, 1:20 RET

2000-01 Fleer Premium Vince Carter Rookie Remnants

This three-card insert was randomly inserted into 2000-01 Fleer products. The set includes a Vince Carter floor card (numbered to 100), a Vince Carter floor/jersey card (numbered to 15), and finally an autographed Vince Carter floor/jersey card (numbered 1/1).
FLOOR: 100 CARDS IN EACH RELEASE
FLOOR/GJ: 15 CARDS IN EACH RELEASE
FLOOR/GJ AU: 1 CARD IN EACH RELEASE
RANDOM INSERTS IN HOBBY PACKS
NNO Vince Carter FLR/100 12.50 30.00
NNO Vince Carter FLR JSY/15 20.00 50.00

2000-01 Fleer Premium Name Game

Randomly inserted in packs at one in 24, this 15-card set features players who have become "household names". Card backs carry a "NG" prefix.
COMPLETE SET (15) 25.00 50.00
STATED ODDS 1:24
NG1 Vince Carter 2.50 6.00
NG2 Allen Iverson 2.50 6.00
NG3 Shaquille O'Neal 3.00 8.00
NG4 Jason Kidd 2.00 5.00
NG5 Jason Williams 1.25 3.00
NG6 Glenn Robinson 1.00 2.50
NG7 Karl Malone 1.50 4.00
NG8 Reggie Miller 1.25 3.00
NG9 Hakeem Olajuwon 1.50 4.00
NG10 Lamar Odom 1.00 2.50
NG11 Tim Duncan 2.50 6.00
NG12 Grant Hill 1.50 4.00
NG13 Kobe Bryant 5.00 12.00
NG14 Tracy McGrady 2.00 5.00
NG15 Kevin Garnett 2.00 5.00

2000-01 Fleer Premium Name Game Premium

ATED PRINT RUN 50 SERIAL #'d SETS
NG1 Vince Carter 25.00 60.00
NG2 Allen Iverson 25.00 60.00
NG3 Shaquille O'Neal 30.00 80.00
NG4 Jason Kidd 20.00 50.00
NG5 Jason Williams 12.00 30.00
NG6 Glenn Robinson 10.00 25.00
NG7 Karl Malone 15.00 40.00
NG8 Reggie Miller 20.00 50.00
NG9 Hakeem Olajuwon 15.00 40.00
NG10 Lamar Odom 10.00 25.00

2000-01 Fleer Premium Skilled Artists

Randomly inserted in packs at one in 12, this 15-card set features players who use a combination of skill and creative direction to become quick strike artists. Card backs carry a "SA" prefix.
COMPLETE SET (15) 10.00 20.00
STATED ODDS 1:12 HOB, 1:15 RET
SA1 Vince Carter 1.25 3.00
SA2 Steve Francis .50 1.25
SA3 Paul Pierce .60 1.50
SA4 Gary Payton .60 1.50
SA5 Jason Williams .60 1.50
SA6 Larry Hughes .50 1.25
SA7 Tim Duncan 1.25 3.00
SA8 Kobe Bryant 2.50 6.00
SA9 Chris Webber .60 1.50
SA10 Tracy McGrady 1.00 2.50
SA11 Dirk Nowitzki 1.00 2.50
SA12 Elton Brand .60 1.50
SA13 Andre Miller .50 1.25
SA14 Ray Allen .60 1.50
SA15 Shareef Abdur-Rahim .50 1.25

2000-01 Fleer Premium Skilled Artists Premium

STATED PRINT RUN 100 SERIAL #'d SETS
SA1 Vince Carter 20.00 50.00
SA2 Steve Francis 8.00 20.00
SA3 Paul Pierce 10.00 25.00
SA4 Gary Payton 10.00 25.00
SA5 Jason Williams 10.00 25.00
SA6 Chris Webber 10.00 25.00

2000-01 Fleer Premium Skylines

Randomly inserted in packs at one in 144, this 10-card set features NBA players against the skyline of the city they play in. Card backs carry a "SL" prefix.
COMPLETE SET (10) 25.00 60.00
STATED ODDS 1:144 HOB, 1:288 RET
SL1 Vince Carter 4.00 10.00
SL2 Allen Iverson 4.00 10.00
SL3 Kobe Bryant 8.00 20.00
SL4 Latrell Sprewell 1.50 4.00
SL5 Elton Brand 2.00 5.00
SL6 Grant Hill 2.50 6.00
SL7 Steve Francis 1.50 4.00
SL8 Richard Hamilton 1.50 4.00
SL9 Gary Payton 2.00 5.00
SL10 David Robinson 3.00 8.00

2000-01 Fleer Premium Sole Train

Randomly inserted in packs at one in six, this 15-card set features players who carry their teams, night in and night out. Card backs carry a "ST" prefix.
COMPLETE SET (15) 4.00 10.00
STATED ODDS 1:6 HOB, 1:8 RET
ST1 Vince Carter .75 2.00
ST2 Marcus Camby .30 .75
ST3 Wally Szczerbiak .30 .75
ST4 Lamar Odom .30 .75
ST5 Shaquille O'Neal 1.00 2.50
ST6 Antoine Walker .30 .75
ST7 Eddie Jones .40 1.00
ST8 Larry Hughes .30 .75
ST9 Baron Davis .40 1.00
ST10 Mike Bibby .40 1.00
ST11 Elton Brand .40 1.00
ST12 Kevin Garnett .60 1.50
ST13 Allen Iverson .75 2.00
ST14 Tim Duncan .75 2.00
ST15 Grant Hill .50 1.25

2000-01 Fleer Premium Sole Train Premium

STATED PRINT RUN 50 SERIAL #'d SETS
ST1 Vince Carter 15.00 40.00
ST2 Marcus Camby 6.00 15.00
ST3 Wally Szczerbiak 6.00 15.00
ST4 Lamar Odom 6.00 15.00
ST5 Shaquille O'Neal 40.00 100.00
ST6 Antoine Walker 6.00 15.00
ST7 Eddie Jones 8.00 20.00
ST8 Larry Hughes 6.00 15.00
ST9 Baron Davis 8.00 20.00
ST10 Mike Bibby 8.00 20.00

2001-02 Fleer Premium

Released in December 2001, This 185-card base set is standard size and contains 150 veterans as well as 35 rookies. The cards are borderless with a white background. A color action shot of the featured player graces the front of the card with his name running along the top of the card and his corresponding team name and position running down the right-hand side. The Rookie Cards (151-185) have a stated print run of 1500 sets.
COMPLETE SET (185) 100.00 200.00
COMP.SET w/o SP's (1-150) 15.00 40.00
151-185 PRINT RUN 1500 SER.#'d SETS
1 Shareef Abdur-Rahim .25 .60
2 Charlie Ward .20 .50
3 Anfernee Hardaway .50 1.25
4 Robert Horry .25 .60
5 Michael Jordan 2.50 6.00
6 Trajan Langdon .20 .50
7 Dan Majerle .30 .75
8 Tracy McGrady .50 1.25
9 Alonzo Mourning .40 1.00
10 Gary Payton .30 .75
11 Erick Barkley .20 .50
12 Jerry Stackhouse .25 .60
13 Vince Carter .50 1.25
14 Speedy Claxton .20 .50
15 DerMarr Johnson .20 .50
16 Bryon Russell .20 .50
17 Derrick Coleman .25 .60
18 Kevin Willis .20 .50
19 Dirk Nowitzki .50 1.25
20 Derek Anderson .20 .50
21 Tim Hardaway .30 .75
22 Avery Johnson .25 .60
23 Quincy Lewis .20 .50
24 Shawn Marion .25 .60
25 Joe Smith .25 .60
26 Tim Thomas .20 .50
27 Bonzi Wells .20 .50
28 Ron Artest .30 .75
29 Elton Brand .30 .75
30 Mateen Cleaves .20 .50
31 Marcus Fizer .20 .50
32 Ervin Johnson .20 .50
33 Mark Madsen .20 .50
34 Andre Miller .25 .60
35 Nazr Mohammed .20 .50
36 Dikembe Mutombo .30 .75
37 Ben Wallace .25 .60
38 Scottie Pippen .50 1.25
39 Theo Ratliff .20 .50
40 Hedo Turkoglu .25 .60
41 Alvin Williams .20 .50
42 Corey Maggette .25 .60
43 Steve Francis .25 .60
44 Dean Garrett .20 .50
45 Wally Szczerbiak .25 .60
46 Brent Barry .20 .50
47 Vlade Divac .25 .60
48 LaPhonso Ellis .25 .60
49 Tyrone Hill .20 .50
50 Toni Kukoc .30 .75
51 George Lynch .20 .50
52 Antonio McDyess .25 .60
53 Paul Pierce .30 .75
54 Mitch Richmond .25 .60
55 Latrell Sprewell .25 .60
56 Otis Thorpe .25 .60
57 Ray Allen .30 .75
58 Mike Bibby .30 .75
59 P.J. Brown .20 .50
60 Allan Houston .25 .60
61 Stephon Marbury .25 .60
62 Aaron McKie .20 .50
63 Reggie Miller .30 .75
64 Eduardo Najera .20 .50
65 Eddie Robinson .20 .50
66 John Stockton .40 1.00
67 Chris Webber .30 .75
68 Kenny Anderson .25 .60
69 Alan Henderson .20 .50
70 Dan Langhi .20 .50
71 Rashard Lewis .30 .75
72 Donyell Marshall .20 .50
73 Charles Oakley .25 .60
74 Stephen Jackson .25 .60
75 Clarence Weatherspoon .20 .50
76 David Wesley .20 .50
77 Kobe Bryant 1.25 3.00
78 Tom Gugliotta .20 .50
79 Darius Miles .20 .50
80 Cuttino Mobley .20 .50
81 Jason Terry .30 .75
82 Shandon Anderson .20 .50
83 Antonio Daniels .20 .50
84 Larry Hughes .25 .60
85 Raef LaFrentz .20 .50
86 Kenyon Martin .30 .75
87 Lamar Odom .25 .60
88 Jermaine O'Neal .25 .60
89 Glenn Robinson .25 .60
90 Damon Stoudamire .25 .60
91 Eddie House .20 .50
92 Antonio Davis .20 .50
93 Rick Fox .20 .50
94 Allen Iverson .60 1.50
95 Chris Mihm .20 .50
96 Hakeem Olajuwon .40 1.00
97 Clifford Robinson .20 .50
98 Derek Fisher .25 .60
99 Joel Przybilla .20 .50
100 Sean Rooks .20 .50
101 Jason Kidd .50 1.25
102 Antoine Walker .25 .60
103 Jason Williams .25 .60
104 Jamal Mashburn .25 .60
105 Courtney Alexander .20 .50
106 Vin Baker .25 .60
107 Chauncey Billups .30 .75
108 Marcus Camby .25 .60
109 Kevin Garnett .50 1.25
110 Juwan Howard .25 .60
111 Marc Jackson .20 .50
112 Karl Malone .40 1.00
113 Ricky Davis .25 .60
114 Desmond Mason .25 .60
115 Jerome Moiso .20 .50
116 Steve Nash .50 1.25
117 Quentin Richardson .25 .60
118 Peja Stojakovic .30 .75
119 Rasheed Wallace .30 .75
120 Travis Best .20 .50
121 Terrell Brandon .20 .50
122 Austin Croshere .20 .50
123 Tony Delk .20 .50
124 Anthony Mason .20 .50
125 Patrick Ewing .40 1.00
126 Brian Grant .20 .50
127 Bobby Jackson .20 .50
128 Eddie Jones .25 .60
129 Popeye Jones .20 .50
130 Brevin Knight .20 .50
131 Mike Miller .25 .60
132 Shaquille O'Neal .75 2.00
133 Morris Peterson .20 .50
134 Mookie Blaylock .20 .50
135 David Robinson .50 1.25
136 John Starks .20 .50
137 Stromile Swift .20 .50
138 Nick Van Exel .25 .60
139 Keith Van Horn .25 .60
140 Antawn Jamison .30 .75
141 Kurt Thomas .20 .50
142 Sam Cassell .25 .60
143 Tim Duncan .60 1.50
144 Baron Davis .30 .75
145 Jerome Williams .20 .50
146 Michael Finley .30 .75
147 Richard Hamilton .25 .60
148 Grant Hill .40 1.00
149 Jalen Rose .25 .60
150 Steve Smith .25 .60
151 Kwame Brown RC 1.25 3.00
152 Jeryl Sasser RC .75 2.00
153 Shane Battier RC 2.50 6.00
154 Gilbert Arenas RC 2.00 5.00
155 Jarron Collins RC 1.25 3.00
156 Jamaal Tinsley RC 1.25 3.00
157 Brandon Armstrong RC .75 2.00
158 Michael Bradley RC .75 2.00
159 Tyson Chandler RC 2.00 5.00
160 Joseph Forte RC .75 2.00
161 Brendan Haywood RC 1.25 3.00
162 Joe Johnson RC 1.50 4.00
163 Vladimir Radmanovic RC 1.25 3.00
164 Gerald Wallace RC 1.50 4.00
165 Steven Hunter RC 1.00 2.50
166 Richard Jefferson RC 2.00 5.00
167 DeSagana Diop RC 1.00 2.50
168 Terence Morris RC 1.25 3.00
169 Jason Richardson RC 1.50 4.00
170 Jeff Trepagnier RC .75 2.00
171 Kirk Haston RC .75 2.00
172 Eddy Curry RC 1.25 3.00
173 Eddie Griffin RC 1.00 2.50
174 Omar Cook RC 1.25 3.00
175 Pau Gasol RC 4.00 10.00
176 Troy Murphy RC 1.25 3.00
177 Trenton Hassell RC 1.00 2.50
178 Kedrick Brown RC .75 2.00
179 Zeljko Rebraca RC 1.25 3.00
180 Tony Parker RC 5.00 12.00
181 Rodney White RC .75 2.00
182 Jason Collins RC 1.00 2.50
183 Samuel Dalembert RC 1.25 3.00
184 Zach Randolph RC 2.00 5.00
185 Will Solomon RC 1.25 3.00

2001-02 Fleer Premium Star Rubies

*RUBY STARS: 8X TO 20X BASE CARD HI
1-150 PRINT RUN 100 SER.#'d SETS
*RUBY RCs: 2X TO 5X BASE CARD HI
151-185 PRINT RUN 50 SER.#'d SETS
5 Michael Jordan 75.00 200.00
9 Alonzo Mourning 10.00 25.00
67 Chris Webber 8.00 20.00
77 Kobe Bryant 40.00 100.00

2001-02 Fleer Premium Commanding Respect

Inserted at stated odds of one in 20, this 25 card set features players whose mere presence on the court brings respect from their opponents.
COMPLETE SET (25) 30.00 60.00
STATED ODDS 1:20
1 Shaquille O'Neal 2.50 6.00
2 Tim Duncan 2.00 5.00
3 Marc Jackson .60 1.50
4 Kevin Garnett 1.50 4.00
5 Kobe Bryant 4.00 10.00
6 Chris Webber 1.00 2.50
7 Michael Jordan 8.00 20.00
8 Dirk Nowitzki 1.50 4.00
9 Ray Allen 1.00 2.50
10 Courtney Alexander .60 1.50
11 David Robinson 1.50 4.00
12 Darius Miles .60 1.50
13 Baron Davis 1.00 2.50
14 Tracy McGrady 1.50 4.00
15 Vince Carter 1.50 4.00
16 Antawn Jamison 1.00 2.50
17 Jerry Stackhouse .75 2.00
18 Allen Iverson 2.00 5.00
19 Jason Kidd 1.50 4.00
20 Antoine Walker .75 2.00
21 Karl Malone 1.25 3.00
22 Grant Hill 1.25 3.00
23 Rasheed Wallace 1.00 2.50
24 Anfernee Hardaway 1.50 4.00
25 Steve Francis .75 2.00

2001-02 Fleer Premium Commanding Respect Premium Patches

STATED PRINT RUN 75 SER.#'d SETS
AH Anfernee Hardaway 25.00 60.00
AI Allen Iverson 30.00 80.00
AW Antoine Walker 12.00 30.00
BD Baron Davis 15.00 40.00
CW Chris Webber 20.00 50.00
DM Darius Miles 10.00 25.00
GH Grant Hill 20.00 50.00
JK Jason Kidd 25.00 60.00
KM Karl Malone 20.00 50.00
MM Mike Miller 12.00 30.00
RA Ray Allen 15.00 40.00
RW Rasheed Wallace 15.00 40.00
SF Steve Francis 12.00 30.00
TM Tracy McGrady 20.00 50.00
VC Vince Carter 20.00 50.00

2001-02 Fleer Premium Rookie Revolution

Inserted at stated odds at one in ten, this 10-card set features some of the highest selected draft picks of the 2002 NBA draft. These players were deemed to have the best chance of being long term NBA stars.
COMPLETE SET (10) 8.00 20.00
STATED ODDS 1:10
1 Kwame Brown .75 2.00
2 Eddy Curry .75 2.00
3 Tyson Chandler 1.25 3.00
4 Pau Gasol 2.50 6.00
5 Joe Johnson 1.00 2.50
6 Michael Bradley .50 1.25
7 Jason Richardson 1.00 2.50
8 DeSagana Diop .60 1.50
9 Troy Murphy .75 2.00
10 Jamaal Tinsley .75 2.00

2001-02 Fleer Premium Rookie Revolution Autographs

STATED PRINT RUN 50 SER. #'d SETS
NNO Eddy Curry 10.00 25.00
NNO Michael Bradley 4.00 10.00
NNO Kwame Brown 6.00 15.00
NNO Joe Johnson 15.00 40.00

2001-02 Fleer Premium Solid Performers

Inserted one in every 20 packs, this 30 card set features some of the NBA's most consistent performers.
COMPLETE SET (30) 30.00 80.00
STATED ODDS 1:20
1 Tracy McGrady 1.50 4.00
2 John Stockton 1.25 3.00
3 Dirk Nowitzki 1.50 4.00
4 Antawn Jamison 1.00 2.50
5 Scottie Pippen 1.50 4.00
6 Morris Peterson .60 1.50
7 Ray Allen 1.00 2.50
8 Antoine Walker .75 2.00
9 Anfernee Hardaway 1.50 4.00
10 Michael Jordan 8.00 20.00
11 Jerry Stackhouse .75 2.00
12 Karl Malone 1.25 3.00
13 Jason Kidd 1.50 4.00
14 Chris Webber 1.00 2.50
15 Vince Carter 1.50 4.00
16 Allen Iverson 2.00 5.00
17 Courtney Alexander .60 1.50
18 Darius Miles .60 1.50
19 Steve Francis .75 2.00
20 Grant Hill 1.25 3.00
21 Rasheed Wallace 1.00 2.50
22 Kenyon Martin 1.00 2.50
23 Shawn Marion .75 2.00
24 Elton Brand 1.00 2.50
25 Jason Terry 1.00 2.50
26 Kobe Bryant 4.00 10.00
27 Tim Duncan 2.00 5.00
28 Kevin Garnett 1.50 4.00
29 Reggie Miller 1.00 2.50
30 Shaquille O'Neal 2.50 6.00

2001-02 Fleer Premium Solid Performers Premium Jerseys

Issued at stated odds of one in 24, this 21 card set is a partial parallel to the Solid Performers insert set. These cards feature a game worn jersey swatch on them in addition to the player's photo and information.
STATED ODDS 1:24
AH Anfernee Hardaway 5.00 12.00
AI Allen Iverson 6.00 15.00
AW Antoine Walker 2.50 6.00
CW Chris Webber 3.00 8.00
DM Darius Miles 2.00 5.00
EB Elton Brand 3.00 8.00
GH Grant Hill 4.00 10.00
JK Jason Kidd 5.00 12.00
JS Jerry Stackhouse 2.50 6.00
JS John Stockton 4.00 10.00
JT Jason Terry 3.00 8.00
KM Karl Malone 4.00 10.00
MA Kenyon Martin 3.00 8.00
MM Mike Miller 2.50 6.00
MP Morris Peterson 2.00 5.00
RA Ray Allen 3.00 8.00
RW Rasheed Wallace 3.00 8.00
SF Steve Francis 2.50 6.00
SM Shawn Marion 2.50 6.00
TM Tracy McGrady 5.00 12.00
VC Vince Carter 5.00 12.00

2001-02 Fleer Premium Vertical Heights

Issued at stated odds of one in 10, these 25 cards feature players known for their ability to dunk a basketball.
COMPLETE SET (25) 15.00 40.00
STATED ODDS 1:10
1 Darius Miles .50 1.25
2 Tracy McGrady 1.25 3.00
3 Allen Iverson 1.50 4.00
4 Baron Davis .75 2.00
5 Desmond Mason .60 1.50
6 Antoine Walker .60 1.50
7 Jerry Stackhouse .60 1.50
8 Michael Finley .75 2.00
9 Eddie Jones .60 1.50
10 Steve Francis .60 1.50
11 David Robinson 1.25 3.00
12 Antawn Jamison .75 2.00
13 Karl Malone 1.00 2.50
14 Michael Jordan 6.00 15.00
15 Vince Carter 1.25 3.00
16 Chris Webber .75 2.00
17 Latrell Sprewell .60 1.50
18 Ray Allen .75 2.00
19 Grant Hill 1.00 2.50
20 Dirk Nowitzki 1.25 3.00
21 Kobe Bryant 3.00 8.00
22 Shaquille O'Neal 2.00 5.00
23 Kevin Garnett 1.25 3.00
24 Tim Duncan 1.50 4.00
25 Stephon Marbury .60 1.50

2001-02 Fleer Premium Vertical Heights Shoes

Randomly inserted in packs, these four cards are a partial parallel for the Vertical Heights insert set. These cards contain a piece of a game-worn shoe and have a stated print run of 100 serial numbered sets.
STATED PRINT RUN 100 SER. #'d SETS
NNO Vince Carter 15.00 40.00
NNO Antoine Walker 8.00 20.00
NNO Jerry Stackhouse 8.00 20.00
NNO Lamar Odom 8.00 20.00

2002-03 Fleer Premium

Released in early October 2002, Fleer Premium consists of a 140-card set divided up into 15 All NBA Team cards, numbers 1-15, which have red white and blue trim across the bottom, 11 All Rookie Team cards, numbers 16-26, which have white backgrounds, 84 Veteran player cards, numbers 27-110, which have gold foil backgrounds, and 30 Rookies, numbers 111-140, which say "Premium Prospects" along the left side of the card and are sequentially numbered to 1500. All cards feature borders which are blue along the outside, then white inside, and have gold foil highlights. Premium was packaged in five card packs with a suggested retail price of $2.99 and boxes contained 24 packs.
COMP.SET w/o SP's (110) 15.00 40.00
111-140 PRINT RUN 1500 SER.#'d SETS
1 Tracy McGrady .50 1.25
2 Tim Duncan .60 1.50
3 Shaquille O'Neal .75 2.00
4 Jason Kidd .50 1.25
5 Kobe Bryant 1.25 3.00
6 Kevin Garnett .50 1.25
7 Chris Webber .30 .75
8 Dirk Nowitzki .50 1.25
9 Gary Payton .30 .75
10 Allen Iverson .50 1.25
11 Ben Wallace .25 .60
12 Jermaine O'Neal .25 .60
13 Dikembe Mutombo .30 .75
14 Paul Pierce .30 .75
15 Steve Nash .40 1.00
16 Pau Gasol .40 1.00
17 Jason Richardson .30 .75
18 Tony Parker .40 1.00
19 Andrei Kirilenko .30 .75
20 Shane Battier .30 .75
21 Jamaal Tinsley .20 .50
22 Richard Jefferson .30 .75
23 Joe Johnson .25 .60
24 Eddie Griffin .20 .50
25 Zeljko Rebraca .20 .50
26 Vladimir Radmanovic .20 .50
27 Damon Stoudamire .25 .60
28 Eddie Jones .25 .60
29 Tyson Chandler .30 .75
30 Karl Malone .40 1.00
31 David Wesley .20 .50
32 Steve Francis .25 .60
33 Hakeem Olajuwon .40 1.00
34 Baron Davis .25 .60
35 Antonio McDyess .25 .60
36 Mike Bibby .30 .75
37 Bonzi Wells .20 .50
38 Ray Allen .30 .75
39 Doug Christie .20 .50
40 Richard Hamilton .25 .60
41 Grant Hill .40 1.00
42 Elton Brand .30 .75
43 Gilbert Arenas .30 .75
44 Vlade Divac .25 .60
45 Sam Cassell .25 .60
46 Jalen Rose .25 .60
47 Peja Stojakovic .30 .75
48 Glenn Robinson .25 .60
49 Ricky Davis .25 .60
50 Antonio Daniels .20 .50
51 Tim Thomas .20 .50
52 Andre Miller .25 .60
53 Stephon Marbury .25 .60
54 Robert Horry .25 .60
55 Tony Delk .20 .50
56 David Robinson .50 1.25
57 Radoslav Nesterovic .20 .50
58 Lamond Murray .20 .50
59 Brent Barry .20 .50
60 Wally Szczerbiak .25 .60
61 Lee Nailon .20 .50
62 Rashard Lewis .30 .75
63 Kenyon Martin .25 .60
64 Michael Finley .30 .75
65 John Stockton .40 1.00
66 Allan Houston .25 .60
67 Terrell Brandon .20 .50
68 Donyell Marshall .20 .50
69 Marcus Camby .25 .60
70 Cuttino Mobley .20 .50
71 Shawn Marion .25 .60
72 Jason Williams .25 .60
73 Rodney Rogers .20 .50
74 Scottie Pippen .50 1.25
75 Brian Grant .20 .50
76 Clifford Robinson .20 .50
77 Antoine Walker .25 .60
78 Michael Dickerson .20 .50
79 Latrell Sprewell .25 .60
80 Ron Artest .30 .75
81 Shareef Abdur-Rahim .25 .60
82 Michael Jordan 2.50 6.00
83 Mike Miller .25 .60
84 Corey Maggette .25 .60
85 Antawn Jamison .30 .75
86 Rasheed Wallace .30 .75
87 Alonzo Mourning .40 1.00
88 Eddy Curry .20 .50
89 Derrick Coleman .25 .60
90 Joe Smith .25 .60
91 Darius Miles .20 .50
92 Nick Van Exel .25 .60
93 Derek Fisher .25 .60
94 Nazr Mohammed .20 .50
95 Morris Peterson .20 .50
96 Jamal Mashburn .25 .60
97 Jerry Stackhouse .25 .60
98 Kwame Brown .20 .50
99 Darrell Armstrong .20 .50
100 Reggie Miller .30 .75
101 Desmond Mason .25 .60
102 Antonio Davis .20 .50
103 Elden Campbell .20 .50
104 Voshon Lenard .20 .50
105 Eric Snow .20 .50
106 Lamar Odom .25 .60
107 Toni Kukoc .30 .75
108 Vince Carter .50 1.25
109 Keith Van Horn .25 .60
110 Juwan Howard .25 .60
111 Jay Williams RC 1.50 4.00
112 Yao Ming RC 3.00 8.00
113 Mike Dunleavy RC 1.50 4.00
114 Drew Gooden RC 1.50 4.00
115 Nikoloz Tskitishvili RC 1.00 2.50
116 DaJuan Wagner RC 1.25 3.00
117 Nene Hilario RC 1.50 4.00
118 Chris Wilcox RC 1.25 3.00
119 Amare Stoudemire RC 2.00 5.00
120 Caron Butler RC 1.50 4.00
121 Melvin Ely RC 1.25 3.00
122 Marcus Haislip RC 1.25 3.00
123 Jared Jeffries RC 1.25 3.00
124 Fred Jones RC 1.25 3.00
125 Bostian Nachbar RC 1.25 3.00
126 Jiri Welsch RC 1.25 3.00
127 Juan Dixon RC 1.50 4.00
128 Curtis Borchardt RC 1.00 2.50
129 Ryan Humphrey RC 1.25 3.00
130 Kareem Rush RC 1.25 3.00
131 Qyntel Woods RC 1.25 3.00
132 Casey Jacobsen RC 1.25 3.00
133 Tayshaun Prince RC 2.00 5.00
134 Carlos Boozer RC 1.50 4.00
135 Frank Williams RC 1.00 2.50
136 John Salmons RC 1.50 4.00
137 Chris Jefferies RC 1.00 2.50
138 Dan Dickau RC 1.25 3.00
139 Manu Ginobili RC 4.00 10.00
140 Roger Mason RC 1.25 3.00

2002-03 Fleer Premium Emerald

*STARS: 2.5X TO 6X BASE CARD HI
*RCs: 1X TO 2.5X BASE CARD HI
PRINT RUN 300 SER.#'d SETS

2002-03 Fleer Premium Star Rubies

*STARS: 4X TO 10X BASE CARD HI
*RCs: 1.5X TO 4X BASE CARD HI
PRINT RUN 100 SER.#'d SETS
82 Michael Jordan 75.00 150.00
87 Alonzo Mourning 6.00 15.00

2002-03 Fleer Premium A Cut Above

Randomly inserted in packs at the rate of one in 120, this ten card set features a horizontal design with full color player photos on the left and a white background with a circular swatch of game-used memorabilia on the right. Fleer confirmed Steve Francis and DerMarr Johnson as short prints and only 250 of each were produced. A Ruby version sequentially numbered to 100 was also included randomly in packs.
STATED ODDS 1:120
*RUBY: .75X TO 2X A CUT ABOVE HI
RUBY PRINT RUN 100 SER.#'d SETS
1 Keith Van Horn 2.50 6.00
2 Vince Carter 5.00 12.00
3 Steve Francis/250 2.50 6.00
4 Grant Hill 4.00 10.00
5 DerMarr Johnson/250 2.00 5.00
6 Jamal Mashburn 2.50 6.00
7 Lamar Odom 2.50 6.00
8 Quentin Richardson 2.50 6.00
9 Richard Hamilton 2.50 6.00
10 Jason Terry 2.50 6.00

2002-03 Fleer Premium Court Collection

Randomly inserted in packs at the rate of one in 175, this 10-card set features a horizontal design with a basketball court background, black and white player portrait photos on the left and a circular swatch of game used memorabilia on the right. Fleer confirmed Keyon Dooling as a short-print with only 250 cards made, and Wally Szczerbiak as a short-print with 125 cards made. A Ruby version was also inserted in packs and is sequentially numbered to 100.
STATED ODDS 1:175
*RUBY: .75X TO 2X COURT COLL.HI
RUBY PRINT RUN 100 SER.#'d SETS
1 Shareef Abdur-Rahim 2.50 6.00
2 Keyon Dooling/250 2.00 5.00
3 Rashard Lewis 3.00 8.00
4 Shawn Marion 2.50 6.00
5 Tracy McGrady 5.00 12.00
6 Alonzo Mourning 4.00 10.00
7 John Stockton 4.00 10.00
8 Wally Szczerbiak/125 2.50 6.00
9 Desmond Mason 2.50 6.00
10 Corey Maggette 2.50 6.00

2002-03 Fleer Premium Gear

Randomly seeded at one in 288, this nine card set is horizontally designed with full color player action photos on the left and a white right side with a circular swatch of game used memorabilia. The border between the color photo and the white side, as well as around the swatch of memorabilia, are shaped to look like a gear. Fleer confirmed Karl Malone and Morris Peterson as short-prints with 125 and 50 copies available respectively. A Ruby version was issued as well where cards are sequentially numbered to 100.
STATED ODDS 1:288
*RUBY: .75X TO 2X GEAR HI
RUBY PRINT RUN 100 SER.#'d SETS
1 Anfernee Hardaway 5.00 12.00
2 Vince Carter 5.00 12.00
3 Antawn Jamison 3.00 8.00
4 Karl Malone/125 4.00 10.00
5 Kenyon Martin 2.50 6.00
6 Andre Miller 2.50 6.00
7 Mike Miller 2.50 6.00
8 Dikembe Mutombo 3.00 8.00
9 Morris Peterson/50 2.00 5.00

2002-03 Fleer Premium Power

Randomly inserted in packs, this 10-card set feature full color player action photos set against a colored background to match the player's team color. The top 1/3 of the card is in white and all cards contain bronze foil highlights. Each card is sequentially numbered to 1000. A Ruby version was issued as well where the cards are sequentially numbered to 100.
PRINT RUN 1000 SERIAL #'d SETS

1 Tim Duncan 2.50 6.00
2 Kobe Bryant 5.00 12.00
3 Ben Wallace 1.00 2.50
4 Michael Jordan 10.00 25.00
5 Shaquille O'Neal 3.00 8.00
6 Vince Carter 2.00 5.00
7 Kevin Garnett 2.00 5.00
8 Chris Webber 1.25 3.00
9 Karl Malone 1.50 4.00
10 Elton Brand 1.25 3.00

2002-03 Fleer Premium Power Ruby

*RUBY: 1X TO 2.5X POWER HI
PRINT RUN 100 SER.#'d SETS

2002-03 Fleer Premium Prime Time

Randomly seeded in packs, this 15-card set features full color player action photos set against a background that is colored to match the player's team colors on the top half and white on the bottom. Cards contain silver foil highlights and are sequentially numbered to 1500. A Ruby version was also issued in packs and is sequentially numbered to 100.

COMPLETE SET (15) 10.00 25.00
PRINT RUN 1500 SERIAL #'d SETS
*RUBY: 1.25X TO 3X PRIME TIME HI
RUBY PRINT RUN 100 SER.#'d SETS
1 Dirk Nowitzki 1.50 4.00
2 Vince Carter 1.50 4.00
3 Allen Iverson 1.50 4.00
4 Ray Allen 1.00 2.50
5 Darius Miles .60 1.50
6 Chris Webber 1.00 2.50
7 Elton Brand 1.00 2.50
8 Jason Kidd 1.50 4.00
9 Paul Pierce 1.00 2.50
10 Baron Davis .75 2.00
11 Stephon Marbury .75 2.00
12 Jerry Stackhouse .75 2.00
13 David Robinson 1.50 4.00
14 Gary Payton 1.00 2.50
15 Antoine Walker .75 2.00

2002-03 Fleer Premium Prime Time Game Used

STATED ODDS 1:75
*RUBY: .75X TO 2X PT GAME USED HI
RUBY PRINT RUN 100 SER.#'d SETS
1 Vince Carter 5.00 12.00
2 Allen Iverson 5.00 12.00
3 Ray Allen 3.00 8.00
4 Darius Miles 2.00 5.00
5 Chris Webber 3.00 8.00
6 Elton Brand 3.00 8.00
7 Jason Kidd 5.00 12.00
8 Paul Pierce 3.00 8.00
9 Baron Davis 2.50 6.00
10 Stephon Marbury 2.50 6.00
11 Jerry Stackhouse 2.50 6.00
12 David Robinson 5.00 12.00
13 Gary Payton 3.00 8.00
14 Antoine Walker 2.50 6.00

2002-03 Fleer Premium Skylines

Randomly inserted in packs, this 20-card set has a horizontal card design with white borders on the top and the bottom and a strip in the middle showing the skyline of the featured player's team city. Full color player action shots are set in front on the right side of the card. Each card is sequentaill numbered to 2500. A Ruby version was inserted into packs as well and cards are sequentially numbered to 100.

PRINT RUN 2500 SERIAL #'D SETS
1 Michael Jordan 10.00 25.00
2 Shaquille O'Neal 3.00 8.00
3 Vince Carter 2.00 5.00
4 Kevin Garnett 2.00 5.00
5 Allen Iverson 2.00 5.00
6 Dirk Nowitzki 2.00 5.00
7 Darius Miles .75 2.00
8 Tracy McGrady 2.00 5.00
9 Chris Webber 1.25 3.00
10 Steve Francis 1.00 2.50
11 Jason Kidd 2.00 5.00
12 Stephon Marbury 1.00 2.50
13 Paul Pierce 1.25 3.00
14 Ray Allen 1.25 3.00
15 Kobe Bryant 5.00 12.00
16 Jay Williams 1.25 3.00
17 DaJuan Wagner 1.00 2.50
18 Yao Ming 2.50 6.00
19 Jared Jeffries 1.00 2.50
20 Amare Stoudemire 1.50 4.00

2002-03 Fleer Premium Skylines Ruby

*RUBY: 1X TO 2.5X SKYLINES HI
PRINT RUN 100 SER.#'d SETS
1 Michael Jordan 50.00 120.00

2002-03 Fleer Premium Triple Threats

Randomly seeded, this 10-card set features full-color player action photos set against an one-color portrait photo in the background. The words "3X Threats" appears on the card front in silver foil, and each card is sequentially numbered to 250. A Ruby version was also issued where cards are sequentially numbered to 100.

PRINT RUN 250 SERIAL #'D SETS
1 Allen Iverson 4.00 10.00
2 Tracy McGrady 4.00 10.00
3 Steve Francis 2.00 5.00
4 Ray Allen 2.50 6.00
5 Tim Duncan 5.00 12.00
6 Kobe Bryant 6.00 15.00
7 Michael Jordan 20.00 50.00
8 Shaquille O'Neal 6.00 15.00
9 Vince Carter 4.00 10.00
10 Kevin Garnett 4.00 10.00

2002-03 Fleer Premium Triple Threats Ruby

*RUBY: .5X TO 1.25X TRIPLE THREATS HI
PRINT RUN 100 SER.#'d SETS
7 Michael Jordan 60.00 150.00

2011-12 Fleer Retro

COMPLETE SET (83) 25.00 60.00
1 Michael Jordan 3.00 8.00
2 LeBron James 2.00 5.00
3 Walt Frazier .50 1.25
4 Larry Johnson .60 1.50
5 Hakeem Olajuwon .60 1.50
6 Candace Parker .75 2.00
7 Christian Laettner .40 1.00
8 Hal Greer .40 1.00
9 Jerry West .60 1.50
10 Dennis Rodman 1.00 2.50
11 Anfernee Hardaway 1.25 3.00
12 Gail Goodrich .40 1.00
13 George Gervin .50 1.25
14 Elgin Baylor .50 1.25
15 Bill Walton .50 1.25
16 Larry Bird 1.25 3.00
17 Rick Barry .40 1.00
18 James Worthy .60 1.50
19 Bill Laimbeer .40 1.00
20 Tim Hardaway .50 1.25
21 David Robinson .75 2.00
22 Adrian Dantley .40 1.00
23 Alonzo Mourning .60 1.50
24 Magic Johnson 1.25 3.00
25 Julius Erving .75 2.00
26 Mark Jackson .40 1.00
27 Bill Cartwright .40 1.00
28 Bill Russell .75 2.00
29 B.J. Armstrong .50 1.25
30 Bob McAdoo .40 1.00
31 Cazzie Russell .40 1.00
32 Brad Daugherty .40 1.00
33 Clyde Drexler .60 1.50
34 Danny Manning .40 1.00
35 John Havlicek .60 1.50
36 Grant Hill .75 2.00
37 Jim Jackson .30 .75
38 David Thompson .40 1.00
39 Rudy Tomjanovich .40 1.00
40 Reggie Theus .40 1.00
41 Freddie Lewis .30 .75
42 Kenny Smith .40 1.00
43 Bill Sharman .50 1.25
44 Lonnie Shelton .30 .75
45 Toni Kukoc .50 1.25
46 Sam Cassell .40 1.00
47 Glen Rice .40 1.00
48 Darrell Griffith .30 .75
49 Steve Nash .50 1.25
50 Chris Paul .60 1.50
51 Tristan Thompson RS 1.00 2.50
52 Jonas Valanciunas RS 1.00 2.50
53 Bismack Biyombo RS .75 2.00
54 Jimmer Fredette RS .50 1.25
55 Klay Thompson RS 2.50 6.00
56 Alec Burks RS .75 2.00
57 Markieff Morris RS .75 2.00
58 Marcus Morris RS .60 1.50
59 Kawhi Leonard RS 12.00 30.00
60 Nikola Vucevic RS .75 2.00
61 Chris Singleton RS .50 1.25
62 Tobias Harris RS .75 2.00
63 Scotty Hopson RS .50 1.25
64 Nolan Smith RS .50 1.25
65 Reggie Jackson RS .75 2.00
66 MarShon Brooks RS .60 1.50
67 JaJuan Johnson RS .50 1.25
68 Norris Cole RS .75 2.00
69 Cory Joseph RS .60 1.50
70 Justin Harper RS .60 1.50
71 Shelvin Mack RS .50 1.25
72 Tyler Honeycutt RS .60 1.50
73 Jordan Williams RS .50 1.25
74 Chandler Parsons RS .75 2.00
75 Jon Leuer RS .60 1.50
76 Malcolm Lee RS .60 1.50
77 Charles Jenkins RS .60 1.50
78 Travis Leslie RS .60 1.50
79 Keith Benson RS .60 1.50
80 Josh Selby RS .60 1.50
81 E'Twaun Moore RS 1.00 2.50
82 Demetri McCamey RS .60 1.50
83 Durrell Summers RS .50 1.25

2011-12 Fleer Retro 1961-62

STATED ODDS 1:100 PACKS
ALL BACKGROUND VARIATIONS SAME VALUE
BR1 Bill Russell 8.00 20.00
DR1 David Robinson 8.00 20.00
HO1 Hakeem Olajuwon 6.00 15.00
JE1 Julius Erving 8.00 20.00
JO1 Magic Johnson 12.00 30.00
JW1 Jerry West 6.00 15.00
LB1 Larry Bird 15.00 40.00
LJ1 LeBron James 20.00 50.00
MJ1 Michael Jordan 60.00 150.00
WO1 James Worthy 6.00 15.00

2011-12 Fleer Retro 1961-62 Autographs

RANDOM INSERTS IN PACKS
ALL BACKGROUND VARIATIONS SAME VALUE
BR1 Bill Russell 100.00 200.00
DR1 David Robinson 250.00 500.00
HO1 Hakeem Olajuwon 75.00 150.00
JE1 Julius Erving EXCH
JO1 Magic Johnson 250.00 500.00
LB1 Larry Bird
LJ1 LeBron James EXCH 200.00 400.00
MJ1 Michael Jordan 500.00 1000.00
WO1 James Worthy 100.00 200.00

2011-12 Fleer Retro 1986-87

COMPLETE SET (15) 15.00 40.00
STATED ODDS 1:20 PACKS
AD Adrian Dantley 1.50 4.00
AM Alonzo Mourning 5.00 12.00
BW Bill Walton 2.00 5.00
CD Clyde Drexler 2.50 6.00
CP Chris Paul 2.50 6.00
DM Danny Manning 1.50 4.00
DR Dennis Rodman 4.00 10.00
EB Elgin Baylor 2.00 5.00
GG George Gervin 2.00 5.00
GH Grant Hill 2.50 6.00
GO Gail Goodrich 1.50 4.00
JH John Havlicek 2.50 6.00
LJ Larry Johnson 2.50 6.00
SN Steve Nash 2.00 5.00
WF Walt Frazier 2.00 5.00

2011-12 Fleer Retro 1986-87 Autographs

RANDOM INSERTS IN PACKS
AD Adrian Dantley 8.00 20.00
AM Alonzo Mourning
BW Bill Walton 25.00 60.00
CD Clyde Drexler 20.00 50.00
CP Chris Paul 20.00 50.00
DR Dennis Rodman 75.00 150.00
GG George Gervin 12.00 30.00
GH Grant Hill EXCH 150.00 300.00
GO Gail Goodrich
JH John Havlicek 30.00 80.00
LJ Larry Johnson 40.00 100.00

2011-12 Fleer Retro 1987-88

COMPLETE SET (20) 12.00 30.00
STATED ODDS 1:10 PACKS
AH Anfernee Hardaway 3.00 8.00
BA B.J. Armstrong 1.25 3.00
BL Bill Laimbeer 1.00 2.50
BM Bob McAdoo 1.00 2.50
BS Bill Sharman 1.25 3.00
CL Christian Laettner 1.00 2.50
CR Cazzie Russell 1.00 2.50
CW Chet Walker 1.00 2.50
DG Darrell Griffith .75 2.00
DT David Thompson 1.00 2.50
HG Hal Greer 1.00 2.50
JJ Jim Jackson .75 2.00
KS Kenny Smith 1.00 2.50
MJ Mark Jackson 1.00 2.50
PA Candace Parker 1.50 4.00
RB Rick Barry 1.00 2.50
RT Reggie Theus 1.00 2.50
SC Sam Cassell 1.00 2.50
TH Tim Hardaway 1.25 3.00
TO Rudy Tomjanovich 1.00 2.50

2011-12 Fleer Retro 1987-88 Autographs

RANDOM INSERTS IN PACKS
AH Anfernee Hardaway 30.00 80.00
BA B.J. Armstrong 12.00 30.00
BL Bill Laimbeer 12.00 30.00
BM Bob McAdoo 20.00 50.00
CL Christian Laettner 15.00 40.00
CR Cazzie Russell 10.00 25.00
CW Chet Walker 10.00 25.00
DT David Thompson 12.00 30.00
HG Hal Greer
JJ Jim Jackson 10.00 25.00
MJ Mark Jackson 10.00 25.00
PA Candace Parker 15.00 40.00
RT Reggie Theus 10.00 25.00
SC Sam Cassell
TH Tim Hardaway 15.00 40.00
TO Rudy Tomjanovich 10.00 25.00

2011-12 Fleer Retro 1988-89

COMPLETE SET (25) 15.00 40.00
STATED ODDS 1:5 PACKS
AB Alec Burks 1.00 2.50
BB Bismack Biyombo 1.00 2.50
BD Brad Daugherty .75 2.00
CJ Cory Joseph .75 2.00
CS Chris Singleton .60 1.50
FL Freddie Lewis .60 1.50
HA Tobias Harris 1.00 2.50
JF Jimmer Fredette .60 1.50
JH Justin Harper .75 2.00
JJ JaJuan Johnson .60 1.50
JV Jonas Valanciunas- 1.25 3.00
KL Kawhi Leonard 12.00 30.00
KT Klay Thompson 3.00 8.00
LS Lonnie Shelton .60 1.50
MM Marcus Morris .75 2.00
MO Markieff Morris 1.00 2.50
MP MarShon Brooks .75 2.00
MR Micheal Ray Richardson .75 2.00
NS Nolan Smith .60 1.50
NV Nikola Vucevic 1.00 2.50
RH Robert Horry .75 2.00
RJ Reggie Jackson 1.00 2.50
TH Tyler Honeycutt .75 2.00
TK Toni Kukoc 1.00 2.50
TT Tristan Thompson 1.25 3.00

2011-12 Fleer Retro 1988-89 Autographs

RANDOM INSERTS IN PACKS
AB Alec Burks 10.00 25.00
BB Bismack Biyombo 10.00 25.00
CJ Cory Joseph 8.00 20.00
CS Chris Singleton 6.00 15.00
FL Freddie Lewis 6.00 15.00
HA Tobias Harris 10.00 25.00
JF Jimmer Fredette 12.00 30.00
JH Justin Harper 8.00 20.00
JJ JaJuan Johnson 6.00 15.00
JV Jonas Valanciunas 20.00 50.00
KL Kawhi Leonard 60.00 150.00
KT Klay Thompson 30.00 80.00
LS Lonnie Shelton 6.00 15.00
NS Nolan Smith 6.00 15.00
RH Robert Horry 15.00 40.00
RJ Reggie Jackson 10.00 25.00
TH Tyler Honeycutt 8.00 20.00
TT Tristan Thompson 12.00 30.00

2011-12 Fleer Retro A Cut Above

ATED ODDS 1:144 PACKS
1 Jimmer Fredette 4.00 10.00
2 Grant Hill 8.00 20.00
3 George Gervin 6.00 15.00
4 Alonzo Mourning 8.00 20.00
5 Hakeem Olajuwon 8.00 20.00
6 Clyde Drexler 12.00 30.00
7 Larry Bird 15.00 40.00
8 Julius Erving 10.00 25.00
9 Elgin Baylor 6.00 15.00
10 Magic Johnson 15.00 40.00
11 David Robinson 10.00 25.00
12 Michael Jordan 75.00 150.00
13 James Worthy 8.00 20.00
14 Tim Hardaway 6.00 15.00
15 John Havlicek 8.00 20.00
16 Bill Russell 10.00 25.00
17 Steve Nash 6.00 15.00
18 Anfernee Hardaway 15.00 40.00
19 Dennis Rodman 12.00 30.00
20 LeBron James 30.00 80.00
21 Walt Frazier 6.00 15.00
22 Bill Walton 6.00 15.00
23 Larry Johnson 8.00 20.00
24 Chris Paul 8.00 20.00
25 Jerry West 8.00 20.00

2011-12 Fleer Retro Autographics 1996-97

RANDOM INSERTS IN PACKS
AD Adrian Dantley 5.00 12.00
AJ Avery Johnson 6.00 15.00
AM Alonzo Mourning 40.00 80.00
BR Bill Russell 100.00 200.00
CC Cynthia Cooper 8.00 20.00
CD Clyde Drexler 15.00 40.00
CJ Cory Joseph 3.00 8.00
CR Cazzie Russell 4.00 10.00
CS Chris Singleton 2.50 6.00
CW Chet Walker 4.00 10.00
DA Dana Altman 10.00 25.00
DR David Robinson 20.00 50.00
DT David Thompson 8.00 20.00
GA Greg Anthony 8.00 20.00
GH Grant Hill EXCH 125.00 250.00
HG Hal Greer 5.00 12.00
HO Hakeem Olajuwon 30.00 80.00
JA LeBron James 300.00 600.00
JC Jim Calhoun 12.00 30.00
JD Jamie Dixon
JE Julius Erving 30.00 60.00
JF Jimmer Fredette 6.00 15.00
JH John Havlicek 25.00 60.00
JO Michael Jordan 600.00 1000.00
JS Jerry Sloan 8.00 20.00
JW James Worthy 25.00 60.00
LB Larry Bird 100.00 175.00
LJ Larry Johnson 12.00 30.00
LS Lonnie Shelton 3.00 8.00
MB Mike Brey 3.00 8.00
MF Mark Few 6.00 15.00
MJ Magic Johnson 50.00 125.00
PA Chris Paul 25.00 60.00
RH Robert Horry 6.00 15.00
RJ Reggie Jackson 4.00 10.00
RO Dennis Rodman 40.00 100.00
RT Reggie Theus 4.00 10.00
SA Steve Alford 5.00 12.00
SC Sam Cassell 4.00 10.00
TH Tim Hardaway 8.00 20.00
TM Thad Matta 12.00 30.00
TO Rudy Tomjanovich 4.00 10.00
TS Tubby Smith
WE Jerry West
WF Walt Frazier 10.00 25.00

2011-12 Fleer Retro Autographics 1997-98

RANDOM INSERTS IN PACKS
AM Alonzo Mourning 50.00 125.00
BB Bismack Biyombo 4.00 10.00
BD Billy Donovan 30.00 80.00
BM Bob McAdoo 12.00 30.00
BR Bo Ryan 10.00 25.00
BW Bruce Weber 4.00 10.00
CC Cynthia Cooper 8.00 20.00
CP Chris Paul 30.00 80.00
CR Cazzie Russell 4.00 10.00
DM Demetri McCamey 3.00 8.00
DR David Robinson 40.00 100.00
DS Durrell Summers 2.50 6.00
DT David Thompson 6.00 15.00
FL Freddie Lewis 3.00 8.00
HG Hal Greer 5.00 12.00
JB Jim Boeheim 30.00 80.00
JC Jeff Capel III 4.00 10.00
JE Julius Erving 40.00 100.00
JF Jimmer Fredette 6.00 15.00
JH Justin Harper 3.00 8.00
JJ JaJuan Johnson 2.50 6.00
JO Michael Jordan
JS Jack Sikma 3.00 8.00
JW James Worthy 25.00 60.00
LA Larry Johnson 12.00 30.00
LB Larry Bird 100.00 175.00
LJ LeBron James 300.00 600.00
LS Lonnie Shelton 3.00 8.00
MH Matt Howard 4.00 10.00
MJ Magic Johnson
MR Micheal Ray Richardson 3.00 8.00
NS Nolan Smith 2.50 6.00
RH Robert Horry 8.00 20.00
RO Dennis Rodman 50.00 125.00
RT Reggie Theus 4.00 10.00
RU Bill Russell 75.00 150.00
SC Sam Cassell 4.00 10.00
SF Steve Fisher 6.00 15.00
SL Jerry Sloan 8.00 20.00
TH Tobias Harris 4.00 10.00
TK Toni Kukoc 25.00 60.00
TO Rudy Tomjanovich 4.00 10.00
TP Terry Porter 6.00 15.00
TT Tristan Thompson 4.00 10.00
WF Walt Frazier 10.00 25.00

2011-12 Fleer Retro Autographics 1998-99

RANDOM INSERTS IN PACKS
AD Adrian Dantley 6.00 15.00
AH Anfernee Hardaway 8.00 20.00
AJ Avery Johnson 4.00 10.00
AM Alonzo Mourning 40.00 100.00
BB Bismack Biyombo 3.00 8.00
BH Bob Huggins 8.00 20.00
BM Bob McAdoo 12.00 30.00
BR Bill Russell
CC Cynthia Cooper 6.00 15.00
CP Chris Paul 30.00 80.00
CR Cazzie Russell 4.00 10.00
CW Chet Walker 3.00 8.00
DR David Robinson 30.00 80.00
DT David Thompson 8.00 20.00
GH Grant Hill EXCH 100.00 200.00
GW Gary Williams 10.00 25.00
HG Hal Greer 5.00 12.00
HO Ben Howland 3.00 8.00
JB John Beilein 4.00 10.00
JE Julius Erving 30.00 60.00
JF Jimmer Fredette 6.00 15.00
JH John Havlicek 25.00 60.00
JJ JaJuan Johnson 2.00 5.00
JO Magic Johnson 50.00 125.00
JS Jerry Sloan 6.00 15.00
JW James Worthy 25.00 60.00
LA Larry Johnson 15.00 40.00
LB Larry Bird
LJ LeBron James 200.00 400.00
LS Lonnie Shelton 2.50 6.00
MB MarShon Brooks 8.00 20.00
MH Matt Howard 3.00 8.00
MJ Michael Jordan 400.00 700.00
MM Markieff Morris 3.00 8.00
MP Matt Painter 5.00 12.00
OL Hakeem Olajuwon 25.00 60.00
PA Candace Parker 15.00 40.00
RH Robert Horry 10.00 25.00
RT Reggie Theus 3.00 8.00
SM Sean Miller 4.00 10.00
ST John Starks 12.00 30.00
TH Tyler Honeycutt 2.50 6.00
TK Toni Kukoc 12.00 30.00
TO Rudy Tomjanovich 4.00 10.00
WE Jerry West 30.00 80.00
WF Walt Frazier 10.00 25.00

2011-12 Fleer Retro Autographics 1999-00

RANDOM INSERTS IN PACKS
AD Adrian Dantley 5.00 12.00
AM Alonzo Mourning 30.00 80.00
BB Bismack Biyombo 3.00 8.00
BC Bobby Cremins 4.00 10.00
BM Bob McAdoo
BR Bill Russell 50.00 125.00
BS Bill Self 12.00 30.00
CC Cynthia Cooper 5.00 12.00
CD Clyde Drexler 25.00 60.00
CP Chris Paul 30.00 80.00
CR Cazzie Russell 3.00 8.00
CS Chris Singleton 2.00 5.00
CW Chet Walker 3.00 8.00
DM Demetri McCamey 2.50 6.00
DR David Robinson
DT David Thompson 6.00 15.00
FL Freddie Lewis 3.00 8.00
GG George Gervin 6.00 15.00
GH Grant Hill 30.00 80.00
HA John Havlicek
HD Homer Drew 4.00 10.00
HG Hal Greer 6.00 15.00
HO Hakeem Olajuwon 30.00 80.00
JE Julius Erving EXCH 40.00 100.00
JF Jimmer Fredette 12.00 30.00
JH Justin Harper 2.50 6.00
JO Magic Johnson 50.00 125.00
JS Jerry Sloan 10.00 25.00
JW Jay Wright 15.00 40.00
KB Keith Benson 2.50 6.00
LA Larry Johnson 30.00 80.00
LB Larry Bird 100.00 175.00
LJ LeBron James 300.00 600.00
LS Lonnie Shelton 2.50 6.00
MJ Michael Jordan
MM Mike Montgomery 4.00 10.00
RH Robert Horry 6.00 15.00
RM Rick Majerus 6.00 15.00
RT Rudy Tomjanovich 5.00 12.00
SG Seth Greenberg 4.00 10.00
SH Scotty Hopson 2.00 5.00
TH Tobias Harris 3.00 8.00
TI Tim Hardaway 8.00 20.00
TP Terry Porter 6.00 15.00
WF Walt Frazier 10.00 25.00
WO James Worthy 25.00 60.00

2011-12 Fleer Retro Autographs

RANDOM INSERTS IN PACKS
1 Michael Jordan 200.00 400.00
2 LeBron James 125.00 250.00
3 Walt Frazier 6.00 15.00
4 Larry Johnson 12.00 30.00
5 Hakeem Olajuwon 12.00 50.00
6 Candace Parker
8 Hal Greer 8.00 20.00
9 Jerry West
10 Dennis Rodman 10.00 25.00
11 Anfernee Hardaway 20.00 50.00
12 Gail Goodrich 20.00 50.00
13 George Gervin 6.00 15.00
14 Elgin Baylor 15.00 40.00
15 Bill Walton 10.00 25.00
16 Larry Bird 50.00 125.00
17 Rick Barry 15.00 40.00
18 James Worthy 10.00 25.00
19 Bill Laimbeer 5.00 12.00
20 Tim Hardaway 6.00 15.00
21 David Robinson 12.00 30.00
22 Adrian Dantley 4.00 10.00
23 Alonzo Mourning 8.00 20.00
24 Magic Johnson 30.00 80.00
25 Julius Erving 30.00 80.00
26 Mark Jackson 4.00 10.00
27 Bill Cartwright
28 Bill Russell 50.00 125.00
29 B.J. Armstrong 8.00 20.00
30 Bob McAdoo 6.00 15.00
31 Cazzie Russell 4.00 10.00
33 Clyde Drexler 20.00 50.00
34 Danny Manning 6.00 15.00
35 John Havlicek 15.00 40.00
36 Grant Hill 20.00 50.00
37 Jim Jackson 6.00 15.00
38 David Thompson 8.00 20.00
39 Rudy Tomjanovich 4.00 10.00
40 Reggie Theus 4.00 10.00
41 Freddie Lewis 4.00 10.00
42 Kenny Smith 4.00 10.00
43 Bill Sharman 10.00 25.00
44 Lonnie Shelton 4.00 10.00
45 Toni Kukoc 12.00 30.00
46 Sam Cassell 4.00 10.00
47 Glen Rice 10.00 25.00
48 Darrell Griffith 4.00 10.00
49 Steve Nash
50 Chris Paul 25.00 60.00
51 Tristan Thompson RS 4.00 10.00
52 Jonas Valanciunas RS 25.00 60.00
53 Bismack Biyombo RS 3.00 8.00
54 Jimmer Fredette RS 6.00 15.00
55 Klay Thompson RS 50.00 120.00
56 Alec Burks RS 3.00 8.00
57 Markieff Morris RS 3.00 8.00
58 Marcus Morris RS 2.50 6.00
59 Kawhi Leonard RS 60.00 150.00
60 Nikola Vucevic RS 3.00 8.00
61 Chris Singleton RS 2.00 5.00
62 Tobias Harris RS 3.00 8.00
63 Scotty Hopson RS 2.00 5.00
64 Nolan Smith RS 2.00 5.00
65 Reggie Jackson RS 3.00 8.00
66 MarShon Brooks RS 2.50 6.00
67 JaJuan Johnson RS 2.00 5.00
68 Norris Cole RS 3.00 8.00
69 Cory Joseph RS 2.50 6.00
70 Justin Harper RS 2.50 6.00
71 Shelvin Mack RS 2.00 5.00
72 Tyler Honeycutt RS 2.50 6.00
73 Jordan Williams RS 2.00 5.00
74 Chandler Parsons RS 3.00 8.00
75 Jon Leuer RS 2.50 6.00
76 Malcolm Lee RS 2.50 6.00
77 Charles Jenkins RS 2.50 6.00
78 Travis Leslie RS 2.50 6.00
79 Keith Benson RS 2.50 6.00
80 Josh Selby RS 2.50 6.00
81 E'Twaun Moore RS 4.00 10.00
82 Demetri McCamey RS 2.50 6.00
83 Durrell Summers RS 2.00 5.00

2011-12 Fleer Retro Big Men on Court

STATED ODDS 1:180 PACKS
1 Michael Jordan 90.00 150.00
2 LeBron James 50.00 120.00
3 Magic Johnson 15.00 40.00
4 Larry Bird 15.00 40.00
5 Bill Russell 10.00 25.00
6 Julius Erving 10.00 25.00
7 David Robinson 10.00 25.00
8 Hakeem Olajuwon 8.00 20.00
9 Alonzo Mourning 8.00 20.00
10 Anfernee Hardaway 15.00 40.00
11 Chris Paul 8.00 20.00
12 Grant Hill 8.00 20.00
13 Walt Frazier 6.00 15.00
14 James Worthy 8.00 20.00
15 Steve Nash 12.00 30.00

2011-12 Fleer Retro Competitive Advantage

STATED ODDS 1:144 PACKS
1 Michael Jordan 50.00 125.00
2 Magic Johnson 8.00 20.00
3 LeBron James 25.00 60.00
4 Larry Bird 10.00 25.00
5 Bill Russell 6.00 15.00
6 Julius Erving 6.00 15.00
7 David Robinson 6.00 15.00
8 Jimmer Fredette 2.00 5.00
9 Anfernee Hardaway 10.00 25.00
10 George Gervin 4.00 10.00
11 Hakeem Olajuwon 5.00 12.00
12 Jerry West 6.00 15.00
13 David Thompson 5.00 12.00
14 Larry Johnson 5.00 12.00
15 Grant Hill 8.00 20.00
16 Chris Paul 5.00 12.00
17 Steve Nash 6.00 15.00
18 Clyde Drexler 5.00 12.00
19 James Worthy 6.00 15.00
20 Alonzo Mourning 6.00 15.00

2011-12 Fleer Retro Flair Showcase

STATED PRINT RUN 150 SER.#'d SETS
1 Michael Jordan 60.00 120.00
2 LeBron James 15.00 40.00
3 Alonzo Mourning 5.00 12.00
4 Bill Russell 6.00 15.00
5 Chris Paul 5.00 12.00
6 Clyde Drexler 5.00 12.00
7 David Robinson 6.00 15.00
8 Grant Hill 10.00 25.00
9 Hakeem Olajuwon 10.00 25.00
10 James Worthy 5.00 12.00
11 Jerry West 5.00 12.00
12 John Havlicek 5.00 12.00
13 Julius Erving 6.00 15.00
14 Larry Bird 10.00 25.00
15 Larry Johnson 5.00 12.00
16 Magic Johnson 10.00 25.00
17 Steve Nash 10.00 25.00
18 Walt Frazier 4.00 10.00
19 Bob McAdoo 3.00 8.00
20 Adrian Dantley 3.00 8.00
21 Cazzie Russell 3.00 8.00
22 Christian Laettner 8.00 20.00
23 Danny Manning 3.00 8.00
24 Darrell Griffith 2.50 6.00
25 Dennis Rodman 8.00 20.00
26 Elgin Baylor 6.00 15.00
27 Gail Goodrich 3.00 8.00
28 George Gervin 4.00 10.00
29 Anfernee Hardaway 10.00 25.00
30 Jim Jackson 2.50 6.00
31 Candace Parker 8.00 20.00
32 Rick Barry 3.00 8.00
33 Tim Hardaway 4.00 10.00
34 David Thompson 3.00 8.00
35 Bill Walton 4.00 10.00
36 Glen Rice 3.00 8.00
37 Toni Kukoc 4.00 10.00
38 Micheal Ray Richardson 3.00 8.00
39 Chet Walker 3.00 8.00
40 Terry Porter 2.50 6.00
41 Kawhi Leonard 25.00 60.00
42 Jimmer Fredette 2.50 6.00
43 Bill Cartwright 3.00 8.00
44 Bill Laimbeer 3.00 8.00
45 Bobby Hurley 6.00 15.00
46 Brad Daugherty 3.00 8.00
47 Hal Greer 3.00 8.00
48 Reggie Theus 3.00 8.00
49 Robert Horry 3.00 8.00
50 Sam Cassell 3.00 8.00
51 Dominique Wilkins 5.00 12.00
52 Karl Malone 5.00 12.00
53 Chandler Parsons 4.00 10.00
54 MarShon Brooks 3.00 8.00
55 Jon Leuer 3.00 8.00
56 Alec Burks 4.00 10.00
57 Tristan Thompson 5.00 12.00
58 Markieff Morris 4.00 10.00
59 Norris Cole 4.00 10.00
60 Klay Thompson 12.00 30.00

2011-12 Fleer Retro Golden Touch

STATED ODDS 1:180 PACKS
1 Michael Jordan 50.00 120.00
2 LeBron James 20.00 50.00
3 Magic Johnson 8.00 20.00
4 Julius Erving 5.00 12.00
5 Hakeem Olajuwon 4.00 10.00
6 David Robinson 5.00 12.00
7 Steve Nash 3.00 8.00
8 Chris Paul 4.00 10.00
9 Larry Bird 8.00 20.00
10 Bill Russell 5.00 12.00
11 Jerry West 4.00 10.00
12 Grant Hill 6.00 15.00
13 James Worthy 4.00 10.00
14 Anfernee Hardaway 8.00 20.00
15 Jimmer Fredette 2.00 5.00

2011-12 Fleer Retro Intimidation Nation

STATED ODDS 1:180 PACKS
1 Grant Hill 5.00 12.00
2 George Gervin 4.00 10.00
3 Alonzo Mourning 5.00 12.00
4 Clyde Drexler 5.00 12.00
5 Hakeem Olajuwon 5.00 12.00
6 Larry Bird 10.00 25.00
7 Darrell Griffith 2.50 6.00
8 Julius Erving 6.00 15.00
9 Magic Johnson 10.00 25.00
10 David Robinson 6.00 15.00
11 David Thompson 3.00 8.00
12 Michael Jordan 100.00 200.00
13 James Worthy 5.00 12.00
14 Jim Jackson 2.50 6.00
15 Bill Russell 6.00 15.00
16 Steve Nash 4.00 10.00
17 Elgin Baylor 4.00 10.00
18 Dennis Rodman 8.00 20.00
19 Walt Frazier 4.00 10.00
20 LeBron James 40.00 100.00
21 Bill Walton 4.00 10.00
22 Larry Johnson 5.00 12.00
23 Tim Hardaway 4.00 10.00
24 Chris Paul 5.00 12.00
25 Jerry West 5.00 12.00
26 Danny Manning 3.00 8.00
27 Bob McAdoo 3.00 8.00
28 Adrian Dantley 3.00 8.00
29 John Havlicek 5.00 12.00
30 Reggie Theus 3.00 8.00
31 Chet Walker 3.00 8.00
32 Bill Laimbeer 3.00 8.00
33 Jimmer Fredette 2.50 6.00
34 Kawhi Leonard 20.00 50.00
35 Anfernee Hardaway 10.00 25.00

2011-12 Fleer Retro Jambalaya

STATED ODDS 1:360 PACKS
1 Michael Jordan 1000.00 1600.00
2 LeBron James 500.00 800.00
3 Bill Russell 30.00 80.00
4 Chris Paul 50.00 125.00
5 Grant Hill 50.00 120.00
6 Dominique Wilkins 25.00 60.00
7 David Robinson 30.00 80.00
8 Hakeem Olajuwon 25.00 60.00
9 James Worthy 25.00 60.00
10 Julius Erving 30.00 80.00
11 Larry Bird 50.00 125.00
12 Magic Johnson 100.00 200.00
13 Anfernee Hardaway 75.00 150.00
14 Dennis Rodman 40.00 100.00
15 Larry Johnson 25.00 60.00
16 Clyde Drexler 25.00 60.00
17 Alonzo Mourning 25.00 60.00
18 Walt Frazier 20.00 50.00
19 John Havlicek 20.00 50.00
20 Karl Malone 30.00 80.00
21 Jerry West 50.00 120.00

2011-12 Fleer Retro Metal Championship Hardware

STATED ODDS 1:90 PACKS
1 Michael Jordan 30.00 80.00
2 LeBron James 15.00 40.00
3 Magic Johnson 10.00 25.00
4 Bill Walton 4.00 10.00
5 Danny Manning 3.00 8.00
6 David Thompson 3.00 8.00
7 Larry Johnson 5.00 12.00
8 James Worthy 5.00 12.00
9 Grant Hill 5.00 12.00
10 Bill Russell 6.00 15.00
11 Christian Laettner 3.00 8.00
12 Glen Rice 3.00 8.00
13 Darrell Griffith 2.50 6.00
14 Gail Goodrich 3.00 8.00
15 John Havlicek 5.00 12.00

2011-12 Fleer Retro Michael Jordan Buybacks

STATED PRINT RUN ONE SERIAL #'d SET

2011-12 Fleer Retro Noyz Boyz

STATED ODDS 1:144 PACKS
1 Bill Walton 4.00 10.00
2 Alonzo Mourning 5.00 12.00
3 Bill Russell 6.00 15.00
4 Chris Paul 5.00 12.00
5 Anfernee Hardaway 10.00 25.00
6 Clyde Drexler 5.00 12.00
7 David Robinson 6.00 15.00
8 David Thompson 8.00 20.00
9 Dennis Rodman 8.00 20.00
10 Grant Hill 5.00 12.00
11 Hakeem Olajuwon 5.00 12.00
12 James Worthy 5.00 12.00
13 Jerry West 5.00 12.00
14 Jim Jackson 2.50 6.00
15 Jimmer Fredette 2.50 6.00
16 Julius Erving 6.00 15.00
17 Kawhi Leonard 50.00 120.00
18 Larry Bird 10.00 25.00
19 Larry Johnson 5.00 12.00
20 LeBron James 50.00 120.00
21 Magic Johnson 10.00 25.00
22 Tim Hardaway 4.00 10.00
23 Michael Jordan 100.00 250.00
24 Steve Nash 4.00 10.00
25 Walt Frazier 4.00 10.00

2011-12 Fleer Retro Precious Metal Gems Red

RANDOM INSERTS IN PACKS
STATED PRINT RUN 150 SER.#'d SETS
UNPRICED GREEN PRINT RUN 10 SETS
1 Michael Jordan 100.00 200.00
2 Mark Jackson 5.00 12.00
3 Hakeem Olajuwon 12.00 30.00
4 LeBron James 100.00 200.00
5 Clyde Drexler 8.00 20.00
6 David Robinson 10.00 25.00
7 Christian Laettner 5.00 12.00
8 Jim Jackson 4.00 10.00
9 Adrian Dantley 5.00 12.00
10 Reggie Theus 5.00 12.00
11 John Havlicek 8.00 20.00
12 Dennis Rodman 15.00 40.00
13 Gail Goodrich 5.00 12.00
14 Danny Manning 5.00 12.00
15 Bob McAdoo 5.00 12.00
16 Walt Frazier 6.00 15.00
17 Bill Laimbeer 5.00 12.00
18 Hal Greer 5.00 12.00
19 Bill Cartwright 5.00 12.00
20 Rudy Tomjanovich 5.00 12.00
21 Bill Russell 10.00 25.00
22 Tim Hardaway 6.00 15.00
23 Cazzie Russell 5.00 12.00
24 David Thompson 5.00 12.00
25 Darrell Griffith 4.00 10.00
26 Rick Barry 5.00 12.00
27 George Gervin 20.00 50.00
28 Elgin Baylor 6.00 15.00
29 Alonzo Mourning 30.00 80.00
30 Bill Walton 6.00 15.00
31 Larry Johnson 8.00 20.00
32 Magic Johnson 15.00 40.00
33 Julius Erving 10.00 25.00
34 Jimmer Fredette 4.00 10.00
35 John Starks 15.00 40.00
36 Bill Sharman 6.00 15.00
37 Larry Bird 15.00 40.00
38 Grant Hill 20.00 50.00
39 Steve Nash 6.00 15.00
40 James Worthy 15.00 40.00

2011-12 Fleer Retro Precious Metal Gems Blue

*BLUE: .5X TO 1.2X BASE HI
STATED PRINT RUN 50 SER.#'d SETS
1 Michael Jordan 800.00 1500.00
4 LeBron James 200.00 400.00

2011-12 Fleer Retro Ultra Court Masters

STATED ODDS 1:90 PACKS
1 Michael Jordan 60.00 150.00
2 LeBron James 40.00 100.00
3 Larry Bird 8.00 20.00
4 Magic Johnson 8.00 20.00
5 Bill Russell 5.00 12.00
6 Julius Erving 5.00 12.00
7 David Robinson 5.00 12.00
8 Hakeem Olajuwon 4.00 10.00
9 Clyde Drexler 4.00 10.00
10 Grant Hill 4.00 10.00
11 Steve Nash 3.00 8.00
12 Chris Paul 4.00 10.00
13 Larry Johnson 4.00 10.00
14 Alonzo Mourning 4.00 10.00
15 James Worthy 4.00 10.00
16 David Thompson 2.50 6.00
17 Danny Manning 2.50 6.00
18 Jimmer Fredette 2.00 5.00
19 George Gervin 3.00 8.00
20 Anfernee Hardaway 8.00 20.00
21 Adrian Dantley 2.50 6.00
22 Walt Frazier 3.00 8.00
23 Bill Walton 3.00 8.00
24 Tim Hardaway 3.00 8.00
25 Jim Jackson 2.00 5.00

2011-12 Fleer Retro Ultra Stars

STATED ODDS 1:180 PACKS
1 Michael Jordan 40.00 100.00
2 LeBron James 20.00 50.00
3 Larry Bird 12.00 30.00
4 Magic Johnson 12.00 30.00
5 Bill Russell 8.00 20.00
6 Julius Erving 8.00 20.00
7 David Robinson 8.00 20.00
8 Hakeem Olajuwon 6.00 15.00
9 Jerry West 6.00 15.00
10 Grant Hill 15.00 40.00
11 Steve Nash 6.00 15.00
12 Chris Paul 10.00 25.00
13 Jimmer Fredette 1.50 4.00
14 John Havlicek 6.00 15.00
15 Alonzo Mourning 8.00 20.00
16 Clyde Drexler 6.00 15.00
17 Dennis Rodman 10.00 25.00
18 Larry Johnson 8.00 20.00
19 James Worthy 6.00 15.00

20 Tim Hardaway 5.00 12.00
21 Walt Frazier 5.00 12.00
22 Elgin Baylor 5.00 12.00
23 George Gervin 5.00 12.00
24 Anfernee Hardaway 12.00 30.00
25 Bill Walton 5.00 12.00

2012-13 Fleer Retro

ATED RS ODDS 1:3 HOBBY
1 Michael Jordan 3.00 8.00
2 LeBron James 2.00 5.00
3 Jason Kidd .50 1.25
4 Dominique Wilkins .60 1.50
5 Karl Malone .60 1.50
6 Bill Walton .50 1.25
7 Allen Iverson .60 1.50
8 Paul Pierce .50 1.25
9 Ray Allen .50 1.25
10 Grant Hill .60 1.50
11 Hakeem Olajuwon .60 1.50
12 Bernard King .40 1.00
13 Isiah Thomas .50 1.25
14 Dennis Rodman 1.00 2.50
15 Reggie Miller .50 1.25
16 Bill Russell .75 2.00
17 David Robinson .75 2.00
18 Jim Jackson .30 .75
19 Larry Johnson .60 1.50
20 Nate Thurmond .40 1.00
21 Alonzo Mourning .60 1.50
22 Anfernee Hardaway 1.25 3.00
23 Glen Rice .40 1.00
24 Tim Hardaway .50 1.25
25 Walt Frazier .50 1.25
26 Larry Bird 1.25 3.00
27 John Havlicek .60 1.50
28 Nick Van Exel .50 1.25
29 Danny Manning .40 1.00
30 Spud Webb .40 1.00
31 Jamal Mashburn .50 1.25
32 David Thompson .40 1.00
33 Micheal Ray Richardson .40 1.00
34 Harold Miner .30 .75
35 Mark Price .50 1.25
36 Jeff Hornacek .40 1.00
37 Toni Kukoc .50 1.25
38 A.C. Green .50 1.25
39 Spencer Haywood .30 .75
40 Sean Elliott .50 1.25
41 Allan Houston .40 1.00
42 Dave Cowens .30 .75
43 Cheryl Miller .50 1.25
44 Christian Laettner .40 1.00
45 Magic Johnson 1.25 3.00
46 Mark A. Jackson .40 1.00
47 Vinny Del Negro .30 .75
48 Clyde Drexler .60 1.50
49 Gary Payton .50 1.25
50 Julius Erving .75 2.00
51 Meyers Leonard RS .60 1.50
52 Jeremy Lamb RS .75 2.00
53 Kendall Marshall RS .50 1.25
54 Moe Harkless RS .75 2.00
55 Tyler Zeller RS .60 1.50
56 Andrew Nicholson RS .50 1.25
57 Evan Fournier RS .75 2.00
58 Jared Cunningham RS .50 1.25
59 Miles Plumlee RS .50 1.25
60 Arnett Moultrie RS .50 1.25
61 Bernard James RS .50 1.25
62 Jae Crowder RS .60 1.50
63 Draymond Green RS 2.50 6.00
64 Quincy Acy RS .50 1.25
65 Khris Middleton RS .75 2.00
66 Will Barton RS .60 1.50
67 Tyshawn Taylor RS .50 1.25
68 Darius Miller RS .50 1.25
69 Kevin Murphy RS .50 1.25
70 Darius Johnson-Odom RS .50 1.25
71 Robbie Hummel RS .50 1.25
72 Robert Sacre RS .50 1.25
73 Wesley Witherspoon RS .50 1.25
74 William Buford RS .50 1.25
75 Ricardo Ratliffe RS .50 1.25
76 John Shurna RS .50 1.25
77 Tomas Satoransky RS .50 1.25
78 Justin Hamilton RS .60 1.50
79 JaMychal Green RS .50 1.25
80 Kris Joseph RS .50 1.25

2012-13 Fleer Retro 96-97 Flair Legacy Row 1

STATED PRINT RUN 150 SER.#'d SETS
96FL1 Julius Erving 5.00 12.00
96FL2 Michael Jordan 30.00 80.00
96FL3 Bob McAdoo 2.50 6.00
96FL4 Wilt Chamberlain 6.00 15.00
96FL5 Danny Manning 2.50 6.00
96FL6 Mark Price 3.00 8.00
96FL7 Magic Johnson 8.00 20.00
96FL8 Tony Gwynn 3.00 8.00
96FL9 Clyde Drexler 4.00 10.00
96FL10 Gary Payton 3.00 8.00
96FL11 LeBron James 25.00 60.00
96FL12 Shawn Bradley 2.00 5.00
96FL13 Elvin Hayes 3.00 8.00
96FL14 Allen Iverson 4.00 10.00
96FL15 Jamal Mashburn 3.00 8.00
96FL16 Nick Van Exel 3.00 8.00
96FL17 Allan Houston 2.50 6.00
96FL18 Antoine Walker 2.50 6.00
96FL19 Toni Kukoc 3.00 8.00
96FL20 David Robinson 5.00 12.00
96FL21 Larry Johnson 4.00 10.00
96FL22 Lou Hudson 3.00 8.00
96FL23 John Havlicek 4.00 10.00
96FL24 Grant Hill 4.00 10.00
96FL25 Isiah Thomas 3.00 8.00
96FL26 Bill Walton 3.00 8.00
96FL27 Reggie Miller 3.00 8.00
96FL28 Derrick Coleman 3.00 8.00
96FL29 Bill Laimbeer 2.50 6.00
96FL30 Sean Elliott 3.00 8.00
96FL31 Spud Webb 2.50 6.00
96FL32 Larry Bird 6.00 15.00
96FL33 Paul Pierce 3.00 8.00
96FL34 Bernard King 2.50 6.00
96FL35 Bill Russell 5.00 12.00
96FL36 Nate Thurmond 2.50 6.00
96FL37 Anfernee Hardaway 6.00 15.00
96FL38 Walt Frazier 3.00 8.00
96FL39 Jason Kidd 3.00 8.00
96FL40 Dennis Rodman 4.00 10.00
96FL41 Cheryl Miller 3.00 8.00
96FL42 Karl Malone 4.00 10.00
96FL43 Jeff Hornacek 2.50 6.00
96FL44 Alonzo Mourning 4.00 10.00
96FL45 Ray Allen 3.00 8.00
96FL46 Bobby Hurley 3.00 8.00
96FL47 Dominique Wilkins 4.00 10.00
96FL48 Hakeem Olajuwon 4.00 10.00
96FL49 A.C. Green 3.00 8.00
96FL50 Robert Horry 2.50 6.00

2012-13 Fleer Retro 96-97 Lucky 13

ATED ODDS 1:20 HOBBY
1 Meyers Leonard 2.00 5.00
2 Kendall Marshall 1.50 4.00
3 Tyler Zeller 2.00 5.00
4 Evan Fournier 2.50 6.00
5 Miles Plumlee 1.50 4.00
6 Tomas Satoransky 1.50 4.00
7 Bernard James 1.50 4.00
8 Draymond Green 8.00 20.00
9 Khris Middleton 2.50 6.00
10 Tyshawn Taylor 1.50 4.00
11 Kevin Murphy 1.50 4.00
12 Kris Joseph 1.50 4.00
13 Robbie Hummel 1.50 4.00

2012-13 Fleer Retro 96-97 Lucky 13 Autographs

OVERALL 96/97 L13 AU ODDS 1:240
EXCHANGE DEADLNE 5/31/2015
1 Meyers Leonard 4.00 10.00
2 Kendall Marshall 3.00 8.00
3 Tyler Zeller 4.00 10.00
4 Evan Fournier 5.00 12.00
5 Miles Plumlee 3.00 8.00
6 Tomas Satoransky 3.00 8.00
7 Bernard James 3.00 8.00
8 Draymond Green 15.00 40.00
9 Khris Middleton 5.00 12.00
10 Tyshawn Taylor EXCH 3.00 8.00
11 Kevin Murphy 3.00 8.00
12 Kris Joseph 3.00 8.00
13 Robbie Hummel 3.00 8.00

2012-13 Fleer Retro 96-97 Molten Metal

STATED ODDS 1:120 HOBBY
1 Magic Johnson 6.00 15.00
2 Gary Payton 2.50 6.00
3 LeBron James 25.00 60.00
4 Allen Iverson 10.00 25.00
5 Ray Allen 2.50 6.00
6 Dennis Rodman 10.00 25.00
7 Larry Johnson 3.00 8.00
8 Wilt Chamberlain 5.00 12.00
9 Karl Malone 3.00 8.00
10 Bill Russell 4.00 10.00
11 Grant Hill 4.00 10.00
12 Reggie Miller 2.50 6.00
13 Isiah Thomas 2.50 6.00
14 David Robinson 4.00 10.00
15 Hakeem Olajuwon 3.00 8.00
16 Paul Pierce 2.50 6.00
17 Julius Erving 4.00 10.00
18 Jason Kidd 2.50 6.00
19 Larry Bird 6.00 15.00
20 Michael Jordan 60.00 150.00

2012-13 Fleer Retro 96-97 Tradition Thrill Seekers

STATED ODDS 1:120 HOBBY
1 Isiah Thomas 4.00 10.00
2 Wilt Chamberlain 8.00 20.00
3 Reggie Miller 8.00 20.00
4 Larry Bird 10.00 25.00
5 Grant Hill 20.00 50.00
6 Allen Iverson 10.00 25.00
7 David Robinson 6.00 15.00
8 Larry Johnson 5.00 12.00
9 Paul Pierce 4.00 10.00
10 Bill Russell 6.00 15.00
11 Dominique Wilkins 5.00 12.00
12 Michael Jordan 60.00 120.00
13 Dennis Rodman 8.00 20.00
14 LeBron James 40.00 80.00
15 Magic Johnson 10.00 25.00
16 Gary Payton 4.00 10.00
17 Julius Erving 6.00 15.00
18 Anfernee Hardaway 10.00 25.00
19 Jason Kidd 10.00 25.00
20 Karl Malone 5.00 12.00

2012-13 Fleer Retro 97-98 EX 2001 Essential Credentials Future

PRINT RUNS B/WN 1-42 COPIES PER
EX1 Michael Jordan/42 300.00 500.00
EX2 Reggie Miller/41 30.00 60.00
EX3 A.C. Green/40 10.00 25.00
EX4 Mark Price/39 15.00 40.00
EX5 David Robinson/38 10.00 25.00
EX6 Clyde Drexler/37 15.00 40.00
EX7 Bernard King/36 6.00 15.00
EX8 Grant Hill/35 15.00 40.00
EX9 David Thompson/34 6.00 15.00
EX10 Elvin Hayes/33 8.00 20.00
EX11 Bill Walton/32 12.00 30.00
EX12 Allan Houston/31 15.00 40.00
EX13 Dennis Rodman/30 20.00 50.00
EX14 Tim Hardaway/29 8.00 20.00
EX15 Walt Frazier/28 10.00 25.00
EX16 Jason Kidd/27 20.00 50.00
EX17 Anfernee Hardaway/26 25.00 60.00
EX18 Spud Webb/25 15.00 40.00
EX19 Christian Laettner/24 15.00 40.00
EX20 John Havlicek/23 20.00 50.00
EX21 Mark A. Jackson/22 12.00 30.00
EX22 Karl Malone/21 20.00 50.00
EX23 Tony Gwynn/20 40.00 80.00

2012-13 Fleer Retro 97-98 EX 2001 Essential Credentials Now

PRINT RUNS B/WN 1-42 COPIES PER
NO PRICING ON QTY 19 OR LESS
EX20 John Havlicek/20 20.00 50.00
EX21 Mark A. Jackson/21 12.00 30.00
EX22 Karl Malone/22 40.00 80.00
EX23 Tony Gwynn/23 40.00 80.00
EX24 Julius Erving/24 50.00 100.00
EX25 Gary Payton/25 40.00 80.00
EX26 Ray Allen/26 40.00 100.00
EX27 Larry Johnson/27 15.00 40.00
EX28 Paul Pierce/28 30.00 60.00
EX29 Magic Johnson/29 30.00 60.00
EX30 Isiah Thomas/30 10.00 25.00
EX31 Derrick Coleman/31 30.00 60.00
EX32 Dominique Wilkins/32 15.00 40.00
EX33 Wilt Chamberlain/33 30.00 60.00
EX34 Allen Iverson/34 60.00 150.00
EX35 Danny Manning/35 12.00 30.00
EX36 Hakeem Olajuwon/36 20.00 50.00
EX37 Alonzo Mourning/37 12.00 30.00
EX38 Bill Russell/38 40.00 80.00
EX39 Antoine Walker/39 10.00 25.00
EX40 Jamal Mashburn/40 10.00 25.00
EX41 Larry Bird/41 20.00 50.00
EX42 LeBron James/42 150.00 300.00

2012-13 Fleer Retro 97-98 Flair Legacy Row 0

STATED PRINT RUN 100 SER.#'d SETS
97FL1 Dominique Wilkins 5.00 12.00
97FL2 Bill Russell 6.00 15.00
97FL3 Paul Pierce 4.00 10.00
97FL4 Grant Hill 10.00 25.00
97FL5 Isiah Thomas 4.00 10.00
97FL6 Dennis Rodman 8.00 20.00
97FL7 Walt Frazier 4.00 10.00
97FL8 Lou Hudson 4.00 10.00
97FL9 Julius Erving 6.00 15.00
97FL10 Anfernee Hardaway 12.00 30.00
97FL11 Nick Van Exel 4.00 10.00
97FL12 David Robinson 8.00 20.00
97FL13 Nate Thurmond 3.00 8.00
97FL14 Mark A. Jackson 3.00 8.00
97FL15 Clyde Drexler 5.00 12.00
97FL16 Bill Walton 4.00 10.00
97FL17 Tony Gwynn 6.00 15.00
97FL18 Ray Allen 4.00 10.00
97FL19 Tim Hardaway 4.00 10.00
97FL20 Robert Horry 3.00 8.00
97FL21 Cheryl Miller 4.00 10.00
97FL22 Allen Iverson 20.00 50.00
97FL23 Bernard King 3.00 8.00
97FL24 Eddie Jones 3.00 8.00
97FL25 Antoine Walker 3.00 8.00
97FL26 Danny Manning 3.00 8.00
97FL27 Jamal Mashburn 4.00 10.00
97FL28 Rod Strickland 4.00 10.00
97FL29 Gary Payton 4.00 10.00
97FL30 Muggsy Bogues 3.00 8.00
97FL31 Larry Johnson 5.00 12.00
97FL32 Magic Johnson 10.00 25.00
97FL33 Allan Houston 3.00 8.00
97FL34 Alonzo Mourning 5.00 12.00
97FL35 Jeff Hornacek 3.00 8.00
97FL36 Elvin Hayes 4.00 10.00
97FL37 Mark Price 4.00 10.00
97FL38 Karl Malone 6.00 15.00
97FL39 Hakeem Olajuwon 5.00 12.00
97FL40 Reggie Miller 4.00 10.00
97FL41 Harold Miner 2.50 6.00
97FL42 LeBron James 30.00 80.00
97FL43 Larry Bird 6.00 15.00
97FL44 Adrian Dantley 3.00 8.00
97FL45 Wilt Chamberlain 6.00 15.00
97FL46 A.C. Green 4.00 10.00
97FL47 Jason Kidd 6.00 15.00
97FL48 Michael Jordan 150.00 300.00
97FL49 Spud Webb 3.00 8.00
97FL50 Dave Cowens 2.50 6.00

2012-13 Fleer Retro 97-98 Fleer EX 2001

STATED ODDS 1:10 HOBBY
EX1 Michael Jordan 12.00 30.00
EX2 Reggie Miller 1.50 4.00
EX3 A.C. Green 1.50 4.00
EX4 Mark Price 1.50 4.00
EX5 David Robinson 2.50 6.00
EX6 Clyde Drexler 2.00 5.00
EX7 Bernard King 1.25 3.00
EX8 Grant Hill 2.00 5.00
EX9 David Thompson 1.25 3.00
EX10 Elvin Hayes 1.50 4.00
EX11 Bill Walton 1.50 4.00
EX12 Allan Houston 1.25 3.00
EX13 Dennis Rodman 3.00 8.00
EX14 Tim Hardaway 1.50 4.00
EX15 Walt Frazier 1.50 4.00
EX16 Jason Kidd 1.50 4.00
EX17 Anfernee Hardaway 4.00 10.00
EX18 Spud Webb 1.25 3.00
EX19 Christian Laettner 1.25 3.00
EX20 John Havlicek 2.00 5.00
EX21 Mark A. Jackson 1.25 3.00
EX22 Karl Malone 2.00 5.00
EX23 Tony Gwynn 1.50 4.00
EX24 Julius Erving 2.50 6.00
EX25 Gary Payton 1.50 4.00
EX26 Ray Allen 1.50 4.00
EX27 Larry Johnson 2.00 5.00
EX28 Paul Pierce 1.50 4.00
EX29 Magic Johnson 4.00 10.00
EX30 Isiah Thomas 1.50 4.00
EX31 Derrick Coleman 1.50 4.00
EX32 Dominique Wilkins 2.00 5.00
EX33 Wilt Chamberlain 3.00 8.00
EX34 Allen Iverson 2.00 5.00
EX35 Danny Manning 1.25 3.00
EX36 Hakeem Olajuwon 2.00 5.00
EX37 Alonzo Mourning 2.00 5.00
EX38 Bill Russell 2.50 6.00
EX39 Antoine Walker 1.25 3.00
EX40 Jamal Mashburn 1.50 4.00
EX41 Larry Bird 4.00 10.00
EX42 LeBron James 6.00 15.00

2012-13 Fleer Retro 97-98 Metal Universe Precious Metal Gems

STATED PRINT RUN 100 SER.#'d SETS
97PM1 Bernard King 5.00 12.00
97PM2 Bill Russell 20.00 50.00
97PM3 Mookie Blaylock 8.00 20.00
97PM4 Lou Hudson 6.00 15.00
97PM5 Magic Johnson 15.00 40.00
97PM6 Ray Allen 15.00 40.00
97PM7 Reggie Miller 6.00 15.00
97PM8 Spencer Haywood 4.00 10.00
97PM9 Walt Frazier 6.00 15.00
97PM10 Jeff Hornacek 5.00 12.00
97PM11 Spud Webb 5.00 12.00
97PM12 Alonzo Mourning 8.00 20.00
97PM13 Larry Bird 15.00 40.00
97PM14 Allan Houston 5.00 12.00
97PM15 Shawn Bradley 4.00 10.00
97PM16 Nate Thurmond 5.00 12.00
97PM17 Christian Laettner 5.00 12.00
97PM18 David Robinson 10.00 25.00
97PM19 Dennis Rodman 5.00 12.00
97PM20 Karl Malone 10.00 25.00
97PM21 Elvin Hayes 6.00 15.00
97PM22 Toni Kukoc 8.00 20.00
97PM23 Anfernee Hardaway 30.00 60.00
97PM24 Antoine Walker 6.00 15.00
97PM25 Mark Price 6.00 15.00
97PM26 Wilt Chamberlain 12.00 30.00
97PM27 Danny Manning 10.00 25.00
97PM28 Nick Van Exel 6.00 15.00
97PM29 Larry Johnson 8.00 20.00
97PM30 Dominique Wilkins 8.00 20.00
97PM31 Hakeem Olajuwon 12.00 30.00
97PM32 Dave Cowens 4.00 10.00
97PM33 Gary Payton 15.00 40.00
97PM34 Isiah Thomas 6.00 15.00
97PM35 LeBron James 75.00 150.00
97PM36 David Thompson 5.00 12.00
97PM37 Jason Kidd 10.00 25.00
97PM38 Paul Pierce 15.00 40.00
97PM39 Tim Hardaway 6.00 15.00
97PM40 A.C. Green 6.00 15.00
97PM41 John Havlicek 5.00 12.00
97PM42 Grant Hill 8.00 20.00
97PM43 Allen Iverson 20.00 50.00
97PM44 Mark A. Jackson 5.00 12.00
97PM45 Clyde Drexler 12.00 30.00
97PM46 Julius Erving 10.00 25.00
97PM47 Cheryl Miller 6.00 15.00
97PM48 Bill Walton 6.00 15.00
97PM49 Tony Gwynn 8.00 20.00
97PM50 Michael Jordan 200.00 400.00

2012-13 Fleer Retro 97-98 Ultra

ATED ODDS 1:5 HOBBY
ULT1 Ray Allen .75 2.00
ULT2 Reggie Miller .75 2.00
ULT3 Nick Van Exel .75 2.00
ULT4 Spud Webb .60 1.50
ULT5 Lou Hudson .75 2.00
ULT6 A.C. Green .75 2.00
ULT7 Antoine Walker .60 1.50
ULT8 Danny Manning .60 1.50
ULT9 Bill Walton .75 2.00
ULT10 Alonzo Mourning 1.00 2.50
ULT11 Anfernee Hardaway 2.00 5.00
ULT12 Larry Bird 2.00 5.00
ULT13 John Havlicek 1.00 2.50
ULT14 Derrick Coleman .75 2.00
ULT15 Hakeem Olajuwon 1.00 2.50
ULT16 Allan Houston .60 1.50
ULT17 David Robinson 1.25 3.00
ULT18 Muggsy Bogues .60 1.50
ULT19 Clyde Drexler 1.00 2.50
ULT20 Harold Miner .50 1.25
ULT21 Bernard King .60 1.50
ULT22 Bill Russell 1.25 3.00
ULT23 Magic Johnson 2.00 5.00
ULT24 Karl Malone 1.00 2.50
ULT25 David Thompson .60 1.50
ULT26 Larry Johnson 1.00 2.50
ULT27 Tony Gwynn .75 2.00
ULT28 Dennis Rodman 1.50 4.00
ULT29 Isiah Thomas .75 2.00
ULT30 Eddie Jones .60 1.50
ULT31 Cheryl Miller .75 2.00
ULT32 Gary Payton .75 2.00
ULT33 Allen Iverson 1.00 2.50
ULT34 Paul Pierce .75 2.00
ULT35 Christian Laettner .60 1.50
ULT36 Jason Kidd .75 2.00
ULT37 Walt Frazier .75 2.00
ULT38 Dominique Wilkins 1.00 2.50
ULT39 Michael Jordan 5.00 12.00
ULT40 Grant Hill 1.00 2.50
ULT41 LeBron James 3.00 8.00
ULT42 Julius Erving 1.25 3.00
ULT43 Micheal Ray Richardson .60 1.50
ULT44 Wilt Chamberlain 1.50 4.00
ULT45 Jamal Mashburn .75 2.00
ULT46 Meyers Leonard .60 1.50
ULT47 Jeremy Lamb .75 2.00
ULT48 Kendall Marshall .50 1.25
ULT49 Moe Harkless .75 2.00
ULT50 Tyler Zeller .60 1.50

2012-13 Fleer Retro 97-98 Ultra Court Masters

STATED ODDS 1:180 HOBBY
1 Magic Johnson 10.00 25.00
2 Bill Russell 6.00 15.00
3 Reggie Miller 12.00 30.00
4 Isiah Thomas 4.00 10.00
5 Michael Jordan 50.00 120.00
6 LeBron James 30.00 60.00
7 Wilt Chamberlain 8.00 20.00
8 Larry Bird 10.00 25.00
9 Allen Iverson 10.00 25.00
10 Anfernee Hardaway 10.00 25.00
11 Julius Erving 6.00 15.00
12 Ray Allen 4.00 10.00
13 Elvin Hayes 4.00 10.00
14 Grant Hill 12.00 30.00
15 David Robinson 6.00 15.00
16 Karl Malone 6.00 15.00
17 Dominique Wilkins 5.00 12.00
18 Jason Kidd 8.00 20.00
19 Walt Frazier 4.00 10.00
20 Paul Pierce 4.00 10.00
21 Hakeem Olajuwon 5.00 12.00

2012-13 Fleer Retro 97-98 Ultra Platinum Medallion

STATED PRINT RUN 100 SER.#'d SETS
ULT1 Ray Allen 4.00 10.00
ULT2 Reggie Miller 4.00 10.00
ULT3 Nick Van Exel 4.00 10.00
ULT4 Spud Webb 3.00 8.00
ULT5 Lou Hudson 4.00 10.00
ULT6 A.C. Green 4.00 10.00
ULT7 Antoine Walker 3.00 8.00
ULT8 Danny Manning 3.00 8.00
ULT9 Bill Walton 4.00 10.00
ULT10 Alonzo Mourning 5.00 12.00
ULT11 Anfernee Hardaway 10.00 25.00
ULT12 Larry Bird 10.00 25.00
ULT13 John Havlicek 5.00 12.00
ULT14 Derrick Coleman 6.00 15.00
ULT15 Hakeem Olajuwon 5.00 12.00
ULT16 Allan Houston 3.00 8.00
ULT17 David Robinson 6.00 15.00
ULT18 Muggsy Bogues 3.00 8.00
ULT19 Clyde Drexler 5.00 12.00
ULT20 Harold Miner 2.50 6.00
ULT21 Bernard King 3.00 8.00
ULT22 Bill Russell 6.00 15.00
ULT23 Magic Johnson 10.00 25.00
ULT24 Karl Malone 5.00 12.00
ULT25 David Thompson 3.00 8.00
ULT26 Larry Johnson 5.00 12.00
ULT27 Tony Gwynn 8.00 20.00
ULT28 Dennis Rodman 8.00 20.00
ULT29 Isiah Thomas 4.00 10.00
ULT30 Eddie Jones 3.00 8.00
ULT31 Cheryl Miller 4.00 10.00
ULT32 Gary Payton 4.00 10.00
ULT33 Allen Iverson 5.00 12.00
ULT34 Paul Pierce 4.00 10.00
ULT35 Christian Laettner 3.00 8.00
ULT36 Jason Kidd 6.00 15.00
ULT37 Walt Frazier 4.00 10.00
ULT38 Dominique Wilkins 5.00 12.00
ULT39 Michael Jordan 75.00 150.00
ULT40 Grant Hill 8.00 20.00
ULT41 LeBron James 25.00 60.00
ULT42 Julius Erving 6.00 15.00
ULT43 Micheal Ray Richardson 3.00 8.00
ULT44 Wilt Chamberlain 8.00 20.00
ULT45 Jamal Mashburn 4.00 10.00
ULT46 Meyers Leonard 3.00 8.00
ULT47 Jeremy Lamb 4.00 10.00
ULT48 Kendall Marshall 2.50 6.00
ULT49 Moe Harkless 4.00 10.00
ULT50 Tyler Zeller 3.00 8.00

2012-13 Fleer Retro 97-98 Ultra Starring Role

STATED ODDS 1:180 HOBBY
1 Larry Bird 8.00 20.00
2 Bill Russell 5.00 12.00
3 Dominique Wilkins 4.00 10.00
4 Anfernee Hardaway 8.00 20.00
5 Karl Malone 4.00 10.00
6 Magic Johnson 8.00 20.00
8 Wilt Chamberlain 6.00 15.00
9 Hakeem Olajuwon 4.00 10.00
10 Ray Allen 3.00 8.00
11 Reggie Miller 5.00 12.00
12 Paul Pierce 6.00 15.00
13 LeBron James 15.00 40.00
14 Grant Hill 10.00 25.00
15 Larry Johnson 4.00 10.00
16 David Robinson 10.00 25.00
17 Michael Jordan 60.00 150.00
18 Jason Kidd 6.00 15.00
19 Clyde Drexler 6.00 15.00
20 Allen Iverson 4.00 10.00
21 Julius Erving 5.00 12.00

2012-13 Fleer Retro 97-98 Z-Force Big Men on Court

ATED ODDS 1:120 HOBBY
1 BMOC Alonzo Mourning 3.00 8.00
2 BMOC David Robinson 4.00 10.00
3 BMOC Isiah Thomas 2.50 6.00
4 BMOC Larry Bird 6.00 15.00
5 BMOC Paul Pierce 2.50 6.00
6 BMOC Ray Allen 2.50 6.00
7 BMOC Grant Hill 3.00 8.00
8 BMOC Anfernee Hardaway 6.00 15.00
9 BMOC Magic Johnson 6.00 15.00
10 BMOC Larry Johnson 3.00 8.00
11 BMOC Bill Russell 4.00 10.00
12 BMOC Julius Erving 4.00 10.00
13 BMOC Allen Iverson 3.00 8.00
14 BMOC Karl Malone 3.00 8.00
15 BMOC Michael Jordan 40.00 100.00
16 BMOC LeBron James 20.00 50.00
17 BMOC Reggie Miller 2.50 6.00
18 BMOC Gary Payton 2.50 6.00
19 BMOC Jason Kidd 2.50 6.00
20 BMOC Wilt Chamberlain 5.00 12.00

2012-13 Fleer Retro 97-98 Z-Force Rave

ATED PRINT RUN 399 SER.#'d SETS
Z1 Isiah Thomas 1.50 4.00
Z2 Dennis Rodman 3.00 8.00
Z3 Larry Bird 4.00 10.00
Z4 John Havlicek 2.00 5.00
Z5 Dominique Wilkins 2.00 5.00
Z6 David Robinson 2.50 6.00
Z7 Muggsy Bogues 1.25 3.00
Z8 Mookie Blaylock 1.00 2.50
Z9 Larry Johnson 2.00 5.00
Z10 Danny Manning 1.25 3.00
Z11 Dave Cowens 1.00 2.50
Z12 Cheryl Miller 1.50 4.00
Z13 Allen Iverson 2.00 5.00
Z14 Nate Thurmond 1.25 3.00
Z15 Elvin Hayes 1.50 4.00
Z16 Lou Hudson 1.50 4.00
Z17 Antoine Walker 1.25 3.00
Z18 A.C. Green 1.50 4.00
Z19 Bill Walton 1.50 4.00
Z20 Magic Johnson 4.00 10.00
Z21 Ray Allen 1.50 4.00
Z22 Jamal Mashburn 1.50 4.00
Z23 Tony Gwynn 1.50 4.00
Z24 Jason Kidd 1.50 4.00
Z25 Hakeem Olajuwon 2.00 5.00
Z26 Hal Greer 1.25 3.00
Z27 Paul Pierce 1.50 4.00
Z28 Wilt Chamberlain 3.00 8.00
Z29 Shawn Bradley 1.00 2.50
Z30 Bill Laimbeer 1.25 3.00
Z31 Grant Hill 2.00 5.00
Z32 Karl Malone 2.00 5.00
Z33 Michael Jordan 15.00 40.00
Z34 Alonzo Mourning 2.00 5.00
Z35 Nick Van Exel 1.50 4.00
Z36 Clyde Drexler 2.00 5.00
Z37 Eddie Jones 1.25 3.00
Z38 Gary Payton 1.50 4.00
Z39 Allan Houston 1.25 3.00
Z40 Bill Russell 2.50 6.00
Z41 David Thompson 1.25 3.00
Z42 Julius Erving 2.50 6.00
Z43 Walt Frazier 1.50 4.00
Z44 Mark Price 1.50 4.00
Z45 Reggie Miller 1.50 4.00
Z46 Spencer Haywood 1.00 2.50
Z47 Harold Miner 1.00 2.50
Z48 Bernard King 1.25 3.00
Z49 Anfernee Hardaway 4.00 10.00
Z50 LeBron James 12.00 30.00

2012-13 Fleer Retro 97-98 Z-Force Super Rave

*SUPER RAVE: 1.2X TO 3X BASIC
STATED PRINT RUN 50 SER.#'d SETS
Z2 Dennis Rodman 12.00 30.00
Z6 David Robinson 12.00 30.00
Z8 Mookie Blaylock 15.00 40.00
Z13 Allen Iverson 15.00 40.00
Z21 Ray Allen 8.00 20.00
Z24 Jason Kidd 30.00 60.00
Z31 Grant Hill 10.00 25.00
Z33 Michael Jordan 150.00 300.00
Z38 Gary Payton 10.00 25.00
Z44 Mark Price 10.00 25.00
Z45 Reggie Miller 12.00 30.00
Z49 Anfernee Hardaway 12.00 30.00

2012-13 Fleer Retro 98-99 Lucky 13

STATED ODDS 1:40 HOBBY
1LT Jeremy Lamb 3.00 8.00
2LT Moe Harkless 3.00 8.00
3LT Andrew Nicholson 2.00 5.00
4LT Jared Cunningham 2.00 5.00
5LT Arnett Moultrie 2.00 5.00
6LT Jae Crowder 2.50 6.00
7LT Quincy Acy 2.00 5.00
8LT Will Barton 2.50 6.00
9LT Darius Miller 2.00 5.00
10LT Darius Johnson-Odom 2.00 5.00
11LT Justin Hamilton 2.50 6.00
12LT Robert Sacre 2.00 5.00
13LT William Buford 2.00 5.00

2012-13 Fleer Retro 98-99 Lucky 13 Autographs

OVERALL 98/99 L13 AU ODDS 1:240
EXCHANGE DEADLNE 5/31/2015
1LT Jeremy Lamb EXCH 5.00 12.00
2LT Moe Harkless 5.00 12.00
3LT Andrew Nicholson 3.00 8.00
4LT Jared Cunningham 3.00 8.00
5LT Arnett Moultrie 3.00 8.00
6LT Jae Crowder 4.00 10.00
7LT Quincy Acy 3.00 8.00
8LT Will Barton 4.00 10.00
9LT Darius Miller 6.00 15.00
10LT Darius Johnson-Odom 3.00 8.00
11LT Justin Hamilton 4.00 10.00
12LT Robert Sacre 3.00 8.00
13LT William Buford 3.00 8.00

2012-13 Fleer Retro 98-99 Metal Universe Precious Metal Gems

STATED PRINT RUN 50 SER.#'d SETS
98PM1 Elvin Hayes 6.00 15.00
98PM2 Mark Price 12.00 30.00
98PM3 Muggsy Bogues 10.00 25.00
98PM4 Dave Cowens 4.00 10.00
98PM5 Walt Frazier 6.00 15.00
98PM6 Alonzo Mourning 10.00 25.00
98PM7 Danny Manning 5.00 12.00
98PM8 Anfernee Hardaway 50.00 125.00
98PM9 Jason Kidd 20.00 50.00
98PM10 Spud Webb 5.00 12.00
98PM11 Larry Bird 15.00 40.00
98PM12 John Havlicek 8.00 20.00
98PM13 Nick Van Exel 6.00 15.00
98PM14 Robert Horry 5.00 12.00
98PM15 Reggie Miller 20.00 50.00
98PM16 Spencer Haywood 4.00 10.00
98PM17 Chet Walker 5.00 12.00
98PM18 Gary Payton 15.00 40.00
98PM19 Cheryl Miller 6.00 15.00
98PM20 Jeff Hornacek 5.00 12.00
98PM21 David Robinson 10.00 25.00
98PM22 Vinny Del Negro 4.00 10.00
98PM23 Michael Jordan 250.00 500.00
98PM24 Wilt Chamberlain 30.00 80.00
98PM25 Allan Houston 5.00 12.00
98PM26 Dominique Wilkins 8.00 20.00
98PM27 Micheal Ray Richardson 5.00 12.00
98PM28 Karl Malone 25.00 60.00
98PM29 Isiah Thomas 6.00 15.00
98PM30 Jamal Mashburn 6.00 15.00
98PM31 Dennis Rodman 12.00 30.00
98PM32 Tony Gwynn 12.00 30.00
98PM33 Lou Hudson 6.00 15.00
98PM34 Bill Russell 10.00 25.00
98PM35 A.C. Green 6.00 15.00
98PM36 Grant Hill 12.00 30.00
98PM37 LeBron James 100.00 200.00
98PM38 Nate Thurmond 5.00 12.00
98PM39 Julius Erving 15.00 40.00
98PM40 Paul Pierce 12.00 30.00
98PM41 Allen Iverson 30.00 80.00
98PM42 Bill Walton 6.00 15.00
98PM43 Bernard King 5.00 12.00
98PM44 Antoine Walker 10.00 25.00
98PM45 Christian Laettner 15.00 40.00
98PM46 Hakeem Olajuwon 8.00 20.00
98PM47 Clyde Drexler 25.00 60.00
98PM48 Magic Johnson 12.00 30.00
98PM49 Ray Allen 20.00 50.00
98PM50 Larry Johnson 15.00 40.00

2012-13 Fleer Retro 98-99 Tradition Playmakers Theater

STATED PRINT RUN 100 SER.#'d SETS
1PT Jason Kidd 4.00 10.00
2PT Ray Allen 4.00 10.00
3PT Grant Hill 5.00 12.00
4PT Elvin Hayes 4.00 10.00
5PT Allen Iverson 5.00 12.00
6PT Isiah Thomas 4.00 10.00
7PT Larry Bird 10.00 25.00
8PT Paul Pierce 4.00 10.00
9PT Karl Malone 5.00 12.00
10PT Julius Erving 6.00 15.00
11PT Anfernee Hardaway 10.00 25.00
12PT Magic Johnson 10.00 25.00
13PT David Robinson 6.00 15.00
14PT Michael Jordan 75.00 200.00
15PT Wilt Chamberlain 8.00 20.00
16PT Bill Russell 6.00 15.00
17PT Walt Frazier 4.00 10.00
18PT LeBron James 30.00 80.00
19PT Bernard King 3.00 8.00
20PT Reggie Miller 4.00 10.00
21PT Hakeem Olajuwon 5.00 12.00

2012-13 Fleer Retro 99-00 Flair Showcase Fresh Ink

OUP A ODDS 1:8975 HOBBY
GROUP B ODDS 1:1007 HOBBY
GROUP C ODDS 1:756 HOBBY
GROUP D ODDS 1:308 HOBBY
GROUP E ODDS 1:179 HOBBY
GROUP F ODDS 1:36 HOBBY
EXCHANGE DEADLNE 5/31/2015
SFIAD Adrian Dantley E 3.00 8.00
SFIAH Anfernee Hardaway B 20.00 50.00
SFIAI Allen Iverson B 25.00 60.00
SFIAM Alonzo Mourning C 15.00 40.00
SFIBD Brad Daugherty F 3.00 8.00
SFIBL Bill Laimbeer F 3.00 8.00
SFIBM Bob McAdoo F 6.00 15.00
SFIBR Bill Russell B 40.00 100.00
SFICD Clyde Drexler C 12.00 30.00
SFICM Cheryl Miller C 4.00 10.00
SFIDM Danny Manning D 6.00 15.00
SFIDR David Robinson B 15.00 40.00
SFIDW Dominique Wilkins B 10.00 25.00
SFIEJ Eddie Jones F 3.00 8.00
SFIFL Fat Lever F 3.00 8.00
SFIGH Grant Hill B 15.00 40.00
SFIHM Harold Miner F 2.50 6.00
SFIHO Allan Houston F 3.00 8.00
SFIIT Isiah Thomas C 10.00 25.00
SFIJA LeBron James B 125.00 250.00
SFIJC Jared Cunningham F 2.50 6.00
SFIJE Julius Erving B 40.00 80.00
SFIJJ Jim Jackson F 2.50 6.00
SFIJK Jason Kidd D 12.00 30.00
SFIJM Jamal Mashburn E 4.00 10.00
SFIJO Michael Jordan A
SFIKM Khris Middleton F 4.00 10.00
SFILB Larry Bird B 50.00 100.00
SFILJ Larry Johnson B
SFILS Lonnie Shelton F 4.00 10.00
SFIMA Karl Malone C 20.00 50.00
SFIMB Muggsy Bogues F 3.00 8.00
SFIMC Michael Cooper E 3.00 8.00
SFIMG Mike Glover F 3.00 8.00
SFIMJ Magic Johnson B 40.00 80.00
SFIML Meyers Leonard E 3.00 8.00
SFIMP Miles Plumlee F 2.50 6.00
SFINT Nate Thurmond D 3.00 8.00
SFIOC Olek Czyz F 3.00 8.00
SFIOL Hakeem Olajuwon C 12.00 30.00
SFIPP Paul Pierce D 8.00 20.00
SFIPR Mark Price F 4.00 10.00
SFIRA Ray Allen C 12.00 30.00
SFIRH Robbie Hummel F 2.50 6.00
SFIRM Reggie Miller A
SFIRO Robert Horry F 3.00 8.00
SFISH Spencer Haywood D 2.50 6.00
SFISW Spud Webb 3.00 8.00
SFITH Tim Hardaway E 4.00 10.00
SFIWB Will Barton F 3.00 8.00

2012-13 Fleer Retro 99-00 Focus Fresh Ink

GROUP A ODDS 1:10,770 HOBBY
GROUP B ODDS 1:798 HOBBY
GROUP C ODDS 1:453 HOBBY
GROUP D ODDS 1:308 HOBBY
GROUP E ODDS 1:33 HOBBY
EXCHANGE DEADLNE 5/31/2015
FFIAH Anfernee Hardaway C 15.00 40.00
FFIAI Allen Iverson B 40.00 80.00
FFIBJ Bernard James E 2.50 6.00
FFIBK Bernard King E 3.00 8.00
FFIBL Bill Laimbeer E 3.00 8.00
FFIBR Bill Russell B 40.00 100.00
FFICD Clyde Drexler B 15.00 40.00
FFICM Cheryl Miller C 4.00 10.00
FFIDC Dave Cowens C 2.50 6.00
FFIDM Danny Manning C 8.00 20.00
FFIDR David Robinson B 15.00 40.00
FFIDT David Thompson D 3.00 8.00
FFIDW Dominique Wilkins C 8.00 20.00
FFIEJ Eddie Jones C 6.00 15.00
FFIGH Grant Hill C 20.00 50.00
FFIGR Glen Rice E 3.00 8.00
FFIHM Harold Miner D 6.00 15.00
FFIIT Isiah Thomas B 6.00 15.00
FFIJC Jae Crowder E 3.00 8.00
FFIJE Julius Erving B 30.00 60.00
FFIJH Jeff Hornacek E 3.00 8.00
FFIJJ Jim Jackson E 2.50 6.00
FFIJM Jamal Mashburn E 4.00 10.00
FFIJO Magic Johnson B 50.00 100.00
FFIJS John Shurna E 2.50 6.00
FFIJW Jo Jo White E 3.00 8.00
FFIKJ Kris Joseph E 2.50 6.00
FFIKM Kevin Murphy E 2.50 6.00
FFILB Larry Bird B 40.00 80.00
FFILH Lou Hudson E 4.00 10.00
FFILJ LeBron James B 100.00 250.00
FFILS Lonnie Shelton E 4.00 10.00
FFIMA Karl Malone B 20.00 50.00
FFIMH Moe Harkless E 4.00 10.00
FFIMJ Michael Jordan A
FFIMR Micheal Ray Richardson E 3.00 8.00
FFINT Nate Thurmond E 3.00 8.00
FFIOC Olek Czyz E 3.00 8.00
FFIPP Paul Pierce D 10.00 25.00
FFIRA Ray Allen C 12.00 30.00
FFIRH Robert Horry E 3.00 8.00
FFIRM Reggie Miller B 50.00 100.00
FFIRO Dennis Rodman D 10.00 25.00
FFIRR Ricardo Ratliffe E 2.50 6.00
FFIRS Robert Sacre E 2.50 6.00
FFIRT Reggie Theus E 3.00 8.00
FFISE Sean Elliott C 4.00 10.00
FFISH Spencer Haywood A 2.50 6.00
FFITZ Tyler Zeller E 3.00 8.00
FFIWF Walt Frazier D 4.00 10.00

2012-13 Fleer Retro 99-00 Mystique Fresh Ink

OUP A ODDS 1:8975 HOBBY
GROUP B ODDS 1:917 HOBBY
GROUP C ODDS 1:173 HOBBY
GROUP D ODDS 1:133 HOBBY
GROUP E ODDS 1:43 HOBBY
EXCHANGE DEADLNE 5/31/2015
MFIAD Adrian Dantley E 3.00 8.00
MFIAH Anfernee Hardaway C 15.00 40.00
MFIAI Allen Iverson B 30.00 60.00
MFIAM Arnett Moultrie E 2.50 6.00
MFIBK Bernard King D 3.00 8.00
MFIBM Bob McAdoo E 6.00 15.00
MFIBR Bill Russell B 40.00 100.00
MFICD Clyde Drexler C 12.00 30.00
MFICM Cheryl Miller C 4.00 10.00
MFICW Chet Walker E 3.00 8.00
MFIDR David Robinson B 15.00 40.00
MFIDT David Thompson C 3.00 8.00
MFIDW Dominique Wilkins C 8.00 20.00
MFIEF Evan Fournier E 4.00 10.00
MFIGH Grant Hill C 12.00 30.00
MFIHA Justin Hamilton E 3.00 8.00
MFIIT Isiah Thomas C 6.00 15.00
MFIJE Julius Erving B EXCH 30.00 60.00
MFIJG JaMychal Green E 2.50 6.00
MFIJH John Havlicek C EXCH 12.00 30.00
MFIJJ Jim Jackson D 2.50 6.00
MFIJL Jeremy Lamb C 4.00 10.00
MFIJO Michael Jordan A 350.00 600.00
MFIKM Karl Malone B 15.00 40.00
MFILB Larry Bird B 30.00 60.00
MFILJ LeBron James B 125.00 250.00
MFILS Lonnie Shelton D 4.00 10.00
MFIMA Mark A. Jackson D 3.00 8.00
MFIMJ Magic Johnson B 40.00 80.00
MFIMO Alonzo Mourning C 10.00 25.00
MFIMP Mark Price E 6.00 15.00
MFIMR Micheal Ray Richardson E 3.00 8.00
MFIMW Mark West D 2.50 6.00
MFINT Nate Thurmond D 3.00 8.00
MFINV Nick Van Exel E 4.00 10.00
MFIPP Paul Pierce C 8.00 20.00
MFIPR Pooh Richardson E 2.50 6.00
MFIQA Quincy Acy E 2.50 6.00
MFIRA Ray Allen C 8.00 20.00
MFIRE Bryant Reeves E 2.50 6.00
MFIRM Reggie Miller A 40.00 80.00
MFIRO Dennis Rodman C 8.00 20.00
MFISB Shawn Bradley D 2.50 6.00
MFISE Sean Elliott D 4.00 10.00
MFISN Swen Nater E 3.00 8.00
MFISW Spud Webb E 3.00 8.00
MFITT Tyshawn Taylor E 2.50 6.00
MFIWB William Buford E 2.50 6.00
MFIWF Walt Frazier D 4.00 10.00

2012-13 Fleer Retro 99-00 Mystique Raise the Roof

STATED PRINT RUN 100 SER.#'d SETS
1RR Dominique Wilkins 6.00 15.00
2RR Karl Malone 6.00 15.00
3RR Allen Iverson 12.00 30.00
4RR Michael Jordan 75.00 200.00
5RR LeBron James 30.00 80.00
6RR Paul Pierce 10.00 25.00
7RR Grant Hill 12.00 30.00
8RR David Robinson 10.00 25.00
9RR Magic Johnson 12.00 30.00
10RR Julius Erving 8.00 20.00
11RR Reggie Miller 5.00 12.00
12RR Isiah Thomas 5.00 12.00
13RR Ray Allen 5.00 12.00
14RR Jason Kidd 10.00 25.00
15RR Bill Russell 8.00 20.00
16RR Wilt Chamberlain 10.00 25.00
17RR Larry Bird 12.00 30.00
18RR Anfernee Hardaway 12.00 30.00
19RR Clyde Drexler 6.00 15.00
20RR Hakeem Olajuwon 6.00 15.00
21RR Jamal Mashburn 5.00 12.00

2012-13 Fleer Retro 99-00 Ultra Fresh Ink

GROUP A ODDS 1:11,967 HOBBY
GROUP B ODDS 1:3590 HOBBY
GROUP C ODDS 1:1026 HOBBY
GROUP D ODDS 1:359 HOBBY
GROUP E ODDS 1:116 HOBBY
GROUP F ODDS 1:35 HOBBY
EXCHANGE DEADLNE 5/31/2015
UFIAD Adrian Dantley F 3.00 8.00
UFIAG A.C. Green F 4.00 10.00
UFIAH Allan Houston F 3.00 8.00
UFIAI Allen Iverson C 50.00 100.00
UFIAM Alonzo Mourning D 6.00 15.00
UFIAN Andrew Nicholson F 2.50 6.00

UFIBD Brad Daugherty F 3.00 8.00
UFIBH Bobby Hurley F 4.00 10.00
UFIBL Bill Laimbeer F 3.00 8.00
UFIBM Bob McAdoo F 5.00 12.00
UFICD Clyde Drexler C 10.00 25.00
UFICH Connie Hawkins E 4.00 10.00
UFICW Chet Walker E 3.00 8.00
UFIDA Danny Manning D 5.00 12.00
UFIDG Draymond Green F 12.00 30.00
UFIDJ Darius Johnson-Odom F 2.50 6.00
UFIDM Darius Miller F 2.50 6.00
UFIDR David Robinson C 12.00 30.00
UFIGH Grant Hill D 12.00 30.00
UFIGS Garrett Stutz F 2.50 6.00
UFIHG Hal Greer F 8.00 20.00
UFIHM Harold Miner E 2.50 6.00
UFIHO Hakeem Olajuwon D 15.00 40.00
UFIIT Isiah Thomas D 6.00 15.00
UFIJA Mark A. Jackson E 3.00 8.00
UFIJE Julius Erving A 40.00 80.00
UFIJG JaMychal Green F 2.50 6.00
UFIJH John Havlicek B EXCH 10.00 25.00
UFIJM Jamal Mashburn F 4.00 10.00
UFIJO Magic Johnson C 30.00 60.00
UFIKM Kendall Marshall F 2.50 6.00
UFILA Larry Johnson B 8.00 20.00
UFILB Larry Bird C 30.00 80.00
UFILJ LeBron James C 125.00 250.00
UFILS Lonnie Shelton E 4.00 10.00
UFIMA Karl Malone C 20.00 50.00
UFIMC Michael Cooper F 3.00 8.00
UFIMJ Michael Jordan A
UFIMP Mark Price E 4.00 10.00
UFIMW Maalik Wayns F 4.00 10.00
UFINV Nick Van Exel F 4.00 10.00
UFIPP Paul Pierce E 8.00 20.00
UFIRA Ray Allen D 12.00 30.00
UFIRM Reggie Miller B 20.00 50.00
UFIRT Reggie Theus E 3.00 8.00
UFITH Tim Hardaway E 4.00 10.00
UFITK Toni Kukoc F 4.00 10.00
UFITS Tomas Satoransky E 2.50 6.00
UFIVD Vinny Del Negro E 2.50 6.00
UFIWW Wesley Witherspoon F 2.50 6.00

2012-13 Fleer Retro Autographs

GROUP A ODDS 1:16,569 HOBBY
GROUP B ODDS 1:2595 HOBBY
GROUP C ODDS 1:206 HOBBY
GROUP D ODDS 1:176 HOBBY
GROUP E ODDS 1:77 HOBBY
GROUP A RS ODDS 1:194 HOBBY
GROUP B RS ODDS 1:9 HOBBY
EXCHANGE DEADLNE 5/31/2015
1 Michael Jordan C 300.00 400.00
2 LeBron James C 100.00 200.00
3 Jason Kidd B 10.00 25.00
4 Dominique Wilkins C 15.00 40.00
5 Karl Malone C 12.00 30.00
6 Bill Walton D 10.00 25.00
7 Allen Iverson C 40.00 80.00
8 Paul Pierce C 10.00 25.00
9 Ray Allen C 12.00 30.00
10 Grant Hill C 12.00 30.00
11 Hakeem Olajuwon C 15.00 40.00
12 Bernard King E 3.00 8.00
13 Isiah Thomas C 10.00 25.00
14 Dennis Rodman C 10.00 25.00
15 Reggie Miller A 40.00 80.00
16 Bill Russell C 40.00 100.00
17 David Robinson C 15.00 40.00
18 Jim Jackson D 2.50 6.00
19 Larry Johnson C 12.50 30.00
20 Nate Thurmond D 3.00 8.00
21 Alonzo Mourning C 12.00 30.00
22 Anfernee Hardaway C 12.00 30.00
23 Glen Rice D 3.00 8.00
24 Tim Hardaway E 4.00 10.00
25 Walt Frazier D 4.00 10.00
26 Larry Bird C 40.00 80.00
27 John Havlicek C EXCH 10.00 25.00
28 Nick Van Exel D 4.00 10.00
29 Danny Manning E 3.00 8.00
30 Spud Webb E 3.00 8.00
31 Jamal Mashburn B 12.00 30.00
32 David Thompson E 3.00 8.00
33 Micheal Ray Richardson E 3.00 8.00
34 Harold Miner E 2.50 6.00
35 Mark Price E 4.00 10.00
36 Jeff Hornacek E 3.00 8.00
37 Toni Kukoc E 5.00 12.00
38 A.C. Green E 4.00 10.00
39 Spencer Haywood D 2.50 6.00
40 Sean Elliott C 6.00 15.00
41 Allan Houston E 3.00 8.00
42 Dave Cowens D 2.50 6.00
43 Cheryl Miller E 6.00 15.00
44 Christian Laettner D 3.00 8.00
45 Magic Johnson C 15.00 40.00
46 Mark A. Jackson D 3.00 8.00
47 Vinny Del Negro E 2.50 6.00
48 Clyde Drexler C 8.00 20.00
50 Julius Erving B 30.00 60.00
51 Meyers Leonard RS B 3.00 8.00
52 Jeremy Lamb RS B 4.00 10.00
53 Kendall Marshall RS B 2.50 6.00
54 Moe Harkless RS B 4.00 10.00
55 Tyler Zeller RS B 3.00 8.00
56 Andrew Nicholson RS B 2.50 6.00
57 Evan Fournier RS B 4.00 10.00
58 Jared Cunningham RS B 2.50 6.00
59 Miles Plumlee RS B 2.50 6.00
60 Arnett Moultrie RS B 2.50 6.00
61 Bernard James RS B 2.50 6.00
62 Jae Crowder RS B 3.00 8.00
63 Draymond Green RS B 20.00 50.00
64 Quincy Acy RS B 2.50 6.00
65 Khris Middleton RS B 4.00 10.00
66 Will Barton RS B 3.00 8.00
67 Tyshawn Taylor RS B 2.50 6.00
68 Darius Miller RS B 2.50 6.00
69 Kevin Murphy RS B 2.50 6.00
70 Darius Johnson-Odom RS B 2.50 6.00
71 Robbie Hummel RS B 2.50 6.00
72 Robert Sacre RS B 2.50 6.00
73 Wesley Witherspoon RS B 2.50 6.00
74 William Buford RS B 2.50 6.00
75 Ricardo Ratliffe RS A 2.50 6.00
76 John Shurna RS B 2.50 6.00
77 Tomas Satoransky RS B 2.50 6.00
78 Justin Hamilton RS B 3.00 8.00
79 JaMychal Green RS B 2.50 6.00
80 Kris Joseph RS B 2.50 6.00

2013-14 Fleer Retro

COMPLETE SET (60) 6.00 15.00
1 Allen Iverson .40 1.00
2 Rajon Rondo .30 .75
3 Glenn Robinson .25 .60
4 Dennis Rodman .60 1.50
5 Elvin Hayes .30 .75
6 Donyell Marshall .20 .50
7 Calbert Cheaney .20 .50
8 Antoine Walker .25 .60
9 David Thompson .25 .60
10 Kerry Kittles .20 .50
11 Grant Hill .40 1.00
12 Dominique Wilkins .40 1.00
13 Tim Hardaway .30 .75
14 Alonzo Mourning .40 1.00
15 Anfernee Hardaway .75 2.00
16 Jason Kidd .30 .75
17 Kenny Anderson .25 .60
18 Paul George .40 1.00
19 Isiah Thomas .30 .75
20 Bill Walton .30 .75
21 Danny Manning .25 .60
22 Jay Williams .20 .50
23 Larry Johnson .40 1.00
24 Jerry Lucas .30 .75
25 Joe Smith .25 .60
26 James Harden .50 1.25
27 Otis Birdsong .25 .60
28 Derek Harper .25 .60
29 Sam Perkins .20 .50
30 Bill Russell .50 1.25
31 David Robinson .50 1.25
32 Reggie Miller .30 .75
33 Hakeem Olajuwon .40 1.00
34 Larry Bird .75 2.00
35 Clyde Drexler .40 1.00
36 Julius Erving .50 1.25
37 Karl Malone .40 1.00
38 Christian Laettner .25 .60
39 LeBron James 1.25 3.00
40 Michael Jordan 2.50 6.00
41 Mason Plumlee .50 1.25
42 Jamaal Franklin .30 .75
43 Shane Larkin .30 .75
44 Lucas Nogueira .30 .75
45 Isaiah Canaan .30 .75
46 Tim Hardaway Jr. .50 1.25
47 Giannis Antetokounmpo 4.00 10.00
48 Livio Jean-Charles .30 .75
49 Archie Goodwin .40 1.00
50 Solomon Hill .30 .75
51 Andre Roberson .30 .75
52 Dennis Schroeder .50 1.25
53 Skylar Diggins 1.00 2.50
54 Grant Jerrett .30 .75
55 Rudy Gobert .60 1.50
56 Allen Crabbe .40 1.00
57 Tony Snell .40 1.00
58 Reggie Bullock .40 1.00
59 Sergey Karasev .30 .75
60 Deshaun Thomas .30 .75

2013-14 Fleer Retro '92-93 Fleer Final Four Stars

STATED ODDS 1:36
1 Antoine Walker 2.00 5.00
2 Bill Laimbeer 2.00 5.00
3 Bill Russell 4.00 10.00
4 Bill Walton 2.50 6.00
5 Calbert Cheaney 1.50 4.00
6 Cheryl Miller 2.50 6.00
7 Christian Laettner 2.00 5.00
8 Corliss Williamson 1.50 4.00
9 Danny Manning 2.00 5.00
10 David Thompson 2.00 5.00
11 Elvin Hayes 2.50 6.00
12 Glen Rice 2.00 5.00
13 Grant Hill 3.00 8.00
14 Hakeem Olajuwon 3.00 8.00
15 Isiah Thomas 2.50 6.00
16 Jamal Mashburn 2.50 6.00
17 Jerry Lucas 2.50 6.00
18 Peyton Siva 1.50 4.00
19 Keith Smart 2.50 6.00
20 Larry Bird 6.00 15.00
21 Larry Johnson 3.00 8.00
22 Kendall Gill 1.50 4.00
23 Ron Mercer 1.50 4.00
24 Michael Jordan 15.00 40.00
25 Sean Elliott 2.50 6.00

2013-14 Fleer Retro '92-93 Fleer Final Four Stars Autographs

PRINT RUNS B/WN 15-25 COPIES PER
NO PRICING ON QTY 15
EXCHANGE DEADLINE 3/28/2016
5 Calbert Cheaney/25 12.00 30.00
13 Grant Hill/25 20.00 50.00
14 Hakeem Olajuwon/25
15 Isiah Thomas/25 15.00 40.00
17 Jerry Lucas/25 20.00 50.00
21 Larry Johnson/25 12.00 30.00
25 Sean Elliott/25 15.00 40.00

2013-14 Fleer Retro '92-93 Fleer Rookie Sensations Autographs

GROUP A ODDS 1:2448
GROUP B ODDS 1:429
GROUP C ODDS 1:233
GROUP D ODDS 1:147
EXCHANGE DEADLINE 3/28/2016
RS1 Mason Plumlee C 4.00 10.00
RS5 Tim Hardaway Jr. C 4.00 10.00
RS9 Reggie Bullock D 3.00 8.00
RS12 Grant Jerrett B 2.50 6.00
RS13 Ricardo Ledo A 2.50 6.00
RS15 Mike Muscala 4.00 10.00
RS18 Giannis Antetokounmpo B 50.00 120.00
RS22 Nemaja Nedovic 2.50 6.00

2013-14 Fleer Retro '92-93 Fleer Team Leaders

STATED ODDS 1:90
1 Grant Hill 2.50 6.00
2 Allen Iverson 2.50 6.00
3 Otis Birdsong 1.50 4.00
4 Hakeem Olajuwon 2.50 6.00
5 Isiah Thomas 2.00 5.00
6 Larry Bird 5.00 12.00
7 Danny Manning 1.50 4.00
8 Dominique Wilkins 2.50 6.00
9 Karl Malone 2.50 6.00
10 Julius Erving 3.00 8.00
11 Anfernee Hardaway 5.00 12.00
12 James Harden 3.00 8.00
13 David Robinson 3.00 8.00
14 David Thompson 1.50 4.00
15 Michael Jordan 25.00 60.00
16 Glenn Robinson 1.50 4.00
17 Dennis Rodman 4.00 10.00
18 LeBron James 8.00 20.00
19 Bill Walton 2.00 5.00
20 Larry Johnson 2.50 6.00

2013-14 Fleer Retro '92-93 Fleer Team Leaders Autographs

PRINT RUNS B/WN 15-25 COPIES PER
NO PRICING ON QTY 15 OR LESS
EXCHANGE DEADLINE 3/28/2016
1 Grant Hill/25 50.00 120.00
4 Hakeem Olajuwon/25 30.00 80.00
5 Isiah Thomas/25 20.00 50.00
8 Dominique Wilkins/25
9 Karl Malone/25 25.00 60.00
13 David Robinson/25 20.00 50.00
15 Michael Jordan/15
18 LeBron James/25 150.00 300.00
20 Larry Johnson/25 20.00 50.00

2013-14 Fleer Retro '92-93 Ultra Michael Jordan Career Highlights

COMMON CARD 3.00 8.00
STATED ODDS 1:60

2013-14 Fleer Retro '93-94 Ultra All Rookie Series Autographs

GROUP A ODDS 1:490
GROUP B ODDS 1:270
EXCHANGE DEADLINE 3/28/2016
ARS1 Tim Hardaway Jr. A 4.00 10.00
ARS2 Skylar Diggins B 12.00 30.00

2013-14 Fleer Retro '93-94 Ultra Power in the Key

STATED ODDS 1:60
1 Alonzo Mourning 3.00 8.00
2 Bill Russell 4.00 10.00
3 Buck Williams 1.50 4.00
4 Danny Manning 2.00 5.00
5 David Robinson 4.00 10.00
6 Dennis Rodman 5.00 12.00
7 Elvin Hayes 2.50 6.00
8 Hakeem Olajuwon 3.00 8.00
9 Jerry Lucas 2.50 6.00
10 Karl Malone 3.00 8.00
11 Larry Johnson 3.00 8.00
12 LeBron James 10.00 25.00
13 Michael Jordan 20.00 50.00
14 Antoine Walker 2.00 5.00
15 Bill Walton 2.50 6.00
16 Julius Erving 4.00 10.00
17 Corliss Williamson 1.50 4.00
18 Sam Perkins 1.50 4.00
19 Bill Laimbeer 2.00 5.00
20 Theo Ratliff 1.50 4.00

2013-14 Fleer Retro '93-94 Ultra Scoring Kings

STATED ODDS 1:60
1 Allan Houston 2.00 5.00
2 Allen Iverson 3.00 8.00
3 Bill Russell 4.00 10.00
4 Reggie Miller 2.50 6.00
5 Calbert Cheaney 1.50 4.00
6 Danny Manning 2.00 5.00
7 David Robinson 4.00 10.00
8 Dominique Wilkins 3.00 8.00
9 Elvin Hayes 2.50 6.00
10 Clyde Drexler 3.00 8.00
11 Hakeem Olajuwon 3.00 8.00
12 Julius Erving 4.00 10.00
13 Karl Malone 3.00 8.00
14 Larry Bird 6.00 15.00
15 Larry Johnson 3.00 8.00
16 LeBron James 12.00 30.00
17 Magic Johnson 6.00 15.00
18 Michael Jordan 50.00 125.00
19 Otis Birdsong 2.00 5.00
20 Grant Hill 3.00 8.00

2013-14 Fleer Retro '94-95 SkyBox Emotion N-Tense

STATED ODDS 1:120
1 Larry Johnson 3.00 8.00
2 Reggie Miller 2.50 6.00
3 Clyde Drexler 3.00 8.00
4 LeBron James 20.00 50.00
5 Bill Russell 4.00 10.00
6 Rajon Rondo 2.50 6.00
7 Michael Jordan 30.00 80.00
8 David Robinson 4.00 10.00
9 Magic Johnson 6.00 15.00
10 Anfernee Hardaway 6.00 15.00
11 Julius Erving 4.00 10.00
12 Karl Malone 3.00 8.00
13 Dominique Wilkins 3.00 8.00
14 Paul George 3.00 8.00
15 Larry Bird 6.00 15.00
16 James Harden 4.00 10.00
17 Hakeem Olajuwon 3.00 8.00
18 Alonzo Mourning 3.00 8.00
19 Allen Iverson 3.00 8.00
20 Grant Hill 3.00 8.00

2013-14 Fleer Retro '95-96 Metal Universe

STATED ODDS 1:10
221 Jason Kidd .40 1.00
222 Grant Hill .50 1.25
223 Jay Williams .25 .60
224 Allen Iverson .50 1.25
225 Alonzo Mourning .50 1.25
226 Kenny Anderson .30 .75
227 Hakeem Olajuwon .50 1.25
228 Jerry Stackhouse .30 .75
229 Paul George .50 1.25
230 Isiah Thomas .40 1.00
231 Larry Bird 1.00 2.50
232 Rajon Rondo .40 1.00
233 Karl Malone .50 1.25
234 Joe Smith .30 .75
235 Julius Erving .60 1.50
236 Anfernee Hardaway 1.00 2.50
237 Clyde Drexler .50 1.25
238 David Robinson .60 1.50
239 Dominique Wilkins .50 1.25
240 Michael Jordan 8.00 20.00
241 Jerry Lucas .40 1.00
242 John Havlicek .50 1.25
243 Glenn Robinson .30 .75
244 Bill Russell .60 1.50
245 James Harden .60 1.50
246 Dennis Rodman .75 2.00
247 LeBron James 1.50 4.00
248 Reggie Miller .40 1.00
249 Larry Johnson .50 1.25
250 Tim Hardaway .40 1.00

2013-14 Fleer Retro '95-96 Metal Universe Precious Metal Gems Blue

*PMG BLUE: 8X TO 20X BASIC
STATED PRINT RUN 50 SER.#'d SETS
221 Jason Kidd 15.00 40.00
223 Jay Williams 10.00 25.00
224 Allen Iverson 25.00 60.00
225 Alonzo Mourning 15.00 40.00
228 Jerry Stackhouse 20.00 50.00
247 LeBron James 50.00 120.00
248 Reggie Miller 15.00 40.00

2013-14 Fleer Retro '95-96 Metal Universe Precious Metal Gems Red

*PMG RED: 5X TO 12X BASIC
STATED PRINT RUN 150 SER.#'d SETS
224 Allen Iverson 10.00 25.00
228 Jerry Stackhouse 10.00 25.00
229 Paul George 20.00 50.00
247 LeBron James 30.00 80.00

2013-14 Fleer Retro '95-96 Metal Universe Maximum Metal

STATED ODDS 1:60
1 Larry Johnson 3.00 8.00
2 Grant Hill 3.00 8.00
3 Allen Iverson 3.00 8.00
4 Hakeem Olajuwon 3.00 8.00
5 Larry Bird 6.00 15.00
6 Jason Kidd 2.50 6.00
7 Rajon Rondo 2.50 6.00
8 Karl Malone 3.00 8.00
9 Jerry Stackhouse 2.00 5.00
10 Julius Erving 4.00 10.00
11 Anfernee Hardaway 6.00 15.00
12 Magic Johnson 6.00 15.00
13 David Robinson 4.00 10.00
14 Michael Jordan 15.00 40.00
15 Clyde Drexler 3.00 8.00
16 Bill Russell 4.00 10.00
17 LeBron James 10.00 25.00
18 Reggie Miller 2.50 6.00
19 Paul George 3.00 8.00
20 James Harden 4.00 10.00

2013-14 Fleer Retro '95-96 SkyBox Premium Meltdown

STATED ODDS 1:60
M1 Jason Kidd 2.50 6.00
M2 Reggie Miller 2.50 6.00
M3 Clyde Drexler 3.00 8.00
M4 LeBron James 10.00 25.00
M5 Dennis Rodman 5.00 12.00
M6 Bill Russell 4.00 10.00
M7 Michael Jordan 15.00 40.00
M8 David Robinson 4.00 10.00
M9 Magic Johnson 6.00 15.00
M10 Julius Erving 4.00 10.00
M11 Karl Malone 3.00 8.00
M12 Rajon Rondo 2.50 6.00
M13 Jerry Stackhouse 2.00 5.00
M14 Larry Bird 6.00 15.00
M15 Hakeem Olajuwon 3.00 8.00
M16 James Harden 4.00 10.00
M17 Allen Iverson 3.00 8.00
M18 Grant Hill 3.00 8.00
M19 Paul George 3.00 8.00
M20 Tim Hardaway Jr. 2.50 6.00

2013-14 Fleer Retro '95-96 Ultra

STATED ODDS 1:6
161 Christian Laettner .30 .75
162 Grant Hill .50 1.25
163 Allen Iverson .50 1.25
164 Alonzo Mourning .50 1.25
165 Hakeem Olajuwon .50 1.25
166 Isiah Thomas .40 1.00
167 Larry Bird 1.00 2.50
168 Ron Mercer .25 .60
169 Rajon Rondo .40 1.00
170 Karl Malone .50 1.25
171 Joe Smith .30 .75
172 Julius Erving .60 1.50
173 Anfernee Hardaway 1.00 2.50
174 Jerry Stackhouse .30 .75
175 David Robinson .60 1.50
176 Sam Perkins .25 .60
177 Michael Jordan 3.00 8.00
178 Dominique Wilkins .50 1.25
179 LaPhonso Ellis .25 .60
180 Jason Kidd .40 1.00
181 Jerry Lucas .40 1.00
182 Glenn Robinson .30 .75
183 James Harden .60 1.50
184 Bill Russell .60 1.50
185 Dennis Rodman .75 2.00
186 LeBron James 1.50 4.00
187 Reggie Miller .40 1.00
188 Larry Johnson .50 1.25
189 Paul George .50 1.25
190 Clyde Drexler .50 1.25
191 Grant Jerrett .25 .60
192 Nemanja Nedovic .25 .60
193 Mason Plumlee .40 1.00
194 Jamaal Franklin .25 .60
195 Shane Larkin .25 .60
196 Isaiah Canaan .25 .60
197 Tim Hardaway Jr. .40 1.00
198 Livio Jean-Charles .25 .60
199 Archie Goodwin .30 .75
200 Skylar Diggins .75 2.00
201 Andre Roberson .25 .60
202 Sergey Karasev .25 .60
203 Erick Green .30 .75
204 Ryan Kelly .25 .60
205 Peyton Siva .25 .60
206 Solomon Hill .25 .60
207 Lucas Nogueira .25 .60
208 Giannis Antetokounmpo 3.00 8.00
209 Brandon Paul .25 .60
210 Allen Crabbe .30 .75
211 Will Clyburn .25 .60
212 Adonis Thomas .25 .60
213 Rudy Gobert .50 1.25
214 Pierre Jackson .25 .60
215 Reggie Bullock .30 .75
216 Tony Snell .30 .75
217 Deshaun Thomas .25 .60
218 Lorenzo Brown .25 .60
219 Phil Pressey .25 .60
220 Dennis Schroeder .40 1.00

2013-14 Fleer Retro '95-96 Ultra Autographs

GROUP A ODDS 1:1200
GROUP B ODDS 1:1262
GROUP C ODDS 1:233
EXCHANGE DEADLINE 3/28/2016
161 Christian Laettner C 6.00 15.00
162 Grant Hill B 12.00 30.00
165 Hakeem Olajuwon A
166 Isiah Thomas B
167 Larry Bird A
170 Karl Malone A 30.00 60.00
174 Jerry Stackhouse A
175 David Robinson A 15.00 40.00
177 Michael Jordan A
178 Dominique Wilkins B
181 Jerry Lucas C 4.00 10.00
183 James Harden B 10.00 25.00
184 Bill Russell A 40.00 80.00
185 Dennis Rodman A 8.00 20.00
186 LeBron James A
188 Larry Johnson A
189 Paul George A 20.00 50.00
197 Tim Hardaway Jr. C 4.00 10.00
200 Skylar Diggins C 4.00 10.00
208 Giannis Antetokounmpo C 30.00 80.00

2013-14 Fleer Retro '96-97 SkyBox Autographics

GROUP A ODDS 1:6800
GROUP B ODDS 1:621
GROUP C ODDS 1:378
EXCHANGE DEADLINE 3/28/2016
96AUAE Alex English D 4.00 10.00
96AUDC Dave Cowens D 3.00 8.00
96AUDM Donyell Marshall D 3.00 8.00
96AUEJ Eddie Jones B 4.00 10.00
96AUJH James Harden A 15.00 40.00
96AUJL Jerry Lucas C 6.00 15.00
96AUSA Stacey Augmon C 3.00 8.00
96AUWI Jay Williams B 3.00 8.00

2013-14 Fleer Retro '96-97 SkyBox Premium

STATED ODDS 1:3
61 Robert Horry .30 .75
62 Jason Kidd .40 1.00
63 Corliss Williamson .25 .60
64 Shawn Bradley .25 .60
65 Donyell Marshall .25 .60
66 Bo Kimble .25 .60
67 Grant Hill .50 1.25
68 Jay Williams .25 .60
69 Dave Cowens .25 .60
70 Allen Iverson .50 1.25
71 Alonzo Mourning .50 1.25
72 Kenny Anderson .30 .75
73 Elvin Hayes .40 1.00
74 Otis Birdsong .30 .75
75 Hakeem Olajuwon .50 1.25
76 Derek Harper .30 .75
77 Tim Hardaway .40 1.00
78 Calbert Cheaney .25 .60
79 Keith Smart .40 1.00
80 Isiah Thomas .40 1.00
81 Larry Bird 1.00 2.50
82 Danny Manning .30 .75
83 Dominique Wilkins .50 1.25
84 Rajon Rondo .40 1.00
85 Antoine Walker .30 .75
86 Karl Malone .50 1.25
87 Buck Williams .25 .60
88 Joe Smith .30 .75
89 Julius Erving .60 1.50
90 Anfernee Hardaway 1.00 2.50
91 Magic Johnson 1.00 2.50
92 Glen Rice .30 .75
93 Micheal Ray Richardson .30 .75
94 David Robinson .60 1.50
95 Spud Webb .30 .75
96 David Thompson .30 .75
97 Toni Kukoc .40 1.00
98 James Harden .60 1.50
99 Paul George .50 1.25
100 Sam Perkins .25 .60
101 Michael Jordan 3.00 8.00
102 John Havlicek .50 1.25
103 Jerry Lucas .40 1.00
104 Jerry Stackhouse .30 .75
105 Clyde Drexler .50 1.25
106 Bill Russell .60 1.50
107 Alex English .30 .75
108 Dennis Rodman .75 2.00
109 LeBron James 1.50 4.00
110 Stacey Augmon .25 .60
111 Allan Houston .30 .75
112 Bill Walton .40 1.00
113 Reggie Miller .40 1.00
114 Theo Ratliff .25 .60
115 Larry Johnson .50 1.25
116 Mason Plumlee .40 1.00
117 Skylar Diggins .75 2.00
118 Shane Larkin .25 .60
119 Lucas Nogueira .25 .60
120 Tim Hardaway Jr. .40 1.00

2013-14 Fleer Retro '96-97 SkyBox Premium Star Rubies

*STAR RUBY: 2.5X TO 6X BASIC
STATED PRINT RUN 150 SER.#'d SETS
70 Allen Iverson 8.00 20.00
109 LeBron James 12.00 30.00

2013-14 Fleer Retro '96-97 SkyBox Premium Golden Touch

STATED ODDS 1:120
1 Grant Hill 3.00 8.00
2 Allen Iverson 3.00 8.00
3 Alonzo Mourning 3.00 8.00
4 Hakeem Olajuwon 3.00 8.00
5 Isiah Thomas 2.50 6.00
6 Larry Bird 6.00 15.00
7 Rajon Rondo 2.50 6.00
8 Karl Malone 3.00 8.00
9 Julius Erving 4.00 10.00
10 Anfernee Hardaway 6.00 15.00
11 Magic Johnson 6.00 15.00
12 Jason Kidd 2.50 6.00
13 David Robinson 4.00 10.00
14 Michael Jordan 75.00 150.00
15 Dominique Wilkins 3.00 8.00
16 Bill Russell 4.00 10.00
17 LeBron James 10.00 25.00
18 Clyde Drexler 3.00 8.00
19 Reggie Miller 2.50 6.00
20 James Harden 4.00 10.00

2013-14 Fleer Retro '97-98 Metal Universe

STATED ODDS 1:10
251 Skylar Diggins 1.25 3.00
252 Giannis Antetokounmpo 5.00 12.00
253 Lucas Nogueira .40 1.00
254 Dennis Schroeder .60 1.50
255 Shane Larkin .40 1.00
256 Sergey Karasev .40 1.00
257 Tony Snell .50 1.25
258 Mason Plumlee .60 1.50
259 Solomon Hill .40 1.00
260 Tim Hardaway Jr. .60 1.50
261 Reggie Bullock .50 1.25
262 Andre Roberson .40 1.00
263 Rudy Gobert .75 2.00
264 Livio Jean-Charles .40 1.00
265 Archie Goodwin .50 1.25
266 Nemanja Nedovic .40 1.00
267 Allen Crabbe .50 1.25
268 Isaiah Canaan .40 1.00
269 Grant Jerrett .40 1.00
270 Jamaal Franklin .40 1.00
271 Pierre Jackson .40 1.00
272 Ricardo Ledo .40 1.00
273 Mike Muscala .60 1.50
274 Erick Green .50 1.25
275 Ryan Kelly .40 1.00
276 Lorenzo Brown .40 1.00
277 Peyton Siva .40 1.00
278 Deshaun Thomas .40 1.00
279 C.J. Leslie .40 1.00
280 Seth Curry 1.25 3.00

2013-14 Fleer Retro '97-98 Metal Universe Precious Metal Gems Blue

*PMG BLUE: 6X TO 15X BASIC
STATED PRINT RUN 50 SER.#'d SETS
254 Dennis Schroeder 15.00 40.00

2013-14 Fleer Retro '97-98 Metal Universe Precious Metal Gems Red

*PMG RED: 3X TO 8X BASIC
STATED PRINT RUN 150 SER.#'d SETS
254 Dennis Schroeder 12.00 30.00

2013-14 Fleer Retro '97-98 SkyBox Autographics

GROUP A ODDS 1:12,240
GROUP B ODDS 1:3060
GROUP C ODDS 1:2448
GROUP D ODDS 1:612
EXCHANGE DEADLINE 3/28/2016
97AUAG A.C. Green A
97AUAH Allan Houston E 4.00 10.00
97AUAW Antoine Walker D 6.00 15.00
97AUEH Elvin Hayes E 5.00 12.00
97AUGH Grant Hill C 20.00 50.00
97AUHO Hakeem Olajuwon B 20.00 50.00
97AUKA Kenny Anderson E 4.00 10.00
97AUKM Karl Malone B 40.00 80.00

2013-14 Fleer Retro '97-98 SkyBox Premium

STATED ODDS 1:10
121 Grant Hill .50 1.25
122 Allen Iverson .50 1.25
123 Alonzo Mourning .50 1.25
124 Hakeem Olajuwon .50 1.25
125 Isiah Thomas .40 1.00
126 Larry Bird 1.00 2.50
127 Rajon Rondo .40 1.00
128 Karl Malone .50 1.25
129 Julius Erving .60 1.50
130 Anfernee Hardaway 1.00 2.50
131 Magic Johnson 1.00 2.50
132 David Robinson .60 1.50
133 Michael Jordan 3.00 8.00
134 Paul George .50 1.25
135 James Harden .60 1.50
136 Bill Russell .60 1.50
137 Dennis Rodman .75 2.00
138 LeBron James 1.50 4.00
139 Reggie Miller .40 1.00
140 Larry Johnson .50 1.25

2013-14 Fleer Retro '97-98 SkyBox Premium Star Rubies

*STAR RUBY: 4X TO 10X BASIC
STATED PRINT RUN 50 SER.#'d SETS
121 Grant Hill 12.00 30.00
122 Allen Iverson 15.00 40.00
131 Magic Johnson 6.00 15.00
133 Michael Jordan 75.00 150.00
134 Paul George 12.00 30.00
138 LeBron James 30.00 80.00
139 Reggie Miller 12.00 30.00

2013-14 Fleer Retro '97-98 Ultra Star Power Supreme

STATED ODDS 1:216
1SPS Grant Hill 4.00 10.00
2SPS Allen Iverson 4.00 10.00
3SPS Alonzo Mourning 4.00 10.00
4SPS Dominique Wilkins 4.00 10.00
5SPS Paul George 4.00 10.00
6SPS Hakeem Olajuwon 4.00 10.00
7SPS Isiah Thomas 3.00 8.00
8SPS Larry Bird 8.00 20.00
9SPS James Harden 5.00 12.00
10SPS Antoine Walker 2.50 6.00
11SPS Julius Erving 5.00 12.00
12SPS Anfernee Hardaway 8.00 20.00
13SPS Clyde Drexler 4.00 10.00
14SPS Glen Rice 2.50 6.00
15SPS David Robinson 5.00 12.00
16SPS Michael Jordan 100.00 200.00
17SPS Bill Russell 5.00 12.00
18SPS LeBron James 40.00 100.00
19SPS Jerry Stackhouse 2.50 6.00
20SPS Larry Johnson 4.00 10.00
21SPS Jason Kidd 3.00 8.00

2013-14 Fleer Retro '98 Ultra Exclamation Points

STATED ODDS 1:216
1EP Allen Iverson 4.00 10.00
2EP Alonzo Mourning 4.00 10.00
3EP Anfernee Hardaway 8.00 20.00
4EP Bill Russell 5.00 12.00
5EP Dominique Wilkins 4.00 10.00
6EP James Harden 5.00 12.00
7EP David Robinson 5.00 12.00
8EP Reggie Miller 3.00 8.00
9EP Jason Kidd 3.00 8.00
10EP Paul George 4.00 10.00
11EP Grant Hill 4.00 10.00
12EP Hakeem Olajuwon 4.00 10.00
13EP Isiah Thomas 3.00 8.00
14EP Julius Erving 5.00 12.00
15EP Karl Malone 4.00 10.00
16EP Larry Bird 8.00 20.00
17EP Larry Johnson 4.00 10.00
18EP LeBron James 20.00 50.00
19EP Jerry Stackhouse 2.50 6.00
20EP Michael Jordan 100.00 200.00
21EP Rajon Rondo 3.00 8.00

2013-14 Fleer Retro '98-99 SkyBox Autographics

GROUP A ODDS 1:15,300
GROUP B ODDS 1:6120
GROUP C ODDS 1:2448
GROUP D ODDS 1:612
EXCHANGE DEADLINE 3/28/2016
98AUBL Bill Laimbeer E 4.00 10.00
98AUCC Calbert Cheaney E 3.00 8.00
98AUCL Christian Laettner D 4.00 10.00
98AUDM Danny Manning D 10.00 25.00
98AUJH James Harden A
98AUJL Jerry Lucas C
98AUPG Paul George B 40.00 80.00

2013-14 Fleer Retro '98-99 SkyBox Premium

STATED ODDS 1:10
141 Grant Hill .50 1.25
142 Allen Iverson .50 1.25
143 Alonzo Mourning .50 1.25
144 Hakeem Olajuwon .50 1.25
145 Isiah Thomas .40 1.00
146 Larry Bird 1.00 2.50
147 Rajon Rondo .40 1.00
148 Karl Malone .50 1.25
149 Julius Erving .60 1.50
150 Anfernee Hardaway 1.00 2.50
151 Magic Johnson 1.00 2.50
152 David Robinson .60 1.50
153 Michael Jordan 3.00 8.00
154 Paul George .50 1.25
155 James Harden .60 1.50
156 Bill Russell .60 1.50
157 Dennis Rodman
158 LeBron James 1.50 4.00
159 Reggie Miller .40 1.00
160 Larry Johnson .50 1.25

2013-14 Fleer Retro '98-99 SkyBox Premium Star Rubies

*STAR RUBY: 4X TO 10X BASIC
STATED PRINT RUN 50 SER.#'d SETS
141 Grant Hill 12.00 30.00
142 Allen Iverson 15.00 40.00
151 Magic Johnson 6.00 15.00
153 Michael Jordan 75.00 150.00
158 LeBron James 60.00 120.00
159 Reggie Miller 12.00 30.00

2013-14 Fleer Retro '99-00 SkyBox Autographics

GROUP A ODDS 1:3060
GROUP B ODDS 1:2448
GROUP C ODDS 1:816
GROUP D ODDS 1:816
EXCHANGE DEADLINE 3/28/2016
99AUCM Cheryl Miller C 5.00 12.00
99AUDS Detlef Schrempf D 5.00 12.00
99AUHM Harold Miner D 3.00 8.00
99AUIT Isiah Thomas B 12.00 30.00
99AUKM Karl Malone A 40.00 80.00
99AURO Dennis Rodman A 12.00 30.00

2013-14 Fleer Retro '99-00 SkyBox Prime Time Autographs

PRINT RUNS B/WN 15-25 COPIES PER
NO PRICING ON QTY 15
EXCHANGE DEADLINE 3/28/2016
4PTV Alonzo Mourning/25 EXCH 50.00 100.00
5PTV Dominique Wilkins/25 15.00 40.00
6PTV Hakeem Olajuwon/25 15.00 40.00
7PTV Larry Bird/25 EXCH 60.00 150.00
10PTV Julius Erving/25 40.00 100.00
11PTV Anfernee Hardaway/25 50.00 120.00
13PTV David Robinson/25 20.00 50.00
15PTV Michael Jordan/15
16PTV James Harden/25 15.00 40.00
18PTV LeBron James/25 250.00 350.00

2013-14 Fleer Retro '99-00 SkyBox Prime Time Rookie Autographs

STATED PRINT RUN 60 SER.#'d SETS
EXCHANGE DEADLINE 3/28/2016
3PT Tim Hardaway Jr./45
4PT Ryan Kelly/60 10.00 25.00
5PT Andre Roberson/60 4.00 10.00
9PT Dennis Schroeder/60 20.00 50.00
10PT G.Antetokounmpo/60 50.00 120.00
15PT Allen Crabbe/99 5.00 12.00
16PT Skylar Diggins/60 12.00 30.00
17PT Jamaal Franklin/99 4.00 10.00

2013-14 Fleer Retro '00-01 Fleer Autographics

GROUP A ODDS 1:4080
GROUP B ODDS 1:600
GROUP C ODDS 1:360
GROUP D ODDS 1:188
GROUP E ODDS 1:60
GROUP F ODDS 1:34
EXCHANGE DEADLINE 3/28/2016
00AUAE Alex English E 4.00 10.00
00AUAM Alonzo Mourning C 12.00 30.00
00AUBJ B.J. Young F 3.00 8.00
00AUBK Bo Kimble F 3.00 8.00
00AUBP Brandon Paul 3.00 8.00
00AUBR Bill Russell A 40.00 100.00
00AUCC Calbert Cheaney F 3.00 8.00
00AUCM Cheryl Miller D 5.00 12.00
00AUDC Dave Cowens D 3.00 8.00
00AUDM Donyell Marshall F 3.00 8.00
00AUDR David Robinson B 12.00 30.00
00AUDS Dennis Schroeder E 5.00 12.00
00AUEH Elias Harris 4.00 10.00
00AUGH Grant Hill C 10.00 25.00
00AUHA Tim Hardaway E 5.00 12.00
00AUHM Harold Miner F 3.00 8.00
00AUHO Hakeem Olajuwon B 20.00 50.00
00AUIT Isiah Thomas C 12.00 30.00
00AUJA LeBron James A 150.00 250.00
00AUJL Jerry Lucas D 5.00 12.00
00AUJO Michael Jordan B 300.00 500.00
00AUJW Jay Williams D 3.00 8.00
00AUKK Kerry Kittles F 3.00 8.00
00AUKM Karl Malone B 15.00 40.00
00AUKS Keith Smart B
00AULB Larry Bird B 40.00 80.00
00AULJ Larry Johnson C 15.00 40.00
00AUMJ Magic Johnson B 40.00 80.00
00AUMR Micheal Ray Richardson F 4.00 10.00
00AUOB Otis Birdsong B 4.00 10.00
00AUPS Peyton Siva F 3.00 8.00
00AURH Robert Horry E 4.00 10.00
00AURO Dennis Rodman C 12.00 30.00
00AURR Rajon Rondo C 12.00 30.00
00AUSA Stacey Augmon C 10.00 25.00
00AUSB Shawn Bradley F 3.00 8.00
00AUSD Skylar Diggins D 6.00 15.00
00AUSL Shane Larkin E 3.00 8.00
00AUTH Tim Hardaway Jr. E 5.00 12.00
00AUTK Toni Kukoc E 5.00 12.00
00AUTR Theo Ratliff F 3.00 8.00

2013-14 Fleer Retro Autographs

GROUP A ODDS 1:2720
GROUP B ODDS 1:862
GROUP C ODDS 1:480
GROUP D ODDS 1:272
GROUP E ODDS 1:77
GROUP F ODDS 1:58
GROUP G ODDS 1:26
EXCHANGE DEADLINE 3/28/2016
4 Dennis Rodman C 10.00 25.00
5 Elvin Hayes G 4.00 10.00
6 Donyell Marshall G 2.50 6.00
7 Calbert Cheaney G 2.50 6.00
8 Antoine Walker G 3.00 8.00
9 David Thompson E 3.00 8.00
10 Kerry Kittles G 2.50 6.00
11 Grant Hill D 15.00 40.00
12 Dominique Wilkins C 5.00 12.00
13 Tim Hardaway G 4.00 10.00
14 Alonzo Mourning C 6.00 15.00
17 Kenny Anderson E 3.00 8.00
18 Paul George B 25.00 60.00
19 Isiah Thomas C 12.00 30.00
21 Danny Manning E 3.00 8.00
22 Jay Williams G 2.50 6.00
23 Larry Johnson C 8.00 20.00
24 Jerry Lucas F 5.00 12.00
26 James Harden B EXCH 15.00 40.00
27 Otis Birdsong G 3.00 8.00
29 Sam Perkins B 12.00 30.00
30 Bill Russell A 30.00 80.00
31 David Robinson B 15.00 40.00
33 Hakeem Olajuwon B 12.00 30.00
34 Larry Bird A 40.00 80.00
37 Karl Malone B 12.00 30.00
38 Christian Laettner G 6.00 15.00
39 LeBron James A 150.00 250.00
40 Michael Jordan A
41 Mason Plumlee E 4.00 10.00
42 Jamaal Franklin G 2.50 6.00
43 Shane Larkin E 2.50 6.00
45 Isaiah Canaan F 2.50 6.00
46 Tim Hardaway Jr. E 8.00 20.00
47 Giannis Antetokounmpo F 40.00 100.00
48 Livio Jean-Charles F 2.50 6.00
49 Archie Goodwin E 3.00 8.00

50 Solomon Hill D 2.50 6.00
52 Dennis Schroeder D 4.00 10.00
53 Skylar Diggins D 6.00 15.00
54 Grant Jerrett F 2.50 6.00
58 Reggie Bullock F 3.00 8.00
60 Deshaun Thomas F 2.50 6.00

2001-02 Fleer Shoebox

This 180 card set was issued in February, 2002. In keeping with the name of the product, the packs were inserted into a "Converse All-Star" style shoe box. The first 150 cards of this set featured veterans while the last 30 cards feature some leading NBA rookies. Those Rookie Cards (151-180) had a stated print run of 2500 serial numbered sets.

COMP.SET w/o SP's (150) 10.00 25.00
151-180 PRINT RUN 2500 SERIAL #'d SETS
1 Tariq Abdul-Wahad .20 .50
2 Glen Rice .25 .60
3 Derek Anderson .20 .50
4 Desmond Mason .25 .60
5 Al Harrington .25 .60
6 Mitch Richmond .25 .60
7 Felipe Lopez .20 .50
8 Andre Miller .25 .60
9 Jerry Stackhouse .25 .60
10 Jalen Rose .25 .60
11 Lindsey Hunter .20 .50
12 Tim Thomas .20 .50
13 Wally Szczerbiak .25 .60
14 Vince Carter .50 1.25
15 Nick Van Exel .25 .60
16 Jon Barry .20 .50
17 Aaron McKie .20 .50
18 Iakovos Tsakalidis .20 .50
19 Chris Webber .30 .75
20 Karl Malone .40 1.00
21 Shareef Abdur-Rahim .25 .60
22 Baron Davis .30 .75
23 Michael Doleac .20 .50
24 Jermaine O'Neal .25 .60
25 Elton Brand .30 .75
26 Glenn Robinson .25 .60
27 Tracy McGrady .50 1.25
28 Allen Iverson .60 1.50
29 Anfernee Hardaway .50 1.25
30 Scot Pollard .20 .50
31 David Robinson .50 1.25
32 John Stockton .40 1.00
33 Jason Williams .25 .60
34 Voshon Lenard .20 .50
35 Shaquille O'Neal .75 2.00
36 Grant Hill .40 1.00
37 Shawn Marion .25 .60
38 Vin Baker .25 .60
39 Raef LaFrentz .20 .50
40 Steve Francis .25 .60
41 Michael Dickerson .20 .50
42 Hedo Turkoglu .25 .60
43 Patrick Ewing .40 1.00
44 Dirk Nowitzki .50 1.25
45 Keyon Dooling .20 .50
46 Marcus Camby .25 .60
47 Bonzi Wells .20 .50
48 Tim Duncan .60 1.50
49 Jamaal Magloire .20 .50
50 Rick Fox .20 .50
51 Kendall Gill .20 .50
52 Michael Redd .30 .75
53 Keith Van Horn .25 .60
54 Eric Snow .20 .50
55 Theo Ratliff .20 .50
56 Clifford Robinson .20 .50
57 Moochie Norris .20 .50
58 Alonzo Mourning .40 1.00
59 Joe Smith .25 .60
60 Brent Barry .20 .50
61 Alvin Williams .20 .50
62 Antoine Walker .25 .60
63 Antonio McDyess .25 .60
64 Derek Fisher .25 .60
65 Ron Mercer .20 .50
66 Hakeem Olajuwon .40 1.00
67 Jamal Crawford .30 .75
68 Chris Mihm .20 .50
69 Ben Wallace .25 .60
70 Brian Grant .20 .50
71 Kevin Garnett .50 1.25
72 Shandon Anderson .20 .50
73 Shawn Bradley .20 .50
74 Danny Fortson .20 .50
75 Jeff McInnis .20 .50
76 LaPhonso Ellis .25 .60
77 Sam Cassell .25 .60
78 Rasheed Wallace .30 .75
79 Malik Rose .20 .50
80 Jahidi White .20 .50
81 Milt Palacio .20 .50
82 Tim Hardaway .30 .75
83 Antonio Daniels .20 .50
84 Tyronn Lue .20 .50
85 Cuttino Mobley .20 .50
86 DerMarr Johnson .20 .50
87 Lamond Murray .20 .50
88 Larry Hughes .25 .60
89 Reggie Miller .30 .75
90 Lorenzen Wright .20 .50
91 Eddie Jones .25 .60
92 Anthony Mason .20 .50
93 Todd MacCulloch .20 .50
94 Speedy Claxton .20 .50
95 Mateen Cleaves .20 .50
96 Gary Payton .30 .75
97 Morris Peterson .20 .50
98 Mike Miller .25 .60
99 Hanno Mottola .20 .50
100 Steve Nash .50 1.25
101 Stromile Swift .20 .50
102 Ray Allen .30 .75
103 Mark Jackson .25 .60
104 Stephon Marbury .25 .60
105 Mike Bibby .30 .75
106 Rashard Lewis .30 .75
107 Jason Kidd .50 1.25
108 P.J. Brown .20 .50
109 Kobe Bryant 1.25 3.00
110 Tom Gugliotta .20 .50
111 Richard Hamilton .25 .60
112 Antawn Jamison .30 .75
113 Lamar Odom .25 .60
114 Kurt Thomas .20 .50
115 Robert Horry .25 .60
116 Dikembe Mutombo .30 .75
117 Tony Delk .20 .50
118 Peja Stojakovic .30 .75
119 Donyell Marshall .20 .50
120 Paul Pierce .30 .75
121 Michael Finley .30 .75
122 Quentin Richardson .25 .60
123 Kenyon Martin .30 .75
124 Allan Houston .25 .60
125 Scottie Pippen .50 1.25
126 Steve Smith .25 .60
127 Bryon Russell .20 .50
128 James Posey .20 .50
129 Terrell Brandon .20 .50
130 Toni Kukoc .30 .75
131 Stephen Jackson .25 .60
132 Marc Jackson .20 .50
133 Kelvin Cato .20 .50
134 Travis Best .20 .50
135 David Wesley .20 .50
136 Anthony Carter .20 .50
137 Michael Jordan 2.50 6.00
138 Darrell Armstrong .20 .50
139 Matt Harpring .20 .50
140 Antonio Davis .20 .50
141 Courtney Alexander .20 .50
142 Jamal Mashburn .25 .60
143 Jason Terry .30 .75
144 Marcus Fizer .20 .50
145 Juwan Howard .25 .60
146 Darius Miles .20 .50
147 Latrell Sprewell .25 .60
148 Damon Stoudamire .25 .60
149 John Starks .20 .50
150 Jumaine Jones .20 .50
151 Kedrick Brown RC .50 1.25
152 Trenton Hassell RC .60 1.50
153 Kwame Brown RC .75 2.00
154 Terence Morris RC .75 2.00
155 Richard Jefferson RC 1.25 3.00
156 Vladimir Radmanovic RC .75 2.00
157 Brandon Armstrong RC .50 1.25
158 Kirk Haston RC .50 1.25
159 Eddie Griffin RC .60 1.50
160 Steven Hunter RC .60 1.50
161 Troy Murphy RC .75 2.00
162 Andrei Kirilenko RC 1.25 3.00
163 Jeryl Sasser RC .50 1.25
164 Michael Bradley RC .50 1.25
165 Rodney White RC .50 1.25
166 Loren Woods RC .50 1.25
167 Zach Randolph RC 1.25 3.00
168 Joe Johnson RC 1.00 2.50
169 Eddy Curry RC .75 2.00
170 Jason Richardson RC 1.00 2.50
171 DeSagana Diop RC .60 1.50
172 Jamaal Tinsley RC .75 2.00
173 Pau Gasol RC 2.50 6.00
174 Jason Collins RC .60 1.50
175 Zeljko Rebraca RC .75 2.00
176 Shane Battier RC 1.50 4.00
177 Gerald Wallace RC 1.00 2.50
178 Joseph Forte RC .50 1.25
179 Tyson Chandler RC 1.25 3.00
180 Tony Parker RC 3.00 8.00

2001-02 Fleer Shoebox Footprints

*FOOT.STARS: 5X TO 12X BASE CARD HI
*FOOT.RCs: 2X TO 5X BASE CARD HI
PRINT RUN 150 SERIAL #'d SETS
137 Michael Jordan 40.00 100.00

2001-02 Fleer Shoebox NBA Flight School

Inserted at stated odds of one in 12 packs, this 20 cards insert sets honors some of the NBA's leading dunkers.

COMPLETE SET (20) 20.00 40.00
STATED ODDS 1:12
1 Richard Hamilton .60 1.50
2 Kobe Bryant 3.00 8.00
3 Michael Jordan 6.00 15.00
4 Desmond Mason .60 1.50
5 Antoine Walker .60 1.50
6 Baron Davis .75 2.00
7 Steve Francis .60 1.50
8 Elton Brand .75 2.00
9 Lamar Odom .60 1.50
10 Kevin Garnett 1.25 3.00
11 Latrell Sprewell .60 1.50
12 Tracy McGrady 1.25 3.00
13 Shawn Marion .60 1.50
14 Chris Webber .75 2.00
15 Vince Carter 1.25 3.00
16 Tim Duncan 1.50 4.00
17 Morris Peterson .50 1.25
18 Karl Malone 1.00 2.50
19 Jerry Stackhouse .60 1.50
20 Darius Miles .50 1.25

2001-02 Fleer Shoebox NBA Flight School Cadet

Inserted at stated odds of one in 63, this is a partial parallel to the Flight School insert set. These cards are differentiated from the standard insert by the game-worn jersey swatch. A Captain version of NBA Flight School was also issued. These cards are sequentially numbered to 75.

STATED ODDS 1:63
*CAPTAIN: 1.25X TO 3X CADET HI
CAPTAIN PRINT RUN 75 SER.#'d SETS
1 Richard Hamilton 2.50 6.00
2 Desmond Mason 2.50 6.00
3 Antoine Walker 2.50 6.00
4 Baron Davis 3.00 8.00
5 Steve Francis 2.50 6.00
6 Elton Brand 3.00 8.00
7 Lamar Odom 2.50 6.00
8 Tracy McGrady 5.00 12.00
9 Shawn Marion 2.50 6.00
10 Chris Webber 3.00 8.00
11 Vince Carter 5.00 12.00
12 Morris Peterson 2.00 5.00
13 Karl Malone 4.00 10.00
14 Jerry Stackhouse 2.50 6.00
15 Darius Miles 2.00 5.00

2001-02 Fleer Shoebox Sole of the Game

Inserted at stated odds of one in 144, these 15 cards feature key NBA players including a Larry Bird tribute.

COMPLETE SET (15) 50.00 100.00
STATED ODDS 1:144
1 Karl Malone 2.50 6.00
2 Dirk Nowitzki 3.00 8.00
3 Ray Allen 2.00 5.00
4 Shaquille O'Neal 5.00 12.00
5 Antoine Walker 1.50 4.00
6 Grant Hill 2.50 6.00
7 Steve Francis 1.50 4.00
8 Kobe Bryant 8.00 20.00
9 Michael Jordan 20.00 50.00
10 Larry Bird 15.00 40.00
11 Darius Miles 1.25 3.00
12 Chris Webber 2.00 5.00
13 Allen Iverson 4.00 10.00
14 Rasheed Wallace 2.00 5.00
15 Vince Carter 3.00 8.00

2001-02 Fleer Shoebox Sole of the Game Ball

Randomly inserted in packs, this is a partial parallel to the Sole of the Game insert set. These cards have a stated print run of 300 serial numbered sets and contain a piece of basketball used in a game by the featured player.

STATED PRINT RUN 300 SERIAL #'d SETS
1 Ray Allen 5.00 12.00
2 Vince Carter 8.00 20.00
3 Steve Francis 4.00 10.00
4 Grant Hill 6.00 15.00
5 Allen Iverson 10.00 25.00
6 Karl Malone 6.00 15.00
7 Darius Miles 3.00 8.00
8 Dirk Nowitzki 8.00 20.00
9 Antoine Walker 4.00 10.00
10 Rasheed Wallace 5.00 12.00
11 Chris Webber 6.00 15.00

2001-02 Fleer Shoebox Sole of the Game Jersey

Randomly inserted in packs, this is a partial parallel to the Sole of the Game insert set. These cards have a stated print run of 200 serial numbered sets and contain a game-worn jersey piece used in a game by the featured player. Some players uniforms were not available in time for inclusion in packs and they were issued as redemptions.

STATED PRINT RUN 200 SERIAL #'d SETS
1 Ray Allen 4.00 10.00
2 Vince Carter 6.00 15.00
3 Steve Francis 3.00 8.00
4 Grant Hill 5.00 12.00
5 Allen Iverson 8.00 20.00
6 Karl Malone 5.00 12.00
7 Darius Miles 2.50 6.00
8 Dirk Nowitzki 6.00 15.00
9 Larry Bird 15.00 40.00
10 Antoine Walker 3.00 8.00
11 Rasheed Wallace 4.00 10.00

2001-02 Fleer Shoebox Sole of the Game Shoe

Randomly inserted in packs, this is a partial parallel to the Sole of the Game insert set. These cards have a stated print run of 100 serial numbered sets and contain a game-worn shoe piece used in a game by the featured player. Some players uniforms were not available in time for inclusion in packs and they were issued as redemptions.

STATED PRINT RUN 100 SERIAL #'d SETS
1 Ray Allen 10.00 25.00
2 Larry Bird 15.00 40.00
3 Vince Carter 15.00 40.00
5 Grant Hill 12.00 30.00
6 Allen Iverson 20.00 50.00
7 Karl Malone 15.00 40.00
8 Darius Miles 6.00 15.00
9 Dirk Nowitzki 15.00 40.00
12 Rasheed Wallace 10.00 25.00
13 Chris Webber 10.00 25.00

2001-02 Fleer Shoebox Sole of the Game Triple

Randomly inserted in packs, this is a partial parallel to the Sole of the Game insert set. These cards have a stated print run of 50 serial numbered sets and contain a piece of basketball used in a game by the featured player. This 11 card set contains a piece of game-worn shoe, patch and basketball from the featured player.

STATED PRINT RUN 50 SERIAL #'d SETS
1 Ray Allen 20.00 50.00
2 Vince Carter 30.00 80.00
3 Steve Francis 15.00 40.00
4 Grant Hill 25.00 60.00
5 Allen Iverson 40.00 100.00
6 Karl Malone 30.00 80.00
7 Darius Miles 12.00 30.00
8 Dirk Nowitzki 30.00 80.00

2001-02 Fleer Shoebox Tougher Than Leather

Inserted at stated odds of one in 36, these 20 cards feature players known for their physical play on the court.

COMPLETE SET (20) 25.00 50.00
STATED ODDS 1:36
1 Alonzo Mourning 1.50 4.00
2 Antonio McDyess 1.00 2.50
3 Paul Pierce 1.25 3.00
4 Peja Stojakovic 1.25 3.00
5 Dirk Nowitzki 2.00 5.00
6 Allen Iverson 2.50 6.00
7 Marcus Camby 1.00 2.50
8 Tracy McGrady 2.00 5.00
9 Kenyon Martin 1.25 3.00
10 Dikembe Mutombo 1.25 3.00
11 Rasheed Wallace 1.25 3.00
12 David Robinson 2.00 5.00
13 Shareef Abdur-Rahim 1.00 2.50
14 Glenn Robinson 1.00 2.50
15 Vince Carter 2.00 5.00
16 Antoine Walker 1.00 2.50
17 Trajan Langdon .75 2.00
18 Scottie Pippen 2.00 5.00
19 Eddie Jones 1.00 2.50
20 Lamar Odom 1.00 2.50

2001-02 Fleer Shoebox Tougher Than Leather Shoes

STATED PRINT RUN 100 SERIAL #'d SETS
1 Alonzo Mourning 12.00 30.00
2 Antonio McDyess 6.00 15.00
3 Eddie Jones 6.00 15.00
5 Dirk Nowitzki 12.00 30.00
6 Marcus Camby 6.00 15.00
7 Tracy McGrady 12.00 30.00
8 Kenyon Martin 8.00 20.00
9 Dikembe Mutombo 8.00 20.00
10 Rasheed Wallace 8.00 20.00
11 David Robinson 12.00 30.00
12 Shareef Abdur-Rahim 6.00 15.00
13 Glenn Robinson 6.00 15.00
14 Vince Carter 12.00 30.00
14A Vince Carter AU 25.00 50.00
15 Antoine Walker 6.00 15.00
16 Allen Iverson 15.00 40.00
17 Scottie Pippen 12.00 30.00
18 Peja Stojakovic 8.00 20.00
19 Trajan Langdon 5.00 12.00
20 Lamar Odom 6.00 15.00

2000-01 Fleer Showcase

The 2000-01 Fleer Showcase product released in March, 2001 and featured a 121-card base set. The base set was broken into tiers as follows: Base Veterans (1-90) and Rookies (91-121) that were broken into three tiers. Tier 1 91-100 were serial numbered to 500, Tier 2 101-110 were serial numbered to 1500, and Tier 3 111-121 were serial numbered to 2000. Each pack contained five cards, and carried a suggested retail price of $4.99.

COMPLETE SET w/o RCs (90) 12.50 30.00
91-100/121: PRINT RUN 500 #'d SETS
101-110: PRINT RUN 1500 #'d SETS
111-121: PRINT RUN 2000 #'d SETS
1 Vince Carter .75 2.00
2 Lamar Odom .30 .75
3 Larry Hughes .30 .75
4 Brian Grant .25 .60
5 Bryon Russell .25 .60
6 Allan Houston .30 .75
7 Juwan Howard .30 .75
8 Cuttino Mobley .25 .60
9 Keith Van Horn .30 .75
10 Mike Bibby .40 1.00
11 Jerome Williams .25 .60
12 Ray Allen .40 1.00
13 Antonio Davis .25 .60
14 Adrian Griffin .25 .60
15 Dan Majerle .40 1.00
16 Rasheed Wallace .40 1.00
17 Antonio McDyess .30 .75
18 Tim Thomas .25 .60
19 Theo Ratliff .25 .60
20 Charles Oakley .30 .75
21 Nick Van Exel .30 .75
22 Glenn Robinson .30 .75
23 Cal Bowdler .25 .60
24 Raef LaFrentz .25 .60
25 Terrell Brandon .25 .60
26 Allen Iverson .75 2.00
27 Patrick Ewing .50 1.25
28 Ron Artest .40 1.00
29 Michael Olowokandi .25 .60
30 Derek Anderson .25 .60
31 Dirk Nowitzki .60 1.50
32 Wally Szczerbiak .30 .75
33 Gary Payton .40 1.00
34 Michael Finley .40 1.00
35 Chauncey Billups .40 1.00
36 Jason Kidd .60 1.50
37 Rashard Lewis .40 1.00
38 Andre Miller .30 .75
39 Kevin Garnett .60 1.50
40 Tim Duncan .75 2.00
41 Jalen Rose .30 .75
42 Marcus Camby .30 .75
43 Richard Hamilton .30 .75
44 Austin Croshere .25 .60
45 Latrell Sprewell .30 .75
46 Shawn Marion .30 .75
47 Jahidi White .25 .60
48 Elton Brand .40 1.00
49 Reggie Miller .40 1.00
50 David Robinson .60 1.50
51 Trajan Langdon .25 .60
52 Jonathan Bender .25 .60
53 Antonio Daniels .25 .60
54 Jason Terry .40 1.00
55 Eddie Jones .40 1.00
56 Mitch Richmond .30 .75
57 Antoine Walker .30 .75
58 Robert Horry .30 .75
59 Tracy McGrady .60 1.50
60 Scottie Pippen .60 1.50
61 Jerry Stackhouse .30 .75
62 Zydrunas Ilgauskas .30 .75
63 Toni Kukoc .40 1.00
64 Karl Malone .50 1.25
65 Baron Davis .40 1.00
66 Shaquille O'Neal 1.00 2.50
67 Vlade Divac .30 .75
68 Eddie Robinson .25 .60
69 Dion Glover .25 .60
70 Jason Williams .40 1.00
71 Steve Francis .30 .75
72 Glen Rice .30 .75
73 Clifford Robinson .25 .60
74 Shareef Abdur-Rahim .30 .75
75 Hakeem Olajuwon .50 1.25
76 Paul Pierce .40 1.00
77 Tim Hardaway .40 1.00
78 Darrell Armstrong .25 .60
79 Bonzi Wells .25 .60
80 Antawn Jamison .40 1.00
81 Stephon Marbury .30 .75
82 Tony Delk .25 .60
83 Michael Dickerson .25 .60
84 Jamal Mashburn .30 .75
85 Kobe Bryant 1.50 4.00
86 Grant Hill .50 1.25
87 Chris Webber .40 1.00
88 Vonteego Cummings .25 .60
89 Jamie Feick .25 .60
90 John Stockton .50 1.25
91 Kenyon Martin RC 8.00 20.00
92 Stromile Swift RC 3.00 8.00
93 Darius Miles RC 3.00 8.00
94 Marcus Fizer RC 3.00 8.00
95 Mike Miller RC 5.00 12.00
96 DerMarr Johnson RC 2.50 6.00
97 Chris Mihm RC 2.50 6.00
98 Jamal Crawford RC 8.00 20.00
99 Joel Przybilla RC 2.50 6.00
100 Keyon Dooling RC 3.00 8.00
101 Jerome Moiso RC 1.25 3.00
102 Etan Thomas RC 2.00 5.00
103 Courtney Alexander RC 1.50 4.00
104 Mateen Cleaves RC 1.50 4.00
105 Jason Collier RC 2.00 5.00
106 Hedo Turkoglu RC 3.00 8.00
107 Desmond Mason RC 2.50 6.00
108 Quentin Richardson RC 2.00 5.00
109 Jamaal Magloire RC 2.00 5.00
110 Speedy Claxton RC 2.00 5.00
111 Morris Peterson RC 1.50 4.00
112 Donnell Harvey RC 1.25 3.00
113 DeShawn Stevenson RC 1.50 4.00
114 Dalibor Bagaric RC 1.25 3.00
115 Mamadou N'Diaye RC 1.00 2.50
116 Erick Barkley RC 1.00 2.50
117 Mark Madsen RC 1.50 4.00
118 Chris Porter RC 1.00 2.50
119 Brian Cardinal RC 1.25 3.00
120 Iakovos Tsakalidis RC 1.00 2.50
121 Marc Jackson RC 2.50 6.00

2000-01 Fleer Showcase Legacy Collection

*STARS: 15X TO 40X BASE CARD HI
*RCs 91-100/121: .75X TO 2X BASE HI
*RCs 101-110: 1.25X TO 3X BASE HI
*RCs 111-120: 1.5X TO 4X BASE HI
STATED PRINT RUN 50 SERIAL #'d SETS

2000-01 Fleer Showcase Avant Card

Randomly inserted in packs, each card in this 20-card set features an original piece of art (by Gerry Thomas) mounted in a card frame. Card backs carry a "AC" prefix. Please note that there wer only 201 of each card produced.

STATED PRINT RUN 201 SERIAL #'d SETS
AC1 Vince Carter 10.00 25.00
AC2 Lamar Odom 4.00 10.00
AC3 Kobe Bryant 20.00 50.00
AC4 Kevin Garnett 8.00 20.00
AC5 Steve Francis 4.00 10.00
AC6 Jason Williams 5.00 12.00
AC7 Eddie Jones 5.00 12.00
AC8 Grant Hill 6.00 15.00
AC9 Elton Brand 5.00 12.00
AC10 Shaquille O'Neal 12.00 30.00
AC11 Allen Iverson 10.00 25.00
AC12 Tim Duncan 10.00 25.00
AC13 Jason Kidd 8.00 20.00
AC14 Kenyon Martin 12.00 30.00
AC15 Stromile Swift 5.00 12.00
AC16 Darius Miles 5.00 12.00
AC17 Marcus Fizer 5.00 12.00
AC18 Mike Miller 8.00 20.00
AC19 Jamal Crawford 12.00 30.00
AC20 Mateen Cleaves 4.00 10.00

2000-01 Fleer Showcase Vince Carter Rookie Remnants

This three-card insert was randomly inserted into 2000-01 Fleer products. The set includes a Vince Carter floor card (numbered to 100), a Vince Carter floor/jersey card (numbered to 15), and finally an autographed Vince Carter floor/jersey card (numbered 1/1).

RANDOM INSERTS IN HOBBY PACKS
NNO Vince Carter FLR JSY/15 20.00 50.00
NNO Vince Carter FLR/100 12.50 30.00

2000-01 Fleer Showcase ELEMENTary

Randomly inserted in packs at one in 48, this 10-card set compares your favorite NBA stars to elements on the periodical chart. Card backs carry an "E" prefix.

COMPLETE SET (10) 20.00 40.00
STATED ODDS 1:48
E1 Vince Carter 2.50 6.00
E2 Lamar Odom 1.00 2.50
E3 Kevin Garnett 2.00 5.00
E4 Steve Francis 1.00 2.50
E5 Grant Hill 1.50 4.00
E6 Eddie Jones 1.25 3.00
E7 Jason Williams 1.25 3.00
E8 Kobe Bryant 5.00 12.00
E9 Allen Iverson 2.50 6.00
E10 Shaquille O'Neal 3.00 8.00

2000-01 Fleer Showcase HIStory

Randomly inserted into packs at one in 24, this 10-card insert set tells the story of how ten players made it to the NBA. Card backs carry an "H" prefix.

COMPLETE SET (10) 12.50 25.00
STATED ODDS 1:24
H1 Vince Carter 1.50 4.00
H2 Lamar Odom .60 1.50
H3 Kobe Bryant 3.00 8.00
H4 Shaquille O'Neal 2.00 5.00
H5 Kevin Garnett 1.25 3.00
H6 Allen Iverson 1.50 4.00
H7 Steve Francis .60 1.50
H8 Eddie Jones .75 2.00
H9 Jason Williams .75 2.00
H10 Michael Finley .75 2.00

2000-01 Fleer Showcase In the Paint

Randomly inserted in packs at one in 110, this 26-card insert offers a piece of a hand-painted basketball from a top 2000-01 NBA rookie. Card backs carry an "P" prefix.

STATED ODDS 1:110
P1 Kenyon Martin 5.00 12.00
P2 Stromile Swift 2.00 5.00
P3 Darius Miles 2.00 5.00
P4 Marcus Fizer 2.00 5.00
P5 Mike Miller 3.00 8.00
P6 DerMarr Johnson 1.50 4.00
P7 Chris Mihm 1.50 4.00
P8 Joel Przybilla 1.50 4.00
P9 Keyon Dooling 2.00 5.00
P10 Jerome Moiso 1.25 3.00
P11 Etan Thomas 2.00 5.00
P12 Courtney Alexander 1.50 4.00
P13 Mateen Cleaves 1.50 4.00
P14 Jason Collier 2.00 5.00
P15 Hedo Turkoglu 3.00 8.00
P16 Desmond Mason 2.50 6.00
P17 Quentin Richardson 2.00 5.00
P18 Jamaal Magloire 2.00 5.00
P19 Speedy Claxton 2.00 5.00
P20 Morris Peterson 2.00 5.00
P21 Donnell Harvey 1.50 4.00
P22 DeShawn Stevenson 2.00 5.00
P23 Dalibor Bagaric 1.50 4.00
P24 Mamadou N'Diaye 1.25 3.00
P25 Erick Barkley 1.25 3.00
P26 Mark Madsen 2.00 5.00

2000-01 Fleer Showcase Showstoppers

Randomly inserted in packs at one in six, this 20-card set features players who are worth the price of admission themselves. Card backs carry a "S" prefix.

COMPLETE SET (20) 6.00 15.00
STATED ODDS 1:6
S1 Vince Carter 1.00 2.50
S2 Lamar Odom .40 1.00
S3 Tracy McGrady .75 2.00
S4 Karl Malone .60 1.50
S5 Scottie Pippen .75 2.00
S6 Antawn Jamison .50 1.25
S7 Chris Webber .50 1.25
S8 Allan Houston .40 1.00
S9 Baron Davis .50 1.25
S10 Rashard Lewis .50 1.25
S11 Jerry Stackhouse .40 1.00
S12 Ray Allen .50 1.25
S13 Keith Van Horn .40 1.00
S14 Tim Duncan 1.00 2.50
S15 Shareef Abdur-Rahim .40 1.00
S16 Jalen Rose .40 1.00
S17 Gary Payton .50 1.25
S18 Andre Miller .40 1.00
S19 Paul Pierce .50 1.25
S20 Antonio McDyess .40 1.00

2000-01 Fleer Showcase To Air is Human

Randomly inserted in packs at one in 12, this 15-card set features high-flyers that don't make mistakes when the game is on the line. Card backs carry a "TA" prefix.

COMPLETE SET (15) 6.00 15.00
STATED ODDS 1:12
TA1 Vince Carter 1.25 3.00
TA2 Lamar Odom .50 1.25
TA3 Grant Hill .75 2.00
TA4 Shareef Abdur-Rahim .50 1.25
TA5 Michael Finley .60 1.50
TA6 Larry Hughes .50 1.25
TA7 Latrell Sprewell .50 1.25
TA8 Tracy McGrady 1.00 2.50
TA9 Ray Allen .60 1.50
TA10 Desmond Mason .75 2.00
TA11 Kenyon Martin 1.50 4.00
TA12 Morris Peterson .60 1.50
TA13 Stromile Swift .60 1.50
TA14 DerMarr Johnson .50 1.25
TA15 Mike Miller 1.00 2.50

2001-02 Fleer Showcase

Issued in January, 2002 this 123 card set features a mix of rookie and veteran players. Cards numbered 87-91 featured special art cards of key superstars and were printed to a stated print run of 500 serial numbered sets. In addition, the rookie cards were also broken down into several levels with cards 92 through 97 also having a stated print run of 500 serial numbered sets. Cards 98 through 112 have a stated print run of 1000 serial numbered sets and cards 113-122 have a stated print run of 1500 serial numbered sets. Card 123, Wang ZhiZhi was also accorded the Avant treatment and his card was issued to a stated print run 500 serial numbered cards. In addition, Vince Carter signed 150 cards of his card number 87. That card is not considered part of the complete set.

COMPLETE SET (123) 150.00 300.00
COMP.SET w/o SP's (86) 20.00 50.00
AVANT PRINT RUN 500 SER.#'d SETS
92-97 PRINT RUN 500 SER.#'d SETS
98-112 PRINT RUN 1000 SER.#'d SETS
113-122 PRINT RUN 1500 SER.#'d SETS
UNPRICED MASTERPIECE PRINT RUN ONE SET
1 Grant Hill .50 1.25
2 Elton Brand .40 1.00
3 Sam Cassell .30 .75
4 John Stockton .50 1.25
5 James Posey .25 .60
6 Eddie Jones .30 .75
7 Damon Stoudamire .30 .75
8 Nick Van Exel .30 .75
9 Brian Grant .25 .60
10 Mike Miller .30 .75
11 Steve Smith .30 .75
12 Michael Finley .40 1.00
13 Peja Stojakovic .40 1.00
14 DerMarr Johnson .25 .60
15 Reggie Miller .40 1.00
16 Quentin Richardson .30 .75
17 Latrell Sprewell .30 .75
18 Richard Hamilton .30 .75
19 Michael Doleac .25 .60
20 Derek Fisher .30 .75
21 Marcus Camby .30 .75
22 Stephon Marbury .30 .75
23 Bryon Russell .25 .60
24 Jumaine Jones .25 .60
25 Anfernee Hardaway .60 1.50
26 P.J. Brown .25 .60
27 Marc Jackson .25 .60
28 Dikembe Mutombo .40 1.00
29 Andre Miller .30 .75
30 Robert Horry .30 .75
31 Tom Gugliotta .25 .60
32 David Robinson .60 1.50
33 Ron Mercer .25 .60
34 Shawn Marion .30 .75
35 Ron Artest .40 1.00
36 Jason Williams .30 .75
37 Scottie Pippen .60 1.50
38 Jerry Stackhouse .30 .75
39 Stromile Swift .25 .60
40 Rasheed Wallace .40 1.00
41 Alonzo Mourning .50 1.25
42 Eddie Robinson .25 .60
43 Shareef Abdur-Rahim .30 .75
44 Wally Szczerbiak .30 .75
45 Antonio Davis .25 .60
46 Glen Rice .30 .75
47 Jason Kidd .60 1.50
48 Gary Payton .40 1.00
49 Steve Nash .60 1.50
50 Lamar Odom .30 .75
51 Glenn Robinson .30 .75
52 Mike Bibby .40 1.00
53 Hakeem Olajuwon .50 1.25
54 Theo Ratliff .25 .60
55 Kenyon Martin .40 1.00
56 Jamal Mashburn .30 .75
57 Larry Hughes .30 .75
58 Speedy Claxton .25 .60
59 Rashard Lewis .40 1.00
60 Raef LaFrentz .25 .60
61 Antonio Daniels .25 .60
62 Jason Terry .40 1.00
63 Jalen Rose .30 .75
64 Terrell Brandon .25 .60
65 Karl Malone .50 1.25
66 Antonio McDyess .30 .75
67 Anthony Carter .25 .60
68 Tim Hardaway .40 1.00
69 Antoine Walker .30 .75
70 Cuttino Mobley .25 .60
71 Allan Houston .30 .75
72 Desmond Mason .30 .75
73 Kurt Thomas .25 .60
74 Juwan Howard .30 .75
75 Tim Thomas .25 .60
76 Tracy McGrady .60 1.50
77 Dirk Nowitzki .60 1.50
78 Tim Duncan .75 2.00
79 Chris Webber .40 1.00
80 Steve Francis .30 .75
81 Paul Pierce .40 1.00
82 Darius Miles .25 .60
83 Ray Allen .40 1.00
84 Baron Davis .40 1.00
85 Antawn Jamison .40 1.00
86 Michael Jordan 4.00 10.00
87 Vince Carter AVANT 4.00 10.00
87A Vince Carter AU/150 60.00 150.00
88 Kobe Bryant AVANT 10.00 25.00
89 Allen Iverson AVANT 5.00 12.00
90 Kevin Garnett AVANT 4.00 10.00
91 Shaquille O'Neal AVANT 6.00 15.00
92 Kwame Brown AVANT RC 5.00 12.00
93 Eddie Griffin AVANT RC 4.00 10.00
94 Eddy Curry AVANT RC 5.00 12.00
95 Shane Battier AVANT RC 10.00 25.00
96 Joe Johnson AVANT RC 6.00 15.00
97 Tyson Chandler AVANT RC 8.00 20.00
98 Jason Richardson RC 1.50 4.00
99 Zach Randolph RC 2.00 5.00
100 Rodney White RC .75 2.00
101 Pau Gasol RC 4.00 10.00
102 Jamaal Tinsley RC 1.25 3.00
103 Troy Murphy RC 1.25 3.00
104 Richard Jefferson RC 2.00 5.00
105 DeSagana Diop RC 1.00 2.50
106 Joseph Forte RC .75 2.00
107 Gerald Wallace RC 1.50 4.00
108 Loren Woods RC .75 2.00
109 Jason Collins RC 1.00 2.50
110 Jeryl Sasser RC .75 2.00
111 Zeljko Rebraca RC 1.25 3.00
112 Kirk Haston RC .75 2.00
113 Kedrick Brown RC .75 2.00
114 Steven Hunter RC 1.00 2.50
115 Michael Bradley RC .75 2.00
116 Brandon Armstrong RC .75 2.00
117 Samuel Dalembert RC 1.25 3.00
118 Primoz Brezec RC 1.25 3.00
119 Andrei Kirilenko RC 2.00 5.00
120 Vladimir Radmanovic RC 1.25 3.00
121 Ratko Varda RC 1.25 3.00
122 Brendan Haywood RC 1.25 3.00
123 Wang Zhizhi AVANT 2.00 5.00

2001-02 Fleer Showcase Legacy

*STARS 1-86: 12X TO 30X BASE CARD HI
*AVANT STARS: 2X TO 5X BASE CARD HI
*AVANT RCs: .75X TO 2X BASE CARD HI
*RCs 97-122: 3X TO 8X BASE CARD HI
PRINT RUN 50 SER.#'d SETS
25 Anfernee Hardaway 30.00 80.00
86 Michael Jordan 175.00 350.00

2001-02 Fleer Showcase Beasts of the East

IRandomly inserted in packs at the rate of one in 26, this 15-card set features the words "Beasts of the East" along the top of the card with player action photos centered on the card front with a swatch of game worn memorabilia.

STATED ODDS 1:24
1 Vince Carter 5.00 12.00
1A Vince Carter AU/225 20.00 50.00
2 Allen Iverson 6.00 15.00
3 Alonzo Mourning 4.00 10.00
4 Paul Pierce 3.00 8.00
5 Tracy McGrady 5.00 12.00
6 Keith Van Horn 2.50 6.00
7 Antoine Walker 2.50 6.00
8 Richard Hamilton 2.50 6.00
9 Andre Miller 2.50 6.00
10 Dikembe Mutombo 3.00 8.00
11 Mike Miller 2.50 6.00
12 Kenyon Martin 3.00 8.00
13 Baron Davis 3.00 8.00
14 Ray Allen 3.00 8.00

2001-02 Fleer Showcase Best of the West

Randomly inserted in packs at the stated odds of one in 26, this 15-card set features the words "Best of the West" along the top of the card with player action photos centered on the card front with a swatch of game worn memorabilia.

STATED ODDS 1:24
1 Terrell Brandon 2.00 5.00
2 Karl Malone 4.00 10.00
3 Lamar Odom 2.50 6.00
4 Darius Miles 2.00 5.00
5 David Robinson 5.00 12.00
6 Chris Webber 3.00 8.00
7 Gary Payton 3.00 8.00
8 Steve Francis 2.50 6.00
9 Desmond Mason 2.50 6.00
10 Elton Brand 3.00 8.00
11 Shawn Marion 2.50 6.00
12 John Stockton 4.00 10.00
13 Antawn Jamison 3.00 8.00
14 Antonio McDyess 2.50 6.00
15 Jason Williams 2.50 6.00

2001-02 Fleer Showcase Rival Revival

Randomly inserted in packs, this five card set features top NBA rivals with player photos and a game jersey swatch from each. Cards have a stated print run of 100 serial numbered sets.

STATED PRINT RUN 100 SERIAL #'d SETS
1 V.Carter/T.McGrady 10.00 25.00
2 V.Carter/A.Jamison 8.00 20.00
3 V.Carter/A.Iverson 12.50 30.00
4 D.Robinson/D.Mutombo 10.00 25.00
5 D.Miles/K.Martin 8.00 20.00

2002-03 Fleer Showcase

Released in mid December 2002, Fleer Showcase consists of a 148-card set divided up as follows: 100 Row 3 Veteran Cards, numbers 1-100, 12 Row 2 Veteran Avant Cards, numbers 101-112, six Row 0 Veteran Avant Cards sequentially numbered to 1000, numbers 113-118, six Row 0 Rookie Avant Cards sequentially numbered to 500, numbers 119-124, and 24 Row 1 Rookie Cards sequentially numbered to 1500, card numbers 125-148. Base Row 3 and Row 1 cards have an embossed picture frame border with color's set to match the featured player's team colors with the team name, player name, and Fleer Showcase logo in bronze foil. Backgrounds are white with one-color minimalist portrait shots of players and full color action photos are set in front. Row 2 Avant cards have the embossed border and an embedded metallic photo that takes up the entire card front. Row 2 Avant Cards are highlighted with silver foil. Row 1 Avant Cards feature the same embossed border, but are cut with a glossy metallic photo of the player embedded on the left half of the card only and are highlighted with blue foil. Showcase was packaged in five card packs which carried a suggested retail price of $4.99, and boxes contained 24 packs.

COMP.SET w/o SP's (100) 12.50 30.00
113-118 PRINT RUN 1000 SER.#'d SETS
119-124 PRINT RUN 500 SER.#'d SETS
125-148 PRINT RUN 1500 SER.#'d SETS
UNPRICED MASTERPIECE PRINT RUN ONE SET
1 Michael Jordan 3.00 8.00
2 Shareef Abdur-Rahim .30 .75
3 Jalen Rose .30 .75
4 Antonio McDyess .30 .75
5 Malik Rose .25 .60
6 Juwan Howard .30 .75
7 Jason Williams .30 .75
8 Darrell Armstrong .25 .60
9 Karl Malone .50 1.25
10 Jason Terry .30 .75
11 David Wesley .25 .60
12 David Robinson .60 1.50
13 Gary Payton .40 1.00
14 Quentin Richardson .30 .75
15 Allan Houston .30 .75
16 Alvin Williams .25 .60
17 Jamal Mashburn .30 .75
18 Theo Ratliff .25 .60
19 Tyson Chandler .40 1.00
20 Gilbert Arenas .40 1.00
21 Dikembe Mutombo .40 1.00
22 Calbert Cheaney .25 .60
23 Rodney Rogers .25 .60
24 Shane Battier .40 1.00
25 Mike Miller .30 .75
26 John Stockton .50 1.25
27 Mengke Bateer .25 .60
28 Andre Miller .30 .75
29 Sam Cassell .30 .75
30 Anfernee Hardaway .60 1.50
31 Keith Van Horn .30 .75
32 Tony Battie .25 .60
33 Derek Fisher .30 .75
34 Grant Hill .50 1.25
35 Andrei Kirilenko .40 1.00
36 Toni Kukoc .40 1.00
37 Jerry Stackhouse .30 .75
38 Latrell Sprewell .30 .75

39 Morris Peterson .25 .60
40 Darius Miles .25 .60
41 Eddie Jones .30 .75
42 Stephon Marbury .30 .75
43 Brent Barry .25 .60
44 DeShawn Stevenson .25 .60
45 Brian Grant .25 .60
46 Derrick Coleman .30 .75
47 Richard Hamilton .30 .75
48 Jason Richardson .40 1.00
49 Kerry Kittles .25 .60
50 Desmond Mason .30 .75
51 Stromile Swift .25 .60
52 Richard Jefferson .40 1.00
53 Vladimir Radmanovic .25 .60
54 Lamond Murray .25 .60
55 Troy Murphy .30 .75
56 Kenyon Martin .30 .75
57 Vlade Divac .30 .75
58 Chris Mihm .25 .60
59 Eddie Griffin .25 .60
60 Marc Jackson .25 .60
61 Peja Stojakovic .40 1.00
62 Vin Baker .30 .75
63 Cuttino Mobley .25 .60
64 Joe Smith .30 .75
65 Damon Stoudamire .30 .75
66 Eddy Curry .25 .60
67 Alonzo Mourning .50 1.25
68 Aaron McKie .25 .60
69 Kwame Brown .25 .60
70 Raef LaFrentz .25 .60
71 Jermaine O'Neal .30 .75
72 Terrell Brandon .25 .60
73 Bonzi Wells .25 .60
74 Steve Nash .50 1.25
75 Jamaal Tinsley .25 .60
76 Wally Szczerbiak .30 .75
77 Scottie Pippen .60 1.50
78 Michael Finley .40 1.00
79 Reggie Miller .40 1.00
80 Glenn Robinson .30 .75
81 Rasheed Wallace .40 1.00
82 Antoine Walker .30 .75
83 Robert Horry .30 .75
84 Kurt Thomas .25 .60
85 Antonio Davis .25 .60
86 Nick Van Exel .30 .75
87 Al Harrington .30 .75
88 Tony Delk .25 .60
89 Joe Johnson .30 .75
90 Chauncey Billups .40 1.00
91 P.J. Brown .25 .60
92 Tony Parker .50 1.25
93 Antawn Jamison .40 1.00
94 Courtney Alexander .25 .60
95 Kenny Anderson .30 .75
96 Clifford Robinson .25 .60
97 Lamar Odom .30 .75
98 Anthony Carter .25 .60
99 Shawn Marion .30 .75
100 Hedo Turkoglu .30 .75
101 Paul Pierce AVANT 1.00 2.50
102 Dirk Nowitzki AVANT 1.50 4.00
103 Ben Wallace AVANT .75 2.00
104 Steve Francis AVANT .75 2.00
105 Pau Gasol AVANT 1.25 3.00
106 Ray Allen AVANT 1.00 2.50
107 Kevin Garnett AVANT 1.50 4.00
108 Jason Kidd AVANT 1.50 4.00
109 Baron Davis AVANT .75 2.00
110 Mike Bibby AVANT 1.00 2.50
111 Chris Webber AVANT 1.00 2.50
112 Tim Duncan AVANT 2.00 5.00
113 Kobe Bryant AVANT 6.00 15.00
114 Shaquille O'Neal AVANT 4.00 10.00
115 Tracy McGrady AVANT 2.50 6.00
116 Allen Iverson AVANT 2.50 6.00
117 Vince Carter AVANT 2.50 6.00
118 Elton Brand AVANT 1.50 4.00
119 Jay Williams AVANT RC 2.50 6.00
120 Yao Ming AVANT RC 5.00 12.00
121 Mike Dunleavy AVANT RC 2.50 6.00
122 DaJuan Wagner AVANT RC 2.00 5.00
123 Caron Butler AVANT RC 2.50 6.00
124 Drew Gooden AVANT RC 2.50 6.00
125 Manu Ginobili RC 5.00 12.00
126 Mehmet Okur RC 2.00 5.00
127 Nene Hilario RC 2.00 5.00
128 Nikoloz Tskitishvili RC 1.25 3.00
129 Tayshaun Prince RC 2.50 6.00
130 Bostjan Nachbar RC 1.50 4.00
131 Fred Jones RC 1.50 4.00
132 Melvin Ely RC 1.50 4.00
133 Chris Wilcox RC 1.50 4.00
134 Kareem Rush RC 1.50 4.00
135 Marcus Haislip RC 1.50 4.00
136 Frank Williams RC 1.25 3.00
137 Ryan Humphrey RC 1.50 4.00
138 John Salmons RC 2.00 5.00
139 Casey Jacobsen RC 1.50 4.00
140 Amare Stoudemire RC 2.50 6.00
141 Qyntel Woods RC 1.50 4.00
142 Chris Jefferies RC 1.25 3.00
143 Juan Dixon RC 2.00 5.00
144 Jared Jeffries RC 1.50 4.00
145 Lonny Baxter RC 1.25 3.00
146 Dan Dickau RC 1.50 4.00
147 Carlos Boozer RC 2.00 5.00
148 Vincent Yarbrough RC 1.25 3.00

2002-03 Fleer Showcase Legacy

*1-100 STARS: 5X TO 12X BASE CARD HI
PRINT RUN 100 SERIAL #'d SETS
*101-112 AVANT: 3X TO 8X BASE AVANT HI
*113-118 AVANT: 2X TO 5X BASE HI
*119-124 AVANT RCs: 1.5X TO 4X BASE HI
101-124 PRINT RUN 50 SER.#'d SETS
*125-148 RCs: 1.25X TO 3X BASE CARD HI
125-148 PRINT RUN 100 SER.#'d SETS
67 Alonzo Mourning 10.00 25.00
112 Tim Duncan AVANT 25.00 60.00

2002-03 Fleer Showcase Avant Card Materials

Randomly seeded in packs, this eight card set parallels the base Avant Card design enhanced with a swatch of jersey on the right side of the card. Each card is sequentially numbered to 202.
PRINT RUN 202 SERIAL #'d SETS
ACM1 Tracy McGrady 8.00 20.00
ACM2 Allen Iverson 8.00 20.00
ACM3 Vince Carter 8.00 20.00
ACM4 Elton Brand 5.00 12.00
ACM5 Yao Ming 10.00 25.00
ACM6 DaJuan Wagner 4.00 10.00
ACM7 Caron Butler 5.00 12.00
ACM8 Drew Gooden 5.00 12.00

2002-03 Fleer Showcase Avant Card SRO

Randomly seeded in packs, this 12-card set parallels the base Avant Card design enhanced with a full metallic gold background. Each card is sequentially numbered to 50, and the letters, "SRO" appear on the back of the card below the number rather than Row 2 or Row 0.
*SRO: 1.25X TO 3X BASE HI 6.00 15.00
PRINT RUN 50 SERIAL #'d SETS

2002-03 Fleer Showcase Basketball's Best

Randomly inserted in packs at the rate of one in eight, this 30-card set features a horizontal design where the background contains a colored wood effect towards the bottom, full color player action photos appear on the left, and the player's team logo appears in the upper right of the card. All cards have gray borders and silver foil highlights.
COMPLETE SET (30) 15.00 40.00
STATED ODDS 1:8
BB1 Vince Carter 1.00 2.50
BB2 Allen Iverson 1.00 2.50
BB3 Jason Kidd 1.00 2.50
BB4 Tracy McGrady 1.00 2.50
BB5 Ben Wallace .50 1.25
BB6 Baron Davis .50 1.25
BB7 Paul Pierce .60 1.50
BB8 Andre Miller .50 1.25
BB9 Jermaine O'Neal .50 1.25
BB10 Kevin Garnett 1.00 2.50
BB11 Pau Gasol .75 2.00
BB12 Dirk Nowitzki 1.00 2.50
BB13 Jason Terry .50 1.25
BB14 Tony Parker .75 2.00
BB15 Kobe Bryant 2.50 6.00
BB16 Mike Bibby .60 1.50
BB17 Steve Nash .75 2.00
BB18 Michael Jordan 5.00 12.00
BB19 Mike Miller .50 1.25
BB20 Kenyon Martin .50 1.25
BB21 Shareef Abdur-Rahim .50 1.25
BB22 Elton Brand .60 1.50
BB23 Grant Hill .75 2.00
BB24 Lamar Odom .50 1.25
BB25 Corey Maggette .50 1.25
BB26 Richard Jefferson .60 1.50
BB27 Keith Van Horn .50 1.25
BB28 Quentin Richardson .50 1.25
BB29 Andrei Kirilenko .60 1.50
BB30 Darius Miles .40 1.00

2002-03 Fleer Showcase Basketball's Best Memorabilia

Inserted in packs at the rate of one in 10, this 23-card set parallels the design of the base Basketball's Best insert but is enhanced with a swatch of game used memorabilia in the place of the team logo.
STATED ODDS 1:10
*GOLD: .75X TO 2X HI
GOLD: STATED PRINT RUN 100 SER.#'d SETS
BBM1 Vince Carter JSY 5.00 12.00
BBM2 Allen Iverson JSY 5.00 12.00
BBM3 Jason Kidd JSY 5.00 12.00
BBM4 Tracy McGrady Short 5.00 12.00
BBM5 Ben Wallace JSY 2.50 6.00
BBM6 Paul Pierce JSY 3.00 8.00
BBM7 Andre Miller JSY 2.50 6.00
BBM8 Jermaine O'Neal JSY 2.50 6.00
BBM9 Kevin Garnett JSY 5.00 12.00
BBM10 Jason Terry JSY 2.50 6.00
BBM11 Steve Nash JSY 4.00 10.00
BBM12 Mike Miller Short 2.50 6.00
BBM13 Kenyon Martin WU 2.50 6.00
BBM14 Shareef Abdur-Rahim Short 2.50 6.00
BBM15 Elton Brand WU 3.00 8.00
BBM16 Grant Hill Short 4.00 10.00
BBM17 Lamar Odom WU 2.50 6.00
BBM18 Corey Maggette WU 2.50 6.00
BBM19 Richard Jefferson WU 3.00 8.00
BBM20 Keith Van Horn WU 2.50 6.00
BBM21 Quentin Richardson JSY 2.50 6.00
BBM22 Andrei Kirilenko JSY 3.00 8.00
BBM23 Darius Miles Short 2.00 5.00
BAS1 Vince Carter AU/400 12.00 30.00

2002-03 Fleer Showcase Vince Carter Legacy Collection

Randomly inserted in packs, this 15-card set highlights the career of Vince Carter. Each card has brown borders, red banners along the top and bottom of the card, silver foil highlights, and sequential numbering to 1000.
COMPLETE SET (15) 20.00 50.00
COMMON CARD (VCL1-VCL15) 2.50 6.00
PRINT RUN 1000 SERIAL #'d SETS

2002-03 Fleer Showcase Vince Carter Legacy Collection Game-Worn

Randomly seeded in packs at the rate of one in 48, this three card set utilizes the same design but is enhanced with a piece of game memorabilia.
STATED ODDS 1:48
VCG1 Vince Carter Warm 8.00 20.00
VCG2 Vince Carter JSY 10.00 25.00

2003-04 Fleer Showcase

Released in August 2003, this 130-card set is divided up into 90 veteran player cards, 10 veteran shortprints (cards 91-100) where no odds were ever given, but appear to be approximately five times tougher than regular base cards and 30 rookies sequentially numbered to 1000. Base cards feature a background black and white portrait photo with a full-color action photo in the foreground and the player's number in the lower right corner. Showcase was packaged in 16-pack boxes of five cards each and carried a suggested retail price of $5.49.
COMP.SET w/o SP's (100) 15.00 40.00
101-130 PRINT RUN 1000 SER.#'d SETS
UNPRICED MASTERPIECE PRINT RUN ONE SET
1 Jason Richardson .50 1.25
2 Andrei Kirilenko .50 1.25
3 Steve Francis .40 1.00
4 Shareef Abdur-Rahim .40 1.00
5 Ben Wallace .40 1.00
6 Predrag Drobnjak .30 .75
7 Jalen Rose .40 1.00
8 Rashard Lewis .50 1.25
9 Darius Miles .30 .75
10 Bobby Jackson .30 .75
11 Steve Nash .60 1.50
12 Gilbert Arenas .40 1.00
13 Aaron McKie .30 .75
14 Reggie Miller .50 1.25
15 Elton Brand .50 1.25
16 Allan Houston .40 1.00
17 Pau Gasol .50 1.25
18 Jamaal Magloire .30 .75
19 Eddie Jones .40 1.00
20 Richard Jefferson .40 1.00
21 Wally Szczerbiak .40 1.00
22 Antonio McDyess .40 1.00
23 Michael Redd .50 1.25
24 Grant Hill .60 1.50
25 Jason Williams .40 1.00
26 Rasheed Wallace .50 1.25
27 Andre Miller .40 1.00
28 Peja Stojakovic .50 1.25
29 Cuttino Mobley .30 .75
30 David Robinson .75 2.00
31 Richard Hamilton .40 1.00
32 Morris Peterson .30 .75
33 Karl Malone .60 1.50
34 Zydrunas Ilgauskas .40 1.00
35 Jerry Stackhouse .40 1.00
36 Eddy Curry .30 .75
37 Sam Cassell .40 1.00
38 Troy Hudson .30 .75
39 Jason Terry .40 1.00
40 Kenyon Martin .40 1.00
41 Bonzi Wells .30 .75
42 Donnell Harvey .30 .75
43 Tracy McGrady .60 1.50
44 Allen Iverson .75 2.00
45 Jermaine O'Neal .40 1.00
46 Larry Hughes .40 1.00
47 Scottie Pippen .75 2.00
48 Antonio Davis .30 .75
49 Chris Webber .50 1.25
50 Vladimir Radmanovic .30 .75
51 Glenn Robinson .40 1.00
52 Antoine Walker .50 1.25
53 Ricky Davis .40 1.00
54 Michael Finley .50 1.25
55 Nick Van Exel .40 1.00
56 Tayshaun Prince .40 1.00
57 Antawn Jamison .40 1.00
58 Jamal Mashburn .40 1.00
59 Jamaal Tinsley .30 .75
60 Kerry Kittles .30 .75
61 Derek Fisher .40 1.00
62 Radoslav Nesterovic .30 .75
63 Mike Miller .40 1.00
64 Gary Payton .50 1.25
65 Brian Grant .30 .75
66 Baron Davis .40 1.00
67 Shane Battier .40 1.00
68 Latrell Sprewell .40 1.00
69 Keith Van Horn .40 1.00
70 Eddie Griffin .30 .75
71 Stephon Marbury .40 1.00
72 Chauncey Billups .50 1.25
73 Shawn Marion .40 1.00
74 Juwan Howard .40 1.00
75 Mike Bibby .50 1.25
76 DaJuan Wagner .30 .75
77 Tony Parker .50 1.25
78 Tyson Chandler .40 1.00
79 Ray Allen .50 1.25
80 Matt Harpring .30 .75
81 Kwame Brown .30 .75
82 Troy Murphy .30 .75
83 Ron Artest .50 1.25
84 Corey Maggette .40 1.00
85 Tony Delk .30 .75
86 Jamal Crawford .50 1.25
87 Vince Carter .75 2.00
88 Kevin Garnett .75 2.00
89 Jason Kidd .75 2.00
90 Paul Pierce .50 1.25
91 Nene SP 1.00 2.50
92 Drew Gooden SP 1.00 2.50
93 Caron Butler SP 1.00 2.50
94 Manu Ginobili SP 1.50 4.00
95 Dirk Nowitzki SP 2.00 5.00
96 Yao Ming SP 2.50 6.00
97 Amare Stoudemire SP 1.50 4.00
98 Kobe Bryant SP 5.00 12.00
99 Tim Duncan SP 2.00 5.00
100 Shaquille O'Neal SP 3.00 8.00
101 T.J. Ford RC 1.50 4.00
102 Chris Bosh RC 3.00 8.00
103 Boris Diaw RC 2.00 5.00
104 Luke Ridnour RC 1.50 4.00
105 Zoran Planinic RC 1.25 3.00
106 Josh Howard RC 2.00 5.00
107 Darko Milicic RC 1.50 4.00
108 Dahntay Jones RC 1.50 4.00
109 Mike Sweetney RC 1.25 3.00
110 Kirk Hinrich RC 2.00 5.00
111 Marcus Banks RC 1.25 3.00
112 Travis Outlaw RC 1.50 4.00
113 Brian Cook RC 1.25 3.00
114 Mario Austin RC 2.00 5.00
115 Dwyane Wade RC 6.00 15.00
116 Chris Kaman RC 2.00 5.00
117 Zarko Cabarkapa RC 1.25 3.00
118 Ndudi Ebi RC 1.25 3.00
119 Mickael Pietrus RC 1.50 4.00
120 Carmelo Anthony RC 6.00 15.00
121 Kendrick Perkins RC 1.50 4.00
122 Troy Bell RC 1.25 3.00
123 Maciej Lampe RC 1.25 3.00
124 Carlos Delfino RC 1.50 4.00
125 Leandro Barbosa RC 2.00 5.00
126 Sofoklis Schortsanitis RC 1.25 3.00
127 Reece Gaines RC 1.25 3.00
128 Nick Collison RC 1.50 4.00
129 David West RC 2.00 5.00
130 LeBron James RC 60.00 150.00

2003-04 Fleer Showcase Legacy

*LEGACY SINGLES: 2.5X TO 6X BASE HI
*LEGACY SPs: 1.25X TO 3X BASE HI
*LEGACY RCs: 1.25X TO 3X BASE HI
STATED PRINT RUN 125 SER.#'d SETS
98 Kobe Bryant 25.00 60.00
130 LeBron James 175.00 400.00

2003-04 Fleer Showcase Basketball's Best

Inserted in packs at the rate of one in 24, this 10-card set features a horizontal design with colored borders along the top and bottom and a white midde. Player black and white portraits appear on the left and a full color player action photo is centered.
COMPLETE SET (10) 8.00 20.00
STATED ODDS 1:24
1 Shaquille O'Neal 2.50 6.00
2 Amare Stoudemire 1.25 3.00
3 Jermaine O'Neal .75 2.00
4 Tim Duncan 1.50 4.00
5 Jason Richardson 1.00 2.50
6 Steve Francis .75 2.00
7 Ben Wallace .75 2.00
8 Chris Webber 1.00 2.50
9 DaJuan Wagner .60 1.50
10 Yao Ming 2.00 5.00

2003-04 Fleer Showcase Basketball's Best Memorabilia

Randomly seeded, this 25-card set parallels the design of the Basketball's Best insert enhanced with a circular swatch of jersey on the right side of the card. A gold version was also inserted and these cards are sequentially numbered to 50.
STATED PRINT RUN 375 SER. #'d SETS
*GOLD: 1.25X TO 3X BEST MEM.HI
GOLD PRINT RUN 50 SER.#'d SETS
1 Yao Ming 5.00 12.00
2 Steve Francis 2.00 5.00
3 Amare Stoudemire 3.00 8.00
4 Elton Brand 2.50 6.00
5 Paul Pierce 2.50 6.00
6 Tracy McGrady 3.00 8.00
7 Allen Iverson 4.00 10.00
8 Dirk Nowitzki 4.00 10.00
9 Antawn Jamison 2.00 5.00
10 Drew Gooden 2.00 5.00
11 DaJuan Wagner 2.00 5.00
12 David Robinson 4.00 10.00
13 Jermaine O'Neal 2.00 5.00
14 Stephon Marbury 2.00 5.00
15 Kevin Garnett 4.00 10.00
16 Jason Kidd 4.00 10.00
17 Vince Carter 4.00 10.00
18 Karl Malone 3.00 8.00
19 Tony Parker 2.50 6.00
20 Peja Stojakovic 2.50 6.00
21 Reggie Miller 2.50 6.00
22 Jason Richardson 2.50 6.00
23 Ray Allen 2.50 6.00
24 Jerry Stackhouse 2.00 5.00
25 Latrell Sprewell 2.00 5.00

2003-04 Fleer Showcase Hot Hands

Inserted at the rate of one in 288, this 10-card set places a full-color player action photo against the backdrop of a player's hands around an NBA basketball.
COMPLETE SET (10) 20.00 40.00
STATED ODDS 1:288
1 Tracy McGrady 3.00 8.00
2 Kobe Bryant 10.00 25.00
3 Allen Iverson 4.00 10.00
4 Dirk Nowitzki 4.00 10.00
5 Jason Kidd 4.00 10.00
6 Vince Carter 4.00 10.00
7 Steve Francis 2.00 5.00
8 Paul Pierce 2.50 6.00
9 Jason Richardson 2.50 6.00
10 Amare Stoudemire 3.00 8.00

2003-04 Fleer Showcase Hot Hands Game-Used

STATED PRINT RUN 375 SER. #'d SETS
1 Tracy McGrady 4.00 10.00
2 Allen Iverson 5.00 12.00
3 Dirk Nowitzki 5.00 12.00
4 Jason Kidd 5.00 12.00
5 Vince Carter 5.00 12.00
6 Jerry Stackhouse 2.50 6.00
7 Paul Pierce 3.00 8.00
8 Stephon Marbury 2.50 6.00
9 Steve Francis 2.50 6.00
10 Peja Stojakovic 3.00 8.00
11 Caron Butler 2.50 6.00
12 Reggie Miller 3.00 8.00
13 Jason Richardson 3.00 8.00
14 Ray Allen 3.00 8.00
15 Amare Stoudemire 4.00 10.00

2003-04 Fleer Showcase Sweet Sigs

Randomly seeded and sequentially numbered, this 18-card set features a horizontal design with a small player portrait style photo in the upper right hand corner of the card and a centered embedded cut signature.
PRINT RUNS LISTED BELOW
SGAM Amare Stoudemire/300 6.00 15.00
SGBC Brian Cook/800 2.50 6.00
SGCA Carmelo Anthony/400 12.00 30.00
SGEC Eddy Curry/540 2.50 6.00
SGJO J.O'Neal/760 6.00 15.00
SGKB Kwame Brown/390 4.00 10.00
SGKM Kenyon Martin/690 3.00 8.00
SGMG Manu Ginobili/555 10.00 25.00
SGMP Mickael Pietrus/800 3.00 8.00
SGMS Mike Sweetney/800 2.50 6.00
SGPS Peja Stojakovic/760 6.00 15.00
SGSA S.Abdur-Rahim/760 4.00 10.00
SGSF Steve Francis/760 6.00 15.00
SGTB Troy Bell/800 2.50 6.00
SGTJ Dahntay Jones/800 3.00 8.00
SGTM Tracy McGrady/380 12.50 30.00
SGTP Tayshaun Prince/760 3.00 8.00

2003-04 Fleer Showcase Sweet Stitch

Inserted in packs at the rate of one in 12, this 10-card set features a centered full-color player portrait style photo framed by an NBA Basketball background.
COMPLETE SET (10) 6.00 15.00
STATED ODDS 1:12
1 Yao Ming 1.25 3.00
2 Kevin Garnett 1.00 2.50
3 Kobe Bryant 2.50 6.00
4 Elton Brand .60 1.50
5 DaJuan Wagner .40 1.00
6 Karl Malone .75 2.00
7 Antawn Jamison .50 1.25
8 Stephon Marbury .50 1.25
9 Michael Finley .60 1.50
10 Drew Gooden .50 1.25
11 David Robinson 1.00 2.50

2003-04 Fleer Showcase Sweet Stitch Game-Used

Inserted in packs randomly at the rate of one in 13, this 10-card set parallels the design of the base Sweet Stitch insert set enhanced with a skinny rectangular jersey swatch below the picture. A patch version was also inserted and is sequentially numbered to 50.
STATED ODDS 1:31
*PATCHES: 1.25X TO 3X GAME USE HI
PATCH PRINT RUN 50 SER.#'d SETS
1 Yao Ming 5.00 12.00
2 Kevin Garnett 4.00 10.00
4 Elton Brand 2.50 6.00
5 DaJuan Wagner 2.00 5.00
6 Karl Malone 3.00 8.00
7 Antawn Jamison 2.00 5.00
8 Stephon Marbury 2.00 5.00
9 Michael Finley 2.50 6.00
10 Drew Gooden 2.00 5.00

2004-05 Fleer Showcase

Released in August 2004, Fleer Showcase's base set consists of 120 cards, where cards 1-90 feature veteran players anc cards 91-120 feature rookies that are randomly numbered to either 199, 499 or 699. Base cards are printed on foil board and feature a head-shot photo of the player in the background and a full-color action photo in the foreground. Flair was packaged in both Hobby and Retail formats with Hobby boxes containing 16 packs of five cards each and retail containing 24 packs of four cards each.
COMP.SET w/o SP's (90) 15.00 40.00
UNPRICED MASTERPIECE PRINT RUN ONE SET
1 Kirk Hinrich .25 .60
2 Shaquille O'Neal .75 2.00
3 Allen Iverson .50 1.25
4 Carlos Arroyo .20 .50
5 Darko Milicic .20 .50
6 Sam Cassell .25 .60
7 Peja Stojakovic .30 .75
8 Ben Wallace .25 .60
9 T.J. Ford .20 .50
10 Chris Webber .30 .75
11 LeBron James 2.00 5.00
12 Karl Malone .40 1.00
13 Glenn Robinson .25 .60
14 Jarvis Hayes .20 .50
15 Bob Sura .20 .50
16 Yao Ming .60 1.50
17 Baron Davis .25 .60
18 Rashard Lewis .30 .75
19 Carlos Boozer .25 .60
20 Pau Gasol .30 .75
21 Tim Duncan .50 1.25
22 Gilbert Arenas .25 .60
23 Dajuan Wagner .20 .50
24 Bonzi Wells .20 .50
25 Dirk Nowitzki .50 1.25
26 Jason Williams .25 .60
27 Amare Stoudemire .25 .60
28 Gerald Wallace .25 .60
29 Corey Maggette .25 .60
30 Tim Thomas .20 .50
31 Andrei Kirilenko .25 .60
32 Steve Nash .40 1.00
33 Caron Butler .25 .60
34 Shawn Marion .25 .60
35 Michael Finley .30 .75
36 Dwyane Wade .50 1.25
37 Joe Johnson .25 .60
38 Carmelo Anthony .60 1.50
39 Lamar Odom .25 .60
40 Darius Miles .20 .50
41 Mike Dunleavy .25 .60
42 Jason Kidd .50 1.25
43 Manu Ginobili .40 1.00
44 Jason Richardson .30 .75
45 Latrell Sprewell .25 .60
46 Willie Green .20 .50
47 Theron Smith .20 .50
48 Elton Brand .30 .75
49 Tracy McGrady .40 1.00
50 Matt Harpring .20 .50
51 Eddy Curry .20 .50
52 Chris Kaman .25 .60
53 Drew Gooden .20 .50
54 Stephen Jackson .25 .60
55 Mickael Pietrus .25 .60
56 Kenyon Martin .25 .60
57 Tony Parker .30 .75
58 Paul Pierce .30 .75
59 Cuttino Mobley .20 .50
60 Jamal Mashburn .25 .60
61 Luke Ridnour .25 .60
62 Jamal Crawford .30 .75
63 Kobe Bryant 1.25 3.00
64 Keith Bogans .20 .50
65 Jerry Stackhouse .25 .60
66 Ricky Davis .25 .60
67 Jermaine O'Neal .25 .60
68 Jamaal Magloire .20 .50
69 Vince Carter .50 1.25
70 Jason Kapono .20 .50
71 Ron Artest .30 .75
72 Allan Houston .25 .60
73 Chris Bosh .30 .75
74 Rasheed Wallace .30 .75
75 Kevin Garnett .50 1.25
76 Mike Bibby .30 .75
77 Jason Terry .25 .60
78 Steve Francis .25 .60
79 Richard Jefferson .25 .60
80 Ray Allen .30 .75
81 Andre Miller .25 .60
82 Desmond Mason .25 .60
83 Zach Randolph .25 .60
84 Marcus Banks .20 .50
85 Reggie Miller .30 .75
86 Stephon Marbury .25 .60
87 Jalen Rose .25 .60
88 Nene .25 .60
89 Michael Redd .25 .60
90 Shareef Abdur-Rahim .25 .60
91 Emeka Okafor/199 RC 4.00 10.00
92 Jameer Nelson/199 RC 5.00 12.00
93 Dwight Howard/199 RC 10.00 25.00
94 Josh Smith/199 RC 5.00 12.00
95 Pavel Podkolzin/699 RC 1.25 3.00
96 Shaun Livingston/199 RC 5.00 12.00
97 Andre Iguodala/199 RC 6.00 15.00
98 Luol Deng/199 RC 5.00 12.00
99 Delonte West/699 RC 2.00 5.00
100 Andris Biedrins/699 RC 1.25 3.00
101 Sasha Vujacic/499 RC 2.50 6.00
102 Kris Humphries/499 RC 2.50 6.00
103 Ben Gordon/199 RC 5.00 12.00
104 Robert Swift/499 RC 1.50 4.00
105 Al Jefferson/499 RC 3.00 8.00
106 Sergei Monia/499 RC 1.50 4.00
107 Devin Harris/499 RC 2.00 5.00
108 Luke Jackson/499 RC 1.50 4.00
109 Anderson Varejao/499 RC 2.00 5.00
110 Sebastian Telfair/199 RC 4.00 10.00
111 Josh Childress/199 RC 4.00 10.00
112 J.R. Smith/499 RC 2.50 6.00
113 Viktor Khryapa/699 RC 1.25 3.00
114 Rafael Araujo/499 RC 1.50 4.00
115 Dorell Wright/499 RC 2.50 6.00
116 Ha Seung-Jin/699 RC 2.00 5.00
117 Tony Allen/699 RC 2.00 5.00
118 Kirk Snyder/699 RC 1.25 3.00
119 Chris Duhon/699 RC 2.00 5.00
120 Beno Udrih/699 RC 1.50 4.00

2004-05 Fleer Showcase Legacy

*LEGACY SINGLES: 4X TO 10X BASE HI
*RC/199: .3X TO .75X BASE CARD HI
*RC/499: .6X TO 1.5X BASE CARD HI
*RC/699: .75X TO 2X BASE CARD HI
PRINT RUN 125 SER.#'d SETS
11 LeBron James 30.00 80.00
63 Kobe Bryant 30.00 60.00

2004-05 Fleer Showcase Feature Film

Inserted in packs, this 15-card set is horizontally designed with a white background on the left and a film cell of the player on the right. Each card is sequentially numbered to 50. Two patch parallels were also issued for this set. Both feature premium jersey patch swatches with one serially numbered to 25 and the other numbered to 10.
PRINT RUN 50 SER.#'d SETS
PATCH PRINT RUN 25 SER.#'d SETS
1 Allen Iverson 12.00 30.00
2 Kobe Bryant 30.00 80.00
3 Vince Carter 12.00 30.00
4 Kevin Garnett 12.00 30.00
5 LeBron James 50.00 125.00
6 Carmelo Anthony 15.00 40.00
7 Tracy McGrady 10.00 25.00
8 Shaquille O'Neal 20.00 50.00
9 Tim Duncan 12.00 30.00
10 Yao Ming 15.00 40.00
11 Jason Kidd 12.00 30.00
12 Karl Malone 10.00 25.00
13 Amare Stoudemire 6.00 15.00
14 Chris Bosh 8.00 20.00
15 Ray Allen 8.00 20.00

2004-05 Fleer Showcase Hot Hands

Seeded in Hobby packs at the rate of one in 192 and Retail at the rate of one in 480, this 15-card set is die cut in the shape of a flame where full-color player action photos are centered.
STATED ODDS 1:192 H, 1:480 R
*PATCH: .5X TO 1.25X BASE HI
PATCH PRINT RUN 50 SER.#'d SETS
UNPRICED PATCH PAR.PRINT RUN 15 SETS
1 Yao Ming 25.00 60.00
2 Shaquille O'Neal 40.00 100.00
3 LeBron James 300.00 600.00
4 Carmelo Anthony 25.00 60.00
5 Dwyane Wade 20.00 50.00
6 Vince Carter 20.00 50.00
7 Kobe Bryant 150.00 300.00
8 Tim Duncan 25.00 60.00
9 Baron Davis 10.00 25.00
10 Manu Ginobili 20.00 50.00
11 Ron Artest 12.00 30.00
12 Ben Wallace 10.00 25.00
13 Andrei Kirilenko 10.00 25.00
14 Mike Bibby 12.00 30.00
15 Allen Iverson 30.00 80.00

2004-05 Fleer Showcase Playmakers

Inserted in packs at the rate of one in four for Hobby and one in eight for Retail, this 20-card set features a gray background, colors to match the player's team along the bottom and lower left and right sides and an action photo.
COMPLETE SET (20) 10.00 25.00
STATED ODDS 1:4 H, 1:8 R
1 Jermaine O'Neal .40 1.00
2 Gary Payton .50 1.25
3 Kenyon Martin .40 1.00
4 Tony Parker .50 1.25
5 Chris Bosh .50 1.25
6 Dwyane Wade .75 2.00
7 Ben Wallace .40 1.00
8 Jason Kidd .75 2.00
9 Tracy McGrady .60 1.50
10 Kevin Garnett .75 2.00
11 Kobe Bryant 2.00 5.00
12 LeBron James 3.00 8.00
13 Paul Pierce .50 1.25
14 Stephon Marbury .40 1.00
15 Manu Ginobili .60 1.50
16 Amare Stoudemire .40 1.00
17 Reggie Miller .50 1.25
18 Dirk Nowitzki .75 2.00
19 Jason Richardson .50 1.25
20 Steve Francis .40 1.00

2004-05 Fleer Showcase Playmakers Jerseys

Inserted in Hobby packs at the rate of one in 96 and Retail packs at the rate of one in 26, this 18-card set parallels the Playmakers set enhanced with a jersey swatch in the lower left hand corner. Four parallel sets were issued, a Jersey version featuring silver foil and sequential numbering to 300, a Jersey version featuring gold foil and sequential numbering to 100 and a Jeresy version featuring a name plate swatch and sequential numbering to 50. There is also a one of one masterpiece.
STATED ODDS 1:96 H, 1:26 R
*JERSEY 300: .5X TO 1.25X BASE JSY HI
*JERSEY 100: .6X TO 1.5X BASE JSY HI
AS Amare Stoudemire 2.00 5.00
BW Ben Wallace 2.00 5.00
CB Chris Bosh 2.50 6.00
DN Dirk Nowitzki 4.00 10.00
DW Dwyane Wade 4.00 10.00
GP Gary Payton 2.50 6.00
JK Jason Kidd 4.00 10.00
JO Jermaine O'Neal 2.00 5.00
JR Jason Richardson 2.50 6.00
KG Kevin Garnett 4.00 10.00
KM Kenyon Martin 2.00 5.00
MG Manu Ginobili 3.00 8.00
PP Paul Pierce 2.50 6.00
RM Reggie Miller 2.50 6.00
SF Steve Francis 2.00 5.00
SM Stephon Marbury 2.00 5.00
TM Tracy McGrady 3.00 8.00
TP Tony Parker 2.50 6.00

2004-05 Fleer Showcase Playmakers Jerseys Nameplates

*NAMEPLATE: 1X TO 2.5X BASE JSY HI
PRINT RUN 50 SER.#'d SETS
RM Reggie Miller 10.00 25.00

2004-05 Fleer Showcase Playmakers Jerseys Numbers

STATED PRINT RUN ONE TO 41 SETS
SOME NOT PRICED DUE TO SCARCITY
AS Amare Stoudemire/32 15.00 40.00
DN Dirk Nowitzki/41 10.00 25.00
GP Gary Payton/20 10.00 25.00
JR Jason Richardson/23 10.00 25.00
MG Manu Ginobili/20 10.00 25.00
PP Paul Pierce/34 10.00 25.00
RM Reggie Miller/31 12.50 30.00

2004-05 Fleer Showcase Playmakers Jerseys Win Total

STATED PRINT RUN 21 TO 61 SETS
AS Amare Stoudemire/29 4.00 10.00
BW Ben Wallace/54 4.00 10.00
CB Chris Bosh/33 5.00 12.00
DN Dirk Nowitzki/52 8.00 20.00
DW Dwyane Wade/42 8.00 20.00
GP Gary Payton/56 5.00 12.00
JK Jason Kidd/47 8.00 20.00
JO Jermaine O'Neal/61 4.00 10.00
JR Jason Richardson/37 5.00 12.00
KG Kevin Garnett/58 8.00 20.00
KM Kenyon Martin/47 4.00 10.00
MG Manu Ginobili/57 6.00 15.00
PP Paul Pierce/36 5.00 12.00
RM Reggie Miller/61 5.00 12.00
SF Steve Francis/45 4.00 10.00
SM Stephon Marbury/39 4.00 10.00
TM Tracy McGrady/21 6.00 15.00
TP Tony Parker/57 5.00 12.00

2004-05 Fleer Showcase Signatures

Randomly inserted, this set is horizontally designed with a player photo on the left above a cut signature. Silver foil lines run along a strip through the middle of the card, and these are sequentially numbered to 150 unless noted in the checklist. A Blue foil parallel was also issued, in which cards are sequentially numbered to either 75 or 99.
PRINT RUN 71 TO 150 SER.#'d SETS
*BLUE: .5X TO 1.25X BASE SIG HI
BLUE PRINT RUN 75 TO 99 SETS
AM Andre Miller/150 4.00 10.00
AV Anderson Varejao/150 3.00 8.00
BG Ben Gordon/150 10.00 25.00
CA Carmelo Anthony/150 15.00 40.00
CB Carlos Boozer/150 4.00 10.00
CD Carlos Delfino/150 2.50 6.00
CD Chris Duhon/150 4.00 10.00
CM Corey Maggette/150 4.00 10.00
DH Devin Harris/150 3.00 8.00
DM Darius Miles/150 4.00 10.00
DW Dwyane Wade/150 30.00 80.00
DW2 Dorell Wright/150 4.00 10.00
DW3 David West/150 4.00 10.00
GP Gary Payton/112 10.00 25.00
HS Ha Seung-Jin/150 4.00 10.00
JC Josh Childress/150 3.00 8.00
JH Josh Howard/150 4.00 10.00
JK Jason Kidd/150 10.00 25.00
JN Jameer Nelson/150 8.00 20.00
JO Jermaine O'Neal/150 6.00 15.00
JS Josh Smith/150 12.50 30.00
JS Jerry Stackhouse/150 4.00 10.00
KB Kwame Brown/150 4.00 10.00
KH Kris Humphries/150 4.00 10.00
KS Kirk Snyder/150 2.50 6.00
LD Luol Deng/150 8.00 20.00
LJ Luke Jackson/150 2.50 6.00
LO Lamar Odom/150 5.00 12.00
MB Mike Bibby/150 5.00 12.00
PP Pavel Podkolzin/150 2.50 6.00
PS Peja Stojakovic/100 8.00 20.00
RA Rafael Araujo/150 2.50 6.00
SL Shaun Livingston/150 4.00 10.00
SM Shawn Marion/150 6.00 15.00
ST Sebastian Telfair/150 3.00 8.00
TB Troy Bell/150 4.00 10.00
TP Tony Parker/71 6.00 15.00
VC Vince Carter/150 12.00 30.00
CBO Chris Bosh/150 6.00 15.00
DJW Dajuan Wagner/150 4.00 10.00
JRS J.R. Smith/150 10.00 25.00

2004-05 Fleer Showcase Signatures Jerseys

PRINT RUNS LISTED BELOW
SOME UNPRICED DUE TO SCARCITY
UNPRICED PATCH PRINT RUN ONE SET
AS Amare Stoudemire/32 20.00 50.00
CA Carmelo Anthony/15 40.00 100.00
DM Darius Miles/23 10.00 25.00
GP Gary Payton/20 25.00 60.00
JS Jerry Stackhouse/42 10.00 25.00
SM Shawn Marion/31 12.50 30.00

2004-05 Fleer Showcase Supreme Showcase

Inserted in Hobby packs at the rate of one in 16 and Retail packs at the rate of one in 24, this 24-card set utilizes a design similar to that of the Signatures set.
COMPLETE SET (20) 10.00 25.00
STATED ODDS 1:16 H, 1:24 R
1 Carmelo Anthony 1.25 3.00
2 Yao Ming 1.25 3.00
3 Carlos Boozer .50 1.25
4 Vince Carter 1.00 2.50
5 Dwyane Wade 1.00 2.50
6 Dirk Nowitzki 1.00 2.50
7 Josh Howard .60 1.50
8 Steve Francis .50 1.25
9 Paul Pierce .60 1.50
10 Amare Stoudemire .50 1.25
11 Peja Stojakovic .60 1.50
12 Shaquille O'Neal 1.50 4.00
13 Tim Duncan 1.00 2.50
14 Kevin Garnett 1.00 2.50
15 Stephon Marbury .50 1.25
16 Tracy McGrady .75 2.00
17 Allen Iverson 1.00 2.50
18 Ray Allen .60 1.50
19 Ben Wallace .50 1.25
20 Jason Kidd 1.00 2.50

2004-05 Fleer Showcase Supreme Showcase Jerseys

Randomly inserted in packs, this 20-card set parallels the base Supreme Showcase set enhanced with a swatch of jersey and sequential numbering to 300. Several different parallel versions were produced for this set: Jerseys numbered to 100, All-Star numbered to 45, All-Star patches numbered to 10 and master piece one of ones.
PRINT RUN 300 SER.#'d SETS
*JERSEY 100: .5X TO 1.25X BASE JSY HI
*JERSEY ALL-STAR: .6X TO 1.5X BASE JSY HI
ALL-STAR PRINT RUN 45 SER.#'d SETS
*JERSEY POINTS: .6X TO 1.5X BASE HI
POINTS PRINT RUN 19 TO 62 SETS
AI Allen Iverson 4.00 10.00
AS Amare Stoudemire 2.00 5.00
BW Ben Wallace 2.00 5.00
CA Carmelo Anthony 5.00 12.00
CB Carlos Boozer 2.00 5.00
DN Dirk Nowitzki 4.00 10.00
DW Dwyane Wade 4.00 10.00
JH Josh Howard 2.50 6.00
JK Jason Kidd 4.00 10.00
KG Kevin Garnett 4.00 10.00
PP Paul Pierce 2.50 6.00
PS Peja Stojakovic 2.50 6.00
RA Ray Allen 2.50 6.00
SF Steve Francis 2.00 5.00
SM Stephon Marbury 2.00 5.00
SO Shaquille O'Neal 6.00 15.00
TD Tim Duncan 4.00 10.00
TM Tracy McGrady 3.00 8.00
VC Vince Carter 4.00 10.00
YM Yao Ming 5.00 12.00

2004-05 Fleer Showcase Supreme Showcase Jerseys Numbers

*NUMBER PATCH: 1X TO 2.5X BASE HI
STATED PRINT RUN ONE TO 41 SETS
SOME NOT PRICED DUE TO SCARCITY
AS Amare Stoudemire/32 5.00 12.00
DN Dirk Nowitzki/41 10.00 25.00
KG Kevin Garnett/21 10.00 25.00
PP Paul Pierce/34 6.00 15.00
RA Ray Allen/34 10.00 25.00
SO Shaquille O'Neal/32 15.00 40.00
VC Vince Carter/15 10.00 25.00

1996-97 Fleer Sprite

This 40-card set was issued as a dual promotion for Fleer/SkyBox and Sprite available exclusively through

7-Eleven convenience stores. For a limited time, with each purchase of Sprite customers received a free pack containing 3 cards from the set along with a checklist (with Grant Hill on the front) and a $.25 coupon on any Fleer or SkyBox product. Randomly inserted was a 10-card Hill tribute set that is listed after the base set. The cards are identical to the 1996-97 Fleer design, except the gold foil text is in yellow and the numbering is different on the back. Notable first year cards of Allen Iverson, Kobe Bryant, Stephon Marbury, Antoine Walker, Shareef Abdur-Rahim and Kerry Kittles.

COMPLETE SET (40) 15.00 40.00
1 Dikembe Mutombo .60 1.50
2 Steve Smith .50 1.25
3 Antoine Walker 1.00 2.50
4 Anthony Mason .40 1.00
5 Toni Kukoc .60 1.50
6 Terrell Brandon .40 1.00
7 Jim Jackson .40 1.00
8 Jason Kidd 1.00 2.50
9 Oliver Miller .40 1.00
10 Antonio McDyess .60 1.50
11 Grant Hill 1.00 2.50
12 Joe Smith .50 1.25
13 Charles Barkley 1.00 2.50
14 Clyde Drexler .75 2.00
15 Reggie Miller .75 2.00
16 Brent Barry .50 1.25
17 Kobe Bryant 5.00 12.00
18 Nick Van Exel .60 1.50
19 Alonzo Mourning .75 2.00
20 Ray Allen 2.50 6.00
21 Vin Baker .50 1.25
22 Kevin Garnett 1.50 4.00
23 Stephon Marbury 1.50 4.00
24 Kerry Kittles .60 1.50
25 Patrick Ewing .75 2.00
26 Larry Johnson .60 1.50
27 Anfernee Hardaway 1.00 2.50
28 Allen Iverson 3.00 8.00
29 Arvydas Sabonis .50 1.25
30 Mitch Richmond .60 1.50
31 Vinny Del Negro .40 1.00
32 Gary Payton .60 1.50
33 Detlef Schrempf .60 1.50
34 Marcus Camby 1.00 2.50
35 Damon Stoudamire .50 1.25
36 Karl Malone .75 2.00
37 John Stockton .75 2.00
38 Shareef Abdur-Rahim 1.00 2.50
39 Juwan Howard .50 1.25
40 Chris Webber .75 2.00
NNO Grant Hill Checklist .40 1.00

1996-97 Fleer Sprite Grant Hill

Randomly inserted into packs of Fleer Sprite, this 10-card set features action shots of Fleer/SkyBox Spokesman Grant Hill. The fronts dawn the Fleer/SkyBox logo in the upper-left corner and Sprite and NBA logos in the bottom-left. Card backs have "Grant Hill Special Issue" in yellow letters at the top followed by themed biographical information. The cards are numbered as "X of 10".

COMPLETE SET (10) 4.00 10.00
COMMON CARD (1-10) .60 1.50

1996-97 Fleer Sprite Australian

This 40 card set is very similar to the 96-97 Fleer Sprite issue. The cards were released with Sprite and other than numbering differences are the same as the American Fleer issue.

COMPLETE SET (40) 40.00 80.00
1 Kenny Anderson 1.50 4.00
2 Chris Mills 1.25 3.00
3 Antonio McDyess 2.00 5.00
4 Joe Smith 1.50 4.00
5 Vin Baker 1.50 4.00
6 Ed O'Bannon 1.25 3.00
7 Anfernee Hardaway 3.00 8.00
8 Kevin Johnson 2.00 5.00
9 Mitch Richmond 2.00 5.00
10 Detlef Schrempf 2.00 5.00
11 John Stockton 2.50 6.00
12 Glen Rice 2.00 5.00
13 Clyde Drexler 2.50 6.00
14 Vlade Divac 2.00 5.00
15 Derek Harper 1.50 4.00
16 Charles Barkley 3.00 8.00
17 Hersey Hawkins 1.25 3.00
18 Karl Malone 2.50 6.00
19 Chris Webber 2.50 6.00
20 Alonzo Mourning 2.50 6.00
21 Clarence Weatherspoon 1.25 3.00
22 Dino Radja 1.25 3.00
23 Scottie Pippen 3.00 8.00
24 Jason Kidd 3.00 8.00
25 Grant Hill 3.00 8.00
26 Sam Cassell 1.50 4.00
27 Brian Williams 1.25 3.00
28 Tom Gugliotta 1.25 3.00
29 John Starks 1.50 4.00
30 Clifford Robinson 1.25 3.00
31 David Robinson 3.00 8.00
32 Damon Stoudamire 1.50 4.00
33 Greg Anthony 1.25 3.00
34 Toni Kukoc 2.00 5.00
35 Christian Laettner 1.50 4.00
36 Rik Smits 1.50 4.00
37 Tim Hardaway 2.00 5.00
38 Nick Anderson 1.25 3.00
39 Sean Elliott 2.00 5.00
40 Juwan Howard 1.50 4.00

2004-05 Fleer Sweet Sigs

Released in October 2004, the Sweet Sigs base showcases veteran players on cards 1-75 and rookies on cards 76-100 which are sequentially numbered to 999. Base cards feature a centered action photo with tan borders and red highlights. Sweet Sigs also marks the first product with Shaquille O'Neal in a Miami Heat jersey. Sweet Sigs was packaged for bot Hobby and retail where both featured six cards per pack, but hobby boxes had 12 packs and retail boxes had 24.

COMP.SET w/o SP's (75) 15.00 40.00
76-100 RC PRINT RUN 999 SER.#'d SETS
1 Kirk Hinrich .25 .60
2 Ron Artest .30 .75
3 T.J. Ford .20 .50
4 Stephon Marbury .25 .60
5 Antawn Jamison .25 .60
6 Jason Richardson .30 .75
7 Dwyane Wade .50 1.25
8 Shawn Marion .25 .60
9 Jermaine O'Neal .25 .60
10 Ricky Davis .25 .60
11 Richard Hamilton .25 .60
12 Karl Malone .40 1.00
13 Jason Williams .25 .60
14 Lamar Odom .25 .60
15 Allan Houston .25 .60
16 Allen Iverson .50 1.25
17 Peja Stojakovic .30 .75
18 Jarvis Hayes .20 .50
19 Stephen Jackson .25 .60
20 Richard Jefferson .25 .60
21 Jahidi White .20 .50
22 Carmelo Anthony .60 1.50
23 Baron Davis .25 .60
24 Dajuan Wagner .20 .50
25 Nene .25 .60
26 Ben Wallace .25 .60
27 Latrell Sprewell .25 .60
28 Ray Allen .30 .75
29 Andrei Kirilenko .25 .60
30 Antoine Walker .30 .75
31 Marcus Banks .20 .50
32 Pau Gasol .30 .75
33 Tony Parker .30 .75
34 Vince Carter .50 1.25
35 Mike Bibby .30 .75
36 Jim Jackson .20 .50
37 Shaquille O'Neal .75 2.00
38 Bonzi Wells .20 .50
39 Paul Pierce .30 .75
40 Jason Kapono .20 .50
41 Reggie Miller .30 .75
42 Drew Gooden .20 .50
43 Shareef Abdur-Rahim .25 .60
44 Chris Bosh .30 .75
45 Steve Nash .40 1.00
46 Elton Brand .30 .75
47 Kevin Garnett .50 1.25
48 Kenyon Martin .25 .60
49 Jamal Crawford .30 .75
50 Dirk Nowitzki .50 1.25
51 Yao Ming .60 1.50
52 Jamaal Magloire .20 .50
53 Tim Duncan .50 1.25
54 Gilbert Arenas .25 .60
55 Steve Francis .25 .60
56 Corey Maggette .25 .60
57 Caron Butler .25 .60
58 Michael Redd .25 .60
59 Kyle Korver .25 .60
60 Amare Stoudemire .25 .60
61 Carlos Boozer .25 .60
62 Darko Milicic .20 .50
63 Kobe Bryant 1.25 3.00
64 Tracy McGrady .40 1.00
65 Zach Randolph .25 .60
66 Luke Ridnour .25 .60
67 Carlos Arroyo .20 .50
68 Michael Finley .30 .75
69 Mickael Pietrus .25 .60
70 Darius Miles .20 .50
71 Chris Webber .30 .75
72 Eddy Curry .20 .50
73 Jason Kidd .50 1.25
74 Manu Ginobili .40 1.00
75 LeBron James 2.00 5.00
76 Emeka Okafor RC 1.25 3.00
77 Rafael Araujo RC 1.00 2.50
78 Andre Iguodala RC 2.00 5.00
79 Kris Humphries RC 1.50 4.00
80 Kevin Martin RC 2.00 5.00
81 Delonte West RC 1.50 4.00
82 Pavel Podkolzin RC 1.00 2.50
83 Al Jefferson RC 2.00 5.00
84 Shaun Livingston RC 1.50 4.00
85 Luke Jackson RC 1.00 2.50
86 Dorell Wright RC 1.50 4.00
87 Andris Biedrins RC 1.00 2.50
88 Sasha Vujacic RC 1.50 4.00
89 Jameer Nelson RC 1.50 4.00
90 Dwight Howard RC 3.00 8.00
91 Robert Swift RC 1.00 2.50
92 Josh Childress RC 1.25 3.00
93 Luol Deng RC 1.50 4.00
94 J.R. Smith RC 1.50 4.00
95 Kirk Snyder RC 1.00 2.50
96 Josh Smith RC 1.50 4.00
97 Devin Harris RC 1.25 3.00
98 Viktor Khryapa RC 1.00 2.50
99 Ben Gordon RC 1.50 4.00
100 Sebastian Telfair RC 1.25 3.00

2004-05 Fleer Sweet Sigs Parallel

*1-75 PAR.SINGLES: 2X TO 5X BASE HI
*76-100 PAR.RC's: 1X TO 2X BASE HI
PRINT RUN 99 SER.#'d SETS
POSITION PARALLEL SER.#'d

2004-05 Fleer Sweet Sigs Autographs

Randomly seeded, this 51-card set is horizontally designed with white borders and a clouded sky background. A small oval with a player portrait photo above a signed swatch of basketball. Each card is individually numbered with print runs listed in the checklist. Masterpiece one of ones were inserted also.

STATED PRINT RUN 50 TO 200 SETS
N Nene/200 4.00 10.00
AB Andris Biedrins/200 2.50 6.00
AJ Al Jefferson/200 15.00 40.00
AS Amare Stoudemire/200 8.00 20.00
AW Antoine Walker/50 10.00 25.00
BG Ben Gordon/200 15.00 30.00
CA Carmelo Anthony/150 20.00 50.00
CB Chris Bosh/150 8.00 20.00
DH Devin Harris/200 3.00 8.00
DW Dwyane Wade/150 30.00 80.00
EB Elton Brand/100 6.00 15.00
EC Eddy Curry/200 4.00 10.00
GA Gilbert Arenas/150 4.00 10.00
GP Gary Payton/50 12.50 30.00
JC Josh Childress/200 3.00 8.00
JH Josh Howard/200 4.00 10.00
JK Jason Kidd/50 15.00 40.00
JN Jameer Nelson/200 8.00 20.00
JS Jerry Stackhouse/150 6.00 15.00
KS Kirk Snyder/200 2.50 6.00
LD Luol Deng/150 10.00 25.00
LJ Luke Jackson/200 2.50 6.00
LO Lamar Odom/150 6.00 15.00
MB Mike Bibby/150 10.00 25.00
MD Mike Dunleavy/200 4.00 10.00
MS Mike Sweetney/200 4.00 10.00
PP Paul Pierce/50 15.00 40.00
RJ Richard Jefferson/200 4.00 10.00
RS Robert Swift/140 2.50 6.00
SF Steve Francis/50 8.00 20.00
SL Shaun Livingston/200 4.00 10.00
SM Stephon Marbury/50 8.00 20.00
ST Sebastian Telfair/200 3.00 8.00
TM Tracy McGrady/50 15.00 40.00
VC Vince Carter/150 12.50 30.00
YT Yuta Tabuse/149 4.00 10.00
ZR Zach Randolph/200 4.00 10.00
CAB Caron Butler/200 4.00 10.00
DAV David West/150 4.00 10.00
DEL Delonte West/150 6.00 15.00
DOR Dorell Wright/150 4.00 10.00
HSJ Ha Seung-Jin/99 4.00 10.00
JAS Jason Richardson/200 4.00 10.00
JON Jermaine O'Neal/100 10.00 25.00
JOS Josh Smith/200 8.00 20.00
JRS J.R. Smith/200 4.00 10.00
KEY Kenyon Martin/200 6.00 15.00
PAV Pavel Podkolzin/200 2.50 6.00
RAF Rafael Araujo/200 2.50 6.00
TAY Tayshaun Prince/200 6.00 15.00
TJF T.J. Ford/150 4.00 10.00

2004-05 Fleer Sweet Sigs Autographs Draft Pick

Randomly inserted in packs, this 50-card set parallels the base Autographs set enhanced with sequential numbering to match the player's draft pick number.

STATED PRINT RUN ONE TO 46 SETS
MOST NOT PRICED DUE TO SCARCITY
AJ Al Jefferson/15 40.00 100.00
JH Josh Howard/29 10.00 25.00
ZR Zach Randolph/19 10.00 25.00
DOR Dorell Wright/19 8.00 20.00
JOS Josh Smith/17 20.00 50.00
DEL Delonte West/24 15.00 40.00
JON Jermaine O'Neal/17 15.00 40.00
JRS J.R. Smith/18 20.00 50.00
HSJ Ha Seung-Jin/46 10.00 25.00

2004-05 Fleer Sweet Sigs Autographs Draft Year

Randomly inserted in packs, this 50-card set parallels the base Autographs set enhanced with gold foil highlights and sequential numbering to match the player's draft year. Anything after 2000 is marked with just a single number.

STATED PRINT RUN ONE TO 99 SETS
MOST NOT PRICED DUE TO SCARCITY
AW Antoine Walker/96 8.00 20.00
EB Elton Brand/99 8.00 20.00
GP Gary Payton/90 12.00 30.00
JK Jason Kidd/94 12.50 30.00
JS Jerry Stackhouse/95 8.00 20.00
LO Lamar Odom/99 8.00 20.00
MB Mike Bibby/98 12.50 30.00
PP Paul Pierce/98 12.50 30.00
SF Steve Francis/99 8.00 20.00
SM Stephon Marbury/96 8.00 20.00
TM Tracy McGrady/97 12.50 30.00
VC Vince Carter/98 15.00 40.00
JON Jermaine O'Neal/96 10.00 25.00

2004-05 Fleer Sweet Sigs Hardcourt Heroics

Randomly inserted in Hobby and Retail packs at the rate of one in six, this 25-card set features a horizontal design with a basketball court in the background. Player photos appear on the right side and the card is highlighted with red foil.

COMPLETE SET (25) 10.00 25.00
STATED ODDS 1:6
1 Vince Carter .60 1.50
2 Kevin Garnett .60 1.50
3 Carmelo Anthony .75 2.00
4 Ben Wallace .30 .75
5 Steve Francis .30 .75
6 Richard Hamilton .30 .75
7 Paul Pierce .40 1.00
8 Kobe Bryant 1.50 4.00
9 Chris Webber .40 1.00
10 Jason Richardson .40 1.00
11 Stephon Marbury .30 .75
12 Jermaine O'Neal .30 .75
13 Shaquille O'Neal 1.00 2.50
14 Allen Iverson .60 1.50
15 Tony Parker .40 1.00
16 Dwyane Wade .60 1.50
17 Mike Bibby .40 1.00
18 Tracy McGrady .50 1.25
19 Pau Gasol .40 1.00
20 Dirk Nowitzki .60 1.50
21 Tim Duncan .60 1.50
22 Jason Kidd .60 1.50
23 Yao Ming .75 2.00
24 Amare Stoudemire .30 .75
25 LeBron James 2.50 6.00

2004-05 Fleer Sweet Sigs Hardcourt Heroics Jerseys

Randomly inserted, this 20-card set parallels the base Hardcourt Heroics set enhanced with a square swatch of jersey in the lower left corner and silver foil highlights. Cards are sequentially numbered to varying amounts.

PRINT RUNS LISTED IN CHECKLIST
AI Allen Iverson/250 4.00 10.00
BW Ben Wallace 2.00 5.00
CA Carmelo Anthony/184 5.00 12.00
DN Dirk Nowitzki/35 8.00 20.00
DW Dwyane Wade 4.00 10.00
JK Jason Kidd/215 4.00 10.00
JO Jermaine O'Neal/74 2.00 5.00
KG Kevin Garnett/223 4.00 10.00
MB Mike Bibby/55 2.50 6.00
PG Pau Gasol/110 2.50 6.00
PP Paul Pierce/250 2.50 6.00
SF Steve Francis/40 8.00 20.00
SM Stephon Marbury/175 2.00 5.00
SO Shaquille O'Neal/200 6.00 15.00
TD Tim Duncan/124 4.00 10.00
TM Tracy McGrady/235 3.00 8.00
VC Vince Carter 4.00 10.00
YM Yao Ming/35 10.00 25.00

2004-05 Fleer Sweet Sigs Hardcourt Heroics Jerseys Retail

Randomly inserted at one in 24 Retail packs, this 20-card set parallels the base Hardcourt Heroics set enhanced with a square swatch of jersey in the lower left corner and red foil highlights.

*RETAIL: .4X TO 1X BASE HI 2.00 5.00

2004-05 Fleer Sweet Sigs Hardcourt Heroics Jerseys Dual

Randomly inserted, this 20-card set parallels the base Hardcourt Heroics set enhanced with two players and two square swatches of jersey. Cards are numbered to varying amounts.

STATED PRINT RUN 2 TO 29 SETS
MOST NOT PRICED DUE TO SCARCITY
CP V.Carter/P.Pierce/29 20.00 50.00
FW S.Francis/D.Wade/18 20.00 50.00
GA K.Garnett/Carmelo/25 20.00 50.00
MK S.Marbury/J.Kidd/22 20.00 50.00

2004-05 Fleer Sweet Sigs Hardcourt Heroics Jerseys Quad

Randomly inserted, this 20-card set parallels the base Hardcourt Heroics set enhanced with four players and four jerseys. Cards are numbered to varying amounts.

STATED PRINT RUN 9 TO 42 SETS
MOST NOT PRICED DUE TO SCARCITY
BPGA Bibby/Parker/KG/Melo/42 25.00 60.00
IMCP AI/T-Mac/Vince/Pierce/28 40.00 100.00
WNOG Webb/Dirk/J.O'Neal/Pau/33 40.00 100.00

2004-05 Fleer Sweet Sigs Hardcourt Heroics Patches

Randomly inserted, this 20-card set parallels the base Hardcourt Heroics set enhanced with a square swatch of jersey patch in the lower left corner and gold foil highlights. Each card is sequentially numbered to 50.

*PATCH: 1.25X TO 3X BASE HI
PRINT RUN 50 SER.#'d SETS
UNPRICED MASTERPIECE PRINT RUN ONE SET
AI Allen Iverson 20.00 50.00
YM Yao Ming 15.00 40.00

2004-05 Fleer Sweet Sigs Hardcourt Heroics Patches Black

PRINT RUNS LISTED IN CHECKLIST
MOST NOT PRICED DUE TO SCARCITY
BW Ben Wallace/35 6.00 15.00
CA Carmelo Anthony/15 15.00 40.00
DN Dirk Nowitzki/34 12.00 30.00
KG Kevin Garnett/21 12.00 30.00
TD Tim Duncan/21 12.00 30.00
TM Tracy McGrady/32 10.00 25.00

2004-05 Fleer Sweet Sigs Sweet Stitches Jerseys

Randomly inserted in packs, this 30-card set places a player action photo on the right of the card and a faded basketball in the background on the left. In the lower left hand corner of the card there is a circular swatch of jersey. The cards are numbered to varying amounts.

PRINT RUN LISTED IN CHECKLIST
SOME NOT PRICED DUE TO SCARCITY
N Nene/19 4.00 10.00
AH Allan Houston/123 2.00 5.00
AS Amare Stoudemire/159 2.00 5.00
CB Chris Bosh/175 2.50 6.00
CW Chris Webber/129 3.00 8.00
DN Dirk Nowitzki/115 4.00 10.00
DW Dwyane Wade/137 4.00 10.00
EC Eddy Curry/113 1.50 4.00
GA Gilbert Arenas/89 2.00 5.00
JK Jason Kidd/136 4.00 10.00
JR Jason Richardson/64 2.50 6.00
JS Jerry Stackhouse/114 2.00 5.00
KG Kevin Garnett/95 4.00 10.00
KM Karl Malone/113 3.00 8.00
LS Latrell Sprewell/26 10.00 25.00
PG Pau Gasol/174 2.50 6.00
RH Richard Hamilton/103 2.00 5.00
RJ Richard Jefferson/143 2.00 5.00
SF Steve Francis/26 10.00 25.00
SM Stephon Marbury/101 2.00 5.00
SN Steve Nash/132 3.00 8.00
SO Shaquille O'Neal/151 6.00 15.00
TD Tim Duncan/163 4.00 10.00
TM Tracy McGrady/171 3.00 8.00
YM Yao Ming/152 5.00 12.00

2004-05 Fleer Sweet Sigs Sweet Stitches Jerseys Retail

Randomly inserted in Retail packs at the rate of one in 108, this 30-card set parallels the base Sweet Stitches Jerseys set enhanced with red foil highlights.

N Nene SP 2.00 5.00
AH Allan Houston 2.00 5.00
AS Amare Stoudemire SP 2.00 5.00
BW Ben Wallace 2.00 5.00
CA Carmelo Anthony SP 5.00 12.00
CB Chris Bosh SP 2.50 6.00
CM Corey Maggette 2.00 5.00
CW Chris Webber 2.50 6.00
DN Dirk Nowitzki 4.00 10.00
DW Dwyane Wade 4.00 10.00
EC Eddy Curry 1.50 4.00
GA Gilbert Arenas 2.00 5.00
JK Jason Kidd 4.00 10.00
JR Jason Richardson SP 2.50 6.00
JS Jerry Stackhouse 2.00 5.00
KG Kevin Garnett 4.00 10.00
KM Karl Malone SP 3.00 8.00
LS Latrell Sprewell 2.00 5.00
MG Manu Ginobili 3.00 8.00
PG Pau Gasol SP 2.50 6.00
RH Richard Hamilton 2.00 5.00
RJ Richard Jefferson 2.00 5.00
SF Steve Francis SP 2.00 5.00
SM Stephon Marbury 2.00 5.00
SN Steve Nash 3.00 8.00
SO Shaquille O'Neal 6.00 15.00
TD Tim Duncan 4.00 10.00
TM Tracy McGrady 3.00 8.00
VC Vince Carter SP 4.00 10.00
YM Yao Ming SP 5.00 12.00

2004-05 Fleer Sweet Sigs Sweet Stitches Patches

Randomly inserted in packs, this 30-card set parallels the base Sweet Stitches Jerseys set enhanced with a patch swatch, gold foil and sequential numbering to 50.

*PATCH: 1X TO 2.5X BASE HI
PRINT RUN 50 SER.#'d SETS
UNPRICED MASTERPIECE PRINT RUN ONE SET
N Nene 5.00 12.00
BW Ben Wallace 5.00 12.00
CA Carmelo Anthony 12.00 30.00
CM Corey Maggette 5.00 12.00
CW Chris Webber 10.00 25.00
LS Latrell Sprewell 5.00 12.00
MG Manu Ginobili 8.00 20.00
SF Steve Francis 5.00 12.00
VC Vince Carter 10.00 25.00

2004-05 Fleer Sweet Sigs Sweet Stitches Patches Black

PRINT RUNS LISTED IN CHECKLIST
SOME NOT PRICED DUE TO SCARCITY
N Nene/40 5.00 12.00
AS Amare Stoudemire/17 6.00 15.00
BW Ben Wallace/42 5.00 12.00
CA Carmelo Anthony/44 12.00 30.00
CB Chris Bosh/19 8.00 20.00
DN Dirk Nowitzki/28 12.00 30.00
GA Gilbert Arenas/40 5.00 12.00
JK Jason Kidd/33 10.00 25.00
JR Jason Richardson/36 6.00 15.00
JS Jerry Stackhouse/28 6.00 15.00
KG Kevin Garnett/35 10.00 25.00
KM Karl Malone/23 10.00 25.00
LS Latrell Sprewell/38 5.00 12.00
MG Manu Ginobili/41 8.00 20.00
PG Pau Gasol/27 8.00 20.00
RH Richard Hamilton/18 6.00 15.00
RJ Richard Jefferson/43 5.00 12.00
SF Steve Francis/36 5.00 12.00
SM Stephon Marbury/39 5.00 12.00
SO Shaquille O'Neal/31 20.00 50.00
TD Tim Duncan/23 12.00 30.00
TM Tracy McGrady/26 10.00 25.00
VC Vince Carter/15 12.00 30.00

2004-05 Fleer Sweet Sigs Sweet Stitches Jerseys Quad

Randomly inserted and numbered to varying amounts, this 10-card set features four players and four swatches of jersey and resembles the design of the base Sweet Stitches Jerseys set.

PRINT RUNS LISTED BELOW
SOME NOT PRICED DUE TO SCARCITY
ANGS Melo/Nene/KG/Spree/30 40.00 80.00
BCAS Bosh/VC/Arenas/Stack/33 25.00 60.00
MFDG Yao/Francis/TD/Manu/18 40.00 80.00
MODG Malone/Shaq/TD/Manu/31 50.00 100.00
MSGA T-Mac/Amare/KG/Melo/25 20.00 50.00

2004-05 Fleer Sweet Sigs Sweet Stroke

Inserted in both Hobby and Retail packs at the rate of one in 12, this 15-card set places players in shooting poses on a tan and brown bordered card with red lettering for the player's name.

COMPLETE SET (15) 8.00 20.00
STATED ODDS 1:12
1 Dwyane Wade .75 2.00
2 Allen Iverson .75 2.00
3 Peja Stojakovic .50 1.25
4 Tony Parker .50 1.25
5 Ray Allen .50 1.25
6 Reggie Miller .50 1.25
7 Kevin Garnett .75 2.00
8 Dirk Nowitzki .75 2.00
9 Tim Duncan .75 2.00
10 Kobe Bryant 2.00 5.00
11 Tracy McGrady .60 1.50
12 Michael Finley .50 1.25
13 LeBron James 3.00 8.00
14 Baron Davis .40 1.00
15 Steve Nash .60 1.50

2004-05 Fleer Sweet Sigs Sweet Stroke Jerseys

Randomly seeded, this 12-card set parallels the look of the base Sweet Stroke Jerseys set enhanced with a square swatch of jersey in the lower left corner. Cards are sequentially numbered to varying amounts.

PRINT RUNS LISTED IN CHECKLIST
AI Allen Iverson/143 4.00 10.00
BD Baron Davis/224 2.00 5.00
DW Dwyane Wade/250 6.00 15.00
KG Kevin Garnett/197 4.00 10.00
MF Michael Finley/21 6.00 15.00
PS Peja Stojakovic/216 2.50 6.00
RA Ray Allen/238 2.50 6.00
RM Reggie Miller/163 2.50 6.00
SN Steve Nash/15 8.00 20.00
TD Tim Duncan/99 4.00 10.00
TM Tracy McGrady/200 3.00 8.00
TP Tony Parker/112 2.50 6.00

2004-05 Fleer Sweet Sigs Sweet Stroke Jerseys Retail

Randomly inserted in Retail packs at the rate of one in 108, this 12-card set parallels the base Sweet Stroke Jerseys set enhanced with red foil highlights.

*RETAIL: .4X TO 1X BASE HI 2.00 5.00

2004-05 Fleer Sweet Sigs Sweet Stroke Jerseys Quad

Randomly inserted, this six card set utilizes the look of the Sweet Stroke insert but combines four players and four jerseys. The cards are sequentially numbered to varying amounts.

PRINT RUNS LISTED IN CHECKLIST
MIGD T-Mac/AI/KG/B.Davis/35 40.00 100.00
WAMM Wade/T-Mac/Miller/Allen/29 30.00 80.00
WIMB Wade/AI/R.Miller/B.Davis/35 30.00 80.00

2004-05 Fleer Sweet Sigs Sweet Stroke Patches

Randomly inserted in packs, this 12-card set parallels the base Sweet Stroke Jerseys set enhanced with a patch swatch, gold foil and sequential numbering to 50.

*PATCH: 1X TO 2.5X BASE HI
PRINT RUN 50 SER.#'d SETS
UNPRICED MASTERPIECE PRINT RUN ONE SET
DW Dwyane Wade 10.00 25.00
RM Reggie Miller 12.50 30.00

2004-05 Fleer Sweet Sigs Sweet Stroke Patches Black

Randomly inserted in packs, this 12-card set parallels the base Sweet Stroke Jerseys set enhanced with two patch swatches, black foil and all cards are sequentially numbered to varying amounts.

PRINT RUNS LISTED IN CHECKLIST
SOME NOT PRICED DUE TO SCARCITY
AI Allen Iverson/37 12.00 30.00
BD Baron Davis/69 5.00 12.00
DW Dwyane Wade/19 12.00 30.00
KG Kevin Garnett/21 12.00 30.00
RA Ray Allen/59 6.00 15.00
RM Reggie Miller/31 12.50 30.00
TD Tim Duncan/32 12.00 30.00
TM Tracy McGrady/62 8.00 20.00
TP Tony Parker/29 8.00 20.00

2004-05 Fleer Throwbacks

Released in March 2005, Fleer Throwbacks boasts a 100-card set featuring 65 veteran player cards, 11 rookies serially numbered to 50 (cards 66-76) and 24 rookie jersey cards serially numbered to 499. Base cards have a colored border with black horizontal stripes and rookie jersey cards have a square swatch of jersey centered towards the bottom of the card. Both Hobby and Retal packs contain five cards and Hobby boxes contain 15 packs while Retail boxes have 24.

COMP.SET w/o RC's (65) 15.00 40.00
66-76 RC PRINT RUN 50 SER.#'d SETS
77-100 JSY RC PRINT RUN 499 #'d SETS
UNPRICED ONE OF ONE PARALLEL EXISTS
1 Baron Davis .25 .60
2 Willie Green .20 .50
3 Allen Iverson .50 1.25
4 Jason Williams .25 .60
5 Kevin Garnett .50 1.25
6 Jason Richardson .30 .75
7 Lamar Odom .25 .60
8 Ben Wallace .25 .60
9 Steve Nash .40 1.00
10 Kobe Bryant 1.25 3.00
11 Kenyon Martin .25 .60
12 Jermaine O'Neal .25 .60
13 Tracy McGrady .40 1.00
14 Darko Mililic .20 .50
15 Pau Gasol .30 .75
16 Darius Miles .20 .50
17 Ray Allen .30 .75
18 Michael Redd .25 .60
19 Chris Bosh .30 .75
20 Peja Stojakovic .30 .75
21 Tim Duncan .50 1.25
22 Corey Maggette .25 .60
23 LeBron James 2.00 5.00
24 Antoine Walker .30 .75
25 Stephon Marbury .25 .60
26 Carlos Boozer .25 .60
27 Jason Kapono .20 .50
28 Grant Hill .40 1.00
29 Mike Bibby .30 .75
30 Jamaal Magloire .20 .50
31 Rashard Lewis .30 .75
32 Jason Kidd .50 1.25
33 Al Harrington .25 .60
34 Steve Francis .25 .60
35 Kirk Hinrich .25 .60
36 Amare Stoudemire .25 .60
37 Gilbert Arenas .25 .60
38 Allan Houston .25 .60
39 Eddy Curry .20 .50
40 Latrell Sprewell .25 .60
41 Mickael Pietrus .25 .60
42 Zach Randolph .25 .60
43 Shaquille O'Neal .75 2.00
44 Jason Terry .25 .60
45 Richard Hamilton .25 .60
46 Karl Malone .40 1.00
47 Elton Brand .30 .75
48 Richard Jefferson .25 .60
49 Andrei Kirilenko .25 .60
50 Reggie Miller .30 .75
51 Yao Ming .60 1.50
52 Gary Payton .30 .75
53 Dirk Nowitzki .50 1.25
54 Dwyane Wade .50 1.25
55 Carmelo Anthony .60 1.50
56 Tony Parker .30 .75
57 T.J. Ford .20 .50
58 Vince Carter .50 1.25
59 Paul Pierce .30 .75
60 Drew Gooden .20 .50
61 Antawn Jamison .25 .60
62 Manu Ginobili .40 1.00
63 Chris Webber .30 .75
64 Shawn Marion .25 .60
65 Jerry Stackhouse .25 .60
66 Andris Biedrins RC 2.00 5.00
67 Robert Swift RC 2.00 5.00
68 Pavel Podkolzin RC 2.00 5.00
69 Kevin Martin RC 4.00 10.00
70 Beno Udrih RC 2.50 6.00
71 David Harrison RC 2.00 5.00
72 Victor Khryapa RC 2.00 5.00
73 Jackson Vroman RC 2.00 5.00
74 Emeka Okafor RC 2.50 6.00
75 Andre Emmett RC 2.00 5.00
76 Andres Nocioni RC 3.00 8.00
77 Dwight Howard JSY RC 5.00 12.00
78 Ben Gordon JSY RC 2.50 6.00
79 Shaun Livingston JSY RC 2.50 6.00
80 Devin Harris JSY RC 2.00 5.00
81 Josh Childress JSY RC 2.00 5.00
82 Luol Deng JSY RC 2.50 6.00
83 Rafael Araujo JSY RC 1.50 4.00
84 Andre Iguodala JSY RC 3.00 8.00
85 Luke Jackson JSY RC 1.50 4.00
86 Sebastian Telfair JSY RC 2.00 5.00
87 Kris Humphries JSY RC 2.50 6.00
88 Al Jefferson JSY RC 3.00 8.00
89 Kirk Snyder JSY RC 1.50 4.00
90 Josh Smith JSY RC 2.50 6.00
91 J.R. Smith JSY RC 2.50 6.00
92 Dorell Wright JSY RC 2.50 6.00
93 Jameer Nelson JSY RC 2.50 6.00
94 Chris Duhon JSY RC 2.50 6.00
95 Delonte West JSY RC 2.50 6.00
96 Tony Allen JSY RC 2.50 6.00
97 Anderson Varejao JSY RC 2.00 5.00
98 Lionel Chalmers JSY RC 2.50 6.00
99 Bernard Robinson JSY RC 2.00 5.00
100 Trevor Ariza JSY RC 2.50 6.00

2004-05 Fleer Throwbacks 100

*1-65 SINGLES: 2X TO 5X BASE HI
STATED PRINT RUN 100 SER.#'d SETS

2004-05 Fleer Throwbacks 50

*1-65 SINGLES: 3X TO 8X BASE HI
STATED PRINT RUN 50 SER.#'d SETS

2004-05 Fleer Throwbacks 25

*1-65 SINGLES: 6X TO 15X BASE HI
*66-76 SINGLES: .75X TO 2X BASE
*77-100 SINGLES: 1X TO 2.5X BASE HI
STATED PRINT RUN 25 SER.#'d SETS

2004-05 Fleer Throwbacks Defining Authentic

Inserted in Hobby packs at the rate of one in 15 and retail packs at the rate of one in 24, these cards place faded color action photos on a bordered card.

COMPLETE SET (22) 12.50 30.00
STATED ODDS 1:15 H 1:24 R
1 Shaquille O'Neal 1.50 4.00
2 Tim Duncan 1.00 2.50
3 Tracy McGrady .75 2.00
4 Vince Carter 1.00 2.50
5 Yao Ming 1.25 3.00
6 Allen Iverson 1.00 2.50
7 Amare Stoudemire .50 1.25
8 Carmelo Anthony 1.25 3.00
9 Jason Kidd 1.00 2.50
10 Jermaine O'Neal .50 1.25
11 Jason Richardson .60 1.50
12 Kevin Garnett 1.00 2.50
13 Paul Pierce .60 1.50
14 Peja Stojakovic .60 1.50
15 Dirk Nowitzki 1.00 2.50
16 Kenyon Martin .50 1.25
17 Dwyane Wade 1.00 2.50
18 Steve Francis .50 1.25
19 Kobe Bryant 2.50 6.00
20 LeBron James 4.00 10.00

2004-05 Fleer Throwbacks Defining Authentic Jerseys

STATED ODDS 1:15 H, 1:29 R
*JERSEY 99: .5X TO 1.25X BASE HI
*JERSEY/PATCH: 1.25X TO 3X BASE HI
JERSEY/PATCH PRINT RUN 25 SETS
AI Allen Iverson 4.00 10.00
AS Amare Stoudemire 2.00 5.00
CA Carmelo Anthony 5.00 12.00
DN Dirk Nowitzki 4.00 10.00
DW Dwyane Wade 6.00 15.00
JK Jason Kidd 4.00 10.00
JO Jermaine O'Neal 2.00 5.00
JR Jason Richardson 2.50 6.00
KG Kevin Garnett 4.00 10.00
KM Kenyon Martin 2.00 5.00
PP Paul Pierce 2.50 6.00
PS Peja Stojakovic 2.50 6.00
SF Steve Francis 2.00 5.00
SM Stephon Marbury 2.00 5.00
SN Steve Nash 3.00 8.00
SO Shaquille O'Neal 6.00 15.00
TD Tim Duncan 4.00 10.00
TM Tracy McGrady 3.00 8.00
VC Vince Carter 4.00 10.00
YM Yao Ming 5.00 12.00

2004-05 Fleer Throwbacks Defining Authentic Jerseys Dual

Randomly inserted in packs, this 15-card set parallels the design of the base Defining Authentic Jerseys set with two players and two swatches of Jersey. Each card is sequentially numbered to 99. One of ones were also inserted in packs. Jersey and Patch cards were printed as well and two versions exist, one serially numbered to 25 and the other done in a one of one format.

PRINT RUN 99 SER.#'d SETS
1 Y.Ming/T.Duncan 8.00 20.00
2 T.McGrady/V.Carter 8.00 20.00
3 S.Marbury/A.Iverson 8.00 20.00
4 J.Kidd/P.Pierce 8.00 20.00
5 A.Iverson/V.Carter 10.00 25.00
7 D.Nowitzki/P.Stojakovic 8.00 20.00
8 A.Stoudemire/S.Nash 8.00 20.00
9 J.Kidd/K.Martin 6.00 15.00
10 T.McGrady/S.Francis 6.00 15.00
11 S.O'Neal/D.Wade 15.00 40.00
12 C.Anthony/K.Martin 6.00 15.00
13 T.McGrady/Y.Ming 8.00 20.00
14 C.Anthony/D.Wade 10.00 25.00
15 S.O'Neal/J.O'Neal 8.00 20.00

2004-05 Fleer Throwbacks Defining Authentic Jerseys and Patch Dual

Randomly inserted in packs, this 20-card set parallels the design of the base Defining Authentc set enhanced with two players, two square swatches of jersey and is sequentially numbered to 25.

PRINT RUN 25 SER.#'d SETS
UNPRICED ONE OF ONE's EXIST
AM C.Anthony/K.Martin 25.00 60.00
DG T.Duncan/K.Garnett 30.00 80.00
KM J.Kidd/K.Martin 25.00 60.00
KP J.Kidd/P.Pierce 25.00 60.00
MC T.McGrady/V.Carter 30.00 80.00
MD Y.Ming/T.Duncan 25.00 60.00
MF T.McGrady/S.Francis 25.00 60.00
MI S.Marbury/A.Iverson 25.00 60.00
MM T.McGrady/Y.Ming 25.00 60.00
NS D.Nowitzki/P.Stojakovic 30.00 80.00
OO S.O'Neal/J.O'Neal 30.00 80.00
OW S.O'Neal/D.Wade 40.00 100.00
SN A.Stoudemire/S.Nash 25.00 60.00

2004-05 Fleer Throwbacks Defining Authentic Jerseys Autographs

Randomly inserted in packs, this 30-card set parallels the design of the base Defining Authentc set enhanced with a square swatch of jersey and an autograph where cards are sequentially numbered to between 149 and 449.

PRINT RUNS FROM 149 TO 449 #'d SETS
UNPRICED PARALLEL PRINT RUN ONE SET
AJ Al Jefferson/149 6.00 15.00
BG Ben Gordon/249 5.00 12.00
CB Chauncey Billups/149 8.00 20.00
CD Chris Duhon/249 5.00 12.00
DH Devin Harris/149 4.00 10.00
DW2 Delonte West/149 5.00 12.00
EC Eddy Curry/249 3.00 8.00
GA Gilbert Arenas/199 4.00 10.00
JH Josh Howard/249 5.00 12.00
JS2 J.R. Smith/249 5.00 12.00
MD Marquis Daniels/249 3.00 8.00
NC Nick Collison/249 4.00 10.00
RA Rafael Araujo/449 3.00 8.00
TA Tony Allen/249 5.00 12.00
TF T.J. Ford/149 3.00 8.00
VC Vince Carter/249 8.00 20.00
YT Yuta Tabuse/449 5.00 12.00

2004-05 Fleer Throwbacks Defining Authentic Jerseys Autographs Numbers

Randomly inserted in packs, this 30-card set parallels the design of the base Defining Authentc set enhanced with a square swatch of jersey and an autograph where cards are numbered to the featured players jersey number.

PRINT RUNS LISTED IN CHECKLIST
MOST UNPRICED DUE TO SCARCITY
CA Carmelo Anthony/15 40.00 100.00
DH Devin Harris/34 15.00 40.00
JS Josh Smith/42 25.00 60.00
JS2 J.R. Smith/23 20.00 50.00
LJ Luke Jackson/33 12.50 30.00
RA Rafael Araujo/55 10.00 25.00

2004-05 Fleer Throwbacks Defining Authentic Jerseys Autographs Silver

PRINT RUNS LISTED IN CHECKLIST
SOME NOT PRICED DUE TO SCARCITY
AJ Al Jefferson/50 12.00 30.00
BG Ben Gordon/50 15.00 40.00
CA Carmelo Anthony/50 25.00 60.00
CB Chauncey Billups/50 10.00 25.00
CD Chris Duhon/149 10.00 25.00
DH Devin Harris/50 8.00 20.00
DW Dwyane Wade/25 75.00 150.00
DW2 Delonte West/50 10.00 25.00
EC Eddy Curry/50 8.00 20.00
GA Gilbert Arenas/50 8.00 20.00
JH Josh Howard/149 8.00 20.00
JK Jason Kidd/25 20.00 50.00
JO Jermaine O'Neal/25 12.00 30.00
JS2 J.R. Smith/50 10.00 25.00
KM Kenyon Martin/25 20.00 50.00
LD Luol Deng/25 10.00 25.00
NC Nick Collison/149 8.00 20.00
RA Rafael Araujo/199 8.00 20.00
SL Shaun Livingston/50 10.00 25.00
SM Stephon Marbury/25 20.00 50.00
TA Tony Allen/199 10.00 25.00
TF T.J. Ford/50 8.00 20.00
VC Vince Carter/99 15.00 40.00
YT Yuta Tabuse/149 10.00 25.00

2004-05 Fleer Throwbacks Hardwood Classics

Randomly inserted in Hobby packs at the rate of one in 90 and Retail at the rate of one in 288, this 15-card set is horizontally designed with a white background and a full color player portrait head shot on the left and a black and white full body shot on the right.

COMPLETE SET (15) 15.00 40.00
STATED ODDS 1:90 H, 1:288 R
1 Elton Brand 2.00 5.00
2 Lamar Odom 1.50 4.00
3 Carlos Boozer 1.50 4.00
4 Andrei Kirilenko 1.50 4.00
5 Zach Randolph 1.50 4.00
6 Darius Miles 1.25 3.00
7 Ben Wallace 1.50 4.00
8 Richard Hamilton 1.50 4.00
9 Pau Gasol 2.00 5.00
10 Chris Bosh 2.00 5.00
11 Baron Davis 1.50 4.00
12 Mike Bibby 2.00 5.00
13 Manu Ginobili 2.50 6.00
14 Tony Parker 2.00 5.00
15 Richard Jefferson 1.50 4.00

2004-05 Fleer Throwbacks Hardwood Classics Jerseys

PRINT RUN 99 SER.#'d SETS
AK Andrei Kirilenko 2.50 6.00
BD Baron Davis 2.50 6.00

BW Ben Wallace 2.50 6.00
CB Charles Barkley 20.00 50.00
CB Carlos Boozer 2.50 6.00
CB Chris Bosh 3.00 8.00
DM Darius Miles 2.00 5.00
DR David Robinson 15.00 40.00
IT Isiah Thomas 8.00 20.00
KA Kareem Abdul-Jabbar 10.00 25.00
LB Larry Bird 40.00 80.00
LE Lamar Odom 2.50 6.00
MB Mike Bibby 3.00 8.00
MG Manu Ginobili 4.00 10.00
PE Patrick Ewing 15.00 40.00
PG Pau Gasol 3.00 8.00
RH Richard Hamilton 2.50 6.00
RJ Richard Jefferson 2.50 6.00
WF Walt Frazier 10.00 25.00
ZR Zach Randolph 2.50 6.00

2004-05 Fleer Throwbacks Hardwood Classics Jerseys and Patch

Randomly inserted in packs, this 22-card set parallels the design of the base Hardwood Classics set enhanced with two swatches of memorabilia and sequential numbering to the featured player's jersey number.
PRINT RUNS LISTED IN CHECKLIST
MOST NOT PRICED DUE TO SCARCITY
1 Elton Brand/42 8.00 20.00
4 Andrei Kirilenko/47 6.00 15.00
5 Zach Randolph/50 6.00 15.00
6 Darius Miles/23 6.00 15.00
8 Richard Hamilton/32 6.00 15.00
9 Pau Gasol/16 12.50 30.00
16 Kareem Abdul-Jabbar/33 25.00 60.00
17 Charles Barkley/34 75.00 150.00
18 David Robinson/50 20.00 50.00
21 Larry Bird/33 30.00 80.00
22 Patrick Ewing/33 25.00 60.00
23 Scottie Pippen/33 30.00 80.00

2004-05 Fleer Throwbacks Hardwood Classics Jerseys Dual

Randomly inserted in packs, this 22-card set parallels the design of the base Hardwood Classics set enhanced with two players and two swatches of jersey. Each card is serially numbered to 50. One of one Jerseys Dual cards were inserted along with Patches Dual serially numbered to 25.
PRINT RUN 50 SER.#'d SETS
*PATCH DUAL: .75X TO 2X BASE HI
PATCH DUAL PRINT RUN 25 SER.#'d SETS
BB C.Boozer/E.Brand 6.00 15.00
BK C.Boozer/A.Kirilenko 6.00 15.00
BO E.Brand/L.Odom 6.00 15.00
DB B.Davis/M.Bibby 6.00 15.00
GB P.Gasol/C.Bosh 8.00 20.00
GG P.Gasol/M.Ginobili 8.00 20.00
GP M.Ginobili/T.Parker 8.00 20.00
JH R.Jefferson/R.Hamilton 6.00 15.00
RM Z.Randolph/D.Miles 6.00 15.00
WH B.Wallace/R.Hamilton 8.00 20.00

2004-05 Fleer Throwbacks Hardwood Classics Jerseys Autographs

Randomly inserted in packs, this 22-card set parallels the design of the base Hardwood Classics set enhanced with both a jersey and an autograph. Cards were numbered to either 149 or 249.
PRINT RUNS LISTED IN CHECKLIST
UNPRICED ONE OF ONE's EXIST
AB Andris Biedrins/249 6.00 15.00
AK Andrei Kirilenko/249 6.00 15.00
DW Dorell Wright/149 6.00 15.00
GG George Gervin 10.00 25.00
JC Josh Childress/249 6.00 15.00
KH Kris Humphries/249 6.00 15.00

2004-05 Fleer Throwbacks Hardwood Classics Jerseys Autographs Numbers

Randomly inserted in packs, this 22-card set parallels the design of the base Hardwood Classics set enhanced with both a jersey and an autograph. Cards were numbered to the featured player's jersey number.
PRINT RUNS LISTED IN CHECKLIST
SOME NOT PRICED DUE TO SCARCITY
AB Andris Biedrins/15 12.50 30.00
AK Andrei Kirilenko/47 25.00 60.00
BW2 Bill Walton/32 15.00 40.00
DM Darius Miles/23 10.00 25.00
EB Elton Brand/42 10.00 25.00
GG George Gervin/44 15.00 40.00
KH Kris Humphries/43 10.00 25.00
RH Richard Hamilton/32 15.00 40.00

2004-05 Fleer Throwbacks Hardwood Classics Jerseys Autographs Silver

PRINT RUNS LISTED IN CHECKLIST
AK Andrei Kirilenko/149 8.00 20.00
BS Byron Scott/249 8.00 20.00
BW Bill Walton/249 8.00 20.00
CB Carlos Boozer/50 8.00 20.00
CB2 Chris Bosh/25 10.00 25.00
DW Dorell Wright/50 8.00 20.00
GG George Gervin/200 15.00 40.00
JC Josh Childress/50 8.00 20.00
KH Kris Humphries/199 8.00 20.00
MC Maurice Cheeks/249 8.00 20.00
RH Richard Hamilton/149 10.00 25.00
ZR Zach Randolph/149 10.00 25.00

2004-05 Fleer Throwbacks Hardwood Classics Jerseys Redemption

Randomly inserted in Hobby packs at the rate of one in 667, this set consists of 20 different redemption cards for Mitchell and Ness throw back jerseys. Four different "Jersey of Your Choice" cards were also inserted where the obtainer gets to pick the jersey.
STATED ODDS 1:667
1 Dave Debusschere 20.00 50.00
2 Bill Russell 50.00 100.00
3 Bill Russell 50.00 100.00
4 George Gervin 40.00 100.00
5 Larry Bird 60.00 120.00
7 George Mikan 25.00 60.00
9 Magic Johnson 25.00 60.00
13 Bill Bradley 20.00 50.00
17 Jersey of Your Choice #1 100.00 200.00

2004-05 Fleer Throwbacks Nostalgia

Randomly inserted in packs, this 15-card set is horizontally designed with a player image in the center and color higlights to match team colors on the left and the right. Cards are all sequentially numbered to the year each player was drafted. A gold version was also produced and is numbered with only the last two digits of the year the player was drafted.
COMPLETE SET (15) 12.50 30.00
PRINT RUNS FROM 1985 TO 2003 SETS
*GOLD/85-98: 1.25X TO 3X BASE HI
SOME GOLD UNPRICED DUE TO SCARCITY
1 Allen Iverson/1996 1.25 3.00
2 Kobe Bryant/1996 3.00 8.00
3 Shaquille O'Neal/1992 2.00 5.00
4 Karl Malone/1985 1.00 2.50
5 Kevin Garnett/1995 1.25 3.00
6 LeBron James/2003 5.00 12.00
7 Carmelo Anthony/2003 1.50 4.00
8 Dwyane Wade/2003 1.25 3.00
9 Baron Davis/1999 .60 1.50
10 Jason Kidd/1994 1.25 3.00
11 Tracy McGrady/1997 1.00 2.50
12 Paul Pierce/1998 .75 2.00
13 Yao Ming/2002 1.50 4.00
14 Vince Carter/1998 1.25 3.00
15 Ben Wallace/1996 .60 1.50

2002-03 Fleer Tradition

Released in late December 2002, Fleer Tradition boasts a 300-card set divided up into 270 veteran players and 30 triple-player rookie cards. The base cards feature an old-school look on corregated cardboard with white borders and framing around the photo in colors that match the player's team colors. Names and positions are in the upper left hand corner, and the team logo is in the upper right. The rookie card are set up like 1980-81 Topps in a horizontal tri-player format-except the perforations are printed on the card front. Tradition was packaged in nine card packs which carried a suggested retail price of $1.49, and boxes contained 40 packs. The PROMO card of Caron Butler listed at the end of the set was given away in Dallas at The American Airlines Center on November 30th to the first 12,000 fans through the gate.
COMPLETE SET (300) 30.00 80.00
1 Shareef Abdur-Rahim .20 .50
2 Dion Glover .15 .40
3 Theo Ratliff .15 .40
4 Nazr Mohammed .15 .40
5 Ira Newble .15 .40
6 Alan Henderson .15 .40
7 Vin Baker .20 .50
8 Tony Battie .15 .40
9 Eric Williams .15 .40
10 Shammond Williams .15 .40
11 Walter McCarty .15 .40
12 Bruno Sundov .15 .40
13 Donyell Marshall .15 .40
14 Marcus Fizer .15 .40
15 Eddie Robinson .15 .40
16 Trenton Hassell .15 .40
17 Ricky Davis .20 .50
18 Jumaine Jones .15 .40
19 Chris Mihm .15 .40
20 Zydrunas Ilgauskas .20 .50
21 Tyrone Hill .15 .40
22 Adrian Griffin .15 .40
23 Nick Van Exel .20 .50
24 Raef LaFrentz .15 .40
25 Eduardo Najera .15 .40
26 Shawn Bradley .15 .40
27 Evan Eschmeyer .15 .40
28 Walt Williams .15 .40
29 Raja Bell .20 .50
30 Marcus Camby .20 .50
31 Donnell Harvey .15 .40
32 Kenny Satterfield .15 .40
33 Rodney White .15 .40
34 Chris Whitney .15 .40
35 Clifford Robinson .15 .40
36 Zeljko Rebraca .15 .40
37 Corliss Williamson .15 .40
38 Chucky Atkins .15 .40
39 Jon Barry .15 .40
40 Michael Curry .15 .40
41 Erick Dampier .15 .40
42 Danny Fortson .15 .40
43 Adonal Foyle .15 .40
44 Troy Murphy .20 .50
45 Bob Sura .15 .40
46 Moochie Norris .15 .40
47 Kenny Thomas .15 .40
48 Terence Morris .15 .40
49 Glen Rice .20 .50
50 Maurice Taylor .15 .40
51 Erick Strickland .15 .40
52 Al Harrington .20 .50
53 Ron Artest .25 .60
54 Austin Croshere .15 .40
55 Ron Mercer .15 .40
56 Brad Miller .20 .50
57 Lamar Odom .20 .50
58 Keyon Dooling .15 .40
59 Corey Maggette .20 .50
60 Michael Olowokandi .15 .40
61 Stanislav Medvedenko .15 .40
62 Rick Fox .15 .40
63 Derek Fisher .20 .50
64 Samaki Walker .15 .40
65 Robert Horry .20 .50
66 Mark Madsen .15 .40
67 Wesley Person .15 .40
68 Michael Dickerson .15 .40
69 Lorenzen Wright .15 .40
70 Brevin Knight .15 .40
71 Travis Best .15 .40
72 Brian Grant .15 .40
73 Eddie Jones .20 .50
74 LaPhonso Ellis .20 .50
75 Anthony Carter .15 .40
76 Tim Thomas .15 .40
77 Toni Kukoc .25 .60
78 Anthony Mason .15 .40
79 Ervin Johnson .15 .40
80 Joel Przybilla .15 .40
81 Rod Strickland .15 .40
82 Terrell Brandon .15 .40
83 Anthony Peeler .15 .40
84 Joe Smith .20 .50
85 Gary Trent .15 .40
86 Rasho Nesterovic .15 .40
87 Loren Woods .15 .40
88 Felipe Lopez .15 .40
89 Dikembe Mutombo .25 .60
90 Rodney Rogers .15 .40
91 Jason Collins .15 .40
92 Kerry Kittles .15 .40
93 Lucious Harris .15 .40
94 Aaron Williams .15 .40
95 Jamal Mashburn .20 .50
96 David Wesley .15 .40
97 Elden Campbell .15 .40
98 Jerome Moiso .15 .40
99 P.J. Brown .15 .40
100 George Lynch .15 .40
101 Robert Traylor .15 .40
102 Antonio McDyess .20 .50
103 Kurt Thomas .15 .40
104 Clarence Weatherspoon .15 .40
105 Charlie Ward .15 .40
106 Lavor Postell .15 .40
107 Shandon Anderson .15 .40
108 Michael Doleac .15 .40
109 Othella Harrington .15 .40
110 Darrell Armstrong .15 .40
111 Steven Hunter .15 .40
112 Pat Garrity .15 .40
113 Horace Grant .20 .50
114 Jacque Vaughn .15 .40
115 Jeryl Sasser .15 .40
116 Todd MacCulloch .15 .40
117 Greg Buckner .15 .40
118 Eric Snow .15 .40
119 Samuel Dalembert .15 .40
120 Monty Williams .15 .40
121 Stephon Marbury .20 .50
122 Anfernee Hardaway .40 1.00
123 Tom Gugliotta .15 .40
124 Iakovos Tsakalidis .15 .40
125 Bo Outlaw .15 .40
126 Damon Stoudamire .20 .50
127 Jeff McInnis .15 .40
128 Derek Anderson .15 .40
129 Antonio Daniels .15 .40
130 Dale Davis .15 .40
131 Zach Randolph .20 .50
132 Bobby Jackson .15 .40
133 Chris Webber .25 .60
134 Vlade Divac .20 .50
135 Keon Clark .15 .40
136 Doug Christie .15 .40
137 Scot Pollard .15 .40
138 Mengke Bateer .15 .40
139 David Robinson .40 1.00
140 Steve Smith .20 .50
141 Malik Rose .15 .40
142 Speedy Claxton .15 .40
143 Danny Ferry .15 .40
144 Brent Barry .15 .40
145 Joseph Forte .15 .40
146 Vladimir Radmanovic .15 .40
147 Kenny Anderson .20 .50
148 Predrag Drobnjak .15 .40
149 Calvin Booth .15 .40
150 Ansu Sesay .15 .40
151 Voshon Lenard .15 .40
152 Lamond Murray .15 .40
153 Antonio Davis .15 .40
154 Lindsey Hunter .15 .40
155 Michael Bradley .15 .40
156 Jerome Williams .15 .40
157 Alvin Williams .15 .40
158 Mamadou N'Diaye .15 .40
159 Raul Lopez .25 .60
160 John Stockton .30 .75
161 Mark Jackson .20 .50
162 DeShawn Stevenson .15 .40
163 Calbert Cheaney .15 .40
164 Matt Harpring .15 .40
165 Jarron Collins .15 .40
166 Tyronn Lue .15 .40
167 Bryon Russell .15 .40
168 Larry Hughes .20 .50
169 Brendan Haywood .15 .40
170 Christian Laettner .20 .50
171 Glenn Robinson .20 .50
172 Tony Delk .15 .40
173 Antoine Walker .20 .50
174 Jalen Rose .20 .50
175 Jamal Crawford .25 .60
176 DeSagana Diop .15 .40
177 Michael Finley .25 .60
178 Dirk Nowitzki .40 1.00
179 Juwan Howard .20 .50
180 Chauncey Billups .25 .60
181 Richard Hamilton .20 .50
182 Antawn Jamison .25 .60
183 Steve Francis .20 .50
184 Eddie Griffin .15 .40
185 Jonathan Bender .15 .40
186 Reggie Miller .25 .60
187 Elton Brand .25 .60
188 Marco Jaric .25 .60
189 Kobe Bryant 1.00 2.50
190 Shaquille O'Neal .60 1.50
191 Jason Williams .20 .50
192 Stromile Swift .15 .40
193 Alonzo Mourning .30 .75
194 Malik Allen .15 .40
195 Sam Cassell .20 .50
196 Ray Allen .25 .60
197 Wally Szczerbiak .20 .50
197B Vince Carter Promo 1.00 2.50
198 Jason Kidd .40 1.00
199 Kenyon Martin .20 .50
200 Courtney Alexander .15 .40
201 Baron Davis .20 .50
202 Allan Houston .20 .50
203 Grant Hill .30 .75
204 Aaron McKie .15 .40
205 Keith Van Horn .20 .50
206 Shawn Marion .20 .50
207 Joe Johnson .20 .50
208 Scottie Pippen .40 1.00
209 Rasheed Wallace .25 .60
210 Peja Stojakovic .25 .60
211 Hedo Turkoglu .20 .50
212 Tony Parker .30 .75
213 Tim Duncan .50 1.25
214 Gary Payton .25 .60
215 Desmond Mason .20 .50
216 Vince Carter .40 1.00
217 Karl Malone .30 .75
218 Andrei Kirilenko .25 .60
219 Jerry Stackhouse .20 .50
220 Michael Jordan 2.00 5.00
221 DerMarr Johnson .15 .40
222 Kedrick Brown .15 .40
223 Eddy Curry .15 .40
224 Tyson Chandler .25 .60
225 Darius Miles .15 .40
226 Wang ZhiZhi .15 .40
227 James Posey .15 .40
228 Ben Wallace .20 .50
229 Jason Richardson .25 .60
230 Gilbert Arenas .25 .60
231 Eddie Griffin .15 .40
232 Jermaine O'Neal .20 .50
233 Quentin Richardson .20 .50
234 Devean George .15 .40
235 Shane Battier .25 .60
236 Pau Gasol .30 .75
237 Eddie House .15 .40
238 Michael Redd .20 .50
239 Troy Hudson .15 .40
240 Richard Jefferson .25 .60
241 Jamal Magloire .15 .40
242 Mike Miller .20 .50
243 Joe Johnson .20 .50
244 Ruben Patterson .15 .40
245 Gerald Wallace .20 .50
246 Tony Parker .30 .75
247 Rashard Lewis .25 .60
248 Morris Peterson .15 .40
249 Andrei Kirilenko .25 .60
250 Kwame Brown .15 .40
251 Jason Terry .20 .50
252 Paul Pierce .25 .60
253 Darius Miles .15 .40
254 Steve Nash .30 .75
255 Cuttino Mobley .15 .40
256 Jamaal Tinsley .15 .40
257 Andre Miller .20 .50
258 Shaquille O'Neal .60 1.50
259 Kobe Bryant 1.00 2.50
260 Kevin Garnett .40 1.00
261 Kenyon Martin .20 .50
262 Latrell Sprewell .20 .50
263 Tracy McGrady .40 1.00
264 Allen Iverson .40 1.00
265 Shawn Marion .20 .50
266 Bonzi Wells .15 .40
267 Mike Bibby .25 .60
268 Tim Duncan .50 1.25
269 Vince Carter .40 1.00
270 Michael Jordan 2.00 5.00
271 Ming/Williams/Dunlvy RC 1.50 4.00
272 Ginobili/Prince/Giricek RC 1.50 4.00
273 Jeffries RC/Williams RC/Pargo RC 1.00 2.50
274 Wilcox RC/Dixon RC/Baxter RC 1.00 2.50
275 Wagnr RC/Dickau RC/Ginbili RC 1.00 2.50
276 Ely RC/Jefferies RC/Maddox RC 1.00 2.50
277 Evans RC/Brmer RC/Williams RC 1.00 2.50
278 Butler RC/Haislip RC/Hmphry RC 1.00 2.50
279 Archbld RC/Burke RC/Huffmn RC 1.00 2.50
280 Goodn/Amare/Woods RC 1.50 4.00
281 Nachbr RC/Welsch RC/Savovic RC 1.00 2.50
282 Borchrdt RC/Jacobsn RC/Gadzu RC 1.00 2.50
283 Clancy RC/Okur RC/Sampson RC 1.00 2.50
284 Prince/Rush/Salmons RC 1.25 3.00
285 Ming/Tskitishvili/Hilario RC 1.50 4.00
286 Wagner RC/Woods RC/Slay RC 1.00 2.50
287 Ely RC/Haislip RC/Jones RC 1.00 2.50
288 Butler/Ginobili/Haislip RC 1.25 3.00
289 Mason RC/Yrbrogh RC/Dickau RC 1.00 2.50
290 Murray RC/Owens RC/Parker RC 1.00 2.50
291 Butler RC/Pargo RC/Giricek RC 1.00 2.50
292 Goodn RC/Tskitish RC/Wagnr RC 1.00 2.50
293 Hilario/Wilcox/Amare RC 2.00 5.00
294 Jay Will RC/Hmphry RC/Woods RC 1.00 2.50
295 Ming/Stoudemire/Rush RC 4.00 10.00
296 Tskitishvili RC/Butler RC/Dixon RC 1.00 2.50
297 Wilcox RC/Jones RC/Nachbar RC 1.00 2.50
298 Dunlvy RC/Hilario RC/Jacobsn RC 1.00 2.50
299 Jeffries RC/Dixon RC/Gooden RC 1.00 2.50
300 Boozer RC/Jay Will RC/Dunlvy RC 1.00 2.50
PROMO Caron Butler PROMO 1.00 2.50

2002-03 Fleer Tradition Crystal

*STARS: 3X TO 8X BASE CARD HI
*RCs: 1.25X TO 3X BASE CARD HI
PRINT RUN 199 SERIAL #'d SETS

2002-03 Fleer Tradition All-Stars

Randomly seeded in packs at the rate of one in 20, this 10-card set highlights NBA All-Stars on a horizontal card design with the layout of a pair of Converse All-Stars. The laces apper on the right side of the card, and the Fleer All-Star log appears on the left. A Sneak Edition version was also issued in packs where the card singles are sequentially numbered to 50.
COMPLETE SET (10) 8.00 20.00
STATED ODDS 1:20
*SNEAK ED: 4X TO 10X ALL-STARS HI
SNEAK ED.PRINT RUN 50 SER.#'d SETS
AS1 Vince Carter 1.00 2.50
AS2 Tim Duncan 1.25 3.00
AS3 Tracy McGrady 1.00 2.50
AS4 Michael Jordan 5.00 12.00
AS5 Shaquille O'Neal 1.50 4.00
AS6 Pau Gasol .75 2.00
AS7 Kevin Garnett 1.00 2.50
AS8 Kobe Bryant 2.50 6.00
AS9 Jason Richardson .60 1.50
AS10 Dirk Nowitzki 1.00 2.50

2002-03 Fleer Tradition Heads Up

Randomly seeded in packs at the rate of one in 10, this 10-card set has white borders, a colored border around the picture to match the player's team colors, and true life photos of the player's heads are oversized and mounted on a comically drawn smaller body.
COMPLETE SET (10) 4.00 10.00
STATED ODDS 1:10
HU1 Baron Davis .50 1.25
HU2 Jason Terry .50 1.25
HU3 Ben Wallace .50 1.25
HU4 Paul Pierce .60 1.50
HU5 Bonzi Wells .40 1.00
HU6 Allen Iverson 1.00 2.50
HU7 Vince Carter 1.00 2.50
HU8 Quentin Richardson .50 1.25
HU9 Eddy Curry .40 1.00
HU10 Darius Miles .40 1.00

2002-03 Fleer Tradition Heads Up Game-Used

PRINT RUN UP TO 100 SETS/PLAYER
AI Allen Iverson 10.00 25.00
BW Bonzi Wells 4.00 10.00
BW Ben Wallace 5.00 12.00
DM Darius Miles 4.00 10.00
EC Eddy Curry 4.00 10.00
JT Jason Terry 5.00 12.00
PP Paul Pierce 6.00 15.00
QR Quentin Richardson 5.00 12.00

2002-03 Fleer Tradition Playground Rules

Inserted in packs at the rate of one in eight, this 30-card set features a horizontal design that places full color rookie player photos agains a brick wall on the right side and the words "Playground Rules" and the player's name in silver foil on the left.
COMPLETE SET (30) 15.00 40.00
STATED ODDS 1:8
PR1 Yao Ming 1.25 3.00
PR2 Fred Jones .50 1.25
PR3 Ryan Humphrey .50 1.25
PR4 Drew Gooden .60 1.50
PR5 Nikoloz Tskitishvili .40 1.00
PR6 Caron Butler .60 1.50
PR7 DaJuan Wagner .50 1.25
PR8 Nene Hilario .60 1.50
PR9 Qyntel Woods .50 1.25
PR10 Jared Jeffries .50 1.25
PR11 Casey Jacobsen .50 1.25
PR12 Marcus Haislip .50 1.25
PR13 Kareem Rush .50 1.25
PR14 Melvin Ely .50 1.25
PR15 Steve Logan .60 1.50
PR16 Amare Stoudemire .75 2.00
PR17 John Salmons .60 1.50
PR18 Chris Jefferies .40 1.00
PR19 Juan Dixon .60 1.50
PR20 Carlos Boozer .60 1.50
PR21 Roger Mason .50 1.25
PR22 Manu Ginobili 1.50 4.00
PR23 Tayshaun Prince .75 2.00
PR24 Chris Wilcox .50 1.25
PR25 Bostjan Nachbar .50 1.25
PR26 Jiri Welsch .50 1.25
PR27 Dan Dickau .50 1.25
PR28 Jay Williams .60 1.50
PR29 Mike Dunleavy .60 1.50
PR30 Frank Williams .40 1.00

2002-03 Fleer Tradition Road to the NBA

Randomly inserted in packs at the rate of one in 40, this 10-card set showcases a horizontal card design with player's centered over their team's logo and a background colored to match the player's team colors. A gray banner is arched across the top of the card containing the set name in yellow, and the contours of the card and the player's name appear in silver toil.
COMPLETE SET (10) 8.00 20.00
STATED ODDS 1:40
RTN1 Jerry Stackhouse .75 2.00
RTN2 Rasheed Wallace 1.00 2.50
RTN3 Allen Iverson 1.50 4.00
RTN4 Kevin Garnett 1.50 4.00
RTN5 Shawn Marion .75 2.00
RTN6 Chris Webber 1.00 2.50
RTN7 Glenn Robinson .75 2.00
RTN8 Antawn Jamison 1.00 2.50
RTN9 Dirk Nowitzki 1.50 4.00
RTN10 Vince Carter 1.50 4.00

2002-03 Fleer Tradition Road to the NBA Game-Used

STATED ODDS 1:240
RTN1 Jerry Stackhouse 3.00 8.00
RTN3 Allen Iverson 6.00 15.00
RTN4 Kevin Garnett 6.00 15.00
RTN5 Shawn Marion 3.00 8.00
RTN6 Chris Webber 4.00 10.00
RTN7 Glenn Robinson 3.00 8.00
RTN8 Antawn Jamison 4.00 10.00
RTN9 Dirk Nowitzki 6.00 15.00
RTN10 Vince Carter 6.00 15.00

2002-03 Fleer Tradition School Ties

Inserted in packs at the rate of one in 20, this 10-card set places either two or three players on the same card who share the same college alma mater. The cards themselves are in the form of the old black and white bound note books where the top of the card has sharp corners (the spine) and the bottom of the card has rounded corners.
COMPLETE SET (10) 8.00 20.00
STATED ODDS 1:20
ST1 J.Stockton/D.Dickau 1.25 3.00
ST2 A.McDyess/L.Sprewell 1.25 3.00
ST3 M.Miller/J.Williams 1.00 2.50
ST4 K.Van Horn/A.Miller 1.00 2.50
ST5 J.Kidd/S.Abdur-Rahim 1.25 3.00
ST6 R.Jefferson/Terry/Bibby 1.00 2.50
ST7 Carter/Jordan/J.Stack 4.00 10.00
ST8 Rose/Howard/Webber 2.50 6.00
ST9 Mutmbo/Mourning/A.I. 1.25 3.00
ST10 Brand/G.Hill/S.Battier 1.00 2.50

2002-03 Fleer Tradition School Ties Game-Used Dual or Triple

Randomly inserted in packs, this nine card set parallels the base School Ties enhanced with two or three swatches of memorabilia-one for each player where the jerseys and such were available. These swatches are circular shaped and appear below the player's picture. Each card is sequentially numbered to 100. Card number ST2 does not exist.
CARDS LISTED W/BASE INSERT #SCHEME
PRINT RUN 100 SERIAL #'d SETS
ST1 Stocktn JSY/Dicku Shorts 6.00 15.00
ST3 Miller Shorts/Williams Jkt 4.00 10.00
ST4 V.Horn Pants/Miller Shorts 4.00 10.00
ST5 Kidd Shorts/A-Rahim JSY 8.00 20.00
ST6 Jeff.Jkt/Terry Jkt/Bibb Pnts 5.00 12.00
ST7 Carter Jkt/MJ/Stack.Pants 15.00 40.00
ST8 Rose JSY/Hwrd/Web.Pants 5.00 12.00
ST9 Mtmbo.Jkt/Zo.JSY/AI.Shorts 8.00 20.00
ST10 Brnd Shts/Hill JSY/Bttier Jkt 6.00 15.00

2002-03 Fleer Tradition School Ties Game-Used Singles

Randomly inserted in packs at the rate of one in 23, this 21-card set parallels the base School Ties insert set enhanced with one circular swatch of game used memorabilia. Some of the pairs and or trio's have multiple variations. Also note, card number ST2 does not exist.
CARDS LISTED W/BASE INSERT #SCHEME
STATED ODDS 1:23
ST1A Stockton JSY/Dickau 4.00 10.00
ST1B Stockton/Dickau Shorts 3.00 8.00
ST3A Miller Shorts/Williams 3.00 8.00
ST3B Miller/Williams Jacket 3.00 8.00
ST4A K.V.Horn Pants/A.Miller 3.00 8.00
ST4B K.V.Horn/A.Miller Shorts 3.00 8.00
ST5A Kidd Shorts/S.A-Rahim 5.00 12.00
ST5B Kidd/S.A-Rahim JSY 3.00 8.00
ST6A Jeffersn Jkt/Terry/Bibby 3.00 8.00
ST6B Jeffersn/Terry Jkt/Bibby 3.00 8.00
ST6C Jeffersn/Terry/Bibby Pnts 3.00 8.00
ST7A Carter Jacket/MJ/Stack 5.00 12.00
ST7B Carter/MJ/Stack Pants 4.00 10.00
ST8A Rose JSY/Howrd/Webb 3.00 8.00
ST8B Rose/Howrd/Webb Pnts 3.00 8.00
ST9A Mutombo Jkt/ZO/A.I. 3.00 8.00
ST9B Mutom./Mourn JSY/A.I. 4.00 10.00
ST9C Mutom./Mourn./A.I. Short 5.00 12.00
ST10A Brand Shorts/Hill/Battier 3.00 8.00
ST10B Brand/Hill JSY/Battier 4.00 10.00
ST10C Brand/Hill/Battier Jacket 3.00 8.00

2003-04 Fleer Tradition

Issued in late October/early September 2003, this 300-card set is divided into 260 veteran players, including subset cards from numbers 221-260, 30 rookie cards, numbers 261-290 and inserted at the rate of one in three, and 10 tri-cards featuring three rookie players on each. Tradition was packaged in 36-pack boxes where packs contained 10 cards and carried a suggested retail price of $1.49.
COMP.SET w/o RC's (260) 15.00 40.00
221-260 SUBSETS SAME VALUE AS BASE
261-290 RC STATED ODDS 1:3
291-300 TRIPLE STATED ODDS 1:18
1 Shareef Abdur-Rahim .20 .50
2 Vince Carter .40 1.00
3 Kevin Garnett .40 1.00
4 Bobby Jackson .15 .40
5 Courtney Alexander .15 .40
6 Tracy McGrady .30 .75
7 Paul Pierce .25 .60
8 Sam Cassell .20 .50
9 Maurice Taylor .15 .40
10 Pat Garrity .15 .40
11 Casey Jacobsen .15 .40
12 Malik Allen .15 .40
13 Aaron McKie .15 .40
14 Tyson Chandler .20 .50
15 Scottie Pippen .40 1.00
16 Jason Terry .20 .50
17 Pau Gasol .25 .60
18 Antawn Jamison .20 .50
19 Stanislav Medvedenko .15 .40
20 Ray Allen .25 .60
21 James Posey .15 .40
22 Calbert Cheaney .15 .40
23 Devean George .15 .40
24 Tim Thomas .15 .40
25 Marko Jaric .15 .40
26 Ron Mercer .15 .40
27 Rafer Alston .15 .40
28 Tayshaun Prince .20 .50
29 Doug Christie .15 .40
30 Kendall Gill .15 .40
31 Kurt Thomas .15 .40
32 Richard Jefferson .20 .50
33 Darius Miles .15 .40
34 Kenny Anderson .20 .50
35 Keon Clark .15 .40
36 Vladimir Radmanovic .15 .40
37 Kenny Thomas .15 .40
38 Manu Ginobili .30 .75
39 Jared Jeffries .15 .40
40 Brad Miller .20 .50
41 Derek Anderson .15 .40
42 Zach Randolph .20 .50
43 Speedy Claxton .15 .40
44 Jamaal Tinsley .15 .40
45 Gordan Giricek .15 .40
46 Joe Johnson .20 .50
47 Mike Miller .20 .50
48 Shandon Anderson .15 .40
49 Theo Ratliff .15 .40
50 Derrick Coleman .20 .50
51 Dion Glover .15 .40
52 Nikoloz Tskitishvili .15 .40
53 Jumaine Jones .15 .40
54 Gilbert Arenas .20 .50
55 Reggie Miller .25 .60
56 Michael Redd .25 .60
57 Jason Collins .15 .40
58 Drew Gooden .20 .50
59 Hedo Turkoglu .20 .50
60 Eddie Jones .20 .50
61 Andre Miller .20 .50
62 Darrell Armstrong .15 .40
63 Glen Rice .15 .40
64 Jarron Collins .15 .40
65 Nick Van Exel .20 .50
66 Brian Grant .15 .40
67 Shawn Kemp .25 .60
68 Yao Ming .50 1.25
69 Ron Artest .25 .60
70 Jamal Crawford .25 .60
71 Jason Richardson .25 .60
72 Eddie Griffin .15 .40
73 Keith Van Horn .20 .50
74 Jason Kidd .40 1.00
75 Cuttino Mobley .15 .40
76 Brent Barry .15 .40
77 Eddy Curry .15 .40
78 Quentin Richardson .20 .50
79 Dajuan Wagner .15 .40
80 Tom Gugliotta .15 .40
81 Andrei Kirilenko .25 .60
82 Shane Battier .20 .50
83 Alonzo Mourning .30 .75
84 Clifford Robinson .15 .40
85 Erick Dampier .15 .40
86 Antoine Walker .25 .60
87 Marcus Haislip .15 .40
88 Kerry Kittles .15 .40
89 Lonny Baxter .15 .40
90 Troy Murphy .15 .40
91 Glenn Robinson .20 .50
92 Ricky Davis .20 .50
93 Richard Hamilton .20 .50
94 Ben Wallace .20 .50
95 Toni Kukoc .25 .60
96 Raja Bell .20 .50
97 Dikembe Mutombo .25 .60
98 Eddie Robinson .15 .40
99 Antonio Davis .15 .40
100 Anfernee Hardaway .40 1.00
101 Rasheed Wallace .25 .60
102 Christian Laettner .20 .50
103 Eduardo Najera .15 .40
104 Jonathan Bender .15 .40
105 Rodney Rogers .15 .40
106 Baron Davis .20 .50
107 Chris Webber .25 .60
108 Matt Harpring .15 .40
109 Raef LaFrentz .15 .40
110 Steve Nash .30 .75
111 Travis Best .15 .40
112 Tony Delk .15 .40
113 Malik Rose .15 .40
114 Al Harrington .20 .50
115 Bonzi Wells .15 .40
116 Voshon Lenard .15 .40
117 Radoslav Nesterovic .15 .40
118 Mike Bibby .25 .60
119 Dan Dickau .15 .40
120 Jalen Rose .20 .50
121 Lucious Harris .15 .40
122 David Wesley .15 .40
123 Rashard Lewis .25 .60
124 Ira Newble .15 .40
125 Chauncey Billups .25 .60
126 Kareem Rush .15 .40
127 Michael Dickerson .15 .40
128 Walt Williams .15 .40
129 Donnell Harvey .15 .40
130 Tyronn Lue .15 .40
131 Carlos Boozer .20 .50
132 Moochie Norris .15 .40
133 John Salmons .20 .50
134 Vlade Divac .20 .50
135 Shammond Williams .15 .40
136 Brendan Haywood .15 .40
137 George Lynch .15 .40
138 Dirk Nowitzki .40 1.00
139 Bruce Bowen .15 .40
140 Brian Skinner .15 .40
141 Juan Dixon .15 .40
142 Eric Williams .15 .40
143 Grant Hill .30 .75
144 Corey Maggette .20 .50
145 Earl Boykins .15 .40
146 Lamar Odom .20 .50
147 Keyon Dooling .15 .40
148 Joe Smith .20 .50
149 Corliss Williamson .15 .40
150 Robert Horry .20 .50
151 Jamaal Magloire .15 .40
152 Mehmet Okur .20 .50
153 Elton Brand .25 .60
154 Steve Smith .20 .50
155 Predrag Drobnjak .15 .40
156 Allan Houston .20 .50
157 Jerome Williams .15 .40
158 Karl Malone .30 .75
159 Michael Olowokandi .15 .40
160 Terrell Brandon .15 .40
161 Eric Snow .15 .40
162 Tim Duncan .40 1.00
163 Juwan Howard .20 .50
164 Jason Williams .20 .50
165 Stephon Marbury .20 .50
166 J.R. Bremer .15 .40
167 Shaquille O'Neal .60 1.50
168 Mike Dunleavy .20 .50
169 Latrell Sprewell .20 .50
170 Troy Hudson .15 .40
171 Alvin Williams .15 .40
172 Shawn Marion .20 .50
173 Jermaine O'Neal .20 .50
174 P.J. Brown .15 .40
175 Howard Eisley .15 .40
176 Jerry Stackhouse .20 .50
177 Qyntel Woods .15 .40
178 Larry Hughes .20 .50
179 Donyell Marshall .15 .40
180 Greg Ostertag .15 .40
181 Kwame Brown .15 .40
182 Reggie Evans .15 .40
183 DeShawn Stevenson .15 .40
184 Lorenzen Wright .15 .40
185 Lindsey Hunter .15 .40
186 Kenyon Martin .20 .50
187 Kobe Bryant 1.00 2.50
188 Scott Padgett .15 .40
189 Michael Finley .25 .60
190 Peja Stojakovic .25 .60
191 Zydrunas Ilgauskas .20 .50
192 Vincent Yarbrough .15 .40
193 Jamal Mashburn .20 .50
194 Smush Parker .15 .40
195 Caron Butler .20 .50
196 Derek Fisher .20 .50
197 Damon Stoudamire .20 .50
198 Nene Hilario .20 .50
199 Allen Iverson .40 1.00
200 Anthony Mason .15 .40
201 Rasual Butler .15 .40
202 Tony Parker .25 .60
203 Marcus Fizer .15 .40
204 Amare Stoudemire .30 .75
205 Marc Jackson .15 .40
206 Desmond Mason .20 .50
207 Marcus Camby .20 .50
208 Ruben Patterson .15 .40
209 Bob Sura .15 .40
210 Rick Fox .15 .40
211 Jim Jackson .15 .40
212 Walter McCarty .15 .40
213 Gary Payton .25 .60
214 Elden Campbell .15 .40
215 Steve Francis .20 .50
216 Stromile Swift .15 .40
217 Stephen Jackson .20 .50
218 Antonio McDyess .20 .50
219 Morris Peterson .15 .40
220 Wally Szczerbiak .20 .50
221 Tim Duncan AW .40 1.00
222 Amare Stoudemire AW .30 .75
223 Bobby Jackson AW .15 .40
224 Ben Wallace AW .20 .50
225 Gilbert Arenas AW .20 .50
226 Tracy McGrady AW .30 .75
227 Kobe Bryant AW 1.00 2.50
228 Kevin Garnett AW .40 1.00
229 Shaquille O'Neal AW .60 1.50
230 Yao Ming AW .50 1.25
231 Stephon Marbury BS .20 .50
232 Ron Artest BS .25 .60
233 Troy Hudson BS .15 .40
234 Ray Allen BS .25 .60
235 Matt Harpring BS .15 .40
236 Jermaine O'Neal BS .20 .50
237 Jason Kidd BS .40 1.00
238 Jason Williams BS .20 .50
239 Zydrunas Ilgauskas BS .20 .50
240 Jamal Mashburn BS .20 .50
241 Yao Ming BS .50 1.25
242 Peja Stojakovic BS .25 .60
243 Tony Parker BS .25 .60
244 Caron Butler BS .20 .50
245 Amare Stoudemire BS .30 .75
246 Troy Murphy BS .15 .40
247 Nene Hilario BS .20 .50
248 Allen Iverson BS .40 1.00
249 Kobe Bryant BS 1.00 2.50
250 Tim Duncan BS .40 1.00
251 Tracy McGrady BS .30 .75
252 Kevin Garnett BS .40 1.00
253 Drew Gooden BS .20 .50
254 Kenyon Martin BS .20 .50
255 Dirk Nowitzki BS .40 1.00
256 Paul Pierce BS .25 .60
257 Steve Francis BS .20 .50
258 Steve Nash BS .30 .75
259 Gary Payton BS .25 .60
260 Chris Webber BS .25 .60
261 LeBron James RC 25.00 60.00
262 Darko Milicic RC .50 1.25
263 Carmelo Anthony RC 2.00 5.00
264 Chris Bosh RC 1.00 2.50
265 Dwyane Wade RC 2.00 5.00
266 Chris Kaman RC .60 1.50
267 Kirk Hinrich RC .60 1.50
268 T.J. Ford RC .50 1.25
269 Mike Sweetney RC .40 1.00
270 Mickael Pietrus RC .50 1.25
271 Jarvis Hayes RC .40 1.00
272 Nick Collison RC .50 1.25
273 Marcus Banks RC .40 1.00
274 Luke Ridnour RC .50 1.25
275 Reece Gaines RC .40 1.00
276 Troy Bell RC .40 1.00
277 Zarko Cabarkapa RC .40 1.00
278 David West RC .60 1.50
279 Luke Walton RC .60 1.50
280 Dahntay Jones RC .50 1.25
281 Boris Diaw RC .60 1.50
282 Zoran Planinic RC .40 1.00
283 Travis Outlaw RC .50 1.25
284 Brian Cook RC .40 1.00
285 Jason Kapono RC .40 1.00
286 Ndudi Ebi RC .40 1.00
287 Kendrick Perkins RC .50 1.25
288 Leandro Barbosa RC .60 1.50
289 Josh Howard RC .60 1.50
290 Maciej Lampe RC .40 1.00
291 James/Darko/Melo 10.00 25.00
292 Sweetney/Bosh/Hayes 1.50 4.00
293 Hinrich/Collison/Kaman 1.25 3.00
294 Sweetney/West/Cook 1.25 3.00
295 Kaman/Bosh/Darko 1.50 4.00
296 Ford/Wade/Hinrich 2.50 6.00

297 Pietrus/Jones/Gaines 1.25 3.00
298 Ford/Banks/Ridnour 1.25 3.00
299 Pietrus/Zarko/Hayes 1.25 3.00
300 LeBron/Melo/Wade 15.00 40.00

2003-04 Fleer Tradition Crystal

*CRYSTAL SINGLES: 6X TO 15X BASE HI
1-260 PRINT RUN 175 SERIAL #'d SETS
*CRYSTAL RC's: 3X TO 8X BASE CARD HI
261-290 PRINT RUN 125 SERIAL #'d SETS
*CRYSTAL TRIPLE: 4X TO 10X BASE HI
291-300 PRINT RUN 50 SERIAL #'d SETS
261 LeBron James 150.00 400.00
300 James/Melo/Wade 100.00 250.00

2003-04 Fleer Tradition Draft Day Rookie

*261-290 DRAFT DAY: 1.5X TO 4X BASE HI
*291-300 DRAFT DAY: .75X TO 2X BASE HI
DRAFT DAY CARDS ARE #'s 261-300
STATED PRINT RUN 375 SERIAL #'d SETS
300 James/Melo/Wade 40.00 100.00

2003-04 Fleer Tradition Heads Up

Inserted in packs at the rate of one in 12, this 10-card set features a horizontal design with a full color player photo on the right and white borders.

COMPLETE SET (10) 4.00 10.00
STATED ODDS 1:12
1 Kwame Brown .60 1.50
2 Scottie Pippen 1.50 4.00
3 Tim Thomas .60 1.50
4 Stephen Jackson .75 2.00
5 Allen Iverson 1.50 4.00
6 Richard Hamilton .75 2.00
7 Jermaine O'Neal .75 2.00
8 Elton Brand 1.00 2.50
9 Antoine Walker 1.00 2.50
10 Drew Gooden .75 2.00

2003-04 Fleer Tradition Heads Up Game Used

Randomly seeded, this 10-card set parallels the base Heads Up insert set enhanced with a swatch of game-worn headband on the left side of the card. Each card is sequentially numbered.

PRINT RUN LISTED IN CHECKLIST
HUCA Carmelo Anthony/50 25.00 60.00
HUCB Chris Bosh/55 12.00 30.00
HUDW Dwyane Wade/65 25.00 60.00
HUKB Kwame Brown/40 8.00 20.00
HULR Luke Ridnour/55 6.00 15.00
HUMB Marcus Banks/50 5.00 12.00
HUMP Mickael Pietrus/50 6.00 15.00
HURG Reece Gaines/55 5.00 12.00
HUTB Troy Bell 5.00 12.00
HUTT Tim Thomas/60 8.00 20.00

2003-04 Fleer Tradition Milestones

Inserted at one in 144, this 10-card set features a horizontal design with a color player action photo on the right set against a black and white background. The left side has a solid color and a floating head portrait of the player.

COMPLETE SET (10) 15.00 40.00
STATED ODDS 1:144
1 Karl Malone 2.00 5.00
2 Kobe Bryant 6.00 15.00
3 Paul Pierce 1.50 4.00
4 Tracy McGrady 2.00 5.00
5 Kevin Garnett 2.50 6.00
6 Allen Iverson 2.50 6.00
7 Tim Duncan 2.50 6.00
8 Shaquille O'Neal 4.00 10.00
9 Vince Carter 2.50 6.00
10 Chris Webber 1.50 4.00

2003-04 Fleer Tradition Playground Rules

Inserted at one in six, this 20-card set places a color player action shot against a diagonally split background with the player's portrait showing in the top half.

COMPLETE SET (20) 10.00 25.00
STATED ODDS 1:6
1 LeBron James 6.00 15.00
2 Darko Milicic .50 1.25
3 Carmelo Anthony 2.00 5.00
4 Chris Bosh 1.00 2.50
5 Dwyane Wade 2.00 5.00
6 Chris Kaman .60 1.50
7 Kirk Hinrich .60 1.50
8 T.J. Ford .50 1.25
9 Mike Sweetney .40 1.00
10 Jarvis Hayes .40 1.00
11 Mickael Pietrus .50 1.25
12 Nick Collison .50 1.25
13 Marcus Banks .40 1.00
14 Luke Ridnour .50 1.25
15 Reece Gaines .40 1.00
16 Troy Bell .40 1.00
17 Zarko Cabarkapa .40 1.00
18 David West .60 1.50
19 Travis Outlaw .50 1.25
20 Dahntay Jones .50 1.25

2003-04 Fleer Tradition Rookie Hats Off

Randomly seeded and sequentially numbered to 180, this 12-card set places players and a swatch of the hat they wore on draft day on each card.

PRINT RUN 180 SER.#'d SETS
RHOCA Carmelo Anthony 15.00 40.00
RHOCB Chris Bosh 8.00 20.00
RHOCK Chris Kaman 5.00 12.00
RHODJ Dahntay Jones 4.00 10.00
RHODW Dwyane Wade 12.00 30.00
RHOJH Jarvis Hayes 3.00 8.00
RHOMJ Maciej Lampe 3.00 8.00
RHOMS Mike Sweetney 3.00 8.00
RHORG Reece Gaines 3.00 8.00
RHOSV Slavko Vranes 3.00 8.00
RHOZC Zarko Cabarkapa 3.00 8.00
RHOZP Zoran Planinic 3.00 8.00

2003-04 Fleer Tradition Throwback Threads

Inserted at one in 36, this 10-card set places full color player portrait photos on a card with black borders.

COMPLETE SET (10) 8.00 20.00
STATED ODDS 1:36
1 Carmelo Anthony 3.00 8.00
2 Luke Walton 1.00 2.50
3 Chris Kaman 1.00 2.50
4 Travis Outlaw .75 2.00
5 Kirk Hinrich 1.00 2.50
6 T.J. Ford .75 2.00
7 Brian Cook .60 1.50
8 Jarvis Hayes .60 1.50
9 Mickael Pietrus .75 2.00
10 Nick Collison .75 2.00

2003-04 Fleer Tradition Throwback Threads Event Worn

Randomly inserted, this 11-card set parallels the design of the base Thowback Threads insert enhanced with a swatch of from Mitchell and Ness throwback jerseys that were worn by the player at an event or photo shoot. No insert odds were given for this set, and these cards are not serial numbered.

RANDOM INSERTS IN PACKS
*COMBO: 1.25X TO 3X BASE JSY HI
COMBO PRINT RUN 150 SETS
BC Brian Cook 1.50 4.00
CA Carmelo Anthony 8.00 20.00
CK Chris Kaman 2.50 6.00
DW David West 2.50 6.00
JH Jarvis Hayes 1.50 4.00
LR Luke Ridnour 2.00 5.00
LW Luke Walton 2.50 6.00
MB Marcus Banks 1.50 4.00
MP Mickael Pietrus 2.00 5.00
MS Mike Sweetney 1.50 4.00
TO Travis Outlaw 2.00 5.00

2003-04 Fleer Tradition Throwback Threads Dual Event Worn

Randomly inserted and sequentially numbered to 299, this five-card set parallels the design of the base Thowback Threads insert set enhanced with a horizontal design, a second player and two swatches from Mitchell and Ness throwback jerseys that were worn by the player at an event or photo shoot.

PRINT RUN 299 SERIAL #'d SETS
BCCK B.Cook/C.Kaman 5.00 12.00
CADW C.Anthony/D.West 8.00 20.00
LWTO L.Walton/T.Outlaw 5.00 12.00
MPJH M.Pietrus/J.Hayes 5.00 12.00
MSMB M.Sweetney/M.Banks 5.00 12.00

2003-04 Fleer Tradition All-Star Game

COMPLETE SET (13) 20.00 50.00
ANNCD PRINT RUN OF 2004 COPIES PER
1 Carmelo Anthony 5.00 12.00
2 Luke Walton 1.50 4.00
3 Jason Kidd 2.50 6.00
4 Allen Iverson 2.50 6.00
5 Tracy McGrady 2.00 5.00
6 Steve Francis 1.25 3.00
7 Kevin Garnett 2.50 6.00
8 Chris Kaman 1.50 4.00
9 Shaquille O'Neal 4.00 10.00
10 Dwyane Wade 5.00 12.00
11 Yao Ming 3.00 8.00
12 Amara Stoudemire 2.00 5.00
13 Vince Carter 2.50 6.00

2004-05 Fleer Tradition

Released in December 2004, Tradition boasts a 268-card base set divided up as follows: cadrs 1-208 are veterans, cards 209-220 are Award Winners, cards 221-20 are inserted at one in four and feature rookies, and cards 251-268 are inserted at one in 18 and are rookie trios. Base cards have a red border and a tan background. Tradition was offered in both Hobby and Retail formats where both packs contain 10 cards, but Hobby is packaged in 36 pack boxes and Retail is packaged in 24 pack boxes.

COMP.SET w/o RC's (220) 20.00 50.00
RC STATED ODDS 1:4
TRIO STATED ODDS 1:18
1 Jonathan Bender .15 .40
2 Boris Diaw .20 .50
3 Eddie Robinson .15 .40
4 Jason Richardson .25 .60
5 Bonzi Wells .15 .40
6 Elden Campbell .15 .40
7 P.J. Brown .15 .40
8 Ray Allen .25 .60
9 Theron Smith .15 .40
10 Darko Milicic .15 .40
11 Bob Sura .15 .40
12 Sam Cassell .20 .50
13 Cuttino Mobley .15 .40
14 Andrei Kirilenko .20 .50
15 Raef LaFrentz .15 .40
16 Aleksandar Pavlovic .15 .40
17 Carmelo Anthony .50 1.25
18 Mickael Pietrus .20 .50
19 James Posey .15 .40
20 Nazr Mohammed .15 .40
21 Jalen Rose .20 .50
22 Jiri Welsch .15 .40
23 Drew Gooden .15 .40
24 Nene .20 .50
25 Troy Murphy .15 .40
26 Mike Miller .20 .50
27 T.J. Ford .15 .40
28 Allan Houston .20 .50
29 Donyell Marshall .15 .40
30 Chris Crawford .15 .40
31 Eric Snow .15 .40
32 Marcus Camby .20 .50
33 Devean George .15 .40
34 Eric Williams .15 .40
35 Kurt Thomas .15 .40
36 Rashard Lewis .25 .60
37 Alvin Williams .15 .40
38 David West .20 .50
39 Shawn Marion .20 .50
40 Mark Blount .15 .40
41 Dikembe Mutombo .25 .60
42 Stephen Jackson .20 .50
43 Rasual Butler .15 .40
44 Michael Redd .20 .50
45 Jason Kidd .40 1.00
46 Malik Rose .15 .40
47 Chris Bosh .25 .60
48 Antonio Daniels .15 .40
49 Doug Christie .15 .40
50 Stephon Marbury .20 .50
51 Gary Payton .25 .60
52 Michael Finley .25 .60
53 Ben Wallace .20 .50
54 Jason Williams .20 .50
55 Michael Olowokandi .15 .40
56 Steve Francis .20 .50
57 Chris Webber .25 .60
58 Tim Duncan .40 1.00
59 Carlos Arroyo .15 .40
60 Eddie House .15 .40
61 Mike Bibby .25 .60
62 Tony Parker .25 .60
63 Matt Harpring .15 .40
64 Richard Hamilton .20 .50
65 Corey Maggette .20 .50
66 Damon Jones .15 .40
67 Keith Bogans .15 .40
68 Willie Green .15 .40
69 Kirk Hinrich .20 .50
70 Jerry Stackhouse .20 .50
71 Chris Kaman .20 .50
72 Lamar Odom .20 .50
73 Dwyane Wade .40 1.00
74 Kevin Garnett .40 1.00
75 Allen Iverson .40 1.00
76 Theo Ratliff .15 .40
77 Shareef Abdur-Rahim .20 .50
78 Gilbert Arenas .20 .50
79 Jamal Sampson .15 .40
80 Josh Howard .25 .60
81 Latrell Sprewell .20 .50
82 Kyle Korver .20 .50
83 Brad Miller .20 .50
84 Rasho Nesterovic .15 .40
85 Larry Hughes .20 .50
86 Eddy Curry .15 .40
87 Rasheed Wallace .25 .60
88 Chris Wilcox .15 .40
89 Mark Madsen .15 .40
90 Kenny Thomas .15 .40
91 Zach Randolph .20 .50
92 Juan Dixon .15 .40
93 Tyson Chandler .20 .50
94 Stromile Swift .15 .40
95 Udonis Haslem .15 .40
96 Jason Collins .15 .40
97 Glenn Robinson .20 .50
98 Darius Miles .15 .40
99 Jared Jeffries .15 .40
100 Bobby Jackson .15 .40
101 Jahidi White .15 .40
102 Dirk Nowitzki .40 1.00
103 Wally Szczerbiak .20 .50
104 John Salmons .20 .50
105 Kwame Brown .15 .40
106 Jason Kapono .15 .40
107 Chauncey Billups .25 .60
108 Shane Battier .20 .50
109 Samuel Dalembert .15 .40
110 Manu Ginobili .30 .75
111 Anfernee Hardaway .60 1.50
112 Yao Ming .50 1.25
113 Eric Piatkowski .15 .40
114 Vlade Divac .20 .50
115 Ron Mercer .15 .40
116 Quentin Richardson .20 .50
117 Derek Anderson .15 .40
118 Jarvis Hayes .15 .40
119 Antonio Davis .15 .40
120 Erick Dampier .15 .40
121 Antonio McDyess .20 .50
122 Fred Jones .15 .40
123 Damon Stoudamire .20 .50
124 Jason Collier .15 .40
125 Frank Williams .15 .40
126 Kobe Bryant 1.00 2.50
127 Keith Van Horn .20 .50
128 Darrell Armstrong .15 .40
129 Steve Nash .30 .75
130 Nick Collison .20 .50
131 Ricky Davis .20 .50
132 Tracy McGrady .30 .75
133 Shaquille O'Neal .60 1.50
134 Desmond Mason .20 .50
135 Richard Jefferson .20 .50
136 Casey Jacobsen .15 .40
137 Ronald Murray .15 .40
138 Rafer Alston .15 .40
139 Tony Delk .15 .40
140 LeBron James 1.50 4.00
141 Earl Boykins .15 .40
142 Speedy Claxton .15 .40
143 Jamaal Tinsley .15 .40
144 Elton Brand .25 .60
145 Jamaal Magloire .15 .40
146 Jamal Crawford .25 .60
147 Peja Stojakovic .25 .60
148 Bruce Bowen .15 .40
149 Paul Pierce .25 .60
150 Jason Terry .20 .50
151 Kenyon Martin .20 .50
152 Maurice Taylor .15 .40
153 Toni Kukoc .25 .60
154 Aaron Williams .15 .40
155 Tony Battie .15 .40
156 Leandro Barbosa .25 .60
157 Carlos Boozer .20 .50
158 Brevin Knight .15 .40
159 Marquis Daniels .15 .40
160 Jim Jackson .15 .40
161 Caron Butler .20 .50
162 Troy Hudson .15 .40
163 DeShawn Stevenson .15 .40
164 Nick Van Exel .20 .50
165 Antawn Jamison .20 .50
166 Marcus Banks .15 .40
167 Derek Fisher .20 .50
168 Juwan Howard .20 .50
169 Reggie Miller .25 .60
170 Joe Smith .20 .50
171 Alonzo Mourning .30 .75
172 Mike Sweetney .15 .40
173 Mehmet Okur .20 .50
174 Brent Barry .15 .40
175 Al Harrington .20 .50
176 Dajuan Wagner .15 .40
177 Voshon Lenard .15 .40
178 Jermaine O'Neal .20 .50
179 Bobby Simmons .15 .40
180 Karl Malone .30 .75
181 Dan Gadzuric .15 .40
182 David Wesley .15 .40
183 Tim Thomas .15 .40
184 Amare Stoudemire .20 .50
185 Morris Peterson .15 .40
186 Fred Hoiberg .15 .40
187 Jeff McInnis .15 .40
188 Andre Miller .20 .50
189 Mike Dunleavy .20 .50
190 Ron Artest .25 .60
191 Kerry Kittles .15 .40
192 Baron Davis .20 .50
193 Vince Carter .40 1.00
194 Gerald Wallace .20 .50
195 Tayshaun Prince .20 .50
196 Marko Jaric .15 .40
197 Luke Walton .15 .40
198 Eddie Jones .20 .50
199 Hedo Turkoglu .20 .50
200 Joe Johnson .20 .50
201 Vladimir Radmanovic .15 .40
202 Gordan Giricek .15 .40
203 Antoine Walker .25 .60
204 Zydrunas Ilgauskas .20 .50
205 Clifford Robinson .15 .40
206 Pau Gasol .25 .60
207 Jamal Mashburn .20 .50
208 Luke Ridnour .20 .50
209 Kevin Garnett AW .50 1.25
210 LeBron James AW 2.00 5.00
211 Jason Kidd AW .50 1.25
212 Kobe Bryant AW 1.25 3.00
213 Shaquille O'Neal AW .75 2.00
214 Tim Duncan AW .50 1.25
215 Ron Artest AW .30 .75
216 Dwyane Wade AW .50 1.25
217 Kirk Hinrich AW .25 .60
218 Chris Bosh AW .30 .75
219 Carmelo Anthony AW .60 1.50
220 Antawn Jamison AW .25 .60
221 Dwight Howard RC 1.50 4.00
222 Emeka Okafor RC .60 1.50
223 Ben Gordon RC .75 2.00
224 Shaun Livingston RC .75 2.00
225 Devin Harris RC .60 1.50
226 Josh Childress RC .60 1.50
227 Luol Deng RC .75 2.00
228 Rafael Araujo RC .50 1.25
229 Andre Iguodala RC 1.00 2.50
230 Luke Jackson RC .50 1.25
231 Andris Biedrins RC .50 1.25
232 Robert Swift RC .50 1.25
233 Sebastian Telfair RC .60 1.50
234 Kris Humphries RC .75 2.00
235 Al Jefferson RC 1.00 2.50
236 Kirk Snyder RC .50 1.25
237 Josh Smith RC .75 2.00
238 J.R. Smith RC .75 2.00
239 Dorell Wright RC .75 2.00
240 Jameer Nelson RC .75 2.00
241 Pavel Podkolzine RC .50 1.25
242 Nenad Krstic RC .75 2.00
243 Andres Nocioni RC .75 2.00
244 Delonte West RC .75 2.00
245 Tony Allen RC .75 2.00
246 Kevin Martin RC 1.00 2.50
247 Sasha Vujacic RC .75 2.00
248 Beno Udrih RC .60 1.50
249 David Harrison RC .50 1.25
250 Anderson Varejao RC .60 1.50
251 Okafor/Gordon/Howard 2.50 6.00
252 Howard/Kasun RC/Nelson 1.25 4.00
253 Allen/Jefferson/West 3.00 8.00
254 Deng/Duhon/Gordon 2.50 6.00
255 Nocioni/Martin/Telfair 1.50 4.00
256 Childress/Ivey RC/Smith 1.50 4.00
257 Harris/Nelson/Telfair 1.25 4.00
258 Chlmrs RC/Burks RC/Emm RC 1.50 4.00
259 Deng/Duhon RC/Pickett RC 1.50 4.00
260 Childress/Jackson/Iguodala 1.50 4.00
261 Livingston/Howard/Swift 1.25 3.00
262 Smith/Jefferson/Telfair 1.50 4.00
263 Livingston/Wright/Smith 1.25 3.00
264 Reed RC/Vroman RC/Ramos RC 1.50 4.00
265 Podkolzin/Biedrins/Krstic 1.50 4.00
266 Vujacic/Tabuse RC/Udrih
267 Araujo/Humphries/Snyder 1.50 4.00
268 Robinson RC/Sow RC/Ariza RC 1.25 3.00

2004-05 Fleer Tradition Blue

*BLUE: .5X TO 1.25X BASE HI

2004-05 Fleer Tradition Crystal

*CRYSTAL STARS: 2X TO 5X BASE HI
*CRYSTAL AW: 1.5X TO 4X BASE HI
PRINT RUN 150 SER.#'d SETS
*CRYSTAL RCs: 2X TO 5X BASE HI
*CRYSTAL TRIO: 3X TO 8X BASE HI
TRIO PRINT RUN 25 SETS

2004-05 Fleer Tradition Draft Day Rookies

*221-250 DRAFT: .75X TO 2X BASE HI
*251-268 DRAFT TRIO: .75X TO 2X BASE HI
PRINT RUN 375 SER.#'d SETS

2004-05 Fleer Tradition Green

*GREEN: .6X TO 1.5X BASE HI

2004-05 Fleer Tradition Classic Combinations

Randomly inserted, this 20-card set is horizontally designed and pairs two players from the same team. Pictures on the card are in black and white and there are Red highlights along the bottom. Each card is serially numbered to 250.

PRINT RUN 250 SER.#'d SETS
1 S.O'Neal/D.Wade 3.00 8.00
2 C.Anthony/K.Martin 2.50 6.00
3 K.Bryant/L.Odom 4.00 10.00
4 Y.Ming/T.McGrady 2.50 6.00
5 A.Houston/S.Marbury 1.00 2.50
6 S.Francis/D.Howard 2.50 6.00
7 K.Hinrich/B.Gordon 1.25 3.00
8 E.Brand/C.Maggette 1.25 3.00
9 P.Pierce/G.Payton 1.25 3.00
10 A.Iverson/A.Iguodala 2.00 5.00
11 L.James/L.Jackson 4.00 10.00
12 B.Davis/J.R.Smith 1.25 3.00
13 D.Nowitzki/D.Harris 2.00 5.00
14 A.Kirilenko/C.Boozer 1.00 2.50
15 B.Wallace/R.Wallace 1.25 3.00
16 R.Miller/J.O'Neal 1.25 3.00
17 A.Stoudemire/S.Nash 1.50 4.00
18 K.Garnett/L.Sprewell 2.00 5.00
19 J.Kidd/R.Jefferson 2.00 5.00
20 T.Duncan/M.Ginobili 2.00 5.00

2004-05 Fleer Tradition Hardcourt Tributes

Inserted in both Hobby and Retail at one in six packs, this 20-card set places a close up photo on a silver background that is shaped like a shield.

COMPLETE SET (20) 12.50 30.00
STATED ODDS 1:6
1 Allen Iverson 1.00 2.50
2 Jason Kidd 1.00 2.50
3 Dwyane Wade 1.00 2.50
4 Kenyon Martin .50 1.25
5 Pau Gasol .60 1.50
6 Carmelo Anthony 1.25 3.00
7 Paul Pierce .60 1.50
8 Tracy McGrady .75 2.00
9 Shaquille O'Neal 1.50 4.00
10 Stephon Marbury .50 1.25
11 Steve Francis .50 1.25
12 Yao Ming 1.25 3.00
13 Peja Stojakovic .60 1.50
14 Kevin Garnett 1.00 2.50
15 Tim Duncan 1.00 2.50
16 Dirk Nowitzki 1.00 2.50
17 Vince Carter 1.00 2.50
18 Jason Richardson .60 1.50
19 Kobe Bryant 2.50 6.00
20 LeBron James 4.00 10.00

2004-05 Fleer Tradition Hardcourt Tributes Jerseys

Inserted in Hobby packs at the rate of one in 102 and Retail at the rate of one in 192, this 20-card set utilizes the design of the base Hardcourt Tributes set enhanced with a square swatch of jersey.

STATED ODDS 1:102 H, 1:192 R
*PATCHES: 1X TO 2.5X BASE HI
PATCH PRINT RUN 50 SER.#'d SETS
1 Allen Iverson 4.00 10.00
2 Jason Kidd 4.00 10.00
3 Dwyane Wade 4.00 10.00
4 Kenyon Martin 2.00 5.00
5 Pau Gasol 2.50 6.00
6 Carmelo Anthony 5.00 12.00
7 Paul Pierce 2.50 6.00
8 Tracy McGrady 3.00 8.00
9 Shaquille O'Neal 6.00 15.00
10 Stephon Marbury 2.00 5.00
11 Steve Francis 2.00 5.00
12 Yao Ming 5.00 12.00
13 Peja Stojakovic 2.50 6.00
14 Kevin Garnett 4.00 10.00
15 Tim Duncan 4.00 10.00
16 Dirk Nowitzki 4.00 10.00
17 Vince Carter 4.00 10.00
18 Jason Richardson 2.50 6.00
19 Amare Stoudemire 2.00 5.00
20 Ben Wallace 2.00 5.00

2004-05 Fleer Tradition Rookie Hats Off

Randomly seeded, this 15-card set features a horizontal design with a black border along the top, a yellow border along the bottom and a green background. Player portrait photos in their Draft Day Hats appear on the right and a swatch of the hat from the picture appears in the upper left. Each card is sequentially numbered to 100.

PRINT RUN 100 SER.#'d SETS
1 Dwight Howard 15.00 40.00
2 Ben Gordon 6.00 15.00
3 Shaun Livingston 6.00 15.00
4 Devin Harris 5.00 12.00
5 Josh Childress 5.00 12.00
6 Luol Deng 6.00 15.00
7 Rafael Araujo 4.00 10.00
8 Andre Iguodala 8.00 20.00
9 Andris Biedrins 4.00 10.00
10 Kirk Snyder 4.00 10.00
11 Josh Smith 6.00 15.00
12 Jameer Nelson 6.00 15.00
13 Pavel Podkolzin 4.00 10.00
15 Beno Udrih 5.00 12.00

2004-05 Fleer Tradition Rookie Throwback Threads Jerseys

Inserted in Hobby packs at one in 112 and Retail at one in 240, this 24-card set parallels the look of the Rookie Hats Off insert but has a blue background and a swatch of jersey. Several other versions of this set were issued: Ball swatches are inserted one in 216 Hobby and one in 480 Retail, Headband swatches are inserted one in 612 Hobby and one in 960 Retail, Jersey and Ball swatches are serially numbered to 50 and Jersey and Headband swatches are serially numbered to 25.

STATED ODDS 1:112 H, 1:240 R
*BALL: .5X TO 1.25X BASE HI
BALL STATED ODDS 1:216 H 1:480 R
*HEADBAND: 1.25X TO 3X BASE HI
HEADBAND STATED ODDS 1:612 H, 1:960 R
*JERSEY/BALL: 1.5X TO 4X BASE HI
JERSEY/BALL PRINT RUN 50 SER.#'d SETS
*JSY/HEADBAND: 2X TO 5X BASE HI
JSY/HEADBAND PRINT RUN 25 SETS
1 Dwight Howard 5.00 12.00
2 Ben Gordon 2.50 6.00
3 Shaun Livingston 2.50 6.00
4 Devin Harris 2.00 5.00
5 Josh Childress 2.00 5.00
6 Luol Deng 2.50 6.00
7 Andre Iguodala 3.00 8.00
8 Rafael Araujo 1.50 4.00
9 Luke Jackson 1.50 4.00
10 Sebastian Telfair 2.00 5.00
11 Kris Humphries 2.50 6.00
12 Al Jefferson 3.00 8.00
13 Kirk Snyder 1.50 4.00
14 Josh Smith 2.50 6.00
15 J.R. Smith 2.50 6.00
16 Dorell Wright 2.50 6.00
17 Jameer Nelson 2.50 6.00
18 Delonte West 2.50 6.00
19 Tony Allen 2.50 6.00
20 Anderson Varejao 2.00 5.00
21 Lionel Chalmers 2.50 6.00
22 Chris Duhon 2.50 6.00
23 Bernard Robinson 2.00 5.00
24 Trevor Ariza 2.50 6.00

2004-05 Fleer Tradition Rookie Throwback Threads Dual

Inserted randomly, this 12-card set parallels the look of the Rookie Hats Off set but with a red background, sequential numbering to 100, two players, one on each side and two jerseys in the center of the card.

PRINT RUN 100 SER.#'d SETS
*PATCHES: .6X TO 1.5X BASE HI
PATCH PRINT RUN 75 SER.#'d SETS
1 B.Gordon/L.Deng 6.00 15.00
2 D.Howard/J.Nelson 8.00 20.00
3 J.Childress/J.Smith 6.00 15.00
4 A.Jefferson/T.Allen 5.00 12.00
5 S.Livingston/L.Chalmers 5.00 12.00
6 A.Iguodala/T.Ariza 8.00 20.00
7 K.Humphries/K.Snyder 5.00 12.00
8 D.Harris/C.Duhon 6.00 15.00
10 A.Varejao/B.Robinson 5.00 12.00
11 R.Araujo/L.Jackson 5.00 12.00
12 J.Nelson/D.West 5.00 12.00

2004-05 Fleer Tradition Signing Day

Inserted in Retail packs at the rate of one in 24, this 15-card set has white borders and a tan background and player photos are set against their new team logo. A Chrome parallel was inserted also and is sequentially numbered to 50.

COMPLETE SET (15) 10.00 25.00
STATED ODDS 1:24 RETAIL
*CHROME: 1.25X TO 3X BASE HI
CHROME PRINT RUN 50 SER.#'d SETS
1 Dwight Howard 1.50 4.00
2 Emeka Okafor .60 1.50
3 Ben Gordon .75 2.00
4 Shaun Livingston .75 2.00
5 Devin Harris .60 1.50
6 Josh Childress .60 1.50
7 Luol Deng .75 2.00
8 Andre Iguodala 1.00 2.50
9 Luke Jackson .50 1.25
10 Andris Biedrins .50 1.25
11 Robert Swift .50 1.25
12 Sebastian Telfair .60 1.50
13 Josh Smith .75 2.00
14 J.R. Smith .75 2.00
15 Jameer Nelson .75 2.00

2004-05 Fleer Tradition USA Basketball

Randomly inserted, this 13-card set features members of the USA basketball team on a card that is heavy with red white and blue and is serially numbered to 99.

PRINT RUN 99 SER.#'d SETS
1 LeBron James 25.00 60.00
2 Carmelo Anthony 8.00 20.00
3 Tim Duncan 5.00 12.00
4 Shawn Marion 2.50 6.00
5 Allen Iverson 5.00 12.00
6 Dwyane Wade 5.00 12.00
7 Amare Stoudemire 2.50 6.00
8 Richard Jefferson 2.50 6.00
9 Stephon Marbury 2.50 6.00
10 Carlos Boozer 2.50 6.00
11 Lamar Odom 2.50 6.00
12 Emeka Okafor 2.50 6.00
13 Larry Brown 4.00 10.00

2000-01 Fleer Triple Crown

The 2000-01 Fleer Triple Crown product was released in March, 2001 and featured a 241-card base set that was broken into tiers as follows: Rookies (1-40, 241), and Base Veterans (41-240). Please note that cards 1-40 and 241 were short-printed at the rate of one in four packs. Each pack contained 10 cards, and carried a suggested retail price of $1.99.

COMPLETE SET w/o RC (200) 12.50 25.00
RC SUBSET: STATED ODDS 1:4
1 Quentin Richardson RC .40 1.00
2 Khalid El-Amin RC .25 .60
3 Courtney Alexander RC .30 .75
4 Mike Penberthy RC .40 1.00
5 DerMarr Johnson RC .30 .75
6 A.J. Guyton RC .25 .60
7 Erick Barkley RC .25 .60
8 Jamal Crawford RC 1.00 2.50
9 Hedo Turkoglu RC .60 1.50
10 Michael Redd RC 1.00 2.50
11 Stromile Swift RC .40 1.00
12 Eddie House RC .30 .75
13 Keyon Dooling RC .40 1.00
14 Lavor Postell RC .25 .60
15 Mateen Cleaves RC .30 .75
16 Morris Peterson RC .40 1.00
17 DeShawn Stevenson RC .40 1.00
18 Darius Miles RC .40 1.00
19 Hanno Mottola RC .25 .60
20 Jerome Moiso RC .25 .60
21 Desmond Mason RC .50 1.25
22 Jason Collier RC .40 1.00
23 Ruben Wolkowyski RC .25 .60
24 Eduardo Najera RC .40 1.00
25 Kenyon Martin RC 1.00 2.50
26 Marcus Fizer RC .40 1.00
27 Etan Thomas RC .40 1.00
28 Mark Madsen RC .40 1.00
29 Pepe Sanchez RC .40 1.00
30 Brian Cardinal RC .30 .75
31 Chris Porter RC .25 .60
32 Dan Langhi RC .25 .60
33 Mike Miller RC .60 1.50
34 Chris Mihm RC .30 .75
35 Mamadou N'Diaye RC .25 .60
36 Dragan Tarlac RC .25 .60
37 Iakovos Tsakalidis RC .25 .60
38 Stephen Jackson RC .60 1.50
39 Jamaal Magloire RC .40 1.00
40 Joel Przybilla RC .30 .75
41 Adrian Griffin .15 .40
42 Allan Houston .20 .50
43 Mahmoud Abdul-Rauf .15 .40
44 Avery Johnson .20 .50
45 Damon Stoudamire .20 .50
46 Jim Jackson .15 .40
47 Jason Williams .25 .60
48 Jason Kidd .40 1.00
49 Ray Allen .25 .60
50 Baron Davis .25 .60
51 Mark Jackson .20 .50
52 Darrick Martin .15 .40
53 Derek Fisher .25 .60
54 Anthony Peeler .15 .40
55 Vince Carter .50 1.25
56 Tim Hardaway .25 .60
57 Richard Hamilton .20 .50
58 Malik Rose .15 .40
59 Antonio Daniels .15 .40
60 Lindsey Hunter .15 .40
61 William Avery .15 .40
62 Reggie Miller .25 .60
63 Shareef Abdur-Rahim .20 .50
64 Travis Best .15 .40
65 John Stockton .30 .75
66 Kenny Anderson .20 .50
67 Trajan Langdon .15 .40
68 Sam Cassell .20 .50
69 Chucky Atkins .15 .40
70 Laron Profit .15 .40
71 Andre Miller .20 .50
72 Erick Strickland .15 .40
73 Ron Artest .25 .60
74 Kobe Bryant 1.00 2.50
75 Ricky Davis .20 .50
76 Allen Iverson .50 1.25
77 Steve Smith .20 .50
78 Alvin Williams .15 .40
79 Randy Brown .15 .40
80 Michael Dickerson .15 .40
81 Tyronn Lue .15 .40
82 Bonzi Wells .15 .40
83 Felipe Lopez .15 .40
84 Steve Francis .20 .50
85 Jaren Jackson .15 .40
86 Anthony Carter .15 .40
87 Mitch Richmond .20 .50
88 Sherman Douglas .15 .40
89 Cuttino Mobley .15 .40
90 Mario Elie .15 .40
91 Tariq Abdul-Wahad .15 .40
92 Ron Mercer .15 .40
93 Jalen Rose .20 .50
94 Mike Bibby .25 .60
95 Voshon Lenard .15 .40
96 Derek Anderson .15 .40
97 Kendall Gill .15 .40
98 Muggsy Bogues .20 .50
99 Eddie Jones .25 .60
100 Larry Hughes .20 .50
101 Latrell Sprewell .20 .50
102 Stephon Marbury .20 .50
103 Eric Piatkowski .15 .40
104 Brevin Knight .15 .40
105 Isaiah Rider .20 .50
106 Wesley Person .15 .40
107 Nick Van Exel .20 .50
108 Dell Curry .15 .40
109 Tony Delk .15 .40
110 Glen Rice .20 .50
111 Bobby Jackson .15 .40
112 Kerry Kittles .15 .40
113 John Starks .20 .50
114 Gary Payton .25 .60
115 Mookie Blaylock .15 .40
116 David Wesley .15 .40
117 Rod Strickland .15 .40
118 Terrell Brandon .15 .40
119 Steve Nash .40 1.00
120 Moochie Norris .15 .40
121 Eric Snow .15 .40
122 Chauncey Billups .25 .60
123 Darrell Armstrong .15 .40
124 Ron Harper .20 .50
125 Dion Glover .15 .40
126 Vin Baker .20 .50
127 Terry Mills .15 .40
128 Joe Smith .20 .50
129 Kurt Thomas .15 .40
130 Dirk Nowitzki .40 1.00
131 Sean Elliott .25 .60
132 Jerome Williams .15 .40
133 Larry Johnson .25 .60
134 LaPhonso Ellis .20 .50
135 Pat Garrity .15 .40
136 Lawrence Funderburke .15 .40
137 Elton Brand .25 .60
138 Rashard Lewis .25 .60
139 Shawn Kemp .25 .60
140 Elden Campbell .15 .40
141 Christian Laettner .20 .50
142 Al Harrington .20 .50
143 Billy Owens .15 .40
144 Wally Szczerbiak .20 .50
145 Jonathan Bender .15 .40
146 Karl Malone .30 .75
147 Andrew DeClercq .15 .40
148 Danny Manning .15 .40
149 Antoine Walker .20 .50
150 Jason Caffey .15 .40
151 P.J. Brown .15 .40
152 Matt Harpring .15 .40
153 Mark Strickland .15 .40
154 Theo Ratliff .15 .40
155 Ruben Patterson .15 .40
156 Tom Gugliotta .15 .40
157 Derrick Coleman .20 .50
158 Lorenzen Wright .15 .40
159 Tracy McGrady .40 1.00
160 Quincy Lewis .15 .40
161 Tony Battie .15 .40
162 Keith Van Horn .20 .50
163 Paul Pierce .25 .60
164 Glenn Robinson .20 .50
165 John Wallace .15 .40
166 Popeye Jones .15 .40
167 Kevin Garnett .40 1.00
168 Donyell Marshall .15 .40
169 Michael Finley .25 .60
170 Nick Anderson .15 .40
171 Danny Fortson .15 .40
172 Keon Clark .15 .40
173 Juwan Howard .20 .50
174 Brian Grant .15 .40
175 Marcus Camby .20 .50
176 Scottie Pippen .40 1.00
177 Shawn Marion .20 .50
178 Lamar Odom .20 .50
179 Charles Oakley .20 .50
180 Tim James .15 .40
181 Eric Williams .15 .40
182 Tim Duncan .50 1.25
183 Andrae Patterson .15 .40
184 Toni Kukoc .25 .60
185 Chris Mullin .25 .60
186 Alan Henderson .15 .40
187 Maurice Taylor .15 .40
188 Chris Webber .25 .60
189 Jamal Mashburn .20 .50
190 Rodney Rogers .15 .40
191 Loy Vaught .15 .40
192 Carlos Rogers .15 .40
193 Grant Hill .30 .75
194 George Lynch .15 .40
195 Antonio McDyess .20 .50
196 Tim Thomas .15 .40
197 Roshown McLeod .15 .40
198 Antawn Jamison .25 .60
199 Clifford Robinson .15 .40
200 Corey Maggette .20 .50
201 Horace Grant .20 .50
202 David Benoit .15 .40
203 Cedric Ceballos .15 .40
204 Antonio Davis .15 .40
205 Lamond Murray .15 .40
206 Jerry Stackhouse .20 .50
207 Jermaine O'Neal .20 .50
208 Anthony Mason .15 .40
209 Cedric Henderson .15 .40
210 Corliss Williamson .15 .40
211 Austin Croshere .15 .40
212 Radoslav Nesterovic .15 .40
213 Hakeem Olajuwon .30 .75
214 Nazr Mohammed .15 .40
215 David Robinson .40 1.00
216 Jeff McInnis .15 .40
217 Brad Miller .20 .50
218 Evan Eschmeyer .15 .40
219 Jelani McCoy .15 .40
220 Sean Rooks .15 .40
221 Dikembe Mutombo .25 .60
222 Othella Harrington .15 .40
223 John Amaechi .15 .40
224 Erick Dampier .15 .40
225 Calvin Booth .15 .40
226 Adonal Foyle .15 .40
227 Michael Doleac .15 .40
228 Michael Olowokandi .15 .40
229 Matt Geiger .15 .40
230 Vlade Divac .20 .50
231 Bryant Reeves .15 .40
232 Shaquille O'Neal .60 1.50
233 Todd Fuller .15 .40
234 Arvydas Sabonis .20 .50
235 Jim McIlvaine .15 .40
236 Isaac Austin .15 .40
237 Raef LaFrentz .15 .40
238 Rasheed Wallace .25 .60
239 Kelvin Cato .15 .40
240 Patrick Ewing .30 .75
241 Marc Jackson RC .30 .75

2000-01 Fleer Triple Crown Vince Carter Rookie Remnants

This three-card insert was randomly inserted into 2000-01 Fleer products. The set includes a Vince Carter floor card (numbered to 100), a Vince Carter floor/jersey card (numbered to 15), and finally an autographed Vince Carter floor/jersey card (numbered 1/1).

RANDOM INSERTS IN HOBBY PACKS
NNO Vince Carter FLR JSY/15 20.00 50.00
NNO Vince Carter FLR/100 12.50 30.00

2000-01 Fleer Triple Crown Crown Jewels

Randomly inserted in packs at one in 84, this 15-card set highlights the marquee players that the fans say is well worth the admission price. Card backs carry a "CJ" prefix.

COMPLETE SET (15) 40.00 100.00
STATED ODDS 1:84
CJ1 Kevin Garnett 3.00 8.00
CJ2 Lamar Odom 1.50 4.00
CJ3 Allen Iverson 4.00 10.00
CJ4 Marcus Fizer 2.00 5.00
CJ5 Shaquille O'Neal 5.00 12.00
CJ6 Steve Francis 1.50 4.00
CJ7 Paul Pierce 2.00 5.00

CJ8 Elton Brand 2.00 5.00
CJ9 Chris Webber 2.00 5.00
CJ10 Tim Duncan 4.00 10.00
CJ11 Kobe Bryant 8.00 20.00
CJ12 Grant Hill 2.50 6.00
CJ13 Kenyon Martin 5.00 12.00
CJ14 Darius Miles 2.00 5.00
CJ15 Vince Carter 4.00 10.00

2000-01 Fleer Triple Crown Heir Force 01

Randomly inserted into packs at one in 10, this 15-card set features players that are so popular, they could almost hitch a ride on Air Force One. Card backs carry a "HF" prefix.

COMPLETE SET (15) 10.00 20.00
STATED ODDS 1:10
HF1 Kenyon Martin 1.50 4.00
HF2 Stromile Swift .60 1.50
HF3 Darius Miles .60 1.50
HF4 Courtney Alexander .50 1.25
HF5 Marcus Fizer .60 1.50
HF6 Keyon Dooling .60 1.50
HF7 Steve Francis .50 1.25
HF8 Elton Brand .60 1.50
HF9 Lamar Odom .50 1.25
HF10 Wally Szczerbiak .50 1.25
HF11 Vince Carter 1.25 3.00
HF12 Antawn Jamison .60 1.50
HF13 Jason Williams .60 1.50
HF14 Tim Duncan 1.25 3.00
HF15 Kobe Bryant 2.50 6.00

2000-01 Fleer Triple Crown Scoring Kings

STATED PRINT RUN 100 SERIAL #'d SETS
SK1 Vince Carter 12.00 30.00
SK2 Shaquille O'Neal 15.00 40.00
SK3 Allen Iverson 12.00 30.00
SK4 Grant Hill 8.00 20.00
SK5 Chris Webber 6.00 15.00
SK6 Glenn Robinson 5.00 12.00
SK7 Lamar Odom 5.00 12.00
SK8 Gary Payton 6.00 15.00
SK9 Eddie Jones 6.00 15.00
SK10 Latrell Sprewell 5.00 12.00

2000-01 Fleer Triple Crown Scoring Menace

Randomly inserted in packs at one in 24, this 10-card set highlights players that can score with the best of them. Card backs carry a "SM" prefix.

COMPLETE SET (10) 7.50 15.00
STATED ODDS 1:24
SM1 Vince Carter 1.50 4.00
SM2 Shaquille O'Neal 2.00 5.00
SM3 Allen Iverson 1.50 4.00
SM4 Grant Hill 1.00 2.50
SM5 Chris Webber .75 2.00
SM6 Glenn Robinson .60 1.50
SM7 Lamar Odom .60 1.50
SM8 Gary Payton .75 2.00
SM9 Eddie Jones .75 2.00
SM10 Latrell Sprewell .60 1.50

2000-01 Fleer Triple Crown Shoot Arounds

Randomly inserted in packs at one in 72, each card in this 16-card set contains a swatch of pre-game warm-ups that the players actually wore. Cards are listed below in alphabetical order for convenience.

STATED ODDS 1:72
1 Vince Carter 6.00 15.00
2 Keyon Dooling 3.00 8.00
3 Grant Hill 4.00 10.00
4 Allen Iverson 8.00 20.00
5 Jason Kidd 5.00 12.00
6 Shawn Marion 2.50 6.00
7 Tracy McGrady 5.00 12.00
8 Chris Mihm 2.50 6.00
9 Darius Miles 3.00 8.00
10 Andre Miller 2.50 6.00
11 Mike Miller 5.00 12.00
12 Hanno Mottola 2.00 5.00
13 Lamar Odom 2.50 6.00
14 Quentin Richardson 3.00 8.00
15 John Stockton 4.00 10.00

2000-01 Fleer Triple Crown Triple Threats

Randomly inserted in packs at one in 5, this 15-card set highlights players that can shoot, pass, and rebound. Card backs carry a "TT" prefix.

COMPLETE SET (15) 4.00 10.00
STATED ODDS 1:5
TT1 Vince Carter .75 2.00
TT2 Jason Kidd .60 1.50
TT3 Gary Payton .40 1.00
TT4 Scottie Pippen .60 1.50
TT5 Hakeem Olajuwon .50 1.25
TT6 Kevin Garnett .60 1.50
TT7 Steve Francis .30 .75
TT8 Antoine Walker .30 .75
TT9 Andre Miller .30 .75
TT10 Chris Webber .40 1.00
TT11 Lamar Odom .30 .75
TT12 Tim Duncan .75 2.00
TT13 Grant Hill .50 1.25
TT14 David Robinson .60 1.50
TT15 Michael Finley .40 1.00

2000 Fleer Tuff Stuff Vince Carter

This card was released by Tuff Stuff in conjunction with Fleer magazine. The card features a facsimile autograph of superstar Vince Carter. The back of the card states that "This card contains a facsimile signature of Toronto Raptors star Vince Carter".

NNO Vince Carter 1.25 3.00

1996 Fleer USA

The 1996 Fleer USA set was issued in one series totalling 52 cards. The 3-card packs retailed for $4.99 each during the summer of 1996. Each pack contained two super-premium and one lenticular card which resulted in the super-premium cards being triple-printed. The set contains the topical subsets: In the Beginning (1-10), By the Numbers (11-20), Defining Moment (21-30), Masters of the Game (31-40), Around the World (41-50). Each Around the World, In the Beginning and Defining Moments card features the lenticular technology with rotating images of the earth, pulsating player images and a USA/5-ring logo that changes color. Each By the Numbers and Masters of the Game card features super-premium UV-coating, foil-stamping and printing on thick, 20-point stock.

COMPLETE SET (52) 20.00 50.00
1 Anfernee Hardaway IB 1.00 2.50
2 Grant Hill IB 1.00 2.50
3 Karl Malone IB .75 2.00
4 Reggie Miller IB .75 2.00
5 Hakeem Olajuwon IB .75 2.00
6 Shaquille O'Neal IB 1.50 4.00
7 Scottie Pippen IB 1.00 2.50
8 David Robinson IB 1.00 2.50
9 Glenn Robinson IB .50 1.25
10 John Stockton IB .75 2.00
11 Anfernee Hardaway BN .50 1.25
12 Grant Hill BN .50 1.25
13 Karl Malone BN .40 1.00
14 Reggie Miller BN .40 1.00
15 Hakeem Olajuwon BN .40 1.00
16 Shaquille O'Neal BN .75 2.00
17 Scottie Pippen BN .50 1.25
18 David Robinson BN .50 1.25
19 Glenn Robinson BN .25 .60
20 John Stockton BN .40 1.00
21 Anfernee Hardaway DM 1.00 2.50
22 Grant Hill DM 1.00 2.50
23 Karl Malone DM .75 2.00
24 Reggie Miller DM .75 2.00
25 Hakeem Olajuwon DM .75 2.00
26 Shaquille O'Neal DM 1.50 4.00
27 Scottie Pippen DM 1.00 2.50
28 David Robinson DM 1.00 2.50
29 Glenn Robinson DM .50 1.25
30 John Stockton DM .75 2.00
31 Anfernee Hardaway MAS .50 1.25
32 Grant Hill MAS .50 1.25
33 Karl Malone MAS .40 1.00
34 Reggie Miller MAS .40 1.00
35 Hakeem Olajuwon MAS .40 1.00
36 Shaquille O'Neal MAS .75 2.00
37 Scottie Pippen MAS .50 1.25
38 David Robinson MAS .50 1.25
39 Glenn Robinson MAS .25 .60
40 John Stockton MAS .40 1.00
41 Anfernee Hardaway AW 1.00 2.50
42 Grant Hill AW 1.00 2.50
43 Karl Malone AW .75 2.00
44 Reggie Miller AW .75 2.00
45 Hakeem Olajuwon AW .75 2.00
46 Shaquille O'Neal AW 1.50 4.00
47 Scottie Pippen AW 1.00 2.50
48 David Robinson AW 1.00 2.50
49 Glenn Robinson AW .50 1.25
50 John Stockton AW .75 2.00
51 Team USA CL 51/52 1.25 3.00
52 Team USA CL 1.25 3.00

1996 Fleer USA Heroes

Randomly inserted exclusively into hobby packs at a rate of one in 18, this 10-card set features the 10 original members of the 1996 USAB men's basketball team in a special die-cut design with the top left of the card clipped as the player is silhouetted across the American flag and extended out beyond the natural border of the card.

COMPLETE SET (10) 40.00 100.00
1 Anfernee Hardaway 8.00 20.00
2 Grant Hill 8.00 20.00
3 Karl Malone 6.00 15.00
4 Reggie Miller 6.00 15.00
5 Hakeem Olajuwon 6.00 15.00
6 Shaquille O'Neal 12.00 30.00
7 Scottie Pippen 8.00 20.00
8 David Robinson 8.00 20.00
9 Glenn Robinson 4.00 10.00
10 John Stockton 6.00 15.00

1996 Fleer USA Wrapper Exchange

Collectors were offered the chance to receive this special 12-card exchange set by sending in 15 wrappers (along with $3.00 for postage and handling). The 12 cards consisted of three lenticular, two super-premium and one Heroes insert of both Charles Barkley and Mitch Richmond.

COMPLETE SET (12) 4.00 10.00
M1 Charles Barkley ITB 1.00 2.50
M2 Mitch Richmond ITB .60 1.50
M3 Charles Barkley BTN .50 1.25
M4 Mitch Richmond BTN .30 .75
M5 Charles Barkley ATW 1.00 2.50
M6 Mitch Richmond ATW .60 1.50
M7 Charles Barkley MAS .50 1.25
M8 Mitch Richmond MAS .30 .75
M9 Charles Barkley DM 1.00 2.50
M10 Mitch Richmond DM .60 1.50
M11 Charles Barkley Heroes 1.50 4.00
M12 Mitch Richmond Heroes 1.00 2.50

2001 Fleer Viva Vince Carter

Given away at a Vince Carter basketball camp in Spain, this card was originally printed unautographed, hence that is how it is cataloged. Vince Carter did sign several, possibly the majority for camp givaways, but it is uncertain as to how many he did in fact sign, and no representative was present to certify the autographs. The front features bright colors and the words, "Viva Vince Carter," while the back, in spanish, is a checklist of basketball fundamental skills.

1 Vince Carter 1.50 4.00

2001 Fleer WNBA

The 2001 Fleer WNBA product was released in June, 2001 and featured a 165-card base set. Each pack contained ten cards, and carried a suggested retail price of $1.49.

COMP.SET w/o RC (165) 10.00 25.00
1 Lisa Leslie .75 2.00
2 Andrea Stinson .30 .75
3 Tammy Jackson .15 .40
4 Nicky McCrimmon RC .20 .50
5 Vickie Johnson .25 .60
6 Maria Stepanova .15 .40
7 Michelle Edwards .30 .75
8 Tausha Mills .15 .40
9 Edwina Brown .20 .50
10 Jurgita Streimikyte .15 .40
11 Keitha Dickerson RC .20 .50
12 Taj McWilliams-Franklin .15 .40
13 DeMya Walker .15 .40
14 Adrienne Goodson .15 .40
15 Eva Nemcova .25 .60
16 Danielle McCulley RC .20 .50
17 Shannon Johnson .15 .40
18 Margo Dydek .25 .60
19 Mery Andrade .15 .40
20 Marlies Askamp .15 .40
21 Adrain Williams .15 .40
22 Sonja Henning .15 .40
23 Astou Ndiaye-Diatta .25 .60
24 Latasha Byears .25 .60
25 Kate Paye RC .20 .50
26 Yolanda Griffith .50 1.25
27 Kate Starbird .25 .60
28 Jennifer Rizzotti .40 1.00
29 Umeki Webb .15 .40
30 Tari Phillips .15 .40
31 Tully Bevilaqua RC .30 .75
32 Murriel Page .20 .50
33 Tricia Bader Binford .15 .40
34 Sheryl Swoopes 1.00 2.50
35 Debbie Black .25 .60
36 Teresa Weatherspoon .60 1.50
37 Alisa Burras .15 .40
38 Stacey Lovelace RC .50 1.25
39 Helen Darling .20 .50
40 Tina Thompson .50 1.25
41 Katrina Colleton .15 .40
42 Tamika Whitmore .15 .40
43 Sylvia Crawley .15 .40
44 Jamie Redd RC .20 .50
45 Tracy Reid .25 .60
46 Janeth Arcain .15 .40
47 Stacy Frese RC .30 .75
48 Grace Daley .15 .40
49 Bridget Pettis .15 .40
50 Katy Steding .15 .40
51 Beth Cunningham .15 .40
52 Vicki Hall RC .20 .50
53 Amaya Valdemoro .20 .50
54 Milena Flores .15 .40
55 Sue Wicks .25 .60
56 Michelle Marciniak .25 .60
57 Tracy Henderson .15 .40
58 Kisha Ford .15 .40
59 Jannon Roland .15 .40
60 Vanessa Nygaard RC .20 .50
61 Pollyanna Johns RC .20 .50
62 Gordana Grubin .15 .40
63 Shantia Owens .15 .40
64 Cintia Dos Santos .15 .40
65 Lynn Pride .15 .40
66 Robin Threatt RC .20 .50
67 Claudia Maria das Neves RC .20 .50
68 Chantel Tremitiere .15 .40
69 Betty Lennox .50 1.25
70 Ruthie Bolton-Holifield .50 1.25
71 Korie Hlede .25 .60
72 Dominique Canty .25 .60
73 Alicia Thompson .15 .40
74 Kristin Folkl .25 .60
75 Elaine Powell .15 .40
76 Cindy Blodgett .25 .60
77 Charlotte Smith .15 .40
78 Mwadi Mabika .15 .40
79 Marina Ferragut RC .30 .75
80 Brandy Reed .25 .60
81 Quacy Barnes .15 .40
82 Chamique Holdsclaw 1.00 2.50
83 Dawn Staley .40 1.00
84 Nekeshia Henderson RC .20 .50
85 Rhonda Mapp .20 .50
86 Becky Hammon 1.00 2.50
87 Edna Campbell .20 .50
88 Nikki McCray .40 1.00
89 Anna DeForge .15 .40
90 Rita Williams .20 .50
91 Andrea Lloyd Curry .15 .40
92 Nykesha Sales .25 .60
93 Stacy Clinesmith RC .30 .75
94 LaTonya Johnson .15 .40
95 Markita Aldridge .15 .40
96 Shalonda Enis .15 .40
97 Wendy Palmer .40 1.00
98 Tamecka Dixon .25 .60
99 Katie Smith .50 1.25
100 Tonya Edwards .15 .40
101 Lady Hardmon .15 .40
102 Dalma Ivanyi .15 .40
103 Tiffany Travis RC .30 .75
104 Tiffani Johnson RC .20 .50
105 DeLisha Milton .15 .40
106 Rebecca Lobo .50 1.25
107 Michele Timms .50 1.25
108 Andrea Garner RC .20 .50
109 Andrea Nagy .25 .60
110 Summer Erb .15 .40
111 Ukari Figgs .15 .40
112 Jennifer Gillom .40 1.00
113 Kedra Holland-Corn .15 .40
114 Natalie Williams .30 .75
115 Clarisse Machanguana .15 .40
116 E.C. Hill RC .20 .50
117 Lisa Harrison .25 .60
118 Tangela Smith .15 .40
119 Vicky Bullett .25 .60
120 Ann Wauters .20 .50
121 Marla Brumfield RC .20 .50
122 Carla McGhee .15 .40
123 Sophia Witherspoon .25 .60
124 Tamicha Jackson .15 .40
125 Kara Wolters .20 .50
126 Maylana Martin .20 .50
127 Tiffany McCain RC .30 .75
128 Naomi Mulitauaopele .15 .40
129 Chasity Melvin .15 .40
130 Stephanie McCarty .30 .75
131 Sheri Sam .15 .40
132 Adrienne Johnson .25 .60
133 Jennifer Azzi .50 1.25
134 Allison Feaster .20 .50
135 Elena Tornikidou RC .20 .50
136 Sonja Tate .15 .40
137 Michelle Brogan RC .20 .50
138 Ticha Penicheiro .40 1.00
139 Keisha Anderson .15 .40
140 Merlakia Jones .25 .60
141 Monica Maxwell .15 .40
142 Kristen Rasmussen RC .30 .75
143 Stacey Thomas .15 .40
144 Kamila Vodichkova .15 .40
145 Angie Braziel .25 .60
146 Olympia Scott-Richardson .15 .40
147 Vedrana Grgin RC .20 .50
148 Shanele Stires .15 .40
149 Coquese Washington .15 .40
150 Crystal Robinson .15 .40
151 Texlan Quinney .15 .40
152 Michelle Cleary RC .20 .50
153 La'Keshia Frett .15 .40
154 Jessie Hicks .15 .40
155 Katrina Hibbert .15 .40
156 Cass Bauer .25 .60
157 Jessica Bibby .15 .40
158 Shea Mahoney RC .20 .50
159 Charmin Smith .25 .60
160 Oksana Zakauluzhnaya .15 .40
161 Tonya Washington .20 .50
162 Rushia Brown .15 .40
163 Amy Herrig RC .20 .50
164 Tara Williams .20 .50
165 Sandy Brondello .40 1.00
166 Tammy Sutton-Brown RC 5.00 12.00
167 Kelly Miller RC 5.00 12.00
168 Penny Taylor RC 8.00 20.00
169 Kelly Santos RC 5.00 12.00
170 Deanna Nolan RC 5.00 12.00
171 Jae Kingi RC 5.00 12.00
172 Amanda Lassiter RC 5.00 12.00
173 Trisha Stafford-Odom RC 5.00 12.00
174 Tynesha Lewis RC 5.00 12.00
175 Tamika Catchings RC 8.00 20.00
176 Kelly Schumacher RC 5.00 12.00
177 Niele Ivey RC 5.00 12.00
178 Nicole Levandusky RC 5.00 12.00
179 Wendy Willits RC 5.00 12.00
180 Ruth Riley RC 6.00 15.00
181 Levys Torres RC 5.00 12.00
182 Janell Burse RC 5.00 12.00
183 Svetlana Abrosimova RC 5.00 12.00
184 Erin Buescher RC 5.00 12.00
185 Georgia Schweitzer RC 5.00 12.00
186 Camille Cooper RC 5.00 12.00
187 Brooke Wyckoff RC 8.00 20.00
188 Jaclyn Johnson RC 5.00 12.00
189 Tawona Alehaleem RC 5.00 12.00
190 Katie Douglas RC 8.00 20.00
191 Jaynetta Saunders RC 5.00 12.00
192 Kristen Veal RC 5.00 12.00
193 Jenny Mowe RC 5.00 12.00
194 Jackie Stiles RC 15.00 40.00
195 LaQuanda Barksdale RC 5.00 12.00
196 Lauren Jackson RC 20.00 50.00
197 Semeka Randall RC 5.00 12.00
198 Michaela Pavlickova RC 5.00 12.00
199 Marie Ferdinand RC 5.00 12.00
200 Shea Ralph RC 5.00 12.00
201 Cara Consuegra RC 5.00 12.00
202 Tamara Stocks RC 5.00 12.00
203 Coco Miller RC 5.00 12.00
204 Helen Luz RC 5.00 12.00

2001 Fleer WNBA Autographics

Randomly inserted into packs at one in 144, this insert set features autographs of the WNBA hottest players. Please note that the cards have been listed below in alphabetical order for convenience.

COMPLETE SET (6) 60.00 120.00
STATED ODDS 1:144
EXTRA PRINT RUN 50 SER.#'d SETS
PLUS UNPRICED DUE TO SCARCITY
1 Jennifer Azzi 6.00 15.00
2 Betty Lennox 6.00 15.00
3 Lisa Leslie 10.00 25.00
4 Katie Smith 6.00 15.00
6 Sheryl Swoopes 6.00 15.00
5 Natalie Williams 6.00 15.00

2001 Fleer WNBA Autographics Extra

*EXTRA: .75X TO 2X AUTOGRAPHICS HI

2001 Fleer WNBA Award Winners

Randomly inserted into packs at one in 30, this 10-card set focuses on some of the more prolific players from the 2000 WNBA season. Card backs carry an "AW" prefix.

COMPLETE SET (10) 10.00 25.00
AW1 Sheryl Swoopes 4.00 10.00
AW2 Natalie Williams 1.25 3.00
AW3 Lisa Leslie 3.00 8.00
AW4 Ticha Penicheiro 1.50 4.00
AW5 Tina Thompson 2.00 5.00
AW6 Katie Smith 2.00 5.00
AW7 Yolanda Griffith 2.00 5.00
AW8 Teresa Weatherspoon 2.50 6.00
AW9 Betty Lennox 2.00 5.00
AW10 Tari Phillips .60 1.50

2001 Fleer WNBA Global Game

Randomly inserted into packs at one in 6, this 20-card insert set focuses on players that would dominate the game no matter what part of the world they were playing in. Card backs carry a "GG" prefix.

COMPLETE SET (20) 8.00 20.00
GG1 Janeth Arcain .40 1.00
GG2 Marlies Askamp .40 1.00
GG3 Mery Andrade .40 1.00
GG4 Tully Bevilaqua .60 1.50
GG5 Margo Dydek .60 1.50
GG6 Gordana Grubin .40 1.00
GG7 Mwadi Mabika .40 1.00
GG8 Andrea Nagy .60 1.50
GG9 Astou Ndiaye-Diatta .60 1.50
GG10 Eva Nemcova .60 1.50
GG11 Ticha Penicheiro 1.00 2.50
GG12 Maria Stepanova .40 1.00
GG13 Michele Timms 1.25 3.00
GG14 Kamila Vodichkova .40 1.00
GG15 Ann Wauters .50 1.25
GG16 Yolanda Griffith 1.25 3.00
GG17 Chamique Holdsclaw 2.50 6.00
GG18 Katie Smith 1.25 3.00
GG19 Nikki McCray 1.00 2.50
GG20 Natalie Williams .75 2.00

2001 Fleer WNBA Starting Five

Randomly inserted into packs at one in 12, this 15-card insert set focuses on players that you can find in the starting lineup almost every night. Card backs carry a "SF" prefix.

COMPLETE SET (15) 12.50 30.00
SF1 Vicky Bullett .75 2.00
SF2 Andrea Stinson 1.00 2.50
SF3 Merlakia Jones .75 2.00
SF4 Eva Nemcova .75 2.00
SF5 Janeth Arcain .50 1.25
SF6 Sheryl Swoopes 3.00 8.00
SF7 Tina Thompson 1.50 4.00
SF8 Lisa Leslie 2.50 6.00
SF9 Mwadi Mabika .50 1.25
SF10 Rebecca Lobo 1.50 4.00
SF11 Sue Wicks .75 2.00
SF12 Teresa Weatherspoon 2.00 5.00
SF13 Michele Timms 1.50 4.00
SF14 Marlies Askamp .50 1.25
SF15 Ruthie Bolton-Holifield 1.50 4.00

2001 Fleer WNBA Supreme Court

Randomly inserted into packs at one in 18, this 10-card insert set focuses on players that dominate the court. Card backs carry a "SC" prefix.

COMPLETE SET (10) 12.50 30.00
SC1 Chamique Holdsclaw 3.00 8.00
SC2 Natalie Williams 1.00 2.50
SC3 Betty Lennox 1.50 4.00
SC4 Yolanda Griffith 1.50 4.00
SC5 Sheryl Swoopes 3.00 8.00
SC6 Tina Thompson 1.50 4.00
SC7 Lisa Leslie 2.50 6.00
SC8 Jennifer Gillom 1.25 3.00
SC9 Ticha Penicheiro 1.25 3.00
SC10 Michele Timms 1.50 4.00

2001 Fleer Hersey WNBA

COMPLETE SET (12) 6.00 15.00
1 Chamique Holdsclaw 2.00 5.00
2 Sonja Henning .30 .75
3 Wendy Palmer .60 1.50
4 Brandy Reed .30 .75
5 Teresa Weatherspoon 1.00 2.50
6 Shannon Johnson .30 .75
7 Natalie Williams .60 1.50
8 Sophia Witherspoon .30 .75
9 Lisa Leslie 1.25 3.00
10 Katie Smith 1.00 2.50
11 Andrea Stinson .60 1.50
12 Kara Wolters .30 .75

1996-97 Fleer/SkyBox Jerry Stackhouse Sample

This unique sample two-card set features Jerry Stackhouse on the left card against a colorful red, blue and black background with the player's name running vertically along the bottom in white letters. The back of the card is not numbered and featues some biographical information on Stackhouse. The right portion of the card is a survey form that if completed by June 15, 1997 and sent it with three wrappers from any Fleer or SkyBox basketball card product, could be sent in for a limited edition Grant Hill jumbo card. Both cards are not-numbered and priced below. The Hill jumbo card is not considered a part of the set.

1 Jerry Stackhouse 1.25 3.00
2 Grant Hill Jumbo 4.00 10.00

1999 Fleer/SkyBox Dunkography

This one oversized card was sent to dealers commemorating the signing of both Vince Carter and Lamar Odom as company spokesmen. The card front features both Carter and Odom dunking against a "sky" background. The card is serially numbered to 3000 on the front. The NNO card back carries player information.

NNO Vince Carter 8.00 20.00
Lamar Odom

1971-72 Floridians McDonald's

This ten-card set of ABA Miami Floridians was sponsored by McDonald's. The cards measure approximately 2 1/2" by 4", including a 1/2" tear-off tab at the bottom. The bottom tab admitted one 14-or-under child to the game with each regular price adult ticket. Prices below refer to cards with tabs intact. The fronts feature color action player photos with rounded corners and black borders. The backs have player information, rules governing the free youth tickets, and an offer to receive an ABA basketball in exchange for a set of ten different Floridian tickets. The cards are unnumbered and are checklisted below in alphabetical order.

COMPLETE SET (10) 300.00 600.00
1 Warren Armstrong 40.00 80.00
2 Mack Calvin 40.00 80.00
3 Ron Franz 30.00 60.00
4 Ira Harge 30.00 60.00
5 Larry Jones 30.00 60.00
6 Willie Long 30.00 60.00
7 Sam Robinson 30.00 60.00
8 Al Tucker 30.00 60.00
9 George Tinsley 30.00 60.00
10 Lonnie Wright 30.00 60.00

1991 Foot Locker Slam Fest

This 30-card standard-size set was issued by Foot Locker in three ten-card series to commemorate the "Foot Locker Slam Fest" dunk contest televised during halftimes of NBC college basketball games through March 10, 1991. Each set contained two Domino's Pizza coupons and a 5.00 discount coupon on any purchase of 50.00 or more at Foot Locker. The set was released in substantial quantity after the promotional coupons expired. The fronts feature both posed and action photos enclosed in an arch like double red borders. The card top carries a blue border with "Foot Locker" in blue print on a white background. Beneath the photo appears "Limited Edition" and the player's name. The backs present career highlights, card series, and numbers placed within an arch of double red borders. The player's name and team name appear in black lettering at the bottom. The cards are numbered on the back; the card numbering below adds the number 10 to each card number in the second series and 20 to each card number in the third series.

COMPLETE SET (30) 2.00 5.00
11 Wilt Chamberlain BK 1.20 3.00
12 Cal Ramsey BK .02 .05
14 John Havlicek BK .40 1.00
15 Calvin Murphy BK .04 .10
16 Nate Thurmond BK .10 .25
17 John Havlicek BK .40 1.00
21 Jerry Lucas BK .10 .25
23 Elvin Hayes BK .10 .25
26 Earl Monroe BK .10 .25
29 Wilt Chamberlain BK .40 1.00
and Company

1985 Fournier Ases del Baloncesto

This set of 33 playing cards was produced in Spain. It is a card game similar to "Go Fish" and features mostly Spanish players who played in the Spanish Basketball League in 1985. Jimmy Wright and David Russell are two Americans included in this set. The cards came in a cardboard box, measure the standard size and have rounded corners. The fronts have color action player photos with the player's name and position, team name, the player's height and age beneath. The backs carry an orange and white pattern. Players from following teams are included in this set: Real Madrid C.F., Licor 43 Santa Coloma, Caja De Alava, Estudiantes Caja Postal, Forum Valladolid, R.C.D. Espanol-Juver, Cai Zaragoza, Breogan Caixa Galicia, Ron Negrita Juventud, and F.C. Barcelona.

COMPLETE SET (33) 30.00 80.00
1a Juan A. Corbalan 1.25 3.00
1b Fernando Martin 1.25 3.00
1c Fernando Romay 1.25 3.00
1d Lopez Iturriaga 1.25 3.00
2a Jordi Freixanet 1.25 3.00
2b Joaquin Costa 1.25 3.00
2c Miguel Angel Pou 1.25 3.00
2d Inaki Garayalde 1.25 3.00
3a Pedro Rodriguez 1.25 3.00
3b David Russell 4.00 10.00
3c Fco. Javier Lafuente 1.25 3.00
3d Alberto Ortega 1.25 3.00
4a Oscar Pena 1.25 3.00
4b Jose A. Alonso 1.25 3.00
4c Joaquin Salvo 1.25 3.00
4d Albert Illa 1.25 3.00
5a Francisco J. Zapata 1.25 3.00
5b Claude Riley 1.25 3.00
5c Jose Luis Diaz 1.25 3.00
5d Herminio San Epifanio 1.25 3.00
6a Manuel Sanchez 1.25 3.00
6b Jimmy Wright 2.50 6.00
6c Suso Fernandez 1.25 3.00
6d Pepe Collins 1.25 3.00
7a Jose Maria Margall 1.25 3.00
7b Jordi Villacampa 1.25 3.00
7c Jose A. Montero 1.25 3.00
7d Andres Jimenez 1.25 3.00
8a J.A. San Epifanio 1.25 3.00
8b Chico Sibilio 1.25 3.00
8c Ignacio Solozabal 1.25 3.00
8d Arturo S. Seara 1.25 3.00
NNO Title Card 2.00 5.00

1988 Fournier NBA Estrellas

This 33-card set was produced in Spain by Fournier and showcases many of the NBA hottest stars. The cards were distributed exclusively in cello-wrapped factory-sealed complete sets. The cards measure approximately 2 1/8" by 3 7/16" and have rounded corners. The fronts feature borderless high glossy action player photos; in the white stripe below the picture, player statistics are given. The entire area of the card backs displays the NBA logo in red, white, and blue (indicating that the set was licensed by the NBA for distribution in Spain). The cards are numbered on the front in the upper left corner. The card backs were written in Spanish. The set features Danny Manning's first professional card in addition to an early Muggsy Bogues issue.

COMPLETE SET (33) 12.50 30.00
1 Larry Bird 1.25 3.00
2 Robert Parish .30 .75
3 Kevin McHale .60 1.50
4 Magic Johnson 1.25 3.00
5 Kareem Abdul-Jabbar .75 2.00
6 Byron Scott .40 1.00
7 Isiah Thomas .60 1.50
8 Adrian Dantley .20 .50
9 Dominique Wilkins .60 1.50
10 Spud Webb .20 .50
11 Clyde Drexler .60 1.50
12 Terry Porter .20 .50
13 Mark Aguirre .20 .50
14 Muggsy Bogues .40 1.00
15 Patrick Ewing .75 2.00
16 Karl Malone 1.00 2.50
17 Charles Barkley 1.25 3.00
18 Ron Harper .40 1.00
19 Alex English .40 1.00
20 Xavier McDaniel .20 .50
21 Jeff Malone .20 .50
22 Michael Jordan 6.00 15.00
23 Hakeem Olajuwon 1.00 2.50
24 Ralph Sampson .20 .50
25 Buck Williams .20 .50
26 Chuck Person .20 .50
27 Alvin Robertson .20 .50
28 Tom Chambers .20 .50
29 Paul Pressey .20 .50
30 Danny Manning .60 1.50
31 LaSalle Thompson .20 .50
32 John Stockton 1.25 3.00
NNO Michael Jordan Rules 4.00 10.00

1988 Fournier NBA Estrellas Stickers

This ten-sticker set was produced in Spain by Fournier as a random insert with its regular set as only a portion of the sets contained a sticker insert. The stickers measure approximately 1" by 1 1/4" and picture the player from the chest up. The stickers come in a sealed pouch which is semi-transparent. The easiest stickers to find are Larry Bird, Magic Johnson, and Michael Jordan. The stickers are unnumbered and are listed below in alphabetical order.

COMPLETE SET (10) 300.00 500.00
1 Kareem Abdul-Jabbar 30.00 80.00
2 Mark Aguirre 20.00 50.00
3 Larry Bird DP 8.00 20.00
4 Magic Johnson DP 8.00 20.00
5 Michael Jordan DP 30.00 75.00
6 Moses Malone 25.00 60.00
7 Kevin McHale 25.00 60.00
8 Robert Parish 25.00 60.00
9 Isiah Thomas 25.00 60.00
10 James Worthy 25.00 60.00

1963 Gad Fun Cards

This set of 1963 Fun Cards were issued by a sports illustrator by the name of Gad from Minneapolis, Minnesota. The cards are printed on cardboard stock paper. The borderless fronts have black and white line drawings. A fun sport's fact or player career statistic is depicted in the drawing. The backs of the first six cards display numbers used to play the game explained on card number 6. The other backs carry a cartoon with a joke or riddle. Copyright information is listed on the lower portion of the card.

COMPLETE SET (84) 37.50 75.00
76 Buffalo Germans .25 .50
Basketball Squad

1998 GE David Robinson Phone Cards

Produced by General Electric, this 5-card set features different action shots of David Robinson on five different prepaid units of phone time. The units available were 30, 60, 75, 90 and 120. Callers could also use the phone card to listen to different messages from Robinson - or even leave him a message. The different units were priced as follows: 30 at $9.90, 60 at $19.80, 75 at $24.75, 90 at $29.70 and 120 at $39.60. The phone cards expire six months from first use or by June 30th, 1999. Prices below reflect cards with phone time intact. Used cards are priced at 20% of the listed value. The cards below are not numbered and listed alphabetically.

COMPLETE SET (5) 40.00 100.00
1 David Robinson 30 units 4.00 10.00
2 David Robinson 60 units 8.00 20.00
3 David Robinson 75 units 10.00 25.00
4 David Robinson 90 units 12.50 30.00
5 David Robinson 120 units 15.00 40.00

1971-72 Globetrotters Cocoa Puffs 28

This 1971-72 Harlem Globetrotters set was produced for Cocoa Puffs cereal by Fleer and contains 28 standard size cards. The cards were issued inside specially marked cereal boxes with four consecutively numbered cards per box. The card fronts have full color pictures with facsimile autographs. The card backs are subtitled "Cocoa Puffs presents the magicians of basketball and have black printing on gray card stock and feature biographical sketches and other interesting information about the Globetrotters. The cards are numbered on back X of 28.

COMPLETE SET (28) 90.00 180.00
1 Geese Ausbie and 8.00 20.00
Curly Neal
2 Neal and Meadowlark 5.00 12.00
3 Meadowlark is Safe 4.00 10.00
4 Meadowlark Lemon 3.00 8.00
Curly Neal and
Geese Ausbie
5 Mel Davis and 2.00 5.00
Bill Meggett
6 Geese Ausbie 3.00 8.00
Meadowlark Lemon
and Curly Neal
7 Geese Ausbie 3.00 8.00
Meadowlark Lemon
and Curly Neal
8 Mel Davis and 2.50 6.00
Curly Neal
9 Meadowlark Lemon 3.00 8.00
Curly Neal and
Geese Ausbie
10 Curly Neal 3.00 8.00
Meadowlark Lemon and
Mel Davis
11 Football Routine 2.00 5.00
12 1970-71 Highlights 2.00 5.00
13 Pabs Robertson 2.00 5.00
14 Bobby Joe Mason 2.00 5.00
15 Pabs Robertson 2.00 5.00
16 Clarence Smith 2.00 5.00
17 Clarence Smith 2.00 5.00
18 Hubert (Geese) Ausbie 2.50 6.00
19 Hubert(Geese) Ausbie 2.50 6.00
(Two balls)
20 Bobby Hunter 2.00 5.00
21 Bobby Hunter 2.00 5.00
(One leg up)
22 Meadowlark Lemon 3.00 8.00
(Three balls)
23 Meadowlark Lemon 4.00 10.00
24 Freddie (Curly) Neal 3.00 8.00
25 Freddie (Curly) Neal 3.00 8.00
(Three paint brushes)
26 Meadowlark Lemon 4.00 10.00
(Palming two balls)
27 Mel Davis 2.00 5.00
(Leaning over with ball)
28 Freddie Curly Neal 7.50 15.00

1971-72 Globetrotters 84

The 1971-72 Harlem Globetrotters set was produced by Fleer and sold in wax packs. The set contains 84 standard size cards. The card fronts have full color pictures. The card backs have black printing on gray card stock and feature biographical sketches and other interesting information about the Globetrotters. The cards are numbered on back "X" of 84. A Globetrotter Emblem sticker was inserted in each wax pack.

COMPLETE SET (85) 75.00 150.00
1 Bob Showboat Hall 5.00 12.00
2 Bob Showboat Hall .75 2.00
(kicking ball)
3 Bob Showboat Hall .75 2.00
(passing behind back)
4 Pabs Robertson .75 2.00
5 Pabs Robertson .75 2.00
6 Pabs Robertson .75 2.00
7 Pabs Robertson .75 2.00
8 Pabs Robertson .75 2.00
9 Meadowlark Lemon 2.50 6.00
(kicking behind back)
10 Meadowlark Lemon 2.50 6.00
(rolling ball on arm)
11 Meadowlark Lemon 2.50 6.00
(palming two balls)
12 Meadowlark Lemon 2.50 6.00
(ball on neck)
13 Meadowlark Lemon 2.50 6.00
(three balls)
14 Meadowlark Lemon 2.50 6.00
(three balls in front)
15 Meadowlark Lemon 2.50 6.00
(three balls)
16 Meadowlark Lemon 2.50 6.00
(dribbling two balls)
17 Meadowlark Lemon 2.50 6.00
(with cap)
18 Curley Neal 2.50 6.00
Meadowlark Lemon and
Mel Davis
19 Football Play 2.50 6.00
(Meadowlark centering)
20 Meadowlark Lemon 2.50 6.00
(hooking)
21 Hubert Geese Ausbie 1.00 2.50
(balls between legs)
22 Hubert Geese Ausbie 1.00 2.50
(ball under arm)
23 Hubert Geese Ausbie 1.00 2.50
(ball on finger)
24 Hubert Geese Ausbie 1.00 2.50
(ball behind back)
25 Hubert Geese Ausbie 1.00 2.50
(no ball)
26 Geese Ausbie and 2.00 5.00
(Curly Neal with confetti)
27 Freddie Curly Neal 2.50 6.00
(artist)
28 Freddie Curly Neal 2.50 6.00
(sitting on ball)
29 Freddie Curly Neal 2.50 6.00
(two balls on head)
30 Mel Davis and 1.50 4.00
Freddie Curly Neal
31 Freddie Curly Neall 2.50 6.00
(smiling)
32 Freddie CurlyNeal 2.50 6.00
(looking to side)
33 Mel Davis .75 2.00
(looking down)
34 Mel Davis .75 2.00
(ready to shoot)
35 Mel Davis .75 2.00
(ball in hand)
36 Mel Davis .75 2.00
(ball over head)
37 Mel Davis and .75 2.00
Bill Meggett
(leap frog)
38 Mel Davis .75 2.00
(ball on knee)
39 Bobby Joe Mason .75 2.00
(ball under arm)
40 Bobby Joe Mason .75 2.00
(ball between legs)
41 Bobby Joe Mason .75 2.00
(passing behind back)
42 Bobby Joe Mason and .75 2.00
(Frank Stephens
43 Bobby Joe Mason .75 2.00
(ball to side)
44 Bobby Joe Mason .75 2.00
(ready to shoot)
45 Clarence Smith .75 2.00
(three balls between legs)
46 Clarence Smith .75 2.00
(on bike)
47 Clarence Smith .75 2.00
(ball at ear)
48 Clarence Smith .75 2.00
(dribbling on side)

49 Jerry Venable .75 2.00
50 Frank Stephens (hands in front) .75 2.00
51 Frank Stephens (ball on finger) .75 2.00
52 Frank Stephens (waiting for ball) .75 2.00
53 Frank Stephens (ball in hand) .75 2.00
54 Theodis Ray Lee (ball on hip) .75 2.00
55 Theodis Ray Lee (ball between knees) .75 2.00
56 Jerry Venable (palming ball) .75 2.00
57 Doug Himes (ball in air) .75 2.00
58 Doug Himes (ball behind back) .75 2.00
59 Bill Meggett (dribbling two balls) .75 2.00
60 Bill Meggett (ready to shoot) .75 2.00
61 Vincent White (ball on hip) .75 2.00
62 Vincent White (kicking ball) .75 2.00
63 Pablo and Showboat .75 2.00
64 Meadowlark Lemon 2.50 6.00
Curly Neal
and Geese Ausbie balls behind back)
65 Curley Neal 2.50 6.00
Quarterback
66 Ausbie, Meadowlark, 2.50 6.00
and Neal (looking at ball)
67 Curly Neal 2.50 6.00
Meadowlark Lemon
68 Football Routine 1.00 2.50
69 Meadowlark To Neal 2.50 6.00
To Ausbie
70 Meadowlark Is Safe 2.50 6.00
At The Plate
71 1970-71 Highlights 1.00 2.50
(baseball act)
72 1970-71 Highlights 2.50 6.00
(Lemon and Neal)
73 Bobby Hunter (ball on hip) .75 2.00
74 Bobby Hunter (ball in hand) .75 2.00
75 Bobby Hunter (ball on shoulder) .75 2.00
76 Bobby Hunter (ball in air) .75 2.00
77 Bobby Hunter (passing between legs) .75 2.00
78 Jackie Jackson (ball on hip) 1.00 2.50
79 Jackie Jackson (ball behind back) 1.00 2.50
80 Jackie Jackson (ball in air) 1.00 2.50
81 Jackie Jackson/ ball on finger) 1.00 2.50
82 The Globetrotters 1.00 2.50
83 The Globetrotters 1.00 2.50
84 Dallas Thornton 2.50 6.00
NNO Globetrotter Official 1.50 4.00
Peel-off Team
Emblem Sticker

1971-72 Globetrotters Phoenix Candy

%This eight-card set was issued as unnumbered cards on the back panels of Phoenix Candy boxes. The cards measure approximately 4 7/8" by 2 1/2" whereas the box measures approximately 3 1/4" by 6 1/2". The year of issue is assumed from the 71 over 72 inside a "clock face" on the box flap. Complete boxes are valued at 1.5 times the prices listed below.

COMPLETE SET (8) 175.00 350.00
1 J.C. Gipson 20.00 40.00
2 Bob Showboat Hall 20.00 40.00
3 Leon Hillard 20.00 40.00
4 Meadowlark Lemon 50.00 100.00
5 Freddie(Curly) Neal 40.00 80.00
6 Pablo Robertson 20.00 40.00
7 National Unit 25.00 50.00
(Team picture)
8 International Unit 25.00 50.00
(Team picture)

1974 Globetrotters Wonder Bread

ix of the twenty-five cards in this set depict Harlem Globetrotters. All cards were randomly inserted inside loaves of Wonder Bread and feature Hanna-Barbera TV cartoon show characters. The fronts feature a multi-color Globetrotter cartoon. The backs carry a lesson in how to do a magic trick. The cards are numbered on the back "X in a series of 25."

COMPLETE SET (6) 25.00 50.00
3 Curley Neal 7.50 15.00
B.J. Mason
4 Curley Neal 7.50 15.00
Geese Ausbie
5 J.C. Gipson 2.50 6.00
14 Pablo Robertson 2.50 6.00
16 Meadowlark and Granny 5.00 10.00
20 J.C. Gipson and Granny 2.50 6.00

1980 Globetrotters

This six photo set features black and white glossy 8" x10" s. The photo backs are blank, and the set is not numbered, therefore appear alphabetically.

COMPLETE SET (6) 10.00 20.00
1 Geese Ausbie 1.50 4.00
2 Geese Ausbie 2.00 5.00
Curly Neal
Nate Branch
3 Nate Branch 1.25 3.00
4 Billy Ray Hobley 1.25 3.00
5 Curly Neal 2.50 6.00
6 Dallas Thornton 1.50 4.00
Fred Neal
Hubert Ausbie
Nate Branch
General Lee Holman
Billy Ray Hobley
Robert Paige
Lionel Garrett
Reggie Franklin
Eddie Fields

1985 Globetrotters

Issued on the back of the 1985 Harlem Globetrotters yearbook, this 11-card set features color fronts with white borders. Card backs feature the player's name in a red bar with their vitals listed in a light blue bar. The cards were not perforated. The cards are numbered below by the player's jersey number.

COMPLETE SET (11) 8.00 20.00
12 Billy Ray Hobley .75 2.00
14 Larry Rivers .75 2.00
15 Clyde Austin .75 2.00
17 Ovie Dotson .75 2.00
18 Jimmy Blacklock .75 2.00
22 Fred Neal 2.50 6.00
26 Osborne Lockhart .75 2.00
29 Harold Hubbard .75 2.00
30 Robert Paige .75 2.00
35 Hubert Ausbie 1.25 3.00
41 Sweet Lou Dunbar 1.25 3.00

1992 Globetrotters Promos

Produced by Comic Images, this six-card promo set previews the design of the 1992 Globetrotters 90 set. The cards measure the standard size. In contrast to the regular set, the front of each card is enhanced by a mosaic of silver metallic geometric shapes that reflect light when the card is tilted. The white backs display "Trotters' Trivia" printed in blue with the team name in large red block letters above. All the text is enclosed in a blue rectangle with blue stars running down each side.

COMPLETE SET (6) 6.00 15.00
P1 All-Time Greats 1.25 3.00
Sixty-Fifth Anniversary
P2 Globetrotting 1.50 4.00
Fred (Curly) Neal
Alan Alda
P3 Famous Feats 1.50 4.00
Fred (Curly) Neal
P4 Media Darlings 2.00 5.00
Mickey Mouse
Fred (Curly) Neal
P5 Honoraries 1.25 3.00
Team Photo
P6 First City 2.00 5.00
Goldie Hawn

1992 Globetrotters

Produced by Comic Images to celebrate the Harlem Globetrotters' Sixty-Fifth Anniversary, this 90-card standard-size set features black-and-white and color photos of Harlem Globetrotters from the inception of the team to the present. The white backs display "Trotters' Trivia" printed in blue with the team name in large red block letters above. All of the text is enclosed in a blue rectangle with blue stars running down each side.

COMPLETE SET (90) 5.00 12.00
1 Abe Saperstein .20 .50
2 In The Beginning .08 .25
3 Hinckley, Illinois .08 .25
4 What's In A Name .08 .25
5 Uniforms .08 .25
6 International Competition .08 .25
7 A Tie .08 .25
8 Hard Times .08 .25
9 Black and White .08 .25
10 Courting Success .08 .25
11 First Tournament .08 .25
12 World Champions .08 .25
13 Tricks and Treats .20 .50
Lynette Woodard)
14 Individual Talents .08 .25
15 For The Boys .08 .25
16 Globetrotting .08 .25
17 The Big Screen .08 .25
18 The Small Screen .08 .25
19 Goodwill Ambassadors .08 .25
20 Leaving Their Mark .08 .25
21 Traveling Troubles .08 .25
22 Have Court Will Travel .08 .25
23 The NBA .08 .25
24 Magic Powers .08 .25
25 Almost Perfect .08 .25
26 The End Of An Era .08 .25
27 Celluloid Heroes .08 .25
28 Star Power .08 .25
29 Sweet Georgia Brown .08 .25
30 The Year Of The Woman .20 .50
Lynette Woodard
31 Quotable Curly .20 .50
Fred (Curly) Neal
32 Honorary Globie Speaks .08 .25
33 Whoopi For The Trotters .20 .50
34 Globie Recollections .08 .25
35 A B'Ball Oscar .20 .50
Bob Hope
36 Singing Their Praises 8.00 .25
37 Hurray For Hollywood .08 .25
Geese Ausbie
38 The Early Signs .08 .25
39 Fast Forward .08 .25
40 A Losing Streak .08 .25
41 Pioneering Prankster .08 .25
42 Changing Of The Guard .08 .25
43 Breaking In .08 .25
44 Trickster In Training .20 .50
Meadowlark Lemon
45 Wearing Many Hats .08 .25
46 Beating The Odds .08 .25
Boid Buie
47 Double Take .08 .25
Lance CudJoe
Lawrence CudJoe
48 Sweetwater .08 .25
49 Founding Father .08 .25
50 Fanciful First .08 .25
Inman Jackson
51 Ernest Aughburns .08 .25
52 Clyde Austin .08 .25
53 J.B. Brown .08 .25
54 Michael Douglas .08 .25
55 Sherwin Durham .08 .25
56 Billy Ray Hobley .20 .50
57 Curley Johnson .08 .25
58 Jolette Law .08 .25
59 Derick Polk .08 .25
60 James(Twiggy) Sanders .08 .25
61 Donald(Clyde) Sinclair .08 .25
62 Antoine Scott .08 .25
63 Sweet Lou Dunbar .08 .25
64 Osbourne Lockhart .08 .25
65 Lifelong Dream .20 .50
Lynette Woodard
66 A Real Show-Off .08 .25
Clyde Austin
67 Competition .08 .25
Jimmy Blacklock
68 A Blend Of Old And New .08 .25
Ovie Dotson
69 Globie Spirit .08 .25
Harold Hubbard
70 Carrying The Torch .20 .50
Curly Neal
71 Geese Ausbie .08 .25
72 Fred(Curly) Neal .20 .50
73 Go, Curly, Go .20 .50
74 Larry(Gator) Rivers .08 .25
75 Off Season .08 .25
76 Sore Losers .08 .25
Washington Generals
(Team photo)
77 Ovie Dotson .08 .25
78 Come On In .08 .25
79 Practice Makes Perfect .08 .25
80 Trotters' 1st Trip .08 .25
81 Winningest Team .08 .25
82 City Slickers .08 .25
83 You Win Some... .08 .25
84 From Russia, With Love .08 .25
85 Hold Your Fire .08 .25
86 What A Crowd .08 .25
87 Destined For Greatness .08 .25
88 A Fantastic First .08 .25
89 A Higher Calling .20 .50
Gerald Ford
NNO Checklist Card .08 .25

1996 Globetrotters Real Action

Issued by Real Action; these 10 cards feature members of the Harlem Globetrotters. These cards, although they measure the standard size, are folded out and "pop-outs" of the featured players can be removed from the card. This set was also sponsored by Denny's. Since these cards are unnumbered, we have sequenced them in alphabetical order.

COMPLETE SET (11) 8.00 20.00
1 Arnold Bernard 1.25 3.00
2 Rodney English 1.50 4.00
3 Paul Gaffney 1.25 3.00
4 Barry Hardy 1.25 3.00
5 Curley Johnson 1.50 4.00
6 Reggie Perkins 1.25 3.00
7 Reggie Phillips 1.25 3.00
8 Trazel Silvers 1.25 3.00
9 Clyde Sinclair 1.25 3.00
10 Wun Versher 1.25 3.00
XX Display Card .25 .60

2001 Greats of the Game

Released in September 2001, this 100-card base set offers a crisp, classic design on standard size cards. The cards stand out with a white background and spotlights on former collegiate players wearing their prospective team jerseys. The Fleer logo is found in the upper right-hand corner. The player's name and college team name run horizontal under the player's photo. The base set contains one subset: Queens of the Court that pays homage to some of the greatest lady hoopsters of all time. Greats of the Game was packaged in 24 pack boxes with each pack containing five cards.

COMPLETE SET (84) 20.00 50.00
1 Adolph Rupp .40 1.00
2 Alonzo Mourning .50 1.25
3 Antawn Jamison .40 1.00
4 Antoine Walker .30 .75
5 Bill Walton .40 1.00
6 Bob Cousy .60 1.50
7 Bob Lanier .30 .75
8 Bobby Cremins .25 .60
9 Bobby Hurley .25 .60
10 Bobby Knight .50 1.25
11 Cazzie Russell .30 .75
12 Charlie Ward .25 .60
13 Christian Laettner .75 2.00
14 Clyde Drexler .50 1.25
15 Danny Ainge .40 1.00
16 Danny Ferry .75 2.00
17 Danny Manning .75 2.00
18 Darrell Griffith .25 .60
19 Dave Cowens .25 .60
20 David Robinson .60 1.50
21 David Thompson .30 .75
22 Dean Smith .40 1.00
23 Don Haskins .40 1.00
24 Eddie Jones .30 .75
25 Elvin Hayes .40 1.00
26 Gene Keady .30 .75
27 George Mikan .75 2.00
28 Glen Rice .30 .75
29 Hakeem Olajuwon .50 1.25
30 Isiah Thomas .40 1.00
31 Jalen Rose .30 .75
32 Jamal Mashburn .30 .75
33 James Worthy .50 1.25
34 Jerry Stackhouse .30 .75
35 Jerry Lucas .40 1.00
36 Jerry Tarkanian .40 1.00
37 Jerry West .50 1.25
38 Jim Valvano .60 1.50
39 Joe Smith .30 .75
40 John Thompson
41 John Havlicek .50 1.25
42 John Wooden .50 1.25
43 John Lucas .40 1.00
44 Kareem Abdul-Jabbar .60 1.50
45 Keith Van Horn .30 .75
46 Kent Benson .40 1.00
47 Kerry Kittles .25 .60
48 Lamar Odom .40 1.00
49 Larry Bird 1.00 2.50
50 Larry Johnson .40 1.00
51 Lefty Driesell .75 2.00
52 Lenny Wilkens .40 1.00
53 Lou Carnesecca .25 .60
54 Marques Johnson .30 .75
55 Mateen Cleaves .60 1.50
56 Mike Bibby .40 1.00
57 Mike Krzyzewski .60 1.50
58 Mychal Thompson .30 .75
59 Nate Archibald .30 .75
60 Pat Riley .50 1.25
61 Paul Arizin .40 1.00
62 Pete Maravich 1.00 2.50
63 Phil Ford .40 1.00
64 Ralph Sampson .30 .75
65 Ray Meyer .40 1.00
66 Rick Pitino .60 1.50
67 Rick Barry .30 .75
68 Rollie Massimino .25 .60
69 Sam Jones .40 1.00
70 Sidney Moncrief .25 .60
71 Spud Webb .30 .75
72 Steve Alford .40 1.00
73 Vince Carter .60 1.50
74 Walt Frazier .40 1.00
75 Wilt Chamberlain .75 2.00
76 Carol Blazejowski QC 1.00 2.50
77 Cynthia Cooper QC 1.00 2.50
78 Chamique Holdsclaw QC 1.00 2.50
79 Lisa Leslie QC 1.00 2.50
80 Nancy Lieberman QC 1.00 2.50
81 Rebecca Lobo QC 1.00 2.50
82 Cheryl Miller QC 1.00 2.50
83 Sheryl Swoopes QC 1.00 2.50
84 Marcus Camby .30 .75

2001 Greats of the Game All-American Collection

Randomly inserted in packs at a rate of one in six, this 14-card insert set features some of the greatest All-Americans to play the game. The standard size cards are horizontally designed. The player's photo is set in the center of the card with logos surrounding him in three of the four corners of the card. The All-American logo is found in the lower left-hand corner, the Fleer logo is found in the upper left-hand corner, and the player's college team logo is found in the upper right-hand corner. The fourth corner contains the player's college position and that is found in the lower right-hand corner.

COMPLETE SET (14) 8.00 20.00
STATED ODDS 1:6
1 Hakeem Olajuwon .75 2.00
2 Vince Carter 1.00 2.50
3 James Worthy .75 2.00
4 David Thompson .50 1.25
5 Paul Arizin .60 1.50
6 George Mikan 1.25 3.00
7 Bob Cousy 1.00 2.50
8 Steve Alford .60 1.50
9 Kent Benson .60 1.50
10 Isiah Thomas .60 1.50
11 Wilt Chamberlain 1.25 3.00
12 Marques Johnson .50 1.25
13 Bill Walton .60 1.50
14 Jerry West .75 2.00

2001 Greats of the Game All-American Collection Autographs

STATED PRINT RUNS LISTED BELOW
AAC1 Hakeem Olajuwon/84 75.00 150.00
AAC2 Vince Carter/98 40.00 80.00
AAC3 James Worthy/82 60.00 120.00
AAC4 David Thompson/77 20.00 50.00
AAC5 Paul Arizin/50 20.00 50.00
AAC6 George Mikan/46 175.00 350.00
AAC7 Bob Cousy/50 30.00 60.00
AAC8 Steve Alford/87 30.00 60.00
AAC9 Kent Benson/77 20.00 50.00
AAC12 Marques Johnson/77 20.00 50.00
AAC13 Bill Walton/74 30.00 80.00

2001 Greats of the Game Autographs

Randomly inserted in packs at the rate of one in 12, this 67-card set utilizes the base set design enhanced with authentic player autographs. There were several short printed cards issued with this set, and those appear below with print runs after the player name.

STATED ODDS 1:12
1 Kareem Abdul-Jabbar 30.00 80.00
2 Danny Ainge 8.00 20.00
3 Steve Alford 12.00 30.00
4 Nate Archibald 10.00 25.00
5 Paul Arizin 12.00 30.00
6 Rick Barry 8.00 20.00
7 Kent Benson 8.00 20.00
8 Mike Bibby 8.00 20.00
9 Larry Bird/200 150.00 300.00
10 Carol Blazejowski 10.00 25.00
11 Vince Carter 12.00 30.00
12 Mateen Cleaves 8.00 20.00
13 Cynthia Cooper 8.00 20.00
14 Bob Cousy 25.00 60.00
15 Dave Cowens 6.00 15.00
16 Clyde Drexler 10.00 25.00
17 Danny Ferry 8.00 20.00
18 Phil Ford 8.00 20.00
19 Walt Frazier 8.00 20.00
20 Darrell Griffith 8.00 20.00
21 John Havlicek/200 30.00 80.00
22 Elvin Hayes 8.00 20.00
23 Chamique Holdsclaw 30.00 80.00
24 Bobby Hurley 6.00 15.00
25 Antawn Jamison 8.00 20.00
26 Larry Johnson 10.00 25.00
27 Marques Johnson 8.00 20.00
28 Eddie Jones 8.00 20.00
29 Sam Jones 10.00 25.00
30 Kerry Kittles 8.00 20.00
31 Bobby Knight 30.00 80.00
32 Christian Laettner 20.00 50.00
33 Bob Lanier 8.00 20.00
34 Lisa Leslie 8.00 20.00
35 Nancy Lieberman-Cline 8.00 20.00
36 Jerry Lucas 6.00 15.00
37 John Lucas 8.00 20.00
38 Danny Manning 12.00 30.00
39 Jamal Mashburn 8.00 20.00
40 George Mikan/300 100.00 200.00
41 Cheryl Miller 10.00 25.00
42 Sidney Moncrief 8.00 20.00
43 Alonzo Mourning 12.50 30.00
45 Hakeem Olajuwon 15.00 40.00
46 Rick Pitino 15.00 40.00
47 Glen Rice 6.00 15.00
48 Pat Riley/150 30.00 80.00
49 David Robinson 30.00 80.00
50 Jalen Rose 10.00 25.00
51 Cazzie Russell 8.00 20.00
52 Ralph Sampson 8.00 20.00
53 Joe Smith 8.00 20.00
54 Jerry Stackhouse 10.00 25.00
55 Sheryl Swoopes 15.00 30.00
56 Isiah Thomas/219 15.00 30.00
57 David Thompson 8.00 20.00
58 Mychal Thompson 8.00 20.00
59 Keith Van Horn 6.00 15.00
60 Antoine Walker 8.00 20.00
61 Bill Walton 10.00 25.00
62 Charlie Ward 8.00 20.00
63 Spud Webb 8.00 20.00
64 Jerry West 20.00 50.00
65 Lenny Wilkens 8.00 20.00
66 John Wooden/300 75.00 150.00
67 James Worthy 15.00 40.00

2001 Greats of the Game Coach's Corner

Randomly inserted in packs at a rate of one in 10, this 16-card insert set features some of the most successful college coaches. The standard size cards include a color photo of the coach, his name, and the team he coached. The team's logo can also be found in the lower right-hand corner.

COMPLETE SET (16) 15.00 40.00
STATED ODDS 1:10
CC1 Lou Carnesecca 1.00 2.50
CC2 Bobby Cremins 1.00 2.50
CC3 Lefty Driesell 3.00 8.00
CC4 Don Haskins 1.00 2.50
CC5 Mike Krzyzewski 3.00 8.00
CC6 Rollie Massimino 1.00 2.50
CC7 Ray Meyer 1.00 2.50
CC8 Rick Pitino 2.50 6.00
CC9 Adolph Rupp 2.50 6.00
CC10 Dean Smith 2.50 6.00
CC11 Jerry Tarkanian 1.00 2.50
CC12 John Thompson 1.00 2.50
CC13 Bobby Knight 1.00 2.50
CC14 John Wooden 2.00 5.00
CC15 Jim Valvano 2.00 5.00
CC16 Gene Keady 1.00 2.50

2001 Greats of the Game Coach's Corner Autographs

STATED PRINT RUN 100 SERIAL #'d SETS
CC2 Bobby Cremins 15.00 40.00
CC3 Lefty Driesell 25.00 60.00
CC4 Don Haskins 15.00 40.00
CC5 Mike Krzyzewski 200.00 500.00
CC6 Rollie Massimino 20.00 50.00
CC7 Ray Meyer 15.00 40.00
CC8 Rick Pitino 20.00 50.00
CC10 Dean Smith 50.00 100.00
CC11 Jerry Tarkanian 20.00 50.00
CC12 John Thompson 60.00 150.00
CC13 Bobby Knight 40.00 100.00
CC14 John Wooden 100.00 200.00

2001 Greats of the Game Feel the Game Classics

Randomly inserted in packs at a rate of one in 24, this 25-card insert set offers circular game-used swatches from some of the legendary names in collegiate basketball history. Vince Carter and Bobby Knight have several different versions, and the type of memorabilia on the card has be added after the player name in the listings below.

STATED ODDS 1:24
1 Rick Barry 4.00 10.00
2 Larry Bird 12.00 30.00
3 Lou Carnasecca 4.00 10.00
4 Vince Carter JSY R 6.00 15.00
5 Vince Carter Shorts R 6.00 15.00
6 Vince Carter WU 6.00 15.00
7 Vince Carter Shirt 6.00 15.00
8 Vince Carter JSY H 6.00 15.00
9 Vince Carter Shorts H 6.00 15.00
10 V.Carter J-Short R/150 8.00 20.00
11 V.Carter J-Short H/150 8.00 20.00
12 V.Carter WU-Shirt/200 8.00 20.00
13 V.Carter J-Shor-Shir R/50 15.00 40.00
14 V.Carter J-Shor-Shir H/50 15.00 40.00
15 V.Carter J-Shor-WU H/75 12.00 30.00
16 V.Carter J-Shor-WU R/75 12.00 30.00
17 V.Carter J-Shor-Shir-WU H/15 20.00 50.00
18 V.Carter J-Shor-Shir-WU R/15 20.00 50.00
20 Larry Johnson 4.00 10.00
21 Bobby Knight Ball 10.00 25.00
22 Bobby Knight Shirt 10.00 25.00
23 Pete Maravich 30.00 80.00
24 Isaiah Rider 4.00 10.00
25 Bill Walton 4.00 10.00

2001 Greats of the Game Feel the Game Hardwood Classics

Randomly inserted in packs at a rate of one 24, this 20-card insert set offers circular swatches of a game floor set next to player photos.

STATED ODDS 1:24
1 Steve Alford 3.00 8.00
2 Marcus Camby 3.00 8.00
4 Mateen Cleaves 3.00 8.00
6 Phil Ford SP 10.00 25.00
7 Antawn Jamison 3.00 8.00
8 Larry Johnson 3.00 8.00
9 Gene Keady 3.00 8.00
10 Bobby Knight 5.00 12.00
11 Mike Krzyzewski 6.00 15.00
13 Danny Manning 3.00 8.00
14 Glen Rice 3.00 8.00
15 Glenn Robinson 3.00 8.00
16 Jalen Rose 3.00 8.00
18 Sheryl Swoopes 3.00 8.00
19 Antoine Walker 3.00 8.00
20 Charlie Ward 3.00 8.00

2001 Greats of the Game Player of the Year

This 10-card insert set was randomly inserted in packs at a rate of one in 24. The standard size cards feature Player of the Year winners. The cards have a heading reading, "Player of the Year". There is an action shot of the featured player in the foreground of the card with a pencil sketching of him in the background.

COMPLETE SET (10) 15.00 40.00
STATED ODDS 1:24
POY1 Christian Laettner 5.00 12.00
POY2 Elvin Hayes 1.50 4.00
POY3 Larry Bird 6.00 15.00
POY4 Joe Smith 1.50 4.00
POY5 Cazzie Russell 1.50 4.00
POY6 Antawn Jamison 1.50 4.00
POY7 Danny Manning 2.50 6.00
POY8 David Robinson 1.50 4.00
POY9 Jerry Lucas 1.50 4.00
POY10 Kareem Abdul-Jabbar 2.50 6.00

2001 Greats of the Game Player of the Year Autographs

STATED PRINT RUNS LISTED BELOW
POY1 Christian Laettner/91 30.00 80.00
POY2 Elvin Hayes/68 20.00 50.00
POY3 Larry Bird/79 100.00 200.00
POY4 Joe Smith/95 12.50 30.00
POY5 Cazzie Russell/66 40.00 100.00
POY6 Antawn Jamison/98 12.50 30.00
POY7 Danny Manning/88 12.50 30.00
POY8 David Robinson/87 40.00 100.00
POY10 Kareem Abdul-Jabbar/69 60.00 150.00

2005-06 Greats of the Game

Released in June 2005, Greats of the game features retired players and veterans on cards 1-91, coaches on cards 92-100, autographed rookies serially numbered to 99 on cards 101-152 and rookies serially numbered to 99 on cards 153-169. Base veteran and retired player cards have brown borders while the rookies have silver borders. Greats was packaged in 15-pack boxes of five cards each and carried an initial SRP of $9.99.

COMP.SET w/o SP's (100) 15.00 40.00
101-169 PRINT RUN 99 SER.#'d SETS
1 Earl Monroe .60 1.50
2 World Free .50 1.25
3 James Worthy .60 1.50
4 Bob McAdoo .50 1.25
5 Connie Hawkins .60 1.50
6 John Starks .50 1.25
7 Byron Scott .50 1.25
8 Brad Daugherty .50 1.25
9 Chris Ford .60 1.50
10 Jamaal Wilkes .60 1.50
11 Julius Erving 1.00 2.50
12 Joe Carroll .60 1.50
13 Bill Laimbeer .50 1.25
14 Bill Walton .60 1.50
15 Brian Winters .60 1.50
16 David Robinson 1.00 2.50
17 Horace Grant .60 1.50
18 Bob Pettit .60 1.50
19 Dan Roundfield .60 1.50
20 Kenny Walker .40 1.00
21 Kenny Smith .50 1.25
22 Thurl Bailey .40 1.00
23 Cedric Maxwell .40 1.00
24 Joe Dumars .50 1.25
25 Adrian Dantley .50 1.25
26 Dale Ellis .40 1.00
27 John Stockton 1.25 3.00
28 Bob Lanier .60 1.50
29 Bernard King .50 1.25
30 Jerry Lucas .60 1.50
31 Bill Russell 1.25 3.00
32 Hal Greer .50 1.25
33 Billy Cunningham .60 1.50
34 Jack Sikma .50 1.25
35 Michael Cooper .50 1.25
36 David Thompson .50 1.25
37 Kareem Abdul-Jabbar 1.00 2.50
38 Bill Sharman .60 1.50
39 George Gervin .60 1.50
40 Kiki Vandeweghe .50 1.25
41 Calvin Murphy .50 1.25
42 Darryl Dawkins .40 1.00
43 Vern Mikkelsen .60 1.50
44 Dee Brown .50 1.25
45 Dennis Rodman 1.25 3.00
46 Bobby Jones .50 1.25
47 Hakeem Olajuwon .75 2.00
48 Alvin Robertson .60 1.50
49 Dennis Johnson .50 1.25
50 Clyde Drexler .75 2.00
51 Anthony Mason .50 1.25
52 Larry Bird 1.50 4.00
53 LeBron James 2.50 6.00
54 Magic Johnson 1.50 4.00
55 Manute Bol .60 1.50
56 Mookie Blaylock .40 1.00
57 Mark Eaton .40 1.00
58 Kevin McHale .75 2.00
59 Maurice Cheeks .40 1.00
60 Maurice Lucas .60 1.50
61 Michael Jordan 5.00 12.00
62 Michael Ray Richardson .50 1.25
63 B.J. Armstrong .60 1.50
64 ML Carr .60 1.50
65 Muggsy Bogues .50 1.25
66 Nate Archibald .50 1.25
67 Glen Rice .60 1.50
68 Nate Thurmond .50 1.25
69 Norm Nixon .40 1.00
70 Bob Love .60 1.50
71 Paul Arizin .60 1.50
72 Ralph Sampson .50 1.25
73 Rolando Blackman .50 1.25
74 Reggie Theus .50 1.25
75 Mitch Richmond .60 1.50
76 Robert Parish .60 1.50
77 Paul Westphal .60 1.50
78 Sam Perkins .40 1.00
79 Scottie Pippen 1.00 2.50
80 Sean Elliott .60 1.50
81 Spud Webb .50 1.25
82 Steve Kerr .60 1.50
83 Tom Chambers .50 1.25
84 Walt Bellamy .50 1.25
85 Walt Frazier .60 1.50
86 Jeff Hornacek .50 1.25
87 Danny Manning .50 1.25
88 Wes Unseld .60 1.50
89 Geoff Petrie .60 1.50
90 Xavier McDaniel .40 1.00
91 Chris Mullin .60 1.50
92 Buck Williams CC .40 1.00
93 Dave Bing CC .60 1.50
94 John Havlicek CC .60 1.50
95 Karl Malone CC .75 2.00
96 Artis Gilmore CC .50 1.25
97 Doug Moe CC .60 1.50
98 Doug Collins CC .60 1.50
99 Chuck Daly CC .60 1.50
100 Bob Knight CC .75 2.00
101 Alex Acker AU RC 5.00 12.00
102 Amir Johnson AU RC 8.00 20.00
103 Andray Blatche AU RC 8.00 20.00
104 Andrew Bogut AU RC 20.00 50.00
105 Andrew Bynum AU RC 6.00 15.00
106 Antoine Wright AU RC 6.00 15.00
107 Yaroslav Korolev AU RC 5.00 12.00
108 Bracey Wright AU RC 5.00 12.00
109 Brandon Bass AU RC 6.00 15.00
110 C.J. Miles AU RC 8.00 20.00
111 Channing Frye AU RC 8.00 20.00
112 Charlie Villanueva AU RC 5.00 12.00
113 Chris Paul AU RC 100.00 250.00
114 Chris Taft AU RC 6.00 15.00
115 Chuck Hayes AU RC 8.00 20.00
116 Daniel Ewing AU RC 6.00 15.00
117 Danny Granger AU RC 10.00 25.00
118 David Lee AU RC 8.00 20.00
119 Deron Williams AU RC 15.00 40.00
120 Dijon Thompson AU RC 5.00 12.00
121 Ersan Ilyasova AU RC 8.00 20.00
122 Francisco Garcia AU RC 6.00 15.00
123 Gerald Green AU RC 8.00 20.00
124 Hakim Warrick AU RC 6.00 15.00
125 Ike Diogu AU RC 5.00 12.00
126 Jarrett Jack AU RC 8.00 20.00
127 Jason Maxiell AU RC 6.00 15.00
128 Joey Graham AU RC 6.00 15.00
129 Johan Petro AU RC 5.00 12.00
130 Julius Hodge AU RC 5.00 12.00
131 Lawrence Roberts AU RC 5.00 12.00
132 Linas Kleiza AU RC 5.00 12.00
133 Louis Williams AU RC 8.00 20.00
134 Luther Head AU RC 6.00 15.00
135 Martell Webster AU RC 6.00 15.00
136 M.Andriuskevicius AU RC 5.00 12.00
137 Marvin Williams AU RC 8.00 20.00
138 Monta Ellis AU RC 20.00 50.00
139 Nate Robinson AU RC 6.00 15.00
140 Orien Greene AU RC 6.00 15.00
141 Rashad McCants AU RC 6.00 15.00
142 Raymond Felton AU RC 8.00 20.00
143 Robert Whaley AU RC 5.00 12.00
144 Ronny Turiaf AU RC 8.00 20.00
145 Ryan Gomes AU RC 6.00 15.00
146 Salim Stoudamire AU RC 6.00 15.00
147 Sarunas Jasikevicius AU RC 8.00 20.00
148 Sean May AU RC 5.00 12.00
149 Stephen Graham AU RC 8.00 20.00
150 Travis Diener AU RC 5.00 12.00
151 Von Wafer AU RC 5.00 12.00
152 Wayne Simien AU RC 5.00 12.00
153 Shavlik Randolph RC 2.50 6.00
154 Alan Anderson RC 2.00 5.00
155 Andre Owens RC 2.00 5.00
156 Anthony Roberson RC 2.50 6.00
157 Arvydas Macijauskas RC 2.00 5.00
158 Boniface N'Dong RC 3.00 8.00
159 Devin Green RC 3.00 8.00
160 Donell Taylor RC 2.00 5.00
161 Earl Barron RC 2.50 6.00
162 Esteban Batista RC 2.00 5.00
163 Fabricio Oberto RC 2.50 6.00
164 Rawle Marshall RC 2.00 5.00
165 James Singleton RC 2.00 5.00
166 Jose Calderon RC 3.00 8.00
167 Josh Powell RC 2.50 6.00
168 Kevin Burleson RC 3.00 8.00
169 Ronnie Price RC 2.50 6.00

2005-06 Greats of the Game Autographs

Randomly seeded in packs, this 68-card set is horizontally designed with player images on the left, logos on the right and player autographs along the bottom on a "hardwood" background. Though the cards are not serially numbered, Upper Deck did release some announce print runs. See checklist for details.

APPROXIMATELY TWO PER BOX
UNPRICED GOLD PRINT RUN 10 SETS
GGAD Adrian Dantley 6.00 15.00
GGAR Alvin Robertson 4.00 10.00
GGBA B.J. Armstrong 6.00 15.00
GGBD Brad Daugherty 4.00 10.00
GGBJ Bobby Jones 6.00 15.00
GGBK Bernard King/248* 6.00 15.00
GGBL Bill Laimbeer 6.00 15.00
GGBM Bob McAdoo 6.00 15.00
GGBO Muggsy Bogues/185* 10.00 25.00
GGBP Bob Pettit 12.00 30.00
GGBR Bill Russell/30* 200.00 400.00
GGBS Byron Scott/250* 6.00 15.00
GGBW Bill Walton/250* 6.00 15.00
GGCD Clyde Drexler/109* 25.00 50.00
GGCF Chris Ford 6.00 15.00
GGCH Connie Hawkins 6.00 15.00
GGCO Michael Cooper 6.00 15.00
GGDA Chuck Daly/84* 20.00 50.00
GGDB Dee Brown 4.00 10.00
GGDC Doug Collins 4.00 10.00
GGDD Darryl Dawkins 6.00 15.00
GGDE Dale Ellis 4.00 10.00
GGDJ Dennis Johnson/236* 25.00 60.00
GGDM Doug Moe 4.00 10.00
GGDR David Robinson/62* 75.00 200.00
GGDT David Thompson 6.00 15.00
GGFR Walt Frazier/63* 12.00 30.00
GGGG George Gervin/250* 10.00 25.00
GGHG Hal Greer 6.00 15.00
GGHO Hakeem Olajuwon/62* 50.00 100.00
GGJE Julius Erving/30* 75.00 150.00
GGJH Jeff Hornacek 6.00 15.00
GGJS John Starks/250* 12.00 30.00
GGJW Jamaal Wilkes 6.00 15.00
GGKA Kareem Abdul-Jabbar/30* 150.00 300.00
GGKV Kiki Vandeweghe 4.00 10.00
GGKW Kenny Walker 6.00 15.00
GGLB Larry Bird/40* 75.00 150.00
GGLJ LeBron James/30* 200.00 450.00
GGMA Magic Johnson/40* 60.00 120.00
GGMC Maurice Cheeks 6.00 15.00
GGME Mark Eaton 6.00 15.00
GGML Maurice Lucas 6.00 15.00
GGMR Michael Ray Richardson 6.00 15.00
GGMX Cedric Maxwell/250* 10.00 25.00
GGNA Nate Archibald/250* 8.00 20.00
GGNN Norm Nixon 4.00 10.00
GGNT Nate Thurmond 6.00 15.00
GGPA Paul Arizin 10.00 25.00
GGPW Paul Westphal/87* 10.00 25.00
GGRD Dennis Rodman/112* 50.00 120.00
GGRO Dan Roundfield 6.00 15.00
GGRS Ralph Sampson/230* 6.00 15.00
GGRT Reggie Theus 4.00 10.00
GGSE Sean Elliott/184* 15.00 40.00
GGSH Bill Sharman 12.00 30.00
GGSI Jack Sikma 6.00 15.00
GGSK Steve Kerr 6.00 15.00
GGSP Sam Perkins/184* 4.00 10.00
GGST John Stockton/40* 60.00 120.00
GGSW Spud Webb/234* 6.00 15.00
GGTC Tom Chambers 6.00 15.00
GGVM Vern Mikkelsen 25.00 60.00
GGWB Walt Bellamy/248* 10.00 25.00
GGWF World Free 6.00 15.00
GGWI Brian Winters 4.00 10.00
GGWU Wes Unseld 6.00 15.00
GGXM Xavier McDaniel 6.00 15.00

2005-06 Greats of the Game Gold

*1-100 GOLD: 1.25X TO 3X BASE HI
1-100 PRINT RUN 99 SER.#'d SETS
*101-152 GOLD AU: .6X TO 1.5X BASE HI
*153-169 GOLD: .75X TO 2X BASE HI
113 Chris Paul AU 300.00 600.00

2005-06 Greats of the Game Great Cuts

Limited to three serially numbered copies per card, this set places cut signatures of some of the NBA's greatest players on each card.

2009-10 Greats of the Game

COMPLETE SET (163) 30.00 60.00
1 Mark Jackson .25 .60
2 Freddie Lewis .30 .75
3 Brad Daugherty .25 .60
4 John Stockton .50 1.25
5 Shareef Abdur-Rahim .25 .60
6 Michael Jordan 2.50 6.00
7 Larry Johnson .30 .75
8 B.J. Armstrong .30 .75
9 Hakeem Olajuwon .40 1.00
10 Sam Perkins .20 .50
11 Steve Kerr .30 .75
12 Julius Erving .50 1.25
13 John Havlicek .30 .75
14 Clyde Lovellette .30 .75
15 Danny Manning .25 .60
16 Isiah Thomas .30 .75
17 Kevin Pittsnogle .20 .50
18 Clyde Drexler .40 1.00
19 Bill Cartwright .25 .60
20 Jerry West .40 1.00
21 Darrell Walker .30 .75
22 Pat Riley .30 .75
23 Cazzie Russell .25 .60
24 Lionel Hollins .30 .75
25 George Karl .30 .75
26 Terry Porter .20 .50
27 Jack Sikma .25 .60
28 Adrian Dantley .25 .60
29 Billy Donovan .40 1.00
30 Micheal Ray Richardson .25 .60
31 Hal Greer .25 .60
32 Terry Cummings .25 .60
33 Rick Mahorn .20 .50
34 Larry Nance .25 .60
35 Oscar Robertson .30 .75
36 James Harden RC 1.50 4.00
37 Horace Grant .30 .75

38 Steve Alford .30 .75
39 Magic Johnson .75 2.00
40 LeBron James 1.25 3.00
41 Yao Ming .40 1.00
42 Larry Bird .75 2.00
43 Tito Horford .30 .75
44 Ricky Rubio RC .50 1.25
45 George Gervin .30 .75
46 Gail Goodrich .25 .60
47 Chet Walker .25 .60
48 Vlade Divac .30 .75
49 Thurl Bailey .20 .50
50 Dominique Wilkins .40 1.00
51 Bob Lanier .25 .60
52 Bill Sharman .30 .75
53 Don Nelson .30 .75
54 Ron Harper .30 .75
55 Bernard King .25 .60
56 Robert Parish .30 .75
57 Elgin Baylor .30 .75
58 Dave Cowens .20 .50
59 Dennis Rodman .60 1.50
60 Rod Hundley .30 .75
61 Bill Walton .30 .75
62 David Thompson .25 .60
63 Bill Laimbeer .25 .60
64 Bob McAdoo .25 .60
65 Kareem Abdul-Jabbar .50 1.25
66 Bill Russell .50 1.25
67 Alonzo Mourning .40 1.00
68 Jerry Sloan .30 .75
69 Avery Johnson .25 .60
70 Bobby Hurley .30 .75
71 Moses Malone .30 .75
72 Chris Mullin .30 .75
73 Derrick Rose .50 1.25
74 Stacey Augmon .20 .50
75 Darrell Griffith .20 .50
76 Danny Ferry .20 .50
77 Michael Cooper .25 .60
78 Brandon Roy .30 .75
79 Bob Pettit .30 .75
80 David Robinson .50 1.25
81 Sam Cassell .25 .60
82 Glen Rice .25 .60
83 Calbert Cheaney .30 .75
84 Christian Laettner .25 .60
85 Mateen Cleaves .20 .50
86 Derrick Rose GD 1.00 2.50
87 Yao Ming GD .75 2.00
88 Brandon Roy GD .60 1.50
89 LeBron James GD 2.50 6.00
90 James Harden GD 3.00 8.00
91 Michael Jordan GD 5.00 12.00
92 Michael Cooper GD .50 1.25
93 Moses Malone GD .60 1.50
94 Kevin Pittsnogle GD .40 1.00
95 Chris Mullin GD .60 1.50
96 Alonzo Mourning GD .75 2.00
97 Horace Grant GD .60 1.50
98 Larry Nance GD .50 1.25
99 Larry Bird GD 1.50 4.00
100 Julius Erving GD 1.00 2.50
101 Tito Horford GD .60 1.50
102 George Gervin GD .60 1.50
103 Red Hundley GD .60 1.50
104 Mateen Cleaves GD .40 1.00
105 Calbert Cheaney GD .60 1.50
106 Brandon Roy BMC .75 2.00
107 Calbert Cheaney BMC .75 2.00
108 Bill Cartwright BMC .60 1.50
109 Danny Ferry BMC .50 1.25
110 Danny Manning BMC .60 1.50
111 Darrell Walker BMC .75 2.00
112 Bill Laimbeer BMC .60 1.50
113 LeBron James BMC 3.00 8.00
114 Derrick Rose BMC 1.25 3.00
115 Hakeem Olajuwon BMC 1.00 2.50
116 Horace Grant BMC .75 2.00
117 James Harden BMC 4.00 10.00
118 Bill Russell BMC 1.25 3.00
119 Larry Bird BMC 2.00 5.00
120 Larry Johnson BMC .75 2.00
121 Michael Jordan BMC 6.00 15.00
122 Bill Walton BMC .75 2.00
123 Shareef Abdur-Rahim BMC .60 1.50
124 Sam Perkins BMC .50 1.25
125 J.West/K.Pittsnogle 1.25 3.00
126 B.Walton/K.Abdul-Jabbar 1.50 4.00
127 L.Johnson/S.Augmon 1.00 2.50
128 D.Cowens/S.Cassell .75 2.00
129 D.Thompson/T.Bailey .75 2.00
130 M.Johnson/M.Cleaves 2.50 6.00
131 B.Cartwright/B.Russell 1.50 4.00
132 B.Hurley/D.Ferry 1.00 2.50
133 H.Grant/L.Nance 1.00 2.50
134 C.Laettner/D.Ferry .75 2.00
135 F.Lewis/L.Hollins 1.00 2.50
136 C.Russell/G.Rice .75 2.00
137 B.Armstrong/D.Nelson 1.00 2.50
138 A.Dantley/B.Laimbeer .75 2.00
139 C.Mullin/M.Jackson 1.00 2.50
140 B.McAdoo/G.Karl 1.00 2.50
141 C.Lovellette/D.Manning 1.00 2.50
142 C.Drexler/H.Olajuwon 1.25 3.00
143 Dave Cowens OS .50 1.25
144 Bernard King OS .60 1.50
145 Mark Jackson OS .60 1.50
146 Danny Ferry OS .50 1.25
147 Darrell Griffith OS .50 1.25
148 Cazzie Russell OS .60 1.50
149 George Karl OS .75 2.00
150 Sam Perkins OS .50 1.25
151 Julius Erving OS 1.25 3.00
152 Larry Bird OS 2.00 5.00
153 Isiah Thomas OS .75 2.00
154 Michael Jordan OS 6.00 15.00
155 Freddie Lewis OS .75 2.00
156 John Stockton OS 1.25 3.00
157 Pat Riley OS .75 2.00
158 Jack Sikma OS .60 1.50
159 Oscar Robertson OS .75 2.00
160 Chris Mullin OS .75 2.00
161 George Gervin OS .75 2.00
162 Bill Walton OS .75 2.00
163 Kareem Abdul-Jabbar OS 1.25 3.00

2009-10 Greats of the Game 199

*GREATS 199 1-85: 1.5X TO 4X BASE HI
*GREATS 199 86-105: .75X TO 2X BASE HI
*GREATS 199 106-124: .6X TO 1.5X BASE HI
*GREATS 199 125-142: .75X TO 2X BASE HI
*GREATS 199 143-163: .6X TO 1.5X BASE HI
STATED PRINT RUN 199 SER.#'d SETS

2009-10 Greats of the Game 50

*GREATS 50 1-85: 4X TO 10X BASE HI
*GREATS 50 86-105: 2X TO 5X BASE HI
*GREATS 50 106-124: 1.5X TO 4X BASE HI
*GREATS 50 125-142: 1.5X TO 4X BASE HI
*GREATS 50 143-163: 1.5X TO 4X BASE HI
PRINT RUN 50 SER.#'d SETS

2009-10 Greats of the Game Autographs

STATED ODDS 1:8
86-163 UNPRICED PRINT RUN 10 SETS
1 Mark Jackson 5.00 12.00
2 Freddie Lewis 4.00 10.00
4 John Stockton 25.00 60.00
5 Shareef Abdur-Rahim 4.00 10.00
6 Michael Jordan 100.00 200.00
8 B.J. Armstrong 5.00 12.00
10 Sam Perkins SP 20.00 50.00
11 Steve Kerr 4.00 10.00
12 Julius Erving SP 40.00 80.00
13 John Havlicek 20.00 40.00
15 Danny Manning 8.00 20.00
17 Kevin Pittsnogle 4.00 10.00
19 Bill Cartwright 8.00 20.00
20 Jerry West 20.00 50.00
21 Darrell Walker 4.00 10.00
22 Pat Riley 20.00 50.00
25 George Karl SP 40.00 80.00
26 Terry Porter 8.00 20.00
27 Jack Sikma 4.00 10.00
28 Adrian Dantley 4.00 10.00
29 Bill Donovan 15.00 30.00
30 Michael Ray Richardson 4.00 10.00
31 Hal Greer 5.00 12.00
32 Terry Cummings 5.00 12.00
33 Rick Mahorn 5.00 12.00
34 Larry Nance 6.00 15.00
35 Oscar Robertson 60.00 120.00
36 James Harden 25.00 60.00
37 Horace Grant 15.00 30.00
38 Steve Alford 5.00 12.00
39 Magic Johnson SP 100.00 200.00
40 LeBron James 125.00 250.00
41 Yao Ming 15.00 30.00
42 Larry Bird 40.00 100.00
43 Tito Horford 4.00 10.00
44 Ricky Rubio 40.00 100.00
45 George Gervin 15.00 30.00
46 Gail Goodrich 10.00 25.00
47 Chet Walker 8.00 20.00
48 Vlade Divac 6.00 15.00
49 Thurl Bailey 5.00 12.00
50 Dominique Wilkins 15.00 30.00
51 Bob Lanier 8.00 20.00
52 Bill Sharman 20.00 40.00
53 Don Nelson 10.00 25.00
54 Ron Harper 8.00 20.00
55 Bernard King 5.00 12.00
57 Elgin Baylor 12.50 30.00
59 Dennis Rodman 20.00 50.00
60 Rod Hundley 10.00 25.00
61 Bill Walton 8.00 20.00
62 David Thompson 6.00 15.00
63 Bill Laimbeer 6.00 15.00
64 Bob McAdoo 15.00 40.00
66 Bill Russell SP 75.00 150.00
67 Alonzo Mourning 25.00 50.00
68 Jerry Sloan 8.00 20.00
69 Avery Johnson 4.00 10.00
70 Bobby Hurley 6.00 15.00
71 Moses Malone 10.00 25.00
72 Chris Mullin 15.00 40.00
73 Derrick Rose 30.00 60.00
75 Darrell Griffith 4.00 10.00
76 Danny Ferry 4.00 10.00
77 Michael Cooper 4.00 10.00
78 Brandon Roy 8.00 20.00
79 Bob Pettit SP 40.00 100.00
81 Sam Cassell 5.00 12.00
82 Glen Rice 8.00 20.00
83 Calbert Cheaney 4.00 10.00
84 Christian Laettner 10.00 25.00
85 Mateen Cleaves 4.00 10.00

2009-10 Greats of the Game Memorable Monikers

STATED PRINT RUN 15 SER.#'d SETS
UNPRICED DUAL PRINT RUN 5 SER.#'d SETS
MBD Billy Donovan 15.00 30.00
MBL Bill Laimbeer 10.00 25.00
MBR Brandon Roy 10.00 25.00
MCW Chet Walker 15.00 30.00
MGG George Gervin 10.00 25.00
MHA Ron Harper 25.00 50.00
MHU Rod Hundley 15.00 30.00
MJA LeBron James 200.00 400.00
MJE Julius Erving 40.00 100.00
MMR Micheal Ray Richardson 10.00 25.00
MSC Sam Cassell 15.00 30.00
MYM Yao Ming 30.00 80.00

2009-10 Greats of the Game Old School Swatches

STATED ODDS 1:16 PACKS
OS1 Adrian Dantley 2.00 5.00
OS2 Magic Johnson 6.00 15.00
OS3 Alonzo Mourning 3.00 8.00
OS4 Larry Bird 6.00 15.00
OS5 Bernard King 2.00 5.00
OS6 Bill Laimbeer 2.00 5.00
OS7 Bill Russell 8.00 20.00
OS8 Bill Walton 2.50 6.00
OS9 Michael Jordan 15.00 40.00
OS10 Walt Frazier 2.50 6.00
OS11 Clyde Drexler 3.00 8.00
OS12 Stacey Augmon 3.00 8.00
OS14 David Robinson 4.00 10.00
OS15 Dennis Rodman 5.00 12.00
OS16 George Gervin 2.50 6.00
OS17 Hakeem Olajuwon 3.00 8.00
OS18 Horace Grant 2.50 6.00
OS19 Isiah Thomas 3.00 8.00
OS20 LeBron James 8.00 20.00
OS21 Micheal Ray Richardson 2.00 5.00
OS22 Steve Francis 2.50 6.00
OS23 Michael Cooper 2.00 5.00
OS24 Jerry West 6.00 15.00
OS25 John Stockton 4.00 10.00
OS26 James Worthy SP 5.00 12.00
OS27 Julius Erving 6.00 15.00
OS28 Kareem Abdul-Jabbar 6.00 15.00
OS29 Vlade Divac 2.50 6.00
OS30 Steve Kerr 2.50 6.00
OS31 Moses Malone 2.50 6.00
OS32 Rick Fox 2.50 6.00
OS33 Oscar Robertson 5.00 12.00
OS34 Pat Riley 4.00 10.00
OS35 Robert Parish 2.50 6.00
OS36 Sam Cassell 2.00 5.00

1995-96 Grizzlies/Topps

Produced by the Topps Company, this 9-card set commemorated the Vancouver Grizzlies inaugural season. Card fronts are identical to the 1995-96 Topps regular issue, but each contains a special expansion gold-foil logo. Cards were originally supposed to be renumbered 10-18, but the numbers on the backs were identical to that of the basic set.

COMPLETE SET (9) 3.00 8.00
10 Byron Scott UER .50 1.25
Numbered 175
11 Blue Edwards UER .40 1.00
Numbered 177
12 Antonio Harvey UER .40 1.00
Numbered 236
13 Kenny Gattison UER .40 1.00
Numbered 180
14 Gerald Wilkins UER .40 1.00
Numbered 174
15 Greg Anthony UER .40 1.00
Numbered 178
16 Lawrence Moten UER .40 1.00
Numbered 231
17 Bryant Reeves UER 1.25 3.00
Numbered 202
18 Checklist .40 1.00

2001-02 Grizzlies Topps

Released by Topps, this nine-card set features a horizontal design with the Grizzlies logo in the background and was given away during the 2001-02 season.

COMPLETE SET (9) 1.50 4.00
VG1 Shareef Abdur-Rahim .40 1.00
VG3 Michael Dickerson .30 .75
VG4 Othella Harrington .30 .75
VG5 Bryant Reeves .30 .75
VG6 Damon Jones .30 .75
VG7 Isaac Austin .30 .75
VG8 Stromile Swift .30 .75
VG9 Tony Massenburg .30 .75
VG10 Grant Long .30 .75

2009-10 Hall of Fame

COMPLETE SET (149) 75.00 150.00
PRINT RUN 599 SER.#'d SETS
UNPRICED MARBLE PRINT RUN ONE SET
1 Kareem Abdul-Jabbar 2.50 6.00
2 Nate Archibald 1.25 3.00
3 Paul Arizin 1.50 4.00
4 Rick Barry 1.25 3.00
5 Elgin Baylor 1.50 4.00
6 John Beckman 1.50 4.00
7 Walt Bellamy 1.25 3.00
8 Dave Bing 1.50 4.00
9 Larry Bird 4.00 10.00
10 Carol Blazejowski 1.50 4.00
11 Al Cervi 1.50 4.00
12 Wilt Chamberlain 3.00 8.00
13 Cynthia Cooper 2.00 5.00
14 Bob Cousy 2.50 6.00
15 Dave Cowens 1.00 2.50
16 Billy Cunningham 1.50 4.00
17 Adrian Dantley 1.25 3.00
18 Bob Davies 1.50 4.00
19 Dave DeBusschere 1.50 4.00
20 Anne Donovan 1.50 4.00
21 Clyde Drexler 2.00 5.00
22 Joe Dumars 1.50 4.00
23 Alex English 1.25 3.00
24 Patrick Ewing 2.00 5.00
25 Walt Frazier 1.50 4.00
26 Joe Fulks 2.00 5.00
27 Harry Gallatin 1.50 4.00
28 Pop Gates 2.00 5.00
29 George Gervin 1.50 4.00
30 Tom Gola 1.50 4.00
31 Gail Goodrich 1.25 3.00
32 Hal Greer 1.25 3.00
33 Cliff Hagan 1.25 3.00
34 John Havlicek 1.50 4.00
35 Connie Hawkins 1.50 4.00
36 Elvin Hayes 1.50 4.00
37 Tom Heinsohn 1.50 4.00
38 Bailey Howell 1.50 4.00
39 Dan Issel 1.25 3.00
40 Buddy Jeannette 1.50 4.00
41 Dennis Johnson 1.25 3.00
42 Magic Johnson 4.00 10.00
43 Neil Johnston 1.50 4.00
44 K.C. Jones 1.50 4.00
45 Sam Jones 2.00 5.00
46 Bob Lanier 1.25 3.00
47 Nancy Lieberman 2.00 5.00
48 Clyde Lovellette 1.50 4.00
49 Jerry Lucas 1.50 4.00
50 Pete Maravich 2.50 6.00
51 Bob McAdoo 1.25 3.00
52 Kevin McHale 1.50 4.00
53 Ed Macauley 1.50 4.00
54 Karl Malone 2.00 5.00
55 Moses Malone 1.50 4.00
56 Slater Martin 1.50 4.00
57 Ann Meyers 1.50 4.00
58 George Mikan 3.00 8.00
59 Vern Mikkelsen 1.50 4.00
60 Cheryl Miller 1.50 4.00
61 Earl Monroe 1.50 4.00
62 Calvin Murphy 1.25 3.00
63 Hakeem Olajuwon 2.00 5.00
64 James Naismith 1.50 4.00
65 Robert Parish 1.50 4.00
66 Drazen Petrovic 3.00 8.00
67 Bob Pettit 1.50 4.00
68 Andy Phillip 2.00 5.00
69 Jim Pollard 2.00 5.00
70 Scottie Pippen 3.00 8.00
71 Frank Ramsey 1.50 4.00
72 Willis Reed 1.50 4.00
73 Arnie Risen 1.50 4.00
74 Oscar Robertson 1.50 4.00
75 David Robinson 2.50 6.00
76 Bill Russell 2.50 6.00
77 Dolph Schayes 1.50 4.00
78 Bill Sharman 1.50 4.00
79 John Stockton 2.50 6.00
80 Maurice Stokes 1.50 4.00
81 Isiah Thomas 1.50 4.00
82 David Thompson 1.25 3.00
83 Nate Thurmond 1.25 3.00
84 Jack Twyman 1.50 4.00
85 Wes Unseld 1.50 4.00
86 Bill Walton 1.50 4.00
87 Bobby Wanzer 1.00 2.50
88 Jerry West 2.00 5.00
89 Lenny Wilkens 1.50 4.00
90 Dominique Wilkins 2.00 5.00
91 Lynette Woodard 1.50 4.00
92 John Wooden 2.00 5.00
93 James Worthy 2.00 5.00
94 George Yardley 1.50 4.00
95 Phog Allen 1.50 4.00
96 Red Auerbach 2.00 5.00
97 Jim Boeheim 1.50 4.00
98 Larry Brown 1.50 4.00
99 Lou Carnesecca 1.50 4.00
100 Jody Conradt 2.00 5.00
101 Denny Crum 1.50 4.00
102 Chuck Daly 1.50 4.00
103 Ed Diddle 1.50 4.00
104 Clarence Gaines 1.50 4.00
105 Alex Hannum 1.50 4.00
106 Red Holzman 1.50 4.00
107 Hank Iba 1.50 4.00
108 Phil Jackson 2.00 5.00
109 Bob Knight 2.00 5.00
110 Mike Krzyzewski 2.00 5.00
111 John Kundla 1.50 4.00
112 Al McGuire 1.50 4.00
113 Ray Meyer 1.50 4.00
114 Jack Ramsay 1.50 4.00
116 Adolph Rupp 1.50 4.00
117 Jerry Sloan 1.50 4.00
118 Dean Smith 2.00 5.00
119 C. Vivian Stringer 1.50 4.00
120 Pat Summitt 12.00 30.00
121 John Thompson
122 Roy Williams 1.50 4.00
123 Meadowlark Lemon 1.50 4.00
124 Wilt Chamberlain 3.00 8.00
125 Lenny Wilkens 1.50 4.00
126 Marques Haynes 1.50 4.00
127 Oscar Robertson 1.50 4.00
128 Abe Saperstein 2.00 5.00
129 Harry Flournoy 1.50 4.00
130 Nevil Shed 1.50 4.00
131 David Lattin 2.00 5.00
132 Willie Worsley 1.50 4.00
133 Orsten Artis 1.50 4.00
134 Willie Cager 2.00 5.00
135 Don Haskins 2.00 5.00
136 Hubie Brown 1.50 4.00
137 Walter Brown 1.50 4.00
138 Jerry Colangelo 2.00 5.00
139 Chick Hearn 1.50 4.00
140 Pete Newell 1.50 4.00
141 Amos Alonzo Stagg 1.50 4.00
142 Chuck Taylor 1.50 4.00
143 Dick Vitale 2.00 5.00
144 Larry O'Brien 1.50 4.00
145 Nat Holman 2.00 5.00
146 Paul Endacott 1.50 4.00
147 Bud Foster 1.50 4.00
148 1960 USA Oly BK Team 2.00 5.00
149 1992 USA Oly BK Team 3.00 8.00
150 Bob Kurland 1.50 4.00

2009-10 Hall of Fame Black Border

*BLACK: .6X TO 1.5X BASE HI
BLACK PRINT RUN 199 SER.#'d SETS

2009-10 Hall of Fame Dream Team

COMPLETE SET (9) 25.00 50.00
PRINT RUN 349 SER.#'d SETS
*BLACK: .5X TO 1.25X BASE HI
BLACK PRINT RUN 199 SER.#'d SETS
UNPRICED MARBLE PRINT RUN ONE SET
1 Larry Bird 8.00 20.00
2 Magic Johnson 8.00 20.00
3 Clyde Drexler 4.00 10.00
4 Karl Malone 4.00 10.00
5 David Robinson 5.00 12.00
6 John Stockton 5.00 12.00
7 Patrick Ewing 4.00 10.00
8 Chris Mullin 3.00 8.00
9 Scottie Pippen 6.00 15.00

2009-10 Hall of Fame Dream Team Game Threads

STATED PRINT RUN 500 TO 1075 SETS
1 Larry Bird/975 10.00 25.00
2 Magic Johnson/750 12.00 30.00
3 Clyde Drexler/650 8.00 20.00
4 Karl Malone/1075 6.00 15.00
5 David Robinson/900 8.00 20.00
6 John Stockton/500 8.00 20.00
7 Patrick Ewing/975 8.00 20.00
8 Chris Mullin/600 6.00 15.00
9 Scottie Pippen/875 8.00 20.00

2009-10 Hall of Fame Dream Team Game Threads Prime

STATED PRINT RUN 99 SER.#'d SETS
1 Larry Bird 40.00 100.00
2 Magic Johnson 30.00 80.00
3 Clyde Drexler 30.00 80.00
4 Karl Malone 30.00 80.00
5 David Robinson 30.00 80.00
6 John Stockton 30.00 80.00
7 Patrick Ewing 30.00 80.00
8 Chris Mullin 30.00 80.00
9 Scottie Pippen 40.00 100.00

2009-10 Hall of Fame Dream Team Marks of Fame

STATED PRINT RUN 44 TO 49 SER.#'d SETS
1 Larry Bird/49 250.00 450.00
2 Magic Johnson/44 200.00 400.00
3 Clyde Drexler/49 125.00 250.00
6 John Stockton/49 125.00 250.00
8 Chris Mullin/49 75.00 150.00
9 Scottie Pippen/49 250.00 500.00

2009-10 Hall of Fame Famed Cuts

STATED PRINT RUN ONE TO 20 SER.#'d SETS
MOST NOT PRICED DUE TO SCARCITY
2 Clarence Gaines/20 60.00 150.00

2009-10 Hall of Fame Famed Fabrics

STATED PRINT RUN 20 TO 599 SER.#'d SETS
UNPRICED PRIME PRINT RUN 10 SETS
1 Alex English/325 2.50 6.00
2 Tom Heinsohn/99 3.00 8.00
3 Bob Lanier/399 2.50 6.00
4 Clyde Drexler/599 4.00 10.00
5 Larry Bird/20 25.00 50.00
6 Dave Cowens/149 5.00 12.00
7 Dominique Wilkins/549 4.00 10.00
9 Hakeem Olajuwon/399 4.00 10.00
10 Isiah Thomas/325 3.00 8.00
11 Joe Dumars/250 3.00 8.00
12 Dennis Johnson/325 4.00 10.00
13 Karl Malone/599 4.00 10.00
14 Kevin McHale/399 4.00 10.00
15 Magic Johnson/250 6.00 15.00
16 Patrick Ewing/599 4.00 10.00
17 John Stockton/99 6.00 15.00
18 George Mikan/99 12.00 30.00
19 Dan Issel/99 2.50 6.00
20 Robert Parish/549 3.00 8.00
21 Kareem Abdul-Jabbar/99 6.00 15.00
22 Scottie Pippen/599 6.00 15.00

2009-10 Hall of Fame Famed Signatures

STATED PRINT RUN 10 TO 899 SER.#'d SETS
1 Kareem Abdul-Jabbar/50 75.00 150.00
2 Nate Archibald/499 6.00 15.00
3 Rick Barry/489 6.00 15.00
4 Elgin Baylor/199 10.00 25.00
6 Carol Blazejowski/899 6.00 15.00
7 Cynthia Cooper/499 6.00 15.00
9 Dave Cowens/499 8.00 20.00
10 Adrian Dantley/499 6.00 15.00
11 Anne Donovan/899 6.00 15.00
12 Joe Dumars/399 6.00 15.00
13 Alex English/499 6.00 15.00
14 Walt Frazier/394 6.00 15.00
15 Harry Gallatin/699 6.00 15.00
16 George Gervin/398 8.00 20.00
17 Tom Gola/899 10.00 25.00
18 Gail Goodrich/499 6.00 15.00
19 Hal Greer/499 8.00 20.00
20 Cliff Hagan/499 6.00 15.00
21 John Havlicek/199 12.00 30.00
22 Connie Hawkins/599 6.00 15.00
23 Elvin Hayes/364 6.00 15.00
24 Bailey Howell/599 6.00 15.00
25 K.C. Jones/399 12.00 30.00
27 Bob Lanier/499 6.00 15.00
28 Nancy Lieberman/496 6.00 15.00
29 Bob McAdoo/391 8.00 20.00
30 Kevin McHale/100 40.00 100.00
33 Ann Meyers/499 8.00 20.00
35 Cheryl Miller/499 6.00 15.00
36 Earl Monroe/399 10.00 25.00
37 Hakeem Olajuwon/299 12.00 30.00
38 Robert Parish/499 8.00 20.00
39 Willis Reed/499 10.00 25.00
40 Oscar Robertson/99 50.00 120.00
42 Bill Russell/99 75.00 150.00
43 Bill Sharman/499 8.00 20.00
44 Isiah Thomas/499 10.00 25.00
45 David Thompson/599 6.00 15.00
46 Nate Thurmond/499 10.00 25.00
47 Wes Unseld/492 8.00 20.00
48 Bill Walton/249 10.00 25.00
49 Lenny Wilkens/499 6.00 15.00
50 Dominique Wilkins/199 10.00 25.00
51 James Worthy/249 12.00 30.00
58 Pat Summitt/599 50.00 120.00
60 Harry Flournoy/899 6.00 15.00
61 Nevil Shed/899 6.00 15.00
62 David Lattin/890 6.00 15.00
63 Orsten Artis/899 6.00 15.00
64 Willie Cager/899 6.00 15.00
65 Willie Worsley/850 6.00 15.00

2009-10 Hall of Fame High Class

MPLETE SET (5) 10.00 25.00
STATED PRINT RUN 399 SER.#'d SETS
*BLACK: .6X TO 1.5X BASE HI
BLACK PRINT RUN 199 SER.#'d SETS
UNPRICED MARBLE PRINT RUN ONE SET
1 George Mikan 3.00 8.00
2 Bill Russell 2.50 6.00
3 Jerry West 2.00 5.00
4 Pete Maravich 2.50 6.00
5 Magic Johnson 4.00 10.00

2009-10 Hall of Fame High Praise

COMPLETE SET (9) 15.00 30.00
STATED PRINT RUN 399 SER.#'d SETS
1 Kareem Abdul-Jabbar 2.50 6.00
2 Oscar Robertson 1.50 4.00
3 Gail Goodrich 1.25 3.00
4 Bill Walton 1.50 4.00
5 Dominique Wilkins 2.00 5.00
6 Phil Jackson 2.00 5.00
7 David Robinson 2.50 6.00
8 Larry Bird 4.00 10.00
9 Wilt Chamberlain 3.00 8.00

2009-10 Hall of Fame Monikers

STATED PRINT RUN 10 TO 299 SER.#'d SETS
SOME UNPRICED DUE TO SCARCITY
1 Larry Bird/10
2 Walt Frazier/99 15.00 40.00
3 Nancy Lieberman/198 8.00 20.00
4 Dominique Wilkins/25 25.00 60.00
5 Bob Cousy/25 100.00 200.00
6 Elvin Hayes/99 15.00 40.00
7 George Gervin/199 15.00 40.00
8 Nate Archibald/299 8.00 20.00
9 Harry Gallatin/299 10.00 25.00
10 Connie Hawkins/199 8.00 20.00
11 Earl Monroe/199 10.00 25.00
12 Robert Parish/149 8.00 20.00
13 Jerry West/25 60.00 150.00
14 Hakeem Olajuwon/49 25.00 60.00
15 Oscar Robertson/25 100.00 225.00
16 John Havlicek/49 60.00 150.00
17 Nate Thurmond/199 12.50 30.00
18 Carol Blazejowski/299 8.00 20.00
19 Cynthia Cooper/294 8.00 20.00
20 Adrian Dantley/199 8.00 20.00
22 Clyde Drexler/99 15.00 40.00
23 Calvin Murphy/299 8.00 20.00
24 David Thompson/149 8.00 20.00
25 Isiah Thomas/99 10.00 25.00

2009-10 Hall of Fame Scoring Legends

COMPLETE SET (20) 20.00 40.00
STATED PRINT RUN 399 SER.#'d SETS
*BLACK: .6X TO 1.5X BASE HI
BLACK PRINT RUN 199 SER.#'d SETS
UNPRICED MARBLE PRINT RUN ONE SET
1 Kareem Abdul-Jabbar 2.50 6.00
2 Moses Malone 1.50 4.00
3 Dan Issel 1.25 3.00
4 Elvin Hayes 1.50 4.00
5 Oscar Robertson 1.50 4.00
6 Dominique Wilkins 2.00 5.00
7 George Gervin 1.50 4.00
8 John Havlicek 1.50 4.00
9 Rick Barry 1.25 3.00
10 Jerry West 2.00 5.00
11 Magic Johnson 4.00 10.00
12 Isiah Thomas 1.50 4.00
13 Lenny Wilkens 1.50 4.00
14 Bob Cousy 2.50 6.00
15 Nate Archibald 1.25 3.00
16 Bill Russell 2.50 6.00
17 Robert Parish 1.50 4.00
18 Nate Thurmond 1.25 3.00
19 Walt Bellamy 1.25 3.00
20 Wes Unseld 1.50 4.00

2009-10 Hall of Fame Scoring Legends Game Threads

STATED PRINT RUN 25 TO 249 SER.#'d SETS
1 Kareem Abdul-Jabbar/249 6.00 15.00
3 Dan Issel/249 2.50 6.00
6 Dominique Wilkins/249 4.00 10.00
8 John Havlicek/25 10.00 25.00
9 Rick Barry/49 2.50 6.00
11 Magic Johnson/249 6.00 15.00
12 Isiah Thomas/199 3.00 8.00
17 Robert Parish/249 3.00 8.00

2009-10 Hall of Fame Scoring Legends Game Threads Prime

STATED PRINT RUN 25 SER.#'d SETS
1 Kareem Abdul-Jabbar 8.00 20.00
3 Dan Issel 6.00 15.00
6 Dominique Wilkins 6.00 15.00
8 John Havlicek 12.00 30.00
9 Rick Barry 6.00 15.00
11 Magic Johnson 15.00 40.00
12 Isiah Thomas 15.00 40.00
17 Robert Parish 8.00 20.00

1968-74 Hall of Fame Bookmarks

These bookmarks commemorate individuals who were elected to the Basketball Hall of Fame. The cards were probably issued year after year (with additions) by the Hall of Fame book store. They measure approximately 2 7/16" by 6 3/8". The top of the front has a blue-tinted 2 1/8" by 2 5/16 "mug shot" of the individual on paper stock. In blue lettering the individual's name and a brief biography are printed below the picture. The backs are blank and the cards are unnumbered. The last seven cards listed below were inducted in 1969 (47-48), 1970 (49-51), 1972 (52), and 1974 (53); there are some slight style and size differences in these later issue cards compared to the first 46 cards in the set.

COMPLETE SET (53) 150.00 300.00
1 Forrest C. Allen .60 1.50
2 Arnold J. Auerbach 1.25 3.00
3 Clair F. Bee .60 1.50
4 Bernhard Borgmann .20 .50
5 Walter A. Brown .20 .50
6 John W. Bunn .20 .50
7 Howard G. Cann .20 .50
8 H. Clifford Carlson .20 .50
9 Everett S. Dean .20 .50
10 Forrest S. DeBernardi .20 .50
11 Henry G. Dehnert .20 .50
12 Harold E. Foster .20 .50
13 Amory T. Gill .20 .50
14 Victor A. Hanson .20 .50
15 Edward J. Hickox .20 .50
16 Paul D. Hinkle .20 .50
17 Howard A. Hobson .20 .50
18 Nat Holman .75 2.00
19 Charles D. Hyatt .20 .50
20 Henry P. Iba .60 1.50
21 Edward S. Irish .25 .60
22 Alvin F. Julian .20 .50
23 Matthew P. Kennedy .20 .50
24 Robert A. Kurland .40 1.00
25 Ward L. Lambert .60 1.50
26 Joe Lapchick .40 1.00
27 Kenneth D. Loeffler .20 .50
28 Angelo Luisetti .50 1.25
29 Ed Macauley .50 1.25
30 Branch McCracken .25 .60
31 George Mikan 2.00 5.00
32 William G. Mokray .20 .50
33 Charles C. Murphy .60 1.50
34 James Naismith 1.25 3.00
35 Andy Phillip .40 1.00
36 John S. Roosma .20 .50
37 Adolph F. Rupp 1.50 4.00
38 John D. Russell .20 .50
39 Arthur A. Schabinger .20 .50
40 Amos Alonzo Stagg 1.25 3.00
41 Charles H. Taylor .20 .50
42 John A. Thompson .20 .50
43 David Tobey .20 .50
44 Oswald Tower .20 .50
45 David H. Walsh .20 .50
46 John R. Wooden 2.00 5.00
47 Bernard Carnevale 8.00 20.00
48 Bob Davies 12.00 30.00
49 Bob Cousy 25.00 60.00
50 Bob Pettit 15.00 40.00
51 Abraham M. Saperstein 20.00 50.00
52 Adolph Schayes 15.00 40.00
53 Bill Russell 40.00 100.00

2005 Hardwood Heroes NBA Medallions

Created by Activa Promotions, this 30-card set features NBA stars on Medallion coins. The cards were distributed via both 7-11 stores and USA Today. The coins were available, one per day, from April 25, 2005 through June 3, 2005. There was also a color collectors album available to house the medallions.

COMPLETE SET (30) 25.00 60.00
1 Ray Allen 1.25 3.00
2 Carmelo Anthony 2.00 5.00
3 Elton Brand 1.25 3.00
4 Kobe Bryant 5.00 12.00
5 Vince Carter 1.50 4.00
6 Tim Duncan 1.50 4.00
7 Steve Francis 1.25 3.00
8 Kevin Garnett 2.00 5.00
9 Pau Gasol 1.25 3.00
10 Kirk Hinrich 1.25 3.00
11 Allen Iverson 1.50 4.00
12 LeBron James 5.00 12.00
13 Antawn Jamison 1.25 3.00
14 Jason Kidd 1.50 4.00
15 Andrei Kirilenko 1.25 3.00
16 Stephon Marbury 1.25 3.00
17 Tracy McGrady 1.50 4.00
18 Yao Ming 1.50 4.00
19 Steve Nash 1.50 4.00
20 Dirk Nowitzki 1.50 4.00
21 Jermaine O'Neal 1.25 3.00
22 Shaquille O'Neal 2.00 5.00
23 Emeka Okafor 1.25 3.00
24 Tony Parker 1.25 3.00
25 Paul Pierce 1.50 4.00
26 Jason Richardson 1.25 3.00
27 Peja Stojakovic 1.25 3.00
28 Amare Stoudemire 1.50 4.00
29 Dwyane Wade 3.00 8.00
30 Ben Wallace 1.25 3.00

1959-60 Hawks Busch Bavarian

These black and white photo-like cards were sponsored by Busch Bavarian Beer and feature members of the St. Louis Hawks. The cards are blank backed and measure approximately 4" by 5". The cards show a facsimile autograph of the player on a drop-out background. The set is dated by the fact that 1959-60 was John McCarthy's first year with the St. Louis Hawks.

COMPLETE SET (5) 400.00 800.00
1 Sihugo Green 100.00 200.00
2 Cliff Hagan 125.00 250.00
3 Clyde Lovellette 125.00 250.00
4 John McCarthy 75.00 150.00
5 Bob Pettit 250.00 450.00

1978-79 Hawks Coke/WPLO

This rather unattractive 14-card set was sponsored by V-103/WPLO radio and Coca-Cola, and they were given out at 7-Eleven stores. The cards are printed on thin cardboard stock and measure approximately 3 by 4 1/4". The fronts feature a black and white pen and ink drawing of the player's head, with the Hawks' and Coke logos in the lower corners in red. The back has a career summary and the sponsor's "V-103 Disco Stereo" at the bottom. The cards are unnumbered and are checklisted below in alphabetical order.

COMPLETE SET (14) 25.00 50.00
1 Hubie Brown CO 5.00 12.00
2 Charlie Criss 2.00 5.00
3 John Drew 2.00 5.00
4 Mike Fratello CO 3.00 8.00
5 Jack Givens 3.00 8.00
6 Steve Hawes 1.25 3.00
7 Armond Hill 1.50 4.00
8 Eddie Johnson 2.00 5.00
9 Frank Layden CO 3.00 8.00
10 Butch Lee 1.25 3.00
11 Tom McMillen 2.50 6.00
12 Tree Rollins 2.50 6.00
13 Dan Roundfield 1.50 4.00
14 Rick Wilson 1.25 3.00

1961 Hawks Essex Meats

The 1961 Essex Meats set contains 14 standard-size cards featuring the St. Louis Hawks. The fronts picture a posed black and white photo of the player with his name at the bottom of the card in bold-faced type. The backs of this white-stock card feature the player's name, brief physical data and biographical information. The cards are unnumbered and give no indication of the producer on the card. The cards were distributed by Bonnie Brands. The catalog designation for the set is F175. The Sihugo Green was reportedly short printed.

COMP.SET w/o SP (13) 200.00 400.00
1 Barney Cable 6.00 15.00
2 Al Ferrari 6.00 15.00
3 Larry Foust 6.00 15.00
4 Cliff Hagan 25.00 45.00
5 Sihugo Green SP 60.00 150.00
6 Vern Hatton 10.00 20.00
7 Cleo Hill 6.00 15.00
8 Fred LaCour 6.00 15.00
9 Fuzzy Levane CO 8.00 20.00
10 Clyde Lovellette 25.00 45.00
11 John McCarthy 6.00 15.00
12 Shellie McMillon 6.00 15.00
13 Bob Pettit 45.00 90.00
14 Bobby Sims 6.00 15.00

1979-80 Hawks Majik Market

The 1979-80 Majik Market/Coca-Cola Atlanta Hawks set contains 15 cards on thin white stock. Cards are approximately 3" by 4 1/4". The fronts of the cards include a crude, black line drawing of the player, the player's name and, in red, a Coke logo and a stylized Hawks logo. The backs contain biographical data and a summary of the player's activity during the 1978-79 season. The Majik Market logo and the call letters V-103/WPLO are printed in red on the back of the cards. Most collectors consider the set quite unattractive and poorly produced. The cards are unnumbered and are checklisted below in alphabetical order.

COMPLETE SET (15) 25.00 50.00
1 Hubie Brown CO 3.00 8.00
2 John Brown 1.25 3.00
3 Charlie Criss 2.00 5.00
4 John Drew 2.00 5.00
5 Mike Fratello ACO 2.50 6.00
6 Jack Givens 2.50 6.00
7 Steve Hawes 1.50 4.00
8 Armond Hill 1.50 4.00
9 Eddie Johnson 2.00 5.00
10 Jimmy McElroy 1.25 3.00
11 Tom McMillen 2.50 6.00
12 Sam Pellom 1.25 3.00
13 Tree Rollins 2.50 6.00
14 Dan Roundfield 2.00 5.00
15 Brendan Suhr ACO 1.50 4.00

1986-87 Hawks Pizza Hut

The 1986-87 Atlanta Hawks Team Photo Night (January 30, 1987) set was sponsored by Pizza Hut. This photo album was distributed to fans attending the Atlanta Hawks home game. It consists of three sheets, each measuring approximately 8 1/4" by 11" and joined together to form one continuous sheet. The first sheet features a team photo of the Hawks. While the second sheet presents two rows of five cards each, the third sheet presents eight additional player cards, with the remaining two slots filled in by Pizza Hut coupons. After perforation, the cards measure approximately 2 1/4" by 3 3/4". The card front features a color player portrait, with a red border on white card stock. The player's name and position are given below the picture, along with the team and Pizza Hut logos. The backs present career statistics in a horizontal format. The cards are unnumbered and checklisted below in the order they appear in the album, with coaching staff listed first and then the players in alphabetical order.

COMPLETE SET (18) 15.00 40.00
1 Mike Fratello CO 1.25 3.00
2 Willis Reed ACO 1.50 4.00
3 Brendan Suhr ACO .40 1.00
4 Brian Hill ACO 1.00 2.50
5 Joe O'Toole TR .40 1.00
6 John Battle .60 1.50
7 Antoine Carr 1.00 2.50
8 Scott Hastings .75 2.00
9 Jon Koncak .75 2.00
10 Cliff Levingston .75 2.00

11 Mike McGee	.75	2.00
12 Doc Rivers	2.50	6.00
13 Tree Rollins	.75	2.00
14 Spud Webb	2.00	5.00
15 Dominique Wilkins	8.00	20.00
16 Gus Williams	.75	2.00
17 Kevin Willis	2.50	6.00
18 Randy Wittman	1.25	3.00

1987-88 Hawks Pizza Hut

The 1987-88 Atlanta Hawks Team Photo Night set was sponsored by Pizza Hut. This photo album was distributed to fans attending the Atlanta Hawks home game on March 11, 1988. The set consists of three sheets, each measuring approximately 8 1/4" by 11" and joined together to form one continuous sheet. The first sheet features a team photo of the Hawks. While the second sheet presents two rows of five cards each, the third sheet presents seven additional player cards, with the remaining three slots filled in by Pizza Hut coupons. After perforation, the cards measure approximately 2 3/16" by 3 3/4". The card front features a color action player photo, with a red border on white card stock. The player's name and position are given below the picture, along with the team and Pizza Hut logos. The back presents career statistics in a horizontal format. The cards are unnumbered and checklisted below in the order they appear in the album.

COMPLETE SET (17)	25.00	60.00
1 Mike Fratello CO	1.50	4.00
2 Brendan Suhr ASST	.75	2.00
3 Brian Hill ASST	1.00	2.50
4 Don Chaney ASST	.75	2.00
5 Joe O'Toole TR	.40	1.00
6 John Battle	.60	1.50
7 Antoine Carr	1.25	3.00
8 Scott Hastings	.75	2.00
9 Jon Koncak	.75	2.00
10 Cliff Levingston	1.00	2.50
11 Doc Rivers	3.00	8.00
12 Tree Rollins	1.00	2.50
13 Chris Washburn	.75	2.00
14 Spud Webb	3.00	8.00
15 Dominique Wilkins	8.00	20.00
16 Kevin Willis	2.50	6.00
17 Randy Wittman	2.00	5.00

1968-69 Hawks Team Issue

Measuring 8" by 10", this seven photo set was released featuring the 1968-69 Atlanta Hawks. Each photo features a posed shot with the player's name in the lower left-hand corner and the team name in the lower right. Each photo is in black and white with blank backs. The photos are not numbered and listed below in alphabetical order.

COMPLETE SET (7)	20.00	40.00
1 Zelmo Beaty	5.00	10.00
2 Joe Caldwell	3.00	8.00
3 Jim Davis	2.50	6.00
4 Dennis Hamilton	2.50	6.00
5 Skip Harlicka	2.50	6.00
6 George Lehmann	3.00	8.00
7 Don Ohl	3.00	8.00

1969-70 Hawks Team Issue

This 10-photo team issue set was released to the press for the Atlanta Hawks' 1969-70 season. The photos measure 8" x 10", are black and white and are blank-backed. All that appears on the photo is a player close-up or action shot set against a white background and the player's name and "Atlanta Hawks" at the bottom. The photos are checklisted below in alphabetical order.

COMPLETE SET (10)	30.00	60.00
1 Butch Beard	3.00	8.00
2 Bill Bridges	2.50	6.00
3 Joe Caldwell	2.50	6.00
4 Jim Davis	2.00	5.00
5 Gary Gregor	2.00	5.00
6 Richie Guerin CO	2.50	6.00
7 Walt Hazzard	5.00	10.00
8 Lou Hudson	6.00	12.00
9 Don Ohl	2.00	5.00
10 Grady O'Malley	2.00	5.00

1972-73 Hawks Team Issue

Measuring 8" by 10", this 9-photo set features members of the 1972-73 Atlanta Hawks. Half of the set features a two-shot front and the other half features one large posed shot. All of the photos are in black and white. The backs are blank and not numbered, thus, listed below in alphabetical order.

COMPLETE SET (9)	17.50	35.00
1 Don Adams	1.50	4.00
2 Walt Bellamy	3.00	8.00
3 Bob Christian	1.25	3.00
4 Herm Gilliam	1.25	3.00
5 Jeff Halliburton	1.25	3.00
6 Lou Hudson	3.00	8.00
7 Tom Payne	1.50	4.00
8 George Trapp	1.25	3.00
9 Jim Washington	1.25	3.00

1977-78 Hawks Team Issue

These 12 photos, which are black and white glossies and measure 8" by 10" feature members of the 1977-78 Atlanta Hawks. Since these photos are unnumbered, we have sequenced them in alphabetical order.

COMPLETE SET (12)	12.50	25.00
1 Hubie Brown HEAD CO	1.50	4.00
2 John Brown	.75	2.00
3 Charles Criss	1.00	2.50
4 John Drew	1.00	2.50
5 Steve Hawes	.75	2.00
6 Armond Hill	1.00	2.50
7 Eddie Johnson	.75	2.00
8 Ollie Johnson	.75	2.00
9 Tom McMillen	1.50	4.00
10 Tony Robertson	.75	2.00
11 Wayne Rollins	1.00	2.50
12 Mike Fratello ACO Frank Layden ACO	1.50	4.00

1978-79 Hawks Team Issue

This 4 1/2" x 6" set was produced for the Atlanta Hawks during the 1978-79 season. The set features 11 full-colored cards of the team's players.

COMPLETE SET (11)	20.00	50.00
1 John Drew	2.50	6.00
2 Eddie Johnson	2.50	6.00
3 Dan Roundfield	3.00	8.00
4 Tree Rollins	3.00	8.00
5 Butch Lee	3.00	8.00
6 Jack Givens	3.00	8.00
7 Tom McMillen	3.00	8.00
8 Armond Hill	2.00	5.00
9 Steve Hawes	2.00	5.00
10 Charlie Criss	2.00	5.00
11 Rick Wilson	2.00	5.00

1993-94 Heat Bookmarks

Measuring 2 1/2" by 8", these four bookmarks were sponsored by the Miami Herald. The color action photo on the top portion is framed by a black inner border and a orangish-yellow outer border. The remainder of the front has biography, a "Join the Winning Team! Read" slogan, as well as team and sponsor logos. In black print on a white background, the back carries ten "Heat Tips For Reading With Children." The bookmarks are unnumbered and checklisted below in alphabetical order.

COMPLETE SET (4)	1.60	4.00
1 Grant Long	.40	1.00
2 Harold Miner	.40	1.00
3 Rony Seikaly	.40	1.00
4 Steve Smith	.75	2.00

2001-02 Hawks Topps

Released by Topps, this set features a horizontal design with the Atlanta Hawks logo in the background. Our information on this set is incomplete. If you have further information about this product, please contact us at basketballmag@beckett.com.

COMPLETE SET (11)	2.00	5.00
AH2 Hanno Mottola	.30	.75
AH4 Alan Henderson	.30	.75
AH6 Anthony Johnson	.30	.75
AH7 Chris Crawford	.30	.75
AH9 Roshown McLeod	.30	.75
AH10 DerMarr Johnson	.30	.75
AH11 Cal Bowdler	.30	.75
AH12 Lorenzen Wright	.30	.75
AH13 Dion Glover	.30	.75
AH14 Jason Terry	.50	1.25
NNO Atlanta Hawks	.25	.60

1989-90 Heat Publix

This 15-card set was distributed in Publix stores in the greater Miami area. The cards measure approximately 2" by 3 1/2" and feature members of the Miami Heat. The fronts feature a color action player photo, with the player's name and position in the stripe below the picture. The back has biographical and statistical information. The cards are unnumbered and are checklisted below in alphabetical order. The set features early cards of Glen Rice and Rony Seikaly among others.

COMPLETE SET (15)	40.00	100.00
1 Terry Davis	2.00	5.00
2 Sherman Douglas	6.00	15.00
3 Kevin Edwards	3.00	8.00
4 Tony Fiorentino CO	2.00	5.00
5 Tellis Frank	2.00	5.00
6 Scott Haffner	2.00	5.00
7 Grant Long	6.00	15.00
8 Heat Mascot	1.50	4.00
9 Glen Rice	15.00	40.00
10 Ron Rothstein CO	5.00	12.00
11 Rony Seikaly	6.00	15.00
12 Rory Sparrow	2.50	6.00
13 Jon Sundvold	2.50	6.00
14 Billy Thompson	3.00	8.00
15 Dave Wohl CO	3.00	8.00

1990-91 Heat Publix

This 16-card set was sponsored by Domino's Pizza, Dixie, and Bumble Bee Tuna and features members of the Miami Heat. The cards were issued in a sheet that contains 16 player cards and four manufacturers' coupons; after perforation, the cards and coupons alike measure the standard size (2 1/2" by 3 1/2"). The front features a color action player photo on a black background. The team logo appears in the upper right corner, while the player's name appears in white lettering below the picture. The back has biographical and statistical information. The cards are unnumbered and are checklisted below as they are listed on the panel, in alphabetical order with coaches at the end.

COMPLETE SET (16)	8.00	20.00
1 Keith Askins	.60	1.50
2 Willie Burton	.60	1.50
3 Bimbo Coles	.75	2.00
4 Terry Davis	.40	1.00
5 Sherman Douglas	.75	2.00
6 Kevin Edwards	.75	2.00
7 Alec Kessler	.40	1.00
8 Grant Long	1.25	3.00
9 Alan Ogg	.40	1.00
10 Glen Rice	3.00	8.00
11 Rony Seikaly	1.25	3.00
12 Jon Sundvold	.40	1.00
13 Billy Thompson	.75	2.00
14 Ron Rothstein CO	1.25	3.00
15 Dave Wohl CO	1.25	3.00
16 Tony Fiorentino CO	.40	1.00

2008-09 Heat Upper Deck

COMPLETE SET (14)	2.50	6.00
1 Dwayne Wade	.50	1.25
2 Shawn Marion	.25	.60
3 Udonis Haslem	.20	.50
4 Yakhouba Diawara	.20	.50
5 Dorell Wright	.20	.50
6 Daequan Cook	.20	.50
7 Chris Quinn	.20	.50
8 Mark Blount	.20	.50
9 Marcus Banks	.20	.50
10 Alonzo Mourning	.40	1.00
11 Michael Beasley	.30	.75
12 Mario Chalmers	.30	.75
13 Erik Spoelstra CO	.20	.50
14 Glen Rice	.25	.60

1910 Helmar Premiums

These premiums were drawn by reknowned artist Hamilton King who originally illustrated advertistments for Coca Cola around 1900. These images are known as the "Women in Athletic Costumes" series. Smokers could redeem coupons for these lithographs either on card stock, on satin or on bookbinding leather. There was also a gift slip which checklisted all the premiums available from the tobacco company, which also listed the number of coupons required for each specific type of premum.

COMPLETE SET	2500.00	5000.00
1 Card Stock	200.00	400.00
2 Individual Satin	400.00	800.00
3 Leather	1000.00	2000.00
4 Satin Pillow Top	1500.00	3000.00

Eight Women shown including Basketball Girl

1997 Highland Mint Legends Mint-Cards

Highland Mint produced its own brand of professional basketball Mint-Cards, known as Hardcourt Legends. Each card contained 4.25 Troy Ounces of .999 silver, bronze, or 24K gold-plated .999 silver. The initial suggested retail price was $50 for bronze, $235 for silver, and $500 or $650 for gold. The cards were packaged in a lucite display case in an album. The enclosed certificate of authenticity carries the serial number. The cards are checklisted below alphabetically; the mintage figures for each card are also listed.

COMPLETE SET (7)	400.00	800.00
1 Kareem Abdul-Jabbar 95 S/1000	150.00	225.00
2 Kareem Abdul-Jabbar 95 B/5000	20.00	35.00
3 Larry Bird 95 G/500	250.00	450.00
4 Larry Bird 95 S/1000	150.00	225.00
5 Larry Bird 95 B/5000	20.00	35.00
6 Jerry West 95 S/500	150.00	225.00
7 Jerry West 95 B/2500	20.00	35.00

1997 Highland Mint Magnum Series Medallions

Measuring 2 1/2" in diameter and encased in a 6" by 5" velvet box, these larger medallions feature Bulls' megastar Michael Jordan. The relief on these medallions are 10 times greater than the regular medallions. The silver version include 4 Troy Ounces of .999 silver.

COMPLETE SET (2)	100.00	200.00
1 Michael Jordan Silver 750	175.00	250.00
2 Michael Jordan Bronze 3000	15.00	30.00

1997 Highland Mint Mini Mint-Cards

These mini Mint-Cards are not replicas but feature Highland Mint's own design. They are one-quarter scale of regular Mint-Cards. The high relief on the fronts is four times greater than that used on regular Mint-Cards. The backs display text and statistics. Each card is individually-numbered, includes a certificate of authenticity, and is packaged in a leather display box. Mini Mint-Cards were issued as a matching set with the cards displayed side by side. Both cards carry the same serial number. The mintage is given below with reference to silver and bronze versions. The suggested retail price was $150.00 for the silver, and $65.00 for the bronze.

COMPLETE SET (4)	100.00	250.00
1 Grant Hill Jason Kidd Silver 1000	40.00	100.00
2 Grant Hill Jason Kidd Bronze 5000	15.00	30.00
3 Michael Jordan Michael Jordan Silver 1000	75.00	150.00
4 Michael Jordan Michael Jordan Bronze 5000	20.00	50.00

1997 Highland Mint Mint-Cards Fleer/Hoops/UD

These Highland Mint cards are metal replicas of already issued Fleer, Hoops and Upper Deck cards. All these standard size replicas contain 4.25 Troy Ounces of .999 silver, bronze, or 24K gold plated .999 silver metal. Suggested retail are 50.00 for bronze and 235.00 for silver. Each card includes a certificate of authenticity, and is packaged in a numbered album and a three-piece Lucite display. The cards are checklisted below alphabetically; the final mintage figures for each card are also listed.

COMPLETE SET (19)	1200.00	2000.00
1 Charles Barkley 86-87 S/1000	150.00	200.00
2 Charles Barkley 86-87 B/5000	12.50	30.00
3 Anfernee Hardaway 93-94UD S/500	150.00	200.00
4 Anfernee Hardaway 93-94UD B/2500	12.50	30.00
5 Anfernee Hardaway 93-94UDSE S/500	150.00	200.00
6 Anfernee Hardaway 93-94UDSE B/2500	10.00	25.00
7 Magic Johnson 90-91 S/1000	150.00	200.00
8 Magic Johnson 90-91 B/5000	20.00	35.00
9 Michael Jordan 91-92 G/500	250.00	450.00
10 Michael Jordan 91-92 S/1000	175.00	250.00
11 Michael Jordan 91-92 B/5000	20.00	50.00
12 Hakeem Olajuwon 86-87 S/250	150.00	200.00
13 Hakeem Olajuwon 86-87 B/1500	10.00	25.00
14 David Robinson 89-90 S/1000	150.00	200.00
15 David Robinson 89-90 B/5000	20.00	35.00
16 Jerry Stackhouse 95-96 S/500	150.00	200.00
17 Jerry Stackhouse 95-96 B/2500	10.00	25.00
18 Damon Stoudamire 95-96 S/500	150.00	200.00
19 Damon Stoudamire 95-96 B/2500	10.00	25.00

1997 Highland Mint Mint-Coins

These medallions feature the player's likeness, name, uniform number, and signature on one side, with career statistics on the reverse side. Each includes one Troy Ounce of .999 silver, bronze, or 24K gold plated .999 silver metal. The medallions are checklisted below alphabetically.

COMPLETE SET (31)	900.00	1500.00
1 Larry Bird Silver 7500	30.00	50.00
2 Chicago Bulls 70 Wins Silver 2500	30.00	50.00
3 Chicago Bulls Division Silver 1000	30.00	50.00
4 Chicago Bulls Conference Silver 5000	30.00	50.00
5 Chicago Bulls Finals Silver 7500	30.00	50.00
6 Chicago Bulls Finals Gold Signature 1500	35.00	60.00
7 Chicago Bulls Seattle SuperSonics Conference Silver 500	30.00	50.00
8 Kevin Garnett Silver 7500	30.00	50.00
9 Anfernee Hardaway Gold Signature 1500	30.00	50.00
10 Anfernee Hardaway Silver 7500	30.00	50.00
11 Anfernee Hardaway Bronze 25000	2.50	6.00
12 Allen Iverson Silver 3000	30.00	50.00
13 Larry Johnson Silver 7500	30.00	50.00
14 Michael Jordan Gold 100	400.00	800.00
15 Michael Jordan Gold Signature 1000	30.00	50.00
16 Michael Jordan Silver 7500	30.00	50.00
17 Michael Jordan Bronze 25000	5.00	12.00
18 Shawn Kemp Silver 7500	30.00	50.00
19 Orlando Magic Silver 5000	30.00	50.00
20 Orlando Magic Div. Silver 1000	30.00	50.00
21 Scottie Pippen Silver 7500	30.00	50.00
22 Mitch Richmond Gold Signature 1000	30.00	50.00
23 Dennis Rodman Red hair Silver 7500	30.00	50.00
24 Dennis Rodman Green hair Bronze 12500	2.50	6.00
25 Dennis Rodman Yellow hair Bronze 12500	2.50	6.00
26 Dennis Rodman 3-coin set Bronze 2500	20.00	40.00
27 San Antonio Spurs Div. Silver 1000	30.00	50.00
28 Seattle Supersonics Div. Silver 1000	30.00	50.00
29 Seattle Supersonics Conf. Silver 5000	30.00	50.00
30 John Stockton Silver 7500	30.00	50.00
31 Nick Van Exel Silver 7500	30.00	50.00

1997 Highland Mint Sandblast Mint-Cards

These Highland Mint cards are metal replicas of already issued Pinnacle cards. All these standard size replicas contain approximately 4.25 ounces of .999 silver or bronze metal and feature a "sandblast" background that accents the shiny surface of the player's likeness. Suggested retail are 60.00 for bronze and 250.00 for silver. Each card includes a certificate of authenticity, and is packaged in a numbered album and a three-piece Lucite display. The cards are checklisted below alphabetically; the final mintage figures for each card are also listed.

COMPLETE SET (2)	100.00	175.00
1 Grant Hill 96 S/500	150.00	200.00
2 Grant Hill 96 B/2500	15.00	30.00

2001 Highland Mint Shaquille O'Neal Promo

This card was given out to members of the hobby media to promote the upcoming Highland Mint products for the 2000-01 NBA Season. This card is unnumbered and contains a swatch of jersey used in the 1999-00 NBA Finals. The actual card is slabbed in a very thick plastic holder.

NNO Shaquille O'Neal Jsy	30.00	65.00

1994-95 Hoop Magazine/Mother's Cookies

Sponsored by Mother's Cookies, Hoop Magazine featured 8 1/2" by 11" cards of NBA stars. At participating arenas, fans who purchased a Hoop game program also received one of 27 different jumbo cards. One star from each NBA team is represented in the set. The fronts display color action player photos inside a black border. The player's name appears in the top wider black border, and the team logo is overprinted on the picture. In red and purple print, the back carries an advertisement for Mother's Cookies. The photos are numbered "No. X/27" on the front in the lower right corner.

COMPLETE SET (27)	40.00	100.00
1 Mookie Blaylock	1.50	4.00
2 Dee Brown	1.50	4.00
3 Alonzo Mourning	3.00	8.00
4 B.J. Armstrong	1.50	4.00
5 Mark Price	2.50	6.00
6 Jason Kidd	5.00	12.00
7 Dikembe Mutombo	2.50	6.00
8 Joe Dumars	2.50	6.00
9 Latrell Sprewell	3.00	8.00
10 Hakeem Olajuwon	4.00	10.00
11 Reggie Miller	4.00	10.00
12 Loy Vaught	1.50	4.00
13 Vlade Divac	2.50	6.00
14 Glen Rice	2.50	6.00
15 Vin Baker	2.50	6.00
16 Isaiah Rider	2.50	6.00
17 Kenny Anderson	2.00	5.00
18 Patrick Ewing	4.00	10.00
19 Shaquille O'Neal	6.00	15.00
20 Clarence Weatherspoon	1.50	4.00
21 Charles Barkley	4.00	10.00
22 Clyde Drexler	5.00	12.00
23 Mitch Richmond	2.50	6.00
24 David Robinson	4.00	10.00
25 Gary Payton	2.50	6.00
26 John Stockton	4.00	10.00
27 Calbert Cheaney	1.50	4.00

1995-96 Hoop Magazine/Mother's Cookies

Sponsored by Mother's Cookies, Hoop Magazine featured 8 1/2" by 11" cards of NBA stars. At participating arenas, fans who purchased a Hoop game program also received one of 29 jumbo cards. One star from each NBA team is represented in the set. The fronts feature glossy color player photos framed by black borders. The player's name appears in either the top or bottom borders in team color-coded lettering; the team logo is overprinted on the picture. In red and purple print, the backs carry a Mother's Cookies advertisement. The jumbo cards are numbered "x/29" on the front at the lower right corner.

COMPLETE SET (29)	175.00	350.00
1 Craig Ehlo	1.50	4.00
2 Eric Montross	1.50	4.00
3 Larry Johnson	2.50	6.00
4 Michael Jordan	100.00	250.00
5 Terrell Brandon	1.50	4.00
6 Jim Jackson	1.50	4.00
7 Mahmoud Abdul-Rauf	1.50	4.00
8 Allan Houston	2.00	5.00
9 Tim Hardaway	2.50	6.00
10 Clyde Drexler	3.00	8.00
11 Rik Smits	2.00	5.00
12 Lamond Murray	1.50	4.00
13 Vlade Divac	2.50	6.00
14 Glen Rice	2.50	6.00
15 Glenn Robinson	2.00	5.00
16 Tom Gugliotta	1.50	4.00
17 Ed O'Bannon	2.00	5.00
18 Patrick Ewing	3.00	8.00
19 Anfernee Hardaway	4.00	10.00
20 Jerry Stackhouse	8.00	20.00
21 Kevin Johnson	2.50	6.00
22 Rod Strickland	1.50	4.00
23 Mitch Richmond	2.50	6.00
24 Avery Johnson	2.00	5.00
25 Detlef Schrempf	2.50	6.00
26 Damon Stoudamire	6.00	15.00
27 Karl Malone	3.00	8.00
28 Greg Anthony	1.50	4.00
29 Juwan Howard	2.50	6.00

1995-96 Hoop Magazine/Mother's Cookies Award Winners

Cards from this over-sized set were distributed in issues of Hoop magazine and sold at selected arenas throughout the nation during the 1995-96 campaign. Each card represents a different Award Winner from the 1994-95 campaign.

COMPLETE SET (7)	10.00	25.00
1 David Robinson	4.00	10.00
2 Jason Kidd	4.00	10.00
3 Grant Hill	4.00	10.00
4 Dana Barros	1.50	4.00
5 Anthony Mason	1.50	4.00
6 Del Harris CO	1.50	4.00
7 Dikembe Mutombo	2.50	6.00

1989-90 Hoops

The 1989-90 Hoops set contains 352 standard-size cards. The cards were issued in two series of 300 and 52 cards. Hoops' initial venture in the basketball market helped spark the basketball card boom of 1989-90. The cards were issued in 15-card packs. The fronts feature color action player photos, bordered by a basketball lane in one of the team's colors. On a white card face the player's name appears in black lettering above the picture. The backs have head shots of the players, biographical information and statistics printed on a pale yellow background with white borders. The cards are numbered on the back. The key Rookie Card in this set is David Robinson (138). This is his lone Rookie Card. Beware of Robinson counterfeits which are distinguishable primarily by comparison to a real card or under magnification. Other Rookie Cards of note include Hersey Hawkins, Jeff Hornacek, Kevin Johnson, Steve Kerr, Reggie Lewis, Dan Majerle, Danny Manning, Mitch Richmond, Rik Smits and Rod Strickland. The second series features the premier cards of the expansion teams (Minnesota and Orlando), traded players, a special NBA Championship card of the Detroit Pistons and a Robinson In Action (310) card. Since the original Detroit Pistons World Champs card (No. 353A) was so difficult for collectors to find in packs, Hoops produced another edition (353B) of the card that was available direct from the company free of charge. If a collector wished to acquire two or more from the company, additional copies were available for 35 cents per card. The set is considered complete with the less difficult version. The short prints (SP below) in the first series are those cards which were dropped to make room for the new second series cards on the printing sheet.

COMPLETE SET (352)	12.50	25.00
COMPLETE SERIES 1 (300)	10.00	20.00
COMPLETE SERIES 2 (52)	2.50	5.00
BEWARE ROBINSON 138 COUNTERFEIT		
1 Joe Dumars	.08	.25
2 Tree Rollins	.02	.10
3 Kenny Walker	.02	.10
4 Mychal Thompson	.02	.10
5 Alvin Robertson SP	.08	.25
6 Vinny Del Negro RC	.08	.25
7 Greg Anderson SP	.08	.25
8 Rod Strickland RC	.30	.75
9 Ed Pinckney	.02	.10
10 Dale Ellis	.02	.10
11 Chuck Daly CO RC	.08	.25
12 Eric Leckner	.02	.10
13 Charles Davis	.02	.10
14 Cotton Fitzsimmons CO	.02	.10
15 Byron Scott	.02	.10
16 Derrick Chievous	.02	.10
17 Reggie Lewis RC	.10	.30
18 Jim Paxson	.02	.10
19 Tony Campbell RC	.02	.10
20 Rolando Blackman	.02	.10
21 Michael Jordan AS	.60	1.50
22 Cliff Levingston	.02	.10
23 Roy Tarpley	.02	.10
24 Harold Pressley UER	.02	.10
25 Larry Nance	.02	.10
26 Chris Morris RC	.02	.10
27 Bob Hansen UER	.02	.10
28 Mark Price AS	.02	.10
29 Reggie Miller	.25	.60
30 Karl Malone	.15	.40
31 Sidney Lowe SP	.08	.25
32 Ron Anderson	.02	.10
33 Mike Gminski	.02	.10
34 Scott Brooks RC	.08	.25
35 Kevin Johnson RC	.20	.50
36 Mark Bryant RC	.02	.10
37 Rik Smits RC	.10	.30
38 Tim Perry RC	.02	.10
39 Ralph Sampson	.02	.10
40 Danny Manning UER RC	.10	.30
41 Kevin Edwards RC	.02	.10
42 Paul Mokeski	.02	.10
43 Dale Ellis AS	.02	.10
44 Walter Berry	.02	.10
45 Chuck Person	.02	.10
46 Rick Mahorn SP	.10	.30
47 Joe Kleine	.02	.10
48 Brad Daugherty AS	.02	.10
49 Mike Woodson	.02	.10
50 Brad Daugherty	.02	.10
51 Shelton Jones SP	.08	.25
52 Michael Adams	.02	.10
53 Wes Unseld CO	.02	.10
54 Rex Chapman RC	.08	.25
55 Kelly Tripucka	.02	.10
56 Rickey Green	.02	.10
57 Frank Johnson SP	.08	.25
58 Johnny Newman RC	.02	.10
59 Billy Thompson	.02	.10
60 Stu Jackson CO	.02	.10
61 Walter Davis	.02	.10
62 Brian Shaw SP UER RC	.10	.30
63 Gerald Wilkins	.02	.10
64 Armon Gilliam	.02	.10
65 Maurice Cheeks SP	.10	.30
66 Jack Sikma	.02	.10
67 Harvey Grant RC	.08	.25
68 Jim Lynam CO	.02	.10
69 Clyde Drexler AS	.02	.10
70 Xavier McDaniel	.02	.10
71 Danny Young	.02	.10
72 Fennis Dembo	.02	.10
73 Mark Acres SP	.08	.25
74 Brad Lohaus SP RC	.08	.25
75 Manute Bol	.02	.10
76 Purvis Short	.02	.10
77 Allen Leavell	.02	.10
78 Johnny Dawkins SP	.08	.25
79 Paul Pressey	.02	.10
80 Patrick Ewing	.08	.25
81 Bill Wennington RC	.15	.40
82 Danny Schayes	.02	.10
83 Derek Smith	.02	.10
84 Moses Malone AS	.02	.10
85 Jeff Malone	.02	.10
86 Otis Smith SP RC	.08	.25
87 Trent Tucker	.02	.10
88 Robert Reid	.02	.10
89 John Paxson	.02	.10
90 Chris Mullin	.08	.25
91 Tom Garrick RC	.02	.10
92 Willis Reed CO SP UER	.10	.30
93 Dave Corzine SP	.08	.25
94 Mark Alarie	.02	.10
95 Mark Aguirre	.02	.10
96 Charles Barkley AS	.07	.20
97 Sidney Green SP	.08	.25
98 Kevin Willis	.02	.10
99 Dave Hoppen	.02	.10
100 Terry Cummings SP	.10	.30
101 Dwayne Washington SP	.08	.25
102 Larry Brown CO	.02	.10
103 Kevin Duckworth	.02	.10
104 Uwe Blab SP	.08	.25
105 Terry Porter	.02	.10
106 Craig Ehlo RC	.08	.25
107 Don Casey CO	.02	.10
108 Pat Riley CO	.08	.25
109 John Salley	.02	.10
110 Charles Barkley	.15	.40
111 Sam Bowie SP	.10	.30
112 Earl Cureton	.02	.10
113 Craig Hodges UER	.02	.10
114 Benoit Benjamin	.02	.10
115A S.Webb 9/27/89 ERR SP	.08	.25
115B S.Webb 9/26/85 COR	.02	.10
116 Karl Malone AS	.08	.25
117 Sleepy Floyd	.02	.10
118 Hot Rod Williams	.02	.10
119 Michael Holton	.02	.10
120 Alex English	.02	.10
121 Dennis Johnson	.02	.10
122 Wayne Cooper SP	.08	.25
123A Don Chaney CO	.02	.10
123B Don Chaney CO	.02	.10
124 A.C. Green	.02	.10
125 Adrian Dantley	.02	.10
126 Del Harris CO	.08	.25
127 Dick Harter CO	.02	.10
128 Reggie Williams RC	.02	.10
129 Bill Hanzlik	.02	.10
130 Dominique Wilkins	.08	.25
131 Herb Williams	.02	.10
132 Steve Johnson SP	.08	.25
133 Alex English AS	.02	.10
134 Darrell Walker	.02	.10
135 Bill Laimbeer	.02	.10
136 Fred Roberts RC	.02	.10
137 Hersey Hawkins RC	.15	.40
138 David Robinson SP RC	4.00	10.00
139 Brad Sellers SP	.08	.25
140 John Stockton	.25	.60
141 Grant Long RC	.02	.10
142 Marc Iavaroni SP	.08	.25
143 Steve Alford SP RC	.10	.30
144 Jeff Lamp SP	.08	.25
145 Buck Williams SP UER	.10	.30
146 Mark Jackson AS	.02	.10
147 Jim Petersen	.02	.10
148 Steve Stipanovich SP	.10	.30
149 Sam Vincent SP RC	.10	.30
150 Larry Bird	.40	1.00
151 Jon Koncak RC	.02	.10
152 Olden Polynice RC	.08	.25
153 Randy Breuer	.02	.10
154 John Battle RC	.02	.10
155 Mark Eaton	.02	.10
156 Kevin McHale AS UER	.02	.10
157 Jerry Sichting SP	.08	.25
158 Pat Cummings SP	.08	.25
159 Patrick Ewing AS	.02	.10
160 Mark Price	.02	.10
161 Jerry Reynolds CO	.02	.10
162 Ken Norman RC	.08	.25
163 John Bagley SP UER	.08	.25
164 Christian Welp SP	.08	.25
165 Reggie Theus SP	.10	.30
166 Magic Johnson AS	.15	.40
167 John Long UER	.02	.10
168 Larry Smith SP	.08	.25
169 Charles Shackleford RC	.02	.10
170 Tom Chambers	.02	.10
171A John MacLeod CO SP ERR	.08	.25
171B John MacLeod CO COR	.02	.10
172 Ron Rothstein CO	.02	.10
173 Joe Wolf	.02	.10
174 Mark Eaton AS	.02	.10
175 Jon Sundvold	.02	.10
176 Scott Hastings SP	.08	.25
177 Isiah Thomas AS	.02	.10
178 Hakeem Olajuwon AS	.08	.25
179 Mike Fratello CO	.02	.10
180 Hakeem Olajuwon	.15	.40
181 Randolph Keys	.02	.10
182 Richard Anderson UER	.02	.10
183 Dan Majerle RC	.10	.30
184 Derek Harper	.02	.10
185 Robert Parish	.02	.10
186 Ricky Berry SP	.08	.25
187 Michael Cooper	.02	.10
188 Vinnie Johnson	.02	.10
189 James Donaldson	.02	.10
190 Clyde Drexler UER	.08	.25
191 Jay Vincent SP	.08	.25
192 Nate McMillan	.02	.10
193 Kevin Duckworth AS	.02	.10
194 Ledell Eackles RC	.02	.10
195 Eddie Johnson	.02	.10
196 Terry Teagle	.02	.10
197 Tom Chambers AS	.02	.10
198 Joe Barry Carroll	.02	.10
199 Dennis Hopson RC	.02	.10
200 Michael Jordan	1.25	3.00
201 Jerome Lane RC	.02	.10
202 Greg Kite RC	.02	.10
203 David Rivers SP	.08	.25
204 Sylvester Gray	.02	.10
205 Ron Harper	.02	.10
206 Frank Brickowski	.02	.10
207 Rory Sparrow	.02	.10
208 Gerald Henderson	.02	.10
209 Rod Higgins UER	.02	.10
210 James Worthy	.08	.25
211 Dennis Rodman	.40	1.00
212 Ricky Pierce	.02	.10
213 Charles Oakley	.02	.10
214 Steve Colter	.02	.10
215 Danny Ainge	.02	.10
216 Lenny Wilkens CO UER	.02	.10
217 Larry Nance AS	.02	.10
218 Muggsy Bogues	.02	.10
219 James Worthy AS	.02	.10
220 Lafayette Lever	.02	.10
221 Quintin Dailey SP	.08	.25
222 Lester Conner	.02	.10
223 Jose Ortiz	.02	.10
224 Micheal Williams SP UER RC	.10	.30
225 Wayman Tisdale	.02	.10
226 Mike Sanders SP	.08	.25
227 Jim Farmer SP	.08	.25
228 Mark West	.02	.10
229 Jeff Hornacek RC	.10	.30
230 Chris Mullin AS	.02	.10
231 Vern Fleming	.02	.10
232 Kenny Smith	.02	.10
233 Derrick McKey	.02	.10
234 Dominique Wilkins AS	.02	.10
235 Willie Anderson RC	.02	.10
236 Keith Lee SP	.08	.25
237 Buck Johnson RC	.02	.10
238 Randy Wittman	.02	.10
239 Terry Catledge SP	.08	.25
240 Bernard King	.02	.10
241 Darrell Griffith	.02	.10
242 Horace Grant	.02	.10
243 Rony Seikaly RC	.10	.30
244 Scottie Pippen	.60	1.50
245 Michael Cage UER	.02	.10
246 Kurt Rambis	.02	.10
247 Morlon Wiley SP RC	.08	.25
248 Ronnie Grandison	.02	.10
249 Scott Skiles SP RC	.15	.40
250 Isiah Thomas	.08	.25
251 Thurl Bailey	.02	.10
252 Doc Rivers	.02	.10
253 Stuart Gray SP	.08	.25
254 John Williams	.02	.10
255 Bill Cartwright	.02	.10
256 Terry Cummings AS	.02	.10
257 Rodney McCray	.02	.10
258 Larry Krystkowiak RC	.02	.10
259 Will Perdue RC	.15	.40
260 Mitch Richmond RC	.50	1.25
261 Blair Rasmussen	.02	.10
262 Charles Smith RC	.08	.25
263 Tyrone Corbin SP RC	.08	.25
264 Kelvin Upshaw	.02	.10
265 Otis Thorpe	.02	.10
266 Phil Jackson CO	.08	.25
267 Jerry Sloan CO	.08	.25
268 John Shasky	.02	.10
269A B.Bickerstaff CO SP ERR	.08	.25
269B B.Bickerstaff CO COR	.02	.10
270 Magic Johnson	.30	.75
271 Vernon Maxwell RC	.08	.25
272 Tim McCormick	.02	.10
273 Don Nelson CO	.02	.10
274 Gary Grant RC	.02	.10
275 Sidney Moncrief SP	.08	.25
276 Roy Hinson	.02	.10
277 Jimmy Rodgers CO	.02	.10
278 Antoine Carr	.02	.10
279A Orlando Woolridge ERR	.08	.25
279B Orlando Woolridge COR	.02	.10
280 Kevin McHale	.08	.25
281 LaSalle Thompson	.02	.10
282 Detlef Schrempf	.02	.10
283 Doug Moe CO	.02	.10
284A James Edwards	.02	.10
284B James Edwards	.02	.10
285 Jerome Kersey	.02	.10
286 Sam Perkins	.02	.10
287 Sedale Threatt	.02	.10
288 Tim Kempton SP	.08	.25
289 Mark McNamara	.02	.10
290 Moses Malone	.08	.25
291 Rick Adelman CO UER	.02	.10
292 Dick Versace CO	.02	.10
293 Alton Lister SP	.08	.25
294 Winston Garland	.02	.10
295 Kiki Vandeweghe	.02	.10
296 Brad Davis	.02	.10
297 John Stockton AS	.08	.25
298 Jay Humphries	.02	.10
299 Dell Curry	.02	.10
300 Mark Jackson	.02	.10
301 Morlon Wiley	.02	.10
302 Reggie Theus	.02	.10
303 Otis Smith	.02	.10
304 Tod Murphy RC	.02	.10
305 Sidney Green	.02	.10
306 Shelton Jones	.02	.10
307 Mark Acres	.02	.10
308 Terry Catledge	.02	.10
309 Larry Smith	.02	.10
310 David Robinson IA	.75	2.00
311 Johnny Dawkins	.02	.10
312 Terry Cummings	.02	.10
313 Sidney Lowe	.02	.10
314 Bill Musselman CO	.02	.10
315 Buck Williams UER	.02	.10
316 Mel Turpin	.02	.10
317 Scott Hastings	.02	.10
318 Scott Skiles	.02	.10
319 Tyrone Corbin	.02	.10
320 Maurice Cheeks	.02	.10
321 Matt Guokas CO	.02	.10
322 Jeff Turner	.02	.10
323 David Wingate	.02	.10
324 Steve Johnson	.02	.10
325 Alton Lister	.02	.10
326 Ken Bannister	.02	.10
327 Bill Fitch CO UER	.02	.10
328 Sam Vincent	.02	.10
329 Larry Drew	.02	.10
330 Rick Mahorn	.02	.10
331 Christian Welp	.02	.10
332 Brad Lohaus	.02	.10
333 Frank Johnson	.02	.10
334 Jim Farmer	.02	.10
335 Wayne Cooper	.02	.10
336 Mike Brown RC	.02	.10
337 Sam Bowie	.02	.10
338 Kevin Gamble RC	.02	.10
339 Jerry Ice Reynolds RC	.02	.10
340 Mike Sanders	.02	.10
341 Bill Jones UER	.02	.10
342 Greg Anderson	.02	.10
343 Dave Corzine	.02	.10
344 Micheal Williams UER	.02	.10
345 Jay Vincent	.02	.10
346 David Rivers	.02	.10
347 Caldwell Jones UER	.02	.10
348 Brad Sellers	.02	.10
349 Scott Roth	.02	.10
350 Alvin Robertson	.02	.10
351 Steve Kerr RC	.40	1.00
352 Stuart Gray	.02	.10
353A Pistons Champions SP	1.50	4.00
353B Pistons Champions UER	.20	.50

1989-90 Hoops Checklists

Hoops made available two different checklists to collectors, primarily by phone request. The checklists are not actually cards but are more like folded four-panel booklets, although when folded they do measure 2 1/2" by 3 1/2". The production on these was rather limited.

COMPLETE SET (2)	1.60	4.00
COMMON CARD (1-2)	.80	2.00

1990-91 Hoops

The complete 1990-91 Hoops basketball set contains 440 standard-size cards. The set was distributed in two series of 336 and 104 cards, respectively. The cards were issued in 15-card plastic-wrap packs which came 36 to a box. On the front the color action player photo appears in the shape of a basketball lane, bordered by gold on the All-Star cards (1-26) and by silver on the regular issues (27-331, 336). The player's name and the stripe below the picture are printed in one of the team's colors. The team logo at the lower right corner rounds out the card face. The back of the regular issue has a color head shot and biographical information as well as college and pro statistics, framed by a basketball lane. The set is arranged alphabetically according to teams. Subsets are Coaches (305-331/343-354), NBA Finals (337-342), Team Checklists (355-381), Inside Stuff (382-385), Stay in School (386-387), Don't Foul Out (388-389), Lottery Selections (390-400), and Updates (401-438). Some of the All-Star cards (card numbers 2, 6, and 8) can be found with or without a printing mistake, i.e., no T in the trademark logo on the card back. A few of the cards (card numbers 14, 66, 144, and 279) refer to the player as "all America" rather than "All America". The following cards can be found with or without a black line under the card number, height, and birthplace: 20, 23, 24, 29, and 87. Rookie Cards of note included in the set are Nick Anderson, Mookie Blaylock, Derrick Coleman, Vlade Divac, Sean Elliott, Kendall Gill, Tim Hardaway, Chris Jackson, Shawn Kemp, Gary Payton, Drazen Petrovic, Glen Rice, Clifford Robinson and Dennis Scott. The short prints (SP below) in the first series are those cards which were dropped to make room for the new second series cards on the printing sheet.

COMPLETE SET (440) 7.50 15.00
COMPLETE SERIES 1 (336) 5.00 10.00
COMPLETE SERIES 2 (104) 2.50 5.00
1 Charles Barkley AS SP .08 .25
2 Larry Bird AS SP .25 .60
3 Joe Dumars AS SP .05 .15
4 Patrick Ewing AS SP UER .08 .25
5 Michael Jordan AS SP UER .75 2.00
6 Kevin McHale AS SP .02 .10
7 Reggie Miller AS SP .05 .15
8 Robert Parish AS SP .02 .10
9 Scottie Pippen AS SP .25 .60
10 Dennis Rodman AS SP .15 .40
11 Isiah Thomas AS SP .05 .15
12 Dominique Wilkins AS SP .05 .15
13A AS CL: ERR NNO SP .08 .25
13B AS CL: COR SP .02 .10
14 Rolando Blackman AS SP .02 .10
15 Tom Chambers AS SP .02 .10
16 Clyde Drexler AS SP .02 .10
17 A.C. Green AS SP .02 .10
18 Magic Johnson AS SP .20 .50
19 Kevin Johnson AS SP .05 .15
20 Lafayette Lever AS SP .02 .10
21 Karl Malone AS SP .08 .25
22 Chris Mullin AS SP .05 .15
23 Hakeem Olajuwon AS SP .08 .25
24 David Robinson AS SP .20 .50
25 John Stockton AS SP .08 .25
26 James Worthy AS SP .05 .15
27 John Battle .02 .10
28 Jon Koncak .02 .10
29 Cliff Levingston SP .02 .10
30 John Long SP .02 .10
31 Moses Malone .05 .15
32 Doc Rivers .02 .10
33 Kenny Smith SP .02 .10
34 Alexander Volkov RC .02 .10
35 Spud Webb .02 .10
36 Dominique Wilkins .05 .15
37 Kevin Willis .02 .10
38 John Bagley .02 .10
39 Larry Bird .25 .60
40 Kevin Gamble .02 .10
41 Dennis Johnson SP .02 .10
42 Joe Kleine .02 .10
43 Reggie Lewis .02 .10
44 Kevin McHale .02 .10
45 Robert Parish .02 .10
46 Jim Paxson SP .02 .10
47 Ed Pinckney .02 .10
48 Brian Shaw .05 .15
49 Richard Anderson SP .02 .10
50 Muggsy Bogues .02 .10
51 Rex Chapman .05 .15
52 Dell Curry .02 .10
53 Kenny Gattison RC .02 .10
54 Armon Gilliam .02 .10
55 Dave Hoppen .02 .10
56 Randolph Keys .02 .10
57 J.R. Reid RC .02 .10
58 Robert Reid SP .02 .10
59 Kelly Tripucka .02 .10
60 B.J. Armstrong RC .02 .10
61 Bill Cartwright .02 .10
62 Charles Davis SP .02 .10
63 Horace Grant .02 .10
64 Craig Hodges .02 .10
65 Michael Jordan .75 2.00
66 Stacey King RC .02 .10
67 John Paxson .02 .10
68 Will Perdue .02 .10
69 Scottie Pippen .25 .60
70 Winston Bennett .02 .10
71 Chucky Brown RC .02 .10
72 Derrick Chievous .02 .10
73 Brad Daugherty .02 .10
74 Craig Ehlo .02 .10
75 Steve Kerr .05 .15
76 Paul Mokeski SP .02 .10
77 John Morton .02 .10
78 Larry Nance .02 .10
79 Mark Price .02 .10
80 Hot Rod Williams .02 .10
81 Steve Alford .02 .10
82 Rolando Blackman .02 .10
83 Adrian Dantley SP .02 .10
84 Brad Davis .02 .10
85 James Donaldson .02 .10
86 Derek Harper .02 .10
87 Sam Perkins SP .02 .10
88 Roy Tarpley .02 .10
89 Bill Wennington SP .02 .10
90 Herb Williams .02 .10
91 Michael Adams .02 .10
92 Joe Barry Carroll SP .02 .10
93 Walter Davis UER .02 .10
94 Alex English SP .02 .10
95 Bill Hanzlik .02 .10
96 Jerome Lane .02 .10
97 Lafayette Lever SP .02 .10
98 Todd Lichti RC .02 .10
99 Blair Rasmussen .02 .10
100 Danny Schayes SP .02 .10
101 Mark Aguirre .02 .10
102 William Bedford RC .02 .10
103 Joe Dumars .05 .15
104 James Edwards .02 .10
105 Scott Hastings .02 .10
106 Gerald Henderson SP .02 .10
107 Vinnie Johnson .02 .10
108 Bill Laimbeer .02 .10
109 Dennis Rodman .15 .40
110 John Salley .02 .10
111 Isiah Thomas UER .05 .15
112 Manute Bol SP .02 .10
113 Tim Hardaway RC .40 1.00
114 Rod Higgins .02 .10
115 Sarunas Marciulionis RC .02 .10
116 Chris Mullin UER .05 .15
117 Jim Petersen .02 .10
118 Mitch Richmond .07 .20
119 Mike Smrek .02 .10
120 Terry Teagle SP .02 .10
121 Tom Tolbert RC .02 .10
122 Christian Welp SP .02 .10
123 Byron Dinkins SP .02 .10
124 Eric (Sleepy) Floyd .02 .10
125 Buck Johnson .02 .10
126 Vernon Maxwell .02 .10
127 Hakeem Olajuwon .08 .25
128 Larry Smith .02 .10
129 Otis Thorpe .02 .10
130 Mitchell Wiggins SP .02 .10
131 Mike Woodson .02 .10
132 Greg Dreiling RC .02 .10
133 Vern Fleming .02 .10
134 Rickey Green SP .02 .10
135 Reggie Miller .07 .20
136 Chuck Person .02 .10
137 Mike Sanders .02 .10
138 Detlef Schrempf .02 .10
139 Rik Smits .05 .15
140 LaSalle Thompson .02 .10
141 Randy Wittman .02 .10
142 Benoit Benjamin .02 .10
143 Winston Garland .02 .10
144 Tom Garrick .02 .10
145 Gary Grant .02 .10
146 Ron Harper .02 .10
147 Danny Manning .02 .10
148 Jeff Martin .02 .10
149 Ken Norman .02 .10
150 David Rivers SP .02 .10
151 Charles Smith .02 .10
152 Joe Wolf SP .02 .10
153 Michael Cooper SP .02 .10
154 Vlade Divac UER RC .15 .40
155 Larry Drew .02 .10
156 A.C. Green .02 .10
157 Magic Johnson .20 .50
158 Mark McNamara SP .02 .10
159 Byron Scott .02 .10
160 Mychal Thompson .02 .10
161 Jay Vincent SP .02 .10
162 Orlando Woolridge SP .02 .10
163 James Worthy .05 .15
164 Sherman Douglas RC .05 .15
165 Kevin Edwards .02 .10
166 Tellis Frank SP .02 .10
167 Grant Long .02 .10
168 Glen Rice RC .25 .60
169A Rony Seikaly Athens .02 .10
169B Rony Seikaly Beirut .02 .10
170 Rory Sparrow SP .02 .10
171A Jon Sundvold .02 .10
171B Billy Thompson .02 .10
172A Billy Thompson .02 .10
172B Jon Sundvold .02 .10
173 Greg Anderson .02 .10
174 Jeff Grayer RC .02 .10
175 Jay Humphries .02 .10
176 Frank Kornet .02 .10
177 Larry Krystkowiak .02 .10
178 Brad Lohaus .02 .10
179 Ricky Pierce .02 .10
180 Paul Pressey SP .02 .10
181 Fred Roberts .02 .10
182 Alvin Robertson .02 .10
183 Jack Sikma .02 .10
184 Randy Breuer .02 .10
185 Tony Campbell .02 .10
186 Tyrone Corbin .02 .10
187 Sidney Lowe SP .02 .10
188 Sam Mitchell RC .02 .10
189 Tod Murphy .02 .10
190 Pooh Richardson RC .02 .10
191 Scott Roth SP .02 .10
192 Brad Sellers SP .02 .10
193 Mookie Blaylock RC .08 .25
194 Sam Bowie .02 .10
195 Lester Conner .02 .10
196 Derrick Gervin .02 .10
197 Jack Haley RC .02 .10
198 Roy Hinson .02 .10
199 Dennis Hopson SP .02 .10
200 Chris Morris .02 .10
201 Purvis Short SP .02 .10
202 Maurice Cheeks .02 .10
203 Patrick Ewing .05 .15
204 Stuart Gray .02 .10
205 Mark Jackson .02 .10
206 Johnny Newman SP .02 .10
207 Charles Oakley .02 .10
208 Trent Tucker .02 .10
209 Kiki Vandeweghe .02 .10
210 Kenny Walker .02 .10
211 Eddie Lee Wilkins .02 .10
212 Gerald Wilkins .02 .10
213 Mark Acres .02 .10
214 Nick Anderson RC .08 .25
215 Michael Ansley UER .02 .10
216 Terry Catledge .02 .10
217 Dave Corzine SP .02 .10
218 Sidney Green SP .02 .10
219 Jerry Reynolds .02 .10
220 Scott Skiles .02 .10
221 Otis Smith .02 .10
222 Reggie Theus SP .02 .10
223A S.Vincent w/M.Jordan 1.50 4.00
223B Sam Vincent .02 .10
224 Ron Anderson .02 .10
225 Charles Barkley .08 .25
226 Scott Brooks SP UER .02 .10
227 Johnny Dawkins .02 .10
228 Mike Gminski .02 .10
229 Hersey Hawkins .02 .10
230 Rick Mahorn .02 .10
231 Derek Smith SP .02 .10
232 Bob Thornton .02 .10
233 Kenny Battle RC .02 .10
234A Tom Chambers Forward .02 .10
234B Tom Chambers Guard .02 .10
235 Greg Grant SP RC .02 .10
236 Jeff Hornacek .02 .10
237 Eddie Johnson .02 .10
238A Kevin Johnson Guard .05 .15
238B Kevin Johnson Forward .05 .15
239 Dan Majerle .05 .15
240 Tim Perry .02 .10
241 Kurt Rambis .02 .10
242 Mark West .02 .10
243 Mark Bryant .02 .10
244 Wayne Cooper .02 .10
245 Clyde Drexler .05 .15
246 Kevin Duckworth .02 .10
247 Jerome Kersey .02 .10
248 Drazen Petrovic RC .05 .15
249A Terry Porter ERR .20 .50
249B Terry Porter COR .02 .10
250 Clifford Robinson RC .08 .25
251 Buck Williams .02 .10
252 Danny Young .02 .10
253 Danny Ainge SP UER .02 .10
254 Randy Allen SP .02 .10
255 Antoine Carr .02 .10
256 Vinny Del Negro SP .02 .10
257 Pervis Ellison SP RC .02 .10
258 Greg Kite SP .02 .10
259 Rodney McCray SP .02 .10
260 Harold Pressley SP .02 .10
261 Ralph Sampson .02 .10
262 Wayman Tisdale .02 .10
263 Willie Anderson .02 .10
264 Uwe Blab SP .02 .10
265 Frank Brickowski SP .02 .10
266 Terry Cummings .02 .10
267 Sean Elliott RC .10 .30
268 Caldwell Jones SP .02 .10
269 Johnny Moore SP .02 .10
270 David Robinson .20 .50
271 Rod Strickland .05 .15
272 Reggie Williams .02 .10
273 David Wingate SP .02 .10
274 Dana Barros UER RC .05 .15
275 Michael Cage UER .02 .10
276 Quintin Dailey .02 .10
277 Dale Ellis .02 .10
278 Steve Johnson SP .02 .10
279 Shawn Kemp RC .60 1.50
280 Xavier McDaniel .02 .10
281 Derrick McKey .02 .10
282 Nate McMillan .02 .10
283 Olden Polynice .02 .10
284 Sedale Threatt .02 .10
285 Thurl Bailey .02 .10
286 Mike Brown .02 .10
287 Mark Eaton UER .02 .10
288 Blue Edwards RC .02 .10
289 Darrell Griffith .02 .10
290 Bobby Hansen SP .02 .10
291 Eric Leckner SP .02 .10
292 Karl Malone .08 .25
293 Delaney Rudd .02 .10
294 John Stockton .07 .20
295 Mark Alarie .02 .10
296 Ledell Eackles SP .02 .10
297 Harvey Grant .02 .10
298A Tom Hammonds No Star RC .02 .10
298B Tom Hammonds Star RC .02 .10
299 Charles Jones RC .02 .10
300 Bernard King .02 .10
301 Jeff Malone SP .02 .10
302 Mel Turpin SP .02 .10
303 Darrell Walker .02 .10
304 John Williams .02 .10
305 Bob Weiss CO .02 .10
306 Chris Ford CO .02 .10
307 Gene Littles CO .02 .10
308 Phil Jackson CO .05 .15
309 Lenny Wilkens CO .02 .10
310 Richie Adubato CO .02 .10
311 Doug Moe CO SP .02 .10
312 Chuck Daly CO .02 .10
313 Don Nelson CO .02 .10
314 Don Chaney CO .02 .10
315 Dick Versace CO .02 .10
316 Mike Schuler CO .02 .10
317 Pat Riley CO SP .05 .15
318 Ron Rothstein CO .02 .10
319 Del Harris CO .02 .10
320 Bill Musselman CO .02 .10
321 Bill Fitch CO .02 .10
322 Stu Jackson CO .02 .10
323 Matt Guokas CO .02 .10
324 Jim Lynam CO .02 .10
325 Cotton Fitzsimmons CO .02 .10
326 Rick Adelman CO .02 .10
327 Dick Motta CO .02 .10
328 Larry Brown CO .02 .10
329 K.C. Jones CO .02 .10
330 Jerry Sloan CO .02 .10
331 Wes Unseld CO .02 .10
332 Checklist 1 SP .02 .10
333 Checklist 2 SP .02 .10
334 Checklist 3 SP .02 .10
335 Checklist 4 SP .02 .10
336 Danny Ferry SP RC .10 .30
337 D.Rodman FIN .05 .15
338 D.Rodman/B.Williams FIN .05 .15
339 Joe Dumars FIN .05 .15
340 J.Kersey/I.Thomas FIN .02 .10
341A Pistons Win ERR w/o .02 .10
341B Pistons Win COR Sports .02 .10
342 Pistons Back to Back UER .02 .10
343 K.C. Jones CO .02 .10
344 Wes Unseld CO .02 .10
345 Don Nelson CO .02 .10
346 Bob Weiss CO .02 .10
347 Chris Ford CO .02 .10
348 Phil Jackson CO .05 .15
349 Lenny Wilkens CO .02 .10
350 Don Chaney CO .02 .10
351 Mike Dunleavy CO .02 .10
352 Matt Guokas CO .02 .10
353 Rick Adelman CO .02 .10
354 Jerry Sloan CO .02 .10
355 Dominique Wilkins TC .02 .10
356 Larry Bird TC .10 .30
357 Rex Chapman TC .02 .10
358 Michael Jordan TC .40 1.00
359 Mark Price TC .02 .10
360 Rolando Blackman TC .02 .10
361 Michael Adams TC UER .02 .10
362 Joe Dumars TC UER .02 .10
363 Chris Mullin TC .02 .10
364 Hakeem Olajuwon TC .05 .15
365 Reggie Miller TC .05 .15
366 Danny Manning TC .02 .10
367 Magic Johnson TC UER .08 .25
368 Rony Seikaly TC .02 .10
369 Alvin Robertson TC .02 .10
370 Pooh Richardson TC .02 .10
371 Chris Morris TC .02 .10
372 Patrick Ewing TC .02 .10
373 Nick Anderson TC .05 .15
374 Charles Barkley TC .05 .15
375 Kevin Johnson TC .02 .10
376 Clyde Drexler TC .02 .10
377 Wayman Tisdale TC .02 .10
378 David Robinson TC .08 .25
378B David Robinson TC half .10 .30
379 Xavier McDaniel TC .02 .10
380 Karl Malone TC .05 .15
381 Bernard King TC .02 .10
382 M.Jordan Playground .40 1.00
383 Karl Malone Lights .05 .15
384 V.Divac Marciulionis .02 .10
385 M.Johnson M.Jordan .40 1.00
386 Johnny Newman SIS .02 .10
387 Dell Curry SIS .02 .10
388 Patrick Ewing DFO .02 .10
389 Isiah Thomas DFO .02 .10
390 Derrick Coleman LS RC .10 .30
391 Gary Payton LS RC .60 1.50
392 Chris Jackson LS RC .02 .10
393 Dennis Scott LS RC .07 .20
394 Kendall Gill LS RC .10 .30
395 Felton Spencer LS RC .02 .10
396 Lionel Simmons LS RC .02 .10
397 Bo Kimble LS RC .02 .10
398 Willie Burton LS RC .02 .10
399 Rumeal Robinson LS RC .02 .10
400 Tyrone Hill LS RC .02 .10
401 Tim McCormick U .02 .10
402 Sidney Moncrief U .02 .10
403 Johnny Newman U .02 .10
404 Dennis Hopson U .02 .10
405 Cliff Levingston U .02 .10
406A Danny Ferry U ERR .10 .30
406B Danny Ferry U COR .05 .15
407 Alex English U .02 .10
408 Lafayette Lever U .02 .10
409 Rodney McCray U .02 .10
410 Mike Dunleavy U CO .02 .10
411 Orlando Woolridge U .02 .10
412 Joe Wolf U .02 .10
413 Tree Rollins U .02 .10
414 Kenny Smith U .02 .10
415 Sam Perkins U .02 .10
416 Terry Teagle U .02 .10
417 Frank Brickowski U .02 .10
418 Danny Schayes U .02 .10
419 Scott Brooks U .02 .10
420 Reggie Theus U .02 .10
421 Greg Grant U .02 .10
422 Paul Westhead U CO .02 .10
423 Greg Kite U .02 .10
424 Manute Bol U .02 .10
425 Rickey Green U .02 .10
426 Ed Nealy U .02 .10
427 Danny Ainge U .02 .10
428 Bobby Hansen U .02 .10
429 Eric Leckner U .02 .10
430 Rory Sparrow U .02 .10
431 Bill Wennington U .02 .10
432 Paul Pressey U .02 .10
433 David Greenwood U .02 .10
434 Mark McNamara U .02 .10
435 Sidney Green U .02 .10
436 Dave Corzine U .02 .10
437 Jeff Malone U .02 .10
438 Pervis Ellison U .02 .10
439 Checklist 5 .02 .10
440 Checklist 6 .02 .10
NNO D.Robinson/ART NoStats .50 1.25
NNO D.Robinson/ART Stats 2.50 6.00

1991-92 Hoops Prototypes

This ten-card set measures the standard size. The fronts features color action player photos, with differing color borders in one of the team's colors. The player's name appears above the picture, and the team logo overlays the lower left corner of the picture. In a horizontal format the back has a head shot of the player, biographical information, and college and pro statistics. The words "Prototype" are written in block lettering across the back.

COMPLETE SET (10) 12.00 30.00
3 Sidney Moncrief 1.25 3.00
9 Larry Bird 6.00 15.00
18 Muggsy Bogues 1.50 4.00
120 Alvin Robertson 1.25 3.00
135 Chris Dudley 1.25 3.00
142 Charles Oakley 1.50 4.00
150 Jerry Reynolds 1.25 3.00
159 Armon Gilliam 1.25 3.00
204 Sedale Threatt 1.25 3.00
210 Jeff Malone 1.25 3.00

1991-92 Hoops Prototypes 00

This ten-card set measures the standard size (2 1/2" by 3 1/2"). The fronts features color action player photos, with differing color borders in one of the team's colors. The player's name appears above the picture, and the team logo overlays the lower left corner of the picture. In a horizontal format the back has a head shot of the player, biographical information, and college and pro statistics. The words "Prototype" are written in block lettering across the back. The cards are numbered on the back as 001, 002, etc.

COMPLETE SET (10) 60.00 150.00
1 Clyde Drexler 6.00 15.00
2 Patrick Ewing 6.00 15.00
3 Magic Johnson 8.00 20.00
4 Michael Jordan 20.00 50.00
4B Michael Jordan Metal 150.00 300.00
5 Karl Malone 10.00 25.00
6 Hakeem Olajuwon 6.00 15.00
7 Charles Barkley AS 6.00 15.00
8 Magic Johnson AS 8.00 20.00
9 Karl Malone AS 10.00 25.00
10 Dominique Wilkins AS 4.00 10.00

1991-92 Hoops

The complete 1991-92 Hoops basketball set contains 590 standard-size cards. The set was released in two series of 330 and 260 cards, respectively. For the first time, second series packs contained only second series cards. The fronts feature color action player photos, with different color borders on a white card face. The player's name is printed in black lettering in the upper left corner, and the team logo is superimposed over the lower left corner of the picture. In a horizontal format the backs have color head shots and biographical information on the left side, while the right side presents college and pro statistics. The cards are numbered on the back and checklisted below alphabetically within team order. Subsets are Coaches (221-247), All-Stars East (248-260), All-Stars West (261-273), Teams (274-300), Centennial Card honoring James Naismith (301), Inside Stuff (302-305), League Leaders (306-313), Milestones (314-318), NBA yearbook (319-324), Public Service messages (325-327/544/545), Supreme Court (449-502), Art Cards (503-529), Active Leaders (530-537), NBA Hoops Tribune (538-543), Draft Picks (546-556), USA Basketball 1976 (557), USA Basketball 1984 (558-564), USA Basketball 1988 (565-574) and USA Basketball 1992 (575-588). Rookie Cards of note include Kenny Anderson, Stacey Augmon, Terrell Brandon, Larry Johnson, Anthony Mason, Dikembe Mutombo, Steve Smith, and John Starks. A short-printed Naismith card, numbered CC1, was inserted into wax packs. It features a colorized photo of Dr. Naismith standing between two peach baskets like those used in the first basketball game. The back narrates the invention of the game of basketball. An unnumbered Centennial card featuring the Centennial logo was also available via a mail-in offer. Second series packs featured a randomly inserted Gold Foil USA Basketball logo card. A special individually numbered (out of 10,000) "Head of the Class" (showing the top six draft picks from 1991) card was made available to the first 10,000 fans requesting one along with three wrappers from each series of 1991-92 Hoops cards. The card is numbered "of 10,000" and features tiny pictures of the top six players selected in the 1991 NBA draft.

COMPLETE SET (590) 12.50 25.00
COMPLETE SERIES 1 (330) 5.00 10.00
COMPLETE SERIES 2 (260) 7.50 15.00
1 John Battle .02 .10
2 Moses Malone UER .08 .25
3 Sidney Moncrief .02 .10
4 Doc Rivers .02 .10
5 Rumeal Robinson UER .02 .10
6 Spud Webb .02 .10
7 Dominique Wilkins .08 .25
8 Kevin Willis .02 .10
9 Larry Bird .40 1.00
10 Dee Brown .02 .10
11 Kevin Gamble .02 .10
12 Joe Kleine .02 .10
13 Reggie Lewis .02 .10
14 Kevin McHale .02 .10
15 Robert Parish .02 .10
16 Ed Pinckney .02 .10
17 Brian Shaw .02 .10
18 Muggsy Bogues .02 .10
19 Rex Chapman .02 .10
20 Dell Curry .02 .10
21 Kendall Gill .02 .10
22 Mike Gminski .02 .10
23 Johnny Newman .02 .10
24 J.R. Reid .02 .10
25 Kelly Tripucka .02 .10
26 B.J. Armstrong UER .02 .10
27 Bill Cartwright .02 .10
28 Horace Grant .02 .10
29 Craig Hodges .02 .10
30 Michael Jordan 1.25 3.00
31 Stacey King .02 .10
32 Cliff Levingston .02 .10
33 John Paxson .02 .10
34 Scottie Pippen .30 .75
35 Chucky Brown .02 .10
36 Brad Daugherty .02 .10
37 Craig Ehlo .02 .10
38 Danny Ferry .02 .10
39 Larry Nance .02 .10
40 Mark Price .02 .10
41 Darnell Valentine .02 .10
42 Hot Rod Williams .02 .10
43 Rolando Blackman .02 .10
44 Brad Davis .02 .10
45 James Donaldson .02 .10
46 Derek Harper .02 .10
47 Fat Lever .02 .10
48 Rodney McCray .02 .10
49 Roy Tarpley .02 .10
50 Herb Williams .02 .10
51 Michael Adams .02 .10
52 Chris Jackson UER .02 .10
53 Jerome Lane .02 .10
54 Todd Lichti .02 .10
55 Blair Rasmussen .02 .10
56 Reggie Williams .02 .10
57 Joe Wolf .02 .10
58 Orlando Woolridge .02 .10
59 Mark Aguirre .02 .10
60 Joe Dumars .08 .25
61 James Edwards .02 .10
62 Vinnie Johnson .02 .10
63 Bill Laimbeer .02 .10
64 Dennis Rodman .20 .50
65 John Salley .02 .10
66 Isiah Thomas .08 .25
67 Tim Hardaway .15 .40
68 Rod Higgins .02 .10
69 Tyrone Hill .02 .10
70 Alton Lister .02 .10
71 Sarunas Marciulionis .02 .10
72 Chris Mullin .08 .25
73 Mitch Richmond .08 .25
74 Tom Tolbert .02 .10
75 Eric(Sleepy) Floyd .02 .10
76 Buck Johnson .02 .10
77 Vernon Maxwell .02 .10
78 Hakeem Olajuwon .15 .40
79 Kenny Smith .02 .10
80 Larry Smith .02 .10
81 Otis Thorpe .02 .10
82 David Wood RC .02 .10
83 Vern Fleming .02 .10
84 Reggie Miller .08 .25
85 Chuck Person .02 .10
86 Mike Sanders .02 .10
87 Detlef Schrempf .02 .10
88 Rik Smits .02 .10
89 LaSalle Thompson .02 .10
90 Micheal Williams .02 .10
91 Winston Garland .02 .10
92 Gary Grant .02 .10
93 Ron Harper .02 .10
94 Danny Manning .02 .10
95 Jeff Martin .02 .10
96 Ken Norman .02 .10
97 Olden Polynice .02 .10
98 Charles Smith .02 .10
99 Vlade Divac .02 .10
100 A.C. Green .02 .10
101 Magic Johnson .30 .75
102 Sam Perkins .02 .10
103 Byron Scott .02 .10
104 Terry Teagle .02 .10
105 Mychal Thompson .02 .10
106 James Worthy .08 .25
107 Willie Burton .02 .10
108 Bimbo Coles .02 .10
109 Terry Davis .02 .10
110 Sherman Douglas .02 .10
111 Kevin Edwards .02 .10
112 Alec Kessler .02 .10
113 Glen Rice .08 .25
114 Rony Seikaly .02 .10
115 Frank Brickowski .02 .10
116 Dale Ellis .02 .10
117 Jay Humphries .02 .10
118 Brad Lohaus .02 .10
119 Fred Roberts .02 .10
120 Alvin Robertson .02 .10
121 Danny Schayes .02 .10
122 Jack Sikma .02 .10
123 Randy Breuer .02 .10
124 Tony Campbell .02 .10
125 Tyrone Corbin .02 .10
126 Gerald Glass .02 .10
127 Sam Mitchell .02 .10
128 Tod Murphy .02 .10
129 Pooh Richardson .02 .10
130 Felton Spencer .02 .10
131 Mookie Blaylock .02 .10
132 Sam Bowie .02 .10
133 Jud Buechler .02 .10
134 Derrick Coleman .02 .10
135 Chris Dudley .02 .10
136 Chris Morris .02 .10
137 Drazen Petrovic .02 .10
138 Reggie Theus .02 .10
139 Maurice Cheeks .02 .10
140 Patrick Ewing .08 .25
141 Mark Jackson .02 .10
142 Charles Oakley .02 .10
143 Trent Tucker .02 .10
144 Kiki Vandeweghe .02 .10
145 Kenny Walker .02 .10
146 Gerald Wilkins .02 .10
147 Nick Anderson .02 .10
148 Michael Ansley .02 .10
149 Terry Catledge .02 .10
150 Jerry Reynolds .02 .10
151 Dennis Scott .02 .10
152 Scott Skiles .02 .10
153 Otis Smith .02 .10
154 Sam Vincent .02 .10
155 Ron Anderson .02 .10
156 Charles Barkley .15 .40
157 Manute Bol .02 .10
158 Johnny Dawkins .02 .10
159 Armon Gilliam .02 .10
160 Rickey Green .02 .10
161 Hersey Hawkins .02 .10
162 Rick Mahorn .02 .10
163 Tom Chambers .02 .10
164 Jeff Hornacek .02 .10
165 Kevin Johnson .08 .25
166 Andrew Lang .02 .10
167 Dan Majerle .02 .10
168 Xavier McDaniel .02 .10
169 Kurt Rambis .02 .10
170 Mark West .02 .10
171 Danny Ainge .02 .10
172 Mark Bryant .02 .10
173 Walter Davis .02 .10
174 Clyde Drexler .08 .25
175 Kevin Duckworth .02 .10
176 Jerome Kersey .02 .10
177 Terry Porter .02 .10
178 Clifford Robinson .02 .10
179 Buck Williams .02 .10
180 Anthony Bonner .02 .10
181 Antoine Carr .02 .10
182 Duane Causwell .02 .10
183 Bobby Hansen .02 .10
184 Travis Mays .02 .10
185 Lionel Simmons .02 .10
186 Rory Sparrow .02 .10
187 Wayman Tisdale .02 .10
188 Willie Anderson .02 .10
189 Terry Cummings .02 .10
190 Sean Elliott .02 .10
191 Sidney Green .02 .10
192 David Greenwood .02 .10
193 Paul Pressey .02 .10
194 David Robinson .20 .50
195 Dwayne Schintzius .02 .10
196 Rod Strickland .08 .25
197 Benoit Benjamin .02 .10
198 Michael Cage .02 .10
199 Eddie Johnson .02 .10
200 Shawn Kemp .25 .60
201 Derrick McKey .02 .10
202 Gary Payton .25 .60
203 Ricky Pierce .02 .10
204 Sedale Threatt .02 .10
205 Thurl Bailey .02 .10
206 Mike Brown .02 .10
207 Mark Eaton .02 .10
208 Blue Edwards UER .02 .10
209 Darrell Griffith .02 .10
210 Jeff Malone .02 .10
211 Karl Malone .15 .40
212 John Stockton .08 .25
213 Ledell Eackles .02 .10
214 Pervis Ellison .02 .10
215 A.J. English .02 .10
216 Harvey Grant .02 .10
217 Charles Jones .02 .10
218 Bernard King .02 .10
219 Darrell Walker .02 .10
220 John Williams .02 .10
221 Bob Weiss CO .02 .10
222 Chris Ford CO .02 .10
223 Gene Littles CO .02 .10
224 Phil Jackson CO .08 .25
225 Lenny Wilkens CO .02 .10
226 Richie Adubato CO .02 .10
227 Paul Westhead CO .02 .10
228 Chuck Daly CO .02 .10
229 Don Nelson CO .02 .10
230 Don Chaney CO .02 .10
231 Bob Hill CO UER RC .02 .10
232 Mike Schuler CO .02 .10
233 Mike Dunleavy CO .02 .10
234 Kevin Loughery CO .02 .10
235 Del Harris CO .02 .10
236 Jimmy Rodgers CO .02 .10
237 Bill Fitch CO .02 .10
238 Pat Riley CO .02 .10
239 Matt Guokas CO .02 .10
240 Jim Lynam CO .02 .10
241 Cotton Fitzsimmons CO .02 .10
242 Rick Adelman CO .02 .10
243 Dick Motta CO .02 .10
244 Larry Brown CO .02 .10
245 K.C. Jones CO .02 .10
246 Jerry Sloan CO .02 .10
247 Wes Unseld CO .02 .10
248 Charles Barkley AS .08 .25
249 Brad Daugherty AS .02 .10
250 Joe Dumars AS .02 .10
251 Patrick Ewing AS .02 .10
252 Hersey Hawkins AS .02 .10
253 Michael Jordan AS .60 1.50
254 Bernard King AS .02 .10
255 Kevin McHale AS .02 .10
256 Robert Parish AS .02 .10
257 Ricky Pierce AS .02 .10
258 Alvin Robertson AS .02 .10
259 Dominique Wilkins AS .02 .10
260 Chris Ford CO AS .02 .10
261 Tom Chambers AS .02 .10
262 Clyde Drexler AS .02 .10
263 Kevin Duckworth AS .02 .10
264 Tim Hardaway AS .08 .25
265 Kevin Johnson AS .02 .10
266 Magic Johnson AS .15 .40
267 Karl Malone AS .08 .25
268 Chris Mullin AS .02 .10
269 Terry Porter AS .02 .10
270 David Robinson AS .08 .25
271 John Stockton AS .02 .10
272 James Worthy AS .02 .10
273 Rick Adelman CO AS .02 .10
274 Atlanta Hawks TC UER .02 .10
275 Boston Celtics TC UER .02 .10
276 Charlotte Hornets TC .02 .10
277 Chicago Bulls TC .02 .10
278 Cleveland Cavaliers TC .02 .10
279 Dallas Mavericks TC .02 .10
280 Denver Nuggets TC .02 .10
281 Detroit Pistons TC UER .02 .10
282 Golden State Warriors TC .02 .10
283 Houston Rockets TC .02 .10
284 Indiana Pacers TC .02 .10
285 Los Angeles Clippers TC .02 .10
286 Los Angeles Lakers TC .02 .10
287 Miami Heat TC .02 .10
288 Milwaukee Bucks TC .02 .10
289 Minnesota Timberwolves TC .02 .10
290 New Jersey Nets TC .02 .10
291 New York Knicks TC UER .02 .10
292 Orlando Magic TC .02 .10
293 Philadelphia 76ers TC .02 .10
294 Phoenix Suns TC .02 .10
295 Portland Trail Blazers TC .02 .10
296 Sacramento Kings TC .02 .10
297 San Antonio Spurs TC .02 .10
298 Seattle Supersonics TC .02 .10
299 Utah Jazz TC .02 .10
300 Washington Bullets TC .02 .10
301 Naismith CENT .02 .10
302 Kevin Johnson IS .02 .10
303 Reggie Miller IS .02 .10
304 Hakeem Olajuwon IS .08 .25
305 Robert Parish IS .02 .10
306 M.Jordan/K.Malone LL .40 1.00
307 3-Point FG Percent .02 .10
308 R.Miller/J.Malone LL .02 .10
309 Olajuwon/D.Robinson LL .08 .25
310 Steals League Leaders .02 .10
311 D.Robinson/Rodman LL .20 .50
312 J.Stockton/M.Johnson LL .02 .10
313 Field Goal Percent .02 .10
314 Larry Bird MS UER .20 .50
315 A.English/M.Malone MS UER .02 .10
316 Magic Johnson MS .15 .40
317 Michael Jordan MS .60 1.50
318 Moses Malone MS .02 .10
319 Larry Bird YB .20 .50
320 Maurice Cheeks YB .02 .10
321 Magic Johnson YB .15 .40
322 Bernard King YB .02 .10
323 Moses Malone YB .02 .10
324 Robert Parish YB .02 .10
325 All-Star Jam .02 .10
326 All-Star Jam .02 .10
327 David Robinson DON'T .08 .25
328 Checklist 1 .02 .10
329 Checklist 2 UER .02 .10
330 Checklist 3 UER .02 .10
331 Maurice Cheeks .02 .10
332 Duane Ferrell .02 .10
333 Jon Koncak .02 .10
334 Gary Leonard .02 .10
335 Travis Mays .02 .10
336 Blair Rasmussen .02 .10
337 Alexander Volkov .02 .10
338 John Bagley .02 .10
339 Rickey Green UER .02 .10
340 Derek Smith .02 .10
341 Stojko Vrankovic .02 .10
342 Anthony Frederick RC .02 .10
343 Kenny Gattison .02 .10
344 Eric Leckner .02 .10
345 Will Perdue .02 .10
346 Scott Williams RC .02 .10
347 John Battle .02 .10
348 Winston Bennett .02 .10
349 Henry James .02 .10
350 Steve Kerr .02 .10
351 John Morton .02 .10
352 Terry Davis .02 .10
353 Randy White .02 .10
354 Greg Anderson .02 .10
355 Anthony Cook .02 .10
356 Walter Davis .02 .10
357 Winston Garland .02 .10
358 Scott Hastings .02 .10
359 Marcus Liberty .02 .10
360 William Bedford .02 .10
361 Lance Blanks .02 .10
362 Brad Sellers .02 .10
363 Darrell Walker .02 .10
364 Orlando Woolridge .02 .10
365 Vincent Askew RC .02 .10
366 Mario Elie RC .08 .25
367 Jim Petersen .02 .10
368 Matt Bullard RC .02 .10
369 Gerald Henderson .02 .10
370 Dave Jamerson .02 .10
371 Tree Rollins .02 .10
372 Greg Dreiling .02 .10
373 George McCloud .02 .10
374 Kenny Williams .02 .10
375 Randy Wittman .02 .10
376 Tony Brown .02 .10
377 Lanard Copeland .02 .10
378 James Edwards .02 .10
379 Bo Kimble .02 .10
380 Doc Rivers .02 .10
381 Loy Vaught .02 .10
382 Elden Campbell .08 .25
383 Jack Haley .02 .10
384 Tony Smith .02 .10
385 Sedale Threatt .02 .10
386 Keith Askins RC .02 .10
387 Grant Long .02 .10
388 Alan Ogg .02 .10
389 Jon Sundvold .02 .10
390 Lester Conner .02 .10
391 Jeff Grayer .02 .10
392 Steve Henson .02 .10
393 Larry Krystkowiak .02 .10
394 Moses Malone .08 .25
395 Scott Brooks .02 .10
396 Tellis Frank .02 .10
397 Doug West .02 .10
398 Rafael Addison RC .02 .10
399 Dave Feitl RC .02 .10
400 Tate George .02 .10
401 Terry Mills RC .08 .25
402 Tim McCormick .02 .10
403 Xavier McDaniel .02 .10
404 Anthony Mason RC .20 .50

405 Brian Quinnett .02 .10
406 John Starks RC .08 .25
407 Mark Acres .02 .10
408 Greg Kite .02 .10
409 Jeff Turner .02 .10
410 Morlon Wiley .02 .10
411 Dave Hoppen .02 .10
412 Brian Oliver .02 .10
413 Kenny Payne .02 .10
414 Charles Shackleford .02 .10
415 Mitchell Wiggins .02 .10
416 Jayson Williams .08 .25
417 Cedric Ceballos .02 .10
418 Negele Knight .02 .10
419 Andrew Lang .02 .10
420 Jerrod Mustaf .02 .10
421 Ed Nealy .02 .10
422 Tim Perry .02 .10
423 Alaa Abdelnaby .02 .10
424 Wayne Cooper .02 .10
425 Danny Young .02 .10
426 Dennis Hopson .02 .10
427 Les Jepsen .02 .10
428 Jim Les RC .02 .10
429 Mitch Richmond .08 .25
430 Dwayne Schintzius .02 .10
431 Spud Webb .02 .10
432 Jud Buechler .02 .10
433 Antoine Carr .02 .10
434 Tom Garrick .02 .10
435 Sean Higgins RC .02 .10
436 Avery Johnson .02 .10
437 Tony Massenburg .02 .10
438 Dana Barros .02 .10
439 Quintin Dailey .02 .10
440 Bart Kofoed RC .02 .10
441 Nate McMillan .02 .10
442 Delaney Rudd .02 .10
443 Michael Adams .02 .10
444 Mark Alarie .02 .10
445 Greg Foster .02 .10
446 Tom Hammonds .02 .10
447 Andre Turner .02 .10
448 David Wingate .02 .10
449 Dominique Wilkins SC .02 .10
450 Kevin Willis SC .02 .10
451 Larry Bird SC .20 .50
452 Robert Parish SC .02 .10
453 Rex Chapman SC .02 .10
454 Kendall Gill SC .02 .10
455 Michael Jordan SC .60 1.50
456 Scottie Pippen SC .15 .40
457 Brad Daugherty SC .02 .10
458 Larry Nance SC .02 .10
459 Rolando Blackman SC .02 .10
460 Derek Harper SC .02 .10
461 Chris Jackson SC .02 .10
462 Todd Lichti SC .02 .10
463 Joe Dumars SC .02 .10
464 Isiah Thomas SC .02 .10
465 Tim Hardaway SC .08 .25
466 Chris Mullin SC .02 .10
467 Hakeem Olajuwon SC .08 .25
468 Otis Thorpe SC .02 .10
469 Reggie Miller SC .02 .10
470 Detlef Schrempf SC .02 .10
471 Ron Harper SC .02 .10
472 Charles Smith SC .02 .10
473 Magic Johnson SC .15 .40
474 James Worthy SC .02 .10
475 Sherman Douglas SC .02 .10
476 Rony Seikaly SC .02 .10
477 Jay Humphries SC .02 .10
478 Alvin Robertson SC .02 .10
479 Tyrone Corbin SC .02 .10
480 Pooh Richardson SC .02 .10
481 Sam Bowie SC .02 .10
482 Derrick Coleman SC .02 .10
483 Patrick Ewing SC .02 .10
484 Charles Oakley SC .02 .10
485 Dennis Scott SC .02 .10
486 Scott Skiles SC .02 .10
487 Charles Barkley SC .08 .25
488 Hersey Hawkins SC .02 .10
489 Tom Chambers SC .02 .10
490 Kevin Johnson SC .02 .10
491 Clyde Drexler SC .02 .10
492 Terry Porter SC .02 .10
493 Lionel Simmons SC .02 .10
494 Wayman Tisdale SC .02 .10
495 Terry Cummings SC .02 .10
496 David Robinson SC .08 .25
497 Shawn Kemp SC .08 .25
498 Ricky Pierce SC .02 .10
499 Karl Malone SC .08 .25
500 John Stockton SC .02 .10
501 Harvey Grant SC .02 .10
502 Bernard King SC .02 .10
503 Travis Mays Art .02 .10
504 Kevin McHale Art .02 .10
505 Muggsy Bogues Art .02 .10
506 Scottie Pippen Art .15 .40
507 Brad Daugherty Art .02 .10
508 Derek Harper Art .02 .10
509 Chris Jackson Art .02 .10
510 Isiah Thomas Art .02 .10
511 Tim Hardaway Art .08 .25
512 Otis Thorpe Art .02 .10
513 Chuck Person Art .02 .10
514 Ron Harper Art .02 .10
515 James Worthy Art .02 .10
516 Sherman Douglas Art .02 .10
517 Dale Ellis Art .02 .10
518 Tony Campbell Art .02 .10
519 Derrick Coleman Art .02 .10
520 Gerald Wilkins Art .02 .10
521 Scott Skiles Art .02 .10
522 Manute Bol Art .02 .10
523 Tom Chambers Art .02 .10
524 Terry Porter Art .02 .10
525 Lionel Simmons Art .02 .10
526 Sean Elliott Art .02 .10
527 Shawn Kemp Art .08 .25
528 John Stockton Art .02 .10
529 Harvey Grant Art .02 .10
530 Michael Adams AL .02 .10
531 Charles Barkley AL .08 .25
532 Larry Bird AL .20 .50
533 Maurice Cheeks AL .02 .10
534 Mark Eaton AL .02 .10
535 Magic Johnson AL .15 .40
536 Michael Jordan AL .60 1.50
537 Moses Malone AL .02 .10
538 Sam Perkins FIN .02 .10
539 S.Pippen/J.Worthy FIN .08 .25
540 Vlade Divac FIN .02 .10
541 John Paxson FIN .02 .10
542 Michael Jordan FIN .60 1.50
543 Michael Jordan FIN .60 1.50
544 Otis Smith SIS .02 .10
545 Jeff Turner SIS .02 .10
546 Larry Johnson RC .40 1.00
547 Kenny Anderson RC .20 .50
548 Billy Owens RC .08 .25
549 Dikembe Mutombo RC .40 1.00
550 Steve Smith RC .40 1.00
551 Doug Smith RC .02 .10
552 Luc Longley RC .08 .25
553 Mark Macon RC .02 .10
554 Stacey Augmon RC .08 .25
555 Brian Williams RC .08 .25
556 Terrell Brandon RC .30 .75
557 Walter Davis USA .02 .10
558 Vern Fleming USA .02 .10
559 Joe Kleine USA .02 .10
560 Jon Koncak USA .02 .10
561 Sam Perkins USA .02 .10
562 Alvin Robertson USA .02 .10
563 Wayman Tisdale USA .02 .10
564 Jeff Turner USA .02 .10
565 Willie Anderson USA .02 .10
566 Stacey Augmon USA .08 .25
567 Bimbo Coles USA .02 .10
568 Jeff Grayer USA .02 .10
569 Hersey Hawkins USA .02 .10
570 Dan Majerle USA .02 .10
571 Danny Manning USA .02 .10
572 J.R. Reid USA .02 .10
573 Mitch Richmond USA .20 .50
574 Charles Smith USA .02 .10
575 Charles Barkley USA .30 .75
576 Larry Bird USA .75 2.00
577 Patrick Ewing USA .20 .50
578 Magic Johnson USA .60 1.50
579 Michael Jordan USA 3.00 8.00
580 Karl Malone USA .30 .75
581 Chris Mullin USA .08 .25
582 Scottie Pippen USA .60 1.50
583 David Robinson USA .40 1.00
584 John Stockton USA .20 .50
585 Chuck Daly CO USA .02 .10
586 Lenny Wilkens CO USA .02 .10
587 P.J.Carlesimo CO USA RC .02 .10
588 Mike Krzyzewski CO USA RC .15 .40
589 Checklist Card 1 .02 .10
590 Checklist Card 2 .02 .10
CC1 Naismith Special .40 1.00
XX Head of the Class 10.00 20.00
NNO Centennial Sendaway Card .20 .50
NNO Team USA Title Card .40 1.00

1991-92 Hoops All-Star MVP's

This six-card standard-size insert set commemorates the most valuable player of the NBA All-Star games from 1986 to 1991. Two cards were inserted in each second series rack pack. On a white card face, the front features non-action color photos framed by either a blue (7, 9, 12) or red (8, 10, 11) border. The top thicker border is jagged and displays the player's name, while the year the award was received appears in a colored box in the lower left corner. The backs have the same design and feature a color action photo from the All-Star game. The cards are numbered on the back by Roman numerals.

COMPLETE SET (6) 10.00 20.00
7 Isiah Thomas .50 1.25
8 Tom Chambers .08 .25
9 Michael Jordan 6.00 15.00
10 Karl Malone .75 2.00
11 Magic Johnson 1.50 4.00
12 Charles Barkley .75 2.00

1991-92 Hoops Slam Dunk

This six-card standard size insert set of "Slam Dunk Champions" features the winners of the All-Star weekend slam dunk competition from 1984 to 1991. The cards were issued two per first series 47-card rack pack. The front has a color photo of the player dunking the ball, with royal blue borders on a white card face. The player's name appears in orange lettering in a purple stripe above the picture, and the year the player won is given in a "Slam Dunk Champion" emblem overlaying the lower left corner of the picture. The design of the back is similar to the front, only with an extended caption on a yellow-green background. A drawing of a basketball entering a rim appears at the upper left corner. The cards are numbered on the back by Roman numerals.

COMPLETE SET (6) 7.50 15.00
1 Larry Nance .20 .50
2 Dominique Wilkins .50 1.25
3 Spud Webb .20 .50
4 Michael Jordan 8.00 20.00
5 Kenny Walker .08 .25
6 Dee Brown .08 .25

1992-93 Hoops Prototypes

Consisting of seven standard-size cards in a cello pack, this advance-run card pack was issued to preview the design of the forthcoming Hoops regular series issue. Additional packs could be obtained through a mail-in offer for 1.00 for postage and handling, with a limit of one pack per address while supplies lasted. Card number 1 carries an advertisement for 1992-93 Hoops Series I; card numbers 2-4 are identical to their regular issue counterparts (card numbers 153, 309, and 229 respectively), except that these prototype cards are unnumbered. After the advertisement card, the cards are listed below in alphabetical order by player's last name. Series II singles follow Series I.

COMPLETE SET (7) 1.25 3.00
1 1992-93 Series I (Advertisement) .25 .60
2 Patrick Ewing Series 1 .60 1.50
3 Magic Johnson Series 1 .60 1.50
4 John Stockton Series 1 .50 1.25
5 1992-93 Series II Advertisement .25 .60
6 Magic Johnson Series 2 .60 1.50
7 David Robinson Series 2 .50 1.25

1992-93 Hoops

The complete 1992-93 Hoops basketball set contains 490 standard-size cards. The set was released in two series of 350 and 140 cards, respectively. Both series packs contained 12 cards each with a suggested retail price of 79 cents each. Reported production quantities were 20,000 20-box wax cases of the first series and approximately 14,000 20-box wax cases of the second series. The basic card fronts display color action player photos surrounded by white borders. A color stripe reflecting one of the team's colors cuts across the picture and the player's name is printed vertically in a transparent stripe bordering the left side of the picture. The horizontally oriented backs carry a color head shot, biography, career highlights, and complete statistics (college and pro). The cards are checklisted below alphabetically according to teams. Subsets include Coaches (239-265), Team cards (266-292), NBA All-Stars East (293-305), NBA All-Stars West (306-319), League Leaders (320-327), Magic Moments (328-331), NBA Inside Stuff (332-333), NBA Stay in School (334-335), Basketball Tournament of the Americas (336-347) and Trivia (481-485). Rookie cards, scattered throughout the set, have a gold rather than a ghosted white stripe. The team logo appears in the lower left corner and intersects a team color-coded stripe that contains the player's position. The horizontal backs show a white background and include statistics (collegiate and pro), biographies, and career summaries. A close-up photo is at the upper left. Rookie Cards of note include Tom Gugliotta, Robert Horry, Christian Laettner, Alonzo Mourning, Shaquille O'Neal, Bobby Phills, Latrell Sprewell and Clarence Weatherspoon. A Magic Johnson "Commemorative Card" and a Patrick Ewing "Ultimate Game" card were randomly inserted in first series foil packs. One-thousand of each were autographed. The odds of pulling an autographed card were one in 14,400 packs. Also randomly inserted into second series foil packs were a Patrick Ewing Art card (reported odds were one per 21 packs), a Chicago Bulls Championship card (reported odds were one per 32 packs) and a John Stockton "Ultimate Game" card (reported odds were one per 92 packs). Stockton autographed 1,633 of these cards (reported odds were one per 5,732 packs). Also randomly inserted into first series packs was a USA Basketball Team card. A Barcelona Plastic card was also randomly inserted in first series packs at a rate of approximately one per 720 packs. This card is priced and listed with the 1992 Skybox USA set where it was originally available.

COMPLETE SET (490) 17.50 35.00
COMPLETE SERIES 1 (350) 7.50 15.00
COMPLETE SERIES 2 (140) 10.00 20.00
AC1: SER.2 STATED ODDS 1:21
SU1: SER.2 STATED ODDS 1:92, 1:5,732 AU
TR1: SER.2 STATED ODDS 1:32
BAR.PLASTIC: SER.1 STATED ODDS 1:720
MAGIC AU: SER.1 STATED ODDS 1:14,400
EWING AU: SER.1 STATED ODDS: 1:14,400
1 Stacey Augmon .02 .10
2 Maurice Cheeks .02 .10
3 Duane Ferrell .02 .10
4 Paul Graham .02 .10
5 Jon Koncak .02 .10
6 Blair Rasmussen .02 .10
7 Rumeal Robinson .02 .10
8 Dominique Wilkins .08 .25
9 Kevin Willis .02 .10
10 Larry Bird .40 1.00
11 Dee Brown .02 .10
12 Sherman Douglas .02 .10
13 Rick Fox .02 .10
14 Kevin Gamble .02 .10
15 Reggie Lewis .02 .10
16 Kevin McHale .08 .25
17 Robert Parish .02 .10
18 Ed Pinckney UER .02 .10
19 Muggsy Bogues .02 .10
20 Dell Curry .02 .10
21 Kenny Gattison .02 .10
22 Kendall Gill .02 .10
23 Mike Gminski .02 .10
24 Larry Johnson .10 .30
25 Johnny Newman .02 .10
26 J.R. Reid .02 .10
27 B.J. Armstrong .02 .10
28 Bill Cartwright .02 .10
29 Horace Grant .02 .10
30 Michael Jordan 1.25 3.00
31 Stacey King .02 .10
32 John Paxson .02 .10
33 Will Perdue .02 .10
34 Scottie Pippen .30 .75
35 Scott Williams .02 .10
36 John Battle .02 .10
37 Terrell Brandon .08 .25
38 Brad Daugherty .02 .10
39 Craig Ehlo .02 .10
40 Danny Ferry .02 .10
41 Henry James .02 .10
42 Larry Nance .02 .10
43 Mark Price .02 .10
44 Hot Rod Williams .02 .10
45 Rolando Blackman .02 .10
46 Terry Davis .02 .10
47 Derek Harper .02 .10
48 Mike Iuzzolino .02 .10
49 Fat Lever .02 .10
50 Rodney McCray .02 .10
51 Doug Smith .02 .10
52 Randy White .02 .10
53 Herb Williams .02 .10
54 Greg Anderson .02 .10
55 Winston Garland .02 .10
56 Chris Jackson .02 .10
57 Marcus Liberty .02 .10
58 Todd Lichti .02 .10
59 Mark Macon .02 .10
60 Dikembe Mutombo .10 .30
61 Reggie Williams .02 .10
62 Mark Aguirre .02 .10
63 William Bedford .02 .10
64 Joe Dumars .08 .25
65 Bill Laimbeer .02 .10
66 Dennis Rodman .20 .50
67 John Salley .02 .10
68 Isiah Thomas .08 .25
69 Darrell Walker .02 .10
70 Orlando Woolridge .02 .10
71 Victor Alexander .02 .10
72 Mario Elie .02 .10
73 Chris Gatling .02 .10
74 Tim Hardaway .10 .30
75 Tyrone Hill .02 .10
76 Alton Lister .02 .10
77 Sarunas Marciulionis .02 .10
78 Chris Mullin .08 .25
79 Billy Owens .02 .10
80 Matt Bullard .02 .10
81 Sleepy Floyd .02 .10
82 Avery Johnson .02 .10
83 Buck Johnson .02 .10
84 Vernon Maxwell .02 .10
85 Hakeem Olajuwon .15 .40
86 Kenny Smith .02 .10
87 Larry Smith .02 .10
88 Otis Thorpe .02 .10
89 Dale Davis .02 .10
90 Vern Fleming .02 .10
91 George McCloud .02 .10
92 Reggie Miller .08 .25
93 Chuck Person .02 .10
94 Detlef Schrempf .02 .10
95 Rik Smits .02 .10
96 LaSalle Thompson .02 .10
97 Micheal Williams .02 .10
98 James Edwards .02 .10
99 Gary Grant .02 .10
100 Ron Harper .02 .10
101 Danny Manning .02 .10
102 Ken Norman .02 .10
103 Olden Polynice .02 .10
104 Doc Rivers .02 .10
105 Charles Smith .02 .10
106 Loy Vaught .02 .10
107 Elden Campbell .02 .10
108 Vlade Divac .02 .10
109 A.C. Green .02 .10
110 Sam Perkins .02 .10
111 Byron Scott .02 .10
112 Tony Smith .02 .10
113 Terry Teagle .02 .10
114 Sedale Threatt .02 .10
115 James Worthy .08 .25
116 Willie Burton .02 .10
117 Bimbo Coles .02 .10
118 Kevin Edwards .02 .10
119 Alec Kessler .02 .10
120 Grant Long .02 .10
121 Glen Rice .08 .25
122 Rony Seikaly .02 .10
123 Brian Shaw .02 .10
124 Steve Smith .10 .30
125 Frank Brickowski .02 .10
126 Dale Ellis .02 .10
127 Jeff Grayer .02 .10
128 Jay Humphries .02 .10
129 Larry Krystkowiak .02 .10
130 Moses Malone .08 .25
131 Fred Roberts .02 .10
132 Alvin Robertson .02 .10
133 Danny Schayes .02 .10
134 Thurl Bailey .02 .10
135 Scott Brooks .02 .10
136 Tony Campbell .02 .10
137 Gerald Glass .02 .10
138 Luc Longley .02 .10
139 Sam Mitchell .02 .10
140 Pooh Richardson .02 .10
141 Felton Spencer .02 .10
142 Doug West .02 .10
143 Rafael Addison .02 .10
144 Kenny Anderson .08 .25
145 Mookie Blaylock .02 .10
146 Sam Bowie .02 .10
147 Derrick Coleman .02 .10
148 Chris Dudley .02 .10
149 Terry Mills .02 .10
150 Chris Morris .02 .10
151 Drazen Petrovic .02 .10
152 Greg Anthony .02 .10
153 Patrick Ewing .08 .25
154 Mark Jackson .02 .10
155 Anthony Mason .08 .25
156 Xavier McDaniel .02 .10
157 Charles Oakley .02 .10
158 John Starks .02 .10
159 Gerald Wilkins .02 .10
160 Nick Anderson .02 .10
161 Terry Catledge .02 .10
162 Jerry Reynolds .02 .10
163 Stanley Roberts .02 .10
164 Dennis Scott .02 .10
165 Scott Skiles .02 .10
166 Jeff Turner .02 .10
167 Sam Vincent .02 .10
168 Brian Williams .02 .10
169 Ron Anderson .02 .10
170 Charles Barkley .15 .40
171 Manute Bol .02 .10
172 Johnny Dawkins .02 .10
173 Armon Gilliam .02 .10
174 Hersey Hawkins .02 .10
175 Brian Oliver .02 .10
176 Charles Shackleford .02 .10
177 Jayson Williams .02 .10
178 Cedric Ceballos .02 .10
179 Tom Chambers .02 .10
180 Jeff Hornacek .02 .10
181 Kevin Johnson .08 .25
182 Negele Knight .02 .10
183 Andrew Lang .02 .10
184 Dan Majerle .02 .10
185 Tim Perry .02 .10
186 Mark West .02 .10
187 Alaa Abdelnaby .02 .10
188 Danny Ainge .02 .10
189 Clyde Drexler .08 .25
190 Kevin Duckworth .02 .10
191 Jerome Kersey .02 .10
192 Robert Pack .02 .10
193 Terry Porter .02 .10
194 Clifford Robinson .02 .10
195 Buck Williams .02 .10
196 Anthony Bonner .02 .10
197 Duane Causwell .02 .10
198 Pete Chilcutt .02 .10
199 Dennis Hopson .02 .10
200 Mitch Richmond .08 .25
201 Lionel Simmons .02 .10
202 Wayman Tisdale .02 .10
203 Spud Webb .02 .10
204 Willie Anderson .02 .10
205 Antoine Carr .02 .10
206 Terry Cummings .02 .10
207 Sean Elliott .02 .10
208 Sidney Green .02 .10
209 David Robinson .15 .40
210 Rod Strickland .08 .25
211 Greg Sutton .02 .10
212 Dana Barros .02 .10
213 Benoit Benjamin .02 .10
214 Michael Cage .02 .10
215 Eddie Johnson .02 .10
216 Shawn Kemp .20 .50
217 Derrick McKey .02 .10
218 Nate McMillan .02 .10
219 Gary Payton .20 .50
220 Ricky Pierce .02 .10
221 David Benoit .02 .10
222 Mike Brown .02 .10
223 Tyrone Corbin .02 .10
224 Mark Eaton .02 .10
225 Blue Edwards .02 .10
226 Jeff Malone .02 .10
227 Karl Malone .15 .40
228 Eric Murdock .02 .10
229 John Stockton .08 .25
230 Michael Adams .02 .10
231 Rex Chapman .02 .10
232 Ledell Eackles .02 .10
233 Pervis Ellison .02 .10
234 A.J. English .02 .10
235 Harvey Grant .02 .10
236 Charles Jones .02 .10
237 LaBradford Smith .02 .10
238 Larry Stewart .02 .10
239 Bob Weiss CO .02 .10
240 Chris Ford CO .02 .10
241 Allan Bristow CO .02 .10
242 Phil Jackson CO .02 .10
243 Lenny Wilkens CO .02 .10
244 Richie Adubato CO .02 .10
245 Dan Issel CO .02 .10
246 Ron Rothstein CO .02 .10
247 Don Nelson CO .02 .10
248 Rudy Tomjanovich CO .02 .10
249 Bob Hill CO .02 .10
250 Larry Brown CO .02 .10
251 Randy Pfund CO RC .02 .10
252 Kevin Loughery CO .02 .10
253 Mike Dunleavy CO .02 .10
254 Jimmy Rodgers CO .02 .10
255 Chuck Daly CO .02 .10
256 Pat Riley CO .02 .10
257 Matt Guokas CO .02 .10
258 Doug Moe CO .02 .10
259 Paul Westphal CO .02 .10
260 Rick Adelman CO .02 .10
261 Garry St. Jean CO RC .02 .10
262 Jerry Tarkanian CO RC .02 .10
263 George Karl CO .02 .10
264 Jerry Sloan CO .02 .10
265 Wes Unseld CO .02 .10
266 Atlanta Hawks TC .02 .10
267 Boston Celtics TC .02 .10
268 Charlotte Hornets TC .02 .10
269 Chicago Bulls TC .02 .10
270 Cleveland Cavaliers TC .02 .10
271 Dallas Mavericks TC .02 .10
272 Denver Nuggets TC .02 .10
273 Detroit Pistons TC .02 .10
274 Golden State Warriors TC .02 .10
275 Houston Rockets TC .02 .10
276 Indiana Pacers TC .02 .10
277 Los Angeles Clippers TC .02 .10
278 Los Angeles Lakers TC .02 .10
279 Miami Heat TC .02 .10
280 Milwaukee Bucks TC .02 .10
281 Minnesota Timberwolves TC .02 .10
282 New Jersey Nets TC .02 .10
283 New York Knicks TC .02 .10
284 Orlando Magic TC .02 .10
285 Philadelphia 76ers TC .02 .10
286 Phoenix Suns TC .02 .10
287 Portland Trail Blazers TC .02 .10
288 Sacramento Kings TC .02 .10
289 San Antonio Spurs TC .02 .10
290 Seattle Supersonics TC .02 .10
291 Utah Jazz TC .02 .10
292 Washington Bullets TC .02 .10
293 Michael Adams AS .02 .10
294 Charles Barkley AS .08 .25
295 Brad Daugherty AS .02 .10
296 Joe Dumars AS .02 .10
297 Patrick Ewing AS .02 .10
298 Michael Jordan AS .60 1.50
299 Reggie Lewis AS .02 .10
300 Scottie Pippen AS .15 .40
301 Mark Price AS .02 .10
302 Dennis Rodman AS .08 .25
303 Isiah Thomas AS .02 .10
304 Kevin Willis AS .02 .10
305 Phil Jackson CO AS .02 .10
306 Clyde Drexler AS .02 .10
307 Tim Hardaway AS .08 .25
308 Jeff Hornacek AS .02 .10
309 Magic Johnson AS .15 .40
310 Dan Majerle AS .02 .10
311 Karl Malone AS .08 .25
312 Chris Mullin AS .02 .10
313 Dikembe Mutombo AS .08 .25
314 Hakeem Olajuwon AS .08 .25
315 David Robinson AS .08 .25
316 John Stockton AS .02 .10
317 Otis Thorpe AS .02 .10
318 James Worthy AS .02 .10
319 Don Nelson CO AS .02 .10
320 M.Jordan/K.Malone LL .40 1.00
321 D.Barros/D.Petrovic LL .02 .10
322 M.Price/L.Bird LL .10 .30
323 D.Robinson/Olajuwon LL .08 .25
324 J.Stockton/M.Williams LL .08 .25
325 D.Rodman/K.Willis LL .08 .25
326 J.Stockton/K.Johnson LL .08 .25
327 B.Williams/O.Thorpe LL .02 .10
328 Magic Moments 1980 .08 .25
329 Magic Moments 1985 .08 .25
330 Magic Moments 87 and 88 .08 .25
331 Magic Numbers .08 .25
332 Drazen Petrovic IS .02 .10
333 Patrick Ewing IS .02 .10
334 David Robinson STAY .08 .25
335 Kevin Johnson STAY .02 .10
336 Charles Barkley USA .08 .25
337 Larry Bird USA .20 .50
338 Clyde Drexler USA .02 .10
339 Patrick Ewing USA .02 .10
340 Magic Johnson USA .15 .40
341 Michael Jordan USA .60 1.50
342 Christian Laettner USA RC .20 .50
343 Karl Malone USA .08 .25
344 Chris Mullin USA .02 .10
345 Scottie Pippen USA .15 .40
346 David Robinson USA .08 .25
347 John Stockton USA .02 .10
348 Checklist 1 .02 .10
349 Checklist 2 .02 .10
350 Checklist 3 .02 .10
351 Mookie Blaylock .07 .20
352 Adam Keefe RC .02 .10
353 Travis Mays .02 .10
354 Morlon Wiley .02 .10
355 Joe Kleine .02 .10
356 Bart Kofoed .02 .10
357 Xavier McDaniel .02 .10
358 Tony Bennett RC .02 .10
359 Tom Hammonds .02 .10
360 Kevin Lynch .02 .10
361 Alonzo Mourning RC 1.00 2.50
362 Rodney McCray .02 .10
363 Trent Tucker .02 .10
364 Corey Williams RC .02 .10
365 Steve Kerr .07 .20
366 Jerome Lane .02 .10
367 Bobby Phills RC .15 .40
368 Mike Sanders .02 .10
369 Gerald Wilkins .02 .10
370 Donald Hodge .02 .10
371 Brian Howard RC .02 .10
372 Tracy Moore RC .02 .10
373 Sean Rooks RC .02 .10
374 Kevin Brooks .02 .10
375 LaPhonso Ellis RC .15 .40
376 Scott Hastings .02 .10
377 Robert Pack .02 .10
378 Bryant Stith RC .07 .20
379 Robert Werdann RC .02 .10
380 Lance Blanks .02 .10
381 Terry Mills .02 .10
382 Isaiah Morris RC .02 .10
383 Olden Polynice .02 .10
384 Brad Sellers .02 .10
385 Jud Buechler .02 .10
386 Jeff Grayer .02 .10
387 Byron Houston RC .02 .10
388 Keith Jennings RC .02 .10
389 Latrell Sprewell RC 1.25 3.00
390 Scott Brooks .02 .10
391 Carl Herrera .02 .10
392 Robert Horry RC .15 .40
393 Tree Rollins .02 .10
394 Kennard Winchester .02 .10
395 Greg Dreiling .02 .10
396 Sean Green .02 .10
397 Sam Mitchell .02 .10
398 Pooh Richardson .02 .10
399 Malik Sealy RC .07 .20
400 Kenny Williams .02 .10
401 Jaren Jackson RC .07 .20
402 Mark Jackson .07 .20
403 Stanley Roberts .02 .10
404 Elmore Spencer RC .02 .10
405 Kiki Vandeweghe .02 .10
406 John Williams .02 .10
407 Randy Woods RC .02 .10
408 Alex Blackwell RC .02 .10
409 Duane Cooper RC .02 .10
410 Anthony Peeler RC .07 .20
411 Keith Askins .02 .10
412 Matt Geiger RC .07 .20
413 Harold Miner RC .07 .20
414 John Salley .02 .10
415 Alaa Abdelnaby .02 .10
416 Todd Day RC .07 .20
417 Blue Edwards .02 .10
418 Brad Lohaus .02 .10
419 Lee Mayberry RC .02 .10
420 Eric Murdock .02 .10
421 Christian Laettner .30 .75
422 Bob McCann RC .02 .10
423 Chuck Person .02 .10
424 Chris Smith RC .02 .10
425 Gundars Vetra RC .02 .10
426 Micheal Williams .02 .10
427 Chucky Brown .02 .10
428 Tate George .02 .10
429 Rick Mahorn .02 .10
430 Rumeal Robinson .02 .10
431 Jayson Williams .07 .20
432 Eric Anderson RC .02 .10
433 Rolando Blackman .02 .10
434 Tony Campbell .02 .10
435 Hubert Davis RC .07 .20
436 Bo Kimble .02 .10
437 Doc Rivers .07 .20
438 Charles Smith .02 .10
439 Anthony Bowie .02 .10
440 Litterial Green RC .02 .10
441 Greg Kite .02 .10
442 Shaquille O'Neal RC 3.00 8.00
443 Donald Royal .02 .10
444 Greg Grant .02 .10
445 Jeff Hornacek .07 .20
446 Andrew Lang .02 .10
447 Kenny Payne .02 .10
448 Tim Perry .02 .10
449 Clarence Weatherspoon RC .15 .40
450 Danny Ainge .07 .20
451 Charles Barkley .25 .60
452 Tim Kempton .02 .10
453 Oliver Miller RC .07 .20
454 Mark Bryant .02 .10
455 Mario Elie .07 .20
456 Dave Jamerson RC .02 .10
457 Tracy Murray RC .07 .20
458 Rod Strickland .15 .40
459 Vincent Askew .02 .10
460 Randy Brown .02 .10
461 Marty Conlon .02 .10
462 Jim Les .02 .10
463 Walt Williams RC .15 .40
464 William Bedford .02 .10
465 Lloyd Daniels RC .02 .10
466 Vinny Del Negro .02 .10
467 Dale Ellis .02 .10
468 Larry Smith .02 .10
469 David Wood .02 .10
470 Rich King .02 .10
471 Isaac Austin RC .07 .20
472 John Crotty RC .02 .10
473 Stephen Howard RC .02 .10
474 Jay Humphries .02 .10
475 Larry Krystkowiak .02 .10
476 Tom Gugliotta RC .50 1.25
477 Buck Johnson .02 .10
478 Don MacLean RC .02 .10
479 Doug Overton .02 .10
480 Brent Price RC .07 .20
481 David Robinson TRV .15 .40
482 Magic Johnson TRV .25 .60
483 John Stockton TRV .07 .20
484 Patrick Ewing TRV .07 .20
485 D.Rob/Ew/Stock/Mag TRV .15 .40
486 John Stockton STAY .07 .20
487 Ahmad Rashad .07 .20
488 Rookie Checklist .02 .10
489 Checklist 1 .02 .10
490 Checklist 2 .02 .10
AC1 P.Ewing Art Card .20 .50
SU1 J.Stockton Game AU 30.00 80.00
SU1 J.Stockton Game .60 1.50
TR1 M.Jordan/C.Drexler FIN 1.25 3.00
NNO M.Johnson Comm .40 1.00
NNO M.Johnson Comm AU 100.00 200.00
NNO P.Ewing Game .20 .50
NNO P.Ewing Game AU 50.00 100.00

1992-93 Hoops Draft Redemption

A "Lottery Exchange Card" randomly inserted (reportedly at a rate of one per 360 packs) in 1992-93 Hoops first series 12-card foil packs entitled the collector to receive this NBA Draft Redemption Lottery Exchange set. It consists of ten standard size cards of the top 1992 NBA Draft Picks. The first eleven players drafted are represented, with the exception of Jim Jackson, the late-signing fourth pick. Insert sets began to be mailed out during the week of January 4, 1993, and the redemption period expired on March 31, 1993. According to SkyBox International media releases a total of 25,876 sets were released to the public; 24,461 Lottery Exchange cards were redeemed. An additional 415 sets were claimed through a second chance drawing (selected from 149,166 mail-in entries). Finally, 1,000 more sets were released for public relations and promotional use. A reserve of 1,000 sets were held for replacement of damaged sets and 500 sets were kept for SkyBox International archives. In the color photos on the fronts, the players appear in dress attire in front of a gray studio background, except for cards C and J. The player's name is printed in white in a hardwood floor border design at the bottom of the card. A NBA Draft icon overlaps the border and the photo. A one inch tall hardwood design number at the upper left corner indicates the order the players were drafted. The horizontal backs display white backgrounds with a similar hardwood stripe containing the player's name across the top. A shadowed close-up photo is displayed next to college statistics and a player profile. The cards are lettered on the back. Sets still in the factory-sealed bags are valued at a premium of up to 20 percent above the complete set price below.

COMPLETE SET (10) 15.00 30.00
EXCH.CARD: SER.1 STATED ODDS 1:360
A Shaquille O'Neal 15.00 40.00
B Alonzo Mourning 4.00 10.00
C Christian Laettner 1.50 4.00
D LaPhonso Ellis 1.25 3.00
E Tom Gugliotta 2.50 6.00
F Walt Williams .75 2.00
G Todd Day .75 2.00
H Clarence Weatherspoon .75 2.00
I Adam Keefe .75 2.00
J Robert Horry 1.25 3.00
NNO Stamped Redemp.Card .40 1.00
NNO Unstamped Redemp.Card 1.25 3.00

1992-93 Hoops Magic's All-Rookies

This 10-card standard size set was randomly inserted into Hoops second series 12-card foil packs. They were inserted at a rate of one in 30 packs. The set features Magic Johnson's selections of the top rookies from the 1992-93 season. The cards show color action player photos and have a gold foil stripe containing the player's name down the left edge and a thinner stripe across the bottom printed with the city's name. The Magic's All-Rookie Team logo appears in the lower left corner. The backs display a small close-up picture of Magic Johnson in a yellow Los Angeles Lakers' warm-up jacket. A yellow stripe down the left edge contains the set name (Magic's All-Rookie Team) and the card number. The white background is printed in black with Magic's evaluation of the player.

COMPLETE SET (10) 25.00 60.00
SER.2 STATED ODDS 1:30
1 Shaquille O'Neal 12.00 30.00
2 Alonzo Mourning 6.00 15.00
3 Christian Laettner 2.00 5.00
4 LaPhonso Ellis 1.25 3.00
5 Tom Gugliotta 1.50 4.00
6 Walt Williams 1.25 3.00
7 Todd Day 1.25 3.00
8 Clarence Weatherspoon 1.25 3.00
9 Robert Horry 2.00 5.00
10 Harold Miner 1.25 3.00

1992-93 Hoops More Magic Moments

Randomly inserted (at a reported rate of one card per 195 packs) into 1992-93 Hoops second series 12-card packs, this three-card standard-size set commemorates Magic Johnson's return to training camp and pre-season game action. Each card features a color player photo bordered in white. Team color-coded bars and lettering accent the picture on the left edge and below, and a team color-coded star overwritten with the words "More Magic" appears at the lower left corner. Over ghosted photos similar or identical to the front photos, the backs summarize Magic's return, his performance in his first game, his performance in his last game, and his decision to retire again. The cards are numbered on the back with an "M" prefix.

COMPLETE SET (3) 45.00 70.00
COMMON MAGIC (M1-M3) 15.00 25.00
SER.2 STATED ODDS 1:195

1992-93 Hoops Supreme Court

This 10-card, standard-size set was randomly inserted (at a reported rate of one card per 11 packs) in Hoops second series 12-card foil packs and features color action player photos on the front. A gold foil stripe frames the pictures which are surrounded by a hardwood floor design. The player's name is printed in gold foil down the left side. A gray and burnt-orange logo printed with the words "Supreme Court 1992-93" appears in the lower left corner. A purple stripe containing the phrase "The Fan's Choice" runs across the bottom of the picture. Hoops promoted The Supreme Court Sweepstakes, which offered fans the opportunity to select the ten players who appeared in this subset. The backs are white with black print. A small color player photo with rounded corners is displayed next to a personal profile. The cards are numbered on the back with an "SC" prefix.

COMPLETE SET (10) 15.00 30.00
SER.2 STATED ODDS 1:11
SC1 Michael Jordan 4.00 10.00
SC2 Scottie Pippen 2.00 5.00
SC3 David Robinson 1.00 2.50
SC4 Patrick Ewing .60 1.50
SC5 Clyde Drexler .60 1.50
SC6 Karl Malone 1.00 2.50
SC7 Charles Barkley 1.00 2.50
SC8 John Stockton .60 1.50
SC9 Chris Mullin .60 1.50
SC10 Magic Johnson 1.00 2.50

1993-94 Hoops Promo Panel

Hoops issued this nine-card sheet to promote the 1993-94 Hoops regular issue. The standard-size cards were issued on a perforated sheet. The fronts feature full-bleed glossy color player photos. Each player's name and team logo appear in team-colors along a ghosted band at the bottom. The back presents a color head shot of the player with a team-color shadow box border at the top right corner. The player's name and a short biography are printed on a hardwood floor design at the top. Below, the player's college and NBA statistics, displayed in separate tables on a white background, round out the card. The individual cards on the sheet are unnumbered and checklisted below in alphabetical order.

NNO Hoops panel 2.00 5.00
Joe Dumars
Patrick Ewing
Tim Hardaway
Dan Majerle
Jeff Malone
Xavier McDaniel
Reggie Miller
David Robinson

1993-94 Hoops Prototypes

Distributed beginning in July 1993 to promote the September 1993 release of its 300-card first series, these standard-size (2 1/2" by 3 1/2") promo cards feature full-bleed glossy color player photos on the fronts. Each player's name and team logo appear in team colors along a ghosted band at the bottom. The back presents a color head shot of the player in a small rectangle bordered with a team color in the top right corner; alongside is his jersey number and position within a team-colored bar. The player's name and a short biography are printed on a hardwood floor design at the top. Below, the player's college and NBA stats, displayed in separate tables on a white background, round out the card. The cards are unnumbered and checklisted below in alphabetical order.

COMPLETE SET (7) 1.20 3.00
1 Jim Jackson .15 .40
2 Larry Johnson .20 .50
3 Karl Malone .25 .60
4 Harold Miner .12 .30
5 Dikembe Mutombo .20 .50

6 Shaquille O'Neal .75 2.00
7 Cover Card .12 .30

1993-94 Hoops

This 421-card standard-size set was issued in separate series of 300 and 121 cards. Cards were distributed in 13-card foil (12 basic cards plus one gold card) and 26-card jumbo (24 basic and two gold cards) packs. Cards feature full-bleed glossy color player photos on the fronts. Each player's name and team logo appear in team colors along a ghosted band at the bottom. The back presents a color head shot of the player in a small rectangle bordered with a team color in the top right corner. Alongside is his jersey number and position within a team-colored bar. The player's name and a short biography are printed on a hardwood floor design at the top. Below, the player's college and NBA stats, displayed in separate tables on a white background, round out the card. The cards are numbered on the back and listed alphabetically within team order. Subsets are Coaches (230-256), All-Stars (257-282), League Leaders (283-290), Boys and Girls Club (291), Hoops Tribune (292-297), and Checklists (298-300/419-420). Rookie Cards of note include Vin Baker, Anfernee Hardaway, Jamal Mashburn, Nick Van Exel and Chris Webber.

COMPLETE SET (421) 10.00 20.00
COMPLETE SERIES 1 (300) 6.00 12.00
COMPLETE SERIES 2 (121) 4.00 8.00
SUBSET CARDS SAME VALUE AS BASE CARDS
DR1: SER.2 STATED ODDS 1:18
BOTH AUs: SER.2 STATED ODDS 1:13,886
BEWARE COUNTERFEIT BIRD/MAGIC AU
1 Stacey Augmon .07 .20
2 Mookie Blaylock .05 .15
3 Duane Ferrell .05 .15
4 Paul Graham .05 .15
5 Adam Keefe .05 .15
6 Blair Rasmussen .05 .15
7 Dominique Wilkins .12 .30
8 Kevin Willis .05 .15
9 Alaa Abdelnaby .05 .15
10 Dee Brown .05 .15
11 Sherman Douglas .05 .15
12 Rick Fox .05 .15
13 Kevin Gamble .05 .15
14 Joe Kleine .05 .15
15 Xavier McDaniel .05 .15
16 Robert Parish .10 .25
17 Tony Bennett .05 .15
18 Muggsy Bogues .07 .20
19 Dell Curry .05 .15
20 Kenny Gattison .05 .15
21 Kendall Gill .05 .15
22 Larry Johnson .10 .25
23 Alonzo Mourning .15 .40
24 Johnny Newman .05 .15
25 B.J. Armstrong .05 .15
26 Bill Cartwright .07 .20
27 Horace Grant .07 .20
28 Michael Jordan 1.00 2.50
29 Stacey King .05 .15
30 John Paxson .07 .20
31 Will Perdue .05 .15
32 Scottie Pippen .20 .50
33 Scott Williams .05 .15
34 Moses Malone .10 .25
35 John Battle .05 .15
36 Terrell Brandon .07 .20
37 Brad Daugherty .07 .20
38 Craig Ehlo .05 .15
39 Danny Ferry .05 .15
40 Larry Nance .07 .20
41 Mark Price .10 .25
42 Gerald Wilkins .05 .15
43 John Williams .05 .15
44 Terry Davis .05 .15
45 Derek Harper .07 .20
46 Donald Hodge .05 .15
47 Mike Iuzzolino .05 .15
48 Jim Jackson .07 .20
49 Sean Rooks .05 .15
50 Doug Smith .05 .15
51 Randy White .05 .15
52 Mahmoud Abdul-Rauf .05 .15
53 LaPhonso Ellis .05 .15
54 Marcus Liberty .05 .15
55 Mark Macon .05 .15
56 Dikembe Mutombo .10 .25
57 Robert Pack .05 .15
58 Bryant Stith .05 .15
59 Reggie Williams .05 .15
60 Mark Aguirre .07 .20
61 Joe Dumars .10 .25
62 Bill Laimbeer .07 .20
63 Terry Mills .05 .15
64 Olden Polynice .05 .15
65 Alvin Robertson .05 .15
66 Dennis Rodman .20 .50
67 Isiah Thomas .10 .25
68 Victor Alexander .05 .15
69 Tim Hardaway .10 .25
70 Tyrone Hill .05 .15
71 Byron Houston .05 .15
72 Sarunas Marciulionis .05 .15
73 Chris Mullin .10 .25
74 Billy Owens .05 .15
75 Latrell Sprewell .15 .40
76 Scott Brooks .05 .15
77 Matt Bullard .05 .15
78 Carl Herrera .05 .15
79 Robert Horry .10 .25
80 Vernon Maxwell .05 .15
81 Hakeem Olajuwon .12 .30
82 Kenny Smith .07 .20
83 Otis Thorpe .05 .15
84 Dale Davis .05 .15
85 Vern Fleming .05 .15
86 George McCloud .05 .15
87 Reggie Miller .12 .30
88 Sam Mitchell .05 .15
89 Pooh Richardson .05 .15
90 Detlef Schrempf .10 .25
91 Malik Sealy .05 .15
92 Rik Smits .07 .20
93 Gary Grant .05 .15
94 Ron Harper .07 .20
95 Mark Jackson .07 .20
96 Danny Manning .07 .20
97 Ken Norman .05 .15
98 Stanley Roberts .05 .15
99 Elmore Spencer .05 .15
100 Loy Vaught .05 .15
101 John Williams .05 .15
102 Randy Woods .05 .15
103 Benoit Benjamin .05 .15
104 Elden Campbell .05 .15
105 Doug Christie UER .05 .15
106 Vlade Divac .10 .25
107 Anthony Peeler .05 .15
108 Tony Smith .05 .15
109 Sedale Threatt .05 .15
110 James Worthy .12 .30
111 Bimbo Coles .05 .15
112 Grant Long .05 .15
113 Harold Miner .05 .15
114 Glen Rice .10 .25
115 John Salley .05 .15
116 Rony Seikaly .05 .15
117 Brian Shaw .05 .15
118 Steve Smith .07 .20
119 Anthony Avent .05 .15
120 Jon Barry .05 .15
121 Frank Brickowski .05 .15
122 Todd Day .05 .15
123 Blue Edwards .05 .15
124 Brad Lohaus .05 .15
125 Lee Mayberry .05 .15
126 Eric Murdock .05 .15
127 Derek Strong RC .15 .40
128 Thurl Bailey .05 .15
129 Christian Laettner .07 .20
130 Luc Longley .07 .20
131 Marlon Maxey .05 .15
132 Chuck Person .07 .20
133 Chris Smith .05 .15
134 Doug West .05 .15
135 Micheal Williams .05 .15
136 Rafael Addison .05 .15
137 Kenny Anderson .07 .20
138 Sam Bowie .05 .15
139 Chucky Brown .05 .15
140 Derrick Coleman .07 .20
141 Chris Morris .05 .15
142 Rumeal Robinson .05 .15
143 Greg Anthony .05 .15
144 Rolando Blackman .07 .20
145 Hubert Davis .05 .15
146 Patrick Ewing .12 .30
147 Anthony Mason .05 .15
148 Charles Oakley .07 .20
149 Doc Rivers .07 .20
150 Charles Smith .05 .15
151 John Starks .07 .20
152 Nick Anderson .05 .15
153 Anthony Bowie .05 .15
154 Litterial Green .05 .15
155 Shaquille O'Neal .40 1.00
156 Donald Royal .05 .15
157 Dennis Scott .05 .15
158 Scott Skiles .05 .15
159 Tom Tolbert .05 .15
160 Jeff Turner .05 .15
161 Ron Anderson .05 .15
162 Johnny Dawkins .05 .15
163 Hersey Hawkins .05 .15
164 Jeff Hornacek .07 .20
165 Andrew Lang .05 .15
166 Tim Perry .05 .15
167 Clarence Weatherspoon .05 .15
168 Danny Ainge .10 .25
169 Charles Barkley .15 .40
170 Cedric Ceballos .07 .20
171 Richard Dumas .05 .15
172 Kevin Johnson .10 .25
173 Dan Majerle .10 .25
174 Oliver Miller .05 .15
175 Mark West .05 .15
176 Clyde Drexler .12 .30
177 Kevin Duckworth .05 .15
178 Mario Elie .05 .15
179 Dave Johnson .05 .15
180 Jerome Kersey .05 .15
181 Tracy Murray .05 .15
182 Terry Porter .05 .15
183 Clifford Robinson .05 .15
184 Rod Strickland .05 .15
185 Buck Williams .05 .15
186 Anthony Bonner .05 .15
187 Randy Brown .05 .15
188 Duane Causwell .05 .15
189 Pete Chilcutt .05 .15
190 Mitch Richmond .10 .25
191 Lionel Simmons .05 .15
192 Wayman Tisdale .05 .15
193 Spud Webb .07 .20
194 Walt Williams .05 .15
195 Willie Anderson .05 .15
196 Antoine Carr .05 .15
197 Terry Cummings .07 .20
198 Lloyd Daniels .05 .15
199 Sean Elliott .10 .25
200 Dale Ellis .05 .15
201 Avery Johnson .07 .20
202 J.R. Reid .05 .15
203 David Robinson .15 .40
204 Dana Barros .05 .15
205 Michael Cage .05 .15
206 Eddie Johnson .05 .15
207 Shawn Kemp .12 .30
208 Derrick McKey .05 .15
209 Nate McMillan .05 .15
210 Gary Payton .12 .30
211 Sam Perkins .05 .15
212 Ricky Pierce .05 .15
213 David Benoit .05 .15
214 Tyrone Corbin .05 .15
215 Mark Eaton .05 .15
216 Jay Humphries .05 .15
217 Jeff Malone .05 .15
218 Karl Malone .12 .30
219 John Stockton .12 .30
220 Michael Adams .05 .15
221 Rex Chapman .05 .15
222 Pervis Ellison .05 .15
223 Harvey Grant .05 .15
224 Tom Gugliotta .07 .20
225 Don MacLean .05 .15
226 Doug Overton .05 .15
227 Brent Price .05 .15
228 LaBradford Smith .05 .15
229 Larry Stewart .05 .15
230 Lenny Wilkens CO .10 .25
231 Chris Ford CO .10 .25
232 Allan Bristow CO .10 .25
233 Phil Jackson CO .20 .50
234 Mike Fratello CO .10 .25
235 Quinn Buckner CO .10 .25
236 Dan Issel CO .10 .25
237 Don Chaney CO .10 .25
238 Don Nelson CO .10 .25
239 Rudy Tomjanovich CO .10 .25
240 Larry Brown CO .10 .25
241 Bob Weiss CO .10 .25
242 Randy Pfund CO .10 .25
243 Kevin Loughery CO .10 .25
244 Mike Dunleavy CO .10 .25
245 Sidney Lowe CO .10 .25
246 Chuck Daly CO .10 .25
247 Pat Riley CO .15 .40
248 Brian Hill CO .10 .25
249 Fred Carter CO .10 .25
250 Paul Westphal CO .10 .25
251 Rick Adelman CO .10 .25
252 Garry St. Jean CO .10 .25
253 John Lucas CO .10 .25
254 George Karl CO .10 .25
255 Jerry Sloan CO .10 .25
256 Wes Unseld CO .10 .25
257 Michael Jordan AS .75 2.00
258 Isiah Thomas AS .10 .25
259 Scottie Pippen AS .20 .50
260 Larry Johnson AS .10 .25
261 Dominique Wilkins AS .12 .30
262 Joe Dumars AS .10 .25
263 Mark Price AS .10 .25
264 Shaquille O'Neal AS .40 1.00
265 Patrick Ewing AS .12 .30
266 Larry Nance AS .07 .20
267 Detlef Schrempf AS .10 .25
268 Brad Daugherty AS .07 .20
269 Charles Barkley AS .15 .40
270 Clyde Drexler AS .12 .30
271 Sean Elliott AS .10 .25
272 Tim Hardaway AS .10 .25
273 Shawn Kemp AS .12 .30
274 Dan Majerle AS .10 .25
275 Karl Malone AS .12 .30
276 Danny Manning AS .07 .20
277 Hakeem Olajuwon AS .12 .30
278 Terry Porter AS .05 .15
279 David Robinson AS .15 .40
280 John Stockton AS .12 .30
281 East Team Photo .40 1.00
282 West Team Photo .15 .40
283 Jordan/Wilkins/Malone LL .75 2.00
284 Rodman/O'Neal/Mut LL .40 1.00
285 Ceballos/Daug/Davis LL .07 .20
286 Stock/Hardaway/Skiles L .50 1.25
287 Price/A-Rauf/L.Johnson L .10 .25
288 Arm/Mullin/Smith LL .10 .25
289 Jordan/Blaylock/Stock LL .75 2.00
290 Olajuwon/O'Neal/Mut LL .40 1.00
291 D.Robinson BOYS/GIRLS .15 .40
292 B.J. Armstrong TRIB .05 .15
293 Scottie Pippen TRIB .20 .50
294 Kevin Johnson TRIB .10 .25
295 Charles Barkley TRIB .15 .40
296 Richard Dumas TRIB .05 .15
297 Horace Grant TRIB .20 .50
298 David Robinson CL .15 .40
299 David Robinson CL .15 .40
300 David Robinson CL .15 .40
301 Craig Ehlo .05 .15
302 Jon Koncak .05 .15
303 Andrew Lang .05 .15
304 Chris Corchiani .05 .15
305 Acie Earl RC .15 .40
306 Dino Radja RC .15 .40
307 Scott Burrell RC .15 .40
308 Hersey Hawkins .05 .15
309 Eddie Johnson .05 .15
310 David Wingate .05 .15
311 Corie Blount RC .15 .40
312 Steve Kerr .07 .20
313 Toni Kukoc RC .40 1.00
314 Pete Myers .05 .15
315 Jay Guidinger .05 .15
316 Tyrone Hill .05 .15
317 Gerald Madkins RC .15 .40
318 Chris Mills RC .15 .40
319 Bobby Phills .05 .15
320 Lucious Harris RC .15 .40
321 Popeye Jones RC .15 .40
322 Fat Lever .07 .20
323 Jamal Mashburn RC .25 .60
324 Darren Morningstar RC .15 .40
325 Kevin Brooks .05 .15
326 Tom Hammonds .05 .15
327 Darnell Mee RC .15 .40
328 Rodney Rogers RC .15 .40
329 Brian Williams .05 .15
330 Greg Anderson .05 .15
331 Sean Elliott .10 .25
332 Allan Houston RC .30 .75
333 Lindsey Hunter RC .15 .40
334 David Wood UER .05 .15
335 Jud Buechler .05 .15
336 Chris Gatling .05 .15
337 Josh Grant RC .15 .40
338 Jeff Grayer .05 .15
339 Keith Jennings .05 .15
340 Avery Johnson .07 .20
341 Chris Webber RC .75 2.00
342 Sam Cassell RC .30 .75
343 Mario Elie .05 .15
344 Eric Riley RC .15 .40
345 Antonio Davis RC .20 .50
346 Scott Haskin RC .15 .40
347 Gerald Paddio .05 .15
348 LaSalle Thompson .05 .15
349 Ken Williams .05 .15
350 Mark Aguirre .07 .20
351 Terry Dehere RC .15 .40
352 Henry James .05 .15
353 Sam Bowie .05 .15
354 George Lynch RC .15 .40
355 Kurt Rambis .07 .20
356 Nick Van Exel RC .30 .75
357 Trevor Wilson .05 .15
358 Keith Askins .05 .15
359 Manute Bol .05 .15
360 Willie Burton .05 .15
361 Matt Geiger .05 .15
362 Alec Kessler .05 .15
363 Vin Baker RC .25 .60
364 Ken Norman .05 .15
365 Danny Schayes .05 .15
366 Mike Brown .05 .15
367 Isaiah Rider RC .25 .60
368 Benoit Benjamin .05 .15
369 P.J. Brown RC .15 .40
370 Kevin Edwards .05 .15
371 Armon Gilliam .05 .15
372 Rick Mahorn .05 .15
373 Dwayne Schintzius .05 .15
374 Rex Walters RC .15 .40
375 Jayson Williams .05 .15
376 Eric Anderson .05 .15
377 Anthony Bonner .05 .15
378 Tony Campbell .05 .15
379 Herb Williams .05 .15
380 Anfernee Hardaway RC .75 2.00
381 Greg Kite .05 .15
382 Larry Krystkowiak .05 .15
383 Todd Lichti .05 .15
384 Dana Barros .05 .15
385 Shawn Bradley RC .15 .40
386 Greg Graham RC .15 .40
387 Warren Kidd RC .15 .40
388 Eric Leckner .05 .15
389 Moses Malone .10 .25
390 A.C. Green .07 .20
391 Frank Johnson .05 .15
392 Joe Kleine .05 .15
393 Malcolm Mackey RC .15 .40
394 Jerrod Mustaf .05 .15
395 Mark Bryant .05 .15
396 Chris Dudley .05 .15
397 Harvey Grant .05 .15
398 James Robinson RC .15 .40
399 Reggie Smith .05 .15
400 Randy Brown .05 .15
401 Bobby Hurley RC .15 .40
402 Jim Les .05 .15
403 Vinny Del Negro .05 .15
404 Sleepy Floyd .05 .15
405 Dennis Rodman .20 .50
406 Chris Whitney RC .15 .40
407 Vincent Askew .05 .15
408 Kendall Gill .05 .15
409 Ervin Johnson RC .15 .40
410 Rich King .05 .15
411 Detlef Schrempf .10 .25
412 Tom Chambers .07 .20
413 John Crotty .05 .15
414 Felton Spencer .05 .15
415 Luther Wright RC .15 .40
416 Calbert Cheaney RC .15 .40
417 Kevin Duckworth .05 .15
418 Gheorghe Muresan RC .15 .40
419 David Robinson CL .15 .40
420 David Robinson CL .15 .40
421 David Robinson CL .15 .40
DR1 D.Robinson Comm .15 .40
MB1 Magic/Bird Comm .20 .50
MB1A Magic/Bird Comm AU 100.00 250.00
NNO D.Robinson Comm AU 20.00 50.00
NNO D.Robinson Exp.Vouch. 4.00 10.00
NNO Magic/Bird Exp.Vouch. 15.00 30.00

1993-94 Hoops Fifth Anniversary Gold

COMPLETE SET (423) 30.00 60.00
COMPLETE SERIES 1 (301) 17.50 35.00
COMPLETE SERIES 2 (122) 12.50 25.00
*STARS: 1X TO 2.5X BASE CARD HI
*RCs: .75X TO 2X BASE HI

1993-94 Hoops Admiral's Choice

Randomly inserted in second series 13-card foil and 26-card jumbo packs at a rate of one in 12, this five-card standard-size set features David Robinson's selection of the best starting five players in the game today. The cards have borderless fronts with color player photos. The player's name appears in gold-foil lettering at the top. The white back features a color player photo on the left with the player profile on the right. The cards are numbered on the back with an "AC" prefix.

COMPLETE SET (5) 1.00 2.50
SER.2 STATED ODDS 1:12
AC1 Shawn Kemp .20 .50
AC2 Derrick Coleman .12 .30
AC3 Kenny Anderson .12 .30
AC4 Shaquille O'Neal .60 1.50
AC5 Chris Webber .75 2.00

1993-94 Hoops David's Best

Inserted into one in every ten first series 1993-94 Hoops 13-card foil packs, these UV-coated cards feature color action photos of David Robinson against featured opponents. The "David's Best" logo runs across the bottom of the card in "golden crystal-foil" lettering. The back of the cards present Robinson's stat line from the selected game and a brief synopsis of the highlights. The cards are numbered on the back with a "DB" prefix.

COMPLETE SET (5) 1.00 2.50
COMMON CARD (DB1-DB5) .30 .75
SER.1 STATED ODDS 1:10

1993-94 Hoops Draft Redemption

For the second consecutive year, a redemption card was randomly inserted into series one packs at a rate of one in 360. The card could be sent in for this 11-card standard-size set by March 31, 1994. The cards feature a full-color head photo on the front. The player's name appears centered at the top in gold foil. The player's draft number also appears in gold foil at the upper right. The horizontal back features a color player head shot on the left, with player statistics and biography alongside on the right. The cards are numbered on the back with an "LP" prefix and sequenced in draft lottery order.

COMPLETE SET (11) 12.00 30.00
EXCH.CARD: SER.1 STATED ODDS 1:360
LP1 Chris Webber 5.00 12.00
LP2 Shawn Bradley .60 1.50
LP3 Anfernee Hardaway 5.00 12.00
LP4 Jamal Mashburn 1.25 3.00
LP5 Isaiah Rider 1.25 3.00
LP6 Calbert Cheaney .60 1.50
LP7 Bobby Hurley .60 1.50
LP8 Vin Baker 1.00 2.50
LP9 Rodney Rogers .60 1.50
LP10 Lindsey Hunter .60 1.50
LP11 Allan Houston 2.00 5.00
NNO Redeemed Draft Card .08 .25
NNO Unredeemed Draft Card .60 1.50

1993-94 Hoops Face to Face

Randomly inserted in first series 13-card foil packs at a rate of one in 20, these 12 standard-size cards feature a standout rookie from 1992-93 on one side and a veteran All-Star with similar skills on the other. The full-bleed glossy color player action photos on both sides are reproduced over metallic-type backgrounds. On both sides, the Face to Face logo and the player's name appears at the bottom. The cards are numbered on the second side with an "FTF" prefix.

COMPLETE SET (12) 6.00 15.00
SER.1 STATED ODDS 1:20
1 S.O'Neal/D.Robinson 1.50 4.00
2 A.Mourning/P.Ewing .60 1.50
3 C.Laettner/S.Kemp .50 1.25
4 J.Jackson/C.Drexler .50 1.25
5 L.Ellis/L.Johnson .40 1.00
6 C.Weatherspoon/C.Barkley .60 1.50
7 T.Gugliotta/K.Malone .50 1.25
8 W.Williams/M.Johnson 1.00 2.50
9 R.Horry/S.Pippen .75 2.00
10 H.Miner/M.Jordan 3.00 8.00
11 Todd Day/C.Mullin .40 1.00
12 R.Dumas/D.Wilkins .50 1.25

1993-94 Hoops Magic's All-Rookies

Randomly inserted in second-series 13-card foil and 26-card jumbo packs at a rate of one in 30, this 10-card standard size set features Magic Johnson's projected All-Rookie team for 1993-94. The borderless front features a full-color action shot with the player's name in a gold-foil strip at the bottom. The borderless back features an italicized player profile written by Magic Johnson set against a ghosted background photo of Magic.

COMPLETE SET (10) 12.00 30.00
SER.2 STATED ODDS 1:30
1 Chris Webber 4.00 10.00
2 Shawn Bradley .75 2.00
3 Anfernee Hardaway 4.00 10.00
4 Jamal Mashburn 1.25 3.00
5 Isaiah Rider 1.25 3.00
6 Calbert Cheaney .75 2.00
7 Bobby Hurley .75 2.00
8 Vin Baker 1.25 3.00
9 Lindsey Hunter .75 2.00
10 Toni Kukoc 2.00 5.00

1993-94 Hoops Scoops

Randomly inserted in second series 13-card foil packs, this 28-card set measures the standard size. Photos feature unique above the rim photography of a star player from each of the 27 NBA teams. Cards are either horizontal or vertical. The player's name, his team's name, and logo appear in a black bar under the photo, while the NBA Hoops Scoops logo appears in the upper right or left corner. On a white background, the backs carry trivia questions about the teams. The cards are numbered on the back with an "HS" prefix. These cards are as plentiful as the regular issue cards.

COMPLETE SET (28) 1.25 3.00
RANDOM INSERTS IN SER.2 PACKS
*GOLD CARDS: .75X TO 2X HI COLUMN
HS1 Dominique Wilkins .12 .30
HS2 Robert Parish .10 .25
HS3 Alonzo Mourning .15 .40
HS4 Scottie Pippen .20 .50
HS5 Larry Nance .07 .20
HS6 Derek Harper .07 .20
HS7 Reggie Williams .05 .15
HS8 Bill Laimbeer .07 .20
HS9 Tim Hardaway .10 .25
HS10 Hakeem Olajuwon UER .12 .30
HS11 LaSalle Thompson .05 .15
HS12 Danny Manning .07 .20
HS13 James Worthy .12 .30
HS14 Grant Long .05 .15
HS15 Blue Edwards .05 .15
HS16 Christian Laettner .07 .20
HS17 Derrick Coleman .07 .20
HS18 Patrick Ewing .12 .30
HS19 Nick Anderson .05 .15
HS20 Clarence Weatherspoon .05 .15
HS21 Charles Barkley .15 .40
HS22 Clifford Robinson .05 .15
HS23 Lionel Simmons .05 .15
HS24 David Robinson .15 .40
HS25 Shawn Kemp .12 .30
HS26 Karl Malone .12 .30
HS27 Rex Chapman .05 .15
HS28 Answer Card .05 .15

1993-94 Hoops Supreme Court

Randomly inserted into second series 13-card foil and 26-card jumbo packs, this 11-card standard-size set reflects the All-NBA team as chosen by media members that report on the hobby. Card fronts feature full-color action player photos set against a wood grain vertical bar with the player's name centered at the top in silver-foil lettering. The backs carry color player action shots along the left side and player statistics along the right side. The cards are numbered on the back with an "SC" prefix.

COMPLETE SET (11) 2.00 5.00
SER.2 STATED ODDS 1:11
SC1 Charles Barkley .25 .60
SC2 David Robinson .25 .60
SC3 Patrick Ewing .20 .50
SC4 Shaquille O'Neal .60 1.50
SC5 Larry Johnson .20 .50
SC6 Karl Malone .20 .50
SC7 Alonzo Mourning .25 .60
SC8 John Stockton .20 .50
SC9 Hakeem Olajuwon UER .20 .50
SC10 Scottie Pippen .30 .75
SC11 Michael Jordan 1.25 3.00

1994-95 Hoops Preview

This standard-size card previews the design of the 1994-95 Hoops regular series. The front features a full-bleed color action player photo. A team color-coded stripe cuts across the bottom of the picture and carries the player's name, position, and Hoops logo. The back has a color headshot, biography, statistics (collegiate and pro), and player profile. The card is unnumbered.

NNO David Robinson .75 2.00

1994-95 Hoops Promo Sheet

Measuring 7" by 10 1/2", this promo sheet was issued to preview the second series of the 1994-95 Hoops set. The perforated sheet consists of six cards, with an advertisement on a strip attached to the left edge. The cards are identical their regular issue counterparts except that the card numbers have been omitted. Cards are priced individually due to the large number of sheets that were seperated.

COMPLETE SET (6) 1.00 2.50
1 Jason Kidd 1.00 2.50
2 Donyell Marshall .20 .50
3 Eric Montross .15 .40
Rodney Rogers
4 Alonzo Mourning .25 .60
5 John Starks .15 .40
6 Dennis Rodman .40 1.00

1994-95 Hoops

The 450 standard-size cards comprising the '94-95 Hoops set were distributed in two separate series of 300 and 150 cards each. Cards were issued in 12-card hobby and retail packs (suggested retail price first series $0.99, second series $1.19) and 24-card retail jumbo packs. All second series packs contained at least one insert card (12-card packs had one insert and 24-card jumbo packs had two). Cards feature borderless color player action shots on the front. The player's name, position, and team name appear in white lettering within a team colored stripe near the bottom. The white back carries a color player head shot at the upper left, with the player's name and brief biography appearing alongside to the right. Statistics and career highlights follow below. The cards are numbered on the back and grouped alphabetically within teams. Subsets include All-Stars (224-251), League Leaders (252-258), Award Winners (259-265), Tribune (266-273), Coaches (274-295/383-388), Team Cards (391-420), Top This (421-430) and Gold Mine (431-450). A special Shaquille O'Neal Press Sheet (featuring 100 of his previously issued Hoops and SkyBox cards in an uncut poster-size format) was available by sending in thirty-two first series wrappers along with a check or money order for $1.50. As a special bonus 100 Press Sheets were autographed by O'Neal and randomly mailed out to collectors who responded to the promotion, which expired on March 1st, 1995. A special Grant Hill Commemorative card was available by sending in two second series wrappers along with a check or money order for $3.00 before the June 15th expiration date. Rookie Cards of note include Grant Hill, Juwan Howard, Eddie Jones, Jason Kidd and Glenn Robinson.

COMPLETE SET (450) 10.00 25.00
COMPLETE SERIES 1 (300) 5.00 12.00
COMPLETE SERIES 2 (150) 5.00 12.00
SUBSET CARDS SAME VALUE AS BASE
1 Stacey Augmon .12 .30
2 Mookie Blaylock .10 .25
3 Doug Edwards .10 .25
4 Craig Ehlo .10 .25
5 Jon Koncak .10 .25
6 Danny Manning .12 .30
7 Kevin Willis .10 .25
8 Dee Brown .10 .25
9 Sherman Douglas .10 .25
10 Acie Earl .10 .25
11 Kevin Gamble .10 .25
12 Xavier McDaniel .10 .25
13 Robert Parish .15 .40
14 Dino Radja .10 .25
15 Tony Bennett .10 .25
16 Muggsy Bogues .12 .30
17 Scott Burrell .10 .25
18 Dell Curry .10 .25
19 Hersey Hawkins .10 .25
20 Eddie Johnson .10 .25
21 Larry Johnson .15 .40
22 Alonzo Mourning .20 .50
23 B.J. Armstrong .10 .25
24 Corie Blount .10 .25
25 Bill Cartwright .12 .30
26 Horace Grant .12 .30
27 Toni Kukoc .20 .50
28 Luc Longley .12 .30
29 Pete Myers .10 .25
30 Scottie Pippen .30 .75
31 Scott Williams .10 .25
32 Terrell Brandon .10 .25
33 Brad Daugherty .12 .30
34 Tyrone Hill .10 .25
35 Chris Mills .10 .25
36 Larry Nance .12 .30
37 Bobby Phills .10 .25
38 Mark Price .15 .40
39 Gerald Wilkins .10 .25
40 John Williams .10 .25
41 Terry Davis .10 .25
42 Lucious Harris .10 .25
43 Jim Jackson .10 .25
44 Popeye Jones .10 .25
45 Tim Legler .10 .25
46 Jamal Mashburn .15 .40
47 Sean Rooks .10 .25
48 Mahmoud Abdul-Rauf .10 .25
49 LaPhonso Ellis .10 .25
50 Dikembe Mutombo .15 .40
51 Robert Pack .10 .25
52 Rodney Rogers .10 .25
53 Bryant Stith .10 .25
54 Brian Williams .10 .25
55 Reggie Williams .10 .25
56 Greg Anderson .10 .25
57 Joe Dumars .15 .40
58 Sean Elliott .15 .40
59 Allan Houston .15 .40
60 Lindsey Hunter .10 .25
61 Mark Macon .10 .25
62 Terry Mills .10 .25
63 Victor Alexander .10 .25
64 Chris Gatling .10 .25
65 Tim Hardaway .15 .40
66 Avery Johnson .12 .30
67 Sarunas Marciulionis .10 .25
68 Chris Mullin .15 .40
69 Billy Owens .10 .25
70 Latrell Sprewell .20 .50
71 Chris Webber .25 .60
72 Matt Bullard .10 .25
73 Sam Cassell .15 .40
74 Mario Elie .10 .25
75 Carl Herrera .10 .25
76 Robert Horry .15 .40
77 Vernon Maxwell .10 .25
78 Hakeem Olajuwon .20 .50
79 Kenny Smith .12 .30
80 Otis Thorpe .10 .25
81 Antonio Davis .10 .25
82 Dale Davis .10 .25
83 Vern Fleming .10 .25
84 Scott Haskin .10 .25
85 Derrick McKey .10 .25
86 Reggie Miller .20 .50
87 Byron Scott .12 .30
88 Rik Smits .12 .30
89 Haywoode Workman .10 .25
90 Terry Dehere .10 .25
91 Harold Ellis .10 .25
92 Gary Grant .10 .25
93 Ron Harper .12 .30
94 Mark Jackson .12 .30
95 Stanley Roberts .10 .25
96 Loy Vaught .10 .25
97 Dominique Wilkins .20 .50
98 Elden Campbell .10 .25
99 Doug Christie .10 .25
100 Vlade Divac .15 .40
101 Reggie Jordan .10 .25
102 George Lynch .10 .25
103 Anthony Peeler .10 .25
104 Sedale Threatt .10 .25
105 Nick Van Exel .15 .40
106 James Worthy .20 .50
107 Bimbo Coles .10 .25
108 Matt Geiger .10 .25
109 Grant Long .10 .25
110 Harold Miner .10 .25
111 Glen Rice .15 .40
112 John Salley .10 .25
113 Rony Seikaly .10 .25
114 Brian Shaw .10 .25
115 Steve Smith .12 .30
116 Vin Baker .15 .40
117 Jon Barry .10 .25
118 Todd Day .10 .25
119 Lee Mayberry .10 .25
120 Eric Murdock .10 .25
121 Ken Norman .10 .25
122 Mike Brown .10 .25
123 Stacey King .10 .25
124 Christian Laettner .12 .30
125 Chuck Person .12 .30
126 Isaiah Rider .15 .40
127 Chris Smith .10 .25
128 Doug West .10 .25
129 Micheal Williams .10 .25
130 Kenny Anderson .12 .30
131 Benoit Benjamin .10 .25
132 P.J. Brown .10 .25
133 Derrick Coleman .12 .30
134 Kevin Edwards .10 .25
135 Armon Gilliam .10 .25
136 Chris Morris .10 .25
137 Rex Walters .10 .25
138 David Wesley .10 .25
139 Greg Anthony .10 .25
140 Anthony Bonner .10 .25
141 Hubert Davis .10 .25
142 Patrick Ewing .20 .50
143 Derek Harper .12 .30
144 Anthony Mason .10 .25
145 Charles Oakley .12 .30
146 Charles Smith .10 .25
147 John Starks .12 .30
148 Nick Anderson .10 .25
149 Anthony Avent .10 .25
150 Anthony Bowie .10 .25
151 Anfernee Hardaway .25 .60
152 Shaquille O'Neal .40 1.00
153 Donald Royal .10 .25
154 Dennis Scott .10 .25
155 Scott Skiles .10 .25
156 Jeff Turner .10 .25
157 Dana Barros .10 .25
158 Shawn Bradley .10 .25
159 Greg Graham .10 .25
160 Warren Kidd .10 .25
161 Eric Leckner .10 .25
162 Jeff Malone .10 .25
163 Tim Perry .10 .25
164 Clarence Weatherspoon .10 .25
165 Danny Ainge .15 .40
166 Charles Barkley .25 .60
167 Cedric Ceballos .10 .25
168 A.C. Green .12 .30
169 Kevin Johnson .15 .40
170 Malcolm Mackey .10 .25
171 Dan Majerle .15 .40
172 Oliver Miller .10 .25
173 Mark West .10 .25
174 Clyde Drexler .20 .50
175 Chris Dudley .10 .25
176 Harvey Grant .10 .25
177 Tracy Murray .10 .25
178 Terry Porter .10 .25
179 Clifford Robinson .10 .25
180 James Robinson .10 .25
181 Rod Strickland .10 .25
182 Buck Williams .10 .25
183 Duane Causwell .10 .25
184 Bobby Hurley .10 .25
185 Olden Polynice .10 .25
186 Mitch Richmond .15 .40
187 Lionel Simmons .10 .25
188 Wayman Tisdale .10 .25
189 Spud Webb .12 .30
190 Walt Williams .10 .25
191 Willie Anderson .10 .25
192 Lloyd Daniels .10 .25
193 Vinny Del Negro .10 .25
194 Dale Ellis .10 .25
195 J.R. Reid .10 .25
196 David Robinson .25 .60
197 Dennis Rodman .30 .75
198 Kendall Gill .10 .25
199 Ervin Johnson .10 .25
200 Shawn Kemp .15 .40
201 Chris King .10 .25
202 Nate McMillan .10 .25
203 Gary Payton .15 .40
204 Sam Perkins .10 .25
205 Ricky Pierce .10 .25
206 Detlef Schrempf .15 .40
207 David Benoit .10 .25
208 Tom Chambers .12 .30
209 Tyrone Corbin .10 .25
210 Jeff Hornacek .12 .30
211 Karl Malone .20 .50
212 Bryon Russell .10 .25
213 Felton Spencer .10 .25
214 John Stockton .20 .50
215 Luther Wright .10 .25
216 Michael Adams .10 .25
217 Mitchell Butler .10 .25
218 Rex Chapman .10 .25
219 Calbert Cheaney .10 .25
220 Pervis Ellison .10 .25
221 Tom Gugliotta .10 .25
222 Don MacLean .10 .25
223 Gheorghe Muresan .10 .25
224 Kenny Anderson AS .12 .30
225 B.J. Armstrong AS .10 .25
226 Mookie Blaylock AS .10 .25
227 Derrick Coleman AS .12 .30
228 Patrick Ewing AS .20 .50
229 Horace Grant AS .12 .30
230 Alonzo Mourning AS .20 .50
231 Shaquille O'Neal AS .40 1.00
232 Charles Oakley AS .12 .30
233 Scottie Pippen AS .30 .75
234 Mark Price AS .15 .40
235 John Starks AS .12 .30
236 Dominique Wilkins AS .20 .50
237 East Team .10 .25
238 Charles Barkley AS .25 .60
239 Clyde Drexler AS .20 .50
240 Kevin Johnson AS .15 .40
241 Shawn Kemp AS .15 .40
242 Karl Malone AS .20 .50
243 Danny Manning AS .12 .30
244 Hakeem Olajuwon AS .20 .50
245 Gary Payton AS .15 .40
246 Mitch Richmond AS .15 .40
247 Clifford Robinson AS .10 .25
248 David Robinson AS .25 .60
249 Latrell Sprewell AS .20 .50
250 John Stockton AS .20 .50
251 West Team .10 .25
252 Murray/Arm/Miller LL .10 .25
253 Stock/Bogues/Blay LL .10 .25
254 Mutombo/Olaj/D.Rob LL .15 .40
255 Rauf/Miller/Pierce LL .10 .25
256 Rodman/O'Neal/Willis LL .15 .40
257 D.Rob/O'Neal/Olaj LL .15 .40
258 McM/Pip/Blaylock LL .15 .40
259 Chris Webber AW .25 .60
260 Hakeem Olajuwon AW .20 .50
261 Hakeem Olajuwon AW .20 .50
262 Dell Curry AW .10 .25
263 Scottie Pippen AW .30 .75
264 Anfernee Hardaway AW .25 .60
265 Don MacLean AW .10 .25
266 Hakeem Olajuwon FIN .20 .50
267 Derek Harper FIN .12 .30
268 Sam Cassell FIN .15 .40
269 Hakeem Olajuwon TRIB .20 .50
270 P.Ewing/Olajuwon FIN .15 .40
271 Carl Herrera FIN .10 .25
272 Vernon Maxwell FIN .10 .25
273 Hakeem Olajuwon FIN .20 .50
274 Lenny Wilkens CO .15 .40
275 Chris Ford CO .10 .25
276 Allan Bristow CO .10 .25
277 Phil Jackson CO .15 .40
278 Mike Fratello CO .15 .40
279 Dick Motta CO .10 .25
280 Dan Issel CO .15 .40
281 Don Chaney CO .10 .25
282 Don Nelson CO .15 .40
283 Rudy Tomjanovich CO .15 .40
284 Larry Brown CO .15 .40

285 Del Harris CO UER .10 .25
286 Kevin Loughery CO .10 .25
287 Mike Dunleavy CO .10 .25
288 Sidney Lowe CO .10 .25
289 Pat Riley CO .15 .40
290 Brian Hill CO .10 .25
291 John Lucas CO .10 .25
292 Paul Westphal CO .10 .25
293 Garry St. Jean CO .10 .25
294 George Karl CO .15 .40
295 Jerry Sloan CO .15 .40
296 Magic Johnson COMM .40 1.00
297 Denzel Washington SPEC .15 .40
298 Checklist .10 .25
299 Checklist .10 .25
300 Checklist .10 .25
301 Sergei Bazarevich RC .15 .40
302 Tyrone Corbin .10 .25
303 Grant Long .10 .25
304 Ken Norman .10 .25
305 Steve Smith .12 .30
306 Blue Edwards .10 .25
307 Greg Minor RC .15 .40
308 Eric Montross RC .12 .30
309 Dominique Wilkins .20 .50
310 Michael Adams .10 .25
311 Darrin Hancock RC .12 .30
312 Robert Parish .15 .40
313 Ron Harper .12 .30
314 Dickey Simpkins RC .12 .30
315 Michael Cage .10 .25
316 Tony Dumas RC .15 .40
317 Jason Kidd RC .75 2.00
318 Roy Tarpley .10 .25
319 Dale Ellis .10 .25
320 Jalen Rose RC .40 1.00
321 Bill Curley RC .10 .25
322 Grant Hill RC .75 2.00
323 Oliver Miller .10 .25
324 Mark West .10 .25
325 Tom Gugliotta .10 .25
326 Ricky Pierce .10 .25
327 Carlos Rogers RC .12 .30
328 Clifford Rozier RC .10 .25
329 Rony Seikaly .10 .25
330 Tim Breaux .10 .25
331 Duane Ferrell .10 .25
332 Mark Jackson .12 .30
333 Lamond Murray RC .15 .40
334 Bo Outlaw RC .15 .40
335 Eric Piatkowski RC .20 .50
336 Pooh Richardson .10 .25
337 Malik Sealy .10 .25
338 Cedric Ceballos .10 .25
339 Eddie Jones RC .50 1.25
340 Anthony Miller RC .15 .40
341 Kevin Gamble .10 .25
342 Brad Lohaus .10 .25
343 Billy Owens .10 .25
344 Khalid Reeves RC .12 .30
345 Kevin Willis .10 .25
346 Eric Mobley RC .10 .25
347 Johnny Newman .10 .25
348 Ed Pinckney .10 .25
349 Glenn Robinson RC .30 .75
350 Howard Eisley RC .15 .40
351 Donyell Marshall RC .15 .40
352 Yinka Dare RC .10 .25
353 Charlie Ward RC .15 .40
354 Monty Williams RC .12 .30
355 Horace Grant .12 .30
356 Brian Shaw .10 .25
357 Brooks Thompson RC .12 .30
358 Derrick Alston RC .10 .25
359 B.J.Tyler RC .10 .25
360 Scott Williams .10 .25
361 Sharone Wright RC .12 .30
362 Antonio Lang RC .15 .40
363 Danny Manning .12 .30
364 Wesley Person RC .15 .40
365 Wayman Tisdale .10 .25
366 Trevor Ruffin RC .10 .25
367 Aaron McKie RC .15 .40
368 Brian Grant RC .25 .60
369 Michael Smith RC .10 .25
370 Sean Elliott .15 .40
371 Avery Johnson .12 .30
372 Chuck Person .12 .30
373 Bill Cartwright .12 .30
374 Sarunas Marciulionis .10 .25
375 Dontonio Wingfield RC .15 .40
376 Antoine Carr .10 .25
377 Jamie Watson RC .10 .25
378 Juwan Howard RC .25 .60
379 Jim McIlvaine RC .12 .30
380 Scott Skiles .10 .25
381 Anthony Tucker RC .10 .25
382 Chris Webber .25 .60
383 Bill Fitch CO .15 .40
384 Bill Blair CO .10 .25
385 Butch Beard CO .10 .25
386 P.J. Carlesimo CO .10 .25
387 Bob Hill CO .10 .25
388 Jim Lynam CO .10 .25
389 Checklist 4 .10 .25
390 Checklist 5 .10 .25
391 Atlanta Hawks TC .10 .25
392 Boston Celtics TC .10 .25
393 Charlotte Hornets TC .10 .25
394 Chicago Bulls TC .10 .25
395 Cleveland Cavaliers TC .10 .25
396 Dallas Mavericks TC .10 .25
397 Denver Nuggets TC .10 .25
398 Detroit Pistons TC .10 .25
399 Golden State Warriors TC .10 .25
400 Houston Rockets TC .10 .25
401 Indiana Pacers TC .10 .25
402 Los Angeles Clippers TC .10 .25
403 Los Angeles Lakers TC .10 .25
404 Miami Heat TC .10 .25
405 Milwaukee Bucks TC .10 .25
406 Minnesota Timberwolves TC .10 .25
407 New Jersey Nets TC .10 .25
408 New York Knicks TC .10 .25
409 Orlando Magic TC .10 .25
410 Philadelphia 76ers TC .10 .25
411 Phoenix Suns TC .10 .25
412 Portland Trail Blazers TC .10 .25
413 Sacramento Kings TC .10 .25
414 San Antonio Spurs TC .10 .25
415 Seattle Supersonics TC .10 .25
416 Utah Jazz TC .10 .25
417 Washington Bullets TC .10 .25
418 Toronto Raptors TC .10 .25
419 Vancouver Grizzlies TC .10 .25
420 NBA Logo Card .10 .25
421 G.Rob/C.Webber TOP .15 .40
422 J.Kidd/S.Bradley TOP .40 1.00
423 G.Hill/A.Hardaway TOP .40 1.00
424 D.Marshall/J.Mashburn TO .10 .25
425 J.Howard/I.Rider TOP .12 .30
426 S.Wright/C.Cheaney TOP .10 .25
427 L.Murray/B.Hurley TOP .10 .25
428 B.Grant/V.Baker TOP .12 .30
429 E.Montross/R.Rogers TOP .10 .25
430 E.Jones/L.Hunter TOP .25 .60
431 Craig Ehlo GM .10 .25
432 Dino Radja GM .10 .25
433 Toni Kukoc GM .20 .50
434 Mark Price GM .15 .40
435 Latrell Sprewell GM .20 .50
436 Sam Cassell GM .15 .40
437 Vernon Maxwell GM .10 .25
438 Haywoode Workman GM .10 .25
439 Harold Ellis GM .10 .25
440 Cedric Ceballos GM .10 .25
441 Vlade Divac GM .15 .40
442 Nick Van Exel GM .15 .40
443 John Starks GM .12 .30
444 Scott Williams GM .10 .25
445 Clifford Robinson GM .10 .25
446 Spud Webb GM .12 .30
447 Avery Johnson GM .12 .30
448 Dennis Rodman GM .30 .75
449 Sarunas Marciulionis GM .10 .25
450 Nate McMillan GM .10 .25
PR1 Grant Hill PROMO 4.00 10.00
NNO Shaq Sheet Wrap.Exch. AU 200.00 400.00
NNO G.Hill Wrapper Exch. 1.50 4.00
NNO Shaq Sheet Wrap.Exch. 15.00 30.00

1994-95 Hoops Big Numbers

Randomly inserted in first series hobby and retail foil packs at a rate of one in 30, this 12 standard-size set features color player action cutouts on their black horizontal and borderless fronts. The player's name and a number representing his Big Number accomplishment appear in silver-foil lettering offset to one side. The white horizontal back carries a color player head shot at the right, with a description of his Big Number accomplishment appearing alongside. The cards are numbered on the back with a "BN" prefix.

COMPLETE SET (12) 15.00 40.00
SER.1 STATED ODDS 1:30
*RAINBOW CARDS: EQUAL VALUE TO SILVER
ONE RAINBOW PER SER.1 RETAIL PACK
BN1 David Robinson 2.00 5.00
BN2 Jamal Mashburn 1.25 3.00
BN3 Hakeem Olajuwon 1.50 4.00
BN4 Patrick Ewing 1.50 4.00
BN5 Shaquille O'Neal 3.00 8.00
BN6 Latrell Sprewell 1.50 4.00
BN7 Chris Webber 2.00 5.00
BN8 Anfernee Hardaway 2.00 5.00
BN9 Scottie Pippen 2.50 6.00
BN10 Isaiah Rider 1.25 3.00
BN11 Alonzo Mourning 1.50 4.00
BN12 Charles Barkley 2.00 5.00

1994-95 Hoops Draft Redemption

For the third straight year, a redemption card was randomly inserted into first series packs at a rate of one in 360. The card could be sent in for this 11-card standard size set on or before the June 15th, 1995 deadline. The cards feature a full-color player photo cut out against a computer-generated background with a big number (corresponding to the player's draft selection) zooming out of the side. This set is sequenced in draft order.

COMPLETE SET (11) 8.00 20.00
EXCH.CARD: SER.1 STATED ODDS 1:360
1 Glenn Robinson 1.00 2.50
2 Jason Kidd 2.50 6.00
3 Grant Hill 2.50 6.00
4 Donyell Marshall .50 1.25
5 Juwan Howard .75 2.00
6 Sharone Wright .40 1.00
7 Lamond Murray .50 1.25
8 Brian Grant .75 2.00
9 Eric Montross .40 1.00
10 Eddie Jones 1.50 4.00
11 Carlos Rogers .40 1.00
NNO Expired Exch.Card .40 1.00

1994-95 Hoops Magic's All-Rookies

Randomly inserted into all second series packs (12-card hobby and retail packs at a rate of one in twelve, 24-card retail jumbo packs at an approximate rate of slightly greater than one per pack), cards from this 12-card standard-size set feature a selection of top rookies from the 1994-95 season. The fronts have a color action photo with different color backgrounds for each card with designs in them. The word "Magic's" is in the upper right corner and "All-Rookie" is three-dimensonally encompassing the player. The backs have a picture of Magic Johnson holding the card showing the front. On the left side it says "Magic's All-Rookie Team" and the their is player commentary at the bottom.

COMPLETE SET (10) 5.00 12.00
SER.2 STATED ODDS 1:12
*FOIL CARDS: 1.25X TO 3X HI COLUMN
FOIL SER.2 STATED ODDS 1:36
*JUMBO CARDS: .75X TO 2X HI COLUMN
JUMBO ONE PER SER.2 HOBBY BOX
AR1 Glenn Robinson .60 1.50
AR2 Jason Kidd 1.50 4.00
AR3 Grant Hill 1.50 4.00
AR4 Donyell Marshall .30 .75
AR5 Juwan Howard .50 1.25
AR6 Sharone Wright .25 .60
AR7 Brian Grant .50 1.25
AR8 Eddie Jones 1.00 2.50
AR9 Jalen Rose .75 2.00
AR10 Wesley Person .30 .75

1994-95 Hoops Power Ratings

Inserted one per pack into all second series packs, cards from this 54-card standard-size set feature a selection of the top players in the NBA. Cards feature a photo of the player silhouetted over flame-thrower graphics. Backs present a second photo and colorful bar chart of the players stats in seven key categories. Two players per team were included in this set.

COMPLETE SET (54) 3.00 8.00
ONE PER SERIES 2 PACK
PR1 Mookie Blaylock .12 .30
PR2 Stacey Augmon .15 .40
PR3 Dino Radja .12 .30
PR4 Dominique Wilkins .25 .60
PR5 Larry Johnson .20 .50
PR6 Alonzo Mourning .25 .60
PR7 Toni Kukoc .25 .60
PR8 Scottie Pippen .40 1.00
PR9 John Williams .12 .30
PR10 Mark Price .20 .50
PR11 Jim Jackson .12 .30
PR12 Jamal Mashburn .20 .50
PR13 Dale Ellis .12 .30
PR14 LaPhonso Ellis .12 .30
PR15 Joe Dumars .20 .50
PR16 Lindsey Hunter .12 .30
PR17 Latrell Sprewell .25 .60
PR18 Chris Mullin .20 .50
PR19 Vernon Maxwell .12 .30
PR20 Hakeem Olajuwon .25 .60
PR21 Mark Jackson .15 .40
PR22 Reggie Miller .25 .60
PR23 Pooh Richardson .12 .30
PR24 Loy Vaught .12 .30
PR25 Vlade Divac .20 .50
PR26 Nick Van Exel .20 .50
PR27 Glen Rice .20 .50
PR28 Billy Owens .12 .30
PR29 Vin Baker .20 .50
PR30 Eric Murdock .12 .30
PR31 Christian Laettner .15 .40
PR32 Isaiah Rider .20 .50
PR33 Kenny Anderson .15 .40
PR34 Derrick Coleman .15 .40
PR35 Patrick Ewing .25 .60
PR36 John Starks .15 .40
PR37 Nick Anderson .12 .30
PR38 Anfernee Hardaway .30 .75
PR39 Shawn Bradley .12 .30
PR40 Clarence Weatherspoon .12 .30
PR41 Charles Barkley .30 .75
PR42 Kevin Johnson .20 .50
PR43 Clyde Drexler .25 .60
PR44 Clifford Robinson .12 .30
PR45 Mitch Richmond .20 .50
PR46 Olden Polynice .12 .30
PR47 Sean Elliott .20 .50
PR48 Chuck Person .15 .40
PR49 Shawn Kemp .20 .50
PR50 Gary Payton .20 .50
PR51 Jeff Hornacek .15 .40
PR52 Karl Malone .25 .60
PR53 Rex Chapman .12 .30
PR54 Don MacLean .12 .30

1994-95 Hoops Predators

Randomly inserted into all second series packs (one in every twelve 12-card packs and two per 24-card jumbo pack), cards from this 8-card standard-size set feature eight league leaders from the 1993-94 season. Design is very similar to the Power Ratings inserts. The set is sequenced in alphabetical order. There was also a Jumbo card of the David Robinson Predator inserted into Series 2 Sam's boxes. That card is listed below at the end of the set.

COMPLETE SET (8) 1.25 3.00
SER.2 STATED ODDS 1:12
P1 Mahmoud Abdul-Rauf .20 .50
P2 Dikembe Mutombo .30 .75
P3 Shaquille O'Neal .75 2.00
P4 Tracy Murray .20 .50
P5 David Robinson .50 1.25
P6 Dennis Rodman .60 1.50
P7 Nate McMillan .20 .50
P8 John Stockton .40 1.00
NNO David Robinson Jumbo .40 1.00

1994-95 Hoops Supreme Court

Randomly inserted in first series hobby and retail packs at a rate of one in four, the 50 standard-size parallel cards comprising the '94-95 Hoops Supreme Court set feature a selection of the top stars within the basic issue first series Hoops set. Unlike the regular issue cards, each Supreme Court insert features a special embossed gold-foil logo on the card front. The cards are also numbered on the back with an "SC" prefix.player head shot at the upper left, with the player's name and brief biography appearing alongside to the right. Statistics and career highlights follow below. The cards are numbered on the back with an "SC" prefix.

COMPLETE SET (50) 8.00 20.00
SER.1 STATED ODDS 1:4
SC1 Mookie Blaylock .15 .40
SC2 Danny Manning .20 .50
SC3 Dino Radja .15 .40
SC4 Larry Johnson .25 .60
SC5 Alonzo Mourning .30 .75
SC6 B.J. Armstrong .15 .40
SC7 Horace Grant .20 .50
SC8 Toni Kukoc .30 .75
SC9 Brad Daugherty .20 .50
SC10 Mark Price .25 .60
SC11 Jim Jackson .15 .40
SC12 Jamal Mashburn .25 .60
SC13 Dikembe Mutombo .25 .60
SC14 Joe Dumars .25 .60
SC15 Lindsey Hunter .15 .40
SC16 Tim Hardaway .25 .60
SC17 Chris Mullin .25 .60
SC18 Sam Cassell .25 .60
SC19 Hakeem Olajuwon .30 .75
SC20 Reggie Miller .30 .75
SC21 Dominique Wilkins .30 .75
SC22 Nick Van Exel .25 .60
SC23 Harold Miner .15 .40
SC24 Steve Smith .20 .50
SC25 Vin Baker .25 .60
SC26 Christian Laettner .20 .50
SC27 Isaiah Rider .25 .60
SC28 Kenny Anderson .20 .50
SC29 Derrick Coleman .20 .50
SC30 Patrick Ewing .30 .75
SC31 John Starks .20 .50
SC32 Anfernee Hardaway .40 1.00
SC33 Shaquille O'Neal .60 1.50
SC34 Shawn Bradley .15 .40
SC35 Clarence Weatherspoon .15 .40
SC36 Charles Barkley .40 1.00
SC37 Kevin Johnson .25 .60
SC38 Oliver Miller .15 .40
SC39 Clyde Drexler .30 .75
SC40 Clifford Robinson .15 .40
SC41 Mitch Richmond .25 .60
SC42 Bobby Hurley .15 .40
SC43 David Robinson .40 1.00
SC44 Dennis Rodman .50 1.25
SC45 Gary Payton .25 .60
SC46 Shawn Kemp .25 .60
SC47 John Stockton .30 .75
SC48 Karl Malone .30 .75
SC49 Calbert Cheaney .15 .40
SC50 Tom Gugliotta .15 .40

1995-96 Hoops National Promos

A cello pack containing these standard-size promo cards was given away at the SkyBox booth during the 16th National Sports Collectors Convention in St. Louis. The set consists of two regular issue cards (2, 6) and four subset cards (1, 3-5). They are identical to their regular issue counterparts except for the absence of numbering. The cards are checklisted below in alphabetical order.

COMPLETE SET (7) 1.25 3.00
1 Kenny Anderson .25 .60
2 Vin Baker .25 .60
3 A.C. Green .25 .60
4 Jason Kidd .50 1.25
5 Glen Rice .30 .75
6 Rony Seikaly .20 .50
7 Title Card .20 .50

1995-96 Hoops Promo Sheet 1

Measuring 7" by 10 1/2", this promo sheet was issued to preview the first series of the 1995-96 Hoops set. The perforated sheet consists of six cards, with an advertisement on a strip attached to the left edge. The cards are identical their regular issue counterparts except that the card numbers have been omitted. With the exception of the Majerle card, the rest of the cards are from insert sets. The cards are priced individually due to the high number of sheets torn apart.

COMPLETE SET (6) 1.25 3.00
1 Eddie Jones .40 1.00
2 Detlef Schrempf .40 1.00
3 Dan Majerle .40 1.00
4 Juwan Howard .40 1.00
5 Larry Johnson .40 1.00
6 Scott Burrell .25 .60

1995-96 Hoops Promo Sheet 2

Measuring 7" by 10 1/2", this promo sheet was issued to preview the second series of the 1995-96 Hoops set. The perforated sheet consists of six cards, with an advertisement on a strip attached to the left edge. The cards are identical their regular issue counterparts except that the card numbers have been omitted. The cards are priced individually due to the high number of sheets torn apart.

COMPLETE SET (6) 2.00 5.00
1 Anfernee Hardaway .60 1.50
2 John Stockton .50 1.25
3 Antonio McDyess .50 1.25
4 Charles Barkley .60 1.50
5 John Salley .25 .60
6 Glenn Robinson .30 .75

1995-96 Hoops

The 1995-96 Hoops basketball set was issued in two series of 250 and 150 standard-size cards respectively for a total of 400. Series one cards were issued in 12-card hobby and retail packs (SRP $1.29) and 20-card retail jumbo packs (SRP $1.99). Series two cards were issued in 8-card hobby and retail packs for $.99 each. Fronts have a full-color action photo with the player's name in gold foil surrounded by his team's color. The backs have a color photo with pro and college career statitistics. Cards are grouped alphabetically within teams. The following subsets are featured: Coaches (171-197), Sizzlin' Sophs (198-207), Milestones (208-217), Buzzer Beaters (218-227), Pipeline (228-232), Class Acts (233-242), Triple Threats (243-247), Player/Coach Updates (291-333), Coaches (334-337), Expansion Teams (338-357), Earthshakers (358-372), Rock/House (373-387) and Wicked Dishes (388-397). A special Grant Hill Tribute card, featuring a clear acetate center, was randomly inserted into one in every 360 series one packs. All insert cards feature 3-D technology. A pair of Grant Hill 3-D glasses was available by sending in two first series wrappers and a check or money order for $3.50. In addition, a limited edition Grant Hill Commemorative Co-Rookie of the Year card was available by sending in a check or money order for $9.95 plus two series one wrappers. Both promotions were detailed on first series wrappers and both expired December 31, 1995. Rookie Cards of note in this set include Michael Finley, Kevin Garnett, Antonio McDyess, Joe Smith, Jerry Stackhouse and Damon Stoudamire.

COMPLETE SET (400) 15.00 40.00
COMPLETE SERIES 1 (250) 10.00 25.00
COMPLETE SERIES 2 (150) 6.00 15.00
SUBSET CARDS SAME VALUE AS BASE CARDS
HILL TRIB: SER.1 STATED ODDS 1:360
1 Stacey Augmon .12 .30
2 Mookie Blaylock .10 .25
3 Craig Ehlo .10 .25
4 Andrew Lang .10 .25
5 Grant Long .10 .25
6 Ken Norman .10 .25
7 Steve Smith .12 .30
8 Dee Brown .10 .25
9 Sherman Douglas .10 .25
10 Pervis Ellison .10 .25
11 Eric Montross .10 .25
12 Dino Radja .10 .25
13 Dominique Wilkins .20 .50
14 Muggsy Bogues .12 .30
15 Scott Burrell .10 .25
16 Dell Curry .10 .25
17 Hersey Hawkins .10 .25
18 Larry Johnson .15 .40
19 Alonzo Mourning .20 .50
20 B.J. Armstrong .10 .25
21 Michael Jordan 1.25 3.00
22 Toni Kukoc .15 .40
23 Will Perdue .10 .25
24 Scottie Pippen .25 .60
25 Dickey Simpkins .10 .25
26 Terrell Brandon .10 .25
27 Tyrone Hill .10 .25
28 Chris Mills .10 .25
29 Bobby Phills .10 .25
30 Mark Price .15 .40
31 John Williams .10 .25
32 Tony Dumas .10 .25
33 Jim Jackson .10 .25
34 Popeye Jones .10 .25
35 Jason Kidd .25 .60
36 Jamal Mashburn .15 .40
37 Roy Tarpley .10 .25
38 Mahmoud Abdul-Rauf .10 .25
39 LaPhonso Ellis .10 .25
40 Dikembe Mutombo .15 .40
41 Robert Pack .10 .25
42 Rodney Rogers .10 .25
43 Jalen Rose .20 .50
44 Bryant Stith .10 .25
45 Joe Dumars .15 .40
46 Grant Hill .25 .60
47 Allan Houston .12 .30
48 Lindsey Hunter .10 .25
49 Oliver Miller .10 .25
50 Terry Mills .10 .25
51 Chris Gatling .10 .25
52 Tim Hardaway .15 .40
53 Donyell Marshall .10 .25
54 Chris Mullin .15 .40
55 Carlos Rogers .10 .25
56 Clifford Rozier .10 .25
57 Rony Seikaly .10 .25
58 Latrell Sprewell .15 .40
59 Sam Cassell .15 .40
60 Clyde Drexler .20 .50
61 Robert Horry .12 .30
62 Vernon Maxwell .10 .25
63 Hakeem Olajuwon .20 .50
64 Kenny Smith .12 .30
65 Dale Davis .10 .25
66 Mark Jackson .12 .30
67 Derrick McKey .10 .25
68 Reggie Miller .20 .50
69 Byron Scott .12 .30
70 Rik Smits .12 .30
71 Terry Dehere .10 .25
72 Lamond Murray .10 .25
73 Eric Piatkowski .12 .30
74 Pooh Richardson .10 .25
75 Malik Sealy .10 .25
76 Loy Vaught .10 .25
77 Elden Campbell .10 .25
78 Cedric Ceballos .10 .25
79 Vlade Divac .15 .40
80 Eddie Jones .15 .40
81 Sedale Threatt .10 .25
82 Nick Van Exel .15 .40
83 Bimbo Coles .10 .25
84 Harold Miner .10 .25
85 Billy Owens .10 .25
86 Khalid Reeves .10 .25
87 Glen Rice .15 .40
88 Kevin Willis .10 .25
89 Vin Baker .12 .30
90 Marty Conlon .10 .25
91 Todd Day .10 .25
92 Eric Mobley .10 .25
93 Eric Murdock .10 .25
94 Glenn Robinson .12 .30
95 Winston Garland .10 .25
96 Tom Gugliotta .10 .25
97 Christian Laettner .12 .30
98 Isaiah Rider .15 .40
99 Sean Rooks .10 .25
100 Doug West .10 .25
101 Kenny Anderson .12 .30
102 Benoit Benjamin .10 .25
103 Derrick Coleman .12 .30
104 Kevin Edwards .10 .25
105 Armon Gilliam .10 .25
106 Chris Morris .10 .25
107 Patrick Ewing .20 .50
108 Derek Harper .12 .30
109 Anthony Mason .10 .25
110 Charles Oakley .12 .30
111 Charles Smith .10 .25
112 John Starks .12 .30
113 Monty Williams .10 .25
114 Nick Anderson .10 .25
115 Horace Grant .12 .30
116 Anfernee Hardaway .25 .60
117 Shaquille O'Neal .40 1.00
118 Dennis Scott .10 .25
119 Brian Shaw .10 .25
120 Dana Barros .10 .25
121 Shawn Bradley .10 .25
122 Willie Burton .10 .25
123 Jeff Malone .10 .25
124 Clarence Weatherspoon .10 .25
125 Sharone Wright .10 .25
126 Charles Barkley .25 .60
127 A.C. Green .12 .30
128 Kevin Johnson .15 .40
129 Dan Majerle .15 .40
130 Danny Manning .12 .30
131 Elliot Perry .10 .25
132 Wesley Person .10 .25
133 Chris Dudley .10 .25
134 Clifford Robinson .10 .25
135 James Robinson .10 .25
136 Rod Strickland .10 .25
137 Otis Thorpe .10 .25
138 Buck Williams .10 .25
139 Brian Grant .12 .30
140 Olden Polynice .10 .25
141 Mitch Richmond .15 .40
142 Michael Smith .10 .25
143 Spud Webb .12 .30
144 Walt Williams .10 .25
145 Vinny Del Negro .10 .25
146 Sean Elliott .15 .40
147 Avery Johnson .12 .30
148 Chuck Person .12 .30
149 David Robinson .25 .60
150 Dennis Rodman .30 .75
151 Kendall Gill .10 .25
152 Ervin Johnson .10 .25
153 Shawn Kemp .15 .40
154 Nate McMillan .10 .25
155 Gary Payton .15 .40
156 Detlef Schrempf .15 .40
157 Dontonio Wingfield .10 .25
158 David Benoit .10 .25
159 Jeff Hornacek .12 .30
160 Karl Malone .20 .50
161 Felton Spencer .10 .25
162 John Stockton .20 .50
163 Jamie Watson .10 .25
164 Rex Chapman .10 .25
165 Calbert Cheaney .10 .25
166 Juwan Howard .15 .40
167 Don MacLean .10 .25
168 Gheorghe Muresan .10 .25
169 Scott Skiles .10 .25
170 Chris Webber .20 .50
171 Lenny Wilkens CO .12 .30
172 Allan Bristow CO .10 .25
173 Phil Jackson CO .15 .40
174 Mike Fratello CO .10 .30
175 Dick Motta CO .10 .25
176 Bernie Bickerstaff CO .10 .25
177 Doug Collins CO .10 .25
178 Rick Adelman CO .10 .25
179 Rudy Tomjanovich CO .12 .30
180 Larry Brown CO .12 .30
181 Bill Fitch CO .10 .25
182 Del Harris CO .10 .25
183 Mike Dunleavy CO .10 .25
184 Bill Blair CO .10 .25
185 Butch Beard CO .10 .25
186 Pat Riley CO .15 .40
187 Brian Hill CO .10 .25
188 John Lucas CO .12 .30
189 Paul Westphal CO .10 .25
190 P.J. Carlesimo CO .10 .25
191 Garry St. Jean CO .10 .25
192 Bob Hill CO .10 .25
193 George Karl CO .12 .30
194 Brendan Malone CO .10 .25
195 Jerry Sloan CO .12 .30
196 Kevin Pritchard CO .10 .25
197 Jim Lynam CO .10 .25
198 Brian Grant SS .12 .30
199 Grant Hill SS .25 .60
200 Juwan Howard SS .15 .40
201 Eddie Jones SS .15 .40
202 Jason Kidd SS .25 .60
203 Donyell Marshall SS .10 .25
204 Eric Montross SS .10 .25
205 Glenn Robinson SS .12 .30
206 Jalen Rose SS .20 .50
207 Sharone Wright SS .10 .25
208 Dana Barros MS .10 .25
209 Joe Dumars MS .15 .40
210 A.C. Green MS .12 .30
211 Grant Hill MS .25 .60
212 Karl Malone MS .20 .50
213 Reggie Miller MS .20 .50
214 Glen Rice MS .15 .40
215 John Stockton MS .20 .50
216 Lenny Wilkens MS .12 .30
217 Dominique Wilkins MS .20 .50
218 Kenny Anderson BB .12 .30
219 Mookie Blaylock BB .10 .25
220 Larry Johnson BB .15 .40
221 Shawn Kemp BB .15 .40
222 Toni Kukoc BB .15 .40
223 Jamal Mashburn BB .15 .40
224 Glen Rice BB .15 .40
225 Mitch Richmond BB .15 .40
226 Latrell Sprewell BB .15 .40
227 Rod Strickland BB .10 .25
228 M.Adams/D.Martin PL .10 .25
229 C.Ehlo/J.Harmon PL .10 .25
230 M.Elie/G.McCloud PL .10 .25
231 A.Mason/C.Brown PL .10 .25
232 J.Starks/T.Legler PL .12 .30
233 Muggsy Bogues CA .12 .30
234 Joe Dumars CA .15 .40
235 LaPhonso Ellis CA .10 .25
236 Patrick Ewing CA .20 .50
237 Grant Hill CA .25 .60
238 Kevin Johnson CA .15 .40
239 Dan Majerle CA .15 .40
240 Karl Malone CA .20 .50
241 Hakeem Olajuwon CA .20 .50
242 David Robinson CA .25 .60
243 Dana Barros TT .10 .25
244 Scott Burrell TT .10 .25
245 Reggie Miller TT .20 .50
246 Glen Rice TT .15 .40
247 John Stockton TT .20 .50
248 Checklist #1 .10 .25
249 Checklist #2 .10 .25
250 Checklist #3 .10 .25
251 Alan Henderson RC .15 .40
252 Junior Burrough RC .15 .40
253 Eric Williams RC .15 .40
254 George Zidek RC .12 .30
255 Jason Caffey RC .15 .40
256 Donny Marshall RC .15 .40
257 Bob Sura RC .12 .30
258 Loren Meyer RC .10 .25
259 Cherokee Parks RC .12 .30
260 Antonio McDyess RC .20 .50
261 Theo Ratliff RC .25 .60
262 Lou Roe RC .15 .40
263 Andrew DeClercq RC .15 .40
264 Joe Smith RC .20 .50
265 Travis Best RC .15 .40
266 Brent Barry RC .25 .60
267 Frankie King RC .15 .40
268 Sasha Danilovic RC .15 .40
269 Kurt Thomas RC .15 .40
270 Shawn Respert RC .12 .30
271 Jerome Allen RC .15 .40
272 Kevin Garnett RC 1.25 3.00
273 Ed O'Bannon RC .12 .30
274 David Vaughn RC .15 .40
275 Jerry Stackhouse RC .50 1.25
276 Mario Bennett RC .12 .30
277 Michael Finley RC .50 1.25
278 Randolph Childress RC .12 .30
279 Arvydas Sabonis RC .30 .75
280 Gary Trent RC .15 .40
281 Tyus Edney RC .15 .40
282 Corliss Williamson RC .15 .40
283 Cory Alexander RC .15 .40
284 Sherrell Ford RC .12 .30
285 Jimmy King RC .15 .40
286 Damon Stoudamire RC .40 1.00
287 Greg Ostertag RC .15 .40
288 Lawrence Moten RC .15 .40
289 Bryant Reeves RC .12 .30
290 Rasheed Wallace RC .50 1.25
291 Spud Webb .12 .30
292 Dana Barros .10 .25
293 Rick Fox .10 .25
294 Kendall Gill .10 .25
295 Khalid Reeves .10 .25
296 Glen Rice .15 .40
297 Luc Longley .12 .30
298 Dennis Rodman .30 .75
299 Dan Majerle .15 .40
300 Lorenzo Williams .10 .25
301 Dale Ellis .10 .25
302 Reggie Williams .10 .25
303 Otis Thorpe .10 .25
304 B.J. Armstrong .10 .25
305 Pete Chilcutt .10 .25
306 Mario Elie .10 .25
307 Antonio Davis .10 .25
308 Ricky Pierce .10 .25
309 Rodney Rogers .10 .25
310 Brian Williams .10 .25
311 Corie Blount .10 .25
312 George Lynch .10 .25
313 Alonzo Mourning .20 .50
314 Lee Mayberry .10 .25
315 Terry Porter .10 .25
316 P.J. Brown .10 .25
317 Hubert Davis .10 .25
318 Charlie Ward .10 .25
319 Jon Koncak .10 .25
320 Derrick Coleman .12 .30
321 Richard Dumas .10 .25
322 Vernon Maxwell .10 .25
323 Wayman Tisdale .10 .25
324 Dontonio Wingfield .10 .25
325 Tyrone Corbin .10 .25
326 Bobby Hurley .10 .25
327 Will Perdue .10 .25
328 J.R. Reid .10 .25
329 Hersey Hawkins .10 .25
330 Sam Perkins .10 .25
331 Adam Keefe .10 .25
332 Chris Morris .10 .25
333 Robert Pack .10 .25
334 M.L. Carr CO .10 .25
335 Pat Riley CO .15 .40
336 Don Nelson CO .12 .30
337 Brian Winters CO .10 .25
338 Willie Anderson ET .10 .25
339 Acie Earl ET .10 .25
340 Jimmy King ET .10 .25
341 Oliver Miller ET .10 .25
342 Tracy Murray ET .10 .25
343 Ed Pinckney ET .10 .25
344 Alvin Robertson ET .10 .25
345 Carlos Rogers ET .10 .25
346 John Salley ET .10 .25
347 Damon Stoudamire ET .25 .60
348 Zan Tabak ET .10 .25
349 Greg Anthony ET .10 .25
350 Blue Edwards ET .10 .25
351 Kenny Gattison ET .10 .25
352 Antonio Harvey ET .10 .25
353 Chris King ET .10 .25
354 Darrick Martin ET .10 .25
355 Lawrence Moten ET .10 .25
356 Bryant Reeves ET .07 .20
357 Byron Scott ET .12 .30
358 Michael Jordan ES 1.25 3.00
359 Dikembe Mutombo ES .15 .40
360 Grant Hill ES .25 .60
361 Robert Horry ES .12 .30
362 Alonzo Mourning ES .20 .50
363 Vin Baker ES .12 .30
364 Isaiah Rider ES .15 .40
365 Charles Oakley ES .12 .30
366 Shaquille O'Neal ES .40 1.00
367 Jerry Stackhouse ES .30 .75
368 Clarence Weatherspoon ES .10 .25
369 Charles Barkley ES .25 .60
370 Sean Elliott ES .15 .40
371 Shawn Kemp ES .15 .40
372 Chris Webber ES .20 .50
373 Spud Webb RH .12 .30
374 Muggsy Bogues RH .12 .30
375 Toni Kukoc RH .15 .40
376 Dennis Rodman RH .30 .75
377 Jamal Mashburn RH .15 .40
378 Jalen Rose RH .20 .50
379 Clyde Drexler RH .20 .50
380 Mark Jackson RH .12 .30
381 Cedric Ceballos RH .10 .25
382 Nick Van Exel RH .15 .40
383 John Starks RH .12 .30
384 Vernon Maxwell RH .10 .25
385 Shawn Kemp RH .15 .40
386 Gary Payton RH .15 .40
387 Karl Malone RH .20 .50
388 Mookie Blaylock WD .10 .25
389 Muggsy Bogues WD .12 .30
390 Jason Kidd WD .25 .60
391 Tim Hardaway WD .15 .40
392 Nick Van Exel WD .15 .40
393 Kenny Anderson WD .12 .30
394 Anfernee Hardaway WD .25 .60
395 Rod Strickland WD .10 .25
396 Avery Johnson WD .12 .30
397 John Stockton WD .20 .50
398 Grant Hill SPEC .25 .60
399 Checklist (251-367) .10 .25
400 Checklist (368-400/Ins.) .10 .25
NNO G.Hill Co-ROY 5.00 12.00
NNO G.Hill Sweepstakes .30 .75
NNO G.Hill Tribute 10.00 25.00

1995-96 Hoops Block Party

Randomly inserted into all first series packs at an approximate rate of one in two packs, these 25 standard-size cards highlight the top shot-blockers in the NBA. The fronts have a full-color action photo with a multi-colored, computer-generated background and the words "Block Party" at the top in gold-foil. The backs have a color photo on the left side with a similar background to the front with player information and statistics on the right.

COMPLETE SET (25) 3.00 8.00
SER.1 STATED ODDS 1:2 HOBBY/RETAIL
1 Oliver Miller .20 .50
2 Dennis Rodman .60 1.50
3 Scottie Pippen .50 1.25
4 Dikembe Mutombo .30 .75
5 Vlade Divac .30 .75
6 Brian Grant .25 .60
7 Alonzo Mourning .40 1.00
8 Hakeem Olajuwon .40 1.00
9 Patrick Ewing .40 1.00
10 Shawn Kemp .30 .75
11 Vin Baker .25 .60
12 Horace Grant .25 .60
13 Dale Davis .20 .50
14 Juwan Howard .30 .75
15 Eddie Jones .30 .75
16 Eric Montross .20 .50
17 Tyrone Hill .20 .50
18 Tom Gugliotta .20 .50
19 Shawn Bradley .20 .50
20 Dan Majerle .30 .75
21 Loy Vaught .20 .50
22 Donyell Marshall .20 .50
23 Chris Webber .40 1.00
24 Derrick Coleman .25 .60
25 Walt Williams .20 .50

1995-96 Hoops Grant Hill Dunks/Slams

Cards D1-D5 were randomly inserted exclusively into one in every 36 first series 12-card hobby packs, while cards S1-S5 were randomly inserted exclusively into one in every 36 first series retail 12-card packs. All cards are foil-coated, featuring an assortion of Grant Hill dunking and slamming photos. The fronts each carry an oversized letter, so that cards D1-D5 spell out "DUNK!!!," and cards S1-S5 spell out "SLAM!". All cards are designed to be viewed through special Grant Hill 3-D glasses which were available through an on-wrapper offer.

COMPLETE SET (10) 10.00 20.00
COMPLETE DUNKS SET (5) 5.00 12.00
COMPLETE SLAMS SET (5) 5.00 12.00
COMMON DUNK/SLAM (D1-D5) 1.50 4.00
DUNK: SER.1 STATED ODDS 1:36 RETAIL
SLAM: SER.1 STATED ODDS 1:36 HOBBY

1995-96 Hoops Grant's All-Rookies

Randomly inserted in all second series packs at a rate of one in 64, this 10-card standard-size set continues the tradition of the Magic's All-Rookies sets featured in earlier Hoops products. New spokesperson Grant Hill replaces Magic Johnson, picking 10 players who may follow in his own footsteps. Hill is pictured alongside the featured rookie on the horizontal fronts. The left side of the card contains a silver hologram strip with "Top 10" cut out to give the card a 3-D look when viewed with the Grant Hill 3-D glasses. Backs carry another full color cutout shot of the player set against the borderless color background. The "Top 10" logo is once again placed on the back. The player's name is printed across the top in gold and a player profile is printed in white. The set is sequenced in alphabetical order by team.

COMPLETE SET (10) 20.00 50.00
SER.2 STATED ODDS 1:64 HOBBY/RETAIL
AR1 Cherokee Parks .60 1.50
AR2 Antonio McDyess 1.00 2.50
AR3 Theo Ratliff 1.25 3.00
AR4 Joe Smith 1.00 2.50
AR5 Shawn Respert .60 1.50
AR6 Kevin Garnett 6.00 15.00
AR7 Ed O'Bannon .60 1.50
AR8 Jerry Stackhouse 2.50 6.00
AR9 Damon Stoudamire 2.00 5.00
AR10 Rasheed Wallace 2.50 6.00

1995-96 Hoops HoopStars

Randomly inserted in all second series packs at a rate of one in 16, this 12-card standard-size set presents top players on multi-colored cards featuring color foils for the HoopStars logo and player name. The set is sequenced in alphabetical order by team.

COMPLETE SET (12) 6.00 15.00
SER.2 STATED ODDS 1:16 HOBBY/RETAIL
HS1 Scottie Pippen 1.25 3.00
HS2 Jim Jackson .50 1.25
HS3 Antonio McDyess .50 1.25
HS4 Clyde Drexler 1.00 2.50
HS5 Alonzo Mourning 1.00 2.50
HS6 Glenn Robinson .60 1.50
HS7 Patrick Ewing 1.00 2.50
HS8 Anfernee Hardaway 1.25 3.00
HS9 Shawn Kemp .75 2.00
HS10 Karl Malone 1.00 2.50
HS11 Juwan Howard .75 2.00
HS12 Rasheed Wallace 1.25 3.00

1995-96 Hoops Hot List

Randomly inserted in second series hobby packs only at a rate of one in 32, this 10-card standard-size set features full-bleed fronts with a full-color player cutout set against a blue foil background. Player's name is printed vertically in copper foil on a purple foil strip. HOT is printed diagonally across the front. Backs feature a full-color action shot with the player's stats printed below the photo. The set is sequenced in alphabetical order by team.

COMPLETE SET (10) 15.00 40.00
SER.2 STATED ODDS 1:32 HOBBY
1 Michael Jordan 12.00 30.00
2 Jason Kidd 2.00 5.00
3 Jamal Mashburn 1.25 3.00
4 Grant Hill 2.00 5.00
5 Joe Smith .75 2.00
6 Hakeem Olajuwon 1.50 4.00
7 Glenn Robinson 1.00 2.50
8 Shaquille O'Neal 4.00 10.00
9 Jerry Stackhouse 2.00 5.00
10 David Robinson 2.00 5.00

1995-96 Hoops Number Crunchers

Randomly inserted into all first series packs at an approximate rate of one in two packs, these 25 standard-size cards highlight players that attained notable statistical achievements during the 1994-95 season. The fronts have a color-action photo with the player's number in a multi-color background and the word "Crunchers" spelled out on a tic-tac-toe board in the lower left corner in gold-foil. The backs have a color-action photo with a huge multi-colored ball in the background along with player information and statistics.

COMPLETE SET (25) 4.00 10.00
SER.1 STATED ODDS 1:2 HOBBY/RETAIL
1 Michael Jordan 2.00 5.00
2 Shaquille O'Neal .50 1.25
3 Grant Hill .30 .75
4 Detlef Schrempf .20 .50
5 Kenny Anderson .15 .40
6 Anfernee Hardaway .30 .75
7 Latrell Sprewell .20 .50
8 Jamal Mashburn .20 .50
9 Nick Van Exel .20 .50
10 Charles Barkley .30 .75
11 Mitch Richmond .20 .50
12 David Robinson .30 .75
13 Gary Payton .20 .50
14 Rod Strickland .12 .30
15 Glenn Robinson .15 .40
16 Reggie Miller .25 .60
17 Karl Malone .25 .60
18 Jim Jackson .12 .30
19 Clyde Drexler .25 .60
20 Glen Rice .20 .50
21 Isaiah Rider .20 .50
22 Cedric Ceballos .12 .30
23 John Stockton .25 .60
24 Jason Kidd .30 .75
25 Mookie Blaylock .12 .30

1995-96 Hoops Power Palette

Randomly inserted in second series retail packs only at a rate of one in 32, this 10-card set is a parallel version of the Hoops SkyView insert. Unlike the acetate-centered SkyView cards, the more common Power Palette's feature metallic foil backgrounds.

COMPLETE SET (10) 15.00 40.00
SER.2 STATED ODDS 1:32 RETAIL
1 Michael Jordan 12.00 30.00
2 Jason Kidd 1.50 4.00
3 Grant Hill 1.50 4.00
4 Joe Smith 1.25 3.00
5 Hakeem Olajuwon 1.25 3.00
6 Glenn Robinson .75 2.00
7 Anfernee Hardaway 1.50 4.00
8 Shaquille O'Neal 2.50 6.00
9 Jerry Stackhouse 3.00 8.00
10 Charles Barkley 1.50 4.00

1995-96 Hoops SkyView

Randomly inserted in all second series packs at a rate of one in 480, cards from this 10-card standard-size set are extra-thick and replace two basic issue cards in the pack. The front of the card presents a die-cut action photo over a multi-color plastic acetate window. The set is sequenced in alphabetical order by team.

COMPLETE SET (10) 75.00 200.00
SER.2 STATED ODDS 1:480 HOBBY/RETAIL
SV1 Michael Jordan 60.00 150.00
SV2 Jason Kidd 4.00 10.00
SV3 Grant Hill 4.00 10.00
SV4 Joe Smith 3.00 8.00
SV5 Hakeem Olajuwon 3.00 8.00
SV6 Glenn Robinson 2.00 5.00
SV7 Anfernee Hardaway 12.00 30.00
SV8 Shaquille O'Neal 6.00 15.00
SV9 Jerry Stackhouse 6.00 15.00
SV10 Charles Barkley 4.00 10.00

1995-96 Hoops Slamland

Inserted into all second series packs at a rate of one per pack, cards from this 50-card standard-size set showcase top stars printed over one of five different animated "Slamland" backgrounds. The card fronts feature the player's name, area of expertise and a distinctive foil-stamped Slamland designation. The set is sequenced in alphabetical order by team.

COMPLETE SET (50) 3.00 8.00
ONE PER SER.2 PACK
SL1 Stacey Augmon .12 .30
SL2 Steve Smith .12 .30
SL3 Eric Montross .10 .25
SL4 Dino Radja .10 .25
SL5 Dell Curry .10 .25
SL6 Larry Johnson .15 .40
SL7 Scottie Pippen .25 .60
SL8 Dennis Rodman .30 .75
SL9 Tyrone Hill .10 .25
SL10 Jim Jackson .10 .25
SL11 Jamal Mashburn .15 .40
SL12 Dikembe Mutombo .15 .40
SL13 Joe Dumars .15 .40
SL14 Grant Hill .25 .60
SL15 Allan Houston .12 .30
SL16 Donyell Marshall .10 .25
SL17 Latrell Sprewell .15 .40
SL18 Sam Cassell .15 .40
SL19 Hakeem Olajuwon .20 .50
SL20 Reggie Miller .20 .50
SL21 Loy Vaught .10 .25
SL22 Vlade Divac .15 .40
SL23 Eddie Jones .15 .40
SL24 Alonzo Mourning .20 .50
SL25 Kevin Willis .10 .25
SL26 Vin Baker .12 .30
SL27 Glenn Robinson .12 .30
SL28 Tom Gugliotta .10 .25
SL29 Kenny Anderson .12 .30
SL30 Derrick Coleman .12 .30
SL31 Patrick Ewing .20 .50
SL32 John Starks .12 .30
SL33 Dennis Scott .10 .25
SL34 Jerry Stackhouse .50 1.25
SL35 Charles Barkley .25 .60
SL36 Kevin Johnson .15 .40
SL37 Danny Manning .12 .30
SL38 Clifford Robinson .10 .25
SL39 Brian Grant .12 .30
SL40 Mitch Richmond .15 .40
SL41 Walt Williams .10 .25
SL42 David Robinson .25 .60
SL43 Gary Payton .15 .40
SL44 Detlef Schrempf .15 .40
SL45 Damon Stoudamire .40 1.00
SL46 Karl Malone .20 .50
SL47 John Stockton .20 .50
SL48 Bryant Reeves .12 .30
SL49 Juwan Howard .15 .40
SL50 Chris Webber .20 .50

1995-96 Hoops Top Ten

Randomly inserted into all first series packs at an approximate rate of one in 12, these 10 standard-size cards feature a selection of former lottery picks that are on their way to or have already attained great success in the NBA. The fronts are laid out horizontally with a color-action photo and a wide strip down the left side that reads "Top" with 10 in the middle of the O. The background on each card is different and has a multi-colored cloudy look. The backs have the same background as the front with a color-action photo and player information at the top.

COMPLETE SET (10) 10.00 25.00
SER.1 STATED ODDS 1:12 HOBBY/RETAIL
AR1 Shaquille O'Neal 2.00 5.00
AR2 Grant Hill 1.25 3.00
AR3 Chris Webber 1.00 2.50
AR4 Jamal Mashburn .75 2.00
AR5 Anfernee Hardaway 1.25 3.00
AR6 Alonzo Mourning 1.00 2.50
AR7 Michael Jordan 5.00 12.00
AR8 Charles Barkley 1.25 3.00
AR9 Glenn Robinson .60 1.50
AR10 Jason Kidd 1.25 3.00

1996-97 Hoops

The 1996-97 Hoops set was issued in two series. The first series had a total of 200 cards, while the second series contained 150. Both series had 9-card packs that carried a suggested retail price of $1.29 each. Card fronts contain a full bleed action shot with the player's name written in gold foil diagonally across the bottom right. Card backs have a small photo of the player in the top left corner with complete college and pro statistics as well as biographical information. The cards are grouped alphabetically within team order. Some Rookie Cards that were included in the second series were Shareef Abdur-Rahim, Kobe Bryant, Marcus Camby, Allen Iverson, Stephon Marbury and Antoine Walker. Also, a Grant Hill Z-Force Preview card was randomly inserted into series one packs at a rate of one in 360 packs. It previewed the inaugural edition of SkyBox Z-Force. A non-numbered two-card promo sheet was also issued which featured a regular issue Grant Hill card and a HIPnotized Jerry Stackhouse.

COMPLETE SET (350) 17.50 35.00
COMPLETE SERIES 1 (200) 7.50 15.00
COMPLETE SERIES 2 (150) 10.00 20.00
HILL Z-F: SER.1 STATED ODDS 1:360 H/R
1 Stacey Augmon .12 .30
2 Mookie Blaylock .10 .25
3 Alan Henderson .10 .25
4 Christian Laettner .12 .30
5 Grant Long .10 .25
6 Steve Smith .12 .30
7 Dana Barros .10 .25
8 Todd Day .10 .25
9 Rick Fox .10 .25
10 Eric Montross .10 .25
11 Dino Radja .10 .25
12 Eric Williams .10 .25
13 Kenny Anderson .12 .30
14 Scott Burrell .10 .25
15 Dell Curry .10 .25
16 Matt Geiger .10 .25
17 Larry Johnson .15 .40
18 Glen Rice .15 .40
19 Ron Harper .12 .30
20 Michael Jordan 1.25 3.00
21 Steve Kerr .12 .30
22 Toni Kukoc .15 .40
23 Luc Longley .12 .30
24 Scottie Pippen .25 .60
25 Dennis Rodman .30 .75
26 Terrell Brandon .10 .25
27 Danny Ferry .10 .25
28 Tyrone Hill .10 .25
29 Chris Mills .10 .25
30 Bobby Phills .10 .25
31 Bob Sura .10 .25
32 Tony Dumas .10 .25
33 Jim Jackson .10 .25
34 Popeye Jones .10 .25
35 Jason Kidd .25 .60
36 Jamal Mashburn .12 .30
37 George McCloud .10 .25
38 Cherokee Parks .10 .25
39 Mahmoud Abdul-Rauf .10 .25
40 LaPhonso Ellis .10 .25
41 Antonio McDyess .15 .40
42 Dikembe Mutombo .15 .40
43 Jalen Rose .12 .30
44 Bryant Stith .10 .25
45 Joe Dumars .15 .40
46 Grant Hill .25 .60
47 Allan Houston .12 .30
48 Lindsey Hunter .10 .25
49 Terry Mills .10 .25
50 Theo Ratliff .10 .25
51 Otis Thorpe .10 .25
52 B.J. Armstrong .10 .25
53 Donyell Marshall .10 .25
54 Chris Mullin .15 .40
55 Joe Smith .12 .30
56 Rony Seikaly .10 .25
57 Latrell Sprewell .15 .40
58 Mark Bryant .10 .25
59 Sam Cassell .12 .30
60 Clyde Drexler .20 .50
61 Mario Elie .10 .25
62 Robert Horry .12 .30
63 Hakeem Olajuwon .20 .50
64 Travis Best .10 .25
65 Antonio Davis .10 .25
66 Mark Jackson .12 .30
67 Derrick McKey .10 .25
68 Reggie Miller .20 .50
69 Rik Smits .12 .30
70 Brent Barry .12 .30
71 Terry Dehere .10 .25
72 Pooh Richardson .10 .25
73 Rodney Rogers .10 .25
74 Loy Vaught .10 .25
75 Brian Williams .10 .25
76 Elden Campbell .10 .25
77 Cedric Ceballos .10 .25
78 Vlade Divac .15 .40
79 Eddie Jones .15 .40
80 Anthony Peeler .10 .25
81 Nick Van Exel .15 .40
82 Sasha Danilovic .10 .25
83 Tim Hardaway .15 .40
84 Alonzo Mourning .20 .50
85 Kurt Thomas .10 .25
86 Walt Williams .10 .25
87 Vin Baker .12 .30
88 Sherman Douglas .10 .25
89 Johnny Newman .10 .25
90 Shawn Respert .10 .25
91 Glenn Robinson .12 .30
92 Kevin Garnett .40 1.00
93 Tom Gugliotta .10 .25
94 Andrew Lang .10 .25
95 Sam Mitchell .10 .25
96 Isaiah Rider .12 .30
97 Shawn Bradley .10 .25
98 P.J. Brown .10 .25
99 Chris Childs .10 .25
100 Armon Gilliam .10 .25
101 Ed O'Bannon .10 .25
102 Jayson Williams .10 .25
103 Hubert Davis .10 .25
104 Patrick Ewing .20 .50
105 Anthony Mason .10 .25
106 Charles Oakley .12 .30
107 John Starks .12 .30
108 Charlie Ward .10 .25
109 Nick Anderson .10 .25
110 Horace Grant .12 .30
111 Anfernee Hardaway .25 .60
112 Shaquille O'Neal .40 1.00
113 Dennis Scott .10 .25
114 Brian Shaw .10 .25
115 Derrick Coleman .12 .30
116 Vernon Maxwell .10 .25
117 Trevor Ruffin .10 .25
118 Jerry Stackhouse .20 .50
119 Clarence Weatherspoon .10 .25
120 Charles Barkley .25 .60
121 Michael Finley .20 .50
122 A.C. Green .12 .30
123 Kevin Johnson .15 .40
124 Danny Manning .12 .30
125 Wesley Person .10 .25
126 John Williams .10 .25
127 Harvey Grant .10 .25
128 Aaron McKie .10 .25
129 Clifford Robinson .10 .25
130 Arvydas Sabonis .12 .30
131 Rod Strickland .10 .25
132 Gary Trent .10 .25
133 Tyus Edney .10 .25
134 Brian Grant .12 .30
135 Billy Owens .10 .25
136 Olden Polynice .10 .25
137 Mitch Richmond .15 .40
138 Corliss Williamson .10 .25
139 Vinny Del Negro .10 .25
140 Sean Elliott .15 .40
141 Avery Johnson .12 .30
142 Chuck Person .12 .30
143 David Robinson .25 .60
144 Charles Smith .10 .25
145 Sherrell Ford .10 .25
146 Hersey Hawkins .10 .25
147 Shawn Kemp .15 .40
148 Nate McMillan .10 .25
149 Gary Payton .15 .40
150 Detlef Schrempf .15 .40
151 Oliver Miller .10 .25
152 Tracy Murray .10 .25
153 Carlos Rogers .10 .25
154 Damon Stoudamire .12 .30
155 Zan Tabak .10 .25
156 Sharone Wright .10 .25
157 Antoine Carr .10 .25
158 Jeff Hornacek .12 .30
159 Adam Keefe .10 .25
160 Karl Malone .20 .50
161 Chris Morris .10 .25
162 John Stockton .20 .50
163 Greg Anthony .10 .25
164 Blue Edwards .10 .25
165 Chris King .10 .25
166 Lawrence Moten .10 .25
167 Bryant Reeves .10 .25
168 Byron Scott .12 .30
169 Calbert Cheaney .10 .25
170 Juwan Howard .12 .30
171 Tim Legler .10 .25
172 Gheorghe Muresan .10 .25
173 Rasheed Wallace .20 .50
174 Chris Webber .20 .50
175 Steve Smith BF .12 .30
176 Michael Jordan BF 1.25 3.00
177 Scottie Pippen BF .25 .60
178 Dennis Rodman BF .30 .75
179 Allan Houston BF .12 .30
180 Hakeem Olajuwon BF .20 .50
181 Patrick Ewing BF .20 .50
182 Anfernee Hardaway BF .25 .60
183 Shaquille O'Neal BF .40 1.00
184 Charles Barkley BF .25 .60
185 Arvydas Sabonis BF .12 .30
186 David Robinson BF .25 .60
187 Shawn Kemp BF .15 .40
188 Gary Payton BF .15 .40
189 Karl Malone BF .20 .50
190 Kenny Anderson PLA .12 .30
191 Toni Kukoc PLA .15 .40
192 Brent Barry PLA .12 .30
193 Cedric Ceballos PLA .10 .25
194 Shawn Bradley PLA .10 .25
195 Charles Oakley PLA .12 .30
196 Dennis Scott PLA .10 .25
197 Clifford Robinson PLA .10 .25
198 Mitch Richmond PLA .15 .40
199 Checklist .10 .25
200 Checklist .10 .25
201 Dikembe Mutombo .15 .40
202 Dee Brown .10 .25
203 David Wesley .10 .25
204 Vlade Divac .15 .40
205 Anthony Mason .10 .25
206 Chris Gatling .10 .25
207 Eric Montross .10 .25
208 Ervin Johnson .10 .25
209 Stacey Augmon .12 .30
210 Joe Dumars .15 .40
211 Grant Hill .25 .60
212 Charles Barkley .25 .60
213 Jalen Rose .12 .30
214 Lamond Murray .10 .25
215 Shaquille O'Neal .40 1.00
216 P.J. Brown .10 .25
217 Dan Majerle .15 .40
218 Armon Gilliam .10 .25
219 Andrew Lang .10 .25
220 Kevin Garnett .40 1.00
221 Tom Gugliotta .10 .25
222 Cherokee Parks .10 .25
223 Doug West .10 .25
224 Kendall Gill .10 .25
225 Robert Pack .10 .25
226 Allan Houston .12 .30
227 Larry Johnson .15 .40
228 Rony Seikaly .10 .25
229 Gerald Wilkins .10 .25
230 Michael Cage .10 .25
231 Lucious Harris .10 .25
232 Sam Cassell .12 .30
233 Robert Horry .12 .30
234 Kenny Anderson .12 .30
235 Isaiah Rider .12 .30
236 Rasheed Wallace .20 .50
237 Mahmoud Abdul-Rauf .10 .25
238 Vernon Maxwell .10 .25
239 Dominique Wilkins .20 .50
240 Jim McIlvaine .10 .25
241 Hubert Davis .10 .25
242 Popeye Jones .10 .25
243 Walt Williams .10 .25
244 Karl Malone .20 .50
245 John Stockton .20 .50
246 Anthony Peeler .10 .25
247 Tracy Murray .10 .25
248 Rod Strickland .10 .25
249 Lenny Wilkens CO .15 .40
250 M.L. Carr CO .15 .40
251 Dave Cowens CO .15 .40
252 Phil Jackson CO .15 .40
253 Mike Fratello CO .15 .40
254 Jim Cleamons CO .15 .40
255 Dick Motta CO .15 .40
256 Doug Collins CO .15 .40
257 Rick Adelman CO .15 .40
258 Rudy Tomjanovich CO .15 .40
259 Larry Brown CO .15 .40
260 Bill Fitch CO .15 .40
261 Del Harris CO .15 .40
262 Pat Riley CO .15 .40
263 Chris Ford CO .15 .40
264 Flip Saunders CO .15 .40
265 John Calipari CO .15 .40
266 Jeff Van Gundy CO .15 .40
267 Brian Hill CO .15 .40
268 Johnny Davis CO .15 .40
269 Danny Ainge CO .15 .40
270 P.J. Carlesimo CO .15 .40
271 Garry St. Jean CO .15 .40
272 Bob Hill CO .15 .40
273 George Karl CO .15 .40
274 Darrell Walker CO .15 .40
275 Jerry Sloan CO .15 .40
276 Brian Winters CO .15 .40
277 Jim Lynam CO .15 .40
278 Shareef Abdur-Rahim RC .25 .60
279 Ray Allen RC .60 1.50
280 Shandon Anderson RC .12 .30
281 Kobe Bryant RC 4.00 10.00
282 Marcus Camby RC .25 .60
283 Erick Dampier RC .15 .40
284 Emanual Davis RC .15 .40
285 Tony Delk RC .15 .40
286 Brian Evans RC .15 .40
287 Derek Fisher RC .20 .50
288 Todd Fuller RC .10 .25
289 Dean Garrett RC .15 .40
290 Reggie Geary RC .15 .40
291 Darvin Ham RC .15. .40
292 Othella Harrington RC .15 .40
293 Shane Heal RC .15 .40
294 Mark Hendrickson RC .15 .40
295 Allen Iverson RC .75 2.00
296 Dontae' Jones RC .15 .40
297 Kerry Kittles RC .15 .40
298 Priest Lauderdale RC .10 .25
299 Matt Maloney RC .12 .30
300 Stephon Marbury RC .40 1.00
301 Walter McCarty RC .15 .40
302 Jeff McInnis RC .15 .40
303 Martin Muursepp RC .10 .25
304 Steve Nash RC .75 2.00
305 Moochie Norris RC .15 .40
306 Jermaine O'Neal RC .25 .60
307 Vitaly Potapenko RC .12 .30
308 Virginius Praskevicius RC .15 .40
309 Roy Rogers RC .12 .30
310 Malik Rose RC .20 .50
311 James Scott RC .15 .40
312 Antoine Walker RC .25 .60
313 Samaki Walker RC .12 .30
314 Ben Wallace RC .75 2.00
315 John Wallace RC .15 .40
316 Jerome Williams RC .12 .30
317 Lorenzen Wright RC .12 .30
318 Charles Barkley ST .25 .60
319 Derrick Coleman ST .12 .30
320 Michael Finley ST .20 .50
321 Stephon Marbury ST .20 .50
322 Reggie Miller ST .20 .50
323 Alonzo Mourning ST .20 .50
324 Shaquille O'Neal ST .40 1.00
325 Gary Payton ST .15 .40
326 Dennis Rodman ST .30 .75
327 Damon Stoudamire ST .12 .30
328 Vin Baker CBG .12 .30
329 Clyde Drexler CBG .20 .50
330 Patrick Ewing CBG .20 .50
331 Anfernee Hardaway CBG .25 .60
332 Grant Hill CBG .25 .60
333 Juwan Howard CBG .12 .30
334 Larry Johnson CBG .15 .40
335 Michael Jordan CBG 1.25 3.00
336 Shawn Kemp CBG .15 .40
337 Jason Kidd CBG .25 .60
338 Karl Malone CBG .20 .50
339 Reggie Miller CBG .20 .50
340 Hakeem Olajuwon CBG .20 .50
341 Scottie Pippen CBG .25 .60
342 Mitch Richmond CBG .15 .40
343 David Robinson CBG UER .25 .60
344 Dennis Rodman CBG .30 .75
345 Joe Smith CBG .12 .30
346 Jerry Stackhouse CBG .20 .50
347 John Stockton CBG .20 .50
348 Jerry Stackhouse BG .20 .50
349 Checklist (201-350/inserts) .10 .25
350 Checklist (inserts) .10 .25
NNO G.Hill/J.Stackhouse Promo 1.00 2.50
NNO G.Hill Z-Force Preview 4.00 10.00

1996-97 Hoops Silver

COMPLETE SET (98) 25.00 50.00
*SILVER: 1.5X TO 4X BASE CARD HI
ONE PER SPECIAL SER.1 RETAIL PACK

1996-97 Hoops Fly With

Randomly inserted in series two retail packs only at a rate of one in 24, this 10-card set focuses on the high-flying acrobats of ten NBA players. Cards feature clear plastic stock and a cloud background on the fronts.

COMPLETE SET (10) 10.00 25.00
SER.2 STATED ODDS 1:24 RETAIL
1 Charles Barkley 2.50 6.00
2 Juwan Howard 1.25 3.00
3 Jason Kidd 2.50 6.00
4 Alonzo Mourning 2.00 5.00
5 Gary Payton 1.50 4.00
6 David Robinson 2.50 6.00
7 Dennis Rodman 3.00 8.00
8 Joe Smith 1.25 3.00
9 Jerry Stackhouse 2.00 5.00
10 Damon Stoudamire 1.25 3.00

1996-97 Hoops Grant's All-Rookies

Randomly inserted in all series two packs at a rate of one in 360, this 11-card set features the SkyView technology as Grant Hill selects his picks for the best rookies from the 1996-97 class. Despite no serial numbering, the stated print run for the set was 996 of each card.

COMPLETE SET (11) 100.00 200.00
SER.2 STATED ODDS 1:360 HOBBY/RETAIL
STATED PRINT RUN 996 SETS
1 Shareef Abdur-Rahim 4.00 10.00
2 Ray Allen 10.00 25.00
3 Kobe Bryant 60.00 150.00
4 Marcus Camby 4.00 10.00
5 Grant Hill 4.00 10.00
6 Allen Iverson 12.00 30.00
7 Kerry Kittles 2.50 6.00
8 Stephon Marbury 6.00 15.00
9 Antoine Walker 4.00 10.00
10 Samaki Walker 2.00 5.00
11 Lorenzen Wright 2.00 5.00

1996-97 Hoops Head to Head

Randomly inserted at a rate of one in 24 packs, this 10-card set features dual-player cards of either teammates or young players. Card fronts contain action photos of both players and the logo "Head to Head" in gold foil at the bottom of the card. In addition, the logo and both of the player's first names are treated with a diamond-like element. Card backs are divided into four quadrants with two of them featuring action shots and the other two featuring a brief commentary on each player. Card backs are numbered with a "HH" prefix.

COMPLETE SET (10) 10.00 25.00
SER.1 STATED ODDS 1:24 HOBBY/RETAIL
HH1 L.Johnson/G.Rice .75 2.00
HH2 M.Jordan/S.Pippen 6.00 15.00
HH3 J.Kidd/G.Hill 1.25 3.00
HH4 C.Drexler/H.Olajuwon 1.00 2.50
HH5 V.Baker/G.Robinson .60 1.50
HH6 A.Hardaway/S.O'Neal 2.00 5.00
HH7 A.McDyess/Stackhouse 1.00 2.50
HH8 S.Elliott/D.Robinson 1.25 3.00
HH9 J.Smith/D.Stoudamire .60 1.50
HH10 K.Malone/J.Stockton 1.00 2.50

1996-97 Hoops HIPnotized

Randomly inserted at a rate of one in four packs, this 20-card set features some of the top players in the game. Card fronts are full bleed action shots with a swirling background. The logo "HIPnotized" and the player's last name are in gold foil. Card backs are horizontal with statistical and biographical information as well as a having a brief commentary next to the photo. Cards are numbered with a "H" prefix.

COMPLETE SET (20) 5.00 12.00
SER.1 STATED ODDS 1:4 HOBBY/RETAIL
H1 Steve Smith .40 1.00
H2 Dana Barros .30 .75
H3 Larry Johnson .50 1.25
H4 Dennis Rodman 1.00 2.50
H5 Terrell Brandon .30 .75
H6 Jason Kidd .75 2.00
H7 Grant Hill .75 2.00
H8 Clyde Drexler .60 1.50
H9 Reggie Miller .60 1.50
H10 Alonzo Mourning .60 1.50
H11 Glenn Robinson .40 1.00
H12 Patrick Ewing .60 1.50
H13 Shaquille O'Neal 1.25 3.00
H14 Jerry Stackhouse .60 1.50
H15 Charles Barkley .75 2.00
H16 Clifford Robinson .30 .75
H17 Mitch Richmond .50 1.25
H18 David Robinson .75 2.00
H19 Gary Payton .50 1.25
H20 Juwan Howard .40 1.00

1996-97 Hoops Hot List

Randomly inserted in series two hobby packs only at a rate of one in 48, this 20-card set features a flamed front on clear plastic stock.

COMPLETE SET (20) 75.00 150.00
SER.2 STATED ODDS 1:48 HOBBY
1 Vin Baker 2.00 5.00
2 Patrick Ewing 3.00 8.00
3 Michael Finley 3.00 8.00
4 Kevin Garnett 6.00 15.00
5 Anfernee Hardaway 4.00 10.00
6 Grant Hill 4.00 10.00
7 Allan Houston 2.00 5.00
8 Michael Jordan 30.00 80.00
9 Shawn Kemp 2.50 6.00
10 Christian Laettner 2.00 5.00
11 Karl Malone 3.00 8.00
12 Antonio McDyess 2.50 6.00
13 Reggie Miller 3.00 8.00
14 Hakeem Olajuwon 3.00 8.00
15 Shaquille O'Neal 8.00 20.00
16 Scottie Pippen 4.00 10.00
17 Mitch Richmond 2.50 6.00
18 Isaiah Rider 2.00 5.00
19 Rod Strickland 1.50 4.00
20 Chris Webber 3.00 8.00

1996-97 Hoops Rookie Headliners

Randomly inserted at a rate of one in 72 hobby packs, this 10-card set focuses on some of the best rookies from the 1995-96 class. Card fronts are designed similar to a game ticket with both the left and right borders in gold foil. The action shot of the player is located between the two borders and the player's last name is in gold foil on top of the photo. Card backs have a shot of the player in the middle of the card against a light gold background along with a brief commentary on the player. The player's rookie statistics are located along the left border. Card backs are numbered as "X of 10".

COMPLETE SET (10) 15.00 40.00
SER.1 STATED ODDS 1:72 HOBBY
1 Antonio McDyess 2.50 6.00
2 Joe Smith 2.00 5.00
3 Brent Barry 2.00 5.00
4 Kevin Garnett 6.00 15.00
5 Jerry Stackhouse 3.00 8.00
6 Michael Finley 3.00 8.00
7 Arvydas Sabonis 2.00 5.00
8 Tyus Edney 1.50 4.00
9 Damon Stoudamire 2.00 5.00
10 Bryant Reeves 1.50 4.00

1996-97 Hoops Rookies

Randomly inserted in all series two packs at one in six, this 30-card set focuses on the season's best first year players. Card fronts carry a gold foiled background.

COMPLETE SET (30) 12.00 30.00
SER.2 STATED ODDS 1:6 HOBBY/RETAIL
1 Shareef Abdur-Rahim 1.00 2.50
2 Ray Allen 2.50 6.00
3 Kobe Bryant 6.00 15.00
4 Marcus Camby 1.00 2.50
5 Erick Dampier .60 1.50
6 Emanual Davis .60 1.50
7 Tony Delk .60 1.50
8 Brian Evans .60 1.50
9 Derek Fisher .75 2.00
10 Todd Fuller .40 1.00
11 Othella Harrington .60 1.50
12 Allen Iverson 3.00 8.00
13 Dontae' Jones .60 1.50
14 Kerry Kittles .60 1.50
15 Priest Lauderdale .40 1.00
16 Matt Maloney .50 1.25
17 Stephon Marbury 1.50 4.00
18 Walter McCarty .60 1.50
19 Jeff McInnis .60 1.50
20 Martin Muursepp .40 1.00
21 Steve Nash 3.00 8.00
22 Moochie Norris .60 1.50
23 Jermaine O'Neal 1.00 2.50
24 Vitaly Potapenko .50 1.25
25 Roy Rogers .50 1.25
26 Antoine Walker 1.00 2.50
27 Samaki Walker .50 1.25
28 John Wallace .60 1.50
29 Jerome Williams .50 1.25
30 Lorenzen Wright .50 1.25

1996-97 Hoops Starting Five

Randomly inserted in all series two packs at one in 12, this 29-card set features each team's starting five. Card fronts feature a full shot of the team's primary player with the other four starters in gold boxes at the bottom of the card.

COMPLETE SET (29) 15.00 30.00
SER.2 STATED ODDS 1:12 HOBBY/RETAIL
1 Mookie Blaylock/Hawks .60 1.50
2 Dino Radja/Celtics .40 1.00
3 Glen Rice/Hornets .60 1.50
4 Michael Jordan/Bulls 6.00 15.00
5 Tyrone Hill/Cavs .50 1.25
6 Jason Kidd/Mavs 1.00 2.50
7 Antonio McDyess/Nuggets .60 1.50
8 Grant Hill/Pistons 1.00 2.50
9 Joe Smith/Warriors .60 1.50
10 Hakeem Olajuwon/Rockets 1.00 2.50
11 Reggie Miller/Pacers .75 2.00
12 Rodney Rogers/Clippers .40 1.00
13 Shaquille O'Neal/Lakers 1.50 4.00
14 Alonzo Mourning/Heat .75 2.00
15 Ray Allen/Bucks 1.25 3.00
16 Kevin Garnett/T'wolves .75 2.00
17 Jayson Williams/Nets .40 1.00
18 Patrick Ewing/Knicks .75 2.00
19 Anfernee Hardaway/Magic 1.00 2.50
20 Jerry Stackhouse/76ers 1.50 4.00
21 Danny Manning/Suns .75 2.00
22 Isaiah Rider/Blazers .75 2.00
23 Mitch Richmond/Kings .60 1.50
24 David Robinson/Spurs 1.00 2.50
25 Shawn Kemp/Sonics .60 1.50
26 D.Stoudamire/Raptors 1.00 2.50
27 Karl Malone/Jazz .75 2.00
28 Bryant Reeves/Grizzlies .50 1.25
29 Juwan Howard/Bullets .75 2.00

1996-97 Hoops Superfeats

Randomly inserted at a rate of one in 36 retail packs, this 10-card set features players who had super "feats" during the 1995-96 NBA season. Card fronts feature a colorful background with a full color action shot of the player on top. The player's name and the logo "Superfeats" are treated with gold foil. Card backs feature another action shot of the player and a brief commentary on the extraordinary achievements the player had the previous season. Card backs are also numbered as "X of 10".

COMPLETE SET (10) 20.00 50.00
SER.1 STATED ODDS 1:36 RETAIL
1 Michael Jordan 10.00 25.00
2 Jason Kidd 3.00 8.00
3 Grant Hill 3.00 8.00
4 Hakeem Olajuwon 2.50 6.00
5 Alonzo Mourning 2.50 6.00
6 Anthony Mason 1.25 3.00
7 Anfernee Hardaway 3.00 8.00
8 Jerry Stackhouse 2.50 6.00
9 Shawn Kemp 2.00 5.00
10 Damon Stoudamire 1.50 4.00

1997-98 Hoops

The 1997-98 Hoops set was released in two series, with each 165-card series distributed in 10-card packs with a suggested retail price of $.99. Card fronts feature color player images on computer graphic treatment backgrounds. The set includes the League Leaders subset (1-8) and two checklist cards (164-165). The backs carry player information and statistics. A Grant Hill promo card was issued to preview the product. It is priced below.

COMPLETE SET (330) 15.00 40.00
COMPLETE SERIES 1 (165) 6.00 15.00
COMPLETE SERIES 2 (165) 10.00 25.00
SUBSET CARDS HALF VALUE
1 Michael Jordan LL .60 1.50
2 Dennis Rodman LL .15 .40
3 Mark Jackson LL .05 .15
4 Shawn Bradley LL .05 .15
5 Glen Rice LL .07 .20
6 Mookie Blaylock LL .05 .15
7 Gheorghe Muresan LL .05 .15
8 Mark Price LL .07 .20
9 Tyrone Corbin .10 .25
10 Christian Laettner .12 .30
11 Priest Lauderdale .10 .25
12 Dikembe Mutombo .15 .40
13 Steve Smith .12 .30
14 Todd Day .10 .25
15 Rick Fox .10 .25
16 Brett Szabo .10 .25
17 Antoine Walker .15 .40
18 David Wesley .10 .25
19 Muggsy Bogues .12 .30
20 Dell Curry .10 .25
21 Tony Delk .10 .25
22 Anthony Mason .10 .25
23 Glen Rice .15 .40
24 Malik Rose .10 .25
25 Steve Kerr .12 .30
26 Toni Kukoc .15 .40
27 Luc Longley .12 .30
28 Robert Parish .15 .40
29 Scottie Pippen .25 .60
30 Dennis Rodman .30 .75
31 Terrell Brandon .10 .25
32 Danny Ferry .10 .25
33 Tyrone Hill .10 .25
34 Bobby Phills .10 .25
35 Vitaly Potapenko .10 .25
36 Shawn Bradley .10 .25
37 Sasha Danilovic .10 .25
38 Derek Harper .12 .30
39 Martin Muursepp .10 .25
40 Robert Pack .10 .25
41 Khalid Reeves .10 .25
42 Vincent Askew .10 .25
43 Dale Ellis .10 .25
44 LaPhonso Ellis .10 .25
45 Antonio McDyess .12 .30
46 Bryant Stith .10 .25
47 Joe Dumars .15 .40
48 Grant Hill .25 .60
49 Lindsey Hunter .10 .25
50 Aaron McKie .10 .25
51 Theo Ratliff .12 .30
52 Scott Burrell .10 .25
53 Todd Fuller .10 .25
54 Chris Mullin .15 .40
55 Mark Price .15 .40
56 Joe Smith .12 .30
57 Latrell Sprewell .15 .40
58 Clyde Drexler .20 .50
59 Mario Elie .10 .25
60 Othella Harrington .10 .25
61 Matt Maloney .10 .25
62 Hakeem Olajuwon .20 .50
63 Kevin Willis .10 .25
64 Travis Best .10 .25
65 Erick Dampier .10 .25
66 Antonio Davis .10 .25
67 Dale Davis .10 .25
68 Mark Jackson .12 .30
69 Reggie Miller .20 .50
70 Brent Barry .12 .30
71 Darrick Martin .10 .25
72 Bo Outlaw .10 .25
73 Loy Vaught .10 .25
74 Lorenzen Wright .10 .25
75 Kobe Bryant .75 2.00
76 Derek Fisher .15 .40
77 Robert Horry .12 .30
78 Eddie Jones .15 .40
79 Travis Knight .10 .25
80 George McCloud .10 .25
81 Shaquille O'Neal .40 1.00
82 P.J. Brown .10 .25
83 Tim Hardaway .15 .40
84 Voshon Lenard .10 .25
85 Jamal Mashburn .12 .30
86 Alonzo Mourning .20 .50
87 Ray Allen .20 .50
88 Vin Baker .12 .30
89 Sherman Douglas .10 .25
90 Armon Gilliam .10 .25
91 Glenn Robinson .12 .30
92 Kevin Garnett .25 .60
93 Dean Garrett .10 .25
94 Tom Gugliotta .10 .25
95 Stephon Marbury .20 .50
96 Doug West .10 .25
97 Chris Gatling .10 .25
98 Kendall Gill .10 .25
99 Kerry Kittles .10 .25
100 Jayson Williams .10 .25
101 Chris Childs .10 .25
102 Patrick Ewing .20 .50
103 Allan Houston .12 .30
104 Larry Johnson .15 .40
105 Charles Oakley .12 .30
106 John Starks .12 .30
107 John Wallace .10 .25
108 Nick Anderson .10 .25
109 Horace Grant .12 .30
110 Anfernee Hardaway .25 .60
111 Rony Seikaly .10 .25
112 Derek Strong .10 .25
113 Derrick Coleman .12 .30
114 Allen Iverson .30 .75
115 Doug Overton .10 .25
116 Jerry Stackhouse .15 .40
117 Rex Walters .10 .25
118 Cedric Ceballos .10 .25
119 Kevin Johnson .15 .40
120 Jason Kidd .25 .60
121 Steve Nash .30 .75
122 Wesley Person .10 .25
123 Kenny Anderson .12 .30
124 Jermaine O'Neal .12 .30
125 Isaiah Rider .12 .30
126 Arvydas Sabonis .12 .30
127 Gary Trent .10 .25
128 Tyus Edney .10 .25
129 Brian Grant .10 .25
130 Olden Polynice .10 .25
131 Mitch Richmond .15 .40
132 Corliss Williamson .10 .25
133 Vinny Del Negro .10 .25
134 Sean Elliott .15 .40
135 Avery Johnson .12 .30
136 Will Perdue .10 .25
137 Dominique Wilkins .20 .50
138 Craig Ehlo .10 .25
139 Hersey Hawkins .10 .25
140 Shawn Kemp .15 .40
141 Jim McIlvaine .10 .25
142 Sam Perkins .10 .25
143 Detlef Schrempf .15 .40
144 Marcus Camby .15 .40
145 Doug Christie .10 .25
146 Popeye Jones .10 .25
147 Damon Stoudamire .12 .30
148 Walt Williams .10 .25
149 Jeff Hornacek .12 .30
150 Karl Malone .20 .50
151 Greg Ostertag .10 .25
152 Bryon Russell .10 .25
153 John Stockton .20 .50
154 Shareef Abdur-Rahim .15 .40
155 Greg Anthony .10 .25
156 Anthony Peeler .10 .25
157 Bryant Reeves .10 .25
158 Roy Rogers .10 .25
159 Calbert Cheaney .10 .25
160 Juwan Howard .12 .30
161 Gheorghe Muresan .10 .25
162 Rod Strickland .10 .25
163 Chris Webber .15 .40
164 Checklist .10 .25
165 Checklist .10 .25
166 Tim Duncan RC .75 2.00
167 Chauncey Billups RC .50 1.25
168 Keith Van Horn RC .25 .60
169 Tracy McGrady RC .60 1.50

170 John Thomas RC .10 .25
171 Tim Thomas RC .20 .50
172 Ron Mercer RC .20 .50
173 Scot Pollard RC .15 .40
174 Jason Lawson RC .15 .40
175 Keith Booth RC .12 .30
176 Adonal Foyle RC .12 .30
177 Bubba Wells RC .15 .40
178 Derek Anderson RC .15 .40
179 Rodrick Rhodes RC .12 .30
180 Kelvin Cato RC .12 .30
181 Serge Zwikker RC .15 .40
182 Ed Gray RC .15 .40
183 Brevin Knight RC .15 .40
184 Alvin Williams RC .15 .40
185 Paul Grant RC .10 .25
186 Austin Croshere RC .12 .30
187 Chris Crawford RC .15 .40
188 Anthony Johnson RC .15 .40
189 James Cotton RC .15 .40
190 James Collins RC .15 .40
191 Tony Battie RC .15 .40
192 Tariq Abdul-Wahad RC .12 .30
193 Danny Fortson RC .15 .40
194 Maurice Taylor RC .15 .40
195 Bobby Jackson RC .20 .50
196 Charles Smith RC .12 .30
197 Johnny Taylor RC .12 .30
198 Jerald Honeycutt RC .15 .40
199 Marko Milic RC .15 .40
200 Anthony Parker RC .15 .40
201 Jacque Vaughn RC .12 .30
202 Antonio Daniels RC .15 .40
203 Charles O'Bannon RC .15 .40
204 God Shammgod RC .15 .40
205 Kebu Stewart RC .15 .40
206 Mookie Blaylock .10 .25
207 Chucky Brown .10 .25
208 Alan Henderson .10 .25
209 Dana Barros .10 .25
210 Tyus Edney .10 .25
211 Travis Knight .10 .25
212 Walter McCarty .10 .25
213 Vlade Divac .15 .40
214 Matt Geiger .10 .25
215 Bobby Phills .10 .25
216 J.R. Reid .10 .25
217 David Wesley .10 .25
218 Scott Burrell .10 .25
219 Ron Harper .12 .30
220 Michael Jordan 1.25 3.00
221 Bill Wennington .10 .25
222 Mitchell Butler .10 .25
223 Zydrunas Ilgauskas .15 .40
224 Shawn Kemp .15 .40
225 Wesley Person .10 .25
226 Shawnelle Scott RC .15 .40
227 Bob Sura .10 .25
228 Hubert Davis .10 .25
229 Michael Finley .15 .40
230 Dennis Scott .10 .25
231 Erick Strickland RC .12 .30
232 Samaki Walker .10 .25
233 Dean Garrett .10 .25
234 Priest Lauderdale .10 .25
235 Eric Williams .10 .25
236 Grant Long .10 .25
237 Malik Sealy .10 .25
238 Brian Williams .10 .25
239 Muggsy Bogues .12 .30
240 Bimbo Coles .10 .25
241 Brian Shaw .10 .25
242 Joe Smith .12 .30
243 Latrell Sprewell .15 .40
244 Charles Barkley .25 .60
245 Emanual Davis .10 .25
246 Brent Price .10 .25
247 Reggie Miller .20 .50
248 Chris Mullin .15 .40
249 Jalen Rose .12 .30
250 Rik Smits .12 .30
251 Mark West .10 .25
252 Lamond Murray .10 .25
253 Pooh Richardson .10 .25
254 Rodney Rogers .10 .25
255 Stojko Vrankovic .10 .25
256 Jon Barry .10 .25
257 Corie Blount .10 .25
258 Elden Campbell .10 .25
259 Rick Fox .10 .25
260 Nick Van Exel .12 .30
261 Isaac Austin .10 .25
262 Dan Majerle .15 .40
263 Terry Mills .10 .25
264 Mark Strickland RC .15 .40
265 Terrell Brandon .10 .25
266 Tyrone Hill .10 .25
267 Ervin Johnson .10 .25
268 Andrew Lang .10 .25
269 Elliot Perry .10 .25
270 Chris Carr .10 .25
271 Reggie Jordan .10 .25
272 Sam Mitchell .10 .25
273 Stanley Roberts .10 .25
274 Michael Cage .10 .25
275 Sam Cassell .12 .30
276 Lucious Harris .10 .25
277 Kerry Kittles .10 .25
278 Don MacLean .10 .25
279 Chris Dudley .10 .25
280 Chris Mills .10 .25
281 Charlie Ward .10 .25
282 Buck Williams .10 .25
283 Herb Williams .10 .25
284 Derek Harper .12 .30
285 Mark Price .15 .40
286 Gerald Wilkins .10 .25
287 Allen Iverson .30 .75
288 Jim Jackson .10 .25
289 Eric Montross .10 .25
290 Jerry Stackhouse .15 .40
291 Clarence Weatherspoon .10 .25
292 Tom Chambers .12 .30
293 Rex Chapman .10 .25
294 Danny Manning .12 .30
295 Antonio McDyess .12 .30
296 Clifford Robinson .10 .25
297 Stacey Augmon .12 .30
298 Brian Grant .10 .25
299 Rasheed Wallace .15 .40
300 Mahmoud Abdul-Rauf .10 .25
301 Terry Dehere .10 .25
302 Billy Owens .10 .25
303 Michael Smith .10 .25
304 Cory Alexander .10 .25
305 Chuck Person .12 .30
306 David Robinson .25 .60
307 Charles Smith .10 .25
308 Monty Williams .10 .25
309 Vin Baker .12 .30
310 Jerome Kersey .10 .25
311 Nate McMillan .10 .25
312 Gary Payton .15 .40
313 Eric Snow .10 .25
314 Carlos Rogers .10 .25
315 Zan Tabak .10 .25
316 John Wallace .10 .25
317 Sharone Wright .10 .25
318 Shandon Anderson .10 .25
319 Antoine Carr .10 .25
320 Howard Eisley .10 .25
321 Chris Morris .10 .25
322 Pete Chilcutt .10 .25
323 George Lynch .10 .25
324 Chris Robinson .15 .40
325 Otis Thorpe .10 .25
326 Harvey Grant .10 .25
327 Darvin Ham .10 .25
328 Juwan Howard .12 .30
329 Ben Wallace .12 .30
330 Chris Webber .15 .40
NNO Grant Hill Promo .60 1.50

1997-98 Hoops Chairman of the Boards

Randomly inserted into series two packs at a rate of one in 9, this 10-card set focuses on some of the players considered the best rebounders in the NBA. The card fronts carry 100% etched silver foil. Card backs carry a "CB" prefix.

COMPLETE SET (10) 4.00 10.00
SER.2 STATED ODDS 1:9 HOBBY/RETAIL
CB1 Shaquille O'Neal 1.25 3.00
CB2 Dikembe Mutombo .50 1.25
CB3 Dennis Rodman 1.00 2.50
CB4 Patrick Ewing .60 1.50
CB5 Charles Barkley .75 2.00
CB6 Karl Malone .60 1.50
CB7 Rasheed Wallace .50 1.25
CB8 Chris Webber .50 1.25
CB9 Tim Duncan 1.25 3.00
CB10 Kevin Garnett .75 2.00

1997-98 Hoops Chill with Hill

Randomly inserted in series one packs at a rate of one in 10, this 10-card set features candid photos of Grant Hill on foil backgrounds which present a photographic essay in a day in his life.

COMPLETE SET (10) 4.00 10.00
COMMON HILL (1-10) .60 1.50
SER.1 STATED ODDS 1:10 HOB/RET

1997-98 Hoops Dish N Swish

Randomly inserted in series one retail packs only at a rate of one in 18, this 10-card set features the top point guards in the league who are adept at both passing and shooting.

COMPLETE SET (10) 12.00 30.00
SER.1 STATED ODDS 1:18 RETAIL
DS1 Mookie Blaylock .60 1.50
DS2 Terrell Brandon .60 1.50
DS3 Anfernee Hardaway 1.50 4.00
DS4 Allen Iverson 2.00 5.00
DS5 Michael Jordan 10.00 25.00
DS6 Jason Kidd 1.50 4.00
DS7 Stephon Marbury 1.25 3.00
DS8 Gary Payton 1.00 2.50
DS9 John Stockton 1.25 3.00
DS10 Damon Stoudamire .75 2.00

1997-98 Hoops Frequent Flyer Club

Randomly inserted in series one hobby packs only at a rate of one in 36, this 20-card set features color photos of players with great dunking ability on a cloud background. The horizontal cards are printed on a special foil-stamped card with rounded corners. Card backs are numbered with a "FF" prefix.

SER.1 STATED ODDS 1:36 HOBBY
*UPGRADE: 1.5X TO 4X BASE FREQ FLYER
UPGRADE: SER.1 STATED ODDS 1:360 HOB
FF1 Christian Laettner 1.50 4.00
FF2 Antoine Walker 2.00 5.00
FF3 Glen Rice 2.00 5.00
FF4 Michael Jordan 20.00 50.00
FF5 Dennis Rodman 4.00 10.00
FF6 Grant Hill 3.00 8.00
FF7 Latrell Sprewell 2.00 5.00
FF8 Charles Barkley 3.00 8.00
FF9 Kobe Bryant 12.00 30.00
FF10 Shaquille O'Neal 5.00 12.00
FF11 Ray Allen 2.50 6.00
FF12 Kevin Garnett 3.00 8.00
FF13 Kerry Kittles 1.25 3.00
FF14 Anfernee Hardaway 3.00 8.00
FF15 Jerry Stackhouse 2.00 5.00
FF16 Cedric Ceballos 1.25 3.00
FF17 Shawn Kemp 2.00 5.00
FF18 Marcus Camby 2.00 5.00
FF19 Juwan Howard 1.50 4.00
FF20 Chris Webber 2.00 5.00

1997-98 Hoops Great Shots

Inserted one per series two pack, this 30-card set features some of the best NBA players on mini-posters that measure 5"x7".

COMPLETE SET (30) 2.50 6.00
ONE PER SERIES 2 PACK
1 Dikembe Mutombo .10 .25
2 Antoine Walker .10 .25
3 Glen Rice .10 .25
4 Dennis Rodman .20 .50
5 D.Anderson/B.Knight .10 .25
6 Michael Finley .10 .25
7 Fortson/Battie/Jackson .12 .30
8 Grant Hill .15 .40
9 Joe Smith .07 .20
10 Charles Barkley .15 .40
11 Reggie Miller .12 .30
12 Lamond Murray .05 .15
13 Kobe Bryant .50 1.25
14 Alonzo Mourning .12 .30
15 Ray Allen .12 .30
16 Kevin Garnett .15 .40
17 Stephon Marbury .15 .40
18 Kerry Kittles .05 .15
19 Patrick Ewing .12 .30
20 Anfernee Hardaway .15 .40
21 Allen Iverson .20 .50
22 Jason Kidd .15 .40
23 Rasheed Wallace .10 .25
24 Mitch Richmond .10 .25
25 David Robinson .10 .25
26 Gary Payton .10 .25
27 Damon Stoudamire .07 .20
28 John Stockton .12 .30
29 Shareef Abdur-Rahim .10 .25
30 Chris Webber .10 .25

1997-98 Hoops High Voltage

Randomly inserted in series two hobby packs at a rate of one in 36, this 20-card set features fan favorites who can electrify a crowd. Card fronts carry a holofoil background. Card backs are numbered with a "HV" prefix.

SER.2 STATED ODDS 1:36 HOBBY
HV1 Kobe Bryant 15.00 40.00
HV2 Eddie Jones 2.00 5.00
HV3 Ray Allen 2.50 6.00
HV4 Anfernee Hardaway 8.00 20.00
HV5 Grant Hill 3.00 8.00
HV6 Shareef Abdur-Rahim 2.00 5.00
HV7 Marcus Camby 2.00 5.00
HV8 Allen Iverson 4.00 10.00
HV9 Kerry Kittles 1.25 3.00
HV10 Kevin Garnett 4.00 10.00
HV11 Stephon Marbury 2.50 6.00
HV12 Chris Webber 2.00 5.00
HV13 Antoine Walker 2.00 5.00
HV14 Michael Jordan 125.00 300.00
HV15 Tim Duncan 5.00 12.00
HV16 Dennis Rodman 8.00 20.00
HV17 Scottie Pippen 3.00 8.00
HV18 Shawn Kemp 2.00 5.00
HV19 Hakeem Olajuwon 2.50 6.00
HV20 Karl Malone 2.50 6.00

1997-98 Hoops High Voltage 500

*STARS: 4X TO 10X HI COLUMN
STATED PRINT RUN 500 SERIAL #'d SETS
HV1 Kobe Bryant 400.00 800.00
HV2 Eddie Jones 25.00 60.00
HV3 Ray Allen 60.00 150.00
HV12 Chris Webber 60.00 150.00
HV14 Michael Jordan 800.00 1200.00
HV16 Dennis Rodman 75.00 200.00
HV17 Scottie Pippen 50.00 120.00
HV19 Hakeem Olajuwon 60.00 150.00

1997-98 Hoops HOOPerstars

Randomly inserted in series one packs at a rate of one in 288, this 10-card die cut set features the best and brightest NBA stars on etched foil backgrounds. Card backs are numbered with a "H" prefix.

COMPLETE SET (10) 75.00 150.00
SER.1 STATED ODDS 1:288 HOBBY/RETAIL
H1 Michael Jordan 125.00 300.00
H2 Grant Hill 6.00 15.00
H3 Shaquille O'Neal 10.00 25.00
H4 Ray Allen 5.00 12.00
H5 Stephon Marbury 5.00 12.00
H6 Anfernee Hardaway 8.00 20.00
H7 Allen Iverson 8.00 20.00
H8 Shawn Kemp 4.00 10.00
H9 Marcus Camby 4.00 10.00
H10 Shareef Abdur-Rahim 4.00 10.00

1997-98 Hoops 911

Randomly inserted in series two packs at a rate of one in 288, this 10-card set features a two-piece card with some of the NBA's best "emergency" players. The card is contained in a lazer-cut sleeve. Card backs are numbered with a "N" prefix.

COMPLETE SET (10) 125.00 300.00
SER.2 STATED ODDS 1:288 HOB/RET
N1 Michael Jordan 100.00 250.00
N2 Grant Hill 8.00 20.00
N3 Shawn Kemp 5.00 12.00
N4 Stephon Marbury 8.00 20.00
N5 Damon Stoudamire 4.00 10.00
N6 Shaquille O'Neal 12.00 30.00
N7 Shareef Abdur-Rahim 5.00 12.00
N8 Allen Iverson 10.00 25.00
N9 Antoine Walker 5.00 12.00
N10 Anfernee Hardaway 8.00 20.00

1997-98 Hoops Rock the House

Randomly inserted in series two retail packs at a rate of one in 18, this 10-card set features some of the NBA's most crowd pleasing players. Card backs are numbered with a "RH" prefix.

COMPLETE SET (10) 15.00 40.00
SER.2 STATED ODDS 1:18 RETAIL
RH1 Anfernee Hardaway 2.00 5.00
RH2 Stephon Marbury 1.50 4.00
RH3 Grant Hill 2.00 5.00
RH4 Shaquille O'Neal 3.00 8.00
RH5 Kerry Kittles .75 2.00
RH6 Michael Jordan 30.00 80.00
RH7 Ray Allen 1.50 4.00
RH8 Damon Stoudamire 1.00 2.50
RH9 Kevin Garnett 2.00 5.00
RH10 Shawn Kemp 1.25 3.00

1997-98 Hoops Rookie Headliners

Randomly inserted in series one packs at a rate of one in 48, this 10-card set showcases the top rookies from the 1996-97 season with silhouetted action shots and a portrait shot on foil with a newspaper print background. Card backs are numbered with a "RH" prefix.

COMPLETE SET (10) 15.00 30.00
SER.1 STATED ODDS 1:48 HOBBY/RETAIL
RH1 Antoine Walker 1.50 4.00
RH2 Matt Maloney 1.00 2.50
RH3 Kobe Bryant 8.00 20.00
RH4 Ray Allen 2.00 5.00
RH5 Stephon Marbury 2.00 5.00
RH6 Kerry Kittles 1.00 2.50
RH7 John Wallace 1.00 2.50
RH8 Allen Iverson 3.00 8.00
RH9 Marcus Camby 1.50 4.00
RH10 Shareef Abdur-Rahim 1.50 4.00

1997-98 Hoops Talkin' Hoops

Inserted one in every series one pack, this 30-card set features color player photos of top NBA players with a commentary on the player by NBC personality Bill Walton. Card backs are numbered with a "TH" prefix.

COMPLETE SET (30) 4.00 10.00
ONE PER SER.1 PACK
1 Christian Laettner .15 .40
2 Antoine Walker .20 .50
3 Glen Rice .20 .50
4 Dennis Rodman .40 1.00
5 Scottie Pippen .30 .75
6 Terrell Brandon .12 .30
7 Michael Finley .20 .50
8 Grant Hill .30 .75
9 Joe Smith .15 .40
10 Charles Barkley .30 .75
11 Hakeem Olajuwon .25 .60
12 Reggie Miller .25 .60
13 Loy Vaught .12 .30
14 Shaquille O'Neal .50 1.25
15 Kobe Bryant 1.00 2.50
16 Kevin Garnett .30 .75
17 Tom Gugliotta .12 .30
18 Kerry Kittles .12 .30
19 John Wallace .10 .25
20 Patrick Ewing .15 .40
21 Jerry Stackhouse .25 .60
22 David Robinson .30 .75
23 Gary Payton .20 .50
24 Shawn Kemp .20 .50
25 Damon Stoudamire .15 .40
26 John Stockton .25 .60
27 Karl Malone .25 .60
28 Shareef Abdur-Rahim .20 .50
29 Juwan Howard .15 .40
30 Chris Webber .20 .50

1997-98 Hoops Top of the World

Randomly inserted in series two packs at a rate of one in 48, this 15-card set features 15 of the top rookies from the 1997 draft class. Card backs are numbered with a "TW" prefix.

COMPLETE SET (15) 12.00 30.00
SER.2 STATED ODDS 1:48 HOB/RET
TW1 Tim Duncan 5.00 12.00
TW2 Tim Thomas 1.00 2.50
TW3 Tony Battie .75 2.00
TW4 Keith Van Horn 1.25 3.00
TW5 Antonio Daniels .75 2.00
TW6 Derek Anderson .75 2.00
TW7 Chauncey Billups 2.50 6.00
TW8 Tracy McGrady 3.00 8.00
TW9 Danny Fortson .75 2.00
TW10 Austin Croshere .60 1.50
TW11 Tariq Abdul-Wahad .60 1.50
TW12 Adonal Foyle .60 1.50
TW13 Rodrick Rhodes .60 1.50
TW14 Ron Mercer 1.00 2.50
TW15 Charles Smith .60 1.50

1998-99 Hoops Promo Sheet

This promo sheet was distributed to dealers and hobby contacts to promote the 98/9 Hoops Basketball product. The sheet features 6 promo cards that carry a "Sample" designation on the back of each card.

1 Grant Hill .60 1.50
2 Kevin Garnett .60 1.50
3 Tim Duncan .75 2.00
4 Allen Iverson .75 2.00
5 Keith Van Horn .40 1.00
6 Shaquille O'Neal 1.00 2.50

1998-99 Hoops

The 1998-99 Hoops set consists of 167 standard size cards. The 12-card packs retail for a suggested price of $1.29. The fronts carry color action photos of NBA players in the foreground with an enlarged version of the photo in the background. The backs provide current statistics as well as what the featured player likes to do when he's not on the court. The set contains the subset Steppin' Out (156-165).

COMPLETE SET (167) 10.00 20.00
UNPRICED STARTING FIVE SERIAL #'d TO 5
1 Kobe Bryant .60 1.50
2 Glenn Robinson .12 .30
3 Derek Anderson .10 .25
4 Terry Dehere .10 .25
5 Jalen Rose .12 .30
6 Zydrunas Ilgauskas .15 .40
7 Scott Williams .10 .25
8 Toni Kukoc .15 .40
9 John Stockton .20 .50
10 Kevin Garnett .25 .60
11 Jerome Williams .10 .25
12 Anthony Mason .10 .25
13 Harvey Grant .10 .25
14 Mookie Blaylock .10 .25
15 Tyrone Hill .10 .25
16 Dale Davis .10 .25
17 Eric Washington .10 .25
18 Aaron McKie .10 .25
19 Jermaine O'Neal .15 .40
20 Anfernee Hardaway .25 .60
21 Derrick Coleman .12 .30
22 Allan Houston .12 .30
23 Michael Jordan 1.25 3.00
24 Jason Kidd .25 .60
25 Tyrone Corbin .10 .25
26 Jacque Vaughn .10 .25
27 Bobby Jackson .10 .25
28 Chris Anstey .10 .25
29 Brent Barry .12 .30
30 Shareef Abdur-Rahim .15 .40
31 Jeff Hornacek .12 .30
32 Ed Gray .10 .25
33 Grant Hill .25 .60
34 Steve Smith .12 .30
35 Rony Seikaly .10 .25
36 Mark Jackson .12 .30
37 Shawn Bradley .10 .25
38 Corie Blount .10 .25
39 Erick Dampier .10 .25
40 Kerry Kittles .10 .25
41 David Wesley .10 .25
42 Horace Grant .12 .30
43 Bobby Hurley .10 .25
44 Tariq Abdul-Wahad .10 .25
45 Brian Williams .10 .25
46 Ray Allen .20 .50
47 Kenny Anderson .12 .30
48 Rodrick Rhodes .10 .25
49 Greg Foster .10 .25
50 Tim Duncan .30 .75
51 Steve Nash .25 .60
52 Kelvin Cato .10 .25
53 Donyell Marshall .10 .25
54 Marcus Camby .12 .30
55 Kevin Willis .10 .25
56 Michael Finley .15 .40
57 Muggsy Bogues .12 .30
58 Mark Price .15 .40
59 Larry Johnson .15 .40
60 Karl Malone .20 .50
61 Greg Ostertag .10 .25
62 Sean Elliott .15 .40
63 Johnny Taylor .10 .25
64 Howard Eisley .10 .25
65 Chris Childs .10 .25
66 Walt Williams .10 .25
67 Tracy Murray .10 .25
68 Patrick Ewing .20 .50
69 Olden Polynice .10 .25
70 Allen Iverson .30 .75
71 David Robinson .25 .60
72 Calbert Cheaney .10 .25
73 Lamond Murray .10 .25
74 Scot Pollard .10 .25
75 Alonzo Mourning .20 .50
76 Tracy McGrady .25 .60
77 Jim McIlvaine .10 .25
78 Bob Sura .10 .25
79 Anthony Peeler .10 .25
80 Keith Van Horn .15 .40
81 Maurice Taylor .10 .25
82 Charles Smith .10 .25
83 Dikembe Mutombo .15 .40
84 Nick Anderson .10 .25
85 Austin Croshere .10 .25
86 Armon Gilliam .10 .25
87 Eddie Jones .15 .40
88 Glen Rice .12 .30
89 Sam Cassell .12 .30
90 Stephon Marbury .20 .50
91 Elliot Perry UER .10 .25
92 Jamal Mashburn .12 .30
93 Adonal Foyle .10 .25
94 Avery Johnson .12 .30
95 Micheal Williams .10 .25
96 Danny Fortson .10 .25
97 Brevin Knight .10 .25
98 Ron Harper .12 .30
99 Chauncey Billups .20 .50
100 Shaquille O'Neal .40 1.00
101 Brent Price .10 .25
102 Tim Thomas .15 .40
103 Khalid Reeves .10 .25
104 Chris Gatling .10 .25
105 Terry Cummings .12 .30
106 Vin Baker .12 .30
107 Bryant Reeves .10 .25
108 John Starks .12 .30
109 Juwan Howard .12 .30
110 Antoine Walker .15 .40
111 Rodney Rogers .10 .25
112 Nick Van Exel .12 .30
113 Chris Whitney .10 .25
114 Bobby Phills .10 .25
115 Travis Knight .10 .25
116 Robert Horry .12 .30
117 Erick Strickland .10 .25
118 Dontae Jones .10 .25
119 Tony Battie .12 .30
120 Lindsey Hunter .10 .25
121 Reggie Miller .20 .50
122 John Wallace .10 .25
123 Ron Mercer .12 .30
124 Antonio Daniels .10 .25
125 Paul Grant .10 .25
126 Voshon Lenard .10 .25
127 Shawn Kemp .15 .40
128 Antonio Davis .10 .25
129 Hakeem Olajuwon .20 .50
130 Danny Manning .12 .30
131 Bimbo Coles .10 .25
132 Tim Hardaway .15 .40
133 Lorenzo Williams .10 .25
134 Dan Majerle .15 .40
135 Bryant Stith .10 .25
136 Randy Brown .10 .25
137 Hubert Davis .10 .25
138 Gary Payton .15 .40
139 Rasheed Wallace .15 .40
140 Chris Robinson .10 .25
141 Doug Christie .10 .25
142 Brian Grant .10 .25
143 Isaiah Rider .12 .30
144 Kendall Gill .10 .25
145 Lorenzen Wright .10 .25
146 Ervin Johnson .10 .25
147 Monty Williams .10 .25
148 Keith Closs .10 .25
149 Tony Delk .10 .25
150 Hersey Hawkins .10 .25
151 Dean Garrett .10 .25
152 Cedric Henderson .10 .25
153 Detlef Schrempf .15 .40
154 Dana Barros .10 .25
155 Dee Brown .10 .25
156 Jayson Williams SO .10 .25
157 Charles Barkley SO .25 .60
158 Damon Stoudamire SO .12 .30
159 Scottie Pippen SO .25 .60
160 Joe Smith SO .12 .30
161 Antonio McDyess SO .12 .30
162 Jerry Stackhouse SO .15 .40
163 Dennis Rodman SO .30 .75
164 Shaquille O'Neal SO .40 1.00
165 Grant Hill SO .25 .60
166 Checklist .10 .25
167 Checklist .10 .25

1998-99 Hoops Bams

The 1998-99 Hoops Bams set consists of 10 cards and is an insert to the 1998-99 Hoops base set. The cards are randomly inserted in packs and each card is serially numbered to 250. The fronts feature ten of the game's most fearsome dunkers and is silver holo foil-stamped.

STATED PRINT RUN 250 SERIAL #'d SETS
1 Michael Jordan 1000.00 1700.00
2 Kobe Bryant 175.00 350.00
3 Allen Iverson 50.00 120.00
4 Shaquille O'Neal 75.00 200.00
5 Tim Duncan 75.00 200.00
6 Shareef Abdur-Rahim 10.00 25.00
7 Keith Van Horn 10.00 25.00
8 Grant Hill 50.00 120.00
9 Anfernee Hardaway 75.00 200.00
10 Kevin Garnett 40.00 100.00

1998-99 Hoops Slam Bams

*STARS: 1.25X TO 3X BAMS INSERT
STATED PRINT RUN 100 SERIAL #'d SETS
1 Michael Jordan 2000.00 3200.00
2 Kobe Bryant 1000.00 2000.00
3 Allen Iverson 200.00 500.00

1998-99 Hoops Freshman Flashback

The 1998-99 Hoops Freshman Flashback set consists of 10 cards and is an insert to the 1998-99 Hoops base set. The cards are randomly inserted in packs and are serially numbered to 1,000. The fronts feature black and white head and shoulder photos of the top 1997-98 rookies.

COMPLETE SET (10) 40.00 80.00
STATED PRINT RUN 1000 SERIAL #'d SETS
1 Tim Duncan 12.00 30.00
2 Keith Van Horn 6.00 15.00
3 Tim Thomas 6.00 15.00
4 Antonio Daniels 4.00 10.00
5 Brevin Knight 4.00 10.00
6 Danny Fortson 4.00 10.00
7 Maurice Taylor 4.00 10.00
8 Chauncey Billups 8.00 20.00
9 Bobby Jackson 4.00 10.00
10 Derek Anderson 4.00 10.00

1998-99 Hoops Prime Twine

The 1998-99 Hoops Prime Twine set consists of 10 cards and is an insert to the 1998-99 Hoops base set. The cards are randomly inserted in packs and are serially numbered to 500. The fronts feature color action photos of an NBA player in the foreground going up for the uniquely designed basket in the background. Each card is die-cut on the outside and gold foil-stamped on the inside.

STATED PRINT RUN 500 SERIAL #'d SETS
1 Dennis Rodman 75.00 200.00
2 Allen Iverson 75.00 200.00
3 Karl Malone 75.00 200.00
4 Antonio McDyess 20.00 50.00
5 Damon Stoudamire 30.00 80.00
6 Eddie Jones 25.00 60.00
7 Scottie Pippen 60.00 150.00
8 Shawn Kemp 30.00 80.00
9 Antoine Walker 25.00 60.00
10 Stephon Marbury 30.00 80.00

1998-99 Hoops Pump Up The Jam

The 1998-99 Hoops Pump Up The Jam set consists of 10 cards and is an insert to the 1998-99 Hoops base set. The cards are randomly inserted in packs at a rate of one in 4. The fronts carry a color action photo of the featured player in the foreground with a shoulder and head shot of the player in the background. The card is designed to resemble a movie poster with the player's credits written along the bottom of the card.

COMPLETE SET (10) 4.00 10.00
STATED ODDS 1:4 HOB/RET
1 Stephon Marbury .40 1.00
2 Allen Iverson .60 1.50
3 Grant Hill .50 1.25
4 Kobe Bryant 1.25 3.00
5 Michael Jordan 2.50 6.00
6 Antoine Walker .30 .75
7 Shareef Abdur-Rahim .30 .75
8 Shawn Kemp .30 .75
9 Anfernee Hardaway .50 1.25
10 Antonio McDyess .25 .60

1998-99 Hoops Rejectors

The 1998-99 Hoops Rejectors set consists of 10 cards and is an insert to the 1998-99 Hoops base set. The cards are randomly inserted in packs and serially numbered to 2,500. The fronts feature color action photos printed on gold foil-stamped cards. Running along the left side of the card are four smaller individual color photos of the featured player.

COMPLETE SET (10) 30.00 60.00
STATED PRINT RUN 2500 SERIAL #'d SETS
1 Dikembe Mutombo 2.50 6.00
2 Marcus Camby 2.00 5.00
3 Shaquille O'Neal 8.00 20.00
4 Tim Duncan 5.00 12.00
5 Shawn Bradley 1.50 4.00
6 Chris Webber 2.50 6.00
7 Patrick Ewing 3.00 8.00
8 Kevin Garnett 4.00 10.00
9 David Robinson 4.00 10.00
10 Michael Stewart 1.50 4.00

1998-99 Hoops Shout Outs

The 1998-99 Hoops Shout Outs set consists of 30 cards and is an insert to the 1998-99 Hoops base set. The cards are inserted one per pack. The fronts feature full color photos of the players expressing themselves against a white background.

COMPLETE SET (30) 4.00 10.00
STATED ODDS: ONE PER PACK
1 Shareef Abdur-Rahim .15 .40
2 Chauncey Billups .20 .50
3 Terrell Brandon UER .10 .25
4 Patrick Ewing .20 .50
5 Michael Finley .15 .40
6 Adonal Foyle .10 .25
7 Kevin Garnett .25 .60
8 Anfernee Hardaway .25 .60
9 Tim Hardaway .15 .40
10 Grant Hill .25 .60
11 Tim Thomas .15 .40
12 Bobby Jackson .10 .25
13 Michael Jordan 1.25 3.00
14 Shawn Kemp .15 .40
15 Jason Kidd .25 .60
16 Karl Malone .20 .50
17 Stephon Marbury .20 .50
18 Anthony Mason .10 .25
19 Reggie Miller .20 .50
20 Dikembe Mutombo .15 .40
21 Kobe Bryant .60 1.50
22 Hakeem Olajuwon .20 .50
23 Gary Payton .15 .40
24 Michael Stewart .10 .25
25 David Robinson .25 .60
26 Maurice Taylor .10 .25
27 Keith Van Horn .15 .40
28 Antoine Walker .15 .40
29 Rasheed Wallace .15 .40
30 Juwan Howard .12 .30

1999-00 Hoops

The 1999-00 Hoops set was released as a 185-card set that featured 117 player cards, 48 sophomore sensation cards and 20 rookie cards. There was only one series offered. Each pack contained 12-cards and carried a suggested retail price of $1.29.

COMPLETE SET (185) 15.00 30.00
UNPRICED STARTING FIVE SERIAL #'d TO 5
1 Paul Pierce .25 .60
2 Ray Allen .20 .50
3 Jason Williams .25 .60
4 Sean Elliott .20 .50
5 Al Harrington .20 .50
6 Bobby Phills .12 .30
7 Tyronn Lue .12 .30
8 James Cotton .12 .30
9 Anthony Peeler .12 .30
10 LaPhonso Ellis .12 .30
11 Voshon Lenard .12 .30
12 Kornel David RC .15 .40
13 Michael Finley .20 .50
14 Danny Fortson .12 .30
15 Antawn Jamison .20 .50
16 Reggie Miller .20 .50
17 Shaquille O'Neal .50 1.25
18 P.J. Brown .12 .30
19 Roshown McLeod .12 .30
20 Larry Johnson .20 .50
21 Rashard Lewis .20 .50
22 Tracy McGrady .30 .75
23 Peja Stojakovic .20 .50
24 Tracy Murray .12 .30
25 Gary Payton .20 .50
26 Ricky Davis .20 .50
27 Kobe Bryant .75 2.00
28 Avery Johnson .15 .40
29 Kevin Garnett .30 .75
30 Charles Jones RC .12 .30
31 Brevin Knight .12 .30
32 Lindsey Hunter .12 .30
33 Felipe Lopez .12 .30
34 Rik Smits .20 .50
35 Maurice Taylor .12 .30
36 Corey Benjamin .12 .30
37 Ervin Johnson .12 .30
38 Steve Smith .12 .30
39 Austin Croshere .12 .30
40 Matt Geiger .12 .30
41 Tom Gugliotta .12 .30
42 Radoslav Nesterovic RC .20 .50
43 Juwan Howard .15 .40
44 Keon Clark .12 .30
45 Latrell Sprewell .20 .50
46 George Lynch .12 .30
47 Greg Ostertag .12 .30
48 J.R. Henderson .12 .30
49 Kerry Kittles .12 .30
50 Matt Harpring .12 .30
51 Duane Causwell .12 .30
52 Andrae Patterson .12 .30
53 Jerry Stackhouse .20 .50
54 Adonal Foyle .12 .30
55 Bryce Drew .12 .30
56 Chris Childs .12 .30
57 Charles Smith .12 .30
58 Rony Seikaly .12 .30
59 Chauncey Billups .20 .50
60 Grant Hill .25 .60
61 Marlon Garnett RC .20 .50
62 Tim Hardaway .20 .50
63 Vlade Divac .20 .50
64 Chris Gatling .12 .30
65 Glenn Robinson .15 .40
66 Michael Olowokandi .12 .30
67 Elliot Perry .12 .30
68 Howard Eisley .12 .30
69 Glen Rice .20 .50
70 Marcus Camby .15 .40
71 Theo Ratliff .15 .40
72 Brian Skinner .12 .30
73 Kenny Anderson .15 .40
74 Jamal Mashburn .15 .40
75 Vladimir Stepania .12 .30
76 Jayson Williams .12 .30
77 Brian Grant .12 .30
78 Raef LaFrentz .15 .40
79 John Starks .15 .40
80 Mike Bibby .20 .50
81 Stephon Marbury .15 .40
82 Armon Gilliam .12 .30
83 Sam Jacobson .12 .30
84 Derrick Coleman .15 .40
85 Allan Houston .15 .40
86 Miles Simon .12 .30
87 Allen Iverson .40 1.00
88 Derek Anderson .12 .30
89 Chris Anstey .12 .30
90 Larry Hughes .15 .40
91 Vitaly Potapenko .12 .30
92 Cherokee Parks .12 .30
93 Donyell Marshall .12 .30
94 Danny Manning .15 .40
95 Bryon Russell .12 .30
96 Randell Jackson .12 .30
97 Antoine Walker .20 .50
98 Dirk Nowitzki .40 1.00
99 Karl Malone .25 .60
100 Vince Carter .40 1.00
101 Eddie Jones .20 .50
102 Bryant Stith .12 .30
103 Korleone Young .12 .30
104 Tim Duncan .40 1.00
105 Jerome Kersey .12 .30
106 Bonzi Wells .12 .30
107 Wesley Person .12 .30
108 Steve Nash .30 .75
109 Tyrone Nesby RC .15 .40
110 Doug Christie .15 .40
111 David Robinson .30 .75
112 Ruben Patterson .12 .30
113 Dikembe Mutombo .20 .50
114 Ron Mercer .15 .40
115 Elden Campbell .12 .30
116 Kevin Willis .12 .30
117 Hakeem Olajuwon .25 .60
118 Shawn Kemp .20 .50
119 Eric Montross .12 .30
120 Shareef Abdur-Rahim .15 .40
121 Bob Sura .12 .30
122 James Robinson .12 .30
123 Shawn Bradley .12 .30
124 Robert Traylor .12 .30
125 Dean Garrett .12 .30
126 Keith Van Horn .15 .40
127 Patrick Ewing .25 .60
128 Isaac Austin .12 .30
129 Jason Kidd .30 .75
130 Isaiah Rider .15 .40
131 Jerome James RC .20 .50
132 John Stockton .25 .60
133 Jason Caffey .12 .30
134 Bryant Reeves .12 .30
135 Michael Dickerson .12 .30
136 Chris Mullin .20 .50
137 Rasheed Wallace .20 .50
138 Cuttino Mobley .12 .30
139 Antonio McDyess .15 .40
140 Chris Webber .20 .50
141 Jelani McCoy .12 .30
142 Damon Stoudamire .15 .40
143 Gerald Brown .20 .50
144 Cory Carr .12 .30
145 Brent Barry .15 .40
146 Alan Henderson .12 .30
147 Nazr Mohammed .12 .30
148 Bison Dele .12 .30
149 Scottie Pippen .30 .75
150 Michael Doleac .12 .30
151 Nick Anderson .12 .30
152 Alonzo Mourning .25 .60
153 Jahidi White .12 .30
154 Jalen Rose .15 .40
155 Brad Miller .15 .40
156 Andrew DeClercq .12 .30
157 Erick Strickland .12 .30
158 Toni Kukoc .20 .50
159 Pat Garrity .12 .30
160 Bobby Jackson .12 .30
161 Steve Kerr .15 .40
162 Toby Bailey .12 .30
163 Charles Oakley .15 .40
164 Rod Strickland .12 .30
165 Rodrick Rhodes .12 .30
166 Ron Artest RC .40 1.00
167 William Avery RC .15 .40
168 Elton Brand RC .50 1.25
169 Baron Davis RC .50 1.25
170 John Celestand RC .12 .30
171 Jumaine Jones RC .15 .40
172 Andre Miller RC .40 1.00
173 Lee Nailon RC .20 .50
174 James Posey RC .20 .50
175 Jason Terry RC .30 .75
176 Kenny Thomas RC .20 .50
177 Steve Francis RC .50 1.25
178 Wally Szczerbiak RC .40 1.00
179 Richard Hamilton RC .40 1.00
180 Jonathan Bender RC .60 1.50
181 Shawn Marion RC .40 1.00
182 A.Radojevic RC .12 .30
183 Tim James RC .12 .30
184 Trajan Langdon RC .12 .30
185 Corey Maggette RC .30 .75

1999-00 Hoops Build Your Own Card

Randomly inserted in packs at one in four, this 10-card set features an opportunity for collectors to build their own insert set. Collectors had the opportunity to select from three different fronts and three different backs for each of the ten players.

COMPLETE SET (10) 8.00 20.00
1 Tim Duncan 1.50 4.00
2 Keith Van Horn .60 1.50
3 Vince Carter 1.50 4.00
4 Grant Hill 1.00 2.50
5 Shaquille O'Neal 2.00 5.00
6 Kevin Garnett 1.25 3.00
7 Allen Iverson 1.50 4.00
8 Jason Williams 1.00 2.50
9 Kobe Bryant 3.00 8.00
10 Paul Pierce 1.00 2.50

1999-00 Hoops Build Your Own Card Redemptions

STATED PRINT RUN 250 SER.#'d SETS
ONLY ONE CARD IS LISTED PER PLAYER
1a T.Duncan Ball/Body 40.00 100.00
1b T.Duncan Ball/Head 40.00 100.00
1c T.Duncan Ball/Horiz 40.00 100.00
1d T.Duncan No Ball/Body 40.00 100.00
1e T.Duncan No Ball/Head 40.00 100.00
1f T.Duncan No Ball/Horiz 40.00 100.00
1g T.Duncan Shoot/Body 40.00 100.00
1h T.Duncan Shoot/Head 40.00 100.00
1i T.Duncan Shoot/Horiz 40.00 100.00
2a K.Van Horn Ball/Body 15.00 40.00
2b K.Van Horn Ball/Head 15.00 40.00
2c K.Van Horn Ball/Horiz 15.00 40.00
2d K.Van Horn No Ball/Body 15.00 40.00
2e K.Van Horn No Ball/Head 15.00 40.00
2f K.Van Horn No Ball/Horiz 15.00 40.00
2g K.Van Horn Shoot/Body 15.00 40.00
2h K.Van Horn Shoot/Head 15.00 40.00
2i K.Van Horn Shoot/Horiz 15.00 40.00
3a V.Carter Ball/Body 40.00 100.00
3b V.Carter Ball/Head 40.00 100.00
3c V.Carter Ball/Horiz 40.00 100.00
3d V.Carter No Ball/Body 40.00 100.00
3e V.Carter No Ball/Head 40.00 100.00
3f V.Carter No Ball/Horiz 40.00 100.00
3g V.Carter Shoot/Body 40.00 100.00
3h V.Carter Shoot/Head 40.00 100.00
3i V.Carter Shoot/Horiz 40.00 100.00
4a G.Hill Ball/Body 60.00 150.00
4b G.Hill Ball/Head 60.00 150.00
4c G.Hill Ball/Horiz 60.00 150.00
4d G.Hill No Ball/Body 60.00 150.00
4e G.Hill No Ball/Head 60.00 150.00
4f G.Hill No Ball/Horiz 60.00 150.00
4g G.Hill Shoot/Body 60.00 150.00
4h G.Hill Shoot/Head 60.00 150.00
4i G.Hill Shoot/Horiz 60.00 150.00
5a S.O'Neal Ball/Body 50.00 125.00
5b S.O'Neal Ball/Head 50.00 125.00
5c S.O'Neal Ball/Horiz 50.00 125.00
5d S.O'Neal No Ball/Body 50.00 125.00
5e S.O'Neal No Ball/Head 50.00 125.00
5f S.O'Neal No Ball/Horiz 50.00 125.00
5g S.O'Neal Shoot/Body 50.00 125.00
5h S.O'Neal Shoot/Head 50.00 125.00
5i S.O'Neal Shoot/Horiz 50.00 125.00
6a K.Garnett Ball/Body 30.00 80.00
6b K.Garnett Ball/Head 30.00 80.00
6c K.Garnett Ball/Horiz 30.00 80.00
6d K.Garnett No Ball/Body 30.00 80.00
6e K.Garnett No Ball/Head 30.00 80.00
6f K.Garnett No Ball/Horiz 30.00 80.00
6g K.Garnett Shoot/Body 30.00 80.00
6h K.Garnett Shoot/Head 30.00 80.00
6i K.Garnett Shoot/Horiz 30.00 80.00
7a A.Iverson Ball/Body 40.00 100.00
7b A.Iverson Ball/Head 40.00 100.00
7c A.Iverson Ball/Horiz 40.00 100.00
7d A.Iverson No Ball/Body 40.00 100.00
7e A.Iverson No Ball/Head 40.00 100.00
7f A.Iverson No Ball/Horiz 40.00 100.00
7g A.Iverson Shoot/Body 40.00 100.00
7h A.Iverson Shoot/Head 40.00 100.00
7i A.Iverson Shoot/Horiz 40.00 100.00
8a J.Williams Ball/Body 30.00 80.00
8b J.Williams Ball/Head 30.00 80.00
8c J.Williams Ball/Horiz 30.00 80.00
8d J.Williams No Ball/Body 30.00 80.00
8e J.Williams No Ball/Head 30.00 80.00
8f J.Williams No Ball/Horiz 30.00 80.00
8g J.Williams Shoot/Body 30.00 80.00
8h J.Williams Shoot/Head 30.00 80.00
8i J.Williams Shoot/Horiz 30.00 80.00
9a K.Bryant Ball/Body 80.00 200.00
9b K.Bryant Ball/Head 80.00 200.00
9c K.Bryant Ball/Horiz 80.00 200.00
9d K.Bryant No Ball/Body 80.00 200.00
9e K.Bryant No Ball/Head 80.00 200.00
9f K.Bryant No Ball/Horiz 80.00 200.00
9g K.Bryant Shoot/Body 80.00 200.00
9h K.Bryant Shoot/Head 80.00 200.00
9i K.Bryant Shoot/Horiz 80.00 200.00
10a P.Pierce Ball/Body 25.00 60.00
10b P.Pierce Ball/Head 25.00 60.00
10c P.Pierce Ball/Horiz 25.00 60.00
10d P.Pierce No Ball/Body 25.00 60.00
10e P.Pierce No Ball/Head 25.00 60.00
10f P.Pierce No Ball/Horiz 25.00 60.00
10g P.Pierce Shoot/Body 25.00 60.00
10h P.Pierce Shoot/Head 25.00 60.00
10i P.Pierce Shoot/Horiz 25.00 60.00

1999-00 Hoops Calling Card

Randomly inserted in packs at one in eight, this 15-card set features signature moves from some of the best in the NBA. Card backs carry a "CC" prefix.

COMPLETE SET (15) 5.00 12.00
STATED ODDS 1:8 HOB/RET
CC1 Kobe Bryant 2.00 5.00
CC2 Kevin Garnett .75 2.00
CC3 Tim Hardaway .50 1.25
CC4 Grant Hill .60 1.50
CC5 Allen Iverson 1.00 2.50
CC6 Karl Malone .60 1.50
CC7 Shawn Kemp .50 1.25
CC8 Stephon Marbury .40 1.00
CC9 Shaquille O'Neal 1.25 3.00
CC10 Hakeem Olajuwon .60 1.50
CC11 Ray Allen .50 1.25
CC12 Damon Stoudamire .40 1.00
CC13 Jason Williams .60 1.50
CC14 Keith Van Horn .40 1.00
CC15 Dikembe Mutombo .50 1.25

1999-00 Hoops Dunk Mob

Randomly inserted in packs at one in 144, this 10-card set highlights some of the league's best dunkers on a silver holo-foil stamped card. Card backs carry a "DM" prefix.

COMPLETE SET (10) 25.00 60.00
STATED ODDS 1:144 HOB/RET
DM1 Shaquille O'Neal 10.00 25.00
DM2 Stephon Marbury 3.00 8.00
DM3 Paul Pierce 5.00 12.00
DM4 Antawn Jamison 4.00 10.00
DM5 Michael Olowokandi 2.50 6.00
DM6 Scottie Pippen 6.00 15.00
DM7 Antonio McDyess 3.00 8.00
DM8 Vince Carter 8.00 20.00
DM9 Ron Mercer 3.00 8.00
DM10 Shawn Kemp 4.00 10.00

1999-00 Hoops Name Plates

Randomly inserted in packs at one in four, this 10-card set features a die cut and embossed card modeled after vanity license plates featuring NBA players that have prominent nicknames. Card backs carry a "NP" prefix.

COMPLETE SET (10) 2.00 5.00
STATED ODDS 1:4 HOB/RET
NP1 Shareef Abdur-Rahim .20 .50
NP2 Allen Iverson .50 1.25
NP3 Karl Malone .30 .75
NP4 Gary Payton .25 .60
NP5 Hakeem Olajuwon .30 .75
NP6 Glenn Robinson .20 .50
NP7 Kevin Garnett .40 1.00
NP8 Anfernee Hardaway .40 1.00
NP9 David Robinson .40 1.00
NP10 Shaquille O'Neal .60 1.50

1999-00 Hoops Pure Players

Randomly inserted in packs, this 10-card set features a profile of top NBA players on silver plastic stock with orange foil type. The cards are serially numbered to 500. Card backs carry a "PP" prefix.

STATED PRINT RUN 500 SERIAL #'d SETS
PP1 Tim Duncan 25.00 60.00
PP2 Keith Van Horn 10.00 25.00
PP3 Stephon Marbury 10.00 25.00
PP4 Grant Hill 15.00 40.00
PP5 Kobe Bryant 100.00 250.00
PP6 Kevin Garnett 40.00 100.00
PP7 Allen Iverson 40.00 100.00
PP8 Antoine Walker 12.00 30.00
PP9 Shareef Abdur-Rahim 10.00 25.00
PP10 Anfernee Hardaway 20.00 50.00

1999-00 Hoops Pure Players 100%

*STARS: .75X TO 2X VALUE
STATED PRINT RUN 100 SERIAL #'d SETS

1999-00 Hoops Y2K Corps

Randomly inserted in packs at one in 16, this 10-card set features the top rookies from last year. The cards are set against an embossed and silver foil-stamped backing. Card backs carry a "BB" prefix.

COMPLETE SET (10) 3.00 8.00
STATED ODDS 1:16 HOB/RET
BB1 Michael Olowokandi .40 1.00
BB2 Mike Bibby .60 1.50
BB3 Jason Williams .75 2.00
BB4 Dirk Nowitzki 1.25 3.00
BB5 Vince Carter 1.25 3.00
BB6 Robert Traylor .40 1.00
BB7 Larry Hughes .50 1.25
BB8 Paul Pierce .75 2.00
BB9 Matt Harpring .40 1.00
BB10 Michael Dickerson .40 1.00

2004-05 Hoops

Released in April, 2005, this is the return of Hoops, a brand that has been on hiatus since 1999-00. The 197-card set divides into 165 veteran cards, seven Hoops History cards serially numbered to 1989 (card numbers 166-175) and 25 rookie cards serially numbered to 1750 (card numbers 176-200). Base cards are borderless and feature a strip along the bottom with the player's information. Hoops was packaged in 24-pack boxes of five cards each. Upon release, packs carried a SRP of $1.99.

COMP.SET w/o SP's (165) 15.00 40.00
176-200 RC PRINT RUN 1750 SER.#'d SETS
CARDS 168-170 NOT RELEASED
1 Dwyane Wade .40 1.00
2 Vince Carter .40 1.00
3 Luke Walton .15 .40
4 Alonzo Mourning .30 .75
5 Antoine Walker .25 .60
6 Jerry Stackhouse .20 .50
7 Chris Wilcox .15 .40
8 Udonis Haslem .15 .40
9 Michael Redd .20 .50
10 Darius Miles .15 .40
11 Jarvis Hayes .15 .40
12 Kirk Hinrich .20 .50
13 Tayshaun Prince .20 .50
14 Caron Butler .20 .50
15 Sam Cassell .20 .50
16 Kurt Thomas .15 .40
17 Bruce Bowen .15 .40
18 Jared Jeffries .15 .40
19 Keith Bogans .15 .40
20 Chauncey Billups .25 .60
21 Lamar Odom .20 .50
22 Fred Hoiberg .15 .40
23 Cuttino Mobley .15 .40
24 Manu Ginobili .30 .75
25 Juan Dixon .15 .40
26 Predrag Drobnjak .15 .40
27 Nene .20 .50
28 Elton Brand .25 .60
29 Rasual Butler .15 .40
30 Nick Van Exel .20 .50
31 Carlos Arroyo .15 .40
32 Zydrunas Ilgauskas .20 .50
33 Troy Murphy .15 .40
34 Jason Williams .20 .50
35 Jason Kidd .40 1.00
36 Samuel Dalembert .15 .40
37 Vladimir Radmanovic .15 .40
38 Kenny Anderson .20 .50
39 Kenyon Martin .20 .50
40 Jamaal Tinsley .15 .40
41 Damon Jones .15 .40
42 Shareef Abdur-Rahim .20 .50
43 Ricky Davis .20 .50
44 Earl Boykins .15 .40
45 Austin Croshere .15 .40
46 Keith Van Horn .20 .50
47 Theo Ratliff .15 .40
48 Mehmet Okur .20 .50
49 Paul Pierce .25 .60
50 Marcus Camby .20 .50
51 Stephen Jackson .20 .50
52 Maurice Williams .20 .50
53 Brad Miller .20 .50
54 Carlos Boozer .20 .50
55 Dirk Nowitzki .40 1.00
56 Dikembe Mutombo .25 .60
57 James Posey .15 .40
58 Baron Davis .20 .50
59 Shawn Marion .20 .50
60 Ronald Murray .15 .40
61 Gary Payton .25 .60
62 Andre Miller .20 .50
63 Reggie Miller .25 .60
64 Zaza Pachulia .15 .40
65 Bobby Jackson .15 .40
66 Peja Stojakovic .25 .60
67 Jiri Welsch .15 .40
68 Darko Milicic .15 .40
69 Ron Artest .25 .60
70 T.J. Ford .15 .40
71 Andrei Kirilenko .20 .50
72 Jason Kapono .15 .40
73 Jermaine O'Neal .20 .50
74 Desmond Mason .20 .50
75 Chris Webber .25 .60
76 Morris Peterson .15 .40
77 Ben Wallace .20 .50
78 Antonio Davis .15 .40
79 Slava Medvedenko .15 .40
80 Brian Scalabrine .15 .40
81 Jamal Crawford .25 .60
82 Josh Howard .25 .60
83 Tyson Chandler .20 .50
84 Rasheed Wallace .25 .60
85 Chris Mihm .15 .40
86 Latrell Sprewell .20 .50
87 Mike Sweetney .15 .40
88 Robert Horry .20 .50
89 Michael Finley .25 .60
90 Bostjan Nachbar .15 .40
91 Allan Houston .20 .50
92 Joe Johnson .20 .50
93 Jalen Rose .20 .50
94 Marquis Daniels .15 .40
95 Tyronn Lue .15 .40
96 Stephon Marbury .20 .50
97 Quentin Richardson .20 .50
98 Chris Bosh .25 .60
99 Dajuan Wagner .15 .40
100 Derek Fisher .20 .50
101 Devean George .15 .40
102 Zoran Planinic .15 .40
103 Corliss Williamson .15 .40
104 Brent Barry .15 .40
105 Drew Gooden .15 .40
106 Clifford Robinson .15 .40
107 Shane Battier .20 .50
108 P.J. Brown .15 .40
109 Willie Green .15 .40
110 Nick Collison .20 .50
111 Al Harrington .20 .50
112 Carmelo Anthony .50 1.25
113 Corey Maggette .20 .50
114 Eddie Jones .20 .50
115 Zach Randolph .20 .50
116 Raja Bell .20 .50
117 Jeff McInnis .15 .40
118 Yao Ming .50 1.25
119 Brian Cardinal .15 .40
120 Jamaal Magloire .15 .40
121 Kyle Korver .20 .50
122 Luke Ridnour .20 .50
123 Jason Terry .20 .50
124 Maurice Taylor .15 .40
125 Bonzi Wells .15 .40
126 David West .20 .50
127 Amare Stoudemire .20 .50
128 Ray Allen .25 .60
129 Eddy Curry .15 .40
130 Richard Hamilton .20 .50
131 Kobe Bryant 1.00 2.50
132 Kevin Garnett .40 1.00
133 Steve Francis .20 .50
134 Tim Duncan .40 1.00
135 Larry Hughes .20 .50
136 LeBron James 1.50 4.00
137 Adonal Foyle .15 .40
138 Pau Gasol .25 .60
139 Richard Jefferson .20 .50
140 Allen Iverson .40 1.00
141 Antonio Daniels .15 .40
142 Eric Williams .15 .40
143 Primoz Brezec .15 .40
144 Jason Richardson .25 .60
145 Chris Kaman .20 .50
146 Troy Hudson .15 .40
147 Hedo Turkoglu .20 .50
148 Tony Parker .25 .60
149 Gilbert Arenas .20 .50
150 Eric Snow .15 .40
151 Tracy McGrady .30 .75
152 Stromile Swift .15 .40
153 Dan Dickau .15 .40
154 Steve Nash .30 .75
155 Rashard Lewis .25 .60
156 Gerald Wallace .20 .50
157 Mike Dunleavy .20 .50
158 Bobby Simmons .15 .40
159 Wally Szczerbiak .20 .50
160 Grant Hill .30 .75
161 Mike Bibby .25 .60
162 Antawn Jamison .20 .50
163 Antonio McDyess .20 .50
164 Shaquille O'Neal .60 1.50
165 Rafer Alston .15 .40
166 Charles Barkley HH 4.00 10.00
167 David Robinson HH 4.00 10.00
171 Larry Bird HH 6.00 15.00
172 Scottie Pippen HH 4.00 10.00
173 Isiah Thomas HH 2.50 6.00
174 Kevin McHale HH 3.00 8.00
175 Dominique Wilkins HH 3.00 8.00
176 Josh Childress RC 1.00 2.50
177 Josh Smith RC 1.25 3.00
178 Al Jefferson RC 1.50 4.00
179 Delonte West RC 1.25 3.00
180 Tony Allen RC 1.25 3.00
181 Emeka Okafor RC 1.00 2.50
182 Bernard Robinson RC 1.00 2.50
183 Ben Gordon RC 1.25 3.00
184 Luol Deng RC 1.25 3.00
185 Andres Nocioni RC 1.25 3.00
186 Luke Jackson RC .75 2.00
187 Devin Harris RC 1.00 2.50
188 Andris Biedrins RC .75 2.00
189 Shaun Livingston RC 1.25 3.00
190 Dorell Wright RC 1.25 3.00
191 J.R. Smith RC 1.25 3.00
192 Trevor Ariza RC 1.25 3.00
193 Dwight Howard RC 2.50 6.00
194 Jameer Nelson RC 1.25 3.00
195 Andre Iguodala RC 1.50 4.00
196 Sebastian Telfair RC 1.00 2.50
197 Kevin Martin RC 1.50 4.00
198 David Harrison RC .75 2.00
199 Rafael Araujo RC .75 2.00
200 Kirk Snyder RC .75 2.00

2004-05 Hoops 100

*1-165 SINGLES: 3X TO 8X BASE HI
*166-175 HH: .6X TO 1.5X BASE HI
*176-200 RC's: .75X TO 2X BASE HI
PRINT RUN 100 SER.#'d SETS

2004-05 Hoops Autographs

Randomly seeded, this 25-card set parallels the look of the base Hoops set enhanced with a cut signature. Each card is serially numbered to 75. A parallel version of this set serially numbered to 25 was also inserted.

PRINT RUN 75 SER.#'d SETS
*AUTO 25: .6X TO 1.5X BASE HI
AB Andris Biedrins 3.00 8.00
BG Ben Gordon 5.00 12.00
CB2 Carlos Boozer 5.00 12.00
DH David Harrison 3.00 8.00
DW David West 6.00 15.00
KK Kyle Korver 10.00 25.00
LD Luol Deng 5.00 12.00
LJ Luke Jackson 3.00 8.00
LR Luke Ridnour 5.00 12.00
MD Marquis Daniels 5.00 12.00
PS Peja Stojakovic 12.00 30.00
RH Richard Hamilton 10.00 25.00
SB Shane Battier 5.00 12.00

2004-05 Hoops Great Shots

Randomly inserted at the rage of one in 72 packs, this 10-card set utilizes a horizontal design where player images appear on the right against a black and red colored background.

COMPLETE SET (10) 10.00 25.00
STATED ODDS 1:72
1 Kobe Bryant 3.00 8.00
2 LeBron James 5.00 12.00
3 Carmelo Anthony 1.50 4.00
4 Ben Wallace .60 1.50
5 Tim Duncan 1.25 3.00
6 Kevin Garnett 1.25 3.00
7 Jason Kidd 1.25 3.00
8 Yao Ming 1.50 4.00
9 Amare Stoudemire .60 1.50
10 Dwyane Wade 1.25 3.00

2004-05 Hoops Great Shots Jerseys

Randomly inserted in packs, this eight-card set parallels the base Great Shots insert enhanced with a square swatch of jersey on the left side of the card. The background is blue, as is the border around the jersey. A Green version containing a small green foil emblem was issued for some players, and a patch version sequentially numbered to 25 was also inserted.

STATED ODDS 1:144
*GREEN: .4X TO 1X BASE JSY HI
GREEN: RANDOM INSERTS IN PACKS
*PATCH: 1X TO 2.5X BASE HI
PATCH PRINT RUN 25 SER.#'d SETS
AS Amare Stoudemire 2.00 5.00
BW Ben Wallace 2.00 5.00
CA Carmelo Anthony 5.00 12.00
DW Dwyane Wade 4.00 10.00
JK Jason Kidd 4.00 10.00
KG Kevin Garnett 4.00 10.00
TD Tim Duncan 4.00 10.00
YM Yao Ming 5.00 12.00

2004-05 Hoops Hot List

Inserted in packs at one in 10, this 15-card set features a tan wood-looking background with player images on the right and the words Hot List on the left. The "o" from hot list is on fire.

COMPLETE SET (15) 8.00 20.00
STATED ODDS 1:10
1 Dwyane Wade .75 2.00
2 LeBron James 3.00 8.00
3 Kobe Bryant 2.00 5.00
4 Shaquille O'Neal 1.25 3.00
5 Michael Redd .40 1.00
6 Tracy McGrady .60 1.50
7 Richard Hamilton .40 1.00
8 Tony Parker .50 1.25
9 Allen Iverson .75 2.00
10 Chris Webber .50 1.25
11 Paul Pierce .50 1.25
12 Jermaine O'Neal .40 1.00
13 Pau Gasol .50 1.25
14 Zach Randolph .40 1.00
15 Andrei Kirilenko .40 1.00

2004-05 Hoops Hot List Jerseys

Randomly inserted in packs at the rate of one in 144, this 13-card set parallels the base Hot List set enhanced with a swatch of jersey in the letter "o" from the words, Hot List.

STATED ODDS 1:144
UNPRICED PATCH PRINT RUN 10 SETS
AI Allen Iverson 4.00 10.00
AK Andrei Kirilenko 2.00 5.00
CW Chris Webber 2.50 6.00
DW Dwyane Wade 4.00 10.00
JO Jermaine O'Neal 2.00 5.00
MR Michael Redd 2.00 5.00
RH Richard Hamilton 2.00 5.00
SO Shaquille O'Neal 6.00 15.00
TM Tracy McGrady 3.00 8.00
ZR Zach Randolph 2.00 5.00

2004-05 Hoops Nameplates

Randomly inserted in packs, this 30-card set is horizontally designed with a player photo on the left side of the card and a square swatch from the name plate on the back of the player's jersey. Cards are all sequentially numbered. An autographed version also serially numbered to 25 were also produced.

PRINT RUNS LISTED IN CHECKLIST
PLATES 25 NOT PRICED DUE TO SCARCITY
UNPRICED AU PRINT RUN 25 SETS
AI Allen Iverson/49 10.00 25.00
AS Amare Stoudemire/43 5.00 12.00
CA Carmelo Anthony/48 12.00 30.00
CK Chris Kaman/40 5.00 12.00
KG Kevin Garnett/48 10.00 25.00
LD Luol Deng/26 8.00 20.00
MD Mike Dunleavy/48 5.00 12.00
MG Manu Ginobili/49 8.00 20.00
MS Mike Sweetney/47 5.00 12.00
RJ Richard Jefferson/50 5.00 12.00
SC Sam Cassell/28 6.00 15.00
VC Vince Carter/45 10.00 25.00

2004-05 Hoops Nameplates Dual

Randomly inserted in packs, this 15-card set parallels the design of the Nameplates insert with two players and two swatches of name plate. Each card is sequentially numbered to 25.

PRINT RUN 25 SER.#'d SETS
BD C.Boozer/L.Deng 15.00 40.00
DN B.Davis/J.Nelson 10.00 25.00
IG A.Iverson/K.Garnett 20.00 50.00
JM R.Jefferson/K.Martin 10.00 25.00
KL C.Kaman/S.Livingston 10.00 25.00
MS D.Milicic/P.Stojakovic 10.00 25.00
SG L.Sprewell/K.Garnett 12.00 30.00

2004-05 Hoops Nameplates Triple

Randomly inserted in packs, this 15-card set parallels the design of the Nameplates insert with three players and three swatches of name plate. Each card is sequentially numbered to 13.

PRINT RUN 13 SER.#'d SETS
GCS KG/Cassell/Sprewell 30.00 80.00
KSD Kaman/Stoj/Dunleavy 12.00 30.00

2004-05 Hoops Supreme Court

Inserted in packs at one in eight, this 20-card set centers player photos on a brown background with the words, Supreme Court, appearing along the top.

COMPLETE SET (20) 12.50 30.00
STATED ODDS 1:8
1 Kobe Bryant 2.00 5.00
2 LeBron James 3.00 8.00
3 Shaquille O'Neal 1.25 3.00
4 Ben Wallace .40 1.00
5 Yao Ming 1.00 2.50
6 Vince Carter .75 2.00
7 Tim Duncan .75 2.00
8 Kevin Garnett .75 2.00
9 Carmelo Anthony 1.00 2.50
10 Richard Jefferson .40 1.00
11 Dwyane Wade .75 2.00
12 Steve Francis .40 1.00
13 Dirk Nowitzki .75 2.00
14 Allen Iverson .75 2.00
15 Jermaine O'Neal .40 1.00
16 Corey Maggette .40 1.00
17 Paul Pierce .50 1.25
18 Baron Davis .40 1.00
19 Ray Allen .50 1.25
20 Jason Richardson .50 1.25

2004-05 Hoops Supreme Court Jerseys

Randomly inserted in packs, this 18-card set parallels the base Supreme Court insert enhanced with a swatch of jersey on the right side of the card. A Green version containing a small green foil emblem was issued for some players, and a patch version sequentially numbered to 25 was also inserted.

STATED ODDS 1:72
*GREEN: .4X TO 1X BASE JSY HI
GREEN: RANDOM INSERTS IN PACKS
*PATCH: 1X TO 2.5X BASE HI
PATCH PRINT RUN 25 SER.#'d SETS
AI Allen Iverson 4.00 10.00
BW Ben Wallace 2.00 5.00
CA Carmelo Anthony 5.00 12.00
CM Corey Maggette 2.00 5.00
DN Dirk Nowitzki 4.00 10.00
DW Dwyane Wade 4.00 10.00
JR Jason Richardson 2.50 6.00
KG Kevin Garnett 4.00 10.00
PP Paul Pierce 2.50 6.00
RA Ray Allen 2.50 6.00
RJ Richard Jefferson 2.00 5.00
SO Shaquille O'Neal 6.00 15.00
TD Tim Duncan 4.00 10.00
VC Vince Carter 4.00 10.00
YM Yao Ming 5.00 12.00

2005-06 Hoops

Issued in February 2007, this 184-card set features veteran players on cards 1-142 and rookie players on cards 143-184. The base design is borderless with full color player images and a color bar across the bottom in team colors featuring the player's name and team logo. Hoops was packaged in 24-pack boxes where packs contain five cards and carried an initial SRP of $1.99.

COMPLETE SET (184) 20.00 50.00
1 Josh Childress .20 .50
2 Al Harrington .20 .50
3 Josh Smith .20 .50
4 Tony Delk .15 .40
5 Joe Johnson .20 .50
6 Al Jefferson .20 .50
7 Paul Pierce .25 .60
8 Ricky Davis .20 .50
9 Tony Allen .15 .40
10 Dan Dickau .15 .40
11 Keith Bogans .15 .40
12 Emeka Okafor .20 .50
13 Kareem Rush .15 .40
14 Gerald Wallace .20 .50
15 Primoz Brezec .15 .40
16 Ben Gordon .20 .50
17 Luol Deng .20 .50
18 Kirk Hinrich .20 .50
19 Chris Duhon .15 .40
20 Michael Jordan 2.00 5.00
21 LeBron James 1.00 2.50
22 Larry Hughes .20 .50
23 Donyell Marshall .15 .40
24 Drew Gooden .20 .50
25 Zydrunas Ilgauskas .20 .50
26 Erick Dampier .15 .40
27 Jason Terry .20 .50
28 Josh Howard .25 .60
29 Dirk Nowitzki .40 1.00
30 Jerry Stackhouse .20 .50
31 Carmelo Anthony .50 1.25
32 Marcus Camby .20 .50
33 Nene .20 .50
34 Kenyon Martin .20 .50
35 Chauncey Billups .25 .60
36 Richard Hamilton .20 .50
37 Ben Wallace .20 .50
38 Rasheed Wallace .25 .60
39 Tayshaun Prince .20 .50
40 Baron Davis .20 .50
41 Mike Dunleavy .20 .50
42 Mickael Pietrus .20 .50
43 Jason Richardson .25 .60
44 Tracy McGrady .30 .75
45 Yao Ming .30 .75
46 Stromile Swift .15 .40
47 Bob Sura .15 .40
48 Jermaine O'Neal .20 .50
49 Ron Artest .25 .60
50 Fred Jones .15 .40
51 Stephen Jackson .20 .50
52 Corey Maggette .20 .50
53 Elton Brand .25 .60
54 Shaun Livingston .15 .40
55 Chris Wilcox .15 .40
56 Chris Kaman .20 .50
57 Kobe Bryant 1.00 2.50
58 Lamar Odom .20 .50
59 Kwame Brown .15 .40
60 Luke Walton .15 .40
61 Devean George .15 .40
62 Pau Gasol .25 .60
63 Shane Battier .20 .50
64 Bobby Jackson .15 .40
65 Eddie Jones .20 .50
66 Lorenzen Wright .15 .40
67 Shaquille O'Neal .50 1.25
68 Dwyane Wade .40 1.00
69 Antoine Walker .20 .50
70 Jason Williams .20 .50
71 James Posey .15 .40
72 T.J. Ford .15 .40
73 Dan Gadzuric .15 .40
74 Desmond Mason .15 .40
75 Michael Redd .20 .50
76 Kevin Garnett .40 1.00
77 Sam Cassell .20 .50
78 Eddie Griffin .15 .40
79 Wally Szczerbiak .20 .50
80 Michael Olowokandi .15 .40
81 Jeff McInnis .15 .40
82 Vince Carter .40 1.00
83 Jason Kidd .40 1.00
84 Richard Jefferson .20 .50
85 Clifford Robinson .15 .40
86 P.J. Brown .15 .40
87 Jamaal Magloire .15 .40
88 J.R. Smith .20 .50
89 Speedy Claxton .15 .40
90 Jamal Crawford .25 .60
91 Stephon Marbury .20 .50
92 Quentin Richardson .20 .50
93 Mike Sweetney .15 .40
94 Malik Rose .15 .40
95 Steve Francis .20 .50
96 Dwight Howard .20 .50
97 Keyon Dooling .15 .40
98 Grant Hill .30 .75
99 Jameer Nelson .15 .40
100 Allen Iverson .40 1.00
101 Samuel Dalembert .15 .40
102 Chris Webber .25 .60
103 Andre Iguodala .20 .50
104 Kyle Korver .20 .50
105 Steve Nash .30 .75
106 Shawn Marion .20 .50
107 Amare Stoudemire .20 .50
108 Kurt Thomas .15 .40
109 Darius Miles .15 .40
110 Zach Randolph .20 .50
111 Sebastian Telfair .20 .50
112 Ruben Patterson .15 .40
113 Joel Przybilla .15 .40
114 Mike Bibby .25 .60
115 Peja Stojakovic .25 .60
116 Brad Miller .20 .50
117 Bonzi Wells .15 .40
118 Tim Duncan .40 1.00
119 Manu Ginobili .25 .60
120 Tony Parker .25 .60
121 Robert Horry .20 .50
122 Bruce Bowen .15 .40
123 Ray Allen .25 .60
124 Rashard Lewis .25 .60
125 Vladimir Radmanovic .15 .40
126 Luke Ridnour .20 .50
127 Reggie Evans .15 .40
128 Chris Bosh .25 .60
129 Morris Peterson .15 .40
130 Rafer Alston .15 .40
131 Rafael Araujo .15 .40
132 Jalen Rose .25 .60
133 Carlos Boozer .20 .50
134 Gordan Giricek .15 .40
135 Matt Harpring .15 .40
136 Andrei Kirilenko .20 .50
137 Mehmet Okur .15 .40
138 Gilbert Arenas .20 .50
139 Antawn Jamison .20 .50
140 Caron Butler .20 .50
141 Antonio Daniels .15 .40
142 Brendan Haywood .15 .40
143 Sarunas Jasikevicius RC .75 2.00
144 Ryan Gomes RC .60 1.50
145 Andray Blatche RC .75 2.00
146 Bracey Wright RC .50 1.25
147 Louis Williams RC .75 2.00
148 Martynas Andriuskevicius RC .50 1.25
149 Chris Taft RC .60 1.50
150 Monta Ellis RC 1.00 2.50
151 Travis Diener RC .50 1.25
152 Ersan Ilyasova RC .75 2.00
153 Yaroslav Korolev RC .50 1.25
154 C.J. Miles RC .75 2.00
155 Brandon Bass RC .60 1.50
156 Daniel Ewing RC .60 1.50
157 Salim Stoudamire RC .60 1.50
158 David Lee RC .75 2.00
159 Wayne Simien RC .50 1.25
160 Linas Kleiza RC .50 1.25
161 Jason Maxiell RC .60 1.50
162 Johan Petro RC .50 1.25
163 Luther Head RC .60 1.50
164 Francisco Garcia RC .60 1.50
165 Jarrett Jack RC .75 2.00
166 Nate Robinson RC .75 2.00
167 Julius Hodge RC .50 1.25
168 Hakim Warrick RC .60 1.50
169 Gerald Green RC .75 2.00
170 Danny Granger RC 1.00 2.50
171 Joey Graham RC .60 1.50
172 Antoine Wright RC .60 1.50
173 Rashad McCants RC .60 1.50
174 Sean May RC .50 1.25
175 Andrew Bynum RC .60 1.50
176 Ike Diogu RC .50 1.25
177 Channing Frye RC .75 2.00
178 Charlie Villanueva RC .75 2.00
179 Martell Webster RC .60 1.50
180 Raymond Felton RC .75 2.00
181 Chris Paul RC 3.00 8.00
182 Deron Williams RC 1.00 2.50
183 Marvin Williams RC .75 2.00
184 Andrew Bogut RC 1.00 2.50

2005-06 Hoops Genuine Coverage

Randomly inserted in packs, this 41-card set features full color player photos and swatches of memorabilia. SP information was provided by Upper Deck.

RANDOM INSERTS IN PACKS
GCAH Al Harrington 2.00 5.00
GCAK Andrei Kirilenko 2.00 5.00
GCAM Antonio McDyess 2.00 5.00
GCAS Amare Stoudemire SP 2.00 5.00
GCBD Baron Davis 2.00 5.00
GCCA Caron Butler 2.00 5.00
GCCB Carlos Boozer 2.00 5.00
GCCM Corey Maggette 2.00 5.00
GCCW Chris Webber 2.50 6.00
GCDA Darko Milicic 2.00 5.00
GCDF Derek Fisher 2.00 5.00
GCDG Devean George 2.00 5.00
GCDM Darius Miles 2.00 5.00
GCDN Dirk Nowitzki 4.00 10.00
GCDW David Wesley 2.00 5.00
GCJJ Joe Johnson 2.00 5.00
GCJT Jason Terry 2.00 5.00
GCKB Kwame Brown 2.00 5.00
GCKG Kevin Garnett SP 4.00 10.00
GCKT Kurt Thomas 2.00 5.00
GCLJ LeBron James SP 10.00 25.00
GCME Carmelo Anthony 5.00 12.00
GCMG Manu Ginobili 2.50 6.00
GCNE Nene 2.00 5.00
GCNK Nenad Krstic 2.00 5.00
GCQR Quentin Richardson 2.00 5.00
GCRA Rafael Araujo 2.00 5.00
GCRL Rashard Lewis 2.50 6.00
GCRW Rasheed Wallace 2.50 6.00
GCSA Shareef Abdur-Rahim 2.00 5.00
GCSB Shane Battier 2.00 5.00
GCSC Sam Cassell 2.00 5.00
GCSD Samuel Dalembert 2.00 5.00
GCSF Steve Francis 2.00 5.00
GCSM Shawn Marion 2.00 5.00
GCSS Stromile Swift 2.00 5.00
GCTC Tyson Chandler 2.00 5.00
GCTD Tim Duncan 4.00 10.00
GCTM Tracy McGrady 3.00 8.00
GCUH Udonis Haslem 1.50 4.00
GCWS Wally Szczerbiak 2.00 5.00

2005-06 Hoops HoopScripts

Inserted at approximately one per box, this 33-card set is horizontally designed with a player photo on the left, his jersey number on the right and an autograph sticker over the number.

APPROXIMATELY ONE PER BOX
HSAA Alex Acker 2.50 6.00
HSAB Andray Blatche 4.00 10.00
HSAJ Amir Johnson 4.00 10.00
HSBB Brandon Bass 3.00 8.00
HSBW Bracey Wright 2.50 6.00
HSCM C.J. Miles 4.00 10.00
HSDH Dwight Howard SP 12.50 30.00
HSDL David Lee 4.00 10.00
HSDT Dijon Thompson 2.50 6.00
HSEI Ersan Ilyasova 4.00 10.00
HSFG Francisco Garcia 3.00 8.00
HSGG Gerald Green 4.00 10.00
HSID Ike Diogu 2.50 6.00
HSJG Joey Graham 3.00 8.00
HSJH Julius Hodge 2.50 6.00
HSJJ Jarrett Jack 4.00 10.00
HSJM Jason Maxiell 3.00 8.00
HSJP Johan Petro 2.50 6.00
HSJS James Singleton 2.50 6.00
HSLH Luther Head 3.00 8.00
HSLJ LeBron James SP 100.00 200.00
HSLK Linas Kleiza 2.50 6.00
HSLR Lawrence Roberts 2.50 6.00
HSLW Louis Williams 4.00 10.00
HSMA Martynas Andriuskevicius 2.50 6.00
HSMW Martell Webster 3.00 8.00
HSNR Nate Robinson 4.00 10.00
HSOG Orien Greene 3.00 8.00
HSRF Raymond Felton 4.00 10.00
HSRG Ryan Gomes 3.00 8.00
HSRM Rashad McCants 3.00 8.00
HSRW Robert Whaley 2.50 6.00
HSVW Von Wafer 2.50 6.00

2005-06 Hoops LBJ Profiles

Inserted at approximately eight per box, this 30-card set showcases highlights from LeBron James' career. Cards are horizontally designed with a red area containing text on the left and an action photo on the right.

COMPLETE SET (30) 12.50 30.00
COMMON CARD (LBJ1-LBJ30) .75 2.00
APPROXIMATELY EIGHT PER BOX

2005-06 Hoops MJ Profiles

Inserted at approximately eight per box, this 30-card set showcases highlights from Michael Jordan's career. Cards are horizontally designed with a red area containing text on the left and an action photo on the right.

COMPLETE SET (30) 15.00 40.00
COMMON CARD (MJ1-MJ30) 1.25 3.00
APPROXIMATELY EIGHT PER BOX

2011-12 Hoops

COMPLETE SET (278) 25.00 60.00
UNPRICED AP BLACK PRINT RUN ONE SET
1 Jamal Crawford .30 .75
2 Kirk Hinrich .25 .60
3 Al Horford .25 .60
4 Joe Johnson .25 .60
5 Marvin Williams .25 .60
6 Josh Smith .25 .60
7 Ray Allen .30 .75
8 Brandon Bass .25 .60
9 Glen Davis .20 .50
10 Kevin Garnett .50 1.25
11 Jeff Green .25 .60
12 Jermaine O'Neal .25 .60
13 Troy Murphy .20 .50
14 Paul Pierce .30 .75
15 Rajon Rondo .30 .75
16 D.J. Augustin .20 .50
17 Kwame Brown .20 .50
18 DeSagana Diop .20 .50
19 Eduardo Najera .20 .50
20 Tyrus Thomas .20 .50
21 Omer Asik .25 .60
22 Carlos Boozer .25 .60
23 Ronnie Brewer .25 .60
24 Rasual Butler .20 .50
25 Luol Deng .25 .60
26 Kyle Korver .25 .60
27 Joakim Noah .25 .60
28 Derrick Rose .40 1.00
29 Baron Davis .25 .60
30 Semih Erden .20 .50
31 Daniel Gibson .25 .60
32 Luke Harangody .20 .50
33 Antawn Jamison .25 .60
34 Anderson Varejao .20 .50
35 J.J. Barea .30 .75
36 Rodrigue Beaubois .20 .50
37 Caron Butler .25 .60
38 Brian Cardinal .20 .50
39 Tyson Chandler .25 .60
40 Rudy Fernandez .20 .50
41 Dominique Jones .20 .50
42 Jason Kidd .30 .75
43 Ian Mahinmi .20 .50
44 Shawn Marion .30 .75
45 Dirk Nowitzki .40 1.00
46 DeShawn Stevenson .20 .50
47 Chris Andersen .25 .60
48 Danilo Gallinari .25 .60
49 Nene .25 .60
50 Ty Lawson .20 .50
51 Corey Brewer .20 .50
52 Andre Miller .25 .60
53 Timofey Mozgov .20 .50
54 Austin Daye .20 .50
55 Ben Gordon .25 .60
56 Richard Hamilton .25 .60
57 Jonas Jerebko .20 .50
58 Tracy McGrady .30 .75
59 Tayshaun Prince .30 .75
60 DaJuan Summers .20 .50
61 Charlie Villanueva .20 .50
62 Ben Wallace .25 .60
63 Terrico White .20 .50
64 Stephen Curry 1.25 3.00
65 Monta Ellis .25 .60
66 David Lee .20 .50

67 Jeremy Lin 1.25 3.00
68 Andris Biedrins .20 .50
69 Ekpe Udoh .20 .50
70 Chase Budinger .20 .50
71 Goran Dragic .25 .60
72 Jordan Hill .20 .50
73 Kevin Martin .25 .60
74 Patrick Patterson .20 .50
75 Luis Scola .25 .60
76 Hasheem Thabeet .20 .50
77 Darren Collison .25 .60
78 Mike Dunleavy Jr. .20 .50
79 T.J. Ford .20 .50
80 Danny Granger .25 .60
81 Tyler Hansbrough .25 .60
82 George Hill .25 .60
83 Josh McRoberts .20 .50
84 Brandon Rush .20 .50
85 Lance Stephenson .25 .60
86 Al-Farouq Aminu .25 .60
87 Ike Diogu .20 .50
88 Randy Foye .20 .50
89 Eric Gordon .25 .60
90 Blake Griffin .30 .75
91 DeAndre Jordan .30 .75
92 Chris Kaman .25 .60
93 Ryan Gomes .20 .50
94 Mo Williams .25 .60
95 Metta World Peace .30 .75
96 Matt Barnes .20 .50
97 Steve Blake .20 .50
98 Kobe Bryant 1.25 3.00
99 Andrew Bynum .20 .50
100 Derrick Caracter .20 .50
101 Derek Fisher .25 .60
102 Pau Gasol .30 .75
103 Lamar Odom .25 .60
104 Darrell Arthur .20 .50
105 Shane Battier .25 .60
106 Marc Gasol .30 .75
107 Rudy Gay .30 .75
108 O.J. Mayo .20 .50
109 Zach Randolph .25 .60
110 Ishmael Smith .20 .50
111 Greivis Vasquez .25 .60
112 Sam Young .20 .50
113 Joel Anthony .20 .50
114 Mike Bibby .25 .60
115 Chris Bosh .30 .75
116 Mario Chalmers .25 .60
117 Juwan Howard .25 .60
118 Udonis Haslem .20 .50
119 LeBron James 1.25 3.00
120 Mike Miller .25 .60
121 Dexter Pittman .20 .50
122 Dwyane Wade .60 1.50
123 Jon Brockman .20 .50
124 Carlos Delfino .20 .50
125 Drew Gooden .25 .60
126 Ersan Ilyasova .20 .50
127 Stephen Jackson .25 .60
128 Brandon Jennings .20 .50
129 Luc Mbah a Moute .20 .50
130 Larry Sanders .20 .50
131 Beno Udrih .20 .50
132 Andrew Bogut .25 .60
133 Michael Beasley .20 .50
134 Wayne Ellington .20 .50
135 Lazar Hayward .20 .50
136 Kevin Love .30 .75
137 Darko Milicic .20 .50
138 Brad Miller .25 .60
139 Nikola Pekovic .25 .60
140 Luke Ridnour .25 .60
141 Ricky Rubio .30 .75
142 Martell Webster .25 .60
143 Jordan Farmar .20 .50
144 Sundiata Gaines .20 .50
145 Anthony Morrow .20 .50
146 Damion James .20 .50
147 Brook Lopez .25 .60
148 Brandan Wright .20 .50
149 Kris Humphries .20 .50
150 Johan Petro .20 .50
151 Deron Williams .25 .60
152 Trevor Ariza .20 .50
153 Carl Landry .20 .50
154 David West .25 .60
155 Jason Smith .20 .50
156 Jarrett Jack .25 .60
157 Emeka Okafor .25 .60
158 Chris Paul .40 1.00
159 Quincy Pondexter .20 .50
160 Carmelo Anthony .40 1.00
161 Chauncey Billups .30 .75
162 Derrick Brown .20 .50
163 Anthony Carter .20 .50
164 Landry Fields .25 .60
165 Toney Douglas .20 .50
166 Amare Stoudemire .25 .60
167 Jerome Jordan RC .30 .75
168 Cole Aldrich .20 .50
169 Nick Collison .25 .60
170 Kevin Durant .75 2.00
171 James Harden .50 1.25
172 Serge Ibaka .25 .60
173 B.J. Mullens .20 .50
174 Eric Maynor .20 .50
175 Russell Westbrook .75 2.00
176 Ryan Anderson .25 .60
177 Chris Duhon .20 .50
178 Dwight Howard .25 .60
179 Jameer Nelson .20 .50
180 J.J. Redick .30 .75
181 Jason Richardson .30 .75
182 Hedo Turkoglu .25 .60
183 Craig Brackins .20 .50
184 Elton Brand .30 .75
185 Andre Iguodala .25 .60
186 Jason Kapono .20 .50
187 Jodie Meeks .25 .60
188 Evan Turner .20 .50
189 Louis Williams .25 .60
190 Thaddeus Young .20 .50
191 Michael Redd .25 .60
192 Vince Carter .40 1.00
193 Channing Frye .25 .60
194 Grant Hill .40 1.00
195 Marcin Gortat .25 .60
196 Steve Nash .30 .75
197 Hakim Warrick .25 .60
198 LaMarcus Aldridge .30 .75
199 Marcus Camby .20 .50
200 Raymond Felton .25 .60
201 Wesley Matthews .20 .50
202 Greg Oden .25 .60
203 Armon Johnson .20 .50
204 Gerald Wallace .25 .60
205 Elliot Williams .20 .50
206 DeMarcus Cousins .30 .75
207 Samuel Dalembert .20 .50
208 Tyreke Evans .20 .50
209 Francisco Garcia .20 .50
210 Donte Greene .20 .50
211 Jason Thompson .20 .50
212 Marcus Thornton .20 .50
213 Hassan Whiteside .30 .75
214 DeJuan Blair .20 .50
215 Da'Sean Butler .20 .50
216 Tim Duncan .50 1.25
217 Manu Ginobili .30 .75
218 Richard Jefferson .25 .60
219 Matt Bonner .20 .50
220 Gary Neal .25 .60
221 Tony Parker .30 .75
222 Tiago Splitter .25 .60
223 Solomon Alabi .20 .50
224 Leandro Barbosa .25 .60
225 Andrea Bargnani .25 .60
226 Jose Calderon .20 .50
227 Ed Davis .20 .50
228 DeMar DeRozan .30 .75
229 Amir Johnson .20 .50
230 Raja Bell .25 .60
231 C.J. Miles .25 .60
232 Jeremy Evans .20 .50
233 Derrick Favors .25 .60
234 Devin Harris .20 .50
235 Gordon Hayward .30 .75
236 Al Jefferson .25 .60
237 Earl Watson .20 .50
238 Paul Millsap .25 .60
239 Mehmet Okur .20 .50
240 Andray Blatche .20 .50
241 Trevor Booker .20 .50
242 Jordan Crawford .20 .50
243 Josh Howard .25 .60
244 Ronny Turiaf .20 .50
245 Rashard Lewis .25 .60
246 JaVale McGee .25 .60
247 John Wall .40 1.00
248 Derrick Rose .40 1.00
249 Dwyane Wade .60 1.50
250 LeBron James 1.25 3.00
251 Chris Bosh .30 .75
252 Amare Stoudemire .25 .60
253 Dwight Howard .25 .60
254 Kevin Garnett .50 1.25
255 Paul Pierce .30 .75
256 Rajon Rondo .30 .75
257 Ray Allen .30 .75
258 Kobe Bryant 1.25 3.00
259 Chris Paul .40 1.00
260 Carmelo Anthony .40 1.00
261 Dirk Nowitzki .40 1.00
262 Kevin Durant .75 2.00
263 Tim Duncan .50 1.25
264 Blake Griffin .30 .75
265 Pau Gasol .30 .75
266 Deron Williams .25 .60
267 Manu Ginobili .30 .75
268 Kobe Bryant 1.25 3.00
269 Blake Griffin .30 .75
270 Kevin Durant .75 2.00
271 Dirk Nowitzki .40 1.00
272 LeBron James 1.25 3.00
273 Derrick Rose .40 1.00
274 Chris Paul .40 1.00
275 Paul Pierce .30 .75
276 Carmelo Anthony .40 1.00
277 Kevin Love .30 .75
278 Kobe Bryant 1.25 3.00
279 Dallas Mavericks SP 8.00 20.00
BG1 B.Griffin Blake Superior 50.00 120.00
KB1 K.Bryant Black Mamba 60.00 150.00

2011-12 Hoops Artist's Proofs
*ARTIST PROOF: 2.5X TO 6X BASE HI
RANDOM INSERTS IN PACKS
67 Jeremy Lin 10.00 25.00

2011-12 Hoops Glossy
*GLOSSY: 1.5X TO 4X BASE HI
RANDOM INSERTS IN PACKS

2011-12 Hoops 89-90 Buyback Autographs
RANDOM INSERTS IN PACKS
70 Xavier McDaniel 20.00 50.00
120 Alex English 15.00 40.00
125 Adrian Dantley 20.00 50.00
310 David Robinson 125.00 225.00
311 Dale Ellis

2011-12 Hoops A Night to Remember
COMPLETE SET (20) 12.00 30.00
RANDOM INSERTS IN PACKS
1 Wilt Chamberlain 1.25 3.00
2 Dwight Howard .50 1.25
3 Magic Johnson 1.50 4.00
4 Kobe Bryant 2.50 6.00
5 Bill Russell 1.00 2.50
6 Magic Johnson 1.50 4.00
7 Wilt Chamberlain 1.25 3.00
8 Wilt Chamberlain 1.25 3.00
9 Ray Allen .60 1.50
10 Elgin Baylor .60 1.50
11 John Stockton 1.00 2.50
12 Hakeem Olajuwon .75 2.00
13 Dwyane Wade 1.25 3.00
14 Ray Allen .60 1.50
15 Bob Cousy 1.00 2.50
16 Scott Skiles .50 1.25
17 Mark Eaton .40 1.00
18 Rick Barry .50 1.25
19 Jason Terry .50 1.25
20 Vince Carter .75 2.00

2011-12 Hoops Action Photos
COMPLETE SET (25) 10.00 25.00
RANDOM INSERTS IN PACKS
1 Derrick Rose .60 1.50
2 JaVale McGee .40 1.00
3 Paul Pierce .50 1.25
4 LeBron James 2.00 5.00
5 Dwight Howard .40 1.00
6 Carmelo Anthony .60 1.50
7 Gary Neal .40 1.00
8 Dirk Nowitzki .60 1.50
9 Kevin Love .50 1.25
10 Al Horford .40 1.00
11 Amare Stoudemire .40 1.00
12 Steve Nash .50 1.25
13 John Wall .60 1.50
14 Chris Paul .60 1.50
15 Kevin Durant 1.25 3.00
16 Pau Gasol .50 1.25
17 Tyson Chandler .40 1.00
18 Rajon Rondo .50 1.25
19 Nene .40 1.00
20 Deron Williams .40 1.00
21 Blake Griffin .50 1.25
22 Stephen Curry 2.00 5.00
23 Marc Gasol .50 1.25
24 Kobe Bryant 2.00 5.00
25 Dwyane Wade 1.00 2.50

2011-12 Hoops Autographs
RANDOM INSERTS IN PACKS
SOME SP's UNPRICED DUE TO SCARCITY
4 Joe Johnson SP 6.00 15.00
11 Jeff Green SP 5.00 12.00
16 D.J. Augustin SP 5.00 12.00
18 DeSagana Diop 2.50 6.00
21 Omer Asik SP 8.00 20.00
22 Carlos Boozer SP 10.00 25.00
23 Ronnie Brewer SP 25.00 60.00
25 Luol Deng SP 20.00 50.00
27 Joakim Noah SP 12.00 30.00
28 Derrick Rose SP 125.00 250.00
30 Semih Erden 2.50 6.00
31 Daniel Gibson SP 15.00 40.00
32 Luke Harangody 2.50 6.00
33 Antawn Jamison SP 5.00 12.00
34 Anderson Varejao 2.50 6.00
35 J.J. Barea 6.00 15.00
36 Rodrigue Beaubois 2.50 6.00
37 Caron Butler SP 20.00 50.00
41 Dominique Jones 2.50 6.00
43 Ian Mahinmi 3.00 8.00
45 Dirk Nowitzki SP 75.00 200.00
47 Chris Andersen SP 15.00 40.00
48 Danilo Gallinari SP 5.00 12.00
53 Timofey Mozgov SP 5.00 12.00
54 Austin Daye SP 5.00 12.00
55 Ben Gordon SP 5.00 12.00
56 Richard Hamilton SP 10.00 25.00
57 Jonas Jerebko SP 5.00 12.00
58 Tracy McGrady SP 40.00 100.00
60 DaJuan Summers 2.50 6.00
61 Charlie Villanueva SP 5.00 12.00
63 Terrico White 2.50 6.00
64 Stephen Curry SP 75.00 200.00
65 Monta Ellis SP 12.00 30.00
66 David Lee SP 5.00 12.00
67 Jeremy Lin 30.00 80.00
69 Ekpe Udoh SP 5.00 12.00
70 Chase Budinger SP 6.00 15.00
71 Goran Dragic SP 6.00 15.00
72 Jordan Hill 2.50 6.00
73 Kevin Martin SP 10.00 25.00
74 Patrick Patterson 4.00 10.00
75 Luis Scola SP 5.00 12.00
76 Hasheem Thabeet 2.50 6.00
78 Mike Dunleavy Jr. SP 5.00 12.00
79 T.J. Ford SP 5.00 12.00
80 Danny Granger SP 12.00 30.00
81 Tyler Hansbrough SP 5.00 12.00
82 George Hill SP 8.00 20.00
85 Lance Stephenson 6.00 15.00
88 Randy Foye 2.50 6.00
90 Blake Griffin SP 40.00 100.00
92 Chris Kaman SP 5.00 12.00
93 Ryan Gomes SP 5.00 12.00
94 Mo Williams SP 5.00 12.00
98 Kobe Bryant SP 125.00 250.00
99 Andrew Bynum SP 12.00 30.00
100 Derrick Caracter 2.50 6.00
101 Derek Fisher SP 8.00 20.00
103 Lamar Odom SP 10.00 25.00
105 Shane Battier SP 8.00 20.00
107 Rudy Gay SP 60.00 150.00
108 O.J. Mayo SP 6.00 15.00
109 Zach Randolph SP 8.00 20.00
110 Ishmael Smith 2.50 6.00
111 Greivis Vasquez 2.50 6.00
112 Sam Young 2.50 6.00
114 Mike Bibby SP 5.00 12.00
115 Chris Bosh SP 25.00 60.00
121 Dexter Pittman SP 5.00 12.00
123 Jon Brockman 2.50 6.00
127 Stephen Jackson SP 40.00 80.00
130 Larry Sanders 2.50 6.00
131 Beno Udrih SP 5.00 12.00
132 Andrew Bogut SP 6.00 15.00
133 Michael Beasley SP 8.00 20.00
134 Wayne Ellington 2.50 6.00
135 Lazar Hayward SP 5.00 12.00
136 Kevin Love SP 40.00 100.00
137 Darko Milicic SP 6.00 15.00
139 Nikola Pekovic 10.00 25.00
140 Luke Ridnour SP 5.00 12.00
144 Sundiata Gaines SP 5.00 12.00
146 Damion James SP 5.00 12.00
147 Brook Lopez SP 12.00 30.00
149 Kris Humphries 4.00 10.00
151 Deron Williams SP 15.00 40.00
152 Trevor Ariza SP 5.00 12.00
153 Carl Landry 2.50 6.00
157 Emeka Okafor SP 5.00 12.00
158 Chris Paul SP 100.00 200.00
159 Quincy Pondexter SP 5.00 12.00
160 Carmelo Anthony SP 25.00 60.00
161 Chauncey Billups SP 15.00 40.00
162 Derrick Brown SP 5.00 12.00
164 Landry Fields SP 5.00 12.00
165 Toney Douglas SP 5.00 12.00
167 Jerome Jordan 2.50 6.00
168 Cole Aldrich 2.50 6.00
170 Kevin Durant SP 125.00 250.00
173 B.J. Mullens 2.50 6.00
175 Russell Westbrook SP 50.00 120.00
179 Jameer Nelson SP 5.00 12.00
180 J.J. Redick 5.00 12.00
182 Hedo Turkoglu SP 5.00 12.00
183 Craig Brackins SP 5.00 12.00
187 Jodie Meeks 3.00 8.00
189 Louis Williams SP 5.00 12.00
192 Vince Carter SP 25.00 60.00
193 Channing Frye SP 5.00 12.00
194 Grant Hill SP 75.00 150.00
196 Steve Nash SP 50.00 120.00
197 Hakim Warrick SP 5.00 12.00
198 LaMarcus Aldridge SP 10.00 25.00
199 Marcus Camby SP 8.00 20.00
200 Raymond Felton SP 8.00 20.00
201 Wesley Matthews SP 5.00 12.00
203 Armon Johnson 2.50 6.00
204 Gerald Wallace SP 6.00 15.00
205 Elliot Williams 2.50 6.00
206 DeMarcus Cousins SP 12.00 30.00
207 Samuel Dalembert 2.50 6.00
208 Tyreke Evans SP 20.00 50.00
210 Donte Greene 2.50 6.00
213 Hassan Whiteside 10.00 25.00
214 DeJuan Blair SP 8.00 20.00
215 Da'Sean Butler 2.50 6.00
220 Gary Neal SP 8.00 20.00
221 Tony Parker SP 15.00 40.00
222 Tiago Splitter SP 8.00 20.00
223 Solomon Alabi 2.50 6.00
225 Andrea Bargnani SP 8.00 20.00
226 Jose Calderon 2.50 6.00
227 Ed Davis 2.50 6.00
228 DeMar DeRozan SP 6.00 15.00
229 Amir Johnson 2.50 6.00
232 Jeremy Evans 2.50 6.00
233 Derrick Favors SP 5.00 12.00
234 Devin Harris SP 15.00 40.00
235 Gordon Hayward SP 12.00 30.00
236 Al Jefferson SP 5.00 12.00
238 Paul Millsap 2.50 6.00
241 Trevor Booker SP 5.00 12.00
242 Jordan Crawford SP 5.00 12.00
243 Josh Howard SP 5.00 12.00
246 JaVale McGee SP 10.00 25.00
248 Derrick Rose SP 30.00 80.00
251 Chris Bosh SP 25.00 60.00
258 Kobe Bryant SP 100.00 225.00
259 Chris Paul SP 60.00 150.00
261 Dirk Nowitzki SP 75.00 200.00
262 Kevin Durant SP 125.00 250.00
264 Blake Griffin SP 40.00 100.00
266 Deron Williams SP 12.00 30.00
268 Kobe Bryant SP 125.00 250.00
269 Blake Griffin SP 80.00 200.00
270 Kevin Durant SP 125.00 250.00
271 Dirk Nowitzki SP 75.00 200.00
273 Derrick Rose SP 30.00 80.00
274 Chris Paul SP 100.00 200.00
277 Kevin Love SP 40.00 100.00
278 Kobe Bryant SP 100.00 200.00

2011-12 Hoops BIGS
COMPLETE SET (15) 12.00 30.00
RANDOM INSERTS IN RETAIL PACKS
1 Dwight Howard 1.00 2.50
2 Tim Duncan 2.00 5.00
3 Andrew Bynum .75 2.00
4 Al Jefferson 1.00 2.50
5 Tyson Chandler 1.00 2.50
6 Kevin Love 1.25 3.00
7 Zach Randolph 1.00 2.50
8 Andrew Bogut 1.00 2.50
9 Nene 1.00 2.50
10 Brook Lopez 1.00 2.50
11 Joakim Noah 1.00 2.50
12 Amare Stoudemire 1.00 2.50
13 Andrea Bargnani 1.00 2.50
14 Al Horford 1.00 2.50
15 Samuel Dalembert .75 2.00

2011-12 Hoops Courtside
COMPLETE SET (15) 10.00 25.00
RANDOM INSERTS IN PACKS
1 Kobe Bryant 2.00 5.00
2 LeBron James 2.00 5.00
3 Chris Paul .60 1.50
4 Dwight Howard .40 1.00
5 Kevin Durant 1.25 3.00
6 Blake Griffin .50 1.25
7 Carmelo Anthony .60 1.50
8 Kevin Love .50 1.25
9 Steve Nash .50 1.25
10 Dwyane Wade 1.00 2.50
11 Dirk Nowitzki .60 1.50
12 Derrick Rose .60 1.50
13 Tony Parker .50 1.25
14 Deron Williams .40 1.00
15 Paul Pierce .50 1.25

2011-12 Hoops Dreams
COMPLETE SET (9) 4.00 10.00
RANDOM INSERTS IN PACKS
1 John Wall .60 1.50
2 DeMarcus Cousins .50 1.25
3 James Harden .75 2.00
4 Blake Griffin .50 1.25
5 Landry Fields .40 1.00
6 Stephen Curry 2.00 5.00
7 Jordan Crawford .30 .75
8 Tyreke Evans .30 .75
9 Darren Collison .40 1.00

2011-12 Hoops Hall of Fame Heroes
COMPLETE SET (20) 12.00 30.00
RANDOM INSERTS IN PACKS
1 Bill Russell 1.00 2.50
2 Jerry West .75 2.00
3 Oscar Robertson .75 2.00
4 Walt Bellamy .50 1.25
5 Nate Thurmond .50 1.25
6 Elgin Baylor .60 1.50
7 John Havlicek .75 2.00
8 Willis Reed .60 1.50
9 Magic Johnson 1.50 4.00
10 Bob Lanier .50 1.25
11 Wilt Chamberlain 1.25 3.00
12 Larry Bird 1.50 4.00
13 Karl Malone .75 2.00
14 David Robinson 1.00 2.50
15 Rick Barry .50 1.25
16 Dolph Schayes .60 1.50
17 Bill Walton .60 1.50
18 George Gervin .60 1.50
19 John Stockton 1.00 2.50
20 Pete Maravich 1.00 2.50

2011-12 Hoops Private Signings
STATED PRINT RUN 49 TO 299 SETS
1 Al Jefferson 12.00 30.00
2 Chauncey Billups 12.00 30.00
3 Zach Randolph 15.00 40.00
4 Lamar Odom 40.00 80.00
5 Louis Williams 12.00 30.00
6 Rudy Gay 10.00 25.00
7 Jose Calderon 12.00 30.00
8 George Hill 12.00 30.00
9 Stephen Jackson 15.00 40.00
10 Joe Johnson 10.00 25.00
11 Marcus Camby 10.00 25.00

2011-12 Hoops Slam Dunk Champion
COMPLETE SET (15) 8.00 20.00
RANDOM INSERTS IN PACKS
1 Larry Nance .50 1.25
2 Dominique Wilkins .75 2.00
3 Spud Webb .50 1.25
4 Kenny Walker .40 1.00
5 Dominique Wilkins .75 2.00
6 Cedric Ceballos .40 1.00
7 Brent Barry .40 1.00
8 Kobe Bryant 2.50 6.00
9 Vince Carter .75 2.00
10 Jason Richardson .60 1.50
11 Josh Smith .50 1.25
12 Nate Robinson .60 1.50
13 Dwight Howard .50 1.25
14 Nate Robinson .60 1.50
15 Blake Griffin .60 1.50

2012-13 Hoops
COMPLETE SET (300) 25.00 60.00
UNPRICED AP BLACK PRINT RUN ONE SET
1 Avery Bradley .25 .60
2 Brandon Bass .20 .50
3 Kevin Garnett .50 1.25
4 Paul Pierce .30 .75
5 Rajon Rondo .30 .75
6 Ray Allen .30 .75
7 Doc Rivers CO .30 .75
8 Deron Williams .25 .60
9 Brook Lopez .25 .60
10 Kris Humphries .20 .50
11 Anthony Morrow .20 .50
12 Jordan Farmar .20 .50
13 Gerald Wallace .25 .60
14 Avery Johnson CO .25 .60
15 Amare Stoudemire .25 .60
16 Carmelo Anthony .40 1.00
17 Landry Fields .20 .50
18 Tyson Chandler .25 .60
19 Jeremy Lin .30 .75
20 Steve Novak .20 .50
21 Mike Woodson CO .30 .75
22 Andre Iguodala .25 .60
23 Jodie Meeks .25 .60
24 Jrue Holiday .30 .75
25 Louis Williams .25 .60
26 Elton Brand .30 .75
27 Evan Turner .20 .50
28 Spencer Hawes .20 .50
29 Doug Collins CO .30 .75
30 Andrea Bargnani .25 .60
31 DeMar DeRozan .30 .75
32 Gary Forbes .20 .50
33 Jose Calderon .20 .50
34 Linas Kleiza .20 .50
35 Ed Davis .20 .50
36 Dwane Casey CO .30 .75
37 Dirk Nowitzki .40 1.00
38 Rodrigue Beaubois .20 .50
39 Shawn Marion .25 .60
40 Jason Kidd .30 .75
41 Jason Terry .25 .60
42 Vince Carter .40 1.00
43 Ian Mahinmi .20 .50
44 Rick Carlisle CO .30 .75
45 Kyle Lowry .25 .60
46 Kevin Martin .25 .60
47 Luis Scola .25 .60
48 Chase Budinger .20 .50
49 Patrick Patterson .20 .50
50 Goran Dragic .25 .60
51 Kevin McHale CO .30 .75
52 Marc Gasol .30 .75
53 Mike Conley .25 .60
54 O.J. Mayo .20 .50
55 Rudy Gay .30 .75
56 Zach Randolph .25 .60
57 Lester Hudson .20 .50
58 Dante Cunningham .20 .50
59 Lionel Hollins CO .30 .75
60 Emeka Okafor .25 .60
61 Carl Landry .20 .50
62 Chris Kaman .25 .60
63 Eric Gordon .25 .60
64 Greivis Vasquez .25 .60
65 Trevor Ariza .20 .50
66 Monty Williams CO .30 .75
67 DeJuan Blair .20 .50
68 Boris Diaw .25 .60
69 Manu Ginobili .30 .75
70 Tim Duncan .50 1.25
71 Tony Parker .30 .75
72 Danny Green .25 .60
73 Gregg Popovich CO .30 .75
74 Carlos Boozer .25 .60
75 Derrick Rose .40 1.00
76 Joakim Noah .25 .60
77 Luol Deng .25 .60
78 Richard Hamilton .25 .60
79 Taj Gibson .25 .60
80 Ronnie Brewer .25 .60
81 Tom Thibodeau CO .30 .75
82 Alonzo Gee .20 .50
83 Anderson Varejao .20 .50
84 Antawn Jamison .25 .60
85 Daniel Gibson .25 .60
86 Byron Scott CO .25 .60
87 Ben Gordon .25 .60
88 Greg Monroe .25 .60
89 Rodney Stuckey .25 .60
90 Tayshaun Prince .25 .60
91 Jonas Jerebko .20 .50
92 Lawrence Frank CO .30 .75
93 Danny Granger .25 .60
94 David West .25 .60
95 Paul George .40 1.00
96 Roy Hibbert .25 .60
97 Darren Collison .25 .60
98 George Hill .25 .60
99 A.J. Price .20 .50
100 Frank Vogel CO .30 .75
101 Brandon Jennings .20 .50
102 Drew Gooden .25 .60
103 Monta Ellis .25 .60
104 Ersan Ilyasova .20 .50
105 Mike Dunleavy .20 .50
106 Luc Mbah a Moute .20 .50
107 Scott Skiles CO .25 .60
108 Arron Afflalo .25 .60
109 Danilo Gallinari .20 .50
110 Ty Lawson .20 .50
111 Wilson Chandler .25 .60
112 JaVale McGee .25 .60
113 Andre Miller .25 .60
114 Timofey Mozgov .20 .50
115 George Karl CO .30 .75
116 Kevin Love .30 .75
117 Luke Ridnour .25 .60
118 Michael Beasley .20 .50
119 Nikola Pekovic .20 .50
120 Ricky Rubio .30 .75
121 Wesley Johnson .25 .60
122 J.J. Barea .25 .60
123 Rick Adelman CO .30 .75
124 LaMarcus Aldridge .30 .75
125 Nicolas Batum .25 .60
126 Wesley Matthews .20 .50
127 Jonny Flynn .20 .50
128 J.J. Hickson .20 .50
129 Jamal Crawford .30 .75
130 Raymond Felton .25 .60
131 Kaleb Canales CO .30 .75
132 Derek Fisher .25 .60
133 James Harden .50 1.25
134 Kendrick Perkins .20 .50
135 Kevin Durant .75 2.00
136 Russell Westbrook .75 2.00
137 Serge Ibaka .25 .60
138 Daequan Cook .20 .50
139 Nick Collison .25 .60
140 Scott Brooks CO .20 .50
141 Al Jefferson .25 .60
142 DeMarre Carroll .20 .50
143 Gordon Hayward .30 .75
144 Paul Millsap .30 .75
145 Derrick Favors .25 .60
146 Josh Howard .25 .60
147 Tyrone Corbin CO .30 .75
148 Al Horford .25 .60
149 Jeff Teague .25 .60
150 Joe Johnson .25 .60
151 Josh Smith .25 .60
152 Tracy McGrady .30 .75
153 Marvin Williams .25 .60
154 Zaza Pachulia .20 .50
155 Larry Drew CO .30 .75
156 LeBron James 1.25 3.00
157 Dwyane Wade .50 1.25
158 Chris Bosh .30 .75
159 Mario Chalmers .25 .60
160 Joel Anthony .20 .50
161 Udonis Haslem .20 .50
162 Shane Battier .25 .60
163 Erik Spoelstra CO .30 .75
164 Dwight Howard .25 .60
165 Hedo Turkoglu .25 .60
166 J.J. Redick .30 .75
167 Jameer Nelson .20 .50
168 Jason Richardson .30 .75
169 Ryan Anderson .25 .60
170 Glen Davis .20 .50
171 Chris Duhon .20 .50
172 John Wall .40 1.00
173 Trevor Booker .20 .50
174 Jordan Crawford .20 .50
175 Nene .25 .60
176 Kevin Seraphin .20 .50
177 Rashard Lewis .25 .60
178 Randy Wittman CO .30 .75
179 Andrew Bogut .25 .60
180 Stephen Curry 1.25 3.00
181 David Lee .20 .50
182 Dorell Wright .20 .50
183 Nate Robinson .20 .50
184 Brandon Rush .20 .50
185 Richard Jefferson .25 .60
186 Mark Jackson CO .25 .60
187 Blake Griffin .30 .75
188 Chauncey Billups .30 .75
189 Chris Paul .40 1.00
190 Mo Williams .25 .60
191 Nick Young .25 .60
192 Eric Bledsoe .25 .60
193 DeAndre Jordan .30 .75
194 Caron Butler .25 .60
195 Vinny Del Negro CO .20 .50
196 Ramon Sessions .25 .60
197 Andrew Bynum .20 .50
198 Kobe Bryant 1.25 3.00
199 Metta World Peace .30 .75
200 Pau Gasol .30 .75
201 Matt Barnes .20 .50
202 Devin Ebanks .20 .50
203 Mike Brown CO .30 .75
204 Shannon Brown .20 .50
205 Marcin Gortat .25 .60
206 Grant Hill .40 1.00
207 Robin Lopez .20 .50
208 Steve Nash .30 .75
209 Channing Frye .25 .60
210 Alvin Gentry CO .30 .75
211 Marcus Thornton .20 .50
212 DeMarcus Cousins .30 .75
213 Tyreke Evans .20 .50
214 Terrence Williams .20 .50
215 Jason Thompson .20 .50
216 John Salmons .25 .60
217 Keith Smart CO .30 .75
218 Gerald Henderson .20 .50
219 Corey Maggette .25 .60
220 D.J. Augustin .20 .50
221 Byron Mullens .20 .50
222 Mike Dunlap CO .30 .75
223 Kyrie Irving RC 3.00 8.00
224 Derrick Williams RC .40 1.00
225 Enes Kanter RC .50 1.25
226 Tristan Thompson RC .60 1.50
227 Jan Vesely RC .40 1.00
228 Bismack Biyombo RC .40 1.00
229 Brandon Knight RC .60 1.50
230 Kemba Walker RC 1.25 3.00
231 Jimmer Fredette RC .40 1.00
232 Klay Thompson RC 2.50 6.00
233 Alec Burks RC .60 1.50
234 Markieff Morris RC .60 1.50
235 Marcus Morris RC .50 1.25
236 Kawhi Leonard RC 3.00 8.00
237 Nikola Vucevic RC .60 1.50
238 Iman Shumpert RC .60 1.50
239 Chris Singleton RC .40 1.00
240 Tobias Harris RC .60 1.50
241 Nolan Smith RC .40 1.00
242 Kenneth Faried RC .60 1.50
243 Reggie Jackson RC .60 1.50
244 MarShon Brooks RC .50 1.25
245 Jordan Hamilton RC .40 1.00
246 JaJuan Johnson RC .40 1.00
247 Norris Cole RC .40 1.00
248 Cory Joseph RC .40 1.00
249 Jimmy Butler RC 2.00 5.00
250 Isaiah Thomas RC 1.00 2.50
251 Charles Jenkins RC .40 1.00
252 Chandler Parsons RC .60 1.50
253 Lavoy Allen RC .40 1.00
254 Jeremy Tyler RC .40 1.00
255 Jon Leuer RC .50 1.25
256 Jeremy Pargo RC .40 1.00
257 Greg Stiemsma RC .40 1.00
258 Andrew Goudelock RC .40 1.00
259 Josh Harrellson RC .40 1.00
260 Elliot Williams .20 .50
261 Vernon Macklin RC .50 1.25
262 Mickell Gladness RC .50 1.25
263 Jordan Williams RC .50 1.25
264 Terrel Harris RC .40 1.00
265 Josh Selby RC .40 1.00
266 DeAndre Liggins RC .50 1.25
267 Jerome Jordan .20 .50
268 Derrick Byars .20 .50
269 Tyler Honeycutt RC .40 1.00
270 Justin Harper RC .40 1.00
271 Shelvin Mack RC .50 1.25
272 Trey Thompkins RC .40 1.00
273 Julyan Stone RC .40 1.00
274 Walker Russell RC .50 1.25
275 Anthony Davis RC 3.00 8.00
276 Michael Kidd-Gilchrist RC .60 1.50
277 Bradley Beal RC 1.00 2.50
278 Dion Waiters RC .60 1.50
279 Thomas Robinson RC .50 1.25
280 Damian Lillard RC 2.50 6.00
281 Harrison Barnes RC 1.00 2.50
282 Terrence Ross RC .60 1.50
283 Andre Drummond RC 1.00 2.50
284 Austin Rivers RC .60 1.50
285 Meyers Leonard RC .50 1.25
286 Jeremy Lamb RC .60 1.50
287 John Henson RC .60 1.50
288 Moe Harkless RC .60 1.50
289 Tyler Zeller RC .50 1.25
290 Evan Fournier RC .60 1.50
291 Perry Jones RC .40 1.00
292 Bernard James RC .40 1.00
293 Quincy Acy RC .40 1.00
294 Quincy Miller RC .40 1.00
295 2012 West All-Stars .40 1.00
296 2012 East All-Stars .40 1.00
297 Serge Ibaka .25 .60
298 Rajon Rondo .30 .75
299 Chris Paul .40 1.00
300 Dwight Howard .25 .60
KD1 K.Durant Durantula 60.00 150.00
MH1 Miami Heat SP 12.00 30.00

2012-13 Hoops Artist's Proofs
*VETS: 2X TO 5X BASE HI
*RCs: 1X TO 2.5X BASE HI
RANDOM INSERTS IN PACKS
223 Kyrie Irving 15.00 40.00
275 Anthony Davis 12.00 30.00
280 Damian Lillard 15.00 40.00
295 2012 West All-Stars 2.50 6.00
296 2012 East All-Stars 2.50 6.00

2012-13 Hoops Glossy
*VETS: 1.5X TO 4X BASE HI
*RCs: .5X TO 1.25X BASE HI
RANDOM INSERTS IN PACKS
223 Kyrie Irving 8.00 20.00
275 Anthony Davis 6.00 15.00

2012-13 Hoops 89-90 Buyback Autographs
RANDOM INSERTS IN PACKS
39 Ralph Sampson 20.00 50.00
108 Pat Riley
138 David Robinson
178 Hakeem Olajuwon AS 50.00 125.00
180 Hakeem Olajuwon
183 Dan Majerle 35.00 70.00
244 Scottie Pippen 125.00 225.00
271 Vernon Maxwell 25.00 60.00

2012-13 Hoops Action Photos
COMPLETE SET (20) 8.00 20.00
RANDOM INSERTS IN PACKS
1 Kobe Bryant 2.00 5.00
2 Kevin Durant 1.25 3.00
3 LeBron James 2.00 5.00
4 Dwyane Wade .75 2.00
5 Kevin Love .50 1.25
6 Dwight Howard .40 1.00
7 Derrick Rose .60 1.50
8 Chris Paul .60 1.50
9 Dirk Nowitzki .60 1.50
10 Russell Westbrook 1.25 3.00
11 Carmelo Anthony .60 1.50
12 Amare Stoudemire .40 1.00
13 Paul Pierce .50 1.25
14 Blake Griffin .50 1.25
15 LaMarcus Aldridge .50 1.25
16 Rajon Rondo .50 1.25
17 Serge Ibaka .40 1.00
18 Andrew Bynum .30 .75
19 James Harden .75 2.00
20 Chris Bosh .50 1.25

2012-13 Hoops Autographs
NDOM INSERTS IN PACKS
1 Avery Bradley SP 10.00 25.00
2 Brandon Bass 2.50 6.00
7 Doc Rivers CO 15.00 40.00
9 Brook Lopez SP 15.00 40.00
14 Avery Johnson CO 5.00 12.00
15 Amare Stoudemire SP 25.00 60.00
17 Landry Fields 2.50 6.00
19 Jeremy Lin SP 40.00 80.00
20 Steve Novak 2.50 6.00
24 Jrue Holiday SP 5.00 12.00
27 Evan Turner SP 5.00 12.00
30 Andrea Bargnani SP 5.00 12.00
32 Gary Forbes 2.50 6.00
33 Jose Calderon 2.50 6.00
37 Dirk Nowitzki SP
40 Jason Kidd SP
42 Vince Carter SP 40.00 80.00
44 Rick Carlisle CO SP 20.00 50.00
45 Kyle Lowry 3.00 8.00
46 Kevin Martin SP 5.00 12.00
47 Luis Scola 3.00 8.00
48 Chase Budinger 2.50 6.00
49 Patrick Patterson 2.50 6.00
50 Goran Dragic 5.00 12.00
51 Kevin McHale CO SP 15.00 40.00
53 Mike Conley 4.00 10.00
56 Zach Randolph SP 20.00 50.00
57 Lester Hudson 2.50 6.00
58 Dante Cunningham 2.50 6.00
60 Emeka Okafor SP 5.00 12.00
63 Eric Gordon SP 10.00 25.00
67 DeJuan Blair 2.50 6.00
68 Boris Diaw 3.00 8.00
72 Danny Green 2.50 6.00
76 Joakim Noah SP 8.00 20.00
78 Richard Hamilton SP 10.00 25.00
79 Taj Gibson 3.00 8.00
80 Ronnie Brewer 2.50 6.00
84 Antawn Jamison SP 8.00 20.00
85 Daniel Gibson 2.50 6.00
86 Byron Scott CO SP 5.00 12.00
87 Ben Gordon SP
88 Greg Monroe 2.50 6.00
90 Tayshaun Prince SP 5.00 12.00
95 Paul George SP 15.00 40.00
96 Roy Hibbert SP
98 George Hill 3.00 8.00
99 A.J. Price 2.50 6.00
103 Monta Ellis SP 5.00 12.00
104 Ersan Ilyasova 2.50 6.00
108 Arron Afflalo 3.00 8.00
109 Danilo Gallinari SP 5.00 12.00
111 Wilson Chandler 3.00 8.00
113 Andre Miller 3.00 8.00
116 Kevin Love SP 15.00 40.00
117 Luke Ridnour 2.50 6.00
120 Ricky Rubio SP 15.00 40.00
121 Wesley Johnson SP 5.00 12.00
127 Jonny Flynn 2.50 6.00
129 Jamal Crawford 5.00 12.00
134 Kendrick Perkins 5.00 12.00
135 Kevin Durant SP 100.00 200.00
136 Russell Westbrook SP 60.00 150.00
142 DeMarre Carroll 2.50 6.00
143 Gordon Hayward SP
144 Paul Millsap 2.50 6.00
145 Derrick Favors SP 5.00 12.00
146 Josh Howard SP 5.00 12.00
148 Al Horford SP 8.00 20.00
149 Jeff Teague 3.00 8.00
161 Udonis Haslem 2.50 6.00
162 Shane Battier SP 10.00 25.00
166 J.J. Redick SP
173 Trevor Booker 2.50 6.00
174 Jordan Crawford SP 5.00 12.00
176 Kevin Seraphin 2.50 6.00
179 Andrew Bogut SP 20.00 50.00
180 Stephen Curry SP 60.00 150.00
187 Blake Griffin SP 20.00 50.00
188 Chauncey Billups SP 10.00 25.00
189 Chris Paul SP EXCH 40.00 100.00
190 Mo Williams SP 8.00 20.00
192 Eric Bledsoe 6.00 15.00
198 Kobe Bryant SP 100.00 200.00
200 Pau Gasol SP
202 Devin Ebanks SP 5.00 12.00
205 Marcin Gortat 8.00 20.00
207 Robin Lopez 2.50 6.00
208 Steve Nash SP 40.00 100.00
209 Channing Frye SP 5.00 12.00
211 Marcus Thornton SP
212 DeMarcus Cousins SP 25.00 60.00
214 Terrence Williams 2.50 6.00

218 Gerald Henderson 2.50 6.00
223 Kyrie Irving 60.00 120.00
224 Derrick Williams 2.50 6.00
225 Enes Kanter 3.00 8.00
226 Tristan Thompson 4.00 10.00
227 Jan Vesely 2.50 6.00
228 Bismack Biyombo 2.50 6.00
229 Brandon Knight 4.00 10.00
230 Kemba Walker 8.00 20.00
231 Jimmer Fredette 2.50 6.00
232 Klay Thompson 15.00 40.00
233 Alec Burks 4.00 10.00
234 Markieff Morris 4.00 10.00
235 Marcus Morris 3.00 8.00
236 Kawhi Leonard 60.00 150.00
238 Iman Shumpert 4.00 10.00
239 Chris Singleton 2.50 6.00
240 Tobias Harris 4.00 10.00
241 Nolan Smith 2.50 6.00
242 Kenneth Faried 4.00 10.00
243 Reggie Jackson 4.00 10.00
244 MarShon Brooks 3.00 8.00
245 Jordan Hamilton 2.50 6.00
246 JaJuan Johnson 2.50 6.00
247 Norris Cole 2.50 6.00
248 Cory Joseph 2.50 6.00
249 Jimmy Butler 20.00 50.00
250 Isaiah Thomas 20.00 50.00
251 Charles Jenkins 2.50 6.00
252 Chandler Parsons 4.00 10.00
253 Lavoy Allen 2.50 6.00
254 Jeremy Tyler 2.50 6.00
255 Jon Leuer 3.00 8.00
257 Greg Stiemsma 2.50 6.00
258 Andrew Goudelock 2.50 6.00
259 Josh Harrellson 2.50 6.00
261 Vernon Macklin 3.00 8.00
263 Jordan Williams 3.00 8.00
265 Josh Selby 2.50 6.00
266 DeAndre Liggins 3.00 8.00
268 Derrick Byars 2.50 6.00
269 Tyler Honeycutt 2.50 6.00
271 Shelvin Mack 3.00 8.00
272 Trey Thompkins 2.50 6.00
275 Anthony Davis 100.00 200.00
276 Michael Kidd-Gilchrist 4.00 10.00
277 Bradley Beal 20.00 50.00
278 Dion Waiters 4.00 10.00
279 Thomas Robinson 3.00 8.00
281 Harrison Barnes 10.00 25.00
282 Terrence Ross 4.00 10.00
283 Andre Drummond 15.00 40.00
284 Austin Rivers 4.00 10.00
285 Meyers Leonard 3.00 8.00
286 Jeremy Lamb 4.00 10.00
287 John Henson 4.00 10.00
288 Moe Harkless 4.00 10.00
289 Tyler Zeller 3.00 8.00
290 Evan Fournier 4.00 10.00
291 Perry Jones 2.50 6.00
292 Bernard James 2.50 6.00
293 Quincy Acy 2.50 6.00
294 Quincy Miller 2.50 6.00
298 Rajon Rondo SP
299 Chris Paul SP EXCH 40.00 100.00

2012-13 Hoops Board Members

MPLETE SET (20) 6.00 15.00
RANDOM INSERTS IN PACKS
1 Kevin Love .50 1.25
2 Dwight Howard .40 1.00
3 Andrew Bynum .30 .75
4 Kris Humphries .30 .75
5 Blake Griffin .50 1.25
6 DeMarcus Cousins .50 1.25
7 Pau Gasol .50 1.25
8 Marc Gasol .50 1.25
9 Marcin Gortat .40 1.00
10 Tyson Chandler .40 1.00
11 Joakim Noah .40 1.00
12 Greg Monroe .40 1.00
13 Josh Smith .40 1.00
14 Al Jefferson .40 1.00
15 David Lee .30 .75
16 Tim Duncan .75 2.00
17 Kevin Durant 1.25 3.00
18 LeBron James 2.00 5.00
19 DeAndre Jordan .50 1.25
20 LaMarcus Aldridge .50 1.25

2012-13 Hoops Courtside

COMPLETE SET (20) 8.00 20.00
RANDOM INSERTS IN PACKS
1 Chris Paul .60 1.50
2 Tony Parker .50 1.25
3 Antawn Jamison .40 1.00
4 Derrick Rose .60 1.50
5 Rajon Rondo .50 1.25
6 Dwyane Wade .75 2.00
7 John Wall .60 1.50
8 Steve Nash .50 1.25
9 David Lee .30 .75
10 Ricky Rubio .50 1.25
11 Kevin Love .50 1.25
12 Russell Westbrook 1.25 3.00
13 Deron Williams .40 1.00
14 LeBron James 2.00 5.00
15 Kobe Bryant 2.00 5.00
16 Kevin Durant 1.25 3.00
17 Blake Griffin .50 1.25
18 LaMarcus Aldridge .50 1.25
19 Dwight Howard .40 1.00
20 Dirk Nowitzki .60 1.50

2012-13 Hoops Draft Night

COMPLETE SET (20) 15.00 40.00
RANDOM INSERTS IN PACKS
1 Anthony Davis 5.00 12.00
2 Michael Kidd-Gilchrist 1.00 2.50
3 Bradley Beal 1.50 4.00
4 Dion Waiters 1.00 2.50
5 Thomas Robinson .75 2.00
6 Damian Lillard 4.00 10.00
7 Harrison Barnes 1.50 4.00
8 Terrence Ross 1.00 2.50
9 Andre Drummond 1.50 4.00
10 Austin Rivers 1.00 2.50
11 Meyers Leonard .75 2.00
12 Jeremy Lamb 1.00 2.50
13 John Henson 1.00 2.50
14 Moe Harkless 1.00 2.50
15 Tyler Zeller .75 2.00
16 Evan Fournier 1.00 2.50
17 Perry Jones .60 1.50
18 Bernard James .60 1.50
19 Quincy Acy .60 1.50
20 Quincy Miller .60 1.50

2012-13 Hoops Draft Night Autographs

RANDOM INSERTS IN PACKS
1 Anthony Davis 125.00 300.00
2 Michael Kidd-Gilchrist 5.00 12.00
3 Bradley Beal 50.00 120.00
4 Dion Waiters 5.00 12.00
5 Thomas Robinson 4.00 10.00
7 Harrison Barnes 15.00 40.00
8 Terrence Ross 5.00 12.00
9 Andre Drummond 15.00 40.00
10 Austin Rivers 5.00 12.00
11 Meyers Leonard 4.00 10.00
12 Jeremy Lamb 5.00 12.00
13 John Henson 5.00 12.00
14 Moe Harkless 5.00 12.00
15 Tyler Zeller 4.00 10.00
16 Evan Fournier 5.00 12.00
17 Perry Jones 3.00 8.00
18 Bernard James 3.00 8.00
19 Quincy Acy 3.00 8.00
20 Quincy Miller 3.00 8.00

2012-13 Hoops Franchise Greats

COMPLETE SET (20) 30.00 80.00
RANDOM INSERTS IN PACKS
1 Magic Johnson 4.00 10.00
2 Kareem Abdul-Jabbar 2.50 6.00
3 Shaquille O'Neal 3.00 8.00
4 Wilt Chamberlain 3.00 8.00
5 Larry Bird 4.00 10.00
6 John Havlicek 2.00 5.00
7 Bill Russell 2.50 6.00
8 Patrick Ewing 2.00 5.00
9 Julius Erving 2.50 6.00
10 Scottie Pippen 3.00 8.00
11 John Stockton 2.50 6.00
12 Karl Malone 2.00 5.00
13 Dominique Wilkins 2.00 5.00
14 Isiah Thomas 1.50 4.00
15 Hakeem Olajuwon 2.00 5.00
16 Kobe Bryant 6.00 15.00
17 Dirk Nowitzki 2.00 5.00
18 Paul Pierce 1.50 4.00
19 Tim Duncan 2.50 6.00
20 Kevin Durant 4.00 10.00

2012-13 Hoops Kobe's All-Rookie Team

RANDOM INSERTS IN PACKS
1 Isaiah Thomas 10.00 25.00
2 Kyrie Irving 30.00 80.00
3 Derrick Williams 4.00 10.00
4 Kemba Walker 12.00 30.00
5 Jimmer Fredette 4.00 10.00
6 Markieff Morris 6.00 15.00
7 Kenneth Faried 6.00 15.00
8 Brandon Knight 6.00 15.00
9 Kawhi Leonard 30.00 80.00
10 MarShon Brooks 5.00 12.00
11 Klay Thompson 25.00 60.00
12 Iman Shumpert 6.00 15.00
13 Chandler Parsons 6.00 15.00
14 Bismack Biyombo 4.00 10.00
15 Tristan Thompson 6.00 15.00
16 Ricky Rubio 15.00 40.00
17 Norris Cole 4.00 10.00
18 Alec Burks 6.00 15.00
19 Gustavo Ayon 4.00 10.00
20 Nikola Vucevic 6.00 15.00
21 Ivan Johnson 4.00 10.00
22 Enes Kanter 5.00 12.00
23 Lavoy Allen 4.00 10.00
24 Greg Stiemsma 4.00 10.00
25 Josh Harrellson 4.00 10.00
26 Darius Morris 4.00 10.00
27 Daniel Orton 4.00 10.00
28 E'Twaun Moore 4.00 10.00
29 Andrew Goudelock 4.00 10.00
30 Tobias Harris 10.00 25.00

2012-13 Hoops Rising Stars

COMPLETE SET (9) 8.00 20.00
RANDOM INSERTS IN BLISTER PACKS
1 Blake Griffin .75 2.00
2 Ricky Rubio .75 2.00
3 Russell Westbrook 2.00 5.00
4 John Wall 1.00 2.50
5 Jeremy Lin .75 2.00
6 Kevin Love .75 2.00
7 Derrick Rose 1.00 2.50
8 Avery Bradley .60 1.50
9 Tyreke Evans .50 1.25

2012-13 Hoops Rookie Impact

COMPLETE SET (28) 12.00 30.00
RANDOM INSERTS IN PACKS
1 Kyrie Irving 2.50 6.00
2 Brandon Knight .50 1.25
3 MarShon Brooks .40 1.00
4 Klay Thompson 2.00 5.00
5 Kemba Walker 1.00 2.50
6 Isaiah Thomas .75 2.00
7 Kenneth Faried .50 1.25
8 Chandler Parsons .50 1.25
9 Iman Shumpert .50 1.25
10 Derrick Williams .30 .75
11 Tristan Thompson .50 1.25
12 Kawhi Leonard 2.50 6.00
13 Jimmer Fredette .30 .75
14 Markieff Morris .50 1.25
15 Alec Burks .50 1.25
16 Norris Cole .30 .75
17 Josh Harrellson .30 .75
18 Gustavo Ayon .30 .75
19 Charles Jenkins .30 .75
20 Bismack Biyombo .30 .75
21 Jan Vesely .30 .75
22 Jimmy Butler 1.50 4.00
23 Enes Kanter .40 1.00
24 Jeremy Tyler .30 .75
25 Ricky Rubio .50 1.25
26 Tobias Harris .50 1.25
27 Andrew Goudelock .30 .75
28 Lavoy Allen .30 .75

2012-13 Hoops Rookie Impact Autographs

RANDOM INSERTS IN PACKS
1 Kyrie Irving 100.00 250.00
2 Brandon Knight 5.00 12.00
3 MarShon Brooks 4.00 10.00
4 Klay Thompson 25.00 60.00
5 Kemba Walker 15.00 40.00
6 Isaiah Thomas 25.00 60.00
7 Kenneth Faried 5.00 12.00
8 Chandler Parsons 5.00 12.00
9 Iman Shumpert 5.00 12.00
10 Derrick Williams 3.00 8.00
11 Tristan Thompson 5.00 12.00
12 Kawhi Leonard 30.00 80.00
13 Jimmer Fredette 3.00 8.00
14 Markieff Morris 5.00 12.00
15 Alec Burks 5.00 12.00
16 Norris Cole 3.00 8.00
17 Josh Harrellson 3.00 8.00
18 Gustavo Ayon 3.00 8.00
19 Charles Jenkins 3.00 8.00
20 Bismack Biyombo 3.00 8.00
21 Jan Vesely 3.00 8.00
22 Jimmy Butler 15.00 40.00
23 Enes Kanter 4.00 10.00
24 Jeremy Tyler 3.00 8.00
26 Tobias Harris 5.00 12.00
27 Andrew Goudelock 3.00 8.00
28 Lavoy Allen 3.00 8.00

2012-13 Hoops Spark Plugs

COMPLETE SET (20) 4.00 10.00
RANDOM INSERTS IN PACKS
1 James Harden .75 2.00
2 Jason Terry .40 1.00
3 Manu Ginobili .50 1.25
4 Joakim Noah .40 1.00
5 Tyson Chandler .40 1.00
6 Anderson Varejao .30 .75
7 Steve Novak .30 .75
8 Chase Budinger .30 .75
9 Shane Battier .40 1.00
10 Mo Williams .40 1.00
11 Al Harrington .40 1.00
12 Louis Williams .40 1.00
13 J.R. Smith .40 1.00
14 Glen Davis .30 .75
15 Tyler Hansbrough .40 1.00
16 Thaddeus Young .30 .75
17 O.J. Mayo .30 .75
18 George Hill .40 1.00
19 Jamal Crawford .50 1.25
20 Avery Bradley .40 1.00

2013-14 Hoops

COMPLETE SET (301) 25.00 60.00
1 Al Horford .25 .60
2 Steve Nash .30 .75
3 Jrue Holiday .30 .75
4 Pau Gasol .30 .75
5 John Jenkins .20 .50
6 Spencer Hawes .20 .50
7 Steve Blake .20 .50
8 Lavoy Allen .20 .50
9 Kobe Bryant 1.25 3.00
10 DeMar DeRozan .30 .75
11 Avery Bradley .25 .60
12 Darrell Arthur .20 .50
13 Evan Turner .20 .50
14 Jordan Hill .20 .50
15 Jason Terry .25 .60
16 Thaddeus Young .20 .50
17 Marc Gasol .30 .75
18 Glen Davis .20 .50
19 Jamal Crawford .30 .75
20 Amir Johnson .20 .50
21 Jeff Green .25 .60
22 Mike Conley .25 .60
23 Nikola Vucevic .25 .60
24 Matt Barnes .20 .50
25 Jordan Crawford .20 .50
26 Jason Richardson .30 .75
27 Quincy Pondexter .20 .50
28 Tobias Harris .25 .60
29 Eric Bledsoe .25 .60
30 Kawhi Leonard .50 1.25
31 Brook Lopez .25 .60
32 Tayshaun Prince .25 .60
33 Serge Ibaka .25 .60
34 DeAndre Jordan .30 .75
35 Deron Williams .25 .60
36 Channing Frye .25 .60
37 Tony Wroten .20 .50
38 Thabo Sefolosha .20 .50
39 Caron Butler .25 .60
40 Gary Neal .25 .60
41 Kris Humphries .20 .50
42 Zach Randolph .25 .60
43 Jeremy Lamb .20 .50
44 Blake Griffin .30 .75
45 Tornike Shengelia .20 .50
46 Goran Dragic .25 .60
47 Chris Bosh .30 .75
48 Arron Afflalo .20 .50
49 Roy Hibbert .25 .60
50 Cory Joseph .20 .50
51 Michael Kidd-Gilchrist .30 .75
52 Dwyane Wade .50 1.25
53 Jameer Nelson .20 .50
54 Louis Williams .25 .60
55 Kemba Walker .30 .75
56 Kendall Marshall .25 .60
57 Joel Anthony .20 .50
58 Maurice Harkless .20 .50
59 Paul George .40 1.00
60 Tony Parker .30 .75
61 Ramon Sessions .25 .60
62 LeBron James 1.25 3.00
63 Reggie Jackson .25 .60
64 Orlando Johnson .20 .50
65 Kevin Garnett .50 1.25
66 Luis Scola .25 .60
67 Mike Miller .25 .60
68 Russell Westbrook .75 2.00
69 Lance Stephenson .25 .60
70 Tim Duncan .50 1.25
71 Jimmy Butler .30 .75
72 Shane Battier .25 .60
73 Kevin Durant .75 2.00
74 George Hill .25 .60
75 Carlos Boozer .25 .60
76 Marcin Gortat .25 .60
77 Norris Cole .20 .50
78 Nick Collison .25 .60
79 Patrick Beverley .20 .50
80 Matt Bonner .20 .50
81 Joakim Noah .25 .60
82 Udonis Haslem .20 .50
83 Steve Novak .20 .50
84 Omer Asik .25 .60
85 Kirk Hinrich .25 .60
86 Marcus Morris .20 .50
87 Ray Allen .30 .75
88 Kendrick Perkins .20 .50
89 Jeremy Lin .30 .75
90 Danny Green .25 .60
91 Luol Deng .25 .60
92 Rashard Lewis .25 .60
93 Pablo Prigioni .20 .50
94 James Harden .50 1.25
95 Anderson Varejao .20 .50
96 Markieff Morris .20 .50
97 Mario Chalmers .25 .60
98 Raymond Felton .25 .60
99 Chandler Parsons .25 .60
100 Marcus Thornton .20 .50
101 C.J. Miles .25 .60
102 Ersan Ilyasova .20 .50
103 Iman Shumpert .20 .50
104 Carlos Delfino .20 .50
105 Kyrie Irving .60 1.50
106 Damian Lillard .60 1.50
107 John Henson .25 .60
108 Tyson Chandler .25 .60
109 Draymond Green .40 1.00
110 John Salmons .25 .60
111 Nene .25 .60
112 Luc Mbah a Moute .20 .50
113 Carmelo Anthony .40 1.00
114 David Lee .20 .50
115 Dirk Nowitzki .40 1.00
116 LaMarcus Aldridge .30 .75
117 Larry Sanders .20 .50
118 Marcus Camby .25 .60
119 Kent Bazemore .25 .60
120 Jimmer Fredette .20 .50
121 Jae Crowder .25 .60
122 Kevin Seraphin .20 .50
123 Amar'e Stoudemire .25 .60
124 Stephen Curry 1.25 3.00
125 Vince Carter .40 1.00
126 Nicolas Batum .25 .60
127 Derrick Williams .20 .50
128 Ryan Anderson .25 .60
129 Klay Thompson .40 1.00
130 Isaiah Thomas .30 .75
131 Danilo Gallinari .20 .50
132 J.J. Barea .25 .60
133 John Wall .40 1.00
134 Harrison Barnes .25 .60
135 Evan Fournier .25 .60
136 Victor Claver .20 .50
137 Kevin Love .30 .75
138 Robin Lopez .20 .50
139 Andrew Bogut .25 .60
140 DeMarcus Cousins .30 .75
141 JaVale McGee .25 .60
142 Andray Blatche .20 .50
143 Eric Gordon .25 .60
144 Rodney Stuckey .25 .60
145 Ty Lawson .20 .50
146 Wesley Matthews .20 .50
147 Jared Dudley .20 .50
148 Darius Miller .20 .50
149 Jonas Jerebko .20 .50
150 Will Barton .20 .50
151 Andre Drummond .30 .75
152 Ricky Rubio .30 .75
153 Brian Roberts .20 .50
154 Greg Monroe .25 .60
155 Wilson Chandler .25 .60
156 Trevor Booker .20 .50
157 Anthony Davis .60 1.50
158 Austin Rivers .25 .60
159 Brandon Knight .25 .60
160 Chuck Hayes .20 .50
161 Jonas Valanciunas .25 .60
162 Derrick Favors .25 .60
163 Bradley Beal .30 .75
164 Kyle Lowry .25 .60
165 Alec Burks .20 .50
166 Terrence Ross .25 .60
167 Alexey Shved .20 .50
168 Gordon Hayward .30 .75
169 Rudy Gay .30 .75
170 Emeka Okafor .25 .60
171 Enes Kanter .20 .50
172 Landry Fields .20 .50
173 Greivis Vasquez .25 .60
174 Tristan Thompson .25 .60
175 Jan Vesely .20 .50
176 Quincy Acy .20 .50
177 Chris Andersen .25 .60
178 Jeff Teague .25 .60
179 Marco Belinelli .20 .50
180 Jeremy Evans .20 .50
181 Tyreke Evans .20 .50
182 Derrick Rose .40 1.00
183 Chris Copeland .20 .50
184 Andrei Kirilenko .25 .60
185 Chris Paul .40 1.00
186 Kenneth Faried .25 .60
187 J.R. Smith .25 .60
188 Nick Young .30 .75
189 Jarrett Jack .25 .60
190 Chauncey Billups .30 .75
191 Tony Allen .20 .50
192 Richard Jefferson .25 .60
193 Elton Brand .30 .75
194 Dorell Wright .20 .50
195 Manu Ginobili .30 .75
196 Shawn Marion .25 .60
197 Gerald Henderson .20 .50
198 Chris Kaman .25 .60
199 Ben Gordon .25 .60
200 Paul Pierce .30 .75
201 Martell Webster .20 .50
202 Tiago Splitter .25 .60
203 Francisco Garcia .20 .50
204 Tyler Hansbrough .25 .60
205 Earl Clark .20 .50
206 J.J. Redick .30 .75
207 Nikola Pekovic .20 .50
208 Kevin Martin .25 .60
209 Andrew Nicholson .20 .50
210 DeJuan Blair .20 .50
211 Trevor Ariza .20 .50
212 Andris Biedrins .20 .50
213 David West .25 .60
214 Dwight Howard .25 .60
215 Mike Dunleavy .20 .50
216 Chase Budinger .20 .50
217 Boris Diaw .25 .60
218 Gerald Wallace .25 .60
219 Brendan Haywood .20 .50
220 D.J. Augustin .20 .50
221 Al Jefferson .25 .60
222 J.J. Hickson .20 .50
223 Brandon Rush .20 .50
224 Andrea Bargnani .25 .60
225 Dion Waiters .25 .60
226 Monta Ellis .25 .60
227 Paul Millsap .30 .75
228 Arnett Moultrie .20 .50
229 Rajon Rondo .30 .75
230 Samuel Dalembert .20 .50
231 Brandon Bass .20 .50
232 Danny Granger .25 .60
233 Kwame Brown .20 .50
234 Kenyon Martin .25 .60
235 Jason Smith .20 .50
236 Brandon Jennings .20 .50
237 Wesley Johnson .25 .60
238 Marvin Williams .25 .60
239 Courtney Lee .25 .60
240 Mo Williams .25 .60
241 Josh Smith .25 .60
242 Nate Robinson .20 .50
243 Kyle Korver .25 .60
244 Taj Gibson .25 .60
245 Byron Mullens .20 .50
246 Andre Iguodala .25 .60
247 Carl Landry .20 .50
248 Zaza Pachulia .20 .50
249 Devin Harris .20 .50
250 O.J. Mayo .20 .50
251 Corey Brewer .20 .50
252 Andrew Bynum .20 .50
253 Jerryd Bayless .25 .60
254 Metta World Peace .30 .75
255 Al-Farouq Aminu .25 .60
256 Darren Collison .25 .60
257 Randy Foye .20 .50
258 Jason Maxiell .20 .50
259 Brandan Wright .20 .50
260 Jose Calderon .20 .50
261 Anthony Bennett RC .50 1.25
262 Victor Oladipo RC .75 2.00
263 Otto Porter RC .60 1.50
264 Cody Zeller RC .50 1.25
265 Alex Len RC .50 1.25
266 Nerlens Noel RC .75 2.00
267 Ben McLemore RC .50 1.25
268 Kentavious Caldwell-Pope RC .60 1.50
269 Trey Burke RC .50 1.25
270 C.J. McCollum RC 1.00 2.50
271 M.Carter-Williams RC .60 1.50
272 Steven Adams RC .60 1.50
273 Kelly Olynyk RC .50 1.25
274 Shabazz Muhammad RC .50 1.25
275 G.Antetokounmpo RC 5.00 12.00
276 Ray McCallum RC .40 1.00
277 Dennis Schroeder RC .60 1.50
278 Shane Larkin RC .40 1.00
279 Sergey Karasev RC .40 1.00
280 Tony Snell RC .50 1.25
281 Gorgui Dieng RC .50 1.25
282 Mason Plumlee RC .60 1.50
283 Solomon Hill RC .40 1.00
284 Tim Hardaway Jr. RC .60 1.50
285 Reggie Bullock RC .50 1.25
286 Andre Roberson RC .40 1.00
287 Rudy Gobert RC .75 2.00
288 Archie Goodwin RC .50 1.25
289 Allen Crabbe RC .50 1.25
290 Carrick Felix RC .40 1.00
291 Isaiah Canaan RC .40 1.00
292 Glen Rice Jr. RC .40 1.00
293 Tony Mitchell RC .40 1.00
294 Grant Jerrett RC .40 1.00
295 Jeff Withey RC .40 1.00
296 Jamaal Franklin RC .40 1.00
297 Phil Pressey RC .40 1.00
298 Peyton Siva RC .40 1.00
299 Ryan Kelly RC .40 1.00
300 Erik Murphy RC .40 1.00
301 Miami Heat Champions 3.00 8.00

2013-14 Hoops Artist's Proofs

*AP VETS: 2X TO 5X BASE HI
*AP RCs: 1X TO 2.5X BASE HI

2013-14 Hoops Blue

*BLUE VETS: .75X TO 2X BASE HI
*BLUE RCs: .75X TO 2X BASE HI

2013-14 Hoops Gold

*GOLD VETS: .6X TO 1.5X BASE HI
*GOLD RCs: .6X TO 1.5X BASE HI

2013-14 Hoops Red

*RED VETS: 1X TO 2.5X BASE HI
*RED RCs: 1X TO 2.5X BASE HI

2013-14 Hoops Red Backs

*RED BACK VETS: .6X TO 1.5X BASE HI
*RED BACK RCs: .6X TO 1.5X BASE HI

2013-14 Hoops Above the Rim

1 Kawhi Leonard 4.00 10.00
2 Anthony Davis 5.00 12.00
3 Andre Iguodala 2.00 5.00
4 Paul George 3.00 8.00
5 Dwyane Wade 4.00 10.00
6 JaVale McGee 2.00 5.00
7 Gerald Green 2.00 5.00
8 Zach Randolph 2.00 5.00
9 Tyson Chandler 2.00 5.00
10 Kevin Durant 6.00 15.00
11 LeBron James 10.00 25.00
12 Kenneth Faried 2.00 5.00
13 Russell Westbrook 6.00 15.00
14 Harrison Barnes 2.00 5.00
15 Carmelo Anthony 3.00 8.00
16 Kobe Bryant 10.00 25.00
17 Joakim Noah 2.00 5.00
18 Jeremy Evans 1.50 4.00
19 Bradley Beal 2.50 6.00
20 Michael Kidd-Gilchrist 2.50 6.00
21 Andre Drummond 2.50 6.00
22 Blake Griffin 2.50 6.00
23 J.R. Smith 2.00 5.00
24 Terrence Ross 2.00 5.00
25 Vince Carter 3.00 8.00

2013-14 Hoops Action Shots

COMPLETE SET (25) 5.00 12.00
1 Jrue Holiday .50 1.25
2 Dwyane Wade .75 2.00
3 Kevin Durant 1.25 3.00
4 Manu Ginobili .50 1.25
5 Ty Lawson .30 .75
6 Joe Johnson .40 1.00
7 Kevin Garnett .75 2.00
8 Harrison Barnes .40 1.00
9 Brandon Knight .40 1.00
10 Dirk Nowitzki .60 1.50
11 Tyreke Evans .30 .75
12 Kobe Bryant 2.00 5.00
13 LeBron James 2.00 5.00
14 Iman Shumpert .30 .75
15 Kevin Love .50 1.25
16 Derrick Favors .40 1.00
17 Joakim Noah .40 1.00
18 Mike Conley .40 1.00
19 Damian Lillard 1.00 2.50
20 Kemba Walker .50 1.25
21 Jimmy Butler .50 1.25
22 DeMar DeRozan .50 1.25
23 John Wall .60 1.50
24 Larry Sanders .30 .75
25 Paul George .60 1.50

2013-14 Hoops Authentics

PRIME PRINT RUNS B/WN 1-25 COPIES PER
NO PRIME PRICING ON QTY 20 OR LESS
1 Kobe Bryant 8.00 20.00
2 Al Jefferson 2.50 6.00
3 Blake Griffin 3.00 8.00
4 Carmelo Anthony 4.00 10.00
5 Danny Granger 2.50 6.00
6 David Lee 2.00 5.00
7 DeQuan Jones 2.00 5.00
8 Devin Harris 2.00 5.00
9 Ekpe Udoh 2.00 5.00
10 Glen Davis 2.00 5.00
11 Hedo Turkoglu 2.50 6.00
12 Tristan Thompson 2.50 6.00
13 Jeff Teague 2.50 6.00
14 Joe Johnson 2.50 6.00
15 John Wall 4.00 10.00
16 Kevin Garnett 5.00 12.00
17 Kyle Lowry 2.50 6.00
18 LeBron James 12.00 30.00
19 Luol Deng 2.50 6.00
20 Marcus Camby 2.50 6.00
21 Michael Beasley 2.00 5.00
22 Pablo Prigioni 2.00 5.00
23 Stephen Curry 6.00 15.00
24 Tim Duncan 5.00 12.00
25 Pau Gasol 3.00 8.00
26 Amar'e Stoudemire 2.50 6.00
27 Brandon Jennings 2.00 5.00
28 Caron Butler
29 Danny Green 2.50 6.00
30 David West 2.50 6.00
31 Derrick Favors 2.50 6.00
32 Drew Gooden 2.50 6.00
33 Emeka Okafor 2.50 6.00
34 Goran Dragic 2.50 6.00
35 J.J. Barea 2.50 6.00
36 Jason Kidd
37 Jeremy Lin 3.00 8.00
38 Joel Anthony 2.00 5.00
39 Jonas Jerebko 2.00 5.00
40 Kevin Martin 2.50 6.00
41 Lamar Odom 2.50 6.00
42 Will Barton 2.00 5.00
43 Manu Ginobili 3.00 8.00
44 Bradley Beal 3.00 8.00
45 Monta Ellis 2.50 6.00
46 Paul Pierce 3.00 8.00
47 Steve Nash 3.00 8.00
48 Tony Parker 3.00 8.00
49 Kyrie Irving 6.00 15.00
50 Dirk Nowitzki 4.00 10.00
51 Andre Iguodala 2.50 6.00
52 Brook Lopez 2.50 6.00
53 Chris Bosh 3.00 8.00
54 Dante Cunningham 2.00 5.00
55 DeMar DeRozan 3.00 8.00
56 Derrick Rose
57 Dwight Howard 2.50 6.00
58 Evan Turner 2.00 5.00
59 Gordon Hayward 3.00 8.00
60 J.R. Smith 2.50 6.00
61 Jason Terry 5.00 12.00
62 Lavoy Allen 2.00 5.00
63 Joel Freeland 2.00 5.00
64 Kent Bazemore 5.00 12.00
65 Avery Bradley 2.50 6.00
66 LaMarcus Aldridge 3.00 8.00
67 Louis Williams
68 Marc Gasol 3.00 8.00
69 Anthony Davis 6.00 15.00
70 Nene 2.50 6.00
71 Richard Hamilton 2.50 6.00
72 Brandon Knight 2.50 6.00
73 Viacheslav Kravtsov 2.00 5.00
74 Taj Gibson 2.50 6.00
75 Kevin Love 3.00 8.00
76 Andre Drummond 3.00 8.00
77 Carlos Delfino 2.00 5.00
78 Daniel Gibson 2.50 6.00
79 Tyreke Evans 2.00 5.00
80 DeMarcus Cousins 3.00 8.00
81 DeShawn Stevenson 2.00 5.00
82 Dwyane Wade 5.00 12.00
83 Gerald Wallace 2.50 6.00
84 Grant Hill
85 Jameer Nelson
86 JaVale McGee 2.50 6.00
87 Joakim Noah
88 John Lucas III
89 Ty Lawson 2.00 5.00
90 Kris Humphries 2.00 5.00
91 Landry Fields 2.00 5.00
92 Luis Scola 2.50 6.00
93 Marcin Gortat 6.00 15.00
94 Austin Rivers 2.50 6.00
95 O.J. Mayo 2.00 5.00
96 Serge Ibaka 2.50 6.00
97 Al Horford 2.50 6.00
98 Kevin Durant 6.00 15.00
99 Darren Collison 2.50 6.00
100 Tyson Chandler 2.50 6.00

2013-14 Hoops Autographs

EXCHANGE DEADLINE 4/28/2015
1 Gustavo Ayon
2 Jeff Taylor 3.00 8.00
3 Brandon Knight 4.00 10.00
4 Derrick Williams 3.00 8.00
5 Maurice Harkless 3.00 8.00
6 Kim English 3.00 8.00
7 Enes Kanter
8 Donatas Motiejunas 3.00 8.00
9 Julyan Stone 3.00 8.00
10 James Anderson 3.00 8.00
11 Ekpe Udoh 3.00 8.00
12 Boris Diaw 3.00 8.00
13 Kyle Korver 3.00 8.00
14 Ben Gordon
15 Lance Stephenson 5.00 12.00
16 Kevin Love
17 Xavier Henry 5.00 12.00
18 Andrei Kirilenko 5.00 12.00
19 Jason Terry
20 Antawn Jamison 4.00 10.00
21 Carl Landry 3.00 8.00
22 Khris Middleton 3.00 8.00
23 Tyreke Evans 3.00 8.00
24 Kwame Brown 3.00 8.00
25 Dahntay Jones 3.00 8.00
26 C.J. Watson 4.00 10.00
27 Marcus Thornton 3.00 8.00
28 Joe Johnson 8.00 20.00
29 Jeff Green 4.00 10.00
30 Josh Smith 4.00 10.00
31 Patrick Patterson 4.00 10.00
32 John Salmons 3.00 8.00
33 Brandon Rush 3.00 8.00
34 Chris Wilcox 5.00 12.00
35 DeMarre Carroll 3.00 8.00
36 Chase Budinger 3.00 8.00
37 Wesley Matthews
38 Marreese Speights 3.00 8.00
39 Lance Thomas 3.00 8.00
40 Mike Scott 3.00 8.00
41 Maalik Wayns 3.00 8.00
42 Jan Vesely 4.00 10.00
43 Tony Wroten 4.00 10.00
44 DeAndre Liggins 3.00 8.00
45 Jon Leuer 3.00 8.00
46 Patrick Beverley 3.00 8.00
47 Jordan Hamilton 3.00 8.00
48 Justin Holiday 3.00 8.00
49 Kendall Marshall
50 Kyle O'Quinn 3.00 8.00
51 Dante Cunningham 3.00 8.00
52 Maurice Taylor 4.00 10.00
53 Travis Best 3.00 8.00
54 Terry Dehere 3.00 8.00
55 Todd Day 3.00 8.00
56 Marcus Liberty 3.00 8.00
57 Hot Rod Williams 3.00 8.00
58 James Robinson 3.00 8.00
59 John Wallace 5.00 12.00
60 Eric Murdock 3.00 8.00
61 Tracy Murray 3.00 8.00
62 Trent Tucker 5.00 12.00
63 Mahmoud Abdul-Rauf 10.00 25.00
64 Craig Hodges 3.00 8.00
65 Michael Bantom 3.00 8.00
66 Jerome Williams 4.00 10.00
67 Greg Minor 4.00 10.00
68 Greg Buckner 3.00 8.00
69 Ish Smith 3.00 8.00
70 Charlie Bell 3.00 8.00
71 Jared Jeffries 3.00 8.00
72 Jannero Pargo 3.00 8.00
73 Marquis Daniels 3.00 8.00
74 Chris Whitney 5.00 12.00
75 Elliot Williams 3.00 8.00
76 Viacheslav Kravtsov 3.00 8.00
77 Nando De Colo 4.00 10.00
78 Herb Williams 3.00 8.00
79 Rory Sparrow 3.00 8.00
80 Otis Birdsong 3.00 8.00
81 Dale Ellis 3.00 8.00
82 Chucky Brown 4.00 10.00
83 Mickael Pietrus 5.00 12.00
84 John Lucas III 3.00 8.00
85 Eric Maynor 5.00 12.00
86 P.J. Tucker 3.00 8.00
87 Greg Stiemsma 3.00 8.00
88 Keith Bogans 5.00 12.00
89 Sebastian Telfair 4.00 10.00
90 Diante Garrett 3.00 8.00
91 Josh Akognon 5.00 12.00
92 DeSagana Diop 3.00 8.00
93 C.J. Miles 3.00 8.00
94 Ronnie Price 3.00 8.00
95 Elgin Baylor 8.00 20.00
96 Kenny Smith 3.00 8.00
97 Jonas Jerebko
98 Andray Blatche
99 Gary Payton 8.00 20.00
100 Luis Scola 4.00 10.00
101 Tyson Chandler 5.00 12.00
102 Dorell Wright
103 Blake Griffin 12.00 30.00
104 Emeka Okafor
105 Luke Ridnour 3.00 8.00
106 Allan Houston 5.00 12.00
107 Chris Andersen
108 Jason Kidd 6.00 15.00
109 Rajon Rondo 15.00 40.00
110 Kobe Bryant 90.00 150.00
111 Kevin Durant 50.00 120.00
112 Kyrie Irving 30.00 80.00
113 Juwan Howard 4.00 10.00
114 Grant Hill
115 Doc Rivers
116 Alonzo Mourning 8.00 20.00
117 Mark Jackson 5.00 12.00
118 Isiah Thomas 12.00 30.00
119 Bob Lanier 8.00 20.00
120 Greg Ostertag 5.00 12.00
121 Sidney Moncrief 3.00 8.00
122 Harrison Barnes 4.00 10.00
123 Wes Unseld
124 Marcin Gortat 6.00 15.00
125 Mario Chalmers
126 Goran Dragic 6.00 15.00
127 Jared Dudley 3.00 8.00
128 Earl Clark
129 Jared Sullinger 4.00 10.00
130 Dominique Wilkins 10.00 25.00
131 James Johnson 3.00 8.00
132 David Robinson 20.00 50.00
133 Jordan Hill 5.00 12.00
134 Deron Williams 4.00 10.00
135 Chris Bosh 6.00 15.00
136 James Worthy 12.00 30.00
137 Toni Kukoc
138 Andrea Bargnani 3.00 8.00
139 Raymond Felton
140 Kelly Tripucka 8.00 20.00
141 Rick Fox 10.00 25.00
142 Nate Thurmond 8.00 20.00
143 J.R. Smith 6.00 15.00
144 J.J. Redick
145 Dikembe Mutombo 12.00 30.00
146 David West 8.00 20.00
147 Andrew Bogut 8.00 20.00
148 Tiago Splitter 4.00 10.00
149 Jarrett Jack
150 Ryan Anderson 3.00 8.00
151 Connie Hawkins 6.00 15.00
152 MarShon Brooks 4.00 10.00
153 Nicolas Batum 5.00 12.00
154 Byron Mullens 3.00 8.00
155 Corey Brewer 4.00 10.00
156 Michael Cooper 4.00 10.00
157 Jay Williams 6.00 15.00
158 Steve Kerr 6.00 15.00
159 Eric Gordon 4.00 10.00
160 Michael Finley 6.00 15.00
161 Kawhi Leonard 12.00 30.00
162 Lou Amundson 3.00 8.00
163 Jamaal Tinsley
164 Ricky Davis 3.00 8.00
165 Marvin Williams 3.00 8.00
166 Ersan Ilyasova 3.00 8.00
167 Royce White 3.00 8.00
168 Tobias Harris 5.00 12.00
169 Kyle Lowry 3.00 8.00
170 Kenneth Faried 6.00 15.00
171 Jamaal Franklin 4.00 10.00
172 Giannis Antetokounmpo 60.00 150.00
173 Ian Clark 5.00 12.00
174 Ray McCallum 5.00 12.00
175 Dennis Schroeder 6.00 15.00
176 Peyton Siva 3.00 8.00
177 Erik Murphy 4.00 10.00
178 Grant Jerrett 4.00 10.00
179 Shane Larkin 3.00 8.00
180 Isaiah Canaan 3.00 8.00
181 Archie Goodwin 4.00 10.00
182 Trey Burke 5.00 12.00
183 Jeff Withey 4.00 10.00
184 Anthony Bennett 4.00 10.00
185 Victor Oladipo 6.00 15.00
186 Solomon Hill 5.00 12.00
187 Rudy Gobert 6.00 15.00
188 Ben McLemore 4.00 10.00
189 Otto Porter 12.00 30.00
190 Ryan Kelly 5.00 12.00
191 Nate Wolters 4.00 10.00
192 Allen Crabbe 3.00 8.00
193 Alex Len 4.00 10.00
194 Steven Adams 6.00 15.00
195 Mason Plumlee 5.00 12.00
196 Reggie Bullock 3.00 8.00
197 Michael Carter-Williams 6.00 15.00
198 Shabazz Muhammad 4.00 10.00
199 Cody Zeller 4.00 10.00
200 Nerlens Noel 6.00 15.00

2013-14 Hoops Autographs Blue

*RED p/r 99-100: .5X TO 1.2X BASIC
*RED p/r 49-50: .5X TO 1.2X BASIC
*RED p/r 25: .6X TO 1.5X BASIC
PRINT RUNS B/WN 10-100 COPIES PER
NO PRICING ON QTY 10
EXCHANGE DEADLINE 4/28/2015
110 Kobe Bryant/25 100.00 175.00
111 Kevin Durant/25 60.00 150.00

2013-14 Hoops Autographs Red

*RED p/r 75-199: .5X TO 1.2X BASIC
*RED p/r 40-50: .5X TO 1.2X BASIC
*RED p/r 25: .6X TO 1.5X BASIC
PRINT RUNS B/WN 10-199 COPIES PER
NO PRICING ON QTY 10
EXCHANGE DEADLINE 4/28/2015
110 Kobe Bryant/25 100.00 175.00
111 Kevin Durant/25 60.00 150.00

2013-14 Hoops Board Members
COMPLETE SET (25) 5.00 12.00
1 Joakim Noah .40 1.00
2 Kevin Love .50 1.25
3 DeMarcus Cousins .50 1.25
4 Al Horford .40 1.00
5 Dwight Howard .40 1.00
6 Marc Gasol .50 1.25
7 Blake Griffin .50 1.25
8 Tyson Chandler .40 1.00
9 Anderson Varejao .30 .75
10 Carlos Boozer .40 1.00
11 Reggie Evans .30 .75
12 Nikola Vucevic .40 1.00
13 Pau Gasol .50 1.25
14 Marcin Gortat .40 1.00
15 Tristan Thompson .40 1.00
16 Anthony Davis 1.00 2.50
17 Greg Monroe .40 1.00
18 David Lee .30 .75
19 Omer Asik .40 1.00
20 LeBron James 2.00 5.00
21 Tim Duncan .75 2.00
22 Roy Hibbert .40 1.00
23 Andre Drummond .50 1.25
24 Larry Sanders .30 .75
25 Zach Randolph .40 1.00

2013-14 Hoops Class Action
COMPLETE SET (25) 6.00 15.00
1 Damian Lillard 1.00 2.50
2 Kyrie Irving 1.00 2.50
3 Paul George .60 1.50
4 Blake Griffin .50 1.25
5 Derrick Rose .60 1.50
6 Kevin Durant 1.25 3.00
7 LaMarcus Aldridge .50 1.25
8 Chris Paul .60 1.50
9 Dwight Howard .40 1.00
10 LeBron James 2.00 5.00
11 Amar'e Stoudemire .40 1.00
12 Tony Parker .50 1.25
13 Jamal Crawford .50 1.25
14 Shawn Marion .40 1.00
15 Dirk Nowitzki .60 1.50
16 Tim Duncan .75 2.00
17 Kobe Bryant 2.00 5.00
18 Kevin Garnett .75 2.00
19 Jason Kidd .50 1.25
20 Sam Cassell .40 1.00
21 Shaquille O'Neal 1.00 2.50
22 Larry Johnson .60 1.50
23 Gary Payton .50 1.25
24 Shawn Kemp .75 2.00
25 Mitch Richmond .50 1.25

2013-14 Hoops Courtside
COMPLETE SET (20) 5.00 12.00
1 Kobe Bryant 2.00 5.00
2 LeBron James 2.00 5.00
3 Kevin Durant 1.25 3.00
4 Blake Griffin .50 1.25
5 Dwyane Wade .75 2.00
6 Kyrie Irving 1.00 2.50
7 Russell Westbrook 1.25 3.00
8 Paul Pierce .50 1.25
9 Carmelo Anthony .60 1.50
10 Rajon Rondo .50 1.25
11 James Harden .75 2.00
12 Stephen Curry 2.00 5.00
13 Ricky Rubio .50 1.25
14 Brandon Jennings .30 .75
15 Klay Thompson .60 1.50
16 Paul George .60 1.50
17 Tony Parker .50 1.25
18 Marc Gasol .50 1.25
19 Kenneth Faried .40 1.00
20 Chris Paul .60 1.50
21 Deron Williams .40 1.00
22 Bradley Beal .50 1.25
23 Andre Drummond .50 1.25
24 Mike Conley .40 1.00
25 Jeremy Lin .50 1.25

2013-14 Hoops Dreams
COMPLETE SET (25) 6.00 15.00
1 Andrew Nicholson .40 1.00
2 Isaiah Thomas .60 1.50
3 Reggie Jackson .50 1.25
4 Larry Sanders .40 1.00
5 Greivis Vasquez .50 1.25
6 Jared Sullinger .40 1.00
7 Brandon Knight .50 1.25
8 Bradley Beal .60 1.50
9 Lance Stephenson .50 1.25
10 Eric Bledsoe .50 1.25
11 Nikola Vucevic .50 1.25
12 John Jenkins .40 1.00
13 Michael Kidd-Gilchrist .60 1.50
14 Marquis Teague .40 1.00
15 Jimmy Butler .60 1.50
16 Dion Waiters .50 1.25
17 Draymond Green .75 2.00
18 Harrison Barnes .50 1.25
19 Norris Cole .40 1.00
20 Malcolm Lee .40 1.00
21 Brian Roberts .40 1.00
22 Tobias Harris .50 1.25
23 Damian Lillard 1.25 3.00
24 Kawhi Leonard 1.00 2.50
25 Perry Jones .40 1.00

2013-14 Hoops Hall of Fame Heroes
COMPLETE SET (25) 8.00 20.00
1 Isiah Thomas .60 1.50
2 Bob McAdoo .50 1.25
3 Drazen Petrovic .60 1.50
4 Clyde Drexler .75 2.00
5 Hakeem Olajuwon .75 2.00
6 Bill Walton .60 1.50
7 Calvin Murphy .50 1.25
8 Julius Erving 1.00 2.50
9 Dave Cowens .40 1.00
10 Wes Unseld .60 1.50
11 Billy Cunningham .60 1.50
12 Sam Jones .60 1.50
13 Dave DeBusschere .60 1.50
14 Oscar Robertson .75 2.00
15 Wilt Chamberlain 1.25 3.00
16 Earl Monroe .60 1.50
17 Bernard King .50 1.25
18 Joe Dumars .60 1.50
19 Adrian Dantley .50 1.25
20 David Robinson 1.00 2.50
21 Gus Johnson .60 1.50
22 Scottie Pippen 1.25 3.00
23 Artis Gilmore .50 1.25
24 Jamaal Wilkes .60 1.50
25 Gary Payton .60 1.50

2013-14 Hoops Highlights
1 Kobe Bryant 30.00 80.00
2 Miami Heat 40.00 80.00
3 Kevin Garnett 20.00 50.00
4 Stephen Curry 20.00 50.00
5 Steve Nash 40.00 80.00

2013-14 Hoops Kobe All Rookie Team
1 Anthony Bennett 5.00 12.00
2 Victor Oladipo 8.00 20.00
3 Otto Porter 6.00 15.00
4 Cody Zeller 5.00 12.00
5 Alex Len 5.00 12.00
6 Nerlens Noel 8.00 20.00
7 Ben McLemore 5.00 12.00
8 Kentavious Caldwell-Pope 6.00 15.00
9 Trey Burke 5.00 12.00
10 C.J. McCollum 10.00 25.00
11 Michael Carter-Williams 6.00 15.00
12 Shabazz Muhammad 5.00 12.00
13 Tim Hardaway Jr. 6.00 15.00

2013-14 Hoops Spark Plugs
COMPLETE SET (24) 4.00 10.00
1 Jamal Crawford .50 1.25
2 Kevin Martin .40 1.00
3 Ryan Anderson .40 1.00
4 Taj Gibson .40 1.00
5 Nate Robinson .30 .75
6 Wilson Chandler .40 1.00
7 Alexey Shved .30 .75
8 Steve Novak .30 .75
9 Nick Young .50 1.25
10 Jared Dudley .30 .75
11 Gerald Green .40 1.00
12 Jimmy Butler .50 1.25
13 Derrick Favors .40 1.00
14 Terrence Ross .40 1.00
15 Manu Ginobili .50 1.25
16 Marcus Thornton .30 .75
17 Reggie Jackson .40 1.00
18 J.J. Barea .40 1.00
19 Norris Cole .30 .75
20 Quincy Pondexter .30 .75
21 MarShon Brooks .40 1.00
22 Jason Terry .40 1.00
23 Louis Williams .40 1.00
24 Jarrett Jack .40 1.00

2014-15 Hoops
MPLETE SET (300) 25.00 60.00
1 Al Horford .25 .60
2 Austin Rivers .25 .60
3 Deron Williams .25 .60
4 Nikola Vucevic .25 .60
5 Jimmy Butler .30 .75
6 Markieff Morris .20 .50
7 JaVale McGee .25 .60
8 DeMarcus Cousins .30 .75
9 Stephen Curry 1.25 3.00
10 Jonas Valanciunas .25 .60
11 Dennis Schroder .25 .60
12 Tim Hardaway Jr. .20 .50
13 Marc Gasol .30 .75
14 Victor Oladipo .25 .60
15 Derrick Rose .40 1.00
16 Marcus Morris .20 .50
17 Kenneth Faried .25 .60
18 Carl Landry .20 .50
19 Andre Iguodala .25 .60
20 Tyler Hansbrough .25 .60
21 Jeff Teague .25 .60
22 Amar'e Stoudemire .30 .75
23 Mason Plumlee .25 .60
24 Arron Afflalo .20 .50
25 Taj Gibson .25 .60
26 Miles Plumlee .20 .50
27 Ty Lawson .20 .50
28 Derrick Williams .20 .50
29 Andrew Bogut .25 .60
30 Chuck Hayes .20 .50
31 Paul Millsap .30 .75
32 Tyson Chandler .25 .60
33 Paul Pierce .30 .75
34 Maurice Harkless .20 .50
35 Joakim Noah .25 .60
36 Damian Lillard .60 1.50
37 Randy Foye .20 .50
38 Ray McCallum .20 .50
39 Klay Thompson .40 1.00
40 Steve Novak .20 .50
41 Kyle Korver .25 .60
42 J.R. Smith .25 .60
43 Joe Johnson .25 .60
44 Andrew Nicholson .20 .50
45 Mike Dunleavy .20 .50
46 LaMarcus Aldridge .30 .75
47 Wilson Chandler .25 .60
48 Tiago Splitter .25 .60
49 Harrison Barnes .25 .60
50 Enes Kanter .20 .50
51 Louis Williams .25 .60
52 Andrea Bargnani .25 .60
53 Andrei Kirilenko .25 .60
54 Nerlens Noel .25 .60
55 D.J. Augustin .20 .50
56 Nicolas Batum .25 .60
57 J.J. Hickson .20 .50
58 Tim Duncan .50 1.25
59 Kobe Bryant 1.25 3.00
60 Trey Burke .20 .50
61 Pero Antic .20 .50
62 Giannis Antetokounmpo .60 1.50
63 Mirza Teletovic .20 .50
64 Tony Wroten .20 .50
65 Kyrie Irving .60 1.50
66 C.J. McCollum .30 .75
67 Timofey Mozgov .20 .50
68 Tony Parker .30 .75
69 Kevin Martin .25 .60
70 Derrick Favors .25 .60
71 Jared Sullinger .20 .50
72 Iman Shumpert .20 .50
73 Al Jefferson .25 .60
74 Michael Carter-Williams .20 .50
75 Tristan Thompson .25 .60
76 Wesley Matthews .20 .50
77 Josh Smith .25 .60
78 Kawhi Leonard .50 1.25
79 J.J. Barea .25 .60
80 Gordon Hayward .30 .75
81 Brandon Bass .20 .50
82 Nick Collison .25 .60
83 Kemba Walker .30 .75
84 Thaddeus Young .20 .50
85 Anthony Bennett .20 .50
86 Dorell Wright .20 .50
87 Brandon Jennings .20 .50
88 Manu Ginobili .30 .75
89 Chase Budinger .20 .50
90 Alec Burks .20 .50
91 Kelly Olynyk .20 .50
92 Russell Westbrook .75 2.00
93 Gerald Henderson .20 .50
94 Jason Richardson .30 .75
95 Dion Waiters .25 .60
96 Dwight Howard .25 .60
97 Andre Drummond .30 .75
98 Marco Belinelli .20 .50
99 Alexey Shved .20 .50
100 Jeremy Evans .20 .50
101 Shelvin Mack .20 .50
102 Robin Lopez .20 .50
103 Jae Crowder .20 .50
104 Terrence Jones .25 .60
105 Lance Stephenson .25 .60
106 Jamal Crawford .30 .75
107 Kosta Koufos .20 .50
108 Kevin Love .30 .75
109 Jason Smith .20 .50
110 Brandon Knight .25 .60
111 Kris Humphries .20 .50
112 Kyle Lowry .25 .60
113 DeJuan Blair .20 .50
114 Mo Williams .25 .60
115 Evan Turner .20 .50
116 Blake Griffin .30 .75
117 LeBron James 1.25 3.00
118 Kevin Garnett .50 1.25
119 Carmelo Anthony .40 1.00
120 O.J. Mayo .20 .50
121 Shaun Livingston .20 .50
122 John Salmons .25 .60
123 Samuel Dalembert .20 .50
124 Donatas Motiejunas .20 .50
125 Danny Granger .25 .60
126 Chris Bosh .30 .75
127 DeAndre Jordan .30 .75
128 Tayshaun Prince .25 .60
129 Shane Larkin .20 .50
130 Carlos Boozer .25 .60
131 Raymond Felton .25 .60
132 Richard Jefferson .25 .60
133 Devin Harris .20 .50
134 Roy Hibbert .25 .60
135 Jordan Hill .20 .50
136 Matt Barnes .20 .50
137 Dwyane Wade .50 1.25
138 Mike Conley .25 .60
139 Caron Butler .25 .60
140 Khris Middleton .25 .60
141 Kirk Hinrich .25 .60
142 Marvin Williams .25 .60
143 Jordan Crawford .25 .60
144 David West .25 .60
145 Pau Gasol .30 .75
146 Chris Paul .40 1.00
147 Francisco Garcia .20 .50
148 Zach Randolph .25 .60
149 Thabo Sefolosha .20 .50
150 John Henson .25 .60
151 Luol Deng .25 .60
152 Marcin Gortat .25 .60
153 Steve Blake .20 .50
154 George Hill .25 .60
155 Jodie Meeks .25 .60
156 J.J. Redick .30 .75
157 Mario Chalmers .25 .60
158 Courtney Lee .25 .60
159 Jameer Nelson .20 .50
160 Z. Pachulia/X.Henry .20 .50
161 Anderson Varejao .20 .50
162 Trevor Ariza .20 .50
163 Chandler Parsons .25 .60
164 Paul George .40 1.00
165 Chris Kaman .25 .60
166 Jared Dudley .20 .50
167 Udonis Haslem .20 .50
168 Tony Allen .20 .50
169 Kyle O'Quinn .20 .50
170 Ricky Rubio .30 .75
171 Spencer Hawes .20 .50
172 Draymond Green .40 1.00
173 Patrick Beverley .20 .50
174 Luis Scola .25 .60
175 Wesley Johnson .25 .60
176 Darren Collison .25 .60
177 Shawne Williams .20 .50
178 Henry Sims RC .20 .50
179 Norris Cole .20 .50
180 Corey Brewer .20 .50
181 Brandan Wright .20 .50
182 James Harden .50 1.25
183 C.J. Watson .20 .50
184 Omer Asik .25 .60
185 K.Marshall/C.Copeland .20 .50
186 Nate Wolters .25 .60
187 Nick Young .25 .60
188 Chris Andersen .25 .60
189 James Anderson .20 .50
190 Nikola Pekovic .20 .50
191 Jeremy Lin .30 .75
192 Dirk Nowitzki .40 1.00
193 Omri Casspi .20 .50
194 Ian Mahinmi .20 .50
195 Mike Miller .25 .60
196 Steve Nash .30 .75
197 Brian Roberts .20 .50
198 Ersan Ilyasova .20 .50
199 Hollis Thompson .25 .60
200 Gorgui Dieng .20 .50
201 Jeff Green .25 .60
202 Serge Ibaka .25 .60
203 Michael Kidd-Gilchrist .25 .60
204 Eric Bledsoe .25 .60
205 Tyler Zeller .25 .60
206 Thomas Robinson .20 .50
207 Kentavious Caldwell-Pope .20 .50
208 Boris Diaw .25 .60
209 Eric Gordon .25 .60
210 Bradley Beal .30 .75
211 Rajon Rondo .30 .75
212 Kevin Durant .75 2.00
213 Cody Zeller .20 .50
214 Alex Len .20 .50
215 Jarrett Jack .25 .60
216 Ben McLemore .20 .50
217 Greg Monroe .25 .60
218 Danny Green .25 .60
219 Al-Farouq Aminu .20 .50
220 Otto Porter .25 .60
221 Avery Bradley .25 .60
222 Steven Adams .25 .60
223 Josh McRoberts .20 .50
224 Gerald Green .25 .60
225 Jose Calderon .20 .50
226 Rudy Gay .30 .75
227 Kyle Singler .20 .50
228 Patty Mills .30 .75
229 Jrue Holiday .25 .60
230 John Wall .40 1.00
231 Gerald Wallace .25 .60
232 Kendrick Perkins .20 .50
233 Ramon Sessions .25 .60
234 Goran Dragic .25 .60
235 Vince Carter .40 1.00
236 Jason Thompson .20 .50
237 R.Stuckey/L.avoy Allen .20 .50
238 Amir Johnson .20 .50
239 Ryan Anderson .20 .50
240 Nene .25 .60
241 Joel Anthony .20 .50
242 Reggie Jackson .20 .50
243 Bismack Biyombo .20 .50
244 Archie Goodwin .20 .50
245 Monta Ellis .25 .60
246 Jason Terry .25 .60
247 Will Bynum .20 .50
248 DeMar DeRozan .30 .75
249 Tyreke Evans .20 .50
250 Martell Webster .20 .50
251 Brook Lopez .25 .60
252 Tobias Harris .25 .60
253 Tony Snell .20 .50
254 Channing Frye .25 .60
255 Danilo Gallinari .20 .50
256 Isaiah Thomas .30 .75
257 David Lee .20 .50
258 Terrence Ross .25 .60
259 Anthony Davis .60 1.50
260 Trevor Booker .20 .50
261 Andrew Wiggins RC 2.00 5.00
262 Jabari Parker RC 1.00 2.50
263 Joel Embiid RC 2.00 5.00
264 Aaron Gordon RC 1.00 2.50
265 Dante Exum RC .60 1.50
266 Marcus Smart RC .60 1.50
267 Julius Randle RC 1.00 2.50
268 Nik Stauskas RC .50 1.25
269 Noah Vonleh RC .50 1.25
270 Elfrid Payton RC .60 1.50
271 Doug McDermott RC .60 1.50
272 Zach LaVine RC 1.00 2.50
273 T.J. Warren RC .60 1.50
274 Adreian Payne RC .50 1.25
275 James Young RC .40 1.00
276 Tyler Ennis RC .40 1.00
277 Gary Harris RC .60 1.50
278 Mitch McGary RC .40 1.00
279 Jordan Adams RC .40 1.00
280 Rodney Hood RC .60 1.50
281 Shabazz Napier RC .50 1.25
282 P.J. Hairston RC .40 1.00
283 C.J. Wilcox RC .40 1.00
284 Jusuf Nurkic RC .60 1.50
285 Kyle Anderson RC .60 1.50
286 K.J. McDaniels RC .50 1.25
287 Joe Harris RC .40 1.00
288 Cleanthony Early RC .40 1.00
289 Jarnell Stokes RC .40 1.00
290 Johnny O'Bryant RC .40 1.00
291 Cory Jefferson RC .40 1.00
292 Spencer Dinwiddie RC .50 1.25
293 Jerami Grant RC .40 1.00
294 Glenn Robinson III RC .40 1.00
295 Nick Johnson RC .40 1.00
296 Markel Brown RC .40 1.00
297 Bruno Caboclo RC .50 1.25
298 Cameron Bairstow RC .40 1.00
299 Alec Brown RC .40 1.00
300 Thanasis Antetokounmpo RC .50 1.25

2014-15 Hoops Artist's Proofs
*AP VETS/99: 2X TO 5X BASIC
*AP RC/99: 2X TO 5X BASIC
RANDOM INSERTS IN PACKS
STATED PRINT RUN 99 SER.#'d SETS
117 LeBron James 15.00 40.00
261 Andrew Wiggins 30.00 80.00
262 Jabari Parker 25.00 60.00
263 Joel Embiid 12.00 30.00
265 Dante Exum 20.00 50.00

2014-15 Hoops Blue
*BLUE VETS/349: 1X TO 2.5X BASIC
*BLUE RC/349: 1X TO 2.5X BASIC
RANDOM INSERTS IN PACKS
STATED PRINT RUN 349 SER.#'d SETS
261 Andrew Wiggins 12.00 30.00
262 Jabari Parker 10.00 25.00

2014-15 Hoops Gold
*GOLD VETS: .6X TO 1.5X BASIC
*GOLD RC: .6X TO 1.5X BASIC
RANDOM INSERTS IN PACKS

2014-15 Hoops Green
*GREEN VETS: .6X TO 1.5X BASIC
*GREEN RC: .6X TO 1.5X BASIC
RANDOM INSERTS IN PACKS

2014-15 Hoops Red Backs
*RED BK VETS: .6X TO 1.5X BASIC
*RED BK RC: .6X TO 1.5X BASIC
RANDOM INSERTS IN PACKS

2014-15 Hoops Silver
*SILVER VETS/399: 1X TO 2.5X BASIC
*SILVER RC/399: 1X TO 2.5X BASIC
RANDOM INSERTS IN PACKS
STATED PRINT RUN 399 SER.#'d SETS

2014-15 Hoops Authentics
RANDOM INSERTS IN PACKS
*PRIME/25: .75X TO 2X BASE HI
1 Luis Scola 2.50 6.00
2 Andrew Bogut 2.50 6.00
3 Austin Rivers 2.50 6.00
4 Dirk Nowitzki 4.00 10.00
5 Tim Duncan 6.00 15.00
6 Nick Young 2.50 6.00
7 O.J. Mayo 2.00 5.00
8 Monta Ellis 2.50 6.00
9 Pau Gasol 3.00 8.00
10 Kobe Bryant 8.00 20.00
11 Paul Pierce 3.00 8.00
12 Rajon Rondo 3.00 8.00
13 Randy Foye 2.00 5.00
14 Raymond Felton 2.50 6.00
15 Ryan Anderson 2.00 5.00
16 Shane Battier 2.50 6.00
17 Steve Nash 3.00 8.00
18 Tayshaun Prince 2.50 6.00
19 Tiago Splitter 2.50 6.00
20 Kevin Durant 6.00 15.00
21 Manu Ginobili 3.00 8.00
22 Tyler Hansbrough 2.50 6.00
23 Tyson Chandler 2.50 6.00
24 Wilson Chandler 2.50 6.00
25 Blake Griffin 4.00 10.00
26 Zach Randolph 2.50 6.00
27 Al Jefferson 2.50 6.00
28 Amar'e Stoudemire 3.00 8.00
29 Andre Drummond 3.00 8.00
30 Andre Iguodala 2.50 6.00

2014-15 Hoops Blast from the Past Memorabilia
RANDOM INSERTS IN PACKS
*PRIME/17-25: .75X TO 2X BASIC
1 Andrea Bargnani 2.50 6.00
2 Andrew Bogut 2.50 6.00
3 Devin Harris 2.00 5.00
4 Dwight Howard 2.50 6.00
5 Elton Brand 3.00 8.00
6 Eric Bledsoe 2.50 6.00
7 Jermaine O'Neal 2.50 6.00
8 Joe Johnson 2.50 6.00
9 Kevin Martin 2.50 6.00
10 Luis Scola 2.50 6.00
11 Marcus Thornton 2.00 5.00
12 Mike Miller 2.50 6.00
13 Nene 2.50 6.00
14 Nick Young 2.50 6.00
15 Tayshaun Prince 2.50 6.00
16 Ray Allen 3.00 8.00
17 Tracy McGrady 3.00 8.00
18 Vince Carter 4.00 10.00
19 Aaron Brooks 2.00 5.00
20 Andray Blatche 2.00 5.00
21 Andre Miller 2.50 6.00
22 Beno Udrih 2.00 5.00
23 Boris Diaw 2.50 6.00
24 Brandon Jennings 2.00 5.00
25 Carl Landry 2.00 5.00
26 Carlos Boozer 2.50 6.00
27 Chris Bosh 3.00 8.00
28 Chris Kaman 2.50 6.00
29 Danilo Gallinari 2.00 5.00
30 Darren Collison 2.50 6.00
31 David West 2.50 6.00
32 Eric Gordon 2.50 6.00
33 Gerald Wallace 2.50 6.00
34 Greivis Vasquez 2.50 6.00
35 Hedo Turkoglu 2.50 6.00
36 J.J. Barea 2.50 6.00
37 Jason Richardson 3.00 8.00
38 JaVale McGee 2.50 6.00
39 Jose Calderon 2.00 5.00
40 Amar'e Stoudemire 3.00 8.00

2014-15 Hoops Champions
RANDOM INSERTS IN PACKS
1 San Antonio Spurs 12.00 30.00
2 San Antonio Spurs 12.00 30.00

2014-15 Hoops Champions Trophy Portraits
STATED PRINT RUN 99 SER.#'d SETS
1 Kawhi Leonard 8.00 20.00
2 Marco Belinelli 12.00 30.00
3 Splttr/Gnbl/Diaw/Mills 15.00 40.00
4 Danny Green 8.00 20.00
5 Tim Duncan 8.00 20.00
6 Tony Parker 8.00 20.00
7 Matt Bonner 12.00 30.00
8 Parker/Duncan/Manu 12.00 30.00

2014-15 Hoops Class Action
COMPLETE SET (15) 6.00 15.00
RANDOM INSERTS IN PACKS
*AP/99: 1.2X TO 3X BASE HI
1 Michael Carter-Williams .30 .75
2 Anthony Davis 1.00 2.50
3 Klay Thompson .60 1.50
4 John Wall .60 1.50
5 Kevin Love .50 1.25
6 Joakim Noah .40 1.00
7 Rajon Rondo .50 1.25
8 Deron Williams .40 1.00
9 Andre Iguodala .40 1.00
10 Carmelo Anthony .60 1.50
11 Yao Ming .60 1.50
12 Baron Davis .40 1.00
13 Vince Carter .60 1.50
14 Tracy McGrady .50 1.25
15 Allen Iverson .60 1.50

2014-15 Hoops Class Action Holo Green
*HOLO GREEN: 3X TO 8X BASE HI
RANDOM INSERTS IN PACKS
STATED PRINT RUN 25 SER.#'d SETS
15 Allen Iverson 15.00 40.00

2014-15 Hoops Courtside
COMPLETE SET (20) 8.00 20.00
RANDOM INSERTS IN PACKS
1 Manu Ginobili .50 1.25
2 Rajon Rondo .50 1.25
3 Dwyane Wade .75 2.00
4 Ricky Rubio .50 1.25
5 Tony Parker .50 1.25
6 Michael Carter-Williams .30 .75
7 John Wall .60 1.50
8 Blake Griffin .50 1.25
9 Kevin Durant 1.25 3.00
10 Chris Paul .60 1.50
11 Derrick Rose .60 1.50
12 Russell Westbrook 1.25 3.00
13 James Harden .75 2.00
14 Damian Lillard 1.00 2.50
15 Monta Ellis .40 1.00
16 Victor Oladipo .40 1.00
17 Kyrie Irving 1.00 2.50
18 DeMar DeRozan .50 1.25
19 Paul George .60 1.50
20 Stephen Curry 2.00 5.00

2014-15 Hoops Dreams
COMPLETE SET (10) 12.00 30.00
RANDOM INSERTS IN PACKS
1 Jabari Parker 1.25 3.00
2 Dante Exum .75 2.00
3 Andrew Wiggins 2.50 6.00
4 Marcus Smart .75 2.00
5 Aaron Gordon 1.25 3.00
6 Joel Embiid 2.50 6.00
7 Julius Randle 1.25 3.00
8 Doug McDermott .75 2.00
9 Shabazz Napier .60 1.50
10 Thanasis Antetokounmpo .60 1.50

2014-15 Hoops End 2 End
MPLETE SET (15) 8.00 20.00
RANDOM INSERTS IN PACKS
1 Dwight Howard .40 1.00
2 Kevin Garnett .75 2.00
3 Blake Griffin .50 1.25
4 Kyrie Irving 1.00 2.50
5 Damian Lillard 1.00 2.50
6 LeBron James 2.00 5.00
7 Kevin Durant 1.25 3.00
8 Anthony Davis 1.00 2.50
9 Dirk Nowitzki .60 1.50
10 Tim Duncan .75 2.00
11 Kevin Love .50 1.25
12 Kobe Bryant 2.00 5.00
13 Chris Bosh .50 1.25
14 Paul Pierce .50 1.25
15 Dwyane Wade .75 2.00

2014-15 Hoops Faces of the Future
MPLETE SET (20) 12.00 30.00
RANDOM INSERTS IN PACKS
1 Anthony Davis 1.25 3.00
2 Victor Oladipo .50 1.25
3 Kyrie Irving 1.25 3.00
4 Michael Carter-Williams .40 1.00
5 Damian Lillard 1.25 3.00
6 Nerlens Noel .50 1.25
7 Klay Thompson .75 2.00
8 Giannis Antetokounmpo 1.25 3.00
9 Kawhi Leonard 1.00 2.50
10 Trey Burke .40 1.00
11 Andrew Wiggins 2.00 5.00
12 Jabari Parker 1.00 2.50
13 Joel Embiid 2.00 5.00
14 Aaron Gordon 1.00 2.50
15 Dante Exum .60 1.50
16 Julius Randle 1.00 2.50
17 Shabazz Napier .50 1.25
18 Marcus Smart .60 1.50
19 Noah Vonleh .50 1.25
20 Doug McDermott .60 1.50

2014-15 Hoops Fast Lane
COMPLETE SET (20) 8.00 20.00
RANDOM INSERTS IN PACKS
1 John Wall .75 2.00
2 Jason Kidd .60 1.50
3 Kyrie Irving 1.25 3.00
4 Allen Iverson .75 2.00
5 Stephen Curry 2.50 6.00
6 Tony Parker .60 1.50
7 Kyle Lowry .50 1.25
8 Deron Williams .50 1.25
9 Damian Lillard 1.25 3.00
10 Kemba Walker .60 1.50
11 Derrick Rose .75 2.00
12 Magic Johnson 1.50 4.00
13 Isaiah Thomas .60 1.50
14 Isiah Thomas .60 1.50
15 Chris Paul .75 2.00
16 Ricky Rubio .60 1.50
17 Goran Dragic .50 1.25
18 Russell Westbrook 1.50 4.00
19 Mike Conley .50 1.25
20 John Stockton 1.00 2.50

2014-15 Hoops Finals MVP
STATED PRINT RUN 99 SER.#'d SETS
1 Kawhi Leonard 25.00 60.00

2014-15 Hoops Freshman Fabrics
RANDOM INSERTS IN PACKS
*PRIME/25: .75X TO 2X BASE HI
1 Bruno Caboclo 2.50 6.00
2 Nik Stauskas 2.50 6.00
3 Rodney Hood 3.00 8.00
4 Doug McDermott 8.00 20.00
5 Kyle Anderson 3.00 8.00
6 Andrew Wiggins 6.00 15.00
7 Adreian Payne 2.50 6.00
8 Joel Embiid 10.00 25.00
9 Tyler Ennis 2.00 5.00
10 Marcus Smart 3.00 8.00
11 Mitch McGary 2.00 5.00
12 Noah Vonleh 2.50 6.00
13 Shabazz Napier 2.50 6.00
14 Zach LaVine 5.00 12.00
15 Cleanthony Early 2.00 5.00
16 Jabari Parker 5.00 12.00
17 James Young 2.00 5.00
18 Aaron Gordon 5.00 12.00
19 Gary Harris 3.00 8.00
20 Julius Randle 5.00 12.00
21 Jordan Adams 3.00 8.00
22 Elfrid Payton 3.00 8.00
23 P.J. Hairston 2.00 5.00
24 T.J. Warren 3.00 8.00
25 Glenn Robinson III 2.00 5.00

2014-15 Hoops Freshman Fabrics Prime
*PRIME: .75X TO 2X BASE HI
RANDOM INSERTS IN PACKS
STATED PRINT RUN 25 SER.#'d SETS
16 Jabari Parker 40.00 100.00

2014-15 Hoops Great SIGnificance
RANDOM INSERTS IN PACKS
1 Otto Porter 5.00 12.00
2 Kentavious Caldwell-Pope 4.00 10.00
3 Cody Zeller 4.00 10.00
4 Alex Len 4.00 10.00
7 Nerlens Noel 5.00 12.00
10 C.J. McCollum 6.00 15.00
11 Anthony Bennett 4.00 10.00
13 Gal Mekel 4.00 10.00
15 Ray McCallum 4.00 10.00
16 Phil Pressey 4.00 10.00
22 Thaddeus Young 4.00 10.00
27 Ryan Anderson 4.00 10.00
29 Jason Thompson 4.00 10.00
34 Allan Houston 5.00 12.00
40 Vinny Del Negro 8.00 20.00
41 George Gervin 8.00 20.00
47 Walt Bellamy 5.00 12.00
48 Ralph Sampson 8.00 20.00
49 Victor Oladipo 5.00 12.00
50 Dominique Wilkins 8.00 20.00
53 Steven Adams 5.00 12.00
55 Luigi Datome 4.00 10.00
57 Brandan Wright 4.00 10.00
58 Ryan Kelly 4.00 10.00
60 Bobby Jones 12.00 30.00
62 Carl Landry 4.00 10.00
63 Erik Murphy 4.00 10.00
66 Greg Buckner 4.00 10.00
71 Andrew Wiggins 50.00 120.00
72 Jabari Parker 25.00 60.00
73 Joel Embiid 40.00 100.00
74 Aaron Gordon 10.00 25.00
75 Dante Exum 6.00 15.00
76 Marcus Smart 6.00 15.00
77 Julius Randle 10.00 25.00
78 Nik Stauskas 5.00 12.00
79 Noah Vonleh 5.00 12.00
80 Elfrid Payton 6.00 15.00
81 Doug McDermott 6.00 15.00
82 Zach LaVine 15.00 40.00
83 T.J. Warren 6.00 15.00
84 Adreian Payne 5.00 12.00
85 James Young 4.00 10.00
86 Tyler Ennis 4.00 10.00
87 Gary Harris 6.00 15.00
88 Mitch McGary 4.00 10.00
89 Jordan Adams 4.00 10.00
90 Rodney Hood 6.00 15.00
91 Shabazz Napier 5.00 12.00
92 P.J. Hairston 4.00 10.00
93 C.J. Wilcox 4.00 10.00
94 Kyle Anderson 6.00 15.00
95 Joe Harris 4.00 10.00
96 Cleanthony Early 4.00 10.00
97 Glenn Robinson III 4.00 10.00
98 Spencer Dinwiddie 5.00 12.00
99 Markel Brown 4.00 10.00
100 Russ Smith 4.00 10.00

2014-15 Hoops High Honors
MPLETE SET (25) 12.00 30.00
RANDOM INSERTS IN PACKS
1 James Harden 1.00 2.50
2 Magic Johnson 1.25 3.00
3 Kareem Abdul-Jabbar .75 2.00
4 Kevin Durant 1.25 3.00
5 Derrick Rose .60 1.50
6 Goran Dragic .40 1.00
7 Dwight Howard .40 1.00
8 LeBron James 2.00 5.00
9 Dennis Rodman 1.00 2.50
10 Steve Nash .50 1.25
11 Shaquille O'Neal 1.00 2.50
12 Larry Bird 1.25 3.00
13 Wilt Chamberlain 1.00 2.50
14 Michael Carter-Williams .30 .75
15 Vince Carter .60 1.50
16 Jamal Crawford .50 1.25
17 Dikembe Mutombo .50 1.25
18 Kobe Bryant 2.00 5.00
19 Bill Walton .50 1.25
20 Tim Duncan .75 2.00
21 Oscar Robertson .60 1.50
22 Kyrie Irving 1.00 2.50
23 Dirk Nowitzki .60 1.50
24 Joakim Noah .40 1.00
25 Allen Iverson .60 1.50

2014-15 Hoops Highlights
RANDOM INSERTS IN PACKS
1 Carmelo Anthony 6.00 15.00
2 Kevin Durant 5.00 12.00
3 Dirk Nowitzki 3.00 8.00

2014-15 Hoops Hot Signatures
RANDOM INSERTS IN PACKS
1 Otto Porter 3.00 8.00
2 Kentavious Caldwell-Pope 2.50 6.00
3 Cody Zeller 2.50 6.00
4 Alex Len 2.50 6.00
5 Shabazz Muhammad 3.00 8.00
6 Jason Terry 3.00 8.00
7 Nerlens Noel 3.00 8.00
8 Earl Monroe 4.00 10.00
9 Artis Gilmore 3.00 8.00
10 C.J. McCollum 6.00 15.00
11 Anthony Bennett 2.50 6.00
12 Peja Stojakovic 4.00 10.00
13 Michael Finley 4.00 10.00
14 Ben Gordon 3.00 8.00
15 Tayshaun Prince 3.00 8.00
16 Horace Grant 4.00 10.00
17 Dan Majerle 3.00 8.00
18 George Hill 3.00 8.00
19 Gal Mekel 2.50 6.00
20 Gorgui Dieng 2.50 6.00
21 Kevin Durant 50.00 120.00
22 Kurt Rambis 2.50 6.00
23 Brent Barry 2.50 6.00
24 Jason Thompson 2.50 6.00
25 Derrick Williams 2.50 6.00
26 Miroslav Raduljica 2.50 6.00
27 Brandon Knight 3.00 8.00
28 Carrick Felix 2.50 6.00
29 Pero Antic 2.50 6.00
30 Arnett Moultrie 2.50 6.00
31 Kyle O'Quinn 2.50 6.00
32 Ray McCallum 2.50 6.00
33 Nemanja Nedovic 2.50 6.00
34 Thabo Sefolosha 2.50 6.00
35 Phil Pressey 2.50 6.00
36 Danny Green 3.00 8.00
37 Mike Muscala 2.50 6.00
38 Terry Porter 2.50 6.00
39 Matthew Dellavedova 3.00 8.00
40 Ryan Kelly 2.50 6.00
41 Elvin Hayes 4.00 10.00
42 Bismack Biyombo 2.50 6.00
43 Allen Crabbe 2.50 6.00
44 Trey Burke 2.50 6.00
45 Allan Houston 3.00 8.00
46 Walt Frazier 6.00 15.00
47 Dwight Buycks 2.50 6.00
48 Danny Manning 3.00 8.00
49 Adrian Dantley 3.00 8.00
50 Caron Butler 3.00 8.00
51 Richard Jefferson 3.00 8.00
52 John Thompson 6.00 15.00
53 Bill Sharman 4.00 10.00
54 George McGinnis 2.50 6.00
55 Jon Leuer 2.50 6.00
56 Walt Bellamy 3.00 8.00
57 Steve Novak 2.50 6.00
58 Gerald Wallace 3.00 8.00
59 Ben McLemore 2.50 6.00
60 Michael Carter-Williams 2.50 6.00
61 Victor Oladipo 3.00 8.00
62 Kobe Bryant 75.00 150.00
64 Ryan Anderson 2.50 6.00
65 Dennis Schroder 3.00 8.00
66 Andrew Wiggins 50.00 120.00
67 Jabari Parker 25.00 60.00
68 Joel Embiid 40.00 100.00
69 Aaron Gordon 6.00 15.00
70 Dante Exum 4.00 10.00
71 Marcus Smart 4.00 10.00
72 Julius Randle 12.00 30.00
73 Nik Stauskas 3.00 8.00
74 Noah Vonleh 3.00 8.00
75 Elfrid Payton 4.00 10.00
76 Doug McDermott 4.00 10.00
77 Zach LaVine 6.00 15.00
78 T.J. Warren 4.00 10.00
79 Adreian Payne 3.00 8.00
80 James Young 2.50 6.00
81 Tyler Ennis 2.50 6.00
82 Gary Harris 4.00 10.00
83 Mitch McGary 2.50 6.00
84 Jordan Adams 2.50 6.00
85 Rodney Hood 4.00 10.00
86 Bruno Caboclo 3.00 8.00
87 Shabazz Napier 3.00 8.00
88 P.J. Hairston 2.50 6.00
89 C.J. Wilcox 2.50 6.00
90 Kyle Anderson 4.00 10.00
91 Joe Harris 2.50 6.00
92 Cleanthony Early 2.50 6.00
93 Jarnell Stokes 2.50 6.00
94 Spencer Dinwiddie 3.00 8.00
95 Glenn Robinson III 2.50 6.00
96 Markel Brown 2.50 6.00
97 Russ Smith 2.50 6.00
98 Xavier Thames 2.50 6.00
99 Cory Jefferson 2.50 6.00
100 Alec Brown 2.50 6.00

2014-15 Hoops Hot Signatures Red
*RED HOT: .6X TO 1.5X BASIC
RANDOM INSERTS IN PACKS
STATED PRINT RUN 25 SER.#'d SETS
62 Kobe Bryant 100.00 200.00

2014-15 Hoops Kobe's All Rookie Team
RANDOM INSERTS IN PACKS
1 Andrew Wiggins 15.00 40.00
2 Jabari Parker 8.00 20.00
3 Aaron Gordon 8.00 20.00
4 Dante Exum 5.00 12.00
5 Marcus Smart 5.00 12.00
6 Julius Randle 8.00 20.00
7 Nik Stauskas 4.00 10.00
8 Noah Vonleh 4.00 10.00
9 Elfrid Payton 5.00 12.00
10 Doug McDermott 5.00 12.00
11 Tyler Ennis 3.00 8.00
12 Shabazz Napier 4.00 10.00

2014-15 Hoops Lights Camera Action
COMPLETE SET (46) 20.00 50.00
RANDOM INSERTS IN PACKS
1 Chris Paul .60 1.50
2 Dirk Nowitzki .60 1.50
3 Joe Johnson .40 1.00
4 Klay Thompson .60 1.50
5 Michael Carter-Williams .30 .75
6 Stephen Curry 2.00 5.00
7 Vince Carter .60 1.50
8 LaMarcus Aldridge .50 1.25
9 Rajon Rondo .50 1.25
10 Kenneth Faried .40 1.00
11 Jeff Teague .40 1.00
12 Derrick Rose .60 1.50
13 Brandon Jennings .30 .75
14 Al Horford .40 1.00
15 DeAndre Jordan .50 1.25
16 Goran Dragic .40 1.00
17 Kevin Garnett .75 2.00
18 Paul George .60 1.50
19 Tony Parker .50 1.25
20 Anthony Davis 1.00 2.50
21 DeMar DeRozan .50 1.25
22 Dwight Howard .40 1.00
23 Bradley Beal .50 1.25
24 John Wall .60 1.50
25 Kyrie Irving 1.00 2.50
26 Manu Ginobili .50 1.25
27 Pau Gasol .50 1.25
28 Russell Westbrook 1.25 3.00
29 Victor Oladipo .40 1.00
30 Tim Duncan .75 2.00
31 Ricky Rubio .50 1.25
32 Paul Pierce .50 1.25
33 Monta Ellis .40 1.00
34 LeBron James 2.00 5.00
35 Kobe Bryant 2.00 5.00
36 Carmelo Anthony .60 1.50
36 Kevin Love .50 1.25
37 Blake Griffin .50 1.25
38 Chris Bosh .50 1.25
39 Damian Lillard 1.00 2.50
40 DeMarcus Cousins .50 1.25
41 Dwyane Wade .75 2.00
42 James Harden .75 2.00
43 Joakim Noah .40 1.00
44 Kemba Walker .50 1.25
45 Kevin Durant 1.25 3.00

2014-15 Hoops Matchups
RANDOM INSERTS IN PACKS
1 K.Bryant/L.James 2.00 5.00
2 D.Nowitzki/T.Duncan .75 2.00
3 D.Williams/C.Paul .60 1.50
4 B.Griffin/Z.Randolph .50 1.25
5 K.Bryant/T.McGrady 2.00 5.00
6 D.DeRozan/D.Williams .50 1.25
7 R.Westbrook/T.Parker 1.25 3.00
8 K.Durant/L.James 2.00 5.00
9 C.Anthony/D.Wade .75 2.00
10 R.Rubio/S.Nash .50 1.25
11 M.Carter-Williams/V.Oladipo .40 1.00
12 S.Curry/C.Paul 2.00 5.00
13 K.Bryant/K.Durant 2.00 5.00
14 K.Irving/S.Curry 2.00 5.00
15 A.Iverson/J.Kidd .60 1.50
16 S.O'Neal/H.Olajuwon 1.00 2.50
17 D.Wilkins/L.Bird 1.25 3.00
18 B.Russell/W.Chamberlain 1.00 2.50
19 L.Bird/M.Johnson 1.25 3.00
20 K.Malone/S.Pippen 1.00 2.50

2014-15 Hoops Matchups Holo Artist's Proof
*HOLO AP: 1.2X TO 3X BASE HI
RANDOM INSERTS IN PACKS
STATED PRINT RUN 99 SER.#'d SETS
1 K.Bryant/L.James 8.00 20.00
8 K.Durant/L.James 8.00 20.00

2014-15 Hoops Matchups Holo Green
*HOLO GREEN: 2.5X TO 6X BASE HI
RANDOM INSERTS IN PACKS
STATED PRINT RUN 25 SER.#'d SETS
15 A.Iverson/J.Kidd 12.00 30.00

2014-15 Hoops Moments of Greatness
COMPLETE SET (25) 12.00 30.00
RANDOM INSERTS IN PACKS
1 Al Jefferson .50 1.25
2 Elgin Baylor .60 1.50
3 Dwight Howard .50 1.25
4 Latrell Sprewell .50 1.25
5 LeBron James 2.50 6.00
6 DeAndre Jordan .60 1.50
7 Anthony Davis 1.25 3.00
8 Spud Webb .50 1.25
9 Terrence Ross .50 1.25
10 Andre Drummond .60 1.50
11 LaMarcus Aldridge .60 1.50
12 Magic Johnson 1.50 4.00
13 Rajon Rondo .60 1.50
14 Kendall Gill .40 1.00
15 Kevin Love .60 1.50
16 Victor Oladipo .50 1.25
17 Chris Paul .75 2.00
18 Kobe Bryant 2.50 6.00
19 Corey Brewer .40 1.00
20 Bill Russell 1.00 2.50
21 Timofey Mozgov .40 1.00
22 Damian Lillard 1.25 3.00
23 Michael Carter-Williams .40 1.00
24 Kevin Garnett 1.00 2.50
25 Kevin Durant 1.50 4.00

2014-15 Hoops Picture Perfect
COMPLETE SET (30) 8.00 20.00
RANDOM INSERTS IN PACKS
1 Stephen Curry 2.00 5.00
2 Kevin Garnett .75 2.00
3 Dwight Howard .40 1.00
4 Russell Westbrook 1.25 3.00
5 Blake Griffin .50 1.25
6 James Harden
7 Kevin Durant 1.25 3.00
8 Kobe Bryant 2.00 5.00
9 Manu Ginobili .50 1.25
10 Dirk Nowitzki .60 1.50
11 Tony Parker .50 1.25
12 Rajon Rondo .50 1.25
13 Damian Lillard 1.00 2.50
14 Anthony Davis 1.00 2.50
15 LaMarcus Aldridge .50 1.25
16 John Wall .60 1.50
17 Tim Duncan .75 2.00
18 Joakim Noah .40 1.00
19 Dwyane Wade .75 2.00
20 Kevin Love .50 1.25
21 Chris Bosh .50 1.25
22 Pau Gasol .50 1.25
23 LeBron James 2.00 5.00
24 Kyrie Irving 1.00 2.50
25 Carmelo Anthony .60 1.50
26 Paul George .60 1.50
27 Chris Paul .60 1.50
28 Michael Carter-Williams .30 .75
29 Vince Carter .60 1.50
30 Derrick Rose .60 1.50

2014-15 Hoops Picture Perfect Holo Artist's Proof
*HOLO AP: 1.2X TO 3X BASE HI
RANDOM INSERTS IN PACKS
STATED PRINT RUN 99 SER.#'d SETS
23 LeBron James 8.00 20.00

2014-15 Hoops Picture Perfect Holo Green
*HOLO GREEN: 3X TO 8X BASE HI
RANDOM INSERTS IN PACKS
STATED PRINT RUN 25 SER.#'d SETS
23 LeBron James 20.00 50.00

2014-15 Hoops Rise and Shine Memorabilia
RANDOM INSERTS IN PACKS
*PRIME/25: .75X TO 2X BASE HI
1 Andrew Wiggins 10.00 25.00
2 Jabari Parker 5.00 12.00
3 Joel Embiid 10.00 25.00
4 Aaron Gordon 5.00 12.00
6 Marcus Smart 3.00 8.00
7 Julius Randle 5.00 12.00
8 Nik Stauskas 2.50 6.00
9 Noah Vonleh 2.50 6.00
10 Elfrid Payton 3.00 8.00
11 Doug McDermott 3.00 8.00
12 Zach LaVine 5.00 12.00
13 T.J. Warren 3.00 8.00
14 Adreian Payne 2.50 6.00
15 James Young 2.00 5.00
16 Tyler Ennis 2.00 5.00
17 Gary Harris 3.00 8.00
18 Mitch McGary 2.00 5.00
19 Jordan Adams 2.00 5.00
20 Rodney Hood 3.00 8.00
21 Shabazz Napier 2.50 6.00
22 Russ Smith 2.00 5.00
23 P.J. Hairston 2.00 5.00
24 C.J. Wilcox 2.00 5.00
25 Bruno Caboclo 2.50 6.00
26 Kyle Anderson 3.00 8.00
27 K.J. McDaniels 2.50 6.00
28 Cleanthony Early 2.00 5.00
29 Glenn Robinson III 2.00 5.00
30 Jarnell Stokes 2.00 5.00

2014-15 Hoops Road to the Finals
1-50 PRINT RUN 2014 SER.#'d SETS
51-72 PRINT RUN 999 SER.#'d SETS
73-84 PRINT RUN 299 SER.#'d SETS
1 Joe Johnson R1 .60 1.50
2 DeMar DeRozan R1 .75 2.00
3 Joe Johnson R1 .60 1.50
4 Kyle Lowry R1 .60 1.50
5 Kyle Lowry R1 .60 1.50
6 Deron Williams R1 .60 1.50
7 Paul Pierce R1 .75 2.00
8 Jeff Teague R1 .60 1.50
9 Paul George R1 1.00 2.50
10 Kyle Korver R1 .60 1.50
11 Paul George R1 1.00 2.50
12 Mike Scott R1 .50 1.25
13 David West R1 .60 1.50
14 Paul George R1 1.00 2.50
15 Dwyane Wade R1 1.25 3.00
16 LeBron James R1 3.00 8.00
17 LeBron James R1 3.00 8.00
18 LeBron James R1 3.00 8.00
19 Nene R1 .60 1.50
20 Bradley Beal R1 .75 2.00
21 Mike Dunleavy R1 .50 1.25
22 Trevor Ariza R1 .50 1.25
23 John Wall R1 1.00 2.50
24 Klay Thompson R1 1.00 2.50
25 Blake Griffin R1 .75 2.00
26 DeAndre Jordan R1 .75 2.00
27 Stephen Curry R1 3.00 8.00
28 DeAndre Jordan R1 .75 2.00
29 Stephen Curry R1 3.00 8.00
30 Chris Paul R1 1.00 2.50
31 Kevin Durant R1 2.00 5.00
32 Zach Randolph R1 .60 1.50
33 Mike Conley R1 .60 1.50
34 Reggie Jackson R1 .50 1.25
35 Mike Miller R1 .50 1.25
36 Kevin Durant R1 2.00 5.00
37 Russell Westbrook R1 2.00 5.00
38 Tim Duncan R1 1.25 3.00
39 Shawn Marion R1 .60 1.50
40 Vince Carter R1 1.00 2.50
41 Boris Diaw R1 .60 1.50
42 Tony Parker R1 .75 2.00
43 Monta Ellis R1 .60 1.50
44 Tony Parker R1 .75 2.00
45 LaMarcus Aldridge R1 .75 2.00
46 LaMarcus Aldridge R1 .75 2.00
47 Troy Daniels R1 .50 1.25
48 LaMarcus Aldridge R1 .75 2.00
49 Dwight Howard R1 .60 1.50
50 Damian Lillard R1 1.50 4.00
51 Ray Allen R2 .60 1.50
52 LeBron James R2 4.00 10.00
53 Joe Johnson R2 .60 1.50
54 LeBron James R2 4.00 10.00
55 Ray Allen R2 1.00 2.50
56 Tony Parker R2 1.00 2.50
57 Kawhi Leonard R2 1.50 4.00
58 Tony Parker R2 1.00 2.50
59 Nicolas Batum R2 .75 2.00
60 Patty Mills R2 1.00 2.50
61 Trevor Ariza R2 .60 1.50
62 Roy Hibbert R2 .75 2.00
63 David West R2 .75 2.00
64 Paul George R2 1.25 3.00
65 Marcin Gortat R2 .75 2.00
66 David West R2 .75 2.00
67 Chris Paul R2 1.25 3.00
68 Kevin Durant R2 2.50 6.00
69 Russell Westbrook R2 2.50 6.00
70 Darren Collison R2 .75 2.00
71 Russell Westbrook R2 2.50 6.00
72 Kevin Durant R2 2.50 6.00
73 Paul George CF 1.50 4.00
74 Dwyane Wade CF 2.00 5.00
75 Ray Allen CF 1.50 4.00
76 LeBron James CF 5.00 12.00
77 Paul George CF 1.50 4.00
78 Chris Bosh CF 1.25 3.00
79 Manu Ginobili CF 1.25 3.00
80 Danny Green CF 1.00 2.50
81 Serge Ibaka CF 1.00 2.50
82 Russell Westbrook CF 3.00 8.00
83 Tim Duncan CF 6.00 15.00
84 Kawhi Leonard CF 2.00 5.00

2014-15 Hoops Road to the Finals NBA Championship
RANDOM INSERTS IN PACKS
STATED PRINT RUN 199 SER.#'d SETS
1 Tim Duncan 10.00 25.00
2 LeBron James 8.00 20.00
3 Kawhi Leonard 12.00 30.00
4 Kawhi Leonard 12.00 30.00
5 Manu Ginobili 2.00 5.00

2014-15 Hoops Rookie Remembrance Memorabilia
RANDOM INSERTS IN PACKS
*PRIME/25: .75X TO 2X BASE HI
1 Harrison Barnes 2.50 6.00
2 Anthony Davis 6.00 15.00
3 Klay Thompson 4.00 10.00
4 Jonas Valanciunas 2.50 6.00
5 Kyrie Irving 6.00 15.00
6 Dion Waiters 2.50 6.00
7 Tristan Thompson 2.50 6.00
8 Markieff Morris 2.00 5.00
9 Kawhi Leonard 5.00 12.00
10 Reggie Jackson 2.00 5.00
11 Nikola Vucevic 2.50 6.00
12 Enes Kanter 2.00 5.00
13 Kemba Walker 3.00 8.00
14 Jared Sullinger 2.00 5.00
15 Michael Kidd-Gilchrist 2.50 6.00
16 Isaiah Thomas 3.00 8.00
17 Kenneth Faried 2.50 6.00
18 Andre Drummond 3.00 8.00
19 Bradley Beal 3.00 8.00
20 Ben McLemore 2.00 5.00
21 Kelly Olynyk 2.00 5.00
22 Giannis Antetokounmpo 6.00 15.00
23 Michael Carter-Williams 2.00 5.00
24 Trey Burke 2.00 5.00
25 Victor Oladipo 2.50 6.00

2014-15 Hoops Shining Stars
COMPLETE SET (20) 8.00 20.00
RANDOM INSERTS IN PACKS
1 Kevin Durant 1.25 3.00
2 Rajon Rondo .50 1.25
3 Russell Westbrook 1.25 3.00
4 Paul George .60 1.50
5 Dwyane Wade .75 2.00
6 Derrick Rose .60 1.50
7 LeBron James 2.00 5.00
8 Anthony Davis 1.00 2.50
9 Dirk Nowitzki .60 1.50
10 Stephen Curry 2.00 5.00
11 Blake Griffin .50 1.25
12 Kyrie Irving 1.00 2.50
13 Chris Paul .60 1.50
14 Kevin Love .50 1.25
15 Tim Duncan .75 2.00
16 Damian Lillard 1.00 2.50
17 Tony Parker .50 1.25
18 James Harden .75 2.00
19 Kobe Bryant 2.00 5.00
20 Dwight Howard .40 1.00

2014-15 Hoops Shining Stars Holo Artist's Proof
*HOLO AP: 1.2X TO 3X BASE HI
RANDOM INSERTS IN PACKS
STATED PRINT RUN 99 SER.#'d SETS
7 LeBron James 8.00 20.00

2014-15 Hoops Shining Stars Holo Green
*HOLO GREEN: 3X TO 8X BASE HI
RANDOM INSERTS IN PACKS
STATED PRINT RUN 25 SER.#'d SETS
7 LeBron James 20.00 50.00

2014-15 Hoops Trading Places
COMPLETE SET (20) 6.00 15.00
RANDOM INSERTS IN PACKS
1 D.Rodman/W.Perdue 1.00 2.50
2 J.Mashburn/E.Jones .50 1.25
3 A.Iverson/A.Miller .60 1.50
4 J.Starks/L.Sprewell .40 1.00
5 G.Payton/R.Allen .50 1.25
6 C.Paul/E.Gordon .60 1.50
7 A.Dantley/M.Aguirre .40 1.00
8 K.Bryant/V.Divac 2.00 5.00
9 J.Redick/E.Bledsoe .50 1.25
10 N.Noel/J.Holiday .40 1.00
11 T.McGrady/S.Francis .50 1.25
12 R.Horry/C.Ceballos .40 1.00
13 P.Gasol/M.Gasol .50 1.25
14 G.Green/L.Scola .40 1.00
15 J.Kidd/M.Finley .50 1.25
16 S.Marion/S.O'Neal 1.00 2.50
17 A.Jamison/V.Carter .60 1.50
18 A.Mourning/G.Rice .60 1.50
19 R.Gay/G.Vasquez .50 1.25
20 B.Jennings/B.Knight .40 1.00

2015-16 Hoops
COMPLETE SET (300) 25.00 60.00
1 Ersan Ilyasova .20 .50
2 Josh Smith .25 .60
3 James Harden .50 1.25
4 Langston Galloway .20 .50
5 Aaron Brooks .20 .50
6 Mike Dunleavy .20 .50
7 Bradley Beal .30 .75
8 Quincy Pondexter .20 .50
9 Dante Exum .25 .60
10 Taj Gibson .25 .60
11 Evan Fournier .25 .60
12 Jrue Holiday .20 .50
13 Jared Dudley .20 .50
14 LeBron James 1.25 3.00
15 Aaron Gordon .25 .60
16 Mike Muscala .20 .50
17 Brandon Bass .20 .50
18 Rajon Rondo .30 .75
19 Darren Collison .20 .50
20 Terrence Jones .25 .60
21 Evan Turner .20 .50
22 Julius Randle .30 .75
23 Jared Sullinger .20 .50
24 Lou Williams .25 .60
25 Al-Farouq Aminu .20 .50
26 Tim Hardaway Jr. .20 .50
27 Brandon Jennings .20 .50
28 Randy Foye .20 .50
29 Shane Larkin .20 .50
30 Terrence Ross .20 .50
31 Gary Harris .20 .50
32 Jusuf Nurkic .20 .50
33 Jarrett Jack .25 .60
34 Isaiah Canaan .25 .60
35 Al Horford .25 .60
36 Mirza Teletovic .20 .50
37 Brandon Knight .25 .60
38 Archie Goodwin .20 .50
39 David West .25 .60
40 Thabo Sefolosha .20 .50
41 George Hill .25 .60
42 Kawhi Leonard .50 1.25
43 Jason Smith .20 .50
44 Luis Scola .25 .60
45 Al Jefferson .25 .60
46 Monta Ellis .25 .60
47 Brian Roberts .20 .50
48 Raymond Felton .25 .60
49 DeAndre Jordan .30 .75
50 Thaddeus Young .20 .50
51 Gerald Green .25 .60
52 Kemba Walker .30 .75
53 Jason Terry .25 .60
54 Luol Deng .20 .50
55 Alan Anderson .20 .50
56 Nene .20 .50
57 Brook Lopez .25 .60
58 Reggie Jackson .25 .60
59 DeMar DeRozan .30 .75
60 Tim Duncan .50 1.25
61 Gerald Henderson .20 .50
62 Kenneth Faried .25 .60
63 Jeff Green .25 .60
64 Manu Ginobili .30 .75
65 Alec Burks .20 .50
66 Nerlens Noel .25 .60
67 C.J. McCollum .30 .75
68 Ricky Rubio .25 .60
69 DeMarcus Cousins .30 .75
70 Timofey Mozgov .20 .50
71 Giannis Antetokounmpo .60 1.50
72 Kent Bazemore .25 .60
73 Jeff Teague .20 .50
74 Marc Gasol .25 .60
75 Alex Len .20 .50
76 Nick Collison .20 .50
77 Quincy Acy .20 .50
78 Robert Covington .20 .50
79 DeMarre Carroll .20 .50
80 T.J. Warren .25 .60
81 Goran Dragic .25 .60
82 Kentavious Caldwell-Pope .25 .60
83 Jerami Grant .20 .50
84 Marcin Gortat .20 .50
85 Alexis Ajinca .20 .50
86 Nick Young .20 .50
87 Cleanthony Early .20 .50
88 Robin Lopez .20 .50
89 Dennis Schroder .25 .60
90 Tobias Harris .25 .60
91 Gordon Hayward .30 .75
92 Kevin Durant .75 2.00
93 Jeremy Evans .20 .50
94 Marco Belinelli .20 .50
95 Amir Johnson .20 .50
96 Nicolas Batum .25 .60
97 Carmelo Anthony .40 1.00
98 Rodney Hood .25 .60
99 Deron Williams .25 .60
100 Tony Allen .25 .60
101 Gorgui Dieng .20 .50
102 Kevin Garnett .50 1.25
103 Jeremy Lamb .20 .50
104 Marcus Morris .20 .50
105 Anderson Varejao .20 .50
106 Nikola Mirotic .25 .60
107 Chandler Parsons .25 .60
108 Rodney Stuckey .20 .50
109 Derrick Favors .20 .50
110 Tony Parker .30 .75
111 Greg Monroe .25 .60
112 Kevin Love .25 .60
113 Jimmy Butler .30 .75
114 Marcus Smart .30 .75
115 Andre Drummond .30 .75
116 Nikola Vucevic .25 .60
117 Channing Frye .25 .60
118 Roy Hibbert .25 .60
119 Derrick Rose .40 1.00
120 Tony Wroten .20 .50
121 Greivis Vasquez .20 .50
122 Kevin Martin .20 .50
123 J.J. Hickson .20 .50
124 Mario Chalmers .20 .50
125 Andre Iguodala .25 .60
126 Noah Vonleh .20 .50
127 Chase Budinger .20 .50
128 Rudy Gay .25 .60
129 Derrick Williams .20 .50
130 Trevor Ariza .20 .50
131 Harrison Barnes .25 .60
132 Kevin Seraphin .20 .50
133 J.J. Redick .30 .75
134 Markieff Morris .20 .50
135 Andre Roberson .20 .50
136 Norris Cole .20 .50
137 Chris Andersen .20 .50
138 Rudy Gobert .30 .75
139 Devin Harris .20 .50
140 Trevor Booker .20 .50
141 Hassan Whiteside .30 .75
142 Khris Middleton .25 .60
143 Joakim Noah .25 .60
144 Marreese Speights .20 .50
145 Andrew Bogut .25 .60
146 O.J. Mayo .20 .50
147 Chris Bosh .30 .75
148 Russell Westbrook .75 2.00
149 Dion Waiters .20 .50
150 Trey Burke .20 .50
151 Sergey Karasev .20 .50
152 Kirk Hinrich .20 .50
153 Jodie Meeks .20 .50
154 Martell Webster .20 .50
155 Andrew Wiggins .50 1.25
156 Omer Asik .20 .50
157 Chris Kaman .20 .50
158 Ryan Anderson .20 .50
159 Dirk Nowitzki .40 1.00
160 Tristan Thompson .25 .60
161 Henry Sims .20 .50
162 Klay Thompson .40 1.00
163 Joe Ingles .20 .50
164 Marvin Williams .20 .50
165 Anthony Davis .60 1.50
166 Omri Casspi .20 .50
167 Chris Paul .40 1.00
168 Serge Ibaka .25 .60
169 Donald Sloan .20 .50
170 Ty Lawson .20 .50
171 Hollis Thompson .20 .50
172 Kobe Bryant 1.25 3.00
173 Joe Johnson .25 .60
174 Mason Plumlee .25 .60
175 Thomas Robinson .20 .50
176 Otto Porter .25 .60
177 C.J. Miles .20 .50
178 Shabazz Muhammad .25 .60
179 Draymond Green .40 1.00
180 Tyler Zeller .20 .50
181 Ian Mahinmi .20 .50
182 Kosta Koufos .20 .50
183 JaKarr Sampson .20 .50
184 Matt Barnes .20 .50
185 Arron Afflalo .20 .50
186 Patrick Beverley .20 .50
187 Cody Zeller .20 .50
188 Shabazz Napier .20 .50
189 Dwight Howard .25 .60
190 Tyreke Evans .20 .50
191 Iman Shumpert .20 .50
192 Josh McRoberts .20 .50
193 John Henson .20 .50
194 Matt Bonner .20 .50
195 Austin Rivers .20 .50
196 Patrick Patterson .20 .50
197 Corey Brewer .20 .50
198 Shaun Livingston .20 .50
199 Dwight Powell .20 .50
200 Tyson Chandler .25 .60
201 Isaiah Thomas .30 .75
202 Kyle Korver .25 .60
203 John Wall .40 1.00
204 Matthew Dellavedova .25 .60
205 Avery Bradley .25 .60
206 Patty Mills .30 .75
207 Cory Joseph .20 .50
208 Shelvin Mack .20 .50
209 Dwyane Wade .50 1.25
210 Victor Oladipo .25 .60
211 J.J. Barea .25 .60
212 Kyle Lowry .25 .60
213 Jonas Valanciunas .25 .60
214 Will Barton .20 .50
215 Ben McLemore .20 .50
216 Pau Gasol .20 .50
217 Courtney Lee .25 .60
218 Solomon Hill .20 .50
219 Ed Davis .20 .50
220 Vince Carter .40 1.00
221 J.R. Smith .20 .50
222 Kyrie Irving .60 1.50
223 Jordan Clarkson .20 .50
224 Meyers Leonard .20 .50
225 Bismack Biyombo .20 .50
226 Paul George .40 1.00
227 Damian Lillard .60 1.50
228 Spencer Dinwiddie .20 .50
229 Elfrid Payton .20 .50
230 Wesley Matthews .20 .50
231 Jabari Parker .40 1.00
232 LaMarcus Aldridge .25 .60
233 Wesley Johnson .30 .75
234 Michael Carter-Williams .25 .60
235 Blake Griffin .30 .75
236 Paul Millsap .20 .50
237 Danilo Gallinari .25 .60
238 Spencer Hawes .25 .60
239 Enes Kanter .25 .60
240 Wilson Chandler .25 .60
241 Jamal Crawford .30 .75
242 Lance Stephenson .25 .60
243 Jose Calderon .20 .50
244 Michael Kidd-Gilchrist .25 .60
245 Bojan Bogdanovic .20 .50
246 Paul Pierce .30 .75
247 Danny Green .25 .60
248 Stephen Curry 1.25 3.00
249 Eric Bledsoe .25 .60
250 Zach LaVine .30 .75
251 Jameer Nelson .20 .50
252 Lance Thomas .20 .50
253 Leandro Barbosa .25 .60
254 Mike Conley .25 .60
255 Boris Diaw .20 .50
256 P.J. Tucker .30 .75
257 Dante Cunningham .20 .50
258 Steven Adams .25 .60
259 Eric Gordon .25 .60
260 Zach Randolph .25 .60
261 Kristaps Porzingis RC 1.50 4.00
262 Walter Tavares RC .50 1.25
263 Trey Lyles RC .60 1.50
264 Pierre Jackson RC .40 1.00
265 D'Angelo Russell RC 1.50 4.00
266 Jarell Martin RC .50 1.25
267 Stanley Johnson RC .50 1.25
268 Devin Booker RC 2.00 5.00
269 Rashad Vaughn RC .40 1.00
270 Kevon Looney RC .50 1.25
271 R.J. Hunter RC .60 1.50
272 Myles Turner RC .60 1.50
273 Pat Connaughton RC .40 1.00
274 Terry Rozier RC .60 1.50
275 Bobby Portis RC .60 1.50
276 Willie Cauley-Stein RC .60 1.50
277 Jordan Mickey RC .40 1.00
278 Montrezl Harrell RC .50 1.25
279 Andrew Harrison RC .40 1.00
280 Jahlil Okafor RC .75 2.00
281 Frank Kaminsky RC .60 1.50
282 Dakari Johnson RC .40 1.00
283 Kelly Oubre Jr. RC .60 1.50
284 Nemanja Bjelica RC .50 1.25
285 Mario Hezonja RC .60 1.50
286 Chris McCullough RC .40 1.00
287 Jerian Grant RC .50 1.25
288 Cameron Payne RC .60 1.50
289 Karl-Anthony Towns RC 3.00 8.00
290 Justin Anderson RC .60 1.50
291 Larry Nance Jr. RC .60 1.50
292 Delon Wright RC .60 1.50
293 Tyus Jones RC .60 1.50
294 Emmanuel Mudiay RC .75 2.00
295 Anthony Brown RC .40 1.00
296 Sam Dekker RC .60 1.50
297 Darrun Hilliard RC .40 1.00
298 Rakeem Christmas RC .50 1.25
299 Rondae Hollis-Jefferson RC .50 1.25
300 Justise Winslow RC .60 1.50

2015-16 Hoops Artist Proof
*AP: 2X TO 5X BASIC
*AP RC: 2X TO 5X BASIC
RANDOM INSERTS IN PACKS
STATED PRINT RUN 99 SER.#'d SETS
265 D'Angelo Russell 25.00 60.00
289 Karl-Anthony Towns 30.00 80.00

2015-16 Hoops Gold
*GOLD: .75X TO 2X BASIC
*GOLD RC: .75X TO 2X BASIC
RANDOM INSERTS IN PACKS

2015-16 Hoops Green
*GREEN: 1X TO 2.5X BASIC
*GREEN RC: 1X TO 2.5X BASIC
RANDOM INSERTS IN PACKS
289 Karl-Anthony Towns 10.00 25.00

2015-16 Hoops Red
*RED: 1.5X TO 4X BASIC
*RED RC: 1.5X TO 4X BASIC
RANDOM INSERTS IN PACKS
STATED PRINT RUN 299 SER.#'d SETS

2015-16 Hoops Red Backs
*RED BACK: .6X TO 1.5X BASIC
*RED BACK RC: .6X TO 1.5X BASIC
RANDOM INSERTS IN PACKS

2015-16 Hoops Silver
*SILVER: 1.5X TO 4X BASIC
*SILVER RC: 1.5X TO 4X BASIC
RANDOM INSERTS IN PACKS
STATED PRINT RUN 299 SER.#'d SETS

2015-16 Hoops Action Shots
RANDOM INSERTS IN PACKS
1 Andrew Wiggins 1.00 2.50
2 James Harden 1.00 2.50
3 Chris Paul .75 2.00
4 Damian Lillard 1.25 3.00
5 Blake Griffin .60 1.50
6 Stephen Curry 2.50 6.00
7 Russell Westbrook 1.50 4.00
8 Carmelo Anthony .75 2.00
9 Kobe Bryant 2.50 6.00
10 Derrick Rose .75 2.00
11 Kevin Durant 1.50 4.00
12 LeBron James 2.50 6.00
13 Anthony Davis 1.25 3.00
14 Kyrie Irving 1.25 3.00
15 Tony Parker .60 1.50
16 John Wall .75 2.00
17 Klay Thompson .75 2.00

2015-16 Hoops Birds Eye View
RANDOM INSERTS IN PACKS
*AP/99: .6X TO 1.5X BASIC
1 John Wall .75 2.00
2 Carmelo Anthony .75 2.00
3 DeMarcus Cousins .60 1.50
4 Derrick Rose .75 2.00
5 Jimmy Butler .60 1.50
6 James Harden 1.00 2.50
7 Bradley Beal .60 1.50
8 LeBron James 2.50 6.00
9 Dirk Nowitzki .75 2.00
10 Chris Paul .75 2.00
11 Kyrie Irving 1.25 3.00
12 Stephen Curry 2.50 6.00
13 DeMar DeRozan .60 1.50
14 Russell Westbrook 1.50 4.00
15 Klay Thompson .75 2.00
16 Kobe Bryant 2.50 6.00
17 Andrew Wiggins 1.00 2.50
18 Kevin Durant 1.50 4.00
19 Damian Lillard 1.25 3.00
20 Anthony Davis 1.25 3.00
21 Dwyane Wade 1.00 2.50
22 Blake Griffin .60 1.50
23 Kawhi Leonard 1.00 2.50
24 Tony Parker .60 1.50
25 DeAndre Jordan .60 1.50

2015-16 Hoops Birds Eye View Holo Green
*HOLO GREEN: .75X TO 2X BASIC
RANDOM INSERTS IN PACKS
STATED PRINT RUN 25 SER.#'d SETS
8 LeBron James 12.00 30.00
16 Kobe Bryant 12.00 30.00

2015-16 Hoops Champions
RANDOM INSERTS IN PACKS
83 Golden State Warriors 6.00 15.00
84 Golden State Warriors 6.00 15.00

2015-16 Hoops Champions Trophy Portraits
RANDOM INSERTS IN PACKS
STATED PRINT RUN 99 SER.#'d SETS
85 Stephen Curry 20.00 50.00
86 Klay Thompson 20.00 50.00
87 Andre Iguodala 8.00 20.00
88 Draymond Green 12.00 30.00
89 Harrison Barnes 8.00 20.00
90 Shaun Livingston 6.00 15.00
91 Leandro Barbosa 6.00 15.00
92 David Lee 6.00 15.00
93 Andrew Bogut 8.00 20.00
94 Steve Kerr 10.00 25.00
95 Thompson/Curry 20.00 50.00
96 Iguodala/Green 20.00 50.00
97 Dell Curry 30.00 80.00
Stephen Curry
98 Marreese Speights 6.00 15.00
99 Iguodala/Russell 15.00 40.00
100 Stephen Curry 20.00 50.00

2015-16 Hoops Courtside
RANDOM INSERTS IN PACKS
1 Kevin Durant 1.50 4.00
2 LeBron James 2.50 6.00
3 Anthony Davis 1.25 3.00
4 Kyrie Irving 1.25 3.00
5 Kawhi Leonard 1.00 2.50
6 John Wall .75 2.00
7 Russell Westbrook 1.50 4.00
8 Derrick Rose .75 2.00
9 Kobe Bryant 2.50 6.00
10 James Harden 1.00 2.50
11 Damian Lillard 1.25 3.00
12 Chris Paul .75 2.00
13 Blake Griffin .60 1.50
14 Stephen Curry 2.50 6.00
15 Tony Parker .60 1.50
16 Carmelo Anthony .75 2.00
17 Klay Thompson .75 2.00
18 Jimmy Butler .60 1.50
19 Andrew Wiggins 1.00 2.50
20 Bradley Beal .60 1.50

2015-16 Hoops Courtside Holo Green
*HOLO GREEN: .75X TO 2X BASIC
RANDOM INSERTS IN PACKS
STATED PRINT RUN 25 SER.#'d SETS
2 LeBron James 12.00 30.00
9 Kobe Bryant 12.00 30.00

2015-16 Hoops Double Trouble
RANDOM INSERTS IN PACKS
1 B.Beal/J.Wall .75 2.00
2 L.James/K.Irving 2.50 6.00
3 K.Durant/R.Westbrook 1.50 4.00
4 T.Duncan/T.Parker 1.00 2.50
5 P.Gasol/D.Rose .75 2.00
6 K.Thompson/S.Curry 2.50 6.00
7 B.Griffin/C.Paul .75 2.00
8 C.Bosh/D.Wade 1.00 2.50
9 J.Harden/D.Howard 1.00 2.50
10 A.Wiggins/Z.LaVine 1.00 2.50

2015-16 Hoops Dreams
RANDOM INSERTS IN PACKS
1 D'Angelo Russell 2.00 5.00
2 Emmanuel Mudiay .75 2.00
3 Mario Hezonja .60 1.50
4 Willie Cauley-Stein .75 2.00
5 Frank Kaminsky .75 2.00
6 Karl-Anthony Towns 4.00 10.00
7 Jahlil Okafor 1.00 2.50
8 Kristaps Porzingis 2.00 5.00
9 Justise Winslow .75 2.00
10 Jerian Grant .50 1.25

2015-16 Hoops Dreams Holo Artist Proof
*AP: 1.2X TO 3X BASIC
RANDOM INSERTS IN PACKS
STATED PRINT RUN 99 SER.#'d SETS
6 Karl-Anthony Towns 20.00 50.00
7 Jahlil Okafor 8.00 20.00

2015-16 Hoops Dreams Holo Green
*HOLO GREEN: 5X TO 12X BASIC
RANDOM INSERTS IN PACKS
STATED PRINT RUN 25 SER.#'d SETS

2015-16 Hoops End 2 End
RANDOM INSERTS IN PACKS
1 Kyrie Irving 1.25 3.00
2 Stephen Curry 2.50 6.00
3 Russell Westbrook 1.50 4.00
4 Klay Thompson .75 2.00
5 Kobe Bryant 2.50 6.00
6 Bradley Beal .60 1.50
7 Kevin Durant 1.50 4.00
8 Damian Lillard 1.25 3.00
9 LeBron James 2.50 6.00
10 Chris Paul .75 2.00
11 John Wall .75 2.00
12 Tony Parker .60 1.50
13 Derrick Rose .75 2.00
14 Andrew Wiggins 1.00 2.50
15 James Harden 1.00 2.50

2015-16 Hoops Faces of the Future
RANDOM INSERTS IN PACKS
1 Mario Hezonja .50 1.25
2 Willie Cauley-Stein .60 1.50
3 Frank Kaminsky .60 1.50
4 Myles Turner .60 1.50
5 Karl-Anthony Towns 3.00 8.00
6 Cameron Payne .50 1.25
7 D'Angelo Russell 1.50 4.00
8 Sam Dekker .50 1.25
9 Emmanuel Mudiay .60 1.50
10 Rondae Hollis-Jefferson .50 1.25
11 Devin Booker 2.00 5.00
12 Justise Winslow .60 1.50
13 Trey Lyles .60 1.50
14 Delon Wright .50 1.25
15 Jahlil Okafor .75 2.00
16 Tyus Jones .60 1.50
17 Kristaps Porzingis 1.50 4.00
18 Kelly Oubre Jr. .50 1.25
19 Jerian Grant .40 1.00
20 Justin Anderson .50 1.25

2015-16 Hoops Finals MVP
RANDOM INSERTS IN PACKS
STATED PRINT RUN 99 SER.#'d SETS
82 Andre Iguodala 8.00 20.00

2015-16 Hoops Ginormous Signatures
TWO AUTOS PER HOBBY BOX
EXCHANGE DEADLINE 4/14/2017
1 Christian Laettner
2 David Robinson 15.00 40.00
3 Dominique Wilkins
4 Kemba Walker
5 Gary Payton
6 Hakeem Olajuwon
7 Isiah Thomas
8 Joe Dumars
9 Thomas Robinson 6.00 15.00
10 Julius Erving
11 Kenny Anderson
12 Kyrie Irving
13 Larry Bird
14 Markieff Morris 6.00 15.00
15 Vinny Del Negro

2015-16 Hoops Great SIGnificance
RANDOM INSERTS IN PACKS
EXCHANGE DEADLINE 4/14/2017
1 Julius Randle 8.00 20.00
2 Jerami Grant 2.50 6.00
3 Michael Carter-Williams 2.50 6.00
4 Alex Len 2.50 6.00
5 Oscar Robertson
6 C.J. McCollum 4.00 10.00
7 Dwight Powell 2.50 6.00
8 Cody Zeller 2.50 6.00
9 Terry Cummings
10 Lorenzo Brown 2.50 6.00
12 Jerry West 15.00 40.00
13 Michael Kidd-Gilchrist
14 Allen Iverson 50.00 120.00
15 Otto Porter 3.00 8.00
16 Cameron Bairstow 2.50 6.00
17 Robert Covington 2.50 6.00
18 Dante Exum 3.00 8.00
20 Isaiah Canaan 3.00 8.00
21 Kentavious Caldwell-Pope
22 John Stockton
23 Mike Muscala 2.50 6.00
24 Anthony Bennett 2.50 6.00
25 Cleanthony Early 2.50 6.00
26 Carl Landry 2.50 6.00
27 Scott Skiles 3.00 8.00
28 Devyn Marble 2.50 6.00
30 James Ennis 2.50 6.00
32 Jordan Clarkson 4.00 10.00
33 Billy Paultz 4.00 10.00
34 Anthony Davis 25.00 60.00
35 Phil Pressey 2.50 6.00
37 Shabazz Muhammad 3.00 8.00
38 Erick Green 2.50 6.00
39 Mark Landsberger 2.50 6.00
40 James Michael McAdoo 2.50 6.00
42 Josh Huestis 2.50 6.00
43 Nerlens Noel
44 Ben McLemore
45 Ray McCallum 2.50 6.00
46 Charles Oakley 6.00 15.00
47 Shaquille O'Neal
48 Glenn Robinson III 4.00 10.00
49 Trey Burke 2.50 6.00
51 Matthew Dellavedova 3.00 8.00
52 Julius Erving 30.00 60.00
53 Noah Vonleh 2.50 6.00
54 Blake Griffin
55 Ricky Pierce 2.50 6.00
56 Chucky Brown 2.50 6.00
57 Steve Novak 2.50 6.00
58 Grant Jerrett 2.50 6.00
59 Victor Oladipo 3.00 8.00
60 Jeff Withey 2.50 6.00
61 Karl-Anthony Towns 100.00 250.00
62 D'Angelo Russell 20.00 50.00
63 Jahlil Okafor 15.00 40.00
64 Emmanuel Mudiay 15.00 40.00
65 Kristaps Porzingis 60.00 150.00
67 Justise Winslow 10.00 25.00
68 Willie Cauley-Stein 15.00 40.00
69 Stanley Johnson 8.00 20.00
70 Frank Kaminsky 8.00 20.00
71 Devin Booker 20.00 50.00
72 Myles Turner 8.00 20.00
73 Jerian Grant 2.50 6.00
74 Trey Lyles 4.00 10.00
75 Cameron Payne 3.00 8.00
76 Delon Wright 3.00 8.00
77 Rashad Vaughn 2.50 6.00

78 Kelly Oubre Jr. 3.00 8.00
79 Sam Dekker 3.00 8.00
80 Terry Rozier 3.00 8.00
81 Rondae Hollis-Jefferson 3.00 8.00
82 Bobby Portis 4.00 10.00
83 Justin Anderson 3.00 8.00
84 Jarell Martin 3.00 8.00
85 R.J. Hunter 2.50 6.00
86 Anthony Brown 2.50 6.00
87 Tyus Jones 4.00 10.00
88 Chris McCullough 2.50 6.00
89 Jordan Mickey 2.50 6.00
90 Larry Nance Jr. 4.00 10.00
91 Montrezl Harrell 3.00 8.00
92 Dakari Johnson 2.50 6.00
94 Pat Connaughton 2.50 6.00
95 Rakeem Christmas 2.50 6.00
96 Richaun Holmes 3.00 8.00
97 Seth Curry 12.00 30.00
99 Lamar Patterson 2.50 6.00
100 Joe Young 3.00 8.00

2015-16 Hoops High Flyers

RANDOM INSERTS IN PACKS
*AP/99: .6X TO 1.5X BASIC
1 LeBron James 2.50 6.00
2 Tracy McGrady .60 1.50
3 Spud Webb .50 1.25
4 Anfernee Hardaway 1.50 4.00
5 Julius Erving 1.00 2.50
6 Dwyane Wade 1.00 2.50
7 Shawn Kemp 1.00 2.50
8 Scottie Pippen 1.25 3.00
9 Kobe Bryant 2.50 6.00
10 Zach LaVine .60 1.50
11 Dwight Howard .50 1.25
12 Shaquille O'Neal 1.25 3.00
13 Blake Griffin .60 1.50
14 Grant Hill .75 2.00
15 Dominique Wilkins .75 2.00

2015-16 Hoops High Flyers Holo Green

*HOLO GREEN: .75X TO 2X BASIC
RANDOM INSERTS IN PACKS
STATED PRINT RUN 25 SER.#'d SETS
1 LeBron James 12.00 30.00
9 Kobe Bryant 12.00 30.00

2015-16 Hoops Highlights

RANDOM INSERTS IN PACKS
1 LeBron James 5.00 12.00
2 Kobe Bryant 5.00 12.00
3 Klay Thompson 1.50 4.00
4 Kyrie Irving 2.50 6.00
5 Stephen Curry 5.00 12.00

2015-16 Hoops Hot Signatures

TWO AUTOS PER HOBBY BOX
*RED HOT/25: .6X TO 1.5X BASIC
EXCHANGE DEADLINE 4/14/2017
1 Kyrie Irving EXCH 20.00 50.00
2 Gary Payton 10.00 25.00
3 Nerlens Noel 6.00 15.00
4 Jerry West 20.00 50.00
5 Ricky Pierce 2.50 6.00
6 Alex Len 2.50 6.00
7 Dwyane Wade 25.00 60.00
8 Blake Griffin 12.00 30.00
9 Julius Erving 25.00 60.00
10 Clyde Drexler 10.00 25.00
11 Matthew Dellavedova 5.00 12.00
12 Hakeem Olajuwon 10.00 25.00
13 Noah Vonleh 2.50 6.00
14 Joel Embiid 10.00 25.00
15 Ricky Rubio 8.00 20.00
16 Allen Iverson 50.00 120.00
17 Tarik Black 2.50 6.00
18 C.J. McCollum 6.00 15.00
19 Julius Randle 10.00 25.00
20 Cody Zeller 2.50 6.00
21 Michael Carter-Williams 2.50 6.00
22 Lorenzo Brown 2.50 6.00
23 Oscar Robertson 25.00 60.00
24 John Stockton 15.00 40.00
25 Dwight Powell 2.50 6.00
26 Andrew Wiggins 25.00 60.00
27 Quincy Acy 2.50 6.00
28 Cameron Bairstow 2.50 6.00
29 Kentavious Caldwell-Pope 3.00 8.00
30 Dante Exum 3.00 8.00
31 Michael Kidd-Gilchrist 3.00 8.00
32 James Ennis 2.50 6.00
33 Otto Porter 3.00 8.00
34 John Wall 20.00 50.00
35 Robert Covington 2.50 6.00
36 Anthony Bennett 2.50 6.00
37 Ray McCallum 2.50 6.00
38 Carl Landry 2.50 6.00
39 Kevin Durant 50.00 120.00
40 David Robinson 15.00 40.00
41 Mike Muscala 2.50 6.00
42 James Michael McAdoo 2.50 6.00
43 Pau Gasol 8.00 20.00
44 Jordan Clarkson 4.00 10.00
45 Shabazz Muhammad 3.00 8.00
46 Anthony Davis 50.00 120.00
47 Trey Burke 2.50 6.00
48 Carmelo Anthony 10.00 25.00
49 Kevin McHale 10.00 25.00
50 Dennis Rodman 15.00 40.00
51 Mason Plumlee 3.00 8.00
52 James Worthy 10.00 25.00
53 Phil Pressey 2.50 6.00
54 Josh Huestis 2.50 6.00
55 Shaquille O'Neal 40.00 100.00
56 Ben McLemore 2.50 6.00
57 Victor Oladipo 3.00 8.00
58 Chris Webber 50.00 120.00
59 Kobe Bryant 75.00 200.00
60 Erick Green 2.50 6.00
61 Karl-Anthony Towns 60.00 150.00
62 D'Angelo Russell 8.00 20.00
63 Jahlil Okafor 5.00 12.00
64 Emmanuel Mudiay 4.00 10.00
65 Kristaps Porzingis 30.00 80.00
67 Justise Winslow 8.00 20.00
68 Willie Cauley-Stein 4.00 10.00
69 Stanley Johnson 3.00 8.00
70 Frank Kaminsky 4.00 10.00
71 Devin Booker 40.00 100.00
72 Myles Turner 12.00 30.00
73 Jerian Grant 2.50 6.00
74 Trey Lyles 4.00 10.00
75 Cameron Payne 3.00 8.00
76 Delon Wright 3.00 8.00
77 Rashad Vaughn 2.50 6.00
78 Kelly Oubre Jr. 3.00 8.00
79 Sam Dekker 3.00 8.00
80 Terry Rozier 3.00 8.00
81 Rondae Hollis-Jefferson 3.00 8.00
82 Bobby Portis 4.00 10.00
83 Justin Anderson 3.00 8.00
84 Jarell Martin 3.00 8.00
85 R.J. Hunter 2.50 6.00
86 Anthony Brown 2.50 6.00
87 Branden Dawson 2.50 6.00
88 Chris McCullough 2.50 6.00
89 Jordan Mickey 2.50 6.00
90 Larry Nance Jr. 4.00 10.00
91 Montrezl Harrell 3.00 8.00
92 Dakari Johnson 2.50 6.00
93 Darrun Hilliard 2.50 6.00
94 Pat Connaughton 2.50 6.00
95 Rakeem Christmas 2.50 6.00
97 Seth Curry 10.00 25.00
99 Tyus Jones 6.00 15.00
100 Lamar Patterson 2.50 6.00

2015-16 Hoops Kobe's All Rookie Team

RANDOM INSERTS IN PACKS
1 Emmanuel Mudiay 6.00 15.00
2 Jerian Grant 5.00 12.00
3 Mario Hezonja 5.00 12.00
4 Devin Booker 20.00 50.00
5 Frank Kaminsky 6.00 15.00
6 Trey Lyles 6.00 15.00
7 Karl-Anthony Towns 30.00 80.00
8 Jahlil Okafor 8.00 20.00
9 D'Angelo Russell 15.00 40.00
10 Kristaps Porzingis 15.00 40.00
11 Willie Cauley-Stein 6.00 15.00
12 Justise Winslow 6.00 15.00

2015-16 Hoops Lights Camera Action

RANDOM INSERTS IN PACKS
1 Jimmy Butler .60 1.50
2 Jabari Parker .75 2.00
3 Dirk Nowitzki .75 2.00
4 Victor Oladipo .50 1.25
5 DeMar DeRozan .60 1.50
6 Magic Johnson 1.50 4.00
7 Andrew Wiggins 1.00 2.50
8 Dwyane Wade 1.00 2.50
9 John Wall .75 2.00
10 DeAndre Jordan .60 1.50
11 James Harden 1.00 2.50
12 Elfrid Payton .50 1.25
13 Chris Paul .75 2.00
14 Kyle Lowry .50 1.25
15 Russell Westbrook 1.50 4.00
16 Shaquille O'Neal 1.25 3.00
17 Kevin Durant 1.50 4.00
18 Blake Griffin .60 1.50
19 Carmelo Anthony .75 2.00
20 Eric Bledsoe .50 1.25
21 Bradley Beal .60 1.50
22 Gordon Hayward .60 1.50
23 Kyrie Irving 1.25 3.00
24 Allen Iverson .75 2.00
25 Klay Thompson .75 2.00
26 Chris Webber .60 1.50
27 Damian Lillard 1.25 3.00
28 Kawhi Leonard 1.00 2.50
29 DeMarcus Cousins .60 1.50
30 Jeff Teague .50 1.25
31 LeBron James 2.50 6.00
32 Nikola Vucevic .50 1.25
33 Stephen Curry 2.50 6.00
34 Larry Bird 1.50 4.00
35 Kobe Bryant 2.50 6.00
36 Latrell Sprewell .50 1.25
37 Anthony Davis 1.25 3.00
38 Tony Parker .60 1.50
39 Derrick Rose .75 2.00
40 Michael Carter-Williams .40 1.00

2015-16 Hoops Picture Perfect

RANDOM INSERTS IN PACKS
1 Blake Griffin .60 1.50
2 Kawhi Leonard 1.00 2.50
3 Tony Parker .60 1.50
4 Russell Westbrook 1.50 4.00
5 Klay Thompson .75 2.00
6 Kobe Bryant 2.50 6.00
7 Andrew Wiggins 1.00 2.50
8 Kevin Durant 1.50 4.00
9 Damian Lillard 1.25 3.00
10 Anthony Davis 1.25 3.00
11 Stephen Curry 2.50 6.00
12 John Wall .75 2.00
13 Carmelo Anthony .75 2.00
14 Derrick Rose .75 2.00
15 Giannis Antetokounmpo 1.25 3.00
16 James Harden 1.00 2.50
17 Jabari Parker .75 2.00
18 LeBron James 2.50 6.00
19 Chris Paul .75 2.00
20 Kyrie Irving 1.25 3.00

2015-16 Hoops Rise N Shine Memorabilia

RANDOM INSERTS IN PACKS
*PRIME/25: .75X TO 2X BASE HI
1 Anthony Brown 2.00 5.00
2 Emmanuel Mudiay 3.00 8.00
3 Kristaps Porzingis 10.00 25.00
4 Chris McCullough 2.00 5.00
5 Jerian Grant 2.00 5.00
6 Devin Booker 10.00 25.00
7 Bobby Portis 3.00 8.00
8 Justise Winslow 3.00 8.00
9 Terry Rozier 2.50 6.00
10 Karl-Anthony Towns 6.00 15.00
11 Jarell Martin 2.50 6.00
12 Stanley Johnson 2.50 6.00
13 Montrezl Harrell 2.50 6.00
14 Tyler Harvey 2.00 5.00
15 Cameron Payne 2.50 6.00
16 Rondae Hollis-Jefferson
17 Myles Turner 3.00 8.00
18 D'Angelo Russell 6.00 15.00
19 Dakari Johnson 2.00 5.00
20 Joe Young 2.50 6.00
21 Frank Kaminsky 3.00 8.00
22 Jordan Mickey 2.00 5.00
23 Willie Cauley-Stein 3.00 8.00
24 Justin Anderson 2.50 6.00
25 Kelly Oubre Jr. 2.50 6.00
26 Tyus Jones 3.00 8.00
27 Trey Lyles 3.00 8.00
28 Sam Dekker 2.50 6.00
29 Jahlil Okafor 5.00 12.00
30 R.J. Hunter 2.00 5.00
31 Josh Huestis 2.00 5.00
32 Rakeem Christmas
33 Richaun Holmes 2.50 6.00
34 Pat Connaughton 2.00 5.00
35 Walter Tavares 2.00 5.00

2015-16 Hoops Road to the Finals

1-41 PRINT RUN 2015 SER.#'d SETS
42-66 PRINT RUN 999 SER.#'d SETS
67-75 PRINT RUN 499 SER.#'d SETS
76-81 PRINT RUN 199 SER.#'d SETS
RANDOM INSERTS IN PACKS
1 Paul Pierce R1 .75 2.00
2 Stephen Curry R1 3.00 8.00
3 Derrick Rose R1 1.00 2.50
4 James Harden R1 1.25 3.00
5 Kyrie Irving R1 1.50 4.00
6 Kyle Korver R1 .60 1.50
7 Beno Udrih R1 .50 1.25
8 Blake Griffin R1 .75 2.00
9 Joakim Noah R1 .60 1.50
10 Klay Thompson R1 1.00 2.50
11 Josh Smith R1 .60 1.50
12 LeBron James R1 3.00 8.00
13 John Wall R1 1.00 2.50
14 Al Horford R1 .60 1.50
15 Mike Conley R1 .75 2.00
16 Tim Duncan R1 1.25 3.00
17 LeBron James R1 3.00 8.00
18 Derrick Rose R1 1.00 2.50
19 Stephen Curry R1 3.00 8.00
20 James Harden R1 1.25 3.00
21 John Wall R1 1.00 2.50
22 Kawhi Leonard R1 1.25 3.00
23 Brook Lopez R1 .60 1.50
24 Jerryd Bayless R1 .60 1.50
25 Stephen Curry R1 3.00 8.00
26 Marc Gasol R1 .75 2.00
27 Monta Ellis R1 .60 1.50
28 LeBron James R1 3.00 8.00
29 Blake Griffin R1 .75 2.00
30 Marcin Gortat R1 .60 1.50
31 Deron Williams R1 .60 1.50
32 Michael Carter-Williams R1 .50 1.25
33 Damian Lillard R1 1.50 4.00
34 Dwight Howard R1 .60 1.50
35 Tim Duncan R1 1.25 3.00
36 Al Horford R1 .60 1.50
37 Marc Gasol R1 .75 2.00
38 Mike Dunleavy R1 .50 1.25
39 Blake Griffin R1 .75 2.00
40 Paul Millsap R1 .75 2.00
41 Chris Paul R1 1.00 2.50
42 Bradley Beal R2 1.00 2.50
43 Stephen Curry R2 4.00 10.00
44 Pau Gasol R2 1.00 2.50
45 Blake Griffin R2 1.00 2.50
46 DeMarre Carroll R2 .60 1.50
47 Mike Conley R2 1.00 2.50
48 LeBron James R2 4.00 10.00
49 James Harden R2 1.50 4.00
50 Derrick Rose R2 1.25 3.00
51 Austin Rivers R2 .75 2.00
52 Paul Pierce R2 1.00 2.50
53 Marc Gasol R2 1.00 2.50
54 LeBron James R2 4.00 10.00
55 DeAndre Jordan R2 1.00 2.50
56 Jeff Teague R2 .75 2.00
57 Stephen Curry R2 4.00 10.00
58 LeBron James R2 4.00 10.00
59 James Harden R2 1.50 4.00
60 Al Horford R2 .75 2.00
61 Klay Thompson R2 1.25 3.00
62 Josh Smith R2 .75 2.00
63 Matthew Dellavedova R2 .75 2.00
64 DeMarre Carroll R2 .60 1.50
65 Stephen Curry R2 4.00 10.00
66 James Harden R2 1.50 4.00
67 Stephen Curry CF 6.00 15.00
68 J.R. Smith CF 1.25 3.00
69 Stephen Curry CF 6.00 15.00
70 LeBron James CF 6.00 15.00
71 Stephen Curry CF 6.00 15.00
72 LeBron James CF 6.00 15.00
73 James Harden CF 2.50 6.00
74 Kyrie Irving CF 3.00 8.00
75 Klay Thompson CF 2.00 5.00
76 Stephen Curry F 8.00 20.00
77 LeBron James F 8.00 20.00
78 LeBron James F 8.00 20.00
79 Andre Iguodala F 1.50 4.00
80 Stephen Curry F 8.00 20.00
81 Draymond Green F 2.50 6.00

2015-16 Hoops Rookie Remembrance Memorabilia

RANDOM INSERTS IN PACKS
*PRIME/25: .75X TO 2X BASE HI
1 Alec Burks 2.00 5.00
2 Alex Len 2.00 5.00
3 Andre Drummond 3.00 8.00
4 Anthony Bennett
5 Archie Goodwin 2.00 5.00
6 Ben McLemore 2.00 5.00
7 Bradley Beal 3.00 8.00
8 C.J. McCollum 3.00 8.00
9 Cody Zeller 2.00 5.00
10 Dennis Schroder 2.50 6.00
11 Dion Waiters
12 Draymond Green 4.00 10.00
13 Enes Kanter 2.00 5.00
14 Evan Fournier 2.50 6.00
15 Giannis Antetokounmpo 6.00 15.00
16 Gorgui Dieng 2.00 5.00
17 Harrison Barnes 2.50 6.00
18 Iman Shumpert 2.00 5.00
19 Isaiah Thomas
20 Jared Sullinger 2.00 5.00
21 Jimmy Butler 3.00 8.00
22 John Henson 2.50 6.00
23 Jonas Valanciunas 2.50 6.00
24 Kawhi Leonard 5.00 12.00
25 Kelly Olynyk 2.00 5.00
26 Kemba Walker 3.00 8.00
27 Kenneth Faried 2.50 6.00
28 Kentavious Caldwell-Pope 2.50 6.00
29 Khris Middleton 2.50 6.00
30 Klay Thompson 4.00 10.00
31 Kyrie Irving 6.00 15.00
32 Marcus Morris 2.00 5.00
33 Markieff Morris 2.00 5.00
34 Mason Plumlee 2.50 6.00
35 Maurice Harkless 2.00 5.00
36 Michael Carter-Williams 2.00 5.00
37 Michael Kidd-Gilchrist
38 Nerlens Noel 2.50 6.00
39 Norris Cole 2.00 5.00
40 Otto Porter 2.50 6.00
41 Reggie Jackson
42 Terrence Jones 2.50 6.00
43 Terrence Ross
44 Thomas Robinson 2.00 5.00
45 Tim Hardaway Jr.
46 Tobias Harris 2.50 6.00
47 Tony Wroten 2.00 5.00
48 Trey Burke 2.00 5.00
49 Tristan Thompson 2.50 6.00
50 Victor Oladipo 2.50 6.00

2015-16 Hoops Swat Team

RANDOM INSERTS IN PACKS
1 Anthony Davis 1.25 3.00
2 Rudy Gobert .60 1.50
3 DeAndre Jordan .60 1.50
4 Serge Ibaka .50 1.25
5 Andre Drummond .60 1.50
6 Tim Duncan 1.00 2.50
7 Pau Gasol .60 1.50
8 Nerlens Noel .50 1.25
9 Marc Gasol .60 1.50
10 Gorgui Dieng .40 1.00
11 Hakeem Olajuwon .75 2.00
12 Dikembe Mutombo .60 1.50
13 Kareem Abdul-Jabbar 1.00 2.50
14 David Robinson 1.00 2.50
15 Shaquille O'Neal 1.25 3.00

2015-16 Hoops Team Leaders

RANDOM INSERTS IN PACKS
*AP/99: .6X TO 1.5X BASIC
1 Andrew Wiggins 1.00 2.50
2 Nikola Vucevic .50 1.25
3 Khris Middleton .50 1.25
4 Kawhi Leonard 1.00 2.50
5 DeMar DeRozan .60 1.50
6 Stephen Curry 2.50 6.00
7 Nerlens Noel .50 1.25
8 DeMarcus Cousins .60 1.50
9 Russell Westbrook 1.50 4.00
10 John Wall .75 2.00
11 LeBron James 2.50 6.00
12 James Harden 1.00 2.50
13 George Hill .50 1.25
14 Chandler Parsons .50 1.25
15 Marcus Smart .50 1.25
16 DeAndre Jordan .60 1.50
17 Carmelo Anthony .75 2.00
18 Kobe Bryant 2.50 6.00
19 Rudy Gobert .60 1.50
20 Dwyane Wade 1.00 2.50
21 Pau Gasol .60 1.50
22 Zach Randolph .50 1.25
23 Andre Drummond .60 1.50
24 Anthony Davis 1.25 3.00
25 Brook Lopez .50 1.25
26 Eric Bledsoe .50 1.25
27 Damian Lillard 1.25 3.00
28 Jeff Teague .50 1.25
29 Kenneth Faried .50 1.25
30 Kemba Walker .60 1.50

2015-16 Hoops Team Leaders Holo Green

*HOLO GREEN: .75X TO 2X BASIC
RANDOM INSERTS IN PACKS
STATED PRINT RUN 25 SER.#'d SETS
11 LeBron James 12.00 30.00
18 Kobe Bryant 12.00 30.00

2015-16 Hoops Triple Double

RANDOM INSERTS IN PACKS
1 Chris Paul .75 2.00
2 Rajon Rondo .60 1.50
3 Kyle Lowry .50 1.25
4 Michael Carter-Williams .40 1.00
5 Kobe Bryant 2.50 6.00
6 Tim Duncan 1.00 2.50
7 Rajon Rondo .60 1.50
8 Eric Bledsoe .50 1.25
9 Rajon Rondo .60 1.50
10 Michael Carter-Williams .40 1.00
11 James Harden 1.00 2.50
12 Eric Bledsoe .50 1.25
13 Kobe Bryant 2.50 6.00
14 Draymond Green .75 2.00
15 Al Horford .50 1.25
16 Russell Westbrook 1.50 4.00
17 Hassan Whiteside .50 1.25
18 Michael Carter-Williams .40 1.00
19 Russell Westbrook 1.50 4.00
20 Tyreke Evans .40 1.00
21 James Harden 1.00 2.50
22 Russell Westbrook 1.50 4.00
23 Evan Turner .50 1.25
24 Russell Westbrook 1.50 4.00
25 George Hill .50 1.25
26 Russell Westbrook 1.50 4.00
27 Ricky Rubio .60 1.50
28 Russell Westbrook 1.50 4.00
29 James Harden 1.00 2.50
30 Russell Westbrook 1.50 4.00
31 Russell Westbrook 1.50 4.00
32 Kyle Lowry .50 1.25
33 Reggie Jackson .50 1.25
34 Elfrid Payton .50 1.25
35 Elfrid Payton .50 1.25
36 Russell Westbrook 1.50 4.00
37 Evan Turner .50 1.25
38 Reggie Jackson .50 1.25
39 Evan Turner .50 1.25
40 DeMarcus Cousins .60 1.50
41 Russell Westbrook 1.50 4.00
42 DeMarcus Cousins .60 1.50
43 LeBron James 2.50 6.00
44 Russell Westbrook 1.50 4.00
45 LeBron James 2.50 6.00
46 James Harden 1.00 2.50

2016-17 Hoops

COMPLETE SET (300) 25.00 60.00
1 Jahlil Okafor .25 .60
2 Nerlens Noel .25 .60
3 Robert Covington .20 .50
4 Joel Embiid .50 1.25
5 Ish Smith .20 .50
6 Giannis Antetokounmpo .60 1.50
7 Jabari Parker .40 1.00
8 Khris Middleton .25 .60
9 Greg Monroe .25 .60
10 Tyler Ennis .20 .50
11 Derrick Rose .40 1.00
12 Jimmy Butler .30 .75
13 Bobby Portis .20 .50
14 Nikola Mirotic .25 .60
15 Doug McDermott .25 .60
16 Pau Gasol .30 .75
17 LeBron James 1.25 3.00
18 Kyrie Irving .60 1.50
19 Kevin Love .30 .75
20 Mike Dunleavy .20 .50
21 Matthew Dellavedova .25 .60
22 Tristan Thompson .25 .60
23 Isaiah Thomas .30 .75
24 Avery Bradley .25 .60
25 Jae Crowder .25 .60
26 Marcus Smart .25 .60
27 Evan Turner .20 .50
28 Jared Sullinger .20 .50
29 Chris Paul .40 1.00
30 Blake Griffin .30 .75
31 DeAndre Jordan .30 .75
32 J.J. Redick .30 .75
33 Jamal Crawford .30 .75
34 Jeff Green .25 .60
35 Mike Conley .25 .60
36 Marc Gasol .30 .75
37 Zach Randolph .25 .60
38 Matt Barnes .20 .50
39 Brandan Wright .20 .50
40 Paul Millsap .30 .75
41 Dennis Schroder .25 .60
42 Kent Bazemore .25 .60
43 Al Horford .25 .60
44 Kyle Korver .25 .60
45 Dwyane Wade .50 1.25
46 Chris Bosh .30 .75
47 Luol Deng .25 .60
48 Goran Dragic .25 .60
49 Hassan Whiteside .25 .60
50 Jeremy Lin .30 .75
51 Kemba Walker .30 .75
52 Frank Kaminsky .25 .60
53 Nicolas Batum .25 .60
54 Al Jefferson .25 .60
55 Gordon Hayward .30 .75
56 Rudy Gobert .30 .75
57 Rodney Hood .25 .60
58 Derrick Favors .25 .60
59 Alec Burks .20 .50
60 DeMarcus Cousins .30 .75
61 Rajon Rondo .30 .75
62 Rudy Gay .30 .75
63 Willie Cauley-Stein .25 .60
64 Darren Collison .25 .60
65 Carmelo Anthony .40 1.00
66 Kristaps Porzingis .60 1.50
67 Jerian Grant .20 .50
68 Arron Afflalo .20 .50
69 Derrick Williams .20 .50
70 D'Angelo Russell .40 1.00
71 Jordan Clarkson .25 .60
72 Julius Randle .30 .75
73 Larry Nance Jr. .25 .60
74 Brandon Bass .20 .50
75 Victor Oladipo .25 .60
76 Mario Hezonja .20 .50
77 Aaron Gordon .25 .60
78 Nikola Vucevic .25 .60
79 Elfrid Payton .25 .60
80 Dirk Nowitzki .40 1.00
81 Justin Anderson .25 .60
82 Deron Williams .25 .60
83 Chandler Parsons .25 .60
84 Zaza Pachulia .20 .50
85 Brook Lopez .25 .60
86 Thaddeus Young .20 .50
87 Rondae Hollis-Jefferson .20 .50
88 Bojan Bogdanovic .20 .50
89 Jarrett Jack .25 .60
90 Emmanuel Mudiay .25 .60
91 Danilo Gallinari .25 .60
92 Kenneth Faried .25 .60
93 Nikola Jokic .30 .75
94 Will Barton .20 .50
95 Paul George .40 1.00
96 Myles Turner .25 .60
97 Monta Ellis .25 .60
98 George Hill .25 .60
99 Ian Mahinmi .20 .50
100 Anthony Davis .60 1.50
101 Ryan Anderson .25 .60
102 Jrue Holiday .25 .60
103 Tyreke Evans .20 .50
104 Eric Gordon .25 .60
105 Jeff Withey .20 .50
106 Reggie Jackson .25 .60
107 Stanley Johnson .20 .50
108 Tobias Harris .25 .60
109 Kentavious Caldwell-Pope .25 .60
110 Kyle Lowry .25 .60
111 DeMar DeRozan .30 .75
112 Jonas Valanciunas .25 .60
113 DeMarre Carroll .20 .50
114 Bismack Biyombo .20 .50
115 Cory Joseph .20 .50
116 James Harden .50 1.25
117 Dwight Howard .25 .60
118 Sam Dekker .25 .60
119 Trevor Ariza .20 .50
120 Clint Capela .20 .50
121 Kawhi Leonard .50 1.25
122 LaMarcus Aldridge .30 .75
123 Tony Parker .30 .75
124 Kyle Anderson .20 .50
125 Manu Ginobili .30 .75
126 Devin Booker .50 1.25
127 Eric Bledsoe .25 .60
128 Brandon Knight .25 .60
129 Alex Len .20 .50
130 Tyson Chandler .25 .60
131 Russell Westbrook .75 2.00
132 Steven Adams .25 .60
133 Enes Kanter .20 .50
134 Serge Ibaka .25 .60
135 Cameron Payne .20 .50
136 Dion Waiters .25 .60
137 Karl-Anthony Towns .75 2.00
138 Andrew Wiggins .50 1.25
139 Kevin Garnett .50 1.25
140 Zach LaVine .30 .75
141 Ricky Rubio .30 .75
142 Shabazz Muhammad .25 .60
143 Damian Lillard .60 1.50
144 C.J. McCollum .25 .60
145 Al-Farouq Aminu .25 .60
146 Mason Plumlee .25 .60
147 Ed Davis .20 .50
148 Stephen Curry 1.25 3.00
149 Klay Thompson .40 1.00
150 Draymond Green .40 1.00
151 Andre Drummond .30 .75
152 Harrison Barnes .25 .60
153 Andrew Bogut .25 .60
154 John Wall .40 1.00
155 Markieff Morris .20 .50
156 Bradley Beal .30 .75
157 Marcin Gortat .25 .60
158 Kelly Oubre Jr. .20 .50
159 Justise Winslow .25 .60
160 Trey Lyles .25 .60
161 Nik Stauskas .20 .50
162 Jerami Grant .20 .50
163 Isaiah Canaan .25 .60
164 John Henson .25 .60
165 Rashad Vaughn .20 .50
166 Michael Carter-Williams .20 .50
167 Cristiano Felicio .20 .50
168 E'Twaun Moore .20 .50
169 Aaron Brooks .20 .50
170 Channing Frye .25 .60
171 Iman Shumpert .20 .50
172 Richard Jefferson .25 .60
173 Mo Williams .25 .60
174 Kelly Olynyk .20 .50
175 Terry Rozier .25 .60
176 Jordan Mickey .20 .50
177 Tyler Zeller .25 .60
178 Paul Pierce .30 .75
179 Austin Rivers .25 .60
180 Cole Aldrich .20 .50
181 Luc Mbah a Moute .20 .50
182 Vince Carter .40 1.00
183 Chris Andersen .25 .60
184 Tony Allen .20 .50
185 Thabo Sefolosha .20 .50
186 Walter Tavares .20 .50
187 Kirk Hinrich .25 .60
188 Tyler Johnson .20 .50
189 Josh Richardson .20 .50
190 Gerald Green .25 .60
191 Michael Kidd-Gilchrist .25 .60
192 Courtney Lee .25 .60
193 Marvin Williams .25 .60
194 Trey Burke .20 .50
195 Dante Exum .25 .60
196 Joe Ingles .20 .50
197 Seth Curry .30 .75
198 Marco Belinelli .20 .50
199 Ben McLemore .20 .50
200 Lance Thomas .20 .50
201 Jose Calderon .20 .50
202 Robin Lopez .20 .50
203 Marcelo Huertas .20 .50
204 Lou Williams .25 .60
205 Tarik Black .20 .50
206 Evan Fournier .25 .60
207 Brandon Jennings .20 .50
208 Ersan Ilyasova .20 .50
209 J.J. Barea .25 .60
210 Salah Mejri .20 .50
211 Wesley Matthews .20 .50
212 Greivis Vasquez .25 .60
213 Chris McCullough .20 .50
214 Trevor Booker .20 .50
215 Jusuf Nurkic .20 .50
216 Wilson Chandler .25 .60
217 D.J. Augustin .20 .50
218 Joe Young .20 .50
219 Jordan Hill .20 .50
220 Rodney Stuckey .20 .50
221 Terrence Jones .25 .60
222 Omer Asik .25 .60
223 Langston Galloway .20 .50
224 Marcus Morris .20 .50
225 Jodie Meeks .25 .60
226 Joel Anthony .20 .50
227 Patrick Patterson .20 .50
228 Norman Powell .20 .50
229 Delon Wright .20 .50
230 Michael Beasley .20 .50
231 Jason Terry .25 .60
232 Corey Brewer .20 .50
233 Boban Marjanovic .20 .50
234 David Lee .20 .50
235 Danny Green .25 .60
236 David West .25 .60
237 Archie Goodwin .20 .50
238 T.J. Warren .25 .60
239 P.J. Tucker .20 .50
240 Kevin Durant .75 2.00
241 Andre Roberson .20 .50
242 Anthony Morrow .20 .50
243 Randy Foye .20 .50
244 Tyus Jones .20 .50
245 Gorgui Dieng .20 .50
246 Adreian Payne .20 .50
247 Brandon Rush .20 .50
248 Allen Crabbe .20 .50
249 Meyers Leonard .20 .50
250 Gerald Henderson .20 .50
251 Shaun Livingston .20 .50
252 Leandro Barbosa .20 .50
253 Marreese Speights .20 .50
254 Festus Ezeli .20 .50
255 Otto Porter .25 .60
256 Nene .25 .60
257 Jared Dudley .20 .50
258 Ramon Sessions .25 .60
259 Udonis Haslem .20 .50
260 Jason Smith .20 .50
261 Ben Simmons RC 2.50 6.00
262 Brandon Ingram RC 2.50 6.00
263 Jaylen Brown RC 1.50 4.00
264 Dragan Bender RC .50 1.25
265 Kris Dunn RC 1.25 3.00
266 Buddy Hield RC 1.00 2.50
267 Jamal Murray RC 1.25 3.00
268 Marquese Chriss RC 1.00 2.50
269 Jakob Poeltl RC .50 1.25
270 Thon Maker RC 1.25 3.00
271 Domantas Sabonis RC .60 1.50
272 Taurean Prince RC .60 1.50
273 Denzel Valentine RC .50 1.25
274 Wade Baldwin IV RC .40 1.00
275 Henry Ellenson RC .50 1.25
276 Malik Beasley RC .40 1.00
277 Caris LeVert RC .50 1.25
278 DeAndre' Bembry RC .40 1.00
279 Malachi Richardson RC .50 1.25
280 T. Luwawu-Cabarrot RC .75 2.00
281 Tomas Satoransky RC .40 1.00
282 Brice Johnson RC .40 1.00
283 Pascal Siakam RC .40 1.00
284 Skal Labissiere RC .60 1.50
285 Dejounte Murray RC .75 2.00
286 Damian Jones RC .40 1.00
287 Deyonta Davis RC .40 1.00
288 Ivica Zubac RC .60 1.50
289 Cheick Diallo RC .40 1.00
290 Tyler Ulis RC 1.25 3.00
291 Malcolm Brogdon RC 1.00 2.50
292 Chinanu Onuaku RC .40 1.00
293 Patrick McCaw RC .75 2.00
294 Diamond Stone RC .40 1.00
295 Isaiah Whitehead RC .40 1.00
296 Demetrius Jackson RC .40 1.00
297 A.J. Hammons RC .40 1.00
298 Michael Gbinije RC .40 1.00
299 Dario Saric RC 1.25 3.00
300 Kay Felder RC .40 1.00

2016-17 Hoops Artist Proof

*ARTIST PROOF: 4X TO 10X BASIC
*ARTIST PROOF RC: 4X TO 10X BASIC
RANDOM INSERTS IN PACKS
STATED PRINT RUN 25 SER.#'d SETS
261 Ben Simmons 75.00 200.00

2016-17 Hoops Blue

*BLUE: .75X TO 2X BASIC
*BLUE RC: .75X TO 2X BASIC
RANDOM INSERTS IN PACKS
261 Ben Simmons 20.00 50.00

2016-17 Hoops Blue Checkerboard

*BLUE CHECK: 2X TO 5X BASIC
*BLUE CHECK RC: 2X TO 5X BASIC
RANDOM INSERTS IN PACKS
STATED PRINT RUN 75 SER.#'d SETS
261 Ben Simmons 50.00 120.00

2016-17 Hoops Green

*GREEN: 1.2X TO 3X BASIC
*GREEN RC: 1.2X TO 3X BASIC
RANDOM INSERTS IN PACKS
STATED PRINT RUN 149 SER.#'d SETS
261 Ben Simmons 40.00 100.00

2016-17 Hoops Orange

*ORANGE: 4X TO 10X BASIC
*ORANGE RC: 4X TO 10X BASIC
RANDOM INSERTS IN PACKS
STATED PRINT RUN 25 SER.#'d SETS
261 Ben Simmons 75.00 200.00

2016-17 Hoops Orange Explosion

*ORANGE EXP: 2X TO 5X BASIC
*ORANGE EXP RC: 2X TO 5X BASIC
RANDOM INSERTS IN PACKS
STATED PRINT RUN 75 SER.#'d SETS
261 Ben Simmons 50.00 120.00
270 Thon Maker 10.00 25.00

2016-17 Hoops Red

*RED: 2.5X TO 6X BASIC
*RED RC: 2.5X TO 6X BASIC
RANDOM INSERTS IN PACKS
STATED PRINT RUN 49 SER.#'d SETS
261 Ben Simmons 60.00 150.00

2016-17 Hoops Red Backs

*RED BACK: .6X TO 1.5X BASIC
*RED BACK RC: .6X TO 1.5X BASIC
RANDOM INSERTS IN PACKS

2016-17 Hoops Red Checkerboard

*RED CHECK: 5X TO 12X BASIC
*RED CHECK RC: 5X TO 12X BASIC
RANDOM INSERTS IN PACKS
STATED PRINT RUN 15 SER.#'d SETS
261 Ben Simmons 100.00 250.00

2016-17 Hoops Silver

*SILVER: 1.5X TO 4X BASIC
*SILVER RC: 1.5X TO 4X BASIC
RANDOM INSERTS IN PACKS
STATED PRINT RUN 99 SER.#'d SETS
261 Ben Simmons 40.00 100.00
262 Brandon Ingram 15.00 40.00

2016-17 Hoops Teal

*TEAL: 2.5X TO 6X BASIC
*TEAL RC: 2.5X TO 6X BASIC
RANDOM INSERTS IN PACKS
STATED PRINT RUN 49 SER.#'d SETS
261 Ben Simmons 60.00 150.00

2016-17 Hoops Teal Explosion

*TEAL EXP: 1X TO 2.5X BASIC
*TEAL EXP RC: 1X TO 2.5X BASIC
RANDOM INSERTS IN PACKS
261 Ben Simmons 30.00 80.00

2016-17 Hoops Action Shots

RANDOM INSERTS IN PACKS
1 Stephen Curry 2.00 5.00
2 John Wall .60 1.50
3 Brandon Knight .40 1.00
4 James Harden .75 2.00
5 Jonas Valanciunas .40 1.00
6 Andre Drummond .50 1.25
7 DeMarcus Cousins .50 1.25
8 Chris Paul .60 1.50
9 Alec Burks .30 .75
10 Jamal Crawford .50 1.25
11 Zach LaVine .50 1.25
12 Kevin Love .50 1.25
13 Marc Gasol .50 1.25
14 Hassan Whiteside .40 1.00
15 Kemba Walker .50 1.25
16 Julius Randle .50 1.25
17 Jabari Parker .60 1.50
18 Jimmy Butler .50 1.25
19 Avery Bradley .40 1.00
20 Elfrid Payton .40 1.00

2016-17 Hoops Birds Eye View

RANDOM INSERTS IN PACKS
1 LeBron James 2.00 5.00
2 Andrew Wiggins .75 2.00
3 Zach LaVine .50 1.25
4 Aaron Gordon .40 1.00
5 DeAndre Jordan .50 1.25
6 Blake Griffin .50 1.25
7 Giannis Antetokounmpo 1.00 2.50
8 John Wall .60 1.50
9 Andre Iguodala .40 1.00
10 Russell Westbrook 1.25 3.00
11 Norman Powell .30 .75
12 Kenneth Faried .40 1.00
13 Justise Winslow .40 1.00
14 Kristaps Porzingis 1.00 2.50
15 Andre Drummond .50 1.25
16 Kawhi Leonard .75 2.00
17 Rudy Gay .50 1.25
18 Jordan Clarkson .40 1.00
19 Paul Millsap .50 1.25
20 Jimmy Butler .50 1.25
21 Hassan Whiteside .40 1.00
22 Paul George .60 1.50
23 Anthony Davis 1.00 2.50
24 Justin Anderson .40 1.00
25 Rodney Hood .40 1.00

2016-17 Hoops Birds Eye View Artist Proof

*ARTIST PROOF: 1.2X TO 3X BASIC
RANDOM INSERTS IN PACKS
STATED PRINT RUN 25 SER.#'d SETS
1 LeBron James 12.00 30.00

2016-17 Hoops Champions

RANDOM INSERTS IN PACKS
1 Cleveland Cavaliers 12.00 30.00

2016-17 Hoops Champions Trophy Portraits

RANDOM INSERTS IN PACKS
STATED PRINT RUN 99 SER.#'d SETS
1 Kobe Bryant 40.00 100.00
2 Stephen Curry 30.00 80.00
3 LeBron James 50.00 125.00
4 David Robinson 15.00 40.00
5 Dirk Nowitzki 15.00 40.00
6 Shaquille O'Neal 25.00 60.00
7 Kevin Garnett 30.00 80.00
8 Tony Parker 12.00 30.00
9 Dwyane Wade 20.00 50.00
10 Magic Johnson 25.00 60.00
11 Larry Bird 25.00 60.00

2016-17 Hoops Courtside

RANDOM INSERTS IN PACKS
1 John Wall .60 1.50
2 Draymond Green .60 1.50
3 Damian Lillard 1.00 2.50
4 Karl-Anthony Towns 1.25 3.00
5 Russell Westbrook 1.25 3.00
6 Kawhi Leonard .75 2.00
7 James Harden .75 2.00
8 Kyle Lowry .40 1.00
9 Andre Drummond .50 1.25
10 Anthony Davis 1.00 2.50
11 Paul George .60 1.50
12 Dirk Nowitzki .60 1.50
13 Jimmy Butler .50 1.25
14 Kristaps Porzingis 1.00 2.50
15 DeMarcus Cousins .50 1.25
16 Kemba Walker .50 1.25
17 Devin Booker .75 2.00
18 Blake Griffin .50 1.25
19 LeBron James 2.00 5.00
20 Giannis Antetokounmpo 1.00 2.50

2016-17 Hoops Courtside Artist Proof

*ARTIST PROOF: 1.2X TO 3X BASIC
RANDOM INSERTS IN PACKS
STATED PRINT RUN 25 SER.#'d SETS
19 LeBron James 12.00 30.00

2016-17 Hoops Double Trouble
RANDOM INSERTS IN PACKS
1 C.Anthony/K.Porzingis 1.00 2.50
2 M.Ellis/P.George .60 1.50
3 A.Drummond/R.Jackson .50 1.25
4 C.McCollum/D.Lillard 1.00 2.50
5 K.Thompson/S.Curry 2.00 5.00
6 D.Booker/E.Bledsoe .75 2.00
7 N.Jokic/E.Mudiay .50 1.25
8 A.Wiggins/K.Towns 1.25 3.00
9 B.Griffin/C.Paul .60 1.50
10 L.James/K.Irving 2.00 5.00

2016-17 Hoops Dreams
RANDOM INSERTS IN PACKS
*ARTIST PROOF/25: 1.2X TO 3X BASIC
1 Kyrie Irving 1.00 2.50
2 Stephen Curry 2.00 5.00
3 Karl-Anthony Towns 1.25 3.00
4 Giannis Antetokounmpo 1.00 2.50
5 John Wall .60 1.50
6 Damian Lillard 1.00 2.50
7 Anthony Davis 1.00 2.50
8 Devin Booker .75 2.00
9 Kristaps Porzingis 1.00 2.50
10 D'Angelo Russell .60 1.50

2016-17 Hoops End 2 End
RANDOM INSERTS IN PACKS
1 Blake Griffin .50 1.25
2 Rudy Gay .50 1.25
3 Kyrie Irving 1.00 2.50
4 Jimmy Butler .50 1.25
5 Marcus Smart .40 1.00
6 Jeremy Lin .50 1.25
7 Dennis Schroder .40 1.00
8 Jordan Clarkson .40 1.00
9 Aaron Gordon .40 1.00
10 Jrue Holiday .40 1.00
11 Reggie Jackson .40 1.00
12 Russell Westbrook 1.25 3.00
13 Draymond Green .60 1.50
14 John Wall .60 1.50
15 Dwyane Wade .75 2.00

2016-17 Hoops Faces of the Future
RANDOM INSERTS IN PACKS
1 Karl-Anthony Towns 1.25 3.00
2 Kristaps Porzingis 1.00 2.50
3 Jahlil Okafor .40 1.00
4 Devin Booker .75 2.00
5 Justise Winslow .40 1.00
6 D'Angelo Russell .60 1.50
7 Andrew Wiggins .75 2.00
8 Jabari Parker .60 1.50
9 Joel Embiid .75 2.00
10 Aaron Gordon .40 1.00
11 Julius Randle .50 1.25
12 Nikola Jokic .50 1.25
13 Victor Oladipo .40 1.00
14 Kentavious Caldwell-Pope .40 1.00
15 C.J. McCollum .40 1.00
16 Steven Adams .40 1.00
17 Giannis Antetokounmpo 1.00 2.50
18 Dennis Schroder .40 1.00
19 Rudy Gobert .50 1.25
20 Myles Turner .40 1.00

2016-17 Hoops Finals MVP
RANDOM INSERTS IN PACKS
1 LeBron James 75.00 200.00

2016-17 Hoops Great SIGnificance
RANDOM INSERTS IN PACKS
EXCHANGE DEADLINE 4/12/2018
1 Cody Zeller 3.00 8.00
2 Dwight Powell 3.00 8.00
3 Aaron Harrison 3.00 8.00
4 Walter Tavares 3.00 8.00
5 Allen Crabbe 3.00 8.00
6 Alex Len 3.00 8.00
7 Jonas Valanciunas 4.00 10.00
8 Rashad Vaughn 3.00 8.00
9 Matthew Dellavedova 4.00 10.00
10 Kelly Olynyk 3.00 8.00
11 Bobby Portis 3.00 8.00
12 Festus Ezeli 3.00 8.00
13 Jason Terry 4.00 10.00
14 Michael Kidd-Gilchrist 4.00 10.00
15 Deron Williams 4.00 10.00
16 Jonathon Simmons 5.00 12.00
17 Michael Carter-Williams 3.00 8.00
18 Dennis Schroder 4.00 10.00
19 Donatas Motiejunas 3.00 8.00
20 Kent Bazemore 4.00 10.00
21 Raul Neto 3.00 8.00
22 Cristiano Felicio 3.00 8.00
23 Clint Capela 3.00 8.00
24 Gorgui Dieng 3.00 8.00
25 Draymond Green 6.00 15.00
26 Ed Davis 3.00 8.00
27 Nikola Jokic 5.00 12.00
28 Paul Millsap 5.00 12.00
29 DeMarre Carroll 3.00 8.00
30 Andrew Bogut 4.00 10.00
31 Zaza Pachulia 3.00 8.00
32 Sam Dekker 4.00 10.00
33 Goran Dragic 4.00 10.00
34 Carmelo Anthony 12.00 30.00
35 Jusuf Nurkic 3.00 8.00
36 Norman Powell 3.00 8.00
37 Larry Nance Jr. 4.00 10.00
38 Shabazz Muhammad 4.00 10.00
39 Khris Middleton 4.00 10.00
40 Marcelo Huertas 3.00 8.00
41 Avery Bradley 4.00 10.00
42 C.J. McCollum 5.00 12.00
43 Montrezl Harrell 3.00 8.00
44 Devin Harris 3.00 8.00
45 Gary Harris 4.00 10.00
46 Jarell Martin 3.00 8.00
47 T.J. McConnell 3.00 8.00
48 Seth Curry 8.00 20.00
49 Gerald Henderson 3.00 8.00
50 Otto Porter 4.00 10.00
51 Jerami Grant 3.00 8.00
52 Sasha Kaun 3.00 8.00
53 Spencer Hawes 3.00 8.00
54 Tony Allen 3.00 8.00
55 R.J. Hunter 3.00 8.00
57 Anthony Davis 25.00 60.00
58 Pau Gasol 5.00 12.00
59 Tyus Jones 3.00 8.00
60 Timofey Mozgov 3.00 8.00
64 Lamar Patterson 3.00 8.00
65 Ian Clark 3.00 8.00
66 E'Twaun Moore 3.00 8.00
67 Reggie Bullock 3.00 8.00
68 James Ennis 3.00 8.00
69 Josh Huestis 3.00 8.00
70 Ray McCallum 3.00 8.00
71 JaKarr Sampson 3.00 8.00
72 Jeff Withey 3.00 8.00
73 Jason Thompson 3.00 8.00
74 Jason Smith 3.00 8.00
75 Tyler Ennis 3.00 8.00
76 James Johnson 3.00 8.00
77 Terrence Jones 4.00 10.00
78 Robert Covington 3.00 8.00
79 Dante Exum 4.00 10.00
80 Salah Mejri 3.00 8.00
81 James Young 3.00 8.00
82 Richaun Holmes 3.00 8.00
83 Kris Humphries 3.00 8.00
84 Joel Embiid 12.00 30.00
85 Brandon Bass 3.00 8.00
86 Amir Johnson 3.00 8.00
87 Chris McCullough 3.00 8.00
88 James Michael McAdoo 3.00 8.00
89 Lance Thomas 3.00 8.00
90 Willie Cauley-Stein 4.00 10.00
91 Shabazz Napier 3.00 8.00
92 Jordan Clarkson 4.00 10.00
93 Wilson Chandler 4.00 10.00
94 Norris Cole 3.00 8.00
95 Kyle Singler 3.00 8.00
96 Mo Williams 4.00 10.00
97 Nick Young 4.00 10.00
98 Trey Burke 3.00 8.00
99 Tobias Harris 4.00 10.00
100 Isaiah Canaan 4.00 10.00

2016-17 Hoops High Flyers
RANDOM INSERTS IN PACKS
*ARTIST PROOF/25: 1.2X TO 3X BASIC
1 DeMarcus Cousins .50 1.25
2 Zach LaVine .50 1.25
3 Aaron Gordon .40 1.00
4 Jabari Parker .60 1.50
5 Julius Randle .50 1.25
6 Andrew Wiggins .75 2.00
7 DeMar DeRozan .50 1.25
8 Will Barton .30 .75
9 Eric Bledsoe .40 1.00
10 Mason Plumlee .40 1.00
11 James Harden .75 2.00
12 Kentavious Caldwell-Pope .40 1.00
13 Blake Griffin .50 1.25
14 Jahlil Okafor .40 1.00
15 Marcus Smart .40 1.00

2016-17 Hoops Highlights
RANDOM INSERTS IN PACKS
1 Tim Duncan .75 2.00
2 Stephen Curry 2.00 5.00
3 Kobe Bryant 2.00 5.00
4 Russell Westbrook 1.25 3.00
5 Dwyane Wade .75 2.00
6 Andre Drummond .50 1.25
7 Anthony Davis 1.00 2.50
8 Stephen Curry 2.00 5.00
9 Hassan Whiteside .40 1.00
10 Rajon Rondo .50 1.25
11 Aaron Gordon .40 1.00
12 LeBron James 2.00 5.00
13 Klay Thompson .60 1.50
14 DeMarcus Cousins .50 1.25
15 Dirk Nowitzki .60 1.50
16 Emmanuel Mudiay .40 1.00
17 Kristaps Porzingis 1.00 2.50
18 Karl-Anthony Towns 1.25 3.00
19 D'Angelo Russell .60 1.50
20 Devin Booker .75 2.00

2016-17 Hoops Hot Signatures
RANDOM INSERTS IN PACKS
EXCHANGE DEADLINE 4/12/2018
*RED/25: .5X TO 1.2X BASIC
1 Cody Zeller 3.00 8.00
2 Dwight Powell 3.00 8.00
3 T.J. McConnell 3.00 8.00
4 Aaron Harrison 3.00 8.00
5 Walter Tavares 3.00 8.00
6 Allen Crabbe 3.00 8.00
7 Alex Len 3.00 8.00
8 Jonas Valanciunas 4.00 10.00
9 Robert Covington 3.00 8.00
10 Rashad Vaughn 3.00 8.00
11 Matthew Dellavedova 4.00 10.00
12 Kelly Olynyk 3.00 8.00
13 Seth Curry 12.00 30.00
14 Bobby Portis 3.00 8.00
15 Festus Ezeli 3.00 8.00
16 Jason Terry 4.00 10.00
17 Michael Kidd-Gilchrist 4.00 10.00
18 Deron Williams 4.00 10.00
19 Jarell Martin 3.00 8.00
20 Jonathon Simmons 5.00 12.00
21 Michael Carter-Williams 3.00 8.00
22 Devin Harris 3.00 8.00
23 Gary Harris 4.00 10.00
24 Dennis Schroder 4.00 10.00
25 Donatas Motiejunas 3.00 8.00
26 Kent Bazemore 4.00 10.00
27 Raul Neto 3.00 8.00
28 Cristiano Felicio 3.00 8.00
29 Clint Capela 3.00 8.00
30 C.J. McCollum 5.00 12.00
31 Gorgui Dieng 3.00 8.00
32 Tyler Ennis 3.00 8.00
33 Marcelo Huertas 3.00 8.00
34 Ed Davis 3.00 8.00
35 Avery Bradley 4.00 10.00
36 Shabazz Muhammad 4.00 10.00
37 Larry Nance Jr. 4.00 10.00
38 Norman Powell 3.00 8.00
39 Gerald Henderson 3.00 8.00
40 Khris Middleton 4.00 10.00
41 Luis Scola 4.00 10.00
42 Paul Millsap 5.00 12.00
43 Nikola Jokic 15.00 40.00
44 Otto Porter 4.00 10.00
45 DeMarre Carroll 3.00 8.00
46 Jerami Grant 3.00 8.00
47 Andrew Bogut 4.00 10.00
48 Zaza Pachulia 3.00 8.00
49 Goran Dragic 4.00 10.00
50 Sam Dekker 4.00 10.00
51 Salah Mejri 3.00 8.00
52 Boban Marjanovic 3.00 8.00
54 Ian Clark 3.00 8.00
55 Eric Bledsoe 4.00 10.00
56 Emmanuel Mudiay 4.00 10.00
57 Anthony Davis 25.00 60.00
58 Kyrie Irving EXCH 20.00 50.00
59 Kevin Durant 60.00 150.00
60 Andrew Wiggins 20.00 50.00

2016-17 Hoops Hot Signatures Rookies
RANDOM INSERTS IN PACKS
EXCHANGE DEADLINE 4/12/2018
*RED/25: .6X TO 1.5X BASIC
1 Brandon Ingram 60.00 150.00
2 Jaylen Brown 15.00 40.00
3 Dragan Bender 10.00 25.00
4 Kris Dunn 15.00 40.00
5 Buddy Hield 15.00 40.00
6 Jamal Murray 12.00 30.00
7 Marquese Chriss 12.00 30.00
8 Jakob Poeltl 4.00 10.00
9 Thon Maker 15.00 40.00
10 Domantas Sabonis 5.00 12.00
11 Taurean Prince 5.00 12.00
12 Denzel Valentine 4.00 10.00
13 Wade Baldwin IV 3.00 8.00
14 Henry Ellenson 8.00 20.00
15 Malik Beasley 3.00 8.00
16 DeAndre' Bembry 3.00 8.00
17 Malachi Richardson 4.00 10.00
18 T. Luwawu-Cabarrot 6.00 15.00
19 Brice Johnson 3.00 8.00
20 Pascal Siakam 3.00 8.00
21 Skal Labissiere 8.00 20.00
22 Damian Jones 5.00 12.00
23 Deyonta Davis 5.00 12.00
24 Cheick Diallo 3.00 8.00
25 Tyler Ulis 12.00 30.00
26 Patrick McCaw 10.00 25.00
28 Demetrius Jackson 3.00 8.00
29 Kay Felder 3.00 8.00
30 Ivica Zubac 8.00 20.00
31 Malcolm Brogdon 15.00 40.00
32 A.J. Hammons 3.00 8.00
33 Diamond Stone 3.00 8.00
34 Gary Payton II 4.00 10.00
35 Caris LeVert 6.00 15.00
37 Ron Baker 10.00 25.00
39 Ben Bentil 3.00 8.00
40 Anthony Barber 4.00 10.00

2016-17 Hoops Kobe 2K Hoops
RANDOM INSERTS IN PACKS
11 Kobe Bryant 2.00 5.00
12 Kobe Bryant 2.00 5.00
13 Kobe Bryant 2.00 5.00
14 Kobe Bryant 2.00 5.00
15 Kobe Bryant 2.00 5.00
16 Kobe Bryant 2.00 5.00
17 Kobe Bryant 2.00 5.00
18 Kobe Bryant 2.00 5.00
19 Kobe Bryant 2.00 5.00
20 Kobe Bryant 2.00 5.00

2016-17 Hoops Kobe Bryant Tribute
RANDOM INSERT IN PACKS
1 Kobe Bryant 8.00 20.00

2016-17 Hoops Lights Camera Action
RANDOM INSERTS IN PACKS
1 Giannis Antetokounmpo 1.00 2.50
2 Khris Middleton .40 1.00
3 Jimmy Butler .50 1.25
4 Kevin Love .50 1.25
5 Kyrie Irving 1.00 2.50
6 Isaiah Thomas .50 1.25
7 Marcus Smart .40 1.00
8 Chris Paul .60 1.50
9 DeAndre Jordan .50 1.25
10 Marc Gasol .50 1.25
11 Kristaps Porzingis 1.00 2.50
12 Dennis Schroder .40 1.00
13 Paul Millsap .50 1.25
14 Carmelo Anthony .60 1.50
15 Goran Dragic .40 1.00
16 Chris Bosh .50 1.25
17 Reggie Jackson .40 1.00
18 Gordon Hayward .50 1.25
19 DeMarcus Cousins .50 1.25
20 D'Angelo Russell .60 1.50
21 Aaron Gordon .40 1.00
22 Dirk Nowitzki .60 1.50
23 Brook Lopez .40 1.00
24 Emmanuel Mudiay .40 1.00
25 Paul George .60 1.50
26 Jrue Holiday .40 1.00
27 Kentavious Caldwell-Pope .40 1.00
28 Jonas Valanciunas .40 1.00
29 Kyle Lowry .40 1.00
30 James Harden .75 2.00
31 Kawhi Leonard .75 2.00
32 Tony Parker .50 1.25
33 Devin Booker .75 2.00
34 Steven Adams .40 1.00
35 Russell Westbrook 1.25 3.00
36 Andrew Wiggins .75 2.00
37 Damian Lillard 1.00 2.50
38 Klay Thompson .60 1.50
39 Draymond Green .60 1.50
40 John Wall .60 1.50

2016-17 Hoops One on One
RANDOM INSERTS IN PACKS
1 C.Anthony/L.James 2.00 5.00
2 D.Lillard/J.Wall 1.00 2.50
3 K.Towns/A.Davis 1.25 3.00
4 A.Wiggins/J.Parker .75 2.00
5 M.Turner/P.Millsap .50 1.25
6 K.Leonard/J.Harden .75 2.00
7 R.Jackson/R.Westbrook 1.25 3.00
8 D.Nowitzki/K.Porzingis 1.00 2.50
9 S.Curry/B.Griffin 2.00 5.00
10 L.James/D.Green 2.00 5.00

2016-17 Hoops Picture Perfect
RANDOM INSERTS IN PACKS
1 DeAndre Jordan .50 1.25
2 Carmelo Anthony .60 1.50
3 Kyrie Irving 1.00 2.50
4 Rudy Gay .50 1.25
5 Jahlil Okafor .40 1.00
6 Jabari Parker .60 1.50
7 Jordan Clarkson .40 1.00
8 Derrick Rose .60 1.50
9 Isaiah Thomas .50 1.25
10 Gordon Hayward .50 1.25
11 Monta Ellis .40 1.00
12 LaMarcus Aldridge .50 1.25
13 Devin Booker .75 2.00
14 Klay Thompson .60 1.50
15 Zach LaVine .50 1.25
16 Kevin Durant 1.25 3.00
17 C.J. McCollum .40 1.00
18 Dennis Schroder .40 1.00
19 Kenneth Faried .40 1.00
20 Jeremy Lin .50 1.25

2016-17 Hoops Road to the Finals
1-44 PRINT RUN 2016 SER.#'d SETS
45-66 PRINT RUN 999 SER.#'d SETS
67-79 PRINT RUN 499 SER.#'d SETS
80-86 PRINT RUN 199 SER.#'d SETS
RANDOM INSERTS IN PACKS
1 Kyrie Irving R1 1.25 3.00
2 LeBron James R1 2.50 6.00
3 Kevin Love R1 .60 1.50
4 J.R. Smith R1 .50 1.25
5 Al Horford R1 .50 1.25
6 Kyle Korver R1 .50 1.25
7 Isaiah Thomas R1 .60 1.50
8 Marcus Smart R1 .50 1.25
9 Jeff Teague R1 .50 1.25
10 Paul Millsap R1 .60 1.50
11 Luol Deng R1 .50 1.25
12 Dwyane Wade R1 1.00 2.50
13 Jeremy Lin R1 .60 1.50
14 Kemba Walker R1 .60 1.50
15 Marvin Williams R1 .50 1.25
16 Goran Dragic R1 .50 1.25
17 Hassan Whiteside R1 .50 1.25
18 Paul George R1 .75 2.00
19 Jonas Valanciunas R1 .50 1.25
20 Kyle Lowry R1 .50 1.25
21 Ian Mahinmi R1 .40 1.00
22 DeMar DeRozan R1 .60 1.50
23 Myles Turner R1 .50 1.25
24 DeMar DeRozan R1 .60 1.50
25 Stephen Curry R1 2.50 6.00
26 Klay Thompson R1 .75 2.00
27 James Harden R1 1.00 2.50
28 Draymond Green R1 .75 2.00
29 Shaun Livingston R1 .40 1.00
30 Chris Paul R1 .75 2.00
31 DeAndre Jordan R1 .60 1.50
32 Damian Lillard R1 1.25 3.00
33 Al-Farouq Aminu R1 .50 1.25
34 C.J. McCollum R1 .50 1.25
35 Mason Plumlee R1 .50 1.25
36 Russell Westbrook R1 1.50 4.00
37 Raymond Felton R1 .50 1.25
38 Russell Westbrook R1 1.50 4.00
39 Enes Kanter R1 .40 1.00
40 Steven Adams R1 .50 1.25
41 Kawhi Leonard R1 1.00 2.50
42 Patty Mills R1 .60 1.50
43 LaMarcus Aldridge R1 .60 1.50
44 Tony Parker R1 .60 1.50
45 LeBron James R2 3.00 8.00
46 J.R. Smith R2 .60 1.50
47 Channing Frye R2 .60 1.50
48 Kevin Love R2 .75 2.00
49 Goran Dragic R2 .60 1.50
50 Kyle Lowry R2 .60 1.50
51 Jonas Valanciunas R2 .60 1.50
52 Dwyane Wade R2 1.25 3.00
53 DeMar DeRozan R2 .75 2.00
54 Goran Dragic R2 .60 1.50
55 Kyle Lowry R2 .60 1.50
56 Klay Thompson R2 1.00 2.50
57 Draymond Green R2 1.00 2.50
58 Damian Lillard R2 1.50 4.00
59 Stephen Curry R2 3.00 8.00
60 Harrison Barnes R2 .60 1.50
61 LaMarcus Aldridge R2 .75 2.00
62 Russell Westbrook R2 2.00 5.00
63 Kawhi Leonard R2 1.25 3.00
64 Kevin Durant R2 2.00 5.00
65 Steven Adams R2 .60 1.50
66 Kevin Durant R2 2.00 5.00
67 LeBron James CF 4.00 10.00
68 Kyrie Irving CF 2.00 5.00
69 DeMar DeRozan CF 1.00 2.50
70 Kyle Lowry CF .75 2.00
71 Kevin Love CF 1.00 2.50
72 LeBron James CF 4.00 10.00
73 Kevin Durant CF 2.50 6.00
74 Stephen Curry CF 4.00 10.00
75 Russell Westbrook CF 2.50 6.00
76 Serge Ibaka CF .75 2.00
77 Klay Thompson CF 1.25 3.00
78 Draymond Green CF 1.25 3.00
79 Stephen Curry CF 4.00 10.00
80 Shaun Livingston F 20.00 50.00
81 Draymond Green F 8.00 20.00
82 LeBron James F 30.00 80.00
83 Stephen Curry F 10.00 25.00
84 Kyrie Irving F 20.00 50.00
85 LeBron James F 30.00 80.00
86 LeBron James F 30.00 80.00

2016-17 Hoops Rookie Remembrance Memorabilia
RANDOM INSERTS IN PACKS
*PRIME/25: .75X TO 2X BASIC
1 Brandon Knight 2.50 6.00
2 Gorgui Dieng 2.00 5.00
3 Jerami Grant 2.00 5.00
4 Jeff Withey 2.00 5.00
5 Allen Crabbe 2.00 5.00
6 Tyler Zeller 2.50 6.00
7 Derrick Williams 2.00 5.00
8 Isaiah Canaan 2.50 6.00
9 Ryan Kelly 2.00 5.00
10 Dennis Schroder 2.50 6.00
11 E'Twaun Moore 2.00 5.00
12 Andre Roberson 2.00 5.00
13 Shabazz Muhammad 2.50 6.00
14 K.J. McDaniels 2.00 5.00
15 James Young 2.00 5.00
16 Tyler Ennis 2.00 5.00
17 Cody Zeller 2.00 5.00
18 Shane Larkin 2.00 5.00
19 Cleanthony Early 2.00 5.00
20 Kentavious Caldwell-Pope 2.50 6.00
21 Noah Vonleh 2.00 5.00
22 Alex Len 2.00 5.00
23 Nerlens Noel 2.50 6.00
24 T.J. Warren 2.50 6.00
25 Mitch McGary 2.00 5.00
26 C.J. McCollum 2.50 6.00
27 Alec Burks 2.00 5.00
28 Gary Harris 2.50 6.00
29 Julius Randle 3.00 8.00
30 Shabazz Napier 2.00 5.00
31 Otto Porter 2.50 6.00
32 Will Barton 2.00 5.00
33 Joel Embiid 5.00 12.00
34 Tony Snell 2.00 5.00
35 Mason Plumlee 2.50 6.00
36 Doug McDermott 2.50 6.00
37 Nik Stauskas 2.00 5.00
38 Rodney Hood 2.50 6.00
39 Steven Adams 2.50 6.00
40 Aaron Gordon 2.50 6.00
41 Trey Burke 2.00 5.00
42 Ben McLemore 2.00 5.00
43 Jabari Parker 4.00 10.00
44 Michael Carter-Williams 2.00 5.00
45 Victor Oladipo 2.50 6.00
46 Marcus Smart 2.50 6.00
47 Archie Goodwin 2.00 5.00
48 Giannis Antetokounmpo 6.00 15.00
49 Zach LaVine 3.00 8.00
50 Andrew Wiggins 5.00 12.00
51 Aaron Harrison 2.00 5.00
52 Andre Drummond 3.00 8.00
53 Dante Exum 2.50 6.00
54 Elfrid Payton 2.50 6.00
55 Glenn Robinson III 2.00 5.00
56 James Ennis 2.00 5.00
57 Jerian Grant 2.00 5.00
58 Kelly Olynyk 2.00 5.00
59 Kyle Anderson 2.00 5.00
60 Trey Lyles 2.50 6.00

2016-17 Hoops Sparkplugs
RANDOM INSERTS IN PACKS
1 Jamal Crawford .50 1.25
2 Will Barton .30 .75
3 Ryan Anderson .40 1.00
4 Enes Kanter .30 .75
5 Dennis Schroder .40 1.00
6 Evan Turner .30 .75
7 Jeremy Lamb .30 .75
8 Aaron Brooks .30 .75
9 Dwight Powell .30 .75
10 Stanley Johnson .30 .75
11 Andre Iguodala .40 1.00
12 Justise Winslow .40 1.00
13 Victor Oladipo .40 1.00
14 Allen Crabbe .30 .75
15 Cory Joseph .30 .75

2016-17 Hoops Swat Team
RANDOM INSERTS IN PACKS
1 Myles Turner .40 1.00
2 Hassan Whiteside .40 1.00
3 DeAndre Jordan .50 1.25
4 Nerlens Noel .40 1.00
5 Paul Millsap .50 1.25
6 Karl-Anthony Towns 1.25 3.00
7 Rudy Gobert .50 1.25
8 Kristaps Porzingis 1.00 2.50
9 DeMarcus Cousins .50 1.25
10 Robin Lopez .30 .75
11 Jerami Grant .30 .75
12 Anthony Davis 1.00 2.50
13 John Henson .40 1.00
14 Brook Lopez .40 1.00
15 Andrew Bogut .40 1.00

2016-17 Hoops Team Leaders
RANDOM INSERTS IN PACKS
*ARTIST PROOF/25: 1.2X TO 3X BASIC
1 Jahlil Okafor .40 1.00
2 Jimmy Butler .50 1.25
3 Khris Middleton .40 1.00
4 LeBron James 2.00 5.00
5 Isaiah Thomas .50 1.25
6 DeAndre Jordan .50 1.25
7 Zach Randolph .40 1.00
8 Paul Millsap .50 1.25
9 Hassan Whiteside .40 1.00
10 Kemba Walker .50 1.25
11 Rudy Gobert .50 1.25
12 DeMarcus Cousins .50 1.25
13 Kristaps Porzingis 1.00 2.50
14 Julius Randle .50 1.25
15 Elfrid Payton .40 1.00
16 Dirk Nowitzki .60 1.50
17 Brook Lopez .40 1.00
18 Emmanuel Mudiay .40 1.00
19 Paul George .60 1.50
20 Anthony Davis 1.00 2.50
21 Andre Drummond .50 1.25
22 Kyle Lowry .40 1.00
23 James Harden .75 2.00
24 LaMarcus Aldridge .50 1.25
25 Eric Bledsoe .40 1.00
26 Russell Westbrook 1.25 3.00
27 Karl-Anthony Towns 1.25 3.00
28 Damian Lillard 1.00 2.50
29 Stephen Curry 2.00 5.00
30 John Wall .60 1.50

2016-17 Hoops Tip Off
RANDOM INSERTS IN PACKS
1 Warriors/Cavaliers 1.25 3.00
2 Warriors/Thunder .75 2.00
3 Cavaliers/Raptors .75 2.00
4 Thunder/Spurs .75 2.00
5 Warriors/Trail Blazers .75 2.00
6 Cavaliers/Hawks .75 2.00
7 Pacers/Raptors .75 2.00
8 Celtics/Hawks .75 2.00
9 Grizzlies/Spurs .75 2.00
10 K.Bryant/L.James 2.00 5.00
11 Clippers/Bucks .75 2.00
12 Pacers/Heat .75 2.00
13 Nuggets/Timberwolves .75 2.00
14 Pacers/Raptors .75 2.00
15 Lakers/Pacers .75 2.00

1990 Hoops 100 Superstars
This 100-card standard-size set is a partial remake of the 1989-90 Hoops set. The pictures used are the same. This set was primarily sold through the Sears catalog. The backs have a head shot in the same format as the front, as well as biographical and statistical information (only up through the 1988-89 season) on a pale yellow background. However, they differ from the Hoops issue in the yellow coloring on the card fronts and a new card numbering system. The cards are numbered on the back and arranged alphabetically according to teams as follows: Atlanta Hawks (1-4), Boston Celtics (5-8), Charlotte Hornets (9-11), Chicago Bulls (12-15), Cleveland Cavaliers (16-19), Dallas Mavericks (20-23), Denver Nuggets (24-26), Detroit Pistons (27-30), Golden State Warriors (31-34), Houston Rockets (35-38), Indiana Pacers (39-42), Los Angeles Clippers (43-46), Los Angeles Lakers (47-50), Miami Heat (51-53), Milwaukee Bucks (54-57), Minnesota Timberwolves (58-60), New Jersey Nets (61-63), New York Knicks (64-67), Orlando Magic (68-70), Philadelphia 76ers (71-74), Phoenix Suns (75-78), Portland Trail Blazers (79-82), Sacramento Kings (83-85), San Antonio Spurs (86-88), Seattle Supersonics (89-92), Utah Jazz (93-96), and Washington Bullets (97-100).

COMP.FACT SET (100) 6.00 15.00
1 Doc Rivers .20 .50
2 Dominique Wilkins .40 1.00
3 Spud Webb .20 .50
4 Moses Malone .20 .50
5 Reggie Lewis .20 .50
6 Larry Bird .75 2.00
7 Kevin McHale .40 1.00
8 Robert Parish .20 .50
9 Muggsy Bogues .30 .75
10 Rex Chapman .20 .50
11 Kelly Tripucka .07 .10
12 Michael Jordan 2.00 5.00
13 Scottie Pippen .75 2.00
14 John Paxson .15 .40
15 Bill Cartwright .15 .40
16 Mark Price .30 .75
17 Larry Nance .20 .50
18 Hot Rod Williams .07 .10
19 Brad Daugherty .07 .20
20 Derek Harper .20 .50
21 Rolando Blackman .20 .50
22 Sam Perkins .20 .50
23 James Donaldson .07 .10
24 Michael Adams .07 .10
25 Lafayette Lever .07 .10
26 Alex English .20 .50
27 Isiah Thomas .40 1.00
28 Joe Dumars .40 1.00
29 Bill Laimbeer .30 .75
30 Dennis Rodman .50 1.25
31 Mitch Richmond .60 1.50
32 Chris Mullin .30 .75
33 Manute Bol .20 .50
34 Rod Higgins .07 .10
35 Sleepy Floyd .07 .10
36 Otis Thorpe .07 .20
37 Buck Johnson .07 .10
38 Hakeem Olajuwon .40 1.00
39 Vern Fleming .07 .10
40 Reggie Miller .40 1.00
41 Chuck Person .07 .20
42 Rik Smits .30 .75
43 Benoit Benjamin .07 .10
44 Charles Smith .08 .25
45 Gary Grant .07 .10
46 Danny Manning .50 1.25
47 Magic Johnson .60 1.50
48 Byron Scott .20 .50
49 A.C. Green .20 .50
50 James Worthy .30 .75
51 Kevin Edwards .07 .10
52 Rory Sparrow .07 .10
53 Rony Seikaly .07 .20
54 Jay Humphries .07 .10
55 Alvin Robertson .07 .20
56 Ricky Pierce .07 .20
57 Jack Sikma .07 .20
58 Tyrone Corbin .07 .10
59 Sidney Lowe .07 .10
60 Steve Johnson .07 .10
61 Dennis Hopson .07 .10
62 Chris Morris .07 .20
63 Roy Hinson .07 .10
64 Mark Jackson .30 .75
65 Gerald Wilkins .07 .10
66 Charles Oakley .07 .20
67 Patrick Ewing .40 1.00
68 Reggie Theus .20 .50
69 Sam Vincent .07 .10
70 Terry Catledge .07 .10
71 Hersey Hawkins .30 .75
72 Johnny Dawkins .07 .10
73 Charles Barkley .40 1.00
74 Mike Gminski .07 .20
75 Kevin Johnson .40 1.00
76 Jeff Hornacek .40 1.00
77 Tom Chambers .20 .50
78 Eddie Johnson .07 .20
79 Terry Porter .20 .50
80 Clyde Drexler .40 1.00
81 Jerome Kersey .07 .10
82 Kevin Duckworth .07 .10
83 Danny Ainge .30 .75
84 Rodney McCray .07 .10
85 Wayman Tisdale .20 .50
86 Willie Anderson .07 .20
87 Terry Cummings .15 .40
88 David Robinson .75 2.00
89 Dale Ellis .07 .20
90 Derrick McKey .07 .20
91 Xavier McDaniel .07 .10
92 Michael Cage .07 .10
93 John Stockton .60 1.50
94 Karl Malone .60 1.50
95 Thurl Bailey .07 .10
96 Mark Eaton .07 .20
97 Jeff Malone .07 .10
98 Darrell Walker .07 .10
99 Bernard King .20 .50
100 John Williams .07 .20

1991 Hoops 100 Superstars
This 100-card set is a partial remake of the 1990-91 Hoops set, and it was primarily sold through the Sears catalog. The standard-size cards use the same pictures. The backs have a color headshot, with biographical and statistical information (only up through the 1989-90 season) in a basketball lane format. However, these cards differ from the regular Hoops issue in the gold coloring on the card fronts and a new numbering system. The players are arranged alphabetically within teams, and the teams are arranged alphabetically as follows: Atlanta Hawks (1-4), Boston Celtics (5-9), Charlotte Hornets (10-11), Chicago Bulls (12-16), Cleveland Cavaliers (17-19), Dallas Mavericks (20-24), Denver Nuggets (25-26), Detroit Pistons (27-31), Golden State Warriors (32-34), Houston Rockets (35-38), Indiana Pacers (39-41), Los Angeles Clippers (42-45), Los Angeles Lakers (46-51), Miami Heat (52-54), Milwaukee Bucks (55-57), Minnesota Timberwolves (58-60), New Jersey Nets (61-63), New York Knicks (64-67), Orlando Magic (68-70), Philadelphia 76ers (71-74), Phoenix Suns (75-79), Portland Trail Blazers (80-83), Sacramento Kings (84-85), San Antonio Spurs (86-90), Seattle Supersonics (91-93), Utah Jazz (94-97), and Washington Bullets (98-100).

COMP.FACT SET (100) 20.00 50.00
1 Moses Malone .40 1.00
2 Doc Rivers .40 1.00
3 Spud Webb .25 .60
4 Dominique Wilkins 1.25 3.00
5 Larry Bird 2.50 6.00
6 Reggie Lewis .40 1.00
7 Kevin McHale .50 1.25
8 Robert Parish .40 1.00
9 Brian Shaw .25 .60
10 Muggsy Bogues .40 1.00
11 Johnny Newman .15 .40
12 Horace Grant .40 1.00
13 Michael Jordan 6.00 15.00
14 Scottie Pippen 2.00 5.00
15 Brad Daugherty .15 .40
16 Craig Ehlo .15 .40
17 Larry Nance .40 1.00
18 Mark Price .60 1.50
19 Hot Rod Williams .15 .40
20 Rolando Blackman .40 1.00
21 James Donaldson .15 .40
22 Derek Harper .40 1.00
23 Fat Lever .15 .40
24 Roy Tarpley .15 .40
25 Michael Adams .15 .40
26 Orlando Woolridge .15 .40
27 Joe Dumars .75 2.00
28 Bill Laimbeer .75 2.00
29 Vinnie Johnson .40 1.00
30 Dennis Rodman 1.25 3.00
31 Isiah Thomas 1.25 3.00
32 Chris Mullin .75 2.00
33 Tim Hardaway .75 2.00
34 Mitch Richmond .75 2.00
35 Sleepy Floyd .15 .40
36 Hakeem Olajuwon 1.00 2.50
37 Kenny Smith .40 1.00
38 Otis Thorpe .25 .60
39 Reggie Miller 1.25 3.00
40 Chuck Person .15 .40
41 Detlef Schrempf .30 .75
42 Danny Manning .30 .75
43 Ken Norman .15 .40
44 Ron Harper .40 1.00
45 Charles Smith .15 .40
46 Vlade Divac .40 1.00
47 A.C. Green .40 1.00
48 Magic Johnson 2.00 5.00
49 Byron Scott .60 1.50
50 James Worthy .75 2.00
51 Sam Perkins .30 .75
52 Rony Seikaly .40 1.00
53 Sherman Douglas .15 .40
54 Glen Rice .75 2.00
55 Jay Humphries .15 .40
56 Alvin Robertson .15 .40
57 Jack Sikma .15 .40
58 Tony Campbell .15 .40
59 Tyrone Corbin .15 .40
60 Pooh Richardson .15 .40
61 Roy Hinson .15 .40
62 Chris Morris .15 .40
63 Reggie Theus .30 .75
64 Maurice Cheeks .30 .75
65 Patrick Ewing 1.00 2.50
66 Mark Jackson .40 1.00
67 Charles Oakley .25 .60
68 Nick Anderson .25 .60
69 Terry Catledge .15 .40
70 Scott Skiles .30 .75
71 Charles Barkley 1.50 4.00
72 Johnny Dawkins .25 .60
73 Hersey Hawkins .25 .60
74 Rick Mahorn .15 .40
75 Tom Chambers .25 .60
76 Jeff Hornacek .40 1.00
77 Kevin Johnson .40 1.00
78 Dan Majerle .40 1.00
79 Mark West .15 .40
80 Clyde Drexler 1.25 3.00
81 Terry Porter .20 .50
82 Jerome Kersey .15 .40
83 Buck Williams .30 .75
84 Antoine Carr .15 .40
85 Wayman Tisdale .15 .40
86 Willie Anderson .15 .40
87 Terry Cummings .25 .60
88 Paul Pressey .15 .40
89 David Robinson 2.00 5.00
90 Rod Strickland .25 .60
91 Michael Cage .15 .40
92 Shawn Kemp .75 2.00
93 Derrick McKey .15 .40
94 Thurl Bailey .15 .40
95 Jeff Malone .15 .40
96 Karl Malone 1.50 4.00
97 John Stockton 2.00 5.00
98 Harvey Grant .15 .40
99 Bernard King .30 .75
100 Darrell Walker .15 .40

1992 Hoops 100 Superstars
This 100-card standard-size set is a partial remake of the 1991-92 Hoops set, and it was primarily sold through the Sears catalog. It is by far the toughest of the Hoops 100 Superstars sets issued between 1990 and 1992. The cards feature color action player photos framed by team color-coded borders against a copper card face. The player's name appears in the copper margin at the top. The horizontal backs are white and display a small player picture framed in the team's primary color. Biographical information appears below the photo. The player's college statistics and NBA record are included along with career highlights. The cards are numbered on the back, grouped alphabetically within teams, and checklisted below according to teams as follows: Atlanta Hawks (1-3), Boston Celtics (4-8), Charlotte Hornets (9-12), Chicago Bulls (13-16), Cleveland Cavaliers (17-20), Dallas Mavericks (21-23), Denver Nuggets (24-26), Detroit Pistons (27-30), Golden State Warriors (31-33), Houston Rockets (34-36), Indiana Pacers (37-39), Los Angeles Clippers (40-43), Los Angeles Lakers (44-49), Miami Heat (50-52), Milwaukee Bucks (53-56), Minnesota Timberwolves (57-60), New Jersey Nets (61-63), New York Knicks (64-68), Orlando Magic (69-71), Philadelphia 76ers (72-75), Phoenix Suns (76-78), Portland Trail Blazers (79-81), Sacramento Kings (82-85), San Antonio Spurs (86-89), Seattle Supersonics (90-92), Utah Jazz (93-96), and Washington Bullets (97-100).

COMP.FACT SET (100) 50.00 125.00
1 Rumeal Robinson .25 .60
2 Dominique Wilkins 2.50 6.00
3 Kevin Willis .50 1.25
4 Larry Bird 6.00 15.00
5 Dee Brown .25 .60
6 Kevin Gamble .25 .60
7 Kevin McHale 1.50 4.00
8 Robert Parish 1.00 2.50
9 Dell Curry .25 .60
10 Muggsy Bogues 1.00 2.50
11 Kendall Gill .50 1.25
12 Johnny Newman .25 .60
13 Horace Grant 1.00 2.50
14 Michael Jordan 10.00 25.00
15 John Paxson 1.00 2.50
16 Scottie Pippen 4.00 10.00
17 Brad Daugherty .25 .60
18 Larry Nance .60 1.50
19 Mark Price 1.00 2.50
20 Hot Rod Williams .25 .60
21 Rolando Blackman .75 2.00
22 Derek Harper .75 2.00
23 Rodney McCray .25 .60
24 Chris Jackson .25 .60
25 Todd Lichti .25 .60
26 Orlando Woolridge .25 .60
27 Joe Dumars 1.25 3.00
28 Bill Laimbeer 1.00 2.50
29 Dennis Rodman 3.00 8.00
30 Isiah Thomas 2.50 6.00
31 Tim Hardaway 1.50 4.00
32 Sarunas Marciulionis .50 1.25
33 Chris Mullin 1.25 3.00
34 Hakeem Olajuwon 2.00 5.00
35 Kenny Smith .50 1.25
36 Otis Thorpe .50 1.25
37 Reggie Miller 2.00 5.00
38 Chuck Person .25 .60
39 Detlef Schrempf .50 1.25
40 Ron Harper .75 2.00
41 Danny Manning .75 2.00
42 Ken Norman .25 .60
43 Charles Smith .25 .60
44 Vlade Divac .75 2.00
45 A.C. Green .75 2.00
46 Magic Johnson 5.00 12.00
47 Sam Perkins .75 2.00
48 Byron Scott .75 2.00
49 James Worthy 1.50 4.00
50 Kevin Edwards .25 .60
51 Glen Rice 1.00 2.50
52 Rony Seikaly .25 .60
53 Dale Ellis .25 .60
54 Jay Humphries .25 .60
55 Moses Malone .75 2.00
56 Alvin Robertson .25 .60
57 Tony Campbell .25 .60
58 Sam Mitchell .25 .60
59 Pooh Richardson .25 .60
60 Felton Spencer .25 .60
61 Mookie Blaylock .50 1.25
62 Sam Bowie .50 1.25
63 Derrick Coleman .50 1.25
64 Patrick Ewing 2.00 5.00
65 Xavier McDaniel .25 .60

66 Charles Oakley .50 1.25
67 Kiki Vandeweghe .75 2.00
68 Gerald Wilkins .40 1.00
69 Terry Catledge .25 .60
70 Dennis Scott .40 1.00
71 Scott Skiles .50 1.25
72 Charles Barkley 4.00 10.00
73 Johnny Dawkins .25 .60
74 Armon Gilliam .25 .60
75 Hersey Hawkins .50 1.25
76 Tom Chambers .75 2.00
77 Jeff Hornacek .75 2.00
78 Kevin Johnson 1.00 2.50
79 Clyde Drexler 2.50 6.00
80 Jerome Kersey .50 1.25
81 Terry Porter .40 1.00
82 Mitch Richmond 1.25 3.00
83 Lionel Simmons .25 .60
84 Wayman Tisdale .25 .60
85 Spud Webb .75 2.00
86 Antoine Carr .25 .60
87 Sean Elliott 1.00 2.50
88 David Robinson 4.00 10.00
89 Rod Strickland .25 .60
90 Shawn Kemp 2.00 5.00
91 Gary Payton 2.00 5.00
92 Ricky Pierce .25 .60
93 Blue Edwards .25 .60
94 Jeff Malone .25 .60
95 Karl Malone 5.00 12.00
96 John Stockton 6.00 15.00
97 Michael Adams .25 .60
98 Pervis Ellison .25 .60
99 Harvey Grant .25 .60
100 Bernard King .75 2.00

1990 Hoops Action Photos

These large action photos are taken from the NBA's official photo library and were primarily sold through retail outlets and toy stores. Original suggested retail price was $1.49 per card, but the photos did not sell well and were eventually closed out nationwide at around twenty-five cents each. The fronts feature an approximately 8" by 10" borderless color glossy player photo with biographical information, statistics, and career highlights on the back. The team logo, player's name, and NBA logo appear in different color stripes below each picture. Each photo is individually wrapped and is accompanied by an offer to order five-photo team sets for $7.50 each. The complete set includes a special "Superstar Set" (1-22) and five players from each of the NBA's 27 teams. These unnumbered photos are checklisted below alphabetically according to teams as follows: Atlanta (23-27), Boston (28-32), Charlotte (33-37), Chicago (38-42), Cleveland (43-47), Dallas (48-52), Denver (53-57), Detroit (58-62), Golden State (63-67), Houston (68-72), Indiana (73-77), LA. Clippers (78-82), L.A. Lakers (83-87), Miami (88-92), Milwaukee (93-97), Minnesota (98-102), New Jersey (103-107), New York (108-112), Orlando (113-117), Philadelphia (118-122), Phoenix (123-127), Portland (128-132), Sacramento (133-137), San Antonio (138-142), Seattle (143-147), Utah (148-152), and Washington (153-157).

COMPLETE SET (160) 30.00 75.00
1 Michael Adams .50 1.25
2 Danny Ainge .50 1.25
3 Willie Anderson .50 1.25
4 Michael Ansley .50 1.25
5 Thurl Bailey .50 1.25
6 Charles Barkley .75 2.00
7 Charles Barkley .75 2.00
8 John Battle .50 1.25
9 Larry Bird 1.50 4.00
10 Larry Bird 1.50 4.00
11 Rolando Blackman .50 1.25
12 Muggsy Bogues .50 1.25
13 Manute Bol .50 1.25
14 Mark Bryant .50 1.25
15 Michael Cage .50 1.25
16 Tony Campbell .50 1.25
17 Bill Cartwright .50 1.25
18 Terry Catledge .50 1.25
19 Tom Chambers .50 1.25
20 Tom Chambers .50 1.25
21 Rex Chapman .50 1.25
22 Maurice Cheeks .50 1.25
23 Lester Conner .50 1.25
24 Michael Cooper .50 1.25
25 Tyrone Corbin .50 1.25
26 Dave Corzine .50 1.25
27 Terry Cummings .50 1.25
28 Dell Curry .50 1.25
29 Brad Daugherty .50 1.25
30 Brad Davis .50 1.25
31 Johnny Dawkins .50 1.25
32 James Donaldson .50 1.25
33 Sherman Douglas .50 1.25
34 Clyde Drexler .75 2.00
35 Clyde Drexler .75 2.00
36 Kevin Duckworth .50 1.25
37 Joe Dumars .50 1.25
38 Joe Dumars .50 1.25
39 Mark Eaton .50 1.25
40 Scottie Pippen 1.50 4.00
40 Kevin Edwards .50 1.25
41 Blue Edwards .50 1.25
42 Craig Ehlo .50 1.25
43 Sean Elliott .75 2.00
44 Dale Ellis .50 1.25
45 Dale Ellis .50 1.25
46 Alex English .50 1.25
47 Alex English .50 1.25
48 Patrick Ewing .75 2.00
49 Patrick Ewing .75 2.00
50 Vern Fleming .50 1.25
51 Mike Gminski .50 1.25
52 Gary Grant .50 1.25
53 A.C. Green .50 1.25
54 Sidney Green .50 1.25
55 Tim Hardaway 1.25 3.00
56 Derek Harper .50 1.25
57 Ron Harper .50 1.25
58 Hersey Hawkins .50 1.25
59 Rod Higgins .50 1.25
60 Roy Hinson .50 1.25
61 Dennis Hopson .50 1.25
62 Jeff Hornacek .50 1.25
63 Jay Humphries .50 1.25
64 Mark Jackson .50 1.25
65 Mark Jackson .50 1.25
66 Buck Johnson .50 1.25
67 Dennis Johnson .50 1.25
68 Eddie Johnson .50 1.25
69 Kevin Johnson .50 1.25
70 Magic Johnson 1.25 3.00
71 Magic Johnson 1.25 3.00
72 Charles Jones .50 1.25
73 Michael Jordan 3.00 8.00
74 Michael Jordan 3.00 8.00
75 Jerome Kersey .50 1.25
76 Bernard King .50 1.25
77 Stacey King .50 1.25
78 Bill Laimbeer .50 1.25
79 Fat Lever .50 1.25
80 Reggie Lewis .50 1.25
81 Grant Long .50 1.25
82 Sidney Lowe .50 1.25
83 John Lucas .50 1.25
84 Rick Mahorn .50 1.25
85 Jeff Malone .50 1.25
86 Karl Malone .75 2.00
87 Karl Malone .75 2.00
88 Moses Malone .50 1.25
89 Moses Malone .50 1.25
90 Danny Manning .50 1.25
91 Rodney McCray .50 1.25
92 Xavier McDaniel .50 1.25
93 Kevin McHale .50 1.25
94 Kevin McHale .50 1.25
95 Derrick McKey .50 1.25
96 Nate McMillan .50 1.25
97 Reggie Miller .75 2.00
98 Sam Mitchell .50 1.25
99 Chris Morris .50 1.25
100 Chris Mullin .50 1.25
101 Chris Mullin .50 1.25
102 Larry Nance .50 1.25
103 Johnny Newman .50 1.25
104 Ken Norman .50 1.25
105 Charles Oakley .50 1.25
106 Hakeem Olajuwon .75 2.00
107 Hakeem Olajuwon .75 2.00
108 Robert Parish .50 1.25
109 John Paxson .50 1.25
110 Sam Perkins .50 1.25
111 Chuck Person .50 1.25
112 Ricky Pierce .50 1.25
114 Terry Porter .50 1.25
115 Paul Pressey .50 1.25
116 Harold Pressley .50 1.25
117 Mark Price .50 1.25
118 Mark Price .50 1.25
119 Blair Rasmussen .50 1.25
120 J.R. Reid .50 1.25
121 Jerry Reynolds .50 1.25
122 Pooh Richardson .50 1.25
123 Mitch Richmond .50 1.25
124 Doc Rivers .50 1.25
125 Alvin Robertson .50 1.25
126 David Robinson 1.25 3.00
127 David Robinson 1.25 3.00
128 Dennis Rodman 1.25 3.00
129 John Salley .50 1.25
130 Danny Schayes .50 1.25
131 Byron Scott .50 1.25
132 Rony Seikaly .50 1.25
133 Charles Shackleford .50 1.25
134 Jack Sikma .50 1.25
135 Charles Smith .50 1.25
136 Kenny Smith .50 1.25
137 Rik Smits .50 1.25
138 Rory Sparrow .50 1.25
139 John Stockton .75 2.00
140 John Stockton .75 2.00
141 Reggie Theus .50 1.25
142 Isiah Thomas .50 1.25
143 Isiah Thomas .50 1.25
144 LaSalle Thompson .50 1.25
145 Otis Thorpe .50 1.25
146 Wayman Tisdale .50 1.25
147 Kelly Tripucka .50 1.25
148 Sam Vincent .50 1.25
149 Darrell Walker .50 1.25
150 Spud Webb .50 1.25
151 Mark West .50 1.25
152 Mitchell Wiggins .50 1.25
153 Dominique Wilkins .50 1.25
154 Dominique Wilkins .50 1.25
155 Gerald Wilkins .50 1.25
156 John Williams .50 1.25
157 John Williams .50 1.25
158 James Worthy .50 1.25
159 James Worthy .50 1.25
160 Michael Jordan
Driving to basket

2011 Hoops All-Star Game

These cards were distributed via a wrapper redemption during the NBA All-Star Jam Session in Los Angeles in February 2011. The card fronts feature the All-Star logo.

COMPLETE SET (4) 10.00 20.00
AS-BG Blake Griffin 5.00 12.00
AS-JW John Wall 6.00 15.00
AS-KB Kobe Bryant 5.00 12.00
AS-KD Kevin Durant 2.00 5.00

1989-90 Hoops All-Star Panels

This 24-card set commemorates the February 1990 NBA All-Star Game and Weekend in Miami. It was issued in four panels of six cards each, with two cards per row inserted in the official All-Star Game program. The number listed adjacent to the player's name below is the panel number for reference although the panels themselves are not numbered. Reportedly 15,000 sets were produced. After perforation, the cards measure the standard size. The front features a color action player photo, entramed by a red arch with white stars on white card stock. Inside a thin red border the back has player statistics and career summary. The cards are numbered on the back with the same numbers as in the regular series, but the numbers are not consecutive. The cards are exactly identical to the regular issue All-Star cards and hence have the same values in the same shape. Keeping the insert intact is highly recommended.

COMPLETE SET (4) 8.00 20.00
1 Panel 1 3.00 8.00
2 Panel 2 3.00 8.00
3 Panel 3 3.00 8.00
4 Panel 4 4.00 10.00

1990-91 Hoops All-Star Panels

These five panels were issued one per All-Star program at the 1991 NBA All-Star game. Each perforated sheet consists of six standard-size cards, arranged in three rows with two cards per row. The color action player photos on the fronts were taken during the 1990 All-Star game in Miami on Feb. 11, 1990. These pictures have the typical Hoops "basketball lane" design and are gold-bordered. Cards picture All-Stars on the East squad are accented by a blue star and a blue stripe carrying a row ofwhite stars; likewise, cards picturing All-Stars on the West squad have a red star and stripe. On a white background with a gray star, the backs carry statistics and player profile. Neither the panels nor the cards are numbered. The cards are checklisted below according to panels, beginning in the upper left corner.

COMPLETE SET (5) 10.00 25.00
1 Panel 1 2.50 6.00
2 Panel 2 3.00 8.00
3 Panel 3 1.50 4.00
4 Panel 4 2.50 6.00
5 Panel 5 3.00 8.00

1989-90 Hoops Announcers

In 1989-90, Hoops issued cards for use as business cards to certain announcers (broadcasters). Reportedly between 200 and 1000 cards were printed of each announcer. Reportedly Rick Barry signed 100 of his cards for sale into the organized hobby. The standard-size cards have the same design as the regular issue, with a color photo in the shape of basketball lane. The back contains biographical information. We have checklisted these unnumbered cards below in alphabetical order.

COMP.SET w/o BARRY (40) 50.00 120.00
1 Al Albert 2.00 5.00
2 Marv Albert 3.00 8.00
3 Steve Albert 2.00 5.00
4 John Andarise 2.00 5.00
5 Jim Barnett 2.00 5.00
6A Rick Barry
6B Rick Barry AU 75.00 200.00
7 Ron Boone 2.00 5.00
8 Hubie Brown 3.00 8.00
9 James Brown 2.00 5.00
10 Larry Burnett 2.00 5.00
11 Kevin Calabro 2.00 5.00
12 Jim Durham 2.00 5.00
13 Kevin Harlan 2.00 5.00
14 Bill Hazen 2.00 5.00
15 Chick Hearn 8.00 20.00
16 Steve Holman 2.00 5.00
17 Rod Hundley 3.00 8.00
18 Jim Irwin 2.00 5.00
19 Dan Issel 3.00 8.00
20 Steve Jones 2.00 5.00
21 Clark Kelllogg 2.00 5.00
22 John Kerr 3.00 8.00
23 Pat Lafferty 2.00 5.00
24 Stu Lantz 2.00 5.00
25 Steve Martin 2.00 5.00
26 Al McCoy 2.00 5.00
27 John McGlocklin 2.00 5.00
28 Gil McGregor 2.00 5.00
29 Brent Musburger 2.00 5.00
30 Pat O'Brien 2.00 5.00
31 Greg Papa 2.00 5.00
32 Jim Paschke 2.00 5.00
33 Steve Physioc 2.00 5.00
34A Bill Raftery 2.00 5.00
34B Bill Raftery 2.00 5.00
CBS Sports
35 Eric Reid 2.00 5.00
36 Sam Smith 2.00 5.00
37 Dick Stockton 2.00 5.00
38 Ron Thulin 2.00 5.00
39 Dick Van Arsdale 2.00 5.00
40 Lesley Visser 2.00 5.00

1990-91 Hoops Announcers

The 1990-91 edition of Hoops Announcer or Broadcaster cards feature 57 announcers from various radio and TV stations. The main radio announcer for each NBA team is represented, and the cards were given to announcers to serve as business cards. The standard-size cards feature a color shot of the announcer inside a basketball lane design. The card face is silver, and the color stripe below the picture intersects a circular-shaped logo with the TV or radio station call letters. The back has biographical information on the sportcaster and a TV or radio advertisement. The cards are unnumbered and checklisted below in alphabetical order. Production quantities for each card were reportedly 250 to 1000 per announcer.

COMPLETE SET (58) 900.00 1800.00
1 Marv Albert 15.00 40.00
2 Steve Albert 12.50 30.00
3 John Andarise 12.50 30.00
4 Jerry Baker 12.50 30.00
5 Jim Barnett 12.50 30.00
6 Jim Barniak 12.50 30.00
7 Rick Barry 60.00 150.00
8 Ron Boone 12.50 30.00
9 Mark Boyle 12.50 30.00
10 Hubie Brown 20.00 50.00
11 Kevin Calabro 12.50 30.00
12 Harry Caray III 12.50 30.00
13 Skip Caray 20.00 50.00
14 Doug Collins 20.00 50.00
15 Chet Coppock 12.50 30.00
16 Bob Costas 25.00 60.00
17 Jim Durham 12.50 30.00
18 Dick Enberg 25.00 60.00
19 Jim Foley 12.50 30.00
20 Mike Fratello 20.00 50.00
21 Gary Gerould 12.50 30.00
22 Jack Givens 15.00 40.00
23 Mike Gorman 12.50 30.00
24 Tom Hanneman 12.50 30.00
25 Kevin Harlan 12.50 30.00
26 Dick Harter 12.50 30.00
27 Fred Hickman 15.00 40.00
28 Steve Holman 12.50 30.00
29 Jay Howard 12.50 30.00
30 Jim Irwin 12.50 30.00
31 Dan Issel 50.00 120.00
32 Ernie Johnson Jr. 25.00 60.00
33 Steve Jones 15.00 40.00
34 Johnny (Red) Kerr 24.00 60.00
35 Jeff Kingery 12.50 30.00
36 Ralph Lawler 15.00 40.00
37 Joe McConnell 12.50 30.00
38 L. Allen McCoy 12.50 30.00
39 Jonathan Miller 12.50 30.00
40 Bob Neal 12.50 30.00
41 Glenn Ordway 12.50 30.00
42 M. John Proctor 12.50 30.00
43 Ed Randall 12.50 30.00
44 Mike Rice 12.50 30.00
45 Pat Riley 50.00 120.00
46 Andrew Rosenberg 12.50 30.00
47 Tommy Roy 12.50 30.00
48 Tim James Roye 12.50 30.00
49 Craig Sager 20.00 50.00
(Play-by-play)
50 Craig Sager 20.00 50.00
(Biography)
51 Bill Schonely 12.50 30.00
52 Charles Slowes 12.50 30.00
53 David Steele 12.50 30.00
54 Hannah Storm 20.00 50.00
55 Ron Thulin 12.50 30.00
56 Gerry Vaillancourt 12.50 30.00
57 Pete Van Wieren 12.50 30.00
58 William Worrell 12.50 30.00

1991 Hoops Larry Bird Video

This standard-size card was enclosed in cellophane and included as an insert with the "Larry Bird - Basketball Legend" VHS video tape. The front has a color photo of Bird shooting the basketball, with the Boston Garden parquet floor serving as the border on the front and back. The lower right corner of the picture is cut off to allow space for the team logo. The back has a color close-up photo, a street sign from the intersection of Main St. and Larry Bird Blvd., and career highlights within a drawing of Indiana's borders. The NBA Hoops logo appears on the card front. The card is unnumbered.

NNO Larry Bird 6.00 15.00

1990-91 Hoops CollectABooks

These card-size "books" measure approximately 2 1/2" by 3 3/8". The set was issued in four different boxes, with 12 different mini-books in each box. Each book consists of eight pages, including the front and back covers. The front cover features a borderless color player photo, with the player's above the picture in the team's color stripe. Pages 2 and 3 have a color "mug shot" of the player, biographical information, team logo, and career highlights. A color stripe runs across the bottom of each page, with the team name in white lettering. Pages 4 and 5 have a "personal story" about the player. Page 6 has career statistics (college and pro), while page 7 features a borderless color action photo. The top half of the back cover has another color player photo, with a player quote below the picture. An additional special collect-a-book chronicles the Detroit Piston's march to consecutive NBA World Championships. It was available free to consumers only through an offer on second series 1990-91 Hoops packs; fans could receive two booklets free, and additional booklets could be purchased for 50 cents each. The eight-page Pistons booklet features four color photos of the Pistons' top players, a three-page story recapping the team's 1989 and 1990 championship seasons, and playoff statistics for each player. The front cover shows several Piston players with the Larry O'Brien Trophy, while the back cover features Thomas and Dumars, MVP's of the 1989 and 1990 NBA Finals respectively.

COMPLETE SET (48) 6.00 15.00
1 Sam Bowie .05 .15
2 Tom Chambers .10 .30
3 Clyde Drexler .40 1.00
4 Michael Jordan 2.00 5.00
5 Karl Malone .60 1.50
6 Kevin McHale .20 .50
7 Reggie Miller .40 1.00
8 Mark Price .20 .50
9 Mitch Richmond .40 1.00
10 Doc Rivers .10 .30
11 Rony Seikaly .10 .30
12 Wayman Tisdale .05 .15
13 Charles Barkley .40 1.00
14 Terry Cummings .10 .30
15 Patrick Ewing .40 1.00
16 Terry Porter .10 .30
17 Danny Manning .10 .30
18 Larry Nance .10 .30
19 Robert Parish .10 .30
20 Chuck Person .10 .30
21 Ricky Pierce .05 .15
22 John Stockton .60 1.50
23 Isiah Thomas .20 .50
24 Spud Webb .10 .30
25 Michael Adams .05 .15
26 Muggsy Bogues .10 .30
27 Joe Dumars .20 .50
28 Hersey Hawkins .10 .30
29 Magic Johnson .50 1.25
30 Bernard King .10 .30
31 Chris Mullin .20 .50
32 Charles Oakley .10 .30
33 Alvin Robertson .05 .15
34 David Robinson .50 1.25
35 Dominique Wilkins .30 .75
36 Buck Williams .10 .30
37 Larry Bird .75 2.00
38 Rolando Blackman .05 .15
39 Mark Eaton .10 .30
40 Kevin Johnson .20 .50
41 J.R. Reid .05 .15
42 Xavier McDaniel .05 .15
43 Hakeem Olajuwon .40 1.00
44 Scottie Pippen .60 1.50
45 Pooh Richardson .10 .30
46 Dennis Rodman .50 1.25
47 Charles Smith .05 .15
48 James Worthy .20 .50
XX Detroit Pistons .20 .50

1999-00 Hoops Decade

The 1999-00 Hoops Decade set was released as a 180-card set. There was only one series offered. Each pack contained 10 cards and carried a suggested retail price of $1.49.

COMPLETE SET (180) 20.00 40.00
1 David Robinson .30 .75
2 Mookie Blaylock .12 .30
3 Jaren Jackson .12 .30
4 Andre Miller RC .40 1.00
5 Michael Olowokandi .12 .30
6 Glenn Robinson .15 .40
7 Steve Smith .15 .40
8 Eric Snow .15 .40
9 Antoine Walker .20 .50
10 Nick Anderson .12 .30
11 Jonathan Bender RC .20 .50
12 Sean Elliott .20 .50
13 Danny Fortson .12 .30
14 Adonal Foyle .12 .30
15 Richard Hamilton RC .40 1.00
16 Shawn Kemp .20 .50
17 Christian Laettner .15 .40
18 Rashard Lewis .20 .50
19 Danny Manning .15 .40
20 Mitch Richmond .20 .50
21 Shawn Bradley .12 .30
22 Tim Duncan .40 1.00
23 Tim Hardaway .20 .50
24 Antawn Jamison .20 .50
25 Jeff Hornacek .15 .40
26 Jumaine Jones RC .15 .40
27 Corey Maggette RC .30 .75
28 Vitaly Potapenko .12 .30
29 Jerry Stackhouse .20 .50
30 Jason Terry RC .30 .75
31 Baron Davis RC .50 1.25
32 Matt Harpring .12 .30
33 Glen Rice .20 .50
34 Vladimir Stepania .12 .30
35 Jayson Williams .12 .30
36 Wally Szczerbiak RC .40 1.00
37 Michael Doleac .12 .30
38 Hersey Hawkins .12 .30
39 Allan Houston .15 .40
40 Hakeem Olajuwon .25 .60
41 Damon Stoudamire .15 .40
42 Jelani McCoy .12 .30
43 A.Radojevic RC .12 .30
44 Cal Bowdler RC .12 .30
45 Tyronn Lue .12 .30
46 Andrae Patterson .12 .30
47 Karl Malone .25 .60
48 Alonzo Mourning .25 .60
49 Vince Carter .40 1.00
50 Darrell Armstrong .12 .30
51 Terrell Brandon .12 .30
52 John Celestand RC .12 .30
53 Grant Hill .25 .60
54 Stephon Marbury .15 .40
55 Tracy McGrady .30 .75
56 Reggie Miller .20 .50
57 Clifford Robinson .12 .30
58 Arvydas Sabonis .15 .40
59 William Avery RC .15 .40
60 Calbert Cheaney .12 .30
61 Jermaine Jackson RC .20 .50
62 Allen Iverson .40 1.00
63 Larry Johnson .20 .50
64 Toni Kukoc .20 .50
65 Raef LaFrentz .15 .40
66 Isaiah Rider .15 .40
67 Jeff Foster RC .20 .50
68 Juwan Howard .15 .40
69 Kerry Kittles .12 .30
70 Brevin Knight .12 .30
71 Voshon Lenard .12 .30
72 Latrell Sprewell .20 .50
73 Maurice Taylor .12 .30
74 Chris Webber .20 .50
75 Jerome Williams .12 .30
76 Scott Padgett RC .15 .40
77 Vin Baker .15 .40
78 Chris Childs .12 .30
79 Erick Dampier .12 .30
80 Anfernee Hardaway .30 .75
81 Jamal Mashburn .15 .40
82 Todd Fuller .12 .30
83 Eric Piatkowski .15 .40
84 Gary Trent .12 .30
85 Kevin Garnett .30 .75
86 Chris Mullin .20 .50
87 Charles Oakley .15 .40
88 Detlef Schrempf .15 .40
89 Elton Brand RC .50 1.25
90 Patrick Ewing .25 .60
91 Devean George RC .20 .50
92 Brian Grant .12 .30
93 Larry Hughes .15 .40
94 Dan Majerle .20 .50
95 Shawn Marion RC .40 1.00
96 Cuttino Mobley .12 .30
97 Paul Pierce .25 .60
98 Bryant Reeves .12 .30
99 Keith Van Horn .15 .40
100 Corliss Williamson .12 .30
101 Tariq Abdul-Wahad .12 .30
102 Brent Barry .15 .40
103 Elden Campbell .12 .30
104 Mark Jackson .15 .40
105 Lamond Murray .12 .30
106 Bryon Russell .12 .30
107 Jason Williams .25 .60
108 Ray Allen .20 .50
109 Ron Artest RC .40 1.00
110 Charles Barkley .30 .75
111 Cedric Ceballos .12 .30
112 Jason Kidd .30 .75
113 Donyell Marshall .12 .30
114 John Stockton .25 .60
115 Mike Bibby .20 .50
116 Ricky Davis .20 .50
117 Steve Francis RC .50 1.25
118 Tom Gugliotta .12 .30
119 Laron Profit RC .15 .40
120 Joe Smith .15 .40
121 Doug Christie .15 .40
122 Kenny Anderson .15 .40
123 Michael Dickerson .12 .30
124 Zydrunas Ilgauskas .15 .40
125 Bobby Jackson .12 .30
126 Quincy Lewis RC .12 .30
127 Shandon Anderson .12 .30
128 Bo Outlaw .12 .30
129 Scottie Pippen .30 .75
130 Rodney Rogers .12 .30
131 Rik Smits .20 .50
132 Chauncey Billups .20 .50
133 Chris Crawford .12 .30
134 Kornel David RC .15 .40
135 Tony Delk .12 .30
136 Kendall Gill .12 .30
137 Trajan Langdon RC .20 .50
138 Ron Mercer .15 .40
139 Othella Harrington .12 .30
140 Gheorghe Muresan .12 .30
141 Isaac Austin .12 .30
142 Dion Glover RC .15 .40
143 Avery Johnson .15 .40
144 Antonio McDyess .15 .40
145 Steve Nash .30 .75
146 Tyrone Nesby RC .15 .40
147 Shaquille O'Neal .50 1.25
148 James Posey RC .20 .50
149 Rod Strickland .12 .30
150 Kobe Bryant .75 2.00
151 Michael Finley .20 .50
152 Anthony Mason .12 .30
153 Dikembe Mutombo .20 .50
154 John Starks .15 .40
155 Kenny Thomas RC .20 .50
156 Matt Geiger .12 .30
157 Tim James RC .12 .30
158 Eddie Jones .20 .50
159 Lamar Odom RC .50 1.25
160 Nick Van Exel .15 .40
161 Sam Cassell .15 .40
162 Vonteego Cummings RC .12 .30
163 Lindsey Hunter .12 .30
164 Dirk Nowitzki .40 1.00
165 Gary Payton .20 .50
166 Shareef Abdur-Rahim .15 .40
167 Jalen Rose .15 .40
168 Robert Traylor .12 .30
169 Derek Anderson .12 .30
170 Corey Benjamin .12 .30
171 Marcus Camby .15 .40
172 Vlade Divac .20 .50
173 Mario Elie .12 .30
174 Felipe Lopez .12 .30
175 Rafer Alston RC .25 .60
176 Antonio Davis .12 .30
177 Howard Eisley .12 .30
178 Theo Ratliff .15 .40
179 Tim Thomas .15 .40
180 Rasheed Wallace .20 .50

1999-00 Hoops Decade Hoopla

*HOOPLA: 1.25X TO 3X BASE CARD HI
STATED ODDS 1:3

1999-00 Hoops Decade Hoopla Plus

*PLUS: 6X TO 15X BASE CARD HI
STATED ODDS 1:30

1999-00 Hoops Decade Draft Day Dominance

Randomly inserted in packs at one in thirty-two, this 10 card set features a dominant player from each of the last 10 NBA Draft classes on a card design from the Hoops card of that year. Card backs carry a "DD" prefix.

COMPLETE SET (10) 8.00 20.00
STATED ODDS 1:32
*PARALLEL: .75X TO 2X HI COLUMN
PARALLEL: PRINT RUN 1989 SERIAL #'d SETS
DD1 David Robinson 1.50 4.00
DD2 Gary Payton 1.00 2.50
DD3 Dikembe Mutombo 1.00 2.50
DD4 Shaquille O'Neal 2.50 6.00
DD5 Anfernee Hardaway 1.50 4.00
DD6 Grant Hill 1.25 3.00
DD7 Antonio McDyess .75 2.00
DD8 Kobe Bryant 4.00 10.00
DD9 Keith Van Horn .75 2.00
DD10 Vince Carter 2.00 5.00

1999-00 Hoops Decade Genuine Coverage

Randomly inserted into packs at one in 893, this 10-card insert set features twelve different memorabilia cards featuring pieces of game-worn uniforms from each of the player's early days.

STATED ODDS 1:893
1 Shareef Abdur-Rahim 8.00 20.00
2 Ray Allen 10.00 25.00
3 Patrick Ewing 12.00 30.00
4 Grant Hill 15.00 40.00
5 Juwan Howard 8.00 20.00
6 Antonio McDyess 8.00 20.00
7 Hakeem Olajuwon 12.00 30.00
8 David Robinson 15.00 40.00
9 Keith Van Horn 8.00 20.00
10 Antoine Walker 10.00 25.00

1999-00 Hoops Decade New Style

Randomly inserted in packs at one in eighteen, this 15-card set features 15 rookies who will blend their style of game into the NBA of the new millennium on 100% silver holofoil stmped cards. Card backs carry a "NS" prefix.

COMPLETE SET (15) 4.00 10.00
STATED ODDS 1:18
*PARALLEL: 1X TO 2.5X HI COLUMN
PARALLEL: PRINT RUN 1989 SERIAL #'d SETS
NS1 Steve Francis .75 2.00
NS2 Lamar Odom .75 2.00
NS3 Wally Szczerbiak .60 1.50
NS4 Elton Brand .75 2.00
NS5 Baron Davis .75 2.00
NS6 Corey Maggette .50 1.25
NS7 Trajan Langdon .30 .75
NS8 Cal Bowdler .20 .50
NS9 Richard Hamilton .60 1.50
NS10 Ron Artest .60 1.50
NS11 Jason Terry .50 1.25
NS12 Jonathan Bender .30 .75
NS13 Andre Miller .60 1.50
NS14 Shawn Marion .60 1.50
NS15 William Avery .25 .60

1999-00 Hoops Decade Retrospection Collection

Randomly inserted in packs at 1 in 108, this 10-card set features 10 players on a Skyview design from Hoops' past. Card backs carry a "RC" prefix.

COMPLETE SET (10) 60.00 150.00
STATED ODDS 1:108
PARALLEL: PRINT RUN 89 SER.#'d SETS
RC1 Kevin Garnett 5.00 12.00
RC2 Kobe Bryant 12.00 30.00
RC3 Allen Iverson 6.00 15.00
RC4 Vince Carter 6.00 15.00
RC5 Jason Williams 4.00 10.00
RC6 Ron Mercer 2.50 6.00
RC7 Tim Duncan 6.00 15.00
RC8 Anfernee Hardaway 5.00 12.00
RC9 Scottie Pippen 5.00 12.00
RC10 Shaquille O'Neal 8.00 20.00

1999-00 Hoops Decade Up Tempo

Randomly inserted in packs at one in nine packs, this 15-card set features 15 players that can step up their game at any given moment on 100% silver holofoil stamped cards. Card backs carry a "UT" prefix.

COMPLETE SET (15) 5.00 12.00
STATED ODDS 1:9
*PARALLEL: 2X TO 5X HI COLUMN
PARALLEL: PRINT RUN 1989 SERIAL #'d SETS
UT1 Allen Iverson .75 2.00
UT2 Kevin Garnett .60 1.50
UT3 Shaquille O'Neal 1.00 2.50
UT4 Tim Duncan .75 2.00
UT5 Stephon Marbury .30 .75
UT6 Keith Van Horn .30 .75
UT7 Paul Pierce .50 1.25
UT8 Vince Carter .75 2.00
UT9 Antawn Jamison .40 1.00
UT10 Larry Hughes .30 .75
UT11 Jason Williams .50 1.25
UT12 Antoine Walker .40 1.00
UT13 Grant Hill .50 1.25
UT14 Steve Francis 1.00 2.50
UT15 Lamar Odom 1.00 2.50

2014 Hoops Draft

AW Andrew Wiggins 10.00 25.00
DE Dante Exum 5.00 12.00
DM Doug McDermott 8.00 20.00
JB Jabari Parker 8.00 20.00
JE Joel Embiid 5.00 12.00
JR Julius Randle 6.00 15.00

2013 Hoops Franchise Greats All-Star Game

COMPLETE SET (6) 10.00 25.00
1 Kobe Bryant 6.00 15.00
2 Blake Griffin 3.00 8.00
3 Kevin Durant 5.00 12.00
4 Deron Williams 1.25 3.00
5 James Harden 2.00 5.00
6 Hakeem Olajuwon 2.00 5.00

1993-94 Hoops Gold Medal Bread

These 49 standard-size cards were produced by Hoops for Gold Medal Bread, and were inserted in its products. The card design is nearly identical to the regular 1993-94 Hoops set. The fronts feature borderless glossy color player action shots, with the player's name and team logo appearing in team colors along a ghosted band at the bottom. The back presents a color head shot of the player in a small rectangle bordered with a team color at the upper right. Alongside is his jersey number and position within a team-colored bar. The player's name and a short biography are printed on a hardwood floor design at the top. Below, the player's college and NBA stats, displayed in separate tables on a white background, round out the card. The cards are unnumbered and checklisted below in alphabetical order.

COMPLETE SET (49) 40.00 100.00
1 B.J. Armstrong 1.00 2.50
2 Thurl Bailey 1.00 2.50
3 Rolando Blackman 1.25 3.00
4 Mookie Blaylock 1.00 2.50
5 Muggsy Bogues 1.25 3.00
6 Anthony Bowie 1.00 2.50
7 Chucky Brown 1.00 2.50
8 Dee Brown 1.00 2.50
9 Duane Causwell 1.00 2.50
10 Cedric Ceballos 1.25 3.00
11 Rex Chapman 1.00 2.50
12 Bimbo Coles 1.00 2.50
13 Tyrone Corbin 1.00 2.50
14 Terry Cummings 1.25 3.00
15 Todd Day 1.00 2.50
16 Joe Dumars 1.50 4.00
17 Mark Eaton 1.00 2.50
18 Vern Fleming 1.00 2.50
19 Kevin Gamble 1.00 2.50
20 Kendall Gill 1.00 2.50
21 Tom Gugliotta 1.25 3.00
22 Derek Harper 1.25 3.00
23 Ron Harper 1.25 3.00
24 Hersey Hawkins 1.00 2.50
25 Tyrone Hill 1.00 2.50
26 Adam Keefe 1.00 2.50
27 Shawn Kemp 2.00 5.00
28 Jerome Kersey 1.00 2.50
29 Stacey King 1.00 2.50
30 Luc Longley 1.25 3.00
31 Moses Malone 1.50 4.00
32 Anthony Mason 1.00 2.50
33 Vernon Maxwell 1.00 2.50
34 Xavier McDaniel 1.00 2.50
35 Oliver Miller 1.00 2.50
36 Sam Mitchell 1.00 2.50
37 Chris Morris 1.00 2.50
38 Dikembe Mutombo 1.50 4.00
39 Billy Owens 1.00 2.50
40 Robert Parish 1.50 4.00
41 Sam Perkins 1.00 2.50
42 Olden Polynice 1.00 2.50
43 Terry Porter 1.00 2.50
44 J.R. Reid 1.00 2.50
45 Rony Seikaly 1.00 2.50
46 Lionel Simmons 1.00 2.50
47 Scott Skiles 1.00 2.50
48 Sedale Threatt 1.00 2.50
49 Loy Vaught 1.00 2.50

2000-01 Hoops Hot Prospects

The 2000-01 Hoops Hot Prospects set was released in November 2000 as a 145-card set. The set features 120 Veterans (1-120), and 25 Rookies (121-145) each numbered to 1000. Each pack contained 5 cards, and carried a suggested retail price of $5.99.

COMPLETE SET w/o RC (120) 15.00 40.00
RCs: PRINT RUN 1000 SERIAL #'d SETS
1 Vince Carter .75 2.00
2 Wesley Person .25 .60
3 Juwan Howard .30 .75
4 Rodney Rogers .25 .60
5 Tim Duncan .75 2.00
6 Rasheed Wallace .40 1.00
7 Anthony Peeler .25 .60
8 John Amaechi .25 .60
9 Tim Hardaway .40 1.00
10 Mark Jackson .30 .75
11 Latrell Sprewell .30 .75
12 Kevin Garnett .60 1.50
13 Alonzo Mourning .50 1.25
14 Jerome Williams .25 .60
15 Anfernee Hardaway .60 1.50
16 Clifford Robinson .25 .60
17 Mike Bibby .40 1.00
18 Allen Iverson .75 2.00
19 Terrell Brandon .25 .60
20 Jerry Stackhouse .30 .75
21 Brian Grant .25 .60
22 Lamond Murray .25 .60
23 Nick Anderson .25 .60
24 Alan Henderson .25 .60
25 Bryon Russell .25 .60
26 Elton Brand .40 1.00
27 Antawn Jamison .40 1.00
28 Mitch Richmond .30 .75
29 Marcus Camby .30 .75
30 Raef LaFrentz .25 .60
31 Damon Stoudamire .30 .75
32 Vin Baker .30 .75
33 Allan Houston .30 .75
34 Doug Christie .25 .60
35 Stephon Marbury .30 .75
36 Tim Thomas .25 .60
37 Tracy McGrady .60 1.50
38 Shareef Abdur-Rahim .30 .75
39 Eddie Jones .40 1.00
40 Glenn Robinson .30 .75
41 Sam Cassell .30 .75
42 Dan Majerle .40 1.00
43 Maurice Taylor .25 .60
44 Anthony Mason .25 .60
45 Dirk Nowitzki .60 1.50
46 Kobe Bryant 1.50 4.00
47 Kerry Kittles .25 .60
48 Derrick Coleman .30 .75
49 Cuttino Mobley .25 .60
50 Nick Van Exel .30 .75
51 LaPhonso Ellis .30 .75
52 Kendall Gill .25 .60
53 Hakeem Olajuwon .50 1.25
54 Rashard Lewis .40 1.00
55 Dale Davis .25 .60
56 Keith Van Horn .30 .75
57 Michael Finley .40 1.00
58 Othella Harrington .25 .60
59 Gary Payton .40 1.00
60 Michael Dickerson .25 .60
61 Voshon Lenard .25 .60
62 Patrick Ewing .50 1.25
63 Ron Mercer .25 .60
64 Kenny Anderson .30 .75
65 Shaquille O'Neal 1.00 2.50
66 Tariq Abdul-Wahad .25 .60
67 Antonio Davis .25 .60
68 Rick Fox .25 .60
69 Lamar Odom .30 .75
70 Derek Anderson .25 .60
71 Vitaly Potapenko .25 .60
72 Karl Malone .50 1.25

73 Wally Szczerbiak .30 .75
74 Jason Williams .40 1.00
75 Steve Francis .30 .75
76 John Starks .30 .75
77 Ron Artest .40 1.00
78 Grant Hill .50 1.25
79 Theo Ratliff .25 .60
80 Antonio McDyess .30 .75
81 Antoine Walker .30 .75
82 Sean Elliott .40 1.00
83 Ruben Patterson .25 .60
84 Ray Allen .40 1.00
85 Tom Gugliotta .25 .60
86 Scottie Pippen .60 1.50
87 Jim Jackson .25 .60
88 Joe Smith .30 .75
89 Reggie Miller .40 1.00
90 Richard Hamilton .30 .75
91 Paul Pierce .40 1.00
92 Mookie Blaylock .25 .60
93 Glen Rice .30 .75
94 P.J. Brown .25 .60
95 Avery Johnson .30 .75
96 John Stockton .50 1.25
97 Tyrone Hill .25 .60
98 Tracy Murray .25 .60
99 Darrell Armstrong .25 .60
100 Steve Smith .30 .75
101 Shawn Kemp .40 1.00
102 Jalen Rose .30 .75
103 Vonteego Cummings .25 .60
104 Larry Hughes .30 .75
105 Charles Oakley .30 .75
106 Rod Strickland .25 .60
107 Christian Laettner .30 .75
108 Baron Davis .40 1.00
109 Jamal Mashburn .30 .75
110 Lindsey Hunter .25 .60
111 Toni Kukoc .40 1.00
112 Austin Croshere .25 .60
113 Chris Webber .40 1.00
114 Vlade Divac .30 .75
115 Andre Miller .30 .75
116 Larry Johnson .40 1.00
117 Jason Kidd .60 1.50
118 David Robinson .60 1.50
119 Donyell Marshall .25 .60
120 Jason Terry .40 1.00
121 Kenyon Martin JSY RC 5.00 12.00
122 Stromile Swift JSY RC 2.00 5.00
123 Chris Mihm JSY RC 1.50 4.00
124 Marcus Fizer JSY RC 2.00 5.00
125 Courtney Alexander JSY RC 1.50 4.00
126 Darius Miles JSY RC 2.00 5.00
127 Jerome Moiso JSY RC 1.25 3.00
128 Joel Przybilla JSY RC 1.50 4.00
129 DerMarr Johnson JSY RC 1.50 4.00
130 Mike Miller JSY RC 3.00 8.00
131 Quentin Richardson JSY RC 2.00 5.00
132 Morris Peterson JSY RC 2.00 5.00
133 Speedy Claxton JSY RC 2.00 5.00
134 Keyon Dooling JSY RC 2.00 5.00
135 Mark Madsen JSY RC 2.00 5.00
136 Mateen Cleaves JSY RC 1.50 4.00
137 Etan Thomas JSY RC 2.00 5.00
138 Jason Collier JSY RC 2.00 5.00
139 Erick Barkley JSY RC 1.25 3.00
140 Desmond Mason JSY RC 2.50 6.00
141 Mamadou N'Diaye JSY RC 1.25 3.00
142 DeShawn Stevenson JSY RC 2.00 5.00
143 Donnell Harvey JSY RC 1.50 4.00
144 Jamaal Magloire JSY RC 2.00 5.00
145 Hedo Turkoglu JSY RC 3.00 8.00

2000-01 Hoops Hot Prospects A'la Carter

Randomly inserted into retail packs at one in five, this 20-card set features various cards of Vince Carter. Card backs carry an "AC" prefix.

COMPLETE SET (20) 12.00 30.00
COMMON CARD (AC1-AC20) .75 2.00
STATED ODDS 1:5 RETAIL

2000-01 Hoops Hot Prospects Vince Carter First In Flight

Some Vince Carter "special" cards were inserted into packs called First In Flight. The Game Jersey version was numbered to 250, the Shooting Shirt was numbered to 750 and the Warm-ups were numbered to 1000. All versions had autographed variations numbered to 15.

AU'S NOT PRICED DUE TO SCARCITY
1 V.Carter JSY/250 15.00 40.00
3 V.Carter Shirt/750 12.50 30.00
5 V.Carter WU/1000 10.00 25.00

2000-01 Hoops Hot Prospects Vince Carter Rookie Remnants

This three-card insert was randomly inserted into 2000-01 Fleer products. The set includes a Vince Carter floor card (numbered to 100), a Vince Carter floor/jersey card (numbered to 15), and finally an autographed Vince Carter floor/jersey card (numbered 1/1).

NNO Vince Carter FLR JSY/15 20.00 50.00
NNO Vince Carter FLR/100 12.50 30.00

2000-01 Hoops Hot Prospects Determined

Randomly inserted into packs at one in 12 packs, this 10-card insert features players that are determined to win. Card backs carry a "D" prefix.

COMPLETE SET (10) 4.00 10.00
STATED ODDS 1:12 HOB, 1:20 RET
D1 Vince Carter .75 2.00
D2 Lamar Odom .30 .75
D3 Steve Francis .30 .75
D4 Kobe Bryant 1.50 4.00
D5 Jason Williams .40 1.00
D6 Karl Malone .50 1.25
D7 Allen Iverson .75 2.00
D8 Elton Brand .40 1.00
D9 Tim Duncan .75 2.00
D10 Kevin Garnett .60 1.50

2000-01 Hoops Hot Prospects Genuine Coverage

Randomly inserted into packs at one in 96, this 17-card insert features game-worn sneaker cards of superstars such as Shaquille O'Neal, Lamar Odom, Eddie Jones and Vince Carter. Card backs carry a "GC" prefix.

STATED ODDS 1:96 RETAIL
GC1 Lamar Odom 4.00 10.00
GC2 Antoine Walker 4.00 10.00
GC3 Shaquille O'Neal 15.00 40.00
GC4 Darrell Armstrong 3.00 8.00
GC5 Larry Hughes 4.00 10.00
GC6 Marcus Camby 4.00 10.00
GC7 Nick Van Exel 4.00 10.00
GC8 Michael Dickerson 3.00 8.00
GC9 Baron Davis 5.00 12.00
GC10 Vince Carter 10.00 25.00
GC11 Mike Bibby 5.00 12.00
GC12 Wally Szczerbiak 4.00 10.00
GC13 Jerry Stackhouse 4.00 10.00
GC14 Eddie Jones 5.00 12.00
GC15 Shawn Kemp 8.00 20.00
GC16 Rick Fox 3.00 8.00
GC17 Jamal Mashburn 4.00 10.00

2000-01 Hoops Hot Prospects Originals

Randomly inserted into packs at one in 24, this 10-card insert gives the classic Hoops design a modern makeover as 10 NBA stars are portrayed on these brilliant die-cut cards. Card backs carry a "H" prefix.

COMPLETE SET (10) 10.00 25.00
STATED ODDS 1:24 HOB, 1:48 RET
H1 Vince Carter 2.00 5.00
H2 Tim Duncan 2.00 5.00
H3 Kevin Garnett 1.50 4.00
H4 Kobe Bryant 4.00 10.00
H5 Lamar Odom .75 2.00
H6 Steve Francis .75 2.00
H7 Shaquille O'Neal 2.50 6.00
H8 David Robinson 1.50 4.00
H9 Grant Hill 1.25 3.00
H10 Allen Iverson 2.00 5.00

2000-01 Hoops Hot Prospects Rookie Headliners

Randomly inserted into packs at one in eight, this 15-card insert features rookies that are sure to make headlines this upcoming season. Card backs carry a "RH" prefix.

COMPLETE SET (15) 3.00 8.00
STATED ODDS 1:8 HOB, 1:16 RET
1 Kenyon Martin .75 2.00
2 Stromile Swift .30 .75
3 Darius Miles .30 .75
4 Jerome Moiso .20 .50
5 Chris Mihm .25 .60
6 Marcus Fizer .30 .75
7 Courtney Alexander .25 .60
8 DerMarr Johnson .25 .60
9 Mike Miller .50 1.25
10 Quentin Richardson .30 .75
11 Morris Peterson .30 .75
12 Keyon Dooling .30 .75
13 Mateen Cleaves .25 .60
14 Etan Thomas .30 .75
15 Jamal Crawford .75 2.00

2001-02 Hoops Hot Prospects

Released in late November 2001, this 108-card base set is standard size and borderless. The background is designed to resemble that of a hardwood court. The featured player's number is represented in the upper left-hand and right-hand corners. The featured player's name runs along the center bottom of the card with the Hoops logo just above it. The set contains 80 veterans and 28 rookies. The rookies contain a swatch of jersey and are sequentially numbered to 1000 unless noted in the set listing below by /300 which are numberd to 300.

COMP.SET w/o SP's (80) 15.00 40.00
RC PRINT RUN 300 OR 1000 SERIAL #'d SETS
1 Vince Carter .60 1.50
2 John Stockton .50 1.25
3 Steve Smith .30 .75
4 Kevin Garnett .60 1.50
5 Larry Hughes .30 .75
6 Ron Mercer .25 .60
7 Marcus Fizer .25 .60
8 Rashard Lewis .40 1.00
9 Mike Miller .30 .75
10 Darius Miles .25 .60
11 Michael Finley .40 1.00
12 Marcus Camby .30 .75
13 Morris Peterson .25 .60
14 Shawn Marion .30 .75
15 Alonzo Mourning .50 1.25
16 Jamal Mashburn .30 .75
17 Michael Jordan 3.00 8.00
18 Jason Williams .30 .75
19 Latrell Sprewell .30 .75
20 Reggie Miller .40 1.00
21 Glenn Robinson .30 .75
22 Steve Francis .30 .75
23 Antoine Walker .30 .75
24 Stromile Swift .25 .60
25 Damon Stoudamire .30 .75
26 Allan Houston .30 .75
27 Kobe Bryant 1.50 4.00
28 Dirk Nowitzki .60 1.50
29 Iakovos Tsakalidis .25 .60
30 Gary Payton .40 1.00
31 Allen Iverson .75 2.00
32 Eddie Jones .30 .75
33 Mateen Cleaves .25 .60
34 Nick Van Exel .30 .75
35 Terrell Brandon .25 .60
36 Wally Szczerbiak .30 .75
37 Jalen Rose .30 .75
38 Elton Brand .40 1.00
39 DerMarr Johnson .25 .60
40 Peja Stojakovic .40 1.00
41 Jason Kidd .60 1.50
42 Sam Cassell .30 .75
43 Cuttino Mobley .25 .60
44 Toni Kukoc .40 1.00
45 DeShawn Stevenson .25 .60
46 David Robinson .60 1.50
47 Grant Hill .50 1.25
48 Shaquille O'Neal 1.00 2.50
49 Andre Miller .30 .75
50 Corey Maggette .30 .75
51 Jason Terry .40 1.00
52 Aaron McKie .25 .60
53 Eddie House .25 .60
54 Steve Nash .60 1.50
55 Clifford Robinson .25 .60
56 Chris Webber .40 1.00
57 Kenyon Martin .40 1.00
58 Jermaine O'Neal .30 .75
59 Baron Davis .40 1.00
60 Mitch Richmond .30 .75
61 Antawn Jamison .40 1.00
62 Paul Pierce .40 1.00
63 Shareef Abdur-Rahim .30 .75
64 Rasheed Wallace .40 1.00
65 Ray Allen .40 1.00
66 Lamar Odom .30 .75
67 Chris Mihm .25 .60
68 Raef LaFrentz .25 .60
69 Patrick Ewing .50 1.25
70 Tracy McGrady .60 1.50
71 Derek Fisher .30 .75
72 Jerry Stackhouse .30 .75
73 Antonio McDyess .30 .75
74 Karl Malone .50 1.25
75 Dikembe Mutombo .40 1.00
76 Hakeem Olajuwon .50 1.25
77 David Wesley .25 .60
78 Courtney Alexander .25 .60
79 Tim Duncan .75 2.00
80 Stephon Marbury .30 .75
81 Kwame Brown JSY RC 3.00 8.00
82 Tyson Chandler JSY RC 5.00 12.00
83 Pau Gasol JSY RC 10.00 25.00
84 Eddy Curry JSY RC 3.00 8.00
85 J.Richardson JSY/300 RC 6.00 15.00
86 Shane Battier JSY RC 6.00 15.00
87 Eddie Griffin JSY/300 RC 4.00 10.00
88 DeSagana Diop JSY RC 2.50 6.00
89 Rodney White JSY RC 2.00 5.00
90 Joe Johnson JSY/300 RC 6.00 15.00
91 Kedrick Brown JSY/300 RC 3.00 8.00
92 V.Radmanovic JSY RC 3.00 8.00
93 Richard Jefferson JSY RC 5.00 12.00
94 Troy Murphy JSY RC 3.00 8.00
95 Steven Hunter JSY RC 2.50 6.00
96 Kirk Haston JSY RC 2.00 5.00
97 Michael Bradley JSY RC 2.00 5.00
98 Jason Collins JSY RC 2.50 6.00
99 Zach Randolph JSY RC 5.00 12.00
100 Brendan Haywood JSY RC 3.00 8.00
101 Joseph Forte JSY RC 2.00 5.00
102 Jeryl Sasser JSY RC 2.00 5.00
103 B.Armstrong JSY/300 RC 3.00 8.00
104 Andrei Kirilenko JSY RC 5.00 12.00
105 Primos Brezec JSY RC 3.00 8.00
106 S.Dalembert JSY/300 RC 5.00 12.00
107 Jamaal Tinsley JSY RC 3.00 8.00
108 Tony Parker JSY RC 10.00 25.00

2001-02 Hoops Hot Prospects Rookie Autographs

PRINT RUN 100 SERIAL #'d SETS
81 Kwame Brown JSY AU 10.00 25.00
84 Eddy Curry JSY AU 10.00 25.00
90 Joe Johnson JSY AU 12.00 30.00
91 Kedrick Brown JSY AU 6.00 15.00
97 Michael Bradley JSY AU 6.00 15.00

2001-02 Hoops Hot Prospects Certified Cuts

Randomly inserted in packs at a rate of 1:44, this 11-card insert set features autographed cards of NBA players that look as though they have signed on the line of a personal check. The cards are horizontally designed, standard size, and borderless. A color head shot of the featured player sits above the signature with his corresponding team logo in the upper left-hand corner.

STATED ODDS 1:64
1 Kwame Brown 5.00 12.00
2 Eddy Curry 5.00 12.00
3 Kedrick Brown 3.00 8.00
4 Joe Johnson 8.00 20.00
5 Michael Bradley 3.00 8.00
6 Richard Jefferson 8.00 20.00
7 Brendan Haywood 5.00 12.00
8 Kirk Haston 3.00 8.00
9 Omar Cook 5.00 12.00
10 Vince Carter 20.00 50.00
11 Larry Bird 100.00 200.00

2001-02 Hoops Hot Prospects Hot Materials

This 43-card insert set is randomly inserted in packs at a rate of 1:7. The cards offer swatches of the featured player's game-used jerseys. The swatches set atop a jersey designed background with the player's team name and number standing out behind a color action shot of the player.

STATED ODDS 1:8
1 Vince Carter 5.00 12.00
2 Darius Miles 2.00 5.00
3 Stephon Marbury 2.50 6.00
4 John Stockton 4.00 10.00
5 Steve Francis 2.50 6.00
6 Tracy McGrady 5.00 12.00
7 Lamar Odom 2.50 6.00
8 Corey Maggette 2.50 6.00
9 Stromile Swift 2.00 5.00
10 Morris Peterson 2.00 5.00
11 Jason Kidd 5.00 12.00
12 Karl Malone 4.00 10.00
13 Baron Davis 3.00 8.00
14 Gary Payton 3.00 8.00
15 Paul Pierce 3.00 8.00
16 Desmond Mason 2.50 6.00
17 Dikembe Mutombo 3.00 8.00
18 Mike Miller 2.50 6.00
19 Craig Claxton 2.00 5.00
20 Antoine Walker 2.50 6.00
21 Allen Iverson 6.00 15.00
22 Reggie Miller 4.00 10.00
23 Chris Webber 3.00 8.00
24 Shawn Marion 2.50 6.00
25 Allan Houston 2.50 6.00
26 Kenyon Martin 3.00 8.00
27 Alonzo Mourning 4.00 10.00
28 Grant Hill 4.00 10.00
29 Kwame Brown 2.00 5.00
30 Tyson Chandler 3.00 8.00
31 Eddy Curry 2.00 5.00
32 Shane Battier 4.00 10.00
33 Eddie Griffin 1.50 4.00
34 Rodney White 1.25 3.00
35 Pau Gasol 6.00 15.00
36 Vladimir Radmanovic 2.00 5.00
37 Richard Jefferson 3.00 8.00
38 Steven Hunter 1.50 4.00
39 Kirk Haston 1.25 3.00
40 Michael Bradley 1.25 3.00
41 Jason Collins 1.50 4.00
42 Zach Randolph 3.00 8.00
43 Brendan Haywood 2.00 5.00

2001-02 Hoops Hot Prospects Hot Tandems

Serially #'d to 100, this 43-card insert set highlights dual players with swatches of their game-worn jerseys. The horizontally designed, standard size cards have each featured player, along with his team number, on the left-hand and right-hand sides of the card.

PRINT RUN 100 SERIAL #'d SETS
1 V.Carter/T.McGrady 10.00 25.00
2 K.Brown/E.Curry 6.00 15.00
3 K.Malone/J.Stockton 6.00 15.00
4 D.Diop/S.Swift 6.00 15.00
5 S.Battier/S.Swift 6.00 15.00
6 P.Pierce/A.Walker 8.00 20.00
7 E.Griffin/J.Kidd 6.00 15.00
8 R.White/S.Francis 6.00 15.00
9 M.Miller/M.Bradley 6.00 15.00
10 T.Chandler/D.Miles 8.00 20.00
11 S.Marbury/J.Kidd 10.00 25.00
12 A.Iverson/V.Carter 10.00 25.00
13 A.Iverson/D.Miles 8.00 20.00
14 R.Miller/B.Davis 8.00 20.00
15 C.Webber/K.Malone 8.00 20.00
16 A.Mourning/D.Mutombo 10.00 25.00
17 K.Martin/L.Odom 6.00 15.00
18 A.Houston/R.Miller 6.00 15.00
19 G.Hill/T.McGrady 6.00 15.00
20 P.Gasol/C.Webber 10.00 25.00
21 D.Mutombo/S.Claxton 6.00 15.00
22 G.Hill/S.Francis 10.00 25.00
23 G.Payton/S.Marbury 6.00 15.00
24 V.Radmanovic/D.Mason 6.00 15.00
25 S.Marion/D.Mason 6.00 15.00
26 R.Jefferson/K.Martin 6.00 15.00
27 K.Haston/B.Davis 6.00 15.00
28 V.Carter/M.Peterson 10.00 25.00
29 V.Carter/L.Odom 10.00 25.00
30 V.Carter/D.Miles 10.00 25.00
31 V.Carter/K.Brown 8.00 20.00
32 V.Carter/C.Webber 10.00 25.00
33 A.Iverson/J.Kidd 10.00 25.00
34 E.Griffin/D.Miles 6.00 15.00
35 E.Curry/E.Griffin 6.00 15.00
36 E.Griffin/K.Brown 6.00 15.00
37 A.Iverson/S.Claxton 10.00 25.00
38 T.Chandler/E.Curry 6.00 15.00
39 T.Chandler/K.Brown 6.00 15.00
40 S.Battier/T.Chandler 8.00 20.00
41 S.Battier/K.Brown 6.00 15.00
42 G.Hill/R.Miller 10.00 25.00
43 C.Webber/D.Miles 8.00 20.00

2001-02 Hoops Hot Prospects Inside Vince Carter

This special 10-card insert set has a different memorabilia items for each Vince Carter card. All cards are sequentially numbered. Autographed versions of each card were also inserted and sequentially numbered to 15.

PRINT RUNS LISTED BELOW
1 V.Carter JSY H/1000 6.00 15.00
2 V.Carter JSY R/900 6.00 15.00
3 V.Carter WARM/800 6.00 15.00
4 V.Carter SHIRT/700 6.00 15.00
5 V.Carter HS FLOOR/600 8.00 20.00
6 V.Carter UNC JSY/500 10.00 25.00
7 V.Carter BALL/400 8.00 20.00
8 V.Carter USA JSY/300 10.00 25.00
9 V.Carter FLOOR/200 12.00 30.00
10 V.Carter SHOE/100 25.00 60.00

2001-02 Hoops Hot Prospects Inside Vince Carter Autographs

PRINT RUN 15 SERIAL #'d SETS
1 V.Carter JSY H 75.00 150.00
2 V.Carter JSY R 75.00 150.00
3 V.Carter WARM 75.00 150.00
4 V.Carter SHIRT 75.00 150.00
5 V.Carter HS FLOOR 75.00 150.00
6 V.Carter UNC JSY 100.00 200.00
7 V.Carter BALL 100.00 200.00
8 V.Carter USA JSY 75.00 150.00
9 V.Carter FLOOR 75.00 150.00
10 V.Carter SHOE 100.00 200.00

2002-03 Hoops Hot Prospects

Release in early November 2002, Hoops Hot Prospects showcases a 116-card set divided up into 80 veteran player cards, 29 Jersey Rookie cards sequentially numbered to 500, card numbers 81-108, six Rookie Cards sequentially numbered to 900, card numbers 109-114, and five Rookie Cards sequentially numbered to 1500, card numbers 115-120. Base cards have borders on all sides, solid colors appear along the top, the left, and the right side, while a basketball looking border is along the bottom. The card backgrounds are done in a one-color scale and appear metallic. Rookie Jersey cards have a close-up portrait style photo towards the top, and a square jersey swatch centered towards the bottom. Hoops was packaged in five-card packs where boxes contained 15 packs.

COMP.SET w/o SP's (80) 20.00 50.00
81-108 PRINT RUN 500 SER.#'d SETS
109-114 PRINT RUN 900 SER.#'d SETS
115-120 PRINT RUN 1500 SER.#'d SETS
1 Vince Carter .60 1.50
2 Chris Webber .40 1.00
3 Latrell Sprewell .30 .75
4 Brian Grant .25 .60
5 Jerry Stackhouse .30 .75
6 Joe Smith .30 .75
7 Jason Terry .30 .75
8 Shawn Marion .30 .75
9 Wally Szczerbiak .30 .75
10 Reggie Miller .40 1.00
11 Steve Nash .50 1.25
12 Karl Malone .50 1.25
13 Damon Stoudamire .30 .75
14 Jamal Mashburn .30 .75
15 Kobe Bryant 1.50 4.00
16 Paul Pierce .40 1.00
17 Tony Parker .50 1.25
18 Mike Miller .30 .75
19 Sam Cassell .30 .75
20 Eddie Griffin .25 .60
21 Jason Williams .30 .75
22 Jason Richardson .40 1.00
23 Antoine Walker .30 .75
24 Tim Duncan .75 2.00
25 Baron Davis .30 .75
26 Glenn Robinson .30 .75
27 Darius Miles .25 .60
28 Dirk Nowitzki .60 1.50
29 John Stockton .50 1.25
30 Allen Iverson .60 1.50
31 Richard Jefferson .40 1.00
32 Rick Fox .25 .60
33 Ben Wallace .30 .75
34 Michael Jordan 3.00 8.00
35 Rasheed Wallace .40 1.00
36 Alonzo Mourning .50 1.25
37 Steve Francis .30 .75
38 Jalen Rose .30 .75
39 Rashard Lewis .40 1.00
40 Tracy McGrady .60 1.50
41 David Wesley .25 .60
42 Pau Gasol .50 1.25
43 Antawn Jamison .40 1.00
44 Shareef Abdur-Rahim .30 .75
45 Mike Bibby .40 1.00
46 Dikembe Mutombo .40 1.00
47 Kevin Garnett .60 1.50
48 Elton Brand .40 1.00
49 Lamond Murray .25 .60
50 Morris Peterson .25 .60
51 Joe Johnson .30 .75
52 Kenyon Martin .30 .75
53 Shaquille O'Neal 1.00 2.50
54 Antonio McDyess .30 .75
55 Vin Baker .30 .75
56 Marcus Camby .30 .75
57 Ray Allen .40 1.00
58 Jermain O'Neal 1.00 2.50
59 Eddy Curry .25 .60
60 David Robinson .60 1.50
61 Clifford Robinson .25 .60
62 Rodney Rogers .25 .60
63 Peja Stojakovic .40 1.00
64 Allan Houston .30 .75
65 Shane Battier .40 1.00
66 Jamaal Tinsley .25 .60
67 Michael Finley .40 1.00
68 Kenny Anderson .30 .75
69 Stephon Marbury .30 .75
70 Terrell Brandon .25 .60
71 Lamar Odom .30 .75
72 Raef LaFrentz .25 .60
73 Jamaal Magloire .25 .60
74 Bonzi Wells .25 .60
75 Jason Kidd .60 1.50
76 Cuttino Mobley .25 .60
77 Tyson Chandler .40 1.00
78 Gary Payton .40 1.00
79 Grant Hill .50 1.25
80 Eddie Jones .30 .75
81 Yao Ming JSY RC 8.00 20.00
82 Fred Jones JSY RC 3.00 8.00
83 Ryan Humphrey JSY RC 3.00 8.00
84 Drew Gooden JSY RC 4.00 10.00
85 Nikoloz Tskitishvili JSY RC 2.50 6.00
86 Caron Butler JSY RC 4.00 10.00
87 Vincent Yarbrough JSY RC 2.50 6.00
88 DaJuan Wagner JSY RC 3.00 8.00
89 Nene Hilario JSY RC 4.00 10.00
90 Qyntel Woods JSY RC 3.00 8.00
91 Jared Jeffries JSY RC 3.00 8.00
92 Casey Jacobsen JSY RC 3.00 8.00
93 Marcus Haislip JSY RC 3.00 8.00
94 Kareem Rush JSY RC 3.00 8.00
95 Predrag Savovic JSY RC 3.00 8.00
96 Melvin Ely JSY RC 3.00 8.00
97 Steve Logan JSY RC 4.00 10.00
98 Amare Stoudemire JSY RC 5.00 12.00
99 John Salmons JSY RC 4.00 10.00
100 Chris Jefferies JSY RC 2.50 6.00
101 Juan Dixon JSY RC 4.00 10.00
102 Carlos Boozer JSY RC 4.00 10.00
103 Roger Mason JSY RC 3.00 8.00
104 Rod Grizzard JSY RC 2.50 6.00
105 Tayshaun Prince JSY RC 5.00 12.00
106 Chris Wilcox JSY RC 3.00 8.00
107 Sam Clancy JSY RC 3.00 8.00
108 Dan Gadzuric JSY RC 3.00 8.00
109 Dan Dickau/900 RC 1.50 4.00
110 Jay Williams/900 RC 2.00 5.00
111 Mike Dunleavy/900 RC 2.00 5.00
112 Robert Archibald/900 RC 1.25 3.00
113 Curtis Borchardt/900 RC 1.25 3.00
114 Bostian Nachbar/900 RC 1.50 4.00
115 Jiri Welsch/1500 RC 1.50 4.00
116 Frank Williams/1500 RC 1.25 3.00
117 Rasual Butler/1500 RC 2.00 5.00
118 Tamar Slay/1500 RC 1.25 3.00
119 Ronald Murray/1500 RC 2.00 5.00
120 Corsley Edwards/1500 RC 1.50 4.00

2002-03 Hoops Hot Prospects Certified Cuts

Seeded in packs at the rate of one in 142, this 16-card set uses a horizontal card design, contains embedded cut signatures, a small portrait photo of the player and the player's team logo.

STATED ODDS 1:142
1 Vince Carter 12.00 30.00
2 Shareef Abdur-Rahim 8.00 20.00
4 Kwame Brown 8.00 20.00
5 Joe Johnson 12.00 30.00
6 Michael Bradley 8.00 20.00
7 Eddy Curry 10.00 25.00
9 Cuttino Mobley 8.00 20.00
10 Matt Harpring 8.00 20.00
11 Brian Grant 8.00 20.00
12 Tracy McGrady 40.00 80.00
13 Antonio McDyess 10.00 25.00
14 Larry Hughes 10.00 25.00

2002-03 Hoops Hot Prospects Class Of

Randomly inserted in packs at the rate of one in 15, this 20-card set pairs players from the same draft year on this horizontally designed card. Each player is separated by white borders and a white line down the middle of the card, and every card has silver foil highlights.

STATED ODDS 1:15
1 K.Martin/D.Miles 1.50 4.00
2 K.Van Horn/T.McGrady 2.00 5.00
3 S.Francis/B.Davis 1.50 4.00
4 A.Iverson/S.Marbury 2.00 5.00
5 J.Tinsley/P.Gasol 1.50 4.00
6 G.Robinson/J.Kidd 2.00 5.00
7 H.Turkoglu/Q.Richardson 1.50 4.00
8 D.Robinson/R.Miller 2.00 5.00
9 D.Nowitzki/V.Carter 3.00 8.00
10 R.Allen/A.Walker 1.50 4.00
11 M.Miller/S.Claxton 1.50 4.00
12 J.Jeffries/D.Wagner 1.50 4.00
13 J.Richardson/T.Parker 2.00 5.00
14 L.Odom/A.Kirilenko 1.50 4.00
15 W.Szczerbiak/E.Brand 1.50 4.00
16 A.Stoudemire/D.Gooden 2.00 5.00
17 S.Marion/J.Terry 1.50 4.00
18 S.Nash/P.Stojakovic 2.00 5.00
19 P.Pierce/V.Carter 2.50 6.00
20 C.Butler/Y.Ming 2.50 6.00

2002-03 Hoops Hot Prospects Class Of Jerseys

INT RUN 375 SERIAL #'d SETS
1 K.Martin/D.Miles 5.00 12.00
2 K.Van Horn/T.McGrady 8.00 20.00
3 S.Francis/B.Davis 6.00 15.00
4 A.Iverson/S.Marbury 8.00 20.00
5 J.Tinsley/P.Gasol 5.00 12.00
6 G.Robinson/J.Kidd 6.00 15.00
7 H.Turkoglu/Q.Richardson 5.00 12.00
8 D.Robinson/R.Miller 10.00 25.00
9 D.Nowitzki/V.Carter 12.00 30.00
10 R.Allen/A.Walker 5.00 12.00
11 M.Miller/S.Claxton 5.00 12.00
12 J.Jeffries/D.Wagner 5.00 12.00
13 J.Richardson/T.Parker 6.00 15.00
14 L.Odom/A.Kirilenko 5.00 12.00
15 W.Szczerbiak/E.Brand 5.00 12.00
16 A.Stoudemire/D.Gooden 6.00 15.00
17 S.Marion/J.Terry 5.00 12.00
18 S.Nash/P.Stojakovic 5.00 12.00
19 P.Pierce/V.Carter 10.00 25.00
20 C.Butler/Y.Ming 8.00 20.00

2002-03 Hoops Hot Prospects Hot Materials

Inserted in packs at the rate of one in eight, this 45-card set is horizontally designed and places full color player action photos on the left side of the card and a swatch of game worn memorabilia on the right side. The card background is set to match the featured player's jersey colors. A Red Hot Materials parallel set was also inserted where cards are sequentially numbered to 50.

STATED ODDS 1:8
*RED HOT: 1X TO 2.5X HOT MAT.HI
RED HOT PRINT RUN 50 SER.#'d SETS
1 Vince Carter 4.00 10.00
2 Steve Francis 2.00 5.00
3 Hedo Turkoglu 2.00 5.00
4 Baron Davis 2.00 5.00
5 Dikembe Mutombo 2.50 6.00
6 Allen Iverson 4.00 10.00
7 Pau Gasol 3.00 8.00
8 Keith Van Horn 2.00 5.00
9 Lamar Odom 2.00 5.00
10 Jason Kidd 4.00 10.00
11 Paul Pierce 2.50 6.00
12 Speedy Claxton 1.50 4.00
13 Steve Nash 3.00 8.00
14 Alonzo Mourning 3.00 8.00
15 Elton Brand 2.50 6.00
16 Corey Maggette 2.00 5.00
17 Jason Richardson 2.50 6.00
18 Desmond Mason 2.00 5.00
19 Antoine Walker 2.00 5.00
20 Cuttino Mobley 1.50 4.00
21 Richard Jefferson 2.50 6.00
22 Darius Miles 1.50 4.00
23 Tracy McGrady 4.00 10.00
24 Peja Stojakovic 2.50 6.00
25 Gary Payton 2.50 6.00
26 Mike Miller 2.00 5.00
27 Tony Parker 3.00 8.00
28 Kenyon Martin 2.00 5.00
29 Yao Ming 5.00 12.00
30 Amare Stoudemire 3.00 8.00
31 Dan Dickau 2.00 5.00
32 Drew Gooden 2.50 6.00
33 Nikoloz Tskitishvili 1.50 4.00
34 Caron Butler 2.50 6.00
35 Fred Jones 2.00 5.00
36 DaJuan Wagner 2.00 5.00
37 Nene Hilario 2.50 6.00
38 Qyntel Woods 2.00 5.00
39 Jared Jeffries 2.00 5.00
40 Tayshaun Prince 3.00 8.00
41 Marcus Haislip 2.00 5.00
42 Kareem Rush 2.00 5.00
43 Ryan Humphrey 2.00 5.00
44 Melvin Ely 2.00 5.00
45 Carlos Boozer 2.50 6.00

2002-03 Hoops Hot Prospects Hot Tandems

Inserted in packs, this 43-card set parallels the design of the Hot Materials set, but instead places two players and two swatches of game used memorabilia on the card front. Each different side is colored to match the featured player's uniform colors, and cards are sequentially numbered to 100. A Red Hot Tandems parallel set was also inserted into packs where singles are sequentially numbered to 10.

PRINT RUN 100 SERIAL #'d SETS
ASTERISK NEVER INSERTED IN PACKS
1 V.Carter/S.Francis 10.00 25.00
2 V.Carter/Y.Ming 12.50 30.00
3 V.Carter/T.McGrady 10.00 25.00
4 V.Carter/D.Wagner 6.00 15.00
5 V.Carter/P.Pierce 10.00 25.00
6 H.Turkoglu/P.Stojakovic 6.00 15.00
7 T.McGrady/A.Iverson 10.00 25.00
8 B.Davis/C.Mobley 6.00 15.00
9 D.Mutombo/N.Hilario 6.00 15.00
10 A.Iverson/Y.Ming 8.00 20.00
11 P.Gasol/R.Humphrey 6.00 15.00
13 L.Odom/D.Miles 6.00 15.00
14 R.Jefferson/J.Kidd 8.00 20.00
15 C.Mobley/S.Francis 6.00 15.00
16 G.Payton/T.Parker 8.00 20.00
17 M.Miller/K.Martin 6.00 15.00
18 D.Gooden/C.Boozer 6.00 15.00
19 M.Ely/M.Haislip 6.00 15.00
20 Q.Woods/A.Stoudemire 8.00 20.00
21 C.Butler/F.Jones 6.00 15.00
22 J.Jeffries/N.Hilario 6.00 15.00
23 A.Stoudemire/D.Miles 8.00 20.00
24 R.Jefferson/C.Butler 6.00 15.00
25 D.Wagner/K.Rush 6.00 15.00
26 T.Parker/J.Kidd 8.00 20.00
27 P.Gasol/D.Nowitzki 8.00 20.00
28 B.Davis/K.Rush 6.00 15.00
29 S.Nash/D.Nowitzki 10.00 25.00
30 C.Boozer/E.Brand 6.00 15.00
31 A.Mourning/D.Mutombo 8.00 20.00
32 M.Ely/E.Brand 6.00 15.00
34 K.Van Horn/K.Martin 6.00 15.00
35 R.Humphrey/P.Stojakovic 6.00 15.00
36 L.Odom/C.Maggette 6.00 15.00
37 H.Turkoglu/N.Tskitishvili 6.00 15.00
38 J.Richardson/P.Pierce 6.00 15.00
39 J.Richardson/D.Gooden 6.00 15.00
40 M.Haislip/Q.Woods 6.00 15.00
41 F.Jones/A.Walker 6.00 15.00
42 A.Walker/G.Payton 6.00 15.00
43 M.Miller/C.Jacobsen 6.00 15.00

2002-03 Hoops Hot Prospects Stat Tracker

Randomly inserted in packs, this 10-card set showcases top players of the NBA in full color action with borders on the left and right set to match the featured player's team colors. Originally Fleer released that the print number was supposed to be 750, however, each player's card is sequentially numbered to a different number.

PRINT RUNS LISTED BELOW
1 Vince Carter/57 8.00 20.00
2 Michael Jordan/60 100.00 200.00
3 Kobe Bryant/80 20.00 50.00
4 Shaquille O'Neal/67 12.00 30.00
5 Kevin Garnett/79 8.00 20.00
6 Allen Iverson 8.00 20.00
7 Tracy McGrady/74 8.00 20.00
8 Tim Duncan/82 10.00 25.00
10 Dirk Nowitzki/76 8.00 20.00

2002-03 Hoops Hot Prospects Supreme Court

Inserted in packs at the rate of one in seven, this 15-card set features top rookies on a horizontally designed card. Backgrounds are set to match the player's team colors and places a full color action photo on top of a close-up portrait shot on the left side and the team logo on the right.

COMPLETE SET (15) 12.50 30.00
STATED ODDS 1:7
1 Melvin Ely .75 2.00
2 Jay Williams 1.00 2.50
3 Mike Dunleavy 1.00 2.50
4 Drew Gooden 1.00 2.50
5 Nikoloz Tskitishvili .60 1.50
6 Caron Butler 1.00 2.50
7 Chris Wilcox .75 2.00
8 DaJuan Wagner .75 2.00
9 Nene Hilario 1.00 2.50
10 Qyntel Woods .75 2.00
11 Jared Jeffries .75 2.00
12 Juan Dixon 1.00 2.50
13 Amare Stoudemire 1.25 3.00
14 Kareem Rush .75 2.00
15 Bostjan Nachbar .75 2.00

2002-03 Hoops Hot Prospects Triple Patch

Randomly seeded in packs, this 15-card set places three players on a horizontally designed card. Each player appears with his own background color and a square swatch of a patch from game-used memorabilia. Each card is sequentially numbered to 75.

PRINT RUN 75 SERIAL #'d SETS
1 Kidd/Francis/McGrady 25.00 60.00
2 Iverson/Carter/Pierce 40.00 100.00
3 Richardson/Jefferson/Miles 15.00 40.00
4 Davis/Gasol/Odom 15.00 40.00
5 Nash/Mourning/Brand 15.00 40.00
6 Walker/Stojakovic/Payton 25.00 60.00
7 Parker/Martin/Turkoglu 20.00 50.00
8 Mutombo/Van Horn/Claxton 15.00 40.00
9 Maggette/Mason/Mobley 15.00 40.00
10 Miller/Ming/Wagner 20.00 50.00
11 Stoudemire/Dickau/Gooden 20.00 50.00
12 Butler/Woods/Jeffries 15.00 40.00
13 Rush/Ely/Tskitishvili 15.00 40.00
14 Jones/Hilario/Prince 15.00 40.00
15 Haislip/Humphrey/Boozer 15.00 40.00

2003-04 Hoops Hot Prospects

Released in December 2003, this 117-card set is comprised of 80 veteran player cards, six autographed rookie cards (numbers 81-87) sequentially numbered to 600, seven jersey rookie cards (numbers 88-94) sequentially numbered to 500, 17 autographed jersey rookie cards (numbers 95-111) sequentially numbered to 400, and six rookie cards sequentially numbered to 1000 (numbers 112-117). Hoops Hot Prospects was packaged in 15-pack boxes of five cards each and carried a suggested retail price of $7.99.

COMP.SET w/o SP's 15.00 40.00
AU RC PRINT RUN 600 SER.#'d SETS
JSY RC PRINT RUN 500 SER.#'d SETS
JSY AU RC PRINT RUN 400 SER.#'d SETS
112-117 RC PRINT RUN 1000 SER.#'d SETS
UNPRICED WHITE HOT PRINT RUN ONE SET
1 Shareef Abdur-Rahim .30 .75
2 Mike Bibby .40 1.00
3 Allan Houston .30 .75
4 Pau Gasol .40 1.00
5 Tayshaun Prince .30 .75
6 Darius Miles .25 .60
7 Ray Allen .40 1.00
8 Amare Stoudemire .50 1.25
9 Latrell Sprewell .30 .75
10 Jamaal Tinsley .25 .60
11 Nene .30 .75
12 Matt Harpring .25 .60
13 Bonzi Wells .25 .60
14 Alonzo Mourning .50 1.25
15 Elton Brand .40 1.00
16 Paul Pierce .40 1.00
17 Tony Parker .40 1.00
18 Glenn Robinson .30 .75
19 Marcus Haislip .25 .60
20 Eddie Griffin .25 .60
21 Jamaal Magloire .25 .60
22 Gilbert Arenas .30 .75
23 Antoine Walker .40 1.00
24 Manu Ginobili .50 1.25
25 Jamal Mashburn .30 .75
26 Michael Redd .40 1.00
27 Ron Artest .40 1.00
28 Steve Nash .50 1.25
29 Andrei Kirilenko .40 1.00
30 Stephon Marbury .30 .75
31 Richard Jefferson .30 .75
32 Kobe Bryant 1.50 4.00
33 Cuttino Mobley .25 .60
34 Juan Dixon .25 .60
35 Rasheed Wallace .40 1.00
36 Eddie Jones .30 .75
37 Steve Francis .30 .75
38 Dajuan Wagner .25 .60
39 Vladimir Radmanovic .25 .60
40 Drew Gooden .30 .75
41 Baron Davis .30 .75
42 Mike Miller .30 .75
43 Jason Richardson .40 1.00
44 Dan Dickau .25 .60
45 Chris Webber .40 1.00
46 Kenny Thomas .25 .60
47 Kevin Garnett .60 1.50
48 Reggie Miller .40 1.00
49 Dirk Nowitzki .60 1.50
50 Vince Carter .60 1.50
51 Zach Randolph .30 .75
52 Jason Kidd .60 1.50
53 Shaquille O'Neal 1.00 2.50
54 Nikoloz Tskitishvili .25 .60
55 Jerry Stackhouse .30 .75
56 Tracy McGrady .50 1.25
57 Desmond Mason .30 .75
58 Yao Ming .75 2.00
59 Jalen Rose .30 .75
60 Tim Duncan .60 1.50
61 Ben Wallace .30 .75
62 Mike Dunleavy .30 .75
63 Peja Stojakovic .40 1.00
64 Keith Van Horn .30 .75
65 Karl Malone .50 1.25
66 Jermaine O'Neal .30 .75
67 Michael Finley .40 1.00
68 Morris Peterson .25 .60
69 Shawn Marion .30 .75
70 John Salmons .30 .75
71 Chris Wilcox .25 .60
72 Rodney White .25 .60
73 Kwame Brown .25 .60
74 Bobby Jackson .25 .60
75 Kenyon Martin .30 .75
76 Antawn Jamison .30 .75
77 Eddy Curry .25 .60
78 Bruce Bowen .25 .60
79 Allen Iverson .60 1.50
80 Caron Butler .30 .75
81 Boris Diaw AU RC 4.00 10.00
82 Quinton Ross AU RC 4.00 10.00
83 Matt Carroll AU RC 2.50 6.00
84 Travis Hansen AU RC 2.50 6.00
85 Zaur Pachulia AU RC 4.00 10.00
86 Zarko Cabarkapa AU RC 2.50 6.00
87 Maciej Lampe AU RC 2.50 6.00
88 Ndudi Ebi JSY RC 3.00 8.00
89 Jarvis Hayes JSY RC 3.00 8.00
90 Steve Blake JSY RC 4.00 10.00
91 Keith Bogans JSY RC 3.00 8.00
92 Reece Gaines JSY RC 3.00 8.00
93 Chris Kaman JSY RC 5.00 12.00
94 Slavko Vranes JSY RC 3.00 8.00
95 C.Anthony JSY AU RC 50.00 100.00
96 Troy Bell JSY AU RC 4.00 10.00
97 Travis Outlaw JSY AU RC 5.00 12.00
98 M.Sweetney JSY AU RC 4.00 10.00
99 Dahntay Jones JSY AU RC 5.00 12.00
100 Chris Bosh JSY AU RC 15.00 40.00
101 Brian Cook JSY AU RC 4.00 10.00
102 Luke Ridnour JSY AU RC 5.00 12.00
103 David West JSY AU RC 6.00 15.00
104 M.Banks JSY AU RC 4.00 10.00
105 K.Perkins JSY AU RC 5.00 12.00
106 L.Barbosa JSY AU RC 6.00 15.00
107 M.Pietrus JSY AU RC 5.00 12.00
108 D.Wade JSY AU RC 50.00 120.00
109 Josh Howard JSY AU RC 6.00 15.00
110 J.Kapono JSY AU RC 4.00 10.00
111 Luke Walton JSY AU RC 6.00 15.00
112 LeBron James RC 50.00 120.00
113 T.J. Ford RC 1.50 4.00
114 Zoran Planinic RC 1.25 3.00
115 Darko Milicic RC 1.50 4.00

116 Kirk Hinrich RC 2.00 5.00
117 Nick Collison RC 1.50 4.00

2003-04 Hoops Hot Prospects Cream of the Crop

Inserted in packs at the rate of one in five, this 15-card set features a horizontal design where the new rookie's photo is centered and framed in tan.

COMPLETE SET (15) 15.00 40.00
STATED ODDS 1:5
1 LeBron James 12.00 30.00
2 Mike Sweetney .50 1.25
3 Chris Bosh 1.25 3.00
4 Darko Milicic .60 1.50
5 Nick Collison .60 1.50
6 Luke Ridnour .60 1.50
7 Kirk Hinrich .75 2.00
8 Carmelo Anthony 2.50 6.00
9 Chris Kaman .75 2.00
10 Mickael Pietrus .60 1.50
11 Jarvis Hayes .50 1.25
12 Reece Gaines .50 1.25
13 Dwyane Wade 2.50 6.00
14 Marcus Banks .50 1.25
15 T.J. Ford .60 1.50

2003-04 Hoops Hot Prospects Hot Materials

andomly inserted in packs, this 30-card set is horizontally designed and has an all-black background. Player images appear on the left in full color and a swatch of game worn memorabilia appears in the upper right corner. Each card is sequentially numbered to 500. Red and white versions were inserted also, where red cards are sequentially numbered to 50 and white cards are one of one's.

PRINT RUN 500 SER.#'d SETS
*RED SINGLES: .75X TO 2X HI COLUMN
RED PRINT RUN 50 SER.#'d SETS
1 Carmelo Anthony 8.00 20.00
2 Dwyane Wade 8.00 20.00
3 Mickael Pietrus 2.00 5.00
4 Mike Sweetney 1.50 4.00
5 Chris Bosh 4.00 10.00
6 Chris Kaman 2.50 6.00
7 Tayshaun Prince 2.00 5.00
8 Amare Stoudemire 3.00 8.00
9 Paul Pierce 2.50 6.00
10 Tony Parker 2.50 6.00
11 Manu Ginobili 3.00 8.00
12 Steve Nash 3.00 8.00
13 Steve Francis 2.00 5.00
14 Jason Richardson 2.50 6.00
15 Kevin Garnett 4.00 10.00
16 Dirk Nowitzki 4.00 10.00
17 Vince Carter 4.00 10.00
18 Jason Kidd 4.00 10.00
19 Tracy McGrady 3.00 8.00
20 Yao Ming 5.00 12.00
21 Ben Wallace 2.00 5.00
22 Kenyon Martin 2.00 5.00
23 Allen Iverson 4.00 10.00
24 Caron Butler 2.00 5.00
25 Shaquille O'Neal 6.00 15.00
26 Baron Davis 2.00 5.00
27 Drew Gooden 2.00 5.00
28 Michael Redd 2.50 6.00
29 Bonzi Wells 2.00 5.00
30 Mike Dunleavy 2.00 5.00

2003-04 Hoops Hot Prospects Hot Tandems

Randomly inserted in packs, this 25-card set utilizes the design of the hot materials cards with pictures of both players and two swatches of game worn memorabilia. Each card is squentially numbered to 100. Red and white versions of this set were also inserted. Red cards are sequentially numbered to 10 and white cards are numbered one of one.

PRINT RUN 100 SER.#'d SETS
1 C.Anthony/D.Wade 25.00 60.00
2 M.Pietrus/M.Sweetney 5.00 12.00
3 C.Bosh/C.Kaman 8.00 20.00
4 Amare/Y.Ming 12.50 30.00
5 T.Prince/B.Wallace 5.00 12.00
6 J.Rich/M.Dunleavy 5.00 12.00
7 K.Garnett/D.Nowitzki 8.00 20.00
8 M.Redd/B.Wells 5.00 12.00
9 T.Parker/M.Ginobili 8.00 20.00
10 T.McGrady/D.Gooden 6.00 15.00
11 B.Davis/S.Francis 5.00 12.00
12 V.Carter/A.Iverson 10.00 25.00
13 S.Nash/J.Kidd 8.00 20.00
14 K.Martin/S.O'Neal 8.00 20.00
15 P.Pierce/C.Butler 6.00 15.00
16 C.Anthony/T.McGrady 20.00 40.00
17 C.Bosh/V.Carter 10.00 25.00
18 Amare/K.Garnett 8.00 20.00
19 Y.Ming/A.Iverson 10.00 25.00
20 D.Nowitzki/K.Martin 6.00 15.00
21 B.Wallace/S.O'Neal 15.00 30.00
22 J.Rich/M.Pietrus 5.00 12.00
23 T.Parker/S.Nash 6.00 15.00
24 J.Kidd/B.Davis 6.00 15.00
25 T.Prince/D.Gooden 5.00 12.00

2003-04 Hoops Hot Prospects Player Graphs

Released originally as a replacement for autograph redemptions Fleer was unable to fulfill, many of these Vince Carter cards hit the secondary market after the summer 2005 Fleer auction following the company's bankruptcy and closing of business, leading us to believe most copies were not issued through the mail, but were purchased at that auction.

PN Nene 8.00 20.00
PVC Vince Carter 15.00 40.00

2003-04 Hoops Hot Prospects Sweet Selections

Randomly inserted at the rate of one in 15, this 10-card set pairs draft picks and which spot they were taken. The draft number appears on the bottom of this horizontally designed card and two player pictures appear above it one on the left and the other right.

COMPLETE SET (10) 10.00 25.00
STATED ODDS 1:15
1 Y.Ming/A.Iverson 2.50 6.00
2 J.Richardson/R.Allen 1.50 4.00
3 P.Gasol/B.Davis 1.50 4.00
4 Amare/S.Marion 2.00 5.00
5 S.O'Neal/T.Duncan 2.50 6.00
6 T.Chandler/S.Francis 1.50 4.00
7 V.Carter/K.Garnett 2.50 6.00
8 J.Kidd/G.Payton 2.00 5.00
9 D.Miles/S.Abdur-Rahim 1.50 4.00
10 D.Nowitzki/T.McGrady 2.00 5.00

2003-04 Hoops Hot Prospects Sweet Selections Game Used

Randomly seeded, this ten-card set parallels the base Sweet Selections set enhanced with swatches of game used material from each player and sequential numbering to 375.

PRINT RUN 375 SER.#'d SETS
1 Y.Ming/A.Iverson 8.00 20.00
2 J.Richardson/R.Allen 4.00 10.00
3 P.Gasol/B.Davis 4.00 10.00
4 Amare/S.Marion 5.00 12.00
5 S.O'Neal/T.Duncan 10.00 25.00
6 T.Chandler/S.Francis 4.00 10.00
7 V.Carter/K.Garnett 8.00 20.00
8 J.Kidd/G.Payton 6.00 15.00
9 D.Miles/S.Abdur-Rahim 4.00 10.00
10 D.Nowitzki/T.McGrady 6.00 15.00

2003-04 Hoops Hot Prospects Triple Patches

Randomly inserted in packs, this 15-card set utilizes the design of the hot materials set with three player photos along the top and three swatches of game-worn material patches along the bottom. Each card is sequentially numbered to 50. A white one of one version was also produced.

PRINT RUN 50 SER.#'d SETS
1 Melo/Wade/Pietrus 50.00 120.00
2 Sweetney/Bosh/Kaman 30.00 80.00
3 Amare/Ming/Prince 30.00 80.00
4 Manu/Nash/Francis 30.00 80.00
5 KG/Nowitzki/Vince 30.00 80.00
6 T-Mac/K-Mart/Iverson 40.00 100.00
7 Pierce/Parker/J-Rich 30.00 80.00
8 Wallace/Butler/Shaq 30.00 80.00
9 Wells/Dunleavy/Gooden 25.00 60.00
10 Kidd/B.Davis/Redd 30.00 80.00
11 Melo/Vince/T-Mac 40.00 100.00
12 Amare/KG/Nowitzki 30.00 80.00
13 Iverson/Pierce/J-Rich 30.00 80.00
14 Ming/Wallace/Kaman 25.00 60.00
15 Nash/Francis/Kidd 25.00 60.00

2003 Hoops Hot Prospects All-Star Game

Produced by Fleer for distribution at the 2003 NBA Jam Session All-Star Game show in Atlanta, this six card set features the top rookies of the 2002 NBA draft and utilize the same base design as 2002-03 Hoops Hot Prospects. Only 2500 total sets were produced and were available to collectors who purchased and opened five packs of Fleer Products at the Fleer show booth.

COMPLETE SET (6) 15.00 40.00
1 Yao Ming 8.00 20.00
2 Drew Gooden 2.50 6.00
3 Caron Butler 2.50 6.00
4 Amare Stoudemire 6.00 15.00
5 Nene Hilario 2.00 5.00
6 DaJuan Wagner 1.50 4.00

2004-05 Hoops Hot Prospects

Released in November 2004, Hoops Hot Prospects boasts a 110-card checklist divided up into 70 veteran players, 20 jersey autographed rookies serially numbered to either 150 or 350 (cards 71-90), 10 jersey rookies serially numbered to 350 (cards 91-100) and 10 rookie cards serially numbered to 1000 (cards 101-110). Base veteran cards feature white borders and foil backgrounds, while rookies have white borders and a player portrait photo towards the top. In the case of cards that have jerseys, the jersey is right below the photo, and in the case of cards that have autographs, the autograph is at the bottom of the card. Hoops was offered for both Hobby and Retail were all packs containted five cards, but Hobby was released with 15 packs per box and Retail with 24.

COMP.SET w/o SP's (70) 15.00 40.00
71-90 PRINT RUNS LISTED IN CHECKLIST
91-99 PRINT RUN 350 SER.#'d SETS
100-110 PRINT RUN 1000 SER.#'d SETS
UNPRICED WHITE HOT PRINT RUN ONE SET
1 Dwyane Wade .60 1.60
2 Chris Bosh .40 1.00
3 Peja Stojakovic .40 1.00
4 Darius Miles .25 .60
5 Drew Gooden .25 .60
6 Latrell Sprewell .30 .75
7 Caron Butler .30 .75
8 Shaquille O'Neal 1.00 2.50
9 Reggie Miller .40 1.00
10 Corey Maggette .30 .75
11 Tracy McGrady .50 1.25
12 Ben Wallace .30 .75
13 Steve Nash .50 1.25
14 Paul Pierce .40 1.00
15 Jarvis Hayes .25 .60
16 Ray Allen .40 1.00
17 Chris Webber .40 1.00
18 Amare Stoudemire .30 .75
19 Pau Gasol .40 1.00
20 Jermaine O'Neal .30 .75
21 Yao Ming .75 2.00
22 Richard Hamilton .30 .75
23 Kirk Hinrich .30 .75
24 Antoine Walker .40 1.00
25 Carlos Arroyo .25 .60
26 Luke Ridnour .30 .75
27 Mike Bibby .40 1.00
28 Tim Duncan .60 1.50
29 Shareef Abdur-Rahim .30 .75
30 Willie Green .25 .60
31 Jamaal Magloire .25 .60
32 Stephen Jackson .30 .75
33 Karl Malone .50 1.25
34 Elton Brand .40 1.00
35 Jason Richardson .40 1.00
36 Steve Francis .30 .75
37 Jason Kidd .60 1.50
38 Kevin Garnett .60 1.50
39 Jason Williams .30 .75
40 Ron Artest .40 1.00
41 Darko Milicic .25 .60
42 Carmelo Anthony .75 2.00
43 Carlos Boozer .30 .75
44 Michael Finley .40 1.00
45 Marcus Fizer .25 .60
46 Ricky Davis .30 .75
47 Andrei Kirilenko .30 .75
48 Tony Parker .40 1.00
49 Shawn Marion .30 .75
50 Allan Houston .30 .75
51 Kenyon Martin .30 .75
52 T.J. Ford .25 .60
53 Nene .30 .75
54 LeBron James 2.50 6.00
55 Eddy Curry .25 .60
56 Jason Terry .30 .75
57 Vince Carter .60 1.50
58 Zach Randolph .30 .75
59 Allen Iverson .60 1.50
60 Stephon Marbury .30 .75
61 Richard Jefferson .30 .75
62 Baron Davis .30 .75
63 Michael Redd .30 .75
64 Lamar Odom .30 .75
65 Kobe Bryant 1.50 4.00
66 Mickael Pietrus .30 .75
67 Dirk Nowitzki .60 1.50
68 Dajuan Wagner .25 .60
69 Jason Kapono .25 .60
70 Antawn Jamison .30 .75
71 B.Gordon JSY AU/350 RC 6.00 15.00
72 S.Livingston JSY AU/350 RC 6.00 20.00
73 Devin Harris JSY AU/150 RC 5.00 12.00
74 J.Childress JSY AU/150 RC 5.00 12.00
75 Luol Deng JSY AU/150 RC 12.00 30.00
76 R.Araujo JSY AU/350 RC 4.00 10.00
77 L.Jackson JSY AU/150 RC 4.00 10.00
78 Andris Biedrins JSY AU RC 4.00 10.00
79 Y.Tabuse JSY AU/350 RC 6.00 15.00
80 S.Telfair JSY AU/350 RC 5.00 12.00
81 K.Humphries JSY AU/350 RC 6.00 15.00
82 Kirk Snyder JSY AU/150 RC 4.00 10.00
83 Josh Smith JSY AU/150 RC 6.00 15.00
84 J.R. Smith JSY AU/350 RC 6.00 15.00
85 D.Wright JSY AU/350 RC 6.00 15.00
86 J.Nelson JSY AU/350 RC 6.00 15.00
87 D.West JSY AU/350 RC 6.00 15.00
88 Tony Allen JSY AU/350 RC 6.00 15.00
89 Seung-Jin JSY AU/350 RC 6.00 15.00
90 Al Jefferson JSY AU/150 RC 8.00 20.00
91 Dwight Howard JSY RC 10.00 25.00
92 Andre Iguodala JSY RC 6.00 15.00
93 Jackson Vroman JSY RC 3.00 8.00
94 Lionel Chalmers JSY RC 5.00 12.00
95 Kevin Martin JSY RC 6.00 15.00
96 Sasha Vujacic JSY RC 5.00 12.00
97 Andre Emmett JSY RC 3.00 8.00
98 David Harrison JSY RC 3.00 8.00
99 Anderson Varejao JSY RC 4.00 10.00
100 Chris Duhon JSY RC 5.00 12.00
101 Emeka Okafor RC 1.50 4.00
102 Viktor Khryapa RC 1.25 3.00
103 Peter John Ramos RC 1.25 3.00
104 Sergei Monia RC 1.25 3.00
105 Beno Udrih RC 1.50 4.00
106 Pavel Podkolzin RC 1.25 3.00
107 Trevor Ariza RC 2.00 5.00
108 Royal Ivey RC 1.50 4.00
109 Bernard Robinson RC 1.50 4.00
110 Robert Swift RC 1.25 3.00

2004-05 Hoops Hot Prospects Red Hot

*1-70 RED: 2X TO 5X BASE HI
*71-90 RED: 1X TO 2.5X BASE HI
*91-100 RED: .6X TO 1.5X BASE HI
*101-110 RED: .75X TO 2X BASE HI
PRINT RUN 50 SER.#'d SETS

2004-05 Hoops Hot Prospects Alumni Ink

Randomly inserted in packs, this 10-card set features a hinged card that opens up on the inside with one player and his autograph on one side and another on the other. Both autographs are cut signatures and the cards are limited to 50 copies. Also released was a Red Hot set serially numbered to 10 and a White Hot set numbered one of one.

PRINT RUN 50 SER.#'d SETS
CJ V.Carter/A.Jamison 30.00 60.00
KA J.Kidd/S.Abdur-Rahim 25.00 60.00
MB S.Marbury/C.Bosh 15.00 40.00
RR Z.Randolph/J.Richardson 15.00 40.00
WN D.West/J.Nelson 15.00 40.00
WP A.Walker/T.Prince 15.00 40.00

2004-05 Hoops Hot Prospects Double Team

Inserted in Hobby packs at the rate of one in 45 and Retail at the rate of one in 96, this 13-card set is horizontally designed and pictures the featured player on the left in his NBA uniform and on the right in his Team USA uniform.

COMPLETE SET (13) 12.50 30.00
STATED ODDS 1:45 H, 1:96 R
AI Allen Iverson 1.25 3.00
AS Amare Stoudemire .60 1.50
CA Carmelo Anthony 1.50 4.00
CB Carlos Boozer .60 1.50
DW Dwyane Wade 1.25 3.00
EO Emeka Okafor .60 1.50
LB Larry Brown 2.50 6.00
LJ LeBron James 5.00 12.00
LO Lamar Odom .60 1.50
RJ Richard Jefferson .60 1.50
SM Stephon Marbury .60 1.50
SM Shawn Marion .60 1.50
TD Tim Duncan 1.25 3.00

2004-05 Hoops Hot Prospects Double Team Jerseys

Limited to 100 serially numbered copies, this 10-card set parallels the look of the base Double Team insert but instead of having an image of the player in his Team USA jersey, it includes a swatch of NBA memorabilia and USA memorabilia. Eight parallel sets were issued as well, Red Hot serially numbered to 25, White Hot numbered one of one, Patches serially numbered to 50, Patch Red Hot serially numbered to 10, Patch White Hot numbered one of one, Patch Autographs serially numbered to 25, Patch Autographs Red Hot serially numbered to five and Patch Autographs White Hot numbered one of one.

PRINT RUN 100 SER.#'d SETS
*RED HOT: .6X TO 1.5X BASE HI
RED HOT PRINT RUN 25 SER.#'d SETS
*PATCH SINGLES: 1.25X TO 3X BASE JSY HI
PATCH PRINT RUN 50 SER.#'d SETS
AI Allen Iverson 5.00 12.00
AS Amare Stoudemire 2.50 6.00
CA Carmelo Anthony 6.00 15.00
CB Carlos Boozer 2.50 6.00
DW Dwyane Wade 5.00 12.00
LO Lamar Odom 2.50 6.00
RJ Richard Jefferson 2.50 6.00
SM Shawn Marion 2.50 6.00
SM Stephon Marbury 3.00 8.00
TD Tim Duncan 6.00 15.00

2004-05 Hoops Hot Prospects Double Team Patches Autographs

Randomly inserted in packs, this 10-card set parallels the base Double Team Jerseys insert set enhanced with patch swatches, an autograph and sequential numbering to 25.

PRINT RUN 25 SER.#'d SETS
UNPRICED RED HOT PRINT RUN 5 SETS
UNPRICED WHITE HOT PRINT RUN ONE SET
CA Carmelo Anthony 75.00 200.00
RJ Richard Jefferson 15.00 40.00
SM Stephon Marbury 40.00 100.00

2004-05 Hoops Hot Prospects Draft Rewind

Inserted in both Hobby and Retail packs at the rate of one in five, this 30-card set is horizontally designed with player's likenesses featured on the left in scale color to match their team's main color and the team's logo in a white box on the right.

COMPLETE SET (30) 10.00 25.00
STATED ODDS 1:5
1 Dwyane Wade .60 1.50
2 Lamar Odom .30 .75
3 Peja Stojakovic .40 1.00
4 Shaquille O'Neal 1.00 2.50
5 Reggie Miller .40 1.00
6 Tracy McGrady .50 1.25
7 Steve Nash .50 1.25
8 Paul Pierce .40 1.00
9 Ray Allen .40 1.00
10 Dirk Nowitzki .60 1.50
11 Amare Stoudemire .30 .75
12 Pau Gasol .40 1.00
13 Jermaine O'Neal .30 .75
14 Yao Ming .75 2.00
15 Kirk Hinrich .30 .75
16 Tim Duncan .60 1.50
17 Karl Malone .50 1.25
18 Mike Bibby .40 1.00
19 Steve Francis .30 .75
20 Jason Kidd .60 1.50
21 Kevin Garnett .60 1.50
22 Darko Milicic .25 .60
23 Carmelo Anthony .75 2.00
24 Tony Parker .40 1.00
25 Kenyon Martin .30 .75
26 LeBron James 2.50 6.00
27 Vince Carter .60 1.50
28 Allen Iverson .60 1.50
29 Stephon Marbury .30 .75
30 Kobe Bryant 1.50 4.00

2004-05 Hoops Hot Prospects Draft Rewind Jerseys

Randomly seeded in packs, this 28-card set parallels the base Draft Rewind set enhanced with a swatch of jersey on the right side. Each card is sequentially numbered to a random amount. Two parallel sets were inserted as well: Red Hot which is sequentially numbered to 10 and White Hot which is done in one of one format.

STATED PRINT RUN 101 TO 117 SETS
AI Allen Iverson/101 5.00 12.00
AS Amare Stoudemire/109 2.50 6.00
CA Carmelo Anthony/103 6.00 15.00
DM Darko Milicic/102 2.00 5.00
DN Dirk Nowitzki/109 5.00 12.00
DW Dwyane Wade/105 5.00 12.00
JK Jason Kidd/102 5.00 12.00
JO Jermaine O'Neal/117 2.50 6.00
KG Kevin Garnett/105 5.00 12.00
KH Kirk Hinrich/107 2.50 6.00
KM Karl Malone/103 4.00 10.00
KM Kenyon Martin/101 2.50 6.00
LO Lamar Odom/104 2.50 6.00
MB Mike Bibby/102 3.00 8.00
PG Pau Gasol/103 3.00 8.00
PP Paul Pierce/110 3.00 8.00
PS Peja Stojakovic/114 3.00 8.00
RA Ray Allen/105 3.00 8.00
RM Reggie Miller/111 3.00 8.00
SF Steve Francis/102 2.50 6.00
SM Stephon Marbury/104 2.50 6.00
SN Steve Nash/115 4.00 10.00
SO Shaquille O'Neal/101 8.00 20.00
TD Tim Duncan/101 5.00 12.00
TM Tracy McGrady/109 4.00 10.00
TP Tony Parker/128 3.00 8.00
VC Vince Carter/105 5.00 12.00
YM Yao Ming/101 6.00 15.00

2004-05 Hoops Hot Prospects Draft Rewind Patches

PRINT RUNS LISTED IN CHECKLIST
MOST NOT PRICED DUE TO SCARCITY
AS Amare Stoudemire/19 6.00 15.00
CA Carmelo Anthony/13 15.00 40.00
DN Dirk Nowitzki/19 12.00 30.00
DW Dwyane Wade/15 15.00 40.00
JO Jermaine O'Neal/27 6.00 15.00
LO Lamar Odom/14 6.00 15.00
PG Pau Gasol/13 8.00 20.00
PP Paul Pierce/20 8.00 20.00
PS Peja Stojakovic/24 8.00 20.00
SM Stephon Marbury/14 8.00 20.00
TM Tracy McGrady/19 10.00 25.00
TP Tony Parker/38 8.00 20.00
VC Vince Carter/15 12.00 30.00

2004-05 Hoops Hot Prospects Hot Materials

Serially numbered to 500, this 35-card set features white borders, player action photos, accent colors to match the player's team colors and a square swatch of jersey centered towards the bottom of the card. Two parallels versions were released for this set: Red Hot sequentially numbered to 50 and White Hot in a one of one format.

PRINT RUN 500 SER.#'d SETS
*RED SINGLES: .6X TO 1.5X BASE JSY HI
RED HOT PRINT RUN 50 SER.#'d SETS
AI Allen Iverson 4.00 10.00
AS Amare Stoudemire 2.00 5.00
BD Baron Davis 2.00 5.00
BG Ben Gordon 2.50 6.00
BW Ben Wallace 2.00 5.00
CA Carmelo Anthony 5.00 12.00
CB Chris Bosh 2.50 6.00
DH Devin Harris 2.00 5.00
DH2 Dwight Howard 5.00 12.00
DM Darko Milicic 2.00 5.00
DN Dirk Nowitzki 4.00 10.00
DW Dwyane Wade 6.00 15.00
JC Josh Childress 2.00 5.00
JK Jason Kidd 4.00 10.00
JO Jermaine O'Neal 2.00 5.00
JR Jason Richardson 2.50 6.00
KG Kevin Garnett 4.00 10.00
KH Kirk Hinrich 2.00 5.00
LD Luol Deng 2.50 6.00
LO Lamar Odom 2.00 5.00
MB Mike Bibby 2.50 6.00
PG Pau Gasol 2.50 6.00
PP Paul Pierce 2.50 6.00
PS Peja Stojakovic 2.50 6.00
RA Ray Allen 2.50 6.00
RJ Richard Jefferson 2.00 5.00
SF Steve Francis 2.00 5.00
SL Shaun Livingston 2.50 6.00
SM Stephon Marbury 2.00 5.00
SM2 Shawn Marion 2.00 5.00
SO Shaquille O'Neal 6.00 15.00
TD Tim Duncan 4.00 10.00
TM Tracy McGrady 3.00 8.00
VC Vince Carter 4.00 10.00
YM Yao Ming 5.00 12.00

2004-05 Hoops Hot Prospects Notable Newcomers

Inserted in both Hobby and Retail packs at the rate of one in 15, this 15-card set places player portrait photos in the upper left hand corner of the card in blue, and a stripe across the middle of a mostly white background.

COMPLETE SET (15) 12.00 30.00
STATED ODDS 1:15
1 Dwight Howard 1.50 4.00
2 Emeka Okafor .60 1.50
3 Ben Gordon .75 2.00
4 Shaun Livingston .75 2.00
5 Devin Harris .60 1.50
6 Josh Childress .60 1.50
7 Luol Deng .75 2.00
8 Andre Iguodala 1.00 2.50
9 Luke Jackson .50 1.25
10 Sebastian Telfair .60 1.50
11 Kris Humphries .75 2.00
12 Al Jefferson 1.00 2.50
13 LeBron James 5.00 12.00
14 Carmelo Anthony 1.50 4.00
15 Dwyane Wade 1.25 3.00

2004-05 Hoops Hot Prospects Notable Notations

Randomly seeded in packs, this nine-card set parallels the design of the Notable Notations insert set enhanced with a cut signature at the bottom of the the card and sequential numbering to 50.

PRINT RUN 50 SER.#'d SETS
AJ Al Jefferson 10.00 25.00
BG Ben Gordon 8.00 20.00
CA Carmelo Anthony 20.00 50.00
DH Devin Harris 6.00 15.00
JC Josh Childress 6.00 15.00
KH Kris Humphries 8.00 20.00
LJ Luke Jackson 5.00 12.00
SL Shaun Livingston 8.00 20.00
ST Sebastian Telfair 6.00 15.00

1991-92 Hoops McDonald's

Four-card cello packs, featuring three NBA cards and one Olympic team card, were distributed at participating McDonald's restaurants with the purchase of any Extra Value Meal, or for 49 cents with any other purchase. A specially marked instant winner card replaced a regular card in one in 20,000 packs, and the holder of this card received the complete 70-card "Superstar" set. After the termination of the promotion many of the excess remaining 70-card sets found their way into the hobby and are now much easier to find. The standard-size cards display color action photos enclosed by different color borders on a white card face. The horizontally oriented backs have a color head shot as well as biographical and statistical information. The set divides into three sections and is checklisted below as follows: player cards (1-50 listed alphabetically according to teams), USA Olympic basketball team (51-62), and Chicago Bulls (63-70 available only in the Chicago area).

COMPLETE SET (70) 10.00 25.00
COMPLETE NAT.SET (62) 6.00 15.00
COMPLETE BULLS SET (8) 2.40 6.00
1 Dominique Wilkins .20 .50
2 Larry Bird .50 1.25
3 Kevin McHale .15 .40
4 Robert Parish .15 .40
5 Michael Jordan 1.50 4.00
6 John Paxson .05 .05
7 Scottie Pippen .50 1.25
8 Brad Daugherty .05 .05
9 Rolando Blackman .05 .05
10 Derek Harper .05 .15
11 Joe Dumars .07 .20
12 Bill Laimbeer .05 .15
13 Isiah Thomas .07 .20
14 Tim Hardaway .30 .75
15 Chris Mullin .07 .20
16 Hakeem Olajuwon .30 .75
17 Reggie Miller .30 .75
18 Chuck Person .05 .05
19 Charles Smith .05 .05
20 Vlade Divac .05 .15
21 James Worthy .08 .25
22 Rony Seikaly .05 .05
23 Alvin Robertson .05 .05
24 Pooh Richardson .05 .05
25 Derrick Coleman .08 .25
26 Patrick Ewing .30 .75
27 Xavier McDaniel .05 .05
28 Dennis Scott .05 .15
29 Scott Skiles .05 .05
30 Charles Barkley .30 .75
31 Hersey Hawkins .05 .15
32 Tom Chambers .05 .05
33 Kevin Johnson .10 .30
34 Clyde Drexler .30 .75
35 Terry Porter .05 .05
36 Buck Williams .05 .15
37 Mitch Richmond .30 .75
38 Lionel Simmons .05 .05
39 Terry Cummings .05 .05
40 Sean Elliott .05 .15
41 David Robinson .30 .75
42 Shawn Kemp .25 .60
43 Ricky Pierce .05 .05
44 Karl Malone .50 1.25
45 John Stockton .50 1.25
46 Bernard King .05 .15
47 Larry Johnson .30 .75
48 Dikembe Mutombo .40 1.00
49A Billy Owens ERR .40 1.00
49B Billy Owens COR .07 .20
50 Kenny Anderson .05 .15
51 Charles Barkley USA .40 1.00
52 Larry Bird USA .60 1.50
53 Patrick Ewing USA .40 1.00
54 Magic Johnson USA .40 1.00
55 Michael Jordan USA 2.00 5.00
56 Karl Malone USA .50 1.25
57 Chris Mullin USA .20 .50
58 Scottie Pippen USA .50 1.25
59 David Robinson USA .40 1.00
60 John Stockton USA .50 1.25
61 Chuck Daly CO USA .40 1.00
62 USAB Team .40 1.00
63 B.J. Armstrong .30 .75
64 Bill Cartwright .30 .75
65 Horace Grant .40 1.00
66 Craig Hodges .30 .75
67 Stacey King .30 .75
68 Cliff Levingston .30 .75
69 Will Perdue .30 .75
70 Scott Williams .30 .75

1994-95 Hoops NSCC Sheet

Given away at the National Sports Collectors Convention (August 2, 4-7, 1994), this promotional sheet measures approximately 7 1/2" by 12". After perforation, each card measures the standard size. The cards preview the design of the 1994-95 Hoops series. The fronts display full-bleed color action photos. A team color-coded stripe cuts across the bottom and carries the player's name, team logo, and position. The backs carry a color headshot, biography, statistics, and player profile. A mustard stripe beneath the last row of cards has a gold foil seal indicating the serial number and the production total (20,000). The individual cards on the sheet are unnumbered and ordered below as they are arranged on the sheet.

NNO Hoops panel 2.00 5.00
Dino Radja
Scott Burrell
Anfernee Hardaway
Latrell Sprewell
Jim Jackson
Hakeem Olajuwon
Vin Baker
Gheorghe Muresan

1994-95 Hoops Schick

As part of a second quarter promotion by Schick Shaving Products Group, a division of the Warner-Lambert Co., this 30-card set features 29 of the NBA's top rookies. The checklist card, which completes the set, features Donyell Marshall shaving with the official NBA Tracer razor on its front. Three cards were available in each specially-marked package of Tracer 5 and 10 pack refills. The package also included a special mail-in offer card whereby the collector received the complete set by sending in three proofs-of-purchase plus 2.50 for postage and handling. The offer expired 12/31/95 or while supplies lasted. These cards have the same design as their regular issue counterparts, except that the word "Rookie" and the player's name on the fronts are in gold (rather than gold-foil) lettering. Also these cards are unnumbered and thus listed below in alphabetical order.

COMPLETE SET (30) 12.00 30.00
1 Sergei Bazarevich .75 2.00
2 Bill Curley .50 1.25
3 Tony Dumas .75 2.00
4 Brian Grant 1.25 3.00
5 Darrin Hancock .60 1.50
6 Grant Hill 4.00 10.00
7 Eddie Jones 2.50 6.00
8 Jason Kidd 4.00 10.00
9 Aaron McKie .75 2.00
10 Donyell Marshall .75 2.00
11 Anthony Miller .75 2.00
12 Greg Minor .75 2.00
13 Eric Mobley .50 1.25
14 Eric Montross .60 1.50
15 Lamond Murray .75 2.00
16 Eric Piatkowski 1.00 2.50
17 Wesley Person .75 2.00
18 Khalid Reeves .60 1.50
19 Glenn Robinson 1.50 4.00
20 Carlos Rogers .60 1.50
21 Jalen Rose 2.00 5.00
22 Clifford Rozier .50 1.25
23 Dickey Simpkins .60 1.50
24 Brooks Thompson .60 1.50
25 Anthony Tucker .50 1.25
26 B.J. Tyler .50 1.25
27 Charlie Ward .75 2.00
28 Monty Williams .60 1.50
29 Sharone Wright .60 1.50
30 Donyell Marshall CL .75 2.00
Shaving)

1993-94 Hoops Sheets

The fronts feature borderless glossy color player action shots, with the player's name and team logo appearing in team colors along a ghosted band at the bottom. The back presents a color head shot of the player in a small rectangle bordered with a team color at the upper right. Alongside is his jersey number and position within a team-colored bar. The player's name and a short biography are printed on a hardwood floor design at the top. Below, the player's college and NBA stats, displayed in separate tables on a white background, round out the card. The cards are unnumbered and checklisted below in alphabetical order.

COMPLETE SET (6) 12.00 30.00
1 B.J. Armstrong 4.00 10.00
Bill Cartwright
Horace Grant
Phil Jackson
Stacy King
John Paxson
Will Perdue
Scottie Pippen
Scott Williams
2 Greg Anderson 2.50 6.00
Don Chaney CO
Joe Dumars
Sean Elliott
Allan Houston
Lindsey Hunter
Terry Mills
Olden Polynice
Isiah Thomas
David Wood
3 Kenny Anderson 2.50 6.00
Derrick Coleman
Chris Morris
Chuck Daly CO
Rick Mahorn
Jayson Williams
Kevin Edwards
Armon Gilliam
Dwayne Schintzius
Chucky Brown
Benoit Benjamin
Rex Walters
4 Greg Anthony 2.50 6.00
Patrick Ewing
Charles Oakley
Charles Smith
John Starks
5 Danny Ainge 3.00 8.00
Charles Barkley
Cedric Ceballos
A.C. Green
Kevin Johnson
Dan Majerle
Oliver Miller
Mark West
Paul Westphal CO
6 Nick Anderson 4.00 10.00
Anthony Bowie
Shaquille O'Neal
Donald Royal
Scott Skiles
Jeff Turner

1994-95 Hoops Sheets

Distributed one per customer on game nights at various NBA arenas, these perforated sheets consist of standard-size cards and vary in size, depending on the number cards featured. On some sheets, one or more card slots have sponsors' advertisements rather than player cards. The fronts feature borderless glossy color player action shots, with the player's name and team logo appearing in a team color-coded bar at the bottom. The back presents a color head shot of the player, along with biography, statistics and profile. The cards are unnumbered and checklisted below in alphabetical order.

COMPLETE SET (18) 30.00 80.00
1 Stacey Augmon 2.50 6.00
Mookie Blaylock
Tyrone Corbin
Craig Ehlo
Jon Koncak
Andrew Lang
Ken Norman
Steve Smith
Lenny Wilkens CO
2 Michael Adams 2.50 6.00
Tony Bennett
Muggsy Bogues
Scott Burrell
Dell Curry
Kenny Gattison
Darrin Hancock
Hersey Hawkins
Larry Johnson
Alonzo Mourning
Robert Parish
David Wingate
3 Muggsy Bogues 2.50 6.00
Dell Curry
Hersey Hawkins
Larry Johnson
Alonzo Mourning
4 Michael Adams 2.50 6.00
Tony Bennett
Muggsy Bogues
Scott Burrell
Dell Curry
Kenny Gattison
Hersey Hawkins
Larry Johnson
Alonzo Mourning
Robert Parish
David Wingate
5 B.J. Armstrong 3.00 8.00
Corie Blount
Phil Jackson
Steve Kerr
Toni Kukoc
Luc Longley
Scottie Pippen
Bill Wennington
6 Terry Davis 3.00 8.00
Tony Dumas
Lucious Harris
Jim Jackson
Popeye Jones
Jason Kidd
Jamal Mashburn
Dick Motta CO
7 Mahmoud Abdul-Rauf 2.50 6.00
LaPhonso Ellis
Dan Issel CO
Dikembe Mutombo
Robert Pack
Rodney Rogers
Bryant Stith
Brian Williams
Reggie Williams
8 Don Chaney CO 5.00 12.00
Bill Curley
Joe Dumars
Grant Hill
Allan Houston
Lindsey Hunter
Mark Macon
Oliver Miller
Terry Mills
Mark West
9 Bill Blair CO 2.50 6.00
Mike Brown
Stacey King
Christian Laettner
Donyell Marshall
Isaiah Rider
Doug West
Michael Williams
10 Greg Anthony 3.00 8.00
Anthony Bonner
Hubert Davis
Patrick Ewing
Derek Harper
Anthony Mason
Charles Oakley
Charles Smith
John Starks
Herb Williams
11 Nick Anderson 5.00 12.00
Anthony Bowie
Horace Grant
Anfernee Hardaway
Shaquille O'Neal
Tree Rollins
Donald Royal
Dennis Scott
Brian Shaw
Brooks Thompson
Jeff Turner
12 Danny Ainge 4.00 10.00
Charles Barkley
A.C. Green
Kevin Johnson
Joe Kleine
Dan Majerle
Danny Manning
Elliot Perry
Wesley Person
Wayman Tisdale
13 P.J. Carlesimo CO 4.00 10.00
Clyde Drexler
Chris Dudley
Harvey Grant
Jerome Kersey
Tracy Murray
Terry Porter
Clifford Robinson
James Robinson
14 Vincent Askew 3.00 8.00
Bill Cartwright
Ervin Johnson
George Karl CO
Shawn Kemp
Sarunas Marciulionis
Nate McMillan
Gary Payton
Sam Perkins
Detlef Schrempf
Dontonio Wingfield
15 David Benoit 2.50 6.00
Tom Chambers
John Crotty
Jeff Hornacek
Karl Malone
Byron Russell
Jerry Sloan CO
Felton Spencer
John Stockton
16 Mitchell Butler 2.50 6.00
Rex Chapman
Calbert Cheaney
Don MacClean
Gheorghe Muresan
Scott Skiles

Chris Webber
Team Card
17 Mitchell Butler 4.00 10.00
Rex Chapman
Calbert Cheaney
Kevin Duckworth
Juwan Howard
Don MacLean
Jim McIlvaine
Gheorghe Muresan
Scott Skiles
Kenny Walker
Chris Webber
18 Mitchell Butler 4.00 10.00
Rex Chapman
Calbert Cheaney
Kevin Duckworth
Juwan Howard
Don MacLean
Jim McIlvaine
Gheorghe Muresan
Scott Skiles
Kenny Walker
Chris Webber

1995-96 Hoops Sheets

The fronts feature borderless glossy color player action shots, with the player's name and team logo along a "torn-out" band at the bottom. The back presents a a color action shot along the left border. The player's name and a short biography are printed against a white background. The cards are unnumbered and checklisted below in alphabetical order.

COMPLETE SET (13) 15.00 40.00
1 Lenny Wilkens CO 2.00 5.00
Stacey Augmon
Mookie Blaylock
Craig Ehlo
Alan Henderson
Andrew Lang
Grant Long
Ken Norman
Steve Smith
Spud Webb
2 Muggsy Bogues 2.00 5.00
Kendall Gill
Glen Rice
Scott Burrell
Larry Johnson
Dell Curry
George Zidek
Khalid Reeves
3 Phil Jackson CO 4.00 10.00
Jason Caffey
Michael Jordan
Toni Kukoc
Luc Longley
Scottie Pippen
Dennis Rodman
Dickey Simpkins
4 Grant Hill 2.50 6.00
Joe Dumars
Terry Mills
Allan Houston
Lindsey Hunter
Theo Ratliff
Otis Thorpe
Doug Collins CO
5 Sedale Threatt 2.50 6.00
Frankie King
Nick Van Exel
Vlade Divac
Cedric Ceballos
Eddie Jones
George Lynch
Elden Campbell
Corie Blount
Del Harris CO
6 Shawn Bradley 2.00 5.00
Kevin Edwards
Rick Mahorn
Kendall Gill
P.J. Brown
Butch Beard CO
Armon Gilliam
Ed O'Bannon
Chris Childs
Yinka Dare
Jayson Williams
7 Patrick Ewing 2.00 5.00
Charles Oakley
John Starks
Anthony Mason
Don Nelson CO
Derek Harper
Charles Smith
Herb Williams
Hubert Davis
8 Nick Anderson 2.50 6.00
Anthony Bowie
Horace Grant
Anfernee Hardaway
Jon Koncak
Shaquille O'Neal
Donald Royal
Dennis Scott
Brian Shaw
Jeff Turner
David Vaughn
9 Elliot Perry 2.00 5.00
A.C. Green
Wayman Tisdale
Mario Bennett
Charles Barkley
Danny Manning
Wesley Person
Michael Finley
Kevin Johnson
10 Clifford Robinson 2.00 5.00
Rod Strickland
Chris Dudley
Arvydas Sabonis
Buck Williams
James Robinson
P.J. Carlesimo CO
Randolph Childress
Gary Trent
Dontonio Wingfield
11 Mitch Richmond 2.00 5.00
Olden Polynice
Brian Grant
Michael Smith
Tyus Edney
Bobby Hurley
Corliss Williamson
Garry St. Jean CO
12 David Benoit 3.00 8.00
Jeff Hornacek
Karl Malone
Felton Spencer
John Stockton
Adam Keefe
Jerry Sloan CO
13 Mitchell Butler 2.50 6.00
Calbert Cheaney
Juwan Howard
Tim Legler
Jim McIlvaine
Gheorghe Muresan
Robert Pack
Brent Price
Mark Price
Rasheed Wallace
Chris Webber

1996-97 Hoops Sheets

Distributed one per customer on game nights at various NBA arenas, these perforated sheets consist of standard-size cards and vary in size, depending on the number cards featured. On some sheets, one or more card slots have sponsors' advertisements rather than player cards. The fronts feature borderless glossy color player action shots, with the player's name and team logo appearing at the bottom. The gold-foil is missing from these cards versus their regular Hoops cards. The back presents the player's biography, statistics and profile. The cards are unnumbered and checklisted below in alphabetical order. Currently, we only have the two sheets checklisted. More will be added as we get them checklisted.

COMPLETE SET (2) 8.00 20.00
1A Byron Scott 8.00 20.00
Nick Van Exel
Shaquille O'Neal
Del Harris
Derek Fisher
Kobe Bryant
Robert Horry
Sean Rooks
Eddie Jones
Jerome Kersey
Elden Campbell
1B Byron Scott LA .40 1.00
1C Nick Van Exel LA .40 1.00
1D Shaquille O'Neal LA .75 2.00
1E Del Harris LA .40 1.00
1F Derek Fisher LA .75 2.00
1G Robert Horry LA .40 1.00
1H Kobe Bryant LA 3.00 8.00
1I Sean Rooks LA .40 1.00
1J Eddie Jones LA .40 1.00
1K Jerome Kersey LA .40 1.00
1L Elden Campbell LA .40 1.00
2A Wesley Person 1.50 4.00
John Williams
Danny Manning
Kevin Johnson
2B Wesley Person SUNS .40 1.00
2C John Williams SUNS .40 1.00
2D Danny Manning SUNS .40 1.00
2E Kevin Johnson SUNS .40 1.00

2002-03 Hoops Stars

Released in early January 2003, Hoops Stars features a 200-card set divided up into 170 veteran cards and 30 rookie cards. Base cards feature a color player photo centered on a patterned background which is made to look like a basketball court on the right and combination of colors and true life background on the left. Each card is highlighted with silver foil. Hoops Stars was packaged in 20-pack boxes with 19 packs containing 10 cards and one Superstar pack containing five cards with different color foil versions of base and insert cards for a roster that consists of 25 different players. Hoops Stars packs carried an SRP of $2.99.

COMP.SET w/o RC's (170) 12.50 30.00
1 Tracy McGrady .50 1.25
2 Kevin Garnett .50 1.25
3 Allen Iverson .50 1.25
4 Keith Van Horn .25 .60
5 Kwame Brown .20 .50
6 Alan Henderson .20 .50
7 Kenny Anderson .25 .60
8 Antoine Walker .25 .60
9 Tony Delk .20 .50
10 Tony Battie .20 .50
11 Wally Szczerbiak .25 .60
12 Paul Pierce .30 .75
13 Glenn Robinson .25 .60
14 Tim Thomas .20 .50
15 Vince Carter .50 1.25
16 Pau Gasol .40 1.00
17 Eddy Curry .20 .50
18 Darrell Armstrong .20 .50
19 Sam Cassell .25 .60
20 Darius Miles .20 .50
21 Jason Richardson .30 .75
22 Elton Brand .30 .75
23 Michael Jordan 2.50 6.00
24 Andre Miller .25 .60
25 Anfernee Hardaway .50 1.25
26 Steve Nash .40 1.00
27 Ron Artest .30 .75
28 Raef LaFrentz .20 .50
29 Troy Hudson .20 .50
30 Rasheed Wallace .30 .75
31 Ricky Davis .25 .60
32 Juwan Howard .25 .60
33 Steve Francis .25 .60
34 Shaquille O'Neal .75 2.00
35 James Posey .20 .50
36 DeShawn Stevenson .20 .50
37 Clifford Robinson .20 .50
38 Jerry Stackhouse .25 .60
39 Chauncey Billups .30 .75
40 Mike Bibby .30 .75
41 Dirk Nowitzki .50 1.25
42 Corliss Williamson .20 .50
43 Antawn Jamison .30 .75
44 Jamal Mashburn .25 .60
45 Danny Fortson .20 .50
46 Reggie Miller .30 .75
47 Scottie Pippen .50 1.25
48 Donnell Harvey .20 .50
49 Moochie Norris .20 .50
50 Corey Maggette .25 .60
51 Eddie Griffin .20 .50
52 Karl Malone .40 1.00
53 Maurice Taylor .20 .50
54 Al Harrington .25 .60
55 Kenyon Martin .25 .60
56 Nick Van Exel .25 .60
57 Jermaine O'Neal .25 .60
58 Anthony Mason .20 .50
59 Jamaal Tinsley .20 .50
60 Chris Mihm .20 .50
61 Lamar Odom .25 .60
62 Cuttino Mobley .20 .50
63 Michael Olowokandi .20 .50
64 Michael Finley .30 .75
65 Anthony Peeler .20 .50
66 Mengke Bateer .20 .50
67 Rick Fox .20 .50
68 Steve Smith .25 .60
69 Robert Horry .25 .60
70 Devean George .20 .50
71 Jason Williams .25 .60
72 Stromile Swift .20 .50
73 Marcus Fizer .20 .50
74 Michael Dickerson .20 .50
75 Shane Battier .30 .75
76 Larry Hughes .25 .60
77 Brian Skinner .20 .50
78 Eddie Jones .25 .60
79 Malik Allen .20 .50
80 Ray Allen .30 .75
81 Jumaine Jones .20 .50
82 Donyell Marshall .20 .50
83 Toni Kukoc .30 .75
84 Michael Redd .25 .60
85 Ron Mercer .20 .50
86 Terrell Brandon .20 .50
87 Latrell Sprewell .25 .60
88 Kobe Bryant 1.25 3.00
89 Kurt Thomas .20 .50
90 Rasho Nesterovic .20 .50
91 Shareef Abdur-Rahim .25 .60
92 Eduardo Najera .20 .50
93 Jamaal Magloire .20 .50
94 Antonio Davis .20 .50
95 Rodney Rogers .20 .50
96 Jason Collins .20 .50
97 Marcus Camby .25 .60
98 Joe Smith .25 .60
99 Richard Jefferson .30 .75
100 Gilbert Arenas .30 .75
101 Courtney Alexander .20 .50
102 David Wesley .20 .50
103 Baron Davis .25 .60
104 Elden Campbell .20 .50
105 Jason Kidd .50 1.25
106 P.J. Brown .20 .50
107 Rashard Lewis .30 .75
108 Alvin Williams .20 .50
109 Kerry Kittles .20 .50
110 Charlie Ward .20 .50
111 Kedrick Brown .20 .50
112 Shandon Anderson .20 .50
113 Grant Hill .40 1.00
114 Tyson Chandler .30 .75
115 Brent Barry .20 .50
116 Travis Best .20 .50
117 Mike Miller .25 .60
118 Aaron McKie .20 .50
119 Theo Ratliff .20 .50
120 Todd MacCulloch .20 .50
121 Trenton Hassell .20 .50
122 Vin Baker .25 .60
123 Dion Glover .20 .50
124 Stephon Marbury .25 .60
125 Ben Wallace .25 .60
126 Glen Rice .25 .60
127 Joe Johnson .25 .60
128 Chris Webber .30 .75
129 Damon Stoudamire .25 .60
130 Voshon Lenard .20 .50
131 Troy Murphy .25 .60
132 Desmond Mason .25 .60
133 Ruben Patterson .20 .50
134 John Stockton .40 1.00
135 Bobby Jackson .20 .50
136 Shawn Marion .25 .60
137 Jarron Collins .20 .50
138 Tom Gugliotta .20 .50
139 Doug Christie .20 .50
140 Zeljko Rebraca .20 .50
141 Tim Duncan .60 1.50
142 David Robinson .50 1.25
143 Tony Parker .40 1.00
144 Derek Fisher .25 .60
145 Speedy Claxton .20 .50
146 Eric Snow .20 .50
147 Gary Payton .30 .75
148 Pat Garrity .20 .50
149 Joseph Forte .20 .50
150 Derek Anderson .20 .50
151 Vladimir Radmanovic .20 .50
152 Samuel Dalembert .20 .50
153 Allan Houston .25 .60
154 Jalen Rose .25 .60
155 Dikembe Mutombo .30 .75
156 Jerome Williams .20 .50
157 Antonio McDyess .25 .60
158 Morris Peterson .20 .50
159 Bonzi Wells .20 .50
160 Hedo Turkoglu .25 .60
161 Gerald Wallace .25 .60
162 Andrei Kirilenko .30 .75
163 Matt Harpring .20 .50
164 Peja Stojakovic .30 .75
165 Zydrunas Ilgauskas .25 .60
166 Richard Hamilton .25 .60
167 Brian Grant .20 .50
168 Christian Laettner .25 .60
169 Jason Terry .25 .60
170 Alonzo Mourning .40 1.00
171 Yao Ming RC 2.00 5.00
172 Jay Williams RC 1.00 2.50
173 Mike Dunleavy RC 1.00 2.50
174 Chris Wilcox RC .75 2.00
175 Amare Stoudemire RC 1.25 3.00
176 Fred Jones RC .75 2.00
177 Caron Butler RC 1.00 2.50
178 Melvin Ely RC .75 2.00
179 Drew Gooden RC 1.00 2.50
180 DaJuan Wagner RC .75 2.00
181 Jared Jeffries RC .75 2.00
182 Nikoloz Tskitishvili RC .60 1.50
183 Nene Hilario RC 1.00 2.50
184 Dan Dickau RC .75 2.00
185 Marcus Haislip RC .75 2.00
186 Gordan Giricek RC 1.00 2.50
187 Jiri Welsch RC .75 2.00
188 Juan Dixon RC 1.00 2.50
189 Curtis Borchardt RC .60 1.50
190 Ryan Humphrey RC .75 2.00
191 Kareem Rush RC .75 2.00
192 Qyntel Woods RC .75 2.00
193 Casey Jacobsen RC .75 2.00
194 Tayshaun Prince RC 1.25 3.00
195 Frank Williams RC .60 1.50
196 Pat Burke RC .60 1.50
197 Chris Jefferies RC .60 1.50
198 Carlos Boozer RC 1.00 2.50
199 Manu Ginobili RC 2.50 6.00
200 Vincent Yarbrough RC .60 1.50

2002-03 Hoops Stars Five-Star

*STARS: 2.5X TO 6X BASE CARD HI
*RCs: .6X TO 1.5X BASE CARD HI
PRINT RUN 299 SERIAL #'d SETS

2002-03 Hoops Stars Platinum

*STARS: 4X TO 10X BASE CARD HI
*RC's: 1.25X TO 3X BASE CARD HI
INSERTED INTO SUPERSTARS PACKS
PRINT RUN 100 SERIAL #'d SETS
SKIP-NUMBERED SET
23 Michael Jordan 30.00 80.00
34 Shaquille O'Neal 8.00 20.00
88 Kobe Bryant 12.00 30.00
141 Tim Duncan 6.00 15.00
172 Jay Williams 3.00 8.00
173 Mike Dunleavy 3.00 8.00

2002-03 Hoops Stars Red

*STARS: 1.25X TO 3X BASE CARD HI
*RCs: .4X TO 1X BASE CARD HI
INSERTED INTO SUPERSTAR PACKS
SKIP-NUMBERED SET
1 Tracy McGrady 1.50 4.00
2 Kevin Garnett 1.50 4.00
3 Allen Iverson 1.50 4.00
12 Paul Pierce 1.00 2.50
15 Vince Carter 1.50 4.00
16 Pau Gasol 1.25 3.00
20 Darius Miles .60 1.50
21 Jason Richardson 1.00 2.50
23 Michael Jordan 25.00 60.00
33 Steve Francis .75 2.00
34 Shaquille O'Neal 2.50 6.00
40 Mike Bibby 1.00 2.50
41 Dirk Nowitzki 1.50 4.00
52 Karl Malone 1.25 3.00
88 Kobe Bryant 4.00 10.00
103 Baron Davis .75 2.00
105 Jason Kidd 1.50 4.00
141 Tim Duncan 2.00 5.00
171 Yao Ming 2.00 5.00
172 Jay Williams 1.00 2.50
173 Mike Dunleavy 1.00 2.50
177 Caron Butler 1.00 2.50
179 Drew Gooden 1.00 2.50
180 DaJuan Wagner .75 2.00

2002-03 Hoops Stars Future Stars

Randomly inserted in packs at the rate of one in 10, this 15-card set uses a horizontal design with photos of top rookies on the left side of the card, a colored strip across the middle set to match the player's team colors and silver foil highlights. A Blue version of this set was inserted into the box-topper Super Star packs.

COMPLETE SET (15) 10.00 25.00
STATED ODDS 1:10
*BLUE: .6X TO 1.5X FUTURE STAR HI
BLUE RANDOM INSERTS IN BOX-TOPPER
FS1 Yao Ming 1.50 4.00
FS2 Jay Williams .75 2.00
FS3 Mike Dunleavy .75 2.00
FS4 Chris Wilcox .60 1.50
FS5 Amare Stoudemire 1.00 2.50
FS6 Fred Jones .60 1.50
FS7 Caron Butler .75 2.00
FS8 Melvin Ely .60 1.50
FS9 Drew Gooden .75 2.00
FS10 DaJuan Wagner .60 1.50
FS11 Jared Jeffries .60 1.50
FS12 Nikoloz Tskitishvili .50 1.25
FS13 Nene Hilario .75 2.00
FS14 Dan Dickau .60 1.50
FS15 Juan Dixon .75 2.00

2002-03 Hoops Stars Future Stars Game-Used

Randomly inserted in packs at the rate of one in 52, this 11-card set parallels the design of the base Future Stars insert set enhanced with a swatch of game-used shoot shirt on the right side of the card.

STATED ODDS 1:52
FSGU1 Chris Wilcox 2.00 5.00
FSGU2 Amare Stoudemire 3.00 8.00
FSGU3 Fred Jones 2.00 5.00
FSGU4 Caron Butler 2.50 6.00
FSGU5 Melvin Ely 2.00 5.00
FSGU6 Drew Gooden 2.50 6.00
FSGU7 DaJuan Wagner 2.00 5.00
FSGU8 Jared Jeffries 2.00 5.00
FSGU9 Nene Hilario 2.50 6.00
FSGU11 Juan Dixon 2.50 6.00

2002-03 Hoops Stars Raising Up

Randomly inserted in packs at the rate of one in five, this 25-card set places player photos on a blue streaky background with sweeping color mixed in to match the player's team colors. Each card contains silver foil highlights. A Blue version of this set was inserted into the box-topper Super Star packs.

COMPLETE SET (25) 15.00 40.00
STATED ODDS 1:5
*BLUE: .6X TO 1.5X RAISING UP HI
BLUE RANDOM INSERTS IN BOX TOPPER
RU1 Jason Kidd 1.00 2.50
RU2 Kevin Garnett 1.00 2.50
RU3 Vince Carter 1.00 2.50
RU4 Baron Davis .50 1.25
RU5 Paul Pierce .60 1.50
RU6 Dirk Nowitzki 1.00 2.50
RU7 Shaquille O'Neal 1.50 4.00
RU8 Michael Jordan 5.00 12.00
RU9 Tim Duncan 1.25 3.00
RU10 Allen Iverson 1.00 2.50
RU11 Jason Richardson .60 1.50
RU12 Pau Gasol .75 2.00
RU13 Steve Francis .50 1.25
RU14 Kobe Bryant 2.50 6.00
RU15 Mike Bibby .60 1.50
RU16 Grant Hill .75 2.00
RU17 Tracy McGrady 1.00 2.50
RU18 Karl Malone .75 2.00
RU19 Darius Miles .40 1.00
RU20 Jay Williams .60 1.50
RU21 Mike Dunleavy .60 1.50
RU22 Drew Gooden .60 1.50
RU23 DaJuan Wagner .50 1.25
RU24 Caron Butler .60 1.50
RU25 Yao Ming 1.25 3.00

2002-03 Hoops Stars Raising Up Game-Used

Randomly inserted in packs, this 15-card set parallels the design from the base Raising Up set enhanced with a swatch of game used memorabilia. Several different types of memorabilia were used and are notated below in the checklist. Each card is sequentially numbered to 250.

STATED PRINT RUN 250 SERIAL #'d SETS
RUGU1 Jason Kidd Pants 5.00 12.00
RUGU2 Kevin Garnett Jacket 5.00 12.00
RUGU3 Vince Carter JSY 5.00 12.00
RUGU4 Paul Pierce Pants 3.00 8.00
RUGU5 Allen Iverson JSY 6.00 15.00
RUGU6 Pau Gasol Jacket 4.00 10.00
RUGU7 Steve Francis Shorts 2.50 6.00
RUGU8 Grant Hill JSY 4.00 10.00
RUGU9 Tracy McGrady JSY 5.00 12.00
RUGU10 Karl Malone Pants 4.00 10.00
RUGU11 Darius Miles JSY 2.00 5.00
RUGU12 Drew Gooden Shorts 3.00 8.00
RUGU13 DaJuan Wagner Shorts 2.50 6.00
RUGU14 Caron Butler Shorts 3.00 8.00
RUGU15 Yao Ming JSY 6.00 15.00

2002-03 Hoops Stars Rare Air

Randomly seeded in packs at the rate of one in 30, this 20-card set fatures full color action photos set against a background that looks like a clouded sky on the top and the top of the key towards the bottom. Each card is highlighted with silver foil. A Blue version of this set was inserted into the box-topper Super Star packs.

COMPLETE SET (20) 20.00 50.00
STATED ODDS 1:30
*BLUE: .6X TO 1.5X RARE AIR HI
BLUE RANDOM INSERTS IN BOX TOPPER
RA1 Jason Kidd 2.00 5.00
RA2 Kevin Garnett 2.00 5.00
RA3 Vince Carter 2.00 5.00
RA4 Baron Davis 1.00 2.50
RA5 Paul Pierce 1.25 3.00
RA6 Dirk Nowitzki 2.00 5.00
RA7 Shaquille O'Neal 3.00 8.00
RA8 Michael Jordan 10.00 25.00
RA9 Tim Duncan 2.50 6.00
RA10 Allen Iverson 2.00 5.00
RA11 Jason Richardson 1.25 3.00
RA12 Pau Gasol 1.50 4.00
RA13 Steve Francis 1.00 2.50
RA14 Kobe Bryant 5.00 12.00
RA15 Mike Bibby 1.25 3.00
RA16 Grant Hill 1.50 4.00
RA17 Tracy McGrady 2.00 5.00
RA18 Karl Malone 1.50 4.00
RA19 Darius Miles .75 2.00
RA20 Latrell Sprewell 1.00 2.50

2002-03 Hoops Stars Rare Air Game-Used

Randomly inserted in packs at the rate of one in 52,, this 10-card set parallels the design of the base Rare Air insert set enhanced with a swatch of game used memorabilia. Different types of memorabilia were used, so they are notated below with the checklist.

STATED ODDS 1:52
RAGU1 Jason Kidd Jacket 5.00 12.00
RAGU2 Kevin Garnett JSY 5.00 12.00
RAGU3 Vince Carter JSY 5.00 12.00
RAGU4 Paul Pierce Jacket 3.00 8.00
RAGU5 Dirk Nowitzki JSY 5.00 12.00
RAGU6 Allen Iverson Pants 5.00 12.00
RAGU7 Pau Gasol Pants 4.00 10.00
RAGU8 Grant Hill Pants 4.00 10.00
RAGU9 Tracy McGrady Pants 5.00 12.00
RAGU10 Karl Malone JSY 4.00 10.00

2002-03 Hoops Stars Star Gazing

Randomly inserted in packs at the rate of one in 20, this 25-card set showcases a horizontal design where a player photo appears on the left of the card and the right side of the card is die cut around a silver foil star in the upper right hand corner. Background start as basketball texture on the left and shift to colors that match the featured player's team colors on the right. A Blue version of this set was inserted into the box-topper Super Star packs.

COMPLETE SET (25) 20.00 50.00
STATED ODDS 1:20
*BLUE: .6X TO 1.5X STAR GAZE HI
BLUE RANDOM INSERTS IN BOX TOPPER
SG1 Jason Kidd 1.50 4.00
SG2 Kevin Garnett 1.50 4.00
SG3 Vince Carter 1.50 4.00
SG4 Baron Davis .75 2.00
SG5 Paul Pierce 1.00 2.50
SG6 Dirk Nowitzki 1.50 4.00
SG7 Shaquille O'Neal 2.50 6.00
SG8 Michael Jordan 8.00 20.00
SG9 Tim Duncan 2.00 5.00
SG10 Allen Iverson 1.50 4.00
SG11 Jason Richardson 1.00 2.50
SG12 Pau Gasol 1.25 3.00
SG13 Steve Francis .75 2.00
SG14 Kobe Bryant 4.00 10.00
SG15 Mike Bibby 1.00 2.50
SG16 Grant Hill 1.25 3.00
SG17 Tracy McGrady 1.50 4.00
SG18 Karl Malone 1.25 3.00
SG19 Darius Miles .60 1.50
SG20 Jay Williams 1.00 2.50
SG21 Mike Dunleavy 1.00 2.50
SG22 Drew Gooden 1.00 2.50
SG23 DaJuan Wagner .75 2.00
SG24 Caron Butler 1.00 2.50
SG25 Yao Ming 2.00 5.00

2002-03 Hoops Stars Star Gazing Game-Used

Randomly seeded in packs, this 12-card set parallels the set design from the base Star Gazing insert enhanced with a swatch of game used memorabilia. Several different types of memorabilia were used and are notated below in the checklist. Each card is sequentially numbered to 50.

PRINT RUN 50 SERIAL #'d SETS
AI Allen Iverson JSY 10.00 25.00
CB Caron Butler JSY 6.00 15.00
DG Drew Gooden Shorts 6.00 15.00
DN Dirk Nowitzki JSY 10.00 25.00
DW DaJuan Wagner Shorts 5.00 12.00
JK Jason Kidd Shorts 10.00 25.00
KG Kevin Garnett JSY 10.00 25.00
MB Mike Bibby JSY 6.00 15.00
PG Pau Gasol Jacket 8.00 20.00
PP Paul Pierce JSY 6.00 15.00
TM Tracy McGrady JSY 10.00 25.00
VC Vince Carter JSY 10.00 25.00

2002-03 Hoops Stars Superstars Game-Used

Randomly inserted in the one-per-box Superstars pack, this 19-card set parallels the base set design enhanced with a swatch of game used memorabilia. Several different types of memorabilia were used and these are noted in the checklist below. Cards contain no foil highlights.

INSERTED INTO SUPERSTAR PACKS
AI Allen Iverson JSY 5.00 12.00
BD Baron Davis Pants 2.50 6.00
CB Caron Butler Shirt 3.00 8.00
DG Drew Gooden Shirt 3.00 8.00
DM Darius Miles Jacket 2.00 5.00
DN Dirk Nowitzki JSY 5.00 12.00
DW DaJuan Wagner Shirt 2.50 6.00
GH Grant Hill Jacket 4.00 10.00
JK Jason Kidd Jacket 5.00 12.00
JR Jason Richardson Pants 3.00 8.00
KG Kevin Garnett JSY 5.00 12.00
KM Karl Malone Pants 4.00 10.00
MB Mike Bibby Jacket 3.00 8.00
PG Pau Gasol Jacket 4.00 10.00
PP Paul Pierce Jacket 3.00 8.00
SF Steve Francis JSY 2.50 6.00
TM Tracy McGrady Pants 5.00 12.00
VC Vince Carter JSY 5.00 12.00
YM Yao Ming JSY 6.00 15.00

2012-13 Hoops Taco Bell

1 Avery Bradley .50 1.25
2 Kevin Garnett 1.00 2.50
3 Paul Pierce .60 1.50
4 Rajon Rondo .60 1.50
5 Jared Sullinger .50 1.25
6 Deron Williams .50 1.25
7 Brook Lopez .50 1.25
8 Kris Humphries .40 1.00
9 Joe Johnson .50 1.25
10 Gerald Wallace .50 1.25
11 Amare Stoudemire .50 1.25
12 Carmelo Anthony .75 2.00
13 Iman Shumpert .60 1.50
14 Tyson Chandler .50 1.25
15 Jason Kidd .60 1.50
16 Andrew Bynum .40 1.00
17 Jrue Holiday .60 1.50
18 Thaddeus Young .40 1.00
19 Evan Turner .40 1.00
20 Spencer Hawes .40 1.00
21 Andrea Bargnani .50 1.25
22 DeMar DeRozan .60 1.50
23 Landry Fields .40 1.00
24 Jose Calderon .40 1.00
25 Linas Kleiza .40 1.00
26 Dirk Nowitzki .75 2.00
27 Rodrigue Beaubois .40 1.00
28 Shawn Marion .50 1.25
29 Vince Carter .75 2.00
30 Delonte West .40 1.00
31 Jeremy Lamb .60 1.50
32 Kevin Martin .50 1.25
33 Terrence Jones .50 1.25
34 Jeremy Lin .60 1.50
35 Earl Boykins .40 1.00
36 Marc Gasol .60 1.50
37 Mike Conley .50 1.25
38 Rudy Gay .60 1.50
39 Zach Randolph .50 1.25
40 Lester Hudson .40 1.00
41 Anthony Davis 8.00 20.00
42 Lance Thomas .40 1.00
43 Austin Rivers .60 1.50
44 Eric Gordon .50 1.25
45 Greivis Vasquez .50 1.25
46 DeJuan Blair .40 1.00
47 Boris Diaw .50 1.25
48 Manu Ginobili .60 1.50
49 Tim Duncan 1.00 2.50
50 Tony Parker .60 1.50
51 Carlos Boozer .50 1.25
52 Derrick Rose .75 2.00
53 Joakim Noah .50 1.25
54 Luol Deng .50 1.25
55 Richard Hamilton .50 1.25
56 Kyrie Irving 5.00 12.00
57 Anderson Varejao .40 1.00
58 Dion Waiters .60 1.50
59 Daniel Gibson .50 1.25
60 Omri Casspi .40 1.00
61 Andre Drummond 1.00 2.50
62 Greg Monroe .50 1.25
63 Rodney Stuckey .50 1.25
64 Tayshaun Prince .50 1.25
65 Brandon Knight .60 1.50
66 Danny Granger .50 1.25
67 David West .50 1.25
68 Paul George .75 2.00
69 Roy Hibbert .50 1.25
70 George Hill .50 1.25
71 Brandon Jennings .40 1.00
72 Drew Gooden .50 1.25
73 Monta Ellis .50 1.25
74 Ersan Ilyasova .40 1.00
75 Mike Dunleavy .40 1.00
76 Danilo Gallinari .40 1.00
77 Ty Lawson .40 1.00
78 Andre Iguodala .50 1.25
79 JaVale McGee .50 1.25
80 Andre Miller .50 1.25
81 Kevin Love .60 1.50
82 Luke Ridnour .50 1.25
83 Ricky Rubio .60 1.50
84 Wesley Johnson .50 1.25
85 J.J. Barea .50 1.25
86 LaMarcus Aldridge .60 1.50
87 Nicolas Batum .50 1.25
88 Wesley Matthews .40 1.00
89 Jonny Flynn .40 1.00
90 J.J. Hickson .40 1.00
91 James Harden 1.00 2.50
92 Kendrick Perkins .40 1.00
93 Kevin Durant 1.50 4.00
94 Russell Westbrook 1.50 4.00
95 Serge Ibaka .50 1.25
96 Al Jefferson .50 1.25
97 DeMarre Carroll .40 1.00
98 Gordon Hayward .60 1.50
99 Paul Millsap .60 1.50
100 Derrick Favors .50 1.25
101 Al Horford .50 1.25
102 Jeff Teague .50 1.25
103 John Jenkins .40 1.00
104 Josh Smith .50 1.25
105 Erick Dampier .40 1.00
106 LeBron James 2.50 6.00
107 Dwyane Wade 1.00 2.50
108 Chris Bosh .60 1.50
109 Mario Chalmers .50 1.25
110 Ray Allen .60 1.50
111 Andrew Nicholson .40 1.00
112 Hedo Turkoglu .50 1.25
113 J.J. Redick .60 1.50
114 Jameer Nelson .40 1.00
115 Glen Davis .40 1.00
116 John Wall .75 2.00
117 Trevor Booker .40 1.00
118 Jordan Crawford .40 1.00
119 Nene .50 1.25
120 Kevin Seraphin .40 1.00
121 Andrew Bogut .50 1.25
122 Stephen Curry 2.50 6.00
123 David Lee .40 1.00
124 Harrison Barnes 1.00 2.50
125 Festus Ezeli .50 1.25
126 Blake Griffin .60 1.50
127 Chauncey Billups .60 1.50
128 Chris Paul .75 2.00
129 Eric Bledsoe .50 1.25
130 DeAndre Jordan .60 1.50
131 Steve Nash .60 1.50
132 Dwight Howard .50 1.25
133 Kobe Bryant 2.50 6.00
134 Metta World Peace .60 1.50
135 Pau Gasol .60 1.50
136 Shannon Brown .40 1.00
137 Marcin Gortat .50 1.25
138 Markieff Morris .60 1.50
139 Kendall Marshall .40 1.00
140 Channing Frye .50 1.25
141 Jimmer Fredette .40 1.00
142 Marcus Thornton .40 1.00
143 DeMarcus Cousins .60 1.50
144 Tyreke Evans .40 1.00
145 Thomas Robinson .50 1.25
146 Gerald Henderson .40 1.00
147 Michael Kidd-Gilchrist .60 1.50
148 Byron Mullens .40 1.00
149 Bismack Biyombo .40 1.00
150 Kemba Walker 1.25 3.00

1990-91 Hoops Team Night Sheets

These team sheets were given out during a series of "NBA HOOPS Nights," which took place primarily between February and April at NBA arenas across the country. Fans attending the game on those nights received a free perforated 12-card sheet featuring NBA Hoops cards of the hometown team's top players. On some sheets, a few of the card slots are sponsors' coupons or advertisements rather than player cards. It was reported that generally between 10,000 and 20,000 card sheets were given away during these promotions. Many of the teams distributed additional card sheets through locally sponsored in-store promotions. The only team not participating was the Sacramento Kings. The Lakers set was actually issued as three panels of three cards plus a Taco Bell game card; only the Teagle card differs from his regular Hoops Series I card, which showed him with the Golden State Warriors. As part of the fourth annual McDonald's Open, the Knicks sheet was distributed to 20,000 youngsters attending a special "Kids Clinic" held October 12, 1990 in Barcelona, Spain. The Knicks team sheet also comes in a second version; after Stuart Gray was traded, another 10,000 new sets were made without Gray but with the additions of Brian Quinnett and John Starks. The Timberwolves cards were issued in four two-card vertical panels with one Burger King coupon per panel. The Supersonics sheet also comes in four versions; one pair of versions (Coke or Combos) has Dale Ellis and Olden Polynice, but after they were traded, reportedly 10,000 new sets were produced which included instead Ricky Pierce and Benoit Benjamin. The Utah Jazz cards were never issued as a sheet but cut into individual cards. All of these 12-card perforated sheets feature standard-size individual cards. The fronts feature color action player photos within a free-throw lane border of silver. Below the picture on a team-color coded bar are the words "NBA Hoops" with the team logo appearing in the lower right corner. The player's name and position are printed in team colors on the upper left edge. The backs sport a similar free-throw lane border with a small head shot of the player located in the upper right portion. The player's biography, college and NBA statistics are provided in separate charts with a brief career summary listed at the bottom. Cards marked with an asterisk are different from their regular issue Hoops card. The cards are unnumbered and checklisted below in alphabetical order.

COMPLETE SET (26) 80.00 200.00
1 John Battle 2.50 6.00
Jon Koncak
Moses Malone
Tim McCormick
Sidney Moncrief
Doc Rivers
Rumeal Robinson
Spud Webb
Dominique Wilkins
Kevin Willis
2 Larry Bird 4.00 10.00
Chris Ford CO
Kevin Gamble
Joe Kleine
Reggie Lewis
Kevin McHale
Robert Parish
Ed Pinckney
Brian Shaw
3 Muggsy Bogues 2.50 6.00
Rex Chapman
Dell Curry
Kenny Gattison
Mike Gminski *
Randolph Keys
Gene Littles CO
Johnny Newman
Robert Reid
Kelly Tripucka
4 B.J. Armstrong 5.00 12.00
Bill Cartwright
Horace Grant
H.Grant
S.Pippen *
Dennis Hopson
Michael Jordan
Stacey King
Cliff Levingston
John Paxson
Will Perdue
Scottie Pippen
5 Winston Bennett 2.50 6.00
Chucky Brown
Brad Daugherty
Craig Ehlo
Danny Ferry
Steve Kerr
Larry Nance
Mark Price
Len Wilkens CO
Hot Rod Williams
6 Richie Adubato CO 2.50 6.00
Alex English
Rolando Blackman
Brad Davis
James Donaldson
Derek Harper
Fat Lever
Rodney McCray
Roy Tarpley
Randy White *
Herb Williams
7 Michael Adams 2.50 6.00
Walter Davis
Bill Hanzlik
Chris Jackson
Jerome Lane
Todd Lichti
Blair Rasmussen
Paul Westhead CO
Joe Wolf
Orlando Woolridge
8 Mark Aguirre 3.00 8.00
William Bedford
Chuck Daly CO
Joe Dumars
James Edwards
Scott Hastings
Vinnie Johnson
Bill Laimbeer
Dennis Rodman
John Salley
Isiah Thomas
9 Tim Hardaway 4.00 10.00

Rod Higgins
Tyrone Hill
Sarunas Marciulionis
Chris Mullin
Don Nelson CO
Jim Petersen
Mitch Richmond
Mike Smrek
Tom Tolbert
10 Don Chaney CO 4.00 10.00
Sleepy Floyd
Buck Johnson
Vernon Maxwell
Hakeem Olajuwon
Kenny Smith
Larry Smith
Otis Thorpe
11 Greg Dreiling * 2.50 6.00
Vern Fleming *
George McCloud *
Reggie Miller *
Chuck Person *
Mike Sanders *
Detlef Schrempf *
Rik Smits *
LaSalle Thompson *
Randy Wittman *
12 Benoit Benjamin 2.50 6.00
Winston Garland
Tom Garrick
Gary Grant
Ron Harper
Bo Kimble
Danny Manning
Jeff Martin
Ken Norman
Mike Schuler CO
Charles Smith
13 Vlade Divac S2 3.00 8.00
Mike Dunleavy CO S3
A.C. Green S2
Magic Johnson S3
Sam Perkins S2
Byron Scott S1
Terry Teagle S1 *
Mychal Thompson S3
James Worthy S1
14 Willie Burton 2.50 6.00
Sherman Douglas
Kevin Edwards
Grant Long
Glen Rice
Ron Rothstein CO
Rony Seikaly
Jon Sundvold
Billy Thompson
15 Greg Anderson 2.50 6.00
Frank Brickowski
Jeff Grayer
Del Harris CO
Jay Humphries
Frank Kornet
Brad Lohaus
Ricky Pierce
Fred Roberts
Alvin Robertson
Dan Schayes
Jack Sikma
16 Randy Breuer S3 2.50 6.00
Scott Brooks S4
Tony Campbell S3
Tyrone Corbin S4
Sam Mitchell S2
Tod Murphy S2
Bill Musselman CO S1
Pooh Richardson S1
17 Charles Chips 2.50 6.00
Mookie Blaylock
Sam Bowie
Derrick Coleman
Lester Conner
Bill Fitch CO
Derrick Gervin
Jack Haley
Roy Hinson
Chris Morris
Reggie Theus
18A Maurice Cheeks 10.00 25.00
Patrick Ewing
Stuart Gray
Mark Jackson
Charles Oakley
Trent Tucker
Kiki Vandeweghe
Kenny Walker
Eddie Lee Wilkins
Gerald Wilkins
18B Maurice Cheeks 5.00 12.00
Patrick Ewing
Mark Jackson
Charles Oakley
Brian Quinnett
John Starks
Trent Tucker
Kiki Vandeweghe
Kenny Walker
Eddie Lee Wilkins
Gerald Wilkins
19 Mark Acres 2.50 6.00
Nick Anderson
Michael Ansley
Terry Catledge
Matt Guokas CO
Greg Kite
Jerry Reynolds
Dennis Scott
Scott Skiles
Otis Smith
Sam Vincent
20 Ron Anderson 3.00 8.00
Charles Barkley
Manute Bol
Johnny Dawkins
Armon Gilliam *
Hersey Hawkins
Jim Lynam CO
Rick Mahorn
21 Ken Battle 8.00 20.00
Tom Chambers
Cotton Fitzsimmons CO
Jeff Hornacek
Kevin Johnson
Dan Majerle
Ed Nealy
Tim Perry
Kurt Rambis
Mark West
22 Rick Adelman CO 10.00 25.00
Danny Ainge
Mark Bryant
Wayne Cooper
Clyde Drexler
Kevin Duckworth
Jerome Kersey
Drazen Petrovic
Terry Porter
Cliff Robinson
Buck Williams
Danny Young
23 Willie Anderson 5.00 12.00
Larry Brown CO
Terry Cummings
Sean Elliott
David Greenwood
Paul Pressey
David Robinson
Rod Strickland
The Coyote (Mascot)
Brad Townsend
Buck Harvey/89-90 Midwest Div.Champs
24A Dana Barros 4.00 10.00
Michael Cage
Quintin Dailey
Dale Ellis
Eddie Johnson *
Shawn Kemp
Derrick McKey
Nate McMillan
Gary Payton
Olden Polynice
Sedale Threatt
24B Combos 4.00 10.00
Dana Barros
Michael Cage
Quintin Dailey
Dale Ellis
Eddie Johnson *
Shawn Kemp
Derrick McKey
Nate McMillan
Gary Payton
Olden Polynice
Sedale Threatt
24C Dana Barros 4.00 10.00
Benoit Benjamin
Michael Cage
Quintin Dailey
Eddie Johnson *
Shawn Kemp
Derrick McKey
Nate McMillan
Gary Payton
Ricky Pierce
Sedale Threatt
24D Dana Barros 4.00 10.00
Benoit Benjamin
Michael Cage
Quintin Dailey
Eddie Johnson *
Shawn Kemp
Derrick McKey
Nate McMillan
Gary Payton
Ricky Pierce
Sedale Threatt
25 Thurl Bailey 5.00 12.00
Mike Brown
Mark Eaton
Blue Edwards
Darrell Griffith
Jeff Malone
Karl Malone
Delaney Rudd
Jerry Sloan CO
John Stockton
26 Mark Alarie 2.50 6.00
Pervis Ellison
Harvey Grant
Tom Hammonds
Charles Jones
Bernard King
Wes Unseld CO
Darrell Walker
John Williams

1991-92 Hoops Team Night Sheets

These 12-card perforated sheets feature standard-size cards. On some sheets, a few of the card slots have sponsors' coupons or advertisements rather than player cards. The fronts feature color action player photos with team-color coded borders on a white card face. The player's name is printed in black lettering in the upper left corner, and the team logo is superimposed over the lower left corner of the picture. In a horizontal format the backs have color head shots and biographical information on the left side, while the right side presents college and pro statistics. The cards are unnumbered and checklisted below in alphabetical order.

COMPLETE SET (27) 60.00 150.00
1 Stacey Augmon 3.00 8.00
Maurice Cheeks
Jon Koncak
Blair Rasmussen
Rumeal Robinson
Alexander Volkov
Bob Weiss CO
Dominique Wilkins
Kevin Willis
2 John Bagley 4.00 10.00
Larry Bird
Dee Brown
Kevin Gamble
Joe Kleine
Reggie Lewis
Kevin McHale
Robert Parish
Ed Pinckney
3 Muggsy Bogues 3.00 8.00
Rex Chapman
Dell Curry
Kenny Gattison
Kendall Gill
Mike Gminski
Hugo (Mascot)
Larry Johnson
Eric Leckner
Johnny Newman
J.R. Reid
4A B.J. Armstrong 5.00 12.00
Bill Cartwright
Horace Grant
Bobby Hansen
Craig Hodges
Michael Jordan
Stacey King
Cliff Levingston
John Paxson
Will Perdue
Scottie Pippen
Scott Williams
4B B.J. Armstrong 5.00 12.00
Bill Cartwright
Horace Grant
Bobby Hansen
Craig Hodges
Michael Jordan
Stacey King
Cliff Levingston
John Paxson
Will Perdue
Scottie Pippen
Mark Randall
5 John Battle 3.00 8.00
Winston Bennett
Terrell Brandon
Brad Daugherty
Craig Ehlo
Danny Ferry
Henry James
Steve Kerr
Larry Nance
Mark Price
Lenny Wilkens CO
John Williams
6 Richie Adubato CO 2.50 6.00
Rolando Blackman
Brad Davis
Terry Davis
James Donaldson
Derek Harper
Fat Lever
Rodney McCray
Doug Smith
Randy White
Herb Williams
7 Cadillac Anderson 2.50 6.00
Walter Davis
Winston Garland
Chris Jackson
Marcus Liberty
Todd Lichti
Mark Macon
Dikembe Mutombo
Paul Westhead CO
Reggie Williams
8 Mark Aguirre 3.00 8.00
William Bedford
Chuck Daly CO
Joe Dumars
Bill Laimbeer
Dennis Rodman
John Salley
Brad Sellers
Isiah Thomas
Darrell Walker
Orlando Woolridge
9 Vincent Askew 2.50 6.00
Mario Elie
Tim Hardaway
Rod Higgins
Tyrone Hill
Alton Lister
Sarunas Marciulionis
Chris Mullin
Don Nelson CO
Jim Petersen
Tom Tolbert
10 Don Chaney CO 3.00 8.00
Eric Floyd
Dave Jamerson
Buck Johnson
Vernon Maxwell
Hakeem Olajuwon
Kenny Smith
Larry Smith
Otis Thorpe
11 Greg Dreiling 2.50 6.00
Vern Fleming
George McCloud
Reggie Miller
Chuck Person
Detlef Schrempf
Rik Smits
LaSalle Thompson
Micheal Williams
Randy Wittman
12 James Edwards 2.50 6.00
Gary Grant
Ron Harper
Bo Kimble
Danny Manning
Ken Norman
Olden Polynice
Doc Rivers
Mike Schuler CO
Charles Smith
Loy Vaught
13 Elden Campbell 2.50 6.00
Vlade Divac
A.C. Green
Jack Haley
Sam Perkins
Byron Scott
Tony Smith
Sedale Threatt
James Worthy
14 Keith Askins 2.50 6.00
Willie Burton
Bimbo Coles
Kevin Edwards
Alec Kessler
Grant Long
Glen Rice
Rony Seikaly
Brian Shaw
Steve Smith
15 Frank Brickowski 3.00 8.00
Dale Ellis
Jeff Grayer
Jay Humphries
Larry Krystkowiak
Brad Lohaus
Moses Malone
Fred Roberts
Alvin Robertson
Dan Schayes
Snickers USA Olympic Team 1992 with Steve Henson and Lester Conner
16 Randy Breuer 2.50 6.00
Scott Brooks
Tony Campbell
Luc Longley
Sam Mitchell
Pooh Richardson
Felton Spencer
Doug West
17 Rafael Addison 2.50 6.00
Kenny Anderson
Mookie Blaylock
Sam Bowie
Derrick Coleman
Chris Dudley
Tate George
Terry Mills
Chris Morris
Drazen Petrovic
18 Greg Anthony 3.00 8.00
Anthony Mason
Patrick Ewing
Mark Jackson
Tim McCormick
Xavier McDaniel
Charles Oakley
Brian Quinnett
John Starks
Kiki Vandeweghe
Gerald Wilkins
19 Mark Acres 2.50 6.00
Nick Anderson
Terry Catledge
Greg Kite
Jerry Reynolds
Dennis Scott
Scott Skiles
Otis Smith
Jeff Turner
Sam Vincent
Brian Williams
20 Ron Anderson 2.50 6.00
Charles Barkley
Manute Bol
Johnny Dawkins
Armon Gilliam
Hersey Hawkins
Jim Lynam CO
Charles Shackleford
21 Cedric Ceballos 2.50 6.00
Tom Chambers
Cotton Fitzsimmons CO
Jeff Hornacek
Kevin Johnson
Negele Knight
Andrew Lang
Dan Majerle
Tim Perry
22 Alaa Abdelnaby 3.00 8.00
Danny Ainge
Mark Bryant
Wayne Cooper
Clyde Drexler
Kevin Duckworth
Jerome Kersey
Terry Porter
Cliff Robinson
Buck Williams
Danny Young
23 Anthony Bonner 2.50 6.00
Randy Brown
Duane Causwell
Pete Chilcutt
Dennis Hopson
Les Jepsen
Jim Les
Mitch Richmond
Dwayne Schintzius
Lionel Simmons
Wayman Tisdale
Spud Webb
24 Willie Anderson 3.00 8.00
Antoine Carr
Terry Cummings
Coby Dietrick and with Dave Barnett ANN
Sean Elliott
Sidney Green
Paul Pressey
David Robinson
David Robinson (Portrait)
Rod Strickland
Greg Sutton
25 Dana Barros 3.00 8.00
Benoit Benjamin
Michael Cage
Marty Conlon
Eddie Johnson
Shawn Kemp
Rich King
Derrick McKey
Nate McMillan
Gary Payton
Ricky Pierce
26 David Benoit 4.00 10.00
Mike Brown
Tyrone Corbin
Mark Eaton
Blue Edwards
Jeff Malone
Karl Malone
Eric Murdock
Delaney Rudd
Jerry Sloan CO
John Stockton
27 Michael Adams 2.50 6.00
Mark Alarie
Ledell Eackles
Pervis Ellison
A.J. English
Greg Foster
Harvey Grant
Tom Hammonds
Charles Jones
Bernard King
Wes Unseld CO

1999 Hoops WNBA

Released for the first time by Fleer/SkyBox, this 110-card set was distributed in 10-card packs that carried a suggested retail price of $1.29. The set contained the following subsets: 7 Future Phenomenons, 8 League Leaders, 6 Postseason Rewind and 2 checklists.

COMPLETE SET (110) 6.00 15.00
1 Cynthia Cooper PR .60 1.50
2 Houston vs. Phoenix PR .20 .50
3 Houston vs. Phoenix PR .20 .50
4 Houston vs. Phoenix PR .20 .50
5 Houston vs. Charlotte PR .20 .50
6 Phoenix vs. Cleveland PR .20 .50
7 Cynthia Cooper .60 1.50
Jennifer Gillom
Nikki McCray
Lisa Leslie
8 Lisa Leslie .50 1.25
Cindy Brown
Jennifer Gillom
Margo Dydek
9 Isabelle Fijalkowski .10 .25
Janice Braxton
Michelle Griffiths
Razija Mujanovic
10 Eva Nemcova .15 .40
Cynthia Cooper
Penny Toler
Suzie McConnell Serio
11 Sandy Brondello .40 1.00
Eva Nemcova
Bridget Pettis
Cynthia Cooper
12 Ticha Penicheiro .50 1.25
Suzie McConnell Serio
Teresa Weatherspoon
Michele Timms
13 Teresa Weatherspoon .40 1.00
Kim Perrot
Sheryl Swoopes
Ticha Penicheiro
14 Margo Dydek .40 1.00
Lisa Leslie
Tangela Smith
Vicky Bullett
15 Andrea Kuklova .20 .50
16 Christy Smith .20 .50
17 Penny Moore .30 .75
18 Octavia Blue RC .20 .50
19 Vickie Johnson .30 .75
20 Latasha Byears .30 .75
21 Vicky Bullett .30 .75
22 Franthea Price RC .20 .50
23 Tina Thompson .75 2.00
24 Teresa Weatherspoon .75 2.00
25 Maria Stepanova RC .20 .50
26 Merlakia Jones .30 .75
27 Razija Mujanovic RC .20 .50
28 Rhonda Mapp .25 .60
29 Kristi Harrower RC .30 .75
30 Penny Toler .30 .75
31 Margo Dydek RC .75 2.00
32 Kim Perrot .60 1.50
33 Cindy Brown .40 1.00
34 Eva Nemcova .30 .75
35 Quacy Barnes .20 .50
36 Tracy Reid RC .40 1.00
37 Chantel Tremitiere .20 .50
38 Lady Hardmon .20 .50
39 Michelle Griffiths RC .40 1.00
40 Sheryl Swoopes 1.25 3.00
41 Sandy Brondello RC .75 2.00
42 Andrea Stinson .40 1.00
43 Marlies Askamp RC .30 .75
44 Rachael Sporn RC .30 .75
45 Nikki McCray .60 1.50
46 Andrea Congreaves .20 .50
47 Toni Foster .30 .75
48 Kim Williams .20 .50
49 Carla Porter RC .30 .75
50 Jamila Wideman .30 .75
51 Isabelle Fijalkowski .20 .50
52 Korie Hlede RC .60 1.50
53 Tora Suber .30 .75
54 Sue Wicks .30 .75
55 Coquese Washington RC .40 1.00
56 Sharon Manning .20 .50
57 Tammy Jackson .20 .50
58 Tangela Smith .20 .50
59 Suzie McConnell-Serio .50 1.25
60 Lisa Leslie 1.00 2.50
61 Wendy Palmer .50 1.25
62 Adia Barnes RC .30 .75
63 La'Shawn Brown RC .20 .50
64 Janeth Arcain .20 .50
65 Ruthie Bolton-Holifield .60 1.50
66 Bridget Pettis .20 .50
67 Pamela McGee .30 .75
68 Rebecca Lobo .60 1.50
69 Cindy Blodgett RC .60 1.50
70 Rita Williams .25 .60
71 Mwadi Mabika .20 .50
72 Sophia Witherspoon .30 .75
73 Janice Braxton .20 .50
74 Cynthia Cooper 1.25 3.00
75 Tammi Reiss .30 .75
76 Umeki Webb .20 .50
77 Kym Hampton .30 .75
78 LaTonya Johnson RC .30 .75
79 Michele Timms .60 1.50
80 Kisha Ford .20 .50
81 Monica Lamb RC .30 .75
82 Keri Chaconas RC .20 .50
83 Elena Baranova .50 1.25
84 Linda Burgess .20 .50
85 Tamecka Dixon .30 .75
86 Heidi Burge .20 .50
87 Michelle Edwards .40 1.00
88 Yolanda Moore RC .20 .50
89 Ticha Penicheiro RC 1.00 2.50
90 A.Santos de Oliveira RC .30 .75
91 Rushia Brown .20 .50
92 Lynette Woodard .40 1.00
93 Katrina Colleton RC .20 .50
94 Bridgette Gordon .20 .50
95 Jennifer Gillom .50 1.25
96 Murriel Page .30 .75
97 Olympia Scott-Richardson .20 .50
98 Adrienne Johnson RC .60 1.50
99 Gergana Branzova FP RC .20 .50
100 Allison Feaster FP RC .50 1.25
101 Brandy Reed FP RC .60 1.50
102 Katie Smith FP RC .75 2.00
103 Natalie Williams FP RC .60 1.50
104 Jennifer Azzi FP RC .75 2.00
105 Chamique Holdsclaw FP RC 2.00 5.00
106 Dawn Staley FP RC .75 2.00
107 Nykesha Sales FP RC .60 1.50
108 Kristin Folkl FP RC .50 1.25
109 Checklist .20 .50
110 Checklist .20 .50

1999 Hoops WNBA Autographics

Randomly inserted in packs at one in 144, this 14-card set features autographs from some of the top names in the WNBA. The cards feature black autographs only.

STATED ODDS 1:144
*BLUE CENTURY MARKS: 1.25X TO 3X HI
BLUE: PRINT RUN 50 SERIAL #'d SETS
1 Cynthia Cooper 30.00 80.00
2 Kristin Folkl 12.00 30.00
3 Bridgette Gordon 5.00 12.00
4 Lisa Leslie 25.00 60.00
5 Suzie McConnell-Serio 12.00 30.00
6 Nikki McCray 15.00 40.00
7 Nykesha Sales 10.00 25.00
8 Dawn Staley 12.00 30.00
9 Andrea Stinson 10.00 25.00
10 Sheryl Swoopes 30.00 80.00
11 Michele Timms 15.00 40.00
12 Penny Toler 8.00 20.00
13 Teresa Weatherspoon 20.00 50.00

1999 Hoops WNBA Award Winners

Randomly inserted in packs at one in 24, this 10-card set features All-WNBA First and Second team players on a matte silver and silver holographic foil stamped card.

COMPLETE SET (10) 20.00 50.00
1 Tina Thompson 4.00 10.00
2 Sheryl Swoopes 6.00 15.00
3 Jennifer Gillom 2.50 6.00
4 Cynthia Cooper 6.00 15.00
5 Suzie McConnell-Serio 2.50 6.00
6 Cindy Brown 2.00 5.00
7 Eva Nemcova 1.50 4.00
8 Lisa Leslie 5.00 12.00
9 Andrea Stinson 2.00 5.00
10 Teresa Weatherspoon 4.00 10.00

1999 Hoops WNBA Building Blocks

Randomly inserted in packs at one in four, this 8-card set features top WNBA stars. The cards are on a matte silver-foil.

COMPLETE SET (8) 3.00 8.00
1 Dawn Staley 1.00 2.50
2 Rebecca Lobo .75 2.00
3 Tracy Reid .50 1.25
4 Korie Hlede .75 2.00
5 Ticha Penicheiro 1.25 3.00
6 Tammi Reiss .40 1.00
7 Nikki McCray .75 2.00
8 Jennifer Gillom .60 1.50

1999 Hoops WNBA Talk of the Town

Randomly inserted in packs at one in 12, this 12-card set features a player from each WNBA team pictured against a cityscape of her team's city. The cards also feature gold-foil stamping.

COMPLETE SET (12) 10.00 25.00
1 Cynthia Cooper 3.00 8.00
2 Michele Timms 1.50 4.00
3 Suzie McConnell-Serio 1.25 3.00
4 Lisa Leslie 2.50 6.00
5 Andrea Stinson 1.00 2.50
6 Elena Baranova 1.25 3.00
7 Cindy Brown 1.00 2.50
8 Teresa Weatherspoon 2.00 5.00
9 Nikki McCray 1.50 4.00
10 Ruthie Bolton-Holifield 1.50 4.00
11 Nykesha Sales 1.50 4.00
12 Kristin Folkl 1.25 3.00

1992-93 Hornets Hive Five

The 1992-93 Hornets Hive Five set consists of five numbered Charlotte Hornets player cards with matching lapel pins, and six game cards. The five player cards were available through Fast Fare convenience stores and Crown gasoline stations in North Carolina, South Carolina, and Georgia. The game cards were distributed free to customers and consisted of five Charlotte Hornet Honeybee Cheerleaders and one mascot card (Hugo the Hornet). The player cards measure approximately 2 1/2" by 5 1/8". The fronts feature color action player photos with the set title, "The Hive Five", printed above the picture. On a border below the photo appears the player's name and team number. Below the border is the team logo and sponsors' logos. The back displays a player head shot with biography listed vertically along the left edge. The cards are numbered on the back. The six game cards measure approximately 2" by 4". The fronts carry a portrait of the cheerleaders bordered by the words "Charlotte Honey Bees" above and below with an outer border. The bottom section of the card contains three scratch-off basketball designs with the possiblity to win a prize by matching two prizes. Prizes include autographed player Hive Five set, a team jacket, a team jersey, a team hat, Dutchess Honey Bun, and popcorn. The game cards are unnumbered and listed below alphabetically.

COMPLETE SET (11) 6.00 15.00
1 Larry Johnson 1.50 4.00
2 Kendall Gill 1.25 3.00
3 Muggsy Bogues 1.25 3.00
4 Dell Curry .75 2.00
5 Alonzo Mourning 3.00 8.00
NNO Hugo the Hornet .20 .50
NNO Kim Bailey .20 .50
NNO Paris Floyd .20 .50
NNO Michelle Lee .20 .50
NNO Angela Pooser .20 .50
NNO Tara Wood .20 .50

1992-93 Hornets Standups

Issued in four sets of three each, these stand-ups were given away, one set per customer, with a purchase at Charlotte area Burger King restaurants during the 1992-93 basketball season. The 12 stand-ups measure approximately 4" by 8 7/8" and feature color action cut-outs on purplish backgrounds. The player's facsimile autograph appears across the photo. The white back carries the player's name, biography, and statistics. The logos for Burger King, Coca-Cola, WJZY Radio, and the Hornets also appear on the front and back. The stand-ups are arranged below by set number, Set 1 (1-3), Set 2 (4-6), Set 3 (7-9), Set 4 (10-12), and listed alphabetically within each set.

COMPLETE SET (12) 20.00 50.00
1 Tony Bennett 1.50 4.00
2 Dell Curry 2.00 5.00
3 Alonzo Mourning 6.00 15.00
4 Muggsy Bogues 3.00 8.00
5 Mike Gminski 1.50 4.00
6 Johnny Newman 1.50 4.00
7 Kenny Gattison 1.50 4.00
8 Kendall Gill 2.50 6.00
9 David Wingate 1.50 4.00
10 Sidney Green 1.50 4.00
11 Larry Johnson 3.00 8.00
12 Kevin Lynch 1.50 4.00

2008-09 Hot Prospects

This set was released on October 14, 2008. The base set consists of 162 cards. Cards 1-110 feature veterans, with cards 91-110 serial numbered of 499. Cards 111-136 are rookie cards featuring jersey swatches and autographs, serial numbered of 399, and cards 137-142 are similar but serial numbered to 199. Cards 143-156 are autographed rookie cards serial numbered of 199, and cards 157-162 are basic rookie cards serial numbered of 199.

COMP.SET w/o SPs (90) 10.00 25.00
DRAFT PRINT RUN 499 SER.#'d SETS
111-136 PRINT RUN 399 SER.#'d SETS
137-142 PRINT RUN 199 SER.#'d SETS
143-162 PRINT RUN 199 SER.#'d SETS
UNPRICED WHITE PRINT RUN ONE SET
1 LaMarcus Aldridge .40 1.00
2 Ray Allen .40 1.00
3 Carmelo Anthony .50 1.25
4 Gilbert Arenas .30 .75
5 Ron Artest .40 1.00
6 Mike Bibby .30 .75
7 Chauncey Billups .40 1.00
8 Andrew Bogut .30 .75
9 Carlos Boozer .30 .75
10 Chris Bosh .40 1.00
11 Elton Brand .40 1.00
12 Corey Brewer .30 .75
13 Kobe Bryant 1.50 4.00
14 Caron Butler .30 .75
15 Jose Calderon .25 .60
16 Marcus Camby .25 .60
17 Vince Carter .50 1.25
18 Mike Conley Jr. .30 .75
19 Daequan Cook .25 .60
20 Jamal Crawford .40 1.00
21 Baron Davis .30 .75
22 Luol Deng .30 .75
23 Tim Duncan .60 1.50
24 Mike Dunleavy .30 .75
25 Kevin Durant 1.00 2.50
26 Francisco Garcia .25 .60
27 Kevin Garnett .60 1.50
28 Pau Gasol .40 1.00
29 Rudy Gay .40 1.00
30 Daniel Gibson .30 .75
31 Manu Ginobili .40 1.00
32 Ben Gordon .30 .75
33 Danny Granger .30 .75
34 Jeff Green .30 .75
35 Richard Hamilton .30 .75
36 Al Harrington .30 .75
37 Al Horford .40 1.00
38 Dwight Howard .30 .75
39 Josh Howard .30 .75
40 Andre Iguodala .30 .75
41 Allen Iverson .50 1.25
42 Stephen Jackson .30 .75
43 LeBron James 1.50 4.00
44 Antawn Jamison .30 .75
45 Al Jefferson .30 .75
46 Richard Jefferson .30 .75
47 Yi Jianlian .40 1.00
48 Joe Johnson .30 .75
49 Chris Kaman .30 .75
50 Jason Kidd .40 1.00
51 Kyle Korver .30 .75
52 Rashard Lewis .30 .75
53 Corey Maggette .30 .75
54 Stephon Marbury .30 .75
55 Shawn Marion .30 .75
56 Kevin Martin .30 .75
57 Rashad McCants .25 .60
58 Tracy McGrady .40 1.00
59 Andre Miller .30 .75
60 Yao Ming .50 1.25
61 Jamario Moon .25 .60
62 Steve Nash .40 1.00
63 Joakim Noah .30 .75
64 Andres Nocioni .25 .60
65 Dirk Nowitzki .50 1.25
66 Jermaine O'Neal .30 .75
67 Shaquille O'Neal .75 2.00
68 Greg Oden .30 .75
69 Emeka Okafor .30 .75
70 Tony Parker .40 1.00
71 Chris Paul .50 1.25
72 Paul Pierce .40 1.00
73 Zach Randolph .30 .75
74 Michael Redd .30 .75
75 Jason Richardson .40 1.00
76 Brandon Roy .40 1.00
77 Luis Scola .30 .75
78 Peja Stojakovic .40 1.00
79 Amare Stoudemire .30 .75
80 Hedo Turkoglu .30 .75
81 Dwyane Wade .60 1.50
82 Ben Wallace .30 .75
83 Gerald Wallace .30 .75
84 Rasheed Wallace .40 1.00
85 Luke Walton .25 .60
86 David West .30 .75
87 Chris Wilcox .25 .60
88 Deron Williams .30 .75
89 Sean Williams .30 .75
90 Thaddeus Young .30 .75
91 Ray Allen .75 2.00
92 Carmelo Anthony 1.00 2.50
93 Chauncey Billups .75 2.00
94 Kobe Bryant 3.00 8.00
95 Vince Carter 1.00 2.50
96 Baron Davis .60 1.50
97 Tim Duncan 1.25 3.00
98 Kevin Garnett 1.25 3.00
99 Pau Gasol .75 2.00
100 Dwight Howard .60 1.50
101 Allen Iverson 1.00 2.50
102 LeBron James 3.00 8.00
103 Michael Jordan 6.00 15.00
104 Tracy McGrady .75 2.00
105 Yao Ming 1.00 2.50
106 Steve Nash .75 2.00
107 Joakim Noah .60 1.50
108 Dirk Nowitzki 1.00 2.50
109 Shaquille O'Neal 1.50 4.00
110 Dwyane Wade 1.25 3.00
111 Kyle Weaver JSY AU RC 4.00 10.00
112 Joe Alexander JSY AU RC 4.00 10.00
113 D.J. Augustin JSY AU RC 5.00 12.00
114 Brook Lopez JSY AU RC 4.00 10.00
115 Jerryd Bayless JSY AU RC 5.00 12.00
116 Jason Thompson JSY AU RC 4.00 10.00
117 Brandon Rush JSY AU RC 5.00 12.00
118 Anthony Randolph JSY AU RC 4.00 10.00
119 Robin Lopez JSY AU RC 6.00 15.00
120 Marreese Speights JSY AU RC 5.00 12.00
121 Roy Hibbert JSY AU RC 6.00 15.00
122 Javale McGee JSY AU RC 8.00 20.00
123 J.J. Hickson JSY AU RC 5.00 12.00
124 Ryan Anderson JSY AU RC 5.00 12.00
125 Courtney Lee JSY AU RC 5.00 12.00
126 Kosta Koufos JSY AU RC 5.00 12.00
127 George Hill JSY AU RC 6.00 15.00
128 Darrell Arthur JSY AU RC 5.00 12.00
129 Donte Greene JSY AU RC 4.00 10.00
130 Sonny Weems JSY AU RC 4.00 10.00
131 J.R. Giddens JSY AU RC 4.00 10.00
132 Walter Sharpe JSY AU RC 4.00 10.00
133 Joey Dorsey JSY AU RC 4.00 10.00
134 Mario Chalmers JSY AU RC 6.00 15.00
135 DeAndre Jordan JSY AU RC 8.00 20.00
136 Patrick Ewing Jr JSY AU RC 4.00 10.00
137 Derrick Rose JSY AU RC 25.00 60.00
138 M.Beasley JSY AU RC 12.00 30.00
139 O.J. Mayo JSY AU RC 12.00 30.00
140 R.Westbrook JSY AU RC 125.00 300.00
141 Kevin Love JSY AU RC 30.00 80.00
142 Eric Gordon JSY AU RC 10.00 25.00
143 Luc Richard Mbah A Moute AU RC 4.00 10.00
144 James Mays AU RC 5.00 12.00
145 Sonny Weems AU 3.00 8.00
146 Chris Douglas-Roberts AU RC 3.00 8.00
147 Deron Washington AU RC 3.00 8.00
148 David Padgett AU RC 5.00 12.00
149 Bill Walker AU RC 3.00 8.00
150 Malik Hairston AU RC 3.00 8.00
151 Richard Hendrix AU RC 3.00 8.00
152 DeVon Hardin AU RC 3.00 8.00
153 Darnell Jackson AU RC 3.00 8.00
154 Maarty Leunen AU RC 3.00 8.00
155 Mike Taylor AU RC 3.00 8.00
156 James Gist AU RC 3.00 8.00
157 Sean Singletary RC 3.00 8.00
158 Joe Crawford RC 3.00 8.00
159 Trent Plaisted RC 3.00 8.00
160 Shan Foster RC 3.00 8.00

161 Juan Palacios RC 5.00 12.00
162 Jaycee Carroll RC 5.00 12.00

2008-09 Hot Prospects Blue

*1-110 BLUE: .5X TO 1.25X BASE HI
RANDOM INSERTS IN PACKS
111 Kyle Weaver 1.00 2.50
112 Joe Alexander 1.00 2.50
113 D.J. Augustin 1.25 3.00
115 Jerryd Bayless 1.25 3.00
116 Jason Thompson 1.00 2.50
117 Brandon Rush 1.25 3.00
118 Anthony Randolph 1.00 2.50
119 Robin Lopez 1.50 4.00
120 Marreese Speights 1.25 3.00
121 Roy Hibbert 1.50 4.00
122 Javale McGee 2.00 5.00
123 J.J. Hickson 1.25 3.00
124 Ryan Anderson 1.25 3.00
125 Courtney Lee 1.25 3.00
126 Kosta Koufos 1.25 3.00
127 George Hill 1.50 4.00
128 Darrell Arthur 1.25 3.00
129 Donte Greene 1.00 2.50
130 Sonny Weems 1.00 2.50
131 J.R. Giddens 1.00 2.50
132 Walter Sharpe 1.00 2.50
133 Joey Dorsey 1.00 2.50
134 Mario Chalmers 1.50 4.00
135 DeAndre Jordan 2.00 5.00
136 Patrick Ewing Jr. 1.00 2.50
137 Derrick Rose 6.00 15.00
138 Michael Beasley 1.50 4.00
139 O.J. Mayo 1.50 4.00
140 Russell Westbrook 12.00 30.00
141 Kevin Love 5.00 12.00
142 Eric Gordon 2.50 6.00
143 Luc Richard Mbah A Moute .75 2.00
144 James Mays 1.00 2.50
145 Sonny Weems .60 1.50
146 Chris Douglas-Roberts .60 1.50
147 Deron Washington .60 1.50
148 David Padgett 1.00 2.50
149 Bill Walker .60 1.50
150 Malik Hairston .60 1.50
151 Richard Hendrix .60 1.50
152 DeVon Hardin .60 1.50
153 Darnell Jackson .60 1.50
154 Maarty Leunen .60 1.50
155 Mike Taylor .60 1.50
156 James Gist .60 1.50
157 Sean Singletary .60 1.50
158 Joe Crawford .60 1.50
159 Trent Plaisted .60 1.50
160 Shan Foster .60 1.50
161 Juan Palacios 1.00 2.50
162 Jaycee Carroll 1.00 2.50

2008-09 Hot Prospects Red

*1-90 RED: 3X TO 8X BASE HI
*91-110 RED: 1.5X TO 4X BASE HI
*111-162 RED: .75X TO 2X BASE HI
RED PRINT RUN 25 SER.#'d SETS
13 Kobe Bryant 20.00 50.00
103 Michael Jordan 40.00 100.00

2008-09 Hot Prospects Alumni Mates

COMPLETE SET (20) 10.00 25.00
APPROXIMATE ODDS 1:6
AM1 G.Arenas/R.Jefferson 1.50 4.00
AM2 J.Kidd/S.Abdur-Rahim 1.50 4.00
AM3 S.Battier/C.Boozer 1.50 4.00
AM4 D.Majerle/C.Kaman 1.50 4.00
AM5 A.Horford/J.Noah 1.50 4.00
AM6 D.Mutombo/A.Mourning 3.00 8.00
AM7 W.Bellamy/E.Gordon 1.50 4.00
AM8 M.Beasley/R.Blackman 2.00 5.00
AM9 S.O'Neal/G.Davis 3.00 8.00
AM10 D.Rose/S.Williams 2.50 6.00
AM11 J.Richardson/Z.Randolph 1.50 4.00
AM12 V.Carter/A.Jamison 2.50 6.00
AM13 A.Dantley/B.Laimbeer 1.50 4.00
AM14 M.Conley/G.Oden 1.50 4.00
AM15 K.Durant/L.Aldridge 2.00 5.00
AM16 R.Allen/R.Hamilton 1.50 4.00
AM17 J.Erving/M.Camby 2.00 5.00
AM18 K.Abdul-Jabbar/B.Walton 2.00 5.00
AM19 B.Sharman/O.Mayo 1.50 4.00
AM20 D.West/J.Posey 1.50 4.00

2008-09 Hot Prospects Cream of the Crop

COMPLETE SET (30) 12.00 30.00
APPROXIMATE ODDS 1:6
CC1 Brandon Roy .75 2.00
CC2 Chris Paul 1.00 2.50
CC3 LeBron James 3.00 8.00
CC4 Amare Stoudemire .60 1.50
CC5 Joe Johnson .60 1.50
CC6 Tony Parker .75 2.00
CC7 Gilbert Arenas .60 1.50
CC8 Michael Redd .60 1.50
CC9 Richard Hamilton .60 1.50
CC10 Shawn Marion .60 1.50
CC11 Manu Ginobili .75 2.00
CC12 Dirk Nowitzki 1.00 2.50
CC13 Paul Pierce .75 2.00
CC14 Tracy McGrady .75 2.00
CC15 Kobe Bryant 3.00 8.00
CC16 Steve Nash .75 2.00
CC17 Rasheed Wallace .75 2.00
CC18 Larry Johnson .75 2.00
CC19 Detlef Schrempf .75 2.00
CC20 Vlade Divac .75 2.00
CC21 Mitch Richmond .75 2.00
CC22 Scottie Pippen 1.25 3.00
CC23 David Robinson 1.25 3.00
CC24 Chris Mullin .75 2.00
CC25 Karl Malone 1.00 2.50
CC26 Isiah Thomas .75 2.00
CC27 Kevin McHale 1.00 2.50
CC28 Larry Bird 2.00 5.00
CC29 Oscar Robertson .75 2.00
CC30 Wilt Chamberlain 1.50 4.00

2008-09 Hot Prospects Draft Day Postmarks

STATED PRINT RUN 50 SER#'d SETS
DDAA Alexis Ajinca 5.00 12.00
DDAD Darrell Arthur 6.00 15.00
DDAR Anthony Randolph 5.00 12.00
DDBL Brook Lopez 10.00 25.00
DDBR Brandon Rush 6.00 15.00
DDCD Chris Douglas-Roberts 5.00 12.00
DDDA D.J. Augustin 6.00 15.00
DDDG Danilo Gallinari 12.00 30.00
DDDR Derrick Rose 30.00 80.00
DDDW D.J. White 6.00 15.00
DDEG Eric Gordon 12.00 30.00
DDGR Donte Greene 5.00 12.00
DDJA Joe Alexander 5.00 12.00
DDJB Jerryd Bayless 6.00 15.00
DDJD Joey Dorsey 5.00 12.00
DDJG J.R. Giddens 5.00 12.00
DDJH J.J. Hickson 6.00 15.00
DDJM Javale McGee 10.00 25.00
DDJT Jason Thompson 5.00 12.00
DDKK Kosta Koufos 6.00 15.00
DDKL Kevin Love 25.00 60.00
DDLM Luc Richard Mbah A Moute 6.00 15.00
DDMB Michael Beasley 8.00 20.00
DDMC Mario Chalmers 8.00 20.00
DDOJ O.J. Mayo 8.00 20.00
DDPE Patrick Ewing Jr 5.00 12.00
DDRA Ryan Anderson 6.00 15.00
DDRH Roy Hibbert 8.00 20.00
DDRL Robin Lopez 8.00 20.00
DDRW Russell Westbrook 125.00 300.00

2008-09 Hot Prospects Hot Materials

COMBINED AU/MEM ODDS 1:9
*RED: .75X TO 2X BASE HI
RED PRINT RUN 25 SER.#'d SETS
UNPRICED PATCH PRINT RUN ONE SET
HMAB Andrew Bogut 2.00 5.00
HMAI Allen Iverson 3.00 8.00
HMAS Amare Stoudemire 2.00 5.00
HMBR Brandon Roy 2.50 6.00
HMCA Carmelo Anthony 3.00 8.00
HMCB Caron Butler 2.00 5.00
HMDG Danny Granger 2.00 5.00
HMDH Dwight Howard 2.00 5.00
HMDN Dirk Nowitzki 3.00 8.00
HMEO Emeka Okafor 2.00 5.00
HMJJ Joe Johnson 2.00 5.00
HMJK Jason Kidd 2.50 6.00
HMKB Kobe Bryant 8.00 20.00
HMKD Kevin Durant 6.00 15.00
HMKG Kevin Garnett 4.00 10.00
HMLJ LeBron James 6.00 15.00
HMMB Mike Bibby 2.00 5.00
HMPG Pau Gasol 2.50 6.00
HMRA Ray Allen 2.50 6.00
HMRH Richard Hamilton 2.00 5.00
HMRJ Richard Jefferson 2.00 5.00
HMRW Rasheed Wallace 2.50 6.00
HMSB Shane Battier 2.00 5.00
HMSM Shawn Marion 2.00 5.00
HMSN Steve Nash 2.50 6.00
HMSO Shaquille O'Neal 5.00 12.00
HMTD Tim Duncan 4.00 10.00
HMTP Tayshaun Prince 2.00 5.00
HMVC Vince Carter 3.00 8.00
HMYM Yao Ming 3.00 8.00

2008-09 Hot Prospects Hot Tandems

COMPLETE SET (20) 8.00 20.00
APPROXIMATE ODDS 1:6
HT1 L.Bird/P.Pierce 2.00 5.00
HT2 M.Jordan/S.Pippen 4.00 10.00
HT3 A.Iverson/C.Anthony 1.50 4.00
HT4 I.Thomas/J.Dumars 1.25 3.00
HT5 C.Billups/R.Hamilton 1.25 3.00
HT6 J.Kidd/D.Nowitzki 1.25 3.00
HT7 T.McGrady/Y.Ming 1.50 4.00
HT8 C.Drexler/H.Olajuwon 2.00 5.00
HT9 M.Johnson/K.Bryant 3.00 8.00
HT10 M.Redd/R.Jefferson 1.25 3.00
HT11 C.Paul/D.West 2.00 5.00
HT12 P.Ewing/W.Reed 1.50 4.00
HT13 P.Jackson/B.Bradley 1.25 3.00
HT14 J.Erving/W.Chamberlain 3.00 8.00
HT15 S.Nash/A.Stoudemire 2.00 5.00
HT16 B.Roy/G.Oden 1.25 3.00
HT17 G.Gervin/D.Robinson 2.00 5.00
HT18 K.Durant/J.Green 1.50 4.00
HT19 J.Stockton/K.Malone 2.00 5.00
HT20 G.Arenas/A.Jamison 1.25 3.00

2008-09 Hot Prospects NBA Game Issue Jerseys

PRINT RUN 149 SER.#'d SETS
*RED: .75X TO 2X BASE HI
RED PRINT RUN 25 SER.#'d SETS
UNPRICED PATCH PRINT RUN ONE SET
NBAAB Andrew Bynum 1.50 4.00
NBAAI Allen Iverson 3.00 8.00
NBAAS Amare Stoudemire 2.00 5.00
NBABA Andrea Bargnani 2.00 5.00
NBABD Baron Davis 2.00 5.00
NBABR Brandon Roy 2.50 6.00
NBABU Caron Butler 2.00 5.00
NBACA Carmelo Anthony 3.00 8.00
NBACB Carlos Boozer 2.00 5.00
NBADH Dwight Howard 2.00 5.00
NBADN Dirk Nowitzki 3.00 8.00
NBADW Deron Williams 2.00 5.00
NBAGA Gilbert Arenas 2.00 5.00
NBAJH Josh Howard 2.00 5.00
NBAJJ Joe Johnson 2.00 5.00
NBAJK Jason Kidd 2.50 6.00
NBAJR Jason Richardson 2.50 6.00
NBAKB Kobe Bryant 8.00 20.00
NBAKG Kevin Garnett 4.00 10.00
NBALJ LeBron James 8.00 20.00
NBAMB Mike Bibby 2.00 5.00
NBAMJ Michael Jordan 20.00 50.00
NBAPG Pau Gasol 2.50 6.00
NBARG Rudy Gay 2.50 6.00
NBASM Shawn Marion 2.00 5.00
NBASN Steve Nash 2.50 6.00
NBASO Shaquille O'Neal 6.00 15.00
NBATD Tim Duncan 4.00 10.00
NBATP Tony Parker 2.50 6.00
NBAYM Yao Ming 3.00 8.00

2008-09 Hot Prospects Numbers Game Autographs Jerseys

CARDS #'d TO PLAYER JSY #
SOME UNPRICED DUE TO SCARCITY
UNPRICED RED PRINT RUN 5 SETS
UNPRICED PATCH PRINT RUN ONE SET
NGAB Andrew Bynum/17 15.00 40.00
NGAH Al Horford/15 20.00 40.00
NGBW Bill Walton/32 10.00 25.00
NGCA Carmelo Anthony/15 20.00 40.00
NGCK Chris Kaman/35 6.00 15.00
NGDG Danny Granger/33 12.00 30.00
NGDH Dwight Howard/12 40.00 70.00
NGDM Desmond Mason/24 10.00 25.00
NGDR David Robinson/50 40.00 100.00
NGEO Emeka Okafor/50 6.00 15.00
NGJS John Stockton/12 75.00 150.00
NGKB Kobe Bryant/24 125.00 250.00
NGKD Kevin Durant/35 75.00 200.00
NGLJ LeBron James/23 150.00 300.00
NGMA Donyell Marshall/42 6.00 15.00
NGMG Corey Maggette/50 6.00 15.00
NGRF Raymond Felton/20 8.00 20.00
NGRJ Richard Jefferson/24 8.00 20.00
NGSB Shane Battier/31 6.00 15.00
NGTP Tayshaun Prince/22 8.00 20.00
NGTT Tyrus Thomas/24 8.00 20.00
NGVC Vince Carter/15 20.00 50.00
NGYM Yao Ming/11 30.00 80.00

2008-09 Hot Prospects Property of Jerseys

ATED PRINT RUN 199 SER.#'d SETS
*RED: .75X TO 2X BASE HI
RED PRINT RUN 25 SER.#'d SETS
UNPRICED PATCH PRINT RUN ONE SET
POAB Andrew Bogut 2.00 5.00
POAI Andre Iguodala 2.00 5.00
POAJ Antawn Jamison 2.00 5.00
POBO Chris Bosh 2.50 6.00
POBW Ben Wallace 2.00 5.00
POCB Chauncey Billups 2.50 6.00
POCK Chris Kaman 2.00 5.00
POCM Corey Maggette 2.00 5.00
POCP Chris Paul 3.00 8.00
PODG Daniel Gibson 2.00 5.00
PODW Dwyane Wade 4.00 10.00
POEB Elton Brand 2.50 6.00
POGR Danny Granger 2.00 5.00
POGW Gerald Wallace 2.00 5.00
POJC Jose Calderon 6.00 15.00
POJJ Joe Johnson 2.00 5.00
POJR Jason Richardson 2.50 6.00
POKD Kevin Durant 6.00 15.00
POKG Kevin Garnett 4.00 10.00
POKM Kevin Martin 2.00 5.00
POLJ LeBron James 8.00 20.00
POMB Mike Bibby 2.00 5.00
POMG Manu Ginobili 2.50 6.00
POPG Pau Gasol 2.50 6.00
PORJ Richard Jefferson 2.00 5.00
PORL Rashard Lewis 2.00 5.00
PORW Rasheed Wallace 2.50 6.00
POSB Shane Battier 2.00 5.00
POSM Shawn Marion 2.00 5.00
POWI Deron Williams 2.00 5.00

2008-09 Hot Prospects Rookie Materials Autographs Patches

COMBINED AU/MEM ODDS 1:9
RMAD Darrell Arthur 6.00 15.00
RMAR Anthony Randolph 5.00 12.00
RMBL Brook Lopez 10.00 25.00
RMBR Brandon Rush 6.00 15.00
RMBW Bill Walker 5.00 12.00
RMCD Chris Douglas-Roberts 5.00 12.00
RMDA Darnell Jackson 5.00 12.00
RMDG Danilo Gallinari 12.00 30.00
RMDJ D.J. Augustin 6.00 15.00
RMDR Derrick Rose 75.00 150.00
RMDW D.J. White 6.00 15.00
RMEG Eric Gordon 12.00 30.00
RMGH George Hill 8.00 20.00
RMGR Donte Greene 5.00 12.00
RMJA Joe Alexander 5.00 12.00
RMJB Jerryd Bayless 6.00 15.00
RMJC Joe Crawford 5.00 12.00
RMJD Joey Dorsey 5.00 12.00
RMJG J.R. Giddens 5.00 12.00
RMJH J.J. Hickson 6.00 15.00
RMJM JaVale McGee 10.00 25.00
RMJO DeAndre Jordan 15.00 40.00
RMJT Jason Thompson 5.00 12.00
RMKK Kosta Koufos 6.00 15.00
RMKL Kevin Love 25.00 60.00
RMKW Kyle Weaver 5.00 12.00
RMLM Luc Richard Mbah A Moute 6.00 15.00
RMMB Michael Beasley 8.00 20.00
RMMC Mario Chalmers 8.00 20.00
RMMH Malik Hairston 5.00 12.00
RMMS Marreese Speights 6.00 15.00
RMOM O.J. Mayo 8.00 20.00
RMPE Patrick Ewing Jr 5.00 12.00
RMRA Ryan Anderson 6.00 15.00
RMRH Roy Hibbert 8.00 20.00
RMRL Robin Lopez 8.00 20.00
RMSS Sean Singletary 5.00 12.00
RMSW Sonny Weems 5.00 12.00
RMWA Deron Washington 5.00 12.00
RMWS Walter Sharpe 5.00 12.00

2008-09 Hot Prospects Supreme Court

COMPLETE SET (20) 10.00 25.00
APPROXIMATE ODDS 1:6
SC1 Mike Bibby .60 1.50
SC2 Ray Allen .75 2.00
SC3 Michael Jordan 6.00 15.00
SC4 LeBron James 3.00 8.00
SC5 Jason Kidd .75 2.00
SC6 Chauncey Billups .75 2.00
SC7 Shane Battier .60 1.50
SC8 Tracy McGrady .75 2.00
SC9 Elton Brand .75 2.00
SC10 Kobe Bryant 3.00 8.00
SC11 Derek Fisher .60 1.50
SC12 Dwyane Wade 1.25 3.00
SC13 Dwight Howard .60 1.50
SC14 Andre Miller .60 1.50
SC15 Steve Nash .75 2.00
SC16 Greg Oden .60 1.50
SC17 Tony Parker .75 2.00
SC18 Jeff Green .60 1.50
SC19 Chris Bosh .75 2.00
SC20 Antawn Jamison .60 1.50

2008-09 Hot Prospects Sweet Selections Autographs

STATED PRINT RUN 25 SER.#'d SETS
UNPRICED RED PRINT RUN 5 SETS
UNPRICED SPECTRUM PRINT RUN ONE SET
SSAJ Antawn Jamison 8.00 20.00
SSAM Alonzo Mourning 30.00 80.00
SSBW Bill Walton 15.00 30.00
SSCB Chauncey Billups 8.00 20.00
SSCP Chris Paul 20.00 50.00
SSDG Darrell Griffith 8.00 20.00
SSDH Dwight Howard 12.00 30.00
SSDR David Robinson 30.00 80.00
SSDT David Thompson 8.00 20.00
SSDW Dominique Wilkins 25.00 50.00
SSHO Hakeem Olajuwon 20.00 50.00
SSJA LeBron James 100.00 200.00
SSJK Jason Kidd 15.00 40.00
SSKD Kevin Durant 75.00 150.00
SSLJ Larry Johnson 12.00 30.00
SSMO Sidney Moncrief 8.00 20.00
SSRR Micheal Ray Richardson 8.00 20.00
SSYM Yao Ming 15.00 30.00

1980-81 Hustle Chicago/La-Z-Boy Team Issue

This team-issued photo measures approximately 8 3/4" by 11" and feature black and white player portraits on one sheet. The player's name is listed below the photo. The sheet contains portraits of the Chicago Hustle from the Women's Professional Basketball Team Association. The backs contains a La-Z-Boy advertisement.The photo is unnumbered.

1 B.Caldwell 12.50 25.00
B.Candler
S.Digitale
R.Easterling
J.Fincher
D.Geils
B.Gleason CO
P.Hodgson
P.Kilday
L.Matthews
P.Mayo
C.McWhorter
I.Nissen
C.Steele TR
E.White

1972-73 Icee Bear

The 1972-73 Icee Bear set contains 20 player cards each measuring approximately 3" by 5". The cards are printed on thin stock. The fronts feature color facial pictures, and the backs show brief biographical information. The set may have been printed in 1973-74 or perhaps later as they were available in the Seattle area as late as summer 1974. The cards were reportedly distributed one card with each Icee Bear Slurpee purchased. There are four cards that are more difficult to find than the other 16; these four are listed as SP's in the checklist below.

COMPLETE SET (20) 100.00 175.00
1 Kareem Abdul-Jabbar 15.00 30.00
2 Dennis Awtrey 1.25 3.00
3 Tom Boerwinkle 2.00 5.00
4 Austin Carr SP 3.00 8.00
5 Wilt Chamberlain 20.00 40.00
6 Archie Clark SP 15.00 40.00
7 Dave DeBusschere 3.00 8.00
8 Walt Frazier SP 6.00 12.00
9 John Havlicek 7.50 15.00
10 Connie Hawkins 5.00 10.00
11 Bob Love 2.00 5.00
12 Jerry Lucas 4.00 10.00
13 Pete Maravich SP 35.00 65.00
14 Calvin Murphy 2.00 5.00
15 Oscar Robertson 10.00 20.00
16 Jerry Sloan 3.00 8.00
17 Wes Unseld 2.50 6.00
18 Dick Van Arsdale 1.25 3.00
19 Jerry West 15.00 30.00
20 Sidney Wicks 3.00 8.00

2000 IMAX Michael Jordan Postcards

These two postcards were given out at IMAX theatres and other participating stores. The set features two Michael Jordan postcards that are advertisements for two made for television movies.

COMPLETE SET (2) 4.00 10.00

2012-13 Immaculate Collection

1-100 PRINT RUN 99 SER.#'d SETS
101-200 STATED PRINT RUN 99 SER.#'d SETS
PREMIUM PATCHES MAY SELL FOR MORE
EXCHANGE DEADLINE 5/4/2015
1 Al Horford 2.50 6.00
2 Louis Williams 2.50 6.00
3 Dominique Wilkins 4.00 10.00
4 Paul Pierce 3.00 8.00
5 Kevin Garnett 5.00 12.00
6 Rajon Rondo 3.00 8.00
7 Larry Bird 8.00 20.00
8 Reggie Lewis 3.00 8.00
9 Deron Williams 2.50 6.00
10 Joe Johnson 2.50 6.00
11 Gerald Henderson 2.00 5.00
12 Ben Gordon 2.50 6.00
13 Ramon Sessions 2.50 6.00
14 Derrick Rose 4.00 10.00
15 Joakim Noah 2.50 6.00
16 Scottie Pippen 6.00 15.00
17 Dennis Rodman 6.00 15.00
18 Anderson Varejao 2.00 5.00
19 Wayne Ellington 2.00 5.00
20 Dirk Nowitzki 4.00 10.00
21 Vince Carter 4.00 10.00
22 O.J. Mayo 2.00 5.00
23 Shawn Marion 2.50 6.00
24 Andre Iguodala 2.50 6.00
25 Ty Lawson 2.00 5.00
26 Alex English 2.50 6.00
27 Greg Monroe 2.50 6.00
28 Isiah Thomas 3.00 8.00
29 Joe Dumars 3.00 8.00
30 Stephen Curry 12.00 30.00
31 David Lee 2.00 5.00
32 Chris Mullin 3.00 8.00
33 Tim Hardaway 3.00 8.00
34 James Harden 5.00 12.00
35 Jeremy Lin 3.00 8.00
36 Hakeem Olajuwon 4.00 10.00
37 Yao Ming 4.00 10.00
38 David West 2.50 6.00
39 Paul George 4.00 10.00
40 Tyler Hansbrough 2.50 6.00
41 Chris Paul 4.00 10.00
42 Blake Griffin 3.00 8.00
43 Grant Hill 4.00 10.00
44 Kobe Bryant 15.00 40.00
45 Steve Nash 3.00 8.00
46 Dwight Howard 2.50 6.00
47 George Mikan 6.00 15.00
48 Wilt Chamberlain 6.00 15.00
49 Shaquille O'Neal 6.00 15.00
50 Zach Randolph 2.50 6.00
51 Marc Gasol 3.00 8.00
52 Mike Conley 2.50 6.00
53 LeBron James 15.00 40.00
54 Dwyane Wade 5.00 12.00
55 Chris Bosh 3.00 8.00
56 Chris Andersen 2.50 6.00
57 Brandon Jennings 2.00 5.00
58 Monta Ellis 2.50 6.00
59 Eric Gordon 2.50 6.00
60 Ryan Anderson 2.50 6.00
61 Greivis Vasquez 2.50 6.00
62 Kevin Love 3.00 8.00
63 Andrei Kirilenko 2.50 6.00
64 Ricky Rubio 3.00 8.00
65 Carmelo Anthony 4.00 10.00
66 Jason Kidd 3.00 8.00
67 Tyson Chandler 2.50 6.00
68 Amar'e Stoudemire 2.50 6.00
69 Kevin Martin 2.50 6.00
70 Kevin Durant 12.00 30.00
71 Russell Westbrook 8.00 20.00
72 Arron Afflalo 2.50 6.00
73 Serge Ibaka 2.50 6.00
74 Jameer Nelson 2.00 5.00
75 Jrue Holiday 3.00 8.00
76 Evan Turner 2.00 5.00
77 Julius Erving 5.00 12.00
78 Moses Malone 3.00 8.00
79 Allen Iverson 6.00 15.00
80 Anfernee Hardaway 8.00 20.00
81 Goran Dragic 2.50 6.00
82 Luis Scola 2.50 6.00
83 Kevin Johnson 3.00 8.00
84 LaMarcus Aldridge 3.00 8.00
85 J.J. Hickson 2.00 5.00
86 DeMarcus Cousins 3.00 8.00
87 Tyreke Evans 2.00 5.00
88 Tim Duncan 5.00 12.00
89 Tony Parker 3.00 8.00
90 Manu Ginobili 3.00 8.00
91 David Robinson 5.00 12.00
92 Sean Elliott 3.00 8.00
93 Rudy Gay 3.00 8.00
94 DeMar DeRozan 3.00 8.00
95 Al Jefferson 2.50 6.00
96 Pete Maravich 5.00 12.00
97 John Stockton 5.00 12.00
98 John Wall 4.00 10.00
99 Martell Webster 2.00 5.00
100 Nene 2.50 6.00
101 K.Irving JSY AU RC 300.00 600.00
102 Derrick Williams JSY AU RC 6.00 15.00
103 Enes Kanter JSY AU RC 25.00 60.00
104 T. Thompson JSY AU RC 25.00 60.00
105 J.Valanciunas JSY AU RC 20.00 50.00
106 Jan Vesely JSY AU RC 6.00 15.00
107 B. Biyombo JSY AU RC 8.00 20.00
108 B.Knight JSY AU RC 10.00 25.00
109 K.Walker JSY AU RC 40.00 100.00
110 Jimmer Fredette JSY AU RC 6.00 15.00
111 Alec Burks JSY AU RC 10.00 25.00
112 K.Leonard JSY AU RC 600.00 900.00
113 N.Vucevic JSY AU RC 25.00 60.00
114 Iman Shumpert JSY AU RC 15.00 40.00
115 Chris Singleton JSY AU RC 6.00 15.00
116 T.Harris JSY AU RC 30.00 80.00
117 Donatas Motiejunas JSY AU RC 8.00 20.00
118 Nolan Smith JSY AU RC 6.00 15.00
119 K.Faried JSY AU RC 10.00 25.00
120 R.Jackson JSY AU RC 25.00 60.00
121 MarShon Brooks JSY AU RC 8.00 20.00
122 Jordan Hamilton JSY AU RC 6.00 15.00
123 N.Cole JSY AU RC 6.00 15.00
124 Cory Joseph JSY AU RC EXCH 6.00 15.00
125 J.Butler JSY AU RC 150.00 300.00
126 Kyle Singler JSY AU RC 6.00 15.00
127 C.Parsons JSY AU RC 30.00 80.00
128 Darius Morris JSY AU RC 6.00 15.00
129 Malcolm Lee JSY AU RC 6.00 15.00
130 D.Lillard JSY AU 300.00 500.00
131 Lavoy Allen JSY AU RC 6.00 15.00
132 E'Twaun Moore JSY AU RC 6.00 15.00
133 I.Thomas JSY AU RC 200.00 500.00
134 A.Davis JSY AU RC 1200.00 1600.00
135 M.Kidd-Gilchrist JSY AU RC 25.00 60.00
136 B.Beal JSY AU RC 75.00 200.00
137 D.Waiters JSY AU RC EXCH 30.00 80.00
138 Thomas Robinson JSY AU RC 10.00 25.00
139 H.Barnes JSY AU RC 75.00 200.00
140 Terrence Ross JSY AU RC 10.00 25.00
141 A.Drummond JSY AU RC 50.00 120.00
142 A.Rivers JSY AU RC 15.00 40.00
143 Meyers Leonard JSY AU RC 8.00 20.00
144 J.Lamb JSY AU RC 10.00 25.00
145 Kendall Marshall JSY AU RC 6.00 15.00
146 J.Henson JSY AU RC EXCH 15.00 40.00
147 M.Harkless JSY AU RC 8.00 20.00
148 Royce White JSY AU RC 6.00 15.00
149 Tyler Zeller JSY AU RC 8.00 20.00
150 T.Jones JSY AU RC EXCH 20.00 50.00
151 Andrew Nicholson JSY AU RC 6.00 15.00
152 Evan Fournier JSY AU RC 25.00 60.00
153 J.Sullinger JSY AU RC EXCH 25.00 60.00
154 Fab Melo JSY AU RC 6.00 15.00
155 Jared Cunningham JSY AU RC 6.00 15.00
156 Miles Plumlee JSY AU RC 6.00 15.00
157 Arnett Moultrie JSY AU RC 6.00 15.00
158 Marquis Teague JSY AU RC 6.00 15.00
159 Bernard James JSY AU RC 6.00 15.00
160 Jae Crowder JSY AU RC 15.00 40.00
161 D.Green JSY AU RC 300.00 600.00
162 O.Johnson JSY AU RC 6.00 15.00
163 Quincy Acy JSY AU RC 6.00 15.00
164 Khris Middleton JSY AU RC 10.00 25.00
165 Will Barton JSY AU RC 12.00 30.00
166 Doron Lamb JSY AU RC 6.00 15.00
167 Kim English JSY AU RC 6.00 15.00
168 Tyshawn Taylor JSY AU RC EXCH 6.00 15.00
169 Kevin Murphy JSY AU RC 6.00 15.00
170 Kyle O'Quinn JSY AU RC 6.00 15.00
171 Tornike Shengelia JSY AU RC 6.00 15.00
172 Robert Sacre JSY AU RC 6.00 15.00
173 Lance Thomas JSY AU RC 6.00 15.00
174 Gustavo Ayon JSY AU RC 6.00 15.00
175 Greg Stiemsma JSY AU RC 6.00 15.00
176 DeQuan Jones JSY AU RC 6.00 15.00
177 Chris Copeland JSY AU RC 6.00 15.00
178 Brian Roberts JSY AU RC 6.00 15.00
179 Victor Claver JSY AU RC 8.00 20.00
180 K.Thompson JSY AU RC 300.00 600.00
181 Mirza Teletovic JSY AU RC 15.00 40.00
182 Kent Bazemore JSY AU RC 15.00 40.00
183 Pablo Prigioni JSY RC 3.00 8.00
184 Markieff Morris JSY RC 5.00 12.00
185 Marcus Morris JSY RC 4.00 10.00
186 Ivan Johnson JSY RC 3.00 8.00
187 D.Lillard JSY RC 30.00 80.00
188 John Jenkins JSY RC 3.00 8.00
189 Tony Wroten JSY RC 4.00 10.00
190 Perry Jones JSY RC 3.00 8.00
191 Quincy Miller JSY RC 3.00 8.00
192 Mike Scott JSY RC 3.00 8.00
193 Darius Miller JSY RC 3.00 8.00
194 Alexey Shved AU RC 3.00 8.00
195 Julyan Stone AU RC 3.00 8.00
196 Nando De Colo AU RC 3.00 8.00
197 Jon Leuer AU RC 8.00 20.00
198 Jeff Taylor AU RC 3.00 8.00
199 DeAndre Liggins AU RC 4.00 10.00
200 Viacheslav Kravtsov AU RC EXCH 3.00 8.00

2012-13 Immaculate Collection Gold

*GOLD: .75X TO 2X BASIC
STATED PRINT RUN 25 SER.#'d SETS
44 Kobe Bryant 40.00 100.00
53 LeBron James 40.00 100.00
70 Kevin Durant 40.00 80.00

2012-13 Immaculate Collection Numbers Parallel

*NUM.101-182 p/r 40-100: .4X TO 1X BASIC
*NUM.101-182 p/r 15-35: .6X TO 1.5X BASIC
*NUM.183-193 p/r 44-100: .4X TO 1X BASIC
*NUM.183-193 p/r 15-32: .6X TO 1.5X BASIC
*NUM.194-200 p/r 44-55: .4X TO 1X BASIC
*NUM.194-200 p/r 22-30: .6X TO 1.5X BASIC
PRINT RUNS B/WN 1-100 COPIES PER
NO PRICING ON QTY 15 OR LESS
PREMIUM PATCHES MAY SELL FOR MORE
EXCHANGE DEADLINE 5/4/2015
3 Dominique Wilkins/21 20.00 50.00
4 Paul Pierce/34 10.00 25.00
7 Larry Bird/33 25.00 60.00
8 Reggie Lewis/35 15.00 40.00
16 Scottie Pippen/33 60.00 150.00
17 Dennis Rodman/91 20.00 50.00
18 Anderson Varejao/17 6.00 15.00
19 Wayne Ellington/21 6.00 15.00
20 Dirk Nowitzki/41 25.00 60.00
21 Vince Carter/25 25.00 60.00
22 O.J. Mayo/32 6.00 15.00
23 Shawn Marion/30 8.00 20.00
30 Stephen Curry/30 30.00 80.00
32 Chris Mullin/17 25.00 60.00
36 Hakeem Olajuwon/34 20.00 50.00
38 David West/21 8.00 20.00
39 Paul George/24 125.00 250.00
40 Tyler Hansbrough/50 8.00 20.00
42 Blake Griffin/32 10.00 25.00
43 Grant Hill/33 20.00 50.00
44 Kobe Bryant/24 150.00 300.00
49 Shaquille O'Neal/34 20.00 50.00
50 Zach Randolph/50 8.00 20.00
51 Marc Gasol/33 10.00 25.00
60 Ryan Anderson/33 8.00 20.00
61 Greivis Vasquez/21 30.00 80.00
62 Kevin Love/42 15.00 40.00
63 Andrei Kirilenko/47 8.00 20.00
69 Kevin Martin/23 8.00 20.00
70 Kevin Durant/35 50.00 120.00
71 Russell Westbrook/100 25.00 60.00
85 J.J. Hickson/21 6.00 15.00
88 Tim Duncan/21 30.00 80.00
90 Manu Ginobili/20 25.00 60.00
91 David Robinson/50 25.00 60.00
92 Sean Elliott/32 15.00 40.00
93 Rudy Gay/22 12.00 30.00
95 Al Jefferson/25 8.00 20.00
96 Pete Maravich/44 60.00 150.00
100 Nene/42 8.00 20.00
103 Enes Kanter JSY AU/100 20.00 50.00
105 J.Valanciunas JSY AU/17 75.00 150.00
106 Jan Vesely JSY AU/24 10.00 25.00
107 Bismack Biyombo JSY AU/100 8.00 20.00
109 Kemba Walker JSY AU/15 200.00 400.00
114 Iman Shumpert JSY AU/21 30.00 80.00
115 Chris Singleton JSY AU/31 10.00 25.00
117 D.Motiejunas JSY AU/20 15.00 40.00
119 Kenneth Faried JSY AU/35 100.00 200.00
120 Reggie Jackson JSY AU/15 60.00 120.00
126 Kyle Singler JSY AU/25 25.00 60.00
127 C.Parsons JSY AU/25 100.00 250.00
131 Lavoy Allen JSY AU/50 8.00 20.00
132 E'Twaun Moore JSY AU/55 6.00 15.00
133 Isaiah Thomas JSY AU/22 400.00 800.00
134 A.Davis JSY AU/23 2000.00 3000.00
138 Thomas Robinson JSY AU/41 20.00 50.00
139 H.Barnes JSY AU/40 150.00 300.00
142 Austin Rivers JSY AU/25 40.00 100.00
146 John Henson JSY AU/31 25.00 60.00
147 M.Harkless JSY AU/21 30.00 80.00
148 Royce White JSY AU/30 10.00 25.00
149 Tyler Zeller JSY AU/40 8.00 20.00
151 A.Nicholson JSY AU/44 12.00 30.00
152 Evan Fournier JSY AU/94 30.00 80.00
158 Marquis Teague JSY AU/25 25.00 60.00
161 D.Green JSY AU/23 600.00 900.00
164 Khris Middleton JSY AU/32 30.00 80.00
167 Kim English JSY AU/24 10.00 25.00
168 Tyshawn Taylor JSY AU/41 10.00 25.00
169 Kevin Murphy JSY AU/55 6.00 15.00
171 Tornike Shengelia JSY AU/20 10.00 25.00
172 Robert Sacre JSY AU/50 6.00 15.00
173 Lance Thomas JSY AU/42 6.00 15.00
174 Gustavo Ayon JSY AU/19 10.00 25.00
175 Greg Stiemsma JSY AU/34 10.00 25.00
176 DeQuan Jones JSY AU/20 10.00 25.00
178 Brian Roberts JSY AU/22 15.00 40.00
179 Victor Claver JSY AU/18 10.00 25.00
181 Mirza Teletovic JSY AU/33 15.00 40.00
182 Kent Bazemore JSY AU/20 15.00 40.00
185 Marcus Morris JSY/15 8.00 20.00
186 Ivan Johnson JSY/44 6.00 15.00
191 Quincy Miller JSY/30 5.00 12.00
192 Mike Scott JSY/32 5.00 12.00
196 Nando De Colo AU/22 5.00 12.00
197 Jon Leuer AU/30 6.00 15.00
198 Jeff Taylor AU/44 3.00 8.00
199 DeAndre Liggins AU/25 8.00 20.00
200 Viacheslav Kravtsov AU/55 3.00 8.00

2012-13 Immaculate Collection All Star Lineage Autographs

PRINT RUNS B/WN 1-19 COPIES PER
NO PRICING ON QTY 15 OR LESS
EXCHANGE DEADLINE 5/4/2015
KA Kareem Abdul-Jabbar/19 150.00 250.00

2012-13 Immaculate Collection Caps

PRINT RUNS B/WN 9-60 COPIES PER
NO PRICING ON QTY 12 OR LESS
AD Anthony Davis/42 150.00 250.00
AM Arnett Moultrie/60 6.00 15.00
AN Andrew Nicholson/31 15.00 40.00
AR Austin Rivers/24 10.00 25.00
BB Bradley Beal/30 25.00 60.00
BJ Bernard James/30 6.00 15.00
BK Brandon Knight/40 15.00 40.00
DD Andre Drummond/19 15.00 40.00
DW Derrick Williams/60 6.00 15.00
DW Dion Waiters/17 20.00 50.00
EF Evan Fournier/18 15.00 40.00
FM Fab Melo/30 12.00 30.00
HB Harrison Barnes/60 15.00 40.00
JC Jared Cunningham/30 15.00 40.00
JC Jae Crowder/30 20.00 50.00
JH John Henson/30 20.00 50.00
JL Jeremy Lamb/60 10.00 25.00
JS Jared Sullinger/27 8.00 20.00
JV Jonas Valanciunas/51 10.00 25.00
KF Kenneth Faried/25 10.00 25.00
KI Kyrie Irving/24 150.00 250.00
KM Kendall Marshall/18 6.00 15.00
KT Klay Thompson/30 40.00 100.00
LE Kawhi Leonard/29 40.00 100.00
MH Maurice Harkless/30 8.00 20.00
MK Michael Kidd-Gilchrist/29 15.00 40.00
ML Meyers Leonard/36 8.00 20.00
MP Miles Plumlee/60 12.00 30.00
MT Marquis Teague/32 6.00 15.00
NC Norris Cole/31 6.00 15.00
PJ Perry Jones/18 20.00 50.00
RS Robert Sacre/45 12.00 30.00
TH Tobias Harris/30 10.00 25.00
TJ Terrence Jones/32 8.00 20.00
TR Terrence Ross/41 20.00 50.00
TR Thomas Robinson/31 8.00 20.00
TT Tristan Thompson/18 12.00 30.00

2012-13 Immaculate Collection Inscriptions

PRINT RUNS B/WN 5-99 COPIES PER
NO PRICING ON QTY 25 OR LESS
EXCHANGE DEADLINE 5/4/2015
AB Alec Burks/99 6.00 15.00
AD Anthony Davis/25 250.00 500.00
AE Alex English/99 5.00 12.00
AH Anfernee Hardaway/99 20.00 50.00
AM Arnett Moultrie/99 4.00 10.00
AN Andrew Nicholson/99 4.00 10.00
AR Austin Rivers/99 6.00 15.00
AS Alexey Shved/99 4.00 10.00
BB Bradley Beal/99 20.00 50.00
BG Blake Griffin/25 40.00 100.00
BK Bernard King/99 5.00 12.00
BK Brandon Knight/99 5.00 12.00
BL Bill Laimbeer/99 5.00 12.00
BR Brandon Rush/99 4.00 10.00
BR Brian Roberts/99 4.00 10.00
BS Byron Scott/99 5.00 12.00
CC Chris Copeland/99 4.00 10.00
CD Clyde Drexler/25 20.00 50.00
CJ Cory Joseph/99
CM Chris Mullin/99
CO Charles Oakley/99 6.00 15.00
CP Chandler Parsons/99 6.00 15.00
CS Chris Singleton/99 4.00 10.00
DD Andre Drummond/99 12.00 30.00
DD Darryl Dawkins/99 4.00 10.00
DW Derrick Williams/99 4.00 10.00
DW Dion Waiters/99
DW Dominique Wilkins/25 10.00 25.00
EC Earl Clark/99 4.00 10.00
GG George Gervin/99 6.00 15.00
GH Grant Hill/25 30.00 60.00
GR Glen Rice/99 5.00 12.00
GS Greg Stiemsma/99 4.00 10.00
HB Harrison Barnes/99 12.00 30.00
HO Hakeem Olajuwon/25 20.00 50.00
IS Iman Shumpert/99 6.00 15.00
IT Isaiah Thomas/99 30.00 80.00
JC Jordan Crawford/99
JC Jae Crowder/99 5.00 12.00
JE Julius Erving/25 50.00 100.00
JF Jimmer Fredette/99 4.00 10.00
JH James Harden/99 50.00 120.00
JJ Jim Jackson/99 4.00 10.00
JR Jalen Rose/99 6.00 15.00
JS John Starks/99 5.00 12.00
JS Julyan Stone/99 4.00 10.00
JS John Stockton/50 40.00 100.00
JV Jonas Valanciunas/99 6.00 15.00
JW Jerry West/25 40.00 80.00
KA Kenny Anderson/99 5.00 12.00
KA Kareem Abdul-Jabbar/25 50.00 100.00
KB Kent Bazemore/99 6.00 15.00
KB Kobe Bryant/99 100.00 250.00
KD Kevin Durant/99 75.00 150.00
KI Kyrie Irving/99 60.00 150.00
KM Kevin Murphy/99 4.00 10.00
KS Kyle Singler/99 4.00 10.00
KW Kemba Walker/99 20.00 50.00
LB Larry Bird/99 40.00 100.00
LE Kawhi Leonard/99 100.00 250.00
LJ Larry Johnson/99 8.00 20.00
LN Larry Nance/99 5.00 12.00
LT Lance Thomas/99 4.00 10.00
MB MarShon Brooks/99 5.00 12.00
MB Muggsy Bogues/99 8.00 20.00
MC Mario Chalmers/99
MC Michael Cooper/99 5.00 12.00
MC Maurice Cheeks/99 4.00 10.00
MJ Magic Johnson/25 EXCH 40.00 80.00
MK Michael Kidd-Gilchrist/99 6.00 15.00
MP Mark Price/99 6.00 15.00
MP Miles Plumlee/99
MR Micheal Ray Richardson/99 5.00 12.00
MR Mitch Richmond/99 6.00 15.00
MT Marquis Teague/99 4.00 10.00
MT Mirza Teletovic/99 5.00 12.00
NB Nicolas Batum/99 5.00 12.00
NC Norris Cole/99 6.00 15.00
ND Nando De Colo/99 4.00 10.00
NV Nikola Vucevic/99 6.00 15.00
QA Quincy Acy/99 4.00 10.00
RJ Reggie Jackson/99 6.00 15.00
RS Robert Sacre/99 4.00 10.00
RW Royce White/99 4.00 10.00
SC Stephen Curry/99 75.00 200.00
SE Sean Elliott/99 6.00 15.00
SW Spud Webb/99 5.00 12.00
TH Tim Hardaway/99 8.00 20.00
TK Toni Kukoc/99 8.00 20.00
TP Terry Porter/99 6.00 15.00
TR Thomas Robinson/25 5.00 12.00
TR Terrence Ross/99 8.00 20.00
TS Tornike Shengelia/99 4.00 10.00
TT Tristan Thompson/99 6.00 15.00
VC Vince Carter/50 12.00 30.00
VC Victor Claver/99 4.00 10.00
VK Viacheslav Kravtsov/99 EXCH 4.00 10.00
WB Will Barton/99

2012-13 Immaculate Collection Logos

PRINT RUNS B/WN 6-38 COPIES PER
NO PRICING ON QTY 15 OR LESS
PREMIUM PATCHES MAY SELL FOR MORE
AB Andrew Bogut/20 40.00 100.00
AN Andrew Nicholson/17
AS Amar'e Stoudemire/16 50.00 120.00
CA Carmelo Anthony/21 50.00 120.00
CP Chris Paul/26 75.00 200.00
CP Chandler Parsons/24 30.00 60.00
DD DeMar DeRozan/28 25.00 60.00
DG Danny Green/16 30.00 80.00
DW David West/36 20.00 50.00
EK Enes Kanter/23 20.00 50.00
GH Grant Hill/24 60.00 150.00
HB Harrison Barnes/20 40.00 100.00
IS Iman Shumpert/25 20.00 50.00
IT Isaiah Thomas/28 30.00 80.00
JB Jimmy Butler/17 50.00 120.00
JF Jimmer Fredette/25 25.00 60.00
JN Joakim Noah/17 60.00 150.00
KD Kevin Durant/19 150.00 300.00
KF Kenneth Faried/21 60.00 150.00
KG Kevin Garnett/21 75.00 200.00
KH Kirk Hinrich/26 40.00 100.00
KI Kyrie Irving/21 150.00 400.00
KM Karl Malone/38 50.00 120.00
KT Klay Thompson/19 150.00 300.00
LD Luol Deng/18 20.00 50.00
MB MarShon Brooks/21 20.00 50.00
MT Marquis Teague/25 40.00 100.00
OM O.J. Mayo/20 25.00 60.00
PE Patrick Ewing/16 90.00 150.00
PJ Perry Jones/17 20.00 50.00
RA Ray Allen/26 50.00 120.00
RG Rudy Gay/19 30.00 80.00
RH Roy Hibbert/21 30.00 80.00
RR Ricky Rubio/24 50.00 120.00
RR Rajon Rondo/16 60.00 150.00
RS Robert Sacre/20 15.00 40.00
RW Russell Westbrook/17 50.00 100.00
SO Shaquille O'Neal/36 150.00 400.00
TC Tyson Chandler/16 20.00 40.00
TR Terrence Ross/28 20.00 50.00
TZ Tyler Zeller/16 20.00 50.00
VC Vince Carter/38 200.00 400.00

2012-13 Immaculate Collection Numbers Patches
PRINT RUNS B/WN 4-36 COPIES PER
NO PRICING ON QTY 15 OR LESS
PREMIUM PATCHES MAY SELL FOR MORE
BR Brian Roberts/21 10.00 25.00
AD Anthony Davis/23 250.00 400.00
AJ Amir Johnson/16 10.00 25.00
AM Arnett Moultrie/24 10.00 25.00
AN Andrew Nicholson/20 10.00 25.00
AR Austin Rivers/20
BG Blake Griffin/23 75.00 150.00
BL Bill Laimbeer/16 12.00 30.00
BL Brook Lopez/18
CA Chris Andersen/18 12.00 30.00
CP Chandler Parsons/31 20.00 50.00
DD DeMar DeRozan/18 50.00 120.00
DG Danny Green/18 12.00 30.00
DH Dwight Howard/17 50.00 120.00
DN Dirk Nowitzki/19 60.00 150.00
DW Deron Williams/19 30.00 80.00
DW David West/34 12.00 30.00
DY Dwyane Wade/19 100.00 200.00
EF Evan Fournier/23 12.00 30.00
EK Enes Kanter/18 12.00 30.00
GH Grant Hill/28 60.00 150.00
GH Gordon Hayward/31 20.00 50.00
HB Harrison Barnes/16 40.00 100.00
IS Iman Shumpert/30 30.00 80.00
IT Isaiah Thomas/36 30.00 80.00
JB Jimmy Butler/31 50.00 120.00
JD Joe Dumars/18 25.00 60.00
JF Jimmer Fredette/36 15.00 40.00
JH John Henson/20 20.00 50.00
JH Jrue Holiday/18 20.00 50.00
JJ Joe Johnson/15 12.00 30.00
JK Jason Kidd/21 75.00 150.00
JN Jameer Nelson/18 20.00 50.00
JN Joakim Noah/32 30.00 80.00
JS Jared Sullinger/17 12.00 30.00
JV Jonas Valanciunas/20 20.00 50.00
KB Kobe Bryant/32 300.00 800.00
KD Kevin Durant/25 150.00 300.00
KF Kenneth Faried/21 15.00 40.00
KG Kevin Garnett/18 60.00 150.00
KH Kirk Hinrich/27 25.00 60.00
KM Karl Malone/23 20.00 50.00
KM Kendall Marshall/26
KS Kyle Singler/29 10.00 25.00
KW Kemba Walker/18
LD Luol Deng/21 20.00 50.00
LE Kawhi Leonard/25 80.00 200.00
ME Monta Ellis/18 12.00 30.00
MG Manu Ginobili/36 50.00 100.00
MH Maurice Harkless/18 20.00 50.00
MK Michael Kidd-Gilchrist/19 12.00 30.00
MT Marquis Teague/35 15.00 40.00
NC Norris Cole/28 25.00 60.00
OM O.J. Mayo/24 10.00 25.00
PE Patrick Ewing/36 60.00 150.00
PP Paul Pierce/34 40.00 100.00
RA Ray Allen/25 50.00 120.00
RG Rudy Gay/29 15.00 40.00
RH Roy Hibbert/21 30.00 80.00
RR Rajon Rondo/21 50.00 120.00
SN Steve Nash/32 25.00 60.00
SO Shaquille O'Neal/32 125.00 300.00
TC Tyson Chandler/18 20.00 50.00
TD Tim Duncan/33 100.00 200.00
TL Ty Lawson/19 30.00 80.00
TP Tony Parker/21 60.00 150.00
TR Terrence Ross/18 15.00 40.00
TS Tiago Splitter/34 12.00 30.00
TT Tristan Thompson/19 40.00 100.00
TZ Tyler Zeller/25 15.00 40.00
VC Vince Carter/21 75.00 200.00
ZR Zach Randolph/18 12.00 30.00

2012-13 Immaculate Collection Patch Autographs
PRINT RUNS B/WN 50-100 COPIES PER
EXCHANGE DEADLINE 5/4/2015
PREMIUM PATCHES MAY SELL FOR MORE
AB Alec Burks/100 10.00 25.00
AD Anthony Davis/100 400.00 800.00
AE Alex English/100 8.00 20.00
AI Andre Iguodala/100 12.00 30.00
AM Alonzo Mourning/75 40.00 100.00
AM Arnett Moultrie/100 6.00 15.00
AN Andrew Nicholson/100 8.00 20.00
AR Austin Rivers/100 12.00 30.00
BB Bradley Beal/100 40.00 100.00
BG Blake Griffin/100 50.00 120.00
BK Brandon Knight/100 20.00 50.00
BL Brook Lopez/100 8.00 20.00
BR Brian Roberts/100 8.00 20.00
CC Chris Copeland/100 6.00 15.00
CD Clyde Drexler/75 30.00 80.00
CJ Cory Joseph/100
CM Chris Mullin/100 20.00 50.00
CP Chandler Parsons/100 25.00 60.00
CS Chris Singleton/100 6.00 15.00
DA Darrell Arthur/100
DD Andre Drummond/100 40.00 100.00
DW Dion Waiters/100 EXCH
DW Derrick Williams/100 10.00 25.00
DW Dominique Wilkins/80 40.00 80.00
EF Evan Fournier/100 10.00 25.00
FE Festus Ezeli/100 8.00 20.00
FM Fab Melo/100 6.00 15.00
GH Grant Hill/100 20.00 50.00
GM Greg Monroe/100 6.00 15.00
HB Harrison Barnes/100 50.00 120.00
HO Hakeem Olajuwon/100 40.00 100.00
IS Iman Shumpert/100 10.00 25.00
IT Isaiah Thomas/100 100.00 250.00
JE Julius Erving/100 50.00 120.00
JF Jimmer Fredette/100 8.00 20.00
JH Jordan Hamilton/100 6.00 15.00
JH John Henson/100 EXCH
JH James Harden/100 100.00 250.00
JH J.J. Hickson/100
JJ Joe Johnson/100 15.00 40.00
JJ Jim Jackson/100 10.00 25.00
JK Jason Kidd/100 25.00 60.00
JN Joakim Noah/100
JN Jameer Nelson/100 6.00 15.00
JS Jared Sullinger/100 EXCH
JS John Stockton/50 50.00 120.00
JV Jonas Valanciunas/100 15.00 40.00
KA Kareem Abdul-Jabbar/50 50.00 120.00
KA Kenny Anderson/100 6.00 15.00
KB Kobe Bryant/100 150.00 400.00
KD Kevin Durant/100 100.00 250.00
KE Kim English/100 6.00 15.00
KF Kenneth Faried/100 30.00 80.00
KI Kyrie Irving/100 250.00 500.00
KL Kyle Lowry/100 20.00 50.00
KL Kevin Love/75 30.00 80.00
KM Kevin Murphy/100 6.00 15.00
KM Kevin Martin/100 6.00 15.00
KM Khris Middleton/100 20.00 50.00
KM Kendall Marshall/100 6.00 15.00
KS Kyle Singler/100 8.00 20.00
KT Klay Thompson/100 125.00 300.00
KW Kemba Walker/100 15.00 40.00
LA LaMarcus Aldridge/100 15.00 40.00
LB Larry Bird/50 75.00 150.00
LE Kawhi Leonard/100 400.00 800.00
LN Larry Nance/100 10.00 25.00
LT Lance Thomas/100 6.00 15.00
MA Mark Aguirre/100 6.00 15.00
MB MarShon Brooks/100 8.00 20.00
MH Maurice Harkless/100 12.00 30.00
MJ Magic Johnson/50 EXCH 60.00 150.00
MK Michael Kidd-Gilchrist/100 10.00 25.00
ML Meyers Leonard/100 8.00 20.00
MP Mark Price/100 20.00 50.00
MP Miles Plumlee/100 10.00 25.00
MR Mitch Richmond/100 20.00 50.00
MT Marquis Teague/100 8.00 20.00
NC Norris Cole/100 10.00 25.00
NV Nikola Vucevic/100 20.00 50.00
PJ Perry Jones/100 10.00 25.00
QA Quincy Acy/100 6.00 15.00
RA Ryan Anderson/100 6.00 15.00
RJ Reggie Jackson/100 20.00 50.00
RS Robert Sacre/100 6.00 15.00
RW Royce White/100 6.00 15.00
SC Stephen Curry/100 250.00 500.00
SE Sean Elliott/100 12.00 30.00
SN Steve Nash/50 30.00 80.00
TC Tyson Chandler/100 10.00 25.00
TG Taj Gibson/100 8.00 20.00
TH Tim Hardaway/100 12.00 30.00
TH Tobias Harris/100 12.00 30.00
TJ Terrence Jones/100
TL Ty Lawson/100 15.00 40.00
TR Terrence Ross/100 25.00 60.00
TR Thomas Robinson/100 8.00 20.00
TT Tristan Thompson/100 EXCH 15.00 40.00
TZ Tyler Zeller/100 8.00 20.00
VC Vince Carter/100 20.00 50.00

2012-13 Immaculate Collection Patch Autographs Red
*RED: .5X TO 1.2X BASIC
PRINT RUNS B/WN 2-25 COPIES PER
EXCHANGE DEADLINE 5/4/2015
PREMIUM PATCHES MAY SELL FOR MORE
AD Anthony Davis/25 1000.00 2000.00
LE Kawhi Leonard/25 1000.00 2000.00

2012-13 Immaculate Collection Jumbo Patch Autographs
PRINT RUNS B/WN 15-75 COPIES PER
NO PRICING ON QTY 15
EXCHANGE DEADLINE 5/4/2015
PREMIUM PATCHES MAY SELL FOR MORE
*RED: .5X TO 1.2X BASIC
AB Alec Burks/75 25.00 60.00
AB Andrew Bogut/75 20.00 50.00
AD Anthony Davis/75 1700.00 2200.00
AI Andre Iguodala/75 20.00 50.00
AM Andre Miller/75 10.00 25.00
AM Arnett Moultrie/75 10.00 25.00
AN Andrew Nicholson/75 12.00 30.00
AR Austin Rivers/75 25.00 60.00
BB Bradley Beal/75 150.00 400.00
BB Bismack Biyombo/75 10.00 25.00
BG Blake Griffin/50 125.00 250.00
BJ Bernard James/75 10.00 25.00
BK Brandon Knight/75 30.00 80.00
BR Brian Roberts/55 10.00 25.00
CA Chris Andersen/25 100.00 200.00
CB Chris Bosh/75 30.00 80.00
CJ Cory Joseph/75
CM Chris Mullin/75 30.00 80.00
CP Chandler Parsons/75 30.00 80.00
CS Chris Singleton/75 10.00 25.00
DD Andre Drummond/75 75.00 200.00
DH Dwight Howard/75 15.00 40.00
DL Doron Lamb/75 10.00 25.00
DR Dennis Rodman/50 60.00 150.00
DW Derrick Williams/75 10.00 25.00
DW Dion Waiters/75 EXCH 50.00 120.00
DY Draymond Green/75 300.00 500.00
DY Dwyane Wade/25 125.00 300.00
EF Evan Fournier/75 15.00 40.00
EK Enes Kanter/75 15.00 40.00
FM Fab Melo/75 10.00 25.00
GH George Hill/50 20.00 50.00
GH Gordon Hayward/75 30.00 80.00
GR Glen Rice/35 30.00 80.00
HB Harrison Barnes/75 150.00 400.00
IS Iman Shumpert/75 15.00 40.00
IH Isaiah Thomas/75 150.00 300.00
JB Jimmy Butler/75 200.00 400.00
JC Jared Cunningham/75 10.00 20.00
JC Jae Crowder/75 20.00 50.00
JF Jimmer Fredette/75 15.00 40.00
JH John Henson/75 EXCH
JH James Harden/40
JH Jordan Hamilton/75 10.00 25.00
JH J.J. Hickson/75
JJ Joe Johnson/55 20.00 50.00
JK Jason Kidd/75 100.00 200.00
JN Joakim Noah/75
JN Jameer Nelson/75 10.00 25.00
JR J.J. Redick/75 40.00 100.00
JS Jared Sullinger/75 EXCH
JV Jonas Valanciunas/75 20.00 50.00
JV Jan Vesely/75 10.00 25.00
KA Kareem Abdul-Jabbar/30 250.00 400.00
KA Kenny Anderson/65 15.00 40.00
KB Kobe Bryant/75 800.00 1200.00
KD Kevin Durant/75 500.00 800.00
KF Kenneth Faried/75 25.00 60.00
KI Kyrie Irving/75 500.00 1000.00
KL Kevin Love/75 40.00 100.00
KM Kevin Murphy/75 10.00 25.00
KM Khris Middleton/75 50.00 120.00
KM Kendall Marshall/75 12.00 30.00
KO Kyle O'Quinn/75 10.00 25.00
KS Kyle Singler/75 10.00 25.00
KT Klay Thompson/75 300.00 600.00
KW Kemba Walker/75 50.00 120.00
LA Lavoy Allen/75 10.00 25.00
LA LaMarcus Aldridge/75 40.00 100.00
LE Kawhi Leonard/75 600.00 1200.00
LP Miles Plumlee/75 12.00 30.00
LT Lance Thomas/75 10.00 25.00
MB MarShon Brooks/75 12.00 30.00
MC Mike Conley/25 25.00 60.00
MH Maurice Harkless/75 15.00 40.00
MK Michael Kidd-Gilchrist/75 30.00 80.00
ML Meyers Leonard/75 12.00 30.00
MP Mark Price/35 100.00 250.00
MT Marquis Teague/75 10.00 25.00
NC Norris Cole/75 12.00 30.00
NS Nolan Smith/75
NV Nikola Vucevic/75 20.00 50.00
OJ Orlando Johnson/75 10.00 25.00
QA Quincy Acy/75 10.00 25.00
RJ Reggie Jackson/75 40.00 100.00
RS Robert Sacre/75 12.00 30.00
RW Royce White/75 10.00 25.00
SC Stephen Curry/50 300.00 600.00
SN Steve Nash/75 100.00 200.00
TC Tyson Chandler/75 12.00 30.00
TH Tobias Harris/75 15.00 40.00
TJ Terrence Jones/75
TR Terrence Ross/75 25.00 60.00
TR Thomas Robinson/75 15.00 40.00
TS Tiago Splitter/75 12.00 30.00
TT Tristan Thompson/75 20.00 50.00
TZ Tyler Zeller/75 12.00 30.00
VC Vince Carter/75 75.00 150.00
WB Will Barton/75 25.00 60.00

2012-13 Immaculate Collection Quads
PRINT RUNS B/WN 10-50 COPIES PER
NO PRICING QTY ON 10
1 Lopez/Williams/Wallace/Johnson 2.50 6.00
2 Kobe/Gasol/Peace/How 12.00 30.00
3 Garn/Pierce/Rondo/Brad 5.00 12.00
4 Durant/Ibaka/Martin/Jack 8.00 20.00
5 Robins/Butler/Booz/Noah 10.00 25.00
6 Fredette/Cousins/Evans/Thomas 5.00 12.00
7 Jennings/Ellis/Ilyasova/Henson 3.00 8.00
8 Leon/Ginob/Dunc/Parker 15.00 40.00
9 Law/Faried/McGee/Iguod 3.00 8.00
10 Holiday/Turner/Allen/Young 3.00 8.00
11 Anthony Davis 25.00 60.00
12 Kyrie Irving 12.00 30.00
13 Bradley Beal 5.00 12.00
14 Kawhi Leonard 15.00 40.00
15 Kenneth Faried 3.00 8.00
16 Dion Waiters 3.00 8.00
17 Andre Drummond 5.00 12.00
18 Damian Lillard 12.00 30.00
19 Harrison Barnes 5.00 12.00
20 Tristan Thompson 3.00 8.00
21 Davis/Beal/Kidd-Gil/Waiters 15.00 40.00
22 Irving/Willi/Kant/Thomp 10.00 25.00
23 Paul/Willi/Felt/Robin 4.00 10.00
24 Hens/Barnes/Marsh/Zel 5.00 12.00
25 Durant/Ald/Thomp/Brad 8.00 20.00
26 Battier/Boozer/Deng/Hill 10.00 25.00
27 Mann/Pierce/Robin/Mor 10.00 25.00
28 Wall/Rub/Westb/Will 8.00 20.00
29 Nowitz/Dunc/Garn/Gasol 8.00 20.00
30 Thom/Stock/Jack/Kidd 8.00 20.00
31 Irving/Lillard 15.00 40.00
32 Kidd/Hill 10.00 25.00
33 Durant/Bryant 20.00 50.00
34 Nowitzki/Garnett 8.00 20.00
35 Irving/Knight 8.00 20.00
36 Drex/Bird/Mullin/Pip 20.00 50.00
37 Ewing/Malone/Robin/Shaq 12.00 30.00
38 George/Hill/James/Wade 30.00 80.00
39 Dunc/Park/Rand/Conley 5.00 12.00
40 James/Bosh/Dunc/Ginob 12.00 30.00

2012-13 Immaculate Collection Veteran Patch Autographs
PRINT RUNS BW/N 5-99 COPIES PER
NO PRICING ON QTY 15 OR LESS
EXCHANGE DEADLINE 5/4/2015
PREMIUM PATCHES MAY SELL FOR MORE
AB Andrew Bogut/25 12.00 30.00
AH Anfernee Hardaway/25 75.00 150.00
BG Blake Griffin/25 100.00 250.00
BJ Brandon Jennings/25
BK Bernard King/25 12.00 30.00
187 Brandon Knight/25 30.00 80.00
BL Brook Lopez/25 15.00 40.00
CB Chris Bosh/25 30.00 80.00
CD Clyde Drexler/25 75.00 150.00
CM Chris Mullin/25 30.00 80.00
DG Danilo Gallinari/25 12.00 30.00
DH Dwight Howard/25 25.00 60.00
DL Damian Lillard/99 300.00 500.00
DM Danny Manning/25 12.00 30.00
DR David Robinson/25 100.00 200.00
.187 Dennis Rodman/25 60.00 150.00
DW Deron Williams/25 30.00 80.00
DW Dominique Wilkins/25 30.00 80.00
GG George Gervin/25 20.00 50.00
GH Grant Hill/25 30.00 80.00
GP Gary Payton/25 50.00 120.00
HO Hakeem Olajuwon/25 75.00 150.00
IT Isiah Thomas/25 30.00 80.00
JD Joe Dumars/25 20.00 50.00
JE Julius Erving/25 75.00 200.00
JF Jimmer Fredette/25 15.00 40.00
JH Jrue Holiday/25 12.00 30.00
JK Jason Kidd/25 50.00 120.00
JN Joakim Noah/25
JS John Starks/25 25.00 60.00
JS John Stockton/25 60.00 150.00
JW James Worthy/25 100.00 250.00
KB Kobe Bryant/25 300.00 800.00
KD Kevin Durant/25 150.00 400.00
KI Kyrie Irving/25 400.00 800.00
KL Kevin Love/25 40.00 100.00
KW Kemba Walker/25 50.00 120.00
LE Kawhi Leonard/25 125.00 250.00
LJ Larry Johnson/25 50.00 120.00
MB MarShon Brooks/25 12.00 30.00
MJ Magic Johnson/25 100.00 200.00
MR Mitch Richmond/25 15.00 40.00
NC Norris Cole/25 12.00 30.00
PG Paul George/25 150.00 300.00
RP Robert Parish/25 12.00 30.00
SN Steve Nash/25 75.00 150.00
SP Scottie Pippen/25 200.00 400.00
TH Tim Hardaway/25 25.00 60.00
TL Ty Lawson/25 20.00 50.00
TT Tristan Thompson/25 EXCH
VC Vince Carter/25 60.00 150.00
YM Yao Ming/25 60.00 150.00

2012-13 Immaculate Collection Rookie Red
*RED 101-182: .6X TO 1.5X BASIC
*RED 183-200: .5X TO 1.2X BASIC
PRINT RUNS B/WN 12-25 COPIES PER
NO COPELAND PRICING AVAILABLE
EXCHANGE DEADLINE 5/4/2015
151 Andrew Nicholson/25 12.00 30.00
187 Damian Lillard/25 50.00 120.00

2012-13 Immaculate Collection Multisport Patch Autographs
PRINT RUNS B/WN 5-25 COPIES PER
NO PRICING ON QTY 10 OR LESS
EXCHANGE DEADLINE 5/4/2015
134D Martin Brodeur/25 75.00 150.00
134H Dwight Gooden/25 20.00 50.00
134K Brett Hull/25 30.00 80.00
134N Patrick Kane/25 40.00 100.00
134O Henrik Lundqvist/25 20.00 50.00
134R Alex Ovechkin/25 125.00 250.00
134S Jonathan Quick/25 30.00 80.00
134U Cal Ripken Jr./25 75.00 150.00
134V Patrick Roy/25 75.00 150.00
134W Nolan Ryan/25 100.00 200.00
134X Joe Sakic/25
134ZB Ozzie Smith/25 60.00 120.00
134ZC Jonathan Toews/25 75.00 150.00
134ZD Nail Yakupov/25

2012-13 Immaculate Collection The Immaculate Collection Standard
PRINT RUNS B/WN 5-75 COPIES PER
NO PRICING ON QTY 15 OR LESS
AA Arron Afflalo/75 3.00 8.00
AD Anthony Davis/75 60.00 150.00
AH Anfernee Hardaway/25 20.00 50.00
AM Alonzo Mourning/75 5.00 12.00
AR Austin Rivers/75 4.00 10.00
AS Amar'e Stoudemire/75 3.00 8.00
BB Bradley Beal/75 10.00 25.00
BG Blake Griffin/75 4.00 10.00
BJ Brandon Jennings/75 2.50 6.00
BK Brandon Knight/75 4.00 10.00
BL Brook Lopez/75 3.00 8.00
CA Chris Andersen/75 10.00 25.00
CA Carmelo Anthony/75 8.00 20.00
CB Chris Bosh/75 4.00 10.00
CD Clyde Drexler/75 6.00 15.00
CP Chris Paul/75 10.00 25.00
DC DeMarcus Cousins/75 4.00 10.00
DD DeMar DeRozan/75 4.00 10.00
DD Andre Drummond/75 6.00 15.00
DH Dwight Howard/75 3.00 8.00
DJ DeAndre Jordan/75 4.00 10.00
DL David Lee/75 2.50 6.00
DL Damian Lillard/75 12.00 30.00
DM Danny Manning/75 3.00 8.00
DN Dirk Nowitzki/75 6.00 15.00
DR Derrick Rose/65 5.00 12.00
DR Dennis Rodman/60 15.00 40.00
DW Derrick Williams/75 2.50 6.00
DW Dion Waiters/75 4.00 10.00
DY Dwyane Wade/75 10.00 25.00
GG George Gervin/25 12.00 30.00
GH Grant Hill/75 5.00 12.00
GM George Mikan/50 30.00 80.00
HB Harrison Barnes/75 6.00 15.00
HO Hakeem Olajuwon/75 8.00 20.00
IS Iman Shumpert/75 4.00 10.00
IT Isaiah Thomas/75 6.00 15.00
JB Jimmy Butler/75 10.00 25.00
JC Jose Calderon/75 2.50 6.00
JF Jimmer Fredette/75 2.50 6.00
JH Jrue Holiday/75 4.00 10.00
JH James Harden/75 6.00 15.00
JJ Joe Johnson/75 3.00 8.00
JK Jason Kidd/75 8.00 20.00
JL Jeremy Lamb/75 4.00 10.00
JL Jeremy Lin/75 12.00 30.00
JR J.J. Redick/75 4.00 10.00
JS Josh Smith/75 3.00 8.00
JS Jared Sullinger/75 3.00 8.00
JV Jonas Valanciunas/75 4.00 10.00
JW John Wall/75 8.00 20.00
KB Kobe Bryant/75 40.00 100.00
KD Kevin Durant/75 10.00 25.00
KF Kenneth Faried/75 4.00 10.00
KG Kevin Garnett/75 8.00 20.00
KI Kyrie Irving/75 15.00 40.00
KL Kevin Love/75 4.00 10.00
KM Karl Malone/75 5.00 12.00
KT Klay Thompson/75 40.00 100.00
KW Kemba Walker/75 8.00 20.00
LA LaMarcus Aldridge/75 4.00 10.00
LB Larry Bird/75 10.00 25.00
LB LeBron James/75 50.00 100.00
LE Kawhi Leonard/75 8.00 20.00
MG Marc Gasol/75 4.00 10.00
MG Manu Ginobili/75 4.00 10.00
MK Michael Kidd-Gilchrist/75 4.00 10.00
MM Markieff Morris/75 4.00 10.00
OM O.J. Mayo/75 2.50 6.00
PE Patrick Ewing/75 8.00 20.00
PG Pau Gasol/75 6.00 15.00
PP Paul Pierce/75 4.00 10.00
RA Ray Allen/75 6.00 15.00
RG Rudy Gay/75 4.00 10.00
RL Reggie Lewis/75 8.00 20.00
RR Ricky Rubio/75 4.00 10.00
RR Rajon Rondo/75 4.00 10.00
RW Russell Westbrook/75 10.00 25.00
SC Stephen Curry/75 15.00 40.00
SE Sean Elliott/75 4.00 10.00
SI Serge Ibaka/75 3.00 8.00
SO Shaquille O'Neal/75 12.00 30.00
SP Scottie Pippen/50 15.00 40.00
TC Tyson Chandler/75 3.00 8.00
TD Tim Duncan/75 8.00 20.00
TJ Terrence Jones/75 6.00 15.00
TL Ty Lawson/75 2.50 6.00
TP Tony Parker/75 6.00 15.00
TR Thomas Robinson/75 3.00 8.00
TR Terrence Ross/75 4.00 10.00
TT Tristan Thompson/75 4.00 10.00
TZ Tyler Zeller/75 3.00 8.00
VC Vince Carter/75 6.00 15.00

2012-13 Immaculate Collection Trios
PRINT RUNS B/WN 10-99 COPIES PER
NO PRICING ON QTY 15 OR LESS
1 Laimbeer/Lanier/Cartwright/99 2.50 6.00
2 Griffin/Paul/Jordan/99 10.00 25.00
3 Anthony/Smith/Amare/99 4.00 10.00
4 Dunc/Parker/Gino/99 12.00 30.00
5 Wade/Bosh/James/99 20.00 50.00
6 Olaj/Mourning/Shaq/99 10.00 25.00
7 Durant/Westb/Sefo/99 8.00 20.00
8 Bryant/Gasol/How/99 10.00 25.00
9 Lillard/Davis/Kidd-Gil/99 12.00 30.00
10 Irving/Thom/Faried/99 20.00 50.00
11 Pierce/Rondo/Garn/99 10.00 25.00
12 Rose/Noah/Robin/99 10.00 25.00
13 Bryant/James/Paul/99 15.00 40.00
14 Carter/Carter/Carter/99 12.00 30.00
15 Gasol/Randolph/Allen/99 3.00 8.00
17 Wade/Will/Rondo/99 5.00 12.00
18 Westb/Paul/Harden/99 6.00 15.00
19 Griffin/Curry/Harden/99 12.00 30.00
20 Bird/McHale/Parish/99 12.00 30.00
21 Kareem/Malone/Bryant/25 12.00 30.00
22 Muto/Ewing/Hibbert/99 6.00 15.00
23 Valanciunas/Ilgauskas/Motiejunas/99 3.00 8.00
24 Batum/Parker/Fournier/99 3.00 8.00
25 Nene/Splitter/Varejao/99 2.50 6.00
26 Ginobili/Prigioni/Scola/99 3.00 8.00
27 Biyombo/Ibaka/Muto/25 20.00 50.00
28 Conley/Sulling/Turner/99 2.50 6.00
29 Green/Richardson/Smith/99 10.00 25.00
30 Anthony/Durant/Bryant/99 12.00 30.00
31 Holiday/Love/Collison/99 3.00 8.00
32 Allen/Butler/Drum/99 5.00 12.00
33 Kareem/Wilk/Allen/50 8.00 20.00
35 Lee/Noah/Beal/99 5.00 12.00
36 Pierce/Gooden/Morris/99 3.00 8.00
37 Davis/Cous/Kidd-Gil/99 10.00 25.00
38 Evans/Rose/Hard/99 12.00 30.00
39 Felton/Anth/Chandler/99 4.00 10.00
40 Williams/Johnson/Lopez/99 2.50 6.00
41 Rose/Griffin/Wall/99 12.00 30.00
42 Irving/Williams/Kanter/99 6.00 15.00
43 Davis/Kidd-Gil/Beal/99 15.00 40.00
44 Robin/Richard/Griffin/99 3.00 8.00
45 Nowitzki/Pierce/Irving/99 15.00 40.00
46 Murphy/Olaju/Drexler/75 10.00 25.00
47 Robin/Pip/Stockton/99 10.00 25.00
48 Johnson/Drexler/Mullin/35 12.00 30.00
49 Bird/Malone/Ewing/99 10.00 25.00
50 Cole/Shumpert/Butler/99 10.00 25.00
51 Ewing/Shaq/Robin/99 8.00 20.00
52 Bosh/Gasol/Duncan/99 5.00 12.00
53 Dikembe Mutombo 6.00 15.00
54 Teague/Jack/Wrot/99 3.00 8.00
55 Drum/Henson/Sull/99 5.00 12.00
56 Lee/Curry/Thomp/99 25.00 60.00
57 Waiters/Beal/Rivers/99 5.00 12.00
58 Irving/Thomp/Butler/99 15.00 40.00
59 Dragic/Collison/Jennings/99 2.50 6.00
60 Leon/Barnes/Faried/99 6.00 15.00

2013-14 Immaculate Collection
100 PRINT RUN 99 SER.#'d SETS
101-150 PRINT RUN 99 SER.#'d SETS
151-200 PRINT RUN 75 SER.#'d SETS
PREMIUM PATCHES MAY SELL FOR MORE
EXCHANGE DEADLINE 3/3/2016
1 Paul George 2.50 6.00
2 Jeremy Lin 2.00 5.00
3 Dion Waiters 1.50 4.00
4 Anfernee Hardaway 5.00 12.00
5 DeMar DeRozan 2.00 5.00
6 David Lee 1.25 3.00
7 Rajon Rondo 2.00 5.00
8 LeBron James 12.00 30.00
9 Nicolas Batum 1.50 4.00
10 Gerald Henderson 1.25 3.00
11 Roy Hibbert 1.50 4.00
12 Dirk Nowitzki 2.50 6.00
13 Luol Deng 1.50 4.00
14 Allen Iverson 2.50 6.00
15 Kyle Lowry 1.50 4.00
16 Goran Dragic 1.50 4.00
17 Jared Sullinger 1.25 3.00
18 Dwyane Wade 3.00 8.00
19 Kenneth Faried 1.50 4.00
20 Kemba Walker 2.00 5.00
21 Lance Stephenson 1.50 4.00
22 Monta Ellis 1.50 4.00
23 Brandon Knight 1.50 4.00
24 Shaquille O'Neal 4.00 10.00
25 Terrence Ross 1.50 4.00
26 Gerald Green 1.50 4.00
27 Evan Turner 1.25 3.00
28 Chris Bosh 2.00 5.00
29 Ty Lawson 1.25 3.00
30 Arron Afflalo 1.25 3.00
31 Joakim Noah 1.50 4.00
32 Vince Carter 2.50 6.00
33 John Henson 1.50 4.00
34 David Robinson 3.00 8.00
35 Kevin Garnett 3.00 8.00
36 Channing Frye 1.50 4.00
37 Thaddeus Young 1.25 3.00
38 Paul Millsap 2.00 5.00
39 Nate Robinson 1.25 3.00
40 Jameer Nelson 1.25 3.00
41 Carlos Boozer 1.50 4.00
42 Zach Randolph 1.50 4.00
43 O.J. Mayo 1.25 3.00
44 Dennis Rodman 4.00 10.00
45 Paul Pierce 2.00 5.00
46 Kobe Bryant 12.00 30.00
47 Spencer Hawes 1.25 3.00
48 Al Horford 1.50 4.00
49 Kevin Love 2.00 5.00
50 Nikola Vucevic 1.50 4.00
51 Derrick Rose 2.50 6.00
52 Mike Conley 1.50 4.00
53 Blake Griffin 2.00 5.00
54 Wilt Chamberlain 4.00 10.00
55 Deron Williams 1.50 4.00
56 Pau Gasol 2.00 5.00
57 Kevin Durant 5.00 12.00
58 Kyle Korver 1.50 4.00
59 Kevin Martin 1.50 4.00
60 Tony Parker 2.00 5.00
61 Brandon Jennings 1.25 3.00
62 Marc Gasol 2.00 5.00
63 Chris Paul 2.50 6.00
64 Tracy McGrady 2.00 5.00
65 Iman Shumpert 1.25 3.00
66 Steve Nash 2.00 5.00
67 Serge Ibaka 1.50 4.00
68 John Wall 2.50 6.00
69 Ricky Rubio 2.00 5.00
70 Tim Duncan 3.00 8.00
71 Greg Monroe 1.50 4.00
72 Anthony Davis 4.00 10.00
73 J.J. Redick 2.00 5.00
74 Larry Bird 5.00 12.00
75 Carmelo Anthony 2.50 6.00
76 Rudy Gay 2.00 5.00
77 Russell Westbrook 5.00 12.00
78 Bradley Beal 2.00 5.00
79 Richard Jefferson 1.50 4.00
80 Manu Ginobili 2.00 5.00
81 Andre Drummond 2.00 5.00
82 Ryan Anderson 1.50 4.00
83 Stephen Curry 6.00 15.00
84 Magic Johnson 5.00 12.00
85 Tyson Chandler 1.50 4.00
86 Isaiah Thomas 2.00 5.00
87 LaMarcus Aldridge 2.00 5.00
88 Marcin Gortat 1.50 4.00
89 Gordon Hayward 2.00 5.00
90 James Harden 3.00 8.00
91 Kyrie Irving 4.00 10.00
92 Jrue Holiday 2.00 5.00
93 Klay Thompson 2.50 6.00
94 Julius Erving 3.00 8.00
95 Jeff Green 1.50 4.00
96 DeMarcus Cousins 2.00 5.00
97 Damian Lillard 4.00 10.00
98 Al Jefferson 1.50 4.00
99 Enes Kanter 1.25 3.00
100 Dwight Howard 1.50 4.00
101 D.Schroder JSY AU RC 75.00 200.00
102 Ricky Ledo JSY AU RC 6.00 15.00
103 Glen Rice Jr. JSY AU RC 6.00 15.00
104 Shane Larkin JSY AU RC 6.00 15.00
105 Kelly Olynyk JSY AU RC 12.00 30.00
106 Tony Mitchell JSY AU RC 6.00 15.00
107 Alex Len JSY AU RC EXCH 12.00 30.00
108 M.Dellavedova JSY AU RC 30.00 80.00
109 Archie Goodwin JSY AU RC 15.00 40.00
110 Otto Porter JSY AU RC 50.00 120.00
111 Erik Murphy JSY AU RC 6.00 15.00
112 Rudy Gobert JSY AU RC 125.00 250.00
113 Isaiah Canaan JSY AU RC 6.00 15.00
114 Solomon Hill JSY AU RC 8.00 20.00
115 Caldwell-Pope JSY AU RC 50.00 120.00
116 Tony Snell JSY AU RC 8.00 20.00
117 Allen Crabbe JSY AU RC 20.00 50.00
118 MCW JSY AU RC 30.00 80.00
119 Ben McLemore JSY AU RC 20.00 50.00
120 Peyton Siva JSY AU RC 6.00 15.00
121 Gal Mekel JSY AU RC 6.00 15.00
122 Ryan Kelly JSY AU RC 6.00 15.00
123 Jamaal Franklin JSY AU RC 6.00 15.00
124 Steven Adams JSY AU RC 20.00 50.00
125 Luigi Datome JSY AU RC 6.00 15.00
126 Trey Burke JSY AU RC 8.00 20.00
127 Andre Roberson JSY AU RC 6.00 15.00
128 Nate Wolters JSY AU RC 8.00 20.00
129 C.J. McCollum JSY AU RC 75.00 200.00
130 Ray McCallum JSY AU RC 6.00 15.00
131 Antetokounmpo JSY AU RC 2200.00 3000.00
132 S.Muhammad JSY AU RC 20.00 50.00
133 Gorgui Dieng JSY AU RC 20.00 50.00
134 T.Hardaway Jr. JSY AU RC 40.00 100.00
135 Mason Plumlee JSY AU RC 10.00 25.00
136 Victor Oladipo JSY AU RC 100.00 250.00
137 A.Bennett JSY AU RC 8.00 20.00
138 Nerlens Noel JSY AU RC 60.00 150.00
139 Cody Zeller JSY AU RC 12.00 30.00
140 Reggie Bullock JSY AU RC 8.00 20.00
141 Pero Antic AU RC 4.00 10.00
142 Sergey Karasev AU RC 4.00 10.00
143 Jeff Withey AU RC 4.00 10.00
144 Dwight Buycks AU RC 4.00 10.00
145 Ian Clark AU RC 25.00 60.00
146 Nemanja Nedovic AU RC 4.00 10.00
147 Raduljica AU RC EXCH 5.00 12.00
148 Phil Pressey AU RC 5.00 12.00
149 Carrick Felix AU RC 4.00 10.00
150 Vitor Faverani AU RC 4.00 10.00
151 Enes Kanter JSY AU/75 6.00 15.00
152 C.Anthony JSY AU/75 40.00 100.00
153 Isiah Thomas JSY AU/75 20.00 50.00
154 S.Curry JSY AU/75 EXCH 200.00 400.00
155 A.Mourning JSY AU/75 EX 30.00 80.00
156 Abdul-Jabbar JSY AU/75 EX 50.00 100.00
157 Bill Laimbeer JSY AU/75 8.00 20.00
158 Kevin Love JSY AU/75 20.00 50.00
159 David Robinson JSY AU/75 30.00 80.00
160 LaMarcus Aldridge JSY AU/75 10.00 25.00
161 Robert Parish JSY AU/75 10.00 25.00
162 Gary Payton JSY AU/75 30.00 80.00
163 Jared Sullinger JSY AU/75 EXCH 6.00 15.00
164 Tony Parker JSY AU/75 30.00 80.00
165 A. Drummond JSY AU/75 30.00 80.00
166 Karl Malone JSY AU/75 40.00 100.00
167 Bradley Beal JSY AU/75 15.00 40.00
168 K. McHale JSY AU/75 EXCH 15.00 40.00
169 Deron Williams JSY AU/75 12.00 30.00
170 Larry Bird JSY AU/75 60.00 150.00
171 Goran Dragic JSY AU/75 10.00 25.00
172 Ryan Anderson JSY AU/75 20.00 50.00
173 Jerry Lucas JSY AU/75 15.00 40.00
174 Tracy McGrady JSY AU/75 40.00 100.00
175 Andre Iguodala JSY AU/75 12.00 30.00
176 Kelly Tripucka JSY AU/75 6.00 15.00
177 Chris Andersen JSY AU/75 20.00 50.00
178 Chris Mullin JSY AU/75 15.00 40.00
179 Dikembe Mutombo JSY AU/75 15.00 40.00
180 Larry Johnson JSY AU/75 15.00 40.00
181 Greg Monroe JSY AU/75 8.00 20.00
182 Scottie Pippen JSY AU/75 75.00 150.00
183 Anthony Davis JSY AU/75 100.00 250.00
184 Tyson Chandler JSY AU/75 10.00 25.00
185 A. Hardaway JSY AU/75 40.00 100.00
186 Kenneth Faried JSY AU/75 10.00 25.00
187 Manu Ginobili JSY AU/75 40.00 100.00
188 Kobe Bryant JSY AU/75 150.00 250.00
189 D. Wilkins JSY AU/75 15.00 40.00
190 Magic Johnson JSY AU/75 50.00 120.00
191 Olajuwon JSY AU/75 30.00 80.00
192 S. O'Neal JSY AU/75 100.00 200.00
193 John Starks JSY AU/75 12.00 30.00
194 Sidney Moncrief JSY AU/75 10.00 25.00
195 Bernard King JSY AU/75 8.00 20.00
196 Kevin Durant JSY AU/75 125.00 250.00
197 Darrell Griffith JSY AU/75 6.00 15.00
198 Kyrie Irving JSY AU/75 75.00 150.00
199 Elgin Baylor JSY AU/75 20.00 50.00
200 Dwight Howard JSY AU/75 20.00 50.00

2013-14 Immaculate Collection Autographs Jersey Number
*JSY NUM p/r 26-55: .6X TO 1.5X BASIC
*JSY NUM p/r 15-25: .75X TO 2X BASIC
RANDOM INSERTS IN PACKS
PRINT RUNS B/WN 1-55 COPIES PER
NO PRICING ON QTY 14 OR LESS
EXCHANGE DEADLINE 3/3/2016
107 Alex Len JSY AU/21 40.00 100.00
116 Tony Snell JSY AU/20 100.00 200.00
119 Ben McLemore JSY AU/16 60.00 150.00
131 Antetokounmpo JSY AU/34 3000.00 4000.00
154 Stephen Curry JSY AU/30 500.00 800.00
155 A. Mourning JSY AU/33 60.00 150.00
156 Abdul-Jabbar JSY AU/33 150.00 300.00
158 Kevin Love JSY AU/42 60.00 120.00
162 Gary Payton JSY AU/20 150.00 300.00
168 Kevin McHale JSY AU/32 40.00 100.00
170 Larry Bird JSY AU/33 200.00 400.00
178 Chris Mullin JSY AU/17 40.00 100.00
182 Scottie Pippen JSY AU/33 200.00 400.00
183 Anthony Davis JSY AU/23 300.00 600.00
187 Manu Ginobili JSY AU/20 150.00 300.00
188 Kobe Bryant JSY AU/24 1000.00 1500.00
190 M. Johnson JSY AU/32 250.00 350.00
191 Olajuwon JSY AU/34 60.00 150.00
192 S. O'Neal JSY AU/34 400.00 600.00
196 Kevin Durant JSY AU/35 400.00 800.00

2013-14 Immaculate Collection Christmas Day Materials
RANDOM INSERTS IN PACKS
STATED PRINT RUN 85 SER.#'d SETS
1 James Harden 8.00 20.00
2 Dwyane Wade 6.00 15.00
3 Tim Duncan 8.00 20.00
4 Jodie Meeks 4.00 10.00
5 Joakim Noah 4.00 10.00
6 Kevin Durant 12.00 30.00
7 Kevin Garnett 6.00 15.00
8 J.R. Smith 4.00 10.00
9 Chris Paul 6.00 15.00
10 Klay Thompson 6.00 15.00
11 Dwight Howard 4.00 10.00
12 LeBron James 20.00 50.00
13 Tony Parker 6.00 15.00
14 Pau Gasol 5.00 12.00
15 Jimmy Butler 5.00 12.00
16 Russell Westbrook 6.00 15.00
17 Deron Williams 4.00 10.00
18 Tyson Chandler 4.00 10.00
19 DeAndre Jordan 5.00 12.00
20 David Lee 3.00 8.00
21 Jeremy Lin 5.00 12.00
22 Chris Bosh 5.00 12.00
23 Kawhi Leonard 10.00 25.00
24 Nick Young 5.00 12.00
25 Carlos Boozer 4.00 10.00
26 Serge Ibaka 6.00 15.00
27 Paul Pierce 5.00 12.00
28 Tim Hardaway Jr. 5.00 12.00
29 Jamal Crawford 5.00 12.00
30 Andrew Bogut 4.00 10.00
31 Chandler Parsons 4.00 10.00
32 Ray Allen 6.00 15.00
33 Manu Ginobili 6.00 15.00
34 Xavier Henry 3.00 8.00
35 Kirk Hinrich 4.00 10.00
36 Reggie Jackson 4.00 10.00
37 Reggie Evans 3.00 8.00
38 Amar'e Stoudemire 4.00 10.00
39 Blake Griffin 6.00 15.00
40 Harrison Barnes 4.00 10.00
41 Terrence Jones 4.00 10.00
42 Mario Chalmers 4.00 10.00
43 Darren Collison 4.00 10.00
44 Stephen Curry 25.00 60.00
45 D.J. Augustin 3.00 8.00
46 Jeremy Lamb 3.00 8.00
47 Mirza Teletovic 3.00 8.00
48 Iman Shumpert 3.00 8.00
49 Jordan Hill 3.00 8.00
50 Andre Iguodala 4.00 10.00

2013-14 Immaculate Collection Elite Scorers Club Signatures
RANDOM INSERTS IN PACKS
PRINT RUNS B/WN 49-60 COPIES PER
EXCHANGE DEADLINE 3/3/2016
1 Jerry West/49 25.00 60.00
2 Dan Issel/60 5.00 12.00
3 Kobe Bryant/49 125.00 250.00
4 Carmelo Anthony/60 30.00 80.00
5 Shaquille O'Neal/49 100.00 200.00
6 David Robinson/49 25.00 60.00
7 Larry Bird/49 40.00 100.00
8 Vince Carter/49 15.00 40.00
9 Allen Iverson/49 100.00 200.00
10 John Havlicek/49 20.00 50.00
11 Karl Malone/49 30.00 80.00
12 Oscar Robertson/49 40.00 100.00
13 Julius Erving/49 40.00 100.00
14 Kevin Durant/49 60.00 150.00
15 Adrian Dantley/60 5.00 12.00

2013-14 Immaculate Collection HOF Heroes Signatures
RANDOM INSERTS IN PACKS
PRINT RUNS B/WN 49-60 COPIES PER
EXCHANGE DEADLINE 3/3/2016
1 David Thompson/60 5.00 12.00
2 David Robinson/49 25.00 60.00
3 Kareem Abdul-Jabbar/49 30.00 80.00
4 Dominique Wilkins/49 12.00 30.00
5 Walt Frazier/60 10.00 25.00
6 Gary Payton/49 25.00 60.00
7 Robert Parish/60 10.00 25.00
8 Artis Gilmore/60 5.00 12.00
9 Kevin McHale/49 12.00 30.00
10 Dennis Rodman/49 30.00 80.00
11 Dan Issel/60 5.00 12.00
12 Hakeem Olajuwon/49 20.00 50.00
13 Bill Walton/60 12.00 30.00
14 Joe Dumars/60 6.00 15.00
15 Elgin Baylor/49 12.00 30.00
16 Bernard King/60 10.00 25.00
17 Magic Johnson/49 40.00 100.00
18 Arvydas Sabonis/60 15.00 40.00
19 Larry Bird/49 40.00 100.00
20 Scottie Pippen/49 50.00 120.00
21 Gail Goodrich/60 8.00 20.00
22 Adrian Dantley/60 5.00 12.00
23 James Worthy/49 12.00 30.00
24 Julius Erving/49 40.00 100.00
25 Jerry West/49 25.00 60.00
26 Isiah Thomas/60 12.00 30.00
27 Jamaal Wilkes/60 8.00 20.00
28 Chris Mullin/60 12.00 30.00
29 Oscar Robertson/49 40.00 100.00
30 Karl Malone/60 30.00 80.00

2013-14 Immaculate Collection Immaculate Standard Materials
RANDOM INSERTS IN PACKS
PRINT RUNS B/WN 5-75 COPIES PER
NO PRICING ON QTY 10 OR LESS
1 Hakeem Olajuwon/49 8.00 20.00
2 Reggie Jackson/75 3.00 8.00
4 Zydrunas Ilgauskas/75 3.00 8.00
5 Kobe Bryant/75 15.00 40.00
6 Dwight Howard/49 3.00 8.00
7 Shaquille O'Neal/49 15.00 40.00
8 Andray Blatche/75 2.50 6.00
9 John Wall/75 5.00 12.00
10 Dikembe Mutombo/75 6.00 15.00
11 Kevin McHale/25 10.00 25.00
12 Thabo Sefolosha/75 2.50 6.00
14 Walter Berry/75 2.50 6.00
15 Pau Gasol/75 4.00 10.00
16 Chris Kaman/75 3.00 8.00
17 Shaquille O'Neal/49 15.00 40.00
18 Anfernee Hardaway/49 15.00 40.00
19 Michael Beasley/75 2.50 6.00
20 Jimmy Butler/75 12.00 30.00
21 Magic Johnson/25 15.00 40.00
22 Nate Thurmond/25 20.00 50.00
23 Jeremy Lin/75 8.00 20.00
24 Sean Elliott/75 4.00 10.00
25 Kevin Love/75 4.00 10.00
26 Tracy McGrady/49 6.00 15.00
27 Clyde Drexler/75 6.00 15.00
28 Brandon Bass/75 2.50 6.00
29 Andrew Bynum/75 2.50 6.00
30 Jodie Meeks/75 3.00 8.00
31 Larry Bird/75 12.00 30.00
32 Chris Morris/75 2.50 6.00
33 Fat Lever/49 3.00 8.00
34 Kenneth Faried/49 3.00 8.00
35 Norris Cole/75 2.50 6.00
36 Greg Monroe/75 3.00 8.00
37 Ray Allen/75 10.00 25.00
38 Carlos Boozer/75 3.00 8.00
39 DeMar DeRozan/75 4.00 10.00
40 Jordan Hill/75 2.50 6.00
41 Robert Parish/25 10.00 25.00
42 Hal Greer/49 10.00 25.00
43 Tyson Chandler/75 3.00 8.00
44 Omer Asik/75 3.00 8.00
45 Derek Fisher/75 3.00 8.00
46 Grant Hill/75 5.00 12.00
47 Carmelo Anthony/49 6.00 15.00
48 Chandler Parsons/75 3.00 8.00
49 Karl Malone/40 8.00 20.00
50 Kendrick Perkins/75 2.50 6.00
51 Larry Johnson/49 8.00 20.00
52 Lou Hudson/49 2.50 6.00
53 Raymond Felton/75 3.00 8.00
54 Serge Ibaka/49 3.00 8.00
55 Joe Johnson/75 3.00 8.00
56 James Jones/75 2.50 6.00
57 Kevin Durant/75 10.00 25.00
58 DeAndre Jordan/75 4.00 10.00
59 John Stockton/25 12.00 30.00
60 Kirk Hinrich/75 3.00 8.00
61 Larry Johnson/75 8.00 20.00
64 Shane Battier/75 6.00 15.00
65 Dirk Nowitzki/75 6.00 15.00
66 Joe Dumars/75 4.00 10.00
67 Kevin Garnett/75 6.00 15.00

68 Donatas Motiejunas/75 3.00 8.00
69 Udonis Haslem/75 2.50 6.00
70 Luol Deng/75 3.00 8.00
71 Bill Cartwright/49 3.00 8.00
72 Bob Lanier/49 3.00 8.00
73 Jermaine O'Neal/75 3.00 8.00
74 Steve Nash/25 8.00 20.00
75 Shaquille O'Neal/49 12.00 30.00
76 Greivis Vasquez/75 3.00 8.00
77 Paul Pierce/75 4.00 10.00
78 JaVale McGee/75 3.00 8.00
79 David Robinson/49 25.00 60.00
80 Mario Chalmers/75 3.00 8.00
81 Kareem Abdul-Jabbar/25 20.00 50.00
82 Brad Daugherty/75 3.00 8.00
83 Gail Goodrich/75 3.00 8.00
84 Tracy McGrady/49 6.00 15.00
85 Chris Bosh/75 4.00 10.00
86 Jared Sullinger/75 2.50 6.00
87 Dwyane Wade/75 6.00 15.00
88 Jason Kidd/75 4.00 10.00
90 Matt Barnes/75 2.50 6.00
91 John Havlicek/49 8.00 20.00
92 Gus Williams/75 2.50 6.00
93 Iman Shumpert/75 2.50 6.00
94 Moses Malone/49 4.00 10.00
95 Scottie Pippen/75 12.00 30.00
96 Alex English/49 3.00 8.00
97 Al Horford/75 3.00 8.00
98 Jeremy Lamb/75 2.50 6.00
99 Julius Erving/25 20.00 50.00
100 Nick Collison/75 3.00 8.00

2013-14 Immaculate Collection Ink

RANDOM INSERTS IN PACKS
PRINT RUNS B/WN 60-99 COPIES PER
EXCHANGE DEADLINE 3/3/2016
1 John Wall/60 20.00 50.00
2 Phil Jackson/60 25.00 60.00
3 Joe Johnson/75 4.00 10.00
4 Thaddeus Young/99 3.00 8.00
5 Michael Finley/75 5.00 12.00
6 Alexey Shved/99 3.00 8.00
7 George Karl/75 8.00 20.00
8 John Lucas/99 5.00 12.00
9 Clark Kellogg/99 5.00 12.00
10 Earl Monroe/60 12.00 30.00
11 Luis Scola/99 4.00 10.00
12 Jonas Valanciunas/99 4.00 10.00
13 Derrick Williams/75 3.00 8.00
14 Theo Ratliff/99 3.00 8.00
15 Peja Stojakovic/75 5.00 12.00
16 Darrell Griffith/99 3.00 8.00
17 Kenny Smith/75 4.00 10.00
18 Jimmer Fredette/99 3.00 8.00
19 Eddie Jones/99 6.00 15.00
20 Thabo Sefolosha/99 3.00 8.00
21 Jason Kidd/60 12.00 30.00
22 Al-Farouq Aminu/99 4.00 10.00
23 Christian Laettner/75 4.00 10.00
24 Vin Baker/99 3.00 8.00
25 Walt Bellamy/99 4.00 10.00
26 Bruce Bowen/99 3.00 8.00
27 Andrei Kirilenko/75 4.00 10.00
28 Arvydas Sabonis/99 8.00 20.00
29 Chet Walker/99 4.00 10.00
30 Danny Green/99 4.00 10.00
31 Elgin Baylor/60 10.00 25.00
32 Amir Johnson/99 3.00 8.00
33 Al Horford/75 4.00 10.00
34 Marvin Williams/99 4.00 10.00
35 Brandon Knight/75 4.00 10.00
36 Buck Williams/99 3.00 8.00
37 Don Nelson/75 10.00 25.00
38 Rodney Stuckey/99 4.00 10.00
39 Dwight Howard/60 4.00 10.00
40 Horace Grant/99 8.00 20.00
41 Clyde Drexler/60 12.00 30.00
42 Adrian Smith/99 3.00 8.00
43 Willis Reed/75 10.00 25.00
44 Luc Longley/99 4.00 10.00
45 Gail Goodrich/75 6.00 15.00
46 Bill Laimbeer/99 4.00 10.00
47 Bill Sharman/99 10.00 25.00
48 Connie Hawkins/99 5.00 12.00
49 Scott Skiles/99 4.00 10.00
50 Greg Anthony/99 3.00 8.00
51 John Havlicek/60 20.00 50.00
52 Dave Cowens/60 6.00 15.00
53 Artis Gilmore/75 6.00 15.00
54 Cedric Ceballos/99 6.00 15.00
55 Danny Manning/75 4.00 10.00
56 Antoine Walker/99 4.00 10.00
57 Devin Harris/75 3.00 8.00
58 Bailey Howell/99 8.00 20.00
59 Jared Dudley/99 3.00 8.00
60 Jo Jo White/99 4.00 10.00
61 Ray Allen/60 15.00 40.00
62 Dan Issel/99 4.00 10.00
63 Bernard King/75 4.00 10.00
65 Avery Johnson/75 4.00 10.00
66 Dale Davis/99 3.00 8.00
67 Luol Deng/75 4.00 10.00
68 Billy Paultz/99 5.00 12.00
69 Dirk Nowitzki/60 40.00 100.00
70 Kurt Rambis/99 3.00 8.00
71 Kevin Love/60 15.00 40.00
72 Maurice Harkless/99 3.00 8.00
73 Chris Mullin/75 8.00 20.00
74 Dick Van Arsdale/99 4.00 10.00
75 John Thompson/75 20.00 50.00
76 David Robinson/60 15.00 40.00
77 Steve Francis/75 4.00 10.00
78 Kenneth Faried/75 4.00 10.00
79 John Stockton/60 20.00 50.00
80 Chase Budinger/99 3.00 8.00
81 Tony Parker/75 12.00 30.00
82 Brandan Wright/99 3.00 8.00
83 Walt Frazier/75 8.00 20.00
84 Tom Van Arsdale/99 4.00 10.00
85 Jerry Lucas/75 5.00 12.00
86 Bradley Beal/75 10.00 25.00
87 Mike Conley/99 4.00 10.00
88 Shane Battier/75 4.00 10.00
89 Anthony Davis/60 40.00 100.00
90 Wayne Embry/99 8.00 20.00

2013-14 Immaculate Collection Multisport Autographs

RANDOM INSERTS IN PACKS
STATED PRINT RUN 10-25
EXCHANGE DEADLINE 3/3/2016
1 Ryne Sandberg EXCH 75.00 150.00
2 Cal Ripken Jr. EXCH 75.00 150.00
3 Jose Abreu EXCH 60.00 120.00
4 Greg Maddux EXCH 40.00 100.00
5 Frank Thomas 40.00 100.00
6 Roger Clemens EXCH 40.00 100.00
7 Johnny Manziel EXCH 30.00 80.00
8 Brett Favre EXCH 125.00 250.00
9 Peyton Manning EXCH 150.00 250.00
10 Bo Jackson/10 100.00 200.00

2013-14 Immaculate Collection Patches

RANDOM INSERTS IN PACKS
PRINT RUNS B/WN 1-50 COPIES PER
NO PRICING ON QTY 13 OR LESS
4 Anthony Davis/23 30.00 80.00
5 Dirk Nowitzki/41 15.00 40.00
7 Stephen Curry/30 20.00 50.00
8 Tim Duncan/21 30.00 80.00
10 Larry Bird/33 20.00 50.00
13 Paul Pierce/34 10.00 25.00
19 Paul George/24 15.00 40.00
20 Magic Johnson/32 15.00 40.00
22 Karl Malone/32 15.00 40.00
24 Kevin Durant/35 30.00 80.00
27 Harrison Barnes/40 15.00 40.00
29 Blake Griffin/32 25.00 60.00
30 Kevin McHale/32 10.00 25.00
31 Kevin Love/42 10.00 25.00
33 Kemba Walker/15 10.00 25.00
36 DeMarcus Cousins/15 20.00 50.00
40 Kareem Abdul-Jabbar/33 20.00 50.00
42 David Robinson/50 15.00 40.00
46 Isaiah Thomas/22 10.00 25.00
49 Kobe Bryant/24 75.00 200.00
50 Dominique Wilkins/21 20.00 50.00

2013-14 Immaculate Collection Player Caps

RANDOM INSERTS IN PACKS
PRINT RUNS B/WN 45-99 COPIES PER
PREMIUM PATCHES MAY SELL FOR MORE
1 Shabazz Muhammad/99 6.00 15.00
2 Kentavious Caldwell-Pope/84 4.00 10.00
3 Tim Hardaway Jr./80 4.00 10.00
4 Alex Len/73 3.00 8.00
5 Mason Plumlee/75 4.00 10.00
6 Archie Goodwin/45 3.00 8.00
7 Nerlens Noel/79 5.00 12.00
8 Cody Zeller/75 3.00 8.00
9 Reggie Bullock/70 3.00 8.00
10 Isaiah Canaan/70 2.50 6.00
11 Solomon Hill/72 2.50 6.00
12 C.J. McCollum/79 6.00 15.00
13 Trey Burke/99 3.00 8.00
14 Andre Roberson/74 2.50 6.00
15 M.Carter-Williams/60 4.00 10.00
16 Ben McLemore/75 3.00 8.00
17 Otto Porter/90 4.00 10.00
18 G.Antetokounmpo/99 20.00 50.00
19 Ryan Kelly/69 2.50 6.00
20 Kelly Olynyk/60 3.00 8.00
21 Steven Adams/75 12.00 30.00
22 Glen Rice Jr./60 2.50 6.00
23 Victor Oladipo/75 5.00 12.00
24 Anthony Bennett/73 3.00 8.00
25 Jeff Withey/78 2.50 6.00

2013-14 Immaculate Collection Premium Autograph Patches

RANDOM INSERTS IN PACKS
STATED PRINT RUN 25 SER.#'d SETS
EXCHANGE DEADLINE 3/3/2016
PREMIUM PATCHES MAY SELL FOR MORE
1 Anthony Bennett 15.00 40.00
2 Ben McLemore 15.00 40.00
3 Alonzo Mourning 100.00 200.00
4 Bradley Beal 125.00 250.00
5 C.J. McCollum 175.00 350.00
6 Isiah Thomas 30.00 80.00
7 Andre Iguodala 30.00 80.00
8 Greg Monroe 20.00 50.00
9 Kiki Vandeweghe 15.00 40.00
10 Thaddeus Young 12.00 30.00
11 Shaquille O'Neal 300.00 600.00
12 Chandler Parsons 50.00 120.00
13 Giannis Antetokounmpo 1800.00 2200.00
14 Stephen Curry 400.00 800.00
15 Dee Brown 12.00 30.00
16 Jimmer Fredette 30.00 80.00
17 Jamal Mashburn 20.00 50.00
18 Tony Parker 100.00 200.00
19 Kelly Olynyk 15.00 40.00
20 Mason Plumlee 20.00 50.00
21 Sidney Moncrief 25.00 60.00
22 Dikembe Mutombo 40.00 100.00
23 Anthony Mason 15.00 40.00
24 Al Horford 15.00 40.00
25 Dennis Rodman 40.00 100.00
26 Enes Kanter 12.00 30.00
27 Michael Carter-Williams 20.00 50.00
28 Iman Shumpert 12.00 30.00
29 Larry Johnson 50.00 120.00
30 Nate Wolters 15.00 40.00
31 Tracy McGrady 100.00 200.00
32 Nerlens Noel 75.00 200.00
33 Fred Brown 12.00 30.00
34 LaMarcus Aldridge 60.00 150.00
35 Dominique Wilkins 60.00 120.00
36 Kawhi Leonard 200.00 300.00
37 Jerry Lucas 30.00 80.00
38 Nikola Vucevic 15.00 40.00
39 Larry Nance 15.00 40.00
40 Jared Sullinger 12.00 30.00
41 Vince Carter 50.00 120.00
42 Jason Richardson
43 Avery Johnson 15.00 40.00
44 Otto Porter 60.00 150.00
45 Harrison Barnes 100.00 200.00
46 Steve Nash 100.00 200.00
47 Nick Young 40.00 100.00
48 John Stockton 100.00 250.00
49 Monta Ellis 15.00 40.00
50 Tayshaun Prince 15.00 40.00
51 Kobe Bryant 800.00 1200.00
52 Jason Terry 15.00 40.00
53 Paul George 100.00 200.00
54 Bernard King 15.00 40.00
55 Gail Goodrich 15.00 40.00
56 Isaiah Thomas 20.00 50.00
57 Kareem Abdul-Jabbar 150.00 300.00
58 Kevin Durant 350.00 700.00
59 Steven Adams 20.00 50.00
60 Allen Iverson 600.00 900.00
61 Kenneth Faried 30.00 80.00
62 Joakim Noah 50.00 100.00
63 Bill Laimbeer 15.00 40.00
64 Baron Davis 15.00 40.00
65 Gary Payton 50.00 120.00
66 Deron Williams 30.00 80.00
67 Karl Malone 100.00 200.00
68 Chris Andersen 200.00 300.00
69 Dwight Howard 75.00 150.00
70 Anderson Varejao 12.00 30.00
71 Blake Griffin 100.00 200.00
72 John Starks 50.00 120.00
73 Andre Drummond 20.00 50.00
74 Tim Hardaway Jr. 75.00 200.00
75 Grant Hill 50.00 120.00
76 Tyson Chandler 25.00 60.00
77 Kelly Tripucka 12.00 30.00
78 Ryan Anderson 15.00 40.00
79 Tony Snell 15.00 40.00
80 Bill Cartwright 12.00 30.00
81 Kyrie Irving 200.00 400.00
82 Norm Nixon 12.00 30.00
83 Clyde Drexler
84 Derrick Favors 15.00 40.00
85 Jeff Green 15.00 40.00
87 Kevin McHale 30.00 80.00
88 Spencer Hawes 12.00 30.00
89 Robert Parish 30.00 80.00
90 Kevin Love 250.00 350.00
91 Brandon Bass 12.00 30.00
92 Steve Mix 12.00 30.00
93 Darrell Griffith 12.00 30.00
94 Hakeem Olajuwon 100.00 200.00
95 Gordon Hayward 40.00 100.00
96 Maurice Harkless 25.00 60.00
97 Kevin Willis 20.00 50.00
98 Trey Burke 15.00 40.00
99 Victor Oladipo 60.00 150.00
100 Terry Cummings 15.00 40.00

2013-14 Immaculate Collection Quad Materials

NDOM INSERTS IN PACKS
PRINT RUNS B/WN 10-25 COPIES PER
NO PRICING ON QTY 10
1 Hrfrd/Krvr/Mllsp/Tg/25 8.00 20.00
2 Walker/Kidd-Gilchrist/Jefferson 5.00 12.00
Henderson/25
3 Crtr/Nwtzk/Cldrn/Ells/25 12.00 30.00
4 Jennings/Monroe/Drummond/Smith/25 5.00 12.00
5 Brns/Thmpsn/Igul/Crry/25 10.00 25.00
6 Prsns/Hwrd/Hrdn/Ln/25 12.00 30.00
7 Stphnsn/Grg/Wst/Hbbrt/25 10.00 25.00
8 Wd/Jms/Alln/Bsh/25 30.00 80.00
9 Anthn/Fltn/Chndlr/Stdmr/25 6.00 15.00
10 Jcksn/Wstbrk/Ibk/Drnt/25 10.00 25.00
11 Lnrd/Gnbl/Prkr/Dncn/25 25.00 60.00
12 DRzn/Vlcns/Lwry/Rss/25 8.00 20.00
13 Dvs/Wtrs/Kdd-Glchrst/Bl/25 8.00 20.00
14 Vlncns/Kntr/Irvng/Thmpsn/25 15.00 40.00
15 Csns/Fvrs/Wll/Grg/25 6.00 15.00
16 Hrdn/Rb/Grffn/Evns/25 6.00 15.00
17 Affl/Hlid/Lv/Wstbrk/25 6.00 15.00
18 Bzr/Hll/Irvng/Bttr/25 12.00 30.00
19 Brdly/Thmpsn/Drnt/Aldrdg/25 8.00 20.00
20 Cldrn/Gsl/Gsl/Rb/25 8.00 20.00
21 Pl/Mln/Grffn/Stcktn/25 12.00 30.00
22 Hwrd/Hrdn/Brnt/O'Nl/25 15.00 40.00
23 Pytn/Drnt/Wstbrk/Kmp/25 20.00 50.00
24 Rc/Rc Jr./Hrdwy/Hrdwy Jr./25 10.00 25.00
26 Bl/Brdl/Smpsn/Mng/25 12.00 30.00
27 Brynt/Abdl-Jbbr/Jhnsn/O'Nl/25 40.00 100.00
28 Crtwght/Okly/Wlkr/Ewng/25 12.00 30.00
29 Rbnsn/Rdmn/Rvrs/Jhnsn/25 20.00 50.00
30 Jhnsn/Jffrsn/Mrnng/Hndrsn/25 25.00 60.00
31 Bnntt/Oldpo/Zllr/Prtr/25 6.00 15.00
32 McLmr/Nl/Ln/Cldwll-Pp/25 6.00 15.00
33 McCllm/Crtr-Wllms/Adms/Brk/25 6.00 15.00
34 Anttknmp/Olnk/Schrdr/Mhmmd/25 40.00 100.00
35 Wthy/Nl/Gdwn/McLmr/25 6.00 15.00
36 Dng/Brk/Sv/Hrdwy/25 6.00 15.00
37 Schrdr/Gbrt/Anttknmp/Adms/25 15.00 40.00
38 Hrdwy/Brk/Crtr-Wllms/Oldp/25 15.00 40.00
39 Oldp/Olnk/Prtr/Brk/25 6.00 15.00
40 Schrdr/Crtr-Wllms/Wltrs/Brk/25 20.00 50.00

2013-14 Immaculate Collection Scorers Club Autographs

RANDOM INSERTS IN PACKS
PRINT RUNS B/WN 49-60 COPIES PER
EXCHANGE DEADLINE 3/3/2016
1 Vince Carter/49 20.00 50.00
2 Oscar Robertson/49 40.00 100.00
3 Gary Payton/49 15.00 40.00
4 Paul George/49 25.00 60.00
5 Kareem Abdul-Jabbar/49 30.00 80.00
6 Kevin Durant/49 100.00 200.00
7 Jerry West/49 25.00 60.00
8 Robert Parish/60 10.00 25.00
9 Kobe Bryant/49 125.00 250.00
10 Clyde Drexler/49 15.00 40.00
11 Shaquille O'Neal/49 60.00 150.00
12 Dominique Wilkins/49 20.00 50.00
13 Larry Bird/49 40.00 100.00
14 Allen Iverson/49 125.00 250.00
15 Bernard King/60 5.00 12.00
16 Karl Malone/49 30.00 80.00
17 Artis Gilmore/60 5.00 12.00
18 Julius Erving/49 40.00 100.00
19 Adrian Dantley/60 5.00 12.00
20 Baron Davis/60 5.00 12.00
21 Tracy McGrady/49 50.00 120.00
22 George Gervin/60 15.00 40.00
23 Rick Barry/60 10.00 25.00
24 David Robinson/49 25.00 60.00
25 Tom Chambers/60 5.00 12.00

2013-14 Immaculate Collection Sole of the Game

RANDOM INSERTS IN PACKS
PRINT RUNS B/WN 4-55 COPIES PER
NO PRICING ON QTY 10 OR LESS
1 Deron Williams/30 25.00 60.00
2 M.Carter-Williams/35 30.00 80.00
3 David Robinson/45 40.00 100.00
4 Scottie Pippen/45 100.00 200.00
5 John Stockton/25 40.00 100.00
6 Kyrie Irving/40 100.00 200.00
8 Kevin Durant/50 100.00 250.00
9 Anfernee Hardaway/40 50.00 120.00
10 LeBron James/45 300.00 400.00
11 Kevin Garnett/15 150.00 250.00
12 Victor Oladipo/35 30.00 80.00
13 Carmelo Anthony/25 60.00 150.00
14 Trey Burke/35 25.00 60.00
15 Alonzo Mourning/45 50.00 120.00
16 Blake Griffin/40 40.00 100.00
17 Shaquille O'Neal/55 60.00 150.00
18 Dirk Nowitzki/40 50.00 120.00
19 Patrick Ewing/30 40.00 100.00
20 Anthony Davis/45 100.00 200.00
21 Shawn Marion/30 20.00 50.00
22 Stephen Curry/30 150.00 300.00
23 Kobe Bryant/40 250.00 350.00
24 Michael Kidd-Gilchrist/35 20.00 50.00
25 Larry Johnson/30 50.00 120.00
27 Grant Hill/35 30.00 80.00
28 Derrick Rose/33 125.00 250.00

2013-14 Immaculate Collection Team Logos

RANDOM INSERTS IN PACKS
PRINT RUNS B/WN 1-40 COPIES PER
NO PRICING ON QTY 10 OR LESS
5 Al Jefferson/18 30.00 80.00
7 David Lee/22 90.00 150.00
8 Anthony Bennett/16 12.00 30.00
18 Victor Oladipo/21 50.00 120.00
20 Steven Adams/40 15.00 40.00
28 Shabazz Muhammad/36 15.00 40.00
30 Kelly Olynyk/33 20.00 50.00
38 Cody Zeller/15 20.00 50.00
40 G.Antetokounmpo/17 100.00 250.00
41 Patrick Ewing/15 100.00 200.00
44 Luis Scola/18 25.00 60.00
46 Russell Westbrook/18 100.00 200.00
48 Alex Len/20 30.00 80.00
50 Dennis Schroder/36 20.00 50.00
54 Luol Deng/28 12.00 30.00
58 Nerlens Noel/23 50.00 120.00
60 Gorgui Dieng/40 12.00 30.00
66 Terrence Ross/15 25.00 60.00
68 Ben McLemore/40 12.00 30.00
78 Kentavious Caldwell-Pope/40 15.00 40.00
80 Tim Hardaway Jr./37 30.00 80.00
90 Archie Goodwin/28 12.00 30.00
95 Danny Granger/35 12.00 30.00
98 C.J. McCollum/39 30.00 80.00
100 Nate Wolters/40 12.00 30.00

2013-14 Immaculate Collection Team Logos Numbers

RANDOM INSERTS IN PACKS
PRINT RUNS B/WN 1-50 COPIES PER
NO PRICING ON QTY 14 OR LESS
2 James Harden/18 40.00 100.00
5 Al Jefferson/24 30.00 80.00
6 Pau Gasol/15 60.00 150.00
8 Anthony Bennett/50 12.00 30.00
10 M.Carter-Williams/50 20.00 50.00
12 Jason Collins/23 10.00 25.00
18 Victor Oladipo/50 25.00 60.00
20 Steven Adams/50 15.00 40.00
22 Jimmy Butler/21 30.00 80.00
28 Shabazz Muhammad/50 12.00 30.00
30 Kelly Olynyk/50 15.00 40.00
35 Blake Griffin/21 40.00 100.00
37 Derrick Favors/28 12.00 30.00
38 Cody Zeller/50 12.00 30.00
39 Shaquille O'Neal/23 100.00 200.00
40 G.Antetokounmpo/50 40.00 100.00
48 Alex Len/50 12.00 30.00
50 Dennis Schroder/50 15.00 40.00
54 Luol Deng/50 12.00 30.00
58 Nerlens Noel/50 40.00 100.00
60 Gorgui Dieng/50 20.00 50.00
63 John Stockton/18 40.00 100.00
64 Manu Ginobili/38 30.00 80.00
66 Terrence Ross/23 12.00 30.00
68 Ben McLemore/50 25.00 60.00
70 Mason Plumlee/50 15.00 40.00
74 Marc Gasol/28 30.00 80.00
76 Tim Duncan/42 60.00 150.00
78 Kentavious Caldwell-Pope/50 15.00 40.00
80 Tim Hardaway Jr./50 20.00 50.00
84 Michael Kidd-Gilchrist/19 15.00 40.00
88 Trey Burke/50 12.00 30.00
90 Archie Goodwin/50 12.00 30.00
92 Al Horford/15
95 Danny Granger/27 12.00 30.00
96 Zach Randolph/18 12.00 30.00
98 C.J. McCollum/50 25.00 60.00
100 Nate Wolters/50 12.00 30.00

2013-14 Immaculate Collection The Greatest Autographs

RANDOM INSERTS IN PACKS
PRINT RUNS B/WN 49-60 COPIES PER
EXCHANGE DEADLINE 3/3/2016
1 George Gervin/60 12.00 30.00
2 James Worthy/49 EXCH 12.00 30.00
3 Karl Malone/49 20.00 50.00
4 Shaquille O'Neal/49 75.00 150.00
5 Nate Thurmond/60 8.00 20.00
6 Bill Russell/49 50.00 120.00
7 Kareem Abdul-Jabbar/49 30.00 80.00
8 Larry Bird/49 40.00 100.00
9 Wes Unseld/49 6.00 15.00
10 John Havlicek/49 20.00 50.00
11 Allen Iverson/49 125.00 250.00
12 Kevin McHale/49 10.00 25.00
13 Oscar Robertson/49 40.00 100.00
14 Robert Parish/60 10.00 25.00
15 Dolph Schayes/60 8.00 20.00
16 Nate Archibald/60 10.00 25.00
17 Bill Walton/60 15.00 40.00
18 Magic Johnson/49 40.00 100.00
19 Dwyane Wade/60 30.00 80.00
20 Scottie Pippen/49 50.00 120.00
21 Rick Barry/49 12.00 30.00
22 Isiah Thomas/49 12.00 30.00
23 Julius Erving/49 30.00 80.00
24 Jerry West/49 20.00 50.00
25 Jerry Lucas/60 10.00 25.00
26 Hakeem Olajuwon/49 20.00 50.00
27 David Robinson/49 25.00 60.00
28 Elgin Baylor/49 6.00 15.00
29 John Stockton/49 25.00 60.00
30 Walt Frazier/49 12.00 30.00

2013-14 Immaculate Collection Trios Materials

RANDOM INSERTS IN PACKS
PRINT RUNS B/WN 10-49 COPIES PER
NO PRICING ON QTY 10
1 Teague/Horford/Korver/49 3.00 8.00
2 Rnd/Brdly/Grn/49 4.00 10.00
3 Wllms/Prc/Grntt/49 6.00 15.00
4 Walker/Jefferson/Kidd-Gilchrist/49 4.00 10.00
5 Butler/Noah/Gibson/49 10.00 25.00
6 Irvng/Wtrs/Thmpsn/49 8.00 20.00
7 Nowitzki/Ellis/Carter/49 5.00 12.00
8 Lawson/McGee/Faried/49 3.00 8.00
9 Drmmnd/Jnnngs/Smth/49 10.00 25.00
10 Igdl/Brns/Crry/49 10.00 25.00
11 Harden/Lin/Howard/49 6.00 15.00
12 Hill/George/Hibbert/49 5.00 12.00
13 Griffin/Paul/Redick/49 10.00 25.00
14 Bryant/Gasol/Nash/49 15.00 40.00
15 Conley/Randolph/Gasol/49 4.00 10.00
16 Wade/Bosh/James/49 20.00 50.00
17 Knight/Sanders/Mayo/49 3.00 8.00
18 Love/Rubio/Brewer/49 4.00 10.00
19 Davis/Evans/Holiday/49 8.00 20.00
20 Fltn/Anthny/Chndlr/49 5.00 12.00
21 Drnt/Wstbrk/Ibk/49 10.00 25.00
22 Aldridge/Batum/Lillard/49 8.00 20.00
23 Cousins/Gay/Thomas/49 4.00 10.00
24 Prkr/Lnrd/Dncn/49 12.00 30.00
25 DeRozan/Lowry/Ross/49 4.00 10.00
26 Fvrs/Kntr/Hywrd/49
27 Wall/Beal/Ariza/49 5.00 12.00
28 Horford/Brewer/Noah/49 6.00 15.00
29 Nwtzk/Prc/Crtr/49 5.00 12.00
30 Paul/Williams/Felton/49 6.00 15.00
31 Dvs/Kdd-Glchrst/Jns/49 8.00 20.00
32 Frd/Irvng/Wkr/49 8.00 20.00
33 Wd/Btlr/Mtthws/49 8.00 20.00
34 Jnnngs/Anthn/Smth/49 5.00 12.00
35 Griffin/Harden/Curry/49 15.00 40.00
36 Felton/Barnes/Lawson/49 3.00 8.00
37 Frye/Lee/Hill/49 3.00 8.00
38 Ginobili/Smith/Harden/49 6.00 15.00
39 Griffin/Irving/Lillard/49 8.00 20.00
40 Teague/Duncan/Paul/49 6.00 15.00
41 Schrdr/Giannis/Adms/49 30.00 80.00
42 Plumlee/Bullock/Kelly/49 4.00 10.00
43 Crtr-Wllms/Brk/Oldp/49 6.00 15.00
44 Giannis/Crtr-Wllms/Olnk/49 6.00 15.00
45 Oladipo/Bennett/Porter/49 6.00 15.00
46 Garnett/Plumlee/Morris/49 6.00 15.00
47 Gibson/Snell/Pippen/49 8.00 20.00
48 Englsh/Lrkn/Nwtzk/49 5.00 12.00
49 Irving/Price/Bennett/49 8.00 20.00
50 King/Wall/Porter/25
51 Mln/McGrd/Wlkns/49 5.00 12.00
52 Brd/McHl/Prsh/49 15.00 40.00
53 Mrnng/Trpck/Jhnsn/49 10.00 25.00
54 Prsh/Glmr/Prd/25 8.00 20.00
55 English/Lever/Vandeweghe/49 3.00 8.00
56 Thms/Jhnsn/Dmrs/20 10.00 25.00
57 Barry/Free/Lucas/20 6.00 15.00
58 Mkn/Abdl-Jbbr/Chmbrln/20 100.00 200.00
59 Oljwn/Drxlr/Hrry/49 12.00 30.00

2014-15 Immaculate Collection

RANDOM INSERTS IN PACKS
STATED PRINT RUN 99 SER.#'d SETS
1 Blake Griffin 2.00 5.00
2 Dwyane Wade 3.00 8.00
3 Al Horford 1.50 4.00
4 Ty Lawson 1.25 3.00
5 Carlos Boozer 1.50 4.00
6 Nerlens Noel 1.50 4.00
7 Rajon Rondo 2.00 5.00
8 Larry Sanders 1.25 3.00
9 Serge Ibaka 1.50 4.00
10 Monta Ellis 1.50 4.00
11 Anthony Davis 4.00 10.00
12 Enes Kanter 1.25 3.00
13 Kevin Garnett 3.00 8.00
14 Tim Duncan 3.00 8.00
15 Brandon Jennings 1.25 3.00
16 Damian Lillard 4.00 10.00
17 Pau Gasol 2.00 5.00
18 Victor Oladipo 1.50 4.00
19 Luis Scola 1.50 4.00
20 Isaiah Thomas 2.00 5.00
21 Paul Millsap 2.00 5.00
22 Jonas Valanciunas 1.50 4.00
23 Andrew Bogut 1.50 4.00
24 Bradley Beal 2.00 5.00
25 LeBron James 15.00 40.00
26 Kevin Durant 5.00 12.00
27 Chris Paul 2.50 6.00
28 Channing Frye 1.50 4.00
29 Al Jefferson 1.50 4.00
30 Kobe Bryant 8.00 20.00
31 LaMarcus Aldridge 2.00 5.00
32 Dirk Nowitzki 2.50 6.00
33 Trey Burke 1.25 3.00
34 Roy Hibbert 1.50 4.00
35 Eric Bledsoe 1.50 4.00
36 Kelly Olynyk 1.25 3.00
37 Chris Bosh 2.00 5.00
38 Kawhi Leonard 3.00 8.00
39 Marc Gasol 2.00 5.00
40 Nikola Vucevic 1.50 4.00
41 Joakim Noah 1.50 4.00
42 DeMarcus Cousins 2.00 5.00
43 Kenneth Faried 1.50 4.00
44 Ricky Rubio 2.00 5.00
45 Goran Dragic 1.50 4.00
46 Jeff Teague 1.50 4.00
47 Tim Hardaway Jr. 1.25 3.00
48 James Harden 3.00 8.00
49 Gordon Hayward 2.00 5.00
50 Kyrie Irving 4.00 10.00
51 Michael Carter-Williams 1.25 3.00
52 Josh Smith 1.50 4.00
53 Luol Deng 1.50 4.00
54 Tony Parker 2.00 5.00
55 Joe Johnson 1.50 4.00
56 Jrue Holiday 1.50 4.00
57 Paul George 2.50 6.00
58 DeMar DeRozan 2.00 5.00
59 Chandler Parsons 1.50 4.00
60 Zach Randolph 1.50 4.00
61 Nicolas Batum 1.50 4.00
62 Lance Stephenson 1.50 4.00
63 Jeremy Lin 2.00 5.00
64 Carmelo Anthony 2.50 6.00
65 Arron Afflalo 1.25 3.00
66 Brandon Knight 1.50 4.00
67 John Wall 2.50 6.00
68 Jared Sullinger 1.25 3.00
69 Ben McLemore 1.25 3.00
70 Stephen Curry 8.00 20.00
71 Thaddeus Young 1.25 3.00
72 Tony Wroten 1.25 3.00
73 Kevin Love 2.00 5.00
74 Mike Conley 1.50 4.00
75 Omer Asik 1.50 4.00
76 Kemba Walker 2.00 5.00
77 Russell Westbrook 5.00 12.00
78 Trevor Ariza 1.25 3.00
79 Rudy Gay 2.00 5.00
80 Derrick Rose 2.50 6.00
81 Iman Shumpert 1.25 3.00
82 Dwight Howard 1.50 4.00
83 Ersan Ilyasova 1.25 3.00
84 Paul Pierce 2.00 5.00
85 Deron Williams 1.50 4.00
86 Nikola Pekovic 1.25 3.00
87 DeAndre Jordan 2.00 5.00
88 Kyle Lowry 1.50 4.00
89 Andre Drummond 2.00 5.00
90 Klay Thompson 2.50 6.00
91 Wilt Chamberlain 4.00 10.00
92 Hakeem Olajuwon 2.50 6.00
93 Larry Bird 5.00 12.00
94 Karl Malone 2.50 6.00
95 Bill Russell 3.00 8.00
96 Kareem Abdul-Jabbar 3.00 8.00
97 Shaquille O'Neal 4.00 10.00
98 David Robinson 3.00 8.00
99 Julius Erving 3.00 8.00
100 Magic Johnson 5.00 12.00
101 A. Wiggins JSY AU RC 500.00 800.00
102 Jabari Parker JSY AU RC 125.00 300.00
103 Julius Randle JSY AU RC 40.00 100.00
104 Joel Embiid JSY AU RC 300.00 600.00
105 Dante Exum JSY AU RC 30.00 80.00
107 Marcus Smart JSY AU RC 20.00 50.00
108 Cleanthony Early JSY AU RC 6.00 15.00
110 Aaron Gordon JSY AU RC 60.00 150.00
111 Elfrid Payton JSY AU RC 40.00 100.00
112 Bruno Caboclo JSY AU RC 8.00 20.00
113 James Ennis JSY AU RC 6.00 15.00
114 Gary Harris JSY AU RC 30.00 80.00
115 Glenn Robinson III JSY AU RC 6.00 15.00
116 Cory Jefferson JSY AU RC 6.00 15.00
118 Russ Smith JSY AU RC 8.00 20.00
119 Zach LaVine JSY AU RC 200.00 400.00
120 Spencer Dinwiddie JSY AU RC 8.00 20.00
121 Rodney Hood JSY AU RC 50.00 120.00
122 T.J. Warren JSY AU RC 30.00 80.00
123 Tyler Ennis JSY AU RC 6.00 15.00
124 Jordan Adams JSY AU RC 6.00 15.00
125 D. McDermott JSY AU RC 15.00 40.00
126 Adreian Payne JSY AU RC 8.00 20.00
127 K.J. McDaniels JSY AU RC 8.00 20.00
128 Nik Stauskas JSY AU RC 8.00 20.00
129 Noah Vonleh JSY AU RC 8.00 20.00
131 Johnny O'Bryant JSY AU RC 6.00 15.00
132 Jarnell Stokes JSY AU RC 6.00 15.00
133 Damien Inglis JSY AU RC 6.00 15.00
134 Markel Brown JSY AU RC 6.00 15.00
136 C.J. Wilcox JSY AU RC 6.00 15.00
137 P.J. Hairston JSY AU RC 6.00 15.00
138 Joe Harris JSY AU RC 6.00 15.00
139 Zoran Dragic AU RC 6.00 15.00
140 Damjan Rudez AU RC 6.00 15.00
141 Jordan Clarkson AU RC 20.00 50.00
143 Lucas Nogueira AU RC 6.00 15.00
145 Erick Green AU RC 6.00 15.00
146 Nikola Mirotic AU RC 20.00 50.00
147 Devyn Marble AU RC 6.00 15.00

2014-15 Immaculate Collection Red

*RED: .6X TO 1.5X BASE HI
RANDOM INSERTS IN PACKS
STATED PRINT RUN 25 SER.#'d SETS
97 Shaquille O'Neal 8.00 20.00

2014-15 Immaculate Collection Rookie Autographs Jersey Number

RANDOM INSERTS IN PACKS
STATED PRINT RUN B/WN 6-92 COPIES PER
NO PRICING ON QTY 11 OR LESS
142 Cameron Bairstow/41 20.00 50.00
143 Lucas Nogueira/92 8.00 20.00
146 Nikola Mirotic/44 40.00 100.00

2014-15 Immaculate Collection Rookie Patch Autographs Jersey Number

*JSY NUMBER: 1.5X TO 4X BASE HI
RANDOM INSERTS IN PACKS
STATED PRINT RUN B/WN 1-36 COPIES PER
NO PRICING ON QTY 14 OR LESS
103 Julius Randle/30 400.00 600.00
107 Marcus Smart/36 100.00 200.00

2014-15 Immaculate Collection Dual Autographs

RANDOM INSERTS IN PACKS
STATED PRINT RUN 49 SER.#'d SETS
DAAA A.Wiggins/A.Bennett 100.00 250.00
DAAJ A.Davis/J.Wall 150.00 400.00
DAAS A.Iguodala/S.Curry 250.00 500.00
DABJ B.Beal/J.Wall 50.00 120.00
DADT D.Exum/T.Burke 15.00 40.00
DAGI G.Dragic/I.Thomas 25.00 60.00
DAGJ Antetokounmpo/J.Parker 250.00 500.00
DAIJ I.Thomas/J.Dumars 50.00 120.00
DAJK J.Randle/K.Bryant 125.00 250.00
DAJK J.Stockton/K.Malone 400.00 600.00
DAMM M.Morris/M.Morris 10.00 25.00
DATD D.Green/T.Parker 40.00 100.00
DAVZ V.Carter/Z.Randolph 40.00 100.00

2014-15 Immaculate Collection Dual Memorabilia

RANDOM INSERTS IN PACKS
STATED PRINT RUN B/WN 25-99 COPIES PER
DMAG Aaron Gordon/99 5.00 12.00
DMAH Anfernee Hardaway/49 8.00 20.00
DMAW Andrew Wiggins/99 10.00 25.00
DMBG Blake Griffin/49 3.00 8.00
DMBK Brandon Knight/49 2.50 6.00
DMCA Carmelo Anthony/99 4.00 10.00
DMCB Chris Bosh/99 3.00 8.00
DMCD Clyde Drexler/25 4.00 10.00
DMCP Chris Paul/49 4.00 10.00
DMDC DeMarcus Cousins/99 3.00 8.00
DMDD DeMar DeRozan/99 3.00 8.00
DMDE Dante Exum/99 3.00 8.00
DMDM Dikembe Mutombo/49 3.00 8.00
DMDN Dirk Nowitzki/99 4.00 10.00
DMDW Dwyane Wade/99 5.00 12.00
DMEB Eric Bledsoe/99 2.50 6.00
DMEP Elfrid Payton/99 3.00 8.00
DMGD Goran Dragic/99 2.50 6.00
DMGH Grant Hill/25 12.00 30.00
DMGM Greg Monroe/99 2.50 6.00
DMGP Gary Payton/99 6.00 15.00
DMHO Hakeem Olajuwon/25 4.00 10.00
DMJB Jimmy Butler/49 6.00 15.00
DMJE Joel Embiid/99 8.00 20.00
DMJH James Harden/99 8.00 20.00
DMJP Jabari Parker/99 5.00 12.00
DMJR Julius Randle/99 5.00 12.00
DMJS Jared Sullinger/99 2.00 5.00
DMJT Jeff Teague/99 2.50 6.00
DMJW John Wall/99 4.00 10.00
DMJY James Young/99 2.00 5.00
DMKA Kareem Abdul-Jabbar/25 12.00 30.00
DMKB Kobe Bryant/99 12.00 30.00
DMKD Kevin Durant/99 6.00 15.00
DMKF Kenneth Faried/99 2.50 6.00
DMKG Kevin Garnett/99 5.00 12.00
DMKI Kyrie Irving/99 6.00 15.00
DMKL Kevin Love/49 3.00 8.00
DMKL Kawhi Leonard/99 5.00 12.00
DMKM K.J. McDaniels/99 2.50 6.00
DMKM Karl Malone/25 4.00 10.00
DMKT Klay Thompson/99 4.00 10.00
DMLB Larry Bird/25 8.00 20.00
DMLJ Larry Johnson/99 4.00 10.00
DMMS Marcus Smart/99 3.00 8.00
DMNB Nicolas Batum/99 2.50 6.00
DMNN Nerlens Noel/99 2.50 6.00
DMPE Patrick Ewing/25 4.00 10.00
DMRR Ricky Rubio/99 3.00 8.00
DMRW Russell Westbrook/99 8.00 20.00
DMSC Stephen Curry/99 25.00 60.00
DMSN Shabazz Napier/99 3.00 8.00
DMSO Shaquille O'Neal/25 6.00 15.00
DMTD Tim Duncan/49 5.00 12.00
DMTE Tyreke Evans/99 2.00 5.00
DMVO Victor Oladipo/99 2.50 6.00
DMZL Zach LaVine/99 5.00 12.00
DMZR Zach Randolph/99 2.50 6.00
DMDMC Doug McDermott/99 3.00 8.00
DMLBJ LeBron James/99 12.00 30.00
DMMCW M.Carter-Williams/99 2.00 5.00
DMMKG Michael Kidd-Gilchrist/99 2.50 6.00

2014-15 Immaculate Collection HOF Heroes Signatures

RANDOM INSERTS IN PACKS
STATED PRINT RUN 75 SER.#'d SETS
1 Gary Payton 10.00 25.00
2 Alonzo Mourning 12.00 30.00
4 Larry Bird 40.00 100.00
5 George Gervin 10.00 25.00
6 Hakeem Olajuwon 20.00 50.00
7 Dennis Rodman 25.00 60.00
8 Walt Frazier 10.00 25.00
9 Jerry West 25.00 60.00
10 Julius Erving 40.00 100.00
11 Clyde Drexler 12.00 30.00
12 John Stockton 30.00 80.00
13 James Worthy 12.00 30.00
15 Willis Reed 15.00 40.00
17 Robert Parish 10.00 25.00
18 Ralph Sampson 8.00 20.00
19 Rick Barry 8.00 20.00
20 Kareem Abdul-Jabbar 40.00 100.00
21 Dan Issel 6.00 15.00
22 David Thompson 8.00 20.00
23 Joe Dumars 10.00 25.00
24 Earl Monroe 10.00 25.00
25 Magic Johnson 30.00 80.00

2014-15 Immaculate Collection Immaculate Standard Materials

RANDOM INSERTS IN PACKS
STATED PRINT RUN B/WN 25-99 COPIES PER
1 LeBron James/50 25.00 60.00
2 Dion Waiters/75 3.00 8.00
3 Pau Gasol/75 4.00 10.00
4 Goran Dragic/50 3.00 8.00
5 Aaron Gordon/75 6.00 15.00
6 T.J. Warren/75 4.00 10.00
7 Jeff Green/75 3.00 8.00
8 Ben McLemore/50 2.50 6.00
9 Karl Malone/50 5.00 12.00
10 Chris Bosh/75 4.00 10.00
11 Luc Longley/50 6.00 15.00
12 Dirk Nowitzki/50 5.00 12.00
13 Ricky Rubio/75 4.00 10.00
14 Grant Hill/50 5.00 12.00
15 Terrence Ross/50 3.00 8.00
16 Al Horford/75 3.00 8.00
17 Jeremy Lin/75 4.00 10.00
18 Bernard King/25 3.00 8.00
19 Kenneth Faried/75 3.00 8.00
20 Marcus Smart/75 4.00 10.00
21 Chris Mullin/25 8.00 20.00
22 Dominique Wilkins/25 5.00 12.00
23 Greg Monroe/75 3.00 8.00
24 Robert Parish/25 4.00 10.00
25 Tim Hardaway Jr./75 2.50 6.00
26 Alex English/25 3.00 8.00
27 Joe Harris/75 2.50 6.00
28 Bill Laimbeer/25 3.00 8.00
29 Kevin Duckworth/75 2.50 6.00
30 Cleanthony Early/75 2.50 6.00
31 Moses Malone/25 4.00 10.00
32 Doug McDermott/75 4.00 10.00
33 Rodney Hood/75 4.00 10.00
34 Hakeem Olajuwon/25 10.00 25.00
35 Tristan Thompson/75 3.00 8.00
36 Alex Len/75 2.50 6.00
37 Joel Embiid/75 12.00 30.00
38 Blake Griffin/25 4.00 10.00
39 Kevin Garnett/75 6.00 15.00
40 Clifford Robinson/75 2.50 6.00
41 Nik Stauskas/75 3.00 8.00
42 Dwyane Wade/75 6.00 15.00
43 Rudy Gay/50 4.00 10.00
45 Tyler Ennis/75 2.50 6.00
46 Allen Iverson/25 25.00 60.00
47 John Starks/25 8.00 20.00
48 Brandon Knight/75 3.00 8.00
49 Kevin Love/25 4.00 10.00
50 Clyde Drexler/25 12.00 30.00
51 Noah Vonleh/75 3.00 8.00
52 Elfrid Payton/75 4.00 10.00
53 Scottie Pippen/25 15.00 40.00
54 Jabari Parker/75 6.00 15.00
55 Tyson Chandler/75 3.00 8.00
56 Alonzo Mourning/75 5.00 12.00
57 John Wall/75 5.00 12.00
58 Brook Lopez/75 3.00 8.00
59 Kevin McHale/25 10.00 25.00
60 Clyde Drexler/25 5.00 12.00
61 Norris Cole/75 2.50 6.00
62 Gary Harris/75 4.00 10.00
63 Shabazz Napier/75 3.00 8.00
64 James Worthy/25 5.00 12.00
65 Walter Davis/75 2.50 6.00
66 Amar'e Stoudemire/75 4.00 10.00
68 Bruno Caboclo/75 3.00 8.00
69 Kobe Bryant/75 15.00 40.00
70 Cody Zeller/75 2.50 6.00
71 Otto Porter/75 3.00 8.00
72 Gary Payton/25 8.00 20.00
73 Shaquille O'Neal/25 30.00 80.00
74 James Young/75 2.50 6.00
75 Zach LaVine/75 6.00 15.00
76 Anderson Varejao/75 2.50 6.00
77 Julius Randle/75 6.00 15.00
78 Larry Bird/25 15.00 40.00
79 Byron Scott/25 3.00 8.00
80 Dante Exum/75 4.00 10.00
81 P.J. Hairston/75 2.50 6.00
83 Shaquille O'Neal/75 8.00 20.00
84 Jared Sullinger/75 2.50 6.00
86 Andrew Wiggins/75 12.00 30.00
87 K.J. McDaniels/75 3.00 8.00
88 Cedric Maxwell/75 2.50 6.00
89 Larry Johnson/50 5.00 12.00
90 David Robinson/25 12.00 30.00
91 Patrick Ewing/50 5.00 12.00
92 Glenn Robinson III/75 2.50 6.00
93 Shaquille O'Neal/25 30.00 80.00
94 Jason Kidd/25 8.00 20.00
96 Anfernee Hardaway/25 15.00 40.00
97 Kareem Abdul-Jabbar/25 15.00 40.00
98 Chris Andersen/75 3.00 8.00
99 Larry Johnson/75 12.00 30.00
100 Dikembe Mutombo/75 4.00 10.00

2014-15 Immaculate Collection Ink

RANDOM INSERTS IN PACKS
STATED PRINT RUN B/WN 49-99 COPIES PER
1 Paul George/49 15.00 40.00
2 Carmelo Anthony/49 25.00 60.00
3 Steve Nash/49 12.00 30.00
4 Ray Allen/49 15.00 40.00
5 Michael Kidd-Gilchrist/49 5.00 12.00
6 Zach Randolph/75 5.00 12.00
7 Bradley Beal/75 6.00 15.00
8 Ben McLemore/75 4.00 10.00
9 Michael Carter-Williams/75 4.00 10.00
10 Brandon Knight/75 4.00 10.00
11 John Stockton/49 10.00 25.00
12 Julius Erving/49 30.00 80.00
13 Jerry West/49 20.00 50.00
14 David Robinson/49 15.00 40.00
15 Pat Riley/49 15.00 40.00
16 Earl Monroe/49 6.00 15.00
17 Kevin McHale/49 12.00 30.00
18 Hakeem Olajuwon/49 15.00 40.00
19 Clyde Drexler/49 10.00 25.00
20 Dennis Rodman/49 15.00 40.00
21 John Havlicek/49 20.00 50.00
22 Elgin Baylor/49 6.00 15.00
23 Gary Payton/49 6.00 15.00
24 James Worthy/49 15.00 40.00
25 Dominique Wilkins/49 12.00 30.00
26 Rick Barry/75 5.00 12.00
27 Sam Jones/75 15.00 40.00
28 Willis Reed/75 12.00 30.00
29 Chris Mullin/75 6.00 15.00
30 Artis Gilmore/75 5.00 12.00
31 Walt Frazier/75 6.00 15.00
32 Don Nelson/75 10.00 25.00
33 George Gervin/75 8.00 20.00
34 Gail Goodrich/75 5.00 12.00

35 Joe Dumars/75 6.00 15.00
36 Dick Vitale/75 10.00 25.00
37 Hal Greer/75 5.00 12.00
38 Nate Thurmond/75 5.00 12.00
39 Robert Parish/75 6.00 15.00
40 Dolph Schayes/75 6.00 15.00
41 Glen Rice/99 5.00 12.00
42 Chet Walker/99 5.00 12.00
43 Dale Ellis/99 4.00 10.00
44 Bonzi Wells/99 4.00 10.00
45 Bob Lanier/75 5.00 10.00
46 Bryon Russell/99 4.00 10.00
47 Earl Lloyd/99 6.00 15.00
48 Connie Hawkins/99 4.00 10.00
49 Marques Johnson/99 5.00 12.00
50 Steve Kerr/75 8.00 20.00
51 Shaquille O'Neal/49 50.00 120.00
52 Yao Ming/49 20.00 50.00
53 Tracy McGrady/49 15.00 40.00
54 Anternee Hardaway/49 15.00 40.00
55 Grant Hill/49 15.00 40.00
56 Christian Laettner/75 8.00 20.00
57 Baron Davis/75 5.00 12.00
58 Brent Barry/75 4.00 10.00
59 Byron Scott/75 5.00 12.00
60 Bill Walton/75 6.00 15.00
61 Latrell Sprewell/75 15.00 40.00
62 Dave Bing/75 15.00 40.00
63 Vinny Del Negro/75 4.00 10.00
64 Kenny Smith/75 5.00 12.00
65 Dikembe Mutombo/99 6.00 15.00
66 Chuck Person/99 5.00 12.00
67 Tim Hardaway/99 5.00 12.00
68 Allan Houston/99 4.00 10.00
69 Toni Kukoc/99 6.00 15.00
70 Kurt Rambis/99 4.00 10.00
71 Adrian Smith/99 5.00 12.00
72 Horace Grant/99 6.00 15.00
73 Scott Brooks/99 5.00 12.00
74 George Karl/99 6.00 15.00
75 Vlade Divac/99 6.00 15.00
76 Chris Paul/49 20.00 50.00
77 Nate Archibald/49 5.00 12.00
78 Goran Dragic/49 4.00 10.00
79 Michael Cooper/49 4.00 10.00
80 Marcin Gortat/49 5.00 12.00
81 Wes Unseld/99 6.00 15.00
82 Elvin Hayes/75 6.00 15.00
83 Karl Malone/49 20.00 50.00
84 Wesley Matthews/99 4.00 10.00
85 Jrue Holiday/49 4.00 10.00
86 Brook Lopez/49 5.00 12.00
87 Bailey Howell/49 6.00 15.00
88 Derrick Favors/75 5.00 12.00
89 Alonzo Mourning/49 12.00 30.00
90 Manu Ginobili/49 12.00 30.00

2014-15 Immaculate Collection Ink Red

*RED: .6X TO 1.5X BASE HI
RANDOM INSERTS IN PACKS
STATED PRINT RUN 25 SER.#'d SETS

2014-15 Immaculate Collection NBA Champions Autographs

RANDOM INSERTS IN PACKS
STATED PRINT RUN 75 SER.#'d SETS
1 Mychal Thompson 8.00 20.00
2 B.J. Armstrong 8.00 20.00
3 Tony Parker 20.00 50.00
5 Clyde Drexler 10.00 25.00
6 Kobe Bryant 100.00 200.00
7 Shaquille O'Neal 30.00 80.00
8 Larry Bird 50.00 120.00
9 Robert Horry 6.00 15.00
10 Jason Terry 6.00 15.00
11 Toni Kukoc 8.00 20.00
12 Dennis Rodman 20.00 50.00
13 Bill Walton 8.00 20.00
14 David Robinson 15.00 40.00
16 Hakeem Olajuwon 15.00 40.00
17 Tiago Splitter 6.00 15.00
18 A.C. Green 8.00 20.00
19 Ray Allen 25.00 60.00
20 Magic Johnson 30.00 80.00

2014-15 Immaculate Collection Patches

RANDOM INSERTS IN PACKS
STATED PRINT RUN B/WN 1-55 COPIES PER
NO PRICING ON QTY 17 OR LESS
PAD Anthony Davis/23 25.00 60.00
PAJ Al Jefferson/25 6.00 15.00
PAM Alonzo Mourning/33 25.00 60.00
PBK Bernard King/30 12.00 30.00
PCZ Cody Zeller/40 5.00 12.00
PDG Draymond Green/23 25.00 60.00
PDM Dikembe Mutombo/55 8.00 20.00
PDN Dirk Nowitzki/41 10.00 25.00
PDR David Robinson/50 12.00 30.00
PGP Gary Payton/20 20.00 50.00
PHO Hakeem Olajuwon/34 10.00 25.00
PJB Jimmy Butler/21 30.00 80.00
PJG Jeff Green/32 6.00 15.00
PJK Jason Kidd/32 20.00 50.00
PKA Kareem Abdul-Jabbar/33 15.00 40.00
PKF Kenneth Faried/35 6.00 15.00
PKK Kyle Korver/26 20.00 50.00
PLB Larry Bird/33 20.00 50.00
PLN Larry Nance/22 6.00 15.00
PNE Nene/42 6.00 15.00
PPE Patrick Ewing/33 15.00 40.00
PPP Paul Pierce/34 8.00 20.00
PRH Roy Hibbert/55 6.00 15.00
PSM Shawn Marion/31 6.00 15.00
PSO Shaquille O'Neal/32 15.00 40.00
PTD Tim Duncan/21 20.00 50.00
PTR Terrence Ross/31 6.00 15.00
PDWE David West/21 6.00 15.00
PDWI Dominique Wilkins/21 10.00 25.00
PGHI Grant Hill/33 10.00 25.00
PKMA Karl Malone/32 10.00 25.00
PKMC Kevin McHale/32 8.00 20.00
PLBJ LeBron James/23 50.00 120.00

2014-15 Immaculate Collection Patches Autographs

RANDOM INSERTS IN PACKS
STATED PRINT RUN B/WN 60-75 COPIES PER
16 Jeff Teague/75 8.00 20.00
PAAL Al Horford/75 8.00 20.00
PABG Blake Griffin/75 30.00 80.00
PABS Byron Scott/75 8.00 20.00
PACA Carmelo Anthony/75 30.00 80.00
PACL Carl Landry/75 6.00 15.00
PADF Derrick Favors/75 8.00 20.00
PADR David Robinson/75 20.00 50.00
PAGD Goran Dragic/75 8.00 20.00
PAIS Iman Shumpert/75 6.00 15.00
PAIT Isiah Thomas/75 12.00 30.00
PAJJ Jim Jackson/75 6.00 15.00
36 Jason Kidd/75 15.00 40.00
PAJW James Worthy/75 20.00 50.00
PAKB Kobe Bryant/75 125.00 250.00
PAKD Kevin Durant/75 100.00 200.00
PAKI Kyrie Irving/75 75.00 150.00
PAKL Kevin Love/75 20.00 50.00
PAKW Kemba Walker/75 12.00 30.00
PALB Larry Bird/75 40.00 100.00
PALS Lance Stephenson/75 8.00 20.00
PAMK Michael Kidd-Gilchrist/75 8.00 20.00
PAMP Mason Plumlee/75 8.00 20.00
PARH Robert Horry/75 8.00 20.00
PARP Robert Parish/75 10.00 25.00
PASO Shaquille O'Neal/75 100.00 200.00
PATB Trey Burke/75 6.00 15.00
PATH Tim Hardaway/75 15.00 40.00
PATM Tracy McGrady/60 50.00 120.00
PATO Tobias Harris/75 8.00 20.00
PAWP Will Perdue/75 6.00 15.00
PAYM Yao Ming/75
PAZI Zydrunas Ilgauskas/60 8.00 20.00
PAAHA Anfernee Hardaway/75 30.00 80.00
PAAHO Allan Houston/75 8.00 20.00
PABLA Bill Laimbeer/75 8.00 20.00
PABLO Brook Lopez/75 8.00 20.00
PADMA Danny Manning/75 8.00 20.00
PADMU Dikembe Mutombo/75 10.00 25.00
PAJWA John Wall/75 40.00 100.00
PAMCW M.Carter-Williams/75 6.00 15.00

2014-15 Immaculate Collection Patches Autographs Jersey Number

*JSY NUMBER: .8X TO 2X BASE HI
RANDOM INSERTS IN PACKS
STATED PRINT RUN B/WN 1-55 COPIES PER
NO PRICING ON QTY 17 OR LESS
PADR David Robinson/50 40.00 100.00
PAKB Kobe Bryant/24 800.00 1200.00

2014-15 Immaculate Collection Player Caps

RANDOM INSERTS IN PACKS
STATED PRINT RUN B/WN 31-39 COPIES PER
PCAG Aaron Gordon/38 6.00 15.00
PCBC Bruno Caboclo/37 4.00 10.00
PCCE Cleanthony Early/39 4.00 10.00
PCDI Damien Inglis/38 4.00 10.00
PCDM Doug McDermott/38 4.00 10.00
PCEP Elfrid Payton/38 6.00 15.00
PCGH Gary Harris/39 6.00 15.00
PCJG Jerami Grant/35 4.00 10.00
PCJH Joe Harris/31 4.00 10.00
PCJP Jabari Parker/38 10.00 25.00
PCJR Julius Randle/35 10.00 25.00
PCJY James Young/37 4.00 10.00
PCKM K.J. McDaniels/35 4.00 10.00
PCMM Mitch McGary/38 4.00 10.00
PCMS Marcus Smart/37 6.00 15.00
PCNV Noah Vonleh/37 5.00 12.00
PCPH P.J. Hairston/37 4.00 10.00
PCRH Rodney Hood/37 6.00 15.00
PCSN Shabazz Napier/38 5.00 12.00
PCTE Tyler Ennis/35 4.00 10.00
PCTW T.J. Warren/35 6.00 15.00
PCZL Zach LaVine/39 10.00 25.00

2014-15 Immaculate Collection Premium Autograph Patches

RANDOM INSERTS IN PACKS
STATED PRINT RUN B/WN 5-25 COPIES PER
NO PRICING ON QTY 18 OR LESS
1 Kobe Bryant/20 800.00 1200.00
2 Kyrie Irving/25 150.00 300.00
3 Kevin Durant/25 300.00 600.00
5 Kareem Abdul-Jabbar/25 150.00 300.00
7 Bernard King/25 25.00 60.00
8 Isiah Thomas/25 40.00 100.00
9 Gary Payton/25 60.00 150.00
10 James Worthy/25 50.00 120.00
11 Eddie Jones/25 50.00 120.00
12 Jim Jackson/25 25.00 60.00
14 Andre Drummond/25 40.00 100.00
15 Trey Burke/25 10.00 25.00
16 Gordon Hayward/25 15.00 40.00
17 Carl Landry/25 10.00 25.00
18 Reggie Jackson/25 50.00 120.00
19 Marcin Gortat/25 25.00 60.00
20 Jason Terry/25 12.00 30.00
21 Magic Johnson/25 150.00 300.00
22 Grant Hill/25 150.00 300.00
23 Clifford Robinson/25 15.00 40.00
24 Dikembe Mutombo/25 75.00 150.00
25 Robert Horry/25 25.00 60.00
26 Byron Scott/25 75.00 150.00
27 Chris Mullin/25 40.00 100.00
28 Anfernee Hardaway/25 150.00 300.00
29 Antoine Walker/25 25.00 60.00
30 Nick Van Exel/25 60.00 150.00
31 Clyde Drexler/25 75.00 150.00
32 Marques Johnson/25 12.00 30.00
34 Tim Hardaway/25 25.00 60.00
36 Jared Sullinger/25 10.00 25.00
37 Shaquille O'Neal/25 200.00 400.00
38 John Stockton/25 75.00 150.00
39 Karl Malone/25 40.00 100.00
41 Larry Bird/25 100.00 200.00
42 Tristan Thompson/25 12.00 30.00
43 Tyreke Evans/25 20.00 50.00
44 Klay Thompson/25 200.00 400.00
47 Hakeem Olajuwon/25 30.00 80.00
48 Michael Kidd-Gilchrist/25 20.00 50.00
49 Eric Gordon/25 12.00 30.00
50 Bradley Beal/25 100.00 200.00
51 John Wall/25 200.00 400.00
52 Stephen Curry/25 500.00 800.00
56 Joe Dumars/25 25.00 60.00
57 David Robinson/25 50.00 120.00
58 Al Horford/25 25.00 60.00
59 Walter Davis/25 40.00 100.00
60 Kevin Love/25 40.00 100.00
64 Mike Conley/25 30.00 80.00
65 Anthony Davis/25 500.00 700.00
67 Danny Green/25 40.00 100.00
69 Enes Kanter/25 20.00 50.00
71 Tyson Chandler/25 15.00 40.00
72 Ben McLemore/25 25.00 60.00
73 M.Carter-Williams/25 30.00 80.00
74 Jeff Green/25 12.00 30.00
75 Nikola Vucevic/25 12.00 30.00
76 Mason Plumlee/25 12.00 30.00
77 Steven Adams/25 25.00 60.00
78 Brook Lopez/25 15.00 40.00
79 Archie Goodwin/25 15.00 40.00
80 Tyler Zeller/25 12.00 30.00
81 Andrew Wiggins/25 900.00 1200.00
82 Jabari Parker/25 400.00 800.00
83 Tyler Ennis/25 20.00 50.00
84 T.J. Warren/25 100.00 250.00
85 Elfrid Payton/25 150.00 300.00
86 Aaron Gordon/25 200.00 400.00
87 Doug McDermott/25 100.00 200.00
88 Marcus Smart/25 100.00 200.00
89 Julius Randle/25 150.00 300.00
90 Cleanthony Early/25 20.00 50.00
91 Zach LaVine/25 400.00 800.00
92 Gary Harris/25 30.00 80.00
93 Adreian Payne/25 30.00 80.00
94 Bruno Caboclo/25 40.00 100.00
95 Joe Harris/25 10.00 25.00
98 Dante Exum/25 75.00 200.00
99 Rodney Hood/25 125.00 250.00
100 Jordan Adams/25 10.00 25.00

2014-15 Immaculate Collection Quad Materials

RANDOM INSERTS IN PACKS
STATED PRINT RUN B/WN 25-49 COPIES PER
31 Anthny/Drnt/Lve/Jms/35 12.00 30.00
32 Pl/Wll/Rbo/Crry/35 25.00 60.00
37 Grdn/Pytn/Vnlh/Npr/49 10.00 25.00
QATL Hrfrd/Tge/Krvr/Mllsp/49 6.00 15.00
QBOS Mxl/Jhn/McHl/Brd/25 15.00 40.00
QBRK Lpz/Wllms/Jhnsn/Plmle/35 15.00 40.00
QCED McDrmtt/Prkr/Hrrs/Dnwdde/49 8.00 20.00
QCHA Jffrsn/Hndrsn/Wlkr/Glchrst/35 6.00 15.00
QCHI Rse/Btlr/Nh/Gbsn/49 10.00 25.00
QCLE Lve/Irvng/Jms/Mrn/49 25.00 60.00
QDAL Prsns/Nwtzki/Ells/Chndlr/49 8.00 20.00
QDEN Afflo/Frd/Lwsn/Chndlr/49 5.00 12.00
QDET Drmmnd/Jnnngs/Mnre/Ppe/35 5.00 12.00
QGSW Bgt/Grn/Thmpsn/Crry/49 25.00 60.00
QHOU Motjns/Hwrd/Hrdn/Arza/35 10.00 25.00
QIND Wst/Scla/Hbbrt/Hll/35 5.00 12.00
QLAC Grffn/Pl/Jrdn/Rdck/35 20.00 50.00
QLAL Jbbr/Brynt/Jhnsn/ONl/25 25.00 60.00
QMEM Gsl/Cnly/Alln/Rndlph/35 15.00 40.00
QMIA And/Bsh/Wde/Chlm/49 10.00 25.00
QMIN Dng/Pkvc/Rbo/Yng/49 8.00 20.00
QNOP Dvs/Grdn/Hldy/Evns/35 12.00 30.00
QNYK Anthny/Cldrn/Lrkn/Hrdwy/49 6.00 15.00
QOKC Drnt/Wstbrk/Ibka/Adms/35 15.00 40.00
QPAD Wlcx/Rndle/Stsks/Wrrn/49 5.00 12.00
QPHI Ivrsn/Grr/Ervng/Mlne/25 20.00 50.00
QPHX Ln/Bldse/Drgc/Mrrs/35 5.00 12.00
QPOR Rbn/Drx/Dckw/Pppn/49 12.00 30.00
QREB Drmmnd/Jrdn/Hwrd/Chndlr/35 20.00 50.00
QRSG Wggns/Exm/Pytn/LVne/49 10.00 25.00
QSAC McLmre/Cllsn/Csns/Gy/35 6.00 15.00
QSAN Lnrd/Gnbli/Dncn/Prkr/35 20.00 50.00
QTOR DRzn/Vlncns/Lwry/Rss/35 6.00 15.00
QWAS Bl/Wll/Grtt/Nne/35 8.00 20.00
QKUUK Wggns/Yng/Embd/Rndle/49 15.00 40.00
QMSMU Hrrs/Rbnsn/McGry/Stsks/49 6.00 15.00

2014-15 Immaculate Collection Rookie Jerseys

RANDOM INSERTS IN PACKS
STATED PRINT RUN 99 SER.#'d SETS
1 Shabazz Napier 3.00 8.00
2 Jabari Parker 6.00 15.00
3 Glenn Robinson III 2.50 6.00
4 K.J. McDaniels 3.00 8.00
5 James Ennis 2.50 6.00
6 Markel Brown 2.50 6.00
7 Elfrid Payton 4.00 10.00
8 C.J. Wilcox 2.50 6.00
9 Bruno Caboclo 3.00 8.00
10 Johnny O'Bryant 2.50 6.00
11 Julius Randle 6.00 15.00
12 Rodney Hood 4.00 10.00
13 James Young 2.50 6.00
14 Zach LaVine 6.00 15.00
15 Aaron Gordon 6.00 15.00
16 Andrew Wiggins 10.00 25.00
17 Cleanthony Early 2.50 6.00
18 Noah Vonleh 3.00 8.00
19 Cory Jefferson 2.50 6.00
20 Gary Harris 4.00 10.00
21 Damien Inglis 2.50 6.00
22 Marcus Smart 4.00 10.00
23 Jerami Grant 2.50 6.00
24 Jarnell Stokes 2.50 6.00
25 P.J. Hairston 2.50 6.00
26 Jordan Adams 2.50 6.00
27 Adreian Payne 3.00 8.00
28 Joe Harris 2.50 6.00
29 Joel Embiid 8.00 20.00
30 Russ Smith 2.50 6.00
31 Doug McDermott 4.00 10.00
32 Kyle Anderson 4.00 10.00
33 Mitch McGary 2.50 6.00
34 Tyler Ennis 2.50 6.00
35 Nik Stauskas 3.00 8.00
36 Dante Exum 6.00 15.00
37 Spencer Dinwiddie 3.00 8.00
38 T.J. Warren 4.00 10.00

2014-15 Immaculate Collection Rookie Jerseys Prime

*PRIME: 1.2X TO 3X BASE HI
RANDOM INSERTS IN PACKS
STATED PRINT RUN 20 SER.#'d SETS
2 Jabari Parker 75.00 150.00
7 Elfrid Payton 40.00 100.00
35 Nik Stauskas 8.00 20.00

2014-15 Immaculate Collection Shadowbox Signatures

RANDOM INSERTS IN PACKS
STATED PRINT RUN B/WN 35-60 COPIES PER
SHAD Anthony Davis/35 100.00 200.00
SHAD Adrian Dantley/49 6.00 15.00
SHAE Alex English/49 6.00 15.00
SHAG Artis Gilmore/49 6.00 15.00
SHAH Anfernee Hardaway/49 40.00 100.00
SHAH Al Horford/49 5.00 12.00
SHAW Antoine Walker/60 5.00 12.00
SHAW Andrew Wiggins/35 200.00 400.00
SHBB Bradley Beal/49 15.00 40.00
SHBR Bill Russell/35 75.00 150.00
SHBW Bill Walton/49 8.00 20.00
SHCD Clyde Drexler/35 25.00 60.00
SHCM Chris Mullin/49 6.00 15.00
SHDE Dante Exum/49 25.00 60.00
SHDI Dan Issel/49 6.00 15.00
SHDM Doug McDermott/49 6.00 15.00
SHDR Dennis Rodman/35 50.00 120.00
SHDR David Robinson/35 20.00 50.00
SHEJ Eddie Jones/60 5.00 12.00
SHGG George Gervin/49 6.00 15.00
SHGH Grant Hill/49 25.00 60.00
SHGP Gary Payton/35 30.00 80.00
SHHO Hakeem Olajuwon/35 15.00 40.00
SHIT Isaiah Thomas/49 10.00 25.00
SHJE Julius Erving/35 40.00 100.00
SHJK Jason Kidd/35 25.00 60.00
SHJP Jabari Parker/35 200.00 400.00
SHJR Julius Randle/49 60.00 150.00
SHJS John Starks/49 5.00 12.00
SHJS John Stockton/35 30.00 80.00
SHJW James Worthy/49 20.00 50.00
SHJW Jerry West/35 30.00 80.00
SHJW John Wall/35 30.00 80.00
SHJY James Young/49 4.00 10.00
SHKB Kobe Bryant/35 150.00 300.00
SHKD Kevin Durant/35 60.00 150.00
SHKI Kyrie Irving/35 40.00 100.00
SHKL Kevin Love/35 20.00 50.00
SHKM Karl Malone/35 40.00 100.00
SHKR Kurt Rambis/49 4.00 10.00
SHLB Larry Bird/35 40.00 100.00
SHMB Muggsy Bogues/60 10.00 25.00
SHMJ Magic Johnson/35 50.00 120.00
SHMP Mark Price/60 6.00 15.00
SHMS Marcus Smart/49 10.00 25.00
SHNS Nik Stauskas/49 5.00 12.00
SHRB Rick Barry/49 6.00 15.00
SHRF Rick Fox/49 5.00 12.00
SHRH Robert Horry/49 10.00 25.00
SHRH Rodney Hood/60 6.00 15.00
SHSC Stephen Curry/49 100.00 250.00
SHSN Shabazz Napier/60 5.00 12.00
SHSN Steve Nash/35 20.00 50.00
SHSO Shaquille O'Neal/35 75.00 150.00
SHSW Spud Webb/60 5.00 12.00
SHTC Tom Chambers/49 5.00 12.00
SHTH Tim Hardaway/60 10.00 25.00
SHTK Toni Kukoc/49 6.00 15.00
SHTL Ty Lawson/49 4.00 10.00
SHTM Tracy McGrady/35 40.00 100.00
SHTP Tony Parker/49 30.00 80.00
SHTW T.J. Warren/49 6.00 15.00
SHTY Thaddeus Young/60 4.00 10.00
SHVC Vince Carter/35 40.00 100.00
SHVD Vlade Divac/60 6.00 15.00
SHVO Victor Oladipo/49 5.00 12.00
SHWF Walt Frazier/49 6.00 15.00
SHZI Zydrunas Ilgauskas/60 5.00 12.00
SHZL Zach LaVine/49 75.00 150.00
SHZR Zach Randolph/49 10.00 25.00
SHMCW M.Carter-Williams/49 4.00 10.00

2014-15 Immaculate Collection Sole of the Game

RANDOM INSERTS IN PACKS
STATED PRINT RUN B/WN 11-30 COPIES PER
NO PRICING ON QTY 19 OR LESS
SGAI Allen Iverson/23 100.00 200.00
SGAW Andrew Wiggins/23 60.00 150.00
SGDW Dominique Wilkins/26 30.00 80.00
SGHO Hakeem Olajuwon/30 40.00 100.00
SGKM Karl Malone/30 30.00 80.00
SGMJ Magic Johnson/26 75.00 150.00
SGMM Moses Malone/20 30.00 80.00
SGRS Ralph Sampson/30 30.00 80.00

2014-15 Immaculate Collection Special Event Jumbo Jerseys

RANDOM INSERTS IN PACKS
STATED PRINT RUN B/WN 4-39 COPIES PER
10 Steven Adams/25 40.00 100.00
12 Donatas Motiejunas/34 15.00 40.00
13 Tarik Black/24 20.00 50.00
15 Jason Terry/26 12.00 30.00
16 Kostas Papanikolaou/32 10.00 25.00
17 Serge Ibaka/20 12.00 30.00
18 Reggie Jackson/24 10.00 25.00
33 Mo Williams/39 12.00 30.00
34 Shabazz Muhammad/38
35 Thaddeus Young/36 10.00 25.00
36 Kevin Martin/36 10.00 25.00
37 Zach LaVine/22 100.00 200.00
38 Nikola Pekovic/37 10.00 25.00
39 Gorgui Dieng/28 10.00 25.00
41 Nick Young/21 15.00 40.00
51 Manu Ginobili/31 40.00 100.00
59 Tiago Splitter/35 12.00 30.00

2014-15 Immaculate Collection Sports Variations Autographs

RANDOM INSERTS IN PACKS
STATED PRINT RUN 25 SER.#'d SETS
SVAJM Joe Montana 100.00 200.00
SVATB T.Bradshaw EXCH 30.00 80.00
SVAMF Marshall Faulk 20.00 50.00
SVAMD M.Ditka EXCH 30.00 80.00
SVACR Cristiano Ronaldo 800.00 1200.00
SVARH R.Henderson EXCH 40.00 100.00
SVAFR F.Robinson EXCH 20.00 50.00
SVAMM M.McGwire EXCH 50.00 120.00
SVABB B.Bonds EXCH 60.00 150.00

2014-15 Immaculate Collection Statistical Standouts Signatures

RANDOM INSERTS IN PACKS
STATED PRINT RUN 49 SER.#'d SETS
1 Joakim Noah
2 Kevin Durant 75.00 150.00
3 Michael Carter-Williams 6.00 15.00
4 Shaquille O'Neal 50.00 120.00
5 Kyle Korver 8.00 20.00
6 Willis Reed 10.00 25.00
7 Dikembe Mutombo 25.00 60.00
8 Alonzo Mourning 25.00 60.00
9 Magic Johnson 25.00 60.00
10 Stephen Curry 75.00 150.00
11 John Wall 40.00 100.00
12 Bernard King 8.00 20.00
13 Charlie Scott 8.00 20.00
14 Blake Griffin 50.00 120.00
15 Tracy McGrady 40.00 100.00
16 Kareem Abdul-Jabbar 30.00 80.00
17 Jason Kidd 20.00 50.00
18 Carmelo Anthony 25.00 60.00
19 Kobe Bryant 100.00 200.00
20 Karl Malone 25.00 60.00

2014-15 Immaculate Collection Team Logos

RANDOM INSERTS IN PACKS
STATED PRINT RUN 1-28 COPIES PER
NO PRICING ON QTY 18 OR LESS
64 Rudy Gay/24 15.00 40.00
98 Tyler Ennis/28 10.00 25.00

2014-15 Immaculate Collection Team Numbers

RANDOM INSERTS IN PACKS
STATED PRINT RUN B/WN 1-50 COPIES PER
NO PRICING ON QTY 18 OR LESS
3 Zach Randolph/23 8.00 20.00
4 Marc Gasol/22 10.00 25.00
6 Grant Hill/24 30.00 80.00
8 Rudy Gobert/24 10.00 25.00
13 Kenneth Faried/21 8.00 20.00
18 Pau Gasol/25 20.00 50.00
23 Chandler Parsons/23 25.00 60.00
33 Kobe Bryant/25 200.00 400.00
36 Al Jefferson/39 20.00 50.00
37 Anthony Davis/20 100.00 200.00
38 Jrue Holiday/21 10.00 25.00
42 Nicolas Batum/21 20.00 50.00
43 Derrick Favors/23 8.00 20.00
44 Gordon Hayward/29 10.00 25.00
48 Al Horford/21 20.00 50.00
50 Thabo Sefolosha/27 6.00 15.00
54 DeMarcus Cousins/21 25.00 60.00
55 Ben McLemore/25 15.00 40.00
56 Vince Carter/22 50.00 120.00
57 Blake Griffin/22 50.00 120.00
63 LeBron James/32 100.00 200.00
64 Rudy Gay/26 10.00 25.00
71 Aaron Gordon/32 15.00 40.00
72 Adreian Payne/40 8.00 20.00
73 Andrew Wiggins/23 200.00 400.00
74 Bruno Caboclo/30 8.00 20.00
75 Cleanthony Early/44 6.00 15.00
76 Damien Inglis/26 6.00 15.00
77 Dante Exum/20 10.00 25.00
78 Doug McDermott/50 10.00 25.00
79 Elfrid Payton/32 30.00 80.00
80 Gary Harris/30 10.00 25.00
81 Glenn Robinson III/28 15.00 40.00
82 Jabari Parker/32 15.00 40.00
83 James Ennis/36 6.00 15.00
84 James Young/42 6.00 15.00
85 Jerami Grant/44 6.00 15.00
86 Joe Harris/40 6.00 15.00
87 Joel Embiid/46 30.00 80.00
88 Julius Randle/46 30.00 80.00
89 K.J. McDaniels/44 8.00 20.00
90 Kyle Anderson/50 10.00 25.00
91 Marcus Smart/50 10.00 25.00
92 Mitch McGary/32 6.00 15.00
93 Nik Stauskas/42 8.00 20.00
94 Noah Vonleh/26 8.00 20.00
95 P.J. Hairston/26 6.00 15.00
96 Rodney Hood/42 10.00 25.00
97 Shabazz Napier/38 10.00 25.00
98 Tyler Ennis/28 6.00 15.00
99 T.J. Warren/32 10.00 25.00
100 Zach LaVine/30 30.00 80.00

2014-15 Immaculate Collection Trio Autographs

RANDOM INSERTS IN PACKS
STATED PRINT RUN 25 SER.#'d SETS
1 Wiggins/Bennett/LaVine 300.00 500.00
2 Davis/Durant/Bryant 1500.00 1800.00
3 Mullin/Richmond/Hardaway 150.00 300.00
4 Wiggins/Parker/Randle 700.00 900.00
5 Robinson III/McGary/Stauskas 75.00 150.00
6 Iguodala/Thompson/Curry 800.00 1000.00

2014-15 Immaculate Collection Trios Materials

RANDOM INSERTS IN PACKS
STATED PRINT RUN B/WN 10-99 COPIES PER
NO PRICING ON QTY 10 OR LESS
2 McHale/Bird/Parish/49 10.00 25.00
7 Love/Irving/James/75 15.00 40.00
8 Dantley/English/Aguirre/49 3.00 8.00
10 Gallinari/Faried/Lawson/75 3.00 8.00
11 English/Mutombo/Lever/49 8.00 20.00
12 Drummond/Monroe/Caldwell-Pope/75 4.00 10.00
13 Laimbeer/Thomas/Dumars/49 4.00 10.00
14 Jefferson/Walker/Kidd-Gilchrist/75 4.00 10.00
15 Green/Thompson/Curry/75 25.00 60.00
20 Jones/Bryant/O'Neal/75 15.00 40.00
23 Andersen/Bosh/Wade/75 6.00 15.00
26 Davis/Holiday/Evans/75 8.00 20.00
28 Starks/Johnson/Ewing/49 12.00 30.00
34 Majerle/Chambers/McDaniel/49 3.00 8.00
36 Robinson/Drexler/Duckworth/49 5.00 12.00
37 McCollum/Aldridge/Batum/75 4.00 10.00
38 McLemore/Cousins/Gay/75 4.00 10.00
39 Robinson/Horry/Duncan/49 12.00 30.00
43 Stockton/Malone/Eaton/49 12.00 30.00
44 Beal/Wall/Porter/75 5.00 12.00
45 Wiggins/Robinson III/LaVine/99 12.00 30.00
48 Caboclo/Inglis/Exum/99 4.00 10.00
52 Harris/Robinson III/Stauskas/99 4.00 10.00
57 McDermott/Parker/Harris/99 6.00 15.00
TADG Wiggins/Exum/Robinson III/99 5.00 12.00
TAES Gordon/Payton/Napier/99 6.00 15.00
TAJJ Wiggins/Embiid/Randle/99 12.00 30.00
TAJM Wiggins/Embiid/Smart/99 12.00 30.00
TATL Horford/Wilkins/Teague/75 5.00 12.00
TBRK Williams/Johnson/Plumlee/75 3.00 8.00
TCDE Early/McDermott/Payton/99 3.00 8.00
TCHI Rose/Butler/Noah/75 5.00 12.00
TGSW Iguodala/Bogut/Lee/75 3.00 8.00
THOU Drexler/Olajuwon/Horry/49 15.00 40.00
TJBK Caboclo/Embiid/McDaniels/99 12.00 30.00
TJJC Early/Young/Randle/99 3.00 8.00
TJNG Robinson III/Randle/Stauskas/99 3.00 8.00
TJPR Parker/Hairston/Hood/99 8.00 20.00
TLAC Griffin/Paul/Jordan/75 5.00 12.00
TLAL Wrthy/Abdl-Jbbr/Jhnsn/49 15.00 40.00
TMCJ Early/Young/Smart/99 3.00 8.00
TMIL Knight/Henson/Mayo/75 3.00 8.00
TMIN Dieng/Pekovic/Rubio/75 3.00 8.00
TMMZ Gasol/Conley/Randolph/75 4.00 10.00
TNYK Anthny/Cldrn/Hrdwy Jr./75 3.00 8.00
TOKC Durant/Westbrook/Ibaka/75 10.00 25.00
TORL Vucevic/Harris/Oladipo/75 3.00 8.00
TORL Hardaway/Scott/O'Neal/49 10.00 25.00
TPHI Collins/Erving/Malone/49 12.00 30.00
TRJK Harris/McDaniels/Hood/99 4.00 10.00
TSEA Schrempf/Payton/Kemp/49 25.00 60.00
TSNP Vonleh/Hairston/Napier/99 3.00 8.00
TTOR DeRozan/Valanciunas/Ross/75 4.00 10.00
TCHH2 Mrnng/Trpcka/Jhnsn/49 12.00 30.00
TDAL2 Nowitzki/Kidd/Finley/49 8.00 20.00
THOU2 Mtjns/Hwrd/Hrdn/75 6.00 15.00
TNYK3 King/Cartwright/Walker/49 15.00 40.00
TPHO2 Len/Bledsoe/Dragic/75 3.00 8.00
TSAS2 Ginobili/Duncan/Parker/75 12.00 30.00

2015-16 Immaculate Collection

RANDOM INSERTS IN PACKS
STATED PRINT RUN 99 SER.#'d SETS
EXCHANGE DEADLINE 3/14/2018
1 Nerlens Noel 1.50 4.00
2 Robert Covington 1.25 3.00
3 Ish Smith 1.25 3.00
4 Jabari Parker 2.50 6.00
5 Khris Middleton 1.50 4.00
6 Michael Carter-Williams 1.25 3.00
7 Jimmy Butler 2.00 5.00
8 Pau Gasol 2.00 5.00
9 Derrick Rose 2.50 6.00
10 Doug McDermott 1.50 4.00
11 LeBron James 8.00 20.00
12 Kevin Love 2.00 5.00
13 Kyrie Irving 4.00 10.00
14 J.R. Smith 1.50 4.00
15 Marcus Smart 1.50 4.00
16 Jared Sullinger 1.25 3.00
17 Isaiah Thomas 2.00 5.00
18 Jae Crowder 1.25 3.00
19 Chris Paul 2.50 6.00
20 J.J. Redick 2.00 5.00
21 Blake Griffin 2.00 5.00
22 DeAndre Jordan 2.00 5.00
23 Marc Gasol 2.00 5.00
24 Mike Conley 2.00 5.00
25 Mario Chalmers 1.50 4.00
26 Paul Millsap 2.00 5.00
27 Al Horford 1.50 4.00
28 Dennis Schroder 1.50 4.00
29 Dwyane Wade 3.00 8.00
30 Hassan Whiteside 1.50 4.00
31 Chris Bosh 2.00 5.00
32 Joe Johnson 1.50 4.00
33 Jeremy Lin 2.00 5.00
34 Kemba Walker 2.00 5.00
35 Al Jefferson 1.50 4.00
36 Derrick Favors 1.50 4.00
37 Rodney Hood 1.50 4.00
38 Gordon Hayward 2.00 5.00
39 DeMarcus Cousins 2.00 5.00
40 Rudy Gay 2.00 5.00
41 Rajon Rondo 2.00 5.00
42 Carmelo Anthony 2.50 6.00
43 Arron Afflalo 1.25 3.00
44 Derrick Williams 1.25 3.00
45 Kobe Bryant 8.00 20.00
46 Jordan Clarkson 2.00 5.00
47 Julius Randle 2.00 5.00
48 Victor Oladipo 1.50 4.00
49 Elfrid Payton 1.50 4.00
50 Nikola Vucevic 1.50 4.00
51 Dirk Nowitzki 2.50 6.00
52 Chandler Parsons 1.50 4.00
53 Wesley Matthews 1.25 3.00
54 Brook Lopez 1.50 4.00
55 Thaddeus Young 1.25 3.00
56 Bojan Bogdanovic 1.25 3.00
57 Kenneth Faried 1.50 4.00
58 Will Barton 1.25 3.00
59 Gary Harris 1.50 4.00
60 Paul George 2.50 6.00
61 George Hill 1.50 4.00
62 Jordan Hill 1.25 3.00
63 Anthony Davis 4.00 10.00
64 Tyreke Evans 1.25 3.00
65 Eric Gordon 1.50 4.00
66 Tobias Harris 1.50 4.00
67 Reggie Jackson 1.50 4.00
68 Andre Drummond 2.00 5.00
69 DeMarre Carroll 1.25 3.00
70 Jonas Valanciunas 1.50 4.00
71 DeMar DeRozan 2.00 5.00
72 Kyle Lowry 1.50 4.00
73 Trevor Ariza 1.25 3.00
74 James Harden 3.00 8.00
75 Jason Terry 1.50 4.00
76 Dwight Howard 1.50 4.00
77 Kawhi Leonard 3.00 8.00
78 Tony Parker 2.00 5.00
79 Manu Ginobili 2.00 5.00
80 Tim Duncan 3.00 8.00
81 T.J. Warren 1.50 4.00
82 Eric Bledsoe 1.50 4.00
83 Brandon Knight 1.50 4.00
84 Serge Ibaka 1.50 4.00
85 Russell Westbrook 5.00 12.00
86 Kevin Durant 5.00 12.00
87 Enes Kanter 1.25 3.00
88 Andrew Wiggins 3.00 8.00
89 Kevin Garnett 3.00 8.00
90 Zach LaVine 2.00 5.00
91 C.J. McCollum 2.00 5.00
92 Gerald Henderson 1.25 3.00
93 Damian Lillard 4.00 10.00
94 Harrison Barnes 1.50 4.00
95 Klay Thompson 2.50 6.00
96 Stephen Curry 8.00 20.00
97 Draymond Green 2.50 6.00
98 John Wall 2.50 6.00
99 Marcin Gortat 1.50 4.00
100 Bradley Beal 2.00 5.00
101 Towns JSY AU/99 RC 600.00 1200.00
102 Jerian Grant JSY AU/99 RC 10.00 25.00
103 Kaminsky JSY AU/99 RC 15.00 40.00
104 Russell JSY AU/99 RC 125.00 300.00
105 Cauley-Stein JSY AU/99 RC 50.00 120.00
106 Jarell Martin JSY AU/99 RC EXCH 8.00 20.00
107 Joe Young JSY AU/99 RC 10.00 25.00
108 Jones JSY AU/99 RC 15.00 40.00
109 Sasha Kaun JSY AU/99 RC 6.00 15.00
110 Okafor JSY AU/99 RC 30.00 80.00
111 Richardson JSY AU/99 RC 25.00 60.00
112 Lyles JSY AU/99 RC 20.00 50.00
113 Cristiano Felicio JSY AU/99 RC 10.00 25.00
114 Anderson JSY AU/99 RC 12.00 30.00
115 Rozier JSY AU/99 RC 20.00 50.00
116 Marcelo Huertas JSY AU 99 RC EXCH 8.00 20.00
117 Mudiay JSY AU/99 RC 40.00 100.00
118 Winslow JSY AU/99 RC 30.00 80.00
119 Johnson JSY AU/99 RC 20.00 50.00
120 Raul Neto JSY AU/99 RC EXCH 6.00 15.00
121 Booker JSY AU/99 RC 400.00 800.00
122 Hollis-Jefferson JSY AU/99 RC 15.00 40.00
123 Dekker JSY AU/99 RC 20.00 50.00
124 Simmons JSY AU/99 RC 40.00 100.00
125 Delon Wright JSY AU/99 RC 8.00 20.00
126 Oubre Jr. JSY AU/99 RC 25.00 60.00
127 Luis Montero JSY AU/99 RC 6.00 15.00
128 Nemanja Bjelica JSY AU/95 RC 10.00 25.00
129 Jordan Mickey JSY AU/99 RC 6.00 15.00
130 Salah Mejri JSY AU/99 RC 6.00 15.00
131 Looney JSY AU/99 RC 8.00 20.00
132 Holmes JSY AU/99 RC 15.00 40.00
133 Jokic JSY AU/99 RC 500.00 1000.00
134 Chris McCullough JSY AU/99 RC 6.00 15.00
135 Porzingis JSY AU/99 RC 300.00 600.00
136 Rakeem Christmas JSY AU/99 RC 6.00 15.00
137 Powell JSY AU/82 RC 30.00 80.00
138 Payne JSY AU/99 RC 8.00 20.00
139 Nance Jr. JSY AU/99 RC 25.00 60.00
140 R.J. Hunter JSY AU/99 RC 6.00 15.00
141 Cliff Alexander JSY AU/99 RC 6.00 15.00
142 Portis JSY AU/99 RC 15.00 40.00
143 Hznja JSY AU/99 RC EXCH 30.00 80.00
144 Pat Connaughton JSY AU/99 RC 6.00 15.00
145 Walter Tavares JSY AU/99 RC 6.00 15.00
146 Anthony Brown JSY AU/99 RC 10.00 25.00
147 Montrezl Harrell JSY AU/99 RC 10.00 25.00
148 Turner JSY AU/99 RC 100.00 250.00
149 Huestis JSY AU/99 RC 6.00 15.00
150 T.J. McConnell JSY AU/99 RC 15.00 40.00

2015-16 Immaculate Collection Bronze

*BRONZE: .6X TO 1.5X BASIC
RANDOM INSERTS IN PACKS
STATED PRINT RUN 49 SER.#'d SETS

2015-16 Immaculate Collection Autographs

RANDOM INSERTS IN PACKS
PRINT RUNS B/WN 32-99 COPIES PER
EXCHANGE DEADLINE 3/14/2018
*BRONZE p/r 30-75: .4X TO 1X BASIC
*BRONZE p/r 25-26: .5X TO 1.2X BASIC
*RED/25: .5X TO 1.2X BASIC
1 Zaza Pachulia/99 4.00 10.00
2 Matthew Dellavedova/99 5.00 12.00
3 Jonas Valanciunas/99 5.00 12.00
4 Draymond Green/99 12.00 30.00
5 Khris Middleton/99 5.00 12.00
6 DeMarre Carroll/99 4.00 10.00
7 Goran Dragic/99 5.00 12.00
8 Eric Bledsoe/99 5.00 12.00
9 Andrew Wiggins/35 25.00 60.00
10 Dirk Nowitzki/35 40.00 100.00
11 Avery Bradley/99 5.00 12.00
12 Dennis Schroder/99 5.00 12.00
13 Gerald Henderson/99 4.00 10.00
14 Anthony Davis/35 30.00 80.00
15 Pau Gasol/35 10.00 25.00
16 Jordan Clarkson/99 8.00 20.00
17 Giannis Antetokounmpo/99 30.00 80.00
18 Al Horford/99 5.00 12.00
19 Nerlens Noel/70 5.00 12.00
20 Gordon Hayward/85 6.00 15.00
21 Nicolas Batum/99 5.00 12.00
22 C.J. McCollum/99 6.00 15.00
23 Gorgui Dieng/99 4.00 10.00
24 Jason Terry/99 5.00 12.00
25 Andrew Bogut/99 5.00 12.00
26 Bobby Portis/99 6.00 15.00
27 Nikola Jokic/99 40.00 100.00
28 Boban Marjanovic/99 5.00 12.00
29 Rondae Hollis-Jefferson/99 5.00 12.00
30 Devin Booker/99 50.00 120.00
31 Jahlil Okafor/49 8.00 20.00
32 Artis Gilmore/99 5.00 12.00
33 James Worthy/35 12.00 30.00
34 John Starks/99 5.00 12.00
35 Charles Oakley/99 5.00 12.00
36 Vinny Del Negro/99 5.00 12.00
37 Peja Stojakovic/99 6.00 15.00
38 Ralph Sampson/45 5.00 12.00
39 Shaquille O'Neal/32 50.00 120.00
40 Allen Iverson/35 40.00 100.00
41 Dikembe Mutombo/99 6.00 15.00
42 David Robinson/35 15.00 40.00
43 Chauncey Billups/99 6.00 15.00
44 Isiah Thomas/99 8.00 20.00
45 Bernard King/99 5.00 12.00
46 Oscar Robertson/35 30.00 80.00
47 George Gervin/99 6.00 15.00
48 Ray Allen/49 12.00 30.00
49 John Stockton/35 25.00 60.00
50 Danny Manning/80 5.00 12.00

2015-16 Immaculate Collection Christmas Day Materials

RANDOM INSERTS IN PACKS
PRINT RUNS B/WN 1-74 COPIES PER
NO PRICING ON QTY 17 OR LESS
PRICING FOR BASIC PATCHES
1 Pau Gasol/61 10.00 25.00
2 Doug McDermott/35 6.00 15.00
4 Eric Gordon/49 6.00 15.00
5 Tyreke Evans/49 5.00 12.00
6 Ryan Anderson/58 6.00 15.00
7 Goran Dragic/39 6.00 15.00
8 Luol Deng/44 10.00 25.00
9 Jonathon Simmons/48 12.00 30.00
10 Jordan Clarkson/40 15.00 40.00
11 Marcelo Huertas/44 6.00 15.00
19 James Harden/20 50.00 120.00
20 Dwight Howard/20 20.00 50.00
21 Clint Capela/74 10.00 25.00
29 Serge Ibaka/42 8.00 20.00
32 Steven Adams/65 25.00 60.00
36 Danny Green/45 15.00 40.00
45 Trevor Ariza/52 8.00 20.00
46 Enes Kanter/43 8.00 20.00
47 Gerald Green/51 8.00 20.00
51 Alonzo Gee/65 5.00 12.00
52 Andre Roberson/67 5.00 12.00
53 Anthony Morrow/43 5.00 12.00
55 Brandon Bass/43 5.00 12.00
56 Corey Brewer/56 5.00 12.00
58 D.J. Augustin/53 5.00 12.00
59 Donatas Motiejunas/46 5.00 12.00
63 Nick Collison/43 6.00 15.00
64 Norris Cole/53 5.00 12.00
65 Omer Asik/55 6.00 15.00
67 Patrick Beverley/64 5.00 12.00
68 Roy Hibbert/57 6.00 15.00
69 Tony Snell/58 5.00 12.00
70 Terrence Jones/40 6.00 15.00
71 Udonis Haslem/59 5.00 12.00
73 Ty Lawson/42 5.00 12.00
74 Jason Terry/50 12.00 30.00

2015-16 Immaculate Collection Dual Autographs

RANDOM INSERTS IN PACKS
PRINT RUNS B/WN 25-49 COPIES PER
EXCHANGE DEADLINE 3/14/2018
1 Russell/Towns/49 200.00 500.00
2 Okafor/Towns/49 150.00 400.00
3 Cly-Stn/Towns/49 150.00 300.00
4 J.Parker/R.Vaughn/49 40.00 100.00
5 D.Booker/B.Knight/49 60.00 150.00
6 D.Wade/S.O'Neal/25 400.00 800.00
7 C.Paul/B.Griffin/25 250.00 400.00
8 A.Davis/K.Durant/25 200.00 400.00
9 Dekker/Kaminsky/49 40.00 100.00
10 E.Mudiay/K.Faried/49 20.00 50.00
11 K.Porzingis/J.Grant/49 75.00 200.00
12 J.Young/M.Turner/49 30.00 80.00
13 M.Harrell/T.Rozier/49 20.00 50.00
14 J.Grant/P.Connaughton/49 15.00 40.00
15 D.Wade/C.Bosh/49 75.00 150.00
16 N.Powell/D.Wright/49 15.00 40.00
17 D.Exum/A.Bogut/49 25.00 60.00
18 D.Exum/J.Ingles/49 30.00 80.00
19 Finley/Nash/49 EXCH 40.00 100.00
20 K.Durant/K.Bryant/49 400.00 600.00
21 K.Love/K.Irving/49 125.00 300.00
22 Russell/Kobe/49 EXCH 400.00 600.00
23 Clrksn/Rssll/49 EXCH 75.00 200.00
24 R.Gay/D.Cousins/49 30.00 80.00
25 E.Payton/M.Hezonja/49 30.00 80.00
26 McGrady/Carter/25 500.00 800.00
27 L.Bird/M.Johnson/25 400.00 800.00
28 Abdul-Jabbar/Magic/25 200.00 400.00
29 K.Bryant/A.Iverson/25
30 Bryant/Anthony/25 300.00 600.00
31 E.Hayes/W.Unseld/49 25.00 60.00
32 I.Thomas/M.Smart/49 30.00 80.00
33 Melo/Porzingis/49 250.00 400.00
34 J.Erving/A.Iverson/25 300.00 600.00
35 Shaq/Hardaway/25 300.00 600.00
36 Hlis-Jffrsn/Jhnsn/49 15.00 40.00
37 J.Winslow/J.Okafor/49 100.00 250.00
38 Gay/Cauley-Stein/49 30.00 80.00
39 Drexler/Olajuwon/49 125.00 300.00
40 M.Hezonja/T.Kukoc/49 40.00 100.00
41 Kobe/Shaq/25 2500.00 3000.00
42 Sprewell/Jackson/49 30.00 80.00
43 B.Knight/T.Warren/49 15.00 40.00
44 M.Jackson/J.Rose/49 20.00 50.00
45 Z.Randolph/M.Conley/49 20.00 50.00
46 A.Horford/D.Schroder/49 EXCH 20.00 50.00
47 N.Bjelica/V.Divac/49 20.00 50.00
48 Porzingis/Towns/49 400.00 800.00
49 McConnell/Okafor/49 25.00 60.00
50 N.Bjelica/N.Jokic/49 30.00 80.00
51 Mudiay/Russell/49 125.00 300.00
52 Stdmre/Stckhse/49 40.00 100.00
53 Robinson/Shaq/25 150.00 300.00
54 Robinson/Elliott/49 30.00 80.00
55 Parker/Robinson/49 75.00 200.00
56 R.Barry/J.Wilkes/49 20.00 50.00
57 D.Cowens/D.Nelson/49 20.00 50.00
58 Stdmre/McGrady/49 50.00 120.00
59 L.Wilkens/C.Hagan/49 20.00 50.00
60 E.Jones/N.Van Exel/49 40.00 100.00

2015-16 Immaculate Collection Dual Memorabilia

RANDOM INSERTS IN PACKS
PRINT RUNS B/WN 25-75 COPIES PER
*PRIME/25: 1X TO 2.5X BASIC
1 Derrick Rose/75 4.00 10.00
2 DeAndre Jordan/75 3.00 8.00
3 Paul Millsap/75 3.00 8.00

4 Tony Parker/75 3.00 8.00
5 Al Horford/75 2.50 6.00
6 Rodney Hood/75 2.50 6.00
7 Kyle Korver/75 2.50 6.00
8 Blake Griffin/75 3.00 8.00
9 Kyle Lowry/75 2.50 6.00
10 Chandler Parsons/75 2.50 6.00
11 Kobe Bryant/75 10.00 25.00
12 Isaiah Thomas/75 5.00 12.00
13 Victor Oladipo/75 2.50 6.00
14 Kemba Walker/75 3.00 8.00
15 Pau Gasol/75 3.00 8.00
16 Al Jefferson/75 2.50 6.00
17 Jeremy Lamb/75 2.00 5.00
18 LeBron James/75 12.00 30.00
19 Shaquille O'Neal/75 6.00 15.00
20 Kyrie Irving/75 6.00 15.00
21 Kevin Love/75 3.00 8.00
22 DeMarre Carroll/75 2.00 5.00
23 Rudy Gobert/75 3.00 8.00
24 Kevin Durant/75 8.00 20.00
25 Tim Duncan/75 5.00 12.00
26 Russell Westbrook/75 10.00 25.00
27 Serge Ibaka/75 2.50 6.00
28 Deron Williams/75 2.50 6.00
29 Jimmy Butler/75 3.00 8.00
30 Reggie Jackson/75 2.50 6.00
31 Damian Lillard/75 6.00 15.00
32 Andre Drummond/75 3.00 8.00
33 Marcus Morris/75 2.00 5.00
34 Elfrid Payton/75 2.50 6.00
35 Nikola Vucevic/75 2.50 6.00
36 DeMar DeRozan/75 3.00 8.00
37 Trey Burke/75 2.00 5.00
38 Gordon Hayward/25 3.00 8.00
39 Josh Smith/75 2.50 6.00
40 Lance Stephenson/75 2.50 6.00
41 Dirk Nowitzki/75 4.00 10.00
42 Manu Ginobili/75 3.00 8.00
43 Michael Beasley/75 2.50 6.00
44 George Hill/75 2.50 6.00
45 Mason Plumlee/75 2.50 6.00
46 Draymond Green/75 4.00 10.00
47 Paul George/75 4.00 10.00
48 Tristan Thompson/75 2.50 6.00
49 Tyler Zeller/75 2.50 6.00

2015-16 Immaculate Collection Dual Patch Autographs

RANDOM INSERTS IN PACKS
PRINT RUNS B/WN 28-75 COPIES PER
EXCHANGE DEADLINE 3/14/2018
DPAABU Alec Burks/50 6.00 15.00
DPAADA Anthony Davis/50 60.00 150.00
DPAAHO Al Horford/50 10.00 25.00
DPAAWI Andrew Wiggins/50 60.00 150.00
DPABBE Bradley Beal/50 20.00 50.00
DPABKN Brandon Knight/50 8.00 20.00
DPABPO Bobby Portis/75 30.00 80.00
DPACPA Cameron Payne/75 8.00 20.00
DPADMU Dikembe Mutombo/35 30.00 80.00
DPADRO Dennis Rodman/35 60.00 150.00
DPAEKA Enes Kanter/50 8.00 20.00
DPAGHA Gordon Hayward/50 12.00 30.00
DPAITH Isiah Thomas/35 25.00 50.00
DPAJCR Jae Crowder/35 12.00 30.00
DPAJRA Julius Randle/50 15.00 40.00
DPAJST John Starks/35 12.00 30.00
DPAJWA John Wall/50 25.00 60.00
DPAJWO James Worthy/31 30.00 80.00
DPAKDU Kevin Durant/50 75.00 200.00
DPAKIR Kyrie Irving/50 60.00 150.00
DPAKOU Kelly Oubre Jr./75 12.00 30.00
DPALBI Larry Bird/35 50.00 120.00
DPAMCW Michael Carter-Williams/50 6.00 15.00
DPAMDE M. Dellavedova/50 8.00 20.00
DPAMJO Magic Johnson/35 50.00 120.00
DPAMTU Myles Turner/75 30.00 80.00
DPANBA Nicolas Batum/50 8.00 20.00
DPARHO Robert Horry/28 10.00 25.00
DPARSA Ralph Sampson/35 8.00 20.00
DPASBA Shane Battier/35 10.00 25.00
DPATHA Tobias Harris/50 8.00 20.00
DPATLY Trey Lyles/75 15.00 40.00
DPATTH Tristan Thompson/50 12.00 30.00
DPAVOL Victor Oladipo/50 12.00 30.00
DPAZLA Zach LaVine/50 30.00 80.00

2015-16 Immaculate Collection Dual Patch Autographs Jersey Number

*JSY NUM p/r 20-91: .75X TO 2X BASIC
RANDOM INSERTS IN PACKS
PRINT RUNS B/WN 2-91 COPIES PER
NO PRICING ON QTY 15 OR LESS
EXCHANGE DEADLINE 3/14/2018
DPADRO Dennis Rodman/91 40.00 100.00

2015-16 Immaculate Collection Ink

RANDOM INSERTS IN PACKS
PRINT RUNS B/WN 50-99 COPIES PER
EXCHANGE DEADLINE 3/14/2018
*RED/25: .5X TO 1.2X BASIC
IKABO Andrew Bogut/99 5.00 12.00
IKABR Avery Bradley/99 5.00 12.00
IKADR Andre Drummond/99 8.00 20.00
IKAHO Allan Houston/99 5.00 12.00
IKAWI Andrew Wiggins/60 30.00 80.00
IKBGR Blake Griffin/60 15.00 40.00
IKBKN Brandon Knight/99 5.00 12.00
IKBPO Bobby Portis/99 6.00 15.00
IKBWA Bill Walton/99 6.00 15.00
IKDBO Devin Booker/99 40.00 100.00
IKDMA Dan Majerle/99 5.00 12.00
IKDMO Donatas Motiejunas/99 4.00 10.00
IKDMU Dikembe Mutombo/50 10.00 25.00
IKDRO Dennis Rodman/60 20.00 50.00
IKDRU D'Angelo Russell/60 20.00 60.00
IKEBL Eric Bledsoe/99 5.00 12.00
IKEFO Evan Fournier/99 5.00 12.00
IKEMU Emmanuel Mudiay/60 8.00 20.00
IKETU Evan Turner/99 5.00 12.00
IKGGE George Gervin/99 6.00 15.00
IKGHA Gary Harris/99 5.00 12.00
IKGOH Gordon Hayward/99 8.00 20.00
IKGHI Grant Hill/60 15.00 40.00
IKJCR Jae Crowder/99 4.00 10.00
IKJIN Joe Ingles/99 4.00 10.00
IKJOK Jahlil Okafor/60 8.00 20.00
IKJRA Julius Randle/99 10.00 25.00
IKJRO Jalen Rose/99 6.00 15.00
IKJTE Jason Terry/99 5.00 12.00
IKJVA Jonas Valanciunas/99 5.00 12.00
IKJWA John Wall/60 15.00 40.00
IKJWI Justise Winslow/99 8.00 20.00
IKKBA Kent Bazemore/99 5.00 12.00
IKKBR Kobe Bryant/60 100.00 250.00
IKKDU Kevin Durant/60 50.00 120.00
IKKFA Kenneth Faried/99 5.00 12.00
IKKIR Kyrie Irving/60 40.00 100.00
IKKLO Kevin Love/60 6.00 15.00
IKKOU Kelly Oubre Jr./99 8.00 20.00
IKKPO Kristaps Porzingis/99 40.00 100.00
IKKTO Karl-Anthony Towns/60 75.00 200.00
IKMGA Marc Gasol/60 20.00 50.00
IKMRI Mitch Richmond/99 10.00 25.00
IKMTU Myles Turner/99 15.00 40.00
IKNBA Nicolas Batum/99 5.00 12.00
IKNVE Nick Van Exel/99 8.00 20.00
IKRAL Ray Allen/60 20.00 50.00
IKRGA Rudy Gay/99 6.00 15.00
IKRHO Robert Horry/99 5.00 12.00
IKRNE Raul Neto/99 4.00 10.00
IKSNA Steve Nash/60 20.00 50.00
IKSON Shaquille O'Neal/60 40.00 100.00
IKTHA Tim Hardaway Jr./99 4.00 10.00
IKTLY Trey Lyles/99 6.00 15.00
IKTMC T.J. McConnell/99 5.00 12.00
IKTMA Tracy McGrady/60 20.00 50.00
IKTRO Terry Rozier/99 5.00 12.00
IKTWA T.J. Warren/99 5.00 12.00
IKWCS Willie Cauley-Stein/99 15.00 40.00
IKZLA Zach LaVine/99 12.00 30.00

2015-16 Immaculate Collection Jumbo Patches Jersey Numbers

RANDOM INSERTS IN PACKS
PRINT RUNS B/WN 8-25 COPIES PER
NO PRICING ON QTY 18 OR LESS
10 Timofey Mozgov/23 8.00 20.00
16 Dante Cunningham/21 5.00 12.00
19 LeBron James/24 150.00 400.00
27 R.J. Hunter/25 5.00 12.00
40 Reggie Evans/25 8.00 20.00
54 Jerian Grant/22 10.00 25.00
57 Marcus Morris/25 8.00 20.00
59 Joakim Noah/25 10.00 25.00
68 Joe Smith/21 10.00 25.00
70 Walter Tavares/23 15.00 40.00
71 Cole Aldrich/20 10.00 25.00
73 Ben McLemore/25 8.00 20.00
76 Mike Scott/25 8.00 20.00
80 Jonas Jerebko/20 20.00 50.00
84 Mo Williams/23 6.00 15.00
90 Nemanja Bjelica/20 6.00 15.00
99 Jordan Mickey/25 8.00 20.00

2015-16 Immaculate Collection Jumbo Patches Team Logos

RANDOM INSERTS IN PACKS
PRINT RUNS B/WN 6-22 COPIES PER
NO PRICING ON QTY 14 OR LESS
45 Tyson Chandler/22 8.00 20.00

2015-16 Immaculate Collection Memorabilia

RANDOM INSERTS IN PACKS
STATED PRINT RUN 99 SER.#'d SETS
*RED/25: 1X TO 2.5X BASIC
1 Nerlens Noel 3.00 8.00
2 Robert Covington 2.00 5.00
3 Jabari Parker 4.00 10.00
4 Michael Carter-Williams 2.00 5.00
5 Derrick Rose 4.00 10.00
6 LeBron James 12.00 30.00
7 Kevin Love 3.00 8.00
8 Kyrie Irving 6.00 15.00
9 Marcus Smart 2.50 6.00
10 Jared Sullinger 2.00 5.00
11 J.J. Redick 3.00 8.00
12 Blake Griffin 3.00 8.00
13 Marc Gasol 3.00 8.00
14 Al Horford 2.50 6.00
15 Dwyane Wade 5.00 12.00
16 Hassan Whiteside 2.50 6.00
17 Kemba Walker 3.00 8.00
18 Al Jefferson 2.50 6.00
19 Derrick Favors 2.50 6.00
20 Rajon Rondo 3.00 8.00
21 Carmelo Anthony 4.00 10.00
22 Arron Afflalo 2.00 5.00
23 Derrick Williams 2.00 5.00
24 Kobe Bryant 12.00 30.00
25 Victor Oladipo 2.50 6.00
26 Chandler Parsons 2.50 6.00
27 Kenneth Faried 2.50 6.00
28 Will Barton 2.00 5.00
29 Gary Harris 2.50 6.00
30 Paul George 4.00 10.00
31 George Hill 2.50 6.00
32 Anthony Davis 6.00 15.00
33 Tyreke Evans 2.00 5.00
34 Reggie Jackson 2.50 6.00
35 Andre Drummond 3.00 8.00
36 DeMar DeRozan 3.00 8.00
37 Kyle Lowry 2.50 6.00
38 James Harden 5.00 12.00
39 Dwight Howard 2.50 6.00
40 Kawhi Leonard 5.00 12.00
41 Tony Parker 3.00 8.00
42 Tim Duncan 5.00 12.00
43 Eric Bledsoe 2.50 6.00
44 Brandon Knight 2.50 6.00
45 Serge Ibaka 2.50 6.00
46 Russell Westbrook 8.00 20.00
47 Andrew Wiggins 5.00 12.00
48 Gerald Henderson 2.00 5.00
49 Damian Lillard 6.00 15.00
50 Stephen Curry 12.00 30.00

2015-16 Immaculate Collection Milestones Autographs

RANDOM INSERTS IN PACKS
PRINT RUNS B/WN 25-50 COPIES PER
EXCHANGE DEADLINE 3/14/2018
1 Kobe Bryant/25 2000.00 2500.00
2 Klay Thompson/25 500.00 800.00
3 Stephen Curry/25 1200.00 1500.00
4 Dwyane Wade/25 600.00 900.00
5 Dikembe Mutombo/50 75.00 200.00
6 Andre Drummond/25 EXCH 150.00 300.00
7 Draymond Green/25 EXCH 250.00 500.00
8 DeMarcus Cousins/25 EXCH 250.00 400.00
9 Jimmy Butler/25 200.00 400.00
10 Anthony Davis/50 150.00 400.00
11 Hassan Whiteside/50 75.00 200.00
12 Steve Kerr/50 EXCH 125.00 250.00
13 Devin Booker/50 400.00 800.00
14 Zach LaVine/50 200.00 400.00
15 Aaron Gordon/50 150.00 300.00

2015-16 Immaculate Collection Patch Autographs

RANDOM INSERTS IN PACKS
PRINT RUNS B/WN 14-99 COPIES PER
NO PRICING ON QTY 19 OR LESS
EXCHANGE DEADLINE 3/14/2018
PAN Nene/60 8.00 20.00
PAAAM Al-Farouq Aminu/60 8.00 20.00
PAADA Anthony Davis/60 60.00 150.00
PAAGI Artis Gilmore/40 10.00 25.00
PAAHO Al Horford/60 10.00 25.00
PAAIV Allen Iverson/40 150.00 300.00
PABBO Bojan Bogdanovic/60 10.00 25.00
PABGR Blake Griffin/60 25.00 60.00
PABKN Brandon Knight/60 8.00 20.00
PACAN Carmelo Anthony/60 30.00 80.00
PACBO Chris Bosh/60 12.00 30.00
PACDR Clyde Drexler/60 20.00 50.00
PACPA Chris Paul/60 30.00 80.00
PADMC Doug McDermott/60 8.00 20.00
PADRO Dennis Rodman/40 40.00 100.00
PADSC Dennis Schroder/60 12.00 30.00
PADWA Dwyane Wade/60 50.00 120.00
PAEBL Eric Bledsoe/60 8.00 20.00
PAEDA Ed Davis/50 6.00 15.00
PAEFO Evan Fournier/60 8.00 20.00
PAEGO Eric Gordon/60 8.00 20.00
PAEKA Enes Kanter/60 6.00 15.00
PAETU Evan Turner/60 8.00 20.00
PAFEZ Festus Ezeli/44 6.00 15.00
PAGHE Gerald Henderson/60 6.00 15.00
PAGHI Grant Hill/60 20.00 50.00
PAHOL Hakeem Olajuwon/60 12.00 30.00
PAJCR Jae Crowder/60 10.00 25.00
PAJER Julius Erving/40 40.00 100.00
PAJHO Jrue Holiday/60 8.00 20.00
PAJRO Jalen Rose/35 10.00 25.00
PAJSM J.R. Smith/51 20.00 50.00
PAJST John Stockton/40 30.00 80.00
PAJTE Jeff Teague/60 8.00 20.00
PAJVA Jonas Valanciunas/60 8.00 20.00
PAJWA John Wall/60 30.00 80.00
PAJWE Jerry West/50 60.00 150.00
PAKBA Kent Bazemore/60
PAKBR Kobe Bryant/60 150.00 300.00
PAKDU Kevin Durant/60 75.00 200.00
PAKIR Kyrie Irving/60 60.00 150.00
PAKLO Kevin Love/60 20.00 50.00
PAKMA Karl Malone/40 30.00 80.00
PALBI Larry Bird/26 60.00 150.00
PAMBR Markel Brown/60 6.00 15.00
PAMCO Mike Conley/60 10.00 25.00
PAMGO Marcin Gortat/60 8.00 20.00
PAMJO Magic Johnson/40 50.00 120.00
PANBA Nicolas Batum/60 8.00 20.00
PANYO Nick Young/60 8.00 20.00
PAOPO Otto Porter/60 8.00 20.00
PAPGE Paul George/99 50.00 120.00
PARGA Rudy Gay/60 12.00 30.00
PARHO Robert Horry/40 12.00 30.00
PARLO Robin Lopez/60 6.00 15.00
PARPA Robert Parish/60 10.00 25.00
PASBA Shane Battier/60 8.00 20.00
PASCU Stephen Curry/60 200.00 400.00
PASNA Steve Nash/60 30.00 80.00
PASON Shaquille O'Neal/40 60.00 150.00
PATAL Tony Allen/60 6.00 15.00
PATWA T.J. Warren/60 10.00 25.00
PAVOL Victor Oladipo/60 8.00 20.00

2015-16 Immaculate Collection Patch Autographs Jersey Number

*JSY NUM p/r 22-91: .5X TO 1.2X BASIC
RANDOM INSERTS IN PACKS
PRINT RUNS B/WN 1-91 COPIES PER
NO PRICING ON QTY 17 OR LESS
EXCHANGE DEADLINE 3/14/2018
PAADA Anthony Davis/23 150.00 300.00
PABGR Blake Griffin/32 50.00 120.00
PACDR Clyde Drexler/22 50.00 120.00
PAGHI Grant Hill/33 40.00 100.00
PAJVA Jonas Valanciunas/58 20.00 50.00
PAKBR Kobe Bryant/24 100.00 1500.00
PAKDU Kevin Durant/35 150.00 400.00
PAKMA Karl Malone/32 75.00 200.00
PAMJO Magic Johnson/32 125.00 300.00
PASCU Stephen Curry/30 500.00 800.00
PASON Shaquille O'Neal/32 200.00 400.00

2015-16 Immaculate Collection Patches Jersey Number

RANDOM INSERTS IN PACKS
PRINT RUNS B/WN 1-50 COPIES PER
NO PRICING ON QTY 15 OR LESS
PJAD Anthony Davis/23 25.00 60.00
PJAJ Al Jefferson/25 5.00 12.00
PJAW Andrew Wiggins/22 60.00 150.00
PJCP Chandler Parsons/25 5.00 12.00
PJDW Derrick Williams/23 4.00 10.00
PJGA Giannis Antetokounmpo/34 20.00 50.00
PJGR Glen Rice/41 5.00 12.00
PJJB Jimmy Butler/21 30.00 80.00
PJKF Kenneth Faried/35 5.00 12.00
PJKM Khris Middleton/22 8.00 20.00
PJLJ LeBron James/23 75.00 200.00
PJMG Marc Gasol/33 6.00 15.00
PJMS Marcus Smart/36 5.00 12.00
PJPP Paul Pierce/34 6.00 15.00
PJRC Robert Covington/33 8.00 20.00
PJRG Rudy Gobert/27 10.00 25.00
PJSC Stephen Curry/30 60.00 150.00
PJTD Tim Duncan/21 30.00 80.00
PJTY Thaddeus Young/30 4.00 10.00
PJZR Zach Randolph/50 5.00 12.00

2015-16 Immaculate Collection Premium Autograph Patches

RANDOM INSERTS IN PACKS
PRINT RUNS B/WN 16-25 COPIES PER
NO PRICING ON QTY 19 OR LESS
EXCHANGE DEADLINE 3/14/2018
PPAN Nene/25 15.00 40.00
PPAABO A. Bogut/25 EXCH 40.00 100.00
PPAABR Avery Bradley/24 20.00 50.00
PPAABR Anthony Brown/25 25.00 60.00
PPAABU Alec Burks/25 6.00 15.00
PPAADR Andre Drummond/25
PPAAHO Al Horford/25 12.00 30.00
PPAAWI Andrew Wiggins/25 150.00 400.00
PPABGR Blake Griffin/25 75.00 200.00
PPABKN Brandon Knight/25 12.00 30.00
PPABPO Bobby Portis/25 75.00 200.00
PPACAN Carmelo Anthony/25 60.00 150.00
PPACBO Chris Bosh/25 15.00 40.00
PPACDR Clyde Drexler/25 100.00 250.00
PPACMC Chris McCullough/25 15.00 40.00
PPACPA Cameron Payne/25 30.00 80.00
PPACWA C.J. Watson/25 6.00 15.00
PPADBO Devin Booker/25 400.00 800.00
PPADGA Danilo Gallinari/25 20.00 50.00
PPADGR Draymond Green/25 75.00 200.00
PPADMO D. Motiejunas/25 12.00 30.00
PPADRO David Robinson/25 50.00 120.00
PPADRO Dennis Rodman/25 75.00 200.00
PPADRU D'Angelo Russell/25 200.00 400.00
PPADSC Dennis Schroder/25 40.00 100.00
PPADWA Dwyane Wade/25 150.00 400.00
PPAEBL Eric Bledsoe/25 20.00 50.00
PPAEFO Evan Fournier/25 8.00 20.00
PPAEMU E. Mudiay/25 60.00 150.00
PPAEPA Elfrid Payton/25 20.00 50.00
PPAETU Evan Turner/25 8.00 20.00
PPAFKA Frank Kaminsky/25 40.00 100.00
PPAGDR Goran Dragic/25 12.00 30.00
PPAGHA Gary Harris/25 20.00 50.00
PPAGHA Gordon Hayward/25 25.00 60.00
PPAGHE Gerald Henderson/25 15.00 40.00
PPAGHI Grant Hill/25 50.00 120.00
PPAHOL Hakeem Olajuwon/25 30.00 80.00
PPAJDU Joe Dumars/25 12.00 30.00
PPAJKI Jason Kidd/25 50.00 120.00
PPAJMA Jamal Mashburn/25 30.00 80.00
PPAJMI Jordan Mickey/25 10.00 25.00
PPAJOK Jahlil Okafor/25 60.00 150.00
PPAJPA Jabari Parker/25 50.00 120.00
PPAJRA Julius Randle/25 20.00 50.00
PPAJRI Josh Richardson/25 30.00 80.00
PPAJSM J.R. Smith/25 20.00 50.00
PPAJST John Stockton/25 40.00 100.00
PPAJTE Jeff Teague/25 12.00 30.00
PPAJVA Jonas Valanciunas/25 20.00 50.00
PPAJWA John Wall/25 40.00 100.00
PPAJWI Justise Winslow/25 100.00 250.00
PPAJYO Joe Young/25 15.00 40.00
PPAKBR Kobe Bryant/25 400.00 1000.00
PPAKDU Kevin Durant/25 250.00 500.00
PPAKFA Kenneth Faried/25 15.00 40.00
PPAKIR Kyrie Irving/25 125.00 250.00
PPAKLO Kevon Looney/25 8.00 20.00
PPAKMA Karl Malone/25 60.00 150.00
PPAKOU Kelly Oubre Jr./25 50.00 120.00
PPAKTH Klay Thompson/25 125.00 300.00
PPAKVH Keith Van Horn/25 15.00 40.00
PPALGA Langston Galloway/25 6.00 15.00
PPAMAG Mark Aguirre/23 8.00 20.00
PPAMCO Mike Conley/25 12.00 30.00
PPAMCW M. Carter-Williams/25 12.00 30.00
PPAMDE M. Dellavedova/25 12.00 30.00
PPAMGA Marc Gasol/25 60.00 150.00
PPAMGO Marcin Gortat/25 20.00 50.00
PPAMHA M. Harkless/25 EXCH 15.00 40.00
PPAMHE Mario Hezonja/25 40.00 100.00
PPAMHU M. Huertas/25 EXCH 20.00 50.00
PPAMPR Mark Price/25 20.00 50.00
PPAMSM Marcus Smart/25 20.00 50.00
PPAMTU Myles Turner/25 150.00 300.00
PPANBA Nicolas Batum/25 15.00 40.00
PPANCO Norris Cole/25 6.00 15.00
PPANVU Nikola Vucevic/25 15.00 40.00
PPANYO Nick Young/22 10.00 25.00
PPARGA Rudy Gay/25 20.00 50.00
PPARHJ R. Hollis-Jefferson/25 40.00 100.00
PPARLO Robin Lopez/25 10.00 25.00
PPASBA Shane Battier/25 20.00 50.00
PPASCU Stephen Curry/25 300.00 800.00
PPASKA Sasha Kaun/25 6.00 15.00
PPASON S. O'Neal/25 EXCH 150.00 300.00
PPATLY Trey Lyles/25 50.00 120.00
PPATMC T.J. McConnell/25 15.00 40.00
PPATMO Timofey Mozgov/25 6.00 15.00
PPATRO Terry Rozier/25 40.00 100.00
PPATTH Tristan Thompson/25 20.00 50.00
PPATYO Thaddeus Young/25 8.00 20.00
PPAVOL Victor Oladipo/25 15.00 40.00
PPAWMA Wesley Matthews/25 15.00 40.00
PPAZPA Zaza Pachulia/19 15.00 40.00
PPAZRA Z. Randolph/25 EXCH 15.00 40.00

2015-16 Immaculate Collection Quad Materials

RANDOM INSERTS IN PACKS
STATED PRINT RUN 49 SER.#'d SETS
QMCHI Rose/Gsl/Btlr/Mrtc 5.00 12.00
QMLAC Grffn/Paul/Jrdn/Prce 5.00 12.00
QMLAL West/Chmbrln/Brnt/O'Nl 25.00 60.00
QMMIN Wggns/Twns/Grntt/LVne 10.00 25.00
QMOKC Wstbrk/Adms/Drnt/Ibka 15.00 40.00
QMORL Fournier/Oladipo/Gordon/Payton 3.00 8.00
QMPOR Drxlr/Lllrd/Dckwrth/Rbnsn 8.00 20.00
QMSAS Dmpr/Rbnsn/Grvn/Dncn 10.00 25.00
QMUTA Favors/Hayward/Hood/Burke 4.00 10.00

2015-16 Immaculate Collection Rookie Patch Autographs Jersey Number

*JSY NUM p/r 20-55: .6X TO 1.5X BASIC
RANDOM INSERTS IN PACKS
PRINT RUNS B/WN 1-55 COPIES PER
NO PRICING ON QTY 17 OR LESS
EXCHANGE DEADLINE 3/14/2018
101 Karl-Anthony Towns/32 2200.00 3000.00
103 Frank Kaminsky/44 25.00 60.00
112 Trey Lyles/41 50.00 120.00
117 Emmanuel Mudiay/1
122 R. Hollis-Jefferson/24 100.00 250.00
140 R.J. Hunter/28 20.00 50.00
148 Myles Turner/33 400.00 600.00

2015-16 Immaculate Collection Rookie Patch Autographs Red

*RED: .5X TO 1.2X BASIC
RANDOM INSERTS IN PACKS
STATED PRINT RUN 25 SER.#'d SETS
EXCHANGE DEADLINE 3/14/2018
101 Karl-Anthony Towns 1500.00 2000.00
102 Jerian Grant 20.00 50.00
103 Frank Kaminsky 25.00 60.00
112 Trey Lyles 40.00 100.00
135 Kristaps Porzingis 500.00 1000.00
139 Larry Nance Jr. 40.00 100.00

2015-16 Immaculate Collection Shadowbox Signatures

RANDOM INSERTS IN PACKS
PRINT RUNS B/WN 60-99 COPIES PER
EXCHANGE DEADLINE 3/14/2018
SSN Nene/99 5.00 12.00
SSAB Avery Bradley/99 5.00 12.00
SSAC Antoine Carr/99 4.00 10.00
SSAD Adrian Dantley/99 5.00 12.00
SSAD Anthony Davis/60 40.00 100.00
SSAE Alex English/99 5.00 12.00
SSAG A.C. Green/99 6.00 15.00
SSAW Andrew Wiggins/60 30.00 80.00
SSBG Blake Griffin/60 20.00 50.00
SSBK Brandon Knight/99 5.00 12.00
SSBM Bob McAdoo/99 8.00 20.00
SSBP Bobby Portis/99 6.00 15.00
SSCB Chris Bosh/60 6.00 15.00
SSCM Calvin Murphy/99 5.00 12.00
SSCP Cameron Payne/99 5.00 12.00
SSDB Devin Booker/99 75.00 200.00
SSDC Dave Cowens/99 4.00 10.00
SSDG Danilo Gallinari/99 5.00 12.00
SSDR D'Angelo Russell/60 50.00 120.00
SSDS Dennis Schroder/99 5.00 12.00
SSDT David Thompson/99 5.00 12.00
SSDW Dwyane Wade/60 30.00 80.00
SSEG Eric Gordon/99 5.00 12.00
SSEM Emmanuel Mudiay/60 20.00 50.00
SSET Evan Turner/99 5.00 12.00
SSGG George Gervin/99 6.00 15.00
SSGH Grant Hill/60 15.00 40.00
SSGH Gerald Henderson/99 4.00 10.00
SSGH Gary Harris/99 5.00 12.00
SSGH Gordon Hayward/99 8.00 20.00
SSHG Horace Grant/99 6.00 15.00
SSJC Jae Crowder/99 4.00 10.00
SSJD Joe Dumars/99 6.00 15.00
SSJE Julius Erving/60 50.00 120.00
SSJG Jerian Grant/99 6.00 15.00
SSJH Jrue Holiday/99 5.00 12.00
SSJK Jason Kidd/60 15.00 40.00
SSJO Jahlil Okafor/60 30.00 80.00
SSJS Jonathon Simmons/99 8.00 20.00
SSJS John Stockton/60 25.00 60.00
SSJS Jerry Stackhouse/99 5.00 12.00
SSJT Jeff Teague/99 5.00 12.00
SSJW John Wall/60 25.00 60.00
SSJY Joe Young/99 5.00 12.00
SSKB Kobe Bryant/60 175.00 350.00
SSKB Kent Bazemore/99 5.00 12.00
SSKD Kevin Durant/60 50.00 120.00
SSKF Kenneth Faried/99 5.00 12.00
SSKI Kyrie Irving/60 50.00 120.00
SSKL Kevon Looney/99 5.00 12.00
SSKM Karl Malone/60 25.00 60.00
SSKO Kelly Oubre Jr./99 8.00 20.00
SSKP Kristaps Porzingis/99 75.00 200.00
SSKT Karl-Anthony Towns/60 125.00 250.00
SSLN Larry Nance Jr./99 15.00 40.00
SSMA Mark Aguirre/99 5.00 12.00
SSMF Michael Finley/99 6.00 15.00
SSMG Marcin Gortat/99 5.00 12.00
SSMJ Mark Jackson/99 5.00 12.00
SSMJ Marques Johnson/99 5.00 12.00
SSMJ Magic Johnson/60 40.00 100.00
SSMP Mason Plumlee/99 5.00 12.00
SSMT Myles Turner/99 40.00 100.00
SSNB Nicolas Batum/99 5.00 12.00
SSNJ Nikola Jokic/99 EXCH 60.00 150.00
SSNP Norman Powell/99 15.00 40.00
SSOR Oscar Robertson/60 30.00 80.00
SSPG Paul George/60 30.00 80.00
SSRF Rick Fox/99 6.00 15.00
SSRH Robert Horry/99 5.00 12.00
SSRH Ron Harper/99 6.00 15.00
SSRH Rondae Hollis-Jefferson/99 5.00 12.00
SSRN Raul Neto/99 4.00 10.00
SSRP Robert Parish/99 6.00 15.00
SSSB Shane Battier/99 8.00 20.00
SSSO Shaquille O'Neal/60 50.00 120.00
SSSW Spud Webb/99 5.00 12.00
SSTH Tim Hardaway/99 6.00 15.00
SSTK Toni Kukoc/99 8.00 20.00
SSTM Tracy McGrady/99 30.00 80.00
SSTM T.J. McConnell/99 5.00 12.00
SSTW T.J. Warren/99 5.00 12.00
SSWF Walt Frazier/99 8.00 20.00
SSZI Zydrunas Ilgauskas/99 5.00 12.00

2015-16 Immaculate Collection Signatures

RANDOM INSERTS IN PACKS
PRINT RUNS B/WN 40-99 COPIES PER
EXCHANGE DEADLINE 3/14/2018
*RED/25: .5X TO 1.2X BASIC
SAA Alvan Adams/99 4.00 10.00
SAB Avery Bradley/99 5.00 12.00
SAB Andrew Bogut/99 5.00 12.00
SAD Andre Drummond/99 8.00 20.00
SAD Anthony Davis/60 30.00 80.00
SAW Andrew Wiggins/60 25.00 60.00
SBG Blake Griffin/60 15.00 40.00
SBR Bill Russell/40 40.00 100.00
SCA Carmelo Anthony/60 20.00 50.00
SDC Dave Cowens/99 4.00 10.00
SDG Draymond Green/99 12.00 30.00
SDR David Robinson/60 20.00 50.00
SDR Dennis Rodman/60 20.00 50.00
SDT David Thompson/99 5.00 12.00
SDW Dwyane Wade/60 30.00 80.00
SEF Evan Fournier/99 5.00 12.00
SEP Elfrid Payton/99 5.00 12.00
SET Evan Turner/99 5.00 12.00
SGD Goran Dragic/99 5.00 12.00
SGG George Gervin/99 6.00 15.00
SGH Grant Hill/60 15.00 40.00
SGH Gordon Hayward/99 6.00 15.00
SHW Hassan Whiteside/99 12.00 30.00
SJC Jae Crowder/99 4.00 10.00
SJE Julius Erving/60 30.00 80.00
SJI Joe Ingles/99 4.00 10.00
SJP Jabari Parker/60 12.00 30.00
SKB Kobe Bryant/60 100.00 200.00
SKD Kevin Durant/60 50.00 120.00
SKI Kyrie Irving/60 30.00 80.00
SKT Klay Thompson/60 25.00 60.00
SMC Michael Carter-Williams/99 4.00 10.00
SPG Pau Gasol/60 10.00 25.00
SRG Rudy Gay/99 6.00 15.00
SSB Sam Bowie/99 4.00 10.00
SSM Sidney Moncrief/99 4.00 10.00
STK Toni Kukoc/99 6.00 15.00
SVO Victor Oladipo/60 5.00 12.00
SWM Wesley Matthews/99 4.00 10.00
SZL Zach LaVine/99 12.00 30.00

2015-16 Immaculate Collection Sneaker Swatches

RANDOM INSERTS IN PACKS
PRINT RUNS B/WN 1-60 COPIES PER
NO PRICING ON QTY 17 OR LESS
3 Carmelo Anthony/60 10.00 25.00
4 Grant Hill/60 15.00 40.00
5 Karl-Anthony Towns/38 25.00 60.00
6 Andrew Wiggins/60 8.00 20.00
7 John Wall/26 10.00 25.00
8 Andre Drummond/60 5.00 12.00
9 Dennis Rodman/32 30.00 80.00
10 Dominique Wilkins/44 12.00 30.00
11 Dwight Howard/60 4.00 10.00
14 Paul Pierce/42 10.00 25.00
15 Ray Allen/52 10.00 25.00
16 Eric Bledsoe/26 4.00 10.00
19 John Stockton/38 10.00 25.00
20 Derrick Rose/60 12.00 30.00
21 Shaquille O'Neal/60 15.00 40.00
22 Dante Exum/56 8.00 20.00
23 Karl Malone/60 10.00 25.00
24 Anfernee Hardaway/44 20.00 50.00
27 Kevin Durant/32 12.00 30.00
29 Robert Horry/27 5.00 12.00
30 Emmanuel Mudiay/56 5.00 12.00

2015-16 Immaculate Collection Sole of the Game

RANDOM INSERTS IN PACKS
PRINT RUNS B/WN 8-25 COPIES PER
NO PRICING ON QTY 18 OR LESS
1 Anthony Davis/25 50.00 125.00
2 Draymond Green/22 30.00 80.00
3 Carmelo Anthony/25 30.00 80.00
4 Grant Hill/25 50.00 120.00
5 Karl-Anthony Towns/20 75.00 200.00
6 Andrew Wiggins/25 40.00 100.00
7 John Wall/25 40.00 100.00
9 Dennis Rodman/25 50.00 125.00
11 Dwight Howard/25 20.00 50.00
12 LaMarcus Aldridge/25 25.00 60.00
13 Magic Johnson/24 60.00 150.00
16 Eric Bledsoe/20 20.00 50.00
18 Spud Webb/22 50.00 120.00
19 John Stockton/25 40.00 100.00
20 Derrick Rose/25 30.00 80.00
22 Dante Exum/25 20.00 50.00
26 D'Angelo Russell/25 60.00 150.00
27 Kevin Durant/25 60.00 150.00
30 Emmanuel Mudiay/25 25.00 60.00

2015-16 Immaculate Collection Standard Materials

RANDOM INSERTS IN PACKS
PRINT RUNS B/WN 13-75 COPIES PER
NO PRICING ON QTY 13
STABR Avery Bradley/75 3.00 8.00
STADA Anthony Davis/75 6.00 15.00
STADR Andre Drummond/75 4.00 10.00
STAHA Anfernee Hardaway/75 8.00 20.00
STAIG Andre Iguodala/75 3.00 8.00
STAMO Alonzo Mourning/75 6.00 15.00
STAWI Andrew Wiggins/75 6.00 15.00
STBGR Blake Griffin/75 4.00 10.00
STBKN Brandon Knight/75 3.00 8.00
STBLO Brook Lopez/75 3.00 8.00
STBPO Bobby Portis/75 4.00 10.00
STCAN Carmelo Anthony/75 5.00 12.00
STCBO Chris Bosh/75 4.00 10.00
STCCA Clint Capela/75 3.00 8.00
STCDR Clyde Drexler/75 5.00 12.00
STCMC C.J. McCollum/75 4.00 10.00
STCPA Chris Paul/75 5.00 12.00
STCPA Chandler Parsons/75 3.00 8.00
STCWE Chris Webber/75 6.00 15.00
STDBO Devin Booker/75 8.00 20.00
STDCA DeMarre Carroll/75 2.50 6.00
STDCO DeMarcus Cousins/75 4.00 10.00
STDDE DeMar DeRozan/75 4.00 10.00
STDGA Danilo Gallinari/75 3.00 8.00
STDGR Draymond Green/75 5.00 12.00
STDHO Dwight Howard/75 3.00 8.00
STDLI Damian Lillard/75 6.00 15.00
STDNO Dirk Nowitzki/75 5.00 12.00
STDRO Derrick Rose/75 5.00 12.00
STDRP David Robinson/75 6.00 15.00
STDWA Dwyane Wade/75 6.00 15.00
STDWI Deron Williams/75 3.00 8.00
STDWI Dominique Wilkins/52 5.00 12.00
STEBL Eric Bledsoe/75 3.00 8.00
STEGO Eric Gordon/75 3.00 8.00
STEMU Emmanuel Mudiay/75 4.00 10.00
STEPA Elfrid Payton/75 3.00 8.00
STFKA Frank Kaminsky/75 4.00 10.00
STGAN G. Antetokounmpo/75 8.00 20.00
STGHA Gordon Hayward/75 4.00 10.00
STITH Isaiah Thomas/75 4.00 10.00
STJBU Jimmy Butler/75 4.00 10.00
STJER Julius Erving/75 6.00 15.00
STJGR Jerian Grant/75 2.50 6.00
STJHA James Harden/75 6.00 15.00
STJHO Jrue Holiday/75 3.00 8.00
STJKI Jason Kidd/75 4.00 10.00
STJOK Jahlil Okafor/75 5.00 12.00
STJPA Jabari Parker/75 5.00 12.00
STJRA Julius Randle/75 4.00 10.00
STJTE Jeff Teague/75 3.00 8.00
STJWA John Wall/75 5.00 12.00
STJWI Justise Winslow/75 4.00 10.00
STKBR Kobe Bryant/75 15.00 40.00
STKCP Kentavious Caldwell-Pope/75 3.00 8.00
STKDU Kevin Durant/75 8.00 20.00
STKFA Kenneth Faried/75 3.00 8.00
STKGA Kevin Garnett/75 6.00 15.00
STKIR Kyrie Irving/75 6.00 15.00
STKLE Kawhi Leonard/75 6.00 15.00
STKLO Kyle Lowry/75 3.00 8.00
STKLO Kevin Love/75 4.00 10.00
STKMC Kevin McHale/75 4.00 10.00
STKMI Khris Middleton/75 3.00 8.00
STKOU Kelly Oubre Jr./75 3.00 8.00
STKTH Klay Thompson/75 5.00 12.00
STKWA Kemba Walker/75 4.00 10.00
STLAL LaMarcus Aldridge/75 4.00 10.00
STLBI Larry Bird/75 8.00 20.00
STLJA LeBron James/75 15.00 40.00
STMCO Mike Conley/75 4.00 10.00
STMEL Monta Ellis/75 3.00 8.00
STMGA Marc Gasol/75 4.00 10.00
STMHE Mario Hezonja/75 3.00 8.00
STNBA Nicolas Batum/75 3.00 8.00
STNNO Nerlens Noel/75 3.00 8.00
STNVU Nikola Vucevic/75 3.00 8.00
STPEW Patrick Ewing/75 5.00 12.00
STPGE Paul George/75 5.00 12.00
STPMI Paul Millsap/75 4.00 10.00
STPPI Paul Pierce/75 4.00 10.00
STRAL Ray Allen/75 4.00 10.00
STRGA Rudy Gay/75 4.00 10.00
STRGO Rudy Gobert/75 4.00 10.00
STRWE Russell Westbrook/75 10.00 25.00
STSCU Stephen Curry/75 15.00 40.00
STSIB Serge Ibaka/75 3.00 8.00
STSJO Stanley Johnson/75 3.00 8.00
STSPI Scottie Pippen/75 10.00 25.00
STTDU Tim Duncan/75 6.00 15.00
STTJO Tyus Jones/75 4.00 10.00
STTLY Trey Lyles/75 4.00 10.00
STTYO Thaddeus Young/75 2.50 6.00
STVOL Victor Oladipo/75 3.00 8.00
STWCH Wilt Chamberlain/75 30.00 80.00
STWCS Willie Cauley-Stein/75 4.00 10.00
STZRA Zach Randolph/75 3.00 8.00

2015-16 Immaculate Collection Trio Autographs

RANDOM INSERTS IN PACKS
PRINT RUNS B/WN 15-25 COPIES PER
NO PRICING ON QTY 15
EXCHANGE DEADLINE 3/14/2018
1 Towns/Jones/Bjelica/25 150.00 250.00
2 Twns/Lyls/Cly-Stn/25 300.00 500.00
3 Smth/Dllvdva/Mzgv/25 30.00 80.00
4 Gnns/Crtr-Wllms/Prkr/25 EXCH 100.00 200.00
5 Grant/Grant/Grant/25 25.00 60.00
6 Kaminsky/Dukan/Dekker/25 EXCH 40.00 100.00
7 Oldpo/Pytn/Hznja/25 25.00 60.00
9 Lnrd/Prkr/Aldrdge/25 EXCH 400.00 800.00
12 Lanier/Johnson/Moncrief/25 40.00 100.00
13 Dandridge/Hayes/Unseld/25 40.00 100.00
14 Lanier/Drummond/Laimbeer/25 40.00 100.00
15 Bryant/Shaq/Horry/25 1200.00 1600.00
16 Motiejunas/Ilgauskas/Valanciunas/25 EXCH 30.00 80.00
17 Jcksn/Hstn/Sprwll/25 150.00 300.00
19 Mshbrn/Kidd/Jcksn/25 200.00 400.00
22 Cwns/Nlsn/Whte/25 50.00 120.00
23 Frazier/Reed/Monroe/25 EXCH 40.00 100.00
25 Brd/Magic/Erving/25 500.00 1000.00

2015-16 Immaculate Collection Trio Materials

RANDOM INSERTS IN PACKS
STATED PRINT RUN 49 SER.#'d SETS
TMATL Korver/Millsap/Horford 4.00 10.00
TMBOS Brdly/Thms/Crwdr 12.00 30.00
TMCHA Walker/Jefferson/Lamb 4.00 10.00
TMCHI Rose/Butler/Gasol 5.00 12.00
TMCLE Irvng/Lve/Jms 30.00 80.00
TMDAL Jackson/Mashburn/Kidd 4.00 10.00
TMDAL Prsns/Wllms/Nwtzki 5.00 12.00
TMDET Drummond/Morris/Jackson 4.00 10.00
TMHOU Drxlr/Oljwn/Horry 8.00 20.00
TMLAC Griffin/Paul/Jordan 5.00 12.00
TMLAL Clrksn/Wrld Pce/Brnt 12.00 30.00
TMOKC Wstbrk/Ibka/Drnt 8.00 20.00
TMORL Payton/Vucevic/Oladipo 3.00 8.00
TMORL Hrdwy/Andrsn/O'Neal 10.00 25.00
TMPOR McCllm/Lllrd/Plmle 6.00 15.00
TMSAS Gnbli/Prkr/Dncn 10.00 25.00
TMTOR DeRozan/Carroll/Lowry 4.00 10.00
TMUTA Hood/Burke/Gobert 4.00 10.00
TMWAS Beal/Porter/Wall 5.00 12.00

1991 Impel U.S. Olympic Hall of Fame

Produced by Impel Marketing Inc., this 90-card set salutes members of the U.S. Olympic Hall of Fame. A portion of the proceeds from the sale of these cards supported the 1992 U.S. Olympic team. The cards were available in 15-card packs, and collectors could obtain a collector's album to display the set for $12.99 plus $3.00 postage and handling. Also the cards were packaged in sets of three, along with a "Medals and Millions" game piece, inside specially-marked multi-packs of Coca-Cola products in a promotion cosponsored by Coca-Cola U.S.A. and CBS. Six cards from the set (Beamon, Fleming, Jenner, Owens, Rudolph, and Spitz) were issued as prototypes in a cello pack; they are unnumbered and clearly marked as such on the backs in the upper right corner. The fronts display a mix of color and black-and-white photos inside a gold inner border. The outer border is light gray, and a red, white, and blue ribbon cuts across the middle of the card. The backs carry a closeup photo, career summary, and career highlights.

COMPLETE SET (90) 6.00 15.00
55 Bill Bradley .20 .50
56 Lucious Jackson .12 .30
57 1964 U.S. Basketball Team .12 .30
Soviet player
58 Bill Bradley .20 .50
59 1964 U.S. Basketball Team Photo .12 .30
60 Lucious Jackson .20 .50
Bill Bradley
61 Henry Iba CO .12 .30
74 Henry Iba .10 .25

1992 Impel U.S. Olympic Hopefuls

COMPLETE SET (110) 8.00 20.00
7 U.S. Olympic Baseball Team .20 .50
8 Charles Barkley BK .40 1.00
9 Larry Bird BK .75 2.00
10 Patrick Ewing BK .30 .75
11 Magic Johnson BK .60 1.50
12 Michael Jordan BK 2.00 5.00
13 Karl Malone BK .40 1.00
14 Chris Mullin BK .20 .50
15 Scottie Pippen BK .50 1.25
16 David Robinson BK .50 1.25
17 John Stockton BK .30 .75
18 U.S. Olympic Basketball Team .10 .25
19 Teresa Edwards BK .10 .25
20 Bridgette Gordon BK .10 .25
21 Andrea Lloyd BK .10 .25
22 Katrina McClain BK .10 .25

1994-95 Imprinted Pins

Produced by Imprinted Products Corporation, this 28-pin set includes the 27 current NBA teams as well as the two new expansion teams, the Toronto Raptors and Vancouver Grizzlies. The pins were packaged in a clam-shell design that allowed consumers to view the team pins.

COMPLETE SET (29) 20.00 50.00
1 Atlanta Hawks .75 2.00
2 Boston Celtics 1.25 3.00
3 Charlotte Hornets .75 2.00
4 Chicago Bulls 1.25 3.00
5 Cleveland Cavaliers .75 2.00
6 Dallas Mavericks .75 2.00
7 Denver Nuggets .75 2.00
8 Detroit Pistons .75 2.00
9 Golden State Warriors .75 2.00
10 Houston Rockets .75 2.00
11 Indiana Pacers .75 2.00
12 Los Angeles Clippers .75 2.00
13 Los Angeles Lakers 1.25 3.00
14 Miami Heat .75 2.00
15 Milwaukee Bucks .75 2.00
16 Minnesota Timberwolves .75 2.00
17 New Jersey Nets .75 2.00
18 New York Knicks 1.25 3.00
19 Orlando Magic 1.25 3.00
20 Philadelphia 76ers .75 2.00
21 Phoenix Suns .75 2.00
22 Portland Trail Blazers .75 2.00
23 Sacramento Kings .75 2.00
24 San Antonio Spurs .75 2.00
25 Seattle Supersonics .75 2.00
26 Toronto Raptors .75 2.00
27 Utah Jazz .75 2.00
28 Vancouver Grizzlies .75 2.00
29 Washington Bullets .75 2.00

2007-08 ITG Ultimate Memorabilia Cityscapes

STATED PRINT RUN 24 SERIAL #'d SETS
2 I.Kovalchuk/D.Wilkins 10.00 25.00

2011 In The Game Canadiana Mega Memorabilia Silver

MM37 Steve Nash L 10.00 20.00

2011 In The Game Canadiana Red

BLUE/50: .75X TO 2X BASIC RED
UNPRICED ONYX ANNOUNCED RUN 5
ANNOUNCED PRINT RUN 180 SETS
41 James Naismith .60 1.50

2012-13 Innovation

101-175 PRINT RUN 349 SER.#'d SETS
176-200 PRINT RUN 349 SER.#'d SETS
1 Serge Ibaka .60 1.50
2 Tony Parker .75 2.00
3 Shawn Marion .60 1.50
4 Jameer Nelson .50 1.25
5 Chris Bosh .75 2.00
6 Taj Gibson .60 1.50
7 Dwight Howard .60 1.50
8 Tyson Chandler .60 1.50
9 Grant Hill 1.00 2.50
10 James Harden 1.25 3.00
11 Nene .60 1.50
12 Kevin Love .75 2.00
13 Dirk Nowitzki 1.00 2.50
14 Raymond Felton .60 1.50
15 O.J. Mayo .50 1.25
16 Jason Kidd .75 2.00
17 Gerald Henderson .50 1.25
18 Russell Westbrook 2.00 5.00
19 LaMarcus Aldridge .75 2.00
20 Ray Allen .75 2.00
21 Jeremy Lin .75 2.00
22 Larry Sanders .50 1.25
23 LeBron James 3.00 8.00
24 Joakim Noah .60 1.50
25 Ersan Ilyasova .50 1.25
26 Steve Novak .50 1.25
27 Andrew Bogut .60 1.50
28 Jrue Holiday .75 2.00
29 Paul George 1.00 2.50
30 Marc Gasol .75 2.00
31 Manu Ginobili .75 2.00
32 Eric Gordon .60 1.50
33 Anderson Varejao .50 1.25
34 Vince Carter 1.00 2.50
35 JaVale McGee .60 1.50
36 Roy Hibbert .60 1.50

37 DeMarcus Cousins .75 2.00
38 Andre Miller .60 1.50
39 Blake Griffin .75 2.00
40 Nicolas Batum .60 1.50
41 John Wall 1.00 2.50
42 Metta World Peace .75 2.00
43 Tim Duncan 1.25 3.00
44 Stephen Curry 3.00 8.00
45 Brandon Jennings .50 1.25
46 Kevin Martin .60 1.50
47 Goran Dragic .60 1.50
48 Ricky Rubio .75 2.00
49 Tyreke Evans .50 1.25
50 Derrick Rose 1.00 2.50
51 Greivis Vasquez .60 1.50
52 Jose Calderon .50 1.25
53 Kobe Bryant 3.00 8.00
54 Marcin Gortat .60 1.50
55 Josh Smith .60 1.50
56 Jeff Teague .60 1.50
57 Rudy Gay .75 2.00
58 Ty Lawson .50 1.25
59 Chris Paul 1.00 2.50
60 David West .60 1.50
61 Paul Pierce .75 2.00
62 Joe Johnson .60 1.50
63 Andre Iguodala .60 1.50
64 Brook Lopez .60 1.50
65 Al Jefferson .60 1.50
66 Dwyane Wade 1.25 3.00
67 Carmelo Anthony 1.00 2.50
68 Ben Gordon .60 1.50
69 Jamal Crawford .75 2.00
70 Deron Williams .60 1.50
71 Greg Monroe .60 1.50
72 Al Horford .60 1.50
73 Rajon Rondo .75 2.00
74 Chauncey Billups .75 2.00
75 Nick Young .60 1.50
76 J.J. Redick .75 2.00
77 Kevin Garnett 1.25 3.00
78 Luol Deng .60 1.50
79 Kyle Lowry .60 1.50
80 Kevin Durant 2.00 5.00
81 Evan Turner .50 1.25
82 David Lee .50 1.25
83 Steve Nash .75 2.00
84 Gordon Hayward .75 2.00
85 Zach Randolph .60 1.50
86 Dominique Wilkins 1.00 2.50
87 Magic Johnson 2.00 5.00
88 Yao Ming 1.00 2.50
89 Shaquille O'Neal 1.50 4.00
90 Scottie Pippen 1.50 4.00
91 Pete Maravich 1.25 3.00
92 Bill Walton .75 2.00
93 David Robinson 1.25 3.00
94 Dennis Rodman 1.50 4.00
95 Hakeem Olajuwon 1.00 2.50
96 Jerry West 1.00 2.50
97 Larry Bird 2.00 5.00
98 Kareem Abdul-Jabbar 1.25 3.00
99 Julius Erving 1.25 3.00
100 Nate Archibald .60 1.50
101 Tyler Zeller RC 1.50 4.00
102 Jimmy Butler RC 6.00 15.00
103 Tristan Thompson RC 2.00 5.00
104 Nikola Vucevic RC 2.00 5.00
105 Mirza Teletovic RC 1.50 4.00
106 E'Twaun Moore RC 1.25 3.00
107 Harrison Barnes RC 3.00 8.00
108 DeAndre Liggins RC 1.50 4.00
109 Kenneth Faried RC 2.00 5.00
110 Enes Kanter RC 1.50 4.00
111 Brian Roberts RC 1.25 3.00
112 Kent Bazemore RC 2.00 5.00
113 Kawhi Leonard RC 10.00 25.00
114 Chandler Parsons RC 2.00 5.00
115 Gustavo Ayon RC 1.25 3.00
116 Jeff Taylor RC 1.25 3.00
117 Klay Thompson RC 8.00 20.00
118 Pablo Prigioni RC 1.25 3.00
119 Nolan Smith RC 1.25 3.00
120 Kim English RC 1.25 3.00
121 Derrick Williams RC 1.25 3.00
122 Miles Plumlee RC 1.25 3.00
123 Michael Kidd-Gilchrist RC 2.00 5.00
124 Kyle Singler RC 1.25 3.00
125 Darius Miller RC 1.25 3.00
126 Isaiah Thomas RC 3.00 8.00
127 Alexey Shved RC 1.25 3.00
128 Jonas Valanciunas RC 2.00 5.00
129 Darius Morris RC 1.25 3.00
130 Alec Burks RC 2.00 5.00
131 Julyan Stone RC 1.25 3.00
132 Kemba Walker RC 4.00 10.00
133 Jae Crowder RC 1.50 4.00
134 Terrence Jones RC 1.50 4.00
135 Evan Fournier RC 2.00 5.00
136 Meyers Leonard RC 1.50 4.00
137 Markieff Morris RC 2.00 5.00
138 Victor Claver RC 1.25 3.00
139 Jeremy Lamb RC 2.00 5.00
140 Jeremy Pargo RC 1.25 3.00
141 Jimmer Fredette RC 1.25 3.00
142 Damian Lillard RC 8.00 20.00
143 Festus Ezeli RC 1.50 4.00
144 Jan Vesely RC 1.25 3.00
145 Iman Shumpert RC 2.00 5.00
146 Tobias Harris RC 2.00 5.00
147 Austin Rivers RC 2.00 5.00
148 Reggie Jackson RC 2.00 5.00
149 Greg Stiemsma RC 1.25 3.00
150 Chris Copeland RC 1.25 3.00
151 Will Barton RC 1.50 4.00
152 Andre Drummond RC 3.00 8.00
153 Anthony Davis RC 10.00 25.00
154 John Henson RC 2.00 5.00
155 Orlando Johnson RC 1.25 3.00
156 Brandon Knight RC 2.00 5.00
157 Andrew Nicholson RC 1.25 3.00
158 Draymond Green RC 6.00 15.00
159 Terrence Ross RC 2.00 5.00
160 MarShon Brooks RC 1.50 4.00
161 Kyrie Irving RC 10.00 25.00
162 Marcus Morris RC 1.50 4.00
163 Lavoy Allen RC 1.25 3.00
164 Thomas Robinson RC 1.50 4.00
165 Jared Cunningham RC 1.25 3.00
166 Jared Sullinger RC 1.50 4.00
167 Nando De Colo RC 1.25 3.00
168 Bradley Beal RC 3.00 8.00
169 Tornike Shengelia RC 1.25 3.00
170 Lance Thomas RC 1.25 3.00
171 Norris Cole RC 1.25 3.00
172 Jordan Hamilton RC 1.25 3.00
173 Kendall Marshall RC 1.25 3.00
174 Dion Waiters RC 2.00 5.00
175 John Jenkins RC 1.25 3.00
176 Kobe Bryant/349 6.00 15.00
177 Tyson Chandler/349 1.25 3.00
178 Ricky Rubio/349 1.50 4.00
179 Deron Williams/349 1.25 3.00
180 John Wall/349 2.00 5.00
181 Chris Paul/349 2.00 5.00
182 Carmelo Anthony/349 2.00 5.00
183 Paul George/349 2.00 5.00
184 Derrick Rose/349 2.00 5.00
185 Kevin Durant/349 4.00 10.00
186 Steve Nash/349 1.50 4.00
187 Dwyane Wade/349 2.50 6.00
188 Kevin Garnett/349 2.50 6.00
189 Joakim Noah/349 1.25 3.00
190 Russell Westbrook/349 4.00 10.00
191 Dirk Nowitzki/349 2.00 5.00
192 LeBron James/349 6.00 15.00
193 Paul Pierce/349 1.50 4.00
194 Andre Iguodala/349 1.25 3.00
195 James Harden/349 2.50 6.00
196 Vince Carter/349 2.00 5.00
197 Kevin Love/349 1.50 4.00
198 Rajon Rondo/349 1.50 4.00
199 Stephen Curry/349 6.00 15.00
200 Blake Griffin/349 1.50 4.00

2012-13 Innovation Red

*RED 101-175: 1.2X TO 3X BASIC
*RED 175-200: 1.5X TO 4X BASIC
STATED PRINT RUN 25 SER.#'d SETS

2012-13 Innovation All Rookies

1 Kyrie Irving 12.00 30.00
2 Bradley Beal 4.00 10.00
3 Andre Drummond 4.00 10.00
4 Anthony Davis 12.00 30.00
5 Kenneth Faried 2.50 6.00
6 Harrison Barnes 4.00 10.00
7 Damian Lillard 10.00 25.00
8 Kemba Walker 5.00 12.00
9 Chandler Parsons 2.50 6.00
10 Dion Waiters 2.50 6.00

2012-13 Innovation Efficiency

1 Joakim Noah 1.25 3.00
2 James Harden 2.50 6.00
3 David Lee 1.00 2.50
4 Blake Griffin 1.50 4.00
5 Carmelo Anthony 2.00 5.00
6 Chris Paul 2.00 5.00
7 LaMarcus Aldridge 1.50 4.00
8 Kevin Love 1.50 4.00
9 Nikola Vucevic 1.50 4.00
10 Rajon Rondo 1.50 4.00
11 Tony Parker 1.50 4.00
12 LeBron James 6.00 15.00
13 Deron Williams 1.25 3.00
14 Russell Westbrook 4.00 10.00
15 Tim Duncan 2.50 6.00

2012-13 Innovation Fine Print Autographs

EXCHANGE DEADLINE 03/04/2015
1 Nikola Pekovic 2.00 5.00
2 Mark Price 3.00 8.00
3 Kevin Durant 50.00 120.00
4 Mario Chalmers 2.50 6.00
5 Jarrett Jack 2.50 6.00
6 Danilo Gallinari 2.00 5.00
7 Ryan Anderson 2.50 6.00
8 Kobe Bryant 75.00 150.00
9 Walt Frazier 8.00 20.00
10 Antawn Jamison 2.50 6.00
11 Cedric Ceballos 2.00 5.00
12 Antoine Walker 2.50 6.00
13 Elvin Hayes 3.00 8.00
14 James Worthy 12.00 30.00
15 Jason Terry 2.50 6.00
16 Jeff Green 2.50 6.00
17 Ed Davis 2.00 5.00
18 Alan Anderson 2.00 5.00
19 Tim Hardaway 8.00 20.00
20 Joel Anthony 2.00 5.00
21 Blake Griffin 20.00 50.00
22 George Gervin 3.00 8.00
23 Nick Anderson 3.00 8.00
24 Arnie Risen 15.00 40.00
25 George McGinnis 2.00 5.00
26 Jerry West 20.00 50.00
27 Patrick Beverley 2.00 5.00
28 Tom Chambers 2.50 6.00
29 Hakeem Olajuwon 10.00 25.00
30 Jim Jackson 2.00 5.00
31 Randy Foye 2.00 5.00
32 Clyde Drexler 10.00 25.00
33 Alex English 2.50 6.00
34 Doug Christie 2.00 5.00
35 Kevin Martin 2.50 6.00
36 Nick Collison 2.50 6.00
37 Greg Monroe 2.50 6.00
38 Wesley Matthews 2.00 5.00
39 Serge Ibaka 2.50 6.00
40 Rick Mahorn 2.00 5.00
41 DeMarcus Cousins 3.00 8.00
42 Nate Archibald 2.50 6.00
43 David Robinson 15.00 40.00
44 Jerryd Bayless 2.50 6.00
45 Anfernee Hardaway 15.00 40.00
46 Jay Williams 2.00 5.00
47 Roy Hibbert 2.50 6.00
48 Chris Bosh 3.00 8.00
49 Tyson Chandler 2.50 6.00
50 J.J. Redick 3.00 8.00
51 Damian Lillard 75.00 150.00

2012-13 Innovation Innovative Ink

EXCHANGE DEADLINE 03/04/2015
1 Chris Bosh 5.00 12.00
2 Steve Nash 20.00 50.00
3 Josh Smith
4 Blake Griffin 12.00 30.00
5 Kobe Bryant 100.00 200.00
6 Ryan Anderson 4.00 10.00
7 George Hill 4.00 10.00
8 J.J. Redick 5.00 12.00
9 Antawn Jamison 4.00 10.00
10 Jarrett Jack 4.00 10.00
11 Gordon Hayward 8.00 20.00
12 Grant Hill 10.00 25.00
13 Andre Iguodala 4.00 10.00
14 Stephen Curry 100.00 200.00
15 Anderson Varejao 3.00 8.00
16 Andre Miller 4.00 10.00
17 Nick Young 4.00 10.00
18 Larry Bird 30.00 80.00
19 Magic Johnson 30.00 80.00
20 Bill Russell 50.00 120.00
21 Chris Mullin 5.00 12.00
22 Bernard King 4.00 10.00
23 Greg Monroe 4.00 10.00
24 Taj Gibson 4.00 10.00
25 Kevin Durant 50.00 120.00
26 Tom Chambers 4.00 10.00
27 Rashard Lewis 4.00 10.00
28 Earl Clark 3.00 8.00
29 Courtney Lee 4.00 10.00
30 Marcus Camby 4.00 10.00
31 Jamaal Wilkes 5.00 12.00
32 Kyle Korver 4.00 10.00
33 Kyle Lowry 4.00 10.00
34 Dan Issel 4.00 10.00
35 Sean Elliott 5.00 12.00
36 Dorell Wright 3.00 8.00
37 Ronnie Brewer 4.00 10.00
38 Tim Hardaway 5.00 12.00
39 Anfernee Hardaway 15.00 40.00
40 Udonis Haslem 3.00 8.00

2012-13 Innovation Innovators

1 Dominique Wilkins 2.00 5.00
2 Kareem Abdul-Jabbar 2.50 6.00
3 Gary Payton 1.50 4.00
4 Shaquille O'Neal 3.00 8.00
5 Allen Iverson 2.00 5.00
6 Bill Russell 2.50 6.00
7 Hakeem Olajuwon 2.00 5.00
8 Bernard King 1.25 3.00
9 David Robinson 2.50 6.00
10 Dennis Rodman 3.00 8.00
11 Ray Allen 1.50 4.00
12 Kevin Garnett 2.50 6.00
13 Kyrie Irving 8.00 20.00
14 Kevin Durant 4.00 10.00
15 Dwyane Wade 2.50 6.00
16 Tim Duncan 2.50 6.00
17 Carmelo Anthony 2.00 5.00
18 LeBron James 6.00 15.00
19 Dirk Nowitzki 2.00 5.00
20 Kobe Bryant 6.00 15.00

2012-13 Innovation Jerseys

PRINT RUNS B/WN 49-199 COPIES PER
1 Joakim Noah/49 3.00 8.00
2 Emeka Okafor/49 3.00 8.00
3 Tony Parker/49 4.00 10.00
4 Goran Dragic/99 3.00 8.00
5 Kevin Durant/99 10.00 25.00
6 Eric Gordon/99 3.00 8.00
7 Ray Allen/49 4.00 10.00
8 Kobe Bryant/99 15.00 40.00
9 James Harden/99 6.00 15.00
10 Dirk Nowitzki/199 5.00 12.00
11 Deron Williams/49 3.00 8.00
12 Al Horford/199 3.00 8.00
13 Mo Williams/99 3.00 8.00
14 Tim Duncan/199 6.00 15.00
15 Jameer Nelson/199 2.50 6.00
16 Tyson Chandler/99 3.00 8.00
17 Ricky Rubio/199 4.00 10.00
18 LeBron James/99 12.00 30.00
19 Dwight Howard/199 3.00 8.00
20 Carl Landry/49 2.50 6.00
21 O.J. Mayo/199 2.50 6.00
22 Brandon Bass/99 2.50 6.00
23 Carlos Boozer/49
24 Derrick Favors/99 3.00 8.00
25 Tyreke Evans/99 2.50 6.00
26 Glen Davis/99 2.50 6.00
27 Marcus Camby/49 3.00 8.00
28 Kevin Love/199 4.00 10.00
29 Dwyane Wade/99 5.00 12.00
30 Jamal Crawford/99 4.00 10.00
31 Stephen Curry/199 10.00 25.00
32 Anderson Varejao/99 2.50 6.00
33 Paul Pierce/99 4.00 10.00
34 Devin Harris/99 2.50 6.00
35 Al Jefferson/99 3.00 8.00
36 DeMarcus Cousins/99 4.00 10.00
37 Arron Afflalo/99 3.00 8.00
38 Kurt Thomas/199 2.50 6.00
39 Andrei Kirilenko/99 3.00 8.00
40 Zach Randolph/199 3.00 8.00
41 DeAndre Jordan/49 4.00 10.00
42 David Lee/99 2.50 6.00
43 Ben Gordon/199 3.00 8.00
44 Kevin Garnett/49 6.00 15.00
45 Nene/149 3.00 8.00
46 Rudy Gay/199 4.00 10.00
47 LaMarcus Aldridge/99 4.00 10.00
48 Serge Ibaka/199 3.00 8.00
49 Jason Kidd/199 4.00 10.00
50 Monta Ellis/49
51 Tayshaun Prince/199 3.00 8.00
52 Blake Griffin/99 4.00 10.00
53 Greg Monroe/49 3.00 8.00
54 Joe Johnson/99 3.00 8.00
55 Rajon Rondo/99 4.00 10.00
56 Derrick Rose/49 5.00 12.00
57 DeMar DeRozan/199 4.00 10.00
58 Marcin Gortat/99
59 Russell Westbrook/149 10.00 25.00
60 Carmelo Anthony/99 5.00 12.00
61 Drew Gooden/199 3.00 8.00
62 Marc Gasol/49 4.00 10.00
63 Paul George/99 10.00 25.00
64 Andre Iguodala/99
65 Brook Lopez/99 3.00 8.00
66 John Wall/199 5.00 12.00
67 Josh Smith/199 3.00 8.00
68 Andrea Bargnani/199 3.00 8.00
69 Luis Scola/99 3.00 8.00
70 Kevin Martin/99 3.00 8.00
71 Amare Stoudemire/199 3.00 8.00
72 Brandon Jennings/199 2.50 6.00
73 Steve Nash/99 4.00 10.00
74 Jeremy Lin/99 4.00 10.00
75 Elton Brand/99 4.00 10.00

2012-13 Innovation Laser Cut

1 Kevin Love 4.00 10.00
2 Tony Parker 4.00 10.00
3 Chris Bosh 4.00 10.00
4 Dwight Howard 3.00 8.00
5 Tyson Chandler 3.00 8.00
6 Grant Hill 5.00 12.00
7 Paul George 5.00 12.00
8 James Harden 6.00 15.00
9 Dirk Nowitzki 5.00 12.00
10 Russell Westbrook 10.00 25.00
11 Marc Gasol 4.00 10.00
12 Ersan Ilyasova 2.50 6.00
13 Eric Gordon 3.00 8.00
14 Jrue Holiday 4.00 10.00
15 LaMarcus Aldridge 4.00 10.00
16 Ray Allen 4.00 10.00
17 Jeremy Lin 4.00 10.00
18 LeBron James 30.00 80.00
19 Joakim Noah 3.00 8.00
20 Vince Carter 5.00 12.00
21 Jonas Valanciunas 4.00 10.00
22 Kemba Walker 8.00 20.00
23 Jimmer Fredette 2.50 6.00
24 Damian Lillard 25.00 60.00
25 Andre Iguodala 3.00 8.00
26 Al Jefferson 3.00 8.00
27 Dwyane Wade 6.00 15.00
28 Andre Drummond 6.00 15.00
29 Harrison Barnes 6.00 15.00
30 DeMarcus Cousins 4.00 10.00
31 Blake Griffin 4.00 10.00
32 Tyreke Evans 2.50 6.00
33 John Wall 5.00 12.00
34 Tim Duncan 6.00 15.00
35 Stephen Curry 15.00 40.00
36 Brandon Jennings 2.50 6.00
37 Carmelo Anthony 5.00 12.00
38 Goran Dragic 3.00 8.00
39 Ricky Rubio 4.00 10.00
40 Kobe Bryant 15.00 40.00
41 Derrick Rose 20.00 50.00
42 David West 3.00 8.00
43 Chris Paul 5.00 12.00
44 Marcin Gortat 3.00 8.00
45 Josh Smith 3.00 8.00
46 Rudy Gay 4.00 10.00
47 Paul Pierce 4.00 10.00
48 Kyrie Irving 20.00 50.00
49 Andrew Nicholson 2.50 6.00
50 Michael Kidd-Gilchrist 4.00 10.00
51 Gordon Hayward 4.00 10.00
52 Zach Randolph 3.00 8.00
53 Dominique Wilkins 5.00 12.00
54 Magic Johnson 10.00 25.00
55 Shaquille O'Neal 8.00 20.00
56 David Robinson 6.00 15.00
57 Anfernee Hardaway 10.00 25.00
58 Larry Bird 15.00 40.00
59 Julius Erving 6.00 15.00
60 Kenneth Faried 4.00 10.00
61 Bradley Beal 6.00 15.00
62 Anthony Davis 20.00 50.00
63 Deron Williams 3.00 8.00
64 Kawhi Leonard 20.00 50.00
65 Chandler Parsons 4.00 10.00
66 Rajon Rondo 4.00 10.00
67 Klay Thompson 15.00 40.00
68 Greg Monroe 3.00 8.00
69 Nikola Vucevic 4.00 10.00
70 Brandon Knight 4.00 10.00
71 Dion Waiters 4.00 10.00
72 Kevin Garnett 6.00 15.00
73 Kevin Durant 10.00 25.00
74 David Lee 2.50 6.00
75 Steve Nash 4.00 10.00

2012-13 Innovation Laser Cut Accomplishments

1 Steve Nash 15.00 40.00
4 Grant Hill 15.00 40.00
9 Rajon Rondo 12.00 30.00
10 Tracy McGrady 12.00 30.00
12 Derrick Rose 15.00 40.00
17 Chris Bosh 5.00 12.00
19 Kyrie Irving 60.00 150.00
22 Blake Griffin 15.00 40.00
24 Tony Parker 6.00 15.00

2012-13 Innovation Passing Grade

1 Steve Nash 1.25 3.00
2 Jason Kidd 1.25 3.00
3 Damian Lillard 5.00 12.00
4 Ricky Rubio 1.25 3.00
5 Jrue Holiday 1.25 3.00
6 Rajon Rondo 1.25 3.00
7 Chris Paul 1.50 4.00
8 Tony Parker 1.25 3.00
9 Deron Williams 1.00 2.50
10 Greivis Vasquez 1.00 2.50

2012-13 Innovation Pride of the NBA

1 LeBron James 8.00 20.00
2 Kobe Bryant 8.00 20.00
3 Anthony Davis 10.00 25.00
4 Kyrie Irving 10.00 25.00
5 Paul Pierce 2.00 5.00
6 Tim Duncan 3.00 8.00
7 Derrick Rose 2.50 6.00
8 Kevin Durant 5.00 12.00
9 Steve Nash 2.00 5.00
10 Rajon Rondo 2.00 5.00

2012-13 Innovation Producers

1 Stephen Curry 6.00 15.00
2 Anderson Varejao 1.00 2.50
3 Steve Nash 1.50 4.00
4 Kevin Durant 4.00 10.00
5 Greivis Vasquez 1.25 3.00
6 Kobe Bryant 6.00 15.00
7 James Harden 2.50 6.00
8 Zach Randolph 1.25 3.00
9 LeBron James 6.00 15.00
10 Russell Westbrook 4.00 10.00
11 David Lee 1.00 2.50
12 Josh Smith 1.25 3.00
13 LaMarcus Aldridge 1.50 4.00
14 Kevin Love 1.50 4.00
15 Carmelo Anthony 2.00 5.00
16 Chris Paul 2.00 5.00
17 Deron Williams 1.25 3.00
18 Greg Monroe 1.25 3.00
19 Blake Griffin 1.50 4.00
20 Tyson Chandler 1.25 3.00

2012-13 Innovation Rookie Autographs

CHANGE DEADLINE 03/04/2015
1 Andre Drummond 8.00 20.00
2 Alexey Shved 3.00 8.00
3 Draymond Green 15.00 40.00
4 Enes Kanter 4.00 10.00
5 Jimmer Fredette 3.00 8.00
6 John Henson 5.00 12.00
7 Klay Thompson 30.00 80.00
8 Kyle Singler 3.00 8.00
9 Nolan Smith 3.00 8.00
10 Orlando Johnson 3.00 8.00
11 Will Barton 4.00 10.00
12 Andrew Nicholson 3.00 8.00
13 DeQuan Jones 3.00 8.00
14 E'Twaun Moore 3.00 8.00
15 Jeremy Pargo 3.00 8.00
16 Jonas Valanciunas 5.00 12.00
17 Kevin Murphy 3.00 8.00
18 Kyrie Irving EXCH 30.00 80.00
19 Nikola Vucevic 5.00 12.00
20 Reggie Jackson 5.00 12.00
21 Khris Middleton 5.00 12.00
22 Alec Burks 5.00 12.00
23 Darius Morris 3.00 8.00
24 Greg Stiemsma 3.00 8.00
25 Jeff Taylor 3.00 8.00
26 Julyan Stone 3.00 8.00
27 Kevin Jones EXCH 3.00 8.00
28 Malcolm Lee 3.00 8.00
29 Kim English 3.00 8.00
30 Robert Sacre 3.00 8.00
31 Tristan Thompson 5.00 12.00
32 Anthony Davis 75.00 150.00
33 Chandler Parsons 5.00 12.00
34 Gustavo Ayon 3.00 8.00
35 Jared Sullinger 4.00 10.00
36 Kemba Walker EXCH 10.00 25.00
37 Kent Bazemore 5.00 12.00
38 MarShon Brooks 4.00 10.00
39 Miles Plumlee 3.00 8.00
40 Terrence Jones 4.00 10.00
41 Tornike Shengelia 3.00 8.00
42 Bradley Beal 8.00 20.00
43 Brandon Knight 5.00 12.00
44 Harrison Barnes 5.00 12.00
45 Mike Scott 3.00 8.00
46 Kendall Marshall 3.00 8.00
47 Kenneth Faried 5.00 12.00
48 Marquis Teague 3.00 8.00
49 Meyers Leonard 4.00 10.00
50 Terrence Ross 5.00 12.00
51 Damian Lillard 125.00 250.00

2012-13 Innovation Rookie Basketballs

PRINT RUNS B/WN 49-199 COPIES PER
1 Lavoy Allen/49 2.00 5.00
2 Bernard James/49 2.00 5.00
3 Terrence Jones/49
4 Bismack Biyombo/99 2.00 5.00
5 Terrence Ross/99 3.00 8.00
6 Fab Melo/49 2.00 5.00
7 Festus Ezeli/49 2.50 6.00
8 Kenneth Faried/99 3.00 8.00
9 Kendall Marshall/49
10 Marcus Morris/99 2.50 6.00
11 Austin Rivers/99 3.00 8.00
12 Thomas Robinson/99 2.50 6.00
13 Markieff Morris/99 3.00 8.00
14 Robert Sacre/49 2.00 5.00
15 Royce White/49 2.00 5.00
16 Bradley Beal/199 5.00 12.00
17 Arnett Moultrie/49
18 Tobias Harris/99 3.00 8.00
19 Brandon Knight/99 3.00 8.00
20 Evan Fournier/99 6.00 15.00
21 Harrison Barnes/199 6.00 15.00
22 Kemba Walker/199 6.00 15.00
23 Khris Middleton/49
24 Will Barton/49
25 John Henson/199 3.00 8.00
26 Jimmer Fredette/99 2.00 5.00
27 Darius Morris/49 2.00 5.00
28 Nolan Smith/49 2.00 5.00
29 Darius Miller/49 2.00 5.00
30 Miles Plumlee/49 2.00 5.00
31 Lance Thomas/49
32 John Jenkins/49
33 Enes Kanter/99 2.50 6.00
34 Iman Shumpert/199 3.00 8.00
35 Kawhi Leonard/199 12.00 30.00
36 Kim English/99 2.00 5.00
37 Jared Sullinger/99
38 Anthony Davis/199 15.00 40.00
39 Chandler Parsons/199 3.00 8.00
40 Marquis Teague/99 2.00 5.00
41 Reggie Jackson/99 3.00 8.00
42 Tony Wroten/49 2.50 6.00
43 Quincy Miller/49 2.00 5.00
44 Tristan Thompson/99 3.00 8.00
45 Andre Drummond/199 5.00 12.00
46 Draymond Green/99 10.00 25.00
47 Isaiah Thomas/99 5.00 12.00
48 Julyan Stone/49
49 Klay Thompson/199 10.00 25.00
50 MarShon Brooks/99 2.50 6.00
51 Andrew Nicholson/49 2.00 5.00
52 Chris Singleton/49
53 Doron Lamb/49 2.00 5.00
54 Jae Crowder/49 2.50 6.00
55 Jordan Hamilton/99 2.00 5.00
56 Kyle Singler/49 2.00 5.00
57 Meyers Leonard/49 2.50 6.00
58 Cory Joseph/99 2.00 5.00
59 Dion Waiters/99 3.00 8.00
60 Jared Cunningham/49 2.00 5.00
61 Jonas Valanciunas/99 3.00 8.00
62 Kyrie Irving/199 12.00 30.00
63 Michael Kidd-Gilchrist/199 3.00 8.00
64 Norris Cole/49 2.00 5.00
65 Jeremy Lamb/99 3.00 8.00
66 Derrick Williams/199 2.00 5.00
67 Quincy Acy/99 2.00 5.00
68 Charles Jenkins/49 2.00 5.00
69 Tyler Zeller/99
70 Alec Burks/49 3.00 8.00

2012-13 Innovation Rookie Innovative Ink

CHANGE DEADLINE 03/04/2015
1 Austin Rivers 6.00 15.00
2 Thomas Robinson 4.00 10.00
3 Terrence Jones 4.00 10.00
4 Kevin Jones 3.00 8.00
5 Bradley Beal 8.00 20.00
6 Tobias Harris 5.00 12.00
7 Terrence Ross 5.00 12.00
8 Kenneth Faried 5.00 12.00
9 Kendall Marshall 3.00 8.00
10 Brandon Knight 5.00 12.00
11 Malcolm Lee 3.00 8.00
12 Harrison Barnes 8.00 20.00
13 Kemba Walker 10.00 25.00
14 Will Barton 4.00 10.00
15 John Henson 5.00 12.00
16 Jimmer Fredette 3.00 8.00
17 Darius Morris 3.00 8.00
18 Mike Scott 3.00 8.00
19 Lance Thomas 3.00 8.00
20 Kevin Murphy 3.00 8.00
21 E'Twaun Moore 3.00 8.00
22 Iman Shumpert 5.00 12.00
23 Kawhi Leonard 60.00 150.00
24 Jared Sullinger 4.00 10.00
25 Anthony Davis 75.00 200.00
26 Chandler Parsons 5.00 12.00
27 Marquis Teague 3.00 8.00
28 Reggie Jackson 5.00 12.00
29 Tristan Thompson 5.00 12.00
30 Andre Drummond 8.00 20.00
31 Khris Middleton 5.00 12.00
32 Isaiah Thomas 30.00 80.00
33 Julyan Stone 3.00 8.00
34 MarShon Brooks 4.00 10.00
35 Andrew Nicholson 3.00 8.00
36 Orlando Johnson 3.00 8.00
37 Alec Burks 5.00 12.00
38 Jae Crowder 4.00 10.00
39 Jordan Hamilton 3.00 8.00
40 Kyle Singler 3.00 8.00
41 Meyers Leonard 4.00 10.00
42 Dion Waiters 5.00 12.00
43 Jeff Taylor 3.00 8.00
44 Kyrie Irving 30.00 80.00
45 Michael Kidd-Gilchrist 5.00 12.00
46 DeQuan Jones 3.00 8.00
47 Greg Stiemsma 3.00 8.00
48 Derrick Williams 3.00 8.00
49 Victor Claver 3.00 8.00
50 Tyler Zeller 4.00 10.00
51 Ben Hansbrough 3.00 8.00
52 Brian Roberts 3.00 8.00
53 Chris Copeland 3.00 8.00
54 Kent Bazemore 5.00 12.00
55 Kim English 3.00 8.00
56 Jonas Valanciunas 5.00 12.00
57 Gustavo Ayon 3.00 8.00
58 Mirza Teletovic 4.00 10.00
59 Nando De Colo 3.00 8.00
60 Alexey Shved 3.00 8.00

2012-13 Innovation Rookie Innovative Ink Gold

*GOLD: .6X TO 1.5X BASIC
STATED PRINT RUN 25 SER.#'d SETS
EXCHANGE DEADLINE 03/04/2015
25 Anthony Davis 125.00 300.00
45 Michael Kidd-Gilchrist 8.00 20.00

2012-13 Innovation Rookie Jumbo Jerseys

PRINT RUNS B/WN 99-199 COPIES PER
1 Brandon Knight/99
2 Terrence Ross/99 3.00 8.00
3 Kenneth Faried/99 3.00 8.00
4 Kendall Marshall/99 2.00 5.00
5 Harrison Barnes/199 6.00 15.00
6 Austin Rivers/199 3.00 8.00
7 Thomas Robinson/199 2.50 6.00
8 Markieff Morris/99 3.00 8.00
9 Bradley Beal/199
10 Kemba Walker/99 6.00 15.00
11 Jared Sullinger/199 2.50 6.00
12 Chandler Parsons/199 3.00 8.00
13 Reggie Jackson/99 3.00 8.00
14 Tyler Zeller/99 2.50 6.00
15 Jimmer Fredette/99 2.00 5.00
16 Derrick Williams/99 2.00 5.00
17 Enes Kanter/99 2.50 6.00
18 Iman Shumpert/99 3.00 8.00
19 Kawhi Leonard/99 15.00 40.00
20 Andre Drummond/199 5.00 12.00
21 Kyrie Irving/199 10.00 25.00
22 Klay Thompson/99 6.00 15.00
23 Tristan Thompson/99 3.00 8.00
24 Anthony Davis/199 15.00 40.00
25 Isaiah Thomas/99 5.00 12.00
26 Jonas Valanciunas/99 3.00 8.00
27 Dion Waiters/199 3.00 8.00
28 Meyers Leonard/99 2.50 6.00
29 Michael Kidd-Gilchrist/199 3.00 8.00
30 Andrew Nicholson/99 2.00 5.00

2012-13 Innovation Stained Glass

1 Vince Carter 4.00 10.00
2 Dwight Howard 2.50 6.00
3 Chauncey Billups 3.00 8.00
4 Ray Allen 3.00 8.00
5 Jeff Green 2.50 6.00
6 Chandler Parsons 3.00 8.00
7 Alexey Shved 2.00 5.00
8 Kevin Durant 8.00 20.00
9 Anthony Davis 20.00 50.00
10 Paul George 4.00 10.00
11 Kevin Martin 2.50 6.00
12 Stephen Curry 12.00 30.00
13 Andre Iguodala 2.50 6.00
14 Derrick Rose 4.00 10.00
15 Kevin Garnett 5.00 12.00
16 Rudy Gay 3.00 8.00
17 J.J. Hickson 2.00 5.00
18 Russell Westbrook 8.00 20.00
19 Steve Nash 3.00 8.00
20 Kirk Hinrich 2.50 6.00
21 Jimmy Butler 10.00 25.00
22 Klay Thompson 12.00 30.00
23 Shawn Marion 2.50 6.00
24 Michael Kidd-Gilchrist 3.00 8.00
25 Avery Bradley 2.50 6.00
26 Jonas Valanciunas 3.00 8.00
27 LaMarcus Aldridge 3.00 8.00
28 Kevin Love 3.00 8.00
29 Pau Gasol 3.00 8.00
30 George Hill 2.50 6.00
31 Jared Sullinger 2.50 6.00
32 David Lee 2.00 5.00
33 O.J. Mayo 2.00 5.00
34 Kemba Walker 6.00 15.00
35 Josh Smith 2.50 6.00
36 DeMar DeRozan 3.00 8.00
37 Damian Lillard 20.00 50.00
38 Ricky Rubio 3.00 8.00
39 Zach Randolph 2.50 6.00
40 Roy Hibbert 2.50 6.00
41 Serge Ibaka 2.50 6.00
42 Greg Monroe 2.50 6.00
43 Dirk Nowitzki 4.00 10.00
44 Ben Gordon 2.50 6.00
45 Al Horford 2.50 6.00
46 Tony Parker 3.00 8.00
47 Marcin Gortat 2.50 6.00
48 Blake Griffin 3.00 8.00
49 Mike Conley 2.50 6.00
50 Andrei Kirilenko 2.50 6.00
51 Chris Paul 4.00 10.00
52 Brandon Knight 3.00 8.00
53 Tristan Thompson 3.00 8.00
54 Brook Lopez 2.50 6.00
55 Nene 2.50 6.00
56 Tim Duncan 5.00 12.00
57 Goran Dragic 2.50 6.00
58 Tyson Chandler 2.50 6.00
59 Brandon Jennings 2.00 5.00
60 Hedo Turkoglu 2.50 6.00
61 Kobe Bryant 25.00 60.00
62 Andre Drummond 5.00 12.00
63 Kyrie Irving 15.00 40.00
64 Joe Johnson 2.50 6.00
65 John Wall 4.00 10.00
66 Manu Ginobili 3.00 8.00
67 Evan Turner 2.00 5.00
68 Austin Rivers 3.00 8.00
69 Monta Ellis 2.50 6.00
70 Jose Calderon 2.00 5.00
71 Danny Granger 2.50 6.00
72 Ty Lawson 2.00 5.00
73 Dion Waiters 3.00 8.00
74 Deron Williams 2.50 6.00
75 Bradley Beal 5.00 12.00
76 Tyreke Evans 2.00 5.00
77 Jrue Holiday 3.00 8.00
78 Amare Stoudemire 2.50 6.00
79 Chris Bosh 3.00 8.00
80 Harrison Barnes 5.00 12.00
81 Jeremy Lin 3.00 8.00
82 Kenneth Faried 3.00 8.00
83 Anderson Varejao 2.00 5.00
84 Rajon Rondo 3.00 8.00
85 Gordon Hayward 3.00 8.00
86 Isaiah Thomas 5.00 12.00
87 Tobias Harris 3.00 8.00
88 Carmelo Anthony 4.00 10.00
89 Dwyane Wade 8.00 20.00
90 Luis Scola 2.50 6.00
91 James Harden 5.00 12.00
92 Andre Miller 2.50 6.00
93 Joakim Noah 2.50 6.00
94 Paul Pierce 3.00 8.00
95 Enes Kanter 2.50 6.00
96 DeMarcus Cousins 3.00 8.00
97 Jameer Nelson 2.00 5.00
98 Jason Kidd 3.00 8.00
99 LeBron James 20.00 50.00
100 Kawhi Leonard 20.00 50.00

2012-13 Innovation Stained Glass Purple

*PURPLE: .6X TO 1.5X BASIC

2012-13 Innovation Stat Line Jerseys

PRINT RUNS B/WN 99-199 COPIES PER
1 Russell Westbrook/199 8.00 20.00
2 Carmelo Anthony/199 4.00 10.00
3 O.J. Mayo/199 2.00 5.00
4 Vince Carter/99 4.00 10.00
5 Marcin Gortat/199 6.00 15.00
6 Kenneth Faried/199 3.00 8.00
7 Kevin Durant/99 8.00 20.00
8 Kyrie Irving/199 8.00 20.00
9 George Hill/199 2.50 6.00
10 Al Horford/199 2.50 6.00
11 Blake Griffin/99 3.00 8.00
12 DeAndre Jordan/199 3.00 8.00
13 Anderson Varejao/149 2.00 5.00
14 Dwight Howard/199 2.50 6.00
15 Josh Smith/199 2.50 6.00
16 J.R. Smith/199 2.50 6.00
17 Kobe Bryant/99 12.00 30.00
18 Kyle Lowry/149 2.50 6.00
19 LaMarcus Aldridge/149 3.00 8.00
20 Al Jefferson/199 2.50 6.00
21 Chris Paul/199 4.00 10.00
22 Damian Lillard/199 12.00 30.00
23 Anthony Davis/199 12.00 30.00
24 Tyson Chandler/99 2.50 6.00
25 Goran Dragic/149 2.50 6.00

2012-13 Innovation Stat Line Jerseys Prime

*PRIME: 2X TO 5X BASIC
PRINT RUNS B/WN 10-25 COPIES PER
NO PRICING ON QTY 15 OR LESS
23 Anthony Davis/25 75.00 150.00

2012-13 Innovation Swat Team

1 Serge Ibaka 1.50 4.00
2 Anthony Davis 10.00 25.00
3 Larry Sanders 1.25 3.00
4 Josh Smith 1.50 4.00
5 Tim Duncan 3.00 8.00
6 Dwight Howard 1.50 4.00
7 JaVale McGee 1.50 4.00
8 Chris Andersen 1.50 4.00
9 Marcus Camby 1.50 4.00
10 Andrei Kirilenko 1.50 4.00
11 Dikembe Mutombo 2.00 5.00
12 Alonzo Mourning 2.50 6.00
13 David Robinson 3.00 8.00
14 Hakeem Olajuwon 2.50 6.00
15 Manute Bol 2.00 5.00

2013-14 Innovation

STATED PRINT RUN 199 SER.#'d SETS
1 Brook Lopez 1.50 4.00
2 Luol Deng 1.50 4.00
3 Andre Iguodala 1.50 4.00
4 Kobe Bryant 10.00 25.00
5 Kevin Love 2.00 5.00
6 Serge Ibaka 1.50 4.00
7 DeMarcus Cousins 2.00 5.00
8 Tim Duncan 3.00 8.00
9 Eric Bledsoe 1.50 4.00
10 Eric Gordon 1.50 4.00
11 Steve Nash 2.00 5.00
12 Jeremy Lin 2.00 5.00
13 Kenneth Faried 1.50 4.00
14 Derrick Rose 2.50 6.00
15 Brandon Bass 1.25 3.00
16 Dirk Nowitzki 2.50 6.00
17 Paul George 2.50 6.00
18 Mike Conley 1.50 4.00
19 Ricky Rubio 2.00 5.00
20 Kevin Durant 5.00 12.00
21 Evan Turner 1.25 3.00
22 Greivis Vasquez 1.50 4.00
23 Enes Kanter 1.25 3.00
24 Damian Lillard 4.00 10.00
25 Iman Shumpert 1.25 3.00
26 Chris Bosh 2.00 5.00
27 Chris Paul 2.50 6.00
28 Andre Drummond 2.00 5.00
29 Kemba Walker 2.00 5.00
30 Al Horford 1.50 4.00
31 Tristan Thompson 1.50 4.00
32 Stephen Curry 8.00 20.00
33 Roy Hibbert 1.50 4.00
34 Marc Gasol 2.00 5.00
35 Anthony Davis 4.00 10.00
36 Nikola Vucevic 1.50 4.00
37 Isaiah Thomas 2.00 5.00
38 Rudy Gay 2.00 5.00
39 Zaza Pachulia 1.25 3.00
40 Paul Pierce 2.00 5.00
41 Bradley Beal 2.00 5.00
42 DeMar DeRozan 2.00 5.00
43 Tiago Splitter 1.50 4.00
44 J.J. Redick 2.00 5.00
45 James Harden 3.00 8.00
46 Ty Lawson 1.25 3.00
47 Jeff Green 1.50 4.00
48 John Wall 2.50 6.00
49 Kyle Lowry 1.50 4.00
50 LaMarcus Aldridge 2.00 5.00
51 Spencer Hawes 1.25 3.00
52 Russell Westbrook 5.00 12.00
53 Kevin Martin 1.50 4.00
54 Dwyane Wade 3.00 8.00
55 Pau Gasol 2.00 5.00
56 Lance Stephenson 1.50 4.00
57 Klay Thompson 2.50 6.00
58 Monta Ellis 1.50 4.00
59 Anderson Varejao 1.25 3.00
60 Michael Kidd-Gilchrist 2.00 5.00
61 Paul Millsap 2.00 5.00
62 Gordon Hayward 2.00 5.00
63 Tony Parker 2.00 5.00
64 Gerald Green 1.50 4.00
65 Arron Afflalo 1.25 3.00
66 Carmelo Anthony 2.50 6.00
67 John Henson 1.50 4.00
68 LeBron James 8.00 20.00
69 Blake Griffin 2.00 5.00
70 Dwight Howard 1.50 4.00
71 Greg Monroe 1.50 4.00
72 Kyrie Irving 4.00 10.00
73 Carlos Boozer 1.50 4.00
74 Joe Johnson 1.50 4.00
75 Jordan Crawford 1.25 3.00
76 C.J. McCollum RC 3.00 8.00
77 Vitor Faverani RC 1.25 3.00
78 Gal Mekel RC 1.25 3.00
79 Otto Porter RC 2.00 5.00
80 Nerlens Noel RC 2.50 6.00
81 Rudy Gobert RC 2.50 6.00
82 G.Antetokounmpo RC 15.00 40.00
83 Steven Adams RC 10.00 25.00
84 Kentavious Caldwell-Pope RC 2.00 5.00
85 Tim Hardaway Jr. RC 2.00 5.00
86 Dennis Schroder RC 2.00 5.00
87 Anthony Bennett RC 1.50 4.00

88 Cody Zeller RC 1.50 4.00
89 Glen Rice Jr. RC 1.25 3.00
90 Alex Len RC 1.50 4.00
91 Mason Plumlee RC 2.00 5.00
92 Ben McLemore RC 1.50 4.00
93 Reggie Bullock RC 1.50 4.00
94 Tony Snell RC 1.50 4.00
95 Shabazz Muhammad RC 1.50 4.00
96 M.Carter-Williams RC 2.00 5.00
97 Victor Oladipo RC 2.50 6.00
98 Trey Burke RC 1.50 4.00
99 Kelly Olynyk RC 1.50 4.00
100 Nate Wolters RC 1.50 4.00

2013-14 Innovation Blue

*BLUE VET: 1X TO 2.5X BASIC
*BLUE RC: 1X TO 2.5X BASIC RC
STATED PRINT RUN 25 SER.#'d SETS
68 LeBron James 30.00 80.00

2013-14 Innovation Purple

*PURPLE VET: .75X TO 2X BASIC
*PURPLE RC: .75X TO 2X BASIC RC
ANNCD PRINT RUN OF 60

2013-14 Innovation All Rookies

1 Ben McLemore 1.25 3.00
2 Archie Goodwin 1.25 3.00
3 Kentavious Caldwell-Pope 1.50 4.00
4 Tim Hardaway Jr. 1.50 4.00
5 Trey Burke 1.25 3.00
6 Anthony Bennett 1.25 3.00
7 C.J. McCollum 2.50 6.00
8 Victor Oladipo 2.00 5.00
9 Michael Carter-Williams 1.50 4.00
10 Otto Porter 1.50 4.00
11 Kelly Olynyk 1.25 3.00
12 Cody Zeller 1.25 3.00
13 Giannis Antetokounmpo 12.00 30.00
14 Alex Len 1.25 3.00
15 Dennis Schroder 1.50 4.00

2013-14 Innovation Digs and Sigs

PRINT RUNS B/WN 15-199 COPIES PER
NO PRICING ON QTY 15
EXCHANGE DEADLINE 12/11/2015
*PRIME: .5X TO 1.2X BASIC
1 Kevin Durant/25
2 Dee Brown/199 4.00 10.00
3 Lavoy Allen/199 4.00 10.00
6 Ray Allen/25 30.00 80.00
9 Deron Williams/25 5.00 12.00
11 Vince Carter/25 30.00 60.00
12 Chris Bosh/25 8.00
13 Kevin Love/25 20.00 50.00
15 LaMarcus Aldridge/15 8.00 20.00
16 Draymond Green/199 12.00 30.00
18 Dwight Howard/25 10.00 25.00
21 Greg Smith/199 4.00 10.00
25 Andre Drummond/25
27 Dirk Nowitzki/25
29 Kyle Singler/199 4.00 10.00
30 Kobe Bryant/25 60.00 150.00
31 Anthony Davis/25
32 Jamal Mashburn/50 6.00 15.00
33 Steve Blake/199 4.00 10.00
34 Karl Malone/25 20.00 50.00
35 Scottie Pippen/25 50.00 120.00
37 Larry Bird/25 50.00 100.00
40 Harrison Barnes/25 5.00 12.00
42 Stephen Curry/25 75.00 200.00
44 John Wall/15 25.00 60.00
47 Marreese Speights/199 4.00 10.00
48 Bradley Beal/25
49 Kareem Abdul-Jabbar/25 40.00 80.00

2013-14 Innovation Digs and Sigs Prime

*PRIME: .5X TO 1.2X BASIC
PRINT RUNS B/WN 10-25 COPIES PER
NO PRICING ON QTY 10
EXCHANGE DEADLINE 12/11/2015

2013-14 Innovation Foundations Ink

PRINT RUNS B/WN 10-199 COPIES PER
NO PRICING ON QTY 10
EXCHANGE DEADLINE 12/11/2015
*PRIME: .5X TO 1.2X BASIC
6 Charlie Bell/199 3.00 8.00
7 Nick Collison/49 4.00 10.00
8 Tim Hardaway/199 5.00 12.00
9 Kenny Anderson/199 4.00 10.00
10 P.J. Tucker/199 3.00 8.00
11 Jeff Malone/199
12 Michael Cooper/199 4.00 10.00
14 Cazzie Russell/199 4.00 10.00
19 Magic Johnson/25 30.00 80.00
24 Dorell Wright/99 3.00 8.00
25 Corey Brewer/125 3.00 8.00
26 Mark Aguirre/99 4.00 10.00
27 Mateen Cleaves/199 3.00 8.00
28 Leonard Truck Robinson/199
29 Jordan Hamilton/199 3.00 8.00
30 Arnett Moultrie/199 3.00 8.00
31 Dale Davis/199 8.00 20.00
32 Dan Issel/99 4.00 10.00
36 Kobe Bryant/35 75.00 150.00
39 Karl Malone/25 50.00 100.00
45 Andrew Nicholson/99
46 Steve Blake/199 3.00 8.00
47 Jerome Williams/199 3.00 8.00
48 Travis Best/199 3.00 8.00
49 Kevin Durant/35
58 Bob Dandridge/199 3.00 8.00
59 Jeff Hornacek/99 4.00 10.00
60 Bobby Jones/199 4.00 10.00
61 Len Elmore/199 3.00 8.00
62 Rex Chapman/199 5.00 12.00
63 Nando De Colo/199 4.00 10.00
64 Larry Bird/25 40.00 80.00
65 Kyrie Irving/40 50.00 100.00
75 Jonas Jerebko/199 3.00 8.00
76 Eddie Johnson/199 3.00 8.00
77 Gary Trent/99 3.00 8.00
78 Raef LaFrentz/199 3.00 8.00
79 Anthony Mason/199 6.00 15.00
80 Cedric Maxwell/199 3.00 8.00
81 Kyle Singler/199 3.00 8.00
82 Travis Outlaw/199 4.00 10.00
92 Udonis Haslem/49 3.00 8.00
93 Marreese Speights/199 3.00 8.00
94 Bill Laimbeer/199 4.00 10.00
95 Lindsey Hunter/199 3.00 8.00
96 Sleepy Floyd/199 3.00 8.00
97 Antonio Davis/199 3.00 8.00
98 Vernon Maxwell/149 3.00 8.00
99 Festus Ezeli/199 3.00 8.00
100 Robert Sacre/199 3.00 8.00

2013-14 Innovation Game Jerseys Autographs

PRINT RUNS B/WN 15-199 COPIES PER
NO PRICING ON QTY 15
EXCHANGE DEADLINE 12/11/2015
1 Kevin Willis/25 4.00 10.00
2 Cazzie Russell/99 5.00 12.00
3 Steve Smith/199 5.00 12.00
4 Kevin Durant/35 40.00 100.00
5 Fat Lever/199 5.00 12.00
6 Sean Elliott/199 6.00 15.00
8 Kyrie Irving/35 40.00 100.00
11 Kiki Vandeweghe/199 EXCH 5.00 12.00
13 Scott Wedman/199 5.00 12.00
17 David Robinson/35 25.00 60.00
21 Fred Brown/199 4.00 10.00
22 Anthony Mason/199 5.00 12.00
23 Spencer Hawes/199 4.00 10.00
25 Rory Sparrow/199 4.00 10.00
26 Kobe Bryant/35 125.00 250.00
28 Kevin Love/25
29 Ricky Pierce/199 4.00 10.00
31 C.J. Watson/199 4.00 10.00
32 Jeff Malone/199 4.00 10.00
33 Larry Nance/199 5.00 12.00
35 Julius Erving/35 30.00 60.00
36 Larry Bird/35 50.00 100.00
37 Vince Carter/25
41 Bill Laimbeer/199 5.00 12.00
42 Jodie Meeks/199 5.00 12.00
43 Eddie Johnson/199 4.00 10.00
44 Brad Daugherty/199 5.00 12.00
45 Magic Johnson/35 40.00 80.00
47 Steve Nash/25 15.00 40.00
48 Anfernee Hardaway/25 40.00 80.00

2013-14 Innovation Game Jerseys Autographs Prime

*PRIME: .5X TO 1.2X BASIC
PRINT RUNS B/WN 10-25 COPIES PER
NO PRICING ON QTY 10
EXCHANGE DEADLINE 12/11/2015
15 Cedric Maxwell/25 12.00 30.00

2013-14 Innovation Juggernauts

1 Brook Lopez 1.25 3.00
2 Marc Gasol 1.50 4.00
3 Serge Ibaka 1.50 4.00
4 Kevin Love 1.50 4.00
5 Kevin Garnett 2.50 6.00
6 Derrick Rose 2.00 5.00
7 Rajon Rondo 1.50 4.00
8 James Harden 2.50 6.00
9 Paul George 2.00 5.00
10 Carmelo Anthony 2.00 5.00
11 Deron Williams 1.25 3.00
12 Kobe Bryant 6.00 15.00
13 Roy Hibbert 1.25 3.00
14 Dwyane Wade 2.50 6.00
15 Al Horford 1.25 3.00
16 Dwight Howard 1.25 3.00
17 Joakim Noah 1.25 3.00
18 Tim Duncan 2.50 6.00
19 Kyrie Irving 3.00 8.00
20 Russell Westbrook 4.00 10.00
21 Blake Griffin 1.50 4.00
22 Chris Paul 2.00 5.00
23 LaMarcus Aldridge 1.50 4.00
24 Tony Parker 1.50 4.00
25 Chris Bosh 1.50 4.00
26 Kevin Durant 4.00 10.00
27 Dirk Nowitzki 2.00 5.00
28 LeBron James 6.00 15.00
29 Stephen Curry 6.00 15.00
30 Anthony Davis 3.00 8.00

2013-14 Innovation Kaboom

1 Rajon Rondo 20.00 50.00
2 Derrick Rose 25.00 60.00
3 Russell Westbrook 50.00 125.00
4 Dirk Nowitzki 25.00 60.00
5 Stephen Curry 80.00 200.00
6 Dwight Howard 15.00 40.00
7 Tim Duncan 30.00 80.00
8 Dwyane Wade 30.00 80.00
9 Kobe Bryant 80.00 200.00
10 James Harden 30.00 80.00
11 Anthony Davis 40.00 100.00
12 John Wall 25.00 60.00
13 Blake Griffin 20.00 50.00
14 Kevin Durant 50.00 125.00
15 Carmelo Anthony 25.00 60.00
16 Kyrie Irving 40.00 100.00
17 Chris Paul 25.00 60.00
18 LeBron James 80.00 200.00
19 Damian Lillard 40.00 100.00
20 Paul Pierce 20.00 50.00

2013-14 Innovation Main Exhibit Signatures

PRINT RUNS B/WN 10-199 COPIES PER
NO PRICING ON QTY 15 OR LESS
EXCHANGE DEADLINE 12/11/2015
1 Ron Harper/75 8.00 20.00
2 Spud Webb/75 4.00 10.00
4 Evan Fournier/199 4.00 10.00
5 Tracy McGrady/25
6 Alexey Shved/199 3.00 8.00
8 Jason Smith/199 3.00 8.00
9 E'Twaun Moore/199 3.00 8.00
11 Kyrie Irving/49 30.00 80.00
12 Ramon Sessions/199 4.00 10.00
14 John Salmons/75 4.00 10.00
15 Kobe Bryant/25 125.00 250.00
18 Kevin Durant/25 60.00 150.00
20 Julius Erving/25 50.00 100.00
22 C.J. Watson/199 3.00 8.00
23 Spencer Haywood/25
24 Darrell Griffith/199 3.00 8.00
26 Chris Mullin/25 10.00 25.00
27 Andray Blatche/75 EXCH 3.00 8.00
28 Elgin Baylor/25 15.00 40.00
31 Zydrunas Ilgauskas/125 4.00 10.00
33 Marcin Gortat/149 10.00 25.00
35 Darryl Dawkins/75 3.00 8.00
36 Isiah Thomas/25 10.00 25.00
40 J.R. Smith/25 12.00 30.00
43 Scottie Pippen/35 50.00 120.00
46 Jack Sikma/199 4.00 10.00
47 Vernon Maxwell/199 3.00 8.00
48 Michael Curry/199 3.00 8.00
49 Lance Stephenson/149 4.00 10.00
51 Rory Sparrow/199 3.00 8.00
53 Rashard Lewis/75 4.00 10.00
55 Luc Longley/199 12.00 30.00

2013-14 Innovation Memorable Memorabilia

PRINT RUNS B/WN 75-299 COPIES PER
*PRIME: .8X TO 2X BASIC
1 Tim Duncan/299 6.00 15.00
2 Rudy Gay/175 4.00 10.00
3 John Henson/149 3.00 8.00
4 Raymond Felton/299 3.00 8.00
5 Rajon Rondo/175 4.00 10.00
6 Andre Drummond/175 4.00 10.00
7 Kevin Garnett/299 5.00 12.00
8 Enes Kanter/175 2.50 6.00
9 Andre Iguodala/125
10 Eric Bledsoe/299 3.00 8.00
11 Kevin Durant/299 6.00 15.00
12 Dwight Howard/299 3.00 8.00
13 Tyson Chandler/299 3.00 8.00
14 Damian Lillard/175 5.00 12.00
15 Evan Turner/99 2.50 6.00
16 Brandon Jennings/99 2.50 6.00
17 Deron Williams/175 3.00 8.00
18 Kevin Love/299 4.00 10.00
19 David Lee/99
20 Kobe Bryant/299 10.00 25.00
21 Monta Ellis/175 3.00 8.00
22 Paul George/299 5.00 12.00
23 Kyrie Irving/99 6.00 15.00
24 O.J. Mayo/299 2.50 6.00
25 Dwyane Wade/299 6.00 15.00
26 Josh Smith/175 3.00 8.00
27 Paul Pierce/299 4.00 10.00
28 Ricky Rubio/99 5.00 12.00
29 LaMarcus Aldridge/149 4.00 10.00
30 DeMarcus Cousins/175 4.00 10.00
31 Kenneth Faried/299 3.00 8.00
32 James Harden/175 6.00 15.00
33 LeBron James/299 10.00 25.00
34 Dirk Nowitzki/299 5.00 12.00
35 Kemba Walker/99
36 Blake Griffin/299 4.00 10.00
37 Derrick Favors/99 3.00 8.00
38 Harrison Barnes/199 3.00 8.00
39 Carmelo Anthony/299 3.00 8.00
40 Anthony Davis/175 8.00 20.00
41 Marc Gasol/175 4.00 10.00
42 Jrue Holiday/175 3.00 8.00
43 Al Jefferson/299 3.00 8.00
44 Zach Randolph/250 3.00 8.00
45 John Wall/299 5.00 12.00
46 Chris Paul/75 5.00 12.00
47 Gordon Hayward/99 4.00 10.00
48 Stephen Curry/175 15.00 40.00
49 Bradley Beal/175 4.00 10.00
50 Goran Dragic/175

2013-14 Innovation Rookie Jumbo Jerseys

STATED PRINT RUN 199 SER.#'d SETS
*PRIME: 1.2X TO 3X BASIC
1 Nate Wolters 3.00 8.00
2 Ben McLemore 5.00 12.00
3 Michael Carter-Williams 6.00 15.00
4 Glen Rice Jr.
5 Steven Adams 4.00 10.00
6 Isaiah Canaan 2.50 6.00
7 C.J. McCollum 6.00 15.00
8 Solomon Hill 2.50 6.00
9 Kentavious Caldwell-Pope 4.00 10.00
10 Victor Oladipo 6.00 15.00
11 Cody Zeller 3.00 8.00
12 Anthony Bennett 3.00 8.00
13 Trey Burke 3.00 8.00
14 Alex Len 3.00 8.00
15 Shabazz Muhammad 3.00 8.00
16 Giannis Antetokounmpo 12.00 30.00
17 Kelly Olynyk 3.00 8.00
18 Andre Roberson 2.50 6.00
19 Tim Hardaway Jr. 4.00 10.00
20 Shane Larkin 2.50 6.00
21 Mason Plumlee 4.00 10.00
22 Nerlens Noel 5.00 12.00
23 Archie Goodwin 3.00 8.00
24 Otto Porter 3.00 8.00
25 Dennis Schroder 8.00 20.00

2013-14 Innovation Rookie Stained Glass

*GOLD: .6X TO 1.5X BASIC
1 Otto Porter
2 Tim Hardaway Jr. 3.00 8.00
3 Mason Plumlee 3.00 8.00
4 Victor Oladipo 4.00 10.00
5 Gal Mekel 2.00 5.00
6 Kentavious Caldwell-Pope 3.00 8.00
7 Cody Zeller 2.50 6.00
8 Ben McLemore 2.50 6.00
9 Michael Carter-Williams 3.00 8.00
10 Nate Wolters 2.50 6.00
11 Rudy Gobert 8.00 20.00
12 Anthony Bennett 2.50 6.00
13 Reggie Bullock 2.50 6.00
14 Kelly Olynyk 2.50 6.00
15 Nerlens Noel 4.00 10.00
16 Dennis Schroder 3.00 8.00
17 Alex Len 2.50 6.00
18 Tony Snell 2.50 6.00
19 Trey Burke 2.50 6.00
20 Vitor Faverani 2.00 5.00
21 Steven Adams 10.00 25.00
22 Glen Rice Jr. 2.00 5.00
23 Shabazz Muhammad 2.00 5.00
24 C.J. McCollum 5.00 12.00
25 Giannis Antetokounmpo 30.00 80.00

2013-14 Innovation Rookies Main Exhibit Signatures

PRINT RUNS B/WN 75-299 COPIES PER
EXCHANGE DEADLINE 12/11/2015
1 Vitor Faverani/299 3.00 8.00
2 Carrick Felix/299 3.00 8.00
3 Solomon Hill/299 3.00 8.00
4 Trey Burke/125 4.00 10.00
5 Sergey Karasev/299 4.00 10.00
6 Toure Murry/299 3.00 8.00
7 Gal Mekel/299 3.00 8.00
8 Mason Plumlee/299 4.00 10.00
9 Shabazz Muhammad/75 4.00 10.00
10 Cody Zeller/75 4.00 10.00
11 Luigi Datome/299 3.00 8.00
12 Ian Clark/299 3.00 8.00
13 Tim Hardaway Jr./299 10.00 25.00
14 Victor Oladipo/75 12.00 30.00
15 Nemanja Nedovic/299 3.00 8.00
16 Gorgui Dieng/299 4.00 10.00
17 Archie Goodwin/299 4.00 10.00
18 G.Antetokounmpo/299 60.00 150.00
19 Ben McLemore/75 4.00 10.00
20 C.J. McCollum/75 20.00 50.00
21 Robert Covington/299 5.00 12.00
22 Shane Larkin/299 3.00 8.00
23 Dennis Schroder/199 3.00 8.00
24 Alex Len/75 3.00 8.00
25 Dwight Buycks/299 3.00 8.00
26 Phil Pressey/299 3.00 8.00
27 Andre Roberson/299 3.00 8.00
28 Kelly Olynyk/299 4.00 10.00
29 Otto Porter/75 5.00 12.00
30 Ray McCallum/299 3.00 8.00
31 Nate Wolters/299 3.00 8.00
32 Glen Rice Jr./199 3.00 8.00
33 Anthony Bennett/75 3.00 8.00
34 Lorenzo Brown/299 3.00 8.00
35 Tony Snell/299 4.00 10.00
36 Isaiah Canaan/299 3.00 8.00
37 Steven Adams/199 8.00 20.00
38 Nerlens Noel/75 8.00 20.00
39 Rudy Gobert/299 12.00 30.00
40 Erik Murphy/299 3.00 8.00
41 M.Carter-Williams/125 5.00 12.00
42 Kentavious Caldwell-Pope/75 6.00 15.00
43 Pero Antic/299 3.00 8.00
44 Miroslav Raduljica/299 3.00 8.00
45 Matthew Dellavedova/299 5.00 12.00

2013-14 Innovation Stained Glass

*GOLD: .75X TO 2X BASIC
1 Luol Deng 1.25 3.00
2 Mike Conley 1.25 3.00
3 LaMarcus Aldridge 1.50 4.00
4 Marc Gasol 1.50 4.00
5 Carmelo Anthony 2.00 5.00
6 DeMarcus Cousins 1.50 4.00
7 Evan Turner 1.00 2.50
8 Anthony Davis 3.00 8.00
9 Kyle Lowry 1.50 4.00
10 Tony Parker 1.50 4.00
11 Kobe Bryant 12.00 30.00
12 Kevin Durant 4.00 10.00
13 Nikola Vucevic 1.25 3.00
14 Russell Westbrook 4.00 10.00
15 LeBron James 12.00 30.00
16 Eric Bledsoe 1.25 3.00
17 Enes Kanter 1.25 3.00
18 Isaiah Thomas 1.50 4.00
19 Spencer Hawes 1.00 2.50
20 Arron Afflalo 1.00 2.50
21 Serge Ibaka 1.25 3.00
22 Greivis Vasquez 1.25 3.00
23 Rudy Gay 1.25 3.00
24 Dwyane Wade 2.50 6.00
25 Dwight Howard 1.50 4.00
26 Steve Nash 1.50 4.00
27 Iman Shumpert 1.00 2.50
28 Zaza Pachulia 1.00 2.50
29 Kevin Martin 1.25 3.00
30 John Henson 1.25 3.00
31 Tim Duncan 2.50 6.00
32 Damian Lillard 3.00 8.00
33 Paul Pierce 1.50 4.00
34 Lance Stephenson 1.25 3.00
35 Kyrie Irving 3.00 8.00
36 Kenneth Faried 1.25 3.00
37 Chris Paul 2.00 5.00
38 Bradley Beal 1.50 4.00
39 Pau Gasol 1.50 4.00
40 Blake Griffin 1.50 4.00
41 Eric Gordon 1.25 3.00
42 Chris Bosh 1.50 4.00
43 DeMar DeRozan 1.50 4.00
44 Monta Ellis 1.25 3.00
45 Joe Johnson 1.25 3.00
46 Brandon Bass 1.00 2.50
47 Kemba Walker 1.50 4.00
48 Tiago Splitter 1.25 3.00
49 Klay Thompson 2.00 5.00
50 Greg Monroe 1.25 3.00
51 Jeremy Lin 1.50 4.00
52 Andre Drummond 1.50 4.00
53 J.J. Redick 1.50 4.00
54 Michael Kidd-Gilchrist 1.50 4.00
55 Brook Lopez 1.25 3.00
56 Paul George 2.00 5.00
57 Tristan Thompson 1.25 3.00
58 James Harden 2.50 6.00
59 Anderson Varejao 1.00 2.50
60 Carlos Boozer 1.25 3.00
61 Al Horford 1.25 3.00
62 Derrick Rose 2.00 5.00
63 Ty Lawson 1.25 3.00
64 Gordon Hayward 1.50 4.00
65 Andre Iguodala 1.50 4.00
66 Ricky Rubio 1.50 4.00
67 Roy Hibbert 1.25 3.00
68 Jeff Green 1.25 3.00
69 Paul Millsap 1.50 4.00
70 Jordan Crawford 1.00 2.50
71 Dirk Nowitzki 2.00 5.00
72 Stephen Curry 10.00 25.00
73 John Wall 2.00 5.00
74 Gerald Green 1.25 3.00
75 Kevin Love 1.50 4.00

2013-14 Innovation Starters

1 76ers 2.50 6.00
2 Celtics 2.50 6.00
3 Amir Johnson 2.00 5.00
DeMar DeRozan
Jonas Valanciunas
Kyle Lowry
Terrence Ross
4 Knicks 2.50 6.00
5 Nets 3.00 8.00
6 Pacers 2.50 6.00
7 Bulls 6.00 15.00
8 Cavaliers 4.00 10.00
9 Andre Drummond 2.00 5.00
Brandon Jennings
Greg Monroe
Josh Smith
Kyle Singler
10 Brandon Knight 1.50 4.00
Ersan Ilyasova
Khris Middleton
Larry Sanders
Nate Wolters
11 Heat 5.00 12.00
12 Al Horford 2.00 5.00
DeMarre Carroll
Jeff Teague
Kyle Korver
Paul Millsap
13 Al Jefferson 2.00 5.00
Gerald Henderson
Josh McRoberts
Kemba Walker
Michael Kidd-Gilchrist
14 Magic 2.50 6.00
15 Wizards 2.50 6.00
16 Trail Blazers 4.00 10.00
17 Timberwolves 2.00 5.00
18 Thunder 5.00 12.00
19 J.J. Hickson 1.50 4.00
Kenneth Faried
Randy Foye
Ty Lawson
Wilson Chandler
20 Jazz 2.00 5.00
21 Warriors 8.00 20.00
22 Clippers 2.50 6.00
23 Channing Frye 1.50 4.00
Eric Bledsoe
Goran Dragic
Miles Plumlee
P.J. Tucker
24 Lakers 8.00 20.00
25 Kings 2.00 5.00
26 Spurs 12.00 30.00
27 Mavericks 2.50 6.00
28 Rockets 3.00 8.00
29 Courtney Lee 2.00 5.00
Marc Gasol
Mike Conley
Tayshaun Prince
Zach Randolph
30 Pelicans 4.00 10.00

2013-14 Innovation Starters Legends

1 00s Lakers 6.00 15.00
2 Spurs 6.00 15.00
3 Rockets 5.00 12.00
4 Pistons 4.00 10.00
5 80s Lakers 10.00 25.00
6 80s Celtics 10.00 25.00
7 70s Celtics 5.00 12.00
8 Heat 6.00 15.00
9 76ers 5.00 12.00
10 60s Celtics 6.00 15.00

2013-14 Innovation Stat Line Jerseys

PRINT RUNS B/WN 49-299 COPIES PER
1 John Wall/125 5.00 12.00
2 Carmelo Anthony/125 5.00 12.00
3 Jrue Holiday/149 4.00 10.00
4 Serge Ibaka/299 3.00 8.00
5 Kevin Durant/299 6.00 15.00
6 Al Jefferson/299 3.00 8.00
7 Stephen Curry/299 15.00 40.00
8 Deron Williams/175 3.00 8.00
9 Kemba Walker/125 4.00 10.00
10 Dirk Nowitzki/175
11 Kevin Love/125 4.00 10.00
12 Dwyane Wade/299 4.00 10.00
13 LaMarcus Aldridge/299 4.00 10.00
14 Russell Westbrook/199 10.00 25.00
15 Monta Ellis/125 3.00 8.00
16 Glen Davis/125 2.50 6.00
17 LeBron James/125 10.00 25.00
18 Ricky Rubio/125 4.00 10.00
19 Damian Lillard/199 5.00 12.00
20 Dion Waiters/199 3.00 8.00
21 DeMarcus Cousins/299 4.00 10.00
22 Josh Smith/125 3.00 8.00
23 Tony Parker/49 10.00 25.00
24 Kevin Garnett/199 5.00 12.00
25 Anthony Davis/175 6.00 15.00

2013-14 Innovation Stat Line Jerseys Prime

*PRIME: 1X TO 2.5X BASIC
PRINT RUNS B/WN 20-25 COPIES PER
12 Dwyane Wade/25 15.00 40.00

2013-14 Innovation Swat Team

1 Anthony Davis 2.50 6.00
2 Larry Sanders .75 2.00
3 Serge Ibaka 1.00 2.50
4 Roy Hibbert 1.00 2.50
5 DeAndre Jordan 1.25 3.00
6 Tyson Chandler 1.00 2.50
7 Josh Smith 1.00 2.50
8 Dwight Howard 1.00 2.50
9 Kevin Garnett 2.00 5.00
10 Tim Duncan 2.00 5.00
11 Bill Russell 2.00 5.00
12 Hakeem Olajuwon 1.50 4.00
13 Kareem Abdul-Jabbar 2.00 5.00
14 Dikembe Mutombo 1.25 3.00
15 Manute Bol 1.25 3.00

2013-14 Innovation Top Notch Autographs

PRINT RUNS B/WN 10-325 COPIES PER
NO PRICING ON QTY 15 OR LESS
EXCHANGE DEADLINE 12/11/2015
1 Theo Ratliff/325 3.00 8.00
4 Kevin Willis/25
5 Vlade Divac/325 5.00 12.00
6 Adrian Smith/199 3.00 8.00
7 Anfernee Hardaway/25 40.00 80.00
8 Kevin Durant/25 125.00 250.00
10 Spencer Hawes/225 3.00 8.00
11 Vin Baker/325 3.00 8.00
12 Amir Johnson/199 3.00 8.00
13 Larry Nance/325 4.00 10.00
16 Mark Aguirre/325 3.00 8.00
18 Anthony Davis/25 50.00 100.00
21 Kenny Anderson/325 4.00 10.00
24 Kyle Singler/325 3.00 8.00
25 Tom Van Arsdale/325 4.00 10.00
26 Mike Conley/325 4.00 10.00
27 Shaquille O'Neal/25 150.00 250.00
30 Kobe Bryant/25 50.00 120.00
31 Steve Smith/325 4.00 10.00
33 Gus Williams/325 3.00 8.00
35 Dick Van Arsdale/325 4.00 10.00
38 Jerry West/25 25.00 60.00
40 Kyrie Irving/25
46 Mahmoud Abdul-Rauf/325 3.00 8.00
51 Darryl Dawkins/199 3.00 8.00
52 Khris Middleton/225 4.00 10.00
53 Clifford Robinson/325 3.00 8.00
55 Rory Sparrow/325 3.00 8.00
56 Jodie Meeks/325 4.00 10.00
57 Grant Hill/25 15.00 40.00
59 Magic Johnson/25 40.00 80.00
61 Jack Sikma/325 4.00 10.00
63 Cazzie Russell/325 4.00 10.00
64 Scott Wedman/325 6.00 15.00
66 Thurl Bailey/325 3.00 8.00
69 Scottie Pippen/25
70 Vince Carter/25 20.00 50.00
71 Buck Williams/325 4.00 10.00
74 Bradley Beal/25 6.00 15.00
75 Rod Strickland/325 4.00 10.00
76 Greg Oden/325 4.00 10.00
81 Luc Longley/325 8.00 20.00
83 Darrell Griffith/325 3.00 8.00
88 DeMarre Carroll/325 3.00 8.00
91 Eddie Johnson/325 4.00 10.00
94 John Starks/325 4.00 10.00
97 Larry Bird/25 50.00 100.00
98 Kenyon Martin/325 4.00 10.00

2013-14 Innovation Top Notch Autographs Gold

*GOLD: .5X TO 1.2X BASIC
PRINT RUNS B/WN 5-25 COPIES PER
NO PRICING ON QTY 10 OR LESS
EXCHANGE DEADLINE 12/11/2015

1950-70 J.D. McCarthy Postcards

This 15-postcard set was released by J.D. McCarthy in the 1950-70's. Each card was produced in black and white and measured 3.25x5.5. Please note that these postcards have blank backs, and are listed below in alphabetical order. This list may be far from complete and because of the wide disparity of years, please note* no pricing is provided. Any further information on cards or pricing would be appreciated.

COMPLETE SET (15)
1 Rick Barry
2 Rick Barry
3 Dave Bing
4 Dave DeBusschere
5 Archie Dees
6 Terry Dischinger
7 Walter Dukes
8 Bailey Howell
9 Bob Lanier
10 Lloyd Love
11 Dick McGuire
12 Eddie Miles
13 Jackie Moreland
14 Gene Shue
15 John Trevsant

1993-94 Jam Session

This 240-card set was issued in 1993 by Fleer and features oversized cards measuring approximately 2 1/2" by 4 3/4". Cards were issued in 12-card packs (36 per box) with a suggested retail pack price of 1.59. One insert card is included in every pack. The full-bleed fronts feature glossy color action player photos. Across the bottom edge of the picture appears a team color-coded bar with the player's name, position and team. The NBA Jam Session logo is superposed on the lower right corner. The backs are divided in half vertically with the left side carrying a second action shot and on the right side a panel with a background that fades from green to white. On the panel appears biography, career highlights, statistics and team logo. The cards are numbered on the back and checklisted below alphabetically within and according to teams. Rookie Cards of note include Anfernee Hardaway, Jamal Mashburn and Chris Webber.

COMPLETE SET (240) 12.00 30.00
1 Stacey Augmon .15 .40
2 Mookie Blaylock .12 .30
3 Doug Edwards RC .25 .60
4 Duane Ferrell .12 .30
5 Paul Graham .12 .30
6 Adam Keefe .12 .30
7 Jon Koncak .12 .30
8 Dominique Wilkins .25 .60
9 Kevin Willis .15 .40
10 Alaa Abdelnaby .12 .30
11 Dee Brown .12 .30
12 Sherman Douglas .12 .30
13 Rick Fox .12 .30
14 Kevin Gamble .12 .30
15 Xavier McDaniel .12 .30
16 Robert Parish .20 .50
17 Muggsy Bogues .15 .40
18 Scott Burrell RC .25 .60
19 Dell Curry .12 .30
20 Kenny Gattison .12 .30
21 Hersey Hawkins .12 .30
22 Eddie Johnson .12 .30
23 Larry Johnson .20 .50
24 Alonzo Mourning .30 .75
25 Johnny Newman .12 .30
26 David Wingate .12 .30
27 B.J. Armstrong .12 .30
28 Corie Blount RC .25 .60
29 Bill Cartwright .15 .40
30 Horace Grant .15 .40
31 Stacey King .12 .30
32 John Paxson .15 .40
33 Michael Jordan 1.50 4.00
34 Scottie Pippen .40 1.00
35 Scott Williams .12 .30
36 Terrell Brandon .15 .40
37 Brad Daugherty .12 .30
38 Danny Ferry .12 .30
39 Tyrone Hill .12 .30
40 Chris Mills RC .25 .60
41 Larry Nance .15 .40
42 Mark Price .20 .50
43 Gerald Wilkins .12 .30
44 John Williams .12 .30
45 Terry Davis .12 .30
46 Derek Harper .15 .40
47 Donald Hodge .12 .30
48 Jim Jackson .15 .40
49 Jamal Mashburn RC .40 1.00
50 Sean Rooks .12 .30
51 Doug Smith .12 .30
52 Mahmoud Abdul-Rauf .12 .30
53 Kevin Brooks .12 .30
54 LaPhonso Ellis .12 .30
55 Mark Macon .12 .30
56 Dikembe Mutombo .20 .50
57 Rodney Rogers RC .25 .60
58 Bryant Stith .12 .30
59 Reggie Williams .12 .30
60 Joe Dumars .20 .50
61 Sean Elliott .15 .40
62 Bill Laimbeer .15 .40
63 Terry Mills .12 .30
64 Olden Polynice .12 .30
65 Alvin Robertson .12 .30
66 Isiah Thomas .20 .50
67 Victor Alexander .12 .30
68 Chris Gatling .12 .30
69 Tim Hardaway .20 .50
70 Byron Houston .12 .30
71 Sarunas Marciulionis .12 .30
72 Chris Mullin .20 .50
73 Billy Owens .12 .30
74 Latrell Sprewell .30 .75
75 Chris Webber RC 1.25 3.00
76 Scott Brooks .12 .30
77 Matt Bullard .12 .30
78 Sam Cassell RC .50 1.25
79 Mario Elie .12 .30
80 Carl Herrera .12 .30
81 Robert Horry .20 .50
82 Vernon Maxwell .12 .30
83 Hakeem Olajuwon .25 .60
84 Kenny Smith .12 .30
85 Otis Thorpe .12 .30
86 Dale Davis .12 .30
87 Vern Fleming .12 .30
88 Scott Haskin RC .12 .30
89 Reggie Miller .25 .60
90 Sam Mitchell .12 .30
91 Pooh Richardson .12 .30
92 Detlef Schrempf .15 .40
93 Malik Sealy .12 .30
94 Rik Smits .15 .40
95 Terry Dehere RC .12 .30
96 Ron Harper .15 .40
97 Mark Jackson .15 .40
98 Danny Manning .15 .40
99 Stanley Roberts .12 .30
100 Loy Vaught .12 .30
101 John Williams .12 .30
102 Sam Bowie .12 .30
103 Elden Campbell .12 .30
104 Doug Christie .20 .50
105 Vlade Divac .15 .40
106 James Edwards .12 .30
107 George Lynch RC .25 .60
108 Anthony Peeler .12 .30
109 Sedale Threatt .12 .30
110 James Worthy .25 .60
111 Bimbo Coles .12 .30
112 Grant Long .12 .30
113 Harold Miner .12 .30
114 Glen Rice .15 .40
115 John Salley .12 .30
116 Rony Seikaly .12 .30
117 Brian Shaw .12 .30
118 Steve Smith .15 .40
119 Anthony Avent .12 .30
120 Vin Baker RC .40 1.00
121 Jon Barry .12 .30
122 Frank Brickowski .12 .30
123 Todd Day .12 .30
124 Blue Edwards .12 .30
125 Brad Lohaus .12 .30
126 Lee Mayberry .12 .30
127 Eric Murdock .12 .30
128 Ken Norman .12 .30
129 Thurl Bailey .12 .30
130 Mike Brown .12 .30
131 Christian Laettner .15 .40
132 Luc Longley .15 .40
133 Chuck Person .15 .40
134 Chris Smith .12 .30
135 Doug West .12 .30
136 Micheal Williams .12 .30
137 Kenny Anderson .15 .40
138 Benoit Benjamin .12 .30
139 Derrick Coleman .15 .40
140 Armon Gilliam .12 .30
141 Rick Mahorn .12 .30
142 Chris Morris .12 .30
143 Rumeal Robinson .12 .30
144 Rex Walters RC .25 .60
145 Greg Anthony .15 .40
146 Rolando Blackman .15 .40
147 Tony Campbell .12 .30
148 Hubert Davis .12 .30
149 Patrick Ewing .25 .60
150 Anthony Mason .15 .40
151 Charles Oakley .15 .40
152 Doc Rivers .15 .40
153 Charles Smith .12 .30
154 John Starks .15 .40
155 Herb Williams .12 .30
156 Nick Anderson .12 .30
157 Anthony Bowie .12 .30
158 Litterial Green .12 .30
159 Anfernee Hardaway RC 1.25 3.00
160 Shaquille O'Neal .75 2.00
161 Donald Royal .12 .30
162 Dennis Scott .12 .30
163 Scott Skiles .12 .30
164 Jeff Turner .12 .30
165 Dana Barros .12 .30
166 Shawn Bradley RC .25 .60
167 Johnny Dawkins .12 .30
168 Greg Graham RC .25 .60
169 Jeff Hornacek .15 .40
170 Moses Malone .20 .50
171 Tim Perry .12 .30
172 Clarence Weatherspoon .12 .30
173 Danny Ainge .15 .40
174 Charles Barkley .30 .75
175 Cedric Ceballos .15 .40
176 A.C. Green .15 .40
177 Frank Johnson .12 .30
178 Kevin Johnson .20 .50
179 Negele Knight .12 .30
180 Malcolm Mackey RC .25 .60
181 Dan Majerle .20 .50
182 Oliver Miller .12 .30
183 Mark West .12 .30
184 Clyde Drexler .25 .60
185 Chris Dudley .12 .30
186 Harvey Grant .12 .30
187 Jerome Kersey .12 .30
188 Terry Porter .12 .30
189 Clifford Robinson .15 .40
190 James Robinson RC .25 .60
191 Rod Strickland .15 .40
192 Buck Williams .15 .40
193 Randy Brown .12 .30
194 Duane Causwell .12 .30
195 Bobby Hurley RC .20 .50
196 Mitch Richmond .25 .60
197 Lionel Simmons .12 .30
198 Wayman Tisdale .15 .40
199 Spud Webb .15 .40
200 Walt Williams .15 .40
201 Willie Anderson .12 .30
202 Antoine Carr .12 .30
203 Terry Cummings .15 .40
204 Lloyd Daniels .12 .30
205 Vinny Del Negro .12 .30
206 Sleepy Floyd .12 .30
207 Avery Johnson .15 .40
208 J.R. Reid .12 .30
209 David Robinson .30 .75
210 Dennis Rodman .40 1.00
211 Michael Cage .12 .30
212 Kendall Gill .15 .40
213 Ervin Johnson RC .25 .60
214 Shawn Kemp .25 .60
215 Derrick McKey .12 .30
216 Nate McMillan .12 .30
217 Gary Payton .25 .60
218 Sam Perkins .15 .40
219 Ricky Pierce .12 .30
220 Isaac Austin .12 .30
221 David Benoit .12 .30
222 Tom Chambers .15 .40
223 Tyrone Corbin .12 .30
224 Mark Eaton .12 .30
225 Jay Humphries .12 .30
226 Jeff Malone .12 .30
227 Karl Malone .25 .60
228 John Stockton .25 .60
229 Luther Wright RC .12 .30
230 Michael Adams .12 .30
231 Calbert Cheaney RC .25 .60
232 Kevin Duckworth .12 .30
233 Pervis Ellison .12 .30
234 Tom Gugliotta .15 .40
235 Buck Johnson .12 .30
236 Doug Overton .12 .30
237 LaBradford Smith .12 .30
238 Larry Stewart .12 .30
239 Checklist .12 .30
240 Checklist .12 .30

1993-94 Jam Session Gamebreakers

Randomly inserted into 12-card packs at a rate of one in four, this eight-card 2 1/2" by 4 3/4" set features some of the NBA's top players. The borderless fronts feature color action cutouts on multicolored backgrounds highlighted by grid lines. The player's name appears in gold foil at the lower left. The back features a color player head shot with a screened background similar to the front. The player's name appears above the photo, career highlights appear below. The cards are numbered on the back as "X of 8."

COMPLETE SET (8) 1.50 4.00
1 Charles Barkley .50 1.25
2 Tim Hardaway .30 .75
3 Kevin Johnson .30 .75
4 Dan Majerle .30 .75
5 Scottie Pippen .60 1.50
6 Mark Price .30 .75
7 John Starks .25 .60
8 Dominique Wilkins .30 .75

1993-94 Jam Session Rookie Standouts

Randomly inserted in 12-card packs at a rate of one in four, this oversized (2 1/2" by 4 3/4") eight-card set features borderless fronts with full-color player action photos. The player's name appears in gold-foil lettering in the lower left corner. The back features a color player action head shot with the player's statistics below. The cards are numbered on the back as "X of 8."

COMPLETE SET (8) 5.00 12.00
1 Vin Baker .75 2.00
2 Shawn Bradley .50 1.25
3 Calbert Cheaney .50 1.25
4 Anfernee Hardaway UER 2.50 6.00
5 Bobby Hurley .50 1.25
6 Jamal Mashburn .75 2.00
7 Rodney Rogers .50 1.25
8 Chris Webber 2.50 6.00

1993-94 Jam Session Second Year Stars

Randomly inserted into Jam Session 12-card packs at a rate of one in four, this eight-card 2 1/2" by 4 3/4" set features some of the NBA's top second-year players. The borderless fronts feature a color action cutout on a rainbow-colored background. The player's name appears in gold foil in the lower right. The back features a color player head shot with screened rainbow background. The players name appears above the photo with a player profile displayed below. The cards are numbered on the back as "X of 8.

COMPLETE SET (8) 1.25 3.00
1 Tom Gugliotta .20 .50
2 Jim Jackson .20 .50
3 Christian Laettner .20 .50
4 Oliver Miller .15 .40
5 Harold Miner .15 .40
6 Alonzo Mourning .40 1.00
7 Shaquille O'Neal 1.00 2.50
8 Walt Williams .15 .40

1993-94 Jam Session Slam Dunk Heroes

Randomly inserted in 12-card Jam Session packs at a rate of one in four, this eight-card 2 1/2" by 4 3/4" set features some of the NBA's top slam dunkers. The borderless fronts feature color action cutouts on multicolored posterized background. The player's name appears vertically in gold foil near the bottom. The back features a color player head shot. The player's name appears above the photo, a player profile is displayed below. The cards are numbered on the back as "X of 8."

COMPLETE SET (8) 3.00 8.00
1 Patrick Ewing .50 1.25
2 Larry Johnson .40 1.00
3 Shawn Kemp .50 1.25
4 Karl Malone .50 1.25
5 Alonzo Mourning .60 1.50
6 Hakeem Olajuwon .50 1.25
7 Shaquille O'Neal 1.50 4.00
8 David Robinson .60 1.50

1993-94 Jam Session Team Night Sheets

These perforated Jam Session sheets were apparently handed out on game nights at various NBA arenas. Some sheets consists of eight cards, arranged in two rows of four each; other sheets had a third row for a total of 12 cards. Other sheets are known to exist (e.g., Orlando); furthermore, some sheets have cards that were created for the team night sheets but were never issued in the basic set (e.g., Kukoc, Hardaway, and Van Exel). If separated, the cards measure 2 1/2" by 4 3/4". The cards have the same design as the regular 1993-94 Jam Session cards, except that they are unnumbered. The sheets are checklisted below in alphabetical order by team name.

COMPLETE SET (9) 12.00 30.00
1 Alaa Abdelnaby 2.00 5.00
Dee Brown
Sherman Douglas
Rick Fox
Kevin Gamble
Xavier McDaniel
Robert Parish 00
Sony (Ad card)
2 Quinn Buckner CO 2.50 6.00
Terry Davis
Lucious Harris
Donald Hodge
Jim Jackson
Popeye Jones
Tom Legler
Fat Lever
Jamal Mashburn
Sean Rooks
Doug Smith
Doritos (Ad Card)
3 B.J. Armstrong 2.50 6.00
Corie Blount
Bill Cartwright
Horace Grant
Phil Jackson CO
Stacey King
Toni Kukoc
John Paxson
Will Perdue
Scottie Pippen
Scott Williams
Rust-oleum (Ad Card)
4 Joe Dumars 2.00 5.00
Sean Elliott
Bill Laimbeer
Terry Mills
Olden Polynice
Isiah Thomas
Pistons Logo
LCI International (Ad card)
5 Larry Brown CO 2.00 5.00
Antonio Davis
Dale Davis
Vern Fleming
Scott Haskin
Derrick McKey
Reggie Miller
Sam Mitchell
Pooh Richardson
Malik Sealy
Rik Smits
Combos Snacks (Ad card)
6 Mark Aguirre 2.00 5.00
Terry Dehere
Gary Grant
Ron Harper
Mark Jackson
Danny Manning
Stanley Roberts
Elmore Spencer
Tom Tolbert
Loy Vaught
Bob Weiss CO
Snickers
Kudos (Ad card)
7 Sam Bowie 2.00 5.00
Elden Campbell
Doug Christie
Vlade Divac
James Edwards
George Lynch
Anthony Peeler
Tony Smith
Sedale Threatt
Nick Van Exel
Team Logo
8 Vin Baker 2.50 6.00
Jon Barry
Frank Brickowski
Todd Day
Blue Edwards
Brad Lohaus
Lee Mayberry
Eric Murdock
Ken Norman
Danny Schayes
Derek Strong
Usinger's (Ad card)
9 Greg Anthony 2.00 5.00
Rolando Blackman
Hubert Davis
Patrick Ewing
Derek Harper
Anthony Mason
Charles Oakley
Charles Smith
John Starks
Herb Williams
WIZ (Two ad cards)

1993-94 Jam Session Ticket Stubs

During the All-Star Weekend, these ticket stub cards were given only to the public. No cards were given out with stubs attached. Without the stubs attached, the cards measure approximately 2 1/2" by 4 3/4". One card was given out during each of the four days of the event: Thursday (Barkley), Friday (Pippen), Saturday (O'Neal), and Sunday (Drexler/Robinson). The fronts feature full-bleed color action player photos except at the bottom where the pictures are edged by a blue fading to red stripe. A Fleer "All Star NBA Jam Session" logo is printed at the lower left. On a white background, the backs contain text describing the conditions governing the use of this ticket. The cards are unnumbered and checklisted below in alphabetical order. Cards found with the stub still intact are valued at five times the values listed below.

COMPLETE SET (4) 6.00 15.00
1 Charles Barkley 2.00 5.00
2 David Robinson 2.00 5.00
3 Shaquille O'Neal 5.00 12.00
4 Scottie Pippen 2.50 6.00

1994-95 Jam Session

The complete 1994-95 Jam Session set consists of 200 oversized (2 1/2" by 4 3/4") cards. The cards were issued in 12-card packs with 36 packs per box. Each pack has one card from one of the four insert sets. Suggested retail price was $1.59 per pack. Cello packs consisting of three player cards and a cover card were given away at McDonald's restaurants in the Phoenix area to promote the Jam Session featured at the NBA All-Star weekend. The fronts have full-bleed color action photos that are tightly cropped so the player takes up a larger percentage of the card than in most sets. The NBA Jam Session logo is superimposed on the lower right corner and the player's name and team is just above it in the teams color. The backs have color-action photos on the right side with statistics and information on the left that is set against the color of the player's team. The entire card is UV coated as are all the insert sets. The cards are numbered on the back and grouped alphabetically within teams. Rookie Cards of note in this set include Grant Hill, Eddie Jones and Jason Kidd.

COMPLETE SET (200) 10.00 25.00
1 Stacey Augmon .20 .50
2 Mookie Blaylock .15 .40
3 Tyrone Corbin .15 .40
4 Craig Ehlo .15 .40
5 Ken Norman .15 .40
6 Kevin Willis .15 .40
7 Dee Brown .15 .40
8 Sherman Douglas .15 .40
9 Acie Earl .15 .40
10 Blue Edwards .15 .40
11 Pervis Ellison .15 .40
12 Rick Fox .15 .40
13 Xavier McDaniel .15 .40
14 Eric Montross RC .20 .50
15 Dino Radja .15 .40
16 Dominique Wilkins .30 .75
17 Michael Adams .15 .40
18 Muggsy Bogues .20 .50
19 Dell Curry .15 .40
20 Kenny Gattison .15 .40
21 Hersey Hawkins .15 .40
22 Larry Johnson .25 .60
23 Alonzo Mourning .30 .75
24 Robert Parish .25 .60
25 B.J. Armstrong .15 .40
26 Ron Harper .20 .50
27 Steve Kerr .20 .50
28 Toni Kukoc .30 .75
29 Pete Myers .15 .40
30 Will Perdue .15 .40
31 Scottie Pippen .50 1.25
32 Terrell Brandon .15 .40
33 Michael Cage .15 .40
34 Brad Daugherty .20 .50
35 Chris Mills .15 .40
36 Bobby Phills .15 .40
37 Mark Price .25 .60
38 Gerald Wilkins .15 .40
39 John Williams .15 .40
40 Jim Jackson .15 .40
41 Jason Kidd RC 1.25 3.00
42 Jamal Mashburn .25 .60
43 Sean Rooks .15 .40
44 Doug Smith .15 .40
45 Mahmoud Abdul-Rauf .15 .40
46 LaPhonso Ellis .15 .40
47 Dikembe Mutombo .25 .60
48 Robert Pack .15 .40
49 Rodney Rogers .15 .40
50 Jalen Rose RC .60 1.50
51 Bryant Stith .15 .40
52 Reggie Williams .15 .40
53 Bill Curley RC .15 .40
54 Joe Dumars .25 .60
55 Grant Hill RC 1.25 3.00
56 Allan Houston .25 .60
57 Lindsey Hunter .15 .40
58 Oliver Miller .15 .40
59 Terry Mills .15 .40
60 Mark West .15 .40
61 Chris Gatling .15 .40
62 Tim Hardaway .25 .60
63 Chris Mullin .25 .60
64 Billy Owens .15 .40
65 Ricky Pierce .15 .40
66 Latrell Sprewell .30 .75
67 Chris Webber .40 1.00
68 Sam Cassell .25 .60
69 Mario Elie .15 .40
70 Carl Herrera .15 .40
71 Robert Horry .25 .60
72 Vernon Maxwell .15 .40
73 Hakeem Olajuwon .30 .75
74 Kenny Smith .20 .50
75 Otis Thorpe .15 .40
76 Antonio Davis .15 .40
77 Dale Davis .15 .40
78 Mark Jackson .20 .50
79 Derrick McKey .15 .40
80 Reggie Miller .30 .75
81 Byron Scott .20 .50
82 Rik Smits .20 .50
83 Haywoode Workman .15 .40
84 Gary Grant .15 .40
85 Pooh Richardson .15 .40
86 Stanley Roberts .15 .40
87 Elmore Spencer .15 .40
88 Loy Vaught .15 .40
89 Elden Campbell .15 .40
90 Cedric Ceballos .15 .40
91 Doug Christie .15 .40
92 Vlade Divac .25 .60
93 Eddie Jones RC .75 2.00
94 George Lynch .15 .40
95 Anthony Peeler .15 .40
96 Nick Van Exel .25 .60
97 James Worthy .30 .75
98 Grant Long .15 .40
99 Harold Miner .15 .40
100 Glen Rice .25 .60
101 John Salley .15 .40
102 Rony Seikaly .15 .40
103 Steve Smith .20 .50
104 Vin Baker .25 .60
105 Jon Barry .15 .40
106 Todd Day .15 .40
107 Lee Mayberry .15 .40
108 Eric Murdock .15 .40
109 Stacey King .15 .40
110 Christian Laettner .20 .50
111 Donyell Marshall RC .25 .60
112 Isaiah Rider .25 .60
113 Doug West .15 .40
114 Micheal Williams .15 .40
115 Kenny Anderson .20 .50
116 P.J. Brown .15 .40
117 Derrick Coleman .20 .50
118 Yinka Dare RC .15 .40
119 Kevin Edwards .15 .40
120 Armon Gilliam .15 .40
121 Chris Morris .15 .40
122 Anthony Bonner .15 .40
123 Hubert Davis .15 .40
124 Patrick Ewing .30 .75
125 Derek Harper .20 .50
126 Anthony Mason .15 .40
127 Charles Oakley .20 .50
128 Doc Rivers .20 .50
129 Charles Smith .15 .40
130 John Starks .20 .50
131 Charlie Ward RC .25 .60
132 Nick Anderson .15 .40
133 Anthony Bowie .15 .40
134 Horace Grant .20 .50
135 Anfernee Hardaway .40 1.00
136 Shaquille O'Neal .60 1.50
137 Dennis Scott .15 .40
138 Jeff Turner .15 .40
139 Dana Barros .15 .40
140 Shawn Bradley .15 .40
141 Johnny Dawkins .15 .40
142 Jeff Malone .15 .40
143 Tim Perry .15 .40
144 Clarence Weatherspoon .15 .40
145 Scott Williams .15 .40
146 Danny Ainge .25 .60
147 Charles Barkley .40 1.00
148 A.C. Green .20 .50
149 Kevin Johnson .25 .60
150 Joe Kleine .15 .40
151 Antonio Lang .25 .60
152 Dan Majerle .25 .60
153 Danny Manning .20 .50
154 Wayman Tisdale .15 .40
155 Clyde Drexler .30 .75
156 Harvey Grant .15 .40
157 Tracy Murray .15 .40
158 Terry Porter .15 .40
159 Clifford Robinson .15 .40
160 Rod Strickland .15 .40
161 Buck Williams .15 .40
162 Bobby Hurley .15 .40
163 Olden Polynice .15 .40
164 Mitch Richmond .25 .60
165 Lionel Simmons .15 .40
166 Spud Webb .20 .50
167 Walt Williams .15 .40
168 Willie Anderson .15 .40
169 Terry Cummings .20 .50
170 Vinny Del Negro .15 .40
171 Sean Elliott .25 .60
172 Avery Johnson .20 .50
173 Chuck Person .20 .50
174 J.R. Reid .15 .40
175 David Robinson .40 1.00
176 Dennis Rodman .50 1.25
177 Bill Cartwright .20 .50
178 Kendall Gill .15 .40
179 Shawn Kemp .25 .60
180 Nate McMillan .15 .40
181 Gary Payton .25 .60
182 Sam Perkins .15 .40
183 Detlef Schrempf .25 .60
184 David Benoit .15 .40
185 Jeff Hornacek .20 .50
186 Jay Humphries .15 .40
187 Karl Malone .30 .75
188 Bryon Russell .15 .40
189 Felton Spencer .15 .40
190 John Stockton .30 .75
191 Mitchell Butler .15 .40
192 Rex Chapman .15 .40
193 Calbert Cheaney .15 .40
194 Tom Gugliotta .15 .40
195 Don MacLean .15 .40
196 Gheorghe Muresan .15 .40
197 Scott Skiles .15 .40
198 Checklist .15 .40
199 Checklist .15 .40
200 Checklist .15 .40

1994-95 Jam Session Flashing Stars

This eight card oversized (2 1/2" by 4 3/4") set was randomly inserted in 12-card packs at a rate of approximately one in two. The set is composed of the flashiest players in the game like Anfernee Hardaway and Reggie Miller. The fronts have full-bleed color action photos similar to the regular set but the background has swirling colors. The player's name and words "Flashing Star" are in gold foil at the bottom. The NBA Jam Session logo is superimposed on the upper right corner. The backs have color action photos and information explaining why he is a "Flashing star." The cards are numbered on the back as "X of 8" and are sequenced in alphabetical order.

COMPLETE SET (8) 2.00 5.00
1 Anfernee Hardaway .75 2.00
2 Robert Horry .50 1.25
3 Dan Majerle .50 1.25
4 Reggie Miller .60 1.50
5 Mitch Richmond .50 1.25
6 Isaiah Rider .50 1.25
7 Latrell Sprewell .60 1.50
8 Dominique Wilkins .60 1.50

1994-95 Jam Session Gamebreakers

This eight card oversized (2 1/2" by 4 3/4") set was randomly inserted in 12-card packs at a rate of one in four. The set is composed of players who can take control of the game. The fronts have full-bleed color action photos similar to the regular set but the background is a basketball going through a net. The player image is also pushed out slightly which can also be seen from the back to give it a 3-D look. The NBA Jam Session logo is superimposed on the upper right corner. The backs have three layers to it. The background has two colors that are different on each card. A full-color action photo of the player is the middle layer. Up front is the player name in the middle and player information is a hazy white box underneath. The cards are numbered on the back as "X of 8" and are sequenced in alphabetical order.

COMPLETE SET (8) 3.00 8.00
1 Charles Barkley .75 2.00
2 Patrick Ewing .60 1.50
3 Karl Malone .60 1.50
4 Alonzo Mourning .60 1.50
5 Hakeem Olajuwon .60 1.50
6 Shaquille O'Neal 1.25 3.00
7 Scottie Pippen 1.00 2.50
8 David Robinson .75 2.00

1994-95 Jam Session Rookie Standouts

This 20-card oversized (2 1/2" by 4 3/4") set was available exclusively via mail. Information on obtaining the set was on the packs and you had to pay $3.95 to receive the set. The wrapper offer expired on June 30th, 1995. The set contains a selection of the top rookies from the 1994-95 season. The fronts have full-bleed color action photos on a painted background with a black and white action photo in the looming behind. The NBA Jam Session logo is superimposed on the upper left corner. The player's name and the "Rookie Standout" with a basketball under it are in gold foil at the bottom of the card. The backs have a full color action photo also on a painted background and information on the rookie particularly about his college career. The cards are numbered on the back as "X of 20" and are sequenced in alphabetical order.

COMPLETE SET (20) 5.00 12.00
1 Brian Grant .40 1.00
2 Grant Hill 1.25 3.00
3 Juwan Howard .40 1.00
4 Eddie Jones .75 2.00
5 Jason Kidd 1.25 3.00
6 Donyell Marshall .25 .60
7 Eric Montross .20 .50
8 Lamond Murray .25 .60
9 Wesley Person .25 .60
10 Khalid Reeves .20 .50
11 Glenn Robinson .50 1.25
12 Carlos Rogers .20 .50
13 Jalen Rose .60 1.50
14 Clifford Rozier .15 .40
15 Dickey Simpkins .20 .50
16 Michael Smith .15 .40
17 Anthony Tucker .15 .40
18 Charlie Ward .25 .60
19 Monty Williams .20 .50
20 Sharone Wright .20 .50

1994-95 Jam Session Second Year Stars

This eight card oversized (2 1/2" by 4 3/4") set was randomly inserted in 12-card packs at a rate of one in four. The set consists of the best rookies from the 93-94 crop. The fronts are laid out horizontally and have full-bleed color action photos. The player is surrounded by a glowing yellow. The background has a close-up of his face from the action shot and copies of the shot in television screens behind that. The bottom says the player's name and "Second Year Star" in gold foil. The backs are laid out vertically with a full color action photo also surrounded by a glowing yellow on the left with player information on the right. The background is the same player photo set in numerous television screens similar to the front. The cards are numbered on the back as "X of 8" and are sequenced in alphabetical order.

COMPLETE SET (8) 2.00 5.00
1 Vin Baker .50 1.25
2 Anfernee Hardaway .75 2.00
3 Lindsey Hunter .30 .75
4 Toni Kukoc .60 1.50
5 Jamal Mashburn .50 1.25
6 Dino Radja .30 .75
7 Isaiah Rider .50 1.25
8 Chris Webber .75 2.00

1994-95 Jam Session Slam Dunk Heroes

Cards from this eight-card oversized (2 1/2" by 4 3/4") set were randomly inserted in packs at a rate of one in 36. The set is made up of players who jam with authority, namely centers and forwards. The cards have a 100% etched foil design. The fronts have a full color action photo with the player's name and the words "Slam Dunk Hero" boxing in a net are at the bottom in gold foil. The backs have a fuller color action photo on the left with player information on the right. The background on both the fronts and backs have a psychedelic look to it with basketballs floating about. The cards are numbered on the back as "X of 8" and are sequenced in alphabetical order.

COMPLETE SET (8) 25.00 60.00
1 Charles Barkley 5.00 12.00
2 Larry Johnson 3.00 8.00
3 Shawn Kemp 3.00 8.00
4 Jamal Mashburn 3.00 8.00
5 Dikembe Mutombo 3.00 8.00
6 Hakeem Olajuwon 4.00 10.00
7 Shaquille O'Neal 8.00 20.00
8 Chris Webber 5.00 12.00

1995-96 Jam Session

The 1995-96 NBA Jam Session regular card set was issued in one series of 118 cards with 2 checklist cards. Cards were distributed in eight card hobby and retail packs carrying a suggested retail price of $1.59. Forty of the cards are titled "Connection Collection" and feature two players that form a unique tandem. The 78 regular cards are full-bleed color player action photos with a strip at the top with the word "JAM" repeating. Backs include a full color action player shot with a screened strip containing the players biography, a short personality profile, a player rating and NBA career summary. The "Connection Collection" cards are borderless with one-color backgrounds and a full-color action player cutout. Backs of the Connection Collection cards feature an extreme vertical and skewed full-color action photo of the player with a player biography, career stats and a short player profile. Cards are grouped alphabetically by team name. There are no Rookie Cards in this set.

COMPLETE SET (120) 10.00 25.00
1 Stacey Augmon CC .20 .50
2 Mookie Blaylock .15 .40
3 Grant Long .15 .40
4 Steve Smith .20 .50
5 Dee Brown CC .15 .40
6 Sherman Douglas .15 .40
7 Eric Montross .15 .40
8 Dino Radja .15 .40
9 Muggsy Bogues CC .20 .50
10 Scott Burrell .15 .40
11 Larry Johnson CC .25 .60
12 Alonzo Mourning .30 .75
13 Michael Jordan CC 2.00 5.00
14 Steve Kerr .20 .50
15 Toni Kukoc CC .25 .60
16 Scottie Pippen .40 1.00
17 Terrell Brandon .15 .40
18 Tyrone Hill .15 .40
19 Mark Price CC .25 .60
20 John Williams .15 .40
21 Jim Jackson .15 .40
22 Popeye Jones CC .15 .40
23 Jason Kidd CC .40 1.00
24 Jamal Mashburn .25 .60
25 Mahmoud Abdul-Rauf .15 .40
26 Dikembe Mutombo CC .25 .60
27 Robert Pack CC .15 .40
28 Jalen Rose .30 .75
29 Joe Dumars CC .25 .60
30 Grant Hill CC .40 1.00
31 Allan Houston .20 .50
32 Terry Mills .15 .40
33 Chris Gatling .15 .40
34 Tim Hardaway CC .25 .60
35 Donyell Marshall .15 .40
36 Chris Mullin CC .25 .60
37 Latrell Sprewell .25 .60
38 Sam Cassell .25 .60
39 Clyde Drexler CC .30 .75
40 Robert Horry .20 .50
41 Hakeem Olajuwon CC .30 .75
42 Kenny Smith .20 .50
43 Dale Davis .15 .40
44 Mark Jackson .20 .50
45 Reggie Miller CC .30 .75
46 Rik Smits .20 .50
47 Lamond Murray .15 .40
48 Pooh Richardson CC .15 .40
49 Malik Sealy .15 .40
50 Loy Vaught .15 .40
51 Cedric Ceballos .15 .40
52 Vlade Divac .25 .60
53 Eddie Jones .25 .60
54 Nick Van Exel .25 .60
55 Billy Owens .15 .40
56 Khalid Reeves .15 .40
57 Glen Rice CC .25 .60
58 Kevin Willis .15 .40
59 Vin Baker .20 .50
60 Todd Day .15 .40
61 Eric Murdock .15 .40
62 Glenn Robinson CC .20 .50
63 Tom Gugliotta .15 .40
64 Christian Laettner CC .20 .50
65 Isaiah Rider CC .25 .60
66 Doug West .15 .40
67 Kenny Anderson .20 .50
68 P.J. Brown .15 .40
69 Derrick Coleman .20 .50
70 Armon Gilliam .15 .40
71 Patrick Ewing CC .30 .75
72 Derek Harper .20 .50
73 Charles Oakley .20 .50
74 John Starks CC .20 .50
75 Horace Grant CC .20 .50
76 Anfernee Hardaway CC .40 1.00
77 Shaquille O'Neal CC .60 1.50
78 Dennis Scott .15 .40
79 Dana Barros CC .15 .40
80 Shawn Bradley .15 .40
81 Clarence Weatherspoon .15 .40
82 Sharone Wright .15 .40
83 Charles Barkley CC .40 1.00
84 Kevin Johnson CC .25 .60
85 Dan Majerle CC .25 .60
86 Wesley Person CC .15 .40
87 Harvey Grant .15 .40
88 Clifford Robinson .15 .40
89 Rod Strickland .15 .40
90 Buck Williams .15 .40
91 Brian Grant .20 .50
92 Olden Polynice .15 .40
93 Mitch Richmond .25 .60
94 Walt Williams .15 .40
95 Sean Elliott .25 .60
96 Avery Johnson .20 .50
97 David Robinson CC .40 1.00
98 Dennis Rodman .50 1.25
99 Shawn Kemp CC .25 .60
100 Nate McMillan .15 .40
101 Gary Payton .25 .60
102 Detlef Schrempf .25 .60
103 Willie Anderson .15 .40
104 Jerome Kersey .15 .40
105 Oliver Miller .15 .40
106 Ed Pinckney CC .15 .40
107 David Benoit .15 .40
108 Jeff Hornacek CC .20 .50
109 Karl Malone CC .30 .75
110 John Stockton .30 .75
111 Greg Anthony .15 .40
112 Benoit Benjamin .15 .40
113 Blue Edwards .15 .40
114 Kenny Gattison .15 .40
115 Calbert Cheaney .15 .40
116 Juwan Howard .25 .60
117 Gheorghe Muresan CC .15 .40
118 Chris Webber CC .30 .75
119 Checklist .15 .40
120 Checklist .15 .40
NNO Grant Hill Foil Tribute 12.50 30.00

1995-96 Jam Session Die Cuts

COMPLETE SET (120) 25.00 60.00
*DIE CUTS: .75X TO 2X HI COLUMN
D13 Michael Jordan CC 10.00 25.00

1995-96 Jam Session Fuel Injectors

Randomly inserted into all packs at a rate of one in 36, these nine cards feature hot stars of the '90s. Borderless fronts have two-toned backgrounds with the player in a full-color action cutout. The player's image has a fuzzy outline, giving it an electric look. A screened box contains the player's biography and a player profile. The player's career summary appears in black type near the bottom of the card. The set is sequenced in alphabetical order.

COMPLETE SET (9) 40.00 80.00
1 Grant Hill 6.00 15.00
2 Larry Johnson 4.00 10.00
3 Eddie Jones 4.00 10.00
4 Jason Kidd 6.00 15.00
5 Hakeem Olajuwon 5.00 12.00
6 Shaquille O'Neal 10.00 25.00
7 Scottie Pippen 6.00 15.00
8 Glenn Robinson 3.00 8.00
9 Latrell Sprewell 4.00 10.00

1995-96 Jam Session Pop-Ups

Seeded at a rate of one per pack these pop-up cards highlight the play of 25 NBA standouts. Fronts feature the player in full-color action with a crowd background printed with horizontal lines. The cards are perforated around the player's image so that it can be separated from the rest of the card, popped out and displayed standing. Card backs give instructions on how to assemble the card for display. The set is sequenced in alphabetical order. Prices below are for mint unperforated cards.

COMPLETE SET (25) 4.00 10.00
1 Kenny Anderson .25 .60
2 Charles Barkley .50 1.25
3 Mookie Blaylock .20 .50
4 Muggsy Bogues .25 .60
5 Shawn Bradley .20 .50
6 Sam Cassell .30 .75
7 Clyde Drexler .40 1.00
8 Brian Grant .25 .60
9 Horace Grant .25 .60
10 Tim Hardaway .30 .75
11 Grant Hill .50 1.25
12 Jim Jackson .20 .50
13 Shawn Kemp .30 .75
14 Christian Laettner .25 .60
15 Dan Majerle .30 .75
16 Eric Montross .20 .50
17 Alonzo Mourning .40 1.00
18 Gheorghe Muresan .20 .50
19 Lamond Murray .20 .50
20 Dikembe Mutombo .30 .75
21 Charles Oakley .25 .60
22 Scottie Pippen .50 1.25
23 Mark Price .30 .75
24 Glen Rice .30 .75
25 Clifford Robinson .20 .50

1995-96 Jam Session Pop-Ups Bonus

Randomly inserted exclusively in retail packs at a rate of one in 24, this five-card set features a selection of NBA stars. The card fronts are borderless with a full-color action shot set against a crowd background with horizontal fading lines. The player's image is perforated for pop-out assembly. The unnumbered backs include instruction for assembly of the cards. The set is sequenced in alphabetical order. Prices below refer to mint unperforated cards.

COMPLETE SET (5) 8.00 20.00
1 Patrick Ewing 3.00 8.00
2 Grant Hill 4.00 10.00
3 Glenn Robinson 2.00 5.00
4 Jason Kidd 4.00 10.00
5 Jerry Stackhouse 4.00 10.00

1995-96 Jam Session Rookies

Randomly inserted in packs at a rate of one in six, cards from this 10-card set highlight the '95-96 freshman crop. Borderless fronts include a full-color player action cutout with stars winding around the player's image. "Rookie" is printed in a spiraling pattern and serves as the background. Numbered backs feature the player in a full-color cutout pose standing on a hovering star and the background continues with the spiraling pattern with the word "rookie". The player's last name appears over his head.

COMPLETE SET (10) 5.00 12.00
1 Joe Smith .60 1.50
2 Antonio McDyess .60 1.50
3 Jerry Stackhouse 1.50 4.00
4 Rasheed Wallace 1.50 4.00
5 Bryant Reeves .40 1.00
6 Shawn Respert .40 1.00
7 Cherokee Parks .40 1.00
8 Alan Henderson .50 1.25
9 George Zidek .40 1.00
10 Sherrell Ford .40 1.00

1995-96 Jam Session Show Stoppers

Randomly inserted exclusively in hobby packs at a rate of one in 48, this set of nine cards is the rarest of the '95-96 Jam Session collection and features some of the game's best players. The full-bleed, fronts show the player in a full-color cutout against a sparkling, etched blue-foil background The players name is stamped in gold foil at the bottom of the card in all caps. A digital image of the player serves as a background and a smaller full-color action player shot appears on the bottom half of the card. The player's biography and profile wrap around the color shot and his NBA totals appear at the bottom of the card. The set is sequenced in alphabetical order and is condition sensitive due to the etched foil edges.

COMPLETE SET (9) 125.00 250.00
1 Anfernee Hardaway 15.00 40.00
2 Grant Hill 15.00 40.00
3 Michael Jordan 60.00 150.00
4 Karl Malone 10.00 25.00
5 Jamal Mashburn 8.00 20.00
6 Reggie Miller 10.00 25.00
7 David Robinson 12.00 30.00
8 John Stockton 10.00 25.00
9 Chris Webber 10.00 25.00

1995 Jam Session Game Test Samples

Jam Session Test Samples was printed as a sample test card that comes from a never produced for distribution card set. The set's designer turned over his design and concept for this issue, and Fleer ran off a "test" batch of approximately 50-60 sets. The samples were returned to the designer. At this point in time, new management at Fleer decided against putting this set into production and distribution. Each card measures 2.50 x 4.75 inches.

COMPLETE SET (14) 350.00 650.00
P1 Michael Jordan 75.00 150.00
P2 Scottie Pippen 25.00 60.00
P3 Anfernee Hardaway 20.00 40.00
P4 Larry Johnson 15.00 30.00
P5 Shaquille O'Neal 40.00 80.00
P6 Alonzo Mourning 20.00 40.00
P7 Grant Hill 20.00 40.00
P8 John Stockton 40.00 80.00
P9 Karl Malone 40.00 80.00
P10 Kevin Johnson 15.00 30.00
P11 Charles Barkley 35.00 70.00
P12 David Robinson 35.00 70.00
P13 Shawn Kemp 20.00 40.00
P14 Jason Kidd 30.00 60.00

1992-93 Jazz Chevron

This set of cards and pins was sponsored by Chevron. Each card measures 2 1/2" by 5 1/4". The larger top portion presents a color action photo edged by thin team color-coded stripes and a gold section. The smaller bottom portion is white and carries the gold player pin and a Chevron advertisement. The backs display a color closeup photo, biography, checklist, and Chevron advertisement.

COMPLETE SET (5) 9.00 18.00
1 Tyrone Corbin .75 2.00
2 John Stockton 3.00 8.00
3 Jeff Malone .75 2.00
4 Tom Chambers 1.25 3.00
5 Karl Malone 3.00 8.00

1989 Jazz Old Home

This 13-card standard-size set of Utah Jazz was sponsored by Old Home bread (and printed by Fleer), and the Old Home company logo appears on both sides of the card. The cards were distributed as an insert one per loaf of bread with a different card featured each week. The color action player photo on the front has rounded corners, and it is superimposed on a background of yellow, green, and purple stripes of varying width. The player's name and team logo appear above the picture, and the words "1989 Collector's Series" below. That statistics on the card backs are complete up through the 1987-88 season. The horizontally oriented backs are printed in pink and red and present biographical and statistical information.

COMPLETE SET (13) 40.00 80.00
1 Thurl Bailey 2.00 5.00
2 Mike Brown 1.00 2.50
3 Mark Eaton 2.00 5.00
4 Darrell Griffith 2.00 5.00
5 Bobby Hansen 1.50 4.00
6 Marc Iavaroni 1.50 4.00
7 Frank Layden CO 2.50 6.00
8 Eric Leckner 1.25 3.00
9 Jim Les 1.25 3.00
10 Karl Malone 12.50 30.00
11 Jose Ortiz 1.50 4.00
12 Scott Roth 1.25 3.00
13 John Stockton 15.00 40.00

1993-94 Jazz Old Home

These 11 standard-size cards were produced by Hoops for Metz Baking Co.'s Old Home Bread, and were inserted in its products. Twenty thousand cards of each player and coach were produced; 200,000 logo cards were also printed up. One player card and one logo card were inserted per loaf. The card design is nearly identical to the regular 1993-94 Hoops set. The fronts feature borderless glossy color player action shots, with the player's name and team logo appearing in team colors along a ghosted band at the bottom. The back presents a color head shot of the player in a small rectangle bordered with a team color at the upper right. Alongside is his jersey number and position within a team-colored bar. The player's name and a short biography are printed on a hardwood floor design at the top. Below, the player's college and NBA stats, displayed in separate tables on a white background, round out the card. The cards are unnumbered and checklisted below in alphabetical order.

COMPLETE SET (11) 15.00 35.00
1 David Benoit .40 1.00
2 Tom Chambers 1.25 3.00
3 Ty Corbin .40 1.00
4 Mark Eaton .40 1.00
5 Jay Humphries .40 1.00
6 Jeff Malone .40 1.00
7 Karl Malone 6.00 15.00
8 Jerry Sloan CO 2.00 5.00
9 Felton Spencer .40 1.00
10 John Stockton 6.00 15.00
11 Logo Card DP .40 1.00

1988-89 Jazz Smokey

The 1988-89 Smokey Utah Jazz set contains eight 8" by 10" (approximately) cards featuring color action photos. The card backs feature a large fire safety cartoon and player information in the form of year-by-year statistics for each NBA regular season and playoffs. The cards are unnumbered and are ordered below alphabetically. The set was sponsored by the Utah Department of State Lands and Forestry and U.S.D.A. Forest Service. The player's name, number, and position are overprinted in white in the lower right corner of each obverse.

COMPLETE SET (8) 45.00 85.00
1 Thurl Bailey 3.00 8.00
2 Mark Eaton 3.00 8.00
3 Bobby Hansen 3.00 8.00
4 Frank Layden CO 3.00 8.00
5 Karl Malone 12.00 30.00
6 Marc Iavaroni 4.00 10.00
7 John Stockton 15.00 40.00
8 Smokey Bear 1.25 3.00

1990-91 Jazz Star

This 12-card set of Utah Jazz measures the standard size. The fronts feature color action shots, with purple borders that wash out in the middle of the card face. The horizontally oriented backs are printed in purple on white and have various kinds of player information.

COMPLETE SET (12) 1.50 4.00
1 Karl Malone .75 2.00
2 John Stockton .75 2.00
3 Mark Eaton .20 .50
4 Blue Edwards .20 .50
5 Thurl Bailey .20 .50
6 Mike Brown .08 .25
7 Jeff Malone .20 .50
8 Andy Toolson .08 .25
9 Darrell Griffith .20 .50
10 Delaney Rudd .08 .25
11 Walter Palmer .08 .25
12 Jerry Sloan CO .20 .50

1975-76 Jazz Team Issue

This 8"x10" set was produced for the New Orleans Jazz during the 1975-76 season. The set features nine black and white cards of the team's players.

COMPLETE SET (9) 12.50 25.00
1 Ron Behagen 1.25 3.00
2 Fred Boyd 1.25 3.00
3 E.C. Coleman 1.25 3.00
4 Aaron James 1.25 3.00
5 Rich Kelley 1.25 3.00
6 Jim McElroy 1.25 3.00
7 Louie Nelson 1.25 3.00
8 Bud Stallworth 1.25 3.00
9 Nate Williams 1.25 3.00

1973-74 Jets Allentown CBA

This crude eight-card set was produced by G.S. Gallery of Allentown, Pennsylvania, whose name and address are listed at the bottom of each card. The cards feature members of the Allentown Jets of the CBA and measure approximately 2 5/8" by 4 1/4". Uncut sheets are available as well. The card fronts are printed in black ink on light-blue construction-paper stock; the card backs are blank. These sets were originally available from the producer for less than 50 cents each in quantity.

COMPLETE SET (8) 15.00 40.00
1 Tony Johnson 2.00 5.00
2 Allie McGuire 3.00 8.00
3 Frank Card 2.00 5.00
4 George Lehmann 2.50 6.00
5 Dennis Bell 2.00 5.00
6 Ken Wilburn 2.00 5.00
7 George Bruns 2.00 5.00
8 Ed Mast 2.50 6.00

1963 Jewish Sports Champions

The 16 cards in this set, measuring roughly 2 2/3" x 3", are cut out of an "Activity Funbook" entitled Jewish Sports Champions. The set pays tribute to famous Jewish athletes from baseball, football, bull fighting to chess. The cards have a green border with a yellow background and a player close-up illustration. Cards that are still attached carry a premium over those that have been cut-out. The cards are unnumbered and listed below in alphabetical order with an assigned sport prefix (BB-baseball, BK- basketball, BX- boxing, FB- football, OT- other).

COMPLETE SET (16) 100.00 200.00
BK1 Nat Holman BK 12.50 25.00
BK2 Dolph Schayes BK 10.00 20.00

1973 Jewish Sports Champions

The 16 cards in this set, measuring roughly 2 2/3" x 3", are cut out of a sequel to the 1968 Activity Funbook. This time, the cards come from a funbook entitled "More Jewish Sports Champions". There are two variations to each card that are valued equally. One has a pink border with a yellow background and blue ink on the player close-up illustration. The other has a blue background and black ink on the player illustration. Cards that are still attached carry a premium over those that have been cut-out. The cards are unnumbered and listed below in alphabetical order.

COMPLETE SET (16) 65.00 125.00
1 Arnold (Red) Auerbach BK 15.00 30.00

1985-86 JMS Game

These standard size cards were issued by J.M.S. in uncut team sheets as part of a table top game and featured nine players each from the Philadelphia 76ers (1-9), Boston Celtics (10-18), and Los Angeles Lakers (19-27). The front features a color action player photo, with a blue border on red background. Player information appears in a white capsule, and statistics are given below the picture in a pink box. In a horizontal format the back has a statistical breakdown year by year and brief biographical information.

COMPLETE SET (27) 50.00 120.00
1 Maurice Cheeks 2.00 5.00
2 Moses Malone 2.50 6.00
3 Bobby Jones 2.00 5.00
4 Charles Barkley 10.00 25.00
5 Julius Erving 8.00 20.00
6 Clint Richardson .75 2.00
7 Andrew Toney 1.25 3.00
8 Sedale Threatt .75 2.00
9 Clem Johnson .75 2.00
10 Bill Walton 3.00 8.00
11 Danny Ainge 2.50 6.00
12 Robert Parish 2.50 6.00
13 Kevin McHale 3.00 8.00
14 Larry Bird 10.00 25.00
15 Dennis Johnson 2.00 5.00
16 Ray Williams .75 2.00
17 Scott Wedman .75 2.00
18 Greg Kite .75 2.00
19 Michael Cooper 1.50 4.00
20 Kareem Abdul-Jabbar 5.00 12.00
21 Jamaal Wilkes 1.50 4.00
22 Bob McAdoo 2.00 5.00
23 James Worthy 3.00 8.00
24 Magic Johnson 8.00 20.00
25 Michael McGee .75 2.00
26 Kurt Rambis 1.50 4.00
27 Byron Scott 2.00 5.00

1994-96 John Deere

Over a three year period, the John Deere tractor company used professional athletes to promote their products and included cards of these athletes in their set. These five cards were issued in 1994 (Ryan and Novacek), 1995 (Jackson and Petty) and 1996 (Larry Bird). For our cataloguing purposes we are sequencing these cards in alphabetical order. Larry Bird signed some cards for this promotion but these cards are so thinly traded that no pricing is available

COMPLETE SET (5) 15.00 40.00
1 Larry Bird 4.00 10.00
AU1 Larry Bird AU

1957-58 Kahn's

The 1957-58 Kahn's Basketball set contains 11 black and white cards. Cards are approximately 3 3/16" by 3 15/16". The backs contain "How To" articles and instructional text. Only Cincinnati Royals players are depicted.

COMPLETE SET (11) 2000.00 3000.00
1 Richard Duckett 75.00 150.00
2 George King 75.00 150.00
3 Clyde Lovellette 300.00 550.00
4 Tom Marshall 75.00 150.00
5 Jim Paxson UER 150.00 275.00
6 Dave Piontek 75.00 150.00
7 Richard Regan 75.00 150.00
8 Dick Ricketts 175.00 275.00
9 Maurice Stokes 300.00 600.00
10 Jack Twyman 300.00 500.00
11 Bobby Wanzer 150.00 275.00

1958-59 Kahn's

The 1958-59 Kahn's Basketball set contains 10 black and white cards. Cards measure approximately 3 1/4" by 3 15/16". The backs feature a short narrative entitled "My Greatest Thrill in Basketball" allegedly written by the player depicted on the front. Only Cincinnati Royals players are depicted. The Sihugo Green card is supposedly a little tougher to find than the other cards in the set.

COMPLETE SET (10) 1000.00 1500.00
1 Arlen Bockhorn 60.00 125.00
2 Archie Dees 60.00 125.00
3 Sihugo Green 100.00 175.00
4 Vern Hatton 80.00 160.00
5 Tom Marshall 60.00 125.00
6 Jack Parr 80.00 160.00
7 Jim Palmer 60.00 125.00
Card lists him as George, his middle name
8 Jim Palmer 60.00 125.00
9 Dave Piontek 60.00 125.00
10 Jack Twyman 200.00 325.00

1959-60 Kahn's

The 1959-60 Kahn's Basketball set features 10 black and white cards. Cards are approximately 3 1/4" by 4". The backs feature descriptive narratives allegedly written by the player depicted on the front. No statistics are featured on the backs. Only Cincinnati Royals players are depicted.

COMPLETE SET (10) 500.00 900.00
1 Arlen Bockhorn 50.00 100.00
2 Wayne Embry 75.00 150.00
3 Tom Marshall 50.00 100.00
4 Med Park 60.00 120.00
5 Dave Piontek 50.00 100.00
6 Hub Reed 50.00 100.00
7 Phil Rollins 50.00 100.00
8 Larry Staverman 50.00 100.00
9 Jack Twyman 100.00 225.00
10 Win Wilfong 50.00 100.00

1960-61 Kahn's

The 1960-61 Kahn's Basketball set features 12 black and white cards. Cards are approximately 3 1/4" by 3 15/16". The backs contain statistical season-by-season records up through the 1959-60 season, player vital statistics, and a short biography of the player's career. The key cards in the set are the first professional cards of Hall of Famers Oscar Robertson and Jerry West. The Lakers' Jerry West is the only non-Cincinnati Royals player depicted and his card does not have any statistical breakdown.

COMPLETE SET (12) 2000.00 3200.00
1 Arlen Bockhorn 30.00 60.00
2 Bob Boozer 45.00 90.00
3 Ralph E. Davis 25.00 60.00
4 Wayne Embry 50.00 100.00
5 Mike Farmer 25.00 60.00
6 Phil Jordan 30.00 60.00
7 Hub Reed 25.00 60.00
8 Oscar Robertson 700.00 1300.00
9 Larry Staverman 25.00 60.00
10 Jack Twyman 75.00 150.00
11 Jerry West 900.00 1500.00
12 Win Wilfong 25.00 60.00

1961-62 Kahn's

The 1961-62 Kahn's Basketball set consists of 13 black and white cards. Cards measure approximately 3 3/16" by 4 1/16". The Lakers' Jerry West is the only non-Cincinnati Royals player depicted and there is also a card of coach Charley Wolf. The backs of the cards are blank; this was the only year the Kahn's basketball cards were blank backed.

COMPLETE SET (13) 1100.00 1600.00
1 Arlen Bockhorn 20.00 50.00
2 Bob Boozer 35.00 75.00
3 Joe Buckhalter 25.00 50.00
4 Wayne Embry 30.00 60.00
5 Bob Nordmann 25.00 50.00
6 Hub Reed 25.00 50.00
7 Oscar Robertson 300.00 600.00
8 Adrian Smith 35.00 75.00
9 Jack Twyman 65.00 125.00
10 Bob Wesenhahn 25.00 50.00
11 Jerry West 400.00 800.00
12 Charley Wolf CO 20.00 50.00
13 Dave Zeller 25.00 50.00

1962-63 Kahn's

The 1962-63 Kahn's Basketball set contains 11 black and white cards. Cards measure approximately 3 1/4" by 4 3/16". Jerry West of the Lakers is the only non-Cincinnati Royals player depicted and there is also a card of Royals' coach Charley Wolf. The backs feature a short biography of the player depicted on the front of the card. The Jerry West card has a picture with no border around it. Cards of Bockhorn, Boozer, Reed, and Twyman are oriented horizontally.

COMPLETE SET (11) 500.00 1000.00
1 Arlen Bockhorn HOR 15.00 40.00
2 Bob Boozer HOR 25.00 50.00
3 Wayne Embry 30.00 55.00
4 Tom Hawkins 30.00 65.00
5 Bud Olsen 15.00 40.00
6 Hub Reed HOR 15.00 40.00
7 Oscar Robertson 150.00 300.00
8 Adrian Smith 25.00 50.00
9 Jack Twyman HOR 40.00 80.00
10 Jerry West 200.00 400.00
11 Charley Wolf CO 15.00 40.00

1963-64 Kahn's

The 1963-64 Kahn's Basketball set contains 13 black and white cards. Cards measure approximately 3 1/4" by 4 3/16". This is the only Kahn's basketball set on which there is a distinctive white border on the fronts of the cards; in this respect the set is similar to the 1963 Kahn's baseball and football sets. A brief biography of the player is contained on the back of the card. Jerry West of the Lakers is the only non-Cincinnati Royals player depicted and there is also a card of coach Jack McMahon. The Jerry West card is identical to that of the previous year except set in smaller type and with the distinctive white border on the front. The cards of Bob Boozer and Jack Twyman are oriented horizontally.

COMPLETE SET (13) 400.00 800.00
1 Jay Arnette 15.00 30.00
2 Arlen Bockhorn 15.00 30.00
3 Bob Boozer HOR 20.00 45.00
4 Wayne Embry 20.00 45.00
5 Tom Hawkins 35.00 55.00
6 Jerry Lucas 60.00 120.00
7 Jack McMahon CO 15.00 30.00
8 Bud Olsen 15.00 30.00
9 Oscar Robertson 100.00 200.00
10 Adrian Smith 15.00 40.00
11 Tom Thacker 15.00 30.00
12 Jack Twyman HOR 30.00 65.00
13 Jerry West 125.00 250.00

1964-65 Kahn's

The 1964-65 Kahn's Basketball set contains 12 full-color subjects on 14 distinct cards. Cards measure approximately 3" by 3 5/8". These cards come in two types distinguishable by the color of the printing on the backs. Type I cards (1-3) have light maroon printing on the backs, while type II (4-12) have black printing on the backs. The fronts are completely devoid of any written material. There are two poses each of Jerry Lucas and Oscar Robertson.

COMPLETE SET (14) 325.00 650.00
1 Happy Hairston 35.00 70.00
2 Jack McMahon CO 15.00 40.00
3 George Wilson 15.00 30.00
4 Jay Arnette 15.00 30.00
5 Arlen Bockhorn 15.00 30.00
6 Wayne Embry 20.00 45.00
7 Tom Hawkins 20.00 50.00
8A Jerry Lucas 40.00 80.00
8B Jerry Lucas 40.00 80.00
9 Bud Olsen 15.00 30.00
10A Oscar Robertson 75.00 150.00
10B Oscar Robertson 75.00 150.00
11 Adrian Smith 15.00 40.00
12 Jack Twyman 30.00 60.00

1965-66 Kahn's

The 1965-66 Kahn's Basketball set contains four full-color cards featuring players of the Cincinnati Royals. Cards in this set measure approximately 3" by 3 9/16". This was the last of the Kahn's Basketball issues and the second in full color. The fronts are devoid of all written material, and the backs are printed in red ink. The "Compliments of Kahn's, The Wiener the World Awaited" slogan appears on the backs of the cards. The set is presumed complete with the following cards.

COMPLETE SET (4) 150.00 300.00
1 Wayne Embry 20.00 40.00
2 Jerry Lucas 40.00 80.00
3 Oscar Robertson 75.00 150.00
4 Jack Twyman 30.00 60.00

1971 Keds KedKards

This set is composed of crude artistic renditions of popular subjects from various sports from 1971 who were apparently celebrity endorsers of Keds shoes. The cards actually form a complete panel on the Keds tennis shoes box. The three different panels are actually different sizes; the Bing panel contains smaller cards. The smaller Bubba Smith shows him without beard and standing straight; the large Bubba shows him leaning over, with beard, and jersey number partially visible. The individual player card portions of the card panels measure approximately 2 15/16" by 2 3/4" and 2 5/16" by 2 3/16" respectively, although it should noted that there are slight size differences among the individual cards even on the same panel. The panel background is colored in black and yellow. On the Bench/Reed card (number 3 below) each player measures approximately 5 1/4" by 3 1/2". A facsimile autograph appears in the upper left corner of each player's drawing. The Bench/Reed was issued with the Keds Champion boys basketball shoe box, printed on the box top with a black broken line around the card to follow when cutting the card out.

COMPLETE SET (3) 112.50 225.00
1BK Dave Bing 30.00 60.00
2BK Willis Reed 30.00 60.00
3BK Willis Reed 30.00 60.00

1991-92 Kellogg's College Greats

The 1991-92 Kellogg's College Basketball Greats set contains 18 standard-size cards. The cards were inserted into boxes of Kellogg's Raisin Bran through the end of March, 1992. The complete set, including a special card holder, was also available for 2.99 with three proofs of purchase from any size box of Kellogg's Raisin Bran. The front design features a color action photo with the player in his college uniform. The pictures are bordered in different colors on different cards, and the words "College Basketball Greats" is written vertically along the left of each card. In a horizontal format, the back presents outstanding achievements of the player and his college statistics.

COMPLETE SET (18) 2.50 6.00
1 Kenny Anderson .20 .50
2 Clyde Drexler .20 .50
3 Wayman Tisdale .08 .25
4 Horace Grant .08 .25
5 Kevin Johnson .08 .25
6 Karl Malone .40 1.00
7 Larry Bird .75 2.00
8 John Stockton .40 1.00
9 Doug Smith .08 .25
10 Mark Price .08 .25
11 Hakeem Olajuwon .30 .75
12 Charles Smith .08 .25
13 Bernard King .08 .25
14 Tim Hardaway .20 .50
15 Spud Webb .08 .25
16 Mark Macon .08 .25
17 Scottie Pippen .50 1.25
18 Gary Payton .40 1.00
xx Album Holder .60 1.50

1993 Kellogg's College Greats Postercards

This ten-card set was manufactured by Star Pics Inc. for Kellogg's. One of these postercards was inserted into specially marked boxes of Kellogg's Raisin Bran. The cards measure the standard size when folded, but the card front can be lifted up to reveal the postercard, a 2 1/2" by 7" full-length action shot of the player. The card fronts, when folded, display close-up color player photos with colorful graphic art backgrounds within white borders. The Kellogg's College Greats logo appears at the upper left. The players' names are printed in border stripes of various colors at the bottom. The backs are white and present player profiles. The words "Kellogg's Raisin Bran Presents" appear at the top. The inside (postercard) features full-length action shots against a graphic art background that is similar to the front. The players' names are printed on bottom border stripes of various colors. The cards are unnumbered and checklisted below in alphabetical order.

COMPLETE SET (10) 3.00 8.00
1 Kareem Abdul-Jabbar 1.00 2.50
2 Teresa Edwards 1.00 2.50
3 Christian Laettner .30 .75
4 Danny Manning .30 .75
5 Cheryl Miller 1.00 2.50
6 Harold Miner .20 .50
7 Chris Mullin .30 .75
8 Scottie Pippen 1.25 3.00
9 David Robinson .75 2.00
10 Isiah Thomas .30 .75

1998-99 Kellogg's NBA/WNBA

COMPLETE SET (56) 3.00 8.00
*SILVER: .4 TO 1X BASE HI
1 Grant Hill .15 .40
2 Dikembe Mutombo .10 .25
3 Mookie Blaylock .05 .15
4 Antoine Walker .10 .25
5 Chauncey Billups .12 .30
6 Glen Rice .10 .25
7 Vlade Divac .10 .25
8 Scott Burrell .05 .15
9 Ron Harper .07 .20
10 Luc Longley .07 .20
11 Samaki Walker .05 .15
12 Michael Finley .10 .25
13 Tony Battie .07 .20
14 Joe Dumars .10 .25
15 Jerry Stackhouse .10 .25
16 Joe Smith .07 .20
17 Hakeem Olajuwon .12 .30
18 Chris Mullin .10 .25
19 Brent Barry .07 .20
20 Eddie Jones .10 .25
21 Kobe Bryant .40 1.00
22 Tim Hardaway .10 .25
23 Terrell Brandon .05 .15
24 Keith Van Horn .10 .25
25 Sam Cassell .07 .20
26 Charlie Ward .05 .15
27 Horace Grant .07 .20
28 Jason Kidd .15 .40
29 Antonio McDyess .07 .20
30 Jermaine O'Neal .10 .25
31 Mitch Richmond .10 .25
32 David Robinson .15 .40
33 Tim Duncan .20 .50
34 Vin Baker .07 .20
35 Marcus Camby .07 .20
36 Damon Stoudamire .07 .20
37 Karl Malone .12 .30
38 John Stockton .12 .30
39 Shareef Abdur-Rahim .10 .25
40 Juwan Howard .07 .20
41 Sheryl Swoopes .20 .50
42 Cynthia Cooper .20 .50
43 Vicky Bullett .05 .15
44 Andrea Stinson .05 .15
45 Michelle Edwards .12 .30
46 Eva Nemcova .05 .15
47 Lisa Leslie .20 .50
48 Tamecka Dixon .05 .15
49 Rebecca Lobo .15 .40
50 Teresa Weatherspoon .12 .30
51 Michele Timms .10 .25
52 Bridget Pettis .05 .15
53 Ruthie Bolton-Holifield .10 .25
54 Bridgette Gordon .05 .15
55 Tammi Reiss .05 .15
56 Wendy Palmer .05 .15

1948 Kellogg's Pep

These small cards measure approximately 1 7/16" by 1 5/8". The card front presents a black and white head-and-shoulders shot of the player, with a white border. The back has the player's name and a brief description of his accomplishments. The cards are unnumbered, but have been assigned numbers below using a sport (BB- baseball, FB- football, BK- basketball, OT- other) prefix. Other Movie Star Kellogg's Pep cards exist, but they are not listed below. The catalog designation for this set is F273-19. An album was also produced to house the set.

COMPLETE SET (20) 700.00 1400.00
BK1 George Mikan 200.00 400.00

1996 Kellogg's Raptors Stoudamire

These 3 3-D "motion" cards were issued in specially marked boxes of Canadian Kellogg's Frosted Flakes. One card was inserted per box, and only three different cards are known to exist. The box does not list a checklist, so information on any other cards would be appreciated.

COMPLETE SET (3) 4.00 10.00
COMMON CARD (1-3) 1.50 4.00

1992 Kellogg's Team USA Posters

Featuring members of the 1992 U.S. Olympic basketball team, this set of five posters was wrapped in a cello pack and placed between the two cereal boxes of a Kellogg's Raisin Bran jumbo pack. Each poster measures approximately 6 3/4" by 9 1/2" and is printed on glossy paper stock. Kellogg's was an official sponsor of the 1992 U.S. Olympic Team. Inside gold borders, the fronts feature color action cutouts set on a dark background with smoke arising from the hardwood floor. Across the top, the player's name appears in gold lettering, with his nickname in red-and-white lettering. The player's facsimile autograph appears in purple ink across each poster. The backs are blank. The posters were produced and designed by Costacos Brothers. The posters are unnumbered and checklisted below in alphabetical order.

COMPLETE SET (5) 10.00 25.00
1 Larry Bird 5.00 12.00
Larry Legend
2 Karl Malone 3.00 8.00
Mailman
3 Chris Mullin 2.00 5.00
Court Warrior
4 David Robinson 3.00 8.00
Admiral
5 John Stockton 4.00 9.00
Playmaker

1988 Kenner Starting Lineup Cards

1 Kareem Abdul-Jabbar 2.00 5.00
2 Michael Adams .75 2.00
3 Mark Aguirre 1.25 3.00
4 Danny Ainge 1.25 3.00
5 Thurl Bailey 5.00 12.00
6 Charles Barkley 2.50 6.00
7 Walter Berry .75 2.00
8 Larry Bird 3.00 8.00
9 Rolando Blackman 1.50 4.00
10 Michael Cage .75 2.00
11 Joe Barry Carroll .75 2.00
12 Tom Chambers .75 2.00
13 Maurice Cheeks .75 2.00
14 Michael Cooper 2.00 5.00
15 Terry Cummings .75 2.00
16 Adrian Dantley 2.00 5.00
17 Brad Daugherty 1.50 4.00
18 Johnny Dawkins .75 2.00
19 Clyde Drexler 1.50 4.00
20 Mark Eaton 5.00 12.00
21 Dale Ellis 1.25 3.00
22 Alex English 1.25 3.00
23 Patrick Ewing 1.50 4.00
24 Sleepy Floyd 1.25 3.00
25 Winston Garland .75 2.00
26 Armon Gilliam .75 2.00
27 Mike Gminski .75 2.00
28 David Greenwood .75 2.00
29 Derek Harper 1.25 3.00
30 Ron Harper 3.00 8.00
31 Rod Higgins .75 2.00
32 Dennis Hopson .75 2.00
33 Jeff Hornacek 1.25 3.00
34 Mark Jackson 1.00 2.50
35 Dennis Johnson 1.00 2.50
36 Eddie Johnson .75 2.00
37 Magic Johnson 2.50 6.00
38 Steve Johnson .75 2.00
39 Vinnie Johnson 1.50 4.00
40 Michael Jordan 8.00 20.00
41 Bernard King .75 2.00
42 Bill Laimbeer 2.00 5.00
43 Lafayette Lever .75 2.00
44 Jeff Malone .75 2.00
45 Karl Malone 10.00 25.00
46 Moses Malone 2.00 5.00
47 Danny Manning 1.00 2.50
48 Rodney McCray 1.50 4.00
49 Xavier McDaniel .75 2.00
50 Kevin McHale 1.00 2.50
51 Derrick McKey .75 2.00
52 Reggie Miller 6.00 15.00
53 Sidney Moncrief 1.50 4.00
54 Chris Mullin 1.50 4.00
55 Hakeem Olajuwon 1.50 4.00
56 Robert Parish 2.00 5.00
57 John Paxon .75 2.00
58 Sam Perkins 1.50 4.00
59 Chuck Person .75 2.00
60 Scottie Pippen 4.00 10.00
61 Terry Porter .75 2.00
62 Paul Pressey .75 2.00
63 Mark Price 4.00 10.00
64 Doc Rivers 1.00 2.50
65 Alvin Robertson .75 2.00
66 Cliff Robinson .75 2.00
67 Ralph Sampson .75 2.00
68 Danny Schayes 1.50 4.00
69 Jack Sikma 1.25 3.00
70 Kenny Smith .75 2.00
71 Steve Stipanovich 1.25 3.00
72 John Stockton 10.00 25.00
73 Isiah Thomas 1.25 3.00
74 Lasalle Thompson .75 2.00
75 Otis Thorpe .75 2.00
76 Wayman Tisdale .75 2.00
77 Kiki Vandeweghe .75 2.00
78 Spud Webb 1.00 2.50
79 Dominique Wilkins 1.50 4.00
80 Gerald Wilkins .75 2.00
81 Buck Williams .75 2.00
82 John Williams 2.00 5.00
83 Reggie Williams .75 2.00
84 Kevin Willis .75 2.00
85 James Worthy 1.50 4.00

1988 Kenner Starting Lineup Unissued Cards

This five-card set was released to hobby dealers in 1988 to promote Kenner's Starting Lineup figures. These cards are unnumbered and are listed below in alphabetical order.

COMPLETE SET (5) 20.00 50.00
1 Muggsy Bogues 6.00 15.00
2 Walter Davis 2.00 5.00
3 Charles Oakley 6.00 15.00
4 Reggie Theus 4.00 10.00
5 Orlando Woolridge 2.00 5.00

1989 Kenner Starting Lineup Cards

1 Rex Chapman 2.50 6.00
2 Dell Curry 2.50 6.00
3 Ron Harper 2.50 6.00
4 Larry Nance 2.50 6.00
5 Kelly Tripucka 2.50 6.00

1989 Kenner Starting Lineup Legends Collection Cards

2 Wilt Chamberlain 2.50 6.00
1 Julius Erving 3.00 8.00
3 John Havlicek 1.50 4.00
4 Oscar Robertson 2.00 5.00

1989 Kenner Starting Lineup One On One Cards

1 Charles Barkley 3.00 8.00
2 Larry Bird 5.00 12.00
3 Patrick Ewing 2.50 6.00
4 Magic Johnson 4.00 10.00
5 Michael Jordan 10.00 25.00
6 Kevin McHale 2.50 6.00
7 Isiah Thomas 2.50 6.00
8 Dominique Wilkins 2.50 6.00

1990 Kenner Starting Lineup Cards

1 Charles Barkley RY 2.00 5.00
1b Charles Barkley 2.00 5.00
2 Larry Bird RY 3.00 8.00
2b Larry Bird 3.00 8.00
3 Tom Chambers RY .75 2.00
3b Tom Chambers .75 2.00
4 Clyde Drexler RY 1.50 4.00
4b Clyde Drexler 1.50 4.00
5 Joe Dumars RY 1.25 3.00
5b Joe Dumars 1.25 3.00
6 Patrick Ewing RY 1.50 4.00
6b Patrick Ewing 1.50 4.00
7 Magic Johnson RY 2.50 6.00
7b Magic Johnson 2.50 6.00
8 Michael Jordan RY 8.00 20.00
8b Michael Jordan 8.00 20.00
9 Karl Malone RY 1.50 4.00
9b Karl Malone 1.50 4.00
10 Chris Mullin RY 1.25 3.00
10b Chris Mullin 1.25 3.00
11 David Robinson RY 2.00 5.00
11b David Robinson 2.00 5.00
12 Byron Scott RY .75 2.00
12b Byron Scott .75 2.00
13 John Stockton RY 1.50 4.00
13b John Stockton 1.50 4.00
14 Isiah Thomas RY 1.25 3.00
14b Isiah Thomas 1.25 3.00
15 Spud Webb RY 1.00 2.50
15b Spud Webb 1.00 2.50
16 Dominique Wilkins RY 1.25 3.00
16b Dominique Wilkins 1.25 3.00
17 James Worthy RY 1.25 3.00
17b James Worthy 1.25 3.00

1991 Kenner Starting Lineup Cards

1 Charles Barkley 1.50 4.00
2 Clyde Drexler 1.25 3.00
3 David Robinson 1.50 4.00
4 Dennis Rodman 2.00 5.00
5 Derrick Coleman 1.00 2.50
6 Dominique Wilkins 1.25 3.00
7 Isiah Thomas 1.00 2.50
8 Joe Dumars 1.00 2.50
9 Kevin Johnson 1.00 2.50
10 Larry Bird 2.50 6.00
11 Magic Johnson 2.00 5.00
12 Michael Jordan Dunk 4.00 10.00
13 Michael Jordan Dribbling 4.00 10.00
14 Patrick Ewing 1.25 3.00
15 Reggie Lewis 1.00 2.50
16 Spud Webb 1.00 2.50

1992 Kenner Starting Lineup Cards

1 Charles Barkley 1.50 4.00
2 Larry Bird 2.50 6.00
3 Manute Bol .75 2.00
4 Dee Brown .75 2.00
5 Derrick Coleman .75 2.00
6 Vlade Divac .75 2.00
7 Clyde Drexler 1.25 3.00
8 Joe Dumars 1.00 2.50
9 Patrick Ewing 1.25 3.00
10 Tim Hardaway 1.00 2.50
11 Kevin Johnson 1.00 2.50
12 Larry Johnson 1.25 3.00
13 Magic Johnson 2.00 5.00
14 Michael Jordan 4.00 10.00
15 Dan Majerle .75 2.00
16 Karl Malone 1.25 3.00
17 Reggie Miller 1.25 3.00
18 Chris Mullin 1.00 2.50
19 Dikembe Mutombo 1.00 2.50
20 Hakeem Olajuwon 1.25 3.00
21 John Paxson .75 2.00
22 Scottie Pippen 2.00 5.00
23 Mark Price 1.00 2.50
24 David Robinson 1.50 4.00
25 Dennis Rodman 2.00 5.00
26 John Stockton 1.25 3.00
27 Isiah Thomas 1.00 2.50

1993 Kenner Starting Lineup Cards

1 Kenny Anderson TSC 1.00 2.50
1b Kenny Anderson Topps .75 2.00
2 Stacey Augmon TSC 1.00 2.50
2b Stacey Augmon Topps .75 2.00
3 Charles Barkley TSC 2.00 5.00
3b Charles Barkley Topps 1.50 4.00
4 Brad Daugherty TSC 1.00 2.50
4b Brad Daugherty Topps .75 2.00
5 Todd Day TSC 1.00 2.50
5b Todd Day Topps .75 2.00
6 Clyde Drexler TSC 1.50 4.00
6b Clyde Drexler Topps 1.25 3.00
7 Sean Elliott TSC 1.25 3.00
7b Sean Elliott Topps 1.00 2.50
8 Patrick Ewing TSC 1.50 4.00
8b Patrick Ewing Topps 1.25 3.00
9 Horace Grant TSC 1.00 2.50
9b Horace Grant Topps .75 2.00
10 Tom Gugliotta TSC 1.00 2.50
10b Tom Gugliotta Topps .75 2.00
11 Tim Hardaway TSC 1.25 3.00
11b Tim Hardaway Topps 1.00 2.50
12 Larry Johnson TSC 1.25 3.00
12b Larry Johnson Topps 1.00 2.50
13 Michael Jordan TSC 5.00 12.00
13b Michael Jordan Topps 4.00 10.00
14 Shawn Kemp TSC 1.25 3.00
14b Shawn Kemp Topps 1.00 2.50
15 Christian Laettner TSC 1.25 3.00
15b Christian Laettner Topps 1.00 2.50
16 Dan Majerle TSC 1.00 2.50
16b Dan Majerle Topps .75 2.00
17 Karl Malone TSC 1.50 4.00
17b Karl Malone Topps 1.25 3.00
18 Alonzo Mourning TSC 2.00 5.00
18b Alonzo Mourning Topps 1.50 4.00
19 Dikembe Mutombo TSC 1.25 3.00
19b Dikembe Mutombo Topps 1.00 2.50
20 Shaquille O'Neal TSC 5.00 12.00
20b Shaquille O'Neal Topps 4.00 10.00
21 Scottie Pippen TSC 2.50 6.00
21b Scottie Pippen Topps 2.00 5.00
22 Terry Porter TSC 1.00 2.50
22b Terry Porter Topps .75 2.00
23 Mark Price TSC 1.25 3.00
23b Mark Price Topps 1.00 2.50
24 Glen Rice TSC 1.25 3.00
24b Glen Rice Topps 1.00 2.50
25 Mitch Richmond TSC 1.25 3.00
25b Mitch Richmond Topps 1.00 2.50
26 David Robinson TSC 2.00 5.00
26b David Robinson Topps 1.50 4.00
27 Detlef Schrempf TSC 1.25 3.00
27b Detlef Schrempf Topps 1.00 2.50
28 John Stockton TSC 1.50 4.00
28b John Stockton Topps 1.25 3.00
29 Dominique Wilkins TSC 1.50 4.00
29b Dominique Wilkins Topps 1.25 3.00

1994 Kenner Starting Lineup Cards

1 B.J. Armstrong .75 2.00
2 Stacey Augmon .75 2.00
3 Charles Barkley 1.50 4.00
4 Shawn Bradley 1.00 2.50
5 Calbert Cheaney 1.00 2.50
6 Derrick Coleman .75 2.00
7 Sean Elliott 1.00 2.50
8 LaPhonso Ellis 1.00 2.50
9 Patrick Ewing 1.25 3.00
10 Anfernee Hardaway 3.00 8.00
11 Jim Jackson 1.00 2.50
12 Larry Johnson 1.00 2.50
13 Shawn Kemp 1.00 2.50
14 Karl Malone 1.25 3.00
15 Jamal Mashburn 1.25 3.00
16 Harold Miner .75 2.00
17 Alonzo Mourning 1.25 3.00
18 Chris Mullin 1.00 2.50
19 Hakeem Olajuwon 1.25 3.00
20 Shaquille O'Neal 2.50 6.00
21 Scottie Pippen 2.00 5.00
22 David Robinson 1.50 4.00
23 Dennis Rodman 2.00 5.00
24 Latrell Sprewell 1.50 4.00
25 Chris Webber 2.50 6.00
26 Dominique Wilkins 1.25 3.00

1995 Kenner Starting Lineup Cards

1 Charles Barkley 1.50 4.00
2 Muggsy Bogues 1.00 2.50
3 Patrick Ewing 1.25 3.00
4 Horace Grant .75 2.00
5 Anfernee Hardaway 1.50 4.00
6 Grant Hill 3.00 8.00
7 Jeff Hornacek .75 2.00
8 Jim Jackson .75 2.00
9 Shawn Kemp 1.00 2.50
10 Jason Kidd 3.00 8.00
11 Toni Kukoc 1.25 3.00
12 Dan Majerle .75 2.00
13 Karl Malone 1.25 3.00
14 Reggie Miller 1.25 3.00
15 Eric Montross .75 2.00
16 Alonzo Mourning 1.25 3.00
17 Hakeem Olajuwon 1.25 3.00
18 Shaquille O'Neal 2.50 6.00
19 Robert Pack .75 2.00
20 Scottie Pippen 2.00 5.00
21 Mark Price 1.00 2.50
22 Cliff Robinson .75 2.00
23 David Robinson 1.50 4.00
24 Glenn Robinson 1.25 3.00
25 Steve Smith 1.00 2.50
26 Latrell Sprewell 1.00 2.50
27 John Starks 1.00 2.50
28 Nick Van Exel 1.00 2.50
29 Clarence Weatherspoon .75 2.00
30 Chris Webber 1.25 3.00
31 Dominique Wilkins 1.25 3.00

1995 Kenner Starting Lineup Timeless Legends Cards

1 Kareem Abdul-Jabbar 1.50 4.00
2 Wilt Chamberlain 2.00 5.00

1996 Kenner Starting Lineup Cards

1 Vin Baker 1.00 2.50
2 Charles Barkley 1.50 4.00
3 Clyde Drexler 1.25 3.00
4 Sean Elliott 1.00 2.50
5 Patrick Ewing 1.25 3.00
6 Kevin Garnett 4.00 10.00
7 Anfernee Hardaway 1.50 4.00
8 Grant Hill 1.50 4.00
9 Tyrone Hill .75 2.00
10 Juwan Howard 1.00 2.50
11 Larry Johnson 1.00 2.50
12 Eddie Jones 1.00 2.50
13 Jason Kidd 1.50 4.00
14 Karl Malone 1.25 3.00
15 Jamal Mashburn 1.00 2.50
16 Antonio McDyess 1.00 2.50
17 Reggie Miller 1.25 3.00
18 Alonzo Mourning 1.25 3.00
19 Hakeem Olajuwon 1.25 3.00
20 Shaquille O'Neal 2.50 6.00
21 Gary Payton 1.00 2.50
22 Scottie Pippen 2.00 5.00
23 Dino Radja .75 2.00
24 Bryant Reeves .75 2.00
25 Pooh Richardson .75 2.00
26 Mitch Richmond 1.00 2.50
27 Cliff Robinson .75 2.00
28 David Robinson 1.50 4.00
29 Glenn Robinson 1.00 2.50
30 Dennis Rodman 2.00 5.00
31 Joe Smith 1.00 2.50
32 Rik Smits .75 2.00
33 Jerry Stackhouse 1.25 3.00
34 Damon Stoudamire 1.25 3.00
NNO Grant Hill 1.50 4.00
Detroit Pistons Exclusive
NNO Grant Hill 1.50 4.00
Kmart Special

1996 Kenner Starting Lineup Extended Series Cards

1 Charles Barkley 1.50 4.00
2 Kobe Bryant 10.00 25.00
3 Grant Hill 1.50 4.00
4 Allen Iverson 4.00 10.00
5 Larry Johnson 1.00 2.50
6 Dikembe Mutombo 1.00 2.50
7 Shaquille O'Neal 2.50 6.00
8 Damon Stoudamire 1.00 2.50

1997 Kenner Starting Lineup Anaheim Convention Cards

1 Jason Kidd 1.50 4.00
w/Traded To Phoenix Line
2 Shaquille O'Neal 2.50 6.00

1997 Kenner Starting Lineup Atlanta Convention Cards

1 Christian Laettner 1.00 2.50
2 Glen Rice 1.00 2.50

1997 Kenner Starting Lineup Cards

1 Shareef Abdur-Rahim 1.25 3.00
2 Ray Allen 2.50 6.00
3 Kenny Anderson .75 2.00
4 Vin Baker .75 2.00
5 Charles Barkley 1.50 4.00
6 Terrell Brandon .75 2.00
7 Marcus Camby 1.25 3.00
8 Vlade Divac .75 2.00
9 Patrick Ewing 1.25 3.00
10 Michael Finley 1.00 2.50
11 Kevin Garnett 2.00 5.00
12 Horace Grant .75 2.00
14 Grant Hill 1.50 4.00
15 Allan Houston 1.00 2.50
16 Juwan Howard .75 2.00
17 Allen Iverson 1.50 4.00
18 Shawn Kemp 1.00 2.50
19 Jason Kidd 1.50 4.00
20 Kerry Kittles .75 2.00
21 Stephon Marbury 1.00 2.50
22 Reggie Miller 1.25 3.00
23 Alonzo Mourning 1.25 3.00
24 Hakeem Olajuwon 1.25 3.00
25 Shaquille O'Neal 2.50 6.00
26 Gary Payton 1.00 2.50
27 Scottie Pippen 2.00 5.00
28 Mitch Richmond 1.00 2.50
29 David Robinson 1.50 4.00
30 Dennis Rodman 2.00 5.00
31 Bill Russell Dunking 2.00 5.00
32 Bill Russell Dribbling 2.00 5.00
33 Steve Smith 1.00 2.50
34 Latrell Sprewell 1.00 2.50
35 John Stockton 1.25 3.00
36 Damon Stoudamire 1.00 2.50
37 Nick Van Exel .75 2.00
38 Loy Vaught .75 2.00
39 Antoine Walker 1.00 2.50
40 Chris Webber 1.25 3.00

1997 Kenner Starting Lineup Classic Doubles Cards

1 Kareem Abdul-Jabbar 1.50 4.00
2 Wilt Chamberlain 2.00 5.00
3 Joe Dumars 1.00 2.50
4 Patrick Ewing 1.25 3.00
5 Karl Malone 1.25 3.00
6 Kevin McHale 1.00 2.50
7 Hakeem Olajuwon 1.25 3.00
8 Willis Reed 1.00 2.50
9 John Stockton 1.25 3.00

1997 Kenner Starting Lineup Edison Convention Cards

1 Larry Johnson 1.00 2.50
2 Jerry Stackhouse 1.00 2.50

1997 Kenner Starting Lineup Timeless Legends Cards

1 Walt Frazier 1.00 2.50
2 Bill Walton 1.00 2.50

1998 Kenner Starting Lineup Cards

1 Vin Baker 1.00 2.50
2 Terrell Brandon .75 2.00
3 Kobe Bryant 4.00 10.00
4 Patrick Ewing 1.25 3.00
5 Kevin Garnett 1.50 4.00
6 Grant Hill 1.50 4.00

7 Allen Iverson	1.50	4.00
8 Magic Johnson	2.00	5.00
9 Shawn Kemp	1.00	2.50
10 Jason Kidd	1.25	3.00
11 Karl Malone	1.25	3.00
12 Stephon Marbury	1.00	2.50
13 Alonzo Mourning	1.25	3.00
14 Shaquille O'Neal	2.50	6.00
15 Dennis Rodman	2.00	5.00
16 Rik Smits	.75	2.00

1985-86 Kings Big League

This skip-numbered standard-sized set was issued during the 1985-86 season by Big League Trading cards. Each card was produced with white borders, and the card backs carry a "A310" suffix.

COMPLETE SET (18)	10.00	25.00
2 Bill Jones	.40	1.00
Frank Hamblen		
3 Joe Axelson	.40	1.00
9 Joe Meriweather	.40	1.00
10 Eddie Nealy	.40	1.00
11 Mark Olberding	.40	1.00
13 LaSalle Thompson	.40	1.00
16 Mike Woodson	.40	1.00
17 Don Buse	.75	2.00
18 Larry Drew	.40	1.00
19 Rick Benner	.40	1.00
Bob Whitsitt		
Sondra Kasserman		
22 Phil Johnson	.40	1.00
23 Kings Team Photo	.75	2.00
24 Sacramento Arena	.40	1.00
25 Eddie Johnson	.75	2.00
26 Mark McNamara	.40	1.00
30 Reggie Theus	2.00	5.00
32 Otis Thorpe	2.00	5.00
33 Peter Verhoeven	.40	1.00

1988-89 Kings Carl's Jr.

The 1988-89 Carl's Jr. Sacramento Kings set contains 12 cards each measuring approximately 2 1/2" by 3 1/2". There are 11 player cards and one coach card in this set. The cards were issued in three strips of four players plus a coupon for savings at Carl's Jr. restaurants before May 31, 1989. Since this set was issued in late spring of 1989, it includes comments and statistics about the 1988-89 season. The set was produced for Carl's Jr. by Sports Marketing Inc. of Redmond, Washington. The cards are unnumbered except for uniform number; they are ordered below by uniform number.

COMPLETE SET (12)	4.00	10.00
2 Michael Jackson	.20	.50
7 Danny Ainge	1.25	3.00
15 Vinny Del Negro	1.00	2.50
21 Harold Pressley	.20	.50
22 Rodney McCray	.40	1.00
23 Wayman Tisdale	.60	1.50
30 Kenny Smith	1.25	3.00
34 Ricky Berry	.20	.50
43 Jim Petersen	.20	.50
50 Ben Gillery	.20	.50
54 Brad Lohaus	.20	.50
NNO Jerry Reynolds CO	.20	.50

1989-90 Kings Carl's Jr.

This 12-card set of Sacramento Kings was sponsored by Carl's Jr. restaurants and issued in three panels, each containing four player cards and one sponsor's coupon. The cards were given away at three different games in strips of four player cards each. After perforation, the player cards measure the standard size. The front features a color action player photo, with red, white, and blue borders on white card stock. The player's name is written between a thin blue stripe and the top border. The team and sponsors' logos overlay the lower corners of the picture, with the year, position, and uniform number below the picture. The back has two team logos in the upper corners, with biographical information and career summary. The cards are unnumbered and checklisted below by uniform number. The set includes an early professional card of Pervis Ellison, the first pick of the 1989 NBA draft. The player groups on the panels were as follows: Michael Jackson, Vinny Del Negro, Wayman Tisdale, and Pervis Ellison; Danny Ainge, Kenny Smith, Randy Allen, and Ralph Sampson; and Harold Pressley, Rodney McCray, Greg Kite, and Jerry Reynolds.

COMPLETE SET (12)	4.00	10.00
2 Michael Jackson	.20	.50
7 Danny Ainge	1.25	3.00
15 Vinny Del Negro	.60	1.50
21 Harold Pressley	.20	.50
22 Rodney McCray	.40	1.00
23 Wayman Tisdale	.40	1.00
30 Kenny Smith	1.00	2.50
32 Greg Kite	.20	.50
40 Randy Allen	.20	.50
42 Pervis Ellison	.60	1.50
50 Ralph Sampson	.40	1.00
NNO Jerry Reynolds CO	.20	.50

1973-74 Kings Linnett

Measuring 8 1/2" by 11", these nine charcoal drawings are facial portraits by noted sports artist Charles Linnett. The player's facsimile autograph is inscribed across the lower right corner. The backs are blank. Three portraits were included in each package, with a suggested retail price of 99 cents. The portraits are unnumbered and checklisted below in alphabetical order. The set is dated by the fact that 1973-74 was John Block's and Ken Durrett's last year with the Kings but Ron Behagen's and Jimmy Walker's first year with the team.

COMPLETE SET (9)	20.00	40.00
1 Nate Archibald	7.50	15.00
2 Ron Behagen	1.00	2.50
3 John Block	2.00	5.00
4 Mike D'Antoni	2.00	5.00
5 Ken Durrett	1.00	2.50
6 Sam Lacey	3.00	8.00
7 Larry McNeill	1.00	2.50
8 Jimmy Walker	3.00	8.00
9 Nate Williams	1.00	2.50

1990-91 Kings Safeway

This 12-card set of Sacramento Kings was sponsored by Safeway stores and issued in three panels, each containing four player cards and one sponsor's coupon. After perforation, the player cards measure the standard size. The front features a color action player photo, with red, white, and blue borders on white card stock. The player's name is written between a thin blue stripe and the top border. The team and sponsors' logos overlay the lower corners of the picture, with the year, position, and uniform number below the picture. The back has two team logos in the upper corners, with biographical information and career summary. The cards are unnumbered and are checklisted below in alphabetical order.

COMPLETE SET (12)	4.00	8.00
1 Anthony Bonner	.30	.75
2 Antoine Carr	.40	1.00
3 Duane Causwell	.40	1.00
4 Steve Colter	.30	.75
5 Bobby Hansen	.40	1.00
6 Eric Leckner	.30	.75
7 Travis Mays	.30	.75
8 Dick Motta CO	.40	1.00
9 Lionel Simmons	.40	1.00
10 Rory Sparrow	.30	.75
11 Wayman Tisdale	.60	1.50
12 Bill Wennington	.40	1.00

1985-86 Kings Smokey

This 15-card set features members of the Sacramento Kings of the NBA. The cards were originally distributed as a perforated sheet along with (and perforated to) a large team photo. The sheet was distributed to fans attending the Kings' Card Night home game. The cards are numbered on the back in the upper right corner. The cards measure approximately 4" by 5 1/2". The card backs contain a fire safety cartoon but minimal information about the player.

COMPLETE SET (16)	10.00	25.00
1 Smokey Emblem	.75	2.00
2 Phil Johnson CO	.75	2.00
3 Frank Hamblen ACO	.75	2.00
Jerry Reynolds ACO		
Bill Jones TR		
4 Smokey Bear	.75	2.00
5 Michael Adams	1.25	3.00
6 Larry Drew	1.00	2.50
7 Carl Henry	1.00	2.50
8 Eddie Johnson	2.00	5.00
9 Rich Kelley	.75	2.00
10 Joe Kleine	1.25	3.00
11 Mark Olberding	.75	2.00
12 Reggie Theus	2.50	6.00
13 LaSalle Thompson	.75	2.00
14 Otis Thorpe	2.50	6.00
15 Terry Tyler	.75	2.00
16 Mike Woodson	1.25	3.00

1986-87 Kings Smokey

This 15-card set features members of the Sacramento Kings of the NBA. The cards were originally distributed as a perforated sheet along with (and perforated to) a large team photo. The sheet was distributed to fans attending the Kings' Card Night home game. Since the cards are unnumbered, they are listed below in alphabetical order. The player's uniform number (given on both sides of the card) is also listed below. The cards measure approximately 2 3/8" by 3". The card backs contain a fire safety cartoon but minimal information about the player.

COMPLETE SET (15)	10.00	25.00
1 Don Buse ACO	.75	2.00
2 Franklin Edwards 10	.75	2.00
3 Eddie Johnson 8	2.00	5.00
4 Bill Jones TR	.75	2.00
5 Joe Kleine 35	1.00	2.50
6 Mark Olberding 53	.75	2.00
7 Harold Pressley 21	.75	2.00
8 Jerry Reynolds CO	.75	2.00
9 Johnny Rogers 32	.75	2.00
10 Derek Smith 18	1.25	3.00
11 Reggie Theus 24	2.00	5.00
12 LaSalle Thompson 41	.75	2.00
13 Otis Thorpe 33	2.00	5.00
14 Terry Tyler 40	.75	2.00
15 Othell Wilson 2	.75	2.00

1975-76 Kings Team Issue

This oversized set was produced for the Kansas City Kings during the 1975-76 season. The set features 10 cards of the team's players and coaches

COMPLETE SET (10)	12.50	25.00
1 Bob Bigelow	1.25	3.00
2 Glenn Hansen	1.25	3.00
3 Ollie Johnson	1.25	3.00
4 Larry McNeill	1.25	3.00
5 Bill Robinzine	1.25	3.00
6 Jimmy Walker	1.50	4.00
7 Lee Winfield	1.25	3.00
8 Richard Washington	1.25	3.00
9 Dan Sparks ACO	1.25	3.00
10 Phil Johnson CO	1.25	3.00

1993-94 Knicks Alamo

Sponsored by Alamo, this 5-card set measures 3 1/2" by 5 1/2" and features the 1993- 94 New York Knicks. The fronts have borderless color action player photos. The backs have a postcard format and carry the player's name and position, the team's logo and address and the sponsor's logo. The cards are unnumbered and checklisted below in alphabetical order.

COMPLETE SET (5)	1.50	4.00
1 Greg Anthony	.40	1.00
2 Anthony Mason	.40	1.00
3 Charles Oakley	.40	1.00
4 Pat Riley CO	1.25	3.00
5 John Starks	.75	2.00

1988-89 Knicks Frito Lay

This 15-card set was sponsored by Frito Lay. The cards were issued in two sheets; after perforation, the cards measure approximately 2 1/2" by 3 1/2". The front design has color action player photos with white borders. The team logo appears in the lower left corner, with the player's name to the right in a yellow stripe. The horizontally oriented backs have blank print on a gray and white background and present biographical and statistical information. The cards are unnumbered and checklisted below in alphabetical order.

COMPLETE SET (15)	20.00	50.00
1 Greg Butler	.40	1.00
2 Patrick Ewing	8.00	20.00
3 Sidney Green	.40	1.00
4 Mark Jackson	4.00	10.00
5 Pete Myers	.75	2.00
6 Johnny Newman	.75	2.00
7 Charles Oakley	1.50	4.00
8 Rick Pitino CO	2.50	6.00
9 Rod Strickland	1.50	4.00
10 Trent Tucker	.75	2.00
11 Kiki Vandeweghe	2.00	5.00
12 Kenny Walker	.75	2.00
13 Eddie Lee Wilkins	.40	1.00
14 Gerald Wilkins	1.25	3.00
15 Frito Lay	.40	1.00
Manufacturer's Coupon		

1984-85 Knicks Getty Photos

These player cards were printed four to a 7" by 9" panel. Though the panel is not actually perforated, black broken lines indicate where the cards could be cut. After cutting, the cards measure approximately 3 1/2" by 4". The front features a borderless color action photo on thin white cardboard stock. In one of the margins that runs alongside the card, a facsimile autograph is written running the length of the card. A one-inch strip at the bottom of each sheet presents the Knicks' and sponsor's logos. The back has the New York Knicks' logo and a sponsor advertisement that reads "Getty. The Proof is at the Pump." The cards are unnumbered and we have checklisted them below in alphabetical order. The set is dated by the fact that 1984-85 was James Bailey, Ken Bannister, Butch Carter, and Pat Cummings' first year with the Knicks.

COMPLETE SET (11)	20.00	50.00
1 James Bailey	1.25	3.00
2 Ken Bannister	1.25	3.00
3 Hubie Brown CO	4.00	9.00
4 Butch Carter	2.00	5.00
5 Pat Cummings	1.50	4.00
6 Ernie Grunfeld	3.00	8.00
7 Bernard King	5.00	12.00
8 Louis Orr	1.50	4.00
9 Rory Sparrow	2.00	5.00
10 Trent Tucker	2.00	5.00
11 Darrell Walker	3.00	8.00

1989-90 Knicks Marine Midland

This 14-card set of New York Knicks was sponsored by Marine Midland Bank. The cards were issued in one sheet with three rows of five cards each, and they measure the standard size after perforation. The 15th slot is filled by the sponsor's advertisement. The front features a color action photo of the player, with orange borders. The upper left corner of the picture is cut out to provide space for the uniform number. The team logo overlays the lower right corner of the picture, and a row of miniature blue triangles run beneath the bottom orange border. In a horizontal format the back is divided into two boxes and presents biographical (on blue) and statistical information. The cards are unnumbered and are checklisted below in alphabetical order.

COMPLETE SET (14)	15.00	40.00
1 Greg Butler	.50	1.25
2 Patrick Ewing	6.00	15.00
3 Mark Jackson	2.50	6.00
4 Stu Jackson CO	.75	2.00
5 Charles Oakley	1.50	4.00
6 Pete Myers	.60	1.50
7 Johnny Newman	.60	1.50
8 Brian Quinnett	.50	1.25
9 Rod Strickland	1.25	3.00
10 Trent Tucker	.60	1.50
11 Kiki Vandeweghe	1.50	4.00
12 Kenny Walker	.75	2.00
13 Gerald Wilkins	.75	2.00
14 Eddie Lee Wilkins	.50	1.25

1970-71 Knicks Photos

This six card oversized set was released during the 1970-71 season, and features such Knick stars as Bill Bradley and Walt Frazier. Please note that these black and white cards measure 8"x10", and have blank backs.

COMPLETE SET (6)	75.00	150.00
1 Dick Barnett	5.00	10.00
2 Bill Bradley	12.00	30.00
3 Dave DeBusschere	15.00	30.00
4 Walt Frazier	20.00	40.00
5 Willis Reed	15.00	30.00
6 Danny Whelan TR	5.00	10.00

1962-63 Knicks Photos

This six card oversized glossy set was released during the 1962-63 season, and features such Knick stars as Willie Naulls. Please note that these black and white cards measure 8"x10", and have the player names stamped on back. Obviously, this checklist is incomplete and all additional information is welcome.

COMPLETE SET (6)	75.00	150.00
1 Dave Budd	10.00	20.00
2 Donnis Butcher	10.00	20.00
3 Knicks Team Photo	20.00	40.00
4 Whitey Martin	10.00	20.00
5 Willie Naulls	25.00	50.00
6 Unknown		

1972-73 Knicks Photos

This two card oversized set was released during the 1972-73 season, and features such Knicks stars as Bill Bradley and Phil Jackson. Please note that these black and white cards measure 8"x10", and have blank backs.

COMPLETE SET (2)	12.50	25.00
1 Dick Barnett	7.50	15.00
Henry Bibby		
Bill Bradley		
Dave DeBusschere		
Walt Frazier		
John Gianelli		
Phil Jackson		
2 Jerry Lucas	5.00	10.00
Dean Meminger		
Earl Monroe		
Willis Reed		
Tom Riker		
Red Holzman CO		

1970-71 Knicks Portraits

Each of these black and white illustrated portraits measure approximately 9" by 12". The player's name and facsimile autograph are also contained on the front. The backs are blank. The photos are unnumbered and listed below alphabetically.

COMPLETE SET (8)	75.00	150.00
1 Dick Barnett	5.00	10.00
2 Dave DeBusschere	12.50	25.00
3 Walt Frazier	20.00	40.00
4 Red Holzman CO	10.00	20.00
5 Willis Reed	15.00	30.00
6 Mike Riordan	5.00	10.00
7 Cazzie Russell	10.00	20.00
8 Dave Stallworth	5.00	10.00

1986-87 Knicks Tickets

These 24 tickets were issued throughout the 1986-87 N.Y. Knicks basketball season. These are the actual ticket stubs that one would use for admission into Madison Square Garden.

COMPLETE SET (24)	25.00	60.00
1 Dick McGuire	1.25	3.00
Joe Lapchick		
Carl Braun		
2 N.Y. Knicks Team Photo	1.50	4.00
3 Hubie Brown	1.50	4.00
4 Rory Sparrow	.75	2.00
5 Dave Stallworth	.75	2.00
6 Bill Bradley	3.00	8.00
7 Jerry Lucas	1.50	4.00
8 Trent Tucker	.75	2.00
9 Walt Frazier	2.50	6.00
10 Willis Reed	2.00	5.00
11 Red Holzman CO	1.50	4.00
12 Mike Riordan	.75	2.00
13 Harry Gallatin	.75	2.00
14 Johnny Green	.75	2.00
15 Kenny Walker	.75	2.00
16 Bill Cartwright	1.25	3.00
17 Butch Beard	.75	2.00
18 Dean Meminger	.75	2.00
19 Mel Hutchins	.75	2.00
20 Phil Jackson	2.50	6.00
21 Pat Cummings	.75	2.00
22 Kenny Sears	1.25	3.00
23 Bernard King	1.50	4.00
24 Howard Komives	.75	2.00

2008-09 Knicks Upper Deck

COMPLETE SET (14)	2.50	6.00
1 Jamal Crawford	.30	.75
2 Stephon Marbury	.25	.60
3 Zach Randolph	.25	.60
4 David Lee	.20	.50
5 Quentin Richardson	.25	.60
6 Nate Robinson	.20	.50
7 Eddy Curry	.20	.50
8 Wilson Chandler	.25	.60
9 Jared Jeffries	.20	.50
10 Mardy Collins	.20	.50
11 Chris Duhon	.20	.50
12 Danilo Gallinari	.50	1.25
13 Mike D'Antoni CO	.20	.50
14 Patrick Ewing	.40	1.00

1996 Kraft Space Jam

COMPLETE SET (15)	6.00	15.00
1 Bugs Bunny	.20	.50
2 Daffy Duck	.20	.50
3 Lola Bunny	.20	.50
4 Marvin the Martian	.20	.50
5 Michael Jordan	2.00	5.00
Green background		
6 Michael Jordan	2.00	5.00
Red background		
7 Michael Jordan	2.00	5.00
Blue background		
8 Monster Bang	.20	.50
9 Monster Pound	.20	.50
10 Nerdluck Bang	.20	.50
11 Nerdluck Pound	.20	.50
12 Slyvester and Tweety	.20	.50
13 Space Jam Logo	.20	.50
14 Swackhammer	.20	.50
15 Tasmanian Devil	.20	.50

2001-02 Lakers American Express

This six-card set was given away at the April 11, 2002 Lakers game versus the Minnesota Timberwolves. These cards measure 5" by 7" and honor great players from the days when the lakers played in Minneapolis. The fronts feature a posed shot of the player while the back can be used as a postcard. Since these cards are unnumbered, we have sequenced them in alphabetical order.

COMPLETE SET (6)	8.00	20.00
1 John Kundla CO	1.25	3.00
2 Clyde Lovellette	1.25	3.00
3 Slater Martin	1.25	3.00
4 George Mikan	3.00	8.00
5 Vern Mikkelsen	1.25	3.00
6 Jim Pollard	1.25	3.00

1982-83 Lakers BASF

This 13-card set was produced by BASF audio and video tapes in a promotional tie-in with the Los Angeles Lakers. The cards were distributed by Big Ben's and The Wherehouse (both chain record and tape stores in southern California), one player per week, with the final card scheduled for distribution during the week of the NBA championship series. The cards measure approximately 5" by 7" and are unnumbered except for uniform number; they are listed below in alphabetical order for convenience. This set can be distinguished from the other two years of BASF Lakers sets in that it is the only year the set was also sponsored by Big Ben's and the only year there were no facsimile autographs on the back. The set features James Worthy's first professional card.

COMPLETE SET (13)	8.00	20.00
1 Kareem Abdul-Jabbar	2.00	5.00
2 Michael Cooper	1.00	2.50
3 Clay Johnson	.60	1.50
4 Magic Johnson	2.50	6.00
5 Eddie Jordan	.75	2.00
6 Mark Landsberger	.60	1.50
7 Bob McAdoo	1.25	3.00
8 Mike McGee	.60	1.50
9 Norm Nixon	1.00	2.50
10 Kurt Rambis	1.50	4.00
11 Jamaal Wilkes	1.00	2.50
12 James Worthy	3.00	8.00
13 Team Card	1.00	2.50

1983-84 Lakers BASF

This 14-card set was produced by BASF audio and video tapes in a promotional tie-in with the Los Angeles Lakers. The cards measure approximately 5" by 7" and are unnumbered except for uniform number; they are listed below in alphabetical order for convenience. This set can be distinguished from the other two years of BASF Lakers sets in that it is the only year the set was referenced on the front of the card as "Switch to BASF". The set features an early Byron Scott card.

COMPLETE SET (14)	10.00	25.00
1 Kareem Abdul-Jabbar	2.00	5.00
2 Michael Cooper	1.00	2.50
3 Calvin Garrett	.60	1.50
4 Magic Johnson	3.00	8.00
5 Mitch Kupchak	.75	2.00
6 Bob McAdoo	1.25	3.00
7 Mike McGee	.60	1.50
8 Swen Nater	.60	1.50
9 Kurt Rambis	1.25	3.00
10 Byron Scott	1.50	4.00
11 Larry Spriggs	.60	1.50
12 Jamaal Wilkes	1.00	2.50
13 James Worthy	1.50	4.00
14 Team Photo	1.25	3.00
(Team roster on back)		

1984-85 Lakers BASF

This 12-card set was produced by BASF audio and video tapes in a promotional tie-in with the Los Angeles Lakers. The cards measure approximately 5" by 7" and are unnumbered except for uniform number; they are listed below in alphabetical order for convenience.

COMPLETE SET (12)	12.00	30.00
1 Kareem Abdul-Jabbar	2.50	6.00
2 Michael Cooper	1.25	3.00
3 Magic Johnson	3.00	8.00
4 Mitch Kupchak	1.00	2.50
5 Ronnie Lester	1.25	3.00
6 Bob McAdoo	1.50	4.00
7 Mike McGee	.60	1.50
8 Kurt Rambis	1.25	3.00
9 Byron Scott	1.25	3.00
10 Larry Spriggs	.75	2.00
10A Jamaal Wilkes	1.50	4.00
11 James Worthy	2.00	5.00
12 Team Photo	2.00	5.00
(Team roster on back)		

1960-61 Lakers Bell Brand

This card measures approximately 6" by 3 1/2" and features Frank Selvy of the Los Angeles Lakers basketball team. The card was inserted one per bag of Bell Brand Potato Chips reportedly midway through the 1960-61 season. The left half of the card features the player whereas the the right side features a 1961 Los Angeles Lakers schedule. The reverse carries a Bell Brand ad along with a coupon offer of a free game ticket with purchase of potato chips. The card is printed in blue ink on heavy white paper stock. The catalog designation is F391-1.

NNO Frank Selvy	400.00	700.00

1961-62 Lakers Bell Brand

The unattractive cards within this ten-card set measure approximately 6" by 3 1/2" and feature members of the Los Angeles Lakers basketball team. The cards were inserted one per bag of Bell Brand Potato Chips. Each player has two versions of his card, once in blue ink on white stock and again in brown ink on cream-tinted stock. The blue-tint versions show a schedule starting with October 27, whereas the brown-tint versions have a schedule starting with December 2. Some veteran collectors feel that the blue-tint versions are touygher to find. The left half of the card features the player whereas the right side features a Bell Brand ad. The reverse has the Los Angeles Lakers schedule behind the player photo and the free ticket offer behind the ad. The catalog designation is F391-2. The key cards in the set are Elgin Baylor and Jerry West.

COMPLETE SET (10)	5000.00	8000.00
1 Elgin Baylor	1500.00	2500.00
2 Ray Felix	200.00	400.00
3 Tom Hawkins	300.00	600.00
4 Rod Hundley	400.00	800.00
5 Howard Joliff	175.00	350.00
6 Rudy LaRusso	250.00	500.00
7 Fred Schaus CO	200.00	600.00
8 Frank Selvy	250.00	450.00
9 Jerry West	2400.00	3000.00
10 Wayne Yates	150.00	300.00

1992 Lakers Chevron Pins

This lapel pin set features five "Laker Legends" who played between 1957 and 1985. The gold-tone pins show the team name and the years the player was with the Lakers printed in purple at the top. A basketball icon makes up the largest portion of the pin with the player's image superimposed on the basketball. The player's name is at the bottom. The pins come attached to a 2 1/2" by 5 1/8" card that is divided into two sections. The top portion resembles a trading card, displaying a color action player photo in a oval shape bordered by thin purple lines. A white banner below the oval contains the team name. Above the picture, on the orange-yellow background, is the word "Legend" in large purple letters. The entire upper portion is bordered by a purple border with ornate corner detailing. The lower portion makes up only one-third of the card and displays the player's name and a purple outline. Within this area is the lapel pin and the sponsor logo. The backs are white and are printed in black with biographical information, statistics, career highlights, and a checklist for the other pins in the set. The cards are unnumbered and checklisted below in alphabetical order.

COMPLETE SET (5)	8.00	20.00
1 Elgin Baylor	2.00	5.00
2 Gail Goodrich	1.25	3.00
3 Rod Hundley	.75	2.00
4 Jerry West	2.50	6.00
5 Jamaal Wilkes	1.25	3.00

1974-75 Lakers Datsun

These 16 blank backed 8 1/4" x 10 1/4" black and white photos were issued during the 1975-75 season to Southern California Datsun dealers. The photos were given out to customers as a promotional offer as well as a Laker game as a complete set with an accompying envelope.

COMPLETE SET (16)	25.00	50.00
1 B.Sharman/J.Barnhill	2.00	5.00
2 P.Newell/L.Creger	1.25	3.00
3 C.Hearn/L.Shackelford	3.00	8.00
4 Lucius Allen	1.25	3.00
5 Zelmo Beaty	1.25	3.00
6 Corky Calhoun	1.25	3.00
7 Gail Goodrich	2.00	5.00
8 Happy Hairston	1.25	3.00
9 Connie Hawkins	2.00	5.00
10 Stu Lantz	1.25	3.00
11 Stan Love	1.25	3.00
12 Pat Riley	3.00	8.00
13 Cazzie Russell	1.50	4.00
14 Elmore Smith	1.25	3.00
15 Kermit Washington	1.25	3.00
16 Brian Winters	1.25	3.00

1985-86 Lakers Denny's Coins

This nine-coin silver-colored set was distributed by Denny's Restaurants. Each coin measures approximately 1 1/2 " in diameter. The fronts feature an embossed image of the player's head, with the team name, player's name, and jersey number circling the edge of the coin. The backs carry the sponsor logo. The coins are unnumbered and checklisted below in alphabetical order.

COMPLETE SET (9)	15.00	40.00
1 Kareem Abdul-Jabbar	4.00	10.00
2 Michael Cooper	1.25	3.00
3 Magic Johnson	6.00	15.00
4 Bob McAdoo	1.25	3.00
5 Mike McGee	.60	1.50
6 Kurt Rambis	1.25	3.00
7 Byron Scott	1.25	3.00
8 Jamaal Wilkes	1.25	3.00
9 James Worthy	2.50	6.00

1993 Lakers Forum

This set features great sports and entertainment personalities who have appeared at the Great Western Forum in Los Angeles during the past 25 years. The set was sponsored by the Los Angeles Times and "Rebuild LA" and celebrates the 25th Anniversary of the Forum with 25,000 sets produced. The set includes one randomly inserted bonus card in each pack of an outstanding Laker basketball player. The bonus cards were numbered on the back with the prefix "BC". The bonus cards were randomly inserted; one could buy five regular sets and still not guarantee a complete insert set. Noted sports artist Terry Smith designed the set. Proceeds from the 12-card sets, originally priced at 25.00 each, were intended to benefit Los Angeles-area Boys and Girls Clubs. The sets were sold at the Forum's box office and concession stands during all Forum events. Sets could also be ordered through Ticketmaster outlets. The cards measure approximately 2 1/2" by 5". The black card fronts have an inner blue border on the left, right, and upper edges. Across the top is a 25th Anniversary design printed on the border with black points along the upper border edge. The name of the highlighted athlete is printed in white with the first name along the left edge and the last name appearing on the bottom edge. The horizontal backs carry a close-up posed shot on the left with a colored panel on the right giving career highlights and significant information pertaining to their appearances at the Great Western Forum.

COMPLETE SET (11)	6.00	15.00
1 Great Western Forum	.10	.25
BC1 Elgin Baylor	5.00	12.00
BC2 Wilt Chamberlain	6.00	15.00
BC3 Jerry West	6.00	15.00
BC4 Kareem Abdul-Jabbar	6.00	15.00
BC5 Magic Johnson HOR	8.00	20.00

1972-73 Lakers Lunch Bags

Measuring 6" by 11", these five paper lunch bags were manufacturered by Mason Hamlin Ind. in 1972. The bags feature blue pencil drawings with the player's name and "Los Angeles" at the bottom of the bag. There are no backs. The bags are not numbered and listed below in alphabetical order.

COMPLETE SET (5)	25.00	50.00
1 Wilt Chamberlain	10.00	20.00
2 Happy Hairston	3.00	8.00
3 Gail Goodrich	5.00	10.00
4 Jim McMillian	2.50	6.00
5 Jerry West	6.00	12.00

1950-51 Lakers Scott's

This 13-card set was sponsored by Scott's Potato Chips as indicated by its logo appearing on the card face. The cards were printed on heavy stock. A complete set was redeemable for tickets to Minneapolis Lakers games and Minneapolis Lakers player photos. The cards measure approximately 2" by 4 1/2" and were distributed in potato chip and cheese potato boxes. The fronts have a cartoon-like drawing of the player in an action pose, with a facsimile autograph below the drawing. The cards are unnumbered and checklisted below in alphabetical order. The Bud Grant in the set also was active as a player in the CFL and later went on to fame as coach of the Minnesota Vikings.

COMPLETE SET (13)	14000.00	21000.00
1 Bobby Doll	300.00	600.00
2 Arnie Ferrin	400.00	800.00
3 Bud Grant	2000.00	2500.00
4 Bob Harrison	400.00	800.00
5 Joey Hutton	300.00	600.00
6 Tony Jaros	300.00	600.00
7 John Kundla CO	400.00	800.00
8 Slater Martin	900.00	1400.00
9 George Mikan	6000.00	12000.00
10 Vern Mikkelsen	1000.00	1600.00
11 Kevin O'Shea	300.00	600.00
12 Jim Pollard	1000.00	1600.00
13 Herm Schaeffer	300.00	600.00

1969-70 Lakers Tickets

Issued as part of the regular admission tickets to Los Angeles Laker home games, there feature players from the Western Conference Champion Los Angeles Lakers. The tickets are not numbered and listed in alphabetical order below.

COMPLETE SET	40.00	80.00
1 Elgin Baylor	12.50	25.00
2 Wilt Chamberlain	15.00	30.00
3 Keith Erickson	5.00	10.00
4 Jerry West	15.00	30.00

2008-09 Lakers Upper Deck

COMPLETE SET (14)	2.50	6.00
1 Kobe Bryant	1.25	3.00
2 Lamar Odom	.25	.60
3 Pau Gasol	.30	.75
4 Andrew Bynum	.20	.50
5 Derek Fisher	.25	.60
6 Luke Walton	.20	.50
7 Vladimir Radmanovic	.20	.50
8 Jordan Farmar	.20	.50
9 Sasha Vujacic	.20	.50
10 Trevor Ariza	.20	.50
11 Chris Mihm	.20	.50
12 Sun Yue	.40	1.00
13 Phil Jackson CO	.30	.75
14 Magic Johnson	.75	2.00

1979-80 Lakers/Kings Alta-Dena

This eight-card set was sponsored by Alta-Dena Dairy, and its logo adorns the bottom of both sides of the card. The cards measure approximately 2 3/4" by 4" and feature color action player photos on the fronts. While the sides of the picture have no borders, green and red-orange stripes border the picture on its top and bottom. The player's name appears in black lettering in the top red-orange stripe. The team logo appears in the bottom red-orange stripe. The back has an offer for youngsters 14-and-under, who could present the complete eight-card set in the souvenir folder to the Forum Box Office and receive a half-price discount on certain tickets to any one of the Lakers and Kings games listed on the reverse of the card. The cards are unnumbered and are checklisted below in alphabetical order. This small set features Los Angeles Kings and Los Angeles Lakers as they were both owned by Jerry Buss. Cards 1-4 are Los Angeles Lakers (NBA) and Cards 5-8 are Los Angeles Kings (NHL). The set must have been planned and produced in the late summer of 1979 since Adrian Dantley was traded to Utah for Spencer Haywood on September 13

COMPLETE SET (8)	10.00	20.00
1 Adrian Dantley	1.25	3.00
2 Don Ford	.40	1.00
3 Kareem Abdul-Jabbar	5.00	12.00
4 Norm Nixon	.75	2.00

1999-00 Las Vegas Silver Bandits

COMPLETE SET (21)	2.50	6.00
1 Team CL	.08	.25
2 Bandit MASCOT	.08	.25
3 Silver Bandit Dancers	.08	.25
4 Radio Crew	.08	.25
5 Patrick Ballinger TR	.08	.25
6 Isaac Burton	.20	.50
7 Harold Ellis	.40	1.00
8 Michael J. Frog	.20	.50
9 Barry Hecker CO	.40	1.00
10 J.R. Henderson	.30	.75
11 Deeandre Hulett	.20	.50
12 Michael Johnson	.20	.50
13 Doug Lee	.20	.50
14 Marcus Liberty	.30	.75
15 Jeff Martin	.30	.75
16 Tim Neverett ANN	.20	.50
17 Eric Schraeder	.20	.50
18 Rolland Todd CO	.20	.50
19 Doug Swenson	.20	.50
20 Mark Wade	.20	.50
21 Rocky Walls	.20	.50

2012-13 Leaf

COMPLETE SET (100)	15.00	40.00
AG1 Artis Gilmore	.50	1.25
AM1 Arnett Moultrie	.40	1.00
AN1 Andrew Nicholson	.40	1.00
AY1 Alex Young	.50	1.25
BB1 Bradley Beal	1.00	2.50
BHS Bob Hurley Sr.	.60	1.50
BJ1 Bernard James	.40	1.00
BR1 Bill Russell	1.00	2.50
CB1 Carol Blazejowski	.60	1.50
CD1 Clyde Drexler	.75	2.00
CH1 Cliff Hagan	.50	1.25
CH2 Connie Hawkins	.60	1.50
CM1 Chris Mullin	.60	1.50
DC1 Dave Cowens	.40	1.00
DC2 Dusan Cantekin	.50	1.25
DG1 Draymond Green	2.00	5.00
DG2 Drew Gordon	.50	1.25
DI1 Dan Issel	.50	1.25
DJO Darius Johnson-Odom	.40	1.00
DL1 Damian Lillard	2.50	6.00
DL2 Doron Lamb	.40	1.00
DR1 Dennis Rodman	1.25	3.00
DS1 Dolph Schayes	.60	1.50
DW1 Dominique Wilkins	.75	2.00
DW2 Dion Waiters	.60	1.50
EB1 Elgin Baylor	.60	1.50
EH1 Elvin Hayes	.60	1.50
EL1 Earl Lloyd	.60	1.50
EU1 Edwin Ubiles	.60	1.50
FA1 Furkan Aldemir	.50	1.25
FE1 Festus Ezeli	.50	1.25
FM1 Fab Melo	.40	1.00
GG1 Gail Goodrich	.50	1.25
GP1 Gary Payton	.60	1.50
HG1 Hal Greer	.50	1.25
HG2 Harry Gallatin	.60	1.50
HP1 Herb Pope	.50	1.25
IK1 Ilkan Karaman	.50	1.25
JC1 Jae Crowder	.50	1.25
JC2 Jared Cunningham	.40	1.00
JC3 Jim Calhoun	.60	1.50
JCB J'Covan Brown	.50	1.25
JG1 Jorge Gutierrez	.50	1.25
JJ1 John Jenkins	.40	1.00
JK1 John Kundla	.60	1.50
JL1 Jeremy Lamb	.60	1.50
JS1 Jerry Sloan	.60	1.50
JS2 John Shurna	.40	1.00
JT1 Jordan Taylor	.60	1.50
JT2 Jeffery Taylor	.40	1.00
JW1 James Worthy	.75	2.00
KE1 Kim English	.40	1.00
KM1 Karl Malone	.75	2.00
KM2 Kendall Marshall	.40	1.00
KM3 Kevin Murphy	.40	1.00
KM4 Khris Middleton	.60	1.50
KOQ Kyle O'Quinn	.40	1.00
LR1 Leon Radosevic	.50	1.25
MD1 Marcus Denmon	.50	1.25
MH1 Marques Haynes	.50	1.25
MH2 Moe Harkless	.60	1.50
MJ1 Magic Johnson	1.50	4.00
ML1 Meyers Leonard	.50	1.25
MM1 Moses Malone	.60	1.50
MP1 Miles Plumlee	.40	1.00
MS1 Mike Scott	.40	1.00
MSB MarShon Brooks	.50	1.25
MT1 Marquis Teague	.40	1.00
NA1 Nate Archibald	.50	1.25
ND1 Nihad Djedovic	.50	1.25
NN1 Nemanja Nedovic	.50	1.25
NO1 Nnemkadi Ogwumike	.60	1.50
NT1 Nate Thurmond	.50	1.25
OC1 Olek Czyz	.50	1.25
OJ1 Orlando Johnson	.40	1.00
PJ3 Perry Jones	.40	1.00
RB1 Rick Barry	.50	1.25
RH1 Robbie Hummel	.40	1.00
RR1 Ricky Rubio	.60	1.50
RS1 Robert Sacre	.40	1.00
RW1 Royce White	.40	1.00
SM1 Scott Machado	.40	1.00
SP1 Scottie Pippen	1.25	3.00
SS1 Sertac Sanli	.50	1.25
TH1 Tu Holloway	.50	1.25
TJ1 Terrence Jones	.50	1.25
TM1 Tony Mitchell	.50	1.25
TP1 The Professor	.50	1.25
TR1 Terrence Ross	.60	1.50
TS1 Tornike Shengelia	.40	1.00
TT1 Tristan Thompson	.60	1.50
TT2 Tyshawn Taylor	.40	1.00
TW1 Tony Wroten	.50	1.25
TZ1 Tomislav Zubcic	.50	1.25
TZ2 Tyler Zeller	.50	1.25
WB1 Will Barton	.50	1.25
WB2 William Buford	.40	1.00
XG1 Xavier Gibson	.50	1.25
YG1 Yancy Gates	.50	1.25
CW11 Chet Walker	.50	1.25

2012-13 Leaf Autographs

RANDOM INSERTS IN RETAIL PACKS

AG1 Artis Gilmore	2.50	6.00
AM1 Arnett Moultrie	2.00	5.00
AN1 Andrew Nicholson	2.00	5.00
AY1 Alex Young	2.50	6.00
BB1 Bradley Beal	5.00	12.00
BJ1 Bernard James	2.00	5.00
CH1 Cliff Hagan	2.50	6.00
CH2 Connie Hawkins	3.00	8.00
DC1 Dave Cowens	4.00	10.00
DG1 Draymond Green	10.00	25.00
DG2 Drew Gordon	2.50	6.00
DJO Darius Johnson-Odom	6.00	15.00
DL1 Damian Lillard	20.00	50.00
DL2 Doron Lamb	6.00	15.00
DR1 Dennis Rodman	6.00	15.00
DW1 Dominique Wilkins	10.00	25.00
DW2 Dion Waiters	10.00	25.00
EH1 Elvin Hayes	3.00	8.00
EU1 Edwin Ubiles	3.00	8.00
FE1 Festus Ezeli	2.50	6.00
FM1 Fab Melo	10.00	25.00
GG1 Gail Goodrich	2.50	6.00
GP1 Gary Payton		
HG1 Hal Greer	2.50	6.00
HP1 Herb Pope	2.50	6.00
JC1 Jae Crowder	2.50	6.00
JC2 Jared Cunningham	2.00	5.00
JC3 Jim Calhoun	10.00	25.00
JCB J'Covan Brown	2.50	6.00
JG1 Jorge Gutierrez	2.50	6.00
JJ1 John Jenkins	2.00	5.00
JL1 Jeremy Lamb	3.00	8.00
JS2 John Shurna	2.00	5.00
JT1 Jordan Taylor	3.00	8.00
JT2 Jeffery Taylor	2.00	5.00
JW1 James Worthy	8.00	20.00
KE1 Kim English	2.00	5.00
KM2 Kendall Marshall	8.00	20.00
KM3 Kevin Murphy	2.00	5.00
KM4 Khris Middleton	3.00	8.00
KOQ Kyle O'Quinn	2.00	5.00
MD1 Marcus Denmon	2.50	6.00
MH2 Moe Harkless	3.00	8.00
ML1 Meyers Leonard	15.00	40.00
MP1 Miles Plumlee	2.00	5.00
MS1 Mike Scott	2.00	5.00
MT1 Marquis Teague	2.00	5.00
NA1 Nate Archibald	2.50	6.00
NO1 Nnemkadi Ogwumike	6.00	15.00
OC1 Olek Czyz	5.00	12.00
OJ1 Orlando Johnson	2.00	5.00
PJ3 Perry Jones	2.00	5.00
RH1 Robbie Hummel	5.00	12.00

RS1 Robert Sacre 2.00 5.00
SM1 Scott Machado 2.00 5.00
TH1 Tu Holloway 2.50 6.00
TJ1 Terrence Jones 2.50 6.00
TR1 Terrence Ross 3.00 8.00
TS1 Tornike Shengelia 2.00 5.00
TT2 Tyshawn Taylor 2.00 5.00
TW1 Tony Wroten 2.50 6.00
TZ1 Tomislav Zubcic 2.50 6.00
TZ2 Tyler Zeller 2.50 6.00
WB1 Will Barton 2.50 6.00
WB2 William Buford 2.00 5.00
YG1 Yancy Gates 2.50 6.00

2011-12 Leaf Best of Basketball Autographs

ONE PER PACK
UNPRICED RED PRINT RUN 5 SETS
UNPRICED PLATE PRINT RUN ONE SET
AG1 Artis Gilmore 5.00 12.00
BH1 Bailey Howell 5.00 12.00
BH2 Bob Hurley Sr. 10.00 25.00
BR1 Bill Russell 40.00 100.00
CB1 Carol Blazejowski 5.00 12.00
CH1 Cliff Hagan 5.00 12.00
DI1 Dan Issel 5.00 12.00
DR1 Dennis Rodman 15.00 40.00
DS1 Dolph Schayes 5.00 12.00
EH1 Elvin Hayes 5.00 12.00
EL1 Earl Lloyd 10.00 25.00
HG1 Harry Gallatin 5.00 12.00
JK1 John Kundla 10.00 25.00
JS1 Jerry Sloan 5.00 12.00
MB1 MarShon Brooks 6.00 15.00
MG1 Marques Haynes 5.00 12.00
MJ1 Magic Johnson 30.00 80.00
ML1 Meadowlark Lemon 15.00 40.00
MM1 Moses Malone 8.00 20.00
NT1 Nate Thurmond 5.00 12.00
OR1 Oscar Robertson 25.00 60.00
RB1 Rick Barry 6.00 15.00
RR1 Ricky Rubio 6.00 15.00
TP1 The Professor 6.00 15.00
TT1 Tristan Thompson 8.00 20.00
SP1A Scottie Pippen 100.00 200.00

2011-12 Leaf Best of Basketball Autographs Green

*GREEN: .5X TO 1.25X HI COLUMN
STATED PRINT RUN 5 TO 25 SER.#'d SETS
SOME UNPRICED DUE TO SCARCITY
EL1 Earl Lloyd/25 15.00 40.00
MB1 MarShon Brooks/25 15.00 40.00
RR1 Ricky Rubio/25 15.00 40.00
TP1 The Professor/25 15.00 40.00
TT1 Tristan Thompson/25 15.00 40.00

2012-13 Leaf Best of Basketball

UNPRICED PLATE PRINT RUN ONE SET
AG1 Artis Gilmore 5.00 12.00
AM1 Ann Meyers 5.00 12.00
AS1 Arvydas Sabonis 40.00 100.00
BM1 Bob McAdoo 6.00 15.00
BW1 Bill Walton 5.00 12.00
CB1 Carol Blazejowski 5.00 12.00
CD1 Clyde Drexler 12.00 30.00
CL1 Clyde Lovellette 5.00 12.00
CW1 Chet Walker 5.00 12.00
DC1 Denise Curry 5.00 12.00
DC2 Denny Crum 5.00 12.00
DL1 Damian Lillard 15.00 40.00
DR1 David Robinson 12.00 30.00
DR2 Dennis Rodman 10.00 25.00
DS1 Dolph Schayes 5.00 12.00
DW1 Dominique Wilkins 8.00 20.00
EH1 Elvin Hayes 5.00 12.00
EL1 Earl Lloyd 12.00 30.00
GG1 Gail Goodrich 5.00 12.00
GG2 George Gervin 5.00 12.00
GP1 Gary Payton 12.50 30.00
HG1 Hal Greer 5.00 12.00
HG3 Horace Grant 8.00 20.00
HO1 Hakeem Olajuwon 12.00 30.00
JC1 Jim Calhoun 5.00 12.00
JW1 Jamaal Wilkes 5.00 12.00
JW2 James Worthy
LB1 Larry Bird 40.00 100.00
LW1 Lenny Wilkens 5.00 12.00
LW2 Lynette Woodard 5.00 12.00
MJ1 Magic Johnson 30.00 60.00
NA1 Nate Archibald 5.00 12.00
NL1 Nancy Lieberman 5.00 12.00
NO1 Nnemkadi Ogwumike
PR1 Pat Riley 10.00 25.00
RB1 Rick Barry 5.00 12.00
RP1 Robert Parish 5.00 12.00
SP1 Scottie Pippen 20.00 50.00
SS1 Sheryl Swoopes 5.00 12.00
SW1 Spud Webb 5.00 12.00
TK1 Toni Kukoc 6.00 15.00

2012-13 Leaf Best of Basketball Green

*GREEN: .5X TO 1.25X HI COLUMN
STATED PRINT RUN 25 SER.#'d SETS
SOME UNPRICED DUE TO SCARCITY
DL1 Damian Lillard 40.00 100.00

2012 Leaf Inscriptions

IAG1 Artis Gilmore 10.00 25.00
IDR1 Dennis Rodman 50.00 120.00
IMJ1 Magic Johnson 40.00 100.00
ISP1 Scottie Pippen 100.00 200.00

2011 Leaf Legends of Sport

STATED PRINT RUN 6-50
NO PRICING ON CARDS #'d TO 12 OR LESS
BA7 Artis Gilmore/15 12.00 30.00
BA11 Bill Russell/20 50.00 120.00
BA28 Elvin Hayes/15 10.00 25.00
BA51 Meadowlark Lemon/50 20.00 50.00
BA57 Moses Malone/15 15.00 40.00
BA60 Oscar Robertson/15 30.00 60.00
BA69 Rick Barry/27 10.00 25.00

2011 Leaf Legends of Sport Award Winners Autographs Bronze

STATED PRINT RUN 10-50
AW1 Artis Gilmore/15 12.00 30.00
AW3 Bill Russell/20 60.00 120.00

2011 Leaf Legends of Sport Cut Signatures

IT3 Isiah Thomas 12.00 30.00

2011 Leaf Legends of Sport Moments of Greatness Autographs Bronze

STATED PRINT RUN 10-50
MG11 Elvin Hayes/15 10.00 25.00
MG29 Rick Barry/26 10.00 25.00

2011 Leaf Legends of Sport Numeration Autographs

STATED PRINT RUN 4-30
NO PRICING ON CARDS #'d TO 12 OR LESS

2011 Leaf Legends of Sport Perennial All-Stars Autographs

STATED PRINT RUN 5-24
NO PRICING ON CARDS #'d TO 13 OR LESS

2012 Leaf Legends of Sport

BAAG1 Artis Gilmore 6.00 15.00
BABB1 Bradley Beal 8.00 20.00
BABR1 Bill Russell
BACD1 Clyde Drexler 25.00 50.00
BACM1 Chris Mullin 10.00 25.00
BACW1 Chet Walker 6.00 15.00
BADL1 Damian Lillard 60.00 120.00
BADR2 Dennis Rodman 20.00 40.00
BADW1 Dominique Wilkins 10.00 25.00
BAEB2 Elgin Baylor 8.00 20.00
BAGG2 Gail Goodrich 8.00 20.00
BAGP1 Gary Payton 10.00 25.00
BAHG2 Harry Gallatin 6.00 15.00
BAHO1 Hakeem Olajuwon 20.00 40.00
BAJW1 James Worthy 10.00 25.00
BAKM1 Karl Malone 25.00 50.00
BALB1 Larry Bird 40.00 80.00
BAMJ1 Magic Johnson 35.00 70.00
BAMM1 Moses Malone 8.00 20.00
BANO1 Nnemkadi Ogwumike 6.00 15.00
BAOR1 Oscar Robertson 25.00 50.00
BARB1 Rick Barry 6.00 15.00
BASP1 Scottie Pippen 50.00 100.00
BASS1 Sheryl Swoopes 6.00 15.00

2012 Leaf Legends of Sport Unsigned Bronze

ANNOUNCED PRINT RUN 70
ONLINE EXCLUSIVE

2012 Leaf Legends of Sport AKA Autographs

AKABB1 Bradley Beal 20.00 40.00
AKACD1 Clyde Drexler 25.00 50.00
AKADL1 Damian Lillard
AKADR2 Dennis Rodman 20.00 40.00
AKADW1 Dominique Wilkins 10.00 25.00
AKAGP1 Gary Payton 10.00 25.00
AKAHO1 Hakeem Olajuwon 20.00 40.00
AKAJW1 James Worthy 10.00 25.00
AKAKM1 Karl Malone 25.00 50.00
AKALB1 Larry Bird 40.00 80.00
AKAOR1 Oscar Robertson 25.00 50.00

2012 Leaf Legends of Sport Award Winners Autographs

AWBB1 Bradley Beal 15.00 40.00
AWDL1 Damian Lillard 100.00 175.00
AWMJ1 Magic Johnson 35.00 70.00
AWSS1 Sheryl Swoopes 6.00 15.00

2012 Leaf Legends of Sport Numerations Autographs

PRINT RUN 5-45
NACD1 Clyde Drexler/22 12.00 30.00
NACW1 Chet Walker/25 6.00 15.00
NADW1 Dominique Wilkins/21 10.00 25.00
NAEB2 Elgin Baylor/22 12.00 30.00
NAGG2 Gail Goodrich/25 8.00 20.00
NAGP1 Gary Payton/20 12.00 30.00
NAHO1 Hakeem Olajuwon/34 25.00 50.00
NAKM1 Karl Malone/32 25.00 50.00
NALB1 Larry Bird/33 50.00 100.00

2012 Leaf Legends of Sport Perennial All-Stars Autographs

PASCD1 Clyde Drexler 25.00 50.00
PASCW1 Chet Walker 6.00 15.00
PASDR2 Dennis Rodman 10.00 25.00
PASDW1 Dominique Wilkins 10.00 25.00
PASGG2 Gail Goodrich 8.00 20.00
PASGP1 Gary Payton 6.00 15.00
PASNO1 Nnemkadi Ogwumike 6.00 15.00

2012 Leaf Legends of Sport Remembering the Games Autographs

RTGSS1 Sheryl Swoopes 6.00 15.00

2012 Leaf Legends of Sport We Are the Champions Autographs

WCDR2 Dennis Rodman 20.00 40.00
WCHO1 Hakeem Olajuwon 20.00 40.00
WCMJ1 Magic Johnson 35.00 70.00
WCRB1 Rick Barry 6.00 15.00
WCSP1 Scottie Pippen 60.00 120.00

2012-13 Leaf Metal

UNPRICED PLATE PRINT RUN ONE SET
BAAD2 Adrian Dantley 4.00 10.00
BAAD3 Anne Donovan 4.00 10.00
BAAG1 Artis Gilmore 4.00 10.00
BAAM3 Ann Meyers 4.00 10.00
BABA1 B.J. Armstrong 4.00 10.00
BABC1 Bob Cousy 30.00 80.00
BABH1 Bailey Howell 5.00 12.00
BABH2 Bob Houbregs 5.00 12.00
BABM1 Bob McAdoo 8.00 20.00
BABM1 Billie Moore 5.00 12.00
BABR1 Bill Russell 25.00 60.00
BABW1 Bill Walton 5.00 12.00
BACB1 Carol Blazejowski 4.00 10.00
BACH1 Cliff Hagan 4.00 10.00
BACL2 Clyde Lovellette 5.00 12.00
BACM1 Chris Mullin 6.00 15.00
BACO1 Charles Oakley 4.00 10.00
BACW1 Chet Walker 4.00 10.00
BACW2 Charlie Ward 4.00 10.00
BADB1 Dave Bing 12.00 30.00
BADC1 Denny Crum 5.00 12.00
BADD1 Darryl Dawkins 4.00 10.00
BADI1 Dan Issel 4.00 10.00
BADL1 Damian Lillard 25.00 60.00
BADN1 Don Nelson 6.00 15.00
BADR2 Dennis Rodman 12.00 30.00
BADR3 David Robinson 12.00 30.00
BADS1 Dolph Schayes 5.00 12.00
BADW1 Dominique Wilkins 6.00 15.00
BAEH1 Elvin Hayes 5.00 12.00
BAEL1 Earl Lloyd 15.00 40.00
BAGA1 Geno Auriemma 10.00 25.00
BAGG1 George Gervin 6.00 15.00
BAGG2 Gail Goodrich 5.00 12.00
BAHG1 Hal Greer 5.00 12.00
BAHG3 Horace Grant 12.00 30.00
BAJC2 Joan Crawford 4.00 10.00
BAJC3 Jody Conradt 4.00 10.00
BAJC4 John Chaney 5.00 12.00
BAJH2 John Havlicek 10.00 25.00
BAJS2 John Salley 4.00 10.00
BAJS4 John Stockton 20.00 50.00
BAJW1 James Worthy 6.00 15.00
BAJW2 Jamaal Wilkes 4.00 10.00
BAKA1 Kenny Anderson 4.00 10.00
BAKM1 Karl Malone 15.00 40.00
BALB1 Larry Bird 25.00 60.00
BALB2 Leon Barmore 4.00 10.00
BALC1 Lou Carnesecca 6.00 15.00
BALJ1 Larry Johnson 6.00 15.00
BALO1 Lute Olson 8.00 20.00
BALW1 Lynette Woodard 4.00 10.00
BALW1 Lenny Wilkens 5.00 12.00
BAMD3 Mel Daniels 5.00 12.00
BAMH1 Marques Haynes 6.00 15.00
BAMJ1 Magic Johnson 20.00 50.00
BANA1 Nate Archibald 5.00 12.00
BAOB1 Otis Birdsong 4.00 10.00
BAPK1 Phil Knight 8.00 20.00
BAPR1 Pat Riley 8.00 20.00
BARB1 Rick Barry 4.00 10.00
BARH1 Robert Horry 4.00 10.00
BARP1 Robert Parish 6.00 15.00
BARR1 Ricky Rubio 12.00 30.00
BARW2 Roy Williams 10.00 25.00
BASJ1 Sam Jones 6.00 15.00
BASK1 Shawn Kemp 12.00 30.00
BASO1 Shaquille O'Neal 30.00 80.00
BASP1 Scottie Pippen 25.00 60.00
BASS1 Sheryl Swoopes 4.00 10.00
BASS3 Satch Sanders 4.00 10.00
BASW1 Spud Webb 4.00 10.00
BATH2 Tom Heinsohn 10.00 25.00
BATK1 Toni Kukoc 5.00 12.00
BAVC1 Van Chancellor 4.00 10.00
BAXM1 Xavier McDaniel 4.00 10.00

2012-13 Leaf Metal Holo

*HOLO: .5X TO 1.2X BASIC
STATED PRINT RUN 50 SER.#'d SETS
BABK1 Bobby Knight 15.00 40.00

2012-13 Leaf Metal Holo Blue

*HOLO BLUE: .6X TO 1.5X BASIC
PRINT RUNS B/WN 15-25 COPIES PER
NO PRICING ON QTY 15

2012-13 Leaf Metal Patrick Ewing Patch Autograph

STATED PRINT RUN 99 SER.#'d SETS
PE2 Patrick Ewing 150.00 300.00

2012-13 Leaf Metal 1960

UNPRICED PLATE PRINT RUN ONE SET
1 Bill Russell 1.00 2.50
2 Bradley Beal 1.00 2.50
4 Damian Lillard 2.50 6.00
5 Dion Waiters .60 1.50
6 Gary Payton .60 1.50
7 Larry Bird 1.50 4.00
8 Magic Johnson 1.50 4.00
9 Moe Harkless .60 1.50
10 Ricky Rubio .60 1.50
11 Shaquille O'Neal 1.25 3.00
12 Tyler Zeller .50 1.25

2012-13 Leaf Metal 1960 Green

*GREEN: 1X TO 2.5X BASIC
STATED PRINT RUN 25 SER.#'d SETS

2012-13 Leaf Metal Faces of the Game Holo

STATED PRINT RUN 50 SER.#'d SETS
UNPRICED PLATE PRINT RUN ONE SET
FGBR1 Bill Russell 30.00 80.00
FGCM1 Chris Mullin 10.00 25.00
FGDL1 Damian Lillard 25.00 60.00
FGDR1 David Robinson 20.00 50.00
FGDR2 Dennis Rodman 15.00 40.00
FGGG1 George Gervin 8.00 20.00
FGJS4 John Stockton 25.00 60.00
FGKM1 Karl Malone 20.00 50.00
FGLB1 Larry Bird 30.00 80.00
FGMJ1 Magic Johnson 25.00 60.00
FGRR1 Ricky Rubio 20.00 50.00
FGSJ1 Sam Jones 8.00 20.00
FGSK1 Shawn Kemp 15.00 40.00
FGSO1 Shaquille O'Neal 30.00 80.00
FGSP1 Scottie Pippen 30.00 80.00
FGSS1 Sheryl Swoopes 4.00 10.00

2012-13 Leaf Metal Faces of the Game Holo Blue

*HOLO BLUE: .5X TO 1.2X BASIC
STATED PRINT RUN 25 SER.#'d SETS

2012-13 Leaf Metal Hoop Matrix

UNPRICED PLATE PRINT RUN TWO SETS
HMBB1 Bradley Beal 1.00 2.50
HMBC1 Bob Cousy 1.00 2.50
HMBR1 Bill Russell 1.00 2.50
HMDL1 Damian Lillard 2.50 6.00
HMDL2 Damian Lillard 2.50 6.00
HMDL3 Damian Lillard 2.50 6.00
HMDR1 David Robinson 1.00 2.50
HMDR2 Dennis Rodman 1.25 3.00
HMDW1 Dion Waiters .60 1.50
HMGP1 Gary Payton .60 1.50
HMJH1 John Havlicek .75 2.00
HMJL1 Jeremy Lamb .60 1.50
HMJS1 John Stockton 1.00 2.50
HMKM1 Karl Malone .75 2.00
HMKM2 Kendall Marshall .40 1.00
HMLB1 Larry Bird 1.50 4.00
HMMH1 Moe Harkless .60 1.50
HMMJ1 Magic Johnson 1.50 4.00
HMPR1 Pat Riley .60 1.50
HMRR1 Ricky Rubio .60 1.50
HMSK1 Shawn Kemp 1.00 2.50
HMSO1 Shaquille O'Neal 1.25 3.00
HMSP1 Scottie Pippen 1.25 3.00
HMTR1 Terrence Ross .60 1.50
HMTZ1 Tyler Zeller .50 1.25

2012-13 Leaf Metal Hoop Matrix Green

*GREEN: .6X TO 1.5X BASIC
STATED PRINT RUN 99 SER.#'d SETS

2012-13 Leaf Metal Hoop Matrix Pink

*PINK: 1.5X TO 4X BASIC
STATED PRINT RUN 25 SER.#'d SETS

2012-13 Leaf Metal Inductions Holo

STATED PRINT RUN 50 SER.#'d SETS
UNPRICED PLATE PRINT RUN ONE SET
IBH1 Bailey Howell 5.00 12.00
IBR1 Bill Russell 40.00 80.00
IBW1 Bill Walton 8.00 20.00
ICM1 Chris Mullin 10.00 25.00
IDI1 Dan Issel 5.00 12.00
IDR1 David Robinson 20.00 50.00
IDW1 Dominique Wilkins 8.00 20.00
IGG2 Gail Goodrich 8.00 20.00
IJW1 James Worthy 10.00 25.00
IKM1 Karl Malone 25.00 60.00
ILB1 Larry Bird 25.00 60.00
IMH1 Marques Haynes 6.00 15.00
IMJ1 Magic Johnson 25.00 60.00
IRB1 Rick Barry 5.00 12.00
ISJ1 Sam Jones 6.00 15.00
ISP1 Scottie Pippen 40.00 100.00

2012-13 Leaf Metal Inductions Holo Blue

*HOLO BLUE: .5X TO 1.2X BASIC
STATED PRINT RUN 25 SER.#'d SETS

2012-13 Leaf Metal Nicknames Holo

STATED PRINT RUN 50 SER.#'d SETS
UNPRICED PLATE PRINT RUN ONE SET
NNDR1 David Robinson 20.00 50.00
NNDR2 Dennis Rodman 15.00 40.00
NNDW1 Dominique Wilkins 10.00 25.00
NNKM1 Karl Malone 30.00 60.00
NNLB1 Larry Bird 40.00 80.00
NNLJ1 Larry Johnson 6.00 15.00

2012-13 Leaf Metal Nicknames Holo Blue

*HOLO BLUE: .5X TO 1.2X BASIC
STATED PRINT RUN 25 SER.#'d SETS

2012-13 Leaf Metal Unsung Heroes Holo

STATED PRINT RUN 50 SER.#'d SETS
UNPRICED PLATE PRINT RUN ONE SET
UHBA1 B.J. Armstrong 5.00 12.00
UHDD1 Darryl Dawkins 5.00 12.00
UHKA1 Kenny Anderson 5.00 12.00
UHLJ1 Larry Johnson 8.00 20.00
UHRH1 Robert Horry 8.00 20.00
UHSK1 Shawn Kemp 20.00 50.00
UHTK1 Toni Kukoc 6.00 15.00

2012-13 Leaf Metal Unsung Heroes Holo Blue

*HOLO BLUE: .5X TO 1.2X BASIC
STATED PRINT RUN 25 SER.#'d SETS

2011 Leaf Muhammad Ali Fans of Ali Autographs Bronze

OVERALL NON-ALI AUTO ODDS TWO PER PACK
CARD FAU7 NOT ISSUED
FAU3 Magic Johnson 40.00 80.00
FAU10 Dennis Rodman 25.00 50.00

2011 Leaf Muhammad Ali Fans of Ali Autographs Gold

STATED PRINT RUN 5 SER. #'d SETS
UNPRICED DUE TO SCARCITY
CARD FAU7 NOT ISSUED

2011 Leaf Muhammad Ali Fans of Ali Autographs Silver

*SILVER: .6X TO 1.2X BRONZE
STATED PRINT RUN 25 SER. #'d SETS
CARD FAU7 NOT ISSUED

2011 Leaf Muhammad Ali Metal Fans of Ali Autographs

FAUM2 Dennis Rodman 15.00 40.00
FAUM9 Magic Johnson 50.00 100.00

2012 Leaf National Convention

AG1 Artis Gilmore .20 .50
CD1 Clyde Drexler .40 1.00
CH1 Cliff Hagan .20 .50
CH2 Connie Hawkins .25 .60
CM1 Chris Mullin .30 .75
DC1 Dave Cowens .20 .50
DR1 Dennis Rodman .75 2.00
DW1 Dominique Wilkins .40 1.00
EB1 Elgin Baylor .20 .50
EH1 Elvin Hayes .20 .50
GG1 Gail Goodrich .20 .50
GP1 Gary Payton .30 .75
HG1 Hal Greer .20 .50
JC3 Jim Calhoun .20 .50
JW1 James Worthy .40 1.00
MJ1 Magic Johnson .75 2.00
NA1 Nate Archibald .20 .50
SP1 Scottie Pippen .60 1.50

2012 Leaf National Convention VIP

COMPLETE SET (5) 5.00 12.00
VIP1 Bradley Beal 1.50 4.00

2014 Leaf National Convention

COMPLETE SET (10) 4.00 10.00
8 Damian Lillard BK .60 1.50
9 Victor Oladipo BK .50 1.25

2015 Leaf National Convention '90 Leaf Acetate

DL1 Damian Lillard 1.25 3.00
MJ1 Magic Johnson 1.50 4.00

2014 Leaf National Convention Andrew Wiggins

COMPLETE SET (5) 4.00 10.00
COMMON WIGGINS 1.00 2.50
ANNOUNCED PRINT RUN 2000

2014 Leaf National Convention Andrew Wiggins Autographs

COMMON WIGGINS AU 60.00 120.00
ANNOUNCED PRINT RUN 20

2014 Leaf Peck and Snyder Promos

COMPLETE SET (45) 15.00 30.00
11 David Robinson BK
15•Giannis Antetokounmpo BK
22•Karl Malone BK
26•Larry Bird BK
28 Magic Johnson BK
39•Shaquille O'Neal BK
45•Victor Oladipo BK

2014 Leaf Q Autographs Silver

*GOLD/25: .5X TO 1.2X BASIC
AAW1 Andrew Wiggins 40.00 100.00
ADR1 Dennis Rodman 20.00 50.00
AGA1 Giannis Antetokounmpo 12.00 30.00
AVO1 Victor Oladipo 6.00 15.00

2014 Leaf Q Memorabilia Autographs Gold

*GOLD: .6X TO 1.5X BASIC
*GOLD BAT: .4X TO 1X BASIC
*GOLD JKT: .4X TO 1X BASIC
*GOLD SHOE: .4X TO 1X BASIC
RANDOM INSERTS IN PACKS
STATED PRINT RUN 25 SER.#'d SETS
SOME NOT PRICED DUE TO LACK OF INFO

2014 Leaf Q Memorabilia Autographs Silver

ASP1 Scottie Pippen Shoes SP 40.00 100.00
ASP2 Scottie Pippen Pants SP 25.00 60.00
AMCM1 Chris Mullin 12.00 30.00
AMDR1 David Robinson Shoes SP 30.00 80.00
AMDR2 David Robinson Jacket 30.00 80.00
AMDW1 Dominique Wilkins SP 30.00 80.00
AMHO1 Hakeem Olajuwon SP 30.00 80.00
AMLB1 Larry Bird SP 100.00 200.00
AMMH1 Marques Haynes 20.00 50.00

2014 Leaf Q Memorabilia Silver

*GOLD/25: .75X TO 2X BASIC
MSO1 Shaquille O'Neal 8.00 20.00

2014 Leaf Q Pure Autographs Charcoal

*BLUE/22-25: .5X TO 1.2X BASIC
PCM1 Chris Mullin 10.00 25.00
PDR2 David Robinson 15.00 40.00
PDW1 Dominique Wilkins SP 20.00 50.00
PGA1 Giannis Antetokounmpo 12.00 30.00
PMJ1 Magic Johnson 20.00 50.00
PSP1 Scottie Pippen 20.00 50.00

2013 Leaf Rookie Retro Genetic Matrix

COMPLETE SET (25) 50.00 100.00
ONE CARD PER ROOKIE RETRO PACK
GMBB1 Bradley Beal 1.50 4.00
GMDL1 Damian Lillard 3.00 8.00
GMDW1 Dion Waiters 2.00 5.00

2013 Leaf Rookie Retro Genetic Matrix Green

*GREEN/50: .6X TO 1.5X BASIC CARDS

2012-13 Leaf Signature

UNPRICED BLUE PRINT RUN 5 TO 10 SETS
UNPRICED PLATE PRINT RUN ONE SET
UNPRICED PURPLE PRINT RUN ONE SET
UNPRICED RED PRINT RUN 5 SETS
AM1 Arnett Moultrie 2.50 6.00
AN1 Andrew Nicholson 2.50 6.00
AY1 Alex Young 3.00 8.00
BB1 Bradley Beal 6.00 15.00
CD1 Clyde Drexler 10.00 25.00
DG1 Draymond Green 12.00 30.00
DG2 Drew Gordon 3.00 8.00
DL1 Damian Lillard 15.00 40.00
DL2 Doron Lamb 2.50 6.00
DR1 Dennis Rodman 8.00 20.00
DW1 Dominique Wilkins 12.00 30.00
DW2 Dion Waiters 6.00 15.00
EU1 Edwin Ubiles 4.00 10.00
FE1 Festus Ezeli 3.00 8.00
FM1 Fab Melo 2.50 6.00
HP1 Herb Pope 3.00 8.00
JC1 Jae Crowder 3.00 8.00
JC2 Jared Cunningham 2.50 6.00
JCB J'Covan Brown 3.00 8.00
JJ1 John Jenkins 2.50 6.00
JL1 Jeremy Lamb 4.00 10.00
JT2 Jeffery Taylor 2.50 6.00
KE1 Kim English 2.50 6.00
KM1 Karl Malone 15.00 40.00
KM2 Kendall Marshall 2.50 6.00
KM4 Khris Middleton 4.00 10.00
MD1 Marcus Denmon 3.00 8.00
MH1 Marques Haynes 6.00 15.00
MH2 Moe Harkless 4.00 10.00
ML1 Meyers Leonard 3.00 8.00
MS1 Mike Scott 2.50 6.00
MT1 Marquis Teague 2.50 6.00
NO1 Nnemkadi Ogwumike 3.00 8.00
OJ1 Orlando Johnson 2.50 6.00
PJ3 Perry Jones 2.50 6.00
RS1 Robert Sacre 2.50 6.00
RW1 Royce White 2.50 6.00
SM1 Scott Machado 2.50 6.00
SP1 Scottie Pippen 40.00 100.00
TH1 Tu Holloway 3.00 8.00
TJ1 Terrence Jones 3.00 8.00
TR1 Terrence Ross 4.00 10.00
TT2 Tyshawn Taylor 2.50 6.00
TW1 Tony Wroten 3.00 8.00
TZ2 Tyler Zeller 3.00 8.00
WB1 Will Barton 3.00 8.00
XG1 Xavier Gibson 3.00 8.00
YG1 Yancy Gates 3.00 8.00

2012-13 Leaf Signature Gold

*GOLD: .6X TO 1.5X BASE HI
STATED PRINT RUN 10 TO 25 SETS
BB1 Bradley Beal 10.00 25.00
FM1 Fab Melo 12.00 30.00
JJ1 John Jenkins 10.00 25.00
NO1 Nnemkadi Ogwumike 8.00 20.00
PJ3 Perry Jones 15.00 40.00
RW1 Royce White 15.00 40.00

2012-13 Leaf Signature Silver

*SILVER: .5X TO 1.25X BASE HI
STATED PRINT RUN 25 TO 99 SETS
BB1 Bradley Beal/99 8.00 20.00
JJ1 John Jenkins/50 10.00 25.00
TT2 Tyshawn Taylor/99 6.00 15.00

2012-13 Leaf Signature All-American Gold

*GOLD: .6X TO 1.5X SILVER
STATED PRINT RUN 25 SER.#'d SETS
NO1 Nnemkadi Ogwumike 6.00 15.00

2012-13 Leaf Signature All-American Silver

STATED PRINT RUN 75 TO 99 SER.#'d SETS
AM1 Arnett Moultrie/99 2.50 6.00
BB1 Bradley Beal/99 6.00 15.00
DL1 Damian Lillard/99 30.00 60.00
DL2 Doron Lamb/99 2.50 6.00
DW2 Dion Waiters/99 4.00 10.00
FM1 Fab Melo/99 2.50 6.00
JL1 Jeremy Lamb/99 4.00 10.00
JT2 Jeffery Taylor/99 2.50 6.00
KM2 Kendall Marshall/99 2.50 6.00
MH2 Moe Harkless/99 4.00 10.00
ML1 Meyers Leonard/99 3.00 8.00
NO1 Nnemkadi Ogwumike/99 4.00 10.00
PJ3 Perry Jones/99 2.50 6.00
TJ1 Terrence Jones/99 3.00 8.00
TR1 Terrence Ross/99 4.00 10.00
TW1 Tony Wroten/99 3.00 8.00
TZ2 Tyler Zeller/75 3.00 8.00

2012-13 Leaf Signature Black and White

RANDOM INSERTS IN PACKS
UNPRICED BLUE PRINT RUN 3 SETS
UNPRICED GOLD PRINT RUN 5 SETS
UNPRICED PURPLE PRINT RUN ONE SET
UNPRICED RED PRINT RUN 2 SETS
UNPRICED SILVER PRINT RUN 10 SETS
BB1 Bradley Beal 8.00 20.00
CD1 Clyde Drexler 15.00 40.00
DL1 Damian Lillard 30.00 80.00
DL2 Doron Lamb 3.00 8.00
DR1 Dennis Rodman 15.00 40.00
DW1 Dominique Wilkins
KM1 Karl Malone 40.00 100.00
KM2 Kendall Marshall 3.00 8.00
NO1 Nnemkadi Ogwumike
PJ3 Perry Jones 3.00 8.00
SP1 Scottie Pippen 100.00 200.00
TJ1 Terrence Jones 4.00 10.00

2012-13 Leaf Signature Droppin' Dimes Gold

*GOLD: .5X TO 1.25X SILVER
STATED PRINT RUN 25 SER.#'d SETS

2012-13 Leaf Signature Droppin' Dimes Silver

STATED PRINT RUN 49 TO 99 SETS
DL1 Damian Lillard/75 30.00 60.00
KM2 Kendall Marshall/99 3.00 8.00
MT1 Marquis Teague/99 3.00 8.00
SM1 Scott Machado/49 3.00 8.00
TT2 Tyshawn Taylor/99 3.00 8.00
TW1 Tony Wroten/99 4.00 10.00

2012-13 Leaf Signature Scottie Pippen Patch Autographs

STATED PRINT RUN ONE TO 99 SETS
SOME UNPRICED DUE TO SCARCITY
SP1 Scottie Pippen/99 40.00 100.00
SP2 Scottie Pippen Blue/25 100.00 200.00

2012-13 Leaf Signature So Money! Gold

*GOLD: .5X TO 1.25X SILVER
STATED PRINT RUN 25 SER.#'d SETS
NO1 Nnemkadi Ogwumike 8.00 20.00

2012-13 Leaf Signature So Money! Silver

STATED PRINT RUN 40 TO 99 SETS
BB1 Bradley Beal/99 8.00 20.00
DL1 Damian Lillard/99 40.00 80.00
DL2 Doron Lamb/99 3.00 8.00
JJ1 John Jenkins/99 8.00 20.00
JL1 Jeremy Lamb/99 5.00 12.00
KM1 Karl Malone/40 25.00 60.00
MH2 Moe Harkless/99 5.00 12.00
MT1 Marquis Teague/99 3.00 8.00
NO1 Nnemkadi Ogwumike/99 4.00 10.00
PJ3 Perry Jones/75 3.00 8.00
TR1 Terrence Ross/99 5.00 12.00
TZ2 Tyler Zeller/75 4.00 10.00

2012-13 Leaf Signature Takin' it to the Hole Gold

*GOLD: .5X TO 1.25X SILVER
STATED PRINT RUN 25 SER.#'d SETS
DG1 Draymond Green 20.00 50.00
NO1 Nnemkadi Ogwumike 8.00 20.00

2012-13 Leaf Signature Takin' it to the Hole Silver

STATED PRINT RUN 99 SER.#'d SETS
AM1 Arnett Moultrie/99 3.00 8.00
AN1 Andrew Nicholson/99 3.00 8.00
BB1 Bradley Beal/99 8.00 20.00
DG1 Draymond Green/49 15.00 40.00
DL1 Damian Lillard/75 20.00 50.00
DW2 Dion Waiters/49 5.00 12.00
JT2 Jeffery Taylor/49 3.00 8.00
MH2 Moe Harkless/49 5.00 12.00
NO1 Nnemkadi Ogwumike/99 4.00 10.00
RW1 Royce White/99 3.00 8.00
TJ1 Terrence Jones/49 4.00 10.00
TR1 Terrence Ross/99 5.00 12.00
WB1 Will Barton/99 4.00 10.00

2013 Leaf Sports Heroes

BAAM2 Ann Meyers 4.00 10.00
BABW1 Bill Walton 6.00 15.00
BACC1 Cynthia Cooper 4.00 10.00
BACD1 Clyde Drexler/17* 12.00 30.00
BACH1 Cliff Hagan 4.00 10.00
BADR1 Dennis Rodman 10.00 25.00
BADW2 Dominique Wilkins 8.00 20.00
BAGG1 George Gervin 5.00 12.00
BAHO1 Hakeem Olajuwon/17* 12.00 30.00
BAJC2 Jim Calhoun 6.00 15.00
BALB1 Larry Bird/5*
BAMJ1 Magic Johnson 15.00 40.00
BAOR1 Oscar Robertson/19*
BAPR1 Pat Riley/7*
BARB1 Rick Barry 5.00 12.00
BARP1 Robert Parish 4.00 10.00
VO Victor Oladipo 15.00 40.00
VO1 Victor Oladipo STATE PRIDE 10.00 25.00

2013 Leaf Sports Heroes Going for the Gold Autographs

*SILVER/25: .5X TO 1.2X BASIC CARDS
GGDR2 David Robinson 20.00 50.00
GGDW2 Dominique Wilkins 8.00 20.00

2013 Leaf Sports Heroes Going for the Gold Autographs Silver

*SILVER: .5X TO 1.2X BASIC CARDS
STATED PRINT RUN 25 SER.#'d SETS

2013 Leaf Sports Heroes Inscriptions Autographs

STATED PRINT RUN 60 SER. #'d SETS
IDL1 Damian Lillard 40.00 80.00

2013 Leaf Sports Heroes Inscriptions Autographs Silver

*SILVER: .5X TO 1.2X BASIC CARDS
STATED PRINT RUN 25 SER.#'d SETS

2013 Leaf Sports Heroes Loyalty Autographs

*SILVER/25: .5X TO 1.2X BASIC CARDS
LMJ1 Magic Johnson 15.00 40.00

2013 Leaf Sports Heroes Loyalty Autographs Silver

*SILVER: .5X TO 1.2X BASIC CARDS
STATED PRINT RUN 25 SER.#'d SETS

2013 Leaf Sports Heroes Pink Ribbon Inscription Autographs

STATED PRINT RUN 60 SER. #'d SETS
DL1 Damian Lillard 50.00 100.00

2013 Leaf Sports Heroes Pink Ribbon Inscription Autographs Silver

*SILVER: .5X TO 1.2X BASIC CARDS
STATED PRINT RUN 25 SER.#'d SETS

2013 Leaf Sports Heroes Springfield's Finest Autographs

SFAM2 Ann Meyers 4.00 10.00
SFAS1 Arvydas Sabonis 15.00 40.00
SFBW1 Bill Walton 8.00 20.00
SFCC1 Cynthia Cooper 4.00 10.00
SFCD1 Clyde Drexler/17* 8.00 20.00
SFCH1 Cliff Hagan 4.00 10.00
SFDR1 Dennis Rodman 10.00 25.00
SFDW2 Dominique Wilkins 10.00 25.00
SFGG1 George Gervin 6.00 15.00
SFGG2 Gail Goodrich 6.00 15.00
SFGP1 Gary Payton 5.00 12.00
SFJC2 Jim Calhoun 5.00 12.00
SFRB1 Rick Barry 5.00 12.00
SFRP1 Robert Parish 6.00 15.00

2013 Leaf Sports Heroes Springfield's Finest Autographs Silver

*SILVER: .5X TO 1.2X BASIC CARDS
STATED PRINT RUN 25 SER.#'d SETS

2013 Leaf Sports Heroes Valiant Damian Lillard Autographs

BADL1 Damian Lillard 20.00 50.00
ROYDL1 Damian Lillard 20.00 50.00

2013 Leaf Sports Heroes Valiant Damian Lillard Autographs Orange

*ORANGE: .5X TO 1.2X BASIC CARDS
STATED PRINT RUN 50 SER.#'d SETS

2013 Leaf Sports Heroes Valiant Damian Lillard Autographs Purple

*PURPLE: .6X TO 1.5X BASIC CARDS
STATED PRINT RUN 25 SER. #'d SETS

2012-13 Leaf Ultimate

UNPRICED GOLD PRINT RUN 10 SER.#'d SETS
UNPRICED PLATE PRINT RUN ONE SER.#'d SET
UNPRICED PURPLE PRINT RUN ONE SER.#'d SET
UNPRICED RED PRINT RUN 5 SER.#'d SETS
AN1 Andrew Nicholson 2.00 5.00
BB1 Bradley Beal 10.00 25.00
BJ1 Bernard James 2.00 5.00
CD1 Clyde Drexler 10.00 25.00
DG1 Draymond Green 10.00 25.00
DL1 Damian Lillard 25.00 60.00
DL2 Doron Lamb 2.00 5.00
DR1 Dennis Rodman 10.00 25.00
DW1 Dominique Wilkins 8.00 20.00
DW2 Dion Waiters 5.00 12.00
EL1 Earl Lloyd 15.00 40.00
FE1 Festus Ezeli 2.50 6.00
FM1 Fab Melo 2.00 5.00
HP1 Herb Pope 2.50 6.00
JC1 Jae Crowder 2.50 6.00
JC2 Jared Cunningham 2.00 5.00
JJ1 John Jenkins 2.00 5.00
JL1 Jeremy Lamb 3.00 8.00
JT2 Jeffery Taylor 2.00 5.00
JW1 James Worthy 8.00 20.00
KE1 Kim English 2.00 5.00
KM1 Karl Malone 15.00 40.00
KM2 Kendall Marshall 2.00 5.00
KM4 Khris Middleton 3.00 8.00
KOQ Kyle O'Quinn 2.00 5.00
MH1 Marques Haynes 6.00 15.00
MH2 Moe Harkless 3.00 8.00
ML1 Meyers Leonard 2.50 6.00
MP1 Miles Plumlee 2.00 5.00
MS1 Mike Scott 2.00 5.00
MT1 Marquis Teague 2.00 5.00
NO1 Nnemkadi Ogwumike 4.00 10.00
OJ1 Orlando Johnson 2.00 5.00
PJ3 Perry Jones 2.00 5.00
RH1 Robbie Hummel 2.00 5.00
RS1 Robert Sacre 2.00 5.00
RW1 Royce White 2.00 5.00
SM1 Scott Machado 2.00 5.00
SP1 Scottie Pippen 25.00 60.00
TJ1 Terrence Jones 2.50 6.00
TR1 Terrence Ross 3.00 8.00
TS1 Tornike Shengelia 2.00 5.00
TT2 Tyshawn Taylor 2.00 5.00
TW1 Tony Wroten 2.50 6.00
TZ2 Tyler Zeller 2.50 6.00
WB1 Will Barton 2.50 6.00

2012-13 Leaf Ultimate Silver

*SILVER: .75X TO 2X BASE HI
STATED PRINT RUN 25 SER.#'d SETS
BB1 Bradley Beal 20.00 50.00
CD1 Clyde Drexler 20.00 50.00
DL1 Damian Lillard 50.00 120.00
DW2 Dion Waiters 25.00 60.00
JW1 James Worthy 15.00 40.00
KM1 Karl Malone 40.00 100.00
MH1 Marques Haynes 8.00 20.00
NO1 Nnemkadi Ogwumike 6.00 15.00

2012-13 Leaf Ultimate Inscriptions

STATED PRINT RUN 25 SER.#'d SETS
DL1 Damian Lillard 50.00 120.00
DR1 Dennis Rodman 40.00 100.00
EL1 Earl Lloyd 12.00 30.00
KM1 Karl Malone 50.00 100.00
MH1 Marques Haynes 8.00 20.00
RS1 Robert Sacre 15.00 40.00

2012-13 Leaf Ultimate Karl Malone Patch Autographs

PRINT RUNS LISTED BELOW
KM1 Karl Malone/99 25.00 60.00
KM2 Karl Malone Blue/25 60.00 120.00

2012-13 Leaf Ultimate Numeration

STATED PRINT RUN 4 TO 91 SETS
UNPRICED PLATE PRINT RUN ONE SER.#'d SET
AN1 Andrew Nicholson/44 6.00 15.00
BB1 Bradley Beal/23 12.00 30.00
DG1 Draymond Green/23 8.00 20.00
DL2 Doron Lamb/20 6.00 15.00
DR1 Dennis Rodman/91 20.00 50.00
DW1 Dominique Wilkins/21 15.00 40.00
FM1 Fab Melo/51 6.00 15.00
JJ1 John Jenkins/23 6.00 15.00
JT2 Jeffery Taylor/44 6.00 15.00
JW1 James Worthy/42 12.00 30.00
KM1 Karl Malone/32 20.00 50.00
MT1 Marquis Teague/25 6.00 15.00
NO1 Nnemkadi Ogwumike/30 6.00 15.00
RW1 Royce White/30 6.00 15.00
SP1 Scottie Pippen/33 75.00 150.00
TR1 Terrence Ross/31 8.00 20.00

2012-13 Leaf Ultimate Rim Rockers

RANDOM INSERTS IN PACKS
UNPRICED GOLD PRINT RUN 10 SER.#'d SETS
UNPRICED PLATE PRINT RUN ONE SER.#'d SET
UNPRICED PURPLE PRINT RUN ONE SER.#'d SET
UNPRICED RED PRINT RUN 5 SER.#'d SETS
AN1 Andrew Nicholson 2.00 5.00
DW1 Dominique Wilkins 8.00 20.00
FM1 Fab Melo 2.00 5.00
JT2 Jeffery Taylor 2.00 5.00
ML1 Meyers Leonard 2.50 6.00
PJ3 Perry Jones 2.00 5.00
TJ1 Terrence Jones 2.50 6.00
TZ2 Tyler Zeller 2.50 6.00

2012-13 Leaf Ultimate Rim Rockers Silver

*SILVER: .75X TO 2X BASE HI
STATED PRINT RUN 25 SER.#'d SETS

2012-13 Leaf Ultimate State Pride

RANDOM INSERTS IN PACKS
UNPRICED GOLD PRINT RUN 10 SER.#'d SETS
UNPRICED PLATE PRINT RUN ONE SER.#'d SET
UNPRICED PURPLE PRINT RUN ONE SER.#'d SET
UNPRICED RED PRINT RUN 5 SER.#'d SETS
BB1 Bradley Beal 6.00 15.00
DG1 Draymond Green 12.00 30.00
DL1 Damian Lillard 20.00 50.00
DL2 Doron Lamb 2.50 6.00
DW2 Dion Waiters 6.00 15.00
JL1 Jeremy Lamb 4.00 10.00
KM2 Kendall Marshall 2.50 6.00
ML1 Meyers Leonard 3.00 8.00
MT1 Marquis Teague 2.50 6.00
NO1 Nnemkadi Ogwumike 4.00 10.00
PJ3 Perry Jones 2.50 6.00
TJ1 Terrence Jones 3.00 8.00
TR1 Terrence Ross 4.00 10.00
TT2 Tyshawn Taylor 6.00 15.00
TW1 Tony Wroten 3.00 8.00
TZ2 Tyler Zeller 3.00 8.00

2012-13 Leaf Ultimate State Pride Silver

*SILVER: .6X TO 1.5X BASE HI
STATED PRINT RUN 25 SER.#'d SETS
DG1 Draymond Green 10.00 25.00
DL1 Damian Lillard 100.00 250.00
DW2 Dion Waiters 25.00 60.00
ML1 Meyers Leonard 12.00 30.00

2012 Leaf Valiant Stars Damian Lillard Autographs

*ORANGE/50: .6X TO 1.5X BASIC
*PURPLE/25: .75X TO 2X BASIC
SDL1 Damian Lillard 12.00 30.00

1992 Lime Rock Larry Bird

This three-card hologram set was produced by Lime Rock Productions and packaged in a black folder displaying a three-dimensional embossed etching of Larry Bird. According to Lime Rock, the production run was 10,000 cases or 250,000 sets, and 2,500 autographed cards were randomly inserted throughout the packaging process (one in every 100 sets). A numbered certificate of authenticity was included with each set. The cards measure the standard size and depict three stages in his career: 1) his passing skill at Indiana State; 2) his patented shooting style at Boston; and 3) posed in a red, white, and blue warm-up in anticipation of his participation in the Summer Olympic games in Barcelona. The backs have color photos and an extended caption summarizing Bird's career.

COMPLETE SET (3) 1.50 4.00
COMMON CARD (1-3) .60 1.50

2009-10 Limited

1-100 PRINT RUN 199 SER.#'d SETS
101-150 PRINT RUN 99 SER.#'d SETS
151-180 PRINT RUN 299 SER.#'d SETS
UNPRICED GOLD PRINT RUN 10 SETS
UNPRICED PLATINUM PRINT RUN ONE SET
1 Andre Iguodala 1.25 3.00
2 Elton Brand 1.50 4.00
3 Samuel Dalembert 1.00 2.50
4 Chris Duhon 1.00 2.50
5 David Lee 1.00 2.50
6 Wilson Chandler 1.25 3.00
7 Kevin Garnett 2.50 6.00
8 Paul Pierce 1.50 4.00
9 Rasheed Wallace 1.50 4.00
10 Ray Allen 1.50 4.00
11 Brook Lopez 1.25 3.00
12 Courtney Lee 1.25 3.00
13 Devin Harris 1.00 2.50
14 Andrea Bargnani 1.25 3.00
15 Chris Bosh 1.50 4.00
16 Hedo Turkoglu 1.25 3.00
17 Ben Wallace 1.25 3.00
18 Richard Hamilton 1.25 3.00
19 Rodney Stuckey 1.00 2.50
20 Tayshaun Prince 1.25 3.00
21 Derrick Rose 2.50 6.00
22 Luol Deng 1.25 3.00
23 Tyrus Thomas 1.00 2.50
24 Daniel Gibson 1.25 3.00
25 LeBron James 6.00 15.00
26 Mo Williams 1.25 3.00
27 Shaquille O'Neal 3.00 8.00
28 Danny Granger 1.25 3.00
29 Jeff Foster 1.00 2.50
30 T.J. Ford 1.00 2.50
31 Andrew Bogut 1.25 3.00
32 Kurt Thomas 1.00 2.50
33 Michael Redd 1.25 3.00
34 Dwight Howard 1.25 3.00
35 Jameer Nelson 1.00 2.50
36 Rashard Lewis 1.25 3.00
37 Vince Carter 2.00 5.00
38 Joe Johnson 1.25 3.00
39 Marvin Williams 1.25 3.00
40 Mike Bibby 1.25 3.00
41 Antawn Jamison 1.25 3.00
42 Caron Butler 1.25 3.00
43 Gilbert Arenas 1.25 3.00
44 Gerald Wallace 1.25 3.00
45 Raymond Felton 1.25 3.00
46 Tyson Chandler 1.25 3.00
47 Dwyane Wade 2.50 6.00
48 Jermaine O'Neal 1.25 3.00
49 Mario Chalmers 1.25 3.00
50 Michael Beasley 1.00 2.50
51 Aaron Brooks 1.00 2.50
52 Shane Battier 1.50 4.00
53 Trevor Ariza 1.00 2.50
54 O.J. Mayo 1.00 2.50
55 Rudy Gay 1.50 4.00
56 Zach Randolph 1.25 3.00
57 Chris Paul 2.00 5.00
58 David West 1.25 3.00
59 Emeka Okafor 1.25 3.00
60 James Posey 1.00 2.50
61 Dirk Nowitzki 2.00 5.00
62 Jason Kidd 1.50 4.00
63 Jason Terry 1.25 3.00
64 Josh Howard 1.25 3.00
65 Antonio McDyess 1.25 3.00
66 Tim Duncan 2.50 6.00
67 Tony Parker 1.50 4.00
68 Brandon Roy 1.50 4.00
69 Greg Oden 1.25 3.00
70 LaMarcus Aldridge 1.50 4.00
71 Rudy Fernandez 1.00 2.50
72 Corey Brewer 1.00 2.50
73 Kevin Love 1.50 4.00
74 Ramon Sessions 1.25 3.00
75 Andrei Kirilenko 1.25 3.00
76 Carlos Boozer 1.25 3.00
77 Deron Williams 1.25 3.00
78 Jeff Green 1.25 3.00
79 Kevin Durant 4.00 10.00
80 Russell Westbrook 4.00 10.00
81 Carmelo Anthony 2.00 5.00
82 Chauncey Billups 1.50 4.00
83 Kenyon Martin 1.25 3.00
84 Derek Fisher 1.25 3.00
85 Kobe Bryant 6.00 15.00
86 Lamar Odom 1.25 3.00
87 Pau Gasol 1.50 4.00
88 Ron Artest 1.50 4.00
89 Andris Biedrins 1.00 2.50
90 Anthony Randolph 1.00 2.50
91 Stephen Jackson 1.25 3.00
92 Amare Stoudemire 1.25 3.00
93 Channing Frye 1.25 3.00
94 Steve Nash 1.50 4.00
95 Baron Davis 1.25 3.00
96 Eric Gordon 1.25 3.00
97 Marcus Camby 1.00 2.50
98 Andres Nocioni 1.00 2.50
99 Kevin Martin 1.25 3.00
100 Spencer Hawes 1.00 2.50
101 Magic Johnson 5.00 12.00
102 Glen Rice 1.50 4.00
103 Wilt Chamberlain 4.00 10.00
104 World B. Free 1.50 4.00
105 Julius Erving 3.00 8.00
106 Alex English 1.50 4.00
107 Al Cervi 2.00 5.00
108 John Salley 1.25 3.00
109 Al Attles 2.00 5.00
110 Maurice Cheeks 1.25 3.00
111 Bob Cousy 3.00 8.00
112 Cazzie Russell 1.50 4.00
113 Dave Bing 2.00 5.00
114 Bob McAdoo 1.50 4.00
115 Albert King 2.00 5.00
116 Alonzo Mourning 2.50 6.00
117 Sleepy Floyd 1.25 3.00
118 John Havlicek 2.00 5.00
119 Gheorghe Muresan 1.25 3.00
120 Sidney Moncrief 1.25 3.00
121 Jamal Mashburn 2.00 5.00
122 Kevin McHale 2.00 5.00
123 Larry Bird 5.00 12.00
124 Vlade Divac 2.00 5.00
125 Sean Elliott 2.00 5.00
126 Chris Ford 2.00 5.00
127 Campy Russell 1.25 3.00
128 Muggsy Bogues 1.50 4.00
129 Elgin Baylor 2.00 5.00
130 Bill Walton 2.00 5.00
131 Rickey Green 2.00 5.00
132 Hal Greer 1.50 4.00
133 Norm Nixon 1.25 3.00
134 Jerry Sloan 2.00 5.00
135 David Robinson 3.00 8.00
136 Darryl Dawkins 1.25 3.00
137 Cliff Hagan 1.50 4.00
138 Clyde Drexler 2.50 6.00
139 Dikembe Mutombo 2.00 5.00
140 Jo Jo White 1.50 4.00
141 LaSalle Thompson 2.00 5.00
142 Michael Cooper 1.50 4.00
143 Shawn Bradley 1.25 3.00
144 Walt Frazier 2.00 5.00
145 Harry Gallatin 2.00 5.00
146 Connie Hawkins 2.00 5.00
147 Moses Malone 2.00 5.00
148 Walt Bellamy 1.50 4.00
149 Pete Maravich 15.00 30.00
150 Bill Russell 3.00 8.00
151 Blake Griffin JSY AU RC 30.00 80.00
152 Hasheem Thabeet JSY AU RC 4.00 10.00
153 James Harden JSY AU RC 60.00 150.00
154 Tyreke Evans JSY AU RC 5.00 12.00
155 Jonny Flynn JSY AU RC 4.00 10.00
156 Stephen Curry JSY AU RC 300.00 600.00
157 Jordan Hill JSY AU RC 5.00 12.00
158 Brandon Jennings JSY AU RC 8.00 20.00
159 Terrence Williams JSY AU RC 4.00 10.00
160 Gerald Henderson JSY AU RC 5.00 12.00
161 Tyler Hansbrough JSY AU RC 5.00 12.00
162 Earl Clark JSY AU RC 5.00 12.00
163 Austin Daye JSY AU RC 4.00 10.00
164 James Johnson JSY AU RC 5.00 12.00
165 Jrue Holiday JSY AU RC 8.00 20.00
166 Ty Lawson JSY AU RC 6.00 15.00
167 Jeff Teague JSY AU RC 6.00 15.00
168 Eric Maynor JSY AU RC 4.00 10.00
169 Darren Collison JSY AU RC 6.00 15.00
170 Omri Casspi JSY AU RC 5.00 12.00
171 B.J. Mullens JSY AU RC 4.00 10.00
172 R.Beaubois JSY AU RC 4.00 10.00
173 Taj Gibson JSY AU RC 6.00 15.00
174 DeMarre Carroll JSY AU RC 5.00 12.00
175 Wayne Ellington JSY AU RC 6.00 15.00
176 Toney Douglas JSY AU RC 4.00 10.00
177 DeJuan Blair JSY AU RC 5.00 12.00
178 Chase Budinger JSY AU RC 5.00 12.00
179 Sam Young JSY AU RC 4.00 10.00
180 Jodie Meeks JSY AU RC 6.00 15.00

2009-10 Limited Silver Spotlight

*1-100 SILVER: 1X TO 2.5X BASE HI
*101-150 SILVER: .75X TO 2X BASE HI
*151-180 SILVER: .75X TO 2X BASE HI
SILVER PRINT RUN 25 SER.#'d SETS
154 Tyreke Evans JSY AU 40.00 100.00
156 Stephen Curry JSY AU 800.00 1200.00

2009-10 Limited Banner Season

COMPLETE SET (20) 25.00 50.00
PRINT RUN 99 SER.#'d SETS
UNPRICED GOLD PRINT RUN 10 SER.#'d SETS
UNPRICED PLATINUM PRINT RUN ONE SET
*SILVER: .75X TO 2X BASE HI
SILVER PRINT RUN 25 SER.#'d SETS
1 Al Jefferson 1.25 3.00
2 Brandon Roy 1.50 4.00
3 Joe Johnson 1.25 3.00
4 Kevin Martin 1.25 3.00
5 Dirk Nowitzki 2.00 5.00
6 Danny Granger 1.25 3.00
7 Tony Parker 1.50 4.00
8 Kobe Bryant 6.00 15.00
9 Dwyane Wade 2.50 6.00
10 LeBron James 6.00 15.00
11 Stephen Jackson 1.25 3.00
12 Dwight Howard 1.25 3.00
13 Chris Paul 2.00 5.00
14 Carmelo Anthony 2.00 5.00
15 Deron Williams 1.25 3.00
16 Kevin Durant 4.00 10.00
17 Chris Bosh 1.50 4.00
18 Devin Harris 1.00 2.50
19 Paul Pierce 1.50 4.00
20 Michael Redd 1.25 3.00

2009-10 Limited Banner Season Materials

STATED PRINT RUN 5 TO 99 SER.#'d SETS
*PRIME: .75X TO 2X BASE HI
PRIME PRINT RUN ONE TO 25 SER.#'d SETS
SOME PRIME UNPRICED DUE TO SCARCITY
1 Al Jefferson/99 2.50 6.00
2 Brandon Roy/99 3.00 8.00
3 Joe Johnson/99 2.50 6.00
5 Dirk Nowitzki/99 4.00 10.00
8 Kobe Bryant/99 8.00 20.00
9 Dwyane Wade/49 5.00 12.00
10 LeBron James/49 10.00 25.00
11 Stephen Jackson/99 2.50 6.00
12 Dwight Howard/99 2.50 6.00
13 Chris Paul/99 4.00 10.00
14 Carmelo Anthony/99 4.00 10.00
15 Deron Williams/49 2.50 6.00
17 Chris Bosh/99 3.00 8.00
19 Paul Pierce/49 3.00 8.00
20 Michael Redd/49 2.50 6.00

2009-10 Limited Banner Season Materials Signatures

STATED PRINT RUN 5 TO 49 SER.#'d SETS
SOME UNPRICED DUE TO SCARCITY
UNPRICED PRIME.SIG PRINT RUN ONE TO 10 SETS
8 Kobe Bryant/49 100.00 200.00

2009-10 Limited Decade Dominance

COMPLETE SET (20) 30.00 60.00
PRINT RUN 99 SER.#'d SETS
UNPRICED GOLD PRINT RUN 10 SER.#'d SETS
UNPRICED PLATINUM PRINT RUN ONE SET
*SILVER: .6X TO 1.5X BASE HI
SILVER PRINT RUN 25 SER.#'d SETS
UNPRICED MATERIAL PRINT RUN 10 SETS
UNPRICED PRIME PRINT RUN ONE TO 10 SETS
UNPRICED PRIME.SIG PRINT RUN 1 TO 5 SETS
1 Jerry West 2.50 6.00
2 Oscar Robertson 2.00 5.00
3 Wilt Chamberlain 4.00 10.00
4 Bill Russell 3.00 8.00
5 Bill Sharman 2.00 5.00
6 Bill Walton 2.00 5.00
7 Willis Reed 2.00 5.00
8 Walt Frazier 2.00 5.00
9 John Havlicek 2.00 5.00
10 Alex English 1.50 4.00
11 Elvin Hayes 2.00 5.00
12 Larry Bird 6.00 15.00
13 Magic Johnson 5.00 12.00
14 Isiah Thomas 2.00 5.00
15 Kareem Abdul-Jabbar 3.00 8.00
16 Dennis Rodman 4.00 10.00
17 Dell Curry 1.25 3.00
18 Kobe Bryant 6.00 15.00
19 LeBron James 6.00 15.00
20 Dirk Nowitzki 2.00 5.00

2009-10 Limited Decade Dominance Materials Signatures

STATED PRINT RUN 10 TO 49 SER.#'d SETS
SOME UNPRICED DUE TO SCARCITY
1 Jerry West/25 30.00 80.00
9 John Havlicek/25 30.00 60.00
10 Alex English/20 15.00 30.00
18 Kobe Bryant/49 100.00 200.00

2009-10 Limited Decade Dominance Signatures

STATED PRINT RUN 5 TO 49 SER.#'d SETS
SOME UNPRICED DUE TO SCARCITY
1 Jerry West/25 20.00 50.00
2 Oscar Robertson/49 25.00 60.00
5 Bill Sharman/49 8.00 20.00
6 Bill Walton/49 8.00 20.00
9 John Havlicek/49 15.00 30.00
10 Alex English/15 10.00 25.00
17 Dell Curry/49 8.00 20.00
18 Kobe Bryant/25 100.00 200.00
20 Dirk Nowitzki/25 40.00 100.00

2009-10 Limited Freshmen Jumbo

STATED PRINT RUN 99 SER.#'d SETS
UNPRICED PRIME PRINT RUN 10 SETS
*NUMBERS: .4X TO 1X JUMBO
NUMBERS PRINT RUN 99 SER.#'d SETS
UNPRICED NUMB.PRIME PRINT RUN 10 SETS
UNPRICED PRIME.SIG PRINT RUN 5 SETS
1 Blake Griffin 10.00 25.00
2 Hasheem Thabeet 1.50 4.00
3 James Harden 12.00 30.00
4 Tyreke Evans 2.00 5.00
5 DeMar DeRozan 6.00 15.00
6 Jonny Flynn 1.50 4.00
7 Stephen Curry 100.00 200.00
8 Jordan Hill 2.00 5.00
9 Brandon Jennings 2.50 6.00
10 Terrence Williams 1.50 4.00
11 Gerald Henderson 2.00 5.00
12 Tyler Hansbrough 2.00 5.00
13 Earl Clark 2.00 5.00
14 Austin Daye 1.50 4.00
15 James Johnson 2.00 5.00
16 Jrue Holiday 3.00 8.00
17 Ty Lawson 2.50 6.00
18 Jeff Teague 2.50 6.00
19 Eric Maynor 1.50 4.00
20 Darren Collison 2.50 6.00
21 Omri Casspi 2.00 5.00
22 B.J. Mullens 1.50 4.00
23 Rodrigue Beaubois 1.50 4.00
24 Taj Gibson 2.50 6.00
25 DeMarre Carroll 2.00 5.00
26 Wayne Ellington 2.50 6.00
27 Toney Douglas 1.50 4.00
28 DeJuan Blair 2.00 5.00
29 Chase Budinger 2.00 5.00
30 Sam Young 1.50 4.00

2009-10 Limited Freshmen Jumbo Jersey Numbers Signatures

STATED PRINT RUN 49 SER.#'d SETS
JUMBO SIGS: .4X TO 1X BASE HI
JUMBO SIGS PRINT RUN 49 SER.#'d SETS
1 Blake Griffin 60.00 150.00
2 Hasheem Thabeet 4.00 10.00
4 Tyreke Evans 12.00 30.00
6 Jonny Flynn 4.00 10.00
7 Stephen Curry 200.00 500.00
8 Jordan Hill 5.00 12.00
9 Brandon Jennings 6.00 15.00
10 Terrence Williams 4.00 10.00
11 Gerald Henderson 5.00 12.00
12 Tyler Hansbrough 5.00 12.00
13 Earl Clark 5.00 12.00
14 Austin Daye 4.00 10.00
15 James Johnson 5.00 12.00
16 Jrue Holiday 8.00 20.00
17 Ty Lawson 6.00 15.00
18 Jeff Teague 6.00 15.00
20 Darren Collison 6.00 15.00
21 Omri Casspi 5.00 12.00
22 B.J. Mullens 4.00 10.00
23 Rodrigue Beaubois 4.00 10.00
24 Taj Gibson 6.00 15.00
25 DeMarre Carroll 5.00 12.00
27 Toney Douglas 4.00 10.00
28 DeJuan Blair 5.00 12.00
29 Chase Budinger 5.00 12.00
30 Sam Young 4.00 10.00

2009-10 Limited Glass Cleaners

COMPLETE SET (20) 30.00 60.00
PRINT RUN 99 SER.#'d SETS
UNPRICED GOLD PRINT RUN 10 SER.#'d SETS
UNPRICED PLATINUM PRINT RUN ONE SET
*SILVER: .75X TO 2X BASE HI
SILVER PRINT RUN 25 SER.#'d SETS
1 Kareem Abdul-Jabbar 2.50 6.00
2 Shaquille O'Neal 3.00 8.00
3 Bill Russell 2.50 6.00
4 Dennis Rodman 3.00 8.00
5 Elvin Hayes 1.50 4.00
6 Kobe Bryant 6.00 15.00
7 Elton Brand 1.50 4.00
8 Dirk Nowitzki 2.00 5.00
9 Tim Duncan 2.50 6.00
10 Nate Thurmond 1.25 3.00
11 Hakeem Olajuwon 2.00 5.00
12 Wes Unseld 1.50 4.00
13 Jermaine O'Neal 1.25 3.00
14 Chris Bosh 1.50 4.00
15 Robert Parish 1.50 4.00
16 Artis Gilmore 1.25 3.00
17 David Robinson 2.50 6.00
18 Pau Gasol 1.50 4.00
19 Dikembe Mutombo 1.50 4.00
20 Moses Malone 1.50 4.00

2009-10 Limited Glass Cleaners Materials

STATED PRINT RUN 49 TO 99 SER.#'d SETS
*PRIME: .75X TO 2X BASE HI
PRIME PRINT RUN ONE TO 25 SER.#'d SETS
SOME PRIME UNPRICED DUE TO SCARCITY
1 Kareem Abdul-Jabbar/49 6.00 15.00
6 Kobe Bryant/99 10.00 25.00
7 Elton Brand/49 3.00 8.00
8 Dirk Nowitzki/99 4.00 10.00
9 Tim Duncan/99 5.00 12.00
11 Hakeem Olajuwon/99 5.00 12.00
13 Jermaine O'Neal/49 2.50 6.00
14 Chris Bosh/99 3.00 8.00
15 Robert Parish/99 4.00 10.00
18 Pau Gasol/99 3.00 8.00
20 Moses Malone/99 4.00 10.00

2009-10 Limited Glass Cleaners Materials Signatures

STATED PRINT RUN 10 TO 49 SER.#'d SETS
SOME UNPRICED DUE TO SCARCITY
UNPRICED PRIME.SIG PRINT RUN 1 TO 5 SETS
6 Kobe Bryant/49 100.00 200.00
15 Robert Parish/25 8.00 20.00

2009-10 Limited Glass Cleaners Signatures

STATED PRINT RUN 49 SER.#'d SETS
1 Kareem Abdul-Jabbar 40.00 80.00
3 Bill Russell 75.00 150.00
4 Dennis Rodman 30.00 80.00
5 Elvin Hayes 8.00 20.00
6 Kobe Bryant 100.00 200.00
7 Elton Brand 8.00 20.00
10 Nate Thurmond 10.00 25.00
12 Wes Unseld 8.00 20.00
13 Jermaine O'Neal 8.00 20.00
14 Chris Bosh 8.00 20.00
15 Robert Parish 10.00 25.00
16 Artis Gilmore 10.00 25.00
18 Pau Gasol 25.00 50.00

2009-10 Limited Jumbo Jersey Numbers Signatures

STATED PRINT RUN 10 TO 49 SER.#'d SETS
SOME UNPRICED DUE TO SCARCITY
NUM.PRIME SIG. PRINT RUN ONE TO 5 SETS
UNPRICED DUE TO SCARCITY
UNPRICED PRIME SIG.PRINT RUN 5 SETS
13 Andre Iguodala/49 6.00 15.00
14 Kobe Bryant/25 125.00 250.00
15 Carlos Boozer/25 6.00 15.00

2009-10 Limited Jumbo Signatures

PRINT RUN 10 TO 25 SER.#'d SETS
SOME UNPRICED DUE TO SCARCITY
14 Kobe Bryant/25 125.00 250.00
15 Carlos Boozer/25 6.00 15.00

2009-10 Limited Monikers Gold

STATED PRINT RUN ONE TO 25 SER.#'d SETS
SOME UNPRICED DUE TO SCARCITY
UNPRICED PLATINUM PRINT RUN ONE SET
13 Devin Harris/25 10.00 25.00
28 Danny Granger/25 6.00 15.00
40 Mike Bibby/25 8.00 20.00
50 Michael Beasley/25 10.00 25.00
52 Shane Battier/25 6.00 15.00
73 Kevin Love/25 10.00 25.00
76 Carlos Boozer/25 6.00 15.00
85 Kobe Bryant/25 125.00 225.00
107 Al Cervi/25 6.00 15.00
109 Al Attles/15 8.00 20.00
111 Bob Cousy/25 25.00 60.00
112 Cazzie Russell/25 8.00 20.00
114 Bob McAdoo/25 20.00 40.00
117 Sleepy Floyd/25 8.00 20.00
120 Sidney Moncrief/25 8.00 20.00
125 Sean Elliott/25 15.00 40.00
127 Campy Russell/25 8.00 20.00
130 Bill Walton/25 8.00 20.00
132 Hal Greer/25 6.00 15.00
138 Clyde Drexler/25 30.00 60.00
145 Harry Gallatin/25 6.00 15.00

2009-10 Limited Monikers Materials

STATED PRINT RUN 10 TO 25 SER.#'d SETS
SOME UNPRICED DUE TO SCARCITY
2 Andre Iguodala/25 8.00 20.00
7 Carlos Boozer/25 8.00 20.00
10 Chris Bosh/25 12.00 30.00
14 David Lee/25 8.00 20.00
15 Deron Williams/25 10.00 25.00
18 Elton Brand/25 8.00 20.00
20 Jason Kidd/25 15.00 30.00
21 Jermaine O'Neal/25 8.00 15.00
23 Kobe Bryant/25 125.00 225.00
25 Michael Beasley/25 15.00 30.00
26 Mike Bibby/25 10.00 25.00
27 Rajon Rondo/25 20.00 50.00
28 Ray Allen/25 30.00 60.00
32 Shane Battier/25 8.00 20.00
36 Alex English/20 15.00 30.00
37 Artis Gilmore/25 12.00 30.00
38 Dikembe Mutombo/25 30.00 75.00
40 Kareem Abdul-Jabbar/25 30.00 60.00
43 Larry Bird/25 40.00 100.00
47 Robert Parish/25 8.00 20.00
48 Dan Issel/25 10.00 25.00

2009-10 Limited Monikers Materials Prime

STATED PRINT RUN ONE TO 25 SER.#'d SETS
SOME UNPRICED DUE TO SCARCITY
37 Artis Gilmore/25 20.00 40.00
48 Dan Issel/25 15.00 30.00

2009-10 Limited Retired Numbers

COMPLETE SET (20) 25.00 50.00
STATED PRINT RUN 99 SER.#'d SETS
UNPRICED GOLD PRINT RUN 10 SER.#'d SETS
UNPRICED PLATINUM PRINT RUN ONE SET
*SILVER: .6X TO 1.5X BASE HI
SILVER PRINT RUN 25 SER.#'d SETS
1 Bill Russell 3.00 8.00
2 Larry Bird 5.00 12.00
3 Bob Love 2.00 5.00
4 Larry Nance 1.50 4.00
5 Alex English 1.50 4.00
6 Isiah Thomas 2.00 5.00
7 Rick Barry 1.50 4.00
8 Clyde Drexler 2.50 6.00
9 Magic Johnson 5.00 12.00
10 Kareem Abdul-Jabbar 3.00 8.00
11 Jerry West 2.50 6.00
12 Oscar Robertson 2.00 5.00
13 Willis Reed 2.00 5.00
14 Julius Erving 3.00 8.00
15 Bill Walton 2.00 5.00
16 Mitch Richmond 2.00 5.00
17 David Robinson 3.00 8.00
18 John Stockton 3.00 8.00
19 Elvin Hayes 2.00 5.00
20 Wes Unseld 2.00 5.00

2009-10 Limited Retired Numbers Materials

STATED PRINT RUN 99 SER.#'d SETS
UNPRICED PRIME PRINT RUN 10 SER.#'d SETS
UNPRICED PRIME.SIG PRINT RUN 5 SETS
2 Larry Bird 10.00 25.00
5 Alex English 3.00 8.00
6 Isiah Thomas 4.00 10.00
8 Clyde Drexler 5.00 12.00
9 Magic Johnson 8.00 20.00
10 Kareem Abdul-Jabbar 8.00 20.00
11 Jerry West 8.00 20.00
14 Julius Erving 6.00 15.00
16 Mitch Richmond 4.00 10.00
18 John Stockton 6.00 15.00

2009-10 Limited Retired Numbers Materials Signatures

STATED PRINT RUN 10 TO 49 SER.#'d SETS
SOME UNPRICED DUE TO SCARCITY
5 Alex English/25 10.00 25.00
8 Clyde Drexler/49 12.00 30.00
11 Jerry West/25 40.00 80.00

2009-10 Limited Retired Numbers Signatures

STATED PRINT RUN ONE TO 25 SER.#'d SETS
SOME UNPRICED DUE TO SCARCITY
5 Alex English/15 10.00 25.00
7 Rick Barry/25 10.00 25.00
8 Clyde Drexler/25 25.00 50.00
11 Jerry West/25 25.00 50.00
12 Oscar Robertson/25 30.00 80.00
13 Willis Reed/25 20.00 40.00
20 Wes Unseld/25 10.00 25.00

2009-10 Limited Team Trademarks

COMPLETE SET (20) 15.00 30.00
STATED PRINT RUN 99 SER.#'d SETS
UNPRICED GOLD PRINT RUN 10 SER.#'d SETS
UNPRICED PLATINUM PRINT RUN ONE SET
*SILVER: 1.25X TO 3X BASE HI
SILVER PRINT RUN 25 SER.#'d SETS
1 Tony Parker 1.00 2.50
2 Kobe Bryant 4.00 10.00
3 Dirk Nowitzki 1.25 3.00
4 Chris Bosh 1.00 2.50
5 Paul Pierce 1.00 2.50
6 Richard Hamilton .75 2.00
7 Yao Ming 1.25 3.00
8 Chris Paul 1.25 3.00
9 Dwight Howard .75 2.00
10 Amare Stoudemire .75 2.00
11 Brandon Roy 1.00 2.50
12 Kevin Love 1.00 2.50
13 Dwyane Wade 1.50 4.00
14 Gilbert Arenas .75 2.00
15 Deron Williams .75 2.00
16 Andre Iguodala .75 2.00
17 Devin Harris .60 1.50
18 Andrew Bogut .75 2.00
19 Carmelo Anthony 1.25 3.00
20 LeBron James 4.00 10.00

2009-10 Limited Team Trademarks Materials

STATED PRINT RUN 10 TO 99 SER.#'d SETS
*PRIME: .75X TO 2X BASE HI
PRIME PRINT RUN ONE TO 25 SETS
SOME PRIME UNPRICED DUE TO SCARCITY
1 Tony Parker/10
2 Kobe Bryant/49 10.00 25.00
3 Dirk Nowitzki/99 4.00 10.00
4 Chris Bosh/99 3.00 8.00
5 Paul Pierce/49 3.00 8.00
6 Richard Hamilton/99 2.50 6.00
7 Yao Ming/99 4.00 10.00
8 Chris Paul/99 4.00 10.00
9 Dwight Howard/99 2.50 6.00
10 Amare Stoudemire/99 2.50 6.00
11 Brandon Roy/99 3.00 8.00
12 Kevin Love/49 3.00 8.00
13 Dwyane Wade/49 5.00 12.00
14 Gilbert Arenas/99 2.50 6.00
15 Deron Williams/49 2.50 6.00
16 Andre Iguodala/99 2.50 6.00
18 Andrew Bogut/99 2.50 6.00
19 Carmelo Anthony/99 4.00 10.00
20 LeBron James/49 10.00 25.00

2009-10 Limited Team Trademarks Materials Prime Signatures

STATED PRINT RUN ONE TO 25 SER.#'d SETS
SOME UNPRICED DUE TO SCARCITY
16 Andre Iguodala/25 8.00 20.00

2009-10 Limited Team Trademarks Materials Signatures

STATED PRINT RUN 5 TO 25 SER.#'d SETS
SOME UNPRICED DUE TO SCARCITY
2 Kobe Bryant/25 100.00 200.00
12 Kevin Love/25 15.00 40.00

2009-10 Limited Threads Prime

STATED PRINT RUN ONE TO 25 SER.#'d SETS
SOME UNPRICED DUE TO SCARCITY
UNPRICED THREADS PRINT RUN 10 SETS
1 Andre Iguodala/25 5.00 12.00
4 Chris Duhon/25 4.00 10.00
5 David Lee/25 4.00 10.00
7 Kevin Garnett/25 10.00 25.00
18 Richard Hamilton/25 5.00 12.00
25 LeBron James/25 25.00 50.00
29 Jeff Foster/25 4.00 10.00
36 Rashard Lewis/25 5.00 12.00
41 Antawn Jamison/25 5.00 12.00
44 Gerald Wallace/25 5.00 12.00
51 Aaron Brooks/25 4.00 10.00
58 David West/25 5.00 12.00
63 Jason Terry/25 5.00 12.00
64 Josh Howard/25 5.00 12.00
66 Tim Duncan/25 10.00 25.00
68 Brandon Roy/25 6.00 15.00
69 Greg Oden/25 5.00 12.00
70 LaMarcus Aldridge/25 6.00 15.00
73 Kevin Love/25 6.00 15.00
75 Andrei Kirilenko/25 5.00 12.00
76 Carlos Boozer/25 5.00 12.00
85 Kobe Bryant/25 25.00 50.00
98 Andres Nocioni/25 4.00 10.00
101 Magic Johnson/25 15.00 30.00
106 Alex English/25 5.00 12.00
122 Kevin McHale/25 8.00 20.00
138 Clyde Drexler/25 15.00 30.00
139 Dikembe Mutombo/25 15.00 30.00

2009-10 Limited Trios

COMPLETE SET (15) 25.00 50.00
STATED PRINT RUN 99 SER.#'d SETS
UNPRICED GOLD PRINT RUN 10 SETS
UNPRICED PLATINUM PRINT RUN ONE SET
*SILVER: .75X TO 2X BASE HI
SILVER PRINT RUN 25 SER.#'d SETS
1 Bryant/Wade/James 6.00 15.00
2 Howard/Robinson/O'Neal 3.00 8.00
3 Paul/Kidd/Nash 2.00 5.00
4 Griffin/Thabeet/Harden 8.00 20.00
5 Evans/Flynn/Curry 15.00 40.00
6 Garnett/Pierce/Allen 2.50 6.00
7 Bird/McHale/Parish 4.00 10.00
8 Artest/Boozer/Brand 1.50 4.00
9 Johnson/Kareem/Cooper 4.00 10.00
10 Granger/Odom/Battier 1.50 4.00
11 Parker/Bibby/Ford 1.50 4.00
12 Frazier/Goodrich/Wilkens 1.50 4.00
13 Russell/Reed/Schayes 2.50 6.00
14 Hayes/Gilmore/Unseld 1.50 4.00
15 West/Robertson/Cousy 2.50 6.00

2009-10 Limited Trios Materials

STATED PRINT RUN 49 SER.#'d SETS
UNPRICED PRIME PRINT RUN 10 SER.#'d SETS
1 Bryant/Wade/James 20.00 50.00
4 Griffin/Thabeet/Harden 12.00 30.00
5 Evans/Flynn/Curry 30.00 80.00
6 Garnett/Pierce/Allen 10.00 25.00
7 Bird/McHale/Parish 20.00 40.00

2009-10 Limited Trios Signatures

STATED PRINT RUN 10 TO 49 SER.#'d SETS
4 Griffin/Thabeet/Harden/49 50.00 120.00
5 Evans/Flynn/Curry/49 150.00 400.00

2010-11 Limited

COMP.SET w/o RCs (150) 125.00 250.00
1-150 STATED PRINT RUN 199 SETS
151-190 RC JSY AU PRINT RUN 249 SETS
UNPRICED PLATINUM PRINT RUN ONE SET
EXCH.EXPIRATION 5/3/2012
1 Nate Robinson 1.00 2.50
2 Paul Pierce 1.50 4.00
3 Rajon Rondo 1.50 4.00
4 Shaquille O'Neal 3.00 8.00
5 Brook Lopez 1.25 3.00
6 Devin Harris 1.00 2.50
7 Travis Outlaw 1.25 3.00
8 Amare Stoudemire 1.25 3.00
9 Danilo Gallinari 1.25 3.00
10 Raymond Felton 1.25 3.00
11 Toney Douglas 1.00 2.50
12 Andre Iguodala 1.25 3.00
13 Elton Brand 1.50 4.00
14 Jrue Holiday 1.50 4.00
15 Louis Williams 1.25 3.00
16 Andrea Bargnani 1.25 3.00
17 DeMar DeRozan 1.50 4.00
18 Jose Calderon 1.00 2.50
19 Carlos Boozer 1.25 3.00
20 Derrick Rose 2.00 5.00
21 Joakim Noah 1.25 3.00
22 Anderson Varejao 1.00 2.50
23 Antawn Jamison 1.25 3.00
24 Mo Williams 1.25 3.00
25 Ben Wallace 1.25 3.00
26 Richard Hamilton 1.25 3.00
27 Rodney Stuckey 1.25 3.00
28 Tracy McGrady 1.50 4.00
29 Danny Granger 1.25 3.00
30 T.J. Ford 1.00 2.50
31 Tyler Hansbrough 1.25 3.00
32 Andrew Bogut 1.25 3.00
33 Brandon Jennings 1.00 2.50
34 Corey Maggette 1.25 3.00
35 Michael Redd 1.25 3.00
36 Al Horford 1.25 3.00
37 Joe Johnson 1.25 3.00
38 Josh Smith 1.25 3.00
39 Gerald Wallace 1.25 3.00
40 Stephen Jackson 1.25 3.00
41 Tyrus Thomas 1.00 2.50
42 Chris Bosh 1.50 4.00
43 Dwyane Wade 2.50 6.00
44 LeBron James 8.00 20.00
45 Mike Miller 1.25 3.00
46 Dwight Howard 1.25 3.00
47 J.J. Redick 1.50 4.00
48 Jason Williams 1.25 3.00
49 Rashard Lewis 1.25 3.00
50 JaVale McGee 1.25 3.00
51 Kirk Hinrich 1.25 3.00
52 Yi Jianlian 1.25 3.00
53 Caron Butler 1.25 3.00
54 Dirk Nowitzki 2.00 5.00
55 Jason Kidd 1.50 4.00
56 Tyson Chandler 1.25 3.00
57 Aaron Brooks 1.00 2.50
58 Kevin Martin 1.25 3.00
59 Shane Battier 1.25 3.00
60 Yao Ming 2.00 5.00
61 Marc Gasol 1.50 4.00
62 O.J. Mayo 1.00 2.50
63 Rudy Gay 1.50 4.00
64 Zach Randolph 1.25 3.00
65 Chris Paul 2.00 5.00
66 Marcus Thornton 1.00 2.50
67 Trevor Ariza 1.00 2.50
68 Manu Ginobili 1.50 4.00
69 Tim Duncan 2.50 6.00
70 Tony Parker 1.50 4.00
71 Carmelo Anthony 2.00 5.00
72 Chauncey Billups 1.50 4.00
73 Chris Andersen 1.25 3.00
74 Jonny Flynn 1.00 2.50
75 Kevin Love 1.50 4.00
76 Michael Beasley 1.00 2.50
77 Brandon Roy 1.50 4.00
78 LaMarcus Aldridge 1.50 4.00
79 Marcus Camby 1.00 2.50
80 James Harden 2.50 6.00
81 Kevin Durant 4.00 10.00
82 Russell Westbrook 4.00 10.00
83 Al Jefferson 1.25 3.00
84 Deron Williams 1.25 3.00
85 Raja Bell 1.25 3.00
86 David Lee 1.00 2.50
87 Monta Ellis 1.25 3.00
88 Stephen Curry 6.00 15.00
89 Baron Davis 1.25 3.00
90 Blake Griffin 1.50 4.00
91 Chris Kaman 1.25 3.00
92 Derek Fisher 1.25 3.00
93 Kobe Bryant 6.00 15.00
94 Pau Gasol 1.50 4.00
95 Grant Hill 2.00 5.00
96 Jason Richardson 1.50 4.00
97 Steve Nash 1.50 4.00
98 Carl Landry 1.00 2.50
99 Samuel Dalembert 1.00 2.50
100 Tyreke Evans 1.00 2.50
101 Alex English 1.25 3.00
102 Alvan Adams 1.00 2.50
103 Artis Gilmore 1.25 3.00
104 Bernard King 1.25 3.00
105 Bill Laimbeer 1.25 3.00
106 Bill Russell 2.50 6.00
107 Bill Sharman 1.50 4.00
108 Bill Walton 1.50 4.00
109 Bob Lanier 1.25 3.00
110 Bob McAdoo 1.25 3.00
111 Bob Pettit 1.50 4.00
112 Calvin Murphy 1.25 3.00
113 Cazzie Russell 1.25 3.00
114 Cedric Maxwell 1.50 4.00
115 Cliff Hagan 1.25 3.00
116 Connie Hawkins 1.50 4.00
117 Darrell Griffith 1.00 2.50
118 Dominique Wilkins 2.00 5.00
119 Elgin Baylor 1.50 4.00
120 Elvin Hayes 1.50 4.00
121 Gail Goodrich 1.25 3.00
122 Gary Payton 1.50 4.00
123 George Gervin 1.50 4.00
124 George Mikan 3.00 8.00
125 Hakeem Olajuwon 2.00 5.00
126 James Worthy 2.00 5.00
127 Jeff Hornacek 1.25 3.00
128 Jerry Lucas 1.50 4.00
129 Jerry Sloan 1.50 4.00
130 Jerry West 2.00 5.00
131 Kareem Abdul-Jabbar 2.50 6.00
132 Karl Malone 2.00 5.00
133 K.C. Jones 1.50 4.00
134 Kelly Tripucka 1.00 2.50
135 Larry Bird 4.00 10.00
136 Lenny Wilkens 1.50 4.00
137 Magic Johnson 4.00 10.00
138 Mark Aguirre 1.25 3.00
139 Nate Archibald 1.25 3.00
140 Nate Thurmond 1.25 3.00
141 Robert Parish 1.50 4.00
142 Walt Frazier 1.50 4.00
143 Wes Unseld 1.50 4.00
144 Willis Reed 1.50 4.00
145 Adrian Dantley 1.25 3.00
146 Bailey Howell 1.50 4.00
147 Chris Mullin 1.50 4.00
148 Clyde Drexler 2.00 5.00
149 Hal Greer 1.25 3.00
150 Harry Gallatin 1.50 4.00
151 Al-Farouq Aminu JSY AU RC 5.00 12.00
152 Andy Rautins JSY AU RC 3.00 8.00
153 Avery Bradley JSY AU RC 6.00 15.00
154 Cole Aldrich JSY AU RC 4.00 10.00
155 Craig Brackins JSY AU RC 3.00 8.00
156 Damion James JSY AU RC 3.00 8.00
157 Daniel Orton JSY AU RC 3.00 8.00
158 Da'Sean Butler JSY AU RC 5.00 12.00
159 D.Cousins JSY AU RC 15.00 40.00
160 Derrick Favors JSY AU RC 6.00 15.00
161 Devin Ebanks JSY AU RC 3.00 8.00
162 Dexter Pittman JSY AU RC 3.00 8.00
163 Dominique Jones JSY AU RC 3.00 8.00
164 Ed Davis JSY AU RC 3.00 8.00
165 Ekpe Udoh JSY AU RC 3.00 8.00
166 Elliot Williams JSY AU RC 3.00 8.00
167 Eric Bledsoe JSY AU RC 6.00 15.00
168 Evan Turner JSY AU RC 4.00 10.00
169 Gani Lawal JSY AU RC 3.00 8.00
170 Gordon Hayward JSY AU RC 8.00 20.00
171 Greg Monroe JSY AU RC 6.00 15.00
172 Greivis Vasquez JSY AU RC 4.00 10.00
173 Hassan Whiteside JSY AU RC 10.00 25.00
174 James Anderson JSY AU RC 3.00 8.00
175 John Wall JSY AU RC 30.00 80.00
176 Jordan Crawford JSY AU RC 4.00 10.00
177 L.Stephenson JSY AU RC 8.00 20.00
178 Larry Sanders JSY AU RC 3.00 8.00
179 Lazar Hayward JSY AU RC 3.00 8.00
180 Luke Babbitt JSY AU RC 4.00 10.00
181 L.Harangody JSY AU RC 3.00 8.00
182 Patrick Patterson JSY AU RC 4.00 10.00
183 Paul George JSY AU RC 30.00 80.00
184 Quincy Pondexter JSY AU RC 3.00 8.00
185 Terrico White JSY AU RC 3.00 8.00
186 Keith Gallon JSY AU RC 3.00 8.00
187 Trevor Booker JSY AU RC 4.00 10.00
188 Wesley Johnson JSY AU RC 3.00 8.00
189 Willie Warren JSY AU RC 3.00 8.00
190 Xavier Henry JSY AU RC 3.00 8.00

2010-11 Limited Gold Spotlight

*1-150 GOLD: .6X TO 1.5X BASE HI
1-150 PRINT RUN 49 SER.#'d SETS
151-190 PRINT RUN 10 SER.#'d SETS
151-190 NOT PRICED DUE TO SCARCITY

2010-11 Limited Silver Spotlight

*1-150 SILVER: .5X TO 1.25X BASE HI
1-150 PRINT RUN 149 SER.#'d SETS
*151-190 SILVER: 1X TO 2.5X BASE HI
151-190 PRINT RUN 25 SER.#'d SETS
159 DeMarcus Cousins JSY AU 50.00 125.00
173 Hassan Whiteside JSY AU 30.00 80.00

2010-11 Limited Banner Season

COMPLETE SET (20) 20.00 50.00
STATED PRINT RUN 149 SER.#'d SETS
*GOLD: .75X TO 2X BASE HI
GOLD PRINT RUN 24 SER.#'d SETS
*SILVER: .6X TO 1.5X BASE HI
SILVER PRINT RUN 49 SER.#'d SETS
UNPRICED PLATINUM PRINT RUN ONE SET
1 Kevin Durant 3.00 8.00
2 LeBron James 6.00 15.00
3 Carmelo Anthony 1.50 4.00
4 Kobe Bryant 5.00 12.00
5 Dwyane Wade 2.00 5.00
6 Monta Ellis 1.00 2.50
7 Dirk Nowitzki 1.50 4.00
8 Danny Granger 1.00 2.50
9 Chris Bosh 1.25 3.00
10 Amare Stoudemire 1.00 2.50
11 Brandon Jennings .75 2.00
12 Joe Johnson 1.00 2.50
13 Derrick Rose 1.50 4.00
14 Zach Randolph 1.00 2.50
15 Kevin Martin 1.00 2.50
16 David Lee .75 2.00
17 Tyreke Evans .75 2.00
18 Brook Lopez 1.00 2.50
19 Deron Williams 1.00 2.50
20 Paul Pierce 1.25 3.00

2010-11 Limited Banner Season Materials

STATED PRINT RUN 25 TO 99 SER.#'d SETS
*PRIME: .75X TO 2X HI
PRIME: PRINT RUN 5 TO 25 SER.#'d SETS
1 Kevin Durant/99 8.00 20.00
2 LeBron James/49 8.00 20.00
3 Carmelo Anthony/99 4.00 10.00
4 Kobe Bryant/99 8.00 20.00
5 Dwyane Wade/99 5.00 12.00
7 Dirk Nowitzki/99 4.00 10.00
8 Danny Granger/25 2.50 6.00
9 Chris Bosh/49 3.00 8.00
10 Amare Stoudemire/99 2.50 6.00
11 Brandon Jennings/99 2.00 5.00
12 Joe Johnson/99 2.50 6.00
13 Derrick Rose/49 4.00 10.00
16 David Lee/49 2.00 5.00
17 Tyreke Evans/25 2.00 5.00
18 Brook Lopez/49 2.50 6.00
19 Deron Williams/99 2.50 6.00
20 Paul Pierce/99 3.00 8.00

2010-11 Limited Banner Season Materials Signatures

STATED PRINT RUN 5 TO 49 SER.#'d SETS
SOME UNPRICED DUE TO SCARCITY
PRIME SIG.PRINT RUN ONE TO 10 SETS
PRIME SIG.UNPRICED DUE TO SCARCITY
4 Kobe Bryant/25 100.00 200.00
11 Brandon Jennings/49 4.00 10.00

2010-11 Limited Decade Dominance
COMPLETE SET (20) 25.00 50.00
STATED PRINT RUN 149 SER.#'d SETS
*GOLD: 1X TO 2.5X BASE HI
GOLD PRINT RUN 24 SER.#'d SETS
*SILVER: .6X TO 1.5X BASE HI
SILVER PRINT RUN 49 SER.#'d SETS
UNPRICED PLATINUM PRINT RUN ONE SET
1 Bob Pettit 1.50 4.00
2 Elgin Baylor 1.50 4.00
3 Lenny Wilkens 1.50 4.00
4 Gail Goodrich 1.25 3.00
5 Earl Monroe 1.50 4.00
6 George Gervin 1.50 4.00
7 David Thompson 1.25 3.00
8 Sidney Moncrief 1.00 2.50
9 Hakeem Olajuwon 2.00 5.00
10 Bernard King 1.25 3.00
11 Isiah Thomas 1.50 4.00
12 Darryl Dawkins 1.00 2.50
13 Patrick Ewing 2.00 5.00
14 Scottie Pippen 3.00 8.00
15 Karl Malone 2.00 5.00
16 Clyde Drexler 2.00 5.00
17 John Stockton 2.50 6.00
18 Kobe Bryant 6.00 15.00
19 Tim Duncan 2.50 6.00
20 Dwyane Wade 2.50 6.00

2010-11 Limited Decade Dominance Materials
STATED PRINT RUN 99 SER.#'d SETS
MAT.PRIME PRINT RUN 5 TO 10 SER.#'d SETS
MAT.PRIME UNPRICED DUE TO SCARCITY
PRIME SIG.PRINT RUN ONE TO 5 SER.#'d SETS
PRIME SIG.UNPRICED DUE TO SCARCITY
9 Hakeem Olajuwon/99 4.00 10.00
10 Bernard King/99 2.50 6.00
13 Patrick Ewing/99 6.00 15.00
14 Scottie Pippen/99 10.00 25.00
15 Karl Malone/99 4.00 10.00
16 Clyde Drexler/99 4.00 10.00
17 John Stockton/99 5.00 12.00
18 Kobe Bryant/99 8.00 20.00
19 Tim Duncan/99 5.00 12.00
20 Dwyane Wade/99 5.00 12.00

2010-11 Limited Decade Dominance Materials Signatures
STATED PRINT RUN ONE TO 25 SER.#'d SETS
SOME UNPRICED DUE TO SCARCITY
9 Hakeem Olajuwon/25 20.00 50.00
14 Scottie Pippen/25 100.00 200.00
17 John Stockton/25 40.00 100.00
18 Kobe Bryant/25 100.00 200.00

2010-11 Limited Decade Dominance Signatures
STATED PRINT RUN 25 TO 99 SER.#'d SETS
1 Bob Pettit/99 6.00 15.00
2 Elgin Baylor/99 EXCH 6.00 15.00
3 Lenny Wilkens/99 6.00 15.00
4 Gail Goodrich/99 6.00 15.00
5 Earl Monroe/99 10.00 25.00
6 George Gervin/99 8.00 20.00
7 David Thompson/99 6.00 15.00
8 Sidney Moncrief/99 6.00 15.00
9 Hakeem Olajuwon/99 20.00 50.00
10 Bernard King/99 6.00 15.00
11 Isiah Thomas/99 EXCH 8.00 20.00
12 Darryl Dawkins/99 8.00 20.00
14 Scottie Pippen/99 75.00 150.00
16 Clyde Drexler/99 15.00 40.00
17 John Stockton/99 35.00 70.00
18 Kobe Bryant/25 100.00 200.00

2010-11 Limited Freshmen Jumbo
STATED PRINT RUN 99 SER.#'d SETS
*NUMBERS: .4X TO 1X BASE HI
NUMBERS PRINT RUN 99 SER.#'d SETS
1 John Wall 12.00 30.00
2 Evan Turner 2.00 5.00
3 Derrick Favors 3.00 8.00
4 Wesley Johnson 1.50 4.00
5 DeMarcus Cousins 8.00 20.00
6 Ekpe Udoh 1.50 4.00
7 Greg Monroe 3.00 8.00
8 Al-Farouq Aminu 2.50 6.00
9 Gordon Hayward 4.00 10.00
10 Paul George 15.00 40.00
11 Cole Aldrich 2.00 5.00
12 Xavier Henry 1.50 4.00
13 Ed Davis 1.50 4.00
14 Patrick Patterson 2.00 5.00
15 Larry Sanders 1.50 4.00
16 Luke Babbitt 2.00 5.00
17 Kevin Seraphin 1.50 4.00
18 Eric Bledsoe 3.00 8.00
19 Avery Bradley 3.00 8.00
20 James Anderson 1.50 4.00
21 Craig Brackins 1.50 4.00
22 Elliot Williams 1.50 4.00
23 Trevor Booker 2.00 5.00
24 Damion James 1.50 4.00
25 Dominique Jones 1.50 4.00
26 Quincy Pondexter 1.50 4.00
27 Jordan Crawford 2.00 5.00
28 Greivis Vasquez 2.00 5.00
29 Daniel Orton 1.50 4.00
30 Lazar Hayward 1.50 4.00

2010-11 Limited Freshmen Jumbo Prime
*PRIME: 1X TO 2.5X BASE HI
STATED PRINT RUN 25 SER.#'d SETS
UNPRICED PRIME SIG.PRINT RUN 10 SETS
*NUMBERS: .4X TO 1X BASE HI
NUMBERS: PRINT RUN 10 TO 25 SETS
UNPRICED NUM.PR.SIG PRINT RUN 10 SETS
1 John Wall 20.00 50.00
2 Evan Turner 5.00 12.00
3 Derrick Favors 8.00 20.00
4 Wesley Johnson 4.00 10.00
5 DeMarcus Cousins 20.00 50.00
6 Ekpe Udoh 4.00 10.00
7 Greg Monroe 8.00 20.00
8 Al-Farouq Aminu 6.00 15.00
9 Gordon Hayward 10.00 25.00
10 Paul George 20.00 50.00
11 Cole Aldrich 5.00 12.00
12 Xavier Henry 4.00 10.00
13 Ed Davis 4.00 10.00
14 Patrick Patterson 5.00 12.00
15 Larry Sanders 4.00 10.00
16 Luke Babbitt 5.00 12.00
17 Kevin Seraphin 4.00 10.00
18 Eric Bledsoe 8.00 20.00
19 Avery Bradley 8.00 20.00
20 James Anderson 4.00 10.00
21 Craig Brackins 4.00 10.00
22 Elliot Williams 4.00 10.00
23 Trevor Booker 5.00 12.00
24 Damion James 4.00 10.00
25 Dominique Jones 4.00 10.00
26 Quincy Pondexter 4.00 10.00
27 Jordan Crawford 5.00 12.00
28 Greivis Vasquez 5.00 12.00
29 Daniel Orton 4.00 10.00
30 Lazar Hayward 4.00 10.00

2010-11 Limited Freshmen Jumbo Signatures
STATED PRINT RUN 99 SER.#'d SETS
*NUMBERS: .4X TO 1X BASE HI
NUMBERS PRINT RUN 99 SER.#'d SETS
1 John Wall 40.00 100.00
2 Evan Turner 5.00 12.00
3 Derrick Favors 8.00 20.00
4 Wesley Johnson 4.00 10.00
5 DeMarcus Cousins 20.00 50.00
6 Ekpe Udoh 4.00 10.00
7 Greg Monroe 6.00 15.00
8 Al-Farouq Aminu 6.00 15.00
9 Gordon Hayward 10.00 25.00
10 Paul George 50.00 120.00
11 Cole Aldrich 5.00 12.00
12 Xavier Henry 4.00 10.00
13 Ed Davis 4.00 10.00
14 Patrick Patterson 5.00 12.00
15 Larry Sanders 4.00 10.00
16 Luke Babbitt 5.00 12.00
17 Kevin Seraphin 4.00 10.00
18 Eric Bledsoe 8.00 20.00
19 Avery Bradley 8.00 20.00
20 James Anderson 4.00 10.00
21 Craig Brackins 4.00 10.00
22 Elliot Williams 4.00 10.00
23 Trevor Booker 5.00 12.00
24 Damion James 4.00 10.00
25 Dominique Jones 4.00 10.00
26 Quincy Pondexter 4.00 10.00
27 Jordan Crawford 5.00 12.00
28 Greivis Vasquez 5.00 12.00
29 Daniel Orton 4.00 10.00
30 Lazar Hayward 4.00 10.00

2010-11 Limited Glass Cleaners
COMPLETE SET (20) 20.00 40.00
STATED PRINT RUN 149 SER.#'d SETS
*GOLD: 1X TO 2.5X BASE HI
GOLD PRINT RUN 24 SER.#'d SETS
*SILVER: .6X TO 1.5X BASE HI
SILVER PRINT RUN 49 SER.#'d SETS
UNPRICED PLATINUM PRINT RUN ONE SET
1 Shaquille O'Neal 2.50 6.00
2 David Lee .75 2.00
3 Chris Bosh 1.25 3.00
4 Carlos Boozer 1.00 2.50
5 Kevin Love 1.25 3.00
6 Lamar Odom 1.00 2.50
7 Jason Kidd 1.25 3.00
8 Elgin Baylor 1.25 3.00
9 Oscar Robertson 1.50 4.00
10 Kevin McHale 1.25 3.00
11 Bill Walton 1.25 3.00
12 Troy Murphy .75 2.00
13 Dave Cowens .75 2.00
14 Mark Eaton .75 2.00
15 Alonzo Mourning 1.50 4.00
16 Elvin Hayes 1.25 3.00
17 Kareem Abdul-Jabbar 2.00 5.00
18 Bill Russell 2.00 5.00
19 Artis Gilmore 1.00 2.50
20 Kobe Bryant 5.00 12.00

2010-11 Limited Glass Cleaners Materials
STATED PRINT RUN 49 TO 99 SER.#'d SETS
PRIME PRINT RUN 5 TO 25 SER.#'d SETS
2 David Lee/49 2.00 5.00
3 Chris Bosh/49 3.00 8.00
4 Carlos Boozer/49 2.50 6.00
5 Kevin Love/99 3.00 8.00
6 Lamar Odom/99 2.50 6.00
7 Jason Kidd/49 4.00 10.00
10 Kevin McHale/99 3.00 8.00
13 Dave Cowens/99 2.00 5.00
14 Mark Eaton/99 2.00 5.00
15 Alonzo Mourning/99 6.00 15.00
19 Artis Gilmore/99 2.50 6.00
20 Kobe Bryant/99 8.00 20.00

2010-11 Limited Glass Cleaners Materials Signatures
STATED PRINT RUN 5 TO 49 SER.#'d SETS
SOME UNPRICED DUE TO SCARCITY
PRIME SIG.PRINT RUN ONE TO FIVE SETS
PRIME SIG.UNPRICED DUE TO SCARCITY
5 Kevin Love/49 15.00 40.00
6 Lamar Odom/49 10.00 25.00
10 Kevin McHale/49 20.00 50.00
13 Dave Cowens/25 10.00 25.00
19 Artis Gilmore/49 10.00 25.00
20 Kobe Bryant/25 100.00 200.00

2010-11 Limited Glass Cleaners Signatures
STATED PRINT RUN 25 TO 99 SER.#'d SETS
2 David Lee/99 EXCH 5.00 12.00
3 Chris Bosh/49 8.00 20.00
4 Carlos Boozer/49 EXCH 6.00 15.00
5 Kevin Love/99 15.00 40.00
6 Lamar Odom/49 8.00 20.00
7 Jason Kidd/49 12.50 30.00
8 Elgin Baylor/49 EXCH 6.00 15.00
9 Oscar Robertson/49 30.00 80.00
10 Kevin McHale/49 20.00 50.00
11 Bill Walton/49 8.00 20.00
13 Dave Cowens/49 6.00 15.00
15 Alonzo Mourning/49 20.00 50.00
16 Elvin Hayes/49 5.00 12.00
17 Kareem Abdul-Jabbar/49 30.00 60.00
18 Bill Russell/25 50.00 120.00
19 Artis Gilmore/99 6.00 15.00
20 Kobe Bryant/25 100.00 200.00

2010-11 Limited Jumbo
STATED PRINT RUN 25 TO 99 SER.#'d SETS
*NUMBERS: .4X TO 1X BASE HI
NUMBERS PRINT RUN 25 TO 99 SETS
PRIME PRINT RUN 5 TO 10 SER.#'d SETS
PRIME UNPRICED DUE TO SCARCITY
NUMBERS PRIME PRINT RUN 5 TO 10 SETS
NUMBERS UNPRICED DUE TO SCARCITY
1 Chris Paul/99 4.00 10.00
2 Dwyane Wade/99 5.00 12.00
3 LeBron James/99 12.00 30.00
4 Kobe Bryant/99 10.00 25.00
5 Kevin Durant/99 8.00 20.00
6 Allen Iverson/49 4.00 10.00
7 Andrew Bogut/99 2.50 6.00
8 Ben Gordon/99 2.50 6.00
9 Carmelo Anthony/99 4.00 10.00
10 Chris Bosh/99 3.00 8.00
11 Deron Williams/99 2.50 6.00
12 Tyreke Evans/25 2.00 5.00
13 Dwight Howard/99 2.50 6.00
14 Tim Duncan/99 5.00 12.00
15 Kevin Garnett/99 5.00 12.00
16 Luol Deng/49 2.50 6.00
17 Gerald Wallace/99 2.50 6.00
18 Alex English/25 2.50 6.00
19 Dominique Wilkins/49 4.00 10.00
20 Patrick Ewing/99 6.00 15.00

2010-11 Limited Jumbo Jersey Numbers Signatures
STATED PRINT RUN 5 TO 25 SER.#'d SETS
SOME UNPRICED DUE TO SCARCITY
PRIME SIG.PRINT RUN ONE TO 5 SER.#'d SETS
PRIME SIG.UNPRICED DUE TO SCARCITY
4 Kobe Bryant/25 100.00 200.00
19 Dominique Wilkins/25 20.00 50.00

2010-11 Limited Jumbo Signatures
STATED PRINT RUN 5 TO 25 SER.#'d SETS
SOME UNPRICED DUE TO SCARCITY
NUMBERS PRINT RUN 5 TO 25 SER.#'d SETS
PRIME SIG.PRINT RUN ONE TO 5 SER.#'d SETS
PRIME SIG.UNPRICED DUE TO SCARCITY
NUMBERS PR.SIG PRINT RUN ONE TO 5 SETS
NUMBERS PR.SIG UNPRICED DUE TO SCARCITY
4 Kobe Bryant/25 150.00 300.00
19 Dominique Wilkins/25 20.00 50.00

2010-11 Limited Monikers Gold
STATED PRINT RUN 5 TO 99 SER.#'d SETS
SOME UNPRICED DUE TO SCARCITY
UNPRICED PLATINUM PRINT RUN ONE SET
6 Devin Harris/49 5.00 12.00
8 Amare Stoudemire/15 25.00 60.00
11 Toney Douglas/99 5.00 12.00
12 Andre Iguodala/99 6.00 15.00
14 Jrue Holiday/99 6.00 15.00
17 DeMar DeRozan/99 8.00 20.00
26 Richard Hamilton/99 6.00 15.00
31 Tyler Hansbrough/99 6.00 15.00
33 Brandon Jennings/25 15.00 40.00
57 Aaron Brooks/99 5.00 12.00
59 Shane Battier/99 5.00 12.00
66 Marcus Thornton/99 5.00 12.00
74 Jonny Flynn/99 5.00 12.00
77 Brandon Roy/49 5.00 12.00
80 James Harden/99 25.00 60.00
83 Al Jefferson/99 6.00 15.00
89 Baron Davis/49 6.00 15.00
90 Blake Griffin/99 30.00 80.00
93 Kobe Bryant/25 100.00 200.00
98 Carl Landry/99 5.00 12.00
100 Tyreke Evans/99 5.00 12.00
101 Alex English/25 6.00 15.00
102 Alvan Adams/49 6.00 15.00
103 Artis Gilmore/49 8.00 20.00
106 Bill Russell/25 50.00 120.00
109 Bob Lanier/49 5.00 12.00
110 Bob McAdoo/49 12.50 30.00
111 Bob Pettit/49 12.50 30.00
113 Cazzie Russell/49 6.00 15.00
115 Cliff Hagan/25 5.00 12.00
118 Dominique Wilkins/49 12.00 30.00
120 Elvin Hayes/49 5.00 12.00
121 Gail Goodrich/49 5.00 12.00
122 Gary Payton/25 20.00 50.00
123 George Gervin/25 8.00 20.00
125 Hakeem Olajuwon/25 15.00 40.00
127 Jeff Hornacek/25 8.00 20.00
133 K.C. Jones/25 10.00 25.00
135 Larry Bird/24 50.00 125.00
136 Lenny Wilkens/49 6.00 15.00
139 Nate Archibald/99 6.00 15.00
140 Nate Thurmond/99 5.00 12.00
141 Robert Parish/25 8.00 20.00
144 Willis Reed/49 6.00 15.00
145 Adrian Dantley/25 6.00 15.00
149 Hal Greer/99 5.00 12.00

2010-11 Limited Monikers Materials
STATED PRINT RUN 5 TO 99 SER.#'d SETS
SOME UNPRICED DUE TO SCARCITY
3 Brandon Jennings/49 10.00 25.00
4 Brandon Roy/49 6.00 15.00
5 Carlos Boozer/25 12.00 30.00
8 Chris Andersen/49 12.00 30.00
10 Chris Kaman/49 6.00 15.00
11 Chris Mullin/25 12.50 30.00
14 Danny Manning/25 12.00 30.00
16 Derek Fisher/49 12.50 30.00
17 Detlef Schrempf/99 6.00 15.00
19 Gary Payton/25 10.00 25.00
20 Glen Rice/99 6.00 15.00
21 Jalen Rose/25 10.00 25.00
23 Jeff Hornacek/25 8.00 20.00
24 Jermaine O'Neal/25 10.00 25.00
25 Joe Dumars/25 10.00 25.00
26 Kareem Abdul-Jabbar/25 50.00 120.00
27 Kelly Tripucka/99 6.00 15.00
28 Kevin Johnson/99 10.00 25.00
29 Kevin Love/99 20.00 50.00
30 Kobe Bryant/25 100.00 200.00
31 Lamar Odom/49 6.00 15.00
32 Larry Johnson/99 10.00 25.00
33 Magic Johnson/25 30.00 80.00
34 Maurice Cheeks/49 6.00 15.00
35 Michael Cage/99 6.00 15.00
36 Pau Gasol/25 12.00 30.00
37 Ray Allen/49 25.00 60.00
38 Robert Parish/25 6.00 15.00
39 Ron Artest/99 10.00 25.00
40 Russell Westbrook/99 30.00 80.00
41 Rudy Fernandez/99 EXCH 6.00 15.00
42 Sam Perkins/25 8.00 20.00
43 Scottie Pippen/25 100.00 200.00
44 Shane Battier/99 8.00 20.00
45 Shawn Bradley/99 6.00 15.00
46 Stephen Curry/99 100.00 200.00
47 Steve Nash/21 20.00 50.00
48 Tony Parker/25 12.50 30.00
49 Tyreke Evans/25 12.50 30.00
50 Vince Carter/25 20.00 50.00

2010-11 Limited Monikers Materials Prime
STATED PRINT RUN ONE TO 25 SER.#'d SETS
SOME UNPRICED DUE TO SCARCITY
4 Brandon Roy/25 10.00 25.00
20 Glen Rice/25 15.00 40.00
27 Kelly Tripucka/25 10.00 25.00
28 Kevin Johnson/25 40.00 100.00
29 Kevin Love/25 30.00 80.00
32 Larry Johnson/25 20.00 50.00
34 Maurice Cheeks/25 10.00 25.00
35 Michael Cage/25 10.00 25.00
37 Ray Allen/25 30.00 80.00
39 Ron Artest/25 20.00 50.00
40 Russell Westbrook/25 75.00 200.00
41 Rudy Fernandez/25 EXCH 10.00 25.00
44 Shane Battier/25 12.00 30.00
45 Shawn Bradley/25 10.00 25.00

2010-11 Limited Next Day Autographs
STATED PRINT RUN 90 TO 99 SER.#'d SETS
1 Ekpe Udoh/99 4.00 10.00
2 Gordon Hayward/99 25.00 60.00
3 Lance Stephenson/99 6.00 15.00
4 Trevor Booker/99 5.00 12.00
6 Paul George/99 150.00 300.00
7 Greg Monroe/90 8.00 20.00
8 Derrick Favors/99 8.00 20.00
9 Gani Lawal/93 4.00 10.00
10 Craig Brackins/99 4.00 10.00
11 Cole Aldrich/99 5.00 12.00
12 Xavier Henry/99 4.00 10.00
13 John Wall/99 100.00 200.00
14 DeMarcus Cousins/99 60.00 150.00
15 Patrick Patterson/99 5.00 12.00
16 Eric Bledsoe/99 20.00 50.00
17 Daniel Orton/99 4.00 10.00
18 Lazar Hayward/99 4.00 10.00
19 Hassan Whiteside/95 12.00 30.00
20 Greivis Vasquez/99 5.00 12.00
21 Elliot Williams/99 4.00 10.00
22 Luke Babbitt/99 5.00 12.00
23 Ed Davis/99 4.00 10.00
24 Luke Harangody/98 4.00 10.00
25 Evan Turner/99 5.00 12.00
26 Willie Warren/99 4.00 10.00
27 Keith Gallon/99 4.00 10.00
28 James Anderson/99 4.00 10.00
29 Dominique Jones/99 4.00 10.00
30 Wesley Johnson/99 4.00 10.00
31 Terrico White/96 4.00 10.00
32 Avery Bradley/99 15.00 40.00
33 Dexter Pittman/97 4.00 10.00
34 Damion James/99 4.00 10.00
35 Larry Sanders/99 6.00 15.00
36 Al-Farouq Aminu/99 6.00 15.00
37 Quincy Pondexter/97 4.00 10.00
38 Da'Sean Butler/99 6.00 15.00
39 Devin Ebanks/99 4.00 10.00
40 Jordan Crawford/99 5.00 12.00
41 Jeremy Lin/99 150.00 400.00

2010-11 Limited Retired Numbers
COMPLETE SET (20) 20.00 40.00
STATED PRINT RUN 149 SER.#'d SETS
*GOLD: 1X TO 2.5X BASE HI
GOLD PRINT RUN 24 SER.#'d SETS
*SILVER: .6X TO 1.5X BASE HI
SILVER PRINT RUN 49 SER.#'d SETS
UNPRICED PLATINUM PRINT RUN ONE SET
1 Bob Pettit 1.50 4.00
2 Mark Price 1.50 4.00
3 Rolando Blackman 1.25 3.00
4 Elgin Baylor 1.50 4.00
5 Nate Archibald 1.25 3.00
6 Darrell Griffith 1.00 2.50
7 Dan Issel 1.25 3.00
8 Al Attles 1.50 4.00
9 Sidney Moncrief 1.00 2.50
10 Earl Monroe 1.50 4.00
11 Mark Eaton 1.00 2.50
12 Tom Heinsohn 1.50 4.00
13 Hakeem Olajuwon 2.00 5.00
14 Gail Goodrich 1.25 3.00
15 George Gervin 1.50 4.00
16 Nate Thurmond 1.25 3.00
17 Joe Dumars 1.50 4.00
18 Calvin Murphy 1.25 3.00
19 Dave Cowens 1.00 2.50
20 Alvan Adams 1.00 2.50

2010-11 Limited Retired Numbers Materials
STATED PRINT RUN 99 SER.#'d SETS
PRIME PRINT RUN 5 TO 10 SER.#'d SETS
PRIME UNPRICED DUE TO SCARCITY
2 Mark Price 5.00 12.00
3 Rolando Blackman 2.50 6.00
6 Darrell Griffith 2.00 5.00
7 Dan Issel 2.50 6.00
11 Mark Eaton 2.00 5.00
13 Hakeem Olajuwon 4.00 10.00
17 Joe Dumars 3.00 8.00
19 Dave Cowens 2.00 5.00
20 Alvan Adams 2.00 5.00

2010-11 Limited Retired Numbers Materials Signatures
STATED PRINT RUN ONE TO 49 SER.#'d SETS
SOME UNPRICED DUE TO SCARCITY
PRIME SIG.PRINT RUN ONE TO 5 SER.#'d SETS
PRIME SIG.UNPRICED DUE TO SCARCITY
2 Mark Price/49 8.00 20.00
3 Rolando Blackman/49 8.00 20.00
7 Dan Issel/49 8.00 20.00
13 Hakeem Olajuwon/25 15.00 40.00
19 Dave Cowens/25 8.00 20.00
20 Alvan Adams/49 8.00 20.00

2010-11 Limited Retired Numbers Signatures
STATED PRINT RUN 49 TO 99 SER.#'d SETS
1 Bob Pettit/99 12.00 30.00
2 Mark Price/99 EXCH 10.00 25.00
3 Rolando Blackman/99 5.00 12.00
4 Elgin Baylor/99 EXCH 5.00 12.00
5 Nate Archibald/99 6.00 15.00
7 Dan Issel/99 8.00 20.00
8 Al Attles/39 EXCH 5.00 12.00
9 Sidney Moncrief/99 5.00 12.00
10 Earl Monroe/99 8.00 20.00
12 Tom Heinsohn/49 EXCH 10.00 25.00
13 Hakeem Olajuwon/99 12.00 30.00
14 Gail Goodrich/99 8.00 20.00
15 George Gervin/99 6.00 15.00
16 Nate Thurmond/99 5.00 12.00
17 Joe Dumars/99 10.00 25.00
18 Calvin Murphy/49 5.00 12.00
19 Dave Cowens/49 5.00 12.00
20 Alvan Adams/99 5.00 12.00

2010-11 Limited Team Trademarks
COMPLETE SET (20) 15.00 30.00
STATED PRINT RUN 149 SER.#'d SETS
*GOLD: 1.5X TO 4X BASE HI
GOLD PRINT RUN 24 SER.#'d SETS
*SILVER: 1X TO 2.5X BASE HI
SILVER PRINT RUN 49 SER.#'d SETS
UNPRICED PLATINUM PRINT RUN ONE SET
1 Al Jefferson .60 1.50
2 Brandon Jennings .50 1.25
3 Brook Lopez .60 1.50
4 David Lee .50 1.25
5 David West .60 1.50
6 Deron Williams .60 1.50
7 Derrick Rose 1.00 2.50
8 Elton Brand .75 2.00
9 Gerald Wallace .60 1.50
10 Jason Kidd .75 2.00
11 Joe Johnson .60 1.50
12 Kevin Durant 2.00 5.00
13 Kevin Martin .60 1.50
14 Kobe Bryant 3.00 8.00
15 LeBron James 4.00 10.00
16 Marc Gasol .75 2.00
17 Monta Ellis .60 1.50
18 Rajon Rondo .75 2.00
19 Steve Nash .75 2.00
20 Vince Carter 1.00 2.50

2010-11 Limited Team Trademarks Materials
STATED PRINT RUN 49 TO 99 SER.#'d SETS
PRIME PRINT RUN 5 TO 25 SER.#'d SETS
1 Al Jefferson 2.50 6.00
2 Brandon Jennings 2.00 5.00
3 Brook Lopez 2.50 6.00
4 David Lee 2.00 5.00
5 David West 2.50 6.00
6 Deron Williams 2.50 6.00
7 Derrick Rose 4.00 10.00
8 Elton Brand 3.00 8.00
9 Gerald Wallace 2.50 6.00
10 Jason Kidd 3.00 8.00
11 Joe Johnson 2.50 6.00
12 Kevin Durant 8.00 20.00
14 Kobe Bryant 10.00 25.00
15 LeBron James 12.00 30.00
16 Marc Gasol 3.00 8.00
18 Rajon Rondo 3.00 8.00
19 Steve Nash 3.00 8.00
20 Vince Carter 4.00 10.00

2010-11 Limited Team Trademarks Materials Prime Signatures
STATED PRINT RUN ONE TO 25 SER.#'d SETS
SOME UNPRICED DUE TO SCARCITY
16 Marc Gasol/25 40.00 100.00

2010-11 Limited Team Trademarks Materials Signatures
STATED PRINT RUN 5 TO 49 SER.#'d SETS
SOME UNPRICED DUE TO SCARCITY
2 Brandon Jennings/49 12.50 30.00
14 Kobe Bryant/25 100.00 200.00
16 Marc Gasol/49 30.00 80.00
18 Rajon Rondo/49 10.00 25.00
19 Steve Nash/25 20.00 50.00
20 Vince Carter/25 20.00 50.00

2010-11 Limited Threads
STATED PRINT RUN 10 TO 199 SER.#'d SETS
SOME UNPRICED DUE TO SCARCITY
2 Paul Pierce/99 3.00 8.00
3 Rajon Rondo/199 3.00 8.00
5 Brook Lopez/99 2.50 6.00
6 Devin Harris/199 2.00 5.00
8 Amare Stoudemire/199 2.50 6.00
11 Toney Douglas/199 2.00 5.00
12 Andre Iguodala/199 2.50 6.00
13 Elton Brand/199 3.00 8.00
14 Jrue Holiday/199 3.00 8.00
16 Andrea Bargnani/199 2.50 6.00
17 DeMar DeRozan/199 3.00 8.00
18 Jose Calderon/199 2.00 5.00
19 Carlos Boozer/199 2.50 6.00
20 Derrick Rose/49 4.00 10.00
21 Joakim Noah/199 2.50 6.00
26 Richard Hamilton/199 2.50 6.00
27 Rodney Stuckey/199 2.50 6.00
29 Danny Granger/25 2.50 6.00
30 T.J. Ford/199 2.00 5.00
31 Tyler Hansbrough/199 2.50 6.00
32 Andrew Bogut/199 2.50 6.00
33 Brandon Jennings/199 2.00 5.00
35 Michael Redd/199 2.50 6.00
36 Al Horford/199 2.50 6.00
37 Joe Johnson/199 2.50 6.00
38 Josh Smith/199 2.50 6.00
39 Gerald Wallace/199 2.50 6.00
42 Chris Bosh/199 3.00 8.00
43 Dwyane Wade/199 5.00 12.00
44 LeBron James/99 10.00 25.00
46 Dwight Howard/199 2.50 6.00
47 J.J. Redick/199 3.00 8.00
48 Jason Williams/199 2.50 6.00
49 Rashard Lewis/199 2.50 6.00
53 Caron Butler/199 2.50 6.00
54 Dirk Nowitzki/199 4.00 10.00
55 Jason Kidd/49 3.00 8.00
59 Shane Battier/199 2.50 6.00
61 Marc Gasol/199 3.00 8.00
62 O.J. Mayo/199 2.00 5.00
63 Rudy Gay/199 3.00 8.00
65 Chris Paul/199 4.00 10.00
68 Manu Ginobili/199 3.00 8.00
69 Tim Duncan/99 5.00 12.00
70 Tony Parker/199 3.00 8.00
71 Carmelo Anthony/199 4.00 10.00
72 Chauncey Billups/199 3.00 8.00
73 Chris Andersen/199 2.50 6.00
74 Jonny Flynn/199 2.00 5.00
75 Kevin Love/199 3.00 8.00
77 Brandon Roy/199 3.00 8.00
78 LaMarcus Aldridge/199 3.00 8.00
79 Marcus Camby/199 2.00 5.00
80 James Harden/199 5.00 12.00
82 Russell Westbrook/199 8.00 20.00
83 Al Jefferson/199 2.50 6.00
84 Deron Williams/199 2.50 6.00
86 David Lee/99 2.00 5.00
88 Stephen Curry/199 12.00 30.00
89 Baron Davis/199 2.50 6.00
90 Blake Griffin/199 6.00 15.00
91 Chris Kaman/199 2.50 6.00
92 Derek Fisher/199 2.50 6.00
93 Kobe Bryant/199 8.00 20.00
94 Pau Gasol/199 3.00 8.00
95 Grant Hill/199 4.00 10.00
96 Jason Richardson/99 3.00 8.00
97 Steve Nash/199 3.00 8.00
101 Alex English/99 2.50 6.00
102 Alvan Adams/199 2.00 5.00
104 Bernard King/199 2.50 6.00
109 Bob Lanier/199 2.50 6.00
117 Darrell Griffith/199 2.00 5.00
118 Dominique Wilkins/99 4.00 10.00
124 George Mikan/99 12.00 30.00
125 Hakeem Olajuwon/199 4.00 10.00
127 Jeff Hornacek/99 2.50 6.00
132 Karl Malone/199 4.00 10.00
137 Magic Johnson/199 6.00 15.00
141 Robert Parish/199 3.00 8.00
147 Chris Mullin/199 3.00 8.00
148 Clyde Drexler/199 4.00 10.00

2010-11 Limited Threads Prime
*PRIME: .75X TO 2X BASE HI
STATED PRINT RUN 5 TO 25 SER.#'d SETS
SOME UNPRICED DUE TO SCARCITY
17 DeMar DeRozan/25 8.00 20.00
48 Jason Williams/25 10.00 25.00
71 Carmelo Anthony/25 12.00 30.00
81 Kevin Durant/25 15.00 40.00
95 Grant Hill/25 12.50 30.00
97 Steve Nash/25 6.00 15.00
104 Bernard King/25 10.00 25.00
118 Dominique Wilkins/25 10.00 25.00
125 Hakeem Olajuwon/25 10.00 25.00
131 Kareem Abdul-Jabbar/25 12.50 30.00
132 Karl Malone/25 12.50 30.00
147 Chris Mullin/25 8.00 20.00

2010-11 Limited Trios
COMPLETE SET (10) 20.00 40.00
STATED PRINT RUN 149 SER.#'d SETS
*GOLD: .75X TO 2X BASE HI
GOLD PRINT RUN 24 SER.#'d SETS
*SILVER: .6X TO 1.5X BASE HI
SILVER PRINT RUN 99 SER.#'d SETS
UNPRICED PLATINUM PRINT RUN ONE SET
1 Bryant/Odom/Gasol 4.00 10.00
2 Jennings/Curry/Evans 2.50 6.00
3 Anthony/Billups/Andersen 1.50 4.00
4 Iverson/Kidd/Nash 3.00 8.00
5 Durant/Bryant/James 6.00 15.00
6 Mikan/Maravich/Chamberlain 5.00 12.00
7 Baylor/Bellamy/Unseld 1.50 4.00
8 Drexler/Thomas/Stockton 5.00 12.00
9 Kareem/Bird/Magic 6.00 15.00
10 Russell/West/Robertson 4.00 10.00

2010-11 Limited Trios Materials
STATED PRINT RUN 49 SER.#'d SETS
UNPRICED PRIME PRINT RUN 5 TO 10 SETS
1 Bryant/Odom/Gasol 10.00 25.00
2 Jennings/Curry/Evans 6.00 15.00
3 Anthony/Billups/Andersen 5.00 12.00
4 Iverson/Kidd/Nash 8.00 20.00
5 Durant/Bryant/James 25.00 60.00
8 Drexler/Thomas/Stockton 10.00 25.00

2010-11 Limited Trios Signatures
STATED PRINT RUN 5 TO 49 SER.#'d SETS
SOME UNPRICED DUE TO SCARCITY
1 Bryant/Odom/Gasol/49 125.00 250.00
2 Jennings/Curry/Evans/49 125.00 250.00

2011-12 Limited
ATED PRINT RUN 299 SER.#'d SETS
UNPRICED PLATINUM PRINT RUN ONE SET
1 Kobe Bryant 6.00 15.00
2 Metta World Peace 1.50 4.00
3 Pau Gasol 1.50 4.00
4 Andrew Bynum 1.00 2.50
5 Derek Fisher 1.25 3.00
6 Chris Bosh 1.50 4.00
7 Dwyane Wade 3.00 8.00
8 LeBron James 6.00 15.00
9 Mario Chalmers 1.25 3.00
10 Shane Battier 1.25 3.00
11 Dirk Nowitzki 2.00 5.00
12 Delonte West 1.00 2.50
13 Jason Kidd 1.50 4.00
14 Jason Terry 1.25 3.00
15 Lamar Odom 1.25 3.00
16 Vince Carter 2.00 5.00
17 Blake Griffin 1.50 4.00
18 Chauncey Billups 1.50 4.00
19 Chris Paul 2.00 5.00
20 Eric Bledsoe 1.50 4.00
21 Caron Butler 1.25 3.00
22 DeAndre Jordan 1.50 4.00
23 Grant Hill 2.00 5.00
24 Hakim Warrick 1.25 3.00
25 Steve Nash 1.50 4.00
26 Marcin Gortat 1.25 3.00
27 David Lee 1.00 2.50
28 Monta Ellis 1.25 3.00
29 Nate Robinson 1.50 4.00
30 Stephen Curry 6.00 15.00
31 James Harden 2.50 6.00
32 Kevin Durant 4.00 10.00
33 Russell Westbrook 4.00 10.00
34 Serge Ibaka 1.25 3.00
35 Nick Collison 1.25 3.00
36 Dwight Howard 1.25 3.00
37 J.J. Redick 1.50 4.00
38 Jason Richardson 1.50 4.00
39 Hedo Turkoglu 1.25 3.00
40 John Wall 2.00 5.00
41 Nick Young 1.25 3.00
42 Andray Blatche 1.00 2.50
43 Kevin Garnett 2.50 6.00
44 Paul Pierce 1.50 4.00
45 Rajon Rondo 1.50 4.00
46 Ray Allen 1.50 4.00
47 Brook Lopez 1.25 3.00
48 Deron Williams 1.25 3.00
49 Kris Humphries 1.00 2.50
50 Mehmet Okur 1.00 2.50
51 J.J. Barea 1.50 4.00
52 Kevin Love 1.50 4.00
53 Ricky Rubio 1.50 4.00
54 Michael Beasley 1.00 2.50
55 DeMarcus Cousins 1.50 4.00
56 Marcus Thornton 1.00 2.50
57 Francisco Garcia 1.00 2.50
58 Tyreke Evans 1.00 2.50
59 Emeka Okafor 1.25 3.00
60 Eric Gordon 1.25 3.00
61 Jarrett Jack 1.25 3.00
62 Chris Kaman 1.25 3.00
63 Jeff Teague 1.25 3.00
64 Joe Johnson 1.25 3.00
65 Josh Smith 1.25 3.00
66 Jerry Stackhouse 1.25 3.00
67 Tracy McGrady 1.50 4.00
68 Mike Conley 1.25 3.00
69 Rudy Gay 1.50 4.00
70 Marc Gasol 1.50 4.00
71 Zach Randolph 1.25 3.00
72 Danny Granger 1.25 3.00
73 Darren Collison 1.25 3.00
74 Roy Hibbert 1.25 3.00
75 George Hill 1.25 3.00
76 Tyler Hansbrough 1.25 3.00
77 Amare Stoudemire 1.25 3.00
78 Jeremy Lin 6.00 15.00
79 Carmelo Anthony 2.00 5.00
80 Tyson Chandler 1.25 3.00
81 LaMarcus Aldridge 1.50 4.00
82 Raymond Felton 1.25 3.00
83 Wesley Matthews 1.00 2.50
84 Andre Iguodala 1.25 3.00
85 Evan Turner 1.00 2.50
86 Jrue Holiday 1.50 4.00
87 Spencer Hawes 1.00 2.50
88 Al Jefferson 1.25 3.00
89 Gordon Hayward 1.50 4.00
90 Paul Millsap 1.25 3.00
91 Raja Bell 1.25 3.00
92 DeJuan Blair 1.00 2.50
93 Manu Ginobili 1.50 4.00
94 Tim Duncan 2.50 6.00
95 Tony Parker 1.50 4.00
96 Carlos Boozer 1.25 3.00
97 Derrick Rose 2.00 5.00
98 Joakim Noah 1.25 3.00
99 Luol Deng 1.25 3.00
100 Chris Andersen 1.25 3.00
101 Danilo Gallinari 1.25 3.00
102 Nene 1.25 3.00
103 Ty Lawson 1.00 2.50
104 Andrea Bargnani 1.25 3.00
105 DeMar DeRozan 1.50 4.00
106 Jose Calderon 1.00 2.50
107 Ed Davis 1.00 2.50
108 Anderson Varejao 1.00 2.50
109 Antawn Jamison 1.25 3.00
110 Daniel Gibson 1.25 3.00
111 Andrew Bogut 1.25 3.00
112 Brandon Jennings 1.00 2.50
113 Stephen Jackson 1.25 3.00
114 Ersan Ilyasova 1.00 2.50
115 Boris Diaw 1.25 3.00
116 D.J. Augustin 1.00 2.50
117 Tyrus Thomas 1.00 2.50
118 Chase Budinger 1.00 2.50
119 Kevin Martin 1.25 3.00
120 Kyle Lowry 1.25 3.00
121 Luis Scola 1.25 3.00
122 Ben Gordon 1.25 3.00
123 Greg Monroe 1.50 4.00
124 Rodney Stuckey 1.25 3.00
125 Tayshaun Prince 1.50 4.00
126 Jerry West 2.00 5.00
127 Pete Maravich 2.50 6.00
128 Scottie Pippen 3.00 8.00
129 Hakeem Olajuwon 2.00 5.00
130 Adrian Dantley 1.25 3.00
131 Tom Chambers 1.25 3.00
132 Larry Bird 4.00 10.00
133 Bernard King 1.25 3.00
134 Moses Malone 1.50 4.00
135 Robert Parish 1.50 4.00
136 Bill Cartwright 1.25 3.00
137 Rolando Blackman 1.25 3.00
138 Bob Lanier 1.25 3.00
139 Walt Frazier 1.50 4.00
140 Elvin Hayes 1.50 4.00
141 Elgin Baylor 1.50 4.00
142 Dave Cowens 1.00 2.50
143 Kareem Abdul-Jabbar 2.50 6.00
144 Nate Thurmond 1.25 3.00
145 Oscar Robertson 2.00 5.00
146 Bill Russell 2.50 6.00
147 Wilt Chamberlain 3.00 8.00
148 Karl Malone 2.00 5.00
149 Magic Johnson 4.00 10.00
150 Isiah Thomas 1.50 4.00
151 George Gervin 1.50 4.00
152 Dikembe Mutombo 1.50 4.00
153 Kevin Willis 1.00 2.50
154 Dennis Rodman 3.00 8.00
155 John Stockton 2.50 6.00
156 Gary Payton 1.50 4.00
157 Anfernee Hardaway 4.00 10.00
158 John Starks 1.25 3.00
159 Wes Unseld 1.50 4.00
160 Rick Mahorn 1.00 2.50
161 Charles Oakley 1.50 4.00
162 Spud Webb 1.25 3.00
163 Larry Johnson 2.00 5.00
164 Julius Erving 2.50 6.00
165 Joe Dumars 1.50 4.00
166 Shawn Kemp 6.00 15.00
167 Nick Van Exel 1.50 4.00
168 Mitch Richmond 1.50 4.00
169 Jeff Hornacek 1.25 3.00
170 David Robinson 2.50 6.00
171 Patrick Ewing 2.00 5.00
172 Clyde Drexler 2.00 5.00
173 Xavier McDaniel 1.00 2.50
174 Alonzo Mourning 2.00 5.00
175 Dominique Wilkins 2.00 5.00
176 James Worthy 2.00 5.00
177 Steve Kerr 1.50 4.00
178 Connie Hawkins 1.50 4.00
179 Darryl Dawkins 1.00 2.50
180 Mark Jackson 1.25 3.00
181 Kurt Rambis 1.00 2.50
182 Earl Monroe 1.50 4.00
183 Maurice Cheeks 1.00 2.50
184 Ernie DiGregorio 1.50 4.00
185 Detlef Schrempf 1.50 4.00
186 Bill Walton 1.50 4.00
187 Artis Gilmore 1.25 3.00
188 Nate Archibald 1.25 3.00
189 David Thompson 1.25 3.00
190 John Havlicek 2.00 5.00
191 Dan Majerle 1.25 3.00
192 Muggsy Bogues 1.25 3.00
193 Tim Hardaway 1.50 4.00
194 Jalen Rose 1.50 4.00
195 Shaquille O'Neal 3.00 8.00
196 Scott Brooks 1.00 2.50
197 Mike Dunleavy Sr. 1.50 4.00
198 Pat Riley 1.50 4.00
199 Kenny Smith 1.25 3.00
200 Alonzo Mourning 2.00 5.00

2011-12 Limited Gold Spotlight
*GOLD STARS: 1.5X TO 4X BASE HI
*GOLD LEGENDS: 1.25X TO 3X HI
STATED PRINT RUN 25 SER.#'d SETS
23 Grant Hill 12.00 30.00
32 Kevin Durant 25.00 60.00
46 Ray Allen 8.00 20.00
51 J.J. Barea 8.00 20.00
152 Dikembe Mutombo 8.00 20.00
163 Larry Johnson 8.00 20.00
166 Shawn Kemp 25.00 60.00
171 Patrick Ewing 12.00 30.00
174 Alonzo Mourning 15.00 40.00
195 Shaquille O'Neal 15.00 40.00
200 Alonzo Mourning 15.00 40.00

2011-12 Limited Silver Spotlight
*SILVER: .6X TO 1.5X BASE HI
STATED PRINT RUN 49 SER.#'d SETS
154 Dennis Rodman 6.00 15.00
166 Shawn Kemp 15.00 40.00
174 Alonzo Mourning 8.00 20.00
195 Shaquille O'Neal 6.00 15.00
200 Alonzo Mourning 8.00 20.00

2011-12 Limited 2011 Draft Pick Redemptions Autographs
RANDOM INSERTS IN PACKS
1 Kyrie Irving 30.00 80.00
XRCA Isaiah Thomas 20.00 50.00
XRCB Shelvin Mack 2.50 6.00
XRCC Alec Burks 4.00 10.00
XRCD Lavoy Allen 4.00 10.00
XRCE MarShon Brooks 3.00 8.00
XRCF Josh Harrellson 4.00 10.00
XRCG Klay Thompson 30.00 80.00
XRCH Brandon Knight 4.00 10.00
XRCI Kemba Walker 6.00 15.00
XRCJ Chris Singleton 2.50 6.00
XRCK Markieff Morris 4.00 10.00
XRCL Marcus Morris 3.00 8.00
XRCM Gustavo Ayon 2.50 6.00
XRCN Kawhi Leonard 40.00 100.00
XRCP Justin Harper 3.00 8.00
XRCQ JaJuan Johnson 2.50 6.00
XRCR Jan Vesely 4.00 10.00
XRCS Kenneth Faried 5.00 12.00
XRCT Norris Cole 4.00 10.00
XRCU Jeremy Tyler 3.00 8.00
XRCV Charles Jenkins 3.00 8.00
XRCW Enes Kanter 5.00 12.00
XRCX Nolan Smith 2.50 6.00
XRCY Jimmy Butler 12.00 30.00

XRCZ Chandler Parsons 4.00 10.00
XRCAA Cory Joseph 3.00 8.00
XRCBB Bismack Biyombo 3.00 8.00
XRCCC Tristan Thompson 6.00 15.00
XRCDD Tobias Harris 4.00 10.00
XRCEE Reggie Jackson 4.00 10.00
XRCFF Iman Shumpert 6.00 15.00
XRCGG Derrick Williams 2.50 6.00
XRCHH Jimmer Fredette 2.50 6.00
XRCII Jordan Hamilton 3.00 8.00

2011-12 Limited 2012 Draft Pick Redemptions

RANDOM INSERTS IN PACKS
1 Anthony Davis 40.00 100.00
2 Michael Kidd-Gilchrist 6.00 15.00
3 Bradley Beal 12.00 30.00
4 Dion Waiters 6.00 15.00
5 Thomas Robinson 4.00 10.00
6 Damian Lillard 20.00 50.00
7 Harrison Barnes 12.00 30.00
8 Terrence Ross 6.00 15.00
9 Andre Drummond 20.00 50.00
10 Austin Rivers 8.00 20.00
11 Meyers Leonard 5.00 12.00
12 Jeremy Lamb 6.00 15.00
13 Kendall Marshall 4.00 10.00
14 John Henson 6.00 15.00
15 Maurice Harkless 6.00 15.00
16 Royce White 4.00 10.00
17 Tyler Zeller 5.00 12.00
18 Terrence Jones 6.00 15.00
19 Andrew Nicholson 4.00 10.00
20 Evan Fournier 6.00 15.00

2011-12 Limited Decade Dominance Materials

STATED PRINT RUN 5 TO 99 SER.#'d SETS
SOME UNPRICED DUE TO SCARCITY
1 Larry Bird/99 8.00 20.00
2 Robert Parish/99 3.00 8.00
3 Artis Gilmore/99 2.50 6.00
4 Dennis Johnson/99 4.00 10.00
5 David Robinson/99 5.00 12.00
6 Alex English/99 2.50 6.00
8 James Worthy/49 5.00 12.00
9 Dennis Rodman/99 6.00 15.00
10 Kevin Johnson/99 3.00 8.00
11 Shaquille O'Neal/99 8.00 20.00
12 Patrick Ewing/99 8.00 20.00
13 Ray Allen/99 5.00 12.00
14 Karl Malone/99 4.00 10.00
15 Clyde Drexler/99 4.00 10.00
16 LeBron James/99 12.00 30.00
17 Dwyane Wade/99 6.00 15.00
18 Kevin Garnett/49 8.00 20.00
19 Tim Duncan/99 5.00 12.00
20 Allen Iverson/25 12.00 30.00

2011-12 Limited Decade Dominance Materials Prime

*PRIME: 1.25X TO 3X BASE HI
STATED PRINT RUN ONE TO 25 SETS
SOME UNPRICED DUE TO SCARCITY
11 Shaquille O'Neal/25 30.00 80.00
15 Clyde Drexler/25 15.00 40.00
18 Kevin Garnett/15 15.00 40.00

2011-12 Limited Decade Dominance Materials Signatures

STATED PRINT RUN 10 TO 49 SER.#'d SETS
SOME UNPRICED DUE TO SCARCITY
UNPRICED PRIME PRINT RUN 5 SETS
3 Robert Parish/49 6.00 15.00
4 Kevin McHale/49 15.00 40.00
5 Joe Dumars/49 10.00 25.00
6 Isiah Thomas/49 12.00 30.00
7 Spencer Haywood/49 6.00 15.00
9 Alex English/49 6.00 15.00
15 Kobe Bryant/49 100.00 200.00
20 Dikembe Mutombo/49 6.00 15.00

2011-12 Limited Decade Dominance Signatures

STATED PRINT RUN 10 TO 99 SER.#'d SETS
SOME UNPRICED DUE TO SCARCITY
1 Wes Unseld/99 6.00 15.00
2 Dave Cowens/99 6.00 15.00
3 Walt Frazier/99 10.00 25.00
4 John Havlicek/25 20.00 50.00
5 Bob McAdoo/99 12.00 30.00
6 Bob Dandridge/99 6.00 15.00
7 Nate Archibald/99 6.00 15.00
8 Bill Walton/99 8.00 20.00
10 George Gervin/99 8.00 20.00
11 Grant Hill/50 75.00 150.00
13 Hakeem Olajuwon/50 20.00 50.00
17 Kobe Bryant/99 100.00 200.00

2011-12 Limited Glass Cleaners Materials

STATED PRINT RUN 49 TO 99 SER.#'d SETS
1 Kobe Bryant/99 10.00 25.00
2 Blake Griffin/99 3.00 8.00
3 Kevin Durant/99 6.00 15.00
4 Joakim Noah/99 2.50 6.00
5 Kevin Love/99 3.00 8.00
6 Marc Gasol/99 3.00 8.00
7 LaMarcus Aldridge/99 3.00 8.00
8 Dwight Howard/99 2.50 6.00
9 Shaquille O'Neal/99 10.00 25.00
10 Moses Malone/49 3.00 8.00
11 Robert Parish/49 3.00 8.00
12 Dennis Rodman/99 6.00 15.00
13 Hakeem Olajuwon/60 4.00 10.00
14 Dikembe Mutombo/99 3.00 8.00
15 Yao Ming/99 4.00 10.00
16 Karl Malone/99 4.00 10.00
17 DeAndre Jordan/99 3.00 8.00
18 Amare Stoudemire/99 2.50 6.00
19 Tyson Chandler/99 2.50 6.00
20 LeBron James/99 12.00 30.00

2011-12 Limited Glass Cleaners Materials Prime

*PRIME: 1.25X TO 3X BASE HI
STATED PRINT RUN 5 TO 25 SER.#'d SETS
SOME UNPRICED DUE TO SCARCITY
14 Dikembe Mutombo/25 15.00 40.00

2011-12 Limited Glass Cleaners Materials Signatures

ATED PRINT RUN 25 TO 49 SER.#'d SETS
1 Kobe Bryant/49 100.00 200.00
2 Blake Griffin/49 50.00 125.00
3 Kevin Durant/49 125.00 225.00
4 Joakim Noah/49 10.00 25.00
5 Kevin Love/49 20.00 50.00
6 Marc Gasol/49 EXCH 12.00 30.00
7 Marcin Gortat/49 8.00 20.00
8 Dirk Nowitzki/25 40.00 100.00
9 Serge Ibaka/49 12.00 30.00
10 A.Varejao/49 6.00 15.00
11 Robert Parish/25 10.00 25.00
12 Dennis Rodman/25 20.00 50.00
13 Hakeem Olajuwon/25 25.00 60.00
14 Dikembe Mutombo/25 15.00 40.00
15 Artis Gilmore/25 8.00 20.00
16 Nate Thurmond/25 6.00 15.00
17 David Robinson/25 40.00 100.00
18 DeMarcus Cousins/49 8.00 20.00
19 Josh Smith/49 5.00 12.00
20 Andrew Bynum/25 5.00 12.00

2011-12 Limited Glass Cleaners Materials Signatures Prime

STATED PRINT RUN 5 TO 25 SER.#'d SETS
SOME UNPRICED DUE TO SCARCITY
4 Joakim Noah/25 15.00 40.00
6 Marc Gasol/15 EXCH 20.00 50.00
7 Marcin Gortat/25 10.00 25.00
9 Serge Ibaka/25 20.00 50.00
10 A.Varejao/25 EXCH 10.00 25.00
18 DeMarcus Cousins/25 15.00 40.00
19 Josh Smith/15 8.00 20.00
20 Andrew Bynum/15 8.00 20.00

2011-12 Limited Glass Cleaners Signatures

STATED PRINT RUN 25 TO 99 SER.#'d SETS
1 Kobe Bryant/50 125.00 250.00
2 Blake Griffin/25 25.00 60.00
3 Kevin Durant/25 125.00 225.00
4 Joakim Noah/49 12.00 30.00
5 Kevin Love/25 30.00 60.00
6 Marc Gasol/99 EXCH 15.00 40.00
7 Marcin Gortat/99 6.00 15.00
8 K.Humphries/99 EXCH 6.00 15.00
9 Serge Ibaka/99 EXCH 10.00 25.00
10 A.Varejao/99 EXCH 6.00 15.00
11 Robert Parish/99 8.00 20.00
12 Dennis Rodman/25 30.00 80.00
13 Hakeem Olajuwon/25 20.00 50.00
14 Dikembe Mutombo/99 12.00 30.00
15 Artis Gilmore/99 6.00 15.00
16 Nate Thurmond/99 6.00 15.00
17 David Robinson/25 20.00 50.00
18 DeMarcus Cousins/99 12.00 30.00
19 Josh Smith/99 6.00 15.00
20 Andrew Bynum/49 12.00 30.00

2011-12 Limited Jumbo

STATED PRINT RUN 49 TO 99 SER.#'d SETS
UNPRICED PRIME PRINT RUN 5 TO 10 SETS
1 LeBron James/49 20.00 50.00
2 Dwyane Wade/49 8.00 20.00
3 Dwight Howard/49 3.00 8.00
4 Kevin Garnett/49 6.00 15.00
5 David Lee/99 2.50 6.00
6 Grant Hill/49 10.00 25.00
7 David West/99 3.00 8.00
8 Manu Ginobili/49 4.00 10.00
9 Jason Terry/49 3.00 8.00
10 O.J. Mayo/99 2.50 6.00
11 Ben Gordon/99 3.00 8.00
12 Joe Johnson/99 3.00 8.00
13 Jrue Holiday/99 4.00 10.00
14 Ryan Anderson/99 3.00 8.00
15 Nick Young/99 3.00 8.00
16 Mo Williams/49 3.00 8.00
17 Pau Gasol/99 4.00 10.00
18 DeMarcus Cousins/99 4.00 10.00
19 Luis Scola/99 3.00 8.00
20 Marcus Thornton/99 2.50 6.00
21 Emeka Okafor/99 3.00 8.00
22 Tim Duncan/49 6.00 15.00
23 Chris Andersen/99 3.00 8.00
24 Michael Beasley/99 2.50 6.00
25 Serge Ibaka/99 3.00 8.00
26 Gerald Wallace/99 3.00 8.00
27 Marcus Camby/99 2.50 6.00
28 Chauncey Billups/99 4.00 10.00
29 Tyson Chandler/99 3.00 8.00
30 Tyler Hansbrough/99 3.00 8.00

2011-12 Limited Jumbo Signatures

STATED PRINT RUN 10 TO 99 SER.#'d SETS
SOME UNPRICED DUE TO SCARCITY
1 Blake Griffin/15 75.00 150.00
2 Deron Williams/15 12.00 30.00
3 Stephen Curry/24 125.00 300.00
4 James Harden/24 EXCH 30.00 80.00
5 Kobe Bryant/24 125.00 225.00
7 Marcus Thornton/99 8.00 20.00
8 Eric Gordon/24 10.00 25.00
9 Ray Allen/15 EXCH 30.00 80.00
10 Jrue Holiday/49 6.00 15.00
11 Joakim Noah/24 8.00 20.00
12 Jeff Teague/99 6.00 15.00
13 Shane Battier/49 6.00 15.00
14 J.J. Redick/49 6.00 15.00
15 Nene/24 EXCH 6.00 15.00
16 Raymond Felton/24 6.00 15.00
17 Gordon Hayward/99 8.00 20.00
18 Rudy Gay/49 EXCH 8.00 20.00
19 DeMar DeRozan/24 8.00 20.00
20 Serge Ibaka/99 EXCH 6.00 15.00

2011-12 Limited Jumbo Signatures Prime

STATED PRINT RUN 5 TO 15 SER.#'d SETS
SOME UNPRICED DUE TO SCARCITY
7 Marcus Thornton/15 12.00 30.00
11 Joakim Noah/15 25.00 60.00
13 Shane Battier/15 12.00 30.00
14 J.J. Redick/15 12.00 30.00
15 Nene/15 EXCH 12.00 30.00
16 Raymond Felton/15
17 Gordon Hayward/15 40.00 100.00

2011-12 Limited Jumbo Jersey Numbers

STATED PRINT RUN 49 TO 99 SER.#'d SETS
1 Dwight Howard/49 3.00 8.00
2 Carmelo Anthony/99 5.00 12.00
3 Boris Diaw/99 3.00 8.00
4 Shawn Marion/99 4.00 10.00
5 Vince Carter/99 5.00 12.00
6 LeBron James/49 15.00 40.00
7 Tim Duncan/99 6.00 15.00
8 Kevin Garnett/99 6.00 15.00
9 Dwyane Wade/99 8.00 20.00
10 DeAndre Jordan/99 4.00 10.00
11 Darren Collison/99 3.00 8.00
12 Danilo Gallinari/99 3.00 8.00
13 Pau Gasol/99 4.00 10.00
14 Nick Young/99 3.00 8.00
15 Devin Harris/99 2.50 6.00
16 Kyle Lowry/99 3.00 8.00
17 Metta World Peace/99 4.00 10.00
18 Mario Chalmers/99 3.00 8.00
19 LaMarcus Aldridge/99 4.00 10.00
20 Lamar Odom/99 3.00 8.00

2011-12 Limited Jumbo Jersey Numbers Prime

*PRIME: 1.5X TO 4X BASE HI
STATED PRINT RUN 14 TO 25 SER.#'d SETS
5 Vince Carter/15 25.00 60.00
7 Tim Duncan/15 50.00 125.00
17 Metta World Peace/15 20.00 50.00

2011-12 Limited Jumbo Jersey Numbers Signatures

STATED PRINT RUN 5 TO 99 SER.#'d SETS
SOME UNPRICED DUE TO SCARCITY
3 Andre Miller/99 5.00 12.00
4 Andrea Bargnani/49 5.00 12.00
5 James Harden/49 15.00 40.00
6 Blake Griffin/25 20.00 50.00
7 Tyson Chandler/25 5.00 12.00
8 Tyreke Evans/25 4.00 10.00
10 Anderson Varejao/49 4.00 10.00
11 Andrew Bogut/99 6.00 15.00
12 Greg Monroe/99 6.00 15.00
13 Paul George/99 25.00 60.00
14 Kevin Love/25 20.00 50.00
15 Ray Allen/15 EXCH
16 Trevor Booker/99 4.00 10.00
17 Wesley Matthews/99 4.00 10.00
18 Derrick Favors/49 5.00 12.00
19 Patrick Patterson/99 4.00 10.00
20 Marc Gasol/25 EXCH 15.00 40.00

2011-12 Limited Jumbo Jersey Numbers Signatures Prime

STATED PRINT RUN 5 TO 25 SER.#'d SETS
SOME UNPRICED DUE TO SCARCITY
3 Andre Miller/25 10.00 25.00
4 Andrea Bargnani/25 10.00 25.00
5 James Harden/25 30.00 80.00
7 Tyson Chandler/25 10.00 25.00
8 Tyreke Evans/25 8.00 20.00
10 Anderson Varejao/25 8.00 20.00
11 Andrew Bogut/25 12.00 30.00
12 Greg Monroe/25 12.00 30.00
16 Trevor Booker/25 8.00 20.00
17 Wesley Matthews/25 8.00 20.00
18 Derrick Favors/25 10.00 25.00
20 Marc Gasol/25 EXCH 30.00 80.00

2011-12 Limited Masterful Marks Signatures

STATED PRINT RUN 10 TO 50 SER.#'d SETS
SOME UNPRICED DUE TO SCARCITY
1 Adrian Dantley/50 5.00 12.00
2 Andre Iguodala/50 5.00 12.00
3 Andre Miller/50 4.00 10.00
4 Anfernee Hardaway/25 20.00 50.00
5 Arron Afflalo/50 4.00 10.00
6 Bill Walton/50 6.00 15.00
7 Blake Griffin/25 40.00 100.00
8 Brook Lopez/50 5.00 12.00
9 Carlos Boozer/50 8.00 20.00
10 Charlie Villanueva/50 4.00 10.00
11 Chase Budinger/50 4.00 10.00
12 Chris Andersen/25 12.00 30.00
13 Chris Paul/25 EXCH 40.00 100.00
14 Daniel Gibson/50 4.00 10.00
15 Danny Manning/50 4.00 10.00
16 Darren Collison/50 6.00 15.00
17 DeAndre Jordan/50 EXCH 6.00 15.00
18 Derek Fisher/50 8.00 20.00
19 Derrick Rose/25 EXCH 125.00 225.00
20 Gordon Hayward/50 8.00 20.00
21 Ian Mahinmi/50 EXCH 4.00 10.00
22 J.J. Barea/50 EXCH 10.00 25.00
23 Roy Hibbert/50 6.00 15.00
24 James Harden/50 20.00 50.00
25 Jason Kidd/25 20.00 50.00
26 Jeremy Lin/50 40.00 100.00
27 Joe Johnson/25 8.00 20.00
28 John Starks/50 12.00 30.00
29 Jordan Crawford/50 5.00 12.00
30 Jordan Farmar/50 EXCH 4.00 10.00
31 Jose Calderon/50 4.00 10.00
32 Kendrick Perkins/50 8.00 20.00
34 Kevin Martin/50 6.00 15.00
35 Kobe Bryant/50 100.00 200.00
36 LaMarcus Aldridge/50 10.00 25.00
37 Luol Deng/50 8.00 20.00
38 Marcin Gortat/50 12.00 30.00
39 Michael Finley/50 6.00 15.00
40 Monta Ellis/50 8.00 20.00
41 Nene/50 EXCH 5.00 12.00
42 Pau Gasol/50 12.00 30.00
43 Deron Williams/50 12.00 30.00
44 Rajon Rondo/25
45 Richard Hamilton/25 10.00 25.00
46 Rodrigue Beaubois/50 8.00 20.00
47 Russell Westbrook/25 40.00 100.00
48 Serge Ibaka/50 EXCH 6.00 15.00
49 Stephen Curry/50 100.00 200.00
50 Zach Randolph/50 6.00 15.00

2011-12 Limited Monikers Materials

STATED PRINT RUN 10 TO 49 SER.#'d SETS
SOME UNPRICED DUE TO SCARCITY
UNPRICED PRIME PRINT RUN ONE TO 5 SETS
1 Kobe Bryant/25 100.00 200.00
4 Brandon Jennings/25 EXCH 12.00 30.00
5 Kevin Love/25 20.00 50.00
6 Russell Westbrook/49 75.00 200.00
7 Andre Iguodala/49 8.00 20.00
8 Greg Monroe/49 8.00 20.00
10 Tyson Chandler/49 8.00 20.00
11 Paul Millsap/49 8.00 20.00
12 Tony Parker/25 10.00 25.00
13 LaMarcus Aldridge/25 10.00 25.00
16 Marc Gasol/49 EXCH 12.00 30.00
17 Danny Granger/15 8.00 20.00
19 Danilo Gallinari/25 8.00 20.00
20 Andrea Bargnani/25 8.00 20.00

2011-12 Limited Potential Signatures

STATED PRINT RUN 25 TO 99 SER.#'d SETS
1 DeMar DeRozan/50 8.00 20.00
2 Greg Monroe/99 5.00 12.00
3 Chase Budinger/99 3.00 8.00
4 Jonas Jerebko/99 3.00 8.00
5 Marco Belinelli/99 3.00 8.00
6 Ed Davis/99 3.00 8.00
7 Eric Bledsoe/99 5.00 12.00
8 Al-Farouq Aminu/99 3.00 8.00
9 Landry Fields/99 4.00 10.00
10 James Harden/50 15.00 40.00
11 Derrick Favors/50 4.00 10.00
12 Evan Turner/25 3.00 8.00
13 Wesley Matthews/99 3.00 8.00
14 Timofey Mozgov/99 3.00 8.00
15 DeMarcus Cousins/50 12.00 30.00
16 Serge Ibaka/99 4.00 10.00
17 Jeremy Lin/99 EXCH 50.00 125.00
18 D.J. Augustin/50 3.00 8.00
19 Trevor Booker/99 3.00 8.00
20 Darren Collison/99 EXCH 4.00 10.00
21 Jrue Holiday/99 6.00 15.00
22 Tyreke Evans/25 3.00 8.00
23 John Wall/25 30.00 80.00
24 Brandon Jennings/25
25 Eric Gordon/99 6.00 15.00
26 Ekpe Udoh/99 3.00 8.00
27 Tyler Hansbrough/50 4.00 10.00
28 Jordan Crawford/99 3.00 8.00
29 George Hill/99 4.00 10.00
30 JaVale McGee/99 4.00 10.00
31 Paul George/99 12.00 30.00
32 Gordon Hayward/99 8.00 20.00
33 Tiago Splitter/99 4.00 10.00
34 Gary Neal/99 EXCH 4.00 10.00
35 Ty Lawson/99 3.00 8.00
36 Marcus Thornton/99 3.00 8.00
37 Blake Griffin/25 20.00 50.00
38 Russell Westbrook/50 40.00 100.00
39 Patrick Patterson/99 3.00 8.00
40 Austin Daye/99 3.00 8.00
41 Marc Gasol/99 EXCH 8.00 20.00
42 Jason Thompson/99 3.00 8.00
43 Greivis Vasquez/99 4.00 10.00
44 Stephen Curry/50 100.00 250.00
45 DeJuan Blair/99 3.00 8.00
46 Gerald Henderson/99 3.00 8.00
47 Terrence Williams/99 3.00 8.00
48 Jodie Meeks/99 4.00 10.00
49 Jeff Teague/99 3.00 8.00
50 Nikola Pekovic/99 4.00 10.00

2011-12 Limited Retired Numbers Materials

STATED PRINT RUN 5 TO 99 SER.#'d SETS
SOME UNPRICED DUE TO SCARCITY
1 Magic Johnson/25 10.00 25.00
2 Kareem Abdul-Jabbar/99 8.00 20.00
5 Patrick Ewing/99 8.00 20.00
6 Hakeem Olajuwon/49 5.00 12.00
7 John Stockton/99 6.00 15.00
8 Alonzo Mourning/99 6.00 15.00
9 Chris Mullin/99 4.00 10.00
10 David Robinson/99 6.00 15.00
11 Mitch Richmond/99 4.00 10.00
12 Julius Erving/99 8.00 20.00
13 Alex English/99 3.00 8.00
14 Dennis Johnson/99 3.00 8.00
15 Kevin McHale/99 4.00 10.00
16 Larry Bird/49 10.00 25.00
17 Sam Jones/99 5.00 12.00
18 Bill Laimbeer/99 3.00 8.00
19 Darrell Griffith/99 2.50 6.00
20 Karl Malone/99 5.00 12.00

2011-12 Limited Retired Numbers Materials Prime

*PRIME: 1X TO 2.5X BASE HI
STATED PRINT RUN ONE TO 25 SER.#'d SETS
SOME UNPRICED DUE TO SCARCITY
5 Patrick Ewing/25 30.00 80.00
11 Mitch Richmond/25 25.00 60.00

2011-12 Limited Retired Numbers Materials Signatures

STATED PRINT RUN 5 TO 49 SER.#'d SETS
SOME UNPRICED DUE TO SCARCITY
2 Chris Mullin/49 8.00 20.00
3 Clyde Drexler/25 30.00 80.00
4 Kevin McHale/25 15.00 40.00
5 Robert Parish/49 8.00 20.00
6 Sam Jones/25 12.00 30.00
7 Isiah Thomas/49 8.00 20.00
9 Joe Dumars/49 5.00 12.00
10 Dominique Wilkins/25 20.00 50.00
11 Scottie Pippen/25 150.00 250.00
12 Magic Johnson/25 40.00 100.00
13 James Worthy/25 25.00 60.00
14 John Stockton/25 40.00 100.00
15 Mark Eaton/49 3.00 8.00
16 Tom Chambers/49 4.00 10.00
17 George Gervin/49 12.00 30.00
19 Dan Issel/49 4.00 10.00
20 Alex English/49 4.00 10.00

2011-12 Limited Retired Numbers Materials Signatures Prime

STATED PRINT RUN ONE TO 25 SER.#'d SETS
SOME UNPRICED DUE TO SCARCITY
2 Chris Mullin/15 20.00 50.00
9 Joe Dumars/25 8.00 20.00
14 John Stockton/15 80.00 160.00
15 Mark Eaton/15 6.00 15.00
16 Tom Chambers/15 8.00 20.00
17 George Gervin/25 12.00 30.00
18 Mark Price/15 75.00 150.00
19 Dan Issel/15 8.00 20.00
20 Alex English/25 8.00 20.00

2011-12 Limited Retired Numbers Signatures

ATED PRINT RUN 25 TO 99 SER.#'d SETS
1 Dave Cowens/50 10.00 25.00
2 Bill Walton/50 12.00 30.00
3 Terry Porter/99 3.00 8.00
4 Rolando Blackman/99 4.00 10.00
5 Joe Dumars/50 8.00 20.00
6 Bob Love/99 4.00 10.00
7 George McGinnis/99 8.00 20.00
8 Bob Pettit/50 10.00 25.00
9 Gail Goodrich/50 8.00 20.00
10 Dominique Wilkins/50 12.00 30.00
11 Earl Monroe/25 15.00 40.00
12 Walt Frazier/50 12.00 30.00
13 K.C. Jones/50 12.00 30.00
14 Wes Unseld/50 10.00 25.00
15 Dan Majerle/99 4.00 10.00
16 Jeff Hornacek/99 4.00 10.00
17 Vlade Divac/99 5.00 12.00
18 George Gervin/50 10.00 25.00
19 Sean Elliott/99 8.00 20.00
20 Lenny Wilkens/50 8.00 20.00

2011-12 Limited Signatures

STATED PRINT RUN 10 TO 99 SER.#'d SETS
SOME UNPRICED DUE TO SCARCITY
UNPRICED PLATINUM PRINT RUN ONE SET
1 Blake Griffin/15 50.00 125.00
2 Rajon Rondo/25
3 Deron Williams/25 6.00 15.00
4 Tyson Chandler/25 8.00 20.00
5 Stephen Jackson/49 5.00 12.00
6 Andrea Bargnani/49 5.00 12.00
7 Monta Ellis/49 8.00 20.00
8 Kobe Bryant/49 100.00 175.00
9 Chris Paul/15 EXCH 40.00 100.00
10 Tyreke Evans/25 6.00 15.00
11 Derrick Rose/15 100.00 200.00
12 Antawn Jamison/49 5.00 12.00
13 Steve Nash/15 30.00 80.00
14 Danny Granger/25 6.00 15.00
15 Ben Gordon/25 6.00 15.00
16 Andre Iguodala/25 6.00 15.00
18 Kevin Martin/49 5.00 12.00
19 Rudy Gay/49 EXCH 6.00 15.00
20 Eric Gordon/49 6.00 15.00
21 Tony Parker/25 10.00 25.00
22 Josh Smith/49 EXCH 5.00 12.00
23 D.J. Augustin/49 5.00 12.00
24 Chris Bosh/15 12.00 30.00
25 Jeremy Lin/25 60.00 150.00
27 Nene/49 EXCH 8.00 20.00
28 Kevin Love/25 15.00 40.00
30 LaMarcus Aldridge/49 8.00 20.00
31 Al Jefferson/25 EXCH 8.00 20.00
32 Bailey Howell/49 5.00 12.00
33 Darryl Dawkins/99 5.00 12.00
34 Nate Archibald/49 5.00 12.00
35 Cedric Maxwell/99 5.00 12.00
36 Chris Mullin/49 10.00 25.00
37 Kurt Rambis/99 8.00 20.00
38 Robert Parish/25 8.00 20.00
39 George Gervin/49 6.00 15.00
40 Detlef Schrempf/99 6.00 15.00
41 Kenny Smith/49 5.00 12.00
42 Bill Walton/25 8.00 20.00
43 Isiah Thomas/25 10.00 25.00
44 Vlade Divac/99 6.00 15.00
45 Tom Chambers/49 5.00 12.00
46 David Robinson/15 30.00 80.00
47 Jeff Hornacek/99 5.00 12.00
48 Joe Dumars/25 10.00 25.00
50 Tim Hardaway/99 8.00 20.00

2011-12 Limited Signatures Gold Spotlight

STATED PRINT RUN 3 TO 24 SER.#'d SETS
SOME UNPRICED DUE TO SCARCITY
5 Stephen Jackson/24 6.00 15.00
6 Andrea Bargnani/15 6.00 15.00
12 Antawn Jamison/24 6.00 15.00
18 Kevin Martin/24 8.00 20.00
19 Rudy Gay/24 EXCH 8.00 20.00
32 Bailey Howell/24 8.00 20.00
33 Darryl Dawkins/24 6.00 15.00
35 Cedric Maxwell/24 6.00 15.00
36 Chris Mullin/24 12.00 30.00
37 Kurt Rambis/24 12.00 30.00
40 Detlef Schrempf/24 6.00 15.00
44 Vlade Divac/24 10.00 25.00
45 Tom Chambers/24 6.00 15.00
47 Jeff Hornacek/24 6.00 15.00
50 Tim Hardaway/24 15.00 40.00

2011-12 Limited Signatures Silver Spotlight

STATED PRINT RUN 5 TO 49 SER.#'d SETS
SOME UNPRICED DUE TO SCARCITY
3 Deron Williams/15 8.00 20.00
5 Stephen Jackson/49 5.00 12.00
6 Andrea Bargnani/25 5.00 12.00
7 Monta Ellis/25 10.00 25.00
8 Kobe Bryant/25 100.00 200.00
12 Antawn Jamison/49 5.00 12.00
18 Kevin Martin/49 5.00 12.00
19 Rudy Gay/49 EXCH 6.00 15.00
20 Eric Gordon/25 8.00 20.00
22 Josh Smith/25 8.00 20.00
23 D.J. Augustin/25 5.00 12.00
25 Jeremy Lin/15 60.00 120.00
27 Nene/25 EXCH 8.00 20.00
30 LaMarcus Aldridge/25 12.00 30.00
32 Bailey Howell/49 5.00 12.00
33 Darryl Dawkins/49 5.00 12.00
34 Nate Archibald/25 6.00 15.00
35 Cedric Maxwell/49 5.00 12.00
36 Chris Mullin/49 10.00 25.00
37 Kurt Rambis/49 10.00 25.00
39 George Gervin/25 8.00 20.00
40 Detlef Schrempf/49 5.00 12.00
41 Kenny Smith/25 5.00 12.00
44 Vlade Divac/49 8.00 20.00
45 Tom Chambers/49 5.00 12.00
47 Jeff Hornacek/49 5.00 12.00
48 Joe Dumars/15 12.00 30.00
50 Tim Hardaway/49 10.00 25.00

2011-12 Limited Team Trademarks Materials

ATED PRINT RUN 75 TO 99 SER.#'d SETS
*PRIME: 1X TO 2.5X HI COLUMN
PRIME PRINT RUN 5 TO 25 SETS
SOME UNPRICED DUE TO SCARCITY
1 Kobe Bryant/75 10.00 25.00
2 Blake Griffin/99 2.50 6.00
3 Carlos Boozer/99 2.00 5.00
4 Rajon Rondo/99 2.50 6.00
5 Carmelo Anthony/99 3.00 8.00
6 Tyreke Evans/99 1.50 4.00
7 Dwyane Wade/99 5.00 12.00
8 Dirk Nowitzki/99 3.00 8.00
9 Danny Granger/99 2.00 5.00
10 David Lee/99 1.50 4.00
11 Tony Parker/99 2.50 6.00
12 Dwight Howard/99 2.00 5.00
13 Al Horford/99 2.00 5.00
14 Kevin Durant/99 6.00 15.00
15 LeBron James/99 10.00 25.00
16 Stephen Jackson/99 2.00 5.00
17 Paul Millsap/99 2.00 5.00
18 Kevin Love/99 2.50 6.00
19 Kevin Garnett/99 4.00 10.00
20 LaMarcus Aldridge/99 2.50 6.00

2011-12 Limited Team Trademarks Materials Signatures

STATED PRINT RUN 25 TO 99 SER.#'d SETS
1 Kobe Bryant/25 100.00 200.00
2 Rudy Gay/99 EXCH 10.00 25.00
3 Ty Lawson/99 EXCH 8.00 20.00
4 Roy Hibbert/99 8.00 20.00
5 James Harden/49 25.00 60.00
6 Tyreke Evans/49 10.00 25.00
7 Deron Williams/49 12.00 30.00
8 Greg Monroe/99 6.00 15.00
9 Stephen Curry/49 75.00 200.00
10 Kevin Love/25 15.00 40.00
11 Serge Ibaka/99 6.00 15.00
12 Kevin Durant/25 125.00 225.00
13 LaMarcus Aldridge/49 10.00 25.00
14 Josh Smith/49 6.00 15.00
15 Blake Griffin/25 25.00 60.00
16 Brandon Jennings/25 EXCH 10.00 25.00
17 Andre Iguodala/49 6.00 15.00
18 DeMarcus Cousins/49 15.00 40.00
19 Kevin Martin/49 6.00 15.00
20 Gordon Hayward/99 6.00 15.00

2011-12 Limited Team Trademarks Materials Signatures Prime

STATED PRINT RUN 5 TO 25 SER.#'d SETS
SOME UNPRICED DUE TO SCARCITY

2011-12 Limited Team Trademarks Signatures

STATED PRINT RUN 10 TO 49 SER.#'d SETS
SOME UNPRICED DUE TO SCARCITY
2 Tyreke Evans/25 12.00 30.00
3 Luol Deng/49 8.00 20.00
4 Al Jefferson/25 8.00 20.00
8 Kobe Bryant/49 75.00 150.00
9 Monta Ellis/49 8.00 20.00
10 Kevin Love/15 25.00 60.00
11 Rajon Rondo/25 12.00 30.00
12 Russell Westbrook/25 40.00 100.00
13 LaMarcus Aldridge/49 10.00 25.00
17 Eric Gordon/49 6.00 15.00
18 Danny Granger/25 8.00 20.00
19 Kevin Martin/49 6.00 15.00
20 Danilo Gallinari/49 EXCH 6.00 15.00

2011-12 Limited Threads

STATED PRINT RUN 49 TO 99 SER.#'d SETS
1 Derrick Rose/99 8.00 20.00
2 Ray Allen/99 5.00 12.00
3 Chris Paul/99 4.00 10.00
4 Dwight Howard/99 2.50 6.00
5 Jason Kidd/99 3.00 8.00
6 Deron Williams/99 2.50 6.00
7 Evan Turner/99 2.00 5.00
8 Kobe Bryant/99 12.00 30.00
9 Amare Stoudemire/99 2.50 6.00
10 Elton Brand/99 3.00 8.00
11 Jose Calderon/99 2.00 5.00
12 Stephen Curry/99 10.00 25.00
13 Steve Nash/99 3.00 8.00
14 Andrew Bynum/99 2.00 5.00
15 DeMarcus Cousins/99 3.00 8.00
16 Joakim Noah/99 2.50 6.00
17 Anderson Varejao/99 2.00 5.00
18 Greg Monroe/99 3.00 8.00
19 Tyler Hansbrough/99 2.50 6.00
20 Manu Ginobili/99 3.00 8.00
21 Tim Duncan/99 5.00 12.00
22 Luis Scola/99 2.50 6.00
23 LeBron James/99 12.00 30.00
24 Dwyane Wade/99 6.00 15.00
25 John Wall/99 4.00 10.00
26 Brandon Jennings/99 2.00 5.00
27 Joe Johnson/99 2.50 6.00
28 D.J. Augustin/99 2.00 5.00
29 Zach Randolph/99 2.50 6.00
30 Emeka Okafor/99 2.50 6.00
31 Jason Terry/99 2.50 6.00
32 Ricky Rubio/99 3.00 8.00
33 Ty Lawson/99 2.00 5.00
34 Paul Pierce/99 3.00 8.00
35 Kevin Durant/99 8.00 20.00
36 James Harden/99 5.00 12.00
37 Kevin Love/99 3.00 8.00
38 LaMarcus Aldridge/99 3.00 8.00
39 Tyreke Evans/99 2.00 5.00
40 Carlos Boozer/99 2.50 6.00
41 Dirk Nowitzki/99 4.00 10.00
42 Paul Millsap/99 2.50 6.00
43 Alonzo Mourning/99 8.00 20.00
44 Derrick Coleman/49 8.00 20.00
45 Clyde Drexler/99 4.00 10.00
46 Dennis Scott/99 2.00 5.00
47 Chuck Person/99 2.50 6.00
48 Glen Rice/99 2.50 6.00
49 Jalen Rose/99 3.00 8.00
50 Karl Malone/99 4.00 10.00

2011-12 Limited Threads Prime

*PRIME: 1X TO 2.5X BASE HI
STATED PRINT RUN 5 TO 25 SER.#'d SETS
SOME UNPRICED DUE TO SCARCITY
11 Jose Calderon/25 8.00 20.00
26 Brandon Jennings/25 10.00 25.00
48 Glen Rice/25 10.00 25.00
49 Jalen Rose/25 12.00 30.00

2011-12 Limited Trios Materials

STATED PRINT RUN 25 TO 49 SER.#'d SETS
UNPRICED SIG PRINT RUN 5 TO 10 SETS
1 Rose/Kobe/Wade/25 30.00 80.00
2 BG/Aldridge/Love/49 8.00 20.00
3 Marion/Nash/Amare/49 10.00 25.00
4 LeBron/Dirk/Durant/25 20.00 50.00
5 Howard/Barg/Bogut/49 8.00 20.00
6 KG/Carmelo/Bosh/49 10.00 25.00
7 Paul/Rondo/Ellis/49 10.00 25.00
8 Wstbrk/Deron/Parker/49 10.00 25.00
9 Hill/Kidd/Allen/25 10.00 25.00
10 Zo/Rice/Shaq/25 10.00 25.00

2011-12 Limited Trios Materials Prime

*PRIME: 1X TO 2.5X HI COLUMN
STATED PRINT RUN 5 TO 15 SER.#'d SETS
SOME UNPRICED DUE TO SCARCITY
5 Howard/Barg/Bogut/15 30.00 80.00
6 KG/Carmelo/Bosh/15 30.00 80.00
9 Hill/Kidd/Allen/15 20.00 50.00
10 Zo/Rice/Shaq/15 60.00 150.00

2011-12 Limited Trophy Case Materials

STATED PRINT RUN 25 TO 99 SER.#'d SETS
1 Derrick Rose/75 4.00 10.00
2 Kobe Bryant/49 15.00 40.00
3 Steve Nash/75 3.00 8.00
4 David Robinson/75 5.00 12.00
5 Hakeem Olajuwon/49 4.00 10.00
6 Blake Griffin/75 3.00 8.00
7 Josh Smith/99 2.50 6.00
8 Vince Carter/99 4.00 10.00
9 Daequan Cook/99 2.00 5.00
10 Glen Rice/99 2.50 6.00
11 Jason Kidd/99 3.00 8.00
12 Deron Williams/99 2.50 6.00
13 Stephen Curry/99 8.00 20.00
14 Kevin Love/99 3.00 8.00
15 Danny Granger/99 2.50 6.00
16 Hedo Turkoglu/99 2.50 6.00
17 Monta Ellis/99 2.50 6.00
18 Tyreke Evans/99 2.00 5.00
19 Isiah Thomas/99 3.00 8.00
20 Tom Chambers/99 2.50 6.00
21 Zydrunas Ilgauskas/99 2.00 5.00
22 Andre Iguodala/99 2.50 6.00
23 David Lee/99 2.00 5.00
24 Daniel Gibson/99 2.50 6.00
25 Kevin Durant/49 8.00 20.00
26 John Wall/99 4.00 10.00
27 Rajon Rondo/99 5.00 12.00
28 Tony Parker/99 3.00 8.00
29 Derek Fisher/99 2.50 6.00
30 Robert Parish/49 3.00 8.00
31 Michael Cooper/99 2.50 6.00
32 Pau Gasol/99 3.00 8.00
33 Joe Dumars/75 3.00 8.00
34 Kevin McHale/75 3.00 8.00
35 Kareem Abdul-Jabbar/25 5.00 12.00
36 Dennis Rodman/75 8.00 20.00
37 Scottie Pippen/75 8.00 20.00
38 Allen Iverson/75 8.00 20.00
39 Eddie Jones/99 2.50 6.00
40 Manu Ginobili/99 3.00 8.00
41 Peja Stojakovic/99 3.00 8.00
42 Quentin Richardson/99 2.50 6.00
43 Dwight Howard/99 2.50 6.00
44 Nate Robinson/99 3.00 8.00
45 Karl Malone/99 5.00 12.00
46 Shaquille O'Neal/49 6.00 15.00
47 Allen Iverson/25 15.00 40.00
48 Kevin Garnett/49 5.00 12.00
49 Dirk Nowitzki/99 4.00 10.00
50 LeBron James/49 12.00 30.00

2011-12 Limited Trophy Case Materials Prime

*PRIME: 1.25X TO 3X BASE HI
STATED PRINT RUN ONE TO 25 SER.#'d SETS
SOME UNPRICED DUE TO SCARCITY
1 Derrick Rose/25 40.00 100.00
8 Vince Carter/25 15.00 40.00
13 Stephen Curry/25 40.00 100.00
21 Zydrunas Ilgauskas/25 12.00 30.00
27 Rajon Rondo/25 20.00 50.00
28 Tony Parker/25 12.00 30.00
29 Derek Fisher/25 10.00 25.00
38 Allen Iverson/15 30.00 80.00
39 Eddie Jones/25 15.00 40.00
47 Allen Iverson/15 30.00 80.00
49 Dirk Nowitzki/25 15.00 40.00

2011-12 Limited Trophy Case Materials Signatures

STATED PRINT RUN 15 TO 49 SER.#'d SETS
1 Derrick Rose/25 100.00 200.00
2 Kobe Bryant/25 125.00 225.00
3 Steve Nash/15 20.00 50.00
4 David Robinson/15 25.00 60.00
5 Hakeem Olajuwon/15 25.00 60.00
6 Blake Griffin/25 30.00 80.00
7 Josh Smith/49 6.00 15.00
8 Vince Carter/15 40.00 100.00
9 Daequan Cook/49 6.00 15.00
10 Glen Rice/49 6.00 15.00
11 Jason Kidd/15 20.00 50.00
12 Deron Williams/15 12.00 30.00
13 Stephen Curry/49 50.00 120.00
14 Kevin Love/15 30.00 80.00
15 Danny Granger/15 6.00 15.00
16 Hedo Turkoglu/49 6.00 15.00
17 Monta Ellis/49 8.00 20.00
18 Tyreke Evans/15 15.00 40.00
19 Isiah Thomas/25 15.00 40.00
20 Tom Chambers/25 6.00 15.00
21 Zydrunas Ilgauskas/49 8.00 20.00
22 Andre Iguodala/49 6.00 15.00
23 David Lee/49 6.00 15.00
24 Daniel Gibson/49 6.00 15.00
25 Kevin Durant/25 100.00 200.00
26 John Wall/15 40.00 100.00
27 Rajon Rondo/15 EXCH
28 Tony Parker/15 25.00 60.00
29 Derek Fisher/49 8.00 20.00
30 Robert Parish/25 10.00 25.00
31 Michael Cooper/49 12.00 30.00
32 Pau Gasol/15 15.00 40.00
33 Joe Dumars/25 6.00 15.00
34 Sam Jones/25 15.00 40.00
35 Bailey Howell/15 15.00 40.00
36 Earl Monroe/15 15.00 40.00
37 Amare Stoudemire/49 12.00 30.00
38 Clyde Drexler/25 20.00 50.00
39 Bill Laimbeer/25 10.00 25.00
40 Dennis Rodman/25 40.00 100.00
41 Ron Harper/49 12.00 30.00
42 Dominique Wilkins/25 12.00 30.00
43 Dikembe Mutombo/25 25.00 60.00
44 Gary Payton/25 15.00 40.00
45 Mark Eaton/49 6.00 15.00
46 Chris Paul/25 EXCH 30.00 80.00
47 Tyreke Evans/25 10.00 25.00
48 Mitch Richmond/25 30.00 80.00
49 Larry Bird/25 50.00 125.00
50 Julius Erving/25 50.00 125.00

2011-12 Limited Trophy Case Materials Signatures Prime

STATED PRINT RUN ONE TO 25 SER.#'d SETS
SOME UNPRICED DUE TO SCARCITY
1 Derrick Rose/15 175.00 350.00
2 Kobe Bryant/15 175.00 350.00
4 David Robinson/15 75.00 150.00
5 Hakeem Olajuwon/15 30.00 80.00
6 Blake Griffin/15 100.00 200.00
7 Josh Smith/25 12.00 30.00
9 Daequan Cook/25 10.00 25.00
10 Glen Rice/25 12.00 30.00
11 Jason Kidd/25 30.00 80.00
13 Stephen Curry/25 50.00 120.00
19 Isiah Thomas/25 15.00 40.00
20 Tom Chambers/15 12.00 30.00
21 Zydrunas Ilgauskas/25 15.00 40.00
22 Andre Iguodala/25 10.00 25.00
23 David Lee/25 10.00 25.00
24 Daniel Gibson/25 10.00 25.00
25 Kevin Durant/15
26 John Wall/25 50.00 125.00
29 Derek Fisher/25 15.00 40.00
30 Robert Parish/15 12.00 30.00
31 Michael Cooper/25 15.00 40.00
33 Joe Dumars/15 15.00 40.00
34 Sam Jones/15 30.00 80.00
37 Amare Stoudemire/25 15.00 40.00
38 Clyde Drexler/25 40.00 70.00
40 Dennis Rodman/15 75.00 200.00
41 Ron Harper/25 30.00 80.00
42 Dominique Wilkins/15 30.00 80.00
43 Dikembe Mutombo/15 50.00 125.00
44 Gary Payton/25 40.00 100.00
45 Mark Eaton/25 10.00 25.00
46 Chris Paul/15 EXCH
47 Tyreke Evans/15 20.00 50.00
48 Mitch Richmond/25 40.00 100.00
50 Julius Erving/15 100.00 175.00

2011-12 Limited Trophy Case Signatures

STATED PRINT RUN 25 TO 49 SER.#'d SETS
1 Derrick Rose/25 EXCH 100.00 200.00
2 Kobe Bryant/25 125.00 225.00
3 Steve Nash/25 35.00 70.00
4 David Robinson/25 30.00 80.00
5 Hakeem Olajuwon/25 12.00 30.00
6 Blake Griffin/25 50.00 125.00
7 Josh Smith/49 6.00 15.00
8 Vince Carter/25 30.00 80.00
9 Daequan Cook/49 6.00 15.00
10 Glen Rice/49 6.00 15.00
11 Jason Kidd/25 10.00 25.00
12 Deron Williams/25 6.00 15.00
13 Stephen Curry/49 15.00 40.00
14 Kevin Love/25 15.00 40.00
15 Danny Granger/25 6.00 15.00
16 Hedo Turkoglu/49 6.00 15.00
17 Monta Ellis/49 6.00 15.00
18 Tyreke Evans/25 6.00 15.00
19 Isiah Thomas/49 8.00 20.00
20 Tom Chambers/49 6.00 15.00
21 Zydrunas Ilgauskas/49 8.00 20.00
22 Andre Iguodala/25 6.00 15.00
23 David Lee/49 6.00 15.00
24 Daniel Gibson/49 6.00 15.00
25 Kevin Durant/25 125.00 250.00
26 John Wall/25 25.00 60.00
27 Rajon Rondo/25 EXCH
28 Tony Parker/25 15.00 40.00
29 Derek Fisher/49 8.00 20.00
30 Robert Parish/49 8.00 20.00
31 Michael Cooper/49 6.00 15.00
32 Pau Gasol/25 12.00 30.00
33 Joe Dumars/49 6.00 15.00
34 Anfernee Hardaway/25 30.00 80.00
35 Ralph Sampson/49 6.00 15.00
36 George Gervin/49 8.00 20.00
37 David Thompson/49 6.00 15.00
38 Lenny Wilkens/49 6.00 15.00
39 Hal Greer/49 6.00 15.00
40 Bill Sharman/49 8.00 20.00
41 Aaron Brooks/49 6.00 15.00
42 Dale Ellis/49 6.00 15.00
43 Mark Price/49 8.00 20.00

44 Jeff Hornacek/49 6.00 15.00
45 Bill Walton/49 6.00 15.00
46 Dave Cowens/49 6.00 15.00
47 Bob McAdoo/49 12.00 30.00
48 Mitch Richmond/49 10.00 25.00
49 Larry Bird/25 50.00 125.00
50 Julius Erving/25 50.00 125.00

2012-13 Limited

COMP.SET w/o RCs (150) 25.00 60.00
AU RC PRINT RUN 199 TO 399 SETS
UNPRICED PLATINUM PRINT RUN ONE SET
1 Paul Pierce .75 2.00
2 Kevin Garnett 1.25 3.00
3 Rajon Rondo .75 2.00
4 Brandon Bass .50 1.25
5 Jason Terry .60 1.50
6 Avery Bradley .60 1.50
7 Brook Lopez .60 1.50
8 Deron Williams .60 1.50
9 Gerald Wallace .60 1.50
10 Joe Johnson .60 1.50
11 Kris Humphries .50 1.25
12 Amare Stoudemire .60 1.50
13 Carmelo Anthony 1.00 2.50
14 J.R. Smith .60 1.50
15 Jason Kidd .75 2.00
16 Marcus Camby .60 1.50
17 Raymond Felton .60 1.50
18 Tyson Chandler .60 1.50
19 Andre Iguodala .60 1.50
20 Evan Turner .50 1.25
21 Jrue Holiday .75 2.00
22 Thaddeus Young .50 1.25
23 Andrea Bargnani .60 1.50
24 DeMar DeRozan .75 2.00
25 Jose Calderon .50 1.25
26 Kyle Lowry .60 1.50
27 Landry Fields .50 1.25
28 Carlos Boozer .60 1.50
29 Derrick Rose 1.00 2.50
30 Joakim Noah .60 1.50
31 John Lucas III .50 1.25
32 Kirk Hinrich .60 1.50
33 Luol Deng .60 1.50
34 Anderson Varejao .50 1.25
35 Daniel Gibson .60 1.50
36 Omri Casspi .50 1.25
37 Corey Maggette .60 1.50
38 Greg Monroe .60 1.50
39 Jason Maxiell .50 1.25
40 Rodney Stuckey .60 1.50
41 Tayshaun Prince .60 1.50
42 D.J. Augustin .50 1.25
43 Danny Granger .60 1.50
44 George Hill .60 1.50
45 Paul George 1.00 2.50
46 Roy Hibbert .60 1.50
47 Brandon Jennings .50 1.25
48 Ersan Ilyasova .50 1.25
49 Monta Ellis .60 1.50
50 Samuel Dalembert .50 1.25
51 Al Horford .60 1.50
52 Jeff Teague .60 1.50
53 Josh Smith .60 1.50
54 Louis Williams .60 1.50
55 Zaza Pachulia .50 1.25
56 Ben Gordon .60 1.50
57 Brendan Haywood .50 1.25
58 Ramon Sessions .60 1.50
59 Tyrus Thomas .50 1.25
60 Chris Bosh .75 2.00
61 Dwyane Wade 1.25 3.00
62 LeBron James 3.00 8.00
63 Mario Chalmers .60 1.50
64 Ray Allen .75* 2.00
65 Shane Battier .60 1.50
66 Dwight Howard .60 1.50
67 Glen Davis .50 1.25
68 J.J. Redick .75 2.00
69 Jameer Nelson .50 1.25
70 Emeka Okafor .60 1.50
71 John Wall 1.00 2.50
72 Jordan Crawford .50 1.25
73 Nene .60 1.50
74 Trevor Ariza .50 1.25
75 Chris Kaman .60 1.50
76 Darren Collison .60 1.50
77 Dirk Nowitzki 1.00 2.50
78 Elton Brand .75 2.00
79 O.J. Mayo .50 1.25
80 Gary Forbes .50 1.25
81 Jeremy Lin .75 2.00
82 Kevin Martin .60 1.50
83 Omer Asik .60 1.50
84 Patrick Patterson .50 1.25
85 Marc Gasol .75 2.00
86 Mike Conley .60 1.50
87 Rudy Gay .75 2.00
88 Tony Allen .50 1.25
89 Zach Randolph .60 1.50
90 Carl Landry .50 1.25
91 Eric Gordon .60 1.50
92 Greivis Vasquez .60 1.50
93 Ryan Anderson .60 1.50
94 Danny Green .60 1.50
95 Gary Neal .60 1.50
96 Manu Ginobili .75 2.00
97 Stephen Jackson .60 1.50
98 Tim Duncan 1.25 3.00
99 Tony Parker .75 2.00
100 Arron Afflalo .60 1.50
101 Corey Brewer .50 1.25
102 JaVale McGee .60 1.50
103 Ty Lawson .50 1.25
104 Andrei Kirilenko .60 1.50
105 Brandon Roy .75 2.00
106 J.J. Barea .60 1.50
107 Kevin Love .75 2.00
108 Ricky Rubio .75 2.00
109 Jonny Flynn .50 1.25
110 LaMarcus Aldridge .75 2.00
111 Nicolas Batum .60 1.50
112 Wesley Matthews .50 1.25
113 James Harden 1.25 3.00
114 Kendrick Perkins .50 1.25
115 Kevin Durant 2.00 5.00
116 Nick Collison .60 1.50
117 Russell Westbrook 2.00 5.00
118 Serge Ibaka .60 1.50
119 Al Jefferson .60 1.50
120 Gordon Hayward .75 2.00
121 Marvin Williams .60 1.50
122 Mo Williams .60 1.50
123 Paul Millsap .75 2.00
124 Andrew Bogut .60 1.50
125 Brandon Rush .50 1.25
126 David Lee .50 1.25
127 Stephen Curry 3.00 8.00
128 Jarrett Jack .60 1.50
129 Blake Griffin .75 2.00
130 Chris Paul 1.00 2.50
131 Eric Bledsoe .60 1.50
132 Grant Hill 1.00 2.50
133 Jamal Crawford .75 2.00
134 Lamar Odom .60 1.50
135 Andrew Bynum .50 1.25
136 Antawn Jamison .60 1.50
137 Kobe Bryant 3.00 8.00
138 Metta World Peace .75 2.00
139 Pau Gasol .75 2.00
140 Steve Nash .75 2.00
141 Wesley Johnson .60 1.50
142 Goran Dragic .60 1.50
143 Luis Scola .60 1.50
144 Marcin Gortat .60 1.50
145 Michael Beasley .50 1.25
146 Aaron Brooks .50 1.25
147 DeMarcus Cousins .75 2.00
148 James Johnson .50 1.25
149 Marcus Thornton .50 1.25
150 Tyreke Evans .50 1.25
151 Thomas Robinson AU/199 RC 4.00 10.00
152 Harrison Barnes AU/199 RC 10.00 25.00
153 Jimmy Butler AU/349 RC 25.00 60.00
154 Norris Cole AU/349 RC 3.00 8.00
155 K.Irving AU/199 RC 30.00 80.00
156 Anthony Davis AU/199 RC 75.00 200.00
157 Bismack Biyombo AU/349 RC 3.00 8.00
158 M.Kidd-Gilchrist AU/199 RC 5.00 12.00
159 Bradley Beal AU/199 RC 12.00 30.00
160 MarShon Brooks AU/349 RC 4.00 10.00
161 Kenneth Faried AU/349 RC 5.00 12.00
162 Dion Waiters AU/299 RC 5.00 12.00
163 Terrence Ross AU/299 RC 5.00 12.00
164 Jimmer Fredette AU/299 RC 3.00 8.00
165 Jordan Hamilton AU/399 RC 3.00 8.00
166 Andre Drummond AU/199 RC 15.00 40.00
167 Austin Rivers AU/199 RC 5.00 12.00
168 Tobias Harris AU/349 RC 5.00 12.00
169 Reggie Jackson AU/349 RC 5.00 12.00
170 Meyers Leonard AU/299 RC 4.00 10.00
171 Jeremy Lamb AU/299 RC 5.00 12.00
172 Enes Kanter AU/306 RC 4.00 10.00
173 Brandon Knight AU/299 RC 5.00 12.00
174 K.Leonard AU/349 RC 60.00 150.00
175 Kendall Marshall AU/349 RC 3.00 8.00
176 John Henson AU/299 RC 5.00 12.00
177 Marc.Morris AU/349 RC EXCH 4.00 10.00
178 Markieff Morris AU/349 RC 5.00 12.00
180 Royce White AU/399 RC EXCH 3.00 8.00
181 Chandler Parsons AU/349 RC 5.00 12.00
182 Iman Shumpert AU/349 RC 5.00 12.00
183 Tyler Zeller AU/349 RC 4.00 10.00
184 Terrence Jones AU/349 RC 4.00 10.00
185 Chris Singleton AU/349 RC 3.00 8.00
186 Nolan Smith AU/349 RC 3.00 8.00
187 A.Nicholson AU/399 RC 3.00 8.00
188 E.Fournier AU/349 RC 5.00 12.00
189 Isaiah Thomas AU/399 RC 30.00 80.00
190 K.Thompson AU/299 RC 30.00 80.00
191 Jared Sullinger AU/199 RC 4.00 10.00
192 Fab Melo AU/349 RC 3.00 8.00
193 Tristan Thompson AU/299 RC 5.00 12.00
194 Jan Vesely AU/349 RC 3.00 8.00
195 John Jenkins AU/349 RC 3.00 8.00
196 J.Cunningham AU/349 RC 3.00 8.00
197 Kemba Walker AU/278 RC 12.00 30.00
198 Derrick Williams AU/199 RC 3.00 8.00
199 Tony Wroten AU/349 RC 4.00 10.00
200 Miles Plumlee AU/399 RC 3.00 8.00
201 Cory Joseph AU/399 RC 3.00 8.00
202 JaJuan Johnson AU/349 RC EXCH 3.00 8.00
203 Arnett Moultrie AU/349 RC 3.00 8.00
204 Perry Jones AU/349 RC EXCH 3.00 8.00
205 Justin Harper AU/399 RC 3.00 8.00
206 Shelvin Mack AU/399 RC 4.00 10.00
207 Marquis Teague AU/349 RC 3.00 8.00
208 Festus Ezeli AU/349 RC 4.00 10.00
209 Gustavo Ayon AU/349 RC 3.00 8.00
210 Charles Jenkins AU/399 RC 3.00 8.00
211 Jeremy Tyler AU/399 RC 3.00 8.00
212 J.Harrellson AU/399 RC 3.00 8.00
213 Jeff Taylor AU/399 RC 3.00 8.00
214 Bernard James AU/399 RC 3.00 8.00
215 Jae Crowder AU/399 RC 4.00 10.00
216 Draymond Green AU/399 RC 15.00 40.00
217 Lavoy Allen AU/349 RC 3.00 8.00
218 Alec Burks AU/349 RC 5.00 12.00
219 Nikola Vucevic AU/349 RC 5.00 12.00
220 Tyler Honeycutt AU/399 RC 3.00 8.00
221 Trey Thompkins AU/399 RC 3.00 8.00
222 Jon Leuer AU/349 RC 4.00 10.00
223 Orlando Johnson AU/399 RC 3.00 8.00
224 Quincy Acy AU/399 RC 3.00 8.00
225 Quincy Miller AU/399 RC 3.00 8.00
226 Darius Morris AU/399 RC 3.00 8.00
227 Malcolm Lee AU/399 RC 3.00 8.00
228 Travis Leslie AU/399 RC 3.00 8.00
229 Khris Middleton AU/399 RC 5.00 12.00
230 Will Barton AU/399 RC 4.00 10.00
231 Tyshawn Taylor AU/399 RC 3.00 8.00
232 Josh Selby AU/399 RC 3.00 8.00
233 Ivan Johnson AU/349 RC EXCH 3.00 8.00
234 Greg Stiemsma AU/399 RC 3.00 8.00
235 Courtney Fortson AU/399 RC 3.00 8.00
236 E'Twaun Moore AU/349 RC 3.00 8.00
237 Doron Lamb AU/399 RC 3.00 8.00
238 Mike Scott AU/380 RC 3.00 8.00
239 Kim English AU/399 RC 3.00 8.00
240 Kyle Singler AU/399 RC 3.00 8.00
241 Darius Miller AU/399 RC 3.00 8.00
242 Kevin Murphy AU/399 RC 3.00 8.00
243 Kyle O'Quinn AU/399 RC 3.00 8.00
244 Kris Joseph AU/399 RC 3.00 8.00
245 D.Jnsn-Odom AU/399 RC 3.00 8.00
246 DeAndre Liggins AU/356 RC 4.00 10.00
247 A.Goudelock AU/399 RC EXCH 3.00 8.00
248 R.Sacre AU/399 RC EXCH 3.00 8.00
249 Tornike Shengelia AU/399 RC EXCH 3.00 8.00
250 Lance Thomas AU/399 RC 3.00 8.00

2012-13 Limited Gold Spotlight

*GOLD: 2.5X TO 6X BASE HI
STATED PRINT RUN 25 SER.#'d SETS
106 J.J. Barea 8.00 20.00
132 Grant Hill 8.00 20.00

2012-13 Limited Silver Spotlight

*SILVER: 1.5X TO 4X BASE HI
STATED PRINT RUN 49 SER.#'d SETS
132 Grant Hill 5.00 12.00

2012-13 Limited Center Stage Materials

STATED PRINT RUN 49 TO 99 SER.#'d SETS
UNPRICED PRIME PRINT RUN ONE TO 10 SETS
1 Kevin Durant/199 8.00 20.00
2 Dwight Howard/199 2.50 6.00
3 Tim Duncan/199 5.00 12.00
4 LeBron James/49 12.00 30.00
5 Kyrie Irving/49 15.00 40.00
6 Tristan Thompson/49 3.00 8.00
7 Amare Stoudemire/199 2.50 6.00
8 Tony Parker/199 3.00 8.00
9 Paul Pierce/49 3.00 8.00
10 Derrick Rose/199 4.00 10.00
11 Rudy Gay/66 3.00 8.00
12 Chris Bosh/199 3.00 8.00
13 Pau Gasol/199 3.00 8.00
14 Dirk Nowitzki/199 4.00 10.00
15 Blake Griffin/199 3.00 8.00
16 Chris Paul/49 6.00 15.00
17 LaMarcus Aldridge/49 3.00 8.00
18 Kevin Love/199 3.00 8.00
19 Deron Williams/199 2.50 6.00
20 David Lee/49 2.00 5.00
21 Brandon Jennings/199 2.00 5.00
22 Josh Smith/49 2.50 6.00
23 Danny Granger/199 2.50 6.00
24 Tyreke Evans/199 2.00 5.00
25 John Wall/49 4.00 10.00
26 Brandon Knight/199 3.00 8.00
27 Tayshaun Prince/49 2.50 6.00
28 DeMar DeRozan/199 3.00 8.00
29 Gordon Hayward/49 3.00 8.00
30 Chandler Parsons/49 10.00 25.00
31 Evan Turner/199 2.00 5.00
32 Marc Gasol/199 3.00 8.00
33 Metta World Peace/199 3.00 8.00
34 Al Horford/199 2.50 6.00
35 Ty Lawson/49 2.00 5.00
36 Jameer Nelson/199 2.00 5.00
37 Joakim Noah/125 2.50 6.00
38 Carmelo Anthony/49 4.00 10.00
39 Carlos Boozer/49 2.50 6.00
40 Rajon Rondo/199 3.00 8.00
41 Andre Iguodala/199 2.50 6.00
42 Stephen Curry/199 8.00 20.00
43 Kawhi Leonard/49 15.00 40.00
44 Greg Monroe/49 2.50 6.00
45 Kevin Garnett/199 5.00 12.00
46 Brook Lopez/199 2.50 6.00
47 Al Jefferson/199 2.50 6.00
48 Wesley Matthews/199 2.00 5.00
49 Jrue Holiday/49 3.00 8.00
50 Jeff Teague/199 2.50 6.00

2012-13 Limited Curtain Call Materials

STATED PRINT RUN 3 TO 199 SER.#'d SETS
UNPRICED PRIME PRINT RUN 2 TO 10 SETS
1 Larry Bird/199 8.00 20.00
2 Scottie Pippen/199 6.00 15.00
3 Shaquille O'Neal/199 8.00 20.00
4 Kareem Abdul-Jabbar/25 6.00 15.00
5 Karl Malone/199 4.00 10.00
6 Danny Ainge/199 3.00 8.00
7 Robert Parish/49 3.00 8.00
8 John Stockton/25 10.00 25.00
9 Dennis Rodman/199 6.00 15.00
10 Kevin McHale/49
11 Hakeem Olajuwon/199 4.00 10.00
12 Ron Harper/199 3.00 8.00
13 Gary Payton/25
14 Patrick Ewing/199 8.00 20.00
15 Derek Fisher/199 2.50 6.00
16 Kobe Bryant/199 8.00 20.00
17 Tim Duncan/199 5.00 12.00
18 Kevin Durant/199 5.00 12.00
19 Tony Parker/199 3.00 8.00
20 Manu Ginobili/199 3.00 8.00
21 Ben Wallace/199 2.50 6.00
22 Paul Pierce/199 3.00 8.00
23 Dirk Nowitzki/199 4.00 10.00
25 Tayshaun Prince/199 2.50 6.00
26 LeBron James/99 12.00 30.00
27 Dwyane Wade/199 5.00 12.00
28 Pau Gasol/199 3.00 8.00
29 David Robinson/199 5.00 12.00
30 Jeff Hornacek/199 2.50 6.00
31 Julius Erving/49 5.00 12.00
32 Clyde Drexler/199 4.00 10.00
33 Isiah Thomas/25
34 Mark Jackson/199 2.50 6.00
36 Michael Cooper/49 2.50 6.00
37 Bill Cartwright/49 2.50 6.00
38 Bill Laimbeer/199 2.50 6.00
39 Joe Dumars/49 3.00 8.00
40 Dikembe Mutombo/199 3.00 8.00
41 Toni Kukoc/49 5.00 12.00
42 John Starks/49 2.50 6.00
43 Alonzo Mourning/199 8.00 20.00
44 Steve Smith/199 2.50 6.00
45 Jason Kidd/199 3.00 8.00
46 Udonis Haslem/199 2.00 5.00
47 Steve Nash/199 4.00 10.00
48 Ray Allen/199 5.00 12.00
49 Kenyon Martin/199 3.00 8.00
50 Hedo Turkoglu/199 2.50 6.00

2012-13 Limited Glass Cleaners Materials

STATED PRINT RUN 10 TO 99 SER.#'d SETS
UNPRICED PRIME PRINT RUN ONE TO 10 SETS
1 Dwight Howard/99 2.50 6.00
2 Kareem Abdul-Jabbar/99 5.00 12.00
3 Kevin Garnett/99 5.00 12.00
4 LeBron James/99 12.00 30.00
5 Marc Gasol/99 3.00 8.00
6 DeMarcus Cousins/99 3.00 8.00
7 Tim Duncan/99 5.00 12.00
8 JaVale McGee/99 2.50 6.00
10 Shawn Marion/99 2.50 6.00
11 Amare Stoudemire/99 2.50 6.00
12 Tristan Thompson/99 3.00 8.00
13 DeAndre Jordan/99 3.00 8.00
14 Derrick Favors/99 2.50 6.00
15 Udonis Haslem/99 2.00 5.00
16 Ed Davis/99 2.00 5.00
17 Patrick Ewing/99 4.00 10.00
18 Karl Malone/99 4.00 10.00
19 Dikembe Mutombo/99 3.00 8.00
20 Shawn Kemp/99 10.00 25.00
21 Shaquille O'Neal/99 8.00 20.00
22 Dennis Rodman/99 6.00 15.00
23 Charles Oakley/99 3.00 8.00
24 Chris Kaman/99 2.50 6.00
25 David West/99 2.50 6.00

2012-13 Limited Glass Cleaners Materials Signatures

STATED PRINT RUN 25 TO 49 SER.#'d SETS
UNPRICED PRIME PRINT RUN 3 TO 10 SETS
1 Charles Oakley/25 15.00 40.00
2 Kevin Durant/25 75.00 150.00
3 Kobe Bryant/49 90.00 150.00
4 Blake Griffin/25 20.00 50.00
5 Alonzo Mourning/25 30.00 60.00
6 Kareem Abdul-Jabbar/25 30.00 80.00
7 Hakeem Olajuwon/49 15.00 40.00
8 David Robinson/25 20.00 50.00
9 Emeka Okafor/49 6.00 15.00
10 Kenneth Faried/49 6.00 15.00
11 Toni Kukoc/49 10.00 25.00
12 Anderson Varejao/49 6.00 15.00
13 Kawhi Leonard/49 40.00 100.00
14 Pau Gasol/25 EXCH 20.00 50.00
15 Zach Randolph/49 6.00 15.00
16 LaMarcus Aldridge/49 8.00 20.00
17 Tristan Thompson/49 10.00 25.00
18 Brook Lopez/49 6.00 15.00
19 Derrick Favors/49 6.00 15.00
20 Charlie Villanueva/49 6.00 15.00
21 Al Jefferson/49 8.00 20.00
22 Joakim Noah/49 12.00 30.00
23 Robert Parish/49 8.00 20.00
24 Chris Bosh/25
25 Anthony Davis/49 125.00 250.00

2012-13 Limited Glass Cleaners Signatures

STATED PRINT RUN 25 TO 199 SER.#'d SETS
1 Kevin Durant/49 50.00 120.00
2 Kevin Love/49 12.00 30.00
3 Andrew Bynum/49 8.00 20.00
4 DeMarcus Cousins/99 12.00 30.00
5 Kris Humphries/199 5.00 12.00
6 Blake Griffin/49 15.00 40.00
7 Pau Gasol/25 EXCH 10.00 25.00
8 Marcin Gortat/199 10.00 25.00
9 Tyson Chandler/49 EXCH
10 Joakim Noah/49 10.00 25.00
11 Greg Monroe/199 5.00 12.00
12 Al Jefferson/49 5.00 12.00
13 Josh Smith/49 5.00 12.00
14 David Lee/99 EXCH 5.00 12.00
15 Marcus Camby/199 5.00 12.00
16 DeAndre Jordan/199 5.00 12.00
17 Chris Bosh/25 30.00 60.00
18 Ersan Ilyasova/199 5.00 12.00
19 Roy Hibbert/199 5.00 12.00
20 Drew Gooden/99 EXCH 5.00 12.00
21 Udonis Haslem/99 5.00 12.00
22 Yao Ming/25 30.00 80.00
23 Dikembe Mutombo/99 6.00 15.00
24 Elgin Baylor/25 10.00 25.00
25 Dave Cowens/49 6.00 15.00

2012-13 Limited Home and Away Materials

STATED PRINT RUN 49 TO 99 SER.#'d SETS
1 Kobe Bryant/99 12.00 30.00
2 Tim Duncan/99 5.00 12.00
3 Blake Griffin/99 3.00 8.00
4 Tony Parker/99 3.00 8.00
5 LeBron James/99 15.00 40.00
6 Kevin Durant/99 8.00 20.00
7 Dirk Nowitzki/99 4.00 10.00
8 Derrick Rose/99 4.00 10.00
9 Paul Pierce/99 3.00 8.00
10 Tyson Chandler/99 2.50 6.00
11 Chris Paul/99 4.00 10.00
12 Shaquille O'Neal/99 6.00 15.00
13 Russell Westbrook/49 8.00 20.00
14 Kevin Love/99 3.00 8.00
15 Vince Carter/99 4.00 10.00
16 Stephen Curry/99 12.00 30.00
17 Andrea Bargnani/99 2.50 6.00
18 Dwyane Wade/99 5.00 12.00
19 Tyreke Evans/99 2.00 5.00
20 Brandon Jennings/99 2.00 5.00
21 LaMarcus Aldridge/99 3.00 8.00
22 Zach Randolph/99 2.50 6.00
23 Kevin Martin/99 2.50 6.00
24 John Wall/99 4.00 10.00
25 Kyrie Irving/99 15.00 40.00

2012-13 Limited Lights Out Materials

STATED PRINT RUN 49 TO 199 SER.#'d SETS
UNPRICED PRIME PRINT RUN 5 TO 10 SETS
1 Dirk Nowitzki/199 5.00 12.00
2 LeBron James/99 10.00 25.00
3 Kevin Durant/199 5.00 12.00
4 Kobe Bryant/99 8.00 20.00
5 Paul Pierce/199 8.00 20.00
6 Carmelo Anthony/199 5.00 12.00
7 Dwyane Wade/199 6.00 15.00
8 Stephen Curry/199 15.00 40.00
9 Manu Ginobili/199 4.00 10.00
10 Ben Gordon/199 3.00 8.00
11 Deron Williams/199 3.00 8.00
12 Joe Johnson/199 3.00 8.00
13 Brandon Jennings/199 2.50 6.00
14 Kevin Love/199 4.00 10.00
15 James Harden/199 6.00 15.00
16 Jason Richardson/199 4.00 10.00
17 Danny Granger/199 3.00 8.00
18 Russell Westbrook/199 10.00 25.00
19 Tony Parker/49 6.00 15.00
20 J.J. Redick/199 8.00 20.00
21 Steve Nash/199 8.00 20.00
22 Ray Allen/199 6.00 15.00
23 Caron Butler/199 3.00 8.00
24 Kyrie Irving/49 15.00 40.00
25 Klay Thompson/49 4.00 10.00
26 Brandon Knight/49 3.00 8.00
27 Derrick Rose/199 6.00 15.00
28 Ryan Anderson/64 3.00 8.00
29 Blake Griffin/199 4.00 10.00
30 Chris Paul/49 5.00 12.00
31 Rudy Gay/199 4.00 10.00
32 Andre Iguodala/199 3.00 8.00
33 Chauncey Billups/199 4.00 10.00
35 Richard Hamilton/90 3.00 8.00
36 Wesley Matthews/199 2.50 6.00
37 Randy Foye/199 2.50 6.00
38 Al Harrington/199 3.00 8.00
39 Dorell Wright/199 2.50 6.00
40 Hedo Turkoglu/199 3.00 8.00
41 Nick Young/199 3.00 8.00
42 Ty Lawson/199 2.50 6.00
43 Shane Battier/199 3.00 8.00
44 Kevin Martin/199 3.00 8.00
45 Jimmer Fredette/199 2.00 5.00
46 D.J. Augustin/199 2.50 6.00
47 Eric Gordon/199 3.00 8.00
48 Brandon Roy/199 4.00 10.00
49 Jameer Nelson/199 2.50 6.00
50 Raymond Felton/199 3.00 8.00

2012-13 Limited Masterful Marks Signatures

STATED PRINT RUN 25 TO 199 SER.#'d SETS
1 Steve Nash/25
2 Deron Williams/25 10.00 25.00
3 Jason Kidd/25 12.00 30.00
4 Kobe Bryant/99 75.00 150.00
5 Brandon Roy/25 5.00 12.00
6 Raymond Felton/99 4.00 10.00
7 Nick Collison/99 4.00 10.00
8 Al Horford/99 4.00 10.00
9 Grant Hill/49 20.00 50.00
10 Darren Collison/99 4.00 10.00
11 Andre Iguodala/99 4.00 10.00
12 LaMarcus Aldridge/49 5.00 12.00
13 James Harden/99 EXCH 15.00 40.00
14 David Lee/99 EXCH 3.00 8.00
15 Ersan Ilyasova/199 3.00 8.00
16 Vlade Divac/199 5.00 12.00
17 Gordon Hayward/199 5.00 12.00
18 Stephen Curry/99 125.00 250.00
19 Marcus Thornton/199 4.00 10.00
20 Antoine Walker/199 4.00 10.00
21 Jordan Crawford/99 3.00 8.00
22 Charles Oakley/99 5.00 12.00
23 Anderson Varejao/99 3.00 8.00
24 O.J. Mayo/49 3.00 8.00
25 Al-Farouq Aminu/99 4.00 10.00
26 Kevin Durant/49 75.00 150.00
27 Joakim Noah/49 5.00 12.00
28 Tony Parker/49 12.00 30.00
29 Kevin Love/49 10.00 25.00
30 Joe Johnson/49 4.00 10.00
31 Brandon Jennings/49 3.00 8.00
32 Derrick Favors/99 4.00 10.00
33 Brook Lopez/99 4.00 10.00
34 Isiah Thomas/99 8.00 20.00
35 Eric Gordon/99 4.00 10.00
36 Ty Lawson/99 3.00 8.00
37 Serge Ibaka/199 4.00 10.00
38 Kevin Martin/99 4.00 10.00
39 Jrue Holiday/99 5.00 12.00
40 Blake Griffin/49 15.00 40.00
41 Mitch Richmond/199 5.00 12.00
42 Dan Majerle/199 4.00 10.00
43 JaVale McGee/99 4.00 10.00
44 Mark Jackson/199 4.00 10.00
45 Jerry West/25 20.00 50.00
46 Antawn Jamison/49 4.00 10.00
47 Delonte West/99 3.00 8.00
48 Steve Novak/99 3.00 8.00
49 Andrew Bogut/99 EXCH 4.00 10.00
50 Drew Gooden/99 EXCH 4.00 10.00

2012-13 Limited Monikers Materials

STATED PRINT RUN 25 TO 99 SER.#'d SETS
1 John Stockton/25 25.00 60.00
2 Amare Stoudemire/49 12.00 30.00
3 Tony Parker/25 15.00 40.00
4 Robert Parish/99 6.00 15.00
5 Tayshaun Prince/99 6.00 15.00
6 Jason Richardson/99 6.00 15.00
7 David Robinson/25 15.00 40.00
8 Kevin Martin/99 4.00 10.00
9 Kevin McHale/25 6.00 15.00
10 Al Jefferson/49 6.00 15.00
11 Kevin Durant/25 75.00 150.00
12 Jalen Rose/99 EXCH 6.00 15.00
13 Joe Dumars/49 6.00 15.00
14 Brandon Knight/99 5.00 12.00
15 LaMarcus Aldridge/49 10.00 25.00
16 Jameer Nelson/49 6.00 15.00
17 Kareem Abdul-Jabbar/49 40.00 100.00
18 Markieff Morris/99 5.00 12.00
19 Derrick Williams/99 3.00 8.00
20 Carlos Boozer/49 6.00 15.00
21 Zach Randolph/49 10.00 25.00
22 David Lee/99 EXCH 8.00 20.00
23 Mark Jackson/99 EXCH 6.00 15.00
24 J.J. Redick/49 8.00 20.00
25 Jimmer Fredette/99 3.00 8.00
26 Blake Griffin/49 30.00 80.00
27 Brook Lopez/49 6.00 15.00
28 Kobe Bryant/99 75.00 150.00
29 Ivan Johnson/99 6.00 15.00
30 Gary Payton/49 12.00 30.00
31 Chandler Parsons/99 5.00 12.00
32 Jeff Teague/99 6.00 15.00
33 Anfernee Hardaway/49 15.00 40.00
34 Luke Ridnour/49 6.00 15.00
35 Beno Udrih/99 3.00 8.00
36 Anthony Mason/99 6.00 15.00
37 Danny Granger/49 6.00 15.00
38 Andre Iguodala/49 8.00 20.00
39 Metta World Peace/49 6.00 15.00
40 Al Horford/49 6.00 15.00
41 Chris Bosh/25 12.00 30.00
42 Toni Kukoc/99 15.00 40.00
43 Luol Deng/49 6.00 15.00
44 Pau Gasol/25
45 Mark Price/99 5.00 12.00
46 Andre Miller/99 6.00 15.00
47 Caron Butler/49 6.00 15.00
48 Ty Lawson/99 3.00 8.00
49 Jerry West/25 25.00 60.00
50 Andrew Bynum/49 10.00 25.00

2012-13 Limited Monikers Materials Prime

*PRIME: .75X TO 2X BASE HI
STATED PRINT RUN 5 TO 25 SER.#'d SETS
SOME UNPRICED DUE TO SCARCITY
4 Robert Parish/25 15.00 40.00

2012-13 Limited Performers Materials

STATED PRINT RUN ONE TO 199 SER.#'d SETS
SOME UNPRICED DUE TO SCARCITY
UNPRICED PRIME PRINT RUN ONE TO 10 SETS
1 Kevin Martin/199 2.50 6.00
2 J.J. Redick/199 6.00 15.00
3 Tyrus Thomas/199 2.00 5.00
4 Grant Hill/199 6.00 15.00
5 Elton Brand/199 3.00 8.00
7 Zach Randolph/199 2.50 6.00
8 Caron Butler/199 2.50 6.00
9 Kevin Garnett/199 5.00 12.00
10 Marc Gasol/199 3.00 8.00
11 LeBron James/199 12.00 30.00
12 Tim Duncan/199 5.00 12.00
13 Dwyane Wade/199 5.00 12.00
14 Dwight Howard/199 2.50 6.00
15 David West/199 2.50 6.00
16 Kirk Hinrich/199 2.50 6.00
17 Shawn Marion/199 2.50 6.00
18 Thaddeus Young/199 2.00 5.00
19 Linas Kleiza/199 2.00 5.00
20 Carmelo Anthony/199 4.00 10.00
21 Amare Stoudemire/199 2.50 6.00
22 Rajon Rondo/199 3.00 8.00
23 Paul Pierce/199 3.00 8.00
24 John Wall/199 4.00 10.00
25 Derrick Rose/199 4.00 10.00
26 Manu Ginobili/199 3.00 8.00
27 Raymond Felton/199 2.50 6.00
28 Kemba Walker/99 5.00 12.00
29 J.J. Barea/199 2.50 6.00
30 DeMar DeRozan/199 3.00 8.00
31 Nick Collison/109 2.50 6.00
32 Glen Davis/199 2.00 5.00
33 George Hill/199 2.50 6.00
34 Josh Smith/199 2.50 6.00
36 Carlos Delfino/199 2.00 5.00
37 Tiago Splitter/199 2.50 6.00
38 Channing Frye/199 2.50 6.00
39 Tyler Hansbrough/199 2.50 6.00
40 Spencer Hawes/199 2.00 5.00
41 Tobias Harris/199 2.50 6.00
42 John Salmons/199 2.50 6.00
44 Tristan Thompson/199 2.50 6.00
45 MarShon Brooks/199 2.00 5.00
46 Udonis Haslem/199 2.00 5.00
47 Wesley Matthews/199 2.00 5.00
48 Ed Davis/199 2.00 5.00
50 Kenneth Faried/25 2.50 6.00

2012-13 Limited Private Signings

RANDOM INSERTS IN PACKS
1 Alex English 6.00 15.00
2 Christian Laettner 15.00 40.00
3 Hakeem Olajuwon 75.00 200.00
4 Rajon Rondo 20.00 50.00

2012-13 Limited Spotlight Signatures

STATED PRINT RUN 10 TO 99 SER.#'d SETS
SOME UNPRICED DUE TO SCARCITY
1 Glen Rice/99 8.00 20.00
2 Magic Johnson/25 40.00 100.00
3 Dirk Nowitzki/15 100.00 200.00
4 Kobe Bryant/49 75.00 150.00
5 Ralph Sampson/99 4.00 10.00
6 Bailey Howell/99 6.00 15.00
7 Blake Griffin/25 15.00 40.00
9 Tyreke Evans/25
10 Luis Scola/99 4.00 10.00
11 Mike Conley/49
12 Chris Kaman/99 4.00 10.00
13 Andrew Bynum/25 3.00 8.00
14 Kevin Durant/25 100.00 200.00
15 Chauncey Billups/25 EXCH 5.00 12.00
16 Delonte West/99 3.00 8.00
17 Greg Monroe/49 4.00 10.00
18 Muggsy Bogues/99 4.00 10.00
19 Marcus Camby/49 4.00 10.00
20 Andrew Bogut/49 4.00 10.00
21 Mario Chalmers/99 EXCH 4.00 10.00
22 DeAndre Jordan/99 5.00 12.00
23 Marcin Gortat/99 4.00 10.00
24 Eric Bledsoe/99 4.00 10.00
25 Avery Bradley/99 4.00 10.00
26 Gerald Wallace/99 4.00 10.00
27 Tayshaun Prince/99 4.00 10.00
28 Steve Nash/25 15.00 40.00
29 Al Jefferson/49 4.00 10.00
30 Zach Randolph/49 4.00 10.00
31 Derek Fisher/49 4.00 10.00
32 Jose Calderon/49 3.00 8.00
33 Stephen Jackson/99 4.00 10.00
34 Kris Humphries/99
35 Julius Erving/25 30.00 80.00
36 Byron Scott/49 4.00 10.00
37 Bill Cartwright/49 4.00 10.00
38 Kevin Willis/99 4.00 10.00
39 Bob Pettit/25 EXCH 6.00 15.00
40 Anfernee Hardaway/49 20.00 50.00
41 Will Bynum/99 3.00 8.00
42 Elgin Baylor/49 8.00 20.00
43 Gary Payton/25 10.00 25.00
44 Bob Lanier/49 4.00 10.00
45 Earl Monroe/25 10.00 25.00
46 Vince Carter/25 30.00 80.00
47 Artis Gilmore/49 4.00 10.00
48 Robert Horry/49 4.00 10.00
49 Chris Bosh/25 12.00 30.00
50 Monta Ellis/49 4.00 10.00

2012-13 Limited Unlimited Potential Signatures

STATED PRINT RUN 49 TO 199 SER.#'d SETS
1 Derrick Favors/99 3.00 8.00
2 Kyrie Irving/199 50.00 120.00
3 MarShon Brooks/199 3.00 8.00
4 Anthony Davis/99 60.00 150.00
5 Brandon Knight/199 4.00 10.00
6 Klay Thompson/99 30.00 80.00
7 Quincy Acy/199 2.50 6.00
8 Isaiah Thomas/199 25.00 60.00
9 Markieff Morris/99 4.00 10.00
10 Ivan Johnson/199 2.50 6.00
11 Thomas Robinson/199 3.00 8.00
12 Kendall Marshall/199 2.50 6.00
13 Chandler Parsons/99 4.00 10.00
14 Michael Kidd-Gilchrist/199 4.00 10.00
15 Tyler Zeller/199 3.00 8.00
16 Andrew Goudelock/199 EXCH 2.50 6.00
17 Dion Waiters/199 EXCH 4.00 10.00
18 Austin Rivers/199 4.00 10.00
19 Andre Drummond/199 10.00 25.00
20 Iman Shumpert/199 4.00 10.00
21 Jeremy Lamb/199 4.00 10.00
22 Kenneth Faried/199 4.00 10.00
23 Meyers Leonard/99 3.00 8.00
24 John Henson/199 4.00 10.00
25 Jonas Valanciunas/199 4.00 10.00
26 Bradley Beal/199 6.00 15.00
27 Tristan Thompson/199 4.00 10.00
28 Jimmer Fredette/199 2.50 6.00
29 Alec Burks/199 4.00 10.00
30 Norris Cole/199 2.50 6.00
31 Enes Kanter/199 3.00 8.00
32 Gustavo Ayon/199 2.50 6.00
33 Royce White/199 2.50 6.00
34 Terrence Ross/199 4.00 10.00
35 Andrew Nicholson/199 2.50 6.00
36 Evan Fournier/199 4.00 10.00
37 Jared Sullinger/199 3.00 8.00
38 Fab Melo/199 2.50 6.00
39 John Jenkins/49 2.50 6.00
40 Jared Cunningham/199 2.50 6.00
41 Tony Wroten/199 3.00 8.00
42 Miles Plumlee/199 2.50 6.00
43 Arnett Moultrie/199 2.50 6.00
44 Perry Jones/199 2.50 6.00
45 Marquis Teague/99 2.50 6.00
46 Festus Ezeli/199 3.00 8.00
47 Bernard James/199 2.50 6.00
48 Draymond Green/199 12.00 30.00
49 Jeff Taylor/199 2.50 6.00
50 Jae Crowder/199 3.00 8.00

2015-16 Limited

STATED PRINT RUN 80 SER.#'d SETS
1 Paul Millsap .75 2.00
2 Gordon Hayward .75 2.00
3 John Wall 1.00 2.50
4 Danilo Gallinari .60 1.50
5 Marc Gasol .75 2.00
6 Jimmy Butler .75 2.00
7 Stephen Curry 3.00 8.00
8 DeMar DeRozan .75 2.00
9 Rajon Rondo .75 2.00
10 Joe Johnson .60 1.50
11 Al Horford .60 1.50
12 Derrick Favors .60 1.50
13 Otto Porter .60 1.50
14 Will Barton .50 1.25
15 Mike Conley .75 2.00
16 Derrick Rose 1.00 2.50
17 Draymond Green 1.00 2.50
18 Kyle Lowry .60 1.50
19 Rudy Gay .75 2.00
20 Brook Lopez .60 1.50
21 Kyle Korver .60 1.50
22 Alec Burks .50 1.25
23 Bradley Beal .75 2.00
24 Kenneth Faried .60 1.50
25 Zach Randolph .60 1.50
26 Pau Gasol .75 2.00
27 Klay Thompson 1.00 2.50
28 DeMarre Carroll .50 1.25
29 DeMarcus Cousins .75 2.00
30 Thaddeus Young .50 1.25
31 Jeff Teague .60 1.50
32 Rodney Hood .60 1.50
33 Marcin Gortat .60 1.50
34 Gary Harris .60 1.50
35 Tony Allen .50 1.25
36 Nikola Mirotic .60 1.50
37 Andre Iguodala .60 1.50
38 Jonas Valanciunas .60 1.50
39 Ben McLemore .50 1.25
40 Jarrett Jack .60 1.50
41 Dennis Schroder .60 1.50
42 Rudy Gobert .75 2.00
43 Nene .60 1.50
44 Jameer Nelson .50 1.25
45 Vince Carter 1.00 2.50
46 Joakim Noah .60 1.50
47 Harrison Barnes .60 1.50
48 Luis Scola .60 1.50
49 Omri Casspi .50 1.25
50 Bojan Bogdanovic .50 1.25
51 Chris Bosh .75 2.00
52 Andrew Wiggins 1.25 3.00
53 Kawhi Leonard 1.25 3.00
54 LeBron James 3.00 8.00
55 James Harden 1.25 3.00
56 Kentavious Caldwell-Pope .60 1.50
57 Blake Griffin .75 2.00
58 Isaiah Thomas .75 2.00
59 Jordan Clarkson .75 2.00
60 Hollis Thompson .50 1.25
61 Goran Dragic .60 1.50
62 Zach LaVine .75 2.00
63 Tony Parker .75 2.00
64 Kevin Love .75 2.00
65 Trevor Ariza .50 1.25
66 Marcus Morris .50 1.25
67 Chris Paul 1.00 2.50
68 Jae Crowder .50 1.25
69 Kobe Bryant 3.00 8.00
70 Jerami Grant .50 1.25
71 Hassan Whiteside .60 1.50
72 Kevin Martin .60 1.50
73 LaMarcus Aldridge .75 2.00
74 Kyrie Irving 1.50 4.00
75 Ty Lawson .50 1.25
76 Andre Drummond .75 2.00
77 DeAndre Jordan .75 2.00
78 Avery Bradley .60 1.50
79 Julius Randle .75 2.00
80 Isaiah Canaan .60 1.50
81 Dwyane Wade 1.25 3.00
82 Ricky Rubio .75 2.00
83 Tim Duncan 1.25 3.00
84 J.R. Smith .60 1.50
85 Dwight Howard .60 1.50
86 Reggie Jackson .60 1.50
87 J.J. Redick .75 2.00
88 Jared Sullinger .50 1.25
89 Roy Hibbert .60 1.50
90 Nerlens Noel .60 1.50
91 Gerald Green .60 1.50
92 Kevin Garnett 1.25 3.00
93 Manu Ginobili .75 2.00
94 Mo Williams .60 1.50
95 Corey Brewer .50 1.25
96 Ersan Ilyasova .50 1.25
97 Paul Pierce .75 2.00
98 Marcus Smart .60 1.50
99 Lou Williams .60 1.50
100 Robert Covington .50 1.25
101 Evan Fournier .60 1.50
102 Damian Lillard 1.50 4.00
103 Deron Williams .60 1.50
104 Paul George 1.00 2.50
105 Eric Gordon .60 1.50
106 Khris Middleton .60 1.50
107 Tyson Chandler .60 1.50
108 Carmelo Anthony 1.00 2.50
109 Nicolas Batum .60 1.50
110 Russell Westbrook 2.00 5.00
111 Tobias Harris .60 1.50
112 C.J. McCollum .75 2.00
113 Zaza Pachulia .50 1.25
114 Monta Ellis .60 1.50
115 Ryan Anderson .60 1.50
116 Giannis Antetokounmpo 1.50 4.00
117 Brandon Knight .60 1.50
118 Jose Calderon .50 1.25
119 Kemba Walker .75 2.00
120 Serge Ibaka .60 1.50
121 Elfrid Payton .60 1.50
122 Al-Farouq Aminu .60 1.50
123 Dirk Nowitzki 1.00 2.50
124 George Hill .60 1.50
125 Anthony Davis 1.50 4.00
126 Greg Monroe .60 1.50
127 Eric Bledsoe .60 1.50
128 Langston Galloway .50 1.25
129 Marvin Williams .60 1.50
130 Dion Waiters .60 1.50
131 Victor Oladipo .60 1.50
132 Mason Plumlee .60 1.50
133 Wesley Matthews .50 1.25
134 C.J. Miles .60 1.50
135 Jrue Holiday .60 1.50
136 Michael Carter-Williams .50 1.25
137 T.J. Warren .60 1.50
138 Robin Lopez .50 1.25
139 Jeremy Lin .75 2.00
140 Kevin Durant 2.00 5.00
141 Nikola Vucevic .60 1.50
142 Ed Davis .50 1.25
143 Chandler Parsons .60 1.50
144 Ian Mahinmi .50 1.25
145 Tyreke Evans .50 1.25
146 Jabari Parker 1.00 2.50
147 Markieff Morris .50 1.25
148 Arron Afflalo .50 1.25
149 Al Jefferson .60 1.50
150 Enes Kanter .50 1.25
151 Frank Kaminsky RC 1.50 4.00
152 Rondae Hollis-Jefferson RC 1.25 3.00
153 Aaron Harrison RC 1.25 3.00
154 Cristiano Felicio RC 1.25 3.00
155 Rashad Vaughn RC 1.00 2.50
156 Richaun Holmes RC 1.25 3.00
157 Jerian Grant RC 1.00 2.50
158 Josh Richardson RC 1.50 4.00
159 D'Angelo Russell RC 5.00 12.00
160 Cliff Alexander RC 1.00 2.50
161 Raul Neto RC 1.00 2.50
162 Delon Wright RC 1.25 3.00
163 Trey Lyles RC 1.50 4.00
164 Tyus Jones RC 1.50 4.00
165 Montrezl Harrell RC 1.25 3.00
166 Jarell Eddie RC 1.50 4.00
167 Stanley Johnson RC 1.25 3.00
168 Norman Powell RC 1.25 3.00
169 Karl-Anthony Towns RC 8.00 20.00
170 Pat Connaughton RC 1.00 2.50
171 Jahlil Okafor RC 2.00 5.00
172 Anthony Brown RC 1.00 2.50
173 Nemanja Bjelica RC 1.25 3.00
174 Luis Montero RC 1.00 2.50
175 R.J. Hunter RC 1.00 2.50
176 Marcelo Huertas RC 1.25 3.00
177 Kristaps Porzingis RC 8.00 20.00
178 Jonathon Simmons RC 1.50 4.00

179 Willie Cauley-Stein RC 1.50 4.00
180 Darrun Hilliard RC 1.00 2.50
181 Justise Winslow RC 1.50 4.00
182 Sam Dekker RC 1.25 3.00
183 Larry Nance Jr. RC 1.50 4.00
184 Jarell Martin RC 1.25 3.00
185 Terry Rozier RC 1.25 3.00
186 Boban Marjanovic RC 5.00 12.00
187 T.J. McConnell RC 1.25 3.00
188 Myles Turner RC 1.50 4.00
189 Mario Hezonja RC 1.25 3.00
190 Sasha Kaun RC 1.00 2.50
191 Devin Booker RC 6.00 15.00
192 Bobby Portis RC 1.50 4.00
193 Justin Anderson RC 1.25 3.00
194 Chris McCullough RC 1.00 2.50
195 Kelly Oubre Jr. RC 1.25 3.00
196 Cameron Payne RC 1.25 3.00
197 Emmanuel Mudiay RC 1.50 4.00
198 Joe Young RC 1.25 3.00
199 Nikola Jokic RC 3.00 8.00
200 Salah Mejri RC 4.00 10.00

2015-16 Limited Gold Spotlight

*GOLD 1-150: 1.5X TO 4X BASIC
*GOLD 151-200: .75X TO 2X BASIC
RANDOM INSERTS IN PACKS
STATED PRINT RUN 25 SER.#'d SETS

2015-16 Limited Silver Spotlight

*SILVER 1-150: .6X TO 1.5X BASIC
*SILVER 151-200: .5X TO 1.2X BASIC
RANDOM INSERTS IN PACKS
STATED PRINT RUN 49 SER.#'d SETS

2015-16 Limited All Star Shorts

RANDOM INSERTS IN PACKS
PRINT RUNS B/WN 146-149 COPIES PER
*PRIME/25: 1.5X TO 4X BASIC
1 LaMarcus Aldridge 3.00 8.00
2 Kyle Korver 2.50 6.00
3 Damian Lillard 5.00 12.00
4 DeMarcus Cousins 3.00 8.00
5 Jeff Teague 2.50 6.00
6 Al Horford 2.50 6.00
7 John Wall 4.00 10.00
8 Paul Millsap 3.00 8.00

2015-16 Limited Decade Dominance Materials

RANDOM INSERTS IN PACKS
PRINT RUNS B/WN 49-149 COPIES PER
*PRIME/25: .75X TO 2X BASIC
1 David Robinson/149 5.00 12.00
2 Kevin Durant/49 6.00 15.00
3 John Stockton/149 5.00 12.00
4 Scottie Pippen/149 6.00 15.00
5 Calvin Murphy/99 2.50 6.00
6 Ben Wallace/149 2.50 6.00
7 Clyde Drexler/149 4.00 10.00
8 Kevin Garnett/149 5.00 12.00
9 Larry Bird/149 6.00 15.00
10 Tim Duncan/149 5.00 12.00
11 Dennis Rodman/149 6.00 15.00
12 LeBron James/149 8.00 20.00
13 Karl Malone/149 4.00 10.00
14 Shaquille O'Neal/149 6.00 15.00
15 Louie Dampier/149 3.00 8.00
16 Dirk Nowitzki/149 4.00 10.00
17 Isiah Thomas/149 3.00 8.00
18 Kobe Bryant/149 10.00 25.00
19 Moses Malone/149 3.00 8.00
20 Tony Parker/149 3.00 8.00
21 Hakeem Olajuwon/149 4.00 10.00
22 Stephen Curry/99 12.00 30.00
23 Patrick Ewing/149 4.00 10.00
24 Allen Iverson/149 4.00 10.00
25 Alex English/149 2.50 6.00
26 Dwyane Wade/149 5.00 12.00
27 Kareem Abdul-Jabbar/149 5.00 12.00
28 Paul Pierce/149 3.00 8.00
29 Clifford Robinson/149 2.00 5.00
30 James Harden/149 5.00 12.00

2015-16 Limited Duos Signatures

RANDOM INSERTS IN PACKS
PRINT RUNS B/WN 10-49 COPIES PER
NO PRICING ON QTY 10
*SILVER/25: .5X TO 1.2X BASIC
1 R.Hunter/T.Rozier/49 5.00 12.00
2 C.McCullough/R.Hollis-Jefferson/49 5.00 12.00
3 M.Harrell/S.Dekker/49 5.00 12.00
4 Russell/Nance Jr./49 25.00 60.00
5 Winslow/Richardson/49 25.00 60.00
6 Jones/Towns/49 75.00 200.00
7 Porzingis/Grant/49 30.00 80.00
8 C.Payne/J.Huestis/49 5.00 12.00
9 Okafor/Noel/49 8.00 20.00
10 Jhnsn/Hlls-Jffrsn/49 5.00 12.00
11 Booker/Lyles/49 25.00 60.00
12 M.Harrell/T.Rozier/49 5.00 12.00
13 J.Grant/P.Connaughton/49 4.00 10.00
14 A.Brown/J.Huestis/49 4.00 10.00
15 R.Christmas/C.McCullough/49 4.00 10.00
16 Dekker/Kaminsky/49 15.00 40.00
17 J.Nurkic/W.Chandler/49 5.00 12.00
18 Drummond/Caldwell-Pope/49 10.00 25.00
19 Paul/Griffin/25 125.00 250.00
21 Nowitzki/Porzingis/25 150.00 300.00
22 M.Price/B.Daugherty/49 6.00 15.00
23 Hamilton/Prince/49 8.00 20.00
24 Ramsey/Sanders/49 12.00 30.00
26 van Arsdale/van Arsdale/49 12.00 30.00
27 L.Nance Jr./L.Nance/49 6.00 15.00
28 D.Manning/R.LaFrentz/49 5.00 12.00
29 Hagan/Ramsey/49 10.00 25.00
30 B.Scott/K.Rambis/49 10.00 25.00
31 Kerr/Johnson/49 12.00 30.00
32 Porter/Drexler/49 15.00 40.00
33 Payton/Hawkins/49 12.00 30.00
34 Johnson/Houston/49 8.00 20.00

2015-16 Limited Glass Cleaners Materials

RANDOM INSERTS IN PACKS
STATED PRINT RUN 149 COPIES PER
*PRIME/25: .75X TO 2X BASIC
1 Tim Duncan 4.00 10.00
2 DeMarcus Cousins 3.00 8.00
3 Andre Drummond 3.00 8.00
4 Zaza Pachulia 2.00 5.00
5 Kevin Love 3.00 8.00
6 Rudy Gobert 3.00 8.00
7 Anthony Davis 5.00 12.00
8 Tristan Thompson 2.50 6.00
9 Pau Gasol 3.00 8.00
10 LaMarcus Aldridge 3.00 8.00
11 Marc Gasol 3.00 8.00
12 Greg Monroe 2.50 6.00
13 Karl-Anthony Towns 8.00 20.00
14 Kristaps Porzingis 6.00 15.00
15 Chris Bosh 3.00 8.00
16 Tyson Chandler 2.50 6.00
17 Zach Randolph 2.50 6.00
18 Derrick Favors 2.50 6.00
19 Blake Griffin 4.00 10.00
20 Julius Randle 3.00 8.00
21 Serge Ibaka 2.50 6.00
22 Nerlens Noel 2.50 6.00
23 Kenneth Faried 2.50 6.00
24 DeAndre Jordan 3.00 8.00
25 Paul Millsap 3.00 8.00
26 Joakim Noah 2.50 6.00
27 Draymond Green 4.00 10.00
28 Mason Plumlee 2.50 6.00
29 Brook Lopez 2.50 6.00
30 Jahlil Okafor 4.00 10.00

2015-16 Limited Material Monikers

RANDOM INSERTS IN PACKS
STATED PRINT RUN 149 COPIES PER
*PRIME/25: 1X TO 2.5X BASIC
1 Carmelo Anthony/149 5.00 12.00
3 Giannis Antetokounmpo/45 20.00 50.00
4 Paul George/49 6.00 15.00
5 Derrick Rose/49 5.00 12.00
6 Paul Pierce/99 4.00 10.00
7 Dirk Nowitzki/149 5.00 12.00
9 Kobe Bryant/149 20.00 50.00
10 Kevin Garnett/149 6.00 15.00
11 Shaquille O'Neal/99 10.00 25.00
12 DeMarcus Cousins/149 4.00 10.00
14 Al Jefferson/99 3.00 8.00
16 Ben Wallace/149 3.00 8.00
17 James Harden/99 6.00 15.00
18 Roy Hibbert/99 3.00 8.00
19 Anthony Davis/99 6.00 15.00
20 Iman Shumpert/99 2.50 6.00
22 Hakeem Olajuwon/99 6.00 15.00
23 Goran Dragic/149 3.00 8.00
24 Jeremy Lin/99 10.00 25.00
25 LeBron James/49 20.00 50.00
26 Steven Adams/99 3.00 8.00
27 Chris Paul/99 5.00 12.00
28 Kawhi Leonard/99 6.00 15.00
29 Dwyane Wade/149 6.00 15.00
30 Deron Williams/99 3.00 8.00
31 Dwight Howard/99 3.00 8.00
32 Clyde Drexler/99 6.00 15.00

2015-16 Limited Phenoms

RANDOM INSERTS IN PACKS
1 Kobe Bryant 5.00 12.00
2 Kevin Durant 3.00 8.00
3 LeBron James 5.00 12.00
4 Anthony Davis 2.50 6.00
5 Carmelo Anthony 1.50 4.00
6 Chris Paul 1.50 4.00
7 Dwyane Wade 2.00 5.00
8 James Harden 2.00 5.00
9 Stephen Curry 5.00 12.00
10 Russell Westbrook 3.00 8.00
11 Blake Griffin 1.25 3.00
12 Andrew Wiggins 2.00 5.00
13 Damian Lillard 2.50 6.00
14 John Wall 1.50 4.00
15 Tim Duncan 2.00 5.00

2015-16 Limited Rookie Jersey Autographs

RANDOM INSERTS IN PACKS
STATED PRINT RUN 99 SER.#'d SETS
1 Karl-Anthony Towns 75.00 200.00
2 D'Angelo Russell 25.00 60.00
3 Jahlil Okafor 12.00 30.00
4 Kristaps Porzingis 30.00 80.00
5 Mario Hezonja 5.00 12.00
6 Willie Cauley-Stein 10.00 25.00
7 Emmanuel Mudiay 12.00 30.00
8 Stanley Johnson 5.00 12.00
9 Frank Kaminsky 6.00 15.00
10 Justise Winslow 12.00 30.00
11 Myles Turner 15.00 40.00
12 Trey Lyles 6.00 15.00
13 Devin Booker 30.00 80.00
14 Cameron Payne 5.00 12.00
15 Kelly Oubre Jr. 5.00 12.00
16 Terry Rozier 5.00 12.00
17 Nikola Jokic 30.00 80.00
18 Salah Mejri 4.00 10.00
19 Jerian Grant 4.00 10.00
20 Delon Wright 5.00 12.00
21 Justin Anderson 5.00 12.00
22 Bobby Portis 6.00 15.00
23 Rondae Hollis-Jefferson 5.00 12.00
24 Tyus Jones 6.00 15.00
25 Jarell Martin 5.00 12.00
26 R.J. Hunter 4.00 10.00
27 Chris McCullough 4.00 10.00
28 Montrezl Harrell 5.00 12.00
29 Jordan Mickey 4.00 10.00
30 Anthony Brown 4.00 10.00
31 Rakeem Christmas 4.00 10.00
32 Richaun Holmes 5.00 12.00
33 Pat Connaughton 4.00 10.00
35 Nemanja Bjelica 5.00 12.00
36 Kevon Looney 5.00 12.00
37 Josh Richardson 6.00 15.00
38 Josh Huestis 4.00 10.00

2015-16 Limited Rookie Jersey Autographs Gold Spotlight

*GOLD: .75X TO 2X BASIC
RANDOM INSERTS IN PACKS
STATED PRINT RUN 25 SER.#'d SETS
34 Joe Young 10.00 25.00

2015-16 Limited Rookie Jersey Autographs Silver Spotlight

*SILVER: .5X TO 1.2X BASIC
RANDOM INSERTS IN PACKS
STATED PRINT RUN 49 SER.#'d SETS
34 Joe Young 6.00 15.00

2015-16 Limited Rookie Phenoms

RANDOM INSERTS IN PACKS
1 Karl-Anthony Towns 10.00 25.00
2 D'Angelo Russell 5.00 12.00
3 Jahlil Okafor 2.50 6.00
4 Kristaps Porzingis 5.00 12.00
5 Mario Hezonja 1.50 4.00
6 Willie Cauley-Stein 2.00 5.00
7 Emmanuel Mudiay 2.00 5.00
8 Stanley Johnson 1.50 4.00
9 Frank Kaminsky 2.00 5.00
10 Justise Winslow 2.00 5.00
11 Myles Turner 2.00 5.00
12 Trey Lyles 2.00 5.00
13 Devin Booker 6.00 15.00
14 Cameron Payne 1.50 4.00
15 Kelly Oubre Jr. 1.50 4.00

2015-16 Limited Signatures

RANDOM INSERTS IN PACKS
PRINT RUNS B/WN 15-99 COPIES PER
NO PRICING ON QTY 15
*SILVER/25: .5X TO 1.2X BASIC
3 Kyrie Irving/35 25.00 60.00
4 Anthony Davis/35 40.00 100.00
5 Chris Paul/35 20.00 50.00
6 Allen Iverson/35 50.00 120.00
7 Chris Webber/99 40.00 100.00
8 Kareem Abdul-Jabbar/35 20.00 50.00
9 Tracy McGrady/99 12.00 30.00
10 Elgin Baylor/99 6.00 15.00
11 James Worthy/99 6.00 15.00
12 Gary Payton/75 10.00 25.00
13 Harrison Barnes/99 6.00 15.00
14 Julius Randle/99 5.00 12.00
15 Bob Lanier/99 4.00 10.00
16 Ben McLemore/99 3.00 8.00
17 Artis Gilmore/99 4.00 10.00
18 Wes Unseld/99 5.00 12.00
19 Walt Frazier/99 5.00 12.00
20 Trey Burke/99 3.00 8.00
21 Brandon Knight/99 4.00 10.00
22 Hal Greer/99 4.00 10.00
23 Dolph Schayes/99 5.00 12.00
24 Lenny Wilkens/99 5.00 12.00
25 Ralph Sampson/99 5.00 12.00
26 Nikola Mirotic/99 4.00 10.00
27 T.J. Warren/99 4.00 10.00
28 Jrue Holiday/99 4.00 10.00
29 Bob McAdoo/99 3.00 8.00
30 Bernard King/99 4.00 10.00
31 Sonny Weems/99 3.00 8.00
32 Jason Smith/99 3.00 8.00
33 Jeff Malone/99 3.00 8.00
34 Kevin Willis/99 3.00 8.00
35 Sam Bowie/99 3.00 8.00
36 Antoine Carr/99 3.00 8.00
37 Cuttino Mobley/99 3.00 8.00
38 Eddie Jones/99 4.00 10.00
39 Rafer Alston/99 3.00 8.00
40 Avery Johnson/99 4.00 10.00
41 Hersey Hawkins/99 3.00 8.00
42 Doug Collins/99 5.00 12.00
43 Spencer Haywood/99 3.00 8.00
44 Jerome Williams/99 3.00 8.00
45 Maurice Cheeks/99 3.00 8.00
46 Harry Gallatin/99 5.00 12.00
47 Jordan Clarkson/99 8.00 20.00
48 T.J. McConnell/99 4.00 10.00
49 Darrun Hilliard/99 3.00 8.00
50 Nemanja Bjelica/99 4.00 10.00
51 Nikola Jokic/99 25.00 60.00
52 Larry Nance Jr./99 5.00 12.00
53 Raul Neto/99 3.00 8.00

2015-16 Limited Team Trademarks

RANDOM INSERTS IN PACKS
STATED PRINT RUN 45-149 COPIES PER
*PRIME/25: .75X TO 2X BASIC
1 Paul Millsap/99 4.00 10.00
2 Isaiah Thomas/99 3.00 8.00
3 Brook Lopez/149 3.00 8.00
4 Nicolas Batum/149 3.00 8.00
5 Derrick Rose/99 6.00 15.00
6 LeBron James/49 12.00 30.00
7 Dirk Nowitzki/149 5.00 12.00
8 Kenneth Faried/149 3.00 8.00
9 Andre Drummond/149 4.00 10.00
10 Stephen Curry/49 25.00 60.00
11 James Harden/99 6.00 15.00
12 Paul George/49 5.00 12.00
13 Chris Paul/149 5.00 12.00
14 Kobe Bryant/149 12.00 30.00
15 Marc Gasol/99 4.00 10.00
16 Dwyane Wade/149 6.00 15.00
17 Giannis Antetokounmpo/45 8.00 20.00
18 Andrew Wiggins/149 6.00 15.00
19 Anthony Davis/149 8.00 20.00
20 Kristaps Porzingis/99 8.00 20.00
21 Kevin Durant/49 8.00 20.00
22 Evan Fournier/149 3.00 8.00
23 Jahlil Okafor/149 5.00 12.00
24 Eric Bledsoe/149 3.00 8.00
25 Damian Lillard/99 6.00 15.00
26 DeMarcus Cousins/149 4.00 10.00
27 Kawhi Leonard/149 6.00 15.00
28 DeMar DeRozan/149 4.00 10.00
29 Rudy Gobert/99 4.00 10.00
30 John Wall/99 5.00 12.00

2015-16 Limited Trios Signatures

RANDOM INSERTS IN PACKS
PRINT RUNS B/WN 10-49 COPIES PER
NO PRICING ON QTY 10
*SILVER/25: .5X TO 1.2X BASIC
1 Mickey/Hunter/Rozier/49 15.00 40.00
3 Cauley-Stein/Towns/Booker/49 150.00 300.00
4 Jones/Okafor/Winslow/49 60.00 150.00
5 Russell/Okafor/Towns/49 150.00 300.00
6 Havlicek/Maxwell/White/49 30.00 80.00
7 Laimbeer/Salley/Mahorn/49 12.00 30.00
9 Jackson/Oakley/Newman/49 8.00 20.00
11 Grant/Grant/Grant/49 12.00 30.00
12 Carter-Williams/Grant/Ennis/49 12.00 30.00
13 Okafor/Holmes/McConnell/49 12.00 30.00

2015-16 Limited Trophy Case Materials

RANDOM INSERTS IN PACKS
STATED PRINT RUN 49-149 COPIES PER
*PRIME/25: .75X TO 2X BASIC
1 Kobe Bryant/149 12.00 30.00
2 Dirk Nowitzki/149 4.00 10.00
3 Andre Iguodala/149 2.50 6.00
4 Karl Malone/149 4.00 10.00
5 Bobby Jackson/149 2.00 5.00
6 Andrew Wiggins/149 5.00 12.00
7 Damian Lillard/99 5.00 12.00
8 Stephen Curry/149 12.00 30.00
9 Ben Wallace/149 2.50 6.00
10 LeBron James/99 12.00 30.00
11 Tony Parker/149 3.00 8.00
12 Grant Hill/149 4.00 10.00
13 Tim Duncan/149 5.00 12.00
14 Kevin Garnett/149 5.00 12.00
15 Tyreke Evans/149 2.00 5.00
16 Michael Carter-Williams/149 2.00 5.00
17 Kawhi Leonard/149 5.00 12.00
18 Kevin Durant/49 6.00 15.00
19 Manu Ginobili/149 3.00 8.00
20 Derrick Rose/149 5.00 12.00

2015-16 Limited Unlimited Potential Materials

RANDOM INSERTS IN PACKS
PRINT RUNS B/WN 99-149 COPIES PER
*PRIME/25: 1.2X TO 3X BASIC
1 Aaron Gordon/149 2.50 6.00
2 Terry Rozier/149 2.50 6.00
3 Noah Vonleh/149 2.00 5.00
4 Justin Anderson/149 2.50 6.00
5 R.J. Hunter/149 2.00 5.00
6 Karl-Anthony Towns/149 10.00 25.00
7 Rakeem Christmas/149 2.00 5.00
8 Willie Cauley-Stein/149 3.00 8.00
9 Nemanja Bjelica/149 2.50 6.00
10 Myles Turner/149 3.00 8.00
11 Doug McDermott/149 2.50 6.00
12 Rodney Hood/149 2.50 6.00
13 Zach LaVine/149 3.00 8.00
14 Bobby Portis/149 3.00 8.00
15 Chris McCullough/149 2.00 5.00
16 D'Angelo Russell/149 6.00 15.00
17 Richaun Holmes/149 2.50 6.00
18 Emmanuel Mudiay/149 3.00 8.00
19 Marcelo Huertas/149 2.50 6.00
20 Trey Lyles/149 3.00 8.00
21 Dante Exum/149 2.50 6.00
22 Salah Mejri/149 2.00 5.00
23 T.J. Warren/149 2.50 6.00
24 Rondae Hollis-Jefferson/149 2.50 6.00
25 Montrezl Harrell/149 2.50 6.00
26 Jahlil Okafor/149 5.00 12.00
27 Pat Connaughton/149 2.00 5.00
28 Stanley Johnson/149 2.50 6.00
29 Andrew Wiggins/149 5.00 12.00
30 Devin Booker/149 6.00 15.00
31 Marcus Smart/149 2.50 6.00
32 Jerian Grant/149 2.00 5.00
33 Jordan Clarkson/149 3.00 8.00
34 Tyus Jones/149 3.00 8.00
35 Jordan Mickey/149 2.00 5.00
36 Kristaps Porzingis/99 10.00 25.00
37 Joe Young/149 2.50 6.00
38 Frank Kaminsky/149 3.00 8.00
39 Jabari Parker/149 4.00 10.00
40 Cameron Payne/149 2.50 6.00
41 Julius Randle/99 3.00 8.00
42 Delon Wright/149 2.50 6.00
43 Langston Galloway/149 2.00 5.00
44 Jarell Martin/149 2.50 6.00
45 Anthony Brown/149 2.00 5.00
46 Mario Hezonja/149 2.50 6.00
47 Raul Neto/149 2.00 5.00
48 Justise Winslow/149 3.00 8.00
49 Elfrid Payton/149 2.50 6.00
50 Kelly Oubre Jr./149 2.50 6.00

2016-17 Limited

JSY AU RC RANDOMLY INSERTED
101-140 PRINT RUN 99 SER.#'d SETS
SPs RANDOMLY INSERTED IN PACKS
1 C.J. McCollum .50 1.25
2 Draymond Green .75 2.00
3 Kyle Lowry .50 1.25
4 Chris Paul .75 2.00
5 Justise Winslow .50 1.25
6 Dwight Howard .50 1.25
7 Jrue Holiday .50 1.25
8 Nicolas Batum .50 1.25
9 Nikola Vucevic .50 1.25
10 Harrison Barnes .50 1.25
11 Al-Farouq Aminu .50 1.25
12 Kentavious Caldwell-Pope .50 1.25
13 DeMar DeRozan .60 1.50
14 Blake Griffin .60 1.50
15 Goran Dragic .50 1.25
16 Paul Millsap .60 1.50
17 Tyreke Evans .40 1.00
18 Kemba Walker .60 1.50
19 Mario Hezonja .40 1.00
20 Emmanuel Mudiay .50 1.25
21 DeMarcus Cousins .60 1.50
22 Patrick Beverley .40 1.00
23 Jonas Valanciunas .50 1.25
24 DeAndre Jordan .60 1.50
25 Hassan Whiteside .50 1.25
26 Kyle Korver .50 1.25
27 Anthony Davis 1.25 3.00
28 Rajon Rondo .60 1.50
29 Evan Fournier .50 1.25
30 Jusuf Nurkic .40 1.00
31 Willie Cauley-Stein .50 1.25
32 Trevor Ariza .40 1.00
33 Derrick Favors .50 1.25
34 D'Angelo Russell .75 2.00
35 Jabari Parker .75 2.00
36 Al Horford .50 1.25
37 Brandon Jennings .40 1.00
38 Dwyane Wade 1.00 2.50
39 Nerlens Noel .50 1.25
40 Nikola Jokic .60 1.50
41 Rudy Gay .60 1.50
42 Ryan Anderson .50 1.25
43 Gordon Hayward .60 1.50
44 Jordan Clarkson .50 1.25
45 Giannis Antetokounmpo 1.25 3.00
46 Isaiah Thomas .60 1.50
47 Carmelo Anthony .75 2.00
48 Jimmy Butler .60 1.50
49 Jahlil Okafor .50 1.25
50 Reggie Jackson .50 1.25
51 Arron Afflalo .40 1.00
52 Jeff Teague .50 1.25
53 Rudy Gobert .60 1.50
54 Julius Randle .60 1.50
55 Michael Carter-Williams .40 1.00
56 Jae Crowder .50 1.25
57 Kristaps Porzingis 1.25 3.00
58 Kyrie Irving 1.25 3.00
59 Joel Embiid 1.00 2.50
60 Tobias Harris .50 1.25
61 Kawhi Leonard 1.00 2.50
62 Monta Ellis .50 1.25
63 John Wall .75 2.00
64 Luol Deng .50 1.25
65 Ricky Rubio .60 1.50
66 Brook Lopez .50 1.25
67 Joakim Noah .50 1.25
68 Tristan Thompson .50 1.25
69 Tyson Chandler .50 1.25
70 Andre Drummond .60 1.50
71 Pau Gasol .60 1.50
72 Paul George .75 2.00
73 Bradley Beal .60 1.50
74 Mike Conley .50 1.25
75 Zach LaVine .60 1.50
76 Jeremy Lin .60 1.50
77 Enes Kanter .40 1.00
78 Kevin Love .60 1.50
79 Devin Booker 1.00 2.50
80 Stephen Curry 2.50 6.00
81 LaMarcus Aldridge .60 1.50
82 Myles Turner .50 1.25
83 Otto Porter .50 1.25
84 Marc Gasol .60 1.50
85 Andrew Wiggins 1.00 2.50
86 Bojan Bogdanovic .40 1.00
87 Victor Oladipo .50 1.25
88 Dirk Nowitzki .75 2.00
89 Eric Bledsoe .50 1.25
90 Kevin Durant 1.50 4.00
91 Tony Parker .60 1.50
92 Paul Pierce .60 1.50
93 Marcin Gortat .50 1.25
94 Chandler Parsons .50 1.25
95 Karl-Anthony Towns 1.50 4.00
96 Roy Hibbert .50 1.25
97 Steven Adams .50 1.25
98 Deron Williams .50 1.25
99 Damian Lillard 1.25 3.00
100 Klay Thompson .75 2.00
101 Taurean Prince JSY AU RC 5.00 12.00
102 DeAndre' Bembry JSY AU RC 3.00 8.00
103 Jaylen Brown JSY AU RC 20.00 50.00
104 Demetrius Jackson JSY AU RC 3.00 8.00
105 Isaiah Whitehead JSY AU RC
106 Caris LeVert JSY AU RC 4.00 10.00
107 D.Valentine JSY AU RC 8.00 20.00
108 Kay Felder JSY AU RC 3.00 8.00
109 A.J. Hammons JSY AU RC 3.00 8.00
110 Jamal Murray JSY AU RC 20.00 50.00
111 Malik Beasley JSY AU RC 3.00 8.00
112 Juan Hernangomez JSY AU RC 4.00 10.00
113 Henry Ellenson JSY AU RC 4.00 10.00
114 Damian Jones JSY AU RC 3.00 8.00
115 P.McCaw JSY AU RC 10.00 25.00
116 Georges Niang JSY AU RC 5.00 12.00
117 Chinanu Onuaku JSY AU RC 3.00 8.00
118 Brice Johnson JSY AU RC 3.00 8.00
119 Diamond Stone JSY AU RC 3.00 8.00
120 B.Ingram JSY AU RC 30.00 80.00
121 Ivica Zubac JSY AU RC 15.00 40.00
122 Wade Baldwin IV JSY AU RC 3.00 8.00
123 Deyonta Davis JSY AU RC 3.00 8.00
124 Thon Maker JSY AU RC 40.00 100.00
125 Kris Dunn JSY AU RC 20.00 50.00
126 Buddy Hield JSY AU RC 20.00 50.00
127 Cheick Diallo JSY AU RC 3.00 8.00
128 D.Sabonis JSY AU RC 5.00 12.00
129 Stephen Zimmerman JSY AU RC 3.00 8.00
130 Lwwu-Cabarrot JSY AU RC 6.00 15.00
131 Dario Saric JSY AU RC 12.00 30.00
132 Dragan Bender JSY AU RC 4.00 10.00
133 M.Chriss JSY AU RC 8.00 20.00
134 Tyler Ulis JSY AU RC 12.00 30.00
135 Georgios Papagiannis JSY AU RC 3.00 8.00
136 Malachi Richardson JSY AU RC
137 Labissiere JSY AU RC 8.00 20.00
138 Dejounte Murray JSY AU RC
139 Jakob Poeltl JSY AU RC 4.00 10.00
140 Pascal Siakam JSY AU RC 3.00 8.00
141 LeBron James SP 6.00 15.00
142 James Harden SP 2.50 6.00
143 Derrick Rose SP 2.00 5.00
144 Russell Westbrook SP 4.00 10.00
145 Ben Simmons SP RC 60.00 150.00
146 Malcolm Brogdon SP RC 4.00 10.00
147 Georgios Papagiannis SP RC 1.00 2.50
148 Willy Hernangomez SP RC 8.00 20.00
149 Ron Baker SP RC 6.00 15.00
150 Alex Abrines SP RC 12.00 30.00

2016-17 Limited Gold Spotlight

*GLD SPTLGHT 1-100: 1.2X TO 3X BASIC
*GLD SPTLGHT 101-140: .6X TO 1.5X BASIC
RANDOM INSERTS IN PACKS
PRINT RUNS B/WN 10-25 COPIES PER
NO PRICING ON QTY 10

2016-17 Limited Red Spotlight

*RED SPOTLIGHT: .6X TO 1.5X BASIC
RANDOM INSERTS IN PACKS
STATED PRINT RUN 99 SER.#'d SETS

2016-17 Limited Silver Spotlight

*SLVR SPTLGHT 1-100: .75X TO 2X BASIC
*SLVR SPTLGHT 101-140: .4X TO 1X BASIC
RANDOM INSERTS IN PACKS
STATED PRINT RUN 49 SER.#'d SETS
131 Dario Saric JSY AU 20.00 50.00

2016-17 Limited Counterparts

RANDOM INSERTS IN PACKS
1 Iverson/Bryant 5.00 12.00
2 Anthony/James 5.00 12.00
3 Olajuwon/O'Neal 3.00 8.00
4 Harden/Paul 2.00 5.00
5 Bird/Johnson 3.00 8.00
6 James/Curry 6.00 15.00
7 Olajuwon/Ewing 1.50 4.00
8 DeRozan/Irving 2.50 6.00
9 Johnson/Erving 3.00 8.00
10 Lillard/Curry 5.00 12.00
11 Kidd/Nash 1.25 3.00
12 Durant/James 5.00 12.00
13 Nash/Parker 1.25 3.00
14 Westbrook/Durant 3.00 8.00
15 Russell/Chamberlain 2.50 6.00
16 Westbrook/Curry 5.00 12.00
17 Robinson/Olajuwon 2.00 5.00
18 Westbrook/Leonard 3.00 8.00
19 Malone/Kemp 2.00 5.00
20 McGrady/Bryant 5.00 12.00

2016-17 Limited Decade Dominance Materials

RANDOM INSERTS IN PACKS
STATED PRINT RUN 99 SER. #'d SETS
1 LeBron James 10.00 25.00
2 Russell Westbrook 4.00 10.00
3 Kobe Bryant 8.00 20.00
4 Allen Iverson 4.00 10.00
5 Shaquille O'Neal 6.00 15.00
6 Magic Johnson 6.00 15.00
7 Stephen Curry 10.00 25.00
8 James Harden 4.00 10.00
9 Kevin Garnett 5.00 12.00
10 Scottie Pippen 8.00 20.00
11 Dan Issel 2.50 6.00
12 Rick Barry 2.50 6.00
13 Anthony Davis 6.00 15.00
14 Dennis Rodman 6.00 15.00
15 Larry Bird 12.00 30.00
16 Andre Drummond 3.00 8.00
17 DeMarcus Cousins 3.00 8.00
18 Alex English 2.50 6.00
19 Anfernee Hardaway 6.00 15.00
20 Paul Pierce 3.00 8.00

2016-17 Limited Limited Jersey Signatures

RANDOM INSERTS IN PACKS
PRINT RUNS B/WN 25-99 COPIES PER
1 Victor Oladipo/99 4.00 10.00
2 Brandon Knight/49
3 Isaiah Thomas/49
4 Kevin Durant/25 75.00 200.00
5 Marcin Gortat/99
6 Alex Len/99 3.00 8.00
7 Clyde Drexler/49 10.00 25.00
8 Devin Harris/99
10 Nikola Mirotic/99 4.00 10.00
11 Maurice Harkless/99 3.00 8.00
12 Chauncey Billups/99 6.00 15.00
13 Justise Winslow/99 4.00 10.00
14 Carmelo Anthony/25 20.00 50.00
15 Nick Van Exel/49
17 Kevin McHale/49 10.00 25.00
18 Frank Kaminsky/99 4.00 10.00
19 Damjan Rudez/99 3.00 8.00
20 Tristan Thompson/99 4.00 10.00
21 P.J. Tucker/99 3.00 8.00
22 Danilo Gallinari/89 4.00 10.00
23 Kenneth Faried/99
24 Chris Paul/25 20.00 50.00
25 Ralph Sampson/99
26 Bobby Portis/99 3.00 8.00
27 Jason Smith/99 3.00 8.00
28 Gary Harris/99 4.00 10.00
29 Brian Roberts/99 3.00 8.00
30 Tyson Chandler/80 4.00 10.00
31 Norman Powell/99 3.00 8.00
32 Danny Manning/99
33 Khris Middleton/99
34 Dwyane Wade/25 25.00 60.00
35 Robert Parish/99 5.00 12.00
36 Cody Zeller/99 3.00 8.00
37 Terrence Jones/99 4.00 10.00
38 Hassan Whiteside/99
39 Tony Snell/99 3.00 8.00
40 Kobe Bryant/25 125.00 250.00
41 Archie Goodwin/99 3.00 8.00
42 Eric Bledsoe/49
43 LaMarcus Aldridge/49 5.00 12.00
44 Dirk Nowitzki/99 50.00 120.00
45 Tobias Harris/99
46 Dante Exum/49 4.00 10.00
47 Dwight Powell/99
48 Jonas Valanciunas/99 4.00 10.00
49 Kyle Anderson/99 3.00 8.00
50 Artis Gilmore/49 6.00 15.00
51 T.J. McConnell/99 5.00 12.00
52 Goran Dragic/49
53 Louis Dampier/99
54 Anthony Davis/25 25.00 60.00
55 Hakeem Olajuwon/49 15.00 40.00
56 Derrick Williams/40 3.00 8.00
57 Kelly Olynyk/99 3.00 8.00
58 Jordan Clarkson/99 4.00 10.00
59 Mario Hezonja/99 3.00 8.00
60 Bernard King/49 4.00 10.00

2016-17 Limited Limited Jersey Signatures Gold Spotlight

*GOLD p/r 25: .5X TO 1.2X BASIC p/r 40-99
RANDOM INSERTS IN PACKS
PRINT RUNS B/WN 5-25 COPIES PER
NO PRICING ON QTY 10 OR LESS
9 Adreian Payne/25 4.00 10.00

2016-17 Limited Limited Jersey Signatures Silver Spotlight

*SILVER p/r 49: .4X TO 1X BASIC p/r 40-99
*SILVER p/r 25: .5X TO 1.2X BASIC p/r 40-99
RANDOM INSERTS IN PACKS
PRINT RUNS B/WN 10-49 COPIES PER
9 Adreian Payne/49 3.00 8.00
16 Andrew Nicholson/49 3.00 8.00

2016-17 Limited Limited Legends Jersey Autographs

RANDOM INSERTS IN PACKS
STATED PRINT RUN 25 SER. #'d SETS
1 Scottie Pippen 50.00 120.00
2 Karl Malone 25.00 60.00
3 Patrick Ewing 75.00 150.00
4 David Robinson 15.00 40.00
5 Hakeem Olajuwon 20.00 50.00
6 Clyde Drexler 12.00 30.00
7 Kevin McHale 12.00 30.00
8 Dennis Rodman 15.00 40.00
9 Kobe Bryant 100.00 250.00
10 Yao Ming 30.00 80.00

2016-17 Limited Limited Rookies

RANDOM INSERTS IN PACKS
1 Malik Beasley .75 2.00
2 Kris Dunn 2.50 6.00
3 Dario Saric 4.00 10.00
4 Marquese Chriss 2.00 5.00
5 Pascal Siakam .75 2.00
6 Taurean Prince 1.25 3.00
7 Denzel Valentine 1.00 2.50
8 Ben Simmons 50.00 120.00
9 Wade Baldwin IV .75 2.00
10 Jaylen Brown 3.00 8.00
11 Caris LeVert 1.00 2.50
12 Buddy Hield 2.00 5.00
13 DeAndre' Bembry .75 2.00
14 Jakob Poeltl 1.00 2.50
15 Skal Labissiere 1.25 3.00
16 Georgios Papagiannis .75 2.00
17 Juan Hernangomez 1.00 2.50
18 Brandon Ingram 5.00 12.00
19 Henry Ellenson 1.00 2.50
20 Dragan Bender 1.00 2.50
21 Malachi Richardson 1.00 2.50
22 Jamal Murray 2.50 6.00
23 Brice Johnson .75 2.00
24 Thon Maker 2.50 6.00
25 Dejounte Murray 5.00 12.00

2016-17 Limited No Limit

STATED ODDS 1:12 HOBBY
1 Carmelo Anthony 3.00 8.00
2 Klay Thompson 3.00 8.00
3 Kawhi Leonard 4.00 10.00
4 Karl-Anthony Towns 6.00 15.00
5 Jimmy Butler 2.50 6.00
6 Stephen Curry 10.00 25.00
7 Andrew Wiggins 4.00 10.00
8 Kevin Durant 6.00 15.00
9 Kristaps Porzingis 5.00 12.00
10 James Harden 4.00 10.00
11 Devin Booker 4.00 10.00
12 Kyrie Irving 5.00 12.00
13 Anthony Davis 5.00 12.00
14 LeBron James 20.00 50.00
15 Russell Westbrook 6.00 15.00

2016-17 Limited Phenoms Jersey Autographs

PRINT RUNS B/WN 25-99 COPIES PER
1 Bill Laimbeer/99 4.00 10.00
2 Hassan Whiteside/99
3 Kevin Durant/25 75.00 200.00
4 Tyson Chandler/49 4.00 10.00
5 Anthony Davis/25 25.00 60.00
7 Andrew Wiggins/49 15.00 40.00
8 Vince Carter/49 12.00 30.00
9 Jason Kidd/49 12.00 30.00
10 Dante Exum/49 4.00 10.00
11 Zydrunas Ilgauskas/99 4.00 10.00
12 Jonas Valanciunas/99 4.00 10.00
13 Carmelo Anthony/25 20.00 50.00
14 Kobe Bryant/25 125.00 250.00
15 Kyrie Irving/25
17 Karl-Anthony Towns/49 50.00 120.00
18 Alex Len/99 3.00 8.00
19 Rashard Lewis/99 4.00 10.00
21 Mark Price/99 5.00 12.00
22 Jordan Clarkson/99 4.00 10.00
23 Chris Paul/25 20.00 50.00
24 Jason Smith/99 3.00 8.00
25 Dwight Howard/25 12.00 30.00
26 Damjan Rudez/99 3.00 8.00
27 D'Angelo Russell/49 15.00 40.00
29 Glen Rice/99 4.00 10.00
30 Devin Harris/99
31 Dennis Scott/99 3.00 8.00
32 Nikola Mirotic/99 4.00 10.00
33 Dwyane Wade/25 25.00 60.00
34 Terrence Jones/99 4.00 10.00
35 Paul George/25
36 Brian Roberts/99 3.00 8.00
37 Kevin Love/49 15.00 40.00
38 Bobby Portis/99 3.00 8.00
39 Dikembe Mutombo/99 5.00 12.00
40 Frank Kaminsky/99 4.00 10.00
41 Kenny Anderson/99
42 Tristan Thompson/99 4.00 10.00
43 Dirk Nowitzki/25 60.00 150.00
44 Dwight Powell/99
45 Pau Gasol/25
47 Deron Williams/99 4.00 10.00
48 Cody Zeller/49 3.00 8.00
49 Shawn Kemp/99 50.00 120.00
50 Gary Harris/99 4.00 10.00

2016-17 Limited Phenoms Jersey Autographs Prime

*PRIME/20-39: .5X TO 1.2X BASIC p/r 49-99
RANDOM INSERTS IN PACKS
PRINT RUNS B/WN 5-39 COPIES PER
NO PRICING ON QTY 10 OR LESS
16 Adreian Payne/39 4.00 10.00
28 Andrew Nicholson/39 4.00 10.00

2016-17 Limited Preparation Jerseys

STATED ODDS 1:24 HOBBY
STATED PRINT RUN 99 SER. #'d SETS
*PRIME/22-29: .75X TO 2X BASIC
1 Stephen Curry 10.00 25.00
2 LeBron James 10.00 25.00
3 Karl-Anthony Towns 5.00 12.00
4 Kenneth Faried 2.50 6.00
5 Kobe Bryant 8.00 20.00
6 Emmanuel Mudiay 2.50 6.00
7 Kyrie Irving 5.00 12.00
8 Andrew Wiggins 5.00 12.00
9 Larry Bird 12.00 30.00
10 Shaquille O'Neal 6.00 15.00

2016-17 Limited Rookie Phenoms Jersey Autographs

STATED PRINT RUN 99 SER. #'d SETS
1 Marquese Chriss 10.00 25.00
2 Henry Ellenson 4.00 10.00
3 Skal Labissiere 5.00 12.00
4 Chinanu Onuaku 3.00 8.00
5 Ivica Zubac 20.00 50.00
6 Taurean Prince 5.00 12.00
7 Kris Dunn 10.00 25.00
8 Isaiah Whitehead 3.00 8.00
9 Stephen Zimmerman 3.00 8.00
10 A.J. Hammons 3.00 8.00
11 Tyler Ulis 10.00 25.00
12 Damian Jones 3.00 8.00
13 Dejounte Murray
14 Brice Johnson 3.00 8.00
15 Wade Baldwin IV 3.00 8.00
16 DeAndre' Bembry 3.00 8.00
17 Buddy Hield 12.00 30.00
18 Caris LeVert 4.00 10.00
19 Timothe Luwawu-Cabarrot 6.00 15.00
20 Jamal Murray 15.00 40.00
21 Georgios Papagiannis 3.00 8.00
22 Patrick McCaw 12.00 30.00
23 Jakob Poeltl 4.00 10.00
24 Diamond Stone 3.00 8.00
25 Deyonta Davis 3.00 8.00
26 Jaylen Brown 20.00 50.00
27 Cheick Diallo 3.00 8.00
28 Denzel Valentine 8.00 20.00
29 Dario Saric 20.00 50.00
30 Malik Beasley 3.00 8.00
31 Malachi Richardson 4.00 10.00
32 Georges Niang 6.00 15.00
33 Pascal Siakam 3.00 8.00
34 Brandon Ingram 30.00 80.00
35 Thon Maker 25.00 60.00
36 Demetrius Jackson 3.00 8.00
37 Domantas Sabonis 8.00 20.00
38 Kay Felder 3.00 8.00
39 Dragan Bender 8.00 20.00
40 Juan Hernangomez 4.00 10.00

2016-17 Limited Rookie Phenoms Jersey Autographs Prime

*PRIME/20-25: .5X TO 1.2X BASIC
RANDOM INSERTS IN PACKS
PRINT RUNS B/WN 10-39 COPIES PER
NO PRICING ON QTY 10 OR LESS
26 Jaylen Brown/39 40.00 100.00

2016-17 Limited Star Factor

RANDOM INSERTS IN PACKS
1 Draymond Green 1.50 4.00
2 Anthony Davis 2.50 6.00
3 Andre Drummond 1.25 3.00
4 Carmelo Anthony 1.50 4.00
5 DeAndre Jordan 1.25 3.00
6 Paul George 1.50 4.00
7 John Wall 1.50 4.00
8 Andrew Wiggins 2.00 5.00
9 Isaiah Thomas 1.25 3.00
10 James Harden 2.00 5.00
11 Ricky Rubio 1.25 3.00
12 LeBron James 15.00 40.00
13 Hassan Whiteside 1.00 2.50
14 Klay Thompson 1.50 4.00
15 Chris Paul 1.50 4.00
16 Jimmy Butler 1.25 3.00
17 DeMarcus Cousins 1.25 3.00
18 Kevin Durant 3.00 8.00
19 Kyle Lowry 1.00 2.50
20 Devin Booker 2.00 5.00
21 Karl-Anthony Towns 3.00 8.00
22 Russell Westbrook 3.00 8.00
23 Giannis Antetokounmpo 2.50 6.00
24 Kawhi Leonard 2.00 5.00
25 Blake Griffin 1.25 3.00
26 Stephen Curry 5.00 12.00
27 Damian Lillard 2.50 6.00
28 Kristaps Porzingis 2.50 6.00
29 Dwight Howard 1.00 2.50
30 Kyrie Irving 2.50 6.00

2016-17 Limited Team Trademarks Jerseys

RANDOM INSERTS IN PACKS
STATED PRINT RUN 99 SER. #'d SETS
*PRIME/23-25: 1X TO 2.5X BASIC
1 Kyle Korver 2.50 6.00
2 Isaiah Thomas 8.00 20.00
3 Brook Lopez 2.50 6.00
4 Nicolas Batum 2.50 6.00
5 Taj Gibson 2.50 6.00
6 Kyrie Irving 5.00 12.00
7 Dirk Nowitzki 4.00 10.00
8 Andre Drummond 3.00 8.00
9 Kenneth Faried 2.50 6.00
10 Andre Iguodala 2.50 6.00
11 James Harden 4.00 10.00
12 Monta Ellis 2.50 6.00
13 Blake Griffin 3.00 8.00
14 Jordan Clarkson 2.50 6.00
15 Zach Randolph 2.50 6.00
16 Udonis Haslem 2.00 5.00
17 Greg Monroe 2.50 6.00
18 Karl-Anthony Towns 5.00 12.00
19 Tyreke Evans 2.00 5.00
20 Carmelo Anthony 4.00 10.00
21 Russell Westbrook 4.00 10.00
22 Mario Hezonja 2.00 5.00
23 Nerlens Noel 2.50 6.00
24 Eric Bledsoe 2.50 6.00
25 Damian Lillard 4.00 10.00

26 DeMarcus Cousins 3.00 8.00
27 Kawhi Leonard 4.00 10.00
28 Kyle Lowry 2.50 6.00
29 Rodney Hood 2.50 6.00
30 John Wall 4.00 10.00

2016-17 Limited Unlimited Potential Materials

RANDOM INSERTS IN PACKS
STATED PRINT RUN 99 SER. #'d SETS
*PRIME/20-39: .75X TO 2X BASIC
1 Buddy Hield 5.00 12.00
2 Georgios Papagiannis 2.00 5.00
3 Marquese Chriss 5.00 12.00
4 Deyonta Davis 2.00 5.00
5 Ivica Zubac 3.00 8.00
6 Dario Saric 6.00 15.00
7 Stephen Zimmerman 2.00 5.00
8 Pascal Siakam 2.00 5.00
9 Dejounte Murray 4.00 10.00
10 Domantas Sabonis 3.00 8.00
11 Caris LeVert 2.50 6.00
12 Patrick McCaw 4.00 10.00
13 Henry Ellenson 2.50 6.00
14 Jaylen Brown 4.00 10.00
15 Taurean Prince 3.00 8.00
16 Malik Beasley 2.00 5.00
17 A.J. Hammons 2.00 5.00
18 Brandon Ingram 6.00 15.00
19 Brice Johnson 2.00 5.00
20 Kay Felder 2.00 5.00
21 Timothe Luwawu-Cabarrot 4.00 10.00
22 Jakob Poeltl 2.50 6.00
23 Skal Labissiere 3.00 8.00
24 Cheick Diallo 2.00 5.00
25 Kris Dunn 4.00 10.00
26 Malachi Richardson 2.50 6.00
27 Tyler Ulis 6.00 15.00
28 Thon Maker 4.00 10.00
29 Wade Baldwin IV 2.00 5.00
30 Dragan Bender 2.50 6.00
31 Jamal Murray 4.00 10.00
32 Diamond Stone 2.00 5.00
33 Chinanu Onuaku 2.00 5.00
34 Denzel Valentine 2.50 6.00
35 Isaiah Whitehead 2.00 5.00
37 Damian Jones 2.00 5.00
38 Demetrius Jackson 2.00 5.00
39 DeAndre' Bembry 2.00 5.00
40 Juan Hernangomez 2.50 6.00

1973-74 Linnett Portraits

Measuring 8 1/2" by 11", these 112 charcoal drawings are facial portraits by noted sports artist Charles Linnett. The player's facsimile autograph is inscribed across the lower right corner. The backs are blank. Three portraits of players from the same team were included in each clear plastic packet. A checklist was also included in each packet, with an offer to order individual player portraits for 50 cents each. Originally, the suggested retail price was 99 cents. In later issues, the price was raised to $1.19. The portraits are unnumbered and listed alphabetically according to teams as follows: Atlanta Hawks (1-10), Boston Celtics (11-22), Buffalo Braves (23-33), Capitol Bullets (34-36), Chicago Bulls (37-43), Cleveland Cavaliers (44-45), Detroit Pistons (46), Golden State Warriors (47-56), Houston Rockets (57-59), Kansas City-Omaha Kings (60-67), Los Angeles Lakers (68-76), Milwaukee Bucks (77-85), New York Knicks (86-96), Philadelphia 76ers (97), Phoenix Suns (98-105), Portland Trail Blazers (106-107), and Seattle Supersonics (108). This listing concludes with four Harlem Globetrotter portraits (109-112).

COMPLETE SET (112) 350.00 700.00
1 Walt Bellamy 2.50 6.00
2 Steve Bracey 2.00 5.00
3 John Brown 2.00 5.00
4 Bob Christian 2.00 5.00
5 Herm Gilliam 2.00 5.00
6 Lou Hudson 2.50 6.00
7 Dwight Jones 2.00 5.00
8 Pete Maravich 12.50 25.00
9 Dale Schlueter 2.00 5.00
10 Jim Washington 2.00 5.00
11 Don Chaney 2.50 6.00
12 Dave Cowens 5.00 10.00
13 Steve Downing 2.00 5.00
14 Hank Finkel 2.00 5.00
15 Phil Hankinson 2.00 5.00
16 John Havlicek 7.50 15.00
17 Steve Kuberski 2.00 5.00
18 Don Nelson 3.00 8.00
19 Paul Silas 2.50 6.00
20 Paul Westphal 5.00 10.00
21 Jo Jo White 2.50 6.00
22 Art Williams 2.00 5.00
23 Ken Charles 2.00 5.00
24 Ernie DiGregorio 3.00 8.00
(Wearing a turtle neck)
25 Ernie DiGregorio 3.00 8.00
(Wearing a t-shirt)
26 Garfield Heard 2.50 6.00
27 Bob Kauffman 2.00 5.00
28 Mike Macaluso 2.00 5.00
29 Bob McAdoo 6.00 12.00
30 Jim McMillian 2.50 6.00
31 Paul Ruffner 2.00 5.00
32 Randy Smith 2.50 6.00
33 Dave Wohl 2.00 5.00
34 Archie Clark 2.50 6.00
35 Elvin Hayes 6.00 12.00
36 Howard Porter 2.50 6.00
37 Dennis Awtrey 2.00 5.00
38 Tom Boerwinkle 2.50 6.00
39 Bob Love 2.50 6.00
40 Jerry Sloan 3.00 8.00
41 Norm Van Lier 2.50 6.00
42 Chet Walker 2.50 6.00
43 Bob Weiss 2.50 6.00
44 Austin Carr 2.50 6.00
45 Lenny Wilkens 3.00 8.00
46 Bob Lanier 5.00 10.00
47 Jim Barnett 2.00 5.00
48 Rick Barry 5.00 10.00
49 Butch Beard 2.50 6.00
50 Derrek Dickey 2.50 6.00
51 Charlie Johnson 2.00 5.00
52 Clyde Lee 2.00 5.00
53 Jeff Mullins 2.50 6.00
54 Clifford Ray 2.00 5.00
55 Cazzie Russell 2.50 6.00
56 Nate Thurmond 3.00 8.00
57 Kevin Kunnert 2.00 5.00
58 Calvin Murphy 3.00 8.00
59 Jimmy Walker 2.50 6.00
60 Nate Archibald 3.00 8.00
61 Ron Behagen 2.00 5.00
62 John Block 2.00 5.00
63 Mike D'Antoni 2.00 5.00
64 Ken Durrett 2.00 5.00
65 Sam Lacey 2.00 5.00
66 Larry McNeill 2.00 5.00
67 Nate Williams 2.00 5.00
68 Bill Bridges 2.00 5.00
69 Mel Counts 2.00 5.00
70 Keith Erickson 2.00 5.00
71 Gail Goodrich 3.00 8.00
72 Happy Hairston 2.50 6.00
73 Jim Price 2.00 5.00
74 Pat Riley 6.00 12.00
75 Elmore Smith 2.00 5.00
76 Jerry West 6.00 12.00
77 Kareem Abdul-Jabbar 10.00 20.00
78 Lucius Allen 2.00 5.00
79 Bob Dandridge 2.50 6.00
80 Mickey Davis 2.00 5.00
81 Terry Driscoll 2.00 5.00
82 Russell Lee 2.00 5.00
83 Jon McGlocklin 2.00 5.00
84 Curtis Perry 2.00 5.00
85 Oscar Robertson 5.00 10.00
86 Henry Bibby 2.50 6.00
87 Bill Bradley 6.00 12.00
88 Dave DeBusschere 3.00 8.00
89 Walt Frazier 5.00 10.00
90 John Gianelli 2.00 5.00
91 Phil Jackson 5.00 10.00
92 Jerry Lucas 3.00 8.00
93 Dean Meminger 2.00 5.00
94 Earl Monroe 3.00 8.00
95 Willis Reed 3.00 8.00
96 Harthorne Wingo 2.00 5.00
97 Tom Van Arsdale 2.50 6.00
98 Mike Bantom 2.00 5.00
99 Corky Calhoun 2.00 5.00
100 Lamar Green 2.00 5.00
101 Clem Haskins 2.00 5.00
102 Connie Hawkins 5.00 10.00
103 Charlie Scott 2.50 6.00
104 Dick Van Arsdale 2.50 6.00
105 Neal Walk 2.00 5.00
106 Geoff Petrie 2.50 6.00
107 Sidney Wicks 3.00 8.00
108 Spencer Haywood 3.00 8.00
109 Geese Ausbie 2.50 6.00
110 Marques Haynes 3.00 8.00
111 Meadowlark Lemon 3.00 8.00
112 Curly Neal 3.00 8.00

1991 Little Basketball Big Leaguers

This 45-card set was included in a book titled "Little Basketball Big Leaguers: Amazing Boyhood Stories of Today's Basketball Stars," published by Little Simon, a division of Simon and Schuster. The book devotes two pages to each player and includes a photograph from their childhood, along with a narrative of how they made it into professional basketball. The cards are located at the back of the book in nine-card perforated sheets that measure 7 1/2" by 10 1/2". If they were separated, the individual cards would measure the standard size (2 1/2" by 3 1/2"). The fronts carry black-and-white head shot of the players taken during childhood. The picture is edged above and below by gold-orange stripes carrying the player's name and the set title respectively. The backs are borderless and have the same gold-orange stripe above and below the data listed. The backs also contain biographical information and a brief career summary. The cards are unnumbered and checklisted below in alphabetical order.

COMPLETE SET (45) 12.00 30.00
1 Danny Ainge .20 .50
2 Charles Barkley .75 2.00
3 Larry Bird 2.00 5.00
4 Rolando Blackman .10 .30
5 Muggsy Bogues .20 .50
6 Sam Bowie .10 .30
7 Brad Daugherty .10 .30
8 Johnny Dawkins .10 .30
9 James Donaldson .10 .30
10 Kevin Duckworth .10 .30
11 Chris Dudley .10 .30
12 A.J. English .10 .30
13 Harvey Grant .20 .50
Horace Grant
14 Jeff Hornacek .20 .50
15 Chris Jackson .10 .30
16 Mark Jackson .20 .50
17 Magic Johnson 1.50 4.00
18 Kevin Johnson .30 .75
19 Michael Jordan 8.00 20.00
20 Greg Kite .10 .30
21 Reggie Lewis .20 .50
22 Kevin McHale .40 1.00
23 Reggie Miller .60 1.50
24 Johnny Newman .10 .30
25 Robert Parish .30 .75
26 John Paxson .10 .30
27 Chuck Person .10 .30
28 Terry Porter .10 .30
29 Mark Price .10 .30
30 J.R. Reid .10 .30
31 Glen Rice .60 1.50
32 Doc Rivers .20 .50
33 Fred Roberts .10 .30
34 Byron Scott .20 .50
35 Jack Sikma .10 .30
36 Kenny Smith .10 .30
37 John Stockton 1.00 2.50
38 Wayman Tisdale .10 .30
39 Kiki Vandeweghe .10 .30
40 Spud Webb .20 .50
41 Dominique Wilkins .40 1.00
42 John Williams .10 .30
43 David Wood .10 .30
44 Orlando Woolridge .10 .30
45 James Worthy .40 1.00

1997 Little Sun Tim Duncan

This commemorative envelope was produced for Tim Duncan's debut night (October 31, 1997) against the Denver Nuggets. Each envelope was produced in a hand-numbered edition of 200 and could be ordered for $12.50 direct from Little Sun. Each envelope is postmarked in Denver, Colorado and features a black-and-white photograph. The front text describes Duncan's debut performance, and inside the envelope is a "stuffer card", which contains that actual box score from the game.

1 Tim Duncan 5.00 12.00

1989-90 Magic Pepsi

This eight-card set of Orlando Magic was sponsored by Pepsi. The standard-size cards feature on the front a posed color player photo, without borders on the sides. While the player's name and team logo appears in the aqua stripe above the picture, the Pepsi logo and the words "'89/'90 Inaugural Season Collector's Card" appear in red stripe below the picture. Also an official sweepstakes entry sticker is attached to each card face. This sticker was to be peeled off and affixed to an official entry form available at participating stores. By collecting four stickers, one was entitled to enter the sweepstakes. The back presents 1988-89 statistics and career highlights, and is printed in black lettering on blue background, with a white stripe at the card bottom. The cards are unnumbered and are checklisted below in alphabetical order. The set features Nick Anderson's first professional card.

COMPLETE SET (8) 15.00 40.00
1 Nick Anderson 6.00 15.00
2 Michael Ansley 2.00 5.00
3 Terry Catledge 2.00 5.00
4 Dave Corzine 2.00 5.00
5 Sidney Green 2.00 5.00
6 Otis Smith 2.00 5.00
7 Sam Vincent 2.00 5.00
8 Stuff the Magic Dragon 2.50 6.00

2001-02 Magic Topps

Produced by Topps in conjunction with AT&T, this seven-card set features a horizontal design with the Magic logo in the background and was given away during the 2001-02 season.

COMPLETE SET (7) 1.25 3.00
OM2 Darrell Armstrong .30 .75
OM3 Michael Doleac .30 .75
OM4 Pat Garrity .30 .75
OM5 Andrew DeClercq .30 .75
OM8 Bo Outlaw .30 .75
OM9 Doc Rivers CO .40 1.00
OM10 John Amaechi .30 .75

2006-07 Magic Upper Deck

COMPLETE SET (15) 5.00 12.00
1 Trevor Ariza .40 1.00
2 Carlos Arroyo .40 1.00
3 James Augustine .40 1.00
4 Tony Battie .40 1.00
5 Keith Bogans .40 1.00
6 Travis Diener .40 1.00
7 Keyon Dooling .40 1.00
8 Pat Garrity .40 1.00
9 Grant Hill 1.00 2.50
10 Dwight Howard 2.00 5.00
11 Darko Milicic .40 1.00
12 Jameer Nelson .60 1.50
13 Bo Outlaw .40 1.00
14 J.J. Redick 1.00 2.50
15 Hedo Turkoglu .40 1.00

2007-08 Magic Upper Deck

COMPLETE SET (15) 5.00 12.00
1 Trevor Ariza .40 1.00
2 Carlos Arroyo .40 1.00
3 James Augustine .40 1.00
4 Tony Battie .40 1.00
5 Keith Bogans .40 1.00
6 Keyon Dooling .40 1.00
7 Pat Garrity .40 1.00
8 Dwight Howard 1.50 4.00
9 Rashard Lewis .60 1.50
10 Jameer Nelson .60 1.50
11 J.J. Redick .40 1.00
12 Hedo Turkoglu .40 1.00
13 Marcin Gortat .40 1.00
14 Adonal Foyle .40 1.00
15 Mascot .40 1.00

2008-09 Magic Upper Deck 20th Anniversary

COMPLETE SET (20) 8.00 20.00
1 Nick Anderson .50 1.25
2 Scott Skiles .50 1.25
3 Otis Smith .50 1.25
4 Anthony Bowie .50 1.25
5 Jeff Turner .50 1.25
6 Donald Royal .50 1.25
7 Shaquille O'Neal 1.50 4.00
8 Dennis Scott .50 1.25
9 Danny Schayes .50 1.25
10 Darrell Armstrong .50 1.25
11 Bo Outlaw .50 1.25
12 Mike Miller .50 1.25
13 Pat Garrity .50 1.25
14 Tracy McGrady 1.00 2.50
15 Grant Hill 1.00 2.50
16 Jameer Nelson .60 1.50
17 Hedo Turkoglu .50 1.25
18 Dwight Howard 1.50 4.00
19 Rashard Lewis .60 1.50
20 Courtney Lee .75 2.00

1989 Magnetables

This set of 35 magnets measure approximately 2" x 3". Reportedly, there are different production numbers for each magnet with more being produced for the bigger stars. The fronts contain color action shots. The player's team name resides at the top right corner and the player's name is towards the bottom. The company that produced the set, Phoenix, is printed at the bottom left along with an NBA copyright and the year 1989.

COMPLETE SET (35) 45.00 90.00
1 Mark Aguirre 1.25 3.00
2 Willie Anderson .75 2.00
3 Charles Barkley 2.50 6.00
4 Larry Bird 3.00 8.00
5 Rolando Blackman 1.25 3.00
6 Tom Chambers 1.25 3.00
7 Clyde Drexler 2.00 5.00
8 Joe Dumars 1.25 3.00
9 Dale Ellis .75 2.00
10 Alex English 1.25 3.00
11 Patrick Ewing 1.50 4.00
12 Roy Hinson .75 2.00
13 Kevin Johnson 1.25 3.00
14 Magic Johnson 3.00 8.00
15 Vinnie Johnson .75 2.00
16 Michael Jordan 8.00 20.00
17 Bernard King 1.25 3.00
18 Bill Laimbeer 1.25 3.00
19 Dan Majerle 1.50 4.00
20 Karl Malone 2.50 6.00
21 Moses Malone 1.25 3.00
22 Kevin McHale 1.50 4.00
23 Chris Mullin 1.50 4.00
24 Ken Norman .75 2.00
25 Hakeem Olajuwon 2.00 5.00
26 Chuck Person .75 2.00
27 Mark Price 1.25 3.00
28 Mitch Richmond 2.50 6.00
29 Dennis Rodman 2.00 5.00
30 Kenny Smith .75 2.00
31 Jon Sundvold .75 2.00
32 Isiah Thomas 1.50 4.00
33 Kelly Tripucka .75 2.00
34 Dominique Wilkins 2.50 6.00
35 James Worthy 1.50 4.00

1987 Marketcom Sports Illustrated

This 20-card white-bordered, multi-sport set measures approximately 3 1/16" by 4 14/16" and features color action photos of players in various sports produced by Marketcom. Cards #1-13 display Baseball players; cards #14-17, Basketball players; cards #18-20, Football players. The backs are blank. The set was issued to promote the Sports Illustrated sticker line. The cards are unnumbered and checklisted below alphabetically within each sport.

COMPLETE SET (20) 60.00 150.00
14 Larry Bird 6.00 15.00
15 Magic Johnson 6.00 15.00
16 Michael Jordan 16.00 40.00
17 Dominique Wilkins 2.00 5.00

1971 Mattel Mini-Records

This set was designed to be played on a special Mattel mini-record player, which is not included in the complete set price. Each black plastic disc, approximately 2 1/2" in diameter, features a recording on one side and a color drawing of the player on the other. The picture appears on a paper disk that is glued onto the smooth unrecorded side of the mini-record. On the recorded side, the player's name and the set's subtitle appear in arcs stamped in the central portion of the mini-record. The hand-engraved player's name appears again along with a production number, copyright symbol, and the Mattel name and year of production in the ring between the central portion of the record and the grooves. The ivory discs are the ones which are double sided and are considered to be tougher than the black discs. They were also known as "Mattel Show 'N Tell". The discs are unnumbered and checklisted below in alphabetical order according to sport

COMPLETE SET (18) 200.00 400.00
BK1 Lew Alcindor 8.00 20.00
BK2 Elgin Baylor 4.00 10.00
BK3 Wilt Chamberlain 6.00 15.00
BK4 Jerry Lucas 2.50 6.00
BK5 Pete Maravich 8.00 20.00
BK6 John Havlicek 4.00 10.00
BK7 Willis Reed 2.50 6.00
BK8 Oscar Robertson 4.00 10.00
BK9 Bill Russell SP 50.00 100.00
BK10 Jerry West 5.00 12.00

1994-95 Mavericks Bookmarks

This set of six bookmarks was jointly sponsored by HSE, Foot Locker, and KLIF 570 AM radio. Each bookmark was given away at a home game during the 1994-95 season. Just 5,000 of each were produced. The bookmarks measure 3" by 10" and have a high-gloss UV coating. A full-bleed purple-tinted action photo appears on the front. The player's name and number appear in green typewritten lettering. The player's signature and uniform number are inscribed across the lower portion of the bookmark. On a black background, the back has a color headshot and biography as well as "college capsule" and "personal capsule" features. The message "Don't Foul Out. Stay in School." completes the back. The bookmarks are numbered on the back.

COMPLETE SET (6) 5.00 12.00
1 Jim Jackson 1.25 3.00
2 Jamal Mashburn 1.25 3.00
3 Jason Kidd 2.50 6.00
4 Popeye Jones .40 1.00
5 Tony Dumas .40 1.00
6 Terry Davis .40 1.00

1988-89 Mavericks Bud Light BLC

The 1988-89 Bud Light Dallas Mavericks set contains 14 standard-size cards comprised of 12 players and two coaches. This set was produced for distribution at the Mavericks "card night" promotion but may not have actually been used by the Mavericks. However the sets do exist within the hobby as the cards were not all destroyed. The set may have been rejected by the Mavericks because of the inclusion of Roy Tarpley and Mark Aguirre; however there is no indication that either the Tarpley or Aguirre cards is any harder to find than the others in the set. The set was produced for the Mavericks by Big League Cards of New Jersey. The set is unnumbered except for uniform numbers on the card backs.

COMPLETE SET (14) 10.00 25.00
12 Derek Harper 1.50 4.00
15 Brad Davis .50 1.25
20 Morlon Wiley .25 .60
22 Rolando Blackman 1.50 4.00
23 Bill Wennington .50 1.50
24 Mark Aguirre 1.50 4.00
32 Detlef Schrempf 3.00 8.00
33 Uwe Blab .25 .60
40 James Donaldson .25 .60
41 Terry Tyler .25 .60
42 Roy Tarpley 1.00 2.50
44 Sam Perkins 1.50 4.00
NNO Richie Adubato ACO .50 1.25
Garfield Heard ACO
NNO John MacLeod CO .50 1.25

1988-89 Mavericks Bud Light Card Night

The 1988-89 Bud Light Dallas Mavericks set contains 13 standard-size cards comprised of 12 players and head coach John MacLeod. This set was produced for distribution at the Mavericks "card night' promotion and is apparently a rework of the set immediately above since Roy Tarpley and Mark Aguirre are not even in this set and many late season acquisitions are noted. It is not known what company produced these cards for the Mavericks and Bud Light. The set is unnumbered except for uniform numbers on the card backs.

COMPLETE SET (13) 6.00 15.00
4 Adrian Dantley 1.25 3.00
12 Derek Harper 1.25 3.00
15 Brad Davis .40 1.00
20 Morlon Wiley .20 .50
21 Anthony Jones .20 .50
22 Rolando Blackman 1.25 3.00
23 Bill Wennington .40 1.00
32 Herb Williams .40 1.00
33 Uwe Blab .20 .50
40 James Donaldson .20 .50
41 Terry Tyler .20 .50
44 Sam Perkins 1.25 3.00
NNO John MacLeod CO .20 .50

1989-90 Mavericks Dr. Pepper

This 13-card standard size set was sponsored by Dr. Pepper and distributed at a Mavs home game. The fronts have color action shots surrounded by a white border. The top dawns two Dr. Pepper logos in each corner and the Mavs logo and the years 1989-1990. The players name along with team name appear at the bottom. The black and white backs have another Dr. Pepper logo, biographical player information and a small description of the player's career highlights. In addition, each card has the same anti-drug message at the bottom. The cards are unnumbered and listed below in alphabetical order.

COMPLETE SET (13) 8.00 20.00
1 Richie Adubato CO .40 1.00
2 Steve Alford 1.25 3.00
3 Rolando Blackman 1.50 4.00
4 Adrian Dantley 1.50 4.00
5 Brad Davis 1.25 3.00
6 James Donaldson .40 1.00
7 Derek Harper 1.50 4.00
8 Anthony Jones .40 1.00
9 Sam Perkins 1.50 4.00
10 Roy Tarpley .40 1.00
11 Bill Wennington .40 1.00
12 Randy White .40 1.00
13 Herb Williams .60 1.50

1987-88 Mavericks Miller Lite

This five-card set of Dallas Mavericks was sponsored by Miller Lite in conjunction with WBAP Radio 820. These oversized cards measure approximately 4" by 6". The front features a borderless color action photo of the player on white card stock. The player's number and name are given below the picture in black lettering, and sponsors' logos in the lower corners complete the card face. The backs are blank. The cards are unnumbered and we have checklisted them below in alphabetical order.

COMPLETE SET (5) 6.00 15.00
1 Mark Aguirre 1.50 4.00
2 Rolando Blackman 1.50 4.00
3 James Donaldson .75 2.00
4 Derek Harper 1.50 4.00
5 Sam Perkins 1.50 4.00

2010-11 Mavericks Panini NBA Champions

This 36-card set commemorates the 2010-11 NBA Champion Dallas Mavericks. Produced by Panini, this set was available through normal distribution channels, as well as through the companies website for an SRP of $20.

COMPLETE SET (36) 12.50 25.00
1 Dirk Nowitzki 1.00 2.50
2 Jason Kidd .75 2.00
3 Jason Terry .60 1.50
4 Tyson Chandler .60 1.50
5 Shawn Marion .60 1.50
6 J.J. Barea .60 1.50
7 DeShawn Stevenson .50 1.25
8 Brendan Haywood .50 1.25
9 Brian Cardinal .50 1.25
10 Caron Butler .60 1.50
11 Peja Stojakovic .75 2.00
12 Ian Mahinmi .75 2.00
13 Corey Brewer .50 1.25
14 Dominique Jones .50 1.25
15 Rodrigue Beaubois .50 1.25
16 Alexis Ajinca .50 1.25
17 Sasha Pavlovic .50 1.25
18 Steve Novak .50 1.25
19 Rick Carlisle CO .50 1.25
20 Playoff Win 1 .50 1.25
21 Playoff Win 2 .50 1.25
22 Playoff Win 3 .50 1.25
23 Playoff Win 4 .50 1.25
24 Playoff Win 5 .50 1.25
25 Playoff Win 6 .50 1.25
26 Playoff Win 7 .50 1.25
27 Playoff Win 8 .50 1.25
28 Playoff Win 9 .50 1.25
29 Playoff Win 10 .50 1.25
30 Playoff Win 11 .50 1.25
31 Playoff Win 12 .50 1.25
32 Playoff Win 13 .50 1.25
33 Playoff Win 14 .50 1.25
34 Playoff Win 15 .50 1.25
35 Playoff Win 16 .50 1.25
36 Dirk Nowitzki MVP 1.00 2.50

2000 Mavericks Rolando Blackman Retirement Sheet

This sheet was passed out at the March 11,2000 Mavericks game to honor all-time Maverick great, Rolando Blackman. The sheet features many different photos of Blackman, and his career statistics are on the back.

1 Rolando Blackman 1.25 3.00

1995-96 Mavericks Taco Bell

The Dallas Mavericks teamed together with Taco Bell Restaurants of Dallas/Fort Worth to issue four postcard-size (3 1/2" by 5") "Triple J" trading cards. Individual cards were cello-wrapped and available at all participating Taco Bell restaurants in the metroplex for 99 cents with any food purchase. Ten cents of every card sold was donated to the West Dallas Community School and the Boys and Girls Clubs of the Metroplex. The production run was 83,000 sets, with a different card being issued each week through February. Against a ghosted photo, the fronts display a caricature of one of the "Triple J Mavericks" by comic book illustrator Larry Webber. The player's name is stamped vertically in royal blue foil along one of the sides. The backs of all four cards can be combined to form a "Triple J" picture of all three players. Finally, a special "Triple" J ad card was distributed at the 1/27/96 Mavericks home game to kick off the promotion. Just 10,000 ad cards were produced; this card is listed below after the other cards.

COMPLETE SET (4) 2.50 6.00
1 Jim Jackson .40 1.00
2 Jason Kidd 1.25 3.00
(NBA Rookie of the Year)
3 Jason Kidd 1.25 3.00
4 Jamal Mashburn .40 1.00
NNO Triple J Ad Card 2.50 6.00

1981-82 Mavericks Team Issue

This 5" x7" set was produced for the Dallas Mavericks during the 1981-82 season. The set features five black and white cards of the team's players and coaches.

COMPLETE SET (5) 8.00 20.00
1 Mark Aguirre 2.50 6.00
2 Brad Davis 2.00 5.00
3 Jim Spanarkel 1.50 4.00
4 Tom LaGarde 1.25 3.00
5 Oliver Mack 1.25 3.00

2001-02 Mavericks Topps

Produced by Topps in association with Minyard Food Stores and Sprite, this 15-card set was given away to the first 10,000 fans at the February 21, 2002 game against the Boston Celtics. The base cards feature white borders with gray and blue framing around full color player action photos.

COMPLETE SET (15) 5.00 12.00
DMAG Adrian Griffin .40 1.00
DMDH Donnell Harvey .40 1.00
DMDN Dirk Nowitzki 1.25 3.00
DMDAN Don Nelson CO .40 1.00
DMDRM Danny Manning .50 1.25
DMEE Evan Eschmeyer .40 1.00
DMEN Eduardo Najera .40 1.00
DMGB Greg Buckner .40 1.00
DMJH Juwan Howard .50 1.25
DMJN Johnny Newman .40 1.00
DMMF Michael Finley .60 1.50
DMSB Shawn Bradley .40 1.00
DMSN Steve Nash 1.00 2.50
DMTH Tim Hardaway .60 1.50
DMWZ Wang Zhizhi .50 1.25

1990-91 McDonald's Jordan Joyner-Kersee

This 16-card set featuring Michael Jordan and Jackie Joyner-Kersee was sponsored by McDonald's restaurants as part of their "Sports Tips" series. The cards of each subject were issued on a 10 7/8" by 8 1/8" perforated sheet (two rows of four cards each) as a special insert in Sports Illustrated for Kids. The two sheets were attached connecting Michael Jordan and 1988 Olympic gold medalist Jackie Joyner-Kersee. After perforation, the cards measure the standard size (2 1/2" by 3 1/2"). The front has a color action photo of Jordan, with four different border stripes on each side of the picture: red above, green below, yellow with black dots on the left, and black , blue candy-stripe on the right. Jordan's autograph is inscribed on the red border, while the card title appears in the green border. The back has a hint on how to perform the move, a training tip, and a nutrition tip. A pink top border stripe and a green bottom border stripe frame this information. The Joyner-Kersee cards are styled similarly. The cards are numbered on both sides; the Joyner-Kersee cards are numbered below using a JK-prefix to distinguish from the similarly numbered Jordan cards.

COMPLETE SET (16) 6.00 15.00
COMMON MJ 1.00 2.50
COMMON JJK .75 2.00

1993-94 McDonald's Lakers Magnets

This 3-card set was given out at participating McDonald's restaurants during the 1993-94 season. The set features three of the L.A. Lakers players on a relatively smaller magnetic card.

COMPLETE SET (3) 6.00 15.00
1 Nick Van Exel 3.00 8.00
2 Doug Christie 1.50 4.00
3 George Lynch 1.50 4.00

1995 McDonald's Looney Tunes All-Star Showdown Cups

This six-cup set was available in McDonald's in 1995 and features NBA Players teamed up with different Looney Tunes characters. The cups are not numbered and listed below in alphabetical order.

COMPLETE SET (6) 5.00 12.00
1 Larry Bird 1.25 3.00
Sylvester
2 Charles Barkley 1.25 3.00
Tasmanian Devil
3 Shawn Kemp .60 1.50
Daffy Duck
4 Michael Jordan 3.00 8.00
Bugs Bunny
5 Larry Johnson .60 1.50
Wile E. Coyote
6 Reggie Miller 1.25 3.00
Road Runner

1994 McDonald's Nothing But Net MVP Cups

This 6-cup set was sponsored by the NBA, Coke and McDonald's and features various MVP's from the past. Each cup contains dates of important games and a quote from the player about the game. The cups are numbered.

COMPLETE SET (6) 7.00 14.00
1 Michael Jordan 2.50 6.00
2 Julius Erving 1.25 3.00
3 Larry Bird 1.25 3.00
4 Moses Malone .75 2.00
5 Charles Barkley 1.00 2.50
6 Bill Walton .75 2.00

1994 McDonald's Nothing But Net MVP Fry Boxes

This set of six MVPs was printed on boxes of McDonald's large fries and endorsed by the NBA. If cut, the cards would measure approximately 3" by 3 7/8". The fronts feature a color action player photo on a white background. The players' names are printed above their photos with the year they were voted MVP. The set title is superposed at the upper right and extends onto the box design. The information on the back is printed on the reverse side of the fries box. The data is not presented in a pie-shaped format. The player's name is printed on a team color-coded, arch-shaped bar at the top. The year (or years) the player was voted MVP is listed below, followed by the player's MVP stats. A head shot, biography and team logo round out the back. The cards are unnumbered and checklisted below in alphabetical order.

COMPLETE SET (6) 8.00 20.00
1 Charles Barkley 1993 MVP 1.50 4.00
2 Larry Bird 1984 MVP 1.50 4.00
3 Julius Erving 1981 MVP 1.50 4.00
4 Michael Jordan 2.50 6.00
1988, 1991, 1992 MVP
5 Moses Malone 1.00 2.50
1979, 1982, 1983 MVP
6 Bill Walton 1978 MVP 1.00 2.50

1992 McDonald's USA Dream Team Cups

This 10-cup set was available at McDonald's during the initial Dream Team Olympics. The cups feature career highlights of each Dream Team member and a facsimile autograph. Each of the cups are numbered. Two other cups were available via redemption (Clyde Drexler and Christian Laettner) and are not numbered. Those cups are not considered part of the set.

COMPLETE SET (10) 10.00 25.00
1 Charles Barkley 1.25 3.00
2 Larry Bird 1.50 4.00
3 Patrick Ewing .75 2.00
4 Magic Johnson 1.50 4.00
5 Michael Jordan 3.00 8.00
6 Karl Malone 1.25 3.00
7 Chris Mullin .75 2.00
8 Scottie Pippen 1.25 3.00
9 David Robinson 1.25 3.00
10 John Stockton 1.50 4.00
NNO Christian Laettner 1.50 4.00
NNO Clyde Drexler 2.50 6.00

1994 McDonald's USA Dream Team 2 Cups

Sponsored by the NBA, Coke and McDonald's, this 13-cup set features members from the USA Dream Team 2. Each cup features career highlights and carries a facsimile autograph. The cups are numbered.

COMPLETE SET (13) 6.00 15.00
1 Isiah Thomas .60 1.50
2 Larry Johnson .60 1.50
3 Shawn Kemp .60 1.50
4 Dan Majerle .60 1.50
5 Dominique Wilkins .75 2.00
6 Derrick Coleman .40 1.00
7 Alonzo Mourning .75 2.00
8 Steve Smith .60 1.50
9 Joe Dumars .60 1.50
10 Mark Price .60 1.50
11 Shaquille O'Neal 2.00 5.00
12 Reggie Miller .75 2.00
13 Tim Hardaway .60 1.50

1994 McDonald's USA Dream Team 2 Fry Boxes

This set of 11 Dream Teamers was printed on boxes of McDonald's large fries and endorsed by the NBA. The fronts feature a color player photo on a red, white and blue background. The players' names are printed above their photos inside one of the white stars. The set title is at the lower right. The information on the back is printed on the reverse side of the fries box. The back lists a schedule of games along with sponser logos for TNT, TBS and NBC. The cards are unnumbered and checklisted below in alphabetical order.

COMPLETE SET (11) 8.00 20.00
1 Derrick Coleman .75 2.00
2 Joe Dumars .75 2.00
3 Tim Hardaway .75 2.00
4 Larry Johnson .75 2.00
5 Shawn Kemp .75 2.00
6 Dan Majerle .75 2.00
7 Reggie Miller 1.50 4.00
8 Alonzo Mourning 1.25 3.00
9 Steve Smith .75 2.00
10 Isiah Thomas 1.25 3.00
11 Dominique Wilkins 1.50 4.00

1993 McDonald's/Footlocker Patrick Ewing

This 1 card set was released at participating McDonald's restaraunts during the 1993-94 season. This card is actually a game card that was good for discounts on Foot Locker prodcuts. Winners either got an autographed Patrick Ewing basketball, season tickets to see the New York Knicks play, 10% of their next purchase at Footlocker, or $50 off their next purchse at Footlocker.

1 Patrick Ewing 8.00 20.00

1995-96 Metal

The 1995-96 premiere issue of Metal basketball by Fleer/SkyBox consists of 220 standard-size cards issued in two separate series of 120 and 100 cards respectively. The eight-card packs carried a suggested retail price of $2.49 each. Borderless fronts feature the player in a full-color action cutout against a multicolored, hand engraved, metallic foil background. Backs picture the player in a full-color action shot with his team's logo printed at the bottom. The only subset is Nuts and Bolts (209-218). Rookie Cards of note include Michael Finley, Kevin Garnett, Antonio McDyess, Joe Smith, Jerry Stackhouse and Damon Stoudamire.

COMPLETE SET (220) 20.00 40.00
COMPLETE SERIES 1 (120) 10.00 20.00
COMPLETE SERIES 2 (100) 10.00 20.00
1 Stacey Augmon .20 .50
2 Mookie Blaylock .15 .40
3 Grant Long .15 .40
4 Steve Smith .20 .50
5 Dee Brown .15 .40
6 Sherman Douglas .15 .40
7 Eric Montross .15 .40
8 Dino Radja .15 .40
9 Muggsy Bogues .20 .50
10 Scott Burrell .15 .40
11 Larry Johnson .25 .60
12 Alonzo Mourning .30 .75
13 Michael Jordan 2.00 5.00
14 Toni Kukoc .25 .60
15 Scottie Pippen .40 1.00
16 Terrell Brandon .15 .40
17 Tyrone Hill .15 .40
18 Mark Price .25 .60
19 John Williams .15 .40
20 Jim Jackson .15 .40
21 Popeye Jones .15 .40
22 Jason Kidd .40 1.00
23 Jamal Mashburn .25 .60
24 Mahmoud Abdul-Rauf .15 .40
25 Dikembe Mutombo .25 .60
26 Robert Pack .15 .40
27 Jalen Rose .30 .75
28 Joe Dumars .25 .60
29 Grant Hill .40 1.00
30 Lindsey Hunter .15 .40
31 Terry Mills .15 .40
32 Tim Hardaway .25 .60
33 Donyell Marshall .15 .40
34 Chris Mullin .25 .60
35 Clifford Rozier .15 .40
36 Latrell Sprewell .25 .60
37 Sam Cassell .25 .60
38 Clyde Drexler .30 .75
39 Robert Horry .20 .50
40 Hakeem Olajuwon .30 .75
41 Kenny Smith .20 .50
42 Dale Davis .15 .40
43 Mark Jackson .20 .50
44 Derrick McKey .15 .40
45 Reggie Miller .30 .75
46 Rik Smits .20 .50
47 Lamond Murray .15 .40
48 Pooh Richardson .15 .40
49 Malik Sealy .15 .40
50 Loy Vaught .15 .40
51 Elden Campbell .15 .40
52 Cedric Ceballos .15 .40
53 Vlade Divac .25 .60
54 Eddie Jones .25 .60
55 Nick Van Exel .25 .60
56 Bimbo Coles .15 .40
57 Billy Owens .15 .40
58 Khalid Reeves .15 .40
59 Glen Rice .25 .60
60 Kevin Willis .15 .40
61 Vin Baker .20 .50
62 Todd Day .15 .40
63 Eric Murdock .15 .40
64 Glenn Robinson .20 .50
65 Tom Gugliotta .15 .40
66 Christian Laettner .20 .50
67 Isaiah Rider .25 .60
68 Kenny Anderson .20 .50
69 P.J. Brown .15 .40
70 Derrick Coleman .20 .50
71 Patrick Ewing .30 .75
72 Anthony Mason .15 .40
73 Charles Oakley .20 .50
74 John Starks .20 .50

1995-96 Metal

75 Nick Anderson .15 .40
76 Horace Grant .20 .50
77 Anfernee Hardaway .40 1.00
78 Shaquille O'Neal .60 1.50
79 Dennis Scott .15 .40
80 Dana Barros .15 .40
81 Shawn Bradley .15 .40
82 Clarence Weatherspoon .15 .40
83 Sharone Wright .15 .40
84 Charles Barkley .40 1.00
85 Kevin Johnson .25 .60
86 Dan Majerle .25 .60
87 Danny Manning .20 .50
88 Wesley Person .15 .40
89 Clifford Robinson .15 .40
90 Rod Strickland .15 .40
91 Otis Thorpe .15 .40
92 Buck Williams .15 .40
93 Brian Grant .20 .50
94 Olden Polynice .15 .40
95 Mitch Richmond .25 .60
96 Walt Williams .15 .40
97 Sean Elliott .25 .60
98 Avery Johnson .20 .50
99 David Robinson .40 1.00
100 Dennis Rodman .50 1.25
101 Shawn Kemp .25 .60
102 Nate McMillan .15 .40
103 Gary Payton .25 .60
104 Detlef Schrempf .25 .60
105 B.J. Armstrong .15 .40
106 Oliver Miller .15 .40
107 John Salley .15 .40
108 David Benoit .15 .40
109 Jeff Hornacek .20 .50
110 Karl Malone .30 .75
111 John Stockton .30 .75
112 Greg Anthony .15 .40
113 Benoit Benjamin .15 .40
114 Byron Scott .20 .50
115 Calbert Cheaney .15 .40
116 Juwan Howard .25 .60
117 Gheorghe Muresan .15 .40
118 Chris Webber .30 .75
119 Checklist .15 .40
120 Checklist .15 .40
121 Stacey Augmon .20 .50
122 Mookie Blaylock .15 .40
123 Alan Henderson RC .25 .60
124 Andrew Lang .15 .40
125 Ken Norman .15 .40
126 Steve Smith .20 .50
127 Dana Barros .15 .40
128 Rick Fox .15 .40
129 Eric Williams RC .25 .60
130 Kendall Gill .15 .40
131 Khalid Reeves .15 .40
132 Glen Rice .25 .60
133 George Zidek RC .20 .50
134 Dennis Rodman .50 1.25
135 Danny Ferry .15 .40
136 Dan Majerle .25 .60
137 Chris Mills .15 .40
138 Bobby Phills .15 .40
139 Bob Sura RC .20 .50
140 Tony Dumas .15 .40
141 Dale Ellis .15 .40
142 Don MacLean .15 .40
143 Antonio McDyess RC .30 .75
144 Bryant Stith .15 .40
145 Allan Houston .20 .50
146 Theo Ratliff RC .40 1.00
147 Otis Thorpe .15 .40
148 B.J. Armstrong .15 .40
149 Rony Seikaly .15 .40
150 Joe Smith RC .30 .75
151 Sam Cassell .25 .60
152 Clyde Drexler .30 .75
153 Robert Horry .20 .50
154 Hakeem Olajuwon .30 .75
155 Antonio Davis .15 .40
156 Ricky Pierce .15 .40
157 Brent Barry RC .40 1.00
158 Terry Dehere .15 .40
159 Rodney Rogers .15 .40
160 Brian Williams .15 .40
161 Magic Johnson .60 1.50
162 Sasha Danilovic RC .25 .60
163 Alonzo Mourning .30 .75
164 Kurt Thomas RC .25 .60
165 Sherman Douglas .15 .40
166 Shawn Respert RC .20 .50
167 Kevin Garnett RC 2.00 5.00
168 Terry Porter .15 .40
169 Shawn Bradley .15 .40
170 Kevin Edwards .15 .40
171 Ed O'Bannon RC .20 .50
172 Jayson Williams .15 .40
173 Derek Harper .20 .50
174 Charles Smith .15 .40
175 Brian Shaw .15 .40
176 Derrick Coleman .20 .50
177 Vernon Maxwell .15 .40
178 Trevor Ruffin .15 .40
179 Jerry Stackhouse RC .75 2.00
180 Michael Finley RC .75 2.00
181 A.C. Green .20 .50
182 John Williams .15 .40
183 Aaron McKie .15 .40
184 Arvydas Sabonis RC .50 1.25
185 Gary Trent RC .25 .60
186 Tyus Edney RC .25 .60
187 Sarunas Marciulionis .15 .40
188 Michael Smith .15 .40
189 Corliss Williamson RC .25 .60
190 Vinny Del Negro .15 .40
191 Hersey Hawkins .15 .40
192 Shawn Kemp .25 .60
193 Gary Payton .25 .60
194 Sam Perkins .15 .40
195 Detlef Schrempf .25 .60
196 Willie Anderson .15 .40
197 Oliver Miller .15 .40
198 Tracy Murray .15 .40
199 Alvin Robertson .15 .40
200 Damon Stoudamire RC .60 1.50
201 Chris Morris .15 .40
202 Greg Anthony .15 .40
203 Blue Edwards .15 .40
204 Eric Murdock .15 .40
205 Bryant Reeves RC .20 .50
206 Byron Scott .20 .50
207 Robert Pack .15 .40
208 Rasheed Wallace RC .75 2.00
209 Anfernee Hardaway NB .20 .50
210 Grant Hill NB .20 .50
211 Larry Johnson NB .12 .30
212 Michael Jordan NB 1.00 2.50
213 Jason Kidd NB .20 .50
214 Karl Malone NB .15 .40
215 Shaquille O'Neal NB .30 .75
216 Scottie Pippen NB .20 .50
217 David Robinson NB .20 .50
218 Glenn Robinson NB .10 .25
219 Checklist .15 .40
220 Checklist .15 .40

1995-96 Metal Silver Spotlight

COMPLETE SET (120) 25.00 60.00
*STARS: 1X TO 2.5X BASE CARD HI
ONE PER SERIES 1 PACK

1995-96 Metal Maximum Metal

Randomly inserted in all series one packs at a rate of one in 36, cards from this 10-card standard-size set highlight some NBA impact players. These cards have a basketball-shaped die cut design and feature a full-color player action cutout on the front. The background is a silver foil diamond-plate basketball going through a hoop. Backs continue with the diamond plate basketball and hoop background and also feature a full-color player cutout. The player's name and a player profile are printed on the back. The set is sequenced in alphabetical order.

COMPLETE SET (10) 15.00 40.00
SER.1 STATED ODDS 1:36 HOBBY/RETAIL
1 Charles Barkley 2.00 5.00
2 Patrick Ewing 1.50 4.00
3 Grant Hill 2.00 5.00
4 Michael Jordan 10.00 25.00
5 Shawn Kemp 1.25 3.00
6 Karl Malone 1.50 4.00
7 Hakeem Olajuwon 1.50 4.00
8 Shaquille O'Neal 3.00 8.00
9 Mitch Richmond 1.25 3.00
10 David Robinson 2.00 5.00

1995-96 Metal Metal Force

Randomly inserted exclusively in second series retail packs at a rate of one in 54, cards from this 15-card set feature a selection of the NBA's top stars and rookies. Each card is made of a clear plastic material and comes with a protective coating on front. Prices provided below refer to unpeeled cards. Peeled cards generally trade for ten to twenty-five percent less.

COMPLETE SET (15) 75.00 150.00
SER.2 STATED ODDS 1:54 RETAIL
1 Vin Baker 3.00 8.00
2 Charles Barkley 6.00 15.00
3 Cedric Ceballos 2.50 6.00
4 Grant Hill 6.00 15.00
5 Larry Johnson 4.00 10.00
6 Magic Johnson 10.00 25.00
7 Shawn Kemp 4.00 10.00
8 Karl Malone 5.00 12.00
9 Jamal Mashburn 4.00 10.00
10 Scottie Pippen 8.00 20.00
11 Glenn Robinson 3.00 8.00
12 Dennis Rodman 8.00 20.00
13 Joe Smith 2.50 6.00
14 Jerry Stackhouse 6.00 15.00
15 Chris Webber 5.00 12.00

1995-96 Metal Molten Metal

Randomly inserted in all series one packs at a rate of one in 72, cards from this 10-card standard-size set feature a selection of up and coming NBA stars. The fronts feature full-color action cutouts set against stamped multicolored laminated foil backgrounds. Borderless backs feature the player in a full-color action cutout and a white box surrounds a player profile which is printed in white type. The set is sequenced in alphabetical order.

COMPLETE SET (10) 40.00 100.00
SER.1 STATED ODDS 1:72 HOBBY/RETAIL
1 Anfernee Hardaway 6.00 15.00
2 Grant Hill 6.00 15.00
3 Robert Horry 3.00 8.00
4 Eddie Jones 4.00 10.00
5 Toni Kukoc 4.00 10.00
6 Jamal Mashburn 4.00 10.00
7 Alonzo Mourning 5.00 12.00
8 Glenn Robinson 3.00 8.00
9 Latrell Sprewell 4.00 10.00
10 Chris Webber 5.00 12.00

1995-96 Metal Rookie Roll Call

Spotlighting the '95-96 rookie class, cards from this 10-card standard-size set were randomly inserted in both series one hobby and retail packs. Though these cards are considered inserts, they were distributed at the same rate as regular issue cards. The cards display hand-engraved, metalized foil designs and are numbered on the back. The set is sequenced in alphabetical order.

COMPLETE SET (10) 2.00 5.00
RANDOM INSERTS IN ALL SER.1 PACKS
*SILV.SPOTLIGHT: 1X TO 2.5X HI COLUMN
RANDOM INSERTS IN ALL SER.1 PACKS
R1 Brent Barry .50 1.25
R2 Antonio McDyess .40 1.00
R3 Ed O'Bannon .25 .60
R4 Cherokee Parks .25 .60
R5 Bryant Reeves .25 .60
R6 Shawn Respert .25 .60
R7 Joe Smith .40 1.00
R8 Jerry Stackhouse 1.00 2.50
R9 Gary Trent .30 .75
R10 Rasheed Wallace 1.00 2.50

1995-96 Metal Scoring Magnets

Randomly inserted exclusively into second series hobby packs at a rate of one in 54, cards from this 8-card set feature a selection of the NBA's top scoring threats. Card fronts have embossed player shots with the card name "Scoring Magnet" in silver foil running vertical along both sides of the player. Card backs contain a brief commentary and are numbered as "X of 8".

COMPLETE SET (8) 30.00 80.00
SER.2 STATED ODDS 1:54 HOBBY
1 Anfernee Hardaway 4.00 10.00
2 Grant Hill 4.00 10.00
3 Magic Johnson 6.00 15.00
4 Michael Jordan 25.00 60.00
5 Jason Kidd 4.00 10.00
6 Hakeem Olajuwon 3.00 8.00
7 Shaquille O'Neal 6.00 15.00
8 David Robinson 4.00 10.00

1995-96 Metal Slick Silver

Randomly inserted exclusively into first series hobby packs at a rate of one in seven, cards from this 10-card standard-size set highlight the league's premier point and shooting guards. The clear acetate cards feature the player in a full-color action shot with a trail of ghost images on the front. Backs feature a player profile printed on the player's reverse silhouette. The set is sequenced in alphabetical order.

COMPLETE SET (10) 25.00 60.00
SER.1 STATED ODDS 1:7 HOBBY/RETAIL
1 Kenny Anderson 1.25 3.00
2 Anfernee Hardaway 2.50 6.00
3 Michael Jordan 15.00 40.00
4 Jason Kidd 2.50 6.00
5 Reggie Miller 2.00 5.00
6 Gary Payton 1.50 4.00
7 Mitch Richmond 1.50 4.00
8 Latrell Sprewell 1.50 4.00
9 John Stockton 2.00 5.00
10 Nick Van Exel 1.50 4.00

1995-96 Metal Stackhouse's Scrapbook

Randomly inserted into one in every 24 second series packs, these two cards continue the eight-card, cross-brand set devoted Fleer spokesperson Jerry Stackhouse. Card #S7 often sells for a premium due to the appearance of Michael Jordan.

COMPLETE SET (2) 3.00 8.00
STATED ODDS 1:24
S7 J.Stackhouse w/Jordan 2.50 6.00
S8 Jerry Stackhouse 1.25 3.00

1995-96 Metal Steel Towers

Randomly inserted exclusively into series one retail and magazine packs at a rate of one in four, cards from this 10-card insert set focus on the leagues top big men. Full-bleed fronts have silver foil backgrounds and are stamped with skyscraper designs. Backs are two-toned according to player's team colors and feature a full-color action shot and a player profile printed next to it. Skyscraper designs also appear in the background on the backs. The set is sequenced in alphabetical order.

COMPLETE SET (10) 5.00 12.00
SER.1 STATED ODDS 1:4 RETAIL
1 Shawn Bradley .60 1.50
2 Vlade Divac 1.00 2.50
3 Patrick Ewing 1.25 3.00
4 Alonzo Mourning 1.25 3.00
5 Dikembe Mutombo 1.00 2.50
6 Hakeem Olajuwon 1.25 3.00
7 Shaquille O'Neal 2.50 6.00
8 David Robinson 1.50 4.00
9 Rik Smits .75 2.00
10 Kevin Willis .60 1.50

1995-96 Metal Tempered Steel

Randomly inserted into all second series packs at a rate of one in 12, cards from this 12-card set feature a selection of top rookies from the 1995-96 season. Card fronts have a colorful foil-etched background with the the "Tempered Steel" logo written in cursive running along the left side. Card backs feature an action shot and a brief commentary next to it. Card backs are numbered as "X of 12".

COMPLETE SET (12) 15.00 30.00
SER.2 STATED ODDS 1:12 HOBBY/RETAIL
1 Sasha Danilovic .75 2.00
2 Tyus Edney .75 2.00
3 Michael Finley 2.50 6.00
4 Kevin Garnett 6.00 15.00
5 Antonio McDyess 1.00 2.50
6 Bryant Reeves .60 1.50
7 Arvydas Sabonis 1.50 4.00
8 Joe Smith 1.00 2.50
9 Jerry Stackhouse 2.50 6.00
10 Damon Stoudamire 2.00 5.00
11 Rasheed Wallace 2.50 6.00
12 Eric Williams .75 2.00

1996-97 Metal

Produced by Fleer/SkyBox, the 1996 Metal set is comprised of 250 cards with eight-card packs carrying a suggested retail price of $2.49. Borderless fronts feature the player in a full-color action cutout against an etched color and silver foil background. The player's name is printed in silver foil and embossed along the right side of the card. Backs picture the player in a full-color action shot with his team's logo printed at the bottom against a "steel" background. The player's name and statistics run vertically along the right side of the card. The cards are grouped alphabetically within teams and checklisted below alphabetically according to team. The Series one Fresh Foundation subset contains the Rookie Cards of Stephon Marbury, Shareef Abdur-Rahim, Ray Allen, Kobe Bryant and Steve Nash. Card #73 (Jerry Stackhouse) was also used for promotional purposes.

COMPLETE SET (250) 25.00 45.00
COMPLETE SERIES 1 (150) 15.00 25.00
COMPLETE SERIES 2 (100) 10.00 20.00
1 Mookie Blaylock .15 .40
2 Christian Laettner .20 .50
3 Steve Smith .20 .50
4 Dana Barros .15 .40
5 Rick Fox .15 .40
6 Dino Radja .15 .40
7 Eric Williams .15 .40
8 Dell Curry .15 .40
9 Matt Geiger .15 .40
10 Glen Rice .25 .60
11 Michael Jordan 2.00 5.00
12 Toni Kukoc .25 .60
13 Luc Longley .20 .50
14 Scottie Pippen .40 1.00
15 Dennis Rodman .50 1.25
16 Terrell Brandon .15 .40
17 Danny Ferry .15 .40
18 Chris Mills .15 .40
19 Bobby Phills .15 .40
20 Bob Sura .15 .40
21 Jim Jackson .15 .40
22 Jason Kidd .40 1.00
23 Jamal Mashburn .20 .50
24 George McCloud .15 .40
25 LaPhonso Ellis .15 .40
26 Antonio McDyess .25 .60
27 Bryant Stith .15 .40
28 Joe Dumars .25 .60
29 Grant Hill .40 1.00
30 Theo Ratliff .15 .40
31 Otis Thorpe .15 .40
32 Chris Mullin .25 .60
33 Joe Smith .20 .50
34 Latrell Sprewell .25 .60
35 Sam Cassell .20 .50
36 Clyde Drexler .30 .75
37 Robert Horry .20 .50
38 Hakeem Olajuwon .30 .75
39 Antonio Davis .15 .40
40 Dale Davis .15 .40
41 Derrick McKey .15 .40
42 Reggie Miller .30 .75
43 Rik Smits .20 .50
44 Brent Barry .20 .50
45 Malik Sealy .15 .40
46 Loy Vaught .15 .40
47 Elden Campbell .15 .40
48 Cedric Ceballos .15 .40
49 Eddie Jones .25 .60
50 Nick Van Exel .25 .60
51 Sasha Danilovic .15 .40
52 Tim Hardaway .25 .60
53 Alonzo Mourning .30 .75
54 Kurt Thomas .15 .40
55 Vin Baker .20 .50
56 Sherman Douglas .15 .40
57 Glenn Robinson .20 .50
58 Kevin Garnett .60 1.50
59 Tom Gugliotta .15 .40
60 Doug West .15 .40
61 Shawn Bradley .15 .40
62 Ed O'Bannon .15 .40
63 Jayson Williams .15 .40
64 Patrick Ewing .30 .75
65 Charles Oakley .20 .50
66 John Starks .20 .50
67 Nick Anderson .15 .40
68 Horace Grant .20 .50
69 Anfernee Hardaway .40 1.00
70 Dennis Scott .15 .40
71 Brian Shaw .15 .40
72 Derrick Coleman .20 .50
73 Jerry Stackhouse .30 .75
74 Clarence Weatherspoon .15 .40
75 Charles Barkley .40 1.00
76 Michael Finley .30 .75
77 Kevin Johnson .25 .60
78 Wesley Person .15 .40
79 Aaron McKie .15 .40
80 Clifford Robinson .15 .40
81 Arvydas Sabonis .20 .50
82 Gary Trent .15 .40
83 Tyus Edney .15 .40
84 Brian Grant .20 .50
85 Billy Owens .15 .40
86 Olden Polynice .15 .40
87 Mitch Richmond .25 .60
88 Vinny Del Negro .15 .40
89 Sean Elliott .25 .60
90 Avery Johnson .20 .50
91 David Robinson .40 1.00
92 Hersey Hawkins .15 .40
93 Shawn Kemp .25 .60
94 Gary Payton .25 .60
95 Sam Perkins .15 .40
96 Detlef Schrempf .25 .60
97 Doug Christie .15 .40
98 Damon Stoudamire .20 .50
99 Sharone Wright .15 .40
100 Jeff Hornacek .20 .50
101 Karl Malone .30 .75
102 John Stockton .30 .75
103 Greg Anthony .15 .40
104 Blue Edwards .15 .40
105 Bryant Reeves .15 .40
106 Juwan Howard .20 .50
107 Gheorghe Muresan .15 .40
108 Chris Webber .30 .75
109 Kenny Anderson OTM .20 .50
110 Stacey Augmon OTM .20 .50
111 Chris Childs OTM .15 .40
112 Vlade Divac OTM .25 .60
113 Allan Houston OTM .20 .50
114 Mark Jackson OTM .20 .50
115 Larry Johnson OTM .25 .60
116 Grant Long OTM .15 .40
117 Anthony Mason OTM .15 .40
118 Dikembe Mutombo OTM .25 .60
119 Shaquille O'Neal OTM .60 1.50
120 Isaiah Rider OTM .20 .50
121 Rod Strickland OTM .15 .40
122 Rasheed Wallace OTM .30 .75
123 Jalen Rose OTM .20 .50
124 Anfernee Hardaway MET .40 1.00
125 Tim Hardaway MET .25 .60
126 Allan Houston MET .20 .50
127 Eddie Jones MET .25 .60
128 Michael Jordan MET 2.00 5.00
129 Reggie Miller MET .30 .75
130 Glen Rice MET .25 .60
131 Mitch Richmond MET .25 .60
132 Steve Smith MET .20 .50
133 John Stockton MET .30 .75
134 Stephon Marbury FF RC .60 1.50
135 Shareef Abdur-Rahim FF RC .40 1.00
136 Ray Allen FF RC 1.00 2.50
137 Kobe Bryant FF RC 4.00 10.00
138 Steve Nash FF RC 1.25 3.00
139 Grant Hill MS .40 1.00
140 Jason Kidd MS .40 1.00
141 Karl Malone MS .30 .75
142 Hakeem Olajuwon MS .30 .75
143 Shaquille O'Neal MS .60 1.50
144 Gary Payton MS .25 .60
145 Scottie Pippen MS .40 1.00
146 Jerry Stackhouse MS .30 .75
147 Damon Stoudamire MS .20 .50
148 Rod Strickland MS .15 .40
149 Checklist (1-102) .15 .40
150 Checklist (103-150/inserts) .15 .40
151 Tyrone Corbin .15 .40
152 Dikembe Mutombo .25 .60
153 Antoine Walker RC .40 1.00
154 David Wesley .15 .40
155 Vlade Divac .25 .60
156 Anthony Mason .15 .40
157 Ron Harper .20 .50
158 Steve Kerr .20 .50
159 Robert Parish .25 .60
160 Tyrone Hill .15 .40
161 Vitaly Potapenko RC .20 .50
162 Sam Cassell .20 .50
163 Chris Gatling .15 .40
164 Samaki Walker RC .20 .50
165 Dale Ellis .15 .40
166 Mark Jackson .20 .50
167 Ervin Johnson .15 .40
168 Grant Hill .40 1.00
169 Lindsey Hunter .15 .40
170 Todd Fuller RC .15 .40
171 Mark Price .25 .60
172 Charles Barkley .40 1.00
173 Othella Harrington RC .25 .60
174 Matt Maloney RC .20 .50
175 Kevin Willis .15 .40
176 Travis Best .15 .40
177 Erick Dampier RC .25 .60
178 Jalen Rose .20 .50
179 Rodney Rogers .15 .40
180 Lorenzen Wright RC .20 .50
181 Kobe Bryant 2.50 6.00
182 Robert Horry .20 .50
183 Shaquille O'Neal .60 1.50
184 P.J. Brown .15 .40
185 Dan Majerle .25 .60
186 Ray Allen .50 1.25
187 Armon Gilliam .15 .40
188 Andrew Lang .15 .40
189 Stephon Marbury .30 .75
190 Stojko Vrankovic .15 .40
191 Kendall Gill .15 .40
192 Kerry Kittles RC .25 .60
193 Robert Pack .15 .40
194 Chris Childs .15 .40
195 Allan Houston .20 .50
196 Larry Johnson .25 .60
197 John Wallace RC .25 .60
198 Rony Seikaly .15 .40
199 Gerald Wilkins .15 .40
200 Lucious Harris .15 .40
201 Allen Iverson RC 1.25 3.00
202 Cedric Ceballos .15 .40
203 Jason Kidd .40 1.00
204 Danny Manning .20 .50
205 Steve Nash .60 1.50
206 Kenny Anderson .20 .50
207 Isaiah Rider .20 .50
208 Rasheed Wallace .30 .75
209 Mahmoud Abdul-Rauf .15 .40
210 Corliss Williamson .15 .40
211 Vernon Maxwell .15 .40
212 Dominique Wilkins .30 .75
213 Craig Ehlo .15 .40
214 Jim McIlvaine .15 .40
215 Marcus Camby RC .40 1.00
216 Hubert Davis .15 .40
217 Walt Williams .15 .40
218 Shandon Anderson RC .20 .50
219 Bryon Russell .15 .40
220 Shareef Abdur-Rahim .20 .50
221 Roy Rogers RC .20 .50
222 Tracy Murray .15 .40
223 Rod Strickland .15 .40
224 Kevin Garnett MET .60 1.50
225 Karl Malone MET .30 .75
226 Alonzo Mourning MET .30 .75
227 Hakeem Olajuwon MET .30 .75
228 Gary Payton MET .25 .60
229 Scottie Pippen MET .40 1.00
230 David Robinson MET .40 1.00
231 Dennis Rodman MET .50 1.25
232 Latrell Sprewell MET .25 .60
233 Jerry Stackhouse MET .30 .75
234 Marcus Camby FF .20 .50
235 Todd Fuller FF .07 .20
236 Allen Iverson FF .60 1.50
237 Kerry Kittles FF .12 .30
238 Roy Rogers FF .10 .25
239 Anfernee Hardaway MS .40 1.00
240 Juwan Howard MS .20 .50
241 Michael Jordan MS 2.00 5.00
242 Shawn Kemp MS .25 .60
243 Gary Payton MS .25 .60
244 Mitch Richmond MS .25 .60
245 Glenn Robinson MS .20 .50
246 John Stockton MS .30 .75
247 Damon Stoudamire MS .20 .50
248 Chris Webber MS .30 .75
249 Checklist .15 .40
250 Checklist .15 .40

1996-97 Metal Precious Metal

*STARS: 12X TO 30X HI COLUMN
*ROOKIES: 6X TO 15X HI
*ROOKIE FF SUBSET: 12X TO 30X HI
SER.2 STATED ODDS 1:36 HOBBY
181 Kobe Bryant 100.00 250.00
241 Michael Jordan MS 75.00 200.00

1996-97 Metal Cyber-Metal

Randomly inserted in all series two packs at a rate of one in 6, this 20-card set features NBA players as "Terminator-type" characters.

COMPLETE SET (20) 20.00 40.00
SER.2 STATED ODDS 1:6 HOBBY/RETAIL
1 Shareef Abdur-Rahim 1.00 2.50
2 Ray Allen 2.50 6.00
3 Vin Baker .75 2.00
4 Charles Barkley 1.50 4.00
5 Kobe Bryant 6.00 15.00
6 Patrick Ewing 1.25 3.00
7 Jason Kidd 1.50 4.00
8 Karl Malone 1.25 3.00
9 Stephon Marbury 1.50 4.00
10 Reggie Miller 1.25 3.00
11 Alonzo Mourning 1.25 3.00
12 Hakeem Olajuwon 1.25 3.00
13 Gary Payton 1.00 2.50
14 Scottie Pippen 1.50 4.00
15 Mitch Richmond 1.00 2.50
16 David Robinson 1.50 4.00
17 Joe Smith .75 2.00
18 Latrell Sprewell 1.00 2.50
19 John Stockton 1.25 3.00
20 Chris Webber 1.25 3.00

1996-97 Metal Decade of Excellence

Randomly inserted in all first series packs at a rate of one in 100, this 10 card set features metalized foil replicas of the 1986-87 Fleer NBA cards. Card backs carry a "M" prefix.

COMPLETE SET (10) 15.00 40.00
SER.1 STATED ODDS 1:100 HOBBY/RETAIL
M1 Clyde Drexler 2.00 5.00
M2 Joe Dumars 1.50 4.00
M3 Derek Harper 1.25 3.00
M4 Michael Jordan 15.00 40.00
M5 Karl Malone 2.00 5.00
M6 Chris Mullin 1.50 4.00
M7 Charles Oakley 1.25 3.00
M8 Sam Perkins 1.00 2.50
M9 Ricky Pierce 1.00 2.50
M10 Buck Williams 1.00 2.50

1996-97 Metal Freshly Forged

Randomly inserted in all series two packs at a rate of one in 24, this 15-card set focuses on younger players and features an original art illustrated background on each card.

COMPLETE SET (15) 25.00 60.00
SER.2 STATED ODDS 1:24 HOBBY/RETAIL
1 Shareef Abdur-Rahim 1.25 3.00
2 Ray Allen 3.00 8.00
3 Kobe Bryant 8.00 12.00
4 Marcus Camby 1.25 3.00
5 Kevin Garnett 3.00 8.00
6 Anfernee Hardaway 2.00 5.00
7 Grant Hill 2.00 5.00
8 Allen Iverson 4.00 10.00
9 Jason Kidd 2.00 5.00
10 Stephon Marbury 2.00 5.00
11 Glenn Robinson 1.00 2.50
12 Joe Smith 1.00 2.50
13 Jerry Stackhouse 1.50 4.00
14 Damon Stoudamire 1.00 2.50
15 Antoine Walker 1.25 3.00

1996-97 Metal Maximum Metal

The first ten cards were randomly inserted in first series hobby packs only at a rate of one in 180. This 10-card set features embossed metalized cards of ten of the fan's favorite impact players. The fronts display color action player images with a metallic foil basketball in the background. The backs carry player information. The final ten cards were randomly inserted in second series retail packs only at a rate of one in 120. These cards feature the same design used in series one.

COMPLETE SET (20) 190.00 375.00
COMPLETE SERIES 1 (10) 150.00 300.00
COMPLETE SERIES 2 (10) 40.00 75.00
1-10: SER.1 STATED ODDS 1:180 HOBBY
11-20: SER.2 STATED ODDS 1:120 RETAIL
1 Charles Barkley 10.00 25.00
2 Anfernee Hardaway 10.00 25.00
3 Grant Hill 12.00 30.00
4 Michael Jordan 100.00 250.00
5 Jason Kidd 10.00 25.00
6 Karl Malone 8.00 20.00
7 Hakeem Olajuwon 8.00 20.00
8 Gary Payton 6.00 15.00
9 David Robinson 10.00 25.00
10 Damon Stoudamire 5.00 12.00
11 Juwan Howard 5.00 12.00
12 Shawn Kemp 8.00 20.00
13 Kerry Kittles 3.00 8.00
14 Stephon Marbury 8.00 20.00
15 Dennis Rodman 12.00 30.00
16 Joe Smith 5.00 12.00
17 Jerry Stackhouse 8.00 20.00
18 John Stockton 8.00 20.00
19 Antoine Walker 5.00 12.00
20 Chris Webber 10.00 25.00

1996-97 Metal Metal Edge

Randomly inserted in all first series packs at a rate of one in 36, this 15-card set features players known for their agressiveness in driving to the basket. The fronts display a color player photo a geometric metallic foil background. The backs carry player information.

COMPLETE SET (15) 35.00 70.00
SER.1 STATED ODDS 1:36 HOBBY/RETAIL
1 Charles Barkley 4.00 10.00
2 Jamal Mashburn 2.00 5.00
3 Alonzo Mourning 3.00 8.00
4 Gary Payton 2.50 6.00
5 Scottie Pippen 4.00 10.00
6 Steve Smith 2.00 5.00
7 Latrell Sprewell 2.50 6.00
8 John Stockton 3.00 8.00
9 Nick Van Exel 2.50 6.00
10 Chris Webber 3.00 8.00
11 Stephon Marbury 3.00 8.00
12 Shareef Abdur-Rahim 2.00 5.00
13 Ray Allen 5.00 12.00
14 Antoine Walker 2.00 5.00
15 Kobe Bryant 12.00 30.00

1996-97 Metal Minted Metal

These redemption cards were randomly inserted into hobby packs of series two at one in 720 packs and were exchangeable for Highland Mint cards. The selected two players are the Fleer Spokesmen, Grant Hill and Jerry Stackhouse. The expiration date for the cards was March 1, 1998. Both players have the following redemptions available: All-Metal 14kt. gold, Gold-plated, Silver and Bronze cards. Both the Gold and the Solid Gold cards for each player are not priced below due to lack of market information.

COMP.BRONZE SET (2) 40.00 80.00
SER.2 STATED ODDS 1:720 HOBBY FOR ANY
1 Grant Hill Bronze 15.00 30.00
2 Jerry Stackhouse Bronze 12.50 25.00
3 Grant Hill Silver 40.00 100.00
4 Jerry Stackhouse Silver 30.00 80.00

1996-97 Metal Molten Metal

The first ten cards were randomly inserted in series one retail packs only at a rate of one in 180. This 10-card set features some of the hottest up and coming stars who have one to three years NBA experience. The fronts display color action player photos on a 3-D background. The backs carry player information. The final twenty cards were randomly inserted in series two hobby packs at a rate of one in 72. The second series cards feature embossed technology.

COMPLETE SET (30) 200.00 400.00
COMPLETE SERIES 1 (10) 75.00 150.00
COMPLETE SERIES 2 (20) 125.00 250.00
1-10: SER.1 STATED ODDS 1:180 RETAIL
11-30: SER.2 STATED ODDS 1:72 HOBBY
1 Michael Finley 12.00 30.00
2 Kevin Garnett 25.00 60.00
3 Anfernee Hardaway 15.00 40.00
4 Grant Hill 15.00 40.00
5 Juwan Howard 8.00 20.00
6 Jason Kidd 15.00 40.00
7 Antonio McDyess 10.00 25.00
8 Joe Smith 8.00 20.00
9 Jerry Stackhouse 12.00 30.00
10 Damon Stoudamire 8.00 20.00
11 Shareef Abdur-Rahim 4.00 10.00
12 Ray Allen 10.00 25.00
13 Charles Barkley 8.00 20.00
14 Terrell Brandon 3.00 8.00
15 Marcus Camby 4.00 10.00
16 Tom Gugliotta 3.00 8.00
17 Allen Iverson 12.00 30.00
18 Michael Jordan 75.00 200.00
19 Kerry Kittles 2.50 6.00
20 Karl Malone 6.00 15.00
21 Hakeem Olajuwon 6.00 15.00
22 Shaquille O'Neal 12.00 30.00
23 Gary Payton 5.00 12.00
24 Scottie Pippen 8.00 20.00
25 David Robinson 8.00 20.00
26 Glenn Robinson 4.00 10.00
27 Joe Smith 4.00 10.00
28 Latrell Sprewell 5.00 12.00
29 Antoine Walker 4.00 10.00
30 Chris Webber 6.00 15.00

1996-97 Metal Net-Rageous

Randomly inserted in all series two packs at a rate of one in 288, this 10-card set features some of the best players in the NBA against a die-cut background.

COMPLETE SET (10) 300.00 600.00
SER.2 STATED ODDS 1:288 HOBBY/RETAIL
1 Kevin Garnett 15.00 40.00
2 Anfernee Hardaway 20.00 50.00
3 Grant Hill 10.00 25.00
4 Juwan Howard 5.00 12.00
5 Michael Jordan 200.00 500.00
6 Shawn Kemp 10.00 25.00
7 Shaquille O'Neal 15.00 40.00
8 Dennis Rodman 15.00 40.00
9 Jerry Stackhouse 8.00 20.00
10 Damon Stoudamire 5.00 12.00

1996-97 Metal Platinum Portraits

Randomly inserted in all series two packs at a rate of one in 96, this 10-card set focuses on NBA stars using up-close profile photography. Card fronts feature a head shot of the player against a silver metalized background.

COMPLETE SET (10) 30.00 80.00
SER.2 STATED ODDS 1:96 HOBBY/RETAIL
1 Charles Barkley 3.00 8.00
2 Kevin Garnett 5.00 12.00
3 Anfernee Hardaway 3.00 8.00
4 Grant Hill 3.00 8.00
5 Michael Jordan 30.00 80.00
6 Shawn Kemp 2.00 5.00
7 Karl Malone 2.50 6.00
8 Shaquille O'Neal 5.00 12.00
9 Hakeem Olajuwon 2.50 6.00
10 Damon Stoudamire 1.50 4.00

1996-97 Metal Power Tools

Randomly inserted in all first series packs at a rate of one in 18, this 10-card set features color action player cutouts of power players on etched foil backgrounds of machine gears. The backs carry player information.

COMPLETE SET (10) 10.00 20.00
SER.1 STATED ODDS 1:18 HOBBY/RETAIL
1 Vin Baker 1.25 3.00
2 Charles Barkley 2.50 6.00
3 Horace Grant 1.25 3.00
4 Juwan Howard 1.25 3.00
5 Larry Johnson 1.50 4.00
6 Shawn Kemp 1.50 4.00
7 Karl Malone 2.00 5.00
8 Antonio McDyess 1.50 4.00
9 Dennis Rodman 3.00 8.00
10 Joe Smith 1.25 3.00

1996-97 Metal Steel Slammin'

Randomly inserted in all first series packs at a rate of one in 72, this 10-card set features the NBA's top slam-dunkers performing their craft on a metal die-cut card. The fronts display a color action player image on a metallic background. The backs carry player information.

COMPLETE SET (10) 60.00 150.00
SER.1 STATED ODDS 1:72 HOBBY/RETAIL
1 Brent Barry 2.50 6.00
2 Clyde Drexler 4.00 10.00
3 Michael Finley 4.00 10.00
4 Kevin Garnett 8.00 20.00
5 Eddie Jones 3.00 8.00
6 Michael Jordan 40.00 100.00
7 Shawn Kemp 3.00 8.00
8 Shaquille O'Neal 8.00 20.00
9 Joe Smith 2.50 6.00
10 Jerry Stackhouse 4.00 10.00

1999-00 Metal

The 1999-00 Metal product was released in April,2000 as a 180-card set. The set features 150 players and 30 rookie subset cards. The rookies are seeded at one in two packs. Each pack contained 10-cards and carried a suggested retail price of 1.99.

COMPLETE SET (180) 15.00 40.00
151-180 STATED ODDS 1:2
1 Vince Carter .40 1.00
2 Stephon Marbury .15 .40
3 David Robinson .30 .75
4 Ray Allen .20 .50
5 P.J. Brown .12 .30
6 Shawn Kemp .20 .50
7 Cedric Ceballos .12 .30
8 Dale Davis .12 .30
9 Rodney Rogers .12 .30
10 Chris Gatling .12 .30
11 Bryant Reeves .12 .30
12 Al Harrington .20 .50
13 Brent Barry .15 .40
14 Brevin Knight .12 .30
15 Radoslav Nesterovic RC .20 .50
16 Tom Gugliotta .12 .30
17 Charles Barkley .30 .75
18 Cuttino Mobley .12 .30
19 Corliss Williamson .12 .30
20 Hersey Hawkins .12 .30
21 Mike Bibby .20 .50
22 Pat Garrity .12 .30
23 Kelvin Cato .12 .30
24 Alan Henderson .12 .30
25 Alvin Williams .12 .30
26 Antonio McDyess .15 .40
27 Damon Stoudamire .15 .40
28 Kerry Kittles .12 .30
29 Michael Olowokandi .12 .30
30 Brent Price .12 .30
31 Fred Hoiberg .12 .30
32 Glenn Robinson .15 .40
33 Hakeem Olajuwon .25 .60
34 Monty Williams .12 .30
35 Terry Porter .12 .30
36 Allen Iverson .40 1.00
37 Juwan Howard .15 .40
38 Mario Elie .12 .30
39 Mookie Blaylock .12 .30
40 Sam Cassell .15 .40
41 Toni Kukoc .20 .50
42 Anthony Mason .12 .30
43 George Lynch .12 .30
44 John Starks .15 .40
45 Malik Rose .12 .30
46 Rod Strickland .12 .30
47 Tim Thomas .15 .40
48 Howard Eisley .12 .30
49 Kenny Anderson .15 .40
50 Kurt Thomas .12 .30
51 Lindsey Hunter .12 .30
52 Rick Fox .12 .30
53 Vlade Divac .20 .50
54 Avery Johnson .15 .40
55 Dale Ellis .12 .30
56 Donyell Marshall .12 .30
57 Elden Campbell .12 .30
58 Larry Hughes .15 .40
59 Mitch Richmond .20 .50
60 Chris Mills .12 .30
61 David Wesley .12 .30
62 Gary Payton .20 .50
63 Isaac Austin .12 .30
64 Robert Traylor .12 .30
65 Theo Ratliff .15 .40
66 Antawn Jamison .20 .50
67 Eddie Jones .20 .50
68 Kevin Garnett .30 .75
69 Matt Geiger .12 .30
70 Vernon Maxwell .12 .30
71 Antonio Davis .12 .30
72 Dirk Nowitzki .40 1.00
73 Johnny Newman .12 .30
74 Maurice Taylor .12 .30
75 Steve Smith .15 .40
76 Derek Anderson .12 .30
77 Doug Christie .15 .40
78 Erick Strickland .12 .30
79 Keith Van Horn .15 .40
80 Luc Longley .15 .40
81 Alonzo Mourning .25 .60
82 Christian Laettner .15 .40
83 Jamal Mashburn .15 .40
84 Jon Barry .12 .30
85 Patrick Ewing .25 .60
86 Shareef Abdur-Rahim .15 .40
87 Vitaly Potapenko .12 .30
88 Darrell Armstrong .12 .30
89 Eric Williams .12 .30
90 Jerome Williams .12 .30
91 Nick Anderson .12 .30
92 Othella Harrington .12 .30
93 Tim Hardaway .20 .50
94 Eric Piatkowski .15 .40
95 Isaiah Rider .15 .40
96 Kendall Gill .12 .30
97 Rasheed Wallace .20 .50
98 Robert Pack .12 .30
99 Tracy McGrady .30 .75
100 Allan Houston .15 .40
101 Brian Grant .12 .30
102 Dikembe Mutombo .20 .50
103 Karl Malone .25 .60
104 Nick Van Exel .15 .40
105 Shaquille O'Neal .50 1.25
106 Chris Anstey .12 .30
107 Michael Dickerson .12 .30
108 Shandon Anderson .12 .30
109 Tariq Adbul-Wahad .12 .30
110 Tim Duncan .40 1.00
111 Voshon Lenard .12 .30
112 Bimbo Coles .12 .30

113 Detlef Schrempf .15 .40
114 John Stockton .25 .60
115 Kobe Bryant .75 2.00
116 Latrell Sprewell .20 .50
117 Raef LaFrentz .15 .40
118 Antoine Walker .20 .50
119 Bryon Russell .12 .30
120 Derek Fisher .20 .50
121 Jason Williams .25 .60
122 Jerry Stackhouse .20 .50
123 Larry Johnson .20 .50
124 Clifford Robinson .12 .30
125 Horace Grant .15 .40
126 Malik Sealy .12 .30
127 Michael Finley .20 .50
128 Rik Smits .20 .50
129 Dell Curry .12 .30
130 Jim Jackson .12 .30
131 Ron Mercer .15 .40
132 Scott Burrell .12 .30
133 Scottie Pippen .30 .75
134 Troy Hudson .20 .50
135 Anfernee Hardaway .30 .75
136 Anthony Peeler .12 .30
137 Jalen Rose .15 .40
138 Lamond Murray .12 .30
139 Ruben Patterson .12 .30
140 Chris Webber .20 .50
141 Glen Rice .20 .50
142 Grant Hill .25 .60
143 Jeff Hornacek .15 .40
144 Marcus Camby .15 .40
145 Paul Pierce .25 .60
146 Bob Sura .12 .30
147 Jason Kidd .30 .75
148 Reggie Miller .20 .50
149 Terrell Brandon .12 .30
150 Vin Baker .15 .40
151 Lamar Odom RC .75 2.00
152 Steve Francis RC .75 2.00
153 Elton Brand RC .75 2.00
154 Wally Szczerbiak RC .60 1.50
155 Adrian Griffin RC .30 .75
156 Andre Miller RC .60 1.50
157 Jason Terry RC .50 1.25
158 Richard Hamilton RC .60 1.50
159 Ron Artest RC .60 1.50
160 Shawn Marion RC .60 1.50
161 James Posey RC .30 .75
162 Greg Buckner RC .30 .75
163 Chucky Atkins RC .30 .75
164 Corey Maggette RC .50 1.25
165 Todd MacCulloch RC .30 .75
166 Baron Davis RC .75 2.00
167 Trajan Langdon RC .30 .75
168 Bruno Sundov RC .30 .75
169 Scott Padgett RC .25 .60
170 Vonteego Cummings RC .20 .50
171 Ryan Bowen RC .30 .75
172 Jonathan Bender RC .30 .75
173 Jermaine Jackson RC .30 .75
174 Devean George RC .30 .75
175 Chris Herren RC .25 .60
176 Rodney Buford RC .30 .75
177 Laron Profit RC .25 .60
178 Mirsad Turkcan RC .30 .75
179 Eddie Robinson RC .30 .75
180 Anthony Carter RC .25 .60

1999-00 Metal Emeralds

*STARS: 2X TO 5X BASE CARD HI
*RCs: .5X TO 1.25X BASE HI
STARS: STATED ODDS 1:4
RCs: STATED ODDS 1:8

1999-00 Metal Vince Carter Scrapbook

Randomly inserted in packs at one in eight, this 10-card set focuses on Vince Carter, with action and casual shots. Card backs carry a "VC" prefix.

COMPLETE SET (10) 12.50 25.00
COMMON CARD (VC1-VC10) 1.50 4.00
STATED ODDS 1:8

1999-00 Metal Genuine Coverage

Randomly inserted in packs at one in 288, this six-card set features swatches of game-used jerseys. The cards are not numbered and listed below in alphabetical order.

STATED ODDS 1:288
1 Vince Carter 12.00 30.00
2 Karl Malone 8.00 20.00
3 Shaquille O'Neal 15.00 40.00
4 Paul Pierce 8.00 20.00
5 John Stockton 8.00 20.00
6 Antoine Walker 6.00 15.00

1999-00 Metal Heavy Metal

Randomly inserted in packs at one in 20, this 10-card set features NBA players against a black and silver background. Card backs carry a "HM" prefix.

COMPLETE SET (10) 8.00 20.00
STATED ODDS 1:20
HM1 Kobe Bryant 2.50 6.00
HM2 Vince Carter 1.25 3.00
HM3 Lamar Odom 1.50 4.00
HM4 Kevin Garnett 1.00 2.50
HM5 Shawn Kemp .60 1.50
HM6 Shareef Abdur-Rahim .50 1.25
HM7 Antonio McDyess .50 1.25
HM8 Tim Duncan 1.25 3.00
HM9 Keith Van Horn .50 1.25
HM10 Shaquille O'Neal 1.50 4.00

1999-00 Metal Platinum Portraits

Randomly inserted in packs at one in four, this 15-card set focuses on the top rookies from 1999. The cards feature an up close portrait shot of each player. Card backs carry a "PP" prefix.

COMPLETE SET (15) 6.00 15.00
STATED ODDS 1:4
PP1 Elton Brand 1.00 2.50
PP2 Lamar Odom 1.00 2.50
PP3 Steve Francis 1.00 2.50
PP4 Richard Hamilton .75 2.00
PP5 Baron Davis 1.00 2.50
PP6 Vonteego Cummings .25 .60
PP7 Corey Maggette .60 1.50
PP8 James Posey .40 1.00
PP9 Shawn Marion .75 2.00
PP10 Wally Szczerbiak .75 2.00
PP11 Jason Terry .60 1.50
PP12 Andre Miller .75 2.00
PP13 Scott Padgett .30 .75
PP14 Trajan Langdon .40 1.00
PP15 Jonathan Bender .40 1.00

1999-00 Metal Rivalries

Randomly inserted in packs at one in four, this 15-card set features some of the great rivalries in the NBA. Card backs carry a "R" prefix.

COMPLETE SET (15) 4.00 10.00
STATED ODDS 1:4
R1 A.Iverson/S.Marbury .50 1.25
R2 J.Kidd/G.Payton .40 1.00
R3 M.Bibby/J.Williams .30 .75
R4 P.Ewing/A.Mourning .30 .75
R5 T.Duncan/K.Garnett .50 1.25
R6 A.Hardaway/K.Bryant 1.00 2.50
R7 C.Barkley/K.Malone .40 1.00
R8 A.McDyess/S.Abdur-Rahim .20 .50
R9 V.Carter/G.Hill .50 1.25
R10 A.Walker/K.Van Horn .25 .60
R11 S.Kemp/E.Brand .60 1.50
R12 S.O'Neal/D.Robinson .60 1.50
R13 R.LaFrentz/D.Nowitzki .50 1.25
R14 S.Francis/J.Stockton .60 1.50
R15 L.Odom/S.Pippen .60 1.50

1999-00 Metal Scoring Magnets

Randomly inserted at one in 20, this 10-card set features the top scoring players in the NBA. The cards feature die cutting on the right side. Card backs carry a "SM" prefix.

COMPLETE SET (10) 4.00 10.00
STATED ODDS 1:20
SM1 Grant Hill .75 2.00
SM2 Stephon Marbury .50 1.25
SM3 Allen Iverson 1.25 3.00
SM4 Ray Allen .60 1.50
SM5 Steve Francis 1.50 4.00
SM6 Ron Mercer .50 1.25
SM7 Paul Pierce .75 2.00
SM8 Latrell Sprewell .60 1.50
SM9 Glenn Robinson .50 1.25
SM10 Eddie Jones .60 1.50

1997-98 Metal Universe

The Metal Universe set was issued in only one series, containing 125 cards that came in nine card packs with a suggested retail price of $2.49. Card fronts contain an action shot of the player with some form of a "cartoon" scene surrouding the player. The player's name is against a silver bar running along the card bottom. Card back contain a photo and statistics.

COMPLETE SET (125) 10.00 25.00
1 Charles Barkley .40 1.00
2 Dell Curry .15 .40
3 Derek Fisher .25 .60
4 Derek Harper .20 .50
5 Avery Johnson .20 .50
6 Steve Smith .20 .50
7 Alonzo Mourning .30 .75
8 Rod Strickland .15 .40
9 Chris Mullin .25 .60
10 Rony Seikaly .15 .40
11 Vin Baker .20 .50
12 Austin Croshere RC .20 .50
13 Vinny Del Negro .15 .40
14 Sherman Douglas .15 .40
15 Priest Lauderdale .15 .40
16 Cedric Ceballos .15 .40
17 LaPhonso Ellis .15 .40
18 Luc Longley .20 .50
19 Brian Grant .15 .40
20 Allen Iverson .50 1.25
21 Anthony Mason .15 .40
22 Bryant Reeves .15 .40
23 Michael Jordan 3.00 8.00
24 Dale Ellis .15 .40
25 Terrell Brandon .15 .40
26 Patrick Ewing .30 .75
27 Allan Houston .20 .50
28 Damon Stoudamire .20 .50
29 Loy Vaught .15 .40
30 Walt Williams .15 .40
31 Shareef Abdur-Rahim .25 .60
32 Mario Elie .15 .40
33 Juwan Howard .20 .50
34 Tom Gugliotta .15 .40
35 Glen Rice .25 .60
36 Isaiah Rider .20 .50
37 Arvydas Sabonis .20 .50
38 Derrick Coleman .20 .50
39 Kevin Willis .15 .40
40 Kendall Gill .15 .40
41 John Wallace .15 .40
42 Tracy McGrady RC 1.00 2.50
43 Travis Best .15 .40
44 Malik Rose .15 .40
45 Anfernee Hardaway .40 1.00
46 Roy Rogers .15 .40
47 Kerry Kittles .15 .40
48 Matt Maloney .15 .40
49 Antonio McDyess .20 .50
50 Shaquille O'Neal .60 1.50
51 George McCloud .15 .40
52 Wesley Person .15 .40
53 Shawn Bradley .15 .40
54 Antonio Davis .15 .40
55 P.J. Brown .15 .40
56 Joe Dumars .25 .60
57 Horace Grant .20 .50
58 Steve Kerr .20 .50
59 Hakeem Olajuwon .30 .75
60 Tim Hardaway .25 .60
61 Toni Kukoc .25 .60
62 Ron Mercer RC .30 .75
63 Gary Payton .25 .60
64 Grant Hill .40 1.00
65 Detlef Schrempf .25 .60
66 Tim Duncan RC 1.25 3.00
67 Shawn Kemp .25 .60
68 Voshon Lenard .15 .40
69 Othella Harrington .15 .40
70 Hersey Hawkins .15 .40
71 Lindsey Hunter .15 .40
72 Antoine Walker .25 .60
73 Jamal Mashburn .20 .50
74 Kenny Anderson .20 .50
75 Todd Day .15 .40
76 Todd Fuller .15 .40
77 Jermaine O'Neal .20 .50
78 David Robinson .40 1.00
79 Erick Dampier .15 .40
80 Keith Van Horn RC .40 1.00
81 Kobe Bryant 1.25 3.00
82 Chris Childs .15 .40
83 Scottie Pippen .40 1.00
84 Marcus Camby .25 .60
85 Danny Ferry .15 .40
86 Jeff Hornacek .20 .50
87 Bo Outlaw .15 .40
88 Larry Johnson .25 .60
89 Tony Delk .15 .40
90 Stephon Marbury .30 .75
91 Robert Pack .15 .40
92 Chris Webber .25 .60
93 Clyde Drexler .30 .75
94 Eddie Jones .25 .60
95 Jerry Stackhouse .25 .60
96 Tyrone Hill .15 .40
97 Karl Malone .30 .75
98 Reggie Miller .30 .75
99 Bryon Russell .15 .40
100 Dale Davis .15 .40
101 Steve Nash .50 1.25
102 Vitaly Potapenko .15 .40
103 Nick Anderson .15 .40
104 Ray Allen .30 .75
105 Sean Elliott .25 .60
106 Dikembe Mutombo .25 .60
107 Dennis Rodman .50 1.25
108 Lorenzen Wright .15 .40
109 Kevin Garnett .40 1.00
110 Christian Laettner .20 .50
111 Mitch Richmond .25 .60
112 Joe Smith .20 .50
113 Jason Kidd .40 1.00
114 Glenn Robinson .20 .50
115 Mark Price .25 .60
116 Mark Jackson .20 .50
117 Bobby Phills .15 .40
118 John Starks .20 .50
119 John Stockton .30 .75
120 Mookie Blaylock .15 .40
121 Dean Garrett .15 .40
122 Olden Polynice .15 .40
123 Latrell Sprewell .25 .60
124 Checklist .15 .40
125 Checklist .15 .40

1997-98 Metal Universe Precious Metal Gems

*STARS: 150X TO 400X BASE CARD HI
*RCs: 150X TO 400X BASE HI
PRINT RUN 100 TOTAL SERIAL #'d SETS
1 Charles Barkley 500.00 1000.00
7 Alonzo Mourning 300.00 600.00
23 Michael Jordan 8000.00 12000.00
26 Patrick Ewing 300.00 600.00
27 Allan Houston 125.00 300.00
28 Damon Stoudamire 125.00 300.00
33 Juwan Howard 125.00 300.00
37 Arvydas Sabonis 150.00 400.00
42 Tracy McGrady 500.00 1000.00
50 Shaquille O'Neal 300.00 600.00
58 Steve Kerr 200.00 500.00
59 Hakeem Olajuwon 175.00 350.00
64 Grant Hill 400.00 800.00
66 Tim Duncan 1000.00 2000.00
78 David Robinson 600.00 1200.00
81 Kobe Bryant 4000.00 8000.00
83 Scottie Pippen 500.00 1000.00
86 Jeff Hornacek 75.00 200.00
88 Larry Johnson 125.00 300.00
92 Chris Webber 150.00 300.00
95 Jerry Stackhouse 200.00 400.00
97 Karl Malone 300.00 600.00
98 Reggie Miller 150.00 300.00
101 Steve Nash 250.00 450.00
106 Dikembe Mutombo 125.00 300.00
107 Dennis Rodman 500.00 1000.00
113 Jason Kidd 250.00 500.00
119 John Stockton 200.00 400.00
123 Latrell Sprewell 150.00 400.00

1997-98 Metal Universe Gold Universe

Randomly inserted in retail packs only at a rate of one in 120, this 10-card set features some of the shining stars of the NBA.

COMPLETE SET (10) 50.00 120.00
STATED ODDS 1:120 RETAIL
1 Damon Stoudamire 6.00 15.00
2 Shawn Kemp 8.00 20.00
3 John Stockton 10.00 25.00
4 Jerry Stackhouse 8.00 20.00
5 John Wallace 5.00 12.00
6 Juwan Howard 6.00 15.00
7 David Robinson 12.00 30.00
8 Gary Payton 8.00 20.00
9 Joe Smith 6.00 15.00
10 Charles Barkley 12.00 30.00

1997-98 Metal Universe Planet Metal

Randomly inserted in packs at a rate of one in 24, this 15-card set focuses on the NBA's best depicted as a universe. Card fronts feature a silver metallic background with a "swirling" planet in the background.

COMPLETE SET (15) 50.00 100.00
STATED ODDS 1:24 HOBBY/RETAIL
1 Michael Jordan 75.00 200.00
2 Allen Iverson 4.00 10.00
3 Kobe Bryant 10.00 25.00
4 Shaquille O'Neal 4.00 10.00
5 Stephon Marbury 2.00 5.00
6 Marcus Camby 1.50 4.00
7 Anfernee Hardaway 3.00 8.00
8 Kevin Garnett 4.00 10.00
9 Shareef Abdur-Rahim 1.50 4.00
10 Dennis Rodman 4.00 10.00
11 Grant Hill 2.50 6.00
12 Hakeem Olajuwon 2.00 5.00
13 David Robinson 2.50 6.00
14 Charles Barkley 4.00 10.00
15 Gary Payton 1.50 4.00

1997-98 Metal Universe Platinum Portraits

Randomly inserted in packs at a rate of one in 288, this 15-card set features NBA stars in a Hall of Fame plaque treatment. The cards feature a matrix-etching the form a picture of the player's face.

STATED ODDS 1:288 HOBBY/RETAIL
1 Michael Jordan 800.00 1200.00
2 Allen Iverson 75.00 200.00
3 Kobe Bryant 150.00 400.00
4 Shaquille O'Neal 60.00 150.00
5 Stephon Marbury 40.00 100.00
6 Marcus Camby 25.00 60.00
7 Anfernee Hardaway 75.00 200.00
8 Kevin Garnett 50.00 120.00
9 Shareef Abdur-Rahim 25.00 60.00
10 Dennis Rodman 75.00 200.00
11 Ray Allen 60.00 150.00
12 Grant Hill 40.00 100.00
13 Kerry Kittles 15.00 40.00
14 Antoine Walker 25.00 60.00
15 Scottie Pippen 75.00 200.00

1997-98 Metal Universe Reebok Chase Bronze

MPLETE SET (15) 2.00 5.00
*GOLD: 1.25X TO 3X BRONZE
*SILVER: .5X TO 1.25X BRONZE
ONE PER SER.1 PACK
5 Avery Johnson .20 .50
6 Steve Smith .20 .50
13 Vinny Del Negro .15 .40
16 Cedric Ceballos .15 .40
20 Allen Iverson .50 1.25
32 Mario Elie .15 .40
50 Shaquille O'Neal .60 1.50
67 Shawn Kemp .25 .60
68 Voshon Lenard .15 .40
74 Kenny Anderson .20 .50
91 Robert Pack .15 .40
93 Clyde Drexler .30 .75
96 Tyrone Hill .15 .40
114 Glenn Robinson .20 .50
116 Mark Jackson .20 .50

1997-98 Metal Universe Silver Slams

Randomly inserted in packs at one in 6, this 20-card set focuses on the young rising stars of the NBA. The cards feature black and white photos of the players against colorful foilboard. Odd numbers are printed on orange, even numbers are printed on purple.

COMPLETE SET (20) 6.00 15.00
STATED ODDS 1:6 HOBBY/RETAIL
1 Ray Allen .75 2.00
2 Kerry Kittles .40 1.00
3 Antoine Walker .60 1.50
4 Scottie Pippen 1.00 2.50
5 Damon Stoudamire .50 1.25
6 Shawn Kemp .60 1.50
7 Jerry Stackhouse .60 1.50
8 John Wallace .40 1.00
9 Juwan Howard .50 1.25
10 Gary Payton .60 1.50
11 Joe Smith .50 1.25
12 Terrell Brandon .40 1.00
13 Hakeem Olajuwon .75 2.00
14 Tom Gugliotta .40 1.00
15 Glen Rice .60 1.50
16 Charles Barkley 1.00 2.50
17 David Robinson 1.00 2.50
18 Patrick Ewing .75 2.00
19 Christian Laettner .50 1.25
20 Chris Webber .60 1.50

1997-98 Metal Universe Titanium

Randomly inserted in hobby packs only at a rate of one in 72, this 20-card set features some of the NBA's most explosive players on die cut cards. The cards are on clear plastic stock with the script in a light-blue foil.

COMPLETE SET (20) 600.00 1200.00
STATED ODDS 1:72 HOBBY
1 Michael Jordan 300.00 600.00
2 Allen Iverson 30.00 80.00
3 Kobe Bryant 50.00 125.00
4 Shaquille O'Neal 20.00 50.00
5 Stephon Marbury 12.00 30.00
6 Marcus Camby 10.00 25.00
7 Anfernee Hardaway 40.00 100.00
8 Kevin Garnett 15.00 40.00
9 Shareef Abdur-Rahim 10.00 25.00
10 Dennis Rodman 30.00 80.00
11 Ray Allen 12.00 30.00
12 Grant Hill 15.00 40.00
13 Kerry Kittles 6.00 15.00
14 Antoine Walker 10.00 25.00
15 Scottie Pippen 20.00 50.00
16 Damon Stoudamire 8.00 20.00
17 Shawn Kemp 12.00 30.00
18 Hakeem Olajuwon 12.00 30.00
19 Jerry Stackhouse 10.00 25.00
20 Juwan Howard 8.00 20.00

1998-99 Metal Universe

The 1998-99 Metal Universe set consists of 125 standard size cards. The 8-card packs retail for a suggested price of $2.69. The fronts feature full color game-action photos with brushed metal backgrounds and an embossed nameplate with the look of forged steel.

COMPLETE SET (125) 12.50 30.00
UNPRICED GEM MASTERS SERIAL #'d TO 1
1 Michael Jordan 2.00 5.00
2 Mario Elie .15 .40
3 Voshon Lenard .15 .40
4 John Starks .20 .50
5 Juwan Howard .20 .50
6 Michael Finley .25 .60
7 Bobby Jackson .15 .40
8 Glenn Robinson .20 .50
9 Antonio McDyess .20 .50
10 Marcus Camby .20 .50
11 Zydrunas Ilgauskas .25 .60
12 LaPhonso Ellis .15 .40
13 Terrell Brandon .15 .40
14 Rex Chapman .15 .40
15 Rod Strickland .15 .40
16 Dennis Rodman .50 1.25
17 Clarence Weatherspoon .15 .40
18 P.J. Brown .15 .40
19 Anfernee Hardaway .40 1.00
20 Dikembe Mutombo .25 .60
21 Gary Trent .15 .40
22 Patrick Ewing .30 .75
23 Sam Mack .15 .40
24 Scottie Pippen .40 1.00
25 Shaquille O'Neal .60 1.50
26 Donyell Marshall .15 .40
27 Bo Outlaw .15 .40
28 Isaiah Rider .20 .50
29 Detlef Schrempf .25 .60
30 Mark Price .25 .60
31 Jim Jackson .15 .40
32 Eddie Jones .25 .60
33 Allen Iverson .50 1.25
34 Corliss Williamson .15 .40
35 Tim Duncan .50 1.25
36 Ron Harper .20 .50
37 Tony Delk .15 .40
38 Derek Fisher .25 .60
39 Kendall Gill .15 .40
40 Theo Ratliff .20 .50
41 Kelvin Cato .15 .40
42 Antoine Walker .25 .60
43 Lamond Murray .15 .40
44 Avery Johnson .20 .50
45 John Stockton .30 .75
46 David Wesley .15 .40
47 Brian Williams .15 .40
48 Elden Campbell .15 .40
49 Sam Cassell .20 .50
50 Grant Hill .40 1.00
51 Tracy McGrady .40 1.00
52 Glen Rice .25 .60
53 Kobe Bryant 1.00 2.50
54 Cherokee Parks .15 .40
55 John Wallace .15 .40
56 Bobby Phills .15 .40
57 Jerry Stackhouse .25 .60
58 Lorenzen Wright .15 .40
59 Stephon Marbury .30 .75
60 Shandon Anderson .15 .40
61 Jeff Hornacek .20 .50
62 Joe Dumars .25 .60
63 Tom Gugliotta .15 .40
64 Johnny Newman .15 .40
65 Kevin Garnett .40 1.00
66 Clifford Robinson .15 .40
67 Dennis Scott .15 .40
68 Anthony Mason .15 .40
69 Rodney Rogers .15 .40
70 Bryon Russell .15 .40
71 Maurice Taylor .15 .40
72 Mookie Blaylock .15 .40
73 Shawn Bradley .15 .40
74 Matt Maloney .15 .40
75 Karl Malone .30 .75
76 Larry Johnson .25 .60
77 Calbert Cheaney .15 .40
78 Steve Smith .20 .50
79 Toni Kukoc .25 .60
80 Reggie Miller .30 .75
81 Jayson Williams .15 .40
82 Gary Payton .25 .60
83 George Lynch .15 .40
84 Wesley Person .15 .40
85 Charles Barkley .40 1.00
86 Tim Hardaway .25 .60
87 Darrell Armstrong .15 .40
88 Rasheed Wallace .25 .60
89 Tariq Abdul-Wahad .15 .40
90 Kenny Anderson .20 .50
91 Chris Mullin .25 .60
92 Keith Van Horn .25 .60
93 Hersey Hawkins .15 .40
94 Billy Owens .15 .40
95 Ron Mercer .20 .50
96 Rik Smits .20 .50
97 David Robinson .40 1.00
98 Derek Anderson .15 .40
99 Danny Fortson .15 .40
100 Jason Kidd .40 1.00
101 Sean Elliott .25 .60
102 Chauncey Billups .30 .75
103 Tyrone Hill .15 .40
104 Alan Henderson .15 .40
105 Chris Anstey .15 .40
106 Hakeem Olajuwon .30 .75
107 Allan Houston .20 .50
108 Bryant Reeves .15 .40
109 Anthony Johnson .15 .40
110 Shawn Kemp .25 .60
111 Brevin Knight .15 .40
112 A.C. Green .20 .50
113 Ray Allen .30 .75
114 Tim Thomas .25 .60
115 Walter McCarty .15 .40
116 Jalen Rose .20 .50
117 Kerry Kittles .15 .40
118 Vin Baker .20 .50
119 Shareef Abdur-Rahim .25 .60
120 Alonzo Mourning .30 .75
121 Joe Smith .20 .50
122 Tracy Murray .15 .40
123 Damon Stoudamire .20 .50
124 Checklist .15 .40
125 Checklist .15 .40
NNO Grant Hill SAMPLE .75 2.00

1998-99 Metal Universe Precious Metal Gems

*STARS: 50X TO 120X BASE CARD HI
STATED PRINT RUN 50 SERIAL #'d SETS
1 Michael Jordan 6000.00 10000.00
24 Scottie Pippen 80.00 200.00
25 Shaquille O'Neal 125.00 300.00
32 Eddie Jones 75.00 150.00
33 Allen Iverson 200.00 400.00
34 Corliss Williamson 40.00 100.00
35 Tim Duncan 80.00 200.00
36 Ron Harper 125.00 250.00
42 Antoine Walker 150.00 300.00
50 Grant Hill 400.00 800.00
51 Tracy McGrady 250.00 500.00
53 Kobe Bryant 2000.00 3000.00
65 Kevin Garnett 100.00 250.00
85 Charles Barkley 200.00 400.00
106 Hakeem Olajuwon 60.00 150.00

1998-99 Metal Universe Grant Hill Blowup

This oversized Metal Universe card features Grant Hill of the Detroit Pistons. The card is listed as a "sample" on the back, and is serial numbered to 10,000.

1 Grant Hill 1.50 4.00

1998-99 Metal Universe Big Ups

The 1998-99 Metal Universe Big Ups set consists of 15 cards and is an insert to the 1998-99 Metal Universe base set. The cards are randomly inserted in packs at a rate of one in 18. The fronts feature full color action photos with a visual background of the planet Earth. The Metal Universe logo sits in the upper left corner.

COMPLETE SET (15) 8.00 20.00
STATED ODDS 1:18
1 Stephon Marbury 1.00 2.50
2 Shareef Abdur-Rahim .75 2.00
3 Scottie Pippen 1.25 3.00
4 Marcus Camby .60 1.50
5 Ray Allen 1.00 2.50
6 Allen Iverson 1.50 4.00
7 Kerry Kittles .50 1.25
8 Dennis Rodman 1.50 4.00
9 Damon Stoudamire .60 1.50
10 Antoine Walker .75 2.00
11 Anfernee Hardaway 1.25 3.00
12 Shawn Kemp .75 2.00
13 Juwan Howard .60 1.50
14 Gary Payton .75 2.00
15 Tim Duncan 1.50 4.00

1998-99 Metal Universe Linchpins

The 1998-99 Metal Universe Linchpins set consists of 10 cards and is an insert to the 1998-99 Metal Universe base set. The cards are randomly inserted in packs at a rate of one in 360. The fronts feature color action player photos silhouetted on a card with laser die-cut pins in the background. The Metal Universe logo is located at the bottom center of the card.

COMPLETE SET (10) 1000.00 1500.00
STATED ODDS 1:360
1 Shaquille O'Neal 50.00 120.00
2 Kobe Bryant 150.00 400.00
3 Kevin Garnett 30.00 80.00
4 Grant Hill 30.00 80.00
5 Shawn Kemp 25.00 60.00
6 Keith Van Horn 12.00 30.00
7 Antoine Walker 12.00 30.00
8 Michael Jordan 800.00 1200.00
9 Gary Payton 20.00 50.00
10 Tim Duncan 40.00 100.00

1998-99 Metal Universe Neophytes

The 1998-99 Metal Universe Neophytes set consists of 15 cards and is an insert to the 1998-99 Metal Universe base set. The cards are randomly inserted in packs at a rate of one in 6. The fronts feature full color game-action photos of the top young stars in the NBA today. The Metal Universe logo is found at the left bottom corner and the featured player's name lines the left side of the gold- and silver-foiled stamped card.

COMPLETE SET (15) 2.50 6.00
STATED ODDS 1:6
1 Antonio Daniels .25 .60
2 Bobby Jackson .25 .60
3 Brevin Knight .25 .60
4 Chauncey Billups .50 1.25
5 Danny Fortson .25 .60
6 Derek Anderson .25 .60
7 Jacque Vaughn .25 .60
8 Keith Van Horn .40 1.00
9 Maurice Taylor .25 .60
10 Michael Stewart .25 .60
11 Ron Mercer .30 .75
12 Tim Thomas .40 1.00
13 Tim Duncan .75 2.00
14 Tracy McGrady .60 1.50
15 Zydrunas Ilgauskas .40 1.00

1998-99 Metal Universe Planet Metal

The 1998-99 Metal Universe Planet Metal set consists of 15 cards and is an insert to the 1998-99 Metal Universe base set. The cards are randomly inserted in packs at a rate of one in 36. The fronts feature full color action photos on top of a uniquely designed space-age die-cut design of the planet Earth. The Metal Universe logo can be found in the lower right corner.

COMPLETE SET (15) 200.00 400.00
STATED ODDS 1:36
1 Michael Jordan 100.00 250.00
2 Antoine Walker 4.00 10.00
3 Scottie Pippen 12.00 30.00
4 Grant Hill 8.00 20.00
5 Dennis Rodman 12.00 30.00
6 Kobe Bryant 25.00 60.00
7 Kevin Garnett 6.00 15.00
8 Shaquille O'Neal 10.00 25.00
9 Stephon Marbury 5.00 12.00
10 Kerry Kittles 2.50 6.00
11 Anfernee Hardaway 10.00 25.00
12 Allen Iverson 12.00 30.00
13 Damon Stoudamire 3.00 8.00
14 Marcus Camby 3.00 8.00
15 Shareef Abdur-Rahim 4.00 10.00

1998-99 Metal Universe Two for Me, Zero for You

The 1998-99 Metal Universe Two For Me set consists of 15 cards and is an insert to the 1998-99 Metal Universe base set. The cards are randomly inserted in packs at a rate of one in 96. The fronts feature a color game-action photo of two NBA players. The right side of the card reads, "Two 4 Me". The Metal Universe logo sits in the upper left corner.

COMPLETE SET (15) 75.00 150.00
STATED ODDS 1:96
1 Kobe Bryant 12.00 30.00
2 Anfernee Hardaway 5.00 12.00
3 Allen Iverson 6.00 15.00
4 Michael Jordan 50.00 120.00
5 Stephon Marbury 4.00 10.00
6 Ron Mercer 2.50 6.00
7 Shareef Abdur-Rahim 3.00 8.00
8 Marcus Camby 2.50 6.00
9 Damon Stoudamire 2.50 6.00
10 Kevin Garnett 5.00 12.00
11 Grant Hill 5.00 12.00
12 Scottie Pippen 5.00 12.00
13 Keith Van Horn 3.00 8.00
14 Dennis Rodman 6.00 15.00
15 Shaquille O'Neal 8.00 20.00

1997-98 Metal Universe Championship Promo Sheet

Released as a six-card sheet, this offered a sneak peek at the basic set design. The sheet was not perforated, but could be cut into individual cards since the backs are numbered. The back of the sheet features information on the basic set and the inserts.

1 Grant Hill 1.25 3.00
Kobe Bryant
Allen Iverson
Keith Van Horn
Kevin Garnett
Tim Duncan

1997-98 Metal Universe Championship

The 1997-98 Metal Universe Championship set was issued in one series totalling 100 cards. The debut set was issued in eight-card packs which carried a suggested retail price of $2.69.

COMPLETE SET (100) 10.00 25.00
1 Shaquille O'Neal .60 1.50
2 Chris Mills .15 .40
3 Tariq Abdul-Wahad RC .20 .50
4 Adonal Foyle RC .20 .50
5 Kendall Gill .15 .40
6 Vin Baker .20 .50
7 Chauncey Billups RC .75 2.00
8 Bobby Jackson RC .30 .75
9 Keith Van Horn RC .40 1.00
10 Avery Johnson .20 .50
11 Juwan Howard .20 .50
12 Steve Smith .20 .50
13 Alonzo Mourning .30 .75
14 Anfernee Hardaway .40 1.00
15 Sean Elliott .25 .60
16 Danny Fortson RC .25 .60
17 John Stockton .30 .75
18 John Thomas RC .15 .40
19 Lorenzen Wright .15 .40
20 Mark Price .25 .60
21 Rasheed Wallace .25 .60
22 Ray Allen .30 .75
23 Michael Jordan 2.00 5.00
24 John Wallace .15 .40
25 Bryant Reeves .15 .40
26 Allen Iverson .50 1.25
27 Antoine Walker .25 .60
28 Terrell Brandon .15 .40
29 Damon Stoudamire .20 .50
30 Antonio Daniels RC .25 .60
31 Corey Beck .25 .60
32 Tyrone Hill .15 .40
33 Grant Hill .40 1.00
34 Tim Thomas RC .30 .75
35 Clifford Robinson .15 .40
36 Tracy McGrady RC 1.00 2.50
37 Chris Webber .25 .60
38 Austin Croshere RC .20 .50
39 Reggie Miller .30 .75
40 Derek Anderson RC .25 .60
41 Kevin Garnett .40 1.00
42 Kevin Johnson .25 .60
43 Antonio McDyess .20 .50
44 Brevin Knight RC .25 .60
45 Charles Barkley .40 1.00
46 Tom Gugliotta .15 .40
47 Jason Kidd .40 1.00
48 Marcus Camby .25 .60
49 God Shammgod RC .25 .60
50 Wesley Person .15 .40
51 Clyde Drexler .30 .75
52 Paul Grant RC .15 .40
53 Rod Strickland .15 .40
54 Tony Delk .15 .40
55 Stephon Marbury .30 .75
56 Detlef Schrempf .25 .60
57 Joe Smith .20 .50
58 Sam Cassell .20 .50
59 Gary Payton .25 .60
60 Chris Crawford RC .25 .60
61 Hakeem Olajuwon .30 .75
62 Dennis Rodman .50 1.25
63 Eddie Jones .25 .60
64 Mitch Richmond .25 .60
65 David Wesley .15 .40
66 Tony Battie RC .25 .60
67 Isaac Austin .15 .40
68 Isaiah Rider .20 .50
69 Jacque Vaughn RC .20 .50
70 Tim Hardaway .25 .60
71 Darrell Armstrong .15 .40
72 Tim Duncan RC 1.25 3.00
73 Glen Rice .25 .60
74 Bubba Wells RC .25 .60
75 Maurice Taylor RC .25 .60
76 Kelvin Cato RC .20 .50
77 Shareef Abdur-Rahim .25 .60
78 Shawn Kemp .25 .60
79 Michael Finley .25 .60
80 Chris Mullin .25 .60
81 Ron Mercer RC .30 .75
82 Brian Williams .15 .40
83 Kerry Kittles .15 .40
84 David Robinson .40 1.00
85 Scottie Pippen .40 1.00
86 Kobe Bryant 1.25 3.00
87 Anthony Johnson RC .25 .60
88 Karl Malone .30 .75
89 Mookie Blaylock .15 .40
90 Joe Dumars .25 .60
91 Patrick Ewing .30 .75
92 Bobby Phills .15 .40
93 Dennis Scott .15 .40
94 Rodney Rogers .15 .40
95 Jim Jackson .15 .40
96 Kenny Anderson .20 .50
97 Jerry Stackhouse .25 .60
98 Larry Johnson .25 .60
99 Checklist .15 .40
100 Checklist .15 .40

1997-98 Metal Universe Championship Precious Metal Gems

*STARS: 75X TO 200X BASE CARD HI
*RCs: 40X TO 100X BASE HI
STATED PRINT RUN 50 SERIAL #'d SETS
1 Shaquille O'Neal 400.00 800.00
13 Alonzo Mourning 75.00 200.00
14 Anfernee Hardaway 800.00 1200.00
17 John Stockton 125.00 250.00
21 Rasheed Wallace 200.00 500.00
23 Michael Jordan 2500.00 5000.00
26 Allen Iverson 150.00 400.00
33 Grant Hill 150.00 300.00
36 Tracy McGrady 175.00 350.00
37 Chris Webber 125.00 225.00
39 Reggie Miller 200.00 400.00
41 Kevin Garnett 200.00 400.00
45 Charles Barkley 150.00 300.00
47 Jason Kidd 100.00 250.00
48 Marcus Camby 60.00 150.00
51 Clyde Drexler 125.00 225.00
61 Hakeem Olajuwon 150.00 300.00
62 Dennis Rodman 400.00 800.00
72 Tim Duncan 1000.00 1400.00
78 Shawn Kemp 100.00 200.00
80 Chris Mullin 100.00 200.00
84 David Robinson 150.00 300.00
85 Scottie Pippen 250.00 500.00
86 Kobe Bryant 1000.00 3000.00
88 Karl Malone 200.00 400.00
91 Patrick Ewing 80.00 200.00
97 Jerry Stackhouse 100.00 250.00

1997-98 Metal Universe Championship All-Millenium Team

Randomly inserted into packs at a rate of one in six, this 20-card set features top veterans and rising stars pictured against etched-foil fronts.

COMPLETE SET (20) 10.00 25.00
STATED ODDS 1:6
1 Stephon Marbury .60 1.50
2 Shareef Abdur-Rahim .50 1.25
3 Karl Malone .60 1.50
4 Scottie Pippen .75 2.00
5 Michael Jordan 4.00 10.00
6 Marcus Camby .50 1.25
7 Kobe Bryant 2.50 6.00
8 Allen Iverson 1.00 2.50
9 Kerry Kittles .30 .75
10 Ray Allen .60 1.50
11 Dennis Rodman 1.00 2.50
12 Damon Stoudamire .40 1.00
13 Antoine Walker .50 1.25
14 Anfernee Hardaway .75 2.00
15 Hakeem Olajuwon .60 1.50
16 Shawn Kemp .50 1.25
17 Antonio Daniels .50 1.25
18 Juwan Howard .40 1.00
19 Gary Payton .50 1.25
20 Tim Duncan 1.25 3.00

1997-98 Metal Universe Championship Championship Galaxy

Randomly inserted into packs at a rate of one in 192, this 15-card set pays tribute to players who currently wear NBA Championship rings and many young players who hope to obtain one in the future. The cards feature a foiled background with a double-etched player image surrounded by a "riveted" border.

COMPLETE SET (15) 500.00 1000.00
STATED ODDS 1:192
1 Michael Jordan 350.00 700.00
2 Allen Iverson 15.00 40.00
3 Kobe Bryant UER 30.00 80.00
4 Shaquille O'Neal 15.00 40.00
5 Stephon Marbury 6.00 15.00
6 Marcus Camby 5.00 12.00
7 Anfernee Hardaway 15.00 40.00
8 Kevin Garnett 15.00 40.00
9 Shareef Abdur-Rahim 5.00 12.00
10 Dennis Rodman 15.00 40.00
11 Grant Hill 8.00 20.00
12 Kerry Kittles 3.00 8.00
13 Antoine Walker 5.00 12.00
14 Scottie Pippen 15.00 40.00
15 Damon Stoudamire 4.00 10.00

1997-98 Metal Universe Championship Future Champions

Randomly inserted into packs at a rate of one in 18, this 15-card set focuses on rookie players. The cards appear three-dimensional with an action photo encased in a copper frame that is die cut at the bottom.
COMPLETE SET (15) 10.00 25.00
STATED ODDS 1:18
1 Tim Duncan 2.50 6.00
2 Tony Battie .50 1.25
3 Keith Van Horn .75 2.00
4 Antonio Daniels .50 1.25
5 Chauncey Billups 1.50 4.00
6 Ron Mercer .60 1.50
7 Tracy McGrady 2.00 5.00
8 Danny Fortson .50 1.25
9 Brevin Knight .50 1.25
10 Derek Anderson .50 1.25
11 Bobby Jackson .60 1.50
12 Jacque Vaughn .40 1.00
13 Tim Thomas .60 1.50
14 Austin Croshere .40 1.00
15 Kelvin Cato .40 1.00

1997-98 Metal Universe Championship Hardware

Randomly inserted into packs at a rate of one in 360, this 15-card set focuses on players who have a shot to one day take home an NBA honor, such as Scoring Champion, Rookie of the Year and MVP. The cards feature dual foils with an embossed background.
COMPLETE SET (15) 400.00 700.00
STATED ODDS 1:360
1 Stephon Marbury 12.00 30.00
2 Shareef Abdur-Rahim 10.00 25.00
3 Shaquille O'Neal 30.00 80.00
4 Scottie Pippen 20.00 50.00
5 Michael Jordan 300.00 600.00
6 Marcus Camby 10.00 25.00
7 Kobe Bryant 75.00 200.00
8 Kevin Garnett 40.00 100.00
9 Kerry Kittles 6.00 15.00
10 Grant Hill 20.00 50.00
11 Dennis Rodman 30.00 80.00
12 Tim Duncan 30.00 80.00
13 Antonio Daniels 6.00 15.00
14 Anfernee Hardaway 20.00 50.00
15 Allen Iverson 30.00 80.00

1997-98 Metal Universe Championship Trophy Case

Randomly inserted into packs at a rate of one in 96, this 10-card set features ten of the best players in the NBA presented on a 3-D sculptured embossed background.
COMPLETE SET (10) 25.00 60.00
STATED ODDS 1:96
1 Kevin Garnett 5.00 12.00
2 Grant Hill 5.00 12.00
3 Damon Stoudamire 2.50 6.00
4 Shaquille O'Neal 8.00 20.00
5 Ray Allen 4.00 10.00
6 Gary Payton 3.00 8.00
7 Shawn Kemp 3.00 8.00
8 Hakeem Olajuwon 4.00 10.00
9 John Stockton 4.00 10.00
10 Antoine Walker 3.00 8.00

1994 Metallic Impressions

Produced by Metallic Impressions for Classic, Inc., this 20-card standard-size set devotes four cards each to five of basketball's best centers. The set is titled "Centers of Attention," and production was limited to 12,500 hobby sets. Each set is accompanied by an individually numbered certificate of authenticity.
COMPLETE SET (20) 15.00 40.00
1 Hakeem Olajuwon 1.00 2.50
2 Hakeem Olajuwon 1.00 2.50
3 Hakeem Olajuwon 1.00 2.50
4 Hakeem Olajuwon 1.00 2.50
5 Patrick Ewing 1.00 2.50
6 Patrick Ewing 1.00 2.50
7 Patrick Ewing 1.00 2.50
8 Patrick Ewing 1.00 2.50
9 Alonzo Mourning 1.00 2.50
10 Alonzo Mourning 1.00 2.50
11 Alonzo Mourning 1.00 2.50
12 Alonzo Mourning 1.00 2.50
13 Dikembe Mutombo .75 2.00
14 Dikembe Mutombo .75 2.00
15 Dikembe Mutombo .75 2.00
16 Dikembe Mutombo .75 2.00
17 Shaquille O'Neal 2.00 5.00
18 Shaquille O'Neal 2.00 5.00
19 Shaquille O'Neal 2.00 5.00
20 Shaquille O'Neal 2.00 5.00

1997 Mexico Wonder Bread

Produced by Wonder Bread in Mexico, and having approval from the NBA, this 40-card set was inserted one per pack of Palitos De Pan tortilla snacks. The cards measure approximately 1 1/2" by 3" and are die cut, so they can stand. The card fronts feature the player's name at both the top and the bottom with the team logo in the upper right-hand corner. The card back features Spanish instructions on making the card stand.
COMPLETE SET (40) 125.00 250.00
1 Dikembe Mutombo 4.00 10.00
2 Mookie Blaylock 2.50 6.00
3 Dino Radja 2.50 6.00
4 Glen Rice 4.00 10.00
5 Toni Kukoc 4.00 10.00
6 Luc Longley 2.50 6.00
7 Terrell Brandon 2.50 6.00
8 A.C. Green 3.00 8.00
9 Antonio McDyess 3.00 8.00
10 Otis Thorpe 2.50 6.00
11 Joe Dumars 3.00 8.00
12 Chris Mullin 4.00 10.00
13 Hakeem Olajuwon 5.00 12.00
14 Charles Barkley 6.00 15.00
15 Rik Smits 3.00 8.00
16 Brent Barry 3.00 8.00
17 Eddie Jones 4.00 10.00
18 Elden Campbell 2.50 6.00
19 Alonzo Mourning 5.00 12.00
20 Tim Hardaway 4.00 10.00
21 Vin Baker 3.00 8.00
22 Tom Gugliotta 2.50 6.00
23 Kevin Garnett 6.00 15.00
24 Jayson Williams 2.50 6.00
25 Allan Houston 3.00 8.00
26 Anfernee Hardaway 6.00 15.00
27 Jerry Stackhouse 4.00 10.00
28 Allen Iverson 8.00 20.00
29 Cedric Ceballos 2.50 6.00
30 Arvydas Sabonis 3.00 8.00
31 Mitch Richmond 4.00 10.00
32 David Robinson 6.00 15.00
33 Avery Johnson 3.00 8.00
34 Gary Payton 4.00 10.00
35 Shawn Kemp 4.00 10.00
36 Damon Stoudamire 4.00 10.00
37 Marcus Camby 4.00 10.00
38 Karl Malone 5.00 12.00
39 Shareef Abdur-Rahim 4.00 10.00
40 Chris Webber 4.00 10.00

2005 Mid Mon Valley Hall of Fame

This set was released in 2005 by the Mid Mon Valley Sports Hall of Fame. Each card features a local sport legend printed on white card stock with a black and white artist's rendering of the featured subject on the front. The cover card proclaims the set as "Series 1 (2001-2005)" inductees.
COMPLETE SET (36) 10.00 20.00
151 Ashley Totedo Women's BK .30 .75
157 Gina Naccarato Women's BK .30 .75

2006 Mid Mon Valley Hall of Fame

This set was released in 2006 by the Mid Mon Valley Sports Hall of Fame. Each card features a local sport legend printed on white card stock with a black and white artist's rendering of the featured subject on the front. The cover card proclaims the set as "Series 2 (1997-2000/2006)" inductees.
COMPLETE SET (36) 10.00 20.00
95 Elmer Benyak BK .30 .75
97 Mouse Chacko BB BK .30 .75
105 Fran LaMendola CO BK .30 .75
114 Dick DiBiaso CO BK .30 .75
117 Don Asmonga CO BK .30 .75

1984-85 Miller Lite/NBA All-Star Charity Classic

This 6 card set was given out in conjunction with a charity half-court 3-on-3 game that was held during halftime of one of the 1984-85 Dallas Mavericks home games. The cards measure approximately 5" by 7" and feature black and white action shots of each player from his NBA career, and also feature sponsor logos from Spalding, Miller Lite, the Dallas Mavericks, and local radio station 98-KZEW. The black text on the backs contain information on the game and an appeal for fans to vote for the upcoming All-Star game in Indianapolis, which was held on February 10, 1985. The cards are unnumbered and are listed below in alphabetical order.
COMPLETE SET (6) 10.00 25.00
1 Connie Hawkins 2.50 6.00
2 Pete Maravich 8.00 20.00
3 Calvin Murphy 1.50 4.00
4 Nate Thurmond 1.50 4.00
5 Paul Westphal 1.50 4.00
6 Jo Jo White 1.50 4.00

2012-13 Momentum

1 Devin Harris .75 2.00
2 Al Horford 1.00 2.50
3 Kyle Korver 1.00 2.50
4 Josh Smith 1.00 2.50
5 Jeff Teague 1.00 2.50
6 John Jenkins RC 1.00 2.50
7 Mike Scott RC 1.00 2.50
8 Pete Maravich 2.00 5.00
9 Dominique Wilkins 1.50 4.00
10 Kevin Garnett 2.00 5.00
11 Jeff Green 1.00 2.50
12 Paul Pierce 1.25 3.00
13 Rajon Rondo 1.25 3.00
14 Brandon Bass .75 2.00
15 Jason Terry 1.00 2.50
16 Jared Sullinger RC 1.25 3.00
17 Larry Bird 3.00 8.00
18 John Havlicek 1.50 4.00
19 Bill Russell 2.00 5.00
20 Deron Williams 1.00 2.50
21 Joe Johnson 1.00 2.50
22 Brook Lopez 1.00 2.50
23 MarShon Brooks RC 1.25 3.00
24 Gerald Wallace 1.00 2.50
25 Kris Humphries .75 2.00
26 Mirza Teletovic RC 1.25 3.00
27 Tyshawn Taylor RC 1.00 2.50
28 Drazen Petrovic 1.25 3.00
29 Gerald Henderson .75 2.00
30 Michael Kidd-Gilchrist RC 1.50 4.00
31 Kemba Walker RC 3.00 8.00
32 Byron Mullens .75 2.00
33 Ramon Sessions 1.00 2.50
34 Bismack Biyombo RC 1.00 2.50
35 Carlos Boozer 1.00 2.50
36 Luol Deng 1.00 2.50
37 Joakim Noah 1.00 2.50
38 Derrick Rose 1.50 4.00
39 Richard Hamilton 1.00 2.50
40 Marquis Teague RC 1.00 2.50
41 Jimmy Butler RC 5.00 12.00
42 Jerry Sloan 1.25 3.00
43 Scottie Pippen 2.50 6.00
44 Reggie Theus 1.00 2.50
45 Kyrie Irving RC 8.00 20.00
46 Anderson Varejao .75 2.00
47 Alonzo Gee .75 2.00
48 C.J. Miles 1.00 2.50
49 Tristan Thompson RC 1.50 4.00
50 Dion Waiters RC 1.50 4.00
51 Tyler Zeller RC 1.25 3.00
52 Mark Price 1.25 3.00
53 Vince Carter 1.50 4.00
54 Chris Kaman 1.00 2.50
55 O.J. Mayo .75 2.00
56 Dirk Nowitzki 1.50 4.00
57 Darren Collison 1.00 2.50
58 Bernard James RC 1.00 2.50
59 Jae Crowder RC 1.25 3.00
60 Shawn Marion 1.00 2.50
61 Rolando Blackman 1.00 2.50
62 Michael Finley 1.25 3.00
63 Danilo Gallinari .75 2.00
64 Andre Iguodala 1.00 2.50
65 Ty Lawson .75 2.00
66 Kenneth Faried RC 1.50 4.00
67 Kosta Koufos .75 2.00
68 Evan Fournier RC 1.50 4.00
69 Quincy Miller RC 1.00 2.50
70 Corey Brewer .75 2.00
71 Fat Lever 1.00 2.50
72 Dan Issel 1.00 2.50
73 Tayshaun Prince 1.00 2.50
74 Brandon Knight RC 1.50 4.00
75 Greg Monroe 1.00 2.50
76 Jason Maxiell .75 2.00
77 Andre Drummond RC 2.50 6.00
78 Kim English RC 1.00 2.50
79 Kyle Singler RC 1.00 2.50
80 Vinnie Johnson 1.25 3.00
81 Dave Bing 1.25 3.00
82 Isiah Thomas 1.25 3.00
83 Stephen Curry 5.00 12.00
84 Klay Thompson RC 6.00 15.00
85 David Lee .75 2.00
86 Jarrett Jack 1.00 2.50
87 Harrison Barnes RC 2.50 6.00
88 Festus Ezeli RC 1.25 3.00
89 Draymond Green RC 5.00 12.00
90 Chris Mullin 1.25 3.00
91 Tim Hardaway 1.25 3.00
92 Sleepy Floyd .75 2.00
93 Jeremy Lin 1.25 3.00
94 James Harden 2.00 5.00
95 Chandler Parsons RC 1.50 4.00
96 Patrick Patterson .75 2.00
97 Omer Asik 1.00 2.50
98 Terrence Jones RC 1.25 3.00
99 Marcus Morris RC 1.25 3.00
100 Clyde Drexler 1.50 4.00
101 Hakeem Olajuwon 1.50 4.00
102 Paul George 1.50 4.00
103 Roy Hibbert 1.00 2.50
104 George Hill 1.00 2.50
105 David West 1.00 2.50
106 Tyler Hansbrough 1.00 2.50
107 Ben Hansbrough RC 1.00 2.50
108 Miles Plumlee RC 1.00 2.50
109 Lance Stephenson 1.00 2.50
110 Detlef Schrempf 1.25 3.00
111 Clark Kellogg 1.25 3.00
112 Blake Griffin 1.25 3.00
113 Chris Paul 1.50 4.00
114 DeAndre Jordan 1.25 3.00
115 Jamal Crawford 1.25 3.00
116 Eric Bledsoe 1.00 2.50
117 Caron Butler 1.00 2.50
118 Grant Hill 1.50 4.00
119 Chauncey Billups 1.25 3.00
120 Danny Manning 1.00 2.50
121 Bob McAdoo 1.00 2.50
122 Kobe Bryant 5.00 12.00
123 Steve Nash 1.25 3.00
124 Dwight Howard 1.00 2.50
125 Pau Gasol 1.25 3.00
126 Antawn Jamison 1.00 2.50
127 Darius Johnson-Odom RC 1.00 2.50
128 Robert Sacre RC 1.00 2.50
129 Jerry West 1.50 4.00
130 Elgin Baylor 1.25 3.00
131 A.C. Green 1.25 3.00
132 Gail Goodrich 1.00 2.50
133 Kareem Abdul-Jabbar 2.00 5.00
134 Magic Johnson 3.00 8.00
135 Wilt Chamberlain 2.50 6.00
136 Tony Allen .75 2.00
137 Mike Conley 1.00 2.50
138 Marc Gasol 1.25 3.00
139 Rudy Gay 1.25 3.00
140 Zach Randolph 1.00 2.50
141 Quincy Pondexter .75 2.00
142 Marreese Speights .75 2.00
143 Darrell Arthur .75 2.00
144 Tony Wroten RC 1.25 3.00
145 LeBron James 5.00 12.00
146 Dwyane Wade 2.00 5.00
147 Chris Bosh 1.25 3.00
148 Ray Allen 1.25 3.00
149 Shane Battier 1.00 2.50
150 Mario Chalmers 1.00 2.50
151 Rashard Lewis 1.00 2.50
152 Norris Cole RC 1.00 2.50
153 Udonis Haslem .75 2.00
154 Mike Miller 1.00 2.50
155 Alonzo Mourning 1.50 4.00
156 Mike Dunleavy .75 2.00
157 Monta Ellis 1.00 2.50
158 Brandon Jennings .75 2.00
159 Ersan Ilyasova .75 2.00
160 Ekpe Udoh .75 2.00
161 John Henson RC 1.50 4.00
162 Doron Lamb RC 1.00 2.50
163 Quinn Buckner 1.25 3.00
164 Bob Lanier 1.00 2.50
165 Oscar Robertson 1.50 4.00
166 Kevin Love 1.25 3.00
167 Ricky Rubio 1.25 3.00
168 Andrei Kirilenko 1.00 2.50
169 Nikola Pekovic .75 2.00
170 Luke Ridnour 1.00 2.50
171 Chase Budinger .75 2.00
172 Derrick Williams RC 1.00 2.50
173 Alexey Shved RC 1.00 2.50
174 Malcolm Lee RC 1.00 2.50
175 Al-Farouq Aminu 1.00 2.50
176 Ryan Anderson 1.00 2.50
177 Anthony Davis RC 8.00 20.00
178 Austin Rivers RC 1.50 4.00
179 Brian Roberts RC 1.00 2.50
180 Darius Miller RC 1.00 2.50
181 Eric Gordon 1.00 2.50
182 Greivis Vasquez 1.00 2.50
183 Robin Lopez .75 2.00
184 Dell Curry .75 2.00
185 Carmelo Anthony 1.50 4.00
186 Amar'e Stoudemire 1.00 2.50
187 Tyson Chandler 1.00 2.50
188 Raymond Felton 1.00 2.50
189 J.R. Smith 1.00 2.50
190 Jason Kidd 1.25 3.00
191 Steve Novak .75 2.00
192 Chris Copeland RC 1.00 2.50
193 Pablo Prigioni RC 1.00 2.50
194 Dave DeBusschere 1.25 3.00
195 Patrick Ewing 1.50 4.00
196 Walt Frazier 1.25 3.00
197 Allan Houston 1.00 2.50
198 Phil Jackson 1.50 4.00
199 Willis Reed 1.25 3.00
200 Kevin Durant 3.00 8.00
201 Russell Westbrook 3.00 8.00
202 Serge Ibaka 1.00 2.50
203 Kevin Martin 1.00 2.50
204 Kendrick Perkins .75 2.00
205 Thabo Sefolosha .75 2.00
206 Nick Collison 1.00 2.50
207 Jeremy Lamb RC 1.50 4.00
208 Perry Jones RC 1.00 2.50
209 Shawn Kemp 2.00 5.00
210 Gary Payton 1.25 3.00
211 Jameer Nelson .75 2.00
212 J.J. Redick 1.25 3.00
213 E'Twaun Moore RC 1.00 2.50
214 Nikola Vucevic RC 1.50 4.00
215 Maurice Harkless RC 1.50 4.00
216 Andrew Nicholson RC 1.00 2.50
217 DeQuan Jones RC 1.00 2.50
218 Kyle O'Quinn RC 1.00 2.50
219 Arron Afflalo 1.00 2.50
220 Anfernee Hardaway 3.00 8.00
221 Jrue Holiday 1.25 3.00
222 Jason Richardson 1.25 3.00
223 Evan Turner .75 2.00
224 Thaddeus Young .75 2.00
225 Andrew Bynum .75 2.00
226 Arnett Moultrie RC 1.00 2.50
227 Maalik Wayns RC 1.50 4.00
228 Hal Greer 1.00 2.50
229 Allen Iverson 1.50 4.00
230 Moses Malone 1.25 3.00
231 Julius Erving 2.00 5.00
232 Goran Dragic 1.00 2.50
233 Shannon Brown .75 2.00
234 Luis Scola 1.00 2.50
235 Marcin Gortat 1.00 2.50
236 Jared Dudley .75 2.00
237 Michael Beasley .75 2.00
238 Markieff Morris RC 1.50 4.00
239 Kendall Marshall RC 1.00 2.50
240 Luke Zeller RC 1.00 2.50
241 Kevin Johnson 1.25 3.00
242 Dan Majerle 1.00 2.50
243 LaMarcus Aldridge 1.25 3.00
244 Nicolas Batum 1.00 2.50
245 Wesley Matthews .75 2.00
246 J.J. Hickson .75 2.00
247 Damian Lillard RC 6.00 15.00
248 Meyers Leonard RC 1.25 3.00
249 Will Barton RC 1.25 3.00
250 Joel Freeland .75 2.00
251 Victor Claver RC 1.00 2.50
252 Bill Walton 1.25 3.00
253 DeMarcus Cousins 1.25 3.00
254 Tyreke Evans .75 2.00
255 Isaiah Thomas RC 2.50 6.00
256 Marcus Thornton .75 2.00
257 Jason Thompson .75 2.00
258 Jimmer Fredette RC 1.00 2.50
259 Thomas Robinson RC 1.25 3.00
260 Nate Archibald 1.00 2.50
261 Tim Duncan 2.00 5.00
262 Tony Parker 1.25 3.00
263 Manu Ginobili 1.25 3.00
264 Gary Neal 1.00 2.50
265 Kawhi Leonard RC 8.00 20.00
266 Danny Green 1.00 2.50
267 Tiago Splitter 1.00 2.50
268 DeJuan Blair .75 2.00
269 Stephen Jackson 1.00 2.50
270 Cory Joseph RC 1.00 2.50
271 Nando De Colo RC 1.00 2.50
272 George Gervin 1.25 3.00
273 David Robinson 2.00 5.00
274 Andrea Bargnani 1.00 2.50
275 Jose Calderon .75 2.00
276 DeMar DeRozan 1.25 3.00
277 Kyle Lowry 1.00 2.50
278 Landry Fields .75 2.00
279 Jonas Valanciunas RC 1.50 4.00
280 Terrence Ross RC 1.50 4.00
281 Quincy Acy RC 1.00 2.50
282 Ed Davis .75 2.00
283 Al Jefferson 1.00 2.50
284 Paul Millsap 1.25 3.00
285 Mo Williams 1.00 2.50
286 Gordon Hayward 1.25 3.00
287 Randy Foye .75 2.00
288 Derrick Favors 1.00 2.50
289 Enes Kanter RC 1.25 3.00
290 Alec Burks RC 1.50 4.00
291 Karl Malone 1.50 4.00
292 John Stockton 2.00 5.00
293 John Wall 1.50 4.00
294 Wes Unseld 1.25 3.00
295 Jordan Crawford .75 2.00
296 Trevor Ariza .75 2.00
297 Chris Singleton RC 1.00 2.50
298 Bradley Beal RC 2.50 6.00
299 Nene 1.00 2.50
300 Elvin Hayes 1.25 3.00

2012-13 Momentum Drive

*DRIVE VET: 1X TO 2.5X BASIC VET
*DRIVE RC: .75X TO 2X BASIC RC
STATED PRINT RUN 49 SER.#'d SETS
247 Damian Lillard 30.00 60.00

2012-13 Momentum Force

*FORCE VET: 1.2X TO 3X BASIC VET
*FORCE RC: 1X TO 2.5X BASIC RC
STATED PRINT RUN 25 SER.#'d SETS
8 Pete Maravich 15.00 40.00
45 Kyrie Irving 25.00 60.00

2012-13 Momentum Autographs

PRINT RUNS B/WN 15-199 COPIES PER
NO PRICING ON QTY 15 OR LESS
EXCHANGE DEADLINE 11/15/2014
1 Kevin Durant/149 50.00 120.00
5 Cedric Maxwell/199 3.00 8.00
6 Kenny Anderson/199 4.00 10.00
9 Mark Price/199 5.00 12.00
10 Eddie Johnson/199 3.00 8.00
11 James Worthy/25 12.00 30.00
13 Rashard Lewis/199 4.00 10.00
14 Tiago Splitter/99 4.00 10.00
15 Greivis Vasquez/199 4.00 10.00
16 Larry Johnson/199 5.00 12.00
18 Dominique Wilkins/35 6.00 15.00
20 Steve Smith/199 4.00 10.00
22 Alonzo Mourning/25 60.00 120.00
27 Chris Mullin/25 10.00 25.00
28 Courtney Lee/199 4.00 10.00
29 Jamaal Tinsley/199 3.00 8.00
31 Kobe Bryant/199 75.00 150.00
33 Dikembe Mutombo/35 5.00 12.00
34 David Robinson/49 12.00 30.00
37 Alex English/25 12.00 30.00
39 Ed Davis/199 3.00 8.00
41 Blake Griffin/99 EXCH 30.00 60.00
42 Larry Bird/49 40.00 80.00
43 Marcus Camby/199 6.00 15.00
49 Rick Mahorn/199 3.00 8.00
51 John Paxson/199 4.00 10.00
55 Dwyane Wade/35 20.00 50.00
56 Muggsy Bogues/199 6.00 15.00
60 Hakeem Olajuwon/35 20.00 50.00
61 Jim Jackson/199 3.00 8.00
62 David Thompson/25 4.00 10.00
63 Ersan Ilyasova/199 3.00 8.00
65 Dennis Scott/199 3.00 8.00
66 Kareem Abdul-Jabbar/99 30.00 80.00
68 Deron Williams/35 10.00 25.00
70 Grant Hill/49 15.00 40.00
71 Cazzie Russell/199 4.00 10.00
74 Mark Jackson/15 6.00 15.00
75 Nick Van Exel/15 10.00 25.00
77 Julius Erving/49 30.00 80.00
78 Anthony Mason/199 3.00 8.00
81 Vince Carter/25 12.00 30.00
82 Scottie Pippen/25 90.00 150.00
84 J.J. Hickson/149 3.00 8.00
85 Michael Cooper/199 4.00 10.00
88 Gordon Hayward/99 5.00 12.00
89 Brandon Rush/199 3.00 8.00
91 Magic Johnson/49 30.00 80.00
93 Byron Mullens/99 3.00 8.00
96 Lance Stephenson/199 4.00 10.00
98 Steve Francis/25 6.00 15.00
100 Bruce Bowen/199 3.00 8.00

2012-13 Momentum Autographs Drive

*DRIVE 49: .5X TO 1.2X BASIC AUTO
*DRIVE 25: .6X TO 1.5X BASIC AUTO
PRINT RUNS B/WN 10-49 COPIES PER
NO PRICING ON QTY 15 OR LESS
EXCHANGE DEADLINE 11/15/2014

2012-13 Momentum Autographs Force

*FORCE: .6X TO 1.5X BASIC AUTO
PRINT RUNS B/WN 5-25 COPIES PER
NO PRICING ON QTY 10 OR LESS
EXCHANGE DEADLINE 11/15/2014

2012-13 Momentum Momentous Rookies Autographs

EXCHANGE DEADLINE 11/15/2014
1 Kawhi Leonard 60.00 150.00
2 Jimmer Fredette 3.00 8.00
3 MarShon Brooks 4.00 10.00
4 Alec Burks 5.00 12.00
5 E'Twaun Moore 3.00 8.00
6 Bradley Beal 8.00 20.00
7 Kyle Singler 3.00 8.00
8 Darius Morris 3.00 8.00
9 Jae Crowder 4.00 10.00
10 Nolan Smith 3.00 8.00
11 Trey Thompkins 3.00 8.00
12 Terrence Jones 4.00 10.00
13 Kemba Walker 10.00 25.00
14 Jimmy Butler 15.00 40.00
15 Meyers Leonard 4.00 10.00
16 Andre Drummond 12.00 30.00
17 Evan Fournier 5.00 12.00
18 Brandon Knight 5.00 12.00
19 Kyrie Irving 50.00 120.00
20 DeAndre Liggins 4.00 10.00
21 Jan Vesely 3.00 8.00
22 Norris Cole 3.00 8.00
23 Tristan Thompson 5.00 12.00
24 Terrence Ross 5.00 12.00
25 Kendall Marshall 3.00 8.00
26 John Henson 5.00 12.00
27 Michael Kidd-Gilchrist 5.00 12.00
28 Andrew Nicholson 3.00 8.00
29 Festus Ezeli 4.00 10.00
30 Chandler Parsons EXCH 5.00 12.00
31 Lance Thomas 3.00 8.00
32 DeQuan Jones 3.00 8.00
33 Jared Cunningham 3.00 8.00
34 Orlando Johnson 3.00 8.00
35 Ivan Johnson 3.00 8.00
36 Thomas Robinson EXCH 4.00 10.00
37 Kenneth Faried 4.00 10.00
38 John Jenkins 3.00 8.00
39 Jon Leuer 4.00 10.00
40 Anthony Davis 75.00 200.00
41 Greg Stiemsma 3.00 8.00
42 Charles Jenkins 3.00 8.00
43 Lavoy Allen 3.00 8.00
44 Derrick Williams 3.00 8.00
45 Jared Sullinger 4.00 10.00
46 Kevin Jones 3.00 8.00
47 Tyler Zeller 4.00 10.00
48 Tobias Harris 5.00 12.00
49 Marquis Teague 3.00 8.00
50 Darius Miller 3.00 8.00
51 Miles Plumlee 3.00 8.00
52 Arnett Moultrie 3.00 8.00
53 Harrison Barnes 10.00 25.00
54 Chris Copeland 3.00 8.00
55 Malcolm Lee 3.00 8.00
56 Dion Waiters 5.00 12.00
57 Jeff Taylor 3.00 8.00
58 Quincy Acy 3.00 8.00
59 Tyshawn Taylor 3.00 8.00
60 Jeremy Tyler 3.00 8.00
61 Nikola Vucevic 5.00 12.00
62 Jonas Valanciunas 5.00 12.00
63 Maurice Harkless 5.00 12.00
64 Austin Rivers 5.00 12.00
65 Iman Shumpert 5.00 12.00
66 Chris Singleton 3.00 8.00
67 Marcus Morris 4.00 10.00
68 Doron Lamb 3.00 8.00
69 Kent Bazemore 5.00 12.00
70 Reggie Jackson 5.00 12.00
71 Will Barton 4.00 10.00
72 Tornike Shengelia 3.00 8.00
73 Bismack Biyombo 3.00 8.00
74 Ben Hansbrough 3.00 8.00
75 Nando De Colo 3.00 8.00
76 Bernard James 3.00 8.00
77 Isaiah Thomas 12.00 30.00
78 Cory Joseph 3.00 8.00
79 Markieff Morris 5.00 12.00
80 Draymond Green 12.00 30.00
81 Jeremy Pargo 3.00 8.00
82 Robert Sacre 3.00 8.00
83 Jordan Hamilton 3.00 8.00
84 Enes Kanter 4.00 10.00
85 Josh Selby 3.00 8.00

2012-13 Momentum Momentous Rookies Autographs Blue

*BLUE: .5X TO 1.2X BASIC
PRINT RUNS B/WN 48-49 COPIES PER
EXCHANGE DEADLINE 11/15/2014

2012-13 Momentum Monumental Marks

INT RUNS B/WN 15-149 COPIES PER
NO PRICING ON QTY 15 OR LESS
EXCHANGE DEADLINE 11/15/2014
3 C.J. Watson/49 3.00 8.00
4 Jerryd Bayless/25 4.00 10.00
5 Luc Longley/99 6.00 15.00
7 Marcus Thornton/25 3.00 8.00
9 Hedo Turkoglu/25 4.00 10.00
15 Tiago Splitter/99 4.00 10.00
16 Jamaal Tinsley/25 8.00 20.00
17 Charles Oakley/149 5.00 12.00
18 Ronnie Brewer/99 4.00 10.00
19 Alex English/35 4.00 10.00
21 Anthony Morrow/99 3.00 8.00
23 Jeff Teague/25 4.00 10.00
25 Andrew Bogut/25 15.00 40.00
26 Taj Gibson/25 8.00 20.00
27 Satch Sanders/25 8.00 20.00
29 Tom Chambers/25 4.00 10.00
30 Mario Chalmers/25 4.00 10.00
32 Muggsy Bogues/149 4.00 10.00
33 J.J. Hickson/25 12.00 30.00
34 Spencer Haywood/99 3.00 8.00
35 A.C. Green/25 15.00 40.00
36 Larry Johnson/99 6.00 15.00
38 Lance Stephenson/149 5.00 12.00
39 Fat Lever/99 4.00 10.00
41 Zydrunas Ilgauskas/99 4.00 10.00
42 Bob Love/49 5.00 12.00
43 Greg Ostertag/49 12.00 30.00
44 Len Elmore/49 3.00 8.00
45 Tyronn Lue/99 3.00 8.00
46 Walt Williams/25 12.00 30.00
47 Scot Pollard/49 3.00 8.00
48 Rod Strickland/99 3.00 8.00
50 Ronny Turiaf/25 12.00 30.00
51 Danny Ferry/49 3.00 8.00
52 Sam Perkins/25 3.00 8.00
54 Timofey Mozgov/149 3.00 8.00
55 Bruce Bowen/49 3.00 8.00
56 Mario Elie/49 3.00 8.00
57 Johan Petro/129 3.00 8.00
58 Jordan Crawford/149 3.00 8.00
59 Keith Erickson/25 10.00 25.00
60 Kwame Brown/49 3.00 8.00
61 Alonzo Gee/129 3.00 8.00
62 Rex Chapman/49 5.00 12.00
65 Stacey Augmon/49 3.00 8.00
66 Brian Grant/99 3.00 8.00
68 Landry Fields/25 3.00 8.00
72 Jason Kidd/25 15.00 40.00
74 Ekpe Udoh/79 3.00 8.00
75 Gordon Hayward/25 5.00 12.00
76 Slick Watts/25 3.00 8.00
77 Danny Green/129 4.00 10.00
79 Glen Rice/25 8.00 20.00
84 Antoine Walker/99 4.00 10.00
85 Dwyane Wade/35 20.00 50.00
87 Corey Brewer/149 3.00 8.00
91 Austin Daye/149 3.00 8.00
93 Marcus Camby/25 6.00 15.00
96 Bill Cartwright/25 12.00 30.00
98 Will Bynum/99 3.00 8.00
100 Tree Rollins/49 3.00 8.00
101 Bonzi Wells/99 3.00 8.00
102 Jerome Williams/99 3.00 8.00
103 Lamond Murray/49 3.00 8.00
104 Isaiah Rider/99 4.00 10.00
105 Darrell Armstrong/49 3.00 8.00
106 Damon Jones/49 3.00 8.00
108 Darryl Dawkins/99 3.00 8.00
109 Bernard King/25 4.00 10.00
111 Michael Bantom/99 3.00 8.00
113 Bo Kimble/149 3.00 8.00
114 Tony Campbell/49 3.00 8.00
115 Dick Barnett/99 5.00 12.00
116 Charlie Ward/49 3.00 8.00
118 Jim Jackson/99 3.00 8.00
119 Alan Anderson/99 3.00 8.00
120 Chris Wilcox/99 10.00 25.00
121 Robert Horry/25 4.00 10.00
124 Anthony Mason/99 6.00 15.00
126 Greivis Vasquez/129 6.00 15.00
127 Ersan Ilyasova/49 3.00 8.00
131 Nick Anderson/99 5.00 12.00
132 Kurt Rambis/25 10.00 25.00
133 Bobby Jackson/99 3.00 8.00
134 Kevin Willis/25 3.00 8.00
137 Mitch Richmond/25 12.00 30.00
138 Tom Gugliotta/99 3.00 8.00
140 Bryant Reeves/49 6.00 15.00
141 Dee Brown/99 3.00 8.00
142 Jonas Jerebko/49 6.00 15.00
143 Kevin Love/25 12.00 30.00
144 Chase Budinger/25 3.00 8.00
145 Rick Mahorn/25 3.00 8.00
146 Trevor Booker/25 3.00 8.00
147 Jason Richardson/25 6.00 15.00
148 J.J. Redick/25 5.00 12.00
153 Brandon Rush/99 3.00 8.00
154 Earl Lloyd/25 10.00 25.00
155 Cedric Ceballos/99 3.00 8.00
156 Adrian Dantley/25 4.00 10.00
161 Mel Davis/99 3.00 8.00
162 Daequan Cook/25 4.00 10.00
164 B.J. Armstrong/25 10.00 25.00
166 Kobe Bryant/149 EXCH 75.00 150.00
167 Blake Griffin/99 EXCH 60.00 60.00
168 Kevin Durant/99 75.00 150.00
171 Vince Carter/35 15.00 40.00
172 Steve Smith/99 4.00 10.00
174 Reggie Theus/49 4.00 10.00
176 Carl Landry/25 20.00 50.00
177 Andray Blatche/25 3.00 8.00
180 Bailey Howell/25 10.00 25.00
181 Gary Payton/25 8.00 20.00
186 Otis Birdsong/49 4.00 10.00
187 Craig Hodges/99 6.00 15.00
188 Truck Robinson/99 5.00 12.00
189 Johnny Newman/99 3.00 8.00
191 Henry Bibby/99 3.00 8.00
193 Klay Thompson/25 20.00 50.00
195 Herb Williams/99 3.00 8.00
196 Victor Claver/149 3.00 8.00
197 Eddie Johnson/99 3.00 8.00
198 Allan Houston/25 4.00 10.00
199 Jason Smith/99 3.00 8.00
200 DeMarre Carroll/149 3.00 8.00
202 Dahntay Jones/49 3.00 8.00
203 Andre Miller/25 4.00 10.00
204 Dan Issel/149 4.00 10.00
206 Larry Bird/25 40.00 100.00
209 Cazzie Russell/99 4.00 10.00
210 Buck Williams/99 3.00 8.00
211 Bryon Russell/49 5.00 12.00
212 Bob Sura/49 3.00 8.00
213 Michael Cooper/99 4.00 10.00
214 Campy Russell/99 3.00 8.00
216 Vin Baker/49 3.00 8.00
217 Chris Ford/25 8.00 20.00
218 Chris Mullin/25 8.00 20.00
220 Detlef Schrempf/49 6.00 15.00
222 Reggie Evans/25 6.00 15.00
226 Toni Kukoc/25 15.00 40.00
227 Brad Daugherty/99 4.00 10.00
228 Vernon Maxwell/99 5.00 12.00
229 Jayson Williams/99 3.00 8.00
230 John Salley/99 3.00 8.00
233 Zaza Pachulia/99 3.00 8.00
234 Walter Berry/79 3.00 8.00
237 David West/25 6.00 15.00
239 John Havlicek/25 40.00 80.00
240 Udonis Haslem/99 3.00 8.00
241 Gerald Henderson/25 3.00 8.00
244 Bobby Jones/49 6.00 15.00
246 Jerry West/25 15.00 40.00
247 Beno Udrih/149 3.00 8.00
248 Kyle Lowry/25 4.00 10.00
249 Earl Clark/49 3.00 8.00
250 Marreese Speights/25 3.00 8.00
252 Roy Hibbert/25 4.00 10.00
254 David Robinson/25 20.00 50.00
255 Richard Jefferson/25 4.00 10.00
256 Marco Belinelli/49 3.00 8.00
258 Maurice Cheeks/49 3.00 8.00
260 Bob McAdoo/25 15.00 40.00
261 Marcin Gortat/25 20.00 50.00
264 Xavier McDaniel/49 3.00 8.00
265 M.L. Carr/49 5.00 12.00
266 Kendrick Perkins/25 3.00 8.00
268 Mark Price/49 15.00 40.00
271 Juwan Howard/25 10.00 25.00
273 Wesley Matthews/149 3.00 8.00
275 Jason Maxiell/129 3.00 8.00
276 Joel Anthony/129 3.00 8.00
277 Sidney Moncrief/99 3.00 8.00
278 Harry Gallatin/25 5.00 12.00
279 Steve Novak/25 3.00 8.00
280 Cedric Maxwell/99 3.00 8.00
281 Derek Anderson/99 3.00 8.00
283 Al Attles/49 5.00 12.00
284 Gus Williams/99 3.00 8.00
285 Louis Williams/99 4.00 10.00
286 Ryan Anderson/99 4.00 10.00
287 Jeff Green/25 8.00 20.00
288 Dave Stallworth/99 3.00 8.00
289 Patrick Patterson/79 3.00 8.00
290 Nikola Pekovic/49 6.00 15.00
291 Marvin Williams/149 4.00 10.00
293 Mark Eaton/49 3.00 8.00
297 Sleepy Floyd/99 3.00 8.00
299 Leandro Barbosa/25 4.00 10.00

2012-13 Momentum Monumental Marks Blue

*BLUE 49: .5X TO 1.2X BASIC AUTO
*BLUE 25: .6X TO 1.5X BASIC AUTO
PRINT RUNS B/WN 10-49 COPIES PER
NO PRICING ON QTY 10 OR LESS
EXCHANGE DEADLINE 11/15/2014

2012-13 Momentum Monumental Marks Red

*RED 25: .6X TO 1.5X BASIC
PRINT RUNS B/WN 5-25 COPIES PER
EXCHANGE DEADLINE 11/15/2014

1976-77 MSA Drinking Cups

This set of MSA (Michael Schacter Associates) Drinking Cups was released in 1976. According to our information, there are relatively few cups that have the MSA credit ONLY. The oval bands that surround the player photo are blue and maize and they are reportedly far rarer than the already rare MSA Circle K variety. This set features some of the top players in the game. Please note that these cups are not numbered and are listed below in alphabetical order.
1 Kareem Abdul-Jabbar 25.00 50.00
2 Alvan Adams 10.00 20.00
3 Nate Archibald 15.00 30.00
4 Dennis Awtrey 10.00 20.00
5 Rick Barry 15.00 30.00
6 Otis Birdsong 10.00 20.00
7 Mike Bratz 10.00 20.00
8 Allan Bristow 10.00 20.00
9 Fred Brown 10.00 20.00
10 Louis Dampier 10.00 20.00
11 Adrian Dantley 15.00 30.00
12 Walter Davis 10.00 20.00
13 John Drew 10.00 20.00
14 Julius Erving 25.00 50.00
15 Walt Frazier 15.00 30.00
16 George Gervin 20.00 40.00
17 Artis Gilmore 15.00 30.00
18 Bob Gross 10.00 20.00
19 John Havlicek 20.00 40.00
20 Elvin Hayes 20.00 40.00
21 Spencer Haywood 15.00 30.00
22 Garfield Heard 10.00 20.00
23 Lionel Hollins 10.00 20.00
24 Dan Issel 15.00 30.00
25 Marques Johnson 10.00 20.00
26 Bernard King 10.00 20.00
27 Billy Knight 10.00 20.00
28 Bob Lanier 15.00 30.00
29 Ron Lee 10.00 20.00
30 Maurice Lucas 10.00 20.00
31 Pete Maravich 30.00 60.00
32 Bob McAdoo 15.00 30.00
33 Earl Monroe 15.00 30.00
34 Calvin Murphy 15.00 30.00
35 Mark Olberding 10.00 20.00
36 Curtis Perry 10.00 20.00
37 Charlie Scott 10.00 20.00
38 Phil Smith 10.00 20.00
39 Ricky Sobers 10.00 20.00
40 David Thompson 15.00 30.00
41 Rudy Tomjanovich 15.00 30.00
42 Dave Twardzik 10.00 20.00
43 Norm Van Lier 10.00 20.00
44 Bill Walton 15.00 30.00
45 Marvin Webster 10.00 20.00
46 Paul Westphal 10.00 20.00

1911 Murad College Series T51

These colorful cigarette cards featured several colleges and a variety of sports and recreations of the day and were issued in packs of Murad Cigarettes. The cards measure approximately 2" by 3". Two variations of each of the first 50 cards were produced; one variation says "College Series" on back, the other, "2nd Series". The drawings on cards of the 2nd Series are slightly different from those of the College Series. There are 6 different series of 25 in the College Series and they are listed here in the order that they appear on the checklist on the cardbacks. There is also a larger version (5" x 8") that was available for the first 25 cards as a premium (catalog designation T6) offer that could be obtained in exchange for 15 Murad cigarette coupons; the offers expired June 30, 1911.
*2ND SERIES: .4X TO 1X COLLEGE SERIES
24 Williams College Basketball 40.00 80.00
35 Northwestern Basketball 40.00 80.00
120 Luther Basketball 40.00 80.00
150 Xavier Basketball 40.00 80.00

1911 Murad College Series Premiums T6

24 Williams College Basketball 300.00 500.00

1974 Nabisco Sugar Daddy

This set of 25 tiny (approximately 1 1/16" by 2 3/4") cards features athletes from a variety of popular pro sports. One card was included in specially marked Sugar Daddy and Sugar Mama candy bars. The cards were designed to be placed on a 18" by 24" poster, which could only be obtained through a mail-in offer direct from Nabisco. The set is referred to as "Pro Faces" as the cards show an enlarged head photo with a small caricature body. Cards 1-10 are football players, cards 11-16 and 22 are hockey players, and cards 17-21 and 23-25 are basketball players. Each card was produced in two printings. The first printing has a copyright date of 1973 printed on the backs (although the cards are thought to have been released in early 1974) and the second printing is missing a copyright date altogether.
COMPLETE SET (25) 75.00 150.00
17 Oscar Robertson 10.00 20.00
18 Spencer Haywood 2.50 5.00
19 Jo Jo White 2.50 5.00

20 Connie Hawkins 5.00 10.00
21 Nate Thurmond 2.50 6.00
23 Chet Walker 2.50 6.00
24 Calvin Murphy 2.50 5.00
25 Kareem Abdul-Jabbar 12.50 25.00

1975 Nabisco Sugar Daddy

This set of 25 tiny (approximately 1 1/16" by 2 3/4") cards features athletes from a variety of popular pro sports. One card was included in specially marked Sugar Daddy and Sugar Mama candy bars. The cards were designed to be placed on a 18" by 24" poster, which could only be obtained through a mail-in offer direct from Nabisco. The set is referred to as "Sugar Daddy All-Stars". As with the set of the previous year, the cards show an enlarged head photo with a small caricature body with a flag background of stars and stripes. This set is referred on the back as Series No. 2 and has a red, white, and blue background behind the picture on the front of the card. Cards 1-10 are pro football players and the remainder are pro basketball (17-21, 23-25) and hockey (11-16, 22) players.

COMPLETE SET (25) 75.00 150.00
17 Jerry Sloan 2.50 6.00
18 Spencer Haywood 2.50 6.00
19 Bob Lanier 3.00 8.00
20 Connie Hawkins 4.00 10.00
21 Geoff Petrie 1.50 4.00
23 Chet Walker 2.00 5.00
24 Bob McAdoo 3.00 8.00
25 Kareem Abdul-Jabbar 10.00 25.00

1976 Nabisco Sugar Daddy 1

This set of 25 tiny (approximately 1 1/16" by 2 3/4") cards features action scenes from a variety of popular sports from around the world. One card was included in specially marked Sugar Daddy and Sugar Mama candy bars. The set is referred to as "Sugar Daddy Sports World - Series 1" on the backs of the cards. The cards are in color with a relatively wide white border around the front of the cards.

COMPLETE SET (25) 40.00 80.00
11 Basketball 5.00 10.00

1976 Nabisco Sugar Daddy 2

This set of 25 tiny (approximately 1 1/16" by 2 3/4") cards features action scenes from a variety of popular sports from around the world. One card was included in specially marked Sugar Daddy and Sugar Mama candy bars. The set is referred to as "Sugar Daddy Sports World - Series 2" on the backs of the cards. The cards are in color with a relatively wide white border around the front of the cards.

COMPLETE SET (25) 40.00 80.00
13 Basketball 5.00 10.00

1997 Nabisco/Post Penny Hardaway Posters

These 11"x17" posters of Anfernee "Penny" Hardaway came exclusively in boxes of Post HoneyComb and Nabisco Frosted Shredded Wheat cereals. Posters one (green border) and two (orange border) were available in HoneyComb and posters three (red border) and four (blue border) were available in Frosted Shredded Wheat.

COMPLETE SET (4) 2.50 6.00
COMMON POSTER (1-4) .75 2.00

2004 National Trading Card Day

This 53-card set (49 basic cards plus four cover cards) was given out in five separate sealed packs (one from each of the following manufacturers: Donruss, Fleer, Press Pass, Topps and Upper Deck). One of the five packs was distributed at no cost to each patron that visited a participating sports card shop on April 3rd, 2004 as part of the National Trading Card Day promotion in an effort to increase awareness of collecting sports cards. The 50-card set is composed of 16 baseball, 9 basketball, 10 football, 4 golf, 5 hockey and 4 NASCAR cards. Of note, first year cards of NBA rookie stars LeBron James and Carmelo Anthony were included respectively within the UD and Fleer packs. An early Alex Rodriguez Yankees card was also highlighted within the Fleer pack.

F1-F9 ISSUED IN FLEER PACK
T1-T12 ISSUED IN TOPPS PACK
DP1-DP6 ISSUED IN DONRUSS PACK
PP1-PP7 ISSUED IN PRESS PASS PACK
UD1-UD15 ISSUED IN UPPER DECK PACK
F7 Vince Carter .30 .75
F8 Carmelo Anthony .40 1.00
F9 Yao Ming .30 .75
T9 Shaquille O'Neal .20 .50
T10 Kirk Hinrich .15 .40
T11 Tracy McGrady .30 .75
UD6 Kevin Garnett .30 .75
UD7 LeBron James .75 2.00
UD8 Michael Jordan 1.00 2.50

2001 NBA All-Star Game

This three card set was handed out at the 2001 NBA All-Star Game, and features cards of Vince Carter, Shaquille O'Neal, and Kobe Bryant. The Vince Carter card was produced by Fleer and pictures Carter dribbling a basketball in front of the White House. The Shaquille O'Neal card was produced by The Topps Company, and features Shaq on his basic Topps Heritage card from 2000-01 with a special "All-Star Game" stamp on the front. Finally, the Kobe Bryant card was produced by Upper Deck and features Kobe going up for a dunk. Please note that all of these cards have a special "2001 All-Star Game" stamp on the front.

COMPLETE SET (3) 5.00 12.00
1 Vince Carter Fleer 2.50 6.00
2 Shaquille O'Neal Topps 1.50 4.00
3 Kobe Bryant Upper Deck 3.00 8.00

1973-74 NBA Players Association

This set contains 40 full-color postcard format cards measuring approximately 3 3/8" by 5 5/8". The front features a borderless posed "action" shot of the player. The back has the player's name at the top, and the NBA Players Association logo. The cards are unnumbered and are checklisted below in alphabetical order. There are ten tougher cards which are marked as SP in the checklist below. The two toughest of these are Mike Newlin and Paul Silas. Walt Bellamy was listed on the checklist, but was never issued, having been replaced by Lou Hudson.

COMPLETE SET (40) 300.00 600.00
1 Lucius Allen 1.50 4.00
2 Dave Bing SP 8.00 20.00
3 Bill Bradley 4.00 10.00
4 Fred Carter SP 7.50 15.00
5 Austin Carr 1.50 4.00
6 Dave Cowens 5.00 10.00
7 Dave DeBusschere 5.00 10.00
8 Ernie DiGregorio 2.50 6.00
9 Gail Goodrich 5.00 10.00
10 Hal Greer 3.00 8.00
11 John Havlicek 7.50 15.00
12 Connie Hawkins 5.00 10.00
13 Spencer Haywood 2.00 5.00
14 Lou Hudson 2.00 5.00
15 Bob Kauffman 1.25 3.00
16 Bob Lanier 4.00 10.00
17 Bob Love 3.00 8.00
18 Jack Marin 2.00 5.00
19 Jim McMillian 2.00 5.00
20 Earl Monroe SP 12.50 25.00
21 Calvin Murphy 3.00 8.00
22 Mike Newlin SP 50.00 100.00
23 Geoff Petrie 2.50 6.00
24 Willis Reed SP 12.50 25.00
25 Rich Rinaldi 1.50 4.00
26 Mike Riordan SP 7.50 15.00
27 Oscar Robertson SP 20.00 40.00
28 Cazzie Russell 2.00 5.00
29 Paul Silas SP 50.00 100.00
30 Jerry Sloan 3.00 8.00
31 Elmore Smith 1.50 4.00
32 Dick Snyder 1.50 4.00
33 Nate Thurmond 3.00 8.00
34 Rudy Tomjanovich 4.00 10.00
35 Wes Unseld 5.00 10.00
36 Dick Van Arsdale SP 10.00 20.00
37 Tom Van Arsdale 1.50 4.00
38 Chet Walker SP 10.00 25.00
39 Jo Jo White 2.50 6.00
40 Len Wilkens 5.00 10.00

1973-74 NBA Players Association 8x10

These ten (approximately) 8" by 10" cards feature full-bleed color posed "action" player photos on the matte-finished fronts. The backs carry the NBA Players Association logo. The cards are unnumbered and checklisted below according to the order sheet. On an order sheet concerning the reprinting of the 1973-74 NBA Players Assn. set, these large photos are mentioned as individual mat finish 8" by 10" pictures.

COMPLETE SET (10) 100.00 200.00
A Dave DeBusschere 10.00 20.00
B John Havlicek 20.00 40.00
C Willis Reed 10.00 20.00
D Ernie DiGregorio 5.00 10.00
E Dave Cowens 10.00 20.00
F Oscar Robertson 20.00 40.00
G Bill Bradley 12.50 25.00
H Jo Jo White 5.00 10.00
I Nate Thurmond 7.50 15.00
J Gail Goodrich 10.00 20.00

2002-03 NBA Showdown

1 Shareef Abdur-Rahim STAR .60 1.50
2 Emanual Davis .20 .50
3 Alan Henderson .20 .50
4 Dermarr Johnson .20 .50
5 Toni Kukoc .30 .75
6 Theo Ratliff .20 .50
7 Jason Terry .25 .60
8 Jacque Vaughn .20 .50
9 Kenny Anderson .25 .60
10 Mark Blount .20 .50
11 Randy Brown .20 .50
12 Milt Palacio .20 .50
13 Paul Pierce STAR .75 2.00
14 Vitaly Potapenko .20 .50
15 Antoine Walker .25 .60
16 Eric Williams .20 .50
17 P.J. Brown .20 .50
18 Elden Campbell .20 .50
19 Baron Davis STAR .60 1.50
20 Bryce Drew .20 .50
21 George Lynch .20 .50
22 Jamaal Magloire .20 .50
23 Jamal Mashburn STAR .60 1.50
24 Jerome Moiso .20 .50
25 Robert Traylor .20 .50
26 David Wesley .20 .50
27 Ron Artest .30 .75
28 Marcus Fizer .20 .50
29 A.J. Guyton .20 .50
30 Fred Hoiberg .20 .50
31 Ron Mercer STAR .50 1.25
32 Brad Miller .25 .60
33 Charles Oakley .25 .60
34 Kevin Ollie .20 .50
35 Eddie Robinson .20 .50
36 Michael Doleac .20 .50
37 Tyrone Hill .20 .50
38 Chris Mihm .20 .50
39 Andre Miller .25 .60
40 Lamond Murray .20 .50
41 Bryant Stith .20 .50
42 Shawn Bradley .20 .50
43 Greg Buckner .20 .50
44 Evan Eschmeyer .20 .50
45 Michael Finley STAR .75 2.00
46 Tim Hardaway .30 .75
47 Juwan Howard .25 .60
48 Danny Manning .25 .60
49 Eduardo Najera
50 Steve Nash .40 1.00
51 Dirk Nowitzki STAR 1.25 3.00
52 Avery Johnson .25 .60
53 Raef Lafrentz .20 .50
54 Voshon Lenard .20 .50
55 George McCloud .20 .50
56 Antonio McDyess STAR .60 1.50
57 James Posey .20 .50
58 Isaiah Rider .25 .60
59 Nick Van Exel STAR .60 1.50
60 Scott Williams .20 .50
61 Chucky Atkins .20 .50
62 Jon Barry .20 .50
63 Michael Curry .20 .50
64 Mikki Moore .20 .50
65 Clifford Robinson .20 .50
66 Jerry Stackhouse STAR .60 1.50
67 Corliss Williamson .20 .50
68 Mookie Blaylock .20 .50
69 Danny Fortson STAR .50 1.25
70 Adonal Foyle .20 .50
71 Larry Hughes .25 .60
72 Marc Jackson .20 .50
73 Antawn Jamison STAR .75 2.00
74 Bob Sura .20 .50
75 Steve Francis STAR .60 1.50
76 Cuttino Mobley STAR .50 1.25
77 Moochie Norris .20 .50
78 Glen Rice .25 .60
79 Maurice Taylor .20 .50
80 Kenny Thomas .20 .50
81 Walt Williams .20 .50
82 Travis Best .20 .50
83 Austin Croshere .20 .50
84 Al Harrington .25 .60
85 Reggie Miller STAR .75 2.00
86 Jermaine O'Neal .25 .60
87 Jalen Rose STAR .60 1.50
88 Elton Brand STAR .75 2.00
89 Corey Maggette .25 .60
90 Jeff McInnis .20 .50
91 Darius Miles .20 .50
92 Lamar Odom STAR .60 1.50
93 Michael Olowokandi .20 .50
94 Eric Piatkowski
95 Quentin Richardson .25 .60
96 Sean Rooks
97 Kobe Bryant STAR 3.00 8.00
98 Derek Fisher
99 Rick Fox .20 .50
100 Robert Horry
101 Lindsey Hunter .20 .50
102 Shaquille O'Neal STAR 2.00 5.00
103 Mitch Richmond .30 .75
104 Brian Shaw .20 .50
105 Isaac Austin .20 .50
106 Michael Dickerson .20 .50
107 Brevin Knight .20 .50
108 Grant Long .20 .50
109 Bryant Reeves .20 .50
110 Stromile Swift .20 .50
111 Jason Williams .25 .60
112 Lorenzen Wright STAR .50 1.25
113 Anthony Carter .20 .50
114 Laphonso Ellis .25 .60
115 Kendall Gill .20 .50
116 Brian Grant .20 .50
117 Eddie House .20 .50
118 Eddie Jones STAR .60 1.50
119 Alonzo Mourning STAR 1.00 2.50
120 Ray Allen STAR .75 2.00
121 Jason Caffey .20 .50
122 Sam Cassell .25 .60
123 Darvin Ham .20 .50
124 Ervin Johnson .20 .50
125 Anthony Mason .20 .50
126 Glenn Robinson STAR .60 1.50
127 Tim Thomas .20 .50
128 Chauncey Billups .30 .75
129 Terrell Brandon STAR .50 1.25
130 Kevin Garnett STAR 1.25 3.00
131 Dean Garrett .20 .50
132 Felipe Lopez .20 .50
133 Radoslav Nesterovic .20 .50
134 Anthony Peeler .20 .50
135 Joe Smith .25 .60
136 Wally Szczerbiak .25 .60
137 Lucious Harris .20 .50
138 Jason Kidd STAR 1.25 3.00
139 Todd MacCulloch .20 .50
140 Kenyon Martin .25 .60
141 Keith Van Horn STAR .60 1.50
142 Aaron Williams .20 .50
143 Shandon Anderson
144 Marcus Camby STAR .60 1.50
145 Othella Harrington
146 Allan Houston .25 .60
147 Mark Jackson .25 .60
148 Latrell Sprewell
149 Kurt Thomas
150 Charlie Ward
151 Clarence Weatherspoon
152 Darrell Armstrong .20 .50
153 Andrew Declercq .20 .50
154 Patrick Ewing .40 1.00
155 Pat Garrity .20 .50
156 Horace Grant .25 .60
157 Grant Hill STAR 1.00 2.50
158 Tracy Mcgrady STAR 1.25 3.00
159 Mike Miller .25 .60
160 Monty Williams .20 .50
161 Derrick Coleman .25 .60
162 Vonteego Cummings .20 .50
163 Matt Geiger .20 .50
164 Matt Harpring .20 .50
165 Allen Iverson STAR 1.25 3.00
166 Aaron McKie .20 .50
167 Dikembe Mutombo STAR .75 2.00
168 Eric Snow .20 .50
169 Tony Delk .20 .50
170 Tom Gugliotta .20 .50
171 Anfernee Hardaway .50 1.25
172 Dan Majerle .30 .75
173 Stephon Marbury STAR .60 1.50
174 Shawn Marion STAR .60 1.50
175 Bo Outlaw .20 .50
176 Rodney Rogers .20 .50
177 Iakovos Tsakalidis .20 .50
178 Derek Anderson .20 .50
179 Dale Davis .20 .50
180 Shawn Kemp .30 .75
181 Ruben Patterson .20 .50
182 Scottie Pippen .50 1.25
183 Damon Stoudamire .25 .60
184 Rasheed Wallace STAR .75 2.00
185 Bonzi Wells STAR .50 1.25
186 Mike Bibby .30 .75
187 Doug Christie .20 .50
188 Vlade Divac .25 .60
189 Bobby Jackson .20 .50
190 Scot Pollard .20 .50
191 Peja Stojakovic STAR .75 2.00
192 Hedo Turkoglu .25 .60
193 Chris Webber STAR .75 2.00
194 Bruce Bowen
195 Antonio Daniels .20 .50
196 Tim Duncan STAR 1.50 4.00
197 Danny Ferry .20 .50
198 Terry Porter .20 .50
199 David Robinson STAR 1.25 3.00
200 Malik Rose
201 Steve Smith
202 Vin Baker
203 Brent Barry .20 .50
204 Calvin Booth .20 .50
205 Rashard Lewis STAR .75 2.00
206 Desmond Mason .25 .60
207 Gary Payton STAR .75 2.00
208 Vince Carter STAR 1.25 3.00
209 Chris Childs .20 .50
210 Keon Clark .20 .50
211 Dell Curry .20 .50
212 Antonio Davis STAR .50 1.25
213 Hakeem Olajuwon .40 1.00
214 Morris Peterson .20 .50
215 Alvin Williams .20 .50
216 Jerome Williams .20 .50
217 Karl Malone STAR 1.00 2.50
218 Donyell Marshall .20 .50
219 Greg Ostertag .20 .50
220 Bryon Russell .20 .50
221 John Starks .60 1.50
222 John Stockton STAR 1.00 2.50
223 Hubert Davis .20 .50
224 Richard Hamilton STAR .60 1.50
225 Christian Laettner .25 .60
226 Tyrone Nesby .20 .50
227 Jahidi White .20 .50
228 Chris Whitney .20 .50

2002-03 NBA Showdown Strategy

S01 3-pointer .20 .50
Jerry Stackhouse
S02 Aggressive Play .40 1.00
Kevin Garnett STAR
S03 Alley-Oop .20 .50
Desmond Mason STAR
S04 And One! .30 .75
Chris Mihm
Grant Hill
S05 Blink and You'll Miss Him .40 1.00
Allen Iverson
S06 Brute Force .60 1.50
Shaquille O'Neal STAR
S07 Clean the Glass .50 1.25
Tim Duncan
S08 Clutch Shot .20 .50
Jalen Rose STAR
S09 Double-Foul .30 .75
Karl Malone
Gary Payton STAR
S10 Drive the Lane .20 .50
John Starks STAR
S11 Find the Open Man .30 .75
Karl Malone STAR
S12 From Way Downtown! .25 .60
Reggie Miller STAR
S13 Half-Court Set .25 .60
Gary Payton
S14 He's Heating Up! .40 1.00
Allen Iverson
S15 Hot Hand .25 .60
Rasheed Wallace
Damon Stoudamire STAR
S16 It's My Job - It's What I Do .30 .75
John Stockton
Wally Szczerbiak STAR
S17 Jumper .40 1.00
Allen Iverson
S18 Killer Crossover .20 .50
Steve Francis STAR
S19 Layup .15 .40
Jerome Moiso
S20 Outside Pick .30 .75
Karl Malone
John Stockton
S21 Power Move .40 1.00
Vince Carter
Tim Thomas
S22 Rimshaker .40 1.00
Vince Carter STAR
S23 Run'N Gun .20 .50
Richard Hamilton
S24 Scrapping in the Paint .15 .40
Kurt Thomas
S25 Slam Dunk .15 .40
Derek Anderson
S26 Starting the Fast Break .30 .75
Grant Hill STAR
S27 Take Two .60 1.50
Shaquille O'Neal
S28 Time-Out .20 .50
Steve Francis
Cuttino Mobley
S29 Tomahawk Dunk 1.00 2.50
Kobe Bryant STAR
S30 Wham Bam Slam! .60 1.50
Shaquille O'Neal STAR
S31 All over the Place .40 1.00
Scottie Pippen STAR
S32 Anticipate the Pass .20 .50
Steve Francis STAR
S33 Boxing Out .20 .50
Steve Francis
Kelvin Cato
S34 Change in Strategy .30 .75
Karl Malone
John Stockton
S35 De-fense! De-fense! .25 .60
Jumaine Jones
Dikembe Mutombo
Eric Snow
Jason Terry
S36 Defensive Stopper .25 .60
Dikembe Mutombo
S37 Get the Crowd Into It! .25 .60
Paul Pierce STAR
S38 Good D! .40 1.00
Kobe Bryant
Scottie Pippen
Wallace
S39 Good Position .20 .50
Kenyon Martin
S40 Guard the Paint .40 1.00
Anthony Mason
Tracy McGrady STAR
S41 Pick His Pocket .20 .50
Steve Francis
S42 Play 'Em Tight .25 .60
Gary Payton
Terrell Brandon STAR
S43 Quick Feet .30 .75
John Stockton
S44 Raising the Bar .20 .50
John Starks
Anthony Peeler STAR
S45 Rejected! .50 1.25
Tim Duncan
S46 Switching Strategies .15 .40
Brian Grant
Anthony Carter
S47 Taking the Charge .15 .40
Antonio Daniels STAR
S48 This is My House! .30 .75
Alonzo Mourning
Joe Smith STAR
S49 Tough Shot .20 .50
Kenyon Martin
Lamond Murray
S50 Turnover .15 .40
Fred Hoiberg
Jon Barry STAR

2008-09 NBA Starting Five

This seven-card set was available through the Starting Five promotion from the NBA and manufactured by both Topps and Upper Deck. The regular cards from Topps feature the 2008-09 Topps Chrome design with an additional "Starting Five" logo on the card front. The regular cards from Upper Deck feature a new design, but also carry a Starting Five logo. Card backs from Upper Deck carry the player's initials, while the Topps cards are not numbered. In addition, autographs of Derrick Rose, Dwayne Wade, Magic Johnson and Michael Jordan were randomly inserted in packs.

1A LeBron James AU 150.00 250.00
Upper Deck
1B LeBron James Black 4.00 10.00
1C LeBron James White 4.00 10.00
DR Derrick Rose 4.00 10.00
MJ Michael Jordan 8.00 20.00
NNO Magic Johnson 2.50 6.00
NNO Magic Johnson AU 100.00 200.00
NNO Greg Oden .75 2.00
NNO Dwyane Wade 1.50 4.00
NNO Dwyane Wade AU
AUDR Derrick Rose AU 200.00 400.00
AUMJ Michael Jordan AU 300.00 500.00

2010-11 NBA Starting Five

This six-card set was available through the Starting Five promotion from the NBA and manufactured by Panini. The regular cards feature the 2010-11 Donruss design with an additional "Starting Five" logo on the card front. Card backs carry the player's initials. In addition, autographs were randomly inserted which were on Playoff Preferred cards.

COMPLETE SET (6) 4.00 10.00
CB Chris Bosh AU
Playoff Preferred
DC DeMarcus Cousins AU 10.00 25.00
Playoff Preferred
DF Derrick Favors AU 8.00 20.00
Playoff Preferred
DH Dwight Howard .30 .75
DW Dwyane Wade .60 1.50
ET Evan Turner AU 10.00 25.00
Playoff Preferred
JW John Wall 2.00 5.00
KB Kobe Bryant 1.50 4.00
KD Kevin Durant 1.00 2.50
LJ LeBron James 2.00 5.00
SC Stephen Curry AU 25.00 60.00
Playoff Preferred
WJ Wesley Johnson AU 6.00 15.00
Playoff Preferred

2012-13 NBA Starting Five

COMPLETE SET (12)
1 Kobe Bryant 1.50 4.00
2 Blake Griffin .40 1.00
3 Kevin Durant 1.00 2.50
4 Kyrie Irving 4.00 10.00
5 Anthony Davis 4.00 10.00
6 Michael Kidd-Gilchrist .75 2.00
7 Thomas Robinson .60 1.50
8 Harrison Barnes 1.25 3.00
9 Derrick Williams .50 1.25
10 Kenneth Faried .75 2.00
11 Austin Rivers .75 2.00
12 Jared Sullinger .60 1.50

2012-13 NBA Starting Five Panini Authentic

1 Kobe Bryant 2.50 6.00
2 Blake Griffin .60 1.50
3 Kevin Durant 1.50 4.00
4 Kyrie Irving 3.00 8.00

2012-13 NBA Starting Five Playmakers

1 Anthony Davis 6.00 15.00
2 Michael Kidd-Gilchrist 1.25 3.00

1971-72 NBA Stickers

This sticker sheet was released during the 1971-72 season, and features team logo stickers of 17 teams. This sheet measures 5.5x9.25 and was done in full color. Please note that this sticker sheet has a blank back.

1 Team Logos 2.00 5.00

1998 NBA Wrapper Rebound Shaquille O'Neal

This promotion was a joint effort between the NBA, Fleer/SkyBox, Topps and Upper Deck. Fans who collected series two wrappers of SkyBox Z-Force, Stadium Club, Ultra and Upper Deck could redeem those for a variety of Shaquille O'Neal collectibles. Collectors could redeem eight wrappers for a facsimile autographed poster, 40 wrappers for an exclusive four-card set featuring one card from each NBA partner, and 200 wrappers for an uncut basketball card sheet. There was also a grand prize of four tickets to an NBA game and O'Neal autographed merchandise. The promotion ran from January 15, 1998 through June 15, 1998. Listed below are the prices for the poster, four-card set and the uncut sheet. The complete set price is for the four-card set only.

COMPLETE SET (4) 12.00 30.00
1 Shaquille O'Neal Fleer 4.00 10.00
2 Shaquille O'Neal SkyBox 4.00 10.00
3 Shaquille O'Neal Topps 4.00 10.00
4 Shaquille O'Neal Upper Deck 4.00 10.00
NNO Shaquille O'Neal Poster 4.00 10.00
NNO Uncut NBA Sheet 15.00 40.00

2007 NBA Valentines

Released by Paper Magic Group in conjunction with the NBA, this set features six valentines measuring 2 1/2" x 4 1/4" an Allen Iverson valentine measuring 4 1/4" x 6 1/4" a tattoo sheet featuring five team logo tattos of all the represented teams (35 total) and a 15" x 19" poster with all seven players in the set placed horizontally next to each other. All these contents were packaged into a single box, and the box carried an initial suggested retail price of $2.99.

NNO Tim Duncan .40 1.00
NNO Allen Iverson .40 1.00
NNO LeBron James .75 2.00
NNO Tracy McGrady .40 1.00
NNO Steve Nash .40 1.00
NNO Dirk Nowitzki .40 1.00
NNO Dwyane Wade .60 1.50
NNO Tattoos .20 .50
NNO Tim Duncan .75 2.00
Allen Iverson
LeBron James
Tracy McGrady
Steve Nash
Dirk Nowitzki
Dwyane Wade
Poster

1969 NBAP Members

These rather unattractive cards, which definitely vary somewhat in size, measure approximately 2 3/4" by 4 1/2". The blank-backed cards feature borderless black-and-white photos and have light blue bottoms. These cards must not have been licensed by the NBA because the red, white and blue NBA logos have been airbrushed out. The cards may have been made from boxes of basketball shoes, possibly Converse. There may also be other cards in the set. Small and large versions of the logo card exist, both of which are almost square and are red, white, and blue. The cards are unummbered and are listed below,in alphabetical order. With some recent discoveries, it is believed that this set was issued into the 1970's as there was a recently discovered Kareem Abdul-Jabbar card. However, with the inclusion of Bill Russell, it becomes obvious that this set was issued over a number of years as Russell retired after the 1968-69 season.

COMPLETE SET (20) 3500.00 5000.00
1 Kareem Abdul-Jabbar 300.00 600.00
2 Elgin Baylor 200.00 400.00
3 Zelmo Beaty 75.00 150.00
4 Bob Boozer 75.00 150.00
5 Bill Bradley 100.00 200.00
6 Wilt Chamberlain 400.00 800.00
7 John Havlicek 200.00 500.00
8 Don Kojis 75.00 150.00
9 Jerry Lucas 100.00 200.00
10 Eddie Miles 75.00 150.00
11 Jeff Mullins 75.00 150.00
12 Willis Reed 100.00 200.00
13 Oscar Robertson 250.00 500.00
14 Bill Russell 400.00 800.00
15 Wes Unseld 100.00 200.00
16 Dick Van Arsdale 75.00 150.00
17 Chet Walker 75.00 150.00
18 Jerry West 400.00 800.00
19 Len Wilkens 100.00 200.00
20 NBAP Logo 75.00 150.00

1984-85 Nets Getty

This 12-card set was produced by Getty and issued in four sheets, with three player cards per sheet. Getty Gas stations distributed the sheets to customers one per week. The sheets measure approximately 8" by 11". Although the sheets are not actually perforated, the black broken lines indicate that the cut cards measure 3 5/8" by 6 3/4". The front features a borderless color action shot, with the player's facsimile autograph below the picture. The player's name and number appear above the picture in block lettering. The New Jersey Nets and Getty logos appear at the bottom of each sheet. The cards are unnumbered and have been listed below in alphabetical order.

COMPLETE SET (12) 15.00 40.00
1 Stan Albeck CO 1.25 3.00
2 Otis Birdsong 2.00 5.00
3 Darwin Cook 1.25 3.00
4 Darryl Dawkins 3.00 8.00
5 Mike Gminski 2.00 5.00
6 Albert King 1.50 4.00
7 Mike O'Koren 1.50 4.00
8 Kelvin Ransey 1.25 3.00
9 M.Ray Richardson 1.50 4.00
10 Jeff Turner 2.00 5.00
11 Buck Williams 3.00 8.00
12 Duncan (Mascot) 1.25 3.00

1990-91 Nets Kayo/Breyers

This 14-card standard-size set of New Jersey Nets was sponsored by Kayo Cards and Breyers Ice Cream. The front features a color action player photo, with a thin red border. The left corner is cut out, and the word "Kayo" appears. The team logo overlays the left bottom corner of the picture, and the player's position and name are given below the picture in black and white lettering on red. The outer border is blue, which washes out as one moves toward the card bottom. The back has biographical information as well as college and pro statistics, enframed by a black border. As on the front, the red outer border washes out. The set features an early professional card of Derrick Coleman.

COMPLETE SET (14) 3.00 8.00
1 Mookie Blaylock .75 2.00
2 Sam Bowie .60 1.50
3 Jud Buechler .40 1.00
4 Derrick Coleman .75 2.00
5 Lester Conner .30 .75
6 Chris Dudley .40 1.00
7 Tate George .30 .75
8 Derrick Gervin .30 .75
9 Jack Haley .30 .75
10 Kirk Lee .30 .75
11 Chris Morris .40 1.00
12 Reggie Theus 1.00 2.50
13 Bill Fitch CO .30 .75
14 Nets Home Schedule .30 .75

1986 Nets Lifebuoy/Star

The 1986 Star Lifebuoy New Jersey Nets set contains 14 cards, one for each of the 12 players, one for Head Coach Dave Wohl, and a checklist card. The set's basic design is identical to those of the Star Company's regular NBA sets. The front borders are royal blue, and the backs show each player's NBA statistics. The cards show a Star '86 logo in the upper right corner. The cards measure approximately 2 1/2" by 3 1/2". The cards are numbered in the upper left corner of the reverse; the numbering corresponds to alphabetical order by player.

COMPLETE SET (14) 5.00 12.00
1 Dave Wohl CO .75 2.00
2 Otis Birdsong .60 1.50
3 Bobby Cattage .40 1.00
4 Darwin Cook .40 1.00
5 Darryl Dawkins 1.50 4.00
6 Mike Gminski .60 1.50
7 Mickey Johnson .40 1.00
8 Albert King .50 1.25
9 Mike O'Koren .50 1.25
10 Kelvin Ransey .40 1.00
11 Micheal Ray Richardson .50 1.25
12 Jeff Turner .75 2.00
13 Buck Williams 1.50 4.00
14 Title Card/ .40 1.00
Checklist on back)

1971-72 Nets New York Team Issue

Each of these team-issued photos measure approximately 8" by 10" and feature black and white player portraits on two sheets. The player's name is listed below the photo. Each sheet contains either six or eight player portraits. The backs are blank. The photos are unnumbered and listed below alphabetically.

COMPLETE SET (2) 12.50 25.00
1 Jim Ard 7.50 15.00
Rick Barry
Jeff Congdon
Joe Depre
Sonny Dove
Jarrett Durham
Manny Leaks
Bill Melchionni
2 Roy Boe PRES 5.00 10.00
Lou Carnesecca CO
Billy Paultz
John Roche
Ollie Taylor
Tom Washington

2001-02 Nets Topps

Released by Topps, this 10-card set features a horizontal design with the Nets logo in the background and was given away during the 2001-02 season.

COMPLETE SET (10) 2.00 5.00
NN1 Stephon Marbury .40 1.00
NN2 Keith Van Horn .40 1.00
NN3 Kendall Gill .30 .75
NN4 Jamie Feick .30 .75
NN5 Stephen Jackson .40 1.00
NN6 Byron Scott .40 1.00
NN7 Johnny Newman .30 .75
NN8 Aaron Williams .30 .75
NN9 Lucious Harris .30 .75
NN10 Kenyon Martin .50 1.25

1974 New York News This Day in Sports

These cards are newspaper clippings of drawings by Hollreiser and are accompanied by textual description highlighting a player's unique sports feat. Cards are approximately 2" X 4 1/4". These are multisport cards and aranged in chronological order.

COMPLETE SET 50.00 120.00
36 Wilt Chamberlain 2.00 4.00
Dec. 6, 1963

1991 Nike Michael Jordan/Spike Lee

This six-card standard-size set was issued by Nike (in complete set form) to depict memorable Nike commercials starring Michael Jordan and Spike Lee. Nike had reportedly planned originally to produce an additional set of cards every three months featuring other world famous athletes in Nike commercials. The cards all have the same horizontally oriented front, with oval-shaped photos of Michael Jordan and Mars Blackmon (the character played by Spike Lee) and a Nike Trading Cards logo. A different quote appears at the top of each card front. The backs are either horizontally or vertically oriented and have either a black and white photo or a commercial advertisement. The cards are numbered on the front.

COMPLETE SET (6) 6.00 15.00
1 Earth/Mars 1988 1.25 3.00
2 High Flying 1989 1.00 2.50
3 Do You Know 1990 1.00 2.50
4 Stay in School 1991 1.00 2.50
5 Genie 1991 1.00 2.50
With Little Richard
6 Michael Jordan Flight 1.25 3.00

1985 Nike

This oversized (slightly larger than 3x5 cards) multisport set was issued by Nike to promote athletic shoe sales. Although the set contains an attractive rookie-season card of Michael Jordan, the fairly plentiful supply has kept the market value quite affordable. Sets were distributed in shrinkwrapped form. The cards are unnumbered and are listed here in alphabetical order.

COMP.FACTORY SET (5) 50.00 125.00
COMPLETE SET (5) 30.00 75.00
2 Michael Jordan 15.00 40.00

1983-85 Nike Poster Cards

The cards in this set measure approximately 5" by 7" and were produced for use by retailers of Nike full-size posters as a promotional counter display. The cards are plastic coated and feature color pictures of players posed in unique settings. The hole at the top was designed so that dealers could attach the cards to the display with a soft plastic fastener provided by Nike. The borders are black. Originally, 27-cards were issued together and others were added later as new posters were created. The backs are plain white and carry the poster name, item number, and the player names (except on group photos). The cards are numbered only by the item number on back and have been listed below according to the final two digits of that number.

COMPLETE SET (43) 125.00 225.00
1 The Supreme Court 3.00 6.00
2 Iceman 5.00 12.00
6 Dr. Dunkenstein 1.25 3.00
19 Moses 3.00 8.00
20 Jam Session 2.00 5.00
25 Silk 2.50 6.00
30 Board Room 2.00 5.00
33 Stormin' Norman 2.00 5.00
34 Secretary of Defense 2.50 6.00
35 Air Force I 5.00 10.00
43 Sir Sid 3.00 8.00
Sidney Moncrief
57 Air Force 10.00 25.00
M.Malone
Barkley
62 Manute Bol Growth Chart 2.50 6.00
68 Shirts and Skins 1.25 3.00

1993 Nike/Warner Michael Jordan

The Nike/Warner Michael Jordan set is comprised of 12 stickers, divided into two series of six stickers each. The first series is dubbed "Aerospace Jordan Trading Stickers," and includes six standard-size stickers. The second series dubbed "The Scream Team," also consists of six stickers. Each series of stickers was issued by Nike and features color pictures of Michael Jordan and characters from Warner Brothers cartoons. The Nike logo appears on each card. The peel-off backs are white. The stickers are unnumbered and checklisted below in alphabetical order according to description within each series: series one (1-6) and series two (7-12).

COMPLETE SET (12) 5.00 12.00
1 Martian .40 1.00
(With basketball)
2 Martian .40 1.00
(The Best on Earth,
The Best on Mars)
3 Martian and his dog .40 1.00
(Hanging from
pulverized planetoid)
4 Michael Jordan .75 2.00
(Palming Martian
by helmet crest)
5 Michael Jordan .75 2.00
(Riding in Bugs'
flying saucer)
6 Porky Pig .40 1.00
(Piloting flying saucer)
7 Aerospace .75 2.00
(Michael Jordan slam
dunking in space)
8 J-J-Just Do It .40 1.00
(Porky Pig in Nikes)
9 Nice Shoes Indeed .40 1.00
(Martian with his dog,
holding a Nike)
10 The Scream Team .75 2.00
(Michael Jordan with Bugs)
11 Warning: .40 1.00
(Martian and
warning message)
12 What's Up Jock .40 1.00
(Bugs slam dunking
in space)

1996 No Fear

This eight-card jumbo-sized set was issued through No Fear. It is a multi-sport set that features a posed color player shot on the front and a white back featuring a slogan by No Fear. The mode of distribution is unclear. The cards are not numbered and checklisted below in alphabetical order.

COMPLETE SET (8) 5.00 12.00
7 Chris Mills BK .40 1.00

1977-78 Nuggets Iron-On

This six item iron-on set was sponsored by Pepsi-Cola, and was released during the 1977-78 season, and features some of the Denver Nugget players and coaches. The iron-ons measure 6 1/4"x11".

COMPLETE SET (6) 20.00 40.00
1 Dan Issel 5.00 10.00
2 Brian Taylor 2.00 5.00
3 Bobby Wilkerson 2.00 5.00
4 Bobby Jones 5.00 10.00

5 Larry Brown CO 3.00 8.00
6 David Thompson 5.00 10.00

1975-76 Nuggets Pepsi Cans

The 1975-76 Nuggets Pepsi Cans feature 15 players, coaches and front office personnel of the Denver Nuggets. The top of the panel that features the player contains the salutation "Congratulations Denver Nuggets", which contains below it a sketch of the player, as well as a facsimile signature and a short biography. These standard-sized aluminum cans then have below the player sketch "75-76 ABA Regular Season Champions". The cans contain no numbering other than jersey numbers, thus the set is listed alphabetically below. Cans opened from the bottom command up to a 25% premium over the prices below.

COMPLETE SET (15) 80.00 160.00
1 Byron Beck 5.00 10.00
2 Larry Brown CO 7.50 15.00
3 Jimmy Foster 3.00 8.00
4 Gus Gerard 3.00 8.00
5 George Irvine 3.00 8.00
6 Dan Issel 12.50 25.00
7 Bobby Jones 10.00 20.00
8 Doug Moe ACO 7.50 15.00
9 Carl Scheer GM 3.00 8.00
10 Ralph Simpson 5.00 10.00
11 Claude Terry 3.00 8.00
12 David Thompson 12.50 25.00
13 Monte Towe 5.00 10.00
14 Marvin Webster 3.00 8.00
15 Chuck Williams 3.00 8.00

1976-77 Nuggets Pepsi Cans

The 1976-77 Nuggets Pepsi Can Issue contains 17 standard-sized aluminum cans which portray players, coaches, and the team trainer. The cans state "Congratulations Denver Nuggets" and have a sketched drawing of the player with a facsimile signature and short biography next to the drawing. Below the drawing the can states "76-77 Midwest Division Champions" and has the NBA logo beside it. The cans contain no number except for players' uniform numbers--they are checklisted alphabetically below. Cans opened from the bottom command up to a 25% premium over the prices below.

COMPLETE SET (17) 60.00 120.00
1 Byron Beck 3.00 8.00
2 Larry Brown CO 5.00 10.00
3 Mack Calvin 3.00 8.00
4 Frank Hamblen ACO 2.00 5.00
5 George Irvine ACO 2.00 5.00
6 Dan Issel 10.00 20.00
7 Bobby Jones 7.50 15.00
8 Ted McClain 2.00 5.00
9 Jim Price 2.00 5.00
10 Carl Scheer GM 2.00 5.00
11 Paul Silas 3.00 8.00
12 Roland Taylor 2.00 5.00
13 David Thompson 10.00 20.00
14 Monte Towe 3.00 8.00
15 Bob Travaglini TR 2.00 5.00
16 Marvin Webster 2.00 5.00
17 Willie Wise 3.00 8.00

1982-83 Nuggets Police

This set contains 14 cards measuring 2 5/8" by 4 1/8" featuring the Denver Nuggets. Backs contain safety tips and are printed with black ink. The set was sponsored by Colorado National Banks, the Denver Nuggets, and the metropolitan area police Juvenile Crime Prevention Bureaus. The cards are unnumbered except for uniform number.

COMPLETE SET (14) 4.00 8.00
2 Alex English 1.25 3.00
7 Billy McKinney .30 .75
21 Rob Williams .30 .75
22 Glen Gondrezick .30 .75
23 T.R. Dunn .30 .75
24 Bill Hanzlik .30 .75
25 Dave Robisch .30 .75
43 James Ray .30 .75
44 Dan Issel 1.00 2.50
53 Rich Kelley .30 .75
55 Kiki Vandeweghe .75 2.00
NNO Carl Scheer Pres/GM .30 .75
NNO Doug Moe CO .40 1.00
NNO Bill Ficke ACO .30 .75
Bob Travaglini TR

1983-84 Nuggets Police

This set contains 14 cards measuring 2 5/8" by 4 1/8" featuring the Denver Nuggets. Backs contain safety tips with black printing. The team name written vertically on the front is distinctive in that "Denver" is in red and "Nuggets" is in blue. The cards are unnumbered except for uniform number.

COMPLETE SET (14) 4.00 8.00
2 Alex English 1.00 2.50
5 Mike Evans .30 .75
21 Rob Williams .30 .75
23 T.R. Dunn .30 .75
24 Bill Hanzlik .30 .75
32 Howard Carter .30 .75
33 Ken Dennard .30 .75
34 Danny Schayes .40 1.00
35 Richard Anderson .30 .75
44 Dan Issel .75 2.00
55 Kiki Vandeweghe .50 1.25
NNO Carl Scheer Pres GM .30 .75
NNO Bill Ficke ACO .30 .75
NNO Doug Moe CO .40 1.00

1985-86 Nuggets Police/Wendy's

The 1985-86 Wendy's Denver Nuggets set contains 12 cards each measuring approximately 2 1/2" by 5". A contest entry form tab is attached to each card (included in the dimensions above). The cards were distributed weekly. As part of the promotion a drawing was held each week for two tickets to Denver Nuggets home games and a free Wendy's meal. The set was also co-sponsored by Continental Airlines and Panasonic. The card fronts have color photos with navy and beige borders. The backs are black and white and have safety tips.

COMPLETE SET (12) 3.00 8.00
1 Alex English .75 2.00
2 Mike Evans .30 .75
3 Bill Hanzlik .30 .75
4 Pete Williams .30 .75
5 Danny Schayes .30 .75
6 Wayne Cooper .30 .75
7 Blair Rasmussen .30 .75
8 Elston Turner 1.25 3.00
9 Lafayette Lever .40 1.00
10 T.R. Dunn .30 .75
11 Willie White .30 .75
12 Calvin Natt .30 .75

1988-89 Nuggets Police/Pepsi

This 12-card set was sponsored by Pepsi, Pizza Hut, and The Children's Hospital of Denver. The cards measure approximately 2 5/8" by 4 1/8". The front features a borderless color action player photo. The player's number and name appear in white lettering in a purple stripe at the top of the card face, while team and sponsor logos appear in the white stripe at the bottom. The back is printed in blue on white and presents a safety tip from the player. The English and Lever variation cards differ only in the safety tip found on the back. The cards are unnumbered but they are numbered on the card front at the top by uniform number. The two Alex English cards and two Fat Lever cards are exactly the same except for the safety tip.

COMPLETE SET (12) 3.00 7.00
2A Alex English .75 2.00
(If someone is hurt in an accident ...)
2B Alex English .75 2.00
(You should never run around ...)
6 Walter Davis .60 1.50
12A Fat Lever .20 .50
(Always wear a helmet when you're ...)
12B Fat Lever .20 .50
(If you're ever in danger& the most ...)
14 Michael Adams .40 1.00
20 Elston Turner .20 .50
24 Bill Hanzlik .20 .50
34 Danny Schayes .30 .75
35 Jerome Lane .20 .50
41 Blair Rasmussen .20 .50
42 Wayne Cooper .20 .50

1988-89 Nuggets Portraits

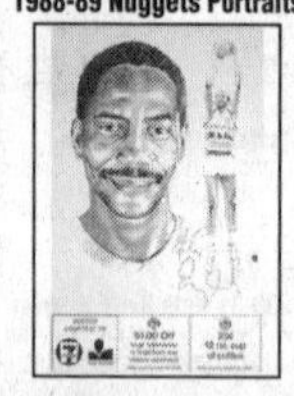

Measuring 11" by 17", these posters featured six members of the 1988-89 Denver Nuggets. Each poster features two black and white drawings of the player (one portrait, one in-action) with a facsimile autograph. The fronts also feature 7-11 coupons. The backs are blank. The posters are not numbered and listed below in alphabetical order.

COMPLETE SET (6) 9.00 18.00
1 Wayne Cooper 1.25 3.00
2 T.R. Dunn 1.25 3.00
3 Alex English 2.50 6.00
4 Fat Lever 1.50 4.00
5 Calvin Natt 1.25 3.00
6 Elston Turner 1.25 3.00
Mike Evans
Bill Hanzlik

1989-90 Nuggets Police/Pepsi

This 12-card set was sponsored by Pepsi, 7/Eleven, and The Children's Hospital of Denver. Beginning in early February, the cards were given out in 7/Eleven stores with Pepsi products. They measure approximately 2 5/8" by 4 1/8". The front features a borderless color action player photo. Two stripes descend from the top of the picture on the right. The longer of the two has alternating black and yellow diagonal sections. In the white stripe appears the player's name and number. The team logo and sponsors' logos appear in the white stripe at the bottom of the card face. The back is printed in lavender on white card stock and presents a safety tip from the player. The cards are unnumbered and checklisted below in alphabetical order.

COMPLETE SET (12) 3.00 8.00
1 Michael Adams .25 .60
2 Walter Davis .60 1.50
3 T.R. Dunn .20 .50
4 Alex English .75 2.00
5 Bill Hanzlik .20 .50
6 Eddie Hughes .20 .50
7 Tim Kempton .20 .50
8 Jerome Lane .20 .50
9 Lafayette Lever .30 .75
10 Todd Lichti .20 .50
11 Blair Rasmussen .20 .50
12 Danny Schayes .30 .75

2002-03 Nuggets Team Issue

Issued through the Denver Nuggets, this 11-card set features members of the 2002-03 Nuggets Squad. Each card boasts full color player action photography on the front of the card and a blank back. These cards measure 3.5" X 5" and are not numbered so they appear in alphabetical order.

COMPLETE SET (11) 6.00 15.00
1 Chris Anderson 1.25 3.00
2 Ryan Bowen .75 2.00
3 Marcus Camby 1.25 3.00
4 Junior Harrington .75 2.00
5 Donnell Harvey .75 2.00
6 Nene Hilario 1.00 2.50
7 Juwan Howard 1.00 2.50
8 Predrag Savovic .75 2.00
9 Nikoloz Tskitishvili .75 2.00
10 Rodney White .75 2.00
11 Vincent Yarbrough .75 2.00

1999 Omni CBA

Produced by Omni, this set features players of the Chinese Basketball Association. Our checklisting information is incomplete. If you have information regarding this set, please email us at basketballmag@beckett.com.

7 Wang ZhiZhi .30 .75
32 Yao Ming 1.50 4.00
36 Mengke Bateer .30 .75

1993-94 Oklahoma City Cavalry CBA

Issued by the Cavalry and sponsored by Lipton Teas, this 14-card set features color photos and a card stock that includes blue borders. The sets were either sold at Cavalry home games or given away as part of a promotional night.

COMPLETE SET (14) 1.50 4.00
1 Isaac Austin .40 1.00
2 Mike Bell .15 .40
3 Henry Bibby CO .60 1.50
4 Mike Bell .15 .40
5 Terry Faggins .15 .40
6 Kermit Holmes .15 .40
7 Steffond Johnson .15 .40
8 Sebastian Neal .15 .40
9 Keith Owens .15 .40
10 Kelsey Weems .15 .40
11 Corey Williams .15 .40
12 Byron Wilson .15 .40
13 Cheerleaders .15 .40
14 Checklist .15 .40

1994 Hakeem Olajuwon Fan Club

Printed on thin card stock, these two standard- size cards were issued to members of the Hakeem the Dream Fan Club. The fronts feature full-bleed color photos, except on the right where a blue stripe carrying the player's name in red lettering edges the picture. The lower left corner has a yellow seal that reads "Most Valuable Player, 1993- 1994 NBA Season." On a black-and-white action cutout, the back of card number one presents "Awards," while that of card number two has "1993-94 Statistics." The cards are unnumbered.

COMPLETE SET (2) 3.00 8.00

1979 Open Pantry

This set is an unnumbered, 12-card issue featuring players from Milwaukee area professional sports teams with five Brewers baseball (1-5), five Bucks basketball (6-10), and two Packers football (11-12). Cards are black and white with red trim and measure approximately 5" by 6". Cards were sponsored by Open Pantry, Lake to Lake, and MACC (Milwaukee Athletes against Childhood Cancer). The cards are unnumbered and hence are listed and numbered below alphabetically within sport.

COMPLETE SET (12) 12.50 25.00
6 Kent Benson 2.00 4.00
7 Junior Bridgeman 2.00 4.00
8 Quinn Buckner 2.50 5.00
9 Marques Johnson 3.00 6.00
10 Jon McGlocklin 2.00 4.00

1991-92 Outlaws Wichita GBA

This 11-card set features the 1991-92 Wichita Outlaws of the Global Basketball Assocation. The cards were produced by Rock's Dugout and printed on thick card stock. Both sides of the standard-size cards are horizontally oriented. Inside marbled burgundy borders, the fronts display a color close-up photo superimposed over a black and white action shot. The backs carry brief biographical information, career summary, and a Rock's Dugout advertisement. Five hundred hand-numbered and uncut sheets were also produced, although these sheets did not include the checklist card.

COMPLETE SET (11) 3.00 8.00
1 Rick Shore .40 1.00
2 Jeff Cummings .40 1.00
3 Brent Dabbs .50 1.25
4 Melvon Foster .50 1.25
5 Paul Guffrovich .40 1.00
6 Tyrone Powell .40 1.00
7 Omar Roland .40 1.00
8 Ricky Ross .40 1.00
9 Robert Spellman .40 1.00
10 Cody Walters .40 1.00
NNO Checklist Card .40 1.00

1971-72 Pacers Volpe Tumblers

This set of Pacers Drinking Cups consists of colorful portraits by distinguished artist Nicholas Volpe. The set features six clear plastic cups that has a paper portrait inserted between the layers of clear plastic. Please note that these cups are not numbered, and are listed below in alphabetical order.

COMPLETE SET (6) 50.00 100.00
1 Mel Daniels 12.50 25.00
2 Bill Keller 7.50 15.00
3 Art Becker 7.50 15.00
4 Bob Netolicky 10.00 20.00
5 Roger Brown 12.50 25.00
6 Rick Mount 10.00 20.00

1971-72 Pacers Volpe Marathon Oil

This set of Marathon Oil Pro Star Portraits consists of colorful portraits by distinguished artist Nicholas Volpe. The cards were part of a gas station promotion. Each portrait measures approximately 7 1/2" by 9 7/8" and features a painting of the player's face on a black background, with an action painting superimposed to the side. A facsimile autograph in white appears at the bottom of the portrait. At the bottom of each portrait is a postcard measuring 7 1/2" by 4" after perforation. While the back of the portrait has offers for a basketball photo album, autographed tumblers, and a poster, the postcard itself may be used to apply for a Marathon credit card. The portraits are unnumbered and checklisted below according to alphabetical order.

COMPLETE SET (12) 40.00 80.00
1 Warren Armstrong 2.50 6.00
2 John Barnhill 2.00 5.00
3 Art Becker 3.00 8.00
4 Roger Brown 3.00 8.00
5A Mel Daniels 5.00 12.00
Releasing ball from both hands
5B Mel Daniels 5.00 12.00
Releasing ball from right hand
6 Earle Higgins 2.00 5.00
7 Bill Keller 5.00 10.00
8 Bob Leonard CO 5.00 10.00
9 Freddie Lewis 3.00 8.00
10 Rick Mount 6.00 12.00
11 Bob Netolicky 3.00 8.00

1971-72 Pacers Team Issue

Each of these team-issued photos measure approximately 8" by 10" and feature black and white player portraits on sheets. Each sheet contains either seven or eight player portraits. The player's name is listed below the photo. The backs are blank. The photos are unnumbered and listed below alphabetically. George McGinnis is featured in his rookie year.

COMPLETE SET (2) 12.50 25.00
1 Roger Brown 7.50 15.00
Wayne Chapman
Mel Daniels
Earle Higgins
Darnell Hillman
Bill Keller
Freddie Lewis
George McGinnis
2 Bob Hooper ACO 5.00 10.00
Bob Leonard CO
Rick Mount
Bob Netolicky
Don Sidle
John Weissert GM
Marv Winkler

1988-89 Pacers Team Issue

The 12 cards in this set are black and white, blank backed and measure approximately 5" x 7". The cards are essentially press photos, but are printed on dull paper stock instead of photo quality. Not listed in the checklist is Julius Erving's appearance on John Long's card. In the card shown above, Erving demonstrates some sort of free jazz dance during his final hurrah in the league.

COMPLETE SET (12) 15.00 40.00
1 Greg Dreiling .75 2.00
2 Vern Fleming 2.00 5.00
3 Anthony Frederick .75 2.00
4 Stuart Gray .75 2.00
5 John Long 2.00 5.00
with Julius Erving
6 Reggie Miller 8.00 20.00
7 Chuck Person 2.50 6.00
8 Scott Skiles 2.50 6.00
9 Everette Stephens .75 2.00
10 Steve Stipanovich .75 2.00
11 Wayman Tisdale 2.50 6.00
12 Herb Williams 2.00 5.00

2009-10 Panini

COMPLETE SET (400) 50.00 120.00
ALL RC VERSIONS SAME VALUE
1 Eddie House .10 .25
2 Glen Davis .10 .25
3 Kendrick Perkins .10 .25
4 Kevin Garnett .25 .60
5 Leon Powe .10 .25
6 Paul Pierce .15 .40
7 Rajon Rondo .15 .40
8 Rasheed Wallace .15 .40
9 Ray Allen .15 .40
10 Stephon Marbury .12 .30
11 Tony Allen .10 .25
12 Bobby Simmons .10 .25
13 Brook Lopez .12 .30
14 Chris Douglas-Roberts .10 .25
15 Courtney Lee .12 .30
16 Devin Harris .10 .25
17 Jarvis Hayes .10 .25
18 Josh Boone .10 .25
19 Keyon Dooling .10 .25
20 Rafer Alston .10 .25
21 Tony Battie .10 .25
22 Yi Jianlian .12 .30
23 Al Harrington .12 .30
24 Chris Duhon .10 .25
25 Danilo Gallinari .12 .30
26 Darko Milicic .10 .25
27 David Lee .10 .25
28 Jared Jeffries .10 .25
29 Larry Hughes .12 .30
30 Nate Robinson .10 .25
31 Wilson Chandler .12 .30
32 Andre Iguodala .12 .30
33 Donyell Marshall .10 .25
34 Elton Brand .15 .40
35 Jason Kapono .10 .25
36 Louis Williams .12 .30
37 Marreese Speights .12 .30
38 Samuel Dalembert .10 .25
39 Thaddeus Young .10 .25
40 Willie Green .10 .25
41 Andrea Bargnani .12 .30
42 Chris Bosh .15 .40
43 Hedo Turkoglu .12 .30
44 Joey Graham .10 .25
45 Jose Calderon .10 .25
46 Pops Mensah-Bonsu .10 .25
47 Quincy Douby .10 .25
48 Reggie Evans .10 .25
49 Devean George .10 .25
50 Antoine Wright .10 .25
51 Jarrett Jack .12 .30
52 Aaron Gray .10 .25
53 Brad Miller .12 .30
54 Derrick Rose .25 .60
55 Joakim Noah .12 .30
56 John Salmons .12 .30
57 Kirk Hinrich .12 .30
58 Luol Deng .12 .30
59 Tyrus Thomas .10 .25
60 Anderson Varejao .10 .25
61 Daniel Gibson .12 .30
62 Delonte West .10 .25
63 Joe Smith .12 .30
64 LeBron James .60 1.50
65 Mo Williams .12 .30
66 Shaquille O'Neal .30 .75
67 Wally Szczerbiak .12 .30
68 Zydrunas Ilgauskas .12 .30
69 Anthony Parker .10 .25
70 Jamario Moon .10 .25
71 Allen Iverson .20 .50
72 Ben Gordon .12 .30
73 Charlie Villanueva .10 .25
74 Fabricio Oberto .10 .25
75 Jason Maxiell .10 .25
76 Kwame Brown .10 .25
77 Chris Wilcox .10 .25
78 Richard Hamilton .12 .30
79 Rodney Stuckey .10 .25
80 Tayshaun Prince .12 .30
81 Will Bynum .10 .25
82 Brandon Rush .10 .25
83 Danny Granger .12 .30
84 Jeff Foster .10 .25
85 Marquis Daniels .10 .25
86 Mike Dunleavy .10 .25
87 Rasho Nesterovic .10 .25
88 Roy Hibbert .12 .30
89 Stephen Graham .10 .25
90 T.J. Ford .10 .25
91 Travis Diener .10 .25
92 Troy Murphy .10 .25
93 Dahntay Jones .10 .25
94 Earl Watson .10 .25
95 Andrew Bogut .12 .30
96 Bruce Bowen .10 .25
97 Joe Alexander .10 .25
98 Keith Bogans .10 .25
99 Kurt Thomas .10 .25
100 Luc Mbah a Moute .10 .25
101 Luke Ridnour .12 .30
102 Michael Redd .12 .30
103 Ramon Sessions .12 .30
104 Al Horford .15 .40
105 Joe Johnson .12 .30
106 Josh Smith .12 .30
107 Marvin Williams .12 .30
108 Maurice Evans .10 .25
109 Mike Bibby .12 .30
110 Ronald Murray .10 .25
111 Solomon Jones .10 .25
112 Jamal Crawford .15 .40
113 Zaza Pachulia .10 .25
114 Boris Diaw .12 .30
115 D.J. Augustin .10 .25
116 DeSagana Diop .10 .25
117 Dontell Jefferson RC .15 .40
118 Gerald Wallace .12 .30
119 Juwan Howard .12 .30
120 Nazr Mohammed .10 .25
121 Raja Bell .12 .30
122 Raymond Felton .12 .30
123 Vladimir Radmanovic .10 .25
124 Tyson Chandler .12 .30
125 Chris Quinn .10 .25
126 Daequan Cook .10 .25
127 Dwyane Wade .25 .60
128 James Jones .15 .40
129 Jermaine O'Neal .12 .30
130 Luther Head .10 .25
131 Mario Chalmers .12 .30
132 Michael Beasley .10 .25
133 Udonis Haslem .10 .25
134 Anthony Johnson .10 .25
135 Dwight Howard .12 .30
136 J.J. Redick .15 .40
137 Jameer Nelson .10 .25
138 Mickael Pietrus .10 .25
139 Rashard Lewis .12 .30
140 Vince Carter .20 .50
141 Brandon Bass .10 .25
142 Matt Barnes .10 .25
143 Andray Blatche .10 .25
144 Antawn Jamison .12 .30
145 Brendan Haywood .10 .25
146 Caron Butler .12 .30
147 DeShawn Stevenson .10 .25
148 Gilbert Arenas .12 .30
149 Mike James .10 .25
150 Mike Miller .12 .30
151 Nick Young .12 .30
152 Randy Foye .10 .25
153 Tim Thomas .10 .25
154 Dirk Nowitzki .20 .50
155 Erick Dampier .10 .25
156 Gerald Green .12 .30
157 James Singleton .10 .25
158 Jason Kidd .15 .40
159 Jason Terry .12 .30
160 Greg Buckner .10 .25
161 Shawn Marion .12 .30
162 Jose Barea .20 .50
163 Josh Howard .12 .30
164 Aaron Brooks .10 .25
165 Brent Barry .10 .25
166 Carl Landry .10 .25
167 Dikembe Mutombo .15 .40
168 Luis Scola .12 .30
169 Shane Battier .15 .40
170 Tracy McGrady .15 .40
171 Trevor Ariza .10 .25
172 Von Wafer .10 .25
173 Yao Ming .20 .50
174 Darius Miles .10 .25
175 Darrell Arthur .12 .30
176 Hakim Warrick .12 .30
177 Marc Gasol .15 .40
178 Mike Conley Jr. .12 .30
179 O.J. Mayo .10 .25
180 Jerry Stackhouse .12 .30
181 Zach Randolph .12 .30
182 Rudy Gay .15 .40
183 Chris Paul .20 .50
184 Emeka Okafor .12 .30
185 David West .12 .30
186 Devin Brown .10 .25
187 James Posey .10 .25
188 Julian Wright .10 .25
189 Morris Peterson .10 .25
190 Peja Stojakovic .15 .40
191 Rasual Butler .10 .25
192 Drew Gooden .12 .30
193 Manu Ginobili .15 .40
194 Matt Bonner .10 .25
195 Michael Finley .15 .40
196 Richard Jefferson .12 .30
197 Roger Mason .10 .25
198 Tim Duncan .25 .60
199 Antonio McDyess .12 .30
200 Tony Parker .15 .40
201 Anthony Carter .10 .25
202 Carmelo Anthony .20 .50
203 Chauncey Billups .15 .40
204 Chris Andersen .12 .30
205 J.R. Smith .12 .30
206 Kenyon Martin .12 .30
207 Linas Kleiza .10 .25
208 Arron Afflalo .10 .25
209 Nene .12 .30
210 Al Jefferson .12 .30
211 Bobby Brown .10 .25
212 Corey Brewer .10 .25
213 Darius Songaila .10 .25
214 Kevin Love .15 .40
215 Rodney Carney .10 .25
216 Quentin Richardson .12 .30
217 Ryan Gomes .10 .25
218 Brandon Roy .15 .40
219 Greg Oden .12 .30
220 Jerryd Bayless .12 .30
221 Joel Przybilla .10 .25
222 LaMarcus Aldridge .15 .40
223 Nicolas Batum .12 .30
224 Rudy Fernandez .10 .25
225 Steve Blake .10 .25
226 Travis Outlaw .12 .30
227 Andre Miller .12 .30
228 D.J. White .10 .25
229 Desmond Mason .10 .25
230 Jeff Green .12 .30
231 Kevin Durant .40 1.00
232 Nenad Krstic .10 .25
233 Nick Collison .12 .30
234 Russell Westbrook .40 1.00
235 Thabo Sefolosha .10 .25
236 Andrei Kirilenko .12 .30
237 C.J. Miles .12 .30
238 Carlos Boozer .12 .30
239 Deron Williams .12 .30
240 Kosta Koufos .10 .25
241 Kyle Korver .12 .30
242 Matt Harpring .10 .25
243 Mehmet Okur .10 .25
244 Paul Millsap .12 .30
245 Ronnie Brewer .12 .30
246 Andris Biedrins .10 .25
247 Anthony Morrow .10 .25
248 Anthony Randolph .10 .25
249 Brandan Wright .10 .25
250 C.J. Watson .10 .25
251 Corey Maggette .12 .30
252 Kelenna Azubuike .10 .25
253 Marco Belinelli .10 .25
254 Monta Ellis .12 .30
255 Acie Law .10 .25
256 Ronny Turiaf .10 .25
257 Stephen Jackson .12 .30
258 Al Thornton .12 .30
259 Baron Davis .12 .30
260 Chris Kaman .12 .30
261 Eric Gordon .12 .30
262 Fred Jones .10 .25
263 Marcus Camby .10 .25
264 Ricky Davis .12 .30
265 Steve Novak .10 .25
266 Sebastian Telfair .10 .25
267 Craig Smith .10 .25
268 Adam Morrison .10 .25
269 Andrew Bynum .10 .25
270 Derek Fisher .12 .30
271 Jordan Farmar .10 .25
272 Josh Powell .10 .25
273 Kobe Bryant .60 1.50
274 Lamar Odom .12 .30
275 Luke Walton .10 .25
276 Pau Gasol .15 .40
277 Ron Artest .15 .40
278 Sasha Vujacic .10 .25
279 Alando Tucker .10 .25
280 Sasha Pavlovic .10 .25
281 Amare Stoudemire .12 .30
282 Ben Wallace .12 .30
283 Goran Dragic RC .30 .75
284 Grant Hill .20 .50
285 Jared Dudley .10 .25
286 Jason Richardson .15 .40
287 Leandro Barbosa .12 .30
288 Channing Frye .12 .30
289 Steve Nash .15 .40
290 Andres Nocioni .10 .25
291 Beno Udrih .10 .25
292 Bobby Jackson .10 .25
293 Francisco Garcia .10 .25
294 Ike Diogu .10 .25
295 Jason Thompson .10 .25
296 Kevin Martin .12 .30
297 Rashad McCants .10 .25
298 Sergio Rodriguez .10 .25
299 Sean May .10 .25
300 Spencer Hawes .10 .25
301 Blake Griffin RC 2.50 6.00
302 Hasheem Thabeet RC .40 1.00
303 James Harden RC 3.00 8.00
304 Tyreke Evans RC .50 1.25
305 Hasheem Thabeet RC .40 1.00
306 Jonny Flynn RC .40 1.00
307 Stephen Curry RC 12.00 30.00
308 Jordan Hill RC .50 1.25
309 DeMar DeRozan RC 1.50 4.00
310 Brandon Jennings RC .60 1.50
311 Terrence Williams RC .40 1.00
312 Gerald Henderson RC .50 1.25
313 Tyler Hansbrough RC .50 1.25
314 Earl Clark RC .50 1.25
315 Austin Daye RC .40 1.00
316 James Johnson RC .50 1.25
317 Jrue Holiday RC .75 2.00
318 Ty Lawson RC .60 1.50
319 Jeff Teague RC .60 1.50
320 Eric Maynor RC .40 1.00
321 Darren Collison RC .60 1.50
322 Blake Griffin RC 2.50 6.00
323 Omri Casspi RC .50 1.25
324 B.J. Mullens RC .40 1.00
325 Rodrigue Beaubois RC .40 1.00
326 Taj Gibson RC .60 1.50
327 DeMarre Carroll RC .50 1.25
328 Wayne Ellington RC .60 1.50
329 Toney Douglas RC .40 1.00
330 Tyreke Evans RC .50 1.25
331 Jeff Pendergraph RC .40 1.00
332 Jermaine Taylor RC .40 1.00
333 Dante Cunningham RC .40 1.00
334 DaJuan Summers RC .40 1.00
335 Sam Young RC .40 1.00
336 DeJuan Blair RC .50 1.25
337 Jon Brockman RC .40 1.00
338 Derrick Brown RC .40 1.00
339 Jodie Meeks RC .60 1.50
340 Patrick Beverley RC .60 1.50
341 Marcus Thornton RC .50 1.25
342 Chase Budinger RC .50 1.25
343 Jack McClinton RC .40 1.00
344 Danny Green RC .75 2.00
345 Taylor Griffin RC .40 1.00
346 A.J. Price RC .40 1.00
347 Jonas Jerebko RC .60 1.50
348 Lester Hudson RC .40 1.00
349 Goran Suton RC .40 1.00
350 Ty Lawson RC .60 1.50
351 Blake Griffin RC 2.50 6.00
352 Hasheem Thabeet RC .40 1.00
353 James Harden RC 3.00 8.00
354 Tyreke Evans RC .50 1.25
355 Jordan Hill RC .50 1.25
356 Jonny Flynn RC .40 1.00
357 Stephen Curry RC 12.00 30.00
358 Jordan Hill RC .50 1.25
359 DeMar DeRozan RC 1.50 4.00
360 Brandon Jennings RC .60 1.50
361 Terrence Williams RC .40 1.00
362 Gerald Henderson RC .50 1.25
363 Tyler Hansbrough RC .50 1.25
364 Earl Clark RC .50 1.25
365 Austin Daye RC .40 1.00
366 James Johnson RC .50 1.25
367 Jrue Holiday RC .75 2.00
368 Ty Lawson RC .60 1.50
369 Jeff Teague RC .60 1.50
370 Eric Maynor RC .40 1.00
371 Darren Collison RC .60 1.50
372 Stephen Curry RC 12.00 30.00
373 Omri Casspi RC .50 1.25
374 B.J. Mullens RC .40 1.00
375 Rodrigue Beaubois RC .40 1.00
376 Taj Gibson RC .60 1.50
377 DeMarre Carroll RC .50 1.25
378 Wayne Ellington RC .60 1.50
379 Toney Douglas RC .40 1.00
380 Tyler Hansbrough RC .50 1.25
381 Jeff Pendergraph RC .40 1.00
382 Jermaine Taylor RC .40 1.00
383 Dante Cunningham RC .40 1.00
384 DaJuan Summers RC .40 1.00
385 Sam Young RC .40 1.00
386 DeJuan Blair RC .50 1.25
387 Jon Brockman RC .40 1.00
388 Derrick Brown RC .40 1.00
389 Jodie Meeks RC .60 1.50
390 Patrick Beverley RC .60 1.50
391 Marcus Thornton RC .50 1.25
392 Chase Budinger RC .50 1.25
393 Jack McClinton RC .40 1.00
394 Danny Green RC .75 2.00
395 Taylor Griffin RC .40 1.00
396 A.J. Price RC .40 1.00
397 Jonas Jerebko RC .60 1.50
398 Lester Hudson RC .40 1.00
399 Goran Suton RC .40 1.00
400 James Harden RC 3.00 8.00

2009-10 Panini Artists Proof

*AP 1-300: 1.25X TO 3X BASE HI
*AP 301-400: 1X TO 2.5X BASE HI
STATED PRINT RUN 199 SER.#'d SETS
301 Blake Griffin 12.50 30.00
322 Blake Griffin 12.50 30.00
351 Blake Griffin 12.50 30.00

2009-10 Panini Glossy

*GLOSSY: 1-300: .75X TO 2X BASE HI
*GLOSSY: 301-400: .6X TO 1.5X BASE HI
RANDOM INSERTS IN PACKS

2009-10 Panini All-Pro Team

COMPLETE SET (20) 8.00 20.00
RANDOM INSERTS IN PACKS
*AP: .75X TO 2X BASE HI
AP PRINT RUN 199 SER.#'d SETS
*GLOSSY: .6X TO 1.5X BASE HI
GLOSSY RANDOM INSERTS IN PACKS
1 LeBron James 2.00 5.00
2 Dirk Nowitzki .60 1.50
3 Dwight Howard .40 1.00
4 Kobe Bryant 2.00 5.00
5 Dwyane Wade .75 2.00
6 Tim Duncan .75 2.00
7 Paul Pierce .50 1.25
8 Yao Ming .60 1.50
9 Brandon Roy .50 1.25
10 Chris Paul .60 1.50
11 Carmelo Anthony .60 1.50
12 Pau Gasol .50 1.25
13 Shaquille O'Neal 1.00 2.50
14 Chauncey Billups .50 1.25
15 Tony Parker .50 1.25
16 Deron Williams .40 1.00
17 Kevin Garnett .75 2.00
18 Chris Bosh .50 1.25
19 Joe Johnson .40 1.00
20 Kevin Durant 1.25 3.00

2009-10 Panini Block Party

COMPLETE SET (10) 5.00 12.00
RANDOM INSERTS IN PACKS
*AP: 1X TO 2.5X BASE HI
AP PRINT RUN 199 SER.#'d SETS
*GLOSSY: .6X TO 1.5X BASE HI
GLOSSY RANDOM INSERTS IN PACKS
1 Dwight Howard .60 1.50
2 Chris Andersen .60 1.50
3 Jermaine O'Neal .60 1.50
4 Yao Ming 1.00 2.50
5 Chris Kaman .60 1.50
6 Joakim Noah .60 1.50
7 Kevin Garnett 1.25 3.00
8 Pau Gasol .75 2.00
9 Amare Stoudemire .60 1.50
10 Dikembe Mutombo .75 2.00

2009-10 Panini Decals

COMPLETE SET (31) 15.00 30.00
RANDOM INSERTS IN PACKS
1 Josh Smith .50 1.25
2 Paul Pierce .60 1.50
3 Gerald Wallace .50 1.25
4 Derrick Rose 1.00 2.50
5 LeBron James 2.50 6.00
6 Dirk Nowitzki .75 2.00
7 Carmelo Anthony .75 2.00
8 Richard Hamilton .60 1.50
9 Stephen Jackson .60 1.50
10 Yao Ming .75 2.00
11 Danny Granger .50 1.25
12 Zach Randolph .60 1.50
13 Kobe Bryant 2.50 6.00
14 O.J. Mayo .40 1.00
15 Dwyane Wade 1.00 2.50
16 Michael Redd .50 1.25
17 Al Jefferson .50 1.25
18 Devin Harris .40 1.00
19 Chris Paul .75 2.00
20 Al Harrington .60 1.50
21 Kevin Durant 1.50 4.00
22 Dwight Howard .50 1.25
23 Andre Iguodala .50 1.25
24 Steve Nash .60 1.50
25 Brandon Roy .60 1.50
26 Kevin Martin .50 1.25
27 Tony Parker .60 1.50
28 Chris Bosh .60 1.50
29 Deron Williams .50 1.25
30 Gilbert Arenas .50 1.25
32 Blake Griffin 2.50 6.00

2009-10 Panini Future Stars

COMPLETE SET (20) 4.00 10.00
RANDOM INSERTS IN PACKS
*AP: 1.25X TO 3X BASE HI
AP PRINT RUN 199 SER.#'d SETS
*GLOSSY: .75X TO 2X BASE HI
GLOSSY RANDOM INSERTS IN PACKS
1 Al Thornton .40 1.00
2 Andrew Bynum .30 .75
3 Charlie Villanueva .30 .75
4 David Lee .30 .75
5 J.J. Redick .50 1.25
6 Jarrett Jack .40 1.00
7 Jeff Green .40 1.00
8 Kelenna Azubuike .30 .75
9 LaMarcus Aldridge .50 1.25
10 Linas Kleiza .30 .75
11 Luis Scola .40 1.00
12 Monta Ellis .40 1.00
13 Nate Robinson .30 .75
14 Nick Young .40 1.00
15 Paul Millsap .40 1.00
16 Rajon Rondo .50 1.25
17 Ronnie Brewer .40 1.00
18 Rudy Gay .50 1.25
19 Ryan Gomes .30 .75
20 Randy Foye .30 .75

2009-10 Panini Glow in the Dark Stickers

COMPLETE SET (30) 3.00 8.00
RANDOM INSERTS IN PACKS
1 Atlanta Hawks .20 .50
2 Boston Celtics .60 1.50
3 Charlotte Bobcats .20 .50
4 Chicago Bulls .40 1.00
5 Cleveland Cavaliers .40 1.00
6 Dallas Mavericks .20 .50
7 Denver Nuggets .20 .50
8 Detroit Pistons .30 .75
9 Golden State Warriors .20 .50
10 Houston Rockets .20 .50
11 Indiana Pacers .20 .50
12 Los Angeles Clippers .20 .50
13 Los Angeles Lakers .60 1.50
14 Memphis Grizzlies .20 .50
15 Miami Heat .20 .50
16 Milwaukee Bucks .20 .50
17 Minnesota Timberwolves .20 .50
18 New Jersey Nets .20 .50
19 New Orleans Hornets .20 .50
20 New York Knicks .40 1.00
21 Oklahoma City Thunder .20 .50
22 Orlando Magic .20 .50
23 Philadelphia 76ers .20 .50
24 Phoenix Suns .20 .50
25 Portland Trail Blazers .20 .50
26 Sacramento Kings .20 .50
27 San Antonio Spurs .30 .75
28 Toronto Raptors .20 .50
29 Utah Jazz .20 .50
30 Washington Wizards .20 .50

2009-10 Panini Headliners
COMPLETE SET (10) 6.00 15.00
RANDOM INSERTS IN PACKS
*AP: 1X TO 2.5X BASE HI
AP PRINT RUN 199 SER.#'d SETS
*GLOSSY: .6X TO 1.5X BASE HI
GLOSSY RANDOM INSERTS IN PACKS
1 Chauncey Billups .60 1.50
2 Nate Robinson .40 1.00
3 Jason Kidd .60 1.50
4 LeBron James 2.50 6.00
5 Derrick Rose 1.00 2.50
6 Dwight Howard .50 1.25
7 LeBron James 2.50 6.00
8 Kobe Bryant 2.50 6.00
9 Pat Riley .60 1.50
10 Blake Griffin 2.50 6.00
8a Kobe Bryant AU/30 125.00 225.00

2009-10 Panini Inscriptions
RANDOM INSERTS IN PACKS
109 Mike Bibby 5.00 12.00
169 Shane Battier 5.00 12.00
301 Blake Griffin 40.00 100.00
303 James Harden 40.00 100.00
304 Tyreke Evans 4.00 10.00
307 Stephen Curry 600.00 800.00
308 Jordan Hill 4.00 10.00
310 Brandon Jennings 5.00 12.00
311 Terrence Williams 3.00 8.00
312 Gerald Henderson 4.00 10.00
313 Tyler Hansbrough 10.00 25.00
314 Earl Clark 4.00 10.00
315 Austin Daye 3.00 8.00
316 James Johnson 4.00 10.00
317 Jrue Holiday 6.00 15.00
319 Jeff Teague 5.00 12.00
321 Darren Collison 5.00 12.00
322 Blake Griffin 75.00 200.00
323 Omri Casspi 4.00 10.00
324 B.J. Mullens 3.00 8.00
325 Rodrigue Beaubois 3.00 8.00
326 Taj Gibson 5.00 12.00
327 DeMarre Carroll 4.00 10.00
329 Toney Douglas 3.00 8.00
330 Tyreke Evans 4.00 10.00
331 Jeff Pendergraph 3.00 8.00
332 Jermaine Taylor 3.00 8.00
333 Dante Cunningham 3.00 8.00
334 DaJuan Summers 3.00 8.00
336 DeJuan Blair 4.00 10.00
337 Jon Brockman 3.00 8.00
338 Derrick Brown 3.00 8.00
339 Jodie Meeks 5.00 12.00
341 Marcus Thornton 4.00 10.00
342 Chase Budinger 4.00 10.00
343 Jack McClinton 3.00 8.00
344 Danny Green 6.00 15.00
345 Taylor Griffin 3.00 8.00
346 A.J. Price 3.00 8.00
348 Lester Hudson 3.00 8.00
349 Goran Suton 3.00 8.00
351 Blake Griffin 75.00 200.00
354 Tyreke Evans 4.00 10.00
355 Jordan Hill 4.00 10.00
357 Stephen Curry 600.00 800.00
358 Jordan Hill 4.00 10.00
360 Brandon Jennings 5.00 12.00
361 Terrence Williams 3.00 8.00
362 Gerald Henderson 4.00 10.00
363 Tyler Hansbrough 10.00 25.00
364 Earl Clark 4.00 10.00
365 Austin Daye 3.00 8.00
366 James Johnson 4.00 10.00
367 Jrue Holiday 6.00 15.00
369 Jeff Teague 5.00 12.00
371 Darren Collison 5.00 12.00
372 Stephen Curry 600.00 800.00
373 Omri Casspi 4.00 10.00
374 B.J. Mullens 3.00 8.00
375 Rodrigue Beaubois 3.00 8.00
376 Taj Gibson 5.00 12.00
377 DeMarre Carroll 4.00 10.00
379 Toney Douglas 3.00 8.00
380 Tyler Hansbrough 10.00 25.00
381 Jeff Pendergraph 3.00 8.00
382 Jermaine Taylor 3.00 8.00
383 Dante Cunningham 3.00 8.00
384 DaJuan Summers 3.00 8.00
386 DeJuan Blair 4.00 10.00
387 Jon Brockman 3.00 8.00
388 Derrick Brown 3.00 8.00
389 Jodie Meeks 5.00 12.00
391 Marcus Thornton 4.00 10.00
392 Chase Budinger 4.00 10.00
393 Jack McClinton 3.00 8.00
394 Danny Green 6.00 15.00
395 Taylor Griffin 3.00 8.00
396 A.J. Price 3.00 8.00
398 Lester Hudson 3.00 8.00
399 Goran Suton 3.00 8.00

2009-10 Panini Jam Masters
COMPLETE SET (10) 6.00 15.00
RANDOM INSERTS IN PACKS
*AP: 1X TO 2.5X BASE HI
AP PRINT RUN 199 SER.#'d SETS
*GLOSSY: .6X TO 1.5X BASE HI
GLOSSY RANDOM INSERTS IN PACKS
1 Tim Duncan 1.25 3.00
2 Shaquille O'Neal 1.50 4.00
3 Dwyane Wade 1.25 3.00
4 LeBron James 3.00 8.00
5 Kobe Bryant 3.00 8.00
6 Danny Granger .60 1.50
7 Nate Robinson .50 1.25
8 Chris Bosh .75 2.00
9 Kevin Durant 2.00 5.00
10 Chris Paul 1.00 2.50

2009-10 Panini Legends of the Game
COMPLETE SET (10) 4.00 10.00
RANDOM INSERTS IN PACKS
*AP: .75X TO 2X BASE HI
AP PRINT RUN 199 SER.#'d SETS
*GLOSSY: .6X TO 1.5X BASE HI
GLOSSY RANDOM INSERTS IN PACKS
1 Jerry West 1.25 3.00
2 John Havlicek 1.00 2.50
3 Bernard King .75 2.00
4 Glen Rice .75 2.00
5 Willis Reed 1.00 2.50
6 Detlef Schrempf 1.00 2.50
7 Dennis Rodman 2.00 5.00
8 Lenny Wilkens 1.00 2.50
9 Bob Cousy 1.50 4.00
10 Sleepy Floyd .60 1.50

2009-10 Panini Legends of the Game Signatures
RANDOM INSERTS IN PACKS
1 Jerry West 20.00 40.00
5 Willis Reed 8.00 20.00
8 Lenny Wilkens 6.00 15.00
10 Sleepy Floyd 6.00 15.00

2009-10 Panini Next Day Signatures
RANDOM INSERTS IN PACKS
1 Austin Daye 20.00 50.00
2 B.J. Mullens 20.00 50.00
3 Blake Griffin 100.00 250.00
4 Brandon Jennings 30.00 80.00
5 Chase Budinger 25.00 60.00
6 DaJuan Summers 20.00 50.00
7 Darren Collison 30.00 80.00
8 DeJuan Blair 25.00 60.00
9 DeMarre Carroll 25.00 60.00
10 Earl Clark 25.00 60.00
11 Eric Maynor 20.00 50.00
12 Gerald Henderson 25.00 60.00
13 Hasheem Thabeet 20.00 50.00
14 James Harden 150.00 300.00
15 James Johnson 10.00 25.00
16 Jeff Pendergraph 20.00 50.00
17 Jeff Teague 30.00 80.00
18 Jermaine Taylor 20.00 50.00
19 Jodie Meeks 20.00 50.00
20 Jonny Flynn 20.00 50.00
21 Jordan Hill 25.00 60.00
22 Jrue Holiday 40.00 100.00
23 Omri Casspi 25.00 60.00
24 Rodrigue Beaubois 20.00 50.00
25 Sam Young 20.00 50.00
26 Stephen Curry 1500.00 2500.00
27 Taj Gibson 30.00 80.00
28 Taylor Griffin 20.00 50.00
29 Terrence Williams 20.00 50.00
30 Toney Douglas 20.00 50.00
31 Ty Lawson 30.00 80.00
32 Tyler Hansbrough 25.00 60.00
33 Tyreke Evans 25.00 60.00
34 Wayne Ellington 30.00 80.00

2009-10 Panini The Franchise
COMPLETE SET (20) 10.00 25.00
RANDOM INSERTS IN PACKS
*AP: .75X TO 2X BASE HI
AP PRINT RUN 199 SER.#'d SETS
*GLOSSY: .6X TO 1.5X BASE HI
GLOSSY RANDOM INSERTS IN PACKS
1 Andre Iguodala .60 1.50
2 Carmelo Anthony 1.00 2.50
3 Chris Paul 1.00 2.50
4 Derrick Rose 1.25 3.00
5 Dirk Nowitzki 1.00 2.50
6 Dwight Howard .60 1.50
7 Dwyane Wade 1.25 3.00
8 Gerald Wallace .60 1.50
9 Josh Smith .60 1.50
10 Kevin Durant 2.00 5.00
11 Kevin Garnett 1.25 3.00
12 Kevin Martin .60 1.50
13 Kobe Bryant 3.00 8.00
14 LeBron James 3.00 8.00
15 Richard Hamilton .60 1.50
16 Rudy Gay .75 2.00
17 Stephen Jackson .60 1.50
18 Steve Nash .75 2.00
19 Tony Parker .75 2.00
20 Yao Ming 1.00 2.50

2012-13 Panini
COMPLETE SET (300) 15.00 40.00
1 Al Horford .15 .40
2 Al Jefferson .15 .40
3 Amare Stoudemire .15 .40
4 Anderson Varejao .12 .30
5 Andray Blatche .12 .30
6 Andre Iguodala .15 .40
7 Andre Miller .15 .40
8 Andrea Bargnani .15 .40
9 Andrei Kirilenko .15 .40
10 Andrew Bogut .15 .40
11 Andrew Bynum .12 .30
12 Antawn Jamison .15 .40
13 Anthony Morrow .12 .30
14 Anthony Randolph .15 .40
15 Alonzo Gee .12 .30
16 Arron Afflalo .15 .40
17 Ben Gordon .15 .40
18 Beno Udrih .12 .30
19 Blake Griffin .20 .50
20 Boris Diaw .15 .40
21 Brandon Bass .12 .30
22 Brandon Rush .12 .30
23 Brandon Jennings .12 .30
24 Brandon Roy .20 .50
25 Brook Lopez .15 .40
26 Carl Landry .12 .30
27 Carlos Boozer .15 .40
28 Carmelo Anthony .25 .60
29 Caron Butler .15 .40
30 Channing Frye .15 .40
31 Chauncey Billups .20 .50
32 Chris Bosh .20 .50
33 Chris Kaman .15 .40
34 Chris Paul .25 .60
35 Corey Brewer .12 .30
36 Courtney Lee .15 .40
37 Daniel Gibson .15 .40
38 Danilo Gallinari .12 .30
39 Danny Granger .15 .40
40 Darren Collison .15 .40
41 David Lee .12 .30
42 David West .15 .40
43 DeAndre Jordan .20 .50
44 DeJuan Blair .12 .30
45 DeMar DeRozan .20 .50
46 DeMarcus Cousins .20 .50
47 Deron Williams .15 .40
48 Derrick Favors .15 .40
49 Derrick Rose .25 .60
50 Marco Belinelli .12 .30
51 Devin Harris .12 .30
52 Dirk Nowitzki .25 .60
53 Drew Gooden .15 .40
54 Dwight Howard .15 .40
55 Dwyane Wade .30 .75
56 Elton Brand .20 .50
57 Emeka Okafor .15 .40
58 Eric Bledsoe .15 .40
59 Eric Gordon .15 .40
60 Eric Maynor .12 .30
61 Ersan Ilyasova .12 .30
62 Evan Turner .12 .30
63 Gerald Wallace .15 .40
64 Gerald Henderson .12 .30
65 Glen Davis .12 .30
66 Goran Dragic .15 .40
67 Gordon Hayward .20 .50
68 Grant Hill .25 .60
69 Greg Monroe .15 .40
70 Greivis Vasquez .15 .40
71 Hedo Turkoglu .15 .40
72 Jameer Nelson .12 .30
73 James Harden .30 .75
74 Jason Kidd .20 .50
75 Jason Richardson .20 .50
76 Jason Terry .15 .40
77 Jason Thompson .12 .30
78 JaVale McGee .15 .40
79 Jeff Green .15 .40
80 Jeff Teague .15 .40
81 Jeremy Lin .20 .50
82 Joakim Noah .15 .40
83 Joe Johnson .15 .40
84 John Salmons .15 .40
85 John Wall .25 .60
86 Jonas Jerebko .12 .30
87 Jose Calderon .12 .30
88 Josh Smith .15 .40
89 J.R. Smith .15 .40
90 Jrue Holiday .20 .50
91 Kendrick Perkins .12 .30
92 Kevin Garnett .30 .75
93 Kirk Hinrich .15 .40
94 Kevin Love .20 .50
95 Kevin Martin .15 .40
96 Kevin Durant .50 1.25
97 Kobe Bryant .75 2.00
98 Kris Humphries .12 .30
99 Kyle Korver .15 .40
100 Kyle Lowry .15 .40
101 Lamar Odom .15 .40
102 LaMarcus Aldridge .20 .50
103 Landry Fields .12 .30
104 LeBron James .75 2.00
105 Louis Williams .15 .40
106 Luc Mbah a Moute .12 .30
107 Luis Scola .15 .40
108 Luol Deng .15 .40
109 Manu Ginobili .20 .50
110 Marc Gasol .20 .50
111 Marcin Gortat .15 .40
112 Marcus Camby .15 .40
113 Marcus Thornton .12 .30
114 Mario Chalmers .15 .40
115 Marreese Speights .12 .30
116 Martell Webster .12 .30
117 Marvin Williams .15 .40
118 Metta World Peace .20 .50
119 Michael Beasley .12 .30
120 Mike Conley .15 .40
121 Mike Miller .15 .40
122 Mike Dunleavy .12 .30
123 Mo Williams .15 .40
124 Monta Ellis .15 .40
125 Nate Robinson .12 .30
126 Nene .15 .40
127 Nick Collison .15 .40
128 Nick Young .15 .40
129 Nicolas Batum .15 .40
130 Nikola Pekovic .12 .30
131 O.J. Mayo .12 .30
132 Patrick Patterson .12 .30
133 Pau Gasol .20 .50
134 Paul Pierce .20 .50
135 Paul George .25 .60
136 Paul Millsap .20 .50
137 Rajon Rondo .20 .50
138 Ramon Sessions .15 .40
139 Ray Allen .20 .50
140 Raymond Felton .15 .40
141 Richard Hamilton .15 .40
142 Richard Jefferson .15 .40
143 Ricky Rubio .20 .50
144 Robin Lopez .12 .30
145 Rodney Stuckey .15 .40
146 Roy Hibbert .15 .40
147 Rudy Gay .20 .50
148 Russell Westbrook .50 1.25
149 Ryan Anderson .15 .40
150 Serge Ibaka .15 .40
151 Shane Battier .15 .40
152 Shannon Brown .12 .30
153 Shawn Marion .15 .40
154 Spencer Hawes .12 .30
155 Stephen Curry .75 2.00
156 Stephen Jackson .15 .40
157 Steve Nash .20 .50
158 Steve Novak .12 .30
159 Steve Blake .12 .30
160 Taj Gibson .15 .40
161 Tayshaun Prince .15 .40
162 Tim Duncan .30 .75
163 Tony Allen .12 .30
164 Tony Parker .20 .50
165 Trevor Ariza .12 .30
166 Ty Lawson .12 .30
167 Tyler Hansbrough .15 .40
168 Tyreke Evans .12 .30
169 Tyrus Thomas .12 .30
170 Tyson Chandler .15 .40
171 Vince Carter .25 .60
172 Wayne Ellington .12 .30
173 Wesley Matthews .12 .30
174 Wilson Chandler .15 .40
175 Zach Randolph .15 .40
176 Adrian Dantley .15 .40
177 Allen Iverson .25 .60
178 Bill Laimbeer .15 .40
179 Chris Webber .20 .50
180 Connie Hawkins .20 .50
181 David Robinson .30 .75
182 Earl Monroe .20 .50
183 Elgin Baylor .20 .50
184 Gary Payton .20 .50
185 George Gervin .20 .50
186 George Mikan .40 1.00
187 James Worthy .25 .60
188 Joe Dumars .20 .50
189 Karl Malone .25 .60
190 Larry Bird .50 1.25
191 Mark Jackson .15 .40
192 Nate Thurmond .15 .40
193 Oscar Robertson .25 .60
194 Pete Maravich .30 .75
195 Shaquille O'Neal .40 1.00
196 Steve Kerr .20 .50
197 Tim Hardaway .20 .50
198 Tom Chambers .15 .40
199 Wes Unseld .20 .50
200 Willis Reed .20 .50
201 Alec Burks RC .40 1.00
202 Brandon Knight RC .40 1.00
203 Dion Waiters RC .40 1.00
204 Iman Shumpert RC .40 1.00
205 Jeremy Tyler RC .25 .60
206 Josh Selby RC .25 .60
207 Klay Thompson RC 1.50 4.00
208 Meyers Leonard RC .30 .75
209 Perry Jones RC .25 .60
210 Tristan Thompson RC .40 1.00
211 Andre Drummond RC .60 1.50
212 Chandler Parsons RC .40 1.00
213 Doron Lamb RC .25 .60
214 Isaiah Thomas RC .60 1.50
215 Jimmer Fredette RC .25 .60
216 Kawhi Leonard RC 2.00 5.00
217 Kyle O'Quinn RC .25 .60
218 Michael Kidd-Gilchrist RC .40 1.00
219 Quincy Acy RC .25 .60
220 Tyler Honeycutt RC .25 .60
221 Andrew Nicholson RC .25 .60
222 Charles Jenkins RC .25 .60
223 Draymond Green RC 1.25 3.00
224 Ivan Johnson RC .25 .60
225 Jimmy Butler RC 1.25 3.00
226 Kemba Walker RC .75 2.00
227 Kyrie Irving RC 2.00 5.00
228 Mike Scott RC .25 .60
229 Reggie Jackson RC .40 1.00
230 Tyler Zeller RC .30 .75
231 Darius Miller RC .25 .60
232 Chris Copeland RC .25 .60
233 Enes Kanter RC .30 .75
234 Jae Crowder RC .30 .75
235 John Henson RC .40 1.00
236 Kendall Marshall RC .25 .60
237 Lance Thomas RC .25 .60
238 Miles Plumlee RC .25 .60
239 Robert Sacre RC .25 .60
240 Tyshawn Taylor RC .25 .60
241 Anthony Davis RC 2.00 5.00
242 Chris Singleton RC .25 .60
243 E'Twaun Moore RC .25 .60
244 Jan Vesely RC .25 .60
245 John Jenkins RC .25 .60
246 Kenneth Faried RC .40 1.00
247 Lavoy Allen RC .25 .60
248 Maurice Harkless RC .40 1.00
249 Royce White RC .25 .60
250 Nando De Colo RC .25 .60
251 Arnett Moultrie RC .25 .60
252 Cory Joseph RC .25 .60
253 Evan Fournier RC .40 1.00
254 Jared Cunningham RC .25 .60
255 Jon Leuer RC .30 .75
256 Kent Bazemore RC .40 1.00
257 Marcus Morris RC .30 .75
258 Nikola Vucevic RC .40 1.00
259 Terrence Jones RC .30 .75
260 Harrison Barnes RC .60 1.50
261 Austin Rivers RC .40 1.00
262 Damian Lillard RC 1.50 4.00
263 Festus Ezeli RC .30 .75
264 Jared Sullinger RC .30 .75
265 Jonas Valanciunas RC .40 1.00
266 Kevin Murphy RC .25 .60
267 Markieff Morris RC .40 1.00
268 Nolan Smith RC .25 .60
269 Terrence Ross RC .40 1.00
270 Will Barton RC .30 .75
271 Bernard James RC .25 .60
272 Darius Johnson-Odom RC .25 .60
273 Greg Stiemsma RC .25 .60
274 Jeff Taylor RC .25 .60
275 Jordan Hamilton RC .25 .60
276 Khris Middleton RC .40 1.00
277 Marquis Teague RC .25 .60
278 Norris Cole RC .25 .60
279 Thomas Robinson RC .30 .75
280 Mirza Teletovic RC .30 .75
281 Bismack Biyombo RC .25 .60
282 Darius Morris RC .25 .60
283 Gustavo Ayon RC .25 .60
284 Jeremy Lamb RC .40 1.00
285 Josh Harrellson RC .25 .60
286 Kim English RC .25 .60
287 MarShon Brooks RC .30 .75
288 Orlando Johnson RC .25 .60
289 Tobias Harris RC .40 1.00
290 Tony Wroten RC .30 .75
291 Bradley Beal RC .60 1.50
292 Derrick Williams RC .25 .60
293 Tornike Shengelia RC .25 .60
294 Brian Roberts RC .25 .60
295 Pablo Prigioni RC .25 .60
296 DeQuan Jones RC .25 .60
297 Alexey Shved RC .25 .60
298 Luke Zeller RC .25 .60
299 Ben Hansbrough RC .25 .60
300 Maalik Wayns RC .40 1.00

2012-13 Panini Gold Knight
*GOLD VET: 1.2X TO 3X BASIC
*GOLD RC: .75X TO 2X BASIC

2012-13 Panini All-Panini
*GOLD: 1.5X TO 4X BASIC
GOLD PRINT RUN 25 SER.#'d SETS
1 Kobe Bryant 4.00 10.00
2 Kevin Durant 2.50 6.00
3 Blake Griffin 1.00 2.50
4 Kyrie Irving 5.00 12.00
5 Anthony Davis 5.00 12.00
6 Kevin Love 1.00 2.50
7 LeBron James 4.00 10.00
8 Rajon Rondo 1.00 2.50
9 Carmelo Anthony 1.25 3.00
10 Deron Williams .75 2.00
11 Chris Paul 1.25 3.00
12 Dirk Nowitzki 1.25 3.00
13 Russell Westbrook 2.50 6.00
14 Paul Pierce 1.00 2.50
15 Derrick Rose 1.25 3.00
16 Jason Kidd 1.00 2.50
17 Dwight Howard .75 2.00
18 Grant Hill 1.25 3.00
19 Joe Johnson .75 2.00
20 Damian Lillard 4.00 10.00
21 Kevin Garnett 1.50 4.00
22 Vince Carter 1.25 3.00
23 Josh Smith .75 2.00
24 Steve Nash 1.00 2.50
25 Dwyane Wade 1.50 4.00
26 James Harden 1.50 4.00
27 O.J. Mayo .60 1.50
28 LaMarcus Aldridge 1.00 2.50
29 Chris Bosh 1.00 2.50
30 Rudy Gay 1.00 2.50
31 Brook Lopez .75 2.00
32 Tim Duncan 1.50 4.00
33 Jrue Holiday 1.00 2.50
34 Stephen Curry 4.00 10.00
35 Tony Parker 1.00 2.50
36 Ricky Rubio 1.00 2.50
37 Marc Gasol 1.00 2.50
38 Kevin Martin .75 2.00
39 Al Horford .75 2.00
40 Greg Monroe .75 2.00
41 Roy Hibbert .75 2.00
42 Al Jefferson .75 2.00
43 Nicolas Batum .75 2.00
44 Zach Randolph .75 2.00
45 Luol Deng .75 2.00
46 Chandler Parsons 1.00 2.50
47 Brandon Jennings .60 1.50
48 Goran Dragic .75 2.00
49 Andrea Bargnani .75 2.00
50 Andre Iguodala .75 2.00
51 Kenneth Faried 1.00 2.50
52 Kawhi Leonard 5.00 12.00
53 Manu Ginobili 1.00 2.50
54 Ray Allen 1.00 2.50
55 Andrei Kirilenko .75 2.00
56 Serge Ibaka .75 2.00
57 Dion Waiters 1.00 2.50
58 Joakim Noah .75 2.00
59 Brandon Knight 1.00 2.50
60 Ty Lawson .60 1.50
61 Pau Gasol 1.00 2.50
62 Tyson Chandler .75 2.00
63 Jeremy Lin 1.00 2.50
64 Michael Kidd-Gilchrist 1.00 2.50
65 Harrison Barnes 1.50 4.00
66 Bradley Beal 1.50 4.00
67 John Wall 1.25 3.00
68 Chauncey Billups 1.00 2.50
69 Amare Stoudemire .75 2.00
70 Klay Thompson 4.00 10.00
71 Tyreke Evans .60 1.50
72 Richard Hamilton .75 2.00
73 Anderson Varejao .60 1.50
74 Thaddeus Young .60 1.50
75 Raymond Felton .75 2.00
76 Metta World Peace 1.00 2.50
77 Paul George 1.25 3.00
78 Jamal Crawford 1.00 2.50
79 Kemba Walker 2.00 5.00
80 David Lee .60 1.50
81 Wesley Matthews .60 1.50
82 Mike Conley .75 2.00
83 Gordon Hayward 1.00 2.50
84 J.J. Hickson .60 1.50
85 Jameer Nelson .60 1.50
86 Jonas Valanciunas 1.00 2.50
87 Jason Terry .75 2.00
88 Shawn Marion .75 2.00
89 DeMarcus Cousins 1.00 2.50
90 Pete Maravich 1.50 4.00
91 Wilt Chamberlain 2.00 5.00
92 Karl Malone 1.25 3.00
93 Jerry West 1.25 3.00
94 Bill Russell 1.50 4.00
95 George Mikan 2.00 5.00
96 Kareem Abdul-Jabbar 1.50 4.00
97 Magic Johnson 2.50 6.00
98 Oscar Robertson 1.25 3.00
99 Shaquille O'Neal 2.00 5.00
100 Julius Erving 1.50 4.00

2012-13 Panini Dress Code Jumbo Jerseys
1 Manu Ginobili 2.50 6.00
2 Jonas Valanciunas 2.50 6.00
3 Tim Duncan 4.00 10.00
4 Al Jefferson 2.00 5.00
5 Bradley Beal 4.00 10.00
6 DeMar DeRozan 2.50 6.00
7 Chris Paul 3.00 8.00
8 John Wall 3.00 8.00
9 Derrick Favors 2.00 5.00
10 Tony Parker 2.50 6.00
11 Andrea Bargnani 2.00 5.00
12 DeMarcus Cousins 2.50 6.00
13 Paul Pierce 2.50 6.00
14 Thomas Robinson 2.00 5.00
15 Dwight Howard 2.00 5.00
17 Tyreke Evans 1.50 4.00
18 Rajon Rondo 2.50 6.00
19 Deron Williams 2.00 5.00
20 LaMarcus Aldridge 2.50 6.00
22 Jameer Nelson 1.50 4.00
23 Dirk Nowitzki 3.00 8.00
24 Steve Nash 2.50 6.00
25 Evan Turner 1.50 4.00
26 Glen Davis 1.50 4.00
27 Channing Frye 2.00 5.00
28 Kevin Durant 6.00 15.00
29 Dwyane Wade 4.00 10.00
30 Carmelo Anthony 3.00 8.00
31 O.J. Mayo 1.50 4.00
32 Kyrie Irving 12.00 30.00
33 Brandon Jennings 1.50 4.00
34 Derrick Rose 3.00 8.00
35 Ricky Rubio 2.50 6.00
36 Monta Ellis 2.00 5.00
37 Austin Rivers 2.50 6.00
38 LeBron James 10.00 25.00
39 Russell Westbrook 6.00 15.00
40 Ray Allen 2.50 6.00
41 Rudy Gay 2.50 6.00
42 Joakim Noah 2.00 5.00
43 Kobe Bryant 10.00 25.00
44 Damian Lillard 10.00 25.00
45 Jrue Holiday 2.50 6.00
46 Blake Griffin 2.50 6.00
47 Gordon Hayward 2.50 6.00
48 Grant Hill 3.00 8.00
49 Michael Kidd-Gilchrist 2.50 6.00

2012-13 Panini Game Jerseys
1 Chris Paul 4.00 10.00
2 John Wall 4.00 10.00
3 George Hill 2.50 6.00
4 Evan Turner 2.00 5.00
5 Dwyane Wade 5.00 12.00
6 Dirk Nowitzki 4.00 10.00
7 Derrick Rose 4.00 10.00
8 Derrick Favors 2.50 6.00
9 Chris Bosh 3.00 8.00
10 Channing Frye 2.50 6.00
11 Carlos Boozer 2.50 6.00
12 Anderson Varejao 2.00 5.00
13 Amare Stoudemire 2.50 6.00
14 Al Jefferson 2.50 6.00
15 Al Horford 2.50 6.00
16 Zach Randolph 2.50 6.00
17 Tyrus Thomas 2.00 5.00
18 Tyreke Evans 2.00 5.00
19 Ty Lawson 2.00 5.00
20 Tayshaun Prince 2.50 6.00
21 Taj Gibson 2.50 6.00
22 Spencer Hawes 2.00 5.00
23 Raymond Felton 2.50 6.00
24 Rajon Rondo 3.00 8.00
25 Pau Gasol 3.00 8.00
26 Mike Conley 2.50 6.00
27 Marc Gasol 3.00 8.00
28 Manu Ginobili 3.00 8.00
29 Luol Deng 2.50 6.00
30 Kirk Hinrich 2.50 6.00
31 Kevin Love 3.00 8.00
32 Kevin Garnett 5.00 12.00
33 Josh Smith 2.50 6.00
34 Glen Davis 2.00 5.00
35 J.J. Redick 3.00 8.00
36 Derrick Williams 2.00 5.00
37 DeMar DeRozan 3.00 8.00
38 David Lee 2.00 5.00
39 Caron Butler 2.50 6.00
40 Brandon Jennings 2.00 5.00
41 Tony Parker 3.00 8.00
42 Tim Duncan 5.00 12.00
43 Andrea Bargnani 2.50 6.00
44 Thaddeus Young 2.00 5.00
45 Hedo Turkoglu 2.50 6.00
46 Jeff Teague 2.50 6.00
47 Jordan Hamilton 2.00 5.00
48 Tyson Chandler 2.50 6.00
49 Danny Granger 2.50 6.00
50 DeMarcus Cousins 3.00 8.00

2012-13 Panini Hall of Fame Signatures
LACK OF PRICING DUE TO MARKET INFO
3 Chris Mullin/99 8.00 20.00
6 Connie Hawkins/99 4.00 10.00
10 Bill Sharman/99 10.00 25.00
11 Larry Bird/25 60.00 120.00
16 Isiah Thomas/99 10.00 25.00
18 Bill Walton/99 10.00 25.00
19 Julius Erving/25 30.00 80.00

2012-13 Panini Heroes of the Hall
COMPLETE SET (25) 12.00 30.00
1 Hakeem Olajuwon 1.00 2.50
2 John Stockton 1.25 3.00
3 Moses Malone .75 2.00
4 Bob McAdoo .60 1.50
5 Lenny Wilkens .75 2.00
6 Walt Frazier .75 2.00
7 Dave Cowens .50 1.25
8 Nate Archibald .60 1.50
9 Bob Lanier .60 1.50
10 Wilt Chamberlain 1.50 4.00
11 Bob Pettit .75 2.00
12 Gail Goodrich .60 1.50
13 Larry Bird 2.00 5.00
14 Calvin Murphy .60 1.50
15 Bill Sharman .75 2.00
16 Bob Cousy 1.25 3.00
17 Dolph Schayes .75 2.00
18 Robert Parish .75 2.00
19 Patrick Ewing 1.00 2.50
20 Dennis Johnson .60 1.50
21 Artis Gilmore .60 1.50
22 Drazen Petrovic .75 2.00
23 Kevin McHale .75 2.00
24 Chris Mullin .75 2.00
25 Magic Johnson 2.00 5.00

2012-13 Panini Knights of the Round
COMMON CARD 3.00 8.00
SEIMISTARS 4.00 10.00
UNLISTED STARS 5.00 12.00
1 LeBron James 25.00 60.00
2 Chris Paul 6.00 15.00
3 Ricky Rubio 5.00 12.00
4 Carmelo Anthony 6.00 15.00
5 Steve Nash 5.00 12.00
6 Dwyane Wade 8.00 20.00
7 Anthony Davis 20.00 50.00
8 Kevin Durant 12.00 30.00
9 John Wall 6.00 15.00
10 Kobe Bryant 20.00 50.00
11 Russell Westbrook 12.00 30.00
12 Rajon Rondo 5.00 12.00
13 Blake Griffin 5.00 12.00
14 Kevin Love 5.00 12.00
15 Derrick Rose 6.00 15.00
16 Tyreke Evans 3.00 8.00
17 Jrue Holiday 5.00 12.00
18 James Harden 8.00 20.00
19 Kyrie Irving 15.00 40.00
20 Dirk Nowitzki 6.00 15.00

2012-13 Panini Matching Numbers
1 B.Griffin/E.Davis .75 2.00
2 Monta Ellis/Jrue Holiday .75 2.00
3 Eric Gordon/DeMar DeRozan .75 2.00
4 K.Durant/K.Faried 2.00 5.00
5 J.Teague/R.Westbrook 2.00 5.00
6 M.Brooks/T.Parker .75 2.00
7 D.Howard/L.Aldridge .75 2.00
8 J.Harden/T.Evans 1.25 3.00
9 R.Rubio/R.Rondo .75 2.00
10 M.Beasley/T.Robinson .60 1.50
11 K.Leonard/T.Sefolosha 4.00 10.00
12 D.Cousins/D.Favors .75 2.00
13 Gordon Hayward/Manu Ginobili .75 2.00
14 Rudy Gay/Anthony Morrow .75 2.00
15 Chris Bosh/Amare Stoudemire .75 2.00
16 D.Wade/B.Beal 1.25 3.00
17 A.Davis/M.Camby 3.00 8.00
18 K.Bryant/P.George 3.00 8.00
19 N.Cole/S.Curry 3.00 8.00
20 D.Rose/G.Dragic 1.00 2.50
21 C.Paul/B.Jennings 1.00 2.50
22 J.Redick/J.Fredette .75 2.00
23 C.Anthony/J.Lin 1.00 2.50
24 J.Smith/K.Garnett 1.25 3.00
25 J.Wall/K.Irving 3.00 8.00

2012-13 Panini Player of the Year
UNLISTED STARS 2.50 6.00
1 Steve Nash 2.50 6.00
2 Dirk Nowitzki 3.00 8.00
3 Kobe Bryant 10.00 25.00
4 Derrick Rose 3.00 8.00
5 LeBron James 10.00 25.00

2012-13 Panini Rated Rookie Signatures
PRINT RUNS B/WN 25-50 COPIES PER
NO PRICING ON MOST DUE TO LACK OF INFO
EXCHANGE DEADLINE 9/06/2014
1 Anthony Davis/50 100.00 200.00
2 Michael Kidd-Gilchrist/50 5.00 12.00
3 Bradley Beal/50 12.00 30.00
4 Dion Waiters/50 5.00 12.00
5 Thomas Robinson/50
6 Harrison Barnes/48 12.00 30.00
7 Terrence Ross/50 5.00 12.00
8 Andre Drummond/50
9 Austin Rivers/50 5.00 12.00
10 Meyers Leonard/50 4.00 10.00
11 John Henson/50 5.00 12.00
12 Maurice Harkless/50 5.00 12.00
13 Royce White/50
14 Tyler Zeller/50 4.00 10.00
15 Jeremy Lamb/49 5.00 12.00
16 Kendall Marshall/50 3.00 8.00
17 Terrence Jones/49
18 Andrew Nicholson/50
19 Evan Fournier/50 5.00 12.00
20 Jared Sullinger/50 4.00 10.00
21 John Jenkins/50 3.00 8.00
22 Fab Melo/50 3.00 8.00
23 Jared Cunningham/50 3.00 8.00
24 Tony Wroten/50 4.00 10.00
25 Miles Plumlee/50 3.00 8.00
26 Arnett Moultrie/50 3.00 8.00
27 Perry Jones/50 3.00 8.00
28 Marquis Teague/50 3.00 8.00
29 Festus Ezeli/50
30 Jeff Taylor/50 3.00 8.00
31 Bernard James/50 3.00 8.00
32 Jae Crowder/50 4.00 10.00
33 Draymond Green/50 12.00 30.00
34 Quincy Acy/50 3.00 8.00
35 Quincy Miller/50
36 Khris Middleton/50 5.00 12.00
37 Doron Lamb/50 3.00 8.00
38 Mike Scott/50
39 Kim English/25
40 Darius Miller/50 3.00 8.00
41 Kyle O'Quinn/49 3.00 8.00
42 Darius Johnson-Odom/50 3.00 8.00
43 Robert Sacre/50 3.00 8.00
44 Jonas Valanciunas/25
45 Kyle Singler/25 3.00 8.00
46 Derrick Williams/50 3.00 8.00
47 Enes Kanter/50 4.00 10.00
48 Tristan Thompson/50 8.00 20.00
49 Bismack Biyombo/50 3.00 8.00
50 Kemba Walker/50 10.00 25.00
51 Klay Thompson/50 20.00 50.00
52 Jimmer Fredette/50 3.00 8.00
53 Alec Burks/50 5.00 12.00
54 Markieff Morris/50 8.00 20.00
55 Marcus Morris/50 4.00 10.00
56 Kawhi Leonard/50 60.00 150.00
57 Iman Shumpert/50 5.00 12.00
58 Chris Singleton/50 3.00 8.00
59 Tobias Harris/50 5.00 12.00
60 Nolan Smith/50
61 Kenneth Faried/50 5.00 12.00
62 Reggie Jackson/50 5.00 12.00
63 MarShon Brooks/50 4.00 10.00
64 Jordan Hamilton/50 3.00 8.00
65 JaJuan Johnson/50 3.00 8.00
66 Norris Cole/50 3.00 8.00
67 Cory Joseph/50 3.00 8.00
68 Jimmy Butler/50 20.00 50.00
69 Shelvin Mack/50 4.00 10.00
70 Tyler Honeycutt/50
71 Kyrie Irving/49 125.00 250.00
72 Trey Thompkins/50 3.00 8.00
73 Chandler Parsons/50 5.00 12.00
74 Jeremy Tyler/50 3.00 8.00
75 Jon Leuer/50
76 Darius Morris/50 5.00 12.00
77 Malcolm Lee/50 3.00 8.00
78 Nikola Vucevic/50 5.00 12.00
79 Josh Selby/50 3.00 8.00
80 Isaiah Thomas/50 30.00 80.00
81 Lavoy Allen/50
82 Ivan Johnson/50 3.00 8.00
83 Lance Thomas/50 3.00 8.00
84 Travis Leslie/50 3.00 8.00
85 Brandon Knight/50

2012-13 Panini Rookie Signatures
EXCHANGE DEADLINE 9/06/2014
1 Kyrie Irving 30.00 80.00
2 Iman Shumpert 4.00 10.00
3 MarShon Brooks 3.00 8.00
4 Kyle Singler 2.50 6.00
5 Chandler Parsons 4.00 10.00
6 Malcolm Lee 2.50 6.00
7 Anthony Davis 75.00 150.00
8 Harrison Barnes 6.00 15.00
9 Jeremy Lamb 4.00 10.00
10 Miles Plumlee 2.50 6.00
11 Quincy Acy 2.50 6.00
12 Tyshawn Taylor 2.50 6.00
13 Draymond Green 10.00 25.00
14 Bernard James 2.50 6.00
15 Perry Jones 2.50 6.00
16 Tyler Zeller 3.00 8.00
17 Jared Sullinger 3.00 8.00
18 Royce White 2.50 6.00
19 Austin Rivers 4.00 10.00
20 Terrence Ross 4.00 10.00
21 Dion Waiters 4.00 10.00
22 Lavoy Allen 2.50 6.00
23 Josh Harrellson 2.50 6.00
24 Jon Leuer 3.00 8.00
25 Jimmy Butler 20.00 50.00
26 Norris Cole 2.50 6.00
27 Kawhi Leonard 50.00 120.00
28 Markieff Morris 4.00 10.00
29 Jimmer Fredette 2.50 6.00
30 Brandon Knight 4.00 10.00
31 Jan Vesely 2.50 6.00
32 Derrick Williams 2.50 6.00
33 Tristan Thompson 4.00 10.00
34 Kemba Walker 8.00 20.00
35 Marcus Morris 3.00 8.00
36 Kenneth Faried 4.00 10.00
37 Cory Joseph 2.50 6.00
38 Darius Morris 2.50 6.00
39 Brian Roberts 2.50 6.00
40 Isaiah Thomas 15.00 40.00
41 Michael Kidd-Gilchrist 4.00 10.00
42 Meyers Leonard 3.00 8.00
43 Jae Crowder 3.00 8.00
44 Quincy Miller 2.50 6.00
45 Doron Lamb 2.50 6.00
46 Darius Miller 2.50 6.00
47 Kris Joseph 2.50 6.00
48 Will Barton 3.00 8.00
49 Andre Drummond 10.00 25.00
50 Lance Thomas 2.50 6.00
51 DeAndre Liggins 3.00 8.00
52 Klay Thompson 30.00 80.00
53 Jonas Valanciunas 4.00 10.00
54 Enes Kanter 3.00 8.00
55 Nikola Vucevic 4.00 10.00
56 Tyler Honeycutt 2.50 6.00
57 Bradley Beal 6.00 15.00
58 Thomas Robinson 3.00 8.00
59 Kendall Marshall 2.50 6.00
60 Marquis Teague 2.50 6.00

2012-13 Panini Signature Inserts
EXCHANGE DEADLINE 9/06/2014
1 Roy Hibbert 3.00 8.00
2 Marcin Gortat 3.00 8.00
3 Jrue Holiday 6.00 15.00
4 Leandro Barbosa 3.00 8.00
5 Kevin Martin 3.00 8.00
6 Goran Dragic
7 Darren Collison EXCH 3.00 8.00
8 Antawn Jamison 3.00 8.00
9 DeAndre Jordan EXCH 4.00 10.00
10 Serge Ibaka 12.00 30.00
11 Kevin Love 4.00 10.00
12 Avery Bradley
13 Anderson Varejao 2.50 6.00
14 Ryan Anderson EXCH 3.00 8.00
15 Andrei Kirilenko 3.00 8.00
16 George Hill 3.00 8.00
17 Luol Deng
18 Kendrick Perkins 2.50 6.00
19 Zach Randolph 3.00 8.00
20 Andre Iguodala 6.00 15.00

2012-13 Panini Spirit of the Game
COMPLETE SET (25) 12.00 30.00
1 Chris Paul 1.00 2.50
2 Jeremy Lin .75 2.00
3 Russell Westbrook 2.00 5.00
4 Rajon Rondo .75 2.00
5 Kyle Lowry .60 1.50
6 Kenneth Faried .75 2.00
7 Jrue Holiday .75 2.00
8 Kevin Love .75 2.00
9 Kawhi Leonard 4.00 10.00
10 LaMarcus Aldridge .75 2.00
11 Josh Smith .60 1.50

12 JaVale McGee .60 1.50
13 Blake Griffin .75 2.00
14 Serge Ibaka .60 1.50
15 Roy Hibbert .60 1.50
16 Louis Williams .60 1.50
17 Derrick Favors .60 1.50
18 DeAndre Jordan .75 2.00
19 Derrick Rose 1.00 2.50
20 Deron Williams .60 1.50
21 Ricky Rubio .75 2.00
22 Michael Beasley .50 1.25
23 Stephen Curry 3.00 8.00
24 Joe Johnson .60 1.50
25 Kemba Walker 1.50 4.00

2013-14 Panini

1 Gerald Wallace .15 .40
2 Brook Lopez .15 .40
3 Carlos Boozer .15 .40
4 Jose Calderon .12 .30
5 Rodney Stuckey .15 .40
6 Dwight Howard .15 .40
7 Jamal Crawford .20 .50
8 Tony Allen
9 Chris Bosh .20 .50
10 Kevin Martin .15 .40
11 Amare Stoudemire .15 .40
12 Serge Ibaka .15 .40
13 Markieff Morris .12 .30
14 LaMarcus Aldridge .20 .50
15 Danny Green .15 .40
16 Gordon Hayward .20 .50
17 DeMarcus Cousins .20 .50
18 Eric Bledsoe .15 .40
19 Thabo Sefolosha .12 .30
20 Eric Gordon .15 .40
21 Michael Beasley .12 .30
22 Chris Kaman .15 .40
23 Lance Stephenson .15 .40
24 Andrew Bogut .15 .40
25 J.J. Hickson .12 .30
26 Kyrie Irving .40 1.00
27 Ben Gordon .15 .40
28 Deron Williams .15 .40
29 Al Horford .15 .40
30 Kemba Walker .20 .50
31 Dion Waiters .15 .40
32 JaVale McGee .15 .40
33 Klay Thompson .25 .60
34 Jeremy Lin .20 .50
35 Chris Paul .25 .60
36 Mike Conley .15 .40
37 Mario Chalmers .15 .40
38 Ricky Rubio .20 .50
39 Tyson Chandler .15 .40
40 Glen Davis .12 .30
41 Marcus Morris .12 .30
42 Isaiah Thomas .20 .50
43 Tim Duncan .30 .75
44 Marvin Williams .15 .40
45 Martell Webster .12 .30
46 Jeff Teague .15 .40
47 Kris Humphries .12 .30
48 Paul Pierce .20 .50
49 Joakim Noah .15 .40
50 Shawn Marion .15 .40
51 Josh Smith .15 .40
52 Harrison Barnes .15 .40
53 George Hill .15 .40
54 Blake Griffin .20 .50
55 John Henson .15 .40
56 Tyreke Evans .12 .30
57 Thaddeus Young .12 .30
58 Wesley Matthews .12 .30
59 Jonas Valanciunas .15 .40
60 Trevor Ariza .12 .30
61 Joe Johnson .15 .40
62 Monta Ellis .15 .40
63 Chandler Parsons .15 .40
64 Nick Young .20 .50
65 Ersan Ilyasova .12 .30
66 Kendrick Perkins .12 .30
67 Terrence Jones .15 .40
68 Tiago Splitter .15 .40
69 Jan Vesely .12 .30
70 Marcus Thornton .12 .30
71 Nikola Vucevic .15 .40
72 Anthony Davis .40 1.00
73 Dwyane Wade .30 .75
74 Roy Hibbert .15 .40
75 Brandon Jennings .12 .30
76 Anderson Varejao .12 .30
77 Andray Blatche .12 .30
78 Jeff Green .15 .40
79 Luol Deng .15 .40
80 Kenneth Faried .15 .40
81 James Harden .30 .75
82 J.J. Redick .20 .50
83 Zach Randolph .15 .40
84 Larry Sanders .12 .30
85 Jrue Holiday .20 .50
86 Arron Afflalo .12 .30
87 Damian Lillard .40 1.00
88 Tony Parker .20 .50
89 Derrick Favors .15 .40
90 Paul Millsap .20 .50
91 Al Jefferson .15 .40
92 Andrei Kirilenko .15 .40
93 Derrick Rose .25 .60
94 Dirk Nowitzki .25 .60
95 Andre Iguodala .15 .40
96 Danny Granger .15 .40
97 Jordan Hill .12 .30
98 Shane Battier .15 .40
99 Kobe Bryant .75 2.00
100 Nikola Pekovic .12 .30
101 Carmelo Anthony .25 .60
102 Evan Turner .12 .30
103 Thomas Robinson .12 .30
104 DeMar DeRozan .20 .50
105 Marcin Gortat .15 .40
106 Danilo Gallinari .12 .30
107 Steve Nash .20 .50
108 J.J. Barea .15 .40
109 Russell Westbrook .50 1.25
110 Jimmer Fredette .12 .30
111 Enes Kanter .12 .30
112 Goran Dragic .15 .40
113 Al-Farouq Aminu .15 .40
114 LeBron James .75 2.00
115 Paul George .25 .60
116 Vince Carter .25 .60
117 Gerald Henderson .12 .30
118 Kyle Lowry .15 .40
119 Jason Richardson .20 .50
120 Iman Shumpert .12 .30
121 O.J. Mayo .12 .30
122 Tayshaun Prince .15 .40
123 David West .15 .40
124 Andre Drummond .20 .50
125 Kirk Hinrich .15 .40
126 Brandon Bass .12 .30
127 Kyle Korver .15 .40
128 Manu Ginobili .20 .50
129 Rajon Rondo .20 .50
130 Andrew Bynum .12 .30
131 David Lee .12 .30
132 Marc Gasol .20 .50
133 Nicolas Batum .15 .40
134 John Wall .25 .60
135 Kevin Garnett .30 .75
136 Ty Lawson .12 .30
137 Luis Scola .15 .40
138 Raymond Felton .15 .40
139 Rudy Gay .20 .50
140 Avery Bradley .15 .40
141 Bradley Beal .20 .50
142 Michael Kidd-Gilchrist .20 .50
143 Richard Jefferson .15 .40
144 Taj Gibson .15 .40
145 Tyler Hansbrough .15 .40
146 Tristan Thompson .15 .40
147 Kawhi Leonard .30 .75
148 Gerald Green .15 .40
149 Greivis Vasquez .15 .40
150 Greg Monroe .15 .40
151 Spencer Hawes .12 .30
152 Stephen Curry .75 2.00
153 Jameer Nelson .12 .30
154 Brandon Knight .15 .40
155 J.R. Smith .15 .40
156 Pau Gasol .20 .50
157 Kevin Durant .50 1.25
158 Kevin Love .20 .50
159 Ray Allen .20 .50
160 DeAndre Jordan .20 .50
161 Kelly Olynyk RC .30 .75
162 Tony Snell RC .30 .75
163 Kentavious Caldwell-Pope RC .40 1.00
164 Solomon Hill RC .25 .60
165 Nate Wolters RC .30 .75
166 Andre Roberson RC .25 .60
167 Nerlens Noel RC .50 1.25
168 C.J. McCollum RC .60 1.50
169 Otto Porter RC .40 1.00
170 Gal Mekel RC .25 .60
171 Mason Plumlee RC .40 1.00
172 Anthony Bennett RC .30 .75
173 Peyton Siva RC .25 .60
174 Reggie Bullock RC .30 .75
175 Shabazz Muhammad RC .30 .75
176 Steven Adams RC .40 1.00
177 Alex Len RC .30 .75
178 Ben McLemore RC .30 .75
179 Vitor Faverani RC .25 .60
180 Luigi Datome RC .25 .60
181 Cody Zeller RC .30 .75
182 Ricky Ledo RC .25 .60
*183 Tony Mitchell RC .25 .60
184 Jamaal Franklin RC .25 .60
185 Jeff Withey RC .25 .60
186 Victor Oladipo RC .50 1.25
187 Archie Goodwin RC .30 .75
188 Trey Burke RC .30 .75
189 Pero Antic RC .25 .60
190 Rudy Gobert RC .50 1.25
191 Erik Murphy RC .25 .60
192 Shane Larkin RC .25 .60
193 Isaiah Canaan RC .25 .60
194 G.Antetokounmpo RC 3.00 8.00
195 Tim Hardaway Jr. RC .40 1.00
196 M.Carter-Williams RC .40 1.00
197 Allen Crabbe RC .30 .75
198 Glen Rice Jr. RC .25 .60
199 Phil Pressey RC .25 .60
200 Nemanja Nedovic RC .25 .60

2013-14 Panini Gold Knights

*GOLD VET: 1.2X TO 3X BASIC
*GOLD RC: .75X TO 2X BASIC

2013-14 Panini All-Panini

*GOLD: .6X TO 1.5X BASIC
1 Carlos Boozer 1.25 3.00
2 Eric Gordon 1.25 3.00
3 Chris Paul 2.00 5.00
4 Josh Smith 1.25 3.00
5 Dwyane Wade 2.50 6.00
6 Arron Afflalo 1.00 2.50
7 Evan Turner 1.00 2.50
8 Kyle Lowry 1.25 3.00
9 John Wall 2.00 5.00
10 Greivis Vasquez 1.25 3.00
11 Dwight Howard 1.25 3.00
12 Lance Stephenson 1.25 3.00
13 Mike Conley 1.25 3.00
14 Harrison Barnes 1.25 3.00
15 Roy Hibbert 1.25 3.00
16 Damian Lillard 3.00 8.00
17 DeMar DeRozan 1.50 4.00
18 Iman Shumpert 1.00 2.50
19 Ty Lawson 1.00 2.50
20 Greg Monroe 1.25 3.00
21 Chris Bosh 1.50 4.00
22 Andrew Bogut 1.25 3.00
23 Ricky Rubio 1.50 4.00
24 George Hill 1.25 3.00
25 Brandon Jennings 1.00 2.50
26 Tony Parker 1.50 4.00
27 Steve Nash 1.50 4.00
28 O.J. Mayo 1.00 2.50
29 Raymond Felton 1.25 3.00
30 Spencer Hawes 1.00 2.50
31 Kevin Martin 1.25 3.00
32 Kyrie Irving 3.00 8.00
33 Tyson Chandler 1.25 3.00
34 Blake Griffin 1.50 4.00
35 Jeff Green 1.25 3.00
36 Al Jefferson 1.25 3.00
37 J.J. Barea 1.25 3.00
38 Andre Drummond 1.50 4.00
39 Rudy Gay 1.50 4.00
40 Stephen Curry 6.00 15.00
41 Amare Stoudemire 1.25 3.00
42 Deron Williams 1.25 3.00
43 Glen Davis 1.00 2.50
44 Joe Johnson 1.25 3.00
45 Luol Deng 1.25 3.00
46 Andrei Kirilenko 1.25 3.00
47 Russell Westbrook 4.00 10.00
48 Kirk Hinrich 1.25 3.00
49 Bradley Beal 1.50 4.00
50 Jameer Nelson 1.00 2.50
51 Serge Ibaka 1.25 3.00
52 Al Horford 1.25 3.00
53 Tim Duncan 2.50 6.00
54 Monta Ellis 1.25 3.00
55 Kenneth Faried 1.25 3.00
56 Derrick Rose 2.00 5.00
57 Enes Kanter 1.00 2.50
58 Manu Ginobili 1.50 4.00
59 Michael Kidd-Gilchrist 1.50 4.00
60 J.R. Smith 1.25 3.00
61 LaMarcus Aldridge 1.50 4.00
62 Kemba Walker 1.50 4.00
63 Jeff Teague 1.25 3.00
64 Chandler Parsons 1.25 3.00
65 Dirk Nowitzki 2.00 5.00
66 James Harden 2.50 6.00
67 Goran Dragic 1.25 3.00
68 Rajon Rondo 1.50 4.00
69 Taj Gibson 1.25 3.00
70 Pau Gasol 1.50 4.00
71 Gordon Hayward 1.50 4.00
72 JaVale McGee 1.25 3.00
73 Paul Pierce 1.50 4.00
74 Tiago Splitter 1.25 3.00
75 J.J. Redick 1.50 4.00
76 Andre Iguodala 1.25 3.00
77 LeBron James 10.00 25.00
78 David Lee 1.00 2.50
79 Tristan Thompson 1.25 3.00
80 Kevin Durant 4.00 10.00
81 DeMarcus Cousins 1.50 4.00
82 Klay Thompson 2.00 5.00
83 Joakim Noah 1.25 3.00
84 Nikola Vucevic 1.25 3.00
85 Zach Randolph 1.25 3.00
86 Kobe Bryant 10.00 25.00
87 Paul George 2.00 5.00
88 Marc Gasol 1.50 4.00
89 Kawhi Leonard 2.50 6.00
90 Kevin Love 1.50 4.00
91 Eric Bledsoe 1.25 3.00
92 Jeremy Lin 1.50 4.00
93 Shawn Marion 1.25 3.00
94 Anthony Davis 3.00 8.00
95 Carmelo Anthony 2.00 5.00
96 Jrue Holiday 1.50 4.00
97 Vince Carter 2.00 5.00
98 Nicolas Batum 1.25 3.00
99 Gerald Green 1.25 3.00
100 Ray Allen 1.50 4.00

2013-14 Panini Bird's Eye View

1 Derrick Rose .40 1.00
2 Victor Oladipo .40 1.00
3 Paul George .40 1.00
4 Pau Gasol .30 .75
5 Eric Gordon .25 .60
6 Tim Duncan .50 1.25
7 Blake Griffin .30 .75
8 Kobe Bryant 1.25 3.00
9 Michael Carter-Williams .30 .75
10 Chris Paul .40 1.00

2013-14 Panini Clipboard Signatures

EXCHANGE DEADLINE 10/09/2015
1 Jeff Hornacek
2 Don Nelson
3 Scott Skiles
4 Jerry West
5 Jason Kidd
6 Byron Scott
7 Maurice Cheeks
8 Tom Heinsohn
9 George Karl 8.00 20.00
10 Kevin McHale
11 Vinny Del Negro
12 Lindsey Hunter 5.00 12.00
13 John Lucas
14 Bill Sharman
15 Dick Vitale 10.00 25.00

2013-14 Panini Energizers Ink

EXCHANGE DEADLINE 10/09/2015
1 Jared Sullinger
2 Vince Carter
3 Andrew Nicholson
4 Xavier Henry
5 Steve Kerr
6 J.R. Smith 6.00 15.00
7 Harrison Barnes 6.00 15.00
8 Andray Blatche
9 Courtney Lee
10 Chris Andersen
11 Marvin Williams
12 Tony Wroten
13 Michael Cooper
14 Ramon Sessions
15 Ricky Pierce

2013-14 Panini Family Business

1 B.Barry/R.Barry .60 1.50
2 D.Curry/S.Curry 3.00 8.00
3 M.Thompson/K.Thompson 1.00 2.50
4 A.Rivers/D.Rivers .75 2.00
5 T.Hardaway/T.Hardaway Jr. .75 2.00
6 G.Rice/G.Rice Jr. .40 1.00
7 L.Walton/B.Walton .75 2.00
8 J.Bryant/K.Bryant 3.00 8.00

2013-14 Panini Favorites

1 James Harden 5.00 12.00
2 LeBron James 20.00 50.00
3 Victor Oladipo 4.00 10.00
4 Ricky Rubio 3.00 8.00
5 Kobe Bryant 12.00 30.00
6 Anthony Davis 6.00 15.00
7 Rajon Rondo 3.00 8.00
8 Carmelo Anthony 4.00 10.00
9 Derrick Rose 4.00 10.00
10 Kevin Durant 8.00 20.00
11 Kyrie Irving 6.00 15.00
12 Michael Carter-Williams 3.00 8.00
13 Dirk Nowitzki 4.00 10.00
14 Damian Lillard 6.00 15.00
15 Stephen Curry 12.00 30.00

2013-14 Panini First Impressions Autographs

EXCHANGE DEADLINE 10/09/2015
1 Kelly Olynyk 4.00 10.00
2 Erik Murphy 3.00 8.00
3 Gal Mekel 3.00 8.00
4 Isaiah Canaan 3.00 8.00
5 Cody Zeller 4.00 10.00
6 Shabazz Muhammad 4.00 10.00
7 Michael Carter-Williams 5.00 12.00
8 Alex Len 4.00 10.00
9 Ben McLemore 4.00 10.00
10 Otto Porter 5.00 12.00
11 Phil Pressey 3.00 8.00
12 Tony Snell 4.00 10.00
13 Tony Mitchell 3.00 8.00
14 Solomon Hill
15 Anthony Bennett 4.00 10.00
16 Victor Oladipo 6.00 15.00
17 Nerlens Noel 6.00 15.00
18 C.J. McCollum 12.00 30.00
19 Trey Burke 4.00 10.00
20 Dennis Schroder 5.00 12.00
21 Mason Plumlee 5.00 12.00
22 Shane Larkin
23 Nemanja Nedovic
24 Ryan Kelly 3.00 8.00
25 Kentavious Caldwell-Pope 5.00 12.00

2013-14 Panini Hall of Fame Signatures

EXCHANGE DEADLINE 10/09/2015
1 Walt Bellamy 4.00 10.00
2 Wes Unseld 10.00 25.00
3 Kevin McHale
4 Dominique Wilkins 8.00 20.00
5 Chris Mullin 10.00 25.00
6 David Robinson 20.00 50.00
7 Dan Issel
8 Adrian Dantley
9 Ralph Sampson
10 Nate Thurmond 4.00 10.00
11 Isiah Thomas 8.00 20.00
12 James Worthy 15.00 40.00
13 Hakeem Olajuwon
14 Elvin Hayes
15 Bill Walton
16 Dennis Rodman 25.00 60.00
17 Jamaal Wilkes
18 David Thompson 4.00 10.00
19 Joe Dumars
20 Robert Parish 10.00 25.00
21 Walt Frazier 5.00 12.00
22 Elgin Baylor 12.00 30.00
23 Gary Payton
24 Artis Gilmore 4.00 10.00
25 Bill Sharman 15.00 40.00
26 Bob McAdoo 4.00 10.00
27 Alex English
28 Hal Greer 4.00 10.00
29 Nate Archibald 10.00 25.00
30 Gail Goodrich 4.00 10.00

2013-14 Panini Insert Signatures

EXCHANGE DEADLINE 10/09/2015
1 Rory Sparrow
2 Danny Manning
3 Michael Finley 12.00 30.00
4 Charlie Bell 3.00 8.00
5 Gary Trent 3.00 8.00
6 Jared Jeffries
7 John Lucas III
8 Chris Whitney 3.00 8.00
9 Chuck Hayes
10 Steve Blake 8.00 20.00
11 Bob Dandridge
12 Jerry Lucas
13 LaMarcus Aldridge
14 Lindsey Hunter 3.00 8.00
15 James Posey 3.00 8.00
16 Greg Buckner 3.00 8.00
17 Bill Willoughby 3.00 8.00
18 Ricky Pierce
19 Ryan Hollins
20 Kenyon Martin 4.00 10.00
21 Fat Lever
22 Kenny Smith
23 Bernard King 10.00 25.00
24 Dale Davis 5.00 12.00
25 Dennis Rodman 20.00 50.00
26 Vlade Divac 5.00 12.00
27 Pearl Washington 3.00 8.00
28 Tree Rollins
29 Travis Outlaw 4.00 10.00
30 Darrell Griffith 3.00 8.00
31 Nick Collison
32 Peja Stojakovic 8.00 20.00
33 Tracy McGrady 8.00 20.00
34 Ronnie Brewer
35 Chris Bosh
36 Walter Berry 3.00 8.00
37 Thurl Bailey
38 Elvin Hayes
39 Greg Stiemsma 3.00 8.00
40 Vernon Maxwell 3.00 8.00
41 Kyle Korver 4.00 10.00
42 Eric Gordon
43 Zydrunas Ilgauskas
44 Chucky Brown 3.00 8.00
45 Kevin Love 15.00 40.00
46 Fred Jones 3.00 8.00
47 Chet Walker 4.00 10.00
48 Ramon Sessions 4.00 10.00
49 Theo Ratliff 3.00 8.00
50 James Jones 3.00 8.00
51 Luis Scola
52 Chris Kaman
53 Jeff Malone
54 Jerome Williams
55 World B. Free 4.00 10.00

2013-14 Panini Knight School

1 Kevin Love .40 1.00
2 Klay Thompson .50 1.25
3 Michael Carter-Williams .40 1.00
4 Damian Lillard .75 2.00
5 Kenneth Faried .30 .75
6 Kyrie Irving .75 2.00
7 Paul George .50 1.25
8 Blake Griffin .40 1.00
9 Rajon Rondo .40 1.00
10 Derrick Rose .50 1.25
11 Russell Westbrook 1.00 2.50
12 James Harden .60 1.50
13 Victor Oladipo .50 1.25
14 Stephen Curry 1.50 4.00
15 Kevin Durant 1.00 2.50

2013-14 Panini Knights of the Round

1 Paul George 8.00 20.00
2 Ricky Rubio 6.00 15.00
3 Dwyane Wade 10.00 25.00
4 John Wall 8.00 20.00
5 Rajon Rondo 6.00 15.00
6 Klay Thompson 8.00 20.00
7 Kevin Love 6.00 15.00
8 James Harden 10.00 25.00
9 Dirk Nowitzki 8.00 20.00
10 LeBron James 25.00 60.00
11 Tony Parker 6.00 15.00
12 Carmelo Anthony 8.00 20.00
13 Anthony Davis 12.00 30.00
14 Kobe Bryant 25.00 60.00
15 Blake Griffin 6.00 15.00
16 Derrick Rose 8.00 20.00
17 Damian Lillard 12.00 30.00
18 Kyrie Irving 12.00 30.00
19 DeMar DeRozan 6.00 15.00
20 Chris Paul 8.00 20.00
21 Monta Ellis 5.00 12.00
22 Kevin Durant 15.00 40.00
23 Stephen Curry 25.00 60.00
24 Russell Westbrook 15.00 40.00

2013-14 Panini Preparation

1 Monta Ellis .50 1.25
2 Chandler Parsons .50 1.25
3 Evan Turner .40 1.00
4 John Wall .75 2.00
5 LeBron James 2.50 6.00
6 Jrue Holiday .60 1.50
7 Mario Chalmers .50 1.25
8 Kevin Durant 1.50 4.00
9 George Hill .50 1.25
10 Dwyane Wade 1.00 2.50
11 Paul George .75 2.00
12 Kevin Garnett 1.00 2.50
13 Daniel Gibson .50 1.25
14 Deron Williams .50 1.25
15 Kyrie Irving 1.25 3.00
16 Jeremy Lin .60 1.50
17 Chris Paul .75 2.00
18 James Harden 1.00 2.50

2013-14 Panini Rated Rookie Signatures

EXCHANGE DEADLINE 10/09/2015
1 Solomon Hill
2 Giannis Antetokounmpo 75.00 200.00
3 Tim Hardaway Jr. 12.00 30.00
4 Michael Carter-Williams 10.00 25.00
5 Allen Crabbe 5.00 12.00
6 Trey Burke 5.00 12.00
7 Kelly Olynyk 5.00 12.00
8 Erik Murphy 4.00 10.00
9 Ricky Ledo 4.00 10.00
10 Peyton Siva
11 Reggie Bullock 5.00 12.00
12 Nate Wolters
13 Andre Roberson 4.00 10.00
14 Nerlens Noel 12.00 30.00
15 C.J. McCollum
16 Glen Rice Jr.
17 Mason Plumlee
18 Tony Snell 5.00 12.00
19 Shane Larkin
20 Tony Mitchell 4.00 10.00
21 Ryan Kelly
22 Shabazz Muhammad 5.00 12.00
23 Steven Adams 30.00 60.00
24 Alex Len 5.00 12.00
25 Ben McLemore 5.00 12.00
26 Otto Porter
27 Cody Zeller
28 Anthony Bennett 5.00 12.00
29 Kentavious Caldwell-Pope
30 Isaiah Canaan 4.00 10.00
31 Jamaal Franklin
32 Jeff Withey
33 Victor Oladipo 8.00 20.00
34 Archie Goodwin 5.00 12.00

2013-14 Panini Rising Tide Autographs

EXCHANGE DEADLINE 10/09/2015
1 Jon Leuer 3.00 8.00
2 Bradley Beal
3 Tyshawn Taylor
4 Nick Young
5 Jeff Withey 3.00 8.00
6 Michael Carter-Williams 5.00 12.00
7 Allen Crabbe 4.00 10.00
8 Jonas Jerebko
9 Pero Antic 3.00 8.00
10 Jimmer Fredette
11 Quincy Acy 3.00 8.00
12 Toure Murry 4.00 10.00
13 Patrick Beverley
14 Kawhi Leonard 15.00 40.00
15 Jamaal Franklin
16 Tim Hardaway Jr. 5.00 12.00
17 Dwight Buycks 3.00 8.00
18 Daniel Orton 3.00 8.00
19 Carrick Felix 3.00 8.00
20 Gordon Hayward 5.00 12.00
21 Andre Drummond
22 Ricky Ledo 3.00 8.00
23 Jared Cunningham 3.00 8.00
24 Goran Dragic
25 Giannis Antetokounmpo 75.00 200.00
26 Andre Roberson 3.00 8.00
27 Rudy Gobert 10.00 25.00
28 Elliot Williams 3.00 8.00
29 Serge Ibaka
30 Nando De Colo 4.00 10.00
31 Greg Monroe
32 Matthew Dellavedova 12.00 30.00
33 Jason Smith 3.00 8.00
34 Jared Sullinger
35 Nate Wolters 4.00 10.00
36 Steven Adams 5.00 12.00
37 Glen Rice Jr. 3.00 8.00
38 Ty Lawson 3.00 8.00
39 Derrick Williams 3.00 8.00
40 Evan Fournier
41 Jrue Holiday
42 DeMarre Carroll 3.00 8.00
43 Lorenzo Brown 3.00 8.00
44 Jordan Hill
45 Gorgui Dieng 4.00 10.00
46 Archie Goodwin 4.00 10.00
47 Hollis Thompson
48 Luigi Datome 8.00 20.00
49 Stephen Curry
50 Arnett Moultrie

2013-14 Panini Rookie Jerseys

MOST NOT PRICED DUE TO LACK OF INFO
1 Isaiah Canaan
2 Andre Roberson
3 Jamaal Franklin
4 Nerlens Noel
5 Jeff Withey 2.00 5.00
6 C.J. McCollum
7 Victor Oladipo
8 Glen Rice Jr. 2.00 5.00
9 Archie Goodwin
10 Mason Plumlee
11 Solomon Hill
12 Tony Snell 2.50 6.00
13 Giannis Antetokounmpo
14 Shane Larkin 2.00 5.00
15 Tim Hardaway Jr. 3.00 8.00
16 Tony Mitchell
17 Michael Carter-Williams 3.00 8.00
18 Ryan Kelly 2.00 5.00
19 Allen Crabbe
20 Shabazz Muhammad
21 Trey Burke
22 Steven Adams
23 Kelly Olynyk
24 Alex Len
25 Erik Murphy
26 Ben McLemore
27 Ricky Ledo
28 Otto Porter 3.00 8.00
29 Peyton Siva
30 Cody Zeller
31 Reggie Bullock
32 Anthony Bennett
33 Nate Wolters 2.50 6.00
34 Kentavious Caldwell-Pope 3.00 8.00

2013-14 Panini Rookie Top 10

1 Michael Carter-Williams .60 1.50
2 Vitor Faverani .40 1.00
3 Nate Wolters .50 1.25
4 Ben McLemore .50 1.25
5 Victor Oladipo .75 2.00
6 Kelly Olynyk .50 1.25
7 Steven Adams .60 1.50
8 Anthony Bennett .50 1.25
9 Cody Zeller .50 1.25
10 Alex Len .50 1.25

2013-14 Panini Superstar Signatures

EXCHANGE DEADLINE 10/09/2015
1 Kobe Bryant 75.00 150.00
2 Kevin Durant EXCH 40.00 100.00
3 Kyrie Irving 150.00 300.00
4 Blake Griffin
5 Anthony Davis 25.00 60.00
6 Tony Parker
7 Steve Nash 50.00 120.00
8 James Harden
9 Jason Kidd 15.00 40.00
10 Tracy McGrady

2010 Panini All-Star Game

These cards were distributed via a wrapper redemption during the NBA All-Star Jam Session in Dallas in February 2010. The card fronts feature the All-Star logo.
COMPLETE SET (14) 20.00 40.00
BG Blake Griffin 8.00 20.00
BJ Brandon Jennings 3.00 8.00
CP Chris Paul 1.00 2.50
DH Dwight Howard 1.00 2.50
DN Dirk Nowitzki 1.00 2.50
DW Dwyane Wade 1.25 3.00
KB Kobe Bryant 3.00 8.00
KD Kevin Durant 2.00 5.00
KG Kevin Garnett 1.00 2.50
LJ LeBron James 3.00 8.00
SN Steve Nash 1.00 2.50
TD Tim Duncan 1.00 2.50
TE Tyreke Evans 4.00 10.00
YM Yao Ming 1.00 2.50

2013 Panini All-Star Game Patches

COMPLETE SET (9)
AD Anthony Davis 25.00 60.00
BG Blake Griffin
DW Deron Williams SP
HO Hakeem Olajuwon
JH James Harden
KD Kevin Durant 12.00 30.00
KI Kyrie Irving
KB1 Kobe Bryant 15.00 40.00
Yellow Jersey
KB2 Kobe Bryant 15.00 40.00
White Jersey

2016-17 Panini Aficionado

COMPLETE SET (150) 30.00 80.00
COMP.SET w/o SP (100) 12.00 30.00
1 Jimmy Butler .50 1.25
2 Anthony Davis 1.00 2.50
3 Elfrid Payton .40 1.00
4 LaMarcus Aldridge .50 1.25
5 Bradley Beal .50 1.25
6 Dwight Howard .40 1.00
7 Henry Ellenson RC .60 1.50
8 Denzel Valentine RC .60 1.50
9 Zach LaVine .50 1.25
10 Chandler Parsons .40 1.00
11 Kenneth Faried .40 1.00
12 Tyreke Evans .30 .75
13 Jahlil Okafor .40 1.00
14 Darren Collison .40 1.00
15 Dario Saric RC 1.50 4.00
16 Dennis Schroder .40 1.00
17 Marquese Chriss RC 1.25 3.00
18 Karl-Anthony Towns 1.25 3.00
19 Nikola Jokic .50 1.25
20 Mike Conley .40 1.00
21 Andre Drummond .50 1.25
22 Kristaps Porzingis 1.00 2.50
23 Nerlens Noel .40 1.00
24 Kawhi Leonard .75 2.00
25 Brandon Ingram RC 3.00 8.00
26 Al Horford .40 1.00
27 Dragan Bender RC .60 1.50
28 Emmanuel Mudiay .40 1.00
29 Andrew Wiggins .75 2.00
30 Julius Randle .50 1.25
31 Tobias Harris .40 1.00
32 Carmelo Anthony .60 1.50
33 Eric Bledsoe .40 1.00
34 Tony Parker .50 1.25
35 Ben Simmons RC 3.00 8.00
36 Isaiah Thomas .50 1.25
37 Malachi Richardson RC .60 1.50
38 Khris Middleton .40 1.00
39 Deron Williams .40 1.00
40 D'Angelo Russell .60 1.50
41 Reggie Jackson .40 1.00
42 Derrick Rose .60 1.50
43 Devin Booker .75 2.00
44 Kyle Lowry .40 1.00
45 Jaylen Brown RC 2.00 5.00
46 Avery Bradley .40 1.00
47 Diamond Stone RC .50 1.25
48 Jabari Parker .60 1.50
49 Dirk Nowitzki .60 1.50
50 Jordan Clarkson .40 1.00
51 Kevin Durant 1.25 3.00
52 Russell Westbrook 1.25 3.00
53 Brandon Knight .40 1.00
54 DeMar DeRozan .50 1.25
55 Domantas Sabonis RC .75 2.00
56 Brook Lopez .40 1.00
57 Kris Dunn RC 1.50 4.00
58 LeBron James 2.00 5.00
59 Giannis Antetokounmpo 1.00 2.50
60 Jamal Crawford .50 1.25
61 Stephen Curry 2.00 5.00
62 Steven Adams .40 1.00
63 Damian Lillard 1.00 2.50
64 Gordon Hayward .50 1.25
65 Buddy Hield RC 1.25 3.00
66 Jeremy Lin .50 1.25
67 Demetrius Jackson RC .50 1.25
68 Kyrie Irving 1.00 2.50
69 Goran Dragic .40 1.00
70 Blake Griffin .50 1.25
71 Klay Thompson .60 1.50
72 Cameron Payne .30 .75
73 C.J. McCollum .40 1.00
74 Rodney Hood .40 1.00
75 Jamal Murray RC 1.50 4.00
76 Nicolas Batum .40 1.00
77 A.J. Hammons RC .50 1.25
78 Justise Winslow .40 1.00
79 Kevin Love .50 1.25
80 Chris Paul .60 1.50
81 James Harden .75 2.00
82 Evan Fournier .40 1.00
83 Allen Crabbe .30 .75
84 Rudy Gobert .50 1.25
85 Taurean Prince .50 1.25
86 Kemba Walker .50 1.25
87 Thon Maker RC 1.50 4.00
88 Hassan Whiteside .40 1.00
89 Rajon Rondo .50 1.25
90 Myles Turner .40 1.00
91 Trevor Ariza .30 .75
92 Aaron Gordon .40 1.00
93 DeMarcus Cousins .50 1.25
94 John Wall .60 1.50
95 Jakob Poeltl RC .60 1.50
96 Michael Kidd-Gilchrist .40 1.00
97 Pascal Siakam RC .50 1.25
98 Dwyane Wade .75 2.00
99 Marc Gasol .50 1.25
100 Paul George .60 1.50
101 Manu Ginobili GR 1.50 4.00
102 Danilo Gallinari GR 1.25 3.00
103 Dirk Nowitzki GR 2.00 5.00
104 Kristaps Porzingis GR 3.00 8.00
105 Boban Marjanovic GR 1.00 2.50
106 Clint Capela GR 1.00 2.50
107 Jordan Clarkson GR 1.25 3.00
108 Marc Gasol GR 1.50 4.00
109 Pau Gasol GR 1.50 4.00
110 Andrew Wiggins GR 2.50 6.00
111 Mario Hezonja GR 1.00 2.50
112 Emmanuel Mudiay GR 1.25 3.00
113 Nicolas Batum GR 1.25 3.00
114 Nikola Mirotic GR 1.25 3.00
115 Ersan Ilyasova GR 1.00 2.50
116 Giannis Antetokounmpo GR 3.00 8.00
117 Ben Simmons GR 6.00 15.00
118 Buddy Hield GR 2.50 6.00
119 Dragan Bender GR 1.25 3.00
120 Juan Hernangomez GR RC .60 1.50
121 Timofey Mozgov GR 1.00 2.50
122 Bojan Bogdanovic GR 1.00 2.50
123 Zaza Pachulia GR 1.00 2.50
124 Jusuf Nurkic GR 1.00 2.50
125 Jonas Valanciunas GR 1.25 3.00
126 Jonas Jerebko GR 1.00 2.50
127 Nik Stauskas GR 1.00 2.50
128 Patty Mills GR 1.50 4.00
129 Mirza Teletovic GR 1.00 2.50
130 Tiago Splitter GR 1.25 3.00
131 Matthew Dellavedova GR 1.25 3.00
132 Joel Embiid GR 2.50 6.00
133 Ricky Rubio GR 1.50 4.00
134 Thabo Sefolosha GR 1.00 2.50
135 Thon Maker GR 3.00 8.00
136 Steven Adams GR 1.25 3.00
137 Marco Belinelli GR 1.00 2.50
138 Omri Casspi GR 1.00 2.50
139 Dennis Schroder GR 1.25 3.00
140 Al Horford GR 1.25 3.00
141 Shaquille O'Neal IN 4.00 10.00
142 Allen Iverson IN 2.00 5.00
143 David Robinson IN 2.50 6.00
144 Scottie Pippen IN 3.00 8.00
145 Wilt Chamberlain IN 3.00 8.00
146 Pete Maravich IN 2.50 6.00
147 Karl Malone IN 2.00 5.00
148 Yao Ming IN 2.00 5.00
149 Patrick Ewing IN 2.00 5.00
150 Bill Russell IN 2.50 6.00

2016-17 Panini Aficionado Artist's Proof

*AP: .75X TO 2X BASIC
*AP RC: .5X TO 1.2X BASIC
*AP 101-150: .5X TO 1.2X BASIC
RANDOM INSERTS IN PACKS
35 Ben Simmons 6.00 15.00

2016-17 Panini Aficionado Artist's Proof Purple

*AP RED: 1.5X TO 4X BASIC
*AP RED RC: 1X TO 2.5X BASIC
*AP RED 101-150: .6X TO 1.5X BASIC
RANDOM INSERTS IN PACKS
STATED PRINT RUN 99 SER.#'d SETS
35 Ben Simmons 12.00 30.00
117 Ben Simmons GR 12.00 30.00

2016-17 Panini Aficionado Authentics

RANDOM INSERTS IN PACKS
PRINT RUNS B/WN 93-175 COPIES PER
*PRIME/25: .75X TO 2X BASIC
1 Blake Griffin/175 2.50 6.00
2 Derrick Rose/175 3.00 8.00
3 Giannis Antetokounmpo/175 5.00 12.00
4 Russell Westbrook/175 6.00 15.00
5 Tim Hardaway Jr./175 1.50 4.00
6 Deron Williams/175 2.00 5.00
7 Damian Lillard/175 5.00 12.00
8 Kentavious Caldwell-Pope/175 2.00 5.00
9 LaMarcus Aldridge/175 2.50 6.00
10 Kyrie Irving/175 5.00 12.00
11 Danilo Gallinari/175 2.00 5.00
12 Terry Rozier/131 2.00 5.00
13 Bojan Bogdanovic/175 1.50 4.00
14 Karl-Anthony Towns/175 6.00 15.00
16 Brook Lopez/175 2.00 5.00
17 Derrick Favors/175 2.00 5.00
18 Kevin Love/175 2.50 6.00
19 Kristaps Porzingis/175 5.00 12.00
20 Monta Ellis/175 2.00 5.00
21 Vince Carter/175 3.00 8.00
22 Terrence Ross/175 2.00 5.00
23 Jeremy Lamb/175 1.50 4.00
24 Ryan Anderson/175 2.00 5.00
25 Dwyane Wade/175 4.00 10.00
26 Noah Vonleh/175 1.50 4.00
27 Jrue Holiday/175 2.00 5.00
28 James Harden/175 4.00 10.00
29 Jimmy Butler/175 2.50 6.00
30 Tony Parker/175 2.50 6.00
31 Cory Joseph/175 1.50 4.00
32 Greg Monroe/175 2.00 5.00
33 Nik Stauskas/175 1.50 4.00
34 Jahlil Okafor/175 2.00 5.00
35 Frank Kaminsky/175 2.00 5.00
36 Jeremy Lin/175 2.50 6.00
37 Nicolas Batum/175 2.00 5.00
38 J.J. Redick/175 2.50 6.00
39 Dirk Nowitzki/175 3.00 8.00
40 Julius Randle/175 2.50 6.00
41 T.J. Warren/175 2.00 5.00
42 Roy Hibbert/175 2.00 5.00
43 Aaron Gordon/175 2.00 5.00
44 Rodney Stuckey/175 1.50 4.00
45 Rodney Hood/175 2.00 5.00
46 Zach Randolph/175 2.00 5.00
47 Norman Powell/175 1.50 4.00
48 George Hill/175 2.00 5.00
49 Carmelo Anthony/175 3.00 8.00
50 Rajon Rondo/175 2.50 6.00
51 Enes Kanter/175 1.50 4.00
52 Tim Frazier/175 1.50 4.00
53 Kawhi Leonard/175 4.00 10.00
54 Kobe Bryant/175 10.00 25.00
55 John Wall/175 3.00 8.00

56 Rudy Gay/175 2.50 6.00
57 Ricky Rubio/175 2.50 6.00
58 Goran Dragic/175 2.00 5.00
59 Andre Iguodala/175 2.00 5.00
60 Jusuf Nurkic/175 1.50 4.00
61 Tyler Zeller/93 2.00 5.00
62 LeBron James/175 15.00 40.00
63 Brandon Knight/175 2.00 5.00
64 Brandon Jennings/175 1.50 4.00
65 Bismack Biyombo/175 1.50 4.00

2016-17 Panini Aficionado Craftwork

RANDOM INSERTS IN PACKS
1 Jimmy Butler .75 2.00
2 LeBron James 3.00 8.00
3 Dennis Schroder .60 1.50
4 Kenneth Faried .60 1.50
5 Kevin Durant 2.00 5.00
6 James Harden 1.25 3.00
7 Blake Griffin .75 2.00
8 Julius Randle .75 2.00
9 Giannis Antetokounmpo 1.50 4.00
10 Brook Lopez .60 1.50
11 Andrew Wiggins 1.25 3.00
12 Anthony Davis 1.50 4.00
13 Derrick Rose 1.00 2.50
14 Russell Westbrook 2.00 5.00
15 Joel Embiid 1.25 3.00
16 T.J. Warren .60 1.50
17 DeMarcus Cousins .75 2.00
18 Tony Parker .75 2.00
19 Kyle Lowry .60 1.50
20 Rudy Gobert .75 2.00
21 Dwyane Wade 1.25 3.00
22 Dirk Nowitzki 1.00 2.50
23 Dwight Howard .60 1.50
24 Andre Drummond .75 2.00
25 Klay Thompson 1.00 2.50
26 Jeff Teague .60 1.50
27 Chris Paul 1.00 2.50
28 Marc Gasol .75 2.00
29 Josh Richardson .50 1.25
30 Jeremy Lin .75 2.00
31 Karl-Anthony Towns 2.00 5.00
32 Jrue Holiday .60 1.50
33 Kristaps Porzingis 1.50 4.00
34 Elfrid Payton .60 1.50
35 Sergio Rodriguez .50 1.25
36 C.J. McCollum .60 1.50
37 Rudy Gay .75 2.00
38 DeMar DeRozan .75 2.00
39 Terrence Ross .60 1.50
40 Bradley Beal .75 2.00
41 Kevin Love .75 2.00
42 Harrison Barnes .60 1.50
43 Isaiah Thomas .75 2.00
44 Reggie Jackson .60 1.50
45 Stephen Curry 3.00 8.00
46 Myles Turner .60 1.50
47 J.J. Redick .75 2.00
48 Mike Conley .60 1.50
49 Jabari Parker 1.00 2.50
50 Kemba Walker .75 2.00
51 Zach LaVine .75 2.00
52 Carmelo Anthony 1.00 2.50
53 Enes Kanter .50 1.25
54 Evan Fournier .60 1.50
55 Devin Booker 1.25 3.00
56 Damian Lillard 1.50 4.00
57 Kawhi Leonard 1.25 3.00
58 Jonas Valanciunas .60 1.50
59 Rodney Hood .60 1.50
60 John Wall 1.00 2.50
61 Kyrie Irving 1.50 4.00
62 Emmanuel Mudiay .60 1.50
63 Jae Crowder .60 1.50
64 Draymond Green 1.00 2.50
65 Ryan Anderson .60 1.50
66 Paul George 1.00 2.50
67 D'Angelo Russell 1.00 2.50
68 Goran Dragic .60 1.50
69 Matthew Dellavedova .60 1.50
70 Nicolas Batum .60 1.50

2016-17 Panini Aficionado Dual Authentics Memorabilia

RANDOM INSERTS IN PACKS
PRINT RUNS B/WN 5-299 COPIES PER
NO PRICING ON QTY 5
*PRIME/25: .75X TO 2X BASIC
1 Korver/Sefolosha/299 2.50 6.00
2 Leonard/Aldridge/299 5.00 12.00
4 Wstbrk/Adams/299 8.00 20.00
6 Lopez/Bogdanovic/299 2.50 6.00
8 Hrdwy/O'Neal/299 8.00 20.00
9 Anthny/Przngs/299 6.00 15.00
10 Cousins/Cauley-Stein/299 3.00 8.00
11 Gasol/Randolph/299 3.00 8.00
12 Wstbrk/Harden/299 8.00 20.00
13 Dirk/Porzingis/299 6.00 15.00
14 Bryant/O'Neal/299 12.00 30.00
15 Wiggins/Towns/299 8.00 20.00
16 Giannis/Parker/299 6.00 15.00
17 Butler/Gibson/299 3.00 8.00
18 Kaminsky/Walker/299 3.00 8.00
19 Redick/Crawford/299 3.00 8.00
20 Irving/James/299 15.00 40.00
21 Hill/Irving/299 6.00 15.00
22 Oubre/Porter/299 2.50 6.00
23 Stcktn/Mlne/299 5.00 12.00
24 McCllm/Lillard/299 6.00 15.00
25 Davis/Wstbrk/299 8.00 20.00
26 Curry/Thmpsn/299 15.00 40.00
27 Williams/Dirk/299 4.00 10.00
28 Bledsoe/Warren/299 2.50 6.00
29 Mudiay/Faried/299 2.50 6.00
30 Okafor/Towns/299 8.00 20.00
31 O'Neal/Mrnng/80 8.00 20.00
32 Oljwn/Drexler/299 4.00 10.00
33 Richmond/Strickland/299 3.00 8.00
35 Hrdwy Jr./Hrdwy/299 3.00 8.00

2016-17 Panini Aficionado Endorsments

RANDOM INSERTS IN PACKS
PRINT RUNS B/WN 53-199 COPIES PER
1 Michael Carter-Williams/149
2 Langston Galloway/199 2.50 6.00
3 James Ennis/199
4 T.J. McConnell/199
5 Allen Crabbe/199
6 Jordan Clarkson/99 5.00 12.00
7 Will Barton/175
8 Jabari Parker/65
9 Dirk Nowitzki/65 50.00 120.00
10 Reggie Jackson/199
11 Justise Winslow/199
12 Andrew Wiggins/60
13 Paul Millsap/60
14 Kevin Durant/99
15 Kyrie Irving/60
16 Jeremy Lin/99
17 Karl-Anthony Towns/99 30.00 80.00
18 Vince Carter/65 10.00 25.00
19 Matthew Dellavedova/199 3.00 8.00
20 Joel Embiid/53 40.00 100.00
22 Victor Oladipo/149 3.00 8.00
23 Tyler Johnson/199 5.00 12.00
24 Julius Randle/99 4.00 10.00
26 Elfrid Payton/99
27 Tim Hardaway/149 6.00 15.00
28 Alonzo Mourning/65
29 Scottie Pippen/65 25.00 60.00
30 Dan Issel/199 3.00 8.00
31 Adrian Dantley/199
32 Calvin Murphy/149 3.00 8.00
33 Rick Barry/85 3.00 8.00
34 Tom Heinsohn/199 12.00 30.00
35 Artis Gilmore/149 3.00 8.00
36 Elvin Hayes/149 4.00 10.00
37 Jamaal Wilkes/90
38 Tom Sanders/199
39 Bob Lanier/145
40 Dennis Rodman/99
41 David Robinson/60
42 Magic Johnson/60
43 Karl Malone/60
44 Hakeem Olajuwon/60 10.00 25.00
45 Junior Bridgeman/199 2.50 6.00
46 Jim Jackson/199 10.00 25.00
47 Dan Majerle/199
48 Jamal Mashburn/199 6.00 15.00
49 Yao Ming/70 30.00 80.00
50 Latrell Sprewell/149

2016-17 Panini Aficionado Endorsments Artist's Proof Bronze

*PROOF BRONZE: .5X TO 1.2X BASIC
RANDOM INSERTS IN PACKS
STATED PRINT RUN 49 SER.#'d SETS
21 Alan Williams 5.00 12.00

2016-17 Panini Aficionado First Impressions Autographs

RANDOM INSERTS IN PACKS
PRINT RUNS B/WN 199-249 COPIES PER
1 Jaylen Brown/199 20.00 50.00
2 Dragan Bender/199 5.00 12.00
3 Marquese Chriss/199
4 Jakob Poeltl/249 3.00 8.00
5 Thon Maker/249 12.00 30.00
6 Domantas Sabonis/249
7 Georgios Papagiannis/249
8 Kris Dunn/199 12.00 30.00
9 Denzel Valentine/249 5.00 12.00
10 Demetrius Jackson/249 5.00 12.00
11 Damian Jones/249 2.50 6.00
12 Henry Ellenson/249 3.00 8.00
13 Wade Baldwin IV/249 2.50 6.00
14 Jamal Murray/199 12.00 30.00
15 Willy Hernangomez/249 15.00 40.00
16 Malik Beasley/249
17 Kay Felder/249 2.50 6.00
18 Brice Johnson/249 2.50 6.00
19 Pascal Siakam/249 2.50 6.00
20 Juan Hernangomez/249
21 Ivica Zubac/249 12.00 30.00
22 Brandon Ingram/199 30.00 80.00
23 Jake Layman/249
24 Georges Niang/249

2016-17 Panini Aficionado First Impressions Autographs Artist's Proof Bronze

*PROOF BRONZE: .5X TO 1.2X BASIC
RANDOM INSERTS IN PACKS
STATED PRINT RUN 49 SER.#'d SETS
25 A.J. Hammons

2016-17 Panini Aficionado Innovators

RANDOM INSERTS IN PACKS
1 Chris Paul 3.00 8.00
2 Carmelo Anthony 3.00 8.00
3 LeBron James 10.00 25.00
4 Stephen Curry 10.00 25.00
5 Russell Westbrook 6.00 15.00
6 Anthony Davis 5.00 12.00
7 Dwyane Wade 4.00 10.00
8 Pete Maravich 4.00 10.00
9 Magic Johnson 6.00 15.00
10 Larry Bird 6.00 15.00

2016-17 Panini Aficionado International Ink

RANDOM INSERTS IN PACKS
PRINT RUNS B/WN 59-249 COPIES PER
1 Dirk Nowitzki/60
2 Yao Ming/60 25.00 60.00
3 Pau Gasol/59
4 Andrew Wiggins/60
5 Tony Parker/70 15.00 40.00
6 Dragan Bender/199 8.00 20.00
7 Jamal Murray/199 12.00 30.00
8 Tristan Thompson/149 6.00 15.00
11 Jakob Poeltl/199 3.00 8.00
12 Nikola Mirotic/199 6.00 15.00
13 Thon Maker/199 20.00 50.00
14 Toni Kukoc/199 6.00 15.00
15 Dario Saric/199 25.00 60.00
16 Zydrunas Ilgauskas/199 3.00 8.00
17 Kristaps Porzingis/199 15.00 40.00
18 Boban Marjanovic/99
19 Juan Hernangomez/249 8.00 20.00
20 T. Luwawu-Cabarrot/249 6.00 15.00
21 Mindaugas Kuzminskas/249
22 Pascal Siakam/249 2.50 6.00
23 Willy Hernangomez/249 15.00 40.00
24 Ivica Zubac/249 6.00 15.00
25 Paul Zipser/249

2016-17 Panini Aficionado International Ink Artist's Proof Bronze

*PROOF BRONZE: .5X TO 1.2X BASIC
RANDOM INSERTS IN PACKS
STATED PRINT RUN 49 SER.#'d SETS
9 Jonas Valanciunas
10 Dikembe Mutombo

2016-17 Panini Aficionado Magic Numbers

RANDOM INSERTS IN PACKS
PROOF: .75X TO 2X BASIC
PROOF RED/99: 1.2X TO 3X BASIC
1 John Wall 1.00 2.50
2 LeBron James 3.00 8.00
3 Karl-Anthony Towns 2.00 5.00
4 Stephen Curry 3.00 8.00
5 Dwyane Wade 1.25 3.00
6 Carmelo Anthony 1.00 2.50
7 Dirk Nowitzki 1.00 2.50
8 Damian Lillard 1.50 4.00
9 Reggie Jackson .60 1.50
10 Paul George 1.00 2.50
11 Isaiah Thomas .75 2.00
12 Kyle Lowry .60 1.50

2016-17 Panini Aficionado Meteor

RANDOM INSERTS IN PACKS
1 Stephen Curry 8.00 20.00
2 Dirk Nowitzki 2.50 6.00
3 LeBron James 20.00 50.00
4 Kawhi Leonard 3.00 8.00
5 Karl-Anthony Towns 5.00 12.00
6 James Harden 3.00 8.00
7 John Wall 2.50 6.00
8 Isaiah Thomas 2.00 5.00
9 D'Angelo Russell 2.50 6.00
10 Jimmy Butler 2.00 5.00
11 Kevin Durant 5.00 12.00
12 Russell Westbrook 5.00 12.00
13 Kyrie Irving 15.00 40.00
14 Devin Booker 3.00 8.00
15 Myles Turner 1.50 4.00
16 Andrew Wiggins 3.00 8.00
17 Damian Lillard 4.00 10.00
18 Chris Paul 2.50 6.00
19 Justise Winslow 1.50 4.00
20 DeMarcus Cousins 2.00 5.00

2016-17 Panini Aficionado Opening Night Preview

*OPENING NIGHT: 2.5X TO 6X BASIC
*OPNNG NGHT RC: 1.5X TO 4X BASIC RC
RANDOM INSERTS IN PACKS
65 Buddy Hield 8.00 20.00

2016-17 Panini Aficionado Power Surge

RANDOM INSERTS IN PACKS
PROOF: .75X TO 2X BASIC
PROOF RED/99: 1.2X TO 3X BASIC
1 Kevin Durant 2.00 5.00
2 Devin Booker 1.25 3.00
3 D'Angelo Russell 1.00 2.50
4 Emmanuel Mudiay .60 1.50
5 James Harden 1.25 3.00
6 Anthony Davis 1.50 4.00
7 DeMar DeRozan .75 2.00
8 Aaron Gordon .60 1.50
9 Zach LaVine .75 2.00
10 Jimmy Butler .75 2.00
11 Russell Westbrook 2.00 5.00
12 Tracy McGrady .75 2.00
13 Kobe Bryant 3.00 8.00
14 Shawn Kemp 1.25 3.00
15 Blake Griffin .75 2.00
16 Dee Brown .50 1.25
17 Spud Webb .60 1.50
18 Dominique Wilkins 1.00 2.50

2016-17 Panini Aficionado Signatures

RANDOM INSERTS IN PACKS
2 Kevin Durant 75.00 200.00
3 Kyrie Irving 40.00 100.00
4 Karl-Anthony Towns 40.00 100.00
6 Chris Paul
7 Anthony Davis 30.00 80.00
10 Andrew Wiggins
11 Bill Russell 60.00 150.00
13 Karl Malone 25.00 60.00
15 Shaquille O'Neal
16 Brandon Ingram
17 Kris Dunn
18 Buddy Hield
19 Jamal Murray 30.00 80.00
20 Jaylen Brown

2016-17 Panini Aficionado Slick Picks

RANDOM INSERTS IN PACKS
PROOF: .6X TO 1.5X BASIC
1 Ben Simmons 3.00 8.00
2 Brandon Ingram 3.00 8.00
3 Jaylen Brown 2.00 5.00
4 Dragan Bender .60 1.50
5 Kris Dunn 1.50 4.00
6 Buddy Hield 1.25 3.00
7 Jamal Murray 1.50 4.00
8 Marquese Chriss 1.25 3.00
9 Jakob Poeltl .60 1.50
10 Thon Maker 1.50 4.00
11 Domantas Sabonis .75 2.00
12 Taurean Prince .75 2.00
13 Georgios Papagiannis .50 1.25
14 Denzel Valentine .60 1.50
15 Juan Hernangomez .60 1.50
16 Wade Baldwin IV .50 1.25
17 Henry Ellenson .60 1.50
18 Malik Beasley .50 1.25
19 Caris LeVert .60 1.50
20 DeAndre' Bembry .50 1.25

2016-17 Panini Aficionado Slick Picks Artist's Proof Purple

*ARTIST PROOF RED: 1X TO 2.5X BASIC
RANDOM INSERTS IN PACKS
STATED PRINT RUN 99 SER.#'d SETS
1 Ben Simmons 20.00 50.00

2016-17 Panini Aficionado Tip-Off

*TIPOFF: 2.5X TO 6X BASIC
*TIPOFF RC: 1.5X TO 4X BASIC RC
RANDOM INSERTS IN PACKS

2011 Panini Black Friday Autographs

Released in November 2011 as part of the Panini Black Friday promotion, these card features autographs on some newly designed cards and/or previously issued items.
BJ Brandon Jennings Adrenalyn 10.00 25.00
KB Kobe Bryant Patch/30* 100.00 200.00
OC Omri Casspi Adrenalyn 3.00 8.00

2012 Panini Black Friday

1-23 CRACKED ICE/25: 6X TO 15X BASE HI
24-50 CRACKED ICE/25: 2.5X TO 6X BASE HI
8 Kobe Bryant 1.00 2.50
9 Blake Griffin .50 1.25
10 Kevin Durant .75 2.00
11 Steve Nash .60 1.50
31 Kyrie Irving/599 4.00 10.00
32 Anthony Davis/599 5.00 12.00
33 Michael Kidd-Gilchrist/599 2.00 5.00
34 Thomas Robinson/599 1.50 4.00
35 Harrison Barnes/599 2.00 5.00
36 Derrick Williams/599 1.25 3.00
37 Kenneth Faried/599 1.25 3.00
38 Austin Rivers/599 1.25 3.00

2012 Panini Black Friday Black Holofoil

CRACKED ICE/25: 3X TO 8X BASE HI
1 Kobe Bryant 2.00 5.00
2 Kevin Durant 1.50 4.00
3 Blake Griffin 1.00 2.50
4 Anthony Davis 2.00 5.00
5 Kyrie Irving 2.00 5.00

2012 Panini Black Friday Gold Border

CRACKED ICE/25*: 4X TO 10X BASE HI
2 Kyrie Irving 2.00 5.00

2012 Panini Black Friday Kings

CRACKED ICE/25: 2X TO 5X BASE HI
6 John Stockton .75 2.00
7 Kareem Abdul-Jabbar 1.25 3.00

2012 Panini Black Friday Rookie Kings

CRACKED ICE/25: 2X TO 5X BASE HI
5 Michael Kidd-Gilchrist 1.50 5.00
6 Austin Rivers 1.25 3.00

2012 Panini Black Friday Rookie Materials Hats

14 Anthony Davis 10.00 25.00
15 Austin Rivers 5.00 12.00
16 Michael Kidd-Gilchrist 5.00 12.00
17 Thomas Robinson 5.00 12.00
18 Harrison Barnes 5.00 12.00
19 Jared Sullinger 5.00 12.00
20 Dion Waiters 5.00 12.00
21 Andre Drummond 5.00 12.00
22 Draymond Green 4.00 10.00
23 Meyers Leonard 3.00 8.00
24 Tyler Zeller 4.00 10.00
25 Fab Melo 4.00 10.00
26 Festus Ezeli 3.00 8.00

2012 Panini Black Friday Rookie Materials Shoes

1 Harrison Barnes 15.00 40.00
2 Jared Sullinger 8.00 20.00

2012 Panini Black Friday Rookie of the Year Materials

ROYKI Kyrie Irving 12.00 30.00

2012 Panini Black Friday Spokesman Jumbo Jerseys

KB Kobe Bryant 15.00 40.00

2012 Panini Black Friday Manufactured Patch Autographs

INSERTS IN BLACK FRIDAY PACKS
AD2 Anthony Davis 75.00 150.00
AD3 Andre Drummond
AR Austin Rivers 10.00 25.00
BB Bradley Beal 20.00 50.00
BK Brandon Knight 12.00 30.00
DW1 Dion Waiters 12.00 30.00
DW2 Derrick Williams 12.00 30.00
HB Harrison Barnes 30.00 80.00
JB2 Jimmy Butler
JF Jimmer Fredette 15.00 40.00
JH John Henson
JS Jared Sullinger
KF Kenneth Faried
MKG Michael Kidd-Gilchrist 30.00 80.00
MT Marquis Teague 8.00 20.00
QA Quincy Acy
TR2 Thomas Robinson 20.00 50.00
TR3 Terrence Ross 8.00 20.00
TT Tristan Thompson 8.00 20.00
NNO Kyrie Irving Black Friday 125.00 250.00

2012 Panini Black Friday Tools of the Trade Towels

1 Anthony Davis 12.00 30.00
2 Michael Kidd-Gilchrist 8.00 20.00
3 Thomas Robinson 10.00 25.00
4 Harrison Barnes 10.00 25.00
5 Terrence Ross 6.00 15.00
6 Austin Rivers 8.00 20.00

2013 Panini Black Friday Inked Autographs

AB Anthony Bennett 12.00 30.00
AL Alex Len 4.00 10.00
BM Ben McLemore 5.00 12.00
CZ Cody Zeller 4.00 10.00
MCW Michael Carter-Williams 20.00 50.00
NN Nerlens Noel 30.00 80.00
OP Otto Porter 5.00 12.00
TB Trey Burke 25.00 60.00
TH Tim Hardaway Jr. 5.00 12.00
VO Victor Oladipo 25.00 60.00

2013 Panini Black Friday

CRACKED ICE/35: 5X TO 12X BASIC CARDS
LAVA FLOW/150: 2X TO 5X BASIC CARDS
2 Kobe Bryant BK 1.25 3.00
6 Kevin Durant BK 1.00 2.50
10 Dwight Howard BK .40 1.00
14 Blake Griffin BK .50 1.25
18 Kevin Garnett BK .50 1.25
22 Kyrie Irving BK .60 1.50
25 Anthony Davis BK .40 1.00
29 C.J. McCollum BK .40 1.00
30 Tim Hardaway Jr. BK .40 1.00
39 Nerlens Noel/299 BK 2.50 6.00
40 Trey Burke/299 BK 2.00 5.00
41 Ben McLemore/299 BK 2.00 5.00
57 Anthony Bennett JSY/99 BK 3.00 8.00
58 Otto Porter JSY/99 BK 2.00 5.00
59 Victor Oladipo JSY/99 BK 4.00 10.00
60 Cody Zeller JSY/99 BK 1.50 4.00
61 Alex Len JSY/99 BK 1.50 4.00

2013 Panini Black Friday Autographs

2 Kobe Bryant
6 Kevin Durant
10 Dwight Howard
14 Blake Griffin
18 Kevin Garnett
22 Kyrie Irving
25 Anthony Davis
29 C.J. McCollum
30 Tim Hardaway Jr.
39 Nerlens Noel
40 Trey Burke
41 Ben McLemore
57 Anthony Bennett
58 Otto Porter
59 Victor Oladipo
60 Cody Zeller
61 Alex Len

2013 Panini Black Friday Collection

CRACKED ICE/35: 4X TO 10X BASIC CARDS
LAVA FLOW/150: 1.5X TO 4X BASIC CARDS
6 LeBron James 1.50 4.00
7 Kobe Bryant 1.50 4.00
8 Anthony Bennett .60 1.50
9 Damian Lillard .75 2.00
10 Tim Duncan .60 1.50
20A DJ Kool .40 1.00
20B DJ Kool AU/49

2013 Panini Black Friday Hot Rookies

ISSUED VIA BLACK FRIDAY PROMOTION
1 Anthony Bennett .60 1.50
2 Trey Burke .50 1.25
3 Nerlens Noel 1.25 3.00
4 Michael Carter-Williams .60 1.50
5 Shabazz Muhammad .50 1.25
6 Cody Zeller .50 1.25
7 Victor Oladipo .75 2.00
8 Kentavious Caldwell-Pope .50 1.25
9 Alex Len .50 1.25
10 Otto Porter .60 1.50

2013 Panini Black Friday Hot Rookies Cracked Ice

*CRACKED ICE: 1.5X TO 4X BASIC
ISSUED VIA BLACK FRIDAY PROMOTION
ANNOUNCED PRINT RUN 35 OR LESS

2013 Panini Black Friday Hot Rookies Lava Flow

*LAVA FLOW: .75X TO 2X BASIC
ISSUED VIA BLACK FRIDAY PROMOTION
ANNOUNCED PRINT RUN 150 OR LESS

2013 Panini Black Friday Jumbo Materials

AD Anthony Davis 6.00 15.00

2013 Panini Black Friday NBA Championship Materials

ISSUED VIA BLACK FRIDAY PROMOTION
1 LeBron James 20.00 50.00
2 Dwyane Wade 6.00 15.00
3 Chris Bosh 3.00 8.00
4 Shane Battier 2.50 6.00
5 Mario Chalmers 2.50 6.00
6 Ray Allen 3.00 8.00

2013 Panini Black Friday Manufactured Patch Autographs

AB Anthony Bennett 40.00 100.00
CJM C.J. McCollum 12.00 30.00
JH James Harden 15.00 40.00
KCP Kentavious Caldwell-Pope 8.00 20.00
SM Shabazz Muhammad
TB Trey Burke 15.00 40.00
VO Victor Oladipo 20.00 50.00

2013 Panini Black Friday Rookie Materials

BK1 Anthony Bennett BK 5.00 12.00
BK2 Michael Carter-Williams BK 10.00 25.00
BK3 Otto Porter BK 3.00 8.00
BK4 Trey Burke BK 5.00 12.00
BK5 Tim Hardaway Jr. BK 4.00 10.00
BK6 Nerlens Noel BK 5.00 12.00
BK7 Kentavious Caldwell-Pope BK 2.50 6.00

2013 Panini Black Friday Rookie Materials Headbands

ISSUED VIA BLACK FRIDAY PROMOTION
1 Anthony Bennett 2.50 6.00
2 Victor Oladipo 3.00 8.00
3 Nerlens Noel 5.00 12.00
4 Trey Burke 2.00 5.00
5 Ben McLemore 2.50 6.00
6 Otto Porter 2.50 6.00

2013 Panini Black Friday Tools of the Trade Materials

ISSUED VIA BLACK FRIDAY PROMOTION
1 Anthony Bennett 2.00 5.00
2 Victor Oladipo 2.50 6.00
3 Alex Len 1.50 4.00
4 C.J. McCollum 2.50 6.00
5 Tim Hardaway Jr. 2.00 5.00
6 Trey Burke 1.50 4.00
KB Kobe Bryant 8.00 20.00

2013 Panini Black Friday VIP

CRACKED ICE/35: 2.5X TO 6X BASIC CARDS
LAVA FLOW/150: 1.2X TO 3X BASIC CARDS
8 Anthony Bennett 1.25 3.00

2014 Panini Black Friday

*1-21 ICE VETS/25: 6X TO 15X BASIC CARDS
*22-50 ICE ROOKIE/25: 2X TO 5X BASIC CARDS/499
*JSY ICE/25: 1.2X TO 3X BASIC JSY/99
1-21 THICK STOCK/50: 1.5X TO 4X BASIC CARDS
22-50 THICK STOCK/50: .8X TO 2X BASIC CARDS
1 LeBron James BK 1.25 3.00
2 Tim Duncan BK .50 1.25
3 Derrick Rose BK .75 2.00
4 Kobe Bryant BK 1.25 3.00
5 Kevin Durant BK 1.00 2.50
6 Blake Griffin BK .50 1.25
22 Nik Stauskas BK .75 2.00
23 Noah Vonleh BK .60 1.50
24 Elfrid Payton BK 1.00 2.50
25 Zach LaVine BK 1.00 2.50
26 Andrew Wiggins BK 2.50 6.00
27 Adreian Payne BK .40 1.00
28 Gary Harris BK .50 1.25
51 Jabari Parker BK JSY 5.00 12.00
52 Joel Embiid BK JSY 4.00 10.00
53 Aaron Gordon BK JSY 3.00 8.00
54 Marcus Smart BK JSY 3.00 8.00
55 Julius Randle BK JSY 4.00 10.00
56 Dante Exum BK JSY 4.00 10.00
57 Shabazz Napier BK JSY 3.00 8.00
58 Doug McDermott BK JSY 3.00 8.00

2014 Panini Black Friday Collection

*CRACKED ICE/25: 4X TO 10X BASIC CARDS
THICK STOCK/50: 1.2X TO 3X BASIC CARDS
5 Andrew Wiggins BK 2.00 5.00
6 Kevin Love BK .60 1.50
7 Lebron James BK 2.00 5.00
8 Tim Duncan BK .75 2.00
22 Carmelo Anthony BK .60 1.50
23 John Wall BK .60 1.50
24 Chris Paul BK .75 2.00
25 Damian Lillard BK 1.00 2.50
26 Rajon Rondo BK .60 1.50
27 Derrick Rose BK 1.25 3.00

2014 Panini Black Friday Collection Autographs

ANNOUNCED PRINT RUN 25 OR LESS
5 Andrew Wiggins BK
6 Kevin Love BK
8 Tim Duncan BK
22 Carmelo Anthony BK 30.00 80.00
23 John Wall BK 20.00 50.00
24 Chris Paul BK
25 Damian Lillard BK
26 Rajon Rondo BK
27 Derrick Rose BK

2014 Panini Black Friday Happy Holidays

COMPLETE SET (15)
CRACKED ICE/25: 1.2X TO 3X BASIC INSERT
8 Doug McDermott BK 3.00 8.00
9 Jabari Parker BK 5.00 12.00
10 Joel Embiid BK 4.00 10.00
11 Julius Randle BK 4.00 10.00
12 Marcus Smart BK 3.00 8.00
13 Shabazz Napier BK 3.00 8.00
14 Andrew Wiggins BK 5.00 12.00
15 Aaron Gordon BK 3.00 8.00

2014 Panini Black Friday Rookie Portraits

*CRACKED ICE/25: 3X TO 8X BASIC CARDS
THICK STOCK/50: 1X TO 2.5X BASIC CARDS
10 Andrew Wiggins BK 2.00 5.00
11 Jabari Parker BK 2.00 5.00
12 Joel Embiid BK 1.00 2.50
13 Aaron Gordon BK .75 2.00
14 Marcus Smart BK .75 2.00
15 Julius Randle BK .75 2.00
16 Dante Exum BK 1.25 3.00
17 Doug McDermott BK .60 1.50

2014 Panini Black Friday Rookie Portraits Autographs

10 Andrew Wiggins BK 75.00 200.00
11 Jabari Parker BK 75.00 200.00
12 Joel Embiid BK 40.00 100.00
13 Aaron Gordon BK 15.00 40.00
14 Marcus Smart BK 15.00 40.00
15 Julius Randle BK 25.00 60.00
16 Dante Exum BK 40.00 100.00
17 Doug McDermott BK 20.00 50.00

2014 Panini Black Friday Manufactured Patch Autographs

MS Marcus Smart
SN Shabazz Napier 10.00 25.00

2014 Panini Black Friday Manufactured Patch Autographs Team Logo

JR Julius Randle 15.00 40.00
MS Marcus Smart 15.00 40.00
SN Shabazz Napier 10.00 25.00

2014 Panini Black Friday Manufactured Patches NBA

AW Andrew Wiggins 4.00 10.00
KB Kobe Bryant 5.00 12.00
KD Kevin Durant 4.00 10.00

2014 Panini Black Friday Rookie Materials Jerseys

*CRACKED ICE/25: 1.2X TO 3X BASIC
1 Dante Exum 2.50 6.00
2 Joel Embiid 6.00 15.00
3 Aaron Gordon 4.00 10.00
4 Shabazz Napier 1.50 4.00
5 Doug McDermott 2.50 6.00
6 Nik Stauskas 2.00 5.00
7 Noah Vonleh 2.00 5.00
8 Elfrid Payton 2.50 6.00
9 Adreian Payne 1.50 4.00
10 Andrew Wiggins 6.00 15.00

2014 Panini Black Friday Rookie Materials Wristbands

*CRACKED ICE/25: 1.2X TO 3X BASIC
1 Jabari Parker 5.00 12.00
2 Julius Randle 3.00 8.00
3 Marcus Smart 2.50 6.00
4 Doug McDermott 2.50 6.00
5 Zach Lavine 3.00 8.00
6 Rodney Hood 2.00 5.00

2014 Panini Black Friday Tools of the Trade Towels

*CRACKED ICE/25: .6X TO 1.5X BASIC
1 Joel Embiid 8.00 20.00
2 Nik Stauskas 2.50 6.00
3 Jabari Parker 6.00 15.00
4 Joe Harris 2.50 6.00
5 Glenn Robinson III 2.00 5.00
6 Zach Lavine 4.00 10.00
7 Shabazz Napier 2.00 5.00
8 Doug McDermott 3.00 8.00
9 Aaron Gordon 5.00 12.00
10 Elfrid Payton 3.00 8.00
11 James Young 2.00 5.00
12 Marcus Smart 3.00 8.00
2 Julius Randle 4.00 10.00

2015 Panini Black Friday

*CRACKED/25: 1X TO 2.5X BASIC CARDS
*THICK/50: .8X TO 2X BASIC CARDS
9 LeBron James 1.25 3.00
10 Derrick Rose .75 2.00
11 Dirk Nowitzki .75 2.00
12 Anthony Davis 1.50 4.00
13 Kobe Bryant 1.50 4.00
14 Andrew Wiggins .75 2.00
15 Stephen Curry .75 2.00
16 Kevin Durant .75 2.00
25 Karl-Anthony Towns 3.00 8.00
26 D'Angelo Russell 1.25 3.00
27 Jahlil Okafor 1.25 3.00
28 Kristaps Porzingis 1.25 3.00
29 Mario Hezonja 1.25 3.00
30 Willie Cauley-Stein 1.25 3.00
31 Emmanuel Mudiay 1.25 3.00
32 Stanley Johnson 1.25 3.00
33 Frank Kaminsky 1.25 3.00
34 Justise Winslow 1.25 3.00

2015 Panini Black Friday Collection

*CRACKED/25: 1X TO 2.5X BASIC CARDS
*THICK/50: .8X TO 2X BASIC CARDS
8 Andrew Wiggins 1.25 3.00
9 Blake Griffin 1.25 3.00
10 D'Angelo Russell 1.25 3.00
11 John Wall 1.25 3.00
12 Klay Thompson 1.25 3.00
13 Karl-Anthony Towns 1.25 3.00
14 Kyrie Irving 1.25 3.00

2015 Panini Black Friday Happy Holidays Materials

*CRACKED/25: .8X TO 2X BASIC HAT
CP Cameron Payne 2.50 6.00
DR D'Angelo Russell 2.50 6.00
FK Frank Kaminsky 2.50 6.00
JO Jahlil Okafor 2.50 6.00
JW Justise Winslow 2.50 6.00
KP Kristaps Porzingis 2.50 6.00
TJ Tyus Jones 2.50 6.00
KAT Karl-Anthony Towns 2.50 6.00
WCS Willie Cauley-Stein 2.50 6.00

2015 Panini Black Friday Manufactured Patches

*CRACKED/25: .8X TO 2X BASIC PATCH
6 Blake Griffin 4.00 10.00
7 Kevin Durant 4.00 10.00
8 Larry Bird 2.50 6.00
9 Magic Johnson 2.50 6.00

2015 Panini Black Friday Rookie Materials Jerseys

*CRACKED/25: .8X TO 2X BASIC JSY
8 Rashad Vaughn 2.50 6.00
9 Karl-Anthony Towns 6.00 15.00
10 D'Angelo Russell 2.50 6.00
11 Jahlil Okafor 2.50 6.00
12 Jerian Grant 2.50 6.00
13 Delon Wright 2.50 6.00
14 Willie Cauley-Stein 2.50 6.00
15 David Johnson 2.50 6.00
16 Tyus Jones 2.50 6.00
17 Frank Kaminsky 2.50 6.00
18 Trey Lyles 2.50 6.00
19 Kelly Oubre Jr. 2.50 6.00
20 Myles Turner 2.50 6.00

2015-16 Panini Black Gold

1 Larry Bird 3.00 8.00
2 Reggie Jackson 1.00 2.50
3 DeAndre Jordan 1.25 3.00
4 Jonas Valanciunas 1.00 2.50
5 Dwyane Wade 2.00 5.00
6 Brook Lopez 1.00 2.50
7 Nicolas Batum 1.00 2.50
8 Rudy Gobert 1.25 3.00
9 Zaza Pachulia .75 2.00
10 LeBron James 8.00 20.00
11 Magic Johnson 3.00 8.00
12 Kentavious Caldwell-Pope 1.00 2.50
13 Rudy Gay 1.25 3.00
14 DeMar DeRozan 1.25 3.00
15 Chris Bosh 1.25 3.00
16 Thaddeus Young .75 2.00
17 Al Jefferson 1.00 2.50
18 Kenneth Faried 1.00 2.50
19 Mike Conley 1.25 3.00
20 Kyrie Irving 2.50 6.00
21 Julius Erving 2.00 5.00
22 Giannis Antetokounmpo 2.50 6.00
23 DeMarcus Cousins 1.25 3.00
24 Kyle Lowry 1.00 2.50
25 Hassan Whiteside 1.00 2.50
26 Nerlens Noel 1.00 2.50
27 John Wall 1.50 4.00
28 Danilo Gallinari 1.00 2.50
29 Marc Gasol 1.25 3.00
30 Kevin Love 1.25 3.00
31 Wilt Chamberlain 2.50 6.00
32 Jabari Parker 1.50 4.00
33 Rajon Rondo 1.25 3.00
34 Avery Bradley 1.00 2.50
35 Al Horford 1.00 2.50
36 Robert Covington .75 2.00
37 Bradley Beal 1.25 3.00
38 Will Barton .75 2.00
39 Zach Randolph 1.00 2.50
40 Jimmy Butler 1.25 3.00
41 Pete Maravich 2.00 5.00
42 Michael Carter-Williams .75 2.00
43 Eric Bledsoe 1.00 2.50
44 Isaiah Thomas 1.25 3.00
45 Paul Millsap 1.25 3.00
46 Isaiah Canaan 1.00 2.50
47 Marcin Gortat 1.00 2.50
48 Andrew Wiggins 2.00 5.00
49 James Harden 2.00 5.00
50 Derrick Rose 1.50 4.00
51 Scottie Pippen 2.50 6.00
52 Stephen Curry 8.00 20.00
53 Brandon Knight 1.00 2.50
54 Jared Sullinger .75 2.00
55 Jeff Teague 1.00 2.50
56 Russell Westbrook 3.00 8.00
57 Tony Parker 1.25 3.00
58 Ricky Rubio 1.25 3.00
59 Trevor Ariza .75 2.00
60 Pau Gasol 1.25 3.00
61 Kareem Abdul-Jabbar 2.00 5.00
62 Klay Thompson 1.50 4.00
63 T.J. Warren 1.00 2.50
64 Carmelo Anthony 1.50 4.00
65 Tobias Harris 1.00 2.50
66 Kevin Durant 3.00 8.00
67 Tim Duncan 2.00 5.00
68 Kevin Garnett 2.00 5.00
69 Dwight Howard 1.00 2.50
70 Paul George 1.50 4.00
71 Allen Iverson 1.50 4.00
72 Draymond Green 1.50 4.00
73 Kobe Bryant 5.00 12.00
74 Arron Afflalo .75 2.00
75 Nikola Vucevic 1.00 2.50
76 Serge Ibaka 1.00 2.50
77 Kawhi Leonard 2.00 5.00
78 Damian Lillard 2.50 6.00
79 Anthony Davis 2.50 6.00
80 George Hill 1.00 2.50
81 John Stockton 2.00 5.00
82 Blake Griffin 1.25 3.00
83 Roy Hibbert 1.00 2.50
84 Robin Lopez .75 2.00
85 Victor Oladipo 1.00 2.50
86 Gordon Hayward 1.25 3.00
87 Dirk Nowitzki 1.50 4.00
88 C.J. McCollum 1.25 3.00
89 Tyreke Evans .75 2.00
90 Monta Ellis 1.00 2.50
91 Chris Webber 1.25 3.00
92 Chris Paul 1.50 4.00
93 Jordan Clarkson 1.25 3.00
94 Joe Johnson 1.00 2.50
95 Kemba Walker 1.25 3.00
96 Derrick Favors 1.00 2.50
97 Deron Williams 1.00 2.50
98 Mason Plumlee 1.00 2.50
99 Eric Gordon 1.00 2.50
100 Andre Drummond 1.25 3.00

2015-16 Panini Black Gold Rare

*RARE: .6X TO 1.5X BASIC
RANDOM INSERTS IN PACKS

2015-16 Panini Black Gold Uncommon

*UNCOMMON: .6X TO 1.5X BASIC
RANDOM INSERTS IN PACKS

2015-16 Panini Black Gold Bronze

*BRONZE: .4X TO 1X BASIC
RANDOM INSERTS IN PACKS

2015-16 Panini Black Gold Gold Discs

RANDOM INSERTS IN PACKS
1 LeBron James 100.00 250.00
2 Stephen Curry 100.00 250.00
3 Kobe Bryant 75.00 200.00
4 Kyrie Irving 30.00 80.00
5 Dwyane Wade 50.00 120.00
6 James Harden 25.00 60.00
7 Tim Duncan 40.00 100.00
8 Russell Westbrook 50.00 120.00
9 Kevin Durant 40.00 100.00
10 Anthony Davis 30.00 80.00

2015-16 Panini Black Gold Golden Jams Materials

RANDOM INSERTS IN PACKS
STATED PRINT RUN 99 SER.#'d SETS
*PRIME/25: 1X TO 2.5X BASIC
1 Aaron Gordon 3.00 8.00
2 Andre Drummond 4.00 10.00
3 Blake Griffin 4.00 10.00
4 Bradley Beal 4.00 10.00
5 Chandler Parsons 3.00 8.00
6 DeAndre Jordan 4.00 10.00
7 DeMar DeRozan 4.00 10.00
8 Gary Harris 3.00 8.00
9 Grant Hill 5.00 12.00
10 Harrison Barnes 3.00 8.00
11 J.R. Smith 3.00 8.00
12 Jimmy Butler 4.00 10.00
13 Jonathon Simmons 4.00 10.00
14 Julius Erving 6.00 15.00
15 Karl-Anthony Towns 10.00 25.00

16 Kemba Walker 4.00 10.00
17 Kenneth Faried 3.00 8.00
18 Kevin Durant 8.00 20.00
19 Kobe Bryant 15.00 40.00
20 Larry Johnson 5.00 12.00
21 LeBron James 15.00 40.00
22 Marcus Smart 3.00 8.00
23 Mario Hezonja 3.00 8.00
24 Nerlens Noel 3.00 8.00
25 Norman Powell 3.00 8.00
26 Rudy Gobert 4.00 10.00
27 Russell Westbrook 8.00 20.00
28 Scottie Pippen 10.00 25.00
29 Victor Oladipo 3.00 8.00
30 Zach LaVine 4.00 10.00

2015-16 Panini Black Gold Golden Opportunity Memorabilia

RANDOM INSERTS IN PACKS
STATED PRINT RUN 199 SER.#'d SETS
*PRIME/25: 1X TO 2.5X BASIC
1 Aaron Gordon 3.00 8.00
2 Alec Burks 2.50 6.00
3 Anthony Davis 6.00 15.00
4 Bobby Portis 4.00 10.00
5 Bradley Beal 4.00 10.00
6 Cameron Payne 3.00 8.00
7 D'Angelo Russell 8.00 20.00
8 Devin Booker 8.00 20.00
9 Emmanuel Mudiay 4.00 10.00
10 Frank Kaminsky 4.00 10.00
11 Gary Harris 3.00 8.00
12 Jahlil Okafor 5.00 12.00
13 James Harden 6.00 15.00
14 Jarell Martin 3.00 8.00
15 Enes Kanter 2.50 6.00
16 Jerian Grant 2.50 6.00
17 Joe Young 3.00 8.00
18 Jonathon Simmons 4.00 10.00
19 Jordan Adams 2.50 6.00
20 Jordan Clarkson 4.00 10.00
21 Josh Richardson 4.00 10.00
22 Jrue Holiday 3.00 8.00
23 Julius Randle 4.00 10.00
24 Justin Anderson 3.00 8.00
25 Justise Winslow 4.00 10.00
26 Karl-Anthony Towns 10.00 25.00
27 Kelly Oubre Jr. 3.00 8.00
28 Kenneth Faried 3.00 8.00
29 Kevon Looney 3.00 8.00
30 Doug McDermott 3.00 8.00
31 Langston Galloway 2.50 6.00
33 Mario Hezonja 3.00 8.00
34 Mitch McGary 2.50 6.00
35 Myles Turner 4.00 10.00
36 Nick Young 3.00 8.00
38 Otto Porter 3.00 8.00
39 Rajon Rondo 4.00 10.00
41 Richaun Holmes 3.00 8.00
42 Rodney Hood 3.00 8.00
43 Rondae Hollis-Jefferson 3.00 8.00
44 Shane Larkin 2.50 6.00
45 Stanley Johnson 3.00 8.00
46 Trey Lyles 4.00 10.00
47 Tyreke Evans 2.50 6.00
48 Victor Oladipo 3.00 8.00
49 Willie Cauley-Stein 4.00 10.00
50 Zach Randolph 3.00 8.00

2015-16 Panini Black Gold Grand Debut Signatures

RANDOM INSERTS IN PACKS
PRINT RUNS B/WN 13-199 COPIES PER
NO PRICING ON QTY 13
EXCHANGE DEADLINE 1/6/2018
1 Tyus Jones/199 6.00 15.00
4 Jahlil Okafor/140 8.00 20.00
5 Emmanuel Mudiay/199 6.00 15.00
6 Boban Marjanovic/199 5.00 12.00
7 Bobby Portis/199 8.00 20.00
8 Jonathon Simmons/199 10.00 25.00
9 Raul Neto/199 4.00 10.00
10 R.J. Hunter/199 4.00 10.00
11 Devin Booker/199 30.00 80.00
12 D'Angelo Russell/124 20.00 50.00
13 Jerian Grant/199 4.00 10.00
14 Stanley Johnson/199 5.00 12.00
15 Larry Nance Jr./199 8.00 20.00
16 Justin Anderson/140 5.00 12.00
17 Myles Turner/199 12.00 30.00
18 Montrezl Harrell/199 5.00 12.00
19 Jordan Mickey/199 4.00 10.00
20 Terry Rozier/100 5.00 12.00
21 Rashad Vaughn/199 4.00 10.00
22 Kelly Oubre Jr./199 5.00 12.00
23 Rondae Hollis-Jefferson/199 5.00 12.00
24 Sam Dekker/199 5.00 12.00
25 Norman Powell/199 5.00 12.00

2015-16 Panini Black Gold Massive Materials

RANDOM INSERTS IN PACKS
PRINT RUNS B/WN 49-199 COPIES PER
1 Al Horford/199 3.00 8.00
2 Al Jefferson/199 3.00 8.00
3 Allen Iverson/99 8.00 20.00
4 Andre Drummond/199 4.00 10.00
5 Avery Bradley/199 3.00 8.00
6 Blake Griffin/199 4.00 10.00
7 Bradley Beal/199 4.00 10.00
8 Brandon Jennings/199 2.50 6.00
9 Chris Bosh/199 4.00 10.00
10 Damian Lillard/99 6.00 15.00
11 Dante Exum/49 3.00 8.00
12 DeAndre Jordan/199 4.00 10.00
13 Devin Booker/199 6.00 15.00
14 Dirk Nowitzki/199 5.00 12.00
15 Dwyane Wade/99 6.00 15.00
16 Gordon Hayward/49 4.00 10.00
17 Grant Hill/149 5.00 12.00
18 James Harden/49 6.00 15.00
19 Joe Johnson/199 3.00 8.00
20 John Stockton/49 6.00 15.00
21 Julius Erving/49 6.00 15.00
22 Karl Malone/49 5.00 12.00
23 Kemba Walker/199 4.00 10.00
24 Kevin Garnett/49 6.00 15.00
25 Kevin Love/199 4.00 10.00
26 Kevin McHale/49 4.00 10.00
27 Kobe Bryant/199 15.00 40.00
28 LaMarcus Aldridge/199 4.00 10.00
29 Marcin Gortat/49 3.00 8.00
30 Marcus Smart/49 3.00 8.00
31 Nerlens Noel/49 3.00 8.00
32 Patrick Ewing/49 6.00 15.00
33 Rajon Rondo/49 4.00 10.00
34 Ricky Rubio/49 4.00 10.00
35 Rudy Gobert/199 4.00 10.00
36 Tony Parker/49 4.00 10.00
37 Victor Oladipo/99 3.00 8.00
38 Alonzo Mourning/49 5.00 12.00
39 Brook Lopez/99 3.00 8.00
40 Chandler Parsons/99 3.00 8.00
41 Deron Williams/49 3.00 8.00
42 Robert Covington/199 2.50 6.00
43 J.J. Redick/199 4.00 10.00
44 Jrue Holiday/199 3.00 8.00
45 Kelly Oubre Jr./199 3.00 8.00
46 Khris Middleton/199 3.00 8.00
47 Kyrie Irving/99 6.00 15.00
48 Lance Stephenson/199 3.00 8.00
49 Thaddeus Young/99 2.50 6.00
50 Trey Lyles/199 4.00 10.00

2015-16 Panini Black Gold Memorabilia

RANDOM INSERTS IN PACKS
STATED PRINT RUN 99 SER.#'d SETS
*PRIME/25: 1X TO 2.5X BASIC
1 Aaron Gordon 3.00 8.00
2 Al Horford 3.00 8.00
3 Al Jefferson 3.00 8.00
4 Allen Iverson 8.00 20.00
5 Andre Drummond 4.00 10.00
6 Avery Bradley 3.00 8.00
7 Blake Griffin 4.00 10.00
8 Bradley Beal 4.00 10.00
9 Brandon Jennings 2.50 6.00
10 Chris Bosh 4.00 10.00
11 Damian Lillard 6.00 15.00
12 Dante Exum 3.00 8.00
13 DeAndre Jordan 4.00 10.00
14 Devin Booker 8.00 20.00
15 Dirk Nowitzki 5.00 12.00
16 Dwyane Wade 6.00 15.00
17 Emmanuel Mudiay 4.00 10.00
18 Gary Harris 3.00 8.00
19 Goran Dragic 3.00 8.00
20 Gordon Hayward 4.00 10.00
21 Grant Hill 5.00 12.00
22 James Harden 6.00 15.00
23 Jerian Grant 2.50 6.00
24 Joe Johnson 3.00 8.00
25 John Stockton 6.00 15.00
26 Jose Calderon 2.50 6.00
27 Julius Erving 6.00 15.00
28 Jusuf Nurkic 2.50 6.00
29 Karl Malone 5.00 12.00
30 Kemba Walker 4.00 10.00
31 Kenneth Faried 3.00 8.00
32 Kevin Garnett 6.00 15.00
33 Kevin Love 4.00 10.00
34 Kevin McHale 4.00 10.00
35 Kobe Bryant 15.00 40.00
36 LaMarcus Aldridge 4.00 10.00
37 Langston Galloway 2.50 6.00
38 Marcin Gortat 3.00 8.00
39 Marcus Smart 3.00 8.00
40 Nerlens Noel 3.00 8.00
41 Patrick Ewing 6.00 15.00
42 Rajon Rondo 4.00 10.00
43 Ricky Rubio 4.00 10.00
44 Rudy Gobert 4.00 10.00
45 Russell Westbrook 8.00 20.00
46 Stephen Curry 20.00 50.00
47 Tim Hardaway Jr. 2.50 6.00
48 Tony Parker 4.00 10.00
49 Tyreke Evans 2.50 6.00
50 Victor Oladipo 3.00 8.00

2015-16 Panini Black Gold Pick and Roll Materials

RANDOM INSERTS IN PACKS
STATED PRINT RUN 99 SER.#'d SETS
*PRIME/25: 1X TO 2.5X BASIC
1 A.Horford/J.Teague 3.00 8.00
2 M.Smart/J.Sullinger 3.00 8.00
3 Rose/Gasol 10.00 25.00
4 Mudiay/Faried 4.00 10.00
5 A.Drummond/R.Jackson 4.00 10.00
6 Green/Curry 20.00 50.00
7 Howard/Harden 6.00 15.00
8 Russell/Randle 6.00 15.00
9 Z.Randolph/M.Conley 4.00 10.00
10 Bosh/Wade 6.00 15.00
11 G.Dieng/R.Rubio 4.00 10.00
12 Davis/Holiday 8.00 20.00
13 Jackson/Ewing 5.00 12.00
14 Westbrook/Ibaka 10.00 25.00
15 N.Vucevic/E.Payton 3.00 8.00
16 A.Len/B.Knight 3.00 8.00
17 A.Stoudemire/S.Nash 4.00 10.00
18 D.Cousins/R.Rondo 4.00 10.00
19 Duncan/Parker 10.00 25.00
20 Stockton/Malone 6.00 15.00

2015-16 Panini Black Gold Rookie Jersey Autographs

RANDOM INSERTS IN PACKS
PRINT RUNS B/WN 65-199 COPIES PER
EXCHANGE DEADLINE 1/6/2018
*PRIME/21-25: 1.2X TO 3X BASIC
1 Karl-Anthony Towns/199 75.00 200.00
2 D'Angelo Russell/199 30.00 80.00
3 Jahlil Okafor/199 12.00 30.00
4 Emmanuel Mudiay/199 6.00 15.00
5 Kristaps Porzingis/199 25.00 60.00
6 Mario Hezonja/199 10.00 25.00
7 Justise Winslow/65 20.00 50.00
8 Willie Cauley-Stein/199 12.00 30.00
9 Tyus Jones/199 8.00 20.00
10 Stanley Johnson/199 5.00 12.00
11 Frank Kaminsky/78 8.00 20.00
12 Devin Booker/199 50.00 120.00
13 Myles Turner/199 12.00 30.00
14 Trey Lyles/199 6.00 15.00
15 Jerian Grant/199 4.00 10.00
16 Kevon Looney/199 5.00 12.00
17 Cameron Payne/118 5.00 12.00
18 Kelly Oubre Jr./199 5.00 12.00
19 Terry Rozier/199 5.00 12.00
20 Rondae Hollis-Jefferson/199 5.00 12.00
21 Bobby Portis/199 4.00 10.00
22 Nikola Jokic/157 40.00 100.00
23 Justin Anderson/199 5.00 12.00
24 R.J. Hunter/199 4.00 10.00
25 Raul Neto/199 4.00 10.00
26 Marcelo Huertas/165 5.00 12.00
27 Anthony Brown/199 4.00 10.00
28 Norman Powell/199 5.00 12.00
29 Sasha Kaun/199 4.00 10.00
30 Pat Connaughton/199 4.00 10.00

2015-16 Panini Black Gold Signatures

RANDOM INSERTS IN PACKS
PRINT RUNS B/WN 60-99 COPIES PER
EXCHANGE DEADLINE 1/6/2018
BGN Nene/99 5.00 12.00
BGAD Anthony Davis/60 40.00 100.00
BGAD Andre Drummond/99 12.00 30.00
BGAH Anfernee Hardaway/75 25.00 60.00
BGAM Alonzo Mourning/60 20.00 50.00
BGAW Andrew Wiggins/60
BGBB Bradley Beal/75 EXCH 12.00 30.00
BGBK Brandon Knight/99 5.00 12.00
BGDE Dante Exum/75 10.00 25.00
BGDG Danny Green/99 5.00 12.00
BGDM Dikembe Mutombo/99 10.00 25.00
BGDR Dennis Rodman/75 25.00 60.00
BGDS Dennis Schroder/99 5.00 12.00
BGEJ Eddie Jones/99 5.00 12.00
BGEP Elfrid Payton/99 12.00 30.00
BGGD Goran Dragic/99 5.00 12.00
BGGH Grant Hill/75 20.00 50.00
BGGH Gordon Hayward/99 12.00 30.00
BGGN Gary Neal/99 5.00 12.00
BGJC Jordan Clarkson/99 EXCH 10.00 25.00
BGJE Julius Erving/60 40.00 100.00
BGJP Jabari Parker/60 12.00 30.00
BGJR Julius Randle/75 10.00 25.00
BGJS John Stockton/60 20.00 50.00
BGJS J.R. Smith/99 EXCH 5.00 12.00
BGJS Jared Sullinger/75 4.00 10.00
BGJW John Wall/60 20.00 50.00
BGKB Kent Bazemore/99 EXCH 5.00 12.00
BGKB Kobe Bryant/60 100.00 250.00
BGKD Kevin Durant/60 60.00 150.00
BGKI Kyrie Irving/60 50.00 120.00
BGKL Kevin Love/75 20.00 50.00
BGKM Karl Malone/60 20.00 50.00
BGKT Klay Thompson/75 30.00 80.00
BGMD M. Dellavedova/99 EXCH 10.00 25.00
BGMJ Mark Jackson/99 5.00 12.00
BGMS Marcus Smart/75 5.00 12.00
BGNM Nikola Mirotic/99 5.00 12.00
BGNS Nik Stauskas/99 4.00 10.00
BGNY Nick Young/99 5.00 12.00
BGRA Ray Allen/75 20.00 50.00
BGRM Ray McCallum/99 4.00 10.00
BGRS Rod Strickland/99 4.00 10.00
BGTM Tracy McGrady/75 20.00 50.00
BGTP Tony Parker/75 25.00 60.00
BGTW T.J. Warren/99 5.00 12.00
BGTY Thaddeus Young/99 4.00 10.00
BGWM Wesley Matthews/99 4.00 10.00
BGABK Alec Burks/99
BGAHF Al Horford/99 5.00 12.00
BGBGF Blake Griffin/60 25.00 60.00
BGCBS Chris Bosh/75 6.00 15.00
BGCJW C.J. Watson/99 4.00 10.00
BGDCL DeMarre Carroll/99 4.00 10.00
BGDMJ Donatas Motiejunas/99 4.00 10.00
BGDPW Dwight Powell/99 4.00 10.00
BGDRS David Robinson/60 25.00 60.00
BGEBS Eric Bledsoe/99 5.00 12.00
BGEMR Earl Monroe/60
BGFEZ Festus Ezeli/99 4.00 10.00
BGGGE George Gervin/75 8.00 20.00
BGGHS Gary Harris/99 5.00 12.00
BGGPT Gary Payton/75 EXCH 6.00 15.00
BGITH Isiah Thomas/99 12.00 30.00
BGJET Jason Terry/99 5.00 12.00
BGJHD Jrue Holiday/75 5.00 12.00
BGJKD Jason Kidd/75 10.00 25.00
BGMGT Marcin Gortat/99 5.00 12.00
BGMHL Maurice Harkless/99 4.00 10.00
BGMJS Magic Johnson/60 30.00 80.00
BGNCL Norris Cole/99 4.00 10.00
BGSON Shaquille O'Neal/60 40.00 100.00
BGTKU Toni Kukoc/99 6.00 15.00
BGVOD Victor Oladipo/75 5.00 12.00
BGZLV Zach LaVine/99 20.00 50.00

2015-16 Panini Black Gold Sizeable Signatures Jerseys

RANDOM INSERTS IN PACKS
STATED PRINT RUN 99 SER.#'d SETS
EXCHANGE DEADLINE 1/6/2018
RSSAB Anthony Brown 5.00 12.00
RSSBP Bobby Portis 12.00 30.00
RSSCP Cameron Payne 6.00 15.00
RSSDB Devin Booker 60.00 150.00
RSSDR D'Angelo Russell EXCH 15.00 40.00
RSSEM Emmanuel Mudiay 8.00 20.00
RSSJG Jerian Grant 6.00 15.00
RSSJO Jahlil Okafor 20.00 50.00
RSSJS Jonathon Simmons 25.00 60.00
RSSJW Justise Winslow 15.00 40.00
RSSKP Kristaps Porzingis 60.00 150.00
RSSKT Karl-Anthony Towns 75.00 200.00
RSSMH Mario Hezonja 6.00 15.00
RSSMH Marcelo Huertas 6.00 15.00
RSSMH Montrezl Harrell 6.00 15.00
RSSMT Myles Turner 15.00 40.00
RSSNB Nemanja Bjelica 8.00 20.00
RSSNJ Nikola Jokic 30.00 80.00
RSSNP Norman Powell 6.00 15.00
RSSRH R.J. Hunter 5.00 12.00
RSSRH Richaun Holmes 6.00 15.00
RSSRN Raul Neto 5.00 12.00
RSSSJ Stanley Johnson 6.00 15.00
RSSTR Terry Rozier 6.00 15.00
RSSWC Willie Cauley-Stein 12.00 30.00

2015-16 Panini Black Gold Sizeable Signatures Jerseys Prime

*PRIME: 1.5X TO 4X BASIC
RANDOM INSERTS IN PACKS
STATED PRINT RUN 25 SER.#'d SETS
EXCHANGE DEADLINE 1/6/2018
RSSDB Devin Booker 150.00 400.00
RSSKP Kristaps Porzingis 300.00 600.00
RSSKT Karl-Anthony Towns 400.00 800.00

2015-16 Panini Black Gold Team Emblems

RANDOM INSERTS IN PACKS
1 Kobe Bryant 75.00 200.00
2 Kristaps Porzingis 20.00 50.00
3 Kevin Durant 30.00 80.00
4 D'Angelo Russell 30.00 80.00
5 Kyrie Irving 40.00 100.00
6 Jahlil Okafor 10.00 25.00
7 Anthony Davis 15.00 40.00
8 Nemanja Bjelica 6.00 15.00
9 LeBron James 75.00 200.00
10 Justise Winslow 12.00 30.00
11 Stephen Curry 100.00 250.00
12 Russell Westbrook 25.00 60.00
13 James Harden 30.00 80.00
14 DeMarcus Cousins 8.00 20.00
15 Chris Paul 20.00 50.00
16 John Wall 10.00 25.00
17 Carmelo Anthony 20.00 50.00
18 Jimmy Butler 20.00 50.00
19 Dwight Howard 6.00 15.00
20 Paul George 20.00 50.00
21 Julius Erving 12.00 30.00
22 Artis Gilmore 6.00 15.00
23 George Gervin 10.00 25.00
24 Connie Hawkins 8.00 20.00
25 David Thompson 10.00 25.00
26 Mack Calvin 5.00 12.00
27 Dan Issel 6.00 15.00
28 George McGinnis 5.00 12.00
29 Louie Dampier 8.00 20.00
30 Larry Brown 8.00 20.00

2015-16 Panini Black Gold Vintage Gold Autographs

RANDOM INSERTS IN PACKS
PRINT RUNS B/WN 28-149 COPIES PER
EXCHANGE DEADLINE 1/6/2018
1 Elvin Hayes/149 6.00 15.00
2 Walt Frazier/55 8.00 20.00
3 Jalen Rose/149 6.00 15.00
4 Jamaal Wilkes/149 6.00 15.00
5 Dan Issel/149 5.00 12.00
6 Tim Hardaway/149 6.00 15.00
7 Glen Rice/115 5.00 12.00
8 George Gervin/149 6.00 15.00
9 Hal Greer/50 5.00 12.00
10 Jason Kidd/65 20.00 50.00
11 Bob McAdoo/70 8.00 20.00
12 David Thompson/149 5.00 12.00
13 Ray Allen/125 12.00 30.00
14 Jerry West/28 25.00 60.00
15 Dennis Rodman/75 25.00 60.00
16 John Stockton/99 20.00 50.00
17 James Worthy/75 10.00 25.00
18 David Robinson/75 20.00 50.00
19 Nate Archibald/99 5.00 12.00
20 Clyde Drexler/65 15.00 40.00
21 Dikembe Mutombo/149 15.00 40.00
22 Grant Hill/105 12.00 30.00
23 John Salley/149 4.00 10.00
24 Steve Smith/149 5.00 12.00
25 Eddie Jones/149 5.00 12.00
26 Charles Oakley/149 5.00 12.00
27 Toni Kukoc/149 8.00 20.00
28 Jo Jo White/125 5.00 12.00
29 Wayne Embry/125 4.00 10.00
30 Ron Harper/125 6.00 15.00
31 Maurice Cheeks/125 4.00 10.00
32 Norm Nixon/99 4.00 10.00
33 Darrell Griffith/99 4.00 10.00
34 Jim Jackson/149 4.00 10.00
35 Bill Laimbeer/149 5.00 12.00
36 Isiah Thomas/125 10.00 25.00
37 Tracy McGrady/75 12.00 30.00
38 Anfernee Hardaway/50 25.00 60.00
39 Tom Heinsohn/149 25.00 60.00
40 Muggsy Bogues/125 5.00 12.00
41 John Starks/149 5.00 12.00
42 Thurl Bailey/149 4.00 10.00
43 Theo Ratliff/49 4.00 10.00
44 Kelly Tripucka/149 4.00 10.00
45 Rolando Blackman/149 5.00 12.00

2012-13 Panini Brilliance

COMPLETE SET (300) 40.00 100.00
1 Al Horford .25 .60
2 Kevin Durant .75 2.00
3 DeShawn Stevenson .20 .50
4 Devin Harris .20 .50
5 Jeff Teague .25 .60
6 Josh Smith .25 .60
7 Kyle Korver .25 .60
8 Kevin Martin .25 .60
9 Avery Bradley .25 .60
10 Brandon Bass .20 .50
11 Courtney Lee .25 .60
12 Jason Terry .25 .60
13 Jeff Green .25 .60
14 Kevin Garnett .50 1.25
15 Leandro Barbosa .25 .60
16 Paul Pierce .30 .75
17 Rajon Rondo .30 .75
18 Andray Blatche .20 .50
19 Brook Lopez .25 .60
20 C.J. Watson .20 .50
21 Serge Ibaka .25 .60
22 Deron Williams .25 .60
23 Gerald Wallace .25 .60
24 Jerry Stackhouse .25 .60
25 Joe Johnson .25 .60
26 Reggie Evans .20 .50
27 Kris Humphries .20 .50
28 Ben Gordon .25 .60
29 Byron Mullens .20 .50
30 Gerald Henderson .20 .50
31 Tyson Chandler .25 .60
32 Ramon Sessions .25 .60
33 Russell Westbrook .75 2.00
34 Carlos Boozer .25 .60
35 Daequan Cook .20 .50
36 Derrick Rose .40 1.00
37 Joakim Noah .25 .60
38 Kirk Hinrich .25 .60
39 Luol Deng .25 .60
40 Marco Belinelli .20 .50
41 Richard Hamilton .25 .60
42 Taj Gibson .25 .60
43 Alonzo Gee .20 .50
44 Anderson Varejao .20 .50
45 Daniel Gibson .25 .60
46 Thabo Sefolosha .20 .50
47 Chris Kaman .25 .60
48 Dahntay Jones .20 .50
49 Darren Collison .25 .60
50 Dirk Nowitzki .40 1.00
51 Elton Brand .30 .75
52 O.J. Mayo .20 .50
53 Shawn Marion .25 .60
54 Vince Carter .40 1.00
55 Andre Iguodala .25 .60
56 Andre Miller .25 .60
57 Corey Brewer .20 .50
58 Danilo Gallinari .20 .50
59 JaVale McGee .25 .60
60 Ty Lawson .20 .50
61 Kendrick Perkins .20 .50
62 Greg Monroe .25 .60
63 Jason Maxiell .20 .50
64 Rodney Stuckey .25 .60
65 Tayshaun Prince .25 .60
66 Will Bynum .20 .50
67 Andrew Bogut .25 .60
68 Andris Biedrins .20 .50
69 Brandon Rush .20 .50
70 Carl Landry .20 .50
71 David Lee .20 .50
72 Stephen Curry 1.25 3.00
73 James Harden .50 1.25
74 Jeremy Lin .30 .75
75 Omer Asik .25 .60
76 Patrick Patterson .20 .50
77 Toney Douglas .20 .50
78 Danny Granger .25 .60
79 George Hill .25 .60
80 Gerald Green .25 .60
81 Lance Stephenson .25 .60
82 Roy Hibbert .25 .60
83 Tyler Hansbrough .25 .60
84 Blake Griffin .30 .75
85 Caron Butler .25 .60
86 Chauncey Billups .30 .75
87 Chris Paul .40 1.00
88 DeAndre Jordan .30 .75
89 Eric Bledsoe .25 .60
90 Grant Hill .40 1.00
91 Jamal Crawford .30 .75
92 Matt Barnes .20 .50
93 Antawn Jamison .25 .60
94 Devin Ebanks .20 .50
95 Earl Clark .20 .50
96 Jodie Meeks .25 .60
97 Dwight Howard .25 .60
98 Kobe Bryant 1.25 3.00
99 Metta World Peace .30 .75
100 Pau Gasol .30 .75
101 Steve Blake .20 .50
102 Steve Nash .30 .75
103 Darrell Arthur .20 .50
104 Jerryd Bayless .25 .60
105 Marc Gasol .30 .75
106 Marreese Speights .20 .50
107 Mike Conley .25 .60
108 Rudy Gay .30 .75
109 Tony Allen .20 .50
110 Wayne Ellington .20 .50
111 Zach Randolph .25 .60
112 Chris Bosh .30 .75
113 Dwyane Wade .50 1.25
114 James Jones .20 .50
115 Joel Anthony .20 .50
116 LeBron James 1.25 3.00
117 Mario Chalmers .25 .60
118 Mike Miller .25 .60
119 Rashard Lewis .25 .60
120 Udonis Haslem .20 .50
121 Beno Udrih .20 .50
122 Brandon Jennings .20 .50
123 Drew Gooden .25 .60
124 Ekpe Udoh .20 .50
125 Ersan Ilyasova .20 .50
126 Larry Sanders .20 .50
127 Luc Mbah a Moute .20 .50
128 Andrei Kirilenko .25 .60
129 Brandon Roy .30 .75
130 J.J. Barea .25 .60
131 Kevin Love .30 .75
132 Luke Ridnour .25 .60
133 Nikola Pekovic .20 .50
134 Ricky Rubio .30 .75
135 Al-Farouq Aminu .25 .60
136 Eric Gordon .25 .60
137 Greivis Vasquez .25 .60
138 Robin Lopez .20 .50
139 Xavier Henry .20 .50
140 Amar'e Stoudemire .25 .60
141 Carmelo Anthony .40 1.00
142 J.R. Smith .25 .60
143 Jason Kidd .30 .75
144 Marcus Camby .25 .60
145 Raymond Felton .25 .60
146 Steve Novak .20 .50
147 Glen Davis .20 .50
148 Hedo Turkoglu .25 .60
149 J.J. Redick .30 .75
150 Jameer Nelson .20 .50
151 Arron Afflalo .25 .60
152 Andrew Bynum .20 .50
153 Evan Turner .20 .50
154 Jason Richardson .30 .75
155 Jrue Holiday .30 .75
156 Nick Young .25 .60
157 Spencer Hawes .20 .50
158 Thaddeus Young .20 .50
159 Goran Dragic .25 .60
160 Jared Dudley .20 .50
161 Jermaine O'Neal .25 .60
162 Luis Scola .25 .60
163 Marcin Gortat .25 .60
164 P.J. Tucker .20 .50
165 Shannon Brown .20 .50
166 J.J. Hickson .20 .50
167 Joel Freeland .20 .50
168 LaMarcus Aldridge .30 .75
169 Nicolas Batum .25 .60
170 Wesley Matthews .20 .50
171 DeMarcus Cousins .30 .75
172 Francisco Garcia .25 .60
173 James Johnson .20 .50
174 Jason Thompson .20 .50
175 John Salmons .25 .60
176 Marcus Thornton .20 .50
177 Tyreke Evans .20 .50
178 Boris Diaw .25 .60
179 Danny Green .25 .60
180 DeJuan Blair .20 .50
181 Manu Ginobili .30 .75
182 Stephen Jackson .25 .60
183 Tiago Splitter .25 .60
184 Tim Duncan .50 1.25
185 Tony Parker .30 .75
186 Alan Anderson .20 .50
187 Amir Johnson .20 .50
188 Andrea Bargnani .25 .60
189 DeMar DeRozan .30 .75
190 Ed Davis .20 .50
191 Kyle Lowry .25 .60
192 Randy Foye .20 .50
193 Al Jefferson .25 .60
194 Derrick Favors .25 .60
195 Gordon Hayward .30 .75
196 Marvin Williams .25 .60
197 Emeka Okafor .25 .60
198 John Wall .40 1.00
199 Jordan Crawford .20 .50
200 Nene .25 .60
201 Adrian Dantley .25 .60
202 Allan Houston .25 .60
203 Allen Iverson .40 1.00
204 B.J. Armstrong .30 .75
205 Bernard King .25 .60
206 Bob McAdoo .25 .60
207 Clyde Drexler .40 1.00
208 Dan Majerle .25 .60
209 Earl Monroe .30 .75
210 Gary Payton .30 .75
211 George Gervin .30 .75
212 Hakeem Olajuwon .40 1.00
213 Horace Grant .30 .75
214 Isiah Thomas .30 .75
215 James Worthy .40 1.00
216 Jeff Hornacek .25 .60
217 John Starks .25 .60
218 John Stockton .50 1.25
219 Larry Bird .75 2.00
220 Mark Aguirre .25 .60
221 Mitch Richmond .30 .75
222 Moses Malone .30 .75
223 Nate McMillian .30 .75
224 Ralph Sampson .25 .60
225 Reggie Theus .25 .60
226 Rick Mahorn .20 .50
227 Sam Cassell .25 .60
228 Sam Perkins .20 .50
229 Shaquille O'Neal .60 1.50
230 Tim Hardaway .30 .75
231 Norris Cole RC .25 .60
232 Alexey Shved RC .25 .60
233 Greg Stiemsma RC .25 .60
234 Anthony Davis RC 2.00 5.00
235 Austin Rivers RC .40 1.00
236 Brian Roberts RC .25 .60
237 Lance Thomas RC .25 .60
238 Chris Copeland RC .25 .60
239 Iman Shumpert RC .40 1.00
240 Jeremy Lamb RC .40 1.00
241 Perry Jones RC .25 .60
242 Reggie Jackson RC .40 1.00
243 Andrew Nicholson RC .25 .60
244 DeQuan Jones RC .25 .60
245 E'Twaun Moore RC .25 .60
246 Gustavo Ayon RC .25 .60
247 Maurice Harkless RC .40 1.00
248 Nikola Vucevic RC .40 1.00
249 John Jenkins RC .25 .60
250 Jared Sullinger RC .30 .75
251 MarShon Brooks RC .30 .75
252 Mirza Teletovic RC .30 .75
253 Tornike Shengelia RC .25 .60
254 Tyshawn Taylor RC .25 .60
255 Kemba Walker RC .75 2.00
256 Michael Kidd-Gilchrist RC .40 1.00
257 Jimmy Butler RC 1.25 3.00
258 Marquis Teague RC .25 .60
259 Dion Waiters RC .40 1.00
260 Kyrie Irving RC 2.00 5.00
261 Tristan Thompson RC .40 1.00
262 Tyler Zeller RC .30 .75
263 Bernard James RC .25 .60
264 Jae Crowder RC .30 .75
265 Kenneth Faried RC .40 1.00
266 Jordan Hamilton RC .25 .60
267 Andre Drummond RC .60 1.50
268 Brandon Knight RC .40 1.00
269 Kyle Singler RC .25 .60
270 Kent Bazemore RC .40 1.00
271 Klay Thompson RC 1.50 4.00
272 Chandler Parsons RC .40 1.00
273 Donatas Motiejunas RC .30 .75
274 Terrence Jones RC .30 .75
275 Miles Plumlee RC .25 .60
276 Orlando Johnson RC .25 .60
277 Darius Morris RC .25 .60
278 Robert Sacre RC .25 .60
279 Ivan Johnson RC .25 .60
280 Tony Wroten RC .30 .75
281 Lavoy Allen RC .25 .60
282 Markieff Morris RC .40 1.00
283 Damian Lillard RC 1.50 4.00
284 Meyers Leonard RC .30 .75
285 Nolan Smith RC .25 .60
286 Will Barton RC .30 .75
287 Thomas Robinson RC .30 .75
288 Kawhi Leonard RC 2.00 5.00
289 Nando De Colo RC .25 .60
290 Jonas Valanciunas RC .40 1.00
291 Quincy Acy RC .25 .60
292 Terrence Ross RC .40 1.00
293 Alec Burks RC .40 1.00
294 Bradley Beal RC .60 1.50
295 Chris Singleton RC .25 .60
296 Pablo Prigioni RC .25 .60
297 John Henson RC .40 1.00
298 Tobias Harris RC .40 1.00
299 Marcus Morris RC .30 .75
300 Viacheslav Kravtsov RC .25 .60

2012-13 Panini Brilliance Starburst

*STARBURST VET: 1.5X TO 4X BASIC
*STARBURST RC: 1.5X TO 4X BASIC RC
260 Kyrie Irving 20.00 50.00
283 Damian Lillard 15.00 40.00

2012-13 Panini Brilliance Accolades

COMPLETE SET (20) 10.00 25.00
1 Jason Kidd .60 1.50
2 Paul Pierce .60 1.50
3 Dirk Nowitzki .75 2.00
4 Kevin Garnett 1.00 2.50
5 Ray Allen .60 1.50
6 Marcus Camby .50 1.25
7 Kobe Bryant 2.50 6.00
8 Grant Hill .75 2.00
9 Steve Nash .60 1.50
10 Andre Miller .50 1.25
11 Vince Carter .75 2.00
12 Tim Duncan 1.00 2.50
13 Shawn Marion .50 1.25
14 Andrei Kirilenko .50 1.25
15 Antawn Jamison .50 1.25
16 Rasheed Wallace .60 1.50
17 Jason Terry .50 1.25
18 Chauncey Billups .60 1.50
19 Jerry Stackhouse .50 1.25
20 LeBron James 2.50 6.00

2012-13 Panini Brilliance Brilliant Beginnings Autographs

EXCHANGE DEADLINE 11/22/2014
1 Alec Burks 5.00 12.00
2 Alexey Shved 3.00 8.00
3 Andre Drummond 8.00 20.00
4 Andrew Nicholson 3.00 8.00
5 Anthony Davis 50.00 120.00
6 Austin Rivers 5.00 12.00
7 Bernard James 3.00 8.00
8 Bismack Biyombo 3.00 8.00
9 Bradley Beal 8.00 20.00
10 Brandon Knight 5.00 12.00
11 Chandler Parsons 5.00 12.00
12 Charles Jenkins 3.00 8.00
13 Chris Singleton 3.00 8.00
14 Darius Morris 3.00 8.00
15 Brian Roberts 3.00 8.00
16 Derrick Williams 3.00 8.00
17 Dion Waiters 5.00 12.00
18 Doron Lamb 3.00 8.00
19 Draymond Green 12.00 30.00
20 Enes Kanter 4.00 10.00
21 E'Twaun Moore 3.00 8.00
22 Evan Fournier 5.00 12.00
23 Gustavo Ayon 3.00 8.00
24 Harrison Barnes 8.00 20.00
25 Iman Shumpert 5.00 12.00
26 Isaiah Thomas 12.00 30.00
27 Jae Crowder 4.00 10.00
28 Jan Vesely 3.00 8.00
29 Tyler Zeller 4.00 10.00
30 Jared Sullinger 4.00 10.00
31 Jeff Taylor 3.00 8.00
32 Tristan Thompson 5.00 12.00
33 Jimmer Fredette 3.00 8.00
34 John Henson 5.00 12.00
35 Jonas Valanciunas 5.00 12.00
36 Jordan Hamilton 3.00 8.00
37 Kawhi Leonard 50.00 120.00
38 Kemba Walker 8.00 20.00
39 Kendall Marshall 3.00 8.00
40 Kenneth Faried 5.00 12.00
41 Kent Bazemore 5.00 12.00
42 Klay Thompson 20.00 50.00
43 Kyrie Irving 30.00 80.00
44 Lance Thomas 3.00 8.00
45 Marquis Teague 3.00 8.00
46 MarShon Brooks 4.00 10.00
47 Maurice Harkless 5.00 12.00
48 Meyers Leonard 4.00 10.00
49 Michael Kidd-Gilchrist 5.00 12.00
50 Tobias Harris 5.00 12.00
51 Nando De Colo 3.00 8.00
52 Nikola Vucevic 5.00 12.00
53 Nolan Smith 3.00 8.00
54 Norris Cole EXCH 3.00 8.00
55 Orlando Johnson 3.00 8.00
56 Quincy Acy 3.00 8.00
57 Robert Sacre 3.00 8.00
58 Will Barton 4.00 10.00
59 Terrence Ross 5.00 12.00
60 Thomas Robinson 4.00 10.00

2012-13 Panini Brilliance City to City Jerseys

PRIME PRINT RUNS 10-25 COPIES PER
NO PRIME PRICING DUE TO SCARCITY
1 Vince Carter 4.00 10.00
2 Dwight Howard 2.50 6.00
3 LeBron James 12.00 30.00
4 Chris Paul 4.00 10.00
5 Carmelo Anthony 4.00 10.00
6 Steve Nash 3.00 8.00
7 Andre Iguodala 2.50 6.00
8 Shaquille O'Neal 6.00 15.00
9 Andrei Kirilenko 2.50 6.00
10 Joe Johnson 2.50 6.00
11 Metta World Peace 3.00 8.00
12 Kyle Lowry 2.50 6.00
13 Ben Gordon 2.50 6.00
14 Andrew Bogut 2.50 6.00
15 Brandon Roy 3.00 8.00
16 Amar'e Stoudemire 2.50 6.00
17 Ray Allen 3.00 8.00
18 Grant Hill 4.00 10.00
19 Stephen Jackson 2.50 6.00

2012-13 Panini Brilliance Game Time Jerseys

PRIME PRINT RUNS 1-25 COPIES PER
NO PRIME PRICING DUE TO SCARCITY
1 Greg Monroe 2.50 6.00
2 Jose Calderon 2.00 5.00
3 Stephen Curry 12.00 30.00
4 Metta World Peace 3.00 8.00
5 J.J. Barea 2.50 6.00
6 Gordon Hayward 3.00 8.00
7 Andrea Bargnani 2.50 6.00
8 Jason Kidd 3.00 8.00
9 Al-Farouq Aminu 2.50 6.00
10 JaVale McGee 2.50 6.00
11 Kevin Love 3.00 8.00
12 Rajon Rondo 3.00 8.00
13 David Lee 2.00 5.00
14 Zach Randolph 2.50 6.00
15 Ryan Anderson 2.50 6.00
16 John Wall 4.00 10.00
17 Kevin Garnett 5.00 12.00
18 Kevin Durant 4.00 10.00
19 Josh Smith 2.50 6.00
20 Ty Lawson 2.00 5.00
21 Steve Novak 2.00 5.00
22 Paul Pierce 3.00 8.00
23 Blake Griffin 3.00 8.00
24 Marc Gasol 3.00 8.00
25 Robin Lopez 2.00 5.00
26 Goran Dragic 2.50 6.00
27 Paul George 4.00 10.00
28 Russell Westbrook 8.00 20.00
29 Al Horford 2.50 6.00
30 Derrick Favors 2.50 6.00
31 Rasheed Wallace 3.00 8.00
32 Derrick Rose 4.00 10.00
33 Grant Hill 4.00 10.00
34 Chris Bosh 3.00 8.00
35 Tyson Chandler 2.50 6.00
36 Luis Scola 2.50 6.00
37 Anderson Varejao 2.00 5.00
38 Glen Davis 2.00 5.00
39 Nene 2.50 6.00
40 Rudy Gay 3.00 8.00
41 David West 2.50 6.00
42 Darren Collison 2.50 6.00
43 Eric Bledsoe 2.50 6.00
44 DeMarcus Cousins 6.00 15.00
45 Kyle Lowry 2.50 6.00
46 LaMarcus Aldridge 3.00 8.00
47 Elton Brand 3.00 8.00
48 Hedo Turkoglu 2.50 6.00
49 Andre Iguodala 2.50 6.00
50 Brandon Roy 3.00 8.00
51 Tim Duncan 5.00 12.00
52 Rodney Stuckey 2.50 6.00
53 Kobe Bryant 12.00 30.00
54 LeBron James 12.00 30.00
55 Al Jefferson 2.50 6.00
56 Tyreke Evans 2.00 5.00
57 Chris Kaman 2.50 6.00
58 J.J. Redick 3.00 8.00
60 Pau Gasol 3.00 8.00
61 Dirk Nowitzki 4.00 10.00
62 Damian Lillard 6.00 15.00
63 Steve Nash 8.00 20.00
64 O.J. Mayo 2.00 5.00
65 J.J. Hickson 2.00 5.00
66 Louis Williams 2.50 6.00
67 Chris Paul 4.00 10.00
68 Bradley Beal 5.00 12.00
69 Marcin Gortat 2.50 6.00
70 Thabo Sefolosha 2.00 5.00
71 Vince Carter 4.00 10.00
72 Anthony Davis 10.00 25.00
73 Emeka Okafor 2.50 6.00
74 Michael Kidd-Gilchrist 3.00 8.00
75 Kenneth Faried 3.00 8.00
76 DeMar DeRozan 3.00 8.00
77 Paul Millsap 3.00 8.00
78 Serge Ibaka 2.50 6.00
79 Eric Gordon 2.50 6.00
80 Jeff Teague 2.50 6.00

2012-13 Panini Brilliance Magic Numbers

COMPLETE SET (15) 10.00 25.00
1 Kobe Bryant 2.50 6.00
2 Blake Griffin .60 1.50
3 Anthony Davis 3.00 8.00
4 James Harden 1.00 2.50
5 Ty Lawson .40 1.00
6 Kyrie Irving 3.00 8.00
7 Kevin Garnett 1.00 2.50
8 John Wall .75 2.00
9 Tim Duncan 1.00 2.50
10 Damian Lillard 2.50 6.00
11 Kevin Love .60 1.50
12 LeBron James 2.50 6.00
13 Jeremy Lin .60 1.50
14 Stephen Curry 2.50 6.00
15 Brandon Knight .60 1.50

2012-13 Panini Brilliance Marks of Brilliance

PRINT RUNS B/WN 25-199 COPIES PER
NO PRICING ON MANY DUE TO SCARCITY
EXCHANGE DEADLINE 11/22/2014
1 Kareem Abdul-Jabbar/199 40.00 100.00
2 Keith Erickson/199 5.00 12.00
4 Kemba Walker/25 10.00 25.00
5 Kenny Anderson/199 4.00 10.00

6 Kevin Durant/199 50.00 120.00
7 Kevin Love/25 10.00 25.00
8 Kevin Martin/25 4.00 10.00
9 Kevin McHale/25 10.00 25.00
11 Klay Thompson/25 20.00 50.00
12 Kobe Bryant/199 75.00 150.00
14 Kwame Brown/199 3.00 8.00
15 Kyle Lowry/199 4.00 10.00
16 LaMarcus Aldridge/25 10.00 25.00
17 Lance Stephenson/199 5.00 12.00
18 Landry Fields/199 3.00 8.00
19 Larry Bird/199 50.00 100.00
20 Larry Johnson/199 4.00 10.00
21 Larry Sanders/199 3.00 8.00
22 Len Elmore/199 3.00 8.00
23 Truck Robinson/199 3.00 8.00
24 Luc Longley/199 4.00 10.00
25 Marcin Gortat/199 4.00 10.00
26 Marco Belinelli/199 EXCH 3.00 8.00
27 Marcus Camby/199 4.00 10.00
29 Leandro Barbosa/199 4.00 10.00
31 Mark Price/199 5.00 12.00
32 Marreese Speights/199 3.00 8.00
33 Maurice Cheeks/199 3.00 8.00
35 Michael Cooper/199 4.00 10.00
38 Muggsy Bogues/199 4.00 10.00
39 Nate Thurmond/25 10.00 25.00
40 Nick Anderson/199 5.00 12.00
41 Nick Collison/199 4.00 10.00
42 Nick Van Exel/25 15.00 40.00
43 Nick Young/25 4.00 10.00
44 Norris Cole/199 3.00 8.00
45 Peja Stojakovic/25 5.00 12.00
46 Rashard Lewis/199 EXCH 4.00 10.00
49 Reggie Theus/199 4.00 10.00
50 Rex Chapman/199 5.00 12.00
52 Rick Mahorn/199 3.00 8.00
53 Robert Horry/25 8.00 20.00
54 Robert Parish/25 5.00 12.00
55 Rod Strickland/199 3.00 8.00
56 Ronnie Brewer/199 4.00 10.00
58 Scottie Pippen/25 40.00 100.00
59 Sean Elliott/199 5.00 12.00
60 Shane Battier/25 4.00 10.00
61 Spencer Haywood/199 3.00 8.00
62 Stephen Curry/25 100.00 200.00
63 Steve Francis/199 4.00 10.00
67 Tiago Splitter/199 4.00 10.00
68 Timofey Mozgov/199 3.00 8.00
71 Tristan Thompson/25 5.00 12.00
72 Tyronn Lue/199 3.00 8.00
73 Udonis Haslem/199 3.00 8.00
74 Vernon Maxwell/199 3.00 8.00
75 Victor Claver/199 3.00 8.00
76 Vin Baker/199 3.00 8.00
77 Vince Carter/25 30.00 60.00
80 Wesley Johnson/25 4.00 10.00
81 Will Bynum/199 3.00 8.00
82 Will Perdue/199 3.00 8.00
83 Zach Randolph/25 4.00 10.00
84 Zaza Pachulia/199 3.00 8.00
85 Zydrunas Ilgauskas/199 4.00 10.00
88 Alan Anderson/199 3.00 8.00
90 Al-Farouq Aminu/199 4.00 10.00
91 Allan Houston/25 4.00 10.00
92 Alonzo Gee/199 3.00 8.00
93 Alonzo Mourning/25 20.00 50.00
94 Andray Blatche/199 3.00 8.00
95 Andre Drummond/25 20.00 50.00
98 Andrea Bargnani/25 4.00 10.00
99 Andrew Bogut/25 4.00 10.00
100 Anfernee Hardaway/25 50.00 120.00
101 Anthony Davis/199 60.00 150.00
102 Anthony Mason/199 6.00 15.00
103 Anthony Morrow/199 3.00 8.00
105 Antonio Davis/199 6.00 15.00
107 Artis Gilmore/25 4.00 10.00
108 Austin Daye/199 3.00 8.00
109 B.J. Armstrong/25 15.00 40.00
110 Bailey Howell/25 8.00 20.00
112 Beno Udrih/199 3.00 8.00
114 Bill Cartwright/25 4.00 10.00
115 Bill Walton/25 6.00 15.00
116 Blake Griffin/199 30.00 80.00
117 Bob Love/199 EXCH 5.00 12.00
119 Bobby Jackson/199 3.00 8.00
120 Bobby Jones/199 6.00 15.00
121 Brad Daugherty/199 4.00 10.00
122 Bradley Beal/25 12.00 30.00
124 Brandon Knight/25 5.00 12.00
127 Brook Lopez/25 4.00 10.00
128 Bruce Bowen/199 3.00 8.00
129 Buck Williams/199 3.00 8.00
130 Byron Mullens/199 3.00 8.00
131 Byron Scott/25 15.00 40.00
132 C.J. Watson/199 3.00 8.00
134 Carl Landry/25 3.00 8.00
137 Cazzie Russell/199 4.00 10.00
138 Cedric Ceballos/199 3.00 8.00
139 Cedric Maxwell/199 3.00 8.00
140 Charles Oakley/199 8.00 20.00
142 Charlie Ward/199 5.00 12.00
143 Chase Budinger/25 3.00 8.00
145 Chris Wilcox/199 3.00 8.00
146 Clyde Drexler/25 30.00 60.00
148 Corey Brewer/199 3.00 8.00
149 Courtney Lee/199 4.00 10.00
150 Dahntay Jones/199 3.00 8.00
151 Dan Issel/199 4.00 10.00
152 Dana Barros/199 3.00 8.00
154 Danny Granger/25 4.00 10.00
155 Danny Green/199 4.00 10.00
156 Danny Manning/25 4.00 10.00
157 Darrell Armstrong/199 3.00 8.00
158 Darryl Dawkins/199 3.00 8.00
159 Dave Cowens/25 8.00 20.00
160 David Robinson/49 15.00 40.00
162 David West/25 4.00 10.00
163 DeMarre Carroll/199 3.00 8.00
164 Dennis Rodman/25 40.00 80.00
165 Dennis Scott/199 3.00 8.00
166 Deron Williams/25 4.00 10.00
167 Derrick Favors/25 4.00 10.00
168 Derrick Williams/25 3.00 8.00
169 Detlef Schrempf/199 5.00 12.00
170 Devin Harris/25 3.00 8.00
171 Dikembe Mutombo/25 12.00 30.00
172 Dominique Wilkins/25 10.00 25.00
173 Dwyane Wade/49 30.00 80.00
174 Yao Ming/25 25.00 60.00
175 Earl Lloyd/25 12.00 30.00
176 Earl Monroe/25 5.00 12.00
177 Ed Davis/199 3.00 8.00
178 Ekpe Udoh/199 3.00 8.00
179 Elgin Baylor/25 10.00 25.00
180 Enes Kanter/25 4.00 10.00
182 Ersan Ilyasova/199 3.00 8.00
183 Fat Lever/199 4.00 10.00
184 J.J. Hickson/199 3.00 8.00
185 J.J. Redick/25 30.00 60.00
186 Jamaal Tinsley/199 3.00 8.00
187 Jamaal Wilkes/25 8.00 20.00
189 James Johnson/199 3.00 8.00
190 James Worthy/25 10.00 25.00
191 Jared Dudley/25 3.00 8.00
192 Jared Sullinger/25 4.00 10.00
193 Jason Kidd/25 20.00 50.00
195 Jason Smith/199 3.00 8.00
196 Jason Terry/25 8.00 20.00
197 Jason Thompson/199 3.00 8.00
199 Jayson Williams/199 3.00 8.00
200 Jeff Teague/199 4.00 10.00
201 Jeremy Evans/199 3.00 8.00
202 Jerome Williams/199 3.00 8.00
203 Jerry West/149 20.00 50.00
204 Jim Jackson/199 3.00 8.00
205 Joakim Noah/25 4.00 10.00
207 Johan Petro/199 3.00 8.00
208 John Havlicek/25 20.00 50.00
209 John Henson/25 5.00 12.00
211 John Stockton/25 25.00 60.00
212 Magic Johnson/199 30.00 80.00
213 Johnny Newman/199 6.00 15.00
214 Jonas Jerebko/199 3.00 8.00
215 Jonas Valanciunas/199 5.00 12.00
216 Jonathan Bender/199 3.00 8.00
217 Jordan Crawford/199 3.00 8.00
218 Josh Smith/25 4.00 10.00
219 Julius Erving/49 40.00 100.00
220 Gail Goodrich/25 4.00 10.00
221 Gary Payton/25 10.00 25.00
222 George Gervin/25 8.00 20.00
223 George Hill/25 4.00 10.00
227 Gordon Hayward/199 5.00 12.00
228 Grant Hill/49 20.00 50.00
229 Greg Monroe/25 4.00 10.00
230 Greg Ostertag/199 4.00 10.00
231 Greivis Vasquez/199 4.00 10.00
232 Hakeem Olajuwon/25 15.00 40.00
234 Harrison Barnes/25 12.00 30.00
236 Henry Bibby/199 3.00 8.00
237 Herb Williams/199 3.00 8.00
238 Iman Shumpert/199 5.00 12.00
239 Isaiah Rider/199 4.00 10.00
240 Isiah Thomas/25 8.00 20.00

2012-13 Panini Brilliance Scorers Inc.

COMPLETE SET (20) 12.00 30.00
1 Dwyane Wade 1.00 2.50
2 Brandon Jennings .40 1.00
3 Paul Pierce .60 1.50
4 LeBron James 2.50 6.00
5 Stephen Curry 2.50 6.00
6 Kobe Bryant 2.50 6.00
7 Kevin Durant 1.50 4.00
8 James Harden 1.00 2.50
9 Russell Westbrook 1.50 4.00
10 O.J. Mayo .40 1.00
11 Carmelo Anthony .75 2.00
12 Kemba Walker 1.25 3.00
13 Jamal Crawford .60 1.50
14 Eric Gordon .50 1.25
15 Monta Ellis .50 1.25
16 Chris Paul .75 2.00
17 Klay Thompson 2.50 6.00
18 J.R. Smith .50 1.25
19 Jrue Holiday .60 1.50
20 Damian Lillard 2.50 6.00

2012-13 Panini Brilliance Spellbound

ALL LETTERS EQUALLY PRICED
1 Russell Westbrook 1.50 4.00
2 Russell Westbrook 1.50 4.00
3 Russell Westbrook 1.50 4.00
4 Russell Westbrook 1.50 4.00
5 Russell Westbrook 1.50 4.00
6 Russell Westbrook 1.50 4.00
7 Russell Westbrook 1.50 4.00
8 Russell Westbrook 1.50 4.00
9 Russell Westbrook 1.50 4.00
10 Kobe Bryant 2.50 6.00
11 Kobe Bryant 2.50 6.00
12 Kobe Bryant 2.50 6.00
13 Kobe Bryant 2.50 6.00
14 Kobe Bryant 2.50 6.00
15 Kobe Bryant 2.50 6.00
16 Kevin Durant 1.50 4.00
17 Kevin Durant 1.50 4.00
18 Kevin Durant 1.50 4.00
19 Kevin Durant 1.50 4.00
20 Kevin Durant 1.50 4.00
21 Kevin Durant 1.50 4.00
22 Kevin Love .60 1.50
23 Kevin Love .60 1.50
24 Kevin Love .60 1.50
25 Kevin Love .60 1.50
26 Anthony Davis 3.00 8.00
27 Anthony Davis 3.00 8.00
28 Anthony Davis 3.00 8.00
29 Anthony Davis 3.00 8.00
30 Anthony Davis 3.00 8.00
31 Blake Griffin .60 1.50
32 Blake Griffin .60 1.50
33 Blake Griffin .60 1.50
34 Blake Griffin .60 1.50
35 Blake Griffin .60 1.50
36 Blake Griffin .60 1.50
37 Blake Griffin .60 1.50
38 LeBron James 2.50 6.00
39 LeBron James 2.50 6.00
40 LeBron James 2.50 6.00
41 LeBron James 2.50 6.00
42 LeBron James 2.50 6.00
43 Dwyane Wade 1.00 2.50
44 Dwyane Wade 1.00 2.50
45 Dwyane Wade 1.00 2.50
46 Dwyane Wade 1.00 2.50
47 Dwight Howard .50 1.25
48 Dwight Howard .50 1.25
49 Dwight Howard .50 1.25
50 Dwight Howard .50 1.25
51 Dwight Howard .50 1.25
52 Dwight Howard .50 1.25
53 Paul Pierce .60 1.50
54 Paul Pierce .60 1.50
55 Paul Pierce .60 1.50
56 Paul Pierce .60 1.50
57 Paul Pierce .60 1.50
58 Paul Pierce .60 1.50
59 Bradley Beal 1.00 2.50
60 Bradley Beal 1.00 2.50
61 Bradley Beal 1.00 2.50
62 Bradley Beal 1.00 2.50
63 Jeremy Lin .60 1.50
64 Jeremy Lin .60 1.50
65 Jeremy Lin .60 1.50
66 Kyrie Irving 3.00 8.00
67 Kyrie Irving 3.00 8.00
68 Kyrie Irving 3.00 8.00
69 Kyrie Irving 3.00 8.00
70 Kyrie Irving 3.00 8.00
71 Kyrie Irving 3.00 8.00
72 Carmelo Anthony .75 2.00
73 Carmelo Anthony .75 2.00
74 Carmelo Anthony .75 2.00
75 Carmelo Anthony .75 2.00
76 Carmelo Anthony .75 2.00
77 Carmelo Anthony .75 2.00
78 Carmelo Anthony .75 2.00
79 Kemba Walker 1.25 3.00
80 Kemba Walker 1.25 3.00
81 Kemba Walker 1.25 3.00
82 Kemba Walker 1.25 3.00
83 Kemba Walker 1.25 3.00
84 Kemba Walker 1.25 3.00
85 Serge Ibaka .50 1.25
86 Serge Ibaka .50 1.25
87 Serge Ibaka .50 1.25
88 Serge Ibaka .50 1.25
89 Serge Ibaka .50 1.25
90 Dion Waiters .60 1.50
91 Dion Waiters .60 1.50
92 Dion Waiters .60 1.50
93 Dion Waiters .60 1.50
94 Dion Waiters .60 1.50
95 Dion Waiters .60 1.50
96 Dion Waiters .60 1.50
97 Derrick Rose .75 2.00
98 Derrick Rose .75 2.00
99 Derrick Rose .75 2.00
100 Derrick Rose .75 2.00

2012-13 Panini Brilliance Springfield

COMPLETE SET (25) 20.00 50.00
1 Bill Russell 1.00 2.50
2 Kevin McHale .60 1.50
3 Larry Bird 1.50 4.00
4 Clyde Drexler .75 2.00
5 Alex English .50 1.25
6 Kareem Abdul-Jabbar 1.00 2.50
7 Hakeem Olajuwon .75 2.00
8 Magic Johnson 1.50 4.00
9 Pete Maravich 1.00 2.50
10 Patrick Ewing .75 2.00
11 Earl Monroe .60 1.50
12 Dominique Wilkins .75 2.00
13 Chris Mullin .60 1.50
14 John Stockton 1.00 2.50
15 David Thompson .50 1.25
16 Isiah Thomas .60 1.50
17 Wes Unseld .60 1.50
18 Bill Walton .60 1.50
19 James Worthy .75 2.00
20 Calvin Murphy .50 1.25
21 Julius Erving 1.00 2.50
22 Joe Dumars .60 1.50
23 David Robinson 1.00 2.50
24 Oscar Robertson .75 2.00
25 Drazen Petrovic .60 1.50

2012-13 Panini Brilliance Team Tomorrow

COMPLETE SET (20) 12.50 30.00
1 Kemba Walker 1.25 3.00
2 MarShon Brooks .50 1.25
3 Dion Waiters .60 1.50
4 Kyrie Irving 3.00 8.00
5 Kenneth Faried .60 1.50
6 Bradley Beal 1.00 2.50
7 Andre Drummond 1.00 2.50
8 Tobias Harris .60 1.50
9 Damian Lillard 2.50 6.00
10 Kawhi Leonard 3.00 8.00
11 Michael Kidd-Gilchrist .60 1.50
12 Tristan Thompson .60 1.50
13 Jared Sullinger .50 1.25
14 Alexey Shved .40 1.00
15 Andrew Nicholson .40 1.00
16 Meyers Leonard .50 1.25
17 Isaiah Thomas 1.00 2.50
18 Thomas Robinson .50 1.25
19 Anthony Davis 3.00 8.00
20 Nikola Vucevic .60 1.50

2010 Panini Century Sports Stamp Autographs

STATED PRINT RUN 5-100
NO PRICING ON QTY 25 OR LESS
12A Bill Walton/36 10.00 25.00
13A Bobby Wanzer/75 6.00 15.00
14A George Gervin/67 6.00 15.00
14B George Gervin/33 8.00 20.00
15A Kevin McHale/33 10.00 25.00
23A Al Cervi/65 6.00 15.00
23B Al Cervi/35 8.00 20.00
28A Elvin Hayes/30 10.00 25.00
29A Bailey Howell/50 10.00 25.00
30A Dan Issel/50 15.00 40.00
31A Clyde Lovellette/75 15.00 40.00
34A Arnie Risen/80 10.00 25.00
35A Dolph Schayes/75 8.00 20.00
36A David Thompson/75 10.00 25.00

2010 Panini Century Sports Stamp Materials

STATED PRINT RUN 1-250
NO PRICING ON QTY 25 OR LESS
2A O.J. Mayo/40 4.00 10.00
2B O.J. Mayo/40 29c 4.00 10.00
3A Derrick Rose/100 4c BK 8.00 20.00
3B Derrick Rose/250 29c 6.00 15.00
3C Derrick Rose/250 4c US Flag 6.00 15.00
4A Michael Beasley/250 4c 3.00 8.00
4B Michael Beasley/250 29c 3.00 8.00
11B Alex English/250 29c 3.00 8.00
17A Wes Unseld/125 4c 3.00 8.00
17B Wes Unseld/125 29c 3.00 8.00
27A Cliff Hagan/250 4c 3.00 8.00
27B Cliff Hagan/250 29c 3.00 8.00
28A Elvin Hayes/250 4c 3.00 8.00
28B Elvin Hayes/250 29c 3.00 8.00
29A Bailey Howell/150 4c 3.00 8.00
29B Bailey Howell/150 29c 3.00 8.00
30A Dan Issel/250 4c 3.00 8.00
30B Dan Issel/250 29c 3.00 8.00
32A Robert Parish/50 5.00 12.00
32B Robert Parish/50 29c 5.00 12.00

2010 Panini Century Sports Stamp Materials Autographs

STATED PRINT RUN 2-50
NO PRICING ON QTY 25 OR LESS
27B Cliff Hagan/40 15.00 40.00

2015-16 Panini Clear Vision

COMP.SET w/o SPs (81) 60.00 150.00
1 Victor Oladipo .50 1.25
2 Kevin Love .60 1.50
3 Wesley Matthews .40 1.00
4 Jabari Parker .75 2.00
5 Chris Paul .75 2.00
6 Kyle Lowry .50 1.25
7 Kobe Bryant 2.50 6.00
8 Nerlens Noel .50 1.25
9 Dwyane Wade 1.00 2.50
10 Andrew Wiggins 1.00 2.50
11 Marcin Gortat .50 1.25
12 Jimmy Butler .60 1.50
13 Marc Gasol .60 1.50
14 Giannis Antetokounmpo 1.25 3.00
15 DeAndre Jordan .60 1.50
16 DeMar DeRozan .60 1.50
17 Jordan Clarkson .60 1.50
18 Robert Covington .40 1.00
19 Paul Millsap .60 1.50
20 Ricky Rubio .60 1.50
21 Kawhi Leonard 1.00 2.50
22 Derrick Rose .75 2.00
23 Mike Conley .60 1.50
24 Greg Monroe .50 1.25
25 Paul Pierce .60 1.50
26 Isaiah Thomas .60 1.50
27 Julius Randle .60 1.50
28 Kevin Durant 1.50 4.00
29 Al Horford .50 1.25
30 Damian Lillard 1.25 3.00
31 Tony Parker .60 1.50
32 Pau Gasol .60 1.50
33 Zach Randolph .50 1.25
34 Stephen Curry 2.50 6.00
35 Brandon Knight .50 1.25
36 Marcus Smart .50 1.25
37 Nicolas Batum .50 1.25
38 Russell Westbrook 1.50 4.00
39 Jeff Teague .50 1.25
40 C.J. McCollum .60 1.50
41 LaMarcus Aldridge .60 1.50
42 Paul George .75 2.00
43 James Harden 1.00 2.50
44 Klay Thompson .75 2.00
45 Eric Bledsoe .50 1.25
46 Carmelo Anthony .75 2.00
47 Kemba Walker .60 1.50
48 Serge Ibaka .50 1.25
49 Tobias Harris .50 1.25
50 Kenneth Faried .50 1.25
51 Tim Duncan 1.00 2.50
52 Monta Ellis .50 1.25
53 Dwight Howard .50 1.25
54 Draymond Green .75 2.00
55 Rajon Rondo .60 1.50
56 Arron Afflalo .40 1.00
57 Jeremy Lin .60 1.50
58 Gordon Hayward .60 1.50
59 Nikola Vucevic .50 1.25
60 Danilo Gallinari .50 1.25
61 Deron Williams .50 1.25
62 Andre Drummond .60 1.50
63 Anthony Davis 1.25 3.00
64 Andre Iguodala .50 1.25
65 DeMarcus Cousins .60 1.50
66 Brook Lopez .50 1.25
67 Chris Bosh .60 1.50
68 Derrick Favors .50 1.25
69 John Wall .75 2.00
70 LeBron James 2.50 6.00
71 Dirk Nowitzki .75 2.00
72 Reggie Jackson .50 1.25
73 Eric Gordon .50 1.25
74 Blake Griffin .60 1.50
75 Rudy Gay .60 1.50
76 Thaddeus Young .40 1.00
77 Goran Dragic .50 1.25
78 Kevin Garnett 1.00 2.50
79 Bradley Beal .60 1.50
80 Kyrie Irving 1.25 3.00
81 Jrue Holiday .50 1.25
82A Karl-Anthony Towns RC 8.00 20.00
82B K.Towns Whte Jsy 10.00 25.00
83 Jonathon Simmons RC 1.50 4.00
84 Kelly Oubre Jr. RC 1.25 3.00
85 Jerian Grant RC 1.00 2.50
86 Myles Turner RC 1.50 4.00
87 Tyus Jones RC 1.50 4.00
88 Mario Hezonja RC 1.25 3.00
89A Raul Neto RC 1.00 2.50
89B Raul Neto 1.25 3.00
Purple jersey
90A Stanley Johnson RC 1.25 3.00
90B Johnson Wht jrsy 1.50 4.00
91 Montrezl Harrell RC 1.25 3.00
92 Trey Lyles RC 1.50 4.00
93 Joe Young RC 1.25 3.00
94 Terry Rozier RC 1.25 3.00
95 Justin Anderson RC 1.25 3.00
96A D'Angelo Russell RC 4.00 10.00
96B D.Russell Prpl Jsy 5.00 12.00
97A T.J. McConnell RC 1.25 3.00
97B T.J. McConnell 1.50 4.00
Blue jersey
98A Willie Cauley-Stein RC 1.50 4.00
98B W.Cauley-Stein Prpl Jsy 2.00 5.00
99 Nikola Jokic RC 2.00 5.00
100 Frank Kaminsky RC 1.50 4.00
101 Marcelo Huertas RC 1.25 3.00
102 Devin Booker RC 5.00 12.00
103 Boban Marjanovic RC 1.25 3.00
104 Rashad Vaughn RC 1.00 2.50
105 Bobby Portis RC 1.50 4.00
106A Jahlil Okafor RC 2.00 5.00
106B J.Okafor Whte Jsy 2.50 6.00
107A Nemanja Bjelica RC 1.25 3.00
107B Nemanja Bjelica 1.50 4.00
White jersey
108A Emmanuel Mudiay RC 1.50 4.00
108B E.Mudiay Blue Jsy 2.00 5.00
109 Larry Nance Jr. RC 1.25 3.00
110A Justise Winslow RC 1.50 4.00
110B Justise Winslow 2.00 5.00
Black jersey
111 R.J. Hunter RC 1.00 2.50
112 Cameron Payne RC 1.25 3.00
113 Richaun Holmes RC 1.25 3.00
114 Sam Dekker RC 1.25 3.00
115 Rondae Hollis-Jefferson RC 1.25 3.00
116A Kristaps Porzingis RC 4.00 10.00
116B K.Porzingis Whte Jsy 5.00 12.00
117A Kobe Bryant RR 5.00 12.00
117B K.Bryant Yllw jersey 6.00 15.00
118A Steve Nash RR 1.25 3.00
118B Steve Nash 1.50 4.00
Purple jersey
119A Anthony Davis RR 2.50 6.00
119B A.Davis Yllw jersey 3.00 8.00
120A Dwight Howard RR 1.00 2.50
120B Dwight Howard 1.25 3.00
Blue jersey
121A Dirk Nowitzki RR 1.50 4.00
121B D.Nowitzki Blue Jsy 2.00 5.00
122A Grant Hill RR 1.50 4.00
122B G.Hill Blue Jsy 2.00 5.00
123A Shaquille O'Neal RR 2.50 6.00
123B S.O'Neal Blk Jsy 3.00 8.00
124A Carmelo Anthony RR 1.50 4.00
124B C.Anthony Whte Jsy 2.00 5.00
125A Gary Payton RR 1.25 3.00
125B Gary Payton 1.50 4.00
Ball in left hand
126A Jason Kidd RR 1.25 3.00
126B Jason Kidd 1.50 4.00
White jersey
127A Kevin Durant RR 3.00 8.00
127B K.Durant Whte Jsy 4.00 10.00
128A Vince Carter RR 1.50 4.00
128B V.Carter Whte Jsy 2.00 5.00
129A Stephen Curry RR 5.00 12.00
129B S.Curry Whte Jsy 6.00 15.00
130A Tony Parker RR 1.25 3.00
130B Tony Parker 1.50 4.00
White jersey
131A Kevin Garnett RR 2.00 5.00
131B K.Garnett Blue Jsy 2.50 6.00
132A Allen Iverson RR 1.50 4.00
132B A.Iverson Red jersey 2.00 5.00
133A Paul Pierce RR 1.25 3.00
133B Paul Pierce 1.50 4.00
Green jersey
134A Chris Webber RR 1.25 3.00
134B Chris Webber 1.50 4.00
White jersey
135A Ray Allen RR 1.25 3.00
135B Ray Allen 1.50 4.00
Purple jersey
136A Chris Paul RR 1.50 4.00
136B C.Paul Blue Jsy 2.00 5.00
137A Kyrie Irving RR 2.50 6.00
137B K.Irving Whte Jsy 3.00 8.00
138A Dwyane Wade RR 2.00 5.00
138B D.Wade Blk Jsy 2.50 6.00
139A Tim Duncan RR 2.00 5.00
139B T.Duncan Whte Jsy 2.50 6.00
140A Chris Bosh RR 1.25 3.00
140B Chris Bosh 1.50 4.00
Red jersey
141A LeBron James RR 5.00 12.00
141B L.James Red jersey 6.00 15.00

2015-16 Panini Clear Vision Blue

*BLUE 1-81: 1.2X TO 3X BASIC
*BLUE 82-116: .5X TO 1.2X BASIC
*BLUE 82-116 VAR: .4X TO 1X BASIC
*BLUE RR: .6X TO 1.5X BASIC
*BLUE RR VAR: .5X TO 1.2X BASIC
RANDOM INSERTS IN PACKS
STATED PRINT RUN 149 SER.#'d SETS

2015-16 Panini Clear Vision Bronze

*BRNZ 1-81: 3X TO 8X BASIC
*BRNZ 82-116: 1.2X TO 3X BASIC
*BRNZ 82-116 VAR: 1X TO 2.5X BASIC
RANDOM INSERTS IN PACKS

2015-16 Panini Clear Vision Purple

*PRPL 1-81: 3X TO 8X BASIC
*PRPL 82-116: 1.2X TO 3X BASIC
*PRPL 82-116 VAR: 1X TO 2.5X BASIC
*PRPL RR: 1.5X TO 4X BASIC
*PRPL RR VAR: 1.2X TO 3X BASIC
RANDOM INSERTS IN PACKS
STATED PRINT RUN 25 SER.#'d SETS

2015-16 Panini Clear Vision Red

*RED 1-81: 1.5X TO 4X BASIC
*RED 82-116: .6X TO 1.5X BASIC
*RED 82-116 VAR: .5X TO 1.2X BASIC
*RED RR: .75X TO 2X BASIC
*RED RR VAR: .6X TO 1.5X BASIC
RANDOM INSERTS IN PACKS
STATED PRINT RUN 99 SER.#'d SETS

2015-16 Panini Clear Vision Clear Vision Signatures

RANDOM INSERTS IN PACKS
PRINT RUNS B/WN 94-119 COPIES PER
*GOLD/25: .5X TO 1.2X BASIC
1 Kobe Bryant/119 100.00 250.00
2 Carmelo Anthony/119 15.00 40.00
3 Chris Paul/119 30.00 80.00
4 Dwyane Wade/119 30.00 80.00
5 Kevin Durant/119 50.00 120.00
7 Anthony Davis/119 30.00 80.00
8 Kyrie Irving/118 30.00 80.00
9 Blake Griffin/119 20.00 50.00
10 Dirk Nowitzki/119 60.00 150.00
11 John Wall/119 15.00 40.00
12 Jabari Parker/119 10.00 25.00
13 Andrew Wiggins/119 25.00 60.00
14 Chris Bosh/118 8.00 20.00
15 Kevin Love/119 8.00 20.00
16 Tony Parker/119 10.00 25.00
17 Vince Carter/99 12.00 30.00
18 Marcus Smart/117 5.00 12.00
19 Julius Randle/102 10.00 25.00
21 Karl-Anthony Towns/115 75.00 200.00
22 D'Angelo Russell/94 20.00 50.00
23 Jahlil Okafor/119 12.00 30.00
24 Emmanuel Mudiay/116 6.00 15.00
25 Kristaps Porzingis/119 50.00 120.00
26 Mario Hezonja/119 5.00 12.00
27 Justise Winslow/119 12.00 30.00
28 Willie Cauley-Stein/99 8.00 20.00

2015-16 Panini Clear Vision Standouts

RANDOM INSERTS IN PACKS
*BLUE/149: .5X TO 1.2X BASIC
*RED/99: .6X TO 1.5X BASIC
*PURPLE/25: 2X TO 5X BASIC
1 LeBron James 3.00 8.00
2 Kevin Durant 2.00 5.00
3 Chris Paul 1.00 2.50
4 Kyrie Irving 1.50 4.00
5 Carmelo Anthony 1.00 2.50
6 Anthony Davis 1.50 4.00
7 Stephen Curry 3.00 8.00
8 Kobe Bryant 3.00 8.00
9 Tim Duncan 1.25 3.00
10 Kevin Garnett 1.25 3.00

2015-16 Panini Clear Vision Visionaries

RANDOM INSERTS IN PACKS
*BLUE/149: .5X TO 1.2X BASIC
*RED/99: .6X TO 1.5X BASIC
*PURPLE/25: 1.2X TO 3X BASIC
1 David Robinson 2.50 6.00
2 Steve Nash 1.50 4.00
3 John Stockton 2.50 6.00
4 Grant Hill 2.00 5.00
5 Allen Iverson 2.00 5.00
6 Clyde Drexler 2.00 5.00
7 Gary Payton 1.50 4.00
8 Hakeem Olajuwon 2.00 5.00
9 Karl Malone 2.00 5.00
10 Tracy McGrady 1.50 4.00
11 Dennis Rodman 3.00 8.00
12 Julius Erving 2.50 6.00
13 Scottie Pippen 3.00 8.00
14 Dominique Wilkins 2.00 5.00
15 Isiah Thomas 1.50 4.00
16 Larry Bird 4.00 10.00
17 Kareem Abdul-Jabbar 2.50 6.00
18 Moses Malone 1.50 4.00
19 Shawn Kemp 2.50 6.00
20 Patrick Ewing 2.00 5.00
21 Jason Kidd 1.50 4.00

2015-16 Panini Clear Vision Visionary Signatures

RANDOM INSERTS IN PACKS
PRINT RUNS B/WN 99-122 COPIES PER
1 Allen Iverson/122 60.00 150.00
2 Alonzo Mourning/99 20.00 50.00
3 Anfernee Hardaway/112 20.00 50.00
4 Clyde Drexler/108 20.00 50.00
5 David Robinson/101 20.00 50.00
6 Dennis Rodman/103 30.00 80.00
7 Dominique Wilkins/110 12.00 30.00
8 Gary Payton/99 30.00 80.00
9 Hakeem Olajuwon/99 20.00 50.00
10 Jason Kidd/99 25.00 60.00
11 Jerry West/112 25.00 60.00
12 Julius Erving/99 30.00 80.00
13 John Stockton/122 20.00 50.00
14 Karl Malone/99 20.00 50.00
16 Larry Bird/99 60.00 120.00
17 Magic Johnson/109 40.00 100.00
18 Oscar Robertson/112 25.00 60.00
19 Shaquille O'Neal/112 50.00 120.00
20 Tracy McGrady/99 40.00 100.00

2015-16 Panini Complete

1 Al Horford .15 .40
2 Jared Sullinger .12 .30
3 Al Jefferson .15 .40
4 Jimmy Butler .20 .50
5 Kevin Love .20 .50
6 Raymond Felton .15 .40
7 Wilson Chandler .15 .40
8 Andre Iguodala .15 .40
9 Clint Capela .15 .40
10 George Hill .15 .40
11 Josh Smith .15 .40
12 Tarik Black .12 .30
13 Chris Andersen .15 .40
14 Jabari Parker .25 .60
15 Nikola Pekovic .12 .30
16 Tyreke Evans .12 .30
17 Enes Kanter .12 .30
18 Nikola Vucevic .15 .40
19 Robert Covington .12 .30
20 Al-Farouq Aminu .15 .40
21 Caron Butler .15 .40
22 David West .20 .50
23 DeMarre Carroll .12 .30
24 Rudy Gobert .20 .50
25 Nene .15 .40
26 Kelly Olynyk .12 .30
27 Cody Zeller .12 .30
28 Joakim Noah .15 .40
29 Kyrie Irving .40 1.00
30 Wesley Matthews .12 .30
31 Andre Drummond .20 .50
32 Andrew Bogut .15 .40
33 Corey Brewer .12 .30
34 Monta Ellis .15 .40
35 Lance Stephenson .15 .40
36 Beno Udrih .12 .30
37 Chris Bosh .20 .50
38 Jerryd Bayless .15 .40
39 Ricky Rubio .20 .50
40 Arron Afflalo .12 .30
41 Kevin Durant .50 1.25
42 Shabazz Napier .12 .30
43 Tony Wroten .12 .30
44 Allen Crabbe .12 .30
45 Darren Collison .15 .40
46 Kawhi Leonard .30 .75
47 Jonas Valanciunas .15 .40
48 Trevor Booker .12 .30
49 Otto Porter .15 .40
50 Marcus Smart .15 .40
51 Jeremy Lamb .12 .30
52 Kirk Hinrich .15 .40
53 LeBron James .75 2.00
54 Zaza Pachulia .12 .30
55 Brandon Jennings .12 .30
56 Draymond Green .25 .60
57 Donatas Motiejunas .12 .30
58 Paul George .25 .60
59 Paul Pierce .20 .50
60 Courtney Lee .15 .40
61 Dwyane Wade .30 .75
62 John Henson .15 .40
63 Shabazz Muhammad .15 .40
64 Carmelo Anthony .25 .60
65 Mitch McGary .12 .30
66 Tobias Harris .15 .40
67 Alex Len .12 .30
68 C.J. McCollum .20 .50
69 DeMarcus Cousins .20 .50
70 Kyle Anderson .12 .30
71 Kyle Lowry .15 .40
72 Trey Burke .12 .30
73 Kyle Korver .15 .40
74 Andrea Bargnani .15 .40
75 Jeremy Lin .20 .50
76 Mike Dunleavy .12 .30
77 Matthew Dellavedova .15 .40
78 Danilo Gallinari .15 .40
79 Aron Baynes RC .25 .60
80 Festus Ezeli .12 .30
81 Dwight Howard .15 .40
82 Rodney Stuckey .15 .40
83 Wesley Johnson .15 .40
84 Jeff Green .15 .40
85 Gerald Green .15 .40
86 Johnny O'Bryant .12 .30
87 Zach LaVine .20 .50
88 Cleanthony Early .12 .30
89 Nick Collison .15 .40
90 Victor Oladipo .15 .40
91 Archie Goodwin .12 .30
92 Damian Lillard .40 1.00
93 Kosta Koufos .12 .30
94 LaMarcus Aldridge .20 .50
95 Patrick Patterson .12 .30
96 Alan Anderson .12 .30
97 Tim Hardaway Jr. .12 .30
98 Bojan Bogdanovic .12 .30
99 Kemba Walker .20 .50
100 Nikola Mirotic .15 .40
101 Mo Williams .15 .40
102 Gary Harris .15 .40
103 Ersan Ilyasova .12 .30
104 C.J. Watson .12 .30
105 Ish Smith .12 .30
106 Shayne Whittington RC .25 .60
107 Jordan Clarkson .20 .50
108 Jordan Adams .12 .30
109 Goran Dragic .15 .40
110 Khris Middleton .15 .40
111 Alexis Ajinca .12 .30
112 Derrick Williams .12 .30
113 Russell Westbrook .50 1.25
114 Furkan Aldemir RC .25 .60
115 Brandon Knight .15 .40
116 Ed Davis .12 .30
117 Marco Belinelli .12 .30
118 Manu Ginobili .20 .50
119 Terrence Ross .15 .40
120 Bradley Beal .20 .50
121 Paul Millsap .20 .50
122 Brook Lopez .15 .40
123 Michael Kidd-Gilchrist .15 .40
124 Pau Gasol .20 .50
125 Timofey Mozgov .12 .30
126 J.J. Hickson .12 .30
127 Jodie Meeks .15 .40
128 Harrison Barnes .15 .40
129 James Harden .30 .75
130 Austin Rivers .15 .40
131 Julius Randle .20 .50
132 Marc Gasol .20 .50
133 Hassan Whiteside .15 .40
134 Michael Carter-Williams .12 .30
135 Anthony Davis .40 1.00
136 Jose Calderon .12 .30
137 Serge Ibaka .15 .40
138 Hollis Thompson .12 .30
139 Eric Bledsoe .15 .40
140 Gerald Henderson .12 .30
141 Omri Casspi .12 .30
142 Matt Bonner .12 .30
143 Alec Burks .12 .30
144 DeJuan Blair .12 .30
145 Thabo Sefolosha .12 .30
146 Jarrett Jack .15 .40
147 Nicolas Batum .15 .40
148 Taj Gibson .15 .40
149 Tristan Thompson .15 .40
150 Jameer Nelson .12 .30
151 Kentavious Caldwell-Pope .15 .40
152 Klay Thompson .25 .60
153 Patrick Beverley .12 .30
154 Blake Griffin .20 .50
155 Kobe Bryant .75 2.00
156 Matt Barnes .12 .30
157 Luol Deng .15 .40
158 O.J. Mayo .12 .30
159 Eric Gordon .15 .40
160 Langston Galloway .12 .30
161 Steven Adams .15 .40
162 Isaiah Canaan .15 .40
163 Markieff Morris .12 .30
164 Mason Plumlee .15 .40
165 Quincy Acy .12 .30
166 Patty Mills .20 .50
167 Dante Exum .15 .40
168 Drew Gooden III .15 .40
169 Avery Bradley .15 .40
170 Joe Johnson .15 .40
171 Spencer Hawes .12 .30
172 Tony Snell .12 .30
173 Chandler Parsons .15 .40
174 Jusuf Nurkic .12 .30
175 Marcus Morris .12 .30
176 Leandro Barbosa .12 .30
177 Terrence Jones .15 .40
178 Chris Paul .25 .60
179 Lou Williams .15 .40
180 Mike Conley .20 .50
181 Mario Chalmers .15 .40
182 Adreian Payne .12 .30
183 Jrue Holiday .15 .40
184 Lou Amundson .12 .30
185 Aaron Gordon .15 .40
186 JaKarr Sampson .12 .30
187 Mirza Teletovic .12 .30
188 Maurice Harkless .12 .30
189 Rajon Rondo .20 .50
190 Tim Duncan .30 .75
191 Derrick Favors .15 .40
192 Gary Neal .15 .40
193 David Lee .12 .30
194 Markel Brown .12 .30
195 Tyler Hansbrough .15 .40
196 Anderson Varejao .12 .30
197 Deron Williams .15 .40
198 Kenneth Faried .15 .40
199 Reggie Jackson .15 .40
200 Marreese Speights .12 .30
201 Trevor Ariza .12 .30
202 Cole Aldrich .12 .30
203 Nick Young .15 .40
204 Tony Allen .12 .30
205 Tyler Johnson RC .30 .75
206 Andrew Wiggins .30 .75
207 Omer Asik .15 .40
208 Robin Lopez .12 .30
209 Andrew Nicholson .12 .30
210 Jerami Grant .12 .30
211 P.J. Tucker .12 .30
212 Meyers Leonard .12 .30
213 Rudy Gay .20 .50
214 Tony Parker .20 .50
215 Gordon Hayward .20 .50
216 Jared Dudley .12 .30
217 Evan Turner .15 .40
218 Shane Larkin .12 .30
219 Derrick Rose .25 .60
220 Iman Shumpert .12 .30
221 Devin Harris .12 .30
222 Nick Johnson .12 .30
223 Spencer Dinwiddie .12 .30
224 Shaun Livingston .12 .30
225 Ty Lawson .12 .30
226 DeAndre Jordan .20 .50
227 Robert Sacre .12 .30
228 Vince Carter .25 .60
229 Chris Copeland .12 .30
230 Gorgui Dieng .12 .30
231 Quincy Pondexter .12 .30
232 Anthony Morrow .12 .30
233 Elfrid Payton .15 .40
234 Nerlens Noel .15 .40
235 T.J. Warren .15 .40
236 Noah Vonleh .12 .30
237 Boris Diaw .15 .40
238 Bruno Caboclo .12 .30
239 Joe Ingles .12 .30
240 John Wall .25 .60
241 Isaiah Thomas .20 .50
242 Thaddeus Young .12 .30
243 Doug McDermott .15 .40
244 J.R. Smith .15 .40
245 Dirk Nowitzki .25 .60
246 Randy Foye .12 .30
247 Steve Blake .12 .30
248 Stephen Curry .75 2.00
249 C.J. Miles .15 .40
250 J.J. Redick .20 .50
251 Roy Hibbert .15 .40
252 Zach Randolph .15 .40
253 Giannis Antetokounmpo .40 1.00
254 Kevin Garnett .30 .75
255 Ryan Anderson .15 .40
256 D.J. Augustin .12 .30
257 Evan Fournier .15 .40
258 Nik Stauskas .12 .30
259 Tyson Chandler .15 .40
260 Ben McLemore .12 .30
261 Danny Green .15 .40
262 DeMar DeRozan .20 .50
263 Rodney Hood .15 .40
264 Marcin Gortat .15 .40
265 Jae Crowder .12 .30
266 Thomas Robinson .12 .30
267 E'Twaun Moore .12 .30
268 James Jones .12 .30
269 J.J. Barea .15 .40

270 Will Barton .12 .30
271 Jeff Teague .15 .40
272 Dennis Schroder .15 .40
273 Chase Budinger .12 .30
274 Jamal Crawford .20 .50
275 Ryan Kelly .12 .30
276 Amar'e Stoudemire .15 .40
277 Greg Monroe .15 .40
278 Kevin Martin .15 .40
279 Dante Cunningham .12 .30
280 Dion Waiters .15 .40
281 Lamar Patterson RC .25 .60
282 Justin Anderson RC .30 .75
283 Larry Nance Jr. RC .40 1.00
284 Jahlil Okafor RC .50 1.25
285 Terran Petteway RC .25 .60
286 Dwight Powell .25 .60
287 Jarell Martin RC .30 .75
288 Pierre Jackson RC .25 .60
289 Walter Tavares RC .25 .60
290 Emmanuel Mudiay RC .40 1.00
291 Josh Richardson RC .40 1.00
292 Richaun Holmes RC .30 .75
293 Jordan Mickey RC .25 .60
294 Darrun Hilliard RC .25 .60
295 Justise Winslow RC .40 1.00
296 Devin Booker RC 1.25 3.00
297 R.J. Hunter RC .25 .60
298 Stanley Johnson RC .30 .75
299 Rashad Vaughn RC .25 .60
300 Cliff Alexander RC .25 .60
301 Terry Rozier RC .30 .75
302 Kevon Looney RC .30 .75
303 Karl-Anthony Towns RC 2.00 5.00
304 Pat Connaughton RC .25 .60
305 Chris McCullough RC .25 .60
306 Sam Dekker RC .30 .75
307 Nemanja Bjelica RC .30 .75
308 Willie Cauley-Stein RC .40 1.00
309 Rondae Hollis-Jefferson RC .30 .75
310 Joe Young RC .30 .75
311 Tyus Jones RC .40 1.00
312 Jonathon Simmons RC .40 1.00
313 Ryan Boatright RC .30 .75
314 Myles Turner RC .40 1.00
315 Jerian Grant RC .25 .60
316 Delon Wright RC .30 .75
317 Aaron Harrison RC .30 .75
318 Rakeem Christmas RC .25 .60
319 Kristaps Porzingis RC 1.00 2.50
320 Norman Powell RC .30 .75
321 Frank Kaminsky RC .40 1.00
322 Branden Dawson RC .25 .60
323 Cameron Payne RC .30 .75
324 Trey Lyles RC .40 1.00
325 Bobby Portis RC .40 1.00
326 Anthony Brown RC .25 .60
327 Mario Hezonja RC .30 .75
328 Kelly Oubre Jr. RC .30 .75
329 Brandon Ashley RC .25 .60
330 D'Angelo Russell RC 1.00 2.50

2015-16 Panini Complete Gold
*GOLD: 5X TO 12X BASIC
*GOLD RC: 2.5X TO 6X BASIC RC
STATED ODDS 1:37 RETAIL

2015-16 Panini Complete Silver
*SILVER: 2.5X TO 6X BASIC
*SILVER RC: 1.2X TO 3X BASIC RC
RANDOM INSERTS IN PACKS

2015-16 Panini Complete Autographs
STATED ODDS 1:220 RETAIL
1 Kobe Bryant
2 Dwyane Wade 15.00 40.00
3 Carmelo Anthony
4 Chris Paul
5 Kevin Durant 40.00 100.00
6 Anthony Davis
7 Blake Griffin
8 Kyrie Irving 25.00 60.00
9 Pau Gasol
10 John Wall 15.00 40.00
11 Jabari Parker
12 James Harden 20.00 50.00
13 Andrew Wiggins
14 Karl-Anthony Towns
15 D'Angelo Russell 25.00 60.00
16 Jahlil Okafor
17 Emmanuel Mudiay 15.00 40.00
18 Kristaps Porzingis 75.00 150.00
19 Mario Hezonja
20 Justise Winslow 12.00 30.00
21 Willie Cauley-Stein 10.00 25.00
22 Stanley Johnson 12.00 30.00
23 Frank Kaminsky 10.00 25.00
24 Devin Booker 20.00 50.00
25 Myles Turner 10.00 25.00
26 Jerian Grant
27 Trey Lyles 12.00 30.00
28 Delon Wright 3.00 8.00
29 Rashad Vaughn 2.50 6.00
30 Cameron Payne 6.00 15.00

2015-16 Panini Complete Away
STATED ODDS 1:112 RETAIL
1 Carmelo Anthony 1.25 3.00
2 Greg Monroe .75 2.00
3 Gordon Hayward 1.00 2.50
4 Eric Bledsoe .75 2.00
5 Vince Carter 1.25 3.00
6 Al Horford .75 2.00
7 Jimmy Butler 1.00 2.50
8 Kemba Walker 1.00 2.50
9 Kyle Lowry .75 2.00
10 Dirk Nowitzki 1.25 3.00
11 Damian Lillard 2.00 5.00
12 Stephen Curry 4.00 10.00
13 Ty Lawson .60 1.50
14 Rajon Rondo 1.00 2.50
15 Kevin Love 1.00 2.50
16 John Wall 1.25 3.00
17 Pau Gasol 1.00 2.50
18 Elfrid Payton .75 2.00
19 DeMar DeRozan 1.00 2.50
20 Tim Duncan 1.50 4.00
21 LaMarcus Aldridge 1.00 2.50
22 Klay Thompson 1.25 3.00
23 Kenneth Faried .75 2.00
24 DeMarcus Cousins 1.00 2.50
25 Kyrie Irving 2.00 5.00
26 Bradley Beal 1.00 2.50
27 Giannis Antetokounmpo 2.00 5.00
28 Victor Oladipo .75 2.00
29 Marcus Smart .75 2.00
30 Tony Parker 1.00 2.50
31 Russell Westbrook 2.50 6.00
32 Blake Griffin 1.00 2.50
33 Andrew Wiggins 1.50 4.00
34 Kobe Bryant 4.00 10.00
35 LeBron James 10.00 25.00
36 Dwyane Wade 1.50 4.00
37 Paul George 1.25 3.00
38 James Harden 1.50 4.00
39 Manu Ginobili 1.00 2.50
40 Anthony Davis 2.00 5.00
41 Kevin Durant 2.50 6.00
42 Chris Paul 1.25 3.00
43 Zach LaVine 1.00 2.50
44 Jeff Teague .75 2.00
45 Derrick Rose 1.25 3.00
46 Chris Bosh 1.00 2.50
47 Andre Drummond 1.00 2.50
48 Dwight Howard .75 2.00
49 Nerlens Noel .75 2.00
50 Marc Gasol 1.00 2.50

2015-16 Panini Complete Court Vision
STATED ODDS 1:40 RETAIL
1 Marcus Smart .50 1.25
2 Emmanuel Mudiay .60 1.50
3 Dante Exum .50 1.25
4 John Wall .75 2.00
5 Kyrie Irving 1.25 3.00
6 Mike Conley .60 1.50
7 Brandon Jennings .40 1.00
8 Chris Paul .75 2.00
9 Kyle Lowry .50 1.25
10 Rajon Rondo .60 1.50
11 Damian Lillard 1.25 3.00
12 Jerian Grant .40 1.00
13 Zach LaVine .60 1.50
14 Kemba Walker .60 1.50
15 Derrick Rose .75 2.00
16 Tony Parker .60 1.50
17 Stephen Curry 2.50 6.00
18 Eric Bledsoe .50 1.25
19 Goran Dragic .50 1.25
20 D'Angelo Russell 1.50 4.00
21 Russell Westbrook 1.50 4.00
22 Jeff Teague .50 1.25
23 Ty Lawson .40 1.00
24 Elfrid Payton .50 1.25
25 Michael Carter-Williams .40 1.00

2015-16 Panini Complete Craftsmen
STATED ODDS 1:562 RETAIL
1 Tony Allen 2.00 5.00
2 Stephen Curry 12.00 30.00
3 LeBron James 12.00 30.00
4 Chris Paul 4.00 10.00
5 Zach LaVine 3.00 8.00
6 DeAndre Jordan 3.00 8.00
7 Kyrie Irving 6.00 15.00
8 DeMarcus Cousins 3.00 8.00
9 Anthony Davis 6.00 15.00
10 Marc Gasol 3.00 8.00

2015-16 Panini Complete Home
STATED ODDS 1:21 RETAIL
1 Carmelo Anthony 1.25 3.00
2 Greg Monroe .75 2.00
3 Gordon Hayward 1.00 2.50
4 Eric Bledsoe .75 2.00
5 Kevin Garnett 1.50 4.00
6 Al Horford .75 2.00
7 Jimmy Butler 1.00 2.50
8 Kemba Walker 1.00 2.50
9 Kyle Lowry .75 2.00
10 Dirk Nowitzki 1.25 3.00
11 Damian Lillard 2.00 5.00
12 Stephen Curry 4.00 10.00
13 Ty Lawson .60 1.50
14 Rajon Rondo 1.00 2.50
15 Kevin Love 1.00 2.50
16 John Wall 1.25 3.00
17 Pau Gasol 1.00 2.50
18 Elfrid Payton .75 2.00
19 DeMar DeRozan 1.00 2.50
20 Tim Duncan 1.50 4.00
21 LaMarcus Aldridge 1.00 2.50
22 Klay Thompson 1.25 3.00
23 Kenneth Faried .75 2.00
24 DeMarcus Cousins 1.00 2.50
25 Kyrie Irving 2.00 5.00
26 Bradley Beal 1.00 2.50
27 Giannis Antetokounmpo 2.00 5.00
28 Victor Oladipo .75 2.00
29 Marcus Smart .75 2.00
30 Tony Parker 1.00 2.50
31 Russell Westbrook 2.50 6.00
32 Blake Griffin 1.00 2.50
33 Andrew Wiggins 1.50 4.00
34 Kobe Bryant 4.00 10.00
35 LeBron James 10.00 25.00
36 Dwyane Wade 1.50 4.00
37 Paul George 1.25 3.00
38 James Harden 1.50 4.00
39 Deron Williams .75 2.00
40 Anthony Davis 2.00 5.00
41 Kevin Durant 2.50 6.00
42 Chris Paul 1.25 3.00
43 Zach LaVine 1.00 2.50
44 Jeff Teague .75 2.00
45 Derrick Rose 1.25 3.00
46 Chris Bosh 1.00 2.50
47 Andre Drummond 1.00 2.50
48 Dwight Howard .75 2.00
49 Nerlens Noel .75 2.00
50 Marc Gasol 1.00 2.50

2015-16 Panini Complete NBA Cares
STATED ODDS 1:40 RETAIL
1 Bob Lanier .50 1.25
2 Dikembe Mutombo .60 1.50
3 Felipe Lopez .40 1.00
5 Tim Duncan 1.00 2.50
6 Kevin Durant 1.50 4.00
7 Russell Westbrook 1.50 4.00
8 Chris Paul .75 2.00
9 Marc Gasol .60 1.50
10 Draymond Green .75 2.00
11 Stephen Curry 2.50 6.00
12 Ryan Anderson .50 1.25
13 LeBron James 2.50 6.00
14 Dwyane Wade 1.00 2.50
15 Pau Gasol .60 1.50
16 Dwight Howard .50 1.25
17 Anthony Davis 1.25 3.00
18 Zach Randolph .50 1.25
19 Damian Lillard 1.25 3.00
20 Kenneth Faried .50 1.25
21 Kyle Korver .50 1.25
22 James Harden 1.00 2.50
23 Michael Carter-Williams .40 1.00
24 Jeremy Lin .60 1.50
25 Klay Thompson .75 2.00

2015-16 Panini Complete Prime Numbers
STATED ODDS 1:563 RETAIL
1 Andre Drummond 3.00 8.00
2 Russell Westbrook 8.00 20.00
3 Kawhi Leonard 5.00 12.00
4 James Harden 5.00 12.00
5 Stephen Curry 12.00 30.00
6 Chris Paul 4.00 10.00
7 Anthony Davis 6.00 15.00
8 John Wall 4.00 10.00
9 Rudy Gobert 3.00 8.00
10 DeAndre Jordan 3.00 8.00

2016-17 Panini Complete
1 Joel Embiid .30 .75
2 Jerryd Bayless .15 .40
3 Robert Covington .12 .30
4 Ben Simmons RC 1.50 4.00
5 Dario Saric RC .75 2.00
6 Jahlil Okafor .15 .40
7 Jerami Grant .12 .30
8 Nerlens Noel .15 .40
9 Richaun Holmes .12 .30
10 Timothe Luwawu-Cabarrot RC .50 1.25
11 Gerald Henderson .12 .30
12 T.J. McConnell .12 .30
13 Anthony Barber .15 .40
14 Giannis Antetokounmpo .40 1.00
15 Malcolm Brogdon RC .60 1.50
16 Michael Carter-Williams .12 .30
17 Matthew Dellavedova .15 .40
18 Tyler Ennis .12 .30
19 John Henson .15 .40
20 Thon Maker RC .75 2.00
21 Khris Middleton .15 .40
22 Greg Monroe .15 .40
23 Jabari Parker .25 .60
24 Miles Plumlee .12 .30
25 Rashad Vaughn .12 .30
26 Mirza Teletovic .12 .30
27 Jimmy Butler .20 .50
28 Isaiah Canaan .15 .40
29 Cristiano Felicio .12 .30
30 Taj Gibson .15 .40
31 Jerian Grant .12 .30
32 Robin Lopez .12 .30
33 Doug McDermott .15 .40
34 Nikola Mirotic .15 .40
35 Bobby Portis .12 .30
36 Rajon Rondo .20 .50
37 Denzel Valentine RC .30 .75
38 Dwyane Wade .30 .75
39 Tony Snell .12 .30
40 Spencer Dinwiddie .12 .30
41 Chris Andersen .15 .40
42 Mike Dunleavy .12 .30
43 Kay Felder RC .25 .60
44 Channing Frye .15 .40
45 Kyrie Irving .40 1.00
46 LeBron James .75 2.00
47 Richard Jefferson .15 .40
48 Kevin Love .20 .50
49 Iman Shumpert .12 .30
50 Tristan Thompson .15 .40
51 J.R. Smith .15 .40
52 James Jones .12 .30
53 Jordan McRae .12 .30
54 Ben Bentil RC .25 .60
55 Avery Bradley .15 .40
56 Jaylen Brown RC 1.00 2.50
57 Jae Crowder .15 .40
58 Gerald Green .15 .40
59 Al Horford .15 .40
60 Demetrius Jackson RC .25 .60
61 R.J. Hunter .12 .30
62 Jordan Mickey .12 .30
63 Kelly Olynyk RC .25 .60
64 Terry Rozier .15 .40
65 Marcus Smart .15 .40
66 Isaiah Thomas .20 .50
67 Brandon Bass .12 .30
68 Jamal Crawford .20 .50
69 Raymond Felton .15 .40
70 Blake Griffin .20 .50
71 Brice Johnson RC .25 .60
72 Wesley Johnson .15 .40
73 DeAndre Jordan .20 .50
74 Chris Paul .25 .60
75 J.J. Redick .20 .50
76 Paul Pierce .20 .50
77 Austin Rivers .15 .40
78 Marreese Speights .12 .30
79 Diamond Stone RC .25 .60
80 Jordan Adams .12 .30
81 Tony Allen .12 .30
82 Wade Baldwin IV RC .25 .60
83 Vince Carter .25 .60
84 Mike Conley .15 .40
85 Deyonta Davis RC .25 .60
86 James Ennis .12 .30
87 Marc Gasol .20 .50
88 Jarell Martin .12 .30
89 Chandler Parsons .15 .40
90 Zach Randolph .15 .40
91 Tony Wroten .12 .30
92 Brandan Wright .12 .30
93 Kent Bazemore .15 .40
94 DeAndre' Bembry RC .25 .60
95 Tim Hardaway Jr. .12 .30
96 Dwight Howard .15 .40
97 Kris Humphries .12 .30
98 Jarrett Jack .15 .40
99 Kyle Korver .15 .40
100 Paul Millsap .20 .50
101 Taurean Prince RC .40 1.00
102 Dennis Schroder .15 .40
103 Thabo Sefolosha .12 .30
104 Walter Tavares .12 .30
105 Mike Scott .12 .30
106 Luke Babbitt .12 .30
107 Chris Bosh .20 .50
108 Goran Dragic .15 .40
109 Wayne Ellington .12 .30
110 Udonis Haslem .12 .30
111 James Johnson .12 .30
112 Tyler Johnson .12 .30
113 Josh Richardson .12 .30
114 Dion Waiters .15 .40
115 Hassan Whiteside .15 .40
116 Derrick Williams .12 .30
117 Justise Winslow .15 .40
118 Josh McRoberts .12 .30
119 Nicolas Batum .15 .40
120 Marco Belinelli .12 .30
121 Aaron Harrison .12 .30
122 Spencer Hawes .12 .30
123 Roy Hibbert .15 .40
124 Frank Kaminsky .15 .40
125 Michael Kidd-Gilchrist .15 .40
126 Jeremy Lamb .12 .30
127 Kemba Walker .20 .50
128 Marvin Williams .15 .40
129 Cody Zeller .12 .30
130 Brian Roberts .12 .30
131 Ramon Sessions .15 .40
132 Joel Bolomboy RC .25 .60
133 Alec Burks .12 .30
134 Boris Diaw .15 .40
135 Dante Exum .15 .40
136 Derrick Favors .15 .40
137 Rudy Gobert .20 .50
138 Gordon Hayward .20 .50
139 George Hill .15 .40
140 Rodney Hood .15 .40
141 Trey Lyles .15 .40
142 Joe Johnson .15 .40
143 Marcus Paige RC .25 .60
144 Jeff Withey .12 .30
145 Raul Neto .12 .30
146 Arron Afflalo .12 .30
147 Matt Barnes .12 .30
148 Omri Casspi .12 .30
149 Willie Cauley-Stein .15 .40
150 Darren Collison .15 .40
151 DeMarcus Cousins .20 .50
152 Rudy Gay .20 .50
153 Skal Labissiere RC .40 1.00
154 Ben McLemore .12 .30
155 Georgios Papagiannis RC .25 .60
156 Malachi Richardson RC .30 .75
157 Isaiah Cousins RC .25 .60
158 Carmelo Anthony .25 .60
159 Ron Baker RC .30 .75
160 Brandon Jennings .12 .30
161 Marshall Plumlee RC .25 .60
162 Courtney Lee .15 .40
163 Joakim Noah .15 .40
164 Kyle O'Quinn .12 .30
165 Kristaps Porzingis .40 1.00
166 Derrick Rose .25 .60
167 Lance Thomas .12 .30
168 Sasha Vujacic .12 .30
169 Justin Holiday RC .25 .60
170 Anthony Brown .12 .30
171 Jose Calderon .12 .30
172 Jordan Clarkson .15 .40
173 Luol Deng .15 .40
174 Marcelo Huertas .12 .30
175 Brandon Ingram RC 1.50 4.00
176 Timofey Mozgov .12 .30
177 Larry Nance Jr. .15 .40
178 Julius Randle .20 .50
179 D'Angelo Russell .25 .60
180 Lou Williams .15 .40
181 Ivica Zubac RC .40 1.00
182 D.J. Augustin .12 .30
183 Bismack Biyombo .12 .30
184 Evan Fournier .15 .40
185 Aaron Gordon .15 .40
186 Jeff Green .15 .40
187 Mario Hezonja .12 .30
188 Serge Ibaka .15 .40
189 C.J. Wilcox .12 .30
190 Jodie Meeks .15 .40
191 Elfrid Payton .15 .40
192 Nikola Vucevic .15 .40
193 C.J. Watson .12 .30
194 Stephen Zimmerman RC .25 .60
195 Dirk Nowitzki .25 .60
196 Harrison Barnes .15 .40
197 Andrew Bogut .15 .40
198 Deron Williams .15 .40
199 Wesley Matthews .12 .30
200 J.J. Barea .15 .40
201 Justin Anderson .15 .40
202 Seth Curry .20 .50
203 Salah Mejri .12 .30
204 Dwight Powell .12 .30
205 A.J. Hammons RC .25 .60
206 Devin Harris .12 .30
207 Quincy Acy .12 .30
208 Anthony Bennett .12 .30
209 Bojan Bogdanovic .12 .30
210 Trevor Booker .12 .30
211 Randy Foye .12 .30
212 Rondae Hollis-Jefferson .12 .30
213 Sean Kilpatrick RC .25 .60
214 Caris LeVert RC .30 .75
215 Jeremy Lin .20 .50
216 Brook Lopez .15 .40
217 Chris McCullough .12 .30
218 Isaiah Whitehead RC .25 .60
219 Luis Scola .15 .40
220 Greivis Vasquez .15 .40
221 Darrell Arthur .12 .30
222 Will Barton .12 .30
223 Malik Beasley RC .25 .60
224 Wilson Chandler .15 .40
225 Kenneth Faried .15 .40
226 Danilo Gallinari .15 .40
227 Gary Harris .15 .40
228 Juan Hernangomez RC .30 .75
229 Nikola Jokic .20 .50
230 Emmanuel Mudiay .15 .40
231 Jamal Murray RC .75 2.00
232 JaKarr Sampson .12 .30
233 Jusuf Nurkic .12 .30
234 Jameer Nelson .12 .30
235 Lavoy Allen .12 .30
236 Aaron Brooks .12 .30
237 Monta Ellis .15 .40
238 Paul George .25 .60
239 Al Jefferson .15 .40
240 C.J. Miles .15 .40
241 Georges Niang RC .25 .60
242 Glenn Robinson III .15 .40
243 Rodney Stuckey .12 .30
244 Jeff Teague .15 .40
245 Myles Turner .15 .40
246 Joe Young .12 .30
247 Thaddeus Young .12 .30
248 Ty Lawson .12 .30
249 Alexis Ajinca .12 .30
250 Omer Asik .15 .40
251 Dante Cunningham .12 .30
252 Anthony Davis .40 1.00
253 Cheick Diallo RC .25 .60
254 Tyreke Evans .12 .30
255 Langston Galloway .12 .30
256 Alonzo Gee .12 .30
257 Lance Stephenson .15 .40
258 Buddy Hield RC .60 1.50
259 Solomon Hill .12 .30
260 Jrue Holiday .15 .40
261 Terrence Jones .15 .40
262 E'Twaun Moore .12 .30
263 Ray McCallum .12 .30
264 Aron Baynes .12 .30
265 Lorenzo Brown .12 .30
266 Reggie Bullock .12 .30
267 Kentavious Caldwell-Pope .15 .40
268 Andre Drummond .20 .50
269 Henry Ellenson RC .30 .75
270 Michael Gbinije RC .25 .60
271 Tobias Harris .15 .40
272 Reggie Jackson .15 .40
273 Stanley Johnson .12 .30
274 Boban Marjanovic .12 .30
275 Marcus Morris .12 .30
276 Ish Smith .12 .30
277 Bruno Caboclo .12 .30
278 DeMarre Carroll .12 .30
279 DeMar DeRozan .20 .50
280 Cory Joseph .12 .30
281 Kyle Lowry .15 .40
282 Patrick Patterson .12 .30
283 Jakob Poeltl RC .30 .75
284 Norman Powell .12 .30
285 Terrence Ross .15 .40
286 Pascal Siakam RC .25 .60
287 Jared Sullinger .12 .30
288 Jonas Valanciunas .15 .40
289 Delon Wright .12 .30
290 Ryan Anderson .15 .40
291 Trevor Ariza .12 .30
292 Michael Beasley .12 .30
293 Patrick Beverley .12 .30
294 Corey Brewer .12 .30
295 Clint Capela .12 .30
296 Sam Dekker .15 .40
297 Eric Gordon .15 .40
298 James Harden .30 .75
299 Chinanu Onuaku .12 .30
300 Nene .15 .40
301 Montrezl Harrell .12 .30
302 Pablo Prigioni .12 .30
303 LaMarcus Aldridge .20 .50
304 Kyle Anderson .12 .30
305 Pau Gasol .20 .50
306 Manu Ginobili .20 .50
307 Danny Green .15 .40
308 Livio Jean-Charles .12 .30
309 David Lee .12 .30
310 Kawhi Leonard .30 .75
311 Kevin Martin .15 .40
312 Patty Mills .20 .50
313 Dejounte Murray RC .50 1.25
314 Tony Parker .20 .50
315 Jonathon Simmons .20 .50
316 Dewayne Dedmon .12 .30
317 Leandro Barbosa .12 .30
318 Dragan Bender RC .30 .75
319 Eric Bledsoe .15 .40
320 Devin Booker .30 .75
321 Tyson Chandler .15 .40
322 Marquese Chriss RC .60 1.50
323 Jared Dudley .12 .30
324 Archie Goodwin .12 .30
325 Brandon Knight .15 .40
326 Alex Len .12 .30
327 P.J. Tucker .12 .30
328 Tyler Ulis RC .75 2.00
329 T.J. Warren .15 .40
330 Steven Adams .15 .40
331 Nick Collison .15 .40
332 Daniel Hamilton RC .25 .60
333 Josh Huestis .12 .30
334 Ersan Ilyasova .12 .30
335 Enes Kanter .12 .30
336 Anthony Morrow .12 .30
337 Mitch McGary .12 .30
338 Victor Oladipo .15 .40
339 Cameron Payne .12 .30
340 Andre Roberson .12 .30
341 Domantas Sabonis RC .40 1.00
342 Russell Westbrook .50 1.25
343 Kyle Singler .12 .30
344 Cole Aldrich .12 .30
345 Nemanja Bjelica .15 .40
346 Gorgui Dieng .12 .30
347 Kris Dunn RC .75 2.00
348 Damjan Rudez .12 .30
349 Jordan Hill .12 .30
350 Tyus Jones .12 .30
351 Zach LaVine .20 .50
352 Andrew Wiggins .30 .75
353 Karl-Anthony Towns .50 1.25
354 Ricky Rubio .20 .50
355 Brandon Rush .12 .30
356 Shabazz Muhammad .15 .40
357 Adreian Payne .12 .30
358 Nikola Pekovic .12 .30
359 Al-Farouq Aminu .15 .40
360 Pat Connaughton .12 .30
361 Allen Crabbe .12 .30
362 Ed Davis .12 .30
363 Festus Ezeli .12 .30
364 Maurice Harkless .12 .30
365 Jake Layman RC .30 .75
366 Meyers Leonard .12 .30
367 Damian Lillard .40 1.00
368 C.J. McCollum .15 .40
369 Evan Turner .12 .30
370 Noah Vonleh .12 .30
371 Mason Plumlee .15 .40
372 Shabazz Napier .12 .30
373 Ian Clark .12 .30
374 Stephen Curry .75 2.00
375 Kevin Durant .50 1.25
376 Draymond Green .25 .60
377 Andre Iguodala .15 .40
378 Damian Jones RC .25 .60
379 Shaun Livingston .12 .30
380 Kevon Looney .15 .40
381 Patrick McCaw RC .50 1.25
382 James Michael McAdoo .12 .30
383 Zaza Pachulia .12 .30
384 Klay Thompson .25 .60
385 Anderson Varejao .12 .30
386 David West .15 .40
387 Bradley Beal .20 .50
388 Trey Burke .12 .30
389 Marcin Gortat .15 .40
390 Danuel House .12 .30
391 Ian Mahinmi .12 .30
392 Sheldon McClellan RC .25 .60
393 Markieff Morris .12 .30
394 Andrew Nicholson .12 .30
395 Kelly Oubre Jr. .12 .30
396 Otto Porter .15 .40
397 Jason Smith .12 .30
398 John Wall .25 .60
399 Marcus Thornton .12 .30
400 Tomas Satoransky RC .25 .60

2016-17 Panini Complete Gold
*GOLD: 5X TO 12X BASIC
*GOLD RC: 2.5X TO 6X BASIC RC
RANDOM INSERTS IN PACKS

2016-17 Panini Complete No Back
*NO BACK: 4X TO 10X BASIC
*NO BACK RC: 2X TO 5X BASIC RC
RANDOM INSERTS IN PACKS

2016-17 Panini Complete Silver
*SILVER: 2X TO 5X BASIC
*SILVER RC: 1X TO 2.5X BASIC RC
RANDOM INSERTS IN PACKS

2016-17 Panini Complete Autographs
RANDOM INSERTS IN PACKS
1 Brandon Ingram 40.00 100.00
2 Jaylen Brown 20.00 50.00
3 Kris Dunn
4 Buddy Hield 6.00 15.00
5 Jamal Murray 15.00 40.00
6 Thon Maker 10.00 25.00
7 Marquese Chriss 8.00 20.00
8 Taurean Prince 4.00 10.00
9 Denzel Valentine 5.00 12.00
10 Malachi Richardson 6.00 15.00
11 Dejounte Murray
12 Jakob Poeltl
13 Dragan Bender 3.00 8.00
14 Caris LeVert
15 Henry Ellenson
16 Dwyane Wade 25.00 60.00
17 Kevin Durant
18 Chris Paul
19 Kyrie Irving 20.00 50.00
20 Anthony Davis 15.00 40.00
21 DeMar DeRozan
22 Kevin Love 10.00 25.00
23 Isaiah Thomas
24 Blake Griffin
25 Dennis Schroder
26 Karl-Anthony Towns 20.00 50.00
27 Andrew Wiggins 15.00 40.00
28 Kristaps Porzingis 20.00 50.00
29 Devin Booker
30 Dirk Nowitzki 15.00 40.00

2016-17 Panini Complete Away
RANDOM INSERTS IN PACKS

2016-17 Panini Complete Complete Players
RANDOM INSERTS IN PACKS
1 Anthony Davis 1.25 3.00
2 LeBron James 2.50 6.00
3 Stephen Curry 2.50 6.00
4 James Harden 1.00 2.50
5 Kevin Durant 1.50 4.00
6 Chris Paul .75 2.00
7 Dwyane Wade 1.00 2.50
8 Carmelo Anthony .75 2.00
9 Kyrie Irving 1.25 3.00
10 Damian Lillard 1.25 3.00
11 Russell Westbrook 1.50 4.00
12 Andre Drummond .60 1.50
13 Dirk Nowitzki .75 2.00
14 DeMar DeRozan .60 1.50
15 Kawhi Leonard 1.00 2.50

2016-17 Panini Complete First Steps
RANDOM INSERTS IN PACKS
1 Juan Hernangomez .50 1.25
2 Denzel Valentine .50 1.25
3 Georgios Papagiannis .40 1.00
4 Taurean Prince .60 1.50
5 Domantas Sabonis .60 1.50
6 Thon Maker 1.25 3.00
7 Jakob Poeltl .50 1.25
8 Marquese Chriss 1.00 2.50
9 Jamal Murray 1.25 3.00
10 Buddy Hield 1.00 2.50
11 Kris Dunn 1.25 3.00
12 Dragan Bender .50 1.25
13 Jaylen Brown 1.50 4.00
14 Brandon Ingram 2.50 6.00
15 Ben Simmons 2.50 6.00

2016-17 Panini Complete Home
RANDOM INSERTS IN PACKS
*AWAY: .75X TO 2X BASIC
1 John Wall 1.25 3.00
2 DeAndre Jordan 1.00 2.50
3 Jimmy Butler 1.00 2.50
4 Dwight Howard .75 2.00
5 Klay Thompson 1.25 3.00
6 LaMarcus Aldridge 1.00 2.50
7 Dirk Nowitzki 1.25 3.00
8 Chris Bosh 1.00 2.50
9 Andrew Wiggins 1.50 4.00
10 Stephen Curry 4.00 10.00
11 Mike Conley .75 2.00
12 DeMarcus Cousins 1.00 2.50
13 LeBron James 4.00 10.00
14 Russell Westbrook 2.50 6.00
15 Chris Paul 1.25 3.00
16 Kyle Lowry .75 2.00
17 Karl-Anthony Towns 2.50 6.00
18 Kristaps Porzingis 2.00 5.00
19 C.J. McCollum .75 2.00
20 Kevin Love 1.00 2.50

2012-13 Panini Contenders
COMP.SET w/o RCs (200) 15.00 40.00
UNPRICED BLACK PRINT RUN ONE SET
UNPRICED GOLD PRINT RUN 5 TO 10 SETS
1 Al Horford .30 .75
2 Al Jefferson .30 .75
3 Al-Farouq Aminu .30 .75
4 Alonzo Gee .25 .60
5 Amare Stoudemire .30 .75
6 Anderson Varejao .25 .60
7 Andre Iguodala .30 .75
8 Andre Miller .30 .75
9 Andrea Bargnani .30 .75
10 Andrei Kirilenko .30 .75
11 John Salmons .30 .75
12 Joe Johnson .30 .75
13 Joakim Noah .30 .75
14 J.J. Hickson .25 .60
15 J.J. Barea .30 .75
16 Jermaine O'Neal .30 .75
17 Jeff Teague .30 .75
18 JaVale McGee .30 .75
19 Jason Thompson .25 .60
20 Jason Terry .30 .75
21 Jason Richardson .40 1.00
22 Steve Blake .25 .60
23 Stephen Jackson .30 .75
24 Stephen Curry 1.50 4.00
25 Spencer Hawes .25 .60
26 Shawn Marion .30 .75
27 Shane Battier .30 .75
28 Serge Ibaka .30 .75
29 Samuel Dalembert .25 .60
30 Ryan Anderson .30 .75
31 Russell Westbrook 1.00 2.50
32 Rudy Gay .40 1.00
33 Ricky Rubio .40 1.00
34 Roy Hibbert .30 .75
35 Rodney Stuckey .30 .75
36 Raymond Felton .30 .75
37 Ray Allen .40 1.00
38 Rashard Lewis .30 .75
39 Randy Foye .25 .60
40 Ramon Sessions .30 .75
41 Rajon Rondo .40 1.00
42 Al Harrington .30 .75
43 Paul Pierce .40 1.00
44 Paul Millsap .40 1.00
45 Paul George .50 1.25
46 Pau Gasol .40 1.00
47 Patrick Patterson .25 .60
48 Omri Casspi .25 .60
49 Omer Asik .30 .75
50 O.J. Mayo .25 .60
51 Nikola Pekovic .25 .60
52 Nicolas Batum .30 .75
53 Nick Young .30 .75
54 Nick Collison .30 .75
55 Nene .30 .75
56 Nate Robinson .25 .60
57 Monta Ellis .30 .75
58 Mo Williams .30 .75
59 Mike Miller .30 .75
60 Mike Dunleavy .25 .60
61 Mike Conley .30 .75
62 Michael Beasley .25 .60
63 Metta World Peace .40 1.00
64 Marvin Williams .30 .75
65 Marreese Speights .25 .60
66 Mario Chalmers .30 .75
67 Marcus Thornton .25 .60
68 Marcus Camby .30 .75
69 Marco Belinelli .25 .60
70 Marcin Gortat .30 .75
71 Marc Gasol .40 1.00
72 Manu Ginobili .40 1.00
73 Luol Deng .30 .75
74 Luke Ridnour .30 .75
75 Luke Harangody .25 .60
76 Luke Babbitt .25 .60
77 Luis Scola .30 .75
78 Louis Williams .30 .75
79 Linas Kleiza .25 .60
80 LeBron James 1.50 4.00
81 Landry Fields .25 .60
82 LaMarcus Aldridge .40 1.00
83 Lamar Odom .30 .75
84 Kyle Lowry .30 .75
85 Kyle Korver .30 .75
86 Kris Humphries .25 .60
87 Kobe Bryant 1.50 4.00
88 Kirk Hinrich .30 .75
89 Kevin Martin .30 .75
90 Kevin Love .40 1.00
91 Kevin Garnett .60 1.50
92 Kevin Durant 1.00 2.50
93 Kendrick Perkins .25 .60
94 Jrue Holiday .40 1.00
95 Josh Smith .30 .75
96 Jose Calderon .25 .60
97 Jordan Crawford .25 .60
98 Leandro Barbosa .30 .75
99 John Wall .50 1.25
100 Trevor Ariza .25 .60
101 Tony Parker .40 1.00
102 Tony Allen .25 .60
103 Timofey Mozgov .25 .60
104 Tim Duncan .60 1.50
105 Thaddeus Young .25 .60
106 Thabo Sefolosha .25 .60
107 Jerry Stackhouse .30 .75
108 Tayshaun Prince .30 .75
109 Taj Gibson .30 .75
110 Steve Nash .40 1.00
111 Jason Kidd .40 1.00
112 Jarrett Jack .30 .75
113 Jeremy Lin .40 1.00
114 James Johnson .25 .60
115 James Harden .60 1.50
116 Jameer Nelson .25 .60
117 J.R. Smith .30 .75
118 J.J. Redick .40 1.00
119 Hedo Turkoglu .30 .75
120 Hakim Warrick .30 .75
121 Greivis Vasquez .30 .75
122 Greg Monroe .30 .75
123 Grant Hill .50 1.25
124 Gordon Hayward .40 1.00
125 Goran Dragic .30 .75
126 Glen Davis .25 .60
127 Gerald Wallace .30 .75
128 Gerald Henderson .25 .60
129 Gerald Green .30 .75
130 George Hill .30 .75
131 Gary Neal .30 .75
132 Toney Douglas .25 .60
133 Evan Turner .25 .60
134 Ersan Ilyasova .25 .60
135 Eric Gordon .30 .75
136 Emeka Okafor .30 .75
137 Elton Brand .40 1.00
138 Ed Davis .25 .60
139 Dwyane Wade .60 1.50
140 Dwight Howard .30 .75
141 Drew Gooden .30 .75
142 Dorell Wright .25 .60
143 Dirk Nowitzki .50 1.25
144 Devin Harris .25 .60
145 Derrick Rose .50 1.25
146 Derrick Favors .30 .75
147 Deron Williams .30 .75
148 DeMarcus Cousins .40 1.00
149 DeMar DeRozan .40 1.00
150 DeJuan Blair .25 .60
151 DeAndre Jordan .40 1.00
152 David West .30 .75
153 David Lee .25 .60
154 Darren Collison .30 .75
155 Darrell Arthur .25 .60
156 Danny Green .30 .75
157 Danny Granger .30 .75
158 Daniel Gibson .30 .75
159 Daequan Cook .25 .60
160 D.J. Augustin .25 .60
161 Courtney Lee .30 .75
162 Corey Maggette .30 .75
163 Corey Brewer .25 .60
164 Chris Paul .50 1.25
165 Chris Kaman .30 .75
166 Chris Bosh .40 1.00
167 Chauncey Billups .40 1.00
168 Chase Budinger .25 .60
169 Charlie Villanueva .25 .60
170 Channing Frye .30 .75
171 Caron Butler .30 .75
172 Carmelo Anthony .50 1.25
173 Carlos Delfino .25 .60
174 Carlos Boozer .30 .75
175 Carl Landry .25 .60
176 C.J. Watson .25 .60
177 Brook Lopez .30 .75
178 Brendan Haywood .25 .60
179 Brandon Rush .25 .60
180 Brandon Roy .40 1.00
181 Brandon Jennings .25 .60
182 Brandon Bass .25 .60
183 Blake Griffin .40 1.00
184 Ben Gordon .30 .75
185 Avery Bradley .30 .75
186 Arron Afflalo .30 .75
187 Anthony Morrow .25 .60
188 Antawn Jamison .30 .75
189 Andrew Bynum .25 .60
190 Andrew Bogut .30 .75
191 Trevor Booker .25 .60
192 Ty Lawson .25 .60
193 Tyreke Evans .25 .60
194 Tyrus Thomas .25 .60
195 Tyson Chandler .30 .75
196 Vince Carter .50 1.25
197 Wesley Matthews .25 .60
198 Will Bynum .25 .60
199 Xavier Henry .25 .60
200 Zach Randolph .30 .75

201 Anthony Davis AU RC 125.00 300.00
202 M.Kidd-Gilchrist AU RC 4.00 10.00
203 Bradley Beal AU RC 12.00 30.00
204 Dion Waiters AU RC EXCH 4.00 10.00
205 Thomas Robinson AU RC 3.00 8.00
206 Harrison Barnes AU RC 12.00 30.00
207 Terrence Ross AU RC 4.00 10.00
208 Andre Drummond AU RC 10.00 25.00
209 Austin Rivers AU RC 4.00 10.00
210 M.Leonard AU RC EXCH 3.00 8.00
211 Jeremy Lamb AU RC 4.00 10.00
212 Kendall Marshall AU RC 2.50 6.00
213 John Henson AU RC 4.00 10.00
214 Moe Harkless AU RC 4.00 10.00
215 Royce White AU RC 2.50 6.00
216 Tyler Zeller AU RC 3.00 8.00
217 Terrence Jones AU RC 3.00 8.00
218 Andrew Nicholson AU RC 2.50 6.00
219 Evan Fournier AU RC 4.00 10.00
220 Jared Sullinger AU RC 3.00 8.00
221 Fab Melo AU RC 2.50 6.00
222 John Jenkins AU RC 2.50 6.00
223 Jared Cunningham AU RC 2.50 6.00
224 Tony Wroten AU RC 3.00 8.00
225 Miles Plumlee AU RC 2.50 6.00
226 Arnett Moultrie AU RC 2.50 6.00
227 Perry Jones AU RC 2.50 6.00
228 Marquis Teague AU RC 2.50 6.00
229 Festus Ezeli AU RC 3.00 8.00
230 Jeff Taylor AU RC 2.50 6.00
231 Bernard James AU RC 2.50 6.00
232 Jae Crowder AU RC 3.00 8.00
233 Draymond Green AU RC 20.00 50.00
234 Orlando Johnson AU RC 2.50 6.00
235 Quincy Acy AU RC 2.50 6.00
236 Quincy Miller AU RC 2.50 6.00
237 Khris Middleton AU RC 4.00 10.00
238 Will Barton AU RC 3.00 8.00
239 Tyshawn Taylor AU RC 2.50 6.00
240 Doron Lamb AU RC 2.50 6.00
241 Mike Scott AU RC 2.50 6.00
242 Kim English AU RC 2.50 6.00
243 Maalik Wayns AU RC 4.00 10.00
244 Darius Miller AU RC 2.50 6.00
245 Kevin Murphy AU RC 2.50 6.00
246 Kyle O'Quinn AU RC 2.50 6.00
247 Kris Joseph AU RC 2.50 6.00
248 Lance Thomas AU RC 2.50 6.00
249 D.Johnson-Odom AU RC 2.50 6.00
250 Kyrie Irving AU RC 60.00 150.00
251 Bismack Biyombo AU RC 2.50 6.00
252 MarShon Brooks AU RC 3.00 8.00
253 Alec Burks AU RC 4.00 10.00
254 Jimmy Butler AU RC 30.00 80.00
255 Norris Cole AU RC 2.50 6.00
256 Kenneth Faried AU RC 4.00 10.00
257 Jimmer Fredette AU RC 2.50 6.00
258 Jordan Hamilton AU RC 2.50 6.00
259 Tobias Harris AU RC 4.00 10.00
260 Reggie Jackson AU RC 4.00 10.00
261 Enes Kanter AU RC 4.00 10.00
262 Brandon Knight AU RC 4.00 10.00
263 Kawhi Leonard AU RC 125.00 300.00
264 Marcus Morris AU RC 3.00 8.00
265 Markieff Morris AU RC EXCH 4.00 10.00
266 Chandler Parsons AU RC 4.00 10.00
267 Iman Shumpert AU RC 4.00 10.00
268 Chris Singleton AU RC 2.50 6.00
269 Nolan Smith AU RC 2.50 6.00
270 Isaiah Thomas AU RC 30.00 80.00
271 Klay Thompson AU RC 50.00 120.00
272 Tristan Thompson AU RC 4.00 10.00
273 Jan Vesely AU RC 2.50 6.00
274 Kemba Walker AU RC 8.00 20.00
275 Derrick Williams AU RC 2.50 6.00
276 Cory Joseph AU RC 2.50 6.00
277 Chris Copeland AU RC 2.50 6.00
278 Gustavo Ayon AU RC 2.50 6.00
279 Charles Jenkins AU RC 2.50 6.00
280 Jeremy Tyler AU RC 2.50 6.00
281 Lavoy Allen AU RC 2.50 6.00
282 Josh Selby AU RC 2.50 6.00
283 Ivan Johnson AU RC 2.50 6.00
284 J.Valanciunas AU RC 4.00 10.00
285 Greg Stiemsma AU RC 2.50 6.00
286 DeAndre Liggins AU RC 3.00 8.00
287 Malcolm Lee AU RC 2.50 6.00
288 Darius Morris AU RC 2.50 6.00
289 Jon Leuer AU RC 3.00 8.00
290 Trey Thompkins AU RC 2.50 6.00
291 D.Motiejunas AU RC 3.00 8.00
292 Tyler Honeycutt AU RC 2.50 6.00
293 Robert Sacre AU RC 2.50 6.00
294 Victor Claver AU RC 2.50 6.00
295 Julyan Stone AU RC 2.50 6.00

2012-13 Panini Contenders Silver

*SILVER: 5X TO 12X BASE HI
STATED PRINT RUN 25 SER.#'d SETS
123 Grant Hill 10.00 25.00

2012-13 Panini Contenders Contemporary Contenders Autographs

STATED PRINT RUN 10 TO 99 SER.#'d SETS
1 Kevin Durant/25
2 Kevin Love/25 15.00 40.00
3 Brook Lopez/49 5.00 12.00
4 Steve Nash/25 40.00 100.00
5 Kobe Bryant/99 75.00 150.00
6 Tony Parker/25 EXCH 12.00 30.00
7 Marcin Gortat/99 15.00 40.00
8 Ray Allen/25
9 James Harden/49 20.00 50.00
10 Josh Smith/49 5.00 12.00
11 LaMarcus Aldridge/25 15.00 40.00
12 Eric Gordon/49
13 Drew Gooden/99 EXCH 4.00 10.00
14 Antawn Jamison/49 8.00 20.00
15 Jason Kidd/25 8.00 20.00
17 Stephen Curry/49 75.00 150.00
18 Tyreke Evans/25 4.00 10.00
19 Ty Lawson/99 5.00 12.00
21 Tyson Chandler/49 8.00 20.00
22 Brandon Rush/99 6.00 15.00
23 Brandon Jennings/49 EXCH 12.00 30.00
24 Mario Chalmers/99 4.00 10.00
25 Grant Hill/25 20.00 50.00
27 Chris Bosh/25 15.00 40.00
28 Andre Iguodala/49 8.00 20.00
29 Kyrie Irving/25 150.00 275.00
30 Stephen Jackson/99 EXCH 4.00 10.00
31 David Lee/49
32 Andrea Bargnani/49 4.00 10.00
33 Jrue Holiday/49
34 Zach Randolph/49 8.00 20.00
36 Andrew Bynum/25
37 Wesley Matthews/99 4.00 10.00
38 David West/49 EXCH 8.00 20.00
39 Roy Hibbert/99 8.00 20.00
40 J.R. Smith/99 12.00 30.00
41 Gordon Hayward/99 8.00 20.00
42 Al-Farouq Aminu/99 4.00 10.00
43 D.J. Augustin/49 4.00 10.00
44 Jameer Nelson/49 4.00 10.00
45 Nick Young/99 EXCH 4.00 10.00
46 Brandon Bass/99 4.00 10.00
48 Goran Dragic/99 4.00 10.00
49 Greivis Vasquez/99 12.00 30.00
50 DeAndre Jordan/99 4.00 10.00

2012-13 Panini Contenders Historic Contenders Autographs

STATED PRINT RUN 10 TO 149 SER.#'d SETS
1 Bill Russell/25 40.00 100.00
2 Magic Johnson/25 40.00 100.00
3 Scottie Pippen/25 125.00 250.00
4 Anfernee Hardaway/49 15.00 40.00
5 Walt Bellamy/49
6 Alvan Adams/149 4.00 10.00
7 Oscar Robertson/25 30.00 80.00
8 George McGinnis/99 6.00 15.00
9 Rick Mahorn/149 4.00 10.00
10 Elgin Baylor/25 8.00 20.00
11 Bob McAdoo/99 10.00 25.00
12 Spencer Haywood/149 4.00 10.00
13 Sleepy Floyd/149 4.00 10.00
14 Jeff Hornacek/149 4.00 10.00
15 Rolando Blackman/99 6.00 15.00
16 Bailey Howell/99 8.00 20.00
17 Otis Birdsong/149 4.00 10.00
18 Sidney Moncrief/99 4.00 10.00
19 Charles Oakley/99 4.00 10.00
20 Cedric Maxwell/99 4.00 10.00
21 Ralph Sampson/149 4.00 10.00
22 Vernon Maxwell/149 6.00 15.00
23 Nick Van Exel/49 20.00 50.00
24 Muggsy Bogues/99 4.00 10.00
25 Kevin Willis/149 4.00 10.00
26 Kareem Abdul-Jabbar/25
27 Bob Love/149 4.00 10.00
28 Kurt Rambis/149 4.00 10.00
29 Spud Webb/149 4.00 10.00
30 Sam Perkins/99 EXCH 6.00 15.00
31 Bill Laimbeer/149 4.00 10.00
32 David Robinson/25 15.00 40.00
33 Larry Bird/25 40.00 100.00
34 Hersey Hawkins/99 EXCH 4.00 10.00
35 Frank Ramsey/99 12.00 30.00
36 Jalen Rose/99 EXCH 8.00 20.00
38 Tom Heinsohn/99 25.00 60.00
39 Kelly Tripucka/99 4.00 10.00
40 Darryl Dawkins/149 4.00 10.00
41 Dan Issel/99 4.00 10.00
42 Alonzo Mourning/25 25.00 60.00
43 Tim Hardaway/99 4.00 10.00
44 Kiki Vandeweghe/149 EXCH 4.00 10.00
45 Bernard King/99 4.00 10.00
46 World B. Free/49 4.00 10.00
47 Robert Horry/49 8.00 20.00
48 Bill Sharman/49 12.00 30.00
49 Paul Silas/99 8.00 20.00
50 Bobby Wanzer/99 4.00 10.00

2012-13 Panini Contenders HOF Contenders

RANDOM INSERTS IN PACKS
1 Carmelo Anthony 6.00 15.00
2 Dwight Howard 4.00 10.00
3 Steve Nash 5.00 12.00
4 Ben Wallace 4.00 10.00
5 Ray Allen 5.00 12.00
6 Jason Kidd 5.00 12.00
7 Dwyane Wade 8.00 20.00
8 LeBron James 20.00 50.00
9 Paul Pierce 5.00 12.00
10 Dirk Nowitzki 6.00 15.00
11 Kevin Garnett 8.00 20.00
12 Kobe Bryant 20.00 50.00
13 Tim Duncan 8.00 20.00
14 Allen Iverson 6.00 15.00
15 Vince Carter 6.00 15.00
16 Kevin Durant 12.00 30.00
17 Derrick Rose 6.00 15.00
18 Chris Paul 6.00 15.00
19 Dikembe Mutombo 5.00 12.00
20 Tony Parker 5.00 12.00
21 Pau Gasol 5.00 12.00
22 Grant Hill 6.00 15.00
23 Manu Ginobili 5.00 12.00
24 Shaquille O'Neal 10.00 25.00
25 Yao Ming 6.00 15.00

2012-13 Panini Contenders Legendary Contenders

COMPLETE SET (50) 30.00 80.00
RANDOM INSERTS IN PACKS
1 Patrick Ewing 1.25 3.00
2 Moses Malone 1.00 2.50
3 Wilt Chamberlain 2.00 5.00
4 Bernard King .75 2.00
5 Shaquille O'Neal 2.00 5.00
6 Karl Malone 1.25 3.00
7 Dikembe Mutombo 1.00 2.50
8 George Mikan 2.00 5.00
9 Bill Laimbeer .75 2.00
10 Clyde Drexler 1.25 3.00
11 Rik Smits 1.00 2.50
12 Shawn Kemp 1.50 4.00
13 Anfernee Hardaway 2.50 6.00
14 George Gervin 1.00 2.50
15 David Thompson .75 2.00
16 Bill Russell 1.50 4.00
17 Gary Payton 1.00 2.50
18 Jeff Malone .60 1.50
19 Julius Erving 1.50 4.00
20 Rolando Blackman .75 2.00
21 Jo Jo White .75 2.00
22 Jerry West 1.25 3.00
23 Bob Pettit 1.00 2.50
24 Rick Barry .75 2.00
25 Elvin Hayes 1.00 2.50
26 Bob Cousy 1.50 4.00
27 Kevin McHale 1.00 2.50
28 Nate Thurmond .75 2.00
29 Dolph Schayes 1.00 2.50
30 Walt Frazier 1.00 2.50
31 Jerry Lucas 1.00 2.50
32 Billy Cunningham 1.00 2.50
33 Dominique Wilkins 1.25 3.00
34 Nate Archibald .75 2.00
35 Connie Hawkins 1.00 2.50
36 James Worthy 1.25 3.00
37 Hal Greer .75 2.00
38 Pete Maravich 1.50 4.00
39 Alonzo Mourning 1.25 3.00
40 Bill Walton 1.00 2.50
41 Joe Dumars 1.00 2.50
42 Chris Webber 1.00 2.50
43 Tim Hardaway 1.00 2.50
44 Chris Mullin 1.00 2.50
45 Mitch Richmond 1.00 2.50
46 Yao Ming 1.25 3.00
47 Toni Kukoc 1.00 2.50
48 Cedric Maxwell .60 1.50
49 Buck Williams .60 1.50
50 Doug Collins 1.00 2.50

2012-13 Panini Contenders Materials

STATED PRINT RUN 10 TO 149 SER.#'d SETS
UNPRICED PRIME PRINT RUN ONE TO 10 SETS
1 Kobe Bryant/99 12.00 30.00
2 Dwyane Wade/99 5.00 12.00
3 LeBron James/99 12.00 30.00
4 Tim Duncan/149 5.00 12.00
5 Kevin Love/49 3.00 8.00
6 Zach Randolph/149 2.50 6.00
7 Raymond Felton/79 2.50 6.00
8 Deron Williams/49 2.50 6.00
9 Stephen Curry/79 12.00 30.00
10 Blake Griffin/79 3.00 8.00
11 Tyreke Evans/79 2.00 5.00
12 Gordon Hayward/79 3.00 8.00
13 Evan Turner/79 2.00 5.00
14 George Hill/79 2.50 6.00
15 Andre Iguodala/79 2.50 6.00
16 Paul Pierce/49 3.00 8.00
17 Kevin Garnett/99 5.00 12.00
18 Brook Lopez/29 2.50 6.00
19 Derrick Rose/49 4.00 10.00
21 Jameer Nelson/149 2.00 5.00
22 Tony Parker/149 3.00 8.00
23 Kevin Martin/149 2.50 6.00
24 Amare Stoudemire/49 2.50 6.00
26 Rudy Gay/49 3.00 8.00
27 Al Jefferson/149 2.50 6.00
28 Josh Smith/149 2.50 6.00
29 Kirk Hinrich/99 2.50 6.00
30 Manu Ginobili/149 3.00 8.00
31 Luol Deng/149 2.50 6.00
32 Rajon Rondo/49 3.00 8.00
33 Marc Gasol/79 3.00 8.00
34 Metta World Peace/99 3.00 8.00
35 Pau Gasol/99 3.00 8.00
36 Chris Paul/49 4.00 10.00
37 Greg Monroe/49 2.50 6.00
38 Shane Battier/99 2.50 6.00
39 J.J. Redick/149 3.00 8.00
40 Serge Ibaka/19 6.00 15.00
41 Tayshaun Prince/149 2.50 6.00
42 Karl Malone/49 4.00 10.00
43 David Lee/149 2.00 5.00
44 Thaddeus Young/79 2.00 5.00
45 Josh Howard/149 2.50 6.00
46 John Wall/49 4.00 10.00
47 Devin Harris/79 2.00 5.00
48 Kyrie Irving/49 12.00 30.00
49 Brandon Knight/49 3.00 8.00
50 MarShon Brooks/149 2.50 6.00
51 David West/49 2.50 6.00
52 Taj Gibson/49 2.50 6.00
53 Patrick Ewing/49 15.00 40.00
54 Caron Butler/79 2.50 6.00
55 Carlos Boozer/149 2.50 6.00
56 Derrick Favors/49 2.50 6.00
57 Hedo Turkoglu/149 2.50 6.00
58 Ben Wallace/149 2.50 6.00
59 Russell Westbrook/49 8.00 20.00
60 Carlos Delfino/149 2.00 5.00
61 Eric Gordon/149 2.50 6.00
62 Hakeem Olajuwon/49 4.00 10.00
63 Ty Lawson/49 2.00 5.00
64 Spencer Hawes/149 2.00 5.00
65 Al Horford/99 2.50 6.00
66 Channing Frye/99 2.50 6.00
67 Danny Granger/99 2.50 6.00
68 Jeff Teague/99 2.50 6.00
69 Brandon Jennings/49 2.00 5.00
71 DeJuan Blair/49 2.00 5.00
72 Wesley Matthews/49 2.00 5.00
74 Daniel Gibson/99 2.50 6.00
75 John Stockton/49 5.00 12.00
76 Ed Davis/149 2.00 5.00
77 James Harden/49 5.00 12.00
79 Gary Neal/99 2.50 6.00
80 Jose Calderon/149 2.00 5.00
81 Jrue Holiday/49 3.00 8.00
82 DeMarcus Cousins/49 3.00 8.00
83 J.J. Barea/49 2.50 6.00
84 Tyson Chandler/49 2.50 6.00
85 Mike Conley/49 2.50 6.00
86 Anderson Varejao/29 2.00 5.00
87 Luke Ridnour/49 2.50 6.00
88 Rodrigue Beaubois/99 2.00 5.00
89 Andrea Bargnani/99 2.50 6.00
90 DeAndre Jordan/79 3.00 8.00
91 Rick Mahorn/49 2.00 5.00
92 Manute Bol/49 3.00 8.00
93 Kenny Anderson/99 2.50 6.00
94 Chris Mullin/49 3.00 8.00
95 Reggie Lewis/99 3.00 8.00
96 Sean Elliott/29 3.00 8.00
97 Alex English/49 2.50 6.00
98 Ron Harper/99 3.00 8.00
99 Kevin McHale/49 3.00 8.00

2012-13 Panini Contenders Playoff Contenders

COMPLETE SET (25) 15.00 40.00
RANDOM INSERTS IN PACKS
1 Tim Duncan 1.25 3.00
2 Kobe Bryant 3.00 8.00
3 Kevin Durant 2.00 5.00
4 LeBron James 3.00 8.00
5 Tony Parker .75 2.00
6 Karl Malone 1.00 2.50
7 Scottie Pippen 1.50 4.00
8 Magic Johnson 2.00 5.00
9 Dennis Rodman 1.50 4.00
10 Paul Pierce .75 2.00
11 Shaquille O'Neal 1.50 4.00
12 Hakeem Olajuwon 1.00 2.50
13 John Stockton 1.25 3.00
14 Robert Horry .60 1.50
15 Jason Kidd .75 2.00
16 Sam Jones .75 2.00
17 Tom Heinsohn .75 2.00
18 Derek Fisher .60 1.50
19 Kareem Abdul-Jabbar 1.25 3.00
20 Danny Ainge .75 2.00
21 Robert Parish .75 2.00
22 Chauncey Billups .75 2.00
23 Bill Russell 1.25 3.00
24 Jerry West 1.00 2.50
25 John Havlicek 1.00 2.50

2012-13 Panini Contenders Rookie Remembrance

COMPLETE SET (35) 20.00 50.00
RANDOM INSERTS IN PACKS
1 Blake Griffin .75 2.00
2 Tyreke Evans .50 1.25
3 Derrick Rose 1.00 2.50
4 Kevin Durant 2.00 5.00
5 Brandon Roy .75 2.00
6 Chris Paul 1.00 2.50
7 Emeka Okafor .60 1.50
8 LeBron James 3.00 8.00
9 Amare Stoudemire .60 1.50
10 Pau Gasol .75 2.00
11 Elton Brand .75 2.00
12 Vince Carter 1.00 2.50
13 Tim Duncan 1.25 3.00
14 Damon Stoudamire .75 2.00
15 Jason Kidd .75 2.00
16 Grant Hill 1.00 2.50
17 Chris Webber .75 2.00
18 Shaquille O'Neal 1.50 4.00
19 Larry Johnson 1.00 2.50
20 Derrick Coleman .75 2.00
21 David Robinson 1.25 3.00
22 Mitch Richmond .75 2.00
23 Mark Jackson .60 1.50
24 Patrick Ewing 1.00 2.50
25 Ralph Sampson .60 1.50
26 Larry Bird 2.00 5.00
27 Bob McAdoo .60 1.50
28 Kareem Abdul-Jabbar 1.25 3.00
29 Wes Unseld .75 2.00
30 Earl Monroe .75 2.00
31 Allen Iverson 1.00 2.50
32 Oscar Robertson 1.00 2.50
33 Wilt Chamberlain 1.50 4.00
34 Elgin Baylor .75 2.00
35 Bob Pettit .75 2.00

2012-13 Panini Contenders ROY Contenders

COMPLETE SET (15) 15.00 40.00
RANDOM INSERTS IN PACKS
1 Andre Drummond 1.25 3.00
2 Anthony Davis 4.00 10.00
3 Austin Rivers .75 2.00
4 Bradley Beal 1.25 3.00
5 Damian Lillard 3.00 8.00
6 Dion Waiters .75 2.00
7 Harrison Barnes 1.25 3.00
8 Jeremy Lamb .75 2.00
9 John Henson .75 2.00
10 Kendall Marshall .50 1.25
11 Meyers Leonard .60 1.50
12 Michael Kidd-Gilchrist .75 2.00
13 Moe Harkless .75 2.00
14 Terrence Ross .75 2.00
15 Thomas Robinson .60 1.50

2012-13 Panini Contenders Statistical Contenders

RANDOM INSERTS IN PACKS
1 LeBron James 2.50 6.00
2 Russell Westbrook 1.50 4.00
3 Kevin Durant 1.50 4.00
4 Kobe Bryant 2.50 6.00
5 Kevin Love .60 1.50
6 Rajon Rondo .60 1.50
7 Steve Nash .60 1.50
8 Chris Paul .75 2.00
9 Ricky Rubio .60 1.50
10 Deron Williams .50 1.25
11 Dwight Howard .50 1.25
12 Andrew Bynum .40 1.00
13 DeMarcus Cousins .60 1.50
14 Kris Humphries .40 1.00
15 Blake Griffin .60 1.50
16 Mike Conley .50 1.25
17 Paul Millsap .60 1.50
18 Derrick Rose .75 2.00
19 Andre Iguodala .50 1.25
20 Iman Shumpert .60 1.50
21 Serge Ibaka .50 1.25
22 Carmelo Anthony .75 2.00
23 DeAndre Jordan .60 1.50
24 Roy Hibbert .50 1.25
25 Marc Gasol .60 1.50

2012-13 Panini Contenders Substantial Signatures Materials

STATED PRINT RUN 10 TO 149 SER.#'d SETS
UNPRICED PRIME PRINT RUN ONE TO 10 SETS
1 Pau Gasol/25 15.00 40.00
3 Kevin Love/25 15.00 40.00
4 Chris Bosh/25 15.00 40.00
5 Chris Paul/25 EXCH 30.00 80.00
6 Al Horford/99 5.00 12.00
7 Kevin Durant/25
8 Jared Dudley/49 4.00 10.00
9 John Wall/25 25.00 60.00
10 Tyler Hansbrough/99 6.00 15.00
11 Vince Carter/49 25.00 60.00
12 Blake Griffin/25 50.00 120.00
13 DeMarcus Cousins/49 12.00 30.00
15 Tayshaun Prince/49 6.00 15.00
16 Brandon Knight/99 6.00 15.00
17 DeJuan Blair/149 EXCH 6.00 15.00
18 Derrick Williams/25 4.00 10.00
19 Kemba Walker/99 12.00 30.00
20 Kevin Martin/99 6.00 15.00
21 Zach Randolph/49 10.00 25.00
22 Tristan Thompson/99 6.00 15.00
23 Derrick Favors/99 5.00 12.00
24 Taj Gibson/149 5.00 12.00
25 Gary Neal/149 EXCH 5.00 12.00
26 Tyreke Evans/99 4.00 10.00
27 David Lee/99 EXCH
28 Udonis Haslem/149 4.00 10.00
29 MarShon Brooks/149 5.00 12.00
30 Kyrie Irving/49 125.00 250.00
31 Ed Davis/149 4.00 10.00
32 Jose Calderon/99 EXCH 6.00 15.00
33 Ty Lawson/49
34 Josh Smith/99 6.00 15.00
35 Norris Cole/149 4.00 10.00
36 Josh Howard/99 EXCH 5.00 12.00
37 Brandon Jennings/49
38 Eric Gordon/49 6.00 15.00
39 Austin Rivers/49 6.00 15.00
40 Andrea Bargnani/49 6.00 15.00
41 Markieff Morris/149 EXCH 6.00 15.00
42 Anthony Davis/25 200.00 400.00
43 Kawhi Leonard/149 100.00 250.00
44 Bradley Beal/99 15.00 40.00
45 Tony Parker/25 15.00 40.00
46 Tobias Harris/149 6.00 15.00
47 Hedo Turkoglu/99 6.00 15.00
50 Bismack Biyombo/149 4.00 10.00
51 Al Jefferson/25 EXCH 5.00 12.00
52 Jimmer Fredette/149 4.00 10.00
53 Channing Frye/149 5.00 12.00
54 Caron Butler/49
55 Jameer Nelson/99 4.00 10.00
56 Wesley Matthews/149 4.00 10.00
57 J.J. Redick/99 12.00 30.00
58 Danny Granger/49 EXCH 6.00 15.00
59 Jrue Holiday/149 6.00 15.00
60 LaMarcus Aldridge/49 12.00 30.00
61 George Hill/149 5.00 12.00
62 Ivan Johnson/149 4.00 10.00
63 Luke Ridnour/99 EXCH 5.00 12.00
65 Shane Battier/25 5.00 12.00
66 Rodrigue Beaubois/149 EXCH 4.00 10.00
67 Brook Lopez/49 5.00 12.00
68 Devin Harris/49 6.00 15.00
69 Jeff Teague/149 5.00 12.00
70 Mark Jackson/49 6.00 15.00
71 Nate Thurmond/25 12.00 30.00
72 Artis Gilmore/49 6.00 15.00
73 Fat Lever/49 6.00 15.00
76 Robert Parish/99 15.00 40.00
78 Larry Johnson/99 12.00 30.00
79 Dikembe Mutombo/49 20.00 50.00
80 Toni Kukoc/49 12.00 30.00
81 Chris Mullin/49 20.00 50.00
82 Bill Laimbeer/49
83 Larry Bird/25 50.00 125.00
84 Danny Manning/49 6.00 15.00
85 Dominique Wilkins/25 12.00 30.00
86 Sean Elliott/149 6.00 15.00
87 Zydrunas Ilgauskas/49 6.00 15.00
88 Alex English/49 6.00 15.00
89 David Robinson/25 50.00 125.00
90 Jeff Hornacek/49 8.00 20.00
91 John Starks/49 12.00 30.00
92 Kareem Abdul-Jabbar/25 40.00 100.00
93 Julius Erving/25
94 Isaiah Thomas/99 50.00 120.00
95 Kendall Marshall/99 4.00 10.00
96 Michael Kidd-Gilchrist/25 6.00 15.00
97 Allan Houston/49 8.00 20.00
99 Mark Price/49 15.00 40.00
100 Thomas Robinson/25 5.00 12.00

2012-13 Panini Contenders Throwback Rookies

RANDOM INSERTS IN PACKS
1 Kobe Bryant
2 LeBron James 50.00 125.00
3 Kevin Garnett 20.00 50.00
4 Dwight Howard 10.00 25.00
5 Dwyane Wade 20.00 50.00
6 Steve Nash 20.00 50.00
7 Deron Williams 10.00 25.00
8 Paul Pierce 20.00 50.00
9 Dirk Nowitzki 15.00 40.00
10 Chris Bosh
11 Pau Gasol
12 LaMarcus Aldridge 12.00 30.00
13 Kareem Abdul-Jabbar 20.00 50.00
14 Larry Bird 15.00 40.00
15 Vince Carter 15.00 40.00
16 Kevin Durant 15.00 40.00
17 Derrick Rose
18 Chris Paul
19 Amare Stoudemire 10.00 25.00
20 Carmelo Anthony 15.00 40.00
21 Tim Duncan 20.00 50.00
22 Jason Kidd 12.00 30.00
23 Grant Hill
24 Magic Johnson
25 Ray Allen

2015-16 Panini Contenders Draft Picks

OVERALL FIVE AUTOS PER HOBBY BOX
1 Aaron Brooks .20 .50
2 Aaron Gordon .25 .60
3 Al Horford .25 .60
4 Al-Farouq Aminu .25 .60
5 Andre Drummond .30 .75
6 Andre Iguodala .25 .60
7 Andrew Bogut .25 .60
8 Andrew Wiggins .50 1.25
9 Anthony Davis .60 1.50
10 Ben Gordon .25 .60
11 Blake Griffin .30 .75
12 Bradley Beal .30 .75
13 Brook Lopez .25 .60
14 Carlos Boozer .25 .60
15 Carmelo Anthony .40 1.00
16 Chandler Parsons .25 .60
17 Channing Frye .25 .60
18 Chris Bosh .30 .75
19 Chris Paul .40 1.00
20 Damian Lillard .60 1.50
21 Darren Collison .25 .60
22 David Lee .20 .50
23 DeAndre Jordan .30 .75
24 DeMar DeRozan .30 .75
25 DeMarcus Cousins .30 .75
26 Deron Williams .25 .60
27 Derrick Favors .25 .60
28 Derrick Rose .40 1.00
29 Doug McDermott .25 .60
30 Draymond Green .40 1.00
31 Dwyane Wade .50 1.25
32 Elfrid Payton .25 .60
33 Eric Bledsoe .25 .60
34 Gary Harris .25 .60
35 Greg Monroe .25 .60
36 Gordon Hayward .30 .75
37 Harrison Barnes .25 .60
38 Hassan Whiteside .25 .60
39 J.J. Redick .30 .75
40 Jabari Brown .25 .60
41 Jabari Parker .40 1.00
42 Jamal Crawford .30 .75
43 James Harden .50 1.25
44 Jimmer Fredette .20 .50
45 Jimmy Butler .30 .75
46 Joakim Noah .25 .60
47 Joe Johnson .25 .60
48 Joel Embiid .50 1.25
49 John Wall .40 1.00
50 Jordan Clarkson .30 .75
51 Jrue Holiday .25 .60
52 Julius Randle .30 .75
53 Kawhi Leonard .50 1.25
54 Kemba Walker .30 .75
55 Kenneth Faried .25 .60
56 Kentavious Caldwell-Pope .25 .60
57 Kevin Durant .75 2.00
58 Kevin Love .30 .75
59 Arron Afflalo .20 .50
60 Kirk Hinrich .25 .60
61 Klay Thompson .40 1.00
62 Kyle Korver .25 .60
63 Kyrie Irving .60 1.50
64 LaMarcus Aldridge .30 .75
65 Marcus Morris .20 .50
66 Marcus Smart .25 .60
67 Markieff Morris .20 .50
68 Mason Plumlee .25 .60
69 Matt Barnes .20 .50
70 Michael Carter-Williams .20 .50
71 Michael Kidd-Gilchrist .25 .60
72 Mike Conley .30 .75
73 Mike Dunleavy .20 .50
74 Mo Williams .25 .60
75 Nerlens Noel .25 .60
76 Nikola Vucevic .25 .60
77 Noah Vonleh .20 .50
78 Paul George .40 1.00
79 Paul Millsap .30 .75
80 Paul Pierce .30 .75
81 Rajon Rondo .30 .75
82 Richard Jefferson .25 .60
83 Rodney Hood .25 .60
84 Roy Hibbert .25 .60
85 Russell Westbrook .75 2.00
86 Shabazz Napier .20 .50
87 Stephen Curry 1.25 3.00
88 Tayshaun Prince .25 .60
89 Tim Duncan .50 1.25
90 Tim Hardaway Jr. .20 .50
91 Trevor Ariza .20 .50
92 Trey Burke .20 .50
93 Ty Lawson .20 .50
94 Tyler Hansbrough .25 .60
95 Tyreke Evans .20 .50
96 Victor Oladipo .25 .60
97 Vince Carter .40 1.00
98 Wesley Matthews .20 .50
99 Zach LaVine .30 .75
100 Zach Randolph .25 .60
101B Hrrsn AU Blue jsy
102A Alan Williams AU 3.00 8.00
Ball at head
102B Alan Williams AU 3.00 8.00
Ball at waist
104A Anthony Brown AU 3.00 8.00
Red jersey
104B Anthony Brown AU 3.00 8.00
Black jersey
105A Portis AU Whte jsy 5.00 12.00
105B Portis AU Red jsy 5.00 12.00
106A Brandon Ashley AU 3.00 8.00
Dribbling
106B Brandon Ashley AU 3.00 8.00
Hands on ball
107A Cameron Payne AU 4.00 10.00
White jersey
107B Cameron Payne AU 4.00 10.00
Yellow jersey
108A Chris McCullough AU 3.00 8.00
Facing right
108B Chris McCullough AU 3.00 8.00
Facing left
109A Aaron White AU 4.00 10.00
Black jersey
109B Aaron White AU 4.00 10.00
White jersey
110A Christian Wood AU 3.00 8.00
Left hand dribbling
110B Christian Wood AU 3.00 8.00
Two hands on ball!
111A Cliff Alexander AU 3.00 8.00
Facing right
111B Cliff Alexander AU 3.00 8.00
Facing left
112A Russell AU Whte jsy 12.00 30.00
112B Russell AU Red jsy 12.00 30.00
113A Dakari Johnson AU 3.00 8.00
Number hidden
113B Dakari Johnson AU 3.00 8.00
Number partially visable
114A Delon Wright AU 4.00 10.00
Dribbling right hand
114B Delon Wright AU 4.00 10.00
Dribbling left hand
115A Booker AU Face left 25.00 60.00
115B Booker AU Face right 25.00 60.00
116A Kmnsky AU Face left 15.00 40.00
116B Kmnsky AU Face right 15.00 40.00
117A J.P. Tokoto AU 4.00 10.00
Blue jersey
117B J.P. Tokoto AU 4.00 10.00
White jersey
118A Okafor AU Face left 12.00 30.00
118B Okafor AU Face right 12.00 30.00
119A Jarell Martin AU 4.00 10.00
Yellow jersey
119B Jarell Martin AU 4.00 10.00
White jersey
120A Jordan Mickey AU 3.00 8.00
Black jersey
120B Jordan Mickey AU 3.00 8.00
White jersey
121A Joe Young AU 4.00 10.00
Yellow jersey
121B Joe Young AU 4.00 10.00
122A Andrsn AU Whte jsy 4.00 10.00
122B Andrsn AU Dark jsy 4.00 10.00
123A Winslow AU Blue jsy 25.00 60.00
123B Winslow AU Whte jsy 25.00 60.00
124A Towns AU Face right 125.00 250.00
124B Towns AU Face left 125.00 250.00
125A Oubre AU Blue jsy 4.00 10.00
125B Oubre AU Whte jsy 4.00 10.00
126A Branden Dawson AU 3.00 8.00
White jersey
126B Branden Dawson AU 3.00 8.00
Green jersey
127A Kevon Looney AU 4.00 10.00
White jersey
127B Kevon Looney AU 4.00 10.00
Blue jersey
128A Michael Frazier II AU 4.00 10.00
White jersey
128B Michael Frazier II AU 4.00 10.00
Blue jersey
129A Michael Qualls AU 5.00 12.00
Dribbling
129B Michael Qualls AU 5.00 12.00
Dunking
130A Montrezl Harrell AU 4.00 10.00
White jersey
130B Montrezl Harrell AU 4.00 10.00
Black jersey
131A Turner AU Ornge jsy 5.00 12.00
131B Turner AU Whte jsy 5.00 12.00
133A Olivier Hanlan AU 3.00 8.00
Left arm out
133B Olivier Hanlan AU 3.00 8.00
Left arm crooked
134A Cook AU Arm down 10.00 25.00
134B Cook AU Arm up 10.00 25.00
135A R.J. Hunter AU 3.00 8.00
Blue jersey
135B R.J. Hunter AU 3.00 8.00
White jersey
136A Rakeem Christmas AU 3.00 8.00
White jersey
136B Rakeem Christmas AU 3.00 8.00
Orange jersey
137A Rashad Vaughn AU 3.00 8.00
Black jersey
137B Rashad Vaughn AU 3.00 8.00
Red jersey
138A Richaun Holmes AU 4.00 10.00
Pointing
138B Richaun Holmes AU 4.00 10.00
Two hands on ball
140A Rondae Hollis-Jefferson AU 4.00 10.00
Blue jersey
140B Rondae Hollis-Jefferson AU 4.00 10.00
Red jersey
141A Dkkr AU Hands on ball 10.00 25.00
141B Dkkr AU Hand on ball 10.00 25.00
142A Jhnsn AU Face forward 15.00 40.00
142B Jhnsn AU Face left 15.00 40.00
144A Rozier AU Whte jsy 4.00 10.00
144B Rozier AU Blck jsy 4.00 10.00
145A Nance Jr. AU Reb 5.00 12.00
145B Nance Jr. AU Drive 5.00 12.00
146A Lyles AU Hands on ball 8.00 20.00
146B Lyles AU Dribble 8.00 20.00
147A Tyler Harvey AU 3.00 8.00
Red jersey
147B Tyler Harvey AU 3.00 8.00
Dark jersey
148A Jones AU Blue jsy 5.00 12.00
148B Jones AU Whte jsy 5.00 12.00
149A Jonathan Holmes AU 3.00 8.00
Orange jersey
149B Jonathan Holmes AU 3.00 8.00
Orange jersey
150A Cly-Stn AU Hands on ball 12.00 30.00
150B Cly-Stn AU Dribble 12.00 30.00
151 Darrun Hilliard AU 3.00 8.00
152 Josh Richardson AU 5.00 12.00
153 Kevin Pangos AU 3.00 8.00
156 Dez Wells AU 3.00 8.00
157 Marcus Thornton AU 3.00 8.00
158 Chasson Randle AU 3.00 8.00
159 Sir'Dominic Pointer AU 3.00 8.00
160 TaShawn Thomas AU 3.00 8.00
161 Christian Wood AU 3.00 8.00
162 Michael Frazier II AU 4.00 10.00
165 Emmanuel Mudiay AU 5.00 12.00
166 Cliff Alexander AU 3.00 8.00
167 Kristaps Porzingis AU 25.00 60.00
168 Mario Hezonja AU 4.00 10.00
169 Aleighsa Welch AU 3.00 8.00
170 Josh Richardson AU 5.00 12.00
171 Ally Malott AU 3.00 8.00
172 Amanda Zahui B. AU 4.00 10.00
173 Amber Orrange AU 3.00 8.00
174 Andrea Hoover AU 3.00 8.00
175 Darrun Hilliard AU 3.00 8.00
176 Betnijah Laney AU 3.00 8.00
177 Brianna Kiesel AU 3.00 8.00
178 Brittany Boyd AU 3.00 8.00
179 Brittany Hrynko AU 3.00 8.00
180 Chelsea Gardner AU 3.00 8.00
181 Cheyenne Parker AU 3.00 8.00
182 Cierra Burdick AU 4.00 10.00
183 Crystal Bradford AU 3.00 8.00
184 Dearica Hamby AU 4.00 10.00
185 Elizabeth Williams AU 3.00 8.00
186 Isabelle Harrison AU 3.00 8.00
187 Kaleena Mosqueda-Lewis AU 3.00 8.00
188 Kiah Stokes AU 4.00 10.00
189 Shannon Scott AU 3.00 8.00
190 Laurin Mincy AU 3.00 8.00
191 Dez Wells AU 3.00 8.00
192 Mimi Mungedi AU 3.00 8.00
193 Natasha Cloud AU 3.00 8.00
194 Nikki Moody AU 3.00 8.00
195 Nneka Enemkpali AU 3.00 8.00
196 Promise Amukamara AU 3.00 8.00
197 Reshanda Gray AU 3.00 8.00
198 Samantha Logic AU 3.00 8.00
199 Shae Kelley AU 3.00 8.00
200 Duje Dukan AU 3.00 8.00

2015-16 Panini Contenders Draft Picks Cracked Ice Ticket

*CRCKD ICE 1-100: 5X TO 12X BASIC
*CRCKD ICE 101-150: .75X TO 2X BASIC
*CRCKD ICE 151-200: .75X TO 2X BASIC
RANDOM INSERTS IN PACKS
OVERALL FIVE AUTOS PER HOBBY BOX
STATED PRINT RUN 23 SER.#'d SETS
101A Hrrsn AU Whte jsy 20.00 50.00
101B Hrrsn AU Blue jsy 20.00 50.00
103A Hrrsn AU No number 10.00 25.00
103B Hrrsn AU Number 10.00 25.00
124A Towns AU Face right 250.00 400.00
124B Towns AU Face left 250.00 400.00
141A Dkkr AU Hands on ball 30.00 80.00
141B Dkkr AU Hand on ball 30.00 80.00
142A Jhnsn AU Face forward 125.00 250.00
142B Jhnsn AU Face left 125.00 250.00
163 Aaron Harrison AU 25.00 60.00
165 Emmanuel Mudiay AU 200.00 400.00
167 Kristaps Porzingis AU 300.00 500.00

2015-16 Panini Contenders Draft Picks Draft Ticket

*DRFT 1-100: 2X TO 5X BASIC
*DRFT 101-150: .5X TO 1.2X BASIC
*DRFT 151-200: .5X TO 1.2X BASIC
RANDOM INSERTS IN PACKS
OVERALL FIVE AUTOS PER HOBBY BOX
STATED PRINT RUN 99 SER.#'d SETS
101A Hrrsn AU Whte jsy 12.00 30.00
101B Hrrsn AU Blue jsy 12.00 30.00
103A Hrrsn AU No number 6.00 15.00
103B Hrrsn AU Number 6.00 15.00
163 Aaron Harrison AU 15.00 40.00

2015-16 Panini Contenders Draft Picks Alumni Ink

OVERALL FIVE AUTOS PER HOBBY BOX
1 Aaron Gordon
2 Al-Farouq Aminu 4.00 10.00
3 Andre Drummond 25.00 60.00
4 Harrison Barnes
5 Jabari Brown 4.00 10.00
6 Jabari Parker
7 Joel Embiid 8.00 20.00
8 Jordan Clarkson 5.00 12.00
9 Jrue Holiday
10 Julius Randle
11 Kentavious Caldwell-Pope 4.00 10.00
12 Victor Oladipo 8.00 20.00
13 Kyle Korver
14 Marcus Smart 6.00 15.00
15 Mason Plumlee 4.00 10.00
16 Michael Carter-Williams 10.00 25.00
17 Michael Kidd-Gilchrist 20.00 50.00
18 Mo Williams 4.00 10.00
19 Nerlens Noel 12.00 30.00
20 Noah Vonleh 3.00 8.00
21 Richard Jefferson
22 Roy Hibbert
23 Tim Hardaway Jr.
24 Trey Burke 3.00 8.00

2015-16 Panini Contenders Draft Picks Class Reunion

APPX.ODDS 1:8 HOBBY
1 Andrew Wiggins .75 2.00
2 Anthony Davis 1.00 2.50
3 Blake Griffin .50 1.25
4 Carmelo Anthony .60 1.50
5 Chris Paul .60 1.50
6 Damian Lillard 1.00 2.50
7 DeMar DeRozan .50 1.25
8 Derrick Rose .60 1.50
9 Dwyane Wade .75 2.00
10 Hassan Whiteside .40 1.00
11 James Harden .75 2.00
12 Jimmy Butler .50 1.25
13 John Wall .60 1.50
14 Kawhi Leonard .75 2.00
15 Kevin Durant 1.25 3.00
16 Kevin Love .50 1.25
17 Klay Thompson .60 1.50
18 Kyrie Irving 1.00 2.50
19 Nerlens Noel .40 1.00
20 Paul George .60 1.50
21 Russell Westbrook 1.25 3.00
22 Stephen Curry 2.00 5.00
23 Tim Duncan .75 2.00
24 Victor Oladipo .40 1.00
25 Zach LaVine .50 1.25

2015-16 Panini Contenders Draft Picks Collegiate Connections
APPX.ODDS 1:8 HOBBY
1 Hlls-Jffrsn/Jhnsn .40 1.00
2 Portis/Qualls .50 1.25
3 McDermott/Korver .40 1.00
4 Parker/Irving 1.00 2.50
5 Okafor/Winslow .60 1.50
6 Beal/Frazier II .50 1.25
7 Wiggins/Embiid .75 2.00
8 Davis/Wall 1.00 2.50
9 Harrison/Harrison .50 1.25
10 Towns/Cauley-Stein 2.50 6.00
11 Booker/Lyles 1.50 4.00
12 Harrell/Rozier .40 1.00
13 Martin/Mickey .40 1.00
14 Wade/Butler .75 2.00
15 Rose/Evans .60 1.50
16 Crawford/Burke .50 1.25
17 Barnes/Carter .60 1.50
18 Russell/Turner 1.25 3.00
19 Brooks/Young .40 1.00
20 Anthony/Carter-Williams .60 1.50
21 Durant/Turner 1.25 3.00
22 Love/Westbrook 1.25 3.00
23 Looney/LaVine .50 1.25
24 Paul/Duncan .75 2.00
25 Kaminsky/Dekker .50 1.25

2015-16 Panini Contenders Draft Picks Collegiate Connections Signatures
OVERALL FIVE AUTOS PER HOBBY BOX
1 Hollis-Jefferson/Johnson 30.00 80.00
2 Portis/Qualls
3 McDermott/Korver
4 Okafor/Winslow
5 Beal/Frazier II 25.00 60.00
6 Wiggins/Embiid
7 Harrison/Harrison
8 Towns/Cauley-Stein
9 Booker/Lyles 60.00 150.00
10 Harrell/Rozier 30.00 80.00
11 Martin/Mickey
12 Russell/Havlicek
13 Brooks/Young
14 Kaminsky/Dekker 50.00 120.00
15 Cook/Jones 40.00 100.00
16 Alexander/Oubre 12.00 30.00
17 Kidd-Gilchrist/Noel 25.00 60.00
18 Johnson/Cauley-Stein
19 McCullough/Christmas
20 Holmes/Turner 30.00 80.00
21 Looney/Wood
22 Vaughn/Drummond
23 Gordon/Johnson
25 Barnes/Tokoto 12.00 30.00

2015-16 Panini Contenders Draft Picks Game Day
APPX.ODDS 1:4 HOBBY
1 Aaron Harrison .50 1.25
2 Alan Williams .40 1.00
3 Andrew Harrison .60 1.50
4 Anthony Brown .40 1.00
5 Bobby Portis .60 1.50
6 Cameron Payne .50 1.25
7 Chris McCullough .40 1.00
8 Aaron White .50 1.25
9 Christian Wood .40 1.00
10 Cliff Alexander .40 1.00
11 D'Angelo Russell 1.50 4.00
12 Dakari Johnson .40 1.00
13 Delon Wright .50 1.25
14 Devin Booker 2.00 5.00
15 Frank Kaminsky .60 1.50
16 Jahlil Okafor .75 2.00
17 Jarell Martin .50 1.25
18 Jordan Mickey .40 1.00
19 Joe Young .50 1.25
20 Justin Anderson .50 1.25
21 Justise Winslow .60 1.50
22 Karl-Anthony Towns 3.00 8.00
23 Kelly Oubre Jr. .50 1.25
24 Branden Dawson .40 1.00
25 Kevon Looney .50 1.25
26 Michael Frazier II .50 1.25
27 Michael Qualls .60 1.50
28 Montrezl Harrell .50 1.25
29 Myles Turner .60 1.50
30 Norman Powell .50 1.25
31 Olivier Hanlan .40 1.00
32 Quinn Cook 1.25 3.00
33 R.J. Hunter .40 1.00
34 Rakeem Christmas .40 1.00
35 Rashad Vaughn .40 1.00
36 Richaun Holmes .50 1.25
37 Robert Upshaw .40 1.00
38 Rondae Hollis-Jefferson .50 1.25
39 Sam Dekker .50 1.25
40 Stanley Johnson .50 1.25
41 Terry Rozier .50 1.25
42 Trey Lyles .60 1.50
43 Tyler Harvey .40 1.00
44 Tyus Jones .60 1.50
45 Larry Nance Jr. .60 1.50
46 Willie Cauley-Stein .60 1.50
47 Darrun Hilliard .40 1.00

2015-16 Panini Contenders Draft Picks Old School Colors
COMPLETE SET (50) 12.00 30.00
RANDOM INSERTS IN PACKS
1 Andrew Wiggins .60 1.50
2 Anthony Davis .75 2.00
3 Blake Griffin .40 1.00
4 Carmelo Anthony .50 1.25
5 Chris Paul .50 1.25
6 Damian Lillard .75 2.00
7 DeMar DeRozan .40 1.00
8 DeMarcus Cousins .40 1.00
9 Derrick Rose .50 1.25
10 Dwyane Wade .60 1.50
11 Hassan Whiteside .30 .75
12 Jabari Parker .50 1.25
13 James Harden .60 1.50
14 Jimmy Butler .40 1.00
15 John Wall .50 1.25
16 Julius Randle .40 1.00
17 Kawhi Leonard .60 1.50
18 Kevin Durant 1.00 2.50
19 Kevin Love .40 1.00
20 Klay Thompson .50 1.25
21 Kyrie Irving .75 2.00
22 Marcus Smart .30 .75
23 Michael Carter-Williams .25 .60
24 Michael Kidd-Gilchrist .30 .75
25 Nerlens Noel .30 .75
26 Paul George .50 1.25
27 Paul Pierce .40 1.00
28 Russell Westbrook 1.00 2.50
29 Stephen Curry 1.50 4.00
30 Tim Duncan .60 1.50
31 Victor Oladipo .30 .75
32 Zach LaVine .40 1.00
33 Aaron Gordon .30 .75
34 Bradley Beal .40 1.00
35 Chris Bosh .40 1.00
36 DeAndre Jordan .40 1.00
37 Joe Johnson .30 .75
38 Nikola Vucevic .30 .75
39 Noah Vonleh .25 .60
40 Shabazz Napier .25 .60
41 Trey Burke .25 .60
42 Vince Carter .50 1.25
43 Andre Iguodala .30 .75
44 Deron Williams .30 .75
45 Derrick Favors .30 .75
46 Doug McDermott .30 .75
47 Gordon Hayward .40 1.00
48 Harrison Barnes .30 .75
49 Jimmer Fredette .25 .60
50 Joel Embiid .60 1.50

2015-16 Panini Contenders Draft Picks Old School Colors Signatures
OVERALL FIVE AUTOS PER HOBBY BOX
1 Aaron Gordon 4.00 10.00
2 Al-Farouq Aminu 4.00 10.00
3 Andre Drummond
4 Ben Gordon 4.00 10.00
5 Harrison Barnes 25.00 60.00
6 Jabari Brown 4.00 10.00
7 Joel Embiid
8 Jordan Clarkson
9 Jrue Holiday
10 Julius Randle
11 Kentavious Caldwell-Pope 4.00 10.00
12 Victor Oladipo 4.00 10.00
13 Kyle Korver 4.00 10.00
14 Marcus Smart 4.00 10.00
15 Mason Plumlee
16 Michael Carter-Williams 10.00 25.00
17 Michael Kidd-Gilchrist
18 Mo Williams 4.00 10.00
19 Nerlens Noel 4.00 10.00
20 Noah Vonleh 3.00 8.00
21 Richard Jefferson
22 Roy Hibbert
23 Tim Hardaway Jr.
24 Trey Burke 3.00 8.00

2015-16 Panini Contenders Draft Picks Passports
RANDOM INSERTS IN PACKS
1 Emmanuel Mudiay .60 1.50
2 Kristaps Porzingis 1.50 4.00
3 Mario Hezonja .50 1.25

2015-16 Panini Contenders Draft Picks School Colors
COMPLETE SET (50) 12.00 30.00
RANDOM INSERTS IN PACKS
1 Aaron Harrison .30 .75
2 Alan Williams .25 .60
3 Andrew Harrison .40 1.00
4 Anthony Brown .25 .60
5 Bobby Portis .40 1.00
6 Brandon Ashley .25 .60
7 Cameron Payne .30 .75
8 Chris McCullough .25 .60
9 Aaron White .30 .75
10 Christian Wood .25 .60
11 Cliff Alexander .25 .60
12 D'Angelo Russell 1.00 2.50
13 Dakari Johnson .25 .60
14 Delon Wright .30 .75
15 Devin Booker 1.25 3.00
16 Frank Kaminsky .40 1.00
17 J.P. Tokoto .30 .75
18 Jahlil Okafor .50 1.25
19 Jarell Martin .30 .75
20 Jordan Mickey .25 .60
21 Joe Young .30 .75
22 Justin Anderson .30 .75
23 Justise Winslow .40 1.00
24 Karl-Anthony Towns 2.00 5.00
25 Kelly Oubre Jr. .30 .75
26 Branden Dawson .25 .60
27 Kevon Looney .30 .75
28 Michael Frazier II .30 .75
29 Michael Qualls .40 1.00
30 Montrezl Harrell .30 .75
31 Myles Turner .40 1.00
32 Norman Powell .30 .75
33 Olivier Hanlan .25 .60
34 Quinn Cook .75 2.00
35 R.J. Hunter .25 .60
36 Rakeem Christmas .25 .60
37 Rashad Vaughn .25 .60
38 Richaun Holmes .30 .75
39 Robert Upshaw .25 .60
40 Rondae Hollis-Jefferson .30 .75
41 Sam Dekker .30 .75
42 Stanley Johnson .30 .75
43 Terran Petteway .25 .60
44 Terry Rozier .30 .75
45 Josh Richardson .40 1.00
46 Trey Lyles .40 1.00
47 Tyler Harvey .25 .60
48 Tyus Jones .40 1.00
49 Larry Nance Jr. .40 1.00
50 Willie Cauley-Stein .40 1.00

2015-16 Panini Contenders Draft Picks School Colors Signatures
OVERALL FIVE AUTOS PER HOBBY BOX
1 Karl-Anthony Towns 150.00 250.00
2 Jahlil Okafor
3 D'Angelo Russell
4 Willie Cauley-Stein 10.00 25.00
5 Justise Winslow 25.00 60.00
6 Devin Booker
7 Stanley Johnson 15.00 40.00
8 Myles Turner
9 Trey Lyles
10 Frank Kaminsky
11 Cameron Payne
12 Sam Dekker
13 Kevon Looney
14 Kelly Oubre Jr.
15 Tyus Jones 12.00 30.00
16 Bobby Portis
17 R.J. Hunter 3.00 8.00
18 Delon Wright
19 Montrezl Harrell 4.00 10.00
20 Rondae Hollis-Jefferson 8.00 20.00
21 Christian Wood
22 Justin Anderson 4.00 10.00
23 Rashad Vaughn
24 Chris McCullough 3.00 8.00
25 Terry Rozier 4.00 10.00

2016-17 Panini Contenders Draft Picks
OVERALL FIVE AUTOS PER HOBBY BOX
1 Aaron Gordon .25 .60
2 Al-Farouq Aminu .25 .60
3 Andre Drummond .30 .75
4 Andre Iguodala .25 .60
5 Andrew Wiggins .50 1.25
6 Anthony Davis .60 1.50
7 Arron Afflalo .20 .50
8 Ben Gordon .25 .60
9 Blake Griffin .30 .75
10 Bobby Portis .20 .50
11 Bradley Beal .30 .75
12 Brook Lopez .25 .60
13 Cameron Payne .20 .50
14 Zach LaVine .30 .75
15 Carmelo Anthony .40 1.00
16 Chris Bosh .30 .75
17 Chris McCullough .20 .50
18 Chris Paul .40 1.00
19 D'Angelo Russell .40 1.00
20 Damian Lillard .60 1.50
21 David Lee .20 .50
22 DeAndre Jordan .30 .75
23 Delon Wright .20 .50
24 DeMar DeRozan .30 .75
25 DeMarcus Cousins .30 .75
26 Deron Williams .25 .60
27 Derrick Favors .25 .60
28 Derrick Rose .40 1.00
29 Devin Booker .50 1.25
30 Doug McDermott .25 .60
31 Draymond Green .40 1.00
32 Dwyane Wade .50 1.25
33 Frank Kaminsky .25 .60
34 Gordon Hayward .30 .75
35 Harrison Barnes .25 .60
36 Hassan Whiteside .25 .60
37 Willie Cauley-Stein .25 .60
38 Jabari Parker .40 1.00
39 Jahlil Okafor .25 .60
40 James Harden .50 1.25
41 Vince Carter .40 1.00
42 Jimmy Butler .30 .75
43 Joakim Noah .25 .60
44 Joe Johnson .25 .60
45 Joel Embiid .50 1.25
46 John Wall .40 1.00
47 Jordan Clarkson .25 .60
48 Josh Richardson .20 .50
49 Jrue Holiday .25 .60
50 Julius Randle .30 .75
51 Justin Anderson .25 .60
52 Justise Winslow .25 .60
53 Karl-Anthony Towns .75 2.00
54 Kawhi Leonard .50 1.25
55 Kelly Oubre Jr. .20 .50
56 Kentavious Caldwell-Pope .25 .60
57 Kevin Durant .75 2.00
58 Kevin Love .30 .75
59 Kevon Looney .25 .60
60 Klay Thompson .40 1.00
61 Kyle Korver .25 .60
62 Kyrie Irving .60 1.50
63 LaMarcus Aldridge .30 .75
64 Larry Nance Jr. .25 .60
65 Marcus Smart .25 .60
66 Mason Plumlee .25 .60
67 Michael Carter-Williams .20 .50
68 Victor Oladipo .25 .60
69 Michael Kidd-Gilchrist .25 .60
70 Mike Conley .25 .60
71 Mo Williams .25 .60
72 Myles Turner .25 .60
73 Nerlens Noel .25 .60
74 Nikola Vucevic .25 .60
75 Noah Vonleh .20 .50
76 Paul George .40 1.00
77 Paul Pierce .30 .75
78 R.J. Hunter .20 .50
79 Rajon Rondo .30 .75
80 Rashad Vaughn .20 .50
81 Richard Jefferson .25 .60
82 Rondae Hollis-Jefferson .20 .50
83 Roy Hibbert .25 .60
84 Russell Westbrook .75 2.00
85 Sam Dekker .25 .60
86 Shabazz Napier .20 .50
87 Stanley Johnson .20 .50
88 Stephen Curry 1.25 3.00
89 Terry Rozier .25 .60
90 Tim Duncan .50 1.25
91 Tim Hardaway Jr. .20 .50
92 Trevor Ariza .20 .50
93 Trey Burke .20 .50
94 Trey Lyles .25 .60
95 Tyreke Evans .20 .50
96 Tyus Jones .20 .50
102A Ingram AU Wht jsy 60.00 150.00
102B Ingram AU Blk jsy 60.00 150.00
103A Murray AU Wht jsy 25.00 60.00
103B Murray AU Blue jsy 25.00 60.00
104A Hield AU Red jsy 25.00 60.00
104B Hield AU Wht jsy 25.00 60.00
105A Henry Ellenson AU 4.00 10.00
Blue jersey
105B Henry Ellenson AU 4.00 10.00
Yellow jersey
106A Dunn AU Gray jsy 10.00 25.00
106B Dunn AU Wht jsy 10.00 25.00
107A Chriss AU Wht jsy 12.00 30.00
107B Chriss AU Prpl jsy 12.00 30.00
108A Brown AU Wht jsy 20.00 50.00
108B Brown AU Ylw jsy 20.00 50.00
109A Jakob Poeltl AU 4.00 10.00
Black jersey
109B Jakob Poeltl AU 4.00 10.00
White jersey
110A Labissiere AU Wht jsy 10.00 25.00
110B Labissiere AU Blue jsy 10.00 25.00
111A Deyonta Davis AU 3.00 8.00
Dribbling
111B Deyonta Davis AU 3.00 8.00
No ball
112A Valentine AU Wht jsy 12.00 30.00
112B Valentine AU Grn jsy 12.00 30.00
113A Ulis AU Blue jsy 12.00 30.00
113B Ulis AU Wht jsy 12.00 30.00
114A Diamond Stone AU 3.00 8.00
Yellow jersey
114B Diamond Stone AU 3.00 8.00
White jersey
115A Murray AU Gld jsy 10.00 25.00
115B Murray AU Blk jsy 10.00 25.00
116A Sabonis AU Ball on side 5.00 12.00
116B Sabonis AU Ball at mid 5.00 12.00
117A Wade Baldwin IV AU 3.00 8.00
White jersey
117B Wade Baldwin IV AU 3.00 8.00
Gold jersey
118A DeAndre Bembry AU 3.00 8.00
Red jersey
118B DeAndre Bembry AU 3.00 8.00
White jersey
119A Stephen Zimmerman AU 3.00 8.00
Two hands on ball
119B Stephen Zimmerman AU 3.00 8.00
Dunking
120A Demetrius Jackson AU 3.00 8.00
120B Demetrius Jackson AU 3.00 8.00
121A Ben Bentil AU 3.00 8.00
Dribbling
121B Ben Bentil AU 3.00 8.00
Ball over head
122A Johnson AU Lt blue jsy 12.00 30.00
122B Johnson AU Blk jsy 12.00 30.00
123A Cheick Diallo AU 3.00 8.00
Ball over head
123B Cheick Diallo AU 3.00 8.00
Ball at hip
124A Malik Beasley AU 3.00 8.00
Red jersey
124B Malik Beasley AU 3.00 8.00
Black jersey
125A LeVert AU Dark jsy 10.00 25.00
125B LeVert AU Wht jsy 10.00 25.00
127A Taurean Prince AU 5.00 12.00
Green jersey
127B Taurean Prince AU 5.00 12.00
Black jersey
128A Richardson AU Orng jsy 6.00 15.00
128B Richardson AU Wht jsy 6.00 15.00
129A McCaw AU Wht jsy 6.00 15.00
129B McCaw AU Blk jsy 6.00 15.00
130A Jarrod Uthoff AU 3.00 8.00
Black jersey
130B Jarrod Uthoff AU 3.00 8.00
White jersey
131A Damian Jones AU 3.00 8.00
Ball at midsection
131B Damian Jones AU 3.00 8.00
Facing right
132A Anthony Barber AU 4.00 10.00
Facing forward
132B Anthony Barber AU 4.00 10.00
Facing left
133A Brogdon AU Dark jsy 10.00 25.00
133B Brogdon AU Wht jsy 10.00 25.00
134A Elgin Cook AU 3.00 8.00
Ball in right hand
134B Elgin Cook AU 3.00 8.00
Ball in left hand
135A Gary Payton II AU 4.00 10.00
Orange jersey
135B Gary Payton II AU 4.00 10.00
White jersey
136A Kay Felder AU 3.00 8.00
Driving
136B Kay Felder AU 3.00 8.00
Making fist
137A Robert Carter AU 3.00 8.00
Ball at midsection
137B Robert Carter AU 3.00 8.00
Ball at head
138A James Webb III AU 3.00 8.00
Ball in right hand
138B James Webb III AU 3.00 8.00
Two hands on ball
139A Baker AU Wht jsy 8.00 20.00
139B Baker AU Ylw jsy 8.00 20.00
140A Jake Layman AU 4.00 10.00
Yellow jersey
140B Jake Layman AU 4.00 10.00
White jersey
141A Paige AU Ball at head 10.00 25.00
141B Paige AU Dribbling 10.00 25.00
142A Jalen Reynolds AU 3.00 8.00
White jersey
142B Jalen Reynolds AU 3.00 8.00
Black jersey
143A Pascal Siakam AU 3.00 8.00
Red jersey
143B Pascal Siakam AU 3.00 8.00
White jersey
144A VanVleet AU Wht jsy 6.00 15.00
144B VanVleet AU Blk jsy 6.00 15.00
146A Tim Quarterman AU 3.00 8.00
White jersey
146B Tim Quarterman AU 3.00 8.00
Yellow jersey
148A Wayne Selden Jr. AU 4.00 10.00
White jersey
148B Wayne Selden Jr. AU 4.00 10.00
Blue jersey
149A Perry Ellis AU 4.00 10.00
White jersey
149B Perry Ellis AU 4.00 10.00
Blue jersey
150A Chinanu Onuaku AU 3.00 8.00
Red jersey
150B Chinanu Onuaku AU 3.00 8.00
White jersey
151 Daniel Hamilton AU 3.00 8.00
152 Rasheed Sulaimon AU 4.00 10.00
153 Rosco Allen AU 3.00 8.00
154 A.J. Hammons AU 3.00 8.00
156 Alex Poythress AU 5.00 12.00
157 Georges Niang AU 6.00 15.00
158 A.J. Hammons AU 3.00 8.00
159 Dorian Finney-Smith AU 4.00 10.00
160 Troy Williams AU 5.00 12.00
161 Danuel House AU 3.00 8.00
162 Devin Williams AU 4.00 10.00
163 David Walker AU 3.00 8.00
164 Rico Gathers AU 3.00 8.00
165 Kyle Wiltjer AU 3.00 8.00
166 Shawn Long AU 3.00 8.00
167 Isaiah Taylor AU 3.00 8.00
168 Yogi Ferrell AU 6.00 15.00
169 Prince Ibeh AU 3.00 8.00
171 Damion Lee AU 3.00 8.00
172 Sheldon McClellan AU 3.00 8.00
173 Joel Bolomboy AU 3.00 8.00
176 Stefan Jankovic AU 3.00 8.00
178 Abdel Nader AU 3.00 8.00
179 Marshall Plumlee AU 3.00 8.00
180 Tre Demps AU 3.00 8.00
181 Nikola Jovanovic AU 3.00 8.00
182 Derrick Jones AU 4.00 10.00
183 Cameron Ridley AU 3.00 8.00
184 Daniel Ochefu AU 3.00 8.00
190 Dragan Bender AU 8.00 20.00
192 Georgios Papagiannis AU 3.00 8.00
193 Timothe Luwawu-Cabarrot AU 6.00 15.00
195 Mindaugas Kuzminskas AU 8.00 20.00
197 Ivica Zubac AU 5.00 12.00
198 Isaia Cordinier AU 3.00 8.00
199 Thon Maker AU 25.00 60.00

2016-17 Panini Contenders Draft Picks Cracked Ice Ticket
*CRCKD ICE 1-96: 5X TO 12X BASIC
*CRCKD ICE 102-199: .75X TO 2X BASIC
OVERALL FIVE AUTOS PER HOBBY BOX
STATED PRINT RUN 23 SER.#'d SETS
102A Ingram AU Wht jsy 150.00 400.00
102B Ingram AU Blk jsy 150.00 400.00
104A Hield AU Red jsy 125.00 300.00
104B Hield AU Wht jsy 125.00 300.00
106A Dunn AU Gray jsy 100.00 250.00
106B Dunn AU Wht jsy 100.00 250.00
113A Ulis AU Blue jsy 75.00 200.00
113B Ulis AU Wht jsy 75.00 200.00

2016-17 Panini Contenders Draft Picks Draft Ticket
*DRFT 1-96: 2X TO 5X BASIC
*DRFT 102-199: .5X TO 1.2X BASIC
OVERALL FIVE AUTOS PER HOBBY BOX
STATED PRINT RUN 99 SER.#'d SETS

2016-17 Panini Contenders Draft Picks Alumni Ink
OVERALL FIVE AUTOS PER HOBBY BOX
1 Andrew Wiggins
2 Anthony Davis
3 Chris Paul
4 Dwyane Wade
5 Kevin Durant
6 Kyrie Irving
7 Shaquille O'Neal
8 Ralph Sampson
9 Magic Johnson
10 Kevin Love
11 James Worthy
12 Gail Goodrich
13 David Robinson
14 Danny Manning 4.00 10.00
15 Carmelo Anthony
18 Draymond Green
19 Gordon Hayward
20 Nikola Vucevic

2016-17 Panini Contenders Draft Picks Class Reunion
1 Ben Simmons 1.50 4.00
2 Brandon Ingram 1.50 4.00
3 Jamal Murray .75 2.00
4 Buddy Hield .60 1.50
5 Henry Ellenson .30 .75
6 Kris Dunn .75 2.00
7 Marquese Chriss .60 1.50
8 Jaylen Brown 1.00 2.50
9 Jakob Poeltl .30 .75
10 Skal Labissiere .40 1.00
11 Deyonta Davis .25 .60
12 Denzel Valentine .30 .75
13 Tyler Ulis .75 2.00
14 Diamond Stone .25 .60
15 Dejounte Murray .50 1.25
16 Domantas Sabonis .40 1.00
17 Wade Baldwin IV .25 .60
18 DeAndre Bembry .30 .75
19 Stephen Zimmerman .25 .60
20 Malachi Richardson .30 .75

2016-17 Panini Contenders Draft Picks Collegiate Connections
1 Murray/Labissiere .75 2.00
2 Murray/Chriss .60 1.50
3 Valentine/Davis .30 .75
4 Bentil/Dunn .75 2.00
5 Simmons/Quarterman 1.50 4.00
6 McCaw/Zimmerman .50 1.25
7 Damian Jones .25 .60
Wade Baldwin IV
8 Diamond Stone .25 .60
Robert Carter
9 Brown/Wallace 1.00 2.50
10 Hield/Cousins .60 1.50
11 Murray/Ulis .75 2.00
12 Cheick Diallo .30 .75
Wayne Selden Jr.
13 Brice Johnson .25 .60
Marcus Paige
14 Daniel Ochefu .40 1.00
Ryan Arcidiacono
15 Ingram/Plumlee 1.50 4.00
16 Sabonis/Wiltjer .40 1.00
17 Jake Layman .30 .75
Robert Carter
18 Fred VanVleet .50 1.25
Ron Baker
19 Rico Gathers .40 1.00
Taurean Prince
20 Malachi Richardson .30 .75
Michael Gbinije

2016-17 Panini Contenders Draft Picks Collegiate Connections Signatures
OVERALL FIVE AUTOS PER HOBBY BOX
1 Murray/Labissiere 50.00 120.00
2 Murray/Chriss
3 Valentine/Davis
4 Bentil/Dunn
6 McCaw/Zimmerman
7 Jones/Baldwin IV 12.00 30.00
8 Stone/Carter 20.00 50.00

2016-17 Panini Contenders Draft Picks Game Day
RANDOM INSERTS IN PACKS
1 Ben Simmons 1.50 4.00
2 Brandon Ingram 1.50 4.00
3 Jamal Murray .75 2.00
4 Buddy Hield .60 1.50
5 Henry Ellenson .30 .75
6 Kris Dunn .75 2.00
7 Marquese Chriss .60 1.50
8 Jaylen Brown 1.00 2.50
9 Jakob Poeltl .30 .75
10 Skal Labissiere .40 1.00
11 Deyonta Davis .25 .60
12 Denzel Valentine .30 .75
13 Tyler Ulis .75 2.00
14 Diamond Stone .25 .60
15 Dejounte Murray .50 1.25
16 Domantas Sabonis .40 1.00
17 Wade Baldwin IV .25 .60
18 DeAndre Bembry .25 .60
19 Stephen Zimmerman .25 .60
20 Malachi Richardson .30 .75

2016-17 Panini Contenders Draft Picks Old School Colors
RANDOM INSERTS IN PACKS
1 Andrew Wiggins .60 1.50
2 Anthony Davis .75 2.00
3 Blake Griffin .40 1.00
4 Carmelo Anthony .50 1.25
5 Chris Paul .50 1.25
6 DeMar DeRozan .40 1.00
7 DeMarcus Cousins .40 1.00
8 James Harden .60 1.50
9 Jimmy Butler .40 1.00
10 John Wall .50 1.25
11 Karl-Anthony Towns 1.00 2.50
12 Kawhi Leonard .60 1.50
13 Kevin Durant 1.00 2.50
14 Klay Thompson .50 1.25
15 Kyrie Irving .75 2.00
16 Myles Turner .30 .75
17 Paul George .50 1.25
18 Russell Westbrook 1.00 2.50
19 Stephen Curry 1.50 4.00

2016-17 Panini Contenders Draft Picks Old School Colors Signatures
OVERALL FIVE AUTOS PER HOBBY BOX
1 Andrew Wiggins
2 Anthony Davis
3 Dwyane Wade
5 Draymond Green
6 James Worthy 6.00 15.00
7 David Robinson
8 Danny Manning
9 Carmelo Anthony
10 Gail Goodrich

2016-17 Panini Contenders Draft Picks School Colors
RANDOM INSERTS IN PACKS
1 Ben Simmons 1.50 4.00
2 Brandon Ingram 1.50 4.00
3 Jamal Murray .75 2.00
4 Buddy Hield .60 1.50
5 Henry Ellenson .30 .75
6 Kris Dunn .75 2.00
7 Marquese Chriss .60 1.50
8 Jaylen Brown 1.00 2.50
9 Jakob Poeltl .30 .75
10 Skal Labissiere .40 1.00
11 Deyonta Davis .25 .60
12 Denzel Valentine .30 .75
13 Tyler Ulis .75 2.00
14 Diamond Stone .25 .60
15 Dejounte Murray .50 1.25
16 Domantas Sabonis .40 1.00
17 Wade Baldwin IV .25 .60
18 DeAndre Bembry .25 .60
19 Stephen Zimmerman .25 .60
20 Malachi Richardson .30 .75

2016-17 Panini Contenders Draft Picks School Colors Signatures
OVERALL FIVE AUTOS PER HOBBY BOX
2 Brandon Ingram
3 Jamal Murray
4 Buddy Hield
5 Henry Ellenson
6 Kris Dunn 60.00 150.00
7 Marquese Chriss
8 Jaylen Brown
9 Jakob Poeltl
10 Skal Labissiere

2012-13 Panini Crusade
COMPLETE SET (100) 20.00 50.00
1 Blake Griffin .50 1.25
2 Chris Paul .60 1.50
3 Grant Hill .60 1.50
4 Dwight Howard .40 1.00
5 Kobe Bryant 2.00 5.00
6 Pau Gasol .50 1.25
7 Steve Nash .50 1.25
8 Marc Gasol .50 1.25
9 Rudy Gay .50 1.25
10 Zach Randolph .40 1.00
11 Chris Bosh .50 1.25
12 Dwyane Wade .75 2.00
13 LeBron James 2.00 5.00
14 Brandon Jennings .30 .75
15 Mike Dunleavy .30 .75
16 Monta Ellis .40 1.00
17 Andrei Kirilenko .40 1.00
18 Kevin Love .50 1.25
19 Ricky Rubio .50 1.25
20 Al-Farouq Aminu .40 1.00
21 Eric Gordon .40 1.00
22 Greivis Vasquez .40 1.00
23 Amar'e Stoudemire .40 1.00
24 Carmelo Anthony .60 1.50
25 Jason Kidd .50 1.25
26 Rasheed Wallace .50 1.25
27 Raymond Felton .40 1.00
28 Kendrick Perkins .30 .75
29 Kevin Durant 1.25 3.00
30 Russell Westbrook 1.25 3.00
31 Serge Ibaka .40 1.00
32 Thabo Sefolosha .30 .75
33 Evan Turner .30 .75
34 Jrue Holiday .50 1.25
35 Nick Young .40 1.00
36 Goran Dragic .40 1.00
37 Jared Dudley .30 .75
38 Marcin Gortat .40 1.00
39 LaMarcus Aldridge .50 1.25
40 Nicolas Batum .40 1.00
41 Wesley Matthews .30 .75
42 DeMarcus Cousins .50 1.25
43 Tyreke Evans .30 .75
44 Manu Ginobili .50 1.25
45 Tim Duncan .75 2.00
46 Tony Parker .50 1.25
47 DeMar DeRozan .50 1.25
48 Kyle Lowry .40 1.00
49 Jose Calderon .30 .75
50 Al Jefferson .40 1.00
51 Gordon Hayward .50 1.25
52 John Wall .60 1.50
53 Jordan Crawford .30 .75
54 Al Horford .40 1.00
55 Josh Smith .40 1.00
56 Kevin Garnett .75 2.00
57 Paul Pierce .50 1.25
58 Rajon Rondo .50 1.25
59 Brook Lopez .40 1.00
60 Deron Williams .40 1.00
61 Gerald Wallace .40 1.00
62 Kris Humphries .30 .75
63 Ben Gordon .40 1.00
64 Gerald Henderson .30 .75
65 Derrick Rose .60 1.50
66 Joakim Noah .40 1.00
67 Luol Deng .40 1.00
68 Taj Gibson .40 1.00
69 Alonzo Gee .30 .75
70 Anderson Varejao .30 .75
71 Dirk Nowitzki .60 1.50
72 Vince Carter .60 1.50
73 Andre Iguodala .40 1.00
74 Ty Lawson .30 .75
75 Greg Monroe .40 1.00
76 Rodney Stuckey .40 1.00
77 Tayshaun Prince .40 1.00
78 David Lee .30 .75
79 Stephen Curry 2.00 5.00
80 James Harden .75 2.00
81 Jeremy Lin .50 1.25
82 Omer Asik .40 1.00
83 David West .40 1.00
84 George Hill .40 1.00
85 Paul George .60 1.50
86 Alexey Shved RC .40 1.00
87 Andre Drummond RC 1.00 2.50
88 Anthony Davis RC 3.00 8.00
89 Bradley Beal RC 1.00 2.50
90 Brandon Knight RC .60 1.50
91 Chandler Parsons RC .60 1.50
92 Damian Lillard RC 2.50 6.00
93 Harrison Barnes RC 1.00 2.50
94 Jared Sullinger RC .50 1.25
95 Kemba Walker RC 1.25 3.00
96 Kenneth Faried RC .60 1.50
97 Klay Thompson RC 2.50 6.00
98 Kyrie Irving RC 3.00 8.00
99 Michael Kidd-Gilchrist RC .60 1.50
100 Tristan Thompson RC .60 1.50

2012-13 Panini Crusade Insert Blue
1 Jared Sullinger 1.50 4.00
2 Anthony Davis 25.00 60.00
3 Will Barton 1.50 4.00
4 Nolan Smith 1.25 3.00
5 Enes Kanter 1.50 4.00
6 Jeff Taylor 1.25 3.00
7 Kevin Murphy 1.25 3.00
8 Klay Thompson 8.00 20.00
9 Draymond Green 6.00 15.00
10 Andrew Nicholson 1.25 3.00
11 Tyler Zeller 1.50 4.00
12 Austin Rivers 2.00 5.00
13 E'Twaun Moore 1.25 3.00
14 Nikola Vucevic 2.00 5.00
15 Kyle Singler 1.25 3.00
16 Nando De Colo 1.25 3.00
17 Kenneth Faried 2.00 5.00
18 Jared Cunningham 1.25 3.00
19 Dion Waiters 2.00 5.00
20 Andre Drummond 3.00 8.00
21 Tristan Thompson 2.00 5.00
22 Bradley Beal 3.00 8.00
23 Evan Fournier 2.00 5.00
24 Tornike Shengelia 1.25 3.00
25 Kyrie Irving 15.00 40.00
26 Jimmer Fredette 1.25 3.00
27 Kendall Marshall 1.25 3.00
28 Jan Vesely 1.25 3.00
29 Derrick Williams 1.25 3.00
30 Fab Melo 1.25 3.00
31 Tobias Harris 2.00 5.00
32 Brandon Knight 2.00 5.00
33 Alexey Shved 1.25 3.00
34 Mirza Teletovic 1.50 4.00
35 Lance Thomas 1.25 3.00
36 Jeremy Lamb 2.00 5.00
37 Kemba Walker 4.00 10.00
38 Jae Crowder 1.50 4.00
39 DeAndre Liggins 1.50 4.00
40 Alec Burks 2.00 5.00
41 Thomas Robinson 1.50 4.00
42 Brian Roberts 1.25 3.00
43 Festus Ezeli 1.50 4.00
44 Miles Plumlee 1.25 3.00
45 Lavoy Allen 1.25 3.00
46 Jimmy Butler 6.00 15.00
47 Kawhi Leonard 10.00 25.00
48 Isaiah Thomas 3.00 8.00
49 Darius Morris 1.25 3.00
50 Orlando Johnson 1.25 3.00
51 Terrence Ross 2.00 5.00
52 Chandler Parsons 2.00 5.00
53 Greg Stiemsma 1.25 3.00
54 Meyers Leonard 1.50 4.00
55 Marcus Morris 1.50 4.00
56 MarShon Brooks 1.50 4.00
57 Jordan Hamilton 1.25 3.00
58 Iman Shumpert 2.00 5.00
59 Darius Miller 1.25 3.00
60 Pablo Prigioni 1.25 3.00
61 Terrence Jones 1.50 4.00
62 Chris Copeland 1.25 3.00
63 Gustavo Ayon 1.25 3.00
64 John Henson 2.00 5.00
65 Markieff Morris 2.00 5.00
66 Norris Cole 1.25 3.00
67 John Jenkins 1.25 3.00
68 Harrison Barnes 3.00 8.00
69 Damian Lillard 12.00 30.00
70 Reggie Jackson 2.00 5.00
71 Dominique Wilkins 2.50 6.00
72 Karl Malone 2.50 6.00
73 Hakeem Olajuwon 2.50 6.00
74 James Worthy 2.50 6.00
75 Larry Bird 5.00 12.00
76 Toni Kukoc 2.00 5.00
77 Rick Mahorn 1.25 3.00
78 Len Elmore 1.25 3.00
79 Julius Erving 3.00 8.00
80 Vlade Divac 2.00 5.00
81 Doc Rivers 2.00 5.00
82 Manute Bol 2.00 5.00
83 Robert Horry 1.50 4.00
84 Jerry West 2.50 6.00
85 Kevin McHale 2.00 5.00
86 Zydrunas Ilgauskas 1.50 4.00
87 Joe Dumars 2.00 5.00
88 Moses Malone 2.00 5.00
89 Allen Iverson 2.50 6.00
90 Wilt Chamberlain 4.00 10.00
91 Gary Payton 2.00 5.00
92 Rod Strickland 1.25 3.00
93 Sam Cassell 1.50 4.00
94 Kareem Abdul-Jabbar 3.00 8.00
95 Bob Cousy 3.00 8.00
96 Mark Price 2.00 5.00
97 Isiah Thomas 2.00 5.00
98 Sidney Moncrief 1.25 3.00
99 Willis Reed 2.00 5.00
100 Horace Grant 2.00 5.00
101 Shawn Kemp 3.00 8.00
102 Wes Unseld 2.00 5.00
103 Steve Francis 1.50 4.00
104 Magic Johnson 5.00 12.00
105 Bill Russell 3.00 8.00
106 Larry Nance 1.50 4.00
107 Dennis Rodman 4.00 10.00
108 Clyde Lovellette 2.00 5.00
109 Patrick Ewing 2.50 6.00
110 Shareef Abdur-Rahim 1.50 4.00
111 Detlef Schrempf 2.00 5.00
112 Chris Webber 2.00 5.00
113 Chris Mullin 2.00 5.00
114 Michael Cooper 1.50 4.00
115 Larry Johnson 2.50 6.00
116 Dell Curry 1.25 3.00
117 Bob Lanier 1.50 4.00
118 Anfernee Hardaway 5.00 12.00
119 John Starks 1.50 4.00
120 Bobby Jackson 1.25 3.00
121 Dolph Schayes 2.00 5.00
122 Tim Hardaway 2.00 5.00
123 A.C. Green 2.00 5.00
124 Nick Van Exel 2.00 5.00
125 Glen Rice 1.50 4.00
126 Michael Finley 2.00 5.00
127 Bill Laimbeer 1.50 4.00
128 Bill Walton 2.00 5.00
129 Jason Kidd 2.00 5.00
130 Cedric Maxwell 1.25 3.00
131 Jeff Hornacek 1.50 4.00
132 Calvin Murphy 1.50 4.00
133 Bob McAdoo 1.50 4.00
134 Shaquille O'Neal 4.00 10.00
135 Anthony Mason 1.50 4.00
136 Jim Jackson 1.25 3.00
137 George Gervin 2.00 5.00

138 Tom Chambers 1.50 4.00
139 Allan Houston 1.50 4.00
140 Bernard King 1.50 4.00
141 John Stockton 3.00 8.00
142 Yao Ming 2.50 6.00
143 Cedric Ceballos 1.25 3.00
144 Pete Maravich 3.00 8.00
145 Alonzo Mourning 2.50 6.00
146 Alex English 1.50 4.00
147 David Robinson 3.00 8.00
148 Kevin Johnson 2.00 5.00
149 Mark Jackson 1.50 4.00
150 Rick Barry 1.50 4.00
151 Kirk Hinrich 1.50 4.00
152 Shawn Marion 1.50 4.00
153 Nene 1.50 4.00
154 Richard Jefferson 1.50 4.00
155 Tiago Splitter 1.50 4.00
156 Kyle Lowry 1.50 4.00
157 Chris Paul 2.50 6.00
158 Kevin Love 2.00 5.00
159 O.J. Mayo 1.25 3.00
160 Brandon Jennings 1.25 3.00
161 LeBron James 10.00 25.00
162 Rasheed Wallace 2.00 5.00
163 Jamal Crawford 2.00 5.00
164 J.R. Smith 1.50 4.00
165 Danny Granger 1.50 4.00
166 Mike Dunleavy 1.25 3.00
167 Dwight Howard 1.50 4.00
168 Kevin Durant 5.00 12.00
169 Tim Duncan 3.00 8.00
170 Grant Hill 2.50 6.00
171 Mike Conley 1.50 4.00
172 Thabo Sefolosha 1.25 3.00
173 Josh Smith 1.50 4.00
174 Arron Afflalo 1.50 4.00
175 Dwyane Wade 3.00 8.00
176 Amar'e Stoudemire 1.50 4.00
177 Stephen Curry 8.00 20.00
178 Kevin Garnett 3.00 8.00
179 Anderson Varejao 1.25 3.00
180 Jarrett Jack 1.50 4.00
181 Tyler Hansbrough 1.50 4.00
182 Marcus Camby 1.50 4.00
183 DeAndre Jordan 2.00 5.00
184 Corey Brewer 1.25 3.00
185 Eric Bledsoe 1.50 4.00
186 Kendrick Perkins 1.25 3.00
187 Deron Williams 1.50 4.00
188 Paul Pierce 2.00 5.00
189 J.J. Hickson 1.25 3.00
190 Patrick Patterson 1.25 3.00
191 Raymond Felton 1.50 4.00
192 Russell Westbrook 5.00 12.00
193 Louis Williams 1.50 4.00
194 Kobe Bryant 8.00 20.00
195 Beno Udrih 1.25 3.00
196 Glen Davis 1.25 3.00
197 Nick Collison 1.50 4.00
198 Carl Landry 1.25 3.00
199 Hedo Turkoglu 1.50 4.00
200 Kevin Martin 1.50 4.00
201 Zaza Pachulia 1.25 3.00
202 Joe Johnson 1.50 4.00
203 Jeff Teague 1.50 4.00
204 Trevor Ariza 1.25 3.00
205 J.J. Redick 2.00 5.00
206 Greivis Vasquez 1.50 4.00
207 Earl Clark 1.25 3.00
208 Jose Calderon 1.25 3.00
209 Larry Sanders 1.25 3.00
210 Andrew Bynum 1.25 3.00
211 Jameer Nelson 1.25 3.00
212 Udonis Haslem 1.25 3.00
213 JaVale McGee 1.50 4.00
214 Thaddeus Young 1.25 3.00
215 Goran Dragic 1.50 4.00
216 Eric Gordon 1.50 4.00
217 Brandon Roy 2.00 5.00
218 Jamaal Tinsley 1.25 3.00
219 Jordan Crawford 1.25 3.00
220 Ty Lawson 1.25 3.00
221 Evan Turner 1.25 3.00
222 LaMarcus Aldridge 2.00 5.00
223 DeMarcus Cousins 2.00 5.00
224 Darrell Arthur 1.25 3.00
225 Derrick Favors 1.50 4.00
226 Nick Young 1.50 4.00
227 P.J. Tucker 1.25 3.00
228 Paul George 2.50 6.00
229 Danny Green 1.50 4.00
230 Jrue Holiday 2.00 5.00
231 Tyreke Evans 1.25 3.00
232 Andrei Kirilenko 1.50 4.00
233 Marc Gasol 2.00 5.00
234 Jason Richardson 2.00 5.00
235 Nicolas Batum 1.50 4.00
236 Shannon Brown 1.25 3.00
237 Brandon Bass 1.25 3.00
238 Blake Griffin 2.00 5.00
239 Tyrus Thomas 1.25 3.00
240 Rudy Gay 2.00 5.00
241 Al Horford 1.50 4.00
242 Marcus Thornton 1.25 3.00
243 Metta World Peace 2.00 5.00
244 Ed Davis 1.25 3.00
245 DeJuan Blair 1.25 3.00
246 John Wall 2.50 6.00
247 Manu Ginobili 2.00 5.00
248 Greg Monroe 1.50 4.00
249 George Hill 1.50 4.00
250 Andrea Bargnani 1.50 4.00
251 Roy Hibbert 1.50 4.00
252 Ersan Ilyasova 1.25 3.00
253 Andre Iguodala 1.50 4.00
254 Zach Randolph 1.50 4.00
255 Chase Budinger 1.25 3.00
256 Tony Parker 2.00 5.00
257 Rodney Stuckey 1.50 4.00
258 Shane Battier 1.50 4.00
259 Andre Miller 1.50 4.00
260 Richard Hamilton 1.50 4.00
261 Rashard Lewis 1.50 4.00
262 Tayshaun Prince 1.50 4.00
263 Amir Johnson 1.25 3.00
264 Al-Farouq Aminu 1.50 4.00
265 Brook Lopez 1.50 4.00
266 Jason Terry 1.50 4.00
267 Gerald Henderson 1.25 3.00
268 Marcin Gortat 1.50 4.00
269 Ray Allen 2.00 5.00
270 Jeremy Lin 2.00 5.00
271 Drew Gooden 1.50 4.00
272 Wilson Chandler 1.50 4.00
273 Ricky Rubio 2.00 5.00
274 Darren Collison 1.50 4.00
275 Spencer Hawes 1.25 3.00
276 Al Jefferson 1.50 4.00
277 Dirk Nowitzki 2.50 6.00
278 Alan Anderson 1.25 3.00
279 Jared Dudley 1.25 3.00
280 Derrick Rose 2.50 6.00
281 Luis Scola 1.50 4.00
282 Marvin Williams 1.50 4.00
283 Vince Carter 2.50 6.00
284 James Harden 3.00 8.00
285 Steve Nash 2.00 5.00
286 Chris Bosh 2.00 5.00
287 Luol Deng 1.50 4.00
288 Linas Kleiza 1.25 3.00
289 Joakim Noah 1.50 4.00
290 David Lee 1.25 3.00
291 Rajon Rondo 2.00 5.00
292 Serge Ibaka 1.50 4.00
293 Taj Gibson 1.50 4.00
294 Gordon Hayward 2.00 5.00
295 Tyson Chandler 1.50 4.00
296 David West 1.50 4.00
297 Caron Butler 1.50 4.00
298 Andrew Bogut 1.50 4.00
299 Carmelo Anthony 2.50 6.00
300 Chauncey Billups 2.00 5.00

2012-13 Panini Crusade Insert Green

*GREEN: 1.5X TO 4X BLUE
STATED PRINT RUN 25 SER.#'d SETS
2 Anthony Davis 60.00 120.00
89 Allen Iverson 25.00 60.00
110 Shareef Abdur-Rahim 12.00 30.00
161 LeBron James 150.00 300.00
168 Kevin Durant 50.00 120.00
194 Kobe Bryant 150.00 300.00

2012-13 Panini Crusade Insert Purple

*PURPLE: 1X TO 2.5X BLUE
STATED PRINT RUN 49 SER.#'d SETS
25 Kyrie Irving 50.00 120.00
161 LeBron James 50.00 120.00
194 Kobe Bryant 50.00 120.00

2012-13 Panini Crusade Insert Red

*RED: .6X TO 1.5X BLUE
STATED PRINT RUN 99 SER.#'d SETS

2012-13 Panini Crusade Knight Court

1 Kobe Bryant 6.00 15.00
2 Jason Kidd 1.50 4.00
3 LeBron James 6.00 15.00
4 Tim Duncan 2.50 6.00
5 Dwyane Wade 2.50 6.00
6 Kevin Love 1.50 4.00
7 James Harden 2.50 6.00
8 Carmelo Anthony 2.00 5.00
9 Derrick Rose 2.00 5.00
10 Russell Westbrook 4.00 10.00
11 Blake Griffin 1.50 4.00
12 Ricky Rubio 1.50 4.00
13 DeMarcus Cousins 1.50 4.00
14 Chris Paul 2.00 5.00
15 Steve Nash 1.50 4.00
16 Stephen Curry 6.00 15.00
17 Joakim Noah 1.25 3.00
18 Amar'e Stoudemire 1.25 3.00
19 Deron Williams 1.25 3.00
20 Kevin Garnett 2.50 6.00
21 Ray Allen 1.50 4.00
22 Greg Monroe 1.25 3.00
23 Zach Randolph 1.25 3.00
24 Dwight Howard 1.25 3.00
25 John Wall 2.00 5.00
26 LaMarcus Aldridge 1.50 4.00
27 Josh Smith 1.25 3.00
28 Tony Parker 1.50 4.00
29 Kevin Durant 4.00 10.00
30 Al Horford 1.25 3.00
31 Vince Carter 2.00 5.00
32 Rajon Rondo 1.50 4.00
33 Al Jefferson 1.25 3.00
34 Chris Bosh 1.50 4.00
35 Pau Gasol 1.50 4.00
36 Manu Ginobili 1.50 4.00
37 Jrue Holiday 1.50 4.00
38 Dirk Nowitzki 2.00 5.00
39 David Lee 1.00 2.50
40 Joe Johnson 1.25 3.00
41 Danny Granger 1.25 3.00
42 Paul Pierce 1.50 4.00
43 Antawn Jamison 1.25 3.00
44 Grant Hill 2.00 5.00
45 Jason Terry 1.25 3.00
46 Chauncey Billups 1.50 4.00
47 Shawn Marion 1.25 3.00
48 Roy Hibbert 1.25 3.00
49 Marc Gasol 1.50 4.00
50 Andrew Bynum 1.00 2.50

2012-13 Panini Crusade Majestic Materials

1 Blake Griffin 3.00 8.00
2 Andre Miller 2.50 6.00
3 Dennis Rodman 6.00 15.00
4 Trevor Ariza 2.00 5.00
5 Tim Duncan 5.00 12.00
6 Jalen Rose 3.00 8.00
7 Doc Rivers 3.00 8.00
8 Earl Monroe 15.00 40.00
9 Ricky Rubio 3.00 8.00
10 Alvan Adams 2.00 5.00
11 Patrick Ewing 4.00 10.00
12 Metta World Peace 3.00 8.00
13 Gary Payton 12.00 30.00
14 Dan Issel 2.50 6.00
15 Glen Rice 2.50 6.00
16 Julius Erving 5.00 12.00
17 Al Jefferson 2.50 6.00
18 Clyde Drexler 4.00 10.00
19 Rasheed Wallace 3.00 8.00
20 Kobe Bryant 12.00 30.00
21 Caron Butler 2.50 6.00
22 Jim Jackson 2.00 5.00
23 Alex English 2.50 6.00
24 Hakeem Olajuwon 4.00 10.00
25 Larry Johnson 4.00 10.00
26 Zydrunas Ilgauskas 2.50 6.00
27 Jason Kidd 3.00 8.00
28 Dwyane Wade 5.00 12.00
29 Paul Millsap 3.00 8.00
30 Chris Kaman 2.50 6.00
31 Amar'e Stoudemire 2.50 6.00
32 David Robinson 5.00 12.00
33 Alonzo Mourning 4.00 10.00
34 Roy Hibbert 2.50 6.00
35 Chris Paul 4.00 10.00
36 Rudy Gay 3.00 8.00
37 James Harden 5.00 12.00
38 Sean Elliott 3.00 8.00
39 Andrei Kirilenko 2.50 6.00
40 Dominique Wilkins 4.00 10.00
41 Jeff Hornacek 2.50 6.00
42 David Lee 2.00 5.00
43 Tyreke Evans 2.00 5.00
44 Zach Randolph 2.50 6.00
45 Marc Gasol 3.00 8.00
46 Lucius Allen 3.00 8.00
47 Dwight Howard 2.50 6.00
48 Detlef Schrempf 3.00 8.00
49 Danny Manning 2.50 6.00
50 Andrew Bogut 2.50 6.00
51 Paul Pierce 3.00 8.00
52 LeBron James 12.00 30.00
53 Nene 2.50 6.00
54 Deron Williams 2.50 6.00
55 Gerald Wallace 2.50 6.00
56 Elton Brand 3.00 8.00
57 Steve Nash 3.00 8.00
58 Stephen Curry 12.00 30.00
59 Dirk Nowitzki 4.00 10.00
60 Jason Terry 2.50 6.00
61 Ty Lawson 2.00 5.00
62 Kevin Durant 8.00 20.00
63 Tim Hardaway 3.00 8.00
64 Derrick Rose 4.00 10.00
65 Rick Mahorn 2.00 5.00
66 Allen Iverson 4.00 10.00
67 Kevin Garnett 5.00 12.00
68 Chris Bosh 3.00 8.00
69 J.J. Redick 3.00 8.00
70 Russell Westbrook 8.00 20.00
71 Drew Gooden 2.50 6.00
72 Rajon Rondo 3.00 8.00
73 Karl Malone 4.00 10.00
74 LaMarcus Aldridge 3.00 8.00
75 Tayshaun Prince 2.50 6.00
76 Vince Carter 4.00 10.00
77 James Worthy 4.00 10.00
78 Kelly Tripucka 2.00 5.00
79 Carmelo Anthony 4.00 10.00
80 Al Horford 2.50 6.00
81 Grant Hill 4.00 10.00
82 Mark Aguirre 2.50 6.00
83 Marcus Camby 2.50 6.00
84 Shawn Marion 2.50 6.00
85 Emeka Okafor 2.50 6.00
86 John Wall 4.00 10.00
87 Manu Ginobili 3.00 8.00
88 Bernard King 2.50 6.00
89 Bill Laimbeer 2.50 6.00
90 Shaquille O'Neal 6.00 15.00
91 Jamaal Wilkes
92 Andre Iguodala 2.50 6.00
93 Kevin Love 3.00 8.00
94 Robert Parish 3.00 8.00
95 Anthony Mason 2.50 6.00
96 Chris Mullin 3.00 8.00
97 Mark Eaton 2.00 5.00
98 Peja Stojakovic 3.00 8.00
99 Shawn Kemp 12.00 30.00
100 Michael Cage 2.00 5.00

2012-13 Panini Crusade Majestic Materials Prime

*PRIME: 1.2X TO 3X BASIC
PRINT RUNS B/WN 1-25 COPIES PER
NO PRICING ON QTY 15 OR LESS

2012-13 Panini Crusade Majestic Signatures

EXCHANGE DEADLINE 12/12/2014
1 Kevin Durant 50.00 120.00
2 Kobe Bryant 100.00 200.00
3 Jared Dudley 3.00 8.00
4 Blake Griffin 12.00 30.00
5 Deron Williams 6.00 15.00
6 Marcus Camby 4.00 10.00
7 Vince Carter 15.00 40.00
8 Andre Iguodala
9 Grant Hill 40.00 80.00
10 Gerald Wallace
11 Jason Kidd 15.00 40.00
12 Andre Miller
13 Marcin Gortat 4.00 10.00
14 Tyson Chandler 4.00 10.00
15 Danny Granger
16 Jason Terry 20.00 50.00
17 Anderson Varejao 3.00 8.00
18 Andrei Kirilenko 4.00 10.00
19 Andrew Bogut 4.00 10.00
20 Kevin Love 15.00 40.00
21 Brook Lopez 4.00 10.00
22 Jeff Green 4.00 10.00
23 Ed Davis 3.00 8.00
24 Tyreke Evans
25 David West 4.00 10.00
26 J.J. Redick 5.00 12.00
27 Joakim Noah 10.00 25.00
28 Greg Monroe 4.00 10.00
29 Ty Lawson 3.00 8.00
30 Stephen Curry EXCH 60.00 150.00
31 Taj Gibson 4.00 10.00
32 Kendrick Perkins 3.00 8.00
33 Kyle Lowry 4.00 10.00
34 Danilo Gallinari 3.00 8.00
35 Nick Collison 4.00 10.00
36 Corey Brewer 3.00 8.00
37 Gordon Hayward 5.00 12.00
38 Rodney Stuckey 4.00 10.00
39 Jeff Teague 4.00 10.00
40 Raymond Felton
41 Ryan Anderson 4.00 10.00
42 DeMarcus Cousins
43 Udonis Haslem 3.00 8.00
44 Gerald Henderson 3.00 8.00
45 Caron Butler 4.00 10.00
46 Jamaal Tinsley 3.00 8.00
47 Jason Thompson 3.00 8.00
48 Kevin Martin 4.00 10.00
49 Jason Maxiell 3.00 8.00
50 Thabo Sefolosha 6.00 15.00
51 Alex English 4.00 10.00
52 Allan Houston 8.00 20.00
53 Alonzo Mourning 20.00 50.00
54 Anfernee Hardaway 40.00 80.00
55 Anthony Mason 4.00 10.00
56 Bernard King 4.00 10.00
57 Bill Walton 8.00 20.00
58 Bob McAdoo 6.00 15.00
59 Bobby Jackson 3.00 8.00
60 Buck Williams 3.00 8.00
61 Cedric Ceballos 3.00 8.00
62 Cedric Maxwell 3.00 8.00
63 Chris Mullin 5.00 12.00
64 Clyde Drexler 12.00 30.00
65 Darryl Dawkins 6.00 15.00
66 David Robinson 15.00 40.00
67 David Thompson 4.00 10.00
68 Dennis Scott 3.00 8.00
69 Detlef Schrempf 5.00 12.00
70 Dikembe Mutombo
71 Dominique Wilkins 12.00 30.00
72 Fat Lever 4.00 10.00
73 Gary Payton 20.00 50.00
74 George Gervin 6.00 15.00
75 Gus Williams 3.00 8.00
76 Hakeem Olajuwon 20.00 50.00
77 Horace Grant 5.00 12.00
78 Julius Erving 40.00 100.00
79 Kurt Rambis 3.00 8.00
80 Larry Bird 40.00 100.00
81 Larry Johnson 6.00 15.00
82 Len Elmore 3.00 8.00
83 Luc Longley 4.00 10.00
84 Mark Price 5.00 12.00
85 Michael Cooper 4.00 10.00
86 Michael Finley 15.00 40.00
87 Nick Anderson 5.00 12.00
88 Walt Bellamy
89 Rick Mahorn 3.00 8.00
90 Sam Cassell 4.00 10.00
91 Sean Elliott 5.00 12.00
92 Sidney Moncrief 3.00 8.00
93 Sleepy Floyd 3.00 8.00
94 Spencer Haywood 3.00 8.00
95 Steve Smith 4.00 10.00
96 Tim Hardaway 6.00 15.00
97 Vernon Maxwell 3.00 8.00
98 Vin Baker 3.00 8.00
99 Walt Frazier 12.00 30.00
100 Will Perdue 3.00 8.00

2012-13 Panini Crusade Majestic Signatures Gold

*GOLD: .6X TO 1.5X BASIC
PRINT RUNS B/WN 10-25 COPIES PER
NO PRICING ON MOST DUE TO SCARCITY
EXCHANGE DEADLINE 12/12/2014
2 Kobe Bryant/25 125.00 250.00

2012-13 Panini Crusade Nobility

1 Paul Pierce 1.50 4.00
2 John Wall 2.00 5.00
3 James Harden 2.50 6.00
4 Kobe Bryant 6.00 15.00
5 Dwight Howard 1.25 3.00
6 Chris Paul 2.00 5.00
7 Carmelo Anthony 2.00 5.00
8 Jason Kidd 1.50 4.00
9 Zach Randolph 1.25 3.00
10 Steve Nash 1.50 4.00
11 Derrick Rose 2.00 5.00
12 LeBron James 6.00 15.00
13 Greg Monroe 1.25 3.00
14 Stephen Curry 6.00 15.00
15 Russell Westbrook 4.00 10.00
16 Tim Duncan 2.50 6.00
17 Rajon Rondo 1.50 4.00
18 Ray Allen 1.50 4.00
19 Blake Griffin 1.50 4.00
20 Dwyane Wade 2.50 6.00
21 Dirk Nowitzki 2.00 5.00
22 Kevin Durant 4.00 10.00
23 Kevin Garnett 2.50 6.00
24 Kevin Love 1.50 4.00
25 Deron Williams 1.25 3.00

2012-13 Panini Crusade Quest Autographs

EXCHANGE DEADLINE 12/12/2014
1 Nikola Vucevic 5.00 12.00
2 Jae Crowder 4.00 10.00
3 Anthony Davis 75.00 150.00
4 Kyrie Irving 40.00 100.00
5 Klay Thompson 40.00 100.00
6 Marquis Teague 3.00 8.00
7 Tristan Thompson 5.00 12.00
8 Alexey Shved 3.00 8.00
9 Bernard James 3.00 8.00
10 Nando De Colo 3.00 8.00
11 Victor Claver 3.00 8.00
12 Brian Roberts 3.00 8.00
13 Jimmy Butler 20.00 50.00
14 Brandon Knight 3.00 8.00
15 Chandler Parsons 5.00 12.00
16 Harrison Barnes 8.00 20.00
17 Jared Sullinger 4.00 10.00
18 Jimmer Fredette 3.00 8.00
19 Andrew Nicholson 3.00 8.00
20 Andre Drummond 8.00 20.00
21 Isaiah Thomas 15.00 40.00
22 Mirza Teletovic 4.00 10.00
23 Lance Thomas 3.00 8.00
24 Bradley Beal 8.00 20.00
25 Michael Kidd-Gilchrist 5.00 12.00
26 Tyler Zeller 4.00 10.00
27 Iman Shumpert 5.00 12.00
28 Jonas Valanciunas 5.00 12.00
29 Kenneth Faried 5.00 12.00
30 Terrence Ross 5.00 12.00
31 Tobias Harris 5.00 12.00
32 Kyle Singler 3.00 8.00
33 Tornike Shengelia 3.00 8.00
34 Robert Sacre 3.00 8.00
35 Kent Bazemore 5.00 12.00
36 Austin Rivers 5.00 12.00
37 Thomas Robinson 4.00 10.00
38 Kemba Walker 10.00 25.00
39 Alec Burks 5.00 12.00
40 Kawhi Leonard 40.00 100.00
41 Doron Lamb 3.00 8.00
42 Darius Morris 3.00 8.00
43 Kendall Marshall 3.00 8.00
44 Will Barton 4.00 10.00
45 MarShon Brooks 4.00 10.00
46 Draymond Green 15.00 40.00
47 Orlando Johnson 3.00 8.00
48 Jeff Taylor 3.00 8.00
49 DeQuan Jones 3.00 8.00
50 Chris Copeland 3.00 8.00
51 John Henson 5.00 12.00
52 Dion Waiters 5.00 12.00
53 Derrick Williams 3.00 8.00
54 Enes Kanter 4.00 10.00
55 Ben Hansbrough 3.00 8.00
56 Greg Stiemsma 3.00 8.00
57 Kevin Jones 3.00 8.00
58 E'Twaun Moore 3.00 8.00
59 Festus Ezeli 4.00 10.00
60 Chris Singleton 3.00 8.00
61 DeAndre Liggins 4.00 10.00
62 Jan Vesely 3.00 8.00
63 Maurice Harkless 5.00 12.00
64 Miles Plumlee 3.00 8.00
65 Nolan Smith 3.00 8.00
66 Norris Cole 3.00 8.00
67 Quincy Acy 3.00 8.00
68 Meyers Leonard 4.00 10.00
69 Jordan Hamilton 3.00 8.00
70 Jon Leuer 4.00 10.00
71 Reggie Jackson 4.00 10.00
72 Lavoy Allen 3.00 8.00
73 Bismack Biyombo 3.00 8.00
74 Evan Fournier 5.00 12.00
75 Earl Clark 3.00 8.00
76 Lance Stephenson 4.00 10.00
77 Joel Anthony 3.00 8.00
78 Marvin Williams 4.00 10.00
79 Jason Smith 3.00 8.00
80 Ronnie Brewer 4.00 10.00
81 Austin Daye 3.00 8.00
82 Chase Budinger 3.00 8.00
83 Courtney Lee 4.00 10.00
84 J.J. Hickson 3.00 8.00
85 George Hill 4.00 10.00
86 Leandro Barbosa 4.00 10.00
87 Mario Chalmers 4.00 10.00
88 Wesley Matthews 3.00 8.00
89 Will Bynum 3.00 8.00
90 Brandon Rush 3.00 8.00
91 Landry Fields 3.00 8.00
92 Alan Anderson 3.00 8.00
93 Anthony Morrow 3.00 8.00
94 Andray Blatche 3.00 8.00
95 Tiago Splitter 4.00 10.00
96 Larry Sanders 3.00 8.00
97 Randy Foye 3.00 8.00
98 Greivis Vasquez 4.00 10.00
99 Byron Mullens 3.00 8.00
100 Ersan Ilyasova 3.00 8.00

2012-13 Panini Crusade Quest Autographs Gold

*GOLD: .6X TO 1.5X BASIC
PRINT RUNS B/WN 10-25 COPIES PER
NO PRICING ON MOST DUE TO SCARCITY
EXCHANGE DEADLINE 12/12/2014

2012-13 Panini Crusade Quest Memorabilia

1 Eric Bledsoe 2.50 6.00
2 Taj Gibson 2.50 6.00
3 Eric Gordon 2.50 6.00
4 Tony Allen 2.00 5.00
5 Robin Lopez 2.00 5.00
6 Tyson Chandler 2.50 6.00
7 Courtney Lee 2.50 6.00
8 Derrick Favors 2.50 6.00
9 DeAndre Jordan 3.00 8.00
10 Luis Scola 2.50 6.00
11 J.J. Barea 2.50 6.00
12 DeMarcus Cousins 3.00 8.00
13 Luke Ridnour 2.50 6.00
14 Jamal Crawford 3.00 8.00
15 Gordon Hayward 3.00 8.00
16 Goran Dragic 2.50 6.00
17 Brook Lopez 2.50 6.00
18 Wesley Matthews 2.00 5.00
19 Hedo Turkoglu 2.50 6.00
20 Brandon Roy 3.00 8.00
21 Tyrus Thomas 2.00 5.00
22 Gerald Henderson 2.00 5.00
23 Marcin Gortat 2.50 6.00
24 Thabo Sefolosha 2.00 5.00
25 Enes Kanter 2.50 6.00
26 Andrea Bargnani 2.50 6.00
27 Jason Maxiell 2.00 5.00
28 Brandon Jennings 2.00 5.00
29 Ryan Anderson 2.50 6.00
30 Michael Beasley 2.00 5.00
31 Anderson Varejao 2.00 5.00
32 Mike Conley 2.50 6.00
33 Serge Ibaka 2.50 6.00
34 Jonas Jerebko 2.00 5.00
35 Anthony Davis 8.00 20.00
36 Xavier Henry 2.00 5.00
37 Evan Fournier 3.00 8.00
38 Kyrie Irving 8.00 20.00
39 DeMar DeRozan 3.00 8.00
40 Jose Calderon 2.00 5.00
41 Linas Kleiza 2.00 5.00
42 Brandon Bass 2.00 5.00
43 Chase Budinger 2.00 5.00
44 Arron Afflalo 2.50 6.00
45 Tristan Thompson 3.00 8.00
46 George Hill 2.50 6.00
47 Kevin Martin 2.50 6.00
48 Landry Fields 2.00 5.00
49 Nicolas Batum 2.50 6.00
50 Nikola Pekovic 2.00 5.00
51 Greg Monroe 2.50 6.00
52 David West 2.50 6.00
53 Glen Davis 2.00 5.00
54 Jameer Nelson 2.00 5.00
55 Markieff Morris 3.00 8.00
56 Thomas Robinson 2.50 6.00
57 Jeremy Lin 12.00 30.00
58 Thaddeus Young 2.00 5.00
59 Ed Davis 2.00 5.00
60 Darrell Arthur 2.00 5.00
61 Michael Kidd-Gilchrist 5.00 12.00
62 Louis Williams 2.50 6.00
63 Draymond Green 6.00 15.00
64 Austin Rivers 3.00 8.00
65 JaVale McGee 2.50 6.00
66 Paul George 4.00 10.00
67 Bismack Biyombo 2.00 5.00
68 Jonas Valanciunas 3.00 8.00
69 Udonis Haslem 2.00 5.00
70 Mo Williams 2.50 6.00
71 Rodney Stuckey 2.50 6.00
72 Jared Sullinger 2.50 6.00
73 Jeff Teague 2.50 6.00
74 Kemba Walker 6.00 15.00
75 Kyle Lowry 2.50 6.00
76 Harrison Barnes 5.00 12.00
77 Josh Smith 2.50 6.00
78 Darren Collison 2.50 6.00
79 Jeff Green 2.50 6.00
80 Kawhi Leonard 5.00 12.00
81 Bradley Beal 5.00 12.00
82 Shane Battier 2.50 6.00
83 Antawn Jamison 2.50 6.00
84 J.J. Hickson 2.00 5.00
85 Ben Gordon 2.50 6.00
86 Devin Harris 2.00 5.00
87 Pau Gasol 3.00 8.00
88 Gary Neal 2.50 6.00
89 Chris Copeland 2.00 5.00
90 Raymond Felton 2.50 6.00
91 Omer Asik 2.50 6.00
92 Carl Landry 2.00 5.00
93 DeShawn Stevenson 2.00 5.00
94 Kris Humphries 2.00 5.00
95 Charlie Villanueva 2.00 5.00
96 Pablo Prigioni 2.00 5.00
97 O.J. Mayo 2.00 5.00
98 Damian Lillard 12.00 30.00
99 Kenneth Faried 5.00 12.00
100 Daniel Gibson 2.50 6.00

2012-13 Panini Crusade Quest Memorabilia Prime

*PRIME: 1.2X TO 3X BASIC
PRINT RUNS B/WN 2-25 COPIES PER
NO PRICING ON QTY 15 OR LESS

2012-13 Panini Crusade Royalty

1 Bill Russell 3.00 8.00
2 Magic Johnson 5.00 12.00
3 Larry Bird 5.00 12.00
4 Dennis Rodman 4.00 10.00
5 Clyde Drexler 2.50 6.00
6 Earl Monroe 2.00 5.00
7 Kareem Abdul-Jabbar 3.00 8.00
8 Patrick Ewing 2.50 6.00
9 John Stockton 3.00 8.00
10 Julius Erving 3.00 8.00
11 Shaquille O'Neal 4.00 10.00
12 Nate Thurmond 1.50 4.00
13 Hal Greer 1.50 4.00
14 Isiah Thomas 2.00 5.00
15 Wes Unseld 2.00 5.00
16 Wilt Chamberlain 4.00 10.00
17 Nate Archibald 1.50 4.00
18 Walt Frazier 2.00 5.00
19 Hakeem Olajuwon 2.50 6.00
20 Jerry West 2.50 6.00
21 Willis Reed 2.00 5.00
22 Oscar Robertson 2.50 6.00
23 Paul Arizin 2.00 5.00
24 Kevin McHale 2.00 5.00
25 Pete Maravich 3.00 8.00

2013-14 Panini Crusade

1 Chris Paul .60 1.50
2 Al Horford .40 1.00
3 Pau Gasol .50 1.25
4 Nikola Vucevic .40 1.00
5 Monta Ellis .40 1.00
6 Tyreke Evans .30 .75
7 Rajon Rondo .50 1.25
8 Carmelo Anthony .60 1.50
9 Kevin Love .50 1.25
10 Andre Drummond .50 1.25
11 J.J. Redick .50 1.25
12 Jeff Teague .40 1.00
13 Steve Nash .50 1.25
14 Jameer Nelson .30 .75
15 Dirk Nowitzki .60 1.50
16 Amir Johnson .30 .75
17 Jeff Green .40 1.00
18 Tyson Chandler .40 1.00
19 Kevin Martin .40 1.00
20 Luol Deng .40 1.00
21 Goran Dragic .40 1.00
22 Nick Young .50 1.25
23 Paul Millsap .50 1.25
24 Tony Parker .50 1.25
25 Shawn Marion .40 1.00
26 Spencer Hawes .30 .75
27 Jordan Crawford .30 .75
28 Andrea Bargnani .40 1.00
29 Derrick Favors .40 1.00
30 Derrick Rose .60 1.50
31 Eric Bledsoe .40 1.00
32 DeMarcus Cousins .50 1.25
33 Kemba Walker .50 1.25
34 Tim Duncan .75 2.00
35 Vince Carter .60 1.50
36 Wesley Matthews .30 .75
37 DeMar DeRozan .50 1.25
38 Damian Lillard 1.00 2.50
39 Enes Kanter .30 .75
40 Carlos Boozer .40 1.00
41 Gerald Green .40 1.00
42 Isaiah Thomas .50 1.25
43 Gerald Henderson .30 .75
44 Manu Ginobili .50 1.25
45 Mike Conley .40 1.00
46 Nicolas Batum .40 1.00
47 Kyle Lowry .40 1.00
48 LaMarcus Aldridge .50 1.25
49 Gordon Hayward .50 1.25
50 Kyrie Irving 1.00 2.50
51 Stephen Curry 2.00 5.00
52 Rudy Gay .50 1.25
53 Al Jefferson .40 1.00
54 Kawhi Leonard .75 2.00
55 Zach Randolph .40 1.00
56 J.J. Hickson .30 .75
57 Evan Turner .30 .75
58 Kevin Durant 1.25 3.00
59 Paul George .60 1.50
60 Dion Waiters .40 1.00
61 Klay Thompson .60 1.50
62 LeBron James 2.00 5.00
63 John Wall .60 1.50
64 James Harden .75 2.00
65 Marc Gasol .50 1.25
66 Ricky Rubio .50 1.25
67 Thaddeus Young .30 .75
68 Russell Westbrook 1.25 3.00
69 David West .40 1.00
70 Tristan Thompson .40 1.00
71 David Lee .30 .75
72 Chris Bosh .50 1.25
73 Marcin Gortat .40 1.00
74 Dwight Howard .40 1.00
75 Eric Gordon .40 1.00
76 Caron Butler .40 1.00
77 Kevin Garnett .75 2.00
78 Serge Ibaka .40 1.00
79 Roy Hibbert .40 1.00
80 O.J. Mayo .30 .75
81 Harrison Barnes .40 1.00
82 Dwyane Wade .75 2.00
83 Bradley Beal .50 1.25
84 Chandler Parsons .40 1.00
85 Anthony Davis 1.00 2.50
86 DeAndre Jordan .50 1.25
87 Paul Pierce .50 1.25
88 Ty Lawson .30 .75
89 Brandon Jennings .30 .75
90 Larry Sanders .30 .75
91 Kobe Bryant 2.00 5.00
92 Ray Allen .50 1.25
93 Arron Afflalo .30 .75
94 Jeremy Lin .50 1.25
95 Jrue Holiday .50 1.25
96 Robin Lopez .30 .75
97 Deron Williams .40 1.00
98 Kenneth Faried .40 1.00
99 Greg Monroe .40 1.00
100 Blake Griffin .50 1.25
101 Nemanja Nedovic RC .40 1.00
102 Ryan Kelly RC .40 1.00
103 Jeff Withey RC .40 1.00
104 Ben McLemore RC .50 1.25
105 Brandon Davies RC .40 1.00
106 Rudy Gobert RC .75 2.00
107 Pero Antic RC .40 1.00
108 Cody Zeller RC .50 1.25
109 Sergey Karasev RC .40 1.00
110 Kentavious Caldwell-Pope RC .60 1.50
111 Isaiah Canaan RC .40 1.00
112 Jamaal Franklin RC .40 1.00
113 Tim Hardaway Jr. RC .60 1.50
114 Victor Oladipo RC .75 2.00
115 Archie Goodwin RC .50 1.25
116 Otto Porter RC .60 1.50
117 Dennis Schroder RC .60 1.50
118 Erik Murphy RC .40 1.00
119 Carrick Felix RC .40 1.00
120 Luigi Datome RC .40 1.00
121 Robert Covington RC .40 1.00
122 G.Antetokounmpo RC 5.00 12.00
123 Steven Adams RC .60 1.50
124 Dwight Buycks RC .40 1.00
125 Alex Len RC .50 1.25
126 Glen Rice Jr. RC .40 1.00
127 Vitor Faverani RC .40 1.00
128 Tony Snell RC .50 1.25
129 Ricky Ledo RC .40 1.00
130 Tony Mitchell RC .40 1.00
131 Solomon Hill RC .40 1.00
132 Miroslav Radulijica RC .40 1.00
133 Andre Roberson RC .40 1.00
134 Gorgui Dieng RC .50 1.25
135 Ian Clark RC .50 1.25
136 C.J. McCollum RC 1.00 2.50
137 Kelly Olynyk RC .50 1.25
138 Anthony Bennett RC .50 1.25
139 Shane Larkin RC .40 1.00
140 Peyton Siva RC .40 1.00
141 Reggie Bullock RC .50 1.25
142 Nate Wolters RC .50 1.25
143 Ray McCallum RC .40 1.00
144 M.Carter-Williams RC .60 1.50
145 Trey Burke RC .50 1.25
146 Lorenzo Brown RC .40 1.00
147 Phil Pressey RC .40 1.00
148 Matthew Dellavedova RC .60 1.50
149 Gal Mekel RC .40 1.00
150 Ognjen Kuzmic RC .40 1.00
151 Hakeem Olajuwon .60 1.50
152 Bill Russell .75 2.00
153 Shaquille O'Neal 1.00 2.50
154 Yao Ming .60 1.50
155 Joe Dumars .50 1.25
156 Lenny Wilkens .50 1.25
157 Robert Horry .40 1.00
158 Clyde Drexler .60 1.50
159 George Gervin .50 1.25
160 Grant Hill .60 1.50
161 Jason Kidd .50 1.25
162 Arvydas Sabonis .40 1.00
163 Larry Johnson .60 1.50
164 Rick Fox .40 1.00
165 Detlef Schrempf .50 1.25
166 Scottie Pippen 1.00 2.50
167 Moses Malone .50 1.25
168 Shawn Kemp .75 2.00
169 Karl Malone .60 1.50
170 Spud Webb .40 1.00
171 Chris Mullin .50 1.25
172 Drazen Petrovic .50 1.25
173 Dave Bing .50 1.25
174 Oscar Robertson .60 1.50
175 Jack Sikma .40 1.00
176 Dennis Johnson .40 1.00
177 Jerry Lucas .50 1.25
178 Isiah Thomas .50 1.25
179 Dominique Wilkins .60 1.50
180 Bernard King .40 1.00
181 Wilt Chamberlain 1.00 2.50
182 John Stockton .75 2.00
183 Dan Majerle .40 1.00
184 Allen Iverson .60 1.50
185 Dennis Rodman 1.00 2.50
186 Nick Van Exel .50 1.25
187 Kareem Abdul-Jabbar .75 2.00
188 Adrian Dantley .40 1.00
189 Alonzo Mourning .60 1.50
190 James Worthy .60 1.50
191 Pete Maravich .75 2.00
192 Vlade Divac .50 1.25
193 Gary Payton .50 1.25
194 John Havlicek .60 1.50
195 David Robinson .75 2.00
196 Larry Bird 1.25 3.00
197 Jerry West .60 1.50
198 Anfernee Hardaway 1.25 3.00
199 Magic Johnson 1.25 3.00
200 Julius Erving .75 2.00

2013-14 Panini Crusade Silver

*SILVER VET: 2X TO 5X BASIC
*SILVER RC: 1.5X TO 4X BASIC RC
STATED PRINT RUN 25 SER.#'d SETS

2013-14 Panini Crusade Apprentice Signatures

EXCHANGE DEADLINE 11/21/2015
1 Shabazz Muhammad 4.00 10.00
2 Kentavious Caldwell-Pope 5.00 12.00
3 Enes Kanter 3.00 8.00
4 Kawhi Leonard 40.00 100.00
5 Steven Adams 5.00 12.00
6 Nerlens Noel 15.00 40.00
7 C.J. McCollum 15.00 40.00
8 Derrick Williams 3.00 8.00
9 Tony Snell 4.00 10.00
10 Ben McLemore 4.00 10.00
11 Harrison Barnes 4.00 10.00
12 Gorgui Dieng 4.00 10.00
13 Stephen Curry 100.00 250.00
14 Trey Burke 4.00 10.00
15 Andre Drummond 8.00 20.00
16 Jason Smith 3.00 8.00
17 Anthony Bennett 4.00 10.00
18 Bradley Beal 8.00 20.00
19 Anthony Davis 40.00 100.00
20 Kelly Olynyk 4.00 10.00
21 Victor Oladipo 6.00 15.00
22 Andrew Nicholson 3.00 8.00
23 Matthew Dellavedova 5.00 12.00
24 Giannis Antetokounmpo 60.00 150.00
25 Michael Carter-Williams 5.00 12.00
26 Khris Middleton 4.00 10.00
27 Phil Pressey 3.00 8.00
28 Patrick Beverley 3.00 8.00
29 Cody Zeller 4.00 10.00
30 Hollis Thompson 4.00 10.00
31 Gal Mekel 3.00 8.00
32 Otto Porter 5.00 12.00
33 Shane Larkin 3.00 8.00
34 Robbie Hummel 3.00 8.00
35 Dwight Buycks 3.00 8.00
36 Mason Plumlee 5.00 12.00
37 Alex Len 4.00 10.00
38 Reggie Jackson 4.00 10.00
39 Danny Green 4.00 10.00
40 Jrue Holiday 5.00 12.00

2013-14 Panini Crusade Apprentice Signatures Silver

*SILVER: .5X TO 1.2X BASIC
PRINT RUNS B/WN 25-49 COPIES PER
EXCHANGE DEADLINE 11/21/2015

2013-14 Panini Crusade Hardwood Homage Autographs

PRINT RUNS B/WN 10-199 COPIES PER
NO PRICING ON QTY 10
EXCHANGE DEADLINE 11/21/2015
1 Bob Dandridge/199 4.00 10.00
2 Kobe Bryant/25 125.00 250.00
8 Dikembe Mutombo/99 6.00 15.00
9 Kenny Anderson/199 5.00 12.00
10 Campy Russell/199 4.00 10.00
11 Larry Johnson/199 8.00 20.00
13 Antawn Jamison/199 5.00 12.00
14 Jason Kidd/25
18 Jalen Rose/199 6.00 15.00
19 Larry Nance/199 5.00 12.00
20 Fat Lever/199 5.00 12.00
21 Mark Aguirre/199 5.00 12.00
23 Kevin Willis/199 4.00 10.00

2013-14 Panini Crusade Hardwood Homage Autographs Silver

*SILVER: .5X TO 1.2X BASIC

PRINT RUNS B/WN 5-25 COPIES PER
NO PRICING ON QTY 10 OR LESS
EXCHANGE DEADLINE 11/21/2015

2013-14 Panini Crusade High Praise Ink

PRINT RUNS B/WN 10-25 COPIES PER
NO PRICING ON QTY 10
EXCHANGE DEADLINE 11/21/2015
2 Karl Malone/25 30.00 60.00
3 Jason Kidd/25 12.00 30.00
4 Anfernee Hardaway/25 20.00 50.00
6 Scottie Pippen/25 30.00 80.00
10 Kevin Durant/25 40.00 100.00
11 Grant Hill/25 25.00 60.00
12 Arvydas Sabonis 4.00 10.00
13 Magic Johnson/25 40.00 100.00
15 Kobe Bryant/25
16 Bob Dandridge 3.00 8.00
17 Larry Bird/25 50.00 120.00
18 Kyrie Irving/25 25.00 60.00

2013-14 Panini Crusade High Praise Ink Silver

*SILVER: .5X TO 1.2X BASIC
PRINT RUNS B/WN 5-49 COPIES PER
NO PRICING ON QTY 10 OR LESS
EXCHANGE DEADLINE 11/21/2015

2013-14 Panini Crusade Insert Blue

*ORANGE: 1X TO 2.5X BASIC
*RED: .5X TO 1.2X BASIC
*TEAL: .6X TO 1.5X BASIC
1 C.J. McCollum 2.00 5.00
2 Toni Kukoc 1.25 3.00
3 Chris Mullin 1.25 3.00
4 Alex English 1.00 2.50
5 Thaddeus Young .75 2.00
6 JaVale McGee 1.00 2.50
7 Joakim Noah 1.00 2.50
8 P.J. Tucker .75 2.00
9 Norris Cole .75 2.00
10 Tiago Splitter 1.00 2.50
11 Vitor Faverani .75 2.00
12 Rick Mahorn .75 2.00
13 Michael Cooper 1.00 2.50
14 David Robinson 2.00 5.00
15 Spencer Hawes .75 2.00
16 Kevin Love 1.25 3.00
17 Derrick Rose 1.50 4.00
18 Miles Plumlee .75 2.00
19 Al Horford 1.00 2.50
20 Boris Diaw 1.00 2.50
21 Gal Mekel .75 2.00
22 Julius Erving 2.00 5.00
23 Larry Johnson 1.50 4.00
24 Tom Gugliotta .75 2.00
25 Tony Wroten .75 2.00
26 Kevin Martin 1.00 2.50
27 Kirk Hinrich 1.00 2.50
28 Klay Thompson 1.50 4.00
29 Jeff Teague 1.00 2.50
30 James Harden 2.00 5.00
31 Otto Porter 1.25 3.00
32 Arvydas Sabonis 1.00 2.50
33 Dell Curry .75 2.00
34 Mark Jackson 1.00 2.50
35 Lavoy Allen .75 2.00
36 Nikola Pekovic .75 2.00
37 Jimmy Butler 1.25 3.00
38 Stephen Curry 5.00 12.00
39 Paul Millsap 1.25 3.00
40 Dwight Howard 1.00 2.50
41 Nerlens Noel 1.50 4.00
42 Doc Rivers 1.25 3.00
43 Bob Lanier 1.00 2.50
44 Rick Barry 1.00 2.50
45 Jason Richardson 1.25 3.00
46 Corey Brewer .75 2.00
47 Kyrie Irving 2.50 6.00
48 David Lee .75 2.00
49 Kyle Korver 1.00 2.50
50 Jeremy Lin 1.25 3.00
51 Rudy Gobert 1.50 4.00
52 Robert Horry 1.00 2.50
53 Anfernee Hardaway 3.00 8.00
54 Drazen Petrovic 1.25 3.00
55 Carmelo Anthony 1.50 4.00
56 Ricky Rubio 1.25 3.00
57 Dion Waiters 1.00 2.50
58 Harrison Barnes 1.00 2.50
59 DeMarre Carroll .75 2.00
60 Chandler Parsons 1.00 2.50
61 Giannis Antetokounmpo 10.00 25.00
62 Jerry West 1.50 4.00
63 John Starks 1.00 2.50
64 Grant Hill 1.50 4.00
65 Andrea Bargnani 1.00 2.50
66 J.J. Barea 1.00 2.50
67 Tristan Thompson 1.00 2.50
68 Andre Iguodala 1.00 2.50
69 Louis Williams 1.00 2.50
70 Patrick Beverley .75 2.00
71 Steven Adams 1.25 3.00
72 Kevin McHale 1.25 3.00
73 Peja Stojakovic 1.25 3.00
74 Dennis Johnson 1.00 2.50
75 J.R. Smith 1.00 2.50
76 Gordon Hayward 1.25 3.00
77 Jarrett Jack 1.00 2.50
78 Andrew Bogut 1.00 2.50
79 Kemba Walker 1.25 3.00
80 Omer Asik 1.00 2.50
81 Kentavious Caldwell-Pope 1.25 3.00
82 Mitch Richmond 1.25 3.00
83 Joe Dumars 1.25 3.00
84 Kelly Tripucka .75 2.00
85 Raymond Felton 1.00 2.50
86 Alec Burks .75 2.00
87 Anderson Varejao .75 2.00
88 Jermaine O'Neal 1.00 2.50
89 Gerald Henderson .75 2.00
90 Terrence Jones 1.00 2.50
91 Tim Hardaway Jr. 1.25 3.00
92 Moses Malone 1.25 3.00
93 A.C. Green 1.25 3.00
94 Robert Parish 1.25 3.00
95 Iman Shumpert .75 2.00
96 Enes Kanter .75 2.00
97 Andrew Bynum .75 2.00
98 Draymond Green 1.50 4.00
99 Ramon Sessions 1.00 2.50
100 Monta Ellis 1.00 2.50
101 Anthony Bennett 1.00 2.50
102 Allen Iverson 1.50 4.00
103 Nick Van Exel 1.25 3.00
104 Jeff Green 1.00 2.50
105 Amare Stoudemire 1.00 2.50
106 Derrick Favors 1.00 2.50
107 O.J. Mayo .75 2.00
108 Kobe Bryant 5.00 12.00
109 Al Jefferson 1.00 2.50
110 Dirk Nowitzki 1.50 4.00
111 Cody Zeller 1.00 2.50
112 Wilt Chamberlain 2.50 6.00
113 Glen Rice 1.00 2.50
114 Jordan Crawford .75 2.00
115 Tyson Chandler 1.00 2.50
116 Richard Jefferson 1.00 2.50
117 John Henson 1.00 2.50
118 Pau Gasol 1.25 3.00
119 Michael Kidd-Gilchrist 1.25 3.00
120 Shawn Marion 1.00 2.50
121 Glen Rice Jr. .75 2.00
122 Gary Payton 1.25 3.00
123 Michael Finley 1.25 3.00
124 Avery Bradley 1.00 2.50
125 LaMarcus Aldridge 1.25 3.00
126 John Lucas III .75 2.00
127 Khris Middleton 1.00 2.50
128 Steve Nash 1.25 3.00
129 Bismack Biyombo .75 2.00
130 Vince Carter 1.50 4.00
131 Alex Len 1.00 2.50
132 Keith Van Horn 1.00 2.50
133 Vernon Maxwell .75 2.00
134 Jared Sullinger .75 2.00
135 Damian Lillard 2.50 6.00
136 Paul George 1.50 4.00
137 Caron Butler 1.00 2.50
138 Nick Young 1.25 3.00
139 John Wall 1.50 4.00
140 Jose Calderon .75 2.00
141 Mason Plumlee 1.25 3.00
142 Kareem Abdul-Jabbar 2.00 5.00
143 Bill Walton 1.25 3.00
144 Wesley Matthews .75 2.00
145 Brandon Bass .75 2.00
146 David West 1.00 2.50
147 Brandon Knight 1.00 2.50
148 Steve Blake .75 2.00
149 Marcin Gortat 1.00 2.50
150 Samuel Dalembert .75 2.00
151 Ben McLemore 1.00 2.50
152 Mark Price 1.25 3.00
153 Jason Kidd 1.25 3.00
154 Rajon Rondo 1.25 3.00
155 Nicolas Batum 1.00 2.50
156 Roy Hibbert 1.00 2.50
157 Ersan Ilyasova .75 2.00
158 Jordan Hill .75 2.00
159 Bradley Beal 1.25 3.00
160 DeJuan Blair .75 2.00
161 Reggie Bullock 1.00 2.50
162 Isiah Thomas 1.25 3.00
163 Cedric Maxwell .75 2.00
164 DeMar DeRozan 1.25 3.00
165 Robin Lopez .75 2.00
166 Lance Stephenson 1.00 2.50
167 Larry Sanders .75 2.00
168 Xavier Henry .75 2.00
169 Trevor Ariza .75 2.00
170 Zach Randolph 1.00 2.50
171 Tony Snell 1.00 2.50
172 Sidney Moncrief .75 2.00
173 Jeff Hornacek 1.00 2.50
174 Kyle Lowry 1.00 2.50
175 Mo Williams 1.00 2.50
176 George Hill 1.00 2.50
177 Blake Griffin 1.25 3.00
178 DeMarcus Cousins 1.25 3.00
179 Nene 1.00 2.50
180 Marc Gasol 1.25 3.00
181 Shabazz Muhammad 1.00 2.50
182 Willis Reed 1.25 3.00
183 Calvin Murphy 1.00 2.50
184 Amir Johnson .75 2.00
185 Kevin Durant 3.00 8.00
186 Luis Scola 1.00 2.50
187 Chris Paul 1.50 4.00
188 Isaiah Thomas 1.25 3.00
189 Martell Webster .75 2.00
190 Mike Conley 1.00 2.50
191 Michael Carter-Williams 1.25 3.00
192 Horace Grant 1.25 3.00
193 Shaquille O'Neal 2.50 6.00
194 Jonas Valanciunas 1.00 2.50
195 Russell Westbrook 3.00 8.00
196 Ian Mahinmi .75 2.00
197 Jamal Crawford 1.25 3.00
198 Jimmer Fredette .75 2.00
199 Arron Afflalo .75 2.00
200 Kosta Koufos .75 2.00
201 Victor Oladipo 1.50 4.00
202 Shawn Kemp 2.00 5.00
203 Jamal Mashburn 1.25 3.00
204 Terrence Ross 1.00 2.50
205 Serge Ibaka 1.00 2.50
206 Brandon Jennings .75 2.00
207 J.J. Redick 1.25 3.00
208 Rudy Gay 1.25 3.00
209 Nikola Vucevic 1.00 2.50
210 Tony Allen .75 2.00
211 Trey Burke 1.00 2.50
212 Steve Francis 1.00 2.50
213 George Gervin 1.25 3.00
214 Tyler Hansbrough 1.00 2.50
215 Reggie Jackson 1.00 2.50
216 Josh Smith 1.00 2.50
217 DeAndre Jordan 1.25 3.00
218 Jason Thompson .75 2.00
219 Jameer Nelson .75 2.00
220 Jon Leuer .75 2.00
221 Kelly Olynyk 1.00 2.50
222 Magic Johnson 3.00 8.00
223 Tom Chambers 1.00 2.50
224 Joe Johnson 1.00 2.50
225 Kendrick Perkins .75 2.00
226 Greg Monroe 1.00 2.50
227 Jared Dudley .75 2.00
228 Derrick Williams .75 2.00
229 Tobias Harris 1.00 2.50
230 Tayshaun Prince 1.00 2.50
231 Nate Wolters 1.00 2.50
232 Bill Russell 2.00 5.00
233 Allan Houston 1.00 2.50
234 Brook Lopez 1.00 2.50
235 Derek Fisher 1.00 2.50
236 Rodney Stuckey 1.00 2.50
237 Antawn Jamison 1.00 2.50
238 LeBron James 5.00 12.00
239 Glen Davis .75 2.00
240 Eric Gordon 1.00 2.50
241 Archie Goodwin 1.00 2.50
242 Larry Nance 1.00 2.50
243 Bernard King 1.00 2.50
244 Paul Pierce 1.25 3.00
245 Thabo Sefolosha .75 2.00
246 Andre Drummond 1.25 3.00
247 Goran Dragic 1.00 2.50
248 Dwyane Wade 2.00 5.00
249 Maurice Harkless .75 2.00
250 Anthony Davis 2.50 6.00
251 Dominique Wilkins 1.50 4.00
252 Dennis Rodman 2.50 6.00
253 John Stockton 2.00 5.00
254 Kevin Garnett 2.00 5.00
255 Ty Lawson .75 2.00
256 Kyle Singler .75 2.00
257 Eric Bledsoe 1.00 2.50
258 Chris Bosh 1.25 3.00
259 Tony Parker 1.25 3.00
260 Jrue Holiday 1.25 3.00
261 Karl Malone 1.50 4.00
262 Patrick Ewing 1.50 4.00
263 Yao Ming 1.50 4.00
264 Jason Terry 1.00 2.50
265 Nate Robinson .75 2.00
266 Chauncey Billups 1.25 3.00
267 Gerald Green 1.00 2.50
268 Ray Allen 1.25 3.00
269 Tim Duncan 2.00 5.00
270 Tyreke Evans .75 2.00
271 Hakeem Olajuwon 1.50 4.00
272 Mahmoud Abdul-Rauf .75 2.00
273 Byron Scott 1.00 2.50
274 Andray Blatche .75 2.00
275 J.J. Hickson .75 2.00
276 Luol Deng 1.00 2.50
277 Marcus Morris .75 2.00
278 Mario Chalmers 1.00 2.50
279 Manu Ginobili 1.25 3.00
280 Ryan Anderson 1.00 2.50
281 James Worthy 1.50 4.00
282 Detlef Schrempf 1.25 3.00
283 Pete Maravich 2.00 5.00
284 Andrei Kirilenko 1.00 2.50
285 Kenneth Faried 1.00 2.50
286 Carlos Boozer 1.00 2.50
287 Markieff Morris .75 2.00
288 Michael Beasley .75 2.00
289 Kawhi Leonard 2.00 5.00
290 Jason Smith .75 2.00
291 Larry Bird 3.00 8.00
292 Tim Hardaway 1.25 3.00
293 Alonzo Mourning 1.50 4.00
294 Evan Turner .75 2.00
295 Danilo Gallinari .75 2.00
296 Taj Gibson 1.00 2.50
297 Channing Frye 1.00 2.50
298 Chris Andersen 1.00 2.50
299 Danny Green 1.00 2.50
300 Al-Farouq Aminu - 1.00 2.50

2013-14 Panini Crusade Insert Orange Die Cut

*ORANGE: 1X TO 2.5X BASIC
STATED PRINT RUN 99 SER.#'d SETS
61 Giannis Antetokounmpo 40.00 100.00
108 Kobe Bryant 50.00 120.00

2013-14 Panini Crusade Insert Purple

*PURPLE: 1.2X TO 3X BASIC
STATED PRINT RUN 49 SER.#'d SETS
61 Giannis Antetokounmpo 50.00 120.00
185 Kevin Durant 40.00 80.00
238 LeBron James 30.00 80.00

2013-14 Panini Crusade Insert Red

*RED: .5X TO 1.2X BASIC
STATED PRINT RUN 349 SER.#'d SETS
61 Giannis Antetokounmpo 20.00 50.00

2013-14 Panini Crusade Insert Teal

*TEAL: .6X TO 1.5X BASIC
STATED PRINT RUN 249 SER.#'d SETS
61 Giannis Antetokounmpo 25.00 60.00

2013-14 Panini Crusade Knight Court

*SILVER: 1.5X TO 4X BASIC
1 DeAndre Jordan .75 2.00
2 Monta Ellis .60 1.50
3 Kevin Durant 2.00 5.00
4 Kyrie Irving 1.50 4.00
5 Derrick Rose 1.00 2.50
6 Kevin Love .75 2.00
7 Al Horford .60 1.50
8 Serge Ibaka .60 1.50
9 Kenneth Faried .60 1.50
10 Greg Monroe .60 1.50
11 Kawhi Leonard 1.25 3.00
12 Jrue Holiday .75 2.00
13 Chris Paul 1.00 2.50
14 James Harden 1.25 3.00
15 Blake Griffin .75 2.00
16 Stephen Curry 3.00 8.00
17 Mike Conley .60 1.50
18 Paul George 1.00 2.50
19 Ty Lawson .50 1.25
20 Andre Drummond .75 2.00
21 George Hill .60 1.50
22 Nikola Vucevic .60 1.50
23 Dwight Howard .60 1.50
24 Anthony Davis 1.50 4.00
25 Russell Westbrook 2.00 5.00
26 LaMarcus Aldridge .75 2.00
27 Luol Deng .60 1.50
28 Brook Lopez .60 1.50
29 Jimmy Butler .75 2.00
30 Rajon Rondo .75 2.00

2013-14 Panini Crusade Majestic Marks

PRINT RUNS B/WN 10-199 COPIES PER
NO PRICING ON QTY 10
EXCHANGE DEADLINE 11/21/2015
*SILVER: .5X TO 1.2X BASIC
1 Kyle Korver/199 4.00 10.00
2 John Havlicek/25 60.00 120.00
5 George McGinnis/199 3.00 8.00
6 Antoine Walker/199 4.00 10.00
7 Kobe Bryant/25 100.00 200.00
9 Andre Iguodala/49
11 John Lucas/199 5.00 12.00
14 David Robinson/25 20.00 50.00
15 Dan Majerle/199 4.00 10.00
16 Larry Bird/25 50.00 100.00
17 Jason Kidd/25 50.00 100.00
19 Bradley Beal/49
21 Nikola Vucevic/199 4.00 10.00
24 Anfernee Hardaway/49 50.00 100.00
25 Darryl Dawkins/199 3.00 8.00
26 Magic Johnson/25 30.00 80.00
27 Anthony Davis/25 40.00 100.00
30 Roy Hibbert/199 4.00 10.00
31 Kenyon Martin/199 4.00 10.00
33 B.J. Armstrong/199 8.00 20.00
34 Kyrie Irving/25 75.00 150.00
35 Cazzie Russell/199 4.00 10.00
36 Julius Erving/25 30.00 80.00
37 Tom Chambers/199 4.00 10.00
38 Stephen Curry/49 75.00 200.00
40 Amir Johnson/199 3.00 8.00
41 Nick Young/199 5.00 12.00
43 Harrison Barnes/49 4.00 10.00
44 Kevin Durant/25 60.00 150.00
45 Muggsy Bogues/199 8.00 20.00
46 Joe Dumars/49 5.00 12.00
47 Kenny Sky Walker/199 3.00 8.00
48 James Harden/49 15.00 40.00
49 Jared Sullinger/49 3.00 8.00
50 Kawhi Leonard/199 30.00 80.00

2013-14 Panini Crusade Majestic Memorabilia

PRINT RUNS B/WN 49-299 COPIES PER
*PRIME: .75X TO 2X BASIC
1 Derrick Favors/99 3.00 8.00
2 Tiago Splitter/299 3.00 8.00
3 Sidney Moncrief/99 2.50 6.00
4 David Robinson/99 6.00 15.00
5 Ricky Rubio/199 5.00 12.00
6 DeMarcus Cousins/199 4.00 10.00
7 Kenny Sky Walker/99 6.00 15.00
8 Kareem Abdul-Jabbar/49
9 Gary Payton/99 4.00 10.00
10 Chris Kaman/299 3.00 8.00
11 Kirk Hinrich /299 3.00 8.00
12 Alex English/99 3.00 8.00
13 Larry Nance/99
14 Robert Horry/99 3.00 8.00
15 Damian Lillard/99 6.00 15.00
16 Kawhi Leonard/149 6.00 15.00
17 John Starks/99 3.00 8.00
18 Larry Bird/49 10.00 25.00
19 Patrick Ewing/49 5.00 12.00
20 John Stockton/99 6.00 15.00
21 Gerald Wallace/299 3.00 8.00
22 Danny Green/199 3.00 8.00
23 Larry Johnson/99 5.00 12.00
24 Kelly Tripucka/99 2.50 6.00
25 Enes Kanter/199 2.50 6.00
26 Brandon Jennings/199 2.50 6.00
27 Charles Oakley/99 4.00 10.00
28 Shaquille O'Neal/99 6.00 15.00
29 Hakeem Olajuwon/99 5.00 12.00
30 Mo Williams/199 3.00 8.00
31 Michael Beasley/199 2.50 6.00
32 Fat Lever/99
33 Shane Battier/299 3.00 8.00
34 Bill Laimbeer/99 3.00 8.00
35 Jeff Teague/49 3.00 8.00
36 Josh Smith/199 3.00 8.00
37 Larry Johnson/99 5.00 12.00
38 Magic Johnson/49 6.00 15.00
39 John Wall/199 5.00 12.00
40 Anderson Varejao/199 2.50 6.00
41 Terrence Ross/99 3.00 8.00
42 Bismack Biyombo/199
43 Rick Mahorn/99 2.50 6.00
44 Shawn Kemp/99 15.00 40.00
45 Andre Iguodala/99 3.00 8.00
46 Jeremy Lin/99 4.00 10.00
47 Iman Shumpert/199 2.50 6.00
48 Kobe Bryant/299 10.00 25.00
49 Shaquille O'Neal /99 6.00 15.00
50 Vince Carter/99
51 Dominique Wilkins/99 5.00 12.00
52 Randy Foye/199 2.50 6.00
53 Pablo Prigioni/299 2.50 6.00
54 Will Perdue/99
55 David Lee/99 2.50 6.00
56 George Hill/199 3.00 8.00
57 Tim Duncan/99 6.00 15.00
58 Kevin Durant/299 8.00 20.00
59 Tracy McGrady/99 4.00 10.00
60 Chris Mullin/99 4.00 10.00
61 Danilo Gallinari/299 2.50 6.00
62 Luis Scola/299 3.00 8.00
63 Evan Fournier/299 3.00 8.00
64 Shawn Bradley/99
65 Mike Conley/99 3.00 8.00
66 Pau Gasol/299 4.00 10.00
67 LeBron James/199 15.00 40.00
68 Scottie Pippen/99 8.00 20.00
69 Dwyane Wade/199 6.00 15.00
70 Amare Stoudemire/299 3.00 8.00
71 Andre Miller/199 3.00 8.00
72 Beno Udrih/299 2.50 6.00
73 Darren Collison/199 3.00 8.00
74 Reggie Lewis/99 8.00 20.00
75 Marc Gasol/199 4.00 10.00
76 Nick Young/99 4.00 10.00
77 Joe Dumars/99 4.00 10.00
78 Kyrie Irving/199 6.00 15.00
79 Clyde Drexler/99 5.00 12.00
80 Tristan Thompson/199 3.00 8.00
81 Thaddeus Young/99
82 Martell Webster/299 2.50 6.00
83 Kevin Love/299 4.00 10.00
84 Kenneth Faried/99 3.00 8.00
85 Zach Randolph/99
86 Tony Parker/99 4.00 10.00
87 Karl Malone/99 5.00 12.00
88 Blake Griffin/199 4.00 10.00
89 Grant Hill/99 5.00 12.00
90 Tayshaun Prince/199 3.00 8.00
91 Gordon Hayward/99
92 James Jones/299 2.50 6.00
93 Kurt Rambis/99 2.50 6.00
94 Dwight Howard/99 3.00 8.00
95 LaMarcus Aldridge/199 4.00 10.00
96 DeMar DeRozan/199 4.00 10.00
97 Kevin McHale/99 4.00 10.00
98 Anthony Davis/99 8.00 20.00
99 Walter Davis/99 2.50 6.00
100 Robert Parish/99 4.00 10.00

2013-14 Panini Crusade Nobility

*SILVER: 1.2X TO 3X BASIC
1 Tony Parker .75 2.00
2 Robert Horry .60 1.50
3 Dennis Rodman 1.50 4.00
4 Isiah Thomas .75 2.00
5 Bob McAdoo .60 1.50
6 Tyson Chandler .60 1.50
7 Anthony Davis 1.50 4.00
8 Russell Westbrook 2.00 5.00
9 LeBron James 3.00 8.00
10 Pau Gasol .75 2.00
11 Tayshaun Prince .60 1.50
12 Glen Rice .60 1.50
13 Hakeem Olajuwon 1.00 2.50
14 Kareem Abdul-Jabbar 1.25 3.00
15 Kevin McHale .75 2.00
16 Kevin Durant 2.00 5.00
17 Damian Lillard 1.50 4.00
18 Dikembe Mutombo .75 2.00
19 Dwyane Wade 1.25 3.00
20 Paul Pierce .75 2.00
21 Manu Ginobili .75 2.00
22 Clyde Drexler 1.00 2.50
23 David Robinson 1.25 3.00
24 Magic Johnson 2.00 5.00
25 Maurice Cheeks .50 1.25
26 Kyrie Irving 1.50 4.00
27 Chris Bosh .75 2.00
28 Kevin Garnett 1.25 3.00
29 Dirk Nowitzki 1.00 2.50
30 Tim Duncan 1.25 3.00
31 Shaquille O'Neal 1.50 4.00
32 Scottie Pippen 1.50 4.00
33 Joe Dumars .75 2.00
34 Larry Bird 2.00 5.00
35 Blake Griffin .75 2.00
36 Rajon Rondo .75 2.00
37 Serge Ibaka .60 1.50
38 Bill Walton .75 2.00
39 Kobe Bryant 3.00 8.00
40 Alonzo Mourning 1.00 2.50

2013-14 Panini Crusade Nobility Silver

*SILVER: 1.2X TO 3X BASIC
STATED PRINT RUN 25 SER.#'d SETS

2013-14 Panini Crusade Quest Autographs

PRINT RUNS B/WN 10-199 COPIES PER
NO PRICING ON QTY 10
EXCHANGE DEADLINE 11/21/2015
*SILVER: .5X TO 1.2X BASIC
1 Jerry West/25 20.00 50.00
2 David Robinson/25 20.00 50.00
4 Steve Blake 3.00 8.00
5 Anthony Davis/25 40.00 100.00
6 Kareem Abdul-Jabbar/25 30.00 80.00
8 Kenny Anderson 4.00 10.00
9 Kobe Bryant/25 100.00 200.00
10 Danny Manning/25
11 Elgin Baylor/49 10.00 25.00
12 Jack Sikma 4.00 10.00
13 Kevin Durant/25 75.00 150.00
16 Larry Nance 4.00 10.00
17 Dennis Rodman/49 15.00 40.00
18 Kyrie Irving/25 30.00 80.00
20 Magic Johnson/25
21 Raef LaFrentz 3.00 8.00
22 Vince Carter/49 12.00 30.00
23 Kyle Korver 4.00 10.00
24 Mark Aguirre 4.00 10.00
25 Larry Bird/25 50.00 100.00
27 Nick Young 6.00 15.00
28 Spud Webb 4.00 10.00
29 Julius Erving/25 30.00 80.00
31 Kevin Willis 3.00 8.00
32 Clifford Robinson 3.00 8.00
33 Karl Malone/25 15.00 40.00
35 Tobias Harris 4.00 10.00
36 Jared Dudley 3.00 8.00
37 Scottie Pippen/25
39 Darryl Dawkins 3.00 8.00

2013-14 Panini Crusade Quest Autographs Silver

*SILVER: .5X TO 1.2X BASIC
PRINT RUNS B/WN 5-25 COPIES PER
NO PRICING ON QTY 5-25 OR LESS
EXCHANGE DEADLINE 11/21/2015

2013-14 Panini Crusade Quest Memorabilia

PRINT RUNS B/WN 15-299 COPIES PER
NO PRICING ON QTY 15
1 Andre Drummond/299 4.00 10.00
2 Kareem Abdul-Jabbar/49 6.00 15.00
3 Blake Griffin/199 4.00 10.00
4 MarShon Brooks/199 3.00 8.00
5 Samuel Dalembert/299 2.50 6.00
6 Norris Cole/299 2.50 6.00
7 Jared Sullinger/299 2.50 6.00
8 O.J. Mayo/299 2.50 6.00
9 Ricky Pierce/99
10 Dirk Nowitzki/299 5.00 12.00
11 Harrison Barnes/99 5.00 12.00
12 Patrick Ewing/49
13 Anthony Davis/99 8.00 20.00
14 John Salmons/199
15 Kevin Garnett/199 5.00 12.00
16 Antawn Jamison/299 3.00 8.00
17 Paul Pierce/199 4.00 10.00
18 Dikembe Mutombo/25 4.00 10.00
19 Deron Williams/99 3.00 8.00
20 James Harden/99 6.00 15.00
21 Steve Nash/49 4.00 10.00
22 Tracy McGrady/99 4.00 10.00
23 Gary Payton/49 4.00 10.00
24 Rashard Lewis/199 3.00 8.00
25 Carmelo Anthony/99
26 Luc Mbah a Moute/199 2.50 6.00
27 Evan Turner/99 2.50 6.00
28 Steve Novak/299
29 Brad Daugherty/49 3.00 8.00
30 Paul George/99 5.00 12.00
31 Iman Shumpert/249 2.50 6.00
32 David Robinson/49 6.00 15.00
33 Larry Bird/49 10.00 25.00
34 Boris Diaw/299 3.00 8.00
35 Vinnie Johnson/99
36 Caron Butler/299 3.00 8.00
37 Nene/99
38 Jordan Farmar/149 2.50 6.00
39 Bill Cartwright/99 3.00 8.00
40 Kevin Love/299 4.00 10.00
41 Tim Duncan/299 6.00 15.00
42 Clyde Drexler/99 5.00 12.00
43 DeJuan Blair/299
44 Scottie Pippen/149 8.00 20.00
45 Anthony Randolph/299 2.50 6.00
46 Brandon Bass/299 2.50 6.00
48 Julius Erving/49 6.00 15.00
49 Mark Jackson/75 3.00 8.00
50 Russell Westbrook/199 5.00 12.00
51 LeBron James/99 10.00 25.00
52 Magic Johnson/49 10.00 25.00
53 Hakeem Olajuwon/99 5.00 12.00
54 Dwyane Wade/99 6.00 15.00
55 Carlos Delfino/299 2.50 6.00
56 Tobias Harris/199 3.00 8.00
57 Udonis Haslem/299 2.50 6.00
58 Andrei Kirilenko/99 3.00 8.00
59 Anthony Mason/99 3.00 8.00
60 Al Horford/99
61 Shaquille O'Neal /99 6.00 15.00
62 Kobe Bryant/199 12.00 30.00
63 Grant Hill/99 5.00 12.00
64 Michael Kidd-Gilchrist/199 4.00 10.00
65 Moses Malone/99 4.00 10.00
66 Ben Gordon/90 3.00 8.00
67 Jerryd Bayless/199 3.00 8.00
68 Terry Cummings/99 3.00 8.00
69 Rory Sparrow/99 2.50 6.00
70 Monta Ellis/99 3.00 8.00
71 Joe Dumars/99 4.00 10.00
72 Kevin Durant/199 8.00 20.00
73 John Wall/199 5.00 12.00
74 Isiah Thomas/49
75 Matt Barnes/299 2.50 6.00
76 Luol Deng /99 3.00 8.00
77 Chris Paul/99 5.00 12.00
78 Norm Nixon/99 2.50 6.00
79 Kiki VanDeWeghe/99 3.00 8.00
80 Bradley Beal/99 4.00 10.00
81 Karl Malone/99 5.00 12.00
82 Vince Carter/99
83 Devin Harris/99
84 Ray Allen/199 4.00 10.00
85 Channing Frye/199 3.00 8.00
86 Nate Robinson/299 2.50 6.00
87 Patty Mills/99 15.00 40.00
88 Dan Majerle/99 3.00 8.00
89 Buck Williams/99
90 Al Jefferson/60 3.00 8.00
91 Kevin McHale/99
92 Kyrie Irving/199 8.00 20.00
93 Jason Richardson/99
94 Kevin Martin/99 3.00 8.00
95 JaVale McGee/299 3.00 8.00
96 David West/199 3.00 8.00
97 Earl Clark/299 2.50 6.00
98 Jeff Malone/99
99 Rajon Rondo/99 4.00 10.00
100 Kemba Walker/99

2013-14 Panini Crusade Quest Memorabilia Prime

*PRIME: .75X TO 2X BASIC
PRINT RUNS B/WN 2-25 COPIES PER
NO PRICING ON QTY 15 OR LESS
47 Maurice Harkless/25 5.00 12.00

2013-14 Panini Crusade Royalty

*SILVER: 1.2X TO 3X BASIC
1 Carmelo Anthony 1.00 2.50
2 Paul George 1.00 2.50
3 Jerry West 1.00 2.50
4 Wilt Chamberlain 1.50 4.00
5 Bill Walton .75 2.00
6 James Worthy 1.00 2.50
7 Cedric Maxwell .50 1.25
8 Kobe Bryant 3.00 8.00
9 Blake Griffin .75 2.00
10 James Harden 1.25 3.00
11 Derrick Rose 1.00 2.50
12 Dirk Nowitzki 1.00 2.50
13 Willis Reed .75 2.00
14 John Havlicek 1.00 2.50
15 Moses Malone .75 2.00
16 Dennis Johnson .60 1.50
17 Grant Hill 1.00 2.50
18 Kevin Durant 2.00 5.00
19 Damian Lillard 1.50 4.00
20 Kevin Love .75 2.00
21 Rudy Gay .75 2.00
22 Steve Nash .75 2.00
23 Kareem Abdul-Jabbar 1.25 3.00
24 Rick Barry .60 1.50
25 Magic Johnson 2.00 5.00
26 Larry Bird 2.00 5.00
27 Anfernee Hardaway 2.00 5.00
28 Kyrie Irving 1.50 4.00
29 Dwight Howard .60 1.50
30 Stephen Curry 3.00 8.00

2013-14 Panini Crusade Sultans of Springfield Signatures

PRINT RUNS B/WN 10-199 COPIES PER
NO PRICING ON QTY 10
EXCHANGE DEADLINE 11/21/2015
*SILVER: .5X TO 1.2X BASIC
3 Bob McAdoo/199 4.00 10.00
4 Kareem Abdul-Jabbar/25 40.00 80.00
5 Karl Malone/25 30.00 60.00
7 Dan Issel/199 4.00 10.00
10 Joe Dumars/75 5.00 12.00
12 Julius Erving/25 50.00 100.00
13 Scottie Pippen/25 75.00 150.00
14 Bernard King/49 4.00 10.00
15 James Worthy/49 15.00 40.00
17 Robert Parish/75 5.00 12.00
22 Magic Johnson/25 50.00 100.00
24 Dennis Rodman/49 25.00 60.00

2014-15 Panini Eminence All Star Signatures Silver

RANDOM INSERTS IN PACKS
PRINT RUNS B/WN 9-10 COPIES PER
SOME NOT PRICED DUE TO SCARCITY
3 Chris Webber/10 250.00 400.00
4 Chris Webber/10 250.00 400.00
8 Chris Bosh/10 90.00 150.00
9 Chris Bosh/10 90.00 150.00
10 Kareem Abdul-Jabbar/10 150.00 300.00
11 Kareem Abdul-Jabbar/10 150.00 300.00
14 Karl Malone/10 125.00 250.00
17 Magic Johnson/10 175.00 350.00
21 Jason Kidd/10 150.00 300.00
22 Jason Kidd/10 150.00 300.00
23 Jason Kidd/10 150.00 300.00
24 Pau Gasol/10 100.00 200.00
25 Pau Gasol/10 100.00 200.00
26 Pau Gasol/10 100.00 200.00
28 Stephen Curry/10 600.00 1000.00
30 David Robinson/10 150.00 300.00
31 Kobe Bryant/10 500.00 1000.00
33 Steve Nash/10 100.00 200.00
34 Steve Nash/10 100.00 200.00
35 Julius Erving/10 200.00 400.00
36 Julius Erving/10 200.00 400.00
37 Julius Erving/10 200.00 400.00
40 Jerry West/10 200.00 400.00
42 Alonzo Mourning/10 125.00 250.00
43 Alonzo Mourning/10 125.00 250.00
44 Chris Paul/10 150.00 300.00
45 Chris Paul/10 150.00 300.00
46 Bill Russell/10 250.00 400.00
48 Ray Allen/10 150.00 300.00
49 Ray Allen/10 150.00 300.00
50 Ray Allen/10 150.00 300.00
54 Shaquille O'Neal/10 200.00 400.00
55 Shaquille O'Neal/10 200.00 400.00
56 Shaquille O'Neal/10 200.00 400.00
57 Shaquille O'Neal/10 200.00 400.00
58 Grant Hill/10 150.00 300.00
59 Grant Hill/10 150.00 300.00
60 Larry Bird/10 175.00 350.00
62 Allen Iverson/10 250.00 500.00
63 Allen Iverson/10 250.00 500.00
64 Allen Iverson/10 250.00 500.00
66 Dwight Howard/10 100.00 200.00
67 Dwight Howard/10 100.00 200.00
68 Dwight Howard/10 100.00 200.00
69 Dwyane Wade/10 175.00 350.00
72 Oscar Robertson/10 100.00 200.00
73 Oscar Robertson/10 100.00 200.00
74 Scottie Pippen/10 200.00 400.00
76 Bill Walton/10 100.00 200.00
77 Wes Unseld/10 100.00 200.00
78 Wes Unseld/10 100.00 200.00
79 Dave Cowens/10 90.00 150.00

2014-15 Panini Eminence Finals MVP Signatures Silver

RANDOM INSERTS IN PACKS
STATED PRINT RUN 10 SER.#'d SETS
SOME NOT PRICED DUE TO SCARCITY
1 Magic Johnson 175.00 350.00
2 Magic Johnson 175.00 350.00
3 Magic Johnson 175.00 350.00
4 Shaquille O'Neal 200.00 400.00
5 Shaquille O'Neal 200.00 400.00
6 Shaquille O'Neal 200.00 400.00
7 Kareem Abdul-Jabbar 150.00 300.00
8 Kareem Abdul-Jabbar 150.00 300.00
9 Larry Bird 175.00 350.00
10 Larry Bird 175.00 350.00
11 Kobe Bryant 500.00 1000.00
12 Kobe Bryant 500.00 1000.00
13 Jerry West 200.00 400.00
15 Hakeem Olajuwon 150.00 300.00
16 Hakeem Olajuwon 150.00 300.00
19 Bill Walton 100.00 200.00
20 Wes Unseld 100.00 200.00

2014-15 Panini Eminence Larry O'Brien Trophy Signatures Silver

RANDOM INSERTS IN PACKS
STATED PRINT RUN 10 SER.#'d SETS
SOME NOT PRICED DUE TO SCARCITY
1 Scottie Pippen 200.00 400.00
2 Scottie Pippen 200.00 400.00
3 Scottie Pippen 200.00 400.00
4 Scottie Pippen 200.00 400.00
5 Scottie Pippen 200.00 400.00
6 Scottie Pippen 200.00 400.00
7 Dwyane Wade 175.00 350.00
8 Dwyane Wade 175.00 350.00
9 Dwyane Wade 175.00 350.00
10 Kareem Abdul-Jabbar 150.00 300.00
11 Kareem Abdul-Jabbar 150.00 300.00
12 Kareem Abdul-Jabbar 150.00 300.00
13 Kareem Abdul-Jabbar 150.00 300.00
14 Kareem Abdul-Jabbar 150.00 300.00
15 Kareem Abdul-Jabbar 150.00 300.00
16 Kobe Bryant 500.00 1000.00
17 Kobe Bryant 500.00 1000.00
18 Kobe Bryant 500.00 1000.00
19 Kobe Bryant 500.00 1000.00
20 Kobe Bryant 500.00 1000.00
21 Larry Bird 175.00 350.00
22 Larry Bird 175.00 350.00
23 Larry Bird 175.00 350.00
24 Magic Johnson 175.00 350.00
25 Magic Johnson 175.00 350.00
26 Magic Johnson 175.00 350.00
27 Magic Johnson 175.00 350.00
28 Magic Johnson 175.00 350.00
29 Shaquille O'Neal 200.00 400.00
30 Shaquille O'Neal 200.00 400.00
31 Shaquille O'Neal 200.00 400.00
32 Shaquille O'Neal 200.00 400.00

2014-15 Panini Eminence MVP Signatures Silver

RANDOM INSERTS IN PACKS
STATED PRINT RUN 10 SER.#'d SETS
SOME NOT PRICED DUE TO SCARCITY
1 Bill Russell 250.00 400.00
2 Bill Russell 250.00 400.00
3 Bill Russell 250.00 400.00
4 Bill Russell 250.00 400.00
5 Bill Russell 250.00 400.00
6 Kareem Abdul-Jabbar 150.00 300.00
7 Kareem Abdul-Jabbar 150.00 300.00
8 Kareem Abdul-Jabbar 150.00 300.00
9 Kareem Abdul-Jabbar 150.00 300.00
10 Kareem Abdul-Jabbar 150.00 300.00
11 Kareem Abdul-Jabbar 150.00 300.00
12 Larry Bird 175.00 350.00
13 Larry Bird 175.00 350.00
14 Larry Bird 175.00 350.00
15 Magic Johnson 175.00 350.00
16 Magic Johnson 175.00 350.00
17 Magic Johnson 175.00 350.00
18 Julius Erving 200.00 400.00
19 Karl Malone 125.00 250.00
20 Karl Malone 125.00 250.00
21 Steve Nash 100.00 200.00
22 Steve Nash 100.00 200.00
23 Shaquille O'Neal 200.00 400.00
25 David Robinson 150.00 300.00
26 Kobe Bryant 500.00 1000.00
27 Hakeem Olajuwon 150.00 300.00
28 Allen Iverson 250.00 500.00
30 Stephen Curry 600.00 1000.00
32 Oscar Robertson 100.00 200.00
33 Bill Walton 100.00 200.00
34 Wes Unseld 100.00 200.00
35 Dave Cowens 90.00 150.00

2015 Immaculate Collection Multisport Autographs

RANDOM INSERTS IN PACKS
PRINT RUNS B/WN 5-25 COPIES PER
NO PRICING ON QTY 10 OR LESS
EXCHANGE DEADLINE 2/26/2017
1 Andrew Wiggins/15 150.00 250.00
2 Jabari Parker/15 100.00 200.00
5 Dante Exum/25 12.00 30.00

2014-15 Panini Excalibur

1 John Wall .50 1.25
2 Brandon Knight .30 .75
3 Nikola Vucevic .30 .75
4 Kyle Lowry .30 .75
5 Monta Ellis .30 .75
6 Michael Carter-Williams .25 .60
7 Stephen Curry 1.50 4.00
8 Serge Ibaka .30 .75
9 Ben McLemore .25 .60
10 Thaddeus Young .25 .60
11 Bradley Beal .40 1.00
12 Giannis Antetokounmpo .75 2.00
13 Victor Oladipo .30 .75
14 Jonas Valanciunas .30 .75
15 Chandler Parsons .30 .75
16 Nerlens Noel .30 .75
17 Harrison Barnes .30 .75
18 Steven Adams .30 .75
19 Rudy Gay .40 1.00
20 Gorgui Dieng .25 .60
21 Paul Pierce .40 1.00
22 Khris Middleton .30 .75
23 Tobias Harris .30 .75
24 Amir Johnson .25 .60
25 Tyson Chandler .30 .75
26 Luc Mbah a Moute .25 .60
27 Draymond Green .50 1.25
28 Kevin Durant 1.00 2.50
29 DeMarcus Cousins .40 1.00
30 Nikola Pekovic .25 .60
31 Marcin Gortat .30 .75
32 O.J. Mayo .25 .60
33 Evan Fournier .25 .60
34 Terrence Ross .30 .75
35 Dirk Nowitzki .50 1.25
36 Robert Covington .25 .60
37 Klay Thompson .50 1.25
38 Russell Westbrook 1.00 2.50
39 Darren Collison .30 .75
40 Ricky Rubio .40 1.00
41 Nene .30 .75
42 Ersan Ilyasova .25 .60
43 Channing Frye .30 .75
44 DeMar DeRozan .40 1.00
45 Rajon Rondo .40 1.00
46 Tony Wroten .25 .60
47 Andrew Bogut .30 .75
48 Reggie Jackson .25 .60
49 Jason Thompson .25 .60
50 Anthony Bennett .25 .60
51 Kemba Walker .40 1.00
52 Kentavious Caldwell-Pope .25 .60
53 Marc Gasol .40 1.00
54 Kevin Garnett .60 1.50

55 Tim Duncan .60 1.50
56 Carmelo Anthony .50 1.25
57 Chris Paul .50 1.25
58 Arron Afflalo .25 .60
59 Kobe Bryant 1.50 4.00
60 Pau Gasol .40 1.00
61 Gerald Henderson .25 .60
62 Andre Drummond .40 1.00
63 Courtney Lee .30 .75
64 Deron Williams .30 .75
65 Tony Parker .40 1.00
66 Jose Calderon .25 .60
67 Blake Griffin .40 1.00
68 Kenneth Faried .30 .75
69 Carlos Boozer .30 .75
70 Derrick Rose .50 1.25
71 Al Jefferson .30 .75
72 Brandon Jennings .25 .60
73 Mike Conley .30 .75
74 Joe Johnson .30 .75
75 Manu Ginobili .40 1.00
76 Jason Smith .25 .60
77 DeAndre Jordan .40 1.00
78 Wilson Chandler .30 .75
79 Jeremy Lin .40 1.00
80 Jimmy Butler .40 1.00
81 Michael Kidd-Gilchrist .30 .75
82 Greg Monroe .30 .75
83 Zach Randolph .30 .75
84 Brook Lopez .30 .75
85 Kawhi Leonard .60 1.50
86 Tim Hardaway Jr. .25 .60
87 J.J. Redick .40 1.00
88 Ty Lawson .25 .60
89 Jordan Hill .25 .60
90 Taj Gibson .30 .75
91 Lance Stephenson .30 .75
92 Kyle Singler .25 .60
93 Vince Carter .50 1.25
94 Jarrett Jack .30 .75
95 Danny Green .30 .75
96 Andrea Bargnani .30 .75
97 Jamal Crawford .40 1.00
98 J.J. Hickson .25 .60
99 Steve Nash .40 1.00
100 Joakim Noah .30 .75
101 Chris Bosh .40 1.00
102 David West .30 .75
103 Dwight Howard .30 .75
104 Jared Sullinger .25 .60
105 Ryan Anderson .25 .60
106 Damian Lillard .75 2.00
107 Markieff Morris .25 .60
108 Gordon Hayward .40 1.00
109 Paul Millsap .40 1.00
110 Kevin Love .40 1.00
111 Luol Deng .30 .75
112 Roy Hibbert .30 .75
113 James Harden .60 1.50
114 Avery Bradley .30 .75
115 Anthony Davis .75 2.00
116 Wesley Matthews .25 .60
117 Marcus Morris .25 .60
118 Derrick Favors .30 .75
119 Kyle Korver .30 .75
120 Kyrie Irving .75 2.00
121 Dwyane Wade .60 1.50
122 Solomon Hill .25 .60
123 Trevor Ariza .25 .60
124 Tyler Zeller .30 .75
125 Jrue Holiday .30 .75
126 LaMarcus Aldridge .40 1.00
127 Eric Bledsoe .30 .75
128 Enes Kanter .25 .60
129 Al Horford .30 .75
130 LeBron James 1.50 4.00
131 Mario Chalmers .30 .75
132 George Hill .30 .75
133 Jason Terry .30 .75
134 Evan Turner .25 .60
135 Tyreke Evans .25 .60
136 Nicolas Batum .30 .75
137 Goran Dragic .30 .75
138 Trey Burke .25 .60
139 Jeff Teague .30 .75
140 Tristan Thompson .30 .75
141 Hassan Whiteside .30 .75
142 Paul George .50 1.25
143 Josh Smith .30 .75
144 Brandon Bass .25 .60
145 Omer Asik .30 .75
146 Robin Lopez .25 .60
147 Isaiah Thomas .40 1.00
148 Alec Burks .25 .60
149 DeMarre Carroll .25 .60
150 Timofey Mozgov .25 .60
151 Jordan Clarkson RC .75 2.00
152 Dante Exum RC .75 2.00
153 Aaron Gordon RC 1.25 3.00
154 Zach LaVine RC 1.25 3.00
155 Jarnell Stokes RC .50 1.25
156 Sim Bhullar RC .50 1.25
157 Jabari Parker RC 1.25 3.00
158 James Young RC .50 1.25
159 C.J. Wilcox RC .50 1.25
160 Cleanthony Early RC .50 1.25
161 Noah Vonleh RC .60 1.50
162 Rodney Hood RC .75 2.00
163 Elfrid Payton RC .75 2.00
164 Adreian Payne RC .60 1.50
165 Russ Smith RC .50 1.25
166 Bruno Caboclo RC .60 1.50
167 Damien Inglis RC .50 1.25
168 Marcus Smart RC .75 2.00
169 Zoran Dragic RC .60 1.50
170 Langston Galloway RC .75 2.00
171 P.J. Hairston RC .50 1.25
172 Joe Ingles RC .50 1.25
173 Clint Capela RC .60 1.50
174 Glenn Robinson III RC .50 1.25
175 Dwight Powell RC .50 1.25
176 Bojan Bogdanovic RC .60 1.50
177 Johnny O'Bryant RC .50 1.25
178 Joel Embiid RC 2.50 6.00
179 Nik Stauskas RC .60 1.50
180 Mitch McGary RC .50 1.25
181 James Ennis RC .50 1.25
182 Elijah Millsap RC .50 1.25
183 Kostas Papanikolaou RC .50 1.25
184 Doug McDermott RC .75 2.00
185 Kyle Anderson RC .75 2.00
186 Cory Jefferson RC .50 1.25
187 Spencer Dinwiddie RC .60 1.50
188 K.J. McDaniels RC .60 1.50
189 Julius Randle RC 1.25 3.00
190 Gary Harris RC .75 2.00
191 Shabazz Napier RC .60 1.50
192 Andrew Wiggins RC 2.50 6.00
193 Jordan Adams RC .50 1.25
194 Nikola Mirotic RC 1.00 2.50
195 JaKarr Sampson RC .50 1.25
196 Markel Brown RC .50 1.25
197 Damjan Rudez RC .50 1.25
198 Jerami Grant RC .50 1.25
199 Tarik Black RC .50 1.25
200 Jusuf Nurkic RC .75 2.00

2014-15 Panini Excalibur Blue

*BLUE 1-150: .75X TO 2X BASIC
*BLUE RC 151-200: .75X TO 2X BASIC RC
RANDOM INSERTS IN PACKS

2014-15 Panini Excalibur Knights Templar

*TEMPLAR 1-150: .6X TO 1.5X BASIC
*TEMPLAR RC 151-200: .6X TO 1.5X BASIC RC
RANDOM INSERTS IN PACKS

2014-15 Panini Excalibur Orange

*ORANGE 1-150: .6X TO 1.5X BASIC
*ORANGE RC 151-200: .6X TO 1.5X BASIC RC
RANDOM INSERTS IN PACKS

2014-15 Panini Excalibur Red

*RED 1-150: .5X TO 1.2X BASIC
*RED RC 151-200: .5X TO 1.2X BASIC RC
RANDOM INSERTS IN PACKS

2014-15 Panini Excalibur Silver

*SILVER 1-150: 1.2X TO 3X BASIC
*SILVER RC 151-200: 1.2X TO 3X BASIC RC
RANDOM INSERTS IN PACKS
STATED PRINT RUN 49 SER.#'d SETS

2014-15 Panini Excalibur Crusade Camouflage

RANDOM INSERTS IN PACKS
*BLUE/149: .5X TO 1.2X BASIC
*RED/99: .6X TO 1.5X BASIC
*PURPLE/75: .75X TO 2X BASIC
*ORANGE/60: .75X TO 2X BASIC
*TEAL/35: 1X TO 2.5X BASIC
1 Serge Ibaka 1.25 3.00
2 Marcin Gortat 1.25 3.00
3 Gorgui Dieng 1.00 2.50
4 Tobias Harris 1.25 3.00
5 Giannis Antetokounmpo 3.00 8.00
6 Dirk Nowitzki 2.00 5.00
7 Kyle Lowry 1.25 3.00
8 Draymond Green 2.00 5.00
9 Michael Carter-Williams 1.00 2.50
10 DeMarcus Cousins 1.50 4.00
11 Reggie Jackson 1.00 2.50
12 Bradley Beal 1.50 4.00
13 Mo Williams 1.25 3.00
14 Victor Oladipo 1.25 3.00
15 O.J. Mayo 1.00 2.50
16 Tyson Chandler 1.25 3.00
17 DeMar DeRozan 1.50 4.00
18 Klay Thompson 2.00 5.00
19 Tony Wroten 1.00 2.50
20 Darren Collison 1.25 3.00
21 Ty Lawson 1.00 2.50
22 Paul Pierce 1.50 4.00
23 Jimmy Butler 1.50 4.00
24 Marc Gasol 1.50 4.00
25 Khris Middleton 1.25 3.00
26 Rajon Rondo 1.50 4.00
27 Jonas Valanciunas 1.25 3.00
28 Harrison Barnes 1.25 3.00
29 Carmelo Anthony 2.00 5.00
30 Ben McLemore 1.00 2.50
31 Arron Afflalo 1.00 2.50
32 Kemba Walker 1.50 4.00
33 Pau Gasol 1.50 4.00
34 Vince Carter 2.00 5.00
35 Greg Monroe 1.25 3.00
36 Kawhi Leonard 2.50 6.00
37 Terrence Ross 1.25 3.00
38 Chris Paul 2.00 5.00
39 Tim Hardaway Jr. 1.00 2.50
40 Kobe Bryant 8.00 20.00
41 Wilson Chandler 1.25 3.00
42 Al Jefferson 1.25 3.00
43 Derrick Rose 2.00 5.00
44 Zach Randolph 1.25 3.00
45 Andre Drummond 1.50 4.00
46 Tim Duncan 2.50 6.00
47 Joe Johnson 1.25 3.00
48 Blake Griffin 1.50 4.00
49 Amare Stoudemire 1.50 4.00
50 Steve Nash 1.50 4.00
51 Kenneth Faried 1.25 3.00
52 Gerald Henderson 1.00 2.50
53 Taj Gibson 1.25 3.00
54 Mike Conley 1.25 3.00
55 Brandon Jennings 1.00 2.50
56 Tony Parker 1.50 4.00
57 Kevin Garnett 2.50 6.00
58 DeAndre Jordan 1.50 4.00
59 Jose Calderon 1.00 2.50
60 Carlos Boozer 1.25 3.00
61 Gordon Hayward 1.50 4.00
62 Lance Stephenson 1.25 3.00
63 Joakim Noah 1.25 3.00
64 Dwight Howard 1.25 3.00
65 Kentavious Caldwell-Pope 1.00 2.50
66 Manu Ginobili 1.50 4.00
67 Deron Williams 1.25 3.00
68 J.J. Redick 1.50 4.00
69 Damian Lillard 3.00 8.00
70 Jordan Hill 1.00 2.50
71 Trey Burke 1.00 2.50
72 Chris Bosh 1.50 4.00
73 Kyrie Irving 3.00 8.00
74 Trevor Ariza 1.00 2.50
75 Paul George 2.00 5.00
76 Danny Green 1.25 3.00
77 Mason Plumlee 1.25 3.00
78 Eric Bledsoe 1.25 3.00
79 LaMarcus Aldridge 1.50 4.00
80 Paul Millsap 1.50 4.00
81 Derrick Favors 1.25 3.00
82 Dwyane Wade 2.50 6.00
83 Kevin Love 1.50 4.00
84 James Harden 2.50 6.00
85 Roy Hibbert 1.25 3.00
86 Anthony Davis 3.00 8.00
87 Jared Sullinger 1.00 2.50
88 Goran Dragic 1.25 3.00
89 Wesley Matthews 1.00 2.50
90 Kyle Korver 1.25 3.00
91 Rudy Gobert 1.50 4.00
92 Luol Deng 1.25 3.00
93 LeBron James 8.00 20.00
94 Donatas Motiejunas 1.00 2.50
95 Solomon Hill 1.00 2.50
96 Ryan Anderson 1.00 2.50
97 Avery Bradley 1.25 3.00
98 Markieff Morris 1.00 2.50
99 Nicolas Batum 1.25 3.00
100 Al Horford 1.25 3.00
101 Thaddeus Young 1.00 2.50
102 Hassan Whiteside 1.25 3.00
103 Shawn Marion 1.25 3.00
104 Monta Ellis 1.25 3.00
105 David West 1.25 3.00
106 Jrue Holiday 1.25 3.00
107 Evan Turner 1.00 2.50
108 Isaiah Thomas 1.50 4.00
109 Kevin Durant 4.00 10.00
110 Jeff Teague 1.25 3.00
111 Ricky Rubio 1.50 4.00
112 Nikola Vucevic 1.25 3.00
113 Brandon Knight 1.25 3.00
114 Chandler Parsons 1.25 3.00
115 Stephen Curry 6.00 15.00
116 Tyreke Evans 1.00 2.50
117 Nerlens Noel 1.25 3.00
118 Rudy Gay 1.50 4.00
119 Russell Westbrook 4.00 10.00
120 John Wall 2.00 5.00
121 George Gervin 1.50 4.00
122 Scottie Pippen 3.00 8.00
123 James Worthy 2.00 5.00
124 Toni Kukoc 1.50 4.00
125 Allen Iverson 2.00 5.00
126 John Stockton 2.50 6.00
127 Baron Davis 1.25 3.00
128 Larry Bird 4.00 10.00
129 Dikembe Mutombo 1.50 4.00
130 Patrick Ewing 2.00 5.00
131 Grant Hill 2.00 5.00
132 Shaquille O'Neal 3.00 8.00
133 Jason Kidd 1.50 4.00
134 Tracy McGrady 1.50 4.00
135 Alonzo Mourning 2.00 5.00
136 Julius Erving 2.50 6.00
137 Clifford Robinson 1.00 2.50
138 Latrell Sprewell 1.25 3.00
139 Dominique Wilkins 2.00 5.00
140 Pete Maravich 2.50 6.00
141 Hakeem Olajuwon 2.00 5.00
142 Shawn Kemp 2.50 6.00
143 Jerry West 2.00 5.00
144 Yao Ming 2.00 5.00
145 Anfernee Hardaway 4.00 10.00
146 Kareem Abdul-Jabbar 2.50 6.00
147 Clyde Drexler 2.00 5.00
148 Magic Johnson 4.00 10.00
149 Drazen Petrovic 1.50 4.00
150 Rony Seikaly 1.00 2.50
151 Isiah Thomas 1.50 4.00
152 Tim Hardaway 1.50 4.00
153 John Havlicek 2.00 5.00
154 Oscar Robertson 2.00 5.00
155 Arvydas Sabonis 1.25 3.00
156 Karl Malone 2.00 5.00
157 David Robinson 2.50 6.00
158 Moses Malone 1.50 4.00
159 Gary Payton 1.50 4.00
160 Dennis Rodman 3.00 8.00
161 Andrew Wiggins 8.00 20.00
162 K.J. McDaniels 1.25 3.00
163 Elfrid Payton 1.50 4.00
164 Bojan Bogdanovic 1.25 3.00
165 Nikola Mirotic 2.00 5.00
166 Zach LaVine 6.00 15.00
167 Jabari Parker 2.50 6.00
168 Jusuf Nurkic 1.50 4.00
169 Dante Exum 1.50 4.00
170 Marcus Smart 1.50 4.00
171 Jordan Clarkson 1.50 4.00
172 Julius Randle 5.00 12.00
173 Joel Embiid 5.00 12.00
174 Jerami Grant 1.00 2.50
175 Shabazz Napier 1.25 3.00
176 Aaron Gordon 2.50 6.00
177 Nik Stauskas 1.25 3.00
178 Noah Vonleh 1.25 3.00
179 Doug McDermott 1.50 4.00
180 James Young 1.00 2.50
181 T.J. Warren 1.50 4.00
182 Gary Harris 1.50 4.00
183 Tyler Ennis 1.00 2.50
184 Bruno Caboclo 1.25 3.00
185 Mitch McGary 1.00 2.50
186 Rodney Hood 1.50 4.00
187 P.J. Hairston 1.00 2.50
188 Kyle Anderson 1.50 4.00
189 Glenn Robinson III 1.25 3.00
190 Cameron Bairstow 1.00 2.50
191 Langston Galloway 1.50 4.00
192 JaKarr Sampson 1.00 2.50
193 Kostas Papanikolaou 1.00 2.50
194 Tarik Black 1.00 2.50
195 Joe Ingles 1.00 2.50
196 Cleanthony Early 1.00 2.50
197 James Ennis 1.00 2.50
198 Zoran Dragic 1.25 3.00
199 Cory Jefferson 1.00 2.50
200 Travis Wear 1.00 2.50

2014-15 Panini Excalibur Dunk Company Jerseys

RANDOM INSERTS IN PACKS
*PRIME/25: 1X TO 2.5X BASIC
1 Jimmy Butler 2.50 6.00
2 Kevin Garnett 4.00 10.00
3 Chandler Parsons 2.00 5.00
4 LeBron James 10.00 25.00
5 Kobe Bryant 10.00 25.00
6 Giannis Antetokounmpo 5.00 12.00
7 Victor Oladipo 2.00 5.00
8 Zach LaVine 4.00 10.00
9 Mason Plumlee 2.00 5.00
10 Andrew Wiggins 6.00 15.00
11 Aaron Gordon 4.00 10.00
12 Adreian Payne 2.00 5.00
13 Bruno Caboclo 2.00 5.00
14 Jabari Parker 6.00 15.00
15 Russell Westbrook 6.00 15.00
16 Terrence Ross 2.00 5.00
17 Blake Griffin 2.50 6.00
18 Dwight Howard 2.00 5.00
19 Derrick Rose 3.00 8.00
20 Kevin Durant 4.00 10.00

2014-15 Panini Excalibur Fresh Faces Die-Cut Jerseys

RANDOM INSERTS IN PACKS
*PRIME/25: 1X TO 2.5X BASIC
1 Jordan Adams 1.50 4.00
2 Kyle Anderson 2.50 6.00
3 Bruno Caboclo 2.00 5.00
4 Cleanthony Early 1.50 4.00
5 Joel Embiid 6.00 15.00
6 Tyler Ennis 1.50 4.00
7 Dante Exum 2.50 6.00
8 Aaron Gordon 4.00 10.00
9 P.J. Hairston 1.50 4.00
10 Gary Harris 2.50 6.00
11 Joe Harris 1.50 4.00
12 Rodney Hood 2.50 6.00
13 Damien Inglis 1.50 4.00
14 Zach LaVine 4.00 10.00
15 K.J. McDaniels 2.00 5.00
16 Doug McDermott 2.50 6.00
17 Mitch McGary 1.50 4.00
18 Shabazz Napier 2.00 5.00
19 Spencer Dinwiddie 2.00 5.00
20 Jabari Parker 6.00 15.00
21 Adreian Payne 2.00 5.00
22 Elfrid Payton 2.50 6.00
23 Julius Randle 4.00 10.00
24 Marcus Smart 2.50 6.00
25 Nik Stauskas 2.00 5.00
26 Noah Vonleh 2.00 5.00
27 T.J. Warren 2.50 6.00
28 Andrew Wiggins 6.00 15.00
29 C.J. Wilcox 1.50 4.00
30 James Young 1.50 4.00

2014-15 Panini Excalibur High Praise Signatures

RANDOM INSERTS IN PACKS
1 George Gervin 8.00 20.00
2 Kevin McHale 8.00 20.00
3 John Stockton 20.00 50.00
4 Terry Cummings 3.00 8.00
5 David Robinson 12.00 30.00
6 Artis Gilmore 3.00 8.00
7 Spud Webb 3.00 8.00
8 Tom Satch Sanders 4.00 10.00
9 Robert Horry 5.00 12.00
10 Grant Hill 12.00 30.00
11 Latrell Sprewell 15.00 40.00
12 Wayne Embry 2.50 6.00
13 Oscar Robertson 40.00 100.00
14 Anthony Mason 3.00 8.00
15 Chris Webber 30.00 80.00
16 Gary Payton 8.00 20.00
17 Tim Hardaway 4.00 10.00
18 Robert Parish 4.00 10.00
19 Joe Dumars 4.00 10.00
20 Dolph Schayes 4.00 10.00
21 Allen Iverson 75.00 150.00
22 Dan Issel 3.00 8.00
23 Karl Malone 20.00 50.00
24 Eddie Jones 3.00 8.00
25 Hakeem Olajuwon 10.00 25.00
26 Bernard King 3.00 8.00
27 John Starks 3.00 8.00
28 Walt Frazier 6.00 15.00
29 Rick Fox 3.00 8.00
30 Clyde Drexler 10.00 25.00

2014-15 Panini Excalibur Juggernauts

RANDOM INSERTS IN PACKS
*BLUE/99: 1.2X TO 3X BASIC
*ORANGE/99: 1.2X TO 3X BASIC
*SILVER/49: 1.5X TO 4X BASIC
1 Stephen Curry 2.00 5.00
2 Kareem Abdul-Jabbar .75 2.00
3 Damian Lillard 1.00 2.50
4 Julius Erving .75 2.00
5 LeBron James 2.00 5.00
6 Tim Duncan .75 2.00
7 Carmelo Anthony .60 1.50
8 Kevin Love .50 1.25
9 Blake Griffin .50 1.25
10 Derrick Rose .60 1.50
11 Jerry West .60 1.50
12 Larry Bird 1.25 3.00
13 Chris Bosh .50 1.25
14 Patrick Ewing .60 1.50
15 Kobe Bryant 2.00 5.00
16 Anthony Davis 1.00 2.50
17 Dwyane Wade .75 2.00
18 Chris Paul .60 1.50
19 Paul Pierce .50 1.25
20 Allen Iverson .60 1.50
21 Russell Westbrook 1.25 3.00
22 Pete Maravich .75 2.00
23 Vince Carter .60 1.50
24 Chris Webber .50 1.25
25 Kevin Durant 1.25 3.00
26 James Harden .75 2.00
27 Dirk Nowitzki .60 1.50
28 Wilt Chamberlain 1.00 2.50
29 Kyrie Irving 1.00 2.50
30 Karl Malone .60 1.50

2014-15 Panini Excalibur Kaboom

RANDOM INSERTS IN PACKS
1 LeBron James 500.00 800.00
2 Kevin Durant 80.00 200.00
3 Kevin Garnett 50.00 125.00
4 Chris Paul 40.00 100.00
5 Tim Duncan 75.00 200.00
6 Dirk Nowitzki 40.00 100.00
7 Vince Carter 40.00 100.00
8 Stephen Curry 125.00 300.00
9 Jimmy Butler 30.00 80.00
10 Blake Griffin 30.00 80.00
11 James Harden 50.00 125.00
12 Dwight Howard 25.00 60.00
13 Kevin Love 30.00 80.00
14 Steve Nash 30.00 80.00
15 Derrick Rose 40.00 100.00
16 Dwyane Wade 60.00 150.00
17 Russell Westbrook 75.00 200.00
18 Carmelo Anthony 40.00 100.00
19 Chris Bosh 30.00 80.00
20 Kobe Bryant 125.00 300.00
21 Anthony Davis 60.00 150.00
22 Tony Parker 30.00 80.00
23 John Wall 40.00 100.00
24 Kyrie Irving 60.00 150.00
25 Damian Lillard 60.00 150.00
26 Pau Gasol 30.00 80.00
27 DeMar DeRozan 30.00 80.00
28 Klay Thompson 40.00 100.00
29 Manu Ginobili 30.00 80.00
30 Rajon Rondo 30.00 80.00
31 Paul George 40.80 100.00
32 Andrew Wiggins 75.00 200.00
33 Jabari Parker 60.00 150.00
34 Allen Iverson 60.00 150.00
35 Shaquille O'Neal 60.00 150.00
36 Karl Malone 40.00 100.00
37 Magic Johnson 80.00 200.00
38 Larry Bird 80.00 200.00
39 Julius Erving 50.00 125.00
40 Kareem Abdul-Jabbar 50.00 125.00
41 Jason Kidd 30.00 80.00
42 Anfernee Hardaway 60.00 150.00
43 Chris Webber 30.00 80.00
44 Patrick Ewing 40.00 100.00
45 Gary Payton 30.00 80.00
46 John Stockton 50.00 125.00
47 Scottie Pippen 60.00 150.00
48 Dominique Wilkins 40.00 100.00
49 Dennis Rodman 60.00 150.00
50 Grant Hill 40.00 100.00

2014-15 Panini Excalibur Knight Court

RANDOM INSERTS IN PACKS
*BLUE/99: 1.2X TO 3X BASIC
*ORANGE/99: 1.2X TO 3X BASIC
*SILVER/49: 1.5X TO 4X BASIC
1 Pau Gasol .50 1.25
2 Kyrie Irving 1.00 2.50
3 Tim Duncan .75 2.00
4 Klay Thompson .60 1.50
5 Dirk Nowitzki .60 1.50
6 John Wall .60 1.50
7 Derrick Rose .60 1.50
8 James Harden .75 2.00
9 Eric Bledsoe .40 1.00
10 Stephen Curry 2.00 5.00
11 Kevin Love .50 1.25
12 Monta Ellis .40 1.00
13 Kobe Bryant 2.00 5.00
14 Jimmy Butler .50 1.25
15 Kevin Garnett .75 2.00
16 Chris Paul .60 1.50
17 Dwight Howard .40 1.00
18 Blake Griffin .50 1.25
19 Russell Westbrook 1.25 3.00
20 Anthony Davis 1.00 2.50
21 DeMarcus Cousins .50 1.25
22 LaMarcus Aldridge .50 1.25
23 Kevin Durant 1.25 3.00
24 Carmelo Anthony .60 1.50
25 Dwyane Wade .75 2.00
26 Jeff Teague .40 1.00
27 Tony Parker .50 1.25
28 Damian Lillard 1.00 2.50
29 Kemba Walker .50 1.25
30 LeBron James 2.00 5.00

2014-15 Panini Excalibur Knights of the Round Die-Cuts

RANDOM INSERTS IN PACKS
1 John Wall 5.00 12.00
2 Kyle Lowry 3.00 8.00
3 Monta Ellis 3.00 8.00
4 Michael Carter-Williams 2.50 6.00
5 Stephen Curry 15.00 40.00
6 Bradley Beal 4.00 10.00
7 Nerlens Noel 3.00 8.00
8 Paul Pierce 4.00 10.00
9 Kevin Durant 10.00 25.00
10 Dirk Nowitzki 5.00 12.00
11 Klay Thompson 5.00 12.00
12 Russell Westbrook 10.00 25.00
13 Ricky Rubio 4.00 10.00
14 Rajon Rondo 4.00 10.00
15 Kevin Garnett 6.00 15.00
16 Tim Duncan 6.00 15.00
17 Carmelo Anthony 5.00 12.00
18 Chris Paul 5.00 12.00
19 Kobe Bryant 40.00 100.00
20 Pau Gasol 4.00 10.00
21 Tony Parker 4.00 10.00
22 Blake Griffin 4.00 10.00
23 Derrick Rose 5.00 12.00
24 Manu Ginobili 4.00 10.00
25 Jeremy Lin 4.00 10.00
26 Jimmy Butler 4.00 10.00
27 Kawhi Leonard 6.00 15.00
28 Vince Carter 5.00 12.00
29 Steve Nash 4.00 10.00
30 Chris Bosh 4.00 10.00
31 Dwight Howard 3.00 8.00
32 Damian Lillard 8.00 20.00
33 Kevin Love 4.00 10.00
34 James Harden 6.00 15.00
35 Anthony Davis 8.00 20.00
36 Kyrie Irving 8.00 20.00
37 Dwyane Wade 6.00 15.00
38 LaMarcus Aldridge 4.00 10.00
39 LeBron James 40.00 100.00
40 Goran Dragic 3.00 8.00
41 Paul George 5.00 12.00
42 Dante Exum 4.00 10.00
43 Zach LaVine 12.00 30.00
44 Jabari Parker 15.00 40.00
45 Elfrid Payton 4.00 10.00
46 Marcus Smart 4.00 10.00
47 Doug McDermott 4.00 10.00
48 Julius Randle 6.00 15.00
49 Andrew Wiggins 40.00 100.00
50 Nikola Mirotic 5.00 12.00

2014-15 Panini Excalibur Majectic Marks Signatures

RANDOM INSERTS IN PACKS
1 Kevin Durant
2 Brad Daugherty 3.00 8.00
3 Gary Payton 4.00 10.00
4 Spud Webb 3.00 8.00
5 Michael Carter-Williams
6 Luc Longley 3.00 8.00
7 Roy Hibbert 3.00 8.00
8 Kendall Gill 2.50 6.00
9 Shaquille O'Neal
10 Lance Stephenson 3.00 8.00
11 Paul George 30.00 80.00
12 Anthony Mason 3.00 8.00
13 Grant Hill 15.00 40.00
14 Mahmoud Abdul-Rauf 2.50 6.00
15 Trey Burke 2.50 6.00
16 Mychal Thompson 2.50 6.00
17 Kurt Rambis 2.50 6.00
18 Donatas Motiejunas 2.50 6.00
19 Carmelo Anthony
20 David Thompson 3.00 8.00
21 Kareem Abdul-Jabbar 25.00 60.00
22 Eddie Jones 3.00 8.00
23 Victor Oladipo 3.00 8.00
24 Bill Laimbeer 3.00 8.00
25 Rick Fox 3.00 8.00
26 Sarunas Marciulionis 2.50 6.00
27 Alex English 3.00 8.00
28 Khris Middleton 3.00 8.00
29 Magic Johnson
30 Cedric Ceballos 2.50 6.00
31 Anthony Davis 50.00 120.00
32 Mark Price 4.00 10.00
33 Ben McLemore
34 Zydrunas Ilgauskas 3.00 8.00
35 Latrell Sprewell 15.00 40.00
36 Michael Cooper 3.00 8.00
37 Adrian Dantley
38 Rudy Gobert 4.00 10.00
39 Julius Erving 25.00 60.00
40 Ricky Pierce 2.50 6.00
41 Kyrie Irving 25.00 60.00
42 Sean Elliott 4.00 10.00
43 Nerlens Noel 3.00 8.00
44 Jack Sikma 3.00 8.00
45 Allan Houston 3.00 8.00
46 Clifford Robinson 2.50 6.00
47 Robert Horry 3.00 8.00
48 Robert Covington 2.50 6.00
49 Karl Malone 20.00 50.00
50 Tim Hardaway Jr. 2.50 6.00

2014-15 Panini Excalibur Nobility

RANDOM INSERTS IN PACKS
*BLUE/99: 1.2X TO 3X BASIC
*ORANGE/99: 1.2X TO 3X BASIC
*SILVER/49: 1.5X TO 4X BASIC
1 Shaquille O'Neal 1.00 2.50
2 Rick Barry .40 1.00
3 Larry Bird 1.25 3.00
4 Willis Reed .50 1.25
5 Manu Ginobili .50 1.25
6 Bill Walton .50 1.25
7 Kawhi Leonard .75 2.00
8 Rajon Rondo .50 1.25
9 Paul Pierce .50 1.25
10 Clyde Drexler .60 1.50
11 Kareem Abdul-Jabbar .75 2.00
12 Tim Duncan .75 2.00
13 Hakeem Olajuwon .60 1.50
14 Robert Horry .40 1.00
15 Chris Bosh .50 1.25
16 Kobe Bryant 2.00 5.00
17 LeBron James 2.00 5.00
18 Alonzo Mourning .60 1.50
19 Tony Parker .50 1.25
20 Dennis Rodman 1.00 2.50
21 Isiah Thomas .50 1.25
22 Kevin Garnett .75 2.00
23 Joe Dumars .50 1.25
24 Moses Malone .50 1.25
25 Jason Kidd .50 1.25
26 Magic Johnson 1.25 3.00
27 Dirk Nowitzki .60 1.50
28 Gary Payton .50 1.25
29 Scottie Pippen 1.00 2.50
30 Dwyane Wade .75 2.00

2014-15 Panini Excalibur Quest Signatures

RANDOM INSERTS IN PACKS
1 Michael Carter-Williams 2.50 6.00
2 Marcus Smart 4.00 10.00
3 Tim Hardaway Jr. 2.50 6.00
4 Trey Burke 2.50 6.00
5 Robert Covington 2.50 6.00
6 Donatas Motiejunas 2.50 6.00
7 K.J. McDaniels 3.00 8.00
8 Reggie Jackson 4.00 10.00
9 Mason Plumlee 3.00 8.00
10 Nikola Mirotic 5.00 12.00
11 Anthony Bennett
12 Joel Embiid 30.00 80.00
13 Lance Stephenson 3.00 8.00
14 Nerlens Noel 3.00 8.00
15 Jordan Clarkson 4.00 10.00
16 Rudy Gobert 4.00 10.00
17 James Ennis 2.50 6.00
18 Taj Gibson 3.00 8.00
19 Victor Oladipo 3.00 8.00
20 Julius Randle 6.00 15.00

2014-15 Panini Excalibur Red White and Blue Jerseys

RANDOM INSERTS IN PACKS
*PRIME/24-25: 1X TO 2.5X BASIC
1 DeMarcus Cousins 2.50 6.00
2 Stephen Curry 12.00 30.00
3 Anthony Davis 5.00 12.00
4 DeMar DeRozan 2.50 6.00
5 Andre Drummond 2.50 6.00
6 Kenneth Faried 2.00 5.00
7 Rudy Gay 2.50 6.00
8 James Harden 8.00 20.00
9 Kyrie Irving 5.00 12.00
10 Mason Plumlee 2.00 5.00
11 Derrick Rose 3.00 8.00
12 Klay Thompson 3.00 8.00
13 Larry Bird 25.00 60.00
14 Karl Malone 20.00 50.00
15 Magic Johnson 25.00 60.00
16 Scottie Pippen 15.00 40.00
17 Clyde Drexler 15.00 40.00
18 David Robinson
19 Chris Mullin
20 Shaquille O'Neal 20.00 50.00

2014-15 Panini Excalibur Ringing Endorsements Jerseys

RANDOM INSERTS IN PACKS
*PRIME/25: 1X TO 2.5X BASIC
1 Kobe Bryant 10.00 25.00
2 Kevin Durant 5.00 12.00
3 Anthony Davis 5.00 12.00
4 Stephen Curry 10.00 25.00
5 James Harden 4.00 10.00
6 LeBron James 6.00 15.00
7 Carmelo Anthony 3.00 8.00
8 Chris Paul 3.00 8.00
9 John Wall 3.00 8.00
10 Derrick Rose 3.00 8.00
11 Jeff Teague 2.00 5.00
12 Klay Thompson 3.00 8.00
13 Blake Griffin 2.50 6.00
14 LaMarcus Aldridge 2.50 6.00
15 Dwyane Wade 4.00 10.00
16 Russell Westbrook 6.00 15.00
17 Kyrie Irving 8.00 20.00
18 Damian Lillard 5.00 12.00
19 Dirk Nowitzki 3.00 8.00
20 Al Horford 2.00 5.00

2014-15 Panini Excalibur Rookie Rampage Autograph Dual Jerseys

RANDOM INSERTS IN PACKS
STATED PRINT RUN 349 SER.#'d SETS
1 Jordan Adams 4.00 10.00
3 Markel Brown 4.00 10.00
5 Spencer Dinwiddie 5.00 12.00
6 Cleanthony Early
7 Joel Embiid 30.00 80.00
8 Tyler Ennis 4.00 10.00
9 Russ Smith 4.00 10.00
10 Aaron Gordon 10.00 25.00
11 Jerami Grant 4.00 10.00
13 Gary Harris 6.00 15.00
16 Damien Inglis 4.00 10.00
18 K.J. McDaniels 5.00 12.00
19 Doug McDermott 6.00 15.00
22 Johnny O'Bryant 4.00 10.00
23 Jabari Parker 25.00 60.00
24 Adreian Payne 5.00 12.00
25 Elfrid Payton 6.00 15.00
26 Julius Randle 25.00 60.00
27 Marcus Smart 4.00 10.00
28 Nik Stauskas 5.00 12.00
29 Jarnell Stokes 4.00 10.00
30 T.J. Warren
31 Andrew Wiggins 100.00 250.00
32 C.J. Wilcox
33 James Young 4.00 10.00

2014-15 Panini Excalibur Rookie Rampage Autograph Dual Jerseys Prime

*PRIME: .6X TO 1.5X BASIC
RANDOM INSERTS IN PACKS
STATED PRINT RUN 25 SER.#'d SETS
4 Bruno Caboclo 8.00 20.00

2014-15 Panini Excalibur Rookie Rampage Autograph Jerseys

RANDOM INSERTS IN PACKS
1 Aaron Gordon 15.00 40.00
2 Adreian Payne 4.00 10.00
3 Andrew Wiggins 40.00 100.00
4 Bruno Caboclo 6.00 15.00
5 C.J. Wilcox 3.00 8.00
6 Cleanthony Early 3.00 8.00
7 Damien Inglis 3.00 8.00
8 Dante Exum 15.00 40.00
9 Doug McDermott 6.00 15.00
10 Elfrid Payton 5.00 12.00
11 Gary Harris 5.00 12.00
12 Jabari Parker 30.00 80.00
13 James Young 3.00 8.00
14 Jarnell Stokes 3.00 8.00
15 Jerami Grant 3.00 8.00
17 Joel Embiid 75.00 200.00
18 Johnny O'Bryant 3.00 8.00
19 Jordan Adams 3.00 8.00
20 Julius Randle 20.00 50.00
21 K.J. McDaniels 4.00 10.00
22 Kyle Anderson 8.00 20.00
23 Marcus Smart 8.00 20.00
24 Markel Brown 3.00 8.00
26 Nik Stauskas 4.00 10.00
30 Spencer Dinwiddie 4.00 10.00
31 T.J. Warren 5.00 12.00
32 Tyler Ennis 3.00 8.00

2014-15 Panini Excalibur Rookie Rampage Autograph Jerseys Prime

*PRIME: .6X TO 1.5X BASIC
RANDOM INSERTS IN PACKS
STATED PRINT RUN 25 SER.#'d SETS
16 Joe Harris 10.00 25.00
27 P.J. Hairston 5.00 12.00
28 Rodney Hood 20.00 50.00
29 Shabazz Napier 6.00 15.00

2014-15 Panini Excalibur Rookie Rampage Autograph Jumbo Jerseys

RANDOM INSERTS IN PACKS
1 Adreian Payne 6.00 15.00
2 Marcus Smart 12.00 30.00
3 James Young 5.00 12.00
4 Markel Brown 5.00 12.00
5 P.J. Hairston 5.00 12.00
6 Doug McDermott 12.00 30.00
8 Gary Harris 8.00 20.00
9 Spencer Dinwiddie 6.00 15.00
10 C.J. Wilcox 5.00 12.00
11 Julius Randle 30.00 80.00
12 Jordan Adams 5.00 12.00
13 Jarnell Stokes 5.00 12.00
15 Damien Inglis
16 Johnny O'Bryant 5.00 12.00
17 Jabari Parker 20.00 50.00
18 Zach LaVine 20.00 50.00
19 Andrew Wiggins
20 Cleanthony Early 5.00 12.00
22 Aaron Gordon 25.00 60.00
23 Elfrid Payton 30.00 80.00
24 Joel Embiid 30.00 80.00
25 Jerami Grant 5.00 12.00
26 K.J. McDaniels 15.00 40.00
27 Tyler Ennis 5.00 12.00
28 T.J. Warren 8.00 20.00
29 Nik Stauskas 6.00 15.00
30 Kyle Anderson 10.00 25.00
31 Bruno Caboclo 10.00 25.00
32 Dante Exum 25.00 60.00
33 Rodney Hood 10.00 25.00

2014-15 Panini Excalibur Rookie Rampage Autograph Jumbo Jerseys Prime

*PRIME: .75X TO 2X BASIC
RANDOM INSERTS IN PACKS
STATED PRINT RUN 25 SER.#'d SETS

2014-15 Panini Excalibur Royalty Jerseys

RANDOM INSERTS IN PACKS
*PRIME/25: 1X TO 2.5X BASIC
1 Avery Johnson 2.00 5.00
2 Tyson Chandler 2.00 5.00
3 Kevin McHale 2.50 6.00
4 Hakeem Olajuwon 3.00 8.00
5 Chris Andersen 2.00 5.00
6 Mark Aguirre 2.00 5.00
7 Boris Diaw 2.00 5.00
8 Byron Scott 2.00 5.00
9 Tayshaun Prince 2.00 5.00
10 Tim Duncan 4.00 10.00
11 Luc Longley 6.00 15.00
12 Danny Green 2.00 5.00
13 Kawhi Leonard 4.00 10.00
14 Robert Horry 2.00 5.00
15 Chris Bosh 2.50 6.00
16 Adrian Dantley 2.00 5.00
17 Kobe Bryant 6.00 15.00
18 James Worthy 3.00 8.00
19 David Robinson 4.00 10.00
20 Robert Parish 2.50 6.00
21 Scottie Pippen
22 Patty Mills 2.50 6.00
23 Tony Parker 2.50 6.00
24 Isiah Thomas 2.50 6.00
25 Dwyane Wade 4.00 10.00
26 Kareem Abdul-Jabbar 4.00 10.00
27 Robert Horry 2.00 5.00
28 Danny Ainge 2.50 6.00
29 Robert Horry 2.00 5.00
30 Julius Erving 4.00 10.00
31 Robert Parish 2.50 6.00
32 Marco Belinelli 1.50 4.00
33 Manu Ginobili 2.50 6.00
34 Bill Laimbeer 2.00 5.00
35 Shane Battier 2.00 5.00
36 Magic Johnson
37 Shaquille O'Neal 5.00 12.00
38 Larry Bird 6.00 15.00
39 Shaquille O'Neal 5.00 12.00
40 Moses Malone 2.50 6.00
41 Clyde Drexler 3.00 8.00
42 Mario Chalmers 2.00 5.00
43 Tiago Splitter 2.00 5.00
44 Joe Dumars 2.50 6.00
45 Dirk Nowitzki 3.00 8.00
46 Kurt Rambis 1.50 4.00
47 Udonis Haslem 1.50 4.00
48 Dennis Johnson 2.00 5.00
49 Ray Allen 2.50 6.00
50 Fred Brown 1.50 4.00

2014-15 Panini Excalibur Slam Inc.

RANDOM INSERTS IN PACKS
*BLUE/99: 1.2X TO 3X BASIC
*ORANGE/99: 1.2X TO 3X BASIC
*SILVER/49: 1.5X TO 4X BASIC
1 Dwight Howard .40 1.00
2 Kobe Bryant 2.00 5.00
3 LeBron James 2.00 5.00
4 DeAndre Jordan .50 1.25
5 DeMar DeRozan .50 1.25
6 Dominique Wilkins .60 1.50
7 Vince Carter .60 1.50
8 Julius Erving .75 2.00
9 Anthony Davis 1.00 2.50
10 Blake Griffin .50 1.25

2014-15 Panini Excalibur Top Flight Jerseys

RANDOM INSERTS IN PACKS
*PRIME/25: 1X TO 2.5X BASIC

1 Damian Lillard 5.00 12.00
2 Larry Nance 2.00 5.00
3 Dwight Howard 2.00 5.00
4 Michael Finley 2.50 6.00
5 Harrison Barnes 2.00 5.00
6 Shawn Kemp 4.00 10.00
7 Aaron Gordon 4.00 10.00
8 Joe Johnson 2.00 5.00
9 Andre Drummond 2.50 6.00
10 Kenny Sky Walker 1.50 4.00
11 DeAndre Jordan 2.50 6.00
12 Larry Johnson 3.00 8.00
13 Dwyane Wade 4.00 10.00
14 Monta Ellis 2.00 5.00
15 J.R. Smith 2.00 5.00
16 Terrence Ross 2.00 5.00
17 Julius Randle 4.00 10.00
18 John Wall 3.00 8.00
19 Anthony Davis 5.00 12.00
20 Kevin Durant 5.00 12.00
21 DeMar DeRozan 2.50 6.00
22 LeBron James 10.00 25.00
23 Julius Erving 6.00 15.00
24 Jimmy Butler 2.50 6.00
25 James Harden 4.00 10.00
26 Victor Oladipo 2.00 5.00
27 Al Horford 2.00 5.00
28 John Starks 2.00 5.00
29 Blake Griffin 2.50 6.00
30 Kobe Bryant 10.00 25.00
31 DeMarcus Cousins 2.50 6.00
32 Marcus Smart 2.50 6.00
33 Giannis Antetokounmpo 5.00 12.00
34 Nick Young 2.00 5.00
35 James Young 1.50 4.00
36 Vince Carter 3.00 8.00
37 Al Jefferson 2.00 5.00
38 Josh Smith 2.00 5.00
39 Chandler Parsons 2.00 5.00
40 Kyrie Irving 6.00 15.00
41 Derrick Rose 3.00 8.00
42 Michael Carter-Williams 1.50 4.00
43 Mason Plumlee 2.00 5.00
44 Russell Westbrook 6.00 15.00
45 Jeff Teague 2.00 5.00
46 Zach LaVine 4.00 10.00
47 Amare Stoudemire 2.50 6.00
48 Kenneth Faried 2.00 5.00
49 Chris Andersen 2.00 5.00
50 LaMarcus Aldridge 2.50 6.00

2015-16 Panini Excalibur

COMPLETE SET (200) 15.00 40.00
1 DeMar DeRozan .30 .75
2 Kyle Lowry .25 .60
3 Luis Scola .25 .60
4 DeMarre Carroll .20 .50
5 Jonas Valanciunas .25 .60
6 Isaiah Thomas .30 .75
7 Jae Crowder .20 .50
8 Jared Sullinger .20 .50
9 Amir Johnson .20 .50
10 Avery Bradley .25 .60
11 Jose Calderon .20 .50
12 Robin Lopez .20 .50
13 Carmelo Anthony .40 1.00
14 Arron Afflalo .20 .50
15 Lance Thomas .20 .50
16 Joe Johnson .25 .60
17 Brook Lopez .25 .60
18 Thaddeus Young .20 .50
19 Jarrett Jack .25 .60
20 Bojan Bogdanovic .20 .50
21 Hollis Thompson .20 .50
22 Nerlens Noel .25 .60
23 Jerami Grant .20 .50
24 Isaiah Canaan .25 .60
25 Robert Covington .20 .50
26 Russell Westbrook .75 2.00
27 Serge Ibaka .25 .60
28 Kevin Durant .75 2.00
29 Dion Waiters .25 .60
30 Steven Adams .25 .60
31 Gordon Hayward .30 .75
32 Rodney Hood .25 .60
33 Derrick Favors .25 .60
34 Trey Burke .20 .50
35 Alec Burks .20 .50
36 C.J. McCollum .30 .75
37 Al-Farouq Aminu .25 .60
38 Damian Lillard .60 1.50
39 Mason Plumlee .25 .60
40 Allen Crabbe .20 .50
41 Kevin Garnett .50 1.25
42 Andrew Wiggins .50 1.25
43 Ricky Rubio .30 .75
44 Gorgui Dieng .20 .50
45 Zach LaVine .30 .75
46 Will Barton .20 .50
47 Danilo Gallinari .25 .60
48 Gary Harris .25 .60
49 Kenneth Faried .25 .60
50 Jameer Nelson .20 .50
51 LeBron James 1.25 3.00
52 Kevin Love .30 .75
53 Kyrie Irving .60 1.50
54 Tristan Thompson .25 .60
55 Matthew Dellavedova .25 .60
56 Jimmy Butler .30 .75
57 Pau Gasol .30 .75
58 Derrick Rose .40 1.00
59 Joakim Noah .25 .60
60 Nikola Mirotic .25 .60
61 Paul George .40 1.00
62 Monta Ellis .25 .60
63 George Hill .25 .60
64 C.J. Miles .25 .60
65 Ian Mahinmi .20 .50
66 Kentavious Caldwell-Pope .25 .60
67 Marcus Morris .20 .50
68 Andre Drummond .30 .75
69 Reggie Jackson .25 .60
70 Ersan Ilyasova .20 .50
71 Khris Middleton .25 .60
72 Giannis Antetokounmpo .60 1.50
73 Greg Monroe .25 .60
74 Michael Carter-Williams .20 .50
75 Jabari Parker .40 1.00
76 Stephen Curry 1.25 3.00
77 Klay Thompson .40 1.00
78 Draymond Green .40 1.00
79 Andre Iguodala .25 .60
80 Harrison Barnes .25 .60
81 DeAndre Jordan .30 .75
82 Blake Griffin .30 .75
83 Chris Paul .40 1.00
84 J.J. Redick .30 .75
85 Paul Pierce .30 .75
86 Rajon Rondo .30 .75
87 Rudy Gay .30 .75
88 Omri Casspi .20 .50
89 DeMarcus Cousins .30 .75
90 Ben McLemore .20 .50
91 Brandon Knight .25 .60
92 Eric Bledsoe .25 .60
93 P.J. Tucker .20 .50
94 T.J. Warren .25 .60
95 Tyson Chandler .25 .60
96 Jordan Clarkson .30 .75
97 Lou Williams .25 .60
98 Roy Hibbert .25 .60
99 Julius Randle .30 .75
100 Kobe Bryant 1.25 3.00
101 Chris Bosh .30 .75
102 Goran Dragic .25 .60
103 Hassan Whiteside .25 .60
104 Dwyane Wade .50 1.25
105 Luol Deng .25 .60
106 Paul Millsap .30 .75
107 Al Horford .25 .60
108 Kyle Korver .25 .60
109 Jeff Teague .25 .60
110 Kent Bazemore .25 .60
111 Tobias Harris .25 .60
112 Evan Fournier .25 .60
113 Elfrid Payton .25 .60
114 Nikola Vucevic .25 .60
115 Victor Oladipo .25 .60
116 Kemba Walker .30 .75
117 Nicolas Batum .25 .60
118 Marvin Williams .25 .60
119 Jeremy Lin .30 .75
120 Al Jefferson .25 .60
121 John Wall .40 1.00
122 Otto Porter .25 .60
123 Marcin Gortat .25 .60
124 Bradley Beal .30 .75
125 Jared Dudley .20 .50
126 Kawhi Leonard .50 1.25
127 LaMarcus Aldridge .30 .75
128 Tony Parker .30 .75
129 Tim Duncan .50 1.25
130 Manu Ginobili .30 .75
131 Wesley Matthews .20 .50
132 Dirk Nowitzki .40 1.00
133 Zaza Pachulia .20 .50
134 Deron Williams .25 .60
135 Chandler Parsons .25 .60
136 Marc Gasol .30 .75
137 Mike Conley .30 .75
138 Vince Carter .40 1.00
139 Jeff Green .25 .60
140 Zach Randolph .25 .60
141 James Harden .50 1.25
142 Dwight Howard .25 .60
143 Trevor Ariza .20 .50
144 Ty Lawson .20 .50
145 Clint Capela .25 .60
146 Eric Gordon .25 .60
147 Anthony Davis .60 1.50
148 Ryan Anderson .25 .60
149 Jrue Holiday .25 .60
150 Tyreke Evans .20 .50
151 Larry Nance Jr. RC .60 1.50
152 Delon Wright RC .50 1.25
153 Trey Lyles RC .60 1.50
154 Salah Mejri RC .40 1.00
155 Kelly Oubre Jr. RC .50 1.25
156 Bobby Portis RC .60 1.50
157 Jahlil Okafor RC .75 2.00
158 Anthony Brown RC .40 1.00
159 Justise Winslow RC .60 1.50
160 Norman Powell RC .50 1.25
161 Raul Neto RC .40 1.00
162 Jarell Martin RC .50 1.25
163 Rondae Hollis-Jefferson RC .50 1.25
164 Luis Montero RC .40 1.00
165 Jonathon Simmons RC .60 1.50
166 Myles Turner RC .60 1.50
167 Karl-Anthony Towns RC 3.00 8.00
168 Stanley Johnson RC .50 1.25
169 Josh Richardson RC .60 1.50
170 Darrun Hilliard RC .40 1.00
171 Nemanja Bjelica RC .50 1.25
172 Sam Dekker RC .50 1.25
173 Mario Hezonja RC .50 1.25
174 Branden Dawson RC .40 1.00
175 Rashad Vaughn RC .40 1.00
176 Montrezl Harrell RC .50 1.25
177 D'Angelo Russell RC 1.50 4.00
178 Justin Anderson RC .50 1.25
179 Emmanuel Mudiay RC .60 1.50
180 Joe Young RC .50 1.25
181 Devin Booker RC 2.00 5.00
182 Jordan Mickey RC .40 1.00
183 Willie Cauley-Stein RC .60 1.50
184 Cliff Alexander RC .40 1.00
185 R.J. Hunter RC .40 1.00
186 Boban Marjanovic RC .50 1.25
187 Kristaps Porzingis RC 1.50 4.00
188 Tyus Jones RC .60 1.50
189 Frank Kaminsky RC .60 1.50
190 Pat Connaughton RC .40 1.00
191 Jerian Grant RC .40 1.00
192 Sasha Kaun RC .40 1.00
193 Richaun Holmes RC .50 1.25
194 Jarell Eddie RC .60 1.50
195 Marcelo Huertas RC .50 1.25
196 Cameron Payne RC .50 1.25
197 T.J. McConnell RC .50 1.25
198 Terry Rozier RC .50 1.25
199 Nikola Jokic RC .75 2.00
200 Aaron Harrison RC .50 1.25

2015-16 Panini Excalibur Gold

*GOID 1-150: 2.5X TO 6X BASIC
*GOLD RC 151-200: 2.5X TO 6X BASIC RC
RANDOM INSERTS IN PACKS
STATED PRINT 25 SER.#'d SETS

2015-16 Panini Excalibur Light Blue

*LT BLUE 1-150: .5X TO 1.2X BASIC
*LT BLUE RC 151-200: .5X TO 1.2X BASIC RC
RANDOM INSERTS IN PACKS

2015-16 Panini Excalibur Silver

*SILVER 1-150: 1X TO 2.5X BASIC
*SILVER RC 151-200: 1X TO 2.5X BASIC RC
RANDOM INSERTS IN PACKS
STATED PRINT 70 SER.#'d SETS

2015-16 Panini Excalibur Class Masters

RANDOM INSERTS IN PACKS
1 LeBron James 5.00 12.00
2 Allen Iverson 1.50 4.00
3 Shaquille O'Neal 2.50 6.00
4 Kyrie Irving 2.50 6.00
5 Derrick Rose 1.50 4.00

2015-16 Panini Excalibur Crusade Camo

RANDOM INSERTS IN PACKS
*BLUE/199: .5X TO 1.2X BASIC
*RED/149: .6X TO 1.5X BASIC
*PURPLE/60: 1X TO 2.5X BASIC
1 Nemanja Bjelica 1.25 3.00
2 Giannis Antetokounmpo 2.00 5.00
3 Patrick Ewing 1.25 3.00
4 DeMarcus Cousins 1.00 2.50
5 Al Horford .75 2.00
6 DeMar DeRozan 1.00 2.50
7 Tim Duncan 1.50 4.00
8 Russell Westbrook 2.50 6.00
9 Jahlil Okafor 1.25 3.00
10 LeBron James 4.00 10.00
11 Devin Booker 3.00 8.00
12 Michael Carter-Williams .60 1.50
13 Dominique Wilkins 1.25 3.00
14 Brandon Knight .75 2.00
15 Elfrid Payton .75 2.00
16 Kyle Lowry .75 2.00
17 Dirk Nowitzki 1.25 3.00
18 Kevin Durant 2.50 6.00
19 Karl-Anthony Towns 8.00 20.00
20 Kevin Love 1.00 2.50
21 Jerian Grant .60 1.50
22 Jabari Parker 1.25 3.00
23 Jason Kidd 1.00 2.50
24 Eric Bledsoe .75 2.00
25 Nikola Vucevic .75 2.00
26 Isaiah Thomas 1.00 2.50
27 Deron Williams .75 2.00
28 Gordon Hayward 1.00 2.50
29 D'Angelo Russell 2.50 6.00
30 Kyrie Irving 2.00 5.00
31 Mario Hezonja .75 2.00
32 Stephen Curry 4.00 10.00
33 Grant Hill 1.25 3.00
34 Jordan Clarkson 1.00 2.50
35 Victor Oladipo .75 2.00
36 Avery Bradley .75 2.00
37 Marc Gasol 1.00 2.50
38 Rodney Hood .75 2.00
39 Kristaps Porzingis 2.50 6.00
40 Jimmy Butler 1.00 2.50
41 Willie Cauley-Stein 1.00 2.50
42 Klay Thompson 1.25 3.00
43 Magic Johnson 2.50 6.00
44 Julius Randle 1.00 2.50
45 Kemba Walker 1.00 2.50
46 Carmelo Anthony 1.25 3.00
47 Mike Conley 1.00 2.50
48 C.J. McCollum 1.00 2.50
49 T.J. McConnell .75 2.00
50 Pau Gasol 1.00 2.50
51 Larry Bird 2.50 6.00
52 Draymond Green 1.25 3.00
53 Anfernee Hardaway 2.50 6.00
54 Kobe Bryant 4.00 10.00
55 Nicolas Batum .75 2.00
56 Arron Afflalo .60 1.50
57 James Harden 1.50 4.00
58 Damian Lillard 2.00 5.00
59 Justise Winslow 1.00 2.50
60 Derrick Rose 1.25 3.00
61 John Stockton 1.50 4.00
62 DeAndre Jordan 1.00 2.50
63 Steve Nash 1.00 2.50
64 Chris Bosh 1.00 2.50
65 John Wall 1.25 3.00
66 Joe Johnson .75 2.00
67 Dwight Howard .75 2.00
68 Kevin Garnett 1.50 4.00
69 Stanley Johnson .75 2.00
70 Paul George 1.25 3.00
71 Karl Malone 1.25 3.00
72 Blake Griffin 1.00 2.50
73 Shawn Kemp 1.50 4.00
74 Hassan Whiteside .75 2.00
75 Bradley Beal 1.00 2.50
76 Brook Lopez .75 2.00
77 Anthony Davis 2.00 5.00
78 Andrew Wiggins 1.50 4.00
79 Emmanuel Mudiay 1.00 2.50
80 Monta Ellis .75 2.00
81 Julius Erving 1.50 4.00
82 Chris Paul 1.25 3.00
83 Ben Wallace .75 2.00
84 Dwyane Wade 1.50 4.00
85 Kawhi Leonard 1.50 4.00
86 Nerlens Noel .75 2.00
87 Jrue Holiday .75 2.00
88 Danilo Gallinari .75 2.00
89 Frank Kaminsky 1.00 2.50
90 Andre Drummond 1.00 2.50
91 Scottie Pippen 2.00 5.00
92 Rajon Rondo 1.00 2.50
93 Dennis Rodman 2.00 5.00
94 Paul Millsap 1.00 2.50
95 Tony Parker 1.00 2.50
96 Robert Covington .60 1.50
97 Tyreke Evans .60 1.50
98 Kenneth Faried .75 2.00
99 Raul Neto .60 1.50
100 Reggie Jackson .75 2.00

2015-16 Panini Excalibur Gamers Jerseys

RANDOM INSERTS IN PACKS
PRINT RUNS B/WN 49-99 COPIES PER
1 Tony Parker/99 3.00 8.00
2 Damian Lillard/99 5.00 12.00
3 Brandon Jennings/99 2.00 5.00
4 DeMarcus Cousins/99 3.00 8.00
5 Kemba Walker/49 3.00 8.00
6 Kyrie Irving/99 5.00 12.00
7 Klay Thompson/49 8.00 20.00
8 James Harden/75 5.00 12.00
9 Marc Gasol/49 3.00 8.00
10 Andrew Wiggins/75 5.00 12.00
11 Rudy Gobert/99 3.00 8.00
12 Blake Griffin/99 3.00 8.00
13 Victor Oladipo/99 2.50 6.00
14 Tim Duncan/75 5.00 12.00
15 Chandler Parsons/49 2.50 6.00
16 Dirk Nowitzki/75 4.00 10.00
17 Monta Ellis/49 2.50 6.00
18 Chris Paul/99 4.00 10.00
19 Elfrid Payton/49 2.50 6.00
20 Kevin Durant/99 5.00 12.00
21 Bojan Bogdanovic/99 2.00 5.00
23 Kawhi Leonard/99 5.00 12.00
24 Marcus Smart/99 2.50 6.00
25 Andre Drummond/74 3.00 8.00

2015-16 Panini Excalibur Head to Toe Signatures

RANDOM INSERTS IN PACKS
STATED PRINT RUN 75 SER.#'d SETS
1 Anthony Brown 4.00 10.00
2 D'Angelo Russell 15.00 40.00
3 Delon Wright 5.00 12.00
4 Jahlil Okafor 8.00 20.00
5 Frank Kaminsky 6.00 15.00
6 Jarell Martin 5.00 12.00
7 Joe Young
8 Jordan Mickey 4.00 10.00
9 Josh Richardson 6.00 15.00
10 Justin Anderson 5.00 12.00
11 Karl-Anthony Towns 60.00 150.00
12 Justise Winslow 6.00 15.00
13 Kelly Oubre Jr. 5.00 12.00
14 Kevon Looney 5.00 12.00
15 Kristaps Porzingis 50.00 120.00
16 Pat Connaughton 4.00 10.00
17 Richaun Holmes 5.00 12.00
18 Rondae Hollis-Jefferson 5.00 12.00
19 Sam Dekker 5.00 12.00
20 Stanley Johnson 5.00 12.00
21 Terry Rozier 5.00 12.00
22 Trey Lyles 6.00 15.00
23 Tyus Jones 6.00 15.00
24 Walter Tavares 4.00 10.00
25 Willie Cauley-Stein 6.00 15.00

2015-16 Panini Excalibur Head to Toe Swatches

RANDOM INSERTS IN PACKS
PRINT RUNS B/WN 10-75 COPIES PER
NO PRICING ON QTY 10
1 Karl Malone/25 8.00 20.00
2 Jerry Stackhouse/75 10.00 25.00
3 Rick Fox/75 5.00 12.00
4 Joe Johnson/75 5.00 12.00
5 Anfernee Hardaway/75 15.00 40.00
6 Grant Hill/75 12.00 30.00
7 Derrick Rose/75 8.00 20.00
8 Joakim Noah/75 5.00 12.00
9 Larry Johnson/75 12.00 30.00
10 Scottie Pippen/25 20.00 50.00
11 Carmelo Anthony/25
12 Kevin Garnett/25 15.00 40.00
13 Dwight Howard/25 5.00 12.00
14 Deron Williams/75 5.00 12.00
15 John Stockton/25 15.00 40.00
16 Gerald Henderson/49 4.00 10.00
17 Tyler Ennis/75 4.00 10.00
18 Patrick Ewing/25
20 Blake Griffin/49 6.00 15.00
23 Anthony Davis/25
24 Michael Kidd-Gilchrist/75 5.00 12.00
25 Shawn Kemp/25 50.00 120.00

2015-16 Panini Excalibur Jamfest

RANDOM INSERTS IN PACKS
*SILVER/70: 1X TO 2.5X BASIC
1 Kobe Bryant 2.00 5.00
2 Dwight Howard .40 1.00
3 Andre Drummond .50 1.25
4 Kevin Durant 1.25 3.00
5 Blake Griffin .50 1.25
6 Russell Westbrook 1.25 3.00
7 Anthony Davis 1.00 2.50
8 Kristaps Porzingis 1.25 3.00
9 Andrew Wiggins .75 2.00
10 LeBron James 2.00 5.00
11 Kawhi Leonard .75 2.00
12 Jimmy Butler .50 1.25
13 Stanley Johnson .40 1.00
14 Mario Hezonja .40 1.00
15 DeAndre Jordan .50 1.25
16 Marc Gasol .50 1.25
17 DeMarcus Cousins .50 1.25
18 Karl-Anthony Towns 2.50 6.00
19 Darryl Dawkins .30 .75
20 Dwyane Wade .75 2.00
21 Julius Erving .75 2.00
22 Dominique Wilkins .60 1.50
23 Shawn Kemp .75 2.00
24 Spud Webb .40 1.00
25 Isaiah Rider .40 1.00
26 Tracy McGrady .50 1.25
27 Dee Brown .30 .75
28 Shaquille O'Neal 1.00 2.50
29 Allen Iverson .60 1.50
30 Clyde Drexler .60 1.50

2015-16 Panini Excalibur Jamfest Gold

*GOLD: 1.5X TO 4X BASIC
RANDOM INSERTS IN PACKS
STATED PRINT RUN 25 SER.#'d SETS
18 Karl-Anthony Towns 25.00 60.00

2015-16 Panini Excalibur Kaboom

RANDOM INSERTS IN PACKS
1 Kobe Bryant 150.00 300.00
2 Kevin Durant 50.00 125.00
3 Kyrie Irving 40.00 100.00
4 John Wall 25.00 60.00
5 Anthony Davis 40.00 100.00
6 Stephen Curry 150.00 300.00
7 Andrew Wiggins 30.00 80.00
8 Chris Paul 25.00 60.00
9 LeBron James 125.00 300.00
10 Tim Duncan 30.00 80.00
11 Derrick Rose 25.00 60.00
12 Russell Westbrook 50.00 125.00
13 James Harden 30.00 80.00
14 Dwyane Wade 30.00 80.00
15 Carmelo Anthony 25.00 60.00
16 Karl-Anthony Towns 250.00 500.00
17 D'Angelo Russell 50.00 125.00
18 Kristaps Porzingis 100.00 250.00
19 Jahlil Okafor 25.00 60.00
20 Patrick Ewing 25.00 60.00
21 Allen Iverson 50.00 120.00
22 Wilt Chamberlain 40.00 100.00
23 Pete Maravich 30.00 80.00
24 Shaquille O'Neal 40.00 100.00
25 Scottie Pippen 40.00 100.00

2015-16 Panini Excalibur Knight School Jerseys

RANDOM INSERTS IN PACKS
PRINT RUNS B/WN 49-99 COPIES PER
*PRIME/25: .75X TO 2X BASIC
1 Rondae Hollis-Jefferson 2.50 6.00
2 Josh Huestis 2.00 5.00
3 Emmanuel Mudiay 3.00 8.00
4 Cameron Payne 2.50 6.00
5 Jahlil Okafor 4.00 10.00
6 D'Angelo Russell 4.00 10.00
7 Devin Booker 4.00 10.00
8 Justise Winslow 3.00 8.00
9 Karl-Anthony Towns 6.00 15.00
10 Trey Lyles 3.00 8.00
11 Richaun Holmes 2.50 6.00
12 Bobby Portis 3.00 8.00
13 Willie Cauley-Stein 3.00 8.00
14 Jordan Mickey 2.00 5.00
15 Kristaps Porzingis 4.00 10.00
16 Terry Rozier 2.50 6.00
17 Frank Kaminsky 3.00 8.00
18 Myles Turner 3.00 8.00
19 Stanley Johnson 2.50 6.00
20 Mario Hezonja 2.50 6.00
21 Kelly Oubre Jr. 2.50 6.00
22 Josh Richardson 3.00 8.00
23 Jerian Grant 2.00 5.00
24 R.J. Hunter 2.00 5.00
25 Justin Anderson 2.50 6.00

2015-16 Panini Excalibur Knight's Templar

*TEMPLAR 1-150: .5X TO 1.2X BASIC
*TEMPLAR RC 151-200: .5X TO 1.2X BASIC RC
RANDOM INSERTS IN PACKS

2015-16 Panini Excalibur Knights of the Round Die Cuts

RANDOM INSERTS IN PACKS
1 D'Angelo Russell 15.00 40.00
2 Anthony Davis 10.00 25.00
3 Patrick Ewing 6.00 15.00
4 Chris Paul 6.00 15.00
5 Pete Maravich 8.00 20.00
6 Derrick Rose 6.00 15.00
7 James Harden 8.00 20.00
8 Kobe Bryant 30.00 80.00
9 Carmelo Anthony 6.00 15.00
10 Kyrie Irving 15.00 40.00
11 Kristaps Porzingis 15.00 40.00
12 Stephen Curry 30.00 80.00
13 Allen Iverson 6.00 15.00
14 LeBron James 30.00 80.00
15 Shaquille O'Neal 12.00 30.00
16 Russell Westbrook 12.00 30.00
17 Dwyane Wade 8.00 20.00
18 Kevin Durant 12.00 30.00
19 Karl-Anthony Towns 25.00 60.00
20 John Wall 6.00 15.00
21 Jahlil Okafor 6.00 15.00
22 Andrew Wiggins 8.00 20.00
23 Wilt Chamberlain 10.00 25.00
24 Tim Duncan 8.00 20.00
25 Scottie Pippen 10.00 25.00

2015-16 Panini Excalibur Memorable Memorabilia

RANDOM INSERTS IN PACKS
1 Nerlens Noel 2.00 5.00
2 Russell Westbrook 6.00 15.00
3 Joe Johnson 2.00 5.00
4 Carmelo Anthony 3.00 8.00
5 Isaiah Thomas 5.00 12.00
6 Derrick Rose 3.00 8.00
7 Reggie Jackson 2.00 5.00
8 Stephen Curry 20.00 50.00
9 Mike Conley 2.50 6.00
10 Kobe Bryant 8.00 20.00
11 Kyle Lowry 2.00 5.00
12 John Wall 3.00 8.00
13 Aaron Gordon 2.00 5.00
14 Rajon Rondo 2.50 6.00
15 Jimmy Butler 2.50 6.00
16 LeBron James 10.00 25.00
17 Dwight Howard 2.00 5.00
18 Paul George 3.00 8.00
19 Zach Randolph 2.00 5.00
20 Anthony Davis 5.00 12.00
21 Gordon Hayward 2.50 6.00
22 Dwyane Wade 4.00 10.00
23 LaMarcus Aldridge 2.50 6.00
24 Bradley Beal 2.50 6.00
25 Kenneth Faried 2.00 5.00

2015-16 Panini Excalibur Monumental Marks

RANDOM INSERTS IN PACKS
PRINT RUNS B/WN 35-299 COPIES PER
1 Chris Paul/35 20.00 50.00
2 Jeff Green/165 3.00 8.00
3 Dirk Nowitzki/35 50.00 120.00
4 Emmanuel Mudiay/149 4.00 10.00
5 Paul George/35 15.00 40.00
6 Frank Kaminsky/99 5.00 12.00
7 Cody Zeller/299 3.00 8.00
8 Tyson Chandler/199 4.00 10.00
9 Kobe Bryant/35 100.00 200.00
10 Tyler Ennis/299 3.00 8.00
11 Dwyane Wade/35 25.00 60.00
12 Ryan Anderson/225 3.00 8.00
13 Blake Griffin/35 20.00 50.00
14 Justise Winslow/49
15 Michael Kidd-Gilchrist/299 3.00 8.00
16 Myles Turner/149 10.00 25.00
17 Dante Exum/199 3.00 8.00
18 Kentavious Caldwell-Pope/149 3.00 8.00
19 Kevin Durant/35 50.00 120.00
20 Gordon Hayward/149 4.00 10.00
21 Anthony Davis/35 30.00 80.00
22 D'Angelo Russell/149 20.00 50.00
23 Kyrie Irving/35 25.00 60.00
24 Tyus Jones/199 4.00 10.00
25 Marcus Smart/115 5.00 12.00
26 Trey Lyles/149 4.00 10.00
27 Al Horford/199 3.00 8.00
28 Trey Burke/199 2.50 6.00
29 Carmelo Anthony/35 15.00 40.00
30 Jose Calderon/146 4.00 10.00

2015-16 Panini Excalibur Old School Swatches

RANDOM INSERTS IN PACKS
PRINT RUNS B/WN 32-99 COPIES PER
1 Rick Fox/99 2.50 6.00
2 Kenny Walker/99 2.00 5.00
3 Shawn Marion/99 2.50 6.00
4 Walter Davis/99 2.00 5.00
5 Ben Wallace/99 2.50 6.00
6 Dominique Wilkins/99 4.00 10.00
7 Calvin Murphy/32 2.50 6.00
8 James Worthy/99 4.00 10.00
9 Mike Bibby/99 2.50 6.00
10 Kenny Anderson/99 2.50 6.00
11 Dennis Rodman/35 5.00 12.00
12 Mark Jackson/99 2.50 6.00
13 Michael Finley/99 3.00 8.00
14 Clyde Drexler/99 4.00 10.00
15 Grant Hill/99 4.00 10.00
16 Karl Malone/99 4.00 10.00
17 Danny Manning/99 2.50 6.00
18 Ray Allen/99 3.00 8.00
19 Danny Ainge/99 3.00 8.00
20 Bernard King/99 2.50 6.00
21 Brad Daugherty/99 2.50 6.00
22 Doug Collins/99 3.00 8.00
23 Dan Issel/99 2.50 6.00
24 Scottie Pippen/99 5.00 12.00
25 Chris Mullin/99 3.00 8.00

2015-16 Panini Excalibur Regal Endorsements

RANDOM INSERTS IN PACKS
PRINT RUNS B/WN 1-300 COPIES PER
NO PRICING ON QTY 15 OR LESS
1 Oscar Robertson/35 30.00 80.00
2 Gail Goodrich/149 5.00 12.00
3 Grant Hill/135 10.00 25.00
4 Shane Battier/200 3.00 8.00
6 Walt Frazier/165 6.00 15.00
7 Scottie Pippen/35 40.00 100.00
8 Cliff Hagan/300 3.00 8.00
10 Don Nelson/234 10.00 25.00
11 Ray Allen/99 12.00 30.00
12 Bobby Wanzer/273 2.50 6.00
13 Anfernee Hardaway/49 20.00 50.00
14 Wes Unseld/200 4.00 10.00
15 Kareem Abdul-Jabbar/35 25.00 60.00
16 Peja Stojakovic/147 4.00 10.00
17 John Stockton/35 30.00 80.00
18 Dolph Schayes/277 4.00 10.00
19 Larry Bird/35 30.00 80.00
20 George Gervin/300 4.00 10.00
21 Tracy McGrady/99 12.00 30.00
22 Slick Watts/260 2.50 6.00
23 Christian Laettner/123 3.00 8.00
24 Isiah Thomas/299 8.00 20.00
25 Allen Iverson/35 30.00 80.00
26 Elvin Hayes/254 4.00 10.00
27 Julius Erving/32 25.00 60.00
28 Calvin Murphy/149 3.00 8.00
29 Karl Malone/35 15.00 40.00
30 Dave Cowens/165 2.50 6.00

2015-16 Panini Excalibur Rookie Rampage Jersey Autographs

RANDOM INSERTS IN PACKS
*PRIME/25: .75X TO 2X BASIC
1 Karl-Anthony Towns 60.00 150.00
2 D'Angelo Russell 20.00 50.00
3 Jahlil Okafor 20.00 50.00
4 Emmanuel Mudiay 6.00 15.00
5 Kristaps Porzingis 40.00 100.00
6 Mario Hezonja 4.00 10.00
7 Justise Winslow
8 Willie Cauley-Stein 8.00 20.00
9 Stanley Johnson 4.00 10.00
10 Frank Kaminsky 5.00 12.00
11 Devin Booker 25.00 60.00
12 Myles Turner 10.00 25.00
13 Trey Lyles 5.00 12.00
14 Jerian Grant 3.00 8.00
15 Cameron Payne 4.00 10.00
16 Delon Wright 4.00 10.00
17 Terry Rozier 4.00 10.00
18 Kelly Oubre Jr. 4.00 10.00
19 Rondae Hollis-Jefferson 4.00 10.00
20 Bobby Portis 5.00 12.00
21 Justin Anderson 4.00 10.00
22 R.J. Hunter 3.00 8.00
23 Jarell Martin 4.00 10.00
24 Anthony Brown 3.00 8.00
25 Jordan Mickey 3.00 8.00
26 Josh Huestis 3.00 8.00
27 Pat Connaughton 3.00 8.00
28 Josh Richardson 5.00 12.00
29 Rakeem Christmas 3.00 8.00
30 Richaun Holmes 4.00 10.00

2015-16 Panini Excalibur Rookie Rampage Jumbo Jersey Autographs

RANDOM INSERTS IN PACKS
*PRIME/21-25: 1.2X TO 3X BASIC
1 Josh Huestis 3.00 8.00
2 Bobby Portis 5.00 12.00
3 Pat Connaughton 3.00 8.00
4 Josh Richardson 5.00 12.00
5 Cameron Payne 4.00 10.00
6 Joe Young 4.00 10.00
7 Jordan Mickey 3.00 8.00
8 R.J. Hunter 3.00 8.00
9 D'Angelo Russell 20.00 50.00
10 Terry Rozier 4.00 10.00
11 Rakeem Christmas 3.00 8.00
12 Anthony Brown 3.00 8.00
13 Justise Winslow
14 Myles Turner 10.00 25.00
15 Trey Lyles 5.00 12.00
16 Chris McCullough 3.00 8.00
17 Mario Hezonja 4.00 10.00
18 Rondae Hollis-Jefferson 4.00 10.00
19 Jarell Martin 4.00 10.00
20 Richaun Holmes 4.00 10.00
21 Kelly Oubre Jr. 4.00 10.00
22 Emmanuel Mudiay 8.00 20.00
23 Willie Cauley-Stein 12.00 30.00
24 Jerian Grant 3.00 8.00
25 Jahlil Okafor 6.00 15.00
26 Delon Wright 4.00 10.00
27 Kristaps Porzingis 30.00 80.00
28 Justin Anderson 4.00 10.00
29 Devin Booker 20.00 50.00
30 Frank Kaminsky 5.00 12.00
31 Karl-Anthony Towns 60.00 150.00
32 Stanley Johnson 8.00 20.00
33 Nemanja Bjelica 4.00 10.00
35 Nikola Jokic 20.00 50.00

2015-16 Panini Excalibur Rookie Rampage Jumbo Jerseys

RANDOM INSERTS IN PACKS
STATED PRINT RUN 49 SER.#'d SETS
*PRIME/25: .75X TO 2X BASIC
1 Trey Lyles 3.00 8.00
2 Jarell Martin 2.50 6.00
3 Josh Huestis 2.00 5.00
4 Willie Cauley-Stein 3.00 8.00
5 Cameron Payne 2.50 6.00
7 D'Angelo Russell 8.00 20.00
8 Frank Kaminsky 3.00 8.00
9 Anthony Brown 2.00 5.00
10 Nemanja Bjelica 2.50 6.00
11 Chris McCullough 2.00 5.00
12 Richaun Holmes 2.50 6.00
13 Bobby Portis 3.00 8.00
14 Jerian Grant 2.00 5.00
15 Joe Young 2.50 6.00
16 Justin Anderson 2.50 6.00
17 Terry Rozier 2.50 6.00
18 Karl-Anthony Towns 12.00 30.00
19 Justise Winslow 3.00 8.00
21 Mario Hezonja 2.50 6.00
22 Kelly Oubre Jr. 2.50 6.00
23 Pat Connaughton 2.00 5.00
24 Jahlil Okafor 4.00 10.00
25 Jordan Mickey 2.00 5.00
26 Devin Booker 10.00 25.00
27 Rakeem Christmas 2.00 5.00
28 Stanley Johnson 2.50 6.00
29 Myles Turner 3.00 8.00
31 Rondae Hollis-Jefferson 2.50 6.00
32 Emmanuel Mudiay 3.00 8.00
33 Josh Richardson 3.00 8.00
34 Delon Wright 2.50 6.00
35 R.J. Hunter 2.00 5.00

2015-16 Panini Excalibur Team 2020

RANDOM INSERTS IN PACKS
*SILVER/70: 1X TO 2.5X BASIC
1 Anthony Davis 1.00 2.50
2 Kyrie Irving 1.00 2.50
3 Andre Drummond .50 1.25
4 Damian Lillard 1.00 2.50
5 Kawhi Leonard .75 2.00
6 Rudy Gobert .50 1.25
7 John Wall .60 1.50
8 DeMarcus Cousins .50 1.25
9 Stephen Curry 2.00 5.00
10 Blake Griffin .50 1.25
11 Giannis Antetokounmpo 1.00 2.50
12 Nikola Mirotic .40 1.00
13 Ricky Rubio .50 1.25
14 Reggie Jackson .40 1.00
15 Nerlens Noel .40 1.00
16 Bradley Beal .50 1.25
17 Jordan Clarkson .50 1.25
18 Tobias Harris .40 1.00
19 Klay Thompson .60 1.50
20 Andrew Wiggins .75 2.00
21 Jabari Parker .60 1.50
22 Elfrid Payton .40 1.00
23 Marcus Smart .40 1.00
24 Aaron Gordon .40 1.00
25 Jusuf Nurkic .30 .75
26 Karl-Anthony Towns 2.50 6.00
27 D'Angelo Russell 1.25 3.00
28 Jahlil Okafor .60 1.50
29 Kristaps Porzingis 1.25 3.00
30 Mario Hezonja .40 1.00
31 Willie Cauley-Stein .50 1.25
32 Emmanuel Mudiay .50 1.25
33 Stanley Johnson .40 1.00
34 Frank Kaminsky .50 1.25
35 Justise Winslow .50 1.25
36 T.J. McConnell .40 1.00
37 Nikola Jokic .60 1.50
38 Raul Neto .30 .75
39 Devin Booker 1.50 4.00
40 Jerian Grant .30 .75

2015-16 Panini Excalibur Team 2020 Gold

*GOLD: 1.5X TO 4X BASIC
RANDOM INSERTS IN PACKS
STATED PRINT RUN 25 SER.#'d SETS
26 Karl-Anthony Towns 25.00 60.00

2015-16 Panini Excalibur Team Titans

RANDOM INSERTS IN PACKS
*SILVER/70: 1X TO 2.5X BASIC
*GOLD/25: 1.5X TO 4X BASIC
1 Karl Malone .60 1.50
2 Magic Johnson 1.25 3.00
3 Dominique Wilkins .60 1.50
4 Kevin McHale .50 1.25
5 Tony Parker .50 1.25
6 John Stockton .75 2.00
7 Kyrie Irving 1.00 2.50
8 Tim Duncan .75 2.00
9 Stephen Curry 2.00 5.00
10 Kobe Bryant 2.00 5.00
11 Hakeem Olajuwon .60 1.50
12 Larry Bird 1.25 3.00
13 Russell Westbrook 1.25 3.00
14 Dwyane Wade .75 2.00
15 Manu Ginobili .50 1.25
16 Dirk Nowitzki .60 1.50
17 Anthony Davis 1.00 2.50
18 David Robinson .75 2.00
19 John Wall .60 1.50
20 Jerry West .60 1.50
21 Patrick Ewing .60 1.50
22 John Havlicek .60 1.50
23 Blake Griffin .50 1.25
24 Bill Russell .75 2.00
25 Kevin Durant 1.25 3.00

2015-16 Panini Excalibur Treasured Ink

RANDOM INSERTS IN PACKS
PRINT RUNS B/WN 15-299 COPIES PER
NO PRICING ON QTY 15
1 Otto Porter/299 3.00 8.00
2 Duje Dukan/299 2.50 6.00
3 C.J. McCollum/199 5.00 12.00
4 Danny Green/175 3.00 8.00
5 Kobe Bryant/35 100.00 200.00
7 Dwyane Wade/35 25.00 60.00
8 Luis Montero/299 2.50 6.00
9 Kyrie Irving/35 30.00 80.00
10 Norman Powell/299 3.00 8.00
11 Alex Len/299 2.50 6.00
12 Branden Dawson/299 2.50 6.00
13 Goran Dragic/249 3.00 8.00
14 Karl-Anthony Towns/99 60.00 150.00
15 Kevin Durant/35 50.00 120.00
16 Stanley Johnson/199 3.00 8.00
17 Anthony Davis/35 30.00 80.00
18 Salah Mejri/299 2.50 6.00
19 Paul George/35 20.00 50.00
20 Sasha Kaun/299 2.50 6.00
21 Bradley Beal/99 5.00 12.00
22 T.J. McConnell/299 3.00 8.00
23 Kevin Martin/299 3.00 8.00
24 Jahlil Okafor/75 15.00 40.00
25 Carmelo Anthony/35 15.00 40.00
26 Devin Booker/199 50.00 120.00
27 Dirk Nowitzki/35 50.00 120.00
28 Larry Nance Jr./299 4.00 10.00
29 Jabari Parker/60 10.00 25.00
30 Boban Marjanovic/199 3.00 8.00
31 Ben McLemore/275 2.50 6.00
32 Robert Covington/299 2.50 6.00
33 Gary Harris/299 3.00 8.00
34 Kristaps Porzingis/99 40.00 100.00
35 Chris Paul/35 20.00 50.00
36 Jerian Grant/199 2.50 6.00
37 Blake Griffin/35 15.00 40.00
38 Gorgui Dieng/299 2.50 6.00
39 Victor Oladipo/199 3.00 8.00
40 Jonathon Simmons/299 4.00 10.00

2016-17 Panini Excalibur

COMPLETE SET (200) 15.00 40.00
1 Dwight Howard .25 .60
2 Paul Millsap .30 .75
3 Tim Hardaway Jr. .20 .50
4 DeAndre' Bembry RC .40 1.00
5 Kent Bazemore .25 .60
6 Taurean Prince RC .60 1.50
7 Isaiah Thomas .30 .75
8 Al Horford .25 .60
9 Jaylen Brown RC 1.50 4.00
10 Gerald Green .25 .60
11 Marcus Smart .25 .60
12 Kelly Olynyk .20 .50
13 Brook Lopez .25 .60
14 Jeremy Lin .30 .75
15 Caris LeVert RC .50 1.25
16 Bojan Bogdanovic .20 .50
17 Isaiah Whitehead RC .40 1.00
18 Trevor Booker .20 .50
19 Kemba Walker .30 .75
20 Nicolas Batum .25 .60
21 Michael Kidd-Gilchrist .25 .60
22 Marco Belinelli .20 .50
23 Miles Plumlee .20 .50
24 Cody Zeller .20 .50
25 Jimmy Butler .30 .75
26 Dwyane Wade .50 1.25
27 Paul Zipser RC .60 1.50
28 Taj Gibson .25 .60
29 Denzel Valentine RC .50 1.25
30 Robin Lopez .20 .50
31 LeBron James 1.25 3.00
32 Kyrie Irving .60 1.50
33 Kay Felder RC .40 1.00
34 Kevin Love .30 .75
35 Tristan Thompson .25 .60
36 Kyle Korver .25 .60

37 Dirk Nowitzki .40 1.00
38 Harrison Barnes .25 .60
39 Yogi Ferrell RC .50 1.25
40 Wesley Matthews .20 .50
41 Devin Harris .20 .50
42 Deron Williams .25 .60
43 Nikola Jokic .30 .75
44 Emmanuel Mudiay .25 .60
45 Jamal Murray RC 1.25 3.00
46 Kenneth Faried .25 .60
47 Juan Hernangomez RC .50 1.25
48 Danilo Gallinari .25 .60
49 Andre Drummond .30 .75
50 Tobias Harris .25 .60
51 Henry Ellenson RC .50 1.25
52 Stanley Johnson .20 .50
53 Michael Gbinije RC .40 1.00
54 Reggie Jackson .25 .60
55 Stephen Curry 1.25 3.00
56 Kevin Durant .75 2.00
57 Klay Thompson .40 1.00
58 Patrick McCaw RC .75 2.00
59 Draymond Green .40 1.00
60 Andre Iguodala .25 .60
61 James Harden .50 1.25
62 Eric Gordon .25 .60
63 Chinanu Onuaku RC .40 1.00
64 Ryan Anderson .25 .60
65 Patrick Beverley .20 .50
66 Clint Capela .20 .50
67 Paul George .40 1.00
68 Monta Ellis .25 .60
69 Georges Niang RC .40 1.00
70 Myles Turner .25 .60
71 Jeff Teague .25 .60
72 Al Jefferson .25 .60
73 Chris Paul .40 1.00
74 Blake Griffin .30 .75
75 DeAndre Jordan .30 .75
76 J.J. Redick .30 .75
77 Diamond Stone RC .40 1.00
78 Jamal Crawford .30 .75
79 Jordan Clarkson .25 .60
80 Brandon Ingram RC 2.50 6.00
81 Julius Randle .30 .75
82 D'Angelo Russell .40 1.00
83 Lou Williams .25 .60
84 Larry Nance Jr. .25 .60
85 Mike Conley .25 .60
86 Deyonta Davis RC .40 1.00
87 Marc Gasol .30 .75
88 Zach Randolph .25 .60
89 Chandler Parsons .25 .60
90 Wade Baldwin IV RC .40 1.00
91 Goran Dragic .25 .60
92 Hassan Whiteside .25 .60
93 Josh Richardson .20 .50
94 Tyler Johnson .20 .50
95 Justise Winslow .25 .60
96 James Johnson .20 .50
97 Giannis Antetokounmpo .60 1.50
98 Malcolm Brogdon RC 1.00 2.50
99 Thon Maker RC 1.25 3.00
100 Jabari Parker .40 1.00
101 Greg Monroe .25 .60
102 Michael Beasley .20 .50
103 Karl-Anthony Towns .75 2.00
104 Andrew Wiggins .50 1.25
105 Kris Dunn RC 1.25 3.00
106 Zach LaVine .30 .75
107 Ricky Rubio .30 .75
108 Shabazz Muhammad .25 .60
109 Anthony Davis .60 1.50
110 Buddy Hield RC 1.00 2.50
111 Jrue Holiday .25 .60
112 Cheick Diallo RC .40 1.00
113 Tyreke Evans .20 .50
114 Solomon Hill .20 .50
115 Carmelo Anthony .40 1.00
116 Derrick Rose .40 1.00
117 Willy Hernangomez RC .50 1.25
118 Kristaps Porzingis .60 1.50
119 Ron Baker RC .50 1.25
120 Courtney Lee .25 .60
121 Russell Westbrook .75 2.00
122 Victor Oladipo .25 .60
123 Steven Adams .25 .60
124 Enes Kanter .25 .60
125 Alex Abrines RC .60 1.50
126 Domantas Sabonis RC .60 1.50
127 Aaron Gordon .25 .60
128 Nikola Vucevic .25 .60
129 Serge Ibaka .25 .60
130 Elfrid Payton .25 .60
131 Evan Fournier .25 .60
132 Jeff Green .25 .60
133 Joel Embiid .50 1.25
134 Ben Simmons RC 2.50 6.00
135 Dario Saric RC 1.25 3.00
136 Nerlens Noel .25 .60
137 Ersan Ilyasova .20 .50
138 T. Luwawu-Cabarrot RC .75 2.00
139 Devin Booker .60 1.50
140 Marquese Chriss RC 1.00 2.50
141 Eric Bledsoe .25 .60
142 Dragan Bender RC .50 1.25
143 Tyson Chandler .20 .50
144 Brandon Knight .25 .60
145 Damian Lillard .60 1.50
146 C.J. McCollum .30 .75
147 Jake Layman RC .50 1.25
148 Allen Crabbe .25 .60
149 Al-Farouq Aminu .20 .50
150 Noah Vonleh .20 .50
151 DeMarcus Cousins .30 .75
152 Darren Collison .25 .60
153 Malachi Richardson RC .50 1.25
154 Willie Cauley-Stein .25 .60
155 Rudy Gay .30 .75
156 Georgios Papagiannis RC .30 .75
157 Kawhi Leonard .50 1.25
158 LaMarcus Aldridge .30 .75
159 Dejounte Murray RC .75 2.00
160 Pau Gasol .30 .75
161 Tony Parker .30 .75
162 Manu Ginobili .30 .75
163 DeMar DeRozan .30 .75
164 Kyle Lowry .30 .75
165 Pascal Siakam RC .40 1.00
166 Jakob Poeltl RC .50 1.25
167 DeMarre Carroll .20 .50
168 Jonas Valanciunas .25 .60
169 Gordon Hayward .30 .75
170 Rudy Gobert .30 .75
171 Derrick Favors .25 .60
172 Joel Bolomboy RC .40 1.00
173 Rodney Hood .25 .60
174 Alec Burks .20 .50
175 John Wall .40 1.00
176 Bradley Beal .30 .75
177 Marcin Gortat .25 .60
178 Tomas Satoransky RC .40 1.00
179 Markieff Morris .20 .50
180 Otto Porter .25 .60
181 Alex English .25 .60
182 Allen Iverson .40 1.00
183 Artis Gilmore .25 .60
184 Shaquille O'Neal .75 2.00
185 Grant Hill .40 1.00
186 Scottie Pippen .60 1.50
187 David Robinson .50 1.25
188 Dave Cowens .20 .50
189 George Gervin .30 .75
190 Hakeem Olajuwon .40 1.00
191 John Havlicek .40 1.00
192 Jerry Lucas .30 .75
193 Lenny Wilkens .30 .75
194 John Stockton .50 1.25
195 Wilt Chamberlain .60 1.50
196 Patrick Ewing .40 1.00
197 Dominique Wilkins .40 1.00
198 Karl Malone .40 1.00
199 Gary Payton .30 .75
200 Charles Oakley .25 .60

2016-17 Panini Excalibur Count
*COUNT: 1.2X TO 3X BASIC
*COUNT RC: .6X TO 1.5X BASIC
RANDOM INSERTS IN PACKS

2016-17 Panini Excalibur Duke
*DUKE: 2X TO 5X BASIC
*DUKE RC: 1X TO 2.5X BASIC
RANDOM INSERTS IN PACKS
STATED PRINT RUN 49 SER.#'d SETS
134 Ben Simmons 30.00 80.00

2016-17 Panini Excalibur Lord
*LORD: 1.2X TO 3X BASIC
*LORD RC: .6X TO 1.5X BASIC
RANDOM INSERTS IN PACKS

2016-17 Panini Excalibur Marquis
*MARQUIS: 1.5X TO 4X BASIC
*MARQUIS RC: .75X TO 2X BASIC
RANDOM INSERTS IN PACKS
STATED PRINT RUN 199 SER.#'d SETS
134 Ben Simmons 10.00 25.00

2016-17 Panini Excalibur Prince
*PRINCE: 1.5X TO 4X BASIC
*PRINCE RC: .75X TO 2X BASIC
RANDOM INSERTS IN PACKS
STATED PRINT RUN 149 SER.#'d SETS
134 Ben Simmons 10.00 25.00

2016-17 Panini Excalibur Squire
RANDOM INSERTS IN PACKS
1 Karl-Anthony Towns 1.50 4.00
2 Anthony Davis 1.25 3.00
3 Ben Simmons 2.50 6.00
4 Brandon Ingram 2.50 6.00
5 Devin Booker 1.00 2.50
6 Kristaps Porzingis 1.25 3.00
7 Patrick McCaw .75 2.00
8 Julius Randle .60 1.50
9 Yogi Ferrell .50 1.25
10 Kris Dunn 1.25 3.00
11 Jaylen Brown 1.50 4.00
12 Buddy Hield 1.00 2.50
13 Myles Turner .50 1.25
14 Andrew Wiggins 1.00 2.50
15 Dario Saric 1.25 3.00

2016-17 Panini Excalibur Squire Red
*RED: .6X TO 1.5X BASIC
RANDOM INSERTS IN PACKS
STATED PRINT RUN 99 SER.#'d SETS
3 Ben Simmons 15.00 40.00

2016-17 Panini Excalibur Viscount
*VISCOUNT: 1.5X TO 4X BASIC
*VISCOUNT RC: .75X TO 2X BASIC
RANDOM INSERTS IN PACKS

2016-17 Panini Excalibur Apprentice Shield Jerseys
RANDOM INSERTS IN PACKS
STATED PRINT RUN 149 SER.#'d SETS
1 Brandon Ingram 8.00 20.00
2 Jaylen Brown 5.00 12.00
3 Dragan Bender 2.50 6.00
4 Kris Dunn 4.00 10.00
5 Buddy Hield 4.00 10.00
6 Jamal Murray 4.00 10.00
7 Marquese Chriss 4.00 10.00
8 Jakob Poeltl 2.50 6.00
9 Thon Maker 4.00 10.00
10 Domantas Sabonis 4.00 10.00
11 Paul Zipser 3.00 8.00
12 Georgios Papagiannis 2.00 5.00
13 Denzel Valentine 2.50 6.00
14 Juan Hernangomez 2.50 6.00
15 Wade Baldwin IV 2.50 6.00
16 Henry Ellenson 2.50 6.00
17 Malik Beasley 2.50 6.00
18 Caris LeVert 2.50 6.00
19 Malachi Richardson 2.50 6.00
20 Timothe Luwawu-Cabarrot 4.00 10.00
21 Brice Johnson 2.00 5.00
22 Pascal Siakam 2.00 5.00
23 Skal Labissiere 3.00 8.00
24 Dejounte Murray 4.00 10.00
25 Damian Jones 2.00 5.00
26 Malcolm Brogdon 4.00 10.00
27 Michael Gbinije 2.00 5.00
28 Georges Niang 2.00 5.00
29 Jake Layman 2.50 6.00
30 Patrick McCaw 4.00 10.00
31 Kay Felder 2.00 5.00
32 Tyler Ulis 4.00 10.00
33 Marshall Plumlee 2.00 5.00
34 Joel Bolomboy 2.00 5.00
35 Ivica Zubac 3.00 8.00

2016-17 Panini Excalibur Apprentice Signature Shield Jerseys
RANDOM INSERTS IN PACKS
1 Brandon Ingram 30.00 80.00
2 Jaylen Brown 12.00 30.00
3 Dragan Bender 6.00 15.00
4 Kris Dunn 8.00 20.00
5 Buddy Hield 8.00 20.00
8 Jakob Poeltl 3.00 8.00
9 Thon Maker 12.00 30.00
10 Domantas Sabonis 4.00 10.00
11 Paul Zipser 4.00 10.00
12 Georgios Papagiannis 2.50 6.00
13 Denzel Valentine 2.50 6.00
14 Juan Hernangomez 3.00 8.00
15 Wade Baldwin IV 2.50 6.00
16 Henry Ellenson 3.00 8.00
17 Malik Beasley 2.50 6.00
18 Caris LeVert 5.00 12.00
20 Timothe Luwawu-Cabarrot 5.00 12.00
21 Brice Johnson 2.50 6.00
22 Pascal Siakam 2.50 6.00
23 Skal Labissiere 8.00 20.00
25 Damian Jones 2.50 6.00
26 Malcolm Brogdon 10.00 25.00
27 Michael Gbinije 2.50 6.00
28 Georges Niang 2.50 6.00
29 Jake Layman 3.00 8.00
30 Patrick McCaw 8.00 20.00
31 Kay Felder 2.50 6.00
33 Marshall Plumlee 2.50 6.00
34 Joel Bolomboy 2.50 6.00
35 Ivica Zubac 5.00 12.00

2016-17 Panini Excalibur Apprentice Signatures
RANDOM INSERTS IN PACKS
STATED PRINT RUN 199 SER.#'d SETS
1 Brandon Ingram 30.00 80.00
2 Jaylen Brown 15.00 40.00
4 Buddy Hield 12.00 30.00
7 Jakob Poeltl 4.00 10.00
8 Thon Maker 10.00 25.00
9 Domantas Sabonis 5.00 12.00
10 Taurean Prince 5.00 12.00
11 Denzel Valentine 4.00 10.00
12 Juan Hernangomez 4.00 10.00
13 Wade Baldwin IV 3.00 8.00
14 Henry Ellenson 4.00 10.00
15 Malik Beasley 3.00 8.00
16 Caris LeVert 4.00 10.00
17 DeAndre' Bembry 3.00 8.00
19 Timothe Luwawu-Cabarrot 6.00 15.00
20 Brice Johnson 3.00 8.00
21 Pascal Siakam 3.00 8.00
22 Skal Labissiere 5.00 12.00
24 Malcolm Brogdon 10.00 25.00
25 Ivica Zubac 5.00 12.00
26 Jake Layman 4.00 10.00
27 Paul Zipser 5.00 12.00
28 Patrick McCaw 8.00 20.00
29 Chinanu Onuaku 3.00 8.00
30 Deyonta Davis 3.00 8.00

2016-17 Panini Excalibur Armory Jerseys
RANDOM INSERTS IN PACKS
STATED PRINT RUN 99 SER.#'d SETS
1 Paul Millsap 3.00 8.00
2 Marcus Smart 2.50 6.00
3 Brook Lopez 2.50 6.00
4 Nicolas Batum 2.50 6.00
5 Dwyane Wade 4.00 10.00
6 Kevin Love 3.00 8.00
7 Harrison Barnes 2.50 6.00
8 Nikola Jokic 3.00 8.00
9 Reggie Jackson 2.50 6.00
10 Draymond Green 4.00 10.00
11 Patrick Beverley 2.00 5.00
12 Myles Turner 2.50 6.00
13 J.J. Redick 3.00 8.00
14 Julius Randle 3.00 8.00
15 Mike Conley 2.50 6.00
16 Goran Dragic 2.50 6.00
17 Jabari Parker 4.00 10.00
18 Ricky Rubio 3.00 8.00
19 Jrue Holiday 2.50 6.00
20 Derrick Rose 4.00 10.00
21 Victor Oladipo 2.50 6.00
22 Aaron Gordon 2.50 6.00
23 Jahlil Okafor 2.50 6.00
24 Eric Bledsoe 2.50 6.00
25 C.J. McCollum 2.50 6.00
26 Rudy Gay 3.00 8.00
27 LaMarcus Aldridge 3.00 8.00
28 Kyle Lowry 2.50 6.00
29 Rudy Gobert 3.00 8.00
30 Markieff Morris 2.00 5.00
31 Jamal Crawford 3.00 8.00
32 Jordan Clarkson 3.00 8.00
33 Marc Gasol 3.00 8.00
34 Hassan Whiteside 2.50 6.00
35 Kristaps Porzingis 4.00 10.00
36 Serge Ibaka 2.50 6.00
37 Pau Gasol 3.00 8.00
38 Bradley Beal 3.00 8.00

2016-17 Panini Excalibur Battlements
RANDOM INSERTS IN PACKS
*RED/99: .6X TO 1.5X BASIC
1 Hassan Whiteside .50 1.25
2 Andre Drummond .60 1.50
3 DeAndre Jordan .60 1.50
4 Dwight Howard .60 1.50
5 Rudy Gobert .60 1.50
6 Anthony Davis 1.25 3.00
7 Karl-Anthony Towns 1.50 4.00
8 Tyson Chandler .50 1.25
9 Marcin Gortat .50 1.25
10 Kevin Love .60 1.50
11 DeMarcus Cousins .60 1.50
12 Russell Westbrook 1.50 4.00
13 Jonas Valanciunas .50 1.25
14 Nikola Vucevic .50 1.25
15 Tristan Thompson .50 1.25
16 Giannis Antetokounmpo 1.25 3.00
17 Joakim Noah .60 1.50
18 Trevor Booker .40 1.00
19 Draymond Green .75 2.00
20 Kevin Durant 1.50 4.00
21 Nikola Jokic .60 1.50
22 Zach Randolph .60 1.50
23 James Harden 1.00 2.50
24 Kenneth Faried .50 1.25
25 Julius Randle .60 1.50
26 Paul Millsap .60 1.50
27 Pau Gasol .60 1.50
28 Steven Adams .50 1.25
29 Michael Kidd-Gilchrist .50 1.25
30 Kawhi Leonard 1.00 2.50

2016-17 Panini Excalibur Calligraphy Autographs
RANDOM INSERTS IN PACKS
STATED PRINT RUN 149 SER.#'d SETS
CALAI Allen Iverson 40.00 100.00
CALBB Bojan Bogdanovic 3.00 8.00
CALBW Bill Willoughby 3.00 8.00
CALDC Dell Curry 3.00 8.00
CALDC DeMarre Carroll
CALDL Damian Lillard 25.00 60.00
CALDS Damon Stoudamire 4.00 10.00
CALDS Dennis Scott 3.00 8.00
CALGH Gary Harris 4.00 10.00
CALGR Glen Rice 4.00 10.00
CALJR Julius Randle 5.00 12.00
CALMG Marc Gasol 5.00 12.00
CALMJ Magic Johnson 25.00 60.00
CALMT Myles Turner 6.00 15.00
CALRA Ryan Anderson 4.00 10.00
CALRF Rick Fox 4.00 10.00
CALRS Ralph Sampson 4.00 10.00
CALSE Sean Elliott 5.00 12.00
CALSK Shawn Kemp 20.00 50.00
CALSW Spud Webb 4.00 10.00
CALTD Tony Delk 3.00 8.00
CALTG Tom Gugliotta 3.00 8.00
CALVB Vin Baker 3.00 8.00
CALZL Zach LaVine 5.00 12.00

2016-17 Panini Excalibur Coat of Arms
RANDOM INSERTS IN PACKS
*BLUE/199: .6X TO 1.5X BASIC
*PURPLE/49: .75X TO 2X BASIC
1 Stephen Curry 5.00 12.00
2 Andrew Wiggins 1.50 4.00
3 Chris Paul 1.25 3.00
4 Kristaps Porzingis 2.00 5.00
5 Kemba Walker 1.00 2.50
6 Karl-Anthony Towns 2.50 6.00
7 Aaron Gordon .75 2.00
8 Nikola Jokic 1.00 2.50
9 Joel Embiid 1.50 4.00
10 Kyrie Irving 2.00 5.00
11 Devin Booker 1.50 4.00
12 D'Angelo Russell 1.25 3.00
13 Damian Lillard 2.00 5.00
14 Dwight Howard .75 2.00
15 DeMarcus Cousins 1.00 2.50
16 Paul George 1.25 3.00
17 Kawhi Leonard 1.50 4.00
18 Giannis Antetokounmpo 2.00 5.00
19 Dirk Nowitzki 1.25 3.00
20 DeMar DeRozan 1.00 2.50
21 Marc Gasol 1.00 2.50
22 James Harden 1.50 4.00
23 Pau Gasol 1.00 2.50
24 Isaiah Thomas 1.00 2.50
25 Gordon Hayward 1.00 2.50
26 Kevin Durant 2.50 6.00
27 Kyle Lowry .75 2.00
28 LeBron James 5.00 12.00
29 Jabari Parker 1.25 3.00
30 C.J. McCollum .75 2.00
31 Klay Thompson 1.25 3.00
32 Russell Westbrook 2.50 6.00
33 Dwyane Wade 1.50 4.00
34 Carmelo Anthony 1.25 3.00
35 Goran Dragic .75 2.00
36 Anthony Davis 2.00 5.00
37 Andre Drummond 1.00 2.50
38 Mike Conley .75 2.00
39 Myles Turner .75 2.00
40 Jeremy Lin 1.00 2.50
41 Ben Simmons 10.00 25.00
42 Brandon Ingram 5.00 12.00
43 Thon Maker 2.00 5.00
44 Jaylen Brown 2.50 6.00
45 Buddy Hield 1.50 4.00
46 Yogi Ferrell .75 2.00
47 Malcolm Brogdon 1.50 4.00
48 Marquese Chriss 1.50 4.00
49 Jamal Murray 2.00 5.00
50 Kris Dunn 2.00 5.00

2016-17 Panini Excalibur Crusade Blue
*BLUE: .6X TO 1.5X BASIC
RANDOM INSERTS IN PACKS
STATED PRINT RUN 149 SER.#'d SETS
1 LeBron James 6.00 15.00
2 Stephen Curry 6.00 15.00
91 Ben Simmons 20.00 50.00
92 Brandon Ingram 8.00 20.00
96 Jaylen Brown 4.00 10.00
97 Jamal Murray 5.00 12.00

2016-17 Panini Excalibur Crusade Orange
*ORANGE: 1.2X TO 3X BASIC
RANDOM INSERTS IN PACKS
STATED PRINT RUN 25 SER.#'d SETS
1 LeBron James 12.00 30.00
2 Stephen Curry 12.00 30.00
91 Ben Simmons 300.00 500.00
92 Brandon Ingram 15.00 40.00
96 Jaylen Brown 8.00 20.00
97 Jamal Murray 10.00 25.00
100 Yogi Ferrell 2.00 5.00

2016-17 Panini Excalibur Crusade Purple
*PURPLE: 1X TO 2.5X BASIC
RANDOM INSERTS IN PACKS
STATED PRINT RUN 49 SER.#'d SETS
1 LeBron James 10.00 25.00
2 Stephen Curry 10.00 25.00
91 Ben Simmons 30.00 80.00
92 Brandon Ingram 12.00 30.00
96 Jaylen Brown 6.00 15.00
97 Jamal Murray 8.00 20.00

2016-17 Panini Excalibur Crusade Red
*RED: .75X TO 2X BASIC
RANDOM INSERTS IN PACKS
STATED PRINT RUN 99 SER.#'d SETS
1 LeBron James 8.00 20.00
2 Stephen Curry 8.00 20.00
91 Ben Simmons 25.00 60.00
92 Brandon Ingram 10.00 25.00
96 Jaylen Brown 5.00 12.00
97 Jamal Murray 6.00 15.00

2016-17 Panini Excalibur Crusade Silver
RANDOM INSERTS IN PACKS
*CAMO: .5X TO 1.2X BASIC
1 LeBron James 3.00 8.00
2 Stephen Curry 3.00 8.00
3 Kevin Durant 2.00 5.00
4 James Harden 1.50 4.00
5 Russell Westbrook 2.00 5.00
6 Anthony Davis 1.50 4.00
7 Isaiah Thomas .75 2.00
8 DeMarcus Cousins .75 2.00
9 DeMar DeRozan .75 2.00
10 Damian Lillard 1.50 4.00
11 Kawhi Leonard 1.50 4.00
12 C.J. McCollum .60 1.50
13 Kyrie Irving 1.50 4.00
14 Giannis Antetokounmpo 1.50 4.00
15 Karl-Anthony Towns 2.00 5.00
16 Jimmy Butler 1.50 4.00
17 Kyle Lowry .60 1.50
18 John Wall 1.00 2.50
19 Carmelo Anthony 1.00 2.50
20 Kemba Walker .75 2.00
21 Paul George 1.00 2.50
22 Andrew Wiggins 1.25 3.00
23 Gordon Hayward .75 2.00
24 Bradley Beal .75 2.00
25 Eric Bledsoe .60 1.50
26 Klay Thompson 1.00 2.50
27 Devin Booker 1.25 3.00
28 Marc Gasol .75 2.00
29 Brook Lopez .60 1.50
30 Harrison Barnes .60 1.50
31 Jabari Parker 1.00 2.50
32 Kevin Love .75 2.00
33 Dirk Nowitzki 1.00 2.50
34 Goran Dragic .60 1.50
35 Mike Conley .60 1.50
36 Dwyane Wade 1.25 3.00
37 Chris Paul 1.00 2.50
38 Paul Millsap .75 2.00
39 Zach LaVine .75 2.00
40 Blake Griffin .75 2.00
41 Kristaps Porzingis 1.50 4.00
42 Lou Williams .60 1.50
43 Derrick Rose 1.00 2.50
44 Avery Bradley .60 1.50
45 LaMarcus Aldridge .75 2.00
46 Eric Gordon .60 1.50
47 Danilo Gallinari .60 1.50
48 Dennis Schroder .60 1.50
49 Evan Fournier .60 1.50
50 Hassan Whiteside .60 1.50
51 Joel Embiid 1.25 3.00
52 Myles Turner .60 1.50
53 Al Horford .60 1.50
54 Nicolas Batum .60 1.50
55 Andre Drummond .75 2.00
56 Zach Randolph .60 1.50
57 Kentavious Caldwell-Pope .60 1.50
58 Dwight Howard .60 1.50
59 DeAndre Jordan .60 1.50
60 Pau Gasol .75 2.00
61 Michael Kidd-Gilchrist .60 1.50
62 Tony Allen .60 1.50
63 Jeff Teague .60 1.50
64 Bojan Bogdanovic .50 1.25
65 Enes Kanter .50 1.25
66 Serge Ibaka .60 1.50
67 J.J. Redick .75 2.00
68 Rudy Gobert .75 2.00
69 Rodney Hood .60 1.50
70 Draymond Green 1.00 2.50
71 Deron Williams .60 1.50
72 Julius Randle .75 2.00
73 Jordan Clarkson .60 1.50
74 Tim Hardaway Jr. .50 1.25
75 Steven Adams .60 1.50
76 Jamal Crawford .75 2.00
77 Jonas Valanciunas .60 1.50
78 Marcin Gortat .60 1.50
79 Victor Oladipo .60 1.50
80 Pete Maravich 1.25 3.00
81 Wilt Chamberlain 1.50 4.00
82 Bill Russell 1.25 3.00
83 George Mikan 1.50 4.00
84 Jerry West 1.00 2.50
85 Scottie Pippen 1.50 4.00
86 Tim Duncan 1.25 3.00
87 Shaquille O'Neal 2.00 5.00
88 Kobe Bryant 3.00 8.00
89 David Robinson 1.25 3.00
90 Allen Iverson 1.50 4.00
91 Ben Simmons 5.00 12.00
92 Brandon Ingram 3.00 8.00
93 Malcolm Brogdon 1.25 3.00
94 Buddy Hield 1.25 3.00
95 Kris Dunn 1.50 4.00
96 Jaylen Brown 2.00 5.00
97 Jamal Murray 1.50 4.00
98 Dario Saric 1.50 4.00
99 Marquese Chriss 1.50 4.00
100 Yogi Ferrell .60 1.50

2016-17 Panini Excalibur Emblem Jerseys
RANDOM INSERTS IN PACKS
STATED PRINT RUN 99 SER.#'d SETS
1 Giannis Antetokounmpo 6.00 15.00
2 Carmelo Anthony 4.00 10.00
3 Jimmy Butler 3.00 8.00
4 DeMarcus Cousins 3.00 8.00
5 Stephen Curry 12.00 30.00
6 Anthony Davis 4.00 10.00
7 DeMar DeRozan 3.00 8.00
8 Andre Drummond 3.00 8.00
9 Kevin Durant 6.00 15.00
10 Paul George 3.00 8.00
11 James Harden 5.00 12.00
12 Kyrie Irving 6.00 15.00
13 LeBron James 12.00 30.00
14 Kawhi Leonard 5.00 12.00
15 Damian Lillard 4.00 10.00
16 Nikola Jokic 3.00 8.00
17 Dirk Nowitzki 4.00 10.00
18 Chris Paul 4.00 10.00
19 Kristaps Porzingis 4.00 10.00
20 Isaiah Thomas 3.00 8.00
21 Klay Thompson 4.00 10.00
22 Karl-Anthony Towns 4.00 10.00
23 Dwyane Wade 4.00 10.00
24 Russell Westbrook 5.00 12.00
25 Hassan Whiteside 2.50 6.00

2016-17 Panini Excalibur Jousting
RANDOM INSERTS IN PACKS
1 LeBron James 2.50 6.00
2 Kawhi Leonard 1.00 2.50
3 Kevin Durant 1.50 4.00
4 Russell Westbrook 1.50 4.00
5 Dirk Nowitzki .75 2.00
6 Dwyane Wade .75 2.00
7 DeMarcus Cousins .60 1.50
8 Joel Embiid .75 2.00
9 Klay Thompson .75 2.00
10 James Harden .75 2.00
11 Damian Lillard 1.25 3.00
12 Stephen Curry 2.00 5.00
13 John Wall .75 2.00
14 Kyrie Irving 1.25 3.00
15 Kevin Love .60 1.50
16 Andre Drummond .60 1.50
17 Karl-Anthony Towns 1.50 4.00
18 Ben Simmons 2.50 6.00
19 Giannis Antetokounmpo 1.25 3.00
20 Anthony Davis 1.25 3.00
21 Wilt Chamberlain 1.25 3.00
22 Bill Russell 1.00 2.50
23 Oscar Robertson .75 2.00
24 Jerry West .75 2.00
25 Larry Bird 1.50 4.00
26 Magic Johnson 1.50 4.00
27 Kobe Bryant 2.50 6.00
Jousting Left
28 Allen Iverson .75 2.00
29 Shaquille O'Neal 1.50 4.00
30 Hakeem Olajuwon .75 2.00

2016-17 Panini Excalibur Jousting Red
*RED: .6X TO 1.5X BASIC
RANDOM INSERTS IN PACKS
STATED PRINT RUN 99 SER.#'d SETS
18 Ben Simmons 8.00 20.00

2016-17 Panini Excalibur Kaboom
RANDOM INSERTS IN PACKS
1 LeBron James 125.00 300.00
2 Stephen Curry 125.00 300.00
3 James Harden 30.00 80.00
4 Russell Westbrook 50.00 120.00
5 Kevin Durant 75.00 200.00
6 Anthony Davis 40.00 100.00
7 DeMarcus Cousins 25.00 60.00
8 Joel Embiid 60.00 150.00
9 Damian Lillard 30.00 80.00
10 Kawhi Leonard 100.00 250.00
11 Jimmy Butler 30.00 80.00
12 Giannis Antetokounmpo 75.00 200.00
13 Karl-Anthony Towns 75.00 200.00
14 John Wall
15 Carmelo Anthony 25.00 60.00
16 Kyrie Irving 50.00 120.00
17 Paul George 25.00 60.00
18 Klay Thompson 50.00 120.00
19 Ben Simmons 300.00 500.00
20 Brandon Ingram 100.00 250.00
21 Buddy Hield 40.00 100.00
22 Tim Duncan 50.00 120.00
23 Kobe Bryant 100.00 250.00
24 Kareem Abdul-Jabbar 40.00 100.00
25 Dominique Wilkins 25.00 60.00

2016-17 Panini Excalibur Knight in Shining Armor
RANDOM INSERTS IN PACKS
*BLUE/199: .6X TO 1.5X BASIC
*PURPLE/49: .75X TO 2X BASIC
1 James Harden 2.50 6.00
2 Russell Westbrook 4.00 10.00
3 Kevin Durant 4.00 10.00
4 Stephen Curry 6.00 15.00
5 LeBron James 6.00 15.00
6 Anthony Davis 3.00 8.00
7 Damian Lillard 3.00 8.00
8 Isaiah Thomas 1.50 4.00
9 DeMarcus Cousins 1.50 4.00
10 Dirk Nowitzki 2.00 5.00
11 Dwyane Wade 2.50 6.00
12 Chris Paul 2.00 5.00
13 Klay Thompson 2.00 5.00
14 Karl-Anthony Towns 4.00 10.00
15 DeMar DeRozan 1.50 4.00
16 Jimmy Butler 1.50 4.00
17 Paul George 2.00 5.00
18 Giannis Antetokounmpo 3.00 8.00
19 Kawhi Leonard 2.50 6.00
20 Kyrie Irving 3.00 8.00
21 C.J. McCollum 1.25 3.00
22 Kyle Lowry 1.25 3.00
23 John Wall 2.00 5.00
24 Carmelo Anthony 2.00 5.00
25 Kemba Walker 1.50 4.00

2016-17 Panini Excalibur Knights Cloak Jerseys
RANDOM INSERTS IN PACKS
*PRIME/25: .75X TO 2X BASIC
1 Kevin Durant 6.00 15.00
2 LeBron James 10.00 25.00
3 Russell Westbrook 6.00 15.00
4 James Harden 4.00 10.00
5 Stephen Curry 10.00 25.00
6 Damian Lillard 5.00 12.00
7 Isaiah Thomas 2.50 6.00
8 DeMarcus Cousins 2.50 6.00
9 Dirk Nowitzki 5.00 12.00
10 Anthony Davis 2.50 6.00
11 Klay Thompson 3.00 8.00
12 Dwyane Wade 4.00 10.00
13 Chris Paul 3.00 8.00
14 DeMar DeRozan 2.50 6.00
15 Karl-Anthony Towns 3.00 8.00
16 Jimmy Butler 2.50 6.00
17 Paul George 3.00 8.00
18 Giannis Antetokounmpo 5.00 12.00
19 Kawhi Leonard 4.00 10.00
20 C.J. McCollum 2.00 5.00
21 Kyrie Irving 5.00 12.00
22 Carmelo Anthony 3.00 8.00
23 John Wall 3.00 8.00
24 Andrew Wiggins 4.00 10.00
25 Kristaps Porzingis 5.00 12.00

2016-17 Panini Excalibur Manuscripts Autographs
RANDOM INSERTS IN PACKS
STATED PRINT RUN 149 SER.#'d SETS
1 C.J. McCollum 8.00 20.00
2 Joel Embiid 20.00 50.00
3 Vince Carter 10.00 25.00
5 Tony Allen 3.00 8.00
6 Ricky Rubio 6.00 15.00
9 Zaza Pachulia 3.00 8.00
11 Zach Randolph 4.00 10.00
12 Marcin Gortat 4.00 10.00
13 Nikola Vucevic 4.00 10.00
14 Danilo Gallinari 4.00 10.00
15 Tristan Thompson 4.00 10.00
16 Tobias Harris 4.00 10.00
17 Dwyane Wade 20.00 50.00
18 Karl-Anthony Towns 30.00 80.00
20 D'Angelo Russell 8.00 20.00
21 Yogi Ferrell 8.00 20.00
22 Buddy Hield 10.00 25.00
23 Malcolm Brogdon 10.00 25.00
24 Brandon Ingram 25.00 60.00
25 Anfernee Hardaway 20.00 50.00
26 Marcus Camby 5.00 12.00
27 Dominique Wilkins 8.00 20.00
28 Kenny Smith 8.00 20.00
29 Kareem Abdul-Jabbar 30.00 80.00
30 Alex English 4.00 10.00
31 Sidney Moncrief 3.00 8.00
32 Jeff Hornacek 4.00 10.00
33 Horace Grant 5.00 12.00
34 Rashard Lewis 4.00 10.00
35 Hakeem Olajuwon 12.00 30.00
36 Alonzo Mourning 12.00 30.00
37 Jo Jo White 4.00 10.00
38 Antoine Carr 3.00 8.00
39 Kobe Bryant 75.00 150.00
40 Jaylen Brown 12.00 30.00

2016-17 Panini Excalibur Run the Gauntlet
RANDOM INSERTS IN PACKS
*RED/99: .6X TO 1.5X BASIC
1 James Harden 1.00 2.50
2 John Wall .75 2.00
3 Russell Westbrook 1.50 4.00
4 LeBron James 2.50 6.00
5 Ricky Rubio .60 1.50
6 Jeff Teague .50 1.25
7 Jrue Holiday .50 1.25
8 Draymond Green .75 2.00
9 Deron Williams .50 1.25
10 Kyle Lowry .60 1.50
11 Rajon Rondo .60 1.50
12 Goran Dragic .50 1.25
13 Isaiah Thomas .60 1.50
14 Stephen Curry 2.50 6.00
15 Dennis Schroder .50 1.25
16 Mike Conley .50 1.25
17 Eric Bledsoe .50 1.25
18 Nicolas Batum .50 1.25
19 Tim Frazier .40 1.00
20 T.J. McConnell .40 1.00
21 Kyrie Irving 1.25 3.00
22 Elfrid Payton .50 1.25
23 Damian Lillard 1.25 3.00
24 Giannis Antetokounmpo 1.25 3.00
25 Kemba Walker .60 1.50

2016-17 Panini Excalibur Signature Knights Autographs
RANDOM INSERTS IN PACKS
1 E'Twaun Moore
2 Trey Lyles 3.00 8.00
3 Sean Kilpatrick
4 Jason Terry 3.00 8.00
5 Victor Oladipo
6 Gordon Hayward 6.00 15.00
7 James Johnson
8 Doug McDermott 8.00 20.00
9 Michael Kidd-Gilchrist
10 Eric Gordon
11 Yogi Ferrell 8.00 20.00
12 J.J. Barea
13 D'Angelo Russell
14 Justise Winslow 3.00 8.00
15 Karl-Anthony Towns 30.00 80.00
16 Larry Nance Jr. 3.00 8.00
17 Chinanu Onuaku
18 Buddy Hield 6.00 15.00
19 Taurean Prince 4.00 10.00
20 Tim Hardaway Jr.
21 Michael Gbinije
22 Willy Hernangomez
23 Diamond Stone
24 Rodney McGruder
25 Joel Bolomboy

2016-17 Panini Excalibur Storm the Castle
RANDOM INSERTS IN PACKS
*BLUE/199: .5X TO 1.2X BASIC
*PURPLE/49: .6X TO 1.5X BASIC
1 Isaiah Thomas 1.50 4.00
2 Jimmy Butler 1.50 4.00
3 Dwyane Wade 2.50 6.00
4 Kyrie Irving 3.00 8.00
5 LeBron James 6.00 15.00
6 Dirk Nowitzki 2.00 5.00
7 Nikola Jokic 1.50 4.00
8 Andre Drummond 1.50 4.00
9 Stephen Curry 6.00 15.00
10 Kevin Durant 4.00 10.00
11 Klay Thompson 2.00 5.00
12 James Harden 2.50 6.00
13 Paul George 2.00 5.00
14 Chris Paul 2.00 5.00
15 Hassan Whiteside 1.25 3.00
16 Giannis Antetokounmpo 3.00 8.00
17 Karl-Anthony Towns 4.00 10.00
18 Anthony Davis 3.00 8.00
19 Carmelo Anthony 2.00 5.00
20 Kristaps Porzingis 3.00 8.00
21 Russell Westbrook 4.00 10.00
22 Damian Lillard 3.00 8.00
23 DeMarcus Cousins 1.50 4.00
24 Kawhi Leonard 2.50 6.00
25 DeMar DeRozan 1.50 4.00

2016-17 Panini Excalibur Storm the Castle Blue
*BLUE: .6X TO 1.5X BASIC
5 LeBron James 12.00 30.00

2016-17 Panini Excalibur Storm the Castle Purple
*PURPLE: .75X TO 2X BASIC
5 LeBron James 15.00 40.00

2016-17 Panini Excalibur Team USA Jerseys
RANDOM INSERTS IN PACKS
STATED PRINT RUN 99 SER.#'d SETS
1 Carmelo Anthony 10.00 25.00
2 Harrison Barnes 4.00 10.00
5 DeMar DeRozan 5.00 12.00
6 Kevin Durant 8.00 20.00
9 Kyrie Irving 8.00 20.00

2012 Panini Father's Day
RANDOM INSERTS IN FATHER'S DAY PACKS
CRACKED ICE/25: 5X TO 12X BASE HI
1 Kobe Bryant 1.00 2.50
2 Blake Griffin .60 1.50
3 Kevin Durant .75 2.00
4 John Wall .50 1.25
5 Dirk Nowitzki 1.25 1.00
6 Derrick Rose .75 2.00

2012 Panini Father's Day Draft Day Hats
RANDOM INSERTS IN FATHERS DAY PACKS
1 DeMarcus Cousins 8.00 20.00
2 Cole Aldrich 4.00 10.00
3 Derrick Favors 6.00 15.00
4 Ekpe Udoh 4.00 10.00
5 Evan Turner 6.00 15.00
6 Gordon Hayward 6.00 15.00
7 Greg Monroe 6.00 15.00
8 Paul George 6.00 15.00
9 Wesley Johnson 5.00 12.00
10 Xavier Henry 5.00 12.00
BG Blake Griffin 12.00 30.00

2012 Panini Father's Day Elements
RANDOM INSERTS IN FATHERS DAY PACKS
CRACKED ICE/25: 5X TO 12X BASE HI
9 Kobe Bryant 1.00 2.50
10 Blake Griffin .60 1.50

2012 Panini Father's Day Kobe Bryant Shoes
RANDOM INSERTS IN FATHERS DAY PACKS
KB1 Kobe Bryant 40.00 70.00
KB2 Kobe Bryant 40.00 70.00

2012 Panini Father's Day Legends
RANDOM INSERTS IN FATHERS DAY PACKS
CRACKED ICE/25: 5X TO 12X BASE HI
3 Larry Bird .75 2.00
4 Magic Johnson .60 1.50

2012 Panini Father's Day NBA Finals Memorabilia
RANDOM INSERTS IN FATHERS DAY PACKS
1 Dirk Nowitzki 20.00 50.00
2 Jason Kidd 20.00 50.00
3 Jason Terry 20.00 50.00
4 LeBron James 50.00 120.00
5 Dwyane Wade 40.00 100.00
MVP Dirk Nowitzki 40.00 100.00
NNO Net Card 50.00 120.00

2012 Panini Father's Day Rookie of the Year Jerseys
RANDOM INSERTS IN FATHERS DAY PACKS
3 Blake Griffin 20.00 50.00

2012 Panini Father's Day Season Highlights
RANDOM INSERTS IN FATHERS DAY PACKS
CRACKED ICE/25: 5X TO 12X BASE HI
1 Kobe Bryant 1.00 2.50
2 Kevin Durant .75 2.00
3 Kevin Durant .75 2.00

2013 Panini Father's Day
CRACKED ICE/25: 4X TO 10X BASIC CARDS
LAVA FLOW/25: 4X TO 10X BASIC CARDS
6 Tim Duncan
10 Derrick Rose
13 Kobe Bryant
14 Kevin Durant
15 Blake Griffin
16 LeBron James
17 Damian Lillard
18 Carmelo Anthony
29 Anthony Davis
30 Kyrie Irving
31 Michael Kidd-Gilchrist
32 Harrison Barnes
33 Andre Drummond
34 Bradley Beal

2013 Panini Father's Day NBA Rookie Materials
1 Kyrie Irving
2 Anthony Davis

2013 Panini Father's Day NBA Rookie Materials Autographs
1 Kyrie Irving
2 Anthony Davis

2013 Panini Father's Day Studio
CRACKED ICE/25: 3X TO 8X BASIC CARDS
LAVA FLOW/25: 3X TO 8X BASIC CARDS
20 Kobe Bryant
21 Kevin Durant

2013 Panini Father's Day Team Pinnacle
CRACKED ICE/25: 3X TO 8X BASIC CARDS
LAVA FLOW/25: 3X TO 8X BASIC CARDS
1 Kobe Bryant/Kyrie Irving
2 LeBron James/Damian Lillard
3 Blake Griffin/Kevin Garnett
12 Anthony Davis/Michael Kidd-Gilchrist

2013-14 Panini Father's Day Jumbo Memorabilia
*CRACKED ICE/25: X TO X BASIC
AL Andrew Luck
BG Blake Griffin
BM Ben McLemore
KB Kobe Bryant
KD Kevin Durant
KI Kyrie Irving
KO Kelly Olynyk
MP Miles Plumlee
MW Michael Carter-Williams
NN Nerlens Noel
SA Steven Adams
VO Victor Oladipo

2013-14 Panini Father's Day March Memories Autographs
STATED PRINT RUN 50 SER.#'d SETS
CD Clyde Drexler 15.00 40.00
CL Christian Laettner 4.00 10.00
DM Danny Manning
JB Jim Boeheim
NR Nolan Richardson 15.00 40.00
RS Ralph Sampson 4.00 10.00

2013-14 Panini Father's Day NBA Draft Combine Jerseys
*CRACKED ICE/25: .6X TO 1.5X BASIC
1 Michael Carter-Williams 2.00 5.00
2 Victor Oladipo 2.50 6.00
3 Trey Burke 1.50 4.00
4 Ben McLemore 1.50 4.00
5 Tim Hardaway Jr. 2.00 5.00
6 Tony Snell 1.50 4.00
7 Kelly Olynyk 1.50 4.00
8 Nate Wolters 1.50 4.00
9 Steven Adams 2.00 5.00
10 Kentavious Caldwell-Pope 2.00 5.00
11 Mason Plumlee 2.00 5.00
12 Shane Larkin 1.25 3.00
13 Otto Porter 2.00 5.00
14 Cody Zeller 1.50 4.00
15 Peyton Siva 1.25 3.00

2013-14 Panini Father's Day NBA Patch Autographs
AB Anthony Bennett 60.00 150.00
CM C.J. McCollum 4.00 10.00
SM Shabazz Muhammad 4.00 10.00
TB Trey Burke 20.00 50.00
TM Tracy McGrady 15.00 40.00
VO Victor Oladipo

2014 Panini Father's Day
COMPLETE SET (55) 20.00 50.00
*1-24 THICK STOCK: 1X TO 2.5X BASIC CARDS
*25-55 THICK STOCK: .5X TO 1.2X BASIC CARDS
*1-24 ICE VETS/25: 5X TO 12X BASIC CARDS
*25-55 ICE ROOKIE/25: 2X TO 5X BASIC CARDS/499
1 Kobe Bryant BK 1.25 3.00
2 Blake Griffin BK .50 1.25
3 Kyrie Irving BK .75
4 Kevin Durant BK 1.00 2.50
5 Stephen Curry BK .50
6 James Harden BK .50
34 Michael Carter-Williams BK 1.00 2.50
35 Victor Oladipo BK 1.00 2.50
36 Trey Burke BK .75 2.00
37 Tim Hardaway Jr. BK .60 1.50
38 Giannis Antetokounmpo BK 1.00 2.50
39 Nerlens Noel BK 1.25 3.00
40 Ben McLemore BK .60 1.50

2014 Panini Father's Day Elements
COMPLETE SET (12) 5.00 12.00
*CRACKED ICE/25: 4X TO 10X BASIC CARDS
*THICK STOCK: 1.2X TO 3X BASIC CARDS
11 Kyrie Irving BK
12 John Wall BK

2014 Panini Father's Day Elite
2 Dante Exum BK

2014 Panini Father's Day Legends
COMPLETE SET (10)
8 Shaquille O'Neal BK
9 Larry Bird BK
10 Magic Johnson BK

2014 Panini Father's Day Rookies
COMPLETE SET (20) 10.00 25.00
*CRACKED ICE/25: 3X TO 8X BASIC CARDS
*THICK STOCK: 1X TO 2.5X BASIC CARDS
R7 Michael Carter-Williams BK
R8 Victor Oladipo BK
R9 Trey Burke BK
R10 Steven Adams BK
R11 Pero Antic BK
R12 Tony Snell BK
R13 Ben McLemore BK

2014 Panini Father's Day Tools of the Trade
*CRACKED ICE/25: 1X TO 2.5X BASIC
DN Dirk Nowitzki 5.00 12.00
MCW Michael Carter-Williams 3.00 8.00

2014 Panini Father's Day Who Do You Collect Jerseys
KB1 Kobe Bryant Ball on Hip
KB2 Kobe Bryant Layup
KB3 Kobe Bryant Two Hands on Ball

2015 Panini Father's Day
9 Kobe Bryant 1.50 4.00
10A Kevin Durant .75 2.00
10B Kevin Durant .75 2.00
11A John Wall .50 1.25
11B John Wall .50 1.25
12 Stephen Curry .75 2.00
13 LeBron James 1.25 3.00
14 Tim Duncan .60 1.50
15 Kevin Garnett .60 1.50
16A Kyrie Irving .75 2.00
16B Kyrie Irving .75 2.00
37 Nikola Mirotic 1.25 3.00
38 Jusuf Nurkic 1.00 2.50
39 Julius Randle 1.00 2.50
40 Joel Embiid 1.00 2.50
51A Andrew Wiggins JSY
51B Andrew Wiggins .75 2.00
52 Dante Exum JSY 2.00 5.00
53 Marcus Smart JSY 2.00 5.00
54A Jabari Parker JSY 2.00 5.00
54B Jabari Parker 1.00 2.50
55A Zach LaVine JSY 2.50 6.00
55B Zach LaVine 1.00 2.50
56 Elfrid Payton JSY 2.00 5.00
57A Doug McDermott JSY 2.00 5.00
57B Doug McDermott 1.00 2.50

2015 Panini Father's Day Elements
9 Zach LaVine 1.00 2.50
10 Russell Westbrook 1.25 3.00
11 Stephen Curry 1.50 4.00
12 Kevin Durant 1.00 2.50
13 Kobe Bryant 1.50 4.00
14 Andrew McCutchen 1.00 2.50

2015 Panini Father's Day Sketch
*THICK: 2X TO 5X BASIC CARDS
*CRACKED/25: 2X TO 5X BASIC CARDS
1 Andrew Wiggins 1.00 2.50
2 Jimmy Butler 1.00 2.50
3 Zach LaVine 1.00 2.50
4 Anthony Davis 1.00 2.50
5 Giannis Antetokounmpo 1.00 2.50

2012-13 Panini Finals Private Signings
PRINT RUNS B/WN 1-25 COPIES PER
NO PRICING ON QTY 10 OR LESS
AH Anfernee Hardaway/10
AI Allen Iverson/5
AM Alonzo Mourning/25 20.00 50.00
BA B.J. Armstrong/10
BC Bob Cousy/5
BL Bill Laimbeer/25
BR Bill Russell
BW Bill Walton/25 10.00 25.00
BW Bill Wennington/25
CB Chris Bosh/25
CB Chauncey Billups/10
CD Clyde Drexler/15 30.00 80.00
DF Derek Fisher/25
DN Don Nelson/25 20.00 50.00
DR Dennis Rodman/15
DR David Robinson/2
DW Dwyane Wade/3
GM George McGinnis/10
HG Horace Grant/25
HO Hakeem Olajuwon/15 40.00 100.00
IT Isiah Thomas/20 20.00 50.00
JD Joe Dumars/5
JE Julius Erving/5
JK1 Jason Kidd/5
JK2 Jason Kidd/5
JS John Stockton/5
JS John Salley/25 6.00 15.00
JW Jerry West/5
JW James Worthy/25 12.00 30.00
KAJ Kareem Abdul-Jabbar/1
KD Kevin Durant/3
KJ Kevin Johnson/10
KM Kevin McHale/10
MC Maurice Cheeks/10
MJ Magic Johnson/2
PG Pau Gasol/10
RA Ray Allen/3
RA Metta World Peace/10
RB Rick Barry/10
RH Ron Harper
RP Robert Parish/25
SK Steve Kerr/25
TC Tyson Chandler/25
TK Toni Kukoc/10
TS Satch Sanders/25 20.00 50.00
WF Walt Frazier/10

2013-14 Panini Finals Private Signings
PRINT RUNS B/WN 2-25 COPIES PER
NO PRICING ON QTY 10 OR LESS
AH Anfernee Hardaway/25 20.00 50.00
AM Alonzo Mourning/15
BL Bill Laimbeer/25 10.00 25.00
BW Bill Walton/25 10.00 25.00
CM Chris Mullin/15
DD Darryl Dawkins/25 4.00 10.00
DR David Robinson/25 15.00 40.00
DW Dominique Wilkins/25
GD Gorgui Dieng/25 8.00 20.00
GH Grant Hill/25 12.00 30.00
HO Hakeem Olajuwon/25 15.00 40.00
JK Jason Kidd/20 10.00 25.00
JW James Worthy/15 10.00 25.00
MP Mason Plumlee/25 10.00 25.00
MR Mitch Richmond/15 20.00 50.00
PA Pero Antic/25 8.00 20.00
SC Stephen Curry/25 40.00 100.00
SN Steve Nash/20 12.00 30.00
SP Scottie Pippen/15 60.00 120.00
TB Trey Burke/15 30.00 60.00
TH Tim Hardaway Jr./15 30.00 60.00
TK Toni Kukoc/20
TS Tony Snell/15
VO Victor Oladipo/15 50.00 100.00

2013-14 Panini Finals Rookie Memorabilia Autographs
STATED PRINT RUN 25 SER.#'d SETS
AB Anthony Bennett 25.00 60.00
AL Alex Len 10.00 25.00
BM Ben McLemore 30.00 60.00
CJM C.J. McCollum 30.00 80.00
CZ Cody Zeller 10.00 25.00
GA Giannis Antetokounmpo 150.00 300.00
KI Kyrie Irving
KO Kelly Olynyk 15.00 40.00
MCW Michael Carter-Williams 30.00 80.00
OP Otto Porter 20.00 50.00
SA Steven Adams 40.00 100.00
SM Shabazz Muhammad 15.00 40.00
TB Trey Burke 30.00 60.00
TH Tim Hardaway Jr. 20.00 50.00
VO Victor Oladipo 40.00 100.00

2014-15 Panini Finals Private Signings
STATED PRINT RUN B/WN 2-25 COPIES PER
NO PRICING ON QTY 15 OR LESS
AP Adrian Payne/25 15.00 40.00
AW Andrew Wiggins/25
BG Blake Griffin/25
BR Bill Russell/25
CB Chris Bosh/25
CM Chris Mullin/25
GG George Gervin/25
GP Gary Payton/25 50.00
HB Harrison Barnes/25
IT Isiah Thomas/25
JC Jordan Clarkson/25 50.00 120.00
JN Jusuf Nurkic/25 15.00 40.00
JO Johnny O'Bryant/25
JP Jabari Parker/25
JR Julius Randle/25
KB Kobe Bryant/25
KD Kevin Durant/25
KI Kyrie Irving/25
KK Kyle Korver/25
LA LaMarcus Aldridge/25
LB Larry Bird/25
MJ Magic Johnson/25
MM Mitch McGary/25 12.00 30.00
MR Mitch Richmond/25
MS Marcus Smart/25
NM Nikola Mirotic/25 25.00 60.00
PG Paul George/25
RB Rick Barry/25
SC Stephen Curry/25 60.00 150.00
SP Scottie Pippen/25
TM Tracy McGrady/25
TT T.J. Warren/25
YM Yao Ming/25
BB2 Bojan Bogdanovic/25 15.00 40.00
CA1 Carmelo Anthony/25
CA2 Chris Andersen/25
DM1 Dikembe Mutombo/25
DM2 Doug McDermott/25
DR1 David Robinson/25
DW1 Dominique Wilkins/25
DW2 Dwyane Wade
GH Grant Hill/25
GH2 Gary Harris/25
JE1 Julius Erving/25
JE2 James Ennis/25 12.00 30.00
JH1 Joe Harris/25 12.00 30.00
JW2 Jerry West/25
JW3 John Wall/5
KA1 Kareem Abdul-Jabbar/25
KA2 Kyle Anderson/25 12.00 30.00
KL1 Kawhi Leonard/25
KL2 Kevin Love/25
KM1 K.J. McDaniels/25 12.00 30.00
KM3 Kevin McHale/25
SN2 Steve Nash/25
SO1 Shaquille O'Neal/25

2012-13 Panini Flawless
STATED PRINT RUN 20 SER.#'d SETS
1 Carlos Boozer 50.00 120.00
2 Chris Bosh 50.00 120.00
3 Eric Gordon 50.00 120.00
4 Gordon Hayward 60.00 150.00
5 Kevin Garnett 125.00 250.00
6 Zach Randolph 50.00 120.00
7 Kevin Love 100.00 200.00
8 Rajon Rondo 100.00 200.00
9 Ricky Rubio 50.00 120.00
10 Andre Iguodala 50.00 120.00
11 Carmelo Anthony 150.00 300.00
12 Chris Paul 175.00 350.00
13 Dwyane Wade 250.00 400.00
14 Greg Monroe 50.00 120.00
15 Kevin Durant 600.00 800.00
16 Vince Carter 125.00 250.00
17 Kobe Bryant 600.00 1200.00
18 Paul Pierce 60.00 150.00
19 Roy Hibbert 50.00 120.00
20 Anderson Varejao 50.00 120.00
21 Brook Lopez 50.00 120.00
22 Danny Granger 50.00 120.00
23 Dwight Howard 100.00 200.00
24 Jameer Nelson 40.00 100.00
25 John Wall 100.00 200.00
26 Tyson Chandler 50.00 120.00
27 LaMarcus Aldridge 60.00 150.00
28 Paul George 300.00 500.00
29 Rudy Gay 40.00 100.00
30 Amar'e Stoudemire 50.00 120.00
31 Brandon Jennings 50.00 120.00
32 David Lee 50.00 120.00
33 Dirk Nowitzki 150.00 300.00
34 James Harden 150.00 300.00
35 Joe Johnson 40.00 100.00
36 Tyreke Evans 60.00 150.00
37 LeBron James 1500.00 2000.00
38 Pau Gasol 50.00 120.00
39 Russell Westbrook 125.00 250.00
40 Al Jefferson 50.00 120.00
41 Blake Griffin 100.00 200.00
42 DeMar DeRozan 100.00 200.00
43 Derrick Rose 250.00 500.00
44 Jason Kidd 60.00 150.00
45 Joakim Noah 50.00 120.00
46 Tony Parker 40.00 100.00
47 Manu Ginobili 50.00 120.00
48 Nick Young 40.00 100.00
49 Shawn Marion 50.00 120.00
50 Al Horford 60.00 150.00
51 Ben Gordon 40.00 100.00
52 DeMarcus Cousins 60.00 150.00
53 Deron Williams 60.00 150.00
54 JaVale McGee 40.00 100.00
55 Jeremy Lin 125.00 250.00
56 Tim Duncan 150.00 300.00
57 Marcin Gortat 40.00 100.00
58 Monta Ellis 50.00 120.00
59 Stephen Curry 200.00 400.00
60 Steve Nash 60.00 150.00
61 Allen Iverson 200.00 400.00
62 Elgin Baylor 60.00 150.00
63 James Worthy 60.00 150.00
64 Pete Maravich 100.00 200.00
65 Yao Ming 100.00 200.00
66 Anfernee Hardaway 125.00 250.00
67 Gary Payton 60.00 150.00
68 Jerry West 60.00 150.00
69 Patrick Ewing 150.00 300.00
70 Wilt Chamberlain 200.00 400.00
71 Bill Russell 150.00 300.00
72 George Gervin 60.00 150.00
73 John Havlicek 60.00 150.00
74 Oscar Robertson 60.00 150.00
75 Willis Reed 60.00 150.00
76 Bob Pettit 50.00 120.00
77 George Mikan 125.00 250.00
78 John Stockton 100.00 200.00
79 Magic Johnson 200.00 400.00
80 Walt Frazier 40.00 100.00
81 David Robinson 60.00 150.00
82 Isiah Thomas 200.00 400.00
83 Julius Erving 125.00 250.00
84 Larry Bird 100.00 200.00
85 Shaquille O'Neal 100.00 200.00
86 Dennis Rodman 50.00 120.00
87 Hakeem Olajuwon 125.00 250.00
88 Kareem Abdul-Jabbar 125.00 250.00
89 Karl Malone 100.00 200.00
90 Scottie Pippen 200.00 400.00
91 Bradley Beal RC 500.00 700.00
92 Brandon Knight RC 150.00 300.00
93 Chandler Parsons RC 300.00 500.00
94 Andre Drummond RC 400.00 600.00
95 Anthony Davis RC 1000.00 1500.00
96 Kyrie Irving RC 1000.00 1500.00
97 Kenneth Faried RC 150.00 300.00
98 Damian Lillard RC 1000.00 1500.00
99 Harrison Barnes RC 300.00 400.00
100 Michael Kidd-Gilchrist RC 200.00 400.00

2012-13 Panini Flawless All-Star Ink
PRINT RUNS B/WN 15-25 COPIES PER
NO PRICING ON QTY 15
1 Magic Johnson/20 75.00 150.00
3 Blake Griffin/20 50.00 120.00
4 Kyrie Irving/20 250.00 500.00
7 Kobe Bryant/20 200.00 300.00
8 Grant Hill/20 50.00 120.00
11 Kevin Durant/20 150.00 300.00
14 Julius Erving/20 50.00 120.00
15 Jerry West/20 40.00 80.00
20 Hakeem Olajuwon/15 30.00 60.00

2012-13 Panini Flawless Greats Autographs
STATED PRINT RUN 20 SER.#'d SETS
1 Yao Ming 40.00 80.00
2 Sam Jones 20.00 50.00
3 Rick Barry 15.00 40.00
4 Larry Johnson 20.00 50.00
5 Kevin McHale 20.00 50.00
6 Gary Payton 50.00 120.00
7 Gail Goodrich 15.00 40.00
8 Clyde Lovellette 15.00 40.00
10 Adrian Dantley 15.00 40.00
11 Walt Frazier 15.00 40.00
12 Sidney Moncrief 15.00 40.00
13 Robert Parish 15.00 40.00
14 Magic Johnson 50.00 120.00
15 John Thompson 25.00 60.00
16 George Gervin 20.00 50.00
17 Dominique Wilkins 20.00 50.00
18 Dan Issel 15.00 40.00
19 Chris Mullin 15.00 40.00
20 Alex English 15.00 40.00
21 Wes Unseld 15.00 40.00
22 Spencer Haywood 15.00 40.00
23 Nate Thurmond 15.00 40.00
24 Mark Eaton 10.00 25.00
25 Larry Bird 75.00 150.00
26 Hal Greer 15.00 40.00
27 Elgin Baylor 20.00 50.00
28 Darryl Dawkins 15.00 40.00
29 Bill Walton 20.00 50.00
30 Anfernee Hardaway 50.00 100.00
31 Willis Reed 20.00 50.00
32 Spud Webb 15.00 40.00
33 Nate Archibald 15.00 40.00
34 Mark Jackson 15.00 40.00
35 John Stockton 40.00 100.00
36 Jeff Hornacek 15.00 40.00
37 Elvin Hayes 15.00 40.00
38 David Thompson 10.00 25.00
39 Bill Russell 75.00 150.00
40 Artis Gilmore 15.00 40.00
41 Tim Hardaway 20.00 50.00
42 Sean Elliott 20.00 50.00
43 Mitch Richmond 15.00 40.00
44 Michael Finley 15.00 40.00
45 John Starks 20.00 50.00
46 John Havlicek 30.00 80.00
47 Dolph Schayes 15.00 40.00
48 Doc Rivers 15.00 40.00
49 Bill Laimbeer 15.00 40.00

2012-13 Panini Flawless Greats Dual Patches Autographs
PRINT RUNS B/WN 15-25 COPIES PER
NO PRICING ON QTY 15
1 Kobe Bryant/25 800.00 1200.00
2 Kareem Abdul-Jabbar/25 150.00 250.00
3 Julius Erving/25 125.00 250.00
4 Grant Hill/20 125.00 250.00
5 David Robinson/25 125.00 250.00
6 Shaquille O'Neal/20 700.00 1000.00
8 Danny Manning/25 30.00 80.00
9 Scottie Pippen/20 400.00 600.00
10 Grant Hill/20 125.00 250.00
11 John Stockton/25 100.00 200.00
13 Artis Gilmore/20 25.00 60.00
14 Clyde Drexler/20 150.00 300.00
15 Larry Bird/20 250.00 350.00
16 Mitch Richmond/20 75.00 150.00
17 Anfernee Hardaway/25 200.00 400.00
18 Ralph Sampson/20 25.00 60.00
19 Robert Parish/20 30.00 80.00
20 Larry Johnson/25 125.00 250.00
21 World B. Free/20 25.00 60.00
22 Calvin Murphy/20 25.00 60.00
23 Bill Laimbeer/20 25.00 60.00
24 Paul Westphal/25 20.00 50.00

2012-13 Panini Flawless Greats Patches Autographs
STATED PRINT RUN 25 SER.#'d SETS
1 Karl Malone 150.00 250.00
2 Larry Johnson 50.00 120.00
3 Earl Monroe 20.00 50.00
4 Mark Jackson 20.00 50.00
5 Robert Parish 20.00 50.00
6 Larry Bird 100.00 200.00
7 Gail Goodrich 25.00 60.00
8 Doc Rivers 50.00 100.00
9 Sean Elliott 25.00 60.00
10 Kevin McHale 40.00 100.00
11 Kiki VanDeWeghe 15.00 40.00
12 Danny Manning 20.00 50.00
14 Julius Erving 100.00 200.00
16 Dan Issel 15.00 40.00
17 Bill Laimbeer 20.00 50.00
18 John Stockton 100.00 200.00
19 Jamaal Wilkes 25.00 50.00
20 Clyde Drexler 50.00 120.00
21 Bob Lanier 20.00 50.00
22 Jerry West 200.00 400.00
23 James Worthy 50.00 100.00
24 Chris Mullin 40.00 100.00
25 Calvin Murphy 25.00 60.00

2012-13 Panini Flawless Hall of Fame Autographs
STATED PRINT RUN 20 SER.#'d SETS
1 Jamaal Wilkes 15.00 40.00
2 Ralph Sampson 15.00 40.00
3 Don Nelson 20.00 50.00
4 Artis Gilmore 15.00 40.00
5 David Robinson 50.00 120.00
6 John Stockton 40.00 100.00
7 Hakeem Olajuwon 30.00 80.00
8 Dominique Wilkins 25.00 60.00
9 Clyde Drexler 40.00 100.00
10 Joe Dumars 15.00 40.00
11 Robert Parish 15.00 40.00
12 Isiah Thomas 25.00 60.00
13 Bob McAdoo 40.00 100.00
14 Gail Goodrich 15.00 40.00
15 Kareem Abdul-Jabbar 50.00 120.00
16 Bill Walton 20.00 50.00
17 Dan Issel 15.00 40.00
18 Earl Monroe 20.00 50.00
19 Wes Unseld 15.00 40.00
20 Willis Reed 20.00 50.00

2012-13 Panini Flawless Inscriptions
PRINT RUNS B/WN 20-25 COPIES PER
1 Zach Randolph/20 15.00 40.00
2 Vince Carter/20 30.00 80.00
3 Kobe Bryant/25 150.00 300.00
4 Kevin Love/20 30.00 80.00
5 Deron Williams/25 20.00 50.00
6 Tobias Harris/20 15.00 40.00
7 Tyson Chandler/20 15.00 40.00
8 Kyrie Irving/25 200.00 400.00
9 Kevin Durant/25 150.00 250.00
10 Chris Bosh/20 25.00 60.00
11 Grant Hill/25 25.00 60.00
12 Tyreke Evans/20 15.00 40.00
13 LaMarcus Aldridge/20 25.00 60.00
14 Andre Drummond/20 100.00 250.00
15 Blake Griffin/20 25.00 60.00
16 Greg Monroe/20 15.00 40.00
17 Tony Parker/20 30.00 80.00
18 Rick Fox/20 12.00 30.00
19 Joakim Noah/20 15.00 40.00
20 Anthony Davis/20 125.00 250.00
21 James Harden/20 50.00 120.00
22 Steve Nash/20 25.00 60.00
23 Stephen Curry/20 75.00 150.00
24 Jason Kidd/20 25.00 60.00
25 Andre Iguodala/20 15.00 40.00

2012-13 Panini Flawless Memorable Marks
PRINT RUNS B/WN 20-25 COPIES PER
1 Hakeem Olajuwon 30.00 80.00
2 Larry Bird 75.00 150.00
3 Magic Johnson 75.00 150.00
4 Jerry West 40.00 80.00
5 Gail Goodrich 15.00 40.00
6 Jamaal Wilkes 15.00 40.00
7 Mark Price 30.00 80.00
8 Kareem Abdul-Jabbar 60.00 150.00
9 Isiah Thomas 25.00 60.00
10 Nate Thurmond 15.00 40.00
11 Glen Rice 20.00 50.00
12 Walt Frazier 15.00 40.00
13 Julius Erving 50.00 120.00
14 Sidney Moncrief 15.00 40.00
15 Calvin Murphy 15.00 40.00
16 Dikembe Mutombo 20.00 50.00
17 Scottie Pippen 125.00 250.00
18 Anfernee Hardaway 60.00 120.00
19 Rick Barry 15.00 40.00
20 Mitch Richmond 25.00 60.00
21 Rolando Blackman 12.00 30.00
22 George Gervin 20.00 50.00
23 Elgin Baylor 20.00 50.00
24 Elvin Hayes 15.00 40.00
25 Alonzo Mourning 60.00 150.00
26 Joe Dumars 15.00 40.00
27 Chris Mullin 15.00 40.00
28 Bill Walton 20.00 50.00
29 Spencer Haywood 15.00 40.00
30 Dolph Schayes 12.00 30.00
31 Connie Hawkins 15.00 40.00
32 Gary Payton 40.00 80.00
33 Larry Johnson 25.00 60.00
34 Sam Jones 20.00 50.00
36 Tim Hardaway 20.00 50.00
37 John Havlicek 20.00 50.00
38 Artis Gilmore 15.00 40.00
39 Nate Archibald 15.00 40.00
40 John Starks 12.00 30.00
41 Spud Webb 15.00 40.00
42 David Robinson 50.00 120.00
43 Bill Russell 75.00 150.00
44 James Worthy 12.00 30.00
45 Robert Parish 15.00 40.00
46 Kobe Bryant 150.00 300.00
47 Kevin Durant 150.00 250.00
48 Kyrie Irving 100.00 200.00
49 Grant Hill 30.00 80.00
50 Blake Griffin 50.00 120.00

2012-13 Panini Flawless Signatures
PRINT RUNS B/WN 20-25 COPIES PER
1 Tyreke Evans/20 15.00 40.00
2 Roy Hibbert/20 15.00 40.00
3 Raymond Felton/20 15.00 40.00
4 Joakim Noah/20 20.00 50.00
5 Jason Kidd/20 25.00 60.00
6 Scottie Pippen/25 100.00 200.00
7 Deron Williams/20 25.00 60.00
8 Anderson Varejao/20 15.00 40.00
9 Stephen Curry/20 200.00 300.00
10 Steve Francis/20 15.00 40.00
11 John Starks/20 15.00 40.00
12 Kenneth Faried/20 20.00 50.00
13 Harrison Barnes/20 25.00 60.00
14 DeMarcus Cousins/20 25.00 60.00
15 Antawn Jamison/20 15.00 40.00
16 Steve Nash/20 25.00 60.00
17 LaMarcus Aldridge/20 20.00 50.00
18 Jose Calderon/20 15.00 40.00
19 James Harden/20 50.00 120.00
20 Goran Dragic/20 25.00 60.00
21 Zach Randolph/20 15.00 40.00
22 Anthony Davis/20 200.00 400.00
23 Tony Parker/20 30.00 80.00
24 Kobe Bryant/25 150.00 300.00
25 Bradley Beal/20 75.00 150.00
26 J.R. Smith/20 20.00 50.00
27 Tyson Chandler/20 15.00 40.00
28 Danny Granger/20 15.00 40.00
29 Blake Griffin/20 60.00 150.00
30 Ty Lawson/20 15.00 40.00
31 Kyrie Irving/25 250.00 500.00
32 Kevin Durant/25 150.00 250.00
33 Greg Monroe/20 15.00 40.00
34 Grant Hill/25 15.00 40.00
35 Karl Malone/25 50.00 100.00
37 Bill Russell/25 75.00 150.00
38 David Robinson/20 50.00 120.00
39 Wes Unseld/20 15.00 40.00
40 Anfernee Hardaway/25 75.00 150.00
41 Clyde Drexler/20 30.00 60.00
42 Kevin McHale/20 20.00 50.00
43 Dominique Wilkins/20 20.00 50.00
44 Julius Erving/20 50.00 120.00
45 Tom Chambers/20 15.00 40.00
46 Larry Bird/20 75.00 150.00
47 Hakeem Olajuwon/20 30.00 80.00
48 Walt Frazier/20 15.00 40.00
49 Jerry West/20 40.00 80.00
50 Elgin Baylor/25 20.00 50.00

2012-13 Panini Flawless Patches
PRINT RUNS B/WN 9-25 COPIES PER
NO PRICING ON QTY 19 OR LESS
1 Russell Westbrook/25 60.00 120.00
2 Amar'e Stoudemire/25 25.00 60.00
3 Andrei Kirilenko/25 20.00 50.00
4 David Lee/25 20.00 50.00
5 David West/25 20.00 50.00
7 Grant Hill/25 50.00 120.00
8 Alex English/25 15.00 40.00
9 LaMarcus Aldridge/25 40.00 100.00
10 Roy Hibbert/25 25.00 60.00
11 Ricky Rubio/25 60.00 150.00
12 Jason Terry/25 15.00 40.00
14 Reggie Lewis/25 75.00 150.00
15 DeMarcus Cousins/25 20.00 50.00
16 Glen Davis/25 15.00 40.00
17 Greg Monroe/25 20.00 50.00
18 Kevin Love/25 30.00 80.00
19 Magic Johnson/25 75.00 150.00
20 Tim Duncan/25 50.00 120.00
21 Ray Allen/25 40.00 100.00
22 Andre Iguodala/25 20.00 50.00
23 Blake Griffin/25 75.00 150.00
24 John Wall/25 50.00 120.00
25 Derrick Favors/25 15.00 40.00
26 Eric Gordon/21 40.00 100.00
27 James Harden/21 40.00 100.00
28 Kevin Garnett/25 40.00 80.00
30 Tony Parker/25 30.00 80.00
31 Rajon Rondo/25 50.00 120.00
32 Al Jefferson/25 15.00 40.00
33 Brandon Jennings/25 20.00 50.00
36 Dwyane Wade/25 150.00 400.00
37 Jeremy Lin/25 75.00 200.00
38 Kevin Durant/25 75.00 150.00
40 Tyreke Evans/25 20.00 50.00
41 Paul Pierce/25 40.00 100.00
42 Manu Ginobili/25 25.00 60.00
43 Carlos Boozer/25 20.00 50.00
44 Carmelo Anthony/25 75.00 150.00
45 Dirk Nowitzki/25 75.00 150.00
46 Dwight Howard/25 50.00 120.00
47 Joakim Noah/25 30.00 80.00
49 O.J. Mayo/25 25.00 60.00
50 LeBron James/25 350.00 700.00
52 Karl Malone/25 30.00 80.00
54 Shaquille O'Neal/22 100.00 200.00
55 David Robinson/24 30.00 80.00
56 Kevin McHale/25 30.00 80.00
58 Manute Bol/25 30.00 80.00
59 Fat Lever/24 30.00 80.00
60 Larry Bird/25 75.00 200.00
61 Gus Williams/25 20.00 50.00
62 John Stockton/25 50.00 120.00
64 Lou Hudson/23 25.00 60.00
67 Hakeem Olajuwon/25 50.00 120.00
70 Jamaal Wilkes/20 40.00 100.00
73 Patrick Ewing/25 100.00 250.00
75 Isiah Thomas/25 25.00 60.00

2012-13 Panini Flawless Patches Autographs
PRINT RUNS B/WN 15-25 COPIES PER
NO PRICING ON QTY 15
2 Kevin Durant/25 300.00 600.00
3 Grant Hill/25 100.00 200.00
4 Alex English/25 30.00 80.00
5 Hakeem Olajuwon/25 60.00 120.00
6 Hal Greer/20 25.00 60.00
7 Jason Kidd/25 60.00 150.00
9 Jeff Hornacek/25 30.00 80.00
10 Joe Dumars/25 40.00 100.00
11 Joe Johnson/25 20.00 50.00
12 LaMarcus Aldridge/25
14 Monta Ellis/25 25.00 60.00
15 Paul George/25 150.00 300.00
16 Raymond Felton/25 25.00 60.00
17 Robert Parish/25 30.00 80.00
18 Jalen Rose/25 25.00 60.00
19 Tom Chambers/25 20.00 50.00
20 Tyson Chandler/25 25.00 60.00
22 Dennis Rodman/25 200.00 300.00
23 Robert Parish/25 30.00 80.00
24 Luol Deng/25 25.00 60.00
25 Tony Parker/25 75.00 150.00
26 Deron Williams/25 30.00 80.00
27 Ron Harper/25 20.00 50.00
28 Derrick Favors/25 30.00 80.00
29 Joakim Noah/25 20.00 50.00
30 Jameer Nelson/25 20.00 50.00
31 Kenneth Faried/25 50.00 120.00
32 Chandler Parsons/25 100.00 200.00
33 Rolando Blackman/25 25.00 60.00
34 Bill Cartwright/25 25.00 60.00
35 Ty Lawson/25 25.00 60.00
39 Doc Rivers/25 30.00 80.00
40 Jeff Teague/25 20.00 50.00
41 Cazzie Russell/25 40.00 100.00
42 Rick Mahorn/25 20.00 50.00
43 Derrick Coleman/25 20.00 50.00
44 Sleepy Floyd/25 25.00 60.00
45 Buck Williams/25 25.00 60.00
48 Chris Bosh/25 40.00 100.00
49 Karl Malone/25 75.00 150.00
50 Damian Lillard/25 600.00 1200.00

2012-13 Panini Flawless Rookie Autographs
STATED PRINT RUN 25 SER.#'d SETS
1 Kenneth Faried 50.00 120.00
2 Kyrie Irving 1000.00 2000.00
3 Anthony Davis 300.00 600.00
4 Iman Shumpert 30.00 80.00
5 Isaiah Thomas 60.00 150.00
6 Kemba Walker 60.00 150.00
7 Harrison Barnes 75.00 150.00
8 Austin Rivers 30.00 80.00
9 Michael Kidd-Gilchrist 50.00 120.00
10 Jared Sullinger 60.00 150.00
11 Kawhi Leonard 200.00 400.00
12 Nikola Vucevic 30.00 80.00
13 Bradley Beal 150.00 300.00
14 Dion Waiters
15 Andre Drummond 150.00 300.00
16 Jonas Valanciunas 40.00 100.00
17 Klay Thompson 250.00 400.00
18 Brandon Knight 30.00 80.00
19 Jimmer Fredette 25.00 60.00
20 Jimmy Butler 150.00 300.00
21 Tobias Harris 40.00 100.00
22 Tristan Thompson 150.00 250.00
23 Chandler Parsons 40.00 100.00
24 Alexey Shved 25.00 60.00
25 Damian Lillard 600.00 1000.00

2012-13 Panini Flawless Rookie Patches
STATED PRINT RUN 25 SER.#'d SETS
1 Harrison Barnes 40.00 100.00
2 Kenneth Faried 30.00 80.00
3 Chandler Parsons 30.00 80.00
4 Damian Lillard 125.00 250.00
5 Klay Thompson 40.00 100.00
6 Andre Drummond 40.00 100.00
7 Jared Sullinger 30.00 80.00
8 Anthony Davis 100.00 200.00
9 Jonas Valanciunas 30.00 80.00
10 Michael Kidd-Gilchrist 30.00 80.00
11 Isaiah Thomas 30.00 80.00
12 Austin Rivers 30.00 80.00
13 Kawhi Leonard 125.00 250.00
14 John Henson 25.00 60.00
15 Iman Shumpert 25.00 60.00
16 Bradley Beal 50.00 120.00
17 Kemba Walker 40.00 100.00
18 Kyrie Irving 125.00 250.00
19 Dion Waiters 30.00 80.00
20 Brandon Knight 20.00 50.00
21 Thomas Robinson 25.00 60.00
22 Tristan Thompson 20.00 50.00
23 Jimmer Fredette 20.00 50.00
24 Kyrie Irving 150.00 300.00
25 Damian Lillard 125.00 250.00

2012-13 Panini Flawless Spokesmen Patches Autographs
PRINT RUNS B/WN 20-25 COPIES PER
1 Kevin Durant/25 200.00 500.00
2 Kobe Bryant/25 250.00 400.00
3 Blake Griffin/20 75.00 150.00
4 Kyrie Irving/25 400.00 800.00
5 Anthony Davis/25 600.00 1000.00
6 Kevin Durant/25 200.00 500.00
7 Kobe Bryant/25 350.00 700.00
8 Blake Griffin/25 75.00 150.00
9 Kyrie Irving/25 350.00 700.00
10 Anthony Davis/20 400.00 800.00

2012-13 Panini Flawless Team Panini Autographs
STATED PRINT RUN 10 SER.#'d SETS
ALL VERSIONS EQUALLY PRICED
1 Kobe Bryant 150.00 300.00
2 Kobe Bryant 150.00 300.00
3 Kobe Bryant 150.00 300.00
4 Kobe Bryant 150.00 300.00
5 Kobe Bryant 150.00 300.00
6 Kobe Bryant 150.00 300.00
7 Kobe Bryant 150.00 300.00
8 Kobe Bryant 150.00 300.00
9 Kobe Bryant 150.00 300.00
10 Kobe Bryant 150.00 300.00
11 Kevin Durant 150.00 300.00
12 Kevin Durant 150.00 300.00
13 Kevin Durant 150.00 300.00
14 Kevin Durant 150.00 300.00
15 Kevin Durant 150.00 300.00
16 Kevin Durant 150.00 300.00
17 Kevin Durant 150.00 300.00
18 Kevin Durant 150.00 300.00
19 Kevin Durant 150.00 300.00
20 Kevin Durant 150.00 300.00
21 Blake Griffin 60.00 120.00
22 Blake Griffin 60.00 120.00
23 Blake Griffin 60.00 120.00
24 Blake Griffin 60.00 120.00
25 Blake Griffin 60.00 120.00
26 Blake Griffin 60.00 120.00
27 Blake Griffin 60.00 120.00
28 Blake Griffin 60.00 120.00
29 Blake Griffin 60.00 120.00
30 Blake Griffin 60.00 120.00
31 Kyrie Irving 125.00 250.00
32 Kyrie Irving 125.00 250.00
33 Kyrie Irving 125.00 250.00
34 Kyrie Irving 125.00 250.00
35 Kyrie Irving 125.00 250.00
36 Kyrie Irving 125.00 250.00
37 Kyrie Irving 125.00 250.00
38 Kyrie Irving 125.00 250.00
39 Kyrie Irving 125.00 250.00
40 Kyrie Irving 125.00 250.00
41 Anthony Davis 300.00 600.00
42 Anthony Davis 300.00 600.00
43 Anthony Davis 300.00 600.00
44 Anthony Davis 300.00 600.00
45 Anthony Davis 300.00 600.00
46 Anthony Davis 300.00 600.00
47 Anthony Davis 300.00 600.00
48 Anthony Davis 300.00 600.00
49 Anthony Davis 300.00 600.00
50 Anthony Davis 300.00 600.00

2012-13 Panini Flawless Team Panini Autographs Emerald
*EMERALD: .6X TO 1.5X BASIC
STATED PRINT RUN 5 SER.#'d SETS
ALL VERSIONS EQUALLY PRICED
31 Kyrie Irving 300.00 600.00

2013-14 Panini Flawless
STATED PRINT RUN 20 SER.#'d SETS
1 Kobe Bryant 400.00 800.00
2A Kevin Durant 500.00 800.00
2B Kevin Durant MVP 500.00 800.00
3 Kyrie Irving 100.00 200.00
4 Blake Griffin 40.00 100.00
5 Anthony Davis 100.00 200.00
6 Carmelo Anthony 175.00 350.00
7 Dwyane Wade 150.00 300.00
8 Chris Paul 50.00 125.00
9 Russell Westbrook 50.00 120.00
10 Tim Duncan 60.00 150.00
11 Tony Parker 25.00 60.00
12 Kevin Love 50.00 120.00
13 Kevin Garnett 100.00 200.00
14 Deron Williams 30.00 80.00
15 Rajon Rondo 40.00 100.00
16 Ricky Rubio 30.00 80.00
17 Andre Drummond 40.00 100.00
18 Brandon Jennings 30.00 80.00
19 Damian Lillard 80.00 200.00
20 LaMarcus Aldridge 40.00 100.00
21 DeMarcus Cousins 40.00 100.00
22 Stephen Curry 300.00 400.00
23 Klay Thompson 50.00 125.00
24 Andre Iguodala 30.00 80.00
25 Pau Gasol 40.00 100.00
26 Goran Dragic 30.00 80.00
27 Eric Bledsoe 30.00 80.00
28 Dirk Nowitzki 50.00 120.00
29 Monta Ellis 30.00 80.00
30 Vince Carter 40.00 100.00
31 LeBron James 200.00 400.00
32 Chris Bosh 40.00 100.00
33 Arron Afflalo 25.00 60.00

34 John Wall
35 Bradley Beal 40.00 100.00
36 Marcin Gortat 25.00 60.00
37 Derrick Rose 50.00 120.00
38 Jimmy Butler 50.00 120.00
39 Joakim Noah 25.00 60.00
40 DeMar DeRozan 40.00 100.00
41 Kyle Lowry 30.00 80.00
42 Paul George 50.00 125.00
43 Roy Hibbert 30.00 80.00
44 Lance Stephenson 30.00 80.00
45 Jeremy Lin 75.00 150.00
46 Dwight Howard
47 James Harden 75.00 150.00
48 Marc Gasol 40.00 100.00
49 Zach Randolph 25.00 60.00
50 Tyson Chandler 40.00 100.00
51 Ty Lawson 30.00 80.00
52 Kenneth Faried 30.00 80.00
53 Gordon Hayward 40.00 100.00
54 Ray Allen 40.00 100.00
55 O.J. Mayo 40.00 100.00
56 Brandon Knight 30.00 80.00
57 Kemba Walker 30.00 80.00
58 Al Jefferson 30.00 80.00
59 Thaddeus Young 25.00 60.00
60 Al Horford 30.00 80.00
61 Paul Millsap 40.00 100.00
62 Chandler Parsons 30.00 80.00
63 Isaiah Thomas 50.00 120.00
64 Paul Pierce 60.00 150.00
65 Manu Ginobili 60.00 150.00
66 Hakeem Olajuwon 100.00 200.00
67 Arvydas Sabonis 30.00 80.00
68 Bill Walton 40.00 100.00
69 Anfernee Hardaway 100.00 250.00
70 Dominique Wilkins 40.00 100.00
71 Bill Russell 60.00 150.00
72 Tim Hardaway 40.00 100.00
73 Alonzo Mourning 50.00 125.00
74 Shaquille O'Neal 80.00 200.00
75 Karl Malone 50.00 125.00
76 Moses Malone 40.00 100.00
77 Scottie Pippen 80.00 200.00
78 Grant Hill 50.00 120.00
79 Kareem Abdul-Jabbar 60.00 150.00
80 John Stockton 50.00 120.00
81 Julius Erving 60.00 150.00
82 Dikembe Mutombo 40.00 100.00
83 Clyde Drexler 50.00 125.00
84 Wilt Chamberlain 80.00 200.00
85 Pete Maravich 50.00 120.00
86 Larry Bird 75.00 150.00
87 Magic Johnson 100.00 250.00
88 Jason Kidd 40.00 100.00
89 Oscar Robertson 60.00 150.00
90 Allen Iverson 250.00 350.00
91 Anthony Bennett RC 30.00 80.00
92 Ben McLemore RC 150.00 300.00
93 Tim Hardaway Jr. RC 100.00 200.00
94 Nerlens Noel RC 100.00 250.00
95 Dennis Schroder RC 125.00 250.00
96 C.J. McCollum RC 150.00 300.00
97A M.Carter-Williams RC 150.00 300.00
97B M.Carter-Williams ROY 125.00 250.00
98 Victor Oladipo RC 250.00 500.00
99 Giannis Antetokounmpo RC 700.00 900.00
100 Trey Burke RC 40.00 100.00

2013-14 Panini Flawless All-Star Achievements Autographs

RANDOM INSERTS IN PACKS
STATED PRINT RUN 20 SER.#'D SETS
1 Kyrie Irving 100.00 250.00
2 Blake Griffin 20.00 50.00
3 Magic Johnson 50.00 125.00
4 Kobe Bryant 250.00 400.00
5 Isiah Thomas 20.00 50.00
6 Allen Iverson 150.00 300.00
7 John Stockton 40.00 100.00
8 Steve Nash 40.00 100.00
9 Kareem Abdul-Jabbar 30.00 80.00
10 Jerry West
11 Clyde Drexler 25.00 60.00
12 Julius Erving 50.00 125.00
13 Jason Kidd 40.00 100.00
14 Chris Bosh
15 Larry Bird 50.00 125.00

2013-14 Panini Flawless Autographs

RANDOM INSERTS IN PACKS
PRINT RUNS B/WN 20-25 COPIES PER
1 Artis Gilmore/20 25.00 60.00
2 Kobe Bryant/25 150.00 300.00
3 Blake Griffin/25 75.00 150.00
4 Jason Kidd/20 20.00 50.00
5 Grant Hill/20 50.00 125.00
6 Anfernee Hardaway/20 50.00 120.00
7 Chris Mullin/20 20.00 50.00
8 Rick Barry/20 15.00 40.00
10 Gary Payton/20 20.00 50.00
11 Allen Iverson/20 125.00 250.00
12 John Havlicek/20 25.00 60.00
13 David Robinson/20 30.00 80.00
14 Bill Russell/25 75.00 200.00
15 Kareem Abdul-Jabbar/25 30.00 80.00
16 Julius Erving/25 30.00 80.00
18 Dennis Rodman/20 40.00 100.00
19 John Wall/25 50.00 120.00
20 Chris Bosh/20 20.00 50.00
21 Tony Parker/20 20.00 50.00
22 Vince Carter/20 25.00 60.00
24 Deron Williams/20
25 Joakim Noah/20 15.00 40.00
26 Chris Andersen/20 40.00 100.00
28 Josh Smith/20 15.00 40.00
29 Manu Ginobili/25 30.00 80.00
30 Mark Aguirre/20 15.00 40.00
31 Jose Calderon/20 12.00 30.00
32 Oscar Robertson/20 50.00 125.00
33 Eric Gordon/20 12.00 30.00
34 Goran Dragic/20 15.00 40.00
35 Marcin Gortat/20 15.00 40.00
36 Harrison Barnes/20 30.00 80.00
37 Dwyane Wade/25 75.00 200.00
38 Baron Davis/20 12.00 30.00
39 George Gervin/20 15.00 40.00
40 Christian Laettner/20 15.00 40.00
41 Kevin Love/25 20.00 50.00
42 Horace Grant/20 12.00 30.00
43 Byron Scott/20 15.00 40.00
44 Robert Horry/20 15.00 40.00
45 Carmelo Anthony/25 40.00 100.00
46 Jerry West/25 25.00 60.00
47 Nick Anderson/20 12.00 30.00
48 Wes Unseld/20 12.00 30.00
51 Chris Webber/25 150.00 300.00

2013-14 Panini Flawless Franchise Greats Autographs

RANDOM INSERTS IN PACKS
STATED PRINT RUN 20 SER.#'D SETS
1 Larry Bird
2 Dominique Wilkins 20.00 50.00
3 Alex English 12.00 30.00
4 Isiah Thomas 15.00 40.00
5 Hakeem Olajuwon 20.00 50.00
6 Kobe Bryant 100.00 200.00
7 Gary Payton 30.00 80.00
8 Walt Frazier 15.00 40.00
9 Karl Malone 40.00 100.00
10 Manu Ginobili
11 Bob McAdoo
12 Terry Porter 10.00 25.00
13 Allen Iverson 150.00 300.00
14 Dick Van Arsdale 12.00 30.00
15 George Gervin 15.00 40.00
16 Blake Griffin 60.00 150.00
17 Baron Davis 12.00 30.00
18 Dwyane Wade 75.00 200.00
19 John Wall 25.00 60.00
20 Stephen Curry 100.00 200.00
21 Oscar Robertson 20.00 50.00

2013-14 Panini Flawless Greats Dual Memorabilia Autographs

RANDOM INSERTS IN PACKS
STATED PRINT RUN 25 SER.#'d SETS
1 David Robinson 75.00 200.00
2 Glen Rice 40.00 100.00
3 Isiah Thomas 30.00 80.00
4 Bill Laimbeer 25.00 60.00
5 Kevin Love 30.00 80.00
6 Larry Johnson 40.00 100.00
7 Steve Nash 30.00 80.00
8 Dwyane Wade 200.00 400.00
9 Deron Williams 25.00 60.00
11 Kobe Bryant 600.00 800.00
12 Kevin Durant 300.00 600.00
13 Anthony Davis 200.00 400.00
14 Carmelo Anthony 100.00 200.00
15 Kyrie Irving 125.00 250.00
16 John Wall 75.00 150.00
17 Grant Hill 75.00 150.00
18 John Stockton 100.00 150.00
19 Shaquille O'Neal 175.00 350.00
20 Tracy McGrady 100.00 200.00
21 Manu Ginobili 125.00 300.00
22 Blake Griffin 75.00 200.00
23 Tony Parker 100.00 200.00
GRPG Paul George

2013-14 Panini Flawless Hall of Fame Autographs Memorabilia

RANDOM INSERTS IN PACKS
STATED PRINT RUN 25 SER.#'d SETS
1 Larry Bird 60.00 150.00
2 Dominique Wilkins 20.00 50.00
3 David Robinson 40.00 100.00
5 Karl Malone 60.00 150.00
6 Gary Payton 50.00 120.00
7 Hakeem Olajuwon 30.00 80.00
8 Alex English 30.00 80.00
9 Clyde Drexler 25.00 60.00
10 Chris Mullin 25.00 60.00
11 Dennis Rodman 30.00 80.00
12 Magic Johnson
13 Gail Goodrich 20.00 50.00
14 Kareem Abdul-Jabbar 75.00 150.00
15 Bob Lanier 20.00 50.00
16 Joe Dumars 25.00 60.00
17 John Stockton 50.00 120.00
18 Kevin McHale 30.00 80.00
19 Isiah Thomas 25.00 60.00
20 Artis Gilmore 20.00 50.00

2013-14 Panini Flawless NBA Signatures

RANDOM INSERTS IN PACKS
PRINT RUNS B/WN 20-25 COPIES PER
1 Dwyane Wade 75.00 150.00
3 Blake Griffin 25.00 60.00
4 Gordon Hayward 12.00 30.00
6 Carmelo Anthony 50.00 125.00
7 John Havlicek 30.00 80.00
8 Manu Ginobili 40.00 100.00
9 Kevin McHale 20.00 50.00
10 LaMarcus Aldridge 20.00 50.00
11 Connie Hawkins 12.00 30.00
12 Andre Drummond 20.00 50.00
13 Stephen Curry 150.00 400.00
14 Mark Aguirre 15.00 40.00
15 Alex English 20.00 50.00
16 Chris Bosh 20.00 50.00
17 Tony Parker 40.00 100.00
18 Anthony Davis 100.00 200.00
19 Artis Gilmore 20.00 50.00
21 Allen Iverson 125.00 250.00
22 Bradley Beal 25.00 60.00
23 Tim Hardaway 25.00 60.00
25 Marcin Gortat 15.00 40.00
26 John Wall 25.00 60.00
27 Andrea Bargnani 12.00 30.00
29 Baron Davis 15.00 40.00
30 Chris Mullin 20.00 50.00
32 Oscar Robertson 40.00 100.00
33 Jon McGlocklin 12.00 30.00
35 Jose Calderon 12.00 30.00
36 Glen Rice 15.00 40.00
37 Byron Scott 12.00 30.00
38 Elgin Baylor 20.00 50.00
39 J.R. Smith 15.00 40.00
40 Mark Jackson 20.00 50.00
41 Sean Elliott
42 David Robinson 30.00 80.00
43 Shaquille O'Neal 75.00 150.00
44 James Worthy 25.00 60.00
45 Anfernee Hardaway 30.00 80.00
46 Gary Payton 25.00 60.00
47 Christian Laettner 12.00 30.00
48 Grant Hill 60.00 150.00
49 Vince Carter 25.00 60.00
50 Kevin Love 20.00 50.00
51 Chris Webber 125.00 250.00

2013-14 Panini Flawless Patch Autographs

RANDOM INSERTS IN PACKS
PRINT RUNS B/WN 20-25 COPIES PER
2 Fred Brown/25 15.00 40.00
3 Rick Barry/25 20.00 50.00
5 Mark Price/25 25.00 60.00
7 Bradley Beal/25 25.00 60.00
8 Josh Smith/25 20.00 50.00
9 LaMarcus Aldridge/25 75.00 150.00
10 Zach Randolph/25 20.00 50.00
11 Tyson Chandler/25 30.00 80.00
12 Kawhi Leonard/25 75.00 150.00
13 Jose Calderon/25 60.00 150.00
14 Vince Carter/25
15 Ty Lawson/25
16 Goran Dragic/25 20.00 50.00
17 Dwyane Wade/25 150.00 400.00
18 Robert Horry/25 20.00 50.00
19 Nick Anderson/25 20.00 50.00
20 Kyle Lowry/25 20.00 50.00
23 John Wall/25 60.00 150.00
24 Allen Iverson/25 300.00 600.00
25 Joakim Noah/25 20.00 50.00
26 Gordon Hayward/25 40.00 100.00
28 Al Horford/25 20.00 50.00
29 Harrison Barnes/25 40.00 100.00
30 Andre Drummond/25 25.00 60.00
31 Carmelo Anthony/25 100.00 200.00
33 Dikembe Mutombo/25 40.00 100.00
34 Grant Hill/25 50.00 120.00
35 Jason Kidd/25 50.00 120.00
36 Manu Ginobili/25 60.00 150.00
37 Kemba Walker/25 25.00 60.00
38 Mark Jackson/25 20.00 50.00
39 Nikola Vucevic/25 40.00 100.00
40 J.R. Smith/25 20.00 50.00
41 Anfernee Hardaway/25 75.00 200.00
42 Eric Gordon/25 20.00 50.00
43 Tyreke Evans/25 20.00 50.00
45 Andrei Kirilenko/25 20.00 50.00
46 Anthony Davis/20 150.00 300.00
47 Kobe Bryant/25 700.00 1000.00
48 Kevin Durant/25 200.00 400.00
49 Kyrie Irving/20 150.00 300.00
50 Kevin Martin/25 15.00 40.00
51 Kevin Love/25 50.00 120.00
52 Jrue Holiday/25 15.00 40.00
53 Stephen Curry/25 75.00 150.00
54 Dominique Wilkins/25 30.00 80.00
55 Kenneth Faried/25 20.00 50.00
56 Chris Webber/25 500.00 700.00
PAPG Paul George/25

2013-14 Panini Flawless Patches

RANDOM INSERTS IN PACKS
PRINT RUNS B/WN 9-25 COPIES PER
NO PRICING ON QTY 15 OR LESS
1 Louie Dampier/25 12.00 30.00
2 LeBron James/25 150.00 300.00
3 Kawhi Leonard/25 75.00 150.00
4 James Harden/25 30.00 80.00
5 Kevin Durant/20 100.00 200.00
7 Vince Carter/20 30.00 80.00
8 Tyson Chandler/25 15.00 40.00
9 Jimmy Butler/25 25.00 60.00
10 Russell Westbrook/25 75.00 150.00
11 Ricky Rubio/20 30.00 80.00
13 Rajon Rondo/25 30.00 80.00
14 Paul George/25 40.00 100.00
15 Patrick Ewing/25 40.00 100.00
16 Monta Ellis/25 15.00 40.00
17 Harrison Barnes/25 20.00 50.00
18 LaMarcus Aldridge/25 30.00 80.00
20 Kyrie Irving/20 60.00 150.00
21 Paul Millsap/20 30.00 80.00
22 Kevin Garnett/20 30.00 80.00
23 Kenneth Faried/25 15.00 40.00
24 Kevin Love/25 20.00 50.00
25 Jrue Holiday/20 12.00 30.00
26 Josh Smith/20 12.00 30.00
27 Jonas Valanciunas/25 15.00 40.00
28 John Wall/20 40.00 100.00
29 Joe Johnson/25 15.00 40.00
30 Eric Bledsoe/25 15.00 40.00
31 Damian Lillard/25 150.00 250.00
32 Nicolas Batum/25 100.00 200.00
33 Brandon Knight/25 20.00 50.00
34 Goran Dragic/20 15.00 40.00
35 Dwight Howard/25 50.00 125.00
36 Chris Paul/25 60.00 150.00
37 Pau Gasol/25 30.00 80.00
38 Dennis Johnson/20 30.00 80.00
39 Kevin McHale/20 15.00 40.00
40 Michael Finley/25 20.00 50.00
41 Chandler Parsons/25 20.00 50.00
42 Stephen Curry/25 125.00 300.00
43 Kobe Bryant/20 150.00 400.00
44 Karl Malone/25 25.00 60.00
45 Kareem Abdul-Jabbar/25 60.00 150.00
46 Larry Bird/25 60.00 150.00
47 DeMar DeRozan/25 30.00 80.00
48 Dwyane Wade/25 25.00 60.00
49 Zach Randolph/25 15.00 40.00
51 Andre Iguodala/25 20.00 50.00
52 Ty Lawson/25 12.00 30.00
53 Bradley Beal/25 20.00 50.00
54 Klay Thompson/20 60.00 150.00
55 Joakim Noah/25 15.00 40.00
56 Blake Griffin/25 75.00 150.00
57 Paul Pierce/25 30.00 80.00
58 Dirk Nowitzki/25 60.00 150.00
59 Andre Drummond/25 20.00 50.00
60 Jeremy Lin/25 60.00 150.00
61 Hakeem Olajuwon/25 25.00 60.00
62 Ray Allen/25 60.00 150.00
63 Tim Duncan/25 60.00 150.00
64 Anthony Davis/25 75.00 150.00
65 Gordon Hayward/25 15.00 40.00
66 Serge Ibaka/25 15.00 40.00
67 O.J. Mayo/25 20.00 50.00
68 DeMarcus Cousins/20 20.00 50.00
69 Kemba Walker/20 20.00 50.00
70 David Robinson/25 30.00 80.00
71 Scottie Pippen/25 150.00 250.00
72 John Stockton/25 30.00 80.00
73 Jason Kidd/25 30.00 80.00
74 James Worthy/25 30.00 80.00
75 Allen Iverson/25 150.00 300.00
76 Larry Johnson/25 40.00 100.00
77 Arron Afflalo/25 15.00 40.00
78 Shawn Kemp/25 40.00 100.00
79 John Starks/20 15.00 40.00
80 Charles Oakley/20 25.00 60.00
81 Joe Dumars/25 20.00 50.00
82 Shawn Bradley/25 12.00 30.00
83 Shawn Marion/20
84 Pat Riley/20 40.00 100.00
85 Alex English/20 20.00 50.00
86 LeBron James/25 100.00 200.00

2013-14 Panini Flawless Retired Numbers Autographs

RANDOM INSERTS IN PACKS
STATED PRINT RUN 20 SER.#'d SETS
1 Dominique Wilkins 20.00 50.00
3 Bill Russell
4 John Havlicek 20.00 50.00
5 Don Nelson 15.00 40.00
6 Karl Malone 30.00 80.00
7 Jason Kidd 30.00 80.00
8 Julius Erving 60.00 150.00
9 Zydrunas Ilgauskas 12.00 30.00
10 Alex English 12.00 30.00
11 David Thompson 12.00 30.00
12 Bob Lanier 12.00 30.00
13 Bill Laimbeer 12.00 30.00
14 Rick Barry 12.00 30.00
16 Clyde Drexler
17 Hakeem Olajuwon 20.00 50.00
18 Gail Goodrich 12.00 30.00
19 Jamaal Wilkes 12.00 30.00
20 Jerry West 25.00 60.00
21 Kareem Abdul-Jabbar 50.00 120.00
23 Oscar Robertson
24 Walt Frazier 15.00 40.00
26 Bobby Jones 12.00 30.00
27 Dan Majerle 12.00 30.00
28 Connie Hawkins
29 Dick Van Arsdale 12.00 30.00
30 Bill Walton 15.00 40.00
31 Terry Porter 10.00 25.00
32 John Stockton 25.00 60.00
34 Avery Johnson 12.00 30.00
35 Sean Elliott 15.00 40.00
37 Spencer Haywood 10.00 25.00
38 Fred Brown 10.00 25.00
39 George Gervin 15.00 40.00
40 Jeff Hornacek 12.00 30.00

2013-14 Panini Flawless Rookie Autographs

RANDOM INSERTS IN PACKS
STATED PRINT RUN 20 SER.#'d SETS
1 Anthony Bennett 20.00 50.00
2 Victor Oladipo 30.00 80.00
3 Trey Burke 20.00 50.00
4 Tim Hardaway Jr. 100.00 200.00
5 Giannis Antetokounmpo 800.00 1200.00
6 Nerlens Noel 40.00 100.00
7 Ben McLemore 20.00 50.00
8 C.J. McCollum 60.00 150.00
9 Michael Carter-Williams 25.00 60.00
10 Steven Adams 30.00 80.00

2013-14 Panini Flawless Rookie Patches

RANDOM INSERTS IN PACKS
STATED PRINT RUN 25 SER.#'d SETS
1 Victor Oladipo 25.00 60.00
2 Kelly Olynyk 15.00 40.00
3 Anthony Bennett 15.00 40.00
4 Tim Hardaway Jr. 20.00 50.00
5 C.J. McCollum 30.00 80.00
6 Ben McLemore 15.00 40.00
7 Trey Burke 15.00 40.00
8 Steven Adams 20.00 50.00
9 Tony Snell 10.00 25.00
10 Michael Carter-Williams 30.00 80.00
11 Reggie Bullock 10.00 25.00
12 Gorgui Dieng 15.00 40.00
13 Dennis Schroder 20.00 50.00
14 Cody Zeller 15.00 40.00
15 Otto Porter 20.00 50.00

2013-14 Panini Flawless Super Signatures

RANDOM INSERTS IN PACKS
PRINT RUNS B/WN 20-25 COPIES PER
2 Kobe Bryant/25 150.00 300.00
3 Kevin Durant/25 100.00 200.00
4 Kyrie Irving/25 75.00 150.00
6 John Wall/25 25.00 60.00
7 Blake Griffin/25 40.00 100.00
8 Anthony Davis/25 100.00 200.00
9 Karl Malone/20 30.00 80.00
10 Kareem Abdul-Jabbar/20 40.00 100.00
12 Bill Russell/25 60.00 150.00
13 Magic Johnson/20 50.00 125.00
14 Larry Bird/25 50.00 125.00
15 Julius Erving/25 30.00 80.00
16 Oscar Robertson/25 50.00 100.00
17 Chris Webber/25 200.00 400.00

2013-14 Panini Flawless Team Panini Autographs

RANDOM INSERTS IN PACKS
STATED PRINT RUN 10 SER.#'D SETS
ALL VERSIONS EQUALLY PRICED
*EMERALD/5: .5X TO 1.2X BASIC
1 Kyrie Irving 150.00 300.00
6 Kobe Bryant 200.00 400.00
11 Kevin Durant 150.00 300.00
16 Anthony Davis 150.00 300.00
21 Trey Burke 25.00 60.00
26 Victor Oladipo 75.00 150.00
31 Michael Carter-Williams 75.00 150.00

2013-14 Panini Flawless Transitions Autographs

RANDOM INSERTS IN PACKS
STATED PRINT RUN 10 SER.#'D SETS
ALL VERSIONS EQUALLY PRICED
*EMERALD/5: .5X TO 1.2X BASIC
TM1 Tracy McGrady 100.00 200.00
SO1 Shaquille O'Neal 150.00 300.00
JE1 Julius Erving 50.00 120.00
TH1 Tim Hardaway 30.00 80.00
DM1 Dikembe Mutombo 40.00 100.00
CW1 Chris Webber 200.00 400.00

2014-15 Panini Flawless Association Autographs

RANDOM INSERTS IN PACKS
PRINT RUNS B/WN 20-25 COPIES PER
*RUBY/15: .5X TO 1.2X BASIC
1 Ricky Rubio/25 25.00 60.00
3 James Harden/25 60.00 150.00
4 Kobe Bryant/20 150.00 300.00
5 Kevin Durant/20 75.00 200.00
6 Kyrie Irving/20 60.00 150.00
7 Kevin Love/20 15.00 40.00
8 Anthony Davis/25 75.00 150.00
9 John Wall/20 30.00 80.00
10 LaMarcus Aldridge/20 20.00 50.00
11 Klay Thompson/20 30.00 80.00
13 Chris Bosh/20 15.00 40.00
14 Chris Andersen/20 8.00 20.00
15 Jerry Stackhouse/20 12.00 30.00
17 DeMarcus Cousins/25 25.00 60.00
18 Chris Paul/20 60.00 150.00
19 Blake Griffin/25 30.00 80.00
21 Trey Burke/20 6.00 15.00
22 Gordon Hayward/20 15.00 40.00
23 Derrick Favors/20 8.00 20.00
24 Jrue Holiday/20 8.00 20.00
27 Victor Oladipo/20 8.00 20.00
29 Tim Hardaway Jr./25 6.00 15.00
30 Carmelo Anthony/20 50.00 120.00
31 Shaquille O'Neal/20 75.00 200.00
32 Bill Russell/20 75.00 200.00
33 Larry Bird/20 40.00 100.00
34 Magic Johnson/20 40.00 100.00
35 Kareem Abdul-Jabbar/20 30.00 80.00
36 Jerry West/20 30.00 80.00
37 Dominique Wilkins/25 15.00 40.00
38 Clyde Drexler/20 25.00 60.00
39 Dolph Schayes/20 10.00 25.00
40 John Stockton/20 50.00 120.00
41 Lenny Wilkens/25 15.00 40.00
42 Glen Rice/20 8.00 20.00
43 Julius Erving/20 50.00 120.00
44 Earl Monroe/20 12.00 30.00
45 Karl Malone/25 30.00 80.00
46 Dennis Rodman/25 40.00 100.00
47 Grant Hill/20 25.00 60.00
48 Anfernee Hardaway/20 40.00 100.00
49 Latrell Sprewell/25 15.00 40.00
50 Tracy McGrady/25 40.00 100.00
51 Bill Walton/25 15.00 40.00
52 Nate Archibald/25 8.00 20.00
53 David Robinson/25 30.00 80.00
54 Jason Kidd/25 15.00 40.00
55 Walt Frazier/25 12.00 30.00
56 Tom Heinsohn/25 12.00 30.00
57 Hal Greer/25 8.00 20.00
58 Tim Hardaway/25 12.00 30.00
59 Muggsy Bogues/25 10.00 25.00
60 Chris Mullin/25 12.00 30.00
61 Giannis Antetokounmpo/25 30.00 80.00
62 Michael Carter-Williams/25 15.00 40.00
63 Reggie Jackson/25 8.00 20.00
64 Kawhi Leonard/25 75.00 200.00
65 Danny Green/25 15.00 40.00
67 Rik Smits/25 20.00 50.00
68 Tobias Harris/25 8.00 20.00
69 Eric Gordon/25 8.00 20.00
71 Kyle Korver/25 8.00 20.00
73 Nene/25 8.00 20.00
74 J.R. Smith/25 8.00 20.00
75 Harrison Barnes/25 8.00 20.00

2014-15 Panini Flawless USA Basketball Autographs Blue

RANDOM INSERTS IN PACKS
STATED PRINT RUN 25 SER.#'d SETS
*RED/25: .4X TO 1X BASIC
*WHITE/25: .4X TO 1X BASIC
1 Chris Mullin 40.00 100.00
2 Christian Laettner 30.00 80.00
3 Anfernee Hardaway 150.00 400.00
4 Grant Hill 60.00 150.00
5 Kyrie Irving 150.00 400.00
6 Hakeem Olajuwon 75.00 200.00
7 Stephen Curry 500.00 800.00
8 Klay Thompson 150.00 300.00
9 Kenneth Faried 25.00 60.00
10 DeMarcus Cousins 50.00 120.00
11 Mason Plumlee 25.00 60.00
12 Andre Drummond 75.00 200.00
13 James Harden 75.00 200.00
15 Tyson Chandler 25.00 60.00
16 Chris Paul 100.00 250.00
17 Chris Bosh 30.00 80.00
18 Gary Payton 30.00 80.00
19 David Robinson 60.00 150.00
20 John Stockton 100.00 250.00
21 Karl Malone 100.00 250.00
22 Larry Bird 150.00 400.00
23 Magic Johnson 125.00 300.00
25 Ray Allen 60.00 150.00
26 Vince Carter 100.00 250.00
27 Tim Hardaway 30.00 80.00
28 Jason Kidd 75.00 200.00
29 Alonzo Mourning 40.00 100.00

2014-15 Panini Flawless Flawless Finishes Autographs

RANDOM INSERTS IN PACKS
STATED PRINT RUN 20 SER.#'d SETS
*RUBY/15: .5X TO 1.2X BASIC
1 Gordon Hayward 15.00 40.00
2 Alonzo Mourning 20.00 50.00
4 Andrew Wiggins
5 Anfernee Hardaway 40.00 100.00
6 Anthony Davis 125.00 250.00
8 Bill Russell 75.00 200.00
9 Bradley Beal 20.00 50.00
10 Carmelo Anthony 50.00 120.00
11 Chris Bosh 15.00 40.00
12 Cliff Hagan 8.00 20.00
13 Dennis Rodman 40.00 100.00
14 James Harden 60.00 150.00
15 Frank Ramsey 20.00 50.00
16 George Gervin 12.00 30.00
18 Rik Smits 8.00 20.00
19 James Worthy 20.00 50.00
20 Jeff Green 25.00 60.00
21 Jerry West 25.00 60.00
22 Jo Jo White 10.00 25.00
23 Joe Dumars 10.00 25.00
25 John Stockton 50.00 120.00
26 John Wall 25.00 60.00
27 Kareem Abdul-Jabbar 30.00 80.00
28 Karl Malone 30.00 80.00
29 Kevin Durant 100.00 200.00
30 DeMarcus Cousins 25.00 60.00
31 Kobe Bryant 150.00 300.00
32 Kyrie Irving 60.00 150.00
33 Larry Bird 40.00 100.00
34 Latrell Sprewell 30.00 80.00
35 Magic Johnson 40.00 100.00
36 Ralph Sampson 8.00 20.00
37 Ray Allen 30.00 80.00
38 Robert Horry 20.00 50.00
39 Shaquille O'Neal 100.00 250.00
40 Stephen Curry 250.00 500.00
41 Klay Thompson 30.00 80.00
42 Steve Kerr 20.00 50.00
45 Tracy McGrady 25.00 60.00
46 Ty Lawson 6.00 15.00
47 Sean Elliott 10.00 25.00
48 Walt Frazier 12.00 30.00
49 Zach LaVine 100.00 250.00
50 Zach Randolph 8.00 20.00

2014-15 Panini Flawless Hall of Fame Autographs

RANDOM INSERTS IN PACKS
STATED PRINT RUN 20 SER.#'d SETS
*RUBY/15: .5X TO 1.2X BASIC
1 Larry Bird 40.00 100.00
2 Magic Johnson 40.00 100.00
3 David Robinson 20.00 50.00
4 Sarunas Marciulionis 10.00 25.00
5 Cliff Hagan 8.00 20.00
6 Larry Brown 8.00 20.00
7 Don Nelson 25.00 60.00
8 Chris Mullin 12.00 30.00
9 Mitch Richmond 25.00 60.00
10 Lenny Wilkens 15.00 40.00
11 Dave Cowens 15.00 40.00
12 Dennis Rodman 40.00 100.00
13 Julius Erving 25.00 60.00
14 George Gervin 12.00 30.00
15 Bernard King 8.00 20.00
16 James Worthy 20.00 50.00
17 Dominique Wilkins 15.00 40.00
18 John Stockton 50.00 120.00
19 Karl Malone 30.00 80.00
20 Gary Payton 15.00 40.00
21 Frank Ramsey 20.00 50.00
22 Ralph Sampson 8.00 20.00
23 Artis Gilmore 15.00 40.00
24 Hakeem Olajuwon 30.00 80.00
25 Clyde Drexler 15.00 40.00

2014-15 Panini Flawless Now and Then Signatures

RANDOM INSERTS IN PACKS
STATED PRINT RUN 20 SER.#'d SETS
*RUBY/15: .5X TO 1.2X BASIC
1 Blake Griffin 30.00 80.00
2 Stephen Curry 150.00 400.00
4 Brook Lopez 8.00 20.00
5 Kevin Durant 100.00 200.00
6 John Wall 30.00 80.00
7 Bradley Beal 20.00 50.00
8 Carmelo Anthony 50.00 120.00
9 DeMarcus Cousins 50.00 120.00
10 Chris Paul 60.00 150.00
11 Anthony Davis 100.00 250.00
12 Eric Gordon 8.00 20.00
13 Tyreke Evans 6.00 15.00
14 Jrue Holiday 8.00 20.00
17 Taj Gibson 8.00 20.00
18 Tayshaun Prince 20.00 50.00
19 Kenneth Faried 15.00 40.00
20 Ty Lawson 6.00 15.00
21 Reggie Jackson 15.00 40.00
23 Harrison Barnes 20.00 50.00
25 Nick Young 12.00 30.00
26 Kyle Korver 8.00 20.00
27 Vince Carter 30.00 80.00
29 Chris Bosh 10.00 25.00
30 Tobias Harris 10.00 25.00
31 LaMarcus Aldridge 20.00 50.00
32 Kawhi Leonard 100.00 250.00
33 Danny Green 15.00 40.00
34 Gordon Hayward 20.00 50.00

2014-15 Panini Flawless Patch Autographs

RANDOM INSERTS IN PACKS
STATED PRINT RUN B/WN 9-25 COPIES PER
NO PRICING ON QTY 11 OR LESS
*RUBY/15: .5X TO 1.2X BASIC
1 Kobe Bryant/25 200.00 500.00
2 Kevin Durant/25 125.00 300.00
3 Blake Griffin/25 15.00 40.00
4 Chris Paul/25 50.00 120.00
5 Ricky Rubio/25 30.00 80.00
7 Larry Bird/25 75.00 200.00
9 Carmelo Anthony/25 20.00 50.00
10 DeMarcus Cousins/25 30.00 80.00
11 Hakeem Olajuwon/25 50.00 120.00
12 Jerry West/25 60.00 150.00
13 John Stockton/25 30.00 80.00
14 John Wall/25 30.00 80.00
15 Adrian Dantley/25 12.00 30.00
16 Andre Drummond/25 15.00 40.00
17 Andrew Wiggins/25 400.00 800.00
18 Antoine Walker/18 12.00 30.00
19 Bradley Beal/25 12.00 30.00
20 Nene/25 12.00 30.00
21 Walter Davis/25 10.00 25.00
22 James Harden/25 50.00 120.00
23 David Robinson/25 40.00 100.00
24 Dikembe Mutombo/15 25.00 60.00
25 Earl Monroe/25 12.00 30.00
26 Grant Hill/25 50.00 120.00
27 J.J. Redick/25 15.00 40.00
28 Kenneth Faried/25 15.00 40.00
30 Kyle Korver/25 15.00 40.00
31 Giannis Antetokounmpo/25 150.00 400.00
32 Zach Randolph/25 12.00 30.00
33 Michael Carter-Williams/25 12.00 30.00
37 Shaquille O'Neal/25 75.00 200.00
40 Victor Oladipo/25 12.00 30.00
42 Karl Malone/25 30.00 80.00
43 Elfrid Payton/25 15.00 40.00
44 LaMarcus Aldridge/25 25.00 60.00
46 Mike Conley/25 12.00 30.00
47 Nick Young/25 12.00 30.00
49 Ray Allen/25 60.00 150.00
50 Robert Parish/25 15.00 40.00
51 Stephen Curry/25 300.00 600.00
52 Tobias Harris/25 12.00 30.00
53 Ty Lawson/25 10.00 25.00
57 Danny Green/25 15.00 40.00
58 Michael Kidd-Gilchrist/25 15.00 40.00
59 Kemba Walker/25 25.00 60.00
61 Tyson Chandler/20 12.00 30.00
62 C.J. McCollum/25 30.00 80.00
63 Trey Burke/18 10.00 25.00
64 Dante Exum/25 50.00 120.00
65 Marcus Smart/25 15.00 40.00

2014-15 Panini Flawless Red White and Blue Triple Autographs

RANDOM INSERTS IN PACKS
STATED PRINT RUN 25 SER.#'d SETS
RWBKCC Paul/Anthony/Bryant 1800.00 2200.00
RWBLMC Johnson/Drexler/Bird
RWBDJK Robinson/Stockton/Malone 700.00 900.00
RWBCCK Mullin/Drexler/Malone 500.00 800.00
RWBSKA Davis/Irving/Curry
RWBHDK Olajuwon/Robinson/Malone
RWBGAG Hardaway/Hill/Payton 500.00 800.00
RWBKKC Durant/Paul/Bryant 1800.00 2200.00

2014-15 Panini Flawless Rookie Autographs

RANDOM INSERTS IN PACKS
STATED PRINT RUN 25 SER.#'d SETS
*RUBY/15: .5X TO 1.2X BASIC
RAAG Aaron Gordon 50.00 120.00
RAAW Andrew Wiggins
RADE Dante Exum 40.00 100.00
RAEP Elfrid Payton 25.00 60.00
RAJC Jordan Clarkson 200.00 400.00
RAJE Joel Embiid 300.00 600.00
RAJN Jusuf Nurkic 20.00 50.00
RAJP Jabari Parker 400.00 600.00
RAJR Julius Randle 75.00 200.00
RALG Langston Galloway 10.00 25.00
RAMS Marcus Smart 30.00 80.00
RASD Spencer Dinwiddie 12.00 30.00
RASN Shabazz Napier 25.00 60.00
RAZL Zach LaVine 100.00 250.00

2014-15 Panini Flawless Super Signatures

RANDOM INSERTS IN PACKS
STATED PRINT RUN 25 SER.#'d SETS
*RUBY/15: .5X TO 1.2X BASIC
1 Kobe Bryant 150.00 300.00
2 Kevin Durant 100.00 200.00
3 Kyrie Irving 60.00 150.00
4 John Wall 30.00 80.00
5 Blake Griffin 30.00 80.00
6 Anthony Davis 125.00 250.00
7 Karl Malone 30.00 80.00
8 Kareem Abdul-Jabbar 30.00 80.00
9 Kenneth Faried 15.00 40.00
10 James Harden 60.00 150.00
11 Rik Smits 10.00 25.00
12 John Stockton 40.00 100.00
13 Bradley Beal 20.00 50.00
15 Jerry Stackhouse 20.00 50.00
16 Tim Hardaway 12.00 30.00
18 Glen Rice 10.00 25.00
19 Jamaal Wilkes 10.00 25.00
20 Chris Paul 60.00 150.00
21 Bill Russell 60.00 150.00
22 Kevin McHale 20.00 50.00
23 Hakeem Olajuwon 30.00 80.00
24 Jason Kidd 20.00 50.00
25 Vince Carter 30.00 80.00
28 Damon Stoudamire 12.00 30.00
29 Bill Walton 12.00 30.00
30 Earl Monroe 15.00 40.00
31 Jerry West 25.00 60.00
32 Joe Dumars 12.00 30.00
33 Jo Jo White 6.00 15.00
34 Andre Drummond 25.00 60.00
35 Frank Ramsey 20.00 50.00
36 Shaquille O'Neal 75.00 200.00
37 Cliff Hagan 8.00 20.00
38 Jrue Holiday 8.00 20.00
39 Rony Seikaly 6.00 15.00
40 Nate Archibald 8.00 20.00
41 Dominique Wilkins 15.00 40.00
42 David Robinson 20.00 50.00
44 Robert Horry 15.00 40.00
45 Sarunas Marciulionis 10.00 25.00
46 Grant Hill 25.00 60.00
47 Dikembe Mutombo 15.00 40.00
48 Dave Cowens 15.00 40.00
49 Byron Scott 8.00 20.00
50 Michael Finley 20.00 50.00

2014-15 Panini Flawless Transitions Autographs

RANDOM INSERTS IN PACKS
STATED PRINT RUN 10 SER.#'d SETS
ALL VERSIONS EQUALLY PRICED
*EMERALD/5: .5X TO 1.2X BASIC
1 Latrell Sprewell 75.00 150.00
2 Latrell Sprewell 75.00 150.00
3 Latrell Sprewell 75.00 150.00
4 Latrell Sprewell 75.00 150.00
8 Chris Paul 75.00 150.00
9 Chris Paul 75.00 150.00
10 Chris Paul 75.00 150.00
11 Chris Paul 75.00 150.00
12 Carmelo Anthony 100.00 200.00
13 Carmelo Anthony 100.00 200.00
14 Carmelo Anthony 100.00 200.00
15 Carmelo Anthony 100.00 200.00
16 Pau Gasol 40.00 100.00
17 Pau Gasol 40.00 100.00
18 Pau Gasol 40.00 100.00
19 Pau Gasol 40.00 100.00
20 Zach Randolph 12.00 30.00
21 Zach Randolph 12.00 30.00
22 Zach Randolph 12.00 30.00
23 Zach Randolph 12.00 30.00
24 Zach Randolph 12.00 30.00
25 Mark Aguirre 12.00 30.00
26 Mark Aguirre 12.00 30.00
27 Mark Aguirre 12.00 30.00
28 Mark Aguirre 12.00 30.00
29 J.J. Redick 20.00 50.00
30 J.J. Redick 20.00 50.00
31 J.J. Redick 20.00 50.00
38 Karl Malone 40.00 100.00
39 Karl Malone 40.00 100.00
40 Karl Malone 40.00 100.00
41 Karl Malone 40.00 100.00
42 Jason Terry 12.00 30.00
43 Jason Terry 12.00 30.00
44 Jason Terry 12.00 30.00
45 Jason Terry 12.00 30.00
46 Jason Terry 12.00 30.00
47 Robert Horry 20.00 50.00
48 Robert Horry 20.00 50.00
49 Robert Horry 20.00 50.00
50 Robert Horry 20.00 50.00
51 Michael Finley 12.00 30.00
52 Michael Finley 12.00 30.00
53 Michael Finley 12.00 30.00
54 Michael Finley 12.00 30.00
55 Michael Finley 12.00 30.00
56 Ray Allen 50.00 120.00
57 Ray Allen 50.00 120.00
58 Ray Allen 50.00 120.00
59 Ray Allen 50.00 120.00
60 Ray Allen 50.00 120.00
61 Ray Allen 50.00 120.00
62 Nate Archibald 12.00 30.00
63 Nate Archibald 12.00 30.00
64 Nate Archibald 12.00 30.00
65 Nate Archibald 12.00 30.00
66 Nate Archibald 12.00 30.00
67 Eddie Jones 15.00 40.00
68 Eddie Jones 15.00 40.00
69 Eddie Jones 15.00 40.00
70 Eddie Jones 15.00 40.00
71 Eddie Jones 15.00 40.00
72 Eddie Jones 15.00 40.00
73 Nick Van Exel 60.00 150.00
74 Nick Van Exel 60.00 150.00
75 Nick Van Exel 60.00 150.00
76 Nick Van Exel 60.00 150.00
77 Nick Van Exel 60.00 150.00
78 Nick Van Exel 60.00 150.00
79 Nick Van Exel 60.00 150.00
80 Robert Parish 15.00 40.00
81 Robert Parish 15.00 40.00
82 Robert Parish 15.00 40.00
83 Robert Parish 15.00 40.00
84 Bill Walton 15.00 40.00
85 Bill Walton 15.00 40.00
86 Bill Walton 15.00 40.00
87 Bill Walton 15.00 40.00
88 Tyreke Evans
89 Tyreke Evans
90 Kevin Love 25.00 60.00
91 Kevin Love 25.00 60.00
92 Kevin Love 25.00 60.00
93 Kevin Love 25.00 60.00
94 Glen Rice 12.00 30.00
95 Glen Rice 12.00 30.00
96 Glen Rice 12.00 30.00
97 Glen Rice 12.00 30.00
98 Glen Rice 12.00 30.00
99 Glen Rice 12.00 30.00
100 Glen Rice 12.00 30.00

2015-16 Panini Flawless

1-150 PRINT RUN 20 SER.#'d SETS
151-170 PRINT RUN 10 SER.#'d SETS
NO PRICING AVAILABLE ON 151-170
1 Kobe Bryant 150.00 400.00
2 Kevin Durant 50.00 120.00
3 Kyrie Irving 40.00 100.00
4 Jimmy Butler 25.00 60.00
5 Damian Lillard 25.00 60.00
6 Dirk Nowitzki 30.00 80.00
7 Eric Bledsoe 10.00 25.00
8 Brandon Knight 10.00 25.00
9 Dwyane Wade 20.00 50.00
10 Chris Bosh 12.00 30.00
11 Paul George 20.00 50.00
12 Monta Ellis 10.00 25.00
13 Russell Westbrook 60.00 150.00
14 Anthony Davis 50.00 120.00
15 Gordon Hayward 12.00 30.00
16 Kemba Walker 12.00 30.00
17 Nicolas Batum 10.00 25.00
18 Lance Stephenson 10.00 25.00
19 LeBron James 150.00 400.00
20 Kevin Love 12.00 30.00
21 Stephen Curry 125.00 300.00
22 Klay Thompson 40.00 100.00
23 Draymond Green 20.00 50.00
24 Kenneth Faried 10.00 25.00
25 James Harden 20.00 50.00
26 Dwight Howard 15.00 40.00
27 Giannis Antetokounmpo 25.00 60.00
28 Jabari Parker 20.00 50.00
29 Chris Paul 15.00 40.00
30 Blake Griffin 12.00 30.00
31 Paul Pierce 12.00 30.00

32 DeMar DeRozan 12.00 30.00
33 Kyle Lowry 10.00 25.00
34 Tim Duncan 75.00 200.00
35 Manu Ginobili 25.00 60.00
36 Tony Parker 15.00 40.00
37 LaMarcus Aldridge 20.00 50.00
38 Jrue Holiday 10.00 25.00
39 Marc Gasol 12.00 30.00
40 Mike Conley 12.00 30.00
41 C.J. McCollum 12.00 30.00
42 Andrew Wiggins 30.00 80.00
43 Zach LaVine 20.00 50.00
44 Greg Monroe 10.00 25.00
45 Carmelo Anthony 20.00 50.00
46 Goran Dragic 10.00 25.00
47 John Wall 20.00 50.00
48 Bradley Beal 12.00 30.00
49 Marcin Gortat 10.00 25.00
50 Brook Lopez 10.00 25.00
51 Thaddeus Young 8.00 20.00
52 Rudy Gobert 12.00 30.00
53 Allen Crabbe 8.00 20.00
54 Al Horford 10.00 25.00
55 Dennis Schroder 12.00 30.00
56 Jeff Teague 10.00 25.00
57 Jeremy Lin 30.00 80.00
58 Derrick Rose 30.00 80.00
59 Pau Gasol 12.00 30.00
60 Hassan Whiteside 15.00 40.00
61 Deron Williams 10.00 25.00
62 Wesley Matthews 8.00 20.00
63 J.R. Smith 15.00 40.00
64 Will Barton 8.00 20.00
65 Danilo Gallinari 10.00 25.00
66 Reggie Jackson 10.00 25.00
67 Andre Drummond 12.00 30.00
68 Kentavious Caldwell-Pope 10.00 25.00
69 Harrison Barnes 10.00 25.00
70 J.J. Redick 12.00 30.00
71 DeAndre Jordan 12.00 30.00
72 Jordan Clarkson 25.00 60.00
73 Lou Williams 10.00 25.00
74 Khris Middleton 10.00 25.00
75 Kevin Garnett 40.00 100.00
76 Ryan Anderson 10.00 25.00
77 Enes Kanter 8.00 20.00
78 Isaiah Thomas 12.00 30.00
79 Avery Bradley 10.00 25.00
80 Jae Crowder 20.00 50.00
81 Arron Afflalo 8.00 20.00
82 Robin Lopez 8.00 20.00
83 Nikola Vucevic 10.00 25.00
84 Victor Oladipo 15.00 40.00
85 Elfrid Payton 10.00 25.00
86 Aaron Gordon 12.00 30.00
87 Ish Smith 8.00 20.00
88 Nerlens Noel 10.00 25.00
89 Rajon Rondo 12.00 30.00
90 DeMarcus Cousins 15.00 40.00
91 Rudy Gay 12.00 30.00
92 DeMarre Carroll 8.00 20.00
93 Rodney Hood 15.00 40.00
94 Alec Burks 8.00 20.00
95 Paul Millsap 12.00 30.00
96 Evan Turner 10.00 25.00
97 Al Jefferson 10.00 25.00
98 Nikola Mirotic 10.00 25.00
99 Doug McDermott 10.00 25.00
100 Tobias Harris 10.00 25.00
101 Trevor Ariza 10.00 25.00
102 Alex Len 8.00 20.00
103 Chandler Parsons 10.00 25.00
104 Zaza Pachulia 8.00 20.00
105 George Hill 10.00 25.00
106 Omri Casspi 8.00 20.00
107 Tristan Thompson 10.00 25.00
108 Zach Randolph 10.00 25.00
109 Norris Cole 8.00 20.00
110 Bojan Bogdanovic 10.00 25.00
111 Dion Waiters 10.00 25.00
112 Serge Ibaka 10.00 25.00
113 Matthew Dellavedova 15.00 40.00
114 Andre Iguodala 20.00 50.00
115 Andrew Bogut 10.00 25.00
116 Kawhi Leonard 50.00 120.00
117 Ricky Rubio 20.00 50.00
118 Patrick Beverley 8.00 20.00
119 Gerald Henderson 8.00 20.00
120 Otto Porter 10.00 25.00
121 Jonas Valanciunas 12.00 30.00
122 Marcus Morris 8.00 20.00
123 Austin Rivers 10.00 25.00
124 Danny Green 10.00 25.00
125 Vince Carter 25.00 60.00
126 Scottie Pippen 60.00 150.00
127 Larry Bird 40.00 100.00
128 Magic Johnson 30.00 80.00
129 Wilt Chamberlain 30.00 80.00
130 Patrick Ewing 20.00 50.00
131 Oscar Robertson 15.00 40.00
132 Shaquille O'Neal 30.00 80.00
133 John Stockton 20.00 50.00
134 Julius Erving 20.00 50.00
135 Pete Maravich 30.00 80.00
136 Karl-Anthony Towns RC 500.00 1000.00
137 D'Angelo Russell RC 300.00 600.00
138 Jahlil Okafor RC 60.00 150.00
139 Kristaps Porzingis RC 500.00 800.00
140 Justise Winslow RC 100.00 250.00
141 Devin Booker RC 350.00 700.00
142 Emmanuel Mudiay RC 100.00 250.00
143 Myles Turner RC 60.00 150.00
144 Bobby Portis RC 40.00 100.00
145 Nikola Jokic RC 200.00 500.00
146 Willie Cauley-Stein RC 40.00 100.00
147 Mario Hezonja RC 100.00 250.00
148 Cameron Payne RC 30.00 80.00
149 Stanley Johnson RC 50.00 120.00
150 Stephen Curry MVP 300.00 500.00

2015-16 Panini Flawless Ruby

*RUBY 1-135/150: .4X TO 1X BASIC
*RUBY 136-149: .4X TO 1X BASIC
RANDOM INSERTS IN PACKS
STATED PRINT RUN 15 SER.#'d SETS

2015-16 Panini Flawless Dual Diamond Memorabilia

RANDOM INSERTS IN PACKS
PRINT RUNS B/WN 16-25 COPIES PER
NO PRICING ON QTY 12 OR LESS
2 Towns/Porzingis/25 60.00 150.00
5 Durant/Westbrook/25 50.00 120.00
7 Leonard/Duncan/25 60.00 150.00
8 McCollum/Lillard/25 30.00 80.00
9 Ellis/George/25 20.00 50.00
10 Cousins/Rondo/25 15.00 40.00
13 Beal/Wall/16 25.00 60.00
15 Love/Westbrook/25 40.00 100.00
16 Russell/Clarkson/25 25.00 60.00
17 Paul/Duncan/25 30.00 80.00
18 Wiggins/Towns/25 150.00 300.00
19 Bird/Johnson/25 30.00 80.00

2015-16 Panini Flawless Dual Diamond Memorabilia Ruby

*RUBY: .4X TO 1X BASIC
RANDOM INSERTS IN PACKS
PRINT RUNS B/WN 12-15 COPIES PER
NO PRICING ON QTY 14 OR LESS
1 Thompson/Curry/15 200.00 400.00
12 Williams/Nowitzki/15 30.00 80.00

2015-16 Panini Flawless Flawless Autographs

RANDOM INSERTS IN PACKS
STATED PRINT RUN 25 SER.#'D SETS
*RUBY/15: .4X TO 1X BASIC
FAAA Alvan Adams 5.00 12.00
FAAB Andrew Bogut 10.00 25.00
FAAB Alec Burks 5.00 12.00
FAAH Anfernee Hardaway 40.00 100.00
FAAW Andrew Wiggins 50.00 120.00
FABG Blake Griffin 20.00 50.00
FABK Brandon Knight 6.00 15.00
FABW Bill Walton 8.00 20.00
FACA Carmelo Anthony 25.00 60.00
FACD Clyde Drexler 15.00 40.00
FACM Cedric Maxwell 5.00 12.00
FACP Chris Paul 30.00 80.00
FADC Dell Curry 8.00 20.00
FADD DeMar DeRozan 12.00 30.00
FADH Dwight Howard 12.00 30.00
FADR David Robinson 25.00 60.00
FADR Dennis Rodman 25.00 60.00
FADS Dennis Scott 5.00 12.00
FADT David Thompson 6.00 15.00
FADW Dwyane Wade 60.00 150.00
FAEB Eric Bledsoe 8.00 20.00
FAET Evan Turner 6.00 15.00
FAGG George Gervin 10.00 25.00
FAGH Grant Hill 20.00 50.00
FAGH Gordon Hayward 8.00 20.00
FAGP Gary Payton 12.00 30.00
FAHO Hakeem Olajuwon 20.00 50.00
FAHW Hassan Whiteside 15.00 40.00
FAIT Isiah Thomas 12.00 30.00
FAJB Junior Bridgeman 5.00 12.00
FAJB Jimmy Butler 50.00 120.00
FAJD Joe Dumars 10.00 25.00
FAJK Jason Kidd 20.00 50.00
FAJM Jamal Mashburn 8.00 20.00
FAJR Jalen Rose 8.00 20.00
FAJS John Stockton 30.00 80.00
FAJS Jerry Stackhouse 12.00 30.00
FAJW John Wall 30.00 80.00
FAJW Jerry West 30.00 80.00
FAJW James Worthy 12.00 30.00
FAKB Kobe Bryant 150.00 300.00
FAKD Kevin Durant 75.00 200.00
FAKI Kyrie Irving 60.00 150.00
FAKL Kevin Love 15.00 40.00
FAKM Karl Malone 20.00 50.00
FAKM Khris Middleton 6.00 15.00
FALA LaMarcus Aldridge 25.00 60.00
FALB Larry Bird 60.00 150.00
FAMD Matthew Dellavedova 10.00 25.00
FAMJ Marques Johnson 6.00 15.00
FAMJ Magic Johnson 40.00 100.00
FAMR Mitch Richmond 10.00 25.00
FAPE Patrick Ewing 125.00 300.00
FAPG Pau Gasol 12.00 30.00
FARA Ray Allen 40.00 100.00
FARH Robert Horry 8.00 20.00
FASP Scottie Pippen 75.00 200.00
FATH Tim Hardaway 8.00 20.00
FATK Toni Kukoc 20.00 50.00
FATW T.J. Warren 6.00 15.00
FAVO Victor Oladipo 10.00 25.00

2015-16 Panini Flawless Now and Then Signatures

RANDOM INSERTS IN PACKS
STATED PRINT RUN 25 SER.#'D SETS
*RUBY/15: .4X TO 1X BASIC
NTAB Andrew Bogut 10.00 25.00
NTAB Avery Bradley 6.00 15.00
NTAW Andrew Wiggins 50.00 120.00
NTBK Brandon Knight 6.00 15.00
NTDD DeMar DeRozan 12.00 30.00
NTDH Dwight Howard 12.00 30.00
NTDW Dwyane Wade 60.00 150.00
NTEB Eric Bledsoe 8.00 20.00
NTEP Elfrid Payton 6.00 15.00
NTET Evan Turner 6.00 15.00
NTHW Hassan Whiteside 15.00 40.00
NTJB Jimmy Butler 50.00 120.00
NTJP Jabari Parker 30.00 80.00
NTJR Julius Randle 12.00 30.00
NTJS Josh Smith 10.00 25.00
NTJS J.R. Smith 10.00 25.00
NTKB Kobe Bryant 400.00 800.00
NTKI Kyrie Irving 60.00 150.00
NTKL Kevin Love 15.00 40.00
NTLA LaMarcus Aldridge 25.00 60.00
NTMC Michael Carter-Williams 8.00 20.00
NTVO Victor Oladipo 10.00 25.00
NTZL Zach LaVine 30.00 80.00
NTZR Zach Randolph 8.00 20.00

2015-16 Panini Flawless Patches

RANDOM INSERTS IN PACKS
PRINT RUNS B/WN 10-25 COPIES PER
NO PRICING ON QTY 12 OR LESS
3 Kevin Durant/25 50.00 120.00
4 Grant Hill/17 15.00 40.00
5 DeAndre Jordan/25 12.00 30.00
6 Marcus Smart/23 8.00 20.00
10 Goran Dragic/21 10.00 25.00
11 Jeremy Lin/25 30.00 80.00
12 Kyle Lowry/23 10.00 25.00
13 Dwyane Wade/25 30.00 80.00
15 Damian Lillard/25 40.00 100.00
16 LeBron James/25 100.00 250.00
17 Isaiah Thomas/25 40.00 100.00
18 DeMarcus Cousins/25 15.00 40.00
19 Vince Carter/25 25.00 60.00
22 Harrison Barnes/23 15.00 40.00
23 Blake Griffin/19 20.00 50.00
24 O.J. Mayo/25 4.00 10.00
27 T.J. Warren/25 12.00 30.00
28 Al Jefferson/25 5.00 12.00
29 Anthony Davis/25 40.00 100.00
30 Kyrie Irving/25 30.00 80.00
31 Pau Gasol/24 12.00 30.00
32 Derrick Rose/25 30.00 80.00
33 Jimmy Butler/25 30.00 80.00
34 Rudy Gobert/25 10.00 25.00
35 Stephen Curry/23 60.00 150.00
36 Russell Westbrook/25 75.00 200.00
39 Aaron Gordon/25 12.00 30.00
41 Jabari Parker/25 20.00 50.00

2015-16 Panini Flawless Patches Ruby

*RUBY: .4X TO 1X BASIC
RANDOM INSERTS IN PACKS
PRINT RUNS B/WN 8-15 COPIES PER
NO PRICING ON QTY 14 OR LESS
7 Marcus Morris/15 4.00 10.00
8 Reggie Jackson/15 12.00 30.00
14 Kevin Love/15 20.00 50.00
20 James Harden/15 25.00 60.00
21 Mike Conley/15 10.00 25.00
37 Rodney Hood/15 8.00 20.00
42 Tyson Chandler/15

2015-16 Panini Flawless Premium Ink

RANDOM INSERTS IN PACKS
STATED PRINT RUN 25 SER.#'D SETS
*RUBY/15: .4X TO 1X BASIC
PIAA Alvan Adams 5.00 12.00
PIAB Alec Burks 5.00 12.00
PIAB Avery Bradley 6.00 15.00
PIAD Anthony Davis 60.00 150.00
PIAH Al Horford 6.00 15.00
PIAI Allen Iverson 75.00 200.00
PIAM Antonio McDyess 8.00 20.00
PIAW Andrew Wiggins 40.00 100.00
PIBG Blake Griffin 25.00 60.00
PIBK Bernard King 6.00 15.00
PIBK Brandon Knight 6.00 15.00
PIBM Boban Marjanovic 10.00 25.00
PIBP Bobby Portis 15.00 40.00
PIBW Bill Walton 10.00 25.00
PICA Carmelo Anthony 25.00 60.00
PICB Chauncey Billups 10.00 25.00
PICB Chris Bosh 8.00 20.00
PICD Clyde Drexler 15.00 40.00
PICM Cedric Maxwell 5.00 12.00
PICP Cameron Payne 6.00 15.00
PICP Chris Paul 30.00 80.00
PIDB Devin Booker 150.00 400.00
PIDC Dell Curry 8.00 20.00
PIDC DeMarre Carroll 5.00 12.00
PIDG Danilo Gallinari 8.00 20.00
PIDH Dwight Howard 20.00 50.00
PIDM Dikembe Mutombo 12.00 30.00
PIDM Dan Majerle 6.00 15.00
PIDR David Robinson 25.00 60.00
PIDR D'Angelo Russell 125.00 300.00
PIDR Dennis Rodman 15.00 40.00
PIDT David Thompson 6.00 15.00
PIDW Dwyane Wade 40.00 100.00
PIEB Eric Bledsoe 8.00 20.00
PIEH Elvin Hayes 8.00 20.00
PIEM Emmanuel Mudiay 40.00 100.00
PIGG George Gervin 10.00 25.00
PIGH Grant Hill 20.00 50.00
PIGH Gordon Hayward 10.00 25.00
PIGP Gary Payton 12.00 30.00
PIHG Horace Grant 10.00 25.00
PIHO Hakeem Olajuwon 20.00 50.00
PIHW Hassan Whiteside 15.00 40.00
PIIT Isiah Thomas 12.00 30.00
PIJB Jimmy Butler 30.00 80.00
PIJD Joe Dumars 8.00 20.00
PIJE Julius Erving 40.00 100.00
PIJK Jason Kidd 20.00 50.00
PIJM Jamal Mashburn 8.00 20.00
PIJO Jahlil Okafor 30.00 80.00
PIJR Jalen Rose 8.00 20.00
PIJR Julius Randle 12.00 30.00
PIJS Jerry Stackhouse 6.00 15.00
PIJS John Stockton 30.00 80.00
PIJS J.R. Smith 10.00 25.00
PIJS John Starks 6.00 15.00
PIJW Jerry West 30.00 80.00
PIJW James Worthy 12.00 30.00
PIJW Justise Winslow 30.00 80.00
PIKB Kobe Bryant 150.00 300.00
PIKD Kevin Durant 60.00 150.00
PIKF Kenneth Faried 6.00 15.00
PIKI Kyrie Irving 40.00 100.00
PIKL Kevin Love 15.00 40.00
PIKM Karl Malone 20.00 50.00
PIKP Kristaps Porzingis 100.00 250.00
PIKT Karl-Anthony Towns 300.00 600.00
PILA LaMarcus Aldridge 25.00 60.00
PILB Larry Bird 50.00 120.00
PIMD Matthew Dellavedova 10.00 25.00
PIMH Mario Hezonja 15.00 40.00
PIMJ Marques Johnson 6.00 15.00
PIMJ Magic Johnson 40.00 100.00
PIMR Mitch Richmond 10.00 25.00
PIMS Marcus Smart 6.00 15.00
PIMT Myles Turner 50.00 120.00
PINJ Nikola Jokic 200.00 500.00
PIPE Patrick Ewing 100.00 250.00
PIPG Pau Gasol 12.00 30.00
PIRA Ray Allen 25.00 60.00
PIRH Robert Horry 8.00 20.00
PISC Stephen Curry 200.00 400.00
PISP Scottie Pippen 60.00 150.00
PITH Tim Hardaway 8.00 20.00
PITK Toni Kukoc 10.00 25.00
PITL Trey Lyles 20.00 50.00
PITM Tracy McGrady 30.00 80.00
PIVO Victor Oladipo 10.00 25.00
PIWC Willie Cauley-Stein 40.00 100.00
PIZL Zach LaVine 30.00 80.00

2015-16 Panini Flawless Rookie Autographs

RANDOM INSERTS IN PACKS
STATED PRINT RUN 25 SER.#'D SETS
*RUBY/15: .4X TO 1X BASIC
RABM Boban Marjanovic 10.00 25.00
RABP Bobby Portis 15.00 40.00
RACP Cameron Payne 12.00 30.00
RADB Devin Booker 200.00 500.00
RADR D'Angelo Russell 125.00 300.00
RAEM Emmanuel Mudiay 50.00 120.00
RAJO Jahlil Okafor 40.00 100.00
RAJW Justise Winslow 60.00 150.00
RAKP Kristaps Porzingis 150.00 300.00
RAKT Karl-Anthony Towns 300.00 600.00
RAMH Mario Hezonja 20.00 50.00
RAMT Myles Turner 50.00 120.00
RANJ Nikola Jokic 200.00 500.00
RATL Trey Lyles 20.00 50.00
RAWC Willie Cauley-Stein 40.00 100.00

2015-16 Panini Flawless Rookie Patches

RANDOM INSERTS IN PACKS
PRINT RUNS B/WN 22-25 COPIES PER
1 Delon Wright/22 5.00 12.00
2 Jahlil Okafor/25 25.00 60.00
3 T.J. McConnell/25 5.00 12.00
4 Richaun Holmes/25 8.00 20.00
5 D'Angelo Russell/25 60.00 150.00
6 Karl-Anthony Towns/25 125.00 250.00
7 Mario Hezonja/25 10.00 25.00
9 Emmanuel Mudiay/25 20.00 50.00
10 Kelly Oubre Jr./25 15.00 40.00
11 Frank Kaminsky/25 10.00 25.00
13 Willie Cauley-Stein/25 20.00 50.00
14 Myles Turner/25 30.00 80.00
16 Stanley Johnson/25 10.00 25.00

2015-16 Panini Flawless Rookie Patches Ruby

*RUBY: .4X TO 1X BASIC
RANDOM INSERTS IN PACKS
STATED PRINT RUN 15 SER.#'d SETS
8 Justise Winslow 25.00 60.00
15 Montrezl Harrell 10.00 25.00

2015-16 Panini Flawless Super Signatures

RANDOM INSERTS IN PACKS
STATED PRINT RUN 25 SER.#'D SETS
*RUBY/15: .4X TO 1X BASIC
SSAB Alec Burks 5.00 12.00
SSAB Andrew Bogut 10.00 25.00
SSAD Anthony Davis 60.00 150.00
SSAH Al Horford 6.00 15.00
SSAH Anfernee Hardaway 40.00 100.00
SSAI Allen Iverson 75.00 200.00
SSBG Blake Griffin 20.00 50.00
SSBK Bernard King 6.00 15.00
SSBM Boban Marjanovic 10.00 25.00
SSBP Bobby Portis 15.00 40.00
SSCA Carmelo Anthony 25.00 60.00
SSCB Chris Bosh 8.00 20.00
SSCD Clyde Drexler 15.00 40.00
SSCP Chris Paul 30.00 80.00
SSCW Chris Webber 75.00 200.00
SSDB Devin Booker 150.00 300.00
SSDC DeMarre Carroll 5.00 12.00
SSDD DeMar DeRozan 15.00 40.00
SSDM Doug McDermott 6.00 15.00
SSDM Dikembe Mutombo 12.00 30.00
SSDM Dan Majerle 6.00 15.00
SSDR D'Angelo Russell 75.00 200.00
SSDR David Robinson 25.00 60.00
SSDS Dennis Scott 5.00 12.00
SSDW Dwyane Wade 30.00 80.00
SSEH Elvin Hayes 8.00 20.00
SSEP Elfrid Payton 6.00 15.00
SSGA Giannis Antetokounmpo 60.00 150.00
SSGH Gordon Hayward 15.00 40.00
SSGH Grant Hill 20.00 50.00
SSGH Gary Harris 6.00 15.00
SSGP Gary Payton 12.00 30.00
SSHO Hakeem Olajuwon 20.00 50.00
SSHW Hassan Whiteside 15.00 40.00
SSIT Isiah Thomas 12.00 30.00
SSJB Jimmy Butler 50.00 120.00
SSJD Joe Dumars 10.00 25.00
SSJE Julius Erving 30.00 80.00
SSJK Jason Kidd 20.00 50.00
SSJO Jahlil Okafor 40.00 100.00
SSJR Julius Randle 12.00 30.00
SSJR Jalen Rose 8.00 20.00
SSJS John Starks 6.00 15.00
SSJS John Stockton 30.00 80.00
SSJS J.R. Smith 10.00 25.00
SSJV Jonas Valanciunas 6.00 15.00
SSJW James Worthy 12.00 30.00
SSJW Jerry West 30.00 80.00
SSKB Kobe Bryant 150.00 300.00
SSKD Kevin Durant 75.00 200.00
SSKI Kyrie Irving 60.00 150.00
SSKL Kevin Love 15.00 40.00
SSKM Khris Middleton 6.00 15.00
SSKM Karl Malone 20.00 50.00
SSKP Kristaps Porzingis 125.00 250.00
SSKT Klay Thompson 60.00 150.00
SSKT Karl-Anthony Towns 250.00 500.00
SSKV Keith Van Horn 6.00 15.00
SSLA LaMarcus Aldridge 12.00 30.00
SSLB Larry Bird 60.00 150.00
SSMC Michael Carter-Williams 8.00 20.00
SSMC Mike Conley 8.00 20.00
SSMD Matthew Dellavedova 10.00 25.00
SSMG Marc Gasol 15.00 40.00
SSMJ Marques Johnson 6.00 15.00
SSMJ Magic Johnson 40.00 100.00
SSMR Mitch Richmond 10.00 25.00
SSPG Pau Gasol 12.00 30.00
SSPM Paul Millsap 8.00 20.00
SSRA Ray Allen 40.00 100.00
SSRH Robert Horry 8.00 20.00
SSSC Stephen Curry 200.00 400.00
SSSP Scottie Pippen 75.00 200.00
SSTH Tim Hardaway 8.00 20.00
SSTM Tracy McGrady 40.00 100.00
SSVO Victor Oladipo 6.00 15.00

2015-16 Panini Flawless Transitions Autographs

RANDOM INSERTS IN PACKS
STATED PRINT RUN 25 SER.#'D SETS
ALL VERSIONS EQUALLY PRICED
TRAB Andrew Bogut 10.00 25.00
TRAB Andrew Bogut 10.00 25.00
TRAB Andrew Bogut 10.00 25.00
TRAM Antonio McDyess 6.00 15.00
TRAM Antonio McDyess 6.00 15.00
TRAM Antonio McDyess 6.00 15.00
TRAM Antonio McDyess 6.00 15.00
TRAM Antonio McDyess 6.00 15.00
TRAM Antonio McDyess 6.00 15.00
TRBK Brandon Knight 6.00 15.00
TRBK Brandon Knight 6.00 15.00
TRBK Brandon Knight 6.00 15.00
TRBK Brandon Knight 6.00 15.00
TRCB Chauncey Billups 20.00 50.00
TRCB Chauncey Billups 20.00 50.00
TRCB Chauncey Billups 20.00 50.00
TRCB Chauncey Billups 20.00 50.00
TRCB Chauncey Billups 20.00 50.00
TRCB Chauncey Billups 20.00 50.00
TRCB Chauncey Billups 20.00 50.00
TRCB Chauncey Billups 20.00 50.00
TRCB Chauncey Billups 20.00 50.00
TRDH Dwight Howard 15.00 40.00
TRDH Dwight Howard 15.00 40.00
TRDH Dwight Howard 15.00 40.00
TREB Eric Bledsoe 8.00 20.00
TREB Eric Bledsoe 8.00 20.00
TREB Eric Bledsoe 8.00 20.00
TREH Elvin Hayes 8.00 20.00
TREH Elvin Hayes 8.00 20.00
TREH Elvin Hayes 8.00 20.00
TRET Evan Turner 6.00 15.00
TRET Evan Turner 6.00 15.00
TRET Evan Turner 6.00 15.00
TRET Evan Turner 6.00 15.00
TRHG Horace Grant 15.00 40.00
TRHG Horace Grant 15.00 40.00
TRHG Horace Grant 15.00 40.00
TRHG Horace Grant 15.00 40.00
TRHW Hassan Whiteside 15.00 40.00
TRHW Hassan Whiteside 15.00 40.00
TRHW Hassan Whiteside 15.00 40.00
TRJM Jamal Mashburn 8.00 20.00
TRJM Jamal Mashburn 8.00 20.00
TRJM Jamal Mashburn 8.00 20.00
TRJM Jamal Mashburn 8.00 20.00
TRJM Jamal Mashburn 8.00 20.00
TRKB Kobe Bryant 250.00 500.00
TRKB Kobe Bryant 250.00 500.00
TRKB Kobe Bryant 250.00 500.00
TRKB Kobe Bryant 250.00 500.00
TRKI Kyrie Irving 60.00 150.00
TRKI Kyrie Irving 60.00 150.00
TRKI Kyrie Irving 60.00 150.00
TRKM Khris Middleton 8.00 20.00
TRKM Khris Middleton 8.00 20.00
TRKM Khris Middleton 8.00 20.00
TRKV Keith Van Horn 6.00 15.00
TRKV Keith Van Horn 6.00 15.00
TRKV Keith Van Horn 6.00 15.00
TRKV Keith Van Horn 6.00 15.00
TRKV Keith Van Horn 6.00 15.00
TRLA LaMarcus Aldridge 15.00 40.00
TRLA LaMarcus Aldridge 15.00 40.00
TRLA LaMarcus Aldridge 15.00 40.00
TRPE Patrick Ewing 125.00 300.00
TRPE Patrick Ewing 125.00 300.00
TRPE Patrick Ewing 125.00 300.00
TRPE Patrick Ewing 125.00 300.00
TRSC Stephen Curry 200.00 400.00
TRSC Stephen Curry 200.00 400.00
TRSC Stephen Curry 200.00 400.00
TRSP Scottie Pippen 75.00 200.00
TRSP Scottie Pippen 75.00 200.00
TRSP Scottie Pippen 75.00 200.00
TRSP Scottie Pippen 75.00 200.00
TRSP Scottie Pippen 75.00 200.00
TRTK Toni Kukoc 20.00 50.00
TRTK Toni Kukoc 20.00 50.00
TRTK Toni Kukoc 20.00 50.00
TRTK Toni Kukoc 20.00 50.00

2014-15 Panini Gala

1-83 PRINT RUN 79 SER.#'d SETS
83-100 PRINT RUN 8 SER.#'d SETS
NO ROOKIE PRICING DUE TO SCARCITY
1 Kobe Bryant 8.00 20.00
2 John Wall 2.50 6.00
3 Goran Dragic 1.50 4.00
4 Victor Oladipo 1.50 4.00
5 Nerlens Noel 1.50 4.00
6 Monta Ellis 1.50 4.00
7 James Harden 3.00 8.00
8 DeMar DeRozan 2.00 5.00
9 Mike Conley 1.50 4.00
10 Dennis Schroeder 2.00 5.00
11 Kevin Durant 5.00 12.00
12 Anthony Davis 4.00 10.00
13 O.J. Mayo 1.25 3.00
14 David West 1.50 4.00
15 Tim Duncan 3.00 8.00
16 Jimmy Butler 2.00 5.00
17 Gordon Hayward 2.00 5.00
18 Zach Randolph 1.50 4.00
19 Markieff Morris 1.25 3.00
20 Avery Bradley 1.50 4.00
21 Draymond Green 2.50 6.00
22 Bradley Beal 2.00 5.00
23 LaMarcus Aldridge 2.00 5.00
24 J.R. Smith 1.50 4.00
25 DeAndre Jordan 2.00 5.00
26 Greg Monroe 1.50 4.00
27 Jeremy Lin 2.00 5.00
28 Kyrie Irving 4.00 10.00
29 Ty Lawson 1.25 3.00
30 Derrick Rose 2.50 6.00
31 Damian Lillard 4.00 10.00
32 Rudy Gay 2.00 5.00
33 Trey Burke 1.25 3.00
34 Luol Deng 1.50 4.00
35 Tyreke Evans 1.25 3.00
36 Joe Johnson 1.50 4.00
37 Klay Thompson 2.50 6.00
38 Nikola Vucevic 1.50 4.00
39 Tim Hardaway Jr. 1.25 3.00
40 Arron Afflalo 1.25 3.00
41 Paul Millsap 2.00 5.00
42 Dwight Howard 1.50 4.00
43 Chandler Parsons 1.50 4.00
44 Blake Griffin 2.00 5.00
45 Tony Parker 2.00 5.00
46 Kemba Walker 2.00 5.00
47 Michael Carter-Williams 1.25 3.00
48 Ricky Rubio 2.00 5.00
49 Jared Sullinger 1.25 3.00
50 Chris Paul 2.50 6.00
51 Kenneth Faried 1.50 4.00
52 Kevin Love 2.00 5.00
53 C.J. Miles 1.50 4.00
54 Andrea Bargnani 1.50 4.00
55 DeMarcus Cousins 2.00 5.00
56 Al Horford 1.50 4.00
57 Brandon Jennings 1.25 3.00
58 Serge Ibaka 1.50 4.00
59 Joakim Noah 1.50 4.00
60 Tyson Chandler 1.50 4.00
61 Dwyane Wade 3.00 8.00
62 Eric Bledsoe 1.50 4.00
63 Deron Williams 1.50 4.00
64 Manu Ginobili 2.00 5.00
65 Jrue Holiday 1.50 4.00
66 Jeff Teague 1.50 4.00
67 Marc Gasol 2.00 5.00
68 Kevin Garnett 3.00 8.00
69 Kyle Lowry 1.50 4.00
70 Stephen Curry 8.00 20.00
71 Paul Pierce 2.00 5.00
72 Russell Westbrook 5.00 12.00
73 Pau Gasol 2.00 5.00
74 Kawhi Leonard 3.00 8.00
75 Carmelo Anthony 2.50 6.00
76 Dirk Nowitzki 2.50 6.00
77 George Hill 1.50 4.00
78 LeBron James 20.00 50.00
79 Al Jefferson 1.50 4.00
80 Lou Williams 1.50 4.00
81 Chris Bosh 2.00 5.00
82 Andre Drummond 2.00 5.00
83 Giannis Antetokounmpo 4.00 10.00

2014-15 Panini Gala Award Winning Autographs

RANDOM INSERTS IN PACKS
PRINT RUNS B/WN 40-60 COPIES PER
INSCRIPTIONS NOT SER.#'d
EXCHANGE DEADLINE 2/19/2017
1 Kevin Durant/40 75.00 150.00
2 Kobe Bryant/40 100.00 200.00
3 Shaquille O'Neal/40 100.00 200.00
5 Magic Johnson/40 40.00 100.00
7 David Robinson/40 15.00 40.00
9 Larry Nance/50 5.00 12.00
12 Tyson Chandler/40 5.00 12.00
13 Dikembe Mutombo/50 12.00 30.00
15 Sidney Moncrief/60 4.00 10.00
16 J.R. Smith/60 10.00 25.00
17 Jason Terry/50 5.00 12.00
18 Clifford Robinson/60 4.00 10.00
19 Bill Walton/50 10.00 25.00
20A Bobby Jones/60 5.00 12.00
20B B.Jones Inscription 30.00 80.00
21 George Karl/50 15.00 40.00
22 Byron Scott/40 8.00 20.00
23 Avery Johnson/40 8.00 20.00
24 Don Nelson/50 20.00 50.00
25 Larry Bird/40 50.00 120.00

2014-15 Panini Gala Cinematic Rookie Signatures

RANDOM INSERTS IN PACKS
STATED PRINT RUN 60 SER.#'d SETS
EXCHANGE DEADLINE 2/19/2017
*JADE/25: .5X TO 1.2X BASIC
1 Andrew Wiggins 150.00 300.00
2 Jabari Parker 20.00 50.00
3 Joel Embiid 25.00 60.00
4 K.J. McDaniels 5.00 12.00
5 Aaron Gordon 15.00 40.00
6 Marcus Smart 8.00 20.00
7 Nikola Mirotic 8.00 20.00
8 Bojan Bogdanovic 5.00 12.00
9 Jarnell Stokes 4.00 10.00
10 Jordan Adams 4.00 10.00
11 Tyler Ennis 4.00 10.00
12 Travis Wear 4.00 10.00
13 Jordan Clarkson 25.00 60.00
15 Bruno Caboclo 5.00 12.00
16 Doug McDermott 6.00 15.00
17 Joe Harris 4.00 10.00
18 James Ennis 4.00 10.00
19 Dante Exum 6.00 15.00
20 Cory Jefferson 4.00 10.00
21 Noah Vonleh 5.00 12.00
22 Julius Randle 10.00 25.00
23 Zach LaVine 30.00 80.00
24 Tarik Black 4.00 10.00
26 Shabazz Napier 5.00 12.00
27 Kyle Anderson 6.00 15.00
28 Elfrid Payton 12.00 30.00
29 Glenn Robinson III 4.00 10.00
30 Nik Stauskas 5.00 12.00

2014-15 Panini Gala Cinematic Signatures

RANDOM INSERTS IN PACKS
PRINT RUNS B/WN 35-60 COPIES PER
INSCRIPTIONS NOT SER.#'d
EXCHANGE DEADLINE 2/19/2017
*JADE/25: .5X TO 1.2X BASIC
1 Kobe Bryant/49 100.00 200.00
2 Kevin Durant/49 75.00 150.00
3 Kyrie Irving/35 30.00 80.00
4 Stephen Curry/35 100.00 200.00
5 John Wall/35 20.00 50.00
6 Anthony Davis/35 60.00 150.00
7 Jeff Green/35 5.00 12.00
9 Vince Carter/49 25.00 60.00
10 Zach Randolph/49 5.00 12.00
12 P.J. Tucker/60 4.00 10.00
13 Jason Terry/60 5.00 12.00
16 Reggie Jackson/60 4.00 10.00
18 Maurice Harkless/60 4.00 10.00
19 Kyle Korver/60 5.00 12.00
20 Alec Burks/60 4.00 10.00
21 Blake Griffin/35 50.00 120.00
22 Mike Conley/35 5.00 12.00
23 Tyson Chandler/49 5.00 12.00
24 Jeff Teague/60 5.00 12.00
26 Mike Muscala/60 4.00 10.00
27 Lance Stephenson/35 5.00 12.00
29 Phil Pressey/60 4.00 10.00
30 DeMarre Carroll/60 4.00 10.00
33 Victor Oladipo/60 5.00 12.00
34 Thaddeus Young/60 4.00 10.00
35 Mason Plumlee/60 5.00 12.00
37 Andrew Nicholson/60 4.00 10.00
38 Tobias Harris/60 5.00 12.00
39 Michael Kidd-Gilchrist/35 5.00 12.00
40 Kevin Love/35 8.00 20.00
41 Harrison Barnes/49
44 Spencer Hawes/60 4.00 10.00
45 Taj Gibson/60 5.00 12.00
46 Derrick Favors/60 5.00 12.00
47 Chris Andersen/49 5.00 12.00
48 Randy Foye/60 4.00 10.00
50 Gordon Hayward/60 8.00 20.00
51 Marcin Gortat/60 5.00 12.00
53A Tim Hardaway/60 8.00 20.00
53B T.Hardaway Inscription 8.00 20.00
54 Bill Walton/60 6.00 15.00
55 Grant Hill/35 25.00 60.00
56 Jason Kidd/49 20.00 50.00
57 Dan Issel/60 5.00 12.00
58 Kendall Gill/60 10.00 25.00
59 Glen Rice/60 5.00 12.00
60 Gary Payton/35 10.00 25.00
61 Isiah Thomas/60 8.00 20.00
63 Antoine Walker/60 5.00 12.00
64 Sean Elliott/60 6.00 15.00
65 Robert Horry/60 8.00 20.00
66 Muggsy Bogues/60 5.00 12.00
67 Jim Jackson/60 4.00 10.00
68 Mychal Thompson/60 4.00 10.00
69 Tracy McGrady/39 25.00 60.00
70 Sam Perkins/35 4.00 10.00

2014-15 Panini Gala Coming Attractions Memorabilia

RANDOM INSERTS IN PACKS
STATED PRINT RUN 35 SER.#'d SETS
*JADE/25: 1.2X TO 3X BASIC
1 Doug McDermott 3.00 8.00
2 Joel Embiid 5.00 12.00
3 Glenn Robinson III 2.00 5.00
4 Marcus Smart 3.00 8.00
5 James Young 2.00 5.00
6 Nik Stauskas 2.50 6.00
7 Aaron Gordon 5.00 12.00
8 Rodney Hood 3.00 8.00
9 Bruno Caboclo 2.50 6.00
10 T.J. Warren 3.00 8.00
11 Elfrid Payton 3.00 8.00
12 Julius Randle 5.00 12.00
13 Jabari Parker 6.00 15.00
14 Markel Brown 2.00 5.00
15 Jerami Grant 2.00 5.00
16 Noah Vonleh 2.50 6.00
17 Adreian Payne 2.50 6.00
18 Shabazz Napier 2.50 6.00
19 Cleanthony Early 2.00 5.00
20 Tyler Ennis 2.00 5.00
21 Gary Harris 3.00 8.00
22 Kyle Anderson 3.00 8.00
23 James Ennis 2.00 5.00
24 Mitch McGary 2.00 5.00
25 Joe Harris 2.00 5.00
26 P.J. Hairston 2.00 5.00
27 Andrew Wiggins 6.00 15.00
28 Spencer Dinwiddie 2.50 6.00
29 Dante Exum 5.00 12.00
30 Zach LaVine 5.00 12.00

2014-15 Panini Gala Double Feature Memorabilia

RANDOM INSERTS IN PACKS
PRINT RUNS B/WN 35-45 COPIES PER
*JADE/25: .75X TO 2X BASIC
1 T.Duncan/T.Parker/49 8.00 20.00
2 D.Howard/J.Harden/35 6.00 15.00
3 J.Stockton/K.Malone/35 10.00 25.00
4 B.Griffin/C.Paul/35 5.00 12.00
5 T.Lawson/K.Faried/35 3.00 8.00
6 A.Horford/J.Teague/49 3.00 8.00
7 K.Bryant/S.Nash/49 15.00 40.00
8 D.Rose/J.Butler/49 5.00 12.00
9 A.Davis/T.Evans/35 6.00 15.00
10 D.Nowitzki/M.Ellis/49 5.00 12.00
11 D.DeRozan/K.Lowry/35 4.00 10.00
12 C.Drexler/H.Olajuwon/35 5.00 12.00
13 P.Ewing/L.Johnson/35 5.00 12.00
14 M.Gasol/Z.Randolph/49 4.00 10.00
15 M.Morris/M.Morris/35 2.50 6.00
16 G.Rice/V.Divac/49 4.00 10.00
17 D.Lillard/L.Aldridge/35 8.00 20.00
18 K.Irving/L.James/49 15.00 40.00
19 K.Durant/R.Westbrook/49 10.00 25.00
20 A.Drummond/B.Jennings/35 4.00 10.00

2014-15 Panini Gala Main Attraction Memorabilia

RANDOM INSERTS IN PACKS
PRINT RUNS B/WN 35-49 COPIES PER
*JADE/15-25: 1.2X TO 3X BASIC
1 DeMarcus Cousins/35 4.00 10.00
2 Kevin Durant/49 6.00 15.00
3 Monta Ellis/35 3.00 8.00
4 Tim Duncan/35 6.00 15.00
5 Jeremy Lin/35 4.00 10.00
6 Roy Hibbert/35 3.00 8.00
7 Joakim Noah/35 3.00 8.00
8 Kobe Bryant/35 12.00 30.00
9 Kyle Lowry/35 3.00 8.00
10 Rajon Rondo/49 4.00 10.00
11 John Wall/35 5.00 12.00
12 Anthony Davis/35 8.00 20.00
13 LaMarcus Aldridge/35 4.00 10.00
14 Chandler Parsons/35 3.00 8.00
15 Jeff Teague/35 3.00 8.00
16 Tobias Harris/49 3.00 8.00
17 Gordon Hayward/35 4.00 10.00
18 Dwyane Wade/35 6.00 15.00
19 Blake Griffin/35 4.00 10.00
20 Grant Hill/49 5.00 12.00
21 James Harden/35 6.00 15.00
22 Dwight Howard/35 3.00 8.00
23 Al Horford/49 3.00 8.00
24 Bradley Beal/35 4.00 10.00
25 Michael Carter-Williams/35 2.50 6.00
26 Dirk Nowitzki/49 5.00 12.00
27 Allen Iverson/49 5.00 12.00
28 Patrick Ewing/49 5.00 12.00
29 Marc Gasol/49 4.00 10.00
30 Russell Westbrook/35 10.00 25.00
31 Ricky Rubio/35 4.00 10.00
32 Kenneth Faried/35 3.00 8.00
33 Manu Ginobili/35 4.00 10.00
34 Jimmy Butler/49 4.00 10.00
35 Chris Andersen/35 3.00 8.00
36 Carmelo Anthony/35 5.00 12.00
37 Ralph Sampson/35 3.00 8.00
38 Chris Paul/35 5.00 12.00
39 Kemba Walker/35 4.00 10.00
40 Derrick Rose/35 6.00 15.00
41 Hakeem Olajuwon/35 5.00 12.00
42 Pau Gasol/35 4.00 10.00
43 Nerlens Noel/35 3.00 8.00
44 Joe Johnson/35 3.00 8.00
45 Taj Gibson/49 3.00 8.00
46 DeMar DeRozan/35 4.00 10.00
47 Damian Lillard/35 6.00 15.00
48 Shaquille O'Neal/35 8.00 20.00
49 Victor Oladipo/35 3.00 8.00
50 Trey Burke/35 2.50 6.00

2014-15 Panini Gala Silver Screen Rookie Signatures

RANDOM INSERTS IN PACKS
STATED PRINT RUN 50 SER.#'d SETS
EXCHANGE DEADLINE 2/19/2017
1 Spencer Dinwiddie 5.00 12.00
2 Jordan Adams 4.00 10.00
3 Andrew Wiggins 75.00 150.00
4 Jabari Parker 20.00 50.00
5 Dante Exum 12.00 30.00
6 Nik Stauskas 5.00 12.00
7 Zach LaVine 20.00 50.00
8 Julius Randle 12.00 30.00
9 Langston Galloway 6.00 15.00
10 Devyn Marble 4.00 10.00
11 Elfrid Payton 6.00 15.00
12 Aaron Gordon 10.00 25.00
13 Shabazz Napier 5.00 12.00
14 Cory Jefferson 4.00 10.00
15 Jordan Clarkson 15.00 40.00
16 Nikola Mirotic 8.00 20.00
17 Johnny O'Bryant 4.00 10.00
18 K.J. McDaniels 5.00 12.00
19 Joe Harris 4.00 10.00
21 Markel Brown 4.00 10.00
22 Travis Wear 4.00 10.00
23 C.J. Wilcox 4.00 10.00
24 Doug McDermott 6.00 15.00
25 Bojan Bogdanovic 5.00 12.00

2014-15 Panini Gala Silver Screen Signatures

RANDOM INSERTS IN PACKS
PRINT RUNS B/WN 35-60 COPIES PER
INSCRIPTIONS NOT SER.#'d
EXCHANGE DEADLINE 2/19/2017
1 Shaquille O'Neal/35 75.00 150.00
3 Maurice Harkless/60 4.00 10.00
6 Dikembe Mutombo/49 8.00 20.00
7 Bill Laimbeer/60 5.00 12.00
8 Vin Baker/60 4.00 10.00
10 Jalen Rose/60 8.00 20.00
11 Kenny Smith/60 5.00 12.00
12A Cedric Maxwell/60 4.00 10.00
12B C.Maxwell Inscription
13 Rick Mahorn/60 4.00 10.00
15 C.J. McCollum/49 10.00 25.00
16 Kelly Olynyk/60 6.00 15.00
17 Mason Plumlee/60 5.00 12.00
18 J.R. Smith/60 5.00 12.00
20 Enes Kanter/60 4.00 10.00
21 Tristan Thompson/60 5.00 12.00
22 John Wall/35 20.00 50.00
23 Bradley Beal/49
24 Deron Williams/35 5.00 12.00
25 Klay Thompson/49 15.00 40.00
26 Troy Daniels/60 4.00 10.00
28 Josh Smith/49 5.00 12.00
30 DeMarre Carroll/60 4.00 10.00
32 Nick Collison/60 5.00 12.00
33 James Jones/60 4.00 10.00
34A Gail Goodrich/49 5.00 12.00
34B G.Goodrich Inscription
35 Bernard King/49 5.00 12.00
36A Bill Cartwright/60 5.00 12.00
36B B.Cartwright Inscription
37 Michael Finley/35 8.00 20.00
38 Keith Van Horn/60 5.00 12.00
39 Magic Johnson/35 40.00 100.00
40 Larry Bird/35 30.00 120.00
41 Byron Scott/35 5.00 12.00
42 A.C. Green/60 10.00 25.00
43A Kenny Anderson/60 5.00 12.00

43B K.Anderson Inscription
44 Ron Harper/60 6.00 15.00
45 Grant Hill/35 25.00 60.00
46 Jason Kidd/35 20.00 50.00
47 Larry Nance/60 5.00 12.00
48 Harvey Grant/60 4.00 10.00
49 Vinny Del Negro/49 5.00 12.00
50 Rick Fox/49 5.00 12.00
51A Bob Dandridge/60 4.00 10.00
51B B.Dandridge Inscription
52 Kiki Vandeweghe/60 5.00 12.00
53 Tom Gugliotta/60 4.00 10.00
54 Toni Kukoc/60 8.00 20.00
55 Mychal Thompson/60 4.00 10.00
56 Doug Collins/49 6.00 15.00
57 Calvin Murphy/35 5.00 12.00
58 Dick Van Arsdale/60 5.00 12.00
59 Campy Russell/60 4.00 10.00
60 Kelly Tripucka/49
61 Phil Chenier/60 4.00 10.00
63A Anfernee Hardaway/35 25.00 60.00
63B A.Hardaway Inscription
64 Allan Houston/49 5.00 12.00
65 Giannis Antetokounmpo/60 15.00 40.00
66 Alec Burks/60 4.00 10.00
67 E'Twaun Moore/60 10.00 25.00
70 Kobe Bryant/49 100.00 200.00
71 Kevin Durant/49 75.00 150.00
72 Kyrie Irving/49 30.00 80.00
73 Stephen Curry/35 100.00 250.00
74 Anthony Davis/35 60.00 150.00
75 Alex Len/49 4.00 10.00

2014-15 Panini Gala Starring Role Signatures

RANDOM INSERTS IN PACKS
PRINT RUNS B/WN 32-60 COPIES PER
INSCRIPTIONS NOT SER.#'d
EXCHANGE DEADLINE 2/19/2017
1 Ty Lawson/47 4.00 10.00
2 Isaiah Thomas/60 25.00 60.00
8 Stephen Curry/40 300.00 600.00
9 Deron Williams/40 5.00 12.00
10 Andre Drummond/40 6.00 15.00
12 Chris Andersen/40 5.00 12.00
15 Jason Terry/50 5.00 12.00
16 Gordon Hayward/60 12.00 30.00
17 Ben McLemore/50 4.00 10.00
18 Blake Griffin/40 25.00 60.00
19 Kyrie Irving/40 30.00 80.00
20 D.J. Augustin/60 4.00 10.00
22 Tony Snell/60 4.00 10.00
25A A.C. Green/60 10.00 25.00
25B A.Green Inscription 50.00 120.00
26 Bernard King/40 5.00 12.00
27 John Starks/60 5.00 12.00
28A Jamaal Wilkes/60 6.00 15.00
28B J.Wilkes Inscription
29 Bob McAdoo/60 5.00 12.00
30 Rick Barry/40 5.00 12.00
31 Jerry Lucas/40 6.00 15.00
32 Toni Kukoc/60 8.00 20.00
33 Danny Manning/32 5.00 12.00
34 Michael Finley/40 8.00 20.00
35 Dave Cowens/50 4.00 10.00
36A Dolph Schayes/50 6.00 15.00
36B Schayes Inscription
37 Walter Davis/60 4.00 10.00
38 Grant Hill/40 25.00 60.00
39 Dominique Wilkins/40 8.00 20.00
40 Jason Kidd/40 20.00 50.00
41 Rony Seikaly/60 4.00 10.00
42 Chris Mullin/50 6.00 15.00
43 George Gervin/50
44 Gary Payton/40 15.00 40.00
45 Mark Aguirre/60 5.00 12.00
46A Alex English/60 5.00 12.00
46B A.English Inscription
47 Rod Strickland/60
49 Clifford Robinson/60 4.00 10.00
50 Steve Smith/60 5.00 12.00

2014-15 Panini Gala World Premiere Autographs

RANDOM INSERTS IN PACKS
STATED PRINT RUN 50 SER.#'d SETS
EXCHANGE DEADLINE 2/19/2017
1 Nik Stauskas 5.00 12.00
2 Andrew Wiggins 75.00 200.00
3 Jabari Parker 50.00 120.00
4 Dante Exum 12.00 30.00
5 Marcus Smart 8.00 20.00
6 Tarik Black 4.00 10.00
7 James Ennis 4.00 10.00
8 Zach LaVine 30.00 80.00
9 Doug McDermott 6.00 15.00
11 Jarnell Stokes 4.00 10.00
12 T.J. Warren 6.00 15.00
13 K.J. McDaniels 5.00 12.00
16 Johnny O'Bryant 4.00 10.00
17 Travis Wear 4.00 10.00
18 Shabazz Napier 5.00 12.00
19 Spencer Dinwiddie 5.00 12.00
20 Langston Galloway 6.00 15.00
21 Nikola Mirotic 15.00 40.00
22 Elfrid Payton 12.00 30.00
23 Aaron Gordon 15.00 40.00
24 Jordan Clarkson 25.00 60.00
25 Kyle Anderson 6.00 15.00

2015-16 Panini Gala

1-120 PRINT RUN 99 SER.#'d SETS
121-150 PRINT RUN 8 SER.#'d SETS
NO ROOKIE PRICING DUE TO SCARCITY
1 Anthony Davis 5.00 12.00
2 Deron Williams 2.00 5.00
3 Elfrid Payton 2.00 5.00
4 James Harden 4.00 10.00
5 Damian Lillard 5.00 12.00
6 Jordan Clarkson 2.50 6.00
7 Rudy Gay 2.50 6.00
8 Marcus Smart 2.00 5.00
9 Ricky Rubio 2.50 6.00
10 Kemba Walker 2.50 6.00
11 Jrue Holiday 2.00 5.00
12 Danilo Gallinari 2.00 5.00
13 Victor Oladipo 2.00 5.00
14 Dwight Howard 2.00 5.00
15 Mason Plumlee 2.00 5.00
16 Julius Randle 2.50 6.00
17 DeMar DeRozan 2.50 6.00
18 Joe Johnson 2.00 5.00
19 Jabari Parker 3.00 8.00
20 Michael Kidd-Gilchrist 2.00 5.00
21 Carmelo Anthony 3.00 8.00
22 Kenneth Faried 2.00 5.00
23 Tobias Harris 2.00 5.00
24 Ty Lawson 1.50 4.00
25 Gerald Henderson 1.50 4.00
26 Mike Conley 2.50 6.00
27 Kyle Lowry 2.00 5.00
28 Brook Lopez 2.00 5.00
29 Giannis Antetokounmpo 5.00 12.00
30 Derrick Rose 3.00 8.00
31 Arron Afflalo 1.50 4.00
32 Gary Harris 2.00 5.00
33 Nikola Vucevic 2.00 5.00
34 Monta Ellis 2.00 5.00
35 Tony Parker 2.50 6.00
36 Zach Randolph 2.00 5.00
37 Jonas Valanciunas 2.00 5.00
38 Avery Bradley 2.00 5.00
39 Michael Carter-Williams 1.50 4.00
40 Pau Gasol 2.50 6.00
41 Robin Lopez 1.50 4.00
42 Andre Drummond 2.50 6.00
43 Isaiah Canaan 2.00 5.00
44 Paul George 3.00 8.00
45 Manu Ginobili 2.50 6.00
46 Marc Gasol 2.50 6.00
47 Trey Burke 1.50 4.00
48 Amir Johnson 1.50 4.00
49 Greg Monroe 2.00 5.00
50 Jimmy Butler 2.50 6.00
51 Langston Galloway 1.50 4.00
52 Reggie Jackson 2.00 5.00
53 Robert Covington 1.50 4.00
54 George Hill 2.00 5.00
55 Kawhi Leonard 4.00 10.00
56 Dwyane Wade 4.00 10.00
57 Gordon Hayward 2.50 6.00
58 Bojan Bogdanovic 1.50 4.00
59 Zach LaVine 2.50 6.00
60 Kyrie Irving 5.00 12.00
61 Russell Westbrook 6.00 15.00
62 Kentavious Caldwell-Pope 2.00 5.00
63 Nerlens Noel 2.00 5.00
64 Chris Paul 3.00 8.00
65 LaMarcus Aldridge 2.50 6.00
66 Chris Bosh 2.50 6.00
67 Rudy Gobert 2.50 6.00
68 Jeff Teague 2.00 5.00
69 DeAndre Jordan 2.50 6.00
70 LeBron James 15.00 40.00
71 Kevin Durant 6.00 15.00
72 Stephen Curry 15.00 40.00
73 Brandon Knight 2.00 5.00
74 Blake Griffin 2.50 6.00
75 Tim Duncan 4.00 10.00
76 Goran Dragic 2.00 5.00
77 John Wall 3.00 8.00
78 Al Horford 2.00 5.00
79 Andre Iguodala 2.00 5.00
80 Kevin Love 2.50 6.00
81 Enes Kanter 1.50 4.00
82 Klay Thompson 3.00 8.00
83 Eric Bledsoe 2.00 5.00
84 Paul Pierce 2.50 6.00
85 Rajon Rondo 2.50 6.00
86 Andrew Wiggins 4.00 10.00
87 Bradley Beal 2.50 6.00
88 Kyle Korver 2.00 5.00
89 Joakim Noah 2.00 5.00
90 Dirk Nowitzki 3.00 8.00
91 Serge Ibaka 2.00 5.00
92 Harrison Barnes 2.00 5.00
93 Tyson Chandler 2.00 5.00
94 Kobe Bryant 15.00 40.00
95 DeMarcus Cousins 2.50 6.00
96 Kevin Garnett 4.00 10.00
97 Marcin Gortat 2.00 5.00
98 Al Jefferson 2.00 5.00
99 Tyreke Evans 1.50 4.00
100 Chandler Parsons 2.00 5.00
101 John Stockton 4.00 10.00
102 Dominique Wilkins 3.00 8.00
103 Kareem Abdul-Jabbar 4.00 10.00
104 Pete Maravich 4.00 10.00
105 Alonzo Mourning 3.00 8.00
106 James Worthy 3.00 8.00
107 Dennis Rodman 5.00 12.00
108 Drazen Petrovic 2.50 6.00
109 Scottie Pippen 5.00 12.00
110 Larry Bird 6.00 15.00
111 Patrick Ewing 3.00 8.00
112 Julius Erving 4.00 10.00
113 Clyde Drexler 3.00 8.00
114 Chris Mullin 2.50 6.00
115 Gary Payton 2.50 6.00
116 Magic Johnson 6.00 15.00
117 Karl Malone 3.00 8.00
118 Isiah Thomas 2.50 6.00
119 David Robinson 4.00 10.00
120 George Gervin 2.50 6.00

2015-16 Panini Gala Action Autographs

RANDOM INSERTS IN PACKS
STATED PRINT RUN 40 SER.#'d SETS
EXCHANGE DEADLINE 12/22/2017
1 Kobe Bryant 125.00 300.00
2 Kevin Durant 50.00 120.00
3 Anthony Davis 25.00 60.00
4 Blake Griffin 20.00 50.00
5 John Wall 15.00 40.00
6 Andrew Wiggins 30.00 80.00
7 Dennis Rodman 15.00 40.00
8 Anfernee Hardaway 30.00 80.00
9 Julius Randle 8.00 20.00
10 Ben McLemore 4.00 10.00
11 Aaron Gordon 5.00 12.00
12 Byron Scott
13 Langston Galloway 4.00 10.00
14 Jonas Valanciunas 5.00 12.00
15 Robert Parish 6.00 15.00
16 Mark Jackson 5.00 12.00
17 Peja Stojakovic 6.00 15.00
18 J.R. Smith 5.00 12.00
20 Nene 5.00 12.00
21 Allan Houston 5.00 12.00
22 Klay Thompson 25.00 60.00
23 Doug McDermott 5.00 12.00
24 Gary Harris 5.00 12.00
25 Mike Conley 6.00 15.00
26 Wilson Chandler 5.00 12.00
27 Mitch Richmond 12.00 30.00
28 Jerry Stackhouse 12.00 30.00
29 Danny Green 5.00 12.00
30 Kenny Walker 4.00 10.00
31 Robert Horry 5.00 12.00
32 Alex English
33 Dennis Schroder 5.00 12.00
34 Antonio McDyess 5.00 12.00
35 Nick Young 5.00 12.00
36 Bill Laimbeer 5.00 12.00
37 Eddie Jones
38 Gary Neal 5.00 12.00
39 Mason Plumlee 5.00 12.00
40 Bojan Bogdanovic 4.00 10.00

2015-16 Panini Gala Award Winning Autographs

RANDOM INSERTS IN PACKS
PRINT RUNS B/WN 30-60 COPIES PER
EXCHANGE DEADLINE 12/22/2017
1 Dwight Howard/30 20.00 50.00
2 Dwyane Wade/30
3 Zach LaVine/50 40.00 100.00
4 Steve Nash/30 EXCH 30.00 80.00
5 Andrew Wiggins/30 10.00 25.00
6 Dennis Rodman/30 30.00 80.00
7 Vince Carter/30 75.00 200.00
8 Gary Payton/30 25.00 60.00
9 Allen Iverson/30 250.00 400.00
10 Larry Brown/30
11 Karl Malone/30
12 Kobe Bryant/30 300.00 500.00
13 Joe Dumars/30 10.00 25.00
14 Glen Rice/60 8.00 20.00
15 Mitch Richmond/60 12.00 30.00
16 Dikembe Mutombo/60 15.00 40.00
17 Michael Cooper/60 4.00 10.00
18 Hakeem Olajuwon/30
19 Blake Griffin/30 50.00 120.00
20 Bob McAdoo/60 12.00 30.00

2015-16 Panini Gala Cinematic Rookie Signatures

RANDOM INSERTS IN PACKS
STATED PRINT RUN 60 SER.#'d SETS
EXCHANGE DEADLINE 12/22/2017
*JADE/25: .6X TO 1.5X BASIC
1 Karl-Anthony Towns 125.00 250.00
2 D'Angelo Russell 20.00 50.00
3 Jahlil Okafor 20.00 50.00
4 Emmanuel Mudiay 12.00 30.00
5 Kristaps Porzingis 50.00 120.00
6 Mario Hezonja 8.00 20.00
7 Justise Winslow 12.00 30.00
8 Willie Cauley-Stein 10.00 25.00
9 Stanley Johnson 6.00 15.00
10 Bobby Portis 6.00 15.00
11 Frank Kaminsky 5.00 12.00
12 Devin Booker 40.00 100.00
13 Myles Turner 12.00 30.00
14 Joe Young 4.00 10.00
15 Jerian Grant 3.00 8.00
16 Trey Lyles 8.00 20.00
17 Delon Wright 4.00 10.00
18 Cameron Payne
19 Norman Powell 4.00 10.00
20 Sam Dekker 6.00 15.00
21 Terry Rozier 4.00 10.00
22 Kelly Oubre Jr. 4.00 10.00
23 Rondae Hollis-Jefferson 4.00 10.00
24 Kevon Looney 4.00 10.00
25 Justin Anderson 5.00 12.00

2015-16 Panini Gala Cinematic Signatures

RANDOM INSERTS IN PACKS
PRINT RUNS B/WN 35-60 COPIES PER
EXCHANGE DEADLINE 12/22/2017
*JADE/25: .6X TO 1.5X p/r 50-60
*JADE/25: .5X TO 1.2X p/r 35-40
1 Chris Paul/40 20.00 50.00
2 Clyde Drexler/40 30.00 80.00
3 Blake Griffin/40 20.00 50.00
4 John Wall/40 15.00 40.00
5 Alonzo Mourning/40 12.00 30.00
6 Andrew Wiggins/40 30.00 80.00
7 Tracy McGrady/40 30.00 80.00
8 Rick Barry/35 5.00 12.00
9 Jason Kidd/40 15.00 40.00
10 Marcus Smart/40 5.00 12.00
11 David Robinson/40 20.00 50.00
13 Victor Oladipo/40 5.00 12.00
14 Julius Randle/40 8.00 20.00
15 Dwyane Wade/40 30.00 80.00
16 Marques Johnson/60 4.00 10.00
17 Joe Dumars/50 5.00 12.00
18 Michael Finley/50 5.00 12.00
19 Dennis Schroder/60 4.00 10.00
20 Anfernee Hardaway/40 30.00 80.00
21 Gary Neal/60 4.00 10.00
22 Courtney Lee/60 4.00 10.00
23 Kenny Smith/50 4.00 10.00
24 Rick Fox/50 6.00 15.00
25 Patrick Patterson/60 3.00 8.00
26 Steve Kerr/50 8.00 20.00
27 Gordon Hayward/60 6.00 15.00
28 Glen Rice/60 4.00 10.00
29 Nene/60 4.00 10.00
30 Kevin Love/40 15.00 40.00
31 Nikola Mirotic/60 4.00 10.00
32 Allan Houston/60 4.00 10.00
33 Joe Ingles/60 3.00 8.00
34 Wilson Chandler/60 4.00 10.00
35 Zach LaVine/60 12.00 30.00
36 A.C. Green/60 5.00 12.00
37 Jerry Stackhouse/60 10.00 25.00
38 Aaron Gordon/60 10.00 25.00
39 Mitch Richmond/60 5.00 12.00
40 Dikembe Mutombo/60 10.00 25.00
41 Doug McDermott/60 4.00 10.00
42 Gary Harris/60 4.00 10.00
43 Giannis Antetokounmpo/60 30.00 80.00
44 Tony Allen/60 3.00 8.00
45 Rolando Blackman/60 5.00 12.00
46 Kyrie Irving/40 30.00 80.00
47 Mo Williams/60 4.00 10.00
48 Elfrid Payton/50 4.00 10.00
49 Thaddeus Young/60 3.00 8.00
50 Timofey Mozgov/60 3.00 8.00
51 Mike Conley/60 5.00 12.00
52 Taj Gibson/60
53 Kenneth Faried/60 4.00 10.00
54 Tom Chambers/60 4.00 10.00
55 Antonio McDyess/60 4.00 10.00
56 Alec Burks/60 3.00 8.00
57 Cuttino Mobley/60 3.00 8.00
58 Damon Stoudamire/60 4.00 10.00
59 Spud Webb/60 4.00 10.00
60 Eddie Jones/60
61 Rafer Alston/60 3.00 8.00
62 Jordan Adams/60 3.00 8.00
63 Gary Payton/40 25.00 60.00
64 Will Barton/60
65 Sam Bowie/60 3.00 8.00
66 Michael Cooper/50 4.00 10.00
67 Anthony Davis/40 40.00 100.00
68 Mason Plumlee/60 4.00 10.00
69 Bojan Bogdanovic/60 3.00 8.00
70 Langston Galloway/60 3.00 8.00
71 Grant Hill/40 20.00 50.00
72 Bradley Beal/40 12.00 30.00
73 Tarik Black/60 3.00 8.00
74 Andre Drummond/50 5.00 12.00
75 K.J. McDaniels/60

2015-16 Panini Gala Coming Attractions Memorabilia

RANDOM INSERTS IN PACKS
PRINT RUNS B/WN 45-60 COPIES PER
*PURPLE/40: .5X TO 1.2X BASIC
*JADE/21-25: .75X TO 2X BASIC
1 Kristaps Porzingis/60 12.00 30.00
2 Justin Anderson/60 2.50 6.00
3 Stanley Johnson/60 2.50 6.00
4 Jarell Martin/60 2.50 6.00
5 Trey Lyles/60 3.00 8.00
6 Montrezl Harrell/60 2.50 6.00
7 Kelly Oubre Jr./60 2.50 6.00
8 Jordan Mickey/60 2.00 5.00
9 Karl-Anthony Towns/60 12.00 30.00
10 Sam Dekker/60 2.50 6.00
11 Mario Hezonja/60 2.50 6.00
12 Bobby Portis/60 3.00 8.00
13 Frank Kaminsky/60 3.00 8.00
14 R.J. Hunter/60 2.00 5.00
15 Devin Booker/60 6.00 15.00
16 Anthony Brown/60 2.00 5.00
17 Terry Rozier/60 2.50 6.00
18 Rakeem Christmas/60 2.00 5.00
19 D'Angelo Russell/45 6.00 15.00
20 Jerian Grant/60 2.00 5.00
21 Willie Cauley-Stein/60 3.00 8.00
22 Rondae Hollis-Jefferson/60 2.50 6.00
23 Justise Winslow/60 3.00 8.00
24 Chris McCullough/60 2.00 5.00
25 Cameron Payne/60 2.50 6.00
26 Joe Young/60 2.50 6.00
27 Nikola Jokic/60 6.00 15.00
28 Pat Connaughton/60 2.00 5.00
29 Jahlil Okafor/60 5.00 12.00
30 Delon Wright/60 2.50 6.00
31 Emmanuel Mudiay/60 3.00 8.00
32 Tyus Jones/60 3.00 8.00
33 Myles Turner/60 3.00 8.00

2015-16 Panini Gala Double Feature Memorabilia

RANDOM INSERTS IN PACKS
PRINT RUNS B/WN 35-60 COPIES PER
*PURPLE/40: .5X TO 1.2X BASIC
*JADE/23-25: .75X TO 2X BASIC
1 K.Duckworth/C.Robinson/60 2.00 5.00
2 Nowitzki/Nash/60 4.00 10.00
3 Schrempf/Payton/60 8.00 20.00
4 Davis/Griffin/60 3.00 8.00
5 D.Favors/T.Burke/60 2.50 6.00
6 Wiggins/Garnett/60 8.00 20.00
7 D.Manning/M.Jackson/60 2.50 6.00
8 Bird/Ainge/60 10.00 25.00
9 Oakley/Ewing/35 8.00 20.00
10 Johnson/Mourning/60 4.00 10.00
11 Duncan/Parker/60 6.00 15.00
12 D.Gallinari/K.Faried/60 2.50 6.00
13 T.Ross/D.DeRozan/60 3.00 8.00
14 K.Bryant/J.Clarkson/60 12.00 30.00
16 Davis/Gordon/60 4.00 10.00
17 A.Gordon/E.Payton/60 2.50 6.00
18 J.Young/M.Smart/60 2.50 6.00
19 Wstbrk/Drnt/60 10.00 25.00
20 Rodman/Pippen/60 10.00 25.00
21 Leonard/Ginobili/60 8.00 20.00
22 A.Dantley/I.Thomas/35 3.00 8.00
23 Stockton/Malone/60 12.00 30.00
24 Wade/O'Neal/60 6.00 15.00
25 Hill/George/60 4.00 10.00
26 Starks/Ewing/60 5.00 12.00
27 A.Adams/W.Davis/60 2.00 5.00
28 K.McHale/R.Lewis/60 3.00 8.00
29 E.Bledsoe/T.Warren/60 2.50 6.00
30 Rose/Butler/60 4.00 10.00
32 H.Olajuwon/C.Drexler/60 10.00 25.00

2015-16 Panini Gala Genregraphs Classics

RANDOM INSERTS IN PACKS
STATED PRINT RUN 25 SER.#'d SETS
EXCHANGE DEADLINE 12/22/2017
1 Larry Bird 40.00 100.00
2 Julius Erving 40.00 100.00
3 Magic Johnson 30.00 80.00
4 Michael Cooper 6.00 15.00
5 Dominique Wilkins 15.00 40.00
6 Hersey Hawkins 5.00 12.00
7 Wes Unseld 8.00 20.00
8 Sam Bowie 5.00 12.00
9 Bob McAdoo 20.00 50.00
10 David Robinson 30.00 80.00
11 Mark Aguirre 6.00 15.00
12 John Stockton 30.00 80.00
13 Karl Malone
14 Steve Kerr 12.00 30.00
15 Dennis Rodman 30.00 80.00
16 Hakeem Olajuwon 15.00 40.00
17 Clyde Drexler 40.00 100.00
18 Jo Jo White
19 Jerry West 20.00 50.00
20 Artis Gilmore 8.00 20.00
21 Nate Archibald 10.00 25.00
22 Calvin Murphy
23 Robert Parish 8.00 20.00
24 Walt Frazier 10.00 25.00
25 Earl Monroe
26 Byron Scott
27 Bill Laimbeer 6.00 15.00
28 Dan Issel 6.00 15.00
29 Anfernee Hardaway 40.00 100.00
30 Gary Payton 30.00 80.00
31 Rick Fox
32 Larry Brown
33 Ralph Sampson 6.00 15.00
34 Jerry Stackhouse 20.00 50.00
35 Marques Johnson 6.00 15.00
36 Dikembe Mutombo 15.00 40.00
37 Bill Walton 8.00 20.00
38 Dave Cowens 5.00 12.00
40 Joe Dumars 8.00 20.00

2015-16 Panini Gala Genregraphs Comedy

RANDOM INSERTS IN PACKS
STATED PRINT RUN 25 SER.#'d SETS
EXCHANGE DEADLINE 12/22/2017
1 Andrew Wiggins 40.00 100.00
2 John Wall 30.00 80.00
3 Kevin Durant 60.00 150.00
4 Tony Allen 5.00 12.00
5 Vlade Divac 8.00 20.00
6 Kevin Love 20.00 50.00
7 J.R. Smith 12.00 30.00
8 Steve Nash 40.00 100.00
9 Zach Randolph 10.00 25.00
10 Kenneth Faried 6.00 15.00
11 Zach LaVine 30.00 80.00
12 Elfrid Payton 6.00 15.00
13 Kobe Bryant 175.00 350.00
14 Magic Johnson 30.00 80.00
15 Grant Hill 25.00 60.00
16 Shaquille O'Neal 40.00 100.00
17 Dikembe Mutombo 15.00 40.00
18 Jason Kidd 20.00 50.00
19 Allen Iverson 175.00 350.00
20 Kyrie Irving 50.00 120.00
21 Blake Griffin 25.00 60.00
22 Anthony Davis 50.00 120.00
23 Damon Stoudamire 10.00 25.00
24 Rick Fox
25 Chris Bosh 12.00 30.00

2015-16 Panini Gala Genregraphs Drama

RANDOM INSERTS IN PACKS
STATED PRINT RUN 25 SER.#'d SETS
EXCHANGE DEADLINE 12/22/2017
1 Kobe Bryant 175.00 350.00
2 Kevin Durant 60.00 150.00
3 Andrew Wiggins 40.00 100.00
4 Anthony Davis 50.00 120.00
5 Vince Carter 40.00 100.00
6 Tracy McGrady 40.00 100.00
7 John Wall 20.00 50.00
8 Julius Randle 10.00 25.00
9 Dante Exum
10 Jrue Holiday 6.00 15.00
11 Zach Randolph 6.00 15.00
12 Klay Thompson 30.00 80.00
13 Bradley Beal 15.00 40.00
14 Tony Parker 25.00 60.00
15 Jabari Parker 30.00 80.00
16 Victor Oladipo 6.00 15.00
17 Zach LaVine 30.00 80.00

2015-16 Panini Gala Genregraphs Thriller

RANDOM INSERTS IN PACKS
STATED PRINT RUN 25 SER.#'d SETS
EXCHANGE DEADLINE 12/22/2017
1 Kevin Durant 60.00 150.00
2 Kobe Bryant 175.00 350.00
3 Kyrie Irving 40.00 100.00
4 John Wall 20.00 50.00
5 Anthony Davis 50.00 120.00
6 Bradley Beal 15.00 40.00
7 Gordon Hayward 10.00 25.00
8 Blake Griffin 25.00 60.00
9 Chris Paul 25.00 60.00
10 Courtney Lee 6.00 15.00
11 Tracy McGrady 40.00 100.00
12 Chris Bosh 12.00 30.00
13 Ray Allen 30.00 80.00
14 Steve Nash 40.00 100.00
15 Robert Horry 6.00 15.00
16 Magic Johnson 30.00 80.00
17 Danny Green 6.00 15.00
18 Alonzo Mourning 15.00 40.00

2015-16 Panini Gala Main Attraction Memorabilia

RANDOM INSERTS IN PACKS
PRINT RUNS B/WN 34-60 COPIES PER
*PURPLE/40: .5X TO 1.2X BASIC
*JADE/20-25: .75X TO 2X BASIC
1 Kevin Durant/60 5.00 12.00
2 Damian Lillard/60 5.00 12.00
3 Markieff Morris/60 2.00 5.00
4 Detlef Schrempf/60 3.00 8.00
5 Rafer Alston/60 2.00 5.00
6 Isaiah Thomas/60 3.00 8.00
7 Terrence Ross/60 2.50 6.00
8 Alex Len/60 2.00 5.00
9 John Starks/60 2.50 6.00
10 Blake Griffin/60 3.00 8.00
11 Kawhi Leonard/60 5.00 12.00
12 Kobe Bryant/60 12.00 30.00
13 LeBron James/60 20.00 50.00
14 Doug McDermott/60 2.50 6.00
15 Richard Hamilton/60 2.50 6.00
16 James Harden/60 5.00 12.00
17 Toni Kukoc/60 3.00 8.00
18 Andrew Bogut/60 2.50 6.00
19 Jordan Clarkson/60 3.00 8.00
20 Brook Lopez/60 2.50 6.00
21 Manute Bol/60 3.00 8.00
22 David Thompson/44 2.50 6.00
23 Mo Williams/60 2.50 6.00
24 Eric Gordon/60 2.50 6.00
25 Ron Harper/34 3.00 8.00
26 Jeff Teague/60 2.50 6.00
27 Wilson Chandler/60 2.50 6.00
28 Avery Bradley/60 2.50 6.00
29 Kenneth Faried/60 2.50 6.00
30 Clifford Robinson/60 2.00 5.00
31 Larry Johnson/60 4.00 10.00
33 Patrick Ewing/60 4.00 10.00
34 Gordon Hayward/60 3.00 8.00
35 Shaquille O'Neal/60 8.00 20.00

2015-16 Panini Gala Primetime Memorabilia

RANDOM INSERTS IN PACKS
STATED PRINT RUN 60 SER.#'d SETS
*PURPLE/40: .5X TO 1.2X BASIC
1 Allen Iverson 4.00 10.00
2 Jimmy Butler 3.00 8.00
3 Carmelo Anthony 4.00 10.00
4 Karl Malone 4.00 10.00
5 David Robinson 5.00 12.00
6 Manu Ginobili 3.00 8.00
7 Dirk Nowitzki 4.00 10.00
8 Scottie Pippen 6.00 15.00
9 Kyrie Irving 6.00 15.00
10 Grant Hill 4.00 10.00
11 Anthony Davis 4.00 10.00
12 John Stockton 5.00 12.00
13 Chris Paul 4.00 10.00
14 Kobe Bryant 12.00 30.00
15 DeMar DeRozan 3.00 8.00
16 Marcus Smart 2.50 6.00
17 Dominique Wilkins 4.00 10.00
18 Steve Nash 3.00 8.00
20 Hakeem Olajuwon 4.00 10.00
21 Chris Bosh 3.00 8.00
22 John Wall 4.00 10.00
23 Clyde Drexler 4.00 10.00
24 LaMarcus Aldridge 3.00 8.00
25 Dennis Rodman 6.00 15.00
27 Dwyane Wade 5.00 12.00
28 Tim Duncan 5.00 12.00
29 Aaron Gordon 2.50 6.00
31 Ben Wallace 2.50 6.00
32 Kareem Abdul-Jabbar 5.00 12.00
33 Danny Manning 2.50 6.00
34 Larry Bird 8.00 20.00
35 Derrick Rose 4.00 10.00
36 Russell Westbrook 8.00 20.00
37 Gary Payton 3.00 8.00
38 Tony Parker 3.00 8.00
40 Jason Kidd 3.00 8.00

2015-16 Panini Gala Primetime Rookie Memorabilia

RANDOM INSERTS IN PACKS
STATED PRINT RUN 60 SER.#'d SETS
*PURPLE/40: .5X TO 1.2X BASIC
*PRIME/24-25: .75X TO 2X BASIC
1 Justise Winslow 3.00 8.00
2 Jarell Martin 2.50 6.00
3 Devin Booker 6.00 15.00
4 Montrezl Harrell 2.50 6.00
5 Karl-Anthony Towns
6 Terry Rozier 2.50 6.00
8 Jerian Grant 2.00 5.00
9 Emmanuel Mudiay 3.00 8.00
10 Bobby Portis 3.00 8.00
11 Myles Turner 3.00 8.00
12 R.J. Hunter 2.00 5.00
13 Cameron Payne 2.50 6.00
14 Anthony Brown 2.00 5.00
15 D'Angelo Russell 8.00 20.00
16 Nemanja Bjelica 2.50 6.00
17 Mario Hezonja 2.50 6.00
18 Delon Wright 2.50 6.00
19 Stanley Johnson 2.50 6.00
20 Rondae Hollis-Jefferson 2.50 6.00
21 Trey Lyles 3.00 8.00
22 Chris McCullough 2.00 5.00
23 Kelly Oubre Jr. 2.50 6.00
24 Joe Young 2.50 6.00
25 Jahlil Okafor 4.00 10.00
26 Sam Dekker 2.50 6.00
27 Willie Cauley-Stein 3.00 8.00
28 Justin Anderson 2.50 6.00
29 Frank Kaminsky 3.00 8.00
30 Tyus Jones 3.00 8.00

2015-16 Panini Gala Red Carpet Signatures

RANDOM INSERTS IN PACKS
STATED PRINT RUN 30 SER.#'d SETS
EXCHANGE DEADLINE 12/22/2017
1 Kobe Bryant 150.00 300.00
2 Chris Paul 30.00 80.00
3 Blake Griffin 20.00 50.00
4 John Wall 20.00 50.00
5 Jabari Parker 20.00 50.00
6 Kevin Love 15.00 40.00
7 Kevin Durant 50.00 120.00
8 Dominique Wilkins 12.00 30.00
9 Nick Young 12.00 30.00
10 Andre Drummond 12.00 30.00
11 Chris Bosh 10.00 25.00
12 Steve Nash 40.00 100.00
13 Victor Oladipo 5.00 12.00
14 Ralph Sampson 5.00 12.00
15 Julius Erving 30.00 80.00
16 Zach LaVine 20.00 50.00
17 Frank Kaminsky 12.00 30.00
18 Shaquille O'Neal 40.00 100.00
19 Walt Frazier 5.00 12.00
20 Justise Winslow 15.00 40.00

2015-16 Panini Gala Signatures

RANDOM INSERTS IN PACKS
STATED PRINT RUN 40 SER.#'d SETS
EXCHANGE DEADLINE 12/22/2017
1 Chris Paul 20.00 50.00
2 Joe Ingles 10.00 25.00
3 Elfrid Payton 5.00 12.00
4 Andrew Wiggins 30.00 80.00
5 Antoine Walker 5.00 12.00
6 Antonio McDyess 5.00 12.00
7 Bill Laimbeer 5.00 12.00
8 Ray Allen 25.00 60.00
9 Mike Conley 6.00 15.00
10 DeMarre Carroll 4.00 10.00
11 Gary Harris 5.00 12.00
12 Tracy McGrady 30.00 80.00
13 Dan Issel 5.00 12.00
14 Jerry West 15.00 40.00
15 Tony Allen 4.00 10.00
16 Doug McDermott 5.00 12.00
17 Dwight Powell 4.00 10.00
18 Eddie Jones
19 Julius Randle 8.00 20.00
20 Giannis Antetokounmpo 40.00 100.00
21 Dennis Schroder 12.00 30.00
22 Nick Van Exel 20.00 50.00
23 Jabari Parker 25.00 60.00
24 Jerami Grant 4.00 10.00
25 Jrue Holiday 5.00 12.00
26 Marques Johnson 5.00 12.00
28 John Wall 15.00 40.00
29 Jordan Adams 4.00 10.00
30 K.J. McDaniels
31 Timofey Mozgov 4.00 10.00
32 Nick Young 5.00 12.00
33 Kenny Smith 5.00 12.00
34 Kevin Love 6.00 15.00
35 Kobe Bryant 125.00 300.00
36 Michael Cooper 5.00 12.00
37 Gary Neal 5.00 12.00
38 Michael Finley 6.00 15.00
39 Kenneth Faried 5.00 12.00
40 Mo Williams 5.00 12.00
41 Antoine Carr 4.00 10.00
42 Jonas Valanciunas 5.00 12.00
43 Mark Aguirre 5.00 12.00
44 Nene 5.00 12.00
45 Rafer Alston 4.00 10.00
46 Hersey Hawkins 4.00 10.00
47 Robert Horry 5.00 12.00
48 Rolando Blackman 6.00 15.00
49 Ron Harper 6.00 15.00
50 Spud Webb 5.00 12.00
51 Will Barton
52 Sam Bowie 4.00 10.00
53 Patrick Patterson 4.00 10.00
54 J.R. Smith 10.00 25.00
55 Tarik Black 4.00 10.00
56 Thaddeus Young 4.00 10.00
57 Tom Chambers 5.00 12.00
58 Tony Delk 5.00 12.00
59 Marcus Smart 5.00 12.00
60 Wilson Chandler 5.00 12.00

2015-16 Panini Gala Silver Screen Autographs

RANDOM INSERTS IN PACKS
PRINT RUNS B/WN 30-60 COPIES PER
EXCHANGE DEADLINE 12/22/2017
1 Kobe Bryant/35 125.00 300.00
2 Kevin Durant/35 75.00 200.00
3 Dwyane Wade/35 30.00 80.00
4 John Stockton/30 25.00 60.00
5 Tracy McGrady/30 30.00 80.00
6 Anthony Davis/35 40.00 100.00
7 Dwight Howard/30
8 Kyrie Irving/35 30.00 80.00
9 Dennis Rodman/35 25.00 60.00
10 Jabari Parker/35 25.00 60.00
11 Andrew Wiggins/35 20.00 50.00
12 Kevin Love/35 15.00 40.00
13 Jrue Holiday/35 5.00 12.00
14 Andre Drummond/35 8.00 20.00
15 Aaron Gordon/35 12.00 30.00
16 Mark Aguirre/60 4.00 10.00
17 Wesley Matthews/60 3.00 8.00
18 Jason Kidd/35 15.00 40.00
19 Mike Conley/60 5.00 12.00
20 Danny Green/60 4.00 10.00
21 Taj Gibson/60
22 Kawhi Leonard/35
23 Jerry Stackhouse/60 3.00 8.00
24 Kenny Walker/60 3.00 8.00
25 Robert Horry/60 4.00 10.00
26 Bill Walton/35 6.00 15.00
27 Dennis Schroder/60 12.00 30.00
28 Tom Chambers/60 4.00 10.00
29 Alec Burks/60 3.00 8.00
30 Kenneth Faried/60 4.00 10.00
31 Jusuf Nurkic/60 3.00 8.00
32 Patrick Patterson/60 3.00 8.00
33 Elfrid Payton/35 5.00 12.00
34 Klay Thompson/60 20.00 50.00
35 Dan Issel/60 4.00 10.00
36 Doug McDermott/60 4.00 10.00
37 Antonio McDyess/60 4.00 10.00
38 Ron Harper/60 5.00 12.00
39 Bill Laimbeer/60 4.00 10.00
40 Eddie Jones/60
41 Rafer Alston/60 3.00 8.00
42 Dino Radja/60 8.00 20.00
43 Cuttino Mobley/60 3.00 8.00
44 Antoine Carr/60 3.00 8.00
45 Keith Van Horn/60 4.00 10.00
46 Damon Stoudamire/60 10.00 25.00
47 Rony Seikaly/60 3.00 8.00
48 Sam Bowie/60 3.00 8.00
49 Tony Delk/60 4.00 10.00
50 Timofey Mozgov/60 3.00 8.00
51 Tony Allen/60 3.00 8.00
52 Sean Elliott/60 5.00 12.00
53 Thaddeus Young/60 3.00 8.00
54 Kendall Gill/60 10.00 25.00
55 Nick Young/60 4.00 10.00
56 Zach LaVine/60 12.00 30.00
57 Michael Finley/35 6.00 15.00
58 Jordan Adams/60 3.00 8.00
59 Rick Barry/35 5.00 12.00
60 Wilson Chandler/60 4.00 10.00
61 Mark Jackson/60 4.00 10.00
62 Dan Majerle/60 4.00 10.00
63 Victor Oladipo/35 5.00 12.00
65 Jerami Grant/60 3.00 8.00
66 J.R. Smith/60 8.00 20.00
67 Dikembe Mutombo/60 10.00 25.00
68 Zach Randolph/35 5.00 12.00
69 Dwight Powell/60 3.00 8.00
70 Michael Cooper/60 4.00 10.00
71 Marques Johnson/35 5.00 12.00
72 Enes Kanter/60 3.00 8.00
74 Nick Van Exel/35 25.00 60.00

2015-16 Panini Gala Silver Screen Rookie Autographs

RANDOM INSERTS IN PACKS
STATED PRINT RUN 60 SER.#'d SETS
EXCHANGE DEADLINE 12/22/2017
1 Karl-Anthony Towns 100.00 250.00
2 D'Angelo Russell 20.00 50.00
3 Jahlil Okafor 20.00 50.00
4 Emmanuel Mudiay 12.00 30.00
5 Kristaps Porzingis 50.00 120.00
6 Mario Hezonja 8.00 20.00
7 Justise Winslow 12.00 30.00
8 Willie Cauley-Stein 8.00 20.00
9 Stanley Johnson
10 Bobby Portis 6.00 15.00
11 Frank Kaminsky 5.00 12.00
12 Devin Booker 60.00 150.00
13 Myles Turner 10.00 25.00
14 Justin Anderson 5.00 12.00
15 Jerian Grant 3.00 8.00
16 Trey Lyles 8.00 20.00
17 Delon Wright 4.00 10.00
18 R.J. Hunter
19 Jarell Martin 4.00 10.00
20 Anthony Brown 3.00 8.00
21 Norman Powell 4.00 10.00
22 Larry Nance Jr. 5.00 12.00
23 Walter Tavares 3.00 8.00
24 Montrezl Harrell
25 Joe Young 4.00 10.00

2015-16 Panini Gala Starring Role Signatures

RANDOM INSERTS IN PACKS
PRINT RUNS B/WN 35-50 COPIES PER
EXCHANGE DEADLINE 12/22/2017
1 Kobe Bryant/35 150.00 300.00
2 Kevin Durant/35 50.00 120.00
3 Anthony Davis/35 40.00 100.00
4 Kyrie Irving/35 30.00 80.00
5 John Wall/35 15.00 40.00
6 Nikola Mirotic/35 8.00 20.00
7 Victor Oladipo/35 5.00 12.00
8 Zach Randolph/35 5.00 12.00
9 Elfrid Payton/35 5.00 12.00
10 Jordan Clarkson/35 12.00 30.00
11 Danny Green/35 5.00 12.00
12 Matthew Dellavedova/35 15.00 40.00
13 Giannis Antetokounmpo/50 20.00 50.00
14 T.J. Warren/35
15 Dennis Schroder/35 12.00 30.00
16 Marcus Smart/35 5.00 12.00
17 Julius Randle/35 8.00 20.00
18 Gordon Hayward/35 8.00 20.00
19 Kevin Love/35 15.00 40.00
20 Blake Griffin/35 20.00 50.00
21 Mike Conley/50 5.00 12.00
22 Kenneth Faried/50 4.00 10.00
23 Norris Cole/50 3.00 8.00
24 Tony Parker/50 15.00 40.00
25 Andre Drummond/50 10.00 25.00
26 Ray Allen/50 20.00 50.00
27 Dominique Wilkins/50 10.00 25.00
28 Nate Archibald/50 6.00 15.00
29 Anfernee Hardaway/50 25.00 60.00
30 Grant Hill/50 20.00 50.00
31 David Robinson/50 20.00 50.00
32 Bill Walton/50 5.00 12.00
33 Wes Unseld/50 5.00 12.00
34 Dave Cowens/50 3.00 8.00
35 Joe Dumars/50 5.00 12.00

2015-16 Panini Gala Studio Swatches

RANDOM INSERTS IN PACKS
STATED PRINT RUN 60 SER.#'d SETS
*PURPLE/40: .5X TO 1.2X BASIC
*PRIME/25: .75X TO 2X BASIC
1 Anderson Varejao 2.00 5.00
2 Danny Green 2.50 6.00
3 LeBron James 20.00 50.00
4 Steven Adams 2.50 6.00
5 Derrick Favors 2.50 6.00
6 James Young 2.00 5.00
7 Kevin Garnett 5.00 12.00
8 Alex Len 2.00 5.00
9 Shane Battier 2.50 6.00
10 Eric Gordon 2.50 6.00
11 Boris Diaw 2.50 6.00
12 DeMar DeRozan 3.00 8.00
13 Darren Collison 2.50 6.00
14 Al Jefferson 2.50 6.00
15 Joe Smith 2.50 6.00
16 John Henson 2.50 6.00
17 Nicolas Batum 2.50 6.00
18 Avery Bradley 2.50 6.00
19 Tim Hardaway Jr. 2.00 5.00
21 Cody Zeller 2.00 5.00
22 Marcus Smart 2.50 6.00
23 David West 3.00 8.00
24 Brandon Jennings 2.00 5.00
25 Jusuf Nurkic 2.00 5.00
26 Aaron Gordon 2.50 6.00
27 Paul George 4.00 10.00
28 Doug McDermott 2.50 6.00
29 Trey Burke 2.00 5.00
30 Stephen Curry 10.00 25.00

2010-11 Panini Gold Standard

STATED PRINT RUN 299 SER.#'d SETS
EWING, MARAVICH, RODMAN HAVE VAR
ALL VAR STILL TOTAL JUST 299 CARDS
UNPRICED BLACK GOLD PRINT RUN ONE SET
EXCH.EXPIRATION 1/14/2013

1 Kevin Durant 3.00 8.00
2 Kobe Bryant 5.00 12.00
3 Derrick Rose 1.50 4.00
4 Paul Pierce 1.25 3.00
5 Ty Lawson .75 2.00
6 Amare Stoudemire 1.00 2.50
7 Deron Williams 1.00 2.50
8 Blake Griffin 1.25 3.00
9 Kevin Love 1.25 3.00
10 Russell Westbrook 3.00 8.00
11 Monta Ellis 1.00 2.50
12 Tim Duncan 2.00 5.00
13 Steve Nash 1.25 3.00
14 Jrue Holiday 1.25 3.00
15 Kevin Martin 1.00 2.50
16 Dirk Nowitzki 1.50 4.00
17 Stephen Jackson 1.00 2.50
18 LeBron James 6.00 15.00
19 Eric Gordon 1.00 2.50
20 Tayshaun Prince 1.00 2.50
21 Derek Fisher 1.00 2.50
22 Vince Carter 1.50 4.00
23 Antawn Jamison 1.00 2.50
24 Tyreke Evans .75 2.00
25 Al Horford 1.00 2.50
26 Danny Granger 1.00 2.50
27 Marcus Camby .75 2.00
28 Rajon Rondo 1.25 3.00
29 Carmelo Anthony 1.50 4.00
30 Michael Beasley .75 2.00
31 Dwight Howard 1.00 2.50
32 Tony Parker 1.25 3.00
33 Chris Bosh 1.25 3.00
34 LaMarcus Aldridge 1.25 3.00
35 Stephen Curry 5.00 12.00
36 Brook Lopez 1.00 2.50
37 Tyson Chandler 1.00 2.50
38 Jason Richardson 1.25 3.00
39 Anderson Varejao .75 2.00
40 Andre Iguodala 1.00 2.50
41 Marc Gasol 1.25 3.00
42 Danilo Gallinari 1.00 2.50
43 Joe Johnson 1.00 2.50
44 DeMar DeRozan 1.25 3.00
45 Devin Harris .75 2.00
46 Andrei Kirilenko 1.00 2.50
47 Brandon Roy 1.25 3.00
48 Raymond Felton 1.00 2.50
49 Pau Gasol 1.25 3.00
50 Dwyane Wade 2.00 5.00
51 Aaron Brooks .75 2.00
52 Zach Randolph 1.00 2.50
53 Jason Terry 1.00 2.50
54 Charlie Villanueva .75 2.00
55 Jeff Green 1.00 2.50
56 Channing Frye 1.00 2.50
57 Al Thornton .75 2.00
58 Manu Ginobili 1.25 3.00
59 David West 1.00 2.50
60 Andrew Bogut 1.00 2.50
61 Jonny Flynn .75 2.00
62 David Lee .75 2.00
63 Tracy McGrady 1.25 3.00
64 Luol Deng 1.00 2.50
65 Elton Brand 1.25 3.00
66 Emeka Okafor 1.00 2.50
67 Kevin Garnett 2.00 5.00
68 Carl Landry .75 2.00
69 Jameer Nelson .75 2.00
70 Joakim Noah 1.00 2.50
71 Chris Kaman 1.00 2.50
72 Rudy Gay 1.25 3.00
73 Richard Jefferson 1.00 2.50
74 Andrea Bargnani 1.00 2.50
75 Jamal Crawford 1.25 3.00
76 Grant Hill 3.00 8.00
77 Lamar Odom 1.00 2.50
78 Paul Millsap 1.00 2.50
79 Luis Scola 1.00 2.50
80 J.R. Smith 1.00 2.50
81 Ray Allen 1.25 3.00
82 Tyler Hansbrough 1.00 2.50
83 Ben Wallace 1.00 2.50
84 J.J. Hickson .75 2.00
85 Al Jefferson 1.00 2.50
86 Jason Kidd 1.25 3.00
87 Luke Ridnour 1.00 2.50
88 Nene 1.00 2.50
89 Sasha Vujacic .75 2.00
90 Rashard Lewis 1.00 2.50
91 D.J. Augustin .75 2.00
92 Ron Artest 1.25 3.00
93 Yao Ming 1.50 4.00
94 Juwan Howard 1.00 2.50
95 Roy Hibbert 1.00 2.50
96 Carlos Boozer 1.00 2.50
97 Wilson Chandler 1.00 2.50
98 DeJuan Blair .75 2.00
99 Shaquille O'Neal 2.50 6.00
100 Chris Paul 1.50 4.00
101 Baron Davis 1.00 2.50
102 Leandro Barbosa 1.00 2.50
103 Josh Smith 1.00 2.50
104 John Salmons 1.00 2.50
105 Hedo Turkoglu 1.00 2.50
106 Ben Gordon 1.00 2.50
107 Gerald Henderson .75 2.00
108 Serge Ibaka 1.00 2.50
109 Shane Battier 1.00 2.50
110 Andrew Bynum .75 2.00
111 Chauncey Billups 1.25 3.00
112 Nick Young 1.00 2.50
113 Dorell Wright .75 2.00
114 Gilbert Arenas 1.00 2.50
115 Darko Milicic .75 2.00
116 Caron Butler 1.00 2.50
117 Zydrunas Ilgauskas 1.00 2.50
118 Trevor Ariza .75 2.00
119 Troy Murphy .75 2.00
120 J.J. Redick 1.25 3.00
121 Gerald Wallace 1.00 2.50
122 Samuel Dalembert .75 2.00
123 Shawn Marion 1.00 2.50
124 Rudy Fernandez .75 2.00
125 Brandon Jennings .75 2.00
126 JaVale McGee 1.00 2.50
127 O.J. Mayo .75 2.00
128 James Harden 2.00 5.00
129 Chris Andersen 1.00 2.50
130 Toney Douglas .75 2.00
131 Glen Davis .75 2.00
132 Richard Hamilton 1.00 2.50
133 George Hill 1.00 2.50
134 Louis Williams 1.00 2.50
135 Al Harrington 1.00 2.50
136 Anthony Morrow .75 2.00
137 Daniel Gibson 1.00 2.50
138 Wesley Matthews .75 2.00
139 Kris Humphries .75 2.00
140 Rodrigue Beaubois .75 2.00
141 A.J. Price .75 2.00
142 Chase Budinger .75 2.00
143 Donte Greene .75 2.00
144 Andre Miller 1.00 2.50
145 Ryan Gomes .75 2.00
146 Jodie Meeks 1.25 3.00
147 Kendrick Perkins .75 2.00
148 Taj Gibson 1.00 2.50
149 Boris Diaw 1.00 2.50
150 Derrick Brown .75 2.00
151 Jeff Teague 1.00 2.50
152 Wayne Ellington 1.00 2.50
153 Terrence Williams .75 2.00
154 Robin Lopez .75 2.00
155 Jermaine O'Neal 1.00 2.50
156 Austin Daye .75 2.00
157 J.J. Barea 1.00 2.50
158 Darren Collison 1.00 2.50
159 Goran Dragic 1.00 2.50
160 Beno Udrih .75 2.00
161 Earl Clark .75 2.00
162 Hakim Warrick 1.00 2.50
163 Sam Young .75 2.00
164 Ronnie Brewer 1.00 2.50
165 Omri Casspi .75 2.00
166 T.J. Ford .75 2.00
167 Chris Douglas-Roberts .75 2.00
168 Eric Maynor .75 2.00
169 James Johnson .75 2.00
170 Patrick Mills 1.25 3.00
171 Mark Jackson 1.25 3.00
172 Chris Webber 1.50 4.00
173 Derek Harper 1.25 3.00
174A Patrick Ewing Knicks 2.00 5.00
174B P.Ewing Magic SP
174C P.Ewing Sonics SP
175 Brad Daugherty 1.25 3.00
176 Kenny Anderson 1.25 3.00
177 Scott Skiles 1.25 3.00
178 Charles Oakley 1.50 4.00
179 Dan Majerle 1.25 3.00
180A Pete Maravich Hawks 2.50 6.00
180B P.Maravich Celtics SP
180C P.Maravich Jazz SP 6.00 15.00
181 Wilt Chamberlain 3.00 8.00
182 Horace Grant 1.50 4.00
183 Glen Rice 1.25 3.00
184 Shawn Kemp 2.50 6.00
185 Jo Jo White 1.25 3.00
186 Jalen Rose 1.50 4.00
187A Dennis Rodman Pistons 6.00 15.00
187B D.Rodman Bulls SP 6.00 15.00
187C D.Rodman Lakers SP 6.00 15.00
187D D.Rodman Mavs SP
187E D.Rodman Spurs SP 6.00 15.00
188 Dave DeBusschere 1.50 4.00
189 Oscar Robertson 2.00 5.00
190 Bill Walton 1.50 4.00
191 Kareem Abdul-Jabbar 2.50 6.00
192 Larry Bird 4.00 10.00
193 Dan Issel 1.25 3.00
194 Doc Rivers 1.50 4.00
195 George McGinnis 1.00 2.50
196 Bill Russell 2.50 6.00
197 Christian Laettner 1.25 3.00
198 Dolph Schayes 1.50 4.00
199 M.L. Carr 1.50 4.00
200 Darryl Dawkins 1.00 2.50
201 David Thompson 1.25 3.00
202 Bob Lanier 1.25 3.00
203 Michael Cooper 1.25 3.00
204 Bernard King 1.25 3.00
205 Bailey Howell 1.50 4.00
206 Al Attles 1.50 4.00
207 Dikembe Mutombo 1.50 4.00
208 Bob McAdoo 1.25 3.00
209 Artis Gilmore 1.25 3.00
210 A.C. Green 1.50 4.00
211 Dominique Wilkins 2.00 5.00
212 Alonzo Mourning 2.00 5.00
213 John Wall AU RC 40.00 100.00
214 Evan Turner AU RC 5.00 12.00
215 Derrick Favors AU RC 8.00 20.00
216 Wesley Johnson AU RC 4.00 10.00
217 DeMarcus Cousins AU RC 25.00 60.00
218 Ekpe Udoh AU RC 4.00 10.00
219 Greg Monroe AU RC 8.00 20.00
220 Al-Farouq Aminu AU RC 6.00 15.00
221 Gordon Hayward AU RC 30.00 80.00
222 Paul George AU RC 60.00 150.00
223 Cole Aldrich AU RC 5.00 12.00
224 Xavier Henry AU RC 4.00 10.00
225 Ed Davis AU RC 4.00 10.00
226 Patrick Patterson AU RC 5.00 12.00
227 Larry Sanders AU RC 4.00 10.00
228 Luke Babbitt AU RC 5.00 12.00
229 Kevin Seraphin AU RC 4.00 10.00
230 Eric Bledsoe AU RC 8.00 20.00
231 Avery Bradley AU RC 8.00 20.00
232 James Anderson AU RC 4.00 10.00
233 Elliot Williams AU RC 4.00 10.00
234 Landry Fields AU RC 5.00 12.00
235 Greivis Vasquez AU RC 5.00 12.00
236 Dominique Jones AU RC 4.00 10.00
237 Gary Neal AU RC 6.00 15.00
238 Daniel Orton AU RC 4.00 10.00
239 Lazar Hayward AU RC 4.00 10.00
240 Devin Ebanks AU RC 4.00 10.00
241 Timofey Mozgov AU RC 6.00 15.00
242 Luke Harangody AU RC 4.00 10.00
243 Omer Asik AU RC 8.00 20.00
244 Eugene Jeter AU RC 6.00 15.00
245 Gary Forbes AU RC 4.00 10.00
246 Nikola Pekovic AU RC 8.00 20.00
247 Jordan Crawford AU RC 5.00 12.00

2010-11 Panini Gold Standard Platinum Gold

*STARS: 2X TO 5X BASE HI
*RETIRED: 1.25X TO 3X BASE HI
*ROOKIES: .75X TO 2X BASE HI
STATED PRINT RUN 25 SER.#'d SETS
76 Grant Hill 15.00 40.00
184 Shawn Kemp 30.00 80.00
212 Alonzo Mourning 12.00 30.00
213 John Wall AU 150.00 300.00
215 Derrick Favors AU 30.00 80.00
217 DeMarcus Cousins AU 50.00 125.00

2010-11 Panini Gold Standard 24-Karat Kobe

COMMON CARD (1-15) 5.00 12.00
STATED PRINT RUN 299 SER.#'d SETS
UNPRICED GOLD RUSH PRINT RUN ONE SET

2010-11 Panini Gold Standard 24-Karat Kobe Materials Signatures

COMMON CARD 100.00 200.00
STATED PRINT RUN 49 SER.#'d SETS

2010-11 Panini Gold Standard 24-Karat Kobe Materials Signatures Prime

COMMON CARD 125.00 250.00
STATED PRINT RUN 24 SER.#'d SETS

2010-11 Panini Gold Standard 24-Karat Kobe Signatures

COMMON CARD 75.00 150.00
STATED PRINT RUN 49 SER.#'d SETS

2010-11 Panini Gold Standard Gold Bars

STATED PRINT RUN 299 SER.#'d SETS
UNPRICED GOLD RUSH PRINT RUN 10 SETS
1 Kevin Durant 5.00 12.00
2 Dwight Howard 1.50 4.00
3 Dwyane Wade 3.00 8.00
4 Kobe Bryant 8.00 20.00
5 LaMarcus Aldridge 2.00 5.00
6 Brandon Jennings 1.25 3.00
7 Kevin Garnett 3.00 8.00
8 Eric Gordon 1.50 4.00
9 Deron Williams 1.50 4.00
10 Kevin Love 2.00 5.00
11 Monta Ellis 1.50 4.00
12 Carmelo Anthony 2.50 6.00
13 Chris Paul 2.50 6.00
14 Kevin Martin 1.50 4.00
15 Derrick Rose 2.50 6.00

2010-11 Panini Gold Standard Gold Bars Materials

STATED PRINT RUN 199 SER.#'d SETS
1 Kevin Durant 8.00 20.00
2 Dwight Howard 2.50 6.00
3 Dwyane Wade 5.00 12.00
4 Kobe Bryant 10.00 25.00
5 LaMarcus Aldridge 3.00 8.00
6 Brandon Jennings 2.00 5.00
7 Kevin Garnett 5.00 12.00
8 Eric Gordon 2.50 6.00
10 Kevin Love 3.00 8.00
11 Monta Ellis 2.50 6.00
13 Chris Paul 4.00 10.00
15 Derrick Rose 4.00 10.00

2010-11 Panini Gold Standard Gold Bars Materials Prime

*PRIME: .75X TO 2X BASE HI
STATED PRINT RUN ONE TO 25 SER.#'d SETS
SOME UNPRICED DUE TO SCARCITY
1 Kevin Durant/25 20.00 50.00

2010-11 Panini Gold Standard Gold Bars Materials Signatures

STATED PRINT RUN 5 TO 49 SER.#'d SETS
SOME UNPRICED DUE TO SCARCITY
4 Kobe Bryant/24 100.00 200.00
5 LaMarcus Aldridge/49 10.00 25.00
8 Eric Gordon/49 8.00 20.00
10 Kevin Love/25 20.00 50.00

2010-11 Panini Gold Standard Gold Bars Materials Signatures Prime

STATED PRINT RUN ONE TO 25 SER.#'d SETS
SOME UNPRICED DUE TO SCARCITY
5 LaMarcus Aldridge/25 15.00 40.00
10 Kevin Love/15 25.00 60.00

2010-11 Panini Gold Standard Gold Bars Signatures

STATED PRINT RUN 5 TO 49 SER.#'d SETS
SOME UNPRICED DUE TO SCARCITY
4 Kobe Bryant/24 100.00 200.00
5 LaMarcus Aldridge/49 8.00 20.00
8 Eric Gordon/40 10.00 25.00
10 Kevin Love/25 15.00 40.00
14 Kevin Martin/49 6.00 15.00

2010-11 Panini Gold Standard Gold Crowns

STATED PRINT RUN 299 SER.#'d SETS
UNPRICED GOLD RUSH PRINT RUN 8 SETS
1 Kevin Durant 3.00 8.00
2 Dwight Howard 1.00 2.50
3 Stephen Curry 15.00 30.00
4 Amare Stoudemire 1.00 2.50
5 Rajon Rondo 1.25 3.00
6 Kevin Love 1.25 3.00
7 Andrew Bogut 1.00 2.50
8 Chris Paul 1.50 4.00
9 Steve Nash 1.25 3.00
10 Kobe Bryant 5.00 12.00
11 Serge Ibaka 1.00 2.50
12 Deron Williams 1.00 2.50
13 Luke Ridnour 1.00 2.50
14 Monta Ellis 1.00 2.50
15 LeBron James 6.00 15.00
16 JaVale McGee 1.00 2.50
17 Emeka Okafor 1.00 2.50
18 Chauncey Billups 1.25 3.00
19 Raymond Felton 1.00 2.50
20 Tyson Chandler 1.00 2.50
21 Russell Westbrook 3.00 8.00
22 Dwyane Wade 2.00 5.00
23 Tim Duncan 2.00 5.00
24 Jose Calderon .75 2.00
25 Pau Gasol 1.25 3.00

2010-11 Panini Gold Standard Gold Crowns Materials

STATED PRINT RUN 99 TO 249 SER.#'d SETS
1 Kevin Durant/249 6.00 15.00
2 Dwight Howard/249 3.00 8.00
3 Stephen Curry/99 15.00 40.00
4 Amare Stoudemire/249 3.00 8.00
5 Rajon Rondo/249 4.00 10.00
6 Kevin Love/249 4.00 10.00
7 Andrew Bogut/249 3.00 8.00
8 Chris Paul/249 5.00 12.00
9 Steve Nash/249 4.00 10.00
10 Kobe Bryant/249 10.00 25.00
11 Serge Ibaka/249 3.00 8.00
13 Luke Ridnour/249 3.00 8.00
14 Monta Ellis/249 3.00 8.00
15 LeBron James/249 12.00 30.00
16 JaVale McGee/249 3.00 8.00
17 Emeka Okafor/249 3.00 8.00
20 Tyson Chandler/249 3.00 8.00
21 Russell Westbrook/249 10.00 25.00
22 Dwyane Wade/249 6.00 15.00
23 Tim Duncan/249 6.00 15.00
24 Jose Calderon/249 2.50 6.00
25 Pau Gasol/249 4.00 10.00

2010-11 Panini Gold Standard Gold Crowns Materials Prime

*PRIME: .6X TO 1.5X BASE HI
STATED PRINT RUN ONE TO 25 SER.#'d SETS
SOME UNPRICED DUE TO SCARCITY
1 Kevin Durant/25 15.00 40.00
9 Steve Nash/25 8.00 20.00
15 LeBron James/25 25.00 60.00

2010-11 Panini Gold Standard Gold Crowns Materials Signatures

STATED PRINT RUN 5 TO 199 SER.#'d SETS
SOME UNPRICED DUE TO SCARCITY
3 Stephen Curry/199 125.00 250.00
5 Rajon Rondo/25 20.00 50.00
6 Kevin Love/49 20.00 50.00
7 Andrew Bogut/199 6.00 15.00
10 Kobe Bryant/24 75.00 150.00
11 Serge Ibaka/199 4.00 10.00
13 Luke Ridnour/199 4.00 10.00
16 JaVale McGee/199 5.00 12.00
17 Emeka Okafor/25 5.00 12.00
20 Tyson Chandler/199 5.00 12.00

2010-11 Panini Gold Standard Gold Crowns Materials Signatures Prime

STATED PRINT RUN 3 TO 25 SER.#'d SETS
SOME UNPRICED DUE TO SCARCITY
3 Stephen Curry/25 175.00 350.00
5 Rajon Rondo/25 25.00 60.00
6 Kevin Love/25 25.00 60.00
7 Andrew Bogut/25 12.00 30.00
10 Kobe Bryant/24 125.00 250.00
11 Serge Ibaka/25 20.00 50.00
13 Luke Ridnour/25 8.00 20.00
16 JaVale McGee/25 8.00 20.00
17 Emeka Okafor/25 8.00 20.00
20 Tyson Chandler/25 10.00 25.00
21 Russell Westbrook/25 60.00 150.00

2010-11 Panini Gold Standard Gold Crowns Signatures

STATED PRINT RUN 5 TO 69 SER.#'d SETS
SOME UNPRICED DUE TO SCARCITY
3 Stephen Curry/69 100.00 200.00
5 Rajon Rondo/25 15.00 40.00
6 Kevin Love/49 12.00 30.00
10 Kobe Bryant/49 90.00 150.00
11 Serge Ibaka/69 8.00 20.00
13 Luke Ridnour/69 4.00 10.00
16 JaVale McGee/69 4.00 10.00
17 Emeka Okafor/49 4.00 10.00
18 Chauncey Billups/25 6.00 15.00
19 Raymond Felton/69 4.00 10.00
20 Tyson Chandler/49 5.00 12.00

2010-11 Panini Gold Standard Gold Medalists

STATED PRINT RUN 299 SER.#'d SETS
UNPRICED GOLD RUSH PRINT RUN 10 SETS
1 Dwight Howard 1.25 3.00
2 Tayshaun Prince 1.25 3.00
3 Michael Redd 1.25 3.00
4 LeBron James 8.00 20.00
5 Dwyane Wade 2.50 6.00
6 Jason Kidd 1.50 4.00
7 Carlos Boozer 1.25 3.00
8 Chris Bosh 1.50 4.00
9 Chris Paul 2.00 5.00
10 Kevin Garnett 2.50 6.00
11 Larry Johnson 2.00 5.00
12 Mark Price 1.50 4.00
13 Shaquille O'Neal 3.00 8.00
14 Steve Smith 1.25 3.00
15 Dan Majerle 1.25 3.00
16 Dominique Wilkins 2.00 5.00
17 Joe Dumars 1.50 4.00
18 Kevin Johnson 1.50 4.00
19 Alonzo Mourning 3.00 8.00
20 David Robinson 3.00 8.00

2010-11 Panini Gold Standard Gold Medalists Materials

STATED PRINT RUN 299 SER.#'d SETS
1 Dwight Howard 3.00 8.00
2 Tayshaun Prince 3.00 8.00
3 Michael Redd 3.00 8.00
4 LeBron James 20.00 50.00
5 Dwyane Wade 6.00 15.00
6 Jason Kidd 4.00 10.00
7 Carlos Boozer 3.00 8.00
8 Chris Bosh 4.00 10.00
9 Chris Paul 5.00 12.00
10 Kevin Garnett 6.00 15.00
11 Larry Johnson 5.00 12.00
12 Mark Price 5.00 12.00
13 Shaquille O'Neal 6.00 15.00
14 Steve Smith 3.00 8.00
15 Dan Majerle 3.00 8.00
16 Dominique Wilkins 5.00 12.00
17 Joe Dumars 4.00 10.00
18 Kevin Johnson 4.00 10.00
19 Alonzo Mourning 5.00 12.00

2010-11 Panini Gold Standard Gold Medalists Materials Prime

*PRIME: 1X TO 2.5X BASE HI
STATED PRINT RUN 25 SER.#'d SETS
4 LeBron James 50.00 125.00
8 Chris Bosh 12.00 30.00
11 Larry Johnson 30.00 80.00
13 Shaquille O'Neal 20.00 50.00
16 Dominique Wilkins 15.00 40.00
17 Joe Dumars 25.00 60.00
18 Kevin Johnson 20.00 50.00

2010-11 Panini Gold Standard Gold Medalists Materials Signatures

STATED PRINT RUN 10 TO 99 SER.#'d SETS
SOME UNPRICED DUE TO SCARCITY
7 Carlos Boozer/49 6.00 15.00
11 Larry Johnson/99 8.00 20.00
12 Mark Price/49 40.00 100.00
14 Steve Smith/99 10.00 25.00
15 Dan Majerle/49 15.00 40.00
17 Joe Dumars/25 12.00 30.00
18 Kevin Johnson/49 20.00 50.00

2010-11 Panini Gold Standard Gold Medalists Materials Signatures Prime

STATED PRINT RUN 5 TO 25 SER.#'d SETS
SOME UNPRICED DUE TO SCARCITY
7 Carlos Boozer/25 12.00 30.00
11 Larry Johnson/25 60.00 150.00
12 Mark Price/25 50.00 125.00
14 Steve Smith/25 30.00 80.00
15 Dan Majerle/25 20.00 50.00
17 Joe Dumars/25 15.00 40.00
18 Kevin Johnson/25 50.00 120.00

2010-11 Panini Gold Standard Gold Medalists Signatures

STATED PRINT RUN 10 TO 199 SER.#'d SETS
SOME UNPRICED DUE TO SCARCITY
7 Carlos Boozer/49 6.00 15.00
12 Mark Price/180 6.00 15.00
14 Steve Smith/49 6.00 15.00
15 Dan Majerle/199 8.00 20.00
17 Joe Dumars/25 20.00 50.00
18 Kevin Johnson/49 20.00 50.00

2010-11 Panini Gold Standard Gold Medalists Signatures Dual

STATED PRINT RUN 5 TO 50 SER.#'d SETS
SOME UNPRICED DUE TO SCARCITY
3 B.Davis/R.Westbrook/50 40.00 100.00
4 M.Bogues/J.Flynn/50 10.00 25.00
5 W.Bellamy/T.Chandler/50 10.00 25.00
6 M.Bibby/S.Curry/50 60.00 150.00
8 J.West/K.Bryant/25 125.00 250.00
9 K.Love/V.Carter/35 30.00 80.00
11 D.Williams/E.Gordon/35 12.00 30.00
12 C.Mullin/C.Laettner/50 12.00 30.00
13 D.Wilkins/D.Majerle/35 20.00 50.00
16 C.Drexler/D.Wilkins/25 60.00 150.00
20 I.Thomas/S.Elliott/50 25.00 60.00

2010-11 Panini Gold Standard Gold Mining

STATED PRINT RUN 299 SER.#'d SETS
UNPRICED GOLD RUSH PRINT RUN 8 SETS
1 Chris Paul 1.50 4.00
2 Bernard King 1.00 2.50
3 Derrick Rose 1.50 4.00
4 Blake Griffin 1.25 3.00
5 Magic Johnson 3.00 8.00
6 Tim Duncan 2.00 5.00
7 Kobe Bryant 5.00 12.00
8 Kareem Abdul-Jabbar 2.00 5.00
9 Stephen Curry 10.00 25.00
10 Dwyane Wade 2.00 5.00
11 Amare Stoudemire 1.00 2.50
12 Oscar Robertson 1.50 4.00
13 Chris Bosh 1.25 3.00
14 Dirk Nowitzki 1.50 4.00
15 Derek Fisher 1.00 2.50
16 Larry Bird 3.00 8.00
17 Kevin Love 1.25 3.00
18 Wilt Chamberlain 2.50 6.00
19 Kevin Durant 3.00 8.00
20 LeBron James 6.00 15.00

2010-11 Panini Gold Standard Gold Mining Materials

STATED PRINT RUN 49 TO 299 SER.#'d SETS
1 Chris Paul/299 4.00 10.00
2 Bernard King/299 2.50 6.00
4 Blake Griffin/299 3.00 8.00
5 Magic Johnson/99 10.00 25.00
6 Tim Duncan/299 5.00 12.00
7 Kobe Bryant/299 10.00 25.00
9 Stephen Curry/99 12.00 30.00
10 Dwyane Wade/299 5.00 12.00
11 Amare Stoudemire/299 2.50 6.00
13 Chris Bosh/299 3.00 8.00
14 Dirk Nowitzki/299 4.00 10.00
15 Derek Fisher/299 2.50 6.00
16 Larry Bird/49 8.00 20.00
17 Kevin Love/299 3.00 8.00
19 Kevin Durant/299 6.00 15.00
20 LeBron James/299 12.00 30.00

2010-11 Panini Gold Standard Gold Mining Materials Prime

*PRIME: .75X TO 2X BASE HI
STATED PRINT RUN ONE TO 25 SER.#'d SETS
SOME UNPRICED DUE TO SCARCITY
14 Dirk Nowitzki/25 12.00 30.00
15 Derek Fisher/25 8.00 20.00
19 Kevin Durant/25 15.00 40.00
20 LeBron James/25 25.00 60.00

2010-11 Panini Gold Standard Gold Mining Materials Signatures

STATED PRINT RUN 3 TO 49 SER.#'d SETS
SOME UNPRICED DUE TO SCARCITY
2 Bernard King/49 6.00 15.00
7 Kobe Bryant/24 100.00 200.00
9 Stephen Curry/49 100.00 200.00
15 Derek Fisher/49 10.00 25.00

2010-11 Panini Gold Standard Gold Mining Materials Signatures Prime

STATED PRINT RUN 3 TO 25 SER.#'d SETS
SOME UNPRICED DUE TO SCARCITY
2 Bernard King/25 15.00 40.00
7 Kobe Bryant/24 150.00 300.00
9 Stephen Curry/25 150.00 300.00
15 Derek Fisher/25 20.00 50.00

2010-11 Panini Gold Standard Gold Mining Signatures

STATED PRINT RUN 3 TO 99 SER.#'d SETS
SOME UNPRICED DUE TO SCARCITY
2 Bernard King/99 5.00 12.00
7 Kobe Bryant/24 100.00 200.00
9 Stephen Curry/99 100.00 250.00
15 Derek Fisher/99 10.00 25.00
17 Kevin Love/25 15.00 40.00

2010-11 Panini Gold Standard Gold Mining Signatures Dual

STATED PRINT RUN 10 TO 50 SER.#'d SETS
SOME UNPRICED DUE TO SCARCITY
1 D.Fisher/P.Gasol/20 20.00 50.00
3 C.Bosh/L.Odom/25 25.00 60.00
6 I.Thomas/J.Dumars/50 20.00 50.00
7 K.Love/D.Granger/50 15.00 40.00
8 J.Noah/T.Chandler/50 15.00 40.00
9 B.King/D.Thompson/50 12.00 30.00
10 J.Rose/J.Howard/50 12.00 30.00

2010-11 Panini Gold Standard Gold NBA Logos

STATED PRINT RUN 5 TO 199 SER.#'d SETS
SOME UNPRICED DUE TO SCARCITY
1 Al Attles/199 6.00 15.00
2 Alex English/199 6.00 15.00
5 Artis Gilmore/199 8.00 20.00
7 Bill Walton/99 10.00 25.00
10 Connie Hawkins/199 8.00 20.00
11 Dave Cowens/99 10.00 25.00
14 Dolph Schayes/99 6.00 15.00
16 Elvin Hayes/99 10.00 25.00
17 Gail Goodrich/99 6.00 15.00
19 George Gervin/99 10.00 25.00
20 Isiah Thomas/99 12.00 30.00
21 Jack Twyman/199 6.00 15.00
22 Jalen Rose/199 6.00 15.00
24 Jeff Hornacek/199 8.00 20.00
30 Kelly Tripucka/199 6.00 15.00
32 Kobe Bryant/99 100.00 200.00
34 Lenny Wilkens/99 8.00 20.00
36 Michael Beasley/25 12.00 30.00
38 Nate Archibald/99 8.00 20.00
41 Rick Barry/199 8.00 20.00
42 Robert Horry/199 10.00 25.00
43 Robert Parish/199 8.00 20.00
44 Rolando Blackman/199 6.00 15.00
45 Sam Perkins/199 6.00 15.00
47 Stephen Curry/199 100.00 250.00
49 Tyreke Evans/25 15.00 40.00
50 Walt Frazier/25 20.00 50.00

2010-11 Panini Gold Standard Gold Nuggets

STATED PRINT RUN 299 SER.#'d SETS
UNPRICED GOLD RUSH PRINT RUN 10 SETS
1 LeBron James 6.00 15.00
2 Kobe Bryant 5.00 12.00
3 Blake Griffin 1.25 3.00
4 Kevin Durant 3.00 8.00
5 Paul Pierce 1.25 3.00
6 Dirk Nowitzki 1.50 4.00
7 Derrick Rose 1.50 4.00
8 Kevin Love 1.25 3.00
9 Tyreke Evans .75 2.00
10 Carmelo Anthony 1.50 4.00
11 Amare Stoudemire 1.00 2.50
12 Dwyane Wade 2.00 5.00
13 Deron Williams 1.00 2.50
14 LaMarcus Aldridge 1.25 3.00
15 Rajon Rondo 1.25 3.00
16 Russell Westbrook 3.00 8.00
17 Brandon Jennings .75 2.00
18 Eric Gordon 1.00 2.50
19 Pau Gasol 1.25 3.00
20 Steve Nash 1.25 3.00
21 Al Jefferson 1.00 2.50
22 D.J. Augustin .75 2.00
23 Raymond Felton 1.00 2.50
24 Kevin Garnett 2.00 5.00
25 Aaron Brooks .75 2.00
26 Chris Paul 1.50 4.00
27 Tim Duncan 2.00 5.00
28 Monta Ellis 1.00 2.50
29 Tracy McGrady 1.25 3.00
30 Dwight Howard 1.00 2.50
31 Andrea Bargnani 1.00 2.50
32 Antawn Jamison 1.00 2.50
33 Joe Johnson 1.00 2.50
34 Lamar Odom 1.00 2.50
35 Tyson Chandler 1.00 2.50
36 Andre Miller 1.00 2.50
37 Devin Harris .75 2.00
38 Roy Hibbert 1.00 2.50
39 Rudy Gay 1.25 3.00
40 David West 1.00 2.50
41 Kevin Martin 1.00 2.50
42 Jameer Nelson .75 2.00
43 Nene 1.00 2.50
44 Al Horford 1.00 2.50
45 Manu Ginobili 1.25 3.00
46 Shaquille O'Neal 2.50 6.00
47 Stephen Curry 10.00 15.00
48 Jeff Green 1.00 2.50
49 Joakim Noah 1.00 2.50
50 Jason Richardson 1.25 3.00

2010-11 Panini Gold Standard Gold Nuggets Materials

STATED PRINT RUN 49 TO 199 SER.#'d SETS
1 LeBron James/199 12.00 30.00
2 Kobe Bryant/199 10.00 25.00
3 Blake Griffin/199 2.50 6.00
4 Kevin Durant/199 6.00 15.00
5 Paul Pierce/199 2.50 6.00
6 Dirk Nowitzki/199 3.00 8.00
7 Derrick Rose/199 3.00 8.00
8 Kevin Love/199 2.50 6.00
9 Tyreke Evans/199 1.50 4.00
11 Amare Stoudemire/199 2.00 5.00
12 Dwyane Wade/199 4.00 10.00
14 LaMarcus Aldridge/199 2.50 6.00
15 Rajon Rondo/199 2.50 6.00
16 Russell Westbrook/199 6.00 15.00
17 Brandon Jennings/199 1.50 4.00
18 Eric Gordon/199 2.00 5.00
19 Pau Gasol/199 2.50 6.00
20 Steve Nash/199 2.50 6.00
21 Al Jefferson/199 2.00 5.00
22 D.J. Augustin/199 1.50 4.00
24 Kevin Garnett/199 4.00 10.00
26 Chris Paul/199 3.00 8.00
27 Tim Duncan/199 4.00 10.00
28 Monta Ellis/199 2.00 5.00
30 Dwight Howard/199 2.00 5.00
31 Andrea Bargnani/199 2.00 5.00
32 Antawn Jamison/199 2.00 5.00
33 Joe Johnson/199 2.00 5.00
34 Lamar Odom/199 2.00 5.00
35 Tyson Chandler/199 2.00 5.00
36 Andre Miller/199 2.00 5.00
39 Rudy Gay/49 2.50 6.00
40 David West/199 2.00 5.00
42 Jameer Nelson/199 1.50 4.00
43 Nene/199 2.00 5.00
44 Al Horford/199 2.00 5.00
45 Manu Ginobili/199 2.50 6.00
46 Shaquille O'Neal/199 5.00 12.00
47 Stephen Curry/99 10.00 25.00
49 Joakim Noah/75 2.00 5.00

2010-11 Panini Gold Standard Gold Nuggets Materials Prime

*PRIME: .75X TO 2X BASE HI
STATED PRINT RUN 10 TO 25 SER.#'d SETS
SOME UNPRICED DUE TO SCARCITY

2010-11 Panini Gold Standard Gold Nuggets Materials Signatures

STATED PRINT RUN 3 TO 99 SER.#'d SETS
SOME UNPRICED DUE TO SCARCITY
2 Kobe Bryant/24 100.00 200.00
8 Kevin Love/25 15.00 40.00
9 Tyreke Evans/25 5.00 12.00
14 LaMarcus Aldridge/25 10.00 25.00
15 Rajon Rondo/25 15.00 40.00
16 Russell Westbrook/25 40.00 100.00
17 Brandon Jennings/25 12.00 30.00
21 Al Jefferson/25 6.00 15.00
22 D.J. Augustin/49 5.00 12.00
31 Andrea Bargnani/25 6.00 15.00
32 Antawn Jamison/25 6.00 15.00
33 Joe Johnson/25 8.00 20.00
36 Andre Miller/49 6.00 15.00
39 Rudy Gay/25 10.00 25.00
42 Jameer Nelson/49 5.00 12.00
44 Al Horford/25 5.00 12.00
47 Stephen Curry/99 75.00 200.00
49 Joakim Noah/25 12.00 30.00

2010-11 Panini Gold Standard Gold Nuggets Materials Signatures Prime

STATED PRINT RUN ONE TO 25 SER.#'d SETS
SOME UNPRICED DUE TO SCARCITY
2 Kobe Bryant/24 150.00 300.00
8 Kevin Love/15 25.00 60.00
14 LaMarcus Aldridge/15 12.00 30.00
15 Rajon Rondo/15 25.00 60.00
16 Russell Westbrook/25 50.00 120.00
21 Al Jefferson/25 10.00 25.00
22 D.J. Augustin/25 8.00 20.00
31 Andrea Bargnani/15 8.00 20.00
32 Antawn Jamison/15 10.00 25.00
33 Joe Johnson/15 12.00 30.00
35 Tyson Chandler/15 10.00 25.00
36 Andre Miller/25 10.00 25.00
42 Jameer Nelson/15 8.00 20.00
44 Al Horford/25 8.00 20.00
47 Stephen Curry/25 125.00 300.00

2010-11 Panini Gold Standard Gold Nuggets Signatures

STATED PRINT RUN ONE TO 99 SER.#'d SETS
SOME UNPRICED DUE TO SCARCITY
2 Kobe Bryant/24 60.00 150.00
8 Kevin Love/25 12.00 30.00
9 Tyreke Evans/25 4.00 10.00
17 Brandon Jennings/49 6.00 15.00
18 Eric Gordon/99 4.00 10.00
21 Al Jefferson/25 6.00 15.00
22 D.J. Augustin/99 4.00 10.00
23 Raymond Felton/49 4.00 10.00
25 Aaron Brooks/99 4.00 10.00
31 Andrea Bargnani/49 4.00 10.00
32 Antawn Jamison/49 5.00 12.00
33 Joe Johnson/25 6.00 15.00
35 Tyson Chandler/49 5.00 12.00
36 Andre Miller/99 5.00 12.00
37 Devin Harris/99 4.00 10.00
38 Roy Hibbert/99 4.00 10.00
39 Rudy Gay/49 8.00 20.00
42 Jameer Nelson/49 4.00 10.00
44 Al Horford/99 4.00 10.00
47 Stephen Curry/99 75.00 200.00
48 Jeff Green/99 5.00 12.00
49 Joakim Noah/25 6.00 15.00

2010-11 Panini Gold Standard Gold Records

STATED PRINT RUN 299 SER.#'d SETS
UNPRICED GOLD RUSH PRINT RUN 10 SETS
1 Ray Allen 1.50 4.00
2 John Stockton 2.50 6.00
3 Wilt Chamberlain 3.00 8.00
4 Hakeem Olajuwon 2.00 5.00
5 Steve Nash 1.50 4.00
6 Mark Eaton 1.00 2.50
7 John Stockton 2.50 6.00
8 Kareem Abdul-Jabbar 2.50 6.00
9 Wilt Chamberlain 3.00 8.00
10 Karl Malone 2.00 5.00
11 Robert Parish 1.50 4.00
12 John Stockton 2.50 6.00
13 Jerry West 2.00 5.00
14 Moses Malone 1.50 4.00
15 Kareem Abdul-Jabbar 2.50 6.00

2010-11 Panini Gold Standard Gold Records Materials

STATED PRINT RUN 49 TO 299 SER.#'d SETS
1 Ray Allen/299 3.00 8.00
2 John Stockton/49 8.00 20.00
5 Steve Nash/299 3.00 8.00
6 Mark Eaton/299 2.00 5.00
7 John Stockton/49 8.00 20.00
8 Kareem Abdul-Jabbar/99 5.00 12.00
10 Karl Malone/299 4.00 10.00
11 Robert Parish/299 3.00 8.00
12 John Stockton/49 8.00 20.00
14 Moses Malone/299 3.00 8.00

2010-11 Panini Gold Standard Gold Records Materials Prime

*PRIME: 1.25X TO 3X BASE HI
STATED PRINT RUN 10 TO 25 SER.#'d SETS
SOME UNPRICED DUE TO SCARCITY
4 Hakeem Olajuwon/25 12.00 30.00
5 Steve Nash/25 15.00 40.00
10 Karl Malone/25 12.00 30.00

2010-11 Panini Gold Standard Gold Records Materials Signatures

STATED PRINT RUN 2 TO 25 SER.#'d SETS
SOME UNPRICED DUE TO SCARCITY
6 Mark Eaton/25 10.00 25.00
11 Robert Parish/25 10.00 25.00

2010-11 Panini Gold Standard Gold Records Materials Signatures Prime

STATED PRINT RUN ONE TO 25 SER.#'d SETS
SOME UNPRICED DUE TO SCARCITY
6 Mark Eaton/25 15.00 40.00
11 Robert Parish/25 20.00 50.00

2010-11 Panini Gold Standard Gold Records Signatures

STATED PRINT RUN 5 TO 99 SER.#'d SETS
SOME UNPRICED DUE TO SCARCITY
6 Mark Eaton/99 6.00 15.00
11 Robert Parish/25 10.00 25.00

2010-11 Panini Gold Standard Gold Rings

STATED PRINT RUN 299 SER.#'d SETS
UNPRICED GOLD RUSH PRINT RUN 8 SETS
1 Magic Johnson 4.00 10.00
2 Tim Duncan 2.50 6.00
3 Rajon Rondo 1.50 4.00
4 Dwyane Wade 2.50 6.00
5 Kobe Bryant 6.00 15.00
6 Scottie Pippen 3.00 8.00
7 Alonzo Mourning 2.00 5.00
8 Isiah Thomas 1.50 4.00
9 Dennis Rodman 3.00 8.00
10 Pau Gasol 1.50 4.00
11 Ray Allen 1.50 4.00
12 Hakeem Olajuwon 2.00 5.00
13 Tony Parker 1.50 4.00
14 Bill Walton 1.50 4.00
15 Kareem Abdul-Jabbar 2.50 6.00
16 Richard Hamilton 1.25 3.00
17 Julius Erving 2.50 6.00
18 Elvin Hayes 1.50 4.00
19 Paul Pierce 1.50 4.00
20 Robert Horry 1.50 4.00

2010-11 Panini Gold Standard Gold Rings Materials

STATED PRINT RUN 49 TO 299 SER.#'d SETS
1 Magic Johnson/99 10.00 25.00
2 Tim Duncan/299 6.00 15.00
3 Rajon Rondo/299 4.00 10.00
4 Dwyane Wade/299 6.00 15.00
5 Kobe Bryant/299 8.00 20.00
6 Scottie Pippen/299 8.00 20.00
7 Alonzo Mourning/299 5.00 12.00
8 Isiah Thomas/199 6.00 15.00
9 Dennis Rodman/49 8.00 20.00
10 Pau Gasol/299 4.00 10.00
11 Ray Allen/299 4.00 10.00
12 Hakeem Olajuwon/299 5.00 12.00

13 Tony Parker/299 4.00 10.00
15 Kareem Abdul-Jabbar/99 6.00 15.00
16 Richard Hamilton/299 3.00 8.00
17 Julius Erving/149 6.00 15.00
19 Paul Pierce/299 4.00 10.00
20 Robert Horry/299 4.00 10.00

2010-11 Panini Gold Standard Gold Rings Materials Prime

*PRIME: .75X TO 2X BASE HI
STATED PRINT RUN 5 TO 25 SER.#'d SETS
SOME UNPRICED DUE TO SCARCITY
6 Scottie Pippen/25 40.00 100.00
7 Alonzo Mourning/25 30.00 80.00
12 Hakeem Olajuwon/25 12.00 30.00

2010-11 Panini Gold Standard Gold Rings Materials Signatures

STATED PRINT RUN 5 TO 49 SER.#'d SETS
SOME UNPRICED DUE TO SCARCITY
3 Rajon Rondo/49 15.00 40.00
5 Kobe Bryant/24 125.00 250.00
8 Isiah Thomas/49 10.00 25.00
9 Dennis Rodman/25 30.00 80.00
11 Ray Allen/25 30.00 60.00
12 Hakeem Olajuwon/25 25.00 60.00
13 Tony Parker/25 12.00 30.00
16 Richard Hamilton/49 6.00 15.00
20 Robert Horry/49 15.00 40.00

2010-11 Panini Gold Standard Gold Rings Materials Signatures Prime

STATED PRINT RUN 3 TO 25 SER.#'d SETS
SOME UNPRICED DUE TO SCARCITY
3 Rajon Rondo/25 25.00 60.00
5 Kobe Bryant/24 150.00 300.00
8 Isiah Thomas/25 12.00 30.00
13 Tony Parker/25 20.00 50.00
16 Richard Hamilton/25 10.00 25.00
20 Robert Horry/25 30.00 80.00

2010-11 Panini Gold Standard Gold Rings Signatures

STATED PRINT RUN 5 TO 69 SER.#'d SETS
SOME UNPRICED DUE TO SCARCITY
3 Rajon Rondo/49 15.00 40.00
5 Kobe Bryant/49 100.00 200.00
7 Alonzo Mourning/25 30.00 80.00
8 Isiah Thomas/49 EXCH 12.00 30.00
9 Dennis Rodman/25 30.00 80.00
12 Hakeem Olajuwon/25 20.00 50.00
13 Tony Parker/49 10.00 25.00
14 Bill Walton/49 10.00 25.00
16 Richard Hamilton/49 6.00 15.00
18 Elvin Hayes/49 6.00 15.00
20 Robert Horry/69 8.00 20.00

2010-11 Panini Gold Standard Gold Rings Signatures Dual

STATED PRINT RUN 10 TO 50 SER.#'d SETS
SOME UNPRICED DUE TO SCARCITY
1 P.Pierce/R.Rondo/20 30.00 80.00
2 I.Thomas/B.Laimbeer/50 EXCH 12.00 30.00
3 R.Rondo/R.Allen/20 25.00 60.00
5 K.Bryant/P.Gasol/50 100.00 200.00
6 K.Bryant/D.Fisher/25 100.00 225.00
7 T.Parker/R.Horry/50 25.00 60.00
8 H.Olajuwon/C.Drexler/20 50.00 120.00
9 C.Billups/R.Hamilton/50 12.00 30.00
10 G.Payton/A.Mourning/20 40.00 100.00

2010-11 Panini Gold Standard Gold Stars

STATED PRINT RUN 299 SER.#'d SETS
UNPRICED GOLD RUSH PRINT RUN 8 SETS
1 Blake Griffin 1.25 3.00
2 Dwight Howard 1.00 2.50
3 Russell Westbrook 3.00 8.00
4 Lamar Odom 1.00 2.50
5 Jonny Flynn .75 2.00
6 Carlos Boozer 1.00 2.50
7 Raymond Felton 1.00 2.50
8 Ray Allen 1.25 3.00
9 Ben Gordon 1.00 2.50
10 Jameer Nelson .75 2.00
11 Dirk Nowitzki 1.50 4.00
12 Marc Gasol 1.25 3.00
13 Monta Ellis 1.00 2.50
14 Shane Battier 1.00 2.50
15 Andre Iguodala 1.00 2.50
16 Andrei Kirilenko 1.00 2.50
17 Nene 1.00 2.50
18 Steve Nash 1.25 3.00
19 Jordan Farmar .75 2.00
20 Andrea Bargnani 1.00 2.50
21 Kevin Durant 3.00 8.00
22 Tyson Chandler 1.00 2.50
23 Derrick Rose 1.50 4.00
24 Kobe Bryant 5.00 12.00
25 Amare Stoudemire 1.00 2.50

2010-11 Panini Gold Standard Gold Stars Materials

STATED PRINT RUN 99 SER.#'d SETS
1 Blake Griffin 2.50 6.00
2 Dwight Howard 2.00 5.00
3 Russell Westbrook 6.00 15.00
4 Lamar Odom 2.00 5.00
5 Jonny Flynn 1.50 4.00
8 Ray Allen 2.50 6.00
9 Ben Gordon 2.00 5.00
10 Jameer Nelson 1.50 4.00
11 Dirk Nowitzki 3.00 8.00
12 Marc Gasol 2.50 6.00
13 Monta Ellis 2.00 5.00
15 Andre Iguodala 2.00 5.00
16 Andrei Kirilenko 2.00 5.00
17 Nene 2.00 5.00
18 Steve Nash 2.50 6.00
20 Andrea Bargnani 2.00 5.00
21 Kevin Durant 6.00 15.00
22 Tyson Chandler 2.00 5.00
23 Derrick Rose 3.00 8.00
24 Kobe Bryant 10.00 25.00
25 Amare Stoudemire 2.00 5.00

2010-11 Panini Gold Standard Gold Stars Materials Prime

*PRIME: .75X TO 2X BASE HI
STATED PRINT RUN 2 TO 25 SER.#'d SETS
SOME UNPRICED DUE TO SCARCITY
11 Dirk Nowitzki/25 10.00 25.00

2010-11 Panini Gold Standard Gold Stars Materials Signatures

STATED PRINT RUN 5 TO 49 SER.#'d SETS
SOME UNPRICED DUE TO SCARCITY
3 Russell Westbrook/25 40.00 100.00
4 Lamar Odom/30 10.00 25.00
5 Jonny Flynn/35 5.00 12.00
9 Ben Gordon/49 5.00 12.00
10 Jameer Nelson/49 5.00 12.00
15 Andre Iguodala/49 6.00 15.00
16 Andrei Kirilenko/25 6.00 15.00
22 Tyson Chandler/20 8.00 20.00
24 Kobe Bryant/15 100.00 200.00

2010-11 Panini Gold Standard Gold Stars Materials Signatures Prime

STATED PRINT RUN 2 TO 25 SER.#'d SETS
SOME UNPRICED DUE TO SCARCITY
5 Jonny Flynn/20 8.00 20.00
9 Ben Gordon/25 8.00 20.00
10 Jameer Nelson/20 8.00 20.00
15 Andre Iguodala/20 8.00 20.00
22 Tyson Chandler/20 12.00 30.00

2010-11 Panini Gold Standard Gold Stars Signatures

STATED PRINT RUN 5 TO 99 SER.#'d SETS
SOME UNPRICED DUE TO SCARCITY
4 Lamar Odom/25 10.00 25.00
5 Jonny Flynn/50 4.00 10.00
6 Carlos Boozer/99 6.00 15.00
7 Raymond Felton/99 4.00 10.00
8 Ray Allen/25 30.00 60.00
10 Jameer Nelson/99 4.00 10.00
14 Shane Battier/99 5.00 12.00
15 Andre Iguodala/99 4.00 10.00
16 Andrei Kirilenko/49 4.00 10.00
20 Andrea Bargnani/25 5.00 12.00
22 Tyson Chandler/49 5.00 12.00
24 Kobe Bryant/24 100.00 200.00

2010-11 Panini Gold Standard Gold Team Logos

STATED PRINT RUN 5 TO 199 SER.#'d SETS
SOME UNPRICED DUE TO SCARCITY
1 Aaron Brooks/199 6.00 15.00
2 Alvan Adams/199 6.00 15.00
4 Andre Iguodala/99 6.00 15.00
5 Andrew Bogut/199 6.00 15.00
6 Andrew Bynum/49 12.00 30.00
7 Baron Davis/49 8.00 20.00
8 Bernard King/199 4.00 10.00
9 Bill Laimbeer/199 8.00 20.00
10 Bill Walton/99 10.00 25.00
11 Billy Cunningham/99 15.00 40.00
13 Boris Diaw/199 6.00 15.00
14 Brandon Jennings/49 12.00 30.00
15 Brook Lopez/99 6.00 15.00
16 Carl Landry/199 6.00 15.00
17 Carlos Boozer/199 10.00 25.00
18 Channing Frye/199 6.00 15.00
20 Danilo Gallinari/199 6.00 15.00
21 David Lee/99 6.00 15.00
22 DeMar DeRozan/199 12.00 30.00
23 Derek Fisher/199 6.00 15.00
26 Elvin Hayes/199 6.00 15.00
27 Emeka Okafor/49 8.00 20.00
28 Eric Gordon/199 8.00 20.00
29 J.J. Barea/199 EXCH 12.00 30.00
30 Jalen Rose/199 6.00 15.00
31 Jeff Green/199 6.00 15.00
32 Joakim Noah/99 12.00 30.00
33 Juwan Howard/199 8.00 20.00
34 Kendrick Perkins/199 4.00 10.00
36 LaMarcus Aldridge/199 20.00 50.00
37 Michael Cooper/199 8.00 20.00
41 Raymond Felton/199 6.00 15.00
42 Russell Westbrook/199 75.00 200.00
43 Stephen Curry/199 100.00 250.00
44 Tony Parker/25 10.00 25.00
45 Tracy McGrady/25 40.00 100.00
47 Walter Berry/199 6.00 15.00
48 Zach Randolph/99 10.00 25.00
49 Tyson Chandler/199 6.00 15.00
50 Robin Lopez/199 6.00 15.00

2010-11 Panini Gold Standard Golden Age

STATED PRINT RUN 299 SER.#'d SETS
UNPRICED GOLD RUSH PRINT RUN 5 SETS
1 Magic Johnson 3.00 8.00
2 Tim Hardaway 1.25 3.00
3 David Robinson 2.00 5.00
4 Dikembe Mutombo 1.25 3.00
5 Jerry West 1.50 4.00
6 Tom Heinsohn 1.25 3.00
7 Dennis Rodman 2.50 6.00
8 Rick Barry 1.00 2.50
9 Bob Lanier 1.00 2.50
10 Oscar Robertson 1.50 4.00
11 Larry Bird 3.00 8.00
12 John Stockton 2.00 5.00
13 Julius Erving 2.00 5.00
14 Hakeem Olajuwon 1.50 4.00
15 David Thompson 1.00 2.50
16 Elvin Hayes 1.25 3.00
17 Walt Bellamy 1.00 2.50
18 Elgin Baylor 1.25 3.00
19 Darryl Dawkins .75 2.00
20 Bill Russell 2.00 5.00

2010-11 Panini Gold Standard Golden Age Materials

STATED PRINT RUN 49 TO 299 SER.#'d SETS
1 Magic Johnson/99 8.00 20.00
2 Tim Hardaway/299 3.00 8.00
4 Dikembe Mutombo/299 3.00 8.00
7 Dennis Rodman/99 6.00 15.00
9 Bob Lanier/99 2.50 6.00
11 Larry Bird/49 8.00 20.00
12 John Stockton/299 5.00 12.00
13 Julius Erving/149 5.00 12.00
14 Hakeem Olajuwon/299 4.00 10.00

2010-11 Panini Gold Standard Golden Age Materials Prime

*PRIME: .75X TO 2X BASE HI
STATED PRINT RUN 5 TO 25 SER.#'d SETS
SOME UNPRICED DUE TO SCARCITY
4 Dikembe Mutombo/25 10.00 25.00
14 Hakeem Olajuwon/25 10.00 25.00

2010-11 Panini Gold Standard Golden Age Materials Signatures

STATED PRINT RUN 3 TO 49 SER.#'d SETS
SOME UNPRICED DUE TO SCARCITY
4 Dikembe Mutombo/49 15.00 40.00
9 Bob Lanier/25 10.00 25.00

2010-11 Panini Gold Standard Golden Age Materials Signatures Prime

STATED PRINT RUN ONE TO 25 SER.#'d SETS
SOME UNPRICED DUE TO SCARCITY
4 Dikembe Mutombo/25 30.00 80.00
6 Tom Heinsohn/25 25.00 60.00
8 Rick Barry/25 20.00 50.00
9 Bob Lanier/25 20.00 50.00

2010-11 Panini Gold Standard Golden Age Signatures

STATED PRINT RUN 2 TO 99 SER.#'d SETS
SOME UNPRICED DUE TO SCARCITY
2 Tim Hardaway/99 10.00 25.00
4 Dikembe Mutombo/99 15.00 40.00
6 Tom Heinsohn/99 20.00 50.00
8 Rick Barry/99 6.00 15.00
9 Bob Lanier/50 5.00 12.00
15 David Thompson/99 5.00 12.00
16 Elvin Hayes/75 6.00 15.00
17 Walt Bellamy/75 5.00 12.00
19 Darryl Dawkins/99 6.00 15.00

2010-11 Panini Gold Standard Golden Age Signatures Dual

STATED PRINT RUN 5 TO 50 SER.#'d SETS
SOME UNPRICED DUE TO SCARCITY
5 D.Dawkins/M.Cheeks/50 10.00 25.00
6 D.Griffith/M.Eaton/50 10.00 25.00
8 A.Dantley/R.Blackman/50 10.00 25.00
10 I.Thomas/J.Dumars/50 20.00 50.00

2010-11 Panini Gold Standard Golden Anniversary

STATED PRINT RUN 299 SER.#'d SETS
UNPRICED GOLD RUSH PRINT RUN 10 SETS
1 Kareem Abdul-Jabbar 2.00 5.00
2 Elgin Baylor 1.25 3.00
3 Rick Barry 1.00 2.50
4 Larry Bird 3.00 8.00
5 Sam Jones 1.25 3.00
6 Oscar Robertson 1.50 4.00
7 Bill Russell 2.00 5.00
8 Jerry West 1.50 4.00
9 Bill Walton 1.25 3.00
10 Lenny Wilkens 1.25 3.00
11 Scottie Pippen 2.50 6.00
12 David Robinson 2.00 5.00
13 Hakeem Olajuwon 1.50 4.00
14 Dolph Schayes 1.25 3.00
15 Julius Erving 2.00 5.00
16 Clyde Drexler 1.50 4.00
17 George Gervin 1.25 3.00
18 Dave Cowens .75 2.00
19 John Havlicek 1.50 4.00
20 Magic Johnson 3.00 8.00

2010-11 Panini Gold Standard Golden Anniversary Materials

STATED PRINT RUN 49 TO 299 SER.#'d SETS
1 Kareem Abdul-Jabbar/99 5.00 12.00
4 Larry Bird/49 8.00 20.00
11 Scottie Pippen/299 8.00 20.00
12 David Robinson/299 5.00 12.00
13 Hakeem Olajuwon/149 4.00 10.00
15 Julius Erving/149 5.00 12.00
16 Clyde Drexler/299 4.00 10.00
17 George Gervin/299 3.00 8.00
18 Dave Cowens/125 2.00 5.00
20 Magic Johnson/99 8.00 20.00

2010-11 Panini Gold Standard Golden Anniversary Materials Prime

*PRIME: .75X TO 2X BASE HI
STATED PRINT RUN ONE TO 25 SER.#'d SETS
SOME UNPRICED DUE TO SCARCITY
11 Scottie Pippen/25 50.00 125.00
13 Hakeem Olajuwon/25 10.00 25.00

2010-11 Panini Gold Standard Golden Anniversary Materials Signatures

STATED PRINT RUN 10 TO 49 SER.#'d SETS
SOME UNPRICED DUE TO SCARCITY
12 David Robinson/49 12.00 30.00
13 Hakeem Olajuwon/25 25.00 60.00
17 George Gervin/49 12.00 30.00

2010-11 Panini Gold Standard Golden Anniversary Materials Signatures Prime

STATED PRINT RUN 5 TO 25 SER.#'d SETS
SOME UNPRICED DUE TO SCARCITY
12 David Robinson/25 40.00 100.00
13 Hakeem Olajuwon/25 30.00 80.00
17 George Gervin/25 15.00 40.00

2010-11 Panini Gold Standard Golden Anniversary Signatures

STATED PRINT RUN 5 TO 49 SER.#'d SETS
SOME UNPRICED DUE TO SCARCITY
2 Elgin Baylor/25 15.00 40.00
3 Rick Barry/49 8.00 20.00
5 Sam Jones/49 12.00 30.00
6 Oscar Robertson/25 40.00 100.00
9 Bill Walton/49 10.00 25.00
10 Lenny Wilkens/49 8.00 20.00
12 David Robinson/25 30.00 80.00
14 Dolph Schayes/49 8.00 20.00
16 Clyde Drexler/25 25.00 60.00
17 George Gervin/30 10.00 25.00
18 Dave Cowens/49 8.00 20.00

2010-11 Panini Gold Standard Golden Anniversary Signatures Dual

STATED PRINT RUN 5 TO 50 SER.#'d SETS
SOME UNPRICED DUE TO SCARCITY
3 D.Robinson/G.Gervin/20 60.00 150.00
4 W.Frazier/E.Monroe/25 25.00 60.00
6 H.Greer/D.Schayes/50 12.00 30.00
7 D.Cowens/R.Parish/50 15.00 40.00
8 E.Hayes/H.Olajuwon/25 30.00 80.00
9 J.Worthy/E.Baylor/25 40.00 100.00
10 S.Moncrief/O.Robertson/25 40.00 100.00
13 W.Frazier/W.Reed/50 25.00 60.00
15 R.Barry/N.Thurmond/50 15.00 40.00

2010-11 Panini Gold Standard Golden Threads

STATED PRINT RUN 299 SER.#'d SETS
1 S.Jones/R.Rondo 1.25 3.00
2 M.Johnson/K.Bryant 12.00 30.00
3 J.Erving/A.Iguodala 2.00 5.00
4 D.Rodman/D.Blair 2.50 6.00
5 R.Blackman/J.Kidd 1.25 3.00
6 W.Frazier/C.Billups 1.25 3.00
7 S.Pippen/D.Rose 5.00 12.00
8 R.Parish/P.Pierce 1.25 3.00
9 A.Mourning/C.Bosh 2.50 6.00
10 W.Reed/A.Stoudemire 1.25 3.00

2010-11 Panini Gold Standard Golden Threads Materials

STATED PRINT RUN 25 TO 299 SER.#'d SETS
2 M.Johnson/K.Bryant/299 12.00 30.00
3 J.Erving/A.Iguodala/99 6.00 15.00
5 R.Blackman/J.Kidd/25 5.00 12.00
8 R.Parish/P.Pierce/299 4.00 10.00
9 A.Mourning/C.Bosh/299 5.00 12.00

2010-11 Panini Gold Standard Golden Threads Materials Prime

*PRIME: 1X TO 2.5X BASE HI
STATED PRINT RUN 3 TO 25 SER.#'d SETS
SOME UNPRICED DUE TO SCARCITY
9 A.Mourning/C.Bosh/25 20.00 50.00

2010-11 Panini Gold Standard Golden Threads Signatures

STATED PRINT RUN 10 TO 25 SER.#'d SETS
SOME UNPRICED DUE TO SCARCITY
1 S.Jones/R.Rondo/25 20.00 50.00
4 D.Rodman/D.Blair/25 20.00 50.00
5 R.Blackman/J.Kidd/25 20.00 50.00
6 W.Frazier/C.Billups/25 20.00 50.00
9 A.Mourning/C.Bosh/25 25.00 60.00

2010-11 Panini Gold Standard Signatures

STATED PRINT RUN 5 TO 299 SER.#'d SETS
SOME UNPRICED DUE TO SCARCITY
2 Kobe Bryant/75 100.00 200.00
5 Ty Lawson/299 4.00 10.00
9 Kevin Love/25 15.00 40.00
15 Kevin Martin/299 4.00 10.00
17 Stephen Jackson/299 4.00 10.00
19 Eric Gordon/299 4.00 10.00
23 Antawn Jamison/199 4.00 10.00
24 Tyreke Evans/25 4.00 10.00
25 Al Horford/99 4.00 10.00
26 Danny Granger/50 5.00 12.00
28 Rajon Rondo/49 12.00 30.00
30 Michael Beasley/25 4.00 10.00
32 Tony Parker/25 15.00 40.00
34 LaMarcus Aldridge/299 6.00 15.00
35 Stephen Curry/299 100.00 250.00
36 Brook Lopez/99 5.00 12.00
37 Tyson Chandler/199 4.00 10.00
40 Andre Iguodala/299 4.00 10.00
42 Danilo Gallinari/299 4.00 10.00
43 Joe Johnson/49 5.00 12.00
44 DeMar DeRozan/299 10.00 25.00
45 Devin Harris/299 4.00 10.00
46 Andrei Kirilenko/199 4.00 10.00
47 Brandon Roy/25 8.00 20.00
48 Raymond Felton/199 4.00 10.00
51 Aaron Brooks/299 4.00 10.00
52 Zach Randolph/49 5.00 12.00
54 Charlie Villanueva/49 4.00 10.00
55 Jeff Green/299 4.00 10.00
56 Channing Frye/220 4.00 10.00
57 Al Thornton/299 4.00 10.00
62 David Lee/199 4.00 10.00
66 Emeka Okafor/25 5.00 12.00
68 Carl Landry/299 4.00 10.00
69 Jameer Nelson/199 4.00 10.00
70 Joakim Noah/99 5.00 12.00
71 Chris Kaman/99 4.00 10.00
74 Andrea Bargnani/49 5.00 12.00
76 Grant Hill/25 125.00 250.00
77 Lamar Odom/25 10.00 25.00
80 J.R. Smith/299 4.00 10.00
82 Tyler Hansbrough/199 5.00 12.00
85 Al Jefferson/49 4.00 10.00
87 Luke Ridnour/199 4.00 10.00
91 D.J. Augustin/299 4.00 10.00
94 Juwan Howard/299 4.00 10.00
95 Roy Hibbert/299 5.00 12.00
98 DeJuan Blair/299 4.00 10.00
101 Baron Davis/49 5.00 12.00
103 Josh Smith/199 4.00 10.00
105 Hedo Turkoglu/299 4.00 10.00
106 Ben Gordon/49 5.00 12.00
107 Gerald Henderson/299 4.00 10.00
108 Serge Ibaka/299 5.00 12.00
109 Shane Battier/149 5.00 12.00
111 Chauncey Billups/23 12.00 30.00
115 Darko Milicic/299 4.00 10.00
116 Caron Butler/49 5.00 12.00
118 Trevor Ariza/49 5.00 12.00
120 J.J. Redick/299 4.00 10.00
121 Gerald Wallace/99 5.00 12.00
122 Samuel Dalembert/299 4.00 10.00
125 Brandon Jennings/149 4.00 10.00
126 JaVale McGee/299 4.00 10.00
128 James Harden/149 15.00 40.00
129 Chris Andersen/25 8.00 20.00
130 Toney Douglas/299 4.00 10.00
132 Richard Hamilton/49 5.00 12.00
133 George Hill/299 5.00 12.00
137 Daniel Gibson/299 4.00 10.00
138 Wesley Matthews/299 5.00 12.00
139 Kris Humphries/49 5.00 12.00
140 Rodrigue Beaubois/299 4.00 10.00
141 A.J. Price/299 4.00 10.00
142 Chase Budinger/299 4.00 10.00
143 Donte Greene/99 4.00 10.00
144 Andre Miller/199 5.00 12.00
145 Ryan Gomes/299 4.00 10.00
146 Jodie Meeks/299 4.00 10.00
147 Kendrick Perkins/99 4.00 10.00
148 Taj Gibson/199 4.00 10.00
149 Boris Diaw/199 4.00 10.00
150 Derrick Brown/299 4.00 10.00
151 Jeff Teague/299 4.00 10.00
152 Wayne Ellington/199 4.00 10.00
153 Terrence Williams/199 4.00 10.00
154 Robin Lopez/149 4.00 10.00
155 Jermaine O'Neal/25 10.00 25.00
156 Austin Daye/299 4.00 10.00
157 J.J. Barea/199 10.00 25.00
158 Darren Collison/299 4.00 10.00
159 Goran Dragic/149 5.00 12.00
160 Beno Udrih/149 4.00 10.00
161 Earl Clark/99 4.00 10.00
162 Hakim Warrick/149 4.00 10.00
163 Sam Young/99 4.00 10.00
164 Ronnie Brewer/199 4.00 10.00
165 Omri Casspi/299 4.00 10.00
166 T.J. Ford/199 4.00 10.00
167 Chris Douglas-Roberts/99 4.00 10.00
168 Eric Maynor/79 4.00 10.00
169 James Johnson/99 4.00 10.00
170 Patrick Mills/99 25.00 60.00
179 Dan Majerle/199 5.00 12.00
183 Glen Rice/299 4.00 10.00
186 Jalen Rose/299 5.00 12.00
190 Bill Walton/49 8.00 20.00
193 Dan Issel/49 5.00 12.00
194 Doc Rivers/49 10.00 25.00
195 George McGinnis/42 4.00 10.00
197 Christian Laettner/25 15.00 40.00
198 Dolph Schayes/49 8.00 20.00
199 M.L. Carr/99 6.00 15.00
200 Darryl Dawkins/99 4.00 10.00
201 David Thompson/99 4.00 10.00
202 Bob Lanier/49 5.00 12.00
204 Bernard King/99 4.00 10.00
205 Bailey Howell/99 4.00 10.00
206 Al Attles/99 4.00 10.00
207 Dikembe Mutombo/49 12.00 30.00
208 Bob McAdoo/99 10.00 25.00
209 Artis Gilmore/99 8.00 20.00
210 A.C. Green/99 8.00 20.00
211 Dominique Wilkins/99 10.00 25.00
212 Alonzo Mourning/99 15.00 40.00

2011-12 Panini Gold Standard

COMMON CARD (1-225) 1.25 3.00
STATED PRINT RUN 299 SER.#'d SETS
170/179/183/210/213/214 HAVE VAR
ALL VAR STILL TOTAL JUST 299 CARDS
UNPRICED BLACK GOLD PRINT RUN ONE SET
UNPRICED PLAT.GOLD PRINT RUN 10 SETS
UNPRICED BULLION PRINT RUN 1 TO 2 SETS
1 Paul Pierce 2.00 5.00
2 LaMarcus Aldridge 2.00 5.00
3 Al Jefferson 1.50 4.00
4 Pau Gasol 2.00 5.00
5 DeMarcus Cousins 2.00 5.00
6 Danilo Gallinari 1.50 4.00
7 Dwight Howard 1.50 4.00
8 Ty Lawson 1.25 3.00
9 Luke Ridnour 1.50 4.00
10 Emeka Okafor 1.50 4.00
11 Ray Allen 2.00 5.00
12 LeBron James 8.00 20.00
13 Eric Gordon 1.50 4.00
14 Nate Robinson 2.00 5.00
15 Kobe Bryant 8.00 20.00
16 Damion James 1.25 3.00
17 Kevin Garnett 3.00 8.00
18 DeJuan Blair 1.25 3.00
19 Jeremy Lin 8.00 20.00
20 Kris Humphries 1.25 3.00
21 Andre Iguodala 1.50 4.00
22 Andrea Bargnani 1.50 4.00
23 Evan Turner 1.25 3.00
24 Carmelo Anthony 2.50 6.00
25 DeAndre Jordan 2.00 5.00
26 Rajon Rondo 2.00 5.00
27 Kevin Durant 5.00 12.00
28 John Wall 2.50 6.00
29 Mo Williams 1.50 4.00
30 Marcin Gortat 1.50 4.00
31 Chauncey Billups 2.00 5.00
32 Tyson Chandler 1.50 4.00
33 Steve Nash 2.00 5.00
34 Caron Butler 1.50 4.00
35 Derek Fisher 1.50 4.00
36 Marcus Thornton 1.25 3.00
37 Jose Calderon 1.25 3.00
38 Zach Randolph 1.50 4.00
39 Grant Hill 3.00 8.00
40 Avery Bradley 2.00 5.00
41 Channing Frye 1.50 4.00
42 Matt Barnes 1.25 3.00
43 Jason Thompson 1.25 3.00
44 Chris Paul 2.50 6.00
45 Tyreke Evans 1.25 3.00
46 Carlos Boozer 1.50 4.00
47 Brandon Rush 1.25 3.00
48 Joakim Noah 1.50 4.00
49 Rudy Gay 2.00 5.00
50 Luol Deng 1.50 4.00
51 Amare Stoudemire 1.50 4.00
52 Taj Gibson 1.50 4.00
53 Anderson Varejao 1.25 3.00
54 Deron Williams 1.50 4.00
55 Antawn Jamison 1.50 4.00
56 Ramon Sessions 1.50 4.00
57 Rodney Stuckey 1.50 4.00
58 Chris Bosh 2.00 5.00
59 Trevor Booker 1.25 3.00
60 Ben Gordon 1.50 4.00
61 Tony Parker 2.00 5.00
62 Danny Granger 1.50 4.00
63 Jodie Meeks 1.50 4.00
64 George Hill 1.50 4.00
65 Ed Davis 1.25 3.00
66 Paul George 2.50 6.00
67 Landry Fields 1.50 4.00
68 Roy Hibbert 1.50 4.00
69 Russell Westbrook 5.00 12.00
70 Thabo Sefolosha 1.25 3.00
71 Darren Collison 1.50 4.00
72 Delonte West 1.25 3.00
73 Jerryd Bayless 1.25 3.00
74 Stephen Jackson 1.50 4.00
75 Dirk Nowitzki 2.50 6.00
76 Tim Duncan 3.00 8.00
77 Drew Gooden 1.50 4.00
78 Shawn Marion 2.00 5.00
79 Brook Lopez 1.50 4.00
80 Kevin Martin 1.50 4.00
81 Manu Ginobili 2.00 5.00
82 Marc Gasol 2.00 5.00
83 Al-Farouq Aminu 1.50 4.00
84 Gary Neal 1.50 4.00
85 Patrick Patterson 1.25 3.00
86 Mike Conley 1.50 4.00
87 Stephen Curry 8.00 20.00
88 Michael Beasley 1.25 3.00
89 Al Harrington 1.50 4.00
90 Larry Sanders 1.25 3.00
91 Ryan Anderson 1.50 4.00
92 Nicolas Batum 1.50 4.00
93 Dwyane Wade 4.00 10.00
94 Gerald Wallace 1.50 4.00
95 Monta Ellis 1.50 4.00
96 Jared Dudley 1.25 3.00
97 Jrue Holiday 2.00 5.00
98 Nick Young 1.50 4.00
99 Nene 1.50 4.00
100 Vince Carter 2.50 6.00
101 Elton Brand 2.00 5.00
102 Andrew Bynum 1.25 3.00
103 Greg Monroe 2.00 5.00
104 Tyler Hansbrough 1.50 4.00
105 Andrew Bogut 1.50 4.00
106 Jeff Teague 1.50 4.00
107 D.J. Augustin 1.25 3.00
108 Jason Terry 1.50 4.00
109 Austin Daye 1.25 3.00
110 Brandon Jennings 1.25 3.00
111 Gordon Hayward 2.00 5.00
112 Kyle Lowry 1.50 4.00
113 Jamal Crawford 2.00 5.00
114 Jason Richardson 2.00 5.00
115 James Harden 3.00 8.00
116 Boris Diaw 1.50 4.00
117 Chris Andersen 1.50 4.00
118 Kevin Love 2.00 5.00
119 Kirk Hinrich 1.50 4.00
120 Shane Battier 1.50 4.00
121 Ersan Ilyasova 1.25 3.00
122 Jason Kidd 2.00 5.00
123 Wesley Matthews 1.25 3.00
124 Serge Ibaka 1.50 4.00
125 Hedo Turkoglu 1.50 4.00
126 Paul Millsap 1.50 4.00
127 JaVale McGee 1.50 4.00
128 Timofey Mozgov 1.25 3.00
129 Nikola Pekovic 1.50 4.00
130 Luis Scola 1.50 4.00
131 Mario Chalmers 1.50 4.00
132 Jameer Nelson 1.25 3.00
133 Tayshaun Prince 2.00 5.00
134 Blake Griffin 2.00 5.00
135 Wesley Johnson 1.50 4.00
136 Derrick Favors 1.50 4.00
137 Kendrick Perkins 1.25 3.00
138 Chase Budinger 1.25 3.00
139 Devin Harris 1.25 3.00
140 Tiago Splitter 1.50 4.00
141 DeMar DeRozan 2.00 5.00
142 Derrick Rose 2.50 6.00
143 Josh Smith 1.50 4.00
144 Ricky Rubio 2.00 5.00
145 Jordan Crawford 1.25 3.00
146 J.J. Redick 2.00 5.00
147 Greivis Vasquez 1.50 4.00
148 Al Horford 1.50 4.00
149 Brandon Bass 1.50 4.00
150 Anthony Morrow 1.25 3.00
151 Baron Davis 1.50 4.00
152 Thaddeus Young 1.25 3.00
153 James Johnson 1.25 3.00
154 Ekpe Udoh 1.25 3.00
155 Metta World Peace 2.00 5.00
156 Michael Redd 1.50 4.00
157 John Salmons 1.50 4.00
158 Omri Casspi 1.25 3.00
159 Richard Hamilton 1.50 4.00
160 Alonzo Gee RC 1.25 3.00
161 J.J. Hickson 1.25 3.00
162 Rodrigue Beaubois 1.25 3.00
163 Marreese Speights 1.25 3.00
164 Xavier Henry 1.25 3.00
165 Reggie Williams 1.50 4.00
166 Raja Bell 1.50 4.00
167 Raymond Felton 1.50 4.00
168 Daequan Cook 1.25 3.00
169 David Lee 1.25 3.00
170A T.McGrady Hawks/149* 5.00 12.00
170B T.McGrady Knicks/11*
170C T.McGrady Magic/45* 12.00 30.00
170D T.McGrady Pistons/9*
170E T.McGrady Raptors/30* 25.00 60.00
170F T.McGrady Rockets/55* 5.00 12.00
171 Joel Anthony 1.25 3.00
172 Tyrus Thomas 1.25 3.00
173 Joe Johnson 1.50 4.00
174 Randy Foye 1.25 3.00
175 Gerald Henderson 1.25 3.00
176 Jack Sikma 1.50 4.00
177 Paul Silas 2.00 5.00
178 Harry Gallatin 2.00 5.00
179A G.Payton Sonics/199* 4.00 10.00
179B G.Payton Bucks/30* 25.00 60.00
179C G.Payton Celtics/25* 25.00 60.00
179D G.Payton Heat/25* 30.00 80.00
179E G.Payton Lakers/20* 25.00 60.00
180 Detlef Schrempf 2.00 5.00
181 John Salley 1.25 3.00
182 Earl Monroe 2.00 5.00
183A B.Walton Blazers/209* 4.00 10.00
183B B.Walton Celtics/40* 20.00 50.00
183C B.Walton LA Clips/30* 12.00 30.00
183D B.Walton SD Clips/20* 15.00 40.00
184 Shawn Kemp 5.00 12.00
185 Wilt Chamberlain 4.00 10.00
186 Dan Issel 1.50 4.00
187 Jerry West 2.50 6.00
188 Bill Russell 3.00 8.00
189 Robert Parish 2.00 5.00
190 Maurice Cheeks 1.25 3.00
191 Allen Iverson 3.00 8.00
192 Anfernee Hardaway 5.00 12.00
193 Horace Grant 2.00 5.00
194 Walt Frazier 2.00 5.00
195 Yao Ming 2.50 6.00
196 Sean Elliott 2.00 5.00
197 Rod Strickland 1.25 3.00
198 Magic Johnson 5.00 12.00
199 Sam Jones 2.00 5.00
200 Tom Sanders 2.00 5.00
201 George Mikan 4.00 10.00
202 Steve Kerr 2.00 5.00
203 Walt Bellamy 1.50 4.00
204 Bruce Bowen 1.25 3.00
205 Larry Johnson 4.00 10.00
206 Cedric Ceballos 1.25 3.00
207 Vlade Divac 2.00 5.00
208 Rex Chapman 2.00 5.00
209 Karl Malone 2.50 6.00
210A S.O'Neal Magic/79* 12.00 30.00
210B S.O'Neal Cavs/50* 10.00 25.00
210C S.O'Neal Celtics/20* 50.00 125.00
210D S.O'Neal Heat/40*
210E S.O'Neal Lakers/70* 12.00 30.00
210F S.O'Neal Suns/40* 40.00 70.00
211 John Starks 1.50 4.00
212 Zydrunas Ilgauskas 1.25 3.00
213A R.Horry Rockets/129* 4.00 10.00
213B R.Horry Lakers/60* 10.00 25.00
213C R.Horry Spurs/40* 12.00 30.00
213D R.Horry Suns/70* 4.00 10.00
214A Mutombo Nuggets/99* 5.00 12.00
214B Mutombo 76ers/30* 12.00 30.00
214C Mutombo Hawks/80* 8.00 20.00
214D Mutombo Knicks/20* 20.00 50.00
214E Mutombo Nets/10*
214F Mutombo Rockets/60* 12.00 30.00
215 Brad Davis 2.00 5.00
216 Jonny Flynn 1.25 3.00
217 Jamal Mashburn 2.00 5.00
218 Marvin Williams 1.50 4.00
219 John Lucas III 1.25 3.00
220 Nick Collison 1.50 4.00
221 J.J. Barea 2.00 5.00
222 Jonas Jerebko 1.25 3.00
223 Danny Green 1.50 4.00
224 Omer Asik 1.50 4.00
225 Dorell Wright 1.25 3.00

2011-12 Panini Gold Standard 14K Autographs

STATED PRINT RUN 25 TO 149 SER.#'d SETS
1 Allan Houston/149 8.00 20.00
2 Robert Parish/49 8.00 20.00
3 Adrian Dantley/149 5.00 12.00
4 Elgin Baylor/74 12.00 30.00
5 Ray Allen/49 EXCH 25.00 60.00
6 Clyde Drexler/49 15.00 40.00
7 Paul Pierce/49 15.00 40.00
8 Gary Payton/49 15.00 40.00
9 Larry Bird/49 50.00 125.00
10 Hal Greer/49 6.00 15.00
11 Walt Bellamy/49 6.00 15.00
12 Bob Pettit/49 10.00 25.00
13 Vince Carter/49 12.00 30.00
14 David Robinson/49 30.00 60.00
15 Mitch Richmond/149 6.00 15.00
16 Tom Chambers/149 5.00 12.00
17 John Stockton/25 50.00 125.00
18 Bernard King/149 5.00 12.00
19 Bob Lanier/49 6.00 15.00
20 Gail Goodrich/49 6.00 15.00
21 Dale Ellis/149 5.00 12.00
22 Scottie Pippen/49 75.00 150.00
23 Isiah Thomas/49 12.00 30.00
24 Bob McAdoo/149 8.00 20.00
25 Antawn Jamison/149 5.00 12.00
26 Mark Aguirre/149 5.00 12.00
27 Dolph Schayes/49 5.00 12.00
28 Glen Rice/149 6.00 15.00
29 Tracy McGrady/25 20.00 50.00
30 World B. Free/49 6.00 15.00
31 Calvin Murphy/49 10.00 25.00
32 Chris Mullin/149 6.00 15.00
33 Lenny Wilkens/49 8.00 20.00
34 Bailey Howell/49 6.00 15.00
35 Magic Johnson/49 20.00 50.00
36 Rolando Blackman/149 5.00 12.00
37 Earl Monroe/49 12.00 30.00
38 Kevin McHale/49 12.00 30.00
39 Michael Finley/149 5.00 12.00
41 Kevin Willis/149 6.00 15.00
42 Spencer Haywood/149 5.00 12.00
43 George McGinnis/149 5.00 12.00
44 Hersey Hawkins/149 5.00 12.00
45 Jason Kidd/25 20.00 50.00
46 Grant Hill/49 30.00 60.00
47 Nate Archibald/49 6.00 15.00
48 Joe Dumars/49 6.00 15.00
49 James Worthy/49 15.00 40.00
50 Billy Cunningham/49 15.00 40.00
51 Steve Nash/25 30.00 60.00
52 Juwan Howard/149 5.00 12.00
53 Rod Strickland/149 5.00 12.00
54 Kiki Vandeweghe/49 6.00 15.00
55 Jack Twyman/99 8.00 20.00
56 Detlef Schrempf/149 8.00 20.00
57 Jeff Hornacek/49 8.00 20.00
58 Terry Porter/149 8.00 20.00
59 Walt Frazier/49 12.00 30.00
60 Tim Hardaway/149 8.00 20.00

2011-12 Panini Gold Standard 14K Memorabilia

STATED PRINT RUN 2 TO 149 SER.#'d SETS
SOME UNPRICED DUE TO SCARCITY
1 LeBron James/99 20.00 50.00
2 Chris Webber/99 10.00 25.00
3 Scottie Pippen/75 10.00 25.00
4 Chauncey Billups/49 5.00 12.00
5 Dennis Johnson/25 6.00 15.00
7 Shawn Marion/99 5.00 12.00
8 Elton Brand/99 5.00 12.00
9 Shawn Kemp/49 40.00 100.00
10 LeBron James/25 30.00 80.00
11 Vince Carter/99 8.00 20.00
12 Carmelo Anthony/149 6.00 15.00
13 Richard Hamilton/25 8.00 20.00
14 Rashard Lewis/99 4.00 10.00
15 Chauncey Billups/99 5.00 12.00
16 Mike Bibby/99 4.00 10.00
17 Jamaal Wilkes/25 15.00 40.00
18 Allan Houston/49 4.00 10.00
19 Dwyane Wade/149 10.00 25.00
21 Andre Miller/99 4.00 10.00
22 Alonzo Mourning/99 12.00 30.00
23 Pau Gasol/99 5.00 12.00
24 Joe Johnson/149 4.00 10.00
25 Eddie Jones/49 12.00 30.00
26 Paul Pierce/149 5.00 12.00
27 David Robinson/49 10.00 25.00
28 Ray Allen/99 6.00 15.00
29 Scottie Pippen/49 12.00 30.00
30 Tracy McGrady/35 5.00 12.00
31 Vince Carter/99 8.00 20.00
32 Tracy McGrady/99 5.00 12.00
33 Jason Terry/99 4.00 10.00
34 Steve Nash/49 6.00 15.00
35 Jason Kidd/49 6.00 15.00
36 Jason Richardson/99 5.00 12.00
37 Robert Parish/49 5.00 12.00
38 Clyde Drexler/49 8.00 20.00
40 Tom Chambers/49 4.00 10.00
41 Grant Hill/99 15.00 40.00
42 Kiki Vandeweghe/99 4.00 10.00
43 Chris Mullin/25 10.00 25.00
44 Mark Aguirre/49 5.00 12.00
45 Joe Dumars/25 5.00 12.00
46 Kevin Willis/49 3.00 8.00
47 Kevin McHale/49 6.00 15.00
48 Earl Monroe/25 30.00 80.00
49 Antawn Jamison/99 4.00 10.00
50 Isiah Thomas/25 10.00 25.00
51 John Stockton/49 12.00 30.00
52 Mitch Richmond/20 20.00 50.00
53 Larry Bird/25 25.00 60.00
55 James Worthy/25 10.00 25.00
57 Glen Rice/49 6.00 15.00

2011-12 Panini Gold Standard 14K Memorabilia Prime

STATED PRINT RUN ONE TO 25 SER.#'d SETS
SOME UNPRICED DUE TO SCARCITY
12 Carmelo Anthony/25 20.00 50.00
19 Dwyane Wade/25 50.00 120.00
26 Paul Pierce/25 10.00 25.00

2011-12 Panini Gold Standard 2011 Draft Pick Redemptions Autographs

RANDOM INSERTS IN PACKS
AB Alec Burks 5.00 12.00
BB Bismack Biyombo 5.00 12.00
BK Brandon Knight 5.00 12.00
CHJ Charles Jenkins 4.00 10.00
CJ Cory Joseph 4.00 10.00
CP Chandler Parsons 5.00 12.00
CS Chris Singleton 3.00 8.00
DW Derrick Williams 3.00 8.00
EK Enes Kanter 6.00 15.00
GA Gustavo Ayon 3.00 8.00
IS Iman Shumpert 8.00 20.00
IT Isaiah Thomas 25.00 60.00
JB Jimmy Butler 10.00 25.00
JF Jimmer Fredette 3.00 8.00
JH Justin Harper 4.00 10.00
JJ JaJuan Johnson 3.00 8.00
JOH Jordan Hamilton 4.00 10.00
JT Jeremy Tyler 4.00 10.00
JV Jan Vesely 5.00 12.00
KF Kenneth Faried 6.00 15.00
KI Kyrie Irving 40.00 100.00
KL Kawhi Leonard 75.00 200.00
KS Kyle Singler 4.00 10.00
KT Klay Thompson 30.00 80.00
KW Kemba Walker 15.00 40.00
LA Lavoy Allen 5.00 12.00
MB MarShon Brooks 4.00 10.00
MCM Marcus Morris 4.00 10.00
MM Markieff Morris 5.00 12.00
NC Norris Cole 5.00 12.00
NS Nolan Smith 3.00 8.00
RJ Reggie Jackson 5.00 12.00
SM Shelvin Mack 3.00 8.00
TH Tobias Harris 5.00 12.00
TT Tristan Thompson 6.00 15.00
XRCF Josh Harrellson 5.00 12.00

2011-12 Panini Gold Standard 2012 Draft Pick Redemptions

RANDOM INSERTS IN PACKS
XRC1 Anthony Davis 25.00 60.00
XRC2 Michael Kidd-Gilchrist 4.00 10.00
XRC3 Bradley Beal 8.00 20.00
XRC4 Dion Waiters 4.00 10.00
XRC5 Thomas Robinson 2.50 6.00
XRC6 Damian Lillard 25.00 60.00
XRC7 Harrison Barnes 10.00 25.00
XRC8 Terrence Ross 4.00 10.00
XRC9 Andre Drummond 5.00 12.00
XRC10 Austin Rivers 5.00 12.00
XRC11 Meyers Leonard 3.00 8.00
XRC12 Jeremy Lamb 4.00 10.00
XRC13 Kendall Marshall 2.50 6.00
XRC14 John Henson 4.00 10.00
XRC15 Maurice Harkless 4.00 10.00
XRC16 Royce White 2.50 6.00

XRC17 Tyler Zeller 3.00 8.00
XRC18 Terrence Jones 4.00 10.00
XRC19 Andrew Nicholson 2.50 6.00
XRC20 Evan Fournier 4.00 10.00
XRC21 Jared Sullinger 4.00 10.00
XRC22 Fab Melo 2.50 6.00
XRC23 John Jenkins 2.50 6.00
XRC24 Jared Cunningham 2.50 6.00
XRC25 Tony Wroten 2.50 6.00
XRC26 Miles Plumlee 3.00 8.00
XRC27 Arnett Moultrie 3.00 8.00
XRC28 Perry Jones 2.50 6.00
XRC29 Marquis Teague 2.50 6.00
XRC30 Festus Ezeli 3.00 8.00

2011-12 Panini Gold Standard 24K Autographs

STATED PRINT RUN 10 TO 149 SER.#'d SETS
SOME UNPRICED DUE TO SCARCITY
1 Kareem Abdul-Jabbar/25 50.00 125.00
2 Julius Erving/25 50.00 125.00
3 Hakeem Olajuwon/25 30.00 80.00
4 Kobe Bryant/49 75.00 150.00
5 Dan Issel/149 6.00 15.00
6 Elvin Hayes/49 6.00 15.00
7 Dirk Nowitzki/25 100.00 175.00
8 Oscar Robertson/25 40.00 100.00
9 Dominique Wilkins/25 15.00 40.00
10 George Gervin/149 8.00 20.00
11 John Havlicek/25 30.00 80.00
12 Alex English/149 6.00 15.00
13 Rick Barry/149 6.00 15.00
14 Jerry West/25 40.00 100.00
15 Shaquille O'Neal/20 100.00 200.00

2011-12 Panini Gold Standard 24K Memorabilia

STATED PRINT RUN 10 TO 149 SER.#'d SETS
SOME UNPRICED DUE TO SCARCITY
1 Kareem Abdul-Jabbar/49 15.00 40.00
2 Karl Malone/49 8.00 20.00
4 Kobe Bryant/149 10.00 25.00
5 Shaquille O'Neal/149 12.00 30.00
6 Moses Malone/49 6.00 15.00
7 Kevin Garnett/149 6.00 15.00
8 Hakeem Olajuwon/49 8.00 20.00
9 Dirk Nowitzki/149 8.00 20.00
10 Dominique Wilkins/149 8.00 20.00
11 George Gervin/149 6.00 15.00
12 Alex English/149 5.00 12.00
13 Jerry West/25 20.00 50.00
14 Patrick Ewing/149 10.00 25.00
15 Shaquille O'Neal/121 12.00 30.00
16 Allen Iverson/30 20.00 50.00

2011-12 Panini Gold Standard 24K Memorabilia Prime

*PRIME: 1X TO 2.5X BASE HI
STATED PRINT RUN 5 TO 25 SER.#'d SETS
SOME UNPRICED DUE TO SCARCITY
4 Kobe Bryant/25 100.00 200.00
14 Patrick Ewing/25 50.00 125.00

2011-12 Panini Gold Standard Black Gold Threads

ATED PRINT RUN 10 TO 149 SER.#'d SETS
SOME UNPRICED DUE TO SCARCITY
UNPRICED PRIME PRINT RUN 1 TO 5 SETS
100 Tony Parker/49 6.00 15.00
BG1 Dirk Nowitzki/149 8.00 20.00
BG2 Brandon Jennings/49 3.00 8.00
BG3 Ricky Rubio/49 20.00 50.00
BG4 Russell Westbrook/149 12.00 30.00
BG5 Shawn Marion/49 5.00 12.00
BG6 Shawn Kemp/49 15.00 40.00
BG7 Stephen Curry/149 25.00 60.00
BG8 Tim Duncan/49 8.00 20.00
BG9 Toni Kukoc/49 8.00 20.00
BG10 Tracy McGrady/49 5.00 12.00
BG11 Tyler Hansbrough/30 4.00 10.00
BG12 LeBron James/149 12.00 30.00
BG13 Dwight Howard/149 4.00 10.00
BG14 Drew Gooden/49 4.00 10.00
BG15 Dwyane Wade/149 10.00 25.00
BG16 Gary Payton/25 10.00 25.00
BG17 Jason Terry/25 6.00 15.00
BG18 Joakim Noah/25 4.00 10.00
BG19 Al Jefferson/149 4.00 10.00
BG20 Alonzo Mourning/49 10.00 25.00
BG21 Amare Stoudemire/49 4.00 10.00
BG22 Andre Iguodala/49 4.00 10.00
BG23 Andrew Bynum/149 3.00 8.00
BG24 Derrick Rose/149 6.00 15.00
BG25 Kobe Bryant/149 12.00 30.00
BG26 Kevin Garnett/49 8.00 20.00
BG27 Kevin Love/49 5.00 12.00
BG28 LaMarcus Aldridge/49 5.00 12.00
BG29 Manu Ginobili/49 6.00 15.00
BG30 Marc Gasol/49 5.00 12.00
BG31 Pau Gasol/49 6.00 15.00
BG32 Paul Pierce/149 8.00 20.00
BG33 Ben Gordon/49 4.00 10.00
BG34 Serge Ibaka/149 4.00 10.00
BG35 David Lee/49 3.00 8.00
BG36 DeMarcus Cousins/149 5.00 12.00
BG37 Andrew Bogut/49 4.00 10.00
BG38 Bill Cartwright/49 4.00 10.00
BG39 Blake Griffin/149 5.00 12.00
BG40 Brendan Haywood/149 3.00 8.00
BG41 Brook Lopez/149 4.00 10.00
BG42 Carlos Boozer/149 4.00 10.00
BG43 Carmelo Anthony/49 8.00 20.00
BG44 Chris Bosh/149 5.00 12.00
BG45 Chris Webber/49 5.00 12.00
BG46 Chuck Hayes/99 3.00 8.00
BG47 Courtney Lee/99 4.00 10.00
BG48 Darren Collison/49 4.00 10.00
BG49 Roy Hibbert/82 4.00 10.00
BG50 Derrick Favors/99 4.00 10.00
BG51 Danny Granger/99 4.00 10.00
BG52 Eddie Jones/49 4.00 10.00
BG53 Evan Turner/149 3.00 8.00
BG54 Glen Davis/99 3.00 8.00
BG55 Grant Hill/99 6.00 15.00
BG56 Greg Monroe/149 5.00 12.00
BG57 James Harden/149 8.00 20.00
BG58 Jason Kidd/99 6.00 15.00
BG59 JaVale McGee/149 4.00 10.00
BG60 Joe Dumars/25 8.00 20.00
BG61 John Wall/149 6.00 15.00
BG62 Jrue Holiday/149 5.00 12.00
BG63 Julius Erving/25 20.00 50.00
BG64 Karl Malone/49 6.00 15.00
BG65 Kevin Durant/149 12.00 30.00
BG66 Kevin Willis/49 3.00 8.00
BG67 Nicolas Batum/149 4.00 10.00
BG68 Luis Scola/99 4.00 10.00
BG69 Luol Deng/99 4.00 10.00
BG70 Tyreke Evans/49 3.00 8.00
BG71 Vince Carter/99 8.00 20.00
BG72 Patrick Ewing/99 10.00 25.00
BG74 Omri Casspi/49 3.00 8.00
BG75 Nick Van Exel/49 12.00 30.00
BG76 Moses Malone/25 8.00 20.00
BG77 Michael Beasley/49 3.00 8.00
BG78 Mario Chalmers/49 4.00 10.00
BG79 Rajon Rondo/49 5.00 12.00
BG80 Josh Smith/99 4.00 10.00
BG81 Rudy Gay/99 5.00 12.00
BG82 Landry Fields/149 4.00 10.00
BG83 Kiki Vandeweghe/99 4.00 10.00
BG84 Kevin Johnson/149 5.00 12.00
BG86 Chris Paul/149 6.00 15.00
BG87 Andrea Bargnani/99 4.00 10.00
BG88 Patrick Patterson/149 3.00 8.00
BG89 Chris Kaman/99 4.00 10.00
BG90 Nene/49 4.00 10.00
BG91 Spencer Hawes/149 3.00 8.00
BG92 Sleepy Floyd/149 5.00 12.00
BG93 Shawn Bradley/99 3.00 8.00
BG94 Alex English/25 8.00 20.00
BG95 Bill Laimbeer/49 4.00 10.00
BG96 Chris Andersen/49 4.00 10.00
BG97 Danilo Gallinari/49 4.00 10.00
BG98 DeMar DeRozan/149 5.00 12.00
BG99 Yao Ming/49 6.00 15.00

2011-12 Panini Gold Standard Gold Rush

STATED PRINT RUN 49 SER.#'d SETS
1 Kobe Bryant 20.00 50.00
2 Paul Pierce 5.00 12.00
3 LaMarcus Aldridge 5.00 12.00
4 Tony Parker 5.00 12.00
5 Tyreke Evans 3.00 8.00
6 Nick Young 4.00 10.00
7 Marc Gasol 5.00 12.00
8 Josh Smith 4.00 10.00
9 Kevin Durant 12.00 30.00
10 Chris Bosh 5.00 12.00
11 Amare Stoudemire 4.00 10.00
12 Kevin Martin 4.00 10.00
13 LeBron James 20.00 50.00
14 James Harden 8.00 20.00
15 Andrew Bogut 4.00 10.00
16 Al Jefferson 4.00 10.00
17 Jason Terry 4.00 10.00
18 Jason Kidd 5.00 12.00
19 Danny Granger 4.00 10.00
20 Dwyane Wade 10.00 25.00
21 Ty Lawson 3.00 8.00
22 Vlade Divac 5.00 12.00
23 John Starks 4.00 10.00
24 Gary Payton 5.00 12.00
25 Blake Griffin 5.00 12.00
26 Stephen Curry 20.00 50.00
27 Jordan Crawford 3.00 8.00
28 Gordon Hayward 5.00 12.00
29 Chris Paul 6.00 15.00
30 Pau Gasol 5.00 12.00
31 Brandon Jennings 3.00 8.00
32 Toni Kukoc 5.00 12.00
33 Landry Fields 4.00 10.00
34 Derrick Rose 6.00 15.00
35 Scottie Pippen 10.00 25.00
36 David Lee 3.00 8.00
37 Vince Carter 6.00 15.00
38 Shawn Marion 5.00 12.00
39 Andre Iguodala 4.00 10.00
40 Andre Miller 4.00 10.00
41 Jrue Holiday 5.00 12.00
42 Earl Monroe 5.00 12.00
43 David Robinson 8.00 20.00
44 Jerry West 6.00 15.00
45 Julius Erving 8.00 20.00
46 Wilt Chamberlain 10.00 25.00
47 Dwight Howard 4.00 10.00
48 George Mikan 10.00 25.00
49 Chris Mullin 5.00 12.00
50 Shaquille O'Neal 10.00 25.00

2011-12 Panini Gold Standard Gold Stars Materials

STATED PRINT RUN 9 TO 149 SER.#'d SETS
SOME UNPRICED DUE TO SCARCITY
1 Kevin Durant/149 8.00 20.00
2 Ricky Rubio/149 10.00 25.00
3 Rajon Rondo/149 5.00 12.00
4 Derrick Rose/149 4.00 10.00
5 LeBron James/149 12.00 30.00
6 Tony Parker/149 3.00 8.00
7 Steve Nash/149 4.00 10.00
8 Dirk Nowitzki/149 4.00 10.00
9 Amare Stoudemire/149 2.50 6.00
10 Chris Paul/149 4.00 10.00
11 Dwight Howard/149 2.50 6.00
12 Dwyane Wade/149 6.00 15.00
13 Deron Williams/149 2.50 6.00
14 Andrea Bargnani/149 2.50 6.00
15 Tim Duncan/149 5.00 12.00
16 Carlos Boozer/149 2.50 6.00
17 Kevin Garnett/149 5.00 12.00
18 Kevin Love/149 3.00 8.00
19 LaMarcus Aldridge/149 3.00 8.00
20 Greg Monroe/149 3.00 8.00
21 Roy Hibbert/149 2.50 6.00
22 Russell Westbrook/149 8.00 20.00
23 Brandon Jennings/149 2.00 5.00
24 Kobe Bryant/149 12.00 30.00
25 Josh Smith/149 2.50 6.00
26 Monta Ellis/149 2.50 6.00
27 Chris Bosh/149 3.00 8.00
28 D.J. Augustin/40 2.50 6.00
29 Al Jefferson/149 2.50 6.00
30 Andrew Bynum/149 2.00 5.00
31 Ryan Anderson/149 2.50 6.00
32 Brook Lopez/149 2.50 6.00
33 Marcin Gortat/149 6.00 15.00
34 John Wall/149 4.00 10.00
35 Tyreke Evans/149 2.00 5.00
36 Kevin Martin/149 2.50 6.00
37 Carmelo Anthony/149 4.00 10.00
38 Paul Pierce/149 3.00 8.00
40 Marcus Thornton/149 2.00 5.00

2011-12 Panini Gold Standard Gold Stars Materials Prime

*PRIME: 1.25X TO 3X BASE HI
STATED PRINT RUN 3 TO 25 SER.#'d SETS
SOME UNPRICED DUE TO SCARCITY
1 Kevin Durant/25 25.00 60.00
2 Ricky Rubio/25 50.00 125.00
6 Tony Parker/25 12.00 30.00
24 Kobe Bryant/15 50.00 125.00
27 Chris Bosh/25 12.00 30.00

2011-12 Panini Gold Standard Golden 50 Materials

STATED PRINT RUN 5 TO 149 SER.#'d SETS
SOME UNPRICED DUE TO SCARCITY
1 James Worthy/25 10.00 25.00
2 Robert Parish/99 6.00 15.00
3 Kevin McHale/99 5.00 12.00
4 Kareem Abdul-Jabbar/25 8.00 20.00
5 Karl Malone/99 6.00 15.00
6 Sam Jones/25 8.00 20.00
7 George Gervin/149 5.00 12.00
8 Patrick Ewing/149 6.00 15.00
9 Shaquille O'Neal/149 10.00 25.00
10 Earl Monroe/149 6.00 15.00
11 Scottie Pippen/149 10.00 25.00
12 Clyde Drexler/149 6.00 15.00
13 David Robinson/99 8.00 20.00
14 Julius Erving/25 12.00 30.00
15 John Stockton/99 8.00 20.00
16 Isiah Thomas/99 5.00 12.00
18 George Mikan/25 15.00 40.00
19 Hakeem Olajuwon/149 6.00 15.00
20 Julius Erving/25 12.00 30.00
21 Shaquille O'Neal/149 10.00 25.00
22 Shaquille O'Neal/57 15.00 40.00
23 Shaquille O'Neal/149 10.00 25.00
24 Scottie Pippen/149 8.00 20.00
25 Clyde Drexler/149 6.00 15.00

2011-12 Panini Gold Standard Golden 50 Materials Prime

*PRIME: 1X TO 2.5X BASE HI
STATED PRINT RUN ONE TO 25 SER.#'d SETS
SOME UNPRICED DUE TO SCARCITY
22 Shaquille O'Neal/25 25.00 60.00

2011-12 Panini Gold Standard Greatest Graphs

STATED PRINT RUN 10 TO 149 SER.#'d SETS
SOME UNPRICED DUE TO SCARCITY
1 John Havlicek/25 30.00 80.00
2 Kareem Abdul-Jabbar/25 75.00 150.00
3 Julius Erving/25 50.00 125.00
4 Lenny Wilkens/149 6.00 15.00
5 Nate Archibald/149 6.00 15.00
6 Rick Barry/25 12.00 30.00
7 Elgin Baylor/49 15.00 40.00
8 Larry Bird/25 50.00 125.00
9 Dave Cowens/149 6.00 15.00
10 Billy Cunningham/149 15.00 40.00
11 Clyde Drexler/25 30.00 80.00
12 Walt Frazier/149 6.00 15.00
13 Hal Greer/149 6.00 15.00
14 Elvin Hayes/149 15.00 40.00
15 Magic Johnson/25 100.00 200.00
16 Sam Jones/25 20.00 50.00
17 Bob Pettit/25 50.00 125.00
18 Kevin McHale/25 30.00 80.00
19 Earl Monroe/25 20.00 50.00
20 Hakeem Olajuwon/25 30.00 80.00
21 Robert Parish/149 6.00 15.00
22 Scottie Pippen/25 125.00 250.00
23 Willis Reed/25 15.00 40.00
24 Oscar Robertson/25 75.00 150.00
25 David Robinson/25 75.00 150.00
27 Dolph Schayes/149 6.00 15.00
29 John Stockton/25 60.00 150.00
30 Isiah Thomas/149 10.00 25.00
31 Nate Thurmond/149 6.00 15.00
32 Wes Unseld/149 6.00 15.00
33 Bill Walton/99 8.00 20.00
35 James Worthy/25 35.00 70.00

2011-12 Panini Gold Standard Hall of Gold Materials

STATED PRINT RUN 5 TO 149 SER.#'d SETS
SOME UNPRICED DUE TO SCARCITY
1 Dominique Wilkins/149 5.00 12.00
2 Dennis Rodman/149 12.00 30.00
3 Clyde Drexler/149 5.00 12.00
4 Joe Dumars/49 4.00 10.00
5 George Gervin/149 4.00 10.00
6 Alex English/149 3.00 8.00
8 Patrick Ewing/149 5.00 12.00
10 Artis Gilmore/25 3.00 8.00
11 David Robinson/149 6.00 15.00
13 James Worthy/25 8.00 20.00
15 Dan Issel/25 3.00 8.00
17 Karl Malone/149 5.00 12.00
18 Kevin McHale/99 4.00 10.00
21 Scottie Pippen/149 8.00 20.00
22 John Stockton/49 8.00 20.00
23 Isiah Thomas/49 4.00 10.00
24 Dennis Johnson/149 3.00 8.00
25 Chris Mullin/49 6.00 15.00

2011-12 Panini Gold Standard Hall of Gold Materials Prime

*PRIME: 1X TO 2.5X BASE HI
STATED PRINT RUN ONE TO 25 SER.#'d SETS
SOME UNPRICED DUE TO SCARCITY
8 Patrick Ewing/25 25.00 60.00

2011-12 Panini Gold Standard Marks of the Hall Autographs

STATED PRINT RUN 10 TO 149 SER.#'d SETS
SOME UNPRICED DUE TO SCARCITY
1 Pat Riley/25 50.00 120.00
2 Kareem Abdul-Jabbar/25 75.00 150.00
3 Nate Archibald/99 6.00 15.00
4 Bobby Wanzer/149 6.00 15.00
5 Elgin Baylor/24 40.00 70.00
7 Dolph Schayes/149 6.00 15.00
8 Bob Pettit/25 25.00 60.00
9 Arnie Risen/149 8.00 20.00
10 Robert Parish/149 10.00 25.00
11 Oscar Robertson/25 75.00 150.00
13 Hal Greer/149 6.00 15.00
14 Frank Ramsey/149 15.00 40.00
15 Willis Reed/25 25.00 60.00
16 John Havlicek/25 40.00 100.00
17 Chris Mullin/149 12.00 30.00
18 Bob McAdoo/149 15.00 40.00
20 Clyde Lovellette/149 12.00 30.00
21 Harry Gallatin/149 6.00 15.00
23 Dan Issel/149 8.00 20.00
26 James Worthy/25 75.00 150.00
27 Dominique Wilkins/25 40.00 100.00
28 Lenny Wilkens/149 6.00 15.00
29 Bill Walton/99 12.00 30.00
30 Wes Unseld/99 8.00 20.00
31 David Thompson/99 6.00 15.00
32 Isiah Thomas/149 EXCH 15.00 40.00
33 John Stockton/25 75.00 200.00
34 Scottie Pippen/25 175.00 325.00
35 Calvin Murphy/149 6.00 15.00
36 Earl Monroe/149 6.00 15.00
37 Bob Lanier/25 25.00 60.00
38 Sam Jones/25 60.00 150.00
39 K.C. Jones/25 50.00 120.00
40 George Gervin/149 10.00 25.00
41 Elvin Hayes/149 8.00 20.00
42 Gail Goodrich/149 6.00 15.00
43 Walt Frazier/99 10.00 25.00
45 Joe Dumars/149 8.00 20.00
46 Dave Cowens/99 5.00 15.00
47 Clyde Drexler/25 60.00 150.00
48 Alex English/99 8.00 20.00
49 Adrian Dantley/149 6.00 15.00
50 Artis Gilmore/25 6.00 15.00

2011-12 Panini Gold Standard Private Signings

RANDOM INSERTS IN PACKS
1 Oscar Robertson 40.00 100.00
2 John Wall 100.00 200.00
3 Elgin Baylor 25.00 60.00
4 Kareem Abdul-Jabbar 75.00 150.00
5 John Stockton 100.00 200.00
6 Magic Johnson 75.00 150.00
7 Kevin Durant 150.00 300.00
8 Julius Erving 50.00 125.00
9 Derrick Rose 175.00 300.00
10 David Robinson 50.00 125.00
11 Bill Russell 75.00 150.00
12 Jerry West 25.00 60.00
13 John Havlicek 30.00 80.00
14 Pat Riley 25.00 60.00
15 Grant Hill 125.00 250.00
16 Toni Kukoc 25.00 60.00

2011-12 Panini Gold Standard Signs of Gold

STATED PRINT RUN 10 TO 149 SER.#'d SETS
SOME UNPRICED DUE TO SCARCITY
1 Chris Paul/25 EXCH 50.00 120.00
4 Andrew Bynum/25 10.00 25.00
5 Russell Westbrook/49 EXCH 50.00 120.00
6 Ray Allen/25 EXCH 20.00 50.00
7 DeMarcus Cousins/49 12.00 30.00
8 Kobe Bryant/49 100.00 200.00
11 Artis Gilmore/49 6.00 15.00
12 Ronnie Brewer/149 4.00 10.00
14 Mike Bibby/49 6.00 15.00
15 Danny Granger/49 6.00 15.00
16 Al Jefferson/49 6.00 15.00
17 David Lee/149 6.00 15.00
18 LaMarcus Aldridge/49 6.00 15.00
19 Jamal Crawford/149 8.00 20.00
20 Joe Johnson/25 6.00 15.00
21 Deron Williams/25 8.00 20.00
22 Jason Kidd/25 25.00 60.00
23 Luol Deng/49 8.00 20.00
24 Andrea Bargnani/49 6.00 15.00
25 Kevin Love/25 25.00 60.00
26 Glen Rice/149 6.00 15.00
27 David Thompson/49 6.00 15.00
28 David Robinson/25 30.00 80.00
29 Paul George/149 15.00 40.00
30 Greg Monroe/149 5.00 12.00
31 Walt Frazier/49 8.00 20.00
33 Detlef Schrempf/149 8.00 20.00
34 Stephen Curry/49 100.00 250.00
35 Tyreke Evans/49 10.00 25.00
36 Marcin Gortat/149 6.00 15.00
37 Kevin Martin/149 4.00 10.00
38 Michael Beasley/49 EXCH 5.00 12.00
39 Blake Griffin/25 50.00 125.00
40 Brandon Jennings/49 EXCH 10.00 25.00
41 Mike Conley/149 4.00 10.00
42 Chauncey Billups/25 4.00 10.00
43 Ty Lawson/149 EXCH 4.00 10.00
44 Tony Parker/25 20.00 50.00
45 O.J. Mayo/149 5.00 12.00
46 Vince Carter/25 30.00 80.00
47 Clyde Drexler/25 12.00 30.00
48 Mo Williams/25 6.00 15.00
49 Jeff Teague/149 4.00 10.00
50 Dikembe Mutombo/49 8.00 20.00
51 James Harden/49 12.00 30.00
52 Serge Ibaka/149 6.00 15.00
53 Juwan Howard/149 5.00 12.00
54 Bernard King/149 4.00 10.00
55 Robert Parish/49 6.00 15.00
56 Mark Price/149 6.00 15.00
57 Danilo Gallinari/49 5.00 12.00
58 Jason Richardson/49 4.00 10.00
59 Andre Iguodala/49 8.00 20.00
60 Grant Hill/25 150.00 300.00
61 George Gervin/49 8.00 20.00
62 World B. Free/49 6.00 15.00
63 Metta World Peace/25 12.00 30.00
64 Spencer Haywood/149 4.00 10.00
65 Gerald Wallace/49 6.00 15.00
66 Dave Cowens/49 8.00 20.00
67 Hal Greer/49 5.00 12.00
68 Delonte West/149 4.00 10.00
69 Shane Battier/49 6.00 15.00
70 Ben Gordon/25 4.00 10.00
71 Kyle Lowry/149 4.00 10.00
72 Ersan Ilyasova/149 6.00 15.00
73 Kris Humphries/149 4.00 10.00
74 Chris Kaman/49 4.00 10.00
75 Trevor Ariza/49 4.00 10.00
76 J.R. Smith/149 5.00 12.00
77 DeJuan Blair/149 EXCH 6.00 15.00
78 DeMar DeRozan/49 8.00 20.00
79 Gordon Hayward/149 6.00 15.00
80 Nick Young/149 6.00 15.00
81 D.J. Augustin/49 4.00 10.00
82 Richard Hamilton/25 4.00 10.00
83 Joakim Noah/49 12.00 30.00
84 Paul Westphal/49 5.00 12.00
85 Jose Calderon/149 5.00 12.00
86 Isiah Thomas/149 10.00 25.00
87 Mitch Richmond/149 6.00 15.00
88 Alonzo Mourning/25 40.00 100.00
89 Xavier Henry/149 6.00 15.00
90 Marc Gasol/25 EXCH 12.00 30.00
91 Tayshaun Prince/49 5.00 12.00
93 Bill Walton/49 8.00 20.00
94 K.C. Jones/25 12.00 30.00
95 Elvin Hayes/25 8.00 20.00
96 Jalen Rose/149 5.00 12.00
97 Jamal Mashburn/149 6.00 15.00
98 James Worthy/49 20.00 50.00
99 Mark Aguirre/149 4.00 10.00
100 Muggsy Bogues/149 8.00 20.00

2011-12 Panini Gold Standard Superscribe Autographs

STATED PRINT RUN 25 TO 149 SER.#'d SETS
1 Stephen Curry/149 75.00 200.00
2 Brandon Jennings/49 EXCH 6.00 15.00
3 DeMar DeRozan/149 8.00 20.00
4 Antawn Jamison/149 4.00 10.00
5 Stephen Jackson/149 8.00 20.00
6 Luis Scola/149 EXCH 6.00 15.00
7 Kevin Love/25 12.00 30.00
8 Kyle Lowry/149 4.00 10.00
9 Ryan Anderson/149 4.00 10.00
10 Roy Hibbert/149 4.00 10.00
11 Tyson Chandler/99 6.00 15.00
12 Paul George/149 40.00 100.00
13 Gary Neal/149 EXCH 4.00 10.00
14 Evan Turner/25 4.00 10.00
15 David Thompson/149 4.00 10.00
16 Jameer Nelson/149 4.00 10.00
17 Channing Frye/149 4.00 10.00
18 Luke Ridnour/149 4.00 10.00
19 Chris Kaman/149 4.00 10.00
20 Jeff Teague/149 4.00 10.00
21 Rajon Rondo/49 EXCH 15.00 40.00
22 Gerald Wallace/49 4.00 10.00
23 Josh Smith/49 8.00 20.00
24 Kobe Bryant/149 100.00 200.00
24A K.Bryant USA Inscription 700.00 1300.00
25 Jrue Holiday/149 4.00 10.00
26 Wesley Matthews/149 4.00 10.00
27 Devin Harris/149 4.00 10.00
28 Shane Battier/149 6.00 15.00
29 Russell Westbrook/49 60.00 150.00
30 Chase Budinger/149 4.00 10.00
31 DeJuan Blair/149 EXCH 4.00 10.00
32 Blake Griffin/49 50.00 125.00
33 Jodie Meeks/149 EXCH 4.00 10.00
34 Caron Butler/49 4.00 10.00
35 Kevin Durant/49 100.00 200.00
36 Landry Fields/149 4.00 10.00
37 Derek Fisher/149 4.00 10.00
38 Rudy Gay/149 EXCH 6.00 15.00
39 Nene/149 EXCH 6.00 15.00
40 Tyler Hansbrough/149 4.00 10.00
41 Ty Lawson/149 4.00 10.00
42 Kris Humphries/149 4.00 10.00
43 Marcin Gortat/149 4.00 10.00
44 DeMarcus Cousins/149 15.00 40.00
45 Eric Gordon/149 4.00 10.00
46 Serge Ibaka/149 EXCH 10.00 25.00
47 Chris Andersen/49 50.00 100.00
48 DeAndre Jordan/149 10.00 25.00
49 Zach Randolph/49 6.00 15.00
50 J.R. Smith/149 4.00 10.00

2012-13 Panini Gold Standard

1-225 PRINT RUN 349 SER.#'d SETS
EXCHANGE DEADLINE 12/26/2014
1 Kevin Love 1.50 4.00
2A Steve Nash
Lakers
2B Steve Nash
Suns
2C Steve Nash
Mavericks
2D Steve Nash
Suns
3 LeBron James 6.00 15.00
4 Carmelo Anthony 2.00 5.00
5 Paul Pierce 1.50 4.00
6 Dirk Nowitzki 2.00 5.00
7 Kevin Durant 4.00 10.00
8 Kobe Bryant 6.00 15.00
9 Dwyane Wade 2.50 6.00
10 Blake Griffin 1.50 4.00
11 James Harden 2.50 6.00
12 Deron Williams 1.25 3.00
13 Ricky Rubio 1.50 4.00
14 Dwight Howard 1.25 3.00
15 Russell Westbrook 4.00 10.00
16 Rajon Rondo 1.50 4.00
17 Ray Allen 1.50 4.00
18A Grant Hill 30.00 80.00
Clippers
18B Grant Hill 12.00 30.00
Magic
18C Grant Hill 10.00 25.00
Suns
18D Grant Hill
Pistons
19 LaMarcus Aldridge 1.50 4.00
20 Chris Bosh 1.50 4.00
21 Tim Duncan 2.50 6.00
22 Tyson Chandler 1.25 3.00
23 Joe Johnson 1.25 3.00
24A Vince Carter
Mavreicks
24B Vince Carter
Suns
24C Vince Carter
Magic
24D Vince Carter
Nets
24E Vince Carter
Raptors
25 Brandon Jennings 1.00 2.50
26 DeMarcus Cousins 1.50 4.00
27 Stephen Curry 6.00 15.00
28 Kevin Garnett 2.50 6.00
29 Chris Paul 2.00 5.00
30 Tyreke Evans 1.00 2.50
31 Andrew Bynum 1.00 2.50
32 Marcin Gortat 1.25 3.00
33 Jeremy Lin 1.50 4.00
34 Derrick Rose 2.00 5.00
35 Ty Lawson 1.00 2.50
36 Al Jefferson 1.25 3.00
37 Tony Parker 1.50 4.00
38 John Wall 2.00 5.00
39 Kevin Martin 1.25 3.00
40 Marc Gasol 1.50 4.00
41 Amar'e Stoudemire 1.25 3.00
42 Josh Smith 1.25 3.00
43 Andrea Bargnani 1.25 3.00
44 Nicolas Batum 1.25 3.00
45 Zach Randolph 1.25 3.00
46A Jason Kidd 12.00 30.00
Knicks
46B Jason Kidd 12.00 30.00
Mavericks
46C Jason Kidd 12.00 30.00
Nets
46D Jason Kidd 12.00 30.00
Suns
46E Jason Kidd 12.00 30.00
Mavericks
47 Luol Deng 1.25 3.00
48 Jrue Holiday 1.50 4.00
49 Danny Granger 1.25 3.00
50 Pau Gasol 1.50 4.00
51 O.J. Mayo 1.00 2.50
52 Corey Brewer 1.00 2.50
53 Anderson Varejao 1.00 2.50
54 Serge Ibaka 1.25 3.00
55 Metta World Peace 1.50 4.00
56 Jordan Crawford 1.00 2.50
57 Jamal Crawford 1.50 4.00
58 Jason Terry 1.25 3.00
59 David West 1.25 3.00
60 Manu Ginobili 1.50 4.00
61 Andre Iguodala 1.25 3.00
62 Evan Turner 1.00 2.50
63 Greg Monroe 1.25 3.00
64 Roy Hibbert 1.25 3.00
65 Rudy Gay 1.50 4.00
66 Chris Kaman 1.25 3.00
67 Joakim Noah 1.25 3.00
68 Gordon Hayward 1.50 4.00
69 JaVale McGee 1.25 3.00
70 Darren Collison 1.25 3.00
71 Mike Conley 1.25 3.00
72 Louis Williams 1.25 3.00
73 Paul George 2.00 5.00
74 Monta Ellis 1.25 3.00
75 Brook Lopez 1.25 3.00
76 Kyle Lowry 1.25 3.00
77 Ryan Anderson 1.25 3.00
78 DeMar DeRozan 1.50 4.00
79 Al Horford 1.25 3.00
80 Arron Afflalo 1.25 3.00
81 Wesley Matthews 1.00 2.50
82 Raymond Felton 1.25 3.00
83 DeAndre Jordan 1.50 4.00
84 Glen Davis 1.00 2.50
85 Brandon Bass 1.00 2.50
86 Jose Calderon 1.00 2.50
87 Goran Dragic 1.25 3.00
88 Ramon Sessions 1.25 3.00
89 Thaddeus Young 1.00 2.50
90 Marcus Thornton 1.00 2.50
91 Paul Millsap 1.50 4.00
92 Nikola Pekovic 1.00 2.50
93 Jameer Nelson 1.00 2.50
94 Richard Hamilton 1.25 3.00
95 J.R. Smith 1.25 3.00
96 Carlos Boozer 1.25 3.00
97 Jeff Teague 1.25 3.00
98 J.J. Redick 1.50 4.00
99 Andrei Kirilenko 1.25 3.00
100 Tayshaun Prince 1.25 3.00
101 Jason Richardson 1.50 4.00
102 J.J. Hickson 1.00 2.50
103 Kirk Hinrich 1.25 3.00
104 Omer Asik 1.25 3.00
105 Nene 1.25 3.00
106 Antawn Jamison 1.25 3.00
107 Chauncey Billups 1.50 4.00
108 Devin Harris 1.00 2.50
109 Mario Chalmers 1.25 3.00
110 Nick Collison 1.25 3.00
111 Darrell Arthur 1.00 2.50
112 Earl Clark 1.00 2.50
113 Taj Gibson 1.25 3.00
114 Shane Battier 1.25 3.00
115 Gerald Wallace 1.25 3.00
116 Gary Neal 1.25 3.00
117 Andre Miller 1.25 3.00
118 Nick Young 1.25 3.00
119 Mo Williams 1.25 3.00
120 Ersan Ilyasova 1.00 2.50
121 Dorell Wright 1.00 2.50
122 J.J. Barea 1.25 3.00
123 Michael Beasley 1.00 2.50
124 Eric Bledsoe 1.25 3.00
125 Ekpe Udoh 1.00 2.50
126 Jared Dudley 1.00 2.50
127 DeJuan Blair 1.00 2.50
128 Thabo Sefolosha 1.00 2.50
129 Mike Miller 1.25 3.00
130 Marcus Camby 1.25 3.00
131 Rodney Stuckey 1.25 3.00
132 Kris Humphries 1.00 2.50
133 Randy Foye 1.00 2.50
134 Tiago Splitter 1.25 3.00
135 Patrick Patterson 1.00 2.50
136 Emeka Okafor 1.25 3.00
137 Steve Novak 1.00 2.50
138 George Hill 1.25 3.00
139 Derrick Favors 1.25 3.00
140 Lamar Odom 1.25 3.00
141 Shannon Brown 1.00 2.50
142 Ben Gordon 1.25 3.00
143 Carl Landry 1.00 2.50
144 Greivis Vasquez 1.25 3.00
145 Stephen Jackson 1.25 3.00
146A Rasheed Wallace
Knicks
146B Rasheed Wallace
Celtics
146C Rasheed Wallace
Pistons
146D Rasheed Wallace
Hawks
146E Rasheed Wallace
Trail Blazers
146F Rasheed Wallace
Bullets
147 Byron Mullens 1.00 2.50
148 Caron Butler 1.25 3.00
149 Robin Lopez 1.00 2.50
150 Gerald Henderson 1.00 2.50
151 Danny Green 1.25 3.00
152 Samuel Dalembert 1.00 2.50
153 Luis Scola 1.25 3.00
154 Shawn Marion 1.25 3.00
155 Elton Brand 1.50 4.00
156 Jerry Stackhouse 1.25 3.00
157 David Lee 1.00 2.50
158 Larry Sanders 1.00 2.50
159 D.J. Augustin 1.00 2.50
160 Al-Farouq Aminu 1.25 3.00
161 Jarrett Jack 1.25 3.00
162 Kyle Korver 1.25 3.00
163 Nate Robinson 1.00 2.50
164 Marco Belinelli 1.00 2.50
165 Mike Dunleavy 1.00 2.50
166 Kevin Seraphin 1.00 2.50
167 Luke Ridnour 1.25 3.00
168 Jeff Green 1.25 3.00
169 Kendrick Perkins 1.00 2.50
170 Matt Barnes 1.00 2.50
171 Chase Budinger 1.00 2.50
172 Linas Kleiza 1.00 2.50
173 Gerald Green 1.25 3.00
174 Brandon Rush 1.00 2.50
175 Ronnie Brewer 1.25 3.00
176 Kosta Koufos 1.00 2.50
177 Marreese Speights 1.00 2.50
178 Ed Davis 1.00 2.50
179 Landry Fields 1.00 2.50
180 Andray Blatche 1.00 2.50
181 C.J. Watson 1.00 2.50
182 Tony Allen 1.00 2.50
183 Damian Lillard RC 6.00 15.00
184 DeShawn Stevenson 1.00 2.50
185 Courtney Lee 1.25 3.00
186 Tyler Hansbrough 1.25 3.00
187 Lance Stephenson 1.25 3.00
188 Jason Smith 1.00 2.50
189 Brandan Wright 1.00 2.50
190 Marvin Williams 1.25 3.00
191 Kareem Abdul-Jabbar 2.50 6.00
192 Larry Bird 4.00 10.00
193 Wilt Chamberlain 3.00 8.00
194 Yao Ming 2.00 5.00
195 Elgin Baylor 1.50 4.00
196 Isiah Thomas 1.50 4.00
197 Magic Johnson 4.00 10.00
198 Oscar Robertson 2.00 5.00
199 Jerry West 2.00 5.00
200 John Havlicek 2.00 5.00
201 Julius Erving 2.50 6.00
202 Bill Russell 2.50 6.00
203 Scottie Pippen 3.00 8.00
204A Anfernee Hardaway
Magic
204B Anfernee Hardaway
Heat
204C Anfernee Hardaway 15.00 40.00
Knicks
204D Anfernee Hardaway 4.00 10.00
Suns
205 Shaquille O'Neal 3.00 8.00
206 Dennis Rodman 3.00 8.00
207 Pete Maravich 2.50 6.00
208 Karl Malone 2.00 5.00
209A Shawn Kemp
Supersonics
209B Shawn Kemp
Cavaliers
209C Shawn Kemp
Magic
209D Shawn Kemp
Blazers
210 Hakeem Olajuwon 2.00 5.00
211 Dikembe Mutombo 1.50 4.00
212 John Stockton 2.50 6.00
213 Gary Payton 1.50 4.00
214 Bob Pettit 1.50 4.00
215 Moses Malone 1.50 4.00
216 Rick Barry 1.25 3.00
217 David Robinson 2.50 6.00
218 Elvin Hayes 1.50 4.00
219 Bob Cousy 2.50 6.00
220 George Mikan 3.00 8.00
221 Patrick Ewing 2.00 5.00
222 Allen Iverson 2.00 5.00
223 Earl Monroe 1.50 4.00
224 Bob Love 1.50 4.00
225 Bill Walton 1.50 4.00
226 A. Drummond JSY AU RC 20.00 50.00
227 Kyrie Irving JSY AU RC 60.00 150.00
228 Anthony Davis JSY AU RC 100.00 250.00
229 Arnett Moultrie JSY AU RC 4.00 10.00
230 M.Kidd-Gilchrist JSY AU RC 6.00 15.00
231 Bernard James JSY AU RC 4.00 10.00
232 Bismack Biyombo JSY AU RC 4.00 10.00
233 Bradley Beal JSY AU RC 25.00 60.00
234 Will Barton JSY AU RC 5.00 12.00
235 Parsons JSY AU RC EXCH 6.00 15.00
236 Chris Copeland JSY AU RC 4.00 10.00
237 Darius Johnson-Odom JSY AU RC 4.00 10.00
238 Darius Miller JSY AU RC 4.00 10.00
239 Darius Morris JSY AU RC 4.00 10.00
240 Austin Rivers JSY AU RC 10.00 25.00
241 D.Williams JSY AU RC EXCH 4.00 10.00
242 Dion Waiters JSY AU RC EXCH 6.00 15.00
243 Kenneth Faried JSY AU RC 6.00 15.00
244 Dray Green JSY AU RC 25.00 60.00
245 Jae Crowder JSY AU RC 5.00 12.00
246 E'Twaun Moore JSY AU RC 4.00 10.00
247 Evan Fournier JSY AU RC 6.00 15.00
248 Fab Melo JSY AU RC 4.00 10.00
249 Festus Ezeli JSY AU RC 5.00 12.00
250 J.Hamilton JSY AU RC EXCH 4.00 10.00
251 H.Barnes JSY AU RC 12.00 30.00
252 I.Shumpert JSY AU RC EXCH 8.00 20.00
253 Isaiah Thomas JSY AU RC 30.00 80.00
254 Ivan Johnson JSY AU RC EXCH 4.00 10.00
255 Marcus Morris JSY AU RC EXCH 5.00 12.00
256 Jan Vesely JSY AU RC 4.00 10.00
257 Jared Cunningham JSY AU RC 4.00 10.00
258 Jared Sullinger JSY AU RC 5.00 12.00
259 Kawhi Leonard JSY AU RC 125.00 300.00
260 Jeremy Pargo JSY AU RC 4.00 10.00
261 Jeremy Tyler JSY AU RC EXCH 4.00 10.00
262 Jimmer Fredette JSY AU RC 4.00 10.00
263 J.Butler JSY AU RC EXCH 30.00 80.00
264 Kevin Murphy JSY AU RC 4.00 10.00
265 John Jenkins JSY AU RC EXCH 4.00 10.00
266 Jonas Valanciunas JSY AU RC 6.00 15.00
267 Jeremy Lamb JSY AU RC 6.00 15.00
268 K.Walker JSY AU RC EXCH 12.00 30.00
269 Kendall Marshall JSY AU RC 4.00 10.00
270 Doron Lamb JSY AU RC 4.00 10.00
271 Thomas Robinson JSY AU RC 5.00 12.00
272 Khris Middleton JSY AU RC 6.00 15.00
273 Kim English JSY AU RC 4.00 10.00
274 Klay Thompson JSY AU RC 40.00 100.00
275 Kris Joseph JSY AU RC 4.00 10.00
276 Andrew Nicholson JSY AU RC 4.00 10.00
277 Lance Thomas JSY AU RC EXCH 4.00 10.00
278 Lavoy Allen JSY AU RC 4.00 10.00
279 Malcolm Lee JSY AU RC 4.00 10.00
280 Nolan Smith JSY AU RC 4.00 10.00
281 Markieff Morris JSY AU RC EXCH 6.00 15.00
282 Marquis Teague JSY AU RC 4.00 10.00
283 MarShon Brooks JSY AU RC 5.00 12.00
284 Meyers Leonard JSY AU RC 5.00 12.00
285 Kyle Singler JSY AU RC 4.00 10.00
286 Mike Scott JSY AU RC EXCH 4.00 10.00
287 Miles Plumlee JSY AU RC EXCH 4.00 10.00
288 Maurice Harkless JSY AU RC 6.00 15.00
289 Nikola Vucevic JSY AU RC 6.00 15.00
290 Enes Kanter JSY AU RC 5.00 12.00
291 Norris Cole JSY AU RC 4.00 10.00
292 Orlando Johnson JSY AU RC 4.00 10.00
293 Perry Jones JSY AU RC 4.00 10.00
294 Quincy Acy JSY AU RC 4.00 10.00
295 Tyler Honeycutt JSY AU RC 4.00 10.00
296 Reggie Jackson JSY AU RC 6.00 15.00
297 Robert Sacre JSY AU RC 4.00 10.00
298 Terrence Jones JSY AU RC 5.00 12.00
299 Terrence Ross JSY AU RC 6.00 15.00
300 Tobias Harris JSY AU RC 6.00 15.00
301 Trey Thompkins JSY AU RC 4.00 10.00
302 Tristan Thompson JSY AU RC 6.00 15.00
303 Tyler Zeller JSY AU RC 5.00 12.00
304 Brandon Knight JSY AU RC 6.00 15.00
305 John Henson JSY AU RC EXCH 6.00 15.00
306 Damian Lillard JSY AU 125.00 250.00

2012-13 Panini Gold Standard Black Gold Threads

PRINT RUNS B/WN 8-199 COPIES PER
NO PRICING ON QTY 10 OR LESS
1 Ricky Rubio/49 5.00 12.00
2 LeBron James/49 20.00 50.00
3 Tim Duncan/149 6.00 15.00
4 Raymond Felton/149 4.00 10.00
5 Paul Pierce/99 8.00 20.00
6 Kareem Abdul-Jabbar/25 12.00 30.00
7 J.R. Smith/99 4.00 10.00
8 Evan Turner/149 3.00 8.00
9 Kevin Love/99 5.00 12.00
10 Kevin Durant/49 15.00 40.00
11 Carmelo Anthony/49 12.00 30.00
12 Jameer Nelson/199 3.00 8.00
13 Kevin McHale/49 8.00 20.00
14 Marc Gasol/149 5.00 12.00
15 Stephen Curry/149 8.00 20.00
16 Greg Monroe/149 4.00 10.00
17 Arron Afflalo/199 4.00 10.00
18 Andrei Kirilenko/149 4.00 10.00
19 Rudy Gay/199 5.00 12.00
20 Rodney Stuckey/199 4.00 10.00
21 Julius Erving/49 10.00 25.00
22 Kobe Bryant/49 20.00 50.00
23 Robert Parish/49 5.00 12.00
24 Marcus Camby/149 4.00 10.00
25 Dwyane Wade/49 10.00 25.00
26 John Wall/149 6.00 15.00
27 Jalen Rose/49 5.00 12.00
28 Kevin Martin/149 4.00 10.00
29 Pau Gasol/149 5.00 12.00
30 Metta World Peace/149 5.00 12.00
31 Dirk Nowitzki/49 6.00 15.00
32 Tayshaun Prince/199 4.00 10.00
33 Derrick Rose/49 20.00 50.00
34 Josh Smith/149 4.00 10.00
35 Kevin Garnett/99 6.00 15.00
36 Alex English/49 4.00 10.00
37 DeMar DeRozan/199 5.00 12.00
38 Ty Lawson/149 3.00 8.00
39 Dominique Wilkins/49
40 Thaddeus Young/199 3.00 8.00
41 Scottie Pippen/49 30.00 60.00
42 Zydrunas Ilgauskas/49 4.00 10.00
43 Blake Griffin/49 5.00 12.00
45 Jason Terry/149 4.00 10.00
46 Robin Lopez/199 3.00 8.00

47 Clyde Drexler/49 6.00 15.00
48 Brandon Roy/99 5.00 12.00
49 Allen Iverson/49 20.00 50.00
50 Tony Parker/49 5.00 12.00
51 J.J. Redick/199 5.00 12.00
52 Joe Dumars/49 5.00 12.00
53 Isiah Thomas/49 5.00 12.00
54 Ron Harper/49 5.00 12.00
55 Chris Mullin/49
56 Amar'e Stoudemire/149 4.00 10.00
57 Alonzo Mourning/49 12.00 30.00
58 Kenneth Faried/99 6.00 15.00
59 Patrick Ewing/99 6.00 15.00
60 Elton Brand/199 5.00 12.00
61 David Lee/149 3.00 8.00
62 Hedo Turkoglu/199 4.00 10.00
63 JaVale McGee/199 4.00 10.00
64 Nene/199 4.00 10.00
66 Jamaal Wilkes/25 20.00 50.00
67 DeMarcus Cousins/149 5.00 12.00
69 Vinnie Johnson/49 5.00 12.00
71 Pablo Prigioni/99 3.00 8.00
72 Steve Novak/199 3.00 8.00
73 DeAndre Jordan/149 5.00 12.00
74 Tyrus Thomas/199 3.00 8.00
75 Alvan Adams/49 3.00 8.00
76 Larry Johnson/49 8.00 20.00
77 Danny Manning/49 4.00 10.00
78 Larry Bird/25 12.00 30.00
79 Michael Kidd-Gilchrist/99 6.00 15.00
80 Andre Iguodala/149 4.00 10.00
81 Kyle Lowry/199 4.00 10.00
82 Al Jefferson/149 4.00 10.00
83 Kemba Walker/99 6.00 15.00
84 Andre Miller/149 4.00 10.00
85 Jose Calderon/199 3.00 8.00
86 Brandon Knight/99 5.00 12.00
87 Gordon Hayward/149 5.00 12.00
88 Ben Gordon/199 4.00 10.00
89 Derrick Favors/199 4.00 10.00
90 Andrea Bargnani/149 4.00 10.00
91 Bismack Biyombo/199 3.00 8.00
92 Ramon Sessions/199 4.00 10.00
93 Reggie Lewis/49 12.00 30.00
94 Gary Payton/49 15.00 40.00
95 Dennis Rodman/25 10.00 25.00
96 Bill Laimbeer/49 4.00 10.00
97 Kenny Anderson/49 4.00 10.00
98 Manu Ginobili/149 5.00 12.00
99 Shawn Bradley/49 6.00 15.00
100 Rajon Rondo/49 5.00 12.00

2012-13 Panini Gold Standard Gold Rush

STATED PRINT RUN 25 SER.#'d SETS
1 Dwyane Wade 10.00 25.00
2 Steve Nash 6.00 15.00
3 Deron Williams 5.00 12.00
4 Chris Paul 8.00 20.00
5 Rajon Rondo 6.00 15.00
6 Russell Westbrook 15.00 40.00
7 Ricky Rubio 15.00 40.00
8 Kyrie Irving 50.00 120.00
9 Stephen Curry 60.00 150.00
10 James Harden 10.00 25.00
11 Tim Duncan 10.00 25.00
12 Dwight Howard 5.00 12.00
13 Brook Lopez 5.00 12.00
14 Chris Bosh 6.00 15.00
15 Al Jefferson 5.00 12.00
16 Joakim Noah 5.00 12.00
17 Marc Gasol 6.00 15.00
18 Pau Gasol 6.00 15.00
19 Zach Randolph 5.00 12.00
20 Serge Ibaka 5.00 12.00
21 Derrick Rose 8.00 20.00
22 Kevin Durant 30.00 80.00
23 LeBron James 60.00 150.00
24 Kobe Bryant 100.00 200.00
25 Joe Johnson 5.00 12.00
26 Luol Deng 5.00 12.00
27 Mario Chalmers 5.00 12.00
28 Carmelo Anthony 20.00 50.00
29 Andre Iguodala 5.00 12.00
30 Paul Pierce 6.00 15.00
31 Amar'e Stoudemire 5.00 12.00
32 Tony Parker 15.00 40.00
33 Kevin Love 6.00 15.00
34 Steve Smith 5.00 12.00
35 O.J. Mayo 4.00 10.00
36 Danny Granger 5.00 12.00
37 Greg Monroe 5.00 12.00
38 Vince Carter 8.00 20.00
39 Ray Allen 6.00 15.00
40 Rudy Gay 6.00 15.00
41 Jrue Holiday 6.00 15.00
42 Monta Ellis 5.00 12.00
43 David Lee 4.00 10.00
44 Raymond Felton 5.00 12.00
45 DeMar DeRozan 6.00 15.00
46 Kemba Walker 12.00 30.00
47 J.R. Smith 5.00 12.00
48 Jamal Crawford 12.00 30.00
49 Paul George 25.00 60.00
50 Klay Thompson 25.00 60.00
51 Al Horford 5.00 12.00
52 Shaquille O'Neal 12.00 30.00
53 Metta World Peace 6.00 15.00
54 DeMarcus Cousins 15.00 40.00
55 Ty Lawson 4.00 10.00
56 Goran Dragic 5.00 12.00
57 Anderson Varejao 4.00 10.00
58 Kenneth Faried 6.00 15.00
59 Roy Hibbert 5.00 12.00
60 Marcin Gortat 20.00 50.00
61 Mike Conley 12.00 30.00
62 Steve Francis 5.00 12.00
63 Shawn Kemp 10.00 25.00
64 Alonzo Mourning 20.00 50.00
65 Allen Iverson 25.00 60.00
66 Isiah Thomas 6.00 15.00
67 Larry Bird 15.00 40.00
68 Horace Grant 6.00 15.00
69 Yao Ming 8.00 20.00
70 Bill Russell 10.00 25.00
71 Wilt Chamberlain 12.00 30.00
72 Pete Maravich 10.00 25.00
73 Patrick Ewing 8.00 20.00
74 David Robinson 10.00 25.00
75 Julius Erving 10.00 25.00
76 Anthony Davis 50.00 120.00
77 Chris Webber 20.00 50.00
78 Vlade Divac 6.00 15.00
79 Hakeem Olajuwon 8.00 20.00
80 Magic Johnson 15.00 40.00
81 Gary Payton 6.00 15.00
82 Karl Malone 8.00 20.00
83 Damian Lillard 75.00 150.00
84 Glen Rice 20.00 50.00
85 Dennis Rodman 12.00 30.00
86 Oscar Robertson 8.00 20.00
87 Moses Malone 6.00 15.00
88 John Stockton 10.00 25.00
89 Michael Kidd-Gilchrist 6.00 15.00
90 Gerald Wallace 5.00 12.00
91 Evan Turner 4.00 10.00
92 Tim Hardaway 6.00 15.00
93 Kevin McHale 6.00 15.00
94 Jerry West 8.00 20.00
95 Kareem Abdul-Jabbar 10.00 25.00
96 Bill Walton 6.00 15.00
97 Bob Cousy 10.00 25.00
98 Clyde Drexler 8.00 20.00
99 LaMarcus Aldridge 6.00 15.00
100 Anfernee Hardaway 15.00 40.00

2012-13 Panini Gold Standard Gold Standard Insert

STATED PRINT RUN 199 SER.#'d SETS
1 Chris Paul 3.00 8.00
2 Dwyane Wade 4.00 10.00
3 Rajon Rondo 2.50 6.00
4 Deron Williams 2.00 5.00
5 Steve Nash 2.50 6.00
6 Derrick Rose 3.00 8.00
7 Russell Westbrook 6.00 15.00
8 Mario Chalmers 2.00 5.00
9 Raymond Felton 2.00 5.00
10 Marc Gasol 2.50 6.00
11 Kobe Bryant 12.00 30.00
12 Kevin Durant 6.00 15.00
13 LeBron James 12.00 30.00
14 James Harden 8.00 20.00
15 Carmelo Anthony 3.00 8.00
16 Damian Lillard 12.00 30.00
17 Tyreke Evans 1.50 4.00
18 Stephen Curry 10.00 25.00
19 LaMarcus Aldridge 2.50 6.00
20 Blake Griffin 2.50 6.00
21 Paul George 8.00 20.00
22 Rudy Gay 2.50 6.00
23 Brandon Jennings 1.50 4.00
24 Tim Duncan 4.00 10.00
25 David Lee 1.50 4.00
26 Kyrie Irving 12.00 30.00
27 Paul Pierce 2.50 6.00
28 Tony Parker 6.00 15.00
29 Monta Ellis 2.00 5.00
30 Jrue Holiday 2.50 6.00
31 Brook Lopez 2.00 5.00
32 Kevin Love 2.50 6.00
33 Chris Bosh 2.50 6.00
34 Dwight Howard 2.00 5.00
35 Klay Thompson 10.00 25.00
36 Joe Johnson 2.00 5.00
37 J.R. Smith 2.00 5.00
38 Dirk Nowitzki 3.00 8.00
39 Serge Ibaka 2.00 5.00
40 Chandler Parsons 2.50 6.00
41 Tyson Chandler 2.00 5.00
42 Anthony Davis 30.00 80.00
43 Danny Granger 2.00 5.00
44 Eric Gordon 2.00 5.00
45 Al Jefferson 2.00 5.00
46 Marcin Gortat 2.00 5.00
47 Amar'e Stoudemire 2.00 5.00
48 David West 2.00 5.00

2012-13 Panini Gold Standard Gold Strike Signatures

PRINT RUNS B/WN 49-249 COPIES PER
EXCHANGE DEADLINE 12/26/2014
1 Derrick Favors/75 4.00 10.00
2 DeMarcus Cousins/75 EXCH 5.00 12.00
3 Al-Farouq Aminu/199 4.00 10.00
4 E'Twaun Moore/249 3.00 8.00
5 Paul George/149 20.00 50.00
6 Ed Davis/249
7 Eric Bledsoe/199 EXCH 6.00 15.00
8 Jordan Crawford/249 EXCH 3.00 8.00
9 Greivis Vasquez/249 4.00 10.00
10 Landry Fields/199 3.00 8.00
11 James Harden/75 50.00 120.00
12 Tyreke Evans/75 3.00 8.00
13 Stephen Curry/75 EXCH 125.00 250.00
14 Gerald Henderson/149 3.00 8.00
15 Brandon Rush/249 3.00 8.00
16 Taj Gibson/149 4.00 10.00
17 DeJuan Blair/49
18 Nando De Colo/249 3.00 8.00
19 Eric Gordon/75 4.00 10.00
20 JaVale McGee/149 EXCH 4.00 10.00
21 Ryan Anderson/249 4.00 10.00
22 DeAndre Jordan/99 5.00 12.00
23 Omer Asik/249 4.00 10.00
24 Goran Dragic/99 10.00 25.00
25 Kyrie Irving/49 50.00 120.00
26 Jeff Teague/199 4.00 10.00
27 Ty Lawson/249 3.00 8.00
28 Alexey Shved/249 3.00 8.00
29 Marcus Thornton/149 3.00 8.00
30 Chase Budinger/149 3.00 8.00
31 Avery Bradley/199 EXCH 4.00 10.00
32 Enes Kanter/249 4.00 10.00
33 Jonas Valanciunas/199 5.00 12.00
34 Jimmer Fredette/199 6.00 15.00
35 Klay Thompson/199 40.00 100.00
36 Kawhi Leonard/249 75.00 200.00
37 Iman Shumpert/249 EXCH 5.00 12.00
38 Tobias Harris/249 5.00 12.00
39 Chandler Parsons/249 EXCH 5.00 12.00
40 Isaiah Thomas/249 25.00 60.00
41 Gordon Hayward/149 12.00 30.00
42 Brandon Knight/75 5.00 12.00
43 Nikola Vucevic/249 5.00 12.00
44 Anthony Davis/49 100.00 200.00
45 Andre Drummond/75 8.00 20.00
46 Harrison Barnes/75 8.00 20.00
47 Kenneth Faried/249 3.00 8.00
48 Nolan Smith/249 3.00 8.00
49 Jordan Hamilton/249 3.00 8.00
50 Norris Cole/249 3.00 8.00
51 MarShon Brooks/249 4.00 10.00
52 Derrick Williams/75 EXCH 3.00 8.00
53 Tristan Thompson/99 5.00 12.00
54 Tiago Splitter/199 4.00 10.00
55 Andray Blatche/199 3.00 8.00
56 Victor Claver/249 3.00 8.00
57 Eric Maynor/249 3.00 8.00
58 Michael Kidd-Gilchrist/49 5.00 12.00
59 Jared Sullinger/75 4.00 10.00
60 Kemba Walker/75 EXCH 12.00 30.00

2012-13 Panini Gold Standard Hall of Gold

STATED PRINT RUN 199 SER.#'d SETS
1 Julius Erving 4.00 10.00
2 Scottie Pippen 5.00 12.00
3 David Robinson 4.00 10.00
4 Larry Bird 6.00 15.00
5 Hakeem Olajuwon 3.00 8.00
6 Isiah Thomas 2.50 6.00
7 Kareem Abdul-Jabbar 4.00 10.00
8 Bob Cousy 4.00 10.00
9 Magic Johnson 6.00 15.00
10 Patrick Ewing 3.00 8.00
11 Bill Russell 4.00 10.00
12 Karl Malone 3.00 8.00
13 Wilt Chamberlain 5.00 12.00
14 Elgin Baylor 2.50 6.00
15 Dave Cowens 1.50 4.00
16 Ralph Sampson 2.00 5.00
17 Bob McAdoo 2.00 5.00
18 Drazen Petrovic 2.50 6.00
19 Frank Ramsey 2.50 6.00
20 John Stockton 4.00 10.00
21 Dennis Rodman 6.00 15.00
22 Joe Dumars 2.50 6.00
23 David Thompson 2.00 5.00
24 Nate Thurmond 2.00 5.00
25 Chet Walker 2.00 5.00
26 James Worthy 3.00 8.00
27 Jerry West 3.00 8.00
28 Arvydas Sabonis 2.50 6.00
29 Chris Mullin 2.50 6.00
30 Oscar Robertson 3.00 8.00
31 Bob Pettit 2.50 6.00
32 Earl Monroe 2.50 6.00
33 Dave Bing 2.50 6.00
34 Bill Bradley 3.00 8.00
35 Clyde Drexler 3.00 8.00
36 George Gervin 2.50 6.00
37 Artis Gilmore 2.00 5.00
38 Harry Gallatin 2.50 6.00
39 Tom Heinsohn 2.50 6.00
40 Dominique Wilkins 3.00 8.00
41 Jamaal Wilkes 2.50 6.00
42 Moses Malone 2.50 6.00
43 Alex English 2.00 5.00
44 Pete Maravich 4.00 10.00
45 Jerry Lucas 2.50 6.00
46 George Mikan 5.00 12.00
47 Robert Parish 2.50 6.00
48 Don Nelson 2.50 6.00

2012-13 Panini Gold Standard Marks of Gold Autographs

PRINT RUNS B/WN 25-149 COPIES PER
EXCHANGE DEADLINE 12/26/2014
1 Joe Johnson/25 8.00 20.00
2 Kobe Bryant/75 100.00 200.00
3 Steve Kerr/49 8.00 20.00
4 Bob Lanier/25 6.00 15.00
5 Mitch Richmond/99 8.00 20.00
6 Fat Lever/149 4.00 10.00
7 Rashard Lewis/99 EXCH 4.00 10.00
8 Darryl Dawkins/149 3.00 8.00
9 Joe Dumars/49 6.00 15.00
10 Kevin Durant/49 60.00 150.00
11 Andre Iguodala/25 4.00 10.00
12 Caron Butler/25
13 Shane Battier/25
14 Kemba Walker/49 10.00 25.00
15 David West/99 6.00 15.00
16 Tayshaun Prince/25 4.00 10.00
17 Rod Strickland/149 6.00 15.00
18 Ersan Ilyasova/99 3.00 8.00
19 Kyle Lowry/99 4.00 10.00
20 Monta Ellis/49 6.00 15.00
21 Tom Gugliotta/149 3.00 8.00
22 Jamaal Wilkes/99 5.00 12.00
23 Al-Farouq Aminu/99 4.00 10.00
24 Tom Chambers/99 4.00 10.00
25 John Paxson/149 6.00 15.00
26 Cedric Ceballos/149 8.00 20.00
27 David Robinson/25 20.00 50.00
28 Arron Afflalo/49 4.00 10.00
29 Metta World Peace/49 10.00 25.00
30 Robert Horry/99 10.00 25.00
31 Kyrie Irving/25 150.00 300.00
32 Detlef Schrempf/99 10.00 25.00
33 Willis Reed/25 12.00 30.00
34 Bradley Beal/49 8.00 20.00
35 Blake Griffin/75 30.00 60.00
36 Corey Brewer/99
37 Dennis Rodman/49 20.00 50.00
38 Ed Davis/99 3.00 8.00
39 Kevin Love/25 12.00 30.00
40 Nick Anderson/99 5.00 12.00
41 James Johnson/99 3.00 8.00
42 Byron Mullens/99 3.00 8.00
43 Wes Unseld/25 6.00 15.00
44 Ben Gordon/25 6.00 15.00
45 Bernard King/99 4.00 10.00
46 Connie Hawkins/99 6.00 15.00
47 Alonzo Gee/99 3.00 8.00
48 Alan Anderson/99 3.00 8.00
49 Luke Ridnour/99 4.00 10.00
50 Adrian Dantley/99 4.00 10.00
51 Antawn Jamison/99 4.00 10.00
52 Udonis Haslem/99 3.00 8.00
53 Nick Collison/99 4.00 10.00
54 Dolph Schayes/49 5.00 12.00
55 Sam Perkins/99 3.00 8.00
56 Dominique Wilkins/25 12.00 30.00
57 Grant Hill/49 30.00 60.00
58 Spud Webb/99 6.00 15.00
59 Dikembe Mutombo/49 12.00 30.00
60 Courtney Lee/99 4.00 10.00
61 Brandon Rush/99 3.00 8.00
62 Tiago Splitter/99 4.00 10.00
63 Lance Stephenson/149 10.00 25.00
64 Jason Thompson/99 EXCH 3.00 8.00
65 Jared Dudley/99 3.00 8.00
66 J.J. Hickson/99 3.00 8.00
67 Jeff Teague/99 4.00 10.00
68 Eric Bledsoe/99 6.00 15.00
69 Greivis Vasquez/99 4.00 10.00
70 Bobby Jackson/99 3.00 8.00
71 Dave Stallworth/99 3.00 8.00
72 Zydrunas Ilgauskas/99 4.00 10.00
73 Harrison Barnes/25 20.00 50.00
74 Charlie Ward/99 6.00 15.00
75 Marcus Camby/99 5.00 12.00
76 Len Elmore/99 8.00 20.00
77 Kevin Martin/49 6.00 15.00
78 Nikola Pekovic/149 3.00 8.00
79 Jordan Crawford/149 EXCH 3.00 8.00
80 Deron Williams/25 10.00 25.00
81 Taj Gibson/99 4.00 10.00
82 Johan Petro/99 5.00 12.00
83 Gerald Wallace/25 4.00 10.00
84 Andrea Bargnani/25
85 Gerald Henderson/99 3.00 8.00
86 Mario Chalmers/99 4.00 10.00
87 Danny Granger/25 6.00 15.00
88 Joel Anthony/99 3.00 8.00
89 John Salmons/99 4.00 10.00
90 Bill Walton/49 5.00 12.00
91 Danny Green/149 6.00 15.00
92 Raymond Felton/49 4.00 10.00
93 World B. Free/49 4.00 10.00
94 Carl Landry/49 3.00 8.00
95 J.J. Redick/49 10.00 25.00
96 Anthony Morrow/99 EXCH 3.00 8.00
97 Dwyane Wade/25 25.00 60.00
98 Kiki Vandeweghe/99 4.00 10.00
99 Brandon Knight/49 5.00 12.00
100 Hakeem Olajuwon/25 20.00 50.00

2012-13 Panini Gold Standard Mother Lode Autographs

PRINT RUNS B/WN 19-99 COPIES PER
NO PRICING ON QTY 20 OR LESS
EXCHANGE DEADLINE 12/26/2014
1 Steve Francis/99 10.00 25.00
2 John Havlicek/25 20.00 50.00
4 Larry Bird/75 50.00 100.00
5 Kareem Abdul-Jabbar/75 50.00 100.00
6 Larry Johnson/99 8.00 20.00
7 Magic Johnson/75 30.00 80.00
8 Brent Barry/75 8.00 20.00
9 Jerry West/75 15.00 40.00
10 Zach Randolph/75 5.00 12.00
11 Alex English/99 5.00 12.00
12 Alonzo Mourning/75 10.00 25.00
13 Micheal Ray Richardson/99 5.00 12.00
14 Kobe Bryant/99 100.00 200.00
15 Brook Lopez/99 5.00 12.00
16 Eric Gordon/99 8.00 20.00
17 Allan Houston/99 5.00 12.00
18 Scottie Pippen/25 100.00 200.00
19 Charles Oakley/99 5.00 12.00
20 Clyde Drexler/75 15.00 40.00
21 Thabo Sefolosha/99 4.00 10.00
22 Blake Griffin/75 15.00 60.00
23 Derrick Favors/99 5.00 12.00
24 Danny Manning/99 5.00 12.00
25 Hakeem Olajuwon/99 20.00 50.00
26 Vince Carter/75 10.00 25.00
27 Dwyane Wade/49 30.00 80.00
28 Michael Finley/99 8.00 20.00
29 Gary Payton/99 12.00 30.00
30 Yao Ming/25 40.00 80.00
31 Artis Gilmore/99 5.00 12.00
32 Kevin Durant/75 100.00 200.00
33 Steve Nash/25 20.00 50.00
34 Isiah Thomas/99 8.00 20.00
35 David Robinson/49 15.00 40.00
36 David Thompson/99 5.00 12.00
37 Jason Kidd/49 15.00 40.00
38 Peja Stojakovic/99 6.00 15.00
39 Allen Iverson/25 200.00 300.00
40 Chris Bosh/99 5.00 12.00
41 Stephen Curry/99 EXCH 150.00 250.00
42 Joakim Noah/99 5.00 12.00
43 Kurt Rambis/99 5.00 12.00
44 Dominique Wilkins/99 10.00 25.00
45 Elgin Baylor/75 12.00 30.00
46 Andre Iguodala/99 5.00 12.00
47 DeMarcus Cousins/99 12.00 30.00
48 LaMarcus Aldridge/99 12.00 30.00
49 Oscar Robertson/25 60.00 150.00
50 Josh Smith/99 5.00 12.00

2012-13 Panini Gold Standard Superscribe Autographs

PRINT RUNS B/WN 10-99 COPIES PER
NO PRICING ON QTY 20 OR LESS
EXCHANGE DEADLINE 12/26/2014
1 James Harden/49 30.00 60.00
2 Grant Hill/49 60.00 120.00
3 Kyrie Irving/25 100.00 200.00
5 Kevin Martin/49 4.00 10.00
7 Muggsy Bogues/99 6.00 15.00
8 Brandon Jennings/25 EXCH 20.00 50.00
9 Luol Deng/25 EXCH 20.00 50.00
10 LaMarcus Aldridge/49 12.00 30.00
11 DeMarcus Cousins/49 EXCH 15.00 40.00
13 Andrei Kirilenko/25 12.00 30.00
14 Goran Dragic/99 8.00 20.00
15 Horace Grant/99 12.00 30.00
16 Anfernee Hardaway/25 125.00 250.00
17 Al-Farouq Aminu/99 5.00 12.00
18 Bob McAdoo/99 8.00 20.00
19 Courtney Lee/99 5.00 12.00
20 Dan Majerle/99 6.00 15.00
21 Dave Cowens/49 6.00 15.00
22 Earl Lloyd/99
23 Ersan Ilyasova/99 5.00 12.00
24 Kobe Bryant/75 100.00 200.00
25 Glen Rice/99 12.00 30.00
27 Mario Chalmers/99 6.00 15.00
29 Toni Kukoc/99 12.00 30.00
30 Lenny Wilkens/49 10.00 20.00
31 Monta Ellis/49 EXCH 10.00 25.00
32 Blake Griffin/75 40.00 80.00
33 Rick Fox/49 4.00 10.00
34 Steve Kerr/49 10.00 25.00
38 Mark Price/99 12.00 30.00
39 Luis Scola/25 12.00 30.00
40 Larry Johnson/99 10.00 25.00

2012-13 Panini Gold Standard White Gold Threads

PRINT RUNS B/WN 25-99 COPIES PER
1 Yao Ming/99 6.00 15.00
2 Paul Pierce/99 8.00 20.00
3 Steve Novak/99 3.00 8.00
4 James Harden/99 6.00 15.00
5 Nate Thurmond/25 30.00 60.00
6 Evan Turner/99 3.00 8.00
7 Brandon Jennings/99 3.00 8.00
8 Danny Manning/99 4.00 10.00
9 Channing Frye/99 4.00 10.00
10 George Hill/99 4.00 10.00
11 Tim Duncan/99 6.00 15.00
12 Patrick Ewing/99 6.00 15.00
13 Ricky Rubio/99 8.00 20.00
14 Andray Blatche/99 3.00 8.00
15 Brook Lopez/99 4.00 10.00
16 Jrue Holiday/99 5.00 12.00
17 Al-Farouq Aminu/99 4.00 10.00
18 Jimmer Fredette/99 3.00 8.00
19 Brandon Knight/99 5.00 12.00
20 Greg Monroe/99 4.00 10.00
21 Josh Smith/99 4.00 10.00
22 Kevin Love/99 5.00 12.00
23 Andrea Bargnani/99 4.00 10.00
24 Mike Dunleavy/99 3.00 8.00
25 Jordan Crawford/99 3.00 8.00
26 Carlos Boozer/99 4.00 10.00
27 Isiah Thomas/49 5.00 12.00
28 Toni Kukoc/99 6.00 15.00
29 DeMarcus Cousins/99 5.00 12.00
30 Thomas Robinson/99 4.00 10.00
31 Dennis Scott/99 3.00 8.00
32 Marc Gasol/99 5.00 12.00
33 Zach Randolph/99 4.00 10.00
34 Ty Lawson/99 3.00 8.00
35 Steve Smith/99 4.00 10.00
36 Ben Gordon/99 4.00 10.00
37 David Lee/99 3.00 8.00
38 Darren Collison/99 4.00 10.00
39 Trevor Booker/99 3.00 8.00
40 LeBron James/99 12.00 30.00
41 Dirk Nowitzki/99 6.00 15.00
42 Jalen Rose/99 5.00 12.00
43 Dwyane Wade/99 8.00 20.00
44 Robert Parish/49 5.00 12.00
45 Pau Gasol/99 5.00 12.00
46 Ed Davis/99 3.00 8.00
47 Chris Paul/99 6.00 15.00
48 John Wall/99 6.00 15.00
49 Wesley Johnson/99 4.00 10.00
50 Tayshaun Prince/99 4.00 10.00

2012-13 Panini Gold Standard Metal

1 Kobe Bryant 10.00 25.00
2 Kevin Durant 6.00 15.00
3 Kyrie Irving 12.00 30.00
4 Blake Griffin 2.50 6.00
5 LeBron James 10.00 25.00
6 Rajon Rondo 2.50 6.00
7 Russell Westbrook 6.00 15.00
8 Kevin Love 2.50 6.00
9 James Harden 4.00 10.00
10 Chris Paul 3.00 8.00
11 Derrick Rose 3.00 8.00
12 Carmelo Anthony 3.00 8.00
13 Dwight Howard 2.00 5.00
14 Zach Randolph 2.00 5.00
15 Tyson Chandler 2.00 5.00
16 Jeremy Lin 2.50 6.00
17 DeMarcus Cousins 2.50 6.00
18 Steve Nash 2.50 6.00
19 Paul Pierce 2.50 6.00
20 John Wall 3.00 8.00
21 Ty Lawson 2.00 5.00
22 Roy Hibbert 2.00 5.00
23 Dirk Nowitzki 3.00 8.00
24 Brandon Jennings 1.50 4.00
25 Luol Deng 2.00 5.00
26 Joe Johnson 2.00 5.00
27 Grant Hill 3.00 8.00
28 Jason Kidd 2.50 6.00
29 Paul George 3.00 8.00
30 Eric Gordon 2.00 5.00
31 J.R. Smith 2.00 5.00
32 Andre Iguodala 2.00 5.00
33 Tim Duncan 4.00 10.00
34 Ricky Rubio 2.50 6.00
35 Klay Thompson 10.00 25.00
36 Kemba Walker 5.00 12.00
37 Raymond Felton 2.00 5.00
38 Josh Smith 2.00 5.00
39 Greg Monroe 2.00 5.00
40 Tyreke Evans 1.50 4.00
41 Brandon Knight 2.50 6.00
42 Tony Parker 2.50 6.00
43 Pau Gasol 2.50 6.00
44 Chandler Parsons 2.50 6.00
45 Kenneth Faried 2.50 6.00
46 Brook Lopez 2.00 5.00
47 Damian Lillard 10.00 25.00
48 Bradley Beal 4.00 10.00
49 Greivis Vasquez 2.00 5.00
50 Dwyane Wade 4.00 10.00
51 Goran Dragic 2.00 5.00
52 Shawn Marion 2.00 5.00
53 Anthony Davis 12.00 30.00
54 Kevin Garnett 4.00 10.00
55 Deron Williams 2.00 5.00
56 Nikola Vucevic 2.50 6.00
57 Metta World Peace 2.50 6.00
58 Marc Gasol 2.50 6.00
59 Vince Carter 3.00 8.00
60 Ray Allen 2.50 6.00
61 Tyler Zeller 2.00 5.00
62 Mario Chalmers 2.00 5.00
63 Thomas Robinson 2.00 5.00
64 Michael Kidd-Gilchrist 2.50 6.00
65 Alexey Shved 1.50 4.00
66 Jared Sullinger 2.00 5.00
67 Harrison Barnes 4.00 10.00
68 Jonas Valanciunas 2.50 6.00
69 Andre Drummond 4.00 10.00
70 Wilt Chamberlain 5.00 12.00
71 Bill Russell 4.00 10.00
72 Pete Maravich 4.00 10.00
73 Anfernee Hardaway 6.00 15.00
74 Allen Iverson 3.00 8.00
75 Yao Ming 3.00 8.00
76 Karl Malone 3.00 8.00
77 John Stockton 4.00 10.00
78 Magic Johnson 6.00 15.00
79 Larry Bird 6.00 15.00
80 Dennis Rodman 5.00 12.00
81 Shaquille O'Neal 5.00 12.00
82 Oscar Robertson 3.00 8.00
83 Elgin Baylor 2.50 6.00
84 Jerry West 3.00 8.00
85 Hakeem Olajuwon 3.00 8.00
86 Julius Erving 4.00 10.00
87 David Robinson 4.00 10.00
88 Bill Walton 2.50 6.00
89 Bob Cousy 4.00 10.00
90 Scottie Pippen 5.00 12.00

2013-14 Panini Gold Standard

226-260 ARE NOT SERIAL NUMBERED
EXCHANGE DEADLINE 8/19/2015
286-310 PRINT RUN 199 SER.#'d SETS
VARIATION PRINT RUN 225 SER.#'d SETS
1 Gordon Hayward 1.50 4.00
2 John Wall 2.00 5.00
3 Louis Williams 1.25 3.00
4 JaVale McGee 1.25 3.00
5 Nikola Vucevic 1.25 3.00
6 Jamal Crawford 1.50 4.00
7 Terrence Ross 1.25 3.00
8 Channing Frye 1.25 3.00
9 Jimmer Fredette 1.00 2.50
10 Danilo Gallinari 1.00 2.50
11 Joakim Noah 1.25 3.00
12 Jason Maxiell 1.00 2.50
13 Austin Rivers 1.25 3.00
14 Tony Wroten 1.00 2.50
15 Larry Sanders 1.00 2.50
16 Kent Bazemore 1.25 3.00
17 Kirk Hinrich 1.25 3.00
18 Arnett Moultrie 1.00 2.50
19 Amir Johnson 1.00 2.50
20 LaMarcus Aldridge 1.50 4.00
21 Andrea Bargnani 1.25 3.00
22 Andrew Bynum 1.00 2.50
23 Marcin Gortat 1.25 3.00
24 Kyrie Irving 3.00 8.00
25 Robert Sacre 1.00 2.50
26 Luke Ridnour 1.25 3.00
27 Greg Oden 1.25 3.00
28 P.J. Tucker 1.00 2.50
29 Kyle Korver 1.25 3.00
30 David West 1.25 3.00
31 Kemba Walker 1.50 4.00
32 George Hill 1.25 3.00
33 Andrew Bogut 1.25 3.00
34 Eric Bledsoe 1.25 3.00
35 Ben Gordon 1.25 3.00
36 Boris Diaw 1.25 3.00
37 Rodney Stuckey 1.25 3.00
38 Kevin Seraphin 1.00 2.50
39 Jrue Holiday 1.50 4.00
40 Dirk Nowitzki 2.00 5.00
41 Bradley Beal 1.50 4.00
42A R.Allen MIA 1.50 4.00
42B R.Allen MIL 6.00 15.00
42C R.Allen SEA 15.00 40.00
42D R.Allen BOS 15.00 40.00
43 Ersan Ilyasova 1.00 2.50
44 Festus Ezeli 1.00 2.50
45 Josh McRoberts 1.00 2.50
46 Ricky Rubio 1.50 4.00
47 Nando De Colo 1.25 3.00
48 Draymond Green 2.00 5.00
49 Bismack Biyombo 1.00 2.50
50 LeBron James 6.00 15.00
51 Will Barton 1.00 2.50
52 Reggie Jackson 1.25 3.00
53 Arron Afflalo 1.00 2.50
54 Kosta Koufos 1.00 2.50
55 Derrick Favors 1.25 3.00
56 Shawn Marion 1.25 3.00
57 J.J. Redick 1.50 4.00
58 Andrei Kirilenko 1.25 3.00
59 Klay Thompson 2.00 5.00
60 Jose Calderon 1.00 2.50
61 Shane Battier 1.25 3.00
62 Kevin Durant 4.00 10.00
63 Blake Griffin 1.50 4.00
64 Marquis Teague 1.00 2.50
65 Tony Parker 1.50 4.00
66 John Jenkins 1.00 2.50
67 Perry Jones 1.00 2.50
68 Harrison Barnes 1.25 3.00
69 Nick Collison 1.25 3.00
70 Udonis Haslem 1.00 2.50
71 Lance Stephenson 1.25 3.00
72 Enes Kanter 1.00 2.50
73 Jae Crowder 1.25 3.00
74 Thabo Sefolosha 1.00 2.50
75 Jared Sullinger 1.00 2.50
76 Goran Dragic 1.25 3.00
77 Marco Belinelli 1.00 2.50
78A D.Howard HOU 1.25 3.00
78B D.Howard LAL
78C D.Howard ORL 4.00 10.00
79 Reggie Evans 1.00 2.50
80 Paul Millsap 1.50 4.00
81 Stephen Curry 6.00 15.00
82 Andray Blatche 1.00 2.50
83 Richard Jefferson 1.25 3.00
84 Brandon Bass 1.00 2.50
85 Thomas Robinson 1.00 2.50
86 DeMar DeRozan 1.50 4.00
87 Wilson Chandler 1.25 3.00
88 Matt Barnes 1.00 2.50
89 Vince Carter 2.00 5.00
90 Earl Clark 1.00 2.50
91 Avery Bradley 1.25 3.00
92 Deron Williams 1.25 3.00
93 Josh Smith 1.25 3.00
94 Jerryd Bayless 1.25 3.00
95 Emeka Okafor 1.25 3.00
96 C.J. Watson 1.00 2.50
97 Jeff Taylor 1.00 2.50
98 Brandon Jennings 1.00 2.50
99 Anderson Varejao 1.00 2.50
100 Matt Bonner 1.00 2.50
101 J.J. Hickson 1.00 2.50
102 Raymond Felton 1.25 3.00
103 Evan Turner 1.00 2.50
104 Amar'e Stoudemire 1.25 3.00
105 Brandon Knight 1.25 3.00
106 Ryan Anderson 1.25 3.00
107 O.J. Mayo 1.00 2.50
108 Markieff Morris 1.00 2.50
109 Derek Fisher 1.25 3.00
110 Paul George 2.00 5.00
111 Jodie Meeks 1.25 3.00
112 Danny Green 1.25 3.00
113 Dion Waiters 1.25 3.00
114 David Lee 1.00 2.50
115 Gerald Green 1.25 3.00
116 Steve Novak 1.00 2.50
117 Jimmy Butler 1.50 4.00
118 Al Horford 1.25 3.00
119 Chris Paul 2.00 5.00
120 Jeff Teague 1.25 3.00
121 Martell Webster 1.00 2.50
122 Luis Scola 1.25 3.00
123 Kris Humphries 1.00 2.50
124 Monta Ellis 1.25 3.00
125 Carlos Boozer 1.25 3.00
126 Miles Plumlee 1.00 2.50
127 Glen Davis 1.00 2.50
128 Trevor Ariza 1.00 2.50
129 E'Twaun Moore 1.00 2.50
130 Zach Randolph 1.25 3.00
131 Elton Brand 1.50 4.00
132 Derrick Rose 2.00 5.00
133 John Henson 1.25 3.00
134 Chris Andersen 1.25 3.00
135 Nicolas Batum 1.25 3.00
136 Jonas Jerebko 1.00 2.50
137 Jason Thompson 1.00 2.50
138 Tiago Splitter 1.25 3.00
139 Danny Granger 1.25 3.00
140 Al-Farouq Aminu 1.25 3.00
141A C.Billups DET 1.50 4.00
141B C.Billups DEN 6.00 15.00
141C C.Billups BOS 6.00 15.00
141D C.Billups TOR
141E C.Billups DEN
141F C.Billups MIN 6.00 15.00
141G C.Billups DET
141H C.Billups NYK
141I C.Billups LAC
142 Wayne Ellington 1.00 2.50
143 Marcus Morris 1.00 2.50
144 Chris Kaman 1.25 3.00
145 DeMarcus Cousins 1.50 4.00
146 Kevin Martin 1.25 3.00
147 Tim Duncan 2.50 6.00
148 Tristan Thompson 1.25 3.00
149 Carlos Delfino 1.00 2.50
150 Kawhi Leonard 2.50 6.00
151 Jordan Hill 1.00 2.50
152 Luc Mbah a Moute 1.00 2.50
153 Pau Gasol 1.50 4.00
154 Greivis Vasquez 1.25 3.00
155 Kendrick Perkins 1.00 2.50
156 Brandan Wright 1.00 2.50
157 Robin Lopez 1.00 2.50
158 Mike Miller 1.25 3.00
159 Nate Robinson 1.00 2.50
160 Jonas Valanciunas 1.25 3.00
161 Kobe Bryant 6.00 15.00
162 Meyers Leonard 1.00 2.50
163 Thaddeus Young 1.00 2.50
164 Russell Westbrook 4.00 10.00
165 Tyreke Evans 1.00 2.50
166 Chandler Parsons 1.25 3.00
167 Taj Gibson 1.25 3.00
168 Terrence Jones 1.25 3.00
169 Corey Brewer 1.00 2.50
170 Iman Shumpert 1.00 2.50
171 Willie Green 1.00 2.50
172 Anthony Davis 3.00 8.00
173 Nene 1.25 3.00
174 Chris Bosh 1.50 4.00
175 Kyle Singler 1.00 2.50
176 John Salmons 1.25 3.00
177 Andrew Nicholson 1.00 2.50
178 Evan Fournier 1.25 3.00
179 Isaiah Thomas 1.50 4.00
180 J.J. Barea 1.25 3.00
181 Donatas Motiejunas 1.25 3.00
182 Wesley Matthews 1.00 2.50
183 Derrick Williams 1.00 2.50
184 C.J. Miles 1.25 3.00
185 Steve Nash 1.50 4.00
186 Aaron Brooks 1.00 2.50
187 Dwyane Wade 2.50 6.00
188 Nick Calathes 1.00 2.50
189 Lavoy Allen 1.00 2.50
190 Metta World Peace 1.50 4.00
191 Jan Vesely 1.00 2.50
192 Kevin Love 1.50 4.00
193 Jason Richardson 1.50 4.00
194 Roy Hibbert 1.25 3.00
195 Marcus Thornton 1.00 2.50
196 Carmelo Anthony 2.00 5.00
197 Brook Lopez 1.25 3.00
198 Damian Lillard 3.00 8.00
199 Jeff Green 1.25 3.00
200 Marc Gasol 1.50 4.00
201 Rajon Rondo 1.50 4.00
202 Spencer Hawes 1.00 2.50
203 Jameer Nelson 1.00 2.50
204A A.Miller DEN 1.25 3.00
204B A.Miller CLE 6.00 15.00
204C A.Miller LAC
204D A.Miller DEN
204E A.Miller PHI
204F A.Miller POR 6.00 15.00
205 Kevin Garnett 2.50 6.00
206 Nikola Pekovic 1.00 2.50
207 Gerald Henderson 1.00 2.50
208 Rudy Gay 1.50 4.00
209 Greg Monroe 1.25 3.00
210 Ty Lawson 1.00 2.50
211 Alonzo Gee 1.00 2.50
212 Kenneth Faried 1.25 3.00
213 DeMarre Carroll 1.00 2.50
214 Serge Ibaka 1.25 3.00
215 Maurice Harkless 1.00 2.50
216 Andre Iguodala 1.25 3.00
217 Kyle Lowry 1.25 3.00
218 James Harden 2.50 6.00
219 Luol Deng 1.25 3.00
220 Dante Cunningham 1.00 2.50
221 Gerald Wallace 1.25 3.00
222 Brian Roberts 1.00 2.50
223 Paul Pierce 1.50 4.00
224 Jeremy Lin 1.50 4.00
225 DeAndre Jordan 1.50 4.00
226 V.Oladipo JSY AU RC 12.00 30.00
227 Archie Goodwin JSY AU RC 4.00 10.00
228 Caldwell-Pope JSY AU RC 5.00 12.00
229 Nate Wolters JSY AU RC 4.00 10.00
230 Isaiah Canaan JSY AU RC 3.00 8.00
231 G.Anttknmp JSY AU RC EXCH 150.00 300.00
232 Carter-Williams JSY AU RC 5.00 12.00
233 Cody Zeller JSY AU RC 4.00 10.00
234 Glen Rice Jr. JSY AU RC 3.00 8.00
235 S.Muhammad JSY AU RC 4.00 10.00
236 Jeff Withey JSY AU RC 3.00 8.00
237 Alex Len JSY AU RC 4.00 10.00
238 Allen Crabbe JSY AU RC 4.00 10.00
239 Reggie Bullock JSY AU RC 4.00 10.00
240 N.Noel JSY AU RC EXCH 6.00 15.00
241 Tony Snell JSY AU RC 4.00 10.00
242 Kelly Olynyk JSY AU RC 4.00 10.00
243 Solomon Hill JSY AU RC 3.00 8.00
244 Andre Roberson JSY AU RC EXCH 3.00 8.00
245 C.J. McCollum JSY AU RC 12.00 30.00
246 Tony Mitchell JSY AU RC 3.00 8.00
247 Mason Plumlee JSY AU RC 5.00 12.00
248 A.Bennett JSY AU RC 4.00 10.00
249 Ricky Ledo JSY AU RC 3.00 8.00
250 Erik Murphy JSY AU RC 3.00 8.00
251 Peyton Siva JSY AU RC 3.00 8.00
252 Hardaway Jr. JSY AU RC 5.00 12.00
253 Dennis Schroder JSY AU RC 5.00 12.00
254 Ryan Kelly JSY AU RC 3.00 8.00
255 B.McLemore JSY AU RC 4.00 10.00
256 Jamaal Franklin JSY AU RC 3.00 8.00
257 Shane Larkin JSY AU RC EXCH 3.00 8.00
258 Steven Adams JSY AU RC 10.00 25.00
259 Trey Burke JSY AU RC 4.00 10.00
260 Otto Porter JSY AU RC 10.00 25.00
261 Omer Asik 1.25 3.00
262 Carl Landry 1.00 2.50
263 Orlando Johnson 1.00 2.50
264 Andre Drummond 1.50 4.00
265 Norris Cole 1.00 2.50
266 Al Jefferson 1.25 3.00
267 Byron Mullens 1.00 2.50
268 Jason Terry 1.25 3.00
269 Michael Kidd-Gilchrist 1.50 4.00
270 Tayshaun Prince 1.25 3.00
271 Joe Johnson 1.25 3.00
272 Mike Conley 1.25 3.00
273 Nick Young 1.50 4.00
274 Marvin Williams 1.25 3.00
275 Ekpe Udoh 1.00 2.50
276 Tyson Chandler 1.25 3.00
277 Eric Gordon 1.25 3.00
278 Devin Harris 1.00 2.50
279 Alec Burks 1.00 2.50
280 Mario Chalmers 1.25 3.00
281 Andris Biedrins 1.00 2.50
282 Tyler Hansbrough 1.25 3.00
283 J.R. Smith 1.25 3.00
284 Manu Ginobili 1.50 4.00
285 Tony Allen 1.00 2.50
286 Shaquille O'Neal 4.00 10.00
287 David Robinson 3.00 8.00
288 Wilt Chamberlain 4.00 10.00
289 Larry Bird 5.00 12.00
290 Magic Johnson 5.00 12.00
291 Hakeem Olajuwon 2.50 6.00
292 Drazen Petrovic 2.00 5.00
293 Walt Frazier 2.00 5.00
294A M.Cheeks PHI 1.25 3.00
294B M.Cheeks SA
294C M.Cheeks NYK
294D M.Cheeks ATL 6.00 15.00
294E M.Cheeks NJN
295 Yao Ming 2.50 6.00
296 George Gervin 2.00 5.00
297 Dominique Wilkins 2.50 6.00
298 Anfernee Hardaway 5.00 12.00
299 Oscar Robertson 2.50 6.00
300 Kevin McHale 2.00 5.00
301 Julius Erving 3.00 8.00
302 Bill Russell 3.00 8.00
303 Alonzo Mourning 2.50 6.00
304 Clyde Drexler 2.50 6.00
305 Jerry West 2.50 6.00
306 Moses Malone 2.00 5.00
307 Karl Malone 2.50 6.00
308 Elgin Baylor 2.00 5.00
309 John Stockton 3.00 8.00
310A M.Finley DAL 2.00 5.00
310B M.Finley PHO 25.00 60.00
310C M.Finley SA 6.00 15.00
310D M.Finley BOS

2013-14 Panini Gold Standard Black Gold Threads

PRINT RUNS B/WN 1-75 COPIES PER
NO PRICING ON QTY 10 OR LESS

1 Dwight Howard/49	4.00	10.00
2 Bill Laimbeer/49	4.00	10.00
3 Dion Waiters/49	4.00	10.00
4 LeBron James/49	20.00	50.00
5 Tristan Thompson/49	6.00	15.00
6 Pau Gasol/49	5.00	12.00
7 Thaddeus Young/20	3.00	8.00
8 Kevin McHale/49	5.00	12.00
9 Brook Lopez/49	4.00	10.00
11 Jeff Green/25	6.00	15.00
12 Andre Miller/20	4.00	10.00
13 Nikola Vucevic/25		
14 Kevin Garnett/25	12.00	30.00
15 Alex English/25		
16 Luol Deng/25	4.00	10.00
17 World B. Free/49	4.00	10.00
18 Chris Paul/25	6.00	15.00
19 Al Horford/25	4.00	10.00
20 Zach Randolph/49	4.00	10.00
21 Ray Allen/25	6.00	15.00
23 Earl Monroe/25	12.00	30.00
24 Paul Pierce/25	5.00	12.00
25 Damian Lillard/49	10.00	25.00
26 Ryan Anderson/25	4.00	10.00
27 Kawhi Leonard/25	15.00	40.00
28 Kareem Abdul-Jabbar/25	8.00	20.00
29 Hakeem Olajuwon/25	8.00	20.00
30 Sidney Moncrief/25	12.00	30.00
31 Rajon Rondo/25	5.00	12.00
32 Roy Hibbert/75	4.00	10.00
33 Jamal Mashburn/25	5.00	12.00
34 Carlos Boozer/25	6.00	15.00
35 Carmelo Anthony/25	12.00	30.00
36 Reggie Lewis/49	6.00	15.00
37 Ralph Sampson/25	4.00	10.00
38 Fat Lever/25	4.00	10.00
40 Russell Westbrook/25		
42 Moses Malone/49	5.00	12.00
43 Vince Carter/20	12.00	30.00
44 Tyson Chandler/25	4.00	10.00
45 Paul Millsap/20	12.00	30.00
46 Blake Griffin/49	5.00	12.00
48 Joakim Noah/25	4.00	10.00
49 Tim Duncan/25	10.00	25.00
50 Monta Ellis/49	4.00	10.00
51 Klay Thompson/49	6.00	15.00
52 J.R. Smith/25	6.00	15.00
53 Mike Conley/25	4.00	10.00
54 Rasheed Wallace/20	12.00	30.00
55 Andrei Kirilenko/25	4.00	10.00
56 Isiah Thomas/25	12.00	30.00
57 David Robinson/49	8.00	20.00
58 Steve Nash/25	15.00	40.00
59 Metta World Peace/25		
60 Bradley Beal/49	5.00	12.00
61 Andre Drummond/25	5.00	12.00
62 Anfernee Hardaway/49	25.00	60.00
63 Robert Horry/49	4.00	10.00
64 John Wall/25	6.00	15.00
66 James Harden/25	8.00	20.00
67 John Stockton/25	15.00	40.00
68 Raymond Felton/25		
69 Jalen Rose/25	5.00	12.00
70 Marc Gasol/49	8.00	20.00
71 Clyde Drexler/49	8.00	20.00
72 Joe Dumars/25	5.00	12.00
73 DeMar DeRozan/25	5.00	12.00
74 Artis Gilmore/25	4.00	10.00
75 Kobe Bryant/25	25.00	60.00
76 Kemba Walker/25	6.00	15.00
77 Serge Ibaka/25		
78 Shaquille O'Neal /49	12.00	30.00
79 Gerald Wallace/25	4.00	10.00
80 Kevin Durant/25	25.00	60.00
81 George Mikan/25	40.00	80.00
82 Chris Bosh/25	6.00	15.00
83 Josh Smith/25	6.00	15.00
84 Deron Williams/25	4.00	10.00
85 Jose Calderon/25	3.00	8.00
86 Dwyane Wade/25		
87 Dirk Nowitzki/25	12.00	30.00
88 Harrison Barnes/49	4.00	10.00
89 LaMarcus Aldridge/49	10.00	25.00
90 Magic Johnson/49	12.00	30.00
91 Kyrie Irving/49	10.00	25.00
92 Manu Ginobili/25	6.00	15.00
93 Ricky Rubio/49	5.00	12.00
94 Larry Bird/49	20.00	50.00
95 Andre Iquodala/49	4.00	10.00
96 Jameer Nelson/49	3.00	8.00
97 Anthony Davis/49	8.00	20.00
98 Patrick Ewing/49	10.00	25.00
99 Dominique Wilkins/49	6.00	15.00
100 Karl Malone/49	6.00	15.00

2013-14 Panini Gold Standard Claim to Fame Duals

STATED PRINT RUN 49 SER.#'d SETS

1 C.Anthony/K.Durant	5.00	12.00
2 D.Howard/N.Vucevic	1.50	4.00
3 R.Rondo/C.Paul	2.50	6.00
4 C.Paul/R.Rubio	2.50	6.00
5 S.Ibaka/L.Sanders	1.50	4.00
6 K.Thompson/S.Curry	8.00	20.00
7 D.Lillard/A.Davis	6.00	15.00
8 K.Faried/K.Leonard	3.00	8.00
9 J.Wall/D.Cousins	2.50	6.00
10 J.Harden/S.Curry	8.00	20.00
11 B.Pettit/D.Wilkins	2.50	6.00
12 B.Russell/L.Bird	5.00	12.00
13 S.O'Neal /W.Chamberlain	4.00	10.00
14 W.Reed/P.Ewing	8.00	20.00
15 K.Malone/J.Stockton	3.00	8.00
16 K.Bryant/K.Garnett	8.00	20.00
17 K.Garnett/T.Duncan	3.00	8.00
18 S.Nash/A.Miller	2.00	5.00
19 C.Paul/M.Peace	2.50	6.00
20 T.Duncan/K.Garnett	3.00	8.00
21 M.Johnson/L.Bird	15.00	40.00
22 J.Erving/M.Malone	3.00	8.00
23 D.Nowitzki/R.Blackman	2.50	6.00
24 B.Russell/D.Cowens	3.00	8.00
25 L.James/O.Robertson	8.00	20.00
26 S.Curry/K.Durant	10.00	25.00
27 R.Rondo/B.Jennings	2.00	5.00
28 N.Vucevic/T.Chandler	1.50	4.00
29 R.Rubio/K.Walker	2.00	5.00
30 J.Noah/R.Hibbert	4.00	10.00
31 A.English/D.Issel	4.00	10.00
32 I.Thomas/J.Dumars	2.00	5.00
33 W.Chamberlain/R.Barry	4.00	10.00
34 H.Olajuwon/C.Murphy	2.50	6.00
35 C.Drexler/T.Porter	5.00	12.00
36 J.Wilkes/R.Sampson	4.00	10.00
37 D.Rodman/C.Mullin	12.00	30.00
38 K.Malone/S.Pippen	4.00	10.00
39 H.Olajuwon/P.Ewing	2.50	6.00
40 D.Wilkins/J.Dumars	2.50	6.00

2013-14 Panini Gold Standard Finals MVP

STATED PRINT RUN 20 SER.#'d SETS

1 LeBron James	75.00	150.00
2 Dirk Nowitzki	15.00	40.00
3 Kobe Bryant	60.00	120.00
4 Paul Pierce	12.00	30.00
5 Tony Parker	20.00	50.00
6 Dwyane Wade	40.00	100.00
7 Tim Duncan	20.00	50.00
8 Chauncey Billups	12.00	30.00
9 Shaquille O'Neal	25.00	60.00
10 Hakeem Olajuwon	15.00	40.00
11 Isiah Thomas	12.00	30.00
12 Joe Dumars	12.00	30.00
13 James Worthy	15.00	40.00
14 Magic Johnson	30.00	80.00
15 Larry Bird	30.00	80.00
16 Kareem Abdul-Jabbar	20.00	50.00
17 Moses Malone	12.00	30.00
18 Bill Walton	12.00	30.00
19 Willis Reed	12.00	30.00
20 Wilt Chamberlain	25.00	60.00

2013-14 Panini Gold Standard Gold Prospects

STATED PRINT RUN 49 SER.#'d SETS

1 Blake Griffin	4.00	10.00
2 Jimmy Butler	4.00	10.00
3 Greg Monroe	3.00	8.00
4 Anthony Davis	8.00	20.00
5 Paul George	15.00	40.00
6 Damian Lillard	8.00	20.00
7 Nikola Vucevic	3.00	8.00
8 Kawhi Leonard	6.00	15.00
9 Kyrie Irving	8.00	20.00
10 Thomas Robinson	2.50	6.00
11 Tristan Thompson	3.00	8.00
12 Kemba Walker	4.00	10.00
13 Kenneth Faried	3.00	8.00
14 Dion Waiters	3.00	8.00
15 Andre Drummond	4.00	10.00
16 Nikola Pekovic	2.50	6.00
17 Isaiah Thomas	4.00	10.00
18 Klay Thompson	5.00	12.00
19 Iman Shumpert	2.50	6.00
20 Michael Kidd-Gilchrist	4.00	10.00
21 Kelly Olynyk	3.00	8.00
22 John Wall	5.00	12.00
23 Victor Oladipo	5.00	12.00
24 Chandler Parsons	3.00	8.00
25 Jonas Valanciunas	3.00	8.00
26 Jonas Jerebko	2.50	6.00
27 Otto Porter	4.00	10.00
28 Derrick Favors	3.00	8.00
29 Ricky Rubio	4.00	10.00
30 Alex Len	3.00	8.00
31 Avery Bradley	3.00	8.00
32 Bradley Beal	4.00	10.00
33 Derrick Williams	2.50	6.00
34 Anthony Bennett	3.00	8.00
35 Harrison Barnes	3.00	8.00
36 Meyers Leonard	2.50	6.00
37 Nerlens Noel	5.00	12.00
38 Cody Zeller	3.00	8.00
39 Greivis Vasquez	3.00	8.00
40 Jared Sullinger	2.50	6.00

2013-14 Panini Gold Standard Gold Records

STATED PRINT RUN 20 SER.#'d SETS

1 Kobe Bryant	100.00	175.00
2 Chris Bosh	10.00	25.00
3 Carmelo Anthony	30.00	80.00
4 Kyrie Irving	20.00	50.00
5 Kevin Garnett		
6 Tim Duncan	25.00	60.00
7 Ricky Rubio		
8 Blake Griffin	30.00	80.00
9 Dwight Howard	20.00	50.00
10 Paul Pierce	15.00	40.00
11 Kevin Durant	75.00	150.00
12 Derrick Rose		
13 Anthony Davis	20.00	50.00
14 Tony Parker		
15 Kenneth Faried		
16 LeBron James	40.00	100.00
17 Damian Lillard	15.00	40.00
18 Russell Westbrook	25.00	60.00
19 Steve Nash		
20 Chris Paul	12.00	30.00

2013-14 Panini Gold Standard Gold Rush

STATED PRINT RUN 20 SER.#'d SETS

1 Kevin Garnett	15.00	40.00
2 J.R. Smith	8.00	20.00
3 Zach Randolph	8.00	20.00
4 Ray Allen	10.00	25.00
5 David Lee	12.00	30.00
6 Luol Deng	8.00	20.00
7 David West	8.00	20.00
8 Pau Gasol	15.00	40.00
9 LaMarcus Aldridge	15.00	40.00
10 Andre Iguodala	8.00	20.00
11 Amar'e Stoudemire	8.00	20.00
12 Chauncey Billups	12.00	30.00
13 Paul Millsap	15.00	40.00
14 Tim Duncan	25.00	60.00
15 Carlos Boozer	8.00	20.00
16 Al Jefferson		
17 Nicolas Batum		
18 Josh Smith	12.00	30.00
19 Paul Pierce	10.00	25.00
20 Gerald Wallace	8.00	20.00
21 Joakim Noah	25.00	60.00
22 Jeff Green	8.00	20.00
23 Andre Miller	8.00	20.00
24 Jose Calderon	6.00	15.00
25 Dwyane Wade	40.00	100.00
26 Danny Granger		
27 Mike Conley		
28 Emeka Okafor	8.00	20.00
29 Dirk Nowitzki	25.00	60.00
30 Thaddeus Young	6.00	15.00
31 Rajon Rondo	10.00	25.00
32 Jameer Nelson	6.00	15.00
33 Steve Nash	20.00	50.00
34 Andrei Kirilenko	8.00	20.00
35 Tyson Chandler	8.00	20.00
36 Ryan Anderson	8.00	20.00
37 Al Horford	8.00	20.00
38 Serge Ibaka	8.00	20.00
39 Dwight Howard	15.00	40.00
40 Anderson Varejao	6.00	15.00
41 Carmelo Anthony	12.00	30.00
42 Marcin Gortat	10.00	25.00
43 Kyrie Irving	40.00	100.00
44 Monta Ellis	8.00	20.00
45 Kobe Bryant		
46 Damian Lillard	20.00	50.00
47 Marc Gasol	10.00	25.00
48 DeMar DeRozan	10.00	25.00
49 Kemba Walker	10.00	25.00
50 Shawn Marion	8.00	20.00
51 Blake Griffin	30.00	80.00
52 Derrick Rose	12.00	30.00
53 Brook Lopez	8.00	20.00
54 Tony Parker	20.00	50.00
55 Brandon Jennings	15.00	40.00
56 Kevin Durant	25.00	60.00
57 Paul George	50.00	120.00
58 Russell Westbrook	25.00	60.00
59 Klay Thompson	12.00	30.00
60 LeBron James	100.00	175.00
61 Kawhi Leonard	15.00	40.00
62 Ty Lawson	6.00	15.00
63 Joe Johnson	8.00	20.00
64 Chris Paul	12.00	30.00
65 Nikola Vucevic	8.00	20.00
66 Tyreke Evans	6.00	15.00
67 Vince Carter	12.00	30.00
68 Ricky Rubio	10.00	25.00
69 Raymond Felton	8.00	20.00
70 Deron Williams	8.00	20.00
71 Anthony Davis	15.00	40.00
72 Manu Ginobili	30.00	60.00
73 Dion Waiters	8.00	20.00
74 James Harden	15.00	40.00
75 Robin Lopez	6.00	15.00
76 Metta World Peace		
77 Tristan Thompson	8.00	20.00
78 Kevin Love	15.00	40.00
79 Roy Hibbert	8.00	20.00
80 Chris Bosh	12.00	30.00

2013-14 Panini Gold Standard Gold Scripts

PRINT RUNS B/WN 3-149 COPIES PER
NO PRICING ON QTY 10 OR LESS
EXCHANGE DEADLINE 8/19/2015

1 D.Cousins/25 EXCH	12.00	30.00
2 Kemba Walker/25 EXCH	8.00	20.00
3 Kevin Willis/49	3.00	8.00
4 Charlie Scott/49	4.00	10.00
6 Kobe Bryant/25 EXCH	100.00	250.00
7 Marvin Williams/49	4.00	10.00
9 Jrue Holiday/25	5.00	12.00
10 Stephen Curry/35	100.00	200.00
11 Brandon Knight/50	4.00	10.00
14 Kevin Durant/35 EXCH	50.00	120.00
15 Festus Ezeli/149	3.00	8.00
16 Patrick Beverley/149	3.00	8.00
17 Andre Miller/100	4.00	10.00
18 Jordan Hamilton/149	3.00	8.00
19 Serge Ibaka/25	8.00	20.00
21 Kyrie Irving/35 EXCH	30.00	80.00
22 Hakeem Olajuwon/25	15.00	40.00
23 Al-Farouq Aminu/25	4.00	10.00
25 J.R. Smith/100	4.00	10.00
26 Joakim Noah/25	4.00	10.00
27 Greivis Vasquez/25	4.00	10.00
28 Greg Monroe/149	4.00	10.00
29 Khris Middleton/149	4.00	10.00
30 Iman Shumpert/25	5.00	12.00
31 Chris Bosh/25	8.00	20.00
32 Donatas Motiejunas/149	4.00	10.00
33 Kent Bazemore/149	4.00	10.00
34 Kawhi Leonard/125	40.00	100.00
35 Andre Drummond/50	10.00	25.00
37 Tom Chambers/49	4.00	10.00
38 Draymond Green/49	6.00	15.00
39 Deron Williams/25	4.00	10.00
41 Michael Finley/25	8.00	20.00
42 Anthony Davis/35	40.00	100.00
43 Luis Scola/35	4.00	10.00
44 Andrei Kirilenko/25		
45 Courtney Lee/149	4.00	10.00
46 Blake Griffin/25	15.00	40.00
47 Perry Jones/49	3.00	8.00
48 Lavoy Allen/49		
49 Alec Burks/49	3.00	8.00
50 P.J. Tucker/49	3.00	8.00

2013-14 Panini Gold Standard Gold Season Autographs

PRINT RUNS B/WN 25-299 COPIES PER
EXCHANGE DEADLINE 8/19/2015

1 Larry Bird/35	40.00	80.00
2 Alonzo Mourning/35	15.00	40.00
3 Magic Johnson/35	25.00	60.00
4 Dikembe Mutombo/100	5.00	12.00
5 Stephen Curry/25	100.00	200.00
6 Elvin Hayes/25	5.00	12.00
7 Allan Houston/100	4.00	10.00
8 Bill Sharman/25	12.00	30.00
9 Antoine Walker/299	4.00	10.00
10 Adrian Dantley/299	4.00	10.00
11 Buck Williams/299	3.00	8.00
12 Kevin Durant/50	40.00	100.00
13 Alex English/299	4.00	10.00
14 Greivis Vasquez/299	4.00	10.00
15 Kyrie Irving/50	40.00	100.00
16 Kareem Abdul-Jabbar/25	50.00	120.00
17 D.Cousins/25 EXCH	12.00	30.00
18 Dennis Rodman/25	40.00	100.00
19 Dan Majerle/249	4.00	10.00
20 Kevin Love/25	12.00	30.00
21 Gary Payton/26		
22 Micheal Ray Richardson/299	4.00	10.00
23 Blake Griffin/25	30.00	80.00
24 Marcus Camby/299	4.00	10.00
25 Kobe Bryant/50 EXCH	125.00	250.00

2013-14 Panini Gold Standard Gold Strike Signatures

PRINT RUNS B/WN 15-299 COPIES PER
EXCHANGE DEADLINE 8/19/2015

1 Kawhi Leonard/100	50.00	120.00
2 Iman Shumpert/250	3.00	8.00
3 J.J. Hickson/299	3.00	8.00
4 Stephen Curry/75	100.00	250.00
5 Jan Vesely/299	3.00	8.00
6 C.Parsons/299 EXCH	4.00	10.00
7 Kevin Love/25	12.00	30.00
8 Dennis Schroder/250	5.00	12.00
9 Ray McCallum/299	3.00	8.00
10 Gal Mekel/299	3.00	8.00
11 MarShon Brooks/298	4.00	10.00
12 Alexey Shved/299	3.00	8.00
13 Robert Sacre/299	3.00	8.00
14 Dwight Howard/25	25.00	60.00
15 Gorgui Dieng/299	4.00	10.00
16 Jared Sullinger/25	3.00	8.00
17 Al-Farouq Aminu/250	4.00	10.00
18 Tobias Harris/250	4.00	10.00
19 Elias Harris/299	4.00	10.00
20 Meyers Leonard/299	3.00	8.00
21 Dwight Buycks/299	3.00	8.00
22 Rudy Gobert/299	15.00	40.00
23 James Harden/25 EXCH	30.00	80.00
24 Phil Pressey/299	3.00	8.00
25 Reggie Jackson/299	4.00	10.00
26 K.Thompson/100 EXCH	30.00	80.00
27 Kyrie Irving/75	40.00	100.00
28 Norris Cole/299	3.00	8.00
29 Tornike Shengelia/299	3.00	8.00
30 Lavoy Allen/299	3.00	8.00
31 Nando De Colo/299	4.00	10.00
32 Kent Bazemore/299	4.00	10.00
33 Jordan Crawford/299	3.00	8.00
34 Brandon Knight/25	4.00	10.00
35 Kenneth Faried/100	4.00	10.00
36 Harrison Barnes/75	10.00	25.00
37 Jimmer Fredette/299	3.00	8.00
38 John Henson/25		
39 Alonzo Gee/299	3.00	8.00
40 Quincy Acy/299	3.00	8.00
41 Greivis Vasquez/299	4.00	10.00
42 Nikola Pekovic/299	3.00	8.00
43 DeMarcus Cousins/15	12.00	30.00
44 Nemanja Nedovic/299	3.00	8.00
45 Isaiah Thomas/299	15.00	40.00
46 Andrew Nicholson/299	3.00	8.00
47 Andre Drummond/75	8.00	20.00
48 Michael Kidd-Gilchrist/25	5.00	12.00
49 Nikola Vucevic/299	4.00	10.00
50 James Anderson/299	3.00	8.00
51 Carrick Felix/299	3.00	8.00
52 Tyreke Evans/15	3.00	8.00
53 Sergey Karasev/299	3.00	8.00
54 Jrue Holiday/25	5.00	12.00
55 Jordan Hamilton/299	3.00	8.00
56 Terrence Ross/150	4.00	10.00
57 Evan Fournier/299	4.00	10.00
58 Enes Kanter/299	3.00	8.00
59 Jonas Valanciunas/299	4.00	10.00
60 Draymond Green/299	12.00	30.00

2013-14 Panini Gold Standard Marks of Gold

PRINT RUNS B/WN 4-99 COPIES PER
NO PRICING ON QTY 10 OR LESS
EXCHANGE DEADLINE 8/19/2015

1 Henry Bibby/49	3.00	8.00
2 James Harden/49	25.00	60.00
5 Maurice Harkless/49	3.00	8.00
6 Orlando Johnson/99	3.00	8.00
7 Kyrie Irving/49	40.00	100.00
8 Eric Gordon/25	4.00	10.00
11 Satch Sanders/25	6.00	15.00
12 Goran Dragic/25	4.00	10.00
13 Tyreke Evans/25	3.00	8.00
14 Andrea Bargnani/25	4.00	10.00
16 Draymond Green/49	6.00	15.00
17 Anthony Davis/35	40.00	100.00
18 Eddie Johnson/49	3.00	8.00
19 Jan Vesely/49	3.00	8.00
20 Michael Kidd-Gilchrist/25	5.00	12.00
21 Juwan Howard/49	4.00	10.00
23 Nick Collison/49	4.00	10.00
24 Vernon Maxwell/49	3.00	8.00
25 Marquis Teague/49	3.00	8.00
26 Kobe Bryant/25 EXCH	125.00	250.00
27 E'Twaun Moore/49	3.00	8.00
28 Kenny Walker/49	3.00	8.00
29 Gail Goodrich/49	4.00	10.00
30 Tony Parker/25	12.00	30.00
31 Chris Andersen/49	8.00	20.00
32 Peja Stojakovic/25	5.00	12.00
33 John Starks/49	10.00	25.00
34 Miles Plumlee/99	3.00	8.00
35 Vince Carter/49	12.00	30.00
38 Derrick Favors/25	4.00	10.00
39 Blake Griffin/25	40.00	100.00
40 Andrew Nicholson/25		
41 Raymond Felton/15		
42 Josh Smith/15	8.00	20.00
43 Kevin Durant/25	75.00	200.00
45 Harrison Barnes/49	10.00	25.00
46 Kenneth Faried/25	4.00	10.00
47 Kurt Rambis/49	3.00	8.00
48 C.J. Watson/49	3.00	8.00

2013-14 Panini Gold Standard Metal

1 Rajon Rondo	2.50	6.00
2 Magic Johnson	5.00	12.00
3 Derrick Rose	3.00	8.00
4 John Havlicek	3.00	8.00
5 Nerlens Noel	3.00	8.00
6 Al Horford	2.00	5.00
7 Larry Bird	6.00	15.00
8 Paul Pierce	2.50	6.00
9 Elvin Hayes	2.50	6.00
10 Kyrie Irving	5.00	12.00
11 Isiah Thomas	2.50	6.00
12 LeBron James	25.00	60.00
13 Bob Cousy	4.00	10.00
14 Anthony Bennett	2.00	5.00
15 Kemba Walker	2.50	6.00
16 Wilt Chamberlain	5.00	12.00
17 Carmelo Anthony	6.00	15.00
18 Jason Kidd	2.50	6.00
19 Josh Smith	2.00	5.00
20 Scottie Pippen	5.00	12.00
21 Alex Len	2.00	5.00
22 Roy Hibbert	2.00	5.00
23 Julius Erving	4.00	10.00
24 Nikola Vucevic	2.00	5.00
25 Willis Reed	2.50	6.00
26 Kevin Garnett	4.00	10.00
27 Anfernee Hardaway	6.00	15.00
28 Michael Carter-Williams	2.50	6.00
29 Larry Sanders	1.50	4.00
30 Walt Frazier	2.50	6.00
31 John Wall	3.00	8.00
32 George Gervin	2.50	6.00
33 Dwyane Wade	4.00	10.00
34 Patrick Ewing	3.00	8.00
35 Ty Lawson	1.50	4.00
36 Shaquille O'Neal	6.00	15.00
37 Stephen Curry	6.00	15.00
38 Gary Payton	2.50	6.00
39 Dirk Nowitzki	3.00	8.00
40 Clyde Drexler	3.00	8.00
41 Deron Williams	2.00	5.00
42 Alonzo Mourning	3.00	8.00
43 Victor Oladipo	3.00	8.00
44 Kevin Love	2.50	6.00
45 Earl Monroe	2.50	6.00
46 Blake Griffin	2.50	6.00
47 Drazen Petrovic	2.50	6.00
48 Brandon Jennings	1.50	4.00
49 Dennis Rodman	5.00	12.00
50 Ben McLemore	2.00	5.08
51 Dwight Howard	2.00	5.00
52 David Robinson	4.00	10.00
53 Kevin Durant	6.00	15.00
54 Maurice Cheeks	1.50	4.00
55 Marc Gasol	2.50	6.00
56 James Worthy	3.00	8.00
57 Chris Bosh	2.50	6.00
58 Bill Russell	4.00	10.00
59 Kobe Bryant	15.00	40.00
60 Bernard King	2.00	5.00
61 Tyreke Evans	1.50	4.00
62 John Stockton	4.00	10.00
63 Chris Paul	3.00	8.00
64 Bill Walton	2.50	6.00
65 Shabazz Muhammad	2.00	5.00
66 Damian Lillard	6.00	15.00
67 Jerry West	3.00	8.00
68 Russell Westbrook	6.00	15.00
69 Adrian Dantley	2.00	5.00
70 Otto Porter	2.50	6.00
71 James Harden	4.00	10.00
72 Alex English	2.00	5.00
73 DeMarcus Cousins	2.50	6.00
74 Dominique Wilkins	3.00	8.00
75 Tony Parker	2.50	6.00
76 Artis Gilmore	2.00	5.00
77 Monta Ellis	2.00	5.00
78 Tim Hardaway	2.50	6.00
79 Steve Nash	2.50	6.00
80 Yao Ming	3.00	8.00
81 Kelly Olynyk	2.00	5.00
82 Anthony Davis	8.00	20.00
83 Chris Mullin	2.50	6.00
84 Tim Duncan	4.00	10.00
85 Karl Malone	3.00	8.00
86 Jeremy Lin	2.50	6.00
87 Dikembe Mutombo	2.50	6.00
88 Cody Zeller	2.00	5.00
89 Manu Ginobili	2.50	6.00
90 Hakeem Olajuwon	3.00	8.00

2013-14 Panini Gold Standard Metal Black

*BLACK: 1.5X TO 4X BASIC

10 Kyrie Irving	40.00	100.00
59 Kobe Bryant	125.00	250.00
82 Anthony Davis	15.00	40.00

2013-14 Panini Gold Standard Mother Lode Autographs

PRINT RUNS B/WN 25-299 COPIES PER
EXCHANGE DEADLINE 8/19/2015

1 Kevin Durant/50	75.00	150.00
2 J.R. Smith/50	4.00	10.00
3 Kenny Walker/249	3.00	8.00
4 Jayson Williams/249	3.00	8.00
5 Satch Sanders/249	5.00	12.00
6 Nick Van Exel/25	12.00	30.00
7 John Havlicek/25	15.00	40.00
8 Gail Goodrich/49	4.00	10.00
9 Terry Porter/249	3.00	8.00
10 Andre Drummond/49	5.00	12.00
11 LaMarcus Aldridge/25	20.00	50.00
12 James Harden/25 EXCH	30.00	80.00
13 Kobe Bryant/25 EXCH	125.00	250.00
14 J.J. Redick/75	5.00	12.00
15 Maalik Wayns/250	3.00	8.00
16 Charlie Ward/299	3.00	8.00
17 Alan Anderson/299	3.00	8.00
18 Tom Gugliotta/225	3.00	8.00
19 Elgin Baylor/25	10.00	25.00
20 Charlie Scott/249	4.00	10.00
21 K.Thompson/149 EXCH	20.00	50.00
22 C.Parsons/249 EXCH	4.00	10.00
23 Stephen Curry/49	100.00	250.00
24 Kyrie Irving/50 EXCH	40.00	100.00
25 Tony Parker/25	30.00	80.00
26 Harrison Barnes/75	10.00	25.00
27 Karl Malone/25	50.00	120.00
28 Sleepy Floyd/249	3.00	8.00
29 Jared Cunningham/299	3.00	8.00
30 Scottie Pippen/25		
31 Vlade Divac/249	5.00	12.00
32 Jarrett Jack/249	4.00	10.00
33 Kenyon Martin/249	4.00	10.00
34 Blake Griffin/25 EXCH	20.00	50.00
35 Tyson Chandler/25	6.00	15.00
36 Anthony Davis/49	40.00	100.00
37 Micheal Ray Richardson/249	4.00	10.00
38 Walt Frazier/25		
39 Anfernee Hardaway/25		
40 Al Horford/25	4.00	10.00
41 Wes Unseld/25		
42 Herb Williams/249	3.00	8.00
43 Danilo Gallinari/25	6.00	15.00
44 George Hill/249	4.00	10.00
45 Nikola Vucevic/249	4.00	10.00
46 James Worthy/25	30.00	80.00
47 Rick Barry/25		
48 Jon Leuer/299	3.00	8.00
49 Muggsy Bogues/249	4.00	10.00
50 David Thompson/299	4.00	10.00

2013-14 Panini Gold Standard Ring Bearers Autographs

PRINT RUNS B/WN 10-299 COPIES PER
NO PRICING ON QTY 10
EXCHANGE DEADLINE 8/19/2015

2 Dwyane Wade/15	75.00	200.00
4 Jon McGlocklin/299	4.00	10.00
5 Mark Landsberger/299	3.00	8.00
6 Kenny Smith/25	5.00	12.00
7 Kareem Abdul-Jabbar/25	30.00	80.00
8 Toni Kukoc/249	5.00	12.00
9 Kobe Bryant/25	125.00	250.00
10 Dennis Rodman/25	15.00	40.00
11 Jason Terry/25	12.00	30.00
13 Joe Dumars/25	15.00	40.00
14 Alonzo Mourning/25	40.00	100.00
15 Sean Elliott/299	5.00	12.00
16 Magic Johnson/25	60.00	150.00
17 Steve Kerr/25	12.00	30.00
18 Hakeem Olajuwon/25	25.00	60.00
19 Tony Parker/25	30.00	80.00
20 Ron Harper/299	5.00	12.00
21 Kurt Rambis/249	3.00	8.00
22 Robert Horry/249 EXCH	4.00	10.00
23 Antoine Walker/299	4.00	10.00
24 Fred Brown/299	3.00	8.00
25 Michael Cooper/299	4.00	10.00

2013-14 Panini Gold Standard Superscribe Autographs

PRINT RUNS B/WN 25-299 COPIES PER
EXCHANGE DEADLINE 8/19/2015

1 Magic Johnson/49	20.00	50.00
2 Jerry Lucas/50	8.00	20.00
3 Eddie Jones/249	4.00	10.00
4 Scottie Pippen/49	90.00	150.00
5 Elgin Baylor/15		
6 John Starks/299	4.00	10.00
7 Adrian Dantley/225	4.00	10.00
8 Chris Andersen/35 EXCH	125.00	250.00
9 Spencer Haywood/299	3.00	8.00
10 Kawhi Leonard/75	50.00	120.00
11 J.J. Redick/99	10.00	25.00
12 Mario Chalmers/75	6.00	15.00
13 Dikembe Mutombo/99	12.00	30.00
14 Tony Parker/25	30.00	60.00
15 Dwight Howard/49	12.00	30.00
16 Kobe Bryant/75 EXCH	125.00	250.00
17 Blake Griffin/25	20.00	50.00
18 John Lucas/225	5.00	12.00
19 Bob Lanier/15	50.00	120.00
20 David Robinson/25	20.00	50.00
21 Jason Terry/25	20.00	50.00
22 Ryan Anderson/199	4.00	10.00
23 World B. Free/25	15.00	40.00
24 Larry Bird/49	50.00	120.00
25 Jamaal Wilkes/25	10.00	25.00
26 Jon McGlocklin/299	4.00	10.00
27 Brook Lopez/15	4.00	10.00
28 James Worthy/15 EXCH	20.00	50.00
29 Kyrie Irving/49	75.00	150.00
30 Kevin Durant/49	60.00	150.00
31 Harrison Barnes/75	4.00	10.00
32 Anfernee Hardaway/50	20.00	50.00
33 Dolph Schayes/25		
34 Kenneth Faried/99	4.00	10.00
35 Spud Webb/299	4.00	10.00
36 James Harden/50 EXCH	30.00	80.00
37 Keith Van Horn/299	4.00	10.00
38 J.R. Smith/99	4.00	10.00
39 Dominique Wilkins/15		
40 Jeff Hornacek/299	4.00	10.00

2013-14 Panini Gold Standard White Gold Threads

PRINT RUNS B/WN 25-199 COPIES PER

1 Deron Williams/99	3.00	8.00
2 World B. Free/49		
3 Vince Carter/99	5.00	12.00
4 Zach Randolph/99	3.00	8.00
5 Andre Iguodala/99	3.00	8.00
6 Kyrie Irving/149	8.00	20.00
7 Mike Conley/149	3.00	8.00
8 Blake Griffin/125	4.00	10.00
9 Josh Smith/75	3.00	8.00
10 Gerald Wallace/75	3.00	8.00
11 Marc Gasol/99	4.00	10.00
12 DeMar DeRozan/149	4.00	10.00
13 Carlos Boozer/149	3.00	8.00
14 Raymond Felton/99	3.00	8.00
15 Hakeem Olajuwon/49	5.00	12.00
16 Kemba Walker/75	4.00	10.00
17 Rajon Rondo/99	4.00	10.00
18 Shaquille O'Neal /99	8.00	20.00
19 Damian Lillard/99	8.00	20.00
20 Artis Gilmore/25	3.00	8.00
21 Steve Nash/125	4.00	10.00
22 Kawhi Leonard/199	6.00	15.00
23 Joakim Noah/149	3.00	8.00
24 Ryan Anderson/75	3.00	8.00
25 Luol Deng/75		
26 Kevin Garnett/199	6.00	15.00
27 Jameer Nelson/99	2.50	6.00
28 Dirk Nowitzki/199	5.00	12.00
29 Al Horford/199	3.00	8.00
30 Amar'e Stoudemire/199	3.00	8.00
31 Ty Lawson/75	2.50	6.00
32 LeBron James/125	15.00	40.00
33 Pau Gasol/199	4.00	10.00
34 Larry Bird/49	12.00	30.00
35 Anfernee Hardaway/49	10.00	25.00
36 Ray Allen/199	4.00	10.00
37 Andre Miller/199	3.00	8.00
38 Clyde Drexler/99	5.00	12.00
39 Manu Ginobili/125	4.00	10.00
40 Joe Dumars/49	4.00	10.00
41 Brook Lopez/149	3.00	8.00
42 Russell Westbrook/99	10.00	25.00
43 Monta Ellis/75	3.00	8.00
44 Ricky Rubio/125	4.00	10.00
45 Carmelo Anthony/199	5.00	12.00
46 Jose Calderon/199	2.50	6.00
47 Andrei Kirilenko/199	3.00	8.00
48 Dwyane Wade/199	6.00	15.00
49 Danny Granger/49	3.00	8.00
50 Serge Ibaka/199	3.00	8.00
51 Magic Johnson/49	10.00	25.00
52 LaMarcus Aldridge/199	4.00	10.00
53 Anthony Davis/199	8.00	20.00
54 Jeff Green/199	3.00	8.00
55 Tim Duncan/199	6.00	15.00
56 Dwight Howard/199	3.00	8.00
57 Tony Parker/99	6.00	15.00
58 Paul Millsap/149	4.00	10.00
59 Kevin Durant/199	10.00	25.00
60 Paul Pierce/199	4.00	10.00
61 J.R. Smith/199	3.00	8.00
62 Klay Thompson/199	5.00	12.00
63 Earl Monroe/49	10.00	25.00
64 Thaddeus Young/50	2.50	6.00
65 Tyson Chandler/199	3.00	8.00

2014-15 Panini Gold Standard

COMPLETE SET (347)
201-266 PRINT RUN B/WN 149-199 COPIES PER
267-299 PRINT RUN 99 SER.#'d SETS
VARIATION PRINT RUN 285 SER.#'d SETS
EXCHANGE DEADLINE 8/19/2015

1 Kawhi Leonard	2.50	6.00
2 Dirk Nowitzki	2.00	5.00
3 DeMarcus Cousins	1.50	4.00
4A Kobe Bryant	6.00	15.00
4B Kobe Bryant VAR	10.00	25.00
5A Damian Lillard	3.00	8.00
5B Damian Lillard VAR	5.00	12.00
6 Kentavious Caldwell-Pope	1.00	2.50
7 Jose Calderon	1.00	2.50
8 Derrick Favors	1.25	3.00
9 David Lee	1.00	2.50
10 Kevin Love	1.50	4.00
11 Amir Johnson	1.00	2.50
12 Zach Randolph	1.25	3.00
13 Ryan Anderson	1.00	2.50
14 Avery Bradley	1.25	3.00
15 Randy Foye	1.00	2.50
16 Andre Iguodala	1.25	3.00
17 Al Jefferson	1.25	3.00
18 Stephen Curry	6.00	15.00
19 Roy Hibbert	1.25	3.00
20A Anthony Davis	3.00	8.00
20B Anthony Davis VAR	5.00	12.00
21 Isaiah Thomas	1.50	4.00
22 Gerald Henderson	1.00	2.50
23A L.James CLE	6.00	15.00
23B L.James CLE	10.00	25.00
23C L.James MIA	10.00	25.00
24 Monta Ellis	1.25	3.00
25 Enes Kanter	1.00	2.50
26 Marc Gasol	1.50	4.00
27A Kyrie Irving	3.00	8.00
27B Kyrie Irving VAR	5.00	12.00
28 Gordon Hayward	1.50	4.00
29 Ersan Ilyasova	1.00	2.50
30 Matt Barnes	1.00	2.50
31 Brandon Knight	1.25	3.00
32 Victor Oladipo	1.25	3.00
33 Tony Parker	1.50	4.00
34 Cody Zeller	1.00	2.50
35 Terrence Ross	1.25	3.00
36 Carlos Boozer	1.25	3.00
37 Bradley Beal	1.50	4.00
38 Ty Lawson	1.00	2.50
39 Tim Duncan	2.50	6.00
40 Channing Frye	1.25	3.00
41 Nicolas Batum	1.25	3.00
42 Joe Johnson	1.25	3.00
43 Jeff Green	1.25	3.00
44 Paul Pierce	1.50	4.00
45 Jamal Crawford	1.50	4.00
46 Norris Cole	1.00	2.50
47 Nerlens Noel	1.25	3.00
48 Jimmy Butler	1.50	4.00
49 Jared Sullinger	1.00	2.50
50 Deron Williams	1.25	3.00
51A P.Gasol CHI	1.50	4.00
51B P.Gasol MEM	2.50	6.00
51C P.Gasol LAL	2.50	6.00
52 DeMar DeRozan	1.50	4.00
53 Klay Thompson	2.00	5.00
54 Kenneth Faried	1.25	3.00
55A Dwyane Wade	2.50	6.00
55B Dwyane Wade VAR	4.00	10.00
56 Kevin Garnett	2.50	6.00
57 Jrue Holiday	1.25	3.00
58 Dion Waiters	1.25	3.00
59 Russell Westbrook	4.00	10.00
60 Arron Afflalo	1.00	2.50
61 Andre Drummond	1.50	4.00
62 Tayshaun Prince	1.25	3.00
63 Al Horford	1.25	3.00
64 Ricky Rubio	6.00	15.00
65A S.Marion CLE	1.25	3.00
65B S.Marion MIA	2.00	5.00
65C S.Marion DAL	2.00	5.00
65D S.Marion TOR	2.00	5.00
65E S.Marion PHO	2.00	5.00
66 Anthony Bennett	1.00	2.50
67 Amar'e Stoudemire	1.50	4.00
68 Steven Adams	1.25	3.00
69 Gerald Green	1.25	3.00
70 Mike Conley	1.25	3.00
71 Manu Ginobili	1.50	4.00
72 J.R. Smith	1.25	3.00
73 Kyle Lowry	1.25	3.00
74 Goran Dragic	1.25	3.00
75 Eric Gordon	1.25	3.00
76 Marco Belinelli	1.00	2.50
77 Lance Stephenson	1.25	3.00
78 Harrison Barnes	1.25	3.00
79 Tobias Harris	1.25	3.00
80A Chris Paul	2.00	5.00
80B Chris Paul VAR	3.00	8.00
81 C.J. McCollum	1.50	4.00
82A Blake Griffin	1.50	4.00
82B Blake Griffin VAR	2.50	6.00
83 Wesley Matthews	1.00	2.50
84 Tristan Thompson	1.25	3.00
85 Tiago Splitter	1.25	3.00
86 Chandler Parsons	1.25	3.00
87 Brandon Jennings	1.00	2.50
88 David West	1.25	3.00
89 Jordan Hill	1.00	2.50
90 Tyson Chandler	1.25	3.00
91 JaVale McGee	1.25	3.00
92 Paul Millsap	1.50	4.00
93 Nikola Pekovic	1.00	2.50
94 Jonas Valanciunas	1.25	3.00
95 Nene	1.25	3.00
96A J.Lin NYK	10.00	25.00
96B J.Lin LAL	2.50	6.00
96C J.Lin HOU	2.50	6.00
96D J.Lin GSW	2.50	6.00
97A James Harden	6.00	15.00
97B James Harden VAR	4.00	10.00
98 Otto Porter	1.25	3.00
99 Nick Young	1.25	3.00
100 Jodie Meeks	1.25	3.00
101 Kemba Walker	1.50	4.00
102 Dwight Howard	1.25	3.00
103 Dennis Schroder	1.25	3.00
104 Danilo Gallinari	1.00	2.50
105 Kyle Korver	1.25	3.00
106A Kevin Durant	4.00	10.00
106B Kevin Durant VAR	6.00	15.00
107 Josh Smith	1.25	3.00
108 Derrick Rose	2.00	5.00
109 DeAndre Jordan	1.50	4.00
110 Kevin Martin	1.25	3.00
111 Anderson Varejao	1.00	2.50
112 Taj Gibson	1.25	3.00
113 Serge Ibaka	1.25	3.00
114 Ben McLemore	1.00	2.50
115 Patrick Beverley	1.00	2.50
116 Andrew Bogut	1.25	3.00
117 Alex Len	1.00	2.50
118 Steve Nash	1.50	4.00
119 Rudy Gay	1.50	4.00
120 Archie Goodwin	1.00	2.50
121 Brook Lopez	1.25	3.00
122 J.J. Redick	1.50	4.00
123 Giannis Antetokounmpo	3.00	8.00
124 Michael Kidd-Gilchrist	1.25	3.00
125 Eric Bledsoe	1.25	3.00
126 Marcin Gortat	1.25	3.00
127 LaMarcus Aldridge	1.50	4.00
128 Greg Monroe	1.25	3.00
129 Michael Carter-Williams	1.00	2.50
130 Luol Deng	1.25	3.00
131 Vince Carter	2.00	5.00
132 Trey Burke	1.00	2.50
133 Corey Brewer	1.00	2.50
134A Carmelo Anthony	2.00	5.00
134B Carmelo Anthony VAR	3.00	8.00
135 Thaddeus Young	1.00	2.50
136 Brandon Bass	1.00	2.50
137 Tyreke Evans	1.00	2.50
138 Tim Hardaway Jr.	1.00	2.50
139 Chris Bosh	1.50	4.00
140 Nikola Vucevic	1.25	3.00
141 John Wall	2.00	5.00
142 Jeff Teague	1.25	3.00
143 Rajon Rondo	1.50	4.00
144 Trevor Ariza	1.00	2.50
145 O.J. Mayo	1.00	2.50
146 Nick Collison	1.25	3.00
147 Joakim Noah	1.25	3.00
148 Paul George	2.00	5.00
149 Tony Wroten	1.00	2.50
150 George Hill	1.25	3.00
151 Robert Horry	1.25	3.00
152 Hakeem Olajuwon	2.00	5.00
153 Tim Hardaway	1.50	4.00
154A A.Iverson PHI	40.00	100.00
154B A.Iverson PHI	3.00	8.00
154C A.Iverson MEM	3.00	8.00
154D A.Iverson DEN	3.00	8.00
154E A.Iverson DET	3.00	8.00
155 John Havlicek	2.00	5.00
156A B.Davis CLE	1.25	3.00
156B B.Davis LAC	2.00	5.00
156C B.Davis CHA	2.00	5.00
156D B.Davis NOH	2.00	5.00
156E B.Davis NYK	2.00	5.00
156F B.Davis GSW	2.00	5.00
157 Kevin McHale	1.50	4.00
158 Clyde Drexler	2.00	5.00
159 Oscar Robertson	2.00	5.00
160 Drazen Petrovic	1.50	4.00
161 Robert Parish	1.50	4.00
162 Isiah Thomas	1.50	4.00
163A Tracy McGrady	1.50	4.00
163B Tracy McGrady VAR	2.50	6.00
164A A.Mourning MIA	2.00	5.00
164B A.Mourning MIA	3.00	8.00
164C A.Mourning CHA	3.00	8.00
164D A.Mourning NJN	3.00	8.00
165 John Stockton	2.50	6.00
166 Bernard King	1.25	3.00
167A Larry Bird	4.00	10.00
167B Larry Bird VAR	6.00	15.00
168 David Robinson	2.50	6.00
169 Patrick Ewing	2.00	5.00
170 Elgin Baylor	1.50	4.00
171A S.Pippen CHI	3.00	8.00
171B S.Pippen CHI	5.00	12.00
171C S.Pippen HOU	5.00	12.00
171D S.Pippen POR	5.00	12.00

172 James Worthy 2.00 5.00
173A Anfernee Hardaway 4.00 10.00
173B Anfernee Hardaway VAR 4.00 10.00
174 Wilt Chamberlain 3.00 8.00
175 Julius Erving 2.50 6.00
176 Bill Russell 2.50 6.00
177A L.Sprewell NYK 1.25 3.00
177B L.Sprewell MIN 2.00 5.00
177C L.Sprewell GSW 2.00 5.00
178 Dennis Rodman 3.00 8.00
179 Pete Maravich 2.50 6.00
180 Gary Payton 1.50 4.00
181A Shaquille O'Neal 3.00 8.00
181B Shaquille O'Neal VAR 5.00 12.00
182 Jason Kidd 1.50 4.00
183 Yao Ming 2.00 5.00
184A C.Webber PHI 2.50 6.00
184B C.Webber WSH 2.50 6.00
184C C.Webber SAC 2.50 6.00
184D C.Webber DET 2.50 6.00
184E C.Webber GSW 2.50 6.00
184F C.Webber WSH 2.50 6.00
185 Kareem Abdul-Jabbar 2.50 6.00
186 Bill Walton 1.50 4.00
187A Magic Johnson 4.00 10.00
187B Magic Johnson VAR 4.00 10.00
188 Dikembe Mutombo 1.50 4.00
189 Phil Jackson 2.00 5.00
190 George Gervin 1.50 4.00
191 Shawn Kemp 2.50 6.00
192 Jerry West 2.00 5.00
193 Arvydas Sabonis 1.25 3.00
194 Karl Malone 2.00 5.00
195 Chris Mullin 1.50 4.00
196 Michael Finley 1.50 4.00
197 Rick Barry 1.25 3.00
198 Grant Hill 2.00 5.00
199 Joe Dumars 1.50 4.00
200 Dominique Wilkins 2.00 5.00
201 A.Wiggins JSY AU/199 RC 60.00 150.00
202 J.Parker JSY AU/199 RC 25.00 60.00
203 J.Randle JSY AU/199 RC 20.00 50.00
204 J.Embiid JSY AU/199 RC 75.00 200.00
205 D.Exum JSY AU/199 RC 6.00 15.00
206 S.Napier JSY AU/199 RC 5.00 12.00
207 M.Smart JSY AU/199 RC 6.00 15.00
208 C.Early JSY AU/199 RC 4.00 10.00
209 J.Young JSY AU/199 RC 4.00 10.00
210 A.Gordon JSY AU/199 RC 10.00 25.00
211 E.Payton JSY AU/199 RC 15.00 40.00
212 B.Caboclo JSY AU/199 RC 5.00 12.00
213 J.Ennis JSY AU/199 RC 4.00 10.00
214 G.Harris JSY AU/199 RC 6.00 15.00
215 G.Robinson III JSY AU/199 RC 4.00 10.00
216 C.Jefferson JSY AU/199 RC 4.00 10.00
217 K.Anderson JSY AU/199 RC 6.00 15.00
218 R.Smith JSY AU/199 RC 4.00 10.00
219 Z.LaVine JSY AU/199 RC 20.00 50.00
220 S.Dinwiddie JSY AU/199 RC 5.00 12.00
221 R.Hood JSY AU/199 RC 6.00 15.00
222 T.Warren JSY AU/199 RC 6.00 15.00
223 T.Ennis JSY AU/199 RC 4.00 10.00
224 J.Adams JSY AU/199 RC 4.00 10.00
225 D.McDermott JSY AU/199 RC 6.00 15.00
226 A.Payne JSY AU/199 RC 5.00 12.00
227 K.McDaniels JSY AU/199 RC 5.00 12.00
228 N.Stauskas JSY AU/199 RC 5.00 12.00
229 N.Vonleh JSY AU/199 RC 5.00 12.00
230 M.McGary JSY AU/199 RC 4.00 10.00
231 J.O'Bryant JSY AU/199 RC 4.00 10.00
232 J.Stokes JSY AU/199 RC 4.00 10.00
233 D.Inglis JSY AU/199 RC 4.00 10.00
234 A.Wiggins JSY AU/149 60.00 150.00
235 J.Parker JSY AU/149 25.00 60.00
236 J.Randle JSY AU/149 20.00 50.00
237 J.Embiid JSY AU/149 50.00 120.00
238 D.Exum JSY AU/149 6.00 15.00
239 S.Napier JSY AU/149 5.00 12.00
240 M.Smart JSY AU/149 6.00 15.00
241 C.Early JSY AU/149 4.00 10.00
242 J.Young JSY AU/149 4.00 10.00
243 A.Gordon JSY AU/149 10.00 25.00
244 E.Payton JSY AU/149 15.00 40.00
245 B.Caboclo JSY AU/149 5.00 12.00
246 J.Ennis JSY AU/149 4.00 10.00
247 G.Harris JSY AU/149 6.00 15.00
248 G.Robinson III JSY AU/149 4.00 10.00
249 C.Jefferson JSY AU/149 4.00 10.00
250 K.Anderson JSY AU/149 6.00 15.00
251 R.Smith JSY AU/149 4.00 10.00
252 Z.LaVine JSY AU/149 20.00 50.00
253 S.Dinwiddie JSY AU/149 5.00 12.00
254 R.Hood JSY AU/149 6.00 15.00
255 T.Warren JSY AU/149 6.00 15.00
256 T.Ennis JSY AU/149 4.00 10.00
257 J.Adams JSY AU/149 4.00 10.00
258 D.McDermott JSY AU/149 6.00 15.00
259 A.Payne JSY AU/149 5.00 12.00
260 K.McDaniels JSY AU/149 5.00 12.00
261 N.Stauskas JSY AU/149 5.00 12.00
262 N.Vonleh JSY AU/149 5.00 12.00
263 M.McGary JSY AU/149 4.00 10.00
264 J.O'Bryant JSY AU/149 4.00 10.00
265 J.Stokes JSY AU/149 4.00 10.00
266 D.Inglis JSY AU/149 4.00 10.00
267 A.Wiggins JSY AU/99 60.00 150.00
268 J.Parker JSY AU/99 25.00 60.00
269 J.Randle JSY AU/99 30.00 80.00
270 J.Embiid JSY AU/99 60.00 150.00
271 D.Exum JSY AU/99 8.00 20.00
272 S.Napier JSY AU/99 6.00 15.00
273 M.Smart JSY AU/99 8.00 20.00
274 C.Early JSY AU/99 5.00 12.00
275 J.Young JSY AU/99 5.00 12.00
276 A.Gordon JSY AU/99 12.00 30.00
277 E.Payton JSY AU/99 20.00 50.00
278 B.Caboclo JSY AU/99 6.00 15.00
279 J.Ennis JSY AU/99 5.00 12.00
280 G.Harris JSY AU/99 8.00 20.00
281 G.Robinson III JSY AU/99 5.00 12.00
282 C.Jefferson JSY AU/99 5.00 12.00
283 K.Anderson JSY AU/99 8.00 20.00
284 R.Smith JSY AU/99 5.00 12.00
285 Z.LaVine JSY AU/99 25.00 60.00
286 S.Dinwiddie JSY AU/99 6.00 15.00
287 R.Hood JSY AU/99 8.00 20.00
288 T.Warren JSY AU/99 8.00 20.00
289 T.Ennis JSY AU/99 5.00 12.00
290 J.Adams JSY AU/99 5.00 12.00
291 D.McDermott JSY AU/99 8.00 20.00
292 A.Payne JSY AU/99 6.00 15.00
293 K.McDaniels JSY AU/99 6.00 15.00
294 N.Stauskas JSY AU/99 6.00 15.00
295 N.Vonleh JSY AU/99 6.00 15.00
296 M.McGary JSY AU/99 5.00 12.00
297 J.O'Bryant JSY AU/99 5.00 12.00
298 J.Stokes JSY AU/99 5.00 12.00
299 D.Inglis JSY AU/99 5.00 12.00

2014-15 Panini Gold Standard Black

*BLACK: 1.2X TO 3X BASE HI
RANDOM INSERTS IN PACKS
27 Kyrie Irving 20.00 50.00
96 Jeremy Lin 20.00 50.00
154 Allen Iverson 12.00 30.00

2014-15 Panini Gold Standard Gold

*GOLD: .8X TO 2X BASE HI
STATED PRINT RUN 79 SER.#'d SETS
27 Kyrie Irving 12.00 30.00
96 Jeremy Lin 3.00 8.00
154 Allen Iverson 4.00 10.00

2014-15 Panini Gold Standard 14K Autographs

STATED PRINT RUN B/WN 99-199 COPIES PER
STATED PRINT RUN B/WN 25-75 COPIES PER
3 Kyrie Irving/25 50.00 120.00
4 Kobe Bryant/25 75.00 150.00
5 Mike Conley/75 6.00 15.00
6 Kendall Gill/199 4.00 10.00
7 Tyler Zeller/199 10.00 25.00
8 Kevin Durant/25 60.00 150.00
9 Larry Bird/25 40.00 100.00
10 Isiah Thomas/50 8.00 20.00
11 George Gervin/35 15.00 40.00
12 Peja Stojakovic/35 8.00 20.00
13 Dan Issel/199 5.00 12.00
14 Marques Johnson/199 5.00 12.00
15 Sam Perkins/99 4.00 10.00
16 Shaquille O'Neal/25 100.00 200.00
17 Spud Webb/199 5.00 12.00
18 Steve Smith/199 5.00 12.00
19 Bill Walton/35 8.00 20.00
20 Satch Sanders/99 6.00 15.00
21 Ralph Sampson/35 6.00 15.00
22 David Thompson/99 5.00 12.00
23 Bradley Beal/35 8.00 20.00
24 Jason Terry/35 6.00 15.00
25 Alex English/99 5.00 12.00
26 Mark Aguirre/99 5.00 12.00
27 Thaddeus Young/199 4.00 10.00

2014-15 Panini Gold Standard AU Autographs

STATED PRINT RUN 79 SER.#'d SETS
1 Kobe Bryant 100.00 200.00
2 Kevin Durant 75.00 150.00
3 Kareem Abdul-Jabbar 40.00 100.00
4 Kyrie Irving 40.00 100.00
5 John Wall 25.00 60.00
6 Kelly Olynyk 10.00 25.00
7 Tim Hardaway Jr. 4.00 10.00
8 Isaiah Thomas 15.00 40.00
9 Andre Drummond 10.00 25.00
10 Bradley Beal 12.00 30.00
11 Nick Van Exel 15.00 40.00
12 Danny Green 5.00 12.00
14 Mychal Thompson 4.00 10.00
16 Iman Shumpert 4.00 10.00
17 Jonas Valanciunas 5.00 12.00
20 Marcin Gortat 5.00 12.00
21 Marvin Williams 5.00 12.00
22 Nick Young 5.00 12.00
24 P.J. Tucker 4.00 10.00
26 Reggie Jackson 8.00 20.00
27 Richard Jefferson 5.00 12.00
29 Stephen Curry 150.00 250.00
30 Steve Blake 4.00 10.00
31 Taj Gibson 5.00 12.00
33 Spencer Hawes 4.00 10.00
35 Tony Parker 20.00 50.00
36 Ty Lawson 4.00 10.00
37 Tom Gugliotta 4.00 10.00
38 Vince Carter 8.00 20.00
39 Archie Goodwin 4.00 10.00
40 Vin Baker 8.00 20.00
41 Wayne Embry 4.00 10.00
43 Adrian Dantley 5.00 12.00
44 Antoine Walker 5.00 12.00
45 Alex English 5.00 12.00
46 Bailey Howell 6.00 15.00
47 Bill Laimbeer 5.00 12.00
48 Joe Dumars 6.00 15.00
51 Bruce Bowen 4.00 10.00
52 Eddie Johnson 4.00 10.00
53 Cedric Maxwell 4.00 10.00
54 Charlie Scott 5.00 12.00
55 Dolph Schayes 6.00 15.00
56 Darryl Dawkins 4.00 10.00
57 Dave Cowens 4.00 10.00
58 Dick Van Arsdale 5.00 12.00
59 Doug Collins 6.00 15.00
61 Fred Brown 4.00 10.00
62 Grant Hill 12.00 30.00
63 Jamal Mashburn 6.00 15.00
65 Jim Jackson 4.00 10.00
66 John Salley 6.00 15.00
67 John Starks 10.00 25.00
68 Keith Van Horn 5.00 12.00
69 Kendall Gill 4.00 10.00
70 David Thompson 5.00 12.00
71 Muggsy Bogues 5.00 12.00
72 Phil Chenier 4.00 10.00
73 Rick Mahorn 4.00 10.00
74 Sam Perkins 4.00 10.00
75 Scott Skiles 5.00 12.00
76 Spud Webb 5.00 12.00
77 Tom Van Arsdale 5.00 12.00
78 Vernon Maxwell 4.00 10.00
79 Vlade Divac 6.00 15.00

2014-15 Panini Gold Standard Black Gold Threads

STATED PRINT RUN B/WN 19-25 COPIES PER
1 Tim Duncan/25 12.00 30.00
2 Alonzo Mourning/25 6.00 15.00
3 Kevin Love/25 5.00 12.00
4 Bradley Beal/25 8.00 20.00
5 John Wall/25 6.00 15.00
6 Dwyane Wade/25 15.00 40.00
7 LeBron James/25 40.00 100.00
8 Kobe Bryant/25 20.00 50.00
9 Kevin Durant/25 12.00 30.00
10 Russell Westbrook/25 12.00 30.00
13 Dirk Nowitzki/25 12.00 30.00
14 Blake Griffin/25 12.00 30.00
15 Chris Paul/25 6.00 15.00
17 Joakim Noah/25 8.00 20.00
18 Brandon Jennings/25 3.00 8.00
19 Victor Oladipo/25 4.00 10.00
20 M.Carter-Williams/25 3.00 8.00
23 Stephen Curry/25 12.00 30.00
24 Deron Williams/25 4.00 10.00
25 Eric Gordon/25 4.00 10.00
26 Paul George/25 6.00 15.00
28 James Harden/25 12.00 30.00
30 DeMar DeRozan/25 5.00 12.00
31 LaMarcus Aldridge/25 8.00 20.00
32 John Stockton/25 12.00 30.00
33 Dominique Wilkins/25 6.00 15.00
34 Kevin McHale/25 5.00 12.00
35 Magic Johnson/25 12.00 30.00
36 Karl Malone/25 6.00 15.00
37 David Robinson/25 5.00 12.00
38 Isiah Thomas/25 5.00 12.00
39 Allen Iverson/25 6.00 15.00
40 Kevin Duckworth/25 3.00 8.00
41 Larry Johnson/25 6.00 15.00
42 Grant Hill/25 6.00 15.00
43 Shaquille O'Neal/25 10.00 25.00
44 Dikembe Mutombo/25 8.00 20.00
45 Antoine Walker/25 4.00 10.00
46 Dan Majerle/25 4.00 10.00
48 Kenneth Faried/25 4.00 10.00
49 Doc Rivers/25 5.00 12.00
50 Mark Jackson/25 4.00 10.00

2014-15 Panini Gold Standard Etched in Gold Autographs

STATED PRINT RUN B/WN 35-99 COPIES PER
2 Dan Issel/99 5.00 12.00
3 Vlade Divac/99 6.00 15.00
5 Jamaal Wilkes/99 6.00 15.00
6 Shaquille O'Neal/35 75.00 150.00
7 Latrell Sprewell/99 20.00 50.00
8 Adrian Dantley/99 5.00 12.00
9 Bobby Jones/99 5.00 12.00
10 Byron Scott/99 5.00 12.00
11 Cedric Maxwell/99 4.00 10.00
12 George Karl/60 6.00 15.00
13 Grant Hill/35 25.00 60.00
14 Jack Sikma/99 5.00 12.00
18 Mark Aguirre/99 5.00 12.00
19 Marques Johnson/99 5.00 12.00
20 Peja Stojakovic/35 6.00 15.00
21 Anfernee Hardaway/35 30.00 80.00

2014-15 Panini Gold Standard Freshly Minted

STATED PRINT RUN 25 SER.#'d SETS
1 Marcus Smart 10.00 25.00
2 Nikola Mirotic 20.00 50.00
3 Julius Randle 15.00 40.00
4 Elfrid Payton 25.00 60.00
5 K.J. McDaniels 15.00 40.00
6 Andrew Wiggins 200.00 400.00
7 Rodney Hood 12.00 30.00
8 T.J. Warren 10.00 25.00
9 Nik Stauskas 8.00 20.00
10 Noah Vonleh 8.00 20.00
11 Jabari Parker 40.00 100.00
12 Doug McDermott 25.00 60.00
13 Nick Johnson 12.00 30.00
14 Dante Exum 30.00 80.00
15 Zach LaVine 40.00 100.00
16 Jordan Adams 12.00 30.00
17 Shabazz Napier 8.00 20.00
18 Aaron Gordon 15.00 40.00
20 Mitch McGary 6.00 15.00
21 Gary Harris 10.00 25.00
22 P.J. Hairston 6.00 15.00
23 Adreian Payne 8.00 20.00
24 Joel Embiid 100.00 200.00
25 Bruno Caboclo 8.00 20.00
26 Cleanthony Early 6.00 15.00
27 C.J. Wilcox 6.00 15.00
28 Johnny O'Bryant 6.00 15.00
29 Glenn Robinson III 6.00 15.00

2014-15 Panini Gold Standard Gold Records

STATED PRINT RUN 25 SER.#'d SETS
1 Robert Parish 15.00 40.00
2 Kareem Abdul-Jabbar 25.00 60.00
3 John Stockton 12.00 30.00
4 Wilt Chamberlain 12.00 30.00
5 Hakeem Olajuwon 20.00 50.00
6 Oscar Robertson 20.00 50.00
7 Ray Allen 15.00 40.00
8 LeBron James 60.00 150.00
9 Kevin Durant 30.00 80.00
10 Artis Gilmore 12.00 30.00
11 Kobe Bryant 60.00 150.00
12 Elgin Baylor 15.00 40.00
13 Carmelo Anthony 30.00 80.00
14 Dave Cowens 10.00 25.00
15 Karl Malone 20.00 50.00
16 Dennis Rodman 20.00 50.00
17 Steve Nash 25.00 60.00
18 George Gervin 15.00 40.00
19 Stephen Curry 40.00 100.00
20 Moses Malone 15.00 40.00
21 Chris Paul 20.00 50.00
22 Dwight Howard 12.00 30.00
23 Scott Skiles 12.00 30.00
24 Michael Carter-Williams 15.00 40.00
25 Nate Archibald 10.00 25.00

2014-15 Panini Gold Standard Gold Rush Autographs

STATED PRINT RUN B/WN 50-199 COPIES PER
1 Isaiah Thomas/199 12.00 30.00
2 Maurice Harkless/199 4.00 10.00
3 Troy Daniels/199 4.00 10.00
4 Gorgui Dieng/199 4.00 10.00
5 M.Carter-Williams/75 4.00 10.00
6 Matthew Dellavedova/199 12.00 30.00
7 Pero Antic/199 4.00 10.00
8 Ryan Kelly/199 4.00 10.00
9 Mike Muscala/199 6.00 15.00
10 Gerald Henderson/199 4.00 10.00
11 Kendall Marshall/199 5.00 12.00
12 P.J. Tucker/199 4.00 10.00
14 Kevin Durant/50 50.00 120.00
15 Steve Blake/199 4.00 10.00
17 Robin Lopez/199 6.00 15.00
18 Taj Gibson/199 5.00 12.00
21 Draymond Green/199 8.00 20.00
22 Kenneth Faried/199 5.00 12.00
24 Jared Sullinger/75 4.00 10.00
25 Bradley Beal/75 10.00 25.00
26 Nate Wolters/199 5.00 12.00
27 Steven Adams/199 5.00 12.00
29 Goran Dragic/99 5.00 12.00
30 G.Antetokounmpo/199 40.00 100.00

2014-15 Panini Gold Standard Gold Scripts

STATED PRINT RUN B/WN 15-199 COPIES PER
NO PRICING ON QTY 15 OR LESS
1 K.J. McDaniels/199 5.00 12.00
2 Rodney Hood/199 6.00 15.00
3 T.J. Warren/199 6.00 15.00
4 Jordan Adams/199 4.00 10.00
5 Glenn Robinson III/199 4.00 10.00
6 Joe Harris/199 4.00 10.00
7 Russ Smith/199 4.00 10.00
8 Gary Harris/199 6.00 15.00
9 C.J. Wilcox/199 4.00 10.00
10 Zach LaVine/199 20.00 50.00
11 Mitch McGary/199 4.00 10.00
12 Dennis Schroder/199 5.00 12.00
13 Gorgui Dieng/199 4.00 10.00
14 Spencer Hawes/199 4.00 10.00
15 Reggie Bullock/199 4.00 10.00
16 P.J. Hairston/199 4.00 10.00
17 Tyler Ennis/99 4.00 10.00
18 Patric Young/199 4.00 10.00
19 Doug McDermott/199 6.00 15.00
20 Johnny O'Bryant/199 4.00 10.00
21 Nerlens Noel/199 5.00 12.00
22 Will Cherry/199 4.00 10.00
23 Erick Green/199 4.00 10.00
24 Jordan Clarkson/199 12.00 30.00
25 Jusuf Nurkic/199 6.00 15.00
26 Cameron Bairstow/199 4.00 10.00
27 Aaron Gordon/125 10.00 25.00
28 James Young/199 4.00 10.00
29 Shabazz Napier/199 5.00 12.00
30 Danny Green/199 5.00 12.00
31 Al-Farouq Aminu/199 4.00 10.00
32 Jason Terry/199 5.00 12.00
33 JaVale McGee/149 5.00 12.00
34 Jeff Green/149 5.00 12.00
35 Evan Fournier/149 4.00 10.00
36 Mason Plumlee/199 5.00 12.00
38 Tristan Thompson/199 5.00 12.00
39 Victor Oladipo/99 5.00 12.00
40 Udonis Haslem/199 4.00 10.00

2014-15 Panini Gold Standard Gold Strike Jersey Autographs

STATED PRINT RUN B/WN 49-199 COPIES PER
1 Nick Anderson/199 5.00 12.00
2 Glen Rice/199 5.00 12.00
3 Bill Laimbeer/199 5.00 12.00
7 Danny Green/149 5.00 12.00
8 Gerald Henderson/99 4.00 10.00
9 James Harden/49 40.00 100.00
10 Jimmy Butler/49 15.00 40.00
11 Jose Calderon/99 4.00 10.00
12 Dennis Schroder/199 5.00 12.00
13 Gorgui Dieng/199 4.00 10.00
14 Cleanthony Early/199 4.00 10.00
15 Russ Smith/199 4.00 10.00
16 Cory Jefferson/199 4.00 10.00
17 Johnny O'Bryant/199 4.00 10.00
18 Doug McDermott/199 6.00 15.00
19 Zach LaVine/199 20.00 50.00
20 T.J. Warren/199 6.00 15.00
21 Rodney Hood/199 6.00 15.00
22 P.J. Hairston/199 4.00 10.00
23 Jordan Adams/199 4.00 10.00
24 Bruno Caboclo/199 5.00 12.00
25 Adreian Payne/199 5.00 12.00
26 Marcus Smart/149 6.00 15.00
27 C.J. Wilcox/199 4.00 10.00
28 James Young/199 4.00 10.00
29 Elfrid Payton/199 6.00 15.00
30 Glenn Robinson III/199 4.00 10.00
31 Gary Harris/199 6.00 15.00
32 Joe Harris/199 4.00 10.00
33 Julius Randle/149 12.00 30.00
34 Markel Brown/199 4.00 10.00
35 James Ennis/199 4.00 10.00
36 Shabazz Napier/199 5.00 12.00
37 Spencer Dinwiddie/199 5.00 12.00
38 Jarnell Stokes/199 4.00 10.00
39 Nik Stauskas/199 5.00 12.00
40 Mitch McGary/199 4.00 10.00

2014-15 Panini Gold Standard Gold Strike Jersey Autographs Prime

*PRIME: .8X TO 2X BASE HI
STATED PRINT RUN 25 SER.#'d SETS
5 Mark Price 15.00 40.00
9 James Harden 50.00 120.00
10 Jimmy Butler 30.00 80.00
12 Dennis Schroder 12.00 30.00
24 Bruno Caboclo 25.00 60.00
31 Gary Harris 20.00 50.00

2014-15 Panini Gold Standard Golden Debuts

STATED PRINT RUN 50 SER.#'d SETS
1 Jusuf Nurkic 8.00 20.00
2 C.J. Wilcox 5.00 12.00
3 Nik Stauskas 6.00 15.00
4 Bruno Caboclo 6.00 15.00
5 Jarnell Stokes 5.00 12.00
6 Andrew Wiggins 75.00 150.00
7 Zach LaVine 12.00 30.00
8 Shabazz Napier 6.00 15.00
9 Dante Exum 12.00 30.00
10 Nick Johnson 5.00 12.00
11 James Young 5.00 12.00
12 Kyle Anderson 8.00 20.00
13 Noah Vonleh 6.00 15.00
14 Mitch McGary 5.00 12.00
15 Spencer Dinwiddie 6.00 15.00
16 Jabari Parker 12.00 30.00
17 T.J. Warren 8.00 20.00
18 Clint Capela 6.00 15.00
19 Marcus Smart 8.00 20.00
20 Markel Brown 5.00 12.00
21 Tyler Ennis 5.00 12.00
22 Cleanthony Early 5.00 12.00
23 Elfrid Payton 8.00 20.00
24 Jordan Adams 5.00 12.00
25 Glenn Robinson III 5.00 12.00
26 Aaron Gordon 12.00 30.00
27 Adreian Payne 6.00 15.00
28 P.J. Hairston 5.00 12.00
29 Julius Randle 12.00 30.00
30 Cory Jefferson 5.00 12.00
31 Gary Harris 8.00 20.00
32 Doug McDermott 8.00 20.00
33 Rodney Hood 8.00 20.00
34 Jordan Clarkson 8.00 20.00
35 Damien Inglis 5.00 12.00

2014-15 Panini Gold Standard Golden Pairs

STATED PRINT RUN 25 SER.#'d SETS
1 T.Duncan/T.Parker 25.00 60.00
2 A.Jefferson/K.Walker 6.00 15.00
3 C.Anthony/I.Shumpert 8.00 20.00
5 K.Durant/R.Westbrook 15.00 40.00
6 D.West/P.George 8.00 20.00
7 K.Thompson/S.Curry 40.00 100.00
8 D.Howard/J.Harden 25.00 60.00
9 D.Nowitzki/M.Ellis 8.00 20.00
10 M.Harkless/V.Oladipo 5.00 12.00
11 B.Griffin/C.Paul 25.00 60.00
12 E.Bledsoe/G.Dragic 5.00 12.00
14 B.Griffin/D.Jordan 15.00 40.00
15 M.Gasol/Z.Randolph 6.00 15.00
16 B.McLemore/D.Cousins 6.00 15.00
17 A.Horford/J.Teague 5.00 12.00
18 B.Beal/J.Wall 20.00 50.00
19 D.Williams/K.Garnett 10.00 25.00
20 C.Bosh/D.Wade 10.00 25.00
21 A.Davis/J.Holiday 12.00 30.00
22 D.DeRozan/K.Lowry 6.00 15.00
23 G.Hayward/T.Burke 6.00 15.00
24 D.Rose/J.Noah 25.00 60.00
25 B.Jennings/J.Smith 12.00 30.00
26 B.Knight/L.Sanders 5.00 12.00
27 K.Faried/T.Lawson 10.00 25.00
28 D.Lillard/L.Aldridge 12.00 30.00
29 J.Richardson/M.Carter-Williams 6.00 15.00
30 A.Bradley/J.Sullinger 5.00 12.00
31 D.Rodman/S.Pippen 75.00 150.00
32 J.Stockton/K.Malone 30.00 80.00
33 I.Thomas/J.Dumars 6.00 15.00
34 T.McGrady/Y.Ming 40.00 100.00
35 A.Hardaway/S.O'Neal 15.00 40.00
36 J.Starks/P.Ewing 8.00 20.00
37 K.McHale/L.Bird 15.00 40.00
38 C.Robinson/K.Duckworth 4.00 10.00
39 K.Bryant/S.O'Neal 25.00 60.00
40 G.Robinson/R.Allen 30.00 80.00
41 D.Robinson/S.Elliott 10.00 25.00
42 C.Mullin/T.Hardaway 25.00 60.00
43 A.Iverson/D.Mutombo 40.00 100.00
44 K.Abdul-Jabbar/M.Johnson 15.00 40.00
45 B.Laimbeer/R.Mahorn 10.00 25.00

2014-15 Panini Gold Standard Golden Quads

STATED PRINT RUN B/WN 9-25 COPIES PER
NO PRICING ON QTY 10 OR LESS
3 Jffrsn/Csns/Hwrd/Nh/25 15.00 40.00
4 Dvs/Grffn/Nwtzki/Aldrdge/25 40.00 100.00
5 Pl/Rse/Wstbrk/Crry/25 80.00 200.00
6 Rse/Nh/Hnrch/Gbsn/25 25.00 60.00
7 Bgt/Le/Thmpsn/Crry/25 80.00 200.00
8 Lnrd/Gnbli/Dncn/Prkr/25 75.00 150.00
9 Grffn/Pl/Jrdn/Rdck/25 75.00 150.00
10 Llrd/Aldrdge/Btm/Mtthws/25 40.00 100.00
11 Bl/Rce/Wll/Nne/25 25.00 60.00
13 Andrsn/Bsh/Wde/Chlmrs/25 100.00 200.00
14 Drnt/Cllsn/Wstbrk/Ibka/20 40.00 100.00
16 Gsl/Cnly/Alln/Rndlph/25 30.00 80.00
18 Grdn/Prkr/Smrt/Vnlh/25 30.00 80.00
19 Wggns/McDrmtt/Rndle/Stsks/25 60.00 150.00
20 Wggns/Pytn/Prkr/LVne/25 60.00 150.00

2014-15 Panini Gold Standard Golden Trios

STATED PRINT RUN B/WN 3-25 COPIES PER
NO PRICING ON QTY 3 OR LESS
2 Gordon/Exum/Smart 15.00 40.00
3 Wiggins/Parker/Randle 75.00 150.00
4 Wiggins/Embiid/Smart 30.00 80.00
5 McDermott/Payton/Stauskas 10.00 25.00
7 Durant/Westbrook/Ibaka 25.00 60.00
8 Rose/Butler/Noah 40.00 100.00
9 Ginobili/Duncan/Parker 40.00 100.00
10 Hill/Bryant/Sacre 40.00 100.00
11 Griffin/Paul/Jordan 50.00 120.00
12 Andersen/Bosh/Wade 40.00 100.00
13 Lee/Thompson/Curry 30.00 80.00
16 Howard/Harden/Jones 40.00 100.00
17 Sullinger/Green/Rondo 10.00 25.00
18 Gasol/Conley/Randolph 20.00 50.00
19 Lillard/Aldridge/Matthews 20.00 50.00
21 Jefferson/Walker/Kidd-Gilchrist 10.00 25.00
22 Wright/Nowitzki/Ellis 30.00 80.00
23 DeRozan/Lowry/Ross 12.00 30.00
24 Lopez/Williams/Johnson 8.00 20.00
25 West/George/Hibbert 12.00 30.00
26 Paul/Wall/Rondo 12.00 30.00
27 Durant/Bryant/James 150.00 300.00
28 Cousins/Howard/Noah 10.00 25.00
29 Davis/Griffin/Duncan 40.00 100.00
30 Wade/Harden/Thompson 40.00 100.00
31 Lillard/Westbrook/Curry 30.00 80.00
32 Anthony/Wade/James 40.00 100.00
33 Erving/Bird/Johnson 75.00 150.00
34 Olajuwon/Malone/Ewing 50.00 120.00

2014-15 Panini Gold Standard Good as Gold Jersey Autographs

STATED PRINT RUN B/WN 35-199 COPIES PER
1 Archie Goodwin/199 4.00 10.00
2 Bradley Beal/49 10.00 25.00
3 Enes Kanter/149 4.00 10.00
4 Chris Copeland/199 4.00 10.00
5 Dennis Rodman/35 20.00 50.00
6 Dennis Schroder/199 5.00 12.00
7 Zydrunas Ilgauskas/199 5.00 12.00
9 Greg Monroe/99 5.00 12.00
10 Isiah Thomas/50 10.00 25.00
12 James Worthy/35 10.00 25.00
13 John Henson/35 4.00 10.00
14 John Wall/35 12.00 30.00
15 Kelly Olynyk/199 4.00 10.00
16 Nate Wolters/199 5.00 12.00
17 Mike Conley/49 5.00 12.00
18 Larry Johnson/199 8.00 20.00
19 Xavier McDaniel/199 4.00 10.00
20 Jordan Hill/49 4.00 10.00
21 Jonas Valanciunas/60 5.00 12.00
22 Jeff Hornacek/149 5.00 12.00
23 Hakeem Olajuwon/35 15.00 40.00
25 Rolando Blackman/149 5.00 12.00

2014-15 Panini Gold Standard Good as Gold Jersey Autographs Prime

*PRIME: .8X TO 2X BASE HI
STATED PRINT RUN 25 SER.#'d SETS
5 Dennis Rodman 30.00 80.00
6 Dennis Schroder 25.00 60.00
14 John Wall 30.00 80.00
22 Jeff Hornacek 12.00 30.00
23 Hakeem Olajuwon 25.00 60.00

2014-15 Panini Gold Standard Marks of Gold Jersey Autographs

STATED PRINT RUN B/WN 49-199 COPIES PER
1 A.C. Green/99 6.00 15.00
2 Anfernee Hardaway/49 20.00 50.00
3 Antoine Walker/199 5.00 12.00
4 Bill Laimbeer/199 5.00 12.00
5 Byron Scott/99 5.00 12.00
6 Carmelo Anthony/49 20.00 50.00
7 Chris Mullin/199 6.00 15.00
8 Dan Majerle/199 5.00 12.00
9 David West/49 5.00 12.00
10 Dikembe Mutombo/99 10.00 25.00
11 Fred Brown/199 4.00 10.00
12 Grant Hill/75 10.00 25.00
13 Harrison Barnes/49 5.00 12.00
14 Jodie Meeks/199 5.00 12.00
15 JaVale McGee/75 5.00 12.00
16 Jeff Green/99 5.00 12.00
18 Alan Anderson/199 4.00 10.00
19 Clifford Robinson/199 4.00 10.00
21 LaMarcus Aldridge/49 15.00 40.00
22 Klay Thompson/75 30.00 80.00
25 M.Carter-Williams/125 4.00 10.00
27 Reggie Jackson/199 6.00 15.00
29 Stephen Curry/49 125.00 250.00
30 Brandan Wright/199 4.00 10.00
31 Thaddeus Young/199 4.00 10.00
32 Tim Hardaway/199 8.00 20.00
33 Tony Snell/199 4.00 10.00
34 Trey Burke/125 4.00 10.00
35 Marques Johnson/199 5.00 12.00

2014-15 Panini Gold Standard Marks of Gold Jersey Autographs Prime

*PRIME: .6X TO 1.5X BASE HI
STATED PRINT RUN B/WN 12-25 SER.#'d SETS
NO PRICING ON QTY 12 OR LESS
1 A.C. Green/25 20.00 50.00
9 David West/25 20.00 50.00
27 Reggie Jackson/25 15.00 40.00
28 Sidney Moncrief/25 12.00 30.00

2014-15 Panini Gold Standard Mother Lode Autographs

STATED PRINT RUN B/WN 35-199 COPIES PER
1 Dan Issel 4.00 10.00
2 Adrian Dantley 4.00 10.00
3 Alex English 4.00 10.00
4 David Thompson 4.00 10.00
5 Arvydas Sabonis 8.00 20.00
6 John Salley 3.00 8.00
7 Jamaal Wilkes 5.00 12.00
8 B.J. Armstrong 8.00 20.00
9 Bruce Bowen 3.00 8.00
10 Charlie Scott 4.00 10.00
11 Chet Walker 4.00 10.00
12 Eddie Jones 4.00 10.00
13 Horace Grant 10.00 25.00
14 Jon McGlocklin 4.00 10.00
15 Mark Price 5.00 12.00
16 Marques Johnson 4.00 10.00
17 Michael Cooper 4.00 10.00
18 Sam Perkins 3.00 8.00
19 Spud Webb 4.00 10.00
20 Tim Hardaway 5.00 12.00
21 Tracy McGrady 25.00 60.00
22 Vlade Divac 5.00 12.00
23 Zydrunas Ilgauskas 4.00 10.00
24 Toni Kukoc 5.00 12.00
25 Robert Horry 4.00 10.00
26 Larry Johnson 6.00 15.00
27 Nick Van Exel 5.00 12.00
28 Bill Walton 5.00 12.00
29 Anfernee Hardaway 20.00 50.00
30 John Stockton 20.00 50.00

2014-15 Panini Gold Standard Newly Minted Memorabilia

STATED PRINT RUN 25 SER.#'d SETS
NMMS Marcus Smart 12.00 30.00
NMRH Rodney Hood 20.00 50.00
NMDM Doug McDermott 10.00 25.00
NMCW C.J. Wilcox 3.00 8.00
NMAP Adreian Payne 10.00 25.00
NMAG Aaron Gordon 8.00 20.00
NMTE Tyler Ennis 8.00 20.00
NMJE Joel Embiid 20.00 50.00
NMJP Jabari Parker 20.00 50.00
NMMM Mitch McGary 15.00 40.00
NMNV Noah Vonleh 4.00 10.00
NMSN Shabazz Napier 4.00 10.00
NMZL Zach LaVine 25.00 60.00
NMCE Cleanthony Early 10.00 25.00
NMJY James Young 3.00 8.00
NMAW Andrew Wiggins 50.00 120.00
NMGH Gary Harris 5.00 12.00
NMDE Dante Exum 25.00 60.00
NMJA Jordan Adams 3.00 8.00
NMEP Elfrid Payton 5.00 12.00
NMPH P.J. Hairston 3.00 8.00

2014-15 Panini Gold Standard Newly Minted Memorabilia Duals

STATED PRINT RUN 25 SER.#'d SETS
1 J.Parker/J.Randle 20.00 50.00
2 J.Young/M.Smart 6.00 15.00
3 C.Jefferson/M.Brown 4.00 10.00
4 N.Vonleh/P.Hairston 5.00 12.00
5 J.Stokes/J.Adams 4.00 10.00
6 J.Ennis/S.Napier 15.00 40.00
7 A.Gordon/E.Payton 10.00 25.00
8 T.Warren/T.Ennis 6.00 15.00
10 A.Wiggins/J.Embiid 100.00 200.00
12 M.Smart/M.Brown 10.00 25.00
13 J.Grant/T.Ennis 4.00 10.00
14 P.Hairston/R.Hood 6.00 15.00
15 C.Jefferson/D.McDermott 6.00 15.00
16 G.Harris/N.Stauskas 6.00 15.00
17 A.Payne/M.McGary 5.00 12.00
18 A.Wiggins/J.Randle 100.00 200.00
20 A.Gordon/Z.LaVine 10.00 25.00
21 A.Wiggins/J.Parker 75.00 150.00
22 A.Gordon/J.Embiid 20.00 50.00
23 D.Exum/M.Smart 15.00 40.00
24 J.Randle/N.Stauskas 10.00 25.00

2014-15 Panini Gold Standard Newly Minted Memorabilia Quads

STATED PRINT RUN 25 SER.#'d SETS
1 Jffrsn/Yng/Smrt/Brwn 12.00 30.00
2 Cbclo/Ealy/Embd/McDnls 40.00 100.00
3 McDrmtt/Prkr/Hrrs/Dnwdde 25.00 60.00
4 Grdn/Pytn/Enns/Npr 20.00 50.00
7 Enns/Vnlh/Hrstn/Npr 25.00 60.00
8 Wggns/Exm/Hod/LVne 40.00 100.00
9 Wlcx/Rndle/Wrrn/Enns 20.00 50.00
11 Prkr/Hrstn/Hod/Wrrn 15.00 40.00
12 Wggns/Yng/Embd/Rndle 40.00 100.00
13 Pyne/Hrrs/McGry/Stsks 12.00 30.00
14 Rbnsn/Yng/Rndle/Stsks 10.00 25.00
15 Prkr/Hrrs/McDnls/Wrrn 20.00 50.00
16 Grdn/Wggns/Prkr/Embd 125.00 250.00
17 Exm/Rndle/Smrt/Stsks 20.00 50.00
18 McDrmtt/Pytn/Vnlh/LVne 20.00 50.00
19 Pyne/Yng/Wrrn/Enns 12.00 30.00
21 Wlcx/Hrstn/Hod/Npr 12.00 30.00
22 Ealy/Ingls/Hrrs/McDnls 30.00 80.00

2014-15 Panini Gold Standard Newly Minted Memorabilia Triples

STATED PRINT RUN 25 SER.#'d SETS
2 Wiggins/Robinson III/LaVine 40.00 100.00
3 Grant/Embiid/McDaniels 20.00 50.00
4 Caboclo/Inglis/Exum 10.00 25.00
5 Robinson/McGary/Stauskas 5.00 12.00
6 Adams/Anderson/LaVine 10.00 25.00
7 Parker/Hairston/Hood 10.00 25.00
8 Grant/Napier/Ennis 5.00 12.00
10 Harris/McDaniels/Warren 12.00 30.00
11 Randle/Smith/Napier 10.00 25.00
12 Jefferson/Smart/Brown 6.00 15.00
14 Gordon/Wilcox/Dinwiddie 10.00 25.00
15 Early/McDermott/Ennis 6.00 15.00
16 Wiggins/Parker/Embiid 40.00 100.00
17 Gordon/Exum/Smart 10.00 25.00
18 Randle/Stauskas/Vonleh 10.00 25.00
19 McDermott/Payton/LaVine 25.00 60.00
20 Payne/Young/Warren 6.00 15.00
21 Caboclo/Harris/Ennis 6.00 15.00
22 Adams/McGary/Hood 6.00 15.00
23 Wilcox/Hairston/Napier 6.00 15.00
24 Wiggins/Parker/Randle 40.00 100.00
25 Wiggins/Exum/Parker 100.00 200.00

2014-15 Panini Gold Standard Ring Bearers Autographs

STATED PRINT RUN B/WN 25-199 COPIES PER
1 Phil Jackson 150.00 300.00
3 Rick Carlisle 15.00 40.00
4 Doc Rivers 10.00 25.00
5 Lenny Wilkens 10.00 25.00
7 Magic Johnson 40.00 100.00
8 Kobe Bryant 150.00 250.00
9 Bill Wennington 8.00 20.00
10 Tony Parker 30.00 80.00
11 Bruce Bowen 6.00 15.00
12 Shaquille O'Neal 100.00 250.00
13 Udonis Haslem 6.00 15.00
14 Antoine Walker 8.00 20.00
15 Derek Anderson 6.00 15.00
16 Gary Payton 25.00 60.00
17 Tiago Splitter 8.00 20.00
18 Robert Horry 8.00 20.00
19 Jason Kidd 30.00 80.00
20 Hakeem Olajuwon 15.00 40.00
21 Kawhi Leonard 60.00 150.00
22 Toni Kukoc 10.00 25.00
23 David Robinson 25.00 60.00
24 Kareem Abdul-Jabbar 25.00 60.00
25 James Worthy 15.00 40.00
26 Ray Allen 30.00 80.00
27 Mark Aguirre 6.00 15.00
28 John Salley 6.00 15.00
29 James Jones 6.00 15.00
30 Sean Elliott 10.00 25.00

2014-15 Panini Gold Standard Rookie Jersey Autographs Prime

*PRIME/25: .75X TO 2X JSY AU/149-199
*PRIME/25: .75X TO 2X JSY AU/99
STATED PRINT RUN 25 SER.#'d SETS
201 Andrew Wiggins 400.00 600.00
202 Jabari Parker 150.00 250.00
205 Dante Exum 40.00 100.00
207 Marcus Smart 25.00 60.00
208 Cleanthony Early 12.00 30.00
210 Aaron Gordon 40.00 100.00
211 Elfrid Payton 50.00 120.00
217 Kyle Anderson 30.00 80.00
219 Zach LaVine 100.00 200.00
220 Spencer Dinwiddie 12.00 30.00
221 Rodney Hood 15.00 40.00
222 T.J. Warren 15.00 40.00
226 Adreian Payne 20.00 50.00
227 K.J. McDaniels 30.00 80.00
238 Dante Exum 30.00 80.00
241 Cleanthony Early 15.00 40.00
242 James Young 20.00 50.00
243 Aaron Gordon 30.00 80.00
244 Elfrid Payton 50.00 120.00
245 Bruno Caboclo 30.00 80.00
247 Gary Harris 15.00 40.00
251 Russ Smith 15.00 40.00
252 Zach LaVine 100.00 200.00
253 Spencer Dinwiddie 15.00 40.00
254 Rodney Hood 20.00 50.00
256 Tyler Ennis 25.00 60.00
258 Doug McDermott 50.00 120.00
259 Adreian Payne 15.00 40.00
260 K.J. McDaniels 30.00 80.00
261 Nik Stauskas 30.00 80.00
264 Johnny O'Bryant 15.00 40.00
266 Damien Inglis 15.00 40.00
269 Julius Randle 75.00 150.00
270 Joel Embiid 75.00 200.00
271 Dante Exum 50.00 120.00
273 Marcus Smart 75.00 150.00
275 James Young 10.00 25.00
276 Aaron Gordon 75.00 150.00
277 Elfrid Payton 75.00 150.00
278 Bruno Caboclo 40.00 100.00
279 James Ennis 30.00 80.00
281 Glenn Robinson III 25.00 60.00
283 Kyle Anderson 30.00 80.00
284 Russ Smith 15.00 40.00
285 Zach LaVine 250.00 500.00
287 Rodney Hood 15.00 40.00
291 Doug McDermott 40.00 100.00
293 K.J. McDaniels 40.00 100.00
295 Noah Vonleh 30.00 80.00
296 Mitch McGary 75.00 150.00

2014-15 Panini Gold Standard Superscribe Autographs

STATED PRINT RUN B/WN 50-199 COPIES PER
1 Victor Oladipo 5.00 12.00
2 Kenneth Faried 8.00 20.00
3 Xavier Henry 4.00 10.00
4 John Wall 20.00 50.00
5 Luigi Datome 4.00 10.00
6 Tony Parker 20.00 50.00
7 Stephen Curry 125.00 250.00
8 Phil Chenier 4.00 10.00
10 Sidney Moncrief 4.00 10.00
11 Toni Kukoc 8.00 20.00
12 Travis Best 5.00 12.00
13 Will Perdue 4.00 10.00
14 World B. Free 5.00 12.00
15 Thabo Sefolosha 4.00 10.00
16 Mychal Thompson 6.00 15.00
17 Archie Goodwin 4.00 10.00
18 Kelly Olynyk 4.00 10.00
19 Ryan Kelly 4.00 10.00
20 Steven Adams 5.00 12.00
21 Tim Hardaway 6.00 15.00
22 Danilo Gallinari 4.00 10.00
23 Mike Conley 5.00 12.00
24 Gorgui Dieng 4.00 10.00
25 Cory Jefferson 4.00 10.00
26 Latrell Sprewell 40.00 100.00
28 Devyn Marble 4.00 10.00
29 Lance Stephenson 5.00 12.00
30 Brook Lopez 5.00 12.00
31 Bradley Beal 6.00 15.00
32 Mike Muscala 4.00 10.00
33 Troy Daniels 4.00 10.00
36 Andre Miller 5.00 12.00
37 Danny Green 5.00 12.00
38 Richard Jefferson 5.00 12.00
39 Robin Lopez 8.00 20.00
40 Michael Kidd-Gilchrist 5.00 12.00

2014-15 Panini Gold Standard Vintage Gold

STATED PRINT RUN 20 SER.#'d SETS
1 Kareem Abdul-Jabbar 15.00 40.00
2 Larry Bird 25.00 60.00
3 Shaquille O'Neal 40.00 100.00
4 David Robinson 15.00 40.00
5 John Stockton 15.00 40.00
6 Julius Erving 15.00 40.00
7 Magic Johnson 25.00 60.00
8 Hakeem Olajuwon 12.00 30.00
9 Patrick Ewing 25.00 60.00
11 Clyde Drexler 12.00 30.00
12 John Havlicek 12.00 30.00
13 Karl Malone 12.00 30.00
14 Scottie Pippen 20.00 50.00
15 Isiah Thomas 10.00 25.00
16 Dominique Wilkins 12.00 30.00
17 Bill Walton 10.00 25.00
18 Nate Thurmond 8.00 20.00
19 Bill Russell 10.00 25.00
20 Tracy McGrady 10.00 25.00
22 Allen Iverson 20.00 50.00
23 Shawn Kemp 25.00 60.00
24 Grant Hill 20.00 50.00
25 Chris Webber 20.00 50.00

2014-15 Panini Gold Standard White Gold Threads

STATED PRINT RUN 49 SER.#'d SETS
1 Tim Duncan 10.00 25.00

4 Eric Bledsoe 5.00 12.00
5 Nikola Vucevic 5.00 12.00
6 LeBron James 25.00 60.00
7 Kevin Love 6.00 15.00
8 Dwight Howard 5.00 12.00
9 Nicolas Batum 5.00 12.00
10 Kemba Walker 4.00 10.00
11 Victor Oladipo 4.00 10.00
13 Josh Smith 5.00 12.00
14 J.R. Smith 5.00 12.00
15 Kelly Olynyk 4.00 10.00
17 Carmelo Anthony 8.00 20.00
19 Tony Parker 6.00 15.00
20 Mike Conley 5.00 12.00
23 Dirk Nowitzki 8.00 20.00
24 Kevin Durant 10.00 25.00
25 Tiago Splitter 5.00 12.00
27 Otto Porter 5.00 12.00
28 Markieff Morris 4.00 10.00
32 Michael Carter-Williams 5.00 12.00
33 Marc Gasol 6.00 15.00
34 Russell Westbrook 15.00 40.00
36 Gary Payton 6.00 15.00
39 Clyde Drexler 15.00 40.00
40 Chris Mullin 6.00 15.00
43 Dikembe Mutombo 6.00 15.00
44 Clifford Robinson 4.00 10.00
47 Yao Ming 8.00 20.00
49 Bobby Jackson 10.00 25.00
50 Michael Finley 4.00 10.00

2014-15 Panini Gold Standard White Gold Threads Prime

*PRIME: .6X TO 1.5X BASE HI
STATED PRINT RUN B/WN 6-25 COPIES PER
NO PRICING ON QTY 6 OR LESS
12 Manu Ginobili/25 25.00 60.00
19 Tony Parker/25 15.00 40.00
27 Otto Porter/25 10.00 25.00
30 Kentavious Caldwell-Pope/25 8.00 20.00
32 M.Carter-Williams/25 8.00 20.00
37 Bill Cartwright/25 6.00 15.00
38 Alvan Adams/25 8.00 20.00
42 Jason Kidd/25 15.00 40.00
50 Michael Finley/25 10.00 25.00

2015-16 Panini Gold Standard

1-200 PRINT RUN 299 SER.#'d SETS
PHT VAR COMBINED P/R OF 299
TEAM VAR COMBINED P/R OF 299
TEAM VAR SP COMBINED P/R OF 299
JSY AU RANDOMLY INSERTED
JSY AU PRINT RUNS B/WN 49-199
EXCHANGE DEADLINE 8/17/2017
1A Curry Black jsy 12.00 30.00
1B Curry White jsy 12.00 30.00
1C Curry Blue jsy 12.00 30.00
2 Tony Parker 1.50 4.00
3 Randy Foye 1.00 2.50
4 Brandon Knight 1.25 3.00
5 Jrue Holiday 1.25 3.00
6A Irving Yellow jsy 3.00 8.00
6B Irving Red jsy 3.00 8.00
6C Irving White jsy 3.00 8.00
7 Jeff Teague 1.25 3.00
8 Ricky Rubio 1.50 4.00
9 Kyle Lowry 1.25 3.00
10 Mike Conley 1.50 4.00
11 Klay Thompson 2.00 5.00
12 Manu Ginobili 1.50 4.00
13 Wilson Chandler 1.25 3.00
14 Eric Bledsoe 1.25 3.00
15 Eric Gordon 1.25 3.00
16A LeBron Yellow jsy 6.00 15.00
16B LeBron White jsy 6.00 15.00
16C LeBron Red jsy 6.00 15.00
17 Kyle Korver 1.25 3.00
18 Zach LaVine 1.50 4.00
19 DeMar DeRozan 1.50 4.00
20 Vince Carter 2.00 5.00
21 Andre Iguodala 1.25 3.00
22 Kawhi Leonard 2.50 6.00
23 Danilo Gallinari 1.25 3.00
24 P.J. Tucker 1.00 2.50
25 Tyreke Evans 1.00 2.50
26 Kevin Love 1.50 4.00
27 Thabo Sefolosha 1.00 2.50
28 Kevin Martin 1.25 3.00
29 Terrence Ross 1.25 3.00
30 Tony Allen 1.00 2.50
31 Draymond Green 2.00 5.00
32 LaMarcus Aldridge 1.50 4.00
33 Kenneth Faried 1.25 3.00
34 Markieff Morris 1.00 2.50
35A A.Davis Red jsy 3.00 8.00
35B A.Davis Blue jsy 3.00 8.00
35C A.Davis White jsy 3.00 8.00
36 Tristan Thompson 1.25 3.00
37 Paul Millsap 1.50 4.00
38A Wiggins Black jsy 2.50 6.00
38B Wiggins Blue jsy 2.50 6.00
38C Wiggins White jsy 2.50 6.00
39 DeMarre Carroll 1.00 2.50
40 Zach Randolph 1.25 3.00
41 Andrew Bogut 1.25 3.00
42 Tim Duncan 2.50 6.00
43 Jusuf Nurkic 1.00 2.50
44 Tyson Chandler 1.25 3.00
45 Omer Asik 1.25 3.00
46 Matthew Dellavedova 1.25 3.00
47 Al Horford 1.25 3.00
48A Garnett T'wolves 2.50 6.00
48B Garnett Celtics 6.00 15.00
48C Garnett Nets SP 50.00 120.00
48D Garnett USA 5.00 12.00
48E Garnett Wolves Blk 5.00 12.00
49 Jonas Valanciunas 1.25 3.00
50 Marc Gasol 1.50 4.00
51 J.J. Redick 1.50 4.00
52 Alec Burks 1.00 2.50
53 Ty Lawson 1.00 2.50
54A Rajon Rondo Kings 1.50 4.00
54B Rajon Rondo Mavericks 3.00 8.00
54C Rajon Rondo Celtics 3.00 8.00
54D Rondo Wildcats SP 25.00 60.00
55 Elfrid Payton 1.25 3.00
56 Reggie Jackson 1.25 3.00
57 Kemba Walker 1.50 4.00
58 Jose Calderon 1.00 2.50
59 Jarrett Jack 1.25 3.00
60 Michael Carter-Williams 1.00 2.50
61A Pierce Clippers 1.50 4.00
61B Pierce Nets SP
61C Pierce Jayhawks SP
61D Pierce Wizards 3.00 8.00
61E Pierce Celtics 3.00 8.00
62 Trey Burke 1.00 2.50
63A Harden Rockets 2.50 6.00
63B Harden Sun Devils SP 40.00 100.00
63C Harden Thunder 5.00 12.00
63D Harden USA SP 40.00 100.00
64 Ben McLemore 1.00 2.50
65 Victor Oladipo 1.25 3.00
66 Brandon Jennings 1.00 2.50
67 Nicolas Batum 1.25 3.00
68 Arron Afflalo 1.00 2.50
69 Joe Johnson 1.25 3.00
70 Giannis Antetokounmpo 3.00 8.00
71A C.Paul Dribbling 2.00 5.00
71B C.Paul Holding ball 2.00 5.00
71C C.Paul Red jsy 2.00 5.00
72 Gordon Hayward 1.50 4.00
73 Trevor Ariza 1.00 2.50
74 Rudy Gay 1.50 4.00
75 Tobias Harris 1.25 3.00
76 Kentavious Caldwell-Pope 1.25 3.00
77 Michael Kidd-Gilchrist 1.25 3.00
78A Carmelo Ornge sleeve 2.00 5.00
78B Carmelo Black sleeve 2.00 5.00
78C Carmelo White jsy 2.00 5.00
79 Bojan Bogdanovic 1.00 2.50
80 Khris Middleton 1.25 3.00
81 Blake Griffin 1.50 4.00
82 Derrick Favors 1.25 3.00
83 Terrence Jones 1.25 3.00
84 DeMarcus Cousins 1.50 4.00
85 Aaron Gordon 1.25 3.00
86 Andre Drummond 1.50 4.00
87 Jeremy Lin 1.50 4.00
88 Langston Galloway 1.00 2.50
89 Thaddeus Young 1.00 2.50
90 Jabari Parker 2.00 5.00
91 DeAndre Jordan 1.50 4.00
92 Rudy Gobert 1.50 4.00
93 Dwight Howard 1.25 3.00
94 Darren Collison 1.25 3.00
95 Nikola Vucevic 1.25 3.00
96 Ersan Ilyasova 1.00 2.50
97 Al Jefferson 1.25 3.00
98 Robin Lopez 1.00 2.50
99 Brook Lopez 1.25 3.00
100 Greg Monroe 1.25 3.00
101A Goran Dragic Heat 1.25 3.00
101B Goran Dragic Suns 2.50 6.00
101C Goran Dragic Rockets 2.50 6.00
102 Marcus Smart 1.25 3.00
103 Jordan Clarkson 1.50 4.00
104A Wall Blue shorts 2.00 5.00
104B Wall White shorts 2.00 5.00
104C Wall Red shorts 2.00 5.00
105A Lillard Red jsy 3.00 8.00
105B Lillard Black jsy 3.00 8.00
106 George Hill 1.25 3.00
107 Deron Williams 1.25 3.00
108 Tony Wroten 1.00 2.50
109A D.Rose Black jsy 2.00 5.00
109B D.Rose Red jsy 2.00 5.00
109C D.Rose White jsy 2.00 5.00
110A Westbrook Orange jsy 4.00 10.00
110B Westbrook Blue jsy 4.00 10.00
110C Westbrook White jsy 4.00 10.00
111A D.Wade Red jsy 2.50 6.00
111B D.Wade Black jsy 2.50 6.00
111C D.Wade White jsy 2.50 6.00
112 Avery Bradley 1.25 3.00
113A Kobe Black jsy 6.00 15.00
113B Kobe Purple jsy 6.00 15.00
113C Kobe Yellow jsy 6.00 15.00
114 Bradley Beal 1.50 4.00
115 Gerald Henderson 1.00 2.50
116 Monta Ellis 1.25 3.00
117 Wesley Matthews 1.00 2.50
118 Robert Covington 1.00 2.50
119 Jimmy Butler 1.50 4.00
120 Dion Waiters 1.25 3.00
121 Luol Deng 1.25 3.00
122 Evan Turner 1.25 3.00
123 Nick Young 1.25 3.00
124 Otto Porter Jr. 1.25 3.00
125 Al-Farouq Aminu 1.25 3.00
126 Paul George 2.00 5.00
127 Chandler Parsons 1.25 3.00
128 Nerlens Noel 1.25 3.00
129 Pau Gasol 1.50 4.00
130A Durant Two hand on ball 4.00 10.00
130B Durant Dribbling 4.00 10.00
130C Durant White jsy 4.00 10.00
131 Chris Bosh 1.50 4.00
132 David Lee 1.00 2.50
133 Julius Randle 1.50 4.00
134 Nene 1.25 3.00
135 Mason Plumlee 1.25 3.00
136 Chase Budinger 1.00 2.50
137A Dirk Dark blue jsy 2.00 5.00
137B Dirk White jsy 2.00 5.00
137C Dirk Blue jsy 2.00 5.00
138 Nik Stauskas 1.00 2.50
139 Nikola Mirotic 1.25 3.00
140 Serge Ibaka 1.25 3.00
141 Hassan Whiteside 1.25 3.00
142 Jared Sullinger 1.00 2.50
143 Roy Hibbert 1.25 3.00
144 Marcin Gortat 1.25 3.00
145 Noah Vonleh 1.00 2.50
146 Jordan Hill 1.00 2.50
147 Devin Harris 1.00 2.50
148 JaKarr Sampson 1.00 2.50
149 Joakim Noah 1.25 3.00
150 Enes Kanter 1.00 2.50
151A Damon Stoudamire Raptors 1.25 3.00
151B Damon Stoudamire Trail Blazers 2.50 6.00
151C Stdmre Spurs SP 40.00 100.00
151D Stdmre Wildcats SP 40.00 100.00
151E Damon Stoudamire Grizzlies 2.50 6.00
152 Jerry West 2.00 5.00
153 Dino Radja 1.00 2.50
154 Kevin McHale 1.50 4.00
155 Grant Hill 2.00 5.00
156 Mike Bibby 1.25 3.00
157 Allen Iverson 2.00 5.00
158 Robert Horry 1.25 3.00
159 Baron Davis 1.25 3.00
160 Steve Kerr 1.50 4.00
161 David Robinson 2.50 6.00
162 John Starks 1.25 3.00
163 Dominique Wilkins 2.00 5.00
164 Larry Bird 4.00 10.00
165 Hakeem Olajuwon 2.00 5.00
166 Patrick Ewing 2.00 5.00
167 Alonzo Mourning 2.00 5.00
168 Rony Seikaly 1.00 2.50
169 Bill Russell 2.50 6.00
170 Tracy McGrady 1.50 4.00
171 Dennis Johnson 1.25 3.00
172 John Stockton 2.50 6.00
173 Drazen Petrovic 1.50 4.00
174 Latrell Sprewell 1.25 3.00
175 Jason Kidd 1.50 4.00
176A Maravich Hawks 2.50 6.00
176B Maravich Tigers SP
176C Maravich Celtics SP 50.00 120.00
176D Maravich Jazz 6.00 15.00
177 Anfernee Hardaway 4.00 10.00
178 Scottie Pippen 3.00 8.00
179 Chris Mullin 1.50 4.00
180 Vlade Divac 1.50 4.00
181 Dennis Rodman 3.00 8.00
182 Julius Erving 2.50 6.00
183 Gary Payton 1.50 4.00
184 Magic Johnson 4.00 10.00
185 Elgin Baylor 1.50 4.00
186 Ralph Sampson 1.25 3.00
187 Antonio McDyess 1.25 3.00
188 Shaquille O'Neal 3.00 8.00
189 Christian Laettner 1.25 3.00
190A Wilt Lakers 3.00 8.00
190B Wilt Jayhawks SP 60.00 150.00
190C Wilt 76ers 20.00 50.00
190D Wilt Phil.Warriors 20.00 50.00
190E Wilt SF Warriors 10.00 25.00
191 Dikembe Mutombo 1.50 4.00
192 Kareem Abdul-Jabbar 2.50 6.00
193 George Gervin 1.50 4.00
194 Michael Redd 1.25 3.00
195A Jerry Stackhouse 76ers 1.25 3.00
195B Jerry Stackhouse Mavericks 2.50 6.00
195C Jerry Stackhouse Pistons 2.50 6.00
195D Jerry Stackhouse Heat 2.50 6.00
195E Jerry Stackhouse Wizards 2.50 6.00
195F Stackhouse Hawks SP 60.00 150.00
195G Stackhouse Nets SP
195H Stackhouse Bucks SP
196 Richard Hamilton 1.25 3.00
197 Arvydas Sabonis 1.25 3.00
198 Shawn Kemp 2.50 6.00
199 Clyde Drexler 2.00 5.00
200 Yao Ming 2.00 5.00
201 Russell JSY AU/199 RC 15.00 40.00
202 Rashad Vaughn JSY AU/199 RC 4.00 10.00
203 Porzingis JSY AU/199 RC 50.00 120.00
204 Delon Wright JSY AU/199 RC 5.00 12.00
205 Kaminsky JSY AU/199 RC 8.00 20.00
206 Chris McCullough JSY AU/199 RC 4.00 10.00
207 Booker JSY AU/199 RC 40.00 100.00
209 Okafor JSY AU/199 RC 8.00 20.00
210 Montrezl Harrell JSY AU/199 RC 5.00 12.00
211 Winslow JSY AU/199 RC 12.00 30.00
212 Jarell Martin JSY AU/199 RC 5.00 12.00
213 Johnson JSY AU/199 RC 5.00 12.00
214 Justin Anderson JSY AU/199 RC 5.00 12.00
215 Dekker JSY AU/199 RC 5.00 12.00
216 Pat Connaughton JSY AU/199 RC 4.00 10.00
217 Lyles JSY AU/199 RC 6.00 15.00
218 Rakeem Christmas JSY AU/199 RC 4.00 10.00
219 Towns JSY AU/199 RC 75.00 200.00
220 Looney JSY AU/199 RC 5.00 12.00
221 Hezonja JSY AU/199 RC 5.00 12.00
222 Payne JSY AU/199 RC 5.00 12.00
223 Kelly Oubre Jr. JSY AU/199 RC 6.00 15.00
224 Anthony Brown JSY AU/199 RC 4.00 10.00
225 Portis JSY AU/199 RC 6.00 15.00
226 Terry Rozier JSY AU/199 RC 6.00 15.00
227 Jerian Grant JSY AU/199 RC 4.00 10.00
228 Rondae Hollis-Jefferson JSY AU/199 RC 5.00 12.00
229 Mudiay JSY AU/199 RC 6.00 15.00
230 R.J. Hunter JSY AU/199 RC 4.00 10.00
231 Cauley-Stein JSY AU/199 RC 12.00 30.00
232 Joe Young JSY AU/199 RC 5.00 12.00
233 Turner JSY AU/199 RC 10.00 25.00
234 Jordan Mickey JSY AU/199 RC 4.00 10.00
235 Richardson JSY AU/199 RC 6.00 15.00
236 Holmes JSY AU/199 RC
237 Jones JSY AU/199 RC 6.00 15.00
238 Walter Tavares JSY AU/199 RC 4.00 10.00
239 Russell JSY AU/149 15.00 40.00
240 Rashad Vaughn JSY AU/149 4.00 10.00
241 Porzingis JSY AU/149 60.00 150.00
242 Delon Wright JSY AU/149 5.00 12.00
243 Jordan Mickey JSY AU/149 4.00 10.00
244 Chris McCullough JSY AU/149 4.00 10.00
245 D.Booker JSY AU/149 40.00 100.00
246 F.Kaminsky JSY AU/149 6.00 15.00
247 Okafor JSY AU/149 8.00 20.00
248 Montrezl Harrell JSY AU/149 5.00 12.00
249 J.Winslow JSY AU/149 10.00 25.00
250 Jarell Martin JSY AU/149 5.00 12.00
251 S.Johnson JSY AU/149 5.00 12.00
252 Justin Anderson JSY AU/149 5.00 12.00
253 S.Dekker JSY AU/149 5.00 12.00
254 Pat Connaughton JSY AU/149 4.00 10.00
255 T.Lyles JSY AU/149 8.00 20.00
256 Rakeem Christmas JSY AU/149 4.00 10.00
257 Towns JSY AU/149 100.00 250.00
258 Rondae Hollis-Jefferson JSY AU/149 5.00 12.00
259 C.Payne JSY AU/149 8.00 20.00
260 Kelly Oubre Jr. JSY AU/149 6.00 15.00
261 Anthony Brown JSY AU/149 4.00 10.00
262 B.Portis JSY AU/149 6.00 15.00
263 Terry Rozier JSY AU/149 5.00 12.00
264 Jerian Grant JSY AU/149 4.00 10.00
265 Richardson JSY AU/149 6.00 15.00
266 Mudiay JSY AU/149 6.00 15.00
267 R.J. Hunter JSY AU/149 4.00 10.00
268 Cauley-Stein JSY AU/149 12.00 30.00
269 Joe Young JSY AU/149 5.00 12.00
270 M.Turner JSY AU/149 10.00 25.00
271 Russell JSY AU/99 20.00 50.00
272 Rashad Vaughn JSY AU/99 4.00 10.00
273 Porzingis JSY AU/99 75.00 150.00
274 Delon Wright JSY AU/99 5.00 12.00
275 Chris McCullough JSY AU/99 4.00 10.00
276 D.Booker JSY AU/99 50.00 120.00
277 F.Kaminsky JSY AU/99 8.00 20.00
278 Okafor JSY AU/99 8.00 20.00
279 Montrezl Harrell JSY AU/99 5.00 12.00
280 J.Winslow JSY AU/99 12.00 30.00
281 Jordan Mickey JSY AU/99 4.00 10.00
282 S.Johnson JSY AU/99 5.00 12.00
283 Justin Anderson JSY AU/99 5.00 12.00
284 S.Dekker JSY AU/99 5.00 12.00
285 Pat Connaughton JSY AU/99 4.00 10.00
286 T.Lyles JSY AU/99 6.00 15.00
287 Rakeem Christmas JSY AU/99 4.00 10.00
288 Towns JSY AU/99 125.00 250.00
289 Rondae Hollis-Jefferson JSY AU/99 5.00 12.00
290 C.Payne JSY AU/99 8.00 20.00
291 Kelly Oubre Jr. JSY AU/99 6.00 15.00
292 Anthony Brown JSY AU/99 4.00 10.00
293 B.Portis JSY AU/99 12.00 30.00
294 Terry Rozier JSY AU/99 6.00 15.00
295 Jerian Grant JSY AU/99 4.00 10.00
296 Mudiay JSY AU/99 6.00 15.00
297 Josh Richardson JSY AU/99 6.00 15.00
298 Cauley-Stein JSY AU/99 12.00 30.00
299 Joe Young JSY AU/99 5.00 12.00
300 M.Turner JSY AU/99 12.00 30.00
301 Russell JSY AU/49 25.00 60.00
302 Rashad Vaughn JSY AU/49 4.00 10.00
303 Porzingis JSY AU/49 75.00 150.00
304 Delon Wright JSY AU/49 5.00 12.00
305 F.Kaminsky JSY AU/49 6.00 15.00
306 Chris McCullough JSY AU/49 4.00 10.00
307 D.Booker JSY AU/49 50.00 120.00
309 Okafor JSY AU/49 8.00 20.00
310 Montrezl Harrell JSY AU/49 5.00 12.00
311 J.Winslow JSY AU/49 6.00 15.00
312 Jarell Martin JSY AU/49 5.00 12.00
313 S.Johnson JSY AU/49 5.00 12.00
314 Justin Anderson JSY AU/49 5.00 12.00
315 S.Dekker JSY AU/49 5.00 12.00
316 Pat Connaughton JSY AU/49 4.00 10.00
317 T.Lyles JSY AU/49 8.00 20.00
318 Rakeem Christmas JSY AU/49 4.00 10.00
319 Towns JSY AU/49 150.00 300.00
320 K.Looney JSY AU/49 5.00 12.00
321 M.Hezonja JSY AU/49 8.00 20.00
322 C.Payne JSY AU/49 8.00 20.00
323 Kelly Oubre Jr. JSY AU/49 6.00 15.00
324 Anthony Brown JSY AU/49 4.00 10.00
325 B.Portis JSY AU/49 12.00 30.00
326 Terry Rozier JSY AU/49 6.00 15.00
327 Jerian Grant JSY AU/49 4.00 10.00
328 Rondae Hollis-Jefferson JSY AU/49 5.00 12.00
329 Mudiay JSY AU/49 6.00 15.00
330 R.J. Hunter JSY AU/49 4.00 10.00
331 Cauley-Stein JSY AU/49 12.00 30.00
332 Joe Young JSY AU/49 5.00 12.00
333 M.Turner JSY AU/49 12.00 30.00
334 Jordan Mickey JSY AU/49 4.00 10.00
335 Josh Richardson JSY AU/49 6.00 15.00
336 R.Holmes JSY AU/49
337 T.Jones JSY AU/49 8.00 20.00
338 Walter Tavares JSY AU/49 4.00 10.00

2015-16 Panini Gold Standard Gold

*GOLD: .6X TO 1.5X BASE HI
RANDOM INSERTS IN PACKS
STATED PRINT RUN 79 SER.#'d SETS

2015-16 Panini Gold Standard 14K Autographs

RANDOM INSERTS IN PACKS
PRINT RUNS B/WN 40-99 COPIES PER
EXCHANGE DEADLINE 8/17/2017
14KAD Anthony Davis/40 50.00 120.00
14KAL Alex Len/40 5.00 12.00
14KAW Andrew Wiggins/40 20.00 50.00
14KBB Bradley Beal/40 12.00 30.00
14KBG Blake Griffin/40 20.00 50.00
14KBW Bill Walton/40 8.00 20.00
14KDI Dan Issel/99 5.00 12.00
14KDW Dwyane Wade/40 40.00 100.00
14KEP Elfrid Payton/40 12.00 30.00
14KGG Gail Goodrich/40 6.00 15.00
14KGH Grant Hill/40 15.00 40.00
14KGH Gordon Hayward/99 10.00 25.00
14KGH Gary Harris/99 5.00 12.00
14KJE James Ennis/99 4.00 10.00
14KJK Jason Kidd/40 20.00 50.00
14KJP Jabari Parker/40 20.00 50.00
14KJR Julius Randle/40 12.00 30.00
14KJW John Wall/40 20.00 50.00
14KKB Kobe Bryant/40 200.00 300.00
14KKD Kevin Durant/40 60.00 150.00
14KMA Mark Aguirre/99 5.00 12.00
14KMF Michael Finley/40 5.00 12.00
14KNC Norris Cole/99 4.00 10.00
14KNV Nick Van Exel/40 10.00 25.00
14KRH Rodney Hood/99 5.00 12.00
14KSN Shabazz Napier/99 4.00 10.00
14KTB Tarik Black/99 4.00 10.00
14KTH Tobias Harris/99 5.00 12.00
14KWF Walt Frazier/40 8.00 20.00

2015-16 Panini Gold Standard AU Autographs

RANDOM INSERTS IN PACKS
STATED PRINT RUN 79 SER.#'d SETS
EXCHANGE DEADLINE 8/17/2017
AUAB Alec Burks 4.00 10.00
AUAD Anthony Davis 40.00 100.00
AUAL Alex Len 4.00 10.00
AUAM Antonio McDyess 5.00 12.00
AUAN Andrew Nicholson 4.00 10.00
AUAW Andrew Wiggins 30.00 80.00
AUBB Bradley Beal 6.00 15.00
AUBBD Bojan Bogdanovic 4.00 10.00
AUBC Bill Cartwright 5.00 12.00
AUBD Brad Daugherty 5.00 12.00
AUBG Blake Griffin 15.00 40.00
AUBL Bill Laimbeer 5.00 12.00
AUBS Byron Scott 5.00 12.00
AUCB Chris Bosh 10.00 25.00
AUCC Cedric Ceballos 4.00 10.00
AUCR Cazzie Russell 5.00 12.00
AUCW C.J. Watson 4.00 10.00
AUDCR DeMarre Carroll 4.00 10.00
AUDC Dave Cowens 4.00 10.00
AUDH Darrun Hilliard 4.00 10.00
AUDI Dan Issel 5.00 12.00
AUDR Dino Radja 12.00 30.00
AUDS Damon Stoudamire 5.00 12.00
AUDSH Dennis Schroder 5.00 12.00
AUED Ed Davis 4.00 10.00
AUEP Elfrid Payton 5.00 12.00
AUGA Giannis Antetokounmpo 50.00 120.00
AUGH Gordon Hayward 6.00 15.00
AUGHR Gary Harris 5.00 12.00
AUGR Glen Rice 5.00 12.00
AUHG Horace Grant 6.00 15.00
AUJC Jordan Clarkson 6.00 15.00
AUJE James Ennis 4.00 10.00
AUJG Jeff Green 5.00 12.00
AUJHR Joe Harris 4.00 10.00
AUJH Jeff Hornacek 5.00 12.00
AUJI Joe Ingles 4.00 10.00
AUJP Jabari Parker 12.00 30.00
AUJV Jonas Valanciunas 5.00 12.00
AUJW John Wall 20.00 50.00
AUJY James Young 4.00 10.00
AUKB Kobe Bryant 100.00 200.00
AUKD Kevin Durant 40.00 100.00
AUKF Kenneth Faried 5.00 12.00
AULG Langston Galloway 4.00 10.00
AULN Larry Nance 5.00 12.00
AUMA Mark Aguirre 5.00 12.00
AUMC Maurice Cheeks 4.00 10.00
AUMCL Mike Conley 6.00 15.00
AUMF Michael Finley 6.00 15.00
AUMH Maurice Harkless 4.00 10.00
AUMJ Marques Johnson 5.00 12.00
AUMP Mason Plumlee 5.00 12.00
AUNA Nate Archibald 5.00 12.00
AUNJ Nikola Jokic 30.00 80.00
AUNM Nikola Mirotic 5.00 12.00
AUNV Nick Van Exel 6.00 15.00
AUPP Patrick Patterson 4.00 10.00
AURA Rafer Alston 4.00 10.00
AURF Rick Fox 5.00 12.00
AURH Robert Horry 5.00 12.00
AURN Raul Neto 6.00 15.00
AURP Robert Parish 6.00 15.00
AURS Ralph Sampson 5.00 12.00
AUSE Sean Elliott 6.00 15.00
AUSS Satch Sanders 6.00 15.00
AUSW Scott Wedman 5.00 12.00
AUTA Tony Allen 4.00 10.00
AUTB Tarik Black 4.00 10.00
AUTD Troy Daniels 4.00 10.00
AUTG Tom Gugliotta 4.00 10.00
AUTM Timofey Mozgov 4.00 10.00
AUWC Wilson Chandler 5.00 12.00
AUWE Wayne Embry 4.00 10.00
AUWF Walt Frazier 6.00 15.00
AUWT Walter Tavares 4.00 10.00

2015-16 Panini Gold Standard Gold Scripts

RANDOM INSERTS IN PACKS
PRINT RUNS B/WN 35-99 COPIES PER
EXCHANGE DEADLINE 8/17/2017
SCAL Alex Len/49 4.00 10.00
SCAM Andre Miller/99 5.00 12.00
SCBB Bojan Bogdanovic/99 4.00 10.00
SCBR Brian Roberts/99 4.00 10.00
SCBW Bill Walton/99 6.00 15.00
SCCL Courtney Lee/99 5.00 12.00
SCCM Calvin Murphy/99 5.00 12.00
SCDC Dave Cowens/99 4.00 10.00
SCDC DeMarre Carroll/99 4.00 10.00
SCDE Dante Exum/49 5.00 12.00
SCDR David Robinson/35 15.00 40.00
SCDS Dennis Schroder/99 5.00 12.00
SCEK Enes Kanter/99 4.00 10.00
SCFE Festus Ezeli/99 4.00 10.00
SCGG Gail Goodrich/99 5.00 12.00
SCGH Gerald Henderson/99 4.00 10.00
SCJC Jordan Clarkson/99 8.00 20.00
SCJE James Ennis/99 4.00 10.00
SCJW Jerry West/35 20.00 50.00
SCJW Jamaal Wilkes/99 6.00 15.00
SCKM Kevin McHale/35 8.00 20.00
SCLG Langston Galloway/99 4.00 10.00
SCMD Matthew Dellavedova/99 5.00 12.00
SCMH Maurice Harkless/99 4.00 10.00
SCMK Michael Kidd-Gilchrist/49 5.00 12.00
SCMP Mason Plumlee/99 5.00 12.00
SCMW Mo Williams/99 5.00 12.00
SCNA Nate Archibald/99 5.00 12.00
SCNS Nik Stauskas/99 4.00 10.00
SCPG Pau Gasol/35 10.00 25.00
SCRG Rudy Gobert/99 6.00 15.00
SCRH Roy Hibbert/99 5.00 12.00
SCRP Robert Parish/99 6.00 15.00
SCRR Ricky Rubio/35 12.00 30.00
SCSC Seth Curry/99 8.00 20.00
SCSM Shabazz Muhammad/49 5.00 12.00
SCTA Tony Allen/99 4.00 10.00
SCTM Timofey Mozgov/99 4.00 10.00
SCVO Victor Oladipo/49 5.00 12.00
SCWF Walt Frazier/99 6.00 15.00

2015-16 Panini Gold Standard Gold Strike Jersey Autographs

RANDOM INSERTS IN PACKS
PRINT RUNS B/WN 30-99 COPIES PER
EXCHANGE DEADLINE 8/17/2017
*PRIME/25: .75X TO 2X BASIC
1 Rashad Vaughn/99 4.00 10.00
2 Mario Hezonja/99 8.00 20.00
3 Mitch McGary/45 4.00 10.00
4 Jusuf Nurkic/99 4.00 10.00
5 Rakeem Christmas/99 4.00 10.00
6 D'Angelo Russell/49 30.00 80.00
7 Andrew Nicholson/99 4.00 10.00
8 Anthony Bennett/49 4.00 10.00
9 Glenn Robinson III/99 4.00 10.00
10 Bernard King/99 5.00 12.00
11 Kelly Oubre Jr./99 6.00 15.00
12 Luol Deng/30 5.00 12.00
13 Robert Sacre/99 4.00 10.00
14 Jared Dudley/99 4.00 10.00
15 Joe Young/99 5.00 12.00
16 Chris Webber/49 50.00 120.00
17 Tony Allen/99 4.00 10.00
18 Victor Oladipo/49 8.00 20.00
19 Kiki Vandeweghe/92 5.00 12.00
20 Kristaps Porzingis/99 60.00 150.00
21 Sam Dekker/99 5.00 12.00
22 Michael Cooper/99 5.00 12.00
23 Montrezl Harrell/99 5.00 12.00
24 Kenny Walker/99 4.00 10.00
25 Terry Rozier/99 5.00 12.00
26 Karl-Anthony Towns/49 125.00 250.00
27 Mo Williams/99 5.00 12.00
28 Harrison Barnes/49 10.00 25.00
29 Norm Nixon/99 4.00 10.00
30 C.J. McCollum/99 10.00 25.00
31 Chris Copeland/99 4.00 10.00
32 Stanley Johnson/99 12.00 30.00
33 Pat Connaughton/99 4.00 10.00
34 Myles Turner/99 12.00 30.00
35 R.J. Hunter/99 4.00 10.00
36 Chris Bosh/49 10.00 25.00
37 Darrell Griffith/99 4.00 10.00
38 Tyreke Evans/49 4.00 10.00
39 Will Perdue/99 4.00 10.00
40 Tyler Ennis/99 4.00 10.00

2015-16 Panini Gold Standard Golden Debuts

RANDOM INSERTS IN PACKS
STATED PRINT RUN 50 SER.#'d SETS
1 Emmanuel Mudiay 4.00 10.00
2 Jerian Grant 2.50 6.00
3 Myles Turner 4.00 10.00
4 Rondae Hollis-Jefferson 3.00 8.00
5 Kelly Oubre Jr. 3.00 8.00
6 R.J. Hunter 2.50 6.00
7 Karl-Anthony Towns 25.00 60.00
8 Jordan Mickey 2.50 6.00
9 Kristaps Porzingis 10.00 25.00
10 Walter Tavares 2.50 6.00
11 Stanley Johnson 3.00 8.00
12 Delon Wright 3.00 8.00
13 Trey Lyles 4.00 10.00
14 Tyus Jones 4.00 10.00
15 Terry Rozier 3.00 8.00
16 Chris McCullough 2.50 6.00
17 D'Angelo Russell 10.00 25.00
18 Mario Hezonja 3.00 8.00
19 Anthony Brown 2.50 6.00
20 Kevon Looney 3.00 8.00
21 Frank Kaminsky 4.00 10.00
22 Justin Anderson 3.00 8.00
23 Devin Booker 15.00 40.00
24 Jarell Martin 3.00 8.00
25 Rashad Vaughn 2.50 6.00
26 Montrezl Harrell 3.00 8.00
27 Jahlil Okafor 5.00 12.00
28 Rakeem Christmas 2.50 6.00
29 Willie Cauley-Stein 4.00 10.00
30 Nemanja Bjelica 3.00 8.00
31 Justise Winslow 4.00 10.00
32 Bobby Portis 4.00 10.00
33 Cameron Payne 3.00 8.00
34 Larry Nance Jr. 4.00 10.00
35 Sam Dekker 3.00 8.00

2015-16 Panini Gold Standard Golden Graphs

RANDOM INSERTS IN PACKS
PRINT RUNS B/WN 35-75 COPIES PER
EXCHANGE DEADLINE 8/17/2017
GGAG A.C. Green/75 6.00 15.00
GGAH Anfernee Hardaway/35 25.00 60.00
GGBW Bill Walton/35 8.00 20.00
GGCH Cliff Hagan/35 6.00 15.00
GGCM Cedric Maxwell/75 4.00 10.00
GGCR Cazzie Russell/75 5.00 12.00
GGDG Danny Green/75 5.00 12.00
GGDR David Robinson/35 20.00 50.00
GGDS Dennis Schroder/75 5.00 12.00
GGJW Jo Jo White/75 5.00 12.00
GGJY James Young/75 4.00 10.00
GGKG Kendall Gill/75 4.00 10.00
GGMC Michael Cage/75 4.00 10.00
GGMJ Magic Johnson/35 25.00 60.00
GGMJ Mark Jackson/35 6.00 15.00
GGNA Nate Archibald/35 6.00 15.00
GGPP Patrick Patterson/75 4.00 10.00
GGRB Rick Barry/35 6.00 15.00
GGRH Ron Harper/75 10.00 25.00
GGRS Rik Smits/75 5.00 12.00
GGSB Sam Bowie/75 4.00 10.00
GGSM Sidney Moncrief/75 4.00 10.00
GGSS Steve Smith/75 5.00 12.00
GGTB Tarik Black/75 4.00 10.00
GGTP Tony Parker/35 20.00 50.00
GGTT Tristan Thompson/35 6.00 15.00
GGVM Vernon Maxwell/75 4.00 10.00

2015-16 Panini Gold Standard Golden Pairs

RANDOM INSERTS IN PACKS
PRINT RUNS B/WN 5-14 COPIES PER
NO PRICING ON QTY 14 OR LESS
1 Iverson/Erving/25 15.00 40.00
2 Griffin/Davis/25 12.00 25.00
3 Johnson/Lopez/25 8.00 20.00
4 Garnett/Wiggins/25
5 Holiday/Davis/25 12.00 30.00
6 Bird/Parish/25 15.00 40.00
7 Vucevic/Harris/25 8.00 20.00
8 Aguirre/Blackman/25 12.00 30.00
9 Payton/Allen/25 15.00 40.00
10 Thompson/Curry/25 75.00 150.00
11 King/Anthony/25 15.00 40.00
12 Bryant/O'Neal/25 125.00 250.00
13 D.Gallinari/K.Faried/25 5.00 12.00
14 Westbrook/Durant/25 25.00 60.00
16 Pippen/Rodman/25 40.00 100.00
17 Hill/Nash/25 25.00 60.00
18 Hill/Dumars/25 15.00 40.00
19 Malone/Stockton/25 30.00 80.00
20 Drexler/Olajuwon/25 25.00 60.00
21 J.Teague/A.Horford/25 5.00 12.00
22 Wade/O'Neal/25 30.00 80.00
25 Oakley/Ewing/25 20.00 50.00

2015-16 Panini Gold Standard Golden Quads

RANDOM INSERTS IN PACKS
PRINT RUNS B/WN 5-25 COPIES PER
NO PRICING ON QTY 5
1 Tge/Mllsp/Hrfrd/Krvr/25 20.00 50.00
2 Bgdnvc/Jack/Jhnsn/Lpz/25 10.00 25.00
3 Jffrsn/Hrstn/Zllr/Wlkr/25 10.00 25.00
4 Btlr/Rose/McDrmtt/Noah/25 20.00 50.00
5 Harris/Nurkic/Gallinari/Faried/25
6 Iguodala/Bogut/Thompson/Curry/25
7 Harden/Howard/Beverley/Jones/25
8 Grffn/Jrdn/Crwfrd/Paul/25 30.00 80.00
9 Gsl/Cnly/Rndlph/Alln/25 12.00 30.00
10 Andrsn/Wade/Bosh/Chlmrs/25 25.00 60.00
12 Wggns/Grntt/Pkvc/Rbo/25 30.00 80.00
13 Drnt/Adms/Wstbrk/Ibka/25 15.00 40.00
14 Vcvc/Hrrs/Oldpo/Pytn/25 20.00 50.00
15 Len/Morris/Warren/Bledsoe/25 5.00 12.00
16 McLmre/Cllsn/Csns/Csspi/25 10.00 25.00
17 Lnrd/Gnbli/Dncn/Prkr/25 25.00 60.00
18 Vlncns/DRzn/Lowry/Ross/25 15.00 40.00
19 Exum/Fvrs/Hywrd/Brke/25 10.00 25.00
21 Mhnm/Grge/Hill/Hill/25 10.00 25.00
22 Clrksn/Brynt/Yng/Scre/25 60.00 150.00
23 Grdn/Hldy/Evns/Dvs/25 12.00 30.00
24 Bird/Lws/Rdja/McHle/25 40.00 100.00
25 Dantley/Laimbeer/Thomas/Dumars/25

2015-16 Panini Gold Standard Golden Trios

RANDOM INSERTS IN PACKS
STATED PRINT RUN 25 SER.#'d SETS
1 Walker/Jefferson/Hairston 6.00 15.00
2 McLmre/Csns/Cllsn 8.00 20.00
3 Igdla/Green/Barnes 12.00 30.00
4 Burke/Favors/Hayward 8.00 20.00
5 Gasol/Conley/Randolph 12.00 30.00
6 Rdmn/Thms/Dmrs 15.00 40.00
7 Starks/Jackson/Ewing 25.00 60.00
8 Robinson/Kerr/Duncan 25.00 60.00
9 Hrfrd/Sflsha/Mllsp 6.00 15.00
10 Mourning/Rice/Johnson 15.00 40.00
11 Nash/Nwtzki/Finley 40.00 100.00
12 Prkr/Ginobili/Duncan 40.00 100.00
13 Paul/Griffin/Jordan 20.00 50.00
14 Beal/Wall/Porter Jr. 12.00 30.00
15 Andersen/Bosh/Wade 15.00 40.00
16 Smith/Drexler/Olajuwon 30.00 80.00
17 Payton/Gordon/Oladipo 30.00 80.00
18 Jnnngs/Cldwll-Pope/Drmmnd 12.00 30.00
19 Bradley/Sullinger/Smart 5.00 12.00
20 Mlne/Hrnck/Socktn 25.00 60.00
21 Gallinari/Nurkic/Faried 5.00 12.00
22 DRzn/Ross/Vlnciuns 15.00 40.00
23 Young/Clarkson/Bryant 60.00 150.00
24 Rbnsn/Dckwrth/Pppn 20.00 50.00
25 Davis/Evans/Holiday 10.00 25.00

2015-16 Panini Gold Standard Good as Gold Jersey Autographs

RANDOM INSERTS IN PACKS
PRINT RUNS B/WN 30-99 COPIES PER
EXCHANGE DEADLINE 8/17/2017
*PRIME/25: .75X TO 2X BASIC
1 Josh Richardson/99 6.00 15.00
2 Manu Ginobili/38 30.00 80.00
3 George Hill/99 5.00 12.00
4 Jrue Holiday/49 5.00 12.00
5 Mitch Richmond/99 6.00 15.00
6 Tayshaun Prince/99 5.00 12.00
7 James Jones/99 4.00 10.00
8 Danilo Gallinari/99 5.00 12.00
9 Jerian Grant/99 4.00 10.00
10 Shabazz Muhammad/99 5.00 12.00
11 Justin Anderson/99 5.00 12.00
12 Marcus Smart/49 8.00 20.00
13 Thabo Sefolosha/99 4.00 10.00
14 Al Horford/99 5.00 12.00
15 Wilson Chandler/99 5.00 12.00
16 Jordan Hill/99 4.00 10.00
17 Devin Booker/99 25.00 60.00
18 Kenny Smith/99 5.00 12.00
19 Jordan Mickey/99 4.00 10.00
20 Kyle Korver/99 5.00 12.00
21 Pat Connaughton/99 4.00 10.00
22 Alex Len/49 5.00 12.00
23 Chase Budinger/99 4.00 10.00
24 Andre Iguodala/98 5.00 12.00
25 Patty Mills/67 10.00 25.00

2015-16 Panini Gold Standard Marks of Gold Jersey Autographs

RANDOM INSERTS IN PACKS
PRINT RUNS B/WN 49-99 COPIES PER
EXCHANGE DEADLINE 8/17/2017
*PRIME/25: .75X TO 2X BASIC
1 Dante Exum/49 5.00 12.00
2 Jack Sikma/99 5.00 12.00
3 Eric Gordon/99 5.00 12.00
4 Donatas Motiejunas/99 4.00 10.00
5 J.R. Smith/75 8.00 20.00
6 Fat Lever/99 5.00 12.00
7 Kurt Rambis/99 4.00 10.00
8 Brad Daugherty/99 5.00 12.00
9 Dennis Rodman/49 20.00 50.00
10 Alan Anderson/99 4.00 10.00
11 Ben McLemore/99 4.00 10.00
12 Rafer Alston/99 4.00 10.00
13 Byron Scott/99 5.00 12.00
14 Jodie Meeks/99 5.00 12.00
15 Nikola Mirotic/99 5.00 12.00
16 Keith Van Horn/99 5.00 12.00
17 Taj Gibson/65 5.00 12.00
18 World B. Free/99 5.00 12.00
19 Grant Hill/49 15.00 40.00
20 Bill Laimbeer/99 5.00 12.00
21 Chris Mullin/99 10.00 25.00
22 Scott Wedman/99 5.00 12.00
23 Joe Dumars/99 6.00 15.00
24 Kent Bazemore/99 10.00 25.00
25 Bill Cartwright/99 5.00 12.00
26 Rik Smits/99 5.00 12.00
27 Cedric Maxwell/99 4.00 10.00
28 Jalen Rose/99 6.00 15.00
29 Richard Hamilton/49 5.00 12.00
30 Dino Radja/84 12.00 30.00
31 Nick Van Exel/99 10.00 25.00
32 Terry Cummings/99 5.00 12.00
33 Rick Fox/99 5.00 12.00
34 K.J. McDaniels/99 5.00 12.00
35 Jason Thompson/99 4.00 10.00

2015-16 Panini Gold Standard Mother Lode Autographs

RANDOM INSERTS IN PACKS
PRINT RUNS B/WN 35-99 COPIES PER
EXCHANGE DEADLINE 8/17/2017
MLAH Anfernee Hardaway/35 20.00 50.00
MLAH Allan Houston/99 5.00 12.00
MLAI Allen Iverson/35 60.00 150.00
MLAM Antonio McDyess/99 5.00 12.00
MLAN Andrew Nicholson/99 4.00 10.00
MLBB Brandon Bass/99 4.00 10.00
MLBC Bruno Caboclo/99 4.00 10.00
MLBS Byron Scott/99 5.00 12.00
MLCR Cazzie Russell/99 5.00 12.00
MLDH Dwight Howard/35 6.00 15.00
MLDM Donatas Motiejunas/99 4.00 10.00
MLDM Dikembe Mutombo/99 6.00 15.00
MLDN Don Nelson/99 10.00 25.00
MLFL Fat Lever/99 5.00 12.00
MLGD Gorgui Dieng/99 4.00 10.00
MLGH George Hill/99 5.00 12.00
MLGH Grant Hill/35 15.00 40.00
MLGK George Karl/99 6.00 15.00
MLGR Glen Rice/49 5.00 12.00
MLHB Henry Bibby/99 4.00 10.00
MLJC Jordan Clarkson/99 6.00 15.00
MLJJ Jim Jackson/99 4.00 10.00
MLJK Jason Kidd/35 12.00 30.00
MLJS Jerry Stackhouse/99 5.00 12.00
MLJS J.R. Smith/99 5.00 12.00
MLJW Jay Williams/99 4.00 10.00
MLKG Kendall Gill/99 4.00 10.00
MLKK Kyle Korver/99 5.00 12.00
MLKM Kevin McHale/35 6.00 15.00
MLLB Larry Brown/99 6.00 15.00
MLLD Luol Deng/99 5.00 12.00
MLLS Lance Stephenson/99 5.00 12.00
MLMC Maurice Cheeks/99 4.00 10.00
MLMD Matthew Dellavedova/99 5.00 12.00
MLMG Manu Ginobili/35 20.00 50.00
MLMM Mike Muscala/99 4.00 10.00
MLNN Norm Nixon/99 4.00 10.00
MLPM Patty Mills/99 10.00 25.00
MLPS Peja Stojakovic/99 6.00 15.00
MLPS Paul Silas/99 6.00 15.00
MLPT P.J. Tucker/99 4.00 10.00
MLRC Robert Covington/99 4.00 10.00
MLRC Rick Carlisle/50 12.00 30.00
MLRG Rudy Gobert/90 6.00 15.00
MLRH Roy Hibbert/99 5.00 12.00
MLRM Ray McCallum/99 4.00 10.00
MLRS Rik Smits/99 5.00 12.00
MLRS Rod Strickland/99 4.00 10.00
MLRT Rudy Tomjanovich/99 5.00 12.00
MLSD Spencer Dinwiddie/99 4.00 10.00
MLSE Sean Elliott/99 6.00 15.00
MLSF Steve Francis/99 5.00 12.00
MLSL Shane Larkin/99 4.00 10.00
MLSW Sonny Weems/99 4.00 10.00
MLTB Trey Burke/50 4.00 10.00
MLTM Tracy McGrady/35 15.00 40.00
MLTM Timofey Mozgov/99 4.00 10.00
MLTS Thabo Sefolosha/99 4.00 10.00
MLVD Vlade Divac/99 6.00 15.00
MLVD Vinny Del Negro/99 5.00 12.00

2015-16 Panini Gold Standard Newly Minted Memorabilia

RANDOM INSERTS IN PACKS
STATED PRINT RUN 25 SER.#'d SETS
1 Kelly Oubre Jr. 5.00 12.00
2 Justise Winslow 6.00 15.00
3 Sam Dekker 5.00 12.00
4 Karl-Anthony Towns 30.00 80.00
5 Justin Anderson 5.00 12.00
6 Kristaps Porzingis 15.00 40.00
7 Tyus Jones 6.00 15.00
8 Willie Cauley-Stein 10.00 25.00
9 Devin Booker 20.00 50.00
10 Stanley Johnson 5.00 12.00
11 Terry Rozier 5.00 12.00
12 Myles Turner 15.00 40.00
13 Jerian Grant 4.00 10.00
14 D'Angelo Russell 15.00 40.00
15 Bobby Portis 6.00 15.00
16 Mario Hezonja 5.00 12.00
17 R.J. Hunter 4.00 10.00
18 Emmanuel Mudiay 6.00 15.00
19 Cameron Payne 5.00 12.00
20 Frank Kaminsky 6.00 15.00
22 Trey Lyles 6.00 15.00
23 Delon Wright 5.00 12.00
24 Jahlil Okafor 12.00 30.00
25 Rondae Hollis-Jefferson 5.00 12.00

2015-16 Panini Gold Standard Newly Minted Memorabilia Duals

RANDOM INSERTS IN PACKS
STATED PRINT RUN 25 SER.#'d SETS
1 S.Johnson/E.Mudiay
2 J.Richardson/J.Winslow
3 J.Grant/P.Connaughton 10.00 25.00
4 C.Payne/J.Huestis 10.00 25.00
5 K.Towns/D.Russell 20.00 50.00
6 T.Rozier/R.Hunter 5.00 12.00
7 Hlls-Jffrsn/Jhnsn 5.00 12.00
8 S.Dekker/M.Harrell 5.00 12.00
9 K.Towns/W.Cauley-Stein 30.00 80.00
10 A.Brown/D.Russell 12.00 30.00
11 M.Harrell/T.Rozier
12 K.Towns/T.Jones
13 A.Brown/J.Huestis 4.00 10.00
14 K.Porzingis/M.Hezonja 15.00 40.00
15 J.Okafor/K.Porzingis 20.00 50.00
16 R.Hollis-Jefferson/C.McCullough 5.00 12.00
17 J.Okafor/J.Winslow 12.00 30.00
18 R.Christmas/M.Turner
19 D.Booker/T.Lyles
20 B.Portis/J.Martin 6.00 15.00
21 J.Martin/J.Mickey 5.00 12.00
22 J.Grant/K.Porzingis 15.00 40.00
23 F.Kaminsky/S.Dekker 15.00 40.00
24 J.Okafor/R.Holmes 12.00 30.00
25 M.Hezonja/W.Cauley-Stein 6.00 15.00

2015-16 Panini Gold Standard Newly Minted Memorabilia Quads

RANDOM INSERTS IN PACKS
STATED PRINT RUN 25 SER.#'d SETS
1 Kaminsky/Winslow/Turner/Lyles
2 Yng/Jhnsn/Wrght/Lny 5.00 12.00
3 Portis/Anderson/Hollis-Jefferson/Jones 6.00 15.00
4 McCullough/Grant/Porzingis/Hollis-Jefferson
5 Twns/Cly-Stn/Kmnsky/Dkkr 20.00 50.00
6 Kmnsky/Hznja/Rchrdsn/Wnsow 6.00 15.00
7 Grnt/Hrrll/Wnslw/Jns 6.00 15.00
8 Connaughton/Mudiay/Lyles/Jones 6.00 15.00
9 Rssll/Okfr/Przngs/Twns 60.00 150.00
10 Anderson/Dekker/Martin/Harrell 5.00 12.00
11 Pyne/Bkr/Obre/Rzer 20.00 50.00
12 Prts/Twns/Mrtn/Cly-Stn 20.00 50.00
13 Harrell/McCullough/Looney/Hunter 5.00 12.00
14 Holmes/Rozier/Wright/Okafor
15 Przngs/Mdy/Hznja/Tvrs 15.00 40.00
16 Pyne/Hsis/Twns/Jns 30.00 80.00
17 Brwn/Hsts/Hlls-Jffrsn/Jhnsn 15.00 40.00
18 Brwn/Rssell/Lny/Cly-Stein 12.00 30.00
19 Mdy/Hznja/Jhnsn/Cly-Stn 10.00 25.00
20 Mdy/Wnslw/Twns/Okfr 50.00 120.00
22 Mrin/Mcky/Towns/Cly-Stn 15.00 40.00
23 Bkr/Twns/Lyles/Cly-Stn 60.00 150.00
24 Prts/Trnr/Chstms/Jhnsn 15.00 40.00
25 McCllgh/Okfr/Andrsn/Rzr 8.00 20.00

2015-16 Panini Gold Standard Newly Minted Memorabilia Triples

RANDOM INSERTS IN PACKS
STATED PRINT RUN 25 SER.#'d SETS
1 Booker/Lyles/Cly-Stein 20.00 50.00
2 Russell/Okafor/Towns 60.00 150.00
3 Russell/Kmnsky/Dekker 25.00 60.00
4 Winslow/Turner/Lyles 15.00 40.00
5 Portis/Martin/Booker 12.00 30.00
6 Wright/Grant/Anderson 5.00 12.00
7 Towns/Cly-Stein/Okafor 25.00 60.00
8 Mickey/Rozier/Hunter 5.00 12.00
10 Okafor/Winslow/Jones 15.00 40.00
11 Rozier/Okafor/Grant 8.00 20.00
12 Przngs/Cly-Stein/Hznja 15.00 40.00
13 Wright/Looney/Johnson 6.00 15.00
14 Payne/Booker/Oubre 12.00 30.00
15 Richardson/Lyles/Mickey 6.00 15.00
16 Portis/Hollis-Jefferson/Jones 6.00 15.00
17 Mudiay/Russell/Hezonja 15.00 40.00
18 Mudiay/Huestis/Payne 8.00 20.00
19 Booker/Lyles/Towns 50.00 120.00
20 Towns/Lyles/Cly-Stein 20.00 50.00
21 Jones/McCullough/Anderson 6.00 15.00
22 Kmnsky/Johnson/Mudiay 15.00 40.00
23 Young/Brown/Hollis-Jefferson 5.00 12.00
25 Mudiay/Hznja/Porzingis 25.00 60.00

2015-16 Panini Gold Standard Ring Bearers Autographs

RANDOM INSERTS IN PACKS
PRINT RUNS B/WN 25-49 COPIES PER
EXCHANGE DEADLINE 8/17/2017
RBAW Antoine Walker/49 8.00 20.00
RBBL Bill Laimbeer/49 6.00 15.00
RBDG Danny Green/49 8.00 20.00
RBDR David Robinson/25 25.00 60.00
RBDW Dwyane Wade/25 60.00 150.00
RBGP Gary Payton/25 12.00 30.00
RBGR Glen Rice/49 5.00 12.00
RBJD Joe Dumars/49 6.00 15.00
RBJM J. Michael McAdoo/25 5.00 12.00
RBJT Jason Terry/25 15.00 40.00
RBKB Kobe Bryant/25 500.00 700.00
RBKM Kevin McHale/25
RBKT Klay Thompson/49 60.00 150.00
RBMA Mark Aguirre/49 5.00 12.00
RBMJ Magic Johnson/25 40.00 100.00
RBRF Rick Fox/49 8.00 20.00
RBRH Robert Horry/49 10.00 25.00
RBSE Sean Elliott/49 6.00 15.00
RBTP Tony Parker/25 40.00 100.00

2015-16 Panini Gold Standard Rookie Jersey Autographs Prime

*PRIME: 1X TO 2.5X BASIC
RANDOM INSERTS IN PACKS
STATED PRINT RUN 25 SER.#'d SETS
EXCHANGE DEADLINE 8/17/2017
201 D'Angelo Russell 150.00 400.00
203 Kristaps Porzingis 300.00 600.00
219 Karl-Anthony Towns 400.00 800.00
233 Myles Turner 60.00 150.00
239 D'Angelo Russell 125.00 300.00
241 Kristaps Porzingis 350.00 700.00
257 Karl-Anthony Towns 400.00 800.00
270 Myles Turner 125.00 300.00
271 D'Angelo Russell 150.00 400.00
273 Kristaps Porzingis 350.00 700.00
288 Karl-Anthony Towns 400.00 800.00
300 Myles Turner 125.00 300.00
301 D'Angelo Russell 150.00 400.00
303 Kristaps Porzingis 350.00 700.00
319 Karl-Anthony Towns 400.00 800.00
333 Myles Turner 125.00 300.00

2015-16 Panini Gold Standard White Gold Threads

RANDOM INSERTS IN PACKS
STATED PRINT RUN 25 SER.#'d SETS
1 Grant Hill 12.00 30.00
2 Damian Lillard 12.00 30.00
3 Marc Gasol 6.00 15.00
4 DeMarcus Cousins 20.00 50.00
5 Michael Redd 5.00 12.00
6 Tim Duncan 25.00 60.00
7 Russell Westbrook 20.00 50.00
8 Manu Ginobili 20.00 50.00
9 Rajon Rondo 6.00 15.00
10 Tony Parker
11 Hakeem Olajuwon 15.00 40.00
12 DeMar DeRozan 10.00 25.00
13 Dwyane Wade
14 John Stockton 30.00 80.00
15 Patrick Ewing 25.00 60.00

2016-17 Panini Gold Standard

1-200 PRINT RUN 269 SER.#'d SETS
SOME VAR NOT PRICED DUE TO SCARCITY
201-238 PRINT RUN 199 SER.#'d SETS
239-269 PRINT RUN 149 SER.#'d SETS
270-300 PRINT RUN 99 SER.#'d SETS
301-338 PRINT RUN 49 SER.#'d SETS
339-373 PRINT RUN 25 SER.#'d SETS
EXCHANGE DEADLINE 6/28/2018
1A Durant Warriors
1B Durant Thunder 4.00 10.00
1C Durant Supersonics
1D Durant Longhorns
2 Emmanuel Mudiay 1.25 3.00
3 Jordan Clarkson 1.25 3.00
4 Brook Lopez 1.25 3.00
5A Kawhi Leonard 2.50 6.00
5B Kawhi Leonard VAR 2.50 6.00
6 John Wall 2.00 5.00
7 Anthony Bennett 1.00 2.50
8 Julius Randle 1.50 4.00
9 Andrew Bogut 1.25 3.00
10 Gary Harris 1.25 3.00
11 Luol Deng 1.25 3.00
12 Bojan Bogdanovic 1.00 2.50
13 Kyle Anderson 1.00 2.50
14 LaMarcus Aldridge 1.50 4.00
15 Lance Thomas 1.00 2.50
16 D'Angelo Russell 2.00 5.00
17 Wesley Matthews 1.00 2.50
18 Dennis Schroder 1.25 3.00
19 Kenneth Faried 1.25 3.00
20 Lou Williams 1.25 3.00
21 Jeremy Lin 1.50 4.00
22 Willie Cauley-Stein 1.25 3.00
23 Manu Ginobili 1.50 4.00
24 Kelly Oubre Jr. 1.00 2.50
25A Kristaps Porzingis 3.00 8.00
25B Kristaps Porzingis VAR 3.00 8.00
26 Paul Pierce 1.50 4.00
27 Harrison Barnes 1.25 3.00
28 Kent Bazemore 1.25 3.00
29 Nikola Jokic 1.50 4.00
30 Chandler Parsons 1.25 3.00
31 Rondae Hollis-Jefferson 1.00 2.50
32 Rudy Gay 1.50 4.00
33 Tony Parker 1.50 4.00
34 Marcin Gortat 1.25 3.00
35 Joakim Noah 1.25 3.00
36 Mike Conley 1.25 3.00
37A Dirk Nowitzki 2.00 5.00
37B Dirk Nowitzki VAR 2.00 5.00
38 Paul Millsap 1.50 4.00
39 Wilson Chandler 1.25 3.00
40 Marc Gasol 1.50 4.00
41 Thomas Robinson 1.00 2.50
42A DeMarcus Cousins 1.50 4.00
42B DeMarcus Cousins VAR 1.50 4.00
43A DeMar DeRozan 1.50 4.00
43B DeMar DeRozan VAR 1.50 4.00
44 Markieff Morris 1.00 2.50
45 Derrick Rose 2.00 5.00
46 J.J. Redick 1.50 4.00
47 Deron Williams 1.25 3.00
48 Al Horford 1.25 3.00
49 Aron Baynes 1.00 2.50
50 DeMarre Carroll 1.00 2.50
51 Cameron Payne 1.00 2.50
52 Darren Collison 1.25 3.00
53A Jamal Crawford Clippers 1.50 4.00
53B Crawford Hawks
53C Jamal Crawford Bulls 1.50 4.00
53D Crawford Warriors
53E Crawford Trail Blazers
53F Crawford Wolverines
53G Jamal Crawford Knicks 1.50 4.00
54 Thabo Sefolosha 1.00 2.50
55A Carmelo Anthony 2.00 5.00
55B Carmelo Anthony VAR 2.00 5.00
55C Anthony Nuggets 2.00 5.00
55D Anthony Orange
56 DeAndre Jordan 1.50 4.00
57 Tristan Thompson 1.25 3.00
58A Isaiah Thomas 1.50 4.00
58B Isaiah Thomas VAR 1.50 4.00
59 Boban Marjanovic 1.00 2.50
60 Vince Carter 2.00 5.00
61 Ersan Ilyasova 1.00 2.50
62 Mason Plumlee 1.25 3.00
63 Jonas Valanciunas 1.25 3.00
64 J.J. Barea 1.25 3.00
65 Solomon Hill 1.00 2.50
66A Chris Paul 2.00 5.00
66B Chris Paul VAR 2.00 5.00
67 Richard Jefferson 1.25 3.00
68 Jae Crowder 1.25 3.00
69 Marcus Morris 1.00 2.50
70 Zach Randolph 1.25 3.00
71A Russell Westbrook 4.00 10.00
71B Russell Westbrook VAR 4.00 10.00
72 Evan Turner 1.00 2.50
73A Kyle Lowry 1.25 3.00
73B Kyle Lowry VAR 1.25 3.00
74 Clint Capela 1.00 2.50
75 Langston Galloway 1.00 2.50
76A Blake Griffin 1.50 4.00
76B Blake Griffin VAR 1.50 4.00
77 Chris Andersen 1.25 3.00
78 Kemba Walker 1.50 4.00
79 Reggie Jackson 1.25 3.00
80 Tyler Johnson 1.00 2.50
81 Steven Adams 1.25 3.00
82A Damian Lillard 3.00 8.00
82B Damian Lillard VAR 3.00 8.00
83 Terrence Ross 1.25 3.00
84 John Henson 1.25 3.00
85 Jrue Holiday 1.25 3.00
86 Thaddeus Young 1.00 2.50
87A LeBron James 8.00 20.00
87B LeBron James VAR 8.00 20.00
88 Michael Kidd-Gilchrist 1.25 3.00
89 Stanley Johnson 1.00 2.50
90 Goran Dragic 1.25 3.00
91 Victor Oladipo 1.25 3.00
92 Allen Crabbe 1.00 2.50
93 Dante Exum 1.25 3.00
94 Gorgui Dieng 1.00 2.50
95A Anthony Davis 3.00 8.00
95B Anthony Davis VAR 3.00 8.00
96A Paul George 2.00 5.00
96B Paul George VAR 2.00 5.00
97A Kyrie Irving 3.00 8.00
97B Kyrie Irving VAR 3.00 8.00
98 Nicolas Batum 1.25 3.00
99 Tobias Harris 1.25 3.00
100 Hassan Whiteside 1.25 3.00
101 Aaron Gordon 1.25 3.00
102 Alex Len 1.00 2.50
103 George Hill 1.25 3.00
104 Joel Embiid 2.50 6.00
105 Alexis Ajinca 1.00 2.50
106 Myles Turner 1.25 3.00
107 Kevin Love 1.50 4.00
108A Wade Bulls
108B Wade Golden Eagles
108C Wade Heat 2.50 6.00
109 Andre Iguodala 1.25 3.00
110 Josh Richardson 1.00 2.50
111 Elfrid Payton 1.25 3.00
112 Eric Bledsoe 1.25 3.00
113 Gordon Hayward 1.50 4.00
114 Alan Williams RC 1.00 2.50
115A Zach LaVine 1.50 4.00
115B Zach LaVine VAR 1.50 4.00
116 Monta Ellis 1.25 3.00
117 Robin Lopez 1.00 2.50
118A Jimmy Butler 1.50 4.00
118B Jimmy Butler VAR 1.50 4.00
119A Draymond Green 2.00 5.00
119B Draymond Green VAR 2.00 5.00
120A Justise Winslow 1.25 3.00
120B Justise Winslow VAR 1.25 3.00
121 Evan Fournier 1.25 3.00
122A Devin Booker 2.50 6.00
122B Devin Booker VAR 2.50 6.00
123 Joe Johnson 1.25 3.00
124 Maurice Harkless 1.00 2.50
125 Ricky Rubio 1.50 4.00
126 Jeff Teague 1.25 3.00
127 Taj Gibson 1.25 3.00
128 Rajon Rondo 1.50 4.00
129A Klay Thompson 2.00 5.00
129B Klay Thompson VAR 2.00 5.00
130A Giannis Antetokounmpo 3.00 8.00
130B G. Antetokounmpo VAR 3.00 8.00
131 Mario Hezonja 1.00 2.50
132 Brandon Knight 1.25 3.00
133A Rodney Hood 1.25 3.00
133B Rodney Hood VAR 1.25 3.00
134 C.J. McCollum 1.25 3.00
135 Shaun Livingston 1.00 2.50
136 Trevor Ariza 1.00 2.50
137 Frank Kaminsky 1.25 3.00
138 Bobby Portis 1.00 2.50
139A Stephen Curry 6.00 15.00
139B Stephen Curry VAR 6.00 15.00
140 Jabari Parker 2.00 5.00
141 Nikola Vucevic 1.25 3.00
142 Robert Covington 1.00 2.50
143 Rudy Gobert 1.50 4.00
144 Ben McLemore 1.00 2.50
145A Karl-Anthony Towns 4.00 10.00
145B Karl-Anthony Towns VAR 4.00 10.00
146 Ryan Anderson 1.25 3.00
147 Cody Zeller 1.00 2.50
148 Marcus Smart 1.25 3.00
149 Zaza Pachulia 1.00 2.50
150 Khris Middleton 1.25 3.00
151 Serge Ibaka 1.25 3.00
152 Nik Stauskas 1.00 2.50
153 Bradley Beal 1.50 4.00
154 Patty Mills 1.50 4.00
155A Andrew Wiggins 2.50 6.00
155B Andrew Wiggins VAR 2.50 6.00
156 Patrick Beverley 1.00 2.50
157 Amir Johnson 1.00 2.50
158 Kyle Korver 1.25 3.00
159 Eric Gordon 1.25 3.00
160 Michael Carter-Williams 1.00 2.50
161 Jahlil Okafor 1.25 3.00
162 Nerlens Noel 1.25 3.00
163 Ian Mahinmi 1.00 2.50
164 Patrick Patterson 1.00 2.50
165 Miles Plumlee 1.00 2.50
166 Jonas Jerebko 1.00 2.50
167A James Harden 2.50 6.00
167B James Harden VAR 2.50 6.00
168 Rodney Stuckey 1.00 2.50
169 Mike Muscala 1.00 2.50
170 Will Barton 1.00 2.50
171A Kobe Bryant 6.00 15.00
171B Kobe Bryant VAR 6.00 15.00
172 David Robinson 2.50 6.00
173 Tracy McGrady 1.50 4.00
174 Larry Johnson 2.00 5.00
175A Scottie Pippen 3.00 8.00
175B Scottie Pippen VAR 3.00 8.00
176 Wilt Chamberlain 3.00 8.00
177A Barry Rockets
177B Barry Nets
177C Barry Oaks
177D Barry Capitols
177E Rick Barry GS Warriors 1.25 3.00
177F Barry SF Warriors
178 Shareef Abdur-Rahim 1.25 3.00
179A Olajuwon Rockets 2.00 5.00
179B Olajuwon Cougars
179C Olajuwon Raptors
180 Pete Maravich 2.50 6.00
181 Shaquille O'Neal 4.00 10.00
182 Dave DeBusschere 1.50 4.00
183A Erving 76ers 2.50 6.00
183B Erving Nets
183C Erving Squires
184 Gary Payton 1.50 4.00
185 Chris Webber 1.50 4.00
186 Larry Bird 4.00 10.00
187 Magic Johnson 4.00 10.00
188A Dikembe Mutombo Nuggets 1.50 4.00
188B Dikembe Mutombo Hawks 1.50 4.00
188C Mutombo Knicks
188D Mutombo 76ers
188E Dikembe Mutombo Rockets 1.50 4.00
188F Mutombo Nets
189 Clyde Drexler 2.00 5.00
190 Anfernee Hardaway 4.00 10.00
191 Connie Hawkins 1.50 4.00
192 Isiah Thomas 1.50 4.00
193 Chris Mullin 1.50 4.00
194A Ben Wallace 1.25 3.00
194B Wallace Bulls
194C Ben Wallace Pistons 1.25 3.00
194D Wallace Magic
194E Wallace Cavaliers
194F Wallace Wizards
195 Jason Kidd 1.50 4.00
196 John Stockton 2.50 6.00
197 Bill Bradley 2.00 5.00
198A Robert Parish Celtics 1.50 4.00
198B Parish Warriors
198C Parish Hornets
198D Parish Bulls
199 Bob Cousy 2.50 6.00
200 Oscar Robertson 2.00 5.00
201 Ingram JSY AU/199 RC 40.00 100.00
202 Brown JSY AU/199 RC 20.00 50.00
203 Bender JSY AU/199 RC 8.00 20.00
204 Dunn JSY AU/199 RC 10.00 25.00
205 Hield JSY AU/199 RC 25.00 60.00
206 Murray JSY AU/199 RC 15.00 40.00
207 Chriss JSY AU/199 RC 15.00 40.00
208 Jakob Poeltl JSY AU/199 RC 4.00 10.00
209 Maker JSY AU/199 RC 15.00 40.00
210 A.J. Hammons JSY AU/199 RC 3.00 8.00
211 Taurean Prince JSY AU/199 RC 5.00 12.00
212 Georgios Papagiannis JSY AU/199 RC 3.00
8.00
213 Valentine JSY AU/199 RC 8.00 20.00
214 Hernangomez JSY AU/199 RC 6.00 15.00
215 Cheick Diallo JSY AU/199 RC 3.00 8.00
216 Wade Baldwin IV JSY AU/199 RC 3.00 8.00
217 Henry Ellenson JSY AU/199 RC 4.00 10.00
218 Malik Beasley JSY AU/199 RC 3.00 8.00
219 LeVert JSY AU/199 RC 6.00 15.00
220 DeAndre' Bembry JSY AU/199 RC 3.00 8.00
221 Malachi Richardson JSY AU/199 RC 4.00 10.00
222 Stephen Zimmerman JSY AU/199 RC 3.00 8.00
223 Lwwu-Cbrrt JSY AU/199 RC 8.00 20.00
224 Brice Johnson JSY AU/199 RC 3.00 8.00
225 Murray JSY AU/199 RC 25.00 60.00
226 Pascal Siakam JSY AU/199 RC 3.00 8.00
227 Labissiere JSY AU/199 RC 12.00 30.00
228 Zubac JSY AU/199 RC 8.00 20.00
229 Jones JSY AU/199 RC 6.00 15.00
230 Deyonta Davis JSY AU/199 RC 3.00 8.00
231 Diamond Stone JSY AU/199 RC 5.00 12.00
232 Ulis JSY AU/199 RC 12.00 30.00
233 Whitehead JSY AU/199 RC 6.00 15.00
234 Demetrius Jackson JSY AU/199 RC 3.00 8.00
235 Brogdon JSY AU/199 RC 15.00 40.00
236 Felder JSY AU/199 RC 6.00 15.00
237 Gary Payton II JSY AU/199 RC 4.00 10.00
238 Saric JSY AU/199 RC 12.00 30.00
239 Ingram JSY AU/149 40.00 100.00
240 Brown JSY AU/149 20.00 50.00
241 Bender JSY AU/149 8.00 20.00
242 Dunn JSY AU/149 10.00 25.00
243 Hield JSY AU/149 25.00 60.00
244 Murray JSY AU/149 15.00 40.00
245 Chriss JSY AU/149 15.00 40.00
246 Jakob Poeltl JSY AU/149 4.00 10.00
247 Maker JSY AU/149 20.00 50.00
248 A.J. Hammons JSY AU/149 3.00 8.00
249 Taurean Prince JSY AU/149 5.00 12.00
250 Valentine JSY AU/149 8.00 20.00
251 Hernangomez JSY AU/149 4.00 10.00
252 Wade Baldwin IV JSY AU/149 3.00 8.00
253 Henry Ellenson JSY AU/149 4.00 10.00
254 Malik Beasley JSY AU/149 3.00 8.00
255 LeVert JSY AU/149 6.00 15.00
256 DeAndre' Bembry JSY AU/149 3.00 8.00
257 Malachi Richardson JSY AU/149 4.00 10.00
258 Lwwu-Cbrrt JSY AU/149 8.00 20.00
259 Brice Johnson JSY AU/149 3.00 8.00
260 Labissiere JSY AU/149 12.00 30.00
261 Jones JSY AU/149 3.00 8.00
262 Deyonta Davis JSY AU/149 3.00 8.00
263 Diamond Stone JSY AU/149 5.00 12.00
264 Ulis JSY AU/149 12.00 30.00
265 Whitehead JSY AU/149 6.00 15.00
266 Demetrius Jackson JSY AU/149 3.00 8.00
267 Brogdon JSY AU/149 20.00 50.00
268 Gary Payton II JSY AU/149 4.00 10.00
269 Saric JSY AU/149 15.00 40.00
270 Ingram JSY AU/99 50.00 120.00
271 Brown JSY AU/99 25.00 60.00
272 Bender JSY AU/99 10.00 25.00
273 Dunn JSY AU/99 12.00 30.00
274 Hield JSY AU/99 30.00 80.00
275 Murray JSY AU/99 20.00 20.00
276 Chriss JSY AU/99 20.00 50.00
277 Jakob Poeltl JSY AU/99 5.00 12.00
278 Maker JSY AU/99 20.00 50.00
279 A.J. Hammons JSY AU/99 4.00 10.00
280 Taurean Prince JSY AU/99 6.00 15.00
281 Valentine JSY AU/99 10.00 25.00
282 Hernangomez JSY AU/99 5.00 12.00
283 Wade Baldwin IV JSY AU/99 4.00 10.00
284 Henry Ellenson JSY AU/99 5.00 12.00
285 Malik Beasley JSY AU/99 4.00 10.00
286 LeVert JSY AU/99 8.00 20.00
287 DeAndre' Bembry JSY AU/99 4.00 10.00
288 Malachi Richardson JSY AU/99 5.00 12.00
289 Lwwu-Cbrrt JSY AU/99 10.00 25.00
290 Brice Johnson JSY AU/99 4.00 10.00
291 Labissiere JSY AU/99 15.00 40.00
292 Jones JSY AU/99 8.00 20.00
293 Deyonta Davis JSY AU/99 4.00 10.00
294 Diamond Stone JSY AU/99 6.00 15.00
295 Ulis JSY AU/99 15.00 40.00
296 Whitehead JSY AU/99 8.00 20.00
297 Demetrius Jackson JSY AU/99 4.00 10.00
298 Brogdon JSY AU/99 25.00 60.00
299 Gary Payton II JSY AU/99 5.00 12.00
300 Saric JSY AU/99 20.00 50.00
301 B. Ingram JSY AU/49 50.00 120.00
302 Brown JSY AU/49 25.00 60.00
303 Bender JSY AU/49 10.00 25.00
304 Dunn JSY AU/49 12.00 30.00
305 Hield JSY AU/49 30.00 80.00
306 Murray JSY AU/49 20.00 50.00
307 Chriss JSY AU/49 20.00 50.00
308 Jakob Poeltl JSY AU/49 5.00 12.00
309 Maker JSY AU/49 50.00 120.00
310 A.J. Hammons JSY AU/49 4.00 10.00
311 Taurean Prince JSY AU/49 6.00 15.00
312 Georgios Papagiannis JSY AU/49 4.00 10.00
313 Valentine JSY AU/49 10.00 25.00
314 Hernangomez JSY AU/49 5.00 12.00
315 Cheick Diallo JSY AU/49 4.00 10.00
316 Wade Baldwin IV JSY AU/49 4.00 10.00
317 Henry Ellenson JSY AU/49 5.00 12.00
318 Malik Beasley JSY AU/49 4.00 10.00
319 LeVert JSY AU/49 8.00 20.00
320 DeAndre' Bembry JSY AU/49 4.00 10.00
321 Malachi Richardson JSY AU/49 5.00 12.00
322 Stephen Zimmerman JSY AU/49 4.00 10.00
323 Lwwu-Cbrrt JSY AU/49 10.00 25.00
324 Brice Johnson JSY AU/49 4.00 10.00
325 Murray JSY AU/49 40.00 100.00
326 Pascal Siakam JSY AU/49 4.00 10.00
327 Labissiere JSY AU/49 15.00 40.00
328 Zubac JSY AU/49 10.00 25.00
329 Jones JSY AU/49 8.00 20.00
330 Deyonta Davis JSY AU/49 4.00 10.00
331 Diamond Stone JSY AU/49 6.00 15.00
332 Ulis JSY AU/49 15.00 40.00
333 Whitehead JSY AU/49 8.00 20.00
334 Demetrius Jackson JSY AU/49 4.00 10.00
335 Brogdon JSY AU/49 25.00 60.00
336 Felder JSY AU/49 8.00 20.00
337 Gary Payton II JSY AU/49 5.00 12.00
338 Saric JSY AU/49 20.00 50.00
339 Brandon Ingram GD 30.00 80.00
340 Ben Simmons GD
341 Jaylen Brown GD 20.00 50.00
342 Kris Dunn GD 15.00 40.00
343 Dragan Bender GD 6.00 15.00
344 Marquese Chriss GD 12.00 30.00
345 Buddy Hield GD 15.00 40.00
346 Jamal Murray GD 15.00 40.00
347 Jakob Poeltl GD 6.00 15.00
348 Thon Maker GD 15.00 40.00
349 Taurean Prince GD 8.00 20.00
350 Domantas Sabonis GD 8.00 20.00
351 Denzel Valentine GD 6.00 15.00
352 Wade Baldwin IV GD 5.00 12.00
353 Henry Ellenson GD 6.00 15.00
354 Caris LeVert GD 6.00 15.00
355 Isaiah Whitehead GD 5.00 12.00
356 Dejounte Murray GD 20.00 50.00
357 Skal Labissiere GD 8.00 20.00
358 Brice Johnson GD 5.00 12.00
359 Malachi Richardson GD 6.00 15.00
360 Malik Beasley GD 5.00 12.00
361 T. Luwawu-Cabarrot GD 10.00 25.00
362 DeAndre' Bembry GD 5.00 12.00
363 Cheick Diallo GD 5.00 12.00
364 Georgios Papagiannis GD 5.00 12.00
365 Juan Hernangomez GD 6.00 15.00
366 Pascal Siakam GD 5.00 12.00
367 Ivica Zubac GD 8.00 20.00
368 Damian Jones GD 5.00 12.00
369 Deyonta Davis GD 5.00 12.00
370 Malcolm Brogdon GD 12.00 30.00
371 Tyler Ulis GD 10.00 25.00
372 Patrick McCaw GD 30.00 80.00
373 Diamond Stone GD 5.00 12.00

2016-17 Panini Gold Standard Gold

*GOLD: .5X TO 1.2X BASE HI
RANDOM INSERTS IN PACKS
STATED PRINT RUN 79 SER.#'d SETS

2016-17 Panini Gold Standard 14K Autographs

RANDOM INSERTS IN PACKS
PRINT RUNS B/WN 25-49 COPIES PER
EXCHANGE DEADLINE 6/28/2018
1 Jimmy Butler/25 30.00 80.00
2 Avery Bradley/49 4.00 10.00
3 Jae Crowder/49 6.00 15.00
4 Dwight Powell/49 3.00 8.00
5 Kyrie Irving/25 40.00 100.00
6 Devin Booker/49 25.00 60.00
7 Kobe Bryant/25 100.00 250.00
8 Kevin Durant/25 75.00 200.00
10 Tom Gugliotta/49 3.00 8.00
11 Tim Hardaway/49 6.00 15.00
12 Cedric Maxwell/49 3.00 8.00
13 John Starks/49 4.00 10.00
14 Robert Horry/49 5.00 12.00
15 Vin Baker/49 3.00 8.00
16 Reggie Jackson/49 4.00 10.00
17 Andrei Kirilenko/49 4.00 10.00
18 Zach LaVine/49 12.00 30.00
19 Clint Capela/49 3.00 8.00
20 Evan Fournier/49 4.00 10.00
21 Evan Turner/49 3.00 8.00
23 Boban Marjanovic/49 5.00 12.00
25 David Robinson/25 30.00 80.00
26 Gary Payton/25 10.00 25.00
27 Sean Elliott/49 5.00 12.00
29 Spud Webb/49 4.00 10.00
30 Jamal Mashburn/49 5.00 12.00

2016-17 Panini Gold Standard AU Autographs

RANDOM INSERTS IN PACKS
STATED PRINT RUN 79 SER.#'d SETS
EXCHANGE DEADLINE 6/28/2018
1 Kevin Durant 60.00 150.00
2 Kyrie Irving 30.00 80.00
3 Carmelo Anthony 20.00 50.00
4 Dwyane Wade 60.00 150.00
5 Chris Paul 25.00 60.00
6 Mike Conley 4.00 10.00
7 Anthony Davis 40.00 100.00
8 Andrew Wiggins 20.00 50.00
9 Blake Griffin 15.00 40.00
10 John Wall 15.00 40.00
12 Karl-Anthony Towns 40.00 100.00
13 Isiah Thomas 10.00 25.00
14 Jimmy Butler 25.00 60.00
16 Tony Parker 20.00 50.00
19 Klay Thompson 25.00 60.00
20 Tobias Harris 4.00 10.00
21 Draymond Green 15.00 40.00
23 Kristaps Porzingis 25.00 60.00
24 Paul Millsap 5.00 12.00
25 Brandon Knight 4.00 10.00
27 Khris Middleton 4.00 10.00
28 Evan Turner 3.00 8.00
29 Jae Crowder 6.00 15.00
30 Matthew Dellavedova 6.00 15.00
31 Michael Carter-Williams 3.00 8.00
33 DeMarre Carroll 3.00 8.00
34 Nikola Vucevic 4.00 10.00
35 Devin Booker 25.00 60.00
36 Myles Turner 10.00 25.00
38 Marcus Smart 4.00 10.00
39 Zach LaVine 12.00 30.00
41 Bobby Portis 3.00 8.00
42 Cameron Payne 3.00 8.00
44 Nemanja Bjelica 4.00 10.00
45 Evan Fournier 10.00 25.00
46 Trey Lyles 4.00 10.00
47 D'Angelo Russell 8.00 20.00
49 Clint Capela 3.00 8.00
50 Thaddeus Young 3.00 8.00
51 Glen Rice 4.00 10.00
52 Dikembe Mutombo 10.00 25.00
53 Horace Grant 8.00 20.00
54 Jo Jo White 8.00 20.00
55 Allan Houston 4.00 10.00
56 Alvan Adams 3.00 8.00
57 Mark Aguirre 4.00 10.00
58 A.C. Green 6.00 15.00
59 Bill Cartwright 4.00 10.00
60 Tom Gugliotta 3.00 8.00
61 Tim Hardaway 6.00 15.00
62 Cedric Maxwell 3.00 8.00
63 Mark Price 8.00 20.00
64 Jim Chones 3.00 8.00
65 Jamal Mashburn 5.00 12.00
66 David Robinson 25.00 60.00
67 Ray Allen 20.00 50.00
68 Alex English 4.00 10.00
69 Dell Curry 5.00 12.00
70 Andrei Kirilenko 4.00 10.00
71 Robert Horry 5.00 12.00
72 Junior Bridgeman 3.00 8.00
73 Gary Payton 8.00 20.00
74 Toni Kukoc 8.00 20.00
75 Patrick Ewing 60.00 150.00
76 John Starks 4.00 10.00
77 Chauncey Billups 5.00 12.00
78 Larry Bird 50.00 120.00
79 Magic Johnson 25.00 60.00

2016-17 Panini Gold Standard Gold Scripts

RANDOM INSERTS IN PACKS
PRINT RUNS B/WN 25-99 COPIES PER
EXCHANGE DEADLINE 6/28/2018
1 Latrell Sprewell/25 8.00 20.00
2 Rashad Vaughn/99 3.00 8.00
3 Kobe Bryant/25 100.00 250.00
4 Tom Heinsohn/99 20.00 50.00
5 Scottie Pippen/25 30.00 80.00
6 Adrian Smith/99 3.00 8.00
7 Tom Van Arsdale/99 4.00 10.00
8 Sean Elliott/99 5.00 12.00
9 Seth Curry/99 10.00 25.00
10 Bob Lanier/25 5.00 12.00
11 Jason Terry/25 5.00 12.00
12 Calvin Murphy/25
13 George Gervin/25 8.00 20.00
14 Yao Ming/25 30.00 80.00
15 Jusuf Nurkic/47 6.00 15.00
16 Jordan Clarkson/25
17 Gail Goodrich/25 5.00 12.00
18 Vince Carter/25 12.00 30.00
19 Mario Chalmers/25 5.00 12.00
20 Brian Grant/99 6.00 15.00
21 Rony Seikaly/99 3.00 8.00
22 Michael Carter-Williams/25 4.00 10.00
23 Junior Bridgeman/99 3.00 8.00
24 Earl Monroe/25
25 Robert Covington/99 3.00 8.00
26 Andrew Nicholson/99 3.00 8.00
27 Joel Embiid/25 40.00 100.00
28 T.J. McConnell/99 3.00 8.00
29 Jahlil Okafor/25 10.00 25.00
30 JaKarr Sampson/99 3.00 8.00
31 Dan Issel/99 4.00 10.00
32 David Thompson/99 4.00 10.00
33 Jalen Rose/25 6.00 15.00
34 Spencer Haywood/99 3.00 8.00
35 Kevin McHale/25 6.00 15.00
36 Paul Millsap/25 6.00 15.00
37 Shawn Kemp/25 30.00 80.00
38 Chuck Person/25
39 Steve Blake/99 3.00 8.00
40 Jim Chones/99 3.00 8.00

2016-17 Panini Gold Standard Gold Standard Autographs

RANDOM INSERTS IN PACKS
PRINT RUNS B/WN 25-75 COPIES PER
EXCHANGE DEADLINE 6/28/2018
1 Jimmy Butler/25 30.00 80.00
2 Kobe Bryant/25 100.00 250.00
3 Kevin Durant/25 75.00 200.00
4 Kyrie Irving/25 40.00 100.00
5 Andrew Wiggins/25 25.00 60.00
6 Nikola Vucevic/75 4.00 10.00
7 Andrei Kirilenko/75 4.00 10.00
8 Draymond Green/25 20.00 50.00
10 Tobias Harris/75 4.00 10.00
11 Adrian Dantley/75 4.00 10.00
12 Chauncey Billups/75 5.00 12.00
13 Bill Walton/75 5.00 12.00
15 Antonio McDyess/75 4.00 10.00
16 Bill Laimbeer/75 4.00 10.00
17 Jeff Hornacek/75 4.00 10.00
18 Kiki Vandeweghe/75 4.00 10.00
19 Spud Webb/75 4.00 10.00
20 Robert Horry/75 5.00 12.00
21 Jo Jo White/75 8.00 20.00

2016-17 Panini Gold Standard Gold Strike Jersey Autographs

RANDOM INSERTS IN PACKS
PRINT RUNS B/WN 25-149 COPIES PER
EXCHANGE DEADLINE 6/28/2018
1 Carmelo Anthony/25 20.00 50.00
2 Kobe Bryant/25
3 Patrick Ewing/25 60.00 150.00
4 Dirk Nowitzki/25 60.00 150.00
5 Kyrie Irving/25 40.00 100.00
6 David Robinson/25 15.00 40.00
7 Karl-Anthony Towns/25 40.00 100.00
8 D'Angelo Russell/25 20.00 50.00
9 Deron Williams/25 5.00 12.00
10 Vince Carter/25 8.00 20.00
11 Alex Len/25 6.00 15.00
12 Tyson Chandler/25 5.00 12.00
13 Michael Carter-Williams/25 4.00 10.00
14 C.J. McCollum/25
15 Tristan Thompson/25
16 Dikembe Mutombo/35 10.00 25.00
17 Reggie Jackson/35
18 Reggie Bullock/149 3.00 8.00
19 Dan Majerle/85 4.00 10.00
20 Jerry Stackhouse/25 5.00 12.00
21 Gary Harris/35 4.00 10.00
22 Langston Galloway/149 3.00 8.00
24 Walter Davis/149 3.00 8.00
25 Bill Laimbeer/149 4.00 10.00
26 Kelly Olynyk/149 3.00 8.00
27 Dwight Powell/149 3.00 8.00
28 Archie Goodwin/149 3.00 8.00
29 T.J. McConnell/149 6.00 15.00
30 Robert Covington/149 3.00 8.00

2016-17 Panini Gold Standard Golden Graphs

RANDOM INSERTS IN PACKS
PRINT RUNS B/WN 25-99 COPIES PER
EXCHANGE DEADLINE 6/28/2018
1 Jimmy Butler/25 25.00 60.00
2 Tobias Harris/49 4.00 10.00
4 Jonas Valanciunas/99 4.00 10.00
5 Chauncey Billups/75 5.00 12.00
6 Reggie Jackson/99 4.00 10.00
7 Mike Conley/99 4.00 10.00
8 Tyus Jones/99 3.00 8.00
9 Avery Bradley/99 4.00 10.00
10 Gary Harris/75 4.00 10.00
11 Evan Turner/99 3.00 8.00
13 DeMarre Carroll/99 3.00 8.00
14 Kevin Durant/25 100.00 250.00
15 Kyrie Irving/25 40.00 100.00
16 Andrew Wiggins/25 25.00 60.00
19 Rondae Hollis-Jefferson/99 3.00 8.00
21 Nate Archibald/49 4.00 10.00
22 Devin Booker/75 25.00 60.00
23 Jamal Mashburn/49 5.00 12.00
24 David Thompson/99 4.00 10.00
25 Alex English/99 4.00 10.00
26 Bob McAdoo/99 4.00 10.00
27 John Stockton/25
28 Dan Issel/99 4.00 10.00
29 Sarunas Marciulionis/99 3.00 8.00
30 Glen Rice/99 4.00 10.00
31 Michael Cooper/99 4.00 10.00
32 Allan Houston/99 4.00 10.00

2016-17 Panini Gold Standard Golden Jumbo Threads

RANDOM INSERTS IN PACKS
STATED PRINT RUN 49 SER.#'d SETS
1 Tim Duncan/49 5.00 12.00
2 Grant Hill/49 5.00 12.00
3 Michael Redd/49 3.00 8.00
4 Shaquille O'Neal/49 10.00 25.00
5 Patrick Ewing/49 5.00 12.00
6 Andrei Kirilenko/49 3.00 8.00
7 Hakeem Olajuwon/49 5.00 12.00
8 Scottie Pippen/49 8.00 20.00
9 Richard Hamilton/49 3.00 8.00
10 Larry Bird/49 10.00 25.00

2016-17 Panini Gold Standard Golden Pairs

RANDOM INSERTS IN PACKS
STATED PRINT RUN 49 SER.#'d SETS
1 A.Gordon/Z.LaVine 4.00 10.00
2 M.Gasol/Z.Randolph 4.00 10.00
3 L.Aldridge/T.Parker 4.00 10.00
4 C.Anthony/L.James 12.00 30.00
5 D.Favors/G.Hayward 4.00 10.00
6 H.Olajuwon/G.Hill 8.00 20.00
7 M.Smart/I.Thomas 4.00 10.00
8 G.Dragic/H.Whiteside 3.00 8.00
9 J.Holiday/K.Love 4.00 10.00
10 P.Millsap/K.Korver 4.00 10.00
11 M.Ellis/P.George 5.00 12.00
12 D.Cousins/R.Gay 4.00 10.00
13 D.Robinson/T.Duncan 10.00 25.00
14 J.Butler/R.Westbrook 10.00 25.00
15 L.James/K.Irving 20.00 50.00
16 J.Okafor/N.Noel 3.00 8.00
17 V.Carter/K.Garnett 6.00 15.00
18 D.Lillard/K.Leonard 8.00 20.00
19 K.Faried/D.Gallinari 3.00 8.00
20 A.Wiggins/K.Towns 10.00 25.00
21 S.Pippen/S.O'Neal 10.00 25.00
22 M.Conley/R.Rubio 4.00 10.00
23 E.Kanter/S.Adams 3.00 8.00
24 A.Mourning/D.Wilkins 6.00 15.00

2016-17 Panini Gold Standard Golden Quads

RANDOM INSERTS IN PACKS
STATED PRINT RUN 49 SER.#'d SETS
1 Ro/Gi/Du/Pa 10.00 25.00
2 Le/An/Bu/Ge 6.00 15.00
3 To/Jo/La/Wi 12.00 30.00
4 Burks/Favors/Hood/Gobert 4.00 10.00
5 Lo/Ja/Sh/Ir 30.00 80.00
6 Ga/Ca/Co/Ra 8.00 20.00
7 Ga/Al/El/Gay 6.00 15.00
8 Ro/Ka/We/Ad 10.00 25.00
9 Ol/Ew/Hi/O'N 10.00 25.00
10 Ha/He/Ba/Co 10.00 25.00
11 Mickey/Rozier/Young/Hunter 3.00 8.00
12 Thomas/Fournier/Smart/Hezonja 4.00 10.00
13 Ha/Ze/Ol/Go 10.00 25.00
15 Gordon/Drummond/Beal/Ross 4.00 10.00
16 Exum/Lamb/Holiday/Dragic 3.00 8.00
17 Bogdanovic/Casspi/Porter/Stuckey 2.50 6.00
18 Okafor/Winslow/Turner/Hollis-Jefferson 3.00
8.00
20 Bi/Pi/Al/Ha 10.00 25.00
21 Mirotic/Vucevic/Noel/Millsap 4.00 10.00
22 Korver/Morris/Gallinari/Neto 3.00 8.00
23 Li/Wh/Po/Ru 8.00 20.00
24 Plumlee/Ariza/Plumlee/Sefolosha 3.00 8.00

2016-17 Panini Gold Standard Golden Trios

RANDOM INSERTS IN PACKS
STATED PRINT RUN 49 SER.#'d SETS
1 Hill/Allen/Duncan 6.00 15.00
2 Anthony/DeRozan/Butler 5.00 12.00
3 Love/Shumpert/James 15.00 40.00
4 Favors/Hood/Gobert 4.00 10.00
5 Carter/Gasol/Randolph 5.00 12.00
6 Leonard/Ginobili/Parker 10.00 25.00
7 Jordan/Walker/Carroll 4.00 10.00
8 Wiggins/Towns/Garnett 25.00 60.00
9 Kanter/Westbrook/Adams 10.00 25.00
10 Randle/Gay/LaVine 4.00 10.00
11 Stuckey/Ellis/George 5.00 12.00
12 Burks/Exum/Hayward 4.00 10.00
13 Beal/Gortat/Porter 4.00 10.00
14 Thomas/Hunter/Smart 4.00 10.00
15 Olajuwon/O'Neal/Ewing 10.00 25.00
16 Hezonja/Gordon/Fournier 3.00 8.00
17 Parker/Aldridge/Irving 6.00 15.00
18 Lillard/Dragic/Conley 5.00 12.00
19 Thompson/Lowry/Griffin 5.00 12.00
20 Drummond/Whiteside/Noel 4.00 10.00
21 Bird/Stockton/Pippen 10.00 25.00
22 Nurkic/Gallinari/Faried 3.00 8.00
23 Bazemore/Millsap/Sefolosha 8.00 20.00
24 Russell/Winslow/Turner 5.00 12.00
25 Oubre Jr./Portis/Hollis-Jefferson 2.50 6.00

2016-17 Panini Gold Standard Good as Gold Jersey Autographs

RANDOM INSERTS IN PACKS
PRINT RUNS B/WN 49-149 COPIES PER
EXCHANGE DEADLINE 6/28/2018
*PRIME/25: 1X TO 2.5X BASIC
1 Brandon Ingram/49 40.00 100.00
2 Juan Hernangomez/149 6.00 15.00
3 Jaylen Brown/49 25.00 60.00
4 Dragan Bender/49 10.00 25.00
5 Cheick Diallo/149 3.00 8.00
6 Kris Dunn/49 10.00 25.00
7 Henry Ellenson/149 4.00 10.00
8 Buddy Hield/49 20.00 50.00
9 Jamal Murray/49 15.00 40.00
10 Malik Beasley/149 3.00 8.00
11 Marquese Chriss/49 12.00 30.00
12 DeAndre' Bembry/149 3.00 8.00
13 Jakob Poeltl/49 4.00 10.00
14 Thon Maker/49 25.00 60.00
15 T. Luwawu-Cabarrot/149 6.00 15.00
16 Pascal Siakam/149 3.00 8.00
17 Ivica Zubac/149 12.00 30.00
18 Demetrius Jackson/149 3.00 8.00
19 Malcolm Brogdon/149 15.00 40.00
20 Kay Felder/149 3.00 8.00

2016-17 Panini Gold Standard Mother Lode Autographs

RANDOM INSERTS IN PACKS
PRINT RUNS B/WN 25-99 COPIES PER
EXCHANGE DEADLINE 6/28/2018
1 Kobe Bryant/25 100.00 250.00
2 T.J. McConnell/99 3.00 8.00
3 Scott Skiles/99 4.00 10.00
4 Hollis Thompson/99 3.00 8.00
5 Bobby Jones/99 4.00 10.00
6 Hersey Hawkins/99 3.00 8.00
7 Satch Sanders/99 5.00 12.00
8 Anthony Bennett/25
9 Scottie Pippen/25 30.00 80.00
10 Toni Kukoc/99 5.00 12.00
11 Reggie Jackson/75 4.00 10.00
12 Terrence Jones/99 4.00 10.00
13 Yao Ming/25 30.00 80.00
14 Vernon Maxwell/99 3.00 8.00
15 Cuttino Mobley/99
16 Jordan Clarkson/49 8.00 20.00

17 Jamaal Wilkes/99 5.00 12.00
18 Eddie Jones/99 4.00 10.00
19 Bob Dandridge/99 3.00 8.00
20 Karl-Anthony Towns/25 40.00 100.00
21 Archie Goodwin/99 3.00 8.00
22 C.J. McCollum/49 8.00 20.00
23 Allen Crabbe/99 3.00 8.00
24 Rod Strickland/99 3.00 8.00
25 Vlade Divac/99 5.00 12.00
26 Michael Kidd-Gilchrist/25 5.00 12.00
27 Steve Francis/27 5.00 12.00
28 C.J. Miles/99 4.00 10.00
29 Cedric Maxwell/88 3.00 8.00
30 Glenn Robinson III/99 3.00 8.00
31 Kendall Gill/99 6.00 15.00
32 Tristan Thompson/25 5.00 12.00
33 Mike Bibby/65 4.00 10.00
34 Latrell Sprewell/49 20.00 50.00
35 Mario Elie/99 3.00 8.00
36 Herb Williams/99 3.00 8.00
37 James Ennis/99 3.00 8.00
38 Chauncey Billups/49 5.00 12.00
39 Dennis Scott/99 3.00 8.00
40 Nick Anderson/99 4.00 10.00
41 Shawn Kemp/75 30.00 80.00
42 Norman Powell/99 3.00 8.00
43 Dante Exum/25 8.00 20.00
44 Thabo Sefolosha/75 3.00 8.00
45 Steve Smith/99 4.00 10.00
46 Spud Webb/99 4.00 10.00
47 Kent Bazemore/86 4.00 10.00
48 Glen Rice/75 4.00 10.00
49 Junior Bridgeman/99 3.00 8.00
50 Johnny Newman/99 3.00 8.00
51 Dick Barnett/99 5.00 12.00
52 Brian Grant/99 6.00 15.00
53 Gail Goodrich/39 4.00 10.00
54 Sidney Moncrief/99 3.00 8.00
55 Spencer Haywood/99 3.00 8.00
56 Michael Carter-Williams/25 4.00 10.00
57 Cazzie Russell/99 4.00 10.00
58 Kiki Vandeweghe/99 4.00 10.00
59 Tony Snell/99 3.00 8.00
60 Frank Ramsey/25 12.00 30.00

2016-17 Panini Gold Standard Newly Minted Memorabilia
RANDOM INSERTS IN PACKS
STATED PRINT RUN 25 SER.#'d SETS
1 Brandon Ingram 15.00 40.00
2 Jaylen Brown 10.00 25.00
3 Kris Dunn 8.00 20.00
4 Dragan Bender 3.00 8.00
5 Buddy Hield 8.00 20.00
6 Jamal Murray 8.00 20.00
7 Marquese Chriss 6.00 15.00
8 Jakob Poeltl 3.00 8.00
9 Thon Maker 8.00 20.00
10 Domantas Sabonis 4.00 10.00
11 Dario Saric 8.00 20.00
12 Georgios Papagiannis 2.50 6.00
13 Denzel Valentine 3.00 8.00
14 Juan Hernangomez 3.00 8.00
15 Wade Baldwin IV 2.50 6.00
16 Henry Ellenson 3.00 8.00
17 Malik Beasley 2.50 6.00
18 Caris LeVert 3.00 8.00
19 Malachi Richardson 3.00 8.00
20 Timothe Luwawu-Cabarrot 5.00 12.00
21 Brice Johnson 2.50 6.00
22 Skal Labissiere 4.00 10.00
23 Dejounte Murray 5.00 12.00
24 Cheick Diallo 2.50 6.00
25 Kay Felder 2.50 6.00

2016-17 Panini Gold Standard Newly Minted Memorabilia Duals
RANDOM INSERTS IN PACKS
STATED PRINT RUN 25 SER.#'d SETS
1 B.Ingram/J.Brown 20.00 50.00
2 D.Bender/G.Papagiannis 5.00 12.00
3 B.Hield/T.Prince 8.00 20.00
4 M.Chriss/D.Murray 10.00 25.00
5 S.Labissiere/J.Murray 12.00 30.00
6 H.Ellenson/K.Dunn 12.00 30.00
7 C.LeVert/D.Valentine 5.00 12.00
8 B.Johnson/D.Stone 4.00 10.00
9 J.Hernangomez/M.Beasley 5.00 12.00
10 P.McCaw/S.Zimmerman 8.00 20.00
11 D.Jones/W.Baldwin IV 4.00 10.00
12 D.Valentine/D.Davis 8.00 20.00
13 J.Murray/T.Ulis 12.00 30.00
14 Luwawu-Cabarrot/Saric 12.00 30.00
15 I.Zubac/B.Ingram 25.00 60.00
16 M.Brogdon/T.Maker 25.00 60.00
17 D.Jackson/J.Brown 12.00 30.00
18 I.Whitehead/C.LeVert 5.00 12.00
19 D.Jones/P.McCaw 12.00 30.00
20 C.Onuaku/G.Payton II 5.00 12.00
21 D.Davis/W.Baldwin IV 4.00 10.00
22 C.Diallo/B.Hield 8.00 20.00
23 P.Siakam/J.Poeltl 5.00 12.00
24 D.Bender/T.Ulis 12.00 30.00
25 D.Saric/D.Sabonis 12.00 30.00

2016-17 Panini Gold Standard Newly Minted Memorabilia Quads
RANDOM INSERTS IN PACKS
STATED PRINT RUN 25 SER.#'d SETS
1 Be/Br/In/Du 15.00 40.00
2 Ma/Sa/Be/Pa 8.00 20.00
3 Hi/Du/Ch/Mu 12.00 30.00
4 Mu/Va/Ba/Br 12.00 30.00
6 Br/Mc/Jo/Ja 12.00 30.00
7 Hield/Poeltl/Diallo/Siakam 10.00 25.00
8 In/Zu/He/Lu 15.00 40.00
9 Pa/Br/Ma/On 8.00 20.00
10 Johnson/Davis/Stone/Baldwin IV 4.00 10.00
11 Ch/Mu/Va/Da 10.00 25.00
12 In/Ch/Be/Zu 15.00 40.00
13 Hi/Va/Du/Mu 12.00 30.00
14 Hammons/Ellenson/Zimmerman/Prince 6.00
15.00
15 Jo/Ri/In/Fe 15.00 40.00
16 Bender/Labissiere/Poeltl/Felder 6.00 15.00
17 Mu/Be/Ul/Du 8.00 20.00
18 Br/Va/Pa/Wh 12.00 30.00
19 LeVert/Bembry/Jhsn/Hield 10.00 25.00
20 Be/Di/Mu/Ri 12.00 30.00
21 Ch/Mc/He/La 10.00 25.00
22 Hammons/Stone/Ellenson/Poeltl 5.00 12.00
23 Si/Fe/Zi/Ma 8.00 20.00
24 Ja/Lu-Ca/On/Pr 8.00 20.00
25 Ul/Sa/Pa/Br 8.00 20.00

2016-17 Panini Gold Standard Newly Minted Memorabilia Triples
RANDOM INSERTS IN PACKS
STATED PRINT RUN 25 SER.#'d SETS
1 Murray/Hernangomez/Beasley 8.00 20.00
2 Bender/Chriss/Ulis 8.00 20.00
3 Richardson/Papagiannis/Labissiere 6.00 15.00
4 Bender/Hernangomez/Papagiannis 5.00 12.00
5 Zubac/Maker/Luwawu-Cabarrot 8.00 20.00
6 Labissiere/Ulis/Murray 12.00 30.00
7 Prince/Hield/Diallo 12.00 30.00
8 Brogdon/Johnson/Jackson 8.00 20.00
9 Ingram/Bender/Brown 12.00 30.00
10 Hield/Murray/Dunn 12.00 30.00
11 Poeltl/Maker/Bender 8.00 20.00
12 Pa/He/Lu-Ca 8.00 20.00
13 Ingram/Hield/Dunn 15.00 40.00
14 Poeltl/Saric/Papagiannis 8.00 20.00
15 LeVert/Valentine/Murray 8.00 20.00
16 Chriss/Prince/Maker 8.00 20.00
17 Murray/Dunn/Baldwin IV 8.00 20.00
19 Johnson/Ellenson/Maker 8.00 20.00
20 Valentine/Ingram/Hield 20.00 50.00
21 Be/He/Lu-Ca 8.00 20.00
22 Ingram/Murray/Murray 20.00 50.00
23 Dunn/Johnson/Valentine 8.00 20.00
24 Stone/Maker/Bender 8.00 20.00
25 Murray/Murray/Brown 12.00 30.00

2016-17 Panini Gold Standard Rookie Jersey Autographs Prime
*PRIME: 1X TO 2.5X BASIC
RANDOM INSERTS IN PACKS
STATED PRINT RUN 25 SER.#'d SETS
EXCHANGE DEADLINE 6/28/2018

2016-17 Panini Gold Standard White Gold Threads
RANDOM INSERTS IN PACKS
STATED PRINT RUN 49 SER.#'d SETS
1 Tim Duncan 5.00 12.00
2 Carmelo Anthony 4.00 10.00
3 LeBron James 12.00 30.00
4 Vince Carter 4.00 10.00
5 Kevin Garnett 5.00 12.00
6 Russell Westbrook 5.00 12.00
7 Grant Hill 4.00 10.00
8 Kawhi Leonard 5.00 12.00
9 Dwyane Wade 5.00 12.00
10 Derrick Rose 4.00 10.00
11 Patrick Ewing 4.00 10.00
12 Shaquille O'Neal 8.00 20.00
13 Thaddeus Young 2.00 5.00
14 Zach LaVine 3.00 8.00
15 Bradley Beal 3.00 8.00

2012 Panini Golden Age
COMP.SET w/o SP's (146) 15.00 40.00
SP ANNCD PRINT RUN OF 92 PER
87 Bill Russell .75 2.00
87SP Bill Russell SP 10.00 25.00
94 Meadowlark Lemon .50 1.25
121 Bill Walton .50 1.25
131 Kareem Abdul-Jabbar .75 2.00
131SP Kareem Abdul-Jabbar SP 6.00 15.00
142 Jerry West .60 1.50

2012 Panini Golden Age Historic Signatures
STATED ODDS 1:24 HOBBY
22 Bill Walton 8.00 20.00
31 Meadowlark Lemon 12.50 30.00

2012 Panini Golden Age Mini Broadleaf Blue Ink
*MINI BLUE: 2.5X TO 6X BASIC

2012 Panini Golden Age Mini Broadleaf Brown Ink
*MINI BROWN: .6X TO 1.5X BASIC
APPX.ODDS ONE PER PACK

2012 Panini Golden Age Mini Crofts Candy Blue Ink
*MINI BLUE: 1.5X TO 4X BASIC

2012 Panini Golden Age Mini Crofts Candy Red Ink
*MINI RED: 1.5X TO 4X BASIC
APPX.ODDS 1:8 HOBBY

2012 Panini Golden Age Mini Ty Cobb Tobacco
*MINI COBB: 2.5X TO 6X BASIC

2012 Panini Golden Age Newark Evening World Supplement
APPX.ODDS 1:24 HOBBY
20 Bill Russell 3.00 8.00
22 Jerry West 3.00 8.00

2013 Panini Golden Age
139 Curly Neal .50 1.25

2013 Panini Golden Age White
*WHITE: 3X TO 8X BASIC
NO WHITE SP PRICING AVAILABLE

2013 Panini Golden Age Delong Gum
COMPLETE SET (30) 40.00 80.00
8 Curly Neal 1.25 3.00

2013 Panini Golden Age Historic Signatures
EXCHANGE DEADLINE 12/26/2014
CN Curly Neal 20.00 50.00

2013 Panini Golden Age Mini American Caramel Blue Back
*MINI BLUE: 1.2X TO 3X BASIC

2013 Panini Golden Age Mini American Caramel Red Back
*MINI RED: 2X TO 5X BASIC

2013 Panini Golden Age Mini Carolina Brights Green Back
*MINI GREEN: .75X TO 2X BASIC

2013 Panini Golden Age Mini Carolina Brights Purple Back
*MINI PURPLE: 2X TO 5X BASIC

2013 Panini Golden Age Mini Nadja Caramels Back
*MINI NADJA: 2X TO 5X BASIC

2013 Panini Golden Age Playing Cards
COMPLETE SET (53) 50.00 100.00
31 Curly Neal 1.25 3.00

2013 Panini Golden Age Tip Top Bread Labels
COMPLETE SET (10) 10.00 25.00
6 Curly Neal 1.00 2.50

2014 Panini Golden Age
COMP.SET w/o SP's (150) 12.00 30.00
79 Geese Ausbie .25 .60
83 Jerry West .40 1.00
90 Marques Haynes .25 .60
101 Bill Russell .50 1.25
135 Artis Gilmore .25 .60
143 George Gervin .30 .75

2014 Panini Golden Age White
*WHITE: 2.5X TO 6X BASIC

2014 Panini Golden Age Mini Croft's Swiss Milk Cocoa
*MINI CROFTS: 2.5X TO 6X BASIC

2014 Panini Golden Age Mini Hindu Brown Back
*MINI HINDU BROWN: 2X TO 5X BASIC

2014 Panini Golden Age Mini Hindu Red Back
*MINI HINDU RED: 2.5X TO 6X BASIC

2014 Panini Golden Age Mini Mono Brand Blue Back
*MINI MONO BLUE: 1.5X TO 4X BASIC

2014 Panini Golden Age Mini Mono Brand Green Back
*MINI MONO GREEN: 1.5X TO 4X BASIC

2014 Panini Golden Age Mini Smith's Mello Mint
*MINI MELLO: 5X TO 12X BASIC

2014 Panini Golden Age First Fifty
*1ST FIFTY: 3X TO 8X BASIC
STATED PRINT RUN 50 SER.#'d SETS

2014 Panini Golden Age Historic Signatures
EXCHANGE DEADLINE 01/02/2016
ART Artis Gilmore 5.00 12.00
AUS Geese Ausbie 5.00 12.00
GRV George Gervin 8.00 20.00
HYN Marques Haynes 5.00 12.00

2014 Panini Golden Age Star Stamps
14 John Havlicek 3.00 8.00
Jerry West
George Gervin
Bill Russell

2016-17 Panini Grand Reserve
COMP.SET w/o AU's (100) 40.00 100.00
JSY AU RC RANDOMLY INSERTED
101-140 PRINT 99 SER.#'d SETS
EXCHANGE DEADLIN 1/19/2019
1 Ben Simmons RC 8.00 20.00
2 Joel Embiid 1.00 2.50
3 Giannis Antetokounmpo 1.25 3.00
4 Jabari Parker .75 2.00
5 Khris Middleton .50 1.25
6 Jimmy Butler .60 1.50
7 Dwyane Wade 1.00 2.50
8 Cameron Payne .40 1.00
9 LeBron James 2.50 6.00
10 Kyrie Irving 1.25 3.00
11 Kevin Love .60 1.50
12 Isaiah Thomas .60 1.50
13 Al Horford .50 1.25
14 Marcus Smart .50 1.25
15 Chris Paul .75 2.00
16 Blake Griffin .60 1.50
17 DeAndre Jordan .60 1.50
18 Marc Gasol .60 1.50
19 Mike Conley .50 1.25
20 Zach Randolph .50 1.25
21 Malcolm Delaney .50 1.25
22 Dennis Schroder .50 1.25
23 Paul Millsap .60 1.50
24 Goran Dragic .50 1.25
25 Hassan Whiteside .50 1.25
26 James Johnson .40 1.00
27 Kemba Walker .60 1.50
28 Michael Kidd-Gilchrist .50 1.25
29 Nicolas Batum .50 1.25
30 Gordon Hayward .60 1.50
31 Rudy Gobert .60 1.50
32 George Hill .50 1.25
33 Darren Collison .50 1.25
34 Willie Cauley-Stein .50 1.25
35 Ben McLemore .40 1.00
36 Carmelo Anthony .75 2.00
37 Kristaps Porzingis 1.25 3.00
38 Derrick Rose .75 2.00
39 D'Angelo Russell .75 2.00
40 Julius Randle .60 1.50
41 Jordan Clarkson .50 1.25
42 Elfrid Payton .50 1.25
43 Aaron Gordon .50 1.25
44 Nikola Vucevic .50 1.25
45 Yogi Ferrell RC 1.50 4.00
46 Dirk Nowitzki .75 2.00
47 Harrison Barnes .50 1.25
48 Jeremy Lin .60 1.50
49 Brook Lopez .50 1.25
50 Sean Kilpatrick .40 1.00
51 Kenneth Faried .50 1.25
52 Emmanuel Mudiay .50 1.25
53 Danilo Gallinari .50 1.25
54 Paul George .75 2.00
55 Jeff Teague .50 1.25
56 Myles Turner .50 1.25
57 Anthony Davis 1.25 3.00
58 DeMarcus Cousins .60 1.50
59 Jrue Holiday .50 1.25
60 Reggie Jackson .50 1.25
61 Kentavious Caldwell-Pope .50 1.25
62 Andre Drummond .60 1.50
63 Kyle Lowry .50 1.25
64 DeMar DeRozan .60 1.50
65 Serge Ibaka .50 1.25
66 James Harden 1.00 2.50
67 Eric Gordon .50 1.25
68 Ryan Anderson .50 1.25
69 Tony Parker .60 1.50
70 LaMarcus Aldridge .60 1.50
71 Kawhi Leonard 1.00 2.50
72 Devin Booker 1.00 2.50
73 Tyson Chandler .50 1.25
74 Eric Bledsoe .50 1.25
75 Russell Westbrook 1.50 4.00
76 Doug McDermott .50 1.25
77 Victor Oladipo .50 1.25
78 Andrew Wiggins 1.00 2.50
79 Karl-Anthony Towns 1.50 4.00
80 Ricky Rubio .60 1.50
81 Damian Lillard 1.25 3.00
82 C.J. McCollum .50 1.25
83 Jusuf Nurkic .40 1.00
84 Stephen Curry 2.50 6.00
85 Kevin Durant 1.50 4.00
86 Draymond Green .75 2.00
87 Klay Thompson .75 2.00
88 John Wall .75 2.00
89 Markieff Morris .40 1.00
90 Otto Porter .50 1.25
91 Bradley Beal .60 1.50
92 Robert Covington .40 1.00
93 Kyle Korver .50 1.25
94 Steven Adams .50 1.25
95 Wesley Matthews .40 1.00
96 Gary Harris .50 1.25
97 Jamal Crawford .60 1.50
98 Jae Crowder .50 1.25
99 DeMarre Carroll .40 1.00
100 Andre Iguodala .50 1.25
101 Ingram JSY AU/99 RC 75.00 200.00
102 Dunn JSY AU/99 RC 20.00 50.00
103 Hield JSY AU/99 RC 25.00 60.00
104 Murray JSY AU/99 RC 30.00 80.00
105 Brown JSY AU/99 RC 30.00 80.00
106 Murray JSY AU/99 RC
107 Kay Felder JSY AU/99 RC 6.00 15.00
108 Stephen Zimmerman JSY AU/99 RC 4.00 10.00
109 Labissiere JSY AU/99 RC 12.00 30.00
110 Richardson JSY AU/99 RC 10.00 25.00
111 Chriss JSY AU/99 RC 15.00 40.00
112 J.Hrnngmz JSY AU/99 RC 10.00 25.00
113 Sabonis JSY AU/99 RC
114 Brogdon JSY AU/99 RC 20.00 50.00
115 Zipser JSY AU/99 RC 12.00 30.00
116 Pascal Siakam JSY AU/99 RC 6.00 15.00
117 W.Hrnngmz JSY AU/99 RC 12.00 30.00
118 Caris LeVert JSY AU/99 RC 6.00 15.00
119 Brice Johnson JSY AU/99 RC 4.00 10.00
120 Maker JSY AU/99 RC 25.00 60.00
121 Plumlee JSY AU/99 RC
122 Jakob Poeltl JSY AU/99 RC 5.00 12.00
123 Jake Layman JSY AU/99 RC 6.00 15.00
124 McCaw JSY AU/99 RC 20.00 50.00
125 Demetrius Jackson JSY AU/99 RC 4.00 10.00
126 Wade Baldwin IV JSY AU/99 RC 4.00 10.00
127 Niang JSY AU/99 RC 4.00 10.00
128 Kuzminskas JSY AU/99 RC 8.00 20.00
129 Isaiah Whitehead JSY AU/99 RC 6.00 15.00
130 Damian Jones JSY AU/99 RC 4.00 10.00
131 Valentine JSY AU/99 RC 10.00 25.00
132 A.J. Hammons JSY AU/99 RC 4.00 10.00
133 Lwwu-Cbrrt JSY AU/99 RC 8.00 20.00
134 Saric JSY AU/99 RC 20.00 50.00
135 Deyonta Davis JSY AU/99 RC 4.00 10.00
136 Zubac JSY AU/99 RC 15.00 40.00
137 Malik Beasley JSY AU/99 RC 6.00 15.00
138 Ulis JSY AU/99 RC 25.00 60.00
139 Cheick Diallo JSY AU/99 RC 6.00 15.00
140 Henry Ellenson JSY AU/99 RC 5.00 12.00

2016-17 Panini Grand Reserve Vintage
*VNTGE: 2.5X TO 6X BASIC
*VNTGE RC: 2X TO 5X BASIC RC
RANDOM INSERTS IN PACKS
1 Ben Simmons 250.00 400.00
9 LeBron James 20.00 50.00
84 Stephen Curry 20.00 50.00

2016-17 Panini Grand Reserve All Systems Go
RANDOM INSERTS IN PACKS
1 Tony Parker 5.00 12.00
2 Mike Conley 4.00 10.00
3 Kyrie Irving 10.00 25.00
4 Isaiah Thomas 5.00 12.00
5 John Wall 6.00 15.00
6 Stephen Curry 25.00 60.00
7 Darren Collison 4.00 10.00
8 D'Angelo Russell 6.00 15.00
9 George Hill 4.00 10.00
10 Emmanuel Mudiay 4.00 10.00
11 Goran Dragic 4.00 10.00
12 Devin Booker 12.00 30.00
13 T.J. McConnell 3.00 8.00
14 Dennis Schroder 4.00 10.00
15 Jimmy Butler 5.00 12.00

2016-17 Panini Grand Reserve Closing Statements
RANDOM INSERTS IN PACKS
1 Kobe Bryant 150.00 400.00
2 Wilt Chamberlain 30.00 80.00
3 Bill Russell 25.00 60.00
4 Larry Bird 40.00 100.00
5 David Robinson 50.00 120.00

2016-17 Panini Grand Reserve Cornerstones Quad Jersey Autographs
RANDOM INSERTS IN PACKS
PRINT RUNS B/WN 35-99 COPIES PER
EXCHANGE DEADLINE 1/19/2019
*QRTZ/30-49: .5X TO 1.2X p/r 75-99
*QRTZ/30-49: .4X TO 1X p/r 35-49
*QRTZ/25: .75X TO 2X p/r 75-99
*QRTZ/25: .6X TO 1.5X p/r 35-49
*GRNTE/20-25: .75X TO 2X p/r 75-99
*GRNTE/20-25: .6X TO 1.5X p/r 35-49
1 Julius Randle/35
2 Myles Turner/99 10.00 25.00
3 Kristaps Porzingis/35 30.00 80.00
4 Karl-Anthony Towns/35 40.00 100.00
5 Clint Capela/99 8.00 20.00
6 Matthew Dellavedova/99 5.00 12.00
7 Devin Booker/75 30.00 80.00
8 Udonis Haslem/99 4.00 10.00
9 J.J. Barea/99 15.00 40.00
10 Elfrid Payton/75 8.00 20.00
11 Bobby Portis/99 4.00 10.00
12 Jimmy Butler/35 20.00 50.00
13 Joel Embiid/35
14 George Hill/99
15 Evan Turner/99 4.00 10.00
16 Kevin Durant/35 100.00 250.00
17 Kyrie Irving/35 40.00 100.00
18 John Wall/35
19 Tony Parker/35 15.00 40.00
20 Kenneth Faried/75 5.00 12.00
21 Evan Fournier/99 5.00 12.00
22 Goran Dragic/75 5.00 12.00
23 Eric Gordon/75 5.00 12.00
24 Michael Kidd-Gilchrist/99 5.00 12.00
25 Ryan Anderson/99 5.00 12.00
26 Carmelo Anthony/35 20.00 50.00
27 Dwyane Wade/35 25.00 60.00
28 Chris Paul/35 15.00 40.00
29 D'Angelo Russell/40 10.00 25.00
30 Anthony Davis/35 30.00 80.00
31 C.J. McCollum/35 10.00 25.00
32 Gordon Hayward/40 15.00 40.00
33 Zach LaVine/99 12.00 30.00
34 Jordan Clarkson/75
35 Luol Deng/99 5.00 12.00
36 Justin Anderson/99 5.00 12.00
37 Nikola Mirotic/75 5.00 12.00
38 Jeremy Lin/35 50.00 120.00
39 Isaiah Thomas/49 15.00 40.00
40 Jrue Holiday/35 6.00 15.00

2016-17 Panini Grand Reserve Difference Makers Autographs
RANDOM INSERTS IN PACKS
PRINT RUNS B/WN 10-99 COPIES PER
NO PRICING ON QTY 10
EXCHANGE DEADLINE 1/19/2019
2 Joe Dumars/75 5.00 12.00
3 Kareem Abdul-Jabbar/25 40.00 100.00
4 James Worthy/35 10.00 25.00
5 Troy Daniels/99 3.00 8.00
7 Isaiah Thomas/75 10.00 25.00
8 Tony Parker/35 25.00 60.00
10 Anthony Davis/25 25.00 60.00
11 Chris Paul/25 20.00 50.00
12 Carmelo Anthony/25 12.00 30.00
13 Dwyane Wade/25 30.00 80.00
15 Kevin Durant/25 75.00 200.00
16 Andrew Wiggins/35 20.00 50.00
17 Karl-Anthony Towns/35 40.00 100.00
18 Alex English/99 4.00 10.00
19 Hakeem Olajuwon/35 15.00 40.00
20 Walt Frazier/75 8.00 20.00
21 Bob Lanier/75 6.00 15.00
22 Oscar Robertson/35 30.00 80.00
23 George Gervin/75 6.00 15.00
24 David Robinson/35 20.00 50.00
25 Cedric Maxwell/99 3.00 8.00
26 Tim Hardaway/99 6.00 15.00
27 Glen Rice/99 4.00 10.00
29 Latrell Sprewell/75 12.00 30.00
30 Yao Ming/35 60.00 150.00
31 Arvydas Sabonis/99 10.00 25.00
33 Justise Winslow/75 5.00 12.00
36 John Wall/35 20.00 50.00
38 Devin Booker/75 25.00 60.00
39 Clint Capela/99 3.00 8.00
40 Elfrid Payton/75 4.00 10.00
41 Tristan Thompson/75 4.00 10.00
42 Jimmy Butler/35
44 Matthew Dellavedova/99 5.00 12.00
45 Nikola Mirotic/75 4.00 10.00
46 Vince Carter/35 25.00 60.00
47 Evan Fournier/99 4.00 10.00
50 Frank Ramsey/75 10.00 25.00

2016-17 Panini Grand Reserve Dominating Performances
RANDOM INSERTS IN PACKS
1 John Wall 1.50 4.00
2 Jimmy Butler 1.25 3.00
3 Kevin Durant 3.00 8.00
4 Kevin Love 1.25 3.00
5 Klay Thompson 1.50 4.00
6 James Harden 2.00 5.00
7 Anthony Davis 2.50 6.00
8 Russell Westbrook 3.00 8.00
9 Isaiah Thomas 1.25 3.00
10 Andrew Wiggins 2.00 5.00
11 Stephen Curry 5.00 12.00
12 Rudy Gobert 1.25 3.00
13 DeAndre Jordan 1.25 3.00
14 Russell Westbrook 3.00 8.00
15 LeBron James 5.00 12.00
16 Giannis Antetokounmpo 2.50 6.00
17 Damian Lillard 2.50 6.00
18 Kyrie Irving 2.50 6.00
19 Anthony Davis 2.50 6.00
20 Andre Drummond 1.25 3.00
21 Kevin Love 1.25 3.00
22 John Stockton 2.00 5.00
23 Draymond Green 1.50 4.00
24 Eric Bledsoe 1.00 2.50
25 Malcolm Brogdon 2.00 5.00
26 Stephen Curry 5.00 12.00
27 Dion Waiters 1.00 2.50
28 Carmelo Anthony 1.50 4.00
29 DeMar DeRozan 1.25 3.00
30 Kyrie Irving 2.50 6.00
31 David Thompson 1.00 2.50
32 Pete Maravich 2.00 5.00
33 Glen Rice 1.00 2.50
34 Gary Payton 1.25 3.00
35 Tim Duncan 2.00 5.00
36 Magic Johnson 3.00 8.00
37 Dennis Rodman 2.50 6.00
38 Shaquille O'Neal 3.00 8.00
39 John Havlicek 1.50 4.00
40 Damon Stoudamire 1.00 2.50
41 Wilt Chamberlain 2.50 6.00
42 Steve Nash 1.25 3.00
43 Shawn Marion 1.00 2.50
44 Vince Carter 1.50 4.00
45 Allen Iverson 1.50 4.00
46 David Robinson 2.00 5.00
47 Larry Bird 3.00 8.00
48 Dominique Wilkins 1.50 4.00
49 Karl Malone 1.50 4.00
50 Hakeem Olajuwon 1.50 4.00

2016-17 Panini Grand Reserve Grand Autographs
RANDOM INSERTS IN PACKS
PRINT RUNS B/WN 35-99 COPIES PER
EXCHANGE DEADLINE 1/19/2019
*GRNTE/25: .6X TO 1.5X p/r 99
*GRNTE/25: .5X TO 1.2X p/r 35-49
1 Buddy Hield/35 10.00 25.00
2 Denzel Valentine/49 5.00 12.00
3 Eric Gordon/49 5.00 12.00
4 Juan Hernangomez/49 8.00 20.00
5 D'Angelo Russell/35
6 Tim Hardaway Jr./99 3.00 8.00
7 Zydrunas Ilgauskas/99 4.00 10.00
8 Frank Ramsey/49 12.00 30.00
9 Kyle Wiltjer/99 3.00 8.00
10 C.J. McCollum/35 12.00 30.00
11 Glen Rice/49 5.00 12.00
12 Allan Houston/99 4.00 10.00
13 DeMarre Carroll/99 3.00 8.00
14 Doug McDermott/99 4.00 10.00
15 Larry Nance/99 4.00 10.00
16 Jason Terry/49 5.00 12.00
17 Trey Lyles/99 4.00 10.00
18 Walter Berry/99 3.00 8.00
19 Gordon Hayward/49 8.00 20.00
20 Alec Burks/99 3.00 8.00
21 Ron Harper/99 5.00 12.00
22 Victor Oladipo/35 5.00 12.00
23 Kenny "Sky" Walker/99 5.00 12.00
24 Dennis Schroder/99 4.00 10.00
25 Dennis Scott/99 3.00 8.00
26 John Starks/99 4.00 10.00
27 Dan Issel/99 4.00 10.00
28 Will Barton/99 3.00 8.00
29 Georgios Papagiannis/49 4.00 10.00
30 Cedric Ceballos/99 3.00 8.00
31 Semaj Christon/99 3.00 8.00
32 Brandon Ingram/35 60.00 150.00
33 Taurean Prince/99 5.00 12.00
34 Cody Zeller/35 4.00 10.00
35 DeAndre' Bembry/99 3.00 8.00
36 Rondae Hollis-Jefferson/99 3.00 8.00
37 Rodney McGruder/99 4.00 10.00
38 Malcolm Delaney/99 4.00 10.00
39 Larry Nance Jr./99 4.00 10.00
40 Dan Majerle/99 5.00 12.00

2016-17 Panini Grand Reserve Hickory Memorabilia
RANDOM INSERTS IN PACKS
STATED PRINT RUN 39 SER.#'d SETS
1 Monta Ellis 12.00 30.00
2 Myles Turner 12.00 30.00
3 Paul George 20.00 50.00
4 Glenn Robinson III 12.00 30.00
5 C.J. Miles 12.00 30.00

2016-17 Panini Grand Reserve Highly Revered Autographs
RANDOM INSERTS IN PACKS
PRINT RUNS B/WN 25-99 COPIES PER
EXCHANGE DEADLINE 1/19/2019
1 Karl-Anthony Towns/35 40.00 100.00
2 Myles Turner/99 5.00 12.00
3 John Wall/35 20.00 50.00
5 Devin Booker/60 25.00 60.00
6 Michael Kidd-Gilchrist/99 4.00 10.00
7 Tristan Thompson/99 4.00 10.00
8 Kevin Durant/25 75.00 200.00
9 Jimmy Butler/35
10 Nikola Mirotic/99 4.00 10.00
11 Oscar Robertson/35 30.00 80.00
12 Bill Walton/99 5.00 12.00
13 Kareem Abdul-Jabbar/35 30.00 80.00
14 Gail Goodrich/99 4.00 10.00
15 Hakeem Olajuwon/35 15.00 40.00
16 Magic Johnson/25 30.00 80.00
17 Larry Bird/25 50.00 120.00
18 Adrian Dantley/99 4.00 10.00
19 James Worthy/49 10.00 25.00
20 Nate Archibald/99 4.00 10.00
21 Arvydas Sabonis/99 10.00 25.00
22 Walt Frazier/60 8.00 20.00
23 Rick Barry/35 8.00 20.00
24 Dave Cowens/99 8.00 20.00

2016-17 Panini Grand Reserve Legendary Cornerstones Quad Jersey Autographs
RANDOM INSERTS IN PACKS
PRINT RUNS B/WN 34-99 COPIES PER
EXCHANGE DEADLINE 1/19/2019
*GRANITE/23-25: .75X TO 2X BASIC
1 Kareem Abdul-Jabbar/35 50.00 120.00
2 David Robinson/35 20.00 50.00
3 Shaquille O'Neal/35
4 Dan Issel/99 5.00 12.00
5 Grant Hill/35 20.00 50.00
6 Bernard King/60 5.00 12.00
7 Louie Dampier/49 5.00 12.00
8 Gary Payton/35 12.00 30.00
9 Arvydas Sabonis/99 10.00 25.00
10 Robert Horry/34 10.00 25.00
11 Vlade Divac/99 6.00 15.00
12 Mark Aguirre/99 5.00 12.00
13 Kenny Smith/60
14 Tim Hardaway/99 10.00 25.00
15 Glen Rice/99 8.00 20.00
17 Jason Kidd/35 20.00 50.00
18 Allen Iverson/35
19 Hakeem Olajuwon/35 20.00 50.00
20 Alex English/99 6.00 15.00

2016-17 Panini Grand Reserve Local Legends Autographs
RANDOM INSERTS IN PACKS
STATED PRINT RUN 25 SER.#'d SETS
EXCHANGE DEADLINE 1/19/2019
1 Larry Bird 50.00 120.00
2 Oscar Robertson 40.00 100.00
3 Allen Iverson 50.00 120.00
4 Magic Johnson 30.00 80.00
5 Kobe Bryant 100.00 200.00
6 Kevin Durant 75.00 200.00
7 Stephen Curry 100.00 250.00
8 Anthony Davis 25.00 60.00
9 John Wall 25.00 60.00
10 Paul George 15.00 40.00

2016-17 Panini Grand Reserve Reserve Materials
RANDOM INSERTS IN PACKS
STATED PRINT RUN 35 SER.#'d SETS
*GRANITE/25: .75X TO 2X BASIC
1 Thabo Sefolosha 2.00 5.00
2 Dwight Howard 2.50 6.00
3 Amir Johnson 2.00 5.00
4 James Young 2.00 5.00
5 Kelly Olynyk 2.00 5.00
6 Rondae Hollis-Jefferson 2.00 5.00
7 LeBron James 15.00 40.00
8 Stephen Curry 15.00 40.00
9 Kevin Durant 8.00 20.00
10 Russell Westbrook 6.00 15.00
11 James Harden 5.00 12.00
12 Jeremy Lamb 2.00 5.00
13 Giannis Antetokounmpo 6.00 15.00
14 Nicolas Batum 2.50 6.00
15 Kemba Walker 3.00 8.00
16 Nikola Mirotic 2.50 6.00
17 Dirk Nowitzki 4.00 10.00
18 Devin Harris 2.00 5.00
19 Wesley Matthews 2.00 5.00
20 Danilo Gallinari 2.50 6.00
21 Jameer Nelson 2.00 5.00
22 Jusuf Nurkic 2.00 5.00
23 Nikola Jokic 3.00 8.00
24 Rudy Gay 3.00 8.00
25 Cory Joseph 2.00 5.00
26 Kyle Lowry 2.50 6.00
27 Bradley Beal 3.00 8.00
28 John Wall 4.00 10.00
29 Trey Burke 2.00 5.00
30 DeMarcus Cousins 3.00 8.00
31 Joakim Noah 2.50 6.00
32 Derrick Rose 4.00 10.00
33 Kristaps Porzingis 4.00 10.00
34 Carmelo Anthony 4.00 10.00
35 Al Horford 2.50 6.00
36 Jeff Teague 2.50 6.00
37 Omri Casspi 2.00 5.00
38 Manu Ginobili 3.00 8.00
39 Marcus Smart 2.50 6.00
40 Harrison Barnes 2.50 6.00
41 Jahlil Okafor 2.50 6.00
42 Kentavious Caldwell-Pope 2.50 6.00
43 Brook Lopez 2.50 6.00
44 Shaun Livingston 2.00 5.00
45 Tyreke Evans 2.00 5.00
46 Jabari Parker 4.00 10.00
47 Willie Cauley-Stein 2.50 6.00
48 Danny Ainge 3.00 8.00
49 Grant Hill 4.00 10.00
50 Patrick Ewing 4.00 10.00
51 Tim Duncan 5.00 12.00
52 David Robinson 5.00 12.00
53 Draymond Green 4.00 10.00
54 Shaquille O'Neal 8.00 20.00
55 Klay Thompson 4.00 10.00
56 DeMar DeRozan 3.00 8.00
57 Cody Zeller 2.00 5.00
58 Greg Monroe 2.50 6.00
59 Derrick Favors 2.50 6.00
60 Vince Carter 4.00 10.00
61 Domantas Sabonis 3.00 8.00
62 Patrick McCaw 4.00 10.00
63 Dejounte Murray 4.00 10.00
64 Jaylen Brown 5.00 12.00
65 Brandon Ingram 6.00 15.00
66 Willy Hernangomez 2.50 6.00
67 Tyler Ulis 5.00 12.00
68 Denzel Valentine 2.50 6.00
69 Wade Baldwin IV 2.00 5.00
70 Juan Hernangomez 2.50 6.00
71 Malcolm Brogdon 4.00 10.00
72 Mindaugas Kuzminskas 2.50 6.00
73 Kay Felder 2.00 5.00
74 Malik Beasley 2.00 5.00
75 Skal Labissiere 3.00 8.00

2016-17 Panini Grand Reserve Reserve Signatures
RANDOM INSERTS IN PACKS
PRINT RUNS B/WN 25-75 COPIES PER
EXCHANGE DEADLINE 1/19/2019
*GRNTE/25: .6X TO 1.5X p/r 75-99
*GRNTE/25: .5X TO 1.2X p/r 35-49
*GRNTE/25: .4X TO 1X p/r 20-25
1 Kevin Durant/25 75.00 200.00
2 Anthony Davis/25 25.00 60.00
3 Karl-Anthony Towns/25 50.00 120.00
4 John Wall/25 25.00 60.00
5 Ricky Rubio/25
6 Tony Parker/25 30.00 80.00
7 Paul George/20 15.00 40.00
8 Buddy Hield/99 8.00 20.00
9 Joel Embiid/49 25.00 60.00
10 Cody Zeller/99 3.00 8.00
11 C.J. McCollum/49 12.00 30.00
12 Zach LaVine/49 10.00 25.00
13 Noah Vonleh/99 3.00 8.00
14 Goran Dragic/35 5.00 12.00
15 George Hill/20 6.00 15.00
16 Michael Kidd-Gilchrist/20 6.00 15.00
17 Gary Harris/75 4.00 10.00
18 Jonas Valanciunas/99 4.00 10.00
19 Jrue Holiday/99 4.00 10.00
20 Tyus Jones/99 3.00 8.00
21 Myles Turner/99 5.00 12.00
22 Danny Green/99 4.00 10.00
23 Jared Dudley/99 3.00 8.00
24 Taurean Prince/99 5.00 12.00
25 Denzel Valentine/99 4.00 10.00
26 Trey Lyles/99 4.00 10.00
27 Nemanja Bjelica/99 4.00 10.00
28 Timofey Mozgov/99 3.00 8.00
29 Tim Hardaway Jr./99 3.00 8.00
30 Matthew Dellavedova/99 5.00 12.00
31 James Johnson/99 3.00 8.00
32 Donatas Motiejunas/99 3.00 8.00
33 Cameron Payne/99 3.00 8.00
34 E'Twaun Moore/99 3.00 8.00
35 Dwight Powell/99 3.00 8.00
36 Justin Holiday/99 3.00 8.00
37 Isaiah Canaan/99 4.00 10.00
38 Deyonta Davis/99 3.00 8.00
39 Brice Johnson/99 3.00 8.00
40 Tarik Black/99 3.00 8.00
41 Lucas Nogueira/99 3.00 8.00
42 C.J. Miles/99
43 Rodney McGruder/99 4.00 10.00
44 Malcolm Delaney/99 4.00 10.00
45 Joe Young/99 3.00 8.00
46 Jake Layman/99 4.00 10.00
47 Boban Marjanovic/99 3.00 8.00
48 Mike Muscala/99 5.00 12.00
49 Sean Kilpatrick/99 3.00 8.00
50 Chasson Randle/99 3.00 8.00

2016-17 Panini Grand Reserve Rookie Cornerstones Quad Jersey Autographs Granite
*GRANITE: .75X TO 2X BASIC
RANDOM INSERTS IN PACKS
STATED PRINT RUN 25 SER.#'d SETS
EXCHANGE DEADLIN 1/19/2019
101 Brandon Ingram 500.00 800.00

2016-17 Panini Grand Reserve Rookie Cornerstones Quad Jersey Autographs Quartz
*QUARTZ: .5X TO 1.2X BASIC
RANDOM INSERTS IN PACKS
STATED PRINT RUN 49 SER.#'d SETS
EXCHANGE DEADLIN 1/19/2019
101 Brandon Ingram 125.00 300.00

2016-17 Panini Grand Reserve Startups
RANDOM INSERTS IN PACKS
1 Dennis Schroder 1.25 3.00
2 Isaiah Thomas 1.50 4.00
3 Malcolm Brogdon 2.50 6.00
4 Yogi Ferrell 1.25 3.00
5 Isaiah Whitehead 1.00 2.50
6 Victor Oladipo 1.25 3.00
7 Kay Felder 1.00 2.50
8 Jaylen Brown 4.00 10.00
9 C.J. McCollum 1.25 3.00
10 Ben McLemore 1.00 2.50
11 Andrew Wiggins 2.50 6.00
12 Jordan Clarkson 1.25 3.00
13 Dejounte Murray 2.00 5.00
14 Wade Baldwin IV 1.00 2.50
15 Tyler Johnson 1.00 2.50
16 Elfrid Payton 1.25 3.00
17 Doug McDermott 1.25 3.00
18 Giannis Antetokounmpo 3.00 8.00
19 Kemba Walker 1.50 4.00
20 Bradley Beal 1.50 4.00

2016-17 Panini Grand Reserve The Ascent Autographs
RANDOM INSERTS IN PACKS
PRINT RUNS B/WN 25-75 COPIES PER
EXCHANGE DEADLINE 1/19/2019
1 Andrew Wiggins/35 20.00 50.00
4 Evan Fournier/75 4.00 10.00
5 Anthony Davis/25 25.00 60.00
6 Eric Bledsoe/75 4.00 10.00
8 Karl-Anthony Towns/35 40.00 100.00
9 Justise Winslow/75 5.00 12.00
11 Kristaps Porzingis/35 40.00 100.00
13 Myles Turner/75 5.00 12.00
14 Tyler Johnson/75 3.00 8.00
15 Allen Crabbe/75 3.00 8.00
18 Clint Capela/75 3.00 8.00
19 Tristan Thompson/75 4.00 10.00
21 Justin Anderson/75 4.00 10.00
22 Robert Covington/75 3.00 8.00
23 Nikola Mirotic/75 4.00 10.00
25 Matthew Dellavedova/75 5.00 12.00
26 John Wall/35 20.00 50.00
27 Kevin Durant/25 75.00 200.00
28 Kyrie Irving/25 30.00 80.00
29 Elfrid Payton/75 4.00 10.00
30 George Hill/75 4.00 10.00
31 Brandon Ingram/35 60.00 150.00
32 Kris Dunn/35 12.00 30.00
33 Jaylen Brown/35 15.00 40.00
34 Buddy Hield/35 10.00 25.00
35 Malcolm Delaney/75 4.00 10.00
36 Rodney McGruder/75 4.00 10.00
37 Kay Felder/75 6.00 15.00
38 Patrick McCaw/75 12.00 30.00
39 Tomas Satoransky/75 3.00 8.00
40 Paul Zipser/75 8.00 20.00
41 Domantas Sabonis/75 5.00 12.00
43 Ron Baker/75 6.00 15.00
44 Pascal Siakam/75 3.00 8.00
45 Willy Hernangomez/75 8.00 20.00
46 Dorian Finney-Smith/75 4.00 10.00
47 Thon Maker/75 15.00 40.00
49 Denzel Valentine/75 4.00 10.00
50 Malcolm Brogdon/75 10.00 25.00

2016-17 Panini Grand Reserve Unbreakable

RANDOM INSERTS IN PACKS
1 James Harden 3.00 8.00
2 Russell Westbrook 5.00 12.00
3 DeMarcus Cousins 2.00 5.00
4 LeBron James 8.00 20.00
5 Giannis Antetokounmpo 4.00 10.00
6 Kevin Durant 5.00 12.00
7 Isaiah Thomas 2.00 5.00
8 Karl-Anthony Towns 5.00 12.00
9 John Wall 2.50 6.00
10 Dennis Schroder 1.50 4.00

2016-17 Panini Grand Reserve Upper Tier Signatures

RANDOM INSERTS IN PACKS
PRINT RUNS B/WN 10-99 COPIES PER
NO PRICING ON QTY 10
EXCHANGE DEADLINE 1/19/2019
2 Shaquille O'Neal/25
3 Magic Johnson/25 30.00 80.00
4 Larry Bird/25 50.00 120.00
5 Hakeem Olajuwon/25 20.00 50.00
6 Kareem Abdul-Jabbar/25 40.00 100.00
7 Alex English/99 4.00 10.00
8 George Gervin/99 6.00 15.00
9 Adrian Dantley/99 4.00 10.00
10 David Thompson/99 4.00 10.00
11 James Worthy/30 10.00 25.00
12 Nate Archibald/99 4.00 10.00
13 Bob Lanier/60 6.00 15.00
14 Damon Stoudamire/99 10.00 25.00
15 Mark Aguirre/99 4.00 10.00
16 Cedric Maxwell/99 3.00 8.00
17 Sidney Moncrief/99 3.00 8.00
18 Horace Grant/99 6.00 15.00
19 Bill Laimbeer/99 6.00 15.00
20 Glen Rice/99 4.00 10.00
21 Latrell Sprewell/99 12.00 30.00
22 Yao Ming/25 75.00 200.00
23 Grant Hill/30 20.00 50.00
24 Frank Ramsey/99 10.00 25.00
25 Spud Webb/99 4.00 10.00
26 Tim Hardaway/99 6.00 15.00
27 Louie Dampier/99 12.00 30.00
28 Arvydas Sabonis/99 10.00 25.00
29 Myles Turner/99 5.00 12.00
30 C.J. McCollum/60 10.00 25.00
31 John Wall/25 25.00 60.00
34 Devin Booker/99 25.00 60.00
35 Elfrid Payton/99 4.00 10.00
36 Zach Randolph/60 4.00 10.00
37 Jimmy Butler/25
39 Kyrie Irving/25 30.00 80.00
40 Kevin Durant/25 100.00 250.00
41 Karl-Anthony Towns/25 50.00 120.00
42 Kristaps Porzingis/60 30.00 80.00
43 Carmelo Anthony/25 12.00 30.00
44 Chris Paul/25 20.00 50.00
45 Dwyane Wade/25 30.00 80.00

2015-16 Panini HV KB20 Unleash the Hero

COMPLETE SET (21) 8.00 20.00
COMMON CARD 1.25 3.00
ONE COMPLETE SET PER BOX

2015-16 Panini HV KB20 Unleash the Hero Black Mamba

*BLACK MAMBA: 20X TO 50X BASIC
RANDOM INSERTS IN PACKS

2015-16 Panini HV KB20 Unleash the Hero Blue Larry O'Brien Trophy

*BLUE: 1X TO 2.5X BASIC
RANDOM INSERTS IN PACKS

2015-16 Panini HV KB20 Unleash the Hero Gold 24

*GOLD: 1.2X TO 3X BASIC
RANDOM INSERTS IN PACKS

2015-16 Panini HV KB20 Unleash the Hero Purple 8

*PURPLE: 1.2X TO 3X BASIC
RANDOM INSERTS IN PACKS

2015-16 Panini HV KB20 Unleash the Hero Red MVP

*RED: 1X TO 2.5X BASIC
RANDOM INSERTS IN PACKS

2015-16 Panini HV KB20 Channel the Villain

COMPLETE SET (21) 8.00 20.00
*VILLAIN: .4X TO 1X HERO
ONE COMPLETE SET PER BOX

2015-16 Panini HV KB20 Channel the Villain Black Mamba

*BLACK MAMBA: 20X TO 50X BASIC
RANDOM INSERTS IN PACKS

2015-16 Panini HV KB20 Channel the Villain Blue Larry O'Brien Trophy

*BLUE: 1X TO 2.5X BASIC
RANDOM INSERTS IN PACKS

2015-16 Panini HV KB20 Channel the Villain Gold 24

*GOLD: 1.2X TO 3X BASIC
RANDOM INSERTS IN PACKS

2015-16 Panini HV KB20 Channel the Villain Purple 8

*PURPLE: 1.2X TO 3X BASIC
RANDOM INSERTS IN PACKS

2015-16 Panini HV KB20 Channel the Villain Red MVP

*RED: 1X TO 2.5X BASIC
RANDOM INSERTS IN PACKS

2012-13 Panini Intrigue

JSY AU RC B/WN 15-199 COPIES PER
NO PRICING ON QTY 15 OR LESS
EXCHANGE DEADLINE 3/18/2015
1 Ty Lawson .25 .60
2 Derrick Rose .50 1.25
3 Alonzo Gee .25 .60
4 Brook Lopez .30 .75
5 Dwyane Wade .60 1.50
6 Anderson Varejao .25 .60
7 Joakim Noah .30 .75
8 Shane Battier .30 .75
9 Deron Williams .30 .75
10 Jason Kidd .40 1.00
11 Dirk Nowitzki .50 1.25
12 Jarrett Jack .30 .75
13 Jeremy Lin .40 1.00
14 Blake Griffin .40 1.00
15 Ekpe Udoh .25 .60
16 Russell Westbrook 1.00 2.50
17 Jrue Holiday .40 1.00
18 Tony Parker .40 1.00
19 Jamaal Tinsley .25 .60
20 Jeff Teague .30 .75
21 Shawn Marion .30 .75
22 Ray Allen .40 1.00
23 Roy Hibbert .30 .75
24 Steve Nash .40 1.00
25 Brandon Jennings .25 .60
26 Kevin Martin .30 .75
27 Marcin Gortat .30 .75
28 Tim Duncan .60 1.50
29 Gordon Hayward .40 1.00
30 Josh Smith .30 .75
31 Luol Deng .30 .75
32 Greg Monroe .30 .75
33 James Harden .60 1.50
34 Pau Gasol .40 1.00
35 Ricky Rubio .40 1.00
36 Kevin Durant 1.00 2.50
37 Luis Scola .30 .75
38 Tiago Splitter .30 .75
39 DeMarre Carroll .25 .60
40 Avery Bradley .30 .75
41 Taj Gibson .30 .75
42 Jose Calderon .25 .60
43 Paul George .50 1.25
44 Kobe Bryant 1.50 4.00
45 Nikola Pekovic .25 .60
46 Kendrick Perkins .25 .60
47 Goran Dragic .30 .75
48 Manu Ginobili .40 1.00
49 Trevor Booker .25 .60
50 Kevin Garnett .60 1.50
51 Ben Gordon .30 .75
52 Stephen Curry 1.50 4.00
53 David West .30 .75
54 Dwight Howard .30 .75
55 Chase Budinger .25 .60
56 Jameer Nelson .25 .60
57 LaMarcus Aldridge .40 1.00
58 Rudy Gay .40 1.00
59 Trevor Ariza .25 .60
60 Paul Pierce .40 1.00
61 Byron Mullens .25 .60
62 Andre Iguodala .30 .75
63 Danny Granger .30 .75
64 Zach Randolph .30 .75
65 Ryan Anderson .30 .75
66 Glen Davis .25 .60
67 J.J. Hickson .25 .60
68 Landry Fields .25 .60
69 John Wall .50 1.25
70 Rajon Rondo .40 1.00
71 Gerald Wallace .30 .75
72 Andre Miller .30 .75
73 Eric Bledsoe .30 .75
74 Mike Conley .30 .75
75 Robin Lopez .25 .60
76 Arron Afflalo .30 .75
77 Tyreke Evans .25 .60
78 Kyle Lowry .30 .75
79 Tyson Chandler .30 .75
80 Amar'e Stoudemire .30 .75
81 Joe Johnson .30 .75
82 LeBron James 1.50 4.00
83 DeAndre Jordan .40 1.00
84 Monta Ellis .30 .75
85 Greivis Vasquez .30 .75
86 Spencer Hawes .25 .60
87 Marcus Thornton .25 .60
88 DeMar DeRozan .40 1.00
89 Steve Novak .25 .60
90 Carmelo Anthony .50 1.25
91 Chris Bosh .40 1.00
92 David Lee .25 .60
93 Chris Paul .50 1.25
94 J.J. Redick .40 1.00
95 Serge Ibaka .30 .75
96 Nick Young .30 .75
97 DeMarcus Cousins .40 1.00
98 Marvin Williams .30 .75
99 Raymond Felton .30 .75
100 Damian Lillard RC 4.00 10.00
101 Jared Sullinger JSY AU/99 RC 5.00 12.00
102 Fab Melo JSY AU/15 RC
103 Kemba Walker JSY AU/15 RC
104 Kevin Murphy JSY AU RC 4.00 10.00
105 Kyle Singler JSY AU/15 RC
106 Marquis Teague JSY AU/25 RC 4.00 10.00
107 Nolan Smith JSY AU/99 RC 4.00 10.00
108 Evan Fournier JSY AU/99 RC 6.00 15.00
109 Mirza Teletovic JSY AU/25 RC 5.00 12.00
110 Iman Shumpert JSY AU/149 RC 6.00 15.00
111 H.Barnes JSY AU/149 RC 10.00 25.00
112 Lavoy Allen JSY AU/199 RC 4.00 10.00
113 Irving JSY AU/199 RC EXCH 40.00 100.00
114 K.Leonard JSY AU/149 RC 75.00 200.00
115 K.Faried JSY AU/125 RC 6.00 15.00
116 Kim English JSY AU RC 4.00 10.00
117 Bradley Beal JSY AU/99 RC 12.00 30.00
118 A.Davis JSY AU/25 RC 125.00 300.00
119 Damian Lillard JSY AU/49 100.00 250.00
120 Meyers Leonard JSY AU/99 RC 5.00 12.00
121 Orlando Johnson JSY AU/99 RC 4.00 10.00
122 T.Robinson JSY AU/49 RC 5.00 12.00
123 Chris Copeland JSY AU/99 RC 4.00 10.00
124 Austin Rivers JSY AU/49 RC 6.00 15.00
125 Chris Singleton JSY AU/15 RC
126 Jae Crowder JSY AU/15 RC
127 Valanciunas JSY AU/199 RC 6.00 15.00
128 Viacheslav Kravtsov JSY AU RC 4.00 10.00
129 Lance Thomas JSY AU RC 4.00 10.00
130 Tornike Shengelia JSY AU/75 RC 4.00 10.00
131 Kent Bazemore JSY AU/199 RC 6.00 15.00
132 Gustavo Ayon JSY AU RC 4.00 10.00
133 Tobias Harris JSY AU/199 RC 6.00 15.00
134 Robert Sacre JSY AU RC 4.00 10.00
135 Victor Claver JSY AU/199 RC 4.00 10.00
136 A.Drummond JSY AU/149 RC 12.00 30.00
137 Brian Roberts JSY AU/199 RC 4.00 10.00
138 M.Brooks JSY AU/199 RC 5.00 12.00
139 Chandler Parsons JSY AU/15 RC
140 Quincy Acy JSY AU/199 RC 4.00 10.00
141 Terrence Jones JSY AU/15 RC
142 Will Barton JSY AU RC 5.00 12.00
143 DeQuan Jones JSY AU/199 RC 4.00 10.00
144 Malcolm Lee JSY AU RC 4.00 10.00
145 Festus Ezeli JSY AU/25 RC
146 N.Vucevic JSY AU/149 RC 6.00 15.00
147 Norris Cole JSY AU/199 RC 4.00 10.00
148 Tyler Zeller JSY AU/49 RC 5.00 12.00
149 Miles Plumlee JSY AU/15 RC
150 Brandon Knight JSY AU/99 RC 6.00 15.00
151 A.Nicholson JSY AU/99 RC 4.00 10.00
152 Michael Kidd-Gilchrist JSY AU/15 RC
153 Terrence Ross JSY AU/15 RC
154 Darius Morris JSY AU RC 4.00 10.00
155 T.Thompson JSY AU/99 RC 6.00 15.00
156 Klay Thompson JSY AU/15 RC
157 Khris Middleton JSY AU RC 6.00 15.00
158 J.Cunningham JSY AU/25 RC
159 R.Jackson JSY AU/49 RC 6.00 15.00
160 John Henson JSY AU/99 RC 6.00 15.00

2012-13 Panini Intrigue Autograph Jerseys

PRINT RUNS B/WN 15-199 COPIES PER
NO PRICING ON QTY 20 OR LESS
EXCHANGE DEADLINE 3/18/2015
3 DeMarcus Cousins/25
4 Alvan Adams/49 4.00 10.00
5 Chase Budinger/49 4.00 10.00
6 James Worthy/25 8.00 20.00
7 Clyde Drexler/25 15.00 40.00
8 Taj Gibson/49 6.00 15.00
9 Anderson Varejao/25
10 Greg Monroe/49 5.00 12.00
11 Kiki Vandeweghe/199 5.00 12.00
12 Ron Harper/199 6.00 15.00
13 Courtney Lee/25
14 Detlef Schrempf/199 8.00 20.00
15 Gail Goodrich/25 5.00 12.00
16 Shawn Bradley/75 4.00 10.00
17 Kevin Love/25 15.00 40.00
18 Mike Conley/25 8.00 20.00
19 James Harden/25 EXCH 30.00 80.00
20 Devin Harris/25 4.00 10.00
21 Chris Kaman/25 5.00 12.00
22 Jason Maxiell/25 4.00 10.00
23 Ty Lawson/25 4.00 10.00
24 Kobe Bryant/49 100.00 200.00
25 Jason Terry/25 8.00 20.00
26 Alan Anderson/25 4.00 10.00
27 Larry Nance/199 5.00 12.00
28 Nick Anderson/99 6.00 15.00
29 Al-Farouq Aminu/25
31 David West/99 5.00 12.00
33 Vince Carter/25 25.00 60.00
34 Rick Mahorn/199 4.00 10.00
38 Andrea Bargnani/25 5.00 12.00
39 Tom Chambers/49
40 Arron Afflalo/25
41 Ryan Anderson/49 5.00 12.00
42 Alonzo Mourning/25
43 George Hill/49 5.00 12.00
44 Brandon Bass/25 4.00 10.00
46 Rodney Stuckey/125 5.00 12.00
47 Carl Landry/25 4.00 10.00
48 Dwyane Wade/49 30.00 80.00
50 Kyle Lowry/99 5.00 12.00
51 Xavier McDaniel/199 4.00 10.00
52 Serge Ibaka/25 8.00 20.00
53 Bernard King/49 10.00 25.00
54 Udonis Haslem/25 6.00 15.00
55 Roy Hibbert/25 5.00 12.00
56 Jeff Green/25 5.00 12.00
57 Andre Miller/25
58 Will Bynum/99
59 Calvin Murphy/25 5.00 12.00
60 Andrei Kirilenko/25 5.00 12.00
61 Gerald Henderson/49 4.00 10.00
62 Landry Fields/99 4.00 10.00
63 Wesley Matthews/49 4.00 10.00
64 Kevin Martin/25 5.00 12.00
65 Marcus Camby/25 5.00 12.00
66 Ekpe Udoh/25 4.00 10.00
67 Danny Manning/25 5.00 12.00
68 Robert Parish/25 8.00 20.00
69 Dan Issel/199 5.00 12.00
70 Andrew Bogut/25 30.00 60.00
71 Hakeem Olajuwon/25 30.00 60.00
72 Greivis Vasquez/25 5.00 12.00
73 Mark Price/99 8.00 20.00
74 Derrick Favors/25 5.00 12.00
75 Bobby Jackson/99 4.00 10.00
76 Kevin Durant/49 90.00 150.00
77 Mark Jackson/25 5.00 12.00
78 Jack Sikma/99 5.00 12.00
79 Grant Hill/49 30.00 60.00
81 Fat Lever/99 5.00 12.00
82 Chris Mullin/49 10.00 25.00
84 Xavier Henry/25 4.00 10.00
85 Jim Jackson/75 4.00 10.00
86 Josh Smith/25 5.00 12.00
87 John Salmons/99 5.00 12.00
88 Tyson Chandler/25
89 Spencer Haywood/99 4.00 10.00
91 Ronny Turiaf/49 4.00 10.00
92 Kelly Tripucka/25 4.00 10.00
94 Carlos Delfino/49 4.00 10.00
95 Caron Butler/25 5.00 12.00
96 Blake Griffin/49 EXCH 20.00 50.00
97 Alex English/49
98 Maurice Cheeks/99 4.00 10.00
100 Steve Novak/25 6.00 15.00

2012-13 Panini Intrigue Dunk Company Autographs

PRINT RUNS B/WN 15-199 COPIES PER
NO PRICING ON QTY 20 OR LESS
EXCHANGE DEADLINE 3/18/2015
1 Harrison Barnes/49 10.00 25.00
2 Blake Griffin/25
3 Kobe Bryant/49 75.00 200.00
4 Kevin Durant/49 60.00 150.00
8 Vince Carter/25 30.00 60.00
9 Dominique Wilkins/49 8.00 20.00
10 Kenneth Faried/49 6.00 15.00
11 Cedric Ceballos/25 12.00 30.00
13 David Robinson/49 15.00 40.00
15 Darryl Dawkins/199 4.00 10.00
16 Tom Chambers/199 5.00 12.00
17 Larry Nance/199 5.00 12.00
18 Spud Webb/199 5.00 12.00
19 Kenny Walker/99 4.00 10.00
20 Larry Johnson/75 12.00 30.00
21 Clyde Drexler/25 20.00 50.00
22 Darrell Griffith/199 4.00 10.00
24 Anthony Davis/25 60.00 120.00

2012-13 Panini Intrigue Fearless Foursomes

PRINT RUNS B/WN 25-49 COPIES PER
1 Ant/Dur/Kobe/James/49 40.00 80.00
2 How/Bran/James/Dunc/49 12.00 30.00
3 Davis/Griffin/Wall/Irvng/49 10.00 25.00
4 Lee/How/Asik/Rand/49
5 Paul/Will/Vasq/Rubio/49 8.00 20.00
6 Noah/Hibb/Ibaka/Dunc/49 10.00 25.00
7 Hard/Walk/Ellis/Westb/49 15.00 40.00
8 Hard/Batum/Ander/Cur/25 25.00 60.00
9 Rob/Rod/Olaj/Ewing/49 10.00 25.00
10 Thom/Kid/Stock/Nash/25

2012-13 Panini Intrigue First Flight Unis

PRINT RUNS B/WN 5-99 COPIES PER
NO PRICING ON QTY 10 OR LESS
1 LeBron James/49
2 Clyde Drexler/99 6.00 15.00
3 Tyrus Thomas/99 3.00 8.00
5 Carmelo Anthony/49 6.00 15.00
6 Shaquille O'Neal/49 12.00 30.00
7 David Lee/49 3.00 8.00
8 Andrei Kirilenko/25 4.00 10.00
9 Monta Ellis/49
10 Deron Williams/99 4.00 10.00
11 Andre Iguodala/25
12 Michael Beasley/99 3.00 8.00
13 Dikembe Mutombo/25 20.00 50.00
14 Amar'e Stoudemire/99
16 Dwight Howard/25
17 Al-Farouq Aminu/99 4.00 10.00
18 Landry Fields/75 3.00 8.00
19 Eric Gordon/25
20 Kevin Martin/25 4.00 10.00
21 Kevin Durant/25 20.00 50.00
22 Grant Hill/99 6.00 15.00
23 Derrick Favors/99 4.00 10.00
24 Jeff Green/99 4.00 10.00
25 JaVale McGee/99 4.00 10.00

2012-13 Panini Intrigue Immortalized Autographs

PRINT RUNS B/WN 15-299 COPIES PER
NO PRICING ON QTY 15 OR LESS
EXCHANGE DEADLINE 3/18/2015
2 Cedric Maxwell/299 4.00 10.00
3 Connie Hawkins/25 12.00 30.00
5 Terry Porter/299 4.00 10.00
8 Bernard King/25
9 George McGinnis/25 8.00 20.00
10 Tom Heinsohn/25 25.00 60.00
12 Nick Anderson/199 6.00 15.00
13 Mitch Richmond/25 15.00 40.00
14 Spud Webb/299 5.00 12.00
15 Adrian Dantley/25 8.00 20.00
16 Rory Sparrow/299 4.00 10.00
17 Larry Nance/199 5.00 12.00
18 Tim Hardaway/299 6.00 15.00
19 Mark Price/249 6.00 15.00
20 Mel Davis/299 4.00 10.00
21 Jack Sikma/299 5.00 12.00
22 Darryl Dawkins/199 4.00 10.00
23 Scott Skiles/299 5.00 12.00
24 Rolando Blackman/199 5.00 12.00
25 Sam Perkins/25 4.00 10.00
26 Bob McAdoo/25 15.00 40.00
27 Satch Sanders/25 10.00 25.00
28 Alex English/25 20.00 50.00
29 Tom Chambers/25 12.00 30.00
30 Kurt Rambis/25 6.00 15.00
31 Buck Williams/299 4.00 10.00
41 Gary Payton/15 20.00 50.00
43 Larry Bird/25 50.00 120.00
44 Magic Johnson/25
45 Vlade Divac/299 6.00 15.00
46 Herb Williams/299 4.00 10.00
47 Muggsy Bogues/299 5.00 12.00
48 Sean Elliott/299 6.00 15.00
49 Cedric Ceballos/299 4.00 10.00
51 Bob Dandridge/299 4.00 10.00
52 Anthony Mason/299 5.00 12.00
53 Charles Oakley/299 6.00 15.00
54 Bill Cartwright/25 12.00 30.00
55 Robert Horry/25
56 Jamaal Wilkes/25 12.50 30.00
57 Horace Grant/25
58 Michael Cage/299 4.00 10.00
60 Mark Aguirre/199 5.00 12.00

2012-13 Panini Intrigue Impact Rookie Autographs

PRINT RUNS B/WN 15-299 COPIES PER
NO PRICING ON QTY 15 OR LESS
EXCHANGE DEADLINE 3/18/2015
1 Harrison Barnes/99 8.00 20.00
3 Iman Shumpert/149 5.00 12.00
4 Alexey Shved/49 3.00 8.00
5 Jordan Hamilton/299 3.00 8.00
6 E'Twaun Moore/249 3.00 8.00
7 Reggie Jackson/49 5.00 12.00
9 Festus Ezeli/149 4.00 10.00
10 MarShon Brooks/199 4.00 10.00
11 Kent Bazemore/299 5.00 12.00
12 Chris Copeland/199 3.00 8.00
13 Mirza Teletovic/25
15 Kendall Marshall/299 3.00 8.00
17 Jared Cunningham/199 EXCH 3.00 8.00
19 Draymond Green/249 15.00 40.00
20 Brian Roberts/299 3.00 8.00
21 Tornike Shengelia/25
25 DeAndre Liggins/299 4.00 10.00
26 Ben Hansbrough/299 3.00 8.00
27 Khris Middleton/299 5.00 12.00
28 Brandon Knight/49 5.00 12.00
29 DeQuan Jones/199 EXCH 3.00 8.00
30 Andre Drummond/99 8.00 20.00
31 Lance Thomas/299 3.00 8.00
32 Orlando Johnson/49 3.00 8.00
34 Jared Sullinger/99 4.00 10.00
35 Nando De Colo/249 3.00 8.00
36 Damian Lillard/25 100.00 250.00
39 Will Barton/199
40 Victor Claver/199 3.00 8.00
41 Viacheslav Kravtsov/199
42 Meyers Leonard/149
43 Kyrie Irving/99 60.00 150.00
44 Kevin Murphy/299 3.00 8.00
45 Bismack Biyombo/299 3.00 8.00
46 Alec Burks/99 5.00 12.00
48 Tyler Zeller/25
50 Robert Sacre/299 3.00 8.00
51 Jonas Valanciunas/99 5.00 12.00
52 Isaiah Thomas/299 20.00 50.00
53 Kawhi Leonard/99 60.00 150.00
55 Mike Scott/299 3.00 8.00
56 John Henson/25 5.00 12.00
57 Darius Morris/299 3.00 8.00
58 Norris Cole/125 3.00 8.00
59 Quincy Acy/279 3.00 8.00
60 Tobias Harris/99 5.00 12.00
61 Jae Crowder/99 EXCH 4.00 10.00
63 Kenneth Faried/99 5.00 12.00
64 Marquis Teague/25 EXCH 3.00 8.00
66 Enes Kanter/25 10.00 25.00
68 Nikola Vucevic/125 5.00 12.00
69 Chandler Parsons/15 15.00 40.00
70 Gustavo Ayon/299 3.00 8.00
72 Bradley Beal/49 8.00 20.00
73 Kim English/299 3.00 8.00
75 Jan Vesely/299 3.00 8.00

2012-13 Panini Intrigue Intriguing Pairs Jerseys

PRINT RUNS B/WN 25-99 COPIES PER
1 Bryant/Irving/99 12.00 30.00
2 Dragic.Scola/25 10.00 25.00
3 Wade/James/99 25.00 60.00
4 M.Gasol/Z.Randolph/25 5.00 12.00
5 Howard/Nash/49
6 Griffin/Paul/49 6.00 15.00
7 J.Harden/J.Lin/49 8.00 20.00
8 A.Drummond/G.Monroe/99 5.00 12.00
9 Irving/Thomp/49
10 D.Williams/G.Wallace/99 4.00 10.00
11 Garnett/Pierce/25
12 A.Horford/J.Noah/25 4.00 10.00
13 B.Beal/J.Wall/25 6.00 15.00
14 Favors/Hayw/25
15 D.DeRozan/T.Ross/25 5.00 12.00
16 J.Fredette/T.Evans/25 3.00 8.00
17 Lillard/Aldridge/49 12.00 30.00
18 Durant/Westb/99 10.00 25.00
19 Anthony/Durant/99 10.00 25.00
20 Davis/Rivers/25 8.00 20.00
21 C.Anthony/T.Chandler/99 5.00 12.00
22 Love/Rubio/25 5.00 12.00
23 Howard/Love/25 10.00 25.00
24 Rubio/Nash/99 5.00 12.00
25 Hill/George/25 10.00 25.00
26 Thompson/Curry/25 20.00 50.00
27 B.Knight/K.Irving/99 10.00 25.00
28 D.Lillard/K.Irving/49 25.00 60.00
29 Howard/Shaq/99 6.00 15.00
30 Walker/Allen/25
31 Griffin/Howard/25 12.00 30.00
32 James/Pierce/25 20.00 50.00
33 Bryant/James/99 12.00 30.00
34 Stoud/Melo/99 6.00 15.00
35 Durant/James/99 20.00 50.00
36 Harden/Curry/99 6.00 15.00
37 Griffin/Duncan/25 8.00 20.00
38 D.Howard/R.Hibbert/99 5.00 12.00
39 B.Jennings/T.Lawson/99 3.00 8.00
40 Lawson/Evans/25 10.00 25.00
41 E.Gordon/R.Westbrook/25 5.00 12.00
42 C.Paul/D.Williams/25 5.00 12.00
43 Bryant/Rondo/99 8.00 20.00
44 J.Kidd/S.Nash/99 5.00 12.00
45 A.Stoudemire/S.Marion/25 4.00 10.00
46 Nicholson/Thomp/25
47 B.Griffin/D.Lee/25
48 Thomas/Crawford/25 12.00 30.00
49 Bogut/Redick/25
50 Barnes/Carter/49 6.00 15.00
51 C.Kaman/D.Nowitzki/99 5.00 12.00
52 Leonard/Elliott/25
53 Durant/Aldridge/99 6.00 15.00
54 Love/Westb/25 12.00 30.00
55 Davis/Irving/99 12.00 30.00
56 B.Gordon/R.Allen/25 5.00 12.00
57 Hill/Irving/99 25.00 60.00
58 D.Collison/K.Love/99 5.00 12.00
59 D.Cousins/J.Wall/25 5.00 12.00
60 DeRozan/Mayo/25

2012-13 Panini Intrigue Intriguing Players

ALL VERSIONS EQUALLY PRICED
1 Kyrie Irving 2.50 6.00
11 Anthony Davis 2.50 6.00
21 Kobe Bryant 2.00 5.00
31 Kevin Durant 1.25 3.00
41 Blake Griffin .50 1.25
51 LeBron James 2.00 5.00
61 Tim Duncan .75 2.00
71 Dirk Nowitzki .60 1.50
81 Dwyane Wade .75 2.00
91 Dwight Howard .40 1.00
101 Rajon Rondo .50 1.25
111 Russell Westbrook 1.25 3.00
121 Derrick Rose .60 1.50
131 Damian Lillard 2.00 5.00
141 Carmelo Anthony .60 1.50
151 Stephen Curry 2.00 5.00
161 Kevin Garnett .75 2.00
171 Chris Paul .60 1.50
181 Paul Pierce .50 1.25
191 John Wall .60 1.50

2012-13 Panini Intrigue Intriguing Players Gold

*GOLD: 8X TO 20X BASIC
STATED PRINT RUN 10 SER.#'d SETS
ALL VERSION EQUALLY PRICED

2012-13 Panini Intrigue Red White and Blue Autographs

PRINT RUNS B/WN 15-299 COPIES PER
NO PRICING ON QTY 15 OR LESS
EXCHANGE DEADLINE 3/18/2015
1 Kevin Durant/125 60.00 150.00
2 Kobe Bryant/99 100.00 200.00
3 Tyson Chandler/25 15.00 40.00
4 Andre Iguodala/25 15.00 40.00
6 Jason Kidd/25
8 Antawn Jamison/99 5.00 12.00
9 Vin Baker/299 4.00 10.00
10 Allan Houston/99 5.00 12.00
11 Alonzo Mourning/25 60.00 150.00
12 Derrick Coleman/199 12.00 30.00
13 Gary Payton/25 40.00 80.00
14 Steve Smith/299 5.00 12.00
15 Tim Hardaway/299 6.00 15.00
16 Anfernee Hardaway/49 50.00 100.00
17 Grant Hill/49 20.00 50.00
22 Chris Mullin/199 6.00 15.00
23 Magic Johnson/25 50.00 100.00
25 Danny Manning/25 5.00 12.00
26 Mitch Richmond/199 6.00 15.00
27 Sam Perkins/199 4.00 10.00
28 Larry Bird/25 60.00 120.00
30 Carlos Boozer/25 12.00 30.00
32 Adrian Dantley/199 5.00 12.00
33 Bobby Jones/299 5.00 12.00
34 Spencer Haywood/299 4.00 10.00
35 Jo Jo White/299 5.00 12.00

2012-13 Panini Intrigue Rookie Memorabilia

STATED PRINT RUN 99 SER.#'d SETS
1 Anthony Davis 8.00 20.00
2 Kenneth Faried 4.00 10.00
3 Jonas Valanciunas 4.00 10.00
4 Kawhi Leonard 6.00 15.00
5 Jae Crowder 3.00 8.00
6 Austin Rivers 4.00 10.00
7 Andre Drummond 6.00 15.00
8 Quincy Acy 2.50 6.00
9 Will Barton 3.00 8.00
10 Tyler Zeller 3.00 8.00
11 Iman Shumpert 4.00 10.00
12 Brandon Knight 4.00 10.00
13 Terrence Ross 4.00 10.00
14 Meyers Leonard 3.00 8.00
15 Tristan Thompson 4.00 10.00
16 John Henson 4.00 10.00
17 Kim English 2.50 6.00
18 Kevin Murphy 2.50 6.00
19 Damian Lillard 5.00 12.00
20 Kyrie Irving 15.00 40.00
21 Norris Cole 2.50 6.00
22 Kyle Singler 2.50 6.00
23 Bradley Beal 6.00 15.00
24 Markieff Morris 4.00 10.00
25 Marquis Teague 2.50 6.00
26 Tony Wroten 3.00 8.00
27 Harrison Barnes 6.00 15.00
28 Chris Singleton 2.50 6.00
29 Perry Jones 2.50 6.00
30 Jimmy Butler 6.00 15.00
31 Dion Waiters 5.00 12.00
32 Klay Thompson 6.00 15.00
33 Andrew Nicholson 2.50 6.00
34 Reggie Jackson 4.00 10.00
35 Michael Kidd-Gilchrist 5.00 12.00
36 John Jenkins 2.50 6.00
37 Orlando Johnson 2.50 6.00
38 Chandler Parsons 5.00 12.00
39 Robert Sacre 2.50 6.00
40 Kemba Walker 5.00 12.00

2012-13 Panini Intrigue Slam Ink

PRINT RUNS B/WN 15-299 COPIES PER
NO PRICING ON QTY 15 OR LESS
EXCHANGE DEADLINE 3/18/2015
2 Blake Griffin/25
3 Kobe Bryant/99 60.00 150.00
4 Kevin Durant/49 60.00 150.00
5 Anthony Davis/25 100.00 200.00
6 Terrence Ross/49 6.00 15.00
7 Kenneth Faried/25
9 Tyson Chandler/25 8.00 20.00
11 Chris Copeland/299 4.00 10.00
12 Harrison Barnes/25 30.00 80.00
13 Taj Gibson/49 EXCH 5.00 12.00
15 Andre Iguodala/25 5.00 12.00
16 Jonas Valanciunas/99 6.00 15.00
17 Michael Kidd-Gilchrist/25 10.00 25.00
19 JaVale McGee/99 5.00 12.00
21 Jerryd Bayless/199 5.00 12.00
22 Maurice Harkless/199 6.00 15.00
23 Tobias Harris/199 6.00 15.00
24 Anthony Randolph/25 EXCH 5.00 12.00
25 Al-Farouq Aminu/199 5.00 12.00
27 J.R. Smith/25 12.00 30.00
28 Jeff Green/25 12.00 30.00
29 Darryl Dawkins/199 4.00 10.00
31 Jason Maxiell/299 4.00 10.00
32 Steve Francis/25 20.00 50.00
33 Alonzo Gee/199 4.00 10.00
34 George Gervin/25 30.00 60.00
35 Dion Waiters/25 20.00 50.00
36 Kenny Walker/199 4.00 10.00
37 Darrell Griffith/199 4.00 10.00
38 Dee Brown/199 8.00 20.00
39 Julius Erving/25
40 Larry Nance/199 5.00 12.00
42 Nick Young/49 5.00 12.00
43 Tristan Thompson/25 EXCH 8.00 20.00
44 Will Barton/299 5.00 12.00
45 John Henson/25 EXCH 10.00 25.00
46 Andre Drummond/49 25.00 60.00
47 Jimmy Butler/199 20.00 50.00
48 Draymond Green/199 20.00 50.00
50 David Thompson/199 5.00 12.00

2012-13 Panini Intrigue Terrific Trios Jerseys

PRINT RUNS B/WN 25-49 COPIES PER
1 Bosh/Wade/James/49 30.00 80.00
2 Griffin/Paul/Hill/49 6.00 15.00
3 Garn/Pierce/Rondo/49 8.00 20.00
4 Melo/Kidd/Chand/49 6.00 15.00
5 Howard/Bryant/Nash/49 10.00 25.00
6 Durant/Martin/Westb/49 10.00 25.00
7 Kirilen/Love/Rubio/49 5.00 12.00
8 DeRozan/Valanciunas/Lowry/49 5.00 12.00
9 Beal/Wall/Nene/49 6.00 15.00
10 Parsons/Harden/Lin/49 10.00 25.00
11 Lopez/Williams/Johnson/49 4.00 10.00
12 Lee/Barnes/Curry/49 15.00 40.00
13 Gasol/Gasol/Rubio/49 15.00 40.00
14 Scola/Ginobili/Prigioni/49 5.00 12.00
15 Fourn/Batum/Parker/49 15.00 40.00
16 Davis/Kidd-Gilt/Jones/49 10.00 25.00
17 Horford/Beal/Noah/49 5.00 12.00
18 Howard/Smith/Garn/49 8.00 20.00
19 Durant/Aldrid/Thomp/49 12.00 30.00
20 Mourning/Rice/Smith/49 15.00 40.00
21 Griffin/Howard/James/25 15.00 40.00
22 Barnes/Felton/Carter/49 5.00 12.00
23 Rivers/Hill/Irving/49 50.00 120.00
24 Melo/Durant/Bryant/49 15.00 40.00
25 Knight/Wall/Rondo/49 6.00 15.00
26 Monroe/Ewing/Hib/49 15.00 40.00
27 Melo/Durant/James/49 20.00 50.00
28 Paul/Will/Rondo/49 6.00 15.00
29 Drum/Okafor/Walk/49 10.00 25.00
30 Iguo/Williams/Terry/49

2012-13 Panini Intrigue Top Flight Unis

PRINT RUNS B/WN 25-99 COPIES PER
1 Dwight Howard/99 3.00 8.00
2 Hakeem Olajuwon/49 5.00 12.00
3 Jimmy Butler/99 8.00 20.00
4 Kevin Garnett/99 6.00 15.00
5 Tyrus Thomas/25 2.50 6.00
6 Kevin Durant/99 5.00 12.00
7 Blake Griffin/99 6.00 15.00
8 Anderson Varejao/99 2.50 6.00
9 Paul Pierce/99 4.00 10.00
10 Clyde Drexler/49 5.00 12.00
11 Dion Waiters/99
12 Harrison Barnes/49 8.00 20.00
13 Jeff Green/25 6.00 15.00
14 Kobe Bryant/99 15.00 40.00
15 Tristan Thompson/25 10.00 25.00
16 Kenneth Faried/25 4.00 10.00
17 Anthony Davis/25 12.00 30.00
18 Amir Johnson/25 2.50 6.00
19 Paul Millsap/25 4.00 10.00
20 Darren Collison/25
21 Dikembe Mutombo/25 12.00 30.00
22 Grant Hill/99 5.00 12.00
23 JaVale McGee/99 3.00 8.00
24 Landry Fields/49 2.50 6.00
25 Thaddeus Young/49 2.50 6.00
26 Kemba Walker/25
27 Bismack Biyombo/99
28 Amar'e Stoudemire/99 3.00 8.00
29 Paul George/49 6.00 15.00
30 Caron Butler/25 3.00 8.00
31 Devin Harris/25 2.50 6.00
32 Gerald Henderson/99 2.50 6.00
33 Jared Sullinger/99 5.00 12.00
34 Luol Deng/25
35 Thabo Sefolosha/99 2.50 6.00
36 Kawhi Leonard/49
37 Andrew Nicholson/99
38 Alex English/99 3.00 8.00
39 Patrick Ewing/49 5.00 12.00
40 Carmelo Anthony/99 5.00 12.00
41 Derrick Favors/25
42 Gerald Wallace/25 3.00 8.00
43 Jan Vesely/99 2.50 6.00
44 LeBron James/49 10.00 25.00
45 Terrence Ross/49
46 Karl Malone/99 5.00 12.00
47 Andrei Kirilenko/49
48 Kevin Martin/49 3.00 8.00
49 Monta Ellis/25
50 Brandon Jennings/25 2.50 6.00
51 Deron Williams/25 3.00 8.00
52 Eric Gordon/99
53 James White/99 2.50 6.00
54 Markieff Morris/99 4.00 10.00
55 Shaquille O'Neal/99 6.00 15.00
56 Jordan Hamilton/99 2.50 6.00
57 Andre Iguodala/25
58 Al-Farouq Aminu/99 3.00 8.00
59 Michael Kidd-Gilchrist/25 6.00 15.00
60 Brandon Bass/49 2.50 6.00
61 DeMar DeRozan/25
62 Ekpe Udoh/49
63 J.J. Hickson/49
64 MarShon Brooks/49
65 Rudy Gay/25
66 John Wall/25 5.00 12.00
67 Andre Drummond/99 5.00 12.00
68 Joakim Noah/49 3.00 8.00
69 Michael Beasley/99 2.50 6.00
70 Bradley Beal/99 5.00 12.00
71 David Lee/25
72 Dwyane Wade/25 6.00 15.00
73 Iman Shumpert/49 4.00 10.00
74 Matt Barnes/99 2.50 6.00
75 Roy Hibbert/25 3.00 8.00

2012-13 Panini Intrigue Winning Ink

PRINT RUNS B/WN 15-299 COPIES PER
NO PRICING ON QTY 15 OR LESS
EXCHANGE DEADLINE 3/18/2015
1 Julius Erving/25 60.00 120.00
2 Robert Parish/25 10.00 25.00
3 Rick Mahorn/299 4.00 10.00
4 David Robinson/25 50.00 100.00
5 Udonis Haslem/49 4.00 10.00
6 Jamaal Wilkes/25
7 Toni Kukoc/25 12.00 30.00
8 Bill Laimbeer/299 5.00 12.00
9 Beno Udrih/299 4.00 10.00
11 Bill Walton/25
12 Dennis Rodman/25 40.00 80.00
13 Mark Aguirre/299 5.00 12.00
14 Antoine Walker/299 5.00 12.00
15 Kobe Bryant/49 100.00 200.00
16 Larry Bird/25
18 Joe Dumars/25 10.00 25.00
19 Gary Payton/25
22 Will Perdue/299 4.00 10.00
23 Bill Cartwright/25 15.00 40.00
24 Alonzo Mourning/25 25.00 60.00
25 Mario Chalmers/25 5.00 12.00
26 A.C. Green/25 12.00 30.00
27 Sean Elliott/199 8.00 20.00
28 B.J. Armstrong/25 10.00 25.00
31 Spencer Haywood/299 4.00 10.00
32 Glen Rice/25 20.00 50.00
33 John Paxson/299 5.00 12.00
34 Bruce Bowen/299 4.00 10.00
35 Tyson Chandler/25
36 Magic Johnson/25 EXCH 40.00 80.00
37 Horace Grant/25 20.00 50.00
38 Clyde Drexler/25 40.00 80.00
39 Michael Finley/25 6.00 15.00
40 Jason Kidd/25 30.00 60.00
42 Rick Fox/25 5.00 12.00
43 Vernon Maxwell/299 4.00 10.00
44 Hakeem Olajuwon/25 30.00 60.00
46 Michael Cooper/299 5.00 12.00
47 Stephen Jackson/25 EXCH 5.00 12.00
48 Luc Longley/299 5.00 12.00
49 Robert Horry/25 12.00 30.00

2013-14 Panini Intrigue

1 Jameer Nelson .25 .60
2 Vince Carter .50 1.25
3 George Hill .30 .75
4 Gerald Green .30 .75
5 Gerald Henderson .25 .60
6 Manu Ginobili .40 1.00
7 Kenneth Faried .30 .75
8 LaMarcus Aldridge .40 1.00
9 Monta Ellis .30 .75
10 Carmelo Anthony .50 1.25
11 Dwight Howard .30 .75
12 DeAndre Jordan .40 1.00
13 Russell Westbrook 1.00 2.50
14 Tyreke Evans .25 .60
15 O.J. Mayo .25 .60
16 Andre Drummond .40 1.00
17 Greivis Vasquez .30 .75
18 Al Horford .30 .75
19 Serge Ibaka .30 .75
20 Rodney Stuckey .30 .75
21 Isaiah Thomas .40 1.00
22 Glen Davis .25 .60
23 Paul Pierce .40 1.00
24 Chris Bosh .40 1.00
25 Harrison Barnes .30 .75
26 Rudy Gay .40 1.00
27 Rajon Rondo .40 1.00
28 Andre Miller .30 .75
29 Marc Gasol .40 1.00
30 Kawhi Leonard .60 1.50
31 LeBron James 1.50 4.00
32 Derrick Favors .30 .75
33 John Wall .50 1.25
34 James Harden .60 1.50
35 Randy Foye .25 .60
36 Andre Iguodala .30 .75
37 Luol Deng .30 .75
38 DeMar DeRozan .40 1.00
39 Kevin Garnett .60 1.50
40 Gordon Hayward .40 1.00
41 Al Jefferson .30 .75
42 Steve Nash .40 1.00
43 Tony Parker .40 1.00
44 Nikola Pekovic .25 .60
45 Shawn Marion .30 .75
46 Evan Turner .25 .60
47 Derrick Rose .50 1.25
48 Bradley Beal .40 1.00
49 Kemba Walker .40 1.00
50 Goran Dragic .30 .75
51 Brandon Jennings .25 .60
52 Deron Williams .30 .75
53 Jason Richardson .40 1.00
54 J.R. Smith .30 .75
55 Anderson Varejao .25 .60
56 Tyson Chandler .30 .75
57 Gerald Wallace .30 .75
58 Nikola Vucevic .30 .75
59 Lance Stephenson .30 .75
60 Dwyane Wade .60 1.50
61 Kobe Bryant 1.50 4.00
62 Marcin Gortat .30 .75
63 Pau Gasol .40 1.00
64 Carlos Boozer .30 .75
65 Paul George .50 1.25
66 Anthony Davis .75 2.00
67 Klay Thompson .50 1.25
68 Nicolas Batum .30 .75
69 Kevin Martin .30 .75
70 Dion Waiters .30 .75
71 Jeremy Lin .40 1.00
72 Paul Millsap .40 1.00
73 Kevin Love .40 1.00
74 DeMarcus Cousins .40 1.00
75 Joakim Noah .30 .75
76 Ricky Rubio .40 1.00
77 Brandon Knight .30 .75
78 Kevin Durant 1.00 2.50
79 Brook Lopez .30 .75
80 Roy Hibbert .30 .75
81 Thaddeus Young .25 .60
82 Blake Griffin .40 1.00
83 Jeff Teague .30 .75

84 Mike Conley .30 .75
85 Eric Bledsoe .30 .75
86 Larry Sanders .25 .60
87 Kyrie Irving .75 2.00
88 Austin Rivers .30 .75
89 Amar'e Stoudemire .30 .75
90 Chris Paul .50 1.25
91 Dirk Nowitzki .50 1.25
92 Ty Lawson .25 .60
93 Damian Lillard .75 2.00
94 Avery Bradley .30 .75
95 Tim Duncan .60 1.50
96 Zach Randolph .30 .75
97 Jrue Holiday .40 1.00
98 Stephen Curry 1.50 4.00
99 Ersan Ilyasova .25 .60
100 Kyle Lowry .30 .75

2013-14 Panini Intrigue '14 Draft X-Change

EXCHANGE DEADLINE 12/12/2015
1 Andrew Wiggins 12.00 30.00
Pick 1
2 Jabari Parker 10.00 25.00
Pick 2
3 Joel Embiid 12.00 30.00
Pick 3
4 Aaron Gordon 10.00 25.00
Pick 4
5 Dante Exum 8.00 20.00
Pick 5
6 Marcus Smart 8.00 20.00
Pick 6
7 Julius Randle 12.00 30.00
Pick 7
8 Nik Stauskas 6.00 15.00
Pick 8
9 Noah Vonleh 6.00 15.00
Pick 9
10 Elfrid Payton 6.00 15.00
Pick 10
11 Doug McDermott 5.00 12.00
Pick 11
12 Dario Saric 8.00 20.00
Pick 12
13 Zach LaVine 8.00 20.00
Pick 13
14 T. J. Warren 8.00 20.00
Pick 14
15 Adreian Payne 6.00 15.00
Pick 15
16 Jusuf Nurkic 8.00 20.00
Pick 16
17 James Young 5.00 12.00
Pick 17
18 Tyler Ennis 5.00 12.00
Pick 18
19 Gary Harris 8.00 20.00
Pick 19
20 Bruno Caboclo 6.00 15.00
Pick 20
21 Mitch McGary 5.00 12.00
Pick 21
22 Jordan Adams 5.00 12.00
Pick 22
23 Rodney Hood 8.00 20.00
Pick 23
24 Shabazz Napier 5.00 12.00
Pick 24
25 Clint Capela 8.00 20.00
Pick 25

2013-14 Panini Intrigue Autograph Jerseys

PRINT RUNS B/WN 12-149 COPIES PER
NO PRICING ON QTY 15 OR LESS
EXCHANGE DEADLINE 10/23/2015
1 DeMarre Carroll/149 4.00 10.00
2 Derrick Williams/25 4.00 10.00
3 Kenyon Martin/149 5.00 12.00
4 Anthony Davis/25 60.00 120.00
6 Darrell Griffith/149 4.00 10.00
8 Kevin Durant/25 50.00 120.00
9 Spencer Haywood/99 4.00 10.00
10 Jason Kidd/25 20.00 50.00
11 John Wall/99 10.00 25.00
13 Kyrie Irving/25
14 Bernard King/49 5.00 12.00
15 Anthony Mason/149 8.00 20.00
16 Fat Lever/149 5.00 12.00
17 James Jones/149 4.00 10.00
18 Ramon Sessions/149 5.00 12.00
19 Eddie Jones/149 10.00 25.00
20 Nick Young/149 8.00 20.00
21 John Stockton/25 40.00 80.00
22 Udonis Haslem/149 4.00 10.00
23 Kevin Love/25 15.00 40.00
24 Tracy McGrady/25 30.00 60.00
26 Brad Daugherty/149 5.00 12.00
27 Ron Harper/149 6.00 15.00
28 Al Horford/25 5.00 12.00
29 John Havlicek/25 40.00 80.00
34 Alex English/75 5.00 12.00
37 Dennis Rodman/25 20.00 50.00
38 Jordan Crawford/149 10.00 25.00
39 Steve Smith/149 5.00 12.00
40 Kenny Anderson/149 5.00 12.00
42 Dwight Howard/25 10.00 25.00
43 Juwan Howard/75 5.00 12.00
44 Mitch Richmond/75 12.00 30.00
46 Tyson Chandler/25 5.00 12.00
49 Tony Parker/25 20.00 50.00
50 Boris Diaw/75 5.00 12.00

2013-14 Panini Intrigue Dual Jersey Autographs

PRINT RUNS B/WN 12-149 COPIES PER
NO PRICING ON QTY 15 OR LESS
EXCHANGE DEADLINE 10/23/2015
1 Dee Brown/99 4.00 10.00
2 Chris Kaman/25 5.00 12.00
3 Al Horford/25 5.00 12.00
4 Reggie Jackson/25 12.00 30.00
5 World B. Free/25 5.00 12.00
6 Ralph Sampson/25 5.00 12.00
7 Andrea Bargnani/49 5.00 12.00
8 Larry Johnson/25 8.00 20.00
9 J.J. Redick/25 12.00 30.00
10 Kyrie Irving/49 60.00 120.00
11 Tracy McGrady/49 20.00 50.00
12 Nick Young/99 10.00 25.00
13 Clyde Drexler/25 20.00 50.00
14 Chuck Person/25 5.00 12.00
15 Artis Gilmore/25 8.00 20.00
16 Jason Terry/25 5.00 12.00
17 Spencer Haywood/99 4.00 10.00
18 Gerald Henderson/25 4.00 10.00
19 Shane Battier/25 15.00 40.00
20 Jae Crowder/99 5.00 12.00
21 Jrue Holiday/25 6.00 15.00
22 Kawhi Leonard/25 60.00 150.00
23 Danny Manning/25 8.00 20.00
24 Alonzo Mourning/25
25 Kareem Abdul-Jabbar/25 40.00 80.00
26 Deron Williams/25 5.00 12.00
27 Evan Fournier/99 5.00 12.00
28 John Lucas/25 6.00 15.00
29 Grant Hill/25 30.00 60.00
30 Andre Iguodala/25 12.00 30.00
31 Ron Harper/75 6.00 15.00
32 Udonis Haslem/99 4.00 10.00
33 Steve Smith/99 5.00 12.00
34 Jayson Williams/99 4.00 10.00
35 Joe Dumars/25 6.00 15.00
36 Kevin Durant/49 75.00 150.00
37 Kobe Bryant/49 100.00 200.00

2013-14 Panini Intrigue Dunk Company Autographs

PRINT RUNS B/WN 12-149 COPIES PER
NO PRICING ON QTY 15 OR LESS
EXCHANGE DEADLINE 10/23/2015
1 Luc Longley/99 4.00 10.00
2 Vlade Divac/99 5.00 12.00
3 Kobe Bryant/25 150.00 250.00
5 Daniel Orton/99 3.00 8.00
6 Nick Collison/99 4.00 10.00
7 Kawhi Leonard/75 50.00 120.00
9 Vince Carter/49 30.00 60.00
10 Iman Shumpert/99 3.00 8.00
14 Darryl Dawkins/99 3.00 8.00
16 Nick Anderson/99 6.00 15.00
17 Mark Aguirre/99 4.00 10.00
18 Tom Chambers/99 8.00 20.00
21 Derrick Coleman/99 5.00 12.00
22 Michael Cooper/99 4.00 10.00
24 Udonis Haslem/99 3.00 8.00
25 Larry Nance/99 4.00 10.00
26 Ron Harper/99 10.00 25.00
28 Toni Kukoc/99 5.00 12.00
29 Kevin Willis/99 3.00 8.00
32 Mahmoud Abdul-Rauf/99 10.00 25.00
33 Greg Monroe/99 4.00 10.00
37 Isaiah Rider/25 15.00 40.00
39 Kenny Walker/99 6.00 12.00
40 Scottie Pippen/25 60.00 150.00
41 Dee Brown/99 6.00 15.00
42 Chris Andersen/49 15.00 40.00
44 Spud Webb/99 4.00 10.00
45 Tyson Chandler/25 4.00 10.00
46 Anfernee Hardaway/49 30.00 60.00
49 Larry Johnson/75 10.00 25.00
50 David Thompson/99 4.00 10.00
51 Tracy McGrady/49 20.00 50.00
52 Kenyon Martin/99 4.00 10.00
53 Jan Vesely/99 3.00 8.00
54 Kevin Love/49 6.00 15.00
55 Connie Hawkins/99 5.00 12.00
57 Vernon Maxwell/99 3.00 8.00
58 Al-Farouq Aminu/99 4.00 10.00
59 Fred Jones/99 3.00 8.00
60 Nick Young/99 5.00 12.00

2013-14 Panini Intrigue Fearless Foursomes

PRINT RUNS B/WN 25-199 COPIES PER
1 Std/Brg/Anth/Fltn/199 8.00 20.00
2 Dvs/Csns/Wll/Glc/199 12.00 30.00
3 Bsh/Wde/Jms/Alln/99 20.00 50.00
4 Le/Brns/Thmp/Crry/149 10.00 25.00
5 Drnt/Wstb/Ibka/Sfl/199 12.00 30.00
6 Vrjo/Wtrs/Jck/Irvng/50 10.00 25.00
7 Bnntt/Zllr/Prtr/Oldpo/199 6.00 15.00
8 Nwtzki/Wde/Brynt/Jms/50 25.00 60.00
9 Grffn/Llrd/Irvng/Evns/25 20.00 50.00
10 Grffn/Drnt/Brynt/Irvng/25 20.00 50.00

2013-14 Panini Intrigue Fearless Foursomes Prime

*PRIME: .6X TO 1.5X BASIC
PRINT RUNS B/WN 2-25 COPIES PER
NO PRICING ON QTY 8 OR LESS
3 Bsh/Wde/Jms/Alln/25 250.00 500.00
8 Nwtzki/Wde/Brynt/Jms/25 50.00 120.00

2013-14 Panini Intrigue First Flight Unis

PRINT RUNS B/WN 99-199 COPIES PER
NO PRICING ON QTY 15 OR LESS
*PRIME: .75X TO 2X BASIC
1 Eric Gordon/199 3.00 8.00
2 David Lee/199 2.50 6.00
3 Vince Carter/199 5.00 12.00
4 Amar'e Stoudemire/199 3.00 8.00
5 JaVale McGee/199 3.00 8.00
6 Andre Iguodala/199 3.00 8.00
7 Derrick Favors/199 3.00 8.00
8 Andrei Kirilenko/199 3.00 8.00
9 Chris Kaman/199 3.00 8.00
10 David West/199 3.00 8.00
11 Dwight Howard/199 3.00 8.00
12 Carl Landry/199 2.50 6.00
13 Jose Calderon/199 2.50 6.00
14 Andray Blatche/199 2.50 6.00
15 Kevin Martin/199 3.00 8.00
16 James Harden/199 6.00 15.00
17 LeBron James/99 15.00 40.00
18 O.J. Mayo/199 2.50 6.00
19 Deron Williams/199 3.00 8.00
20 Danilo Gallinari/199 2.50 6.00
21 Andrew Bynum/199 2.50 6.00
22 Nene/199 3.00 8.00
23 Luis Scola/199 3.00 8.00
24 Samuel Dalembert/199 2.50 6.00
25 Kevin Garnett/149 5.00 12.00

2013-14 Panini Intrigue Hall Dwellers Jersey Autographs

PRINT RUNS B/WN 15-49 COPIES PER
NO PRICING ON QTY 15 OR LESS
EXCHANGE DEADLINE 10/23/2015
3 Julius Erving/25 40.00 100.00
5 Karl Malone/25 40.00 80.00
10 Kareem Abdul-Jabbar/25 50.00 100.00
14 Jerry West/25 60.00 120.00
15 Dan Issel/49 5.00 12.00
19 Scottie Pippen/25 50.00 120.00
20 Arvydas Sabonis/25
22 Alex English/49 10.00 25.00
28 Larry Bird/25 50.00 120.00

2013-14 Panini Intrigue Immortalized Autographs

PRINT RUNS B/WN 15-99 COPIES PER
NO PRICING ON QTY 15 OR LESS
EXCHANGE DEADLINE 10/23/2015
1 Wes Unseld/35 5.00 12.00
2 Muggsy Bogues/99 8.00 20.00
3 Micheal Ray Richardson/99 4.00 10.00
4 Jason Kidd/25 40.00 80.00
5 Clyde Drexler/25 50.00 100.00
6 Spencer Haywood/99 6.00 15.00
7 Nate Thurmond/25 6.00 15.00
8 Tom Chambers/25 12.00 30.00
9 George McGinnis/25 3.00 8.00
10 Fat Lever/99 4.00 10.00
11 Eddie Jones/99 8.00 20.00
13 Toni Kukoc/25 20.00 50.00
14 Bob McAdoo/25 50.00 100.00
15 Kevin McHale/25 30.00 60.00
16 James Worthy/25 12.00 30.00
17 Dan Issel/99 4.00 10.00
20 Tom Gugliotta/99 3.00 8.00
21 Darryl Dawkins/99 3.00 8.00
22 Hakeem Olajuwon/25 12.00 30.00
23 Nick Van Exel/35
24 Earl Monroe/25 30.00 60.00
25 Robert Parish/15
26 Sam Cassell/25 10.00 25.00
28 Elgin Baylor/25 30.00 60.00
29 Dikembe Mutombo/25 20.00 50.00
30 Bernard King/35 12.00 30.00
31 David Robinson/25
32 Rex Chapman/99 5.00 12.00
33 Gary Payton/25 10.00 25.00
34 Tracy McGrady/25 40.00 80.00
35 Michael Cooper/49 4.00 10.00
36 Mitch Richmond/25 30.00 60.00
37 Dennis Rodman/25
38 Eddie Johnson/99
39 Derrick Coleman/25
41 Detlef Schrempf/99 5.00 12.00
42 Dan Majerle/25 12.00 30.00
43 Sleepy Floyd/99 3.00 8.00
44 Grant Hill/25 40.00 80.00
45 Allan Houston/25 4.00 10.00
46 Scottie Pippen/35 50.00 120.00
47 Dana Barros/99 3.00 8.00
48 Michael Finley/35 30.00 60.00
50 Reggie Theus/99 4.00 10.00
51 Jalen Rose/25 40.00 80.00
52 Dominique Wilkins/25 40.00 80.00
53 Karl Malone/35 40.00 80.00
54 Magic Johnson/25
56 Isiah Thomas/35 20.00 50.00
57 Cedric Maxwell/99 3.00 8.00
58 Julius Erving/25 50.00 100.00
59 Sean Elliott/99 5.00 12.00
60 Ron Harper/99 8.00 20.00

2013-14 Panini Intrigue Impact Rookie Autographs

PRINT RUNS B/WN 49-149 COPIES PER
EXCHANGE DEADLINE 10/23/2015
1 Cody Zeller/75 4.00 10.00
2 Peyton Siva/149 3.00 8.00
3 Shabazz Muhammad/75 4.00 10.00
4 M.Carter-Williams/149 5.00 12.00
5 Ben McLemore/49 4.00 10.00
6 Andre Roberson/149 3.00 8.00
7 Matthew Dellavedova/149 5.00 12.00
8 Carrick Felix/149 3.00 8.00
9 Nemanja Nedovic/149 3.00 8.00
10 Jamaal Franklin/149 3.00 8.00
11 Tim Hardaway Jr./149 5.00 12.00
12 Glen Rice Jr./149 3.00 8.00
13 C.J. McCollum/75 12.00 30.00
14 Ricky Ledo/149 3.00 8.00
15 Kelly Olynyk/149 4.00 10.00
16 Anthony Bennett/75 4.00 10.00
17 Kentavious Caldwell-Pope/75 5.00 12.00
18 Rudy Gobert/149 8.00 20.00
19 Tony Snell/149 4.00 10.00
20 Isaiah Canaan/149 3.00 8.00
21 G.Antetokounmpo/149 60.00 150.00
22 Gorgui Dieng/149 8.00 20.00
23 Victor Oladipo/75 8.00 20.00
24 Alex Len/75 4.00 10.00
25 Dennis Schroder/149 5.00 12.00
26 Erik Murphy/149 3.00 8.00
27 Gal Mekel/149 3.00 8.00
28 Solomon Hill/149 3.00 8.00
29 Nate Wolters/149 4.00 10.00
30 Steven Adams/149 12.00 30.00
31 Archie Goodwin/149 4.00 10.00
32 Trey Burke/75 4.00 10.00
33 Mason Plumlee/149 5.00 12.00
34 Shane Larkin/149 3.00 8.00
35 Tony Mitchell/149 3.00 8.00
36 Ryan Kelly/149 3.00 8.00
37 Jeff Withey/149 3.00 8.00
38 Nerlens Noel/49 20.00 50.00
39 Allen Crabbe/149 4.00 10.00
40 Otto Porter/49 5.00 12.00

2013-14 Panini Intrigue Intriguing Pairs Jerseys

PRINT RUNS B/WN 25-199 COPIES PER
*PRIME: .75X TO 2X BASIC
1 K.Hinrich/N.Collison/199 3.00 8.00
2 K.Walker/M.Gilchrist/199 4.00 10.00
3 B.Beal/J.Wall/99 5.00 12.00
4 T.Splitter/T.Duncan/99 6.00 15.00
5 K.Durant/S.Ibaka/199 10.00 25.00
6 K.Bryant/K.Irving/25 15.00 40.00
7 B.McLemore/J.Withey/199 5.00 12.00
8 C.Zeller/O.Porter/199 3.00 8.00
9 T.Hardaway Jr./T.Burke/199 6.00 15.00
10 B.Griffin/J.Redick/169 4.00 10.00
11 D.Lillard/K.Irving/25 8.00 20.00
12 T.Prince/Z.Randolph/49 3.00 8.00
13 E.Ilyasova/J.Henson/199 3.00 8.00
14 L.Allen/T.Young/199 2.50 6.00
15 J.Green/R.Rondo/99 4.00 10.00
16 G.Hill/K.Irving/25 10.00 25.00
17 M.Beasley/U.Haslem/199 2.50 6.00
18 A.Davis/A.Rivers/99 6.00 15.00
19 D.Williams/J.Terry/199 3.00 8.00
20 C.Paul/J.Crawford/25 8.00 20.00
21 A.Bennett/K.Olynyk/199 3.00 8.00
22 R.Ledo/S.Larkin/199 2.50 6.00
23 C.McCollum/M.Williams/199 6.00 15.00
24 M.Gasol/P.Gasol/99 4.00 10.00
25 R.Jackson/R.Westbrook/199 10.00 25.00
26 B.Griffin/K.Durant/199 8.00 20.00
27 D.Wade/M.Chalmers/199 5.00 12.00
28 J.Noah/T.Gibson/199 3.00 8.00
29 B.Bass/J.Sullinger/199 2.50 6.00
30 K.Durant/K.Bryant/199 12.00 30.00
31 A.Nicholson/N.Vucevic/25
32 J.McGee/K.Faried/199 3.00 8.00
33 K.Bryant/S.Nash/25 8.00 20.00
34 C.Zeller/V.Oladipo/199 6.00 15.00
35 A.Goodwin/B.McLemore/199 4.00 10.00
36 H.Barnes/K.Thompson/49 5.00 12.00
37 A.Shved/R.Rubio/99 4.00 10.00
38 J.Harden/J.Lin/99 6.00 15.00
39 C.Bosh/L.James/49 8.00 20.00
40 A.Drummond/C.Villanueva/199 4.00 10.00
41 D.Williams/J.Johnson/199 3.00 8.00
42 D.West/G.Hill/49 3.00 8.00
43 D.Blair/D.Nowitzki/199 5.00 12.00
44 F.Lever/T.Lawson/99 3.00 8.00
45 D.Lee/D.Green/199 5.00 12.00
46 D.Cousins/I.Thomas/99 4.00 10.00
47 A.Bennett/L.Johnson/49 5.00 12.00
48 J.Dumars/K.Pope/99 4.00 10.00
49 A.Iverson/M.Williams/99 5.00 12.00
50 N.De Colo/T.Parker/49 10.00 25.00
51 N.Cole/R.Allen/199 6.00 15.00
52 A.Johnson/D.DeRozan/199 4.00 10.00
53 I.Shumpert/R.Felton/199 3.00 8.00
54 A.Len/N.Noel/199 5.00 12.00
55 M.Gortat/Nene/35 12.00 30.00
56 A.Bennett/V.Oladipo/199 5.00 12.00
57 Marc.Morris/Mark.Morris/199 2.50 6.00
58 A.Goodwin/N.Noel/199 4.00 10.00
59 C.Anthony/J.Smith/99 5.00 12.00
60 E.Murphy/T.Snell/199 3.00 8.00

2013-14 Panini Intrigue Intriguing Players

ALL VERSIONS EQUALLY PRICED
1 LeBron James 2.50 6.00
11 Kevin Durant 1.50 4.00
21 Stephen Curry 2.50 6.00
31 Russell Westbrook 1.50 4.00
41 James Harden 1.00 2.50
51 Carmelo Anthony .75 2.00
61 Kyrie Irving 1.25 3.00
71 Chris Paul .75 2.00
81 Derrick Rose .75 2.00
91 Dwyane Wade 1.00 2.50
101 Dirk Nowitzki .75 2.00
111 Tim Duncan 1.00 2.50
121 Anthony Davis 1.25 3.00
131 Dwight Howard .50 1.25
141 Paul George .75 2.00
151 Kobe Bryant 2.50 6.00
161 Damian Lillard 1.25 3.00
171 Paul Pierce .60 1.50
181 John Wall .75 2.00
191 Tony Parker .60 1.50

2013-14 Panini Intrigue Intriguing Players Die Cuts

*DIE CUT: .75X TO 2X BASIC

2013-14 Panini Intrigue Intriguing Players Die Cuts Gold

*DIE CUT GOLD: 6X TO 15X
STATED PRINT RUN 10 SER.#'d SETS

2013-14 Panini Intrigue Intriguing Players Gold

*DIE CUT: 6X TO 15X
STATED PRINT RUN 10 SER.#'d SETS

2013-14 Panini Intrigue Red White and Blue Autographs

PRINT RUNS B/WN 15-99 COPIES PER
NO PRICING ON QTY 15 OR LESS
EXCHANGE DEADLINE 10/23/2015
1 Tim Hardaway/99 6.00 15.00
2 Kenny Anderson/99 4.00 10.00
3 Rick Mahorn/99 3.00 8.00
4 Jerry Lucas/25
5 Jason Kidd/25 40.00 80.00
8 Larry Bird/25 60.00 120.00
9 Terry Porter/99 3.00 8.00
12 Kendall Gill/99 10.00 25.00
15 Spencer Haywood/99 3.00 8.00
16 Bobby Jones/99 4.00 10.00
17 Kobe Bryant/25 150.00 250.00
18 Bill Russell/25 75.00 150.00
19 Karl Malone/25 30.00 80.00
20 Buck Williams/99 3.00 8.00
21 David Robinson/25 50.00 100.00
24 Scottie Pippen/25 100.00 175.00
25 Jeff Hornacek/99 4.00 10.00
26 Steve Blake/99 8.00 20.00
29 Mark Price/99 20.00 50.00
32 John Starks/99 4.00 10.00
34 Anfernee Hardaway/25 75.00 150.00
35 Charlie Scott/99 4.00 10.00
36 Mark Aguirre/99 4.00 10.00
38 Grant Hill/25 EXCH 50.00 100.00

2013-14 Panini Intrigue Rookie Autographed Memorabilia

PRINT RUNS B/WN 49-149 COPIES PER
EXCHANGE DEADLINE 10/23/2015
1 Tony Mitchell/99 4.00 10.00
2 M.Carter-Williams/99 6.00 15.00
3 Otto Porter/25 10.00 25.00
4 G.Antetokounmpo/99 100.00 250.00
5 Tony Snell/99 5.00 12.00
6 Peyton Siva/99 4.00 10.00
7 Jeff Withey/99 4.00 10.00
8 C.J. McCollum/25 10.00 25.00
9 Kelly Olynyk/99 5.00 12.00
10 Ricky Ledo/99 4.00 10.00
11 Jamaal Franklin/99 4.00 10.00
12 Victor Oladipo/25 8.00 20.00
13 Trey Burke/25 5.00 12.00
14 Isaiah Canaan/99 4.00 10.00
15 Mason Plumlee/99 10.00 25.00
16 Reggie Bullock/99 5.00 12.00
17 Alex Len/25 15.00 40.00
18 Erik Murphy/99 4.00 10.00
19 Andre Roberson/99 4.00 10.00
20 Archie Goodwin/99 5.00 12.00
21 Ben McLemore/25 5.00 12.00
22 Dennis Schroder/99 10.00 25.00
23 Anthony Bennett/25 5.00 12.00
24 Kentavious Caldwell-Pope/25
25 Ryan Kelly/99 4.00 10.00
26 Shabazz Muhammad/25 5.00 12.00
27 Steven Adams/99 6.00 15.00
28 Allen Crabbe/99 5.00 12.00
29 Cody Zeller/25 5.00 12.00
30 Shane Larkin/99 4.00 10.00
31 Solomon Hill/99 4.00 10.00
32 Nate Wolters/99 5.00 12.00
33 Tim Hardaway Jr./99 6.00 15.00
34 Nerlens Noel/25 8.00 20.00
35 Glen Rice Jr./99 4.00 10.00

2013-14 Panini Intrigue Slam Ink

PRINT RUNS B/WN 15-49 COPIES PER
NO PRICING ON QTY 15 OR LESS
EXCHANGE DEADLINE 10/23/2015
1 Lavoy Allen/49
2 Jeff Green/20
3 Derrick Favors/20 4.00 10.00
4 Raef LaFrentz/49
5 Nick Collison/49
6 Jason Richardson/25 EXCH 15.00 40.00
7 Michael Finley/20 EXCH 5.00 12.00
8 Harrison Barnes/20 8.00 20.00
9 George Gervin/20
10 Kenny Smith/20
11 David Thompson/25 12.00 30.00
12 Michael Cooper/49 12.00 30.00
14 Jerome Williams/49
15 Clyde Drexler/20 15.00 40.00
16 Chris Andersen/20
17 John Starks/49 6.00 15.00
18 J.J. Hickson/49 3.00 8.00
19 Terrence Ross/25 4.00 10.00
20 Darryl Dawkins/49 3.00 8.00
21 Cedric Ceballos/49 12.00 30.00
22 Andre Iguodala/20 20.00 50.00
23 Tom Chambers/25 4.00 10.00
24 Allan Houston/20 4.00 10.00
25 Kobe Bryant/25 100.00 200.00
26 Rex Chapman/49 5.00 12.00
27 Artis Gilmore/20
28 Xavier Henry/49 12.00 30.00
29 Spud Webb/49 4.00 10.00
30 Kenny Walker/25 12.00 30.00
31 JaVale McGee/20 10.00 25.00
32 Steve Francis/20
33 Larry Nance/49 6.00 15.00
34 Reggie Jackson/25 20.00 50.00
35 Ralph Sampson/20
36 Jonas Jerebko/49 3.00 8.00
37 Doug Christie/49 8.00 20.00
38 Ron Harper/49 8.00 20.00
39 Dominique Wilkins/20 30.00 60.00
40 Vince Carter/20 40.00 80.00
41 Chase Budinger/25 3.00 8.00
42 Bismack Biyombo/49 3.00 8.00
43 Kawhi Leonard/20 EXCH 60.00 150.00
44 Julius Erving/20 40.00 100.00
45 Tracy McGrady/20
46 Andrew Nicholson/49 3.00 8.00
47 J.R. Smith/25 12.00 30.00
48 Larry Johnson/20 15.00 40.00
49 Dee Brown/49 10.00 25.00
50 Gerald Henderson/25 10.00 25.00

2013-14 Panini Intrigue Terrific Trios

PRINT RUNS B/WN 25-199 COPIES PER
1 Bss/Grn/Rndo/199 4.00 10.00
2 Bltche/Wllms/Jhn/199 3.00 8.00
3 Anth/Smth/Chnd/149 5.00 12.00
4 Rse/Btlr/Hnrch/25 10.00 25.00
5 Bsh/Wde/Jms/199 12.00 30.00
6 Bl/Wll/Arza/199 5.00 12.00
7 Prsns/Hrdn/Ln/199 6.00 15.00
8 Lnrd/Dncn/Prkr/25 10.00 25.00
9 Gllnri/Frd/Lwsn/199 3.00 8.00
10 Shvd/Lve/Rbo/199 4.00 10.00
11 Drnt/Wst/Ibka/199 8.00 20.00
12 Brns/Thmpsn/Crry/149 10.00 25.00
13 Grffn/Pl/Jrdn/49 8.00 20.00
14 Brynt/Gsl/Nsh/199 15.00 40.00
15 Jhn/Chnd/Rndl/199 3.00 8.00
16 Anthny/Bsh/Jms/49 15.00 40.00
17 Pl/Wllms/Fltn/199 5.00 12.00
18 Hrfrd/Nh/Drnt/199 4.00 10.00
19 Gllnri/Lve/Wstbrk/199 10.00 25.00
20 Grffn/Hrdn/Rbo/199 6.00 15.00
21 Shmprt/Lnrd/Wlkr/199 6.00 15.00
22 Dvs/Lllrd/Brns/199 8.00 20.00
23 Bnntt/Prtr/Oldpo/199 5.00 12.00
24 Ln/Zllr/Nl/199 6.00 15.00
25 McLmre/Ppe/Brke/199 5.00 12.00
26 Schrdr/Gian/Adms/199 5.00 12.00
27 Nwtzki/Wde/Dncn/199 6.00 15.00
28 Wll/Irvng/Evns/199 8.00 20.00
29 Dvs/Grffn/Lve/199 10.00 25.00
30 Grffn/Drnt/Brynt/199 15.00 40.00

2013-14 Panini Intrigue Terrific Trios Prime

*PRIME: .75X TO 2X BASIC
PRINT RUNS B/WN 1-25 COPIES PER
NO PRICING ON QTY 15 OR LESS
13 Grffn/Pl/Jrdn/25 20.00 50.00
26 Schrdr/Gian/Adms/25 75.00 150.00
27 Nwtzki/Wde/Dncn/25 20.00 50.00

2013-14 Panini Intrigue Top Flight Unis

PRINT RUNS B/WN 49-199 COPIES PER
*PRIME: .75X TO 2X BASIC
1 Michael Kidd-Gilchrist/49 4.00 10.00
2 Tristan Thompson/49 3.00 8.00
3 DeAndre Jordan/99 4.00 10.00
4 LeBron James/99 15.00 40.00
5 Andrea Bargnani/49 3.00 8.00
6 Nick Young/49
7 Kevin Garnett/99 5.00 12.00
8 Jrue Holiday/49
9 Tiago Splitter/49 3.00 8.00
10 Serge Ibaka/99 3.00 8.00
11 Evan Turner/49 2.50 6.00
12 JaVale McGee/199 3.00 8.00
13 Dirk Nowitzki/199 5.00 12.00
14 Kobe Bryant/199 10.00 25.00
15 Udonis Haslem/99 2.50 6.00
16 Tayshaun Prince/49
17 Blake Griffin/199 4.00 10.00
18 Kyrie Irving/49 8.00 20.00
19 Damian Lillard/49 8.00 20.00
20 Joakim Noah/49 6.00 15.00
21 Courtney Lee/99 6.00 15.00
22 Jamal Crawford/49 4.00 10.00
23 Gordon Hayward/49 4.00 10.00
24 Chris Kaman/49
25 Samuel Dalembert/49
26 Nate Robinson/49 2.50 6.00
27 Rudy Gay/49 4.00 10.00
28 Eric Bledsoe/99 3.00 8.00
29 Andre Iguodala/49 3.00 8.00
30 Thaddeus Young/99 2.50 6.00
31 Gerald Henderson/49 2.50 6.00
32 Norris Cole/199 2.50 6.00
33 Iman Shumpert/49
34 Tobias Harris/49 3.00 8.00
35 Harrison Barnes/49
36 Kirk Hinrich/99 3.00 8.00
37 Brandon Bass/99 2.50 6.00
38 Amar'e Stoudemire/49
39 Jameer Nelson/49 2.50 6.00
40 Joe Johnson/199 3.00 8.00
41 Andre Miller/49
42 Jared Sullinger/49 2.50 6.00
43 Austin Rivers/49 3.00 8.00
44 Channing Frye/49
45 Reggie Jackson/99 3.00 8.00
46 Kevin Love/199 4.00 10.00
47 John Wall/99 5.00 12.00
48 Bismack Biyombo/49 2.50 6.00
49 O.J. Mayo/49 2.50 6.00
50 Andrew Bynum/199 2.50 6.00
51 Chris Paul/99 5.00 12.00
52 Mike Miller/99 3.00 8.00
53 Michael Beasley/49
54 Carmelo Anthony/99 5.00 12.00
55 Glen Davis/49 2.50 6.00
56 Deron Williams/49 3.00 8.00
57 Kenneth Faried/49 3.00 8.00
58 Rodney Stuckey/49 3.00 8.00
59 Kawhi Leonard/49 6.00 15.00
60 Kevin Durant/99 8.00 20.00
61 Draymond Green/49 5.00 12.00
62 Eric Gordon/49 3.00 8.00
63 Luol Deng/49 3.00 8.00
64 Gerald Wallace/99 3.00 8.00
65 J.J. Redick/49 4.00 10.00
66 Dwyane Wade/199 5.00 12.00
67 Raymond Felton/49 3.00 8.00
68 Shane Battier/99 3.00 8.00
69 DeJuan Blair/49 2.50 6.00
70 Paul Pierce/49
71 Alec Burks/49 2.50 6.00
72 Jason Richardson/49 4.00 10.00
73 Tim Duncan/49 6.00 15.00
74 Thabo Sefolosha/99 2.50 6.00
75 Klay Thompson/49 5.00 12.00

2013-14 Panini Intrigue Winning Ink

PRINT RUNS B/WN 15-49 COPIES PER
NO PRICING ON QTY 15 OR LESS
EXCHANGE DEADLINE 10/23/2015
1 Scottie Pippen/20 200.00 300.00
2 Udonis Haslem/49 12.00 30.00
3 Rick Fox/20 40.00 80.00
5 James Jones/49 EXCH 6.00 15.00
6 Joe Dumars/20 30.00 60.00
7 Willis Reed/20 40.00 100.00
8 Robert Parish/20 30.00 60.00
9 Horace Grant/25 40.00 80.00
10 Jerry Lucas/20 30.00 60.00
11 Michael Cooper/49 12.00 30.00
12 George McGinnis/25 20.00 50.00
13 Sean Elliott/49 6.00 15.00
14 Robert Horry/25 EXCH 30.00 60.00
15 Kobe Bryant/20 150.00 250.00
17 Luc Longley/49 15.00 40.00
18 Bill Walton/20 20.00 50.00
19 Kendrick Perkins/25 10.00 25.00
21 Kareem Abdul-Jabbar/20 150.00 250.00
22 Vernon Maxwell/49 10.00 25.00
23 David Robinson/20 25.00 60.00
24 Peja Stojakovic/20 50.00 100.00
25 Glen Rice/25 50.00 100.00
26 Bailey Howell/25 20.00 50.00
27 Jon McGlocklin/49 8.00 20.00
28 Byron Scott/20 40.00 80.00
29 Mark Aguirre/49 15.00 40.00
30 Avery Johnson/20
31 Bobby Jones/49 12.00 30.00
33 Magic Johnson/20 150.00 250.00
34 Bruce Bowen/49 15.00 40.00
35 Toni Kukoc/25 60.00 150.00
36 Nazr Mohammed/49 EXCH 10.00 25.00
37 Sam Cassell/25 EXCH 15.00 40.00
38 Isiah Thomas/20 20.00 50.00
39 Jason Terry/20 20.00 50.00
40 Gail Goodrich/20 20.00 50.00
41 Walt Frazier/20 30.00 60.00
42 Dan Issel/49 10.00 25.00
44 Steve Kerr/20 30.00 60.00
46 Tayshaun Prince/20
47 Spencer Haywood/49 30.00 60.00
48 Nate Archibald/20 15.00 40.00
49 Kevin Willis/25
50 Larry Bird/20 EXCH 40.00 100.00

2012-13 Panini Kobe Anthology

COMMON CARD (1-201) 1.50 4.00
RANDOM INSERTS IN 12-13 PANINI PRODUCTS

2012-13 Panini Kobe Anthology Gold

COMMON CARD (1-200) 10.00 25.00
STATED PRINT RUN 24 SER.#'d SETS

2012-13 Panini Kobe Anthology Platinum

COMMON CARD (1-200) 12.00 30.00
STATED PRINT RUN 8 SER.#'d SETS

2012-13 Panini Kobe Anthology Autographs

COMMON CARD (1-25) 100.00 200.00
STATED PRINT RUN 24 SER.#'d SETS
UNPRICED GOLD PRINT RUN 8 SETS

2012-13 Panini Kobe Anthology Memorabilia

COMMON CARD (1-50) 15.00 40.00
STATED PRINT RUN 24 SER.#'d SETS
*PRIME: .6X TO 1.5X BASIC
PRIME PRINT RUN 8 SETS

2012-13 Panini Kobe Anthology Memorabilia Autographs

COMMON CARD (1-25) 150.00 300.00
STATED PRINT RUN 24 SER.#'d SETS
UNPRICED PRIME PRINT RUN 8 SETS

2014-15 Panini Luxe Autographs

OVERALL THREE AUTOS PER BOX
PRINT RUNS B/WN 40-65 COPIES PER
EXCHANGE DEADLINE 3/2/2017
1 Aaron Gordon/40 10.00 25.00
2 Andrew Wiggins/40 60.00 150.00
3 Elfrid Payton/40 5.00 12.00
4 James Ennis/60 3.00 8.00
5 Bojan Bogdanovic/60 4.00 10.00
6 Damjan Rudez/60 3.00 8.00
8 Zoran Dragic/60 4.00 10.00
9 Jordan Clarkson/60 8.00 20.00
10 T.J. Warren/40 6.00 15.00
11 Kyle Anderson/60 5.00 12.00
12 Nikola Mirotic/40 6.00 15.00
13 Doug McDermott/49 12.00 30.00
14 Spencer Dinwiddie/60 4.00 10.00
15 Joel Embiid/40 40.00 100.00
16 K.J. McDaniels/49 4.00 10.00
17 Jerami Grant/60 3.00 8.00
18 Langston Galloway/60 5.00 12.00
19 Shabazz Napier/60 4.00 10.00
20 Jabari Parker/40 20.00 50.00
21 Johnny O'Bryant/60 3.00 8.00
22 Cory Jefferson/60 3.00 8.00
23 Devyn Marble/60 3.00 8.00
24 Russ Smith/65 3.00 8.00
25 Jarnell Stokes/60 3.00 8.00
26 Lucas Nogueira/60 3.00 8.00
27 Gary Harris/49 5.00 12.00
28 Jusuf Nurkic/49 12.00 30.00
29 Erick Green/60 3.00 8.00
30 Zach LaVine/49 25.00 60.00
31 Rodney Hood/60 8.00 20.00
32 Bruno Caboclo/60 4.00 10.00
33 Marcus Smart/40 10.00 25.00
34 James Young/49 3.00 8.00
35 Dante Exum/40 12.00 30.00
36 Cleanthony Early/40 3.00 8.00
37 Kobe Bryant/40 100.00 200.00
38 Kyrie Irving/40 30.00 80.00
39 Carmelo Anthony/40 25.00 60.00
40 Michael Carter-Williams/40 6.00 15.00
41 Julius Randle/40 15.00 40.00
42 Trey Burke/40 3.00 8.00
43 Michael Kidd-Gilchrist/40 4.00 10.00
44 Tyson Chandler/40 4.00 10.00
46 John Wall/40 12.00 30.00
47 Kelly Olynyk/60 3.00 8.00
48 Tyler Zeller/40 4.00 10.00
49 Kyle Korver/49 6.00 15.00
50 Stephen Curry/40 75.00 200.00
51 Carl Landry/40 3.00 8.00
52 Ben McLemore/40 3.00 8.00
53 Blake Griffin/40 25.00 60.00
54 Goran Dragic/40 4.00 10.00
55 Ty Lawson/40 3.00 8.00
56 LaMarcus Aldridge/40 6.00 15.00
58 Latrell Sprewell/40 15.00 40.00
61 Steven Adams/40 6.00 15.00
62 Giannis Antetokounmpo/49 15.00 40.00
63 Tim Hardaway Jr./49 3.00 8.00
64 Shabazz Muhammad/40 4.00 10.00
65 Tracy McGrady/40 25.00 60.00
66 Mason Plumlee/60 4.00 10.00
67 Rudy Gobert/60 10.00 25.00
68 Brook Lopez/40 4.00 10.00
69 Kevin Durant/40 60.00 150.00
70 Kareem Abdul-Jabbar/40 25.00 60.00
71 Tom Van Arsdale/49 4.00 10.00
72 Rudy Tomjanovich/49 6.00 15.00
73 Scott Brooks/40 3.00 8.00
74 Mark Price/49 10.00 25.00
75 Zydrunas Ilgauskas/49 5.00 12.00
76 Clifford Robinson/49 6.00 15.00
77 Steve Smith/49 4.00 10.00
78 Dikembe Mutombo/40 10.00 25.00
79 Rod Strickland/49 3.00 8.00
80 Cedric Maxwell/49 3.00 8.00
81 Mark Aguirre/40 4.00 10.00
82 Adrian Dantley/40 4.00 10.00
83 Alex English/40 4.00 10.00
84 Horace Grant/40 10.00 25.00
85 Dan Issel/49 4.00 10.00
86 Mychal Thompson/49 3.00 8.00
87 Ron Harper/49 6.00 15.00
88 Michael Finley/40 8.00 20.00
89 Mahmoud Abdul-Rauf/49 10.00 25.00
90 Larry Bird/40 40.00 100.00
91 Hakeem Olajuwon/40 15.00 40.00
92 Magic Johnson/40 30.00 80.00
93 Kevin Love/40 12.00 30.00
94 Steve Nash/40 20.00 50.00
95 George Gervin/40 8.00 20.00
96 Bill Walton/40 5.00 12.00
97 Gary Payton/40 8.00 20.00
98 Clyde Drexler/40 8.00 20.00
99 Bernard King/40 4.00 10.00
100 Scott Skiles/49 4.00 10.00

2014-15 Panini Luxe Autographs Silver

*SILVER: .6X TO 1.5X BASIC
OVERALL THREE AUTOS PER BOX
STATED PRINT RUN 25 SER.#'d SETS
EXCHANGE DEADLINE 3/2/2017

2014-15 Panini Luxe Die Cut Autographs

OVERALL THREE AUTOS PER BOX
PRINT RUNS B/WN 25-60 COPIES PER
EXCHANGE DEADLINE 3/2/2017
1 Kyrie Irving/40 30.00 80.00
2 Kobe Bryant/25 125.00 250.00
3 Kevin Durant/35 60.00 150.00
4 Kevin Love/40 12.00 30.00
5 Carmelo Anthony/35 12.00 50.00
7 Anthony Davis/25 50.00 120.00
8 Trey Burke/40 3.00 8.00
9 Ty Lawson/50 3.00 8.00
11 Andre Drummond/40 6.00 15.00
12 Gordon Hayward/60 6.00 15.00
13 Derrick Favors/40 4.00 10.00
15 Tony Parker/40 20.00 50.00
16 DeMarre Carroll/60 3.00 8.00
18 Isaiah Thomas/60 8.00 20.00
19 Gary Harris/60 5.00 12.00
20 Chris Bosh/40 5.00 12.00
21 Reggie Jackson/60 3.00 8.00
22 Blake Griffin/35 25.00 60.00
23 John Wall/40 15.00 40.00
24 Gary Payton/40 10.00 25.00
25 Clyde Drexler/40 15.00 40.00
26 Jason Kidd/40 15.00 40.00
27 Grant Hill/40 15.00 40.00
28 Jonas Valanciunas/60 4.00 10.00
30 Kenneth Faried/50 4.00 10.00
31 Josh Smith/40 4.00 10.00
35 Mason Plumlee/60 4.00 10.00
36 Enes Kanter/60 3.00 8.00
37 Taj Gibson/60 4.00 10.00
39 Jeff Green/50 4.00 10.00
40 Alec Burks/60 3.00 8.00
41 Erick Green/60 3.00 8.00
42 Zoran Dragic/60 4.00 10.00
43 Jusuf Nurkic/60 5.00 12.00
44 Cory Jefferson/60 3.00 8.00
46 Jarnell Stokes/60 3.00 8.00
47 Bruno Caboclo/60 4.00 10.00
48 Andrew Wiggins/40 125.00 300.00
49 Jabari Parker/40 30.00 80.00
50 Julius Randle/40 20.00 50.00
51 Joel Embiid/40 40.00 100.00
52 Marcus Smart/40 12.00 30.00
53 Zach LaVine/60 30.00 80.00
54 Elfrid Payton/60 5.00 12.00
55 Aaron Gordon/40 15.00 40.00
58 Glenn Robinson III/60 3.00 8.00
59 Jordan Clarkson/60 6.00 15.00
61 James Ennis/60 3.00 8.00
62 Shabazz Napier/60 4.00 10.00
63 Tyler Ennis/40 3.00 8.00
64 T.J. Warren/60 6.00 15.00
65 James Young/60 3.00 8.00
66 Devyn Marble/60 3.00 8.00
68 Dante Exum/40 12.00 30.00
70 P.J. Hairston/60 3.00 8.00
71 Lucas Nogueira/60 3.00 8.00
72 Adreian Payne/60 4.00 10.00
73 Johnny O'Bryant/60 3.00 8.00
74 Nikola Mirotic/50 6.00 15.00
75 Bojan Bogdanovic/60 4.00 10.00
76 World B. Free/50 4.00 10.00
77 Terry Porter/50 3.00 8.00
78 Wayne Embry/60 3.00 8.00
79 Charles Oakley/60 4.00 10.00
80 Horace Grant/50 6.00 15.00
81 Dikembe Mutombo/50 10.00 25.00
82 Bernard King/40 4.00 10.00
83 Julius Erving/35 30.00 80.00
84 Dolph Schayes/50 5.00 12.00
85 Adrian Dantley/60 4.00 10.00
86 Walt Frazier/40 10.00 25.00
87 Dave Cowens/50 6.00 15.00
88 Hal Greer/50 6.00 15.00
89 Mark Aguirre/60 4.00 10.00
90 Latrell Sprewell/50 12.00 30.00
91 Tim Hardaway/60 5.00 12.00
92 Rick Fox/50 4.00 10.00
93 George Karl/50 5.00 12.00
94 Bob Dandridge/60 3.00 8.00
95 Jo Jo White/60 4.00 10.00
96 Tracy McGrady/40 25.00 60.00
97 Shaquille O'Neal/25 50.00 120.00
98 Larry Bird/35 40.00 100.00
99 Keith Van Horn/60 4.00 10.00
100 Eddie Jones/60 4.00 10.00

2014-15 Panini Luxe Memorabilia Autographs

OVERALL THREE AUTOS PER BOX
PRINT RUNS B/WN 30-60 COPIES PER
EXCHANGE DEADLINE 3/2/2017
1 Jabari Parker/49 20.00 50.00
2 Jarnell Stokes/60 5.00 12.00
3 Julius Randle/49 15.00 40.00
4 Andrew Wiggins/49 100.00 250.00
5 Aaron Gordon/49 15.00 40.00
6 Marcus Smart/49 12.00 30.00
7 James Young/60 5.00 12.00
8 Elfrid Payton/49 8.00 20.00
9 Cleanthony Early/60 5.00 12.00
10 Bruno Caboclo/60 6.00 15.00
11 Jordan Adams/60 5.00 12.00

12 James Ennis/60 5.00 12.00
13 Adreian Payne/60
14 Gary Harris/60 8.00 20.00
16 Noah Vonleh/49 8.00 20.00
17 Spencer Dinwiddie/60 6.00 15.00
18 Doug McDermott/60 8.00 20.00
19 Cory Jefferson/60 5.00 12.00
20 Zach LaVine/60 30.00 80.00
22 Johnny O'Bryant/60 5.00 12.00
23 Jerami Grant/60 5.00 12.00
24 Dante Exum/49 8.00 20.00
25 Joel Embiid/49 75.00 200.00
26 Joe Harris/60 5.00 12.00
28 P.J. Hairston/60 5.00 12.00
30 Tyler Ennis/49 5.00 12.00
32 Glenn Robinson III/60 5.00 12.00
33 Russ Smith/60 5.00 12.00
34 T.J. Warren/49 10.00 25.00
35 Shabazz Napier/60 10.00 25.00
36 Larry Bird/35 40.00 100.00
37 Kevin McHale/35 12.00 30.00
38 Clyde Drexler/35 15.00 40.00
39 Alonzo Mourning/35 20.00 50.00
40 Jeff Green/49 6.00 15.00
42 Tim Hardaway Jr./60 5.00 12.00
43 Kyle Korver/35 6.00 15.00
44 Gordon Hayward/49 8.00 20.00
45 Kevin Martin/35 6.00 15.00
46 Andre Drummond/35 8.00 20.00
49 Danilo Gallinari/35 5.00 12.00
50 Charles Oakley/60 6.00 15.00
51 Michael Kidd-Gilchrist/35 6.00 15.00
52 Hakeem Olajuwon/35 15.00 40.00
53 Kevin Love/35 20.00 50.00
54 Clifford Robinson/49 5.00 12.00
55 Michael Finley/35 8.00 20.00
56 Thaddeus Young/60 5.00 12.00
57 Tyson Chandler/35 6.00 15.00
59 Kyrie Irving/35 40.00 100.00
60 Carmelo Anthony/35 20.00 50.00
61 Blake Griffin/35 25.00 60.00
62 Kevin Durant/35 50.00 120.00
63 Kobe Bryant/35 125.00 250.00
64 Karl Malone/35 25.00 60.00
65 John Stockton/35 25.00 60.00
66 James Worthy/35 15.00 40.00
67 Adrian Dantley/49 6.00 15.00
68 Bernard King/35 6.00 15.00
69 Gerald Henderson/49 5.00 12.00
71 Marcin Gortat/49 12.00 30.00
72 John Wall/35 20.00 50.00
74 Ben McLemore/35 5.00 12.00
75 Chris Andersen/35 6.00 15.00
76 Stephen Curry/49 150.00 300.00
78 Reggie Jackson/49 5.00 12.00
79 Spencer Hawes/60 5.00 12.00
80 Mike Conley/35 6.00 15.00
81 Ryan Anderson/49 5.00 12.00
82 Tony Parker/35 20.00 50.00
83 Thabo Sefolosha/30 5.00 12.00
84 Alec Burks/60 5.00 12.00
85 Tiago Splitter/49 6.00 15.00
86 Steve Nash/35 15.00 40.00
87 Harrison Barnes/35 6.00 15.00
89 Andrew Nicholson/60 5.00 12.00
90 Jonas Valanciunas/49 6.00 15.00
91 Joe Dumars/35 8.00 20.00
92 Magic Johnson/35 30.00 80.00
93 Alex English/49 6.00 15.00
94 Brad Daugherty/60 6.00 15.00
95 Tom Chambers/49 6.00 15.00
96 Dan Majerle/49 6.00 15.00
97 Jason Kidd/35 15.00 40.00
98 Xavier McDaniel/60 5.00 12.00
99 Robert Horry/49 6.00 15.00
100 Shaquille O'Neal/35 75.00 150.00

2014-15 Panini Luxe Memorabilia Prime

OVERALL ONE MEM PER BOX
PRINT RUNS B/WN 10-25 COPIES PER
NO PRICING ON QTY 10
EXCHANGE DEADLINE 3/2/2017
1 Manu Ginobili/25 12.00 30.00
2 Jarnell Stokes/25 4.00 10.00
3 Rajon Rondo/25 6.00 15.00
4 Mitch McGary/25 4.00 10.00
5 Detlef Schrempf/25 20.00 50.00
6 Tiago Splitter/25 5.00 12.00
7 Danny Manning/20 5.00 12.00
8 Mario Chalmers/25
9 Joe Johnson/25 5.00 12.00
10 Cory Jefferson/25 4.00 10.00
11 Manute Bol/25 20.00 50.00
12 Jerami Grant/25 4.00 10.00
13 Rick Mahorn/25 4.00 10.00
14 Nik Stauskas/25 5.00 12.00
15 Dikembe Mutombo/25 10.00 25.00
16 Tom Chambers/25 5.00 12.00
17 Derrick Rose/25 8.00 20.00
18 Chris Andersen/25 5.00 12.00
19 Kareem Abdul-Jabbar/25 10.00 25.00
20 Damien Inglis/25 10.00 25.00
21 Markieff Morris/25 4.00 10.00
22 Joe Harris/25 4.00 10.00
23 Robert Horry/25 5.00 12.00
24 Noah Vonleh/25 10.00 25.00
25 Allen Iverson/25 20.00 50.00
27 Earl Monroe/25 6.00 15.00
28 Jeff Teague/25 5.00 12.00
29 Kevin Duckworth/25 4.00 10.00
30 Dante Exum/25 8.00 20.00
31 Matt Barnes/25 4.00 10.00
32 Joel Embiid/25 20.00 50.00
34 P.J. Hairston/25 4.00 10.00
35 Andre Iguodala/25 5.00 12.00
36 Tristan Thompson/25 5.00 12.00
37 Eric Bledsoe/25 5.00 12.00
38 Paul Millsap/25 6.00 15.00
40 Doug McDermott/25 6.00 15.00
41 Monta Ellis/25 5.00 12.00
42 Johnny O'Bryant/25 4.00 10.00
43 Roy Hibbert/25 5.00 12.00
44 Rodney Hood/25 6.00 15.00
45 Anthony Davis/25 12.00 30.00
46 Tyreke Evans/25 4.00 10.00
47 Fat Lever/25 5.00 12.00
48 Kenneth Faried/25 5.00 12.00
49 Kiki Vandeweghe/25 5.00 12.00
50 Elfrid Payton/25 6.00 15.00
51 Moses Malone/25 6.00 15.00
52 Jordan Adams/25 4.00 10.00
53 Russell Westbrook/25 15.00 40.00
54 Shabazz Napier/25 5.00 12.00
55 Bernard King/25 5.00 12.00
56 Vinnie Johnson/25
57 Grant Hill/25 10.00 25.00
58 Aaron Gordon/25 10.00 25.00
59 Kevin Durant/25 25.00 60.00
60 Gary Harris/25 6.00 15.00
61 Nick Young/25 5.00 12.00
62 Julius Randle/25 10.00 25.00
64 Spencer Dinwiddie/25 5.00 12.00
65 Bradley Beal/25 6.00 15.00
66 Walter Davis/25 8.00 20.00
68 Andrew Wiggins/25 20.00 50.00
70 Glenn Robinson III/25 4.00 10.00
71 Nicolas Batum/25 8.00 20.00
72 K.J. McDaniels/25 5.00 12.00
73 Steve Nash/25 10.00 25.00
74 T.J. Warren/25 6.00 15.00
75 Chandler Parsons/25 6.00 15.00
76 Jimmy Butler/25 8.00 20.00
77 Hakeem Olajuwon/25 8.00 20.00
78 Bruno Caboclo/25 5.00 12.00
79 Larry Johnson/25 12.00 30.00
80 Jabari Parker/25 10.00 25.00
81 Norm Nixon/25 4.00 10.00
82 Kyle Anderson/25
83 Terry Cummings/25 5.00 12.00
84 Tyler Ennis/25 4.00 10.00
85 Damian Lillard/25 12.00 30.00
86 Xavier McDaniel/25 6.00 15.00
87 Jeff Hornacek/25 5.00 12.00
88 C.J. Wilcox/25 4.00 10.00
89 LeBron James/25 50.00 120.00
90 James Ennis/25 4.00 10.00
91 Patrick Ewing/25 15.00 40.00
92 Marcus Smart/25 6.00 15.00
93 Thaddeus Young/25 4.00 10.00
94 Zach LaVine/25 10.00 25.00
95 Danny Ainge/25 6.00 15.00
96 Kirk Hinrich/25 5.00 12.00
97 Joakim Noah/25 5.00 12.00
98 Cleanthony Early/25 4.00 10.00
99 Anderson Varejao/25 4.00 10.00
100 James Young/25 4.00 10.00

2015-16 Panini Luxe Autographs

RANDOM INSERTS IN PACKS
PRINT RUNS B/WN 34-75 COPIES PER
EXCHANGE DEADLINE 10/20/2017
1 Karl-Anthony Towns/75 100.00 250.00
2 D'Angelo Russell/75 30.00 80.00
3 Jahlil Okafor/75 15.00 40.00
4 Emmanuel Mudiay/49 15.00 40.00
5 Kristaps Porzingis/49 100.00 250.00
6 Mario Hezonja/49 10.00 25.00
7 Justise Winslow/49 8.00 20.00
8 Willie Cauley-Stein/49 12.00 30.00
9 Stanley Johnson/49 6.00 15.00
10 Frank Kaminsky/49 8.00 20.00
11 Devin Booker/49 60.00 150.00
12 Myles Turner/49 30.00 80.00
13 Jerian Grant/49 5.00 12.00
14 Trey Lyles/49 12.00 30.00
15 Nemanja Bjelica/49 6.00 15.00
16 Cameron Payne/75 5.00 12.00
17 Delon Wright/75
18 Rashad Vaughn/75 4.00 10.00
19 Sam Dekker/75 5.00 12.00
20 Kelly Oubre Jr./75 5.00 12.00
21 Terry Rozier/75 10.00 25.00
22 Rondae Hollis-Jefferson/75 5.00 12.00
23 Nikola Jokic/75 30.00 80.00
24 Bobby Portis/75 6.00 15.00
25 Kevon Looney/75 5.00 12.00
26 Justin Anderson/75 8.00 20.00
27 Jarell Martin/75 5.00 12.00
28 R.J. Hunter/75 4.00 10.00
29 Anthony Brown/75 4.00 10.00
30 Raul Neto/75 6.00 15.00
31 Jordan Mickey/75 10.00 25.00
32 Montrezl Harrell/75 5.00 12.00
33 Larry Nance Jr./75 10.00 25.00
34 Walter Tavares/75 4.00 10.00
35 Josh Richardson/75 6.00 15.00
36 Norman Powell/75 5.00 12.00
37 Jonathon Simmons/75 12.00 30.00
38 Joe Young/75 5.00 12.00
39 Duje Dukan/75 4.00 10.00
41 Kobe Bryant/35 150.00 300.00
42 Chris Paul/35 20.00 50.00
43 Carmelo Anthony/35 40.00 100.00
44 Larry Bird/35 60.00 150.00
45 Julius Erving/35 30.00 80.00
46 Anthony Davis/35 50.00 120.00
47 Kyrie Irving/35 30.00 80.00
48 Alonzo Mourning/35 15.00 40.00
49 John Wall/35 15.00 40.00
50 Jabari Parker/35 15.00 40.00
51 Clyde Drexler/34 10.00 25.00
52 Chris Bosh/49 12.00 30.00
53 Tony Parker/49 10.00 25.00
54 Tracy McGrady/49 30.00 80.00
55 Dominique Wilkins/49 20.00 50.00
56 Victor Oladipo/49 6.00 15.00
57 Anfernee Hardaway/49 30.00 80.00
58 Harrison Barnes/49 8.00 20.00
59 Larry Brown/49 10.00 25.00
60 Andre Drummond/49 8.00 20.00
61 Steve Kerr/49 8.00 20.00
62 Walt Frazier/49 15.00 40.00
63 Byron Scott/49 10.00 25.00
64 Jared Sullinger/49
65 Gail Goodrich/49 6.00 15.00
66 Dave Cowens/49 5.00 12.00
67 Robert Parish/49 8.00 20.00
68 Frank Ramsey/49 10.00 25.00
69 Calvin Murphy/49 6.00 15.00
70 Joe Dumars/49 8.00 20.00
71 Bill Walton/49 8.00 20.00
72 Mark Jackson/49 10.00 25.00
73 Mike Conley/49 8.00 20.00
74 Gordon Hayward/49 8.00 20.00
75 Nikola Mirotic/49 6.00 15.00
76 Danny Green/49 15.00 40.00
77 Chuck Person/49 6.00 15.00
78 Michael Cooper/49 6.00 15.00
79 Wesley Matthews/49
80 Al-Farouq Aminu/49 6.00 15.00
81 Zach LaVine/49 15.00 40.00
82 Bob McAdoo/45 5.00 12.00
83 Kenny Walker/49 5.00 12.00
84 George McGinnis/49 5.00 12.00
85 Marques Johnson/49 6.00 15.00
86 A.C. Green/49 8.00 20.00
87 Mitch Richmond/49 8.00 20.00
88 Doug McDermott/49 6.00 15.00
89 Gary Harris/49 6.00 15.00
90 Giannis Antetokounmpo/49 75.00 200.00
91 DeMarre Carroll/75 4.00 10.00
92 Sonny Weems/75
93 Dennis Schroder/75 8.00 20.00
94 Rony Seikaly/75 4.00 10.00
95 Antonio McDyess/75 5.00 12.00
96 Bobby Jones/75 5.00 12.00
97 Ron Harper/75 6.00 15.00
98 Raef LaFrentz/75 4.00 10.00
99 Tony Delk/75 4.00 10.00
100 Paul Westphal/75 6.00 15.00

2015-16 Panini Luxe Autographs Ruby

*RUBY: .5X TO 1.2X BASIC p/r 75
*RUBY: .4X TO 1X BASIC p/r 34-49
RANDOM INSERTS IN PACKS
PRINT RUNS B/WN 25-49 COPIES PER
EXCHANGE DEADLINE 10/20/2017

2015-16 Panini Luxe Autographs Sapphire

*SAPPHIRE: .5X TO 1.2X BASIC p/r 75
*SAPPHIRE: .4X TO 1X BASIC p/r 34-49
RANDOM INSERTS IN PACKS
PRINT RUNS B/WN 15-25 COPIES PER
NO PRICING ON QTY 15
EXCHANGE DEADLINE 10/20/2017

2015-16 Panini Luxe Crown Jewels Autographs

RANDOM INSERTS IN PACKS
PRINT RUNS B/WN 35-49 COPIES PER
EXCHANGE DEADLINE 10/20/2017
1 Dwyane Wade/35
2 Magic Johnson/35 30.00 80.00
3 Blake Griffin/35 20.00 50.00
4 Steve Nash/35
5 Andrew Wiggins/35 40.00 100.00
6 Jason Kidd/49
7 Klay Thompson/49
8 Gary Payton/49 25.00 60.00
9 Bradley Beal/49
10 Wes Unseld/49
11 Nick Van Exel/49
12 Kenneth Faried/49 12.00 30.00
13 Ralph Sampson/49
14 Elfrid Payton/49 6.00 15.00
15 Nate Archibald/49
16 J.R. Smith/49
17 Dikembe Mutombo/49 8.00 20.00
18 Nene/49
19 Allan Houston/49 6.00 15.00
20 Wilson Chandler/49 12.00 30.00
21 Satch Sanders/49 8.00 20.00
22 Jerry Stackhouse/49
23 John Lucas/49
24 James Young/49
25 Tony Allen/49
26 Thaddeus Young/49
27 Dino Radja/49
28 Scott Wedman/49 6.00 15.00
29 Brad Daugherty/49
30 Rod Strickland/49
31 Norm Nixon/49 5.00 12.00
32 Michael Cage/49
33 Mason Plumlee/49
34 Joe Harris/49
35 Kenny Anderson/49 6.00 15.00
36 Rudy Gay/49
37 Cuttino Mobley/49 5.00 12.00
38 Bojan Bogdanovic/49 5.00 12.00
39 Hersey Hawkins/49 5.00 12.00
40 Joe Ingles/49
41 Shabazz Napier/49
42 Tarik Black/49 5.00 12.00
43 James Ennis/49 5.00 12.00
44 Oscar Robertson/35 30.00 80.00
45 Jeff Green/49
46 Zach Randolph/49
47 Nick Young/49 6.00 15.00
48 Jordan Clarkson/49
49 Taj Gibson/49
50 Enes Kanter/49 5.00 12.00

2015-16 Panini Luxe DeLuxe Autographs

RANDOM INSERTS IN PACKS
STATED PRINT RUN 25 SER.#'d SETS
EXCHANGE DEADLINE 10/20/2017
1 Karl-Anthony Towns 175.00 350.00
2 D'Angelo Russell 60.00 150.00
3 Jahlil Okafor 60.00 150.00
4 Emmanuel Mudiay 8.00 20.00
5 Kristaps Porzingis 20.00 50.00
6 Mario Hezonja 6.00 15.00
7 Justise Winslow 8.00 20.00
8 Willie Cauley-Stein
9 Stanley Johnson 30.00 80.00
10 Frank Kaminsky
11 Devin Booker
12 Myles Turner 60.00 150.00
13 Jerian Grant 5.00 12.00
14 Trey Lyles 8.00 20.00
15 Nemanja Bjelica 10.00 25.00
16 Cameron Payne 20.00 50.00
17 Delon Wright
18 Rashad Vaughn
19 Sam Dekker 6.00 15.00
20 Kelly Oubre Jr.
21 Terry Rozier
22 Rondae Hollis-Jefferson
23 Nikola Jokic
24 Bobby Portis 15.00 40.00
25 Kevon Looney 6.00 15.00
26 Justin Anderson 20.00 50.00
27 Jarell Martin 6.00 15.00
28 R.J. Hunter
29 Anthony Brown
30 Raul Neto
31 Jordan Mickey
32 Montrezl Harrell
33 Larry Nance Jr. 15.00 40.00
34 Walter Tavares
35 Josh Richardson 8.00 20.00
36 Norman Powell
37 Jonathon Simmons
38 Joe Young 12.00 30.00
39 Duje Dukan
41 Kobe Bryant 300.00 500.00
42 Chris Paul 40.00 100.00
43 Carmelo Anthony 40.00 100.00
44 Larry Bird
45 Julius Erving
46 Anthony Davis
47 Kyrie Irving
48 Alonzo Mourning 40.00 100.00
49 John Wall 30.00 80.00
50 Jabari Parker
51 Clyde Drexler 15.00 40.00
52 Chris Bosh
53 Tony Parker
54 Tracy McGrady
55 Dominique Wilkins EXCH 15.00 40.00
56 Victor Oladipo 6.00 15.00
57 Anfernee Hardaway
58 Harrison Barnes
59 Larry Brown 15.00 40.00
60 Andre Drummond
61 Steve Kerr 20.00 50.00
62 Walt Frazier
63 Byron Scott 6.00 15.00
64 Jared Sullinger 12.00 30.00
65 Gail Goodrich 15.00 40.00
66 Dave Cowens
67 Robert Parish
68 Frank Ramsey 20.00 50.00
69 Calvin Murphy
70 Joe Dumars 8.00 20.00
71 Bill Walton
72 Mark Jackson
73 Mike Conley
74 Gordon Hayward 10.00 25.00
75 Nikola Mirotic 10.00 25.00
76 Danny Green 20.00 50.00
77 Chuck Person
78 Michael Cooper
79 Wesley Matthews
80 Al-Farouq Aminu
81 Zach LaVine
82 Bob McAdoo 20.00 50.00
83 Kenny Walker
84 George McGinnis 5.00 12.00
85 Marques Johnson 6.00 15.00
86 A.C. Green
87 Mitch Richmond
88 Doug McDermott 6.00 15.00
89 Gary Harris 6.00 15.00
90 Giannis Antetokounmpo
91 DeMarre Carroll
92 Sonny Weems
93 Dennis Schroder 20.00 50.00
94 Rony Seikaly 5.00 12.00
95 Antonio McDyess
96 Bobby Jones 6.00 15.00
97 Ron Harper
98 Raef LaFrentz 5.00 12.00
99 Tony Delk
100 Paul Westphal

2015-16 Panini Luxe Die Cut Autographs

RANDOM INSERTS IN PACKS
PRINT RUNS B/WN 35-49 COPIES PER
EXCHANGE DEADLINE 10/20/2017
1 Marcus Smart/49
2 Julius Randle/49 15.00 40.00
3 Michael Finley/49 20.00 50.00
4 Michael Carter-Williams/49
5 Cliff Hagan/49 6.00 15.00
7 Lenny Wilkens/49 8.00 20.00
8 Rick Fox/49
9 Antoine Carr/49 5.00 12.00
10 Bojan Bogdanovic/49 5.00 12.00
11 Hersey Hawkins/49 5.00 12.00
12 Joe Ingles/49 5.00 12.00
13 James Ennis/49 5.00 12.00
14 Gerald Henderson/49 5.00 12.00
15 Aaron Gordon/49 12.00 30.00
16 Dennis Rodman/49 15.00 40.00
17 Maurice Harkless/49
19 Shaquille O'Neal/35 30.00 80.00
20 Kevin Durant/35 50.00 120.00
21 Karl Malone/35 20.00 50.00
22 Jerry West/35 30.00 80.00
23 Hakeem Olajuwon/35 15.00 40.00
24 Kevin McHale/49
25 Kevin Love/49 8.00 20.00
26 Grant Hill/49
27 Terry Cummings/49 6.00 15.00
28 Keith Van Horn/49
29 Langston Galloway/49
30 Gary Neal/49
31 Kenny Anderson/49 6.00 15.00
32 Cuttino Mobley/49 5.00 12.00
33 Shabazz Napier/49
34 Tarik Black/49 5.00 12.00
35 Oscar Robertson/35 30.00 80.00
36 Isaiah Thomas/49
37 Marcin Gortat/49
38 Nik Stauskas/49 5.00 12.00
39 Scott Brooks/49 5.00 12.00
40 T.J. Warren/49
41 Norris Cole/49 5.00 12.00
42 Wayne Embry/49 5.00 12.00
43 Bill Cartwright/49
44 Dan Majerle/49 6.00 15.00
45 Timofey Mozgov/49 5.00 12.00
46 Tim Hardaway Jr./49
47 Cazzie Russell/49 6.00 15.00
48 Rafer Alston/49 5.00 12.00
49 Fred Brown/49
50 Will Perdue/49 5.00 12.00

2015-16 Panini Luxe Memorabilia

RANDOM INSERTS IN PACKS
STATED PRINT RUN 99 SER.#'d SETS
1 Zach LaVine/99 4.00 10.00
2 Ricky Rubio/99 4.00 10.00
3 Avery Bradley/99 3.00 8.00
4 Marcus Smart/99 3.00 8.00
5 Evan Turner/99 3.00 8.00
6 Dirk Nowitzki/99 5.00 12.00
7 Matthew Dellavedova/99 3.00 8.00
8 Iman Shumpert/99 2.50 6.00
9 Tristan Thompson/99 3.00 8.00
10 Tiago Splitter/99 3.00 8.00
11 Deron Williams/99 3.00 8.00
12 Andre Iguodala/99 3.00 8.00
13 Gary Neal/99 3.00 8.00
14 Andre Miller/99 3.00 8.00
15 Moses Malone/99 4.00 10.00
16 Kent Bazemore/99 3.00 8.00
17 Thaddeus Young/99 2.50 6.00
18 Nene/99 3.00 8.00
19 T.J. Warren/99 3.00 8.00
20 Lou Williams/99 3.00 8.00
21 Mirza Teletovic/99 2.50 6.00
22 Kevin Love/99 4.00 10.00
23 Luol Deng/99 3.00 8.00
24 Kelly Olynyk/99 2.50 6.00
25 DeMar DeRozan/99 4.00 10.00
26 Damian Lillard/99 6.00 15.00
27 Rajon Rondo/99 4.00 10.00
28 Tobias Harris/99 3.00 8.00
29 Mike Conley/99 4.00 10.00
30 Dwyane Wade/99 6.00 15.00
31 LeBron James/99 10.00 25.00
32 Gary Payton/99 4.00 10.00
33 Serge Ibaka/99 3.00 8.00
34 Andre Drummond/99 4.00 10.00
35 Tyson Chandler/99 3.00 8.00
36 Trey Burke/99 2.50 6.00
37 Dante Exum/99 3.00 8.00
38 Klay Thompson/99 5.00 12.00
39 Russell Westbrook/99 10.00 25.00
40 Dennis Rodman/99 5.00 12.00
41 Kevin Durant/99 6.00 15.00
42 Larry Bird/99 12.00 30.00
43 Mark Jackson/99 3.00 8.00
44 Dan Issel/99 3.00 8.00
45 Chris Andersen/99 3.00 8.00
46 Glenn Robinson/99 3.00 8.00
47 Adreian Payne/99 2.50 6.00
48 Alex Len/99 2.50 6.00
49 Allen Iverson/99 5.00 12.00
50 Jordan Clarkson/99 4.00 10.00
51 Magic Johnson/49 10.00 25.00
52 Alonzo Mourning/99 5.00 12.00
53 Glen Rice/99 3.00 8.00
54 Karl Malone/99 5.00 12.00
55 Shaquille O'Neal/99 5.00 12.00
56 Blake Griffin/99 4.00 10.00
57 John Wall/99 5.00 12.00
58 Kentavious Caldwell-Pope/99 3.00 8.00
59 Ty Lawson/99 2.50 6.00
60 Tony Allen/99 2.50 6.00

2015-16 Panini Luxe Memorabilia Die Cuts Red

RANDOM INSERTS IN PACKS
PRINT RUNS B/WN 85-99 COPIES PER
*BLUE/25: .75X TO 2X BASIC
1 Tim Duncan/99 6.00 15.00
2 Kevin Garnett/99 6.00 15.00
3 Jimmy Butler/99 4.00 10.00
4 Bojan Bogdanovic/99 2.50 6.00
5 Russell Westbrook/99 10.00 25.00
6 Khris Middleton/99 3.00 8.00
7 Kemba Walker/99 4.00 10.00
8 Enes Kanter/99 2.50 6.00
9 Kawhi Leonard/99 6.00 15.00
10 Thaddeus Young/99 2.50 6.00
11 Vince Carter/99 12.00 30.00
12 Festus Ezeli/99 2.50 6.00
13 Kobe Bryant/99 12.00 30.00
14 Harrison Barnes/99 3.00 8.00
15 Kyrie Irving/99 6.00 15.00
16 Joe Johnson/99 3.00 8.00
17 John Wall/99 5.00 12.00
18 Nicolas Batum/99 3.00 8.00
19 Michael Carter-Williams/99 2.50 6.00
20 Paul George/99 5.00 12.00
21 LeBron James/99 12.00 30.00
22 Shane Larkin/99 2.50 6.00
23 Zach Randolph/99 3.00 8.00
24 Andre Drummond/99 4.00 10.00
25 Iman Shumpert/99 2.50 6.00
26 Victor Oladipo/99 3.00 8.00
27 Derrick Favors/99 3.00 8.00
28 Serge Ibaka/99 3.00 8.00
29 Bradley Beal/99 4.00 10.00
30 Andrew Wiggins/99 6.00 15.00
31 Thomas Robinson/99 2.50 6.00
32 Timofey Mozgov/99 2.50 6.00
33 George Hill/99 3.00 8.00
34 Evan Fournier/99 3.00 8.00
35 Marcus Smart/99 3.00 8.00
36 Terrence Jones/99 3.00 8.00
37 Rudy Gay/99 4.00 10.00
38 Marc Gasol/99 4.00 10.00
39 Jordan Clarkson/99 4.00 10.00
40 DeMarcus Cousins/99 4.00 10.00
41 Paul Millsap/99 4.00 10.00
42 Boris Diaw/99 3.00 8.00
43 Damian Lillard/99 6.00 15.00
44 Markieff Morris/99 2.50 6.00
45 Kenneth Faried/99 3.00 8.00
46 Carmelo Anthony/99 5.00 12.00
47 Gordon Hayward/85 4.00 10.00
48 David Lee/99 2.50 6.00
49 Klay Thompson/99 5.00 12.00
50 Jose Calderon/99 2.50 6.00
51 Paul Pierce/99 4.00 10.00
52 Tony Parker/99 4.00 10.00
53 Reggie Jackson/99 3.00 8.00
54 Terrence Ross/99 3.00 8.00
55 Corey Brewer/99 2.50 6.00
56 Anthony Davis/99 6.00 15.00
57 Manu Ginobili/99 4.00 10.00
58 Draymond Green/99 5.00 12.00
59 James Harden/99 6.00 15.00
60 Shabazz Napier/99 2.50 6.00
61 C.J. McCollum/99 4.00 10.00
62 Chris Paul/99 5.00 12.00
63 Eric Gordon/99 3.00 8.00
64 Goran Dragic/99 3.00 8.00
65 Otto Porter/99 3.00 8.00
66 Dwight Howard/99 3.00 8.00
67 Stephen Curry/99 15.00 40.00
68 Greg Monroe/99 3.00 8.00
69 Chris Bosh/99 4.00 10.00
70 Gary Harris/99 3.00 8.00
71 Karl-Anthony Towns/99 12.00 30.00
72 Jahlil Okafor/99 5.00 12.00
73 D'Angelo Russell/99 5.00 12.00
74 Kristaps Porzingis/99 10.00 25.00
75 Mario Hezonja/99 3.00 8.00
76 Frank Kaminsky/99 4.00 10.00
77 Justise Winslow/99 4.00 10.00
78 Jerian Grant/99 2.50 6.00
79 Stanley Johnson/99 3.00 8.00
80 Emmanuel Mudiay/99 4.00 10.00
81 Devin Booker/99 12.00 30.00
82 Willie Cauley-Stein/99 4.00 10.00
83 Jonathon Simmons/99 4.00 10.00
84 Myles Turner/99 4.00 10.00
85 Tyus Jones/99 4.00 10.00
86 Larry Bird/99 8.00 20.00
87 Jason Kidd/99 4.00 10.00
88 Larry Johnson/99 5.00 12.00
89 Joe Smith/99 3.00 8.00
90 Danny Manning/99 3.00 8.00
91 Gary Payton/99 4.00 10.00
92 John Stockton/99 5.00 12.00
93 Scottie Pippen/99 8.00 20.00
94 David Robinson/99 5.00 12.00
95 Shaquille O'Neal/99 8.00 20.00
96 Patrick Ewing/99 5.00 12.00
97 Alonzo Mourning/99 5.00 12.00
98 Grant Hill/99 5.00 12.00
99 Hakeem Olajuwon/99 5.00 12.00
100 Karl Malone/99 5.00 12.00

2015-16 Panini Luxe Memorabilia Prime

*PRIME/17-25: .75X TO 2X BASIC
RANDOM INSERTS IN PACKS
PRINT RUNS B/WN 5-25 COPIES PER
NO PRICING ON QTY 15 OR LESS
49 Allen Iverson/25 60.00 150.00

2015-16 Panini Luxe Rookie Jerseys

RANDOM INSERTS IN PACKS
PRINT RUNS B/WN 30-99 COPIES PER
*PRIME/25: 1X TO 2.5X BASIC
1 Jahlil Okafor/99 5.00 12.00
2 Tyus Jones/99 3.00 8.00
3 Terry Rozier/99 2.50 6.00
4 Pat Connaughton/99 2.00 5.00
5 Norman Powell/99 2.50 6.00
6 Anthony Brown/99 2.00 5.00
7 Frank Kaminsky/99 3.00 8.00
8 Kevon Looney/99 2.50 6.00
9 Justise Winslow/99 3.00 8.00
10 Justin Anderson/99 2.50 6.00
11 Jerian Grant/99 2.00 5.00
12 Trey Lyles/99 3.00 8.00
13 Stanley Johnson/99 2.50 6.00
14 R.J. Hunter/99 2.00 5.00
15 Nikola Jokic/99 4.00 10.00
16 Bobby Portis/99 3.00 8.00
17 Emmanuel Mudiay/99 3.00 8.00
18 Marcelo Huertas/99 2.50 6.00
19 Kelly Oubre Jr./99 2.50 6.00
20 Josh Richardson/99 3.00 8.00
21 Joe Young/99 2.50 6.00
22 Walter Tavares/99 2.00 5.00
23 Sam Dekker/99 2.50 6.00
24 Raul Neto/99 2.00 5.00
25 Nemanja Bjelica/99 2.50 6.00
26 Cameron Payne/99 2.50 6.00
27 Devin Booker/99 5.00 12.00
28 Mario Hezonja/99 2.50 6.00
29 Karl-Anthony Towns/99 12.00 30.00
30 Josh Huestis/99 2.00 5.00
31 Jonathon Simmons/99 3.00 8.00
32 Willie Cauley-Stein/99 3.00 8.00
33 Rondae Hollis-Jefferson/99 2.50 6.00
34 Richaun Holmes/99 2.50 6.00
35 Myles Turner/99 3.00 8.00
36 D'Angelo Russell/99 8.00 20.00
37 Delon Wright/99 2.50 6.00
38 Montrezl Harrell/99 2.50 6.00
39 Kristaps Porzingis/30 8.00 20.00
40 Jordan Mickey/99 2.00 5.00

2015-16 Panini Luxe Rookie Jumbo Jersey Autographs

RANDOM INSERTS IN PACKS
STATED PRINT RUN 35 SER.#'d SETS
EXCHANGE DEADLINE 10/20/2017
*PRIME: .6X TO 1.5X BASIC
1 Karl-Anthony Towns 150.00 250.00
2 D'Angelo Russell 50.00 120.00
3 Jahlil Okafor
4 Emmanuel Mudiay
5 Kristaps Porzingis 50.00 120.00
6 Mario Hezonja 10.00 25.00
7 Justise Winslow
8 Willie Cauley-Stein 10.00 25.00
9 Stanley Johnson 12.00 30.00
10 Tyus Jones 6.00 15.00
11 Frank Kaminsky 6.00 15.00
12 Devin Booker 50.00 120.00
13 Myles Turner 15.00 40.00
14 Jerian Grant 4.00 10.00
15 Trey Lyles 12.00 30.00
16 Cameron Payne 5.00 12.00
17 Delon Wright 5.00 12.00
18 Rashad Vaughn 4.00 10.00
19 Kelly Oubre Jr. 5.00 12.00
20 Sam Dekker 8.00 20.00
21 Terry Rozier
22 Rondae Hollis-Jefferson 5.00 12.00
23 Bobby Portis 10.00 25.00
24 Justin Anderson 6.00 15.00
25 Kevon Looney 5.00 12.00
26 Jarell Martin 5.00 12.00
27 R.J. Hunter 4.00 10.00
28 Jordan Mickey 4.00 10.00
29 Walter Tavares 4.00 10.00
30 Josh Richardson 10.00 25.00
31 Joe Young
32 Pat Connaughton
33 Rakeem Christmas 4.00 10.00

2015-16 Panini Luxe Rookie Memorabilia Autographs

RANDOM INSERTS IN PACKS
STATED PRINT RUN 49 SER.#'d SETS
EXCHANGE DEADLINE 10/20/2017
*PRIME: .6X TO 1.5X BASIC
1 Karl-Anthony Towns 100.00 250.00
2 D'Angelo Russell 15.00 40.00
3 Jahlil Okafor
4 Emmanuel Mudiay 12.00 30.00
5 Kristaps Porzingis 40.00 100.00
6 Mario Hezonja 5.00 12.00
7 Justise Winslow 10.00 25.00
8 Willie Cauley-Stein 15.00 40.00
9 Stanley Johnson 5.00 12.00
10 Tyus Jones 6.00 15.00
11 Frank Kaminsky 6.00 15.00
12 Devin Booker 50.00 120.00
13 Myles Turner 15.00 40.00
14 Jerian Grant 4.00 10.00
15 Trey Lyles 6.00 15.00
16 Cameron Payne 5.00 12.00
17 Delon Wright
18 Rashad Vaughn
19 Kelly Oubre Jr. 5.00 12.00
20 Sam Dekker 5.00 12.00
21 Terry Rozier
22 Rondae Hollis-Jefferson 5.00 12.00
23 Bobby Portis
24 Justin Anderson 5.00 12.00
25 Kevon Looney 5.00 12.00
26 Jarell Martin 5.00 12.00
27 R.J. Hunter 4.00 10.00
28 Jordan Mickey 4.00 10.00
29 Walter Tavares 4.00 10.00
30 Josh Richardson 6.00 15.00
31 Joe Young
32 Pat Connaughton 4.00 10.00
33 Rakeem Christmas 4.00 10.00

2012-13 Panini Marquee

1 Kobe Bryant 1.50 4.00
2 Kevin Durant 1.00 2.50
3 LeBron James 1.50 4.00
4 Goran Dragic .30 .75
5 Chris Paul .50 1.25
6 Derrick Rose .50 1.25
7 Dirk Nowitzki .50 1.25
8 Kevin Love .40 1.00
9 Amare Stoudemire .30 .75
10 Dwight Howard .30 .75
11 Greg Monroe .30 .75
12 Andrew Bogut .30 .75
13 Daniel Gibson .30 .75
14 James Harden .60 1.50
15 John Wall .50 1.25
16 Deron Williams .30 .75
17 Blake Griffin .40 1.00
18 Ben Gordon .30 .75
19 David West .30 .75
20 Eric Gordon .30 .75
21 Andrew Bynum .25 .60
22 Serge Ibaka .30 .75
23 Dwyane Wade .60 1.50
24 Paul Pierce .40 1.00
25 Paul Millsap .40 1.00
26 Brandon Jennings .25 .60
27 DeAndre Jordan .40 1.00
28 Andrea Bargnani .30 .75
29 Stephen Jackson .30 .75
30 DeMarcus Cousins .40 1.00
31 J.J. Hickson .25 .60
32 Luol Deng .30 .75
33 Stephen Curry 1.50 4.00
34 Joe Johnson .30 .75
35 Andre Iguodala .30 .75
36 Roy Hibbert .30 .75
37 Manu Ginobili .40 1.00
38 Carmelo Anthony .50 1.25
39 J.J. Redick .40 1.00
40 Tyrus Thomas .25 .60
41 Kevin Garnett .60 1.50
42 Rudy Gay .40 1.00
43 Rodney Stuckey .30 .75
44 Ryan Anderson .30 .75
45 Al Horford .30 .75
46 Joakim Noah .30 .75
47 O.J. Mayo .25 .60
48 Ray Allen .40 1.00
49 Evan Turner .25 .60
50 Jeremy Lin .40 1.00
51 Danny Granger .30 .75
52 Ricky Rubio .40 1.00
53 Anderson Varejao .25 .60
54 Ersan Ilyasova .25 .60
55 Nene Hilario .30 .75
56 Tyson Chandler .30 .75
57 Tony Parker .40 1.00
58 Kevin Martin .30 .75
59 DeMar DeRozan .40 1.00
60 Wesley Matthews .25 .60
61 JaVale McGee .30 .75
62 Marc Gasol .40 1.00
63 Jason Terry .30 .75
64 Al Jefferson .30 .75
65 Grant Hill .50 1.25
66 Luc Mbah a Moute .25 .60
67 Carl Landry .25 .60
68 Charlie Villanueva .25 .60
69 Steve Nash .40 1.00
70 Daequan Cook .25 .60
71 Hedo Turkoglu .30 .75
72 Brook Lopez .30 .75
73 Andrei Kirilenko .30 .75
74 Al-Farouq Aminu .30 .75
75 Josh Smith .30 .75
76 Tim Duncan .60 1.50
77 Gordon Hayward .40 1.00
78 Carlos Boozer .30 .75
79 David Lee .25 .60
80 Tyreke Evans .25 .60
81 Darren Collison .30 .75
82 Rajon Rondo .40 1.00
83 Emeka Okafor .30 .75
84 Chris Bosh .40 1.00
85 Marcin Gortat .30 .75
86 Ty Lawson .25 .60
87 LaMarcus Aldridge .40 1.00
88 Jason Kidd .40 1.00
89 Danny Green .30 .75
90 Luis Scola .30 .75
91 Pau Gasol .40 1.00
92 Ed Davis .25 .60
93 Zach Randolph .30 .75
94 Paul George .50 1.25
95 Vince Carter .50 1.25
96 Gerald Wallace .30 .75
97 Arron Afflalo .30 .75
98 Louis Williams .30 .75
99 Travis Outlaw .30 .75
100 Thaddeus Young .25 .60
101 Pete Maravich 1.50 4.00
102 Wilt Chamberlain 2.00 5.00
103 Bill Russell 1.50 4.00
104 Patrick Ewing 1.25 3.00
105 Jerry West 1.25 3.00
106 Larry Bird 2.50 6.00
107 Magic Johnson 2.50 6.00
108 Bob Cousy 1.50 4.00
109 George Mikan 2.00 5.00
110 Julius Erving 1.50 4.00
111 Ralph Sampson .75 2.00
112 David Thompson .75 2.00
113 Hakeem Olajuwon 1.25 3.00
114 Kareem Abdul-Jabbar 1.50 4.00
115 Bill Walton 1.00 2.50
116 Isiah Thomas 1.00 2.50
117 Mookie Blaylock .60 1.50
118 Clyde Lovellette 1.00 2.50
119 Scottie Pippen 2.00 5.00
120 Shaquille O'Neal 2.00 5.00
121 Chris Webber 1.00 2.50
122 Jalen Rose 1.00 2.50
123 Elvin Hayes 1.00 2.50
124 Karl Malone 1.25 3.00
125 Drazen Petrovic 1.00 2.50
126 Calvin Murphy .75 2.00
127 John Stockton 1.50 4.00
128 Doug Collins 1.00 2.50
129 Sean Elliott 1.00 2.50
130 David Robinson 1.50 4.00
131 Dolph Schayes 1.00 2.50
132 Dominique Wilkins 1.25 3.00
133 Jamal Mashburn 1.00 2.50
134 Danny Manning .75 2.00
135 Elgin Baylor 1.00 2.50
136 Greg Anthony .60 1.50
137 Cedric Maxwell .60 1.50
138 Mitch Richmond 1.00 2.50
139 Dennis Rodman 2.00 5.00
140 Rolando Blackman .75 2.00
141 Glenn Robinson 1.00 2.50
142 Clyde Drexler 1.25 3.00
143 Jerry Lucas 1.00 2.50
144 Oscar Robertson 1.25 3.00
145 Gary Payton 1.00 2.50
146 Kevin McHale 1.00 2.50
147 Rex Chapman 1.00 2.50
148 Christian Laettner .75 2.00
149 Antoine Walker .75 2.00
150 Allen Iverson 1.25 3.00
151 Damian Lillard RC 3.00 8.00
152 Anthony Davis RC 4.00 10.00
153 Dion Waiters RC .75 2.00
154 Bradley Beal RC 1.25 3.00
155 Michael Kidd-Gilchrist RC .75 2.00
156 Alexey Shved RC .50 1.25
157 Harrison Barnes RC 1.25 3.00
158 Jonas Valanciunas RC .75 2.00
159 Kyle Singler RC .50 1.25
160 Tyler Zeller RC .60 1.50
161 Kyrie Irving RC 5.00 12.00
162 Kemba Walker RC 1.50 4.00
163 Klay Thompson RC 3.00 8.00
164 Brandon Knight RC .75 2.00
165 Kenneth Faried RC .75 2.00
166 Kawhi Leonard RC 5.00 12.00
167 Nikola Vucevic RC .75 2.00
168 Markieff Morris RC .75 2.00
169 Derrick Williams RC .50 1.25
170 Jimmer Fredette RC .50 1.25
171 Austin Rivers RC .75 2.00
172 Jae Crowder RC .60 1.50
173 Jeff Taylor RC .50 1.25
174 Andrew Nicholson RC .50 1.25
175 Brian Roberts RC .50 1.25
176 Andre Drummond RC 1.25 3.00
177 Jared Sullinger RC .60 1.50
178 Terrence Ross RC .75 2.00
179 John Henson RC .75 2.00
180 Thomas Robinson RC .60 1.50
181 Marcus Morris RC .60 1.50
182 Tristan Thompson RC .75 2.00
183 Isaiah Thomas RC 1.25 3.00
184 Tobias Harris RC .75 2.00
185 MarShon Brooks RC .60 1.50
186 Enes Kanter RC .60 1.50
187 Lavoy Allen RC .50 1.25
188 Jimmy Butler RC 2.50 6.00
189 Norris Cole RC .50 1.25
190 Bismack Biyombo RC .50 1.25
191 Doron Lamb RC .50 1.25
192 Meyers Leonard RC .60 1.50

193 Bernard James RC .50 1.25
194 Chris Copeland RC .50 1.25
195 Evan Fournier RC .75 2.00
196 Maurice Harkless RC .75 2.00
197 Draymond Green RC 2.50 6.00
198 Kyle O'Quinn RC .50 1.25
199 Mirza Teletovic RC .60 1.50
200 Festus Ezeli RC .60 1.50
201 Jan Vesely RC .50 1.25
202 Lance Thomas RC .50 1.25
203 Alec Burks RC .75 2.00
204 Ivan Johnson RC .50 1.25
205 Jordan Hamilton RC .50 1.25
206 Kent Bazemore RC .75 2.00
207 Greg Stiemsma RC .50 1.25
208 Reggie Jackson RC .75 2.00
209 Gustavo Ayon RC .50 1.25
210 Charles Jenkins RC .50 1.25
211 Nando De Colo RC .50 1.25
212 Pablo Prigioni RC .50 1.25
213 Kim English RC .50 1.25
214 DeQuan Jones RC .50 1.25
215 Darius Miller RC .50 1.25
216 Luke Zeller RC .50 1.25
217 Perry Jones RC .50 1.25
218 Kendall Marshall RC .50 1.25
219 Tyshawn Taylor RC .50 1.25
220 Terrence Jones RC .60 1.50
221 Chandler Parsons RC .75 2.00
222 Will Barton RC .60 1.50
223 Josh Selby RC .50 1.25
224 DeAndre Liggins RC .60 1.50
225 Iman Shumpert RC .75 2.00
226 Nolan Smith RC .50 1.25
227 Malcolm Lee RC .50 1.25
228 Marquis Teague RC .50 1.25
229 Miles Plumlee RC .50 1.25
230 Orlando Johnson RC .50 1.25
231 Damian Lillard RC 3.00 8.00
232 Anthony Davis RC 4.00 10.00
233 Dion Waiters RC .75 2.00
234 Bradley Beal RC 1.25 3.00
235 Michael Kidd-Gilchrist RC .75 2.00
236 Alexey Shved RC .50 1.25
237 Harrison Barnes RC 1.25 3.00
238 Jonas Valanciunas RC .75 2.00
239 Kyle Singler RC .50 1.25
240 Tyler Zeller RC .60 1.50
241 Kyrie Irving RC 4.00 10.00
242 Kemba Walker RC 1.50 4.00
243 Klay Thompson RC 3.00 8.00
244 Brandon Knight RC .75 2.00
245 Kenneth Faried RC .75 2.00
246 Kawhi Leonard RC 4.00 10.00
247 Nikola Vucevic RC .75 2.00
248 Markieff Morris RC .75 2.00
249 Derrick Williams RC .50 1.25
250 Jimmer Fredette RC .50 1.25
251 Austin Rivers RC .75 2.00
252 Jae Crowder RC .60 1.50
253 Jeff Taylor RC .50 1.25
254 Andrew Nicholson RC .50 1.25
255 Brian Roberts RC .50 1.25
256 Andre Drummond RC 1.25 3.00
257 Jared Sullinger RC .60 1.50
258 Terrence Ross RC .75 2.00
259 John Henson RC .75 2.00
260 Thomas Robinson RC .60 1.50
261 Marcus Morris RC .60 1.50
262 Tristan Thompson RC .75 2.00
263 Isaiah Thomas RC 1.25 3.00
264 Tobias Harris RC .75 2.00
265 MarShon Brooks RC .60 1.50
266 Enes Kanter RC .60 1.50
267 Lavoy Allen RC .50 1.25
268 Jimmy Butler RC 2.50 6.00
269 Norris Cole RC .50 1.25
270 Bismack Biyombo RC .50 1.25
271 Doron Lamb RC .50 1.25
272 Meyers Leonard RC .60 1.50
273 Bernard James RC .50 1.25
274 Chris Copeland RC .50 1.25
275 Evan Fournier RC .75 2.00
276 Maurice Harkless RC .75 2.00
277 Draymond Green RC 2.50 6.00
278 Kyle O'Quinn RC .50 1.25
279 Mirza Teletovic RC .60 1.50
280 Festus Ezeli RC .60 1.50
281 Jan Vesely RC .50 1.25
282 Lance Thomas RC .50 1.25
283 Alec Burks RC .75 2.00
284 Ivan Johnson RC .50 1.25
285 Jordan Hamilton RC .50 1.25
286 Kent Bazemore RC .75 2.00
287 Greg Stiemsma RC .50 1.25
288 Reggie Jackson RC .75 2.00
289 Gustavo Ayon RC .50 1.25
290 Charles Jenkins RC .50 1.25
291 Nando De Colo RC .50 1.25
292 Pablo Prigioni RC .50 1.25
293 Kim English RC .50 1.25
294 DeQuan Jones RC .50 1.25
295 Darius Miller RC .50 1.25
296 Luke Zeller RC .50 1.25
297 Perry Jones RC .50 1.25
298 Kendall Marshall RC .50 1.25
299 Tyshawn Taylor RC .50 1.25
300 Terrence Jones RC .60 1.50
301 Chandler Parsons RC .75 2.00
302 Will Barton RC .60 1.50
303 Josh Selby RC .50 1.25
304 DeAndre Liggins RC .60 1.50
305 Iman Shumpert RC .75 2.00
306 Nolan Smith RC .50 1.25
307 Malcolm Lee RC .50 1.25
308 Marquis Teague RC .50 1.25
309 Miles Plumlee RC .50 1.25
310 Orlando Johnson RC .50 1.25
311 Damian Lillard RC 3.00 8.00
312 Anthony Davis RC 6.00 15.00
313 Dion Waiters RC .75 2.00
314 Bradley Beal RC 1.25 3.00
315 Michael Kidd-Gilchrist RC .75 2.00
316 Alexey Shved RC .50 1.25
317 Harrison Barnes RC 1.25 3.00
318 Jonas Valanciunas RC .75 2.00
319 Kyle Singler RC .50 1.25
320 Tyler Zeller RC .60 1.50
321 Kyrie Irving RC 4.00 10.00
322 Kemba Walker RC 1.50 4.00
323 Klay Thompson RC 3.00 8.00
324 Brandon Knight RC .75 2.00
325 Kenneth Faried RC .75 2.00
326 Kawhi Leonard RC 6.00 15.00
327 Nikola Vucevic RC .75 2.00
328 Markieff Morris RC .75 2.00
329 Derrick Williams RC .50 1.25
330 Jimmer Fredette RC .50 1.25
331 Austin Rivers RC .75 2.00
332 Jae Crowder RC .60 1.50
333 Jeff Taylor RC .50 1.25
334 Andrew Nicholson RC .50 1.25
335 Brian Roberts RC .50 1.25
336 Andre Drummond RC 1.25 3.00
337 Jared Sullinger RC .60 1.50
338 Terrence Ross RC .75 2.00
339 John Henson RC .75 2.00
340 Thomas Robinson RC .60 1.50
341 Marcus Morris RC .60 1.50
342 Tristan Thompson RC .75 2.00
343 Isaiah Thomas RC 1.25 3.00
344 Tobias Harris RC .75 2.00
345 MarShon Brooks RC .60 1.50
346 Enes Kanter RC .60 1.50
347 Lavoy Allen RC .50 1.25
348 Jimmy Butler RC 2.50 6.00
349 Norris Cole RC .50 1.25
350 Bismack Biyombo RC .50 1.25
351 Doron Lamb RC .50 1.25
352 Meyers Leonard RC .60 1.50
353 Bernard James RC .50 1.25
354 Chris Copeland RC .50 1.25
355 Evan Fournier RC .75 2.00
356 Maurice Harkless RC .75 2.00
357 Draymond Green RC 2.50 6.00
358 Kyle O'Quinn RC .50 1.25
359 Mirza Teletovic RC .60 1.50
360 Festus Ezeli RC .60 1.50
361 Jan Vesely RC .50 1.25
362 Lance Thomas RC .50 1.25
363 Alec Burks RC .75 2.00
364 Ivan Johnson RC .50 1.25
365 Jordan Hamilton RC .50 1.25
366 Kent Bazemore RC .75 2.00
367 Greg Stiemsma RC .50 1.25
368 Reggie Jackson RC .75 2.00
369 Gustavo Ayon RC .50 1.25
370 Charles Jenkins RC .50 1.25
371 Nando De Colo RC .50 1.25
372 Pablo Prigioni RC .50 1.25
373 Kim English RC .50 1.25
374 DeQuan Jones RC .50 1.25
375 Darius Miller RC .50 1.25
376 Luke Zeller RC .50 1.25
377 Perry Jones RC .50 1.25
378 Kendall Marshall RC .50 1.25
379 Tyshawn Taylor RC .50 1.25
380 Terrence Jones RC .60 1.50
381 Chandler Parsons RC .75 2.00
382 Will Barton RC .60 1.50
383 Josh Selby RC .50 1.25
384 DeAndre Liggins RC .60 1.50
385 Iman Shumpert RC .75 2.00
386 Nolan Smith RC .50 1.25
387 Malcolm Lee RC .50 1.25
388 Marquis Teague RC .50 1.25
389 Miles Plumlee RC .50 1.25
390 Orlando Johnson RC .50 1.25
391 Damian Lillard RC 10.00 25.00
392 Anthony Davis RC 12.00 30.00
393 Dion Waiters RC 2.50 6.00
394 Bradley Beal RC 4.00 10.00
395 Michael Kidd-Gilchrist RC 2.50 6.00
396 Alexey Shved RC 1.50 4.00
397 Harrison Barnes RC 4.00 10.00
398 Jonas Valanciunas RC 2.50 6.00
399 Kyle Singler RC 1.50 4.00
400 Tyler Zeller RC 2.00 5.00
401 Kyrie Irving RC 20.00 50.00
402 Kemba Walker RC 5.00 12.00
403 Klay Thompson RC 10.00 25.00
404 Brandon Knight RC 2.50 6.00
405 Kenneth Faried RC 2.50 6.00
406 Kawhi Leonard RC 12.00 30.00
407 Nikola Vucevic RC 2.50 6.00
408 Markieff Morris RC 2.50 6.00
409 Derrick Williams RC 1.50 4.00
410 Jimmer Fredette RC 1.50 4.00
411 Austin Rivers RC 2.50 6.00
412 Jae Crowder RC 2.00 5.00
413 Jeff Taylor RC 1.50 4.00
414 Andrew Nicholson RC 1.50 4.00
415 Brian Roberts RC 1.50 4.00
416 Andre Drummond RC 4.00 10.00
417 Jared Sullinger RC 2.00 5.00
418 Terrence Ross RC 2.50 6.00
419 John Henson RC 2.50 6.00
420 Thomas Robinson RC 2.00 5.00
421 Marcus Morris RC 2.00 5.00
422 Tristan Thompson RC 2.50 6.00
423 Isaiah Thomas RC 4.00 10.00
424 Tobias Harris RC 2.50 6.00
425 MarShon Brooks RC 2.00 5.00
426 Enes Kanter RC 2.00 5.00
427 Lavoy Allen RC 1.50 4.00
428 Jimmy Butler RC 8.00 20.00
429 Norris Cole RC 1.50 4.00
430 Bismack Biyombo RC 1.50 4.00
431 Doron Lamb RC 1.50 4.00
432 Meyers Leonard RC 2.00 5.00
433 Bernard James RC 1.50 4.00
434 Chris Copeland RC 1.50 4.00
435 Evan Fournier RC 2.50 6.00
436 Maurice Harkless RC 2.50 6.00
437 Draymond Green RC 8.00 20.00
438 Kyle O'Quinn RC 1.50 4.00
439 Mirza Teletovic RC 2.00 5.00
440 Festus Ezeli RC 2.00 5.00
441 Jan Vesely RC 1.50 4.00
442 Lance Thomas RC 1.50 4.00
443 Alec Burks RC 2.50 6.00
444 Ivan Johnson RC 1.50 4.00
445 Jordan Hamilton RC 1.50 4.00
446 Kent Bazemore RC 2.50 6.00
447 Greg Stiemsma RC 1.50 4.00
448 Reggie Jackson RC 2.50 6.00
449 Gustavo Ayon RC 1.50 4.00
450 Charles Jenkins RC 1.50 4.00
451 Nando De Colo RC 1.50 4.00
452 Pablo Prigioni RC 1.50 4.00
453 Kim English RC 1.50 4.00
454 DeQuan Jones RC 1.50 4.00
455 Darius Miller RC 1.50 4.00
456 Luke Zeller RC 1.50 4.00
457 Perry Jones RC 1.50 4.00
458 Kendall Marshall RC 1.50 4.00
459 Tyshawn Taylor RC 1.50 4.00
460 Terrence Jones RC 2.00 5.00
461 Damian Lillard RC 4.00 10.00
462 Anthony Davis RC 6.00 15.00
463 Dion Waiters RC 1.00 2.50
464 Bradley Beal RC 1.50 4.00
465 Michael Kidd-Gilchrist RC 1.00 2.50
466 Alexey Shved RC .60 1.50
467 Harrison Barnes RC 1.50 4.00
468 Jonas Valanciunas RC 1.00 2.50
469 Kyle Singler RC .60 1.50
470 Tyler Zeller RC .75 2.00
471 Kyrie Irving RC 5.00 12.00
472 Kemba Walker RC 2.00 5.00
473 Klay Thompson RC 4.00 10.00
474 Brandon Knight RC 1.00 2.50
475 Kenneth Faried RC 1.00 2.50
476 Kawhi Leonard RC 5.00 12.00
477 Nikola Vucevic RC 1.00 2.50
478 Markieff Morris RC 1.00 2.50
479 Derrick Williams RC .60 1.50
480 Jimmer Fredette RC .60 1.50
481 Austin Rivers RC 1.00 2.50
482 Jae Crowder RC .75 2.00
483 Jeff Taylor RC .60 1.50
484 Andrew Nicholson RC .60 1.50
485 Brian Roberts RC .60 1.50
486 Andre Drummond RC 1.50 4.00
487 Jared Sullinger RC .75 2.00
488 Terrence Ross RC 1.00 2.50
489 John Henson RC 1.00 2.50
490 Thomas Robinson RC .75 2.00
491 Marcus Morris RC .75 2.00
492 Tristan Thompson RC 1.00 2.50
493 Isaiah Thomas RC 1.50 4.00
494 Tobias Harris RC 1.00 2.50
495 MarShon Brooks RC .75 2.00
496 Enes Kanter RC .75 2.00
497 Lavoy Allen RC .60 1.50
498 Jimmy Butler RC 3.00 8.00
499 Norris Cole RC .60 1.50
500 Bismack Biyombo RC .60 1.50
501 Doron Lamb RC .60 1.50
502 Meyers Leonard RC .75 2.00
503 Bernard James RC .60 1.50
504 Chris Copeland RC .60 1.50
505 Evan Fournier RC 1.00 2.50
506 Maurice Harkless RC 1.00 2.50
507 Draymond Green RC 3.00 8.00
508 Kyle O'Quinn RC .60 1.50
509 Mirza Teletovic RC .75 2.00
510 Festus Ezeli RC .75 2.00
511 Jan Vesely RC .60 1.50
512 Lance Thomas RC .60 1.50
513 Alec Burks RC 1.00 2.50
514 Ivan Johnson RC .60 1.50
515 Jordan Hamilton RC .60 1.50
516 Kent Bazemore RC 1.00 2.50
517 Greg Stiemsma RC .60 1.50
518 Reggie Jackson RC 1.00 2.50
519 Gustavo Ayon RC .60 1.50
520 Charles Jenkins RC .60 1.50
521 Nando De Colo RC .60 1.50
522 Pablo Prigioni RC .60 1.50
523 Kim English RC .60 1.50
524 DeQuan Jones RC .60 1.50
525 Darius Miller RC .60 1.50
526 Luke Zeller RC .60 1.50
527 Perry Jones RC .60 1.50
528 Kendall Marshall RC .60 1.50
529 Tyshawn Taylor RC .60 1.50
530 Terrence Jones RC .75 2.00
531 Chandler Parsons RC 1.00 2.50
532 Will Barton RC .75 2.00
533 Josh Selby RC .60 1.50
534 DeAndre Liggins RC .75 2.00
535 Iman Shumpert RC 1.00 2.50
536 Nolan Smith RC .60 1.50
537 Malcolm Lee RC .60 1.50
538 Marquis Teague RC .60 1.50
539 Miles Plumlee RC .60 1.50
540 Orlando Johnson RC .60 1.50

2012-13 Panini Marquee All-Rookie Team Laser Cut

COMPLETE SET (20) 30.00 60.00
1 Kareem Abdul-Jabbar 1.50 4.00
2 Larry Bird 2.50 6.00
3 Wilt Chamberlain 2.00 5.00
4 Kyrie Irving 5.00 12.00
5 Blake Griffin 1.00 2.50
6 Patrick Ewing 1.25 3.00
7 Shaquille O'Neal 2.00 5.00
8 Grant Hill 1.25 3.00
9 Jason Kidd 1.00 2.50
10 Allen Iverson 1.25 3.00
11 LeBron James 4.00 10.00
12 Kevin Durant 2.50 6.00
13 Chris Paul 1.25 3.00
14 Vince Carter 1.25 3.00
15 Tim Duncan 1.50 4.00
16 David Robinson 1.50 4.00
17 Elgin Baylor 1.00 2.50
18 Derrick Rose 1.25 3.00
19 Amare Stoudemire .75 2.00
20 Chris Webber 1.00 2.50

2012-13 Panini Marquee Champions

COMPLETE SET (20) 30.00 60.00
UNLISTED STARS 1.00 2.50
1 Kobe Bryant 4.00 10.00
2 Bill Russell 1.50 4.00
3 Tim Duncan 1.50 4.00
4 Larry Bird 2.50 6.00
5 Scottie Pippen 2.00 5.00
6 Dirk Nowitzki 1.25 3.00
7 LeBron James 4.00 10.00
8 Hakeem Olajuwon 1.25 3.00
9 Kareem Abdul-Jabbar 1.50 4.00
10 Dwyane Wade 1.50 4.00
11 Isiah Thomas 1.00 2.50
12 David Robinson 1.50 4.00
13 Kevin Garnett 1.50 4.00
14 James Worthy 1.25 3.00
15 Moses Malone 1.00 2.50
16 Dennis Rodman 2.00 5.00
17 John Havlicek 1.25 3.00
18 Horace Grant 1.00 2.50
19 Magic Johnson 2.50 6.00
20 Bill Walton 1.00 2.50

2012-13 Panini Marquee Coach's Autographs

PRINT RUNS B/WN 10-299 COPIES PER
NO JACKSON PRICING AVAILABLE
EXCHANGE DEADLINE 10/10/2014
1 Larry Bird/49 60.00 150.00
2 Bill Russell/46 50.00 100.00
3 Bill Sharman/25 15.00 40.00
4 Kiki VanDeWeghe/299 EXCH 4.00 10.00
5 Dave Cowens/25 10.00 25.00
6 Doc Rivers/25 15.00 40.00
7 Don Nelson/25 12.00 30.00
8 Vinny Del Negro/25 15.00 40.00
9 Maurice Cheeks/299 3.00 8.00
10 George Karl/25 40.00 100.00
11 Harry Gallatin/199 5.00 12.00
12 Isiah Thomas/25 20.00 50.00
13 Pat Riley/49 30.00 60.00
15 Jerry West/49 30.00 60.00
18 Kevin McHale/25 10.00 25.00
19 Lenny Wilkens/25 8.00 20.00
20 Magic Johnson/49 EXCH 20.00 50.00
21 Paul Westphal/299 EXCH 5.00 12.00
23 Byron Scott/25 30.00 60.00
24 Al Attles/299 5.00 12.00
25 Mark Jackson/25 10.00 25.00

2012-13 Panini Marquee Election Night Autographs

PRINT RUNS B/WN 10-299 COPIES PER
EXCHANGE DEADLINE 10/10/2014
1 Kareem Abdul-Jabbar/49 30.00 60.00
2 Dolph Schayes/25
3 Magic Johnson/49 30.00 80.00
4 David Robinson/49 20.00 50.00
5 Hakeem Olajuwon/49 12.00 30.00
6 George Gervin/25 15.00 40.00
7 Scottie Pippen/49 60.00 150.00
8 James Worthy/49
9 Clyde Drexler/49 20.00 50.00
10 Larry Bird/49 75.00 150.00
11 Bob Lanier/25 20.00 50.00
12 Tom Heinsohn/199 15.00 40.00
13 Bill Russell/49 60.00 120.00
14 Jamaal Wilkes/199 5.00 12.00
15 Joe Dumars/25 10.00 25.00
16 Julius Erving/49 40.00 100.00
17 Robert Parish/25
18 Adrian Dantley/199 4.00 10.00
19 Bob McAdoo/199 8.00 20.00
20 Alex English/199 4.00 10.00
21 Jerry West/49 50.00 100.00
22 Artis Gilmore/25
23 Dennis Rodman/49
24 Bailey Howell/199 6.00 15.00
25 Nate Archibald/25 10.00 25.00

2012-13 Panini Marquee Legends Signatures

EXCHANGE DEADLINE 10/10/2014
1 Elgin Baylor SP 10.00 25.00
2 George McGinnis 3.00 8.00
3 Nick Anderson 5.00 12.00
4 Walt Frazier SP 30.00 80.00
5 Muggsy Bogues 4.00 10.00
6 Bill Walton SP 10.00 25.00
7 Michael Finley SP
8 Alonzo Mourning 20.00 50.00
9 Buck Williams 3.00 8.00
10 Elvin Hayes SP
11 Robert Horry 4.00 10.00
12 Alex English 4.00 10.00
13 Hakeem Olajuwon SP 15.00 40.00
14 Michael Cooper 6.00 15.00
15 Robert Parish SP
16 Cedric Maxwell 3.00 8.00
17 Rick Fox SP 50.00 100.00
18 Bruce Bowen 3.00 8.00
19 Luc Longley 4.00 10.00
20 Glen Rice SP 4.00 10.00
21 Tom Sanders 5.00 12.00
22 Steve Smith 4.00 10.00
23 Bailey Howell 6.00 15.00
24 Tom Chambers 4.00 10.00
25 Gary Payton 20.00 50.00
26 Darryl Dawkins 3.00 8.00
27 Walt Bellamy SP 6.00 15.00
28 Magic Johnson 40.00 80.00
29 Julius Erving 25.00 60.00
30 Sam Jones SP 15.00 40.00
31 Sam Perkins 3.00 8.00
32 Nick Van Exel SP 15.00 40.00
33 Leonard Robinson 3.00 8.00
34 Artis Gilmore SP
35 Fat Lever 4.00 10.00
36 Bob Love 5.00 12.00
37 Detlef Schrempf SP
38 James Worthy 12.00 30.00
39 John Starks 4.00 10.00
40 John Havlicek SP 15.00 40.00
41 Bernard King 4.00 10.00
42 Toni Kukoc 15.00 40.00
43 Anfernee Hardaway 20.00 50.00
44 Dave Cowens SP 10.00 25.00
45 Dale Ellis 5.00 12.00
46 Sidney Moncrief 3.00 8.00
47 Zydrunas Ilgauskas 4.00 10.00
48 Bill Cartwright 4.00 10.00
49 Tom Heinsohn 15.00 40.00
50 George Gervin SP 8.00 20.00

2012-13 Panini Marquee Rookie Rivals Leather

1 G.Hill/J.Kidd 2.00 5.00
2 L.James/C.Anthony 6.00 15.00
3 S.O'Neal /A.Mourning 3.00 8.00
4 L.Bird/M.Johnson 4.00 10.00
5 K.Bryant/R.Allen 6.00 15.00
6 V.Carter/P.Pierce 2.00 5.00
7 Wes Unseld 1.50 4.00
Elvin Hayes
8 C.Paul/D.Williams 2.00 5.00
9 D.Rose/R.Westbrook 4.00 10.00
10 A.Davis/D.Lillard 8.00 20.00
11 J.Kidd/G.Hill 2.00 5.00
12 C.Anthony/L.James 6.00 15.00
13 A.Mourning/S.O'Neal 3.00 8.00
14 M.Johnson/L.Bird 4.00 10.00
15 R.Allen/K.Bryant 6.00 15.00
16 P.Pierce/V.Carter 2.00 5.00
17 Elvin Hayes 1.50 4.00
Wes Unseld
18 D.Williams/C.Paul 2.00 5.00
19 R.Westbrook/D.Rose 4.00 10.00
20 D.Lillard/A.Davis 8.00 20.00

2012-13 Panini Marquee Rookie Signatures

EXCHANGE DEADLINE 10/10/2014
1 Kyrie Irving 30.00 80.00
2 Anthony Davis 75.00 150.00
3 Dion Waiters SP EXCH 10.00 25.00
4 Thomas Robinson 4.00 10.00
5 Chandler Parsons 5.00 12.00
6 Michael Kidd-Gilchrist 5.00 12.00
7 Bradley Beal 8.00 20.00
8 Kemba Walker 10.00 25.00
9 Brandon Knight SP
10 Harrison Barnes 6.00 15.00
11 Andre Drummond 8.00 20.00
12 Austin Rivers 5.00 12.00
13 Derrick Williams SP
14 Markieff Morris SP
15 Donatas Motiejunas 4.00 10.00
16 Victor Claver 3.00 8.00
17 Kyle Singler 3.00 8.00
18 John Henson SP
19 Jeremy Lamb SP EXCH 5.00 12.00
20 Kawhi Leonard 50.00 120.00
21 Chris Copeland 3.00 8.00
22 Kenneth Faried 5.00 12.00
23 Klay Thompson 40.00 100.00
24 Jonas Valanciunas 5.00 12.00
25 Nikola Vucevic 5.00 12.00
26 Isaiah Thomas 10.00 25.00
27 Marcus Morris SP EXCH 4.00 10.00
28 Tristan Thompson SP
29 Jimmer Fredette 3.00 8.00
30 Enes Kanter 4.00 10.00
31 Lavoy Allen 3.00 8.00
32 Tobias Harris 5.00 12.00
33 MarShon Brooks SP
34 Jimmy Butler SP 15.00 40.00
35 Bismack Biyombo 3.00 8.00
36 Tyler Zeller 4.00 10.00
37 Andrew Nicholson 3.00 8.00
38 Terrence Ross 5.00 12.00
39 Brian Roberts 3.00 8.00
40 Doron Lamb 3.00 8.00
41 Maurice Harkless 5.00 12.00
42 Jeff Taylor 3.00 8.00
43 Jae Crowder 4.00 10.00
44 Jared Sullinger 4.00 10.00
45 Meyers Leonard 4.00 10.00
46 Alexey Shved 3.00 8.00
47 John Jenkins 3.00 8.00
48 Nando De Colo 3.00 8.00
49 Evan Fournier 5.00 12.00
50 Bernard James 3.00 8.00
51 Terrence Jones 4.00 10.00
52 Draymond Green 20.00 50.00
53 Will Barton 4.00 10.00
54 Festus Ezeli 4.00 10.00
55 Marquis Teague 3.00 8.00
56 Kyle O'Quinn 3.00 8.00
57 DeQuan Jones 3.00 8.00
58 Kent Bazemore 5.00 12.00
59 Shelvin Mack 4.00 10.00
60 Gustavo Ayon 3.00 8.00
61 Khris Middleton 5.00 12.00
62 Fab Melo SP 3.00 8.00
63 Tornike Shengelia 3.00 8.00
64 Arnett Moultrie
65 Julyan Stone 3.00 8.00
66 Cory Joseph SP EXCH 3.00 8.00
67 Kendall Marshall 3.00 8.00
68 Iman Shumpert 5.00 12.00
69 DeAndre Liggins 4.00 10.00
70 Orlando Johnson 3.00 8.00
71 Perry Jones 3.00 8.00
72 Robert Sacre 3.00 8.00
73 Mike Scott 3.00 8.00
74 Nolan Smith 3.00 8.00
75 Charles Jenkins SP 3.00 8.00
76 Ben Hansbrough 3.00 8.00
77 Jon Leuer 4.00 10.00
78 Norris Cole 3.00 8.00
79 Miles Plumlee 3.00 8.00
80 Alec Burks 5.00 12.00
81 Darius Miller 3.00 8.00
82 Greg Stiemsma 3.00 8.00
83 Jan Vesely 3.00 8.00
84 Jared Cunningham 3.00 8.00
85 Kim English 3.00 8.00
86 Lance Thomas 3.00 8.00
87 Chris Singleton 3.00 8.00
88 Quincy Acy SP 3.00 8.00
89 Tyshawn Taylor SP EXCH 3.00 8.00
90 Reggie Jackson 5.00 12.00

2012-13 Panini Marquee Signatures

EXCHANGE DEADLINE 10/10/2014
1 Grant Hill EXCH 60.00 120.00
2 Andrea Bargnani SP 4.00 10.00
3 Joe Johnson SP 10.00 25.00
4 Kobe Bryant 75.00 150.00
5 Zach Randolph SP
6 Ersan Ilyasova 3.00 8.00
7 Greivis Vasquez 6.00 15.00
8 Kevin Durant 60.00 150.00
9 Mario Chalmers SP 8.00 20.00
10 Joakim Noah SP 12.00 30.00
11 Jeff Teague 4.00 10.00
12 Brook Lopez SP
13 Chris Kaman SP
14 Stephen Curry SP
15 Blake Griffin 12.00 30.00
16 Nick Collison 5.00 12.00
17 Metta World Peace SP 6.00 15.00
18 Kevin Martin SP 6.00 15.00
19 Goran Dragic SP
20 LaMarcus Aldridge SP
21 Danny Granger SP
22 Elliot Williams 3.00 8.00
23 Kevin Love 12.00 30.00
24 Ben Gordon SP
25 Darren Collison SP
26 Greg Monroe SP 4.00 10.00
27 Carlos Boozer SP
28 Gordon Hayward 5.00 12.00
29 Danny Green 8.00 20.00
30 Jordan Crawford 3.00 8.00
31 Marcus Thornton 3.00 8.00
32 Andre Iguodala SP 4.00 10.00
33 Courtney Lee 6.00 15.00
34 Tiago Splitter 4.00 10.00
35 Jason Kidd 30.00 60.00
36 Vince Carter 20.00 50.00
37 Raymond Felton SP 4.00 10.00
38 Jason Richardson SP 5.00 12.00
39 Tyreke Evans SP
40 Gerald Henderson 3.00 8.00
41 Andre Miller SP
42 Tyson Chandler SP 5.00 12.00
43 Anderson Varejao SP 3.00 8.00
44 Monta Ellis SP 6.00 15.00
45 Landry Fields 3.00 8.00
46 Ekpe Udoh EXCH 3.00 8.00
47 Corey Brewer 5.00 12.00
48 Thabo Sefolosha SP
49 Hedo Turkoglu SP 4.00 10.00
50 Eric Gordon SP

2012-13 Panini Marquee Slam Dunk Legends

COMPLETE SET (20) 20.00 50.00
1 LeBron James 4.00 10.00
2 Vince Carter 1.25 3.00
3 Kobe Bryant 4.00 10.00
4 Dominique Wilkins 1.25 3.00
5 Clyde Drexler 1.25 3.00
6 Shawn Kemp 1.50 4.00
7 Julius Erving 1.50 4.00
8 Blake Griffin 1.00 2.50
9 Steve Francis .75 2.00
10 Shaquille O'Neal 2.00 5.00
11 Kevin Durant 2.50 6.00
12 David Thompson .75 2.00
13 Dwyane Wade 1.50 4.00
14 Dwight Howard .75 2.00
15 Spud Webb .75 2.00
16 Tom Chambers .75 2.00
17 Brent Barry .60 1.50
18 Larry Nance .75 2.00
19 Darryl Dawkins .60 1.50
20 Amare Stoudemire .75 2.00

2012-13 Panini Marquee Stars of the Night

COMPLETE SET (20) 15.00 40.00
1 Blake Griffin .60 1.50
2 Kobe Bryant 2.50 6.00
3 Kevin Durant 1.50 4.00
4 Kyrie Irving 3.00 8.00
5 Paul Pierce .60 1.50
6 Grant Hill .75 2.00
7 Carmelo Anthony .75 2.00
8 James Harden 1.00 2.50
9 Rajon Rondo .60 1.50
10 Russell Westbrook 1.50 4.00
11 Derrick Rose .75 2.00
12 Kenneth Faried .60 1.50
13 Jeremy Lin .60 1.50
14 Kevin Love .60 1.50
15 Chris Paul .75 2.00
16 Dwight Howard .50 1.25
17 Deron Williams .50 1.25
18 DeMarcus Cousins .60 1.50
19 Stephen Curry 2.50 6.00
20 Dirk Nowitzki .75 2.00

2012 Panini Materials Toronto Fall Expo

5 Terrence Ross SP
6 Quincy Acy 2.50 6.00
7 Jonas Valanciunas 6.00 15.00

2013-14 Panini Toronto Fall Expo

*LAVA FLOW: 1X TO 2.5X BASIC CARDS
22 Anthony Bennett 1.50 4.00

2009 Panini National Convention

*BLUE: .6X TO 1.5X BASE HI
*GOLD: .75X TO 2X BASE HI
*RED: .6X TO 1.5X BASE HI
BG Blake Griffin 10.00 25.00
BW Bill Walton OS .60 1.50
DR Derrick Rose 10.00 25.00
HT Hasheem Thabeet 2.00 5.00
KM Kevin McHale OS .60 1.50
LB Larry Bird OS 2.00 5.00
TH Tyler Hansbrough 3.00 8.00

2009 Panini National Convention Autographs

For the 2009 National Sports Collectors Convention, newly licensed Panini had two of their new spokesman sign at their booth for free. Earlier in the week, Panini gave away trade cards, which served to hold a place in the line for the cardholder, however, both Blake Griffin and Tyler Hansbrough signed many more autographs than just the 150 trade cards that were handed out on the floor.

BG Blake Griffin Fabric 125.00 300.00
HT Hasheem Thabeet Fabric 8.00 20.00
JH James Harden Fabric
OM O.J. Mayo Fabric 15.00 40.00
TH Tyler Hansbrough Fabric 30.00 80.00
BG09 Blake Griffin 40.00 100.00
BG0925 Blake Griffin/25 60.00 150.00
BG0950 Blake Griffin/50 40.00 100.00
TH09 Tyler Hansbrough 20.00 50.00
TH0925 Tyler Hansbrough/25 30.00 80.00
TH0950 Tyler Hansbrough/50 25.00 60.00
NNO Blake Griffin Trade 4.00 10.00
NNO Tyler Hansbrough Trade 2.00 5.00

2011 Panini National Convention VIP

COMPLETE SET (6) 6.00 15.00
*RED: 1.25X TO 3X BASE HI
RED PRINT RUN 25 SER.#'d SETS
UNPRICED BLUE PRINT RUN 10 SETS
UNPRICED GREEN PRINT RUN 5 SETS
VIP 5 AND 6 DO NOT HAVE PARALLELS
VIP1 Kobe Bryant 2.50 6.00
VIP2 Blake Griffin 1.50 4.00
VIP3 John Wall 2.00 5.00
VIP4 Kevin Durant 2.00 5.00
VIP5 Kyrie Irving 4.00 10.00
VIP6 Derrick Williams 1.50 4.00

2012 Panini National Convention

1-20 CRACKED ICE/25: 5X TO 12X BASE HI
21-40 CRACKED ICE/25: 1.5X TO 4X BASE HI
*HOLO 1-20: 1X TO 2.5X BASIC CARDS
*HOLO 21-40: .6X TO 1.5X BASIC CARDS
*1-20 HOLO LAVA: 2X TO 5X BASE HI
*21-40 HOLO LAVA: 1X TO 2.5X BASE HI
UNPRICED PLATE ANNCD PRINT RUN 5 SETS
6 Kobe Bryant 1.00 2.50
7 Blake Griffin .50 1.25
8 Kevin Durant .75 2.00
20 Bill Russell .60 1.50
35 Kyrie Irving/499 8.00 20.00
36 Derrick Williams/499 2.50 6.00
37 Anthony Davis/499 8.00 20.00
38 Michael Kidd-Gilchrist/499 4.00 10.00
39 Thomas Robinson/499 3.00 8.00
40 Harrison Barnes/499 2.50 6.00

2012 Panini National Convention Kings VIP

COMPLETE SET (6) 12.00 30.00
4 Kyrie Irving 4.00 10.00
5 Anthony Davis 4.00 10.00
6 Michael Kidd-Gilchrist 2.50 6.00

2013 Panini National Convention

1-24 CRACKED ICE/25: 4X TO 10X BASIC CARDS
25-47 CRACKED ICE/25: 2X TO 5X BASIC CARDS
*1-24 LAVA FLOW/99: 2.5X TO 6X BASIC CARDS
*25-47 LAVA FLOW/99: 1.2X TO 3X BASIC CARDS
7 Kobe Bryant
8 Dwayne Wade
9 Kevin Durant
10 Kyrie Irving
11 Anthony Davis
12 Blake Griffin
39 Anthony Bennett
45 Trey Burke
46 Nerlens Noel
47 Ben McLemore

2013 Panini National Convention Kings

CRACKED ICE/25: 2.5X TO 6X BASIC CARDS
*LAVA FLOW: 1.5X TO 4X BASIC CARDS
R5 Otto Porter

2013 Panini National Convention RC

CRACKED ICE/25: 2X TO 5X BASIC CARDS
*LAVA FLOW/99: 1.2X TO 3X BASIC CARDS
RC3 Anthony Bennett
RC5 Ben McLemore
RC6 Nerlens Noel

2013 Panini National Convention Team Colors

COMPLETE SET (10) 4.00 10.00
CRACKED ICE/25: 5X TO 12X BASIC CARDS
LAVA FLOW/99: 2.5X TO 6X BASIC CARDS
1 Scottie Pippen
2 Joakim Noah

2013 Panini National Convention VIP

COMPLETE SET (6) 3.00 8.00
5 Ben McLemore
6 Nerlens Noel

2014 Panini National Convention

*1-21 CRACKED ICE VETS/25: 4X TO 10X
*22-50 CRACKED ICE ROOKIE/25: 2X TO 5X
*THICK STOCK: .6X TO 1.5X BASIC CARDS
15 Kobe Bryant BK .80 2.00
16 Kevin Durant BK .60 1.50
17 Blake Griffin BK .50 1.25
18 Kyrie Irving BK .60 1.50
19 LeBron James BK 1.00 2.50
20 John Wall BK .40 1.00
21 Tim Duncan BK .50 1.25
33 Dante Exum BK .60 1.50
34 Andrew Wiggins BK .75 2.00
35 Jabari Parker BK .60 1.50
36 Doug McDermott BK .60 1.50
37 Julius Randle BK .60 1.50
38 Marcus Smart BK .60 1.50
39 Nik Stauskas BK .60 1.50
40 Joel Embiid BK .75 2.00

2014 Panini National Convention City of Cleveland

*THICK STOCK: .6X TO 1.5X BASIC CARDS
*CRACKED ICE/25: 3X TO 8X BASIC CARDS
8 Kyrie Irving BK
9 Dion Waiters BK
10 Anderson Varejao BK

2014 Panini National Convention Legends

*CRACKED ICE/25: 5X TO 12X BASIC CARDS
*THICK STOCK: .6X TO 1.5X BASIC CARDS
8 David Robinson BK
9 Dominique Wilkins BK
10 Julius Erving BK

2014 Panini National Convention VIP

PRIZM BLUE VETS/25: 2.5X TO 6X BASIC CARDS
PRIZM BLUE ROOKIES/25: 1.2X TO 3X
14 Marcus Smart BK
15 Nik Stauskas BK
21 Damian Lillard BK
22 Anthony Bennett BK
23 Otto Porter BK
24 Alex Len BK
32 Trey Burke BK
34 Michael Carter-Williams BK
35 Nerlens Noel BK
39 Victor Oladipo BK
47 Lebron James BK
48 Tim Duncan BK
49 Kawhi Leonard BK
50 Dwyane Wade BK
51 Derrick Rose BK
57 Kobe Bryant BK
58 Kevin Durant BK
59 Blake Griffin BK
60 Kyrie Irving BK
61 James Harden BK
62 Stephen Curry BK
68 Dirk Nowitzki BK
70 Ben McLemore BK
71 Kelly Olynyk BK
72 Paul George BK
73 LaMarcus Aldridge BK
74 Tony Parker BK
75 Manu Ginobili BK
92 Dante Exum BK
93 Andrew Wiggins BK
94 Joel Embiid BK
95 Jabari Parker BK
96 Doug McDermott BK
97 Julius Randle BK

2014 Panini National Convention VIP Rookies

COMPLETE SET (6) 6.00 15.00
5 Dante Exum BK 1.25 3.00
6 Andrew Wiggins BK 3.00 8.00

2015 Panini National Convention

7 Kevin Durant
8 John Wall
9A Stephen Curry
9B Stephen Curry
College photo
10 Kyrie Irving
11 LeBron James
12 Tim Duncan
13 Derrick Rose
14 Kobe Bryant
32A Jahlil Okafor
32B Jahlil Okafor
College photo
33 D'Angelo Russell
34 Trey Lyles
35 Willie Cauley-Stein
36A Karl-Anthony Towns
36B Karl-Anthony Towns
College photo
37 Stanley Johnson
38 Myles Turner
39 Devin Booker
40 Emmanuel Mudiay

2015 Panini National Convention College Legends

*CRACKED ICE/25: 5X TO 12X BASIC CARDS
*THICK STOCK: .6X TO 1.5X BASIC CARDS
13 Blake Griffin
14 Kevin Durant
15 Evan Turner

2015 Panini National Convention Manufactured Patch Autographs

AG Aaron Gordon BK
DM Doug McDermott BK
JP Jabari Parker BK
ZL Zach Lavine BK

2015 Panini National Convention Memorabilia

SJ Stanley Johnson
WC Willie Cauley-Stein

2015 Panini National Convention Team Colors

COMPLETE SET (10) 3.00 8.00
*CRACKED ICE/25: 4X TO 10X BASIC CARDS
BK1 Scottie Pippen
BK2 Joakim Noah
BK3 Jimmy Butler
BK4 Pau Gasol
BK5 Nikola Mirotic

2015 Panini National Convention Tools of the Trade Jerseys

*CRACKED ICE/25: 1X TO 2.5X BASIC JSY
10 Andrew Wiggins
11 Zach LaVine
12 Doug McDermott
13 Marcus Smart
14 Giannis Antetokounmpo
15 Julius Randle

2015 Panini National Convention VIP

COMPLETE SET (6) 3.00 8.00

*CRACKED ICE/25: 5X TO 12X BASIC CARDS
5 Jahlil Okafor BK
6 Karl-Anthony Towns BK

2012-13 Panini National Treasures

1-100 PRINT RUN 99 SER.#'d SETS
101-200 PRINT RUNS B/WN 25-199 PER
PRIME PATCHES MAY SELL FOR PREMIUM
EXCHANGE DEADLINE 01/31/2015
1 Kobe Bryant 12.00 30.00
2 Marc Gasol 3.00 8.00
3 Tony Parker 3.00 8.00
4 Joe Johnson 2.50 6.00
5 Josh Smith 2.50 6.00
6 Kevin Garnett 5.00 12.00
7 LaMarcus Aldridge 3.00 8.00
8 Ray Allen 3.00 8.00
9 Rajon Rondo 3.00 8.00
10 Raymond Felton 2.50 6.00
11 Luol Deng 2.50 6.00
12 Ben Gordon 2.50 6.00
13 Joakim Noah 2.50 6.00
14 LeBron James 20.00 50.00
15 Anderson Varejao 2.00 5.00
16 Jason Kidd 3.00 8.00
17 Dirk Nowitzki 4.00 10.00
18 Jason Terry 2.50 6.00
19 Carmelo Anthony 4.00 10.00
20 Nene 2.50 6.00
21 Tim Duncan 5.00 12.00
22 Monta Ellis 2.50 6.00
23 Goran Dragic 2.50 6.00
24 Kyle Lowry 2.50 6.00
25 Jameer Nelson 2.00 5.00
26 Nikola Pekovic 2.00 5.00
27 Roy Hibbert 2.50 6.00
28 Jarrett Jack 2.50 6.00
29 Chris Kaman 2.50 6.00
30 Greivis Vasquez 2.50 6.00
31 Pau Gasol 3.00 8.00
32 Mike Conley 2.50 6.00
33 Rudy Gay 3.00 8.00
34 Paul Pierce 3.00 8.00
35 Kevin Durant 20.00 50.00
36 Andrew Bogut 2.50 6.00
37 Ramon Sessions 2.50 6.00
38 Al Jefferson 2.50 6.00
39 Kevin Love 3.00 8.00
40 Ryan Anderson 2.50 6.00
41 Brook Lopez 2.50 6.00
42 Tyson Chandler 2.50 6.00
43 Chris Paul 4.00 10.00
44 Danilo Gallinari 2.00 5.00
45 J.R. Smith 2.50 6.00
46 David Lee 2.00 5.00
47 Dwyane Wade 5.00 12.00
48 Russell Westbrook 8.00 20.00
49 Marcin Gortat 2.50 6.00
50 Dwight Howard 2.50 6.00
51 Andre Iguodala 2.50 6.00
52 Louis Williams 2.50 6.00
53 Grant Hill 4.00 10.00
54 Steve Nash 3.00 8.00
55 Jason Richardson 3.00 8.00
56 Amar'e Stoudemire 2.50 6.00
57 Mario Chalmers 2.50 6.00
58 Nicolas Batum 2.50 6.00
59 Zach Randolph 2.50 6.00
60 Kevin Martin 2.50 6.00
61 Rodney Stuckey 2.50 6.00
62 Manu Ginobili 3.00 8.00
63 Derrick Rose 4.00 10.00
64 Andrea Bargnani 2.50 6.00
65 Chris Bosh 3.00 8.00
66 Jose Calderon 2.00 5.00
67 Kris Humphries 2.00 5.00
68 Shawn Marion 2.50 6.00
69 Carlos Boozer 2.50 6.00
70 Paul Millsap 3.00 8.00
71 Deron Williams 2.50 6.00
72 Caron Butler 2.50 6.00
73 Antawn Jamison 2.50 6.00
74 JaVale McGee 2.50 6.00
75 Nick Young 2.50 6.00
76 Blake Griffin 3.00 8.00
77 Ricky Rubio 3.00 8.00
78 Jrue Holiday 3.00 8.00
79 Ty Lawson 2.00 5.00
80 Jeff Teague 2.50 6.00
81 Darren Collison 2.50 6.00
82 James Harden 5.00 12.00
83 Tyreke Evans 2.00 5.00
84 Jeremy Lin 3.00 8.00
85 Stephen Curry 12.00 30.00
86 DeMar DeRozan 3.00 8.00
87 Brandon Jennings 2.00 5.00
88 Gerald Henderson 2.00 5.00
89 Serge Ibaka 2.50 6.00
90 Wesley Matthews 2.00 5.00
91 John Wall 4.00 10.00
92 Evan Turner 2.00 5.00
93 DeMarcus Cousins 3.00 8.00
94 Greg Monroe 2.50 6.00
95 Gordon Hayward 3.00 8.00
96 Paul George 4.00 10.00
97 Jordan Crawford 2.00 5.00
98 Marcus Thornton 2.00 5.00
99 Danny Granger 2.50 6.00
100 Damian Lillard RC 60.00 150.00
101 K.Irving JSY AU/199 RC 1200.00 2000.00
102 D.Will JSY AU/199 RC 15.00 40.00
103 Enes Kanter JSY AU/99 RC 50.00 120.00
104 T.Thompson JSY AU/199 RC 30.00 80.00
105 Jan Vesely JSY AU/99 RC 6.00 15.00
106 B.Biyombo JSY AU/199 RC 25.00 60.00
107 B.Knight JSY AU/199 RC 40.00 100.00
108 K.Walker JSY AU/199 RC 125.00 300.00
109 J.Fredette JSY AU/199 RC 20.00 50.00
110 Thomp JSY AU/199 RC 800.00 1200.00
111 Alec Burks JSY AU/99 RC 30.00 80.00
112 Mkieff Morris JSY AU/99 RC 30.00 80.00
113 Mrcus Morris JSY AU/99 RC 30.00 80.00
114 K.Leonard JSY AU/199 RC 2500.00 3500.00
115 N.Vucevic JSY AU/199 RC 50.00 120.00
116 I.Shumpert JSY AU/199 RC 25.00 60.00
117 Chris Singleton JSY AU/99 RC 6.00 15.00
118 T.Harris JSY AU/199 RC 30.00 80.00
119 Nolan Smith JSY AU/99 RC 6.00 15.00
120 K.Faried JSY AU/199 RC 30.00 80.00
121 R.Jackson JSY AU/99 RC 60.00 150.00
122 MarShon Brooks JSY AU/199 RC 8.00 20.00
123 Jordan Hamilton JSY AU/99 RC 6.00 15.00
124 Lavoy Allen JSY AU/99 RC 6.00 15.00
125 N.Cole JSY AU/199 RC 15.00 40.00
126 Cory Joseph JSY AU/99 RC 30.00 80.00
127 J.Butler JSY AU/199 RC 400.00 800.00
128 Ivan Johnson JSY AU/99 RC EXCH 6.00 15.00
129 C.Parsons JSY AU/199 RC 60.00 120.00
130 J.Valanci JSY AU/199 RC 40.00 100.00
131 Gustavo Ayon JSY AU/99 RC 12.00 30.00
132 I.Thomas JSY AU/199 RC 400.00 800.00
133 Chris Copeland JSY AU/99 RC 6.00 15.00
134 Charles Jenkins AU/99 RC 4.00 10.00
135 DeQuan Jones AU/99 RC 4.00 10.00
136 D.Motiejunas AU/99 RC EXCH 10.00 25.00
137 Julyan Stone AU/99 RC 4.00 10.00
138 Malcolm Lee AU/99 RC EXCH 4.00 10.00
139 Jon Leuer AU/99 RC 5.00 12.00
140 E'Twaun Moore AU/99 RC 4.00 10.00
141 Darius Morris AU/99 RC 4.00 10.00
142 Viacheslav Kravtsov AU/99 RC 4.00 10.00
143 Victor Claver AU/99 RC 4.00 10.00
144 Kyle O'Quinn AU/99 RC 4.00 10.00
145 Maurice Harkless AU/99 RC 20.00 50.00
146 Brian Roberts AU/99 RC 4.00 10.00
147 M.Teletovic AU/99 RC EXCH 12.00 30.00
148 Greg Stiemsma AU/99 RC 4.00 10.00
149 DeAndre Liggins AU/99 RC 5.00 12.00
150 Kent Bazemore AU/99 RC 10.00 25.00
151 A.Davis JSY AU/199 RC 1200.00 2000.00
152 Kidd-Gilch JSY AU/199 RC 30.00 80.00
153 B.Beal JSY AU/199 RC 400.00 800.00
154 D.Waiters JSY AU/199 RC 60.00 150.00
155 T.Robinson JSY AU/199 RC 8.00 20.00
156 D.Green JSY AU/99 RC 800.00 1200.00
157 H.Barnes JSY AU/199 RC 125.00 300.00
158 T.Ross JSY AU/99 RC 75.00 150.00
159 Drmmnd JSY AU/199 RC 125.00 300.00
160 Austin Rivers JSY AU/199 RC 30.00 80.00
161 M.Leonard JSY AU/99 RC 15.00 40.00
162 Jeremy Lamb JSY AU/99 RC 10.00 25.00
163 K.Marshall JSY AU/99 RC 12.00 30.00
164 J.Henson JSY AU/199 RC 20.00 50.00
165 Kyle Singler JSY AU/99 RC 6.00 15.00
166 Jae Crowder JSY AU/99 RC 40.00 100.00
167 Tyler Zeller JSY AU/99 RC 15.00 40.00
168 T.Jones JSY AU/99 RC 40.00 100.00
169 A.Nicholson JSY AU/99 RC 12.00 30.00
170 E.Frnr JSY AU/99 RC 60.00 150.00
171 J.Sullinger JSY AU/199 RC 20.00 50.00
172 Fab Melo JSY AU/99 RC 6.00 15.00
173 John Jenkins JSY AU/99 RC 15.00 40.00
174 Jared Cunningham JSY AU/99 RC 6.00 15.00
175 Tony Wroten JSY AU/99 RC 8.00 20.00
176 Miles Plumlee JSY AU/99 RC 12.00 30.00
177 Arnett Moultrie JSY AU/99 RC 6.00 15.00
178 Perry Jones JSY AU/99 RC 6.00 15.00
179 M.Teague JSY AU/99 RC 6.00 15.00
180 Festus Ezeli JSY AU/99 RC 30.00 80.00
181 A.Shved JSY AU/25 RC 40.00 100.00
182 Quincy Acy JSY AU/99 RC 6.00 15.00
183 Doron Lamb JSY AU/99 RC 6.00 15.00
184 Jeff Taylor AU/99 RC 4.00 10.00
185 Royce White AU/99 RC EXCH 4.00 10.00
186 Draymond Green AU/99 RC 150.00 300.00
187 Orlando Johnson AU/99 RC 4.00 10.00
188 Quincy Miller AU/99 RC 4.00 10.00
189 Khris Middleton AU/99 RC 30.00 80.00
190 Will Barton AU/99 RC 8.00 20.00
191 Tyshawn Taylor AU/99 RC 4.00 10.00
192 Mike Scott AU/99 RC 15.00 40.00
193 Kim English AU/99 RC 4.00 10.00
194 Darius Miller AU/99 RC 4.00 10.00
195 Kevin Murphy AU/99 RC 4.00 10.00
196 Nando De Colo AU/99 RC 4.00 10.00
197 Tornike Shengelia AU/99 RC 4.00 10.00
198 Bernard James AU/99 RC 4.00 10.00
199 Robert Sacre AU/99 RC 4.00 10.00
200 Lance Thomas AU/99 RC 4.00 10.00
201 Damian Lillard JSY AU/99 350.00 700.00

2012-13 Panini National Treasures Silver

*SILVER: .75X TO 2X BASIC
STATED PRINT RUN 25 SER.#'d SETS

2012-13 Panini National Treasures 11 vs. 12 Signatures

PRINT RUNS B/WN 49-99 COPIES PER
EXCHANGE DEADLINE 01/31/2015
1 K.Irving/A.Davis/49 150.00 300.00
2 Williams/Kidd-Gilchrist/49 8.00 20.00
3 B.Beal/I.Shumpert/49 10.00 25.00
4 Thompson/Waiters/99 8.00 20.00
5 Robinson/Faried/49 8.00 20.00
6 M.Leonard/J.Vesely/99 5.00 12.00
7 B.Biyombo/H.Barnes/49 8.00 20.00
8 B.Knight/T.Ross/99 6.00 15.00
9 Walker/Drummond/49 15.00 40.00
10 J.Fredette/A.Rivers/99 8.00 20.00
11 Thompson/Leonard/99 8.00 20.00
12 A.Burks/C.Copeland/99 5.00 12.00
13 M.Morris/K.Marshall/99 6.00 15.00
14 M.Morris/J.Henson/99 5.00 12.00
15 K.Irving/A.Rivers/49 30.00 80.00
16 E.Kanter/A.Davis/49 30.00 80.00
17 C.Parsons/B.Beal/49 12.00 30.00
18 M.Morris/T.Robinson/49 6.00 15.00
19 B.Knight/A.Davis/49 40.00 100.00
20 K.Walker/J.Lamb/99 10.00 25.00
21 N.Smith/A.Rivers/99 8.00 20.00
22 Kanter/Kidd-Gilchrist/49 5.00 12.00
23 T.Robinson/C.Parsons/49 5.00 12.00
24 Thompson/Barnes/99 12.00 30.00
25 Leonard/Harkless/99 20.00 50.00
26 K.Faried/T.Zeller/49 8.00 20.00
27 T.Harris/J.Sullinger/99 5.00 12.00
28 M.Teague/N.Cole/99 6.00 15.00
29 M.Brooks/J.Jenkins/99 5.00 12.00
30 Q.Acy/N.Vucevic/99 8.00 20.00
31 K.Faried/J.Crowder/49 8.00 20.00
32 C.Parsons/H.Barnes/99 10.00 25.00
33 C.Singleton/B.James/99 5.00 12.00
34 C.Parsons/A.Davis/49 25.00 60.00
35 N.Smith/T.Zeller/99 5.00 12.00
36 D.Green/K.Walker/99 8.00 20.00
37 I.Thomas/T.Ross/99 12.00 30.00
38 M.Morris/R.White/99 5.00 12.00
39 Robinson/Valanciunas/49 8.00 20.00
40 Bazemore/Fredette/49 6.00 15.00
41 E.Kanter/T.Jones/49 6.00 15.00
42 Sullinger/Thompson/49 8.00 20.00
43 A.Shved/E.Moore/49 5.00 12.00
44 Thompson/Ross/49 10.00 25.00
45 D.Williams/A.Shved/49 5.00 12.00
46 A.Burks/T.Ross/99 5.00 12.00
47 N.Smith/M.Plumlee/99 5.00 12.00
48 F.Melo/N.Vucevic/99 6.00 15.00
49 Jackson/Teague/99 6.00 15.00
50 M.Leonard/E.Kanter/99 5.00 12.00
51 B.Knight/D.Lamb/49 6.00 15.00
52 Biyombo/Drummond/49 12.00 30.00
53 Hamilton/Harkless/99 5.00 12.00
54 M.Morris/A.Nicholson/99 5.00 12.00
55 M.Teague/K.Walker/49 10.00 25.00
56 M.Brooks/B.Beal/49 10.00 25.00
57 K.Irving/B.Beal/49 40.00 100.00
58 Knight/Kidd-Gilchrist/49 8.00 20.00
59 Leonard/Sullinger/49 20.00 50.00
60 K.Faried/A.Moultrie/49 8.00 20.00
61 Shumpert/Marshall/49 6.00 15.00
62 Fredette/Robinson/49 6.00 15.00
63 Davis/Thompson/49 40.00 100.00
64 T.Harris/A.Shved/49 8.00 20.00
65 K.Irving/D.Waiters/49 30.00 80.00
66 Drummond/Valanciunas/49 12.00 30.00
67 R.Jackson/K.Marshall/99 5.00 12.00
68 N.Smith/C.Copeland/99 5.00 12.00
69 K.English/B.Knight/49 6.00 15.00
70 L.Allen/Q.Acy/99 5.00 12.00
71 D.Green/J.Fredette/99 10.00 25.00
72 A.Burks/E.Fournier/99 6.00 15.00
73 F.Ezeli/J.Valanciunas/99 5.00 12.00
74 C.Singleton/T.Jones/99 5.00 12.00
75 J.Vesely/J.Henson/99 5.00 12.00
76 M.Brooks/J.Cunningham/99 5.00 12.00
77 B.James/K.Singler/99 5.00 12.00
78 Williams/Robinson/49 6.00 15.00
79 Kidd-Gilchrist/Thompson/49 8.00 20.00
80 Fredette/Fournier/99 6.00 15.00
81 J.Vesely/H.Barnes/49 10.00 25.00
82 Thompson/Bazemore/49 12.00 30.00
83 M.Plumlee/L.Allen/99 5.00 12.00
84 Barton/Jackson/99 8.00 20.00
85 K.Leonard/J.Taylor/49 12.00 30.00
86 I.Thomas/D.Lamb/99 10.00 25.00
87 T.Harris/F.Ezeli/49 6.00 15.00
88 G.Ayon/A.Nicholson/99 5.00 12.00
89 B.Beal/B.Knight/49 10.00 25.00
90 K.Marshall/A.Burks/99 5.00 12.00
91 N.Smith/J.Cunningham/99 5.00 12.00
92 I.Johnson/R.White/99 5.00 12.00
93 T.Shengelia/J.Valanciunas/99 5.00 12.00
94 E.Moore/K.English/99 5.00 12.00
95 J.Hamilton/J.Cunningham/99 5.00 12.00
96 Thompson/Waiters/49 15.00 40.00
97 F.Melo/B.Biyombo/99 5.00 12.00
98 M.Scott/T.Harris/99 6.00 15.00
99 Johnson/Shumpert/49 5.00 12.00
100 K.Faried/D.Green/49 12.00 30.00

2012-13 Panini National Treasures 11 vs. 12 Signatures Gold

*GOLD: .5X TO 1.2X BASE/99
*GOLD: .4X TO 1X BASE/49
STATED PRINT RUN 25 SER.#'d SETS
EXCHANGE DEADLINE 01/31/2015
1 K.Irving/A.Davis 200.00 400.00

2012-13 Panini National Treasures 11 vs. 12 Signatures Silver

*SILVER 49: .5X TO 1.2X BASIC/99
*SILVER 49: .4X TO 1X BASIC/49
*SILVER 25: .6X TO 1.5X BASIC/99
*SILVER 25: .5X TO 1.2X BASIC/49
PRINT RUNS B/WN 25-49 COPIES PER
EXCHANGE DEADLINE 01/31/2015

2012-13 Panini National Treasures ABA Legends Signatures

PRINT RUNS B/WN 25-99 COPIES PER
EXCHANGE DEADLINE 1/31/2015
1 Julius Erving/25 75.00 150.00
2 Louie Dampier/99 EXCH 30.00 60.00
3 Dan Issel/99 6.00 15.00
4 Mel Daniels/75 15.00 40.00
5 George Gervin/75 15.00 40.00
6 Ron Boone/75 EXCH 12.00 30.00
7 Freddie Lewis/75 EXCH 6.00 15.00
8 Rick Barry/75 10.00 25.00
9 George Karl/75 6.00 15.00
10 Jimmy Jones/75 6.00 15.00

2012-13 Panini National Treasures Champions Signatures

ODDS B/WN 25-49 COPIES PER
EXCHANGE DEADLINE 01/31/2015
1 Walt Frazier/49 8.00 20.00
2 Magic Johnson/49 EXCH 75.00 150.00
3 Larry Bird/49 60.00 120.00
4 Julius Erving/25 100.00 200.00
5 Clyde Drexler/25 40.00 80.00
6 John Havlicek/25 40.00 80.00
7 Shaquille O'Neal/25 250.00 400.00
8 Chris Bosh/49 12.00 30.00
9 Mark Aguirre/49 8.00 20.00
10 Rick Barry/49 8.00 20.00
11 Toni Kukoc/49 12.00 30.00
12 Bill Walton/49 8.00 20.00
13 Bob McAdoo/49 12.00 30.00
14 Gail Goodrich/49 5.00 12.00
15 Peja Stojakovic/25 EXCH 30.00 60.00
16 Kobe Bryant/49 125.00 250.00
17 Willis Reed/49 12.00 30.00
18 Paul Westphal/49 EXCH 10.00 25.00
19 Hakeem Olajuwon/49 20.00 50.00
20 Nate Archibald/49 8.00 20.00
21 Bill Russell/25 60.00 120.00
22 Kenny Smith/49 8.00 20.00
23 Glen Rice/49 12.00 30.00
24 Jason Kidd/25 60.00 120.00
25 Jerry West/49 75.00 150.00

2012-13 Panini National Treasures Champions Signatures Combos

ODDS B/WN 15-25 COPIES PER
NO PRICING ON QTY 15
EXCHANGE DEADLINE 01/31/2015
1 J.Kidd/D.Nowitzki/25 125.00 250.00
3 J.Erving/M.Cheeks/25 40.00 100.00
4 S.Pippen/P.Jackson/25 600.00 900.00
5 I.Thomas/J.Dumars/25 30.00 80.00
6 T.Parker/D.Robinson/25 40.00 100.00
7 J.Erving/M.Johnson/25 100.00 200.00
8 B.Laimbeer/D.Rodman/25 20.00 50.00
9 B.Pettit/T.Heinsohn/25 20.00 50.00
10 G.Payton/A.Mourning/25 50.00 120.00
11 M.Cooper/B.Scott/25 20.00 50.00
12 D.Nowitzki/L.Bird/25 200.00 300.00
13 Robert Horry/Mario Elie 15.00 40.00
14 Andrew Bynum/Metta World Peace 15.00 40.00
15 R.Hamilton/C.Billups/25 20.00 50.00
16 Cedric Maxwell/Wes Unseld 15.00 40.00
17 P.Westphal/D.Cowens/25 20.00 50.00
18 Robert Parish/Nate Archibald 15.00 40.00
19 B.Armstrong/B.Cartwright/25 30.00 60.00

2012-13 Panini National Treasures Colossal Materials

PRINT RUNS B/WN 25-99 COPIES PER
1 Carmelo Anthony/99 6.00 15.00
2 Carlos Boozer/99 4.00 10.00
3 Rajon Rondo/49 5.00 12.00
4 Serge Ibaka/99 4.00 10.00
5 LeBron James/99 15.00 40.00
6 Ty Lawson/99 3.00 8.00
7 Tony Parker/99 5.00 12.00
8 Dwyane Wade/49 8.00 20.00
9 Kevin Johnson/49 5.00 12.00
10 DeMarcus Cousins/99 5.00 12.00
11 Russell Westbrook/99 6.00 15.00
12 Joakim Noah/49 4.00 10.00
13 Kevin Garnett/49 6.00 15.00
14 Moses Malone/49 5.00 12.00
15 Ricky Rubio/25 5.00 12.00
16 Deron Williams/99 4.00 10.00
17 Michael Cooper/49 4.00 10.00
18 Larry Johnson/49 6.00 15.00
19 John Starks/99 4.00 10.00
20 Chris Webber/49 12.00 30.00

2012-13 Panini National Treasures Colossal Materials Jersey Number Signatures

PRINT RUNS B/WN 10-49 COPIES PER
NO PRICING ON QTY 10
EXCHANGE DEADLINE 1/31/2015
1 Kevin Durant/25 125.00 250.00
2 Kobe Bryant/25 200.00 400.00
3 Blake Griffin/25 60.00 120.00
4 Vince Carter/25 12.00 30.00
5 D.J. Augustin/49 5.00 12.00
6 Kevin Love/49 20.00 50.00
7 Andre Iguodala/49 8.00 20.00
8 Larry Bird/25 60.00 120.00
9 Kevin Martin/49 8.00 20.00
10 Stephen Curry/49 75.00 200.00
11 Jordan Crawford/49 8.00 20.00
12 LaMarcus Aldridge/25 10.00 25.00
13 Tyreke Evans/25 8.00 20.00
14 James Harden/25 30.00 80.00
15 Hakeem Olajuwon/25 30.00 60.00
16 Grant Hill/25 40.00 80.00
18 Al Jefferson/25 10.00 25.00
19 Dikembe Mutombo/25 20.00 50.00
20 Zach Randolph/25 10.00 25.00

2012-13 Panini National Treasures Colossal Materials Jersey Number Signatures Prime

*PRIME: .6X TO 1.5X BASIC
PRINT RUNS B/WN 5-25 COPIES PER
NO PRICING ON QTY 15 OR LESS
EXCHANGE DEADLINE 1/31/2015

2012-13 Panini National Treasures Colossal Materials Jersey Numbers

PRINT RUNS B/WN 49-99 COPIES PER
1 Paul Pierce/49 5.00 12.00
2 Dirk Nowitzki/49 6.00 15.00
3 Rudy Gay/99 5.00 12.00
4 Dennis Rodman/49 15.00 40.00
5 Kobe Bryant/49 20.00 50.00
6 Marcus Thornton/99 3.00 8.00
7 Bill Cartwright/49 4.00 10.00
8 Patrick Ewing/99 6.00 15.00
9 Thaddeus Young/99 3.00 8.00
10 David Lee/99 3.00 8.00
11 Greg Monroe/99 4.00 10.00
12 Karl Malone/49 6.00 15.00
13 Tim Duncan/99 8.00 20.00
14 Jason Terry/99 4.00 10.00
15 Jordan Crawford/49 3.00 8.00
16 Pau Gasol/99 5.00 12.00
17 Artis Gilmore/49 4.00 10.00
18 Steve Nash/99 5.00 12.00
19 Nicolas Batum/49 4.00 10.00
20 Manu Ginobili/99 5.00 12.00

2012-13 Panini National Treasures Colossal Materials Jersey Numbers Prime

*PRIME: .5X TO 1.2X BASIC
PRINT RUNS B/WN 10-25 COPIES PER
NO PRICING ON QTY 15 OR LESS
5 Kobe Bryant/25 60.00 150.00
8 Patrick Ewing/25 20.00 50.00
18 Steve Nash/25 30.00 60.00
19 Nicolas Batum/25 40.00 80.00
20 Manu Ginobili/25 12.00 30.00

2012-13 Panini National Treasures Colossal Materials Prime

*PRIME 25: 1.2X TO 3X BASIC
PRINT RUNS B/WN 10-25 COPIES PER
NO RUBIO PRICING AVAILABLE
5 LeBron James 150.00 250.00
9 Kevin Johnson 40.00 80.00
19 John Starks 20.00 50.00

2012-13 Panini National Treasures Colossal Materials Prime Signatures

*PRIME: 1.2X TO 3X BASIC
PRINT RUNS B/WN 5-25 COPIES PER
NO PRICING ON QTY 10 OR LESS
EXCHANGE DEADLINE 01/31/2015

2012-13 Panini National Treasures Colossal Materials Signatures

ODDS B/WN 10-49 COPIES PER
NO PRICING ON QTY 10 OR LESS
EXCHANGE DEADLINE 01/31/2015
1 Marcin Gortat/49 8.00 20.00
2 Deron Williams/25 15.00 40.00
3 Serge Ibaka/49 12.00 30.00
4 LaMarcus Aldridge/25 12.00 30.00
5 Steve Nash/25 25.00 60.00
6 Alonzo Mourning/25 30.00 80.00
7 Jeff Teague/49 6.00 15.00
8 Luol Deng /49 6.00 15.00
9 Brook Lopez/25 6.00 15.00
10 Mike Conley/49 6.00 15.00
11 Danilo Gallinari/25 10.00 25.00
12 Greg Monroe/49 6.00 15.00
13 Anderson Varejao/49 6.00 15.00
14 Tyreke Evans/25 6.00 15.00
15 Wesley Matthews/49 6.00 15.00
16 Chris Bosh/25 15.00 40.00
18 Jrue Holiday/25 10.00 25.00
20 Dwight Howard/25 30.00 80.00

2012-13 Panini National Treasures Gold Proof Autographs

PRINT RUNS B/WN 10-54 COPIES PER
NO PRICING ON QTY 20 OR LESS
EXCHANGE DEADLINE 1/31/2015
2 Grant Hill/53 EXCH 20.00 50.00
5 Jason Kidd/54 15.00 40.00
9 Kevin Durant/49 EXCH 150.00 250.00
10 Dwyane Wade/49 60.00 150.00
11 Walt Frazier/46 EXCH 8.00 20.00
17 Kevin Durant/49 EXCH 150.00 250.00
19 Mark Aguirre/47 6.00 15.00
25 Blake Griffin/49 EXCH 30.00 80.00

2012-13 Panini National Treasures Jersey Number Autographs

PRINT RUNS B/WN 10-25 COPIES PER
NO PRICING ON QTY 10
EXCHANGE DEADLINE 1/31/2015
101 Kyrie Irving/25 1000.00 2000.00
102 Derrick Williams/25 12.00 30.00
103 Enes Kanter/25 100.00 200.00
104 Tristan Thompson/25 100.00 200.00
105 Jan Vesely/25 12.00 30.00
106 Bismack Biyombo/25 20.00 50.00
107 Brandon Knight/25 100.00 200.00
108 Kemba Walker/25 200.00 400.00
109 Jimmer Fredette/25 30.00 80.00
110 Klay Thompson/25
111 Alec Burks/25 50.00 120.00
112 Markieff Morris/25 50.00 120.00
113 Marcus Morris/25 50.00 120.00
114 Kawhi Leonard/25 2000.00 3000.00
115 Nikola Vucevic/25 150.00 300.00
116 Iman Shumpert/25 30.00 80.00
117 Chris Singleton/25 12.00 30.00
118 Tobias Harris/25 100.00 200.00
119 Nolan Smith/25 40.00 100.00
120 Kenneth Faried/25 50.00 120.00
121 Reggie Jackson/25 500.00 700.00
122 MarShon Brooks/25 75.00 150.00
123 Jordan Hamilton/25 12.00 30.00
124 Lavoy Allen/25 12.00 30.00
125 Norris Cole/25 15.00 40.00
126 Cory Joseph/25 20.00 50.00
127 Jimmy Butler/25 600.00 900.00
128 Ivan Johnson/25 12.00 30.00
129 Chandler Parsons/25 150.00 300.00
130 Jonas Valanciunas/25 100.00 200.00
132 Isaiah Thomas/25 700.00 1200.00
151 Anthony Davis/25 1200.00 2000.00
152 Michael Kidd-Gilchrist/25 125.00 250.00
153 Bradley Beal/25 500.00 800.00
154 Dion Waiters/25 250.00 400.00
155 Thomas Robinson/25 40.00 100.00
156 Draymond Green/25 700.00 1000.00
157 Harrison Barnes/25 500.00 800.00
158 Terrence Ross/25 125.00 250.00
159 Andre Drummond/25 700.00 900.00
160 Austin Rivers/25 75.00 200.00
161 Meyers Leonard/25 20.00 50.00
162 Jeremy Lamb/25 75.00 150.00
163 Kendall Marshall/25 60.00 150.00
164 John Henson/25 50.00 100.00
165 Kyle Singler/25 15.00 40.00
166 Jae Crowder/25 75.00 150.00
167 Tyler Zeller/25 40.00 100.00
168 Terrence Jones/25 50.00 120.00
169 Andrew Nicholson/25 20.00 50.00
170 Evan Fournier/25 60.00 150.00
171 Jared Sullinger/25 125.00 250.00
172 Fab Melo/25 12.00 30.00
173 John Jenkins/25 30.00 80.00
174 Jared Cunningham/25 12.00 30.00
175 Tony Wroten/25 60.00 150.00
176 Miles Plumlee/25 20.00 50.00
177 Arnett Moultrie/25 12.00 30.00
178 Perry Jones/25 60.00 120.00
179 Marquis Teague/25 20.00 50.00
180 Festus Ezeli/25 30.00 80.00
182 Quincy Acy/25 30.00 80.00
183 Doron Lamb/25 12.00 30.00
201 Damian Lilllard/25 1500.00 2000.00

2012-13 Panini National Treasures Matchups Materials

PRINT RUNS B/WN 25-99 COPIES PER
1 K.Bryant/K.Durant/49 12.00 30.00
2 D.Nowitzki/K.Love/49 6.00 15.00
3 P.Gasol/M.Gasol/99 5.00 12.00
4 D.Rose/J.Wall/49 6.00 15.00
5 R.Rondo/C.Paul/49 6.00 15.00
6 R.Westbrook/R.Rondo/49 12.00 30.00
7 A.Bargnani/B.Lopez/99 4.00 10.00
8 D.Cousins/D.Jordan/49 5.00 12.00
9 S.Ibaka/E.Okafor/49 4.00 10.00
10 R.Felton/M.Conley/99 4.00 10.00
11 J.Holiday/B.Jennings/99 5.00 12.00
12 D.Howard/T.Duncan/99 6.00 15.00
13 L.Deng /A.Iguodala/99 4.00 10.00
14 B.Griffin/J.Smith/49 6.00 15.00
15 S.Nash/J.Kidd/49 5.00 12.00
16 T.Chandler/J.Noah/49 4.00 10.00
17 G.Monroe/R.Hibbert/99 4.00 10.00
18 K.Garnett/D.Nowitzki/49 8.00 20.00
19 R.Westbrook/D.Rose/49 12.00 30.00
20 K.Bryant/D.Wade/99 12.00 30.00
21 K.Durant/L.James/49 15.00 40.00
22 P.Pierce/M.Ginobili/99 5.00 12.00
23 C.Paul/D.Rose/49 10.00 25.00
24 T.Duncan/K.Garnett/49 8.00 20.00
25 B.Griffin/K.Love/49 8.00 20.00
26 T.Parker/R.Rubio/49 5.00 12.00
27 D.Williams/S.Nash/49 5.00 12.00
28 K.Durant/C.Anthony/49 10.00 25.00
29 A.Stoudemire/C.Bosh/99 5.00 12.00
30 K.Bryant/L.James/49 25.00 60.00
31 T.Evans/J.Wall/99 6.00 15.00
32 R.Rubio/S.Nash/49 5.00 12.00
33 D.Williams/D.Wade/49 6.00 15.00
34 C.Boozer/D.West/99 4.00 10.00
35 J.Noah/A.Horford/99 4.00 10.00
36 B.Jennings/J.Johnson/99 4.00 10.00
37 J.Anthony/T.Hansbrough/99 4.00 10.00
38 R.Gay/D.Granger/99 5.00 12.00
39 D.Lee/L.Aldridge/49 5.00 12.00
40 K.Martin/D.DeRozan/99 5.00 12.00
41 R.Allen/J.Harden/49 6.00 15.00
42 V.Carter/D.DeRozan/99 6.00 15.00
43 A.Jefferson/M.Gasol/99 5.00 12.00
44 Z.Randolph/L.Aldridge/49 5.00 12.00
45 P.Pierce/K.Bryant/99 12.00 30.00
46 S.Marion/T.Prince/99 4.00 10.00
47 E.Brand/C.Boozer/99 5.00 12.00
48 D.DeRozan/Mayo/99 5.00 12.00
49 R.Felton/T.Lawson/99 4.00 10.00
50 G.Hayward/T.Booker/99 5.00 12.00
51 P.Pierce/L.James/99 12.00 30.00
52 G.Dragic/B.Udrih/99 4.00 10.00
53 T.Duncan/D.Nowitzki/99 8.00 20.00
54 A.Varejao/C.Andersen/99 4.00 10.00
55 K.Durant/D.Gallinari/49 6.00 15.00
56 J.Erving/D.Wilkins/49 8.00 20.00
57 E.Gordon/D.DeRozan/99 5.00 12.00
58 K.Garnett/P.Gasol/49 6.00 15.00
59 D.Gallinari/A.Bargnani/99 4.00 10.00
60 K.Martin/R.Allen/49 5.00 12.00
61 D.Jordan/C.Frye/99 5.00 12.00
62 J.Holiday/J.Teague/99 5.00 12.00
63 C.Andersen/J.Noah/99 4.00 10.00
64 B.Griffin/D.Cousins/49 6.00 15.00
65 L.Deng /C.Anthony/49 6.00 15.00
66 A.Jamison/V.Carter/49 6.00 15.00
67 M.Williams/T.Hansbrough/99 4.00 10.00
68 S.Battier/Redick/99 5.00 12.00
69 R.Rondo/J.Wall/49 6.00 15.00
70 J.Terry/M.Ginobili/49 5.00 12.00
71 T.Evans/D.Rose/49 12.00 30.00
72 M.Thornton/W.Matthews/25 3.00 8.00
73 G.Hayward/C.Landry/99 5.00 12.00
74 D.Nowitzki/P.Gasol/49 6.00 15.00
75 A.Iguodala/R.Gay/49 5.00 12.00
76 L.Aldridge/C.Bosh/49 5.00 12.00
77 D.Granger/J.Johnson/99 4.00 10.00
78 D.Cousins/D.Favors/49 5.00 12.00
79 R.Anderson/C.Frye/75 4.00 10.00
80 A.Jamison/D.Wright/99 4.00 10.00
81 J.Calderon/R.Rubio/99 6.00 15.00
82 H.Turkoglu/T.Ariza/99 4.00 10.00
83 S.Curry/T.Evans/49 10.00 25.00
84 B.Lopez/R.Lopez/99 4.00 10.00
85 Barea/J.Calderon/99 4.00 10.00
86 M.Peace/P.Pierce/99 5.00 12.00
87 C.Anthony/L.James/49 15.00 40.00
88 A.Stoudemire/D.Howard/49 4.00 10.00
89 B.Lopez/R.Hibbert/49 4.00 10.00
90 D.Howard/K.Garnett/49 6.00 15.00
91 T.Lawson/M.Conley/99 4.00 10.00
92 J.Kidd/G.Hill/49 10.00 25.00
93 M.Malone/H.Olajuwon/25 6.00 15.00
94 Y.Ming/S.Bradley/49 10.00 25.00
95 S.O'Neal /T.Duncan/49 10.00 25.00
96 S.O'Neal /Y.Ming/25 10.00 25.00
97 D.Rodman/K.Malone/25 15.00 40.00
98 D.Robinson/P.Ewing/49 10.00 25.00
99 H.Olajuwon/S.O'Neal /25 10.00 25.00
100 P.Ewing/A.Mourning/49 10.00 25.00

2012-13 Panini National Treasures Matchups Materials Prime

*PRIME: .75X TO 2X BASIC
PRINT RUNS B/WN 5-25 COPIES PER
NO PRICING ON QTY 10 OR LESS
51 P.Pierce/L.James/25 30.00 80.00

2012-13 Panini National Treasures Material Treasures

PRINT RUNS B/WN 10-99 COPIES PER
NO CRAWFORD PRICING AVAILABLE
1 Kobe Bryant/49 20.00 50.00
2 Kyrie Irving/99 12.00 30.00
3 Pau Gasol/49 5.00 12.00
4 Blake Griffin/49 5.00 12.00
5 Chris Paul/49 6.00 15.00
6 Caron Butler/99 4.00 10.00
7 Kevin Durant/49 12.00 30.00
8 Russell Westbrook/49 12.00 30.00
9 James Harden/49 6.00 15.00
10 Serge Ibaka/49 4.00 10.00
11 Derrick Rose/49 6.00 15.00
12 Luol Deng /49 4.00 10.00
13 Joakim Noah/49 4.00 10.00
14 Carlos Boozer/49 4.00 10.00
15 Dirk Nowitzki/49 6.00 15.00
16 Jason Terry/49 4.00 10.00
17 Jeremy Lin/49 5.00 12.00
18 Jason Kidd/49 5.00 12.00
19 Kevin Garnett/49 6.00 15.00
20 Paul Pierce/49 5.00 12.00
21 Rajon Rondo/49 5.00 12.00
22 Ray Allen/49 10.00 25.00
23 Dwight Howard/49 6.00 15.00
24 Hedo Turkoglu/99 4.00 10.00
25 J.J. Redick/99 5.00 12.00
26 Josh Smith/49 4.00 10.00
27 Joe Johnson/49 4.00 10.00
28 Al Horford/49 4.00 10.00
29 Danny Granger/49 4.00 10.00
30 Tyler Hansbrough/99 4.00 10.00
31 Darren Collison/99 4.00 10.00
32 David West/49 4.00 10.00
33 Tim Duncan/49 6.00 15.00
34 Tony Parker/49 5.00 12.00
35 Manu Ginobili/49 5.00 12.00
36 Tiago Splitter/99 4.00 10.00
37 Jrue Holiday/99 5.00 12.00
38 Thaddeus Young/99 3.00 8.00
39 Evan Turner/99 3.00 8.00
40 Elton Brand/99 5.00 12.00
41 John Wall/49 6.00 15.00
42 Andray Blatche/99 3.00 8.00
44 Gordon Hayward/99 5.00 12.00
45 Al Jefferson/49 4.00 10.00
46 Devin Harris/99 3.00 8.00
47 Derrick Favors/99 4.00 10.00
48 Carmelo Anthony/49 6.00 15.00
49 Amar'e Stoudemire/49 4.00 10.00
50 Damian Lillard/99 12.00 30.00
51 Landry Fields/99 3.00 8.00
52 Ricky Rubio/49 5.00 12.00
53 Kevin Love/49 5.00 12.00
54 Wesley Johnson/99 4.00 10.00
55 Luke Ridnour/99 4.00 10.00
56 D.J. Augustin/99 3.00 8.00
57 Tyrus Thomas/99 3.00 8.00
58 Antawn Jamison/99 4.00 10.00
59 Anderson Varejao/99 3.00 8.00
60 Daniel Gibson/99 4.00 10.00
61 Tyreke Evans/49 3.00 8.00
62 Marcus Thornton/49 3.00 8.00
63 DeMarcus Cousins/99 5.00 12.00
64 John Salmons/99 4.00 10.00
65 Dwyane Wade/49 6.00 15.00
66 LeBron James/49 20.00 50.00
67 Chris Bosh/49 5.00 12.00
68 Shane Battier/99 4.00 10.00
69 Marc Gasol/49 5.00 12.00
70 Rudy Gay/49 5.00 12.00
71 Zach Randolph/49 4.00 10.00
72 Mike Conley/99 4.00 10.00
73 Trevor Ariza/99 3.00 8.00
74 Andrea Bargnani/49 4.00 10.00
75 DeMar DeRozan/99 5.00 12.00
76 Stephen Curry/99 20.00 50.00
77 Brandon Jennings/49 3.00 8.00
78 Drew Gooden/99 4.00 10.00
79 Carlos Delfino/99 3.00 8.00
80 Kevin Martin/99 4.00 10.00
81 Luis Scola/99 4.00 10.00
82 Goran Dragic/99 4.00 10.00
83 Channing Frye/99 4.00 10.00
84 Steve Nash/49 5.00 12.00
85 Jared Dudley/49 3.00 8.00
86 Grant Hill/49 6.00 15.00
87 Chris Kaman/99 4.00 10.00
88 Deron Williams/49 4.00 10.00
89 Brook Lopez/49 4.00 10.00
90 Kris Humphries/99 3.00 8.00
91 LaMarcus Aldridge/49 6.00 15.00
92 Carl Landry/99 3.00 8.00
93 Raymond Felton/99 4.00 10.00
94 Ty Lawson/49 3.00 8.00
95 Chris Andersen/99 4.00 10.00
96 Danilo Gallinari/99 3.00 8.00
97 Greg Monroe/49 4.00 10.00
98 Tayshaun Prince/99 4.00 10.00
99 George Hill/99 4.00 10.00
100 David Lee/49 3.00 8.00

2012-13 Panini National Treasures Material Treasures Prime

*PRIME: 1.2X TO 3X BASIC
PRINT RUNS B/WN 5-25 COPIES PER
NO PRICING ON QTY 25 OR LESS
1 Kobe Bryant/25 200.00 400.00
2 Kyrie Irving/25 75.00 150.00
11 Derrick Rose/25 75.00 150.00
13 Joakim Noah/25 15.00 40.00
18 Jason Kidd/25 30.00 80.00
22 Ray Allen/25 40.00 80.00
33 Tim Duncan/25 50.00 120.00
53 Kevin Love/25 40.00 100.00
86 Grant Hill/25 50.00 120.00
91 LaMarcus Aldridge/25 40.00 80.00

2012-13 Panini National Treasures NBA Gear Dual

PRINT RUNS B/WN 25-99 COPIES PER
1 J.J. Hickson/99 3.00 8.00
2 LeBron James/99 15.00 40.00
3 John Wall/99 6.00 15.00
4 Serge Ibaka/99 4.00 10.00
5 Paul Pierce/49 5.00 12.00
6 Jordan Crawford/49 3.00 8.00
7 Dwyane Wade/99 6.00 15.00
8 Derrick Rose/99 12.00 30.00
9 Caron Butler/99 4.00 10.00
10 Brandon Jennings/99 3.00 8.00
11 Andrew Bynum/49 3.00 8.00
12 James Harden/99 6.00 15.00
13 Chris Andersen/99 4.00 10.00
14 Chris Kaman/25 4.00 10.00
15 Dirk Nowitzki/49 6.00 15.00
16 Andrea Bargnani/49 4.00 10.00
17 Mo Williams/99 4.00 10.00
18 Jeremy Lin/99 5.00 12.00
19 Jeff Teague/99 4.00 10.00
20 DeJuan Blair/49 3.00 8.00
21 Pau Gasol/99 5.00 12.00
22 Tyler Hansbrough/99 4.00 10.00
23 Raymond Felton/49 4.00 10.00
24 Russell Westbrook/49 6.00 15.00
25 Kris Humphries/99 3.00 8.00
26 Andre Iguodala/99 4.00 10.00
27 Rodrigue Beaubois/99 3.00 8.00
28 Andre Miller/99 4.00 10.00
29 Al Jefferson/49 4.00 10.00
30 Tim Duncan/99 6.00 15.00
31 David Lee/49 3.00 8.00
32 Jrue Holiday/99 5.00 12.00
33 Dwight Howard/99 4.00 10.00
34 Kevin Durant/99 12.00 30.00
35 DeMar DeRozan/99 5.00 12.00
36 O.J. Mayo/99 3.00 8.00
37 Kevin Martin/99 4.00 10.00
38 Ben Gordon/99 4.00 10.00
39 Vince Carter/49 6.00 15.00
40 Darren Collison/99 4.00 10.00
41 Carmelo Anthony/99 6.00 15.00
42 Rajon Rondo/49 5.00 12.00
43 Al Horford/99 4.00 10.00
44 Greg Monroe/99 4.00 10.00
45 Kevin Garnett/49 6.00 15.00
46 Trevor Ariza/99 3.00 8.00
47 J.J. Barea/99 4.00 10.00
48 Luis Scola/99 4.00 10.00
49 Jason Kidd/49 5.00 12.00
50 Landry Fields/99 3.00 8.00

2012-13 Panini National Treasures NBA Gear Dual Prime

*PRIME: .75X TO 2X BASIC
PRINT RUNS B/WN 5-25 COPIES PER
NO PRICING ON QTY 10 OR LESS
13 Chris Andersen/25 40.00 100.00
15 Dirk Nowitzki/25 25.00 60.00
18 Jeremy Lin/25 30.00 80.00
21 Pau Gasol/25 20.00 50.00
33 Dwight Howard/25 25.00 60.00

2012-13 Panini National Treasures NBA Gear Dual Prime Signatures

*PRIME: .75X TO 2X BASIC
PRINT RUNS B/WN 5-25 COPIES PER
NO PRICING ON QTY 10 OR LESS
EXCHANGE DEADLINE 01/31/2015

2012-13 Panini National Treasures NBA Gear Dual Signatures

PRINT RUNS B/WN 10-99 COPIES PER
NO CHALMERS PRICING AVAILABLE
EXCHANGE DEADLINE 01/31/2015
1 Marcin Gortat/49 12.00 30.00
2 Steve Nash/25 30.00 80.00
3 Ray Allen/25 30.00 80.00
4 Blake Griffin/25 40.00 80.00
5 Tyreke Evans/25 8.00 20.00
6 Chris Kaman/25 6.00 15.00
7 Josh Smith/25 8.00 20.00
8 James Harden/25 25.00 60.00
9 Ben Gordon/25 6.00 15.00
10 Joakim Noah/49 6.00 15.00
11 Marcus Thornton/49 6.00 15.00
12 Mike Conley/25 8.00 20.00
13 Chris Bosh/25 15.00 40.00
14 Evan Turner/25 6.00 15.00
15 Gordon Hayward/99 8.00 20.00
16 Andre Iguodala/25 10.00 25.00
17 Hedo Turkoglu/99 6.00 15.00
18 Vince Carter/25 25.00 60.00
19 Danilo Gallinari/49 6.00 15.00
20 Andre Miller/49 6.00 15.00
21 Devin Harris/25 6.00 15.00
22 Wesley Johnson/99 6.00 15.00
23 Deron Williams/25 12.00 30.00
24 Kobe Bryant/49 125.00 250.00
25 Kevin Durant/49 100.00 200.00
26 Emeka Okafor/25 6.00 15.00
27 Tyson Chandler/49 6.00 15.00
28 Tony Parker/25 25.00 60.00
30 Kevin Martin/25 8.00 20.00
31 Richard Hamilton/49 6.00 15.00
32 Kevin Love/49 20.00 50.00
33 Al Jefferson/49 6.00 15.00
34 Monta Ellis/49 6.00 15.00
35 Brandon Jennings/49 8.00 20.00
36 Ty Lawson/49 8.00 20.00
37 Trevor Booker/99 6.00 15.00
38 Andrea Bargnani/25 6.00 15.00
39 Jeff Teague/99 6.00 15.00
40 Antawn Jamison/49 6.00 15.00
41 Eric Gordon/25 8.00 20.00
42 Joe Johnson/49 10.00 25.00
43 Carlos Boozer/49 10.00 25.00
44 Anderson Varejao/49 6.00 15.00
45 Derrick Favors/49 6.00 15.00
46 Greg Monroe/49 6.00 15.00
47 J.R. Smith/49 8.00 20.00
48 Zach Randolph/25 10.00 25.00
49 Grant Hill/25 30.00 80.00
50 LaMarcus Aldridge/25 12.00 30.00

2012-13 Panini National Treasures NBA Gear Trios

PRINT RUNS B/WN 49-99 COPIES PER
1 Joakim Noah/99 4.00 10.00
2 LeBron James/49 20.00 50.00
3 Jason Terry/49 4.00 10.00
4 Al Jefferson/99 4.00 10.00
5 Paul Pierce/49 5.00 12.00
6 Tim Duncan/99 8.00 20.00
7 Dwyane Wade/49 8.00 20.00
8 Ty Lawson/99 3.00 8.00
9 Beno Udrih/99 3.00 8.00
10 Kevin Garnett/49 6.00 15.00
11 Andrea Bargnani/99 4.00 10.00
12 DeMar DeRozan/99 5.00 12.00
13 Shawn Marion/49 4.00 10.00
14 Manu Ginobili/49 5.00 12.00
15 Kobe Bryant/49 20.00 50.00
16 Ricky Rubio/49 6.00 15.00

17 Jose Calderon/99 3.00 8.00
18 Zach Randolph/99 4.00 10.00
19 Amar'e Stoudemire/49 4.00 10.00
20 Rudy Gay/99 5.00 12.00
21 Kevin Martin/99 4.00 10.00
22 Danny Granger/99 4.00 10.00
23 Joe Johnson/99 4.00 10.00
24 Russell Westbrook/99 6.00 15.00
25 Evan Turner/99 3.00 8.00

2012-13 Panini National Treasures NBA Gear Trios Prime
*PRIME: X TO X BASIC
PRINT RUNS B/WN 5-25 COPIES PER
NO PRICING ON QTY 10 OR LESS
1 Joakim Noah/25 20.00 50.00
2 LeBron James/25 100.00 200.00
6 Tim Duncan/25 40.00 100.00
7 Dwyane Wade/25 50.00 100.00
10 Kevin Garnett/25 40.00 80.00
14 Manu Ginobili/25 20.00 50.00
15 Kobe Bryant/25 100.00 200.00
24 Russell Westbrook/25 20.00 50.00

2012-13 Panini National Treasures NBA Gear Trios Prime Signatures
*PRIME: .75X TO 2X BASIC
PRINT RUNS B/WN 5-25 COPIES PER
NO PRICING ON QTY 10 OR LESS
EXCHANGE DEADLINE 01/31/2015
2 Kobe Bryant/25 250.00 500.00
4 Kevin Durant/25 150.00 300.00

2012-13 Panini National Treasures NBA Gear Trios Signatures
PRINT RUNS B/WN 25-99 COPIES PER
EXCHANGE DEADLINE 01/31/2015
2 Kobe Bryant/99 125.00 250.00
3 Tony Parker/49 20.00 50.00
4 Kevin Durant/49 75.00 150.00
5 Chris Bosh/49 12.00 30.00
6 Josh Smith/49 8.00 20.00
7 Blake Griffin/49 20.00 50.00
8 John Wall/25 40.00 100.00
9 Grant Hill/49 30.00 80.00
10 DeMarcus Cousins/49 12.00 30.00
11 Andre Iguodala/49 8.00 20.00
12 Kevin Love/49 15.00 40.00
13 Brook Lopez/49 8.00 20.00
14 Stephen Curry/99 50.00 120.00
15 Tyson Chandler/49 6.00 15.00
16 LaMarcus Aldridge/49 10.00 25.00
17 Danny Granger/49 10.00 25.00
18 Zach Randolph/49 6.00 15.00
19 Wesley Matthews/99 6.00 15.00
20 Serge Ibaka/99 10.00 25.00
21 Gordon Hayward/99 8.00 20.00
22 Eric Gordon/49 6.00 15.00
23 Dwight Howard/25 30.00 80.00
24 Al Horford/49 12.00 30.00
25 Metta World Peace/49 12.00 30.00

2012-13 Panini National Treasures Notable Nicknames
PRINT RUNS B/WN 25-99 COPIES PER
EXCHANGE DEADLINE 1/31/2015
1 Kyrie Irving/49 600.00 1000.00
2 Walt Frazier/99 10.00 25.00
3 James Worthy/49 40.00 100.00
4 Robert Horry/99 12.00 30.00
5 Bill Walton/49 12.00 30.00
6 Kobe Bryant/49 2000.00 2500.00
7 Clyde Drexler/49 50.00 120.00
8 Anthony Davis/25 1000.00 1500.00
9 Nick Van Exel/99 30.00 80.00
10 Anfernee Hardaway/49 200.00 400.00
11 Kenny Smith/99 40.00 100.00
12 Harrison Barnes/49 75.00 200.00
13 Kevin Durant/49 125.00 300.00
14 Toni Kukoc/99 20.00 50.00
15 Cedric Maxwell/99 6.00 15.00
16 Dikembe Mutombo/49 25.00 60.00
17 Kenneth Faried/99 30.00 80.00
18 Julius Erving/25 100.00 200.00
19 Larry Johnson/49 25.00 60.00
20 Marcin Gortat/99 20.00 50.00
21 Dominique Wilkins/49 15.00 40.00
22 Shaquille O'Neal/25 450.00 600.00
23 Jerry West/25 75.00 150.00
24 Serge Ibaka/49 EXCH 20.00 50.00
25 Blake Griffin/49 300.00 600.00

2012-13 Panini National Treasures Springfield Bound Signatures
PRINT RUNS B/WN 49-99 COPIES PER
EXCHANGE DEADLINE 1/31/2015
1 Kobe Bryant/49 150.00 250.00
2 Grant Hill/49 25.00 60.00
3 Vince Carter/99 20.00 50.00
4 Tony Parker/49 20.00 50.00
5 Jason Kidd/49 25.00 60.00
6 Steve Nash/49 30.00 80.00
7 Yao Ming/49 40.00 100.00
8 Chris Bosh/99 EXCH 12.00 30.00
9 Kevin Durant/49 100.00 200.00
10 Dwyane Wade/49 40.00 100.00

2012-13 Panini National Treasures Timeline Materials Custom Names
PRINT RUNS B/WN 25-99 COPIES PER
1 Kevin Durant/49 12.00 30.00
2 Jrue Holiday/99 5.00 12.00
3 Dirk Nowitzki/49 6.00 15.00
4 Emeka Okafor/99 4.00 10.00
5 Andre Iguodala/99 4.00 10.00
6 Deron Williams/99 4.00 10.00
7 Nick Collison/99 4.00 10.00
8 Gordon Hayward/49 5.00 12.00
9 DeMarcus Cousins/49 5.00 12.00
10 Joe Johnson/99 4.00 10.00
11 Kris Humphries/99 3.00 8.00
12 Kevin Garnett/25 8.00 20.00
13 Darren Collison/99 4.00 10.00
14 Tony Parker/49 5.00 12.00
15 Dwight Howard/99 4.00 10.00
16 Damian Lillard/99 10.00 25.00
17 Carlos Boozer/49 4.00 10.00
18 Carmelo Anthony/49 6.00 15.00
19 Russell Westbrook/99 6.00 15.00
20 Metta World Peace/99 5.00 12.00
21 Manu Ginobili/43 5.00 12.00
22 Andrew Bynum/99 3.00 8.00
23 Zach Randolph/99 4.00 10.00
24 Shane Battier/99 4.00 10.00
25 Trevor Booker/99 3.00 8.00

2012-13 Panini National Treasures Timeline Materials Custom Names Prime
21 Manu Ginobili/25 15.00 40.00

2012-13 Panini National Treasures Timeline Materials Custom Names Prime Signatures
*PRIME: .6X TO 1.5X BASIC
PRINT RUNS B/WN 10-25 COPIES PER
NO PRICING ON QTY 10
EXCHANGE DEADLINE 01/31/2015

2012-13 Panini National Treasures Timeline Materials Custom Names Signatures
PRINT RUNS B/WN 25-99 COPIES PER
EXCHANGE DEADLINE 01/31/2015
1 Kevin Durant/49 100.00 200.00
2 LaMarcus Aldridge/49 15.00 40.00
3 Dirk Nowitzki/49 50.00 125.00
4 Emeka Okafor/49 6.00 15.00
5 Andre Iguodala/99 8.00 20.00
6 Tyson Chandler/49 6.00 15.00
7 Michael Kidd-Gilchrist/49 12.00 30.00
8 Gordon Hayward/49 15.00 40.00
9 Derrick Favors/30 8.00 20.00
10 Joe Johnson/99 8.00 20.00
11 Andre Miller/99 6.00 15.00
12 Kobe Bryant/49 125.00 250.00
13 Richard Hamilton/49 8.00 20.00
14 Julius Erving/25 50.00 125.00
15 Shaquille O'Neal/25 60.00 150.00
16 Anderson Varejao/49 6.00 15.00
17 Zach Randolph/99 8.00 20.00
18 David Robinson/49 30.00 80.00
19 Jerry West/25 40.00 100.00
20 John Stockton/25 40.00 100.00
21 Alex English/49 8.00 20.00
22 Elgin Baylor/25 20.00 50.00
23 Nick Van Exel/25 15.00 40.00
24 Kareem Abdul-Jabbar/25 50.00 125.00
25 Yao Ming/25 40.00 100.00

2012-13 Panini National Treasures Timeline Materials Custom Team Nicknames
PRINT RUNS B/WN 15-99 COPIES PER
NO PRICING ON QTY 15
1 LeBron James/99 20.00 50.00
2 Ben Gordon/99 4.00 10.00
3 Derrick Rose/99 10.00 25.00
4 Russell Westbrook/49 6.00 15.00
5 Kobe Bryant/49 20.00 50.00
6 Antawn Jamison/99 4.00 10.00
7 LaMarcus Aldridge/99 5.00 12.00
8 Pau Gasol/99 5.00 12.00
9 Blake Griffin/49 5.00 12.00
10 Tony Parker/49 5.00 12.00
11 Paul Pierce/49 5.00 12.00
12 Dwyane Wade/49 8.00 20.00
13 Amar'e Stoudemire/99 4.00 10.00
14 Andrea Bargnani/99 4.00 10.00
15 David Lee/49 3.00 8.00
16 Tim Duncan/99 8.00 20.00
17 Eric Gordon/99 4.00 10.00
18 Brook Lopez/99 4.00 10.00
19 Ty Lawson/99 3.00 8.00
20 Josh Smith/99 4.00 10.00
21 David West/99 4.00 10.00
22 Steve Nash/49 5.00 12.00
24 Jeremy Lin/99 5.00 12.00
25 Marc Gasol/99 5.00 12.00

2012-13 Panini National Treasures Timeline Materials Custom Team Nicknames Prime
*PRIME: .75X TO 2X BASIC
PRINT RUNS B/WN 10-25 COPIES PER
NO PRICING ON QTY 15 OR LESS
10 Tony Parker/25 15.00 40.00
16 Tim Duncan/25 25.00 60.00

2012-13 Panini National Treasures Timeline Materials Custom Team Nicknames Prime Signatures
*PRIME: .6X TO 1.5X BASIC
PRINT RUNS B/WN 10-25 COPIES PER
NO PRICING ON QTY 15 OR LESS
EXCHANGE DEADLINE 01/31/2015

2012-13 Panini National Treasures Timeline Materials Custom Team Nicknames Signatures
PRINT RUNS B/WN 49-99 COPIES PER
EXCHANGE DEADLINE 01/31/2015
1 Ray Allen/49 20.00 50.00
2 Ben Gordon/99 6.00 15.00
3 Kyrie Irving/49 200.00 400.00
4 James Harden/49 20.00 50.00
5 Kobe Bryant/49 100.00 200.00
6 Harrison Barnes/49 15.00 40.00
7 LaMarcus Aldridge/49 8.00 20.00
8 Kevin Love/49 20.00 50.00
9 Blake Griffin/49 20.00 50.00
10 Tony Parker/49 15.00 40.00
11 Jared Sullinger/49 10.00 25.00
12 Mike Conley/99 6.00 15.00
13 DeMarcus Cousins/49 8.00 20.00
14 Ersan Ilyasova/99 6.00 15.00
15 Andre Drummond/49 40.00 100.00
16 Chris Kaman/99 6.00 15.00
17 Deron Williams/49 15.00 40.00
18 Stephen Curry/49 60.00 150.00
19 Al Jefferson/49 6.00 15.00
20 Brandon Jennings/49 8.00 20.00
21 Grant Hill/49 30.00 60.00
22 Raymond Felton/49 6.00 15.00
23 Steve Nash/49 25.00 60.00
24 J.J. Hickson/99 6.00 15.00
25 Chris Bosh/49 15.00 40.00

2013-14 Panini National Treasures
1-100 PRINT RUN 99 SER.#'d SETS
101-200 PRINT RUNS 99 SER.#'d SETS
PRIME PATCHES MAY SELL FOR PREMIUM
EXCHANGE DEADLINE 1/30/2016
1 Jameer Nelson 1.50 4.00
2 Avery Bradley 2.00 5.00
3 Steve Nash 2.50 6.00
4 Josh Smith 2.00 5.00
5 Dirk Nowitzki 3.00 8.00
6 Russell Westbrook 6.00 15.00
7 Al Horford 2.00 5.00
8 DeMar DeRozan 2.50 6.00
9 Chris Paul 3.00 8.00
10 Derrick Favors 2.00 5.00
11 Nikola Vucevic 2.00 5.00
12 Brandon Bass 1.50 4.00
13 Pau Gasol 2.50 6.00
14 Greg Monroe 2.00 5.00
15 Monta Ellis 2.00 5.00
16 Serge Ibaka 2.00 5.00
17 Kyle Korver 2.00 5.00
18 Kyle Lowry 2.00 5.00
19 DeAndre Jordan 2.50 6.00
20 Enes Kanter 1.50 4.00
21 Tony Parker 2.50 6.00
22 Evan Turner 1.50 4.00
23 DeMarcus Cousins 2.50 6.00
24 Andre Drummond 2.50 6.00
25 Vince Carter 3.00 8.00
26 Ty Lawson 1.50 4.00
27 Jeff Teague 2.00 5.00
28 Jonas Valanciunas 2.00 5.00
29 Stephen Curry 6.00 15.00
30 Paul George 3.00 8.00
31 Tim Duncan 4.00 10.00
32 Spencer Hawes 1.50 4.00
33 Isaiah Thomas 2.50 6.00
34 Luol Deng 2.00 5.00
35 Mike Conley 2.00 5.00
36 Kenneth Faried 2.00 5.00
37 John Wall 3.00 8.00
38 Joe Johnson 2.00 5.00
39 Klay Thompson 3.00 8.00
40 Lance Stephenson 2.00 5.00
41 Kawhi Leonard 4.00 10.00
42 Thaddeus Young 1.50 4.00
43 Rudy Gay 2.50 6.00
44 Kyrie Irving 5.00 12.00
45 Zach Randolph 2.00 5.00
46 Nate Robinson 1.50 4.00
47 Bradley Beal 2.50 6.00
48 Kevin Garnett 4.00 10.00
49 David Lee 1.50 4.00
50 Roy Hibbert 2.00 5.00
51 Manu Ginobili 2.50 6.00
52 LaMarcus Aldridge 2.50 6.00
53 LeBron James 10.00 25.00
54 Dion Waiters 2.00 5.00
55 Marc Gasol 2.50 6.00
56 Kevin Love 2.50 6.00
57 Marcin Gortat 2.00 5.00
58 Paul Pierce 2.50 6.00
59 Harrison Barnes 2.00 5.00
60 Danny Granger 2.00 5.00
61 Dwight Howard 2.00 5.00
62 Damian Lillard 5.00 12.00
63 Dwyane Wade 4.00 10.00
64 Brandon Knight 2.00 5.00
65 Anthony Davis 5.00 12.00
66 Nikola Pekovic 1.50 4.00
67 Kemba Walker 2.50 6.00
68 Carmelo Anthony 3.00 8.00
69 Channing Frye 2.00 5.00
70 Derrick Rose 3.00 8.00
71 Jeremy Lin 2.50 6.00
72 Wesley Matthews 1.50 4.00
73 Chris Bosh 2.50 6.00
74 O.J. Mayo 1.50 4.00
75 Eric Gordon 2.00 5.00
76 Kevin Martin 2.00 5.00
77 Gerald Henderson 1.50 4.00
78 Andrea Bargnani 2.00 5.00
79 Goran Dragic 2.00 5.00
80 Joakim Noah 2.00 5.00
81 James Harden 4.00 10.00
82 Nicolas Batum 2.00 5.00
83 Ray Allen 2.50 6.00
84 Larry Sanders 1.50 4.00
85 Jrue Holiday 2.50 6.00
86 Ricky Rubio 2.50 6.00
87 Al Jefferson 2.00 5.00
88 Iman Shumpert 1.50 4.00
89 Gerald Green 2.00 5.00
90 Carlos Boozer 2.00 5.00
91 Chandler Parsons 2.00 5.00
92 Kevin Durant 6.00 15.00
93 Paul Millsap 2.50 6.00
94 Blake Griffin 2.50 6.00
95 Ryan Anderson 2.00 5.00
96 Gordon Hayward 2.50 6.00
97 Arron Afflalo 1.50 4.00
98 Jeff Green 2.00 5.00
99 Kobe Bryant 10.00 25.00
100 Brandon Jennings 1.50 4.00
101 D. Schroder JSY AU RC 100.00 250.00
102 Luigi Datome JSY AU RC 12.00 30.00
103 Solomon Hill JSY AU RC 15.00 40.00
104 Glen Rice Jr. JSY AU RC 12.00 30.00
105 Tony Mitchell JSY AU RC 12.00 30.00
106 Anthony Bennett JSY AU RC 15.00 40.00
107 Cody Zeller JSY AU RC 20.00 50.00
108 CJ McCollum JSY AU RC 200.00 500.00
109 Caldwell-Pope JSY AU RC 30.00 80.00
110 Kelly Olynyk JSY AU RC 25.00 60.00
111 Shane Larkin JSY AU RC 12.00 30.00
112 Rudy Gobert JSY AU RC 400.00 800.00
113 Hardaway Jr. JSY AU RC 100.00 250.00
114 Nate Wolters JSY AU RC 15.00 40.00
115 Jeff Withey JSY AU RC 12.00 30.00
116 Victor Oladipo JSY AU RC 100.00 250.00
117 Alex Len JSY AU RC EXCH 25.00 60.00
118 Ben McLemore JSY AU RC 75.00 150.00
119 Carter-Williams JSY AU RC 75.00 200.00
120 S.Muhammad JSY AU RC 50.00 120.00
121 Dellavedova JSY AU RC 40.00 100.00
122 Tony Snell JSY AU RC 25.00 60.00
123 Andre Roberson JSY AU RC 12.00 30.00
124 Peyton Siva JSY AU RC 15.00 40.00
125 Gorgui Dieng JSY AU RC 40.00 100.00
126 Otto Porter JSY AU RC 75.00 200.00
127 Nerlens Noel JSY AU RC 150.00 300.00
128 Trey Burke JSY AU RC 15.00 40.00
129 Steven Adams JSY AU RC 30.00 80.00
130 Antetokounmpo JSY AU RC 3500.00 4500.00
131 Gal Mekel JSY AU RC 12.00 30.00
132 Mason Plumlee JSY AU RC 25.00 60.00
133 Archie Goodwin JSY AU RC 30.00 80.00
134 Ray McCallum AU RC 4.00 10.00
135 Pero Antic AU RC 4.00 10.00
136 Jamaal Franklin AU RC 4.00 10.00
137 Ryan Kelly AU RC EXCH 4.00 10.00
138 Ricky Ledo AU RC 4.00 10.00
139 Sergey Karasev AU RC EXCH 4.00 10.00
140 Erik Murphy AU RC 4.00 10.00
141 Isaiah Canaan AU RC 8.00 20.00
142 Dwight Buycks AU RC 4.00 10.00
143 Reggie Bullock AU RC 5.00 12.00
144 Ian Clark AU RC 15.00 40.00
145 Nemanja Nedovic AU RC 4.00 10.00
146 Mike Muscala AU RC 12.00 30.00
147 Allen Crabbe AU RC 5.00 12.00
148 Phil Pressey AU RC 4.00 10.00
149 Carrick Felix AU RC 4.00 10.00
150 Vitor Faverani AU RC 4.00 10.00

2013-14 Panini National Treasures Gold
*GOLD 1-100: 1X TO 2.5X BASIC
*GOLD 101-133: .6X TO 1.5X BASIC
*GOLD 134-150: .5X TO 1.2X BASIC
RANDOM INSERTS IN PACKS
STATED PRINT RUN 25 SER.#'d SETS
EXCHANGE DEADLINE 1/30/2016
116 Victor Oladipo JSY AU 300.00 600.00
130 Giannis Antetokounmpo JSY AU 4000.00 5000.00

2013-14 Panini National Treasures Air Apparent Materials
RANDOM INSERTS IN PACKS
STATED PRINT RUN 99 SER.#'d SETS
*PRIME: .75X TO 2X BASIC
1 Marc Gasol 4.00 10.00
2 Kevin Durant 8.00 20.00
3 Evan Turner 2.50 6.00
4 Stephen Curry 15.00 40.00
5 Kawhi Leonard 6.00 15.00
6 Deron Williams 3.00 8.00
7 Dion Waiters 3.00 8.00
8 Andre Drummond 4.00 10.00
9 Kyrie Irving 8.00 20.00
10 Blake Griffin 4.00 10.00
11 Brandon Knight 3.00 8.00
12 Russell Westbrook 10.00 25.00
13 Goran Dragic 3.00 8.00
14 O.J. Mayo 2.50 6.00
15 Derrick Favors 3.00 8.00
16 Al Jefferson 3.00 8.00
17 Nikola Vucevic 3.00 8.00
18 Kenneth Faried 3.00 8.00
19 Brandon Jennings 2.50 6.00
20 Chris Paul 5.00 12.00
21 Larry Sanders 2.50 6.00
22 Damian Lillard 8.00 20.00
23 Monta Ellis 3.00 8.00
24 LaMarcus Aldridge 4.00 10.00
25 Gordon Hayward 4.00 10.00
26 Michael Kidd-Gilchrist 4.00 10.00
27 Iman Shumpert 6.00 15.00
28 James Harden 6.00 15.00
29 Josh Smith 3.00 8.00
30 LeBron James 12.00 30.00
31 Anthony Davis 8.00 20.00
32 John Wall 5.00 12.00
33 DeMarcus Cousins 4.00 10.00
34 Eric Bledsoe 3.00 8.00
35 Enes Kanter 2.50 6.00
36 Jimmy Butler 4.00 10.00
37 Tobias Harris 3.00 8.00
38 Dwight Howard 3.00 8.00
39 Harrison Barnes 3.00 8.00
40 Kevin Love 4.00 10.00
41 Jrue Holiday 4.00 10.00
42 Al Horford 3.00 8.00
43 Isaiah Thomas 4.00 10.00
44 Bradley Beal 4.00 10.00
45 Jeremy Lin 4.00 10.00
46 Kemba Walker 4.00 10.00
47 Maurice Harkless 2.50 6.00
48 Paul George 5.00 12.00
49 Mike Conley 3.00 8.00
50 Ricky Rubio 4.00 10.00

2013-14 Panini National Treasures Career Materials Trios
RANDOM INSERTS IN PACKS
PRINT RUNS B/WN 49-99 COPIES PER
*PRIME: 1.5X TO 4X BASIC
1 Andre Iguodala/99 5.00 12.00
2 Dan Majerle/99 5.00 12.00
3 Dikembe Mutombo/70 6.00 15.00
4 Dominique Wilkins/99 8.00 20.00
5 Grant Hill/99 8.00 20.00
6 Chris Paul/99 6.00 15.00
7 Kevin Martin/99 5.00 12.00
8 Michael Beasley/95 4.00 10.00
9 Moses Malone/49 6.00 15.00
10 Kiki Vandeweghe/99 5.00 12.00
11 Rashard Lewis/99 5.00 12.00
12 Shaquille O'Neal/49 12.00 30.00
13 Tracy McGrady/49 12.00 30.00
14 Vince Carter/99 8.00 20.00
15 Robert Horry/99 5.00 12.00

2013-14 Panini National Treasures Colossal Materials
RANDOM INSERTS IN PACKS
PRINT RUNS B/WN 25-99 COPIES PER
1 Klay Thompson/99 5.00 12.00
2 Arron Afflalo/99 2.50 6.00
3 Joakim Noah/75 3.00 8.00
4 Manu Ginobili/75 4.00 10.00
5 Amare Stoudemire/99 3.00 8.00
6 Vinnie Johnson/25 4.00 10.00
7 Rajon Rondo/75 4.00 10.00
8 Tim Duncan/75 6.00 15.00
9 John Wall/99 5.00 12.00
10 Dwight Howard/75 8.00 20.00
11 Chris Paul/75 5.00 12.00
12 Reggie Lewis/49 10.00 25.00
13 Xavier McDaniel/49 2.50 6.00
14 Patrick Ewing/99 5.00 12.00
15 Damian Lillard/99 8.00 20.00
16 LeBron James/75 20.00 50.00
17 Russell Westbrook/99 10.00 25.00
18 Kevin Garnett/99 6.00 15.00
19 Carmelo Anthony/75 5.00 12.00
20 Scottie Pippen/99 8.00 20.00
21 Marc Gasol/75 4.00 10.00
22 Moses Malone/49 4.00 10.00
23 Dennis Johnson/25 6.00 15.00
24 Paul Pierce/99 4.00 10.00
25 Jeremy Lin/75 4.00 10.00

2013-14 Panini National Treasures Colossal Materials Signatures
RANDOM INSERTS IN PACKS
STATED PRINT RUN 60 SER.#'d SETS
EXCHANGE DEADLINE 1/30/2016
1 James Harden 20.00 50.00
2 Robert Parish 10.00 25.00
3 John Stockton 30.00 80.00
4 Alex English 6.00 15.00
5 Nicolas Batum EXCH 10.00 25.00
6 Kareem Abdul-Jabbar 50.00 120.00
7 Kevin Durant 100.00 200.00
8 Clyde Drexler 25.00 60.00
9 Blake Griffin 30.00 80.00
10 Stephen Curry 75.00 150.00
11 Dikembe Mutombo 12.00 30.00
12 Scottie Pippen 50.00 120.00
13 Isiah Thomas 20.00 50.00
14 Shaquille O'Neal 75.00 150.00
15 Mark Aguirre 6.00 15.00
16 Tracy McGrady 20.00 50.00
17 Kyrie Irving 75.00 150.00
18 David Robinson 30.00 80.00
19 Anthony Davis 50.00 120.00
20 Magic Johnson 50.00 120.00
21 Kelly Tripucka 5.00 12.00
22 Tyson Chandler 6.00 15.00
23 Tony Parker 20.00 50.00
24 Joe Dumars 10.00 25.00
25 Kobe Bryant 150.00 250.00

2013-14 Panini National Treasures Game Changers Signatures
RANDOM INSERTS IN PACKS
STATED PRINT RUN 60 SER.#'d SETS
EXCHANGE DEADLINE 1/30/2016
1 Tracy McGrady 30.00 80.00
2 Stephen Curry 100.00 250.00
3 Bill Walton 10.00 25.00
4 Kobe Bryant 75.00 150.00
5 Vince Carter 15.00 40.00
6 Magic Johnson 40.00 100.00
7 Karl Malone 30.00 80.00
8 Anthony Davis 40.00 100.00
9 David Robinson 30.00 80.00
10 Chris Bosh 10.00 25.00
11 Jason Kidd 15.00 40.00
12 James Harden 15.00 40.00
13 Ryan Anderson 5.00 12.00
14 Dwyane Wade 25.00 60.00
15 Larry Bird 50.00 120.00
16 Kevin Durant 75.00 200.00
17 Scottie Pippen 40.00 100.00
18 Grant Hill 20.00 50.00
19 Kevin Love 15.00 40.00
20 Bernard King 5.00 12.00
21 Julius Erving 40.00 100.00
22 Kyrie Irving 30.00 80.00
23 Kareem Abdul-Jabbar 40.00 100.00
24 Carmelo Anthony 30.00 80.00
25 Anfernee Hardaway 30.00 80.00
26 Blake Griffin 30.00 80.00

2013-14 Panini National Treasures International Treasures Signatures
RANDOM INSERTS IN PACKS
PRINT RUNS B/WN 35-60 COPIES PER
EXCHANGE DEADLINE 1/30/2016
*GOLD: .5X TO 1.2 BASIC
1 Enes Kanter/60 5.00 12.00
2 Tony Parker/35 25.00 60.00
3 Goran Dragic/60 EXCH 6.00 15.00
4 Luol Deng/35 EXCH 6.00 15.00
5 Nikola Vucevic/60 10.00 25.00
6 Manu Ginobili/60 EXCH 40.00 100.00
7 Kelly Olynyk/60 12.00 30.00
8 Zydrunas Ilgauskas/35 10.00 25.00
9 H.Olajuwon/60 EXCH 15.00 40.00
10 Jonas Valanciunas/60 EXCH 10.00 25.00
11 Rick Fox/35 EXCH 6.00 15.00
12 Toni Kukoc/60 EXCH 12.00 30.00
13 Tiago Splitter/60 EXCH 6.00 15.00
14 Steven Adams/60 20.00 50.00
15 Steve Nash/35 30.00 80.00
16 Yao Ming/35 EXCH 100.00 200.00
17 Anthony Bennett/35 6.00 15.00
18 Detlef Schrempf/60 8.00 20.00
19 G.Antetokounmpo/60 75.00 200.00
20 Vlade Divac/60 8.00 20.00
21 Andrei Kirilenko/35 8.00 20.00
22 Peja Stojakovic/35 EXCH 20.00 50.00
23 Jonas Jerebko/60 5.00 12.00
24 A.Sabonis/60 EXCH 12.00 30.00
25 A.Bargnani/35 EXCH 6.00 15.00
26 Dennis Schroder/60 15.00 40.00
27 Luc Longley/60 6.00 15.00

2013-14 Panini National Treasures Kobe's All-Rookie Selections Signature Materials
RANDOM INSERTS IN PACKS
STATED PRINT RUN 99 SER.#'d SETS
*PRIME: .75X TO 2X BASIC
1 Michael Carter-Williams 10.00 25.00
2 Victor Oladipo 12.00 30.00
3 Giannis Antetokounmpo 75.00 200.00
4 Tim Hardaway Jr. 10.00 25.00
5 C.J. McCollum 15.00 40.00
6 Trey Burke 8.00 20.00
7 Steven Adams 10.00 25.00
8 Ben McLemore 8.00 20.00

2013-14 Panini National Treasures Lasting Legacies Signature Materials
RANDOM INSERTS IN PACKS
PRINT RUNS B/WN 25-99 COPIES PER
EXCHANGE DEADLINE 1/30/2016
*PRIME: .6X TO 1.5X BASIC
1 Chris Mullin/49 10.00 25.00
2 Joe Dumars/49 8.00 20.00
3 Tom Chambers/99 6.00 15.00
4 Mark Price/99 8.00 20.00
5 Manu Ginobili/49 25.00 60.00
6 Gary Payton/49 10.00 25.00
7 Kevin Love/49 15.00 40.00
8 Bernard King/49 6.00 15.00
9 Isiah Thomas/49 15.00 40.00
10 LaMarcus Aldridge/49 15.00 40.00
11 Kurt Rambis/99 5.00 12.00
12 John Havlicek/49 25.00 60.00
13 Tony Parker/49 20.00 50.00
14 Robert Parish/49 10.00 25.00
15 Hakeem Olajuwon/49 20.00 50.00
16 Kevin McHale/49 12.00 30.00
17 Nick Collison/99 6.00 15.00
18 Toni Kukoc/99 EXCH 12.00 30.00
19 James Worthy/49 12.00 30.00
20 Larry Bird/49 50.00 120.00
21 Bailey Howell/49 8.00 20.00
22 John Stockton/49 40.00 100.00
23 Elgin Baylor/49 12.00 30.00
24 Scottie Pippen/49 40.00 100.00
25 Al Horford/49 6.00 15.00
26 Karl Malone/49 30.00 80.00
27 Kobe Bryant/25 150.00 250.00
28 Brad Daugherty/99 6.00 15.00
29 Magic Johnson/49 60.00 150.00
30 Kevin Durant/49 100.00 200.00
31 Udonis Haslem/99 5.00 12.00
32 Kareem Abdul-Jabbar/49 40.00 100.00

2013-14 Panini National Treasures Material Treasures
RANDOM INSERTS IN PACKS
PRINT RUNS B/WN 49-99 COPIES PER
*PRIME: .75X TO 2X BASIC
1 O.J. Mayo/75 2.50 6.00
2 Marc Gasol/99 4.00 10.00
3 Tyson Chandler/99 3.00 8.00
4 Chris Bosh/99 4.00 10.00
5 Robert Parish/75 4.00 10.00
6 Kobe Bryant/99 12.00 30.00
7 Klay Thompson/99 5.00 12.00
8 Al Jefferson/99 3.00 8.00
9 Dwyane Wade/99 6.00 15.00
10 Jimmy Butler/99 4.00 10.00
11 Patrick Ewing/99 5.00 12.00
12 Rajon Rondo/75 4.00 10.00
13 Bradley Beal/99 4.00 10.00
14 Jrue Holiday/99 4.00 10.00
15 Larry Bird/49 10.00 25.00
16 Kevin Durant/99 6.00 15.00
17 Al Horford/99 3.00 8.00
18 Brandon Jennings/99 2.50 6.00
19 Jeremy Lin/75 4.00 10.00
20 Joakim Noah/99 3.00 8.00
21 Paul Pierce/99 4.00 10.00
22 Vinnie Johnson/49 4.00 10.00
23 Paul George/99 5.00 12.00
24 Steve Nash/75 4.00 10.00
25 Kyrie Irving/99 6.00 15.00
26 Magic Johnson/49 10.00 25.00
27 Ricky Pierce/49 2.50 6.00
28 DeMarcus Cousins/99 4.00 10.00
29 Kevin Garnett/99 5.00 12.00
30 Kemba Walker/99 4.00 10.00
31 Scottie Pippen/99 6.00 15.00
32 Xavier McDaniel/99 2.50 6.00
33 Russell Westbrook/99 10.00 25.00
34 Tracy McGrady/99 4.00 10.00
35 Julius Erving/49 8.00 20.00
36 Anthony Davis/99 8.00 20.00
37 Dirk Nowitzki/99 5.00 12.00
38 Dion Waiters/99 3.00 8.00
39 Mark Jackson/49 3.00 8.00
40 Manu Ginobili/75 4.00 10.00
41 Alonzo Mourning/99 5.00 12.00
42 Tim Duncan/75 6.00 15.00
43 Stephen Curry/99 15.00 40.00
44 Amare Stoudemire/99 3.00 8.00
45 Kareem Abdul-Jabbar/49 6.00 15.00
46 Thaddeus Young/49 2.50 6.00
47 Blake Griffin/99 4.00 10.00
48 Doc Rivers/99 4.00 10.00
49 Monta Ellis/99 3.00 8.00
50 Michael Kidd-Gilchrist/99 4.00 10.00
51 Tony Parker/75 4.00 10.00
52 Anfernee Hardaway/49 10.00 25.00
53 Chris Paul/75 5.00 12.00
54 David Robinson/49 6.00 15.00
55 Hakeem Olajuwon/49 5.00 12.00
56 Dikembe Mutombo/49 4.00 10.00
57 Hal Greer/49 3.00 8.00
58 Evan Turner/99 2.50 6.00
59 Pau Gasol/99 4.00 10.00
60 Moses Malone/49 4.00 10.00

2013-14 Panini National Treasures Material Treasures Signatures
RANDOM INSERTS IN PACKS
PRINT RUNS B/WN 35-99 COPIES PER
EXCHANGE DEADLINE 1/30/2016
*PRIME: .6X TO 1.5X BASIC
1 Josh Smith/49 5.00 12.00
2 Avery Johnson/99 5.00 12.00
3 Larry Johnson/49 12.00 30.00
4 Derrick Favors/99 5.00 12.00
5 Nikola Vucevic/49 5.00 12.00
6 Alex English/49 5.00 12.00
7 Bill Cartwright/49 EXCH 5.00 12.00
8 Jason Kidd/49 15.00 40.00
9 Iman Shumpert/99 4.00 10.00
10 Kawhi Leonard/49 20.00 50.00
11 Buck Williams/99 4.00 10.00
12 Danny Green/99 5.00 12.00
13 Larry Nance/99 5.00 12.00
14 Dikembe Mutombo/49 12.00 30.00
15 Michael Finley/99 6.00 15.00
16 Andre Drummond/49 20.00 50.00
17 Goran Dragic/49 EXCH 8.00 20.00
18 Bob Lanier/49 5.00 12.00
19 Isaiah Thomas/99 12.00 30.00
20 Chris Andersen/49 EXCH 10.00 25.00
21 Paul George/35 25.00 60.00
22 Dennis Rodman/35 25.00 60.00
23 Glen Rice/99 5.00 12.00
24 Enes Kanter/49 4.00 10.00
25 Raymond Felton/99 5.00 12.00
26 Gordon Hayward/49 6.00 15.00
27 Anthony Mason/99 5.00 12.00
28 Brad Daugherty/99 6.00 15.00
29 James Worthy/49 12.00 30.00
30 Grant Hill/49 20.00 50.00
31 LaMarcus Aldridge/49 15.00 40.00
32 Deron Williams/49 EXCH 5.00 12.00
33 Mike Conley/49 5.00 12.00
34 Fat Lever/99 5.00 12.00
35 Serge Ibaka/49 5.00 12.00
36 Bernard King/49 5.00 12.00
37 Harrison Barnes/99 5.00 12.00
38 Brandon Knight/99 5.00 12.00
39 Thabo Sefolosha/99 4.00 10.00
40 Chris Mullin/49 12.00 30.00

2013-14 Panini National Treasures NBA Game Gear Dual
RANDOM INSERTS IN PACKS
PRINT RUNS B/WN 25-99 COPIES PER
*PRIME: 1X TO 2.5X BASIC
1 Dwight Howard/99 3.00 8.00
2 James Harden/99 6.00 15.00
3 Joe Dumars/75 4.00 10.00
4 Michael Cooper/99 3.00 8.00
5 LeBron James/99 12.00 30.00
6 Dwyane Wade/99 6.00 15.00
7 DeMarcus Cousins/99 4.00 10.00
8 Kyrie Irving/99 8.00 20.00
9 Dion Waiters/99 3.00 8.00
10 Charles Oakley/75 4.00 10.00
11 Hakeem Olajuwon/49 5.00 12.00
12 Scottie Pippen/75 8.00 20.00
13 Chris Bosh/99 4.00 10.00
14 Udonis Haslem/99 2.50 6.00
15 Bernard King/49 3.00 8.00
16 Bill Cartwright/49 3.00 8.00
17 Marc Gasol/99 4.00 10.00
18 Serge Ibaka/99 3.00 8.00
19 Dominique Wilkins/49 5.00 12.00
20 Tim Duncan/99 6.00 15.00
21 Tony Parker/99 4.00 10.00
22 Brad Daugherty/75 3.00 8.00
23 Mark Price/49 4.00 10.00
24 Magic Johnson/49 10.00 25.00
25 Roy Hibbert/99 3.00 8.00
26 Ray Allen/99 6.00 15.00
27 Norris Cole/99 2.50 6.00
28 Russell Westbrook/99 10.00 25.00
29 DeAndre Jordan/99 4.00 10.00
30 Jared Sullinger/99 2.50 6.00
31 Jeff Green/99 3.00 8.00
32 Monta Ellis/99 3.00 8.00
33 Blake Griffin/99 5.00 12.00
34 Clyde Drexler/49 5.00 12.00
35 Brandon Knight/99 3.00 8.00
36 Larry Johnson/75 5.00 12.00
37 Anfernee Hardaway/75 10.00 25.00
38 Ty Lawson/99 2.50 6.00
39 Kenneth Faried/99 3.00 8.00
40 Larry Bird/49 12.00 30.00
41 Kobe Bryant/99 15.00 40.00
42 Pau Gasol/99 4.00 10.00
43 Patrick Ewing/75 5.00 12.00
44 Alonzo Mourning/75 8.00 20.00
45 Michael Finley/49 4.00 10.00
46 Chris Paul/99 5.00 12.00
47 Brook Lopez/99 3.00 8.00
48 Deron Williams/99 3.00 8.00
49 Gary Payton/49 4.00 10.00
50 Shawn Kemp/75 10.00 25.00
51 Fat Lever/49 3.00 8.00
52 Kareem Abdul-Jabbar/49 8.00 20.00
53 Kevin Love/99 4.00 10.00
54 Ricky Rubio/99 4.00 10.00
55 David Robinson/75 6.00 15.00
56 Kemba Walker/99 4.00 10.00
57 Gordon Hayward/99 4.00 10.00
58 Enes Kanter/99 2.50 6.00
59 Andre Drummond/99 4.00 10.00
60 Greg Monroe/99 3.00 8.00
61 Kevin McHale/75 4.00 10.00
62 Anthony Davis/99 8.00 20.00
63 Dan Majerle/75 3.00 8.00
64 Karl Malone/49 5.00 12.00
65 Walter Berry/99 2.50 6.00
66 Jayson Williams/99 2.50 6.00
67 Elgin Baylor/25 20.00 50.00
68 Jerry West/25 15.00 40.00
69 Dirk Nowitzki/99 5.00 12.00
70 Tyson Chandler/99 3.00 8.00
71 Jason Kidd/49 4.00 10.00
72 Damian Lillard/99 6.00 15.00
73 LaMarcus Aldridge/99 4.00 10.00
74 Paul George/99 5.00 12.00
75 Carmelo Anthony/99 5.00 12.00
76 Taj Gibson/99 3.00 8.00
77 Joakim Noah/99 6.00 15.00
78 John Wall/99 5.00 12.00
79 Bradley Beal/99 4.00 10.00
80 Stephen Curry/99 10.00 25.00
81 Harrison Barnes/99 3.00 8.00
82 James Worthy/49 5.00 12.00
83 Zach Randolph/99 3.00 8.00
84 Kevin Durant/99 10.00 25.00
85 Shaquille O'Neal/75 8.00 20.00

2013-14 Panini National Treasures NBA Game Gear Signatures
RANDOM INSERTS IN PACKS
PRINT RUNS B/WN 30-75 COPIES PER
EXCHANGE DEADLINE 1/30/2016
*PRIME: .6X TO 1.5X BASIC
1 Paul George/75 25.00 60.00
2 Deron Williams/49 8.00 20.00
3 Kenyon Martin/75
4 Harrison Barnes/49 5.00 12.00
5 Ty Lawson/75 4.00 10.00
6 Kobe Bryant/30 100.00 250.00
7 Jodie Meeks/75
8 Andrew Bogut/75 12.00 30.00
9 Kevin Willis/75 4.00 10.00
10 Charles Oakley/75 6.00 15.00
11 Terry Cummings/75 5.00 12.00
12 Derrick Favors/49 5.00 12.00
13 Stephen Curry/49 100.00 250.00
14 Iman Shumpert/75 4.00 10.00
15 Udonis Haslem/75 4.00 10.00
16 Kyrie Irving/49 50.00 120.00
17 John Stockton/35 50.00 120.00
18 Anfernee Hardaway/49 25.00 60.00
19 Kurt Rambis/75 4.00 10.00
20 Chris Bosh/49 10.00 25.00
21 Robert Horry/75 8.00 20.00
22 Dikembe Mutombo/75 10.00 25.00
23 Steve Blake/75 4.00 10.00
24 Isaiah Thomas/75 15.00 40.00
25 Vince Carter/49 20.00 50.00
26 Kevin Durant/49 75.00 200.00
27 Anthony Mason/75 5.00 12.00
28 Ricky Pierce/75 4.00 10.00
29 Larry Johnson/75 10.00 25.00
30 Chris Mullin/49 15.00 40.00
31 Robert Parish/75 15.00 40.00
32 Enes Kanter/75 4.00 10.00
33 Lance Stephenson/75 8.00 20.00
34 J.J. Redick/75 12.00 30.00
35 Zach Randolph/49 5.00 12.00
36 Glen Rice/75 5.00 12.00
37 Jordan Hill/49 4.00 10.00
38 Avery Johnson/75 5.00 12.00
39 Larry Nance/75 5.00 12.00
40 Clyde Drexler/49 15.00 40.00
41 Amir Johnson/75 4.00 10.00
42 Fred Brown/75 4.00 10.00
43 Taj Gibson/75 5.00 12.00
44 Jack Sikma/75 5.00 12.00
45 Jared Sullinger/75 4.00 10.00
46 Anthony Davis/35 75.00 150.00
47 Josh Smith/49 8.00 20.00
48 Bernard King/49 5.00 12.00
49 Mark Price/75 8.00 20.00
50 Jared Dudley/75 4.00 10.00
51 Roy Hibbert/75 5.00 12.00
52 Gail Goodrich/75 5.00 12.00
53 Tayshaun Prince/49 5.00 12.00
54 Jalen Rose/75 6.00 15.00
55 Steve Mix/49 4.00 10.00
56 Al Horford/49 5.00 12.00
57 Bill Cartwright/75
58 Jrue Holiday/49 6.00 15.00
59 Jonas Valanciunas/75
60 Dan Majerle/75 5.00 12.00
61 Scottie Pippen/35 50.00 120.00
62 George Hill/75 5.00 12.00
63 Norm Nixon/75 4.00 10.00
64 James Jones/75 4.00 10.00
65 Bradley Beal/49 10.00 25.00
66 Anderson Varejao/75
67 Kawhi Leonard/75 50.00 120.00
68 Ersan Ilyasova/75 4.00 10.00
69 Mike Conley/75 5.00 12.00
70 Danilo Gallinari/75 4.00 10.00
71 Serge Ibaka/75 EXCH 8.00 20.00
72 Goran Dragic/75 8.00 20.00
73 Thabo Sefolosha/75 4.00 10.00
74 Jayson Williams/75
75 Fat Lever/75 5.00 12.00
76 Andre Drummond/49 10.00 25.00
77 Brook Lopez/49 5.00 12.00
78 Kelly Tripucka/65 4.00 10.00
79 Nick Collison/75 5.00 12.00
80 Danny Granger/49 5.00 12.00
81 Shane Battier/49 5.00 12.00
82 Gordon Hayward/75 12.00 30.00
83 Tom Chambers/75 5.00 12.00
84 Jeff Green/75 5.00 12.00
85 Joe Dumars/75 6.00 15.00
86 Andre Miller/75 5.00 12.00
87 Kemba Walker/75 EXCH 10.00 25.00
88 Buck Williams/49 4.00 10.00
89 Nick Young/75 8.00 20.00
90 Jose Calderon/75 4.00 10.00
91 Shaquille O'Neal/30 100.00 200.00
92 Greg Monroe/75 5.00 12.00
93 Tracy McGrady/49 15.00 40.00
94 Jeff Malone/35 4.00 10.00
95 Tyson Chandler/49 5.00 12.00
96 Andrei Kirilenko/75 5.00 12.00
97 Kenny Walker/75 4.00 10.00
98 Norris Cole/75
99 Nando De Colo/75
100 Raymond Felton/75 5.00 12.00

2013-14 Panini National Treasures NBA Greats Signatures
RANDOM INSERTS IN PACKS
PRINT RUNS B/WN 25-49 COPIES PER
EXCHANGE DEADLINE 1/30/2016
*PRIME: .5X TO 1.2X BASIC

1 Bill Sharman/49 10.00 25.00
2 Jerry West/49 25.00 60.00
3 Gail Goodrich/49 6.00 15.00
4 Tony Parker/49 15.00 40.00
5 Joe Dumars/49 8.00 20.00
6 Clyde Drexler/49 12.00 30.00
7 Spencer Haywood/49 5.00 12.00
8 Rolando Blackman/49 6.00 15.00
9 Walt Frazier/49 8.00 20.00
10 Larry Bird/49 50.00 120.00
11 World B. Free/49 6.00 15.00
12 Earl Monroe/49 8.00 20.00
13 Nate Thurmond/49 8.00 20.00
14 Vince Carter/49 12.00 30.00
15 Walt Bellamy/49 6.00 15.00
16 Jason Kidd/49 8.00 20.00
17 Adrian Dantley/49 6.00 15.00
18 John Stockton/49 25.00 60.00
19 Wayne Embry/49 5.00 12.00
20 Karl Malone/49 25.00 60.00
21 Dirk Nowitzki/49 50.00 120.00
22 Kelly Tripucka/49 5.00 12.00
23 Hal Greer/49 6.00 15.00
24 Wes Unseld/49 8.00 20.00
25 Dave Bing/25 15.00 40.00
26 Dennis Rodman/49 25.00 60.00
27 Jack Sikma/49 6.00 15.00
28 Magic Johnson/49 40.00 100.00
29 Allan Houston/49 6.00 15.00
30 Scottie Pippen/49 40.00 100.00
31 Bill Walton/49 8.00 20.00
32 Steve Nash/49 15.00 40.00
33 Ralph Sampson/49 6.00 15.00
34 Anfernee Hardaway/49 12.00 30.00
35 Michael Finley/49 8.00 20.00
36 Ray Allen/49 20.00 50.00
37 Dan Issel/49 6.00 15.00
38 Julius Erving/49 25.00 60.00
39 Jerry Lucas/49 8.00 20.00
40 Kareem Abdul-Jabbar/49 30.00 80.00

2013-14 Panini National Treasures NBA Materials

RANDOM INSERTS IN PACKS
PRINT RUNS B/WN 45-99 COPIES PER
*PRIME: .75X TO 2X BASIC
1 Bill Laimbeer/45 3.00 8.00
2 Kevin Garnett/99 5.00 12.00
3 Fred Brown/49 2.50 6.00
4 Kyrie Irving/99 6.00 15.00
5 Larry Nance/49 3.00 8.00
6 Paul George/99 5.00 12.00
7 Bradley Beal/99 4.00 10.00
8 Dwyane Wade/99 6.00 15.00
9 Tyson Chandler/99 3.00 8.00
10 Russell Westbrook/99 5.00 12.00
11 Brad Daugherty/99 3.00 8.00
12 Paul Pierce/99 4.00 10.00
13 Fat Lever/49 3.00 8.00
14 Dirk Nowitzki/99 5.00 12.00
15 Louie Dampier/49 4.00 10.00
16 Blake Griffin/99 5.00 12.00
17 Allen Iverson/49 6.00 15.00
18 Kevin Love/99 4.00 10.00
19 Amare Stoudemire/99 3.00 8.00
20 Damian Lillard/99 6.00 15.00
21 John Starks/49 3.00 8.00
22 Monta Ellis/99 3.00 8.00
23 Grant Hill/49 5.00 12.00
24 Kenneth Faried/99 3.00 8.00
25 Manute Bol/75 10.00 25.00
26 Chris Paul/99 5.00 12.00
27 Alonzo Mourning/49 5.00 12.00
28 Ricky Rubio/99 4.00 10.00
29 Raymond Felton/99 3.00 8.00
30 Tim Duncan/99 5.00 12.00
31 Chris Andersen/99 3.00 8.00
32 Stephen Curry/99 15.00 40.00
33 Jeff Malone/49 2.50 6.00
34 James Harden/99 6.00 15.00
35 Serge Ibaka/99 3.00 8.00
36 Kobe Bryant/99 10.00 25.00
37 Larry Johnson/75 5.00 12.00
38 Anfernee Hardaway/75 10.00 25.00
39 Carmelo Anthony/99 5.00 12.00
40 John Wall/99 5.00 12.00
41 Chris Bosh/99 4.00 10.00
42 O.J. Mayo/99 2.50 6.00
43 Klay Thompson/99 5.00 12.00
44 Dwight Howard/99 3.00 8.00
45 Eric Bledsoe/99 3.00 8.00
46 LeBron James/99 12.00 30.00
47 Bill Cartwright/75 3.00 8.00
48 Kevin Durant/99 8.00 20.00
49 Anthony Mason/49 3.00 8.00
50 Al Horford/99 3.00 8.00

2013-14 Panini National Treasures NBA Rookie Materials

RANDOM INSERTS IN PACKS
STATED PRINT RUN 99 SER.#'d SETS
1 Peyton Siva 2.50 6.00
2 Trey Burke 3.00 8.00
3 Mason Plumlee 4.00 10.00
4 Dennis Schroder 4.00 10.00
5 Tony Mitchell 2.50 6.00
6 Rudy Gobert 5.00 12.00
7 Kentavious Caldwell-Pope 4.00 10.00
8 Ben McLemore 3.00 8.00
9 Isaiah Canaan 2.50 6.00
10 Steven Adams 4.00 10.00
11 Archie Goodwin 3.00 8.00
12 Luigi Datome 2.50 6.00
13 Anthony Bennett 3.00 8.00
14 Kelly Olynyk 3.00 8.00
15 Tim Hardaway Jr. 4.00 10.00
16 Victor Oladipo 5.00 12.00
17 Michael Carter-Williams 4.00 10.00
18 Tony Snell 3.00 8.00
19 Otto Porter 4.00 10.00
20 Giannis Antetokounmpo 15.00 40.00
21 Solomon Hill 2.50 6.00
22 Cody Zeller 3.00 8.00
23 Shane Larkin 2.50 6.00
24 Nate Wolters 3.00 8.00
25 Alex Len 3.00 8.00
26 Shabazz Muhammad 3.00 8.00
27 Nerlens Noel 5.00 12.00
28 Gal Mekel 2.50 6.00
29 Glen Rice Jr. 2.50 6.00
30 C.J. McCollum 6.00 15.00

2013-14 Panini National Treasures NBA Rookie Materials Prime

*PRIME: 1X TO 2.5X BASIC
RANDOM INSERTS IN PACKS
STATED PRINT RUN 25 SER.#'d SETS
10 Steven Adams 12.00 30.00
16 Victor Oladipo 20.00 50.00
17 Michael Carter-Williams 20.00 50.00
20 Giannis Antetokounmpo 40.00 100.00

2013-14 Panini National Treasures Night Moves Signature Materials

RANDOM INSERTS IN PACKS
PRINT RUNS B/WN 49-99 COPIES PER
EXCHANGE DEADLINE 1/30/2016
*GOLD: .6X TO 1.5X BASIC
1 Clyde Drexler/49 20.00 50.00
2 Larry Bird/49 40.00 100.00
3 Danny Green/99 8.00 20.00
4 Robert Parish/49 10.00 25.00
5 Harrison Barnes/49 10.00 25.00
6 Tom Chambers/99 5.00 12.00
7 Andre Drummond/49 20.00 50.00
8 Jason Kidd/49 12.00 30.00
9 Michael Finley/99 6.00 15.00
10 Kawhi Leonard/49 50.00 120.00
11 Toni Kukoc/99 10.00 25.00
12 Larry Johnson/49 10.00 25.00
13 Fat Lever/99 5.00 12.00
14 Roy Hibbert/49 5.00 12.00
15 Iman Shumpert/99 4.00 10.00
16 Tony Parker/49 20.00 50.00
17 Anfernee Hardaway/49 25.00 60.00
18 Thaddeus Young/75 4.00 10.00
19 Raymond Felton/49 5.00 12.00
20 Kevin Durant/49 60.00 120.00
21 Taj Gibson/99 5.00 12.00
22 Larry Nance/99 5.00 12.00
23 Goran Dragic/49 8.00 20.00
24 Scottie Pippen/49 50.00 120.00
25 Isaiah Thomas/99 12.00 30.00
26 Tracy McGrady/49 20.00 50.00
27 Anthony Davis/49 60.00 120.00
28 Joe Dumars/49 6.00 15.00
29 Bob Lanier/49 5.00 12.00
30 Kevin Love/49 15.00 40.00
31 Carmelo Anthony/49 50.00 120.00
32 Mark Price/99 6.00 15.00
33 Grant Hill/49 20.00 50.00
34 Serge Ibaka/49 5.00 12.00
35 James Harden/49 30.00 80.00
36 Tyson Chandler/49 5.00 12.00
37 Josh Smith/49 5.00 12.00
38 Anthony Mason/99 4.00 10.00
39 Bradley Beal/49 12.00 30.00
40 Kobe Bryant/49 100.00 200.00
41 Dikembe Mutombo/49 10.00 25.00
42 Mike Conley/49 5.00 12.00
43 Greg Monroe/99 5.00 12.00
44 Shaquille O'Neal/49 75.00 200.00
45 James Jones/99 4.00 10.00
46 Bernard King/49 5.00 12.00
47 Udonis Haslem/99 4.00 10.00
48 Julius Erving/49 40.00 100.00
49 Cedric Maxwell/99 4.00 10.00
50 Enes Kanter/99 4.00 10.00
51 Kurt Rambis/99 4.00 10.00
52 Hakeem Olajuwon/49 20.00 50.00
53 Nick Young/99 6.00 15.00
54 Stephen Curry/49 150.00 300.00
55 Jared Sullinger/49 4.00 10.00
56 Zach Randolph/49 5.00 12.00
57 Bill Cartwright/99
58 Kareem Abdul-Jabbar/49 30.00 80.00
59 Chris Mullin/49 10.00 25.00
60 LaMarcus Aldridge/49 20.00 50.00

2013-14 Panini National Treasures Notable Nicknames

RANDOM INSERTS IN PACKS
STATED PRINT RUN 49 SER.#'d SETS
EXCHANGE DEADLINE 1/30/2016
1 Andre Iguodala 12.00 30.00
2 Dick Van Arsdale 8.00 20.00
3 Fred Brown 15.00 40.00
4 Josh Smith 15.00 40.00
5 Darrell Griffith 12.00 30.00
6 Tracy McGrady 150.00 250.00
7 Nick Van Exel 40.00 100.00
8 Andrei Kirilenko 8.00 20.00
9 Billy Paultz 10.00 25.00
10 Danilo Gallinari 6.00 15.00
11 Robert Parish 12.00 30.00
12 Tom Gugliotta 12.00 30.00
13 Isiah Thomas 20.00 50.00
14 Karl Malone 75.00 150.00
15 Jamaal Wilkes 10.00 25.00
16 Zach Randolph 12.00 30.00
17 Vince Carter 75.00 150.00
18 Sam Perkins 12.00 30.00
19 Dan Majerle 12.00 30.00
20 Andrea Bargnani 8.00 20.00
21 Darryl Dawkins 12.00 30.00
22 Steve Francis 12.00 30.00
23 George Gervin 20.00 50.00
24 Earl Monroe 25.00 60.00
25 John Havlicek 40.00 100.00
26 Goran Dragic 8.00 20.00
27 David Robinson 50.00 120.00
28 Hakeem Olajuwon 40.00 100.00
29 Gus Williams
30 Dwyane Wade EXCH 40.00 100.00

2013-14 Panini National Treasures Scripts

RANDOM INSERTS IN PACKS
STATED PRINT RUN 49 SER.#'d SETS
EXCHANGE DEADLINE 1/30/2016
*GOLD: .5X TO 1.2X BASIC
1 Dolph Schayes 5.00 12.00
2 Ryan Anderson 4.00 10.00
3 Horace Grant 5.00 12.00
4 Tony Parker 20.00 50.00
5 Al Horford 4.00 10.00
6 Cazzie Russell 4.00 10.00
7 Dominique Wilkins 12.00 30.00
8 Bob Love 5.00 12.00
9 Clyde Drexler 12.00 30.00
10 Mike Conley 4.00 10.00
11 Donatas Motiejunas 4.00 10.00
12 Scottie Pippen 30.00 80.00
13 James Worthy 10.00 25.00
14 Tyson Chandler 4.00 10.00
15 Amir Johnson 3.00 8.00
16 Dirk Nowitzki 50.00 120.00
17 Brandon Knight 4.00 10.00
18 Kyle Lowry 4.00 10.00
19 Darrell Griffith 3.00 8.00
20 Nick Collison 4.00 10.00
21 Elgin Baylor 15.00 40.00
22 Steve Francis 6.00 15.00
23 Jared Sullinger 3.00 8.00
24 Vince Carter 12.00 30.00
25 Andre Miller 4.00 10.00
26 Kendrick Perkins 3.00 8.00
27 Chase Budinger 3.00 8.00
28 LaMarcus Aldridge 12.00 30.00
29 Dick Van Arsdale 4.00 10.00
30 Pat Riley 10.00 25.00
31 Gail Goodrich 4.00 10.00
32 Steve Mix 3.00 8.00
33 Jason Terry 4.00 10.00
34 Walt Bellamy 4.00 10.00
35 Anthony Davis 40.00 100.00
36 Karl Malone 25.00 60.00
37 Chris Andersen 12.00 30.00
38 Luol Deng 4.00 10.00
39 Dennis Rodman 12.00 30.00
40 Kevin Durant 60.00 150.00
41 Gus Williams 3.00 8.00
42 Theo Ratliff 3.00 8.00
43 John Hot Rod Williams 3.00 8.00
44 Bill Sharman 8.00 20.00
45 Avery Johnson 4.00 10.00
46 Kevin Love 12.00 30.00
47 Chuck Person 4.00 10.00
48 Maurice Harkless 3.00 8.00
49 Derrick Williams 3.00 8.00
50 Rod Strickland 3.00 8.00

2013-14 Panini National Treasures Signatures

RANDOM INSERTS IN PACKS
PRINT RUNS B/WN 10-99 COPIES PER
NO PRICING ON QTY 10
EXCHANGE DEADLINE 1/30/2016
SIAD Andre Drummond/35 15.00 40.00
SIAD Anthony Davis/49 60.00 150.00
SIAF Al Horford/35 5.00 12.00
SIAG Artis Gilmore/35 5.00 12.00
SIAH Anfernee Hardaway/35 25.00 60.00
SIAH Allan Houston/60 5.00 12.00
SIAJ Amir Johnson/60 4.00 10.00
SIAJ Avery Johnson/35 5.00 12.00
SIAL Andre Miller/60 5.00 12.00
SIBG Bernard King/35 5.00 12.00
SIBK Brandon Knight/35 5.00 12.00
SIBL Bob Lanier/25 8.00 20.00
SIBR Bill Russell/35 50.00 120.00
SICA Chris Andersen/35 25.00 60.00
SICB Chase Budinger/60 4.00 10.00
SICB Chris Bosh/35 12.00 30.00
SICD Clyde Drexler/35 20.00 50.00
SICP Chuck Person/60 5.00 12.00
SICR Clifford Robinson/60 4.00 10.00
SICS Cazzie Russell/60 5.00 12.00
SICW Chet Walker/60 5.00 12.00
SIDA Dick Van Arsdale/60 5.00 12.00
SIDD Dale Davis/60 4.00 10.00
SIDE Derrick Williams/25 4.00 10.00
SIDF Derrick Favors/35 5.00 12.00
SIDG Darrell Griffith/60 4.00 10.00
SIDH Dwight Howard/49 10.00 25.00
SIDM Donatas Motiejunas/60 5.00 12.00
SIDN Dirk Nowitzki/49 50.00 120.00
SIDN Danny Manning/35 5.00 12.00
SIDR David Robinson/25 20.00 50.00
SIDR Dennis Rodman/35 25.00 60.00
SIDS Dolph Schayes/35 6.00 15.00
SIDW Dominique Wilkins/35 15.00 40.00
SIEB Elgin Baylor/35 12.00 30.00
SIEH Elvin Hayes/35
SIGG Gail Goodrich/35 5.00 12.00
SIGP Gary Payton/35 12.00 30.00
SIGW Gus Williams/60 4.00 10.00
SIHG Hal Greer/35 5.00 12.00
SIHG Horace Grant/60 10.00 25.00
SIJD Jared Dudley/60 4.00 10.00
SIJH John Havlicek/25 30.00 80.00
SIJI Jack Sikma/60 5.00 12.00
SIJJ Jo Jo White/60 5.00 12.00
SIJK Jason Kidd/35 20.00 50.00
SIJM Jodie Meeks/60 5.00 12.00
SIJP John Thompson/35 15.00 40.00
SIJS Jared Sullinger/35 4.00 10.00
SIJS John Stockton/35 25.00 60.00
SIJT Jason Terry/35 5.00 12.00
SIJW James Worthy/35 15.00 40.00
SIJW John Hot Rod Williams/60 4.00 10.00
SIKA Kareem Abdul-Jabbar/49 30.00 80.00
SIKC K.C. Jones/25 20.00 50.00
SIKI Kyrie Irving/49 50.00 120.00
SIKK Kyle Korver/60 5.00 12.00
SIKL Kyle Lowry/60 8.00 20.00
SIKL Kevin Love/35 12.00 30.00
SIKM Kevin Martin/35 5.00 12.00
SIKM Karl Malone/49 30.00 80.00
SIKP Kendrick Perkins/60 4.00 10.00
SIKT Kelly Tripucka/35 4.00 10.00
SILA LaMarcus Aldridge/35 10.00 25.00
SILB Larry Bird/35 30.00 80.00
SILD Luol Deng/35 5.00 12.00
SIMC Mike Conley/60 5.00 12.00
SIMF Michael Finley/35 10.00 25.00
SIMH Maurice Harkless/60 4.00 10.00
SIMJ Magic Johnson/35 30.00 80.00
SINA Nate Archibald/35 5.00 12.00
SINC Nick Collison/60 5.00 12.00
SIOR Oscar Robertson/25 25.00 60.00
SIPJ Phil Jackson/35 100.00 250.00
SIPR Pat Riley/35 10.00 25.00
SIPS Peja Stojakovic/35 10.00 25.00
SIRA Ryan Anderson/60 5.00 12.00
SIRS Rod Strickland/60 4.00 10.00
SIRS Ralph Sampson/35 5.00 12.00
SIRW Rory Sparrow/60 4.00 10.00
SISB Shane Battier/25 5.00 12.00
SISF Steve Francis/35 5.00 12.00
SISK Steve Kerr/35 12.00 30.00
SISM Steve Mix/60 4.00 10.00
SISP Scottie Pippen/49 50.00 120.00
SISW Scott Wedman/60 5.00 12.00
SITC Tyson Chandler/35 5.00 12.00
SITG Taj Gibson/60 5.00 12.00
SITM Tracy McGrady/35 20.00 50.00
SITP Tony Parker/35 15.00 40.00
SITR Theo Ratliff/60 4.00 10.00
SITV Tom Van Arsdale/60 5.00 12.00
SIVB Vin Baker/60 4.00 10.00
SIVC Vince Carter/35 12.00 30.00
SIWB Walter Berry/60 4.00 10.00
SIWF Walt Frazier/35 8.00 20.00
SIWF World B. Free/35 5.00 12.00
SIZI Zydrunas Ilgauskas/60 5.00 12.00
SIZR Zach Randolph/35 5.00 12.00

2013-14 Panini National Treasures Sneaker Swatches

RANDOM INSERTS IN PACKS
PRINT RUNS B/WN 2-99 COPIES PER
NO PRICIN ON QTY 10 OR LESS
2 Shawn Marion/75 4.00 10.00
3 Kelly Olynyk/60 10.00 25.00
4 Kevin Garnett/75 6.00 15.00
8 Connie Hawkins/40 5.00 12.00
13 Nate Wolters/99 4.00 10.00
14 Gerald Henderson/99 3.00 8.00
15 Steven Adams/75 5.00 12.00
16 Alonzo Mourning/40 20.00 50.00
18 Shaquille O'Neal/99 12.00 30.00
20 Derrick Rose/65 6.00 15.00
21 C.J. McCollum/60 10.00 25.00
24 David Robinson/20 25.00 60.00
25 Shabazz Muhammad/99 4.00 10.00
26 Larry Johnson/40 20.00 50.00
28 Grant Hill/30 12.00 30.00
29 Dirk Nowitzki/99 10.00 25.00
30 Patrick Ewing/99 10.00 25.00
31 Cody Zeller/99 4.00 10.00
33 Tony Snell/75 8.00 20.00
34 Carmelo Anthony/95 10.00 25.00

2013-14 Panini National Treasures Sneaker Swatches Autographs

RANDOM INSERTS IN PACKS
PRINT RUNS B/WN 30-60 COPIES PER
EXCHANGE DEADLINE 1/30/2016
1 Jimmer Fredette/49 8.00 20.00
2 Kobe Bryant/39 200.00 400.00
3 Vince Carter/60 30.00 80.00
4 Ben McLemore/49 10.00 25.00
5 Victor Oladipo/49 15.00 40.00
6 Steven Adams/60 12.00 30.00
7 John Stockton/55 40.00 100.00
8 Shaquille O'Neal/60 200.00 300.00
9 Larry Johnson/60 20.00 50.00
10 Anfernee Hardaway/30 60.00 150.00
11 Deron Williams/40 10.00 25.00
12 Kyrie Irving/60 100.00 200.00
13 Kevin Durant/60 150.00 300.00
14 C.J. McCollum/60 25.00 60.00
15 Tony Snell/60 10.00 25.00
16 Nerlens Noel/60 30.00 80.00
17 Alonzo Mourning/60 30.00 80.00
18 Connie Hawkins/60 12.00 30.00
19 Grant Hill/60 50.00 120.00
20 Jason Kidd/60 30.00 80.00
21 David Robinson/60 50.00 120.00
22 Blake Griffin/60 30.00 80.00
23 Anthony Bennett/49 10.00 25.00
24 Kelly Olynyk/60 10.00 25.00
25 Tim Hardaway Jr./49 30.00 80.00

2013-14 Panini National Treasures Spanning Time Dual Signatures

RANDOM INSERTS IN PACKS
STATED PRINT RUN 49 SER.#'d SETS
EXCHANGE DEADLINE 1/30/2016
1 D.Williams/J.Kidd 20.00 50.00
2 C.Mullin/H.Barnes 10.00 25.00
3 C.Robinson/L.Aldridge 10.00 25.00
4 M.Daniels/R.Hibbert 10.00 25.00
5 Irving/Price EXCH 90.00 150.00
6 J.West/K.Bryant 125.00 250.00
7 S.Curry/T.Hardaway 100.00 200.00
8 D.Howard/H.Olajuwon 40.00 80.00
9 A.Mourning/A.Davis 75.00 150.00
10 J.Harden/T.McGrady 30.00 80.00

2013-14 Panini National Treasures Springfield Swatches

RANDOM INSERTS IN PACKS
PRINT RUNS B/WN 15-99 COPIES PER
*PRIME: .75X TO 2X BASIC
1 Wilt Chamberlain/15 40.00 100.00
2 Scottie Pippen/99 6.00 15.00
3 Isiah Thomas/49 5.00 12.00
4 James Worthy/49 6.00 15.00
5 Adrian Dantley/25 4.00 10.00
6 Kareem Abdul-Jabbar/49 6.00 15.00
7 Julius Erving/99 10.00 25.00
8 Dennis Johnson/49 4.00 10.00
9 Bob Lanier/99 4.00 10.00
10 Pete Maravich/49 25.00 60.00
11 Hakeem Olajuwon/75 6.00 15.00
12 David Robinson/49 6.00 15.00
13 Nate Thurmond/25 8.00 20.00
14 Jamaal Wilkes/49 5.00 12.00
15 Rick Barry/25 6.00 15.00
16 Clyde Drexler/99 6.00 15.00
17 Patrick Ewing/99 6.00 15.00
18 Magic Johnson/49 10.00 25.00
19 Jerry Lucas/25 12.00 30.00
20 Kevin McHale/75 5.00 12.00
21 Dennis Rodman/49 6.00 15.00
22 Robert Parish/49 5.00 12.00
23 Jerry West/25 20.00 50.00
24 Earl Monroe/49 10.00 25.00
25 Elgin Baylor/25 6.00 15.00
26 Joe Dumars/99 5.00 12.00
27 John Havlicek/99 12.00 30.00
28 Bernard King/75 4.00 10.00
29 Karl Malone/49 6.00 15.00
30 George Mikan/49 12.00 30.00
31 Gary Payton/49 5.00 12.00
32 John Stockton/49 6.00 15.00
33 Dominique Wilkins/49 6.00 15.00
34 Arvydas Sabonis/99 4.00 10.00
35 Larry Bird/49 12.00 30.00
36 Alex English/49 4.00 10.00
37 Bailey Howell/49 5.00 12.00
38 Moses Malone/75 5.00 12.00
39 Sam Jones/49 10.00 25.00
40 Chris Mullin/75 5.00 12.00

2013-14 Panini National Treasures Timelines Materials

RANDOM INSERTS IN PACKS
PRINT RUNS B/WN 49-99 COPIES PER
1 Kobe Bryant/99 12.00 30.00
2 John Stockton/49 6.00 15.00
3 Kevin Love/99 4.00 10.00
4 Karl Malone/49 5.00 12.00
5 Kyrie Irving/99 12.00 30.00
6 Kevin Durant/99 8.00 20.00
7 Dwight Howard/49 3.00 8.00
8 Tim Duncan/49 6.00 15.00
9 Blake Griffin/75 5.00 12.00
10 Ricky Pierce/49 2.50 6.00
11 LeBron James/99 12.00 30.00
12 Tyson Chandler/99 3.00 8.00
13 Ricky Rubio/99 4.00 10.00
14 Tony Parker/49 4.00 10.00
15 Dirk Nowitzki/99 5.00 12.00
16 Russell Westbrook/49 5.00 12.00
17 Paul George/99 5.00 12.00
18 John Wall/99 5.00 12.00
19 Chris Paul/75 5.00 12.00
20 Norm Nixon/49 2.50 6.00
21 Dwyane Wade/99 6.00 15.00
22 Danny Ainge/49 4.00 10.00
23 Carmelo Anthony/75 5.00 12.00
24 Doc Rivers/99 4.00 10.00
25 Kenneth Faried/99 3.00 8.00
26 Damian Lillard/75 6.00 15.00
27 James Harden/99 6.00 15.00
28 Terry Cummings/49 3.00 8.00
29 Shaquille O'Neal/99 12.00 30.00
30 Brad Daugherty/49 3.00 8.00
31 Larry Bird/49 10.00 25.00
32 Magic Johnson/49 10.00 25.00
33 Patrick Ewing/99 5.00 12.00
34 Dikembe Mutombo/99 4.00 10.00
35 Hakeem Olajuwon/49 5.00 12.00
36 Fred Brown/99 2.50 6.00
37 Anthony Davis/99 8.00 20.00
38 Dan Majerle/99 3.00 8.00
39 Mark Price/49 4.00 10.00
40 Xavier McDaniel/99 2.50 6.00

2013-14 Panini National Treasures Timelines Materials Prime

*PRIME: .75X TO 2X BASIC
RANDOM INSERTS IN PACKS
PRINT RUNS B/WN 10-25 COPIES PER
NO PRICING ON QTY 10
6 Kevin Durant/25 30.00 80.00
11 LeBron James/25 75.00 150.00

2013-14 Panini National Treasures X-Factor Materials

RANDOM INSERTS IN PACKS
STATED PRINT RUN 99 SER.#'d SETS
*PRIME: .75X TO 2X BASIC
1 James Harden/99 6.00 15.00
2 Mark Jackson/75 3.00 8.00
3 Hakeem Olajuwon/49 5.00 12.00
4 Karl Malone/49 5.00 12.00
5 Jason Kidd/49 4.00 10.00
6 Kevin Garnett/99 6.00 15.00
7 Steve Nash/99 4.00 10.00
8 David Robinson/99 6.00 15.00
9 Pau Gasol/99 4.00 10.00
10 Kyrie Irving/99 8.00 20.00
11 Allen Iverson/49 5.00 12.00
12 LeBron James/75 10.00 25.00
13 Joe Dumars/99 4.00 10.00
14 Kevin Love/99 4.00 10.00
15 Clyde Drexler/99 5.00 12.00
16 Shaquille O'Neal/49 8.00 20.00
17 Patrick Ewing/99 5.00 12.00
18 Kobe Bryant/99 12.00 30.00
19 Dwyane Wade/99 6.00 15.00
20 Anthony Davis/99 10.00 25.00
21 Kareem Abdul-Jabbar/49 6.00 15.00
22 Larry Bird/49 10.00 25.00
23 Magic Johnson/49 10.00 25.00
24 Tim Duncan/99 6.00 15.00
25 Xavier McDaniel/49 2.50 6.00
26 Dirk Nowitzki/99 5.00 12.00
27 Dominique Wilkins/75 5.00 12.00
28 Kevin Durant/99 8.00 20.00
29 Dwight Howard/99 3.00 8.00
30 Blake Griffin/99 4.00 10.00

2014-15 Panini National Treasures

1-100 PRINT RUN 99 SER.#'d SETS
JSY AU RC p/r B/WN 49-99 COPIES PER
134-186 PRINT RUNS 99 SER.#'d SETS
PRIME PATCHES MAY SELL FOR PREMIUM
EXCHANGE DEADLINE 2/5/2017
1 Arron Afflalo 1.25 3.00
2 LaMarcus Aldridge 2.00 5.00
3 Ryan Anderson 1.25 3.00
4 Giannis Antetokounmpo 4.00 10.00
5 Carmelo Anthony 2.50 6.00
6 Bradley Beal 2.00 5.00
7 Patrick Beverley 1.25 3.00
8 Eric Bledsoe 1.50 4.00
9 Carlos Boozer 1.50 4.00
10 Chris Bosh 2.00 5.00
11 Avery Bradley 1.50 4.00
12 Kobe Bryant 8.00 20.00
13 Trey Burke 1.25 3.00
14 Jimmy Butler 2.00 5.00
15 Michael Carter-Williams 1.25 3.00
16 Darren Collison 1.50 4.00
17 Mike Conley 1.50 4.00
18 DeMarcus Cousins 2.00 5.00
19 Stephen Curry 8.00 20.00
20 Anthony Davis 4.00 10.00
21 Luol Deng 1.50 4.00
22 DeMar DeRozan 2.00 5.00
23 Goran Dragic 1.50 4.00
24 Andre Drummond 2.00 5.00
25 Tim Duncan 3.00 8.00
26 Kevin Durant 5.00 12.00
27 Monta Ellis 1.50 4.00
28 Tyreke Evans 1.25 3.00
29 Derrick Favors 1.50 4.00
30 Marc Gasol 2.00 5.00
31 Pau Gasol 2.00 5.00
32 Rudy Gay 2.00 5.00
33 Marcin Gortat 1.50 4.00
34 Draymond Green 2.50 6.00
35 Blake Griffin 2.00 5.00
36 Tim Hardaway Jr. 1.25 3.00
37 James Harden 3.00 8.00
38 Tobias Harris 1.50 4.00
39 Gordon Hayward 2.00 5.00
40 Roy Hibbert 1.50 4.00
41 Jordan Hill 1.25 3.00
42 Jrue Holiday 1.50 4.00
43 Al Horford 1.50 4.00
44 Dwight Howard 1.50 4.00
45 Serge Ibaka 1.50 4.00
46 Andre Iguodala 1.50 4.00
47 Kyrie Irving 4.00 10.00
48 LeBron James 8.00 20.00
49 Al Jefferson 1.50 4.00
50 Brandon Jennings 1.25 3.00
51 Joe Johnson 1.50 4.00
52 Brandon Knight 1.50 4.00
53 Ty Lawson 1.25 3.00
54 Kawhi Leonard 3.00 8.00
55 Damian Lillard 4.00 10.00
56 Brook Lopez 1.50 4.00
57 Kevin Love 2.00 5.00
58 Kyle Lowry 1.50 4.00
59 Wesley Matthews 1.25 3.00
60 O.J. Mayo 1.25 3.00
61 Paul Millsap 2.00 5.00
62 Markieff Morris 1.25 3.00
63 Shabazz Muhammad 1.50 4.00
64 Joakim Noah 1.50 4.00
65 Dirk Nowitzki 2.50 6.00
66 Victor Oladipo 1.50 4.00
67 Tony Parker 2.00 5.00
68 Chris Paul 2.50 6.00
69 Paul Pierce 2.00 5.00
70 Zach Randolph 1.50 4.00
71 J.J. Redick 2.00 5.00
72 Rajon Rondo 2.00 5.00
73 Derrick Rose 2.50 6.00
74 Dennis Schroder 1.50 4.00
75 Luis Scola 1.50 4.00
76 Amar'e Stoudemire 2.00 5.00
77 Jared Sullinger 1.25 3.00
78 Jeff Teague 1.50 4.00
79 Klay Thompson 2.50 6.00
80 Jonas Valanciunas 1.50 4.00
81 Nikola Vucevic 1.50 4.00
82 Dwyane Wade 3.00 8.00
83 Kemba Walker 2.00 5.00
84 John Wall 2.50 6.00
85 Russell Westbrook 5.00 12.00
86 Deron Williams 1.50 4.00
87 Lou Williams 1.50 4.00
88 Tony Wroten 1.25 3.00
89 Thaddeus Young 1.25 3.00
90 Bill Russell 3.00 8.00
91 Jerry West 2.50 6.00
92 Kareem Abdul-Jabbar 3.00 8.00
93 Scottie Pippen 4.00 10.00
94 Pete Maravich 3.00 8.00
95 Wilt Chamberlain 4.00 10.00
96 Karl Malone 2.50 6.00
97 Larry Bird 5.00 12.00
98 Magic Johnson 5.00 12.00
99 Oscar Robertson 2.50 6.00
100 Shaquille O'Neal 4.00 10.00
101 A.Wiggins JSY AU/99 RC 2000.00 3000.00
102 J.Parker JSY AU/99 RC 800.00 1200.00
103 J.Embiid JSY AU/99 RC 1500.00 2000.00
104 A.Gordon JSY AU/99 RC 250.00 500.00
105 D.Exum JSY AU/99 RC 125.00 300.00
106 M.Smart JSY AU/99 RC 100.00 250.00
107 J.Randle JSY AU/99 RC 200.00 500.00
108 N.Stauskas JSY AU/99 RC 40.00 100.00
109 N.Vonleh JSY AU/99 RC 25.00 60.00
110 E.Payton JSY AU/99 RC 150.00 300.00
111 D.McDermott JSY AU/99 RC 50.00 120.00
112 Z.LaVine JSY AU/99 RC 1200.00 1600.00
113 T. Warren JSY AU/99 RC 125.00 300.00
114 A.Payne JSY AU/99 RC 10.00 25.00
115 J.Young JSY AU/99 RC 12.00 30.00
116 Tyler Ennis JSY AU/99 RC 15.00 40.00
117 Gary Harris JSY AU/99 RC 125.00 300.00
118 B.Caboclo JSY AU/99 RC 60.00 150.00
119 M.McGary JSY AU/99 RC
120 J.Adams JSY AU/99 RC 15.00 40.00
121 R.Hood JSY AU/99 RC 150.00 300.00
122 S.Napier JSY AU/99 RC 20.00 50.00
123 P.Hairston JSY AU/99 RC 12.00 30.00
124 N.Mirotic JSY AU/49 RC 150.00 300.00
125 K.Anderson JSY AU/99 RC 40.00 100.00
126 D.Inglis JSY AU/99 RC 12.00 30.00
127 K.McDaniels JSY AU/99 RC 15.00 40.00
128 Joe Harris JSY AU/99 RC 12.00 30.00
129 C.Early JSY AU/99 RC 12.00 30.00
130 L.Galloway JSY AU/49 RC 30.00 80.00
131 J.O'Bryant JSY AU/99 RC 12.00 30.00
132 S.Dinwiddie JSY AU/99 RC 30.00 80.00
133 T. Wear JSY AU/49 RC 12.00 30.00
134 B.Bogdanovic AU RC 5.00 12.00
135 Jusuf Nurkic AU RC 50.00 120.00
136 J.Michael McAdoo AU RC 8.00 20.00
137 K.Papanikolaou AU RC
138 Jordan Clarkson AU RC 50.00 120.00
139 Tarik Black AU RC 4.00 10.00
140 Erick Green AU RC 4.00 10.00
141 Markel Brown AU RC 4.00 10.00
142 Dwight Powell AU RC 4.00 10.00
143 C.J. Wilcox AU RC 4.00 10.00
144 Damjan Rudez AU RC
145 Cory Jefferson AU RC 4.00 10.00
146 Jarnell Stokes AU RC 4.00 10.00
147 James Ennis AU RC 4.00 10.00
148 Glenn Robinson III AU RC 4.00 10.00
149 Devyn Marble AU RC 4.00 10.00
150 Lucas Nogueira AU RC 4.00 10.00
151 Andrew Wiggins AU 100.00 200.00
152 Jabari Parker AU 25.00 60.00
153 Joel Embiid AU 40.00 100.00
154 Aaron Gordon AU 12.00 30.00
155 Marcus Smart AU 10.00 25.00
156 Julius Randle AU 12.00 30.00
157 Nik Stauskas AU 5.00 12.00
158 Noah Vonleh AU 5.00 12.00
159 Elfrid Payton AU 6.00 15.00
160 D.McDermott AU 6.00 15.00
161 Zach LaVine AU 15.00 40.00
162 T.J. Warren AU 6.00 15.00
163 Adreian Payne AU 6.00 15.00
164 James Young AU 6.00 15.00
165 Tyler Ennis AU 6.00 15.00
166 Gary Harris AU 6.00 15.00
167 Mitch McGary AU
168 Jordan Adams AU 4.00 10.00
169 Rodney Hood AU 6.00 15.00
170 Shabazz Napier AU 5.00 12.00
171 P.J. Hairston AU 4.00 10.00
172 C.J. Wilcox AU 4.00 10.00
173 Kyle Anderson AU 6.00 15.00
174 J.Michael McAdoo AU 5.00 12.00
176 Cleanthony Early AU 4.00 10.00
177 Jarnell Stokes AU 4.00 10.00
178 Johnny O'Bryant AU 4.00 10.00
179 Tarik Black AU 4.00 10.00
180 Spencer Dinwiddie AU 5.00 12.00
181 Jerami Grant AU 4.00 10.00
182 Glenn Robinson III AU 4.00 10.00
183 Markel Brown AU 4.00 10.00
184 Dwight Powell AU 4.00 10.00
185 Jordan Clarkson AU 15.00 40.00
186 Russ Smith AU 4.00 10.00

2014-15 Panini National Treasures Blue

*BLUE: .5X TO 1.2X BASIC
RANDOM INSERTS IN PACKS
STATED PRINT RUN 25 SER.#'d SETS
48 LeBron James 25.00 60.00

2014-15 Panini National Treasures Gold

RANDOM INSERTS IN PACKS
1-100 PRINT RUN 10 SER.#'d SETS
NO PRICING ON 1-100 AVAILABLE
*GOLD 101-133: .6X TO 1.5X BASIC
*GOLD 134-150: .5X TO 1.2X BASIC
101-186 PRINT RUN 25 SER.#'d SETS
EXCHANGE DEADLINE 2/5/2017
104 Aaron Gordon JSY AU 350.00 600.00

2014-15 Panini National Treasures Air Apparent Jersey Autographs

RANDOM INSERTS IN PACKS
PRINT RUNS B/WN 25-49 COPIES PER
EXCHANGE DEADLINE 2/5/2017
AAAB Anthony Bennett/49 4.00 10.00
AAAD Anthony Davis/25 40.00 100.00
AAAG Aaron Gordon/49 12.00 30.00
AAAL Alex Len/49 4.00 10.00
AAAW Andrew Wiggins/35 100.00 200.00
AABB Bradley Beal/49 10.00 25.00
AABK Brandon Knight/49 4.00 10.00
AABM Ben McLemore/49 4.00 10.00
AACE Cleanthony Early/49 4.00 10.00
AACJ Cory Jefferson/49 4.00 10.00
AACM C.J. McCollum/49 12.00 30.00
AACZ Cody Zeller/49 4.00 10.00
AADI Damien Inglis/49 4.00 10.00
AADM Donatas Motiejunas/49 4.00 10.00
AAGA G. Antetokounmpo/49 60.00 150.00
AAGR Glenn Robinson III/49 4.00 10.00
AAHB Harrison Barnes/49 8.00 20.00
AAJA Jordan Adams/49 4.00 10.00
AAJE Joel Embiid/49 75.00 200.00
AAJG Jerami Grant/49 4.00 10.00
AAJO Johnny O'Bryant/49 4.00 10.00
AAJP Jabari Parker/35 50.00 120.00
AAJR Julius Randle/49 15.00 40.00
AAJS Jarnell Stokes/49 4.00 10.00
AAJV Jonas Valanciunas/35 5.00 12.00
AAJW John Wall/25 20.00 50.00
AAJY James Young/49 4.00 10.00
AAKA Kyle Anderson/49 6.00 15.00
AAKC Kentavious Caldwell-Pope/49 3.00 8.00
AAKI Kyrie Irving/25 30.00 80.00
AAKM K.J. McDaniels/49 5.00 12.00
AALS Lance Stephenson/49 5.00 12.00
AAMC Michael Carter-Williams/49 4.00 10.00
AAMP Mason Plumlee/49 5.00 12.00
AAMS Marcus Smart/49 10.00 25.00
AANN Nerlens Noel/49 5.00 12.00
AANS Nik Stauskas/49 5.00 12.00
AANV Noah Vonleh/49 5.00 12.00
AAOP Otto Porter/49 5.00 12.00
AAPG Paul George/25 25.00 60.00
AARJ Reggie Jackson/49 4.00 10.00
AASD Spencer Dinwiddie/49 5.00 12.00
AASH Solomon Hill/49 4.00 10.00
AASM Shabazz Muhammad/49 5.00 12.00
AATB Trey Burke/49 4.00 10.00
AATH Tim Hardaway Jr./49 4.00 10.00
AATT Tristan Thompson/49 5.00 12.00
AAVO Victor Oladipo/49 5.00 12.00
AAJEN James Ennis/49 4.00 10.00

2014-15 Panini National Treasures Air Apparent Jersey Autographs Prime

*PRIME/25: .75X TO 2X
RANDOM INSERTS IN PACKS
PRINT RUNS B/WN 10-25 COPIES PER
NO PRICING ON QTY 10
EXCHANGE DEADLINE 2/5/2017
AATW T.J. Warren/25 10.00 25.00

2014-15 Panini National Treasures Career Materials Trios

RANDOM INSERTS IN PACKS
PRINT RUNS B/WN 35-99 COPIES PER
*PRIME: .75X TO 2X BASIC
CMTAJ Al Jefferson/49 3.00 8.00
CMTAM Alonzo Mourning/99 5.00 12.00
CMTCM Cedric Maxwell/35 2.50 6.00
CMTDC Darren Collison/99 3.00 8.00
CMTDH Dwight Howard/99 3.00 8.00
CMTDM Dikembe Mutombo/40 6.00 15.00
CMTDW Dominique Wilkins/99 5.00 12.00
CMTEG Eric Gordon/99 3.00 8.00
CMTJC Jose Calderon/99 2.50 6.00
CMTJF Jimmer Fredette/99 2.50 6.00
CMTJK Jason Kidd/99 4.00 10.00
CMTKG Kevin Garnett/99 8.00 20.00
CMTLS Luis Scola/99 3.00 8.00
CMTPP Paul Pierce/99 4.00 10.00
CMTRG Rudy Gay/99 4.00 10.00

2014-15 Panini National Treasures Clutch Factor Jersey Autographs

RANDOM INSERTS IN PACKS
PRINT RUNS B/WN 24-75 COPIES PER
EXCHANGE DEADLINE 2/5/2017
CFAD Adrian Dantley/75 5.00 12.00
CFBK Bernard King/49 6.00 15.00
CFBL Bill Laimbeer/75 6.00 15.00
CFCA Chris Andersen/49 10.00 25.00
CFCB Chris Bosh/35 8.00 20.00
CFCD Clyde Drexler/25 20.00 50.00
CFCM Cedric Maxwell/75 5.00 12.00
CFDG Danny Green/75 6.00 15.00
CFDW Dominique Wilkins/49 12.00 30.00
CFEM Earl Monroe/49 12.00 30.00
CFGA G. Antetokounmpo/75 50.00 120.00
CFJD Joe Dumars/49 6.00 15.00
CFJE Julius Erving/35 40.00 100.00
CFJW Jerry West/35 30.00 80.00
CFJWO James Worthy/49 20.00 50.00
CFKA Kareem Abdul-Jabbar/24 30.00 80.00
CFKB Kobe Bryant/35 100.00 200.00
CFKD Kevin Durant/35 75.00 150.00
CFKI Kyrie Irving/35 30.00 80.00
CFKK Kyle Korver/75 6.00 15.00
CFLB Larry Bird/35 50.00 120.00
CFMA Mark Aguirre/75 5.00 12.00
CFRH Robert Horry/75 6.00 15.00
CFRP Robert Parish/49 10.00 25.00
CFSC Stephen Curry/49 100.00 250.00
CFSE Sean Elliott/75 6.00 15.00

2014-15 Panini National Treasures Clutch Factor Jersey Autograhs Prime

*PRIME: .75X TO 2X
RANDOM INSERTS IN PACKS
PRINT RUNS B/WN 5-25 COPIES PER
NO PRICING ON QTY 10 OR LESS
EXCHANGE DEADLINE 2/5/2017
CFSC Stephen Curry/25 300.00 600.00

2014-15 Panini National Treasures Colossal Jerseys

RANDOM INSERTS IN PACKS
STATED PRINT RUN 99 SER.#'d SETS
1 LeBron James 10.00 25.00
2 Kobe Bryant 12.00 30.00
3 Kevin Durant 6.00 15.00
4 Damian Lillard 5.00 12.00
5 Derrick Rose 8.00 20.00
6 Kyrie Irving 8.00 20.00
7 Blake Griffin 4.00 10.00
8 Carmelo Anthony 5.00 12.00
9 Tim Duncan 6.00 15.00
10 John Wall 5.00 12.00
11 Anthony Davis 8.00 20.00
12 Stephen Curry 12.00 30.00
13 Pau Gasol 4.00 10.00
14 James Harden 6.00 15.00
15 Dwyane Wade 5.00 12.00
16 Russell Westbrook 5.00 12.00
17 Marc Gasol 4.00 10.00
18 Kyle Lowry 3.00 8.00
19 Jeff Teague 3.00 8.00
20 Klay Thompson 5.00 12.00
21 Larry Bird 10.00 25.00
22 Karl Malone 6.00 15.00
23 Shaquille O'Neal 8.00 20.00
24 Patrick Ewing 6.00 15.00
25 Hakeem Olajuwon 5.00 12.00

2014-15 Panini National Treasures Colossal Jerseys Signatures

RANDOM INSERTS IN PACKS
PRINT RUNS B/WN 25-49 COPIES PER
CJSAE Alex English/49 6.00 15.00
CJSAW Antoine Walker/49 6.00 15.00
CJSCD Clyde Drexler/25 12.00 30.00
CJSCM Cedric Maxwell/49 5.00 12.00
CJSCR Clifford Robinson/49 8.00 20.00
CJSDR David Robinson/35 20.00 50.00
CJSEK Enes Kanter/49 5.00 12.00
CJSGR Glen Rice/49 6.00 15.00
CJSJD Joe Dumars/35 8.00 20.00
CJSJE Julius Erving/25 50.00 120.00
CJSKB Kobe Bryant/49 125.00 250.00
CJSKD Kevin Durant/25 75.00 150.00
CJSKL Kevin Love/35 15.00 40.00

CJSLB Larry Bird/25 50.00 120.00
CJSSC Stephen Curry/35 175.00 350.00
CJSTH Tim Hardaway/49 8.00 20.00
CJSVC Vince Carter/35 20.00 50.00
CJSZR Zach Randolph/35 6.00 15.00

2014-15 Panini National Treasures Colossal Jerseys Signatures Prime

*PRIME: .75X TO 2X BASIC
RANDOM INSERTS IN PACKS
PRINT RUNS B/WN 5-25 COPIES PER
NO PRICING ON QTY 10 OR LESS
CJSSC Stephen Curry/25 300.00 600.00

2014-15 Panini National Treasures Game Changers Autographs

RANDOM INSERTS IN PACKS
PRINT RUNS B/WN 25-49 COPIES PER
EXCHANGE DEADLINE 2/5/2017
*GOLD: .5X TO 1.2X BASIC p/r 35-49
*GOLD: .4X TO 1X BASIC p/r 25
GCAE Alex English/49 5.00 12.00
GCBK Bernard King/35 5.00 12.00
GCCA Carmelo Anthony/25 25.00 60.00
GCCP Chris Paul/25 40.00 100.00
GCDI Dan Issel/49 5.00 12.00
GCDW Dominique Wilkins/35 10.00 25.00
GCJE Julius Erving/25 30.00 80.00
GCJK Jason Kidd/35 12.00 30.00
GCJW John Wall/35 20.00 50.00
GCKB Kobe Bryant/25 150.00 300.00
GCKD Kevin Durant/25 75.00 150.00
GCKI Kyrie Irving/35 30.00 80.00
GCKL Kevin Love/35 12.00 30.00
GCLB Larry Bird/25 40.00 100.00
GCLS Latrell Sprewell/35 25.00 60.00
GCMA Mark Aguirre/49 5.00 12.00
GCTC Tyson Chandler/35 5.00 12.00
GCTH Tim Hardaway/49 6.00 15.00
GCWF Walt Frazier/35 10.00 25.00

2014-15 Panini National Treasures Gold Logoman Signatures

RANDOM INSERTS IN PACKS
STATED PRINT RUN 49 SER.#'d SETS
EXCHANGE DEADLINE 2/5/2017
GLAD Adrian Dantley/49 8.00 20.00
GLAE Alex English/49 8.00 20.00
GLAG Artis Gilmore/49 8.00 20.00
GLAM Alonzo Mourning/49 30.00 80.00
GLAW Antoine Walker/49 10.00 25.00
GLBK Bernard King/49 8.00 20.00
GLBL Bill Laimbeer/49 10.00 25.00
GLCA Carmelo Anthony/49 30.00 80.00
GLCA Chris Andersen/49 10.00 25.00
GLCB Chris Bosh/49 12.00 30.00
GLCD Clyde Drexler/49 25.00 60.00
GLCH Cliff Hagan/49 8.00 20.00
GLDF Derrick Favors/49 8.00 20.00
GLDI Dan Issel/49 8.00 20.00
GLDW Dominique Wilkins/49 20.00 50.00
GLEK Enes Kanter/49 6.00 15.00
GLGA Giannis Antetokounmpo/49 30.00 80.00
GLGG George Gervin/49 12.00 30.00
GLGG Gail Goodrich/49 8.00 20.00
GLGH Gordon Hayward/49 25.00 60.00
GLGH Grant Hill/49 20.00 50.00
GLGP Gary Payton/49 15.00 40.00
GLIT Isiah Thomas/49 15.00 40.00
GLJE Julius Erving/49 40.00 100.00
GLJK Jason Kidd/49 25.00 60.00
GLJS John Stockton/49 25.00 60.00
GLJW John Wall/49 40.00 100.00
GLKB Kobe Bryant/49 125.00 250.00
GLKD 75.00 150.00
GLKI Kyrie Irving/49 60.00 150.00
GLKK Kyle Korver/49 8.00 20.00
GLKLV Kevin Love/49 25.00 60.00
GLKL Kawhi Leonard/49 60.00 150.00
GLKM Karl Malone/49 30.00 80.00
GLLB Larry Bird/49 50.00 120.00
GLLS Latrell Sprewell/49 15.00 40.00
GLLS Lance Stephenson/49 10.00 25.00
GLMF Michael Finley/49 10.00 25.00
GLMG Marcin Gortat/49 8.00 20.00
GLMJ Magic Johnson/49 40.00 100.00
GLMP Mark Price/49 12.00 30.00
GLMT Mychal Thompson/49 6.00 15.00
GLPG Pau Gasol/49 15.00 40.00
GLRB Rick Barry/49 15.00 40.00
GLRB Rolando Blackman/49 8.00 20.00
GLRR Ricky Rubio/49 40.00 100.00
GLRS Rony Seikaly/49 6.00 15.00
GLRT Rudy Tomjanovich/49 8.00 20.00
GLRW Russell Westbrook/49 60.00 150.00
GLSC Stephen Curry/49 100.00 250.00
GLSO Shaquille O'Neal/49 50.00 120.00
GLTG Taj Gibson/49 8.00 20.00
GLTG Tom Gugliotta/49 6.00 15.00
GLTM Tracy McGrady/49 40.00 100.00
GLTY Thaddeus Young/49 6.00 15.00
GLVC Vince Carter/49 30.00 80.00
GLWF Walt Frazier/49 12.00 30.00
GLXM Xavier McDaniel/49 6.00 15.00
GLZI Zydrunas Ilgauskas/49 8.00 20.00
GLZR Zach Randolph/49 12.00 30.00

2014-15 Panini National Treasures Kobe's All-Rookie Team Selections Signature Materials

RANDOM INSERTS IN PACKS
STATED PRINT RUN 99 SER.#'d SETS
EXCHANGE DEADLINE 2/5/2017
KOBEAG Aaron Gordon 12.00 30.00
KOBEAW Andrew Wiggins 75.00 200.00
KOBEDE Dante Exum 10.00 25.00
KOBEDM Doug McDermott 4.00 10.00
KOBEEP Elfrid Payton 4.00 10.00
KOBEGH Gary Harris 5.00 12.00
KOBEJH Joe Harris 2.50 6.00
KOBEJP Jabari Parker 25.00 60.00
KOBEJY James Young 2.50 6.00
KOBEKM K.J. McDaniels 3.00 8.00
KOBEMS Marcus Smart 10.00 25.00
KOBEPH P.J. Hairston 2.50 6.00
KOBERH Rodney Hood 6.00 15.00
KOBESN Shabazz Napier 3.00 8.00
KOBEZL Zach LaVine 25.00 60.00

2014-15 Panini National Treasures Kobe's All-Rookie Team Selections Signature Materials Prime

*PRIME: .75X TO 2X
RANDOM INSERTS IN PACKS
STATED PRINT RUN 25 SER.#'d SETS
EXCHANGE DEADLINE 2/5/2017

2014-15 Panini National Treasures Lasting Legacies Jersey Autographs

RANDOM INSERTS IN PACKS
PRINT RUNS B/WN 24-75 COPIES PER
EXCHANGE DEADLINE 2/5/2017
*PRIME: .75X TO 2X BASIC
LLAD Adrian Dantley/49 5.00 12.00
LLAI Allen Iverson/25 75.00 150.00
LLBK Bernard King/35 6.00 15.00
LLCD Clyde Drexler/25 20.00 50.00
LLCM Chris Mullin/35 12.00 30.00
LLDR David Robinson/25 20.00 50.00
LLDW Dominique Wilkins/35 12.00 30.00
LLEB Elgin Baylor/35 10.00 25.00
LLEM Earl Monroe/25 15.00 40.00
LLGH Grant Hill/35 20.00 50.00
LLGP Gary Payton/35 12.00 30.00
LLHO Hakeem Olajuwon/25 25.00 60.00
LLJD Joe Dumars/35 6.00 15.00
LLJW James Worthy/35 10.00 25.00
LLJW Jerry West/25 30.00 80.00
LLKA Kareem Abdul-Jabbar/25 30.00 80.00
LLKM Kevin McHale/35 10.00 25.00
LLLB Larry Bird/25 50.00 120.00
LLMA Mark Aguirre/49 5.00 12.00
LLMF Michael Finley/35 6.00 15.00
LLRB Rick Barry/35 10.00 25.00
LLRH Robert Horry/49 6.00 15.00
LLRP Robert Parish/35 10.00 25.00
LLSO Shaquille O'Neal/25 75.00 150.00
LLNVE Nick Van Exel/35 15.00 40.00

2014-15 Panini National Treasures Material Treasures

RANDOM INSERTS IN PACKS
STATED PRINT RUN 99 SER.#'d SETS
*PRIME: .75X TO 2X BASIC
MTAD Anthony Davis 6.00 15.00
MTAD Andre Drummond 4.00 10.00
MTAI Allen Iverson 6.00 15.00
MTAS Amar'e Stoudemire 4.00 10.00
MTBK Bernard King 3.00 8.00
MTBL Brook Lopez 3.00 8.00
MTCA Chris Andersen 3.00 8.00
MTCP Chandler Parsons 3.00 8.00
MTDC Darren Collison 3.00 8.00
MTDG Danilo Gallinari 2.50 6.00
MTDJ DeAndre Jordan 4.00 10.00
MTDR Derrick Rose 8.00 20.00
MTDW Dwyane Wade 5.00 12.00
MTDW Deron Williams 3.00 8.00
MTGH Gordon Hayward 4.00 10.00
MTGP Gary Payton 4.00 10.00
MTIS Iman Shumpert 2.50 6.00
MTJL Jeremy Lin 4.00 10.00
MTJR J.J. Redick 4.00 10.00
MTJS Josh Smith 3.00 8.00
MTJS John Stockton 6.00 15.00
MTKG Kevin Garnett 8.00 20.00
MTKI Kyrie Irving 8.00 20.00
MTKW Kemba Walker 4.00 10.00
MTLJ Larry Johnson 5.00 12.00
MTLL Luc Longley 3.00 8.00
MTMC Michael Carter-Williams 2.50 6.00
MTMC Mario Chalmers 3.00 8.00
MTNB Nicolas Batum 3.00 8.00
MTPM Paul Millsap 4.00 10.00
MTPP Paul Pierce 4.00 10.00
MTRA Ray Allen 5.00 12.00
MTRH Roy Hibbert 3.00 8.00
MTRL Reggie Lewis 4.00 10.00
MTSK Shawn Kemp 8.00 20.00
MTTA Trevor Ariza 2.50 6.00
MTTG Taj Gibson 3.00 8.00
MTTT Tristan Thompson 3.00 8.00
MTTY Thaddeus Young 2.50 6.00
MTWM Wesley Matthews 2.50 6.00

2014-15 Panini National Treasures Material Treasures Signatures

RANDOM INSERTS IN PACKS
PRINT RUNS B/WN 20-49 COPIES PER
EXCHANGE DEADLINE 2/5/2017
*PRIME: .75X TO 2X BASIC
MTSAA Arron Afflalo/49 4.00 10.00
MTSAB Anthony Bennett/35 4.00 10.00
MTSAH Al Horford/35 5.00 12.00
MTSAL Alex Len/35 5.00 12.00
MTSAV Anderson Varejao/49 4.00 10.00
MTSAW Antoine Walker/49 6.00 15.00
MTSBC Bill Cartwright/49 5.00 12.00
MTSBD Brad Daugherty/49 5.00 12.00
MTSBD Baron Davis/35 5.00 12.00
MTSBG Blake Griffin/25 25.00 60.00
MTSBK Brandon Knight/35 4.00 10.00
MTSBL Bill Laimbeer/49 6.00 15.00
MTSBM Ben McLemore/35 5.00 12.00
MTSBS Byron Scott/35 6.00 15.00
MTSCA Carmelo Anthony/25 20.00 50.00
MTSCB Chris Bosh/25 8.00 20.00
MTSCR Clifford Robinson/49 4.00 10.00
MTSDC Doug Collins/49 6.00 15.00
MTSDG Danilo Gallinari/35 4.00 10.00
MTSDH Dwight Howard/25 10.00 25.00
MTSDM Donatas Motiejunas/49 4.00 10.00
MTSGH George Hill/49 5.00 12.00
MTSHB Harrison Barnes/35 8.00 20.00
MTSJC Jose Calderon/49 3.00 8.00
MTSJS John Stockton/25 25.00 60.00
MTSJS John Starks/49 10.00 25.00
MTSJW John Wall/35 12.00 30.00
MTSKA Kenny Anderson/49 5.00 12.00
MTSKB Kobe Bryant/25 100.00 200.00
MTSKD Kevin Durant/25 75.00 150.00
MTSKI Kyrie Irving/35 30.00 80.00
MTSKM Kevin Martin/35 5.00 12.00
MTSKM Karl Malone/20 25.00 60.00
MTSKW Kenny Sky Walker/49 4.00 10.00
MTSLL Luc Longley/49 10.00 25.00
MTSLN Larry Nance/49 5.00 12.00
MTSLS Lance Stephenson/49 5.00 12.00
MTSMG Manu Ginobili/35 15.00 40.00
MTSMP Mason Plumlee/49 5.00 12.00
MTSNN Nerlens Noel/35 5.00 12.00
MTSNT Nate Thurmond/49 6.00 15.00
MTSPG Pau Gasol/35 6.00 15.00
MTSPM Patty Mills/49 10.00 25.00
MTSPW Paul Westphal/49 5.00 12.00
MTSRH Roy Hibbert/49 5.00 12.00
MTSRR Ricky Rubio/35 12.00 30.00
MTSSC Stephen Curry/35 60.00 150.00
MTSTC Tom Chambers/49 5.00 12.00
MTSTE Tyreke Evans/35 4.00 10.00
MTSTG Taj Gibson/49 5.00 12.00
MTSTH Tim Hardaway Jr./49 4.00 10.00
MTSTL Ty Lawson/35 4.00 10.00
MTSTP Tayshaun Prince/35 5.00 12.00
MTSTT Tristan Thompson/35 4.00 10.00
MTSTY Thaddeus Young/35 4.00 10.00
MTSVD Vlade Divac/49 8.00 20.00
MTSVO Victor Oladipo/35 10.00 25.00
MTSWD Walter Davis/49 5.00 12.00
MTSZI Zydrunas Ilgauskas/49 5.00 12.00
MTSZR Zach Randolph/35 5.00 12.00

2014-15 Panini National Treasures NBA Champions Signatures

RANDOM INSERTS IN PACKS
STATED PRINT RUN 49 SER.#'d SETS
EXCHANGE DEADLINE 2/5/2017
NBAAG A.C. Green/49 8.00 20.00
NBABS Byron Scott/49 6.00 15.00
NBACD Clyde Drexler/49 15.00 40.00
NBADC Dave Cowens/49 10.00 25.00
NBADR David Robinson/49 75.00 150.00
NBAGP Gary Payton/49 8.00 20.00
NBAGR Glen Rice/49 6.00 15.00
NBAHO Hakeem Olajuwon/49 20.00 50.00
NBAJE Julius Erving/49 30.00 80.00
NBAJJW Jo Jo White/49 15.00 40.00
NBAJK Jason Kidd/49 25.00 60.00
NBAKB Kobe Bryant/49 150.00 300.00
NBAKM Kevin McHale/49 12.00 30.00
NBALB Larry Bird/49 60.00 150.00
NBAMA Mark Aguirre/49 6.00 15.00
NBAMJ Magic Johnson/49 50.00 120.00
NBARF Rick Fox/49 6.00 15.00
NBARH Robert Horry/49 12.00 30.00
NBASE Sean Elliott/49 8.00 20.00
NBASO Shaquille O'Neal/49 75.00 200.00
NBATP Tony Parker/49 25.00 60.00
NBATS Tiago Splitter/49 6.00 15.00
NBAWF Walt Frazier/49 12.00 30.00

2014-15 Panini National Treasures NBA Game Gear Duals

RANDOM INSERTS IN PACKS
PRINT RUNS b/wn 25-99 COPIES PER
*PRIME: .75X TO 2X BASIC
GGDN Nene/99 3.00 8.00
GGDAA Arron Afflalo/99 2.50 6.00
GGDAB Avery Bradley/99 3.00 8.00
GGDAD Adrian Dantley/25 6.00 15.00
GGDAI Andre Iguodala/99 3.00 8.00
GGDAJ Al Jefferson/99 3.00 8.00
GGDAM Alonzo Mourning/99 5.00 12.00
GGDAV Anderson Varejao/99 2.50 6.00
GGDBB Bradley Beal/99 4.00 10.00
GGDBG Blake Griffin/99 4.00 10.00
GGDBK Brandon Knight/99 3.00 8.00
GGDBM Ben McLemore/99 2.50 6.00
GGDCA Carmelo Anthony/99 5.00 12.00
GGDCR Clifford Robinson/99 2.50 6.00
GGDDA Danny Ainge/99 5.00 12.00
GGDDC DeMarcus Cousins/99 4.00 10.00
GGDDF Derrick Favors/99 3.00 8.00
GGDDG Draymond Green/99 5.00 12.00
GGDDH Dwight Howard/99 3.00 8.00
GGDDL Damian Lillard/99 5.00 12.00
GGDDM Dan Majerle/99 3.00 8.00
GGDDN Dirk Nowitzki/99 5.00 12.00
GGDDR David Robinson/99 5.00 12.00
GGDDS Detlef Schrempf/99 4.00 10.00
GGDEB Eric Bledsoe/99 3.00 8.00
GGDEI Ersan Ilyasova/99 2.50 6.00
GGDGA G. Antetokounmpo/99 8.00 20.00
GGDGD Goran Dragic/99 3.00 8.00
GGDGH Grant Hill/99 5.00 12.00
GGDHO Hakeem Olajuwon/99 5.00 12.00
GGDIT Isaiah Thomas/99 4.00 10.00
GGDJB Jimmy Butler/99 6.00 15.00
GGDJH Jrue Holiday/99 3.00 8.00
GGDJH James Harden/99 6.00 15.00
GGDJW John Wall/99 5.00 12.00
GGDKB Kobe Bryant/99 10.00 25.00
GGDKC Kentavious Caldwell-Pope/99 2.50 6.00
GGDKD Kevin Duckworth/99 2.50 6.00
GGDKD Kevin Durant/99 8.00 20.00
GGDKF Kenneth Faried/99 3.00 8.00
GGDKK Kyle Korver/99 3.00 8.00
GGDKL Kawhi Leonard/99 5.00 12.00
GGDKL Kevin Love/99 4.00 10.00
GGDKM Karl Malone/99 6.00 15.00
GGDLA LaMarcus Aldridge/99 4.00 10.00
GGDLB Larry Bird/99 10.00 25.00
GGDLD Luol Deng/99 3.00 8.00
GGDLJ LeBron James/99 20.00 50.00
GGDMA Mark Aguirre/99 3.00 8.00
GGDMB Michael Beasley/99 2.50 6.00
GGDMB Manute Bol/99 4.00 10.00
GGDMC Mike Conley/99 3.00 8.00
GGDME Monta Ellis/99 3.00 8.00
GGDMG Manu Ginobili/99 4.00 10.00
GGDMG Marcin Gortat/99 3.00 8.00
GGDNN Nerlens Noel/99 3.00 8.00
GGDNP Nikola Pekovic/99 2.50 6.00
GGDNY Nick Young/99 3.00 8.00
GGDOM O.J. Mayo/99 2.50 6.00
GGDPE Patrick Ewing/99 6.00 15.00
GGDPG Pau Gasol/99 4.00 10.00
GGDRG Rudy Gay/99 4.00 10.00
GGDRH Robert Horry/99 3.00 8.00
GGDRR Rajon Rondo/99 4.00 10.00
GGDRW Russell Westbrook/99 6.00 15.00
GGDSA Steven Adams/99 3.00 8.00
GGDSB Shawn Bradley/99 2.50 6.00
GGDSB Shane Battier/99 3.00 8.00
GGDSI Serge Ibaka/99 3.00 8.00
GGDSM Shawn Marion/99 3.00 8.00
GGDSN Steve Nash/99 4.00 10.00
GGDSO Shaquille O'Neal/99 8.00 20.00
GGDTA Tony Allen/99 2.50 6.00
GGDTB Trey Burke/99 2.50 6.00
GGDTC Tyson Chandler/99 3.00 8.00
GGDTD Tim Duncan/99 6.00 15.00
GGDTH Tobias Harris/99 3.00 8.00
GGDTL Ty Lawson/99 2.50 6.00
GGDTP Tony Parker/99 5.00 12.00
GGDTP Tayshaun Prince/99 3.00 8.00
GGDTS Thabo Sefolosha/99 2.50 6.00
GGDTS Tiago Splitter/99 3.00 8.00
GGDVO Victor Oladipo/99 3.00 8.00
GGDWD Walter Davis/99 2.50 6.00
GGDZR Zach Randolph/99 3.00 8.00

2014-15 Panini National Treasures NBA Game Gear Signatures

RANDOM INSERTS IN PACKS
PRINT RUNS B/WN 25-75 COPIES PER
EXCHANGE DEADLINE 2/5/2017
*PRIME: .75X TO 2X BASIC
GGSAB Alec Burks/75 4.00 10.00
GGSAD Adrian Dantley/75 5.00 12.00
GGSAE Alex English/75 5.00 12.00
GGSAH Anfernee Hardaway/35 25.00 60.00
GGSAM Alonzo Mourning/35 12.00 30.00
GGSAW Antoine Walker/75 6.00 15.00
GGSBD Brad Daugherty/75 5.00 12.00
GGSBK Bernard King/49 6.00 15.00
GGSBL Bill Laimbeer/75 6.00 15.00
GGSBS Byron Scott/49 6.00 15.00
GGSCA Chris Andersen/49 5.00 12.00
GGSCA Carmelo Anthony/25 20.00 50.00
GGSCB Chris Bosh/25 8.00 20.00
GGSCD Clyde Drexler/25 20.00 50.00
GGSCM Cedric Maxwell/75 5.00 12.00
GGSCP Chris Paul/25 30.00 80.00
GGSCR Clifford Robinson/75 4.00 10.00
GGSDC DeMarcus Cousins/49
GGSDC Doug Collins/49 6.00 15.00
GGSDG Danny Green/75 6.00 15.00
GGSDI Dan Issel/49 5.00 12.00
GGSDM Danny Manning/49 5.00 12.00
GGSDM Dan Majerle/75 6.00 15.00
GGSDR David Robinson/35 20.00 50.00
GGSEK Enes Kanter/75 4.00 10.00
GGSGA G. Antetokounmpo/75 60.00 150.00
GGSGG George Gervin/49 10.00 25.00
GGSGH Grant Hill/35 20.00 50.00
GGSGP Gary Payton/35 12.00 30.00
GGSGR Glen Rice/75 5.00 12.00
GGSJD Joe Dumars/49 6.00 15.00
GGSJE Julius Erving/25 40.00 100.00
GGSJK Jason Kidd/35 12.00 30.00
GGSJN Joakim Noah/49
GGSJS John Stockton/25 25.00 60.00
GGSJS Jack Sikma/75 5.00 12.00
GGSJW John Wall/35 20.00 50.00
GGSJW Jamaal Wilkes/75 10.00 25.00
GGSKA Abdul-Jabbar/25 30.00 80.00
GGSKA Kenny Anderson/75 5.00 12.00
GGSKB Kobe Bryant/25 100.00 200.00
GGSKD Kevin Durant/25 75.00 150.00
GGSKI Kyrie Irving/25 30.00 80.00
GGSKL Kevin Love/35 15.00 40.00
GGSKM Kevin Martin/49 5.00 12.00
GGSKM Karl Malone/25 25.00 60.00
GGSKR Kurt Rambis/75 5.00 12.00
GGSKV Kiki Vandeweghe/75 6.00 15.00
GGSKW Kenny Sky Walker/75 4.00 10.00
GGSLB Larry Bird/25 50.00 120.00
GGSLL Luc Longley/49 10.00 25.00
GGSLS Lance Stephenson/60 5.00 12.00
GGSMA Mark Aguirre/75 5.00 12.00
GGSMF Michael Finley/49 6.00 15.00
GGSMG Marcin Gortat/49 6.00 15.00
GGSMJ Magic Johnson/35 40.00 100.00
GGSNC Nick Collison/75 5.00 12.00
GGSNVE Nick Van Exel/75 6.00 15.00
GGSPW Paul Westphal/75 5.00 12.00
GGSRB Rick Barry/49 10.00 25.00
GGSRH Robert Horry/75 6.00 15.00
GGSRP Robert Parish/49 10.00 25.00
GGSRW Russell Westbrook/35 60.00 150.00
GGSSC Stephen Curry/35 75.00 200.00
GGSSE Sean Elliott/75 6.00 15.00
GGSSO Shaquille O'Neal/25 75.00 150.00
GGSTC Tyson Chandler/49 5.00 12.00
GGSTC Tom Chambers/75 5.00 12.00
GGSTG Taj Gibson/75 5.00 12.00
GGSTH Tim Hardaway/75 6.00 15.00
GGSTM Tracy McGrady/49 15.00 40.00
GGSTS Tiago Splitter/75 5.00 12.00
GGSTY Thaddeus Young/75 4.00 10.00
GGSVC Vince Carter/35 15.00 40.00
GGSWD Walter Davis/75 5.00 12.00
GGSXM Xavier McDaniel/75 4.00 10.00
GGSZR Zach Randolph/49 5.00 12.00

2014-15 Panini National Treasures NBA Greats Signatures

RANDOM INSERTS IN PACKS
PRINT RUNS B/WN 25-75 COPIES PER
EXCHANGE DEADLINE 2/5/2017
*GOLD: .5X TO 1.2X BASIC p/r 35-75
*GOLD: .4X TO 1X BASIC p/r 25
NBGAD Adrian Dantley/75 5.00 12.00
NBGAE Alex English/75 5.00 12.00
NBGAG Artis Gilmore/75 5.00 12.00
NBGAI Allen Iverson/25 60.00 150.00
NBGBK Bernard King/75 5.00 12.00
NBGBR Bill Russell/25 75.00 150.00
NBGBW Bill Walton/75 6.00 15.00
NBGCD Clyde Drexler/35
NBGCM Chris Mullin/75 10.00 25.00
NBGCW Chris Webber/35 75.00 150.00
NBGDI Dan Issel/75 5.00 12.00
NBGDR Dennis Rodman/49 15.00 40.00
NBGDR David Robinson/35 15.00 40.00
NBGDS Dolph Schayes/75 6.00 15.00
NBGDT David Thompson/75 5.00 12.00
NBGEB Elgin Baylor/49 10.00 25.00
NBGEM Earl Monroe/35 10.00 25.00
NBGGG Gail Goodrich/75 5.00 12.00
NBGGG George Gervin/75 8.00 20.00
NBGGM George McGinnis/75 6.00 15.00
NBGGP Gary Payton/49 10.00 25.00
NBGHO Hakeem Olajuwon/35 12.00 30.00
NBGJD Joe Dumars/75 6.00 15.00
NBGJE Julius Erving/25 30.00 80.00
NBGJS John Stockton/25 20.00 50.00
NBGJW Jerry West/25 25.00 60.00
NBGJW Jamaal Wilkes/75 8.00 20.00
NBGJW James Worthy/49 15.00 40.00
NBGKM Kevin McHale/49 10.00 25.00
NBGMA Mark Aguirre/75 5.00 12.00
NBGMD Mel Daniels/75 6.00 15.00
NBGOR Oscar Robertson/25 50.00 120.00
NBGRP Robert Parish/75 6.00 15.00
NBGSM Sarunas Marciulionis/75 6.00 15.00
NBGSM Sidney Moncrief/75 4.00 10.00
NBGSO Shaquille O'Neal/25 60.00 150.00
NBGTS Tom Satch Sanders/75 10.00 25.00
NBGWF Walt Frazier/75 10.00 25.00
NBGWU Wes Unseld/75 6.00 15.00
NBGJJW Jo Jo White/75 8.00 20.00

2014-15 Panini National Treasures NBA Material

RANDOM INSERTS IN PACKS
STATED PRINT RUN 99 SER.#'d SETS
*PRIME: .75X TO 2X BASIC
NBAAD Adrian Dantley 3.00 8.00
NBAAD Andre Drummond 4.00 10.00
NBAAD Anthony Davis 6.00 15.00
NBABB Bradley Beal 4.00 10.00
NBABG Blake Griffin 4.00 10.00
NBABK Bernard King 3.00 8.00
NBACA Carmelo Anthony 5.00 12.00
NBACP Chris Paul 5.00 12.00
NBADH Dwight Howard 3.00 8.00
NBADJ DeAndre Jordan 4.00 10.00
NBADL Damian Lillard 5.00 12.00
NBADN Dirk Nowitzki 5.00 12.00
NBADR Derrick Rose 8.00 20.00
NBADW Deron Williams 3.00 8.00
NBADW Dwyane Wade 5.00 12.00
NBAGA Giannis Antetokounmpo 8.00 20.00
NBAGH Gordon Hayward 4.00 10.00
NBAGR Glen Rice 3.00 8.00
NBAJB Jimmy Butler 4.00 10.00
NBAJH James Harden 6.00 15.00
NBAJJ Joe Johnson 3.00 8.00
NBAJM Jamal Mashburn 4.00 10.00
NBAJS John Stockton 6.00 15.00
NBAKB Kobe Bryant 10.00 25.00
NBAKD Kevin Durant 6.00 15.00
NBAKK Kyle Korver 3.00 8.00
NBAKL Kevin Love 4.00 10.00
NBAKL Kawhi Leonard 5.00 12.00
NBAKM Karl Malone 6.00 15.00
NBALA LaMarcus Aldridge 4.00 10.00
NBALJ LeBron James 15.00 40.00
NBAME Monta Ellis 3.00 8.00
NBAMG Manu Ginobili 4.00 10.00
NBAMG Marcin Gortat 3.00 8.00
NBANV Nikola Vucevic 3.00 8.00
NBARH Roy Hibbert 3.00 8.00
NBARP Robert Parish 4.00 10.00
NBARR Rajon Rondo 4.00 10.00
NBARS Ralph Sampson 3.00 8.00
NBARW Russell Westbrook 5.00 12.00
NBASK Steve Kerr 4.00 10.00
NBASM Shawn Marion 3.00 8.00
NBASO Shaquille O'Neal 8.00 20.00
NBASP Scottie Pippen 8.00 20.00
NBATB Trey Burke 2.50 6.00
NBATD Tim Duncan 6.00 15.00
NBATP Tony Parker 5.00 12.00
NBAVD Vlade Divac 4.00 10.00
NBAVO Victor Oladipo 3.00 8.00
NBAZR Zach Randolph 3.00 8.00

2014-15 Panini National Treasures NBA Rookie Materials

RANDOM INSERTS IN PACKS
STATED PRINT RUN 99 SER.#'d SETS
*PRIME: .75X TO 2X BASIC
RMAG Aaron Gordon/99 6.00 15.00
RMAP Adreian Payne/99 3.00 8.00
RMAW Andrew Wiggins/99 20.00 50.00
RMBC Bruno Caboclo/99 5.00 12.00
RMCE Cleanthony Early/99 2.50 6.00
RMCJ Cory Jefferson/99 2.50 6.00
RMCW C.J. Wilcox/99 2.50 6.00
RMDE Dante Exum/99 6.00 15.00
RMDM Doug McDermott/99 4.00 10.00
RMEP Elfrid Payton/99 4.00 10.00
RMGH Gary Harris/99 4.00 10.00
RMGR Glenn Robinson III/99 2.50 6.00
RMJE Joel Embiid/99 6.00 15.00
RMJE James Ennis/99 2.50 6.00
RMJG Jerami Grant/99 2.50 6.00
RMJH Joe Harris/99 2.50 6.00
RMJO Johnny O'Bryant/99 2.50 6.00
RMJP Jabari Parker/99 12.00 30.00
RMJR Julius Randle/99 10.00 25.00
RMJS Jarnell Stokes/99 2.50 6.00
RMJY James Young/99 2.50 6.00
RMKA Kyle Anderson/99 15.00 40.00
RMKM K.J. McDaniels/99 3.00 8.00
RMMM Mitch McGary/99 2.50 6.00
RMMS Marcus Smart/99 4.00 10.00
RMNS Nik Stauskas/99 3.00 8.00
RMNV Noah Vonleh/99 3.00 8.00
RMPH P.J. Hairston/99 2.50 6.00
RMRH Rodney Hood/99 4.00 10.00
RMRS Russ Smith/99 2.50 6.00
RMSD Spencer Dinwiddie/99 3.00 8.00
RMSN Shabazz Napier/99 3.00 8.00
RMTE Tyler Ennis/99 2.50 6.00
RMTW T.J. Warren/99 4.00 10.00
RMZL Zach LaVine/99 6.00 15.00

2014-15 Panini National Treasures Night Moves Jersey Autographs

RANDOM INSERTS IN PACKS
PRINT RUNS B/WN 23-49 COPIES PER
EXCHANGE DEADLINE 2/5/2017
*PRIME: .75X TO 2X BASIC
NMAA Arron Afflalo/49 4.00 10.00
NMAD Adrian Dantley/49 5.00 12.00
NMAH Al Horford/35 5.00 12.00
NMAI Allen Iverson/25 75.00 150.00
NMAV Anderson Varejao/49 4.00 10.00
NMBC Bill Cartwright/49 5.00 12.00
NMBK Brandon Knight/35 4.00 10.00
NMBM Ben McLemore/35 5.00 12.00
NMBS Byron Scott/35 6.00 15.00
NMCR Clifford Robinson/49 4.00 10.00
NMDG Danilo Gallinari/35 4.00 10.00
NMDN Dirk Nowitzki/25 75.00 200.00
NMDR David Robinson/25 20.00 50.00
NMDW Dwyane Wade/25 50.00 120.00
NMDW Deron Williams/35 4.00 10.00
NMEM Earl Monroe/25 15.00 40.00
NMGD Goran Dragic/30 8.00 20.00
NMGH George Hill/49 5.00 12.00
NMIT Isiah Thomas/35 10.00 25.00
NMJC Jose Calderon/49 3.00 8.00
NMJK Jason Kidd/35 12.00 30.00
NMJS John Stockton/25 25.00 60.00
NMJS John Starks/49 10.00 25.00
NMJV Jonas Valanciunas/23 6.00 15.00
NMKB Kobe Bryant/25 100.00 200.00
NMKD Kevin Durant/25 60.00 150.00
NMKI Kyrie Irving/25 30.00 80.00
NMKL Kevin Love/35 15.00 40.00
NMKL Kawhi Leonard/25 30.00 80.00
NMKL Kyle Lowry/49 5.00 12.00
NMKM Kevin McHale/35 10.00 25.00
NMKM Kevin Martin/35 5.00 12.00
NMKM Karl Malone/25 25.00 60.00
NMKR Kurt Rambis/49 5.00 12.00
NMKW Kenny Sky Walker/49 4.00 10.00
NMLJ Larry Johnson/35 8.00 20.00
NMLL Luc Longley/49 10.00 25.00
NMLS Lance Stephenson/49 5.00 12.00
NMMC Mike Conley/49 4.00 10.00
NMME Monta Ellis/25 6.00 15.00
NMMF Michael Finley/49 6.00 15.00
NMMG Marcin Gortat/40 6.00 15.00
NMNN Nerlens Noel/35 10.00 25.00
NMNY Nick Young/49 5.00 12.00
NMPG Paul George/25 15.00 40.00
NMPM Patty Mills/49 10.00 25.00
NMPS Peja Stojakovic/35 6.00 15.00
NMRH Roy Hibbert/49 5.00 12.00
NMSB Shane Battier/35 6.00 15.00
NMTC Tom Chambers/49 5.00 12.00
NMTG Taj Gibson/49 5.00 12.00
NMTK Toni Kukoc/49 6.00 15.00
NMTL Ty Lawson/35 4.00 10.00
NMTP Tayshaun Prince/35 5.00 12.00
NMTS Tiago Splitter/35 5.00 12.00
NMTT Tristan Thompson/35 4.00 10.00
NMTY Thaddeus Young/35 4.00 10.00
NMZR Zach Randolph/35 5.00 12.00

2014-15 Panini National Treasures Notable Nicknames

RANDOM INSERTS IN PACKS
STATED PRINT RUN 49 SER.#'d SETS
EXCHANGE DEADLINE 2/5/2017
NNAG A.C. Green 25.00 60.00
NNAM Alonzo Mourning 30.00 80.00
NNBD Bob Dandridge 10.00 25.00
NNCH Cliff Hagan 12.00 30.00
NNCP Chris Paul 150.00 250.00
NNDC DeMarcus Cousins
NNDM Doug McDermott 40.00 100.00
NNGA Giannis Antetokounmpo 75.00 200.00
NNJK Jason Kidd 150.00 250.00
NNJN Jusuf Nurkic
NNJR Julius Randle 25.00 60.00
NNJS John Salley 10.00 25.00
NNKR Kurt Rambis 10.00 25.00
NNLS Latrell Sprewell 60.00 150.00
NNNS Nik Stauskas 12.00 30.00
NNRG Rudy Gobert
NNRS Rony Seikaly 10.00 25.00
NNSC Stephen Curry 200.00 400.00
NNSO Shaquille O'Neal 75.00 150.00
NNXM Xavier McDaniel 10.00 25.00
NNZI Zydrunas Ilgauskas 12.00 30.00

2014-15 Panini National Treasures Scripts

RANDOM INSERTS IN PACKS
PRINT RUNS B/WN 35-75 COPIES PER
EXCHANGE DEADLINE 2/5/2017
*GOLD: .5X TO 1.2X BASIC
SCAG Artis Gilmore/49 5.00 12.00
SCAH Allan Houston/75 5.00 12.00
SCAI Allen Iverson/35 50.00 120.00
SCAJ Avery Johnson/49 5.00 12.00
SCAM Anthony Mason/75 5.00 12.00
SCBD Brad Daugherty/75 5.00 12.00
SCBK Brandon Knight/49 5.00 12.00
SCBK Bernard King/49 5.00 12.00
SCBS Byron Scott/49 5.00 12.00
SCCA Carmelo Anthony/35 20.00 50.00
SCCD Clyde Drexler/35 15.00 40.00
SCCO Charles Oakley/75 5.00 12.00
SCCP Chuck Person/75 5.00 12.00
SCCW Chris Webber/49 75.00 150.00
SCDM Danny Manning/49 5.00 12.00
SCDR David Robinson/49 15.00 40.00
SCDS Dolph Schayes/49 6.00 15.00
SCEJ Eddie Jones/75 6.00 15.00
SCEM Earl Monroe/49 10.00 25.00
SCGG Gail Goodrich/49 5.00 12.00
SCGG George Gervin/49 8.00 20.00
SCGH Grant Hill/49 12.00 30.00
SCGK George Karl/49 6.00 15.00
SCGP Gary Payton/49 10.00 25.00
SCHO Hakeem Olajuwon/49 20.00 50.00
SCJD Joe Dumars/49 6.00 15.00
SCJE Julius Erving/35 30.00 80.00
SCJS John Stockton/35 15.00 40.00
SCJW Jerry West/35 25.00 60.00
SCJW James Worthy/49 12.00 30.00
SCKC Kentavious Caldwell-Pope/49 4.00 10.00
SCKM Kevin Martin/49 5.00 12.00
SCKM Kevin McHale/49 10.00 25.00
SCKR Kurt Rambis/75 4.00 10.00
SCKW Kenny Sky Walker/75 4.00 10.00
SCKW Kevin Willis/75 4.00 10.00
SCMC Michael Carter-Williams/49 4.00 10.00
SCNN Nerlens Noel/49 5.00 12.00
SCOR Oscar Robertson/35 40.00 100.00
SCRF Rick Fox/49 5.00 12.00
SCRP Robert Parish/49 6.00 15.00
SCSS Scott Skiles/75 5.00 12.00
SCTB Trey Burke/49 4.00 10.00
SCTH Tim Hardaway Jr./75 4.00 10.00
SCTS Tom Satch Sanders/75 10.00 25.00
SCVO Victor Oladipo/49 5.00 12.00
SCWD Walter Davis/75 4.00 10.00
SCWF Walt Frazier/49 6.00 15.00
SCWU Wes Unseld/49 6.00 15.00

2014-15 Panini National Treasures Signature Materials

RANDOM INSERTS IN PACKS
PRINT RUNS B/WN 32-75 COPIES PER
EXCHANGE DEADLINE 2/5/2017
*PRIME: .75X TO 2X BASIC
SMAB Alec Burks/75 4.00 10.00
SMBC Bill Cartwright/75 5.00 12.00
SMBD Brad Daugherty/75 5.00 12.00
SMBL Brook Lopez/49 5.00 12.00
SMBS Byron Scott/49 5.00 12.00
SMCA Carmelo Anthony/35 20.00 50.00
SMCO Charles Oakley/75 5.00 12.00
SMCR Clifford Robinson/75 4.00 10.00
SMDC Doug Collins/75 6.00 15.00
SMDC DeMarcus Cousins/49
SMDF Derrick Favors/35 5.00 12.00
SMDG Danilo Gallinari/75 4.00 10.00
SMDM Danny Manning/49 5.00 12.00
SMEK Enes Kanter/75 4.00 10.00
SMGG George Gervin/49 10.00 25.00
SMGH Grant Hill/49 20.00 50.00
SMGH Gordon Hayward/75 8.00 20.00
SMGP Gary Payton/49 12.00 30.00
SMGR Glen Rice/75 5.00 12.00
SMJC Jamal Crawford/75
SMJD Jared Dudley/75 4.00 10.00
SMJG Jeff Green/75 4.00 10.00
SMJJ James Jones/75 4.00 10.00
SMJN Joakim Noah/49
SMJS John Stockton/35 25.00 60.00
SMJS John Starks/32 10.00 25.00
SMJT Jason Thompson/75 4.00 10.00
SMJW John Wall/49 20.00 50.00
SMKA Kenny Anderson/75 5.00 12.00
SMKL Kevin Love/49 15.00 40.00
SMKM Kevin Martin/49 5.00 12.00
SMKM Karl Malone/35 25.00 60.00
SMKV Kiki Vandeweghe/75 5.00 12.00
SMKW Kenny Sky Walker/75 4.00 10.00
SMMC Mike Conley/75 4.00 10.00
SMMF Michael Finley/49 6.00 15.00
SMMG Marcin Gortat/75 5.00 12.00
SMMK Michael Kidd-Gilchrist/49 5.00 12.00
SMNC Nick Collison/75 5.00 12.00
SMRA Ryan Anderson/50 4.00 10.00
SMRF Randy Foye/75 4.00 10.00
SMRW Russell Westbrook/49 60.00 150.00
SMTC Tyson Chandler/49 5.00 12.00
SMTC Tom Chambers/75 5.00 12.00
SMTG Taj Gibson/75 5.00 12.00
SMTS Tiago Splitter/75 5.00 12.00
SMTY Thaddeus Young/75 4.00 10.00
SMVC Vince Carter/49 15.00 40.00
SMWD Walter Davis/75 4.00 10.00
SMXM Xavier McDaniel/75 4.00 10.00
SMZI Zydrunas Ilgauskas/75 5.00 12.00
SMZR Zach Randolph/49 5.00 12.00

2014-15 Panini National Treasures Signatures

RANDOM INSERTS IN PACKS
PRINT RUNS B/WN 35-75 COPIES PER
EXCHANGE DEADLINE 2/5/2017
*GOLD: .5X TO 1.2X BASIC
SAD Anthony Davis/49 40.00 150.00
SAE Alex English/75 5.00 12.00
SAG A.C. Green/75 8.00 20.00
SAH Allan Houston/75 5.00 12.00
SBD Bob Dandridge/75 4.00 10.00
SBK Bernard King/49 5.00 12.00
SBR Bill Russell/35 75.00 150.00
SBS Byron Scott/49 5.00 12.00
SCA Chris Andersen/49 10.00 25.00
SCB Chris Bosh/35 10.00 25.00
SCH Cliff Hagan/49 5.00 12.00
SCM Cedric Maxwell/75 4.00 10.00
SCR Campy Russell/75 4.00 10.00
SCR Cazzie Russell/75 5.00 12.00
SCR Clifford Robinson/75 4.00 10.00
SDB Dee Brown/75 4.00 10.00
SDC Doug Collins/75 6.00 15.00
SDF Derrick Favors/49 5.00 12.00
SDI Dan Issel/75 5.00 12.00
SDR David Robinson/49 15.00 40.00
SDS Dolph Schayes/49 6.00 15.00
SEK Enes Kanter/75 4.00 10.00
SGA Giannis Antetokounmpo/75 25.00 60.00
SGG George Gervin/49 8.00 20.00
SGH Gordon Hayward/75 6.00 15.00
SGK George Karl/49 6.00 15.00
SGP Gary Payton/49 10.00 25.00
SIT Isiah Thomas/49 6.00 15.00
SIT Isaiah Thomas/75 20.00 50.00
SJC Jamal Crawford/75 6.00 15.00
SJD Joe Dumars/49 6.00 15.00
SJE Julius Erving/35 30.00 80.00
SJJ Jim Jackson/75 4.00 10.00
SJK Jason Kidd/49 12.00 30.00
SJN Joakim Noah/49
SJS Josh Smith/49 5.00 12.00
SJS John Starks/75 5.00 12.00
SJS John Stockton/35 15.00 40.00
SJW John Wall/49 20.00 50.00
SJW Jamaal Wilkes/75 8.00 20.00
SJW Jerome Williams/75 4.00 10.00
SKB Kobe Bryant/49 125.00 250.00
SKD Kevin Durant/35 75.00 150.00
SKI Kyrie Irving/49 30.00 80.00
SKK Kyle Korver/75 5.00 12.00
SKL Kevin Love/49 12.00 30.00
SKM Kevin Martin/49 5.00 12.00
SKM Karl Malone/35 30.00 80.00
SKR Kurt Rambis/75 4.00 10.00
SKS Kenny Smith/49 5.00 12.00
SKV Kiki Vandeweghe/75 5.00 12.00
SLN Larry Nance/75 5.00 12.00
SLS Lance Stephenson/75 5.00 12.00
SLS Latrell Sprewell/49 20.00 50.00
SMA Mark Aguirre/75 5.00 12.00
SMB Muggsy Bogues/75 5.00 12.00
SMG Marcin Gortat/49 5.00 12.00
SMT Mychal Thompson/75 4.00 10.00
SPG Pau Gasol/49 15.00 40.00
SRB Rolando Blackman/75 5.00 12.00
SRB Rick Barry/49 10.00 25.00
SRH Robert Horry/75 5.00 12.00
SRL Raef LaFrentz/75 4.00 10.00
SRS Rod Strickland/75 4.00 10.00
SRT Rudy Tomjanovich/75 5.00 12.00
SRW Russell Westbrook/49 75.00 200.00
SSB Scott Brooks/75 4.00 10.00
SSC Stephen Curry/49 100.00 250.00
SSM Sidney Moncrief/75 4.00 10.00
SSO Shaquille O'Neal/35 50.00 120.00
SSS Scott Skiles/75 5.00 12.00
STC Tom Chambers/75 5.00 12.00
STC Tyson Chandler/49 5.00 12.00
STG Tom Gugliotta/75 4.00 10.00
STH Tim Hardaway/75 6.00 15.00
STK Toni Kukoc/75 10.00 25.00
STM Tracy McGrady/49 25.00 60.00
STS Tiago Splitter/75 5.00 12.00
STY Thaddeus Young/75 4.00 10.00
SVC Vince Carter/49 15.00 40.00
SWD Walter Davis/75 4.00 10.00
SWE Wayne Embry/75 4.00 10.00
SXM Xavier McDaniel/75 4.00 10.00
SZI Zydrunas Ilgauskas/75 5.00 12.00
SZR Zach Randolph/49 5.00 12.00
SKLE Kawhi Leonard/49 60.00 150.00

2014-15 Panini National Treasures Sneaker Swatches

RANDOM INSERTS IN PACKS
PRINT RUNS B/WN 1-49 COPIES PER
NO PRICING ON QTY 17 OR LESS
SSAD Anthony Davis/49 15.00 40.00
SSAI Allen Iverson/49 20.00 50.00
SSDW Dominique Wilkins/49 8.00 20.00
SSGH Grant Hill/20 20.00 50.00
SSGP Gary Payton/49 6.00 15.00
SSHO Hakeem Olajuwon/49 8.00 20.00
SSJE Julius Erving/40 10.00 25.00
SSKM Karl Malone/49 8.00 20.00
SSLJ LeBron James/49 60.00 150.00
SSLJ Larry Johnson/49 8.00 20.00
SSMC Michael Carter-Williams/49 4.00 10.00
SSMJ Magic Johnson/49 15.00 40.00
SSMM Moses Malone/49 6.00 15.00
SSRS Ralph Sampson/49 5.00 12.00
SSSC Stephen Curry/45 40.00 100.00
SSSK Shawn Kemp/49 30.00 80.00
SSSO Shaquille O'Neal/49 12.00 30.00
SSSP Scottie Pippen/49 25.00 60.00
SSTB Trey Burke/17 4.00 10.00
SSVO Victor Oladipo/31 5.00 12.00

2014-15 Panini National Treasures Sneaker Swatches Autographs

RANDOM INSERTS IN PACKS
PRINT RUNS B/WN 23-49 COPIES PER
EXCHANGE DEADLINE 2/5/2017
SSAAD Anthony Davis/49 75.00 200.00
SSAAW Andrew Wiggins/35 300.00 600.00
SSACA Carmelo Anthony/43 30.00 80.00
SSADW Dominique Wilkins/49 25.00 60.00
SSAGP Gary Payton/49 20.00 50.00
SSAJD Joe Dumars/49 10.00 25.00
SSAJE Julius Erving/35 50.00 120.00
SSAKB Kobe Bryant/32 150.00 250.00
SSAKM Karl Malone/49 30.00 80.00
SSALJ Larry Johnson/49 12.00 30.00
SSAMC Michael Carter-Williams/49 6.00 15.00
SSAMJ Magic Johnson/49 40.00 100.00
SSAMK Michael Kidd-Gilchrist/23 8.00 20.00
SSARP Robert Parish/30 10.00 25.00
SSASC Stephen Curry/49 200.00 300.00
SSASO Shaquille O'Neal/49 100.00 200.00
SSATB Trey Burke/49 6.00 15.00
SSAVO Victor Oladipo/49 15.00 40.00
SSAYM Yao Ming/33 30.00 80.00

2014-15 Panini National Treasures Spanning Time Dual Signatures

RANDOM INSERTS IN PACKS
PRINT RUNS B/WN 10-49 COPIES PER
NO PRICING ON QTY 10
EXCHANGE DEADLINE 2/5/2017
*GOLD: .5X TO 1.2X BASIC
STAWSN Wiggins/Nash/25 125.00 250.00
STCMKL Maxwell/Leonard/49 20.00 50.00
STCPGP Paul/Payton/25 30.00 80.00
STGHKI Hill/Irving/25 40.00 100.00
STHOAD Olajuwon/Davis/25 100.00 200.00
STLSSC Sprewell/Curry/25 90.00 150.00
STMTKT Thompson/Thompson/45 20.00 50.00
STRRJK Rondo/Kidd/25 40.00 100.00
STTHTH Hardaway/Hardaway Jr./49 10.00 25.00

2014-15 Panini National Treasures Springfield Swatches
RANDOM INSERTS IN PACKS
PRINT RUNS B/WN 35-49 COPIES PER
*PRIME: .75X TO 2X BASIC
SPSAD Adrian Dantley 3.00 8.00
SPSAG Artis Gilmore 10.00 25.00
SPSBK Bernard King 3.00 8.00
SPSDJ Dennis Johnson 3.00 8.00
SPSDM Dikembe Mutombo/35 6.00 15.00
SPSDR David Robinson 5.00 12.00
SPSEB Elgin Baylor 4.00 10.00
SPSEM Earl Monroe 4.00 10.00
SPSGM George Mikan 15.00 40.00
SPSGP Gary Payton 6.00 15.00
SPSHG Hal Greer 6.00 15.00
SPSHO Hakeem Olajuwon 5.00 12.00
SPSIT Isiah Thomas 4.00 10.00
SPSJD Joe Dumars 4.00 10.00
SPSJH John Havlicek 20.00 50.00
SPSJS John Stockton 6.00 15.00
SPSJW James Worthy 5.00 12.00
SPSKA Kareem Abdul-Jabbar 6.00 15.00
SPSKM Karl Malone 6.00 15.00
SPSKM Kevin McHale 6.00 15.00
SPSLB Larry Bird 10.00 25.00
SPSLD Louie Dampier 4.00 10.00
SPSMM Moses Malone 4.00 10.00
SPSNT Nate Thurmond 3.00 8.00
SPSPE Patrick Ewing 6.00 15.00
SPSPM Pete Maravich 25.00 60.00
SPSRB Rick Barry 6.00 15.00
SPSRP Robert Parish 4.00 10.00
SPSRS Ralph Sampson 3.00 8.00
SPSWC Wilt Chamberlain 25.00 60.00

2014-15 Panini National Treasures Timelines
RANDOM INSERTS IN PACKS
PRINT RUNS B/WN 10-99 COPIES PER
*PRIME: .75X TO 2X BASIC
TAD Anthony Davis/99 6.00 15.00
TAG Aaron Gordon/99 6.00 15.00
TAH Al Horford/99 3.00 8.00
TAI Allen Iverson/99 6.00 15.00
TAW Andrew Wiggins/99 20.00 50.00
TBK Bernard King/99 3.00 8.00
TDE Dante Exum/99 6.00 15.00
TDJ DeAndre Jordan/99 4.00 10.00
TDL Damian Lillard/99 5.00 12.00
TDM Dikembe Mutombo/75 4.00 10.00
TDM Doug McDermott/99 4.00 10.00
TDN Dirk Nowitzki/99 5.00 12.00
TDR Derrick Rose/99 8.00 20.00
TDW Dwyane Wade/99 5.00 12.00
TEP Elfrid Payton/99 4.00 10.00
TGM George Mikan/25 30.00 80.00
TGR Glen Rice/99 3.00 8.00
TJB Jimmy Butler/99 4.00 10.00
TJE Joel Embiid/99 15.00 40.00
TJL Jeremy Lin/99 4.00 10.00
TJM Jamal Mashburn/99 4.00 10.00
TJN Joakim Noah/99 3.00 8.00
TJP Jabari Parker/99 8.00 20.00
TJR Julius Randle/99 10.00 25.00
TJS John Stockton/49 6.00 15.00
TKB Kobe Bryant/99 10.00 25.00
TKG Kevin Garnett/99 8.00 20.00
TKM Karl Malone/99 6.00 15.00
TLJ Larry Johnson/99 5.00 12.00
TMM Moses Malone/99 15.00 40.00
TMM Mitch McGary/99 2.50 6.00
TMS Marcus Smart/99 4.00 10.00
TNS Nik Stauskas/99 3.00 8.00
TPE Patrick Ewing/99 6.00 15.00
TPP Paul Pierce/99 4.00 10.00
TRA Ray Allen/99 4.00 10.00
TRP Robert Parish/99 4.00 10.00
TRS Ralph Sampson/99 3.00 8.00
TSD Spencer Dinwiddie/99 3.00 8.00
TSK Shawn Kemp/99 8.00 20.00
TSK Steve Kerr/99 4.00 10.00
TSN Shabazz Napier/99 3.00 8.00
TSO Shaquille O'Neal/99 8.00 20.00
TSP Scottie Pippen/99 8.00 20.00
TTT Tristan Thompson/99 3.00 8.00
TVD Vlade Divac/99 4.00 10.00
TVJ Vinnie Johnson/49 4.00 10.00
TXM Xavier McDaniel/99 2.50 6.00
TZL Zach LaVine/99 6.00 15.00

2015-16 Panini National Treasures
1-100 PRINT RUN 99 SER. #'d SETS
JSY AU RC p/r B/WN 49-99 COPIES
141-157 PRINT RUNS 99 SER.#'d SETS
PRIME PATCHES MAY SELL FOR PREMIUM
EXCHANGE DEADLINE 11/11/2017
1 Kobe Bryant 8.00 20.00
2 Al Horford 1.50 4.00
3 Derrick Favors 1.50 4.00
4 Tim Duncan 3.00 8.00
5 Jusuf Nurkic 1.25 3.00
6 Dwight Howard 1.50 4.00
7 Andre Drummond 2.00 5.00
8 Chris Paul 2.50 6.00
9 DeMar DeRozan 2.00 5.00
10 Julius Randle 2.00 5.00
11 Thaddeus Young 1.25 3.00
12 Tobias Harris 1.50 4.00
13 Andrew Wiggins 3.00 8.00
14 Tony Parker 2.00 5.00
15 Kevin Love 2.00 5.00
16 Trevor Ariza 1.25 3.00
17 Reggie Jackson 1.50 4.00
18 DeAndre Jordan 2.00 5.00
19 Kyle Lowry 1.50 4.00
20 Jordan Clarkson 2.00 5.00
21 Robert Covington 1.25 3.00
22 Victor Oladipo 1.50 4.00
23 Zach LaVine 2.00 5.00
24 Deron Williams 1.50 4.00
25 LeBron James 12.00 30.00
26 Anthony Davis 4.00 10.00
27 Marcus Morris 1.25 3.00
28 Paul Pierce 2.00 5.00
29 Isaiah Thomas 2.00 5.00
30 Chris Bosh 2.00 5.00
31 Nerlens Noel 1.50 4.00
32 Nikola Vucevic 1.50 4.00
33 Ricky Rubio 2.00 5.00
34 Dirk Nowitzki 2.50 6.00
35 Kyrie Irving 4.00 10.00
36 Eric Gordon 1.50 4.00
37 Jabari Parker 2.50 6.00
38 Brandon Knight 1.50 4.00
39 Marcus Smart 1.50 4.00
40 Dwyane Wade 3.00 8.00
41 Isaiah Canaan 1.50 4.00
42 Evan Fournier 1.50 4.00
43 Kevin Garnett 3.00 8.00
44 Zaza Pachulia 1.25 3.00
45 Jimmy Butler 2.00 5.00
46 Ryan Anderson 1.50 4.00
47 Giannis Antetokounmpo 4.00 10.00
48 Tyson Chandler 1.50 4.00
49 Jared Sullinger 1.25 3.00
50 Hassan Whiteside 1.50 4.00
51 Kevin Durant 5.00 12.00
52 Bradley Beal 2.00 5.00
53 Damian Lillard 4.00 10.00
54 Marc Gasol 2.00 5.00
55 Pau Gasol 2.00 5.00
56 Andre Iguodala 1.50 4.00
57 Greg Monroe 1.50 4.00
58 Eric Bledsoe 1.50 4.00
59 Jonas Valanciunas 1.50 4.00
60 Nicolas Batum 1.50 4.00
61 Russell Westbrook 5.00 12.00
62 John Wall 2.50 6.00
63 C.J. McCollum 2.00 5.00
64 Mike Conley 2.00 5.00
65 Derrick Rose 2.50 6.00
66 Enes Kanter 1.25 3.00
67 Stephen Curry 12.00 30.00
68 Rajon Rondo 2.00 5.00
69 Carmelo Anthony 2.50 6.00
70 Kemba Walker 2.00 5.00
71 Serge Ibaka 1.50 4.00
72 Marcin Gortat 1.50 4.00
73 Al-Farouq Aminu 1.50 4.00
74 Zach Randolph 1.50 4.00
75 Paul George 2.50 6.00
76 Marvin Williams 1.50 4.00
77 Draymond Green 2.50 6.00
78 Rudy Gay 2.00 5.00
79 Robin Lopez 1.25 3.00
80 Jeremy Lin 2.00 5.00
81 Rudy Gobert 2.00 5.00
82 Kawhi Leonard 3.00 8.00
83 Danilo Gallinari 1.50 4.00
84 Vince Carter 2.50 6.00
85 George Hill 1.50 4.00
86 Will Barton 1.25 3.00
87 Klay Thompson 2.50 6.00
88 DeMarcus Cousins 2.00 5.00
89 Jose Calderon 1.25 3.00
90 Paul Millsap 2.00 5.00
91 Gordon Hayward 2.00 5.00
92 LaMarcus Aldridge 2.00 5.00
93 Kenneth Faried 1.50 4.00
94 James Harden 3.00 8.00
95 Monta Ellis 1.50 4.00
96 C.J. Miles 1.50 4.00
97 Blake Griffin 2.00 5.00
98 Brook Lopez 1.50 4.00
99 Joe Johnson 1.50 4.00
100 Jeff Teague 1.50 4.00
101 Anthony Towns JSY AU/99 RC 3000.00 5000.00
102 D.Russell JSY AU/99 RC 700.00 1000.00
103 J.Okafor JSY AU/99 RC 200.00 400.00
104 K.Porzingis JSY AU/99 RC 1500.00 2500.00
105 M.Hezonja JSY AU/99 RC 125.00 250.00
106 Cly-Stn JSY AU/99 RC EXCH 150.00 400.00
107 E.Mudiay JSY AU/99 RC EXCH 125.00 300.00
108 S.Johnson JSY AU/99 RC 125.00 300.00
109 Kmnsky JSY AU/99 RC EXCH 50.00 120.00
110 Winslow JSY AU/99 RC EXCH 300.00 500.00
111 M.Turner JSY AU/99 RC 300.00 600.00
112 Trey Lyles JSY AU/99 RC 75.00 200.00
113 D.Booker JSY AU/99 RC 800.00 1500.00
114 C.Payne JSY AU/99 RC 40.00 100.00
115 K.Oubre Jr. JSY AU/99 RC 100.00 250.00
116 Terry Rozier JSY AU/99 RC 40.00 100.00
118 S.Dekker JSY AU/99 RC 50.00 120.00
119 J.Grant JSY AU/99 RC 30.00 80.00
120 Delon Wright JSY AU/99 RC 20.00 50.00
121 J.Anderson JSY AU/99 RC 50.00 120.00
122 B.Portis JSY AU/99 RC 100.00 250.00
123 Hlls-Jffrsn JSY AU/99 RC 50.00 120.00
124 T.Jones JSY AU/99 RC 50.00 120.00
125 Jarell Martin JSY AU/99 RC 20.00 50.00
126 L.Nance Jr. JSY AU/49 RC 50.00 120.00
127 R.J. Hunter JSY AU/99 RC 15.00 40.00
128 Chris McCullough JSY AU/99 RC 15.00 40.00
129 K.Looney JSY AU/99 RC 30.00 80.00
130 Montrezl Harrell JSY AU/99 RC 40.00 100.00
131 Jordan Mickey JSY AU/99 RC 15.00 40.00
132 Anthony Brown JSY AU/99 RC 15.00 40.00
133 Rakeem Christmas JSY AU/99 RC 15.00 40.00
134 Richaun Holmes JSY AU/99 RC 40.00 100.00
135 Pat Connaughton JSY AU/99 RC 15.00 40.00
136 Joe Young JSY AU/99 RC EXCH 20.00 50.00
137 Aaron Harrison JSY AU/49 RC EXCH 20.00 50.00
138 Richardson JSY AU/99 RC 60.00 150.00
139 Walter Tavares JSY AU/99 RC EXCH 15.00 40.00
140 Josh Huestis JSY AU/99 RC 15.00 40.00
141 Branden Dawson AU RC
142 T.J. McConnell AU RC EXCH 10.00 25.00
144 Cliff Alexander AU RC EXCH 6.00 15.00
145 Cristiano Felicio AU RC 5.00 12.00
146 Darrun Hilliard AU RC 4.00 10.00
147 Sasha Kaun AU RC 4.00 10.00
148 Duje Dukan AU RC 4.00 10.00
149 Luis Montero AU RC 4.00 10.00
150 Jonathon Simmons AU RC EXCH 60.00 150.00
151 Nemanja Bjelica AU RC 8.00 20.00
152 Nikola Jokic AU RC 400.00 800.00
153 Norman Powell AU RC 20.00 50.00
154 Salah Mejri AU RC 4.00 10.00
155 Raul Neto AU RC 4.00 10.00
156 Marcelo Huertas AU RC 8.00 20.00
157 Boban Marjanovic AU RC 15.00 40.00

2015-16 Panini National Treasures Silver
*SILVER JSY AU: .5X TO 1.2X BASIC
*SILVER AU: .6X TO 1.5X BASIC
RANDOM INSERTS IN PACKS
STATED PRINT RUN 25 SER.#'d SETS
EXCHANGE DEADLINE 11/11/2017

2015-16 Panini National Treasures Clutch Factor Jersey Autographs
RANDOM INSERTS IN PACKS
PRINT RUNS B/WN 25-49 COPIES PER
EXCHANGE DEADLINE 11/11/2017
*PRIME/22-25: .75X TO 2X BASIC
CFAD Anthony Davis/25 40.00 100.00
CFBB Bradley Beal/49 12.00 30.00
CFBK Bernard King/49 8.00 20.00
CFBL Bill Laimbeer/49 5.00 12.00
CFBW Bill Walton/49 8.00 20.00
CFCB Chris Bosh/25 15.00 40.00
CFCL Christian Laettner/49 10.00 25.00
CFDR Dennis Rodman/49 30.00 80.00
CFIT Isiah Thomas/49 12.00 30.00
CFJE Julius Erving/25 40.00 100.00
CFKB Kobe Bryant/25 150.00 300.00
CFKD Kevin Durant/25 60.00 150.00
CFKI Kyrie Irving/25 40.00 100.00
CFKM Karl Malone/25 20.00 50.00
CFKS Kenny Smith/35 5.00 12.00
CFLB Larry Bird/25 40.00 100.00
CFRA Ray Allen/49 25.00 60.00
CFRA Ryan Anderson/49 5.00 12.00
CFRR Ricky Rubio/49 10.00 25.00
CFSB Shane Battier/49 5.00 12.00
CFSC Stephen Curry/25 200.00 500.00
CFSN Steve Nash/49 20.00 50.00
CFTH Tobias Harris/49 5.00 12.00
CFTP Tony Parker/49 15.00 40.00
CFVC Vince Carter/49 20.00 50.00
CFVD Vlade Divac/49 6.00 15.00
CFBDG Brad Daugherty/49 5.00 12.00
CFDGL Danilo Gallinari/49 5.00 12.00
CFDRS David Robinson/49 20.00 50.00
CFJDM Joe Dumars/49 6.00 15.00
CFJST John Stockton/25 25.00 60.00
CFKAJ Kareem Abdul-Jabbar/25 30.00 80.00
CFKVW Kiki VanDeWeghe/49 5.00 12.00
CFRFX Rick Fox/49 5.00 12.00
CFRPS Robert Parish/49 6.00 15.00
CFSKR Steve Kerr/49 12.00 30.00
CFSON Shaquille O'Neal/25 60.00 150.00
CFTHW Tim Hardaway/49 8.00 20.00
CFTKK Toni Kukoc/49 10.00 25.00
CFWBF World B. Free/49 5.00 12.00

2015-16 Panini National Treasures Colossal Jersey Signatures
RANDOM INSERTS IN PACKS
PRINT RUNS B/WN 12-49 COPIES PER
NO PRICING ON QTY 12
EXCHANGE DEADLINE 11/11/2017
CJAB Anthony Brown/49 6.00 15.00
CJAD Anthony Davis/25 40.00 100.00
CJBG Blake Griffin/25 25.00 60.00
CJCA Carmelo Anthony/25 25.00 60.00
CJDR Dino Radja/35 20.00 50.00
CJEM E. Mudiay/49 EXCH 40.00 100.00
CJFK Frank Kaminsky/49 12.00 30.00
CJGH Gordon Hayward/49 6.00 15.00
CJGP Gary Payton/49 15.00 40.00
CJHO Hakeem Olajuwon/49 20.00 50.00
CJJB Jerryd Bayless/49 5.00 12.00
CJJO Jahlil Okafor/49 20.00 50.00
CJJP Jabari Parker/49 20.00 50.00
CJJR Julius Randle/49 12.00 30.00
CJJW Justise Winslow/49 40.00 100.00
CJJW John Wall/49 20.00 50.00
CJKB Kobe Bryant/25 150.00 300.00
CJKD Kevin Durant/25 60.00 150.00
CJKI Kyrie Irving/25 40.00 100.00
CJKL Kevin Love/49 20.00 50.00
CJKL Kevon Looney/49 6.00 15.00
CJKM Karl Malone/25 25.00 60.00
CJKP Kristaps Porzingis/49 100.00 200.00
CJMD Matthew Dellavedova/49 12.00 30.00
CJMG Marcin Gortat/49 5.00 12.00
CJMH Mario Hezonja/49 15.00 40.00
CJMT Myles Turner/49 25.00 60.00
CJTM Timofey Mozgov/49 4.00 10.00
CJTP Tony Parker/49 20.00 50.00
CJTR Terry Rozier/49 10.00 25.00
CJADR Andre Drummond/49 12.00 30.00
CJBBD Bojan Bogdanovic/49 4.00 10.00
CJCDX Clyde Drexler/49 20.00 50.00
CJCPN Cameron Payne/49 5.00 12.00
CJCPT Bobby Portis/49 12.00 30.00
CJDBK Devin Booker/49 75.00 200.00
CJDRS D'Angelo Russell/49 60.00 150.00
CJDWT Delon Wright/49 6.00 15.00
CJJAN Justin Anderson/49 8.00 20.00
CJJDM Joe Dumars/49 6.00 15.00
CJJGR Jerian Grant/49 8.00 20.00
CJJMK Jordan Mickey/49 6.00 15.00
CJKMT Khris Middleton/49 10.00 25.00
CJKOJ Kelly Oubre Jr./49 10.00 25.00
CJKTH Klay Thompson/49 50.00 120.00
CJLGW Langston Galloway/49 4.00 10.00
CJMCL Mike Conley/49 6.00 15.00
CJMJS Mark Jackson/49 5.00 12.00
CJRHJ R. Hollis-Jefferson/49 10.00 25.00
CJRHP Ron Harper/49 6.00 15.00
CJRJH R.J. Hunter/49 5.00 12.00
CJSJS Stanley Johnson/49 15.00 40.00
CJSON Shaquille O'Neal/25 60.00 150.00
CJTHJ Tim Hardaway Jr./49 4.00 10.00
CJTJS Tyus Jones/49 8.00 20.00
CJTJW T.J. Warren/49 5.00 12.00
CJTLS Trey Lyles/49 10.00 25.00
CJWCS Willie Cauley-Stein/49 25.00 60.00
CJZLV Zach LaVine/49 20.00 50.00

2015-16 Panini National Treasures Colossal Jersey Signatures Prime
*PRIME/25: .75X TO 2X BASIC
RANDOM INSERTS IN PACKS
PRINT RUNS B/WN 9-25 COPIES PER
NO PRICING ON QTY 15 OR LESS
EXCHANGE DEADLINE 11/11/2017
CJFK Frank Kaminsky/25 50.00 120.00
CJJO Jahlil Okafor/25 200.00 400.00
CJKL Kevon Looney/25 75.00 200.00
CJKP Kristaps Porzingis/25 600.00 1200.00
CJMT Myles Turner/25 250.00 500.00
CJCPT Bobby Portis/25 75.00 200.00
CJDBK Devin Booker/25 400.00 800.00
CJDRS D'Angelo Russell/25 400.00 800.00
CJJGR Jerian Grant/25 25.00 60.00
CJKOJ Kelly Oubre Jr./25 60.00 150.00
CJRHJ R. Hollis-Jefferson/25 40.00 100.00
CJSJS Stanley Johnson/25 150.00 300.00
CJTJS Tyus Jones/25 40.00 100.00
CJTLS Trey Lyles/25 150.00 400.00
CJZLV Zach LaVine/25 100.00 200.00

2015-16 Panini National Treasures Colossal Jerseys
RANDOM INSERTS IN PACKS
PRINT RUNS B/WN 49-99 COPIES PER
1 Andre Iguodala/99 5.00 12.00
2 Paul Millsap/60 4.00 10.00
3 Joakim Noah/99 3.00 8.00
4 Tony Parker/99 4.00 10.00
5 Derrick Rose/49 6.00 15.00
6 Kyrie Irving/99 6.00 15.00
7 Nikola Vucevic/99 3.00 8.00
8 Kyle Korver/60 3.00 8.00
9 Andrew Wiggins/99 6.00 15.00
10 Brook Lopez/99 3.00 8.00
11 Tobias Harris/99 3.00 8.00
12 Greg Monroe/99 3.00 8.00
13 Dirk Nowitzki/99 5.00 12.00
14 Chris Paul/60 5.00 12.00
15 Marcus Smart/99 3.00 8.00
16 LeBron James/49 25.00 60.00
17 Kemba Walker/60 4.00 10.00
18 Ty Lawson/60 2.50 6.00
19 Jimmy Butler/60 4.00 10.00
20 Kyle Lowry/99 3.00 8.00
21 DeAndre Jordan/60 4.00 10.00
22 Nerlens Noel/99 3.00 8.00
23 Tim Duncan/99 6.00 15.00
24 LaMarcus Aldridge/99 4.00 10.00
25 Bojan Bogdanovic/99 2.50 6.00
26 Langston Galloway/99 2.50 6.00
27 Russell Westbrook/60 10.00 25.00
28 Damian Lillard/49 6.00 15.00
29 Manu Ginobili/60 4.00 10.00
30 C.J. McCollum/60 4.00 10.00
31 Jeremy Lin/60 4.00 10.00
32 Victor Oladipo/99 3.00 8.00
33 James Harden/60 6.00 15.00
34 Zach Randolph/99 3.00 8.00
35 Jared Sullinger/99 2.50 6.00

2015-16 Panini National Treasures Colossal Jerseys Prime
*PRIME/20-25: .75X TO 2X BASIC
RANDOM INSERTS IN PACKS
PRINT RUNS B/WN 5-25 COPIES PER
NO PRICING ON QTY 13 OR LESS
4 Tony Parker/25 25.00 60.00
23 Tim Duncan/25 30.00 80.00
24 LaMarcus Aldridge/25 30.00 80.00
29 Manu Ginobili/25 20.00 50.00

2015-16 Panini National Treasures Game Changers Autographs
RANDOM INSERTS IN PACKS
PRINT RUNS B/WN 25-49 COPIES PER
EXCHANGE DEADLINE 11/11/2017
GCAD Andre Drummond/49 8.00 20.00
GCAH Allan Houston/49 5.00 12.00
GCAH Anfernee Hardaway/35 30.00 80.00
GCAM Alonzo Mourning/25 20.00 50.00
GCAW Andrew Wiggins/25 40.00 100.00
GCBS Byron Scott/49 5.00 12.00
GCBW Bill Walton/49 6.00 15.00
GCCM Calvin Murphy/49 5.00 12.00
GCDM Danny Manning/49 5.00 12.00
GCDM Dikembe Mutombo/49 12.00 30.00
GCDW Dwyane Wade/25 50.00 120.00
GCEK Enes Kanter/49 4.00 10.00
GCFR Frank Ramsey/49 10.00 25.00
GCJE Julius Erving/25 30.00 80.00
GCJP Jabari Parker/25 20.00 50.00
GCJR Julius Randle/49 10.00 25.00
GCJW James Worthy/49 15.00 40.00
GCKI Kyrie Irving/25 30.00 80.00
GCKL Kevin Love/35 10.00 25.00
GCKM Karl Malone/25 30.00 80.00
GCKR Kurt Rambis/49 4.00 10.00
GCKT Klay Thompson/35 40.00 100.00
GCLB Larry Brown/49 6.00 15.00
GCLW Lenny Wilkens/49 8.00 20.00
GCMC Mike Conley/49 6.00 15.00
GCMR Mitch Richmond/49 8.00 20.00
GCMS Marcus Smart/35 12.00 30.00
GCNA Nate Archibald/49 6.00 15.00
GCRG Rudy Gay/49 8.00 20.00
GCRP Robert Parish/49 6.00 15.00
GCRS Ralph Sampson/49 5.00 12.00
GCSS Satch Sanders/49 12.00 30.00
GCVO Victor Oladipo/35 5.00 12.00
GCWM Wesley Matthews/49 4.00 10.00
GCCAY Carmelo Anthony/25 20.00 50.00
GCDCW Dave Cowens/49 6.00 15.00
GCDMC DeMarre Carroll/49 4.00 10.00
GCDMD Doug McDermott/49 8.00 20.00
GCEHY Elvin Hayes/49 6.00 15.00
GCGAT G. Antetokounmpo/49 40.00 100.00
GCGHW Gordon Hayward/49 6.00 15.00
GCJDM Joe Dumars/49 6.00 15.00
GCJHD Jrue Holiday/49 5.00 12.00
GCJJW Jo Jo White/49 5.00 12.00
GCJKD Jason Kidd/25 12.00 30.00
GCJNK Jusuf Nurkic/49 4.00 10.00
GCKMH Kevin McHale/25 12.00 30.00
GCKSM Kenny Smith/49 5.00 12.00
GCMJS Mark Jackson/49 5.00 12.00
GCNVE Nick Van Exel/49 10.00 25.00
GCTAL Tony Allen/49 4.00 10.00
GCTHS Tobias Harris/49 5.00 12.00
GCTJW T.J. Warren/49 5.00 12.00
GCTMG Tracy McGrady/35 20.00 50.00
GCWCH Wilson Chandler/49 5.00 12.00
GCWFZ Walt Frazier/49 5.00 12.00
GCZLV Zach LaVine/49 15.00 40.00

2015-16 Panini National Treasures Hometown Heroes Autographs
RANDOM INSERTS IN PACKS
PRINT RUNS B/WN 25-75 COPIES PER
EXCHANGE DEADLINE 11/11/2017
HHAD Anthony Davis/25 40.00 100.00
HHAI Allen Iverson/25 150.00 250.00
HHBG Blake Griffin/25 25.00 60.00
HHCP Chris Paul/25 30.00 80.00
HHDW Dwyane Wade/25 60.00 150.00
HHFR Frank Ramsey/75 12.00 30.00
HHGP Gary Payton/49 10.00 25.00
HHJE Julius Erving/25 30.00 80.00
HHJR Julius Randle/75 10.00 25.00
HHJW Jerry West/25 25.00 60.00
HHJW Justise Winslow/75 20.00 50.00
HHKB Kobe Bryant/25 150.00 300.00
HHKD Kevin Durant/25 60.00 150.00
HHKI Kyrie Irving/25 30.00 80.00
HHKM Karl Malone/25 20.00 50.00
HHKM Kevin McHale/49 12.00 30.00
HHLB Larry Bird/25 50.00 120.00
HHMC Mike Conley/75 6.00 15.00
HHMR Mitch Richmond/75 6.00 15.00
HHRP Robert Parish/75 6.00 15.00
HHSC Stephen Curry/25 300.00 500.00
HHSS Satch Sanders/75 10.00 25.00
HHWF Walt Frazier/75 10.00 25.00
HHAHW Anfernee Hardaway/49 20.00 50.00
HHBKG Bernard King/75 5.00 12.00
HHBWT Bill Walton/75 6.00 15.00
HHCAY Carmelo Anthony/25 20.00 50.00
HHCHG Cliff Hagan/75 5.00 12.00
HHDCR DeMarre Carroll/75 4.00 10.00
HHJJW Jo Jo White/75 5.00 12.00
HHJKD Jason Kidd/49 12.00 30.00
HHKAJ Kareem Abdul-Jabbar/25 40.00 100.00
HHMJS Magic Johnson/25 30.00 80.00
HHMST Marcus Smart/49 8.00 20.00
HHNVE Nick Van Exel/75 8.00 20.00
HHRAL Rafer Alston/75 4.00 10.00
HHSBT Shane Battier/75 5.00 12.00
HHSON S. O'Neal/25 EXCH 60.00 150.00
HHTMG Tracy McGrady/49 30.00 80.00
HHMJS2 Mark Jackson/75 5.00 12.00

2015-16 Panini National Treasures International Treasures Autographs
RANDOM INSERTS IN PACKS
PRINT RUNS B/WN 25-75 COPIES PER
EXCHANGE DEADLINE 11/11/2017
ITAW Andrew Wiggins/25 60.00 150.00
ITBB Bojan Bogdanovic/75 6.00 15.00
ITDM Dikembe Mutombo/75 12.00 30.00
ITDW Dominique Wilkins/25 20.00 50.00
ITEK Enes Kanter/75 4.00 10.00
ITEM Emmanuel Mudiay/25 40.00 100.00
ITGA G. Antetokounmpo/75 60.00 150.00
ITJN Jusuf Nurkic/75 6.00 15.00
ITKI Kyrie Irving/25 125.00 250.00
ITKP Kristaps Porzingis/49 100.00 200.00
ITMG Marcin Gortat/75 8.00 20.00
ITMH Mario Hezonja/49 20.00 50.00
ITNB Nemanja Bjelica/75 12.00 30.00
ITNJ Nikola Jokic/75 100.00 250.00
ITRF Rick Fox/49 5.00 12.00
ITRR Ricky Rubio/25 40.00 100.00
ITSN Steve Nash/25 50.00 120.00
ITTP Tony Parker/25 40.00 100.00
ITWT Walter Tavares/75 4.00 10.00
ITDGL Danilo Gallinari/49 5.00 12.00
ITDRJ Dino Radja/75 12.00 30.00
ITHOW Hakeem Olajuwon/49 20.00 50.00
ITMHT Marcelo Huertas/75 6.00 15.00
ITNMT Nikola Mirotic/75 5.00 12.00
ITRNT Raul Neto/75 4.00 10.00
ITRSK Rony Seikaly/75 4.00 10.00
ITSMC Sarunas Marciulionis/75 8.00 20.00
ITTKK Toni Kukoc/75 15.00 40.00
ITTMZ Timofey Mozgov/75 4.00 10.00
ITVDV Vlade Divac/75 10.00 25.00

2015-16 Panini National Treasures Lasting Legacies Jersey Autographs
RANDOM INSERTS IN PACKS
PRINT RUNS B/WN 25-49 COPIES PER
EXCHANGE DEADLINE 11/11/2017
*PRIME/25: .75X TO 2X BASIC
LLAD Anthony Davis/25 50.00 120.00
LLAM Alonzo Mourning/25 20.00 50.00
LLBG Blake Griffin/25 20.00 50.00
LLBW Bill Walton/49 6.00 15.00
LLGH Grant Hill/49 20.00 50.00
LLGP Gary Payton/49 12.00 30.00
LLHO Hakeem Olajuwon/25 20.00 50.00
LLJE Julius Erving/25 40.00 100.00
LLJW John Wall/25 20.00 50.00
LLKB Kobe Bryant/25 150.00 300.00
LLKD Kevin Durant/25 60.00 150.00
LLKI Kyrie Irving/25 30.00 80.00
LLKM Karl Malone/25 25.00 60.00
LLKM Kevin McHale/49 10.00 25.00
LLMJ Mark Jackson/49 5.00 12.00
LLSC Stephen Curry/25 300.00 500.00
LLADL Adrian Dantley/49 5.00 12.00
LLBDT Brad Daugherty/49 5.00 12.00
LLCDX Clyde Drexler/25 20.00 50.00
LLDMG Danny Manning/49 5.00 12.00
LLDMT Dikembe Mutombo/49 10.00 25.00
LLDRJ Dino Radja/49 12.00 30.00
LLJDM Joe Dumars/49 6.00 15.00
LLJKD Jason Kidd/49 15.00 40.00
LLMJS Magic Johnson/25 40.00 100.00
LLRAL Rafer Alston/49 5.00 12.00
LLRHP Ron Harper/49 6.00 15.00
LLRSP Ralph Sampson/49 5.00 12.00
LLSON Shaquille O'Neal/25 60.00 150.00
LLWBF World B. Free/49 5.00 12.00

2015-16 Panini National Treasures Material Treasures
1 Arvydas Sabonis/99 3.00 8.00
2 Dirk Nowitzki/75 5.00 12.00
3 Serge Ibaka/75 3.00 8.00
4 Isiah Thomas/49 4.00 10.00
5 Aaron Gordon/75 3.00 8.00
6 Karl Malone/75 5.00 12.00
7 Kevin McHale/75 4.00 10.00
8 C.J. McCollum/75 4.00 10.00
9 Mark Jackson/49 3.00 8.00
10 Danny Green/75 3.00 8.00
11 Ray Allen/75 4.00 10.00
12 Eric Bledsoe/75 3.00 8.00
13 Shaquille O'Neal/75 6.00 15.00
14 Jeff Teague/75 3.00 8.00
15 Alonzo Mourning/99 5.00 12.00
16 Kawhi Leonard/75 6.00 15.00
17 Larry Bird/75 10.00 25.00
18 Chris Andersen/75 3.00 8.00
19 Michael Redd/75 3.00 8.00
20 David Robinson/75 5.00 12.00
21 Reggie Lewis/75 4.00 10.00
22 Gary Payton/75 4.00 10.00
23 Steve Nash/75 4.00 10.00
24 Jimmy Butler/75 4.00 10.00
25 Alonzo Mourning/99 5.00 12.00
26 Kenneth Faried/75 3.00 8.00
27 Chris Bosh/75 4.00 10.00
28 Larry Johnson/75 5.00 12.00
29 Mike Bibby/75 3.00 8.00
30 DeMar DeRozan/75 4.00 10.00
31 Russell Westbrook/75 5.00 12.00
32 Gordon Hayward/75 4.00 10.00
33 Tim Duncan/75 6.00 15.00
34 John Starks/75 3.00 8.00
35 Blake Griffin/75 4.00 10.00
36 Kevin Durant/49 6.00 15.00
37 Manu Ginobili/75 4.00 10.00
38 Clyde Drexler/75 5.00 12.00
39 Moses Malone/75 4.00 10.00
40 DeMarcus Cousins/75 4.00 10.00
41 Scottie Pippen/75 8.00 20.00
42 Grant Hill/75 5.00 12.00
43 Tony Parker/75 4.00 10.00
44 John Stockton/75 5.00 12.00
45 Bradley Beal/75 4.00 10.00
46 Kevin Garnett/75 5.00 12.00
47 Mark Aguirre/75 3.00 8.00
48 Damian Lillard/49 8.00 20.00
49 Patrick Ewing/75 5.00 12.00
50 Dennis Rodman/75 8.00 20.00

2015-16 Panini National Treasures Material Treasures Prime
*PRIME/25: .75X TO 2X BASIC
RANDOM INSERTS IN PACKS
PRINT RUNS B/WN 10-25 COPIES PER
NO PRICING ON QTY 10
16 Kawhi Leonard/25 20.00 50.00
41 Scottie Pippen/25 25.00 60.00
46 Kevin Garnett/25 20.00 50.00

2015-16 Panini National Treasures Material Treasures Signatures
RANDOM INSERTS IN PACKS
PRINT RUNS B/WN 25-99 COPIES PER
EXCHANGE DEADLINE 11/11/2017
*PRIME/25: .75X TO 2X BASIC
MTSAH Al Horford/99 5.00 12.00
MTSAI Allen Iverson/99 40.00 100.00
MTSBG Blake Griffin/75 20.00 50.00
MTSBK Bernard King/99 5.00 12.00
MTSBS Byron Scott/90 5.00 12.00
MTSCL Christian Laettner/99 5.00 12.00
MTSCM Chris Mullin/75 12.00 30.00
MTSCW Chris Webber/77 40.00 100.00
MTSDN Dirk Nowitzki/99 60.00 150.00
MTSDR D'Angelo Russell/99 40.00 100.00
MTSDR Dennis Rodman/99 15.00 40.00
MTSDR David Robinson/99 15.00 40.00
MTSEM Emmanuel Mudiay/99 10.00 25.00
MTSGH Grant Hill/99 12.00 30.00
MTSHO Hakeem Olajuwon/99 15.00 40.00
MTSJS John Stockton/85 20.00 50.00
MTSJW John Wall/99 15.00 40.00
MTSJW Justise Winslow/99 6.00 15.00
MTSKA Abdul-Jabbar/30 30.00 80.00
MTSKM Karl Malone/72 20.00 50.00
MTSKP Kristaps Porzingis/99 60.00 150.00
MTSKT Karl-Anthony Towns/99 150.00 300.00
MTSMH Mario Hezonja/99 10.00 25.00
MTSPG Paul George/46 25.00 60.00
MTSRA Ray Allen/99 15.00 40.00
MTSRH Richard Hamilton/76 5.00 12.00
MTSRS Ralph Sampson/99 5.00 12.00
MTSSK Steve Kerr/99 8.00 20.00
MTSSP Scottie Pippen/25 50.00 120.00
MTSTB Trey Burke/99 4.00 10.00
MTSVO Victor Oladipo/99 5.00 12.00
MTSCMU Calvin Murphy/99 5.00 12.00
MTSDMA Danny Manning/99 5.00 12.00

2015-16 Panini National Treasures NBA Game Gear Duals
RANDOM INSERTS IN PACKS
PRINT RUNS B/WN 45-75 COPIES PER
1 David Robinson/75 6.00 15.00
2 Russell Westbrook/75 10.00 25.00
3 Scottie Pippen/75 8.00 20.00
4 Derrick Rose/49 5.00 12.00
5 World B. Free/49 3.00 8.00
6 Stephen Curry/49 15.00 40.00
7 Rudy Gobert/75 4.00 10.00
8 Blake Griffin/75 4.00 10.00
9 John Stockton/75 5.00 12.00
10 Andrew Wiggins/75 5.00 12.00
11 Dennis Rodman/75 8.00 20.00
12 Damian Lillard/49 6.00 15.00
13 Ben Wallace/75 3.00 8.00
14 Kyrie Irving/75 5.00 12.00
15 Gail Goodrich/49 3.00 8.00
16 James Harden/75 6.00 15.00
17 Rick Fox/75 3.00 8.00
18 Kobe Bryant/75 12.00 30.00
19 Karl Malone/75 5.00 12.00
20 Anthony Davis/75 6.00 15.00
21 Danny Manning/75 3.00 8.00
22 Tim Duncan/75 6.00 15.00
23 Kevin McHale/75 4.00 10.00
24 LeBron James/49 20.00 50.00
25 Moses Malone/75 4.00 10.00
26 Gordon Hayward/75 4.00 10.00
27 Steve Nash/75 4.00 10.00
28 Dwyane Wade/75 6.00 15.00
29 Grant Hill/75 5.00 12.00
30 Carmelo Anthony/75 5.00 12.00
31 Clyde Drexler/75 5.00 12.00
32 John Wall/75 5.00 12.00
33 Larry Bird/75 10.00 25.00
34 Dirk Nowitzki/75 5.00 12.00
35 Gary Payton/75 4.00 10.00
36 Chris Paul/75 5.00 12.00
37 Cazzie Russell/45 3.00 8.00
38 Derrick Favors/75 3.00 8.00
39 Patrick Ewing/75 5.00 12.00
40 Kevin Durant/49 8.00 20.00

2015-16 Panini National Treasures NBA Game Gear Duals Prime
*PRIME/25: .75X TO 2X BASIC
RANDOM INSERTS IN PACKS
PRINT RUNS B/WN 10-25 COPIES PER
NO PRICING ON QTY 15 OR LESS
18 Kobe Bryant/25 75.00 200.00
22 Tim Duncan/25 20.00 50.00
28 Dwyane Wade/25 20.00 50.00

2015-16 Panini National Treasures NBA Game Gear Signatures
RANDOM INSERTS IN PACKS
PRINT RUNS B/WN 25-49 COPIES PER
EXCHANGE DEADLINE 11/11/2017
*PRIME/25: .75X TO 2X BASIC
GGAD Anthony Davis/25 40.00 100.00
GGAW Andrew Wiggins/25 40.00 100.00
GGBG Blake Griffin/25 20.00 50.00
GGCP Chris Paul/25 30.00 80.00
GGDW Dwyane Wade/25 40.00 100.00
GGEP Elfrid Payton/49 5.00 12.00
GGGH Gordon Hayward/49 6.00 15.00
GGIT Isaiah Thomas/49 25.00 60.00
GGJH Jrue Holiday/49 5.00 12.00
GGJR Julius Randle/49 10.00 25.00
GGJW John Wall/25 20.00 50.00
GGKB Kobe Bryant/25 150.00 250.00
GGKD Kevin Durant/25 60.00 150.00
GGKI Kyrie Irving/25 30.00 80.00
GGKL Kevin Love/25 20.00 50.00
GGKL Kawhi Leonard/49 40.00 100.00
GGKT Klay Thompson/49 40.00 100.00
GGMP Mason Plumlee/49 5.00 12.00
GGRA Ryan Anderson/49 5.00 12.00
GGRG Rudy Gay/49 6.00 15.00
GGSC Stephen Curry/25 250.00 400.00
GGADR Andre Drummond/49 8.00 20.00
GGAGD Aaron Gordon/49 8.00 20.00
GGBJB Bojan Bogdanovic/49 4.00 10.00
GGCAY Carmelo Anthony/25 25.00 60.00
GGDMC DeMarre Carroll/49 6.00 15.00
GGGAT G. Antetokounmpo/49 40.00 100.00
GGJNK Jusuf Nurkic/49 4.00 10.00
GGJPK Jabari Parker/25 15.00 40.00
GGKFR Kenneth Faried/49 5.00 12.00
GGLGW Langston Galloway/49 4.00 10.00
GGMCL Mike Conley/49 6.00 15.00
GGMGT Marcin Gortat/49 5.00 12.00
GGMST Marcus Smart/49 8.00 20.00
GGNMT Nikola Mirotic/49 8.00 20.00
GGTHJ Tim Hardaway Jr./49 4.00 10.00
GGTJW T.J. Warren/49 5.00 12.00
GGVOD Victor Oladipo/49 5.00 12.00
GGWCH Wilson Chandler/49 5.00 12.00
GGZLV Zach LaVine/49 15.00 40.00

2015-16 Panini National Treasures NBA Game Gear Triples
RANDOM INSERTS IN PACKS
PRINT RUNS B/WN 25-49 COPIES PER
*PRIME/25: .75X TO 2X BASIC
1 John Wall/49 5.00 12.00
2 Andrew Wiggins/49 6.00 15.00
3 Chris Paul/49 5.00 12.00
4 James Harden/49 6.00 15.00
5 Patrick Ewing/49 5.00 12.00
6 Anthony Davis/49 6.00 15.00
7 LeBron James/25 50.00 120.00
8 Russell Westbrook/49 10.00 25.00
9 Chandler Parsons/49 3.00 8.00
10 Stephen Curry/25 15.00 40.00
11 Dirk Nowitzki/49 5.00 12.00
12 Damian Lillard/25 6.00 15.00
13 Arron Afflalo/49 2.50 6.00
14 Kobe Bryant/49 20.00 50.00
15 Kevin Durant/25 8.00 20.00
16 Tim Duncan/49 6.00 15.00
17 Moses Malone/49 4.00 10.00
18 Derrick Rose/25 6.00 15.00
19 Dwyane Wade/49 5.00 12.00
20 Blake Griffin/49 4.00 10.00

2015-16 Panini National Treasures NBA Greats Signatures
RANDOM INSERTS IN PACKS
PRINT RUNS B/WN 56-99 COPIES PER
EXCHANGE DEADLINE 11/11/2017
GR8AG Artis Gilmore/99 5.00 12.00
GR8AH Anfernee Hardaway/85 15.00 40.00
GR8BW Bill Walton/99 6.00 15.00
GR8CH Cliff Hagan/99 5.00 12.00
GR8CW Chris Webber/99 30.00 80.00
GR8DB Dave Bing/99 12.00 30.00
GR8EB Elgin Baylor/56 10.00 25.00
GR8EH Elvin Hayes/99 6.00 15.00
GR8FR Frank Ramsey/99 10.00 25.00
GR8GG Gail Goodrich/83 5.00 12.00
GR8HG Hal Greer/99 5.00 12.00
GR8JW Jerry West/99 20.00 50.00
GR8KA K. Abdul-Jabbar/76 25.00 60.00
GR8LW Lenny Wilkens/99 6.00 15.00
GR8OR Oscar Robertson/99 25.00 60.00
GR8SP Scottie Pippen/72 40.00 100.00
GR8WU Wes Unseld/99 6.00 15.00

2015-16 Panini National Treasures NBA Materials
RANDOM INSERTS IN PACKS
PRINT RUNS B/WN 49-99 COPIES PER
1 Jimmy Butler/99 4.00 10.00
2 Darren Collison/99 3.00 8.00
3 Chris Andersen/99 3.00 8.00
4 Kyle Korver/99 3.00 8.00
5 Tim Duncan/99 6.00 15.00
6 Terrence Ross/99 3.00 8.00
7 Bradley Beal/99 4.00 10.00
8 Kyrie Irving/99 6.00 15.00
9 LaMarcus Aldridge/99 4.00 10.00
10 Derrick Rose/49 5.00 12.00
11 Kenneth Faried/99 3.00 8.00
12 Doug McDermott/99 3.00 8.00
13 Kawhi Leonard/99 5.00 12.00
14 Markieff Morris/99 2.50 6.00
15 Blake Griffin/99 4.00 10.00
16 Trey Burke/99 2.50 6.00
17 Kevin Garnett/99 5.00 12.00
18 John Wall/99 5.00 12.00
19 Dirk Nowitzki/99 5.00 12.00
20 Archie Goodwin/99 2.50 6.00
21 Chris Bosh/99 4.00 10.00
22 Evan Fournier/99 3.00 8.00
23 Jeff Teague/99 3.00 8.00
24 Mo Williams/99 3.00 8.00
25 Manu Ginobili/99 4.00 10.00
26 Zach Randolph/99 3.00 8.00
27 Damian Lillard/49 8.00 20.00
28 Anthony Davis/99 6.00 15.00
29 Serge Ibaka/99 3.00 8.00
30 Boris Diaw/99 3.00 8.00
31 DeMar DeRozan/99 4.00 10.00
32 John Henson/99 3.00 8.00
33 Eric Bledsoe/99 3.00 8.00
34 Otto Porter/99 3.00 8.00
35 DeMarcus Cousins/99 4.00 10.00
36 Kevin Durant/49 8.00 20.00
37 Stephen Curry/49 15.00 40.00
38 Aaron Gordon/99 3.00 8.00
39 Brandon Jennings/99 2.50 6.00
40 Russell Westbrook/99 10.00 25.00
41 Kelly Olynyk/99 2.50 6.00
42 Danny Green/99 3.00 8.00
43 Rodney Hood/99 3.00 8.00
44 Tony Parker/99 4.00 10.00
45 Kobe Bryant/99 12.00 30.00
46 Klay Thompson/99 5.00 12.00
47 C.J. McCollum/99 4.00 10.00
48 Danilo Gallinari/99 3.00 8.00
49 Gordon Hayward/99 4.00 10.00
50 Jordan Clarkson/99 4.00 10.00

2015-16 Panini National Treasures NBA Materials Prime
*PRIME/25: .75X TO 2X BASIC
RANDOM INSERTS IN PACKS
PRINT RUNS B/WN 5-25 COPIES PER
NO PRICING ON QTY 10
17 Kevin Garnett/25 40.00 100.00
45 Kobe Bryant/25 50.00 120.00

2015-16 Panini National Treasures NBA Rookie Materials
RANDOM INSERTS IN PACKS
PRINT RUNS B/WN 86-99 COPIES PER
1 Emmanuel Mudiay/99 4.00 10.00
2 Salah Mejri/99 2.50 6.00
3 Cameron Payne/99 3.00 8.00
4 Luis Montero/99 2.50 6.00
5 Marcelo Huertas/99 3.00 8.00
6 Kelly Oubre Jr./99 3.00 8.00
7 Justise Winslow/99 4.00 10.00
8 Cristiano Felicio/99 3.00 8.00
9 Trey Lyles/99 4.00 10.00
10 Nikola Jokic/99 5.00 12.00
11 Frank Kaminsky/99 4.00 10.00
12 Sasha Kaun/99 2.50 6.00
13 Rondae Hollis-Jefferson/99 3.00 8.00
14 Tyus Jones/99 4.00 10.00
15 Jerian Grant/99 2.50 6.00
16 Montrezl Harrell/99 3.00 8.00
17 Kristaps Porzingis/86 10.00 25.00
18 R.J. Hunter/99 2.50 6.00
19 Jahlil Okafor/99 6.00 15.00
20 Raul Neto/99 2.50 6.00
21 Norman Powell/99 3.00 8.00
22 Jonathon Simmons/99 4.00 10.00
23 Cliff Alexander/99 2.50 6.00
24 Nemanja Bjelica/99 3.00 8.00
25 Myles Turner/99 4.00 10.00
26 Stanley Johnson/99 3.00 8.00
27 Bobby Portis/99 4.00 10.00
28 Mario Hezonja/99 3.00 8.00
29 Karl-Anthony Towns/99 12.00 30.00
30 Willie Cauley-Stein/99 4.00 10.00
31 D'Angelo Russell/99 6.00 15.00
32 Pat Connaughton/99 2.50 6.00
33 Terry Rozier/99 3.00 8.00
34 Devin Booker/99 5.00 12.00
35 Justin Anderson/99 3.00 8.00

2015-16 Panini National Treasures NBA Rookie Materials Prime
*PRIME/25: .75X TO 2X BASIC
RANDOM INSERTS IN PACKS
PRINT RUNS B/WN 10-25 COPIES PER
NO PRICING ON QTY 10
17 Kristaps Porzingis/25 40.00 100.00

2015-16 Panini National Treasures Night Moves Jersey Autographs
RANDOM INSERTS IN PACKS
PRINT RUNS B/WN 25-49 COPIES PER

EXCHANGE DEADLINE 11/11/2017
*PRIME/24-25: .75X TO 2X BASIC
NMAD Anthony Davis/25 40.00 100.00
NMAD Andre Drummond/49 10.00 25.00
NMBG Blake Griffin/25 20.00 50.00
NMDR Dino Radja/49 12.00 30.00
NMGH Gordon Hayward/49 6.00 15.00
NMGP Gary Payton/49 10.00 25.00
NMHO Hakeem Olajuwon/25 20.00 50.00
NMJP Jabari Parker/25 15.00 40.00
NMJW John Wall/25 20.00 50.00
NMKB Kobe Bryant/25 150.00 300.00
NMKD Kevin Durant/25 60.00 150.00
NMKI Kyrie Irving/25 30.00 80.00
NMKL Kevin Love/49 15.00 40.00
NMKM Karl Malone/25 20.00 50.00
NMMJ Mark Jackson/49 5.00 12.00
NMADL Adrian Dantley/49 5.00 12.00
NMBJB Bojan Bogdanovic/49 4.00 10.00
NMCAY Carmelo Anthony/25 25.00 60.00
NMCDX Clyde Drexler/25 20.00 50.00
NMJDM Joe Dumars/49 6.00 15.00
NMJRD Julius Randle/49 10.00 25.00
NMKTM Klay Thompson/49 50.00 120.00
NMLGW Langston Galloway/49 4.00 10.00
NMMCL Mike Conley/49 6.00 15.00
NMMGT Marcin Gortat/49 5.00 12.00
NMRHP Ron Harper/49 6.00 15.00
NMSON Shaquille O'Neal/25 60.00 150.00
NMTHJ Tim Hardaway Jr./49 4.00 10.00
NMTJW T.J. Warren/49 5.00 12.00
NMZLV Zach LaVine/49 15.00 40.00

2015-16 Panini National Treasures Notable Nicknames

RANDOM INSERTS IN PACKS
STATED PRINT RUN 25 SER.#'d SETS
EXCHANGE DEADLINE 11/11/2017
NNAI Allen Iverson 200.00 400.00
NNFK Frank Kaminsky 50.00 120.00
NNGH Grant Hill 150.00 300.00
NNJW John Wall 250.00 400.00
NNMH Mario Hezonja 40.00 100.00
NNNB Nemanja Bjelica 50.00 120.00
NNRA Ray Allen 100.00 200.00
NNSJ Stanley Johnson 200.00 400.00
NNSN Steve Nash 75.00 150.00
NNDRS D'Angelo Russell 125.00 300.00
NNKAT Karl-Anthony Towns
NNSON Shaquille O'Neal 150.00 300.00
NNWCS Willie Cauley-Stein 50.00 120.00

2015-16 Panini National Treasures Rookie Jumbo Materials

RANDOM INSERTS IN PACKS
STATED PRINT RUN 99 SER.#'d SETS
1 Marcelo Huertas 3.00 8.00
2 Jerian Grant 2.50 6.00
3 Myles Turner 4.00 10.00
4 Justin Anderson 3.00 8.00
5 Justise Winslow 4.00 10.00
7 Bobby Portis 4.00 10.00
8 Trey Lyles 4.00 10.00
9 Jahlil Okafor 5.00 12.00
10 Karl-Anthony Towns 12.00 30.00
11 Emmanuel Mudiay 4.00 10.00
12 Frank Kaminsky 4.00 10.00
13 Norman Powell 3.00 8.00
14 D'Angelo Russell 6.00 15.00
15 Cameron Payne 3.00 8.00
16 Rondae Hollis-Jefferson 3.00 8.00
17 Cliff Alexander 2.50 6.00
18 Terry Rozier 3.00 8.00
19 Luis Montero 2.50 6.00
20 Tyus Jones 4.00 10.00
21 Nemanja Bjelica 3.00 8.00
22 Devin Booker 6.00 15.00
23 Kelly Oubre Jr. 3.00 8.00
24 Jarell Martin 3.00 8.00
25 Montrezl Harrell 3.00 8.00
26 Stanley Johnson 3.00 8.00
27 Cristiano Felicio 3.00 8.00
28 Delon Wright 3.00 8.00
29 R.J. Hunter 2.50 6.00
30 Mario Hezonja 3.00 8.00
31 Nikola Jokic 5.00 12.00
32 Anthony Brown 2.50 6.00
33 Raul Neto 2.50 6.00
34 Willie Cauley-Stein 4.00 10.00
35 Pat Connaughton 2.50 6.00

2015-16 Panini National Treasures Rookie Jumbo Materials Prime

*PRIME/25: .75X TO 2X BASIC
RANDOM INSERTS IN PACKS
PRINT RUNS B/WN 10-25 COPIES PER
NO PRICING ON QTY 15 OR LESS
9 Jahlil Okafor/25 15.00 40.00
11 Emmanuel Mudiay/25 30.00 80.00
14 D'Angelo Russell/25 20.00 50.00
22 Devin Booker/25 20.00 50.00

2015-16 Panini National Treasures Signature Moves

RANDOM INSERTS IN PACKS
PRINT RUNS B/WN 25-49 COPIES PER
EXCHANGE DEADLINE 11/11/2017
SMAI Allen Iverson 150.00 300.00
SMBG Blake Griffin 20.00 50.00
SMDM Dikembe Mutombo 12.00 30.00
SMDR Dennis Rodman 30.00 80.00
SMDW Dominique Wilkins 12.00 30.00
SMDW Dwyane Wade 60.00 150.00
SMGG George Gervin 15.00 40.00
SMHO Hakeem Olajuwon 20.00 50.00
SMJE Julius Erving 30.00 80.00
SMJS John Stockton 30.00 80.00
SMJW James Worthy 12.00 30.00
SMKB Kobe Bryant 250.00 400.00
SMKL Kevin Love 15.00 40.00
SMKM Kevin McHale 12.00 30.00
SMMJ Mark Jackson 5.00 12.00
SMRA Ray Allen 50.00 120.00
SMSC Stephen Curry 250.00 500.00
SMSN Steve Nash 40.00 100.00
SMTP Tony Parker 20.00 50.00
SMWM Wesley Matthews 4.00 10.00
SMWU Wes Unseld 6.00 15.00
SMCAY Carmelo Anthony 20.00 50.00
SMKAJ Kareem Abdul-Jabbar 50.00 120.00
SMKVW Kiki VanDeWeghe 5.00 12.00
SMRBY Rick Barry 12.00 30.00
SMSMC Sarunas Marciulionis 6.00 15.00
SMSON Shaquille O'Neal 60.00 150.00
SMTHW Tim Hardaway 6.00 15.00
SMTMG Tracy McGrady 40.00 100.00
SMMJS2 Magic Johnson 40.00 100.00

2015-16 Panini National Treasures Signatures

RANDOM INSERTS IN PACKS
PRINT RUNS B/WN 25-75 COPIES PER
EXCHANGE DEADLINE 11/11/2017
SAD Anthony Davis/25 40.00 100.00
SAG Aaron Gordon/49 10.00 25.00
SAH Allan Houston/75 5.00 12.00
SAI Allen Iverson/25 150.00 300.00
SAW Andrew Wiggins/49 30.00 80.00
SBG Blake Griffin/25 20.00 50.00
SBK Bernard King/49 5.00 12.00
SBS Byron Scott/49 5.00 12.00
SCB Chris Bosh/49 8.00 20.00
SCP Chris Paul/25 40.00 100.00
SDH Dwight Howard/25 12.00 30.00
SDM Danny Manning/75 5.00 12.00
SEB Eric Bledsoe/49 6.00 15.00
SEH Elvin Hayes/75 8.00 20.00
SEP Elfrid Payton/75 5.00 12.00
SIT Isaiah Thomas/75 25.00 60.00
SIT Isiah Thomas/75 10.00 25.00
SJE Julius Erving/25 40.00 100.00
SJN Jusuf Nurkic/75 4.00 10.00
SJS Jerry Stackhouse/75 6.00 15.00
SJW Jerry West/25 25.00 60.00
SKB Kobe Bryant/25 150.00 300.00
SKD Kevin Durant/25 60.00 150.00
SKI Kyrie Irving/25 40.00 100.00
SKL Kevin Love/49 12.00 30.00
SKM Karl Malone/25 25.00 60.00
SKT Klay Thompson/49 60.00 150.00
SLB Larry Brown/49 8.00 20.00
SLW Lenny Wilkens/75 10.00 25.00
SMJ Magic Johnson/25 30.00 80.00
SNA Nate Archibald/75 6.00 15.00
SOR Oscar Robertson/25 40.00 100.00
SRG Rudy Gay/75 6.00 15.00
SRP Robert Parish/75 8.00 20.00
SSC Stephen Curry/25 150.00 300.00
SCAY Carmelo Anthony/25 20.00 50.00
SCDX Clyde Drexler/49 12.00 30.00
SCLT Christian Laettner/49 8.00 20.00
SDMD Doug McDermott/75 5.00 12.00
SGAT G. Antetokounmpo/75 60.00 150.00
SKFD Kenneth Faried/75 5.00 12.00
SMCL Mike Conley/75 6.00 15.00
SRSS Ralph Sampson/75 5.00 12.00
SSON Shaquille O'Neal/25 60.00 150.00
STAL Tony Allen/75 4.00 10.00

2015-16 Panini National Treasures Springfield Swatches

RANDOM INSERTS IN PACKS
PRINT RUNS B/WN 25-49 COPIES PER
*PRIME/20-25: .75X TO 2X BASIC
1 George Mikan/49 15.00 40.00
2 Wilt Chamberlain/49 25.00 60.00
3 Jerry Lucas/49 4.00 10.00
4 Elgin Baylor/49 10.00 25.00
5 Hal Greer/49 3.00 8.00
6 Jerry West/49 10.00 25.00
7 Nate Thurmond/49 3.00 8.00
8 Rick Barry/25 3.00 8.00
9 Pete Maravich/49 20.00 50.00
10 Earl Monroe/49 4.00 10.00
11 Bob Lanier/25 3.00 8.00
12 Julius Erving/49 10.00 25.00
13 Bill Walton/49 4.00 10.00
14 Kareem Abdul-Jabbar/49 8.00 20.00
15 Moses Malone/49 4.00 10.00

2015-16 Panini National Treasures Super Swatches

RANDOM INSERTS IN PACKS
PRINT RUNS B/WN 45-99 COPIES PER
1 Andrew Wiggins/99 5.00 12.00
2 DeMarcus Cousins/99 4.00 10.00
3 Chris Paul/75 5.00 12.00
4 Kevin Garnett/99 5.00 12.00
5 Jared Sullinger/99 2.50 6.00
6 James Harden/75 6.00 15.00
7 Chris Bosh/99 4.00 10.00
8 Arron Afflalo/99 2.50 6.00
9 Ty Lawson/75 2.50 6.00
10 Avery Bradley/99 3.00 8.00
11 Greg Monroe/99 3.00 8.00
12 Anthony Davis/75 6.00 15.00
13 Dwyane Wade/99 6.00 15.00
14 Hassan Whiteside/99 3.00 8.00
15 Isaiah Thomas/75 4.00 10.00
16 Gordon Hayward/99 4.00 10.00
17 LeBron James/49 25.00 60.00
18 Tyreke Evans/99 2.50 6.00
19 Damian Lillard/49 6.00 15.00
20 Trey Burke/75 2.50 6.00
21 Nerlens Noel/99 3.00 8.00
22 Goran Dragic/99 3.00 8.00
23 Zach Randolph/99 3.00 8.00
24 Markieff Morris/99 2.50 6.00
25 Evan Turner/99 3.00 8.00
26 Al Horford/99 3.00 8.00
27 Joe Johnson/99 3.00 8.00
28 Ryan Anderson/75 3.00 8.00
29 Jeremy Lin/75 6.00 15.00
30 Jimmy Butler/75 4.00 10.00
31 Dirk Nowitzki/99 5.00 12.00
32 Tim Duncan/99 6.00 15.00
33 Rajon Rondo/99 4.00 10.00
34 Manu Ginobili/75 4.00 10.00
35 Nikola Vucevic/99 3.00 8.00
36 Serge Ibaka/99 3.00 8.00
37 DeAndre Jordan/75 4.00 10.00
38 Carmelo Anthony/99 5.00 12.00
39 Brook Lopez/99 3.00 8.00
40 Ricky Rubio/99 4.00 10.00
41 Victor Oladipo/99 3.00 8.00
42 Trevor Ariza/99 2.50 6.00
43 Derrick Rose/45 6.00 15.00
44 Rudy Gobert/99 4.00 10.00
45 Kemba Walker/99 4.00 10.00
46 Andre Iguodala/99 3.00 8.00
47 Wesley Matthews/99 2.50 6.00
48 Nicolas Batum/99 3.00 8.00
49 Kyle Lowry/99 3.00 8.00
50 Deron Williams/99 3.00 8.00
51 Tony Parker/99 4.00 10.00
52 Kenneth Faried/75 3.00 8.00
53 Marcus Smart/99 3.00 8.00
54 Eric Gordon/99 3.00 8.00
55 Russell Westbrook/75 10.00 25.00
56 Kyrie Irving/75 6.00 15.00
57 Kyle Korver/75 3.00 8.00
58 Eric Bledsoe/99 3.00 8.00
59 C.J. McCollum/99 4.00 10.00
60 Jordan Clarkson/99 4.00 10.00
61 Chandler Parsons/99 3.00 8.00
62 Danilo Gallinari/99 3.00 8.00
63 Josh Smith/99 3.00 8.00
64 Draymond Green/99 5.00 12.00
65 Paul Millsap/99 4.00 10.00

2015-16 Panini National Treasures Super Swatches Prime

*PRIME/20-25: .75X TO 2X BASIC
RANDOM INSERTS IN PACKS
PRINT RUNS B/WN 7-25 COPIES PER
NO PRICING ON QTY 10 OR LESS
4 Kevin Garnett/25 20.00 50.00
32 Tim Duncan/25 20.00 50.00
34 Manu Ginobili/25 15.00 40.00
51 Tony Parker/25 15.00 40.00

2015-16 Panini National Treasures Super Swatches Rookies

RANDOM INSERTS IN PACKS
PRINT RUNS B/WN 25-99 COPIES PER
1 Tyus Jones/99 4.00 10.00
2 R.J. Hunter/99 2.50 6.00
3 Emmanuel Mudiay/99 4.00 10.00
4 Jonathon Simmons/75 4.00 10.00
5 Justin Anderson/99 3.00 8.00
6 Stanley Johnson/99 3.00 8.00
7 Cristiano Felicio/99 3.00 8.00
8 Karl-Anthony Towns/99 12.00 30.00
9 Frank Kaminsky/99 4.00 10.00
10 Pat Connaughton/99 2.50 6.00
11 Jerian Grant/99 2.50 6.00
12 Jahlil Okafor/99 5.00 12.00
13 Salah Mejri/99 2.50 6.00
14 Cliff Alexander/99 2.50 6.00
15 Marcelo Huertas/75 3.00 8.00
16 Bobby Portis/99 4.00 10.00
17 Trey Lyles/99 4.00 10.00
18 Willie Cauley-Stein/99 4.00 10.00
19 Sasha Kaun/99 2.50 6.00
20 Terry Rozier/99 3.00 8.00
21 Montrezl Harrell/99 3.00 8.00
22 Raul Neto/75 2.50 6.00
23 Cameron Payne/99 3.00 8.00
24 Nemanja Bjelica/99 3.00 8.00
25 Kelly Oubre Jr./99 3.00 8.00
26 Mario Hezonja/99 3.00 8.00
27 Nikola Jokic/99 5.00 12.00
28 D'Angelo Russell/99 6.00 15.00
29 Rondae Hollis-Jefferson/99 3.00 8.00
30 Devin Booker/99 6.00 15.00
31 Kristaps Porzingis/25 10.00 25.00
32 Norman Powell/99 3.00 8.00
33 Luis Montero/99 2.50 6.00
34 Myles Turner/99 4.00 10.00
35 Justise Winslow/99 4.00 10.00

2015-16 Panini National Treasures Super Swatches Rookies Prime

*PRIME/25: .75X TO 2X BASIC
RANDOM INSERTS IN PACKS
PRINT RUNS B/WN 10-25 COPIES PER
NO PRICING ON QTY 10
3 Emmanuel Mudiay/25 15.00 40.00

2015-16 Panini National Treasures Timelines

RANDOM INSERTS IN PACKS
PRINT RUNS B/WN 49-99 COPIES PER
*PRIME/25: .75X TO 2X BASIC
1 Chandler Parsons/99 3.00 8.00
2 Tony Parker/99 4.00 10.00
3 Anthony Davis/75 6.00 15.00
4 Russell Westbrook/75 10.00 25.00
5 Deron Williams/99 3.00 8.00
6 Manu Ginobili/75 4.00 10.00
7 Kevin Garnett/99 5.00 12.00
8 Draymond Green/75 5.00 12.00
9 Carmelo Anthony/99 5.00 12.00
10 Kyrie Irving/75 6.00 15.00
11 Jordan Clarkson/99 4.00 10.00
12 Derrick Williams/99 2.50 6.00
13 Goran Dragic/99 3.00 8.00
14 Andrew Wiggins/99 5.00 12.00
15 Kenneth Faried/99 3.00 8.00
16 Dirk Nowitzki/99 5.00 12.00
17 Jared Sullinger/99 2.50 6.00
18 James Harden/75 6.00 15.00
19 Eric Bledsoe/99 3.00 8.00
20 LeBron James/49 15.00 40.00
21 DeMarcus Cousins/99 4.00 10.00
22 Derrick Rose/49 5.00 12.00
23 Tim Duncan/99 6.00 15.00
24 Jimmy Butler/75 4.00 10.00
25 Danilo Gallinari/99 3.00 8.00
26 George Hill/99 3.00 8.00
27 J.R. Smith/99 3.00 8.00
28 Al Horford/99 3.00 8.00
29 Trey Burke/75 2.50 6.00
30 Damian Lillard/49 5.00 12.00

2015-16 Panini National Treasures Treasured Threads

RANDOM INSERTS IN PACKS
PRINT RUNS B/WN 49-99 COPIES PER
1 Hakeem Olajuwon/99 5.00 12.00
2 Herb Williams/99 2.50 6.00
3 Karl Malone/99 5.00 12.00
4 Danny Manning/99 3.00 8.00
5 Ralph Sampson/99 3.00 8.00
6 Ben Wallace/99 3.00 8.00
7 Louie Dampier/99 4.00 10.00
8 Clifford Robinson/99 2.50 6.00
9 Magic Johnson/49 8.00 20.00
10 Reggie Lewis/99 4.00 10.00
11 Arvydas Sabonis/99 3.00 8.00
12 Alonzo Mourning/99 5.00 12.00
13 Brad Daugherty/99 3.00 8.00
14 Clyde Drexler/99 5.00 12.00
15 Grant Hill/99 5.00 12.00
16 Doc Rivers/99 4.00 10.00
17 Patrick Ewing/99 5.00 12.00
18 Jamal Mashburn/99 4.00 10.00
19 Kenny Smith/99 3.00 8.00
20 Alvan Adams/99 2.50 6.00
21 Dominique Wilkins/49 5.00 12.00
22 Larry Johnson/99 5.00 12.00
23 Derrick Coleman/49 4.00 10.00
24 Scottie Pippen/99 6.00 15.00
25 Bill Laimbeer/99 3.00 8.00
26 Kevin McHale/99 4.00 10.00
27 David Thompson/99 3.00 8.00
28 Ray Allen/99 4.00 10.00
29 Shaquille O'Neal/99 6.00 15.00
30 Vlade Divac/99 4.00 10.00
31 Vinnie Johnson/49 4.00 10.00
32 Dennis Rodman/99 6.00 15.00
33 Kevin Duckworth/99 2.50 6.00
34 Mark Aguirre/99 3.00 8.00
35 Isiah Thomas/49 4.00 10.00
36 Larry Bird/99 8.00 20.00
37 David Robinson/99 5.00 12.00
38 Detlef Schrempf/99 4.00 10.00
39 Mark Price/99 4.00 10.00
40 Allen Iverson/99 6.00 15.00

2015-16 Panini National Treasures Treasured Threads Prime

*PRIME/25: .75X TO 2X BASIC
RANDOM INSERTS IN PACKS
PRINT RUNS B/WN 5-25 COPIES PER
NO PRICING ON QTY 15 OR LESS
9 Magic Johnson/25 25.00 60.00
24 Scottie Pippen/25 15.00 40.00

2015-16 Panini National Treasures Treasures of the Hall Autographs

RANDOM INSERTS IN PACKS
PRINT RUNS B/WN 25-49 COPIES PER
EXCHANGE DEADLINE 11/11/2017
THBR Bill Russell/25 60.00 150.00
THBW Bill Walton/49 6.00 15.00
THDR Dennis Rodman/25 20.00 50.00
THGP Gary Payton/49 15.00 40.00
THJE Julius Erving/25 25.00 60.00
THJW Jerry West/25 20.00 50.00
THKM Karl Malone/25 20.00 50.00
THLB Larry Bird/25 40.00 100.00
THLW Lenny Wilkens/49 10.00 25.00
THMJ Magic Johnson/25 30.00 80.00
THOR Oscar Robertson/25 40.00 100.00
THRB Rick Barry/49 8.00 20.00
THRP Robert Parish/49 6.00 15.00
THWU Wes Unseld/49 10.00 25.00
THAMG Alonzo Mourning/25 20.00 50.00
THCHG Cliff Hagan/49 5.00 12.00
THCMY Calvin Murphy/49 5.00 12.00
THDCW Dave Cowens/49 6.00 15.00
THEHY Elvin Hayes/49 6.00 15.00
THHOW Hakeem Olajuwon/25 15.00 40.00
THJDM Joe Dumars/49 6.00 15.00
THKAJ Kareem Abdul-Jabbar/25 30.00 80.00
THKMH Kevin McHale/25 12.00 30.00
THNAB Nate Archibald/49 5.00 12.00
THRSS Ralph Sampson/49 5.00 12.00

2015-16 Panini National Treasures USA Basketball Autographs

RANDOM INSERTS IN PACKS
STATED PRINT RUN 25 SER.#'d SETS
EXCHANGE DEADLINE 11/11/2017
1 Kobe Bryant 800.00 1200.00
2 Shaquille O'Neal 100.00 200.00
3 Carmelo Anthony 125.00 250.00
4 Chris Paul 60.00 150.00
5 Dwyane Wade 200.00 400.00
6 Kevin Durant 150.00 300.00
7 Allen Iverson 250.00 400.00
8 John Stockton 50.00 120.00
9 Magic Johnson 100.00 250.00
10 Larry Bird 100.00 200.00
11 Karl Malone 40.00 100.00
12 Stephen Curry 500.00 800.00
13 Anthony Davis 150.00 300.00
14 Jerry West 50.00 120.00
15 Dwight Howard 20.00 50.00
16 Kyrie Irving 60.00 150.00
17 Oscar Robertson 75.00 200.00
18 Alonzo Mourning 40.00 100.00
19 Hakeem Olajuwon 60.00 150.00
20 David Robinson 50.00 120.00
21 Clyde Drexler 50.00 120.00
22 Jason Kidd 75.00 200.00
23 Chris Bosh 40.00 100.00
24 Kevin Love 25.00 60.00
25 Ray Allen 100.00 250.00
26 Vince Carter 100.00 250.00
27 Gary Payton 50.00 120.00
28 Anfernee Hardaway 60.00 150.00
29 Grant Hill 60.00 150.00
30 Larry Brown 25.00 60.00
31 Christian Laettner 20.00 50.00
32 Allan Houston 25.00 60.00
33 Adrian Dantley 50.00 120.00
34 Dan Majerle EXCH 60.00 150.00
35 Mitch Richmond 40.00 100.00

2015-16 Panini National Treasures USA Basketball Jersey Autographs

RANDOM INSERTS IN PACKS
STATED PRINT RUN 25 SER.#'d SETS
EXCHANGE DEADLINE 11/11/2017
USJAD Andre Drummond 30.00 80.00
USJAM Alonzo Mourning 40.00 100.00
USJBB Bradley Beal 20.00 50.00
USJBG Blake Griffin 25.00 60.00
USJCA Carmelo Anthony 40.00 100.00
USJCB Chris Bosh 20.00 50.00
USJCD Clyde Drexler 40.00 100.00
USJCP Chris Paul 60.00 150.00
USJDH Dwight Howard 20.00 50.00
USJDM Dan Majerle 12.00 30.00
USJDR David Robinson 40.00 100.00
USJDW Dominique Wilkins 25.00 60.00
USJDW Dwyane Wade 75.00 200.00
USJGP Gary Payton 25.00 60.00
USJHO Hakeem Olajuwon 30.00 80.00
USJJK Jason Kidd 30.00 80.00
USJKF Kenneth Faried 12.00 30.00
USJKL Kawhi Leonard 100.00 200.00
USJKM Karl Malone 40.00 100.00
USJKT Klay Thompson 75.00 200.00
USJMJ Magic Johnson 100.00 200.00
USJMP Mason Plumlee 6.00 15.00
USJRA Ray Allen 25.00 60.00
USJRG Rudy Gay 12.00 30.00
USJSO Shaquille O'Neal 100.00 200.00

2016-17 Panini National Treasures

1-100 PRINT RUN 99 SER. #'d SETS
101-150 PRINT RUN 99 SER.#'d SETS
151-200 PRINT RUN B/WN 32-49 COPIES PER
201-206 PRINT RUNS 99 SER.#'d SETS
PRIME PATCHES MAY SELL FOR PREMIUM
EXCHANGE DEADLINE 11/3/2018
1 John Wall 3.00 8.00
2 Dwight Howard 2.00 5.00
3 Dwyane Wade 4.00 10.00
4 Dirk Nowitzki 3.00 8.00
5 Draymond Green 3.00 8.00
6 Myles Turner 2.00 5.00
7 Marc Gasol 2.50 6.00
8 Anthony Davis 5.00 12.00
9 Aaron Gordon 2.00 5.00
10 C.J. McCollum 2.00 5.00
11 Marcin Gortat 2.00 5.00
12 Bradley Beal 2.50 6.00
13 Dennis Schroder 2.00 5.00
14 Nicolas Batum 2.00 5.00
15 Deron Williams 2.00 5.00
16 Kevin Durant 6.00 15.00
17 Paul George 3.00 8.00
18 Mike Conley 2.00 5.00
19 Tim Frazier 1.50 4.00
20 Elfrid Payton 2.00 5.00
21 Damian Lillard 5.00 12.00
22 Otto Porter 2.00 5.00
23 Rudy Gobert 2.50 6.00
24 Paul Millsap 2.50 6.00
25 Jimmy Butler 2.50 6.00
26 Harrison Barnes 2.00 5.00
27 Klay Thompson 3.00 8.00
28 Blake Griffin 2.50 6.00
29 Vince Carter 3.00 8.00
30 Tyreke Evans 1.50 4.00
31 Serge Ibaka 2.00 5.00
32 Evan Turner 1.50 4.00
33 Al Horford 2.00 5.00
34 Gordon Hayward 2.50 6.00
35 Bojan Bogdanovic 1.50 4.00
36 Rajon Rondo 2.50 6.00
37 Emmanuel Mudiay 2.00 5.00
38 Stephen Curry 12.00 30.00
39 Chris Paul 3.00 8.00
40 Giannis Antetokounmpo 5.00 12.00
41 Brandon Jennings 1.50 4.00
42 Joel Embiid 4.00 10.00
43 Kawhi Leonard 4.00 10.00
44 Avery Bradley 2.00 5.00
45 George Hill 2.00 5.00
46 Brook Lopez 2.00 5.00
47 Robin Lopez 1.50 4.00
48 Kenneth Faried 2.00 5.00
49 Eric Gordon 2.00 5.00
50 DeAndre Jordan 2.50 6.00
51 Jabari Parker 3.00 8.00
52 Carmelo Anthony 3.00 8.00
53 Ben Simmons RC 1200.00 1600.00
54 LaMarcus Aldridge 2.50 6.00
55 Isaiah Thomas 2.50 6.00
56 DeMarcus Cousins 2.50 6.00
57 Jeremy Lin 2.50 6.00
58 J.R. Smith 2.00 5.00
59 Nikola Jokic 2.50 6.00
60 James Harden 4.00 10.00
61 Jamal Crawford 2.50 6.00
62 Matthew Dellavedova 2.00 5.00
63 Kristaps Porzingis 5.00 12.00
64 Robert Covington 1.50 4.00
65 Pau Gasol 2.50 6.00
66 Jae Crowder 2.00 5.00
67 Darren Collison 2.00 5.00
68 Trevor Booker 1.50 4.00
69 Kevin Love 2.50 6.00
70 Andre Drummond 2.50 6.00
71 Patrick Beverley 1.50 4.00
72 D'Angelo Russell 3.00 8.00
73 Andrew Wiggins 4.00 10.00
74 Russell Westbrook 6.00 15.00
75 Devin Booker 4.00 10.00
76 Manu Ginobili 2.50 6.00
77 Goran Dragic 2.00 5.00
78 Ben McLemore 1.50 4.00
79 Frank Kaminsky 2.00 5.00
80 Kyrie Irving 5.00 12.00
81 Reggie Jackson 2.00 5.00
82 Jeff Teague 2.00 5.00
83 Julius Randle 2.50 6.00
84 Karl-Anthony Towns 6.00 15.00
85 Steven Adams 2.00 5.00
86 Eric Bledsoe 2.00 5.00
87 Cory Joseph 1.50 4.00
88 Justise Winslow 2.00 5.00
89 Jonas Valanciunas 2.00 5.00
90 Kemba Walker 2.50 6.00
91 LeBron James 12.00 30.00
92 Tobias Harris 2.00 5.00
93 Monta Ellis 2.00 5.00
94 Lou Williams 2.00 5.00
95 Zach LaVine 2.50 6.00
96 Victor Oladipo 2.00 5.00
97 Tyson Chandler 2.00 5.00
98 DeMar DeRozan 2.50 6.00
99 Josh Richardson 1.50 4.00
100 Kyle Lowry 2.00 5.00
101 Bembry JSY AU/99 RC 40.00 100.00
102 Prince JSY AU/99 RC 125.00 300.00
103 Jackson JSY AU/99 RC 25.00 60.00
104 Brown JSY AU/99 RC 700.00 1200.00
105 LeVert JSY AU/99 RC 100.00 250.00
106 Whitehead JSY AU/99 RC EXCH 60.00 150.00
107 Valentine JSY AU/99 RC EXCH 100.00 250.00
108 Felder JSY AU/99 RC 40.00 100.00
109 A.J. Hammons JSY AU/99 RC EXCH 25.00 60.00
110 Murray JSY AU/99 RC 600.00 1000.00
111 Hernangomez JSY AU/99 RC 100.00 250.00
112 Beasley JSY AU/99 RC 100.00 250.00
113 Ellenson JSY AU/99 RC 50.00 120.00
114 Michael Gbinije JSY AU/99 RC 25.00 60.00
115 Jones JSY AU/99 RC 100.00 250.00
116 McCaw JSY AU/99 RC 200.00 400.00
117 Chinanu Onuaku JSY AU/99 RC 25.00 60.00
118 Paul Zipser JSY AU/99 RC 40.00 100.00
119 Georges Niang JSY AU/99 RC 25.00 60.00
120 Johnson JSY AU/99 RC EXCH 100.00 250.00
121 Diamond Stone JSY AU/99 RC EXCH 25.00 60.00
122 Ingram JSY AU/99 RC 1500.00 2500.00
123 Zubac JSY AU/99 RC 200.00 500.00
124 Davis JSY AU/99 RC 60.00 150.00
125 Baldwin IV JSY AU/99 RC 50.00 120.00
126 Brogdon JSY AU/99 RC 300.00 600.00
127 Maker JSY AU/99 RC 500.00 1000.00
128 Dunn JSY AU/99 RC 400.00 800.00
129 Hield JSY AU/99 RC 500.00 1000.00
130 Diallo JSY AU/99 RC 50.00 120.00
131 Marshall Plumlee JSY AU/99 RC 25.00 60.00
132 Hernangomez JSY AU/99 RC 100.00 250.00
133 Sabonis JSY AU/99 RC 75.00 200.00
135 Stephen Zimmerman JSY AU/99 RC 25.00 60.00
136 Saric JSY AU/99 RC 300.00 600.00
137 Lu-Cabarrot JSY AU/99 RC 75.00 200.00
138 Bender JSY AU/99 RC 150.00 400.00
139 Chriss JSY AU/99 RC 350.00 700.00
140 Ulis JSY AU/99 RC EXCH 200.00 400.00
141 Jake Layman JSY AU/99 RC 30.00 80.00
142 Papagiannis JSY AU/99 RC 60.00 150.00
143 Richardson JSY AU/99 RC EXCH 60.00 150.00
144 Labissiere JSY AU/99 RC 350.00 700.00
146 Murray JSY AU/99 RC 500.00 1000.00
147 Poeltl JSY AU/99 RC 50.00 120.00
148 Pascal Siakam JSY AU/99 RC 30.00 80.00
149 Joel Bolomboy JSY AU/99 RC 30.00 80.00
150 Tomas Satoransky JSY AU/99 RC 25.00 60.00
151 DeAndre' Bembry JSY AU/49 20.00 50.00
152 Prince JSY AU/49 100.00 250.00
153 Demetrius Jackson JSY AU/49 20.00 50.00
154 Brown JSY AU/49 200.00 500.00
155 Caris LeVert JSY AU/49 25.00 60.00
156 Whitehead JSY AU/49 EXCH 60.00 150.00
157 Valentine JSY AU/49 EXCH 60.00 150.00
158 Felder JSY AU/49 40.00 100.00
159 A.J. Hammons JSY AU/49 EXCH 20.00 50.00
160 Murray JSY AU/49 350.00 700.00
161 Hernangomez JSY AU/49 75.00 200.00
162 Malik Beasley JSY AU/49 25.00 60.00
163 Henry Ellenson JSY AU/49 25.00 60.00
164 Michael Gbinije JSY AU/49 20.00 50.00
165 Jones JSY AU/49 40.00 100.00
166 McCaw JSY AU/49 125.00 300.00
167 Chinanu Onuaku JSY AU/49 20.00 50.00
168 Zipser JSY AU/49 30.00 80.00
169 Georges Niang JSY AU/49 20.00 50.00
170 Johnson JSY AU/49 EXCH 40.00 100.00
171 Stone JSY AU/49 EXCH
172 Ingram JSY AU/49 700.00 1000.00
173 Zubac JSY AU/49 125.00 300.00
174 Davis JSY AU/49 50.00 120.00
175 Wade Baldwin IV JSY AU/49 25.00 60.00
176 Brogdon JSY AU/49 150.00 300.00
177 Maker JSY AU/49 300.00 600.00
178 Dunn JSY AU/49 150.00 400.00
179 Hield JSY AU/49 300.00 600.00
180 Cheick Diallo JSY AU/49 30.00 80.00
181 Marshall Plumlee JSY AU/49 20.00 50.00
182 Willy Hernangomez JSY AU/49 25.00 60.00
183 Sabonis JSY AU/49 50.00 120.00
185 Stephen Zimmerman JSY AU/49 20.00 50.00
186 Saric JSY AU/32 200.00 500.00
187 Lu-Cabarrot JSY AU/49 125.00 300.00
188 Bender JSY AU/49 125.00 300.00
189 Chriss JSY AU/49 200.00 500.00
190 Ulis JSY AU/49 EXCH 125.00 300.00
191 Jake Layman JSY AU/49 25.00 60.00
192 Papagiannis JSY AU/49 40.00 100.00
193 Richardson JSY AU/49 40.00 100.00
194 Labissiere JSY AU/49 150.00 300.00
196 Murray JSY AU/49 300.00 600.00
197 Poeltl JSY AU/49 40.00 100.00
198 Pascal Siakam JSY AU/49 30.00 80.00
199 Joel Bolomboy JSY AU/49 20.00 50.00
200 Tomas Satoransky JSY AU/49 20.00 50.00
201 Jones Jr. AU/99 RC EXCH 20.00 50.00
202 Bryn Forbes AU/99 RC 50.00 120.00
203 Dorian Finney-Smith AU/99 RC 5.00 12.00
204 Kuzminskas AU/99 RC 6.00 15.00
205 Ron Baker AU/99 RC 12.00 30.00
206 Sheldon McClellan AU/99 RC 4.00 10.00
207 Fred VanVleet AU/99 RC 8.00 20.00
208 Danuel House AU/99 RC 4.00 10.00
209 Malcolm Delaney AU/99 RC 5.00 12.00
210 McGruder AU/99 RC 5.00 12.00

2016-17 Panini National Treasures Bronze

*BRONZE: .6X TO 1.5X BASIC
*BRONZE JSY AU: .5X TO 1.2X BASIC
*BRONZE AU: .5X TO 1.2X BASIC
RANDOM INSERTS IN PACKS
STATED PRINT RUN 25 SER.#'d SETS
EXCHANGE DEADLINE 11/3/2018
53 Ben Simmons 2500.00 3500.00

2016-17 Panini National Treasures All-Decade Materials

RANDOM INSERTS IN PACKS
PRINT RUNS B/WN 15-99 COPIES PER
NO PRICING ON QTY 15
1 Dirk Nowitzki/30 5.00 12.00
2 Kobe Bryant/99 10.00 25.00
3 Tim Duncan/99 6.00 15.00
5 Larry Bird/30 10.00 25.00
6 Magic Johnson/30 10.00 25.00
7 Kareem Abdul-Jabbar/30 10.00 25.00
9 Russell Westbrook/99 8.00 20.00
10 Stephen Curry/30 20.00 50.00
11 Jason Kidd/99 4.00 10.00
12 Shaquille O'Neal/99 10.00 25.00
13 Tony Parker/99 4.00 10.00
14 Kyrie Irving/99 8.00 20.00
15 David Robinson/99 5.00 12.00
16 Karl Malone/99 5.00 12.00
17 Hakeem Olajuwon/30 5.00 12.00
18 Damian Lillard/99 6.00 15.00
19 Vince Carter/99 5.00 12.00

2016-17 Panini National Treasures All-Decade Materials Prime

*PRIME/25: 1X TO 2.5X BASIC
RANDOM INSERTS IN PACKS
PRINT RUNS B/WN 7-25 COPIES PER
NO PRICING ON QTY 7
10 Stephen Curry/25 75.00 200.00

2016-17 Panini National Treasures Century Materials

RANDOM INSERTS IN PACKS
PRINT RUNS B/WN 30-99 COPIES PER
1 Jimmy Butler/30 4.00 10.00
2 Chris Paul/99 5.00 12.00
3 Kevin Durant/99 10.00 25.00
4 Goran Dragic/99 3.00 8.00
5 Dwight Howard/99 3.00 8.00
6 Dirk Nowitzki/30 5.00 12.00
7 Hassan Whiteside/99 3.00 8.00
8 Devin Booker/99 6.00 15.00
9 Patty Mills/99 4.00 10.00
10 Jahlil Okafor/99 3.00 8.00
11 Michael Kidd-Gilchrist/99 3.00 8.00
12 Blake Griffin/99 4.00 10.00
14 Zach Randolph/30 3.00 8.00
16 Deron Williams/99 3.00 8.00
17 Dennis Schroder/99 3.00 8.00
18 Brandon Knight/99 3.00 8.00
19 LaMarcus Aldridge/99 4.00 10.00
20 Otto Porter/99 3.00 8.00
21 Kemba Walker/99 4.00 10.00
22 Thaddeus Young/99 2.50 6.00
23 Tobias Harris/99 3.00 8.00
24 Vince Carter/99 5.00 12.00
25 Giannis Antetokounmpo/99 8.00 20.00
26 Sasha Vujacic/99 2.50 6.00
27 Alex Len/30 2.50 6.00
28 James Young/99 2.50 6.00
29 Kawhi Leonard/99 6.00 15.00
30 John Wall/99 5.00 12.00
31 Cody Zeller/99 2.50 6.00
32 Paul George/99 5.00 12.00
33 Reggie Jackson/30 3.00 8.00
34 Tony Allen/99 2.50 6.00
35 Jabari Parker/99 5.00 12.00
36 Kristaps Porzingis/99 5.00 12.00
37 Serge Ibaka/99 3.00 8.00
38 Jae Crowder/99 3.00 8.00
39 Rudy Gay/99 4.00 10.00
40 Gordon Hayward/99 4.00 10.00
42 Jeff Teague/30 3.00 8.00
43 Andre Drummond/99 4.00 10.00
44 Mike Conley/99 3.00 8.00
45 Andrew Wiggins/99 4.00 10.00
46 Carmelo Anthony/99 5.00 12.00
47 Elfrid Payton/99 3.00 8.00
48 Al Horford/99 3.00 8.00
49 DeMarcus Cousins/99 4.00 10.00
50 Rodney Hood/99 3.00 8.00
51 Rajon Rondo/99 4.00 10.00
52 James Harden/99 6.00 15.00
53 Marc Gasol/99 4.00 10.00
54 Nikola Jokic/99 4.00 10.00
56 Karl-Anthony Towns/99 6.00 15.00
57 Trevor Booker/99 2.50 6.00
58 Aaron Gordon/99 3.00 8.00
59 Ben McLemore/99 2.50 6.00
60 Joe Johnson/99 3.00 8.00
61 Nikola Mirotic/99 3.00 8.00
62 Patrick Beverley/99 2.50 6.00
63 Julius Randle/99 4.00 10.00
64 Kenneth Faried/99 3.00 8.00
65 Frank Kaminsky/99 3.00 8.00
66 Langston Galloway/99 2.50 6.00
67 Victor Oladipo/99 3.00 8.00
68 Luis Scola/99 3.00 8.00
69 Mason Plumlee/99 3.00 8.00
70 Kyle Lowry/30 3.00 8.00
71 Tristan Thompson/99 3.00 8.00
72 Eric Gordon/99 3.00 8.00
73 Jordan Clarkson/30 3.00 8.00
74 Jusuf Nurkic/99 2.50 6.00
75 Paul Millsap/99 4.00 10.00
76 Anthony Davis/99 5.00 12.00
77 Russell Westbrook/99 8.00 20.00
79 Damian Lillard/99 6.00 15.00
80 Jonas Valanciunas/99 3.00 8.00
81 LeBron James/99 15.00 40.00
82 Stephen Curry/30 20.00 50.00
83 D'Angelo Russell/99 5.00 12.00
84 Emmanuel Mudiay/99 3.00 8.00
85 J.J. Barea/99 3.00 8.00
86 Zach LaVine/99 4.00 10.00
87 Isaiah Thomas/99 5.00 12.00
88 Enes Kanter/99 2.50 6.00
89 C.J. McCollum/99 3.00 8.00
90 Tony Parker/99 4.00 10.00
91 Kyrie Irving/99 8.00 20.00
92 Klay Thompson/99 5.00 12.00
93 J.J. Redick/99 4.00 10.00
94 Wesley Matthews/99 2.50 6.00
95 Kyle Korver/99 3.00 8.00
96 Tyreke Evans/99 2.50 6.00
97 Solomon Hill/99 2.50 6.00
98 Brook Lopez/99 3.00 8.00
99 Eric Bledsoe/99 3.00 8.00
100 Iman Shumpert/99 2.50 6.00

2016-17 Panini National Treasures Century Materials Bronze

*BRONZE: 1X TO 2.5X BASIC
RANDOM INSERTS IN PACKS
STATED PRINT RUN 25 SER.#'d SETS
81 LeBron James 75.00 200.00
82 Stephen Curry 75.00 200.00

2016-17 Panini National Treasures Clutch Factor Jersey Autographs

RANDOM INSERTS IN PACKS
PRINT RUNS B/WN 49-75 COPIES PER
EXCHANGE DEADLINE 11/3/2018
1 Carmelo Anthony/49 20.00 50.00
2 Kyrie Irving/49 50.00 120.00
3 Kobe Bryant/49 100.00 250.00
4 Kevin Durant/49 100.00 250.00
5 Stephen Curry/49 125.00 300.00
6 Dirk Nowitzki/49 75.00 200.00
7 Ryan Anderson/75 5.00 12.00
8 David Robinson/49 15.00 40.00
9 Elfrid Payton/75 5.00 12.00
10 Karl-Anthony Towns/49 40.00 100.00
11 Andrew Wiggins/49 25.00 60.00
12 Paul Millsap/75 6.00 15.00
13 Larry Bird/49 50.00 120.00
14 Kelly Tripucka/75 4.00 10.00
15 Devin Booker/75 30.00 80.00
16 Myles Turner/75 8.00 20.00
17 C.J. McCollum/75 10.00 25.00
18 Shawn Marion/75 10.00 25.00
19 Kenneth Faried/75 5.00 12.00
20 Julius Erving/49 40.00 100.00
21 Clyde Drexler/49 20.00 50.00
22 Harrison Barnes/75 6.00 15.00
23 DeMar DeRozan/75 20.00 50.00
24 Jabari Parker/49 15.00 40.00
25 Blake Griffin/49 15.00 40.00
26 Damian Lillard/49 75.00 200.00
27 Mitch Richmond/75 8.00 20.00
28 Patrick Ewing/49 50.00 120.00
29 Kevin Love/49 15.00 40.00
30 Tony Parker/49 12.00 30.00
31 Ricky Rubio/49 10.00 25.00
32 Al Horford/75 5.00 12.00
33 Luol Deng/75 6.00 15.00
34 Jeremy Lin/75 40.00 100.00
35 Shaquille O'Neal/49 60.00 150.00
37 Tim Hardaway/75 10.00 25.00
38 Anthony Davis/49 40.00 100.00
39 Rashard Lewis/75 5.00 12.00
40 Kristaps Porzingis/75 25.00 60.00

2016-17 Panini National Treasures Clutch Factor Jersey Autographs Bronze

*BRONZE: .75X TO 2X BASIC
RANDOM INSERTS IN PACKS
STATED PRINT RUN 25 SER.#'d SETS
EXCHANGE DEADLINE 11/3/2018
5 Stephen Curry/25 400.00 800.00

2016-17 Panini National Treasures Colossal Jersey Autographs

RANDOM INSERTS IN PACKS
PRINT RUNS B/WN 49-60 COPIES PER
EXCHANGE DEADLINE 11/3/2018
1 Tim Hardaway/60 10.00 25.00
2 Alonzo Mourning/49 20.00 50.00
3 Julius Erving/49 40.00 100.00
4 Karl Malone/49 20.00 50.00
5 David Robinson/49 15.00 40.00
6 Detlef Schrempf/60 10.00 25.00
8 Kobe Bryant/49 100.00 250.00
9 Larry Bird/49 50.00 120.00
10 Magic Johnson/49 30.00 80.00
11 Robert Parish/60 8.00 20.00
12 Shaquille O'Neal/49 60.00 150.00
13 Shawn Kemp/60 60.00 150.00
14 Kenny Smith/60 6.00 15.00
15 Dirk Nowitzki/49 75.00 200.00
16 Jeremy Lin/49 40.00 100.00
17 Nicolas Batum/60 5.00 12.00
18 Kevin Love/49 15.00 40.00
19 Langston Galloway/60 4.00 10.00
20 Stephen Curry/49 125.00 300.00
21 Kyrie Irving/49 40.00 100.00
22 Kevin Durant/49 100.00 250.00
23 Kenneth Faried/60 5.00 12.00
24 Will Barton/60 4.00 10.00
25 Justise Winslow/60 6.00 15.00
26 DeMar DeRozan/60 20.00 50.00
27 Damian Lillard/49 60.00 150.00
28 DeMarre Carroll/60 4.00 10.00
29 Bojan Bogdanovic/60 4.00 10.00
30 Luol Deng/60 6.00 15.00
31 Al Horford/60 5.00 12.00
32 Carmelo Anthony/49 20.00 50.00
33 Chris Paul/49 25.00 60.00
34 Dwyane Wade/49 25.00 60.00
35 Doug McDermott/60
36 Mitch Richmond/60 8.00 20.00
37 Alvan Adams/60 4.00 10.00
38 Bernard King/60 10.00 25.00
39 Cedric Maxwell/60 4.00 10.00
40 Patrick Ewing/49 50.00 120.00
41 Kevin McHale/49 15.00 40.00
42 Matthew Dellavedova/60 10.00 25.00
43 Hakeem Olajuwon/49 25.00 60.00
44 Andrew Wiggins/49 25.00 60.00
45 Karl-Anthony Towns/49 40.00 100.00
46 Zach LaVine/60 6.00 15.00
47 Goran Dragic/60 8.00 20.00
48 Gordon Hayward/60 20.00 50.00
49 Blake Griffin/49 15.00 40.00
50 Evan Fournier/60 5.00 12.00
51 Dwight Powell/60 4.00 10.00

52 Reggie Jackson/60 5.00 12.00
53 Tobias Harris/60 5.00 12.00
54 Marc Gasol/49 12.00 30.00
55 Pau Gasol/49 20.00 50.00
56 Mark Price/60 12.00 30.00
57 Jordan Clarkson/60 10.00 25.00
58 Julius Randle/60 8.00 20.00
59 Enes Kanter/60 4.00 10.00
60 Hassan Whiteside/60 12.00 30.00

2016-17 Panini National Treasures Colossal Jersey Autographs Bronze

*BRONZE/22-25: .75X TO 2X BASIC
RANDOM INSERTS IN PACKS
PRINT RUNS B/WN 18-25 COPIES PER
NO PRICING ON QTY 19 OR LESS
EXCHANGE DEADLINE 11/3/2018
2 Alonzo Mourning/25 75.00 200.00
4 Karl Malone/25 50.00 120.00
8 Kobe Bryant/25 800.00 1200.00
12 Shaquille O'Neal/25 400.00 800.00
20 Stephen Curry/25 800.00 1200.00
22 Kevin Durant/25 1000.00 1200.00

2016-17 Panini National Treasures Colossal Materials

RANDOM INSERTS IN PACKS
PRINT RUNS B/WN 30-60 COPIES PER
1 D'Angelo Russell/60 5.00 12.00
2 Kristaps Porzingis/30 5.00 12.00
3 Kevin Durant/30 10.00 25.00
4 Kawhi Leonard/30 6.00 15.00
5 Rudy Gobert/60 4.00 10.00
6 LaMarcus Aldridge/30 4.00 10.00
7 Emmanuel Mudiay/30 3.00 8.00
8 Jimmy Butler/30 4.00 10.00
10 Russell Westbrook/60 8.00 20.00
11 C.J. McCollum/30 3.00 8.00
12 Zach LaVine/60 4.00 10.00
13 Eric Bledsoe/30 3.00 8.00
14 Kyle Lowry/30 3.00 8.00
15 Derrick Rose/30 5.00 12.00
16 Detlef Schrempf/30 4.00 10.00
17 Karl-Anthony Towns/30 6.00 15.00
18 Carmelo Anthony/30 5.00 12.00
19 DeMarre Carroll/30 2.50 6.00
20 Kyrie Irving/30 8.00 20.00
21 Deron Williams/60 3.00 8.00
23 Tobias Harris/30 3.00 8.00
24 DeMar DeRozan/30 6.00 15.00
25 LeBron James/30 40.00 100.00
26 Damian Lillard/30 6.00 15.00
27 Aaron Gordon/30 3.00 8.00
28 Victor Oladipo/30 3.00 8.00
29 Rudy Gay/30 4.00 10.00
30 Monta Ellis/30 3.00 8.00
31 Dirk Nowitzki/30 5.00 12.00
32 Giannis Antetokounmpo/30 8.00 20.00
33 Tim Frazier/60 2.50 6.00
34 Kobe Bryant/30 10.00 25.00
35 Shabazz Muhammad/30 3.00 8.00
36 Shawn Marion/60 3.00 8.00
37 Jabari Parker/30 5.00 12.00
38 Jrue Holiday/30 3.00 8.00
39 DeMarcus Cousins/30 4.00 10.00
40 Goran Dragic/60 3.00 8.00

2016-17 Panini National Treasures Colossal Materials Prime

*PRIME/21-25: 1X TO 2.5X BASIC
RANDOM INSERTS IN PACKS
PRINT RUNS B/WN 10-25 COPIES PER
NO PRICING ON QTY 18 OR LESS
25 LeBron James/25 150.00 400.00

2016-17 Panini National Treasures Colossal Rookie Materials

RANDOM INSERTS IN PACKS
STATED PRINT RUN 60 SER.#'d SETS
*PRIME/25: 1X TO 2.5X BASIC
1 Jaylen Brown 6.00 15.00
2 Kris Dunn 6.00 15.00
3 Malachi Richardson 3.00 8.00
4 Brice Johnson 2.50 6.00
5 Caris LeVert 3.00 8.00
6 Diamond Stone 2.50 6.00
7 Buddy Hield 5.00 12.00
8 Georgios Papagiannis 2.50 6.00
9 Isaiah Whitehead 2.50 6.00
10 Brandon Ingram 8.00 20.00
11 Cheick Diallo 2.50 6.00
12 Jake Layman 3.00 8.00
14 Denzel Valentine 3.00 8.00
15 Ivica Zubac 4.00 10.00
16 Marquese Chriss 6.00 15.00
17 Chinanu Onuaku 2.50 6.00
18 A.J. Hammons 2.50 6.00
19 Deyonta Davis 2.50 6.00
20 Pascal Siakam 2.50 6.00
21 Tyler Ulis 6.00 15.00
22 Patrick McCaw 5.00 12.00
23 Kay Felder 2.50 6.00
24 Wade Baldwin IV 2.50 6.00
25 Domantas Sabonis 4.00 10.00
26 Dragan Bender 3.00 8.00
27 Damian Jones 2.50 6.00
28 Jamal Murray 6.00 15.00
29 Malcolm Brogdon 6.00 15.00
30 Timothe Luwawu-Cabarrot 5.00 12.00
31 Juan Hernangomez 3.00 8.00
32 Thon Maker 10.00 25.00
33 Stephen Zimmerman 2.50 6.00
34 Dario Saric 5.00 12.00
35 Henry Ellenson 3.00 8.00
36 Malik Beasley 2.50 6.00
37 Demetrius Jackson 2.50 6.00
38 Skal Labissiere 4.00 10.00
39 Dejounte Murray 6.00 15.00
40 Jakob Poeltl 3.00 8.00

2016-17 Panini National Treasures Game Gear

RANDOM INSERTS IN PACKS
PRINT RUNS B/WN 30-99 COPIES PER
1 James Harden/99 6.00 15.00
2 Russell Westbrook/49 8.00 20.00
3 Stephen Curry/49 20.00 50.00
4 Damian Lillard/99 6.00 15.00
5 Otto Porter/99 3.00 8.00
6 Andrew Wiggins/99 4.00 10.00
7 Giannis Antetokounmpo/99 8.00 20.00
8 Kobe Bryant/99 10.00 25.00
9 Kyrie Irving/99 8.00 20.00
10 Aaron Gordon/99 3.00 8.00
11 Dennis Schroder/99 3.00 8.00
12 Enes Kanter/99 2.50 6.00
13 Mike Conley/99 3.00 8.00
14 Paul Pierce/99 4.00 10.00
15 Bojan Bogdanovic/99 2.50 6.00
16 John Wall/99 5.00 12.00
17 Tony Parker/99 4.00 10.00
18 Marc Gasol/99 4.00 10.00
19 LeBron James/99 15.00 40.00
20 Kawhi Leonard/99 6.00 15.00
21 D'Angelo Russell/99 5.00 12.00
22 Steven Adams/99 3.00 8.00
24 Thomas Robinson/99 2.50 6.00
25 Jason Terry/99 3.00 8.00
26 Bradley Beal/30 4.00 10.00
27 Goran Dragic/99 3.00 8.00
28 Zach Randolph/99 3.00 8.00
29 Jamal Crawford/99 4.00 10.00
30 Manu Ginobili/99 4.00 10.00
31 Brandon Knight/99 3.00 8.00
32 Trevor Booker/99 2.50 6.00
33 Draymond Green/99 5.00 12.00
34 Brook Lopez/99 3.00 8.00
35 Kevin Durant/99 12.00 30.00
36 Paul George/99 5.00 12.00
37 Jabari Parker/99 5.00 12.00
38 Blake Griffin/99 4.00 10.00
39 Adreian Payne/99 2.50 6.00
40 Monta Ellis/99 3.00 8.00

2016-17 Panini National Treasures Game Gear Autographs

RANDOM INSERTS IN PACKS
PRINT RUNS B/WN 19-49 COPIES PER
NO PRICING ON QTY 19
EXCHANGE DEADLINE 11/3/2018
*PRIME/25: .75X TO 2X BASIC
1 Stanley Johnson/60 4.00 10.00
2 Kristaps Porzingis/75 25.00 60.00
3 Kobe Bryant/25 125.00 300.00
4 Myles Turner/75 8.00 20.00
5 Justise Winslow/49 6.00 15.00
6 Zach LaVine/75 10.00 25.00
7 Norman Powell/99 4.00 10.00
8 Reggie Jackson/49 5.00 12.00
9 Carmelo Anthony/25 25.00 60.00
10 Kevin Love/25 20.00 50.00
11 Victor Oladipo/25 6.00 15.00
12 Mario Hezonja/70 4.00 10.00
13 C.J. McCollum/99 10.00 25.00
14 Devin Booker/75 30.00 80.00
15 Maurice Harkless/99 4.00 10.00
16 Danny Green/99 6.00 15.00
17 Karl-Anthony Towns/25 40.00 100.00
18 Dennis Rodman/25 20.00 50.00
19 Dan Issel/75 5.00 12.00
20 George Hill/75 5.00 12.00
21 Shaquille O'Neal/25 50.00 120.00
22 Karl Malone/25 25.00 60.00
23 Marques Johnson/75 5.00 12.00
24 Jrue Holiday/99 5.00 12.00
25 Solomon Hill/99 4.00 10.00
26 Magic Johnson/25 40.00 100.00
27 Marcus Camby/49 5.00 12.00
29 Kyrie Irving/25 50.00 120.00
30 John Stockton/25 40.00 100.00

2016-17 Panini National Treasures Game Gear Dual Jersey Autographs

RANDOM INSERTS IN PACKS
PRINT RUNS B/WN 25-75 COPIES PER
EXCHANGE DEADLINE 11/3/2018
*PRIME/25: .75X TO 2X BASIC
1 Ryan Anderson/49 5.00 12.00
2 George Hill/49 5.00 12.00
3 Myles Turner/49 8.00 20.00
4 Kobe Bryant/35 100.00 250.00
5 Andrew Wiggins/30 25.00 60.00
6 Langston Galloway/75 4.00 10.00
7 Elfrid Payton/49 5.00 12.00
8 Nikola Vucevic/75 6.00 15.00
9 C.J. McCollum/75 10.00 25.00
10 Evan Turner/49 4.00 10.00
11 Isaiah Thomas/75 25.00 60.00
12 Rondae Hollis-Jefferson/75 4.00 10.00
13 Carmelo Anthony/35 20.00 50.00
14 Kristaps Porzingis/75 25.00 60.00
15 Kenneth Faried/49 5.00 12.00
16 Danilo Gallinari/49 5.00 12.00
18 Dwyane Wade/25 30.00 80.00
19 Blake Griffin/30 15.00 40.00
20 Rashard Lewis/49 5.00 12.00
21 Magic Johnson/35 30.00 80.00
22 Hakeem Olajuwon/35 25.00 60.00
23 Larry Bird/35 50.00 120.00
24 Louie Dampier/49 10.00 25.00
25 Kareem Abdul-Jabbar/35 30.00 80.00

2016-17 Panini National Treasures Game Gear Duals

RANDOM INSERTS IN PACKS
PRINT RUNS B/WN 49-99 COPIES PER
*PRIME/25: 1X TO 2.5X BASIC
1 Dwight Howard/49 3.00 8.00
2 Kyrie Irving/75 8.00 20.00
3 Dirk Nowitzki/49 5.00 12.00
4 Tristan Thompson/75 3.00 8.00
5 Wesley Matthews/75 2.50 6.00
6 Kemba Walker/49 4.00 10.00
7 J.R. Smith/49 3.00 8.00
8 Michael Kidd-Gilchrist/75 3.00 8.00
9 Deron Williams/75 3.00 8.00
10 Jimmy Butler/75 4.00 10.00
11 Russell Westbrook/49 8.00 20.00
12 James Harden/49 6.00 15.00
13 Rudy Gobert/75 4.00 10.00
14 Jonas Valanciunas/75 3.00 8.00
15 Otto Porter/75 3.00 8.00
16 Carmelo Anthony/49 5.00 12.00
17 LaMarcus Aldridge/75 4.00 10.00
18 Marcus Smart/75 3.00 8.00
19 Kenneth Faried/75 3.00 8.00
20 Kristaps Porzingis/75 6.00 15.00
21 Kawhi Leonard/49 6.00 15.00
22 Evan Turner/75 2.50 6.00
23 Nik Stauskas/75 2.50 6.00
24 Thaddeus Young/49 2.50 6.00
25 Kyle Korver/75 3.00 8.00
26 Isaiah Thomas/49 5.00 12.00
27 Karl-Anthony Towns/49 6.00 15.00
28 Anthony Davis/75 8.00 20.00
29 Elfrid Payton/49 3.00 8.00
30 Nikola Vucevic/75 3.00 8.00

2016-17 Panini National Treasures Game Gear Prime

*PRIME: 1X TO 2.5X BASIC
RANDOM INSERTS IN PACKS
STATED PRINT RUN 25 SER.#'d SETS
3 Stephen Curry 75.00 200.00
19 LeBron James 75.00 200.00

2016-17 Panini National Treasures Game Gear Triple Jersey Autographs

RANDOM INSERTS IN PACKS
PRINT RUNS B/WN 25-75 COPIES PER
EXCHANGE DEADLINE 11/3/2018
*PRIME/20-25: .75X TO 2X BASIC
1 Andrew Wiggins/49 25.00 60.00
2 Jabari Parker/49 15.00 40.00
3 Zach LaVine/49 10.00 25.00
4 Khris Middleton/49 10.00 25.00
6 Blake Griffin/35 15.00 40.00
7 Luis Scola/75 5.00 12.00
8 Andre Drummond/49 6.00 15.00
9 Dirk Nowitzki/35 75.00 200.00
10 Tristan Thompson/75 5.00 12.00
11 Michael Carter-Williams/49 4.00 10.00
12 Marcus Camby/75 5.00 12.00
13 Magic Johnson/25 40.00 100.00
14 Shane Battier/75 5.00 12.00
15 Rik Smits/49 10.00 25.00
16 Jason Kidd/49 12.00 30.00
17 Grant Hill/49 15.00 40.00
18 Bill Laimbeer/75 8.00 20.00
19 Brad Daugherty/75 5.00 12.00
20 Kareem Abdul-Jabbar/25 40.00 100.00

2016-17 Panini National Treasures Game Gear Triples

RANDOM INSERTS IN PACKS
PRINT RUNS B/WN 25-49 COPIES PER
1 Nikola Vucevic/49 3.00 8.00
2 Eric Bledsoe/49 3.00 8.00
3 Kawhi Leonard/49 6.00 15.00
4 Kyle Lowry/49 3.00 8.00
5 Rodney Hood/49 3.00 8.00
6 John Wall/49 5.00 12.00
7 Kyrie Irving/49 8.00 20.00
9 Carmelo Anthony/49 5.00 12.00
10 Jrue Holiday/49 3.00 8.00
11 Russell Westbrook/49 8.00 20.00
12 Isaiah Thomas/49 5.00 12.00
13 Jimmy Butler/49 4.00 10.00
14 Dirk Nowitzki/49 5.00 12.00
15 Emmanuel Mudiay/49 3.00 8.00
16 Stephen Curry/49 20.00 50.00
17 Jeff Teague/49 3.00 8.00
18 George Hill/49 3.00 8.00
19 DeAndre Jordan/49 4.00 10.00
20 Jordan Clarkson/25 3.00 8.00

2016-17 Panini National Treasures Game Gear Triples Prime

*PRIME: 1X TO 2.5X BASIC
RANDOM INSERTS IN PACKS
STATED PRINT RUN 25 SER.#'d SETS
16 Stephen Curry 75.00 200.00

2016-17 Panini National Treasures Hometown Heroes

RANDOM INSERTS IN PACKS
PRINT RUNS B/WN 35-75 COPIES PER
EXCHANGE DEADLINE 11/3/2018
*BRONZE/25: .5X TO 1.2X BASIC
1 Carmelo Anthony/35 25.00 60.00
2 Kobe Bryant/35 75.00 200.00
3 Patrick Ewing/35 50.00 120.00
4 Kevin Durant/35 100.00 250.00
5 Karl Malone/35 30.00 80.00
6 John Stockton/35 25.00 60.00
7 Eddie Jones/75 6.00 15.00
8 Michael Cage/75 4.00 10.00
9 Mark Price/75 6.00 15.00
10 DeMar DeRozan/60 12.00 30.00
11 Jo Jo White/75 5.00 12.00
12 Latrell Sprewell/75 12.00 30.00
13 Gary Payton/35 10.00 25.00
14 Ray Allen/35 25.00 60.00
15 Karl-Anthony Towns/35 30.00 80.00
16 Jeremy Lin/35 30.00 80.00
17 Devin Booker/75 30.00 80.00
18 Anthony Davis/35 25.00 60.00
19 Dwyane Wade/35 25.00 60.00
20 Dante Exum/60 10.00 25.00
21 Al Horford/60
22 Khris Middleton/75 5.00 12.00
23 Doug McDermott/75 5.00 12.00
24 Tyler Johnson/75 10.00 25.00
25 Isaiah Thomas/60 20.00 50.00
26 Julius Randle/60 12.00 30.00
27 Aaron Gordon/60 6.00 15.00
28 Jordan Clarkson/75 5.00 12.00
29 Elfrid Payton/75 5.00 12.00
30 Bobby Portis/75 6.00 15.00
31 Larry Bird/35 40.00 100.00
32 Magic Johnson/35 25.00 60.00
33 Shane Battier/60 5.00 12.00
34 Shaquille O'Neal/35 50.00 120.00
35 Gail Goodrich/75 5.00 12.00
36 Alex English/75 5.00 12.00
37 Bernard King/75 5.00 12.00
38 Louie Dampier/75 10.00 25.00
39 Nate Archibald/75 5.00 12.00
40 Dave Cowens/75 10.00 25.00
41 Henry Ellenson/75 12.00 30.00
42 Denzel Valentine/75 12.00 30.00
43 Malachi Richardson/75 5.00 12.00
44 Marquese Chriss/75 25.00 60.00
45 Kris Dunn/60 25.00 60.00
46 Buddy Hield/60 25.00 60.00
47 Jaylen Brown/35 25.00 60.00
48 Isaiah Whitehead/75 8.00 20.00
49 Caris LeVert/75 8.00 20.00
50 Brandon Ingram/35 60.00 150.00

2016-17 Panini National Treasures International Treasures

RANDOM INSERTS IN PACKS
PRINT RUNS B/WN 49-75 COPIES PER
EXCHANGE DEADLINE 11/3/2018
*BRONZE/25: .5X TO 1.2X BASIC
1 Dragan Bender/75 15.00 40.00
2 Thon Maker/75 40.00 100.00
3 Dario Saric/75 30.00 80.00
4 Juan Hernangomez/75 15.00 40.00
5 T. Luwawu-Cabarrot/75 15.00 40.00
6 Willy Hernangomez/75 20.00 50.00
7 Ivica Zubac/75 25.00 60.00
8 Dirk Nowitzki/49 150.00 300.00
9 Pau Gasol/49 25.00 60.00
10 Ricky Rubio/49 20.00 50.00
11 Marc Gasol/49 20.00 50.00
12 Tony Parker/75 20.00 50.00
13 Dante Exum/75 10.00 25.00
14 Danilo Gallinari/75 5.00 12.00
15 Kristaps Porzingis/75 30.00 80.00
16 Goran Dragic/75 5.00 12.00
17 Mario Hezonja/75 4.00 10.00
18 Marcin Gortat/75 6.00 15.00
19 Yao Ming/75 75.00 200.00
20 Toni Kukoc/75 10.00 25.00
21 Evan Fournier/75 5.00 12.00
22 Bojan Bogdanovic/75 10.00 25.00
23 Clint Capela/75 15.00 40.00
24 Nikola Jokic/75 30.00 80.00
25 Dennis Schroder/75 12.00 30.00
26 Buddy Hield/75 30.00 80.00
27 Jamal Murray/75 40.00 100.00
28 Andrew Wiggins/49 25.00 60.00
29 Dikembe Mutombo/75 15.00 40.00
30 Steve Nash/49 25.00 60.00

2016-17 Panini National Treasures Lasting Legacies Jersey Autographs

RANDOM INSERTS IN PACKS
PRINT RUNS B/WN 20-99 COPIES PER
EXCHANGE DEADLINE 11/3/2018
*PRIME/25: .75X TO 2X BASIC
1 Tony Parker/20 25.00 60.00
2 Kyrie Irving/20 50.00 120.00
3 Michael Kidd-Gilchrist/75 5.00 12.00
4 Dirk Nowitzki/20 100.00 250.00
5 Andre Drummond/60 6.00 15.00
6 Paul George/20
7 Blake Griffin/20 20.00 50.00
8 Kobe Bryant/20 125.00 300.00
9 Kevin Durant/20 75.00 200.00
10 Zach Randolph/60 5.00 12.00
11 Anthony Davis/20 50.00 120.00
13 Scottie Pippen/20 40.00 100.00
14 Joe Dumars/60 6.00 15.00
15 Carmelo Anthony/20 25.00 60.00
16 Magic Johnson/20 40.00 100.00
17 Allen Iverson/20 40.00 100.00
18 Shane Battier/99 5.00 12.00
19 Deron Williams/20 6.00 15.00
21 Anfernee Hardaway/20 30.00 80.00
22 Alvan Adams/99 4.00 10.00
23 Tristan Thompson/99 5.00 12.00
24 Udonis Haslem/55 4.00 10.00
25 Mark Aguirre/40 5.00 12.00

2016-17 Panini National Treasures Material Treasures

RANDOM INSERTS IN PACKS
PRINT RUNS B/WN 30-99 COPIES PER
*PRIME/25: 1X TO 2.5X BASIC
2 Blake Griffin 4.00 10.00
3 Kawhi Leonard 6.00 15.00
4 Giannis Antetokounmpo 8.00 20.00
5 Kemba Walker 4.00 10.00
6 Chris Paul 5.00 12.00
7 Reggie Jackson 3.00 8.00
8 Andre Drummond 4.00 10.00
9 Paul George 5.00 12.00
10 Jeff Teague 3.00 8.00
11 Otto Porter 3.00 8.00
12 Jimmy Butler 4.00 10.00
13 Andrew Wiggins 4.00 10.00
14 Jabari Parker 5.00 12.00
15 Cody Zeller 2.50 6.00
16 LaMarcus Aldridge 4.00 10.00
17 Kevin Durant 10.00 25.00
18 Tony Allen 2.50 6.00
19 Mike Conley 3.00 8.00
20 John Wall 5.00 12.00
21 Brandon Knight 3.00 8.00
22 Goran Dragic 3.00 8.00
23 Carmelo Anthony 5.00 12.00
24 Kristaps Porzingis 5.00 12.00
25 James Young 2.50 6.00
26 Dennis Schroder 3.00 8.00
27 Dwight Howard 3.00 8.00
28 Serge Ibaka 3.00 8.00
29 Alex Len 2.50 6.00
30 Deron Williams 3.00 8.00
31 Dirk Nowitzki 5.00 12.00
32 Elfrid Payton 3.00 8.00
33 Jae Crowder 3.00 8.00
34 Sasha Vujacic 2.50 6.00
36 Hassan Whiteside 3.00 8.00
37 Rudy Gay 4.00 10.00
38 Vince Carter 5.00 12.00
39 Zach Randolph 3.00 8.00
40 Al Horford 3.00 8.00
41 Devin Booker 6.00 15.00
42 Gordon Hayward 4.00 10.00
43 Tobias Harris 3.00 8.00
45 Patty Mills 4.00 10.00
46 Thaddeus Young 2.50 6.00
47 Michael Kidd-Gilchrist 3.00 8.00
48 Rodney Hood 3.00 8.00
49 DeMarcus Cousins 4.00 10.00
50 Jahlil Okafor 3.00 8.00

2016-17 Panini National Treasures Material Treasures Signatures

RANDOM INSERTS IN PACKS
PRINT RUNS B/WN 25-99 COPIES PER
EXCHANGE DEADLINE 11/3/2018
*BRONZE/20-25: .75X TO 2X BASIC
1 Mark Aguirre/99 5.00 12.00
2 Cedric Maxwell/99 4.00 10.00
3 Tim Hardaway/99 6.00 15.00
4 Robert Horry/99 6.00 15.00
5 Scottie Pippen/25 40.00 100.00
6 Kiki Vandeweghe/99 5.00 12.00
7 Marcus Camby/99 5.00 12.00
8 Kenny Anderson/99 5.00 12.00
9 Rashard Lewis/99 5.00 12.00
10 Kurt Rambis/99 4.00 10.00
11 Shane Battier/35 5.00 12.00
12 Jeff Malone/99 4.00 10.00
13 Jeff Hornacek/99 5.00 12.00
14 Xavier McDaniel/65 4.00 10.00
15 Chuck Person/99 5.00 12.00
16 Clyde Drexler/25 15.00 40.00
17 Mark Jackson/99 5.00 12.00
18 Anternee Hardaway/35 25.00 60.00
19 Kareem Abdul-Jabbar/25 40.00 100.00
20 Brad Daugherty/99 5.00 12.00
21 Danny Green/99 6.00 15.00
22 Karl-Anthony Towns/25 50.00 120.00
23 Cody Zeller/35 5.00 12.00
24 Victor Oladipo/35 5.00 12.00
25 Langston Galloway/99 4.00 10.00
26 Larry Bird/25 60.00 150.00
27 Andrew Wiggins/25 30.00 80.00
28 Allen Iverson/25 40.00 100.00
29 Magic Johnson/25 40.00 100.00
30 Karl Malone/25 25.00 60.00
31 Dominique Wilkins/35 12.00 30.00
32 Kyrie Irving/25 50.00 120.00
33 Courtney Lee/99 5.00 12.00
34 C.J. McCollum/35 10.00 25.00
35 Kevin Love/35 15.00 40.00
36 Luis Scola/99 5.00 12.00
37 Allen Crabbe/99 4.00 10.00
38 Jeremy Lin/35 30.00 80.00
39 George Hill/99 5.00 12.00
40 Jeff Teague/99 5.00 12.00

2016-17 Panini National Treasures NBA Greats Signatures

RANDOM INSERTS IN PACKS
PRINT RUNS B/WN 25-99 COPIES PER
EXCHANGE DEADLINE 11/3/2018
*BRONZE/25: .4X TO 1X BASE p/r 25
*BRONZE/25: .5X TO 1.2X BASE p/r 99
1 Magic Johnson/25 30.00 80.00
2 Kareem Abdul-Jabbar/25 40.00 100.00
3 Elvin Hayes/99 6.00 15.00
4 Calvin Murphy/99 5.00 12.00
5 Oscar Robertson/25 30.00 80.00
6 Karl Malone/25 25.00 60.00
7 Tom Heinsohn/99 20.00 50.00
8 Kobe Bryant/25 100.00 250.00
9 Alvan Adams/99 4.00 10.00
10 Jeff Hornacek/99 5.00 12.00
11 Mark Aguirre/99 5.00 12.00
12 Mark Price/99 6.00 15.00
13 David Robinson/25 15.00 40.00
14 Nate Archibald/99 5.00 12.00
15 Walt Frazier/99 8.00 20.00
16 Cliff Hagan/99 5.00 12.00
17 Bob Dandridge/99 4.00 10.00
18 Ron Boone/99 4.00 10.00
19 Junior Bridgeman/99 4.00 10.00
20 Kiki Vandeweghe/99 5.00 12.00

2016-17 Panini National Treasures Penmanship

RANDOM INSERTS IN PACKS
PRINT RUNS B/WN 25-99 COPIES PER
EXCHANGE DEADLINE 11/3/2018
*BRONZE/25: .4X TO 1X BASE p/r 25
*BRONZE/25: .5X TO 1.2X BASE p/r 40-99
1 Kobe Bryant/25 100.00 250.00
2 Sarunas Marciulionis/99 4.00 10.00
3 Tom "Satch" Sanders/99 6.00 15.00
4 Vin Baker/99 4.00 10.00
5 Spud Webb/99 5.00 12.00
6 Frank Ramsey/99 10.00 25.00
7 World B. Free/99 5.00 12.00
8 Dell Curry/99 4.00 10.00
9 Chuck Person/99 5.00 12.00
10 Larry Brown/40 6.00 15.00
11 Kurt Rambis/99 4.00 10.00
12 Sam Bowie/99 4.00 10.00
13 Michael Cooper/99 5.00 12.00
14 Cedric Ceballos/99 5.00 12.00
15 Marcus Camby/99 5.00 12.00
16 Horace Grant/99 6.00 15.00
17 Dale Davis/99 4.00 10.00
18 Fat Lever/99 5.00 12.00
19 Antoine Carr/99 4.00 10.00
20 Vlade Divac/99 6.00 15.00
21 Sean Elliott/99 6.00 15.00
22 Mark Price/99 6.00 15.00
23 Antoine Walker/99 5.00 12.00
24 Jamal Mashburn/99 6.00 15.00
25 Antonio McDyess/99 5.00 12.00
26 Cody Zeller/40 4.00 10.00
27 Langston Galloway/99 4.00 10.00
28 Mario Hezonja/40 4.00 10.00
29 Danny Green/99 5.00 12.00
30 Cameron Payne/99 4.00 10.00
31 Kurt Thomas/99 4.00 10.00
32 Nikola Mirotic/99 5.00 12.00
33 Karl-Anthony Towns/25 40.00 100.00
34 DeMar DeRozan/40 12.00 30.00
35 Robert Covington/99 4.00 10.00
36 Jonathon Simmons/99 8.00 20.00
37 Jeremy Lin/40 20.00 50.00
38 Adrian Dantley/99 5.00 12.00
39 Allen Crabbe/99 5.00 12.00
40 Kevon Looney/99 5.00 12.00

2016-17 Panini National Treasures Retro Materials

RANDOM INSERTS IN PACKS
PRINT RUNS B/WN 15-99 COPIES PER
NO PRICING ON QTY 15
1 Shaquille O'Neal/99 10.00 25.00
2 Shaquille O'Neal/30 10.00 25.00
3 Shaquille O'Neal/30 10.00 25.00
4 Dwyane Wade/99 5.00 12.00
5 Kevin Love/99 4.00 10.00
6 Paul Pierce/99 4.00 10.00
7 Paul Pierce/99 4.00 10.00
8 Chris Paul/99 5.00 12.00
9 Al Horford/30 3.00 8.00
10 Tyson Chandler/99 3.00 8.00
11 Tyson Chandler/99 3.00 8.00
12 Pau Gasol/99 4.00 10.00
13 Pau Gasol/99 4.00 10.00
14 Derrick Rose/99 5.00 12.00
15 Dwight Howard/99 3.00 8.00
16 Dwight Howard/99 3.00 8.00
17 Dwight Howard/99 3.00 8.00
18 Vince Carter/30 5.00 12.00
19 Vince Carter/99 5.00 12.00
20 Vince Carter/99 5.00 12.00
21 Luol Deng/99 3.00 8.00
22 Luol Deng/30 3.00 8.00
23 Jeremy Lin/99 4.00 10.00
24 Jeremy Lin/30 4.00 10.00
25 Rajon Rondo/99 4.00 10.00
26 Rajon Rondo/30 4.00 10.00
27 Chris Andersen/99 3.00 8.00
28 Harrison Barnes/99 3.00 8.00
29 Andrew Bogut/99 3.00 8.00
30 Deron Williams/30 3.00 8.00
31 Nene/99 3.00 8.00
32 Nene/99 3.00 8.00
33 Al Jefferson/99 3.00 8.00
34 Chandler Parsons/99 3.00 8.00
35 Chandler Parsons/99 3.00 8.00
36 Joakim Noah/99 3.00 8.00
37 LaMarcus Aldridge/99 4.00 10.00
38 Joe Johnson/99 3.00 8.00
39 Brandon Knight/99 3.00 8.00
40 LeBron James/99 15.00 40.00
41 Tracy McGrady/99 4.00 10.00
42 Grant Hill/30 5.00 12.00
43 Scottie Pippen/99 6.00 15.00
44 Yao Ming/30 6.00 15.00
45 Shane Battier/99 3.00 8.00
46 Patrick Ewing/30 5.00 12.00
47 Magic Johnson/99 8.00 20.00
48 Larry Bird/30 10.00 25.00
49 Kobe Bryant/30 10.00 25.00
50 Julius Erving/30 6.00 15.00

2016-17 Panini National Treasures Retro Materials Bronze

*BRONZE/25: 1X TO 2.5X BASIC
RANDOM INSERTS IN PACKS
PRINT RUNS B/WN 8-25 COPIES PER
NO PRICING ON QTY 18 OR LESS
40 LeBron James/25 75.00 200.00

2016-17 Panini National Treasures Rookie Dual Materials

RANDOM INSERTS IN PACKS
STATED PRINT RUN 60 SER.#'d SETS
*BRONZE/25: 1X TO 2.5X BASIC
1 Jaylen Brown 6.00 15.00
2 Kris Dunn 6.00 15.00
3 Malachi Richardson 3.00 8.00
4 Brice Johnson 2.50 6.00
5 Diamond Stone 2.50 6.00
6 Buddy Hield 5.00 12.00
7 Isaiah Whitehead 2.50 6.00
8 Brandon Ingram 8.00 20.00
9 Cheick Diallo 2.50 6.00
10 Dejounte Murray 6.00 15.00
11 Denzel Valentine 3.00 8.00
12 Marquese Chriss 6.00 15.00
13 A.J. Hammons 2.50 6.00
14 Deyonta Davis 2.50 6.00
15 Pascal Siakam 2.50 6.00
16 Patrick McCaw 5.00 12.00
17 Dragan Bender 3.00 8.00
18 Damian Jones 2.50 6.00
19 Jamal Murray 6.00 15.00
20 Timothe Luwawu-Cabarrot 5.00 12.00
21 Juan Hernangomez 3.00 8.00
22 Thon Maker 10.00 25.00
23 Henry Ellenson 3.00 8.00
24 Malik Beasley 2.50 6.00
25 Jakob Poeltl 3.00 8.00

2016-17 Panini National Treasures Rookie Jumbo Materials

RANDOM INSERTS IN PACKS
PRINT RUNS B/WN 35 COPIES PER
*BRONZE/25: 1X TO 2.5X BASIC
1 Brandon Ingram 8.00 20.00
2 Malik Beasley 2.50 6.00
3 Buddy Hield 5.00 12.00
4 Marquese Chriss 6.00 15.00
5 Jaylen Brown 6.00 15.00
6 Wade Baldwin IV 2.50 6.00
7 Henry Ellenson 3.00 8.00
8 Cheick Diallo 2.50 6.00
9 Tyler Ulis 6.00 15.00
10 Caris LeVert 3.00 8.00
11 Malcolm Brogdon 6.00 15.00
12 Patrick McCaw 5.00 12.00
13 Domantas Sabonis 4.00 10.00
14 Georgios Papagiannis 2.50 6.00
15 Denzel Valentine 3.00 8.00
16 Thon Maker 10.00 25.00
17 Brice Johnson 2.50 6.00
18 Dario Saric 5.00 12.00
19 Skal Labissiere 4.00 10.00
20 Jamal Murray 6.00 15.00
21 Kris Dunn 6.00 15.00
22 Ivica Zubac 4.00 10.00
23 Dragan Bender 3.00 8.00
24 Jakob Poeltl 3.00 8.00
25 Kay Felder 2.50 6.00

2016-17 Panini National Treasures Rookie Materials

RANDOM INSERTS IN PACKS
STATED PRINT RUN 75 SER.#'d SETS
*BRONZE/25: 1X TO 2.5X BASIC
1 Jaylen Brown 6.00 15.00
2 Kris Dunn 6.00 15.00
3 Malachi Richardson 3.00 8.00
4 Brice Johnson 2.50 6.00
5 Diamond Stone 2.50 6.00
6 Buddy Hield 5.00 12.00
7 Isaiah Whitehead 2.50 6.00
8 Brandon Ingram 8.00 20.00
9 Cheick Diallo 2.50 6.00
10 Dejounte Murray 6.00 15.00
11 Denzel Valentine 3.00 8.00
12 Marquese Chriss 6.00 15.00
13 A.J. Hammons 2.50 6.00
14 Deyonta Davis 2.50 6.00
15 Pascal Siakam 2.50 6.00
16 Patrick McCaw 5.00 12.00
17 Dragan Bender 3.00 8.00
18 Damian Jones 2.50 6.00
19 Jamal Murray 6.00 15.00
20 Timothe Luwawu-Cabarrot 5.00 12.00
21 Juan Hernangomez 3.00 8.00
22 Thon Maker 10.00 25.00
23 Henry Ellenson 3.00 8.00
24 Malik Beasley 2.50 6.00
25 Jakob Poeltl 3.00 8.00

2016-17 Panini National Treasures Rookie Triple Materials

RANDOM INSERTS IN PACKS
STATED PRINT RUN 49 SER.#'d SETS
*BRONZE/25: 1X TO 2.5X BASIC
1 Jaylen Brown 6.00 15.00
2 Kris Dunn 6.00 15.00
3 Malachi Richardson 3.00 8.00
4 Brice Johnson 2.50 6.00
5 Diamond Stone 2.50 6.00
6 Buddy Hield 5.00 12.00
7 Isaiah Whitehead 2.50 6.00
8 Brandon Ingram 8.00 20.00
9 Cheick Diallo 2.50 6.00
10 Dejounte Murray 6.00 15.00
11 Denzel Valentine 3.00 8.00
12 Marquese Chriss 6.00 15.00
13 A.J. Hammons 2.50 6.00
14 Deyonta Davis 2.50 6.00
15 Pascal Siakam 2.50 6.00
16 Patrick McCaw 5.00 12.00
17 Dragan Bender 3.00 8.00
18 Damian Jones 2.50 6.00
19 Jamal Murray 6.00 15.00
20 Timothe Luwawu-Cabarrot 5.00 12.00
21 Juan Hernangomez 3.00 8.00
22 Thon Maker 10.00 25.00
23 Henry Ellenson 3.00 8.00
24 Malik Beasley 2.50 6.00
25 Jakob Poeltl 3.00 8.00

2016-17 Panini National Treasures Signatures

RANDOM INSERTS IN PACKS
PRINT RUNS B/WN 35-75 COPIES PER
EXCHANGE DEADLINE 11/3/2018
*BRONZE/25: .5X TO 1.2X BASIC
1 George Gervin/35
2 Ben Wallace/75 30.00 80.00
3 Clyde Drexler/35 15.00 40.00
4 Latrell Sprewell/75 12.00 30.00
5 Karl Malone/35 20.00 50.00
6 John Stockton/35 25.00 60.00
7 Walt Frazier/75 10.00 25.00
9 Mark Aguirre/75 5.00 12.00
10 Adrian Dantley/75 5.00 12.00
11 Detlef Schrempf/75 6.00 15.00
12 Gary Payton/35 10.00 25.00
13 Kobe Bryant/35 75.00 200.00
14 David Robinson/35 20.00 50.00
15 Sean Elliott/75 6.00 15.00
16 Cedric Ceballos/75 5.00 12.00
17 Chauncey Billups/75 10.00 25.00
18 Dan Majerle/75 6.00 15.00
19 Dell Curry/75 4.00 10.00
20 Eddie Jones/75 6.00 15.00
21 Glen Rice/75 6.00 15.00
22 Jo Jo White/75 5.00 12.00
23 Jim Jackson/75 6.00 15.00
24 Bill Laimbeer/75 6.00 15.00
25 Nick Van Exel/75 10.00 25.00
26 Allan Houston/75
27 Tom Gugliotta/75 4.00 10.00
28 Larry Brown/49 8.00 20.00
29 Robert Horry/75 10.00 25.00
30 Vin Baker/75 4.00 10.00
31 Jamal Mashburn/75 6.00 15.00
32 Michael Cooper/75 5.00 12.00
33 Kenny Smith/75 5.00 12.00
34 Spud Webb/75 5.00 12.00
35 Grant Hill/35 25.00 60.00
36 Cedric Maxwell/75 4.00 10.00
37 Vlade Divac/75 6.00 15.00
38 Jeff Hornacek/75 5.00 12.00
39 Sidney Moncrief/75 4.00 10.00
40 Horace Grant/75 6.00 15.00
41 Dennis Rodman/35 25.00 60.00
42 Jerry West/35 20.00 50.00
43 David Thompson/75 5.00 12.00
44 Louie Dampier/75 10.00 25.00
45 Bill Russell/35 60.00 150.00
46 Justise Winslow/75 5.00 12.00
47 Pau Gasol/35 25.00 60.00
48 Jonas Valanciunas/75 5.00 12.00
49 Khris Middleton/75 5.00 12.00
50 Nicolas Batum/75 15.00 40.00
51 Dirk Nowitzki/35 100.00 250.00
52 DeMar DeRozan/49 12.00 30.00
53 Brandon Knight/75 5.00 12.00
54 Chris Paul/35 25.00 60.00
55 Dwyane Wade/35 25.00 60.00
56 Stephen Curry/35 125.00 300.00
57 Kevin Durant/35 100.00 250.00
58 Kyrie Irving/35 50.00 120.00
59 Kevin Love/35 15.00 40.00
60 Andrew Wiggins/35 25.00 60.00
61 Tony Parker/35 15.00 40.00
62 Karl-Anthony Towns/35 30.00 80.00
63 Klay Thompson/49 30.00 80.00
64 Tyler Johnson/75 10.00 25.00
65 Allen Crabbe/75 5.00 12.00
66 Clint Capela/75 4.00 10.00
67 Isaiah Thomas/75 20.00 50.00
68 Jordan Clarkson/75 5.00 12.00
69 Marc Gasol/35 10.00 25.00
70 Bojan Bogdanovic/75 4.00 10.00
71 Ryan Anderson/75 5.00 12.00
72 Dwight Powell/75 4.00 10.00
73 Julius Randle/49 6.00 15.00
74 Bobby Portis/75 6.00 15.00
75 Luol Deng/75 5.00 12.00
76 Danilo Gallinari/75 5.00 12.00
77 Elfrid Payton/75 5.00 12.00
78 Blake Griffin/35 15.00 40.00
79 Devin Booker/75 30.00 80.00
80 Evan Fournier/75 5.00 12.00
81 Jeremy Lin/35 30.00 80.00
82 Marcin Gortat/75 6.00 15.00
83 Nikola Vucevic/75 5.00 12.00
84 Nikola Jokic/75 25.00 60.00
85 Jason Terry/75 5.00 12.00
86 Ricky Rubio/35 10.00 25.00
87 Matthew Dellavedova/75 5.00 12.00
88 Kristaps Porzingis/49 25.00 60.00
89 Myles Turner/75 8.00 20.00
90 Carmelo Anthony/35 25.00 60.00

2016-17 Panini National Treasures Treasured Threads

RANDOM INSERTS IN PACKS
PRINT RUNS B/WN 49-99 COPIES PER
1 Klay Thompson/99 5.00 12.00
2 LeBron James/99 15.00 40.00
3 Jahlil Okafor/49 3.00 8.00
4 Kemba Walker/49 4.00 10.00
5 Kawhi Leonard/49 6.00 15.00
6 Andrew Wiggins/99 4.00 10.00
8 Karl-Anthony Towns/99 6.00 15.00
9 Goran Dragic/99 3.00 8.00
10 Kyrie Irving/49 8.00 20.00
11 Damian Lillard/49 6.00 15.00
12 Devin Booker/99 6.00 15.00
13 Otto Porter/99 3.00 8.00
14 James Young/99 2.50 6.00
15 Rudy Gay/99 4.00 10.00
16 James Harden/99 6.00 15.00
17 Aaron Gordon/99 3.00 8.00
18 Kevin Durant/99 10.00 25.00
19 Tony Parker/49 4.00 10.00
21 Hassan Whiteside/49 3.00 8.00
22 Zach Randolph/99 3.00 8.00
23 Giannis Antetokounmpo/49 8.00 20.00
24 Kristaps Porzingis/99 5.00 12.00
25 DeMarcus Cousins/49 4.00 10.00
26 Kenneth Faried/49 3.00 8.00
27 Chris Paul/99 5.00 12.00
28 Isaiah Thomas/99 5.00 12.00
29 Russell Westbrook/49 8.00 20.00
30 Dirk Nowitzki/49 5.00 12.00
31 Blake Griffin/49 4.00 10.00
32 Tobias Harris/99 3.00 8.00
33 Paul George/49 5.00 12.00
34 Elfrid Payton/49 3.00 8.00
35 Victor Oladipo/49 3.00 8.00
36 Jimmy Butler/49 4.00 10.00
37 Emmanuel Mudiay/49 3.00 8.00
38 Tristan Thompson/99 3.00 8.00
39 Dwight Howard/49 3.00 8.00
40 Michael Kidd-Gilchrist/99 3.00 8.00
41 Vince Carter/99 5.00 12.00
42 John Wall/99 5.00 12.00
43 Carmelo Anthony/49 5.00 12.00
44 Kyle Lowry/49 3.00 8.00
45 D'Angelo Russell/99 5.00 12.00
46 J.J. Redick/49 4.00 10.00
47 Wesley Matthews/99 2.50 6.00
48 Tyreke Evans/99 2.50 6.00
49 Solomon Hill/99 2.50 6.00
50 Brook Lopez/99 3.00 8.00

2016-17 Panini National Treasures Treasured Threads Prime

*PRIME/20-25: 1X TO 2.5X BASIC
RANDOM INSERTS IN PACKS
PRINT RUNS B/WN 5-25 COPIES PER
NO PRICING ON QTY 5
2 LeBron James/25 75.00 200.00

2016-17 Panini National Treasures Treasures of the Hall Autographs

RANDOM INSERTS IN PACKS
PRINT RUNS B/WN 49-75 COPIES PER
EXCHANGE DEADLINE 11/3/2018
*BRONZE/25: .5X TO 1.2X BASIC
1 Bill Russell/49 60.00 150.00
2 Shaquille O'Neal/49 50.00 120.00
3 Allen Iverson/49 75.00 200.00
4 Scottie Pippen/49 50.00 120.00
5 Karl Malone/49 20.00 50.00
6 Magic Johnson/49 25.00 60.00
7 Larry Bird/49 40.00 100.00
8 Oscar Robertson/49 25.00 60.00
9 Alonzo Mourning/49 20.00 50.00
10 David Robinson/49 20.00 50.00
11 Hakeem Olajuwon/49 15.00 40.00
12 Kevin McHale/49 10.00 25.00
13 Dennis Rodman/49 25.00 60.00
14 Clyde Drexler/49 12.00 30.00
15 Gary Payton/49 10.00 25.00
16 James Worthy/49 15.00 40.00
17 Rick Barry/75 5.00 12.00
18 Bob Lanier/75 8.00 20.00
19 Artis Gilmore/75 8.00 20.00
20 Bernard King/75 5.00 12.00

2016-17 Panini National Treasures Tremendous Treasures

RANDOM INSERTS IN PACKS

PRINT RUNS BW/N 30-60 COPIES PER
1 James Harden/60 6.00 15.00
2 Karl-Anthony Towns/60 6.00 15.00
3 Nikola Mirotic/60 3.00 8.00
4 Kyle Lowry/60 3.00 8.00
5 Anthony Davis/60 5.00 12.00
6 Russell Westbrook/60 8.00 20.00
7 LeBron James/60 30.00 80.00
8 Stephen Curry/60 20.00 50.00
9 Kyrie Irving/30 8.00 20.00
10 Iman Shumpert/60 2.50 6.00
11 Rajon Rondo/60 4.00 10.00
12 Trevor Booker/60 2.50 6.00
13 Patrick Beverley/60 2.50 6.00
14 Langston Galloway/60 2.50 6.00
15 Tristan Thompson/60 3.00 8.00
16 Paul Millsap/60 4.00 10.00
17 D'Angelo Russell/60 5.00 12.00
18 Isaiah Thomas/60 5.00 12.00
19 Klay Thompson/60 5.00 12.00
20 Eric Bledsoe/60 3.00 8.00
21 Marc Gasol/60 4.00 10.00
22 Aaron Gordon/60 3.00 8.00
23 Julius Randle/60 4.00 10.00
24 Victor Oladipo/60 3.00 8.00
25 Eric Gordon/60 3.00 8.00
27 Emmanuel Mudiay/60 3.00 8.00
28 Enes Kanter/60 2.50 6.00
29 J.J. Redick/60 4.00 10.00
30 Brook Lopez/60 3.00 8.00
31 Nikola Jokic/30 4.00 10.00
32 Ben McLemore/60 2.50 6.00
33 Frank Kaminsky/60 3.00 8.00
34 Luis Scola/60 3.00 8.00
35 Jordan Clarkson/30 3.00 8.00
36 Damian Lillard/60 6.00 15.00
37 J.J. Barea/60 3.00 8.00
38 C.J. McCollum/60 3.00 8.00
39 Wesley Matthews/60 2.50 6.00
40 Solomon Hill/60 2.50 6.00
41 Nicolas Batum/60 3.00 8.00
42 Joe Johnson/60 3.00 8.00
43 Kenneth Faried/60 3.00 8.00
44 Mason Plumlee/60 3.00 8.00
45 Jusuf Nurkic/60 2.50 6.00
46 Jonas Valanciunas/60 3.00 8.00
47 Zach LaVine/60 4.00 10.00
48 Tony Parker/60 4.00 10.00
49 Kyle Korver/60 3.00 8.00
50 Tyreke Evans/60 2.50 6.00

2016-17 Panini National Treasures Tremendous Treasures Bronze

*BRONZE/20-25: 1X TO 2.5X BASIC
RANDOM INSERTS IN PACKS
PRINT RUNS B/WN 15-25 COPIES PER
NO PRICING ON QTY 15
7 LeBron James/25 75.00 200.00

2014-15 Panini Noir

VET PRINT RUN 70 SER.#'d SETS
RC PRINT RUN 99 SER.#'d SETS
JSY AU PRINT RUN 99 SER.#'d SETS
PATCHES MAY SELL FOR PREMIUM
EXCHANGE DEADLINE 3/16/2017
1 Ty Lawson BW 2.00 5.00
2 Al Horford BW 2.50 6.00
3 Kevin Love BW 3.00 8.00
4 Victor Oladipo BW 2.50 6.00
5 Andre Drummond BW 3.00 8.00
6 Rajon Rondo BW 3.00 8.00
7 Kyle Lowry BW 2.50 6.00
8 Julius Erving BW 5.00 12.00
9 Carmelo Anthony BW 4.00 10.00
10 Brandon Knight BW 2.50 6.00
11 Kenneth Faried BW 2.50 6.00
12 Jeff Teague BW 2.50 6.00
13 LeBron James BW 12.00 30.00
14 Nikola Vucevic BW 2.50 6.00
15 Brandon Jennings BW 2.00 5.00
16 Monta Ellis BW 2.50 6.00
17 DeMar DeRozan BW 3.00 8.00
18 Shaquille O'Neal BW 6.00 15.00
19 LaMarcus Aldridge BW 3.00 8.00
20 DeMarcus Cousins BW 3.00 8.00
21 Kevin Garnett BW 5.00 12.00
22 John Wall BW 4.00 10.00
23 Kyrie Irving BW 6.00 15.00
24 Marc Gasol BW 3.00 8.00
25 Stephen Curry BW 12.00 30.00
26 Tim Duncan BW 5.00 12.00
27 Joe Johnson BW 2.50 6.00
28 Patrick Ewing BW 4.00 10.00
29 Damian Lillard BW 6.00 15.00
30 Rudy Gay BW 3.00 8.00
31 Ricky Rubio BW 3.00 8.00
32 Bradley Beal BW 3.00 8.00
33 Giannis Antetokounmpo BW 6.00 15.00
34 Vince Carter BW 4.00 10.00
35 Klay Thompson BW 4.00 10.00
36 Tony Parker BW 3.00 8.00
37 Deron Williams BW 2.50 6.00
38 Pete Maravich BW 5.00 12.00
39 Kevin Durant BW 8.00 20.00
40 Kobe Bryant BW 20.00 50.00
41 Derrick Rose BW 4.00 10.00
42 Chris Bosh BW 3.00 8.00
43 Michael Carter-Williams BW 2.00 5.00
44 Dwight Howard BW 2.50 6.00
45 Blake Griffin BW 3.00 8.00
46 Anthony Davis BW 6.00 15.00
47 Avery Bradley BW 2.50 6.00
48 Scottie Pippen BW 6.00 15.00
49 Russell Westbrook BW 8.00 20.00
50 Steve Nash BW 3.00 8.00
51 Joakim Noah BW 2.50 6.00
52 Dwyane Wade BW 5.00 12.00
53 Paul George BW 4.00 10.00
54 James Harden BW 5.00 12.00
55 Larry Bird BW 8.00 20.00
56 Chris Paul BW 4.00 10.00
57 Jared Sullinger BW 2.00 5.00
58 Jerry West BW 4.00 10.00
59 Gordon Hayward BW 3.00 8.00
60 Jeremy Lin BW 3.00 8.00
61 Jimmy Butler BW 3.00 8.00
62 Al Jefferson BW 2.50 6.00
63 Roy Hibbert BW 2.50 6.00
64 Dirk Nowitzki BW 4.00 10.00
65 Eric Bledsoe BW 2.50 6.00
66 Magic Johnson BW 8.00 20.00
67 Nerlens Noel BW 2.50 6.00
68 Chris Webber BW 3.00 8.00
69 Trey Burke BW 2.00 5.00
70 Allen Iverson BW 4.00 10.00
71 Marcus Smart BW RC 3.00 8.00
72 Bruno Caboclo BW RC 2.50 6.00
73 James Young BW RC 2.00 5.00
74 Bojan Bogdanovic BW RC 2.50 6.00
75 Doug McDermott BW RC 3.00 8.00
76 Julius Randle BW RC 5.00 12.00
77 Aaron Gordon BW RC 5.00 12.00
78 Gary Harris BW RC 3.00 8.00
79 Cleanthony Early BW RC 2.00 5.00
80 Rodney Hood BW RC 3.00 8.00
81 Glenn Robinson III BW RC 2.00 5.00
82 Nikola Mirotic BW RC 4.00 10.00
83 T.J. Warren BW RC 3.00 8.00
84 Joe Ingles BW RC 2.00 5.00
85 Nik Stauskas BW RC 2.50 6.00
86 Dante Exum BW RC 3.00 8.00
87 Shabazz Napier BW RC 2.50 6.00
88 Mitch McGary BW RC 2.00 5.00
89 K.J. McDaniels BW RC 2.50 6.00
90 Joe Harris BW RC 2.00 5.00
91 Noah Vonleh BW RC 2.50 6.00
92 Jusuf Nurkic BW RC 3.00 8.00
93 Andrew Wiggins BW RC 30.00 80.00
94 Jordan Clarkson BW RC 3.00 8.00
95 James Ennis BW RC 2.00 5.00
96 Kyle Anderson BW RC 3.00 8.00
97 Joel Embiid BW RC 10.00 25.00
98 Jabari Parker BW RC 5.00 12.00
99 Elfrid Payton BW RC 3.00 8.00
100 Zach LaVine BW RC 5.00 12.00
101 Ty Lawson CLR 2.00 5.00
102 Al Horford CLR 2.50 6.00
103 Kevin Love CLR 3.00 8.00
104 Victor Oladipo CLR 2.50 6.00
105 Andre Drummond CLR 3.00 8.00
106 Rajon Rondo CLR 3.00 8.00
107 Kyle Lowry CLR 2.50 6.00
108 Julius Erving CLR 5.00 12.00
109 Carmelo Anthony CLR 4.00 10.00
110 Brandon Knight CLR 2.50 6.00
111 Kenneth Faried CLR 2.50 6.00
112 Jeff Teague CLR 2.50 6.00
113 LeBron James CLR 20.00 50.00
114 Nikola Vucevic CLR 2.50 6.00
115 Brandon Jennings CLR 2.00 5.00
116 Monta Ellis CLR 2.50 6.00
117 DeMar DeRozan CLR 3.00 8.00
118 Shaquille O'Neal CLR 6.00 15.00
119 LaMarcus Aldridge CLR 3.00 8.00
120 DeMarcus Cousins CLR 3.00 8.00
121 Kevin Garnett CLR 5.00 12.00
122 John Wall CLR 4.00 10.00
123 Kyrie Irving CLR 6.00 15.00
124 Marc Gasol CLR 3.00 8.00
125 Stephen Curry CLR 12.00 30.00
126 Tim Duncan CLR 5.00 12.00
127 Joe Johnson CLR 2.50 6.00
128 Patrick Ewing CLR 4.00 10.00
129 Damian Lillard CLR 6.00 15.00
130 Rudy Gay CLR 3.00 8.00
131 Ricky Rubio CLR 3.00 8.00
132 Bradley Beal CLR 3.00 8.00
133 Giannis Antetokounmpo CLR 6.00 15.00
134 Vince Carter CLR 4.00 10.00
135 Klay Thompson CLR 4.00 10.00
136 Tony Parker CLR 3.00 8.00
137 Deron Williams CLR 2.50 6.00
138 Pete Maravich CLR 5.00 12.00
139 Kevin Durant CLR 8.00 20.00
140 Kobe Bryant CLR 20.00 50.00
141 Derrick Rose CLR 4.00 10.00
142 Chris Bosh CLR 3.00 8.00
143 Michael Carter-Williams CLR 2.00 5.00
144 Dwight Howard CLR 2.50 6.00
145 Blake Griffin CLR 3.00 8.00
146 Anthony Davis CLR 6.00 15.00
147 Avery Bradley CLR 2.50 6.00
148 Scottie Pippen CLR 6.00 15.00
149 Russell Westbrook CLR 8.00 20.00
150 Steve Nash CLR 3.00 8.00
151 Joakim Noah CLR 2.50 6.00
152 Dwyane Wade CLR 5.00 12.00
153 Paul George CLR 4.00 10.00
154 James Harden CLR 5.00 12.00
155 Larry Bird CLR 8.00 20.00
156 Chris Paul CLR 4.00 10.00
157 Jared Sullinger CLR 2.00 5.00
158 Jerry West CLR 4.00 10.00
159 Gordon Hayward CLR 3.00 8.00
160 Jeremy Lin CLR 3.00 8.00
161 Jimmy Butler CLR 3.00 8.00
162 Al Jefferson CLR 2.50 6.00
163 Roy Hibbert CLR 2.50 6.00
164 Dirk Nowitzki CLR 4.00 10.00
165 Eric Bledsoe CLR 2.50 6.00
166 Magic Johnson CLR 8.00 20.00
167 Nerlens Noel CLR 2.50 6.00
168 Chris Webber CLR 3.00 8.00
169 Trey Burke CLR 2.00 5.00
170 Allen Iverson CLR 4.00 10.00
171 Marcus Smart CLR RC 3.00 8.00
172 Bruno Caboclo CLR RC 2.50 6.00
173 James Young CLR RC 2.00 5.00
174 Bojan Bogdanovic CLR RC 2.50 6.00
175 Doug McDermott CLR RC 3.00 8.00
176 Julius Randle CLR RC 5.00 12.00
177 Aaron Gordon CLR RC 5.00 12.00
178 Gary Harris CLR RC 3.00 8.00
179 Cleanthony Early CLR RC 2.00 5.00
180 Rodney Hood CLR RC 3.00 8.00
181 Glenn Robinson III CLR RC 2.00 5.00
182 Nikola Mirotic CLR RC 4.00 10.00
183 T.J. Warren CLR RC 3.00 8.00
184 Joe Ingles CLR RC 2.00 5.00
185 Nik Stauskas CLR RC 2.50 6.00
186 Dante Exum CLR RC 3.00 8.00
187 Shabazz Napier CLR RC 2.50 6.00
188 Mitch McGary CLR RC 2.00 5.00
189 K.J. McDaniels CLR RC 2.50 6.00
190 Joe Harris CLR RC 2.00 5.00
191 Noah Vonleh CLR RC 2.50 6.00
192 Jusuf Nurkic CLR RC 3.00 8.00
193 Andrew Wiggins CLR RC 30.00 80.00
194 Jordan Clarkson CLR RC 3.00 8.00
195 James Ennis CLR RC 2.00 5.00
196 Kyle Anderson CLR RC 3.00 8.00
197 Joel Embiid CLR RC 10.00 25.00
198 Jabari Parker CLR RC 5.00 12.00
199 Elfrid Payton CLR RC 3.00 8.00
200 Zach LaVine CLR RC 5.00 12.00
201 McDermott BW JSY AU 15.00 40.00
202 Stauskas BW JSY AU 12.00 30.00
203 James Ennis BW JSY AU 4.00 10.00
204 A.Gordon BW JSY AU 30.00 80.00
205 Shabazz Napier BW JSY AU 5.00 12.00
206 Joel Embiid BW JSY AU 20.00 50.00
207 Spencer Dinwiddie BW JSY AU 6.00 15.00
208 K.J. McDaniels BW JSY AU 5.00 12.00
209 Elfrid Payton BW JSY AU 30.00 80.00
210 M.Smart BW JSY AU 20.00 50.00
211 Robinson BW JSY AU 10.00 25.00
212 Noah Vonleh BW JSY AU 5.00 12.00
213 James Young BW JSY AU 15.00 40.00
214 T.J. Warren BW JSY AU 10.00 25.00
215 Wiggins BW JSY AU 350.00 600.00
216 J.Randle BW JSY AU 30.00 80.00
217 Dante Exum BW JSY AU 12.00 30.00
218 Anderson BW JSY AU 12.00 30.00
219 Gary Harris BW JSY AU 6.00 15.00
221 Parker BW JSY AU 200.00 400.00
222 R.Hood BW JSY AU 12.00 30.00
223 Joe Harris BW JSY AU 4.00 10.00
224 Zach LaVine BW JSY AU 100.00 200.00
225 Caboclo BW JSY AU 5.00 12.00
226 McDermott CLR JSY AU 15.00 40.00
227 Stauskas CLR JSY AU 5.00 12.00
228 James Ennis CLR JSY AU 4.00 10.00
229 A.Gordon CLR JSY AU 30.00 80.00
230 Shabazz Napier CLR JSY AU 5.00 12.00
231 Joel Embiid CLR JSY AU 125.00 300.00
232 Spencer Dinwiddie CLR JSY AU 6.00 15.00
233 K.J. McDaniels CLR JSY AU 5.00 12.00
234 Elfrid Payton CLR JSY AU 30.00 80.00
235 M.Smart CLR JSY AU 20.00 50.00
236 Robinson CLR JSY AU 10.00 25.00
237 Noah Vonleh CLR JSY AU 5.00 12.00
238 James Young CLR JSY AU 6.00 15.00
239 T.J. Warren CLR JSY AU 10.00 25.00
240 Wiggins CLR JSY AU 200.00 400.00
241 J.Randle CLR JSY AU 30.00 80.00
242 Dante Exum CLR JSY AU 12.00 30.00
243 Anderson CLR JSY AU 12.00 30.00
244 Gary Harris CLR JSY AU 6.00 15.00
246 Parker CLR JSY AU 200.00 400.00
247 R.Hood CLR JSY AU 20.00 50.00
248 Joe Harris CLR JSY AU 4.00 10.00
249 Zach LaVine CLR JSY AU 100.00 200.00
250 Caboclo CLR JSY AU 5.00 12.00

2014-15 Panini Noir China Jerseys

RANDOM INSERTS IN PACKS
STATED PRINT RUN 99 SER.#'d SETS
PRIME JSY MAY SELL FOR PREMIUM
*PRIME/25: X TO X BASIC
CJAB Andrew Bogut 10.00 25.00
CJAI Andre Iguodala 10.00 25.00
CJCB Corey Brewer 4.00 10.00
CJDG Draymond Green 20.00 50.00
CJDL David Lee 4.00 10.00
CJDM Donatas Motiejunas 4.00 10.00
CJFE Festus Ezeli 4.00 10.00
CJHB Harrison Barnes 10.00 25.00
CJJH James Harden 25.00 60.00
CJJH Justin Holiday 6.00 15.00
CJJS Josh Smith 5.00 12.00
CJJT Jason Terry 10.00 25.00
CJKM K.J. McDaniels 5.00 12.00
CJKT Klay Thompson 20.00 50.00
CJPB Patrick Beverley 4.00 10.00
CJPP Pablo Prigioni 4.00 10.00
CJSC Stephen Curry 50.00 100.00
CJSL Shaun Livingston 10.00 25.00
CJTA Trevor Ariza 4.00 10.00
CJTJ Terrence Jones 5.00 12.00

2014-15 Panini Noir Spotlight Signatures

RANDOM INSERTS IN PACKS
STATED PRINT RUN 25 SER.#'d SETS
EXCHANGE DEADLINE 3/16/2017
1 Kobe Bryant 2000.00 2500.00
2 Kevin Durant 300.00 500.00
4 Giannis Antetokounmpo 75.00 200.00
5 Mason Plumlee 25.00 60.00
6 Zach LaVine
7 Victor Oladipo 50.00 120.00
8 Kenneth Faried 25.00 60.00
9 Anthony Davis 60.00 150.00
10 Nikola Mirotic 75.00 200.00
11 Chris Paul 200.00 300.00
12 Thaddeus Young 20.00 50.00
14 Ty Lawson 20.00 50.00
15 Russell Westbrook EXCH 200.00 400.00
16 Bradley Beal 50.00 120.00
17 Blake Griffin 150.00 300.00
19 Jusuf Nurkic 30.00 80.00
20 Gary Harris 30.00 80.00

2015-16 Panini Noir

VET PRINT RUN 99 SER.#'d SETS
RC PRINT RUN 99 SER.#'d SETS
JSY AU PRINT RUN 99 SER.#'d SETS
PATCHES MAY SELL FOR PREMIUM
EXCHANGE DEADLINE 1/20/2018
1 Kobe Bryant BW 10.00 25.00
2 Kevin Garnett BW 4.00 10.00
3 Anthony Davis BW 5.00 12.00
4 Victor Oladipo BW 2.00 5.00
5 Damian Lillard BW 5.00 12.00
6 DeMar DeRozan BW 2.50 6.00
7 John Wall BW 3.00 8.00
8 Dwyane Wade BW 4.00 10.00
9 Paul George BW 3.00 8.00
10 Stephen Curry BW 10.00 25.00
11 Will Barton BW 1.50 4.00
12 LeBron James BW 12.00 30.00
13 Derrick Rose BW 3.00 8.00
14 Al Horford BW 2.00 5.00
15 Chris Bosh BW 2.50 6.00
16 Khris Middleton BW 2.00 5.00
17 Arron Afflalo BW 1.50 4.00
18 Nikola Vucevic BW 2.00 5.00
19 C.J. McCollum BW 2.50 6.00
20 Tim Duncan BW 4.00 10.00
21 Bradley Beal BW 2.50 6.00
22 Jordan Clarkson BW 2.50 6.00
23 Monta Ellis BW 2.00 5.00
24 Klay Thompson BW 3.00 8.00
25 Danilo Gallinari BW 2.00 5.00
26 Kyrie Irving BW 5.00 12.00
27 Kemba Walker BW 2.50 6.00
28 Jeff Teague BW 2.00 5.00
29 Mike Conley BW 2.50 6.00
30 Jabari Parker BW 3.00 8.00
31 Norris Cole BW 1.50 4.00
32 Russell Westbrook BW 6.00 15.00
33 T.J. Warren BW 2.00 5.00
34 Kawhi Leonard BW 4.00 10.00
35 Gordon Hayward BW 2.50 6.00
36 DeAndre Jordan BW 2.50 6.00
37 Terrence Jones BW 2.00 5.00
38 Draymond Green BW 3.00 8.00
39 Deron Williams BW 2.00 5.00
40 Kevin Love BW 2.50 6.00
41 Jeremy Lin BW 2.50 6.00
42 Kent Bazemore BW 2.00 5.00
43 Marc Gasol BW 2.50 6.00
44 Giannis Antetokounmpo BW 5.00 12.00
45 Zach LaVine BW 2.50 6.00
46 Kevin Durant BW 6.00 15.00
47 Brandon Knight BW 2.00 5.00
48 Rajon Rondo BW 2.50 6.00
49 Alec Burks BW 1.50 4.00
50 Chris Paul BW 3.00 8.00
51 James Harden BW 4.00 10.00
52 Reggie Jackson BW 2.00 5.00
53 J.J. Barea BW 2.00 5.00
54 Pau Gasol BW 2.50 6.00
55 Thaddeus Young BW 1.50 4.00
56 Isaiah Thomas BW 2.50 6.00
57 Lou Williams BW 2.00 5.00
58 Goran Dragic BW 2.00 5.00
59 Andrew Wiggins BW 4.00 10.00
60 Carmelo Anthony BW 3.00 8.00
61 Nerlens Noel BW 2.00 5.00
62 DeMarcus Cousins BW 2.50 6.00
63 Kyle Lowry BW 2.00 5.00
64 Blake Griffin BW 2.50 6.00
65 Dwight Howard BW 2.00 5.00
66 Andre Drummond BW 2.50 6.00
67 Dirk Nowitzki BW 3.00 8.00
68 Jimmy Butler BW 2.50 6.00
69 Brook Lopez BW 2.00 5.00
70 Jae Crowder BW 1.50 4.00
71 Karl-Anthony Towns BW RC 25.00 60.00
72 D'Angelo Russell BW RC 10.00 25.00
73 Jahlil Okafor BW RC 5.00 12.00
74 Emmanuel Mudiay BW RC 4.00 10.00
75 Kristaps Porzingis BW RC 10.00 25.00
76 Mario Hezonja BW RC 3.00 8.00
77 Justise Winslow BW RC 4.00 10.00
78 Willie Cauley-Stein BW RC 4.00 10.00
79 Stanley Johnson BW RC 3.00 8.00
80 Frank Kaminsky BW RC 4.00 10.00
81 Devin Booker BW RC 12.00 30.00
82 Myles Turner BW RC 4.00 10.00
83 Jerian Grant BW RC 2.50 6.00
84 Marcelo Huertas BW RC 3.00 8.00
85 Cameron Payne BW RC 3.00 8.00
86 Delon Wright BW RC 3.00 8.00
87 Sam Dekker BW RC 3.00 8.00
88 Boban Marjanovic BW RC 3.00 8.00
89 Terry Rozier BW RC 3.00 8.00
90 Bobby Portis BW RC 4.00 10.00
91 Jonathon Simmons BW RC 4.00 10.00
92 Rondae Hollis-Jefferson BW RC 3.00 8.00
93 Raul Neto BW RC 2.50 6.00
94 R.J. Hunter BW RC 2.50 6.00
95 Nikola Jokic BW RC 10.00 25.00
96 Nemanja Bjelica BW RC 3.00 8.00
97 Norman Powell BW RC 3.00 8.00
98 Larry Nance Jr. BW RC 4.00 10.00
99 Montrezl Harrell BW RC 3.00 8.00
100 Rashad Vaughn BW RC 2.50 6.00
101 Kobe Bryant CLR 10.00 25.00
102 Kevin Garnett CLR 4.00 10.00
103 Anthony Davis CLR 5.00 12.00
104 Victor Oladipo CLR 2.00 5.00
105 Damian Lillard CLR 5.00 12.00
106 DeMar DeRozan CLR 2.50 6.00
107 John Wall CLR 3.00 8.00
108 Dwyane Wade CLR 4.00 10.00
109 Paul George CLR 3.00 8.00
110 Stephen Curry CLR 10.00 25.00
111 Will Barton CLR 1.50 4.00
112 LeBron James CLR 12.00 30.00
113 Derrick Rose CLR 3.00 8.00
114 Al Horford CLR 2.00 5.00
115 Chris Bosh CLR 2.50 6.00
116 Khris Middleton CLR 2.00 5.00
117 Arron Afflalo CLR 1.50 4.00
118 Nikola Vucevic CLR 2.00 5.00
119 C.J. McCollum CLR 2.50 6.00
120 Tim Duncan CLR 4.00 10.00
121 Bradley Beal CLR 2.50 6.00
122 Jordan Clarkson CLR 2.50 6.00
123 Monta Ellis CLR 2.00 5.00
124 Klay Thompson CLR 3.00 8.00
125 Danilo Gallinari CLR 2.00 5.00
126 Kyrie Irving CLR 5.00 12.00
127 Kemba Walker CLR 2.50 6.00
128 Jeff Teague CLR 2.00 5.00
129 Mike Conley CLR 2.50 6.00
130 Jabari Parker CLR 3.00 8.00
131 Norris Cole CLR 1.50 4.00
132 Russell Westbrook CLR 6.00 15.00
133 T.J. Warren CLR 2.00 5.00
134 Kawhi Leonard CLR 4.00 10.00
135 Gordon Hayward CLR 2.50 6.00
136 DeAndre Jordan CLR 2.50 6.00
137 Terrence Jones CLR 2.00 5.00
138 Draymond Green CLR 3.00 8.00
139 Deron Williams CLR 2.00 5.00
140 Kevin Love CLR 2.50 6.00
141 Jeremy Lin CLR 2.50 6.00
142 Kent Bazemore CLR 2.00 5.00
143 Marc Gasol CLR 2.50 6.00
144 Giannis Antetokounmpo CLR 5.00 12.00
145 Zach LaVine CLR 2.50 6.00
146 Kevin Durant CLR 6.00 15.00
147 Brandon Knight CLR 2.00 5.00
148 Rajon Rondo CLR 2.50 6.00
149 Alec Burks CLR 1.50 4.00
150 Chris Paul CLR 3.00 8.00
151 James Harden CLR 4.00 10.00
152 Reggie Jackson CLR 2.00 5.00
153 J.J. Barea CLR 2.00 5.00
154 Pau Gasol CLR 2.50 6.00
155 Thaddeus Young CLR 1.50 4.00
156 Isaiah Thomas CLR 2.50 6.00
157 Lou Williams CLR 2.00 5.00
158 Goran Dragic CLR 2.00 5.00
159 Andrew Wiggins CLR 4.00 10.00
160 Carmelo Anthony CLR 3.00 8.00
161 Nerlens Noel CLR 2.00 5.00
162 DeMarcus Cousins CLR 2.50 6.00
163 Kyle Lowry CLR 2.00 5.00
164 Blake Griffin CLR 2.50 6.00
165 Dwight Howard CLR 2.00 5.00
166 Andre Drummond CLR 2.50 6.00
167 Dirk Nowitzki CLR 3.00 8.00
168 Jimmy Butler CLR 2.50 6.00
169 Brook Lopez CLR 2.00 5.00
170 Jae Crowder CLR 1.50 4.00
171 Karl-Anthony Towns CLR RC 25.00 60.00
172 D'Angelo Russell CLR RC 10.00 25.00
173 Jahlil Okafor CLR RC 5.00 12.00
174 Emmanuel Mudiay CLR RC 4.00 10.00
175 Kristaps Porzingis CLR RC 10.00 25.00
176 Mario Hezonja CLR RC 3.00 8.00
177 Justise Winslow CLR RC 4.00 10.00
178 Willie Cauley-Stein CLR RC 4.00 10.00
179 Stanley Johnson CLR RC 3.00 8.00
180 Frank Kaminsky CLR RC 4.00 10.00
181 Devin Booker CLR RC 12.00 30.00
182 Myles Turner CLR RC 4.00 10.00
183 Jerian Grant CLR RC 2.50 6.00
184 Marcelo Huertas CLR RC 3.00 8.00
185 Cameron Payne CLR RC 3.00 8.00
186 Delon Wright CLR RC 3.00 8.00
187 Sam Dekker CLR RC 3.00 8.00
188 Boban Marjanovic CLR RC 3.00 8.00
189 Terry Rozier CLR RC 3.00 8.00
190 Bobby Portis CLR RC 4.00 10.00
191 Jonathon Simmons CLR RC 4.00 10.00
192 Rondae Hollis-Jefferson CLR RC 3.00 8.00
193 Raul Neto CLR RC 2.50 6.00
194 R.J. Hunter CLR RC 2.50 6.00
195 Nikola Jokic CLR RC 10.00 25.00
196 Nemanja Bjelica CLR RC 3.00 8.00
197 Norman Powell CLR RC 3.00 8.00
198 Larry Nance Jr. CLR RC 4.00 10.00
199 Montrezl Harrell CLR RC 3.00 8.00
200 Rashad Vaughn CLR RC 2.50 6.00
201 Towns BW JSY AU 300.00 600.00
202 Russell BW JSY AU 125.00 250.00
203 Okafor BW JSY AU 40.00 100.00
204 Mdy BW JSY AU EXCH 40.00 100.00
205 Porzingis BW JSY AU 200.00 400.00
206 Hezonja BW JSY AU 25.00 60.00
207 Winslow BW JSY AU 30.00 80.00
208 Cly-Stn BW JSY AU 30.00 80.00
209 S.Johnson BW JSY AU 30.00 80.00
210 Kaminsky BW JSY AU 12.00 30.00
211 Booker BW JSY AU 200.00 400.00
212 Turner BW JSY AU 30.00 80.00
213 Jerian Grant BW JSY AU 6.00 15.00
214 Marcelo Huertas BW JSY AU 8.00 20.00
215 Cameron Payne BW JSY AU 10.00 25.00
216 Delon Wright BW JSY AU 10.00 25.00
217 Jarell Martin BW JSY AU 8.00 20.00
218 Cristiano Felicio BW JSY AU 8.00 20.00
219 Rozier BW JSY AU 15.00 40.00
220 Rondae Hollis-Jefferson BW JSY AU 8.00 20.00
221 Portis BW JSY AU 30.00 80.00
222 Cliff Alexander BW JSY AU 6.00 15.00
223 Raul Neto BW JSY AU 6.00 15.00
224 R.J. Hunter BW JSY AU 6.00 15.00
225 Jokic BW JSY AU 100.00 250.00
226 Bjelica BW JSY AU 12.00 30.00
227 Powell BW JSY AU 20.00 50.00
228 Richardson BW JSY AU 30.00 80.00
229 Luis Montero BW JSY AU 6.00 15.00
230 Joe Young BW JSY AU 10.00 25.00
231 Towns CLR JSY AU 300.00 600.00
232 Russell CLR JSY AU 50.00 120.00
233 Okafor CLR JSY AU 40.00 100.00
234 Mdy CLR JSY AU EXCH 40.00 100.00
235 Porzingis CLR JSY AU 200.00 400.00
236 Hezonja CLR JSY AU 25.00 60.00
237 Winslow CLR JSY AU 30.00 80.00
238 Cly-Stn CLR JSY AU 30.00 80.00
239 S.Johnson CLR JSY AU 30.00 80.00
240 Kaminsky CLR JSY AU 12.00 30.00
241 Booker CLR JSY AU 200.00 400.00
242 Turner CLR JSY AU 30.00 80.00
243 Jerian Grant CLR JSY AU 6.00 15.00
244 Marcelo Huertas CLR JSY AU 8.00 20.00
245 Cameron Payne CLR JSY AU 10.00 25.00
246 Delon Wright CLR JSY AU 10.00 25.00
247 Jarell Martin CLR JSY AU 8.00 20.00
248 Cristiano Felicio CLR JSY AU 8.00 20.00
249 Rozier CLR JSY AU 15.00 40.00
250 Rondae Hollis-Jefferson CLR JSY AU 8.00 20.00
251 Portis CLR JSY AU 30.00 80.00
252 Cliff Alexander CLR JSY AU 6.00 15.00
253 Raul Neto CLR JSY AU 6.00 15.00
254 R.J. Hunter CLR JSY AU 6.00 15.00
255 Jokic CLR JSY AU 100.00 250.00
256 Bjelica CLR JSY AU 12.00 30.00
257 Powell CLR JSY AU 20.00 50.00
258 Richardson CLR JSY AU 30.00 80.00
259 Luis Montero CLR JSY AU 6.00 15.00
260 Joe Young CLR JSY AU 10.00 25.00

2015-16 Panini Noir Acetate Materials Prime

RANDOM INSERTS IN PACKS
PRINT RUNS B/WN 10-49 COPIES PER
NO PRICING ON QTY 10
ANAB Avery Bradley/49 5.00 12.00
ANAF Arron Afflalo/49 4.00 10.00
ANAH Al Horford/49 5.00 12.00
ANAJ Al Jefferson/49 5.00 12.00
ANAX Alex Len/25 4.00 10.00
ANBB Bojan Bogdanovic/49 4.00 10.00
ANBP Bobby Portis/49 6.00 15.00
ANCP Cameron Payne/49 5.00 12.00
ANDB Devin Booker/25 25.00 60.00
ANDC DeMarcus Cousins/49 6.00 15.00
ANDG Draymond Green/49 8.00 20.00
ANDJ DeAndre Jordan/25 6.00 15.00
ANDR D'Angelo Russell/49 15.00 40.00
ANDW Delon Wright/49 5.00 12.00
ANEF Evan Fournier/49 5.00 12.00
ANEG Eric Gordon/49 5.00 12.00
ANEM Emmanuel Mudiay/49 6.00 15.00
ANET Evan Turner/25 5.00 12.00
ANFK Frank Kaminsky/49 6.00 15.00
ANGH Grant Hill/49 8.00 20.00
ANGN Gary Neal/49 5.00 12.00
ANHO Hakeem Olajuwon/49 8.00 20.00
ANIT Isaiah Thomas/49 6.00 15.00
ANJA Justin Anderson/49 12.00 30.00
ANJB Jerryd Bayless/49 5.00 12.00
ANJB Jimmy Butler/49 10.00 25.00
ANJC Jae Crowder/49 4.00 10.00
ANJG Jerian Grant/25 4.00 10.00
ANJJ John Jenkins/49 4.00 10.00
ANJJ Joe Johnson/49 5.00 12.00
ANJN Joakim Noah/49 5.00 12.00
ANJO John Stockton/49 10.00 25.00
ANJO Jahlil Okafor/49 6.00 15.00
ANJR Josh Richardson/49 6.00 15.00
ANJS J.R. Smith/49 5.00 12.00
ANJS Jonathon Simmons/49 6.00 15.00
ANJS Jared Sullinger/49 4.00 10.00
ANJW John Wall/49 8.00 20.00
ANJW Justise Winslow/49 6.00 15.00
ANKB Kobe Bryant/49 25.00 60.00
ANKD Kevin Durant/49 12.00 30.00
ANKK Kosta Koufos/49 4.00 10.00
ANKL Kevin Love/25 6.00 15.00
ANKM Karl Malone/49 8.00 20.00
ANKM Khris Middleton/49 5.00 12.00
ANKO Kelly Oubre Jr./49 5.00 12.00
ANKP Kristaps Porzingis/49 15.00 40.00
ANKT Klay Thompson/49 8.00 20.00
ANKT Karl-Anthony Towns/25 30.00 80.00
ANKW Kemba Walker/49 6.00 15.00
ANLB Larry Bird/25
ANLG Langston Galloway/49 4.00 10.00
ANLJ LeBron James/49 25.00 60.00
ANLJ Larry Johnson/25 8.00 20.00
ANLM Luis Montero/49 4.00 10.00
ANLS Lance Stephenson/49 5.00 12.00
ANMG Manu Ginobili/49 6.00 15.00
ANMG Marcin Gortat/49 5.00 12.00
ANMH Mario Hezonja/49 5.00 12.00
ANMS Marcus Smart/49 5.00 12.00
ANMT Myles Turner/49 6.00 15.00
ANNB Nemanja Bjelica/25 5.00 12.00
ANNJ Nikola Jokic/49 12.00 30.00
ANNN Nerlens Noel/25 5.00 12.00
ANNP Norman Powell/49 5.00 12.00
ANNV Nikola Vucevic/49 5.00 12.00
ANOP Otto Porter/49 5.00 12.00
ANPE Patrick Ewing/49
ANPM Paul Millsap/49 6.00 15.00
ANRC Rakeem Christmas/49 4.00 10.00
ANRG Rudy Gay/49 6.00 15.00
ANRG Rudy Gobert/49 6.00 15.00
ANRH Roy Hibbert/49 5.00 12.00
ANRH R.J. Hunter/49 4.00 10.00
ANRH Richaun Holmes/49 5.00 12.00
ANRH Rodney Hood/49 5.00 12.00
ANRJ Rondae Hollis-Jefferson/49 5.00 12.00
ANRL Robin Lopez/49 4.00 10.00
ANRN Raul Neto/49 4.00 10.00
ANRR Ricky Rubio/25 6.00 15.00
ANRW Russell Westbrook/49 15.00 40.00
ANSC Stephen Curry/49 25.00 60.00
ANSD Sam Dekker/25 5.00 12.00
ANSI Serge Ibaka/49 5.00 12.00
ANSJ Stanley Johnson/25 5.00 12.00
ANSL Shane Larkin/49 4.00 10.00
ANSM Salah Mejri/49 4.00 10.00
ANSO Shaquille O'Neal/49 10.00 25.00
ANSP Scottie Pippen/49 15.00 40.00
ANTD Tim Duncan/49 10.00 25.00
ANTH Tobias Harris/49 5.00 12.00
ANTL Trey Lyles/49 6.00 15.00
ANTM Timofey Mozgov/49 4.00 10.00
ANTP Tony Parker/49 6.00 15.00
ANTR Terry Rozier/49 5.00 12.00
ANTY Thaddeus Young/49 4.00 10.00
ANWCS Willie Cauley-Stein/49 6.00 15.00

2015-16 Panini Noir Autograph Materials Prime Black and White

RANDOM INSERTS IN PACKS
PRINT RUNS B/WN 10-75 COPIES PER
NO PRICING ON QTY 10
EXCHANGE DEADLINE 1/20/2018
ABAGD Aaron Gordon/49 20.00 50.00
ABAGW Archie Goodwin/39 6.00 15.00
ABAWG Andrew Wiggins/25
ABBBY Brent Barry/49 6.00 15.00
ABBDT Brad Daugherty/75 8.00 20.00
ABBJB Bojan Bogdanovic/75 6.00 15.00
ABCBO Chris Bosh/25 15.00 40.00
ABCDX Clyde Drexler/25 30.00 80.00
ABCLN Christian Laettner/39 12.00 30.00
ABCMC C.J. McCollum/49 12.00 30.00
ABDMD Doug McDermott/75 8.00 20.00
ABDMG Danny Manning/49 8.00 20.00
ABDRD Dennis Rodman/25 75.00 200.00
ABGHL Grant Hill/49 25.00 60.00
ABGPT Gary Payton/25 25.00 60.00
ABHOW Hakeem Olajuwon/25 40.00 100.00
ABJCD Jose Calderon/25 6.00 15.00
ABJKD Jason Kidd/25 25.00 60.00
ABJVC Jonas Valanciunas/75 8.00 20.00
ABJWL John Wall/25 25.00 60.00
ABKMH Kevin McHale/25 20.00 50.00
ABKOL Kelly Olynyk/75 6.00 15.00
ABMHL Maurice Harkless/75 6.00 15.00
ABMST Marcus Smart/49 8.00 20.00
ABMWL Mo Williams/75 8.00 20.00
ABRAL Ray Allen/25 50.00 120.00
ABRAS Rafer Alston/45 8.00 20.00
ABRRB Ricky Rubio/25 20.00 50.00

2015-16 Panini Noir Autograph Materials Prime Color

RANDOM INSERTS IN PACKS
PRINT RUNS B/WN 5-75 COPIES PER
NO PRICING ON QTY 10 OR LESS
EXCHANGE DEADLINE 1/20/2018
70 Archie Goodwin/39 6.00 15.00
ACAGD Aaron Gordon/49 8.00 20.00
ACAWG Andrew Wiggins/25
ACBBY Brent Barry/49 6.00 15.00
ACBDT Brad Daugherty/75 8.00 20.00
ACBJB Bojan Bogdanovic/75 6.00 15.00
ACCBO Chris Bosh/25 15.00 40.00
ACCDX Clyde Drexler/25 30.00 80.00
ACCLN Christian Laettner/49 12.00 30.00
ACCMC C.J. McCollum/49 12.00 30.00
ACDMD Doug McDermott/75 8.00 20.00
ACDMG Danny Manning/49 8.00 20.00
ACDRD Dennis Rodman/25 75.00 200.00
ACGHL Grant Hill/49 25.00 60.00
ACGPY Gary Payton/25 25.00 60.00
ACHOW Hakeem Olajuwon/25 40.00 100.00
ACJCD Jose Calderon/25 6.00 15.00
ACJKD Jason Kidd/25 25.00 60.00
ACJVC Jonas Valanciunas/75 8.00 20.00
ACJWL John Wall/25 25.00 60.00
ACKMH Kevin McHale/25 20.00 50.00
ACKOL Kelly Olynyk/75 6.00 15.00
ACMHL Maurice Harkless/75 6.00 15.00
ACMST Marcus Smart/49 8.00 20.00
ACMWL Mo Williams/75 8.00 20.00
ACRAL Ray Allen/25 50.00 120.00
ACRAT Rafer Alston/45 8.00 20.00
ACRRB Ricky Rubio/25 20.00 50.00

2015-16 Panini Noir Autographs Black and White

RANDOM INSERTS IN PACKS
PRINT RUNS B/WN 35-60 COPIES PER
EXCHANGE DEADLINE 1/20/2018
*BRONZE/25: .4X TO1X p/r 35
*BRONZE/25: .5X TO1.2X p/r 49-60
NBACG A.C. Green/49 5.00 12.00
NBADR Andre Drummond/49 8.00 20.00
NBADV Anthony Davis/35 30.00 80.00
NBAHF Al Horford/49 4.00 10.00
NBAMG Alonzo Mourning/49 12.00 30.00
NBBGF Blake Griffin/35 20.00 50.00
NBBMA Bob McAdoo/49 4.00 10.00
NBBMJ Boban Marjanovic/60 4.00 10.00
NBBPR Bobby Portis/60 5.00 12.00
NBBWT Bill Walton/49 5.00 12.00
NBCAN Carmelo Anthony/35 25.00 60.00
NBCDX Clyde Drexler/49 10.00 25.00
NBCMB Cuttino Mobley/49 3.00 8.00
NBCPL Chris Paul/35 20.00 50.00
NBCPN Cameron Payne/60 EXCH 4.00 10.00
NBDAR D'Angelo Russell/60 25.00 60.00
NBDBK Devin Booker/60 40.00 100.00
NBDCR DeMarre Carroll 3.00 8.00
NBDGR Danny Green/49 4.00 10.00
NBDHW Dwight Howard/35 10.00 25.00
NBDMD Doug McDermott/49 4.00 10.00
NBDMG Danny Manning/49 4.00 10.00
NBDMJ Dan Majerle/49 4.00 10.00
NBDSD Dennis Schroder/49 8.00 20.00
NBDWD Dwyane Wade/35 20.00 50.00
NBEHS Elvin Hayes/49 5.00 12.00
NBEPT Elfrid Payton/49 4.00 10.00
NBFKA Frank Kaminsky/60 8.00 20.00
NBGAN G. Antetokounmpo/49 50.00 120.00
NBGGR Gail Goodrich/49 4.00 10.00
NBGHW Gordon Hayward/49 5.00 12.00
NBHHK Hersey Hawkins/49 3.00 8.00
NBHOW Hakeem Olajuwon/49 12.00 30.00
NBITM Isaiah Thomas/49 20.00 50.00
NBJDM Joe Dumars/49 5.00 12.00
NBJEV Julius Erving/35 25.00 60.00
NBJGR Jeff Green/49 4.00 10.00
NBJHD Jrue Holiday/49 4.00 10.00
NBJOK Jahlil Okafor/60 10.00 25.00
NBJPK Jabari Parker/49 EXCH 12.00 30.00
NBJRD Julius Randle/49 8.00 20.00
NBJSG Jared Sullinger/49 3.00 8.00
NBJSK John Starks/49 4.00 10.00
NBJWL John Wall/49 15.00 40.00
NBJWS Jerry West/35 20.00 50.00
NBKAT Karl-Anthony Towns/60 75.00 200.00
NBKBR Kobe Bryant/35 100.00 250.00
NBKDR Kevin Durant/35 50.00 120.00
NBKIV Kyrie Irving/35 30.00 80.00
NBKMH Kevin McHale/49 8.00 20.00
NBKML Karl Malone/35 20.00 50.00
NBKPZ Kristaps Porzingis/60 50.00 120.00
NBKTP Klay Thompson/49
NBLNJ Larry Nance Jr./49 5.00 12.00
NBMGT Marcin Gortat/49 4.00 10.00
NBMHT Marcelo Huertas/49 4.00 10.00
NBMJN Magic Johnson/35 30.00 80.00
NBMRM Mitch Richmond/49 5.00 12.00
NBMST Marcus Smart/49 4.00 10.00
NBMTU Myles Turner/60 10.00 25.00
NBNAB Nate Archibald/49 4.00 10.00
NBNBJ Nemanja Bjelica/49 4.00 10.00
NBNJK Nikola Jokic/49 30.00 80.00
NBNMT Nikola Mirotic/49 4.00 10.00
NBNPW Norman Powell/49 4.00 10.00
NBPGR Paul George/35 EXCH 30.00 80.00
NBRNT Raul Neto/49 3.00 8.00
NBRPS Robert Parish/49 5.00 12.00
NBRSP Ralph Sampson/49 4.00 10.00
NBSON Shaquille O'Neal/35 40.00 100.00
NBTHW Tim Hardaway Jr./49 3.00 8.00
NBTJW T.J. Warren/49 4.00 10.00
NBVOD Victor Oladipo/49 4.00 10.00
NBWMT Wesley Matthews/49 3.00 8.00
NBWTV Walter Tavares/49 3.00 8.00
NBZLV Zach LaVine/49 20.00 50.00

2015-16 Panini Noir Autographs Color

RANDOM INSERTS IN PACKS
PRINT RUNS B/WN 35-60 COPIES PER
EXCHANGE DEADLINE 1/20/2018
*BRONZE/25: .4X TO1X p/r 25
*BRONZE/25: .5X TO1.2X p/r 49-60
NCACG A.C. Green/49 5.00 12.00
NCADR Andre Drummond/49 8.00 20.00
NCADV Anthony Davis/25 30.00 80.00
NCAHF Al Horford/49 4.00 10.00
NCAMG Alonzo Mourning/49 12.00 30.00
NCBGF Blake Griffin/25 20.00 50.00
NCBMA Bob McAdoo/49 4.00 10.00
NCBMJ Boban Marjanovic/60 4.00 10.00
NCBPR Bobby Portis/60 5.00 12.00
NCBWT Bill Walton/49 5.00 12.00
NCCAN Carmelo Anthony/25 25.00 60.00
NCCDX Clyde Drexler/49 10.00 25.00
NCCMB Cuttino Mobley/49 3.00 8.00
NCCPL Chris Paul/25 20.00 50.00
NCCPN Cameron Payne/60 EXCH 4.00 10.00
NCDAR D'Angelo Russell/60 25.00 60.00
NCDBK Devin Booker/60 40.00 100.00
NCDCD Doug McDermott/49 4.00 10.00
NCDCR DeMarre Carroll/49 3.00 8.00
NCDGR Danny Green/49 4.00 10.00
NCDHW Dwight Howard/25 10.00 25.00
NCDMG Danny Manning/49 4.00 10.00
NCDMJ Dan Majerle/49 4.00 10.00
NCDSD Dennis Schroder/49 8.00 20.00
NCDWD Dwyane Wade/25 20.00 50.00
NCEHS Elvin Hayes/49 5.00 12.00
NCEPT Elfrid Payton/49 4.00 10.00
NCFKM Frank Kaminsky/60 8.00 20.00
NCGAN G. Antetokounmpo/49 50.00 120.00
NCGGR Gail Goodrich/49 4.00 10.00
NCGHW Gordon Hayward/49 5.00 12.00
NCHHK Hersey Hawkins/49 3.00 8.00
NCHOW Hakeem Olajuwon/49 12.00 30.00
NCITM Isaiah Thomas/49 20.00 50.00
NCJDM Joe Dumars/49 5.00 12.00
NCJEV Julius Erving/25 25.00 60.00
NCJGR Jeff Green/49 4.00 10.00
NCJHD Jrue Holiday/49 4.00 10.00
NCJOK Jahlil Okafor/60 10.00 25.00
NCJPK Jabari Parker/49 EXCH 12.00 30.00
NCJRD Julius Randle/49 8.00 20.00
NCJSG Jared Sullinger/49 3.00 8.00
NCJSK John Starks/49 4.00 10.00
NCJWL John Wall/49 15.00 40.00
NCJWS Jerry West/25 20.00 50.00
NCKAT Karl-Anthony Towns/60 75.00 200.00
NCKBR Kobe Bryant/25 100.00 250.00
NCKDR Kevin Durant/25 50.00 120.00
NCKIR Kyrie Irving/25 30.00 80.00
NCKMH Kevin McHale/49 8.00 20.00
NCKML Karl Malone/25 20.00 50.00
NCKPZ Kristaps Porzingis/60 50.00 120.00
NCKTM Klay Thompson/49
NCLNJ Larry Nance Jr./49 5.00 12.00
NCMGT Marcin Gortat/49 4.00 10.00
NCMHT Marcelo Huertas/49 4.00 10.00
NCMJS Magic Johnson/25 30.00 80.00
NCMRM Mitch Richmond/49 5.00 12.00
NCMST Marcus Smart/49 4.00 10.00
NCMTU Myles Turner/60 10.00 25.00
NCNAB Nate Archibald/49 4.00 10.00
NCNBJ Nemanja Bjelica/49 4.00 10.00
NCNJK Nikola Jokic/49 30.00 80.00
NCNMT Nikola Mirotic/49 4.00 10.00
NCNPW Norman Powell/49 4.00 10.00
NCPGG Paul George/25 EXCH 30.00 80.00
NCRNT Raul Neto/49 3.00 8.00
NCRPS Robert Parish/49 5.00 12.00
NCRSP Ralph Sampson/49 4.00 10.00
NCSON Shaquille O'Neal/25 40.00 100.00
NCTHJ Tim Hardaway Jr./49 3.00 8.00
NCTJW T.J. Warren/49 4.00 10.00
NCVOD Victor Oladipo/49 4.00 10.00
NCWMW Wesley Matthews/49 3.00 8.00
NCWTV Walter Tavares/49 3.00 8.00
NCWUN Wes Unseld/49 8.00 20.00
NCZLV Zach LaVine/49 20.00 50.00

2015-16 Panini Noir Jumbo Materials Prime

RANDOM INSERTS IN PACKS
PRINT RUNS B/WN 10-49 COPIES PER
NO PRICING ON QTY 10
2 Kobe Bryant/25 60.00 150.00
3 Russell Westbrook/49 20.00 50.00
4 Klay Thompson/25 15.00 40.00
6 Jae Crowder/49 4.00 10.00
7 Khris Middleton/49 5.00 12.00
8 LeBron James/25 60.00 150.00
10 Arron Afflalo/49 4.00 10.00
11 Jared Sullinger/25 4.00 10.00
12 Timofey Mozgov/25 4.00 10.00
13 Rodney Hood/49 5.00 12.00
14 Stephen Curry/25 60.00 150.00
15 Robin Lopez/49 4.00 10.00
16 Al Horford/49 5.00 12.00
17 Rudy Gobert/49 8.00 20.00
18 Kemba Walker/49 6.00 15.00
19 Langston Galloway/49 4.00 10.00
20 Paul Millsap/25 6.00 15.00
21 Roy Hibbert/49 5.00 12.00
22 Lance Stephenson/25 5.00 12.00
23 John Jenkins/20 4.00 10.00
24 Kosta Koufos/45 4.00 10.00
25 Thaddeus Young/49 4.00 10.00
27 Draymond Green/25 15.00 40.00
28 Rudy Gay/25 6.00 15.00
29 Shane Larkin/49 4.00 10.00
30 Tim Duncan/49 20.00 50.00
31 Evan Fournier/49 10.00 25.00
32 Serge Ibaka/49 5.00 12.00
34 DeMarcus Cousins/49 6.00 15.00
35 Nikola Vucevic/25 5.00 12.00
37 Tony Parker/49 6.00 15.00
38 Tobias Harris/49 5.00 12.00
39 Manu Ginobili/49 6.00 15.00

41 Kevin Durant/49 12.00 30.00
42 Avery Bradley/49 5.00 12.00
43 John Wall/25 12.00 30.00
46 Marcin Gortat/49 5.00 12.00
47 Eric Gordon/49 5.00 12.00
48 Marcus Smart/49 5.00 12.00
49 Jerryd Bayless/45 5.00 12.00
51 Bojan Bogdanovic/49 4.00 10.00
52 Isaiah Thomas/20 10.00 25.00
53 Otto Porter/49 5.00 12.00
55 Joe Johnson/49 5.00 12.00
58 Grant Hill/49 15.00 40.00
59 John Stockton/25 20.00 50.00
60 Shaquille O'Neal/49 20.00 50.00
62 Patrick Ewing/49 12.00 30.00
63 Karl Malone/25 12.00 30.00
65 Scottie Pippen/25 30.00 80.00

2015-16 Panini Noir Rookie Patches Prime

RANDOM INSERTS IN PACKS
PRINT RUNS B/WN 8-25 COPIES PER
NO PRICING ON QTY 10 OR LESS
2 Justise Winslow/25 6.00 15.00
3 Bobby Portis/25 6.00 15.00
4 Rondae Hollis-Jefferson/25 5.00 12.00
5 D'Angelo Russell/25 15.00 40.00
6 Willie Cauley-Stein/25 6.00 15.00
8 Cliff Alexander/25 4.00 10.00
9 Terry Rozier/25 5.00 12.00
12 Raul Neto/25 4.00 10.00
13 Cristiano Felicio/25 5.00 12.00
16 R.J. Hunter/25 4.00 10.00
19 Myles Turner/25 6.00 15.00
21 Delon Wright/25 5.00 12.00
22 Mario Hezonja/25 5.00 12.00
23 Jerian Grant/25 4.00 10.00
25 Cameron Payne/25 5.00 12.00
26 Kelly Oubre Jr./25 5.00 12.00
28 Josh Richardson/25 6.00 15.00
29 Luis Montero/25 4.00 10.00
30 Rakeem Christmas/25 4.00 10.00
31 Trey Lyles/25 6.00 15.00
32 Justin Anderson/25 12.00 30.00
33 Salah Mejri/25 4.00 10.00
34 Jonathon Simmons/25 6.00 15.00
35 Richaun Holmes/25 5.00 12.00

2015-16 Panini Noir Spotlight Signatures

RANDOM INSERTS IN PACKS
PRINT RUNS B/WN 25-99 COPIES PER
EXCHANGE DEADLINE 1/20/2018
SS Kenneth Faried/49 10.00 25.00
SSAW Andrew Wiggins/49 125.00 250.00
SSCP Chris Paul/49 100.00 250.00
SSDB Devin Booker/49 250.00 400.00
SSDG Danilo Gallinari/49 10.00 25.00
SSEB Eric Bledsoe/49 15.00 40.00
SSEM Mudiay/49 EXCH 75.00 200.00
SSEP Elfrid Payton/49 25.00 60.00
SSGA Giannis/99 EXCH 200.00 400.00
SSGH Gary Harris/99 15.00 40.00
SSHB Harrison Barnes/25 100.00 200.00
SSKI Kyrie Irving/49 200.00 400.00
SSKL Kevin Love/49 25.00 60.00
SSKT Karl-Anthony Towns/49 600.00 900.00
SSTH Tobias Harris/99 10.00 25.00
SSZL Zach LaVine/99 150.00 250.00

2016-17 Panini Noir

1-200 PRINT RUN 79 SER.#'d SETS
RC PRINT RUN 79 SER.#'d SETS
JSY AU PRINT RUN 99 SER.#'d SETS
PATCHES MAY SELL FOR PREMIUM
231-330 PRINT RUN 25 SER.#'d SETS
EXCHANGE DEADLINE 2/19/2019
1 Kevin Durant BW 6.00 15.00
2 Anthony Davis BW 5.00 12.00
3 Chris Paul BW 3.00 8.00
4 Gordon Hayward BW 2.50 6.00
5 C.J. McCollum BW 2.00 5.00
6 Jimmy Butler BW 2.50 6.00
7 Aaron Gordon BW 2.00 5.00
8 Paul George BW 3.00 8.00
9 Brook Lopez BW 2.00 5.00
10 Carmelo Anthony BW 3.00 8.00
11 Zach LaVine BW 2.50 6.00
12 Andre Drummond BW 2.50 6.00
13 Joel Embiid BW 4.00 10.00
14 Dwight Howard BW 2.00 5.00
15 Zach Randolph BW 2.00 5.00
16 Pau Gasol BW 2.50 6.00
17 Marcus Morris BW 1.50 4.00
18 Robert Covington BW 1.50 4.00
19 LeBron James BW 10.00 25.00
20 Devin Booker BW 4.00 10.00
21 Kemba Walker BW 2.50 6.00
22 Karl-Anthony Towns BW 6.00 15.00
23 Kyle Lowry BW 2.00 5.00
24 Gary Harris BW 2.00 5.00
25 Marc Gasol BW 2.50 6.00
26 Tony Parker BW 2.50 6.00
27 Isaiah Thomas BW 2.50 6.00
28 Tyreke Evans BW 1.50 4.00
29 Jordan Clarkson BW 2.00 5.00
30 John Wall BW 3.00 8.00
31 Dirk Nowitzki BW 3.00 8.00
32 Elfrid Payton BW 2.00 5.00
33 Jeff Teague BW 2.00 5.00
34 DeMar DeRozan BW 2.50 6.00
35 Stephen Curry BW 10.00 25.00
36 Eric Bledsoe BW 2.00 5.00
37 Goran Dragic BW 2.00 5.00
38 James Harden BW 4.00 10.00
39 George Hill BW 2.00 5.00
40 Kyrie Irving BW 5.00 12.00
41 Andrew Wiggins BW 4.00 10.00
42 Blake Griffin BW 2.50 6.00
43 Bradley Beal BW 2.50 6.00
44 Klay Thompson BW 3.00 8.00
45 Kawhi Leonard BW 4.00 10.00
46 Paul Millsap BW 2.50 6.00
47 Derrick Rose BW 3.00 8.00
48 Jabari Parker BW 3.00 8.00
49 Nerlens Noel BW 2.00 5.00
50 Victor Oladipo BW 2.00 5.00
51 D'Angelo Russell BW 3.00 8.00
52 Damian Lillard BW 5.00 12.00
53 Dwyane Wade BW 4.00 10.00
54 Russell Westbrook BW 6.00 15.00
55 Mike Conley BW 2.00 5.00
56 Jeremy Lin BW 2.50 6.00
57 Jahlil Okafor BW 2.00 5.00
58 J.J. Redick BW 2.50 6.00
59 Giannis Antetokounmpo BW 5.00 12.00
60 Nikola Jokic BW 2.50 6.00
61 Kristaps Porzingis BW 5.00 12.00
62 Nicolas Batum BW 2.00 5.00
63 Dion Waiters BW 2.00 5.00
64 Myles Turner BW 2.00 5.00
65 Nick Young BW 2.00 5.00
66 Eric Gordon BW 2.00 5.00
67 Kevin Love BW 2.50 6.00
68 Tobias Harris BW 2.00 5.00
69 Seth Curry BW 2.50 6.00
70 Jae Crowder BW 2.00 5.00
71 Brandon Ingram BW RC 12.00 30.00
72 Ben Simmons BW RC 150.00 300.00
73 Jaylen Brown BW RC 8.00 20.00
74 Jamal Murray BW RC 6.00 15.00
75 Malcolm Brogdon BW RC 5.00 12.00
76 Thon Maker BW RC 6.00 15.00
77 Buddy Hield BW RC 5.00 12.00
78 Dario Saric BW RC 6.00 15.00
79 Denzel Valentine BW RC 2.50 6.00
80 Dragan Bender BW RC 2.50 6.00
81 Domantas Sabonis BW RC 3.00 8.00
82 Willy Hernangomez BW RC 2.50 6.00
83 Marquese Chriss BW RC 5.00 12.00
84 Kris Dunn BW RC 6.00 15.00
85 Jakob Poeltl BW RC 2.50 6.00
86 Skal Labissiere BW RC 3.00 8.00
87 Timothe Luwawu-Cabarrot BW RC 4.00 10.00
88 Yogi Ferrell BW RC 2.50 6.00
89 Malik Beasley BW RC 2.50 6.00
90 Juan Hernangomez BW RC 2.50 6.00
91 Wade Baldwin IV BW RC 2.00 5.00
92 Taurean Prince BW RC 3.00 8.00
93 Patrick McCaw BW RC 4.00 10.00
94 Malachi Richardson BW RC 2.50 6.00
95 Tyler Ulis BW RC 6.00 15.00
96 Pascal Siakam BW RC 2.00 5.00
97 Ivica Zubac BW RC 3.00 8.00
98 Henry Ellenson BW RC 2.50 6.00
99 Deyonta Davis BW RC 2.00 5.00
100 Caris LeVert BW RC 2.50 6.00
101 Brown BW JSY AU 50.00 120.00
102 Demetrius Jackson BW JSY AU 5.00 12.00
103 Caris LeVert BW JSY AU 12.00 30.00
104 Valentine BW JSY AU 12.00 30.00
105 Kay Felder BW JSY AU 5.00 12.00
106 Hernangomez BW JSY AU 10.00 25.00
107 Jamal Murray BW JSY AU 75.00 200.00
108 H. Ellenson BW JSY AU 12.00 30.00
109 Isaiah Whitehead BW JSY AU 5.00 12.00
110 Chinanu Onuaku BW JSY AU 5.00 12.00
111 Georges Niang BW JSY AU 5.00 12.00
112 Diamond Stone BW JSY AU 5.00 12.00
113 Brice Johnson BW JSY AU 5.00 12.00
114 Ivica Zubac BW JSY AU 15.00 40.00
115 Ingram BW JSY AU 125.00 300.00
116 Deyonta Davis BW JSY AU 5.00 12.00
117 Wade Baldwin IV BW JSY AU 5.00 12.00
118 Brogdon BW JSY AU 20.00 50.00
119 Thon Maker BW JSY AU 60.00 150.00
120 Kris Dunn BW JSY AU 30.00 80.00
121 Hield BW JSY AU 40.00 100.00
122 Sabonis BW JSY AU 10.00 25.00
123 Stephen Zimmerman BW JSY AU 5.00 12.00
124 Lwwu-Cbrrt BW JSY AU 10.00 25.00
125 Chriss BW JSY AU 40.00 100.00
126 D. Bender BW JSY AU 20.00 50.00
127 Tyler Ulis BW JSY AU 25.00 60.00
128 Labissiere BW JSY AU 25.00 60.00
129 Murray BW JSY AU
130 Pascal Siakam BW JSY AU 5.00 12.00
131 Kevin Durant CLR 6.00 15.00
132 Anthony Davis CLR 5.00 12.00
133 Chris Paul CLR 3.00 8.00
134 Gordon Hayward CLR 2.50 6.00
135 C.J. McCollum CLR 2.00 5.00
136 Jimmy Butler CLR 2.50 6.00
137 Aaron Gordon CLR 2.00 5.00
138 Paul George CLR 3.00 8.00
139 Brook Lopez CLR 2.00 5.00
140 Carmelo Anthony CLR 3.00 8.00
141 Zach LaVine CLR 2.50 6.00
142 Andre Drummond CLR 2.50 6.00
143 Joel Embiid CLR 4.00 10.00
144 Dwight Howard CLR 2.00 5.00
145 Zach Randolph CLR 2.00 5.00
146 Pau Gasol CLR 2.50 6.00
147 Marcus Morris CLR 1.50 4.00
148 Robert Covington CLR 1.50 4.00
149 LeBron James CLR 10.00 25.00
150 Devin Booker CLR 4.00 10.00
151 Kemba Walker CLR 2.50 6.00
152 Karl-Anthony Towns CLR 6.00 15.00
153 Kyle Lowry CLR 2.00 5.00
154 Gary Harris CLR 2.00 5.00
155 Marc Gasol CLR 2.50 6.00
156 Tony Parker CLR 2.50 6.00
157 Isaiah Thomas CLR 2.50 6.00
158 Tyreke Evans CLR 1.50 4.00
159 Jordan Clarkson CLR 2.00 5.00
160 John Wall CLR 3.00 8.00
161 Dirk Nowitzki CLR 3.00 8.00
162 Elfrid Payton CLR 2.00 5.00
163 Jeff Teague CLR 2.00 5.00
164 DeMar DeRozan CLR 2.50 6.00
165 Stephen Curry CLR 10.00 25.00
166 Eric Bledsoe CLR 2.00 5.00
167 Goran Dragic CLR 2.00 5.00
168 James Harden CLR 4.00 10.00
169 George Hill CLR 2.00 5.00
170 Kyrie Irving CLR 5.00 12.00
171 Andrew Wiggins CLR 4.00 10.00
172 Blake Griffin CLR 2.50 6.00
173 Bradley Beal CLR 2.50 6.00
174 Klay Thompson CLR 3.00 8.00
175 Kawhi Leonard CLR 4.00 10.00
176 Paul Millsap CLR 2.50 6.00
177 Derrick Rose CLR 3.00 8.00
178 Jabari Parker CLR 3.00 8.00
179 Nerlens Noel CLR 2.00 5.00
180 Victor Oladipo CLR 2.00 5.00
181 D'Angelo Russell CLR 3.00 8.00
182 Damian Lillard CLR 5.00 12.00
183 Dwyane Wade CLR 4.00 10.00
184 Russell Westbrook CLR 6.00 15.00
185 Mike Conley CLR 2.00 5.00
186 Jeremy Lin CLR 2.50 6.00
187 Jahlil Okafor CLR 2.00 5.00
188 J.J. Redick CLR 2.50 6.00
189 G. Antetokounmpo CLR 5.00 12.00
190 Nikola Jokic CLR 2.50 6.00
191 Kristaps Porzingis CLR 5.00 12.00
192 Nicolas Batum CLR 2.00 5.00
193 Dion Waiters CLR 2.00 5.00
194 Myles Turner CLR 2.00 5.00
195 Nick Young CLR 2.00 5.00
196 Eric Gordon CLR 2.00 5.00
197 Kevin Love CLR 2.50 6.00
198 Tobias Harris CLR 2.00 5.00
199 Seth Curry CLR 2.50 6.00
200 Jae Crowder CLR 2.00 5.00
201 Brandon Ingram CLR RC 12.00 30.00
202 Ben Simmons CLR RC 150.00 300.00
203 Jaylen Brown CLR RC 8.00 20.00
204 Jamal Murray CLR RC 6.00 15.00
205 Malcolm Brogdon CLR RC 5.00 12.00
206 Thon Maker CLR RC 6.00 15.00
207 Buddy Hield CLR RC 5.00 12.00
208 Dario Saric CLR RC 6.00 15.00
209 Denzel Valentine CLR RC 2.50 6.00
210 Dragan Bender CLR RC 2.50 6.00
211 Domantas Sabonis CLR RC 3.00 8.00
212 Willy Hernangomez CLR RC 2.50 6.00
213 Marquese Chriss CLR RC 5.00 12.00
214 Kris Dunn CLR RC 6.00 15.00
215 Jakob Poeltl CLR RC 2.50 6.00
216 Skal Labissiere CLR RC 3.00 8.00
217 Timothe Luwawu-Cabarrot CLR RC 4.00 10.00
218 Yogi Ferrell CLR RC 2.50 6.00
219 Malik Beasley CLR RC 2.00 5.00
220 Juan Hernangomez CLR RC 2.50 6.00
221 Wade Baldwin IV CLR RC 2.00 5.00
222 Taurean Prince CLR RC 3.00 8.00
223 Patrick McCaw CLR RC 4.00 10.00
224 Malachi Richardson CLR RC 2.50 6.00
225 Tyler Ulis CLR RC 6.00 15.00
226 Pascal Siakam CLR RC 2.00 5.00
227 Ivica Zubac CLR RC 3.00 8.00
228 Henry Ellenson CLR RC 2.50 6.00
229 Deyonta Davis CLR RC 2.00 5.00
230 Caris LeVert CLR RC 2.50 6.00
231 Kevin Durant MET 25.00 60.00
232 Kyrie Irving MET 20.00 50.00
233 John Wall MET 12.00 30.00
234 Stephen Curry MET 60.00 150.00
235 Russell Westbrook MET 25.00 60.00
236 James Harden MET 15.00 40.00
237 Towns MET 25.00 60.00
238 Carmelo Anthony MET 12.00 30.00
239 Dwyane Wade MET 15.00 40.00
240 Damian Lillard MET 20.00 50.00
241 Jimmy Butler MET 10.00 25.00
242 Anthony Davis MET 20.00 50.00
243 Kawhi Leonard MET 15.00 40.00
244 Blake Griffin MET 10.00 25.00
245 DeMarcus Cousins MET 10.00 25.00
246 LeBron James MET 60.00 150.00
247 Chris Paul MET 12.00 30.00
248 Paul George MET 12.00 30.00
249 DeMar DeRozan MET 10.00 25.00
250 Nikola Jokic MET 10.00 25.00
251 Isaiah Thomas MET 10.00 25.00
252 Rudy Gobert MET 10.00 25.00
253 Kemba Walker MET 10.00 25.00
254 Marc Gasol MET 10.00 25.00
255 Kyle Lowry MET 8.00 20.00
256 Antetokounmpo MET 20.00 50.00
257 Gordon Hayward MET 10.00 25.00
258 Kevin Love MET 10.00 25.00
259 Klay Thompson MET 12.00 30.00
260 Dirk Nowitzki MET 12.00 30.00
261 Brandon Ingram MET 200.00 400.00
262 Ben Simmons MET 250.00 500.00
263 Malcolm Brogdon MET 15.00 40.00
264 Kris Dunn MET 20.00 50.00
265 Marquese Chriss MET 15.00 40.00
266 Buddy Hield MET 15.00 40.00
267 Thon Maker MET 20.00 50.00
268 Jamal Murray MET 20.00 50.00
269 Jaylen Brown MET 25.00 60.00
270 Denzel Valentine MET 8.00 20.00
271 Yogi Ferrell MET 8.00 20.00
272 Dario Saric MET 20.00 50.00
273 Willy Hernangomez MET 8.00 20.00
274 Isaiah Whitehead MET 6.00 15.00
275 Pascal Siakam MET 6.00 15.00
276 Dragan Bender MET 8.00 20.00
277 Patrick McCaw MET 12.00 30.00
278 Mindaugas Kuzminskas MET 8.00 20.00
279 Paul Zipser MET 10.00 25.00
280 Dejounte Murray MET 12.00 30.00
281 Kobe Bryant MET CC 75.00 200.00
282 Ray Allen MET CC 10.00 25.00
283 Tim Duncan MET CC 15.00 40.00
284 O'Neal MET CC 25.00 60.00
285 Allen Iverson MET CC 12.00 30.00
286 Steve Nash MET CC 10.00 25.00
287 David Robinson MET CC 15.00 40.00
288 Larry Bird MET CC 25.00 60.00
289 Magic Johnson MET CC 25.00 60.00
290 Olajuwon MET CC 12.00 30.00
291 Dikembe Mutombo MET CC 10.00 25.00
292 John Stockton MET CC 15.00 40.00
293 Abdul-Jabbar MET CC 15.00 40.00
294 Karl Malone MET CC 12.00 30.00
295 Gary Payton MET CC 10.00 25.00
296 Yao Ming MET CC 12.00 30.00
297 Grant Hill MET CC 12.00 30.00
298 Jason Kidd MET CC 10.00 25.00
299 Julius Erving MET CC 15.00 40.00
300 Scottie Pippen MET CC 20.00 50.00
301 Kobe Bryant MET ENC 75.00 200.00
302 Rudy Tomjanovich MET ENC 8.00 20.00
303 Chamberlain MET ENC 20.00 50.00
304 LeBron James MET ENC 60.00 150.00
305 Dirk Nowitzki MET ENC 12.00 30.00
306 Magic Johnson MET ENC 25.00 60.00
307 Elgin Baylor MET ENC 10.00 25.00
308 Abdul-Jabbar MET ENC 15.00 40.00
309 Tim Duncan MET ENC 15.00 40.00
310 O'Neal MET ENC 25.00 60.00
311 Kobe Bryant MET ENC 75.00 200.00
312 David Robinson MET ENC 15.00 40.00
313 Bill Russell MET ENC 15.00 40.00
314 Allen Iverson MET ENC 12.00 30.00
315 Dwyane Wade MET ENC 15.00 40.00
316 Spud Webb MET ENC 8.00 20.00
317 Larry Bird MET ENC 25.00 60.00
318 John Havlicek MET ENC 12.00 30.00
319 Willis Reed MET ENC 10.00 25.00
320 Grvn/Thmpsn MET ENC 10.00 25.00
321 Stephen Curry MET ART 500.00 1000.00
322 LeBron James MET ART 400.00 800.00
323 Kevin Durant MET ART 150.00 300.00
324 Kyrie Irving MET ART 60.00 150.00
325 Westbrook MET ART 80.00 200.00
326 James Harden MET ART 50.00 125.00
327 Anthony Davis MET ART 60.00 150.00
328 Towns MET ART 80.00 200.00
329 Ingram MET ART
330 Simmons MET ART

2016-17 Panini Noir Autograph Materials Prime Black and White

RANDOM INSERTS IN PACKS
STATED PRINT RUN 40 SER.#'d SETS
EXCHANGE DEADLINE 2/16/2019
*COLOR/40: .4X TO 1X BASIC
1 Kevin Durant 100.00 250.00
2 Jeremy Lin 50.00 120.00
3 Karl Malone 30.00 80.00
4 Alex English 10.00 25.00
6 Michael Kidd-Gilchrist 6.00 15.00
7 Kyrie Irving 50.00 120.00
8 Evan Turner 10.00 25.00
9 Isaiah Thomas 30.00 80.00
10 Magic Johnson 50.00 120.00
12 Kobe Bryant 125.00 300.00
13 Bobby Portis
14 Kevin Love 12.00 30.00
15 Kenneth Faried 6.00 15.00
16 Vince Carter 40.00 100.00
17 Larry Bird 50.00 120.00
18 Karl-Anthony Towns 100.00 250.00
19 George Hill 6.00 15.00
20 Ryan Anderson 6.00 15.00
21 Jimmy Butler 40.00 100.00
23 Anthony Davis 40.00 100.00
25 Andrew Wiggins 30.00 80.00
26 Jae Crowder 6.00 15.00
27 Luol Deng 10.00 25.00
28 Tobias Harris 6.00 15.00
29 Clint Capela 10.00 25.00
30 John Wall 30.00 80.00
31 Hakeem Olajuwon 25.00 60.00
32 C.J. McCollum 25.00 60.00
33 Bojan Bogdanovic 6.00 15.00
35 Nikola Mirotic 6.00 15.00
36 Myles Turner 12.00 30.00
37 John Stockton 30.00 80.00
38 Grant Hill 30.00 80.00
39 Shaquille O'Neal 60.00 150.00
40 Jordan Clarkson 15.00 40.00

2016-17 Panini Noir Autographs Color

RANDOM INSERTS IN PACKS
PRINT RUNS B/WN 75-99 COPIES PER
EXCHANGE DEADLINE 2/16/2019
*GOLD/25: .5X TO 1.2X BASIC
1 Paul Millsap/75 6.00 15.00
3 Jae Crowder/75 4.00 10.00
4 Bojan Bogdanovic/99 3.00 8.00
5 Jeremy Lin/75 40.00 100.00
6 Michael Kidd-Gilchrist/75 5.00 12.00
7 Bobby Portis/75 8.00 20.00
8 Michael Carter-Williams/75 3.00 8.00
9 Dwyane Wade/75 25.00 60.00
10 Tristan Thompson/99 5.00 12.00
11 Kevin Love/75 10.00 25.00
12 Kyrie Irving/75 40.00 100.00
13 J.J. Barea/99 15.00 40.00
14 Devin Harris/75 3.00 8.00
15 Justin Anderson/75 4.00 10.00
16 Danilo Gallinari/99 4.00 10.00
17 Kenneth Faried/75 4.00 10.00
18 Tobias Harris/75 4.00 10.00
19 Zaza Pachulia/99 5.00 12.00
20 Kevin Durant/75 100.00 250.00
21 Ryan Anderson/75
22 Clint Capela/99 8.00 20.00
23 Myles Turner/75 10.00 25.00
24 Joe Young/99 5.00 12.00
25 Jordan Clarkson/75 12.00 30.00
26 Julius Randle/75 8.00 20.00
27 Luol Deng/99
28 Marc Gasol/75 10.00 25.00
29 Zach Randolph/75
30 Tyler Johnson/99 5.00 12.00
31 Karl-Anthony Towns/75 60.00 150.00
33 Anthony Davis/75 30.00 80.00
34 Jrue Holiday/99
35 Kristaps Porzingis/99 25.00 60.00
36 Justin Holiday/99 3.00 8.00
37 Elfrid Payton/99 6.00 15.00
38 Nikola Vucevic/99 4.00 10.00
39 Alan Williams/99 3.00 8.00
40 Eric Bledsoe/75 6.00 15.00
41 Allen Crabbe/99 3.00 8.00
42 C.J. McCollum/75 12.00 30.00
43 Evan Turner/75 3.00 8.00
44 Pau Gasol/75 12.00 30.00
45 Tony Parker/75 20.00 50.00
46 George Hill/75 4.00 10.00
47 John Wall/75 30.00 80.00
48 Larry Bird/75 40.00 100.00
49 Dennis Rodman/75 25.00 60.00
50 Hakeem Olajuwon/75 20.00 50.00
51 Shaquille O'Neal/75 50.00 120.00
52 Kareem Abdul-Jabbar/75 40.00 100.00
53 Magic Johnson/75 30.00 80.00
54 Jerry West/75 20.00 50.00
55 Alonzo Mourning/75 25.00 60.00
56 Allen Iverson/75 100.00 250.00
57 Bill Walton/75 6.00 15.00
58 George Gervin/75 10.00 25.00
59 Karl Malone/75 25.00 60.00
60 John Stockton/75 20.00 50.00
61 Kobe Bryant/75 125.00 300.00
62 David Robinson/75 25.00 60.00
63 Grant Hill/75 25.00 60.00
64 Jason Kidd/75 20.00 50.00
65 Ray Allen/75 20.00 50.00
66 Isaiah Thomas/75 20.00 50.00
67 Nikola Mirotic/99 6.00 15.00
68 Giannis Antetokounmpo/75 40.00 100.00
69 Reggie Jackson/75 4.00 10.00
70 Marc Gasol/75 10.00 25.00
71 Justise Winslow/99 6.00 15.00
72 Carmelo Anthony/75 25.00 60.00
73 Evan Fournier/75 4.00 10.00
74 Devin Booker/75 20.00 50.00
75 Andrew Wiggins/75 20.00 50.00
76 Marcin Gortat/99 4.00 10.00
77 Dominique Wilkins/75 15.00 40.00
78 Latrell Sprewell/99 25.00 60.00

2016-17 Panini Noir Jumbo Materials

RANDOM INSERTS IN PACKS
PRINT RUNS B/WN 30-99 COPIES PER
*PRIME/21-25: 1X TO 2.5X BASIC
1 Kevin Durant/99 10.00 25.00
2 Kareem Abdul-Jabbar/30
3 Tim Duncan/99 5.00 12.00
4 Carmelo Anthony/99 4.00 10.00
5 Kevin Love/99 3.00 8.00
6 David Robinson/99 6.00 15.00
7 Russell Westbrook/99 6.00 15.00
8 Pau Gasol/99 3.00 8.00
9 Jeremy Lin/99 3.00 8.00
10 DeMarcus Cousins/99 3.00 8.00
11 Kristaps Porzingis/99 5.00 12.00
12 Kawhi Leonard/99 5.00 12.00
13 Blake Griffin/99 3.00 8.00
14 Kevin McHale/40 3.00 8.00
15 Giannis Antetokounmpo/99 6.00 15.00
16 Dennis Rodman/99 6.00 15.00
17 Jimmy Butler/99 3.00 8.00
18 Larry Bird/49 8.00 20.00
19 Joel Embiid/99 5.00 12.00
20 Devin Booker/99 5.00 12.00
21 John Havlicek/30 8.00 20.00
22 Kyrie Irving/99 8.00 20.00
23 Dikembe Mutombo/99 8.00 20.00
24 John Stockton/30 10.00 25.00
25 DeMar DeRozan/99 3.00 8.00
26 Julius Erving/30 5.00 12.00
27 Patrick Ewing/99 4.00 10.00
28 James Worthy/99 4.00 10.00
29 Larry Johnson/99
30 Karl Malone/99 4.00 10.00
31 John Wall/99 4.00 10.00
32 James Harden/99 5.00 12.00
33 Dwyane Wade/99 5.00 12.00
34 Allen Iverson/99 6.00 15.00
35 Karl-Anthony Towns/99 6.00 15.00
36 Clyde Drexler/99 4.00 10.00
37 Myles Turner/75 2.50 6.00
38 Kobe Bryant/99 10.00 25.00
39 Andrew Wiggins/99 5.00 12.00
40 Grant Hill/99 6.00 15.00
41 Paul George/89 4.00 10.00
42 Marc Gasol/99 3.00 8.00
43 D'Angelo Russell/99 4.00 10.00
44 Jason Kidd/99 3.00 8.00
45 Michael Finley/99 3.00 8.00
46 Zach LaVine/99 3.00 8.00
47 Damian Lillard/99 6.00 15.00
48 Jahlil Okafor/99 2.50 6.00
49 Bradley Beal/99 3.00 8.00
50 Tony Parker/99 3.00 8.00
51 Derrick Rose/99 4.00 10.00
52 Anthony Davis/99 6.00 15.00
53 Draymond Green/99 4.00 10.00
54 Chris Paul/99 4.00 10.00
55 Jabari Parker/99 4.00 10.00
56 Ray Allen/99 3.00 8.00
57 Hakeem Olajuwon/99 4.00 10.00
58 Manu Ginobili/99 5.00 12.00
59 Isaiah Thomas/99 3.00 8.00
60 Alex English/99 2.50 6.00
61 Isiah Thomas/99 3.00 8.00
62 Dirk Nowitzki/99 6.00 15.00
63 Bernard King/49 2.50 6.00
64 Gordon Hayward/99 3.00 8.00
65 Dominique Wilkins/99 4.00 10.00
66 Stephen Curry/99 15.00 40.00
67 Joe Dumars/99 3.00 8.00
68 Klay Thompson/99 4.00 10.00
69 Joakim Noah/99 2.50 6.00
70 Dwight Howard/99 2.50 6.00
71 Scottie Pippen/99 6.00 15.00
72 Shaquille O'Neal/48 12.00 30.00
73 Danny Ainge/99 3.00 8.00
74 Harrison Barnes/99 2.50 6.00
75 Magic Johnson/30 8.00 20.00
76 Detlef Schrempf/99 3.00 8.00
77 Mike Conley/99 2.50 6.00
78 Christian Laettner/99 2.50 6.00
79 Zach Randolph/99 2.50 6.00
80 LeBron James/99 15.00 40.00

2016-17 Panini Noir Materials Black and White Prime

1 Dirk Nowitzki/49 10.00 25.00
2 J.J. Barea/49 20.00 50.00
3 Derrick Rose/49 8.00 20.00
4 Joakim Noah/35 3.00 8.00
5 Rondae Hollis-Jefferson/49 2.50 6.00
6 Kawhi Leonard/49 12.00 30.00
7 Manu Ginobili/49 6.00 15.00
8 Tony Parker/49 6.00 15.00
9 Marcus Smart/49 3.00 8.00
10 Avery Bradley/49 3.00 8.00
11 Paul George/49 6.00 15.00
12 Jeff Teague/49 3.00 8.00
13 Willie Cauley-Stein/49 3.00 8.00
14 Rudy Gay/35 4.00 10.00
15 LeBron James/49 30.00 80.00
16 J.R. Smith/49 5.00 12.00
17 Robert Covington/49 2.50 6.00
18 Nerlens Noel/49 3.00 8.00
19 Greg Monroe/49 3.00 8.00
20 John Henson/49 3.00 8.00
21 Nikola Vucevic/49 3.00 8.00
22 Serge Ibaka/49 3.00 8.00
23 Evan Fournier/30 3.00 8.00
24 Tyus Jones/49 2.50 6.00
25 Nemanja Bjelica/49 3.00 8.00
26 Gorgui Dieng/49 2.50 6.00
28 Thabo Sefolosha/25 6.00 15.00
30 Al Horford/49 3.00 8.00
31 Jeremy Lamb/49 2.50 6.00
32 Jimmy Butler/49 5.00 12.00
33 Nikola Mirotic/35 3.00 8.00
34 Richard Jefferson/49 3.00 8.00
35 Danilo Gallinari/49 3.00 8.00
37 Tobias Harris/49 3.00 8.00
39 George Hill/49 3.00 8.00
40 Dwyane Wade/49 10.00 25.00
41 Myles Turner/30 3.00 8.00
42 Julius Randle/25 6.00 15.00
43 Jordan Clarkson/49 5.00 12.00
44 Timofey Mozgov/49 2.50 6.00
45 Marc Gasol/49 4.00 10.00
46 Zach Randolph/49 3.00 8.00
48 Steven Adams/49 8.00 20.00
49 Andre Roberson/49 2.50 6.00
50 Mason Plumlee/49 3.00 8.00
51 Terrence Ross/49 3.00 8.00
52 DeMar DeRozan/49 4.00 10.00
53 Jonas Valanciunas/49 3.00 8.00
54 Alec Burks/49 2.50 6.00
55 Gordon Hayward/49 4.00 10.00
56 Derrick Favors/49 3.00 8.00
57 Bradley Beal/49 4.00 10.00
58 Kelly Oubre Jr./49 2.50 6.00
59 Marcin Gortat/30 3.00 8.00
60 Markieff Morris/35 2.50 6.00
61 Mike Bibby/49 6.00 15.00
62 Danny Ainge/49 4.00 10.00
63 Richard Hamilton/30 3.00 8.00
64 Shawn Marion/49 3.00 8.00
65 Michael Redd/49 3.00 8.00
66 Christian Laettner/49 3.00 8.00
67 Amare Stoudemire/49 5.00 12.00
68 Jason Richardson/49 4.00 10.00
69 Tom Chambers/35 3.00 8.00
70 Kevin Duckworth/49 2.50 6.00

2016-17 Panini Noir Materials Color Prime

*CLR/25-49: .4X TO 1X BASE B/W
RANDOM INSERTS IN PACKS
PRINT RUNS B/WN 8-49 COPIES PER
NO PRICING ON QTY 15 OR LESS
38 Klay Thompson/35 15.00 40.00

2016-17 Panini Noir Rookie Jumbo Materials

RANDOM INSERTS IN PACKS
STATED PRINT RUN 99 SER.#'d SETS
*PRIME/25: 1X TO 2.5X BASIC
1 Brandon Ingram 6.00 15.00
2 Jamal Murray 5.00 12.00
3 Kay Felder 2.00 5.00
4 Jaylen Brown 5.00 12.00
5 Jakob Poeltl 2.50 6.00
6 Denzel Valentine 2.50 6.00
7 Buddy Hield 5.00 12.00
8 Kris Dunn 5.00 12.00
9 Dragan Bender 2.50 6.00
10 Malcolm Brogdon 5.00 12.00
11 Tyler Ulis 5.00 12.00
12 Pascal Siakam 2.00 5.00
13 Dejounte Murray 6.00 15.00
14 Thon Maker 5.00 12.00
15 Timothe Luwawu-Cabarrot 5.00 12.00
16 Patrick McCaw 4.00 10.00
17 Willy Hernangomez 2.50 6.00
18 Marquese Chriss 5.00 12.00
19 Wade Baldwin IV 2.00 5.00
20 Domantas Sabonis 3.00 8.00

2016-17 Panini Noir Rookie Materials Black and White Prime

RANDOM INSERTS IN PACKS
PRINT RUNS B/WN 8-49 COPIES PER
NO PRICING ON QTY 15 OR LESS
*PATCH/20-25: .5X TO 1.2X BASE B/W
1 Demetrius Jackson/99 2.50 6.00
2 Caris LeVert/99 3.00 8.00
3 Denzel Valentine/99 3.00 8.00
4 Kay Felder/99 2.50 6.00
5 A.J. Hammons/99 2.50 6.00
6 Jamal Murray/99 6.00 15.00
7 Juan Hernangomez/99 5.00 12.00
8 Henry Ellenson/61 8.00 20.00
9 Patrick McCaw/99 5.00 12.00
10 Damian Jones/99 2.50 6.00
11 Chinanu Onuaku/76 2.50 6.00
12 Brice Johnson/99 2.50 6.00
13 Diamond Stone/99 2.50 6.00
14 Brandon Ingram/99 15.00 40.00
15 Ivica Zubac/99 4.00 10.00
16 Deyonta Davis/99 2.50 6.00
17 Wade Baldwin IV/99 2.50 6.00
18 Thon Maker/33 20.00 50.00
19 Malcolm Brogdon/99 6.00 15.00
21 Cheick Diallo/99 2.50 6.00
22 Tyler Ulis/99 5.00 12.00
23 Marquese Chriss/35 6.00 15.00
24 Stephen Zimmerman/99 2.50 6.00
26 Skal Labissiere/99 4.00 10.00
27 Malachi Richardson/99 3.00 8.00
28 Dejounte Murray/99 5.00 12.00
29 Isaiah Whitehead/99 2.50 6.00
30 T. Luwawu-Cabarrot/99 5.00 12.00

2016-17 Panini Noir Rookie Materials Color Prime

*CLR/45-99: .4X TO 1X BASE B/W
RANDOM INSERTS IN PACKS
PRINT RUNS B/WN 45-99 COPIES PER
20 Buddy Hield/99 6.00 15.00

2016-17 Panini Noir Rookie Patch Autographs Black and White Horizontal

*BW HOR: .5X TO 1.2X BASIC
RANDOM INSERTS IN PACKS
STATED PRINT RUN 35 SER.#'d SETS
EXCHANGE DEADLINE 2/16/2019

2016-17 Panini Noir Rookie Patch Autographs Color

*CLR: .4X TO 1X BASIC
RANDOM INSERTS IN PACKS
STATED PRINT RUN 75 SER.#'d SETS
EXCHANGE DEADLINE 2/16/2019

2016-17 Panini Noir Rookie Patch Autographs Color Horizontal

*CLR HOR: .5X TO 1.2X BASIC
RANDOM INSERTS IN PACKS
STATED PRINT RUN 35 SER.#'d SETS
EXCHANGE DEADLINE 2/16/2019

2016-17 Panini Noir Spotlight Signatures

RANDOM INSERTS IN PACKS
PRINT RUNS B/WN 75-125 COPIES PER
EXCHANGE DEADLINE 2/16/2019
1 Jamal Murray EXCH 125.00 300.00
2 Dario Saric EXCH 75.00 200.00
3 Joel Embiid/125 125.00 300.00
4 Ricky Rubio/125 50.00 120.00
5 Karl-Anthony Towns/125 150.00 400.00
6 Kobe Bryant/125 900.00 1200.00
7 Kristaps Porzingis/125 125.00 300.00
8 Ray Allen/125 150.00 400.00
9 C.J. McCollum/125 50.00 120.00
10 Damian Lillard EXCH 125.00 300.00
11 Dwyane Wade/125 125.00 300.00
12 Jimmy Butler EXCH 100.00 250.00
13 Tyler Johnson/125 15.00 40.00
14 Dirk Nowitzki/75 500.00 800.00
15 Malik Beasley/125 40.00 100.00
16 Kevin Durant/125 350.00 700.00
17 Stephen Curry EXCH 800.00 1200.00
18 Andrew Wiggins/125 100.00 250.00
19 Eric Gordon/125 30.00 80.00
20 Dikembe Mutombo/125 60.00 150.00
21 Evan Turner EXCH 10.00 25.00
22 Isaiah Thomas EXCH 60.00 150.00

2011-12 Panini Past and Present

MPLETE SET (200) 20.00 50.00
1 LaMarcus Aldridge .40 1.00
2 Ray Allen .40 1.00
3 Chris Andersen .30 .75
4 Carmelo Anthony .50 1.25
5 Shane Battier .30 .75
6 Eric Bledsoe .40 1.00
7 Carlos Boozer .30 .75
8 Chris Bosh .40 1.00
9 Elton Brand .40 1.00
10 Andrew Bynum .25 .60
11 Vince Carter .50 1.25
12 Tyson Chandler .30 .75
13 Darren Collison .30 .75
14 Mike Conley .30 .75
15 Stephen Curry 1.50 4.00
16 Baron Davis .30 .75
17 Brandon Bass .30 .75
18 Luol Deng .30 .75
19 DeMar DeRozan .40 1.00
20 Tim Duncan .60 1.50
21 Kevin Durant 1.00 2.50
22 Monta Ellis .30 .75
23 Raymond Felton .30 .75
24 Derek Fisher .30 .75
25 Kevin Garnett .60 1.50
26 Marc Gasol .40 1.00
27 Pau Gasol .40 1.00
28 Manu Ginobili .40 1.00
29 Marcin Gortat .30 .75
30 Danny Granger .30 .75
31 Blake Griffin .40 1.00
32 James Harden .60 1.50
33 Devin Harris .25 .60
34 Roy Hibbert .30 .75
35 George Hill .30 .75
36 Grant Hill .50 1.25
37 Dwight Howard .30 .75
38 Serge Ibaka .30 .75
39 Andre Iguodala .30 .75
40 LeBron James 1.50 4.00
41 Al Jefferson .30 .75
42 Brandon Jennings .25 .60
43 Joe Johnson .30 .75
44 DeAndre Jordan .40 1.00
45 Jason Kidd .40 1.00
46 Ty Lawson .25 .60
47 Brook Lopez .30 .75
48 Kevin Love .40 1.00
49 Shawn Marion .40 1.00
50 Wesley Matthews .25 .60
51 Tracy McGrady .40 1.00
52 Greg Monroe .40 1.00
53 Steve Nash .40 1.00
54 Nene .30 .75
55 Joakim Noah .30 .75
56 Dirk Nowitzki .50 1.25
57 Chris Paul .50 1.25
58 Tony Parker .40 1.00
59 Paul Pierce .40 1.00
60 Jason Richardson .40 1.00
61 Rajon Rondo .40 1.00
62 Ricky Rubio .40 1.00
63 Josh Smith .30 .75
64 Tiago Splitter .30 .75
65 Amare Stoudemire .30 .75
66 Jason Terry .30 .75
67 Hedo Turkoglu .30 .75
68 Evan Turner .25 .60
69 Ekpe Udoh .25 .60
70 Dwyane Wade .75 2.00
71 David West .30 .75
72 Russell Westbrook 1.00 2.50
73 Deron Williams .30 .75
74 Jeremy Lin .60 1.50
75 Thaddeus Young .25 .60
76 Elgin Baylor .40 1.00
77 Larry Bird 1.00 2.50
78 Julius Erving .60 1.50
79 Patrick Ewing .50 1.25
80 George Gervin .40 1.00
81 John Havlicek .50 1.25
82 Magic Johnson 1.00 2.50
83 Sam Jones .40 1.00
84 Karl Malone .50 1.25
85 Pete Maravich .60 1.50
86 George Mikan .75 2.00
87 Hakeem Olajuwon .50 1.25
88 Shaquille O'Neal .75 2.00
89 Scottie Pippen .75 2.00
90 Willis Reed .40 1.00
91 Oscar Robertson .50 1.25
92 David Robinson .60 1.50
93 Bill Russell .60 1.50
94 John Stockton .60 1.50
95 Isiah Thomas .40 1.00
96 David Thompson .30 .75
97 Wes Unseld .40 1.00
98 Bill Walton .40 1.00
99 Jerry West .50 1.25
100 James Worthy .50 1.25
101 Carmelo Anthony .50 1.25
102 Ray Allen .40 1.00
103 Shane Battier .30 .75
104 Andrea Bargnani .30 .75
105 Michael Beasley .25 .60
106 Chauncey Billups .40 1.00
107 Andrew Bogut .30 .75
108 Carlos Boozer .30 .75
109 Chris Bosh .40 1.00
110 Elton Brand .40 1.00
111 Kobe Bryant 1.50 4.00
112 Tyson Chandler .30 .75
113 DeMarcus Cousins .40 1.00
114 Stephen Curry 1.50 4.00
115 Baron Davis .30 .75
116 Luol Deng .30 .75
117 Tim Duncan .60 1.50
118 Kevin Durant 1.00 2.50
119 Monta Ellis .30 .75
120 Tyreke Evans .25 .60
121 Kevin Garnett .60 1.50
122 Pau Gasol .40 1.00
123 Rudy Gay .40 1.00
124 Eric Gordon .30 .75
125 Danny Granger .30 .75
126 Blake Griffin .40 1.00
127 Richard Hamilton .30 .75
128 Roy Hibbert .30 .75
129 Tyler Hansbrough .30 .75
130 James Harden .60 1.50
131 Devin Harris .25 .60
132 Grant Hill .50 1.25
133 Al Horford .30 .75
134 Dwight Howard .30 .75
135 Serge Ibaka .30 .75
136 Andre Iguodala .30 .75
137 LeBron James 1.50 4.00
138 Stephen Jackson .30 .75
139 Al Jefferson .30 .75
140 Joe Johnson .30 .75
141 Jason Kidd .40 1.00
142 Ty Lawson .25 .60
143 David Lee .25 .60
144 Brook Lopez .30 .75
145 Kevin Love .40 1.00
146 Kyle Lowry .30 .75
147 Shawn Marion .40 1.00
148 Kevin Martin .30 .75
149 Andre Miller .30 .75
150 Paul Millsap .30 .75
151 Steve Nash .40 1.00
152 Jameer Nelson .25 .60
153 Nene .30 .75
154 Joakim Noah .30 .75
155 Dirk Nowitzki .50 1.25
156 Lamar Odom .30 .75
157 Emeka Okafor .30 .75
158 Chris Paul .50 1.25
159 Paul Pierce .40 1.00
160 Zach Randolph .30 .75
161 Rajon Rondo .40 1.00
162 Derrick Rose .50 1.25
163 Luis Scola .30 .75
164 Josh Smith .30 .75
165 Amare Stoudemire .30 .75
166 Rodney Stuckey .30 .75
167 Jeff Teague .30 .75
168 Jason Terry .30 .75
169 Hedo Turkoglu .30 .75
170 Dwyane Wade .75 2.00
171 John Wall .50 1.25
172 Gerald Wallace .30 .75
173 Russell Westbrook 1.00 2.50
174 Deron Williams .30 .75
175 Jeremy Lin .60 1.50
176 Nate Archibald .30 .75
177 B.J. Armstrong .40 1.00
178 Elgin Baylor .40 1.00
179 Rick Barry .30 .75
180 Walt Bellamy .30 .75
181 Bill Cartwright .30 .75
182 Tom Chambers .30 .75
183 Bob Cousy .60 1.50
184 Dave DeBusschere .40 1.00
185 Walt Frazier .40 1.00
186 Harry Gallatin .40 1.00
187 Artis Gilmore .30 .75
188 Phil Jackson .50 1.25
189 K.C. Jones .40 1.00
190 Mitch Kupchak .40 1.00
191 Clyde Lovellette .40 1.00
192 Jerry Lucas .40 1.00
193 Moses Malone .40 1.00
194 Gail Goodrich .30 .75
195 Vern Mikkelsen .40 1.00
196 Bob Pettit .40 1.00
197 Robert Parish .40 1.00
198 Wes Unseld .40 1.00
199 Jo Jo White .30 .75
200 Lenny Wilkens .40 1.00

2011-12 Panini Past and Present 2011 Draft Pick Redemptions Autographs

RANDOM INSERTS IN PACKS
XRCA Isaiah Thomas 20.00 50.00
XRCB Shelvin Mack 3.00 8.00
XRCC Alec Burks 5.00 12.00
XRCD Lavoy Allen 5.00 12.00
XRCE MarShon Brooks 4.00 10.00
XRCF Josh Harrellson 5.00 12.00
XRCG Klay Thompson 25.00 60.00
XRCH Brandon Knight 5.00 12.00
XRCI Kemba Walker 15.00 40.00
XRCJ Chris Singleton 3.00 8.00
XRCK Markieff Morris 5.00 12.00
XRCL Marcus Morris 4.00 10.00
XRCM Gustavo Ayon 3.00 8.00
XRCN Kawhi Leonard 50.00 120.00
XRCO Kyrie Irving 30.00 80.00
XRCP Justin Harper 4.00 10.00
XRCQ JaJuan Johnson 3.00 8.00
XRCR Jan Vesely 5.00 12.00
XRCS Kenneth Faried 6.00 15.00
XRCT Norris Cole 5.00 12.00
XRCU Jeremy Tyler 4.00 10.00
XRCV Charles Jenkins 4.00 10.00
XRCW Enes Kanter 6.00 15.00
XRCX Nolan Smith 3.00 8.00
XRCY Jimmy Butler 10.00 25.00
XRCZ Chandler Parsons 5.00 12.00
XRCAA Cory Joseph 4.00 10.00
XRCBB Bismack Biyombo 5.00 12.00
XRCCC Tristan Thompson 6.00 15.00
XRCDD Tobias Harris 5.00 12.00
XRCEE Reggie Jackson 5.00 12.00
XRCFF Iman Shumpert 8.00 20.00
XRCGG Derrick Williams 3.00 8.00
XRCHH Jimmer Fredette 3.00 8.00
XRCII Jordan Hamilton 4.00 10.00

2011-12 Panini Past and Present 2012 Draft Pick Redemptions

RANDOM INSERTS IN PACKS
1 Anthony Davis 15.00 40.00
2 Michael Kidd-Gilchrist 2.50 6.00
3 Bradley Beal 5.00 12.00
4 Dion Waiters 2.50 6.00
5 Thomas Robinson 1.50 4.00
6 Damian Lillard 15.00 40.00
7 Harrison Barnes 6.00 15.00
8 Terrence Ross 2.50 6.00
9 Andre Drummond 8.00 20.00
10 Austin Rivers 3.00 8.00
11 Meyers Leonard 2.00 5.00
12 Jeremy Lamb 2.50 6.00
13 Kendall Marshall 1.50 4.00
14 John Henson 2.50 6.00
15 Maurice Harkless 2.50 6.00
16 Royce White 1.50 4.00
17 Tyler Zeller 2.00 5.00
18 Terrence Jones 2.50 6.00
19 Andrew Nicholson 1.50 4.00
20 Evan Fournier 2.50 6.00
21 Jared Sullinger 2.50 6.00
22 Fab Melo 1.50 4.00
23 John Jenkins 1.50 4.00
24 Jared Cunningham 1.50 4.00
25 Tony Wroten 1.50 4.00
NNO COMPLETE SET EXCH 200.00 400.00

2011-12 Panini Past and Present Autographs

RANDOM INSERTS IN PACKS
5 Shane Battier 5.00 12.00
6 Eric Bledsoe 5.00 12.00
12 Tyson Chandler 6.00 15.00
14 Mike Conley 6.00 15.00
16 Baron Davis 6.00 15.00
21 Kevin Durant 50.00 120.00
31 Blake Griffin 30.00 80.00
32 James Harden 25.00 60.00
36 Grant Hill 100.00 200.00
38 Serge Ibaka 8.00 20.00
42 Brandon Jennings 5.00 12.00
47 Brook Lopez 5.00 12.00
48 Kevin Love 15.00 40.00
52 Greg Monroe 5.00 12.00
53 Steve Nash 30.00 80.00
56 Dirk Nowitzki 50.00 120.00
61 Rajon Rondo 12.00 30.00
65 Amare Stoudemire 6.00 15.00
68 Evan Turner 5.00 12.00
72 Russell Westbrook 50.00 120.00
74 Jeremy Lin 40.00 100.00
76 Elgin Baylor 12.00 30.00
80 George Gervin 10.00 25.00
83 Sam Jones 8.00 20.00
87 Hakeem Olajuwon 25.00 60.00
91 Oscar Robertson 12.00 30.00
96 David Thompson 5.00 12.00
97 Wes Unseld 10.00 25.00
98 Bill Walton 6.00 15.00
100 James Worthy 20.00 50.00
103 Shane Battier 5.00 12.00
107 Andrew Bogut 5.00 12.00
111 Kobe Bryant 60.00 150.00
112 Tyson Chandler 6.00 15.00
113 DeMarcus Cousins 6.00 15.00
114 Stephen Curry 60.00 150.00
115 Baron Davis 6.00 15.00
126 Blake Griffin 30.00 80.00
127 Richard Hamilton 8.00 20.00
130 James Harden 25.00 60.00
133 Al Horford 5.00 12.00
135 Serge Ibaka 6.00 15.00
144 Brook Lopez 5.00 12.00
145 Kevin Love 10.00 25.00
151 Steve Nash 40.00 100.00
155 Dirk Nowitzki 50.00 120.00
157 Emeka Okafor 5.00 12.00
158 Chris Paul EXCH 30.00 80.00
161 Rajon Rondo 12.00 30.00
162 Derrick Rose EXCH 175.00 350.00
163 Luis Scola 5.00 12.00
165 Amare Stoudemire 12.00 30.00
167 Jeff Teague 5.00 12.00
173 Russell Westbrook 40.00 100.00
175 Jeremy Lin 60.00 120.00
176 Nate Archibald 5.00 12.00
177 B.J. Armstrong 5.00 12.00
178 Elgin Baylor 12.00 30.00
179 Rick Barry 8.00 20.00
182 Tom Chambers 5.00 12.00
185 Walt Frazier 20.00 50.00
186 Harry Gallatin 5.00 12.00
187 Artis Gilmore 8.00 20.00
188 Phil Jackson 300.00 600.00
189 K.C. Jones 15.00 40.00
191 Clyde Lovellette 8.00 20.00
194 Gail Goodrich 8.00 20.00
196 Bob Pettit 8.00 20.00
197 Robert Parish 8.00 20.00
198 Wes Unseld 6.00 15.00
200 Lenny Wilkens 6.00 15.00

2011-12 Panini Past and Present Bread for Energy

COMPLETE SET (50) 25.00 60.00
RANDOM INSERTS IN PACKS
1 Carmelo Anthony 1.00 2.50
2 Leandro Barbosa .60 1.50
3 J.J. Barea .75 2.00
4 Andrea Bargnani .60 1.50
5 Andray Blatche .50 1.25
6 Ronnie Brewer .60 1.50
7 Carlos Boozer .60 1.50
8 Mario Chalmers .60 1.50
9 Darren Collison .60 1.50
10 Stephen Curry 3.00 8.00
11 DeMar DeRozan .75 2.00
12 Kevin Durant 2.00 5.00
13 Tyreke Evans .50 1.25
14 Raymond Felton .60 1.50
15 Landry Fields .60 1.50
16 Danilo Gallinari .60 1.50
17 Kevin Garnett 1.25 3.00
18 Marc Gasol .75 2.00
19 Pau Gasol .75 2.00
20 Taj Gibson .60 1.50
21 Manu Ginobili .75 2.00
22 Devin Harris .50 1.25
23 Gordon Hayward .75 2.00
24 Grant Hill 1.00 2.50
25 Jrue Holiday .75 2.00
26 Al Horford .60 1.50
27 Dwight Howard .60 1.50
28 Stephen Jackson .60 1.50
29 Amir Johnson .50 1.25
30 Carl Landry .50 1.25
31 David Lee .50 1.25
32 Rashard Lewis .60 1.50
33 Corey Maggette .60 1.50
34 Tracy McGrady .75 2.00
35 Joakim Noah .60 1.50
36 Lamar Odom .60 1.50
37 Mehmet Okur .50 1.25
38 Tony Parker .75 2.00
39 J.J. Redick .75 2.00
40 Luke Ridnour .60 1.50
41 Rajon Rondo .75 2.00
42 Derrick Rose 1.00 2.50
43 Jason Terry .60 1.50
44 Dwyane Wade 1.50 4.00
45 John Wall 1.00 2.50
46 Hakim Warrick .60 1.50
47 David West .60 1.50
48 Russell Westbrook 2.00 5.00
49 Deron Williams .60 1.50
50 Anderson Varejao .50 1.25

2011-12 Panini Past and Present Bread for Health

COMPLETE SET (50) 30.00 80.00
RANDOM INSERTS IN PACKS
1 LaMarcus Aldridge .75 2.00
2 Ray Allen .75 2.00
3 Chauncey Billups .75 2.00
4 Andrew Bogut .60 1.50
5 Chris Bosh .75 2.00
6 Elton Brand .75 2.00
7 Kobe Bryant 3.00 8.00
8 Chase Budinger .50 1.25
9 Andrew Bynum .50 1.25
10 Jose Calderon .50 1.25
11 Tyson Chandler .60 1.50
12 DeMarcus Cousins .75 2.00
13 Jamal Crawford .75 2.00
14 Luol Deng .60 1.50
15 Tim Duncan 1.25 3.00
16 Monta Ellis .60 1.50
17 Derek Fisher .60 1.50
18 Rudy Gay .75 2.00
19 Drew Gooden .60 1.50
20 Ben Gordon .60 1.50
21 Danny Granger .60 1.50
22 Blake Griffin .75 2.00
23 James Harden 1.25 3.00
24 Kris Humphries .50 1.25
25 Andre Iguodala .60 1.50
26 Chris Kaman .60 1.50
27 Jason Kidd .75 2.00
28 Jarrett Jack .60 1.50
29 LeBron James 3.00 8.00
30 Antawn Jamison .60 1.50
31 Al Jefferson .60 1.50
32 Brandon Jennings .50 1.25
33 Joe Johnson .60 1.50
34 Brook Lopez .60 1.50
35 Kevin Love .75 2.00
36 Kevin Martin .60 1.50
37 JaVale McGee .60 1.50
38 Andre Miller .60 1.50
39 Greg Monroe .75 2.00
40 Steve Nash .75 2.00
41 Gary Neal .60 1.50
42 Dirk Nowitzki 1.00 2.50
43 Paul Pierce .75 2.00
44 Tayshaun Prince .75 2.00
45 Zach Randolph .60 1.50
46 Brandon Rush .50 1.25
47 Amare Stoudemire .60 1.50
48 Rodney Stuckey .60 1.50
49 Evan Turner .50 1.25
50 D.J. White .50 1.25

2011-12 Panini Past and Present Bread for Life

COMPLETE SET (50) 75.00 150.00
RANDOM INSERTS IN PACKS
1 Elgin Baylor 1.50 4.00
2 Larry Bird 6.00 15.00
3 Wilt Chamberlain 5.00 12.00
4 Phil Chenier 1.00 2.50
5 Maurice Cheeks 1.00 2.50
6 Clyde Drexler 2.00 5.00
7 Dale Ellis 1.00 2.50
8 Sean Elliott 1.50 4.00
9 Julius Erving 2.50 6.00
10 Patrick Ewing 6.00 15.00
11 Harry Gallatin 1.50 4.00
12 A.C. Green 1.50 4.00
13 Anfernee Hardaway 4.00 10.00
14 Ron Harper 1.50 4.00
15 Hersey Hawkins 1.00 2.50
16 Robert Horry 1.25 3.00
17 Mark Jackson 1.25 3.00
18 Magic Johnson 6.00 15.00
19 Dave Cowens 1.00 2.50
20 Bill Laimbeer 1.25 3.00
21 Dan Majerle 1.25 3.00
22 Karl Malone 2.00 5.00
23 Pete Maravich 2.50 6.00
24 Bob McAdoo 1.25 3.00
25 George Mikan 3.00 8.00
26 Alonzo Mourning 6.00 15.00
27 Dikembe Mutombo 1.50 4.00
28 Charles Oakley 1.50 4.00
29 Hakeem Olajuwon 2.00 5.00
30 Shaquille O'Neal 3.00 8.00
31 Robert Parish 1.50 4.00
32 Gary Payton 1.50 4.00
33 Scottie Pippen 3.00 8.00
34 Sam Perkins 1.00 2.50
35 Terry Porter 1.00 2.50
36 Mark Price 1.50 4.00
37 Glen Rice 1.25 3.00
38 Arnie Risen 1.50 4.00
39 Dennis Rodman 3.00 8.00
40 Tree Rollins 1.00 2.50
41 Bill Russell 2.50 6.00
42 Jack Sikma 1.25 3.00
43 Kenny Smith 1.25 3.00
44 Dolph Schayes 1.50 4.00
45 Paul Silas 1.50 4.00
46 Isiah Thomas 1.50 4.00
47 Chet Walker 1.25 3.00
48 Dominique Wilkins 2.00 5.00
49 Lenny Wilkens 1.50 4.00
50 Kevin Willis 1.00 2.50

2011-12 Panini Past and Present Breakout

COMPLETE SET (30) 15.00 40.00
RANDOM INSERTS IN PACKS
1 Blake Griffin .75 2.00
2 John Wall 1.00 2.50
3 DeMarcus Cousins .75 2.00
4 Stephen Curry 3.00 8.00
5 Brandon Jennings .50 1.25
6 Taj Gibson .60 1.50
7 Tyler Hansbrough .60 1.50
8 Tyreke Evans .50 1.25
9 Brook Lopez .60 1.50
10 Eric Gordon .60 1.50
11 Andrew Bynum .50 1.25
12 Derrick Rose 1.00 2.50
13 Russell Westbrook 2.00 5.00
14 Kevin Love .75 2.00
15 DeJuan Blair .50 1.25
16 James Harden 1.25 3.00
17 Jrue Holiday .75 2.00
18 Wesley Matthews .50 1.25
19 Derrick Favors .60 1.50
20 Landry Fields .60 1.50
21 Greg Monroe .75 2.00
22 Jeremy Lin 1.25 3.00
23 Serge Ibaka .60 1.50
24 Eric Bledsoe .75 2.00
25 DeMar DeRozan .75 2.00
26 Gordon Hayward .75 2.00
27 Danilo Gallinari .60 1.50
28 Michael Beasley .50 1.25
29 O.J. Mayo .50 1.25
30 Ricky Rubio .75 2.00

2011-12 Panini Past and Present Breakout Autographs

RANDOM INSERTS IN PACKS
1 Blake Griffin 20.00 50.00
3 DeMarcus Cousins 12.00 30.00
4 Stephen Curry 100.00 250.00
6 Taj Gibson 5.00 12.00
8 Tyreke Evans 5.00 12.00
9 Brook Lopez 5.00 12.00
10 Eric Gordon 5.00 12.00
12 Derrick Rose EXCH 20.00 50.00
13 Russell Westbrook 60.00 150.00
14 Kevin Love 15.00 40.00
15 DeJuan Blair 5.00 12.00
16 James Harden EXCH 20.00 50.00
17 Jrue Holiday 5.00 12.00
18 Wesley Matthews 5.00 12.00
19 Derrick Favors 5.00 12.00
20 Landry Fields 5.00 12.00
21 Greg Monroe 5.00 12.00
22 Jeremy Lin 75.00 200.00
23 Serge Ibaka 5.00 12.00
24 Eric Bledsoe 5.00 12.00
25 DeMar DeRozan 10.00 25.00
26 Gordon Hayward 6.00 15.00
27 Danilo Gallinari 5.00 12.00
28 Michael Beasley 5.00 12.00

2011-12 Panini Past and Present Changing Times

COMPLETE SET (30) 20.00 50.00
RANDOM INSERTS IN PACKS
1 Bill Russell 1.25 3.00
2 Oscar Robertson 1.00 2.50
3 Dolph Schayes .75 2.00
4 Al Attles .75 2.00
5 Bob Cousy 1.25 3.00
6 Lenny Wilkens .75 2.00
7 Harry Gallatin .75 2.00
8 George Mikan 1.50 4.00
9 Clyde Lovellette .75 2.00
10 Julius Erving 1.25 3.00
11 George Gervin .75 2.00
12 Dan Issel .60 1.50
13 David Thompson .60 1.50
14 Artis Gilmore .60 1.50
15 Spencer Haywood .50 1.25
16 Connie Hawkins .75 2.00
17 Mel Daniels .75 2.00
18 Billy Cunningham .75 2.00
19 George McGinnis .50 1.25
20 Bobby Jones .60 1.50
21 Kobe Bryant 3.00 8.00
22 Blake Griffin .75 2.00
23 Kevin Durant 2.00 5.00
24 Chris Paul 1.00 2.50
25 LeBron James 3.00 8.00
26 Dirk Nowitzki 1.00 2.50
27 Derrick Rose 1.00 2.50
28 Kevin Love .75 2.00
29 Marc Gasol .75 2.00
30 Monta Ellis .60 1.50

2011-12 Panini Past and Present Elusive Ink Autographs

RANDOM INSERTS IN PACKS
AA Anthony Avent 4.00 10.00
AC Archie Clark 4.00 10.00
AH Allan Houston 4.00 10.00
AJ Avery Johnson 4.00 12.00
AM Anthony Mason 10.00 25.00
BA B.J. Armstrong 6.00 15.00
BB Brent Barry 5.00 12.00
BD Brad Davis 4.00 10.00
BE Bob Elliott 4.00 10.00
BG Brian Grant 4.00 10.00
BL Bob Love 4.00 10.00
BO Bo Outlaw 4.00 10.00
BR Bryant Reeves 4.00 10.00
BS Bob Sura 4.00 10.00
BW Bill Wennington 6.00 15.00
BW Buck Williams 4.00 10.00
CC Cedric Ceballos 6.00 15.00
CO Charles Oakley 6.00 15.00
DB Dee Brown 4.00 10.00
DC Dell Curry 4.00 10.00
DF Danny Ferry 4.00 10.00
DM Danny Manning 8.00 20.00
GM Gheorghe Muresan 8.00 20.00
HD Hubert Davis 4.00 10.00
HH Hersey Hawkins 4.00 10.00
JM Jamal Mashburn 12.00 30.00
JP John Paxson 6.00 15.00
JS John Starks 6.00 15.00
JS John Salley 4.00 10.00
KA Kenny Anderson 5.00 12.00
KK Kerry Kittles 4.00 10.00
KS Kenny Smith 6.00 15.00
KW Kevin Willis 4.00 10.00
LF Lawrence Funderburke 4.00 10.00
LL Luc Longley 4.00 10.00
LN Larry Nance 4.00 10.00
LS LaBradford Smith 4.00 10.00
LW Luther Wright 4.00 10.00
MA Mark Aguirre 5.00 12.00
MB Muggsy Bogues 6.00 15.00
ME Mario Elie 5.00 12.00
MF Michael Finley 6.00 15.00
MJ Major Jones 4.00 10.00
MR Marv Roberts 4.00 10.00
MW Morlon Wiley 4.00 10.00
NA Nick Anderson 6.00 15.00
OB Otis Birdsong 4.00 10.00
RB Ron Brewer 4.00 10.00
RC Rex Chapman 4.00 10.00
RM Rick Mahorn 6.00 15.00
RS Rory Sparrow 4.00 10.00
RS Rod Strickland 4.00 10.00
RT Reggie Theus 4.00 10.00
SA Stacey Augmon 4.00 10.00
SE Sean Elliott 6.00 15.00
SF Sleepy Floyd 4.00 10.00
SK Steve Kerr 8.00 20.00
SM Scooter McCray 4.00 10.00
SP Scot Pollard 4.00 10.00
TB Thurl Bailey 4.00 10.00
TG Tom Gugliotta 4.00 10.00
TH Tim Hardaway 4.00 10.00
VB Vin Baker 4.00 10.00
WB Willie Burton 4.00 10.00
VDN Vinny Del Negro 4.00 10.00

2011-12 Panini Past and Present Fireworks

COMPLETE SET (20) 25.00 60.00
RANDOM INSERTS IN PACKS
1 Kevin Durant 3.00 8.00
2 LeBron James 5.00 12.00
3 Kobe Bryant 5.00 12.00
4 Dwyane Wade 2.50 6.00
5 Dwight Howard 1.00 2.50
6 Blake Griffin 1.25 3.00
7 Dirk Nowitzki 1.50 4.00
8 Derrick Rose 1.50 4.00
9 Carmelo Anthony 1.50 4.00
10 Amare Stoudemire 1.00 2.50
11 Monta Ellis 1.00 2.50
12 Kevin Garnett 2.00 5.00
13 Kevin Love 1.25 3.00
14 John Wall 1.50 4.00
15 Russell Westbrook 3.00 8.00
16 Rajon Rondo 1.25 3.00
17 Josh Smith 1.00 2.50
18 Jeremy Lin 2.00 5.00
19 Chris Paul 1.50 4.00
20 Tyreke Evans .75 2.00

2011-12 Panini Past and Present Gamers Jerseys

RANDOM INSERTS IN PACKS
1 Amare Stoudemire 3.00 8.00
2 Al Jefferson 3.00 8.00
3 Allan Houston 5.00 12.00
4 Al Horford 3.00 8.00
5 Allen Iverson 12.00 30.00
6 Alonzo Mourning 5.00 12.00
7 Andre Iguodala 3.00 8.00
8 Avery Bradley 4.00 10.00
9 Darren Collison 3.00 8.00
10 Ben Wallace 3.00 8.00
11 Beno Udrih 2.50 6.00
12 Ed Davis 2.50 6.00
13 Blake Griffin 4.00 10.00
14 Bobby Jackson 2.50 6.00
15 Brandon Jennings 2.50 6.00
16 Brendan Haywood 2.50 6.00
17 Brook Lopez 3.00 8.00
18 Carlos Boozer 3.00 8.00
19 Grant Hill 8.00 20.00
20 Charles Oakley 4.00 10.00
21 Charlie Villanueva 2.50 6.00
22 Chris Andersen 3.00 8.00
23 Chris Bosh 4.00 10.00
24 Chris Webber 10.00 25.00
25 Cole Aldrich 2.50 6.00
26 Danny Granger 3.00 8.00
27 DeMar DeRozan 4.00 10.00
28 Damion James 2.50 6.00
29 Daniel Orton 2.50 6.00
30 Danny Manning 3.00 8.00
31 Patrick Ewing 12.00 30.00
32 Derrick Favors 3.00 8.00
33 Ekpe Udoh 2.50 6.00
34 Evan Turner 2.50 6.00
35 Greg Monroe 4.00 10.00
36 Hassan Whiteside 4.00 10.00
37 J.J. Redick 4.00 10.00
38 James Anderson 2.50 6.00
39 Jason Richardson 4.00 10.00
40 Jermaine O'Neal 3.00 8.00
41 Joe Johnson 3.00 8.00
42 John Wall 5.00 12.00
43 John Stockton 6.00 15.00
44 David Robinson 8.00 20.00
45 Kevin Durant 5.00 12.00
46 Kevin Garnett 6.00 15.00
47 Kevin Love 4.00 10.00
48 Gary Neal 3.00 8.00
49 Kobe Bryant 15.00 40.00
50 Lance Stephenson 3.00 8.00
51 Larry Johnson 8.00 20.00
52 Lazar Hayward 2.50 6.00
53 LeBron James 12.00 30.00
54 Landry Fields 3.00 8.00
55 Luke Walton 2.50 6.00
56 Manu Ginobili 4.00 10.00
57 Marcus Camby 2.50 6.00
58 Mario Chalmers 3.00 8.00
59 Marvin Williams 3.00 8.00
60 Mo Williams 3.00 8.00
61 Marc Gasol 4.00 10.00
62 Eric Bledsoe 4.00 10.00
63 Patrick Patterson 2.50 6.00
64 Paul George 5.00 12.00
65 Pau Gasol 4.00 10.00
66 Paul Pierce 8.00 20.00
67 Peja Stojakovic 6.00 15.00
68 Quincy Pondexter 2.50 6.00
69 Raja Bell 3.00 8.00
70 Rajon Rondo 4.00 10.00
71 Ray Allen 8.00 20.00
72 Hedo Turkoglu 3.00 8.00
73 Jeff Teague 3.00 8.00
74 Ramon Sessions 3.00 8.00
75 Reggie Miller 15.00 40.00
76 Robert Parish 4.00 10.00
77 Robin Lopez 2.50 6.00
78 Rodrigue Beaubois 2.50 6.00
79 Stephen Curry 12.00 30.00
80 Ron Harper 4.00 10.00
81 Roy Hibbert 3.00 8.00
82 Rudy Gay 4.00 10.00
83 Russell Westbrook 10.00 25.00
84 Steve Nash 4.00 10.00
85 LaMarcus Aldridge 4.00 10.00
86 Jalen Rose 4.00 10.00
87 Spencer Hawes 2.50 6.00
88 Andrew Bogut 3.00 8.00
89 Tim Duncan 6.00 15.00
90 Toney Douglas 2.50 6.00
91 Tony Parker 4.00 10.00
92 Trevor Booker 2.50 6.00
93 Ty Lawson 2.50 6.00
94 Tyrus Thomas 2.50 6.00
95 Udonis Haslem 2.50 6.00
96 Terrence Williams 2.50 6.00
97 Yao Ming 5.00 12.00
98 Zach Randolph 3.00 8.00
99 Jrue Holiday 4.00 10.00
100 Derrick Rose 5.00 12.00

2011-12 Panini Past and Present Gamers Jerseys Prime

*PRIME: 2.5X TO 6X BASE HI
STATED PRINT RUN ONE TO 25 SETS
SOME UNPRICED DUE TO SCARCITY
62 Eric Bledsoe/15 30.00 80.00

2011-12 Panini Past and Present Modern Marks Autographs

RANDOM INSERTS IN PACKS
1 Kobe Bryant 150.00 300.00
2 Blake Griffin 75.00 150.00
3 Kevin Durant 150.00 300.00
4 Derrick Rose 75.00 150.00
5 Chris Paul 75.00 150.00
6 Kevin Love 12.00 30.00
7 LaMarcus Aldridge 30.00 80.00
8 Stephen Curry 150.00 300.00
9 Marc Gasol 50.00 125.00
10 Andrew Bogut 10.00 25.00

2011-12 Panini Past and Present Raining 3's

COMPLETE SET (20) 20.00 50.00
RANDOM INSERTS IN PACKS
1 Dirk Nowitzki 1.25 3.00
2 Joe Johnson .75 2.00
3 Carmelo Anthony 1.25 3.00
4 Vince Carter 1.25 3.00
5 Paul Pierce 1.00 2.50
6 Kobe Bryant 4.00 10.00
7 Kevin Durant 2.50 6.00
8 Jason Terry .75 2.00
9 LeBron James 4.00 10.00
10 Jeremy Lin 1.50 4.00
11 Derrick Rose 1.25 3.00
12 Jason Richardson 1.00 2.50
13 Ray Allen 1.00 2.50
14 Steve Nash 1.00 2.50
15 Larry Bird 2.50 6.00
16 Robert Horry .75 2.00
17 Allen Iverson 1.25 3.00
18 Dan Majerle .75 2.00
19 Chris Mullin 1.00 2.50
20 John Stockton 1.50 4.00

2011-12 Panini Past and Present Variations

RANDOM INSERTS IN PACKS
1 Ray Allen 3.00 8.00
2 Carmelo Anthony 4.00 10.00
3 Chris Bosh 3.00 8.00
4 Kobe Bryant 12.00 30.00
5 Vince Carter 4.00 10.00
6 Baron Davis 2.50 6.00
7 Tim Duncan 5.00 12.00
8 Kevin Durant 8.00 20.00
9 Kevin Garnett 5.00 12.00
10 Blake Griffin 3.00 8.00
11 Grant Hill 6.00 15.00
12 Dwight Howard 2.50 6.00
13 LeBron James 12.00 30.00
14 DeAndre Jordan 3.00 8.00
15 Jason Kidd 3.00 8.00
16 Kevin Love 3.00 8.00
17 Steve Nash 4.00 10.00
18 Dirk Nowitzki 4.00 10.00
19 Chris Paul 4.00 10.00
20 Paul Pierce 3.00 8.00
21 Rajon Rondo 3.00 8.00
22 Amare Stoudemire 2.50 6.00
23 Dwyane Wade 6.00 15.00
24 Deron Williams 2.50 6.00
25 Metta World Peace 4.00 10.00
26 Larry Bird 8.00 20.00
27 Julius Erving 5.00 12.00
28 Patrick Ewing 6.00 15.00
29 George Gervin 3.00 8.00
30 Magic Johnson 12.00 30.00
31 Karl Malone 4.00 10.00
32 Pete Maravich 5.00 12.00
33 George Mikan 6.00 15.00
34 Shaquille O'Neal 6.00 15.00
35 Scottie Pippen 6.00 15.00
36 Oscar Robertson 4.00 10.00
37 David Robinson 5.00 12.00
38 Bill Russell 5.00 12.00
39 John Stockton 6.00 15.00
40 Isiah Thomas 3.00 8.00
41 David Thompson 2.50 6.00
42 Bill Walton 3.00 8.00
43 Jerry West 4.00 10.00
44 Bob Cousy 5.00 12.00
45 Dave DeBusschere 3.00 8.00
46 Artis Gilmore 2.50 6.00
47 Phil Jackson 4.00 10.00
48 Moses Malone 3.00 8.00
49 Robert Parish 3.00 8.00
50 Wes Unseld 3.00 8.00

2012-13 Panini Past and Present

COMPLETE SET (250) 40.00 80.00
1 Shawn Marion .30 .75
2 David West .30 .75
3 Amare Stoudemire .30 .75
4 Pau Gasol .40 1.00
5 Carmelo Anthony .50 1.25
6 LeBron James 1.50 4.00
7 Dirk Nowitzki .50 1.25
8 Jeremy Lin .40 1.00
9 Tim Duncan .60 1.50
10 Samuel Dalembert .25 .60
11 Paul Pierce .40 1.00
12 DeJuan Blair .25 .60
13 Spencer Hawes .25 .60
14 Rasheed Wallace .40 1.00
15 Luc Mbah a Moute .25 .60
16 Tyreke Evans .25 .60
17 John Wall .50 1.25
18 Kevin Garnett .60 1.50
19 Derrick Rose .50 1.25
20 Ty Lawson .25 .60
21 Marcus Thornton .25 .60
22 James Harden .60 1.50
23 David Lee .25 .60
24 Elton Brand .40 1.00
25 Damon Stoudamire .40 1.00
26 Magic Johnson 1.00 2.50
27 Cedric Ceballos .25 .60
28 Larry Bird 1.00 2.50
29 John Thompson .40 1.00
30 Glen Rice .30 .75
31 Drazen Petrovic .40 1.00
32 Manute Bol .40 1.00
33 Vlade Divac .40 1.00
34 Clyde Drexler .50 1.25
35 Brandon Jennings .25 .60
36 Tony Parker .40 1.00
37 Mo Williams .30 .75
38 Evan Turner .25 .60
39 Steve Blake .25 .60
40 Glen Davis .25 .60
41 Chris Andersen .30 .75
42 Larry Sanders .25 .60
43 Robin Lopez .25 .60
44 Manu Ginobili .40 1.00
45 Leandro Barbosa .30 .75
46 Jrue Holiday .40 1.00
47 Stephen Jackson .30 .75
48 Paul Millsap .40 1.00
49 Jerry Stackhouse .30 .75
50 Dwight Howard .30 .75
51 Greg Monroe .30 .75
52 Gordon Hayward .40 1.00
53 Paul George .50 1.25
54 George Hill .30 .75
55 Blake Griffin .40 1.00
56 Kyle Lowry .30 .75
57 Raymond Felton .30 .75
58 Kevin Durant 1.00 2.50
59 Steve Nash .40 1.00
60 Gerald Wallace .30 .75
61 Kevin Love .40 1.00
62 Jodie Meeks .30 .75
63 Andrew Bogut .30 .75
64 Vince Carter .50 1.25
65 Chris Bosh .40 1.00
66 Grant Hill .50 1.25
67 Mike Conley .30 .75
68 Ricky Rubio .40 1.00
69 Carlos Boozer .30 .75
70 Kobe Bryant 1.50 4.00
71 Chris Kaman .30 .75
72 Ronnie Brewer .30 .75
73 Corey Brewer .25 .60
74 Rashard Lewis .30 .75
75 Danny Granger .30 .75
76 Dwyane Wade .60 1.50
77 Caron Butler .30 .75
78 Goran Dragic .30 .75
79 Rajon Rondo .40 1.00
80 JaVale McGee .30 .75
81 Shane Battier .30 .75
82 Tony Allen .25 .60
83 Antawn Jamison .30 .75
84 Brook Lopez .30 .75
85 Josh Smith .30 .75
86 Brent Barry .25 .60
87 Byron Scott .30 .75
88 Vernon Maxwell .25 .60
89 Reggie Theus .30 .75
90 Chris Mullin .40 1.00
91 Bobby Jackson .25 .60
92 Larry Nance .30 .75
93 Michael Cooper .30 .75
94 Toni Kukoc .40 1.00
95 Robert Horry .30 .75
96 Larry Johnson .50 1.25
97 Connie Hawkins .40 1.00
98 Darryl Dawkins .25 .60
99 Bailey Howell .40 1.00
100 George Gervin .40 1.00
101 Doc Rivers .40 1.00
102 Rod Strickland .25 .60
103 Mitch Richmond .40 1.00
104 Jamal Mashburn .40 1.00
105 Bernard King .30 .75
106 Fat Lever .30 .75
107 Sidney Moncrief .25 .60
108 Dell Curry .25 .60
109 Dominique Wilkins .50 1.25
110 Nate Archibald .30 .75
111 Alex English .30 .75
112 John Stockton .60 1.50
113 Tom Heinsohn .40 1.00
114 Kareem Abdul-Jabbar .60 1.50
115 Antoine Walker .30 .75
116 Hal Greer .30 .75
117 Alonzo Mourning .50 1.25
118 Gary Payton .40 1.00
119 David Robinson .60 1.50
120 Hakeem Olajuwon .50 1.25
121 Moses Malone .40 1.00
122 Wes Unseld .40 1.00
123 Shaquille O'Neal .75 2.00
124 Dikembe Mutombo .40 1.00
125 Anfernee Hardaway 1.00 2.50
126 Chris Paul .50 1.25
127 Mario Chalmers .30 .75
128 Joakim Noah .30 .75
129 Eric Bledsoe .30 .75
130 Joe Johnson .30 .75
131 Tyson Chandler .30 .75
132 Anderson Varejao .25 .60
133 Metta World Peace .40 1.00
134 J.J. Hickson .25 .60
135 Deron Williams .30 .75
136 Taj Gibson .30 .75
137 Kris Humphries .25 .60
138 Jason Richardson .40 1.00
139 Roy Hibbert .30 .75
140 Ersan Ilyasova .25 .60
141 Eric Gordon .30 .75
142 Tyler Hansbrough .30 .75
143 Ryan Anderson .30 .75
144 Stephen Curry 1.50 4.00
145 Chase Budinger .25 .60
146 Hedo Turkoglu .30 .75
147 Tiago Splitter .30 .75
148 Al-Farouq Aminu .30 .75
149 Ben Gordon .30 .75
150 James Anderson .25 .60
151 Pablo Prigioni RC .40 1.00
152 Will Barton RC .50 1.25
153 Greg Stiemsma RC .40 1.00
154 Lavoy Allen RC .40 1.00
155 Tyshawn Taylor RC .40 1.00
156 Festus Ezeli RC .50 1.25
157 Lance Thomas RC .40 1.00
158 Tyler Zeller RC .50 1.25
159 Fab Melo RC .40 1.00
160 Kyrie Irving RC 3.00 8.00
161 Tyler Honeycutt RC .40 1.00
162 Evan Fournier RC .60 1.50
163 Kyle Singler RC .40 1.00
164 Tristan Thompson RC .60 1.50
165 E'Twaun Moore RC .40 1.00
166 Kyle O'Quinn RC .40 1.00
167 Tornike Shengelia RC .40 1.00
168 Enes Kanter RC .50 1.25
169 Mirza Teletovic RC .50 1.25
170 Tony Wroten RC .50 1.25
171 Draymond Green RC 2.00 5.00
172 Klay Thompson RC 2.50 6.00
173 Tobias Harris RC .60 1.50
174 Doron Lamb RC .40 1.00
175 Kim English RC .40 1.00
176 Thomas Robinson RC .50 1.25
177 Donatas Motiejunas RC .50 1.25
178 Khris Middleton RC .60 1.50
179 Terrence Ross RC .60 1.50
180 Dion Waiters RC .60 1.50
181 Kent Bazemore RC .60 1.50
182 Terrence Jones RC .50 1.25
183 Derrick Williams RC .40 1.00
184 Kenneth Faried RC .60 1.50
185 Victor Claver RC .40 1.00
186 DeQuan Jones RC .40 1.00
187 Kendall Marshall RC .40 1.00
188 Royce White RC .40 1.00
189 Darius Morris RC .40 1.00
190 Kemba Walker RC 1.25 3.00
191 Robert Sacre RC .40 1.00
192 DeAndre Liggins RC .50 1.25
193 Kawhi Leonard RC 3.00 8.00
194 Reggie Jackson RC .60 1.50
195 Harrison Barnes RC 1.00 2.50
196 Julyan Stone RC .40 1.00
197 Quincy Miller RC .40 1.00
198 Cory Joseph RC .40 1.00
199 Jeff Taylor RC .40 1.00
200 Quincy Acy RC .40 1.00
201 Chris Singleton RC .40 1.00
202 Jordan Hamilton RC .40 1.00
203 Perry Jones RC .40 1.00
204 Chris Copeland RC .40 1.00
205 Jonas Valanciunas RC .60 1.50
206 Orlando Johnson RC .40 1.00
207 Charles Jenkins RC .40 1.00
208 John Jenkins RC .40 1.00
209 Norris Cole RC .40 1.00
210 Chandler Parsons RC .60 1.50
211 John Henson RC .60 1.50
212 Nolan Smith RC .40 1.00
213 Brian Roberts RC .40 1.00
214 Jimmy Butler RC 2.00 5.00
215 Nikola Vucevic RC .60 1.50
216 Brandon Knight RC .60 1.50
217 Jimmer Fredette RC .40 1.00
218 Nando De Colo RC .40 1.00
219 Bradley Beal RC 1.00 2.50
220 Jeremy Pargo RC .40 1.00
221 Maurice Harkless RC .60 1.50
222 Bismack Biyombo RC .40 1.00
223 Jeremy Lamb RC .60 1.50
224 Miles Plumlee RC .40 1.00
225 Bernard James RC .40 1.00
226 Jared Sullinger RC .50 1.25
227 Mike Scott RC .40 1.00
228 Ben Hansbrough RC .40 1.00
229 Jared Cunningham RC .40 1.00
230 Michael Kidd-Gilchrist RC .60 1.50
231 Austin Rivers RC .60 1.50
232 Jan Vesely RC .40 1.00
233 Meyers Leonard RC .50 1.25
234 Arnett Moultrie RC .40 1.00
235 Jae Crowder RC .50 1.25
236 MarShon Brooks RC .50 1.25
237 Anthony Davis RC 3.00 8.00
238 Ivan Johnson RC .40 1.00
239 Marquis Teague RC .40 1.00
240 Andrew Nicholson RC .40 1.00
241 Isaiah Thomas RC 1.00 2.50
242 Markieff Morris RC .60 1.50
243 Andre Drummond RC 1.00 2.50
244 Iman Shumpert RC .60 1.50
245 Marcus Morris RC .50 1.25
246 Alec Burks RC .60 1.50
247 Gustavo Ayon RC .40 1.00
248 Malcolm Lee RC .40 1.00
249 Damian Lillard RC 2.50 6.00
250 Alexey Shved RC .40 1.00

2012-13 Panini Past and Present Variations

COMMON CARD 1.00 2.50
SEMISTARS 1.25 3.00
UNLISTED STARS 1.50 4.00
1 Kevin Love 1.50 4.00
2 Kevin Durant 4.00 10.00
3 Dwyane Wade 2.50 6.00
4 Rudy Gay 1.50 4.00
5 Derrick Rose 2.00 5.00
6 Steve Nash 1.50 4.00
7 LeBron James 6.00 15.00
8 Kobe Bryant 6.00 15.00
9 Blake Griffin 1.50 4.00
10 Chris Paul 2.00 5.00
11 Carmelo Anthony 2.00 5.00
12 Deron Williams 1.25 3.00
13 Stephen Curry 6.00 15.00
14 LaMarcus Aldridge 1.50 4.00
15 James Harden 2.50 6.00
16 Jrue Holiday 1.50 4.00
17 Jeremy Lin 1.50 4.00
18 Vince Carter 2.00 5.00
19 Rajon Rondo 1.50 4.00
20 Ray Allen 1.50 4.00
21 Eric Gordon 1.25 3.00
22 Kyrie Irving 8.00 20.00
23 Bradley Beal 2.50 6.00
24 Anthony Davis 8.00 20.00
25 Damian Lillard 6.00 15.00
26 Shaquille O'Neal 3.00 8.00
27 Larry Bird 4.00 10.00
28 Mitch Richmond 1.50 4.00
29 Moses Malone 1.50 4.00
30 George Gervin 1.50 4.00
31 Magic Johnson 4.00 10.00
32 Larry Johnson 2.00 5.00
33 Kareem Abdul-Jabbar 2.50 6.00
34 Julius Erving 2.50 6.00
35 John Stockton 2.50 6.00
36 Joe Dumars 1.50 4.00
37 Dominique Wilkins 2.00 5.00
38 Hakeem Olajuwon 2.00 5.00
39 Gary Payton 1.50 4.00
40 Alonzo Mourning 2.00 5.00
41 Drazen Petrovic 1.50 4.00
42 Dikembe Mutombo 1.50 4.00
43 Clyde Drexler 2.00 5.00
44 Chris Mullin 1.50 4.00
45 Charles Oakley 1.50 4.00
46 Anfernee Hardaway 4.00 10.00
47 Nate Archibald 1.25 3.00
48 Fat Lever 1.25 3.00
49 Alex English 1.25 3.00
50 Connie Hawkins 1.50 4.00

2012-13 Panini Past and Present Championship Banners

COMPLETE SET (25)	20.00	50.00
APPX.ODDS 1:10 HOBBY		
1 Tim Duncan	1.50	4.00
2 Dirk Nowitzki	1.25	3.00
3 Kobe Bryant	4.00	10.00
4 Hakeem Olajuwon	1.25	3.00
5 Scottie Pippen	2.00	5.00
6 Isiah Thomas	1.00	2.50
7 Dwyane Wade	1.50	4.00
8 Larry Bird	2.50	6.00
9 Robert Horry	.75	2.00
10 Dennis Rodman	2.00	5.00
11 Shaquille O'Neal	2.00	5.00
12 Manu Ginobili	1.00	2.50
13 Moses Malone	1.00	2.50
14 Kareem Abdul-Jabbar	1.50	4.00
15 Kenny Smith	.75	2.00
16 Tony Parker	1.00	2.50
18 LeBron James	4.00	10.00
18 Joe Dumars	1.00	2.50
19 Bill Russell	1.50	4.00
20 Magic Johnson	2.50	6.00
21 Chris Bosh	1.00	2.50
22 David Robinson	1.50	4.00
23 Luc Longley	.75	2.00
24 James Worthy	1.25	3.00
25 Paul Pierce	1.00	2.50

2012-13 Panini Past and Present Dual Jerseys

1 T.Lawson/R.Felton/99	4.00	10.00
2 A.Bargnani/D.Nowitzki/99	6.00	15.00
3 M.Gasol/P.Gasol/99	5.00	12.00
4 V.Carter/K.Bryant/99	10.00	25.00
5 T.Hansbrough/S.Hawes/99	4.00	10.00
6 G.Hill/J.Calderon/99	4.00	10.00
7 G.Monroe/A.Mourning/99	6.00	15.00
8 S.Pippen/P.Pierce/99	12.00	30.00
9 C.Drexler/A.Iguodala/99	6.00	15.00
10 J.Smith/T.Evans/99	4.00	10.00
11 B.Wallace/M.Camby/99	4.00	10.00
12 D.Robinson/K.Garnett/49	8.00	20.00
13 J.Smith/T.Thomas/99	4.00	10.00
14 K.Irving/D.Rose/99	15.00	40.00
15 T.Thompson/C.Bosh/99	5.00	12.00
16 B.Griffin/K.Malone/49	6.00	15.00
17 L.James/K.Bryant/49	25.00	60.00
18 L.Johnson/D.Favors/49	12.00	30.00
19 T.Duncan/P.Ewing/49	12.00	30.00
20 I.Thomas/C.Paul/49	6.00	15.00

2012-13 Panini Past and Present Dual Jerseys Prime

*PRIME: .75X TO 2X BASIC
STATED PRINT RUN 25 SER.#'d SETS

2012-13 Panini Past and Present Elusive Ink

EXCHANGE DEADLINE 11/01/2014		
1 Rick Fox	4.00	10.00
2 Fat Lever	4.00	10.00
3 Luc Longley	4.00	10.00
4 Jack Sikma	4.00	10.00
5 B.J. Armstrong	5.00	12.00
6 Willis Reed	10.00	25.00
7 Will Perdue	3.00	8.00
8 Dana Barros	3.00	8.00
9 Ray Williams	3.00	8.00
11 George McGinnis	3.00	8.00
12 Horace Grant	5.00	12.00
13 Byron Scott		
14 Glen Rice	4.00	10.00
15 Bob Dandridge	3.00	8.00
16 Tom Gugliotta	3.00	8.00
17 Rod Strickland	3.00	8.00
19 Doug Christie	3.00	8.00
20 Jeff Malone	3.00	8.00
21 Jim Jackson	3.00	8.00
22 Jo Jo White	4.00	10.00
23 Cazzie Russell	4.00	10.00
24 Nate McMillan	5.00	12.00
25 Sam Cassell	4.00	10.00
26 Spud Webb	4.00	10.00
27 Scott Skiles	4.00	10.00
28 Paul Silas	5.00	12.00
29 Brad Daugherty	4.00	10.00
30 Terry Porter	3.00	8.00
31 Christian Laettner	4.00	10.00
32 Charles Oakley	5.00	12.00
33 Vlade Divac	5.00	12.00
34 Herb Williams	3.00	8.00
35 Kendall Gill	3.00	8.00
37 Isaiah Rider	8.00	20.00
39 Jay Williams	3.00	8.00

2012-13 Panini Past and Present Gamers Jerseys

NO PRICING DUE TO LACK OF MARKET INFO		
NO PRIME PRICING DUE TO SCARCITY		
1 Dwyane Wade	5.00	12.00
2 Kevin Durant	8.00	20.00
3 Dirk Nowitzki	4.00	10.00
4 Tayshaun Prince	2.50	6.00
5 Derrick Williams	2.00	5.00
6 Zach Randolph	2.50	6.00
7 Gordon Hayward	3.00	8.00
8 Kevin Love	3.00	8.00
9 Rodney Stuckey	2.50	6.00
10 Arron Afflalo	2.50	6.00
11 Calvin Murphy	2.50	6.00
12 Dominique Wilkins	5.00	12.00
13 Bill Laimbeer	2.50	6.00
14 Alvan Adams	2.00	5.00
15 Larry Johnson	6.00	15.00
16 Hakeem Olajuwon	6.00	15.00
17 Karl Malone	4.00	10.00
18 James Worthy	8.00	20.00
19 Tyreke Evans	2.00	5.00
20 Metta World Peace	3.00	8.00
21 LaMarcus Aldridge	3.00	8.00
22 Andrea Bargnani	2.50	6.00
23 Tim Duncan	5.00	12.00
24 Kobe Bryant	10.00	25.00
25 David Lee	2.00	5.00
26 Glen Davis	2.00	5.00
27 Marc Gasol	3.00	8.00
28 Amare Stoudemire	2.50	6.00
29 John Wall	4.00	10.00
30 Derrick Favors	2.50	6.00

2012-13 Panini Past and Present Hall Marks Autographs

EXCHANGE DEADLINE 11/01/2014		
1 Larry Bird	75.00	150.00
2 Magic Johnson	30.00	80.00
3 David Robinson	25.00	60.00
4 Dennis Rodman	40.00	80.00
5 Scottie Pippen		
6 Hakeem Olajuwon	15.00	40.00
7 James Worthy	12.00	30.00
8 Bob McAdoo EXCH	6.00	15.00
9 Alex English	8.00	20.00
10 George Gervin		
11 Artis Gilmore		
12 Nate Archibald	12.00	30.00
13 David Thompson	6.00	15.00
14 Kareem Abdul-Jabbar	30.00	80.00
15 Bill Walton		
16 Clyde Lovellette		
17 Julius Erving	50.00	100.00
18 Bill Sharman	6.00	15.00
19 Elgin Baylor		
20 Clyde Drexler	15.00	40.00

2012-13 Panini Past and Present Headbands

COMPLETE SET (25)	20.00	50.00
APPX.THREE PER HOBBY BOX		
1 Isaiah Thomas	1.50	4.00
2 Zach Randolph	.75	2.00
3 Corey Brewer	.60	1.50
4 Vince Carter	1.25	3.00
5 Ronnie Brewer	.75	2.00
6 Gerald Wallace	.75	2.00
7 Dwight Howard	.75	2.00
8 Paul Pierce	1.00	2.50
9 Anderson Varejao	.60	1.50
10 Josh Smith	.75	2.00
11 Rasheed Wallace	1.00	2.50
12 LeBron James	4.00	10.00
13 Jared Dudley	.60	1.50
14 DeMarcus Cousins	1.00	2.50
15 Ty Lawson	.60	1.50
16 Carmelo Anthony	1.25	3.00
17 Chris Andersen	.75	2.00
18 Jason Terry	.75	2.00
19 Stephen Jackson	.75	2.00
20 Drew Gooden	.75	2.00
21 Daniel Gibson	.75	2.00
22 Michael Beasley	.60	1.50
23 Reggie Evans	.60	1.50
24 Dirk Nowitzki	1.25	3.00
25 Corey Maggette	.75	2.00

2012-13 Panini Past and Present Modern Marks Autographs

EXCHANGE DEADLINE 11/01/2014		
1 Kobe Bryant	100.00	200.00
2 Kevin Durant	50.00	120.00
3 Blake Griffin EXCH	20.00	50.00
4 Andre Iguodala		
5 Ben Gordon	4.00	10.00
6 Carl Landry		
7 Carlos Boozer EXCH	4.00	10.00
8 Chris Bosh	5.00	12.00
9 David Lee		
11 DeMarcus Cousins		
12 Deron Williams		
13 Eric Gordon		
14 Gordon Hayward	10.00	25.00
15 Grant Hill	25.00	60.00
16 James Harden	30.00	60.00
17 JaVale McGee EXCH	4.00	10.00
18 Joakim Noah		
19 Joe Johnson	10.00	25.00
20 Kendrick Perkins	3.00	8.00
21 Kevin Love	15.00	40.00
22 Kevin Martin	4.00	10.00
23 Stephen Curry EXCH	100.00	250.00
24 Stephen Jackson EXCH	4.00	10.00
25 Steve Nash	50.00	100.00
26 Steve Novak	3.00	8.00
27 Tony Parker	15.00	40.00
28 Vince Carter EXCH	20.00	50.00
29 Zach Randolph		
30 Artis Gilmore	12.00	30.00
31 Dolph Schayes	10.00	25.00
32 Elvin Hayes	10.00	25.00
33 Don Nelson	15.00	40.00
34 Walt Frazier		
35 Kelly Tripucka	3.00	8.00
36 Kyrie Irving	50.00	120.00
37 Anthony Davis	75.00	200.00
38 Kawhi Leonard	40.00	100.00
39 Michael Kidd-Gilchrist	5.00	12.00
40 Dion Waiters EXCH	5.00	12.00

2012-13 Panini Past and Present Raining 3's

COMPLETE SET (15)	15.00	40.00
APPX.ODDS 1:10 HOBBY		
1 Joe Johnson	.75	2.00
2 Jason Terry	.75	2.00
3 Carmelo Anthony	1.25	3.00
4 Damian Lillard	4.00	10.00
5 Ryan Anderson	.75	2.00
6 Kevin Martin	.75	2.00
7 Klay Thompson	4.00	10.00
8 Randy Foye	.60	1.50
9 Kobe Bryant	4.00	10.00
10 Steve Novak	.60	1.50
11 Chandler Parsons	1.00	2.50
12 O.J. Mayo	.60	1.50
13 Stephen Curry	4.00	10.00
14 James Harden	1.50	4.00
15 Nicolas Batum	.75	2.00

2012-13 Panini Past and Present Rise N Shine

ONE PER HOBBY PACK		
1 James Harden	1.00	2.50
2 Alexey Shved	.40	1.00
3 Dwight Howard	.50	1.25
4 Blake Griffin	.60	1.50
5 Kendrick Perkins	.40	1.00
6 Avery Bradley	.50	1.25
7 DeMar DeRozan	.60	1.50
8 Bradley Beal	1.00	2.50
9 Evan Turner	.40	1.00
10 Kevin Durant	1.50	4.00
11 Dirk Nowitzki	.75	2.00
12 Kawhi Leonard	3.00	8.00
13 Goran Dragic	.50	1.25
14 Alonzo Gee	.40	1.00
15 Andre Iguodala	.50	1.25
16 Damian Lillard	2.50	6.00
17 David Lee	.40	1.00
18 Chris Paul	.75	2.00
19 Brandon Jennings	.40	1.00
20 JaVale McGee	.50	1.25
21 Andre Drummond	1.00	2.50
22 Kevin Garnett	1.00	2.50
23 John Wall	.75	2.00
24 Derrick Rose	.75	2.00
25 Marreese Speights	.40	1.00
26 George Hill	.50	1.25
27 Mike Conley	.50	1.25
28 Brandon Knight	.60	1.50
29 Amare Stoudemire	.50	1.25
30 Kevin Love	.60	1.50
31 Jodie Meeks	.50	1.25
32 Joakim Noah	.50	1.25
33 Manu Ginobili	.60	1.50
34 Jae Crowder	.50	1.25
35 Paul George	.75	2.00
36 Al-Farouq Aminu	.50	1.25
37 Anderson Varejao	.40	1.00
38 Rudy Gay	.60	1.50
39 O.J. Mayo	.40	1.00
40 Isaiah Thomas	1.00	2.50
41 Jrue Holiday	.60	1.50
42 Deron Williams	.50	1.25
43 Harrison Barnes	1.00	2.50
44 Chandler Parsons	.60	1.50
45 Michael Kidd-Gilchrist	.60	1.50
46 Carmelo Anthony	.75	2.00
47 Jonas Valanciunas	.60	1.50
48 Jeremy Lin	.60	1.50
49 DeAndre Jordan	.60	1.50
50 Dwyane Wade	1.00	2.50
51 Ricky Rubio	.60	1.50
52 Ben Gordon	.50	1.25
53 Paul Pierce	.60	1.50
54 Al Jefferson	.50	1.25
55 Thomas Robinson	.50	1.25
56 Iman Shumpert	.60	1.50
57 Rajon Rondo	.60	1.50
58 Eric Bledsoe	.50	1.25
59 Greg Monroe	.50	1.25
60 Kobe Bryant	2.50	6.00
61 Al Horford	.50	1.25
62 Kemba Walker	1.25	3.00
63 LeBron James	2.50	6.00
64 Anthony Davis	3.00	8.00
65 Mario Chalmers	.50	1.25
66 Austin Rivers	.60	1.50
67 J.R. Smith	.50	1.25
68 Kevin Martin	.50	1.25
69 Gerald Wallace	.50	1.25
70 Russell Westbrook	1.50	4.00
71 Josh Smith	.50	1.25
72 Kenneth Faried	.60	1.50
73 LaMarcus Aldridge	.60	1.50
74 Derrick Favors	.50	1.25
75 Omer Asik	.50	1.25
76 Roy Hibbert	.50	1.25
77 Ty Lawson	.40	1.00
78 Gordon Hayward	.60	1.50
79 Larry Sanders	.40	1.00
80 Marcin Gortat	.50	1.25
81 Stephen Curry	2.50	6.00
82 Brook Lopez	.50	1.25
83 Mo Williams	.50	1.25
84 Nick Young	.50	1.25
85 Serge Ibaka	.50	1.25
86 Zach Randolph	.50	1.25
87 Taj Gibson	.50	1.25
88 Ray Allen	.60	1.50
89 Eric Gordon	.50	1.25
90 Jameer Nelson	.40	1.00
91 Dion Waiters	.60	1.50
92 Thaddeus Young	.40	1.00
93 Nicolas Batum	.50	1.25
94 Greivis Vasquez	.50	1.25
95 Shawn Marion	.50	1.25
96 Nikola Vucevic	.60	1.50
97 Metta World Peace	.60	1.50
98 Tony Parker	.60	1.50
99 Kyrie Irving	3.00	8.00
100 Jared Sullinger	.50	1.25

2012-13 Panini Past and Present Shattered

APPX.ODDS 1:10 HOBBY		
1 Dominique Wilkins	1.25	3.00
2 Josh Smith	.75	2.00
3 Kevin Garnett	1.50	4.00
4 Gerald Wallace	.75	2.00
5 Byron Mullens	.60	1.50
6 Michael Kidd-Gilchrist	1.00	2.50
7 Steve Francis	.75	2.00
8 Derrick Rose	1.25	3.00
9 Joakim Noah	.75	2.00
10 Brandon Bass	.60	1.50
11 Taj Gibson	.75	2.00
12 Alonzo Gee	.60	1.50
13 Anderson Varejao	.60	1.50
14 Dion Waiters	1.00	2.50
15 Vince Carter	1.25	3.00
16 Andre Iguodala	.75	2.00
17 Corey Brewer	.60	1.50
18 JaVale McGee	.75	2.00
19 David Lee	.60	1.50
20 Harrison Barnes	1.50	4.00
21 James Harden	1.50	4.00
22 Gerald Green	.75	2.00
23 Paul George	1.25	3.00
24 Blake Griffin	1.00	2.50
25 DeAndre Jordan	1.00	2.50
26 Dwight Howard	.75	2.00
27 Kobe Bryant	4.00	10.00
28 Rudy Gay	1.00	2.50
29 Dwyane Wade	1.50	4.00
30 LeBron James	4.00	10.00
31 Larry Sanders	.60	1.50
32 Anthony Davis	5.00	12.00
33 Amare Stoudemire	.75	2.00
34 Tyson Chandler	.75	2.00
35 Kevin Durant	2.50	6.00
36 Russell Westbrook	2.50	6.00
37 Serge Ibaka	.75	2.00
38 Darryl Dawkins	.60	1.50
39 Shawn Marion	.75	2.00
40 Julius Erving	1.50	4.00
41 Shannon Brown	.60	1.50
42 Clyde Drexler	1.25	3.00
43 LaMarcus Aldridge	1.00	2.50
44 Will Barton	.75	2.00
45 George Gervin	1.00	2.50
46 Shawn Kemp	1.50	4.00
47 DeMar DeRozan	1.00	2.50
48 J.R. Smith	.75	2.00
49 Shaquille O'Neal	2.00	5.00
50 Bradley Beal	1.50	4.00

2012-13 Panini Past and Present Shattered Black

APPX.ODDS 1:20 HOBBY		
1 Dominique Wilkins	1.50	4.00
2 Josh Smith	1.00	2.50
3 Kevin Garnett	2.00	5.00
4 Gerald Wallace	1.00	2.50
5 Byron Mullens	.75	2.00
6 Michael Kidd-Gilchrist	1.25	3.00
7 Steve Francis	1.00	2.50
8 Derrick Rose	1.50	4.00
9 Joakim Noah	1.00	2.50
10 Brandon Bass	.75	2.00
11 Taj Gibson	1.00	2.50
12 Alonzo Gee	.75	2.00
13 Anderson Varejao	.75	2.00
14 Dion Waiters	1.25	3.00
15 Vince Carter	1.50	4.00
16 Andre Iguodala	1.00	2.50
17 Corey Brewer	.75	2.00
18 JaVale McGee	1.00	2.50
19 David Lee	.75	2.00
20 Harrison Barnes	2.00	5.00
21 James Harden	2.00	5.00
22 Gerald Green	1.00	2.50
23 Paul George	1.50	4.00
24 Blake Griffin	1.25	3.00
25 DeAndre Jordan	1.25	3.00
26 Dwight Howard	1.00	2.50
27 Kobe Bryant	5.00	12.00
28 Rudy Gay	1.25	3.00
29 Dwyane Wade	2.00	5.00
30 LeBron James	5.00	12.00
31 Larry Sanders	.75	2.00
32 Anthony Davis	6.00	15.00
33 Amare Stoudemire	1.00	2.50
34 Tyson Chandler	1.00	2.50
35 Kevin Durant	3.00	8.00
36 Russell Westbrook	3.00	8.00
37 Serge Ibaka	1.00	2.50
38 Darryl Dawkins	.75	2.00
39 Shawn Marion	1.00	2.50
40 Julius Erving	2.00	5.00
41 Shannon Brown	.75	2.00
42 Clyde Drexler	1.50	4.00
43 LaMarcus Aldridge	1.25	3.00
44 Will Barton	1.00	2.50
45 George Gervin	1.25	3.00
46 Shawn Kemp	2.00	5.00
47 DeMar DeRozan	1.25	3.00
48 J.R. Smith	1.00	2.50
49 Shaquille O'Neal	2.50	6.00
50 Bradley Beal	2.00	5.00

2012-13 Panini Past and Present Signatures

EXCHANGE DEADLINE 11/01/2014		
51 Greg Monroe	4.00	10.00
52 Gordon Hayward	6.00	15.00
53 Paul George		
54 George Hill		
55 Blake Griffin EXCH	12.00	30.00
56 Kyle Lowry	4.00	10.00
57 Raymond Felton		
58 Kevin Durant	50.00	120.00
59 Steve Nash	50.00	100.00
60 Gerald Wallace		
61 Kevin Love	12.00	30.00
62 Jodie Meeks		
63 Andrew Bogut	4.00	10.00
64 Vince Carter	12.00	30.00
65 Chris Bosh		
66 Grant Hill	12.00	30.00
67 Mike Conley	6.00	15.00
68 Ricky Rubio	10.00	25.00
69 Carlos Boozer	4.00	10.00
70 Kobe Bryant	75.00	150.00
71 Chris Kaman	4.00	10.00
72 Ronnie Brewer	4.00	10.00
73 Corey Brewer	3.00	8.00
74 Rashard Lewis		
75 Danny Granger		
76 Dwyane Wade	20.00	50.00
77 Caron Butler		
78 Goran Dragic	4.00	10.00
80 JaVale McGee		
81 Shane Battier	4.00	10.00
82 Tony Allen	3.00	8.00
83 Antawn Jamison		
84 Brook Lopez	4.00	10.00
85 Josh Smith		
86 Brent Barry	8.00	20.00
87 Byron Scott		
88 Vernon Maxwell	6.00	15.00
89 Reggie Theus	4.00	10.00
90 Chris Mullin	5.00	12.00
91 Bobby Jackson	3.00	8.00
92 Larry Nance	4.00	10.00
93 Michael Cooper	4.00	10.00
94 Toni Kukoc	8.00	20.00
95 Robert Horry	4.00	10.00
96 Larry Johnson	4.00	10.00
97 Connie Hawkins	8.00	20.00
98 Darryl Dawkins	3.00	8.00
99 Bailey Howell		
100 George Gervin	6.00	15.00
101 Doc Rivers		
102 Rod Strickland	3.00	8.00
103 Mitch Richmond EXCH	12.00	30.00
104 Jamal Mashburn	5.00	12.00
105 Bernard King	4.00	10.00
106 Fat Lever	4.00	10.00
107 Sidney Moncrief	3.00	8.00
108 Dell Curry	3.00	8.00
109 Dominique Wilkins	12.00	30.00
110 Nate Archibald	4.00	10.00
111 Alex English	4.00	10.00
113 Tom Heinsohn	25.00	60.00
115 Antoine Walker	4.00	10.00
116 Hal Greer	4.00	10.00
117 Alonzo Mourning	8.00	20.00
119 David Robinson	12.00	30.00
120 Hakeem Olajuwon	20.00	50.00
122 Wes Unseld	10.00	25.00
123 Shaquille O'Neal		
124 Dikembe Mutombo	10.00	25.00
125 Anfernee Hardaway	12.00	30.00
127 Mario Chalmers	4.00	10.00
128 Joakim Noah		
129 Eric Bledsoe	4.00	10.00
130 Joe Johnson		
131 Tyson Chandler	8.00	20.00
132 Anderson Varejao		
133 Metta World Peace		
134 J.J. Hickson	3.00	8.00
135 Deron Williams		
136 Taj Gibson	4.00	10.00
137 Kris Humphries		
138 Jason Richardson	5.00	12.00
139 Roy Hibbert	5.00	12.00
140 Ersan Ilyasova	3.00	8.00
141 Eric Gordon	4.00	10.00
142 Tyler Hansbrough		
143 Ryan Anderson		
144 Stephen Curry	60.00	150.00
145 Chase Budinger		
146 Hedo Turkoglu		
147 Tiago Splitter		
148 Al-Farouq Aminu		
149 Ben Gordon	4.00	10.00
150 James Anderson	3.00	8.00
152 Will Barton	4.00	10.00
153 Greg Stiemsma	3.00	8.00
154 Lavoy Allen	3.00	8.00
155 Tyshawn Taylor	3.00	8.00
156 Festus Ezeli	4.00	10.00
157 Lance Thomas	3.00	8.00
158 Tyler Zeller	4.00	10.00
159 Fab Melo EXCH	3.00	8.00
160 Kyrie Irving	40.00	100.00
161 Tyler Honeycutt	3.00	8.00
162 Evan Fournier	5.00	12.00
163 Kyle Singler	3.00	8.00
164 Tristan Thompson	5.00	12.00
165 E'Twaun Moore	3.00	8.00
166 Kyle O'Quinn	3.00	8.00
167 Tornike Shengelia	3.00	8.00
168 Enes Kanter	4.00	10.00
169 Mirza Teletovic	4.00	10.00
170 Tony Wroten	4.00	10.00
171 Draymond Green	20.00	50.00
172 Klay Thompson	20.00	50.00
173 Tobias Harris	5.00	12.00
174 Doron Lamb	3.00	8.00
175 Kim English	3.00	8.00
176 Thomas Robinson	4.00	10.00
177 Donatas Motiejunas	4.00	10.00
178 Khris Middleton	5.00	12.00
179 Terrence Ross		
180 Dion Waiters EXCH	5.00	12.00
181 Kent Bazemore	5.00	12.00
182 Terrence Jones	4.00	10.00
183 Derrick Williams	3.00	8.00
184 Kenneth Faried	5.00	12.00
185 Victor Claver	3.00	8.00
186 DeQuan Jones	3.00	8.00
187 Kendall Marshall	3.00	8.00
188 Royce White	3.00	8.00
189 Darius Morris	3.00	8.00
190 Kemba Walker	10.00	25.00
191 Robert Sacre	3.00	8.00
192 DeAndre Liggins	4.00	10.00
193 Kawhi Leonard	60.00	150.00
194 Reggie Jackson	5.00	12.00
195 Harrison Barnes	6.00	15.00
196 Julyan Stone	3.00	8.00
197 Quincy Miller	3.00	8.00
198 Cory Joseph	3.00	8.00
199 Jeff Taylor	3.00	8.00
200 Quincy Acy	3.00	8.00
201 Chris Singleton		
202 Jordan Hamilton	3.00	8.00
203 Perry Jones		
204 Chris Copeland	3.00	8.00
205 Jonas Valanciunas	5.00	12.00
206 Orlando Johnson	3.00	8.00
207 Charles Jenkins	3.00	8.00
208 John Jenkins	3.00	8.00
209 Norris Cole	3.00	8.00
210 Chandler Parsons	5.00	12.00
211 John Henson	5.00	12.00
212 Nolan Smith	3.00	8.00
213 Brian Roberts	3.00	8.00
214 Jimmy Butler	20.00	50.00
215 Nikola Vucevic	5.00	12.00
216 Brandon Knight	5.00	12.00
217 Jimmer Fredette	3.00	8.00
218 Nando De Colo	3.00	8.00
219 Bradley Beal	8.00	20.00
220 Jeremy Pargo	3.00	8.00
221 Maurice Harkless	5.00	12.00
222 Bismack Biyombo	3.00	8.00
223 Jeremy Lamb	5.00	12.00
224 Miles Plumlee	3.00	8.00
225 Bernard James	3.00	8.00
226 Jared Sullinger	4.00	10.00
227 Mike Scott	3.00	8.00
228 Ben Hansbrough	3.00	8.00
229 Jared Cunningham	3.00	8.00
230 Michael Kidd-Gilchrist	5.00	12.00
231 Austin Rivers	5.00	12.00
232 Jan Vesely	3.00	8.00
233 Meyers Leonard	4.00	10.00
234 Arnett Moultrie	3.00	8.00
235 Jae Crowder	4.00	10.00
236 MarShon Brooks	4.00	10.00
237 Anthony Davis	60.00	150.00
238 Ivan Johnson	3.00	8.00
239 Marquis Teague	3.00	8.00
240 Andrew Nicholson	3.00	8.00
241 Isaiah Thomas	15.00	40.00
242 Markieff Morris	5.00	12.00
243 Andre Drummond	6.00	15.00
244 Iman Shumpert	5.00	12.00
245 Marcus Morris	4.00	10.00
246 Alec Burks	5.00	12.00
247 Gustavo Ayon	3.00	8.00
248 Malcolm Lee	3.00	8.00
250 Alexey Shved	3.00	8.00

2012-13 Panini Past and Present Treads

COMPLETE SET (35)	20.00	50.00
APPX.ODDS 1:4 HOBBY		
1 Chris Paul	1.00	2.50
2 Monta Ellis	.60	1.50
3 Dwight Howard	.60	1.50
4 Harrison Barnes	1.25	3.00
5 Kevin Durant	2.00	5.00
6 LeBron James	3.00	8.00
7 Paul George	1.00	2.50
8 Kevin Love	.75	2.00
9 Vince Carter	1.00	2.50
10 Tim Duncan	1.25	3.00
11 Ricky Rubio	.75	2.00
12 Rudy Gay	.75	2.00
13 Paul Pierce	.75	2.00
14 John Wall	1.00	2.50
15 Dirk Nowitzki	1.00	2.50
16 David Lee	.60	1.50
17 Blake Griffin	.75	2.00
18 Russell Westbrook	2.00	5.00
19 Michael Kidd-Gilchrist	.75	2.00
20 Rajon Rondo	.75	2.00
21 Dwyane Wade	1.25	3.00
22 Andre Iguodala	.60	1.50
23 Anthony Davis	4.00	10.00
24 Kobe Bryant	3.00	8.00
25 Tyreke Evans	.50	1.25
26 Brandon Knight	.75	2.00
27 O.J. Mayo	.50	1.25
28 Deron Williams	.60	1.50
29 Derrick Rose	1.00	2.50
30 Carmelo Anthony	1.00	2.50
31 DeMar DeRozan	.75	2.00
32 Kyrie Irving	4.00	10.00
33 Kevin Garnett	1.25	3.00
34 Damian Lillard	3.00	8.00
35 James Harden	1.25	3.00

2011-12 Panini Preferred

PS PRINT RUN 10 TO 99 SER.#'d SETS
PC PRINT RUN 15 TO 74 SER.#'d SETS
SL PRINT RUN 5 TO 99 SER.#'d SETS
CR PRINT RUN 24 TO 99 SER.#'d SETS
PS STANDS FOR PREFERRED SIGNATURES
PC STANDS FOR PANINIS CHOICE
SL STANDS FOR SILHOUETTE
CR STANDS FOR CROWN ROYALE
UNPRICED BLACK PRINT RUN ONE SET

1 Walt Bellamy PS/25 AU	5.00	12.00
2 Adrian Dantley PS/74 AU	4.00	10.00
3 Al Thornton PS/74 AU	4.00	10.00
4 Alex English PS/74 AU	4.00	10.00
5 Alonzo Mourning PS/25 AU	20.00	50.00
6 Andre Iguodala PS/25 AU	5.00	12.00
7 Andre Miller PS/49 AU	4.00	10.00
8 Andrea Bargnani PS/25 AU	6.00	15.00
9 Andrei Kirilenko PS/25 AU	8.00	20.00
10 Artis Gilmore PS/25 AU	8.00	20.00
11 Bailey Howell PS/74 AU	5.00	12.00
12 Bernard King PS/74 AU	6.00	15.00
13 Bill Cartwright PS/74 AU	6.00	15.00
14 Bill Laimbeer PS/74 AU	4.00	10.00
16 Bill Walton PS/25 AU	10.00	25.00
18 Bob Dandridge PS/74 AU	4.00	10.00
19 Bob McAdoo PS/74 AU	10.00	25.00
20 Brandon Jennings PS/25 AU	10.00	25.00
21 Byron Scott PS/49 AU	6.00	15.00
22 Calvin Murphy PS/25 AU	5.00	12.00
23 Campy Russell PS/74 AU	4.00	10.00
24 Cazzie Russell PS/74 AU	4.00	10.00
25 Cedric Maxwell PS/74 AU	4.00	10.00
26 Charles Oakley PS/74 AU	10.00	25.00
27 Chris Ford PS/74 AU	4.00	10.00
28 Chris Mullin PS/74 AU	10.00	25.00
30 Christian Laettner PS/25 AU	6.00	15.00
31 Clyde Lovellette PS/25 AU	6.00	15.00
32 Connie Hawkins PS/74 AU	8.00	20.00
33 Dan Issel PS/74 AU	5.00	12.00
34 Dan Majerle PS/74 AU	5.00	12.00
35 Darrell Griffith PS/74 AU	4.00	10.00
36 Darren Collison PS/74 AU	4.00	10.00
37 Darryl Dawkins PS/74 AU	5.00	12.00
38 Dave Cowens PS/49 AU	5.00	12.00
40 David Thompson PS/74 AU	4.00	10.00
41 DeMar DeRozan PS/25 AU	6.00	15.00
44 Detlef Schrempf PS/74 AU	8.00	20.00
45 Dikembe Mutombo PS/74 AU	15.00	40.00
46 Dirk Nowitzki PS/15 AU	100.00	175.00
47 Elgin Baylor PS/20 AU	12.00	30.00
48 Elvin Hayes PS/49 AU	5.00	12.00
49 Eric Gordon PS/49 AU	5.00	12.00
50 Frank Ramsey PS/74 AU	6.00	15.00
51 Gail Goodrich PS/25 AU	8.00	20.00
52 George Gervin PS/25 AU	10.00	25.00
53 George McGinnis PS/74 AU	4.00	10.00
54 Grant Hill PS/15 AU	100.00	200.00
55 Hakeem Olajuwon PS/15 AU	30.00	80.00
56 Isiah Thomas PS/25 AU	10.00	25.00
57 James Harden PS/25 AU	30.00	80.00
58 James Worthy PS/15 AU	25.00	60.00
59 Jeff Hornacek PS/74 AU	5.00	12.00
61 Jrue Holiday PS/49 AU	8.00	20.00
65 Kiki Vandeweghe PS/74 AU	4.00	10.00
66 Kobe Bryant PS/49 AU	100.00	200.00
68 Lenny Wilkens PS/25 AU	8.00	20.00
69 Luol Deng PS/25 AU	10.00	25.00
71 Mark Aguirre PS/74 AU	4.00	10.00
72 Mark Eaton PS/74 AU	4.00	10.00
73 Mark Price PS/74 AU	6.00	15.00
74 Maurice Cheeks PS/74 AU	4.00	10.00
75 Michael Cage PS/74 AU	4.00	10.00
76 M.Richmond PS/74 AU	8.00	20.00
77 Monta Ellis PS/49 AU	8.00	20.00
78 Nate Archibald PS/25 AU	8.00	20.00
79 Nate Thurmond PS/25 AU	8.00	20.00
82 Paul Westphal PS/74 AU	4.00	10.00
83 Ralph Sampson PS/74 AU	5.00	12.00
84 Robert Horry PS/49 AU	8.00	20.00
85 Robert Parish PS/25 AU	8.00	20.00
86 Rolando Blackman PS/74 AU	4.00	10.00
87 Sam Perkins PS/74 AU	4.00	10.00
88 Spencer Haywood PS/74 AU	4.00	10.00
89 Stephen Curry PS/49 AU	100.00	200.00
90 Stephen Jackson PS/74 AU	4.00	10.00
91 Steve Smith PS/74 AU	4.00	10.00
92 Tom Heinsohn PS/74 AU	15.00	40.00
93 D.Wilkins PS/25 AU	12.00	30.00
94 Toney Douglas PS/74 AU	4.00	10.00
95 Toni Kukoc PS/74 AU	6.00	15.00
96 Ty Lawson PS/49 AU	4.00	10.00
97 Walt Frazier PS/25 AU	10.00	25.00
98 Zach Randolph PS/25 AU	8.00	20.00
99 Xavier McDaniel PS/74 AU	4.00	10.00
100 World B. Free PS/25 AU	6.00	15.00
101 Walt Bellamy PC/25 AU	6.00	15.00
102 Adrian Dantley PC/74 AU	5.00	12.00
103 A.Thornton PC/74 AU EXCH	5.00	12.00
104 Alex English PC/74 AU	5.00	12.00
105 Alonzo Mourning PC/25 AU	60.00	150.00
106 Andre Iguodala PC/25 AU	6.00	15.00
107 Andre Miller PC/49 AU	5.00	12.00
108 Andrea Bargnani PC/25 AU	6.00	15.00
110 Artis Gilmore PC/25 AU	10.00	25.00
111 Bailey Howell PC/74 AU	5.00	12.00
112 Bernard King PC/74 AU	6.00	15.00
113 Bill Cartwright PC/74 AU	6.00	15.00
114 Bill Laimbeer PC/74 AU	6.00	15.00
115 Bill Russell PC/15 AU	75.00	150.00
116 Bill Walton PC/25 AU	6.00	15.00
117 Blake Griffin PC/25 AU	100.00	200.00
118 Bob Dandridge PC/74 AU	5.00	12.00
119 Bob McAdoo PC/74 AU	6.00	15.00
120 Brandon Jennings PC/25 AU	12.00	30.00
121 Byron Scott PC/74 AU	5.00	12.00
122 Calvin Murphy PC/25 AU	6.00	15.00
123 Campy Russell PC/74 AU	5.00	12.00
124 Cazzie Russell PC/74 AU	5.00	12.00
125 Cedric Maxwell PC/74 AU	5.00	12.00
126 Charles Oakley PC/74 AU	8.00	20.00
127 Chris Ford PC/74 AU	5.00	12.00
128 Chris Mullin PC/74 AU	10.00	25.00
129 Chris Paul PC/25 AU	40.00	100.00
130 Christian Laettner PC/25 AU	8.00	20.00
131 Clyde Lovellette PC/25 AU	6.00	15.00
132 Connie Hawkins PC/74 AU	8.00	20.00
133 Dan Issel PC/74 AU	5.00	12.00
134 Dan Majerle PC/74 AU	6.00	15.00
135 Darrell Griffith PC/74 AU	5.00	12.00
136 Darren Collison PC/74 AU	6.00	15.00
137 Darryl Dawkins PC/74 AU	5.00	12.00
138 Dave Cowens PC/25 AU	10.00	25.00
139 David Robinson PC/25 AU	50.00	125.00
140 David Thompson PC/74 AU	6.00	15.00
141 DeMar DeRozan PC/25 AU	12.00	30.00
142 Dennis Rodman PC/25 AU	30.00	80.00
143 Derrick Rose PC/20 AU	60.00	150.00
144 Detlef Schrempf PC/74 AU	8.00	20.00
145 D.Mutombo PC/74 AU	10.00	25.00
146 Elgin Baylor PC/25 AU	12.00	30.00
147 Elvin Hayes PC/25 AU	6.00	15.00
148 Eric Gordon PC/25 AU	8.00	20.00
149 Frank Ramsey PC/74 AU	6.00	15.00
150 Gail Goodrich PC/25 AU	8.00	20.00
151 George Gervin PC/25 AU	15.00	40.00
152 George McGinnis PC/74 AU	5.00	12.00
153 Grant Hill PC/25 AU	75.00	150.00
154 H.Olajuwon PC/25 AU	30.00	80.00
155 Isiah Thomas PC/25 AU	12.00	30.00
156 James Harden PC/25 AU	20.00	50.00
157 James Worthy PC/25 AU	15.00	40.00
158 Jeff Hornacek PC/74 AU	6.00	15.00
159 John Stockton PC/15 AU	50.00	120.00
160 Jrue Holiday PC/74 AU	8.00	20.00
161 Julius Erving PC/15 AU	50.00	125.00
162 K.Abdul-Jabbar PC/15 AU	50.00	100.00
163 Kevin Durant PC/25 AU	75.00	150.00
164 K.Vandeweghe PC/74 AU EXCH	5.00	12.00
165 Kobe Bryant PC/49 AU	150.00	300.00
166 Larry Bird PC/15 AU	100.00	175.00
167 Lenny Wilkens PC/25 AU	10.00	25.00
168 Luol Deng PC/25 AU	12.00	30.00
169 Magic Johnson PC/15 AU	75.00	150.00
170 Mark Aguirre PC/74 AU	5.00	12.00
171 Mark Eaton PC/74 AU	5.00	12.00
172 Mark Price PC/74 AU	12.00	30.00
173 Maurice Cheeks PC/74 AU	5.00	12.00
174 Michael Cage PC/74 AU	5.00	12.00
175 M.Richmond PC/74 AU	10.00	25.00
176 Monta Ellis PC/49 AU	10.00	25.00
177 Nate Archibald PC/25 AU	12.00	30.00
178 Nate Thurmond PC/25 AU	10.00	25.00
179 Oscar Robertson PC/25 AU	50.00	125.00
180 Pat Riley PC/25 AU	15.00	40.00
181 Paul Westphal PC/74 AU	5.00	12.00
182 Ralph Sampson PC/74 AU	6.00	15.00
183 Robert Horry PC/74 AU	8.00	20.00
184 Robert Parish PC/25 AU	10.00	25.00
185 Rolando Blackman PC/74 AU	6.00	15.00
186 Sam Perkins PC/74 AU	8.00	20.00
187 Spencer Haywood PC/74 AU	5.00	12.00
188 Stephen Curry PC/74 AU	100.00	250.00
189 Stephen Jackson PC/74 AU	5.00	12.00
190 Steve Nash PC/20 AU	20.00	50.00
191 Steve Smith PC/74 AU	5.00	12.00
192 Tom Heinsohn PC/74 AU	8.00	20.00
193 D.Wilkins PC/25 AU	15.00	40.00
194 Toney Douglas PC/74 AU	5.00	12.00
195 Toni Kukoc PC/49 AU	15.00	40.00
196 Ty Lawson PC/49 AU	8.00	20.00
197 Walt Frazier PC/25 AU	10.00	25.00
198 Zach Randolph PC/25 AU	10.00	25.00
199 Xavier McDaniel PC/74 AU	5.00	12.00
200 World B. Free PC/25 AU	8.00	20.00
201 Al Jefferson SL/25 JSY AU	10.00	25.00
202 Thornton SL/49 JSY AU EXCH	10.00	25.00
203 Alex English SL/49 JSY AU	10.00	25.00
204 A.Mourning SL/25 JSY AU	50.00	125.00
205 A.Iguodala SL/49 JSY AU	8.00	20.00
206 A.Bargnani SL/49 JSY AU	10.00	25.00
208 Artis Gilmore SL/25 JSY AU	20.00	50.00
210 Ben Gordon SL/25 JSY AU	12.00	30.00
211 Bernard King SL/24 JSY AU	15.00	40.00
212 Blake Griffin SL/25 JSY AU	175.00	325.00
213 B.Jennings SL/49 JSY AU	8.00	20.00
214 Charles Oakley SL/99 JSY AU	15.00	40.00
215 Chris Paul SL/25 JSY AU	75.00	200.00
216 Clyde Drexler SL/25 JSY AU	50.00	120.00
217 Dan Issel SL/49 JSY AU	6.00	15.00
218 Darrell Griffith SL/49 JSY AU	10.00	25.00
220 D.DeRozan SL/49 JSY AU	15.00	40.00
223 D.Schrempf SL/99 JSY AU	12.00	30.00
224 D.Mutombo SL/49 JSY AU	25.00	60.00
226 Grant Hill SL/25 JSY AU	125.00	250.00
227 H.Olajuwon SL/25 JSY AU	75.00	150.00
228 Isiah Thomas SL/25 JSY AU	30.00	80.00
229 J.Worthy SL/25 JSY AU	50.00	125.00
230 Jason Kidd SL/20 JSY AU	50.00	125.00
234 Kevin Love SL/25 JSY AU	100.00	200.00
235 K.Vandeweghe SL/99 JSY AU	8.00	20.00
236 Kobe Bryant SL/49 JSY AU	250.00	400.00
237 Luol Deng SL/49 JSY AU	8.00	20.00
238 Mark Aguirre SL/49 JSY AU	6.00	15.00
239 Mark Eaton SL/99 JSY AU	10.00	25.00
240 M.Cheeks SL/49 JSY AU	10.00	25.00
241 Michael Cage SL/99 JSY AU	10.00	25.00
242 M.Richmond SL/25 JSY AU	40.00	80.00
243 Monta Ellis SL/49 JSY AU	8.00	20.00
246 Robert Parish SL/49 JSY AU	15.00	40.00
247 S.Curry SL/99 JSY AU	200.00	400.00
248 D.Wilkins SL/25 JSY AU	30.00	80.00
249 Toni Kukoc SL/49 JSY AU	30.00	80.00
250 Ty Lawson SL/49 JSY AU	6.00	15.00
251 Artis Gilmore CR/25 AU	10.00	25.00
252 Bill Walton CR/25 AU	10.00	25.00
253 Dan Issel CR/25 AU	8.00	20.00
254 Darryl Dawkins CR/25 AU	6.00	15.00
255 Dave Cowens CR/25 AU	10.00	25.00
256 David Thompson CR/25 AU	8.00	20.00
257 Elgin Baylor CR/25 AU	15.00	40.00
258 George Gervin CR/25 AU	12.00	30.00
259 Oscar Robertson CR/25 AU	40.00	100.00
260 Walt Frazier CR/24 AU	10.00	25.00
261 Cole Aldrich CR/99 AU	3.00	8.00
262 Al-Farouq Aminu CR/99 AU	3.00	8.00
263 James Anderson CR/99 AU	3.00	8.00
264 Luke Babbitt CR/99 AU	3.00	8.00
265 Eric Bledsoe CR/99 AU	10.00	25.00
266 Trevor Booker CR/99 AU	3.00	8.00
267 Craig Brackins CR/99 AU	3.00	8.00
268 Avery Bradley CR/99 AU	6.00	15.00
269 D.Cousins CR/49 AU	20.00	50.00
270 Jordan Crawford CR/99 AU	3.00	8.00
271 Ed Davis CR/99 AU	3.00	8.00
272 Derrick Favors CR/49 AU	8.00	20.00
273 Landry Fields CR/99 AU	3.00	8.00
274 Paul George CR/99 AU	100.00	200.00
275 Luke Harangody CR/99 AU	3.00	8.00
276 Gordon Hayward CR/99 AU	6.00	15.00
277 Lazar Hayward CR/99 AU	3.00	8.00
278 Xavier Henry CR/99 AU	3.00	8.00
279 Wesley Johnson CR/49 AU	3.00	8.00
280 Greg Monroe CR/99 AU	8.00	20.00
281 Daniel Orton CR/99 AU	3.00	8.00
282 Patrick Patterson CR/99 AU	3.00	8.00
284 Gary Neal CR/99 AU	3.00	8.00
285 Devin Ebanks CR/99 AU	3.00	8.00
286 Evan Turner CR/49 AU	3.00	8.00
287 Ekpe Udoh CR/98 AU	3.00	8.00
288 Greivis Vasquez CR/99 AU	3.00	8.00
289 John Wall CR/49 AU	50.00	125.00
290 Elliot Williams CR/99 AU	3.00	8.00
291 Cole Aldrich PS/99 AU	3.00	8.00
292 Al-Farouq Aminu PS/99 AU	3.00	8.00
293 James Anderson PS/99 AU	3.00	8.00
294 Luke Babbitt PS/99 AU	3.00	8.00
295 Eric Bledsoe PS/99 AU	6.00	15.00
296 Trevor Booker PS/99 AU	3.00	8.00
297 Craig Brackins PS/99 AU	3.00	8.00
298 Avery Bradley PS/99 AU	6.00	15.00
299 D.Cousins PS/49 AU	12.00	30.00
300 Jordan Crawford PS/99 AU	3.00	8.00
301 Ed Davis PS/99 AU	3.00	8.00
302 Derrick Favors PS/49 AU	6.00	15.00
303 Landry Fields PS/99 AU	3.00	8.00
304 Paul George PS/99 AU	25.00	60.00
305 Luke Harangody PS/99 AU	3.00	8.00
306 Gordon Hayward PS/99 AU	6.00	15.00
307 L.Hayward PS/99 AU EXCH	3.00	8.00
308 Xavier Henry PS/99 AU	3.00	8.00
309 Wesley Johnson PS/49 AU	3.00	8.00
310 Greg Monroe PS/99 AU	5.00	12.00
311 Daniel Orton PS/99 AU	3.00	8.00
312 Patrick Patterson PS/99 AU	3.00	8.00
313 Andy Rautins PS/99 AU	3.00	8.00
314 Gary Neal PS/99 AU	3.00	8.00
315 Devin Ebanks PS/99 AU	3.00	8.00
316 Evan Turner PS/49 AU	4.00	10.00
317 Ekpe Udoh PS/99 AU	3.00	8.00
318 Greivis Vasquez PS/99 AU	3.00	8.00
319 John Wall PS/49 AU	40.00	100.00
320 Elliot Williams PS/99 AU	3.00	8.00
321 Cole Aldrich SL/99 JSY AU	6.00	15.00
322 A.Aminu SL/99 JSY AU	6.00	15.00
323 J.Anderson SL/99 JSY AU	6.00	15.00
324 Luke Babbitt SL/99 JSY AU	6.00	15.00
325 Eric Bledsoe SL/99 JSY AU	12.00	30.00
326 Trevor Booker SL/99 JSY AU	6.00	15.00
327 Craig Brackins SL/99 JSY AU	6.00	15.00
328 Avery Bradley SL/99 JSY AU	8.00	20.00
329 D.Cousins SL/49 JSY AU	30.00	80.00
330 Jo.Crawford SL/99 JSY AU	6.00	15.00
331 Ed Davis SL/99 JSY AU	6.00	15.00
332 Derrick Favors SL/49 JSY AU	8.00	20.00
333 Landry Fields SL/99 JSY AU	6.00	15.00
334 Paul George SL/99 JSY AU	40.00	100.00

335 L.Harangody SL/99 JSY AU 6.00 15.00
336 G.Hayward SL/99 JSY AU 15.00 40.00
337 L.Hayward SL/99 JSY AU 6.00 15.00
338 Xavier Henry SL/99 JSY AU 6.00 15.00
339 W.Johnson SL/49 JSY AU 6.00 15.00
340 Greg Monroe SL/99 JSY AU 6.00 15.00
341 Daniel Orton SL/99 JSY AU 6.00 15.00
342 P.Patterson SL/99 JSY AU 6.00 15.00
344 Gary Neal SL/99 JSY AU 6.00 15.00
345 Devin Ebanks SL/99 JSY AU 6.00 15.00
346 Evan Turner SL/49 JSY AU 6.00 15.00
347 Ekpe Udoh SL/99 JSY AU 6.00 15.00
348 G.Vasquez SL/99 JSY AU 6.00 15.00
349 John Wall SL/49 JSY AU 60.00 150.00
350 Elliot Williams SL/99 JSY AU 6.00 15.00

2011-12 Panini Preferred Blue
*BLUE: .5X TO 1.25X HI COLUMN
PS STATED PRINT RUN 5 TO 49 SETS
PC STATED PRINT RUN 6 TO 50 SER.#'d SETS
SOME UNPRICED DUE TO SCARCITY
84 Robert Horry PS/25 AU 12.00 30.00
86 Rolando Blackman PS/25 AU 8.00 20.00
95 Toni Kukoc PS/25 AU 10.00 25.00
106 Andre Iguodala PC/20 AU 6.00 15.00
108 Andrea Bargnani PC/20 AU 6.00 15.00
110 Artis Gilmore PC/20 AU 10.00 25.00
119 Bob McAdoo PC/50 AU 10.00 25.00
138 Dave Cowens PC/20 AU 10.00 25.00
139 David Robinson PC/15 AU 50.00 125.00
140 David Thompson PC/50 AU 6.00 15.00
142 Dennis Rodman PC/25 AU 30.00 80.00
143 Derrick Rose PC/15 AU 60.00 150.00
150 Gail Goodrich PC/20 AU 8.00 20.00
151 George Gervin PC/20 AU 15.00 40.00
153 Grant Hill PC/15 AU 75.00 150.00
154 H.Olajuwon PC/15 AU 30.00 80.00
158 Jeff Hornacek PC/50 AU 8.00 20.00
165 Kobe Bryant PC/50 AU 175.00 350.00
177 Nate Archibald PC/20 AU 12.00 30.00
179 Oscar Robertson PC/15 AU 50.00 125.00
180 Pat Riley PC/15 AU 15.00 40.00
184 Robert Parish PC/20 AU 10.00 25.00
185 R.Blackman PC/35 AU 8.00 20.00
190 Steve Nash PC/15 AU 30.00 80.00
197 Walt Frazier PC/20 AU 10.00 25.00
199 Xavier McDaniel PC/35 AU 8.00 20.00

2011-12 Panini Preferred Emerald
*EMERALD: .4X TO 1X HI COLUMN
PS STATED PRINT RUN 2 TO 75 SER.#'d SETS
PC STATED PRINT RUN 2 TO 5 SER.#'d SETS
SOME UNPRICED DUE TO SCARCITY
299 D.Cousins PS/25 AU 15.00 40.00
302 Derrick Favors PS/25 AU 8.00 20.00
309 Wesley Johnson PS/25 AU 8.00 20.00
319 John Wall PS/25 AU 40.00 100.00

2011-12 Panini Preferred Gold
*GOLD: .5X TO 1.25X HI COLUMN
PC STATED PRINT RUN 5 TO 10 SER.#'d SETS
CR STATED PRINT RUN 10 TO 25 SER.#'d SETS
SOME UNPRICED DUE TO SCARCITY
265 Eric Bledsoe CR/25 AU 15.00 40.00
268 Avery Bradley CR/25 AU 12.00 30.00
276 Gordon Hayward CR/25 AU 12.00 30.00

2011-12 Panini Preferred Silhouettes Prime
STATED PRINT RUN ONE TO 25 SER.#'d SETS
SOME UNPRICED DUE TO SCARCITY
202 Al Thornton/15 EXCH 25.00 60.00
203 Alex English/25 60.00 150.00
205 Andre Iguodala/15 40.00 100.00
213 Brandon Jennings/25 30.00 80.00
214 Charles Oakley/25 50.00 125.00
218 Darrell Griffith/25 40.00 100.00
224 Dikembe Mutombo/25 125.00 225.00
235 Kiki Vandeweghe/25 30.00 80.00
237 Luol Deng/25 30.00 80.00
238 Mark Aguirre/25 20.00 50.00
239 Mark Eaton/15 25.00 60.00
240 Maurice Cheeks/25 75.00 150.00
241 Michael Cage/25 20.00 50.00
242 Mitch Richmond/25 40.00 100.00
243 Monta Ellis/15 50.00 120.00
247 Stephen Curry/25 400.00 800.00
249 Toni Kukoc/25 150.00 300.00
250 Ty Lawson/25 50.00 120.00
321 Cole Aldrich/25 25.00 60.00
322 Al-Farouq Aminu/25 25.00 60.00
323 James Anderson/25 25.00 60.00
326 Trevor Booker/25 25.00 60.00
329 DeMarcus Cousins/25 100.00 200.00
332 Derrick Favors/25 30.00 80.00
333 Landry Fields/25 25.00 60.00
336 Gordon Hayward/25 30.00 80.00
337 Lazar Hayward/24 25.00 60.00
338 Xavier Henry/20 25.00 60.00
340 Greg Monroe/25 25.00 60.00
341 Daniel Orton/25 25.00 60.00
344 Gary Neal/25 25.00 60.00
345 Devin Ebanks/25 25.00 60.00
346 Evan Turner/25 25.00 60.00
347 Ekpe Udoh/25 25.00 60.00
349 John Wall/25 175.00 350.00
350 Elliot Williams/25 25.00 60.00

2011-12 Panini Preferred Silver
*SILVER: .5X TO 1.25X HI COLUMN
STATED PRINT RUN 5 TO 25 SER.#'d SETS
SOME UNPRICED DUE TO SCARCITY
104 Alex English PC/25 AU 8.00 20.00
106 Andre Iguodala PC/15 AU 10.00 25.00
108 Andrea Bargnani PC/15 AU 10.00 25.00
110 Artis Gilmore PC/15 AU 10.00 25.00
112 Bernard King PC/25 AU 10.00 25.00
126 Charles Oakley PC/25 AU 12.00 30.00
145 D.Mutombo PC/25 AU 15.00 40.00
151 George Gervin PC/15 AU 15.00 40.00
155 Isiah Thomas PC/15 AU 20.00 50.00
156 James Harden PC/15 AU 30.00 80.00
160 Jrue Holiday PC/25 AU 12.00 30.00
175 Mitch Richmond PC/25 AU 15.00 40.00
183 Robert Horry PC/25 AU 12.00 30.00
184 Robert Parish PC/15 AU 10.00 25.00
195 Toni Kukoc PC/25 AU 25.00 60.00

2011-12 Panini Preferred All-Star Memorabilia
STATED PRINT RUN 50 TO 199 SER.#'d SETS
1 AI/DR/RR/JK/CP/SN/TP/99 15.00 40.00
2 BG/DW/KD/CA/DN/LJ/DR/199 15.00 40.00
3 RL/XM/DS/GP/SK/RA/KD/79 15.00 40.00
4 LJ/DW/DW/MW/JH/CA/CK/199 15.00 40.00
5 AM/RA/KG/GH/LJ/DR/AH/50 15.00 40.00
6 CM/JS/KM/SP/CL/CD/LB/50 25.00 60.00
7 PE/LB/CD/CM/MJ/KM/JS/50 30.00 80.00
8 CO/EM/LJ/MJ/PE/JS/AS/199 15.00 40.00
9 KB/JO/VC/PP/KG/TM/AI/99 25.00 60.00
10 KJ/MM/SO/KB/DR/HO/KM/50 30.00 80.00

2011-12 Panini Preferred All-Star Memorabilia Prime
STATED PRINT RUN 10 TO 25 SER.#'d SETS
SOME UNPRICED DUE TO SCARCITY
1 AI/DR/RR/JK/CP/SN/TP/25 100.00 200.00
2 BG/DW/KD/CA/DN/LJ/DR/25 150.00 300.00
4 LJ/DW/DW/MW/JH/CA/CK/25 100.00 200.00
5 AM/RA/KG/GH/LJ/DR/AH/25 100.00 200.00
8 CO/EM/LJ/MJ/PE/JS/AS/25 75.00 150.00
9 KB/JO/VC/PP/KG/TM/AI/25 75.00 150.00
10 KJ/MM/SO/KB/DR/HO/KM/25 100.00 200.00

2011-12 Panini Preferred Assists Memorabilia
STATED PRINT RUN 50 TO 199 SER.#'d SETS
1 JS/IT/GP/MJ/MJ/JK/SN/99 20.00 50.00
2 JK/SN/TP/CP/DW/RR/DR/199 12.00 30.00
3 KB/LB/RR/DF/MJ/NV/GP/50 30.00 80.00
4 CB/SC/RW/DW/AM/MW/DR/199 12.00 30.00
5 DR/CB/ME/RR/RW/CP/SC/199 12.00 30.00
6 JS/MP/IT/KJ/MJ/MJ/LB/50 15.00 40.00

2011-12 Panini Preferred Assists Memorabilia Prime
STATED PRINT RUN 5 TO 25 SER.#'d SETS
SOME UNPRICED DUE TO SCARCITY
1 JS/IT/GP/MJ/MJ/JK/SN/25 100.00 200.00
2 JK/SN/TP/CP/DW/RR/DR/25 30.00 80.00
4 CB/SC/RW/DW/AM/MW/DR/25 30.00 80.00
5 DR/CB/ME/RR/RW/CP/SC/25 60.00 150.00

2011-12 Panini Preferred Centers Memorabilia
STATED PRINT RUN 99 TO 199 SER.#'d SETS
1 AB/MG/AV/MG/AB/TM/199 10.00 25.00
2 AS/AB/MO/PG/KL/EO/199 10.00 25.00
3 EO/CA/MC/TC/DH/GO/199 10.00 25.00
4 BC/DR/HO/DM/ME/MB/99 15.00 40.00

2011-12 Panini Preferred Centers Memorabilia Prime
STATED PRINT RUN 10 TO 25 SER.#'d SETS
SOME UNPRICED DUE TO SCARCITY
1 AB/MG/AV/MG/AB/TM/25 30.00 80.00
2 AS/AB/MO/PG/KL/EO/25 30.00 80.00
3 EO/CA/MC/TC/DH/GO/25 40.00 100.00

2011-12 Panini Preferred Decades Memorabilia
STATED PRINT RUN 10 TO 199 SER.#'d SETS
SOME UNPRICED DUE TO SCARCITY
UNPRICED PRIME PRINT RUN 3 TO 10 SETS
2 BL/CM/KM/JW/KV/MC/MA/DJ/25 20.00 50.00
3 PE/MJ/ME/KV/IT/JD/LB/DA/25 30.00 80.00
4 AM/DM/CM/DR/PE/MJ/MP/JS/99 15.00 40.00
5 DM/MR/MJ/LJ/PE/RH/KM/DS/99 12.00 30.00
6 AI/AM/RA/BW/KJ/SK/NV/LJ/199 20.00 50.00
7 KB/SP/AH/AI/TM/PP/VC/SN/199 20.00 50.00
8 CA/MG/TP/PG/DH/JJ/YM/LJ/199 12.00 30.00

2011-12 Panini Preferred Defense Memorabilia
STATED PRINT RUN 25 TO 199 SER.#'d SETS
UNPRICED PRIME PRINT RUN 3 TO 10 SETS
1 PE/RP/DR/MB/KA/DM/HO/50 15.00 40.00
2 SO/KA/PE/WC/DR/AM/YM/25 50.00 120.00
3 JS/BW/CA/EO/TT/TC/AK/199 10.00 25.00
4 JE/KM/PE/SH/MJ/MC/JS/25 25.00 60.00
5 TP/RB/RR/ME/SB/RA/MB/199 10.00 25.00
6 AM/TP/CP/JK/JS/IT/GP/50 12.00 30.00

2011-12 Panini Preferred Forwards Memorabilia
STATED PRINT RUN 125 TO 199 SETS
1 BG/DN/TM/PP/KD/TD/CB/125 20.00 50.00
2 GM/PG/LS/PP/AA/LH/LF/199 10.00 25.00
3 CB/ED/DC/EU/DE/DJ/ET/199 10.00 25.00
4 JN/AI/LA/HT/LO/LD/CA/199 10.00 25.00
5 CM/CP/DC/GR/DS/KW/LJ/125 10.00 25.00
6 KM/SP/KV/DC/TC/CD/DW/125 15.00 40.00

2011-12 Panini Preferred Forwards Memorabilia Prime
STATED PRINT RUN 15 TO 25 SER.#'d SETS
1 BG/DN/TM/PP/KD/TD/CB/25 40.00 80.00
4 JN/AI/LA/HT/LO/LD/CA/25 30.00 80.00
5 CM/CP/DC/GR/DS/KW/LJ/15 75.00 150.00
6 KM/SP/KV/DC/TC/CD/DW/25 125.00 250.00

2011-12 Panini Preferred Inducted Memorabilia
STATED PRINT RUN 50 TO 99 SER.#'d SETS
UNPRICED PRIME PRINT RUN 3 SETS
1 CM/DW/CD/DR/IT/JS/HO/PE/99 20.00 50.00
2 LB/PE/KM/KA/WC/DR/DW/JE/50 50.00 120.00
3 JE/LB/MM/RP/DR/KA/JD/MJ/50 40.00 100.00
4 KM/SP/JD/JS/JW/KM/CM/AE/99 20.00 50.00

2011-12 Panini Preferred Legends Memorabilia
STATED PRINT RUN 50 TO 150 SER.#'d SETS
UNPRICED PRIME PRINT RUN 3 TO 10 SETS
1 GM/SO/KA/EB/MJ/WC/50 50.00 120.00
2 SO/PE/DM/HO/KA/DR/150 20.00 50.00
3 KM/DR/IT/JS/PE/SP/150 20.00 50.00
4 LB/MJ/IT/KA/JE/CD/50 40.00 100.00
5 DA/SO/RP/LB/KM/SJ/50 30.00 80.00
6 AE/PE/KM/RP/MM/BK/150 12.00 30.00

2011-12 Panini Preferred Rebound Memorabilia
STATED PRINT RUN 199 SER.#'d SETS
1 AM/PE/KM/HO/DR/SO/DR 12.00 30.00
2 AS/KD/DH/KL/DN/KG/LJ 15.00 40.00
3 CB/LD/ZR/AJ/DL/MO/CB 10.00 25.00
4 SD/AB/CK/MC/JN/ZI/MG 10.00 25.00
5 NH/LD/AV/KL/TC/DG/SB 10.00 25.00
6 BM/TJ/LA/GO/PM/DW/UH 10.00 25.00

2011-12 Panini Preferred Rebound Memorabilia Prime
STATED PRINT RUN 10 TO 25 SER.#'d SETS
SOME UNPRICED DUE TO SCARCITY
1 AM/PE/KM/HO/DR/SO/DR/25 50.00 120.00
2 AS/KD/DH/KL/DN/KG/LJ/25 90.00 150.00
4 SD/AB/CK/MC/JN/ZI/MG/25 40.00 80.00
5 NH/LD/AV/KL/TC/DG/SB/25 25.00 50.00
6 BM/TJ/LA/GO/PM/DW/UH/25 30.00 60.00

2011-12 Panini Preferred Rookies Memorabilia
STATED PRINT RUN 99 SER.#'d SETS
1 JC/JW/ET/GM/DC/LF 12.00 30.00
2 JW/AR/DC/LS/ET/DF 10.00 25.00
3 EB/JW/ET/EU/DC/LH 10.00 25.00
4 JW/CA/EU/JA/JC/DE 10.00 25.00
5 CB/JW/DP/DC/JL/GN 15.00 40.00
6 JW/DJ/EU/QP/GH/ET 12.00 30.00
7 WJ/JW/GH/QP/EU/LS 10.00 25.00
8 JW/LF/EU/QP/GH/JC 12.00 30.00

2011-12 Panini Preferred Rookies Memorabilia Prime
STATED PRINT RUN 25 SER.#'d SETS
1 JC/JW/ET/GM/DC/LF 25.00 60.00
2 JW/AR/DC/LS/ET/DF 25.00 60.00
3 EB/JW/ET/EU/DC/LH 25.00 60.00
4 JW/CA/EU/JA/JC/DE 25.00 60.00
5 CB/JW/DP/DC/JL/GN 60.00 150.00
6 JW/DJ/EU/QP/GH/ET 25.00 60.00
7 WJ/JW/GH/QP/EU/LS 60.00 150.00
8 JW/LF/EU/QP/GH/JC 25.00 60.00

2011-12 Panini Preferred Slam Dunk Memorabilia
STATED PRINT RUN 99 TO 199 SER.#'d SETS
1 KB/SO/KG/TM/VC/GH/DR/CW/125 30.00 80.00
2 SP/CD/GH/KG/SO/DW/SK/LJ/125 12.00 30.00
3 JE/BG/DW/KB/LJ/VC/DW/CD/99 20.00 50.00
4 BG/AI/RW/TY/JM/TG/DD/SI/199 12.00 30.00
5 YM/TD/LA/AS/DH/PG/KG/SO/125 15.00 40.00
6 KD/JE/KB/DW/LJ/DW/VC/BG/125 20.00 50.00
7 NR/RW/TC/RG/JR/JS/CA/CA/199 12.00 30.00
8 JE/DW/TY/CD/BG/SI/DD/LJ/99 25.00 60.00

2011-12 Panini Preferred Slam Dunk Memorabilia Prime
STATED PRINT RUN 25 SER.#'d SETS
1 KB/SO/KG/TM/VC/GH/DR/CW 75.00 200.00
2 SP/CD/GH/KG/SO/DW/SK/LJ 100.00 250.00
3 JE/BG/DW/KB/LJ/VC/DW/CD 75.00 150.00
4 BG/AI/RW/TY/JM/TG/DD/SI 30.00 80.00
5 YM/TD/LA/AS/DH/PG/KG/SO 100.00 200.00
6 KD/JE/KB/DW/LJ/DW/VC/BG 125.00 250.00
7 NR/RW/TC/RG/JR/JS/CA/CA 30.00 80.00
8 JE/DW/TY/CD/BG/SI/DD/LJ 75.00 200.00

2012-13 Panini Preferred
PC PRINT RUN 20 TO 99 SER.#'d SETS
PS PRINT RUN 20 TO 74 SER.#'d SETS
SL PRINT RUN 8 TO 99 SER.#'d SETS
CR PRINT RUN 25 TO 99 SER.#'d SETS
PS STANDS FOR PREFERRED SIGNATURES
PC STANDS FOR PANINIS CHOICE
SL STANDS FOR SILHOUETTE
CR STANDS FOR CROWN ROYALE
NO PRICING ON QTY 15 OR LESS
EXCHANGE DEADLINE 10/24/2014
1 Al Jefferson PC AU/25 EXCH 6.00 15.00
2 A.Bynum PC AU/25 EXCH 5.00 12.00
3 Anfernee Hardaway PC AU/35 25.00 60.00
4 Antawn Jamison PC AU/50 5.00 12.00
5 Anthony Mason PC AU/74 5.00 12.00
6 Bailey Howell PC AU/74 6.00 15.00
7 Bernard King PC AU/74 5.00 12.00
8 Bill Cartwright PC AU/74 EXCH 5.00 12.00
9 Bill Laimbeer PC AU/74 5.00 12.00
10 Bill Russell PC AU/25 60.00 150.00
11 H.Grant PC AU/74 6.00 15.00
12 Bill Walton PC AU/35 8.00 20.00
13 B.Griffin PC AU/74 EXCH 30.00 80.00
14 Bob McAdoo PC AU/74 5.00 12.00
15 Byron Scott PC AU/25 6.00 15.00
16 Brandon Jennings PC AU/25 5.00 12.00
17 Brandon Rush PC AU/74 EXCH 4.00 10.00
18 Brook Lopez PC AU/35 6.00 15.00
19 Carl Landry PC AU/50 4.00 10.00
20 Chase Budinger PC AU/74 4.00 10.00
21 Chris Bosh PC AU/25 8.00 20.00
22 Chris Paul PC AU/35 EXCH 30.00 80.00
23 Clyde Drexler PC AU/35 10.00 25.00
24 Clyde Lovellette PC AU/25 8.00 20.00
25 Danny Granger PC AU/25 6.00 15.00
26 Darryl Dawkins PC AU/74 4.00 10.00
27 John Paxson PC AU/74 5.00 12.00
28 David Robinson PC AU/50 20.00 50.00
29 Ray Allen PC AU/35 EXCH 20.00 50.00
30 D.Cousins PC AU/25 8.00 20.00
31 Dennis Rodman PC AU/35 15.00 40.00
32 Deron Williams PC AU/50 5.00 12.00
33 Dolph Schayes PC AU/25 8.00 20.00
34 Derrick Favors PC AU/25 6.00 15.00
35 Anderson Varejao PC AU/74 4.00 10.00
36 Doc Rivers PC AU/25 8.00 20.00
37 Kyle Lowry PC AU/74 5.00 12.00
39 Rodney Stuckey PC AU/74 5.00 12.00
40 Gary Payton PC AU/35 8.00 20.00
41 Glen Rice PC AU/74 5.00 12.00
42 G.Hayward PC AU/74 6.00 15.00
43 Grant Hill PC AU/74 25.00 60.00
44 Greg Monroe PC AU/74 5.00 12.00
45 J.Harden PC AU/74 EXCH 10.00 25.00
46 Jason Kidd PC AU/35 8.00 20.00
47 Jerry West PC AU/25 20.00 50.00
48 Joe Johnson PC AU/25 6.00 15.00
49 John Starks PC AU/74 5.00 12.00
50 J.Stockton PC AU/25 EXCH 30.00 80.00
51 Jordan Crawford PC AU/74 EXCH 4.00 10.00
52 Jose Calderon PC AU/50 4.00 10.00
53 Julius Erving PC AU/25 40.00 100.00
54 K.Abdul-Jabbar PC AU/25 40.00 100.00
55 Kenny Anderson PC AU/74 5.00 12.00
56 Kevin Durant PC AU/50 60.00 150.00
57 Kevin Love PC AU/50 6.00 15.00
58 Kobe Bryant PC AU/74 75.00 200.00
59 L.Aldridge PC AU/50 6.00 15.00
60 Landry Fields PC AU/74 4.00 10.00
61 Larry Bird PC AU/25 50.00 120.00
62 L.Johnson PC AU/74 EXCH 8.00 20.00
63 R.Horry PC AU/74 EXCH 5.00 12.00
64 Magic Johnson PC AU/25 40.00 100.00
65 Marcin Gortat PC AU/74 5.00 12.00
66 Mario Chalmers PC AU/74 5.00 12.00
67 Mark Jackson PC AU/35 6.00 15.00
68 Marreese Speights PC AU/74 EXCH 4.00 10.00
69 Michael Finley PC AU/25 8.00 20.00
70 Muggsy Bogues PC AU/74 5.00 12.00
71 Nazr Mohammed PC AU/74 EXCH 4.00 10.00
72 Nick Collison PC AU/74 5.00 12.00
74 Nick Young PC AU/74 5.00 12.00
76 J.Crawford PC AU/50 EXCH 6.00 15.00
77 P.George PC AU/74 EXCH 20.00 50.00
78 Rashard Lewis PC AU/74 EXCH 5.00 12.00
79 Raymond Felton PC AU/25 6.00 15.00
80 Rick Fox PC AU/25 EXCH 6.00 15.00
81 Robert Parish PC AU/25 8.00 20.00
82 R.Beaubois PC AU/74 4.00 10.00
83 Ronnie Brewer PC AU/74 5.00 12.00
84 Ronny Turiaf PC AU/74 4.00 10.00
85 Roy Hibbert PC AU/74 5.00 12.00
86 Sam Perkins PC AU/74 4.00 10.00
87 Scottie Pippen PC AU/35 100.00 250.00
88 Serge Ibaka PC AU/74 5.00 12.00
89 Shane Battier PC AU/25 6.00 15.00
90 Spud Webb PC AU/74 5.00 12.00
92 Thabo Sefolosha PC AU/50 4.00 10.00
93 Tim Hardaway PC AU/74 6.00 15.00
94 Satch Sanders PC AU/74 6.00 15.00
95 Toni Kukoc PC AU/74 6.00 15.00
96 Tony Parker PC AU/35 8.00 20.00
97 Tyreke Evans PC AU/25 5.00 12.00
100 Z.Ilgauskas PC AU/74 5.00 12.00
101 Adrian Dantley PS AU/74 5.00 12.00
102 Alex English PS AU/74 5.00 12.00
103 Al-Farouq Aminu PS AU/74 5.00 12.00
104 Alonzo Mourning PS AU/50 20.00 50.00
108 Bailey Howell PS AU/74 6.00 15.00
109 Bernard King PS AU/74 5.00 12.00
111 B.Griffin PS AU/74 EXCH 20.00 50.00
112 Bob Dandridge PS AU/74 4.00 10.00
113 Bob Love PS AU/74 6.00 15.00
116 Campy Russell PS AU/74 4.00 10.00
118 Cazzie Russell PS AU/74 5.00 12.00
119 Charles Oakley PS AU/74 6.00 15.00
121 Chris Mullin PS AU/74 6.00 15.00
122 Connie Hawkins PS AU/74 6.00 15.00
123 Corey Brewer PS AU/74 4.00 10.00
124 Dan Issel PS AU/74 5.00 12.00
125 D.Majerle PS AU/74 5.00 12.00
126 Danny Green PS AU/74 5.00 12.00
128 Darren Collison PS AU/50 5.00 12.00
130 David Lee PS AU/25 5.00 12.00
131 David Thompson PS AU/74 5.00 12.00
132 Jim Jackson PS AU/74 4.00 10.00
133 Ersan Ilyasova PS AU/74 4.00 10.00
134 John Starks PS AU/74 5.00 12.00
135 Goran Dragic PS AU/74 5.00 12.00
137 Deron Williams PS AU/35 6.00 15.00
138 Detlef Schrempf PS AU/74 6.00 15.00
139 Dikembe Mutombo PS AU/50 6.00 15.00
140 D.Wilkins PS AU/25 10.00 25.00
141 Anderson Varejao PS AU/74 4.00 10.00
142 Ekpe Udoh PS AU/74 4.00 10.00
144 Eric Bledsoe PS AU/74 EXCH 5.00 12.00
146 Fat Lever PS AU/74 5.00 12.00
147 Kurt Rambis PS AU/74 4.00 10.00
149 George Gervin PS AU/25 8.00 20.00
150 George McGinnis PS AU/74 4.00 10.00
152 H.Olajuwon PS AU/25 25.00 60.00
153 Isiah Thomas PS AU/35 8.00 20.00
154 Jamaal Tinsley PS AU/74 4.00 10.00
155 J.Worthy PS AU/50 8.00 20.00
156 Jarrett Jack PS AU/74 5.00 12.00
157 Jason Richardson PS AU/50 6.00 15.00
158 Jeff Green PS AU/50 5.00 12.00
159 Jeff Hornacek PS AU/74 5.00 12.00
160 Jeff Teague PS AU/74 5.00 12.00
161 Jerry West PS AU/25 30.00 80.00
162 Joel Anthony PS AU/74 4.00 10.00
163 Cedric Maxwell PS AU/74 4.00 10.00
164 George Hill PS AU/74 5.00 12.00
165 K.Abdul-Jabbar PS AU/25 40.00 100.00
166 Kevin Durant PS AU/74 60.00 120.00
167 Kevin Love PS AU/50 6.00 15.00
168 Kobe Bryant PS AU/74 60.00 150.00
169 Kris Humphries PS AU/74 4.00 10.00
170 Kyle Korver PS AU/50 5.00 12.00
171 Larry Bird PS AU/25 50.00 120.00
173 Luc Mbah a Moute PS AU/74 4.00 10.00
174 L Deng PS AU/25 EXCH 20.00 50.00
175 Magic Johnson PS AU/25 30.00 80.00
176 Marcus Thornton PS AU/74 4.00 10.00
177 Mark Aguirre PS AU/50 5.00 12.00
178 Mark Eaton PS AU/74 4.00 10.00
179 Mark Price PS AU/74 6.00 15.00
180 Maurice Cheeks PS AU/74 4.00 10.00
181 Ryan Anderson PS AU/74 5.00 12.00
182 Mitch Richmond PS AU/74 6.00 15.00
183 Monta Ellis PS AU/25 6.00 15.00
184 Nate Archibald PS AU/25 6.00 15.00
185 N.Thurmond PS AU/25 EXCH 6.00 15.00
186 Paul Westphal PS AU/73 6.00 15.00
187 R.Sampson PS AU/74 5.00 12.00
188 Rolando Blackman PS AU/74 5.00 12.00
189 Spencer Haywood PS AU/74 4.00 10.00
190 Stephen Curry PS AU/50 30.00 80.00
191 Steve Kerr PS AU/35 8.00 20.00
192 Steve Nash PS AU/25 20.00 50.00
193 Steve Smith PS AU/74 5.00 12.00
194 Taj Gibson PS AU/74 5.00 12.00
195 Tom Heinsohn PS AU/50 6.00 15.00
196 Tony Allen PS AU/25 5.00 12.00
197 Vince Carter PS AU/35 10.00 25.00
200 World B. Free PS AU/25 6.00 15.00
201 Glen Rice SL JSY AU/49 15.00 40.00
204 B.Griffin SL JSY AU/25 EXCH 20.00 50.00
205 H.Olajuwon SL JSY AU/25 75.00 150.00
206 J.Stockton SL JSY AU/25 30.00 80.00
207 Kevin Durant SL JSY AU/25
208 Tony Parker SL JSY AU/49 20.00 50.00
209 R.Parish SL JSY AU/49 10.00 25.00
211 D.Rbnsn SL JSY AU/49 20.00 50.00
212 K.Bryant SL JSY AU/49 200.00 400.00
213 Ron Harper SL JSY AU/25 40.00 80.00
214 Tayshaun Prince SL JSY AU/49 6.00 15.00
215 A.Mourning SL JSY AU/49 50.00 100.00
216 Jalen Rose SL JSY AU/49 10.00 25.00
217 Joe Dumars SL JSY AU/49 8.00 20.00
218 D.Wilkins SL JSY AU/49 15.00 40.00
219 Raymond Felton SL JSY AU/49 8.00 20.00
220 Mark Price SL JSY AU/25 50.00 120.00
223 J.Hornacek SL JSY AU/25 12.00 30.00
224 Jose Calderon SL JSY AU/49 6.00 15.00
228 K.McHale SL JSY AU/25 EXCH 30.00 60.00
229 L.Aldridge SL JSY AU/49 15.00 40.00
230 Taj Gibson SL JSY AU/49 10.00 25.00
231 D.Manning SL JSY AU/25 10.00 25.00
233 Alex English SL JSY AU/25 12.00 30.00
235 H.Turkoglu SL JSY AU/49 6.00 15.00
236 Mark Jackson SL JSY AU/25 15.00 40.00
237 Luol Deng SL JSY AU/25 8.00 20.00
238 Kevin Love SL JSY AU/49 12.00 30.00
239 Derrick Favors SL JSY AU/25 12.00 30.00
240 Mark Aguirre SL JSY AU/25 8.00 20.00
241 E.Monroe SL JSY AU/25 EXCH 30.00 80.00
242 Bill Laimbeer SL JSY AU/25 10.00 25.00
243 C.Person SL JSY AU/25 EXCH 12.00 30.00
244 David Lee SL JSY AU/49 12.00 30.00
245 Maurice Cheeks SL JSY AU/29 8.00 20.00
246 Toni Kukoc SL JSY AU/49 15.00 40.00
247 Nick Van Exel SL JSY AU/49 30.00 60.00
248 Jamaal Wilkes SL JSY AU/25 20.00 50.00
251 Tyler Hansbrough SL JSY AU/49 8.00 20.00
252 Zach Randolph SL JSY AU/49 15.00 40.00
253 Cedric Maxwell SL JSY AU/29 15.00 40.00
255 Ty Lawson SL JSY AU/49 8.00 20.00
259 George Hill SL JSY AU/49 12.00 30.00
260 Steve Smith SL JSY AU/25 12.00 30.00
261 Yao Ming SL JSY AU/49 40.00 100.00
262 Tiago Splitter SL JSY AU/25 10.00 25.00
264 Mike Conley SL JSY AU/25 12.00 30.00
265 Joe Johnson SL JSY AU/49 8.00 20.00
266 Chris Bosh SL JSY AU/49 12.00 30.00
268 Gerald Wallace SL JSY AU/49 15.00 40.00
269 Marcus Camby SL JSY AU/49 10.00 25.00
270 Al-Farouq Aminu SL JSY AU/49 8.00 20.00
273 Ray Allen SL JSY AU/49 40.00 80.00
274 Carl Landry SL JSY AU/49 6.00 15.00
275 Chris Kaman SL JSY AU/49 8.00 20.00
276 Clyde Drexler SL JSY AU/25 90.00 150.00
277 Anderson Varejao SL JSY AU/49 6.00 15.00
278 C.Paul SL JSY AU/49 EXCH 60.00 120.00
279 D.Cousins SL JSY AU/49 10.00 25.00
280 Gary Neal SL JSY AU/49 EXCH 8.00 20.00
281 R.Lewis SL JSY AU/49 EXCH 5.00 12.00
282 Kevin Martin SL JSY AU/49 8.00 20.00
283 Grant Hill SL JSY AU/49 50.00 120.00
284 Artis Gilmore SL JSY AU/25 15.00 40.00
285 Sean Elliott SL JSY AU/49 15.00 40.00
286 A.Jamison SL JSY AU/49 15.00 40.00
287 Tyreke Evans SL JSY AU/49 10.00 25.00
288 A.Iguodala SL JSY AU/49 10.00 25.00
289 E.Gordon SL JSY AU/49 EXCH 6.00 15.00
290 Serge Ibaka SL JSY AU/49 30.00 60.00
291 Darren Collison SL JSY AU/49 5.00 12.00
292 Devin Harris SL JSY AU/45 5.00 12.00
293 E.Bledsoe SL JSY AU/49 EXCH 12.00 30.00
294 Drn.Williams SL JSY AU/25 20.00 50.00
296 J.Nelson SL JSY AU/49 EXCH 8.00 20.00
297 Wesley Matthews SL JSY AU/49 8.00 20.00
298 L.Johnson SL JSY AU/25 30.00 80.00
299 S.Curry SL JSY AU/49 100.00 250.00
300 Brandon Jennings SL JSY AU/49 8.00 20.00
301 Will Barton SL JSY AU/99 6.00 15.00
302 Royce White SL JSY AU/99 6.00 15.00
303 Ter.Jones SL JSY AU/99 12.00 30.00
304 T.Robinson SL JSY AU/99 8.00 20.00
305 Tobias Harris SL JSY AU/99 8.00 20.00
306 Tyler Zeller SL JSY AU/99 10.00 25.00
307 Quincy Miller SL JSY AU/99 5.00 12.00
308 Kim English SL JSY AU/99 5.00 12.00
309 K.Middleton SL JSY AU/99 8.00 20.00
310 K.Faried SL JSY AU/99 8.00 20.00
311 K.Marshall SL JSY AU/99 10.00 25.00
312 J.Sullinger SL JSY AU/99 6.00 15.00
313 Jared Cunningham SL JSY AU/99 5.00 12.00
314 Perry Jones SL JSY AU/99 5.00 12.00
315 Orlando Johnson SL JSY AU/99 5.00 12.00
316 Norris Cole SL JSY AU/99 10.00 25.00
317 Kris Joseph SL JSY AU/99 5.00 12.00
318 K.Walker SL JSY AU/99 30.00 80.00
319 K.Leonard SL JSY AU/99 50.00 120.00
320 John Henson SL JSY AU/99 8.00 20.00
321 Jimmy Butler SL JSY AU/99 30.00 80.00
322 J.Fredette SL JSY AU/99 8.00 20.00
323 J.Lamb SL JSY AU/99 EXCH 12.00 30.00
324 B.James SL JSY AU/99 EXCH 6.00 15.00
325 A.Davis SL JSY AU/99 200.00 300.00
326 Andrew Nicholson SL JSY AU/99 8.00 20.00
327 Kyrie Irving SL JSY AU/99 100.00 200.00
328 Marquis Teague SL JSY AU/99 6.00 15.00
329 MarShon Brooks SL JSY AU/99 8.00 20.00
330 Meyers Leonard SL JSY AU/99 6.00 15.00
331 Kidd-Gilch SL JSY AU/99 12.00 30.00
332 Mike Scott SL JSY AU/99 5.00 12.00
333 Doron Lamb SL JSY AU/99 6.00 15.00
334 M.Harkless SL JSY AU/99 12.00 30.00
335 R.Jackson SL JSY AU/99 12.00 30.00
336 Robert Sacre SL JSY AU/99 6.00 15.00
337 Markieff Morris SL JSY AU/99 6.00 15.00
338 Lavoy Allen SL JSY AU/99 5.00 12.00
339 Lance Thomas SL JSY AU/99 5.00 12.00
340 Josh Selby SL JSY AU/99 5.00 12.00
341 Josh Harrellson SL JSY AU/99 EXCH 5.00 12.00
342 Jordan Hamilton SL JSY AU/99 5.00 12.00
343 J.Valanciunas SL JSY AU/99 12.00 30.00
344 John Jenkins SL JSY AU/99 6.00 15.00
345 Jan Vesely SL JSY AU/99 5.00 12.00
346 Jae Crowder SL JSY AU/99 6.00 15.00
347 Ivan Johnson SL JSY AU/99 5.00 12.00
348 H.Barnes SL JSY AU/99 20.00 50.00
349 Evan Fournier SL JSY AU/99 8.00 20.00
350 E'Twaun Moore SL JSY AU/99 6.00 15.00
351 Enes Kanter SL JSY AU/99 15.00 40.00
352 D.Green SL JSY AU/99 75.00 200.00
353 Marcus Morris SL JSY AU/99 6.00 15.00
354 Dion Waiters SL JSY AU/99 20.00 50.00
355 Derrick Williams SL JSY AU/99 6.00 15.00
356 Darius Morris SL JSY AU/99 6.00 15.00
357 Brandon Knight SL JSY AU/99 6.00 15.00
358 Bradley Beal SL JSY AU/99 30.00 80.00
359 B.Biyombo SL JSY AU/99 8.00 20.00
360 N.Vucevic SL JSY AU/99 12.00 30.00
361 A.Drummond SL JSY AU/99 50.00 120.00
362 Alec Burks SL JSY AU/99 10.00 25.00
363 Tony Wroten SL JSY AU/99 12.00 30.00
364 T.Thompson SL JSY AU/99 10.00 25.00
365 Kyle Singler SL JSY AU/99 8.00 20.00
366 Darius Johnson-Odom SL JSY AU/99 EXCH 5.00 12.00
367 A.Rivers SL JSY AU/99 EXCH 10.00 25.00
368 Arnett Moultrie SL JSY AU/99 5.00 12.00
369 Kyle O'Quinn SL JSY AU/99 5.00 12.00
370 Miles Plumlee SL JSY AU/99 5.00 12.00
371 T.Ross SL JSY AU/99 EXCH 10.00 25.00
372 Quincy Acy SL JSY AU/99 6.00 15.00
373 Iman Shumpert SL JSY AU/99 5.00 12.00
374 Charles Jenkins SL JSY AU/99 5.00 12.00
375 C.Parsons SL JSY AU/99 15.00 40.00
376 Tyler Honeycutt SL JSY AU/99 5.00 12.00
377 Nolan Smith SL JSY AU/99 5.00 12.00
378 Cory Joseph SL JSY AU/99 8.00 20.00
379 Festus Ezeli SL JSY AU/99 6.00 15.00
380 I.Thomas SL JSY AU/99 30.00 80.00
381 Jeremy Pargo SL JSY AU/99 5.00 12.00
382 Will Barton CR AU/99 5.00 12.00
383 Royce White CR AU/99 4.00 10.00
384 Brian Roberts CR AU/99 4.00 10.00
385 Terrence Jones CR AU/99 5.00 12.00
386 Thomas Robinson CR AU/79 5.00 12.00
387 Tobias Harris CR AU/99 6.00 15.00
388 Tyler Zeller CR AU/99 5.00 12.00
389 Quincy Miller CR AU/99 EXCH 4.00 10.00
390 Kim English CR AU/99 4.00 10.00
391 Khris Middleton CR AU/99 6.00 15.00
392 Kenneth Faried CR AU/99 6.00 15.00
393 Kendall Marshall CR AU/99 4.00 10.00
394 Jared Sullinger CR AU/99 5.00 12.00
395 Jared Cunningham CR AU/99 4.00 10.00
396 Perry Jones CR AU/99 4.00 10.00
397 Orlando Johnson CR AU/99 4.00 10.00
398 Norris Cole CR AU/99 4.00 10.00
399 Kris Joseph CR AU/99 4.00 10.00
400 Kemba Walker CR AU/49 12.00 30.00
401 Kawhi Leonard CR AU/99 40.00 100.00
402 John Henson CR AU/99 6.00 15.00
403 Jimmy Butler CR AU/99 20.00 50.00
404 Jimmer Fredette CR AU/99 4.00 10.00
405 Jeremy Lamb CR AU/99 EXCH 6.00 15.00
406 Bernard James CR AU/99 4.00 10.00
407 Anthony Davis CR AU/25 200.00 400.00
408 Andrew Nicholson CR AU/99 4.00 10.00
409 Kyrie Irving CR AU/79 75.00 200.00
410 Marquis Teague CR AU/99 4.00 10.00
411 MarShon Brooks CR AU/99 5.00 12.00
412 Meyers Leonard CR AU/99 5.00 12.00
413 M.Kidd-Gilchrist CR AU/49 6.00 15.00
414 Mike Scott CR AU/99 4.00 10.00
415 Doron Lamb CR AU/99 4.00 10.00
416 Maurice Harkless CR AU/99 6.00 15.00
417 Reggie Jackson CR AU/99 6.00 15.00
418 Robert Sacre CR AU/99 4.00 10.00
419 Markieff Morris CR AU/79 6.00 15.00
420 Chris Copeland CR AU/99 4.00 10.00
421 Lavoy Allen CR AU/99 4.00 10.00
422 Lance Thomas CR AU/99 4.00 10.00
423 Josh Selby CR AU/99 4.00 10.00
424 Josh Harrellson CR AU/99 EXCH 4.00 10.00
425 Jordan Hamilton CR AU/99 4.00 10.00
426 Jonas Valanciunas CR AU/99 6.00 15.00
427 John Jenkins CR AU/99 4.00 10.00
428 Jan Vesely CR AU/99 4.00 10.00
429 Jae Crowder CR AU/99 5.00 12.00
430 Ivan Johnson CR AU/99 4.00 10.00
431 Harrison Barnes CR AU/49 25.00 60.00
432 Fab Melo CR AU/99 4.00 10.00
433 Evan Fournier CR AU/99 6.00 15.00
434 E'Twaun Moore CR AU/99 4.00 10.00
435 Enes Kanter CR AU/99 5.00 12.00
436 Draymond Green CR AU/99 20.00 50.00
437 Marcus Morris CR AU/79 5.00 12.00
438 Dion Waiters CR AU/99 6.00 15.00
439 Derrick Williams CR AU/99 4.00 10.00
440 Darius Morris CR AU/99 4.00 10.00
441 Brandon Knight CR AU/99 6.00 15.00
442 Bradley Beal CR AU/99 10.00 25.00
443 Bismack Biyombo CR AU/99 4.00 10.00
444 Nikola Vucevic CR AU/99 6.00 15.00
445 DeQuan Jones CR AU/99 4.00 10.00
446 A.Drummond CR AU/99 20.00 50.00
447 Alec Burks CR AU/99 6.00 15.00
448 Tony Wroten CR AU/49 5.00 12.00
449 Tristan Thompson CR AU/99 6.00 15.00
450 Kyle Singler CR AU/99 4.00 10.00
451 Darius Johnson Odom CR AU/99 EXCH 4.00 10.00
452 A.Rivers CR AU/79 EXCH 6.00 15.00
453 Arnett Moultrie CR AU/99 4.00 10.00
454 Kyle O'Quinn CR AU/99 4.00 10.00
455 T.Ross CR AU/99 EXCH 6.00 15.00
456 Quincy Acy CR AU/99 4.00 10.00
457 Iman Shumpert CR AU/99 6.00 15.00
458 Charles Jenkins CR AU/99 4.00 10.00
459 Chandler Parsons CR AU/99 6.00 15.00
460 Tyler Honeycutt CR AU/99 4.00 10.00
461 Nolan Smith CR AU/99 4.00 10.00
462 Cory Joseph CR AU/99 4.00 10.00
463 Festus Ezeli CR AU/99 5.00 12.00
464 Isaiah Thomas CR AU/99 20.00 50.00
465 Jeremy Pargo CR AU/99 4.00 10.00
466 Jeremy Tyler CR AU/99 4.00 10.00
467 Kevin Murphy CR AU/99 4.00 10.00
468 Darius Miller CR AU/99 EXCH 4.00 10.00
469 DeAndre Liggins CR AU/99 EXCH 5.00 12.00
470 Greg Stiemsma CR AU/99 4.00 10.00
471 Gustavo Ayon CR AU/99 4.00 10.00
472 Jeff Taylor CR AU/99 4.00 10.00
473 Jon Leuer CR AU/99 5.00 12.00
474 Nando De Colo CR AU/99 4.00 10.00
475 Maalik Wayns CR AU/99 EXCH 6.00 15.00
476 Malcolm Lee CR AU/99 4.00 10.00
477 Trey Thompkins CR AU/99 4.00 10.00
478 Tyshawn Taylor CR AU/99 EXCH 4.00 10.00
479 Chris Singleton CR AU/99 EXCH 4.00 10.00
480 Kent Bazemore CR AU/99 6.00 15.00
481 Miles Plumlee CR AU/99 EXCH 4.00 10.00
482 Will Barton PC AU/99 5.00 12.00
483 Royce White PC AU/99 4.00 10.00
484 Chris Copeland PC AU/99 4.00 10.00
485 Terrence Jones PC AU/99 5.00 12.00
486 Thomas Robinson PC AU/74 5.00 12.00
487 Tobias Harris PC AU/99 6.00 15.00
488 Tyler Zeller PC AU/99 5.00 12.00
489 Quincy Miller PC AU/99 EXCH 4.00 10.00
490 Kim English PC AU/99 4.00 10.00
491 Khris Middleton PC AU/99 6.00 15.00
492 Kenneth Faried PC AU/99 6.00 15.00
493 Kendall Marshall PC AU/99 4.00 10.00
494 Jared Sullinger PC AU/74 5.00 12.00
495 Jared Cunningham PC AU/99 4.00 10.00
496 Perry Jones PC AU/99 4.00 10.00
497 Orlando Johnson PC AU/99 4.00 10.00
498 Norris Cole PC AU/99 4.00 10.00
499 DeQuan Jones PC AU/99 4.00 10.00
500 Kemba Walker PC AU/49 12.00 30.00
501 Kawhi Leonard PC AU/99 40.00 100.00
502 John Henson PC AU/99 6.00 15.00
503 Jimmy Butler PC AU/99 25.00 60.00
504 Jimmer Fredette PC AU/99 4.00 10.00
505 Jeremy Lamb PC AU/99 EXCH 6.00 15.00
506 Bernard James PC AU/99 4.00 10.00
507 Anthony Davis PC AU/25 100.00 250.00
508 Andrew Nicholson PC AU/99 4.00 10.00
509 Kyrie Irving PC AU/25 150.00 300.00
510 Marquis Teague PC AU/99 4.00 10.00
511 MarShon Brooks PC AU/99 5.00 12.00
512 Meyers Leonard PC AU/99 5.00 12.00
513 M.Kidd-Gilchrist PC AU/25 25.00 60.00
514 Mike Scott PC AU/99 4.00 10.00
515 Doron Lamb PC AU/99 4.00 10.00
516 Maurice Harkless PC AU/99 6.00 15.00
517 Reggie Jackson PC AU/99 6.00 15.00
518 Robert Sacre PC AU/99 4.00 10.00
519 Markieff Morris PC AU/99 6.00 15.00
520 Lavoy Allen PC AU/99 4.00 10.00
521 Lance Thomas PC AU/99 4.00 10.00
522 Josh Selby PC AU/99 4.00 10.00
523 Josh Harrellson PC AU/99 EXCH 4.00 10.00
524 Jordan Hamilton PC AU/99 4.00 10.00
525 Jonas Valanciunas PC AU/99 6.00 15.00
526 John Jenkins PC AU/99 4.00 10.00
527 Jan Vesely PC AU/99 4.00 10.00
528 Jae Crowder PC AU/99 5.00 12.00
529 Ivan Johnson PC AU/99 4.00 10.00
530 Harrison Barnes PC AU/74 10.00 25.00
531 Nando De Colo PC AU/99 4.00 10.00
532 Evan Fournier PC AU/99 6.00 15.00
533 E'Twaun Moore PC AU/99 4.00 10.00
534 Enes Kanter PC AU/99 5.00 12.00
535 Draymond Green PC AU/99 30.00 80.00
536 Marcus Morris PC AU/99 5.00 12.00
537 Dion Waiters PC AU/99 6.00 15.00
538 Derrick Williams PC AU/74 4.00 10.00
539 Darius Morris PC AU/99 4.00 10.00
540 Brandon Knight PC AU/99 6.00 15.00
541 Bradley Beal PC AU/99 10.00 25.00
542 Bismack Biyombo PC AU/99 4.00 10.00
543 Nikola Vucevic PC AU/99 6.00 15.00
544 Kris Joseph PC AU/99 4.00 10.00
545 A.Drummond PC AU/74 20.00 50.00
546 Alec Burks PC AU/99 6.00 15.00
547 Tony Wroten PC AU/99 5.00 12.00
548 Tristan Thompson PC AU/99 6.00 15.00
549 Kyle Singler PC AU/99 4.00 10.00
550 Darius Johnson-Odom PC AU/99 EXCH 4.00 10.00
551 Austin Rivers PC AU/99 EXCH 6.00 15.00
552 Arnett Moultrie PC AU/99 4.00 10.00
553 Kyle O'Quinn PC AU/99 4.00 10.00
554 Terrence Ross PC AU/99 EXCH 6.00 15.00
555 Quincy Acy PC AU/99 4.00 10.00
556 Iman Shumpert PC AU/99 6.00 15.00
557 Charles Jenkins PC AU/99 4.00 10.00
558 Chandler Parsons PC AU/99 6.00 15.00
559 Tyler Honeycutt PC AU/99 4.00 10.00
560 Nolan Smith PC AU/99 4.00 10.00
561 Cory Joseph PC AU/99 4.00 10.00
562 Festus Ezeli PC AU/99 5.00 12.00
563 Isaiah Thomas PC AU/99 20.00 50.00
564 Jeremy Pargo PC AU/99 4.00 10.00
565 Jeremy Tyler PC AU/99 4.00 10.00
566 Kevin Murphy PC AU/99 4.00 10.00
567 Darius Miller PC AU/99 EXCH 4.00 10.00
568 DeAndre Liggins PC AU/99 EXCH 5.00 12.00
569 Greg Stiemsma PC AU/99 4.00 10.00
570 Gustavo Ayon PC AU/99 4.00 10.00
571 Jeff Taylor PC AU/99 4.00 10.00
572 Jon Leuer PC AU/99 5.00 12.00
573 Brian Roberts PC AU/99 4.00 10.00
574 Maalik Wayns PC AU/99 EXCH 6.00 15.00
575 Malcolm Lee PC AU/99 4.00 10.00
576 Trey Thompkins PC AU/99 4.00 10.00
577 Tyshawn Taylor PC AU/99 EXCH 4.00 10.00
578 Chris Singleton PC AU/99 EXCH 4.00 10.00
579 Kent Bazemore PC AU/99 6.00 15.00
580 Miles Plumlee PC AU/99 EXCH 4.00 10.00
581 Fab Melo PC AU/99 4.00 10.00
582 D.Lillard CR JSY AU/99 75.00 200.00

2012-13 Panini Preferred Blue
*BLUE: .5X TO 1.2X BASIC
PRINT RUNS BW/N 15-49 COPIES PER
NO PRICING ON QTY 20 OR LESS
EXCHANGE DEADLINE 10/24/2014

2012-13 Panini Preferred 50 Greats Memorabilia
PRINT RUNS B/WN 129-149 COPIES PER
1 G/S/P/E/D/R/O/M/129 15.00 40.00
2 M/O/D/E/T/R/S/P/149 15.00 40.00

2012-13 Panini Preferred All World Memorabilia
STATED PRINT RUN 199 SER.#'d SETS
1 K/V/D/H/B/R/D/G 10.00 25.00
2 G/M/O/M/B/S/G/T 12.00 30.00
3 T/U/B/K/C/N/G/P 12.00 30.00

2012-13 Panini Preferred Awards Memorabilia
STATED PRINT RUN 199 SER.#'d SETS
1 Jam/Ros/Bry/Now/Nash/Garn 20.00 50.00
2 Irv/Grif/Evan/Ros/Dur/Roy 10.00 25.00
3 Hard/Terry/Ginoi/Jack/McH/Kuk 10.00 25.00
4 Wal/How/Gar/Metta/Chan/Mut 10.00 25.00

2012-13 Panini Preferred Boston Memorabilia
PRINT RUNS B/WN 129-149 COPIES PER
1 John/Ron/Pier/Bird/McH/Sul/129 20.00 50.00
2 Gart/Pie/McH/Par/Sul/Ron/199 12.00 30.00

2012-13 Panini Preferred Bryant Memorabilia
STATED PRINT RUN 199 SER.#'d SET
1 Kobe Bryant 30.00 80.00

2012-13 Panini Preferred Buckets Memorabilia
STATED PRINT RUN 199 SER.#'d SETS
1 Har/Bry/Cur/Wes/Pau/Jam/Pie 15.00 40.00
2 Wall/Will/Wes/Ros/Joh/May/Thom 10.00 25.00
3 Thom/Col/Fred/Pri/Sto/All/Gino 12.50 30.00
4 Bry/Thom/Dur/Now/Gino/Ros/Lov 10.00 25.00
5 Gino/Fel/Wal/Wad/Ros/Wall/Cur 10.00 25.00

2012-13 Panini Preferred Celtics Memorabilia
PRINT RUNS B/WN 25-149 COPIES PER
1 Pie/Gar/RonSul/Mel/Ter/Gre/149 12.00 30.00
2 McH/Bir/Par/How/Cha/Pie/Gar/25 12.00 30.00

2012-13 Panini Preferred Center Memorabilia
STATED PRINT RUN 199 SER.#'d SETS
1 Bog/Haw/How/Ola/Rob/O'Ne 10.00 25.00
2 Haw/Kan/Wal/Min/Jef/Spl 15.00 40.00

2012-13 Panini Preferred Champs Memorabilia
STATED PRINT RUN 199 SER.#'d SETS
1 Jon/Jam/Wad/Bos/Col/Has 10.00 25.00
2 Now/Bea/Cha/Kid/But/Mar 10.00 25.00
3 Bry/Gas/Wor/Pea/Byn/Fis/Wal 15.00 40.00

2012-13 Panini Preferred Chicago Memorabilia
PRINT RUNS B/WN 179-199 COPIES PER
1 Har/KukPar/Ros/Noa/Den/Boo/179 15.00 40.00
2 But/Noa/Ros/Gib/Den/Hin/Boo/199 12.00 30.00

2012-13 Panini Preferred Clutch Memorabilia
STATED PRINT RUN 199 SER.#'d SETS
1 Cur/Law/Bry/Bil/Pau/Ron 12.00 30.00
2 Bry/Pau/All/Har/Jen/Eva 12.00 30.00

2012-13 Panini Preferred Decades Memorabilia
PRINT RUNS B/WN 10-199 COPIES PER
2 1970s 20.00 50.00
3 1980s 8.00 20.00
4 1990s 12.00 30.00
5 2000s 12.00 30.00

2012-13 Panini Preferred Defense Memorabilia
STATED PRINT RUN 199 SER.#'d SETS
1 How/Wal/Rod/Dun/Gar/Far/Ran 12.50 30.00
2 Bos/Wad/Ros/Par/Pau/Ron/Metta 12.50 30.00
3 Ola/Mut/Mou/Rod/Rob/How/Cam 12.50 30.00

2012-13 Panini Preferred Detroit Memorabilia
STATED PRINT RUN 199 SER.#'d SETS
1 Dru/Mon/Pri/Mid/Eng/Sin/Stu 10.00 25.00
2 Tri/Kni/Pri/Dru/Mon/Tho/Wal 8.00 20.00
3 Kni/Sin/Wal/Pri/Dru/Tho/Mon 10.00 25.00

2012-13 Panini Preferred Diesel Memorabilia
STATED PRINT RUN 199 SER.#'d SETS
1 Shaquille O'Neal 15.00 40.00

2012-13 Panini Preferred Draft Memorabilia
STATED PRINT RUN 199 SER.#'d SETS
1 Ive/All/Cam/Bry/Nas/Fis/Ilg 15.00 40.00
2 Jam/Ant/Bos/Wad/Kam/Wes/Hin 15.00 40.00
3 Wal/Fav/Cou/Cur/Jen/Law/Tea 10.00 25.00
4 How/Jef/Den/Igu/Smi/Mar/Nel 10.00 25.00
5 Bog/Pau/Wil/Fel/Byn/Gra/Lee 10.00 25.00

2012-13 Panini Preferred Duncan Memorabilia
STATED PRINT RUN 199 SER.#'d SETS
1 Tim Duncan 15.00 40.00

2012-13 Panini Preferred Finals Memorabilia
STATED PRINT RUN 199 SER.#'d SETS
1 Gar/Pie/Ron/Bry/Odo/Gas 15.00 40.00
2 Gin/Dun/Par/Var/Jam/Ilg 15.00 40.00
3 Har/Wes/Dur/Jam/Wad/Bos 15.00 40.00

2012-13 Panini Preferred Forward Memorabilia
STATED PRINT RUN 199 SER.#'d SETS
1 Chas/Ell/Tur/Mul/Pie/Hil/Dur 10.00 25.00
2 Web/Mal/Gar/Dun/Lov/Ald/Lee 15.00 40.00
3 Fav/Dun/Ald/You/Now/Ran/Booz 12.00 30.00
4 Now/Far/Dur/Pip/Jam/Ant/Hil 15.00 40.00

2012-13 Panini Preferred Inducted Memorabilia
PRINT RUNS B/WN 10-129 COPIES PER
1 Dr/Mu/Ro/Pi/Ma/Ro/St/Pa/99 15.00 40.00
2 Ew/Ol/Du/Wi/Dr/Th/Mu/Mc/129 8.00 20.00
4 En/Is/Mo/Ew/Dr/Ge/Ol/Ma/79 15.00 40.00

2012-13 Panini Preferred Knicks Memorabilia
STATED PRINT RUN 199 SER.#'d SETS

1 Ewi/Sto/Kid/Ant/Car/Cam 10.00 25.00
2 Fel/Smi/Cam/CopNov/Ant 12.00 30.00
3 Che/Mon/Ant/Ewi/Sto/Fel 12.50 30.00

2012-13 Panini Preferred Lakers Memorabilia

PRINT RUNS B/WN 129-199 COPIES PER
1 Mo/Sa/Jo/Od/Ga/Pe/Br/199 12.00 30.00
2 Va/Br/Jo/O'N/Pe/Ga/199 12.00 30.00
3 Co/Br/Va/Jo/Pe/O'N/129 15.00 40.00

2012-13 Panini Preferred LeBron Memorabilia

STATED PRINT RUN 199 SER.#'d SETS
1 LeBron James 40.00 80.00

2012-13 Panini Preferred Legends Memorabilia

PRINT RUNS B/WN 10-199 COPIES PER
1 An/Ro/Ri/Sm/Ja/Ho/Sc/199 12.00 30.00
2 Mo/We/O'N/Mu/Ew/Jo/Ma/129 10.00 25.00
4 Ca/Ch/Pr/La/Ha/Wi/Le/99 10.00 25.00

2012-13 Panini Preferred London Memorabilia

STATED PRINT RUN 199 SER.#'d SETS
1 Will/Jam/Har/Bry/Lov/Dur 20.00 50.00

2012-13 Panini Preferred Lottery Memorabilia

STATED PRINT RUN 199 SER.#'d SETS
1 Au/Ro/Be/Lo/Ma/Go/We 12.00 30.00
2 Du/Ho/Co/No/Yo/Gr/Ha 10.00 25.00
3 Gr/Ha/Ev/Cu/De/Je/Ha 12.00 30.00
4 Wa/Fa/Co/Mo/Am/Ha/Tu 10.00 25.00
5 Da/Ki/Wa/Li/Ba/Dr/Ri 10.00 25.00

2012-13 Panini Preferred Match Up Memorabilia

STATED PRINT RUN 199 SER.#'d SETS
1 Dr/Ga/Al/Gr/Je/No/Ro 8.00 20.00
2 Bo/Le/Lo/Co/Du/Ho/Ga 8.00 20.00

2012-13 Panini Preferred New York Memorabilia

STATED PRINT RUN 199 SER.#'d SETS
1 An/Sh/St/Fe/Ca/Co/No 10.00 25.00
2 Ch/Ew/St/Mo/Ma/Ca/Ja 10.00 25.00
3 An/Ja/Ch/Sh/Mo/St/Ki 12.50 30.00

2012-13 Panini Preferred Pistons Memorabilia

PRINT RUNS B/WN 99-129 COPIES PER
1 Ho/Ma/Pr/Dr/Kn/Mo/Ag/99 10.00 25.00
2 Th/Tr/Wa/Ag/La/Ma/Du/129 10.00 25.00

2012-13 Panini Preferred Rebound Memorabilia

STATED PRINT RUN 199 SER.#'d SETS
1 Le/Ra/Ho/Gr/Lo/Ro/Du 10.00 25.00
2 Ro/Gr/O'N/Wa/No/Il/Mu 10.00 25.00
3 Mo/Ma/Ka/Br/Du/O'N/Ol 10.00 25.00

2012-13 Panini Preferred Repeat Memorabilia

STATED PRINT RUN 199 SER.#'d SETS
1 Pip/Kuk/Dre/Ola/Bry/Fis 10.00 25.00
2 O'N/Ola/Coo/Rod/Tho/Wal 12.50 30.00

2012-13 Panini Preferred Rivals Memorabilia

STATED PRINT RUN 199 SER.#'d SETS
1 BOS-MIA 20.00 50.00
3 OKC-LAL 12.00 30.00

2012-13 Panini Preferred Rookie Memorabilia

STATED PRINT RUN 249 SER.#'d SETS
1 Da/Be/Ki/Wa/Ro/Li 12.00 30.00
2 Ir/Le/Wa/Li/Ba/Da 12.00 30.00
3 Va/Le/Ro/Da/Ka/Dr 12.00 30.00
4 Le/Pa/Wil/Ba/Fa/Ki 10.00 25.00
5 Wa/Ir/Kn/Be/Li/Wa 12.00 30.00
6 Fo/Ka/Va/Bi/Ve/Vu 8.00 20.00
7 Kn/Te/Mi/Da/Ki/Jo 10.00 25.00
8 Ma/Ba/He/Ir/Ri/Pl 10.00 25.00
9 Ir/Wi/Ka/Th/Va/Ve 10.00 25.00
10 Da/Ki/Be/Ir/Wil/Ka 12.00 30.00

2012-13 Panini Preferred Silhouettes Prime

*SIL.PRIME: .8X TO 2X BASE HI
RANDOM INSERTS IN PACKS
STATED PRINT RUN B/WN 1-25 COPIES PER
NO PRICING ON QTY 15 OR LESS
208 Tony Parker/25 100.00 200.00
229 LaMarcus Aldridge/25 100.00 200.00
230 Taj Gibson/25 40.00 100.00
235 Hedo Turkoglu/25 30.00 80.00
265 Joe Johnson/20 40.00 100.00
281 Rashard Lewis/25 25.00 60.00
285 Sean Elliott/25 25.00 60.00
291 Darren Collison/25 15.00 40.00
292 Devin Harris/25 15.00 40.00
301 Will Barton/25 40.00 100.00
303 Terrence Jones/25 50.00 120.00
304 Thomas Robinson/25 30.00 80.00
305 Tobias Harris/25 15.00 40.00
306 Tyler Zeller/25 30.00 80.00
307 Quincy Miller/25 15.00 40.00
308 Kim English/25 20.00 50.00
309 Khris Middleton/25 30.00 80.00
310 Kenneth Faried/25 30.00 80.00
311 Kendall Marshall/25 40.00 100.00
312 Jared Sullinger/25 75.00 150.00
314 Perry Jones/25 40.00 100.00
315 Orlando Johnson/25 15.00 40.00
316 Norris Cole/25 100.00 200.00
318 Kemba Walker/25 100.00 250.00
319 Kawhi Leonard/25 250.00 500.00
320 John Henson/24 40.00 100.00
321 Jimmy Butler/25 300.00 500.00
322 Jimmer Fredette/25 30.00 80.00
323 Jeremy Lamb/25 20.00 50.00
325 Anthony Davis/25 1800.00 2000.00
326 Andrew Nicholson/25 50.00 120.00
327 Kyrie Irving/25 800.00 1200.00
328 Marquis Teague/25 20.00 50.00
329 MarShon Brooks/25 25.00 60.00
331 Michael Kidd-Gilchrist/25 40.00 100.00
332 Mike Scott/25 40.00 100.00
334 Maurice Harkless/25 75.00 150.00
335 Reggie Jackson/25 75.00 150.00
336 Robert Sacre/25 25.00 60.00
337 Markieff Morris/25 30.00 80.00
339 Lance Thomas/25 12.00 30.00
346 Jae Crowder/25 25.00 60.00
348 Harrison Barnes/25 100.00 250.00
349 Evan Fournier/25 75.00 150.00
350 E'Twaun Moore/25 10.00 25.00
351 Enes Kanter/25 50.00 120.00
352 Draymond Green/25 300.00 600.00
353 Marcus Morris/25 20.00 50.00
354 Dion Waiters/25 50.00 120.00
357 Brandon Knight/25 50.00 120.00
358 Bradley Beal/25 250.00 500.00
359 Bismack Biyombo/25 25.00 60.00
360 Nikola Vucevic/25 75.00 150.00
361 Andre Drummond/25 125.00 300.00
362 Alec Burks/25 50.00 120.00
363 Tony Wroten/25 40.00 100.00
364 Tristan Thompson/25 75.00 150.00
366 Darius Johnson-Odom/25 12.00 30.00
367 Austin Rivers/25 100.00 200.00
368 Arnett Moultrie/25 12.00 30.00
369 Kyle O'Quinn/25 15.00 40.00
370 Miles Plumlee/25 25.00 60.00
371 Terrence Ross/25 40.00 100.00
375 Chandler Parsons/25 250.00 400.00
377 Nolan Smith/25 40.00 100.00
378 Cory Joseph/25 20.00 50.00
379 Festus Ezeli/25 20.00 50.00
380 Isaiah Thomas/25 125.00 300.00
381 Jeremy Pargo/25 20.00 50.00

2012-13 Panini Preferred Slam Dunk Memorabilia

STATED PRINT RUN 199 SER.#'d SETS
1 De/Ig/Ca/Ja/Wi/Gr/Dr/Ho 12.00 30.00
2 Ri/Ig/Br/Ja/St/Ke/Ca/De 15.00 40.00

2012-13 Panini Preferred Steals Memorabilia

STATED PRINT RUN 199 SER.#'d SETS
1 Con/Smi/Gra/Jam/Igu/Pau 12.50 30.00
2 Rub/Kidd/Ron/Hill/Jen/Smi 10.00 25.00

2012-13 Panini Preferred Veteran Memorabilia

STATED PRINT RUN 199 SER.#'d SETS
1 Pr/Du/Pa/Ga/Ga/Wa/Ro 12.00 30.00
2 Ga/Pi/Gi/Ro/Ha/Gi/Sa 12.00 30.00
3 G/St/Br/Du/Ho/Gr/Bo 12.00 30.00
4 Lo/Du/No/Th/Yo/Fr/Da 20.00 50.00
5 Ne/Ud/Al/Ro/Fe/Ki/Pa 12.00 30.00

2013-14 Panini Preferred

RANDOM INSERTS IN PACKS
PRINT RUNS B/WN 20-99 COPIES PER
EXCHANGE DEADLINE 1/23/2016
1 Larry Johnson PC AU/25 10.00 25.00
2 Vinny Del Negro PC AU/25
3 Phil Chenier PC AU/74 3.00 8.00
4 Marques Johnson PC AU/60
5 Brian Grant PC AU/74
6 Christian Laettner PC AU/25
7 Jay Williams PC AU/35
8 Michael Cooper PC AU/74
9 Billy Paultz PC AU/74 5.00 12.00
10 Bob McAdoo PC AU/60 8.00 20.00
11 Avery Johnson PC AU/25
12 Tom Gugliotta PC AU/60 3.00 8.00
13 Antoine Walker PC AU/74
14 Michael Finley PC AU/35 10.00 25.00
15 Raef LaFrentz PC AU/74
16 George Karl PC AU/25
17 Jerry West PC AU/20 40.00 80.00
18 Clyde Drexler PC AU/20
19 Eddie Johnson PC AU/74 3.00 8.00
20 Dana Barros PC AU/74 3.00 8.00
21 Kelly Tripucka PC AU/25
22 Len Elmore PC AU/74 6.00 15.00
23 Chris Mullin PC AU/25
24 Kenny Anderson PC AU/74 4.00 10.00
25 Clifford Robinson PC AU/74
26 Peja Stojakovic PC AU/25 8.00 20.00
27 Lindsey Hunter PC AU/74 3.00 8.00
28 Danny Manning PC AU/25
29 World B. Free PC AU/25
30 Tracy McGrady PC AU/20
31 Jalen Rose PC AU/25 12.00 30.00
32 Muggsy Bogues PC AU/74 4.00 10.00
33 Fat Lever PC AU/74 4.00 10.00
34 Cedric Maxwell PC AU/74 3.00 8.00
35 Darrell Griffith PC AU/74
36 Darryl Dawkins PC AU/60 3.00 8.00
37 Bobby Jones PC AU/74 4.00 10.00
38 Bill Willoughby PC AU/74 6.00 15.00
39 Dale Davis PC AU/74
40 B.J. Armstrong PC AU/25 12.00 30.00
41 George Gervin PC AU/25 15.00 40.00
42 Travis Best PC AU/74 3.00 8.00
43 Scottie Pippen PC AU/25 60.00 150.00
44 Wayne Embry PC AU/60 3.00 8.00
45 Kenny Smith PC AU/60 4.00 10.00
46 Jamaal Wilkes PC AU/60 5.00 12.00
47 Julius Erving PC AU/20
48 Joe Dumars PC AU/25 8.00 20.00
49 Dan Issel PC AU/74 4.00 10.00
50 Terry Cummings PC AU/74 4.00 10.00
51 P.J. Tucker PC AU/74 3.00 8.00
52 Nick Young PC AU/25 8.00 20.00
53 Carlos Boozer PC AU/25
54 Arron Afflalo PC AU/25
55 Kevin Martin PC AU/25 15.00 40.00
56 Marcin Gortat PC AU/25 30.00 60.00
57 Jrue Holiday PC AU/25
58 Al-Farouq Aminu PC AU/60
59 Andrew Bogut PC AU/25
60 Boris Diaw PC AU/35 15.00 40.00
61 D.J. Augustin PC AU/35 4.00 10.00
62 Marcus Thornton PC AU/35 4.00 10.00
63 Shaquille O'Neal PC AU/20
64 Tobias Harris PC AU/35 5.00 12.00
65 Nikola Vucevic PC AU/35
66 Marreese Speights PC AU/74
67 Josh Smith PC AU/25
68 Jimmer Fredette PC AU/35 4.00 10.00
69 LaMarcus Aldridge PC AU/25 8.00 20.00
70 Tyler Zeller PC AU/60 4.00 10.00
71 Taj Gibson PC AU/35 5.00 12.00
72 Lavoy Allen PC AU/74 3.00 8.00
73 Kevin Durant PC AU/49 75.00 150.00
74 Jared Dudley PC AU/25 5.00 12.00
75 Roy Hibbert PC AU/25
76 Eric Maynor PC AU/74 3.00 8.00
77 Tony Wroten PC AU/74
78 Mike Conley PC AU/25
79 Tayshaun Prince PC AU/25 6.00 15.00
80 Brandan Wright PC AU/60 3.00 8.00
81 Danny Green PC AU/25 6.00 15.00
82 Khris Middleton PC AU/74
83 Courtney Lee PC AU/74
84 Kyrie Irving PC AU/25 30.00 80.00
85 Jonas Valanciunas PC AU/35 5.00 12.00
86 Kemba Walker PC AU/25
87 Quincy Acy PC AU/74 3.00 8.00
88 Patrick Beverley PC AU/74 3.00 8.00
89 Hollis Thompson PC AU/74
90 Danilo Gallinari PC AU/25 5.00 12.00
91 Trevor Booker PC AU/74 3.00 8.00
92 Andre Drummond PC AU/25 12.00 30.00
93 Andrew Nicholson PC AU/60
94 Andrea Bargnani PC AU/25 6.00 15.00
95 John Wall PC AU/20 15.00 40.00
96 Eric Gordon PC AU/25 6.00 15.00
97 Bradley Beal PC AU/25 12.00 30.00
98 Ty Lawson PC AU/25 5.00 12.00
99 Tiago Splitter PC AU/25 6.00 15.00
100 Kendall Marshall PC AU/49 4.00 10.00
101 Andre Roberson PC AU/99 3.00 8.00
102 Rudy Gobert PC AU/75
103 MCW PC AU/49 15.00 40.00
104 Miroslav Raduljica PC AU/99
105 Tony Snell PC AU/49 10.00 25.00
106 Vitor Faverani PC AU/99 3.00 8.00
107 Gal Mekel PC AU/75 3.00 8.00
108 Jeff Withey PC AU/99 3.00 8.00
109 Nemanja Nedovic PC AU/75 3.00 8.00
110 Robert Covington PC AU/99
111 Ian Clark PC AU/99 4.00 10.00
112 Ryan Kelly PC AU/99 3.00 8.00
113 Trey Burke PC AU/35 5.00 12.00
114 Peyton Siva PC AU/99
115 Ricky Ledo PC AU/99
116 Antetokounmpo PC AU/60 125.00 300.00
117 Kentavious Caldwell-Pope PC AU/35 6.00 15.00
118 Erik Murphy PC AU/99
119 Archie Goodwin PC AU/99 4.00 10.00
120 Matthew Dellavedova PC AU/99 5.00 12.00
121 Nate Wolters PC AU/99 8.00 20.00
122 Ben McLemore PC AU/35 5.00 12.00
123 Toure Murry PC AU/99 4.00 10.00
124 Anthony Bennett PC AU/35 5.00 12.00
125 Ray McCallum PC AU/99 3.00 8.00
126 Carrick Felix PC AU/75 3.00 8.00
127 Glen Rice Jr. PC AU/49 3.00 8.00
128 Allen Crabbe PC AU/75 4.00 10.00
129 Otto Porter PC AU/35 6.00 15.00
130 Victor Oladipo PC AU/49 15.00 40.00
131 Dennis Schroder PC AU/75 5.00 12.00
132 Solomon Hill PC AU/99 3.00 8.00
133 Lorenzo Brown PC AU/99 3.00 8.00
134 Kelly Olynyk PC AU/60 4.00 10.00
135 Tim Hardaway Jr. PC AU/49 12.00 30.00
136 Alex Len PC AU/35
137 Shane Larkin PC AU/75 3.00 8.00
138 Pero Antic PC AU/75
139 Mason Plumlee PC AU/75 5.00 12.00
140 Nerlens Noel PC AU/35 8.00 20.00
141 Kyle Singler CR AU/99 3.00 8.00
142 Alan Anderson CR AU/99 3.00 8.00
143 Andrei Kirilenko CR AU/20
144 Evan Fournier CR AU/99
145 Patrick Beverley CR AU/99 6.00 15.00
146 Andre Iguodala CR AU/20 6.00 15.00
147 Kobe Bryant CR AU/35 100.00 200.00
148 Reggie Jackson CR AU/25 15.00 40.00
149 Chris Singleton CR AU/99 3.00 8.00
150 Victor Claver CR AU/99 3.00 8.00
151 Alexey Shved CR AU/49
152 Tony Wroten CR AU/49 3.00 8.00
153 Bradley Beal CR AU/20
154 Wesley Matthews CR AU/25 5.00 12.00
155 P.J. Tucker CR AU/99 3.00 8.00
156 Richard Jefferson CR AU/20 8.00 20.00
157 Will Barton CR AU/99
158 Jared Sullinger CR AU/20 5.00 12.00
159 Mike Scott CR AU/99
160 Khris Middleton CR AU/99
161 Raymond Felton CR AU/20
162 Kawhi Leonard CR AU/25 60.00 150.00
163 Jared Dudley CR AU/25 5.00 12.00
164 Keith Bogans CR AU/99
165 Kevin Martin CR AU/20 6.00 15.00
166 Timofey Mozgov CR AU/99 3.00 8.00
167 Trevor Booker CR AU/99 3.00 8.00
168 Jason Thompson CR AU/25
169 John Salmons CR AU/99 4.00 10.00
170 Brandon Knight CR AU/20 6.00 15.00
171 Jonas Jerebko CR AU/99
172 Arron Afflalo CR AU/20
173 D.J. Augustin CR AU/49 3.00 8.00
174 Brian Roberts CR AU/99
175 Goran Dragic CR AU/25
176 Lavoy Allen CR AU/75 3.00 8.00
177 Marcin Gortat CR AU/25 20.00 50.00
178 MarShon Brooks CR AU/99 4.00 10.00
179 Tiago Splitter CR AU/25
180 Ersan Ilyasova CR AU/25
181 Jason Maxiell CR AU/99 3.00 8.00
182 Antawn Jamison CR AU/20
183 Chris Copeland CR AU/75 3.00 8.00
184 Brandon Bass CR AU/20
185 Randy Foye CR AU/25
186 Chris Andersen CR AU/20
187 Xavier Henry CR AU/25
188 Jason Terry CR AU/20
189 Ryan Anderson CR AU/25
190 Amir Johnson CR AU/99 3.00 8.00
191 H.Olajuwon CR AU/20 50.00 100.00
192 David Robinson CR AU/20 20.00 50.00
193 Steve Smith CR AU/99 4.00 10.00
194 Walt Frazier CR AU/20
195 Jerry Lucas CR AU/25 8.00 20.00
196 Robert Parish CR AU/20
197 Dan Issel CR AU/99 4.00 10.00
198 Dennis Rodman CR AU/20
199 Toni Kukoc CR AU/25 15.00 40.00
200 Nate Archibald CR AU/25
201 Larry Bird CR AU/20 50.00 100.00
202 Gary Payton CR AU/20 15.00 40.00
203 Christian Laettner CR AU/20 6.00 15.00
204 Dale Davis CR AU/99
205 Theo Ratliff CR AU/99 3.00 8.00
206 Phil Chenier CR AU/99 3.00 8.00
207 Campy Russell CR AU/99 3.00 8.00
208 Bill Walton CR AU/25 8.00 20.00
209 Danny Manning CR AU/20 6.00 15.00
210 Mark Price CR AU/99 10.00 25.00
211 Len Elmore CR AU/99 3.00 8.00
212 Scott Wedman CR AU/99 4.00 10.00
213 Fat Lever CR AU/99 4.00 10.00
214 Kevin Willis CR AU/25
215 Bob McAdoo CR AU/25 30.00 60.00
216 Rory Sparrow CR AU/99 3.00 8.00
217 Cazzie Russell CR AU/99 4.00 10.00
218 Nick Van Exel CR AU/20 8.00 20.00
219 Jack Sikma CR AU/99 4.00 10.00
220 Tyronn Lue CR AU/99 3.00 8.00
221 Connie Hawkins CR AU/20
222 Clyde Drexler CR AU/20 40.00 80.00
223 Michael Finley CR AU/20 8.00 20.00
224 Jerry West CR AU/20 30.00 60.00
225 Raef LaFrentz CR AU/99
226 Cedric Ceballos CR AU/99 3.00 8.00
227 S. O'Neal CR AU/20 100.00 200.00
228 Kendall Gill CR AU/99 3.00 8.00
229 Nick Anderson CR AU/99 5.00 12.00
230 Scott Skiles CR AU/99 4.00 10.00
231 Jo Jo White CR AU/99 4.00 10.00
232 Mario Elie CR AU/99 6.00 15.00
233 John Salley CR AU/99 3.00 8.00
234 Glen Rice CR AU/25 6.00 15.00
235 Bill Laimbeer CR AU/99 4.00 10.00
236 Maurice Cheeks CR AU/99 3.00 8.00
237 Horace Grant CR AU/25 20.00 50.00
238 Robert Horry CR AU/25 15.00 40.00
239 Terry Porter CR AU/99 3.00 8.00
240 Arvydas Sabonis CR AU/99 10.00 25.00
241 Nemanja Nedovic CR AU/75 3.00 8.00
242 Phil Pressey CR AU/75 3.00 8.00
243 Anthony Bennett CR AU/25
244 C.J. McCollum CR AU/25 20.00 50.00
245 Trey Burke CR AU/49 4.00 10.00
246 Antetokounmpo CR AU/49 125.00 300.00
247 Ian Clark CR AU/75 4.00 10.00
248 Archie Goodwin CR AU/75
249 Ryan Kelly CR AU/75 3.00 8.00
250 Alex Len CR AU/25 10.00 25.00
251 Victor Oladipo CR AU/49 20.00 50.00
252 Dwight Buycks CR AU/99
253 Andre Roberson CR AU/75 3.00 8.00
254 MCW CR AU/49 12.00 30.00
255 Isaiah Canaan CR AU/75 3.00 8.00
256 Gorgui Dieng CR AU/75 10.00 25.00
257 Tony Mitchell CR AU/75
258 Allen Crabbe CR AU/75 4.00 10.00
259 Otto Porter CR AU/25 12.00 30.00
260 Carrick Felix CR AU/75 3.00 8.00
261 Tim Hardaway Jr. CR AU/60 10.00 25.00
262 Jamaal Franklin CR AU/75
263 Toure Murry CR AU/75 4.00 10.00
264 M.Dellavedova CR AU/75 5.00 12.00
265 S.Muhammad CR AU/25 6.00 15.00
266 Tony Snell CR AU/49 10.00 25.00
267 Rudy Gobert CR AU/75
268 Reggie Bullock CR AU/75
269 Luigi Datome CR AU/75
270 Miroslav Raduljica CR AU/75
271 Gal Mekel CR AU/75
272 Ricky Ledo CR AU/75
273 Peyton Siva CR AU/75
274 Lorenzo Brown CR AU/99 3.00 8.00
275 Cody Zeller CR AU/25
276 Erik Murphy CR AU/75
277 Solomon Hill CR AU/75 3.00 8.00
278 Robert Covington CR AU/75
279 Glen Rice Jr. CR AU/75 8.00 20.00
280 Steven Adams CR AU/49 8.00 20.00
281 Tim Hardaway Jr. RR AU/60 10.00 25.00
282 Vitor Faverani RR AU/99 3.00 8.00
283 Kelly Olynyk RR AU/99 4.00 10.00
284 S.Muhammad RR AU/25
285 Trey Burke RR AU/35
286 MCW RR AU/99 12.00 30.00
287 Steven Adams RR AU/49 8.00 20.00
288 Phil Pressey RR AU/99
289 Otto Porter RR AU/25 10.00 25.00
290 Victor Oladipo RR AU/49 12.00 30.00
291 Ben McLemore RR AU/25 6.00 15.00
292 Nate Wolters RR AU/75 4.00 10.00
293 Alex Len RR AU/25 6.00 15.00
294 Tony Snell RR AU/60 4.00 10.00
295 Dwight Buycks RR AU/99
296 Pero Antic RR AU/99
297 Nerlens Noel RR AU/25 10.00 25.00
298 Mason Plumlee RR AU/99 5.00 12.00
299 Shane Larkin RR AU/99 3.00 8.00
300 Gorgui Dieng RR AU/99 4.00 10.00
301 Karl Malone SL JSY AU/35 75.00 150.00
302 D.Robinson SL JSY AU/25 50.00 100.00
303 Brad Daugherty SL JSY AU/49
304 Anthony Mason SL JSY AU/49 6.00 15.00
305 Fred Brown SL JSY AU/49
306 Chris Mullin SL JSY AU/35 30.00 60.00
307 Grant Hill SL JSY AU/35 50.00 100.00
308 S.O'Neal SL JSY AU/35 150.00 250.00
309 L.Johnson SL JSY AU/35 20.00 50.00
310 Dan Majerle SL JSY AU/35 12.00 30.00
311 John Starks SL JSY AU/49 10.00 25.00
312 Norm Nixon SL JSY AU/49 3.00 8.00
313 D.Wilkins SL JSY AU/25 20.00 50.00
314 Doc Rivers SL JSY AU/35
315 A.Johnson SL JSY AU/35 15.00 40.00
316 Scott Wedman SL JSY AU/49 4.00 10.00
317 Steve Mix SL JSY AU/49 3.00 8.00
318 Gary Payton SL JSY AU/25 40.00 100.00
319 Cedric Maxwell SL JSY AU/49
320 B.Cartwright SL JSY AU/35 8.00 20.00
321 A.Hardaway SL JSY AU/35 50.00 120.00
322 Mark Jackson SL JSY AU/49 4.00 10.00
323 Kiki Vandeweghe SL JSY AU/49 4.00 10.00
324 Rick Barry SL JSY AU/25 10.00 25.00
325 Jeff Malone SL JSY AU/49 3.00 8.00
326 M.Johnson SL JSY AU/35 60.00 120.00
327 Abdul-Jabbar SL JSY AU/35 40.00 100.00
328 Julius Erving SL JSY AU/35 60.00 120.00
329 Xavier McDaniel SL JSY AU/49 3.00 8.00
330 D.Mutombo SL JSY AU/35 30.00 60.00
331 H.Barnes SL JSY AU/35 15.00 40.00
332 Tiago Splitter SL JSY AU/35 12.00 30.00
333 J.Valanciunas SL JSY AU/35
334 Nicolas Batum SL JSY AU/49
335 Danny Green SL JSY AU/49 15.00 40.00
336 Tyson Chandler SL JSY AU/35 5.00 12.00
337 Raymond Felton SL JSY AU/35
338 Kendrick Perkins SL JSY AU/35
339 K.Durant SL JSY AU/35 200.00 300.00
340 Reggie Jackson SL JSY AU/35
341 Ryan Anderson SL JSY AU/35
342 G.Hayward SL JSY AU/35 15.00 40.00
343 A.Davis SL JSY AU/35 50.00 120.00
344 Jrue Holiday SL JSY AU/35
345 Kevin Love SL JSY AU/25 8.00 20.00
346 Ersan Ilyasova SL JSY AU/35
347 Lance Stephenson SL JSY AU/49
348 L.Aldridge SL JSY AU/35 15.00 40.00
349 C.Andersen SL JSY AU/35 30.00 80.00
350 Kobe Bryant SL JSY AU/35 100.00 200.00
351 Nick Young SL JSY AU/35 15.00 40.00
352 Blake Griffin SL JSY AU/25
353 Steve Nash SL JSY AU/35 20.00 50.00
354 Bernard King SL JSY AU/35 5.00 12.00
355 J.Harden SL JSY AU/35 30.00 80.00
356 A.Iguodala SL JSY AU/35 25.00 60.00
357 S.Curry SL JSY AU/35 150.00 250.00
358 Kyrie Irving SL JSY AU/35 150.00 250.00
359 A.Drummond SL JSY AU/35 10.00 25.00
360 Josh Smith SL JSY AU/35
361 J.Calderon SL JSY AU/35 10.00 25.00
362 Jeff Green SL JSY AU/35 12.00 30.00
363 Andrew Bogut SL JSY AU/35
364 Bradley Beal SL JSY AU/35 12.00 30.00
365 Z.Randolph SL JSY AU/35 10.00 25.00
366 Gal Mekel SL JSY AU/99
367 Kelly Olynyk SL JSY AU/60 12.00 30.00
368 V.Oladipo SL JSY AU/75 30.00 80.00
369 MCW SL JSY/75 12.00 30.00
370 Alex Len SL JSY AU/49 12.00 30.00
371 A.Goodwin SL JSY AU/99 10.00 25.00
372 A.Bennett SL JSY AU/49 4.00 10.00
373 Ricky Ledo SL JSY AU/99
374 Tony Snell SL JSY AU/99 10.00 25.00
375 Hardaway Jr. SL JSY AU/60 20.00 50.00
376 Solomon Hill SL JSY AU/99
377 Nerlens Noel SL JSY AU/75 40.00 100.00
378 Trey Burke SL JSY AU/75 4.00 10.00
379 Erik Murphy SL JSY AU/99
380 G.Anttknmpo SL JSY AU/99 200.00 500.00
381 Jeff Withey SL JSY AU/99 3.00 8.00
382 D.Schroder SL JSY AU/99 12.00 30.00
383 Shane Larkin SL JSY AU/60 3.00 8.00
384 Nate Wolters SL JSY AU/99 4.00 10.00
385 Ryan Kelly SL JSY AU/99 3.00 8.00
386 Dellavedova SL JSY AU/99 20.00 50.00
387 Allen Crabbe SL JSY AU/99 4.00 10.00
388 Carrick Felix SL JSY AU/99 3.00 8.00
389 Jamaal Franklin SL JSY AU/99 3.00 8.00
390 Peyton Siva SL JSY AU/99
391 Cody Zeller SL JSY AU/49 8.00 20.00
392 Tony Mitchell SL JSY AU/99
393 M.Plumlee SL JSY AU/60 10.00 25.00
394 Caldwell-Pope SL JSY AU/49 15.00 40.00
395 S.Muhammad SL JSY AU/49 12.00 30.00
396 B.McLemore SL JSY AU/49 15.00 40.00
397 C.McCollum SL JSY AU/49 30.00 80.00
398 S.Adams SL JSY AU/99 6.00 15.00
399 Otto Porter SL JSY AU/49 20.00 50.00
400 Luigi Datome SL JSY AU/99 3.00 8.00
401 Goran Dragic NP AU/20
402 Carlos Boozer NP AU/20
403 Kevin Durant NP AU/25 75.00 150.00
404 Shane Battier NP AU/20
405 Anthony Davis NP AU/20 50.00 100.00
406 Udonis Haslem NP AU/99 3.00 8.00
407 Joakim Noah NP AU/20 6.00 15.00
408 Eric Gordon NP AU/20 6.00 15.00
409 Xavier Henry NP AU/25 5.00 12.00
410 Steve Blake NP AU/99 3.00 8.00
411 Harrison Barnes NP AU/20
412 Kobe Bryant NP AU/25 100.00 200.00
413 Brandon Knight NP AU/20
414 Kyrie Irving NP AU/20 40.00 100.00
415 Ty Lawson NP AU/20 5.00 12.00
416 DeAndre Jordan NP AU/20
417 Brandon Bass NP AU/20
418 Marcin Gortat NP AU/20
419 Gordon Hayward NP AU/20
420 LaMarcus Aldridge NP AU/20
421 Andre Drummond NP AU/20
422 George Hill NP AU/20
423 Tyson Chandler NP AU/20
424 Kemba Walker NP AU/20
425 Roy Hibbert NP AU/20
426 Deron Williams NP AU/20 6.00 15.00
427 Andrea Bargnani NP AU/20 6.00 15.00
428 Tony Parker NP AU/20 40.00 80.00
429 Wesley Matthews NP AU/20 5.00 12.00
430 J.R. Smith NP AU/20
431 Brook Lopez NP AU/20 6.00 15.00
432 Iman Shumpert NP AU/99
433 Kendrick Perkins NP AU/20
434 John Henson NP AU/20
435 James Harden NP AU/20 10.00 25.00
436 Robert Sacre NP AU/99 3.00 8.00
437 Marvin Williams NP AU/99 4.00 10.00
438 Mirza Teletovic NP AU/99
439 Tobias Harris NP AU/20
440 Jared Sullinger NP AU/20
441 Spencer Hawes NP AU/99 3.00 8.00
442 Nicolas Batum NP AU/99
443 Jared Dudley NP AU/99
444 J.J. Redick NP AU/20 12.00 30.00
445 Kendall Marshall NP AU/35 5.00 12.00
446 Robin Lopez NP AU/49
447 Maurice Harkless NP AU/20
448 Isaiah Thomas NP AU/99 5.00 12.00
449 Eric Maynor NP AU/99 3.00 8.00
450 Nick Young NP AU/20
451 Tim Hardaway NP AU/99 5.00 12.00
452 Shaquille O'Neal NP AU/20
453 Will Perdue NP AU/99 3.00 8.00
454 Magic Johnson NP AU/20 20.00 50.00
455 Bill Walton NP AU/20 8.00 20.00
456 Sam Perkins NP AU/20 12.00 30.00
457 Gary Payton NP AU/20 10.00 25.00
458 Connie Hawkins NP AU/20 8.00 20.00
459 Scottie Pippen NP AU/20 75.00 150.00
460 Norm Nixon NP AU/60 3.00 8.00
461 Darrell Griffith NP AU/99 3.00 8.00
462 Grant Hill NP AU/20 15.00 40.00
463 Nate Archibald NP AU/20
464 Rory Sparrow NP AU/99 3.00 8.00
465 Nick Collison NP AU/99 4.00 10.00
466 Julius Erving NP AU/25
467 Vernon Maxwell NP AU/99 3.00 8.00
468 Mark Jackson NP AU/20
469 Larry Bird NP AU/20 50.00 100.00
470 Rolando Blackman NP AU/99 4.00 10.00
471 Muggsy Bogues NP AU/99 4.00 10.00
472 Spud Webb NP AU/99 4.00 10.00
473 Mark Aguirre NP AU/99 4.00 10.00
474 Isiah Thomas NP AU/20 10.00 25.00
475 Sidney Moncrief NP AU/99 3.00 8.00
476 Zydrunas Ilgauskas NP AU/99 4.00 10.00
477 B.J. Armstrong NP AU/20 10.00 25.00
478 George McGinnis NP AU/20
479 Marques Johnson NP AU/99 4.00 10.00
480 Bob Dandridge NP AU/99 3.00 8.00
481 Bobby Jones NP AU/99 4.00 10.00
482 Buck Williams NP AU/99 3.00 8.00
483 Bruce Bowen NP AU/99 3.00 8.00
484 Allan Houston NP AU/20 10.00 25.00
485 Derrick Coleman NP AU/20
486 Vin Baker NP AU/99 3.00 8.00
487 Lindsey Hunter NP AU/99 3.00 8.00
488 Jay Williams NP AU/20
489 Larry Nance NP AU/99 4.00 10.00
490 Michael Cage NP AU/99 3.00 8.00
491 Fred Brown NP AU/99 3.00 8.00
492 Brent Barry NP AU/20
493 Byron Scott NP AU/20
494 Alex English NP AU/20 10.00 25.00
495 George Gervin NP AU/20 25.00 60.00
496 Karl Malone NP AU/20 20.00 50.00
497 Cedric Ceballos NP AU/75 10.00 25.00
498 Wes Unseld NP AU/20
499 Gail Goodrich NP AU/20
500 Walt Frazier NP AU/20 10.00 25.00
501 Kendall Gill PS AU/99 3.00 8.00
502 Jerry Lucas PS AU/20 20.00 50.00
503 Rick Barry PS AU/20
504 Abdul-Jabbar PS AU/20 60.00 120.00
505 Larry Johnson PS AU/25 12.00 30.00
506 M.Abdul-Rauf PS AU/99 6.00 15.00
507 Robert Parish PS AU/20 12.00 30.00
508 Joe Dumars PS AU/20 10.00 25.00
509 Isiah Thomas PS AU/20 10.00 25.00
510 Nate Thurmond PS AU/20
511 Scottie Pippen PS AU/20 75.00 150.00
512 Mark Aguirre PS AU/99 4.00 10.00
513 Adrian Dantley PS AU/35 5.00 12.00
514 Rex Chapman PS AU/99
515 H.Olajuwon PS AU/20 25.00 60.00
516 Alex English PS AU/35 10.00 25.00
517 Dee Brown PS AU/99 3.00 8.00
518 Tom Heinsohn PS AU/25 12.00 30.00
519 Thaddeus Young PS AU/99 3.00 8.00
520 D.Wilkins PS AU/20 12.00 30.00
521 Steve Mix PS AU/99 3.00 8.00
522 Adrian Smith PS AU/99 3.00 8.00
523 George Karl PS AU/20
524 Jon McGlocklin PS AU/75 4.00 10.00
525 Byron Scott PS AU/20 6.00 15.00
526 Tracy McGrady PS AU/20
527 Bernard King PS AU/20
528 John Lucas PS AU/35
529 Luc Longley PS AU/49 8.00 20.00
530 Jerome Williams PS AU/99 3.00 8.00
531 Antonio Davis PS AU/99 3.00 8.00
532 Jack Sikma PS AU/99 4.00 10.00
533 Charlie Scott PS AU/99 4.00 10.00
534 Jalen Rose PS AU/25 8.00 20.00
535 Tom Chambers PS AU/35 5.00 12.00
536 D.Mutombo PS AU/25 25.00 60.00
537 Tom Van Arsdale PS AU/99 4.00 10.00
538 Gail Goodrich PS AU/20
539 Walt Frazier PS AU/20
540 Dick Van Arsdale PS AU/99 4.00 10.00
541 Rolando Blackman PS AU/99 4.00 10.00
542 Anthony Mason PS AU/99 6.00 15.00
543 Grant Hill PS AU/20 25.00 60.00
544 Spud Webb PS AU/99 4.00 10.00
545 Doug Christie PS AU/75
546 A.Hardaway PS AU/20 15.00 40.00
547 Robert Horry PS AU/25 10.00 25.00
548 Billy Paultz PS AU/99 5.00 12.00
549 Brian Grant PS AU/99
550 Mark Price PS AU/99 10.00 25.00
551 Isaiah Thomas PS AU/99 5.00 12.00
552 Travis Outlaw PS AU/99 4.00 10.00
553 Kyle Lowry PS AU/25 6.00 15.00
554 Zach Randolph PS AU/20
555 Alan Anderson PS AU/35
556 Greg Stiemsma PS AU/99 3.00 8.00
557 Patrick Patterson PS AU/99
558 Tyler Zeller PS AU/35
559 C.J. Watson PS AU/99 3.00 8.00
560 James Jones PS AU/99 3.00 8.00
561 Courtney Lee PS AU/25
562 Andrew Nicholson PS AU/75 3.00 8.00
563 Shelvin Mack PS AU/99 3.00 8.00
564 Udonis Haslem PS AU/99 3.00 8.00
565 Nick Collison PS AU/99 4.00 10.00
566 Gordon Hayward PS AU/35 6.00 15.00
567 Gerald Henderson PS AU/35
568 Lance Stephenson PS AU/75
569 Quincy Acy PS AU/99 3.00 8.00
570 Kevin Love PS AU/20
571 Jeff Green PS AU/25 10.00 25.00
572 Goran Dragic PS AU/25
573 Jeff Teague PS AU/35
574 Bernard James PS AU/99 3.00 8.00
575 Al-Farouq Aminu PS AU/35
576 DeAndre Jordan PS AU/25
577 Greg Monroe PS AU/35 5.00 12.00
578 Danny Green PS AU/25
579 Kenyon Martin PS AU/99 4.00 10.00
580 Kyle Korver PS AU/25
581 Tristan Thompson PS AU/20 6.00 15.00
582 Robin Lopez PS AU/49
583 Mike Conley PS AU/25
584 Taj Gibson PS AU/35 10.00 25.00
585 Andre Miller PS AU/25 6.00 15.00
586 Amir Johnson PS AU/99 3.00 8.00
587 Reggie Jackson PS AU/35 5.00 12.00
588 J.R. Smith PS AU/25 12.00 30.00
589 Greg Oden PS AU/99 4.00 10.00
590 Brian Roberts PS AU/99 3.00 8.00
591 Timofey Mozgov PS AU/99 3.00 8.00
592 Joakim Noah PS AU/20
593 Ersan Ilyasova PS AU/35
594 DeMarre Carroll PS AU/99 3.00 8.00
595 Jason Smith PS AU/99 3.00 8.00
596 Boris Diaw PS AU/25 20.00 50.00
597 Marvin Williams PS AU/99 4.00 10.00
598 Harrison Barnes PS AU/20
599 Jose Calderon PS AU/25 10.00 25.00
600 Jodie Meeks PS AU/99 4.00 10.00

2013-14 Panini Preferred Blue

*BLUE p/r 49: .4X TO 1X p/r 60-99
*BLUE p/r 35: .5X TO 1.2X p/r 49-99
*BLUE p/r 25: .6X TO 1.5X p/r 49-60
*BLUE p/r 25: .5X TO 1.2X p/r 35
*BLUE p/r 20: .4X TO 1X p/r 25
RANDOM INSERTS IN PACKS
PRINT RUN B/WN 15-49 COPIES PER
NO PRICING ON QTY 15
EXCHANGE DEADLINE 1/23/2016

2013-14 Panini Preferred Purple

*PURPLE p/r 25: .6X TO 1.5X p/r 49-99
*PURPLE p/r 25: .5X TO 1.2X p/r 35
*PURPLE p/r 25: .4X TO 1X p/r 25
RANDOM INSERTS IN PACKS
PRINT RUN B/WN 10-25 COPIES PER
NO PRICING ON QTY 15 OR LESS
EXCHANGE DEADLINE 1/23/2016
116 G.Anttknmpo PC AU/25 150.00 300.00
529 Luc Longley PS AU/25 10.00 25.00

2013-14 Panini Preferred Silhouettes Prime

RANDOM INSERTS IN PACKS
PRINT RUNS B/WN 10-25 COPIES PER
NO PRICING ON QTY 10
EXCHANGE DEADLINE 1/23/2016
301 Karl Malone/25 200.00 500.00
303 Brad Daugherty/25 30.00 80.00
304 Anthony Mason/25 50.00 120.00
305 Fred Brown/25 25.00 60.00
306 Chris Mullin/25 75.00 200.00
307 Grant Hill/25 125.00 300.00
308 Shaquille O'Neal/25 150.00 400.00
309 Larry Johnson/25 60.00 150.00
310 Dan Majerle/25 30.00 80.00
311 John Starks/25 30.00 80.00
312 Norm Nixon/25 25.00 60.00
314 Doc Rivers/25
315 Avery Johnson/25 30.00 80.00
316 Scott Wedman/25 30.00 80.00
317 Steve Mix/25 25.00 60.00
319 Cedric Maxwell/25 25.00 60.00
320 Bill Cartwright/25 30.00 80.00
321 Anfernee Hardaway/25 75.00 150.00
322 Mark Jackson/25 30.00 80.00
323 Kiki Vandeweghe/25 30.00 80.00
325 Jeff Malone/25 25.00 60.00
326 Magic Johnson/25 125.00 250.00
327 Kareem Abdul-Jabbar/25 300.00 500.00
328 Julius Erving/25 200.00 400.00
329 Xavier McDaniel/25 25.00 60.00
330 Dikembe Mutombo/25 100.00 200.00
331 Harrison Barnes/25 60.00 150.00
332 Tiago Splitter/25 30.00 80.00
334 Nicolas Batum/25
335 Danny Green/25 40.00 100.00
336 Tyson Chandler/25 30.00 80.00
337 Raymond Felton/25
338 Kendrick Perkins/25
339 Kevin Durant/25 600.00 1000.00
340 Reggie Jackson/25 40.00 100.00
341 Ryan Anderson/25 30.00 80.00
342 Gordon Hayward/25 40.00 100.00
343 Anthony Davis/25 200.00 400.00
344 Jrue Holiday/25 40.00 100.00
346 Ersan Ilyasova/25
347 Lance Stephenson/25
348 LaMarcus Aldridge/25 100.00 200.00
349 Chris Andersen/25 300.00 600.00
351 Nick Young/25 60.00 150.00
353 Steve Nash/25 300.00 500.00
354 Bernard King/25 30.00 80.00
355 James Harden/25 150.00 300.00
356 Andre Iguodala/25 30.00 80.00
357 Stephen Curry/25 300.00 500.00
358 Kyrie Irving/25 400.00 800.00
359 Andre Drummond/25 40.00 100.00
360 Josh Smith/25 25.00 60.00
361 Jose Calderon/25 25.00 60.00
363 Andrew Bogut/25
364 Bradley Beal/25 50.00 120.00
365 Zach Randolph/25 30.00 80.00
366 Gal Mekel/25 25.00 60.00
367 Kelly Olynyk/25 40.00 100.00
368 Victor Oladipo/25 75.00 200.00
369 Michael Carter-Williams/25
370 Alex Len/25 30.00 80.00
371 Archie Goodwin/25 30.00 80.00
373 Ricky Ledo/25
374 Tony Snell/25 30.00 80.00
375 Tim Hardaway Jr./25 40.00 100.00
376 Solomon Hill/25 25.00 60.00
377 Nerlens Noel/25 50.00 120.00
378 Trey Burke/25 30.00 80.00
379 Erik Murphy/25
380 G.Antetokounmpo/25 500.00 1000.00
381 Jeff Withey/25 25.00 60.00
382 Dennis Schroder/25 40.00 100.00
383 Shane Larkin/25 25.00 60.00
384 Nate Wolters/25 30.00 80.00
385 Ryan Kelly/25 25.00 60.00
386 Matthew Dellavedova/25 40.00 100.00
387 Allen Crabbe/25 30.00 80.00
388 Carrick Felix/25 25.00 60.00
389 Jamaal Franklin/25 25.00 60.00
390 Peyton Siva/25
391 Cody Zeller/25 30.00 80.00
392 Tony Mitchell/25
393 Mason Plumlee/25 40.00 100.00
394 Kentavious Caldwell-Pope/25 40.00 100.00
395 Shabazz Muhammad/25 30.00 80.00
396 Ben McLemore/25 30.00 80.00
397 C.J. McCollum/25 125.00 300.00
398 Steven Adams/25 40.00 100.00
399 Otto Porter/25 50.00 120.00
400 Luigi Datome/25

2013-14 Panini Preferred Cavaliers Memorabilia

RANDOM INSERTS IN PACKS
STATED PRINT RUN 199 SER.#'d SETS
*PRIME: 1.2X TO 3X BASIC
1 Be/Ma/Ir/Ze/Da/Na/Pr/Th 10.00 25.00

2013-14 Panini Preferred Celtics Memorabilia

RANDOM INSERTS IN PACKS
PRINT RUNS B/WN 99-199 COPIES PER
*PRIME: 1.2X TO 3X BASIC
1 Bi/Mc/Br/Jo/Su/Ro/Pa/199 10.00 25.00
2 Ho/Mc/Pa/Jo/Bi/Le/Mc/99 20.00 50.00

2013-14 Panini Preferred Clippers Memorabilia

RANDOM INSERTS IN PACKS
STATED PRINT RUN 199 SER.#'d SETS
*PRIME: 1.2X TO 3X BASIC
1 Gr/Pa/Jo/Wi/Ri/Hi/Cr/Ha 12.00 30.00
2 Pa/Du/Ba/Bu/Gr/Jo/Re/Cr 12.00 30.00

2013-14 Panini Preferred Decades Memorabilia

RANDOM INSERTS IN PACKS
PRINT RUNS BW/N 99-199 COPIES PER
*PRIME: 1.2X TO 3X BASIC
1 Du/Mc/Iv/No/Br/O'N/Ca/199 15.00 40.00
2 Ew/Pi/Ke/Dr/Ro/St/Ma/99 12.00 30.00
3 En/Th/Bi/Jo/Ma/Ab/Pa/99 15.00 40.00
4 Da/An/Ha/Du/Ir/Ja/Ho/199 20.00 50.00

2013-14 Panini Preferred Europe Memorabilia

RANDOM INSERTS IN PACKS
STATED PRINT RUN 199 SER.#'d SETS
1 Ba/Da/Ga/Ca/Ga/Ru 10.00 25.00
2 Dr/Vu/St/Ku/Te/Ne
3 Di/Sc/Sc/Ba/Pa/No
4 Sa/De/Se/Il/Go/Ka 6.00 15.00

2013-14 Panini Preferred Europe Memorabilia Prime

*PRIME: 1.2X TO 3X BASIC
RANDOM INSERTS IN PACKS
STATED PRINT RUN 25 SER.#'d SETS
3 Diaw/Schroder/Schrempf/Batum/Parker/Nowitzki
40.00 100.00

2013-14 Panini Preferred Finals Memorabilia

RANDOM INSERTS IN PACKS
STATED PRINT RUN 99 SER.#'d SETS
1 Chris Andersen 8.00 20.00
2 Chris Bosh 10.00 25.00
3 Dwyane Wade 12.00 30.00
4 LeBron James 40.00 100.00
5 Mario Chalmers 8.00 20.00
6 Ray Allen 10.00 25.00
7 Danny Green 12.00 30.00
8 Kawhi Leonard 25.00 60.00
9 Manu Ginobili 10.00 25.00
10 Tim Duncan 12.00 30.00
11 Tony Parker 10.00 25.00
12 Tracy McGrady 10.00 25.00

2013-14 Panini Preferred Finals Memorabilia Prime

*PRIME: 1.2X TO 3X BASIC
RANDOM INSERTS IN PACKS
STATED PRINT RUN 25 SER.#'d SETS
3 Dwyane Wade 100.00 250.00
4 LeBron James 125.00 300.00
10 Tim Duncan 125.00 250.00

2013-14 Panini Preferred Houston Memorabilia

RANDOM INSERTS IN PACKS
STATED PRINT RUN 199 SER.#'d SETS
1 Ha/Ca/Be/Jo/Pa/Ho/Li 10.00 25.00
2 Mu/Ha/Li/Ho/Mc/Ba/Dr 12.00 30.00
3 Mu/Ho/Jo/As/Jo/Ol/Mi 10.00 25.00

2013-14 Panini Preferred Houston Memorabilia Prime

*PRIME: 1.2X TO 3X BASIC
RANDOM INSERTS IN PACKS
STATED PRINT RUN 25 SER.#'d SETS

2013-14 Panini Preferred Jumbo Book Memorabilia

RANDOM INSERTS IN PACKS
STATED PRINT RUN 149 SER.#'d SETS
1 Kobe Bryant 12.00 30.00
2 LeBron James 12.00 30.00
3 Tim Duncan 12.00 30.00
4 Kevin Love 8.00 20.00
5 Carmelo Anthony 10.00 25.00
6 Dirk Nowitzki 10.00 25.00
7 Kevin Durant 10.00 25.00
8 Anthony Davis 15.00 40.00
9 Paul George 10.00 25.00
10 Shaquille O'Neal 10.00 25.00
11 Grant Hill 15.00 40.00
12 David Robinson 12.00 30.00

2013-14 Panini Preferred Jumbo Book Memorabilia Prime

*PRIME: 1.2X TO 3X BASIC
RANDOM INSERTS IN PACKS
PRINT RUNS B/WN 10-25 COPIES PER
NO PRICING ON QTY 10

2 LeBron James/25 100.00 250.00
7 Kevin Durant/25 50.00 120.00

2013-14 Panini Preferred Knicks Memorabilia

RANDOM INSERTS IN PACKS
STATED PRINT RUN 199 SER.#'d SETS
*PRIME: 1.2X TO 3X BASIC
1 Sh/Fe/Ch/St/An/Pr 10.00 25.00
2 Oa/Ew/St/An/Jo/Ch 10.00 25.00
3 St/Ew/Ma/Oa/Va/Ja 12.00 30.00
4 Ki/An/St/Ja/Fe/Sm 8.00 20.00

2013-14 Panini Preferred Lake Show Memorabilia

RANDOM INSERTS IN PACKS
PRINT RUNS B/WN 49-199 COPIES PER
*PRIME: 1.2X TO 3X BASIC
1 Hi/Br/Yo/Na/Me/Fa/Ga/He/199 15.00 40.00
2 We/Ab/Ri/O'N/Na/Wo/Br/Co/49 60.00 120.00

2013-14 Panini Preferred One on One Rivalry Memorabilia

RANDOM INSERTS IN PACKS
PRINT RUNS B/WN 99-199 COPIES PER
1 D.Robinson/H.Olajuwon/199 10.00 25.00
2 H.Olajuwon/P.Ewing/199 10.00 25.00
3 J.Erving/L.Bird/99 10.00 25.00
4 K.Bryant/T.McGrady/199 10.00 25.00
5 T.Duncan/S.O'Neal/199 12.00 30.00
6 C.Paul/D.Williams/199 8.00 20.00
7 K.Durant/L.James/199 15.00 40.00
8 L.Bird/M.Johnson/99 15.00 40.00
9 MCW/V.Oladipo/199 8.00 20.00
10 B.McLemore/T.Burke/199 5.00 12.00
11 K.Durant/C.Anthony/199 10.00 25.00
12 P.Pierce/L.James/199 12.00 30.00
13 T.Chambers/K.Malone/199 8.00 20.00
14 M.Jackson/J.Stockton/199 6.00 15.00
15 A.English/B.King/199 5.00 12.00
16 D.Nowitzki/T.Duncan/199 10.00 25.00
17 M.Gasol/P.Gasol/199 6.00 15.00
18 C.Bosh/J.Noah/199 6.00 15.00

2013-14 Panini Preferred One on One Rivalry Memorabilia Prime

*PRIME: 1.2X TO 3X BASIC
RANDOM INSERTS IN PACKS
PRINT RUNS B/WN 10-25 COPIES PER
NO PRICING ON QTY 10

2013-14 Panini Preferred Rookie Memorabilia

RANDOM INSERTS IN PACKS
STATED PRINT RUN 249 SER.#'d SETS
1 Len/Bennett/Zeller/Noel/Porter/Oladipo
2 McCollum/McLemore/Caldwell-Pope/Carter-Williams/Adams/Burke
3 McLemore/Withey/Burke/Zeller/Hardaway/Oladipo
4 McCollum/Hardaway/Oladipo/McLemore/Carter-Williams/Burke
5 Adams/Len/Zeller/Olynyk/Plumlee/Noel
6 Len/Adams/Bennett/Schroder/Mekel/Antetokounmpo
7 Porter/Muhammad/Hill Antetokounmpo/Bullock/Snell
8 Gian/Carter-Willi/Adam/Bur/Oly/Ola 12.00 30.00

2013-14 Panini Preferred Rookie Memorabilia Prime

*PRIME: 1.2X TO 3X BASIC
RANDOM INSERTS IN PACKS
STATED PRINT RUN 25 SER.#'d SETS
1 Len/Ben/Zel/Noe/Por/Ola 40.00 100.00
3 McLemore/Withey/Burke Zeller/Hardaway/Oladipo 25.00 60.00
4 McC/Har/Ola/McL/Car/Bur 40.00 100.00
7 Por/Muh/Hil/Ant/Bul/Sne 30.00 80.00

2013-14 Panini Preferred Rookie Rotation Memorabilia

RANDOM INSERTS IN PACKS
STATED PRINT RUN 249 SER.#'d SETS
1 Michael Carter-Williams 8.00 20.00
2 Ben McLemore 3.00 8.00
3 Shabazz Muhammad
4 Victor Oladipo 5.00 12.00
5 Otto Porter
6 Trey Burke 3.00 8.00
7 C.J. McCollum
8 Giannis Antetokounmpo 30.00 80.00
9 Steven Adams 4.00 10.00
10 Tim Hardaway Jr. 8.00 20.00
11 Anthony Bennett 3.00 8.00
12 Kelly Olynyk 3.00 8.00

2013-14 Panini Preferred Rookie Rotation Memorabilia Prime

*PRIME: 1.2X TO 3X BASIC
RANDOM INSERTS IN PACKS
STATED PRINT RUN 25 SER.#'d SETS

2013-14 Panini Preferred Two on Two Rivalry Memorabilia

RANDOM INSERTS IN PACKS
PRINT RUNS B/WN 49-199 COPIES PER
*PRIME: 1.2X TO 3X BASIC
1 Wad/Hib/Jam/Geo/199 12.00 30.00
2 Dur/Par/Iba/Dun/199 10.00 25.00
3 Sto/Dre/Ola/Mal/199 12.00 30.00
4 Mou/Mas/Joh/Ewi/49 10.00 25.00
5 Lai/Bir/Par/Mah/149 10.00 25.00
6 Dum/Joh/Joh/Abd/99 12.00 30.00
7 Byn/Gar/Bry/Pie/199 12.00 30.00
8 Dun/Sto/Gin/Nas/199 8.00 20.00
9 Mut/Gin/Dun/McG/199 10.00 25.00
10 Var/Jam/But/Jam/99 10.00 25.00
11 Sto/Kuk/Mal/Pip/99 12.00 30.00
12 Ola/Wor/Abd/Sam/49 10.00 25.00
13 Ant/Wil/Gar/Cha/199 8.00 20.00
14 Gri/Bry/Gas/Jor/199 12.00 30.00
15 Dau/Pri/Pip/Kuk/199 8.00 20.00
16 Ant/Jam/Gas/Gas/199 12.00 30.00
17 Dre/Pay/Ola/Kem/199 12.00 30.00

2013-14 Panini Preferred USA Memorabilia

RANDOM INSERTS IN PACKS
PRINT RUNS BW/N 99-199 COPIES PER
1 Mu/Dr/Ma/Jo/Bi/Pi/99 15.00 40.00
2 Ho/O'N/Mo/Ro/Ga/Ja/199 12.00 30.00
3 La/Wi/Du/Ja/An/Pa/199 12.00 30.00
4 Be/Du/Dr/Co/Ha/Cu/199 12.00 30.00

2013-14 Panini Preferred USA Memorabilia Prime

*PRIME: 1.2X TO 3X BASIC
RANDOM INSERTS IN PACKS
STATED PRINT RUN 25 SER.#'d SETS
1 Mn/Dr/Me/Jn/Me/Bd/Pn 50.00 120.00

2013-14 Panini Preferred Warriors Memorabilia

RANDOM INSERTS IN PACKS
PRINT RUNS BW/N 49-199 COPIES PER
*PRIME: 1.2X TO 3X BASIC
1 Ig/Bo/Ba/O'N/Th/Cu/Le/Gr/199 30.00 80.00
2 Ig/Mu/Th/Ba/Ba/Th/Cu/Fr/49 20.00 50.00

2014-15 Panini Preferred

AU PRINT RUNS B/WN 25-99 COPIES PER
SL JSY AU PRINT RUN B/WN 35-99 COPIES PER
OVERALL ODDS THREE AU PER BOX
EXCHANGE DEADLINE 12/17/2016
1 Aaron Gordon RB AU/35 12.00 30.00
2 Andrew Wiggins RB AU/35 75.00 200.00
3 Elfrid Payton RB AU/35 8.00 20.00
4 James Ennis RB AU/99 4.00 10.00
5 Bojan Bogdanovic RB AU/99 5.00 12.00
6 Damjan Rudez RB AU/99 4.00 10.00
8 Zoran Dragic RB AU/99 5.00 12.00
9 Jordan Clarkson RB AU/99 20.00 50.00
10 T.J. Warren RB AU/99 6.00 15.00
12 Nikola Mirotic RB AU/99 4.00 10.00
13 Doug McDermott RB AU/99 6.00 15.00
14 Spencer Dinwiddie RB AU/99 5.00 12.00
16 K.J. McDaniels RB AU/99 5.00 12.00
17 Jerami Grant RB AU/99 4.00 10.00
18 Travis Wear RB AU/99 4.00 10.00
19 Shabazz Napier RB AU/99 5.00 12.00
20 Jabari Parker RB AU/35 40.00 100.00
21 Johnny O'Bryant RB AU/99 4.00 10.00
22 Cory Jefferson RB AU/99 4.00 10.00
23 Devyn Marble RB AU/99 4.00 10.00
24 Russ Smith RB AU/99 4.00 10.00
25 Jarnell Stokes RB AU/99 4.00 10.00
26 Lucas Nogueira RB AU/99 4.00 10.00
27 Gary Harris RB AU/35 8.00 20.00
28 Jusuf Nurkic RB AU/35 8.00 20.00
29 Erick Green RB AU/99 4.00 10.00
30 Glenn Robinson III RB AU/35 5.00 12.00
31 Rodney Hood RB AU/35 8.00 20.00
32 Bruno Caboclo RB AU/35 6.00 15.00
33 Marcus Smart RB AU/35
34 James Young RB AU/35 5.00 12.00
35 Dante Exum RB AU/35 8.00 20.00
36 Kevin Durant RB AU/35 75.00 200.00
37 Kobe Bryant RB AU/35 150.00 250.00
38 Kyrie Irving RB AU/35 50.00 120.00
39 Carmelo Anthony RB AU/35 20.00 50.00
41 Victor Oladipo RB AU/35 6.00 15.00
43 Michael Kidd-Gilchrist RB AU/25 6.00 15.00
44 Otto Porter RB AU/25 6.00 15.00
45 Bradley Beal RB AU/25 10.00 25.00
46 John Wall RB AU/35 30.00 80.00
47 Kelly Olynyk RB AU/99 4.00 10.00
48 Tyler Zeller RB AU/99 5.00 12.00
49 Harrison Barnes RB AU/25 12.00 30.00
50 Stephen Curry RB AU/35 200.00 400.00
51 Carl Landry RB AU/35 5.00 12.00
52 Ben McLemore RB AU/25 10.00 25.00
53 Blake Griffin RB AU/25 30.00 80.00
54 Goran Dragic RB AU/25 6.00 15.00
55 Ty Lawson RB AU/25 5.00 12.00
56 LaMarcus Aldridge RB AU/25 12.00 30.00
57 Udonis Haslem RB AU/35 5.00 12.00
60 Steven Adams RB AU/99 5.00 12.00
61 Giannis Antetokounmpo RB AU/99
62 Tim Hardaway Jr. RB AU/99 4.00 10.00
63 Jason Terry RB AU/25 6.00 15.00
64 Josh Smith RB AU/25 6.00 15.00
66 Mason Plumlee RB AU/99 5.00 12.00
67 Anthony Davis RB AU/35 50.00 120.00
68 Brook Lopez RB AU/25 6.00 15.00
69 Rudy Gobert RB AU/99 6.00 15.00
71 Marques Johnson RB AU/99 5.00 12.00
72 Rudy Tomjanovich RB AU/75 5.00 12.00
73 Scott Brooks RB AU/25 5.00 12.00
74 Mark Price RB AU/99 6.00 15.00
75 Zydrunas Ilgauskas RB AU/99 5.00 12.00
76 Clifford Robinson RB AU/99 6.00 15.00
77 Terry Porter RB AU/99 4.00 10.00
78 Dikembe Mutombo RB AU/25 12.00 30.00
79 Rod Strickland RB AU/99 4.00 10.00
80 Cedric Maxwell RB AU/99 4.00 10.00
81 Mark Aguirre RB AU/99 5.00 12.00
82 Adrian Dantley RB AU/99 5.00 12.00
83 Alex English RB AU/99 5.00 12.00
84 Horace Grant RB AU/25 12.00 30.00
85 Fat Lever RB AU/60 5.00 12.00
87 Ron Harper RB AU/99 6.00 15.00
88 Michael Finley RB AU/25 8.00 20.00
91 Hakeem Olajuwon RB AU/25 15.00 40.00
92 Magic Johnson RB AU/25 30.00 80.00
93 James Worthy RB AU/25 10.00 25.00
94 Steve Nash RB AU/25 20.00 50.00
95 George Gervin RB AU/25 8.00 20.00
96 Bill Walton RB AU/25 8.00 20.00
97 Gary Payton RB AU/25 12.00 30.00
98 Clyde Drexler RB AU/25 10.00 25.00
100 Scott Skiles RB AU/99 5.00 12.00
101 Tim Hardaway Jr. CR AU/75 4.00 10.00
102 Bill Cartwright CR AU/35 6.00 15.00
103 Ty Lawson CR AU/35 5.00 12.00
104 Steve Nash CR AU/35 25.00 60.00
105 Eddie Jones CR AU/75 5.00 12.00
107 Don Nelson CR AU/35 12.00 30.00
108 Alonzo Mourning CR AU/35 20.00 50.00
109 Jeff Malone CR AU/75 4.00 10.00
111 George Gervin CR AU/35 8.00 20.00
112 Tracy McGrady CR AU/35 25.00 60.00
113 Jim Jackson CR AU/75 4.00 10.00
114 Kurt Rambis CR AU/35 5.00 12.00
115 Mark Jackson CR AU/35 6.00 15.00
116 Kevin Love CR AU/35 12.00 30.00
118 Mark Aguirre CR AU/35 6.00 15.00
119 Nate Archibald CR AU/35 6.00 15.00
120 Michael Kidd-Gilchrist CR AU/35 6.00 15.00
121 Mateen Cleaves CR AU/75 4.00 10.00
122 Chase Budinger CR AU/35 5.00 12.00
123 Ralph Sampson CR AU/35 6.00 15.00
124 Grant Hill CR AU/35 20.00 50.00
125 Maurice Cheeks CR AU/75 4.00 10.00
126 Courtney Lee CR AU/35 6.00 15.00
127 Avery Johnson CR AU/35 6.00 15.00
128 Victor Oladipo CR AU/35 6.00 15.00
129 Sean Elliott CR AU/75 6.00 15.00
130 Jonas Valanciunas CR AU/35 6.00 15.00
131 Kyle Korver CR AU/35 6.00 15.00
132 Rick Barry CR AU/35 6.00 15.00
133 Antoine Walker CR AU/75 5.00 12.00
134 Robert Horry CR AU/35 10.00 25.00
135 J.R. Smith CR AU/35 6.00 15.00
136 Zach Randolph CR AU/35 6.00 15.00
137 Spencer Hawes CR AU/75 4.00 10.00
138 Reggie Jackson CR AU/35 5.00 12.00
141 Thaddeus Young CR AU/75 4.00 10.00
142 Jamaal Wilkes CR AU/35 8.00 20.00
143 D. Mutombo CR AU/35 12.00 30.00
145 Timofey Mozgov CR AU/75 6.00 15.00
146 George McGinnis CR AU/35 5.00 12.00
147 Jose Calderon CR AU/35 5.00 12.00
148 Byron Scott CR AU/35 6.00 15.00
149 Bill Laimbeer CR AU/75 5.00 12.00
150 G.Antetokounmpo CR AU/75 60.00 150.00
151 Richard Jefferson CR AU/35 6.00 15.00
152 L. Aldridge CR AU/35 12.00 30.00
153 Dee Brown CR AU/75 4.00 10.00
154 C.J. Watson CR AU/75 4.00 10.00
155 Glen Rice CR AU/35 6.00 15.00
156 Isiah Thomas CR AU/35 10.00 25.00
157 Jack Sikma CR AU/75 5.00 12.00
158 Adrian Smith CR AU/75 5.00 12.00
159 Tiago Splitter CR AU/35 6.00 15.00
160 Walt Frazier CR AU/35 10.00 25.00
161 Larry Nance CR AU/75 5.00 12.00
162 Darryl Dawkins CR AU/75 4.00 10.00
163 Marcin Gortat CR AU/35 10.00 25.00
164 Michael Finley CR AU/35 8.00 20.00
165 Ron Harper CR AU/75 6.00 15.00
167 Toni Kukoc CR AU/35 8.00 20.00
169 Evan Fournier CR AU/75 4.00 10.00
170 Mychal Thompson CR AU/75 4.00 10.00
173 John Starks CR AU/75 5.00 12.00
174 DeMarre Carroll CR AU/75 4.00 10.00
175 Randy Foye CR AU/35
176 Rick Fox CR AU/35 6.00 15.00
177 Troy Daniels CR AU/75 4.00 10.00
178 Alec Burks CR AU/75 4.00 10.00
180 Joe Dumars CR AU/35 8.00 20.00
181 Mirza Teletovic CR AU/75 4.00 10.00
182 Arvydas Sabonis CR AU/75 8.00 20.00
184 Jerry Lucas CR AU/35 8.00 20.00
185 P.J. Tucker CR AU/75 4.00 10.00
187 Tobias Harris CR AU/35 6.00 15.00
188 Dolph Schayes CR AU/35 8.00 20.00
190 Zydrunas Ilgauskas CR AU/75 5.00 12.00
191 Lance Stephenson CR AU/35 6.00 15.00
192 Kevin Martin CR AU/35 6.00 15.00
193 Solomon Hill CR AU/75 4.00 10.00
194 Walter Davis CR AU/75 4.00 10.00
195 Tom Chambers CR AU/35 6.00 15.00
196 Shabazz Muhammad CR AU/35 6.00 15.00
197 Phil Pressey CR AU/75 4.00 10.00
198 Norm Nixon CR AU/75 4.00 10.00
199 Satch Sanders CR AU/35 12.00 30.00
200 Tristan Thompson CR AU/35 6.00 15.00
201 Jabari Parker CR AU/49 RC 50.00 120.00
202 A. Wiggins CR AU/49 RC 125.00 250.00
203 Joel Embiid CR AU/49 RC 60.00 150.00
204 Marcus Smart CR AU/49 RC 6.00 15.00
205 Dante Exum CR AU/49 RC 6.00 15.00
206 Julius Randle CR AU/49 RC 15.00 40.00
207 Aaron Gordon CR AU/49 RC 10.00 25.00
208 Noah Vonleh CR AU/49 RC 5.00 12.00
209 Tyler Ennis CR AU/49 RC 4.00 10.00
211 Elfrid Payton CR AU/49 RC 6.00 15.00
212 Doug McDermott CR AU/49 RC 6.00 15.00
213 James Young CR AU/49 RC 4.00 10.00
214 Jusuf Nurkic CR AU/49 RC 6.00 15.00
215 Zach LaVine CR AU/49 RC 15.00 40.00
216 Glenn Robinson III CR AU/49 RC 4.00 10.00
217 Bojan Bogdanovic CR AU/49 RC 5.00 12.00
218 Damjan Rudez CR AU/49 RC 4.00 10.00
219 Jerami Grant CR AU/49 RC
220 Jordan Adams CR AU/49 RC 4.00 10.00
221 Bruno Caboclo CR AU/49 RC 5.00 12.00
224 Markel Brown CR AU/49 RC 4.00 10.00
225 Lucas Nogueira CR AU/49 RC 4.00 10.00
227 Joe Harris CR AU/49 RC 4.00 10.00
228 Devyn Marble CR AU/49 RC 4.00 10.00
229 Johnny O'Bryant CR AU/49 RC 4.00 10.00
230 J. Clarkson CR AU/49 RC 10.00 25.00
231 Erick Green CR AU/49 RC 4.00 10.00
232 James Ennis CR AU/49 RC 4.00 10.00
233 Nikola Mirotic CR AU/49 RC 15.00 40.00
234 K. Bryant SL JSY AU/35 200.00 400.00
236 C. Anthony SL JSY AU/35 50.00 120.00
237 Kevin Durant SL JSY AU/35 60.00 150.00
238 J. Stockton SL JSY AU/35 30.00 80.00
239 Blake Griffin SL JSY AU/35 25.00 60.00
240 Kyrie Irving SL JSY AU/35 50.00 120.00
241 D. Robinson SL JSY AU/35 20.00 50.00
242 John Wall SL JSY AU/35 20.00 50.00
244 C.Drexler SL JSY AU/35 25.00 60.00
245 H. Olajuwon SL JSY AU/35 20.00 50.00
246 Jason Kidd SL JSY AU/35 20.00 50.00
247 Kevin Love SL JSY AU/35 20.00 50.00
248 Tony Parker SL JSY AU/35 25.00 60.00
249 Michael Kidd-Gilchrist SL JSY AU/35 8.00 20.00
250 Steph Curry SL JSY AU/35 125.00 250.00
251 Chris Andersen SL JSY AU/35 8.00 20.00
254 Tyreke Evans SL JSY AU/35 6.00 15.00
255 Tyson Chandler SL JSY AU/35 8.00 20.00
256 Matthew Dellavedova SL JSY AU/35 8.00 20.00
258 Brent Barry SL JSY AU/35 6.00 15.00
259 Andre Drummond SL JSY AU/35 8.00 20.00
260 Isiah Thomas SL JSY AU/35 10.00 25.00
261 L. Aldridge SL JSY AU/35 20.00 50.00
263 Tobias Harris SL JSY AU/60 6.00 15.00
264 Goran Dragic SL JSY AU/35 8.00 20.00
266 Grant Hill SL JSY AU/35 25.00 60.00
267 Kemba Walker SL JSY AU/35 10.00 25.00
268 Tristan Thompson SL JSY AU/35 8.00 20.00
269 D. Mutombo SL JSY AU/60 12.00 30.00
270 Kenneth Faried SL JSY AU/60 6.00 15.00
271 Carl Landry SL JSY AU/60 5.00 12.00
272 D. Schroder SL JSY AU/60 8.00 20.00
273 Wesley Matthews SL JSY AU/60 5.00 12.00
274 Clifford Robinson SL JSY AU/60 5.00 12.00
276 Robert Horry SL JSY AU/60 6.00 15.00
277 Marques Johnson SL JSY AU/60 6.00 15.00
279 Danny Manning SL JSY AU/60 6.00 15.00
280 Dan Majerle SL JSY AU/60 6.00 15.00
281 Alan Anderson SL JSY AU/60 5.00 12.00
282 Maurice Harkless SL JSY AU/60 5.00 12.00
283 Adrian Dantley SL JSY AU/60 6.00 15.00
284 Nick Young SL JSY AU/60 6.00 15.00
285 Luis Scola SL JSY AU/35 8.00 20.00
286 Archie Goodwin SL JSY AU/60 5.00 12.00
287 Steven Adams SL JSY AU/60 6.00 15.00
289 Timofey Mozgov SL JSY AU/60 5.00 12.00
290 Walter Davis SL JSY AU/60 5.00 12.00
291 Evan Fournier SL JSY AU/60 5.00 12.00
293 Mason Plumlee SL JSY AU/60 6.00 15.00
294 Mirza Teletovic SL JSY AU/60 5.00 12.00
295 G. Hayward SL JSY AU/60 12.00 30.00
296 A. Gordon SL JSY AU/99 RC 20.00 50.00
297 Wiggins SL JSY AU/99 RC 150.00 300.00
298 E. Payton SL JSY AU/99 RC 20.00 50.00
299 James Ennis SL JSY AU/99 RC 5.00 12.00
300 Russ Smith SL JSY AU/99 RC 5.00 12.00
301 Jarnell Stokes SL JSY AU/99 RC 5.00 12.00
303 M. Smart SL JSY AU/99 RC 10.00 25.00
304 Tyler Ennis SL JSY AU/99 RC 5.00 12.00
305 TJ Warren SL JSY AU/99 RC 10.00 25.00
307 Bruno Caboclo SL JSY AU/99 RC 6.00 15.00
308 McDermott SL JSY AU/99 RC 8.00 20.00
309 Spencer Dinwiddie SL JSY AU/99 RC 6.00 15.00
310 Embiid SL JSY AU/99 RC 200.00 400.00
311 K.J. McDaniels SL JSY AU/99 RC 6.00 15.00
312 Jerami Grant SL JSY AU/99 RC 5.00 12.00
314 Shabazz Napier SL JSY AU/99 RC 6.00 15.00
315 J. Parker SL JSY AU/99 RC 60.00 150.00
316 Johnny O'Bryant SL JSY AU/99 RC 5.00 12.00
318 Damien Inglis SL JSY AU/99 RC 5.00 12.00
319 James Young SL JSY AU/99 RC 8.00 20.00
320 D.Exum SL JSY AU/99 RC 15.00 40.00
321 Jordan Adams SL JSY AU/99 RC 5.00 12.00
322 Gary Harris SL JSY AU/99 RC 8.00 20.00
323 R.Hood SL JSY AU/99 RC 10.00 25.00
324 Glenn Robinson III SL JSY AU/99 RC 5.00 12.00
325 J. Randle SL JSY AU/99 RC 20.00 50.00
326 Joe Harris SL JSY AU/99 RC 5.00 12.00
327 Noah Vonleh SL JSY AU/99 RC 6.00 15.00
329 Adreian Payne SL JSY AU/99 RC 6.00 15.00
330 Cory Jefferson SL JSY AU/99 RC 5.00 12.00
331 Markel Brown SL JSY AU/99 RC 5.00 12.00
332 C.J. Wilcox SL JSY AU/99 RC 5.00 12.00
333 Z. LaVine SL JSY AU/99 RC 40.00 100.00
334 A. Wiggins DD AU/49 125.00 250.00
335 Dante Exum DD AU/49 12.00 30.00
336 Jabari Parker DD AU/49 30.00 80.00
337 Marcus Smart DD AU/49 6.00 15.00
338 Shabazz Napier DD AU/49 5.00 12.00
340 Spencer Dinwiddie DD AU/49 5.00 12.00
341 Erick Green DD AU/49 4.00 10.00
342 Jordan Clarkson DD AU/49 20.00 50.00
343 Julius Randle DD AU/49 15.00 40.00
344 Aaron Gordon DD AU/49 10.00 25.00
345 James Ennis DD AU/49 4.00 10.00
346 Zach LaVine DD AU/49 15.00 40.00
347 Gary Harris DD AU/49 6.00 15.00
348 Jusuf Nurkic DD AU/49 6.00 15.00
350 Rodney Hood DD AU/49 6.00 15.00
351 Bojan Bogdanovic DD AU/49 5.00 12.00
352 Nikola Mirotic DD AU/49 25.00 60.00
353 Glenn Robinson III DD AU/49 4.00 10.00
354 Travis Wear DD AU/49 4.00 10.00
355 Devyn Marble DD AU/49 4.00 10.00
356 Elfrid Payton DD AU/49 6.00 15.00
358 Joe Harris DD AU/49 4.00 10.00
359 K.J. McDaniels DD AU/49 5.00 12.00
360 Bruno Caboclo DD AU/49 5.00 12.00
361 C.J. Wilcox DD AU/49 4.00 10.00
362 Jarnell Stokes DD AU/49 4.00 10.00
363 Cory Jefferson DD AU/49 4.00 10.00
364 Noah Vonleh DD AU/49 5.00 12.00
365 Tyler Ennis DD AU/49 4.00 10.00
366 Doug McDermott DD AU/49 6.00 15.00
367 Jabari Parker RR AU/49 RC 40.00 100.00
368 A. Wiggins RR AU/49 RC 125.00 250.00
370 Marcus Smart RR AU/49 RC 6.00 15.00
371 Dante Exum RR AU/49 RC 12.00 30.00
372 Julius Randle RR AU/49 RC 15.00 40.00
373 Aaron Gordon RR AU/49 RC 10.00 25.00
374 Noah Vonleh RR AU/49 RC 5.00 12.00
375 Tyler Ennis RR AU/49 RC 4.00 10.00
377 Elfrid Payton RR AU/49 RC 6.00 15.00
378 T.J. Warren RR AU/49 RC 6.00 15.00
379 C.J. Wilcox RR AU/49 RC 4.00 10.00
380 Zach LaVine RR AU/49 RC 15.00 40.00
381 Adreian Payne RR AU/49 RC 5.00 12.00
382 Damjan Rudez RR AU/49 RC 4.00 10.00
383 Jordan Adams RR AU/49 RC 4.00 10.00
384 Jarnell Stokes RR AU/49 RC 4.00 10.00
385 Shabazz Napier RR AU/49 RC 5.00 12.00
386 Damien Inglis RR AU/49 RC 4.00 10.00
388 Devyn Marble RR AU/49 RC 4.00 10.00
389 Travis Wear RR AU/49 RC 4.00 10.00
390 N. Mirotic RR AU/49 RC 20.00 50.00
391 Markel Brown RR AU/49 RC 4.00 10.00
394 J. Clarkson RR AU/49 RC 20.00 50.00
395 Joe Harris RR AU/49 RC 4.00 10.00
396 Bojan Bogdanovic RR AU/49 RC 5.00 12.00
397 Rodney Hood RR AU/49 RC 6.00 15.00
398 Zoran Dragic RR AU/49 RC 5.00 12.00
399 James Young RR AU/49 RC 4.00 10.00
401 Chris Andersen PS AU/30 12.00 30.00
402 Goran Dragic PS AU/30 6.00 15.00
404 Victor Oladipo PS AU/30 6.00 15.00
405 Mark Aguirre PS AU/30 6.00 15.00
406 Phil Pressey PS AU/30 5.00 12.00
407 Alec Burks PS AU/75 4.00 10.00
408 J.R. Smith PS AU/30 6.00 15.00
409 Anthony Davis PS AU/30 50.00 120.00
410 Mason Plumlee PS AU/35 6.00 15.00
411 Tristan Thompson PS AU/30 6.00 15.00
412 Steve Nash PS AU/30 20.00 50.00
413 Dan Issel PS AU/35 6.00 15.00
414 Tim Hardaway PS AU/75 6.00 15.00
415 Kendall Gill PS AU/35 5.00 12.00
416 Gus Williams PS AU/35 5.00 12.00
417 Thaddeus Young PS AU/35 5.00 12.00
419 Andrew Nicholson PS AU/75 4.00 10.00
421 Enes Kanter PS AU/30 5.00 12.00
423 Derrick Williams PS AU/30 5.00 12.00
424 Derrick Favors PS AU/30 6.00 15.00
425 Rod Strickland PS AU/75 4.00 10.00
427 Steve Smith PS AU/75 5.00 12.00
428 Rick Mahorn PS AU/75 4.00 10.00
429 Phil Chenier PS AU/75 4.00 10.00
430 Paul Westphal PS AU/75 6.00 15.00
431 Mychal Thompson PS AU/75 4.00 10.00
433 Kiki Vandeweghe PS AU/75 5.00 12.00
434 Keith Van Horn PS AU/75 5.00 12.00
435 Eddie Jones PS AU/75 5.00 12.00
436 Doug Collins PS AU/75 6.00 15.00
437 Tom Van Arsdale PS AU/75 5.00 12.00
438 Charlie Scott PS AU/75 5.00 12.00
439 Brian Grant PS AU/75 4.00 10.00
441 Bob Dandridge PS AU/75 4.00 10.00
442 Tom Gugliotta PS AU/75 4.00 10.00
443 Wayne Embry PS AU/30 5.00 12.00
444 John Starks PS AU/75 6.00 15.00
445 Robert Horry PS AU/30 6.00 15.00
446 Alonzo Mourning PS AU/30 25.00 60.00
447 Latrell Sprewell PS AU/30 30.00 80.00
448 Bill Walton PS AU/30 8.00 20.00
449 Grant Hill PS AU/30 20.00 50.00
450 Tracy McGrady PS AU/30 30.00 80.00
451 Zach Randolph PS AU/30 6.00 15.00
452 Josh Smith PS AU/30 6.00 15.00
453 Stephen Curry PS AU/30 150.00 400.00
454 Kawhi Leonard PS AU/30 40.00 100.00
455 Tobias Harris PS AU/30 6.00 15.00
456 Kenneth Faried PS AU/30 6.00 15.00
459 Iman Shumpert PS AU/30 5.00 12.00
461 Lance Stephenson PS AU/30 6.00 15.00
463 Reggie Jackson PS AU/30 5.00 12.00
465 Nick Collison PS AU/75 5.00 12.00
467 Robin Lopez PS AU/75
468 Tyler Zeller PS AU/75 5.00 12.00
469 Maurice Harkless PS AU/75 4.00 10.00
470 Walt Frazier PS AU/30 10.00 25.00
472 Dolph Schayes PS AU/30 8.00 20.00
473 Don Nelson PS AU/30 12.00 30.00
474 George Gervin PS AU/30 8.00 20.00
475 Hal Greer PS AU/30 6.00 15.00
476 James Worthy PS AU/30 10.00 25.00
477 Robert Parish PS AU/30 8.00 20.00
478 Alex English PS AU/30 6.00 15.00
479 David Thompson PS AU/30 6.00 15.00
480 Jason Kidd PS AU/30 15.00 40.00
481 Gary Payton PS AU/30 15.00 40.00
482 Christian Laettner PS AU/30 8.00 20.00
483 Brent Barry PS AU/30 5.00 12.00
484 Michael Finley PS AU/30 12.00 30.00
485 Dave Cowens PS AU/30 5.00 12.00
486 Horace Grant PS AU/30 15.00 40.00
487 Jalen Rose PS AU/30 8.00 20.00
488 Scott Brooks PS AU/30 5.00 12.00
489 Rudy Tomjanovich PS AU/75 5.00 12.00
490 Kevin Love PS AU/30 12.00 30.00
491 Tony Parker PS AU/30 12.00 30.00
492 Muggsy Bogues PS AU/75 8.00 20.00
493 Kenny Smith PS AU/30 6.00 15.00
494 C.Anthony PS AU/30 25.00 60.00
495 Michael Kidd-Gilchrist PS AU/30 6.00 15.00
496 Harrison Barnes PS AU/30 6.00 15.00
497 Tyson Chandler PS AU/30 10.00 25.00
498 John Wall PS AU/30 25.00 60.00
499 Bradley Beal PS AU/30 12.00 30.00
500 Kobe Bryant U AU/50 125.00 250.00
501 Kevin Durant U AU/50 60.00 150.00
502 Kyrie Irving U AU/50 25.00 60.00
503 Anthony Davis U AU/50 75.00 150.00
504 Bradley Beal U AU/50 10.00 25.00
505 John Wall U AU/50 20.00 50.00
506 Tony Parker U AU/50 15.00 40.00
507 Iman Shumpert U AU/50 4.00 10.00
509 Marcin Gortat U AU/50 5.00 12.00
510 Danny Green U AU/50 5.00 12.00
511 Gordon Hayward U AU/50 6.00 15.00
512 Jonas Valanciunas U AU/50 5.00 12.00
514 Lance Stephenson U AU/50 5.00 12.00
515 Reggie Jackson U AU/50 4.00 10.00
517 Corey Brewer U AU/50 4.00 10.00
518 G. Antetokounmpo U AU/50 40.00 100.00
519 Steven Adams U AU/50 5.00 12.00
520 Spencer Hawes U AU/50 4.00 10.00
521 Thaddeus Young U AU/50 4.00 10.00
522 Kelly Olynyk U AU/50 4.00 10.00
524 Lavoy Allen U AU/50 4.00 10.00
525 Gorgui Dieng U AU/50 4.00 10.00
526 Ryan Kelly U AU/50 4.00 10.00
527 Kent Bazemore U AU/50 5.00 12.00
528 P.J. Tucker U AU/50 4.00 10.00
529 Troy Daniels U AU/50 4.00 10.00
530 Mason Plumlee U AU/50 5.00 12.00
531 Enes Kanter U AU/50 4.00 10.00
532 Tobias Harris U AU/50 5.00 12.00
533 Latrell Sprewell U AU/50 25.00 60.00
534 Larry Bird U AU/50 50.00 120.00
535 Magic Johnson U AU/50 30.00 80.00
536 Abdul-Jabbar U AU/50 30.00 80.00
537 Isiah Thomas U AU/50 10.00 25.00
538 Gary Payton U AU/50 10.00 25.00
539 Rick Barry U AU/50 5.00 12.00
540 Alex English U AU/50 5.00 12.00
541 Joe Dumars U AU/50 6.00 15.00
542 George Gervin U AU/50 6.00 15.00
543 Bill Laimbeer U AU/50 5.00 12.00
544 Antoine Walker U AU/50 5.00 12.00
545 Bob McAdoo U AU/50 10.00 25.00
546 Allan Houston U AU/50 5.00 12.00
547 D. Mutombo U AU/50 10.00 25.00
548 Eddie Jones U AU/50 8.00 20.00
550 Jeff Hornacek U AU/50 5.00 12.00
551 Jim Jackson U AU/50 4.00 10.00
552 Muggsy Bogues U AU/50 8.00 20.00
553 Scott Skiles U AU/50 5.00 12.00
554 David Robinson U AU/50 20.00 50.00
555 Tim Hardaway U AU/50 6.00 15.00
556 Kenny Smith U AU/50 5.00 12.00
557 Sidney Moncrief U AU/50 4.00 10.00
558 Mark Aguirre U AU/50 5.00 12.00
559 Adrian Dantley U AU/50 5.00 12.00
560 Jo Jo White U AU/50 5.00 12.00
561 John Salley U AU/50 10.00 25.00
562 Mark Price U AU/50 6.00 15.00
563 Bobby Jones U AU/50 5.00 12.00
564 Doug Collins U AU/50 6.00 15.00
565 Dick Van Arsdale U AU/50 5.00 12.00
566 Aaron Gordon U AU/50 RC 10.00 25.00
567 A. Wiggins U AU/50 RC 75.00 150.00
568 Elfrid Payton U AU/50 RC 6.00 15.00
569 James Ennis U AU/50 RC 4.00 10.00
570 Russ Smith U AU/50 RC 4.00 10.00
572 Marcus Smart U AU/50 RC 6.00 15.00
573 Tyler Ennis U AU/50 RC 4.00 10.00
574 Zoran Dragic U AU/50 RC 5.00 12.00
576 Bruno Caboclo U AU/50 RC 5.00 12.00
577 Doug McDermott U AU/50 RC 6.00 15.00
578 Spencer Dinwiddie U AU/50 RC 5.00 12.00
579 Joel Embiid U AU/50 RC 75.00 200.00
580 K.J. McDaniels U AU/50 RC 5.00 12.00
582 Shabazz Napier U AU/50 RC 5.00 12.00
583 Jabari Parker U AU/50 RC 25.00 60.00
585 Damien Inglis U AU/50 RC 4.00 10.00
586 James Young U AU/50 RC 4.00 10.00
587 Dante Exum U AU/50 RC 15.00 40.00
588 Jordan Adams U AU/50 RC 4.00 10.00
589 Gary Harris U AU/50 RC 6.00 15.00
590 Rodney Hood U AU/50 RC 6.00 15.00
591 Erick Green U AU/50 RC 4.00 10.00
592 Julius Randle U AU/50 RC 15.00 40.00
593 Joe Harris U AU/50 RC 4.00 10.00
594 Noah Vonleh U AU/50 RC 5.00 12.00
596 Adreian Payne U AU/50 RC 5.00 12.00
597 Cory Jefferson U AU/50 RC 4.00 10.00
598 Markel Brown U AU/50 RC 4.00 10.00
599 Zach LaVine U AU/50 RC 20.00 50.00

2014-15 Panini Preferred Purple

*PURPLE: .5X TO 1.2X BASE p/r 49-99
*PURPLE: .4X TO 1.X BASE p/r 25-35
OVERALL ODDS THREE AU PER BOX
STATED PRINT RUN 20 SER.#'d SETS
EXCHANGE DEADLINE 12/17/2016

2014-15 Panini Preferred Silhouettes Prime

*SL PRIME: 2.5X TO 6X BASE p/r 60-99
*SL PRIME: 2X TO 5X BASE p/r 25-35
OVERALL ODDS THREE AU PER BOX
PRINT RUNS B/WN 5-25 COPIES PER
NO PRICING ON QTY 15 OR LESS
EXCHANGE DEADLINE 12/17/2016
234 Kobe Bryant/25 1000.00 2000.00
238 John Stockton/25 200.00 500.00
239 Blake Griffin/25 150.00 300.00
244 Clyde Drexler/25 100.00 200.00
266 Grant Hill/25 100.00 250.00
296 Aaron Gordon/25 200.00 400.00
298 Elfrid Payton/25 250.00 500.00
305 T.J. Warren/25 150.00 300.00
310 Joel Embiid/25
320 Dante Exum/25 200.00 400.00
325 Julius Randle/25 125.00 300.00
333 Zach LaVine/25 300.00 500.00

2014-15 Panini Preferred '14 NBA Finals Game 2 Memorabilia

OVERALL MEM ODDS ONE PER BOX
STATED PRINT RUN 99 SER.#'d SETS
1 Tim Duncan 12.00 30.00
2 Tony Parker 12.00 30.00
3 Kawhi Leonard 10.00 25.00
4 Tiago Splitter 5.00 12.00
5 Danny Green 6.00 15.00
6 Manu Ginobili 8.00 20.00
7 Patty Mills 12.00 30.00
8 Boris Diaw 5.00 12.00
9 Chris Bosh 6.00 15.00
10 Dwyane Wade 8.00 20.00
11 Ray Allen 10.00 25.00
12 Chris Andersen 5.00 12.00
13 Mario Chalmers 5.00 12.00
14 Norris Cole 4.00 10.00
15 Rashard Lewis 5.00 12.00
16 James Jones 4.00 10.00

2014-15 Panini Preferred '14 NBA Finals Game 2 Memorabilia Prime

*PRIME: 2.5X TO 6X BASIC
OVERALL MEM ODDS ONE PER BOX
STATED PRINT RUN 25 SER.#'d SETS
PRICING IS FOR BASIC PATCH CARDS
1 Tim Duncan 250.00 600.00
2 Tony Parker 250.00 600.00
3 Kawhi Leonard 200.00 500.00
6 Manu Ginobili 125.00 300.00

2014-15 Panini Preferred Champs Memorabilia

OVERALL MEM ODDS ONE PER BOX
STATED PRINT RUN 99 SER.#'d SETS
1 Tony Parker 12.00 30.00
2 LeBron James 30.00 80.00
3 Dirk Nowitzki 8.00 20.00
4 Dwyane Wade 8.00 20.00
5 Paul Pierce 8.00 20.00
6 Chris Bosh 5.00 12.00
7 Tim Duncan 25.00 60.00
8 Tayshaun Prince 4.00 10.00
9 Tyson Chandler 4.00 10.00
10 Shaquille O'Neal 15.00 40.00
11 David Robinson 20.00 50.00
12 Hakeem Olajuwon 12.00 30.00

2014-15 Panini Preferred Crazy Eights Memorabilia

OVERALL MEM ODDS ONE PER BOX
STATED PRINT RUN 99 SER.#'d SETS
*PRIME/25: 1.5X TO 4X BASIC
1 R/B/N/H/D/G/G/S 12.00 30.00
2 V/L/I/J/D/M/M/T 20.00 50.00
3 D/G/L/G/B/M/D/P 20.00 50.00
4 I/B/L/G/B/T/S/C 30.00 80.00
5 A/B/W/E/D/C/N/H 6.00 15.00
6 W/D/G/M/P/R/M/L 12.00 30.00
7 B/W/S/G/W/N/P/P 10.00 25.00
8 R/L/D/C/J/W/I/A 10.00 25.00

2014-15 Panini Preferred Playbook Rookie Memorabilia

OVERALL MEM ODDS ONE PER BOX
STATED PRINT RUN 99 SER.#'d SETS
1 Marcus Smart 5.00 12.00
2 Gary Harris 5.00 12.00
3 Noah Vonleh 4.00 10.00
4 Jabari Parker 12.00 30.00
5 Shabazz Napier 4.00 10.00
6 Aaron Gordon 8.00 20.00
7 Joe Harris 3.00 8.00
8 Bruno Caboclo 4.00 10.00
9 Julius Randle 8.00 20.00
10 Doug McDermott 5.00 12.00
11 Nik Stauskas 4.00 10.00
12 Jerami Grant 3.00 8.00
13 Rodney Hood 5.00 12.00
14 James Young 3.00 8.00
15 Zach LaVine 8.00 20.00
16 Andrew Wiggins 12.00 30.00
17 Joel Embiid 8.00 20.00
18 Dante Exum 8.00 20.00
19 T.J. Warren 5.00 12.00
20 Elfrid Payton 5.00 12.00
21 Adreian Payne 4.00 10.00
22 James Ennis 3.00 8.00
23 Kyle Anderson 5.00 12.00
24 Mitch McGary 3.00 8.00
25 Cleanthony Early 3.00 8.00
26 P.J. Hairston 3.00 8.00

2014-15 Panini Preferred Playbook Rookie Memorabilia Prime

*PRIME: 1.5X TO 4X BASIC
OVERALL MEM ODDS ONE PER BOX
STATED PRINT RUN 25 SER.#'d SETS
PRICING IS FOR BASIC PATCH CARDS
15 Zach LaVine 60.00 150.00

2014-15 Panini Preferred Playbook Veteran Memorabilia

OVERALL MEM ODDS ONE PER BOX
STATED PRINT RUN 99 SER.#'d SETS
1 Kobe Bryant 25.00 60.00
2 Chris Bosh 5.00 12.00
3 Kevin Love 10.00 25.00
4 Pau Gasol 5.00 12.00
5 Blake Griffin 5.00 12.00
6 Dirk Nowitzki 10.00 25.00
7 Jimmy Butler 10.00 25.00
8 Dwyane Wade 8.00 20.00
9 Victor Oladipo 4.00 10.00
10 Ricky Rubio 5.00 12.00

2014-15 Panini Preferred Stat Line Memorabilia

OVERALL MEM ODDS ONE PER BOX
STATED PRINT RUN 99 SER.#'d SETS
1 Ricky Rubio 4.00 10.00
2 Klay Thompson 5.00 12.00
3 Kobe Bryant 15.00 40.00
4 Andrew Bogut 3.00 8.00
5 Deron Williams 3.00 8.00
6 Tyreke Evans 2.50 6.00
7 Kyrie Irving 8.00 20.00
8 Anthony Davis 8.00 20.00
9 Joe Johnson 3.00 8.00
10 Dwyane Wade 6.00 15.00
11 Dwight Howard 3.00 8.00
12 Stephen Curry 15.00 40.00
13 James Harden 6.00 15.00
14 Chris Paul 5.00 12.00
15 LaMarcus Aldridge 4.00 10.00
16 Bradley Beal 4.00 10.00
17 Ty Lawson 2.50 6.00
18 John Wall 5.00 12.00
19 Kyle Korver 3.00 8.00
20 DeMarcus Cousins 4.00 10.00

2014-15 Panini Preferred Stat Line Memorabilia Prime

*PRIME: 2.5X TO 6X BASIC
OVERALL MEM ODDS ONE PER BOX
STATED PRINT RUN 25 SER.#'d SETS
PRICING IS FOR BASIC PATCH CARDS
2 Klay Thompson 60.00 150.00
3 Kobe Bryant 150.00 400.00
4 Andrew Bogut 30.00 80.00

2014-15 Panini Preferred Swish Memorabilia

OVERALL MEM ODDS ONE PER BOX
STATED PRINT RUN 99 SER.#'d SETS
1 Kobe Bryant 30.00 80.00
2 Kevin Durant 12.00 30.00
3 Stephen Curry 40.00 100.00
4 Dirk Nowitzki 15.00 40.00
5 James Harden 12.00 30.00
6 Bradley Beal 6.00 15.00

2014-15 Panini Preferred Swish Memorabilia Prime

*PRIME: 2X TO 5X BASIC
OVERALL MEM ODDS ONE PER BOX
STATED PRINT RUN 25 SER.#'d SETS
PRICING IS FOR BASIC PATCH CARDS
1 Kobe Bryant 250.00 400.00
3 Stephen Curry 125.00 400.00

2014-15 Panini Preferred Trending Upward Memorabilia

OVERALL MEM ODDS ONE PER BOX
STATED PRINT RUN 199 SER.#'d SETS
*PRIME/25: .75X TO 2X BASIC
1 Gn/Ws/Em/Pr/Ed/St 6.00 15.00
2 Gn/Pn/Es/Vh/Hn/Nr 3.00 8.00
3 Jn/Yg/Gt/Ed/St/Bn 6.00 15.00
4 Ws/Em/Hs/My/Hd/Le 6.00 15.00
5 Em/Pn/St/Nr/De/Le 3.00 8.00
6 Ws/Hs/Yg/Hs/Ss/Le 6.00 15.00
7 Gn/Jn/O'B/Re/My/Vh 3.00 8.00
8 Co/Ey/Mt/Pr/An/Hd 3.00 8.00
9 Ws/Co/Em/Ed/Ss/Es 6.00 15.00
10 Mt/Pn/Re/Ss/Vh/Le 3.00 8.00

2014-15 Panini Preferred VS 1 on 1 Memorabilia

OVERALL MEM ODDS ONE PER BOX
PRINT RUNS B/WN 25-99 COPIES PER
*PRIME/20-25: 2.5X TO 6X BASIC
1 A.Horford/M.Gasol/49 4.00 10.00
2 D.Rose/S.Curry/99 15.00 40.00
3 D.Rose/R.Rondo/99 8.00 20.00
4 K.Love/L.Aldridge/99 4.00 10.00
5 K.Irving/R.Westbrook/99 10.00 25.00
6 B.Lopez/D.Cousins/99 4.00 10.00
7 A.Jefferson/N.Noel/49 3.00 8.00
8 T.Harris/Z.Randolph/49 3.00 8.00
9 B.Griffin/L.James/99 15.00 40.00
10 C.Paul/T.Lawson/49 5.00 12.00
11 D.Jordan/T.Duncan/99 8.00 20.00
12 D.Green/L.James/99 15.00 40.00
13 B.McLemore/M.Ellis/49 3.00 8.00
14 C.Andersen/D.Williams/49 3.00 8.00
15 L.Aldridge/T.Duncan/99 12.00 30.00
16 K.Durant/R.Gay/99 6.00 15.00
17 J.Johnson/P.Pierce/99 4.00 10.00
18 K.Durant/L.James/99 20.00 50.00
19 L.Bird/M.Johnson/25 50.00 100.00
20 I.Thomas/K.McHale/25 10.00 25.00
21 K.McHale/R.Sampson/25 10.00 25.00
22 D.Mutombo/S.O'Neal/25 20.00 50.00
23 A.Iverson/K.Bryant/49 30.00 80.00
24 D.Lee/N.Noel/49 3.00 8.00
25 D.Williams/D.Wade/99 6.00 15.00
26 D.Jordan/V.Oladipo/99 4.00 10.00
27 L.Scola/P.Millsap/49 4.00 10.00
28 C.Parsons/T.Hardaway Jr./49 3.00 8.00

2015-16 Panini Preferred

SL JSY AU PRINT RUN B/WN 21-99 COPIES PER
AU PRINT RUNS B/WN 40-99 COPIES PER
EXCHANGE DEADLINE 2/17/2018
1 Porzingis SL JSY AU/99 RC 100.00 250.00
2 Cauley-Stein SL JSY AU/99 RC 12.00 30.00
3 Portis SL JSY AU/99 RC 6.00 15.00
4 Richardson SL JSY AU/99 RC 6.00 15.00
5 Marcelo Huertas SL JSY AU/99 RC 5.00 12.00
7 R.J. Hunter SL JSY AU/99 RC EXCH 4.00 10.00
8 Payne SL JSY AU/99 RC 8.00 20.00
9 Anderson SL JSY AU/99 RC 5.00 12.00
10 Hezonja SL JSY AU/99 RC 25.00 60.00
11 Richaun Holmes SL JSY AU/99 RC 5.00 12.00
12 Hollis-Jefferson SL JSY AU/99 RC 10.00 25.00
13 Russell SL JSY AU/99 RC EXCH 50.00 120.00
14 Winslow SL JSY AU/99 RC 25.00 60.00
15 Turner SL JSY AU/99 RC 20.00 50.00
16 Anthony Brown SL JSY AU/99 RC 4.00 10.00
17 Luis Montero SL JSY AU/99 RC 4.00 10.00
18 Delon Wright SL JSY AU/99 RC 5.00 12.00
19 Towns SL JSY AU/99 RC 150.00 300.00
20 Nemanja Bjelica SL JSY AU/99 RC 5.00 12.00
21 Salah Mejri SL JSY AU/99 RC 4.00 10.00
22 Powell SL JSY AU/99 RC 10.00 25.00
23 Booker SL JSY AU/99 RC 60.00 150.00
24 Oubre Jr. SL JSY AU/99 RC 8.00 20.00
25 Jokic SL JSY AU/99 RC 60.00 150.00
26 Johnson SL JSY AU/99 RC 5.00 12.00
27 Kevon Looney SL JSY AU/99 RC 5.00 12.00
28 Mudiay SL JSY AU/99 RC 15.00 40.00
29 Rozier SL JSY AU/99 RC 8.00 20.00
30 Montrezl Harrell SL JSY AU/99 RC 5.00 12.00
31 Frank Kaminsky SL JSY AU/99 RC 6.00 15.00
32 Lyles SL JSY AU/99 RC 12.00 30.00
33 Okafor SL JSY AU/99 RC 20.00 50.00
34 Jerian Grant SL JSY AU/99 RC 4.00 10.00
35 Joe Young SL JSY AU/99 RC 5.00 12.00
36 Simmons SL JSY AU/99 RC 12.00 30.00
37 Jordan Mickey SL JSY AU/99 RC 4.00 10.00
38 Bryant SL JSY AU/40 100.00 250.00
39 Durant SL JSY AU/40 75.00 200.00
40 Irving SL JSY AU/40 40.00 100.00
41 Love SL JSY AU/40 20.00 50.00
42 Wall SL JSY AU/40 20.00 50.00
43 Davis SL JSY AU/40 50.00 120.00
44 Wiggins SL JSY AU/49 30.00 80.00
45 Parker SL JSY AU/40 20.00 50.00
46 Randle SL JSY AU/60 12.00 30.00
47 Marcus Smart SL JSY AU/40 6.00 15.00
48 LaVine SL JSY AU/75 25.00 60.00
49 Robin Lopez SL JSY AU/75 EXCH 4.00 10.00
50 Johnson SL JSY AU/40 40.00 100.00
51 Khris Middleton SL JSY AU/75 5.00 12.00
52 Giannis SL JSY AU/75 40.00 100.00
53 Marcin Gortat SL JSY AU/75 5.00 12.00
54 Evan Fournier SL JSY AU/75 5.00 12.00
55 Eric Gordon SL JSY AU/60 5.00 12.00
56 Donatas Motiejunas SL JSY AU/75 4.00 10.00
57 Olajuwon SL JSY AU/40 25.00 60.00
58 Griffin SL JSY AU/40 25.00 60.00
59 Tobias Harris SL JSY AU/75 5.00 12.00
60 Bojan Bogdanovic SL JSY AU/75 4.00 10.00
61 George SL JSY AU/40 EXCH 25.00 60.00
62 Drexler SL JSY AU/40 15.00 40.00
63 Gary Harris SL JSY AU/75 5.00 12.00
64 Nene SL JSY AU/75 5.00 12.00
65 Brook Lopez SL JSY AU/60 EXCH 5.00 12.00
66 Bosh SL JSY AU/40 12.00 30.00
67 Mourning SL JSY AU/40 15.00 40.00
68 Jonas Valanciunas SL JSY AU/75 5.00 12.00
69 Gary Neal SL JSY AU/75 5.00 12.00
70 Batum SL JSY AU/75 5.00 12.00
71 Whiteside SL JSY AU/60 5.00 12.00
72 Stockton SL JSY AU/40 30.00 80.00
73 Oladipo SL JSY AU/40 10.00 25.00
74 Wesley Matthews SL JSY AU/75 4.00 10.00
75 Walker SL JSY AU/60 6.00 15.00
76 Nikola Vucevic SL JSY AU/75 5.00 12.00
77 Hill SL JSY AU/40 25.00 60.00
78 Payton SL JSY AU/60 10.00 25.00
79 Rudy Gay SL JSY AU/75 EXCH 6.00 15.00
80 Gasol SL JSY AU/40 15.00 40.00
81 Gordon SL JSY AU/60 12.00 30.00
82 Starks SL JSY AU/75 6.00 15.00
83 Mo Williams SL JSY AU/55 5.00 12.00
84 Horford SL JSY AU/75 5.00 12.00
85 Nikola Mirotic SL JSY AU/75 EXCH 5.00 12.00
86 DeMarre Carroll SL JSY AU/60 4.00 10.00
87 Allen SL JSY AU/40 30.00 80.00
88 Smith SL JSY AU/75 15.00 40.00
89 Hayward SL JSY AU/75 12.00 30.00
90 Dellavedova SL JSY AU/75 10.00 25.00
91 Brandon Knight SL JSY AU/60 5.00 12.00
92 Kerr SL JSY AU/21 20.00 50.00
93 Timofey Mozgov SL JSY AU/75 4.00 10.00
94 Doug McDermott SL JSY AU/75 5.00 12.00
95 Zaza Pachulia SL JSY AU/75 4.00 10.00

96 Alec Burks SL JSY AU/75 4.00 10.00
97 Kidd SL JSY AU/40 8.00 20.00
98 Jeff Teague SL JSY AU/50 EXCH 5.00 12.00
99 Bird SL JSY AU/40 40.00 100.00
100 Howard SL JSY AU/40 15.00 40.00
101 Kobe Bryant AU/40 100.00 250.00
102 Kevin Durant AU/40 50.00 120.00
103 Kyrie Irving AU/40 40.00 100.00
104 Gordon Hayward AU/60 12.00 30.00
105 John Wall AU/40 15.00 40.00
106 Anthony Davis AU/40 30.00 80.00
107 Andrew Wiggins AU/40 30.00 80.00
108 Jabari Parker AU/40 12.00 30.00
109 Julius Randle AU/60 12.00 30.00
110 Marcus Smart AU/45 6.00 15.00
111 Zach LaVine AU/99 8.00 20.00
112 Marcin Gortat AU/60 5.00 12.00
113 Blake Griffin AU/40 20.00 50.00
114 Gary Harris AU/99 5.00 12.00
115 Jonas Valanciunas AU/60 5.00 12.00
116 Victor Oladipo AU/45 6.00 15.00
117 Bill Laimbeer AU/99 5.00 12.00
118 Sam Dekker AU/99 5.00 12.00
119 Emmanuel Mudiay AU/45 15.00 40.00
120 Kemba Walker AU/60 8.00 20.00
121 Kristaps Porzingis AU/60 40.00 100.00
122 Donatas Motiejunas AU/99 4.00 10.00
123 Rashad Vaughn AU/99 4.00 10.00
124 Jonathon Simmons AU/99 6.00 15.00
125 Al Horford AU/60 6.00 15.00
126 Jahlil Okafor AU/45 10.00 25.00
127 Jusuf Nurkic AU/99 4.00 10.00
128 Jerian Grant AU/99 4.00 10.00
129 Boban Marjanovic AU/99 5.00 12.00
130 Chris Bosh AU/40 8.00 20.00
131 Alec Burks AU/99 4.00 10.00
132 Norman Powell AU/99 5.00 12.00
134 Nikola Jokic AU/99 25.00 60.00
135 Marcelo Huertas AU/99 5.00 12.00
136 Joe Ingles AU/99 6.00 15.00
137 Cameron Payne AU/99 5.00 12.00
138 Richaun Holmes AU/99 5.00 12.00
139 Festus Ezeli AU/99 4.00 10.00
140 Julius Erving AU/40 30.00 80.00
141 Klay Thompson AU/45 20.00 50.00
142 Matthew Dellavedova AU/99 5.00 12.00
143 Magic Johnson AU/40 25.00 60.00
144 D'Angelo Russell AU/45 30.00 80.00
145 Pau Gasol AU/40 12.00 30.00
146 Devin Booker AU/99 30.00 80.00
147 Rudy Gay AU/60 6.00 15.00
148 Eric Bledsoe AU/60 5.00 12.00
149 Paul Millsap AU/60 6.00 15.00
150 Mario Hezonja AU/60 5.00 12.00
151 Hardaway CR AU/40 25.00 60.00
152 Hill CR AU/40 12.00 30.00
153 Kidd CR AU/40 15.00 40.00
154 Bryant CR AU/40 100.00 250.00
155 Durant CR AU/40 50.00 120.00
156 Irving CR AU/40 40.00 100.00
157 Love CR AU/40 8.00 20.00
158 Wiggins CR AU/40 30.00 80.00
159 Davis CR AU/40 30.00 80.00
160 Griffin CR AU/40 15.00 40.00
161 Marcus Smart CR AU/40 6.00 15.00
162 Julius Randle CR AU/49 8.00 20.00
163 Parker CR AU/40 15.00 40.00
164 Walt Frazier CR AU/49 8.00 20.00
165 Heinsohn CR AU/85 15.00 40.00
166 Isiah Thomas CR AU/49 8.00 20.00
167 Stockton CR AU/40 20.00 50.00
168 Byron Scott CR AU/85 5.00 12.00
169 Robert Horry CR AU/85 5.00 12.00
170 Wall CR AU/40 15.00 40.00
171 Hayward CR AU/85 8.00 20.00
172 Thomas CR AU/85 25.00 60.00
173 Nikola Mirotic CR AU/49 6.00 15.00
174 Gary Harris CR AU/85 5.00 12.00
175 Norris Cole CR AU/85 4.00 10.00
176 LaVine CR AU/85 15.00 40.00
177 Brandon Knight CR AU/85 5.00 12.00
178 Schroder CR AU/85 10.00 25.00
179 Archibald CR AU/85 5.00 12.00
180 Ralph Sampson CR AU/85 5.00 12.00
182 Trey Lyles CR AU/85 6.00 15.00
183 Cauley-Stein CR AU/85 6.00 15.00
184 Anthony Brown CR AU/85 4.00 10.00
185 Cameron Payne CR AU/85 5.00 12.00
186 Russell CR AU/85 25.00 60.00
187 Sasha Kaun CR AU/85 4.00 10.00
188 Booker CR AU/85 40.00 100.00
189 Mudiay CR AU/85 10.00 25.00
190 Frank Kaminsky CR AU/85 6.00 15.00
191 Okafor CR AU/85 20.00 50.00
192 Jerian Grant CR AU/85 4.00 10.00
193 Jokic CR AU/85 25.00 60.00
194 Simmons CR AU/85 8.00 20.00
195 Walter Tavares CR AU/85 4.00 10.00
196 Nemanja Bjelica CR AU/85 5.00 12.00
197 Anderson CR AU/85 8.00 20.00
198 Winslow CR AU/85 12.00 30.00
199 Towns CR AU/85 75.00 200.00
200 Porzingis CR AU/85 40.00 100.00
201 Kobe Bryant UP AU 125.00 300.00
202 Kevin Durant UP AU 60.00 150.00
203 Anthony Davis UP AU 50.00 120.00
204 Blake Griffin UP AU 20.00 50.00
205 Kyrie Irving UP AU 40.00 100.00
206 Pau Gasol UP AU 12.00 30.00
207 Andrew Wiggins UP AU 40.00 100.00
208 John Wall UP AU 12.00 30.00
209 Jabari Parker UP AU 15.00 40.00
210 Andre Drummond UP AU 12.00 30.00
211 Kevin Love UP AU 10.00 25.00
212 Chris Bosh UP AU 6.00 15.00
213 Al Horford UP AU 8.00 20.00
214 Klay Thompson UP AU 30.00 80.00
215 Victor Oladipo UP AU 8.00 20.00
216 Eric Bledsoe UP AU 5.00 12.00
217 Brandon Knight UP AU 5.00 12.00
218 Donatas Motiejunas UP AU 4.00 10.00
219 Jason Terry UP AU 5.00 12.00
220 Dennis Schroder UP AU 6.00 15.00
221 Kemba Walker UP AU 10.00 25.00
222 Paul Millsap UP AU
223 Paul George UP AU 30.00 80.00
224 Julius Randle UP AU 10.00 25.00
225 Jeff Teague UP AU 5.00 12.00
226 Evan Fournier UP AU 8.00 20.00
227 Norris Cole UP AU 4.00 10.00
228 G. Antetokounmpo UP AU 50.00 120.00
229 Jonas Valanciunas UP AU 8.00 20.00
230 T.J. Warren UP AU 5.00 12.00
231 Doug McDermott UP AU 5.00 12.00
232 Wesley Matthews UP AU 4.00 10.00
233 Timofey Mozgov UP AU 4.00 10.00
234 J.R. Smith UP AU 15.00 40.00
235 Marcus Smart UP AU 5.00 12.00
236 Nikola Vucevic UP AU 5.00 12.00
237 Grant Hill UP AU 15.00 40.00
238 Ray Allen UP AU 20.00 50.00
239 Hakeem Olajuwon UP AU 15.00 40.00
240 Larry Bird UP AU 40.00 100.00
241 John Stockton UP AU 30.00 80.00
242 John Starks UP AU 5.00 12.00
243 David Robinson UP AU 20.00 50.00
244 Bill Walton UP AU 6.00 15.00
245 Tom Heinsohn UP AU 25.00 60.00
246 Isiah Thomas UP AU 15.00 40.00
247 Dennis Rodman UP AU 40.00 100.00
248 Walt Frazier UP AU 10.00 25.00
249 Nate Archibald UP AU 6.00 15.00
250 Clyde Drexler UP AU 20.00 50.00
251 Julius Erving UP AU 40.00 100.00
252 Magic Johnson UP AU 30.00 80.00
253 Anfernee Hardaway UP AU 15.00 40.00
254 Tracy McGrady UP AU 25.00 60.00
255 Damon Stoudamire UP AU 5.00 12.00
256 Bobby Jones UP AU 5.00 12.00
257 Robert Horry UP AU 5.00 12.00
258 Shaquille O'Neal UP AU 60.00 150.00
259 Allan Houston UP AU 5.00 12.00
260 Marques Johnson UP AU 5.00 12.00
261 Cedric Ceballos UP AU 4.00 10.00
262 Eddie Jones UP AU 5.00 12.00
263 Cuttino Mobley UP AU 4.00 10.00
264 Bill Laimbeer UP AU 5.00 12.00
265 Jason Kidd UP AU 12.00 30.00
266 Bobby Portis UP AU 10.00 25.00
267 Cameron Payne UP AU 10.00 25.00
268 D'Angelo Russell UP AU 30.00 80.00
269 Delon Wright UP AU 5.00 12.00
270 Devin Booker UP AU 60.00 150.00
271 Emmanuel Mudiay UP AU 10.00 25.00
272 Frank Kaminsky UP AU 10.00 25.00
273 Jahlil Okafor UP AU 40.00 100.00
274 Jerian Grant UP AU 4.00 10.00
275 Joe Young UP AU 5.00 12.00
276 Jonathon Simmons UP AU 8.00 20.00
277 Jordan Mickey UP AU 4.00 10.00
278 Josh Richardson UP AU 12.00 30.00
279 Justin Anderson UP AU 10.00 25.00
280 Justise Winslow UP AU 25.00 60.00
281 Karl-Anthony Towns UP AU 200.00 400.00
282 Kelly Oubre Jr. UP AU 20.00 50.00
283 Kristaps Porzingis UP AU 50.00 120.00
284 Marcelo Huertas UP AU 8.00 20.00
285 Mario Hezonja UP AU 5.00 12.00
286 Myles Turner UP AU 20.00 50.00
287 Nemanja Bjelica UP AU 5.00 12.00
288 Nikola Jokic UP AU 40.00 100.00
290 Richaun Holmes UP AU 5.00 12.00
291 Kevon Looney UP AU 5.00 12.00
292 Walter Tavares UP AU 4.00 10.00
293 Stanley Johnson UP AU 15.00 40.00
294 Terry Rozier UP AU 10.00 25.00
295 Trey Lyles UP AU 12.00 30.00
296 Willie Cauley-Stein UP AU 15.00 40.00
297 Anthony Brown UP AU 4.00 10.00
298 Sam Dekker UP AU 10.00 25.00
299 Luis Montero UP AU 4.00 10.00
300 Norman Powell UP AU 10.00 25.00

2015-16 Panini Preferred Autographs Purple

*PURPLE: .5X TO 1.2X BASE p/r 50-99
*PURPLE: .4X TO 1.X BASE p/r 40-49
PRINT RUNS B/WN 25-49 COPIES PER
EXCHANGE DEADLINE 2/17/2018

2015-16 Panini Preferred Silhouettes Prime

*SL PRIME: 2X TO 5X BASE p/r 50-99
*SL PRIME: 1.5X TO 4X BASE p/r 21-49
RANDOM INSERTS IN PACKS
PRINT RUNS B/WN 5-25 COPIES PER
NO PRICING ON QTY 19 OR LESS
EXCHANGE DEADLINE 2/17/2018
1 Porzingis SL JSY AU/25 1000.00 1500.00
13 Russell SL JSY AU/25 350.00 700.00
14 Winslow SL JSY AU/25 200.00 400.00
19 Towns SL JSY AU/25 1000.00 1500.00
23 Devin Booker SL JSY AU/25 500.00 1000.00
38 Kobe Bryant SL JSY AU/25 600.00 1000.00
39 Kevin Durant SL JSY AU/25 400.00 800.00
50 M. Johnson SL JSY AU/25 300.00 600.00
52 Antetokounmpo SL JSY AU/25 300.00 600.00

2015-16 Panini Preferred '15 NBA Finals

RANDOM INSERTS IN PACKS
STATED PRINT RUN 99 SER.#'d SETS
1 Stephen Curry 40.00 100.00
2 Andre Iguodala 10.00 25.00
3 Klay Thompson 15.00 40.00
4 Harrison Barnes 5.00 12.00
5 Andrew Bogut 5.00 12.00
6 Leandro Barbosa 4.00 10.00
7 Draymond Green 12.00 30.00
8 Festus Ezeli 4.00 10.00
9 Shaun Livingston 8.00 20.00
10 Marreese Speights 4.00 10.00
11 Iman Shumpert 8.00 20.00
12 J.R. Smith 15.00 40.00
13 Timofey Mozgov 4.00 10.00
14 Joe Harris 4.00 10.00
15 Kendrick Perkins 4.00 10.00
16 Tristan Thompson 10.00 25.00
17 Matthew Dellavedova 12.00 30.00
18 Mike Miller 5.00 12.00
19 James Jones 4.00 10.00
20 LeBron James 40.00 100.00

2015-16 Panini Preferred '15 NBA Finals Prime

*PRIME: 2X TO 5X BASIC
RANDOM INSERTS IN PACKS
PRINT RUNS B/WN 19-25 COPIES PER
NO PRICING ON QTY 19
1 Stephen Curry/25 400.00 800.00
2 Andre Iguodala/23 100.00 250.00
3 Klay Thompson/23 200.00 400.00
4 Harrison Barnes/25 50.00 120.00
5 Andrew Bogut/25 75.00 200.00
6 Leandro Barbosa/25 20.00 50.00
7 Draymond Green/25 75.00 200.00
8 Festus Ezeli/25 50.00 120.00
10 Marreese Speights/23 75.00 200.00
20 LeBron James/25 200.00 500.00

2015-16 Panini Preferred Board Members

RANDOM INSERTS IN PACKS
PRINT RUNS B/WN 75-149 COPIES PER
1 Tristan Thompson/149 3.00 8.00
2 Dwight Howard/149 3.00 8.00
3 DeMarcus Cousins/149 4.00 10.00
4 Andre Drummond/149 4.00 10.00
5 DeAndre Jordan/149 4.00 10.00
6 Greg Monroe/149 3.00 8.00
7 Andrew Bogut/149 3.00 8.00
8 Nikola Vucevic/149 3.00 8.00
9 Joakim Noah/149 3.00 8.00
10 Marc Gasol/149 4.00 10.00
11 Shaquille O'Neal/75 10.00 25.00
12 Hakeem Olajuwon/75 6.00 15.00
13 Karl Malone/75 5.00 12.00
14 Tim Duncan/149 6.00 15.00
15 Patrick Ewing/75 5.00 12.00
16 Robert Parish/75 4.00 10.00

2015-16 Panini Preferred Crazy Eights

RANDOM INSERTS IN PACKS
STATED PRINT RUN 149 SER.#'d SETS
1 Hawks 5.00 12.00
2 Cavaliers 20.00 50.00
3 Mavericks 6.00 15.00
4 Warriors 25.00 60.00
5 Rockets 8.00 20.00
6 Clippers 6.00 15.00
7 Knicks 10.00 25.00
8 Thunder 10.00 25.00
9 Spurs 15.00 40.00
11 Celtics 4.00 10.00
12 Magic 4.00 10.00
13 Lakers 20.00 50.00
14 Nets 4.00 10.00

2015-16 Panini Preferred Dual Memorabilia

RANDOM INSERTS IN PACKS
STATED PRINT RUN 199 SER.#'d SETS
1 L.James/S.Curry 50.00 120.00
2 R.Jackson/A.Drummond 4.00 10.00
3 R.Westbrook/J.Harden 10.00 25.00
4 D.Lillard/C.McCollum 5.00 12.00
5 D.Cousins/R.Rondo 4.00 10.00
6 K.Lowry/D.DeRozan 4.00 10.00
7 R.Gobert/D.Favors 4.00 10.00
8 I.Thomas/J.Sullinger 4.00 10.00
9 J.Butler/D.Rose 5.00 12.00
10 D.Williams/C.Parsons 3.00 8.00

2015-16 Panini Preferred Playbook Rookie Jumbo

RANDOM INSERTS IN PACKS
PRINT RUNS B/WN 10-199 COPIES PER
NO PRICING ON QTY 10
2 Bobby Portis/199 4.00 10.00
3 Cameron Payne/199 3.00 8.00
4 Chris McCullough/199 2.50 6.00
5 Devin Booker/199 8.00 20.00
6 Emmanuel Mudiay/199 4.00 10.00
7 Frank Kaminsky/199 4.00 10.00
8 Jarell Martin/199 3.00 8.00
9 Joe Young/199 3.00 8.00
10 Jonathon Simmons/49 4.00 10.00
11 Josh Richardson/199 4.00 10.00
12 Justin Anderson/199 3.00 8.00
13 Kelly Oubre Jr./199 3.00 8.00
14 Kevon Looney/199 3.00 8.00
15 Myles Turner/125 4.00 10.00
16 R.J. Hunter/199 2.50 6.00
17 Rakeem Christmas/199 2.50 6.00
18 Rondae Hollis-Jefferson/199 3.00 8.00
19 Sasha Kaun/199 2.50 6.00
20 Terry Rozier/199 3.00 8.00
21 Trey Lyles/199 4.00 10.00
22 Anthony Brown/199 2.50 6.00
23 Jahlil Okafor/199 5.00 12.00
24 Jerian Grant/199 2.50 6.00
25 Willie Cauley-Stein/199 4.00 10.00
26 Tyus Jones/199 4.00 10.00

2015-16 Panini Preferred Playbook Veteran Jumbo

RANDOM INSERTS IN PACKS
STATED PRINT RUN 99 SER.#'d SETS
1 Monta Ellis 3.00 8.00
2 Kobe Bryant 15.00 40.00
3 Derrick Rose 5.00 12.00
4 DeMarcus Cousins 4.00 10.00
5 Dwyane Wade 6.00 15.00
6 Marc Gasol 4.00 10.00
7 Giannis Antetokounmpo 8.00 20.00
8 Andre Iguodala 3.00 8.00
9 Tim Duncan 6.00 15.00
10 John Wall 5.00 12.00

2015-16 Panini Preferred Quads Relics

RANDOM INSERTS IN PACKS
PRINT RUNS B/WN 49-149 COPIES PER
1 Pistons/149 6.00 15.00
2 Blazers/149 6.00 15.00
3 Lowry/DeRozan 5.00 12.00
Carroll/Valanciunas/149
4 Del/Exu/Mil/Bog/149 8.00 20.00
5 Irv/Bra/Bat/Hil/149 8.00 20.00
6 Wig/Oly/Nic/Tho/149 6.00 15.00
7 Noel/Canaan/Stauskas/Covington/149 4.00 10.00
8 Batum/Fournier/Gobert/Diaw/149 5.00 12.00
9 Gas/Gas/Cal/Rub/149 10.00 25.00
10 Cavaliers/149 20.00 50.00
11 Joh/Bir/Erv/Mal/49 20.00 50.00
12 Jam/Dav/Wig/Wal/149 12.00 30.00

2015-16 Panini Preferred Stat Line Memorabilia

RANDOM INSERTS IN PACKS
STATED PRINT RUN 149 SER.#'d SETS
1 Damian Lillard 8.00 20.00
2 Thaddeus Young 2.50 6.00
3 Dirk Nowitzki 5.00 12.00
4 Tim Duncan 6.00 15.00
5 Rudy Gobert 4.00 10.00
6 Gordon Hayward 4.00 10.00
7 Nikola Vucevic 3.00 8.00
8 Russell Westbrook 10.00 25.00
9 Anthony Davis 8.00 20.00
10 Julius Randle 4.00 10.00
11 James Harden 6.00 15.00
12 Danilo Gallinari 3.00 8.00
13 Klay Thompson 5.00 12.00
14 Kenneth Faried 3.00 8.00
15 Dwyane Wade 5.00 12.00
16 Marc Gasol 4.00 10.00
17 Kemba Walker 4.00 10.00
18 John Wall 5.00 12.00
19 Paul George 5.00 12.00
20 Zach Randolph 3.00 8.00
21 Dwight Howard 3.00 8.00
22 DeMarcus Cousins 4.00 10.00
23 Kevin Love 4.00 10.00
24 LeBron James 15.00 40.00
25 C.J. McCollum 4.00 10.00
26 Rajon Rondo 4.00 10.00

2015-16 Panini Preferred Stat Line Memorabilia Prime

*PRIME: 1.5X TO 4X BASIC
RANDOM INSERTS IN PACKS
STATED PRINT RUN 25 SER.#'d SETS
3 Dirk Nowitzki 40.00 100.00
4 Tim Duncan 40.00 100.00
18 John Wall 30.00 80.00
19 Paul George 40.00 100.00

2015-16 Panini Preferred Trending Upward

RANDOM INSERTS IN PACKS
STATED PRINT RUN 199 SER.#'d SETS
1 Twns/Bkr/Cly-Stn/Lyls 8.00 20.00
2 Okfr/Trnr/Prts/Kmnsky 5.00 12.00
3 Mdy/Rssll/Bkr/Pyne 6.00 15.00
4 Okfr/Wnslw/Grnt/Rzr 5.00 12.00
5 Jhnsn/Wrght/Hlls-Jffrsn/Yng 3.00 8.00
6 Rssll/Brwn/Hrts/Nnce Jr. 6.00 15.00
8 Oubre Jr./Alexander/Kaminsky/Dekker 4.00 10.00
9 Hunter/Mickey/Winslow/Richardson 4.00 10.00
10 Cly-Stn/Prts/Mrtn/Rchrdsn 4.00 10.00

2015-16 Panini Preferred Triple Memorabilia

RANDOM INSERTS IN PACKS
STATED PRINT RUN 99 SER.#'d SETS
1 Duncan/Ginobili/Parker 12.00 30.00
2 Cousins/Gay/Rondo 5.00 12.00
3 James/Irving/Love 25.00 60.00
4 Paul/Jordan/Griffin 8.00 20.00
5 Wall/Beal/Porter 6.00 15.00
6 Smart/Sullinger/Thomas 5.00 12.00
7 Davis/Irving/Wiggins 10.00 25.00
8 Okafor/Winslow/Jones 6.00 15.00
9 Towns/Russell/Okafor 10.00 25.00
10 Towns/Booker/Lyles 12.00 30.00

2015-16 Panini Preferred VS One on One Relics

RANDOM INSERTS IN PACKS
STATED PRINT RUN 99 SER.#'d SETS
1 K.Towns/K.Porzingis 15.00 40.00
2 A.Horford/S.Ibaka 4.00 10.00
3 J.Randle/E.Payton 5.00 12.00
4 L.Aldridge/A.Davis 8.00 20.00
5 K.Walker/J.Clarkson 5.00 12.00
6 K.Durant/K.Bryant 20.00 50.00
7 J.Teague/T.Parker 6.00 15.00
8 P.George/L.James 12.00 30.00
9 C.Bosh/P.George 6.00 15.00
10 D.Green/J.Clarkson 6.00 15.00
11 T.Lyles/K.Towns 8.00 20.00
12 C.Anthony/K.Bryant 12.00 30.00
13 P.Gasol/A.Len 5.00 12.00
14 C.McCollum/M.Carter-Williams 5.00 12.00
15 D.Rose/D.Nowitzki 6.00 15.00
16 V.Oladipo/D.DeRozan 5.00 12.00
17 K.Faried/H.Barnes 4.00 10.00
18 R.Westbrook/K.Bryant 20.00 50.00

2016-17 Panini Preferred

SL JSY AU PRINT RUN B/WN 35-99 COPIES PER
AU PRINT RUNS B/WN 35-99 COPIES PER
EXCHANGE DEADLINE 2/28/2019
1 Jaylen Brown SL JSY AU/99 RC
2 Jamal Murray SL JSY AU/99 RC 30.00 80.00
3 Patrick McCaw SL JSY AU/99 RC 12.00 30.00
4 Brice Johnson SL JSY AU/99 RC 6.00 15.00
5 Wade Baldwin IV SL JSY AU/99 RC 4.00 10.00
6 Cheick Diallo SL JSY AU/99 RC 10.00 25.00
7 Dario Saric SL JSY AU/99 RC 20.00 50.00
8 Tyler Ulis SL JSY AU/99 RC 20.00 50.00
9 Malachi Richardson SL JSY AU/99 RC 8.00 20.00
10 Juan Hernangomez SL JSY AU/99 RC 8.00 20.00
11 Demetrius Jackson SL JSY AU/99 RC 4.00 10.00
12 Malik Beasley SL JSY AU/99 RC 4.00 10.00
13 Chinanu Onuaku SL JSY AU/99 RC 4.00 10.00
14 Ivica Zubac SL JSY AU/99 RC 10.00 25.00
15 Malcolm Brogdon SL JSY AU/99 RC 20.00 50.00
16 Buddy Hield SL JSY AU/99 RC 20.00 50.00
17 Tomas Satoransky SL JSY AU/99 RC 8.00 20.00
18 Jake Layman SL JSY AU/99 RC
19 Dejounte Murray SL JSY AU/99 RC 40.00 100.00
20 AJ Hammons SL JSY AU/99 RC 4.00 10.00
21 Caris LeVert SL JSY AU/99 RC 5.00 12.00
22 Henry Ellenson SL JSY AU/99 RC 8.00 20.00
23 Georges Niang SL JSY AU/99 RC 4.00 10.00
24 Brandon Ingram SL JSY AU/99 RC 60.00 150.00
25 Thon Maker SL JSY AU/99 RC 25.00 60.00
26 Domantas Sabonis SL JSY AU/99 RC
27 Marquese Chriss SL JSY AU/99 RC 10.00 25.00
28 Skal Labissiere SL JSY AU/99 RC
29 Jakob Poeltl SL JSY AU/99 RC
30 Kay Felder SL JSY AU/99 RC 5.00 12.00
31 Isaiah Whitehead SL JSY AU/99 RC 6.00 15.00
32 Damian Jones SL JSY AU/99 RC 6.00 15.00
33 Diamond Stone SL JSY AU/99 RC 6.00 15.00
34 Deyonta Davis SL JSY AU/99 RC 4.00 10.00
35 Kris Dunn SL JSY AU/99 RC 12.00 30.00
36 Stephen Zimmerman 4.00 10.00
SL JSY AU/99 RC
37 Dragan Bender SL JSY AU/99 RC 10.00 25.00
38 Georgios Papagiannis SL JSY AU/99 RC
39 Pascal Siakam SL JSY AU/99 RC 4.00 10.00
40 Denzel Valentine SL JSY AU/99 RC 6.00 15.00
41 Larry Bird SL JSY AU/35
42 Michael Carter 4.00 10.00
Williams SL JSY AU/60
43 Jimmy Butler SL JSY AU/35 15.00 40.00
44 Zach LaVine SL JSY AU/60 10.00 25.00
45 Paul Millsap SL JSY AU/75 10.00 25.00
46 Myles Turner SL JSY AU/60 10.00 25.00
47 Devin Booker SL JSY AU/60
48 Dikembe Mutombo SL JSY AU/60 12.00 30.00
49 Tim Hardaway SL JSY AU/47 12.00 30.00
51 Jordan Clarkson SL JSY AU/75 5.00 12.00
52 Zaza Pachulia SL JSY AU/35
53 Evan Turner SL JSY AU/75
54 Isaiah Thomas SL JSY AU/49 12.00 30.00
55 Julius Randle SL JSY AU/35
56 J.J. Barea SL JSY AU/60
57 Reggie Miller SL JSY AU/75 150.00 300.00
58 Kenny Smith SL JSY AU/60
59 Jae Crowder SL JSY AU/75 5.00 12.00
60 Marc Gasol SL JSY AU/35 12.00 30.00
61 Grant Hill SL JSY AU/35
62 Mario Hezonja SL JSY AU/75 4.00 10.00
63 David Robinson SL JSY AU/50
64 Michael Kidd-Gilchrist SL JSY AU/60 5.00 12.00
65 Zach Randolph SL JSY AU/49
66 Allen Crabbe SL JSY AU/75
67 Toni Kukoc SL JSY AU/45 15.00 40.00
68 Justin Anderson SL JSY AU/60 5.00 12.00
69 Nikola Mirotic SL JSY AU/60
70 Vince Carter SL JSY AU/35
71 Kristaps Porzingis SL JSY AU/49 30.00 80.00
73 Artis Gilmore SL JSY AU/60 6.00 15.00
74 Marcus Camby SL JSY AU/60 6.00 15.00
75 Karl-Anthony Towns SL JSY AU/35
76 C.J. McCollum SL JSY AU/49
77 Mark Price SL JSY AU/38 15.00 40.00
78 Rafer Alston SL JSY AU/60 6.00 15.00
79 Kyrie Irving SL JSY AU/35
80 Jrue Holiday SL JSY AU/75 5.00 12.00
81 Ray Allen SL JSY AU/35 30.00 80.00
82 Goran Dragic SL JSY AU/75 5.00 12.00
83 Harrison Barnes SL JSY AU/75 12.00 30.00
84 Tristan Thompson SL JSY AU/75
85 Langston Galloway SL JSY AU/60 4.00 10.00
86 Tony Parker SL JSY AU/35 12.00 30.00
87 D'Angelo Russell SL JSY AU/75 8.00 20.00
88 Aaron Gordon SL JSY AU/75
89 Kevin Love SL JSY AU/35
90 Anthony Davis SL JSY AU/35 30.00 80.00
91 Kevin Durant SL JSY AU/35 75.00 200.00
92 Andrew Wiggins SL JSY AU/35
93 Rondae Hollis-Jefferson SL JSY AU/75
94 Tobias Harris SL JSY AU/75 6.00 15.00
95 Elfrid Payton SL JSY AU/60
96 George Hill SL JSY AU/60 6.00 15.00
97 Alex English SL JSY AU/60
98 Marques Johnson SL JSY AU/60
99 Kurt Thomas SL JSY AU/60 10.00 25.00
100 Ryan Anderson SL JSY AU/60 5.00 12.00
101 Kenneth Faried AU/35 5.00 12.00
102 Dennis Scott AU/99 3.00 8.00
103 Michael Kidd-Gilchrist AU/35 8.00 20.00
104 Nikola Mirotic AU/35 6.00 15.00
105 Zach LaVine AU/35 12.00 30.00
106 Kyrie Irving AU/35 30.00 80.00
107 Tristan Thompson AU/35 5.00 12.00
108 Kristaps Porzingis AU/35 25.00 60.00
109 J.J. Barea AU/99 10.00 25.00
110 Clint Capela AU/75 5.00 12.00
111 Vlade Divac AU/99 5.00 12.00
112 Ryan Anderson AU/35 5.00 12.00
113 Cedric Ceballos AU/99 6.00 15.00
114 Hersey Hawkins AU/99 3.00 8.00
115 Karl-Anthony Towns AU/35 30.00 80.00
116 Tobias Harris AU/35
117 Langston Galloway AU/99 3.00 8.00
118 Anthony Davis AU/35 40.00 100.00
119 Elfrid Payton AU/35 5.00 12.00
120 Devin Booker AU/35 20.00 50.00
121 Allen Crabbe AU/99 3.00 8.00
122 C.J. McCollum AU/35 10.00 25.00
123 Jrue Holiday AU/35
124 Danilo Gallinari AU/35 5.00 12.00
125 Jonas Valanciunas AU/35 5.00 12.00
126 Evan Turner AU/35
127 Shawn Kemp AU/35 25.00 60.00
128 Latrell Sprewell AU/35 15.00 40.00
129 Dan Majerle AU/49 6.00 15.00
130 Bob McAdoo AU/99 4.00 10.00
131 Jim Chones AU/99 3.00 8.00
132 Larry Nance Jr. AU/99 4.00 10.00
133 Kareem Abdul-Jabbar AU/35 30.00 80.00
134 Magic Johnson AU/35 40.00 100.00
135 Chauncey Billups AU/35 6.00 15.00
136 Rod Strickland AU/99 3.00 8.00
137 Kurt Rambis AU/99 3.00 8.00
138 Rick Fox AU/35 5.00 12.00
139 Kurt Thomas AU/99 3.00 8.00
140 Marcus Camby AU/99 6.00 15.00
141 Alex English CR AU/99 4.00 10.00
142 Isaiah Thomas CR AU/35 20.00 50.00
143 Jae Crowder CR AU/99 4.00 10.00
144 Kenny "Sky" Walker CR AU/49 4.00 10.00
145 Jeff Hornacek CR AU/99 4.00 10.00
146 Chauncey Billups CR AU/35 6.00 15.00
147 Michael Carter-Williams CR AU/35
148 Kyrie Irving CR AU/35 30.00 80.00
149 Kenneth Faried CR AU/35 5.00 12.00
150 Justin Anderson CR AU/99 4.00 10.00
151 Robert Horry CR AU/35 5.00 12.00
152 Reggie Jackson CR AU/60 4.00 10.00
153 Kevin Durant CR AU/35 60.00 150.00
154 Junior Bridgeman CR AU/99 3.00 8.00
155 Clint Capela CR AU/75 5.00 12.00
156 Myles Turner CR AU/99 10.00 25.00
157 Tyler Johnson CR AU/60 3.00 8.00
158 Jordan Clarkson CR AU/35
160 Karl-Anthony Towns CR AU/35 30.00 80.00
161 Zach LaVine CR AU/35 12.00 30.00
162 Sidney Moncrief CR AU/99 3.00 8.00
163 Kristaps Porzingis CR AU/35 25.00 60.00
164 Nikola Vucevic CR AU/35 5.00 12.00
165 Zaza Pachulia CR AU/99 3.00 8.00
166 Joel Embiid CR AU/35 40.00 100.00
167 Michael Cooper CR AU/99 4.00 10.00
168 George Hill CR AU/35 6.00 15.00
169 Langston Galloway CR AU/35 4.00 10.00
170 Larry Bird CR AU/35 40.00 100.00
171 Magic Johnson CR AU/35 40.00 100.00
172 Jalen Rose CR AU/35 6.00 15.00
173 Damon Stoudamire CR AU/99 6.00 15.00
174 Cedric Maxwell CR AU/99 3.00 8.00
175 Mark Aguirre CR AU/99
176 Jim Jackson CR AU/99
177 Kiki VanDeWeghe CR AU/99 4.00 10.00
178 Bill Laimbeer CR AU/99 4.00 10.00
179 Latrell Sprewell CR AU/35 15.00 40.00
180 Cuttino Mobley CR AU/99
181 Dario Saric PC AU/75 12.00 30.00
182 Kris Dunn PC AU/35 15.00 40.00
183 Jamal Murray PC AU/35 30.00 80.00
184 Malcolm Brogdon PC AU/99 12.00 30.00
185 Brandon Ingram PC AU/35 100.00 250.00
186 Kenneth Faried PC AU/35 5.00 12.00
187 Magic Johnson PC AU/35 40.00 100.00
188 Shawn Kemp PC AU/75 20.00 50.00
189 Larry Bird PC AU/35 40.00 100.00
190 Wade Baldwin IV PC AU/99 3.00 8.00
191 Walter Berry PC AU/99 3.00 8.00
192 Devin Booker PC AU/35 20.00 50.00
193 Joel Embiid PC AU/35 40.00 100.00
194 Andrew Wiggins PC AU/35 20.00 50.00
195 Karl-Anthony Towns PC AU/35 30.00 80.00
196 Kyrie Irving PC AU/35 30.00 80.00
197 Jimmy Butler PC AU/35 15.00 40.00
198 Ray Allen PC AU/35
199 Kevin Durant PC AU/35 60.00 150.00
200 Kobe Bryant PC AU/35 100.00 250.00
201 Alex English UP AU/50 5.00 12.00
202 Jalen Rose UP AU/50 6.00 15.00
204 Zach Randolph UP AU/50 8.00 20.00
205 Ray Allen UP AU/50
206 Anthony Davis UP AU/50 40.00 100.00
207 Artis Gilmore UP AU/50 8.00 20.00
208 Bill Laimbeer UP AU/50 5.00 12.00
209 Demetrius Jackson UP AU/50 4.00 10.00
210 Bob McAdoo UP AU/50 5.00 12.00
211 C.J. McCollum UP AU/50 10.00 25.00
212 Michael Cooper UP AU/50 5.00 12.00
213 Cedric Ceballos UP AU/50 8.00 20.00
214 Cedric Maxwell UP AU/50 4.00 10.00
215 Rodney McGruder UP AU/50 5.00 12.00
216 Larry Nance Jr. UP AU/50 5.00 12.00
217 Dejounte Murray UP AU/50 40.00 100.00
218 Dan Majerle UP AU/50 6.00 15.00
219 Dennis Scott UP AU/50 4.00 10.00
220 Devin Booker UP AU/50 20.00 50.00
221 Elfrid Payton UP AU/50 5.00 12.00
222 Paul Millsap UP AU/50 12.00 30.00
223 Evan Turner UP AU/50
224 Goran Dragic UP AU/50 5.00 12.00
225 George Hill UP AU/50 6.00 15.00
226 Grant Hill UP AU/50 25.00 60.00
227 Hersey Hawkins UP AU/50 4.00 10.00
228 Isaiah Thomas UP AU/50 20.00 50.00
229 Kenny "Sky" Walker UP AU/50 8.00 20.00
230 Jae Crowder UP AU/50 5.00 12.00
231 Jeff Hornacek UP AU/50 5.00 12.00
232 Danilo Gallinari UP AU/50 5.00 12.00
233 Jim Chones UP AU/50 4.00 10.00
234 Jim Jackson UP AU/50
235 Julius Randle UP AU/50 12.00 30.00
236 Joel Embiid UP AU/50 40.00 100.00
237 Thon Maker UP AU/50 12.00 30.00
238 Jonas Valanciunas UP AU/50 5.00 12.00
239 Jordan Clarkson UP AU/50
240 Juan Hernangomez UP AU/50
241 Junior Bridgeman UP AU/50 4.00 10.00
242 Justin Anderson UP AU/50 5.00 12.00
243 Kareem Abdul-Jabbar UP AU/50 30.00 80.00
244 Karl-Anthony Towns UP AU/50 30.00 80.00
245 Kenny Smith UP AU/50 5.00 12.00
246 Kevin Durant UP AU/50 60.00 150.00
247 Rod Strickland UP AU/50 4.00 10.00
248 Kiki VanDeWeghe UP AU/50 5.00 12.00
249 Kristaps Porzingis UP AU/50 25.00 60.00
250 Kurt Rambis UP AU/50 4.00 10.00
251 Kurt Thomas UP AU/50 4.00 10.00
252 Marc Gasol UP AU/50 12.00 30.00
253 Malachi Richardson UP AU/50
254 Dikembe Mutombo UP AU/50 15.00 40.00
255 Latrell Sprewell UP AU/50 15.00 40.00
257 Kobe Bryant UP AU/50 300.00 500.00
258 Marcus Camby UP AU/50 8.00 20.00
259 Mark Aguirre UP AU/50
260 Mark Price UP AU/50
261 Shawn Kemp UP AU/50 25.00 60.00
262 Walter Berry UP AU/50 4.00 10.00
263 Nikola Mirotic UP AU/50 6.00 15.00
264 Brice Johnson UP AU/50 4.00 10.00
265 Rick Fox UP AU/50 5.00 12.00
266 Myles Turner UP AU/50 12.00 30.00
267 Ryan Anderson UP AU/50 5.00 12.00
268 Sidney Moncrief UP AU/50 4.00 10.00
269 Tobias Harris UP AU/50
270 Marques Johnson UP AU/50
271 Tristan Thompson UP AU/50 5.00 12.00
272 Tyler Johnson UP AU/50 4.00 10.00
273 Vlade Divac UP AU/50 6.00 15.00
274 Malcolm Delaney UP AU/50
275 Nikola Vucevic UP AU/50 5.00 12.00
276 Dragan Bender UP AU/50
277 Kay Felder UP AU/50 4.00 10.00
278 Dorian Finney-Smith UP AU/50 5.00 12.00
279 Malik Beasley UP AU/50 10.00 25.00
280 Jamal Murray UP AU/50 30.00 80.00
281 Damian Jones UP AU/50
282 Kyle Wiltjer UP AU/50 6.00 15.00
283 Diamond Stone UP AU/50 4.00 10.00
284 Brandon Ingram UP AU/50 100.00 250.00
285 Wade Baldwin IV UP AU/50 4.00 10.00
286 Troy Williams UP AU/50 8.00 20.00
287 Malcolm Brogdon UP AU/50 15.00 40.00
288 Buddy Hield UP AU/50 20.00 50.00
289 Willy Hernangomez UP AU/50 8.00 20.00
290 Ron Baker UP AU/50 12.00 30.00
291 Domantas Sabonis UP AU/50 6.00 15.00
292 Dario Saric UP AU/50 15.00 40.00
293 Marquese Chriss UP AU/50 10.00 25.00
294 Tyler Ulis UP AU/50 12.00 30.00
295 Tim Quarterman UP AU/50
296 Jake Layman UP AU/50 5.00 12.00
297 Pascal Siakam UP AU/50 4.00 10.00
298 Jakob Poeltl UP AU/50 5.00 12.00
299 Tomas Satoransky UP AU/50 4.00 10.00
300 Sheldon Mac UP AU/50

2016-17 Panini Preferred Autographs Blue

*BLUE/25: .6X TO 1.5X p/r 60-99
*BLUE/25: .5X TO 1.2X p/r 35-50
RANDOM INSERTS IN PACKS
PRINT RUNS B/WN 15-25 COPIES PER
NO PRICING ON QTY 15
EXCHANGE DEADLINE 2/28/2019

2016-17 Panini Preferred Autographs Purple

*PURPLE/49: .5X TO 1.2X p/r 60-99
*PURPLE/49: .4X TO 1X p/r 35-50
*PURPLE/25: .6X TO 1.5X p/r 60-99
*PURPLE/25: .5X TO 1.2X p/r 35-50
RANDOM INSERTS IN PACKS
PRINT RUNS B/WN 25-49 COPIES PER
EXCHANGE DEADLINE 2/28/2019

2016-17 Panini Preferred Crown Royale Autographs Blue

*BLUE/25: .6X TO 1.5X p/r 60-99
*BLUE/25: .5X TO 1.2X p/r 35-50
RANDOM INSERTS IN PACKS
PRINT RUNS B/WN 15-25 COPIES PER
NO PRICING ON QTY 15
EXCHANGE DEADLINE 2/28/2019

2016-17 Panini Preferred Crown Royale Autographs Purple

*PURPLE/35-49: .5X TO 1.2X p/r 60-99
*PURPLE/35-49: .4X TO 1X p/r 35-50
*PURPLE/25: .5X TO 1.2X p/r 35-50
RANDOM INSERTS IN PACKS
PRINT RUNS B/WN 25-49 COPIES PER
EXCHANGE DEADLINE 2/28/2019

2016-17 Panini Preferred Panini's Choice Autographs Blue

*BLUE/25: .6X TO 1.5X p/r 60-99
RANDOM INSERTS IN PACKS
PRINT RUNS B/WN 15-25 COPIES PER
NO PRICING ON QTY 15
EXCHANGE DEADLINE 2/28/2019

2016-17 Panini Preferred Panini's Choice Autographs Purple

*PURPLE/49: .5X TO 1.2X p/r 60-99
*PURPLE/25: .5X TO 1.2X p/r 35-50
RANDOM INSERTS IN PACKS
PRINT RUNS B/WN 25-49 COPIES PER
EXCHANGE DEADLINE 2/28/2019

2016-17 Panini Preferred Silhouettes Prime

*SL PRIME: 1.5X TO 4X BASE p/r 50-99
*SL PRIME: 1.2X TO 3X BASE p/r 35-49
RANDOM INSERTS IN PACKS
PRINT RUNS B/WN 3-25 COPIES PER
NO PRICING ON QTY 15 OR LESS
EXCHANGE DEADLINE 2/28/2019
1 Jaylen Brown JSY AU/25 300.00 600.00
2 Jamal Murray JSY AU/25 300.00 600.00
3 Patrick McCaw JSY AU/25 300.00 600.00
24 Brandon Ingram JSY AU/25 400.00 800.00
27 Marquese Chriss JSY AU/25 100.00 250.00
35 Kris Dunn JSY AU/25 100.00 250.00

2016-17 Panini Preferred '16 NBA Finals Memorabilia

RANDOM INSERTS IN PACKS
PRINT RUNS B/WN 3-99 COPIES PER
NO PRICING ON QTY 13 OR LESS
1 Channing Frye/99 8.00 20.00
2 Dahntay Jones/86 10.00 25.00
3 Iman Shumpert/76 10.00 25.00
4 J.R. Smith/99 12.00 30.00
5 James Jones/99 4.00 10.00
6 Kevin Love/99 15.00 40.00
8 LeBron James/31
9 Mo Williams/99 5.00 12.00
10 Richard Jefferson/99 5.00 12.00
11 Tristan Thompson/99 12.00 30.00
12 Andrew Bogut/99 5.00 12.00
13 Brandon Rush/99 4.00 10.00
14 Draymond Green/99
15 Festus Ezeli/99 4.00 10.00
16 Ian Clark/99 6.00 15.00
17 Klay Thompson/99 15.00 40.00
18 Leandro Barbosa/99 4.00 10.00
19 Marreese Speights/99 4.00 10.00

2016-17 Panini Preferred Board Members Memorabilia

RANDOM INSERTS IN PACKS
STATED PRINT RUN 99 SER.#'d SETS
1 Al Horford 3.00 8.00
2 DeAndre Jordan 4.00 10.00
3 Myles Turner 6.00 15.00
4 Bobby Portis 2.50 6.00
5 Nene 3.00 8.00
6 Andre Drummond 4.00 10.00
7 Dirk Nowitzki 5.00 12.00
8 Cody Zeller 2.50 6.00
9 Brook Lopez 3.00 8.00
10 Alexis Ajinca 5.00 12.00
11 DeMarcus Cousins 4.00 10.00
12 Mason Plumlee 3.00 8.00
13 Jahlil Okafor 3.00 8.00
14 Nerlens Noel 3.00 8.00
15 Nikola Vucevic 3.00 8.00
16 Derrick Favors 3.00 8.00

2016-17 Panini Preferred Crazy Eights Memorabilia

RANDOM INSERTS IN PACKS
STATED PRINT RUN 149 SER.#'d SETS
1 Wizards 6.00 15.00
2 Timberwolves 12.00 30.00
3 Nuggets 10.00 25.00
4 Cavaliers 20.00 50.00
5 Hornets 5.00 12.00
6 Celtics 12.00 30.00
7 Raptors 10.00 25.00
8 Kings 8.00 20.00
9 Trail Blazers 10.00 25.00
10 Suns 15.00 40.00
11 Thunder 8.00 20.00
12 Knicks 6.00 15.00
13 Pelicans 6.00 15.00
14 Rockets 8.00 20.00

2016-17 Panini Preferred Dual Memorabilia

RANDOM INSERTS IN PACKS
STATED PRINT RUN 149 SER.#'d SETS
1 Randle/Russell 5.00 12.00
2 Conley/Randolph 3.00 8.00
3 Henson/Monroe 3.00 8.00
4 Chriss/Ulis 6.00 15.00
5 Lillard/McCollum 6.00 15.00
6 Beal/Porter 4.00 10.00
7 Hayward/Favors 4.00 10.00
8 Cauley-Stein/Collison 3.00 8.00
9 George/James 12.00 30.00
10 Durant/Westbrook 12.00 30.00

2016-17 Panini Preferred Playbook Jumbo Memorabilia

RANDOM INSERTS IN PACKS
STATED PRINT RUN 99 SER.#'d SETS
1 Richard Jefferson 3.00 8.00
2 Thaddeus Young 2.50 6.00
3 Dirk Nowitzki 5.00 12.00
4 Rondae Hollis-Jefferson 2.50 6.00
5 LeBron James 30.00 80.00
6 Shawn Marion 3.00 8.00
7 Evan Fournier 3.00 8.00
8 David Robinson 6.00 15.00
9 Tim Duncan 6.00 15.00
10 Shabazz Muhammad 3.00 8.00
11 Joe Smith 3.00 8.00
12 Derrick Rose 5.00 12.00
13 Joakim Noah 5.00 12.00
14 Steven Adams 5.00 12.00
15 Chandler Parsons 3.00 8.00
16 Nemanja Bjelica 3.00 8.00
17 Deron Williams 3.00 8.00
18 Alec Burks 2.50 6.00
19 Carmelo Anthony 5.00 12.00
20 Nicolas Batum 3.00 8.00
21 Manu Ginobili 6.00 15.00
22 Andrew Wiggins 6.00 15.00
23 Wilson Chandler 3.00 8.00
24 Ricky Rubio 4.00 10.00
25 Rudy Gay 4.00 10.00
26 Mason Plumlee 3.00 8.00
27 Brandon Knight 3.00 8.00
28 Noah Vonleh 2.50 6.00
29 Timofey Mozgov 2.50 6.00
31 Victor Oladipo 3.00 8.00
32 Damian Lillard 8.00 20.00
33 Courtney Lee 3.00 8.00
34 Serge Ibaka 3.00 8.00
35 Monta Ellis 3.00 8.00
36 Russell Westbrook 15.00 40.00

2016-17 Panini Preferred Quads Memorabilia

RANDOM INSERTS IN PACKS
STATED PRINT RUN 149 SER.#'d SETS
1 Jms/Crry/Hrdn/Drnt 30.00 80.00
2 Nwtzki/Anthny/Wall/Wade 6.00 15.00
3 Wggns/Twns/Rbo/Lvne 12.00 30.00
4 Love/Beal/Przngs/Dvs 10.00 25.00
5 O'Nl/Brnt/Hill/Drxlr 25.00 60.00
6 Wall/Irvng/Crry/Lllrd 25.00 60.00
7 Lwry/Wlkr/Paul/Wstbrk 12.00 30.00
8 Gnns/Jms/Thms/Btlr 20.00 50.00
9 Grge/Hywrd/Jkc/Hrdn 8.00 20.00
10 Twns/Przngs/Bkr/Rssll 12.00 30.00
12 Nwtzki/Gnns/Dvs/Btlr 10.00 25.00

2016-17 Panini Preferred Rookie Playbook Memorabilia

RANDOM INSERTS IN PACKS
STATED PRINT RUN 99 SER.#'d SETS
1 Malcolm Brogdon 6.00 15.00
2 Patrick McCaw 6.00 15.00
3 Brandon Ingram 15.00 40.00
4 Dragan Bender 4.00 10.00
5 Tyler Ulis 8.00 20.00
6 Domantas Sabonis 5.00 12.00
7 Jaylen Brown 10.00 25.00
8 Pascal Siakam 3.00 8.00
9 Henry Ellenson 4.00 10.00
10 Demetrius Jackson 3.00 8.00
11 Kay Felder 3.00 8.00
12 AJ Hammons 3.00 8.00
13 Chinanu Onuaku 3.00 8.00
14 Wade Baldwin IV 3.00 8.00
15 Juan Hernangomez 4.00 10.00
16 Mindaugas Kuzminskas 4.00 10.00
17 Denzel Valentine 4.00 10.00
18 Isaiah Whitehead 3.00 8.00
19 Dejounte Murray 6.00 15.00
20 Malachi Richardson 4.00 10.00
21 Stephen Zimmerman 3.00 8.00
22 Malik Beasley 3.00 8.00
23 Paul Zipser 5.00 12.00
24 Georges Niang 3.00 8.00
25 Ivica Zubac 5.00 12.00
26 Willy Hernangomez 4.00 10.00
27 Cheick Diallo 3.00 8.00
28 Deyonta Davis 3.00 8.00
29 Marquese Chriss 6.00 15.00
30 Michael Gbinije 3.00 8.00
31 Diamond Stone 3.00 8.00

32 Brice Johnson 3.00 8.00
33 Georgios Papagiannis 3.00 8.00
34 Joel Bolomboy 3.00 8.00
35 Skal Labissiere 5.00 12.00
36 Tomas Satoransky 3.00 8.00

2016-17 Panini Preferred Stat Line Memorabilia

RANDOM INSERTS IN PACKS
PRINT RUNS B/WN 125-149 COPIES PER
1 Avery Bradley/149 3.00 8.00
2 Kyrie Irving/149 8.00 20.00
3 Kevin Love/149 4.00 10.00
4 Kentavious Caldwell-Pope/149 3.00 8.00
5 Andre Drummond/149 4.00 10.00
6 Tobias Harris/149 3.00 8.00
7 DeAndre Jordan/149 4.00 10.00
8 Blake Griffin/149 4.00 10.00
9 Mike Conley/149 3.00 8.00
10 Marc Gasol/125 4.00 10.00
11 Hassan Whiteside/149 3.00 8.00
12 Anthony Davis/149 6.00 15.00
13 Derrick Rose/149 5.00 12.00
14 Steven Adams/149 5.00 12.00
15 Russell Westbrook/149 8.00 20.00
16 Joel Embiid/149 5.00 12.00
17 Jahlil Okafor/149 3.00 8.00
18 DeMar DeRozan/149 4.00 10.00
19 Jonas Valanciunas/149 3.00 8.00
20 Markieff Morris/149 2.50 6.00
21 Dwyane Wade/149 5.00 12.00
22 LeBron James/149 12.00 30.00
23 Stephen Curry/149 12.00 30.00
24 Goran Dragic/149 3.00 8.00
25 Dion Waiters/149 3.00 8.00
26 Hassan Whiteside/149 3.00 8.00

2016-17 Panini Preferred Stat Line Memorabilia Prime

*PRIME: 1.5X TO 4X BASIC
RANDOM INSERTS IN PACKS
PRINT RUNS B/WN 15-25 COPIES PER
NO PRICING ON QTY 15 OR LESS
22 LeBron James/25 75.00 200.00

2016-17 Panini Preferred Trending Upward Memorabilia

RANDOM INSERTS IN PACKS
STATED PRINT RUN 149 SER.#'d SETS
*PRIME/25: 1.5X TO 4X BASIC
1 Brgdn/Dunn/Mkr/Hld 10.00 25.00
2 Ingrm/Brwn/Mkr/Hld 10.00 25.00
3 Ingrm/Stne/Ulis/Dllo 8.00 20.00
4 Brwn/Ppgnns/Vlntne/Dvs 6.00 15.00
5 Brgdn/McCw/Jns/Jhnsn 6.00 15.00
6 Dunn/Bldwn/Rchrdsn/Mrry 8.00 20.00
7 Mrry/Lwwu-Cbrrt/Hrnngmz/Ellnsn 8.00 20.00
8 Bndr/McCw/Jhnsn/Prnce 5.00 12.00
9 Poeltl/Felder/Hammons/Jackson 3.00 8.00
10 LeVert/Whitehead/Onuaku/Zimmerman 3.00 8.00

2016-17 Panini Preferred Triple Memorabilia

RANDOM INSERTS IN PACKS
STATED PRINT RUN 99 SER.#'d SETS
1 Gllnri/Chndlr/Hrrs 12.00 30.00
3 Irvng/Jms/Love 25.00 60.00
4 Btlr/Wade/Rndo 8.00 20.00
5 Walker/Lamb/Zeller 5.00 12.00
6 Horford/Bradley/Smart 5.00 12.00
7 Howard/Hardaway/Schroder 5.00 12.00
8 Crry/Thmpsn/Grn 20.00 50.00
9 DRzn/Lwry/Vlncns 6.00 15.00
10 Lnrd/Gsl/Aldrdge 15.00 40.00

2016-17 Panini Preferred VS One on One Memorabilia

RANDOM INSERTS IN PACKS
STATED PRINT RUN 99 SER.#'d SETS
1 K.Towns/K.Porzingis 12.00 30.00
2 L.James/C.Anthony 30.00 80.00
3 P.George/R.Jackson 6.00 15.00
4 S.Curry/R.Westbrook 20.00 50.00
5 H.Barnes/D.Rose 6.00 15.00
6 Anttknmpo/Turner 12.00 30.00
7 Julius Randle/Al Horford 5.00 12.00
8 J.Wall/D.Schroder 6.00 15.00
9 Thompson/Turner 6.00 15.00
10 J.Parker/A.Gordon 10.00 25.00
11 J.Brown/B.Ingram 15.00 40.00
12 DeRozan/K.Irving 10.00 25.00
13 Zubac/Hrnngmz 6.00 15.00
14 Gobert/Lowry 12.00 30.00
15 Eric Bledsoe/Elfrid Payton 4.00 10.00
16 Gasol/Adams 6.00 15.00
17 Rudy Gay/Andre Drummond 5.00 12.00
18 Hassan Whiteside/Brook Lopez 4.00 10.00

2011 Panini Private Signings CS Exchange

AE Alex English 6.00 15.00
BWL Bill Walton 8.00 20.00
CON Connie Hawkins 6.00 15.00
LWL Lenny Wilkins

2012-13 Panini Prizm

COMPLETE SET (300) 30.00 80.00
UNPRICED PRIZMS GOLD PRINT RUN 10 SETS
1 LeBron James 2.00 5.00
2 Paul Pierce .50 1.25
3 Jrue Holiday .50 1.25
4 Dwight Howard .40 1.00
5 Danny Granger .40 1.00
6 Elton Brand .50 1.25
7 Deron Williams .40 1.00
8 Omer Asik .40 1.00
9 Devin Harris .30 .75
10 DeMarcus Cousins .50 1.25
11 Arron Afflalo .40 1.00
12 Kirk Hinrich .40 1.00
13 LaMarcus Aldridge .50 1.25
14 Thabo Sefolosha .30 .75
15 Amare Stoudemire .40 1.00
16 Andris Biedrins .30 .75
17 Tayshaun Prince .40 1.00
18 Al-Farouq Aminu .40 1.00
19 Chris Paul .60 1.50
20 Andrea Bargnani .40 1.00
21 Martell Webster .30 .75
22 John Wall .60 1.50
23 Matt Bonner .30 .75
24 Kobe Bryant 2.00 5.00
25 Paul Millsap .50 1.25
26 Brendan Haywood .30 .75
27 DeAndre Jordan .50 1.25
28 Andre Iguodala .40 1.00
29 Nicolas Batum .40 1.00
30 Paul George .60 1.50
31 Mike Conley .40 1.00
32 Blake Griffin .50 1.25
33 Kevin Garnett .75 2.00
34 Jeremy Lin .50 1.25
35 Kevin Durant 1.25 3.00
36 Vince Carter .60 1.50
37 Ray Allen .50 1.25
38 Marco Belinelli .30 .75
39 Corey Brewer .30 .75
40 Glen Davis .30 .75
41 Tyson Chandler .40 1.00
42 Eric Gordon .40 1.00
43 Andrew Bogut .40 1.00
44 Tyreke Evans .30 .75
45 Pau Gasol .50 1.25
46 Jose Calderon .30 .75
47 Russell Westbrook 1.25 3.00
48 Ricky Rubio .50 1.25
49 Stephen Jackson .40 1.00
50 Jeff Teague .40 1.00
51 Marc Gasol .50 1.25
52 Hollis Thompson RC .50 1.25
53 Carlos Boozer .40 1.00
54 Grant Hill .60 1.50
55 Al Jefferson .40 1.00
56 Evan Turner .30 .75
57 Kendrick Perkins .30 .75
58 Ramon Sessions .40 1.00
59 Danilo Gallinari .30 .75
60 DeMar Derozan .50 1.25
61 Ryan Anderson .40 1.00
62 Brandon Bass .30 .75
63 Dirk Nowitzki .60 1.50
64 Roy Hibbert .40 1.00
65 Emeka Okafor .40 1.00
66 Channing Frye .40 1.00
67 Wesley Matthews .30 .75
68 Corey Maggette .40 1.00
69 Serge Ibaka .40 1.00
70 Luke Ridnour .40 1.00
71 Carmelo Anthony .60 1.50
72 Stephen Curry 2.00 5.00
73 Luol Deng .40 1.00
74 J.J. Redick .50 1.25
75 Avery Bradley .40 1.00
76 Rudy Gay .50 1.25
77 Dwyane Wade .75 2.00
78 Thaddeus Young .30 .75
79 Brandon Jennings .30 .75
80 Manu Ginobili .50 1.25
81 Jason Kidd .50 1.25
82 Kevin Martin .40 1.00
83 Andrew Bynum .30 .75
84 Kyle Lowry .40 1.00
85 Gordon Hayward .50 1.25
86 Al Harrington .40 1.00
87 Gerald Wallace .40 1.00
88 Antawn Jamison .40 1.00
89 Caron Butler .40 1.00
90 Anderson Varejao .30 .75
91 Nene .40 1.00
92 David Lee .30 .75
93 Shane Battier .40 1.00
94 Jason Thompson .30 .75
95 James Harden .75 2.00
96 Tyrus Thomas .30 .75
97 J.J. Barea .40 1.00
98 Tyler Hansbrough .40 1.00
99 J.J. Hickson .30 .75
100 Louis Williams .40 1.00
101 Tim Duncan .75 2.00
102 Chris Kaman .40 1.00
103 Jodie Meeks .40 1.00
104 Ty Lawson .30 .75
105 Derrick Favors .40 1.00
106 Luis Scola .40 1.00
107 Rajon Rondo .50 1.25
108 Hedo Turkoglu .40 1.00
109 Rodney Stuckey .40 1.00
110 Zach Randolph .40 1.00
111 Steve Novak .30 .75
112 Jon Brockman .30 .75
113 Steve Nash .50 1.25
114 Joakim Noah .40 1.00
115 Chase Budinger .30 .75
116 Chris Bosh .50 1.25
117 Brook Lopez .40 1.00
118 Jordan Crawford .30 .75
119 Luc Mbah a Moute .30 .75
120 Tony Parker .50 1.25
121 Daniel Gibson .40 1.00
122 Chauncey Billups .50 1.25
123 Brandon Rush .30 .75
124 Shawn Marion .40 1.00
125 Al Horford .40 1.00
126 Raja Bell .40 1.00
127 Daequan Cook .30 .75
128 Goran Dragic .40 1.00
129 Ben Gordon .40 1.00
130 Andre Miller .40 1.00
131 Jason Richardson .50 1.25
132 Udonis Haslem .30 .75
133 Jason Terry .40 1.00
134 Nick Collison .40 1.00
135 Kevin Love .50 1.25
136 Marreese Speights .30 .75
137 Toney Douglas .30 .75
138 Charlie Villanueva .30 .75
139 Tiago Splitter .40 1.00
140 George Hill .40 1.00
141 Marcin Gortat .40 1.00
142 Raymond Felton .40 1.00
143 O.J. Mayo .30 .75
144 Ersan Ilyasova .30 .75
145 Derrick Rose .60 1.50
146 Trevor Ariza .30 .75
147 Metta World Peace .50 1.25
148 Mario Chalmers .40 1.00
149 Joe Johnson .40 1.00
150 Josh Smith .40 1.00
151 Wilt Chamberlain 1.00 2.50
152 Pete Maravich .75 2.00
153 Bill Russell .75 2.00
154 Oscar Robertson .60 1.50
155 Hakeem Olajuwon .60 1.50
156 Julius Erving .75 2.00
157 Dennis Rodman 1.00 2.50
158 Maurice Cheeks .30 .75
159 Kareem Abdul-Jabbar .75 2.00
160 Anfernee Hardaway 1.25 3.00
161 David Thompson .40 1.00
162 Horace Grant .50 1.25
163 Larry Bird 1.25 3.00
164 Rolando Blackman .40 1.00
165 Larry Johnson .60 1.50
166 Shaquille O'Neal 1.00 2.50
167 Derrick Coleman .50 1.25
168 Karl Malone .60 1.50
169 Moses Malone .50 1.25
170 Mark Aguirre .40 1.00
171 Rudy Tomjanovich .40 1.00
172 Jerry West .60 1.50
173 George Mikan 1.00 2.50
174 Kelly Tripucka .30 .75
175 David Robinson .75 2.00
176 Scottie Pippen 1.00 2.50
177 Danny Manning .40 1.00
178 Elgin Baylor .50 1.25
179 Charles Oakley .50 1.25
180 Sam Jones .50 1.25
181 Magic Johnson 1.25 3.00
182 Isiah Thomas .50 1.25
183 Bill Laimbeer .40 1.00
184 Patrick Ewing .60 1.50
185 Chris Mullin .50 1.25
186 John Stockton .75 2.00
187 Allen Iverson .60 1.50
188 Dominique Wilkins .60 1.50
189 Tim Hardaway .50 1.25
190 Zydrunas Ilgauskas .40 1.00
191 George Gervin .50 1.25
192 Toni Kukoc .50 1.25
193 James Worthy .60 1.50
194 Vlade Divac .50 1.25
195 Terry Porter .30 .75
196 Bill Walton .50 1.25
197 Shawn Kemp .75 2.00
198 Yao Ming .60 1.50
199 Dikembe Mutombo .50 1.25
200 Alonzo Mourning .60 1.50
201 Kyrie Irving RC 8.00 20.00
202 MarShon Brooks RC .60 1.50
203 Klay Thompson RC 5.00 12.00
204 Alec Burks RC .75 2.00
205 Jimmy Butler RC 2.50 6.00
206 Norris Cole RC .50 1.25
207 Brandon Knight RC .75 2.00
208 Kenneth Faried RC .75 2.00
209 Kawhi Leonard RC 20.00 50.00
210 Reggie Jackson RC .75 2.00
211 Jordan Hamilton RC .50 1.25
212 Jimmer Fredette RC .50 1.25
213 Bismack Biyombo RC .50 1.25
214 Enes Kanter RC .60 1.50
215 Marcus Morris RC .60 1.50
216 Chandler Parsons RC .75 2.00
217 Iman Shumpert RC .75 2.00
218 Markieff Morris RC .75 2.00
219 Tobias Harris RC .75 2.00
220 Chris Singleton RC .50 1.25
221 Nolan Smith RC .50 1.25
222 Isaiah Thomas RC 5.00 12.00
223 Tristan Thompson RC .75 2.00
224 Jan Vesely RC .50 1.25
225 Kemba Walker RC 1.50 4.00
226 Derrick Williams RC .50 1.25
227 Cory Joseph RC .50 1.25
228 JaJuan Johnson RC .50 1.25
229 Justin Harper RC .50 1.25
230 Shelvin Mack RC .60 1.50
231 Gustavo Ayon RC .50 1.25
232 Charles Jenkins RC .50 1.25
233 Jeremy Tyler RC .50 1.25
234 Kyle Singler RC .50 1.25
235 Lavoy Allen RC .50 1.25
236 Anthony Davis RC 15.00 40.00
237 Michael Kidd-Gilchrist RC .75 2.00
238 Bradley Beal RC 1.25 3.00
239 Terrence Ross RC .75 2.00
240 Austin Rivers RC .75 2.00
241 Jeremy Lamb RC .75 2.00
242 Dion Waiters RC .75 2.00
243 Darius Morris RC .50 1.25
244 Thomas Robinson RC .60 1.50
245 Damian Lillard RC 6.00 15.00
246 Harrison Barnes RC 1.25 3.00
247 Andre Drummond RC 1.25 3.00
248 Meyers Leonard RC .60 1.50
249 Kendall Marshall RC .50 1.25
250 John Jenkins RC .50 1.25
251 John Henson RC .75 2.00
252 E'Twaun Moore RC .50 1.25
253 Royce White RC .50 1.25
254 Tyler Zeller RC .60 1.50
255 Terrence Jones RC .60 1.50
256 Andrew Nicholson RC .50 1.25
257 Evan Fournier RC .75 2.00
258 Jared Sullinger RC .60 1.50
259 Fab Melo RC .50 1.25
260 Jared Cunningham RC .50 1.25
261 Festus Ezeli RC .60 1.50
262 Tony Wroten RC .60 1.50
263 Miles Plumlee RC .50 1.25
264 Marquis Teague RC .50 1.25
265 Perry Jones RC .50 1.25
266 Arnett Moultrie RC .50 1.25
267 Nikola Vucevic RC .75 2.00
268 Donald Sloan RC .50 1.25
269 Jon Leuer RC .60 1.50
270 John Shurna RC .50 1.25
271 Andrew Goudelock RC .50 1.25
272 Lance Thomas RC .50 1.25
273 Cory Higgins RC .50 1.25
274 Elliot Williams .30 .75
275 Terrel Harris RC .50 1.25
276 Malcolm Lee RC .50 1.25
277 Jeff Taylor RC .50 1.25
278 Jae Crowder RC .60 1.50
279 Orlando Johnson RC .50 1.25
280 Jonas Valanciunas RC .75 2.00
281 Bernard James RC .50 1.25
282 Draymond Green RC 2.50 6.00
283 Quincy Acy RC .50 1.25
284 Quincy Miller RC .50 1.25
285 Khris Middleton RC .75 2.00
286 Will Barton RC .60 1.50
287 Tyshawn Taylor RC .50 1.25
288 Doron Lamb RC .50 1.25
289 Josh Selby RC .50 1.25
290 Kim English RC .50 1.25
291 Scott Machado RC .50 1.25
292 Kris Joseph RC .50 1.25
293 Julyan Stone RC .50 1.25
294 DeAndre Liggins RC .60 1.50
295 Robert Sacre RC .50 1.25
296 Darrell Arthur .30 .75
297 Kyle O'Quinn RC .50 1.25
298 Darius Miller RC .50 1.25
299 Darius Johnson-Odom RC .50 1.25
300 Greg Stiemsma RC .50 1.25

2012-13 Panini Prizm Prizms

*VETS: 2.5X TO 6X BASE HI
*RETIRED: 2X TO 5X BASE HI
*ROOKIES: 1.5X TO 4X BASE HI
RANDOM INSERTS IN PACKS
1 LeBron James 20.00 50.00
184 Patrick Ewing 4.00 10.00
197 Shawn Kemp 5.00 12.00
201 Kyrie Irving 150.00 400.00
203 Klay Thompson 75.00 200.00
205 Jimmy Butler 40.00 100.00
209 Kawhi Leonard 300.00 600.00
222 Isaiah Thomas 60.00 150.00
236 Anthony Davis 150.00 400.00
238 Bradley Beal 50.00 120.00
245 Damian Lillard 50.00 120.00
246 Harrison Barnes 12.00 30.00
247 Andre Drummond 20.00 50.00
282 Draymond Green 40.00 100.00

2012-13 Panini Prizm Prizms Green

*VETS: 5X TO 12X BASE HI
*RETIRED: 4X TO 10X BASE HI
*ROOKIES: 3X TO 8X BASE HI
RANDOM INSERTS IN RETAIL PACKS
47 Russell Westbrook 10.00 25.00
54 Grant Hill 15.00 40.00
71 Carmelo Anthony 12.00 30.00
72 Stephen Curry 15.00 40.00
77 Dwyane Wade 20.00 50.00
135 Kevin Love 12.00 30.00
160 Anfernee Hardaway 20.00 50.00
166 Shaquille O'Neal 12.00 30.00
176 Scottie Pippen 12.00 30.00
184 Patrick Ewing 8.00 20.00
197 Shawn Kemp 20.00 50.00
200 Alonzo Mourning 12.00 30.00
201 Kyrie Irving 150.00 300.00
203 Klay Thompson 100.00 250.00
209 Kawhi Leonard 400.00 800.00
222 Isaiah Thomas 75.00 200.00
236 Anthony Davis 125.00 300.00
238 Bradley Beal 10.00 25.00
241 Jeremy Lamb 6.00 15.00
245 Damian Lillard 175.00 350.00
247 Andre Drummond 10.00 25.00

2012-13 Panini Prizm Autographs

RANDOM INSERTS IN PACKS
1 Kobe Bryant 100.00 200.00
2 Kevin Durant EXCH 60.00 150.00
3 Blake Griffin 15.00 40.00
4 Kyrie Irving 60.00 150.00
5 Anthony Davis 125.00 250.00
6 Michael Kidd-Gilchrist 4.00 10.00
7 Brandon Knight 4.00 10.00
8 Alex English 3.00 8.00
9 World B. Free 6.00 15.00
10 Kenneth Faried 4.00 10.00
11 Iman Shumpert 4.00 10.00
12 MarShon Brooks 3.00 8.00
13 Austin Rivers 4.00 10.00
14 Meyers Leonard 3.00 8.00
15 Clyde Lovellette 5.00 12.00
16 Gary Payton 15.00 40.00
17 George McGinnis 2.50 6.00
18 Kendall Marshall 2.50 6.00
19 John Starks 3.00 8.00
20 Terrence Ross 8.00 20.00
21 Bernard James 2.50 6.00
22 Reggie Jackson 4.00 10.00
23 Sean Elliott 5.00 12.00
24 Tyler Honeycutt 2.50 6.00
25 Jonas Valanciunas 4.00 10.00
26 Jared Sullinger 3.00 8.00
27 Kenny Anderson 3.00 8.00
28 Marco Belinelli 3.00 8.00
29 Michael Finley 4.00 10.00
30 Peja Stojakovic 5.00 12.00
31 Rex Chapman 4.00 10.00
32 Reggie Theus 3.00 8.00
33 Robert Sacre 2.50 6.00
34 Sidney Moncrief 2.50 6.00
35 Tristan Thompson 4.00 10.00
36 Jimmer Fredette 2.50 6.00
37 Steve Kerr 6.00 15.00
38 Tom Chambers 3.00 8.00
39 Terry Porter 2.50 6.00
40 Nikola Vucevic 6.00 15.00
41 Kemba Walker 12.00 30.00
42 Lance Thomas 2.50 6.00
43 Vlade Divac 4.00 10.00
44 Tyler Zeller 3.00 8.00
45 Zydrunas Ilgauskas 5.00 12.00
46 Tony Wroten 3.00 8.00
47 Ivan Johnson 2.50 6.00
48 Jan Vesely 2.50 6.00
49 Jared Cunningham 2.50 6.00
50 Jeff Hornacek 3.00 8.00
51 Justin Hamilton 3.00 8.00
52 Will Barton 3.00 8.00
53 Kurt Rambis 4.00 10.00
54 Kareem Abdul-Jabbar 30.00 80.00
55 Miles Plumlee 2.50 6.00
56 Lenny Wilkens 6.00 15.00
57 Fab Melo 2.50 6.00
58 Kevin Willis 3.00 8.00
59 Kim English 2.50 6.00
60 Harry Gallatin 4.00 10.00
61 Quincy Miller 2.50 6.00
62 Ralph Sampson 3.00 8.00
63 Thomas Robinson 3.00 8.00
64 Walter Berry 3.00 8.00
65 Nate Archibald 5.00 12.00
66 Lavoy Allen 2.50 6.00
67 Quincy Acy 2.50 6.00
68 John Henson 4.00 10.00
69 Alec Burks 4.00 10.00
70 Allan Houston 6.00 15.00
71 Andrew Goudelock EXCH 2.50 6.00
72 Andrew Nicholson 2.50 6.00
73 Chandler Parsons 4.00 10.00
74 Larry Johnson 15.00 40.00
75 Mike Scott 2.50 6.00
76 DeAndre Liggins 3.00 8.00
77 Norris Cole 2.50 6.00
78 Perry Jones 2.50 6.00
79 Rolando Blackman 3.00 8.00
80 Royce White 2.50 6.00
81 Shelvin Mack 3.00 8.00
82 Terrence Jones 3.00 8.00
83 Tyshawn Taylor 2.50 6.00
84 Evan Fournier 4.00 10.00
85 Charles Jenkins 2.50 6.00
86 Darius Johnson-Odom 2.50 6.00
87 Greg Stiemsma 2.50 6.00
88 Arnett Moultrie 2.50 6.00
89 Bradley Beal 12.00 30.00
90 Jeremy Lamb 4.00 10.00
91 Marquis Teague 2.50 6.00
92 Jeff Taylor 2.50 6.00
93 Festus Ezeli 3.00 8.00
94 Jae Crowder 3.00 8.00
95 Draymond Green 20.00 50.00
96 Dion Waiters 4.00 10.00
97 Chris Singleton 2.50 6.00
98 Jimmy Butler 30.00 80.00
99 Malcolm Lee 2.50 6.00
100 E'Twaun Moore 2.50 6.00

2012-13 Panini Prizm Autographs Prizms

*PRIZMS: 1X TO 2.5X BASE HI
STATED PRINT RUN 25 SER.#'d SETS
1 Kobe Bryant 200.00 400.00
8 Alex English 20.00 50.00
16 Gary Payton 30.00 80.00
41 Kemba Walker 60.00 150.00
54 Kareem Abdul-Jabbar 50.00 120.00
89 Bradley Beal 50.00 120.00

2012-13 Panini Prizm Downtown Bound

COMPLETE SET (25) 20.00 50.00
RANDOM INSERTS IN PACKS
*PRIZMS: 1.25X TO 3X HI COLUMN
*PRIZMS GREEN: 3X TO 8X HI COLUMN
UNPRICED PRIZMS GOLD PRINT RUN 10 SETS
1 Ray Allen 1.00 2.50
2 Dirk Nowitzki 1.25 3.00
3 Steve Novak .60 1.50
4 Steve Nash 1.00 2.50
5 Kevin Durant 2.50 6.00
6 Kobe Bryant 4.00 10.00
7 Stephen Curry 4.00 10.00
8 Dwyane Wade 1.50 4.00
9 LeBron James 4.00 10.00
10 Jeremy Lin 3.00 8.00
11 Brandon Jennings .60 1.50
12 Kevin Love 1.00 2.50
13 Kyrie Irving 5.00 12.00
14 Chris Paul 1.25 3.00
15 Mario Chalmers .75 2.00
16 Ryan Anderson .75 2.00
17 Shane Battier .75 2.00
18 Paul Pierce 1.00 2.50
19 James Harden 1.50 4.00
20 Joe Johnson .75 2.00
21 Russell Westbrook 2.50 6.00
22 Deron Williams .75 2.00
23 Danny Granger .75 2.00
24 Klay Thompson 4.00 10.00
25 Brandon Rush .60 1.50

2012-13 Panini Prizm Finalists

COMPLETE SET (38) 30.00 80.00
RANDOM INSERTS IN PACKS
*PRIZMS: 1X TO 2.5X HI COLUMN
*PRIZMS GREEN: 2.5X TO 6X HI COLUMN
UNPRICED PRIZMS GOLD PRINT RUN 10 SETS
1 Bill Russell 2.00 5.00
2 Bill Laimbeer 1.00 2.50
3 Kareem Abdul-Jabbar 2.00 5.00
4 Scottie Pippen 2.50 6.00
5 Kobe Bryant 5.00 12.00
6 LeBron James 5.00 12.00
7 Dwyane Wade 2.00 5.00
8 Tim Duncan 2.00 5.00
9 David Robinson 2.00 5.00
10 Shaquille O'Neal 2.50 6.00
11 Robert Horry 1.00 2.50
12 Magic Johnson 3.00 8.00
13 Larry Bird 3.00 8.00
14 Dennis Rodman 2.50 6.00
15 Derek Fisher 1.00 2.50
16 Robert Parish 1.25 3.00
17 Kurt Rambis .75 2.00
18 Chris Bosh 1.25 3.00
19 Dirk Nowitzki 1.50 4.00
20 Jason Kidd 1.25 3.00
21 Tyson Chandler 1.00 2.50
22 Mario Chalmers 1.00 2.50
23 Tony Parker 1.25 3.00
24 Chauncey Billups 1.25 3.00
25 Hakeem Olajuwon 1.50 4.00
26 Isiah Thomas 1.25 3.00
27 Joe Dumars 1.25 3.00
28 James Worthy 1.50 4.00
29 Toni Kukoc 1.25 3.00
30 Rajon Rondo 1.25 3.00
31 Paul Pierce 1.25 3.00
32 Kevin Garnett 2.00 5.00
33 Ray Allen 1.25 3.00
34 Manu Ginobili 1.25 3.00
35 Clyde Drexler 1.50 4.00
36 Pau Gasol 1.25 3.00
37 Jason Terry 1.00 2.50
38 Michael Finley 1.25 3.00

2012-13 Panini Prizm Most Valuable Players

COMPLETE SET (25) 25.00 60.00
RANDOM INSERTS IN PACKS
*PRIZMS: 1X TO 2.5X HI COLUMN
UNPRICED PRIZMS GOLD PRINT RUN 10 SETS
1 LeBron James 5.00 12.00
2 Derrick Rose 1.50 4.00
3 Kobe Bryant 5.00 12.00
4 Dirk Nowitzki 1.50 4.00
5 Steve Nash 1.25 3.00
6 Kevin Garnett 2.00 5.00
7 Tim Duncan 2.00 5.00
8 Allen Iverson 1.50 4.00
9 Shaquille O'Neal 2.50 6.00
10 Karl Malone 1.50 4.00
11 David Robinson 2.00 5.00
12 Hakeem Olajuwon 1.50 4.00
13 Magic Johnson 3.00 8.00
14 Larry Bird 3.00 8.00
15 Moses Malone 1.25 3.00
16 Julius Erving 2.00 5.00
17 Kareem Abdul-Jabbar 2.00 5.00
18 Bill Walton 1.25 3.00
19 Bob McAdoo 1.00 2.50
20 Dave Cowens .75 2.00
21 Willis Reed 1.25 3.00
22 Wes Unseld 1.25 3.00
23 Wilt Chamberlain 2.50 6.00
24 Bill Russell 2.00 5.00
25 Oscar Robertson 1.50 4.00

2012-13 Panini Prizm Most Valuable Players Prizms Green

*PRIZMS GREEN: 3X TO 8X BASE HI
RANDOM INSERTS IN RETAIL PACKS
1 LeBron James 50.00 125.00
3 Kobe Bryant 50.00 125.00

2012-13 Panini Prizm USA Basketball

COMPLETE SET (12) 30.00 80.00
RANDOM INSERTS IN PACKS
UNPRICED PRIZMS GOLD PRINT RUN 10 SETS
1 Tyson Chandler 2.50 6.00
2 Kevin Durant 6.00 15.00
3 LeBron James 10.00 25.00
4 Russell Westbrook 8.00 20.00
5 Deron Williams 2.50 6.00
6 Andre Iguodala 2.50 6.00
7 Kobe Bryant 8.00 20.00
8 Kevin Love 3.00 8.00
9 James Harden 5.00 12.00
10 Chris Paul 4.00 10.00
11 Anthony Davis 20.00 50.00
12 Carmelo Anthony 4.00 10.00

2012-13 Panini Prizm USA Basketball Prizms

*PRIZMS: 1.25X TO 3X BASE HI
RANDOM INSERTS IN PACKS
2 Kevin Durant 25.00 60.00
3 LeBron James 40.00 100.00
7 Kobe Bryant 40.00 100.00
11 Anthony Davis 50.00 125.00

2012-13 Panini Prizm USA Basketball Prizms Green

*PRIZMS GREEN: 1.2X TO 3X BASE HI
RANDOM INSERTS IN RETAIL PACKS
2 Kevin Durant 30.00 80.00
3 LeBron James 40.00 100.00
4 Russell Westbrook 30.00 80.00
7 Kobe Bryant 50.00 120.00
8 Kevin Love 10.00 25.00
9 James Harden 8.00 20.00
10 Chris Paul 12.00 30.00
11 Anthony Davis 30.00 80.00
12 Carmelo Anthony 8.00 20.00

2013-14 Panini Prizm

COMPLETE SET (297) 25.00 60.00
1 Kobe Bryant 2.00 5.00
2 Zach Randolph .40 1.00
3 Larry Sanders .30 .75
4 Anthony Davis 1.00 2.50
5 J.R. Smith .40 1.00
6 Carl Landry .30 .75
7 Jamal Crawford .50 1.25
8 Paul George .60 1.50
9 Harrison Barnes .40 1.00
10 Nate Robinson .30 .75
11 Monta Ellis .40 1.00
12 Taj Gibson .40 1.00
13 Ben Gordon .40 1.00
14 Rajon Rondo .50 1.25
15 Jeff Teague .40 1.00
16 Gordon Hayward .50 1.25
17 DeMar DeRozan .50 1.25
18 Jimmer Fredette .30 .75
19 Damian Lillard 1.00 2.50
20 Spencer Hawes .30 .75
21 Arron Afflalo .30 .75
22 Nick Young .50 1.25
23 Chris Bosh .50 1.25
24 Ersan Ilyasova .30 .75
25 Austin Rivers .40 1.00
26 Kenyon Martin .40 1.00
27 Eric Maynor .30 .75
28 Jared Dudley .30 .75
29 Lance Stephenson .40 1.00
30 Draymond Green .60 1.50
31 J.J. Hickson .30 .75
32 Samuel Dalembert .30 .75
33 Luol Deng .40 1.00
34 Al Jefferson .40 1.00
35 Jeff Green .40 1.00
36 Al Horford .40 1.00
37 Marvin Williams .40 1.00
38 Tracy McGrady .50 1.25
39 Jason Thompson .30 .75
40 Markieff Morris .30 .75
41 Lavoy Allen .30 .75
42 Andrew Nicholson .30 .75
43 Pau Gasol .50 1.25
44 Dwyane Wade .75 2.00
45 O.J. Mayo .30 .75
46 Jason Smith .30 .75
47 Metta World Peace .50 1.25
48 Paul Millsap .50 1.25
49 J.J. Redick .50 1.25
50 Danny Granger .40 1.00
51 David Lee .30 .75
52 JaVale McGee .40 1.00
53 Dirk Nowitzki .60 1.50
54 Joakim Noah .40 1.00
55 Paul Pierce .50 1.25
56 Jared Sullinger .30 .75
57 Trevor Ariza .30 .75
58 Enes Kanter .30 .75
59 Tony Parker .50 1.25
60 Greivis Vasquez .40 1.00
61 Marcus Morris .30 .75
62 Jason Richardson .50 1.25
63 Thabo Sefolosha .30 .75
64 Steve Blake .30 .75
65 LeBron James 2.00 5.00
66 John Henson .40 1.00
67 Jrue Holiday .50 1.25
68 Raymond Felton .40 1.00
69 Kevin Seraphin .30 .75
70 DeAndre Jordan .50 1.25
71 Jeremy Lin .50 1.25
72 Andre Iguodala .40 1.00
73 Ty Lawson .30 .75
74 Tyler Zeller .40 1.00
75 Jimmy Butler .50 1.25
76 Kevin Garnett .75 2.00
77 Gerald Wallace .40 1.00
78 Nene .40 1.00
79 Derrick Favors .40 1.00
80 Tim Duncan .75 2.00
81 DeMarcus Cousins .50 1.25
82 Marcin Gortat .40 1.00
83 Evan Turner .30 .75
84 Serge Ibaka .40 1.00
85 Steve Nash .50 1.25
86 Norris Cole .30 .75
87 Kevin Love .50 1.25
88 Ryan Anderson .40 1.00
89 Tyson Chandler .40 1.00
90 Martell Webster .30 .75
91 Chris Paul .60 1.50
92 James Harden .75 2.00
93 Chauncey Billups .50 1.25
94 Kenneth Faried .40 1.00
95 Dion Waiters .40 1.00
96 Derrick Rose .60 1.50
97 Joe Johnson .40 1.00
98 Brandon Bass .30 .75
99 John Wall .60 1.50
100 Tyler Hansbrough .40 1.00
101 Tiago Splitter .40 1.00
102 Thomas Robinson .30 .75
103 Kendall Marshall .40 1.00
104 Tobias Harris .40 1.00
105 Russell Westbrook 1.25 3.00
106 Robert Sacre .30 .75
107 Shane Battier .40 1.00
108 Kevin Martin .40 1.00
109 Tyreke Evans .30 .75
110 Francisco Garcia .30 .75
111 Ryan Hollins .30 .75
112 Blake Griffin .50 1.25
113 Dwight Howard .40 1.00
114 Rodney Stuckey .40 1.00
115 Evan Fournier .40 1.00
116 Tristan Thompson .40 1.00
117 Carlos Boozer .40 1.00
118 Jason Terry .40 1.00
119 Avery Bradley .40 1.00
120 Emeka Okafor .40 1.00
121 Terrence Ross .40 1.00
122 Manu Ginobili .50 1.25
123 Wesley Matthews .30 .75
124 Goran Dragic .40 1.00
125 Nikola Vucevic .40 1.00
126 Ronnie Brewer .40 1.00
127 Marc Gasol .50 1.25
128 Udonis Haslem .30 .75
129 Ricky Rubio .50 1.25
130 Eric Gordon .40 1.00
131 Marcus Camby .40 1.00
132 Arnett Moultrie .30 .75
133 George Hill .40 1.00
134 Chandler Parsons .40 1.00
135 Josh Smith .40 1.00
136 Andre Miller .40 1.00
137 Kyrie Irving 1.00 2.50
138 Michael Kidd-Gilchrist .50 1.25
139 Deron Williams .40 1.00
140 Louis Williams .40 1.00
141 Bradley Beal .50 1.25
142 Rudy Gay .50 1.25
143 Kawhi Leonard .75 2.00
144 Nicolas Batum .40 1.00
145 Eric Bledsoe .40 1.00
146 Maurice Harkless .30 .75
147 Kevin Durant 1.25 3.00
148 Mike Conley .40 1.00
149 Ray Allen .50 1.25
150 Alexey Shved .30 .75
151 Amar'e Stoudemire .40 1.00
152 Bismack Biyombo .30 .75
153 Andrei Kirilenko .40 1.00
154 David West .40 1.00
155 Aaron Brooks .30 .75
156 Greg Monroe .40 1.00
157 Jae Crowder .40 1.00
158 Andrew Bynum .30 .75
159 Kemba Walker .50 1.25
160 Brook Lopez .40 1.00
161 Kyle Korver .40 1.00
162 Alec Burks .30 .75
163 Kyle Lowry .40 1.00
164 Danny Green .40 1.00
165 Meyers Leonard .30 .75
166 Caron Butler .40 1.00
167 Jameer Nelson .30 .75
168 Kendrick Perkins .30 .75
169 Tayshaun Prince .40 1.00
170 Brandon Knight .40 1.00
171 Chase Budinger .30 .75
172 Carmelo Anthony .60 1.50
173 Mike Miller .40 1.00
174 Andray Blatche .30 .75
175 Chris Copeland .30 .75
176 Stephen Curry 2.00 5.00
177 Brandon Jennings .30 .75
178 Vince Carter .60 1.50
179 Anderson Varejao .30 .75
180 Gerald Henderson .30 .75
181 MarShon Brooks .40 1.00
182 John Jenkins .30 .75
183 Jeremy Evans .30 .75
184 Jonas Valanciunas .40 1.00
185 Marcus Thornton .30 .75
186 LaMarcus Aldridge .50 1.25
187 Thaddeus Young .30 .75
188 Glen Davis .30 .75
189 Jeremy Lamb .30 .75
190 Tony Allen .30 .75
191 Carlos Delfino .30 .75
192 Corey Brewer .30 .75
193 Iman Shumpert .30 .75
194 Tony Wroten .30 .75
195 C.J. Miles .40 1.00
196 Roy Hibbert .40 1.00
197 Klay Thompson .60 1.50
198 Andre Drummond .50 1.25
199 Shawn Marion .40 1.00
200 Kirk Hinrich .40 1.00
201 John Stockton .75 2.00
202 Pete Maravich .75 2.00
203 Rolando Blackman .40 1.00
204 Shaquille O'Neal 1.00 2.50
205 Larry Johnson .60 1.50
206 Sean Elliott .50 1.25
207 Dan Majerle .40 1.00
208 Vlade Divac .50 1.25
209 Yao Ming .60 1.50
210 Rick Fox .40 1.00
211 Norm Nixon .30 .75
212 Oscar Robertson .60 1.50
213 Ron Harper .50 1.25
214 Allen Iverson .60 1.50
215 Gary Payton .50 1.25
216 Joe Dumars .50 1.25
217 Detlef Schrempf .50 1.25
218 Jack Sikma .40 1.00
219 Dennis Rodman 1.00 2.50
220 John Havlicek .60 1.50
221 Julius Erving .75 2.00
222 Phil Jackson .60 1.50
223 Scottie Pippen 1.00 2.50
224 Dennis Johnson .40 1.00
225 Nick Van Exel .50 1.25
226 David Robinson .75 2.00
227 Robert Horry .40 1.00
228 Sam Perkins .30 .75
229 Moses Malone .50 1.25
230 Dave DeBusschere .50 1.25
231 Kareem Abdul-Jabbar .75 2.00
232 Larry Bird 1.25 3.00
233 Clyde Drexler .60 1.50
234 Shawn Kemp .75 2.00
235 Nate Archibald .40 1.00
236 Isiah Thomas .50 1.25
237 Manute Bol .50 1.25
238 Adrian Dantley .40 1.00
239 Jerry West .60 1.50
240 George Gervin .50 1.25
241 Karl Malone .60 1.50
242 Magic Johnson 1.25 3.00
243 Dominique Wilkins .60 1.50
244 Alonzo Mourning .60 1.50
245 Grant Hill .60 1.50
246 Tim Hardaway .50 1.25
247 Muggsy Bogues .40 1.00
248 Mark Jackson .40 1.00
249 Lucius Allen .50 1.25
250 Bernard King .40 1.00
251 Walt Frazier .50 1.25
252 James Worthy .60 1.50
253 Anfernee Hardaway 1.25 3.00
254 Hakeem Olajuwon .60 1.50
255 Jason Kidd .50 1.25
256 Chris Mullin .50 1.25
257 Wilt Chamberlain 1.00 2.50
258 Glen Rice .40 1.00
259 B.J. Armstrong .50 1.25
260 Bill Russell .75 2.00
261 Shabazz Muhammad RC .60 1.50
262 Alex Len RC .60 1.50
263 Ben McLemore RC .60 1.50
264 Cody Zeller RC .60 1.50
265 M.Carter-Williams RC .75 2.00
266 Glen Rice Jr. RC .50 1.25
267 Archie Goodwin RC .60 1.50
268 Nate Wolters RC .60 1.50
269 Jamaal Franklin RC .50 1.25
270 Reggie Bullock RC .60 1.50
271 Anthony Bennett RC .60 1.50
272 Kelly Olynyk RC .60 1.50
273 Tony Mitchell RC .50 1.25
274 Isaiah Canaan RC .50 1.25
275 Carrick Felix RC .50 1.25
276 Victor Oladipo RC 1.50 4.00
277 Solomon Hill RC .50 1.25
278 Ricky Ledo RC .50 1.25
279 Shane Larkin RC .50 1.25
280 Ryan Kelly RC .50 1.25
281 Otto Porter RC .75 2.00
282 Trey Burke RC .60 1.50
283 C.J. McCollum RC 1.25 3.00
284 Kentavious Caldwell-Pope RC .75 2.00
285 Nerlens Noel RC 1.00 2.50

286 Dennis Schroder RC .75 2.00
287 Tim Hardaway Jr. RC .75 2.00
288 Mason Plumlee RC .75 2.00
289 Peyton Siva RC .50 1.25
290 G.Antetokounmpo RC 15.00 40.00
291 Steven Adams RC .75 2.00
292 Tony Snell RC .60 1.50
293 Ray McCallum RC .50 1.25
294 Gorgui Dieng RC .60 1.50
295 Allen Crabbe RC .60 1.50
296 Jeff Withey RC .50 1.25
297 Gal Mekel RC .50 1.25

2013-14 Panini Prizm Prizms
*PRIZM VET: 1.5X TO 4X BASIC
*PRIZM RC: 1X TO 2.5X BASIC

2013-14 Panini Prizm Prizms Blue
*BLUE VET: 2.5X TO 6X BASIC
*BLUE RC: 1.5X TO 4X BASIC
8 Paul George 10.00 25.00
65 LeBron James 20.00 50.00
290 Giannis Antetokounmpo 100.00 250.00

2013-14 Panini Prizm Prizms Green
*GREEN VET: 2X TO 5X BASIC
*GREEN RC: 1.2X TO 3X BASIC
290 Giannis Antetokounmpo 100.00 250.00

2013-14 Panini Prizm Prizms Light Blue Die Cut
*LT.BLUE VET: 2.5X TO 6X BASIC
*LT.BLUE RC: 1.5X TO 4X BASIC
STATED PRINT RUN 199 SER.#'d SETS
290 Giannis Antetokounmpo 75.00 200.00

2013-14 Panini Prizm Prizms Orange
*ORANGE VET: 4X TO 10X BASIC
*ORANGE RC: 2.5X TO 6X BASIC
STATED PRINT RUN 60 SER.#'d SETS
65 LeBron James 25.00 60.00
276 Victor Oladipo 15.00 40.00
290 Giannis Antetokounmpo 250.00 500.00

2013-14 Panini Prizm Prizms Purple Die Cut
*PURPLE VET: 5X TO 12X BASIC
*PURPLE RC: 3X TO 8X BASIC
STATED PRINT RUN 49 SER.#'d SETS
65 LeBron James 40.00 100.00
285 Nerlens Noel 15.00 40.00
290 Giannis Antetokounmpo 300.00 600.00

2013-14 Panini Prizm Prizms Red
*RED VET: 2X TO 5X BASIC
*RED RC: 1.2X TO 3X BASIC
287 Tim Hardaway Jr. 6.00 15.00
290 Giannis Antetokounmpo 100.00 250.00

2013-14 Panini Prizm Prizms Red White and Blue Mosaic
*RWB VET: 2.5X TO 6X BASIC
*RWB RC: 1.5X TO 4X BASIC
290 Giannis Antetokounmpo 100.00 250.00

2013-14 Panini Prizm Autographs
EXCHANGE DEADLINE 6/18/2015
1 Otto Porter 10.00 25.00
2 Erik Murphy 2.50 6.00
3 Ryan Kelly 2.50 6.00
4 Kentavious Caldwell-Pope 4.00 10.00
5 Ricky Ledo 2.50 6.00
6 C.J. McCollum 10.00 25.00
7 Michael Carter-Williams 4.00 10.00
8 Anthony Bennett 3.00 8.00
9 Andre Roberson 2.50 6.00
10 Alex Len 3.00 8.00
11 Trey Burke 3.00 8.00
12 Tony Snell 3.00 8.00
13 Victor Oladipo 12.00 30.00
14 Cody Zeller 8.00 20.00
15 Allen Crabbe 3.00 8.00
16 Peyton Siva 2.50 6.00
17 Tim Hardaway Jr. 4.00 10.00
18 Solomon Hill 2.50 6.00
19 Jamaal Franklin 2.50 6.00
20 Jeff Withey 2.50 6.00
21 Ben McLemore 3.00 8.00
22 Steven Adams 8.00 20.00
23 Isaiah Canaan 2.50 6.00
24 Nate Wolters 3.00 8.00
25 Archie Goodwin 3.00 8.00
26 Kelly Olynyk 3.00 8.00
27 Shane Larkin 2.50 6.00
28 Shabazz Muhammad 3.00 8.00
29 Ray McCallum 2.50 6.00
30 Nerlens Noel 15.00 40.00
31 Glen Rice Jr. 2.50 6.00
32 Mason Plumlee 4.00 10.00
33 Giannis Antetokounmpo 75.00 200.00
34 Elias Harris 3.00 8.00
35 Gorgui Dieng 3.00 8.00
36 Dennis Schroder 4.00 10.00
37 Nemanja Nedovic 2.50 6.00
38 Matthew Dellavedova 8.00 20.00
39 Phil Pressey 2.50 6.00
40 Carrick Felix 2.50 6.00
41 Rudy Gobert 12.00 30.00
42 Ian Clark 3.00 8.00
43 Miroslav Raduljica 2.50 6.00
44 C.J. Leslie 2.50 6.00
45 Gal Mekel 2.50 6.00
46 Nick Anderson 4.00 10.00
47 Marcus Camby 3.00 8.00
48 Dee Brown 2.50 6.00
49 Bobby Jones 3.00 8.00
50 Damian Lillard 30.00 80.00
51 Vince Carter 12.00 30.00
52 Kenny Walker 2.50 6.00
53 Tom Chambers 3.00 8.00
54 Tony Parker 8.00 20.00
55 Stephen Curry 100.00 200.00
56 Steve Smith 3.00 8.00
57 Larry Johnson 6.00 15.00
58 Darrell Griffith 2.50 6.00
59 Magic Johnson 40.00 100.00
60 Larry Bird 40.00 100.00
61 Bill Russell 60.00 150.00
62 Blake Griffin 15.00 40.00
63 Lance Thomas 6.00 15.00
64 Kenny Smith 3.00 8.00
65 Mark Aguirre 3.00 8.00
66 Dominique Wilkins 8.00 20.00
67 Deron Williams 3.00 8.00
68 David Robinson 20.00 50.00
69 Harrison Barnes 3.00 8.00
70 Steve Nash 15.00 40.00
71 Jerry West 12.00 30.00
72 Kawhi Leonard 50.00 120.00
73 Kenyon Martin 3.00 8.00
74 Ersan Ilyasova 2.50 6.00
75 Tobias Harris 3.00 8.00
76 Chris Andersen 8.00 20.00
77 Kenneth Faried 3.00 8.00
78 Norm Nixon 2.50 6.00
79 Rick Barry 3.00 8.00
80 Iman Shumpert 4.00 10.00
81 Bernard King 3.00 8.00
82 Nicolas Batum 12.00 30.00
83 LaMarcus Aldridge 12.00 30.00
84 Sean Elliott 4.00 10.00
85 Isiah Thomas 8.00 20.00
86 Jannero Pargo 3.00 8.00
87 Micheal Ray Richardson 3.00 8.00
88 Gail Goodrich 3.00 8.00
89 Michael Finley 4.00 10.00
90 Charlie Scott 3.00 8.00
91 Bill Sharman 6.00 15.00
92 Rory Sparrow 2.50 6.00
93 Wes Unseld 4.00 10.00
94 Ronnie Brewer 3.00 8.00
95 Jamaal Wilkes 4.00 10.00
96 Kendall Marshall 3.00 8.00
97 John Lucas III 2.50 6.00
98 Nate Archibald 8.00 20.00
99 Scottie Pippen 30.00 80.00
100 Raymond Felton 3.00 8.00
101 Byron Scott 6.00 15.00
102 Bill Laimbeer 5.00 12.00
103 J.R. Smith 3.00 8.00
104 J.J. Redick 4.00 10.00
105 Connie Hawkins 4.00 10.00
106 A.C. Green 4.00 10.00
107 Jim Jackson 2.50 6.00
108 Tyson Chandler 3.00 8.00
109 Joe Johnson 3.00 8.00
110 Herb Williams 2.50 6.00
111 Dick Barnett 4.00 10.00
112 Jeff Teague 3.00 8.00
113 Jason Terry 3.00 8.00
114 Rajon Rondo 8.00 20.00
115 Kurt Rambis 2.50 6.00
116 Jason Kidd 12.00 30.00
117 Fred Jones 2.50 6.00
118 Larry Nance 3.00 8.00
119 Danny Green 3.00 8.00
120 Paul Westphal 4.00 10.00
121 Andrea Bargnani 3.00 8.00
122 Danilo Gallinari 2.50 6.00
123 Tiago Splitter 3.00 8.00
124 Dean Meminger 4.00 10.00
125 Kendall Gill 2.50 6.00
126 Alexey Shved 2.50 6.00
127 Dikembe Mutombo 8.00 20.00
128 George Gervin 8.00 20.00
129 Grant Hill 12.00 30.00
130 David West 3.00 8.00
131 Gary Payton 6.00 15.00
132 Josh Smith 3.00 8.00
133 Horace Grant 8.00 20.00
134 Jeff Green 3.00 8.00
135 Ryan Anderson 3.00 8.00
136 Kyle Lowry 3.00 8.00
137 Andre Drummond 4.00 10.00
138 Mark Jackson 3.00 8.00
139 Brandon Roy
140 Kobe Bryant 75.00 150.00
141 Kyrie Irving 30.00 80.00
142 Kevin Durant 50.00 120.00
143 Karl Malone 40.00 80.00
144 Kareem Abdul-Jabbar 40.00 100.00
145 Derrick Williams 2.50 6.00
146 Rex Chapman 4.00 10.00
147 Bradley Beal 10.00 25.00
148 Kenny Anderson 3.00 8.00
149 Kevin Willis 2.50 6.00
150 Bismack Biyombo 2.50 6.00
151 Marvin Williams 3.00 8.00
152 Ricky Davis 3.00 8.00
153 Jared Sullinger 2.50 6.00
154 Maurice Cheeks 2.50 6.00
155 Boris Diaw 6.00 15.00
156 Robert Parish 4.00 10.00
157 Jared Dudley 2.50 6.00
158 B.J. Armstrong 4.00 10.00
159 Brandon Knight
160 Michael Curry 2.50 6.00
161 Zach Randolph 3.00 8.00
162 Anfernee Hardaway 20.00 50.00
163 Kiki Vandeweghe 3.00 8.00
164 Jrue Holiday 6.00 15.00
165 Darryl Dawkins 2.50 6.00
166 Brandon Bass 2.50 6.00
167 Peja Stojakovic 4.00 10.00
168 Draymond Green 8.00 20.00
169 Jack Sikma 3.00 8.00
170 Greg Stiemsma 2.50 6.00
171 Alonzo Mourning 10.00 25.00
172 Sam Cassell 6.00 15.00
173 Dennis Rodman 10.00 25.00
174 Marcin Gortat 10.00 25.00
175 Goran Dragic 3.00 8.00
176 Jeff Ayres 2.50 6.00
177 Al-Farouq Aminu 3.00 8.00
178 Elgin Baylor 10.00 25.00
179 Allan Houston 3.00 8.00
180 Jason Smith 2.50 6.00
181 Luis Scola 3.00 8.00
182 Joe Dumars 4.00 10.00
183 World B. Free 3.00 8.00
184 DeMarre Carroll 6.00 15.00
185 John Salley
186 Michael Cage
187 Andrei Kirilenko
188 Theo Ratliff 2.50 6.00
189 Vinny Del Negro 2.50 6.00
190 John Lucas 4.00 10.00
191 Sleepy Floyd
192 Elvin Hayes 8.00 20.00
193 Tariq Abdul-Wahad 2.50 6.00
194 Reggie Theus 3.00 8.00
195 Bill Walton 4.00 10.00
196 P.J. Tucker 2.50 6.00
197 Keith Bogans 2.50 6.00
198 Dwight Howard 6.00 15.00
199 Nick Van Exel 4.00 10.00
200 James Harden EXCH 30.00 80.00

2013-14 Panini Prizm Autographs Prizms
*PRIZM: .6X TO 1.5X BASIC
STATED PRINT RUN 25 SER.#'d SETS
EXCHANGE DEADLINE 6/18/2015
7 Michael Carter-Williams 15.00 40.00
41 Rudy Gobert 75.00 200.00
50 Damian Lillard 75.00 150.00

2013-14 Panini Prizm Autographs Prizms Blue
*BLUE p/r 75-99: .6X TO 1.5X BASIC
*BLUE p/r 49-50: .75X TO 2X BASIC
*BLUE p/r 25: 1X TO 2.5X BASIC
PRINT RUNS B/WN 5-99 COPIES PER
NO PRICING ON QTY 10 OR LESS
EXCHANGE DEADLINE 6/18/2015

2013-14 Panini Prizm Autographs Prizms Red
*RED p/r 75-99: .6X TO 1.5X BASIC
*RED p/r 49-50: .75X TO 2X BASIC
*RED p/r 25: 1X TO 2.5X BASIC
PRINT RUNS B/WN 5-99 COPIES PER
NO PRICING ON QTY 10 OR LESS
EXCHANGE DEADLINE 6/18/2015

2013-14 Panini Prizm BK HRX
COMPLETE SET (24) 6.00 15.00
1 Alex Len .40 1.00
2 Anthony Bennett .40 1.00
3 Archie Goodwin .40 1.00
4 Ben McLemore .40 1.00
5 C.J. McCollum .75 2.00
6 Cody Zeller .40 1.00
7 Erik Murphy .30 .75
8 Glen Rice Jr. .30 .75
9 Isaiah Canaan .30 .75
10 Jamaal Franklin .30 .75
11 Kelly Olynyk .40 1.00
12 Kentavious Caldwell-Pope .50 1.25
13 Mason Plumlee .50 1.25
14 Michael Carter-Williams .50 1.25
15 Nerlens Noel .60 1.50
16 Otto Porter .50 1.25
17 Ricky Ledo .30 .75
18 Ryan Kelly .30 .75
19 Shabazz Muhammad .40 1.00
20 Shane Larkin .40 1.00
21 Solomon Hill .30 .75
22 Tim Hardaway Jr. .50 1.25
23 Trey Burke .40 1.00
24 Victor Oladipo .60 1.50

2013-14 Panini Prizm Brilliance
1 Tony Parker .75 2.00
2 Steve Nash .75 2.00
3 Jeremy Lin .75 2.00
4 Joe Johnson .60 1.50
5 Paul George
6 Ty Lawson .50 1.25
7 LeBron James 3.00 8.00
8 Kevin Durant 2.00 5.00
9 Kobe Bryant 3.00 8.00
10 Kyrie Irving 1.50 4.00
11 Tyson Chandler .60 1.50
12 Marc Gasol .75 2.00
13 Chandler Parsons .60 1.50
14 Kawhi Leonard 1.25 3.00
15 Joakim Noah .60 1.50
16 Ricky Rubio .75 2.00
17 Danny Green .60 1.50
18 Jimmy Butler .75 2.00
19 Dion Waiters .60 1.50
20 Paul Pierce .75 2.00
21 Chris Andersen .60 1.50
22 Iman Shumpert .50 1.25
23 Rudy Gay .75 2.00
24 Chris Bosh .75 2.00
25 Kevin Garnett 1.25 3.00

2013-14 Panini Prizm Brilliance Prizms
*PRIZM: .75X TO 2X BASIC

2013-14 Panini Prizm Brilliance Prizms Light Blue Die Cut
*LT BLUE: 1.5X TO 4X BASIC
STATED PRINT RUN 199 SER.#'d SETS

2013-14 Panini Prizm Brilliance Prizms Orange
*ORANGE: 2X TO 5X BASIC
STATED PRINT RUN 60 SER.#'d SETS
5 Paul George 10.00 25.00
7 LeBron James 25.00 60.00

2013-14 Panini Prizm Brilliance Prizms Purple Die Cut
*PURPLE: 2.5X TO 6X BASIC
STATED PRINT RUN 49 SER.#'d SETS
5 Paul George 12.00 30.00
7 LeBron James 30.00 80.00
9 Kobe Bryant 40.00 100.00

2013-14 Panini Prizm Dominance
*PRIZM: .75X TO 2X BASIC
*LT BLUE: 1.5X TO 4X BASIC
*ORANGE: 2X TO 5X BASIC
1 LeBron James 3.00 8.00
2 Carmelo Anthony 1.00 2.50
3 Kevin Durant 2.00 5.00
4 Chris Paul 1.00 2.50
5 James Harden 1.25 3.00
6 Kevin Love .75 2.00
7 Kyrie Irving 1.50 4.00
8 Tim Duncan 1.25 3.00
9 Derrick Rose 1.00 2.50
10 Dwight Howard .60 1.50
11 Blake Griffin .75 2.00
12 Rajon Rondo .75 2.00
13 Stephen Curry 3.00 8.00
14 Damian Lillard 1.50 4.00
15 Deron Williams .60 1.50
16 Kenneth Faried .60 1.50
17 Harrison Barnes .60 1.50
18 Bradley Beal .75 2.00
19 Dwyane Wade 1.25 3.00
20 Russell Westbrook 2.00 5.00
21 Vince Carter 1.00 2.50
22 Brook Lopez .60 1.50
23 Dirk Nowitzki 1.00 2.50
24 Kobe Bryant 3.00 8.00
25 Anthony Davis 1.50 4.00

2013-14 Panini Prizm Dominance Prizms
*PRIZM: .75X TO 2X BASIC

2013-14 Panini Prizm Dominance Prizms Purple Die Cut
*PURPLE: 2.5X TO 6X BASIC
STATED PRINT RUN 60 SER.#'d SETS
1 LeBron James 40.00 100.00
24 Kobe Bryant 40.00 100.00

2013-14 Panini Prizm Guard Duty
*PRIZM: .75X TO 2X BASIC
*LT BLUE: 1.5X TO 4X BASIC
*ORANGE: 2X TO 5X BASIC
*PURPLE: 2.5X TO 6X BASIC
1 Chris Paul 1.00 2.50
2 Kyrie Irving 1.50 4.00
3 Russell Westbrook 2.00 5.00
4 Damian Lillard 1.50 4.00
5 John Wall 1.00 2.50
6 James Harden 1.25 3.00
7 Derrick Rose 1.00 2.50
8 Ricky Rubio .75 2.00
9 Stephen Curry 3.00 8.00
10 Steve Nash .75 2.00
11 Dwyane Wade 1.25 3.00
12 Tony Parker .75 2.00
13 Jeremy Lin .75 2.00
14 Rajon Rondo .75 2.00
15 Kobe Bryant 3.00 8.00

2013-14 Panini Prizm Hall Monitors
*PRIZM: .75X TO 2X BASIC
*BLUE: 1X TO 2.5X BASIC
*GREEN: .75X TO 2X BASIC
*LT BLUE: 1.5X TO 4X BASIC
*ORANGE: 2X TO 5X BASIC
*PURPLE: 2.5X TO 6X BASIC
*RED: .75X TO 2X BASIC
1 Gary Payton .75 2.00
2 Scottie Pippen 1.50 4.00
3 Bill Russell 1.25 3.00
4 Karl Malone 1.00 2.50
5 Arvydas Sabonis .60 1.50
6 John Stockton 1.25 3.00
7 David Robinson 1.25 3.00
8 Patrick Ewing 1.00 2.50
9 Magic Johnson 2.00 5.00
10 Drazen Petrovic .75 2.00
11 Moses Malone .75 2.00
12 Pete Maravich 1.25 3.00
13 Wilt Chamberlain 1.50 4.00
14 George Mikan 1.50 4.00
15 Jerry West 1.00 2.50
16 Oscar Robertson 1.00 2.50
17 Earl Monroe .75 2.00
18 Bill Walton .75 2.00
19 John Havlicek 1.00 2.50
20 Elgin Baylor .75 2.00
21 Julius Erving 1.25 3.00
22 Wes Unseld .75 2.00
23 Hakeem Olajuwon 1.00 2.50
24 Larry Bird 2.00 5.00
25 Kareem Abdul-Jabbar 1.25 3.00

2013-14 Panini Prizm Post Season
1 Tyson Chandler .60 1.50
2 Marc Gasol .75 2.00
3 Pau Gasol .75 2.00
4 Dwight Howard .60 1.50
5 Joakim Noah .60 1.50
6 Marcin Gortat .60 1.50
7 Roy Hibbert .60 1.50
8 Blake Griffin .75 2.00
9 Tim Duncan 1.25 3.00
10 Andre Drummond .75 2.00

2013-14 Panini Prizm Post Season Prizms
*PRIZM: .75X TO 2X BASIC

2013-14 Panini Prizm Post Season Prizms Light Blue Die Cut
*LT BLUE: 1.5X TO 4X BASIC
STATED PRINT RUN 199 SER.#'d SETS
6 Marcin Gortat 5.00 12.00

2013-14 Panini Prizm Post Season Prizms Orange
*ORANGE: 2X TO 5X BASIC
STATED PRINT RUN 60 SER.#'d SETS
6 Marcin Gortat 6.00 15.00

2013-14 Panini Prizm Post Season Prizms Purple Die Cut
*PURPLE: 2.5X TO 6X BASIC
STATED PRINT RUN 49 SER.#'d SETS
6 Marcin Gortat 20.00 50.00

2014-15 Panini Prizm
COMPLETE SET (300) 30.00 80.00
1 Damian Lillard .75 2.00
2 Randy Foye .25 .60
3 Enes Kanter .25 .60
4 Terrence Ross .30 .75
5 Jamal Crawford .40 1.00
6 Jordan Hill .25 .60
7 Al Horford .30 .75
8 Kyle Lowry .30 .75
9 Blake Griffin .40 1.00
10 Nene .30 .75
11 Danilo Gallinari .25 .60
12 Mario Chalmers .30 .75
13 Eric Bledsoe .30 .75
14 Thaddeus Young .25 .60
15 Jameer Nelson .25 .60
16 Jose Calderon .25 .60
17 Al Jefferson .30 .75
18 Kyrie Irving .75 2.00
19 Bradley Beal .40 1.00
20 Nerlens Noel .30 .75
21 David West .30 .75
22 Ricky Rubio .40 1.00
23 Eric Gordon .30 .75
24 Tiago Splitter .30 .75
25 James Harden .60 1.50
26 Josh Smith .30 .75
27 Alex Len .25 .60
28 LaMarcus Aldridge .40 1.00
29 Brandon Bass .25 .60
30 Nick Collison .30 .75
31 David Lee .25 .60
32 Roy Hibbert .30 .75
33 Ersan Ilyasova .25 .60
34 Tim Duncan .60 1.50
35 Jared Sullinger .25 .60
36 Jrue Holiday .30 .75
37 Amar'e Stoudemire .40 1.00
38 Lance Stephenson .30 .75
39 Brandon Jennings .25 .60
40 Nick Young .30 .75
41 DeAndre Jordan .40 1.00
42 Rudy Gay .40 1.00
43 George Hill .30 .75
44 Tim Hardaway Jr. .25 .60
45 Jason Terry .30 .75
46 Kawhi Leonard .60 1.50
47 Amir Johnson .25 .60
48 LeBron James 1.50 4.00
49 Brandon Knight .30 .75
50 Nicolas Batum .30 .75
51 DeMar DeRozan .40 1.00
52 Russell Westbrook 1.00 2.50
53 Gerald Green .30 .75
54 Tobias Harris .30 .75
55 JaVale McGee .30 .75
56 Kemba Walker .40 1.00
57 Anderson Varejao .25 .60
58 Brook Lopez .30 .75
59 Luol Deng .30 .75
60 Nikola Vucevic .30 .75
61 DeMarcus Cousins .40 1.00
62 Ryan Anderson .25 .60
63 Gerald Henderson .25 .60
64 Tony Parker .40 1.00
65 Jeff Green .30 .75
66 Kenneth Faried .30 .75
67 Andre Drummond .40 1.00
68 Manu Ginobili .40 1.00
69 C.J. McCollum .40 1.00
70 Nikola Pekovic .25 .60
71 Dennis Schroder .30 .75
72 Serge Ibaka .30 .75
73 Giannis Antetokounmpo .75 2.00
74 Trey Burke .25 .60
75 Jeff Teague .30 .75
76 Kentavious Caldwell-Pope .25 .60
77 Andre Iguodala .30 .75
78 Marc Gasol .40 1.00
79 Carlos Boozer .30 .75
80 Norris Cole .25 .60
81 Deron Williams .30 .75
82 Shawn Marion .30 .75
83 Goran Dragic .30 .75
84 Tristan Thompson .30 .75
85 Jeremy Lin .40 1.00
86 Kevin Durant 1.00 2.50
87 Andrew Bogut .30 .75
88 Marcin Gortat .30 .75
89 Carmelo Anthony .50 1.25
90 O.J. Mayo .25 .60
91 Derrick Favors .30 .75
92 Stephen Curry 1.50 4.00
93 Gordon Hayward .40 1.00
94 Ty Lawson .25 .60
95 Jimmy Butler .40 1.00
96 Kevin Garnett .60 1.50
97 Anthony Bennett .25 .60
98 Marco Belinelli .25 .60
99 Chandler Parsons .30 .75
100 Otto Porter .30 .75
101 Derrick Rose .50 1.25
102 Steve Nash .40 1.00
103 Greg Monroe .30 .75
104 Tyreke Evans .25 .60
105 Joakim Noah .30 .75
106 Kevin Love .40 1.00
107 Anthony Davis .75 2.00
108 Matt Barnes .25 .60
109 Channing Frye .30 .75
110 Pau Gasol .40 1.00
111 Dion Waiters .30 .75
112 Steven Adams .30 .75
113 Harrison Barnes .30 .75
114 Tyson Chandler .30 .75
115 Jodie Meeks .30 .75
116 Kevin Martin .30 .75
117 Archie Goodwin .25 .60
118 Michael Carter-Williams .25 .60
119 Chris Bosh .40 1.00
120 Paul George .50 1.25
121 Dirk Nowitzki .50 1.25
122 Zach Randolph .30 .75
123 Isaiah Thomas .40 1.00
124 Victor Oladipo .30 .75
125 Joe Johnson .30 .75
126 Klay Thompson .50 1.25
127 Arron Afflalo .25 .60
128 Mike Conley .30 .75
129 Chris Paul .50 1.25
130 Paul Millsap .40 1.00
131 Dwight Howard .30 .75
132 Taj Gibson .30 .75
133 J.J. Redick .40 1.00
134 Vince Carter .50 1.25
135 John Wall .50 1.25
136 Kobe Bryant 1.50 4.00
137 Avery Bradley .30 .75
138 Monta Ellis .30 .75
139 Cody Zeller .25 .60
140 Paul Pierce .40 1.00
141 Dwyane Wade .60 1.50
142 Tayshaun Prince .30 .75
143 J.R. Smith .30 .75
144 Wesley Matthews .25 .60
145 Jonas Valanciunas .30 .75
146 Kyle Korver .30 .75
147 Ben McLemore .25 .60
148 Michael Kidd-Gilchrist .30 .75
149 Corey Brewer .25 .60
150 Rajon Rondo .40 1.00
151 Adrian Dantley .30 .75
152 Swen Nater .25 .60
153 Hakeem Olajuwon .50 1.25
154 John Stockton .60 1.50
155 Latrell Sprewell .30 .75
156 Avery Johnson .30 .75
157 Sam Jones .40 1.00
158 George Mikan .75 2.00
159 Rick Barry .30 .75
160 Dikembe Mutombo .40 1.00
161 Tim Hardaway .40 1.00
162 Isiah Thomas .40 1.00
163 Julius Erving .60 1.50
164 Alex English .30 .75
165 Louie Dampier .40 1.00
166 Baron Davis .30 .75
167 Moses Malone .40 1.00
168 Clifford Robinson .25 .60
169 Robert Horry .30 .75
170 Dominique Wilkins .50 1.25
171 Tom Chambers .30 .75
172 James Worthy .50 1.25
173 Kareem Abdul-Jabbar .60 1.50
174 Allan Houston .30 .75
175 Magic Johnson 1.00 2.50
176 Bernard King .30 .75
177 Mychal Thompson .25 .60
178 Clyde Drexler .50 1.25
179 Robert Parish .40 1.00
180 Drazen Petrovic .40 1.00
181 Toni Kukoc .40 1.00
182 Jason Kidd .40 1.00
183 Karl Malone .50 1.25
184 Allen Iverson .50 1.25
185 Mahmoud Abdul-Rauf .25 .60
186 Bill Laimbeer .30 .75
187 Oscar Robertson .50 1.25
188 Rudy Tomjanovich .30 .75
189 Eddie Jones .30 .75
190 Tracy McGrady .40 1.00
191 Jeff Hornacek .30 .75
192 Kenny Smith .30 .75
193 Alonzo Mourning .50 1.25
194 Mark Aguirre .30 .75
195 Bill Russell .60 1.50
196 Patrick Ewing .50 1.25
197 Damon Stoudamire .30 .75
198 Elgin Baylor .40 1.00
199 Sam Perkins .25 .60
200 Vlade Divac .40 1.00
201 Jerry Sloan .40 1.00
202 Kevin McHale .40 1.00
203 Anfernee Hardaway 1.00 2.50
204 Mark Jackson .30 .75
205 Bill Walton .40 1.00
206 Paul Silas .40 1.00
207 Danny Manning .30 .75
208 Sarunas Marciulionis .25 .60
209 Gary Payton .40 1.00
210 Walt Frazier .40 1.00
211 Jerry West .50 1.25
212 Kevin Willis .25 .60
213 Antoine Walker .30 .75
214 Mark Price .40 1.00
215 Bob Cousy .60 1.50
216 Peja Stojakovic .40 1.00
217 Dave Cowens .25 .60
218 Scottie Pippen .75 2.00
219 George Gervin .40 1.00
220 Wilt Chamberlain .75 2.00
221 Joe Dumars .40 1.00
222 Kurt Rambis .25 .60
223 Artis Gilmore .30 .75
224 Maurice Cheeks .25 .60
225 Bob Love .40 1.00
226 Pete Maravich .60 1.50
227 David Robinson .60 1.50
228 Shaquille O'Neal .75 2.00
229 Gheorghe Muresan .25 .60
230 John Havlicek .50 1.25
231 Xavier McDaniel .25 .60
232 Larry Bird 1.00 2.50
233 Michael Cooper .30 .75
234 Arvydas Sabonis .30 .75
235 Byron Scott .30 .75
236 Phil Jackson .50 1.25
237 Dennis Rodman .75 2.00
238 Shawn Kemp .60 1.50
239 Glen Rice .30 .75
240 Yao Ming .50 1.25
241 John Starks .30 .75
242 Larry Johnson .50 1.25
243 Michael Finley .40 1.00
244 Chris Mullin .40 1.00
245 Ralph Sampson .30 .75
246 Detlef Schrempf .40 1.00
247 Spud Webb .30 .75
248 Grant Hill .50 1.25
249 Craig Ehlo .25 .60
250 Austin Carr .40 1.00
251 Andrew Wiggins RC 4.00 10.00
252 Jabari Parker RC 1.00 2.50
253 Joel Embiid RC 5.00 12.00
254 Aaron Gordon RC 1.00 2.50
255 Dante Exum RC .60 1.50
256 Marcus Smart RC .60 1.50
257 Julius Randle RC 1.00 2.50
258 Nik Stauskas RC .50 1.25
259 Noah Vonleh RC .50 1.25
260 Elfrid Payton RC .60 1.50
261 Doug McDermott RC .60 1.50
262 Zach LaVine RC 1.00 2.50
263 T.J. Warren RC .60 1.50
264 Adreian Payne RC .50 1.25
265 James Young RC .40 1.00
266 Tyler Ennis RC .40 1.00
267 Gary Harris RC .60 1.50
268 Mitch McGary RC .40 1.00
269 Jordan Adams RC .40 1.00
270 Rodney Hood RC .60 1.50
271 Shabazz Napier RC .50 1.25
272 P.J. Hairston RC .40 1.00
273 C.J. Wilcox RC .40 1.00
274 James Ennis RC .40 1.00
275 Kyle Anderson RC .60 1.50
276 Joe Harris RC .40 1.00
277 Cleanthony Early RC .40 1.00
278 Jarnell Stokes RC .40 1.00
279 Johnny O'Bryant RC .40 1.00
280 Jusuf Nurkic RC .60 1.50
281 Spencer Dinwiddie RC .50 1.25
282 Jerami Grant RC .40 1.00
283 Glenn Robinson III RC .40 1.00
284 Nick Johnson RC .40 1.00
285 Markel Brown RC .40 1.00
286 Dwight Powell RC .40 1.00
287 Jordan Clarkson RC .60 1.50
288 Russ Smith RC .40 1.00
289 Erick Green RC .40 1.00
290 Patric Young RC .40 1.00
291 Will Cherry RC .40 1.00
292 Devyn Marble RC .40 1.00
293 Bojan Bogdanovic RC .50 1.25
294 Damjan Rudez RC .40 1.00
295 Cory Jefferson RC .40 1.00
296 James Michael McAdoo RC .50 1.25
297 Cameron Bairstow RC .40 1.00
298 Bruno Caboclo RC .50 1.25
299 Damien Inglis RC .40 1.00
300 Nikola Mirotic RC .75 2.00

2014-15 Panini Prizm Prizms
*PRIZM VET: 1.2X TO 3X BASIC
*PRIZM RC: .75X TO 2X BASIC
RANDOM INSERTS IN PACKS
92 Stephen Curry 6.00 15.00
251 Andrew Wiggins 125.00 300.00
252 Jabari Parker 30.00 80.00
253 Joel Embiid 125.00 300.00
254 Aaron Gordon 12.00 30.00
256 Marcus Smart 8.00 20.00
262 Zach LaVine 50.00 120.00
267 Gary Harris 12.00 30.00
270 Rodney Hood 12.00 30.00
280 Jusuf Nurkic 15.00 40.00

2014-15 Panini Prizm Prizms Blue
*PRIZM BLUE VET: 2.5X TO 6X BASIC
*PRIZM BLUE RC: 1.5X TO 4X BASIC
RANDOM INSERTS IN PACKS
STATED PRINT RUN 99 SER.#'d SETS
251 Andrew Wiggins 60.00 150.00
252 Jabari Parker 25.00 60.00
253 Joel Embiid 60.00 150.00
280 Jusuf Nurkic 10.00 25.00

2014-15 Panini Prizm Prizms Blue and Green Mosaic
*PRIZM BGM VET: 1.2X TO 3X BASIC
*PRIZM BGM RC: .75X TO 2X BASIC
RANDOM INSERTS IN PACKS
251 Andrew Wiggins 15.00 40.00
252 Jabari Parker 12.00 30.00
253 Joel Embiid 15.00 40.00
262 Zach LaVine 6.00 15.00

2014-15 Panini Prizm Prizms Blue Mojo
*BLUE MOJO VET: 2.5X TO 6X BASIC
*BLUE MOJO RC: 1.5X TO 4X BASIC
RANDOM INSERTS IN PACKS
48 LeBron James 25.00 60.00
251 Andrew Wiggins 60.00 150.00
280 Jusuf Nurkic 10.00 25.00

2014-15 Panini Prizm Prizms Blue Wave
*BLUE WAVE VET: 2.5X TO 6X BASIC
*BLUE WAVE RC: 1.5X TO 4X BASIC
RANDOM INSERTS IN PACKS
251 Andrew Wiggins 60.00 150.00
252 Jabari Parker 25.00 60.00
253 Joel Embiid 60.00 150.00
280 Jusuf Nurkic 10.00 25.00

2014-15 Panini Prizm Prizms Green
*GREEN VET: 1X TO 2.5X BASIC
*GREEN RC: .6X TO 1.5X BASIC
RANDOM INSERTS IN PACKS
48 LeBron James 8.00 20.00
251 Andrew Wiggins 20.00 50.00
252 Jabari Parker 10.00 25.00
253 Joel Embiid 20.00 50.00
256 Marcus Smart 5.00 12.00
262 Zach LaVine 12.00 30.00

2014-15 Panini Prizm Prizms Light Blue
*LGHT BLUE VET: 3X TO 8X BASIC
*LGHT BLUE RC: 2X TO 5X BASIC
RANDOM INSERTS IN PACKS
STATED PRINT RUN 49 SER.#'d SETS
251 Andrew Wiggins 100.00 250.00
252 Jabari Parker 30.00 80.00
253 Joel Embiid 100.00 250.00
280 Jusuf Nurkic 12.00 30.00

2014-15 Panini Prizm Prizms Orange Die Cut
*PRIZM ORNG VET: 2.5X TO 6X BASIC
*PRIZM ORNG RC: 1.5X TO 4X BASIC
STATED PRINT RUN 139 SER.#'d SETS
251 Andrew Wiggins 20.00 50.00
252 Jabari Parker 8.00 20.00
253 Joel Embiid 25.00 60.00
262 Zach LaVine 8.00 20.00
280 Jusuf Nurkic 8.00 20.00

2014-15 Panini Prizm Prizms Purple Die Cut
*PRIZM PRPLE VET: 2.5X TO 6X BASIC
*PRIZM PRPLE RC: 1.5X TO 4X BASIC
STATED PRINT RUN 139 SER.#'d SETS
251 Andrew Wiggins 20.00 50.00
252 Jabari Parker 8.00 20.00
253 Joel Embiid 25.00 60.00
280 Jusuf Nurkic 8.00 20.00

2014-15 Panini Prizm Prizms Red
*PRIZMS RED VET: 4X TO 10X BASIC
*PRIZMS RED RC: 2.5X TO 6X BASIC
STATED PRINT RUN 49 SER.#'d SETS
251 Andrew Wiggins 100.00 250.00
252 Jabari Parker 30.00 80.00
253 Joel Embiid 100.00 250.00
280 Jusuf Nurkic 15.00 40.00

2014-15 Panini Prizm Prizms Red Pulsar
*PRIZMS RED VET: 5X TO 12X BASIC
*PRIZMS RED RC: 3X TO 8X BASIC
RANDOM INSERTS IN PACKS
STATED PRINT RUN 25 SER.#'d SETS
48 LeBron James 40.00 100.00
136 Kobe Bryant 75.00 150.00
251 Andrew Wiggins 125.00 300.00
252 Jabari Parker 40.00 100.00
253 Joel Embiid 125.00 300.00
261 Doug McDermott 20.00 50.00
280 Jusuf Nurkic 20.00 50.00

2014-15 Panini Prizm Prizms Red White and Blue Pulsar
*RWB PLUSAR VET: 1.5X TO 4X BASIC
*RWB PULSAR RC: 1X TO 2.5X BASIC
RANDOM INSERTS IN PACKS
251 Andrew Wiggins 12.00 30.00
252 Jabari Parker 5.00 12.00
253 Joel Embiid 12.00 30.00

2014-15 Panini Prizm Prizms Yellow and Red Mosaic
*YELLOW RED VET: 1.5X TO 4X BASIC
*YELLOW RED RC: 1X TO 2.5X BASIC
RANDOM INSERTS IN PACKS
251 Andrew Wiggins 12.00 30.00
252 Jabari Parker 5.00 12.00
253 Joel Embiid 12.00 30.00
262 Zach LaVine 6.00 15.00

2014-15 Panini Prizm Autographs Green
1 Nerlens Noel 4.00 10.00
2 Brandan Wright 3.00 8.00
3 Trey Burke 3.00 8.00
4 Gorgui Dieng 3.00 8.00
5 Kobe Bryant 75.00 150.00
6 John Thompson 5.00 12.00
7 Kevin McHale 8.00 20.00
8 Bill Walton 6.00 15.00
9 Victor Oladipo 4.00 10.00
10 David Thompson 4.00 10.00
11 Joe Johnson 4.00 10.00
12 Bill Willoughby 3.00 8.00
13 Brent Barry 3.00 8.00
14 Tim Hardaway Jr. 3.00 8.00
15 Kevin Durant 75.00 150.00
16 Tony Allen 3.00 8.00
17 Hakeem Olajuwon 12.00 30.00
18 Glen Rice 4.00 10.00
19 Cody Zeller 3.00 8.00
20 Steven Adams 4.00 10.00
21 Kentavious Caldwell-Pope 3.00 8.00
22 Greg Oden
23 James Harden 25.00 60.00
24 Jae Crowder 3.00 8.00
25 Dwyane Wade 20.00 50.00
26 Kelly Tripucka 3.00 8.00
27 Jason Kidd 10.00 25.00
28 JaVale McGee 4.00 10.00
29 Otto Porter 6.00 15.00
30 Phil Chenier 3.00 8.00
31 Michael Finley 5.00 12.00
32 Kenny Anderson 4.00 10.00
33 Shabazz Muhammad 6.00 15.00
34 Miroslav Raduljica
35 Karl Malone 20.00 50.00
36 Nate Archibald 4.00 10.00
37 Kevin Love 20.00 50.00
38 Ralph Sampson 10.00 25.00
39 Alex Len 3.00 8.00
40 Brook Lopez 4.00 10.00
41 Nate Thurmond 4.00 10.00
42 Otis Birdsong 4.00 10.00
43 Jason Terry 4.00 10.00
44 Carrick Felix 3.00 8.00
45 Kyrie Irving 25.00 60.00
46 Steve Kerr 6.00 15.00
47 Anthony Bennett 3.00 8.00
48 Kevin Willis 3.00 8.00
49 Derrick Williams 3.00 8.00
50 Jim Jackson 3.00 8.00
51 Monta Ellis 8.00 20.00
52 Michael Cooper 4.00 10.00
53 Gail Goodrich 4.00 10.00
54 Matthew Dellavedova 4.00 10.00
55 John Havlicek 15.00 40.00
56 Jared Sullinger 3.00 8.00
57 Gary Payton 8.00 20.00
58 Kurt Rambis 3.00 8.00
59 Stephen Curry 75.00 200.00
60 Ron Harper 5.00 12.00
61 C.J. McCollum 5.00 12.00
62 Dennis Schroder 4.00 10.00
63 Elvin Hayes 5.00 12.00
64 Phil Pressey 6.00 15.00
65 John Wall 20.00 50.00
66 Peja Stojakovic 5.00 12.00
67 Dominique Wilkins 12.00 30.00
68 Reggie Jackson 3.00 8.00
69 Ben McLemore 3.00 8.00
70 Pearl Washington 3.00 8.00
71 Michael Carter-Williams 3.00 8.00
72 Vitor Faverani 3.00 8.00
73 Jerry Lucas 5.00 12.00
74 Troy Daniels 3.00 8.00
75 Earl Monroe 6.00 15.00
76 Jabari Parker 25.00 60.00
77 Andrew Wiggins 75.00 150.00

78 Julius Randle 15.00 40.00
79 Joel Embiid 60.00 150.00
80 Marcus Smart 12.00 30.00
81 Dante Exum 5.00 12.00
82 Aaron Gordon 8.00 20.00
83 Noah Vonleh 4.00 10.00
84 Gary Harris 5.00 12.00
85 Tyler Ennis 3.00 8.00
86 Nik Stauskas 4.00 10.00
87 Doug McDermott 5.00 12.00
88 Bruno Caboclo 4.00 10.00
89 James Young 3.00 8.00
90 Zach LaVine 10.00 25.00
91 Spencer Dinwiddie 4.00 10.00
92 Mitch McGary 3.00 8.00
93 Rodney Hood 5.00 12.00
94 Cleanthony Early 3.00 8.00
95 Shabazz Napier 4.00 10.00
96 Kyle Anderson 5.00 12.00
97 Adreian Payne 4.00 10.00
98 Elfrid Payton 5.00 12.00
99 T.J. Warren 5.00 12.00
100 C.J. Wilcox 3.00 8.00

2014-15 Panini Prizm Autographs Prizms Blue Pulsar

*BLUE PULSAR: .5X TO 1.2X GREEN
PRINT RUNS B/WN 49-249 COPIES PER
22 Udonis Haslem/149 3.00 8.00
34 Ray McCallum/249 3.00 8.00

2014-15 Panini Prizm Autographs Prizms Purple Pulsar

*PURPLE PULSAR: .5X TO 1.2X BASE HI
PRINT RUNS B/WN 15-49 COPIES PER
NO PRICING ON QTY 15 OR LESS
22 Udonis Haslem/49 4.00 10.00

2014-15 Panini Prizm Autographs Prizms Red Pulsar

*RED p/r 49-149: .5X TO 1.2X GREEN
*RED p/r 25-35: .6X TO 1.5X GREEN
PRINT RUNS B/WN 25-149 COPIES PER
22 Udonis Haslem/99 4.00 10.00

2014-15 Panini Prizm Fireworks

RANDOM INSERTS IN PACKS
1 Blake Griffin 1.25 3.00
2 Kobe Bryant 5.00 12.00
3 Damian Lillard 2.50 6.00
4 LeBron James 5.00 12.00
5 Dirk Nowitzki 1.50 4.00
6 Tony Parker 1.25 3.00
7 James Harden 2.00 5.00
8 Kevin Durant 3.00 8.00
9 Anthony Davis 2.50 6.00
10 Kevin Love 1.25 3.00
11 Chris Paul 1.50 4.00
12 Kyrie Irving 2.50 6.00
13 Derrick Rose 1.50 4.00
14 Russell Westbrook 3.00 8.00
15 Dwyane Wade 2.00 5.00

2014-15 Panini Prizm Freshman Phenoms

COMPLETE SET (10) 10.00 25.00
RANDOM INSERTS IN PACKS
1 Andrew Wiggins 3.00 8.00
2 Jabari Parker 1.50 4.00
3 Joel Embiid 3.00 8.00
4 Aaron Gordon 1.50 4.00
5 Dante Exum 1.00 2.50
6 Marcus Smart 1.00 2.50
7 Julius Randle 1.50 4.00
8 Elfrid Payton 1.00 2.50
9 Doug McDermott 1.00 2.50
10 Shabazz Napier .75 2.00

2014-15 Panini Prizm Jerseys Prizms Blue Mojo

RANDOM INSERTS IN PACKS
1 Blake Griffin 4.00 10.00
2 Matt Barnes 2.50 6.00
3 David Lee 2.50 6.00
4 Raymond Felton 3.00 8.00
5 Rashard Lewis 3.00 8.00
6 Udonis Haslem 2.50 6.00
7 James Jones 2.50 6.00
8 Jeremy Lamb 2.50 6.00
9 Al Horford 3.00 8.00
10 Kendrick Perkins 2.50 6.00
11 Boris Diaw 3.00 8.00
12 Zach Randolph 3.00 8.00
13 David Robinson 6.00 15.00
14 Reggie Jackson 2.50 6.00
15 Gary Payton 4.00 10.00
16 Kevin Durant 10.00 25.00
17 Jared Sullinger 2.50 6.00
18 Jimmy Butler 4.00 10.00
19 Amar'e Stoudemire 4.00 10.00
20 Kevin Garnett 6.00 15.00
21 Carlos Boozer 3.00 8.00
22 Mirza Teletovic 2.50 6.00
23 DeAndre Jordan 4.00 10.00
24 Scottie Pippen 6.00 15.00
25 Grant Hill 5.00 12.00
26 Kyrie Irving 8.00 20.00
27 Jason Kidd 4.00 10.00
28 Jodie Meeks 3.00 8.00
29 Carmelo Anthony 5.00 12.00
30 Kevin Love 4.00 10.00
31 Chandler Parsons 3.00 8.00
32 Norris Cole 2.50 6.00
33 DeMar DeRozan 4.00 10.00
34 Shaquille O'Neal 8.00 20.00
35 Greg Monroe 3.00 8.00
36 Chris Kaman 3.00 8.00
37 Jason Terry 3.00 8.00
38 Joe Johnson 3.00 8.00
39 Andre Iguodala 3.00 8.00
40 Kirk Hinrich 3.00 8.00
41 Chris Bosh 4.00 10.00
42 Patrick Ewing 5.00 12.00
43 Deron Williams 3.00 8.00
44 Taj Gibson 3.00 8.00
45 Harrison Barnes 3.00 8.00
46 Patty Mills 4.00 10.00
47 JaVale McGee 3.00 8.00
48 Jordan Hill 2.50 6.00
49 Andrea Bargnani 3.00 8.00
50 Kobe Bryant 15.00 40.00
51 Clyde Drexler 5.00 12.00
52 Pau Gasol 4.00 10.00
53 Dikembe Mutombo 4.00 10.00
54 Thabo Sefolosha 2.50 6.00
55 J.R. Smith 3.00 8.00
56 Evan Fournier 2.50 6.00
57 Luol Deng 3.00 8.00
58 Kawhi Leonard 6.00 15.00
59 Andrew Bogut 3.00 8.00
60 Marco Belinelli 2.50 6.00
61 Darren Collison 3.00 8.00
62 Paul Pierce 4.00 10.00
63 Dirk Nowitzki 5.00 12.00
64 Tyson Chandler 3.00 8.00
65 Jamal Crawford 4.00 10.00
66 Andrew Wiggins 20.00 50.00
67 Jabari Parker 6.00 15.00
68 Joel Embiid 10.00 25.00
69 Aaron Gordon 4.00 10.00
70 Dante Exum 12.00 30.00
71 Marcus Smart 4.00 10.00
72 Julius Randle 5.00 12.00
73 Nik Stauskas 3.00 8.00
74 Noah Vonleh 3.00 8.00
75 Elfrid Payton 4.00 10.00
76 Doug McDermott 6.00 15.00
77 Zach LaVine 5.00 12.00
78 T.J. Warren 3.00 8.00
79 Adreian Payne 3.00 8.00
80 James Young 3.00 8.00
81 Tyler Ennis 3.00 8.00
82 Gary Harris 3.00 8.00
83 Bruno Caboclo 3.00 8.00
84 Mitch McGary 3.00 8.00
85 Jordan Adams 2.50 6.00
86 Rodney Hood 4.00 10.00
87 Shabazz Napier 4.00 10.00
88 P.J. Hairston 2.50 6.00
89 C.J. Wilcox 2.50 6.00
90 Cory Jefferson 2.50 6.00
91 Kyle Anderson 3.00 8.00
92 K.J. McDaniels 3.00 8.00
93 Joe Harris 3.00 8.00
94 Cleanthony Early 2.50 6.00
95 Jarnell Stokes 2.50 6.00
96 James Ennis 2.50 6.00
97 Spencer Dinwiddie 3.00 8.00
98 Glenn Robinson III 3.00 8.00
99 Russ Smith 2.50 6.00
100 Markel Brown 2.50 6.00

2014-15 Panini Prizm Photo Variations

RANDOM INSERTS IN PACKS
*GREEN/25: 2.5X TO 6X BASIC
1 Dirk Nowitzki 1.25 3.00
2 Russell Westbrook 2.50 6.00
3 Dwyane Wade 1.50 4.00
4 Tim Duncan 1.50 4.00
5 Anthony Davis 2.00 5.00
6 Kevin Durant 2.50 6.00
7 Carmelo Anthony 1.25 3.00
8 Kobe Bryant 4.00 10.00
9 Damian Lillard 2.00 5.00
10 LeBron James 4.00 10.00
11 Dwight Howard .75 2.00
12 Stephen Curry 4.00 10.00
13 James Harden 1.50 4.00
14 Tony Parker 1.00 2.50
15 Blake Griffin 1.00 2.50
16 Kevin Love 1.00 2.50
17 Chris Paul 1.25 3.00
18 Kyrie Irving 2.00 5.00
19 Derrick Rose 1.25 3.00
20 Paul George 1.25 3.00
21 Wilt Chamberlain 2.00 5.00
22 Karl Malone 1.25 3.00
23 Bill Russell 1.50 4.00
24 Kareem Abdul-Jabbar 1.50 4.00
25 Larry Bird 2.50 6.00
26 Magic Johnson 2.50 6.00
27 Scottie Pippen 2.00 5.00
28 David Robinson 1.50 4.00
29 Julius Erving 1.50 4.00
30 Pete Maravich 1.50 4.00
31 Andrew Wiggins 3.00 8.00
32 Jabari Parker 1.50 4.00
33 Joel Embiid 3.00 8.00
34 Aaron Gordon 1.50 4.00
35 Dante Exum 1.00 2.50
36 Marcus Smart 1.00 2.50
37 Julius Randle 1.50 4.00
38 Nik Stauskas .75 2.00
39 Noah Vonleh .75 2.00
40 Elfrid Payton 1.00 2.50
41 Doug McDermott 1.00 2.50
42 Zach LaVine 1.50 4.00
43 T.J. Warren 1.00 2.50
44 Adreian Payne .75 2.00
45 James Young .60 1.50
46 Tyler Ennis .60 1.50
47 Gary Harris 1.00 2.50
48 Bruno Caboclo .75 2.00
49 Mitch McGary .60 1.50
50 Shabazz Napier .75 2.00

2014-15 Panini Prizm Representatives

COMPLETE SET (20) 20.00 50.00
RANDOM INSERTS IN PACKS
*GREEN MOJO: 5X TO 12X BASE HI
1 Kevin Durant 2.50 6.00
2 Kevin Love 1.00 2.50
3 Tony Parker 1.00 2.50
4 Anthony Davis 2.00 5.00
5 Andrei Kirilenko .75 2.00
6 Chris Paul 1.25 3.00
7 Ricky Rubio 1.00 2.50
8 Russell Westbrook 2.50 6.00
9 LeBron James 4.00 10.00
10 Kobe Bryant 4.00 10.00
11 Dwyane Wade 1.50 4.00
12 Carmelo Anthony 1.25 3.00
13 Manu Ginobili 1.00 2.50
14 James Harden 1.50 4.00
15 Marc Gasol 1.00 2.50
16 Magic Johnson 2.50 6.00
17 Larry Bird 2.50 6.00
18 Scottie Pippen 2.00 5.00
19 Patrick Ewing 1.25 3.00
20 Karl Malone 1.25 3.00

2014-15 Panini Prizm Rookie Autographs Prizms

RANDOM INSERTS IN PACKS
PRINT RUNS B/WN 249-499 COPIES PER
*RED/199: .4X TO 1X BASIC
*PURPLE/99: .5X TO 1.2X BASIC
1 Jabari Parker/249 25.00 60.00
2 Andrew Wiggins/249 100.00 150.00
3 Joel Embiid/249 40.00 100.00
4 Marcus Smart/299 5.00 12.00
5 Julius Randle/299 15.00 40.00
6 Dante Exum/299 5.00 12.00
7 Aaron Gordon/349 8.00 20.00
8 Noah Vonleh/349 4.00 10.00
9 Tyler Ennis/349 3.00 8.00
10 Nik Stauskas/349 4.00 10.00
11 Elfrid Payton/399 5.00 12.00
12 T.J. Warren/399 5.00 12.00
13 Doug McDermott/449 5.00 12.00
14 James Young/449 3.00 8.00
15 Gary Harris/449 5.00 12.00
16 Zach LaVine/449 15.00 40.00
17 Glenn Robinson III/449 3.00 8.00
18 Adreian Payne/449 4.00 10.00
19 C.J. Wilcox/449 3.00 8.00
20 Mitch McGary/449 3.00 8.00
21 Shabazz Napier/449 4.00 10.00
22 Jordan Adams/449 3.00 8.00
23 Devyn Marble/499 3.00 8.00
24 Spencer Dinwiddie/449 4.00 10.00
25 Bruno Caboclo/499 4.00 10.00
26 Kyle Anderson/499 5.00 12.00
27 Rodney Hood/499 5.00 12.00
28 P.J. Hairston/499 3.00 8.00
29 Cleanthony Early/499 3.00 8.00
30 Jerami Grant/499 3.00 8.00
31 James Ennis/499 3.00 8.00
32 Jordan Clarkson/499 5.00 12.00
33 Johnny O'Bryant/499 3.00 8.00
34 K.J. McDaniels/499 4.00 10.00
35 Dwight Powell/499 3.00 8.00
36 Markel Brown/499 3.00 8.00
37 Cory Jefferson/499 3.00 8.00
38 Joe Harris/499 3.00 8.00
39 Russ Smith/499 3.00 8.00
40 Lucas Nogueira/499 3.00 8.00

2014-15 Panini Prizm Superstars

COMPLETE SET (5) 10.00 25.00
RANDOM INSERTS IN PACKS
1 LeBron James 2.50 6.00
2 Kobe Bryant 2.50 6.00
3 Kevin Durant 1.50 4.00
4 Kyrie Irving 1.25 3.00
5 Anthony Davis 1.25 3.00

2015-16 Panini Prizm

1 DeMarcus Cousins .40 1.00
2 Marvin Williams .30 .75
3 John Wall .50 1.25
4 Vince Carter .50 1.25
5 Donatas Motiejunas .25 .60
6 Kevin Garnett .60 1.50
7 Aron Baynes .25 .60
8 Tim Hardaway Jr. .25 .60
9 Nik Stauskas .25 .60
10 Michael Kidd-Gilchrist .30 .75
11 Darren Collison .30 .75
12 Al Jefferson .30 .75
13 Marcin Gortat .30 .75
14 Mike Conley .40 1.00
15 Patrick Beverley .25 .60
16 Shabazz Muhammad .30 .75
17 Jae Crowder .25 .60
18 Tiago Splitter .30 .75
19 Jason Thompson .25 .60
20 Jeremy Lin .40 1.00
21 Omri Casspi .25 .60
22 Jordan Hill .25 .60
23 Bradley Beal .40 1.00
24 Zach Randolph .30 .75
25 Josh Smith .30 .75
26 Arron Afflalo .25 .60
27 Cody Zeller .25 .60
28 Al Horford .30 .75
29 Tony Wroten .25 .60
30 Deron Williams .30 .75
31 David West .40 1.00
32 Chase Budinger .25 .60
33 Nene .30 .75
34 Marc Gasol .40 1.00
35 Jason Terry .30 .75
36 Robin Lopez .25 .60
37 Boris Diaw .30 .75
38 Kyle Korver .30 .75
39 Nerlens Noel .30 .75
40 Wesley Matthews .25 .60
41 LaMarcus Aldridge .40 1.00
42 Solomon Hill .25 .60
43 Rasual Butler .25 .60
44 Courtney Lee .30 .75
45 Tyreke Evans .25 .60
46 Derrick Williams .25 .60
47 John Henson .30 .75
48 Paul Millsap .40 1.00
49 Robert Covington .25 .60
50 Dirk Nowitzki .50 1.25
51 Tim Duncan .60 1.50
52 Rodney Stuckey .30 .75
53 Otto Porter .30 .75
54 Gerald Green .30 .75
55 Anthony Davis .75 2.00
56 Carmelo Anthony .50 1.25
57 Kelly Olynyk .25 .60
58 Jeff Teague .30 .75
59 Wesley Johnson .30 .75
60 Chandler Parsons .30 .75
61 Tony Parker .40 1.00
62 Paul George .50 1.25
63 Kris Humphries .25 .60
64 Dwyane Wade .60 1.50
65 Eric Gordon .30 .75
66 Langston Galloway .25 .60
67 Amare Stoudemire .30 .75
68 Dennis Schroder .30 .75
69 Tyson Chandler .30 .75
70 Devin Harris .25 .60
71 Manu Ginobili .40 1.00
72 C.J. Miles .30 .75
73 Ty Lawson .25 .60
74 Chris Bosh .40 1.00
75 Omer Asik .30 .75
76 Jose Calderon .25 .60
77 Tyler Hansbrough .30 .75
78 David Lee .25 .60
79 Eric Bledsoe .30 .75
80 J.J. Barea .30 .75
81 Kawhi Leonard .60 1.50
82 Lance Stephenson .30 .75
83 Wilson Chandler .30 .75
84 Luol Deng .30 .75
85 Ryan Anderson .30 .75
86 Quincy Acy .25 .60
87 Aaron Brooks .25 .60
88 Amir Johnson .25 .60
89 Brandon Knight .30 .75
90 Zaza Pachulia .25 .60
91 Danny Green .30 .75
92 Paul Pierce .40 1.00
93 Kenneth Faried .30 .75
94 Hassan Whiteside .30 .75
95 Jrue Holiday .30 .75
96 Kevin Durant 1.00 2.50
97 Kosta Koufos .25 .60
98 Avery Bradley .30 .75
99 Markieff Morris .25 .60
100 Ersan Ilyasova .25 .60
101 DeMarre Carroll .25 .60
102 Chris Paul .50 1.25
103 Danilo Gallinari .30 .75
104 Mario Chalmers .30 .75
105 Quincy Pondexter .25 .60
106 Russell Westbrook 1.00 2.50
107 Alexis Ajinca .25 .60
108 Tyler Zeller .30 .75
109 P.J. Tucker .25 .60
110 Marcus Morris .25 .60
111 Luis Scola .30 .75
112 Blake Griffin .40 1.00
113 J.J. Hickson .25 .60
114 Chris Andersen .30 .75
115 Kyrie Irving .75 2.00
116 Serge Ibaka .30 .75
117 Tarik Black .25 .60
118 Evan Turner .30 .75
119 Alex Len .25 .60
120 Kentavious Caldwell-Pope .30 .75
121 Kyle Lowry .30 .75
122 DeAndre Jordan .40 1.00
123 Jusuf Nurkic .25 .60
124 Greg Monroe .30 .75
125 LeBron James 1.50 4.00
126 Dion Waiters .30 .75
127 Lavoy Allen .25 .60
128 Jared Sullinger .25 .60
129 T.J. Warren .30 .75
130 Jodie Meeks .30 .75
131 Patrick Patterson .25 .60
132 J.J. Redick .40 1.00
133 Randy Foye .25 .60
134 Greivis Vasquez .30 .75
135 Kevin Love .40 1.00
136 Andre Roberson .25 .60
137 Leandro Barbosa .25 .60
138 Marcus Smart .30 .75
139 Mason Plumlee .30 .75
140 Andre Drummond .40 1.00
141 DeMar DeRozan .40 1.00
142 Jamal Crawford .40 1.00
143 Pau Gasol .40 1.00
144 Giannis Antetokounmpo .75 2.00
145 Tristan Thompson .30 .75
146 Steven Adams .30 .75
147 Alan Anderson .25 .60
148 Wayne Ellington .25 .60
149 Gerald Henderson .25 .60
150 Brandon Jennings .25 .60
151 Jonas Valanciunas .30 .75
152 Brandon Bass .25 .60
153 Jimmy Butler .40 1.00
154 Khris Middleton .30 .75
155 J.R. Smith .30 .75
156 Anthony Morrow .25 .60
157 Thabo Sefolosha .25 .60
158 Shane Larkin .25 .60
159 Noah Vonleh .25 .60
160 Reggie Jackson .30 .75
161 Terrence Ross .30 .75
162 Roy Hibbert .30 .75
163 Joakim Noah .30 .75
164 Jabari Parker .50 1.25
165 Matthew Dellavedova .30 .75
166 Aaron Gordon .30 .75
167 Jarrett Jack .30 .75
168 Thomas Robinson .25 .60
169 Al-Farouq Aminu .30 .75
170 Stephen Curry 1.50 4.00
171 Gordon Hayward .40 1.00
172 Lou Williams .30 .75
173 Derrick Rose .50 1.25
174 O.J. Mayo .25 .60
175 Timofey Mozgov .25 .60
176 Elfrid Payton .30 .75
177 Hollis Thompson .25 .60
178 Joe Johnson .30 .75
179 Damian Lillard .75 2.00
180 Klay Thompson .50 1.25
181 Trey Burke .25 .60
182 Kobe Bryant 1.50 4.00
183 Mike Dunleavy .25 .60
184 Michael Carter-Williams .25 .60
185 Ed Davis .25 .60
186 Tobias Harris .30 .75
187 Tayshaun Prince .30 .75
188 Brook Lopez .30 .75
189 Chris Kaman .30 .75
190 Draymond Green .50 1.25
191 Derrick Favors .30 .75
192 Julius Randle .40 1.00
193 Taj Gibson .30 .75
194 Andrew Wiggins .60 1.50
195 Cory Joseph .25 .60
196 Nikola Vucevic .30 .75
197 Nick Collison .30 .75
198 Markel Brown .25 .60
199 C.J. McCollum .40 1.00
200 Andre Iguodala .30 .75
201 Dante Exum .30 .75
202 Jordan Clarkson .40 1.00
203 Nikola Mirotic .30 .75
204 Zach LaVine .40 1.00
205 Tony Allen .25 .60
206 Victor Oladipo .30 .75
207 Tony Snell .25 .60
208 Bojan Bogdanovic .25 .60
209 Rajon Rondo .40 1.00
210 Andrew Bogut .30 .75
211 Rudy Gobert .40 1.00
212 Nick Young .30 .75
213 James Harden .60 1.50
214 Gorgui Dieng .25 .60
215 Jared Dudley .25 .60
216 Channing Frye .30 .75
217 Caron Butler .30 .75
218 Spencer Hawes .25 .60
219 Marco Belinelli .25 .60
220 Shaun Livingston .25 .60
221 Trevor Booker .25 .60
222 Matt Barnes .25 .60
223 Dwight Howard .30 .75
224 Ricky Rubio .40 1.00
225 James Johnson .25 .60
226 Evan Fournier .30 .75
227 Jameer Nelson .25 .60
228 Nicolas Batum .30 .75
229 Ben McLemore .25 .60
230 Marreese Speights .25 .60
231 Rodney Hood .30 .75
232 Brandan Wright .25 .60
233 Trevor Ariza .25 .60
234 Kevin Martin .30 .75
235 Bismack Biyombo .25 .60
236 Carl Landry .25 .60
237 Joe Ingles .25 .60
238 Kemba Walker .40 1.00
239 Rudy Gay .40 1.00
240 Monta Ellis .30 .75
241 Patrick Ewing .50 1.25
242 Scottie Pippen .75 2.00
243 Alonzo Mourning .50 1.25
244 Tracy McGrady .40 1.00
245 Dennis Rodman .75 2.00
246 Steve Nash .40 1.00
247 Hakeem Olajuwon .50 1.25
248 Magic Johnson 1.00 2.50
249 Kevin McHale .40 1.00
250 Chauncey Billups .40 1.00
251 Drazen Petrovic .40 1.00
252 Tim Hardaway .40 1.00
253 Anfernee Hardaway 1.00 2.50
254 Latrell Sprewell .30 .75
255 Dikembe Mutombo .40 1.00
256 Robert Horry .30 .75
257 Isiah Thomas .40 1.00
258 Jason Williams .30 .75
259 Karl Malone .50 1.25
260 Moses Malone .40 1.00
261 Larry Bird 1.00 2.50
262 Yao Ming .50 1.25
263 Antonio McDyess .30 .75
264 Robert Parish .40 1.00
265 Mike Bibby .30 .75
266 Dino Radja .25 .60
267 Jason Kidd .40 1.00
268 Sam Bowie .25 .60
269 Steve Francis .30 .75
270 Shawn Kemp .60 1.50
271 Jerry Stackhouse .30 .75
272 Rick Fox .30 .75
273 Chris Mullin .40 1.00
274 Darryl Dawkins .25 .60
275 Dominique Wilkins .50 1.25
276 Michael Finley .40 1.00
277 John Stockton .60 1.50
278 James Worthy .50 1.25
279 Mark Eaton .25 .60
280 Jalen Rose .40 1.00
281 Rony Seikaly .25 .60
282 Richard Hamilton .30 .75
283 Clyde Drexler .50 1.25
284 Shaquille O'Neal .75 2.00
285 Gary Payton .40 1.00
286 Allen Iverson .50 1.25
287 Vlade Divac .40 1.00
288 Julius Erving .60 1.50
289 Shareef Abdur-Rahim .30 .75
290 Rik Smits .30 .75
291 Joe Dumars .40 1.00
292 Clifford Robinson .25 .60
293 David Robinson .60 1.50
294 Mark Jackson .30 .75
295 Grant Hill .50 1.25
296 Michael Redd .30 .75
297 Kareem Abdul-Jabbar .60 1.50
298 Eddie Jones .30 .75
299 Dan Majerle .30 .75
300 Maurice Cheeks .25 .60
301 Jarell Martin RC .60 1.50
302 Larry Nance Jr. RC .75 2.00
303 Justin Anderson RC .60 1.50
304 Anthony Brown RC .50 1.25
305 Joe Young RC .60 1.50
306 Jerian Grant RC .50 1.25
307 Ryan Boatright RC .60 1.50
308 Devin Booker RC 5.00 12.00
309 Kelly Oubre Jr. RC .60 1.50
310 Delon Wright RC .60 1.50
311 R.J. Hunter RC .50 1.25
312 Cameron Payne RC .60 1.50
313 Rakeem Christmas RC .50 1.25
314 Frank Kaminsky RC .75 2.00
315 Dakari Johnson RC .50 1.25
316 Emmanuel Mudiay RC .75 2.00
317 Josh Richardson RC .75 2.00
318 Raul Neto RC .50 1.25
319 Aaron Harrison RC .60 1.50
320 Stanley Johnson RC .60 1.50
321 Chris McCullough RC .50 1.25
322 D'Angelo Russell RC 2.00 5.00
323 Richaun Holmes RC .60 1.50
324 Tyus Jones RC .75 2.00
325 Tyler Harvey RC .50 1.25
326 Bobby Portis RC .75 2.00
327 Terran Petteway RC .50 1.25
328 Karl-Anthony Towns RC 6.00 15.00
329 Jahlil Okafor RC 1.00 2.50
330 Rondae Hollis-Jefferson RC .60 1.50
331 Montrezl Harrell RC .60 1.50
332 Rashad Vaughn RC .50 1.25
333 Pat Connaughton RC .50 1.25
334 Trey Lyles RC .75 2.00
335 Nikola Jokic RC 5.00 12.00
336 Justise Winslow RC .75 2.00
337 Norman Powell RC .60 1.50
338 Terry Rozier RC .60 1.50
339 Sam Dekker RC .60 1.50
340 Myles Turner RC .75 2.00
341 Jordan Mickey RC .50 1.25
342 Mario Hezonja RC .60 1.50
343 Andrew Harrison RC .75 2.00
344 Walter Tavares RC .50 1.25
345 Darrun Hilliard RC .50 1.25
346 Kevon Looney RC .60 1.50
347 Branden Dawson RC .50 1.25
348 Kristaps Porzingis RC 4.00 10.00
349 Willie Cauley-Stein RC 1.25 3.00
350 Nemanja Bjelica RC .60 1.50
351 Carmelo Anthony AS .50 1.25
352 LeBron James AS 1.50 4.00
353 Pau Gasol AS .40 1.00
354 John Wall AS .50 1.25
355 Kyle Lowry AS .30 .75
356 Chris Bosh AS .40 1.00
357 Jimmy Butler AS .40 1.00
358 Al Horford AS .30 .75
359 Kyrie Irving AS .75 2.00
360 Kyle Korver AS .30 .75
361 Paul Millsap AS .40 1.00
362 Jeff Teague AS .30 .75
363 Marc Gasol AS .40 1.00
364 Stephen Curry AS 1.50 4.00
365 LaMarcus Aldridge AS .40 1.00
366 DeMarcus Cousins AS .40 1.00
367 Tim Duncan AS .60 1.50
368 Kevin Durant AS 1.00 2.50
369 James Harden AS .60 1.50
370 Damian Lillard AS .75 2.00
371 Dirk Nowitzki AS .50 1.25
372 Chris Paul AS .50 1.25
373 Klay Thompson AS .50 1.25
374 Russell Westbrook AS 1.00 2.50
375 LeBron James ANBA 1.50 4.00
376 Anthony Davis ANBA .75 2.00
377 Stephen Curry ANBA 1.50 4.00
378 James Harden ANBA .60 1.50
379 Marc Gasol ANBA .40 1.00
380 LaMarcus Aldridge ANBA .40 1.00
381 DeMarcus Cousins ANBA .40 1.00
382 Russell Westbrook ANBA 1.00 2.50
383 Chris Paul ANBA .50 1.25
384 Pau Gasol ANBA .40 1.00
385 Blake Griffin ANBA .40 1.00
386 Tim Duncan ANBA .60 1.50
387 Kyrie Irving ANBA .75 2.00
388 Klay Thompson ANBA .50 1.25
389 DeAndre Jordan ANBA .40 1.00
390 Kawhi Leonard ANBA .60 1.50
391 Draymond Green ANBA .50 1.25
392 Tony Allen ANBA .25 .60
393 DeAndre Jordan ANBA .40 1.00
394 Chris Paul ANBA .50 1.25
395 Anthony Davis ANBA .75 2.00
396 Jimmy Butler ANBA .40 1.00
397 Andrew Bogut ANBA .30 .75
398 John Wall ANBA .50 1.25
399 Tim Duncan ANBA .60 1.50
400 Stephen Curry MVP 3.00 8.00

2015-16 Panini Prizm Prizms Flash

*FLASH VET: .75X TO 2X BASE
*FLASH RC: 1X TO 2.5X BASE
*FLASH AS: .75X TO 2X BASE
*FLASH ANBA: .75X TO 2X BASE
*FLASH MVP: .75X TO 2X BASE
1-300 ODDS 1:10 HOBBY
301-350 ODDS 1:55 HOBBY
351-375 ODDS 1:114 HOBBY
376-399 ODDS 1:109 HOBBY
400 ODDS 1:2724 HOBBY
308 Devin Booker 20.00 50.00
328 Karl-Anthony Towns 40.00 100.00
348 Kristaps Porzingis 12.00 30.00

2015-16 Panini Prizm Prizms Green

*GREEN VET: 1X TO 2.5X BASE
*GREEN RC: 1.2X TO 3X BASE
*GREEN AS: 1X TO 2.5X BASE
*GREEN ANBA: 1X TO 2.5X BASE
*GREEN MVP: 1X TO 2.5X BASE
RANDOM INSERTS IN PACKS
308 Devin Booker 25.00 60.00
328 Karl-Anthony Towns 50.00 120.00
335 Nikola Jokic 25.00 60.00
340 Myles Turner 10.00 25.00
348 Kristaps Porzingis 20.00 50.00

2015-16 Panini Prizm Prizms Light Blue

*BLUE VET: 1X TO 2.5X BASIC
*BLUE RC: 1.2X TO 3X BASIC
*BLUE AS: 1X TO 2.5X BASIC
*BLUE ANBA: 1X TO 2.5X BASIC
*BLUE MVP: 1X TO 2.5X BASIC
RANDOM INSERTS IN PACKS
STATED PRINT RUN 199 SER.#'d SETS
182 Kobe Bryant 10.00 25.00
308 Devin Booker 40.00 100.00
328 Karl-Anthony Towns 60.00 150.00
335 Nikola Jokic 30.00 80.00
340 Myles Turner 10.00 25.00
348 Kristaps Porzingis 15.00 40.00

2015-16 Panini Prizm Prizms Mojo

*MOJO VET: 5X TO 12X BASIC
*MOJO RC: 10X TO 25X BASIC
*MOJO AS: 5X TO 12X BASIC
*MOJO ANBA: 5X TO 12X BASIC
*MOJO MVP: 5X TO 12X BASIC
RANDOM INSERTS IN PACKS
STATED PRINT RUN 25 SER.#'d SETS
182 Kobe Bryant 30.00 80.00
308 Devin Booker 150.00 400.00
322 D'Angelo Russell 100.00 250.00
328 Karl-Anthony Towns 300.00 600.00
335 Nikola Jokic 150.00 400.00
340 Myles Turner 100.00 250.00
348 Kristaps Porzingis 150.00 400.00
400 Stephen Curry MVP 50.00 120.00

2015-16 Panini Prizm Prizms Orange

*ORANGE VET: 2.5X TO 6X BASIC
*ORANGE RC: 3X TO 8X BASIC
*ORANGE AS: 2.5X TO 6X BASIC
*ORANGE ANBA: 2.5X TO 6X BASIC
*ORANGE MVP: 2.5X TO 6X BASIC
RANDOM INSERTS IN PACKS
STATED PRINT RUN 65 SER.#'d SETS
182 Kobe Bryant 15.00 40.00
308 Devin Booker 125.00 300.00
322 D'Angelo Russell 30.00 80.00
328 Karl-Anthony Towns 150.00 400.00
335 Nikola Jokic 75.00 200.00
340 Myles Turner 30.00 80.00
348 Kristaps Porzingis 60.00 150.00

2015-16 Panini Prizm Prizms Orange Wave

*ORNGE WAVE VET: 1X TO 2.5X
*ORNGE WAVE RC: 1.2X TO 3X
*ORNGE WAVE AS: 1X TO 2.5X
*ORNGE WAVE ANBA: 1X TO 2.5X
*ORNGE WAVE MVP: 1X TO 2.5X
RANDOM INSERTS IN PACKS
308 Devin Booker 60.00 150.00
328 Karl-Anthony Towns 50.00 120.00
340 Myles Turner 10.00 25.00
348 Kristaps Porzingis 15.00 40.00

2015-16 Panini Prizm Prizms Purple

*PURPLE VET: 1.2X TO 3X BASIC
*PURPLE RC: 1.5X TO 4X BASIC
*PURPLE AS: 1.2X TO 3X BASIC
*PURPLE ANBA: 1.2X TO 3X BASIC
*PURPLE MVP: 1.2X TO 3X BASIC
RANDOM INSERTS IN PACKS
STATED PRINT RUN 99 SER.#'d SETS
182 Kobe Bryant 12.00 30.00
308 Devin Booker 100.00 250.00
322 D'Angelo Russell 25.00 60.00
328 Karl-Anthony Towns 125.00 300.00
335 Nikola Jokic 60.00 150.00
340 Myles Turner 12.00 30.00
348 Kristaps Porzingis 30.00 80.00

2015-16 Panini Prizm Prizms Red White Blue

*RWB VET: 1X TO 2.5X BASE
*RWB RC: 1.2X TO 3X BASE
*RWB AS: 1X TO 2.5X BASE
*RWB ANBA: 1X TO 2.5X BASE
*RWB MVP: 1X TO 2.5X BASE
RANDOM INSERTS IN PACKS
308 Devin Booker 25.00 60.00
322 D'Angelo Russell 4.00 10.00
328 Karl-Anthony Towns 40.00 100.00
335 Nikola Jokic 20.00 50.00
348 Kristaps Porzingis 25.00 60.00

2015-16 Panini Prizm Prizms Ruby Wave

*RUBY VET: 1X TO 2.5X BASE
*RUBY RC: 1.2X TO 3X BASE
*RUBY AS: 1X TO 2.5X BASE
*RUBY ANBA: 1X TO 2.5X BASE
*RUBY MVP: 1X TO 2.5X BASE
RANDOM INSERTS IN PACKS
STATED PRINT RUN 350 SER.#'d SETS
182 Kobe Bryant 8.00 20.00
308 Devin Booker 30.00 80.00
322 D'Angelo Russell 8.00 20.00
328 Karl-Anthony Towns 50.00 120.00
335 Nikola Jokic 20.00 50.00
340 Myles Turner 10.00 25.00
348 Kristaps Porzingis 15.00 40.00

2015-16 Panini Prizm Prizms Silver

*SILVER VET: .6X TO 1.5X BASE
*SILVER RC: .75X TO 2X BASE
*SILVER AS: .6X TO 1.5X BASE
*SILVER ANBA: .6X TO 1.5X BASE
*SILVER MVP: .6X TO 1.5X BASE
1-300 ODDS 1:7 HOBBY
301-350 ODDS 1:41 HOBBY
351-375 ODDS 1:86 HOBBY
376-399 ODDS 1:82 HOBBY
400 ODDS 1:2041 HOBBY
308 Devin Booker 75.00 200.00
316 Emmanuel Mudiay 5.00 12.00
322 D'Angelo Russell 25.00 60.00
328 Karl-Anthony Towns 125.00 300.00
329 Jahlil Okafor 10.00 25.00
335 Nikola Jokic 60.00 150.00
336 Justise Winslow 12.00 30.00
337 Norman Powell 6.00 15.00
340 Myles Turner 30.00 80.00
348 Kristaps Porzingis 75.00 200.00
349 Willie Cauley-Stein 8.00 20.00

2015-16 Panini Prizm Autographs

OVERALL AU ODDS 1:20 HOBBY
EXCHANGE DEADLINE 5/16/2017
1 Otto Porter 3.00 8.00
2 Shabazz Muhammad 3.00 8.00
3 Cody Zeller 2.50 6.00
4 Jerami Grant 2.50 6.00
5 Dante Exum 3.00 8.00
6 Jarnell Stokes 2.50 6.00
7 Langston Galloway 2.50 6.00
8 Bojan Bogdanovic 2.50 6.00
9 C.J. McCollum 8.00 20.00
10 Robert Covington 2.50 6.00
11 Chucky Brown 2.50 6.00
12 Ben McLemore 2.50 6.00
13 Trey Burke 2.50 6.00
14 Alex Len 2.50 6.00
15 Mike Muscala 2.50 6.00
16 Victor Oladipo 3.00 8.00
17 Nerlens Noel 3.00 8.00
18 Robert Sacre 2.50 6.00
19 Michael Carter-Williams 2.50 6.00
20 Kentavious Caldwell-Pope 3.00 8.00
21 Jabari Brown 3.00 8.00
22 Andre Roberson 2.50 6.00
23 Matthew Dellavedova 3.00 8.00
24 Carl Landry 2.50 6.00
25 Mason Plumlee 3.00 8.00
26 Al-Farouq Aminu 3.00 8.00
27 Allen Iverson 40.00 100.00
28 Alan Anderson 2.50 6.00
29 Maurice Harkless 2.50 6.00
30 Brandon Knight 3.00 8.00
31 Cliff Hagan 3.00 8.00
32 Artis Gilmore 3.00 8.00
33 Robert Parish 4.00 10.00
34 Gail Goodrich 3.00 8.00
35 Joe Dumars 4.00 10.00
36 Don Nelson 10.00 25.00
37 Dave Cowens 2.50 6.00
38 Dominique Wilkins 6.00 15.00
39 Raef LaFrentz 2.50 6.00
40 Terry Cummings 3.00 8.00
41 Larry Brown 4.00 10.00
42 Scott Brooks 2.50 6.00
43 Chuck Person 3.00 8.00
44 Mitch Richmond 4.00 10.00
45 Jerry Stackhouse 3.00 8.00
46 Damon Stoudamire 3.00 8.00
47 Dino Radja 2.50 6.00
48 Jeff Malone 2.50 6.00
49 Bobby Jones 3.00 8.00
50 Vernon Maxwell 2.50 6.00
51 Kurt Rambis 2.50 6.00
52 Michael Cage 2.50 6.00
53 John Lucas 4.00 10.00
54 Muggsy Bogues 3.00 8.00
55 Kenny Walker 2.50 6.00
56 Marques Johnson 3.00 8.00
57 Peja Stojakovic 4.00 10.00
58 Vinny Del Negro 3.00 8.00
59 Jabari Parker 10.00 25.00
60 Julius Randle 4.00 10.00
61 Christian Laettner 3.00 8.00
62 Tom Chambers 3.00 8.00
63 Scott Skiles 3.00 8.00
64 Rik Smits 6.00 15.00
65 Steve Mix 2.50 6.00
66 Bill Cartwright 3.00 8.00
67 Adrian Smith 2.50 6.00
68 Sean Elliott 4.00 10.00
69 Keith Van Horn 3.00 8.00
70 George Karl 4.00 10.00
71 Allan Houston 3.00 8.00
72 Noah Vonleh 2.50 6.00
73 Dennis Rodman 10.00 25.00
74 Antoine Walker 3.00 8.00
75 Tracy McGrady 12.00 30.00
76 Nick Van Exel 4.00 10.00
77 Brent Barry 2.50 6.00
78 Aaron Gordon 5.00 12.00
79 Baron Davis 3.00 8.00
80 Kobe Bryant 75.00 150.00
81 Kevin Durant 50.00 120.00
82 Kyrie Irving 20.00 50.00
83 Ricky Rubio 8.00 20.00
84 Anthony Davis 40.00 100.00
85 Andrew Wiggins 20.00 50.00
86 Justin Anderson 3.00 8.00
87 Montrezl Harrell 3.00 8.00
88 Devin Booker 50.00 120.00
89 Sam Dekker 3.00 8.00
90 Willie Cauley-Stein 10.00 25.00
91 Karl-Anthony Towns 75.00 200.00
92 Jahlil Okafor 10.00 25.00
93 Bobby Portis 4.00 10.00
94 Jerian Grant 2.50 6.00
95 Myles Turner 12.00 30.00
96 Justise Winslow 6.00 15.00
97 Jordan Mickey 2.50 6.00
98 Kristaps Porzingis 40.00 100.00
99 Emmanuel Mudiay 6.00 15.00
100 D'Angelo Russell 20.00 50.00

2015-16 Panini Prizm Autographs Prizms Orange

*ORANGE: .5X TO 1.2X BASIC
OVERALL AU ODDS 1:20 HOBBY
STATED PRINT RUN 65 SER.#'d SETS
EXCHANGE DEADLINE 5/16/2017
91 Karl-Anthony Towns 125.00 300.00

2015-16 Panini Prizm Emergent

STATED ODDS 1:17 HOBBY
*GREEN: 2X TO 5X BASIC
*SILVER: 2.5X TO 6X BASIC
1 Jerian Grant .50 1.25
2 Emmanuel Mudiay .75 2.00
3 Bobby Portis .75 2.00
4 Justise Winslow .75 2.00
5 Joe Young .60 1.50
6 Devin Booker 2.50 6.00
7 Raul Neto .50 1.25
8 Karl-Anthony Towns 4.00 10.00
9 Terry Rozier .60 1.50
10 Kristaps Porzingis 2.00 5.00
11 Delon Wright .60 1.50
12 Stanley Johnson .60 1.50
13 Rondae Hollis-Jefferson .60 1.50
14 Myles Turner .75 2.00
15 Nemanja Bjelica .60 1.50

16 Larry Nance Jr. .75 2.00
17 Cameron Payne .60 1.50
18 D'Angelo Russell 2.00 5.00
19 Rashad Vaughn .50 1.25
20 Mario Hezonja .60 1.50
21 Justin Anderson .60 1.50
22 Frank Kaminsky .75 2.00
23 Tyus Jones .75 2.00
24 Trey Lyles .75 2.00
25 Walter Tavares .50 1.25
26 Kelly Oubre Jr. .60 1.50
27 Kevon Looney .60 1.50
28 Jahlil Okafor 1.00 2.50
29 Sam Dekker .60 1.50
30 Willie Cauley-Stein .75 2.00

2015-16 Panini Prizm Fireworks

STATED ODDS 1:15 HOBBY
*GREEN: 1X TO 2.5X BASIC
*SILVER: 1.2X TO 3X BASIC
1 Andre Iguodala .60 1.50
2 Russell Westbrook 2.00 5.00
3 Stephen Curry 3.00 8.00
4 Mike Conley .75 2.00
5 James Harden 1.25 3.00
6 Jabari Parker 1.00 2.50
7 Kyrie Irving 1.50 4.00
8 Joakim Noah .60 1.50
9 LeBron James 3.00 8.00
10 Kobe Bryant 3.00 8.00
11 Tim Duncan 1.25 3.00
12 Kyle Lowry .60 1.50
13 Dwight Howard .60 1.50
14 Goran Dragic .60 1.50
15 Dirk Nowitzki 1.00 2.50
16 Klay Thompson 1.00 2.50
17 Chris Bosh .75 2.00
18 Damian Lillard 1.50 4.00
19 Kevin Durant 2.00 5.00
20 DeMarcus Cousins .75 2.00
21 Anthony Davis 1.50 4.00
22 Blake Griffin .75 2.00
23 John Wall 1.00 2.50
24 DeAndre Jordan .75 2.00
25 Tony Parker .75 2.00
26 Bradley Beal .75 2.00
27 Dwyane Wade 1.25 3.00
28 Derrick Rose 1.00 2.50
29 Chris Paul 1.00 2.50
30 Kawhi Leonard 1.25 3.00
31 Kevin Love .75 2.00
32 Andrew Wiggins 1.25 3.00
33 Carmelo Anthony 1.00 2.50
34 Manu Ginobili .75 2.00
35 Marc Gasol .75 2.00

2015-16 Panini Prizm Point Men

STATED ODDS 1:33 HOBBY
*GREEN: .75X TO 2X BASIC
*SILVER: 1.2X TO 3X BASIC
1 John Wall 1.25 3.00
2 Anfernee Hardaway 2.50 6.00
3 Stephen Curry 4.00 10.00
4 Steve Nash 1.00 2.50
5 Isiah Thomas 1.00 2.50
6 Damon Stoudamire .75 2.00
7 Magic Johnson 2.50 6.00
8 John Stockton 1.50 4.00
9 Derrick Rose 1.25 3.00
10 Russell Westbrook 2.50 6.00
11 Kyrie Irving 2.00 5.00
12 Allen Iverson 1.25 3.00
13 Jason Kidd 1.00 2.50
14 Tony Parker 1.00 2.50
15 Chris Paul 1.25 3.00

2015-16 Panini Prizm Rookie Autographs

OVERALL AU ODDS 1:20 HOBBY
EXCHANGE DEADLINE 5/16/2017
1 Jahlil Okafor 10.00 25.00
2 Karl-Anthony Towns 75.00 200.00
3 Emmanuel Mudiay 8.00 20.00
4 D'Angelo Russell 20.00 50.00
5 Justise Winslow 10.00 25.00
6 Mario Hezonja 3.00 8.00
7 Willie Cauley-Stein 8.00 20.00
8 Kristaps Porzingis 75.00 200.00
9 Stanley Johnson 3.00 8.00
10 Kelly Oubre Jr. 3.00 8.00
11 Myles Turner 15.00 40.00
12 Frank Kaminsky 4.00 10.00
13 Sam Dekker 3.00 8.00
14 Bobby Portis 4.00 10.00
15 Devin Booker 20.00 50.00
16 Trey Lyles 4.00 10.00
17 Jerian Grant 2.50 6.00
18 Kevon Looney 3.00 8.00
19 Tyus Jones 6.00 15.00
20 Rondae Hollis-Jefferson 2.50 6.00
21 Montrezl Harrell 3.00 8.00
23 R.J. Hunter 2.50 6.00
25 Jarell Martin 3.00 8.00
26 Cameron Payne 3.00 8.00
28 Delon Wright 3.00 8.00
29 Justin Anderson 3.00 8.00
31 Richaun Holmes 3.00 8.00
32 Dakari Johnson 2.50 6.00
33 Terry Rozier 3.00 8.00
34 Chris McCullough 2.50 6.00
37 Rashad Vaughn 2.50 6.00
39 Andrew Harrison 4.00 10.00
40 Jordan Mickey 2.50 6.00
41 Anthony Brown 2.50 6.00
42 Norman Powell 3.00 8.00
45 Tyler Harvey 2.50 6.00
49 Aaron Harrison 3.00 8.00
50 Pat Connaughton 2.50 6.00
51 Rakeem Christmas 2.50 6.00
54 Darrun Hilliard 2.50 6.00
55 Branden Dawson 2.50 6.00
58 Joe Young 3.00 8.00
64 Larry Nance Jr. 6.00 15.00
67 Josh Richardson 4.00 10.00

2015-16 Panini Prizm Rookie Autographs Prizms

*PRIZMS: .6X TO 1.5X BASIC
OVERALL AU ODDS 1:20 HOBBY
STATED PRINT RUN 25 SER.#'d SETS
EXCHANGE DEADLINE 5/16/2017

2015-16 Panini Prizm USA Basketball

STATED ODDS 1:25 HOBBY
*GREEN: 1X TO 2.5X BASIC
*SILVER: 1.2X TO 3X BASIC
1 Russell Westbrook 2.00 5.00
2 Rudy Gay .75 2.00
3 Chris Paul 1.00 2.50
4 Kyrie Irving 1.50 4.00
5 Kevin Love .75 2.00
6 DeMarcus Cousins .75 2.00
7 Derrick Rose 1.00 2.50
8 Anthony Davis 1.50 4.00
9 Kevin Durant 2.00 5.00
10 Andre Drummond .75 2.00
11 Kobe Bryant 3.00 8.00
12 James Harden 1.25 3.00
13 Carmelo Anthony 1.00 2.50
14 Mason Plumlee .60 1.50
15 Andre Iguodala .60 1.50
16 Stephen Curry 3.00 8.00
17 Klay Thompson 1.00 2.50
18 DeMar DeRozan .75 2.00
19 LeBron James 3.00 8.00
20 Kenneth Faried .60 1.50

2015-16 Panini Prizm Veteran Autographs

OVERALL AU ODDS 1:20 HOBBY
STATED PRINT RUN 150 SER.#'d SETS
EXCHANGE DEADLINE 5/16/2017
*PRIZMS/25: .6X TO 1.5X BASIC
1 Kobe Bryant 100.00 200.00
2 Kevin Durant 50.00 120.00
3 Kyrie Irving 30.00 80.00
4 Dwyane Wade 25.00 60.00
7 Carmelo Anthony 15.00 40.00
8 Andrew Wiggins 25.00 60.00
9 Bradley Beal EXCH 10.00 25.00
10 Blake Griffin 25.00 60.00
11 Tony Parker 15.00 40.00
12 Klay Thompson 25.00 60.00
13 Jabari Parker 12.00 30.00
14 Anthony Davis 40.00 100.00
15 Kawhi Leonard EXCH 15.00 40.00

2016-17 Panini Prizm

1 Ben Simmons RC 15.00 40.00
2 Dario Saric RC 1.50 4.00
3 T. Luwawu-Cabarrot RC 1.00 2.50
4 Joel Embiid .60 1.50
5 T.J. McConnell .25 .60
6 Robert Covington .25 .60
7 Nerlens Noel .30 .75
8 Jahlil Okafor .30 .75
9 Jerami Grant .25 .60
10 Nik Stauskas .25 .60
11 Jabari Parker .50 1.25
12 Khris Middleton .30 .75
13 Giannis Antetokounmpo .75 2.00
14 Thon Maker RC 1.50 4.00
15 Greg Monroe .30 .75
16 Matthew Dellavedova .30 .75
17 Malcolm Brogdon RC 1.25 3.00
18 John Henson .30 .75
19 Michael Carter-Williams .25 .60
20 Rashad Vaughn .25 .60
21 Jimmy Butler .40 1.00
22 Bobby Portis .25 .60
23 Denzel Valentine RC .60 1.50
24 Dwyane Wade .60 1.50
25 Rajon Rondo .40 1.00
26 Robin Lopez .25 .60
27 Jerian Grant .25 .60
28 Doug McDermott .30 .75
29 Nikola Mirotic .30 .75
30 Taj Gibson .30 .75
31 LeBron James 1.50 4.00
32 Kyrie Irving .75 2.00
33 Kay Felder RC .50 1.25
34 Kevin Love .40 1.00
35 Richard Jefferson .30 .75
36 Tristan Thompson .30 .75
37 Iman Shumpert .25 .60
38 Channing Frye .30 .75
39 J.R. Smith .30 .75
40 Mo Williams .30 .75
41 Al Horford .30 .75
42 Isaiah Thomas .40 1.00
43 Avery Bradley .30 .75
44 Jaylen Brown RC 2.00 5.00
45 Jae Crowder .30 .75
46 Marcus Smart .30 .75
47 Kelly Olynyk .25 .60
48 Ben Bentil RC .50 1.25
49 Terry Rozier .30 .75
50 Jordan Mickey .25 .60
51 Chris Paul .50 1.25
52 Blake Griffin .40 1.00
53 DeAndre Jordan .40 1.00
54 J.J. Redick .40 1.00
55 Diamond Stone RC .50 1.25
56 Brice Johnson RC .50 1.25
57 Jamal Crawford .40 1.00
58 Paul Pierce .40 1.00
59 Marreese Speights .25 .60
60 Brandon Bass .25 .60
61 Mike Conley .30 .75
62 Chandler Parsons .30 .75
63 Marc Gasol .40 1.00
64 Zach Randolph .30 .75
65 Vince Carter .50 1.25
66 Brandan Wright .25 .60
67 Tony Allen .25 .60
68 Wade Baldwin IV RC .50 1.25
69 Deyonta Davis RC .50 1.25
70 James Ennis .25 .60
71 Dwight Howard .30 .75
72 Dennis Schroder .30 .75
73 Paul Millsap .40 1.00
74 Kyle Korver .30 .75
75 Kent Bazemore .30 .75
76 Kris Humphries .25 .60
77 DeAndre' Bembry RC .50 1.25
78 Taurean Prince RC .75 2.00
79 Thabo Sefolosha .25 .60
80 Jarrett Jack .30 .75
81 Hassan Whiteside .30 .75
82 Justise Winslow .30 .75
83 Josh Richardson .25 .60
84 Goran Dragic .30 .75
85 Tyler Johnson .25 .60
86 Chris Bosh .40 1.00
87 Dion Waiters .30 .75
88 Derrick Williams .25 .60
89 Udonis Haslem .25 .60
90 Wayne Ellington .25 .60
91 Kemba Walker .40 1.00
92 Nicolas Batum .30 .75
93 Frank Kaminsky .30 .75
94 Marvin Williams .30 .75
95 Roy Hibbert .30 .75
96 Michael Kidd-Gilchrist .30 .75
97 Jeremy Lamb .25 .60
98 Aaron Harrison .25 .60
99 Marco Belinelli .25 .60
100 Ramon Sessions .30 .75
101 Gordon Hayward .40 1.00
102 Rudy Gobert .40 1.00
103 Derrick Favors .30 .75
104 Dante Exum .30 .75
105 Joe Johnson .30 .75
106 George Hill .30 .75
107 Boris Diaw .30 .75
108 Trey Lyles .30 .75
109 Alec Burks .25 .60
110 Rodney Hood .30 .75
111 DeMarcus Cousins .40 1.00
112 Rudy Gay .40 1.00
113 Georgios Papagiannis RC .50 1.25
114 Skal Labissiere RC .75 2.00
115 Malachi Richardson RC .60 1.50
116 Ben McLemore .25 .60
117 Willie Cauley-Stein .30 .75
118 Matt Barnes .25 .60
119 Arron Afflalo .25 .60
120 Omri Casspi .25 .60
121 Carmelo Anthony .50 1.25
122 Derrick Rose .50 1.25
123 Joakim Noah .30 .75
124 Kristaps Porzingis .75 2.00
125 Courtney Lee .30 .75
126 Brandon Jennings .25 .60
127 Lance Thomas .25 .60
128 Justin Holiday RC .50 1.25
129 Marshall Plumlee RC .50 1.25
130 Kyle O'Quinn .25 .60
131 Brandon Ingram RC 5.00 12.00
132 D'Angelo Russell .50 1.25
133 Timofey Mozgov .25 .60
134 Jordan Clarkson .30 .75
135 Julius Randle .40 1.00
136 Ivica Zubac RC .75 2.00
137 Luol Deng .30 .75
138 Jose Calderon .25 .60
139 Marcelo Huertas .25 .60
140 Lou Williams .30 .75
141 Serge Ibaka .30 .75
142 Nikola Vucevic .30 .75
143 Aaron Gordon .30 .75
144 Evan Fournier .30 .75
145 Bismack Biyombo .25 .60
146 Elfrid Payton .30 .75
147 Mario Hezonja .25 .60
148 Stephen Zimmerman RC .50 1.25
149 Jeff Green .30 .75
150 D.J. Augustin .25 .60
151 Dirk Nowitzki .50 1.25
152 Harrison Barnes .30 .75
153 Andrew Bogut .30 .75
154 Deron Williams .30 .75
155 Justin Anderson .30 .75
156 J.J. Barea .30 .75
157 Seth Curry .40 1.00
158 Salah Mejri .25 .60
159 A.J. Hammons RC .50 1.25
160 Dwight Powell .25 .60
161 Jeremy Lin .40 1.00
162 Isaiah Whitehead RC .50 1.25
163 Brook Lopez .30 .75
164 Bojan Bogdanovic .25 .60
165 Caris LeVert RC .60 1.50
166 Chris McCullough .25 .60
167 Trevor Booker .25 .60
168 Rondae Hollis-Jefferson .25 .60
169 Sean Kilpatrick RC .50 1.25
170 Anthony Bennett .25 .60
171 Danilo Gallinari .30 .75
172 Kenneth Faried .30 .75
173 Emmanuel Mudiay .30 .75
174 Nikola Jokic .40 1.00
175 Jamal Murray RC 1.50 4.00
176 Wilson Chandler .30 .75
177 Jusuf Nurkic .25 .60
178 Gary Harris .30 .75
179 Will Barton .25 .60
180 Darrell Arthur .25 .60
181 Paul George .50 1.25
182 Jeff Teague .30 .75
183 Monta Ellis .30 .75
184 Al Jefferson .30 .75
185 Thaddeus Young .25 .60
186 Myles Turner .30 .75
187 Georges Niang RC .50 1.25
188 Joe Young .25 .60
189 Rodney Stuckey .25 .60
190 C.J. Miles .30 .75
191 Anthony Davis .75 2.00
192 Buddy Hield RC 1.25 3.00
193 Tyreke Evans .25 .60
194 Jrue Holiday .30 .75
195 Omer Asik .30 .75
196 Cheick Diallo RC .50 1.25
197 Terrence Jones .30 .75
198 Alonzo Gee .25 .60
199 Tim Frazier RC .50 1.25
200 Langston Galloway .25 .60
201 Andre Drummond .40 1.00
202 Reggie Jackson .30 .75
203 Kentavious Caldwell-Pope .30 .75
204 Marcus Morris .25 .60
205 Henry Ellenson RC .60 1.50
206 Boban Marjanovic .25 .60
207 Ish Smith .25 .60
208 Tobias Harris .30 .75
209 Michael Gbinije .25 .60
210 Jon Leuer .25 .60
211 DeMar DeRozan .40 1.00
212 Kyle Lowry .30 .75
213 Jonas Valanciunas .30 .75
214 Jared Sullinger .25 .60
215 DeMarre Carroll .25 .60
216 Jakob Poeltl RC .60 1.50
217 Norman Powell .25 .60
218 Cory Joseph .25 .60
219 Patrick Patterson .25 .60
220 Pascal Siakam RC .50 1.25
221 James Harden .60 1.50
222 Michael Beasley .25 .60
223 Patrick Beverley .25 .60
224 Gary Payton II RC .60 1.50
225 Eric Gordon .30 .75
226 Ryan Anderson .30 .75
227 Nene .30 .75
228 Trevor Ariza .25 .60
229 Sam Dekker .30 .75
230 Clint Capela .25 .60
231 Kawhi Leonard .60 1.50
232 Pau Gasol .40 1.00
233 Tony Parker .40 1.00
234 Manu Ginobili .40 1.00
235 LaMarcus Aldridge .40 1.00
236 Dejounte Murray RC 1.50 4.00
237 Danny Green .30 .75
238 Kyle Anderson .25 .60
239 Jonathon Simmons .40 1.00
240 Patty Mills .40 1.00
241 Devin Booker .60 1.50
242 Dragan Bender RC .60 1.50
243 Marquese Chriss RC 1.25 3.00
244 Eric Bledsoe .30 .75
245 Brandon Knight .30 .75
246 Tyler Ulis RC 1.50 4.00
247 Tyson Chandler .30 .75
248 Leandro Barbosa .25 .60
249 T.J. Warren .30 .75
250 Alex Len .25 .60
251 Russell Westbrook 1.00 2.50
252 Steven Adams .30 .75
253 Victor Oladipo .30 .75
254 Enes Kanter .25 .60
255 Domantas Sabonis RC .75 2.00
256 Andre Roberson .25 .60
257 Cameron Payne .25 .60
258 Ersan Ilyasova .25 .60
259 Mitch McGary .25 .60
260 Anthony Morrow .25 .60
261 Ricky Rubio .40 1.00
262 Karl-Anthony Towns 1.00 2.50
263 Andrew Wiggins .60 1.50
264 Kevin Garnett .60 1.50
265 Zach LaVine .40 1.00
266 Kris Dunn RC 1.50 4.00
267 Nikola Pekovic .25 .60
268 Gorgui Dieng .25 .60
269 Cole Aldrich .25 .60
270 Shabazz Muhammad .30 .75
271 Damian Lillard .75 2.00
272 Allen Crabbe .25 .60
273 C.J. McCollum .30 .75
274 Evan Turner .25 .60
275 Festus Ezeli .25 .60
276 Mason Plumlee .30 .75
277 Meyers Leonard .25 .60
278 Al-Farouq Aminu .30 .75
279 Jake Layman RC .60 1.50
280 Ed Davis .25 .60
281 Stephen Curry 1.50 4.00
282 Kevin Durant 1.00 2.50
283 Klay Thompson .50 1.25
284 Draymond Green .50 1.25
285 Andre Iguodala .30 .75
286 Anderson Varejao .25 .60
287 Shaun Livingston .25 .60
288 David West .30 .75
289 Zaza Pachulia .25 .60
290 Patrick McCaw RC 1.00 2.50
291 John Wall .50 1.25
292 Bradley Beal .40 1.00
293 Marcin Gortat .30 .75
294 Kelly Oubre Jr. .25 .60
295 Trey Burke .25 .60
296 Markieff Morris .25 .60
297 Ian Mahinmi .25 .60
298 Otto Porter .30 .75
299 Andrew Nicholson .25 .60
300 Jason Smith .25 .60

2016-17 Panini Prizm Prizms Blue Wave

*BLUE WAVE: 1.2X TO 3X BASIC
*BLUE WAVE RC: 1.2X TO 3X BASIC
RANDOM INSERTS IN PACKS
STATED PRINT RUN 99 SER.#'d SETS
1 Ben Simmons 100.00 250.00
2 Dario Saric 10.00 25.00
14 Thon Maker 20.00 50.00
17 Malcolm Brogdon 20.00 50.00
44 Jaylen Brown 20.00 50.00
78 Taurean Prince 10.00 25.00
114 Skal Labissiere 12.00 30.00
131 Brandon Ingram 50.00 120.00
136 Ivica Zubac 6.00 15.00
175 Jamal Murray 15.00 40.00
192 Buddy Hield 12.00 30.00
236 Dejounte Murray 25.00 60.00
243 Marquese Chriss 12.00 30.00
246 Tyler Ulis 15.00 40.00
266 Kris Dunn 10.00 25.00
290 Patrick McCaw 6.00 15.00

2016-17 Panini Prizm Prizms Green

*GREEN: 1X TO 2.5X BASIC
*GREEN RC: 1X TO 2.5X BASIC
RANDOM INSERTS IN PACKS
1 Ben Simmons 75.00 200.00
2 Dario Saric 8.00 20.00
14 Thon Maker 12.00 30.00
17 Malcolm Brogdon 10.00 25.00
44 Jaylen Brown 15.00 40.00
78 Taurean Prince 4.00 10.00
114 Skal Labissiere 10.00 25.00
131 Brandon Ingram 30.00 80.00
136 Ivica Zubac 4.00 10.00
175 Jamal Murray 15.00 40.00
192 Buddy Hield 10.00 25.00
236 Dejounte Murray 15.00 40.00
243 Marquese Chriss 6.00 15.00
246 Tyler Ulis 8.00 20.00
266 Kris Dunn 6.00 15.00
290 Patrick McCaw 5.00 12.00

2016-17 Panini Prizm Prizms Mojo

*MOJO: 5X TO 12X BASIC
*MOJO RC: .5X TO 12X BASIC
RANDOM INSERTS IN PACKS
STATED PRINT RUN 25 SER.#'d SETS
1 Ben Simmons 1000.00 1200.00
2 Dario Saric 40.00 100.00
14 Thon Maker 60.00 150.00
17 Malcolm Brogdon 50.00 120.00
44 Jaylen Brown 75.00 200.00
78 Taurean Prince 20.00 50.00
114 Skal Labissiere 75.00 200.00
131 Brandon Ingram 125.00 300.00
136 Ivica Zubac 25.00 60.00
165 Caris LeVert 20.00 50.00
175 Jamal Murray 60.00 150.00
192 Buddy Hield 50.00 120.00
236 Dejounte Murray 60.00 150.00
243 Marquese Chriss 40.00 100.00
246 Tyler Ulis 50.00 120.00
266 Kris Dunn 30.00 80.00
290 Patrick McCaw 15.00 40.00

2016-17 Panini Prizm Prizms Orange

*ORANGE: 1.5X TO 4X BASIC
*ORANGE RC: 1.5X TO 4X BASIC
RANDOM INSERTS IN PACKS
STATED PRINT RUN 49 SER.#'d SETS
1 Ben Simmons 300.00 600.00
2 Dario Saric 20.00 50.00
14 Thon Maker 30.00 80.00
17 Malcolm Brogdon 25.00 60.00
44 Jaylen Brown 60.00 150.00
78 Taurean Prince 12.00 30.00
114 Skal Labissiere 30.00 80.00
131 Brandon Ingram 100.00 250.00
136 Ivica Zubac 15.00 40.00
175 Jamal Murray 30.00 80.00
192 Buddy Hield 15.00 40.00
236 Dejounte Murray 30.00 80.00
243 Marquese Chriss 15.00 40.00
246 Tyler Ulis 20.00 50.00
266 Kris Dunn 20.00 50.00
290 Patrick McCaw 8.00 20.00

2016-17 Panini Prizm Prizms Orange Wave

*ORANGE WAVE: 5X TO 12X BASIC
*ORANGE WAVE RC: .5X TO 12X BASIC
RANDOM INSERTS IN PACKS
STATED PRINT RUN 25 SER.#'d SETS
1 Ben Simmons 1000.00 1200.00
2 Dario Saric 40.00 100.00
14 Thon Maker 60.00 150.00
17 Malcolm Brogdon 50.00 120.00
44 Jaylen Brown 75.00 200.00
78 Taurean Prince 20.00 50.00
114 Skal Labissiere 75.00 200.00
131 Brandon Ingram 125.00 300.00
136 Ivica Zubac 20.00 50.00
175 Jamal Murray 60.00 150.00
192 Buddy Hield 50.00 120.00
236 Dejounte Murray 60.00 150.00
243 Marquese Chriss 40.00 100.00
246 Tyler Ulis 50.00 120.00
266 Kris Dunn 30.00 80.00
290 Patrick McCaw 15.00 40.00

2016-17 Panini Prizm Prizms Purple

*PURPLE: 1.2X TO 3X BASIC
*PURPLE RC: 1.2X TO 3X BASIC
RANDOM INSERTS IN PACKS
STATED PRINT RUN 75 SER.#'d SETS
1 Ben Simmons 100.00 250.00
2 Dario Saric 12.00 30.00
14 Thon Maker 20.00 50.00
17 Malcolm Brogdon 20.00 50.00
44 Jaylen Brown 30.00 80.00
78 Taurean Prince 10.00 25.00
114 Skal Labissiere 12.00 30.00
131 Brandon Ingram 60.00 150.00
136 Ivica Zubac 8.00 20.00
175 Jamal Murray 20.00 50.00
192 Buddy Hield 12.00 30.00
236 Dejounte Murray 25.00 60.00
243 Marquese Chriss 12.00 30.00
246 Tyler Ulis 15.00 40.00
266 Kris Dunn 10.00 25.00
290 Patrick McCaw 8.00 20.00

2016-17 Panini Prizm Prizms Ruby Wave

*RUBY WAVE: 1X TO 2.5X BASIC
*RUBY WAVE RC: 1X TO 2.5X BASIC
RANDOM INSERTS IN PACKS
1 Ben Simmons 75.00 200.00
2 Dario Saric 8.00 20.00
14 Thon Maker 12.00 30.00
17 Malcolm Brogdon 10.00 25.00
44 Jaylen Brown 10.00 25.00
78 Taurean Prince 4.00 10.00
114 Skal Labissiere 10.00 25.00
131 Brandon Ingram 25.00 60.00
136 Ivica Zubac 4.00 10.00
175 Jamal Murray 8.00 20.00
192 Buddy Hield 10.00 25.00
236 Dejounte Murray 15.00 40.00
243 Marquese Chriss 6.00 15.00
246 Tyler Ulis 8.00 20.00
290 Patrick McCaw 5.00 12.00

2016-17 Panini Prizm Prizms Silver

*SILVER: .6X TO 1.5X BASIC
*SILVER RC: 1.2X TO 3X BASIC
RANDOM INSERTS IN PACKS
1 Ben Simmons 150.00 400.00
2 Dario Saric 10.00 25.00
14 Thon Maker 20.00 50.00
17 Malcolm Brogdon 15.00 40.00
44 Jaylen Brown 25.00 60.00
78 Taurean Prince 10.00 25.00
114 Skal Labissiere 15.00 40.00
131 Brandon Ingram 75.00 200.00
136 Ivica Zubac 8.00 20.00
175 Jamal Murray 30.00 80.00
192 Buddy Hield 12.00 30.00
236 Dejounte Murray 25.00 60.00
243 Marquese Chriss 12.00 30.00
246 Tyler Ulis 12.00 30.00
266 Kris Dunn 10.00 25.00
290 Patrick McCaw 15.00 40.00

2016-17 Panini Prizm Prizms Starburst

*STARBURST: .75X TO 2X BASIC
*STARBURST RC: .75X TO 2X BASIC
RANDOM INSERTS IN PACKS
1 Ben Simmons 40.00 100.00
2 Dario Saric 3.00 8.00
44 Jaylen Brown 8.00 20.00
131 Brandon Ingram 15.00 40.00
175 Jamal Murray 6.00 15.00
192 Buddy Hield 4.00 10.00
236 Dejounte Murray 8.00 20.00

2016-17 Panini Prizm Prizms Teal Wave

*TEAL WAVE: 5X TO 12X BASIC
*TEAL WAVE RC: .5X TO 12X BASIC
RANDOM INSERTS IN PACKS
STATED PRINT RUN 25 SER.#'d SETS
1 Ben Simmons 1000.00 1200.00
2 Dario Saric 40.00 100.00
14 Thon Maker 60.00 150.00
17 Malcolm Brogdon 50.00 120.00
44 Jaylen Brown 75.00 200.00
78 Taurean Prince 20.00 50.00
114 Skal Labissiere 75.00 200.00
131 Brandon Ingram 125.00 300.00
136 Ivica Zubac 20.00 50.00
175 Jamal Murray 60.00 150.00
192 Buddy Hield 50.00 120.00
236 Dejounte Murray 60.00 150.00
243 Marquese Chriss 40.00 100.00
246 Tyler Ulis 50.00 120.00
266 Kris Dunn 30.00 80.00
290 Patrick McCaw 15.00 40.00

2016-17 Panini Prizm All Day

RANDOM INSERTS IN PACKS
*GREEN: .5X TO 1.2X BASIC
*SILVER: .5X TO 1.2X BASIC
*RUBY: .5X TO 1.2X BASIC
*BLUE/99: .6X TO 1.5X BASIC
*PURPLE/75: .75X TO 2X BASIC
*ORANGE/49: 1X TO 2.5X BASIC
*MOJO/25: 1.5X TO 4X BASIC
*ORNG WAVE/25: 1.5X TO 4X BASIC
*TEAL WAVE/25: 1.5X TO 4X BASIC
1 Kyrie Irving 1.25 3.00
2 Carmelo Anthony .75 2.00
3 Khris Middleton .50 1.25
4 J.J. Redick .60 1.50
5 Kyle Korver .50 1.25
6 Evan Fournier .50 1.25
7 Dirk Nowitzki .75 2.00
8 Paul George .75 2.00
9 James Harden 1.00 2.50
10 Devin Booker 1.00 2.50
11 C.J. McCollum .60 1.50
12 Klay Thompson .75 2.00
13 Stephen Curry 2.50 6.00
14 John Wall .75 2.00
15 Bradley Beal .60 1.50

2016-17 Panini Prizm Autographs

RANDOM INSERTS IN PACKS
*ORANGE/25: .6X TO 1.5X BASIC
1 Brandon Ingram 40.00 100.00
2 Anthony Bennett 3.00 8.00
3 Cody Zeller 3.00 8.00
4 C.J. McCollum 5.00 12.00
5 Lamar Patterson 3.00 8.00
6 James Ennis 3.00 8.00
7 Dwight Powell 3.00 8.00
8 Ray McCallum 3.00 8.00
9 T.J. McConnell 3.00 8.00
10 Walter Tavares 3.00 8.00
11 Allen Crabbe 3.00 8.00
12 Reggie Jackson 4.00 10.00
13 Aaron Harrison 3.00 8.00
14 Kevon Looney 4.00 10.00
15 Tristan Thompson 4.00 10.00
16 Jeff Withey 3.00 8.00
17 Jonas Valanciunas
18 Deron Williams 4.00 10.00
19 Seth Curry 20.00 50.00
20 Rashad Vaughn 3.00 8.00
21 Andrew Nicholson 3.00 8.00
22 Jusuf Nurkic 3.00 8.00
23 Matthew Dellavedova 4.00 10.00
24 Montrezl Harrell
25 Courtney Lee 4.00 10.00
26 Devin Harris 3.00 8.00
27 James Johnson 3.00 8.00
28 Kelly Olynyk 3.00 8.00
29 Skal Labissiere
30 Michael Kidd-Gilchrist 4.00 10.00
31 Alex Len 3.00 8.00
32 E'Twaun Moore 3.00 8.00
33 Justin Hamilton 3.00 8.00
34 Ian Clark 3.00 8.00
35 Josh Huestis 3.00 8.00
36 Frank Kaminsky 4.00 10.00
37 Kelly Oubre Jr. 3.00 8.00
38 Kristaps Porzingis 25.00 60.00
39 Cameron Payne
40 Tobias Harris
41 Bobby Portis 3.00 8.00
42 Luol Deng
43 Willie Cauley-Stein 4.00 10.00
44 Devin Booker
45 Zach Randolph
46 Nikola Vucevic 4.00 10.00
47 Myles Turner
48 Larry Nance Jr. 4.00 10.00
49 Tony Delk
50 Marc Gasol
51 Bill Willoughby 3.00 8.00
52 Vin Baker 3.00 8.00
53 Brian Grant 3.00 8.00
54 Zydrunas Ilgauskas 4.00 10.00
55 Mark Price 6.00 15.00
56 Dan Majerle 4.00 10.00
57 Shane Battier 4.00 10.00
58 Dan Issel 4.00 10.00
59 Cedric Ceballos 3.00 8.00
60 Jim Jackson 3.00 8.00
61 Glen Rice 4.00 10.00
62 Jamal Mashburn 5.00 12.00
63 Dell Curry 3.00 8.00
64 Artis Gilmore 4.00 10.00
65 Brent Barry 3.00 8.00
66 Kurt Rambis 3.00 8.00
67 Vlade Divac 5.00 12.00
68 Dikembe Mutombo 5.00 12.00
69 Toni Kukoc 5.00 12.00
70 Spud Webb 4.00 10.00
71 Jalen Rose 5.00 12.00
72 Tim Hardaway 5.00 12.00
73 Cedric Maxwell 3.00 8.00
74 Josh Richardson 3.00 8.00
75 Jordan Mickey 3.00 8.00
76 Raul Neto
77 Justin Anderson
78 Nikola Jokic
79 Malachi Richardson 4.00 10.00
80 Rondae Hollis-Jefferson 3.00 8.00
81 Kent Bazemore 4.00 10.00
82 Jae Crowder
83 Donatas Motiejunas 3.00 8.00
84 Festus Ezeli 3.00 8.00
85 Trey Lyles 4.00 10.00
86 Patrick Patterson 3.00 8.00
87 Jaylen Brown 20.00 50.00
88 Dragan Bender 6.00 15.00
89 Kris Dunn 10.00 25.00
90 Buddy Hield 15.00 40.00
91 Jamal Murray 25.00 60.00
92 Marquese Chriss 12.00 30.00
93 Jakob Poeltl 4.00 10.00
94 Thon Maker 25.00 60.00
95 Domantas Sabonis 8.00 20.00
96 Taurean Prince 5.00 12.00
97 Denzel Valentine 10.00 25.00
98 Wade Baldwin IV 3.00 8.00
99 Henry Ellenson 4.00 10.00
100 Dejounte Murray 30.00 80.00

2016-17 Panini Prizm Explosion

RANDOM INSERTS IN PACKS
*GREEN: .5X TO 1.2X BASIC
*SILVER: .5X TO 1.2X BASIC
*RUBY: .5X TO 1.2X BASIC
*BLUE/99: .6X TO 1.5X BASIC
*PURPLE/75: .75X TO 2X BASIC
*ORANGE/49: 1X TO 2.5X BASIC
*MOJO/25: 1.5X TO 4X BASIC
*ORNG WAVE/25: 1.5X TO 4X BASIC
*TEAL WAVE/25: 1.5X TO 4X BASIC
1 LeBron James 2.50 6.00
2 Kyrie Irving 1.25 3.00
3 Paul George .75 2.00
4 James Harden 1.00 2.50
5 Jimmy Butler .60 1.50
6 Carmelo Anthony .75 2.00
7 Karl-Anthony Towns 1.50 4.00
8 Chris Paul .75 2.00
9 Klay Thompson .75 2.00
10 Anthony Davis 1.25 3.00
11 Dirk Nowitzki .75 2.00
12 DeMar DeRozan .60 1.50
13 Kawhi Leonard 1.00 2.50
14 LaMarcus Aldridge .60 1.50
15 Russell Westbrook 1.50 4.00
16 Blake Griffin .60 1.50
17 Stephen Curry 2.50 6.00
18 Andrew Wiggins 1.00 2.50
19 Damian Lillard 1.25 3.00
20 John Wall .75 2.00

2016-17 Panini Prizm First Step

RANDOM INSERTS IN PACKS
*GREEN: .5X TO 1.2X BASIC
*SILVER: .5X TO 1.2X BASIC
*RUBY: .5X TO 1.2X BASIC
*BLUE/99: .6X TO 1.5X BASIC
*PURPLE/75: .75X TO 2X BASIC
*ORANGE/49: 1X TO 2.5X BASIC
*MOJO/25: 1.5X TO 4X BASIC
*ORNG WAVE/25: 1.5X TO 4X BASIC
*TEAL WAVE/25: 1.5X TO 4X BASIC
1 Damian Lillard 1.25 3.00
2 Tony Parker .60 1.50
3 Reggie Jackson .50 1.25
4 Stephen Curry 2.50 6.00
5 John Wall .75 2.00
6 LeBron James 2.50 6.00
7 Russell Westbrook 1.50 4.00
8 Isaiah Thomas .60 1.50
9 Andrew Wiggins 1.00 2.50
10 James Harden 1.00 2.50

2016-17 Panini Prizm Go Hard or Go Home

RANDOM INSERTS IN PACKS
*GREEN: .5X TO 1.2X BASIC
*SILVER: .5X TO 1.2X BASIC
*RUBY: .5X TO 1.2X BASIC
*BLUE/99: .6X TO 1.5X BASIC
*PURPLE/75: .75X TO 2X BASIC
*ORANGE/49: 1X TO 2.5X BASIC
*MOJO/25: 1.5X TO 4X BASIC
*ORNG WAVE/25: 1.5X TO 4X BASIC
*TEAL WAVE/25: 1.5X TO 4X BASIC
1 John Wall .75 2.00
2 Damian Lillard 1.25 3.00
3 Anthony Davis 1.25 3.00
4 LeBron James 2.50 6.00
5 Jahlil Okafor .50 1.25
6 Giannis Antetokounmpo 1.25 3.00
7 Jimmy Butler .60 1.50
8 Mike Conley .50 1.25
9 Kyrie Irving 1.25 3.00
10 Isaiah Thomas .60 1.50
11 Chris Paul .75 2.00
12 Justise Winslow .50 1.25
13 Kemba Walker .60 1.50
14 Gordon Hayward .60 1.50
15 DeMarcus Cousins .60 1.50
16 Carmelo Anthony .75 2.00
17 Jordan Clarkson .50 1.25
18 Manu Ginobili .60 1.50
19 Emmanuel Mudiay .50 1.25
20 Jeff Teague .50 1.25
21 Reggie Jackson .50 1.25
22 DeMar DeRozan .60 1.50
23 James Harden 1.00 2.50
24 Tony Parker .60 1.50
25 Brandon Knight .50 1.25
26 Ricky Rubio .60 1.50
27 Draymond Green .75 2.00
28 Bradley Beal .60 1.50
29 Elfrid Payton .50 1.25
30 Eric Bledsoe .50 1.25

2016-17 Panini Prizm Go Hard or Go Home Prizms Orange Wave

*ORANGE WAVE: 1.5X TO 4X BASIC
4 LeBron James 20.00 50.00

2016-17 Panini Prizm Mosaic

COMPLETE SET (100) 60.00 150.00
1 Aaron Gordon .60 1.50
2 Al Horford .60 1.50
3 Andre Drummond .75 2.00
4 Andrew Wiggins 1.25 3.00
5 Anthony Davis 1.50 4.00
6 Ben Simmons 25.00 60.00
7 Blake Griffin .75 2.00
8 Brandon Ingram 5.00 12.00
9 Brook Lopez .60 1.50
10 Buddy Hield 2.00 5.00
11 C.J. McCollum .60 1.50
12 Carmelo Anthony 1.00 2.50
13 Chris Paul 1.00 2.50
14 Damian Lillard 1.50 4.00
15 Dario Saric 2.50 6.00
16 DeAndre Jordan .75 2.00
17 D'Angelo Russell 1.00 2.50
18 DeMar DeRozan .75 2.00
19 DeMarcus Cousins .75 2.00
20 Denzel Valentine 1.00 2.50
21 Derrick Favors .60 1.50
22 Derrick Rose 1.00 2.50
23 Devin Booker 1.25 3.00
24 Dirk Nowitzki 1.00 2.50
25 Domantas Sabonis 1.25 3.00
26 Dragan Bender 1.00 2.50
27 Dwight Howard .60 1.50
28 Dwyane Wade 1.25 3.00
29 Emmanuel Mudiay .60 1.50
30 Eric Bledsoe .60 1.50
31 Eric Gordon .60 1.50
32 Evan Fournier .60 1.50
33 Giannis Antetokounmpo 1.50 4.00
34 Goran Dragic .60 1.50
35 Gordon Hayward .75 2.00
36 Harrison Barnes .60 1.50
37 Hassan Whiteside .60 1.50
38 Henry Ellenson 1.00 2.50
39 Isaiah Thomas .75 2.00
40 Jabari Parker 1.00 2.50
41 Jakob Poeltl 1.00 2.50
42 Jamal Murray 2.50 6.00
43 James Harden 1.25 3.00
44 Jeremy Lin .75 2.00
45 Jaylen Brown 3.00 8.00
46 Jimmy Butler .75 2.00
47 Joel Embiid 1.25 3.00
48 John Wall 1.00 2.50
49 Juan Hernangomez 1.00 2.50
50 Julius Randle .75 2.00
51 Karl-Anthony Towns 2.00 5.00
52 Kawhi Leonard 1.25 3.00
53 Kay Felder .75 2.00
54 Kemba Walker .75 2.00
55 Kenneth Faried .60 1.50
56 Kevin Durant 2.00 5.00
57 Kevin Love .75 2.00
58 Klay Thompson 1.00 2.50
59 Kris Dunn 2.50 6.00
60 Kristaps Porzingis 1.50 4.00
61 Kyle Lowry .60 1.50
62 Kyrie Irving 1.50 4.00
63 LaMarcus Aldridge .75 2.00
64 LeBron James 3.00 8.00
65 Malcolm Brogdon 2.00 5.00
66 Malik Beasley .75 2.00
67 Marc Gasol .75 2.00
68 Marquese Chriss 2.00 5.00
69 Mike Conley .60 1.50
70 Myles Turner .60 1.50
71 Nicolas Batum .60 1.50
72 Pascal Siakam .75 2.00
73 Patrick McCaw 1.50 4.00
74 Pau Gasol .75 2.00
75 Paul George 1.00 2.50
76 Paul Millsap .75 2.00
77 Reggie Jackson .60 1.50
78 Rudy Gay .75 2.00
79 Rudy Gobert .75 2.00
80 Russell Westbrook 2.00 5.00
81 Stephen Curry 3.00 8.00
82 Thon Maker 2.50 6.00
83 Tyler Ulis 2.50 6.00
84 Vince Carter 1.00 2.50
85 Zach LaVine .75 2.00
86 Tristan Thompson .60 1.50

87 Victor Oladipo .60 1.50
88 Nikola Vucevic .60 1.50
89 Bradley Beal .75 2.00
90 J.J. Redick .75 2.00
91 Jordan Clarkson .60 1.50
92 Wilson Chandler .60 1.50
93 Marcin Gortat .60 1.50
94 Nikola Mirotic .60 1.50
95 Taurean Prince 1.25 3.00
96 Rajon Rondo .75 2.00
97 Jeff Teague .60 1.50
98 Sergio Rodriguez .50 1.25
99 Wade Baldwin IV .75 2.00
100 Jonas Valanciunas .60 1.50

2016-17 Panini Prizm Mosaic Blue

*BLUE: .6X TO 1.5X BASIC
*BLUE RC: .6X TO 1.5X BASIC RC
RANDOM INSERTS IN PACKS

2016-17 Panini Prizm Mosaic Camo

*CAMO: 2X TO 5X BASIC
*CAMO RC: 2X TO 5X BASIC RC
RANDOM INSERTS IN PACKS
STATED PRINT RUN 25 SER.#'d SETS
6 Ben Simmons 400.00 800.00
8 Brandon Ingram 75.00 200.00
10 Buddy Hield 25.00 60.00
15 Dario Saric 20.00 50.00
20 Denzel Valentine 15.00 40.00
25 Domantas Sabonis 12.00 30.00
26 Dragan Bender 10.00 25.00
38 Henry Ellenson 20.00 50.00
41 Jakob Poeltl 10.00 25.00
42 Jamal Murray 50.00 120.00
45 Jaylen Brown 60.00 150.00
49 Juan Hernangomez 10.00 25.00
53 Kay Felder 8.00 20.00
59 Kris Dunn 30.00 80.00
64 LeBron James 60.00 150.00
65 Malcolm Brogdon 20.00 50.00
66 Malik Beasley 8.00 20.00
68 Marquese Chriss 30.00 80.00
72 Pascal Siakam 8.00 20.00
73 Patrick McCaw 12.00 30.00
82 Thon Maker 40.00 100.00
83 Tyler Ulis 20.00 50.00
95 Taurean Prince 10.00 25.00
99 Wade Baldwin IV 8.00 20.00

2016-17 Panini Prizm Mosaic Red

COMPLETE SET (100) 100.00 250.00
*RED: .6X TO 1.5X BASIC
*RED RC: .6X TO 1.5X BASIC RC
RANDOM INSERTS IN PACKS

2016-17 Panini Prizm Mosaic Autographs

RANDOM INSERTS IN PACKS
5 Anthony Davis 50.00 120.00
7 Blake Griffin 20.00 50.00
8 Brandon Ingram 50.00 120.00
10 Buddy Hield 12.00 30.00
15 Dario Saric 30.00 80.00
20 Denzel Valentine 5.00 12.00
24 Dirk Nowitzki
25 Domantas Sabonis 6.00 15.00
28 Dwyane Wade 30.00 80.00
38 Henry Ellenson 5.00 12.00
42 Jamal Murray 20.00 50.00
45 Jaylen Brown 25.00 60.00
49 Juan Hernangomez 5.00 12.00
51 Karl-Anthony Towns 60.00 150.00
53 Kay Felder 4.00 10.00
56 Kevin Durant
59 Kris Dunn 12.00 30.00
62 Kyrie Irving 30.00 80.00
65 Malcolm Brogdon 20.00 50.00
66 Malik Beasley 4.00 10.00
72 Pascal Siakam 4.00 10.00
73 Patrick McCaw 8.00 20.00
81 Stephen Curry 100.00 250.00
82 Thon Maker 25.00 60.00
83 Tyler Ulis 15.00 40.00
95 Taurean Prince 6.00 15.00
99 Wade Baldwin IV 4.00 10.00

2016-17 Panini Prizm Rookie Jerseys

RANDOM INSERTS IN PACKS
*SILVER: .5X TO 1.2X BASIC
*GREEN: .5X TO 1.2X BASIC
*ORANGE/25: .75X TO 2X BASIC
2 Brandon Ingram 5.00 12.00
3 Jaylen Brown 5.00 12.00
4 Dragan Bender 2.50 6.00
5 Kris Dunn 4.00 10.00
6 Buddy Hield 5.00 12.00
7 Jamal Murray 6.00 15.00
8 Marquese Chriss 5.00 12.00
9 Jakob Poeltl 2.50 6.00
10 Thon Maker 4.00 10.00
11 Taurean Prince 3.00 8.00
12 Georgios Papagiannis 2.00 5.00
13 Denzel Valentine 4.00 10.00
14 Juan Hernangomez 2.50 6.00
15 Wade Baldwin IV 2.00 5.00
16 Henry Ellenson 2.50 6.00
17 Malik Beasley 2.00 5.00
18 Caris LeVert 2.50 6.00
19 DeAndre' Bembry 2.00 5.00
20 Malachi Richardson 2.50 6.00
21 T. Luwawu-Cabarrot 4.00 10.00
22 Brice Johnson 2.00 5.00
23 Pascal Siakam 2.00 5.00
24 Skal Labissiere 3.00 8.00
25 Dejounte Murray 4.00 10.00
26 Damian Jones 2.00 5.00
27 Deyonta Davis 2.00 5.00
28 Cheick Diallo 2.00 5.00
29 Tyler Ulis 4.00 10.00
30 Patrick McCaw 4.00 10.00
31 Malcolm Brogdon 4.00 10.00
32 Isaiah Whitehead 2.00 5.00
33 Demetrius Jackson 2.00 5.00
34 Kay Felder 2.00 5.00
35 Gary Payton II 2.50 6.00
36 Diamond Stone 2.00 5.00
37 Ivica Zubac 3.00 8.00
38 Chinanu Onuaku 2.00 5.00
39 Stephen Zimmerman 2.00 5.00
40 A.J. Hammons 2.00 5.00
42 Brandon Ingram 8.00 20.00
43 Jaylen Brown 6.00 15.00
44 Dragan Bender 2.50 6.00
45 Kris Dunn 4.00 10.00
46 Buddy Hield 5.00 12.00
47 Jamal Murray 6.00 15.00
48 Marquese Chriss 5.00 12.00
49 Jakob Poeltl 2.50 6.00
50 Thon Maker 4.00 10.00
51 Taurean Prince 3.00 8.00
52 Georgios Papagiannis 2.00 5.00
53 Denzel Valentine 4.00 10.00
54 Juan Hernangomez 2.50 6.00
55 Wade Baldwin IV 2.00 5.00
56 Henry Ellenson 2.50 6.00
57 Malik Beasley 2.00 5.00
58 Caris LeVert 2.50 6.00
59 DeAndre' Bembry 2.00 5.00
60 Malachi Richardson 2.50 6.00
61 T. Luwawu-Cabarrot 4.00 10.00
62 Brice Johnson 2.00 5.00
63 Pascal Siakam 2.00 5.00
64 Skal Labissiere 3.00 8.00
65 Dejounte Murray 4.00 10.00
66 Damian Jones 2.00 5.00
67 Deyonta Davis 2.00 5.00
68 Cheick Diallo 2.00 5.00
69 Tyler Ulis 4.00 10.00
70 Patrick McCaw 4.00 10.00
71 Malcolm Brogdon 4.00 10.00
72 Isaiah Whitehead 2.00 5.00
73 Demetrius Jackson 2.00 5.00
74 Kay Felder 2.00 5.00
75 Gary Payton II 2.50 6.00
76 Diamond Stone 2.00 5.00
77 Ivica Zubac 3.00 8.00
78 Chinanu Onuaku 2.00 5.00
79 Stephen Zimmerman 2.00 5.00
80 A.J. Hammons 2.00 5.00
82 Brandon Ingram 8.00 20.00
83 Jaylen Brown 6.00 15.00
84 Dragan Bender 2.50 6.00
85 Kris Dunn 4.00 10.00
86 Buddy Hield 5.00 12.00
87 Jamal Murray 6.00 15.00
88 Marquese Chriss 5.00 12.00
89 Jakob Poeltl 2.50 6.00
90 Thon Maker 4.00 10.00
91 Taurean Prince 3.00 8.00
92 Georgios Papagiannis 2.00 5.00
93 Denzel Valentine 4.00 10.00
94 Juan Hernangomez 2.50 6.00
95 Wade Baldwin IV 2.00 5.00
96 Henry Ellenson 2.50 6.00
97 Malik Beasley 2.00 5.00
98 Caris LeVert 2.50 6.00
99 DeAndre' Bembry 2.00 5.00
100 Malachi Richardson 2.50 6.00

2016-17 Panini Prizm Rookie Signatures

RANDOM INSERTS IN PACKS
*BLUE/49: .5X TO 1.2X BASIC
1 Brandon Ingram 60.00 150.00
2 Jaylen Brown 20.00 50.00
3 Dragan Bender 8.00 20.00
4 Kris Dunn 10.00 25.00
5 Buddy Hield 20.00 50.00
6 Jamal Murray 25.00 60.00
7 Marquese Chriss 15.00 40.00
8 Jakob Poeltl 4.00 10.00
9 Thon Maker 25.00 60.00
10 Domantas Sabonis 5.00 12.00
11 Taurean Prince 5.00 12.00
12 Georgios Papagiannis 3.00 8.00
13 Denzel Valentine 4.00 10.00
14 Juan Hernangomez 4.00 10.00
15 Wade Baldwin IV 3.00 8.00
16 Henry Ellenson 4.00 10.00
17 Malik Beasley 3.00 8.00
18 Caris LeVert 4.00 10.00
19 DeAndre' Bembry 3.00 8.00
20 Malachi Richardson 4.00 10.00
21 T. Luwawu-Cabarrot 6.00 15.00
22 Brice Johnson 3.00 8.00
23 Pascal Siakam 3.00 8.00
24 Skal Labissiere
25 Dejounte Murray
26 Damian Jones 3.00 8.00
27 Deyonta Davis 3.00 8.00
28 Ivica Zubac 15.00 40.00
29 Cheick Diallo 3.00 8.00
30 Tyler Ulis 20.00 50.00
31 Malcolm Brogdon 25.00 60.00
32 Chinanu Onuaku 3.00 8.00
33 Patrick McCaw 10.00 25.00
34 Diamond Stone 3.00 8.00
35 Stephen Zimmerman
36 Dario Saric 60.00 150.00
37 Isaiah Whitehead
38 Demetrius Jackson 3.00 8.00
39 A.J. Hammons 3.00 8.00
40 Jake Layman 4.00 10.00
41 Georges Niang 3.00 8.00
42 Kay Felder 3.00 8.00
43 Gary Payton II 4.00 10.00
44 Isaiah Cousins 3.00 8.00
45 Ben Bentil 3.00 8.00
46 Ron Baker 10.00 25.00
47 Joel Bolomboy 3.00 8.00
48 Daniel Hamilton 3.00 8.00
49 Sheldon McClellan 3.00 8.00
50 Zach Auguste 3.00 8.00

2016-17 Panini Prizm Sky's the Limit

RANDOM INSERTS IN PACKS
*GREEN: .5X TO 1.2X BASIC
*SILVER: .5X TO 1.2X BASIC
*RUBY: .5X TO 1.2X BASIC
*BLUE/99: .6X TO 1.5X BASIC
*PURPLE/75: .75X TO 2X BASIC
*ORANGE/49: 1X TO 2.5X BASIC
*MOJO/25: 1.5X TO 4X BASIC
*ORNG WAVE/25: 1.5X TO 4X BASIC
*TEAL WAVE/25: 1.5X TO 4X BASIC
1 Zach LaVine .60 1.50
2 Andre Drummond .60 1.50
3 Aaron Gordon .50 1.25
4 LeBron James 2.50 6.00
5 Vince Carter .75 2.00
6 Will Barton .40 1.00
7 Giannis Antetokounmpo 1.25 3.00
8 Terrence Ross .50 1.25
9 John Wall .75 2.00
10 DeAndre Jordan .60 1.50
11 Andre Iguodala .50 1.25
12 Russell Westbrook 1.50 4.00
13 Blake Griffin .60 1.50
14 Andrew Wiggins 1.00 2.50
15 Julius Randle .60 1.50
16 Mason Plumlee .50 1.25
17 Victor Oladipo .50 1.25
18 Paul George .75 2.00
19 Damian Lillard 1.25 3.00
20 Eric Bledsoe .50 1.25
21 Justise Winslow .50 1.25
22 Kristaps Porzingis 1.25 3.00
23 Kenneth Faried .50 1.25
24 Stanley Johnson .40 1.00
25 Anthony Davis 1.25 3.00

2016-17 Panini Prizm Veteran Signatures

RANDOM INSERTS IN PACKS
*BLUE/49: .5X TO 1.2X BASIC
1 Kevin Durant 60.00 120.00
2 Andrew Wiggins 20.00 50.00
3 Kobe Bryant 60.00 150.00
4 Anthony Davis 25.00 60.00
5 Karl-Anthony Towns 50.00 120.00
6 Kristaps Porzingis 25.00 60.00
7 Devin Booker
8 Justise Winslow
9 Myles Turner
10 Klay Thompson 25.00 60.00
11 Kyrie Irving 25.00 60.00
12 D'Angelo Russell 12.00 30.00
13 Dirk Nowitzki 40.00 100.00
14 Draymond Green 10.00 25.00
15 Bobby Portis 3.00 8.00
16 Isaiah Thomas
17 Vince Carter 10.00 25.00
18 Reggie Jackson 4.00 10.00
19 Tony Parker
21 Hassan Whiteside 6.00 15.00
22 Danilo Gallinari
23 Mario Hezonja 3.00 8.00
24 Wesley Matthews
26 Tony Allen
28 Boban Marjanovic 3.00 8.00
29 Zach LaVine
30 Emmanuel Mudiay 4.00 10.00
31 Jonas Valanciunas 4.00 10.00
32 Andrew Bogut 4.00 10.00
33 Dwyane Wade/150 20.00 50.00
34 John Wall
35 C.J. McCollum 5.00 12.00
36 Anthony Bennett 3.00 8.00
37 Cody Zeller 3.00 8.00
38 Dwight Powell 3.00 8.00
39 E'Twaun Moore 3.00 8.00
40 Ian Clark 3.00 8.00
41 James Ennis 3.00 8.00
42 Ray McCallum 3.00 8.00
43 T.J. McConnell 3.00 8.00
44 Alex Len 3.00 8.00
45 Allen Crabbe 3.00 8.00
46 Aaron Harrison 3.00 8.00
47 Tristan Thompson 4.00 10.00
48 Lamar Patterson 3.00 8.00
50 Victor Oladipo 4.00 10.00

2015-16 Panini Revolution

1 John Wall .50 1.25
2 DeMarcus Cousins .40 1.00
3 Elfrid Payton .30 .75
4 Kevin Garnett .60 1.50
5 Mike Conley .40 1.00
6 James Harden .60 1.50
7 Chandler Parsons .30 .75
8 Jeremy Lamb .25 .60
9 Bradley Beal .40 1.00
10 Jeff Teague .30 .75
11 Rajon Rondo .40 1.00
12 Tobias Harris .30 .75
13 Ricky Rubio .40 1.00
14 Zach Randolph .30 .75
15 Terrence Jones .30 .75
16 Deron Williams .30 .75
17 Jeremy Lin .40 1.00
18 Marcin Gortat .30 .75
19 Rudy Gay .40 1.00
20 Victor Oladipo .30 .75
21 Zach LaVine .40 1.00
22 Jordan Clarkson .40 1.00
23 Draymond Green .50 1.25
24 Dirk Nowitzki .50 1.25
25 Kemba Walker .40 1.00
26 Gordon Hayward .40 1.00
27 C.J. McCollum .40 1.00
28 Kevin Durant 1.00 2.50
29 Giannis Antetokounmpo .75 2.00
30 Julius Randle .40 1.00
31 Harrison Barnes .30 .75
32 John Jenkins .25 .60
33 Nicolas Batum .30 .75
34 Rodney Hood .30 .75
35 Damian Lillard .75 2.00
36 Russell Westbrook 1.00 2.50
37 Greg Monroe .30 .75
38 Kobe Bryant 1.50 4.00
39 Klay Thompson .50 1.25
40 Kevin Love .40 1.00
41 Bojan Bogdanovic .25 .60
42 Rudy Gobert .40 1.00
43 Meyers Leonard .25 .60
44 Serge Ibaka .30 .75
45 Jabari Parker .50 1.25
46 Blake Griffin .40 1.00
47 Stephen Curry 1.50 4.00
48 Kyrie Irving .75 2.00
49 Brook Lopez .30 .75
50 DeMar DeRozan .40 1.00
51 Brandon Knight .30 .75
52 Arron Afflalo .25 .60
53 Michael Carter-Williams .25 .60
54 Chris Paul .50 1.25
55 Andre Drummond .40 1.00
56 LeBron James 1.50 4.00
57 Joe Johnson .30 .75
58 Jonas Valanciunas .30 .75
59 Eric Bledsoe .30 .75
60 Carmelo Anthony .50 1.25
61 Chris Andersen .30 .75
62 DeAndre Jordan .40 1.00
63 Kentavious Caldwell-Pope .30 .75
64 Matthew Dellavedova .30 .75
65 Avery Bradley .30 .75
66 Kyle Lowry .30 .75
67 T.J. Warren .30 .75
68 Robin Lopez .25 .60
69 Chris Bosh .40 1.00
70 George Hill .30 .75
71 Reggie Jackson .30 .75
72 Derrick Rose .50 1.25
73 Evan Turner .30 .75
74 Kawhi Leonard .60 1.50
75 Isaiah Canaan .30 .75
76 Anthony Davis .75 2.00
77 Dwyane Wade .60 1.50
78 Monta Ellis .30 .75
79 Gary Harris .30 .75
80 Jimmy Butler .40 1.00
81 Marcus Smart .30 .75
82 Manu Ginobili .40 1.00
83 Nerlens Noel .30 .75
84 Jrue Holiday .30 .75
85 Goran Dragic .30 .75
86 Paul George .50 1.25
87 Kenneth Faried .30 .75
88 Nikola Mirotic .30 .75
89 Al Horford .30 .75
90 Tim Duncan .60 1.50
91 Nik Stauskas .25 .60
92 Tyreke Evans .25 .60
93 Marc Gasol .40 1.00
94 Dwight Howard .30 .75
95 Danilo Gallinari .30 .75
96 Pau Gasol .40 1.00
97 Dennis Schroder .30 .75
98 Tony Parker .40 1.00
99 Aaron Gordon .30 .75
100 Andrew Wiggins .60 1.50
101 D'Angelo Russell RC 1.50 4.00
102 Devin Booker RC 2.00 5.00
103 Josh Richardson RC .60 1.50
104 Myles Turner RC .60 1.50
105 R.J. Hunter RC .40 1.00
106 Aaron Harrison RC .50 1.25
107 Duje Dukan RC .40 1.00
108 Justin Anderson RC .50 1.25
109 Nemanja Bjelica RC .50 1.25
110 Rondae Hollis-Jefferson RC .50 1.25
111 Anthony Brown RC .40 1.00
112 Emmanuel Mudiay RC .60 1.50
113 Justise Winslow RC .60 1.50
114 Nikola Jokic RC .75 2.00
115 Marcelo Huertas RC .50 1.25
116 Boban Marjanovic RC .50 1.25
117 Frank Kaminsky RC .60 1.50
118 Karl-Anthony Towns RC 3.00 8.00
119 Norman Powell RC .50 1.25
120 Sam Dekker RC .50 1.25
121 Bobby Portis RC .60 1.50
122 Jahlil Okafor RC .75 2.00
123 Kelly Oubre Jr. RC .50 1.25
124 Pat Connaughton RC .40 1.00
125 Stanley Johnson RC .50 1.25
126 T.J. McConnell RC .50 1.25
127 Jarell Martin RC .50 1.25
128 Kevon Looney RC .50 1.25
129 Josh Huestis RC .40 1.00
130 Terry Rozier RC .50 1.25
131 Branden Dawson RC .40 1.00
132 Jerian Grant RC .40 1.00
133 Kristaps Porzingis RC 1.50 4.00
134 Rakeem Christmas RC .40 1.00
135 Trey Lyles RC .60 1.50
136 Cameron Payne RC .50 1.25
137 Joe Young RC .50 1.25
138 Larry Nance Jr. RC .60 1.50
139 Rashad Vaughn RC .40 1.00
140 Tyus Jones RC .60 1.50
141 Chris McCullough RC .40 1.00
142 Jonathon Simmons RC .60 1.50
143 Mario Hezonja RC .50 1.25
144 Raul Neto RC .40 1.00
145 Walter Tavares RC .40 1.00
146 Delon Wright RC .50 1.25
147 Jordan Mickey RC .40 1.00
148 Montrezl Harrell RC .50 1.25
149 Richaun Holmes RC .50 1.25
150 Willie Cauley-Stein RC .60 1.50

2015-16 Panini Revolution Angular

*ANG 1-100: 1X TO 2.5X BASIC
*ANG 101-150: .6X TO 1.5X BASIC
STATED ODDS 1:12 PACKS

2015-16 Panini Revolution Cosmic

*COS 1-100: 2.5X TO 6X BASIC
*COS 101-150: 1.5X TO 4X BASIC
RANDOM INSERTS IN PACKS
STATED PRINT RUN 100 SER.#'d SETS

2015-16 Panini Revolution Futura

*FUT 1-100: 5X TO 12X BASIC
*FUT 101-150: 3X TO 8X BASIC
RANDOM INSERTS IN PACKS
STATED PRINT RUN 25 SER.#'d SETS
28 Kevin Durant 20.00 50.00
38 Kobe Bryant 40.00 100.00
56 LeBron James 40.00 100.00
101 D'Angelo Russell 25.00 60.00
118 Karl-Anthony Towns 50.00 120.00
122 Jahlil Okafor 20.00 50.00
133 Kristaps Porzingis 50.00 120.00

2015-16 Panini Revolution Infinite

*INF 1-100: .75X TO 2X BASIC
*INF 101-150: .5X TO 1.2X BASIC
STATED ODDS 1:6 PACKS

2015-16 Panini Revolution Nova

*NOVA 1-100: .75X TO 2X BASIC
*NOVA 101-150: .5X TO 1.2X BASIC
STATED ODDS 1:6 PACKS

2015-16 Panini Revolution Sunburst

*SUN 1-100: 2.5X TO 6X BASIC
*SUN 101-150: 1.5X TO 4X BASIC
RANDOM INSERTS IN PACKS
STATED PRINT RUN 75 SER.#'d SETS
102 Devin Booker 30.00 80.00
118 Karl-Anthony Towns 30.00 80.00

2015-16 Panini Revolution Autographs

STATED ODDS 1:69 PACKS
EXCHANGE DEADLINE 9/23/2017
1 Kobe Bryant 250.00 500.00
2 Kevin Durant 60.00 150.00
3 Kyrie Irving 40.00 100.00
4 Blake Griffin EXCH 20.00 50.00
5 Anthony Davis 60.00 150.00
6 Kevin Love 15.00 40.00
7 Dwyane Wade 125.00 250.00
8 Julius Randle 15.00 40.00
10 John Wall 40.00 100.00
11 Carmelo Anthony 30.00 80.00
12 Zach LaVine 30.00 80.00
13 Andrew Wiggins 30.00 80.00
14 Victor Oladipo 12.00 30.00
16 Tony Parker 30.00 80.00
17 Harrison Barnes 12.00 30.00
18 Kenneth Faried 12.00 30.00
19 Elfrid Payton 12.00 30.00
20 Jabari Parker 25.00 60.00
21 Chris Paul 40.00 100.00
22 Bradley Beal 25.00 60.00
24 Hakeem Olajuwon 20.00 50.00
25 Isiah Thomas 20.00 50.00
26 Grant Hill 20.00 50.00
27 Anfernee Hardaway 30.00 80.00
28 Alonzo Mourning 20.00 50.00
29 Dennis Rodman 40.00 100.00
30 Tracy McGrady 40.00 100.00
31 Jason Kidd 25.00 60.00
32 Gary Payton 20.00 50.00

2015-16 Panini Revolution Icons

STATED ODDS 1:10 PACKS
*COSMIC/100: 1.2X TO 3X BASIC
1 Larry Bird 2.50 6.00
2 Magic Johnson 2.50 6.00
3 Wilt Chamberlain 2.00 5.00
4 Pete Maravich 1.50 4.00
5 Julius Erving 1.50 4.00
6 Gary Payton 1.00 2.50
7 Hakeem Olajuwon 1.25 3.00
8 Dominique Wilkins 1.25 3.00
9 Shaquille O'Neal 2.00 5.00
10 Scottie Pippen 2.00 5.00
11 Bob Cousy 1.50 4.00
12 Bill Russell 1.50 4.00
13 John Stockton 1.50 4.00
14 Karl Malone 1.25 3.00
15 David Robinson 1.50 4.00
16 Oscar Robertson 1.25 3.00
17 Kareem Abdul-Jabbar 1.50 4.00
18 Steve Nash 1.00 2.50
19 Grant Hill 1.25 3.00
20 Patrick Ewing 1.25 3.00
21 Alonzo Mourning 1.25 3.00
22 Allen Iverson 1.25 3.00
23 Yao Ming 1.25 3.00
24 Clyde Drexler 1.25 3.00
25 Jason Kidd 1.00 2.50
26 Walt Frazier 1.00 2.50
27 Dikembe Mutombo 1.00 2.50
28 Shawn Kemp 1.50 4.00
29 Dennis Rodman 2.00 5.00
30 Jerry West 1.25 3.00
31 Chris Mullin 1.00 2.50
32 Nate Archibald .75 2.00
33 Tracy McGrady 1.00 2.50

2015-16 Panini Revolution New Wave

STATED ODDS 1:4 PACKS
*COSMIC/100: 2X TO 5X BASIC
1 Zach LaVine .60 1.50
2 Elfrid Payton .50 1.25
3 Kyle Anderson .40 1.00
4 Victor Oladipo .50 1.25
5 Dennis Schroder .50 1.25
6 Kentavious Caldwell-Pope .50 1.25
7 T.J. Warren .50 1.25
8 C.J. McCollum .60 1.50
9 Kawhi Leonard 1.00 2.50
10 Rodney Hood .50 1.25
11 Bruno Caboclo .40 1.00
12 Jusuf Nurkic .40 1.00
13 Reggie Jackson .50 1.25
14 Bradley Beal .60 1.50
15 Julius Randle .60 1.50
16 Otto Porter .50 1.25
17 Bojan Bogdanovic .40 1.00
18 Jordan Clarkson .60 1.50
19 Nikola Mirotic .50 1.25
20 Archie Goodwin .40 1.00
21 Nikola Jokic .75 2.00
22 Nerlens Noel .50 1.25
23 Anthony Davis 1.25 3.00
24 Jabari Parker .75 2.00
25 Michael Carter-Williams .40 1.00
26 Andrew Wiggins 1.00 2.50
27 Harrison Barnes .50 1.25
28 Marcus Smart .50 1.25
29 Aaron Gordon .50 1.25
30 Gary Harris .50 1.25

2015-16 Panini Revolution Rookie Autographs

STATED ODDS 1:55 PACKS
EXCHANGE DEADLINE 9/23/2017
1 Karl-Anthony Towns 200.00 400.00
2 Jahlil Okafor 12.00 30.00
3 Myles Turner 30.00 80.00
5 Justise Winslow 12.00 30.00
6 Jerian Grant 5.00 12.00
7 Kristaps Porzingis 100.00 250.00
8 Mario Hezonja 6.00 15.00
9 Nemanja Bjelica 6.00 15.00
10 Emmanuel Mudiay 20.00 50.00
11 Willie Cauley-Stein 20.00 50.00
12 Delon Wright 6.00 15.00
13 Bobby Portis 8.00 20.00
14 Sam Dekker 6.00 15.00
15 Devin Booker 100.00 250.00
16 D'Angelo Russell 30.00 80.00
17 Trey Lyles 8.00 20.00
18 Frank Kaminsky 8.00 20.00

2015-16 Panini Revolution Rookie Revolution

STATED ODDS 1:10 PACKS
*COSMIC/100: 1.2X TO 3X BASIC
1 Willie Cauley-Stein 1.00 2.50
2 Rashad Vaughn .60 1.50
3 Karl-Anthony Towns 5.00 12.00
4 Emmanuel Mudiay 1.00 2.50
5 Tyus Jones 1.00 2.50
6 Nemanja Bjelica .75 2.00
7 Justise Winslow 1.00 2.50
8 Devin Booker 3.00 8.00
9 Trey Lyles 1.00 2.50
10 Myles Turner 1.00 2.50
11 Justin Anderson .75 2.00
12 Delon Wright .75 2.00
13 Terry Rozier .75 2.00
14 Mario Hezonja .75 2.00
15 Josh Richardson 1.00 2.50
16 D'Angelo Russell 2.50 6.00
17 Stanley Johnson .75 2.00
18 Kristaps Porzingis 2.50 6.00
19 Jerian Grant .60 1.50
20 Cameron Payne .75 2.00
21 Sam Dekker .75 2.00
22 Jahlil Okafor 1.25 3.00
23 Bobby Portis 1.00 2.50
24 R.J. Hunter .60 1.50
25 Kelly Oubre Jr. .75 2.00

2015-16 Panini Revolution Showstoppers

STATED ODDS 1:64 PACKS
*COSMIC/100: 1.2X TO 3X BASIC
1 Stephen Curry 8.00 20.00
2 Russell Westbrook 5.00 12.00
3 LeBron James 8.00 20.00
4 Tim Duncan 3.00 8.00
5 Kobe Bryant 8.00 20.00
6 Kevin Durant 5.00 12.00
7 James Harden 3.00 8.00
8 Dirk Nowitzki 2.50 6.00
9 Kyrie Irving 4.00 10.00
10 Derrick Rose 2.50 6.00
11 Damian Lillard 4.00 10.00
12 Chris Paul 2.50 6.00

2016-17 Panini Revolution

1 Steven Adams .30 .75
2 LaMarcus Aldridge .40 1.00
3 Ryan Anderson .30 .75
4 Giannis Antetokounmpo .75 2.00
5 Carmelo Anthony .50 1.25
6 Trevor Ariza .25 .60
7 Harrison Barnes .30 .75
8 Nicolas Batum .30 .75
9 Bradley Beal .40 1.00
10 Eric Bledsoe .30 .75
11 Devin Booker .60 1.50
12 Justise Winslow .30 .75
13 Jimmy Butler .40 1.00
14 Kentavious Caldwell-Pope .30 .75
15 Willie Cauley-Stein .30 .75
16 Jordan Clarkson .30 .75
17 Darren Collison .30 .75
18 Mike Conley .30 .75
19 DeMarcus Cousins .40 1.00
20 Stephen Curry 1.50 4.00
21 Anthony Davis .75 2.00
22 DeMar DeRozan .40 1.00
23 Goran Dragic .30 .75
24 Andre Drummond .40 1.00
25 Kevin Durant 1.00 2.50
26 Monta Ellis .30 .75
27 Tyreke Evans .25 .60
28 Kenneth Faried .30 .75
29 Derrick Favors .30 .75
30 Evan Fournier .30 .75
31 Marc Gasol .40 1.00
32 Pau Gasol .40 1.00
33 Paul George .50 1.25
34 Rudy Gobert .40 1.00
35 Aaron Gordon .30 .75
36 Eric Gordon .30 .75
37 Marcin Gortat .30 .75
38 Draymond Green .50 1.25
39 Blake Griffin .40 1.00
40 James Harden .60 1.50
41 Gordon Hayward .40 1.00
42 Jrue Holiday .30 .75
43 Al Horford .30 .75
44 Dwight Howard .30 .75
45 Kyrie Irving .75 2.00
46 LeBron James 1.50 4.00
47 Stanley Johnson .25 .60
48 Nikola Jokic .40 1.00
49 DeAndre Jordan .40 1.00
50 Michael Kidd-Gilchrist .30 .75
51 Brandon Knight .30 .75
52 Zach LaVine .40 1.00
53 Kawhi Leonard .60 1.50
54 Damian Lillard .75 2.00
55 Jeremy Lin .40 1.00
56 Brook Lopez .30 .75
57 Kevin Love .40 1.00
58 Kyle Lowry .30 .75
59 C.J. McCollum .30 .75
60 T.J. McConnell .25 .60
61 Paul Millsap .40 1.00
62 Nikola Mirotic .30 .75
63 Greg Monroe .30 .75
64 Emmanuel Mudiay .30 .75
65 Joakim Noah .30 .75
66 Nerlens Noel .30 .75
67 Dirk Nowitzki .50 1.25
68 Jahlil Okafor .30 .75
69 Victor Oladipo .30 .75
70 Jabari Parker .50 1.25
71 Tony Parker .40 1.00
72 Chandler Parsons .30 .75
73 Chris Paul .50 1.25
74 Kristaps Porzingis .75 2.00
75 Julius Randle .40 1.00
76 Zach Randolph .30 .75
77 J.J. Redick .40 1.00
78 Rajon Rondo .40 1.00
79 Derrick Rose .50 1.25
80 Ricky Rubio .40 1.00
81 D'Angelo Russell .50 1.25
82 Dennis Schroder .30 .75
83 Luis Scola .30 .75
84 Marcus Smart .30 .75
85 Jared Sullinger .25 .60
86 Isaiah Thomas .40 1.00
87 Klay Thompson .50 1.25
88 Tristan Thompson .30 .75
89 Karl-Anthony Towns 1.00 2.50
90 Myles Turner .30 .75
91 Jonas Valanciunas .30 .75
92 Noah Vonleh .25 .60
93 Nikola Vucevic .30 .75
94 Dwyane Wade .60 1.50
95 Kemba Walker .40 1.00
96 John Wall .50 1.25
97 Russell Westbrook 1.00 2.50
98 Hassan Whiteside .30 .75
99 Andrew Wiggins .60 1.50
100 Deron Williams .30 .75
101 Wade Baldwin IV RC .40 1.00
102 Malik Beasley RC .40 1.00
103 DeAndre' Bembry RC .40 1.00
104 Dragan Bender RC .50 1.25
105 Joel Bolomboy RC .40 1.00
106 Malcolm Brogdon RC 1.00 2.50
107 Jaylen Brown RC 1.50 4.00
108 Marquese Chriss RC 1.00 2.50
109 Deyonta Davis RC .40 1.00
110 Cheick Diallo RC .40 1.00
111 Kris Dunn RC 1.25 3.00
112 Henry Ellenson RC .50 1.25
113 Kay Felder RC .40 1.00
114 Michael Gbinije RC .40 1.00
115 A.J. Hammons RC .40 1.00
116 Willy Hernangomez RC .50 1.25
117 Buddy Hield RC 1.00 2.50
118 Brandon Ingram RC 2.50 6.00
119 Demetrius Jackson RC .40 1.00
120 Brice Johnson RC .40 1.00
121 Damian Jones RC .40 1.00
122 Mindaugas Kuzminskas RC .50 1.25
123 Skal Labissiere RC .60 1.50
124 Jake Layman RC .50 1.25
125 Caris LeVert RC .50 1.25
126 T. Luwawu-Cabarrot RC .75 2.00
127 Thon Maker RC 1.25 3.00
128 Patrick McCaw RC .75 2.00
129 Dejounte Murray RC .75 2.00
130 Jamal Murray RC 1.25 3.00
131 Georges Niang RC .40 1.00
132 Chinanu Onuaku RC .40 1.00
133 Georgios Papagiannis RC .40 1.00
134 Ron Baker RC .50 1.25
135 Marshall Plumlee RC .40 1.00
136 Jakob Poeltl RC .50 1.25
137 Taurean Prince RC .60 1.50
138 Malachi Richardson RC .50 1.25
139 Domantas Sabonis RC .60 1.50
140 Dario Saric RC 1.25 3.00
141 Tomas Satoransky RC .40 1.00
142 Pascal Siakam RC .40 1.00
143 Ben Simmons RC 8.00 20.00
144 Diamond Stone RC .40 1.00
145 Tyler Ulis RC 1.25 3.00
146 Denzel Valentine RC .50 1.25
147 Isaiah Whitehead RC .40 1.00
148 Stephen Zimmerman RC .40 1.00
149 Paul Zipser RC .60 1.50
150 Ivica Zubac RC .60 1.50

2016-17 Panini Revolution Astro

*ASTRO: .75X TO 2X BASIC
*ASTRO RC: .75X TO 2X BASIC RC
RANDOM INSERTS IN PACKS

2016-17 Panini Revolution Cosmic

*COSMIC: 2X TO 5X BASIC
*COSMIC RC: 2X TO 5X BASIC RC
RANDOM INSERTS IN PACKS
STATED PRINT RUN 100 SER.#'d SETS
46 LeBron James 20.00 50.00

2016-17 Panini Revolution Fractal

*FRACTAL: 1.2X TO 3X BASIC
*FRACTAL RC: 1.2X TO 3X BASIC RC
RANDOM INSERTS IN PACKS

2016-17 Panini Revolution Futura

*FUTURA: 3X TO 8X BASIC
*FUTURA RC: 3X TO 8X BASIC RC
RANDOM INSERTS IN PACKS
STATED PRINT RUN 25 SER.#'d SETS
46 LeBron James 30.00 80.00
143 Ben Simmons 150.00 400.00

2016-17 Panini Revolution Infinite

*INFINITE: 1X TO 2.5X BASIC
*INFINITE RC: 1X TO 2.5X BASIC RC
RANDOM INSERTS IN PACKS

2016-17 Panini Revolution Sunburst

*SUNBURST: 2.5X TO 6X BASIC
*SUNBURST RC: 2.5X TO 6X BASIC RC
RANDOM INSERTS IN PACKS
STATED PRINT RUN 75 SER.#'d SETS
46 LeBron James 25.00 60.00
143 Ben Simmons 125.00 300.00

2016-17 Panini Revolution Autographs

RANDOM INSERTS IN PACKS
*FUTURA/25: .6X TO 1.5X BASIC
1 Anthony Davis 50.00 120.00
2 Kobe Bryant 150.00 400.00
3 Kyrie Irving 40.00 100.00
4 Kevin Durant 100.00 250.00
6 Vince Carter 30.00 80.00
8 Kevin Love
9 Kristaps Porzingis 30.00 80.00
12 Justise Winslow 8.00 20.00
13 Andrew Wiggins 30.00 80.00
14 Myles Turner 12.00 30.00
15 Karl-Anthony Towns 50.00 120.00
16 Hassan Whiteside
17 Reggie Jackson 5.00 12.00
18 Nikola Jokic 30.00 80.00
19 Zach LaVine 20.00 50.00
20 Josh Richardson
21 James Worthy 12.00 30.00
22 Gary Payton 10.00 25.00
24 Grant Hill 20.00 50.00
25 Ray Allen 30.00 80.00
26 David Robinson 30.00 80.00
27 Patrick Ewing 100.00 250.00
28 John Stockton 25.00 60.00
29 Allen Iverson 100.00 250.00
30 Larry Bird 50.00 120.00
31 Magic Johnson 30.00 80.00
33 Karl Malone 25.00 60.00
34 Dennis Rodman 25.00 60.00
35 Shaquille O'Neal 50.00 120.00

2016-17 Panini Revolution By the Numbers

RANDOM INSERTS IN PACKS
*COSMIC/100: 1.2X TO 3X BASIC
1 Stephen Curry 2.50 6.00
2 James Harden 1.00 2.50
3 Kevin Durant 1.50 4.00
4 DeMarcus Cousins .60 1.50
5 LeBron James 2.50 6.00
6 Damian Lillard 1.25 3.00
7 Anthony Davis 1.25 3.00
8 Russell Westbrook 1.50 4.00
9 DeMar DeRozan .60 1.50
10 Paul George .75 2.00
11 Rajon Rondo .60 1.50
12 Russell Westbrook 1.50 4.00
13 John Wall .75 2.00
14 Chris Paul .75 2.00
15 Ricky Rubio .60 1.50
16 Andre Drummond .60 1.50
17 DeAndre Jordan .60 1.50
18 Dwight Howard .50 1.25
19 Hassan Whiteside .50 1.25
20 DeMarcus Cousins .60 1.50

2016-17 Panini Revolution Revolutionaries

RANDOM INSERTS IN PACKS
*COSMIC/100: 1X TO 2.5X BASIC
1 Bill Russell 3.00 8.00
2 Oscar Robertson 2.50 6.00
3 Jerry West 2.50 6.00
4 Wilt Chamberlain 4.00 10.00
5 Pete Maravich 3.00 8.00
6 Julius Erving 3.00 8.00
7 Larry Bird 5.00 12.00
8 Magic Johnson 5.00 12.00
9 Hakeem Olajuwon 2.50 6.00
10 David Robinson 3.00 8.00
11 Scottie Pippen 4.00 10.00
12 Karl Malone 2.50 6.00
13 Shaquille O'Neal 5.00 12.00
14 Allen Iverson 2.50 6.00
15 Yao Ming 2.50 6.00
16 Kobe Bryant 8.00 20.00

2016-17 Panini Revolution Rookie Autographs

RANDOM INSERTS IN PACKS
*FUTURA/25: .6X TO 1.5X BASIC
1 Brandon Ingram 75.00 200.00
2 Dario Saric 20.00 50.00
3 Jaylen Brown 30.00 80.00
4 Buddy Hield 25.00 60.00
5 Kris Dunn 25.00 60.00
6 Jamal Murray 25.00 60.00
7 Marquese Chriss 12.00 30.00
8 Jakob Poeltl 5.00 12.00
9 Thon Maker 40.00 100.00
10 Caris LeVert 15.00 40.00
11 Dragan Bender
12 Dejounte Murray
13 Denzel Valentine 15.00 40.00
14 Damian Jones 10.00 25.00
15 Juan Hernangomez 8.00 20.00

2016-17 Panini Revolution Rookie Autographs Futura

*FUTURA: .6X TO 1.5X BASIC
RANDOM INSERTS IN PACKS
STATED PRINT RUN 25 SER.#'d SETS
7 Marquese Chriss 30.00 80.00

2016-17 Panini Revolution Rookie Revolution

RANDOM INSERTS IN PACKS
*COSMIC/100: 1.2X TO 3X BASIC
1 Dario Saric 1.25 3.00
2 Brandon Ingram 2.50 6.00
3 Jaylen Brown 1.50 4.00
4 Ben Simmons 2.50 6.00
5 Dragan Bender .50 1.25
6 Kris Dunn 1.25 3.00
7 Buddy Hield 1.00 2.50
8 Jamal Murray 1.25 3.00

9 Marquese Chriss 1.00 2.50
10 Jakob Poeltl .50 1.25
11 Thon Maker 1.25 3.00
12 Domantas Sabonis .60 1.50
13 Taurean Prince .60 1.50
14 Georgios Papagiannis .40 1.00
15 Denzel Valentine .50 1.25
16 Juan Hernangomez .50 1.25
17 Wade Baldwin IV .40 1.00
18 Henry Ellenson .50 1.25
19 Malik Beasley .40 1.00
20 Caris LeVert .50 1.25
21 DeAndre' Bembry .40 1.00
22 Malachi Richardson .50 1.25
23 Timothe Luwawu-Cabarrot .75 2.00
24 Brice Johnson .40 1.00
25 Pascal Siakam .40 1.00
26 Skal Labissiere .60 1.50
27 Dejounte Murray .75 2.00
28 Damian Jones .40 1.00

2016-17 Panini Revolution Showstoppers

RANDOM INSERTS IN PACKS
*COSMIC/100: .75X TO 2X BASIC
1 Carmelo Anthony 2.50 6.00
2 Stephen Curry 8.00 20.00
3 Anthony Davis 4.00 10.00
4 Kevin Durant 5.00 12.00
5 James Harden 3.00 8.00
6 Kyrie Irving 4.00 10.00
7 LeBron James 8.00 20.00
8 Dirk Nowitzki 2.50 6.00
9 Chris Paul 2.50 6.00
10 Karl-Anthony Towns 5.00 12.00
11 Dwyane Wade 3.00 8.00
12 Russell Westbrook 5.00 12.00

2016-17 Panini Revolution Star Gazing

RANDOM INSERTS IN PACKS
*COSMIC/100: 1.2X TO 3X BASIC
1 LaMarcus Aldridge .60 1.50
2 Carmelo Anthony .75 2.00
3 Jimmy Butler .60 1.50
4 DeMarcus Cousins .60 1.50
5 Stephen Curry 2.50 6.00
6 Anthony Davis 1.25 3.00
7 DeMar DeRozan .60 1.50
8 Kevin Durant 1.50 4.00
9 Paul George .75 2.00
10 Blake Griffin .60 1.50
11 James Harden 1.00 2.50
12 Kyrie Irving 1.25 3.00
13 LeBron James 2.50 6.00
14 DeAndre Jordan .60 1.50
15 Kawhi Leonard 1.00 2.50
16 Damian Lillard 1.25 3.00
17 Dirk Nowitzki .75 2.00
18 Chris Paul .75 2.00
19 Derrick Rose .75 2.00
20 Klay Thompson .75 2.00
21 Karl-Anthony Towns 1.50 4.00
22 Dwyane Wade 1.00 2.50
23 John Wall .75 2.00
24 Russell Westbrook 1.50 4.00

2009-10 Panini Season Update

COMPLETE SET (200) 25.00 50.00
UNPRICED PLATINUM PRINT RUN ONE SET
1 Kobe Bryant HL 1.00 2.50
2 Brandon Jennings HL .25 .60
3 Allen/Nowitzki/Duncan HL .40 1.00
4 Kevin Durant HL .60 1.50
5 Rajon Rondo HL .25 .60
6 Ben Gordon HL .20 .50
7 Gasol/Odom/Kobe HL 1.00 2.50
8 Jason Kidd HL .25 .60
9 Vince Carter HL .30 .75
10 NBA All-Star Game HL .25 .60
11 Dwyane Wade HL .40 1.00
12 Malone/Pippen HL .50 1.25
13 Kobe Bryant HL 1.00 2.50
14 Kevin Durant HL .60 1.50
15 Don Nelson HL .25 .60
16 Josh Smith HL .20 .50
17 Tyreke Evans HL .20 .50
18 LeBron James HL 1.00 2.50
19 2010 NBA Lottery HL .25 .60
20 Los Angeles Lakers HL 1.00 2.50
21 Rajon Rondo .25 .60
22 Paul Pierce .25 .60
23 Kevin Garnett .40 1.00
24 Rasheed Wallace .25 .60
25 Glen Davis .15 .40
26 Ray Allen .25 .60
27 Brook Lopez .20 .50
28 Devin Harris .15 .40
29 Courtney Lee .20 .50
30 Chris Douglas-Roberts .15 .40
31 Al Harrington .20 .50
32 David Lee .15 .40
33 Tracy McGrady .25 .60
34 Danilo Gallinari .20 .50
35 Amare Stoudemire SP 4.00 10.00
36 Andre Iguodala .20 .50
37 Louis Williams .20 .50
38 Allen Iverson .30 .75
39 Samuel Dalembert .15 .40
40 Elton Brand .25 .60
41 Thaddeus Young .15 .40
42 Chris Bosh .25 .60
43 Jarrett Jack .20 .50
44 Andrea Bargnani .20 .50
45 Hedo Turkoglu .20 .50
46 Jose Calderon .15 .40
47 Jason Kidd .25 .60
48 Dirk Nowitzki .30 .75
49 Caron Butler .20 .50
50 Jason Terry .20 .50
51 Shawn Marion .20 .50
52 Brendan Haywood .15 .40
53 Aaron Brooks .15 .40
54 Trevor Ariza .15 .40
55 Luis Scola .20 .50
56 Shane Battier .25 .60
57 Kevin Martin .20 .50
58 Zach Randolph .20 .50
59 Rudy Gay .25 .60
60 O.J. Mayo .15 .40
61 Marc Gasol .25 .60
62 Mike Conley Jr. .20 .50
63 Darrell Arthur .20 .50
64 David West .20 .50
65 Emeka Okafor .20 .50
66 Chris Paul .30 .75
67 Peja Stojakovic .25 .60
68 Morris Peterson .15 .40
69 Tim Duncan .40 1.00
70 Manu Ginobili .25 .60
71 George Hill .25 .60
72 Tony Parker .25 .60
73 Richard Jefferson .20 .50
74 Antonio McDyess .20 .50
75 Joakim Noah .20 .50
76 Derrick Rose .40 1.00
77 Kirk Hinrich .20 .50
78 Luol Deng .20 .50
79 Carlos Boozer SP 6.00 15.00
80 Brad Miller .20 .50
81 Antawn Jamison .20 .50
82 LeBron James 1.00 2.50
83 Anderson Varejao .15 .40
84 Shaquille O'Neal .50 1.25
85 Mo Williams .20 .50
86 J.J. Hickson .15 .40
87 Ben Gordon .20 .50
88 Tayshaun Prince .20 .50
89 Richard Hamilton .20 .50
90 Ben Wallace .20 .50
91 Rodney Stuckey .15 .40
92 Jason Maxiell .15 .40
93 Danny Granger .20 .50
94 Roy Hibbert .20 .50
95 Mike Dunleavy .15 .40
96 Troy Murphy .15 .40
97 Dahntay Jones .15 .40
98 Brandon Rush .15 .40
99 Andrew Bogut .20 .50
100 John Salmons .20 .50
101 Luke Ridnour .20 .50
102 Carlos Delfino .15 .40
103 Michael Redd .20 .50
104 Carmelo Anthony .30 .75
105 Chris Andersen .20 .50
106 J.R. Smith .20 .50
107 Nene .20 .50
108 Chauncey Billups .25 .60
109 Al Jefferson .20 .50
110 Kevin Love .25 .60
111 Corey Brewer .15 .40
112 Ryan Gomes .15 .40
113 LaMarcus Aldridge .25 .60
114 Brandon Roy .25 .60
115 Rudy Fernandez .15 .40
116 Andre Miller .20 .50
117 Juwan Howard .20 .50
118 Nicolas Batum .20 .50
119 Kevin Durant .60 1.50
120 Russell Westbrook .60 1.50
121 Jeff Green .20 .50
122 Nenad Krstic .15 .40
123 Nick Collison .20 .50
124 Deron Williams .20 .50
125 Carlos Boozer .20 .50
126 Mehmet Okur .15 .40
127 Paul Millsap .20 .50
128 Andrei Kirilenko .20 .50
129 Monta Ellis .20 .50
130 Anthony Morrow .15 .40
131 Corey Maggette .20 .50
132 C.J. Watson .15 .40
133 Kobe Bryant 1.00 2.50
134 Pau Gasol .25 .60
135 Lamar Odom .20 .50
136 Andrew Bynum .15 .40
137 Ron Artest .25 .60
138 Derek Fisher .20 .50
139 Luke Walton .15 .40
140 Amare Stoudemire .20 .50
141 Steve Nash .25 .60
142 Jason Richardson .25 .60
143 Robin Lopez .15 .40
144 Grant Hill .30 .75
145 Channing Frye .20 .50
146 Spencer Hawes .15 .40
147 Beno Udrih .15 .40
148 Jason Thompson .15 .40
149 Carl Landry .15 .40
150 Donte Greene .15 .40
151 Andres Nocioni .15 .40
152 Josh Smith .20 .50
153 Jamal Crawford .25 .60
154 Al Horford .25 .60
155 Joe Johnson .20 .50
156 Mike Bibby .20 .50
157 Marvin Williams .20 .50
158 Gerald Wallace .20 .50
159 Stephen Jackson .20 .50
160 Raymond Felton .20 .50
161 Boris Diaw .20 .50
162 D.J. Augustin .15 .40
163 Michael Beasley .15 .40
164 Dwyane Wade .40 1.00
165 Jermaine O'Neal .20 .50
166 Udonis Haslem .15 .40
167 Chris Bosh SP 6.00 15.00
168 LeBron James 8.00 20.00
169 Dwight Howard .20 .50
170 Vince Carter .30 .75
171 Rashard Lewis .20 .50
172 J.J. Redick .25 .60
173 Jameer Nelson .15 .40
174 Matt Barnes .15 .40
175 Al Thornton .20 .50
176 Josh Howard .20 .50
177 Randy Foye .15 .40
178 Mike Miller .20 .50
179 Andray Blatche .15 .40
180 Shaun Livingston .15 .40
181 LeBron James AS 1.00 2.50
182 Dwight Howard AS .20 .50
183 Dwyane Wade AS .40 1.00
184 Chris Bosh AS .25 .60
185 Rajon Rondo AS .25 .60
186 Joe Johnson AS .20 .50
187 Paul Pierce AS .25 .60
188 Derrick Rose AS .40 1.00
189 Al Horford AS .25 .60
190 David Lee AS .15 .40
191 Carmelo Anthony AS .30 .75
192 Dirk Nowitzki AS .30 .75
193 Chauncey Billups AS .25 .60
194 Deron Williams AS .20 .50
195 Amare Stoudemire AS .20 .50
196 Pau Gasol AS .25 .60
197 Steve Nash AS .25 .60
198 Kevin Durant AS .60 1.50
199 Chris Kaman AS .20 .50
200 Tim Duncan AS .40 1.00

2009-10 Panini Season Update Gold

*GOLD: 5X TO 12X BASE HI
STATED PRINT RUN 24 SER.#'d SETS
35 Amare Stoudemire 2.50 6.00
79 Carlos Boozer 2.50 6.00
167 Chris Bosh 3.00 8.00
168 LeBron James 20.00 50.00

2009-10 Panini Season Update Silver

*SILVER: 2.5X TO 6X BASE HI
STATED PRINT RUN 99 SER.#'d SETS
35 Amare Stoudemire 1.25 3.00
79 Carlos Boozer 1.25 3.00
167 Chris Bosh 1.50 4.00
168 LeBron James 12.00 30.00

2009-10 Panini Season Update All-Star Patches

COMPLETE SET (5) 25.00 60.00
STATED PRINT RUN 499 SER.#'d SETS
1 Kobe Bryant 12.00 30.00
2 Dirk Nowitzki 6.00 15.00
3 Chris Bosh 6.00 15.00
4 LeBron James 12.00 30.00
5 Dwyane Wade 8.00 20.00

2009-10 Panini Season Update Christmas Cards Materials

INT RUN 499 SER.#'d SETS
*PRIME: .75X TO 2X BASE HI
PRIME PRINT RUN 25 SER.#'d SETS
1 Andre Miller 3.00 8.00
2 Amare Stoudemire 3.00 8.00
3 Anthony Carter 2.50 6.00
4 Arron Afflalo 2.50 6.00
5 Brandon Roy 4.00 10.00
6 Carlos Arroyo 3.00 8.00
7 Carmelo Anthony 5.00 12.00
8 Channing Frye 3.00 8.00
9 Chauncey Billups 4.00 10.00
10 Daequan Cook 2.50 6.00
11 Dorell Wright 2.50 6.00
12 Dwight Howard 3.00 8.00
13 Dwyane Wade 6.00 15.00
14 Earl Clark 3.00 8.00
15 Goran Dragic 8.00 20.00
16 J.J. Redick 4.00 10.00
17 J.R. Smith 3.00 8.00
18 Jameer Nelson 2.50 6.00
19 Jared Dudley 2.50 6.00
20 Jason Richardson 4.00 10.00
21 Jason Williams 3.00 8.00
22 Jeff Pendergraph 2.50 6.00
23 Jermaine O'Neal 3.00 8.00
24 Jerryd Bayless 3.00 8.00
25 Joel Anthony 4.00 10.00
26 LaMarcus Aldridge 4.00 10.00
27 Louis Amundson 2.50 6.00
28 Marcin Gortat 3.00 8.00
29 Mario Chalmers 3.00 8.00
30 Martell Webster 2.50 6.00
31 Matt Barnes 2.50 6.00
32 Michael Beasley 2.50 6.00
33 Mickael Pietrus 2.50 6.00
34 Quentin Richardson 3.00 8.00
35 Rashard Lewis 3.00 8.00
36 Robin Lopez 2.50 6.00
37 Ryan Anderson 3.00 8.00
38 Steve Nash 4.00 10.00
39 Ty Lawson 4.00 10.00
40 Udonis Haslem 2.50 6.00

2009-10 Panini Season Update Lakers Legacy

COMPLETE SET (10) 4.00 10.00
RANDOM INSERTS IN PACKS
1 Kobe Bryant 2.00 5.00
2 Derek Fisher .50 1.25
3 Nick Van Exel .60 1.50
4 Pau Gasol .60 1.50
5 Robert Horry .50 1.25
6 Kareem Abdul-Jabbar 1.00 2.50
7 Gary Payton .60 1.50
8 Luke Walton .40 1.00
9 Lamar Odom .50 1.25
10 Andrew Bynum .40 1.00

2009-10 Panini Season Update Lakers Legacy Jerseys

COMPLETE SET (10) 30.00 80.00
RANDOM INSERTS IN PACKS
1 Kobe Bryant 8.00 20.00
2 Derek Fisher 4.00 10.00
3 Nick Van Exel 4.00 10.00
4 Pau Gasol 4.00 10.00
5 Robert Horry 4.00 10.00
6 Kareem Abdul-Jabbar 10.00 25.00
7 Gary Payton 4.00 10.00
8 Luke Walton 4.00 10.00
9 Lamar Odom 4.00 10.00
10 Andrew Bynum 4.00 10.00

2009-10 Panini Season Update Lakers Legacy Jerseys Prime

*PRIME: 1.25X TO 3X HI COLUMN
STATED PRINT RUN 10 TO 49 SER.#'d SETS
1 Kobe Bryant/49 20.00 50.00
6 Kareem Abdul-Jabbar/49 20.00 50.00
10 Andrew Bynum/15 15.00 40.00

2009-10 Panini Season Update Playoff Debuts

COMPLETE SET (19) 8.00 20.00
RANDOM INSERTS IN PACKS
*GOLD: 2X TO 5X BASE HI
GOLD PRINT RUN 24 SER.#'d SETS
UNPRICED PLATINUM PRINT RUN ONE SET
*SILVER: 1X TO 2.5X BASE HI
SILVER PRINT RUN 99 SER.#'d SETS
1 Kevin Durant 1.50 4.00
2 Brandon Jennings .60 1.50
3 Robin Lopez .40 1.00
4 D.J. Augustin .40 1.00
5 Wesley Matthews .60 1.50
6 Taj Gibson .60 1.50
7 Nate Robinson .40 1.00
8 Russell Westbrook 1.50 4.00
9 Adam Morrison .40 1.00
10 DeJuan Blair .50 1.25
11 Jeff Teague .60 1.50
12 Jeff Pendergraph .40 1.00
13 J.J. Hickson .40 1.00
14 Rodrigue Beaubois .40 1.00
15 Jeff Green .50 1.25
16 Raymond Felton .50 1.25
17 Jamal Crawford .60 1.50
18 Ty Lawson .60 1.50
19 Ryan Anderson .50 1.25

2009-10 Panini Season Update Rookie Challenge

COMPLETE SET (16) 10.00 25.00
RANDOM INSERTS IN PACKS
1 Stephen Curry 15.00 40.00
2 Tyreke Evans .60 1.50
3 Brandon Jennings .75 2.00
4 Anthony Morrow .50 1.25
5 Brook Lopez .60 1.50
6 Danilo Gallinari .60 1.50
7 DeJuan Blair .60 1.50
8 Eric Gordon .60 1.50
9 Jonas Jerebko .75 2.00
10 Jonny Flynn .50 1.25
11 Kevin Love .75 2.00
12 Marc Gasol .75 2.00
13 Michael Beasley .50 1.25
14 O.J. Mayo .50 1.25
15 Omri Casspi .60 1.50
16 Russell Westbrook 2.00 5.00

2009-10 Panini Season Update Rookie Challenge Jerseys

RANDOM INSERTS IN PACKS
UNPRICED PRIME PRINT RUN 5 TO 10 SETS
1 Stephen Curry 40.00 100.00
2 Tyreke Evans 1.50 4.00
3 Brandon Jennings 2.00 5.00
4 Anthony Morrow 2.00 5.00
5 Brook Lopez 2.50 6.00
6 Danilo Gallinari 2.50 6.00
7 DeJuan Blair 1.50 4.00
8 Eric Gordon 2.50 6.00
9 Jonas Jerebko 2.00 5.00
10 Jonny Flynn 1.25 3.00
11 Kevin Love 3.00 8.00
12 Marc Gasol 3.00 8.00
13 Michael Beasley 2.00 5.00
14 O.J. Mayo 2.00 5.00
15 Omri Casspi 1.50 4.00
16 Russell Westbrook 8.00 20.00

2009-10 Panini Season Update Rookie Challenge Jerseys Signatures

STATED PRINT RUN 25 SER.#'d SETS
UNPRICED PRIME PRINT RUN ONE TO 10 SETS
1 Stephen Curry 500.00 900.00
2 Tyreke Evans 6.00 15.00
3 Brandon Jennings 6.00 15.00
7 DeJuan Blair 6.00 15.00
9 Jonas Jerebko 8.00 20.00
10 Jonny Flynn 5.00 12.00
11 Kevin Love 15.00 40.00
13 Michael Beasley 10.00 25.00
15 Omri Casspi 6.00 15.00

2009-10 Panini Season Update Rookie Challenge Signatures

PRINT RUN 49 SER.#'d SETS
1 Stephen Curry 150.00 300.00
2 Tyreke Evans 5.00 12.00
3 Brandon Jennings 6.00 15.00
7 DeJuan Blair 5.00 12.00
9 Jonas Jerebko 6.00 15.00
10 Jonny Flynn 4.00 10.00
11 Kevin Love 12.00 30.00
13 Michael Beasley 8.00 20.00
15 Omri Casspi 5.00 12.00
16 Russell Westbrook 30.00 80.00

2009-10 Panini Season Update Rookie Duals Signatures

STATED PRINT RUN 49 TO 99 SER.#'d SETS
1 B.Griffin/B.Jennings/49 60.00 150.00
2 B.Griffin/S.Curry/49 400.00 800.00
3 B.Griffin/T.Evans/49 60.00 150.00
4 T.Evans/B.Jennings/49 6.00 15.00
5 T.Evans/S.Curry/49 150.00 300.00
6 B.Jennings/S.Curry/49 150.00 300.00
7 S.Curry/D.Collison/49 150.00 300.00
8 B.Griffin/T.Griffin/49 25.00 60.00
9 T.Griffin/E.Clark/99 6.00 15.00
10 J.Harden/S.Ibaka/99 40.00 100.00
11 J.Harden/E.Maynor/99 20.00 50.00
12 S.Ibaka/E.Maynor/99 6.00 15.00
13 J.Harden/B.Mullens/99 15.00 40.00
14 S.Ibaka/B.Mullens/99 6.00 15.00
15 W.Ellington/T.Lawson/99 6.00 15.00
16 J.Flynn/W.Ellington/99 6.00 15.00
17 T.Lawson/J.Flynn/99 6.00 15.00
18 T.Gibson/T.Lawson/99 6.00 15.00
19 T.Gibson/J.Johnson/99 6.00 15.00
20 J.Johnson/J.Teague/99 6.00 15.00
21 T.Gibson/J.Teague/99 8.00 20.00
22 H.Thabeet/D.Carroll/99 6.00 15.00
23 H.Thabeet/S.Young/99 6.00 15.00
24 D.Carroll/S.Young/99 6.00 15.00
25 D.Carroll/D.DeRozan/99 8.00 20.00
26 A.Price/T.Hansbrough/99 6.00 15.00
27 DeRozan/Hansbrough/99 6.00 15.00
28 S.Curry/J.Hill/49 150.00 300.00
29 J.Hill/T.Williams/99 6.00 15.00
30 T.Williams/G.Henderson/99 6.00 15.00
31 J.Harden/T.Williams/99 25.00 60.00
32 J.Holiday/T.Williams/99 6.00 15.00
33 T.Williams/A.Daye/99 6.00 15.00
34 J.Flynn/J.Hill/99 6.00 15.00
35 J.Harden/J.Teague/99 20.00 50.00
36 D.Collison/J.Teague/99 6.00 15.00
37 T.Douglas/L.Hudson/99 6.00 15.00
38 T.Douglas/Ellington/99 6.00 15.00
39 T.Hansbrough/B.Mullens/99 6.00 15.00
40 T.Hansbrough/L.Hudson/99 6.00 15.00
41 R.Beaubois/T.Evans/49 6.00 15.00
42 S.Curry/R.Beaubois/49 150.00 300.00
43 R.Beaubois/O.Casspi/99 6.00 15.00
44 T.Evans/O.Casspi/49 6.00 15.00
45 O.Casspi/J.Pendergraph/99 6.00 15.00
46 J.Jerebko/A.Daye/99 6.00 15.00
47 J.Jerebko/D.Summers/99 6.00 15.00
48 D.Summers/A.Daye/99 6.00 15.00
49 O.Casspi/J.Jerebko/99 6.00 15.00
50 D.Collison/M.Thornton/99 6.00 15.00
51 M.Thornton/D.Brown/99 6.00 15.00
52 J.Holiday/J.Meeks/99 6.00 15.00
53 J.Pendergraph/P.Mills/99 8.00 20.00
54 O.Casspi/J.Brockman/99 6.00 15.00
55 T.Evans/J.Brockman/49 6.00 15.00
56 J.Brockman/T.Griffin/99 6.00 15.00
57 D.Andersen/J.Hill/99 6.00 15.00
58 J.Hill/C.Budinger/99 6.00 15.00
59 J.Taylor/C.Budinger/99 6.00 15.00
60 J.Taylor/D.Andersen/99 6.00 15.00
61 J.Pendergraph/D.Cunningham/99 6.00 15.00
62 D.Cunningham/P.Mills/99 8.00 20.00
63 W.Matthews/S.Gaines/99 6.00 15.00
64 A.Price/J.Meeks/99 6.00 15.00
65 B.Jennings/J.Meeks/49 6.00 15.00
66 D.Blair/D.Summers/99 6.00 15.00
67 D.Blair/E.Clark/99 6.00 15.00
68 D.Blair/J.Johnson/99 6.00 15.00
69 D.DeRozan/D.Blair/99 6.00 15.00
70 H.Thabeet/S.Ibaka/99 6.00 15.00
71 W.Matthews/T.Douglas/99 6.00 15.00
72 W.Ellington/L.Hudson/99 6.00 15.00
73 L.Hudson/S.Gaines/99 6.00 15.00
74 J.Holiday/C.Budinger/99 6.00 15.00
75 R.Beaubois/DeRozan/99 6.00 15.00

2009-10 Panini Season Update Rookie Triples Signatures

STATED PRINT RUN 25 TO 49 SER.#'d SETS
1 Evans/Curry/Jennings/25 250.00 500.00
2 Harden/Maynor/Ibaka/49 50.00 120.00
3 Griffin/Blair/DeRozan/25 100.00 200.00
4 Collison/Beaubois/Flynn/49 15.00 40.00
5 Hill/Budinger/Taylor/49 10.00 25.00
6 Gibson/Lawson/Williams/49 8.00 20.00
7 Hnsbrgh/Price/Hndrsn/49 10.00 25.00
8 Griffin/Griffin/Clark/25 75.00 150.00
9 Daye/Jerebko/Summers/49 10.00 25.00
10 Thabeet/Young/Carroll/49 8.00 20.00
11 Evans/Casspi/Brock/25 30.00 60.00
12 Hnsbrgh/Mullens/Meeks/49 10.00 25.00
13 Collison/Thornton/Brown/49 8.00 20.00
14 Pndrgrph/Cnghm/Mills/49 12.00 30.00
15 Curry/Flynn/Lawson/25 250.00 500.00
16 Clark/Daye/Johnson/49 8.00 20.00
17 Holiday/Teague/Beaubois/49 12.50 30.00
18 Douglas/Hudson/Meeks/49 8.00 20.00
19 Blair/DeRozan/Carroll/49 15.00 30.00
20 Matthews/Douglas/Hudson/49 10.00 25.00
21 Jennings/Collison/Flynn/25 25.00 60.00
22 Williams/Henderson/Teague/49 8.00 20.00
23 Griffin/Thabeet/Harden/25 60.00 150.00
24 Flynn/Clark/Holiday/49 10.00 25.00
25 Hnsbrgh/Elngtn/Lawson/49 25.00 60.00

2009-10 Panini Season Update Signatures

STATED PRINT RUN ONE TO 100 SER.#'d SETS
SOME UNPRICED DUE TO SCARCITY
28 Darryl Dawkins/99 6.00 15.00
33 Mark Price/50 12.50 30.00
34 Mark Price/25 15.00 40.00
35 Robert Horry/50 25.00 60.00
37 Hakeem Olajuwon/50 15.00 30.00
38 Hakeem Olajuwon/25 25.00 50.00
39 Joe Dumars/50 8.00 20.00
40 Joe Dumars/25 10.00 25.00
41 Dominique Wilkins/50 15.00 30.00
42 Dominique Wilkins/25 15.00 40.00
44 Elgin Baylor/25 12.50 30.00
45 Sidney Moncrief/50 6.00 15.00
46 Sidney Moncrief/25 8.00 20.00

2010-11 Panini Season Update

COMPLETE SET (200) 15.00 40.00
EXCH.EXPIRATION 1/20/2013
UNPRICED PLATINUM PRINT RUN ONE SET
1 Glen Davis .15 .40
2 Jeff Green .20 .50
3 Kevin Garnett .40 1.00
4 Paul Pierce .25 .60
5 Rajon Rondo .25 .60
6 Ray Allen .25 .60
7 Shaquille O'Neal .50 1.25
8 Anthony Morrow .15 .40
9 Brook Lopez .20 .50
10 Deron Williams .20 .50
11 Kris Humphries .15 .40
12 Sasha Vujacic .15 .40
13 Travis Outlaw .20 .50
14 Amare Stoudemire .20 .50
15 Carmelo Anthony .30 .75
16 Chauncey Billups .25 .60
17 Ronny Turiaf .15 .40
18 Shawne Williams .15 .40
19 Toney Douglas .15 .40
20 Andre Iguodala .20 .50
21 Andres Nocioni .15 .40
22 Elton Brand .25 .60
23 Jrue Holiday .25 .60
24 Louis Williams .20 .50
25 Spencer Hawes .15 .40
26 Thaddeus Young .15 .40
27 Andrea Bargnani .20 .50
28 DeMar DeRozan .25 .60
29 Jose Calderon .15 .40
30 Leandro Barbosa .20 .50
31 Linas Kleiza .15 .40
32 Sonny Weems .15 .40
33 Carlos Boozer .20 .50
34 Derrick Rose .30 .75
35 Joakim Noah .20 .50
36 Kyle Korver .20 .50
37 Luol Deng .20 .50
38 Ronnie Brewer .20 .50
39 Taj Gibson .20 .50
40 Anderson Varejao .15 .40
41 Antawn Jamison .20 .50
42 Daniel Gibson .20 .50
43 J.J. Hickson .15 .40
44 Baron Davis .20 .50
45 Ramon Sessions .20 .50
46 Austin Daye .15 .40
47 Ben Gordon .20 .50
48 Charlie Villanueva .15 .40
49 Richard Hamilton .20 .50
50 Rodney Stuckey .20 .50
51 Tayshaun Prince .20 .50
52 Tracy McGrady .25 .60
53 Danny Granger .20 .50
54 Darren Collison .20 .50
55 Jeff Foster .15 .40
56 Mike Dunleavy .15 .40
57 Roy Hibbert .20 .50
58 T.J. Ford .15 .40
59 Tyler Hansbrough .20 .50
60 Andrew Bogut .20 .50
61 Brandon Jennings .15 .40
62 Carlos Delfino .15 .40
63 Corey Maggette .20 .50
64 Drew Gooden .20 .50
65 Ersan Ilyasova .20 .50
66 John Salmons .20 .50
67 Luc Mbah a Moute .15 .40
68 Al Horford .20 .50
69 Jamal Crawford .25 .60
70 Jeff Teague .20 .50
71 Joe Johnson .20 .50
72 Josh Smith .20 .50
73 Marvin Williams .20 .50
74 Boris Diaw .20 .50
75 D.J. Augustin .15 .40
76 Gerald Henderson .15 .40
77 Stephen Jackson .20 .50
78 Tyrus Thomas .15 .40
79 Chris Bosh .25 .60
80 Dwyane Wade .40 1.00
81 Eddie House .15 .40
82 LeBron James 1.25 3.00
83 Mike Miller .20 .50
84 Mike Bibby .20 .50
85 Udonis Haslem .15 .40
86 Brandon Bass .15 .40
87 Dwight Howard .20 .50
88 Gilbert Arenas .20 .50
89 Hedo Turkoglu .20 .50
90 J.J. Redick .25 .60
91 Jameer Nelson .15 .40
92 Jason Richardson .25 .60
93 Andray Blatche .15 .40
94 JaVale McGee .20 .50
95 Kirk Hinrich .20 .50
96 Nick Young .20 .50
97 Rashard Lewis .20 .50
98 Caron Butler .20 .50
99 Dirk Nowitzki .30 .75
100 Jason Kidd .25 .60
101 Jason Terry .20 .50
102 Peja Stojakovic .25 .60
103 Corey Brewer .15 .40
104 Shawn Marion .20 .50
105 Tyson Chandler .20 .50
106 Goran Dragic .20 .50
107 Kevin Martin .20 .50
108 Kyle Lowry .20 .50
109 Luis Scola .20 .50
110 Yao Ming .30 .75
111 Marc Gasol .25 .60
112 Shane Battier .20 .50
113 Mike Conley Jr. .25 .60
114 O.J. Mayo .15 .40
115 Rudy Gay .25 .60
116 Zach Randolph .20 .50
117 Chris Paul .30 .75
118 David West .20 .50
119 Emeka Okafor .20 .50
120 Carl Landry .15 .40
121 Trevor Ariza .15 .40
122 DeJuan Blair .15 .40
123 George Hill .20 .50
124 Manu Ginobili .25 .60
125 Richard Jefferson .20 .50
126 Tim Duncan .40 1.00
127 Tony Parker .25 .60
128 Al Harrington .20 .50
129 Arron Afflalo .15 .40
130 Danilo Gallinari .20 .50
131 Raymond Felton .20 .50
132 Wilson Chandler .20 .50
133 Chris Andersen .20 .50
134 J.R. Smith .20 .50
135 Kenyon Martin .20 .50
136 Nene .20 .50
137 Anthony Randolph .15 .40
138 Darko Milicic .15 .40
139 Kevin Love .25 .60
140 Luke Ridnour .20 .50
141 Martell Webster .20 .50
142 Michael Beasley .15 .40
143 Andre Miller .20 .50
144 Gerald Wallace .20 .50
145 Brandon Roy .25 .60
146 LaMarcus Aldridge .25 .60
147 Nicolas Batum .20 .50
148 Rudy Fernandez .15 .40
149 Wesley Matthews .15 .40
150 James Harden .40 1.00
151 Kendrick Perkins .15 .40
152 Kevin Durant .60 1.50
153 Russell Westbrook .60 1.50
154 Serge Ibaka .20 .50
155 Al Jefferson .20 .50
156 Andrei Kirilenko .20 .50
157 C.J. Miles .20 .50
158 Devin Harris .15 .40
159 Paul Millsap .20 .50
160 Raja Bell .20 .50
161 Andris Biedrins .15 .40
162 Al Thornton .15 .40
163 David Lee .15 .40
164 Dorell Wright .15 .40
165 Monta Ellis .20 .50
166 Reggie Williams .25 .60
167 Stephen Curry 1.00 2.50
168 Mo Williams .20 .50
169 Blake Griffin .25 .60
170 Chris Kaman .20 .50
171 Eric Gordon .20 .50
172 Ryan Gomes .15 .40
173 Andrew Bynum .15 .40
174 Derek Fisher .20 .50
175 Kobe Bryant 1.00 2.50
176 Lamar Odom .20 .50
177 Pau Gasol .25 .60
178 Ron Artest .25 .60
179 Channing Frye .20 .50
180 Aaron Brooks .15 .40
181 Grant Hill .30 .75
182 Marcin Gortat .20 .50
183 Steve Nash .25 .60
184 Vince Carter .30 .75
185 Beno Udrih .15 .40
186 Marcus Thornton .15 .40
187 Francisco Garcia .15 .40
188 Omri Casspi .15 .40
189 Samuel Dalembert .15 .40
190 Tyreke Evans .15 .40
191 Blake Griffin .25 .60
192 Ray Allen .25 .60
193 Kobe Bryant 1.00 2.50
194 Kevin Durant .60 1.50
195 Kevin Love .25 .60
196 George Karl .25 .60
197 Blake Griffin .25 .60
198 Derrick Rose .30 .75
199 Lamar Odom .20 .50
200 Kevin Love .25 .60

2010-11 Panini Season Update Gold

*GOLD: 5X TO 12X BASE HI
STATED PRINT RUN 24 SER.#'d SETS
181 Grant Hill 12.50 30.00

2010-11 Panini Season Update Silver

*SILVER: 2.5X TO 6X BASE HI
STATED PRINT RUN 99 SER.#'d SETS
181 Grant Hill 8.00 20.00

2010-11 Panini Season Update All-Stars

COMPLETE SET (25) 8.00 20.00
RANDOM INSERTS IN PACKS
1 Al Horford .30 .75
2 Amare Stoudemire .30 .75
3 Carmelo Anthony .50 1.25
4 Chauncey Billups .40 1.00
5 Chris Bosh .40 1.00
6 Chris Kaman .30 .75
7 David Lee .25 .60
8 Deron Williams .30 .75
9 Derrick Rose .50 1.25
10 Dirk Nowitzki .50 1.25
11 Dwight Howard .30 .75
12 Gerald Wallace .30 .75
13 Jason Kidd .40 1.00
14 Joe Johnson .30 .75
15 Kevin Durant 1.00 2.50
16 Kevin Garnett .60 1.50
17 LeBron James 2.00 5.00
18 Pau Gasol .40 1.00
19 Paul Pierce .40 1.00
20 Rajon Rondo .40 1.00
21 Steve Nash .40 1.00
22 Tim Duncan .60 1.50
23 Zach Randolph .30 .75
24 Kobe Bryant 1.50 4.00
25 Chris Paul .50 1.25

2010-11 Panini Season Update All-Stars Materials

RANDOM INSERTS IN PACKS
UNPRICED PRIME PRINT RUN 10 SETS
1 Al Horford 2.00 5.00
2 Amare Stoudemire 2.00 5.00
3 Carmelo Anthony 3.00 8.00
4 Chauncey Billups 2.50 6.00
5 Chris Bosh 2.50 6.00
6 Chris Kaman 2.00 5.00
7 David Lee 1.50 4.00
8 Deron Williams 2.00 5.00
9 Derrick Rose 3.00 8.00
10 Dirk Nowitzki 3.00 8.00
11 Dwight Howard 2.00 5.00
12 Gerald Wallace 2.00 5.00
13 Jason Kidd 2.50 6.00
14 Joe Johnson 2.00 5.00
15 Kevin Durant 6.00 15.00
16 Kevin Garnett 4.00 10.00
17 LeBron James 10.00 25.00
18 Pau Gasol 2.50 6.00
19 Paul Pierce 2.50 6.00
20 Rajon Rondo 2.50 6.00
21 Steve Nash 2.50 6.00
22 Tim Duncan 4.00 10.00
23 Zach Randolph 2.00 5.00
24 Kobe Bryant 10.00 25.00
25 Chris Paul 3.00 8.00

2010-11 Panini Season Update Green Week Jerseys

STATED PRINT RUN 10 TO 799 SER.#'d SETS
SOME UNPRICED DUE TO SCARCITY
1 Andre Miller/10
2 Anthony Carter/799 2.00 5.00
3 Arron Afflalo/799 2.00 5.00
4 Brandon Bass/799 2.00 5.00
5 Brandon Roy/99 2.50 6.00
6 Caron Butler/25 2.00 5.00
7 Chauncey Billups/50 2.50 6.00
8 Chris Andersen/699 2.00 5.00
9 Dante Cunningham/799 2.00 5.00
10 Dirk Nowitzki/399 3.00 8.00
11 Dwight Howard/99 2.00 5.00
12 J.R. Smith/499 2.00 5.00
13 Jameer Nelson/449 1.50 4.00
14 Jason Terry/649 2.00 5.00
15 Juwan Howard/799 2.00 5.00
16 LaMarcus Aldridge/799 2.50 6.00
17 Marcin Gortat/749 5.00 12.00
18 Martell Webster/799 2.00 5.00
19 Mickael Pietrus/349 2.00 5.00
20 Nene/699 2.00 5.00
21 Nicolas Batum/799 2.00 5.00
22 Rashard Lewis/799 2.00 5.00
23 Rudy Fernandez/749 1.50 4.00
24 Ryan Anderson/799 2.00 5.00
25 Shawn Marion/799 2.00 5.00
26 Ty Lawson/799 1.50 4.00
27 Vince Carter/799 3.00 8.00
28 Erick Dampier/799 2.00 5.00
29 Matt Barnes/799 2.00 5.00
30 Jerryd Bayless/799 2.00 5.00

2010-11 Panini Season Update Green Week Jerseys Prime

*PRIME: 1X TO 2.5X BASE HI
STATED PRINT RUN ONE TO 49 SER.#'d SETS
SOME UNPRICED DUE TO SCARCITY
1 Andre Miller/49 5.00 12.00
8 Chris Andersen/29 8.00 20.00
20 Nene/15 6.00 15.00

2010-11 Panini Season Update Rookie Challenge

COMPLETE SET (15) 5.00 12.00
RANDOM INSERTS IN PACKS
1 DeMarcus Cousins 1.25 3.00
2 Derrick Favors .50 1.25
3 Eric Bledsoe .50 1.25
4 Gary Neal .40 1.00
5 Greg Monroe .50 1.25
6 Landry Fields .30 .75
7 Wesley Johnson .25 .60
8 Brandon Jennings .25 .60
9 DeJuan Blair .25 .60
10 DeMar DeRozan .40 1.00
11 James Harden .60 1.50
12 Jrue Holiday .40 1.00
13 Serge Ibaka .30 .75
14 Stephen Curry 1.50 4.00
15 Wesley Matthews .25 .60

2010-11 Panini Season Update Rookie Challenge Materials

STATED PRINT RUN 799 SER.#'d SETS
UNPRICED PRIME PRINT RUN 5 SETS
1 DeMarcus Cousins 5.00 12.00
2 Derrick Favors 2.00 5.00
3 Eric Bledsoe 2.00 5.00
4 Gary Neal 1.50 4.00
5 Greg Monroe 2.00 5.00
6 Landry Fields 1.25 3.00
7 Wesley Johnson 1.00 2.50
8 Brandon Jennings 1.50 4.00
9 DeJuan Blair 1.50 4.00
10 DeMar DeRozan 2.50 6.00
11 James Harden 4.00 10.00
12 Jrue Holiday 2.50 6.00
13 Serge Ibaka 2.00 5.00
14 Stephen Curry 10.00 25.00
15 Wesley Matthews 1.50 4.00

2010-11 Panini Season Update Rookie Challenge Materials Signatures

STATED PRINT RUN 25 SER.#'d SETS
UNPRICED PRIME PRINT RUN 5 SETS
1 DeMarcus Cousins 25.00 60.00
2 Derrick Favors 10.00 25.00
3 Eric Bledsoe 10.00 25.00
4 Gary Neal 8.00 20.00
5 Greg Monroe 10.00 25.00
6 Landry Fields 6.00 15.00
7 Wesley Johnson 5.00 12.00
8 Brandon Jennings 12.00 30.00
9 DeJuan Blair 8.00 20.00
10 DeMar DeRozan 12.00 30.00
11 James Harden 20.00 50.00
12 Jrue Holiday 10.00 25.00
13 Serge Ibaka 10.00 25.00
14 Stephen Curry 40.00 100.00
15 Wesley Matthews 12.00 30.00

2010-11 Panini Season Update Rookie Challenge Signatures

STATED PRINT RUN 49 SER.#'d SETS
1 DeMarcus Cousins 15.00 40.00
2 Derrick Favors 6.00 15.00
3 Eric Bledsoe 6.00 15.00
4 Gary Neal 5.00 12.00
5 Greg Monroe 6.00 15.00
6 Landry Fields 4.00 10.00
7 Wesley Johnson 3.00 8.00
8 Brandon Jennings 8.00 20.00
9 DeJuan Blair 5.00 12.00
10 DeMar DeRozan 5.00 12.00
11 James Harden 12.00 30.00
12 Jrue Holiday 6.00 15.00
13 Serge Ibaka 6.00 15.00

14 Stephen Curry 60.00 150.00
15 Wesley Matthews 6.00 15.00

2010-11 Panini Season Update Rookie Duals Signatures

STATED PRINT RUN 10 TO 99 SER.#'d SETS
SOME UNPRICED DUE TO SCARCITY
UNPRICED TRIPLE PRINT RUN 10 SETS
4 E.Turner/D.Favors 20.00 50.00
5 E.Turner/D.Cousins 25.00 60.00
6 E.Turner/W.Johnson 10.00 25.00
7 D.Favors/W.Johnson 10.00 25.00
8 D.Favors/D.Cousins 15.00 40.00
9 W.Johnson/D.Cousins 20.00 50.00
10 W.Johnson/E.Udoh 5.00 12.00
12 D.Cousins/G.Monroe 25.00 60.00
13 E.Udoh/G.Monroe 6.00 15.00
14 E.Udoh/A.Aminu 5.00 12.00
15 G.Monroe/A.Aminu 6.00 15.00
16 G.Monroe/G.Hayward 12.00 30.00
17 A.Aminu/G.Hayward 8.00 20.00
18 A.Aminu/P.George 20.00 50.00
19 G.Hayward/P.George 50.00 100.00
20 G.Hayward/C.Aldrich 8.00 20.00
21 P.George/C.Aldrich 25.00 60.00
22 P.George/X.Henry 25.00 60.00
23 C.Aldrich/X.Henry 5.00 12.00
24 C.Aldrich/E.Davis 5.00 12.00
25 X.Henry/E.Davis 5.00 12.00
26 X.Henry/P.Patterson 5.00 12.00
27 P.Patterson/E.Davis 5.00 12.00
28 E.Davis/L.Sanders 5.00 12.00
29 P.Patterson/L.Sanders 8.00 20.00
30 L.Babbitt/E.Williams 5.00 12.00
31 L.Babbitt/A.Johnson 5.00 12.00
32 E.Bledsoe/Warren 6.00 15.00
33 E.Bledsoe/D.Orton 8.00 20.00
34 E.Bledsoe/P.Patterson 10.00 25.00
35 C.Brackins/E.Turner 10.00 25.00
36 T.Booker/J.Crawford 8.00 20.00
37 T.Booker/Seraphin 8.00 20.00
38 D.James/D.Pittman 5.00 12.00
39 D.James/A.Bradley 5.00 12.00
40 A.Bradley/Harangody 5.00 12.00
41 A.Bradley/S.Erden 6.00 15.00
42 D.Jones/Q.Pondexter 5.00 12.00
43 J.Crawford/Seraphin 8.00 20.00
44 G.Vasquez/X.Henry 5.00 12.00
45 G.Vasquez/D.Orton 5.00 12.00
46 D.Orton/L.Hayward 5.00 12.00
47 L.Hayward/W.Johnson 5.00 12.00
48 L.Hayward/N.Pekovic 6.00 15.00
49 Whiteside/D.Cousins 30.00 80.00
50 T.White/G.Monroe 8.00 20.00
51 A.Rautins/L.Fields 5.00 12.00
52 A.Rautins/T.Mozgov 5.00 12.00
53 L.Fields/T.Mozgov 5.00 12.00
54 Stephenson/P.George 30.00 60.00
55 Stephenson/D.Pittman 5.00 12.00
56 D.Ebanks/D.Caracter 5.00 12.00
57 G.Lawal/S.Alabi 5.00 12.00
58 J.Evans/G.Hayward 10.00 25.00
59 G.Neal/G.Forbes 5.00 12.00
60 J.Lin/O.Asik 30.00 80.00
61 J.Lin/E.Udoh 25.00 60.00
62 W.Warren/C.Aldrich 5.00 12.00
63 W.Warren/X.Henry 5.00 12.00
64 J.Anderson/G.Neal 6.00 15.00
65 O.Asik/S.Erden 5.00 12.00
66 D.Jones/J.Crawford 5.00 12.00
67 D.Orton/H.Whiteside 12.00 30.00
68 Whiteside/A.Johnson 12.00 30.00
69 A.Johnson/T.White 5.00 12.00
70 T.White/A.Rautins 5.00 12.00
71 L.Fields/Stephenson 5.00 12.00
72 Stephenson/Ebanks 5.00 12.00
73 D.Ebanks/G.Lawal 5.00 12.00
74 S.Alabi/L.Harangody 5.00 12.00
75 Harangody/Warren 5.00 12.00

2010-11 Panini Season Update Signatures

STATED PRINT RUN 10 TO 299 SER.#'d SETS
SOME UNPRICED DUE TO SCARCITY
2 Jeff Green/199 6.00 15.00
9 Brook Lopez/99 4.00 10.00
11 Kris Humphries/299 3.00 8.00
19 Toney Douglas/299 3.00 8.00
24 Louis Williams/199 3.00 8.00
27 Andrea Bargnani/99 5.00 12.00
28 DeMar DeRozan/25 5.00 12.00
29 Jose Calderon/199 6.00 15.00
32 Sonny Weems/299 3.00 8.00
38 Ronnie Brewer/299 3.00 8.00
41 Antawn Jamison/99 4.00 10.00
42 Daniel Gibson/99 3.00 8.00
46 Austin Daye/299 3.00 8.00
48 Charlie Villanueva/99 3.00 8.00
56 Mike Dunleavy/99 3.00 8.00
57 Roy Hibbert/299 6.00 15.00
58 T.J. Ford/199 3.00 8.00
59 Tyler Hansbrough/99 5.00 12.00
70 Jeff Teague/299 3.00 8.00
72 Josh Smith/99 4.00 10.00
76 Gerald Henderson/299 3.00 8.00
77 Stephen Jackson/199 3.00 8.00
90 J.J. Redick/99 4.00 10.00
91 Jameer Nelson/25 3.00 8.00
94 JaVale McGee/299 3.00 8.00
106 Goran Dragic/99 6.00 15.00
112 Shane Battier/25 6.00 15.00
115 Rudy Gay/299 5.00 12.00
122 DeJuan Blair/299 3.00 8.00
123 George Hill/299 3.00 8.00
131 Raymond Felton/49 3.00 8.00
134 J.R. Smith/299 3.00 8.00
138 Darko Milicic/299 3.00 8.00
140 Luke Ridnour/299 3.00 8.00
143 Andre Miller/299 3.00 8.00
149 Wesley Matthews/299 4.00 10.00
150 James Harden/49 20.00 50.00
152 Kevin Durant/24 75.00 150.00
154 Serge Ibaka/299 6.00 15.00
156 Andrei Kirilenko/99 3.00 8.00
158 Devin Harris/25 5.00 12.00
163 David Lee/25 5.00 12.00
165 Monta Ellis/299 6.00 15.00
167 Stephen Curry/99 60.00 150.00
169 Blake Griffin/15 75.00 150.00
171 Eric Gordon/299 5.00 12.00
172 Ryan Gomes/299 3.00 8.00
175 Kobe Bryant/49 100.00 200.00
180 Aaron Brooks/299 3.00 8.00
185 Beno Udrih/299 3.00 8.00
186 Marcus Thornton/299 3.00 8.00
188 Omri Casspi/299 3.00 8.00
189 Samuel Dalembert/299 3.00 8.00
190 Tyreke Evans/99 10.00 25.00
193 Kobe Bryant/49 100.00 200.00
194 Kevin Durant/24 125.00 250.00

2010-11 Panini Season Update Throwback Threads

STATED PRINT RUN 199 TO 799 SER.#'d SETS
1 Jermaine O'Neal/799 2.50 6.00
2 Dikembe Mutombo/299 3.00 8.00
3 Tracy McGrady/799 3.00 8.00
4 Larry Johnson/299 10.00 25.00
5 Stephen Jackson/499 2.50 6.00
6 Scottie Pippen/399 6.00 15.00
7 Raja Bell/799 2.50 6.00
8 Toni Kukoc/399 3.00 8.00
9 Marcin Gortat/499 5.00 12.00
10 Kelly Tripucka/299 2.00 5.00
11 Jason Kidd/499 3.00 8.00
12 Ron Harper/399 3.00 8.00
13 Amare Stoudemire/199 2.50 6.00
14 Chuck Person/299 2.50 6.00
15 Tyson Chandler/599 2.50 6.00
16 Xavier McDaniel/299 2.00 5.00
17 Raymond Felton/299 2.50 6.00
18 Moses Malone/299 3.00 8.00
19 Trevor Ariza/499 2.00 5.00
20 Tom Chambers/299 2.50 6.00

2010-11 Panini Season Update Throwback Threads Prime

*PRIME: 1X TO 2.5X BASE HI
STATED PRINT RUN 25 TO 49 SER.#'d SETS
9 Marcin Gortat/49 15.00 40.00
12 Ron Harper/49 10.00 25.00

2012-13 Panini Signatures

PRINT RUNS B/WN 10-99 COPIES PER
SOME CARDS ARE NOT SERIAL #'d
NO PRICING ON QTY 15 OR LESS
EXCHANGE DEADLINE 01/24/2014
1A Anthony Davis/49 75.00 150.00
1B Anthony Davis/25 VAR 75.00 150.00
2A Kyrie Irving/49 50.00 120.00
2B Kyrie Irving/25 VAR 60.00 120.00
21 Norris Cole/99 3.00 8.00
23 Tobias Harris/99 5.00 12.00
27 Nando De Colo 3.00 8.00
29 Kent Bazemore 5.00 12.00
31 Orlando Johnson 3.00 8.00
32 Jeff Taylor 3.00 8.00
35 Draymond Green 12.00 30.00
38 Tyler Zeller 4.00 10.00
41 Andrew Nicholson 3.00 8.00
42 Chris Copeland 3.00 8.00
43 Gustavo Ayon 3.00 8.00
45A Jimmy Butler 12.00 30.00
45B Jimmy Butler VAR 12.00 30.00
46 Tornike Shengelia 3.00 8.00
47 Jan Vesely 3.00 8.00
48 Ben Hansbrough 3.00 8.00
50 Mirza Teletovic 6.00 15.00
51 Kyle Singler/99 VAR
52 E'Twaun Moore 3.00 8.00
55 Victor Claver 3.00 8.00
57 Marquis Teague 3.00 8.00
59 Bernard James 3.00 8.00
60 Nolan Smith 3.00 8.00
62 Brian Roberts 3.00 8.00
63 Donatas Motiejunas 4.00 10.00
64 Jared Cunningham 3.00 8.00
65 Viacheslav Kravtsov 3.00 8.00
74 Alan Anderson 3.00 8.00
83 Alonzo Gee/99 3.00 8.00
85 Dorell Wright 3.00 8.00
96 Carlos Delfino 3.00 8.00
98 Corey Brewer 3.00 8.00
105 Johan Petro 3.00 8.00
113 Trevor Booker 3.00 8.00
116 Jason Maxiell 3.00 8.00
119A Marvin Williams 4.00 10.00
119B Marvin Williams VAR/99 4.00 10.00
122A Nick Collison/49 4.00 10.00
123 Nikola Pekovic 3.00 8.00
129 Ronnie Brewer 4.00 10.00
131A Kobe Bryant/75 100.00 200.00
131B Kobe Bryant/49 VAR 100.00 200.00
132A Blake Griffin/49 12.00 30.00
132B Blake Griffin/25 VAR 30.00 80.00
133A Kevin Durant/49 75.00 150.00
138 Doug Christie 3.00 8.00
140 Jim Jackson 3.00 8.00
147 Larry Bird/25 30.00 60.00
157 C.J. Watson 3.00 8.00
161 Anthony Morrow 3.00 8.00
173 Zaza Pachulia 3.00 8.00
174 Toney Douglas 3.00 8.00
176 Luc Mbah a Moute 3.00 8.00
182 Sean Elliott 6.00 15.00
184 Tim Hardaway 8.00 20.00
188 Anthony Mason 4.00 10.00
190 Mark Aguirre 4.00 10.00

2012-13 Panini Signatures Die Cut Autographs

PRINT RUNS B/WN 10-99 COPIES PER
SOME CARDS ARE NOT SERIAL #'d
NO PRICING ON QTY 15 OR LESS
EXCHANGE DEADLINE 01/24/2014
1 Anthony Davis/49 200.00 400.00
2 Kyrie Irving/99 40.00 100.00
27 Nando De Colo 3.00 8.00
29 Kent Bazemore 5.00 12.00
31 Orlando Johnson 3.00 8.00
32 Jeff Taylor 3.00 8.00
35 Draymond Green 25.00 60.00
38 Tyler Zeller 4.00 10.00
41 Andrew Nicholson 3.00 8.00
42 Chris Copeland 3.00 8.00
43 Gustavo Ayon 3.00 8.00
45 Jimmy Butler EXCH 15.00 40.00
46 Tornike Shengelia 3.00 8.00
47 Jan Vesely 3.00 8.00
48 Ben Hansbrough 3.00 8.00
49 Kendall Marshall/25 4.00 10.00
50 Mirza Teletovic 4.00 10.00
52 E'Twaun Moore 3.00 8.00
55 Victor Claver 3.00 8.00
59 Bernard James 3.00 8.00
60 Nolan Smith 3.00 8.00
62 Brian Roberts 3.00 8.00
63 Donatas Motiejunas 4.00 10.00
64 Jared Cunningham 3.00 8.00
65 Viacheslav Kravtsov 3.00 8.00
71 Beno Udrih
74 Alan Anderson 3.00 8.00
83 Alonzo Gee 3.00 8.00
85 Dorell Wright 3.00 8.00
96 Carlos Delfino 3.00 8.00
98 Corey Brewer 3.00 8.00
105 Johan Petro 3.00 8.00
119 Marvin Williams 4.00 10.00
129 Ronnie Brewer 4.00 10.00
131 Kobe Bryant/49 125.00 250.00
132 Blake Griffin/25 15.00 40.00
133 Kevin Durant/49 75.00 150.00
138 Doug Christie 3.00 8.00
140 Jim Jackson 3.00 8.00
147 Larry Bird/25 EXCH 40.00 100.00

2012-13 Panini Signatures Die Cut Autographs Red

PRINT RUNS B/WN 5-49 COPIES PER
NO PRICING ON QTY 15 OR LESS
EXCHANGE DEADLINE 01/24/2014
1 Anthony Davis/25 250.00 500.00
2 Kyrie Irving/25 60.00 150.00
20 Iman Shumpert/25 EXCH 6.00 15.00
22 Alec Burks/49 5.00 12.00
24 Isaiah Thomas/49 8.00 20.00
25 Evan Fournier/49 EXCH
26 Bismack Biyombo/49
27 Nando De Colo/49 3.00 8.00
29 Kent Bazemore/49 5.00 12.00
31 Orlando Johnson/49 3.00 8.00
32 Jeff Taylor/49 3.00 8.00
35 Draymond Green/49 25.00 60.00
38 Tyler Zeller/49
40 Alexey Shved/49 EXCH
41 Andrew Nicholson/49 3.00 8.00
42 Chris Copeland/49
43 Gustavo Ayon/49 3.00 8.00
44 MarShon Brooks/49 EXCH 4.00 10.00
45 Jimmy Butler/49 25.00 60.00
46 Tornike Shengelia/49
47 Jan Vesely/49 3.00 8.00
48 Ben Hansbrough/49 3.00 8.00
50 Mirza Teletovic/49
51 Kyle Singler/49
52 E'Twaun Moore/49 3.00 8.00
54 Jon Leuer/49 4.00 10.00
55 Victor Claver/49 3.00 8.00
59 Bernard James/49 3.00 8.00
60 Nolan Smith/49 3.00 8.00
61 Miles Plumlee/49
62 Brian Roberts/49 3.00 8.00
63 Donatas Motiejunas/49
64 Jared Cunningham/49 3.00 8.00
65 Viacheslav Kravtsov/49 3.00 8.00
71 Beno Udrih/25
74 Alan Anderson/25
83 Alonzo Gee/25 4.00 10.00
85 Dorell Wright/25 4.00 10.00
96 Carlos Delfino/25
98 Corey Brewer/25 4.00 10.00
105 Johan Petro/25 4.00 10.00
116 Jason Maxiell/25
119 Marvin Williams/25
129 Ronnie Brewer/25
131 Kobe Bryant/25 150.00 300.00
133 Kevin Durant/25 100.00 200.00
138 Doug Christie/25 4.00 10.00
140 Jim Jackson/25

2012-13 Panini Signatures Red

PRINT RUNS B/WN 5-49 COPIES PER
SOME CARDS ARE NOT SERIAL #'d
NO PRICING ON QTY 15 OR LESS
EXCHANGE DEADLINE 01/24/2014
1A Anthony Davis/25 100.00 200.00
20 Iman Shumpert/49 EXCH 5.00 12.00
22 Alec Burks/49 5.00 12.00
24 Isaiah Thomas/49 EXCH 8.00 20.00
25 Evan Fournier/49 EXCH 5.00 12.00
26 Bismack Biyombo/49
27 Nando De Colo/49 3.00 8.00
29 Kent Bazemore/49
31 Orlando Johnson/49 3.00 8.00
32 Jeff Taylor/49 3.00 8.00
35 Draymond Green/49 15.00 40.00
38 Tyler Zeller/49 4.00 10.00
40A Alexey Shved/49
40B Alexey Shved/49 VAR
41 Andrew Nicholson/49 3.00 8.00
42 Chris Copeland/49 3.00 8.00
43 Gustavo Ayon/49 3.00 8.00
44 MarShon Brooks/49 EXCH 4.00 10.00
45A Jimmy Butler/49 EXCH 30.00 80.00
45B Jimmy Butler/49 VAR EXCH 30.00 80.00
46 Tornike Shengelia/49
47 Jan Vesely/49 3.00 8.00
48 Ben Hansbrough/49 3.00 8.00
50 Mirza Teletovic/49 6.00 15.00
51 Kyle Singler/49 VAR
52 E'Twaun Moore/49 3.00 8.00
54 Jon Leuer/49 4.00 10.00
55 Victor Claver/49 3.00 8.00
57 Marquis Teague/49 3.00 8.00
59 Bernard James/49 3.00 8.00
60 Nolan Smith/49 3.00 8.00
62 Brian Roberts/49
63 Donatas Motiejunas/49 4.00 10.00
64 Jared Cunningham/49 3.00 8.00
65 Viacheslav Kravtsov/49 3.00 8.00
71 Beno Udrih/49
74 Alan Anderson/49 3.00 8.00
83 Alonzo Gee/49 3.00 8.00
85 Dorell Wright/49 3.00 8.00
96 Carlos Delfino/49 3.00 8.00
98 Corey Brewer/49 3.00 8.00
105 Johan Petro/49 3.00 8.00
116 Jason Maxiell/49 3.00 8.00
119A Marvin Williams/49 4.00 10.00
119B Marvin Williams/25 VAR 5.00 12.00
129 Ronnie Brewer/49 4.00 10.00
131A Kobe Bryant/49 100.00 200.00
131B Kobe Bryant/25 VAR 150.00 300.00
132A Blake Griffin/25 15.00 40.00
133A Kevin Durant/25 100.00 200.00
138 Doug Christie/49 3.00 8.00
140 Jim Jackson/49 3.00 8.00
154 Marco Belinelli/49
157 C.J. Watson/49 3.00 8.00
161 Anthony Morrow/49 3.00 8.00
173 Zaza Pachulia/49 3.00 8.00
174 Toney Douglas/49 3.00 8.00
176 Luc Mbah a Moute/49 3.00 8.00
182 Sean Elliott/49 6.00 15.00
183 Detlef Schrempf/49 5.00 12.00
184 Tim Hardaway/49 8.00 20.00
188 Anthony Mason/49 6.00 15.00
190 Mark Aguirre/49 4.00 10.00

2012-13 Panini Signatures Film Autographs

PRINT RUNS B/WN 10-99 COPIES PER
SOME CARDS ARE NOT SERIAL #'d
NO PRICING ON QTY 20 OR LESS
EXCHANGE DEADLINE 01/24/2014
7 Beno Udrih
11 Alan Anderson/49
24 C.J. Watson/49
28 Alonzo Gee/49 3.00 8.00
30 Anthony Morrow/49
31 Dorell Wright/49
47 Carlos Delfino/49
49 Corey Brewer/49 3.00 8.00
56 Johan Petro/49
59 Greivis Vasquez/49 10.00 25.00
69 Jason Maxiell/49
72 Marvin Williams/49 4.00 10.00
81 Luc Mbah a Moute/49
84 Kobe Bryant/75 125.00 250.00
85 Blake Griffin/25 15.00 40.00
86 Kevin Durant/49 50.00 120.00
88 Toney Douglas/49 3.00 8.00
95 Zaza Pachulia/49 3.00 8.00
99 Jordan Crawford
103 Ian Mahinmi/49 3.00 8.00
108 Jarvis Varnado 4.00 10.00
110 Joel Anthony/49
111 Detlef Schrempf/49 10.00 25.00
114 Antoine Walker/49 15.00 40.00
117 John Starks/49 10.00 25.00
119 Tim Hardaway/49 8.00 20.00
129 Larry Bird/20 75.00 150.00
135 Sean Elliott/49 8.00 20.00
136 Anthony Davis/49 75.00 150.00
137 Kyrie Irving/99 50.00 120.00
155 Iman Shumpert/49 EXCH 10.00 25.00
157 Alec Burks/49 5.00 12.00
162 Nando De Colo 3.00 8.00
164 Kent Bazemore 5.00 12.00
167 Jeff Taylor 3.00 8.00
169 Jae Crowder 4.00 10.00
170 Draymond Green 12.00 30.00
173 Tyler Zeller/49 4.00 10.00
176 Andrew Nicholson/49 3.00 8.00
177 Chris Copeland 3.00 8.00
179 MarShon Brooks/49 EXCH 4.00 10.00
180 Jimmy Butler
181 Tornike Shengelia
182 Jan Vesely/49
183 Ben Hansbrough 3.00 8.00
185 Mirza Teletovic
187 E'Twaun Moore 3.00 8.00
189 Jon Leuer 4.00 10.00
190 Victor Claver
194 Bernard James 3.00 8.00
195 Nolan Smith/49 3.00 8.00
197 Brian Roberts 3.00 8.00
199 Jared Cunningham 3.00 8.00

2012-13 Panini Signatures Film Autographs Red

PRINT RUNS B/WN 4-49 COPIES PER
NO PRICING ON QTY 15 OR LESS
EXCHANGE DEADLINE 01/24/2014
7 Beno Udrih/25
11 Alan Anderson/25
16 Marco Belinelli/25
24 C.J. Watson/25
28 Alonzo Gee/25
30 Anthony Morrow/25 4.00 10.00
31 Dorell Wright/25
47 Carlos Delfino/25
49 Corey Brewer/25 4.00 10.00
56 Johan Petro/25
59 Greivis Vasquez/25 12.00 30.00
69 Jason Maxiell/25
72 Marvin Williams/25 5.00 12.00
81 Luc Mbah a Moute/25
84 Kobe Bryant/49 125.00 250.00
86 Kevin Durant/25 EXCH 100.00 200.00
88 Toney Douglas/25 4.00 10.00
95 Zaza Pachulia/25 4.00 10.00
98 Trevor Booker/25 4.00 10.00
99 Jordan Crawford/25
103 Ian Mahinmi/25
108 Jarvis Varnado/49
110 Joel Anthony/25
111 Detlef Schrempf/25 6.00 15.00
114 Antoine Walker/25 20.00 50.00
117 John Starks/25 12.00 30.00
119 Tim Hardaway/25 10.00 25.00
135 Sean Elliott/25 6.00 15.00
136 Anthony Davis/25 100.00 200.00
137 Kyrie Irving/25 60.00 150.00
155 Iman Shumpert/25 EXCH
157 Alec Burks/25 6.00 15.00
159 Isaiah Thomas/25 10.00 25.00
160 Evan Fournier/25 EXCH
161 Bismack Biyombo/25
162 Nando De Colo/49 3.00 8.00
164 Kent Bazemore/49 5.00 12.00
167 Jeff Taylor/25 4.00 10.00
168 Will Barton/49
169 Jae Crowder/49 4.00 10.00
172 Doron Lamb/49
173 Tyler Zeller/25 5.00 12.00
175 Alexey Shved/49
176 Andrew Nicholson/25 4.00 10.00
177 Chris Copeland/49 3.00 8.00
178 Gustavo Ayon/25
179 MarShon Brooks/25 EXCH
180 Jimmy Butler/49 20.00 50.00
181 Tornike Shengelia/49
182 Jan Vesely/25
183 Ben Hansbrough/49
185 Mirza Teletovic/49
186 Kyle Singler/49
187 E'Twaun Moore/25 4.00 10.00
189 Jon Leuer/49
190 Victor Claver/49
191 DeQuan Jones/49
193 Greg Stiemsma/49
194 Bernard James/25 4.00 10.00
195 Nolan Smith/25
197 Brian Roberts/49 3.00 8.00
199 Jared Cunningham/49 3.00 8.00

2012-13 Panini Signatures Legends

STATED PRINT RUN 25 SER.#'d SETS
ALL VERSIONS EQUALLY PRICED
1 Scottie Pippen 6.00 15.00
11 Allen Iverson 4.00 10.00
21 Shaquille O'Neal 6.00 15.00
31 Gary Payton 3.00 8.00
41 Larry Bird 8.00 20.00
51 Magic Johnson 8.00 20.00
61 David Robinson 5.00 12.00
71 Dominique Wilkins 4.00 10.00
81 Hakeem Olajuwon 8.00 20.00
91 Clyde Drexler 4.00 10.00
101 John Stockton 5.00 12.00
111 Isiah Thomas 3.00 8.00
121 Karl Malone 4.00 10.00
131 James Worthy 4.00 10.00
141 Anfernee Hardaway 8.00 20.00
151 Oscar Robertson 4.00 10.00
161 Drazen Petrovic 20.00 50.00
171 Patrick Ewing 4.00 10.00
181 Yao Ming 4.00 10.00
191 Shawn Kemp 5.00 12.00
201 Alonzo Mourning 10.00 25.00
211 Dennis Rodman 6.00 15.00
221 Kareem Abdul-Jabbar 5.00 12.00
231 Bill Walton 3.00 8.00
241 Julius Erving 5.00 12.00

2012-13 Panini Signatures Legends Green

*GREEN: 1X TO 2.5X BASIC
STATED PRINT RUN 5 SER.#'d SETS
ALL VERSIONS EQUALLY PRICED
11 Allen Iverson 25.00 60.00
91 Clyde Drexler 25.00 60.00
171 Patrick Ewing 25.00 60.00

2012-13 Panini Signatures Rookies

STATED PRINT RUN 25 SER.#'d SETS
ALL VERSIONS EQUALLY PRICED
1 Anthony Davis 20.00 50.00
11 Kyrie Irving 20.00 50.00
21 Damian Lillard 20.00 50.00
31 Andre Drummond 3.00 8.00
41 Bradley Beal 3.00 8.00
51 Kemba Walker 4.00 10.00
61 Chandler Parsons 2.00 5.00
71 Harrison Barnes 3.00 8.00
81 Klay Thompson 12.00 30.00
91 Michael Kidd-Gilchrist 2.00 5.00
101 Brandon Knight 2.00 5.00
111 Alexey Shved 1.25 3.00
121 Derrick Williams 1.25 3.00
131 Dion Waiters 2.00 5.00
141 Jared Sullinger 1.50 4.00

2012-13 Panini Signatures Rookies Green

*GREEN: 1.2X TO 3X BASIC
STATED PRINT RUN 5 SER.#'d SETS
ALL VERSIONS EQUALLY PRICED
11 Kyrie Irving 100.00 200.00

2012-13 Panini Signatures Stars

STATED PRINT RUN 25 SER.#'d SETS
ALL VERSIONS EQUALLY PRICED
1 Kevin Durant 8.00 20.00
11 Derrick Rose 4.00 10.00
21 Russell Westbrook 8.00 20.00
31 Blake Griffin 3.00 8.00
41 Kobe Bryant 12.00 30.00
51 Chris Paul 4.00 10.00
61 Dirk Nowitzki 4.00 10.00
71 John Wall 4.00 10.00
81 Dwight Howard 2.50 6.00
91 Kevin Garnett 5.00 12.00
101 Steve Nash 3.00 8.00
111 James Harden 5.00 12.00
121 Rajon Rondo 3.00 8.00
131 Jeremy Lin 3.00 8.00
141 LeBron James 12.00 30.00
151 Carmelo Anthony 4.00 10.00
161 Chris Bosh 3.00 8.00
171 Amar'e Stoudemire 2.50 6.00
181 Dwyane Wade 5.00 12.00
191 Tim Duncan 5.00 12.00
201 Vince Carter 6.00 15.00
211 Manu Ginobili 3.00 8.00
221 Paul Pierce 3.00 8.00
231 Deron Williams 2.50 6.00
241 Andre Iguodala 2.50 6.00
251 Paul George 6.00 15.00
261 LaMarcus Aldridge 3.00 8.00
271 Kevin Love 3.00 8.00
281 Tony Parker 3.00 8.00
291 Joakim Noah 2.50 6.00
301 Goran Dragic 2.50 6.00
311 Grant Hill 4.00 10.00
321 Stephen Curry 12.00 30.00
331 Danny Granger 2.50 6.00
341 Ricky Rubio 3.00 8.00
351 David Lee 2.00 5.00
361 Zach Randolph 2.50 6.00
371 Ray Allen 2.50 6.00
381 Pau Gasol 3.00 8.00
391 Rudy Gay 3.00 8.00

2012-13 Panini Signatures Stars Green

*GREEN: 1X TO 2.5X BASIC
STATED PRINT RUN 5 SER.#'d SETS
ALL VERSIONS EQUALLY PRICED
1 Kevin Durant 50.00 120.00
181 Dwyane Wade 30.00 60.00
371 Ray Allen 15.00 40.00

2013-14 Panini Signatures

1-200 PRINT RUN 25 SER.#'d SETS
200-300 PRINT RUN 15 SER.#'d SETS
301-400 PRINT RUN 15 SER.#'d SETS
ALL VERSIONS EQUALLY PRICED
1 Kobe Bryant 10.00 25.00
11 Kevin Durant 6.00 15.00
21 Blake Griffin 2.50 6.00
31 Kyrie Irving 5.00 12.00
41 Anthony Davis 5.00 12.00
51 Russell Westbrook 6.00 15.00
61 Chris Paul 3.00 8.00
71 Kevin Love 2.50 6.00
81 Paul George 3.00 8.00
91 LeBron James 10.00 25.00
101 Damian Lillard 5.00 12.00
111 Dirk Nowitzki 3.00 8.00
121 Carmelo Anthony 3.00 8.00
131 James Harden 4.00 10.00
141 Derrick Rose 3.00 8.00
151 Stephen Curry 10.00 25.00
161 DeMar DeRozan 2.50 6.00
171 Dwight Howard 2.00 5.00
181 Dwyane Wade 4.00 10.00
191 Rajon Rondo 2.50 6.00
201 Shaquille O'Neal 6.00 15.00
211 Magic Johnson 8.00 20.00
221 Larry Bird 8.00 20.00
231 Julius Erving 5.00 12.00
241 Grant Hill 6.00 15.00
251 Jason Kidd 3.00 8.00
261 Tracy McGrady 3.00 8.00
271 Kareem Abdul-Jabbar 5.00 12.00
281 Dennis Rodman 6.00 15.00
291 Moses Malone 3.00 8.00
301 M.Carter-Williams RC 3.00 8.00
311 Victor Oladipo RC 4.00 10.00
321 Anthony Bennett RC 2.50 6.00
331 Ben McLemore RC 2.50 6.00
341 Cody Zeller RC 2.50 6.00
351 G.Antetokounmpo RC 30.00 80.00
361 Kentavious Caldwell-Pope RC 3.00 8.00
371 Nate Wolters RC 2.50 6.00
381 Steven Adams RC 3.00 8.00
391 Tim Hardaway Jr. RC 3.00 8.00

2013-14 Panini Signatures Blue

*BLUE 1-200: .6X TO 1.5X BASIC
*BLUE 201-300: .5X TO 1.2X BASIC
*BLUE 301-400: .5X TO 1.2X BASIC
1-200 PRINT RUN 15 SER.#'d SETS
201-400 PRINT RUN 10 SER.#'d SETS

2013-14 Panini Signatures Green

*GREEN 1-200: 1X TO 2.5X BASIC
*GREEN 201-300: .75X TO 2X BASIC
*GREEN 301-400: .75X TO 2X BASIC
1-200 PRINT RUN 5 SER.#'d SETS
201-400 PRINT RUN 3 SER.#'d SETS

2013-14 Panini Signatures Red

*RED 1-200: .75X TO 2X BASIC
*RED 201-300: .6X TO 1.5X BASIC
*RED 301-400: .6X TO 1.5X BASIC
1-200 PRINT RUN 10 SER.#'d SETS
201-400 PRINT RUN 5 SER.#'d SETS

2013-14 Panini Signatures '14 Draft X-Change

EXCHANGE DEADLINE 12/12/2015
1 Andrew Wiggins 8.00 20.00
Pick 1
2 Jabari Parker 3.00 8.00
Pick 2
3 Joel Embiid 8.00 20.00
Pick 3
4 Aaron Gordon 3.00 8.00
Pick 4
5 Dante Exum 2.50 6.00
Pick 5
6 Marcus Smart 2.50 6.00
Pick 6
7 Julius Randle 4.00 10.00
Pick 7
8 Nik Stauskas 2.00 5.00
Pick 8
9 Noah Vonleh 2.00 5.00
Pick 9
10 Elfrid Payton 2.50 6.00
Pick 10
11 Doug McDermott 2.50 6.00
Pick 11
12 Dario Saric 4.00 10.00
Pick 12
13 Zach LaVine 4.00 10.00
Pick 13
14 TJ Warren 1.50 4.00
Pick 14
15 Adreian Payne 2.00 5.00
Pick 15
16 Jusuf Nurkic 2.50 6.00
Pick 16
17 James Young 1.50 4.00
Pick 17
18 Tyler Ennis 1.50 4.00
Pick 18
19 Gary Harris 2.50 6.00
Pick 19
20 Bruno Caboclo 2.00 5.00
Pick 20
21 Mitch McGary 1.50 4.00
Pick 21
22 Jordan Adams 1.50 4.00
Pick 22
23 Rodney Hood 2.50 6.00
Pick 23
24 Shabazz Napier 2.00 5.00
Pick 24
25 Clint Capela 2.50 6.00
Pick 25

2013-14 Panini Signatures Dynamic Ink

PRINT RUNS B/WN 25-249 COPIES PER
EXCHANGE DEADLINE 11/28/2015
2 George Gervin/35
3 Bill Walton/35 8.00 20.00
4 Julius Erving/25 40.00 100.00
5 Christian Laettner/35 4.00 10.00
6 Jodie Meeks/199 4.00 10.00
8 Harrison Barnes/35 12.00 30.00
9 Kenyon Martin/199 4.00 10.00
10 Jonas Valanciunas/99 4.00 10.00
11 Xavier Henry/49 3.00 8.00
12 Chris Copeland/199 3.00 8.00
13 Eric Maynor/199 3.00 8.00
14 Marvin Williams/199 4.00 10.00
16 Tyler Zeller/49 4.00 10.00
17 Orlando Johnson/199 3.00 8.00
18 Trevor Booker/199 3.00 8.00
20 Kevin Love/25 20.00 50.00
21 Jason Thompson/99 3.00 8.00
23 Gerald Henderson/99 3.00 8.00
24 Ersan Ilyasova/99 3.00 8.00
25 Marcin Gortat/75 4.00 10.00
26 Courtney Lee/99 4.00 10.00
28 B.Grant/199 EXCH 3.00 8.00
29 Dana Barros/199 3.00 8.00
31 Tracy McGrady/35 20.00 50.00
32 Kyrie Irving/35 50.00 120.00
33 Kevin Durant/35 50.00 120.00
34 Kobe Bryant/25 125.00 250.00
35 Ryan Anderson/75 4.00 10.00

2013-14 Panini Signatures Endorsements

PRINT RUNS B/WN 25-249 COPIES PER
EXCHANGE DEADLINE 11/28/2015
1 Chet Walker/49
2 Spencer Haywood/249 3.00 8.00
3 Darrell Griffith/249 3.00 8.00
4 Jon McGlocklin/249 6.00 15.00
5 Ron Harper/249 5.00 12.00
6 Anfernee Hardaway/49 12.00 30.00
7 Grant Hill/49 15.00 40.00
8 Eddie Johnson/249 3.00 8.00
10 Juwan Howard/49
11 Connie Hawkins/149 5.00 12.00
12 Jamal Mashburn/175 5.00 12.00
13 Anthony Davis/20
14 Patrick Beverley/249 3.00 8.00
15 Jason Smith/249 3.00 8.00
17 Kevin Love/20
18 Ray Allen/20 15.00 40.00
19 James Jones/249 3.00 8.00
21 Harrison Barnes/25 10.00 25.00
22 Ramon Sessions/249 4.00 10.00
24 Nick Collison/249 4.00 10.00
25 Steve Blake/249 3.00 8.00
26 Nick Young/49 10.00 25.00
28 Dwight Howard/20 20.00 50.00
30 Jordan Crawford/249 3.00 8.00
32 David Thompson/99 4.00 10.00
33 Adrian Dantley/99 4.00 10.00
36 Scottie Pippen/20 60.00 120.00
37 Satch Sanders/99 5.00 12.00
38 Jamaal Wilkes/199 5.00 12.00
40 Marques Johnson/249 4.00 10.00
41 A.C. Green/49 6.00 15.00
43 Bruce Bowen/249 3.00 8.00
44 Keith Van Horn/249 4.00 10.00
45 Jerome Williams/249 3.00 8.00
46 Raef LaFrentz/249 5.00 12.00
47 Vlade Divac/249 5.00 12.00
48 Vernon Maxwell/249 3.00 8.00
49 Jason Kidd/20 20.00 50.00
51 Darryl Dawkins/249 3.00 8.00
52 Fred Jones/249 3.00 8.00
53 Bob Dandridge/249 3.00 8.00
54 Jack Sikma/249 4.00 10.00
55 Chris Andersen/25 50.00 100.00
60 Goran Dragic/35

2013-14 Panini Signatures Film

STATED PRINT RUN 35 SER.#'d SETS
1 Dwyane Wade 4.00 10.00
2 J.J. Hickson 1.50 4.00
3 Ray Allen 2.50 6.00
4 Steve Nash 2.50 6.00
5 Al Horford 2.00 5.00
6 Joakim Noah 2.00 5.00
7 Bradley Beal 2.50 6.00
8 Kevin Martin 2.00 5.00
9 Danny Granger 2.00 5.00
10 Mike Conley 2.00 5.00
11 Enes Kanter 1.50 4.00
12 Raymond Felton 2.00 5.00
13 J.J. Redick 2.50 6.00
14 Taj Gibson 2.00 5.00
15 Al Jefferson 2.00 5.00
16 Joe Johnson 2.00 5.00
17 Brandon Bass 1.50 4.00
18 Klay Thompson 3.00 8.00
19 Monta Ellis 2.00 5.00
20 David Lee 1.50 4.00
21 Eric Bledsoe 2.00 5.00
22 Ricky Rubio 2.50 6.00
23 J.R. Smith 2.00 5.00
24 Tayshaun Prince 2.00 5.00
25 Alec Burks 1.50 4.00
26 John Wall 3.00 8.00
27 Brandon Jennings 1.50 4.00
28 Kobe Bryant 10.00 25.00
29 David West 2.00 5.00
30 Nate Robinson 1.50 4.00
31 Eric Gordon 2.00 5.00
32 Roy Hibbert 2.00 5.00
33 Jameer Nelson 1.50 4.00
34 Thabo Sefolosha 1.50 4.00
35 Alexey Shved 1.50 4.00
36 Jonas Valanciunas 2.00 5.00
37 Brandon Knight 2.00 5.00
38 Kyle Korver 2.00 5.00
39 DeAndre Jordan 2.50 6.00
40 Nene 2.00 5.00
41 Evan Turner 1.50 4.00
42 Rudy Gay 2.50 6.00
43 James Harden 6.00 15.00
44 Thaddeus Young 1.50 4.00
45 Amare Stoudemire 2.00 5.00
46 Josh Smith 2.00 5.00
47 Brook Lopez 2.00 5.00
48 Kyrie Irving 5.00 12.00
49 DeMar DeRozan 2.50 6.00
50 Nick Young 2.50 6.00
51 George Hill 2.00 5.00
52 Russell Westbrook 6.00 15.00
53 Jared Sullinger 1.50 4.00
54 Tiago Splitter 2.00 5.00
55 Anderson Varejao 1.50 4.00
56 Jrue Holiday 2.50 6.00
57 Carlos Boozer 2.00 5.00
58 LaMarcus Aldridge 2.50 6.00
59 DeMarcus Cousins 2.50 6.00
60 Nicolas Batum 2.00 5.00
61 Gerald Henderson 1.50 4.00
62 Ryan Anderson 2.00 5.00
63 Jason Terry 2.00 5.00
64 Tim Duncan 4.00 10.00
65 Andre Drummond 2.50 6.00
66 Kawhi Leonard 4.00 10.00
67 Carmelo Anthony 3.00 8.00
68 Lance Stephenson 2.00 5.00
69 Deron Williams 2.00 5.00
70 Nikola Vucevic 2.00 5.00
71 Serge Ibaka 2.00 5.00
72 Glen Davis 1.50 4.00
73 JaVale McGee 2.00 5.00
74 Tony Parker 2.50 6.00
75 Andre Iguodala 2.00 5.00
76 Kemba Walker 2.50 6.00
77 Caron Butler 2.00 5.00
78 LeBron James 10.00 25.00
79 Derrick Favors 2.00 5.00
80 Pau Gasol 2.50 6.00
81 Goran Dragic 2.00 5.00
82 Shane Battier 2.00 5.00
83 Jeff Green 2.00 5.00
84 Tristan Thompson 2.00 5.00
85 Andrei Kirilenko 2.00 5.00
86 Kenneth Faried 2.00 5.00
87 Chandler Parsons 2.00 5.00
88 Luol Deng 2.00 5.00
89 Paul George 3.00 8.00
90 Derrick Rose 10.00 25.00
91 Gordon Hayward 2.50 6.00
92 Shawn Marion 2.00 5.00
93 Jeff Teague 2.00 5.00
94 Ty Lawson 1.50 4.00
95 Anthony Davis 5.00 12.00
96 Kevin Durant 6.00 15.00
97 Chris Bosh 2.50 6.00
98 Manu Ginobili 2.50 6.00
99 Dion Waiters 2.00 5.00
100 Paul Millsap 2.50 6.00
101 Greg Monroe 2.00 5.00
102 Stephen Curry 10.00 25.00
103 Jeremy Lin 2.50 6.00
104 Tyreke Evans 1.50 4.00
105 Arron Afflalo 1.50 4.00
106 Kevin Garnett 4.00 10.00
107 Chris Paul 3.00 8.00
108 Marc Gasol 2.50 6.00
109 Dirk Nowitzki 3.00 8.00
110 Paul Pierce 2.50 6.00
111 Harrison Barnes 2.00 5.00
112 Steve Blake 1.50 4.00
113 Jimmer Fredette 1.50 4.00
114 Tyson Chandler 2.00 5.00
115 Avery Bradley 2.00 5.00
116 Kevin Love 2.50 6.00
117 Damian Lillard 5.00 12.00
118 Marcin Gortat 2.00 5.00
119 Dwight Howard 2.00 5.00
120 Rajon Rondo 2.50 6.00
121 Iman Shumpert 1.50 4.00
122 Zach Randolph 2.00 5.00
123 Jimmy Butler 2.50 6.00
124 Vince Carter 3.00 8.00
125 Blake Griffin 2.50 6.00
126 Mahmoud Abdul-Rauf 1.50 4.00
127 Scottie Pippen 5.00 12.00
128 Arvydas Sabonis 2.00 5.00
129 Clyde Drexler 3.00 8.00
130 Pete Maravich 4.00 10.00
131 Wilt Chamberlain 5.00 12.00
132 Chris Mullin 2.50 6.00
133 Kareem Abdul-Jabbar 4.00 10.00
134 Michael Cooper 2.00 5.00
135 Karl Malone 3.00 8.00
136 Dan Majerle 2.00 5.00
137 Jason Kidd 2.50 6.00
138 Drazen Petrovic 2.50 6.00
139 Dominique Wilkins 3.00 8.00
140 Robert Parish 2.50 6.00
141 Oscar Robertson 3.00 8.00
142 Tracy McGrady 2.50 6.00
143 Jerry West 3.00 8.00
144 Shawn Kemp 4.00 10.00
145 Isiah Thomas 2.50 6.00
146 Vlade Divac 2.50 6.00
147 Patrick Ewing 3.00 8.00
148 Robert Horry 2.00 5.00
149 George Gervin 2.50 6.00
150 Bernard King 2.00 5.00
151 Larry Bird 6.00 15.00
152 Grant Hill 3.00 8.00
153 Elgin Baylor 2.50 6.00
154 Yao Ming 3.00 8.00
155 John Stockton 4.00 10.00
156 Xavier McDaniel 1.50 4.00
157 Gary Payton 2.50 6.00
158 James Worthy 3.00 8.00

159 Dennis Rodman 5.00 12.00
160 Alonzo Mourning 3.00 8.00
161 Magic Johnson 6.00 15.00
162 Dikembe Mutombo 2.50 6.00
163 Hakeem Olajuwon 3.00 8.00
164 Mark Price 2.50 6.00
165 David Robinson 4.00 10.00
166 Michael Finley 2.50 6.00
167 Allen Iverson 3.00 8.00
168 Julius Erving 4.00 10.00
169 Dennis Johnson 2.00 5.00
170 Joe Dumars 2.50 6.00
171 Shaquille O'Neal 5.00 12.00
172 Anfernee Hardaway 6.00 15.00
173 Moses Malone 2.50 6.00
174 Steve Francis 2.00 5.00
175 Kevin McHale 2.50 6.00
176 Pero Antic 1.50 4.00
177 C.J. McCollum 4.00 10.00
178 Kelly Olynyk 2.00 5.00
179 Anthony Bennett 2.00 5.00
180 Shane Larkin 1.50 4.00
181 Cody Zeller 2.00 5.00
182 Tim Hardaway Jr. 2.50 6.00
183 Nerlens Noel 3.00 8.00
184 Dwight Buycks 1.50 4.00
185 Kentavious Caldwell-Pope 2.50 6.00
186 Nate Wolters 2.00 5.00
187 Michael Carter-Williams 2.50 6.00
188 Shabazz Muhammad 2.00 5.00
189 Victor Oladipo 3.00 8.00
190 Tony Snell 2.00 5.00
191 Alex Len 2.00 5.00
192 Ben McLemore 2.00 5.00
193 Archie Goodwin 2.00 5.00
194 Luigi Datome 1.50 4.00
195 Trey Burke 2.00 5.00
196 Matthew Dellavedova 2.50 6.00
197 Steven Adams 2.50 6.00
198 Giannis Antetokounmpo 20.00 50.00
199 Otto Porter 2.50 6.00
200 Mason Plumlee 2.50 6.00

2013-14 Panini Signatures Film Onyx

*ONYX: .5X TO 1.2X BASIC
STATED PRINT RUN 20 SER.#'d SETS

2013-14 Panini Signatures Film Rookie Autographs

PRINT RUNS B/WN 25-249 COPIES PER
EXCHANGE DEADLINE 11/28/2015
1 M.Carter-Williams/99 5.00 12.00
2 Gal Mekel/249 3.00 8.00
3 Nate Wolters/249 4.00 10.00
4 Dwight Buycks/249 3.00 8.00
5 Kelly Olynyk/249 4.00 10.00
6 Shabazz Muhammad/49 4.00 10.00
7 Otto Porter/25 10.00 25.00
8 Victor Oladipo/99 6.00 15.00
9 Solomon Hill/249 3.00 8.00
10 Tony Snell/199 4.00 10.00
11 Carrick Felix/249 3.00 8.00
12 Trey Burke/99 4.00 10.00
13 Shane Larkin/249 3.00 8.00
14 Alex Len/25 6.00 15.00
15 G.Antetokounmpo/199 EXCH 60.00 150.00
16 Mason Plumlee/249 5.00 12.00
17 Archie Goodwin/249 4.00 10.00
18 Tim Hardaway Jr./249 5.00 12.00
19 Gorgui Dieng/249 4.00 10.00
20 Peyton Siva/249 3.00 8.00
21 Nemanja Nedovic/249 3.00 8.00
22 Phil Pressey/249 3.00 8.00
23 Luigi Datome/249 3.00 8.00
24 Ben McLemore/49 4.00 10.00
25 Cody Zeller/25

2013-14 Panini Signatures Film Veteran Autographs

PRINT RUNS B/WN 25-149 COPIES PER
EXCHANGE DEADLINE 11/28/2015
1 Bradley Beal/49 15.00 40.00
3 Timofey Mozgov/249 3.00 8.00
4 Thabo Sefolosha/35 8.00 20.00
6 Jared Dudley/75 3.00 8.00
7 K.Irving/35 EXCH 50.00 120.00
8 Kevin Durant/45 75.00 150.00
9 K.Bryant/25 EXCH 150.00 250.00
10 Goran Dragic/75 4.00 10.00
11 Andrew Bogut/35 10.00 25.00
12 Kevin Martin/35 4.00 10.00
14 Randy Foye/75 3.00 8.00
15 Deron Williams/25
16 Harrison Barnes/25 8.00 20.00
18 Kawhi Leonard/35 30.00 80.00
19 Andrea Bargnani/35 4.00 10.00
20 Lance Stephenson/249 4.00 10.00
22 Jimmer Fredette/149 3.00 8.00
23 Earl Clark/249 3.00 8.00
24 C.J. Watson/249 3.00 8.00
25 James Anderson/249 3.00 8.00
26 Andre Drummond/35 8.00 20.00
27 Brandon Rush/249 3.00 8.00
28 Corey Brewer/249 3.00 8.00
29 J.J. Redick/35 10.00 25.00
31 Steve Blake/249 3.00 8.00
34 Landry Fields/199 3.00 8.00
35 Boris Diaw/49 10.00 25.00
36 Udonis Haslem/249 8.00 20.00
37 Draymond Green/249 10.00 25.00
38 Jordan Crawford/249 3.00 8.00
39 Patrick Patterson/249 3.00 8.00
40 Christian Laettner/25 10.00 25.00
42 Ronnie Brewer/249 4.00 10.00
43 Ersan Ilyasova/49 3.00 8.00
44 Kyle Korver/35 4.00 10.00
45 Marcin Gortat/35 20.00 50.00
46 Tobias Harris/149 4.00 10.00
47 Brandon Bass/35 3.00 8.00
49 Anthony Davis/35 40.00 80.00
50 Tracy McGrady/35 30.00 80.00
51 Byron Scott/35 4.00 10.00
52 Jason Kidd/35 15.00 40.00
53 Tom Chambers/49 4.00 10.00
54 Dikembe Mutombo/35 15.00 40.00
55 Toni Kukoc/49 20.00 50.00
57 Steve Smith/249 4.00 10.00
58 D.Coleman/49 EXCH 5.00 12.00
59 Jalen Rose/35 10.00 25.00
60 Avery Johnson/35 4.00 10.00
62 Jamal Mashburn/249 5.00 12.00
64 Clyde Drexler/35 30.00 60.00
65 Scottie Pippen/35
66 Luc Longley/249 4.00 10.00
68 Kevin Love/35 20.00 50.00
71 Kareem Abdul-Jabbar/35 40.00 80.00
72 D.Robinson/35 EXCH 25.00 60.00
73 Gary Payton/35 12.00 30.00
74 Anfernee Hardaway/35 40.00 80.00
75 Jarrett Jack/49 4.00 10.00

2013-14 Panini Signatures Franchise Graphs

PRINT RUNS B/WN 25-149 COPIES PER
EXCHANGE DEADLINE 11/28/2015
1 Gordon Hayward/25 20.00 50.00
4 Zach Randolph/25 10.00 25.00
5 Dwight Howard/35 15.00 40.00
6 Jeff Green/35 4.00 10.00
7 Kevin Love/25 12.00 30.00
8 Stephen Curry/25 100.00 250.00
9 Kobe Bryant/25 75.00 200.00
10 Kevin Durant/25 75.00 200.00
11 Chris Bosh/25 10.00 25.00
12 Kawhi Leonard/49 50.00 120.00
13 Jonas Valanciunas/25 6.00 15.00
14 Andre Drummond/25 20.00 50.00
16 Kyrie Irving/35 50.00 120.00
17 Anthony Davis/35 60.00 120.00
20 LaMarcus Aldridge/25 20.00 50.00
21 Victor Oladipo/35 20.00 50.00
22 M.Carter-Williams/49 5.00 12.00
23 G.Antetokounmpo/149 60.00 150.00
24 Alex Len/35 4.00 10.00
25 Ben McLemore/35 4.00 10.00

2013-14 Panini Signatures Hall Hopefuls Signatures

PRINT RUNS B/WN 20-149 COPIES PER
EXCHANGE DEADLINE 11/28/2015
1 Vince Carter/20
2 S.Nash/20 EXCH 40.00 80.00
3 Tony Parker/20
4 Shaquille O'Neal/20
5 Tracy McGrady/20 12.00 30.00
6 Kobe Bryant/20
7 Grant Hill/20 40.00 80.00
8 Jason Kidd/20 30.00 60.00
9 Spencer Haywood/50 3.00 8.00
10 Chris Bosh/20 20.00 50.00
12 Kevin Durant/20 75.00 150.00
13 Tim Hardaway/125 10.00 25.00
14 Mark Aguirre/149 4.00 10.00
15 Alonzo Mourning/20 30.00 60.00

2013-14 Panini Signatures History of the Hall Autographs

PRINT RUNS B/WN 20-99 COPIES PER
EXCHANGE DEADLINE 11/28/2015
1 Jerry West/20
3 Dan Issel/99 4.00 10.00
4 D.Robinson/20 EXCH
5 Kevin McHale/20
6 Bob McAdoo/75 15.00 40.00
7 Jerry Lucas/35 12.00 30.00
8 Walt Frazier/20 12.00 30.00
9 Nate Thurmond/20 12.00 30.00
10 Adrian Dantley/99 4.00 10.00
11 Alex English/99 4.00 10.00
12 Nate Archibald/35 8.00 20.00
13 Dennis Rodman/20 25.00 60.00
14 C.Mullin/20 EXCH 5.00 12.00
15 Bernard King/20 15.00 40.00

2013-14 Panini Signatures Ringing Endorsements

STATED PRINT RUN 20 SER.#'d SETS
EXCHANGE DEADLINE 11/28/2015
1 Scottie Pippen 150.00 250.00
2 Isiah Thomas
3 Hakeem Olajuwon 30.00 60.00
4 Magic Johnson 50.00 100.00
5 Bill Russell 60.00 120.00
6 Chris Bosh 30.00 60.00
7 Kobe Bryant
8 Tony Parker 60.00 120.00
9 Jason Terry 8.00 20.00
10 Tayshaun Prince 8.00 20.00

2013-14 Panini Signatures Rookie Signatures

PRINT RUNS B/WN 99-199 COPIES PER
EXCHANGE DEADLINE 11/28/2015
1 Dwight Buycks/199 3.00 8.00
2 G.Antetokounmpo/199 60.00 150.00
3 M.Carter-Williams/125 5.00 12.00
5 Gorgui Dieng/199 4.00 10.00
6 Andre Roberson/199 3.00 8.00
7 Steven Adams/199 5.00 12.00
8 Archie Goodwin/199 4.00 10.00
10 Lorenzo Brown/199 3.00 8.00
11 Victor Oladipo/99 12.00 30.00
12 Ian Clark/199 4.00 10.00
13 Ray McCallum/199 3.00 8.00
15 Anthony Bennett/125 4.00 10.00
16 Nerlens Noel/99 6.00 15.00
17 Matthew Dellavedova/199 5.00 12.00
18 Carrick Felix/199 3.00 8.00
19 Jamaal Franklin/199 3.00 8.00
20 Toure Murry/199 4.00 10.00
21 Tim Hardaway Jr./199 5.00 12.00
22 Ryan Kelly/199 3.00 8.00
23 Trey Burke/99 4.00 10.00
25 James Southerland/199 3.00 8.00
26 Nate Wolters/199 6.00 15.00
27 Tony Snell/199 4.00 10.00
28 Kelly Olynyk/199 4.00 10.00
29 Phil Pressey/199 3.00 8.00
30 Mason Plumlee/199 5.00 12.00
31 Gal Mekel/199 3.00 8.00
32 Jeff Withey/199 3.00 8.00
33 Peyton Siva/199 3.00 8.00
34 Solomon Hill/199 3.00 8.00
35 Tony Mitchell/199 3.00 8.00
37 Shane Larkin/199 3.00 8.00
38 Dennis Schroder/199 5.00 12.00
39 Erik Murphy/199 3.00 8.00
40 Miroslav Raduljica/199 3.00 8.00

2013-14 Panini Spectra

STATED PRINT RUN 199 SER.#'d SETS
JSY AU RC RANDOMLY INSERTED
EXCHANGE DEADLINE 1/16/2016
1 Derrick Rose 2.00 5.00
2 Monta Ellis 1.25 3.00
3 Jeff Green 1.25 3.00
4 Chris Paul 2.00 5.00
5 Carmelo Anthony 2.00 5.00
6 Kobe Bryant 6.00 15.00
7 Damian Lillard 3.00 8.00
8 Jeff Teague 1.25 3.00
9 Derrick Favors 1.25 3.00
10 Nikola Vucevic 1.25 3.00
11 Luol Deng 1.25 3.00
12 Dirk Nowitzki 2.00 5.00
13 Avery Bradley 1.25 3.00
14 DeAndre Jordan 1.50 4.00
15 Andrea Bargnani 1.25 3.00
16 Steve Nash 1.50 4.00
17 Nicolas Batum 1.25 3.00
18 Paul Millsap 1.50 4.00
19 Enes Kanter 1.00 2.50
20 Jameer Nelson 1.00 2.50
21 Carlos Boozer 1.25 3.00
22 Jose Calderon 1.00 2.50
23 Jared Sullinger 1.00 2.50
24 Goran Dragic 1.25 3.00
25 J.R. Smith 1.25 3.00
26 DeMarcus Cousins 1.50 4.00
27 Ty Lawson 1.00 2.50
28 Kyle Korver 1.25 3.00
29 Paul George 2.00 5.00
30 Tony Parker 1.50 4.00
31 Kyrie Irving 3.00 8.00
32 Shawn Marion 1.25 3.00
33 DeMar DeRozan 1.50 4.00
34 Eric Bledsoe 1.25 3.00
35 Evan Turner 1.00 2.50
36 Isaiah Thomas 1.50 4.00
37 Kenneth Faried 1.25 3.00
38 Kemba Walker 1.50 4.00
39 David West 1.25 3.00
40 Manu Ginobili 1.50 4.00
41 Dion Waiters 1.25 3.00
42 Ryan Anderson 1.25 3.00
43 Kyle Lowry 1.25 3.00
44 Channing Frye 1.25 3.00
45 Thaddeus Young 1.00 2.50
46 Rudy Gay 1.50 4.00
47 Nate Robinson 1.00 2.50
48 Gerald Henderson 1.00 2.50
49 Lance Stephenson 1.25 3.00
50 Tim Duncan 2.50 6.00
51 Tristan Thompson 1.25 3.00
52 Anthony Davis 3.00 8.00
53 Jonas Valanciunas 1.25 3.00
54 Stephen Curry 6.00 15.00
55 Spencer Hawes 1.00 2.50
56 LeBron James 10.00 25.00
57 Kevin Love 1.50 4.00
58 Al Jefferson 1.25 3.00
59 Roy Hibbert 1.25 3.00
60 Kawhi Leonard 2.50 6.00
61 O.J. Mayo 1.00 2.50
62 Jrue Holiday 1.50 4.00
63 Joe Johnson 1.25 3.00
64 Klay Thompson 2.00 5.00
65 Kevin Durant 4.00 10.00
66 Dwyane Wade 2.50 6.00
67 Kevin Martin 1.25 3.00
68 John Wall 2.00 5.00
69 Brandon Jennings 1.00 2.50
70 James Harden 2.50 6.00
71 Caron Butler 1.25 3.00
72 Mike Conley 1.25 3.00
73 Brook Lopez 1.25 3.00
74 David Lee 1.00 2.50
75 Russell Westbrook 4.00 10.00
76 Chris Bosh 1.50 4.00
77 Nikola Pekovic 1.00 2.50
78 Bradley Beal 1.50 4.00
79 Josh Smith 1.25 3.00
80 Dwight Howard 1.25 3.00
81 Brandon Knight 1.25 3.00
82 Zach Randolph 1.25 3.00
83 Paul Pierce 1.50 4.00
84 Harrison Barnes 1.25 3.00
85 Serge Ibaka 1.25 3.00
86 Ray Allen 1.50 4.00
87 Gordon Hayward 1.50 4.00
88 Marcin Gortat 1.25 3.00
89 Greg Monroe 1.25 3.00
90 Chandler Parsons 1.25 3.00
91 Blake Griffin 1.50 4.00
92 Marc Gasol 1.50 4.00
93 Kevin Garnett 2.50 6.00
94 Pau Gasol 1.50 4.00
95 LaMarcus Aldridge 1.50 4.00
96 Al Horford 1.25 3.00
97 Alec Burks 1.00 2.50
98 Arron Afflalo 1.00 2.50
99 Andre Drummond 1.50 4.00
100 Jeremy Lin 1.50 4.00
101 N.Noel JSY AU RC 6.00 15.00
102 K.Olynyk JSY AU RC 4.00 10.00
103 G.Mekel JSY AU RC 3.00 8.00
104 O.Porter JSY AU RC 5.00 12.00
105 N.Wolters JSY AU RC 4.00 10.00
106 M.Plumlee JSY AU RC 5.00 12.00
107 C.McCollum JSY AU RC 8.00 20.00
108 A.Goodwin JSY AU RC 4.00 10.00
109 S.Larkin JSY AU RC 3.00 8.00
110 T.Snell JSY AU RC 4.00 10.00
111 A.Len JSY AU RC 4.00 10.00
112 T.Burke JSY AU RC 4.00 10.00
113 B.McLemore JSY AU RC 4.00 10.00
114 S.Hill JSY AU RC 3.00 8.00
115 R.Gobert JSY AU RC 12.00 30.00
116 K.Caldwell-Pope JSY AU RC 5.00 12.00
117 T.Hardaway Jr. JSY AU RC 5.00 12.00
118 A.Bennett JSY AU RC 4.00 10.00
119 C.Zeller JSY AU RC 4.00 10.00
120 G.Antetokounmpo JSY AU RC 75.00 200.00
121 M.Carter-Williams JSY AU RC 5.00 12.00
122 M.Dellavedova JSY AU RC 5.00 12.00
123 J.Franklin JSY AU RC 3.00 8.00
124 V.Oladipo JSY AU RC 6.00 15.00
125 S.Adams JSY AU RC 5.00 12.00

2013-14 Panini Spectra Blue

*BLUE: .6X TO 1.5X BASIC
RANDOM INSERTS IN PACKS
STATED PRINT RUN 65 SER.#'d SETS

2013-14 Panini Spectra Red Die Cut Variations

*RED DC: 2X TO 5X BASIC
RANDOM INSERTS IN PACKS
STATED PRINT RUN 25 SER.#'d SETS
1 Derrick Rose 60.00 120.00
6 Kobe Bryant 100.00 200.00
50 Tim Duncan 25.00 60.00
56 LeBron James 100.00 200.00

2013-14 Panini Spectra Rookie Jerseys Autographs Light Blue

*LT BLUE: .5X TO 1.2X BASIC
RANDOM INSERTS IN PACKS
PRINT RUNS B/WN 5-99 COPIES PER
NO PRICING ON QTY 5
EXCHANGE DEADLINE 1/16/2016

2013-14 Panini Spectra Rookie Jerseys Autographs Orange

*ORANGE: .6X TO 1.5X BASIC
RANDOM INSERTS IN PACKS
PRINT RUNS B/WN 5-60 COPIES PER
NO PRICING ON QTY 5
EXCHANGE DEADLINE 1/16/2016

2013-14 Panini Spectra All-Stars Jersey Autographs

RANDOM INSERTS IN PACKS
STATED PRINT RUN 125 SER.#'d SETS
EXCHANGE DEADLINE 1/16/2016
17 Brad Daugherty
19 Fat Lever

2013-14 Panini Spectra All-Stars Jersey Autographs Light Blue

RANDOM INSERTS IN PACKS
PRINT RUNS B/WN 25-60 COPIES PER
EXCHANGE DEADLINE 1/16/2016
1 Kobe Bryant/40 100.00 250.00
4 Steve Nash/25 20.00 50.00
5 Tony Parker/25 50.00 100.00
6 Kevin Durant/40 125.00 250.00
7 Kevin Love/25 15.00 40.00
8 Tyson Chandler/25 5.00 12.00
9 Larry Bird/25 50.00 120.00
10 James Harden/25 30.00 60.00
11 Andrei Kirilenko/25 5.00 12.00
13 Kyrie Irving/25 50.00 120.00
15 Caron Butler/25 12.00 30.00
17 Brad Daugherty/60
19 Fat Lever/49 5.00 12.00
21 Tracy McGrady/25 40.00 80.00
22 Al Horford/25 5.00 12.00
23 David Robinson/25 30.00 60.00
24 Jason Kidd/25 20.00 50.00
25 Grant Hill/25 50.00 120.00

2013-14 Panini Spectra All-Stars Jersey Autographs Orange

*ORANGE: .4X TO 1X LT BLUE
RANDOM INSERTS IN PACKS
PRINT RUNS B/WN 15-25 COPIES PER
NO PRICING ON QTY 15
EXCHANGE DEADLINE 1/16/2016

2013-14 Panini Spectra Double Team Jerseys

RANDOM INSERTS IN PACKS
PRINT RUNS B/WN 49-75 COPIES PER
1 K.Garnett/P.Pierce/75 6.00 15.00
2 K.Irving/D.Waiters/75 8.00 20.00
3 D.Nowitzki/M.Ellis/75 5.00 12.00
4 A.Drummond/G.Monroe/75 4.00 10.00
5 S.Curry/H.Barnes/75 6.00 15.00
6 D.Howard/J.Harden/75 10.00 25.00
7 B.Griffin/C.Paul/75 5.00 12.00
8 K.Bryant/P.Gasol/75 12.00 30.00
9 L.James/D.Wade/75 12.00 30.00
10 K.Love/R.Rubio/75 4.00 10.00
11 K.Durant/R.Westbrook/75 10.00 25.00
12 D.Lillard/L.Aldridge/75 12.00 30.00
13 T.Duncan/T.Parker/75 10.00 25.00
14 J.Wall/B.Beal/75 15.00 40.00
15 S.O'Neal /A.Hardaway/49 15.00 40.00
16 L.Bird/K.McHale/49 12.00 30.00
17 P.Ewing/C.Oakley/49 8.00 20.00
18 M.Johnson/K.Abdul-Jabbar/49 15.00 40.00
19 K.Malone/J.Stockton/49 12.00 30.00
20 I.Thomas/J.Dumars/49 4.00 10.00
21 H.Olajuwon/C.Drexler/49 15.00 40.00
22 G.Payton/S.Kemp/49 12.00 30.00
23 A.English/D.Issel/49 3.00 8.00
24 S.Pippen/R.Parish/49 10.00 25.00
25 L.Nance/M.Price/49 4.00 10.00

2013-14 Panini Spectra Hall of Fame Jersey Autographs

RANDOM INSERTS IN PACKS
STATED PRINT RUN 99 SER.#'d SETS
EXCHANGE DEADLINE 1/16/2016
2 Arvydas Sabonis 12.00 30.00
22 Alex English 4.00 10.00

2013-14 Panini Spectra Hall of Fame Jersey Autographs Light Blue

RANDOM INSERTS IN PACKS
PRINT RUNS B/WN 25-60 COPIES PER
EXCHANGE DEADLINE 1/16/2016
1 Larry Bird/20 50.00 100.00
2 Arvydas Sabonis/60 12.00 30.00
3 Rick Barry/20 15.00 40.00
4 Clyde Drexler/20 30.00 60.00
5 Dominique Wilkins/20 12.00 30.00
6 Karl Malone/20 60.00 120.00
7 Scottie Pippen/20 100.00 200.00
8 Gary Payton/20 20.00 50.00
9 David Robinson/20 30.00 60.00
10 Bob Lanier/20 12.00 30.00
11 Gail Goodrich/20 10.00 25.00
12 Joe Dumars/20
13 John Havlicek/20 30.00 80.00
14 Julius Erving/20 50.00 100.00
15 Hakeem Olajuwon/20 30.00 60.00
16 Robert Parish/20 12.00 30.00
17 James Worthy/20 30.00 60.00
18 George Gervin/20 15.00 40.00
19 Kareem Abdul-Jabbar/20 10.00 25.00
21 Dennis Rodman/20 40.00 80.00
22 Alex English/60 5.00 12.00

2013-14 Panini Spectra Indelible Ink Jerseys

RANDOM INSERTS IN PACKS
PRINT RUNS B/WN 75-199 COPIES PER
EXCHANGE DEADLINE 1/16/2016
4 Jack Sikma/199
8 Steve Blake/149
15 Bill Laimbeer/99 6.00 15.00
17 Ryan Anderson/75 4.00 10.00
18 Nick Collison/199
32 George Hill/149
40 Sean Elliott/149 5.00 12.00

2013-14 Panini Spectra Indelible Ink Jerseys Light Blue

RANDOM INSERTS IN PACKS
PRINT RUNS B/WN 25-99 COPIES PER
EXCHANGE DEADLINE 1/16/2016
1 Danny Manning/20
2 Kevin Love/25 40.00 80.00
3 Tony Parker/25 12.00 30.00
4 Jack Sikma/99 5.00 12.00
7 Bradley Beal/25 12.00 30.00
8 Steve Blake/99
9 James Harden/25 20.00 50.00
10 Steve Nash/25 30.00 60.00
11 Kawhi Leonard/75 15.00 40.00
12 Magic Johnson/25 40.00 80.00
13 Dominique Wilkins/25 20.00 50.00
15 Bill Laimbeer/60 5.00 12.00
17 Ryan Anderson/75 5.00 12.00
18 Nick Collison/75
20 Kobe Bryant/40 125.00 250.00
21 Larry Bird/25 50.00 100.00
22 Glen Rice/25 10.00 25.00
23 Anfernee Hardaway/25 60.00 120.00
25 Kyrie Irving/25 60.00 120.00
28 Kevin Durant/40 60.00 150.00
31 Julius Erving/25 30.00 80.00
32 George Hill/99 5.00 12.00
36 Joe Dumars/25 6.00 15.00
40 Sean Elliott/99 6.00 15.00

2013-14 Panini Spectra Indelible Ink Jerseys Orange

*ORANGE: .4X TO 1X LT BLUE
RANDOM INSERTS IN PACKS
PRINT RUNS B/WN 15-60 COPIES PER
NO PRICING ON QTY 15
EXCHANGE DEADLINE 1/16/2016

2013-14 Panini Spectra Jerseys Autographs

RANDOM INSERTS IN PACKS
PRINT RUNS B/WN 49-149 COPIES PER
EXCHANGE DEADLINE 1/16/2016
16 Terry Cummings/149
20 Kenny Sky Walker/49 8.00 20.00
23 Fred Brown/149
26 Tom Chambers/49 4.00 10.00
29 Buck Williams/75
30 Kurt Rambis/49 6.00 15.00
37 Thabo Sefolosha/49 8.00 20.00
45 Jayson Williams/149
49 Brad Daugherty/149
50 Mark Price/75 5.00 12.00

2013-14 Panini Spectra Jerseys Autographs Light Blue

RANDOM INSERTS IN PACKS
PRINT RUNS B/WN 30-75 COPIES PER
EXCHANGE DEADLINE 1/16/2016
8 Jerry West/30 40.00 80.00
10 Kelly Tripucka/30 4.00 10.00
11 Ty Lawson/30 4.00 10.00
14 Shaquille O'Neal 30 75.00 150.00
16 Terry Cummings/75 5.00 12.00
17 Andrei Kirilenko/30 5.00 12.00
18 John Havlicek/30 40.00 80.00
20 Kenny Sky Walker/30 10.00 25.00
22 Kevin Love/30 15.00 40.00
23 Fred Brown/75 4.00 10.00
26 Tom Chambers/30 10.00 25.00
27 Anfernee Hardaway/30 60.00 120.00
29 Buck Williams/49 4.00 10.00
30 Kurt Rambis/30 4.00 10.00
34 Kobe Bryant/30 150.00 250.00
35 Ryan Anderson/30 5.00 12.00
36 Tyson Chandler/30
37 Thabo Sefolosha/30 10.00 25.00
40 Caron Butler/30 5.00 12.00
45 Jayson Williams/75 4.00 10.00
47 Avery Johnson/30 6.00 15.00
48 Josh Smith/30
49 Brad Daugherty/75
50 Mark Price/49 6.00 15.00

2013-14 Panini Spectra Jerseys Autographs Orange

*ORANGE: .4X TO 1X LT BLUE
RANDOM INSERTS IN PACKS
PRINT RUNS B/WN 12-25 COPIES PER
NO PRICING ON QTY 12
EXCHANGE DEADLINE 1/16/2016
48 Josh Smith/20 20.00 50.00

2013-14 Panini Spectra Marks Memorabilia

RANDOM INSERTS IN PACKS
PRINT RUNS B/WN 125-199 COPIES PER
EXCHANGE DEADLINE 1/16/2016
12 Robert Horry/125 4.00 10.00
13 Alex English/199 4.00 10.00
15 Terry Cummings/175
17 Jayson Williams/199

2013-14 Panini Spectra Marks Memorabilia Light Blue

RANDOM INSERTS IN PACKS
PRINT RUNS B/WN 20-99 COPIES PER
EXCHANGE DEADLINE 1/16/2016
4 Hakeem Olajuwon/20 30.00 60.00
5 Gail Goodrich/20 10.00 25.00
6 Larry Johnson/75 10.00 25.00
7 Tracy McGrady/20 40.00 80.00
8 Grant Hill/20 30.00 60.00
12 Robert Horry/49 5.00 12.00
13 Alex English/49
14 Bob Lanier/20 5.00 12.00
15 Terry Cummings/99 5.00 12.00
16 James Worthy/20 15.00 40.00
17 Jayson Williams/99
21 Joe Dumars/20

2013-14 Panini Spectra Marks Memorabilia Orange

*ORANGE: .4X TO 1X LT BLUE
RANDOM INSERTS IN PACKS
PRINT RUNS B/WN 15-60 COPIES PER
NO PRICING ON QTY 15
EXCHANGE DEADLINE 1/16/2016

2013-14 Panini Spectra Materials

RANDOM INSERTS IN PACKS
STATED PRINT RUN 25 SER.#'d SETS
1 Jared Sullinger 2.50 6.00
2 Kevin Durant 15.00 40.00
3 Kenneth Faried 3.00 8.00
4 Tim Duncan 12.00 30.00
5 Paul George
6 Kevin Garnett 6.00 15.00
7 Kobe Bryant 20.00 50.00
8 Stephen Curry 15.00 40.00
9 Kevin Love 4.00 10.00
10 Kemba Walker 4.00 10.00
11 Kyrie Irving 10.00 25.00
12 Russell Westbrook 10.00 25.00
13 James Harden 6.00 15.00
14 John Wall
15 Blake Griffin 12.00 30.00
16 Paul Pierce 4.00 10.00
17 LeBron James 20.00 50.00
18 O.J. Mayo 2.50 6.00
19 Ricky Rubio 4.00 10.00
20 Anthony Davis 10.00 25.00
21 Dirk Nowitzki 10.00 25.00
22 Damian Lillard 10.00 25.00
23 Dwight Howard 3.00 8.00
24 Al Horford 3.00 8.00
25 Chris Paul 5.00 12.00
26 Monta Ellis 3.00 8.00
27 Dwyane Wade 10.00 25.00
28 Bradley Beal 4.00 10.00
29 Carmelo Anthony 5.00 12.00
30 Kawhi Leonard 10.00 25.00

2013-14 Panini Spectra Rookie Jumbo Jerseys

RANDOM INSERTS IN PACKS
STATED PRINT RUN 75 SER.#'d SETS
1 Nate Wolters 3.00 8.00
2 Rudy Gobert 5.00 12.00
3 Steven Adams 5.00 12.00
4 C.J. McCollum 6.00 15.00
5 Tim Hardaway Jr. 4.00 10.00
6 Shane Larkin 2.50 6.00
7 Cody Zeller 3.00 8.00
8 Kelly Olynyk 3.00 8.00
9 Trey Burke 3.00 8.00
10 Matthew Dellavedova 4.00 10.00
11 Otto Porter 4.00 10.00
12 Solomon Hill 2.50 6.00
13 Victor Oladipo 6.00 15.00
14 Luigi Datome 2.50 6.00
15 Mason Plumlee 4.00 10.00
16 Kentavious Caldwell-Pope 4.00 10.00
17 Archie Goodwin 3.00 8.00
18 Anthony Bennett 3.00 8.00
19 Tony Snell 3.00 8.00
20 Giannis Antetokounmpo 20.00 50.00
21 Nerlens Noel 5.00 12.00
22 Alex Len 3.00 8.00
23 Michael Carter-Williams 4.00 10.00
24 Gal Mekel 2.50 6.00
25 Ben McLemore 3.00 8.00

2013-14 Panini Spectra Spectacular Swatch Signatures

RANDOM INSERTS IN PACKS
PRINT RUNS B/WN 75-199 COPIES PER
EXCHANGE DEADLINE 1/16/2016
1 Buck Williams/99
3 Thaddeus Young/199 3.00 8.00
5 Fat Lever/199 4.00 10.00
15 Fred Brown/199 3.00 8.00
18 George Hill/199
19 Kawhi Leonard/75 20.00 50.00
20 Mark Price/175 8.00 20.00
23 Larry Johnson/75 8.00 20.00
27 Alex English/149 6.00 15.00
28 Steve Blake/199
43 Marcin Gortat/175 8.00 20.00
48 Nick Collison/175
49 Kenny Sky Walker/149
57 Anthony Mason/199
61 Brad Daugherty/199
65 Ryan Anderson/75 4.00 10.00
68 Thabo Sefolosha/75 3.00 8.00
72 Tom Chambers/149 4.00 10.00
80 Steve Mix/99 3.00 8.00
90 Kurt Rambis/149
99 Kevin Willis/99 3.00 8.00

2013-14 Panini Spectra Spectacular Swatch Signatures Light Blue

RANDOM INSERTS IN PACKS
PRINT RUNS B/WN 20-60 COPIES PER
EXCHANGE DEADLINE 1/16/2016
1 Buck Williams/60 8.00 20.00
3 Thaddeus Young/60
5 Fat Lever/60 5.00 12.00
6 Tony Parker/20 50.00 100.00
7 Kyrie Irving/20 75.00 150.00
9 Kareem Abdul-Jabbar/20 30.00 80.00
10 Avery Johnson/20 12.00 30.00
12 Scottie Pippen/20 100.00 200.00
15 Fred Brown/60 4.00 10.00
16 Clyde Drexler/20 40.00 80.00
17 Al Horford/20
18 George Hill/60 5.00 12.00
19 Kawhi Leonard/35 20.00 50.00
20 Mark Price/60 12.00 30.00
22 Shaquille O'Neal /20
23 Larry Johnson/35 10.00 25.00
27 Alex English/49 5.00 12.00
28 Steve Blake/60 4.00 10.00
29 Kelly Tripucka/60 4.00 10.00
30 Gary Payton/20 20.00 50.00
32 Stephen Curry/20 150.00 300.00
33 Magic Johnson/20
34 Anthony Davis/20
35 Grant Hill/20 20.00 50.00
41 David Robinson/20 40.00 80.00
42 Tyson Chandler/20 5.00 12.00
43 Marcin Gortat/60 10.00 25.00
45 John Wall/20
48 Nick Collison/60 5.00 12.00
49 Kenny Sky Walker/49 8.00 20.00
52 Steve Nash/20 20.00 50.00
56 Hakeem Olajuwon/20 30.00 60.00
57 Anthony Mason/60 8.00 20.00
60 John Stockton/20
61 Brad Daugherty/60 5.00 12.00
65 Ryan Anderson/35 5.00 12.00
68 Thabo Sefolosha/35 10.00 25.00
70 Kevin Durant/20 100.00 200.00
72 Tom Chambers/49 5.00 12.00
73 Glen Rice/35 10.00 25.00
75 James Harden/20 30.00 60.00
79 Kevin Love/20 40.00 80.00
80 Steve Mix/60 4.00 10.00
82 Tracy McGrady/20
85 Josh Smith/20 5.00 12.00
87 Bob Lanier/20 5.00 12.00
90 Kurt Rambis/49 4.00 10.00
93 Robert Parish/20
95 Karl Malone/20 50.00 100.00
97 Bradley Beal/20 20.00 50.00
99 Kevin Willis/60 4.00 10.00

2013-14 Panini Spectra Spectacular Swatch Signatures Orange

*ORANGE: .4X TO 1X LT BLUE
RANDOM INSERTS IN PACKS
PRINT RUNS B/WN 15-35 COPIES PER
NO PRICING ON QTY 15
EXCHANGE DEADLINE 1/16/2016
19 Kawhi Leonard/20 30.00 60.00

2013-14 Panini Spectra Swatches

RANDOM INSERTS IN PACKS
PRINT RUNS B/WN 15-49 COPIES PER
1 Elgin Baylor/15 3.00 8.00
2 Dan Majerle/49 2.50 6.00
3 Dwight Howard/49 2.50 6.00
4 Rajon Rondo/25 3.00 8.00
5 Shaquille O'Neal /49 6.00 15.00
6 Kevin Garnett/49 5.00 12.00
7 Moses Malone/49 3.00 8.00
8 Russell Westbrook/49 8.00 20.00
9 Patrick Ewing/49 8.00 20.00
10 LeBron James/49 15.00 40.00
11 Brad Daugherty/49 2.50 6.00
12 Jason Kidd/49 8.00 20.00
13 Chris Paul/49 4.00 10.00
14 Kevin Durant/49 8.00 20.00
15 Avery Johnson/49 2.50 6.00
16 Kobe Bryant/49 12.00 30.00
17 Dominique Wilkins/49 4.00 10.00
18 James Harden/49 5.00 12.00
19 Kurt Rambis/49 2.00 5.00
20 Ricky Rubio/49 3.00 8.00
21 Reggie Lewis/49 10.00 25.00
22 Anfernee Hardaway/49 12.00 30.00
23 Dwyane Wade/49 5.00 12.00
24 Kenneth Faried/49 2.50 6.00
25 Joe Dumars/49 3.00 8.00
26 Stephen Curry/49 6.00 15.00
27 Scottie Pippen/49 8.00 20.00
28 John Wall/49 4.00 10.00
29 Robert Horry/49 2.50 6.00
30 Anthony Davis/49 6.00 15.00
31 Tracy McGrady/25 6.00 15.00
32 David Robinson/49 5.00 12.00
33 Carmelo Anthony/49 4.00 10.00
34 Tim Duncan/49 6.00 15.00
35 Fat Lever/49 2.50 6.00
36 Kevin Love/49 3.00 8.00
37 Robert Parish/49 3.00 8.00
38 Blake Griffin/49
39 Larry Johnson/49 4.00 10.00
40 Dirk Nowitzki/49 8.00 20.00
41 Xavier McDaniel/49 2.00 5.00
42 Julius Erving/49 8.00 20.00
43 Kemba Walker/49 3.00 8.00
44 Paul George/49 4.00 10.00
45 Alex English/49 2.50 6.00
46 Kyrie Irving/49 8.00 20.00
47 Clyde Drexler/49 15.00 40.00
48 Paul Pierce/49 3.00 8.00
49 Bill Laimbeer/49 2.50 6.00
50 Damian Lillard/49 6.00 15.00

2013-14 Panini Spectra Threads Autographs

RANDOM INSERTS IN PACKS
PRINT RUNS B/WN 35-149 COPIES PER
EXCHANGE DEADLINE 1/16/2016
*ORANGE: .4X TO 1X LT BLUE
8 Bill Laimbeer/149 4.00 10.00
11 Jeff Malone/149
14 Taj Gibson/125
16 Kenneth Faried/35
17 Andrew Bogut/35
20 Greg Monroe/125
21 Jodie Meeks/149
28 Charles Oakley/149
29 Enes Kanter/125

2013-14 Panini Spectra Threads Autographs Light Blue

RANDOM INSERTS IN PACKS
PRINT RUNS B/WN 25-60 COPIES PER
EXCHANGE DEADLINE 1/16/2016
4 Stephen Curry/25 50.00 120.00
5 Bradley Beal/25 12.00 30.00
6 Kareem Abdul-Jabbar/25 40.00 80.00
8 Bill Laimbeer/25 10.00 25.00
12 Avery Johnson/25
15 David Robinson/25 30.00 60.00
22 Terry Cummings/30 5.00 12.00
23 Robert Horry/60 10.00 25.00
24 Thabo Sefolosha/25 10.00 25.00
25 Gary Payton/25 25.00 60.00
27 Anthony Mason/75
31 John Stockton/25 40.00 80.00
35 Grant Hill/25 40.00 80.00

2014-15 Panini Spectra

1 Zach Randolph 1.25 3.00
2 Kenneth Faried 1.25 3.00
3 Kevin Durant 4.00 10.00
4 Goran Dragic 1.25 3.00
5 Michael Kidd-Gilchrist 1.25 3.00
6 Bradley Beal 1.50 4.00
7 Dwight Howard 1.25 3.00
8 Carmelo Anthony 2.00 5.00
9 Pete Maravich 2.50 6.00
10 Al Horford 1.25 3.00
11 Luol Deng 1.25 3.00
12 David Robinson 2.50 6.00
13 Klay Thompson 2.00 5.00
14 Kawhi Leonard 2.50 6.00
15 Derrick Rose 2.00 5.00
16 Shawn Kemp 2.50 6.00
17 DeAndre Jordan 1.50 4.00
18 Moses Malone 1.50 4.00
19 John Stockton 2.50 6.00
20 Rajon Rondo 1.50 4.00
21 Thaddeus Young 1.00 2.50
22 Eric Bledsoe 1.25 3.00
23 Andre Drummond 1.50 4.00
24 John Havlicek 2.00 5.00
25 Dirk Nowitzki 2.00 5.00
26 Giannis Antetokounmpo 3.00 8.00
27 Magic Johnson 4.00 10.00
28 Trevor Ariza 1.00 2.50
29 Tony Parker 1.50 4.00
30 Dennis Schroder 1.25 3.00
31 Russell Westbrook 4.00 10.00
32 Nick Young 1.25 3.00
33 Damian Lillard 3.00 8.00
34 Joakim Noah 1.25 3.00
35 Omer Asik 1.25 3.00
36 Gordon Hayward 1.50 4.00
37 Jared Sullinger 1.00 2.50
38 Marc Gasol 1.50 4.00
39 Marcin Gortat 1.25 3.00
40 Stephen Curry 6.00 15.00
41 Serge Ibaka 1.25 3.00
42 Shaquille O'Neal 3.00 8.00
43 Lance Stephenson 1.25 3.00
44 LaMarcus Aldridge 1.50 4.00
45 Blake Griffin 1.50 4.00
46 Kyle Lowry 1.25 3.00
47 Chandler Parsons 1.25 3.00
48 Brandon Knight 1.25 3.00
49 Kareem Abdul-Jabbar 2.50 6.00
50 Jeff Green 1.25 3.00
51 Ricky Rubio 1.50 4.00
52 Amar'e Stoudemire 1.50 4.00
53 Brandon Jennings 1.00 2.50
54 Nicolas Batum 1.25 3.00
55 Tim Duncan 2.50 6.00
56 Pau Gasol 1.50 4.00
57 Mike Conley 1.25 3.00
58 Victor Oladipo 1.25 3.00
59 JaVale McGee 1.25 3.00
60 Anthony Davis 3.00 8.00
61 Larry Bird 4.00 10.00
62 Deron Williams 1.25 3.00
63 Hakeem Olajuwon 2.00 5.00
64 Paul George 2.00 5.00
65 Andrea Bargnani 1.25 3.00
66 Tyson Chandler 1.25 3.00
67 Chris Bosh 1.50 4.00
68 Trey Burke 1.00 2.50
69 LeBron James 10.00 25.00
70 Grant Hill 2.00 5.00
71 DeMar DeRozan 1.50 4.00
72 Ty Lawson 1.00 2.50
73 Rudy Gay 1.50 4.00
74 Kobe Bryant 6.00 15.00
75 Clyde Drexler 2.00 5.00
76 Kevin Garnett 2.50 6.00
77 Channing Frye 1.25 3.00
78 Scottie Pippen 3.00 8.00
79 David Lee 1.00 2.50
80 Bill Russell 2.50 6.00
81 John Wall 2.00 5.00
82 Kyrie Irving 3.00 8.00
83 Anfernee Hardaway 4.00 10.00
84 Chris Paul 2.00 5.00
85 Nikola Pekovic 1.00 2.50
86 DeMarcus Cousins 1.50 4.00
87 Al Jefferson 1.25 3.00
88 Dwyane Wade 2.50 6.00
89 Michael Carter-Williams 1.00 2.50
90 Roy Hibbert 1.25 3.00
91 Walt Frazier 1.50 4.00
92 Josh Smith 1.25 3.00
93 Wilt Chamberlain 3.00 8.00
94 Karl Malone 2.00 5.00
95 James Harden 2.50 6.00
96 Elgin Baylor 1.50 4.00
97 Kevin Love 1.50 4.00
98 George Gervin 1.50 4.00
99 Nerlens Noel 1.25 3.00
100 Jeremy Lin 1.50 4.00
101 Jabari Parker JSY AU RC 20.00 50.00
102 A.Wiggins JSY AU RC 60.00 150.00
103 Joel Embiid JSY AU RC 60.00 150.00
104 Marcus Smart JSY AU RC 10.00 25.00
105 Julius Randle JSY AU RC 10.00 25.00

Card	Low	High
106 Aaron Gordon JSY AU RC	10.00	25.00
107 Nik Stauskas JSY AU RC	5.00	12.00
108 Elfrid Payton JSY AU RC	6.00	15.00
109 Doug McDermott JSY AU RC	6.00	15.00
110 Zach LaVine JSY AU RC	15.00	40.00
111 Shabazz Napier JSY AU RC	5.00	12.00
112 Gary Harris JSY AU RC	6.00	15.00
113 Rodney Hood JSY AU RC	6.00	15.00
114 James Ennis JSY AU RC	4.00	10.00
115 Tyler Ennis JSY AU RC	4.00	10.00
116 Noah Vonleh JSY AU RC	5.00	12.00
117 T.J. Warren JSY AU RC	6.00	15.00
118 Johnny O'Bryant JSY AU RC	4.00	10.00
119 C.J. Wilcox JSY AU RC	4.00	10.00
120 Adreian Payne JSY AU RC	5.00	12.00
121 Damien Inglis JSY AU RC	4.00	10.00
122 Jordan Adams JSY AU RC	4.00	10.00
123 Mitch McGary JSY AU RC	4.00	10.00
124 Kyle Anderson JSY AU RC	6.00	15.00
125 Spencer Dinwiddie JSY AU RC	5.00	12.00
126 K.J. McDaniels JSY AU RC	5.00	12.00
127 Joe Harris JSY AU RC	4.00	10.00
128 P.J. Hairston JSY AU RC	4.00	10.00
129 Jarnell Stokes JSY AU RC	4.00	10.00
130 Jerami Grant JSY AU RC	4.00	10.00
131 Cory Jefferson JSY AU RC	4.00	10.00
132 Markel Brown JSY AU RC	4.00	10.00
133 James Young JSY AU RC	4.00	10.00

2014-15 Panini Spectra Prizms Blue

*BLUE VET: .5X TO 1.2X BASE HI
*BLUE RK: .5X TO 1.2X BASE HI
RANDOM INSERTS IN PACKS
STATED PRINT RUN 49 SER.#'d SETS
ROOKIE PRINT RUN 99 SER.#'d SETS

2014-15 Panini Spectra Prizms Red Die Cut

*RED: 1.2X TO 3X BASE HI
RANDOM INSERTS IN PACKS
STATED PRINT RUN 25 SER.#'d SETS

Card	Low	High
29 Tony Parker	25.00	60.00
32 Nick Young	4.00	10.00
75 Clyde Drexler	12.00	30.00
82 Kyrie Irving	40.00	100.00

2014-15 Panini Spectra Double Team Jerseys

RANDOM INSERTS IN PACKS
STATED PRINT RUN B/WN 35-49 COPIES PER

Card	Low	High
DTATL A.Horford/J.Teague/49	4.00	10.00
DTBOS A.Bradley/J.Sullinger/49	4.00	10.00
DTBRK J.Johnson/D.Williams/49	4.00	10.00
DTCHI J.Butler/D.Rose/49	6.00	15.00
DTCLE K.Irving/L.James/49	15.00	40.00
DTDAL D.Nowitzki/M.Ellis/49	10.00	25.00
DTDEN K.Faried/T.Lawson/35	4.00	10.00
DTDET A.Drummond/G.Monroe/49	3.00	8.00
DTGSW K.Thompson/S.Curry/49	20.00	50.00
DTHOU D.Howard/J.Harden/49	8.00	20.00
DTLAC B.Griffin/C.Paul/49	4.00	10.00
DTLAL K.Bryant/S.Nash/49	8.00	20.00
DTMEM M.Gasol/M.Conley/35	5.00	12.00
DTMIA C.Bosh/D.Wade/49	8.00	20.00
DTMIN T.Young/G.Dieng/49	3.00	8.00
DTNYK T.Hardaway/C.Anthony/49	5.00	12.00
DTOKC R.Westbrook/K.Durant/49	10.00	25.00
DTORL V.Oladipo/N.Vucevic/49	4.00	10.00
DTPHX E.Bledsoe/G.Dragic/49	4.00	10.00
DTPOR L.Aldridge/N.Batum/35	12.00	30.00
DTSAC D.Collison/D.Cousins/49	5.00	12.00
DTSAS T.Duncan/T.Parker/49	8.00	20.00
DTTOR D.DeRozan/T.Ross/49	5.00	12.00
DTWAS B.Beal/J.Wall/49	6.00	15.00

2014-15 Panini Spectra Franchise Fabrics

RANDOM INSERTS IN PACKS
STATED PRINT RUN 25 SER.#'d SETS

Card	Low	High
FRAAD Anthony Davis	8.00	20.00
FRAAH Al Horford	3.00	8.00
FRAAI Allen Iverson	5.00	12.00
FRAAM Alonzo Mourning	5.00	12.00
FRAAS Arvydas Sabonis	3.00	8.00
FRAAW Antoine Walker	3.00	8.00
FRABB Bradley Beal	4.00	10.00
FRABD Brad Daugherty	3.00	8.00
FRABG Blake Griffin	4.00	10.00
FRACA Carmelo Anthony	5.00	12.00
FRACB Chris Bosh	4.00	10.00
FRACD Clyde Drexler	5.00	12.00
FRACM Chris Mullin	4.00	10.00
FRACR Clifford Robinson	2.50	6.00
FRADC DeMarcus Cousins	4.00	10.00
FRADD DeMar DeRozan	4.00	10.00
FRADH Dwight Howard	3.00	8.00
FRADM1 Danny Manning	3.00	8.00
FRADM2 Dikembe Mutombo	4.00	10.00
FRADN Dirk Nowitzki	5.00	12.00
FRADR1 David Robinson	6.00	15.00
FRADR2 Derrick Rose	5.00	12.00
FRADW Dominique Wilkins	5.00	12.00
FRAEI Ersan Ilyasova	2.50	6.00
FRAEM Earl Monroe	4.00	10.00
FRAGD Goran Dragic	3.00	8.00
FRAGM Greg Monroe	3.00	8.00
FRAGP Gary Payton	4.00	10.00
FRAHG Hal Greer	3.00	8.00
FRAHO Hakeem Olajuwon	5.00	12.00
FRAJD Joe Dumars	4.00	10.00
FRAJK Jason Kidd	4.00	10.00
FRAJR Jalen Rose	4.00	10.00
FRAJS1 Jared Sullinger	2.50	6.00
FRAJS2 John Stockton	6.00	15.00
FRAJW1 James Worthy	5.00	12.00
FRAJW2 John Wall	5.00	12.00
FRAKA Kareem Abdul-Jabbar	6.00	15.00
FRAKB Kobe Bryant	15.00	40.00
FRAKD Kevin Durant	10.00	25.00
FRAKF Kenneth Faried	3.00	8.00
FRAKG Kevin Garnett	6.00	15.00
FRAKM Karl Malone	5.00	12.00
FRALB Larry Bird	10.00	25.00
FRALBJ LeBron James	15.00	40.00
FRALJ Larry Johnson	5.00	12.00
FRAMC Michael Carter-Williams	2.50	6.00
FRAMF Michael Finley	4.00	10.00
FRAMK Michael Kidd-Gilchrist	3.00	8.00
FRAPE Patrick Ewing	5.00	12.00
FRARH Roy Hibbert	3.00	8.00
FRARL Reggie Lewis	4.00	10.00
FRARR Ricky Rubio	4.00	10.00
FRASC Stephen Curry	15.00	40.00
FRASK Shawn Kemp	6.00	15.00
FRASO Shaquille O'Neal	8.00	20.00
FRATD Tim Duncan	6.00	15.00
FRATM Tracy McGrady	4.00	10.00
FRAVO Victor Oladipo	3.00	8.00
FRAWD Walter Davis	2.50	6.00
FRAYM Yao Ming	5.00	12.00
FRAZR Zach Randolph	3.00	8.00

2014-15 Panini Spectra Freshman Fabrics

RANDOM INSERTS IN PACKS
STATED PRINT RUN 49 SER.#'d SETS

Card	Low	High
FREAG Aaron Gordon	6.00	15.00
FREAP Adreian Payne	2.50	6.00
FREAW Andrew Wiggins	10.00	25.00
FREBC Bruno Caboclo	2.50	6.00
FRECE Cleanthony Early	2.00	5.00
FRECJ Cory Jefferson	2.00	5.00
FRECW C.J. Wilcox	2.00	5.00
FREDE Dante Exum	3.00	8.00
FREDI Damien Inglis	2.00	5.00
FREDM Doug McDermott	3.00	8.00
FREEP Elfrid Payton	3.00	8.00
FREGH Gary Harris	3.00	8.00
FREGR Glenn Robinson III	2.00	5.00
FREJA Jordan Adams	2.00	5.00
FREJE1 James Ennis	2.00	5.00
FREJE2 Joel Embiid	10.00	25.00
FREJG Jerami Grant	2.00	5.00
FREJH Joe Harris	2.00	5.00
FREJO Johnny O'Bryant	2.00	5.00
FREJP Jabari Parker	5.00	12.00
FREJR Julius Randle	5.00	12.00
FREJS Jarnell Stokes	2.00	5.00
FREJY James Young	2.00	5.00
FREKA Kyle Anderson	3.00	8.00
FREKM K.J. McDaniels	2.50	6.00
FREMB Markel Brown	2.00	5.00
FREMM Mitch McGary	2.00	5.00
FREMS Marcus Smart	3.00	8.00
FRENS Nik Stauskas	2.50	6.00
FRENV Noah Vonleh	2.50	6.00
FREPH P.J. Hairston	2.00	5.00
FRERH Rodney Hood	3.00	8.00
FRERS Russ Smith	2.00	5.00
FRESD Spencer Dinwiddie	2.50	6.00
FRESN Shabazz Napier	2.50	6.00
FRETE Tyler Ennis	2.00	5.00
FRETW T.J. Warren	3.00	8.00
FREZL Zach LaVine	5.00	12.00

2014-15 Panini Spectra Global Icons

RANDOM INSERTS IN PACKS

Card	Low	High
1 Luis Scola	12.00	30.00
2 Marcin Gortat	12.00	30.00
3 Andrew Wiggins	200.00	300.00
4 Tony Parker	15.00	40.00
5 Dennis Schroder	12.00	30.00
6 Drazen Petrovic	15.00	40.00
7 Ben Gordon	12.00	30.00
8 Nik Stauskas	12.00	30.00
9 Luigi Datome	10.00	25.00
10 Mirza Teletovic	10.00	25.00
11 Nikola Pekovic	10.00	25.00
12 Joel Embiid	25.00	60.00
13 Festus Ezeli	10.00	25.00
14 Ian Mahinmi	10.00	25.00
15 Yao Ming	20.00	50.00
16 Goran Dragic	12.00	30.00
17 Bismack Biyombo	10.00	25.00
18 Pau Gasol	15.00	40.00
19 Anderson Varejao	10.00	25.00
20 Sergey Karasev	10.00	25.00
21 Peja Stojakovic	15.00	40.00
22 Marc Gasol	15.00	40.00
23 Pablo Prigioni	10.00	25.00
24 Luc Longley	12.00	30.00
25 Lucas Nogueira	10.00	25.00
26 Boris Diaw	12.00	30.00
27 Patrick Ewing	20.00	50.00
28 Jusuf Nurkic	15.00	40.00
29 Kevin Seraphin	10.00	25.00
30 Giannis Antetokounmpo	30.00	80.00
31 Tristan Thompson	12.00	30.00
32 Timofey Mozgov	10.00	25.00
33 Manu Ginobili	15.00	40.00
34 Dirk Nowitzki	20.00	50.00
35 Jonas Valanciunas	12.00	30.00
36 Luc Mbah a Moute	10.00	25.00
37 Nikola Mirotic	20.00	50.00
38 Evan Fournier	10.00	25.00
39 Dikembe Mutombo	15.00	40.00
40 Andrea Bargnani	12.00	30.00
41 Andrew Nicholson	10.00	25.00
42 Rik Smits	12.00	30.00
43 Leandro Barbosa	10.00	25.00
44 Kostas Papanikolaou	10.00	25.00
45 Detlef Schrempf	15.00	40.00
46 Zoran Dragic	12.00	30.00
47 Clint Capela	12.00	30.00
48 Matthew Dellavedova	12.00	30.00
49 Thabo Sefolosha	10.00	25.00
50 Tyler Ennis	10.00	25.00
51 Luol Deng	12.00	30.00
52 Nene	12.00	30.00
53 Gheorghe Muresan	10.00	25.00
54 Cory Joseph	10.00	25.00
55 Rudy Gobert	15.00	40.00
56 Patty Mills	15.00	40.00
57 J.J. Barea	12.00	30.00
58 Bojan Bogdanovic	8.00	20.00
59 Ricky Rubio	15.00	40.00
60 Bruno Caboclo	12.00	30.00
61 Marco Belinelli	10.00	25.00
62 Kelly Olynyk	10.00	25.00
63 Zaza Pachulia	10.00	25.00
64 Jonas Jerebko	10.00	25.00
65 Kyrie Irving	30.00	80.00
66 Nikola Vucevic	12.00	30.00
67 Manute Bol	15.00	40.00
68 Steve Nash	15.00	40.00
69 Nicolas Batum	12.00	30.00
70 Gorgui Dieng	10.00	25.00
71 Arvydas Sabonis	12.00	30.00
72 Mychal Thompson	10.00	25.00
73 Vlade Divac	15.00	40.00
74 Rick Fox	12.00	30.00
75 Donatas Motiejunas	10.00	25.00
76 Steven Adams	12.00	30.00
77 Dante Exum	15.00	40.00
78 Jose Calderon	10.00	25.00
79 Robert Sacre	10.00	25.00
80 Pero Antic	10.00	25.00
81 Ersan Ilyasova	10.00	25.00
82 Tiago Splitter	12.00	30.00
83 Alex Len	10.00	25.00
84 Danilo Gallinari	10.00	25.00
85 Enes Kanter	10.00	25.00
86 Andrew Bogut	8.00	20.00
87 Rony Seikaly	10.00	25.00
88 Swen Nater	10.00	25.00
89 Damjan Rudez	10.00	25.00
90 Omer Asik	12.00	30.00
91 Damien Inglis	10.00	25.00
92 Tim Duncan	30.00	80.00
93 Zydrunas Ilgauskas	12.00	30.00
94 Hedo Turkoglu	12.00	30.00
95 Omri Casspi	10.00	25.00
96 Greivis Vasquez	12.00	30.00
97 Anthony Bennett	10.00	25.00
98 Toni Kukoc	15.00	40.00
99 Al Horford	12.00	30.00
100 Joe Ingles	10.00	25.00

2014-15 Panini Spectra Hall of Fame Autograph Materials

RANDOM INSERTS IN PACKS
STATED PRINT RUN B/WN 35-60 COPIES PER

Card	Low	High
HOFAD Adrian Dantley	6.00	15.00
HOFAG Artis Gilmore	8.00	20.00
HOFAM Alonzo Mourning	20.00	50.00
HOFCD Clyde Drexler	20.00	50.00
HOFDR1 David Robinson	15.00	40.00
HOFDR2 Dennis Rodman	30.00	80.00
HOFDW Dominique Wilkins	12.00	30.00
HOFGG1 Gail Goodrich	15.00	40.00
HOFGG2 George Gervin	15.00	40.00
HOFGP Gary Payton	15.00	40.00
HOFHO Hakeem Olajuwon	20.00	50.00
HOFIT Isiah Thomas	15.00	40.00
HOFJE Julius Erving	25.00	60.00
HOFJS John Stockton	25.00	60.00
HOFJW1 Jamaal Wilkes	10.00	25.00
HOFJW2 James Worthy	12.00	30.00
HOFKA Kareem Abdul-Jabbar	30.00	80.00
HOFKM Karl Malone	30.00	80.00
HOFLB Larry Bird	40.00	100.00
HOFMJ Magic Johnson	40.00	100.00
HOFMR Mitch Richmond	10.00	25.00
HOFRP Robert Parish	10.00	25.00
HOFRS Ralph Sampson	8.00	20.00

2014-15 Panini Spectra Jersey Autographs

RANDOM INSERTS IN PACKS
STATED PRINT RUN B/WN 100-125 COPIES PER

Card	Low	High
1 Andrew Nicholson/125	3.00	8.00
2 Antoine Walker/125	4.00	10.00
3 Brandan Wright/125	3.00	8.00
4 C.J. Watson/125	3.00	8.00
5 C.J. Wilcox/125	3.00	8.00
6 Carl Landry/100	3.00	8.00
7 Clifford Robinson/125	3.00	8.00
8 Cory Jefferson/125	3.00	8.00
9 Dan Issel/125	4.00	10.00
10 Dante Exum/100	5.00	12.00
11 Dikembe Mutombo/100	8.00	20.00
12 Eddie Johnson/125	3.00	8.00
13 Michael Cage/125	3.00	8.00
15 Gary Harris/125	5.00	12.00
16 James Ennis/125	3.00	8.00
17 James Jones/125	3.00	8.00
19 Jarnell Stokes/125	3.00	8.00
21 Joe Harris/125	3.00	8.00
22 Jordan Adams/125	3.00	8.00
23 K.J. McDaniels/125	4.00	10.00
25 Danny Green/100	4.00	10.00
26 Lavoy Allen/125	3.00	8.00
28 Luigi Datome/125	3.00	8.00
29 Mark Price/125	5.00	12.00
30 Markel Brown/125	3.00	8.00
31 Maurice Harkless/125	3.00	8.00
32 Nick Collison/125	4.00	10.00
38 Reggie Jackson/125	3.00	8.00
39 Robert Horry/125	4.00	10.00
40 Robert Parish/100	5.00	12.00
41 Rodney Hood/125	5.00	12.00
42 Russ Smith/125	3.00	8.00
43 Shabazz Napier/125	4.00	10.00
44 Spencer Dinwiddie/125	4.00	10.00
45 Spencer Hawes/125	3.00	8.00
46 Steve Blake/125	3.00	8.00
47 Thaddeus Young/125	3.00	8.00
48 Timofey Mozgov/125	5.00	12.00
50 Zach LaVine/125	12.00	30.00

2014-15 Panini Spectra Jersey Autographs Prizms Orange

*ORANGE: .8X TO 2X BASE HI
RANDOM INSERTS IN PACKS
STATED PRINT RUN 25 SER.#'d SETS

2014-15 Panini Spectra Millenial Memorabilia

RANDOM INSERTS IN PACKS
STATED PRINT RUN B/WN 25-35 COPIES PER

Card	Low	High
MMAB Anthony Bennett/25	3.00	8.00
MMAD Anthony Davis/25	8.00	20.00
MMAD Andre Drummond/35	5.00	12.00
MMAL Alex Len/25	3.00	8.00
MMAW Andrew Wiggins/25	40.00	100.00
MMBB Bradley Beal/35	5.00	12.00
MMBG Blake Griffin/35	5.00	12.00
MMBJ Brandon Jennings/25	3.00	8.00
MMBM Ben McLemore/25	3.00	8.00
MMCM C.J. McCollum/25	5.00	12.00
MMCP Chandler Parsons/25	4.00	10.00
MMCZ Cody Zeller/25	3.00	8.00
MMDC DeMarcus Cousins/35	5.00	12.00
MMDD DeMar DeRozan/35	5.00	12.00
MMDG Draymond Green/35	6.00	15.00
MMDG Danilo Gallinari/25	3.00	8.00
MMDG Danny Green/25	4.00	10.00
MMDR Derrick Rose/35	6.00	15.00
MMGM Greg Monroe/25	4.00	10.00
MMIT Isaiah Thomas/25	8.00	20.00
MMJB Jimmy Butler/35	5.00	12.00
MMJE Joel Embiid/25	8.00	20.00
MMJH Jrue Holiday/35	3.00	8.00
MMJH James Harden/35	8.00	20.00
MMJL Jeremy Lin/25	5.00	12.00
MMJP Jabari Parker/25	6.00	15.00
MMJR Julius Randle/25	8.00	20.00
MMJT Jeff Teague/35	4.00	10.00
MMJV Jonas Valanciunas/25	4.00	10.00
MMJW John Wall/25	6.00	15.00
MMKF Kenneth Faried/35	4.00	10.00
MMKI Kyrie Irving/35	10.00	25.00
MMKL Kawhi Leonard/25	8.00	20.00
MMKT Klay Thompson/25	6.00	15.00
MMKW Kemba Walker/25	5.00	12.00
MMMS Marcus Smart/25	5.00	12.00
MMNP Nikola Pekovic/25	3.00	8.00
MMNV Nikola Vucevic/25	4.00	10.00
MMOP Otto Porter/25	4.00	10.00
MMSA Steven Adams/25	10.00	25.00
MMSC Stephen Curry/35	20.00	50.00
MMSI Serge Ibaka/25	4.00	10.00
MMSM Shabazz Muhammad/25	10.00	25.00
MMTE Tyreke Evans/35	3.00	8.00
MMTG Taj Gibson/25	4.00	10.00
MMTL Ty Lawson/35	3.00	8.00
MMTS Tiago Splitter/25	4.00	10.00
MMTT Tristan Thompson/35	4.00	10.00
MMVO Victor Oladipo/25	4.00	10.00
MMWM Wesley Matthews/25	6.00	15.00

2014-15 Panini Spectra Rookie Jumbo Jerseys

RANDOM INSERTS IN PACKS
STATED PRINT RUN 49 SER.#'d SETS

Card	Low	High
RJJAG Aaron Gordon	4.00	10.00
RJJAP Adreian Payne	4.00	10.00
RJJAW Andrew Wiggins	15.00	40.00
RJJBC Bruno Caboclo	4.00	10.00
RJJCE Cleanthony Early	3.00	8.00
RJJDE Dante Exum	4.00	10.00
RJJDM Doug McDermott	4.00	10.00
RJJEP Elfrid Payton	5.00	12.00
RJJGH Gary Harris	5.00	12.00
RJJGR Glenn Robinson III	3.00	8.00
RJJJA Jordan Adams	3.00	8.00
RJJJE Joel Embiid	8.00	20.00
RJJJH Joe Harris	3.00	8.00
RJJJP Jabari Parker	8.00	20.00
RJJJR Julius Randle	8.00	20.00
RJJJY James Young	3.00	8.00
RJJKM K.J. McDaniels	4.00	10.00
RJJMS Marcus Smart	5.00	12.00
RJJNS Nik Stauskas	4.00	10.00
RJJNV Noah Vonleh	3.00	8.00
RJJRH Rodney Hood	5.00	12.00
RJJSN Shabazz Napier	4.00	10.00
RJJTE Tyler Ennis	3.00	8.00
RJJTW T.J. Warren	5.00	12.00
RJJZL Zach LaVine	8.00	20.00

2014-15 Panini Spectra Spectacular Swatches Signatures

RANDOM INSERTS IN PACKS
STATED PRINT RUN B/WN 35-149 COPIES PER

Card	Low	High
SSAD Adrian Dantley/49	4.00	10.00
SSAE Alex English/49	4.00	10.00
SSAM Alonzo Mourning/35	15.00	40.00
SSAP Adreian Payne/149	4.00	10.00
SSAW Andrew Wiggins/35	125.00	250.00
SSBB Bradley Beal/35	5.00	12.00
SSBL Brook Lopez/35	4.00	10.00
SSBM Ben McLemore/35	3.00	8.00
SSCA1 Carmelo Anthony/35	15.00	40.00
SSCA2 Chris Andersen/35	4.00	10.00
SSCE Cleanthony Early/149	3.00	8.00
SSCL Courtney Lee/49	4.00	10.00
SSCZ Cody Zeller/35	3.00	8.00
SSDB Dee Brown/75	3.00	8.00
SSDC DeMarre Carroll/149	3.00	8.00
SSDE Dante Exum/35	5.00	12.00
SSDF Derrick Favors/35	4.00	10.00
SSDM1 Danny Manning/35	4.00	10.00
SSDM2 Dikembe Mutombo/35	5.00	12.00
SSDR David Robinson/35	15.00	40.00
SSDW Dominique Wilkins/35	12.00	30.00
SSEP Elfrid Payton/49	5.00	12.00
SSGD1 Goran Dragic/35	4.00	10.00
SSGD2 Gorgui Dieng/149	3.00	8.00
SSGH1 Gary Harris/149	5.00	12.00
SSGH2 Gordon Hayward/35	5.00	12.00
SSGH3 Grant Hill/35	15.00	40.00
SSGP Gary Payton/35	10.00	25.00
SSHO Hakeem Olajuwon/35	12.00	30.00
SSIT1 Isaiah Thomas/149	8.00	20.00
SSIT2 Isiah Thomas/35	10.00	25.00
SSJC Jose Calderon/35	6.00	15.00
SSJH Joe Harris/149	3.00	8.00
SSJK Jason Kidd/35	15.00	40.00
SSJL Jerry Lucas/35	8.00	20.00
SSJP Jabari Parker/35	60.00	150.00
SSJR Julius Randle/35	20.00	50.00
SSJS1 Jared Sullinger/35	3.00	8.00
SSJS2 J.R. Smith/35	8.00	20.00
SSJT Jeff Teague/49	4.00	10.00
SSJW John Wall/35	20.00	50.00
SSKA1 Kareem Abdul-Jabbar/35	30.00	80.00
SSKA2 Kenny Anderson/149	4.00	10.00
SSKB Kobe Bryant/35	100.00	200.00
SSKC Kentavious Caldwell-Pope/35	3.00	8.00
SSKD Kevin Durant/35	75.00	150.00
SSKF Kenneth Faried/35	4.00	10.00
SSKI Kyrie Irving/35	40.00	100.00
SSKL Kevin Love/35	15.00	40.00
SSLA LaMarcus Aldridge/35	5.00	12.00
SSLS1 Lance Stephenson/49	4.00	10.00
SSLS2 Luis Scola/35	4.00	10.00
SSMA Mark Aguirre/49	4.00	10.00
SSMC Mike Conley/35	4.00	10.00
SSMF Michael Finley/35	5.00	12.00
SSMJ Marques Johnson/149	4.00	10.00
SSMK Michael Kidd-Gilchrist/35	4.00	10.00
SSMS Marcus Smart/35	5.00	12.00
SSMT Mirza Teletovic/149	3.00	8.00
SSNS Nik Stauskas/35	4.00	10.00
SSNV1 Nick Van Exel/35	8.00	20.00
SSNV2 Noah Vonleh/35	4.00	10.00
SSNY Nick Young/49	4.00	10.00
SSOP Otto Porter/35	4.00	10.00
SSQA Quincy Acy/149	3.00	8.00
SSRH Ron Harper/75	10.00	25.00
SSRL Robin Lopez/149	3.00	8.00
SSRS Robert Sacre/149	3.00	8.00
SSSA Steven Adams/149	4.00	10.00
SSSC Stephen Curry/35	100.00	250.00
SSSE Sean Elliott/49	5.00	12.00
SSSH Spencer Hawes/149	3.00	8.00
SSSM Sidney Moncrief/90	3.00	8.00
SSSN1 Shabazz Napier/149	4.00	10.00
SSSN2 Steve Nash/35	20.00	50.00
SSTC Tyson Chandler/35	4.00	10.00
SSTH Tobias Harris/49	4.00	10.00
SSTS1 Tiago Splitter/35	4.00	10.00
SSTS2 Tony Snell/149	3.00	8.00
SSTW T.J. Warren/49	5.00	12.00
SSTY Thaddeus Young/149	3.00	8.00
SSWD Walter Davis/149	3.00	8.00
SSZL Zach LaVine/149	20.00	50.00

2014-15 Panini Spectra Spectacular Swatches Signatures Prizms Orange

*ORANGE: 1X TO 2.5X BASE HI
RANDOM INSERTS IN PACKS
STATED PRINT RUN 25 SER.#'d SETS

Card	Low	High
SSGH1 Gary Harris	15.00	40.00
SSGH2 Gordon Hayward	15.00	40.00
SSJR Julius Randle	75.00	150.00
SSKA1 Kareem Abdul-Jabbar	50.00	120.00
SSKL Kevin Love	25.00	60.00
SSMJ Marques Johnson	8.00	20.00
SSSN2 Steve Nash	30.00	80.00
SSTL Ty Lawson	15.00	40.00
SSTP Tony Parker	25.00	60.00
SSTW T.J. Warren	20.00	50.00

2014-15 Panini Spectra Superstar Autograph Materials

RANDOM INSERTS IN PACKS
STATED PRINT RUN 35 SER.#'d SETS

Card	Low	High
3 Bradley Beal	12.00	30.00
4 Aaron Gordon	20.00	50.00
5 Julius Randle	20.00	50.00
6 Victor Oladipo	10.00	25.00
9 Grant Hill	20.00	50.00
10 Stephen Curry	60.00	150.00
11 Tony Parker	15.00	40.00
12 Jason Kidd	12.00	30.00
13 Tracy McGrady	20.00	50.00
15 Chris Bosh	12.00	30.00
16 Andrew Wiggins	150.00	300.00
17 Jabari Parker	40.00	100.00
18 John Wall	20.00	50.00
19 Kyrie Irving	40.00	100.00
20 Larry Bird	40.00	100.00
21 Magic Johnson	40.00	100.00
22 Kevin Durant	60.00	150.00
23 Carmelo Anthony	20.00	50.00
25 Kobe Bryant	100.00	200.00

2014-15 Panini Spectra Swatches

RANDOM INSERTS IN PACKS
STATED PRINT RUN B/WN 25-49 COPIES PER

Card	Low	High
SAB Andrew Bogut/35	4.00	10.00
SAG Aaron Gordon/49	8.00	20.00
SAW Andrew Wiggins/49	15.00	40.00
SBC Bruno Caboclo/49	4.00	10.00
SBG Blake Griffin/25	5.00	12.00
SBL Bill Laimbeer/35	4.00	10.00
SCA Chris Andersen/35	3.00	8.00
SCE Cleanthony Early/49	3.00	8.00
SCR Clifford Robinson/35	3.00	8.00
SDC DeMarcus Cousins/25	5.00	12.00
SDE Dante Exum/49	4.00	10.00
SDM1 Dikembe Mutombo/35	10.00	25.00
SDM2 Doug McDermott/49	8.00	20.00
SDN Dirk Nowitzki/25	8.00	20.00
SDW Deron Williams/35	4.00	10.00
SEK Enes Kanter/25	3.00	8.00
SEP Elfrid Payton/49	5.00	12.00
SGD Goran Dragic/25	4.00	10.00
SGH1 Gary Harris/49	5.00	12.00
SGH2 Gerald Henderson/25	3.00	8.00
SGR Glenn Robinson III/49	3.00	8.00
SJE Joel Embiid/49	4.00	10.00
SJH1 James Harden/25	8.00	20.00
SJH2 Joe Harris/49	3.00	8.00
SJH3 John Henson/35	4.00	10.00
SJN Joakim Noah/35	10.00	25.00
SJP Jabari Parker/49	5.00	12.00
SJR Julius Randle/49	6.00	15.00
SJS Jared Sullinger/35	3.00	8.00
SJV Jonas Valanciunas/35	4.00	10.00
SJW John Wall/25	8.00	20.00
SJY James Young/49	3.00	8.00
SKI Kyrie Irving/25	10.00	25.00
SKK Kyle Korver/25	4.00	10.00
SKM K.J. McDaniels/49	4.00	10.00
SMS Marcus Smart/49	3.00	8.00
SNS Nik Stauskas/49	4.00	10.00
SPE Patrick Ewing/25	8.00	20.00
SPH P.J. Hairston/49	3.00	8.00
SRH1 Rodney Hood/49	5.00	12.00
SRH2 Roy Hibbert/35	4.00	10.00
SRR Ricky Rubio/25	3.00	8.00
SSI Serge Ibaka/35	4.00	10.00
SSN1 Steve Nash/25	10.00	25.00
SSN2 Shabazz Napier/49	4.00	10.00
STE Tyreke Evans/35	3.00	8.00
STH Tobias Harris/35	4.00	10.00
STS Tiago Splitter/35	4.00	10.00
SZL Zach LaVine/49	8.00	20.00
SZR Zach Randolph/35	4.00	10.00

2014-15 Panini Spectra Top Tier Threads

RANDOM INSERTS IN PACKS
STATED PRINT RUN B/WN 25-35 COPIES PER

Card	Low	High
TTAD Adrian Dantley/25	3.00	8.00
TTAE Alex English/35	3.00	8.00
TTAH Anfernee Hardaway/25	10.00	25.00
TTAI Allen Iverson/25	5.00	12.00
TTCD Clyde Drexler/35	5.00	12.00
TTDJ Dennis Johnson/25	3.00	8.00
TTDN Dirk Nowitzki/35	5.00	12.00
TTDR1 David Robinson/35	6.00	15.00
TTDR2 Derrick Rose/35	5.00	12.00
TTDW Dwyane Wade/35	6.00	15.00
TTGH Grant Hill/35	5.00	12.00
TTGP Gary Payton/35	4.00	10.00
TTHO Hakeem Olajuwon/25	5.00	12.00
TTJS John Stockton/25	6.00	15.00
TTKA Kareem Abdul-Jabbar/25	6.00	15.00
TTKB Kobe Bryant/35	15.00	40.00
TTKD Kevin Durant/35	10.00	25.00
TTKG Kevin Garnett/35	6.00	15.00
TTKI Kyrie Irving/35	8.00	20.00
TTKL Kevin Love/35	4.00	10.00
TTKM Karl Malone/25	5.00	12.00
TTLB Larry Bird/25	10.00	25.00
TTLJ LeBron James/35	15.00	40.00
TTMM Moses Malone/25	4.00	10.00
TTPE Patrick Ewing/35	5.00	12.00
TTRW Russell Westbrook/35	10.00	25.00
TTSO Shaquille O'Neal/25	8.00	20.00
TTSP Scottie Pippen/25	8.00	20.00
TTTD Tim Duncan/35	6.00	15.00
TTYM Yao Ming/25	5.00	12.00

2014-15 Panini Spectra Triple Double Threads

RANDOM INSERTS IN PACKS
STATED PRINT RUN B/WN 25-49 COPIES PER

Card	Low	High
TDAW Antoine Walker/49	5.00	12.00
TDCD Clyde Drexler/25	8.00	20.00
TDCM Chris Mullin/25	6.00	15.00
TDCW Chris Webber/35	10.00	25.00
TDDM Dikembe Mutombo/25	6.00	15.00
TDDR David Robinson/49	10.00	25.00
TDFL Fat Lever/25	5.00	12.00
TDGH Grant Hill/49	8.00	20.00
TDGP Gary Payton/25	6.00	15.00
TDHO Hakeem Olajuwon/25	8.00	20.00
TDJK Jason Kidd/25	6.00	15.00
TDJN Joakim Noah/25	5.00	12.00
TDLB Larry Bird/49	10.00	25.00
TDLBJ LeBron James/25	25.00	60.00
TDLJ Larry Johnson/25	8.00	20.00
TDMF Michael Finley/35	6.00	15.00
TDMJ1 Magic Johnson/25	15.00	40.00
TDMJ2 Mark Jackson/35	5.00	12.00
TDSC Stephen Curry/49	25.00	60.00
TDTD Tim Duncan/25	10.00	25.00

2015-16 Panini Spectra

1-100 PRINT RUN 215 SER.#'d SETS
JSY AU RC NOT SERIAL NUMBERED
EXCHANGE DEADLINE 12/15/2017

Card	Low	High
1 Russell Westbrook	4.00	10.00
2 Bradley Beal	1.50	4.00
3 Danilo Gallinari	1.25	3.00
4 Zach Randolph	1.25	3.00
5 Andre Drummond	1.50	4.00
6 John Stockton	2.50	6.00
7 DeAndre Jordan	1.50	4.00
8 Shawn Kemp	2.50	6.00
9 DeMar DeRozan	1.50	4.00
10 Paul Millsap	1.50	4.00
11 Serge Ibaka	1.25	3.00
12 Marcin Gortat	1.25	3.00
13 Kenneth Faried	1.25	3.00
14 Dwight Howard	1.25	3.00
15 Reggie Jackson	1.25	3.00
16 Karl Malone	2.00	5.00
17 Rajon Rondo	1.50	4.00
18 Gary Payton	1.50	4.00
19 Kyle Lowry	1.25	3.00
20 Jeff Teague	1.25	3.00
21 Kevin Durant	4.00	10.00
22 Tim Duncan	2.50	6.00
23 Kevin Love	1.50	4.00
24 James Harden	2.50	6.00
25 Giannis Antetokounmpo	3.00	8.00
26 Rudy Gay	1.50	4.00
27 Oscar Robertson	2.00	5.00
28 Steve Nash	1.50	4.00
29 Isaiah Thomas	1.50	4.00
30 Tobias Harris	1.25	3.00
31 Gordon Hayward	1.50	4.00
32 Tony Parker	1.50	4.00
33 LeBron James	10.00	25.00
34 Anthony Davis	3.00	8.00
35 Jabari Parker	2.00	5.00
36 Allen Iverson	2.00	5.00
37 DeMarcus Cousins	1.50	4.00
38 Yao Ming	2.00	5.00
39 Avery Bradley	1.25	3.00
40 Nikola Vucevic	1.25	3.00
41 Derrick Favors	1.25	3.00
42 Kawhi Leonard	2.50	6.00
43 Kyrie Irving	3.00	8.00
44 Tyreke Evans	1.00	2.50
45 Greg Monroe	1.25	3.00
46 Patrick Ewing	2.00	5.00
47 Eric Bledsoe	1.25	3.00
48 Dennis Rodman	3.00	8.00
49 Carmelo Anthony	2.00	5.00
50 Dwyane Wade	2.50	6.00
51 Damian Lillard	3.00	8.00
52 Dirk Nowitzki	2.00	5.00
53 Derrick Rose	2.00	5.00
54 Wilt Chamberlain	3.00	8.00
55 Stephen Curry	6.00	15.00
56 Jason Kidd	1.50	4.00
57 Brandon Knight	1.25	3.00
58 Alonzo Mourning	2.00	5.00
59 Arron Afflalo	1.00	2.50
60 Hassan Whiteside	1.25	3.00
61 C.J. McCollum	1.50	4.00
62 Deron Williams	1.25	3.00
63 Jimmy Butler	1.50	4.00
64 Pete Maravich	2.50	6.00
65 Klay Thompson	2.00	5.00
66 Scottie Pippen	3.00	8.00
67 Kobe Bryant	6.00	15.00
68 Brook Lopez	1.25	3.00
69 Elgin Baylor	1.50	4.00
70 Chris Bosh	1.50	4.00
71 Andrew Wiggins	2.50	6.00
72 Zaza Pachulia	1.00	2.50
73 Pau Gasol	1.50	4.00
74 Magic Johnson	4.00	10.00
75 Draymond Green	2.00	5.00
76 Kareem Abdul-Jabbar	2.50	6.00
77 Latrell Sprewell	1.25	3.00
78 Jordan Clarkson	1.50	4.00
79 Thaddeus Young	1.00	2.50
80 Kemba Walker	1.50	4.00
81 Ricky Rubio	1.50	4.00
82 Marc Gasol	1.50	4.00
83 Paul George	2.00	5.00
84 Larry Bird	4.00	10.00
85 Blake Griffin	1.50	4.00
86 Tracy McGrady	1.50	4.00
87 Julius Randle	1.50	4.00
88 Nerlens Noel	1.25	3.00
89 Shaquille O'Neal	3.00	8.00
90 Nicolas Batum	1.25	3.00
91 Kevin Garnett	2.50	6.00
92 Mike Conley	1.50	4.00
93 Monta Ellis	1.25	3.00
94 Julius Erving	2.50	6.00
95 Chris Paul	2.00	5.00
96 Al Horford	1.25	3.00
97 Bill Russell	2.50	6.00
98 Dominique Wilkins	2.00	5.00
99 Isaiah Canaan	1.25	3.00
100 John Wall	2.00	5.00
101 K.Towns JSY AU RC	75.00	150.00
102 D.Russell JSY AU RC	20.00	50.00
103 J.Okafor JSY AU RC	10.00	25.00
104 E.Mudiay JSY AU RC	5.00	12.00
105 K.Porzingis JSY AU RC	40.00	100.00
106 M.Hezonja JSY AU RC	4.00	10.00
107 J.Winslow JSY AU RC	6.00	15.00
108 Cauley-Stein JSY AU RC	8.00	20.00
109 Tyus Jones JSY AU RC	5.00	12.00
110 Stanley Johnson JSY AU RC	4.00	10.00
111 Frank Kaminsky JSY AU RC	5.00	12.00
112 Devin Booker JSY AU RC	50.00	80.00
113 Myles Turner JSY AU RC	8.00	20.00
114 Trey Lyles JSY AU RC	5.00	12.00
115 Jerian Grant JSY AU RC	3.00	8.00
116 Nemanja Bjelica JSY AU RC	4.00	10.00
117 Cameron Payne JSY AU RC	4.00	10.00
118 Kelly Oubre Jr. JSY AU RC	4.00	10.00
119 Terry Rozier JSY AU RC	4.00	10.00
120 Rondae Hollis-Jefferson JSY AU RC	4.00	10.00
121 Bobby Portis JSY AU RC	5.00	12.00
122 Nikola Jokic JSY AU RC	25.00	60.00
123 Justin Anderson JSY AU RC	4.00	10.00
124 R.J. Hunter JSY AU RC	3.00	8.00
125 Raul Neto JSY AU RC	3.00	8.00
126 Marcelo Huertas JSY AU RC	4.00	10.00
127 Salah Mejri JSY AU RC	3.00	8.00
128 Norman Powell JSY AU RC	4.00	10.00
129 Sasha Kaun JSY AU RC	3.00	8.00
130 Pat Connaughton JSY AU RC	3.00	8.00
131 Richaun Holmes JSY AU RC	4.00	10.00
132 J.Simmons JSY AU RC	15.00	40.00
133 Cristiano Felicio JSY AU RC	4.00	10.00

2015-16 Panini Spectra Prizms Red Die Cut

*RED DC: 2X TO 5X BASIC
RANDOM INSERTS IN PACKS
STATED PRINT RUN 25 SER.#'d SETS

2015-16 Panini Spectra City Limits

RANDOM INSERTS IN PACKS

Card	Low	High
1 Dwight Howard	4.00	10.00
2 Stephen Curry	30.00	80.00
3 Tim Duncan	8.00	20.00
4 Magic Johnson	12.00	30.00
5 Anthony Davis	10.00	25.00
6 Shaquille O'Neal	10.00	25.00
7 Patrick Ewing	12.00	30.00
8 Dwyane Wade	12.00	30.00
9 Russell Westbrook	12.00	30.00
10 Dirk Nowitzki	6.00	15.00
11 Karl Malone	6.00	15.00
12 Scottie Pippen	10.00	25.00
13 James Harden	8.00	20.00
14 Larry Bird	12.00	30.00
15 Allen Iverson	12.00	30.00
16 Chris Paul	6.00	15.00
17 Carmelo Anthony	6.00	15.00
18 Damian Lillard	10.00	25.00
19 John Stockton	8.00	20.00
20 Derrick Rose	6.00	15.00
21 Kevin Durant	12.00	30.00
22 Kobe Bryant	20.00	50.00
23 LeBron James	30.00	80.00
24 Blake Griffin	5.00	12.00
25 Kyrie Irving	15.00	40.00

2015-16 Panini Spectra Franchise Fabrics

RANDOM INSERTS IN PACKS
STATED PRINT RUN 49 SER,#'d SETS

Card	Low	High
1 Jimmy Butler	4.00	10.00
2 Monta Ellis	3.00	8.00
3 Al Horford	3.00	8.00
4 Arron Afflalo	2.50	6.00
5 Chris Paul	5.00	12.00
6 Dennis Rodman	8.00	20.00
7 John Wall	5.00	12.00
8 Omri Casspi	2.50	6.00
9 Rajon Rondo	4.00	10.00
10 Ricky Rubio	4.00	10.00
11 Chandler Parsons	3.00	8.00
12 Mike Conley	4.00	10.00
13 Marc Gasol	4.00	10.00
14 Tony Parker	4.00	10.00
15 Kobe Bryant	15.00	40.00
16 Grant Hill	5.00	12.00
17 Blake Griffin	4.00	10.00
18 Reggie Lewis	4.00	10.00
19 Tim Duncan	6.00	15.00
20 Dennis Schroder	3.00	8.00
21 Kenneth Faried	3.00	8.00
22 Zach Randolph	3.00	8.00
23 LeBron James	15.00	40.00
24 Kyle Lowry	3.00	8.00
25 Andrew Wiggins	6.00	15.00
26 Jalen Rose	4.00	10.00
27 Dwyane Wade	6.00	15.00
28 Scottie Pippen	6.00	15.00
29 Bradley Beal	4.00	10.00
30 Jared Sullinger	2.50	6.00
31 Andre Drummond	4.00	10.00
32 Elfrid Payton	3.00	8.00
33 Dirk Nowitzki	5.00	12.00
34 Rudy Gobert	4.00	10.00
35 Anthony Davis	6.00	15.00
36 John Stockton	6.00	15.00
37 Jabari Parker	5.00	12.00
38 Timofey Mozgov	2.50	6.00
39 Marcus Smart	3.00	8.00
40 Nikola Vucevic	3.00	8.00
41 Chris Bosh	4.00	10.00
42 Nerlens Noel	3.00	8.00
43 Stephen Curry	15.00	40.00
44 George Hill	3.00	8.00
45 Kevin Durant	6.00	15.00
46 Kevin Duckworth	2.50	6.00
47 Carmelo Anthony	5.00	12.00
48 Joakim Noah	3.00	8.00
49 Isaiah Thomas	4.00	10.00
50 Hassan Whiteside	3.00	8.00
51 Klay Thompson	5.00	12.00
52 Eric Bledsoe	3.00	8.00
53 James Harden	6.00	15.00
54 Charles Oakley	3.00	8.00
55 Russell Westbrook	10.00	25.00
56 Manu Ginobili	4.00	10.00
57 DeMarcus Cousins	4.00	10.00
58 Jusuf Nurkic	2.50	6.00
59 Kemba Walker	4.00	10.00
60 Donatas Motiejunas	2.50	6.00
61 Dwight Howard	3.00	8.00
62 Brandon Knight	3.00	8.00
63 Paul George	5.00	12.00
64 Danny Manning	3.00	8.00
65 Damian Lillard	6.00	15.00

2015-16 Panini Spectra Freshman Fabrics

RANDOM INSERTS IN PACKS
STATED PRINT RUN 35 SER,#'d SETS

Card	Low	High
1 Kelly Oubre Jr.	3.00	8.00
2 Karl-Anthony Towns	15.00	40.00
3 Nikola Jokic	5.00	12.00
4 Kristaps Porzingis	8.00	20.00
5 Richaun Holmes	3.00	8.00
6 Jarell Martin	3.00	8.00
7 Montrezl Harrell	3.00	8.00
8 Devin Booker	6.00	15.00
9 Josh Richardson	4.00	10.00
10 Jerian Grant	2.50	6.00
11 Terry Rozier	3.00	8.00
12 D'Angelo Russell	6.00	15.00
13 Salah Mejri	2.50	6.00
14 Mario Hezonja	3.00	8.00
15 Jonathon Simmons	4.00	10.00
16 Stanley Johnson	3.00	8.00
17 Pat Connaughton	2.50	6.00
18 Myles Turner	4.00	10.00
19 Justin Anderson	3.00	8.00
20 Nemanja Bjelica	3.00	8.00
21 Rondae Hollis-Jefferson	3.00	8.00
22 Jahlil Okafor	5.00	12.00
23 Jordan Mickey	2.50	6.00
24 Justise Winslow	4.00	10.00
25 R.J. Hunter	2.50	6.00
26 Frank Kaminsky	4.00	10.00
27 Anthony Brown	2.50	6.00
28 Trey Lyles	4.00	10.00
29 Tyus Jones	4.00	10.00
30 Cameron Payne	3.00	8.00
31 Bobby Portis	4.00	10.00
32 Emmanuel Mudiay	4.00	10.00
34 Willie Cauley-Stein	4.00	10.00
35 Marcelo Huertas	3.00	8.00

2015-16 Panini Spectra Game Time Materials

RANDOM INSERTS IN PACKS
STATED PRINT RUN 49 SER,#'d SETS

Card	Low	High
1 Anthony Davis	6.00	15.00
2 Scottie Pippen	6.00	15.00
3 Al Horford	3.00	8.00
4 Serge Ibaka	3.00	8.00
5 Julius Randle	4.00	10.00
6 Victor Oladipo	3.00	8.00
7 Zach Randolph	3.00	8.00
8 Brad Daugherty	3.00	8.00
9 James Harden	6.00	15.00
10 Isaiah Canaan	3.00	8.00
11 Kevin Durant	6.00	15.00
12 Terrence Ross	3.00	8.00
13 Bojan Bogdanovic	2.50	6.00
14 Andre Iguodala	3.00	8.00
15 Chris Bosh	4.00	10.00
16 LaMarcus Aldridge	4.00	10.00
17 Kyrie Irving	6.00	15.00
18 Clyde Drexler	5.00	12.00
19 Paul George	5.00	12.00
20 Kenny Smith	3.00	8.00
21 Russell Westbrook	10.00	25.00
22 Gary Harris	3.00	8.00
23 Nicolas Batum	3.00	8.00
24 Al Jefferson	3.00	8.00
25 Giannis Antetokounmpo	8.00	20.00
26 DeMarre Carroll	2.50	6.00
27 LeBron James	15.00	40.00
28 Dennis Rodman	8.00	20.00
29 Nerlens Noel	3.00	8.00
30 Larry Bird	10.00	25.00
31 Monta Ellis	3.00	8.00
32 Tobias Harris	3.00	8.00
33 Deron Williams	3.00	8.00
34 DeAndre Jordan	4.00	10.00
35 Tyreke Evans	2.50	6.00

36 Jonas Valanciunas 3.00 8.00
37 Dirk Nowitzki 5.00 12.00
38 Gary Payton 4.00 10.00
39 Kobe Bryant 15.00 40.00
40 Mike Bibby 3.00 8.00
41 John Wall 5.00 12.00
42 Rodney Hood 3.00 8.00
43 Draymond Green 8.00 20.00
44 Kyle Korver 3.00 8.00
45 Jrue Holiday 3.00 8.00
46 DeMarcus Cousins 4.00 10.00
47 Stephen Curry 15.00 40.00
48 Thaddeus Young 2.50 6.00
49 Arvydas Sabonis 3.00 8.00
50 Langston Galloway 2.50 6.00

2015-16 Panini Spectra Indelible Ink Materials

RANDOM INSERTS IN PACKS
PRINT RUNS B/WN 35-60 COPIES PER
EXCHANGE DEADLINE 12/15/2017
*ORANGE: .6X TO 1.5X BASIC
1 Nikola Mirotic/60 5.00 12.00
2 Elfrid Payton/60 5.00 12.00
3 Matthew Dellavedova/60 10.00 25.00
4 Blake Griffin/35 25.00 60.00
5 Donatas Motiejunas/60 4.00 10.00
6 Kyrie Irving/35 40.00 100.00
7 John Wall/35 20.00 50.00
8 Mo Williams/60 5.00 12.00
9 Jonas Valanciunas/60 5.00 12.00
10 Zach LaVine/60 15.00 40.00
11 T.J. Warren/60 5.00 12.00
12 Alec Burks/60 4.00 10.00
13 Gary Harris/60 5.00 12.00
14 Klay Thompson/35 40.00 100.00
15 Tim Hardaway Jr./60 4.00 10.00
16 Marcin Gortat/60 5.00 12.00
17 Thaddeus Young/60 4.00 10.00
18 Kobe Bryant/35 125.00 250.00
19 Kevin Durant/35 60.00 150.00
20 Mason Plumlee/60 5.00 12.00

2015-16 Panini Spectra Marks Memorabilia

RANDOM INSERTS IN PACKS
PRINT RUNS B/WN 35-65 COPIES PER
EXCHANGE DEADLINE 12/15/2017
1 Ray Allen/35 20.00 50.00
2 Jalen Rose/65 6.00 15.00
3 Robert Horry/65 5.00 12.00
4 Isiah Thomas/35 15.00 40.00
5 John Starks/65 5.00 12.00
6 Michael Finley/65 6.00 15.00
7 Gary Payton/35 10.00 25.00
8 Karl Malone/35 25.00 60.00
9 Dennis Rodman/35 25.00 60.00
10 Hakeem Olajuwon/65 15.00 40.00

2015-16 Panini Spectra Materials

RANDOM INSERTS IN PACKS
PRINT RUNS B/WN 28-49 COPIES PER
1 Jeff Teague/49 3.00 8.00
2 Harrison Barnes/49 3.00 8.00
3 Jordan Clarkson/49 4.00 10.00
4 Aaron Gordon/49 3.00 8.00
5 Derrick Rose/49 5.00 12.00
6 Alonzo Mourning/49 5.00 12.00
7 James Harden/49 6.00 15.00
8 Hakeem Olajuwon/49 5.00 12.00
9 Anthony Davis/49 6.00 15.00
10 Patrick Ewing/49 5.00 12.00
11 Marcin Gortat/49 3.00 8.00
12 Derrick Favors/49 3.00 8.00
13 Vince Carter/49 5.00 12.00
14 C.J. McCollum/49 4.00 10.00
15 Kyrie Irving/49 6.00 15.00
16 Bernard King/49 3.00 8.00
17 Paul George/49 5.00 12.00
18 Jeff Malone/28 2.50 6.00
19 Kevin Durant/49 6.00 15.00
20 Richard Hamilton/49 3.00 8.00
21 Joe Johnson/49 3.00 8.00
22 Danilo Gallinari/49 3.00 8.00
23 Goran Dragic/49 3.00 8.00
24 Kawhi Leonard/49 6.00 15.00
25 LeBron James/49 15.00 40.00
26 Christian Laettner/49 3.00 8.00
27 Chris Paul/49 5.00 12.00
28 Karl Malone/49 5.00 12.00
29 Russell Westbrook/49 10.00 25.00
30 Shaquille O'Neal/49 8.00 20.00
31 Kevin Love/49 4.00 10.00
32 Pau Gasol/49 4.00 10.00
33 Michael Carter-Williams/49 2.50 6.00
34 DeMar DeRozan/49 4.00 10.00
35 Dirk Nowitzki/49 5.00 12.00
36 Dante Exum/49 3.00 8.00
37 Kobe Bryant/49 15.00 40.00
38 Kevin Garnett/49 6.00 15.00
39 Damian Lillard/49 6.00 15.00
40 Trey Burke/49 2.50 6.00
41 Brandon Jennings/49 2.50 6.00
42 Rudy Gay/49 4.00 10.00
43 Eric Gordon/49 3.00 8.00
44 Alec Burks/49 2.50 6.00
45 Stephen Curry/49 15.00 40.00
46 Eddie Johnson/35 2.50 6.00
47 Andrew Wiggins/49 6.00 15.00
48 Mark Jackson/49 3.00 8.00
49 John Wall/49 5.00 12.00
50 Chris Andersen/49 3.00 8.00

2015-16 Panini Spectra Rookie Jersey Autographs Prizms Orange

*ORANGE: .6X TO 1.5X BASIC
RANDOM INSERTS IN PACKS
STATED PRINT RUN 25 SER.#'d SETS
EXCHANGE DEADLINE 12/15/2017
101 Karl-Anthony Towns 250.00 400.00
102 D'Angelo Russell 150.00 300.00
105 Kristaps Porzingis 150.00 300.00
108 Willie Cauley-Stein 12.00 30.00
110 Stanley Johnson 30.00 80.00
112 Devin Booker 200.00 400.00
113 Myles Turner 50.00 120.00
121 Bobby Portis 12.00 30.00
122 Nikola Jokic 100.00 200.00
132 Jonathon Simmons 20.00 50.00

2015-16 Panini Spectra Rookie Jumbo Jerseys

RANDOM INSERTS IN PACKS
STATED PRINT RUN 49 SER.#'d SETS
1 Frank Kaminsky 4.00 10.00
2 Jarell Martin 3.00 8.00
3 Jerian Grant 2.50 6.00
4 Terry Rozier 3.00 8.00
5 Karl-Anthony Towns 12.00 30.00
6 Justin Anderson 3.00 8.00
8 Norman Powell 3.00 8.00
9 Willie Cauley-Stein 4.00 10.00
10 Salah Mejri 2.50 6.00
11 Devin Booker 6.00 15.00
12 Sam Dekker 3.00 8.00
13 Nemanja Bjelica 3.00 8.00
14 Rondae Hollis-Jefferson 3.00 8.00
15 D'Angelo Russell 6.00 15.00
16 R.J. Hunter 2.50 6.00
17 Mario Hezonja 3.00 8.00
18 Joe Young 3.00 8.00
19 Tyus Jones 4.00 10.00
20 Luis Montero 2.50 6.00
21 Myles Turner 4.00 10.00
22 Jordan Mickey 2.50 6.00
23 Cameron Payne 3.00 8.00
24 Bobby Portis 4.00 10.00
25 Jahlil Okafor 5.00 12.00
26 Raul Neto 2.50 6.00
27 Justise Winslow 4.00 10.00
28 Pat Connaughton 2.50 6.00
29 Stanley Johnson 3.00 8.00
30 Delon Wright 3.00 8.00
31 Trey Lyles 4.00 10.00
32 Rakeem Christmas 2.50 6.00
33 Kelly Oubre Jr. 3.00 8.00
35 Emmanuel Mudiay 4.00 10.00

2015-16 Panini Spectra Spectacular Swatch Signatures

RANDOM INSERTS IN PACKS
PRINT RUNS B/WN 35-149 COPIES PER
EXCHANGE DEADLINE 12/15/2017
1 Kyrie Irving/35 40.00 100.00
2 Isaiah Thomas/149 25.00 60.00
3 John Wall/35 25.00 60.00
4 Andrew Wiggins/35 25.00 60.00
5 Eric Bledsoe/40 5.00 12.00
6 Gary Harris/149 5.00 12.00
7 Norris Cole/99 4.00 10.00
8 T.J. Warren/149 5.00 12.00
9 Jonas Valanciunas/149 5.00 12.00
10 Gordon Hayward/149 6.00 15.00
11 Festus Ezeli/149 4.00 10.00
12 Blake Griffin/35 20.00 50.00
13 Al Horford/40 6.00 15.00
14 Andrew Bogut/99 5.00 12.00
15 Doug McDermott/149 5.00 12.00
16 Elfrid Payton/99 5.00 12.00
17 Dwight Howard/35 12.00 30.00
18 Victor Oladipo/35 15.00 40.00
19 Tristan Thompson/99 5.00 12.00
20 Klay Thompson/35 30.00 80.00
21 Zach LaVine/149 12.00 30.00
22 Nene/149 5.00 12.00
23 Bojan Bogdanovic/149 4.00 10.00
24 Timofey Mozgov/149 4.00 10.00
25 Kobe Bryant/35 100.00 250.00
26 Alec Burks/99 4.00 10.00
27 Jae Crowder/149 5.00 12.00
28 Marcin Gortat/149 5.00 12.00
29 Dennis Schroder/149 5.00 12.00
30 Dante Exum/35 6.00 15.00
31 David Robinson/35 20.00 50.00
32 Jason Kidd/35 12.00 30.00
33 Dikembe Mutombo/149 10.00 25.00
34 Grant Hill/35 20.00 50.00
35 John Stockton/35 25.00 60.00
36 Karl Malone/35 20.00 50.00
37 Bill Laimbeer/149 5.00 12.00
38 Thaddeus Young/99 4.00 10.00
39 Magic Johnson/35 40.00 100.00
40 Michael Carter-Williams/40 8.00 20.00
42 Jahlil Okafor/35 20.00 50.00
43 Mario Hezonja/99 5.00 12.00
44 Jerian Grant/149 4.00 10.00
45 Nemanja Bjelica/149 5.00 12.00
46 Emmanuel Mudiay/35 12.00 30.00
47 D'Angelo Russell/35 40.00 100.00
48 Karl-Anthony Towns/35 150.00 300.00
49 Willie Cauley-Stein/149 12.00 30.00
50 Myles Turner/149 12.00 30.00

2015-16 Panini Spectra Spectacular Swatch Signatures Prizms Light Blue

*LT.BLUE: .5X TO 1.2X BASIC
RANDOM INSERTS IN PACKS
STATED PRINT RUN 49 SER.#'d SETS
EXCHANGE DEADLINE 12/15/2017
41 Kristaps Porzingis 100.00 200.00

2015-16 Panini Spectra Spectacular Swatch Signatures Prizms Orange

*ORANGE: .6X TO 1.5X BASIC
RANDOM INSERTS IN PACKS
STATED PRINT RUN 25 SER.#'d SETS
EXCHANGE DEADLINE 12/15/2017
41 Kristaps Porzingis 150.00 300.00

2015-16 Panini Spectra Superstar Material Autographs

RANDOM INSERTS IN PACKS
STATED PRINT RUN 30 SER.#'d SETS
EXCHANGE DEADLINE 12/15/2017
1 Kobe Bryant 125.00 250.00
2 Kevin Durant 60.00 150.00
3 Kyrie Irving 40.00 100.00
4 Blake Griffin 30.00 80.00
5 Anthony Davis 50.00 120.00
6 John Wall 30.00 80.00
7 Dwight Howard 12.00 30.00
8 Andrew Wiggins 30.00 80.00
9 Klay Thompson 40.00 100.00
10 Andre Drummond 10.00 25.00
11 Kristaps Porzingis 60.00 150.00
12 Karl-Anthony Towns 150.00 300.00
13 D'Angelo Russell 40.00 100.00
14 Jahlil Okafor 15.00 40.00
15 Emmanuel Mudiay
16 John Stockton 20.00 50.00
17 Karl Malone 20.00 50.00
18 Hakeem Olajuwon 15.00 40.00
19 Magic Johnson 40.00 100.00
20 David Robinson 20.00 50.00

2015-16 Panini Spectra Swatches

RANDOM INSERTS IN PACKS
STATED PRINT RUN 49 SER.#'d SETS
1 Paul George 5.00 12.00
2 Bill Walton 4.00 10.00
3 Damian Lillard 6.00 15.00
4 Kevin McHale 4.00 10.00
5 Rajon Rondo 4.00 10.00
6 Brook Lopez 3.00 8.00
7 Chandler Parsons 3.00 8.00
8 Monta Ellis 3.00 8.00
9 Derrick Rose 5.00 12.00
10 Brandon Knight 3.00 8.00
11 Chris Paul 5.00 12.00
12 Clyde Drexler 5.00 12.00
13 John Wall 5.00 12.00
14 Michael Redd 3.00 8.00
15 Tim Duncan 6.00 15.00
16 O.J. Mayo 2.50 6.00
17 Kenneth Faried 3.00 8.00
18 Marc Gasol 4.00 10.00
19 Kyrie Irving 8.00 20.00
20 T.J. Warren 3.00 8.00
21 Kobe Bryant 15.00 40.00
22 David Robinson 6.00 15.00
23 Blake Griffin 4.00 10.00
24 Rafer Alston 2.50 6.00
25 Bradley Beal 4.00 10.00
26 Ben McLemore 2.50 6.00
27 Andre Drummond 4.00 10.00
28 Zach Randolph 3.00 8.00
29 LeBron James 15.00 40.00
30 Tony Parker 4.00 10.00
31 Andrew Wiggins 6.00 15.00
32 Elton Brand 4.00 10.00
33 Dwyane Wade 6.00 15.00
34 Rory Sparrow 2.50 6.00
35 Marcus Smart 3.00 8.00
36 George Hill 3.00 8.00
37 Reggie Jackson 3.00 8.00
38 Elfrid Payton 3.00 8.00
39 Dirk Nowitzki 5.00 12.00
40 Kyle Lowry 3.00 8.00
41 Anthony Davis 6.00 15.00
42 Herb Williams 2.50 6.00
43 Jabari Parker 5.00 12.00
44 Shaquille O'Neal 8.00 20.00
45 Isaiah Thomas 4.00 10.00
46 Paul Millsap 4.00 10.00
47 Klay Thompson 5.00 12.00
48 Nerlens Noel 3.00 8.00
49 Stephen Curry 15.00 40.00
50 Rudy Gobert 4.00 10.00
51 Kevin Durant 6.00 15.00
52 Joe Smith 3.00 8.00
53 Carmelo Anthony 5.00 12.00
54 Vlade Divac 4.00 10.00
55 Kemba Walker 4.00 10.00
56 Nikola Mirotic 3.00 8.00
57 Dwight Howard 3.00 8.00
58 Eric Bledsoe 3.00 8.00
59 James Harden 6.00 15.00
60 Alvan Adams 2.50 6.00
61 Russell Westbrook 10.00 25.00
62 Keith Van Horn 3.00 8.00
63 DeMarcus Cousins 4.00 10.00
64 Zach LaVine 4.00 10.00
65 Jimmy Butler 4.00 10.00

2016-17 Panini Spectra

JSY AU RC RANDOMLY INSERTED
JSY AU RC PRINT RUN 300 SER.#'d SETS
EXCHANGE DEADLINE 12/28/2018
1 Kevin Durant 3.00 8.00
2 Blake Griffin 1.25 3.00
3 Mike Conley 1.00 2.50
4 Paul George 1.50 4.00
5 Jordan Clarkson 1.00 2.50
6 Giannis Antetokounmpo 2.50 6.00
7 Jae Crowder 1.00 2.50
8 Anthony Davis 2.50 6.00
9 Carmelo Anthony 1.50 4.00
10 Deron Williams 1.00 2.50
11 Russell Westbrook 3.00 8.00
12 Dwight Howard 1.00 2.50
13 Jrue Holiday 1.00 2.50
14 Ersan Ilyasova .75 2.00
15 Kemba Walker 1.25 3.00
16 DeMarcus Cousins 1.25 3.00
17 Patrick Beverley .75 2.00
18 Aaron Gordon 1.00 2.50
19 Lou Williams 1.00 2.50
20 Randy Foye .75 2.00
21 Damian Lillard 2.50 6.00
22 Jared Sullinger .75 2.00
23 Kawhi Leonard 2.00 5.00
24 Thaddeus Young .75 2.00
25 Gordon Hayward 1.25 3.00
26 Nikola Mirotic 1.00 2.50
27 Maurice Harkless .75 2.00
28 Kenneth Faried 1.00 2.50
29 Greg Monroe 1.00 2.50
30 Stephen Curry 5.00 12.00
31 Devin Booker 2.00 5.00
32 Dennis Schroder 1.00 2.50
33 Rudy Gobert 1.25 3.00
34 Julius Randle 1.25 3.00
35 Jeremy Lin 1.25 3.00
36 Andrew Wiggins 2.00 5.00
37 Reggie Jackson 1.00 2.50
38 Elfrid Payton 1.00 2.50
39 Chandler Parsons 1.00 2.50
40 Roy Hibbert 1.00 2.50
41 Tony Parker 1.25 3.00
42 Justise Winslow 1.00 2.50
43 Kevin Love 1.25 3.00
44 Kyle Lowry 1.00 2.50
45 Eric Gordon 1.00 2.50
46 Ty Lawson .75 2.00
47 Chris Paul 1.50 4.00
48 Paul Millsap 1.25 3.00
49 Victor Oladipo 1.00 2.50
50 Derrick Rose 1.50 4.00
51 Nikola Jokic 1.25 3.00
52 Pau Gasol 1.25 3.00
53 Isaiah Thomas 1.25 3.00
54 Enes Kanter .75 2.00
55 Jabari Parker 1.50 4.00
56 Justin Anderson 1.00 2.50
57 Serge Ibaka 1.00 2.50
58 Draymond Green 1.50 4.00
59 Jahlil Okafor 1.00 2.50
60 Ben Simmons RC 50.00 120.00
61 D'Angelo Russell 1.50 4.00
62 Hassan Whiteside 1.00 2.50
63 Michael Kidd-Gilchrist 1.00 2.50
64 Terrence Jones 1.00 2.50
65 Marc Gasol 1.25 3.00
66 Tobias Harris 1.00 2.50
67 Zach LaVine 1.25 3.00
68 Khris Middleton 1.00 2.50
69 Marcus Smart 1.00 2.50
70 Joel Embiid 2.00 5.00
71 Ryan Anderson 1.00 2.50
72 Rudy Gay 1.25 3.00
73 Kyrie Irving 2.50 6.00
74 J.J. Redick 1.25 3.00
75 Brandon Knight 1.00 2.50
76 Klay Thompson 1.50 4.00
77 C.J. McCollum 1.00 2.50
78 Andrew Bogut 1.00 2.50
79 Myles Turner 1.00 2.50
80 George Hill 1.00 2.50
81 Kentavious Caldwell-Pope 1.00 2.50
82 DeMar DeRozan 1.25 3.00
83 Zach Randolph 1.00 2.50
84 Dwyane Wade 2.00 5.00
85 LaMarcus Aldridge 1.25 3.00
86 Emmanuel Mudiay 1.00 2.50
87 Jeff Teague 1.00 2.50
88 Karl-Anthony Towns 3.00 8.00
89 LeBron James 5.00 12.00
90 Tyson Chandler 1.00 2.50
91 Dirk Nowitzki 1.50 4.00
92 Kristaps Porzingis 2.50 6.00
93 DeAndre Jordan 1.25 3.00
94 Frank Kaminsky 1.00 2.50
95 Ricky Rubio 1.25 3.00
96 James Harden 2.00 5.00
97 Goran Dragic 1.00 2.50
98 Avery Bradley 1.00 2.50
99 Andre Drummond 1.25 3.00
100 Jimmy Butler 1.25 3.00
102 D.Saric JSY AU RC EXCH 12.00 30.00
103 P. McCaw JSY AU RC 15.00 40.00
104 Denzel Valentine JSY AU RC 6.00 15.00
105 Thon Maker JSY AU RC 25.00 60.00
106 Dragan Bender JSY AU RC EXCH 10.00 25.00
107 Isaiah Whitehead JSY AU RC 4.00 10.00
108 A.J. Hammons JSY AU RC
109 J.Brown JSY AU RC EXCH 20.00 50.00
110 Caris LeVert JSY AU RC 5.00 12.00
111 M.Brogdon JSY AU RC 15.00 40.00
112 DeAndre' Bembry JSY AU RC 4.00 10.00
113 Skal Labissiere JSY AU RC EXCH 6.00 15.00
114 Deyonta Davis JSY AU RC 4.00 10.00
115 T.Luwawu-Cabarrot JSY AU RC
116 Georges Niang JSY AU RC 4.00 10.00
117 Ivica Zubac JSY AU RC 8.00 20.00
118 B.Ingram JSY AU RC 40.00 100.00
119 Juan Hernangomez JSY AU RC 5.00 12.00
120 Cheick Diallo JSY AU RC 4.00 10.00
121 Malik Beasley JSY AU RC 4.00 10.00
123 Stephen Zimmerman JSY AU RC 4.00 10.00
124 Diamond Stone JSY AU RC 4.00 10.00
125 Tyler Ulis JSY AU RC 10.00 25.00
126 Georgios Papagiannis JSY AU RC 4.00 10.00
127 Jakob Poeltl JSY AU RC 5.00 12.00
128 Brice Johnson JSY AU RC EXCH 4.00 10.00
129 Kay Felder JSY AU RC 4.00 10.00
130 Chinanu Onuaku JSY AU RC 4.00 10.00
132 Demetrius Jackson JSY AU RC 4.00 10.00
133 Taurean Prince JSY AU RC 8.00 20.00
134 Domantas Sabonis JSY AU RC 6.00 15.00
135 Wade Baldwin IV JSY AU RC 4.00 10.00
136 Henry Ellenson JSY AU RC 5.00 12.00
137 J.Murray JSY AU RC EXCH 15.00 40.00
138 Buddy Hield JSY AU RC 15.00 40.00
139 Kris Dunn JSY AU RC 12.00 30.00
140 Damian Jones JSY AU RC 4.00 10.00
141 Pascal Siakam JSY AU RC 4.00 10.00
142 Tomas Satoransky JSY AU RC 4.00 10.00
143 Mindaugas Kuzminskas JSY AU RC 5.00 12.00
144 Ron Baker JSY AU RC 8.00 20.00

2016-17 Panini Spectra Neon Blue

*NEON BLUE 1-100: .75X TO 2X BASIC
*NEON BLUE 101-141: .6X TO 1.5X BASIC
RANDOM INSERTS IN PACKS
1-100 PRINT RUN 60 SER.#'d SETS
101-141 PRINT RUN 99 SER.#'d SETS
EXCHANGE DEADLINE 12/28/2018
1 Kevin Durant 10.00 25.00
60 Ben Simmons 125.00 300.00

2016-17 Panini Spectra Neon Green

*NEON GREEN 1-100: 2X TO 5X BASIC
*NEON GREEN 101-141: .75X TO 2X BASIC
RANDOM INSERTS IN PACKS
STATED PRINT RUN 25 SER.#'d SETS
EXCHANGE DEADLINE 12/28/2018
1 Kevin Durant 30.00 80.00
23 Kawhi Leonard 30.00 80.00
30 Stephen Curry 30.00 80.00
60 Ben Simmons 500.00 1000.00
73 Kyrie Irving 20.00 50.00
89 LeBron James 60.00 150.00

2016-17 Panini Spectra Pink

*PINK 1-100: .75X TO 2X BASIC
*PINK 101-141: .75X TO 2X BASIC
RANDOM INSERTS IN PACKS
PRINT RUNS B/WN 45-49 COPIES PER
EXCHANGE DEADLINE 12/28/2018
1 Kevin Durant 12.00 30.00
60 Ben Simmons 150.00 400.00

2016-17 Panini Spectra Catalysts Materials

RANDOM INSERTS IN PACKS
STATED PRINT RUN 149 SER.#'d SETS
1 Dennis Schroder 2.50 6.00
2 Marcus Smart 2.50 6.00
3 Isaiah Thomas 3.00 8.00
4 Kemba Walker 3.00 8.00
5 Michael Kidd-Gilchrist 2.50 6.00
7 Jimmy Butler 3.00 8.00
8 Kyrie Irving 6.00 15.00
9 Deron Williams 2.50 6.00
10 Harrison Barnes 2.50 6.00
11 Kentavious Caldwell-Pope 2.50 6.00
12 Stephen Curry 12.00 30.00
14 James Harden 4.00 10.00
15 Jeff Teague 2.50 6.00
16 Monta Ellis 2.50 6.00
17 Jamal Crawford 3.00 8.00
18 Chris Paul 4.00 10.00
19 D'Angelo Russell 4.00 10.00
20 Jordan Clarkson 2.50 6.00
21 Mike Conley 2.50 6.00
22 Goran Dragic 2.50 6.00
24 Ricky Rubio 3.00 8.00
26 Derrick Rose 4.00 10.00
29 Eric Bledsoe 2.50 6.00
30 Damian Lillard 4.00 10.00
31 C.J. McCollum 2.50 6.00
32 Darren Collison 2.50 6.00
33 Rudy Gay 3.00 8.00
34 Tony Parker 3.00 8.00
35 Kyle Lowry 2.50 6.00
36 DeMar DeRozan 3.00 8.00
39 John Wall 4.00 10.00
40 Bradley Beal 3.00 8.00

2016-17 Panini Spectra Catalysts Materials Neon Blue

*NEON BLUE: .5X TO 1.2X BASIC
RANDOM INSERTS IN PACKS
PRINT RUNS B/WN 72-99 COPIES PER
13 Patrick Beverley/99 2.50 6.00
37 Alec Burks/99 2.50 6.00

2016-17 Panini Spectra Catalysts Materials Neon Green

*NEON GREEN: 1X TO 2.5X BASIC
RANDOM INSERTS IN PACKS
PRINT RUNS B/WN 11-25 COPIES PER
NO PRICING ON QTY 17 OR LESS
6 Rajon Rondo/25 8.00 20.00
12 Stephen Curry/25 60.00 150.00
25 Tyreke Evans/25 5.00 12.00
27 Victor Oladipo/25 6.00 15.00
28 Elfrid Payton/25 6.00 15.00
37 Alec Burks/25 5.00 12.00

2016-17 Panini Spectra Catalysts Materials Pink

*PINK: .6X TO 1.5X BASIC
RANDOM INSERTS IN PACKS
STATED PRINT RUN 49 SER.#'d SETS
6 Rajon Rondo 5.00 12.00
13 Patrick Beverley 3.00 8.00
23 Matthew Dellavedova 4.00 10.00
25 Tyreke Evans 3.00 8.00
27 Victor Oladipo 4.00 10.00
28 Elfrid Payton 4.00 10.00
37 Alec Burks 3.00 8.00
38 George Hill 4.00 10.00

2016-17 Panini Spectra Global Icons Memorabilia Autographs

RANDOM INSERTS IN PACKS
STATED PRINT RUN 199 SER.#'d SETS
EXCHANGE DEADLINE 12/28/2018
2 Jakob Poeltl 4.00 10.00
7 J.J. Barea 20.00 50.00
8 Thon Maker 12.00 30.00
15 Jonas Valanciunas 4.00 10.00

2016-17 Panini Spectra Global Icons Memorabilia Autographs Neon Blue

*NEON BLUE: .5X TO 1.2X BASIC
RANDOM INSERTS IN PACKS
STATED PRINT RUN 99 SER.#'d SETS
EXCHANGE DEADLINE 12/28/2018
1 Karl-Anthony Towns 50.00 120.00
3 Buddy Hield 12.00 30.00
4 Joel Embiid 30.00 80.00
6 Kristaps Porzingis 20.00 50.00
10 Jamal Murray 20.00 50.00
11 Dragan Bender 6.00 15.00
12 Zaza Pachulia 6.00 15.00
13 Luol Deng 8.00 20.00
14 Danilo Gallinari 5.00 12.00

2016-17 Panini Spectra Global Icons Memorabilia Autographs Neon Green

*NEON GREEN: .75X TO 2X BASIC
RANDOM INSERTS IN PACKS
STATED PRINT RUN 25 SER.#'d SETS
EXCHANGE DEADLINE 12/28/2018
4 Joel Embiid 40.00 100.00

2016-17 Panini Spectra In the Zone Memorabilia Autographs

RANDOM INSERTS IN PACKS
STATED PRINT RUN 149 SER.#'d SETS
EXCHANGE DEADLINE 12/28/2018
4 Dahntay Jones 3.00 8.00
5 Walter Berry 3.00 8.00
6 Brent Barry 3.00 8.00
7 Shane Battier 4.00 10.00
8 Walter Davis 3.00 8.00
12 Denzel Valentine 5.00 12.00
13 Chinanu Onuaku
14 Diamond Stone 3.00 8.00
15 Juan Hernangomez 4.00 10.00
16 Deyonta Davis 3.00 8.00
17 Tobias Harris 4.00 10.00
18 Demetrius Jackson 3.00 8.00
19 Cheick Diallo 3.00 8.00
20 Damian Jones 3.00 8.00
21 Georgios Papagiannis 3.00 8.00
23 Ivica Zubac 8.00 20.00
26 Nemanja Bjelica 4.00 10.00
27 Josh Richardson 3.00 8.00
34 Justin Anderson 4.00 10.00

2016-17 Panini Spectra In the Zone Memorabilia Autographs Neon Blue

*NEON BLUE: .5X TO 1.2X BASIC
RANDOM INSERTS IN PACKS
STATED PRINT RUN 99 SER.#'d SETS
EXCHANGE DEADLINE 12/28/2018
1 Kobe Bryant 100.00 200.00
3 Magic Johnson 30.00 80.00
10 Grant Hill 15.00 40.00
11 Avery Bradley 5.00 12.00
24 Cody Zeller 4.00 10.00
25 C.J. McCollum 8.00 20.00
28 Brandon Knight 5.00 12.00
29 Victor Oladipo 5.00 12.00
31 Marcin Gortat 6.00 15.00
32 Devin Harris 4.00 10.00
33 Andre Drummond 6.00 15.00
35 LaMarcus Aldridge 10.00 25.00

2016-17 Panini Spectra In the Zone Memorabilia Autographs Neon Green

*NEON GREEN: .75X TO 2X BASIC
RANDOM INSERTS IN PACKS
STATED PRINT RUN 25 SER.#'d SETS
EXCHANGE DEADLINE 12/28/2018
11 Avery Bradley 6.00 15.00
24 Cody Zeller 5.00 12.00
25 C.J. McCollum 10.00 25.00
28 Brandon Knight 6.00 15.00
29 Victor Oladipo 6.00 15.00
31 Marcin Gortat 8.00 20.00
32 Devin Harris 5.00 12.00
33 Andre Drummond 8.00 20.00
35 LaMarcus Aldridge 12.00 30.00

2016-17 Panini Spectra Locked In Memorabilia Autographs

RANDOM INSERTS IN PACKS
STATED PRINT RUN 199 SER.#'d SETS
EXCHANGE DEADLINE 12/28/2018
4 Tyler Johnson 5.00 12.00
5 Malcolm Brogdon 10.00 25.00
10 Kay Felder 3.00 8.00
11 Demetrius Jackson 3.00 8.00
21 Michael Kidd-Gilchrist 4.00 10.00
24 Skal Labissiere 8.00 20.00
26 Ron Baker 10.00 25.00
32 Sean Kilpatrick 3.00 8.00
35 Juan Hernangomez 4.00 10.00
37 Thaddeus Young 3.00 8.00
40 Cheick Diallo 3.00 8.00
41 Henry Ellenson 4.00 10.00
44 Norman Powell 3.00 8.00
45 Pascal Siakam 3.00 8.00
46 Tony Allen 3.00 8.00
48 Bojan Bogdanovic 3.00 8.00
52 Steven Adams 4.00 10.00
57 Mason Plumlee 4.00 10.00
58 Allen Crabbe 3.00 8.00

2016-17 Panini Spectra Locked In Memorabilia Autographs Neon Blue

*NEON BLUE: .5X TO 1.2X BASIC
RANDOM INSERTS IN PACKS
STATED PRINT RUN 99 SER.#'d SETS
EXCHANGE DEADLINE 12/28/2018
1 C.J. McCollum 8.00 20.00
3 Kobe Bryant 100.00 200.00
6 Denzel Valentine 6.00 15.00
7 Dwyane Wade 20.00 50.00
8 Kyrie Irving 30.00 80.00
9 Kevin Love 10.00 25.00
13 Blake Griffin 10.00 25.00
14 Diamond Stone 4.00 10.00
16 Marc Gasol 10.00 25.00
17 Jrue Holiday 5.00 12.00
19 Goran Dragic 5.00 12.00
20 Justise Winslow 5.00 12.00
22 George Hill 5.00 12.00
25 Kristaps Porzingis 20.00 50.00
27 Carmelo Anthony 12.00 30.00
28 Julius Randle 6.00 15.00
29 Tristan Thompson 5.00 12.00
31 Jeremy Lin 25.00 60.00
33 Danilo Gallinari 5.00 12.00
34 Jamal Murray 20.00 50.00
36 Jordan Clarkson 5.00 12.00
39 Buddy Hield 12.00 30.00
42 Andre Drummond 6.00 15.00
43 DeMar DeRozan 12.00 30.00
47 Eric Gordon 5.00 12.00
49 Devin Booker 25.00 60.00
50 Eric Bledsoe 6.00 15.00
51 Dragan Bender 6.00 15.00
54 Stephen Curry 125.00 300.00
55 Elfrid Payton 5.00 12.00
59 Klay Thompson 20.00 50.00
60 John Wall 12.00 30.00

2016-17 Panini Spectra Locked In Memorabilia Autographs Neon Green

*NEON GREEN: .75X TO 2X BASIC
RANDOM INSERTS IN PACKS
STATED PRINT RUN 25 SER.#'d SETS
EXCHANGE DEADLINE 12/28/2018
6 Denzel Valentine 8.00 20.00
14 Diamond Stone 5.00 12.00
23 Malachi Richardson 10.00 25.00
27 Carmelo Anthony 15.00 40.00
29 Tristan Thompson 6.00 15.00
36 Jordan Clarkson 6.00 15.00
55 Elfrid Payton 6.00 15.00

2016-17 Panini Spectra Next Era Materials

RANDOM INSERTS IN PACKS
STATED PRINT RUN 149 SER.#'d SETS
1 Brandon Ingram 6.00 15.00
2 Jaylen Brown 4.00 10.00
3 Dragan Bender 2.50 6.00
4 Jamal Murray 4.00 10.00
5 Marquese Chriss 4.00 10.00
6 Jakob Poeltl 2.50 6.00
7 Thon Maker 6.00 15.00
8 Georgios Papagiannis 2.00 5.00
9 Denzel Valentine 2.50 6.00
10 Juan Hernangomez 2.50 6.00
11 Wade Baldwin IV 2.00 5.00
12 Henry Ellenson 2.50 6.00
13 Malik Beasley 2.00 5.00
14 Caris LeVert 2.50 6.00
15 Malachi Richardson 2.50 6.00
17 Brice Johnson 2.00 5.00
18 Pascal Siakam 2.00 5.00
19 Skal Labissiere 3.00 8.00
20 Dejounte Murray 6.00 15.00
21 Damian Jones 2.00 5.00
22 Deyonta Davis 2.00 5.00
23 Ivica Zubac 3.00 8.00
24 Cheick Diallo 2.00 5.00
25 Tyler Ulis 4.00 10.00
26 Malcolm Brogdon 4.00 10.00
27 Chinanu Onuaku 2.00 5.00
28 Patrick McCaw 4.00 10.00
29 Kay Felder 2.00 5.00
30 Andrew Wiggins 5.00 12.00
32 Jabari Parker 4.00 10.00
33 Jahlil Okafor 2.50 6.00
34 Kristaps Porzingis 4.00 10.00
35 D'Angelo Russell 4.00 10.00
36 Myles Turner 2.50 6.00
37 Emmanuel Mudiay 2.50 6.00
39 Devin Booker 5.00 12.00

2016-17 Panini Spectra Next Era Materials Neon Blue

*NEON BLUE: .5X TO 1.2X BASIC
RANDOM INSERTS IN PACKS
STATED PRINT RUN 99 SER.#'d SETS
31 Karl-Anthony Towns 8.00 20.00

2016-17 Panini Spectra Next Era Materials Neon Green

*NEON GREEN: 1X TO 2.5X BASIC
RANDOM INSERTS IN PACKS
STATED PRINT RUN 25 SER.#'d SETS
16 Timothe Luwawu-Cabarrot 10.00 25.00

2016-17 Panini Spectra Next Era Materials Pink

*PINK: .6X TO 1.5X BASIC
RANDOM INSERTS IN PACKS
STATED PRINT RUN 49 SER.#'d SETS
31 Karl-Anthony Towns 10.00 25.00
40 Norman Powell 3.00 8.00

2016-17 Panini Spectra Rising Stars Memorabilia Autographs

RANDOM INSERTS IN PACKS
STATED PRINT RUN 199 SER.#'d SETS
*NEON GREEN/25: .75X TO 2X BASIC
1 Brandon Ingram 40.00 100.00
2 Buddy Hield 12.00 30.00
3 Kris Dunn 8.00 20.00
4 Jaylen Brown 20.00 50.00
5 Malcolm Brogdon 10.00 25.00
6 Tyler Ulis 10.00 25.00
7 Patrick McCaw 10.00 25.00
9 Kay Felder 2.50 6.00
10 Marquese Chriss 8.00 20.00
11 Thon Maker 12.00 30.00
13 Joel Embiid 25.00 60.00
14 Jabari Parker 12.00 30.00
15 Julius Randle 8.00 20.00
17 Kristaps Porzingis 20.00 50.00
18 Devin Booker 30.00 80.00
19 Myles Turner 6.00 15.00
20 Denzel Valentine 6.00 15.00
21 Pascal Siakam 2.50 6.00
22 Zach LaVine 8.00 20.00
24 Malachi Richardson 3.00 8.00
25 Wade Baldwin IV 2.50 6.00

2016-17 Panini Spectra Rising Stars Memorabilia Autographs Neon Blue

*NEON BLUE: .5X TO 1.2X BASIC
RANDOM INSERTS IN PACKS
STATED PRINT RUN 99 SER.#'d SETS
EXCHANGE DEADLINE 12/28/2018
16 Karl-Anthony Towns 50.00 120.00
23 Dario Saric 15.00 40.00

2016-17 Panini Spectra Rising Stars Memorabilia Autographs Neon Green

*NEON GREEN: .75X TO 2X BASIC
RANDOM INSERTS IN PACKS
STATED PRINT RUN 25 SER.#'d SETS
EXCHANGE DEADLINE 12/28/2018
10 Marquese Chriss 25.00 60.00

2016-17 Panini Spectra Spectacular Swatch Autographs

RANDOM INSERTS IN PACKS
STATED PRINT RUN 25-149 SER.#'d SETS
EXCHANGE DEADLINE 12/28/2018
*BLUE/75-99: .5X TO 1.2X p/r 149
*BLUE/75-99: .4X TO 1X p/r 49-99
*PINK/49: .5X TO 1.2X p/r 149
*PINK/49: .4X TO 1X p/r 49-99
*GREEN/25: .6X TO 1.5X p/r 149
*GREEN/25: .5X TO 1.2X p/r 49-99
1 Larry Bird/25 50.00 120.00
2 Denzel Valentine/149 5.00 12.00
3 David Robinson/49 15.00 40.00
4 Junior Bridgeman/149 3.00 8.00
5 Anfernee Hardaway/49 25.00 60.00
6 Damian Jones/149 5.00 12.00
7 Dragan Bender/99 6.00 15.00
9 Kobe Bryant/25 100.00 250.00
12 Tim Hardaway/149 5.00 12.00
13 Ricky Rubio/49 6.00 15.00
14 Kevin Durant/25
15 Jaylen Brown/49 EXCH 50.00 120.00
16 DeAndre' Bembry/149 3.00 8.00
17 C.J. McCollum/99 8.00 20.00
18 Robert Parish/99 6.00 15.00
19 Allen Iverson/25 75.00 200.00
20 Thon Maker/149 15.00 40.00
21 Yao Ming/49 60.00 150.00
22 Taurean Prince/149 5.00 12.00
23 Jimmy Butler/49 20.00 50.00
24 Caris LeVert/149 5.00 12.00
27 Kenny Smith/99 5.00 12.00
29 Carmelo Anthony/25 20.00 50.00
30 Zaza Pachulia/149 5.00 12.00
31 Pau Gasol/49 10.00 25.00
32 Skal Labissiere/149 EXCH 8.00 20.00
33 Marc Gasol/49
34 Demetrius Jackson/149 3.00 8.00
35 Buddy Hield/99 12.00 30.00
36 Brice Johnson/149 EXCH 8.00 20.00
37 Jamal Murray/99 20.00 50.00
39 Karl Malone/25
40 Al-Farouq Aminu/149 4.00 10.00
41 Karl-Anthony Towns/49 75.00 200.00
42 Dennis Scott/149 3.00 8.00
43 Brandon Ingram/49 50.00 120.00
44 Wade Baldwin IV/149 3.00 8.00
45 Kris Dunn/99 12.00 30.00
46 Dan Issel/49
47 Nikola Mirotic/99
48 Jakob Poeltl/149 4.00 10.00
49 Magic Johnson/25 40.00 100.00
50 Cedric Maxwell/149 3.00 8.00
51 Andrew Wiggins/49 20.00 50.00
52 Mark Price/149 5.00 12.00
53 Tony Parker/49
54 Henry Ellenson/149 10.00 25.00
55 Zach Randolph/99 6.00 15.00
56 Diamond Stone/149 3.00 8.00

2016-17 Panini Spectra Spectacular Swatches

RANDOM INSERTS IN PACKS
PRINT RUNS B/WN 134-149 COPIES PER
3 Isaiah Thomas/134 3.00 8.00
8 Kemba Walker/149 3.00 8.00
10 Dwyane Wade/149 4.00 10.00
13 Dirk Nowitzki/149 4.00 10.00
14 Deron Williams/149 2.50 6.00
19 Draymond Green/149 4.00 10.00
20 Stephen Curry/149 15.00 40.00
21 Eric Gordon/149 2.50 6.00
22 James Harden/149 5.00 12.00
23 Paul George/149 4.00 10.00
25 Blake Griffin/149 3.00 8.00
29 Mike Conley/149 2.50 6.00
30 Marc Gasol/149 3.00 8.00
31 Hassan Whiteside/149 2.50 6.00
32 Goran Dragic/149 2.50 6.00
33 Giannis Antetokounmpo/149 6.00 15.00
34 Jabari Parker/149 4.00 10.00
35 Andrew Wiggins/149 5.00 12.00
39 Brandon Jennings/149 2.00 5.00
40 Derrick Rose/149 4.00 10.00
42 Russell Westbrook/149 6.00 15.00
43 Evan Fournier/149 2.50 6.00
44 Serge Ibaka/149 2.50 6.00
46 Nerlens Noel/149 2.50 6.00
48 Eric Bledsoe/149 2.50 6.00
51 DeMarcus Cousins/149 3.00 8.00
52 Willie Cauley-Stein/149 2.50 6.00
54 LaMarcus Aldridge/149 3.00 8.00
56 Tony Parker/149 3.00 8.00
57 DeMar DeRozan/149 3.00 8.00
58 Kyle Lowry/149 2.50 6.00
59 Gordon Hayward/149 3.00 8.00
61 Markieff Morris/149 2.00 5.00
62 Bradley Beal/149 3.00 8.00
63 John Wall/149 4.00 10.00
64 Kevin Love/149 3.00 8.00

2016-17 Panini Spectra Spectacular Swatches Neon Blue

*NEON BLUE: .5X TO 1.2X BASIC
RANDOM INSERTS IN PACKS
PRINT RUNS B/WN 83-99 COPIES PER
1 Dwight Howard/99 3.00 8.00
2 Paul Millsap/99 4.00 10.00
4 Avery Bradley/99 3.00 8.00
5 Rondae Hollis-Jefferson/99 2.50 6.00
6 Brook Lopez/99 3.00 8.00
7 Nicolas Batum/99 3.00 8.00
9 Bobby Portis/99 2.50 6.00
11 LeBron James/99 15.00 40.00
12 Kyrie Irving/99 8.00 20.00
15 Danilo Gallinari/99 3.00 8.00
16 Emmanuel Mudiay/99 3.00 8.00
17 Andre Drummond/99 4.00 10.00
18 Stanley Johnson/99 2.50 6.00
24 Monta Ellis/99 3.00 8.00
26 DeAndre Jordan/99 4.00 10.00
36 Ricky Rubio/99 4.00 10.00
41 Steven Adams/99 10.00 25.00
45 Jahlil Okafor/99 3.00 8.00
55 Kawhi Leonard/99 6.00 15.00
60 Joe Johnson/99 3.00 8.00
65 Jeff Teague/99 3.00 8.00

2016-17 Panini Spectra Spectacular Swatches Neon Green

*NEON GREEN: 1X TO 2.5X BASIC
RANDOM INSERTS IN PACKS
PRINT RUNS B/WN 8-25 COPIES PER
NO PRICING ON QTY 18 OR LESS
4 Avery Bradley/25 6.00 15.00
5 Rondae Hollis-Jefferson/25 5.00 12.00
6 Brook Lopez/25 6.00 15.00
7 Nicolas Batum/25 6.00 15.00
9 Bobby Portis/25 5.00 12.00
11 LeBron James/25 50.00 120.00
13 Dirk Nowitzki/25 12.00 30.00
15 Danilo Gallinari/25 6.00 15.00
16 Emmanuel Mudiay/25 6.00 15.00
17 Andre Drummond/25 8.00 20.00
18 Stanley Johnson/25 5.00 12.00
24 Monta Ellis/25 6.00 15.00

27 Jordan Clarkson/25 6.00 15.00
36 Ricky Rubio/25 8.00 20.00
37 Langston Galloway/25 5.00 12.00
38 Tyreke Evans/25 5.00 12.00
41 Steven Adams/25 20.00 50.00
45 Jahlil Okafor/25 6.00 15.00
47 Brandon Knight/25 6.00 15.00
50 Al-Farouq Aminu/25 6.00 15.00
53 Darren Collison/25 6.00 15.00
60 Joe Johnson/25 6.00 15.00
65 Jeff Teague/20 6.00 15.00

2016-17 Panini Spectra Spectacular Swatches Pink

*PINK: .6X TO 1.5X BASIC
RANDOM INSERTS IN PACKS
PRINT RUNS B/WN 41-49 COPIES PER
1 Dwight Howard/49 4.00 10.00
2 Paul Millsap/49 5.00 12.00
4 Avery Bradley/49 4.00 10.00
5 Rondae Hollis-Jefferson/49 3.00 8.00
6 Brook Lopez/49 4.00 10.00
7 Nicolas Batum/49 4.00 10.00
9 Bobby Portis/49 3.00 8.00
11 LeBron James/49 20.00 50.00
12 Kyrie Irving/49 10.00 25.00
15 Danilo Gallinari/49 4.00 10.00
16 Emmanuel Mudiay/49 4.00 10.00
17 Andre Drummond/49 5.00 12.00
18 Stanley Johnson/49 3.00 8.00
24 Monta Ellis/49 4.00 10.00
26 DeAndre Jordan/49 5.00 12.00
27 Jordan Clarkson/49 4.00 10.00
36 Ricky Rubio/49 5.00 12.00
37 Langston Galloway/49 3.00 8.00
38 Tyreke Evans/49 3.00 8.00
41 Steven Adams/49 12.00 30.00
45 Jahlil Okafor/49 4.00 10.00
47 Brandon Knight/49 4.00 10.00
49 Evan Turner/49 3.00 8.00
50 Al-Farouq Aminu/49 4.00 10.00
53 Darren Collison/49 4.00 10.00
55 Kawhi Leonard/49 8.00 20.00
60 Joe Johnson/49 4.00 10.00
65 Jeff Teague/49 4.00 10.00

2016-17 Panini Spectra Triple Threat Materials

RANDOM INSERTS IN PACKS
STATED PRINT RUN 149 SER.#'d SETS
*NEON BLUE/99: .5X TO 1.2X BASIC
*PINK/49: .6X TO 1.5X BASIC
1 LeBron James 20.00 50.00
5 Al Horford 2.50 6.00
7 Marc Gasol 3.00 8.00
8 Paul Millsap 3.00 8.00
9 Hassan Whiteside 2.50 6.00
11 DeMarcus Cousins 3.00 8.00
12 Carmelo Anthony 4.00 10.00
13 Brandon Ingram 10.00 25.00
15 Malcolm Brogdon 4.00 10.00
16 Paul George 4.00 10.00
17 Anthony Davis 5.00 12.00
18 Dirk Nowitzki 4.00 10.00
19 Devin Booker 5.00 12.00

2016-17 Panini Spectra Triple Threat Materials Neon Green

*NEON GREEN: 1X TO 2.5X BASIC
RANDOM INSERTS IN PACKS
STATED PRINT RUN 25 SER.#'d SETS
14 Jaylen Brown 8.00 20.00

1976 Panini Olympic Stickers

This 300-sticker set celebrate the 1976 Montreal Olympics as well as Olympic athletes from earlier games. Each sticker measures 1 15/16" by 2 11/16", and a collector's album was available for displaying the stickers. The white-bordered stickers have mostly color photos. The player's name appears at the bottom between icons representing the event and the country's flag. The first six stickers are designed to form a composite of Canada, the host country for the summer and winter olympic games. Then follows a subset of men (7-10) who played a role in organizing the olympic games. The next subset is arranged according to olympiad (numbered with Roman numerals) as follows: I. 1896 Athens (11-15); II. 1900 Paris (16-20); III. 1904 St. Louis (21-25); IV. 1908 London (26-30); V. 1912 Stockholm (30-35); VII. 1920 Antwerp (36-40); VIII. 1924 Paris (41-45); IX. 1928 Amsterdam (46-50); X. 1932 Los Angeles (51-55); XI. 1936 Berlin (56-60); XIV. 1948 London (61-65); XV. 1952 Helsinki (66-70); XVI. Melbourne (71-75); XVII. 1960 Rome (76-80); XVIII. 1964 Tokyo (81-85); XIX. 1968 Mexico (86-90); and XX. 1972 Munchen (91-95). After two Canadian stickers (96-97) appear athletes from various countries who participated in the XXI. olympiad (98-300).

COMPLETE SET (300) 50.00 100.00
162 U.S.A. Men's Basketball Team 2.00 4.00
163 S.S.S.R. Men's Basketball Team 2.00 4.00
164 Yugoslavia Men's Basketball Team .13 .25
165 Italy Men's Basketball Team/ .13 .25
166 Brazil Men's Basketball .13 .25
167 Cuba Men's Basketball Team .13 .25
168 Mexico Men's Basketball .13 .25
169 U.S.S.R. Women's BK Team .50 1.00
170 Czechoslovakia Women's BK Team .13 .25
171 Italy Women's Basketball .13 .25

1987 Panini Stickers

138 Magic Johnson
141 Michael Jordan 20.00 50.00

1990-91 Panini Stickers

This set of 180 basketball stickers was produced and distributed by Panini primarily through mass market retailers. The stickers measure 1 15/16" by 2 15/16" and are issued in sheets consisting of three rows of four stickers each. The sheets were included with the sticker album itself. The stickers feature color action photos of the players on a white background. The team name is given in a light blue stripe below the picture, with a basketball icon to the right. The player's name appears at the bottom of the sticker. The stickers are numbered on the back. Stickers 1-162 showcase NBA players according to their teams. The remaining 18 stickers are lettered A-R and feature 1990 NBA All-Stars (A-J); Jordan, Bird, and Olajuwon (K-M); and the 1990 NBA Finals (N-R).

COMPLETE SET (180) 8.00 20.00
1 Magic Johnson .40 1.00
2 Mychal Thompson .08 .25
3 Vlade Divac .15 .40
4 Byron Scott .08 .25
5 James Worthy .20 .50
6 A.C. Green .08 .25
7 Jerome Kersey .08 .25
8 Clyde Drexler .40 1.00
9 Buck Williams .08 .25
10 Kevin Duckworth .08 .25
11 Terry Porter .08 .25
12 Cliff Robinson .15 .40
13 Tom Chambers .08 .25
14 Dan Majerle .15 .40
15 Mark West .08 .25
16 Kevin Johnson .15 .40
17 Jeff Hornacek .15 .40
18 Kurt Rambis .08 .25
19 Nate McMillan .08 .25
20 Shawn Kemp .50 1.25
21 Dale Ellis .08 .25
22 Michael Cage .08 .25
23 Xavier McDaniel .08 .25
24 Derrick McKey .08 .25
25 Manute Bol .08 .25
26 Chris Mullin .20 .50
27 Terry Teagle .08 .25
28 Tim Hardaway .20 .50
29 Sarunas Marciulionis .08 .25
30 Mitch Richmond .40 1.00
31 Gary Grant .08 .25
32 Danny Manning .15 .40
33 Benoit Benjamin .08 .25
34 Ron Harper .15 .40
35 Ken Norman .08 .25
36 Charles Smith .08 .25
37 Harold Pressley .08 .25
38 Antoine Carr .08 .25
39 Danny Ainge .15 .40
40 Wayman Tisdale .08 .25
41 Ralph Sampson .08 .25
42 Vinny Del Negro .08 .25
43 David Robinson .50 1.25
44 Sean Elliott .20 .50
45 Terry Cummings .15 .40
46 Willie Anderson .08 .25
47 Rod Strickland .15 .40
48 Frank Brickowski .08 .25
49 Karl Malone .60 1.50
50 Darrell Griffith .08 .25
51 John Stockton .60 1.50
52 Blue Edwards .08 .25
53 Mark Eaton .08 .25
54 Thurl Bailey .08 .25
55 Rolando Blackman .08 .25
56 Sam Perkins .08 .25
57 James Donaldson .08 .25
58 Herb Williams .08 .25
59 Roy Tarpley .08 .25
60 Derek Harper .08 .25
61 Michael Adams .08 .25
62 Blair Rasmussen .08 .25
63 Jerome Lane .08 .25
64 Walter Davis .08 .25
65 Todd Lichti .08 .25
66 Joe Barry Carroll .08 .25
67 Vernon Maxwell .08 .25
68 Otis Thorpe .08 .25
69 Hakeem Olajuwon .40 1.00
70 Buck Johnson .08 .25
71 Eric (Sleepy) Floyd .08 .25
72 Mitchell Wiggins .08 .25
73 Tony Campbell .08 .25
74 Tod Murphy .08 .25
75 Tyrone Corbin .08 .25
76 Sam Mitchell .08 .25
77 Randy Breuer .08 .25
78 Pooh Richardson .08 .25
79 Rex Chapman .15 .40
80 Dell Curry .08 .25
81 Muggsy Bogues .15 .40
82 J.R. Reid .08 .25
83 Armon Gilliam .08 .25
84 Kelly Tripucka .08 .25
85 Dennis Rodman .50 1.25
86 Joe Dumars .20 .50
87 Isiah Thomas .20 .50
88 Bill Laimbeer .15 .40
89 Vinnie Johnson .08 .25
90 James Edwards .08 .25
91 Michael Jordan 1.50 4.00
92 Stacey King .08 .25
93 Scottie Pippen .60 1.50
94 John Paxson .08 .25
95 Horace Grant .08 .25
96 Craig Hodges .08 .25
97 Brad Lohaus .08 .25
98 Jack Sikma .08 .25
99 Ricky Pierce .08 .25
100 Greg Anderson .08 .25
101 Alvin Robertson .08 .25
102 Jay Humphries .08 .25
103 Mark Price .15 .40
104 Winston Bennett .08 .25
105 Brad Daugherty .08 .25
106 Craig Ehlo .08 .25
107 Larry Nance .08 .25
108 Hot Rod Williams .08 .25
109 Rik Smits .15 .40
110 Chuck Person .08 .25
111 Reggie Miller .40 1.00
112 LaSalle Thompson .08 .25
113 Detlef Schrempf .15 .40
114 Vern Fleming .08 .25
115 Moses Malone .15 .40
116 Doc Rivers .15 .40
117 Dominique Wilkins .25 .60
118 Spud Webb .15 .40
119 Kevin Willis .08 .25
120 Kenny Smith .08 .25
121 Otis Smith .08 .25
122 Sidney Green .08 .25
123 Nick Anderson .08 .25
124 Scott Skiles .08 .25
125 Jerry Reynolds .08 .25
126 Terry Catledge .08 .25
127 Charles Barkley .40 1.00
128 Ron Anderson .08 .25
129 Hersey Hawkins .08 .25
130 Mike Gminski .08 .25
131 Johnny Dawkins .08 .25
132 Rick Mahorn .08 .25
133 Michael Smith .08 .25
134 Reggie Lewis .08 .25
135 Larry Bird 1.00 2.50
136 Kevin McHale .20 .50
137 Joe Kleine .08 .25
138 Robert Parish .15 .40
139 Maurice Cheeks .08 .25
140 Patrick Ewing .40 1.00
141 Charles Oakley .15 .40
142 Gerald Wilkins .08 .25
143 Kenny Walker .15 .40
144 Mark Jackson .08 .25
145 Mark Alarie .08 .25
146 John Williams .08 .25
147 Darrell Walker .08 .25
148 Bernard King .08 .25
149 Harvey Grant .08 .25
150 Ledell Eackles .08 .25
151 Glen Rice .50 1.25
152 Kevin Edwards .08 .25
153 Tellis Frank .08 .25
154 Rony Seikaly .08 .25
155 Billy Thompson .08 .25
156 Sherman Douglas .08 .25
157 Roy Hinson .08 .25
158 Chris Morris .08 .25
159 Lester Conner .08 .25
160 Sam Bowie .08 .25
161 Purvis Short .08 .25
162 Mookie Blaylock .15 .40
A John Stockton AS .25 .60
B Magic Johnson AS .25 .60
C A.C. Green AS .08 .25
D Hakeem Olajuwon AS .25 .60
E James Worthy AS .15 .40
F Isiah Thomas AS .15 .40
G Michael Jordan AS .75 2.00
H Larry Bird AS .40 1.00
I Patrick Ewing AS .25 .60
J Charles Barkley AS .25 .60
K Michael Jordan .75 2.00
L Larry Bird .40 1.00
M Hakeem Olajuwon .25 .60
N NBA Finals .08 .25
O NBA Finals .08 .25
P NBA Finals .08 .25
Q NBA Finals .08 .25
R NBA Finals .08 .25
XX Panini Album .40 1.00

1991-92 Panini Stickers

This set of 192 basketball stickers was produced and distributed by Panini primarily through mass market retailers. Unlike the previous year's issue, these were distributed only in the usual Panini packet of six stickers with 100 packets (suggested retail price of 39 cents) per box. The stickers measure approximately 1 7/8" by 2 15/16". The fronts feature player action shots. The stickers are numbered on the back and checklisted below alphabetically according to teams within the divisions. The set closes with the All-Rookie Team (179-186) and All-NBA 1st Team (187-192).

COMPLETE SET (192) 10.00 25.00
1 NBA Official .08 .25
  Licensed Product Logo
2 1991 NBA Finals Logo .08 .25
3 Chris Mullin .30 .75
4 Mitch Richmond .30 .75
5 Alton Lister .08 .25
6 Tim Hardaway .30 .75
7 Tom Tolbert .08 .25
8 Rod Higgins .08 .25
9 Charles Smith .08 .25
10 Ron Harper .20 .50
11 Olden Polynice .08 .25
12 Ken Norman .08 .25
13 Gary Grant .08 .25
14 Danny Manning .15 .40
15 Sam Perkins .10 .30
16 Vlade Divac .10 .30
17 James Worthy .30 .75
18 Magic Johnson .75 2.00
19 A.C. Green .20 .50
20 Byron Scott .20 .50
21 Kevin Johnson .15 .40
22 Mark West .08 .25
23 Dan Majerle .30 .75
24 Jeff Hornacek .30 .75
25 Xavier McDaniel .08 .25
26 Tom Chambers .20 .50
27 Terry Porter .08 .25
28 Kevin Duckworth .08 .25
29 Clyde Drexler .40 1.00
30 Jerome Kersey .08 .25
31 Buck Williams .15 .40
32 Danny Ainge .20 .50
33 Wayman Tisdale .08 .25
34 Antoine Carr .08 .25
35 Lionel Simmons .08 .25
36 Travis Mays .08 .25
37 Rory Sparrow .08 .25
38 Duane Causwell .08 .25
39 Benoit Benjamin .08 .25
40 Michael Cage .08 .25
41 Derrick McKey .08 .25
42 Shawn Kemp .30 .75
43 Gary Payton .60 1.50
44 Ricky Pierce .08 .25
45 Derek Harper .15 .40
46 James Donaldson .08 .25
47 Randy White .08 .25
48 Rodney McCray .08 .25
49 Alex English .20 .50
50 Rolando Blackman .15 .40
51 Orlando Woolridge .08 .25
52 Todd Lichti .08 .25
53 Chris Jackson .08 .25
54 Blair Rasmussen .08 .25
55 Reggie Williams .08 .25
56 Marcus Liberty .08 .25
57 Hakeem Olajuwon .50 1.25
58 Kenny Smith .08 .25
59 Vernon Maxwell .08 .25
60 Otis Thorpe .10 .30
61 Buck Johnson .08 .25
62 Larry Smith .08 .25
63 Pooh Richardson .08 .25
64 Felton Spencer .08 .25
65 Tod Murphy .08 .25
66 Tyrone Corbin .08 .25
67 Tony Campbell .08 .25
68 Sam Mitchell .15 .40
69 Dennis Scott .10 .30
70 Nick Anderson .10 .30
71 Terry Catledge .08 .25
72 Scott Skiles .20 .50
73 Otis Smith .08 .25
74 Greg Kite .08 .25
75 Terry Cummings .15 .40
76 Rod Strickland .10 .30
77 David Robinson .60 1.50
78 Willie Anderson .08 .25
79 Sean Elliott .20 .50
80 Paul Pressey .08 .25
81 John Stockton .75 2.00
82 Jeff Malone .08 .25
83 Mark Eaton .08 .25
84 Thurl Bailey .08 .25
85 Karl Malone .75 2.00
86 Blue Edwards .08 .25
87 Kevin Johnson .15 .40
88 '91 Western Division .10 .30
89 NBA All-Star Weekend .08 .25
90 Magic Johnson AS .40 1.00
91 Karl Malone AS .40 1.00
92 David Robinson AS .30 .75
93 Chris Mullin AS .20 .50
94 Charles Barkley AS .30 .75
95 '91 Eastern Division .10 .30
96 Michael Jordan AS 1.00 2.50
97 Isiah Thomas AS .30 .75
98 Charles Barkley AS .40 1.00
99 Patrick Ewing AS .30 .75
100 Larry Bird AS .50 1.25
101 Dominique Wilkins .40 1.00
102 Kevin Willis .10 .30
103 John Battle .08 .25
104 Doc Rivers .20 .50
105 Spud Webb .10 .30
106 Moses Malone .15 .40
107 J.R. Reid .08 .25
108 Johnny Newman .08 .25
109 Rex Chapman .15 .40
110 Muggsy Bogues .20 .50
111 Mike Gminski .08 .25
112 Kendall Gill .15 .40
113 Scottie Pippen .60 1.50
114 Bill Cartwright .10 .30
115 John Paxson .10 .30
116 Michael Jordan 1.50 4.00
117 Horace Grant .15 .40
118 B.J. Armstrong .08 .25
119 Brad Daugherty .08 .25
120 Larry Nance .10 .30
121 Hot Rod Williams .08 .25
122 Craig Ehlo .08 .25
123 Darnell Valentine .08 .25
124 Danny Ferry .08 .25
125 Isiah Thomas .40 1.00
126 James Edwards .08 .25
127 Bill Laimbeer .20 .50
128 Vinnie Johnson .08 .25
129 Joe Dumars .30 .75
130 Dennis Rodman .40 1.00
131 Reggie Miller .40 1.00
132 Detlef Schrempf .10 .30
133 Chuck Person .08 .25
134 LaSalle Thompson .08 .25
135 Vern Fleming .08 .25
136 Rik Smits .10 .30
137 Dale Ellis .10 .30
138 Frank Brickowski .08 .25
139 Jay Humphries .08 .25
140 Jack Sikma .08 .25
141 Fred Roberts .08 .25
142 Alvin Robertson .08 .25
143 Robert Parish .20 .50
144 Kevin McHale .30 .75
145 Kevin Gamble .08 .25
146 Larry Bird .75 2.00
147 Reggie Lewis .15 .40
148 Brian Shaw .15 .40
149 Sherman Douglas .08 .25
150 Rony Seikaly .08 .25
151 Glen Rice .30 .75
152 Grant Long .08 .25
153 Billy Thompson .08 .25
154 Willie Burton .08 .25
155 Reggie Theus .10 .30
156 Sam Bowie .10 .30
157 Derrick Coleman .10 .30
158 Drazen Petrovic .60 1.50
159 Mookie Blaylock .10 .30
160 Chris Morris .08 .25
161 Gerald Wilkins .08 .25
162 Charles Oakley .10 .30
163 Patrick Ewing .40 1.00
164 Kiki Vandeweghe .20 .50
165 Maurice Cheeks .15 .40
166 John Starks .20 .50
167 Hersey Hawkins .10 .30
168 Rick Mahorn .08 .25
169 Charles Barkley .50 1.25
170 Rickey Green .08 .25
171 Ron Anderson .08 .25
172 Armon Gilliam .08 .25
173 Bernard King .15 .40
174 Ledell Eackles .08 .25
175 John Williams .08 .25
176 Darrell Walker .08 .25
177 Haywoode Workman .08 .25
178 Harvey Grant .08 .25
179 Derrick Coleman ART .08 .25
180 Dee Brown ART .08 .25
181 Lionel Simmons ART .08 .25
182 Felton Spencer ART .08 .25
183 Dennis Scott ART .08 .25
184 Gary Payton ART .40 1.00
185 Travis Mays ART .08 .25
186 Kendall Gill ART .10 .30
187 All-NBA 1st Team .10 .30
188 Charles Barkley AS .40 1.00
189 Patrick Ewing AS .30 .75
190 Michael Jordan AS 1.00 2.50
191 Karl Malone AS .50 1.25
192 Magic Johnson AS .50 1.25
XX Panini Album 1.25 3.00

1992-93 Panini Stickers

The 192 stickers in this set measure approximately 1 15/16" by 3" and were to be pasted in a 9" by 11" album. The fronts feature color action player photos with white borders. Two team color-coded bars at the top contain the player's name and team. The backs are white and carry the set name, sticker number, and manufacturer logo. Six players from each of the 27 NBA teams are featured. The stickers are numbered on the back and checklisted below according to special subsets and teams.

COMPLETE SET (192) 8.00 20.00
1 Shaquille O'Neal 2.50 6.00
2 Tracy Murray .08 .25
3 Robert Horry .50 1.25
4 Bryant Stith .08 .25
5 Randy Woods .08 .25
6 Adam Keefe .08 .25
7 Byron Houston .08 .25
8 Duane Cooper .08 .25
9 Western Playoffs .08 .25
  (Action scene left)
10 Western Playoffs .08 .25
  (Action scene right)
11 Clyde Drexler .50 1.25
12 Michael Jordan 1.50 4.00
13 Eastern Playoffs .08 .25
  (Action scene left)
14 Eastern Playoffs .08 .25
  (Action scene right)
15 Chicago Bulls Logo .08 .25
16 1992 NBA Finals .40 1.00
  (Action scene
  upper left; Michael Jordan pictured)
17 1992 NBA Finals .40 1.00
  (Action scene
  upper right; Michael Jordan pictured)
18 1992 NBA Finals .40 1.00
  (Action scene
  lower left; Michael Jordan pictured)
19 1992 NBA Finals .40 1.00
  (Action scene
  lower right; Michael Jordan pictured)
20 Michael Jordan MVP 1.50 4.00
21 Tim Hardaway .40 1.00
22 Chris Mullin .40 1.00
23 Billy Owens .08 .25
24 Sarunas Marciulionis .20 .50
25 Jeff Grayer .08 .25
26 Tyrone Hill .08 .25
27 Danny Manning .20 .50
28 Ron Harper .20 .50
29 Ken Norman .08 .25
30 Charles Smith .08 .25
31 Gary Grant .08 .25
32 Doc Rivers .20 .50
33 James Worthy .40 1.00
34 Sam Perkins .20 .50
35 Byron Scott .20 .50
36 Sedale Threatt .08 .25
37 Elden Campbell .08 .25
38 A.C. Green .20 .50
39 Charles Barkley .50 1.25
40 Kevin Johnson .20 .50
41 Tom Chambers .20 .50
42 Dan Majerle .20 .50
43 Mark West .08 .25
44 Danny Ainge .20 .50
45 Buck Williams .20 .50
46 Clyde Drexler .50 1.25
47 Jerome Kersey .08 .25
48 Terry Porter .20 .50
49 Clifford Robinson .08 .25
50 Kevin Duckworth .08 .25
51 Mitch Richmond .30 .75
52 Lionel Simmons .08 .25
53 Wayman Tisdale .08 .25
54 Spud Webb .20 .50
55 Duane Causwell .08 .25
56 Jim Les .08 .25
57 Eddie Johnson .08 .25
58 Ricky Pierce .08 .25
59 Shawn Kemp .30 .75
60 Benoit Benjamin .08 .25
61 Gary Payton .50 1.25
62 Dana Barros .08 .25
63 Herb Williams .08 .25
64 Doug Smith .08 .25
65 Terry Davis .08 .25
66 Derek Harper .20 .50
67 Mike Iuzzolino .08 .25
68 Rodney McCray .08 .25
69 Greg Anderson .08 .25
70 Reggie Williams .08 .25
71 Dikembe Mutombo .40 1.00
72 Mark Macon .08 .25
73 Winston Garland .08 .25
74 Chris Jackson .08 .25
75 Otis Thorpe .08 .25
76 Hakeem Olajuwon .50 1.25
77 Vernon Maxwell .08 .25
78 Kenny Smith .08 .25
79 Avery Johnson .20 .50
80 Sleepy Floyd .08 .25
81 Pooh Richardson .08 .25
82 Tony Campbell .08 .25
83 Thurl Bailey .08 .25
84 Doug West .08 .25
85 Gerald Glass .08 .25
86 Felton Spencer .08 .25
87 David Robinson .50 1.25
88 Terry Cummings .08 .25
89 Sidney Green .08 .25
90 Sean Elliott .20 .50
91 Willie Anderson .08 .25
92 Antoine Carr .08 .25
93 Clyde Drexler FF .30 .75
94 Patrick Ewing FF .25 .60
95 Magic Johnson FF .40 1.00
96 Scottie Pippen FF .30 .75
97 John Stockton FF .40 1.00
98 Tim Hardaway FF .10 .30
99 David Robinson FF .30 .75
100 Karl Malone FF .30 .75
101 Chris Mullin FF .20 .50
102 Michael Jordan FF 1.50 4.00
103 Mark Eaton .08 .25
104 Karl Malone .50 1.25
105 Jeff Malone .08 .25
106 John Stockton .60 1.50
107 David Benoit .08 .25
108 Jay Humphries .08 .25
109 Alvin Robertson .08 .25
110 Moses Malone .20 .50
111 Sam Vincent .08 .25
112 Frank Brickowski .08 .25
113 Fred Roberts .08 .25
114 Blue Edwards .08 .25
115 Stacey Augmon .08 .25
116 Rumeal Robinson .08 .25
117 Paul Graham .08 .25
118 Dominique Wilkins .50 1.25
119 Kevin Willis .08 .25
120 Duane Ferrell .08 .25
121 Tyrone Bogues .15 .40
122 Kendall Gill .08 .25
123 Dell Curry .08 .25
124 Larry Johnson .25 .60
125 Johnny Newman .08 .25
126 J.R. Reid .08 .25
127 Scottie Pippen .75 2.00
128 Michael Jordan 1.50 4.00
129 Bill Cartwright .10 .30
130 Horace Grant .20 .50
131 John Paxson .20 .50
132 B.J. Armstrong .08 .25
133 Mark Price .20 .50
134 Brad Daugherty .08 .25
135 Larry Nance .20 .50
136 Craig Ehlo .15 .40
137 Hot Rod Williams .08 .25
138 Terrell Brandon .10 .30
139 Joe Dumars .40 1.00
140 Isiah Thomas .50 1.25
141 Dennis Rodman .50 1.25
142 Orlando Woolridge .08 .25
143 John Salley .20 .50
144 Bill Laimbeer .20 .50
145 Reggie Miller .50 1.25
146 Detlef Schrempf .20 .50
147 Chuck Person .08 .25
148 Micheal Williams .08 .25
149 Rik Smits .08 .25
150 Vern Fleming .08 .25
151 Lester Conner .08 .25
152 Nick Anderson .08 .25
153 Scott Skiles .15 .40
154 Terry Catledge .08 .25
155 Jerry Reynolds .08 .25
156 Dennis Scott .08 .25
157 Rick Fox .08 .25
158 Reggie Lewis .08 .25
159 Robert Parish .20 .50
160 Kevin Gamble .08 .25
161 Kevin McHale .25 .60
162 John Bagley .08 .25
163 Steve Smith .25 .60
164 Glen Rice .25 .60
165 Grant Long .08 .25
166 Rony Seikaly .08 .25
167 Bimbo Coles .08 .25
168 Willie Burton .08 .25
169 Derrick Coleman .08 .25
170 Drazen Petrovic .40 1.00
171 Sam Bowie .08 .25
172 Chris Morris .08 .25
173 Mookie Blaylock .08 .25
174 Chris Dudley .08 .25
175 Patrick Ewing .40 1.00
176 Mark Jackson .20 .50
177 Xavier McDaniel .08 .25
178 John Starks .15 .40
179 Charles Oakley .08 .25
180 Rolando Blackman .08 .25
181 Hersey Hawkins .08 .25
182 Johnny Dawkins .08 .25
183 Armon Gilliam .08 .25
184 Jeff Hornacek .20 .50
185 Tim Perry .08 .25
186 Andrew Lang .08 .25
187 Pervis Ellison .08 .25
188 Michael Adams .08 .25
189 Harvey Grant .08 .25
190 Ledell Eackles .08 .25
191 A.J. English .08 .25
192 David Wingate .08 .25
XX Panini Album 1.00 2.50

1993-94 Panini Stickers

The 253 stickers in this set measure approximately 2 3/8" by 3 3/8" and were to be pasted in a 9" by 11" album. On a team color-coded background with a black border, the fronts feature slightly tilted color action player photos framed by a thin white border. The team name appears above the photo, while the player's name is under the photo. The team logo is superimposed at the bottom right corner of the photo. The backs are white and carry the set name, sticker number, and manufacturer logo. The stickers are numbered on the back and checklisted below according to teams. In the middle of the album is a poster featuring the 1993 NBA Honor Roll (A-F).

COMPLETE SET (253) 10.00 25.00
1 John Paxson .25 .60
  (top part of photo)
2 John Paxson .25 .60
  (bottom part of photo)
3 Charles Barkley .50 1.25
  (top part of photo)
4 Charles Barkley .50 1.25
  (bottom part of photo)
5 Victor Alexander .20 .50
6 Chris Gatling .20 .50
7 Tim Hardaway .30 .75
8 Warriors Team Logo .20 .50
9 Tyrone Hill .20 .50
10 Sarunas Marciulionis .20 .50
11 Chris Mullin .30 .75
12 Billy Owens .20 .50
13 Latrell Sprewell .50 1.25
14 Gary Grant .20 .50
15 Ron Harper .25 .60
16 Mark Jackson .25 .60
17 Clippers Team Logo .20 .50
18 Danny Manning .25 .60
19 Ken Norman .20 .50
20 Stanley Roberts .20 .50
21 Loy Vaught .20 .50
22 John Williams .20 .50
23 Sam Bowie .20 .50
24 Elden Campbell .20 .50
25 Vlade Divac .30 .75
26 Lakers Team Logo .20 .50
27 A.C. Green .25 .60
28 Anthony Peeler .20 .50
29 Doug Christie .20 .50
30 Sedale Threatt .20 .50
31 James Worthy .40 1.00
32 Danny Ainge .30 .75
33 Charles Barkley .50 1.25
34 Cedric Ceballos .25 .60
35 Suns Team Logo .20 .50
36 Tom Chambers .25 .60
37 Richard Dumas .20 .50
38 Kevin Johnson .30 .75
39 Dan Majerle .30 .75
40 Oliver Miller .20 .50
41 Clyde Drexler .40 1.00
42 Mario Elie .20 .50
43 Harvey Grant .20 .50
44 Trail Blazers Team Logo .20 .50
45 Jerome Kersey .20 .50
46 Terry Porter .20 .50
47 Clifford Robinson .20 .50
48 Rod Strickland .20 .50
49 Buck Williams .20 .50
50 Anthony Bonner .20 .50
51 Duane Causwell .20 .50
52 Kurt Rambis .25 .60
53 Kings Team Logo .20 .50
54 Mitch Richmond .30 .75
55 Lionel Simmons .20 .50
56 Wayman Tisdale .20 .50
57 Spud Webb .25 .60
58 Walt Williams .20 .50
59 Dana Barros .20 .50
60 Eddie Johnson .20 .50
61 Shawn Kemp .40 1.00
62 Supersonics Team Logo .20 .50
63 Derrick McKey .20 .50
64 Nate McMillan .20 .50
65 Gary Payton .40 1.00
66 Sam Perkins .20 .50
67 Ricky Pierce .20 .50
68 Terry Davis .20 .50
69 Derek Harper .25 .60
70 Donald Hodge .20 .50
71 Mavericks Team Logo .20 .50
72 Mike Iuzzolino .20 .50
73 Jim Jackson .25 .60
74 Sean Rooks .20 .50
75 Doug Smith .20 .50
76 Randy White .20 .50
77 LaPhonso Ellis .20 .50
78 Scott Hastings .20 .50
79 Mahmoud Abdul-Rauf .20 .50
80 Nuggets Team Logo .20 .50
81 Marcus Liberty .20 .50
82 Mark Macon .20 .50
83 Dikembe Mutombo .30 .75
84 Robert Pack .20 .50
85 Reggie Williams .20 .50
86 Scott Brooks .20 .50
87 Sleepy Floyd .20 .50
88 Carl Herrera .20 .50
89 Rockets Team Logo .20 .50
90 Robert Horry .30 .75
91 Vernon Maxwell .20 .50
92 Hakeem Olajuwon .40 1.00
93 Kenny Smith .25 .60
94 Otis Thorpe .20 .50
95 Thurl Bailey .20 .50
96 Chris Smith .20 .50
97 Mike Brown .20 .50
98 Timberwolves Team Logo .20 .50
99 Christian Laettner .25 .60
100 Luc Longley .25 .60
101 Chuck Person .25 .60
102 Doug West .20 .50
103 Micheal Williams .20 .50
104 Willie Anderson .20 .50
105 Antoine Carr .20 .50
106 Terry Cummings .25 .60
107 Spurs Team Logo .20 .50
108 Sean Elliott .30 .75
109 Dale Ellis .20 .50
110 Avery Johnson .25 .60
111 J.R. Reid .20 .50
112 David Robinson .50 1.25
113 David Benoit .20 .50
114 Tyrone Corbin .20 .50
115 Mark Eaton .20 .50
116 Jazz Team Logo .20 .50
117 Jay Humphries .20 .50
118 Jeff Malone .20 .50
119 Karl Malone .40 1.00
120 Felton Spencer .20 .50
121 John Stockton .40 1.00
122 Anthony Avent .20 .50
123 Frank Brickowski .20 .50
124 Todd Day .20 .50
125 Bucks Team Logo .20 .50
126 Blue Edwards .20 .50
127 Brad Lohaus .20 .50
128 Moses Malone .30 .75
129 Lee Mayberry .20 .50
130 Eric Murdock .20 .50
131 Stacey Augmon .25 .60
132 Mookie Blaylock .20 .50
133 Duane Ferrell .20 .50
134 Hawks Team Logo .20 .50
135 Steve Henson .20 .50
136 Adam Keefe .20 .50
137 Jon Koncak .20 .50
138 Dominique Wilkins .40 1.00
139 Kevin Willis .20 .50
140 Muggsy Bogues .25 .60
141 Dell Curry .20 .50
142 Kenny Gattison .20 .50
143 Hornets Team Logo .20 .50
144 Kendall Gill .20 .50
145 Larry Johnson .30 .75
146 Alonzo Mourning .50 1.25
147 Johnny Newman .20 .50
148 David Wingate .20 .50
149 B.J. Armstrong .20 .50
150 Bill Cartwright .25 .60
151 Horace Grant .25 .60
152 Bulls Team Logo .20 .50
153 Stacey King .20 .50
154 John Paxson .25 .60
155 Will Perdue .20 .50
156 Scottie Pippen .60 1.50
157 Scott Williams .20 .50
158 Terrell Brandon .25 .60
159 Brad Daugherty .25 .60
160 Craig Ehlo .20 .50
161 Cavaliers Team Logo .20 .50
162 Danny Ferry .20 .50
163 Larry Nance .25 .60
164 Mark Price .30 .75
165 Gerald Wilkins .20 .50
166 Hot Rod Williams .20 .50
167 Mark Aguirre .25 .60
168 Joe Dumars .30 .75
169 Bill Laimbeer .25 .60
170 Pistons Team Logo .20 .50
171 Terry Mills .20 .50
172 Olden Polynice .20 .50
173 Alvin Robertson .20 .50
174 Dennis Rodman .60 1.50
175 Isiah Thomas .30 .75
176 Dale Davis .20 .50
177 Vern Fleming .20 .50
178 Reggie Miller .40 1.00
179 Pacers Team Logo .20 .50
180 Pooh Richardson .20 .50
181 Detlef Schrempf .30 .75
182 Malik Sealy .20 .50
183 Rik Smits .25 .60
184 LaSalle Thompson .20 .50
185 Nick Anderson .20 .50
186 Anthony Bowie .20 .50
187 Shaquille O'Neal 1.25 3.00
188 Magic Team Logo .20 .50
189 Donald Royal .20 .50
190 Dennis Scott .20 .50
191 Scott Skiles .20 .50
192 Tom Tolbert .20 .50
193 Jeff Turner .20 .50
194 Alaa Abdelnaby .20 .50
195 Dee Brown .20 .50
196 Sherman Douglas .20 .50
197 Celtics Team Logo .20 .50
198 Rick Fox .20 .50
199 Kevin Gamble .20 .50
200 Xavier McDaniel .20 .50
201 Robert Parish .30 .75
202 Lorenzo Williams .20 .50
203 Bimbo Coles .20 .50
204 Matt Geiger .20 .50
205 Harold Miner .20 .50
206 Heat Team Logo .20 .50
207 Glen Rice .30 .75
208 John Salley .20 .50
209 Rony Seikaly .20 .50
210 Brian Shaw .20 .50
211 Steve Smith .25 .60
212 Rafael Addison .20 .50
213 Kenny Anderson .25 .60
214 Benoit Benjamin .20 .50
215 Nets Team Logo .20 .50
216 Derrick Coleman .25 .60
217 Chris Dudley .20 .50
218 Rick Mahorn .20 .50
219 Chris Morris .20 .50
220 Rumeal Robinson .20 .50
221 Greg Anthony .20 .50
222 Rolando Blackman .25 .60
223 Patrick Ewing .40 1.00
224 Knicks Team Logo .20 .50
225 Anthony Mason .20 .50
226 Charles Oakley .25 .60
227 Doc Rivers .25 .60
228 Charles Smith .20 .50
229 John Starks .25 .60
230 Ron Anderson .20 .50
231 Johnny Dawkins .20 .50
232 Armon Gilliam .20 .50
233 76ers Team Logo .20 .50
234 Hersey Hawkins .20 .50
235 Jeff Hornacek .25 .60
236 Andrew Lang .20 .50
237 Tim Perry .20 .50
238 Clarence Weatherspoon .20 .50
239 Michael Adams .20 .50
240 Rex Chapman .20 .50
241 Kevin Duckworth .20 .50
242 Bullets Team Logo .20 .50
243 Pervis Ellison .20 .50
244 Tom Gugliotta .25 .60
245 Don MacLean .20 .50
246 Brent Price .20 .50
247 LaBradford Smith .20 .50
A Charles Barkley MVP .50 1.25
B Mahmoud Abdul-Rauf MIP .20 .50
C Shaquille O'Neal ROY 1.25 3.00
D Hakeem Olajuwon Def POY .40 1.00
E John Stockton CV .40 1.00

F Clifford Robinson SM .20 .50
XX Panini Album .75 2.00

1994-95 Panini Stickers

This 230-card sticker set was issued in the United States and most of Europe. Stickers came in 6-card packets and sold for about 49-cents each. In addition to the regularly numbered 220-cards, there is a 10-card 1994 NBA All-Rookie Team subset numbered A-J. Each sticker is slightly smaller than a standard-sized trading cards and each feature full color photos surrounded by a white border, except for the Future Star subset cards scattered throughout the set that feature foil borders.. The backs of each sticker contain a large number and licensing information.

COMPLETE SET (230) 30.00 80.00
1 Toronto Raptors .40 1.00
2 Toronto Raptors .40 1.00
3 Vancouver Grizzlies .40 1.00
4 Vancouver Grizzlies .40 1.00
5 Stacey Augmon .50 1.25
6 Mookie Blaylock .40 1.00
7 Craig Ehlo .40 1.00
8 Duane Ferrell .40 1.00
9 Adam Keefe .40 1.00
10 Andrew Lang .40 1.00
11 Danny Manning .50 1.25
12 Kevin Willis .40 1.00
13 Dee Brown .40 1.00
14 Sherman Douglas .40 1.00
15 Pervis Ellison .40 1.00
16 Rick Fox .40 1.00
17 Kevin Gamble .40 1.00
18 Xavier McDaniel .40 1.00
19 Dino Radja .40 1.00
20 Dominique Wilkins .75 2.00
21 Michael Adams .40 1.00
22 Muggsy Bogues .50 1.25
23 Dell Curry .40 1.00
24 Kenny Gattison .40 1.00
25 Hersey Hawkins .40 1.00
26 Larry Johnson .60 1.50
27 Alonzo Mourning .75 2.00
28 Robert Parish .60 1.50
29 B.J. Armstrong .40 1.00
30 Steve Kerr .50 1.25
31 Toni Kukoc .75 2.00
32 Luc Longley .50 1.25
33 Pete Myers .40 1.00
34 Will Perdue .40 1.00
35 Scottie Pippen 1.25 3.00
36 Bill Wennington .40 1.00
37 Terrell Brandon .40 1.00
38 Michael Cage .40 1.00
39 Brad Daugherty .50 1.25
40 Tyrone Hill .40 1.00
41 Chris Mills .40 1.00
42 Mark Price .60 1.50
43 Gerald Wilkins .40 1.00
44 John Williams .40 1.00
45 Greg Anderson .40 1.00
46 Joe Dumars .60 1.50
47 Allan Houston .60 1.50
48 Lindsey Hunter .40 1.00
49 Eric Leckner .40 1.00
50 Mark Macon .40 1.00
51 Terry Mills .40 1.00
52 Mark West .40 1.00
53 Antonio Davis .40 1.00
54 Dale Davis .40 1.00
55 Mark Jackson .50 1.25
56 Derrick McKey .40 1.00
57 Reggie Miller .75 2.00
58 Byron Scott .50 1.25
59 Rik Smits .50 1.25
60 Haywoode Workman .40 1.00
61 Vernell Bimbo Coles .40 1.00
62 Matt Geiger .40 1.00
63 Grant Long .40 1.00
64 Harold Miner .40 1.00
65 Glen Rice .60 1.50
66 John Salley .40 1.00
67 Rony Seikaly .40 1.00
68 Steve Smith .50 1.25
69 Vin Baker .60 1.50
70 Jon Barry .40 1.00
71 Anthony Cook .40 1.00
72 Todd Day .40 1.00
73 Brad Lohaus .40 1.00
74 Lee Mayberry .40 1.00
75 Eric Murdock .40 1.00
76 Ed Pinckney .40 1.00
77 Kenny Anderson .50 1.25
78 Benoit Benjamin .40 1.00
79 P.J. Brown .40 1.00
80 Derrick Coleman .50 1.25
81 Kevin Edwards .40 1.00
82 Armon Gilliam .40 1.00
83 Chris Morris .40 1.00
84 Rex Walters .40 1.00
85 Greg Anthony .40 1.00
86 Hubert Davis .40 1.00
87 Patrick Ewing .75 2.00
88 Derek Harper .50 1.25
89 Anthony Mason .40 1.00
90 Charles Oakley .50 1.25
91 Charles Smith .40 1.00
92 John Starks .50 1.25
93 Nick Anderson .40 1.00
94 Anthony Avent .40 1.00
95 Horace Grant .50 1.25
96 Anfernee Hardaway 1.00 2.50
97 Shaquille O'Neal 1.50 4.00
98 Donald Royal .40 1.00
99 Dennis Scott .40 1.00
100 Jeff Turner .40 1.00
101 Dana Barros .40 1.00
102 Shawn Bradley .40 1.00
103 Johnny Dawkins .40 1.00
104 Jeff Malone .40 1.00
105 Tim Perry .40 1.00
106 Clarence Weatherspoon .40 1.00
107 Scott Williams .40 1.00
108 Orlando Woolridge .40 1.00
109 Rex Chapman .40 1.00
110 Calbert Cheaney .40 1.00
111 Kevin Duckworth .40 1.00
112 Tom Gugliotta .40 1.00
113 Don MacLean .40 1.00
114 Gheorghe Muresan .40 1.00
115 Brent Price .40 1.00
116 Scott Skiles .40 1.00
117 Tony Campbell .40 1.00
118 Lucious Harris .40 1.00
119 Donald Hodge .40 1.00
120 Jim Jackson .40 1.00
121 Popeye Jones .40 1.00
122 Jamal Mashburn .60 1.50
123 Sean Rooks .40 1.00
124 Doug Smith .40 1.00
125 Mahmoud Abdul-Rauf .40 1.00
126 LaPhonso Ellis .40 1.00
127 Dikembe Mutombo .60 1.50
128 Robert Pack .40 1.00
129 Rodney Rogers .40 1.00
130 Bryant Stith .40 1.00
131 Brian Williams .40 1.00
132 Reggie Williams .40 1.00
133 Victor Alexander .40 1.00
134 Chris Gatling .40 1.00
135 Tim Hardaway .60 1.50
136 Keith Jennings .40 1.00
137 Chris Mullin .60 1.50
138 Billy Owens .40 1.00
139 Latrell Sprewell .75 2.00
140 Chris Webber 1.00 2.50
141 Sam Cassell .60 1.50
142 Mario Elie .40 1.00
143 Carl Herrera .40 1.00
144 Robert Horry .60 1.50
145 Vernon Maxwell .40 1.00
146 Hakeem Olajuwon .75 2.00
147 Kenny Smith .50 1.25
148 Otis Thorpe .40 1.00
149 Terry Dehere .40 1.00
150 Harold Ellis .40 1.00
151 Gary Grant .40 1.00
152 Ron Harper .50 1.25
153 Pooh Richardson .40 1.00
154 Malik Sealy .40 1.00
155 Elmore Spencer .40 1.00
156 Loy Vaught .40 1.00
157 Elden Campbell .40 1.00
158 Doug Christie .40 1.00
159 Vlade Divac .60 1.50
160 Anthony Peeler .40 1.00
161 Tony Smith .40 1.00
162 Sedale Threatt .40 1.00
163 Nick Van Exel .60 1.50
164 James Worthy .75 2.00
165 Thurl Bailey .40 1.00
166 Mike Brown .40 1.00
167 Stacey King .40 1.00
168 Christian Laettner .50 1.25
169 Isaiah Rider .60 1.50
170 Chris Smith .40 1.00
171 Doug West .40 1.00
172 Micheal Williams .40 1.00
173 Danny Ainge .60 1.50
174 Charles Barkley 1.00 2.50
175 Cedric Ceballos .40 1.00
176 A.C. Green .50 1.25
177 Frank Johnson .40 1.00
178 Kevin Johnson .60 1.50
179 Dan Majerle .60 1.50
180 Oliver Miller .40 1.00
181 Mark Bryant .40 1.00
182 Clyde Drexler .75 2.00
183 Harvey Grant .40 1.00
184 Jerome Kersey .40 1.00
185 Terry Porter .40 1.00
186 Clifford Robinson .40 1.00
187 Rod Strickland .40 1.00
188 Buck Williams .40 1.00
189 Randy Brown .40 1.00
190 Olden Polynice .40 1.00
191 Mitch Richmond .60 1.50
192 Lionel Simmons .40 1.00
193 Andre Spencer .40 1.00
194 Wayman Tisdale .40 1.00
195 Spud Webb .50 1.25
196 Walt Williams .40 1.00
197 Willie Anderson .40 1.00
198 Vinny Del Negro .40 1.00
199 Sean Elliott .60 1.50
200 Dale Ellis .40 1.00
201 Avery Johnson .50 1.25
202 Chuck Person .50 1.25
203 David Robinson 1.00 2.50
204 Dennis Rodman 1.25 3.00
205 Kendall Gill .40 1.00
206 Ervin Johnson .40 1.00
207 Shawn Kemp .60 1.50
208 Sarunas Marciulionis .40 1.00
209 Nate McMillan .40 1.00
210 Gary Payton .60 1.50
211 Sam Perkins .40 1.00
212 Detlef Schrempf .60 1.50
213 David Benoit .40 1.00
214 Tyrone Corbin .40 1.00
215 Jeff Hornacek .50 1.25
216 Jay Humphries .40 1.00
217 Karl Malone .75 2.00
218 Felton Spencer .40 1.00
219 John Stockton .75 2.00
220 Luther Wright .40 1.00
A Chris Webber ART 1.00 2.50
B Anfernee Hardaway ART 1.00 2.50
C Vin Baker ART .60 1.50
D Jamal Mashburn ART .60 1.50
E Isaiah Rider ART .60 1.50
F Dino Radja ART .40 1.00
G Nick Van Exel ART .60 1.50
H Toni Kukoc ART .75 2.00
I Lindsey Hunter ART .40 1.00
J Shawn Bradley ART .40 1.00
XX Panini Album .40 1.00

1995-96 Panini Stickers

The 288 stickers in this set measure approximately 2 1/8" by 3" and were to be pasted in a 9" by 10 3/4" album. The fronts feature color action player photos with white borders. The player's name runs vertically down one side of the photo while the team name and logo appear in a bottom corner inside a basketball. The white backs carry the set name, sticker number, and manufacturer logo. The stickers are checklisted below according to teams. The set closes with NBA League Leaders (271-280) NBA Rookie Sensations (281-288).

COMPLETE SET (288) 15.00 40.00
1 Dee Brown .15 .40
2 Sherman Douglas .15 .40
3 Pervis Ellison .15 .40
4 Rick Fox .15 .40
5 Greg Minor .15 .40
6 Celtics Team Logo .15 .40
7 Eric Montross .15 .40
8 Dino Radja .15 .40
9 David Wesley .15 .40
10 Rex Chapman .15 .40
11 Bimbo Coles .15 .40
12 Kevin Gamble .15 .40
13 Matt Geiger .15 .40
14 Billy Owens .15 .40
15 Heat Team Logo .15 .40
16 Khalid Reeves .15 .40
17 Glen Rice .25 .60
18 Kevin Willis .15 .40
19 Kenny Anderson .20 .50
20 P.J. Brown .15 .40
21 Chris Childs .15 .40
22 Derrick Coleman .20 .50
23 Kevin Edwards .15 .40
24 Nets Team Logo .15 .40
25 Armon Gilliam .15 .40
26 Chris Morris .15 .40
27 Jayson Williams .15 .40
28 Anthony Bonner .15 .40
29 Hubert Davis .15 .40
30 Patrick Ewing .30 .75
31 Derek Harper .20 .50
32 Anthony Mason .15 .40
33 Knicks Team Logo .15 .40
34 Charles Oakley .20 .50
35 Charles Smith .15 .40
36 John Starks .20 .50
37 Nick Anderson .15 .40
38 Horace Grant .20 .50
39 Anfernee Hardaway .40 1.00
40 Shaquille O'Neal .60 1.50
41 Donald Royal .15 .40
42 Magic Team Logo .15 .40
43 Dennis Scott .15 .40
44 Brian Shaw .15 .40
45 Jeff Turner .15 .40
46 Derrick Alston .15 .40
47 Dana Barros .15 .40
48 Shawn Bradley .15 .40
49 Willie Burton .15 .40
50 Jeff Malone .15 .40
51 76ers Team Logo .15 .40
52 Clarence Weatherspoon .15 .40
53 Scott Williams .15 .40
54 Sharone Wright .15 .40
55 Mitchell Butler .15 .40
56 Calbert Cheaney .15 .40
57 Juwan Howard .25 .60
58 Don MacLean .15 .40
59 Gheorghe Muresan .15 .40
60 Bullets Team Logo .15 .40
61 Doug Overton .15 .40
62 Scott Skiles .15 .40
63 Chris Webber .30 .75
64 Stacey Augmon .20 .50
65 Mookie Blaylock .15 .40
66 Craig Ehlo .15 .40
67 Andrew Lang .15 .40
68 Grant Long .15 .40
69 Hawks Team Logo .15 .40
70 Ken Norman .15 .40
71 Steve Smith .20 .50
72 Spud Webb .20 .50
73 Tony Bennett .15 .40
74 Muggsy Bogues .20 .50
75 Scott Burrell .15 .40
76 Dell Curry .15 .40
77 Kendall Gill .15 .40
78 Hornets Team Logo .15 .40
79 Larry Johnson .25 .60
80 Alonzo Mourning .30 .75
81 Robert Parish .25 .60
82 Ron Harper .20 .50
83 Michael Jordan 2.00 5.00
84 Steve Kerr .20 .50
85 Toni Kukoc .25 .60
86 Luc Longley .20 .50
87 Bulls Team Logo .15 .40
88 Will Perdue .15 .40
89 Scottie Pippen .40 1.00
90 Bill Wennington .15 .40
91 Terrell Brandon .15 .40
92 Michael Cage .15 .40
93 Danny Ferry .15 .40
94 Tyrone Hill .15 .40
95 Chris Mills .15 .40
96 Cavaliers Team Logo .15 .40
97 Bobby Phills .15 .40
98 Mark Price .25 .60
99 John Williams .15 .40
100 Bill Curley .15 .40
101 Joe Dumars .25 .60
102 Grant Hill .40 1.00
103 Allan Houston .20 .50
104 Lindsey Hunter .15 .40
105 Pistons Team Logo .15 .40
106 Mark Macon .15 .40
107 Terry Mills .15 .40
108 Mark West .15 .40
109 Antonio Davis .15 .40
110 Dale Davis .15 .40
111 Duane Ferrell .15 .40
112 Mark Jackson .20 .50
113 Derrick McKey .15 .40
114 Pacers Team Logo .15 .40
115 Reggie Miller .30 .75
116 Rik Smits .20 .50
117 Haywoode Workman .15 .40
118 Vin Baker .20 .50
119 Jon Barry .15 .40
120 Marty Conlon .15 .40
121 Todd Day .15 .40
122 Lee Mayberry .15 .40
123 Bucks Team Logo .15 .40
124 Eric Mobley .15 .40
125 Eric Murdock .15 .40
126 Glenn Robinson .20 .50
127 Willie Anderson .15 .40
128 B.J. Armstrong .15 .40
129 Acie Earl .15 .40
130 Jerome Kersey .15 .40
131 Tony Massenburg .15 .40
132 Raptors Team Logo .15 .40
133 Oliver Miller .15 .40
134 John Salley .15 .40
135 B.J. Tyler .15 .40
136 Larry Johnson POW .25 .60
137 Shawn Kemp POW .25 .60
138 Karl Malone POW .30 .75
139 Jamal Mashburn POW .25 .60
140 Alonzo Mourning POW .30 .75
141 Hakeem Olajuwon POW .30 .75
142 Shaquille O'Neal POW .60 1.50
143 David Robinson POW .40 1.00
144 Chris Webber POW .30 .75
145 Lucious Harris .15 .40
146 Jim Jackson .15 .40
147 Popeye Jones .15 .40
148 Jason Kidd .40 1.00
149 Jamal Mashburn .25 .60
150 Mavericks Team Logo .15 .40
151 George McCloud .15 .40
152 Roy Tarpley .15 .40
153 Lorenzo Williams .15 .40
154 Mahmoud Abdul-Rauf .15 .40
155 LaPhonso Ellis .15 .40
156 Dikembe Mutombo .25 .60
157 Robert Pack .15 .40
158 Jalen Rose .30 .75
159 Nuggets Team Logo .15 .40
160 Bryant Stith .15 .40
161 Brian Williams .15 .40
162 Reggie Williams .15 .40
163 Chucky Brown .15 .40
164 Sam Cassell .25 .60
165 Clyde Drexler .30 .75
166 Mario Elie .15 .40
167 Carl Herrera .15 .40
168 Rockets Team Logo .15 .40
169 Robert Horry .20 .50
170 Hakeem Olajuwon .30 .75
171 Kenny Smith .20 .50
172 Tom Gugliotta .15 .40
173 Christian Laettner .20 .50
174 Darrick Martin .15 .40
175 Isaiah Rider .25 .60
176 Sean Rooks .15 .40
177 Timberwolves Team Logo .15 .40
178 Chris Smith .15 .40
179 Doug West .15 .40
180 Micheal Williams .15 .40
181 Vinny Del Negro .15 .40
182 Sean Elliott .25 .60
183 Avery Johnson .20 .50
184 Chuck Person .20 .50
185 J.R. Reid .15 .40
186 Spurs Team Logo .15 .40
187 Doc Rivers .20 .50
188 David Robinson .40 1.00
189 Dennis Rodman .50 1.25
190 David Benoit .15 .40
191 Jeff Hornacek .20 .50
192 Adam Keefe .15 .40
193 Karl Malone .30 .75
194 Bryon Russell .15 .40
195 Jazz Team Logo .15 .40
196 Felton Spencer .15 .40
197 John Stockton .30 .75
198 Jamie Watson .15 .40
199 Greg Anthony .15 .40
200 Benoit Benjamin .15 .40
201 Blue Edwards .15 .40
202 Doug Edwards .15 .40
203 Kenny Gattison .15 .40
204 Grizzlies Team Logo .15 .40
205 Antonio Harvey .15 .40
206 Byron Scott .20 .50
207 Larry Stewart .15 .40
208 Chris Gatling .15 .40
209 Tim Hardaway .25 .60
210 Donyell Marshall .15 .40
211 Chris Mullin .25 .60
212 Carlos Rogers .15 .40
213 Warriors Team Logo .15 .40
214 Clifford Rozier .15 .40
215 Rony Seikaly .15 .40
216 Latrell Sprewell .25 .60
217 Terry Dehere .15 .40
218 Harold Ellis .15 .40
219 Lamond Murray .15 .40
220 Bo Outlaw .15 .40
221 Pooh Richardson .15 .40
222 Clippers Team Logo .15 .40
223 Rodney Rogers .15 .40
224 Malik Sealy .15 .40
225 Loy Vaught .15 .40
226 Sam Bowie .15 .40
227 Elden Campbell .15 .40
228 Cedric Ceballos .15 .40
229 Vlade Divac .25 .60
230 Eddie Jones .25 .60
231 Lakers Team Logo .15 .40
232 Anthony Peeler .15 .40
233 Sedale Threatt .15 .40
234 Nick Van Exel .25 .60
235 Charles Barkley .40 1.00
236 A.C. Green .20 .50
237 Kevin Johnson .25 .60
238 Dan Majerle .25 .60
239 Danny Manning .20 .50
240 Suns Team Logo .15 .40
241 Elliot Perry .15 .40
242 Wesley Person .15 .40
243 Wayman Tisdale .15 .40
244 Chris Dudley .15 .40
245 Harvey Grant .15 .40
246 Aaron McKie .15 .40
247 Terry Porter .15 .40
248 Clifford Robinson .15 .40
249 Trail Blazers Team Logo .15 .40
250 Rod Strickland .15 .40
251 Otis Thorpe .15 .40
252 Buck Williams .15 .40
253 Randy Brown .15 .40
254 Brian Grant .20 .50
255 Bobby Hurley .15 .40
256 Olden Polynice .15 .40
257 Mitch Richmond .25 .60
258 Kings Team Logo .15 .40
259 Lionel Simmons .15 .40
260 Michael Smith .15 .40
261 Walt Williams .15 .40
262 Vincent Askew .15 .40
263 Hersey Hawkins .15 .40
264 Shawn Kemp .25 .60
265 Sarunas Marciulionis .15 .40
266 Nate McMillan .15 .40
267 Supersonics Team Logo .15 .40
268 Gary Payton .25 .60
269 Sam Perkins .15 .40
270 Detlef Schrempf .25 .60
271 Chris Gatling LL .15 .40
272 Popeye Jones LL .15 .40
273 Steve Kerr LL .20 .50
274 Karl Malone LL .30 .75
275 Dikembe Mutombo LL .25 .60
276 Shaquille O'Neal LL .60 1.50
277 Scottie Pippen LL .40 1.00
278 Dennis Rodman LL .50 1.25
279 John Stockton LL .30 .75
280 Spud Webb LL .20 .50
281 Brian Grant ROO .20 .50
282 Grant Hill ROO .40 1.00
283 Juwan Howard ROO .25 .60
284 Eddie Jones ROO .25 .60
285 Jason Kidd ROO .40 1.00
286 Eric Montross ROO .15 .40
287 Wesley Person ROO .15 .40
288 Glenn Robinson ROO .20 .50
XX Panini Album .75 2.00

1996-97 Panini Stickers

COMPLETE SET (288) 15.00 40.00
1 NBA Logo .15 .40
2 Eastern Conference Logo .15 .40
3 Western Conference Logo .15 .40
4 Dana Barros .15 .40
5 Dee Brown .15 .40
6 Todd Day .15 .40
7 Rick Fox .15 .40
8 Eric Montross .15 .40
9 Dino Radja .15 .40
10 Boston Celtics Logo .15 .40
11 David Wesley .15 .40
12 Eric Williams .15 .40
13 Keith Askins .15 .40
14 Rex Chapman .15 .40
15 Sasha Danilovic .15 .40
16 Chris Gatling .15 .40
17 Tim Hardaway .25 .60
18 Alonzo Mourning .30 .75
19 Miami Heat Logo .15 .40
20 Kurt Thomas .15 .40
21 Walt Williams .15 .40
22 Shawn Bradley .15 .40
23 P.J. Brown .15 .40
24 Vern Fleming .15 .40
25 Kendall Gill .15 .40
26 Armon Gilliam .15 .40
27 New Jersey Nets Logo .15 .40
28 Ed O'Bannon .15 .40
29 Khalid Reeves .15 .40
30 Jayson Williams .15 .40
31 Willie Anderson .15 .40
32 Chris Childs .15 .40
33 Hubert Davis .15 .40
34 Patrick Ewing .30 .75
35 Derek Harper .20 .50
36 New York Knicks Logo .15 .40
37 Anthony Mason .15 .40
38 Charles Oakley .20 .50
39 John Starks .20 .50
40 Nick Anderson .15 .40
41 Horace Grant .20 .50
42 Anfernee Hardaway .40 1.00
43 Jon Koncak .15 .40
44 Shaquille O'Neal .60 1.50
45 Orlando Magic Logo .15 .40
46 Donald Royal .15 .40
47 Dennis Scott .15 .40
48 Brian Shaw .15 .40
49 Derrick Coleman .20 .50
50 Richard Dumas .15 .40
51 Tony Massenburg .15 .40
52 Vernon Maxwell .15 .40
53 Ed Pinckney .15 .40
54 Trevor Ruffin .15 .40
55 Philadelphia 76ers Logo .15 .40
56 Jerry Stackhouse .30 .75
57 Clarence Weatherspoon .15 .40
58 Calbert Cheaney .15 .40
59 Juwan Howard .20 .50
60 Tim Legler .15 .40
61 Gheorghe Muresan .15 .40
62 Robert Pack .15 .40
63 Washington Bullets Logo .15 .40
64 Brent Price .15 .40
65 Rasheed Wallace .30 .75
66 Chris Webber .30 .75
67 Stacey Augmon .20 .50
68 Mookie Blaylock .15 .40
69 Craig Ehlo .15 .40
70 Alan Henderson .15 .40
71 Christian Laettner .20 .50
72 Atlanta Hawks Logo .15 .40
73 Grant Long .15 .40
74 Sean Rooks .15 .40
75 Steve Smith .20 .50
76 Kenny Anderson .20 .50
77 Scott Burrell .15 .40
78 Dell Curry .15 .40
79 Matt Geiger .15 .40
80 Darrin Hancock .15 .40
81 Larry Johnson .25 .60
82 Glen Rice .25 .60
83 Charlotte Hornets Logo .15 .40
84 George Zidek .15 .40
85 Jud Buechler .15 .40
86 Ron Harper .20 .50
87 Steve Kerr .20 .50
88 Toni Kukoc .25 .60
89 Luc Longley .20 .50
90 Chicago Bulls Logo .15 .40
91 Scottie Pippen .40 1.00
92 Dennis Rodman .50 1.25
93 Bill Wennington .15 .40
94 Terrell Brandon .15 .40
95 Michael Cage .15 .40
96 Danny Ferry .15 .40
97 Tyrone Hill .15 .40
98 Dan Majerle .25 .60
99 Chris Mills .15 .40
100 Bobby Phills .15 .40
101 Cleveland Cavaliers Logo .15 .40
102 Bob Sura .15 .40
103 Joe Dumars .25 .60
104 Grant Hill .40 1.00
105 Allan Houston .20 .50
106 Lindsey Hunter .15 .40
107 Terry Mills .15 .40
108 Detroit Pistons Logo .15 .40
109 Theo Ratliff .15 .40
110 Don Reid .15 .40
111 Otis Thorpe .15 .40
112 Antonio Davis .15 .40
113 Dale Davis .15 .40
114 Mark Jackson .20 .50
115 Derrick McKey .15 .40
116 Reggie Miller .30 .75
117 Ricky Pierce .15 .40
118 Indiana Pacers Logo .15 .40
119 Rik Smits .20 .50
120 Haywoode Workman .15 .40
121 Vin Baker .20 .50
122 Benoit Benjamin .15 .40
123 Terry Cummings .20 .50
124 Sherman Douglas .15 .40
125 Milwaukee Bucks Logo .15 .40
126 Lee Mayberry .15 .40
127 Johnny Newman .15 .40
128 Shawn Respert .15 .40
129 Glenn Robinson .20 .50
130 Doug Christie .15 .40
131 Jimmy King .15 .40
132 Oliver Miller .15 .40
133 Tracy Murray .15 .40
134 Alvin Robertson .15 .40
135 Toronto Raptors Logo .15 .40
136 Carlos Rogers .15 .40
137 Damon Stoudamire .20 .50
138 Sharone Wright .15 .40
139 Mookie Blaylock FG .15 .40
140 Terrell Brandon FG .15 .40
141 Anfernee Hardaway FG .40 1.00
142 Tim Hardaway FG .25 .60
143 Jason Kidd FG .40 1.00
144 Gary Payton FG .25 .60
145 John Stockton FG .30 .75
146 Nick Van Exel FG .25 .60
147 Tony Dumas .15 .40
148 Lucious Harris .15 .40
149 Jim Jackson .15 .40
150 Popeye Jones .15 .40
151 Jason Kidd .40 1.00
152 Dallas Mavericks Logo .15 .40
153 Jamal Mashburn .20 .50
154 George McCloud .15 .40
155 Cherokee Parks .15 .40
156 Mahmoud Abdul-Rauf .15 .40
157 Dale Ellis .15 .40
158 LaPhonso Ellis .15 .40
159 Don MacLean .15 .40
160 Antonio McDyess .25 .60
161 Dikembe Mutombo .25 .60
162 Denver Nuggets Logo .15 .40
163 Jalen Rose .20 .50
164 Bryant Stith .15 .40
165 Chucky Brown .15 .40
166 Mark Bryant .15 .40
167 Sam Cassell .20 .50
168 Pete Chilcutt .15 .40
169 Houston Rockets Logo .15 .40
170 Clyde Drexler .30 .75
171 Mario Elie .15 .40
172 Robert Horry .20 .50
173 Hakeem Olajuwon .30 .75
174 Kevin Garnett .60 1.50
175 Tom Gugliotta .15 .40
176 Andrew Lang .15 .40
177 Darrick Martin .15 .40
178 Sam Mitchell .15 .40
179 Minnesota Timberwolves Logo .15 .40
180 Terry Porter .15 .40
181 Isaiah Rider .20 .50
182 Doug West .15 .40
183 Cory Alexander .15 .40
184 Vinny Del Negro .15 .40
185 Sean Elliott .25 .60
186 Avery Johnson .20 .50
187 Will Perdue .15 .40
188 San Antonio Spurs Logo .15 .40
189 Chuck Person .20 .50
190 David Robinson .40 1.00
191 Charles Smith .15 .40
192 David Benoit .15 .40
193 Antoine Carr .15 .40
194 Jeff Hornacek .20 .50
195 Adam Keefe .15 .40
196 Karl Malone .30 .75
197 Chris Morris .15 .40
198 Utah Jazz Logo .15 .40
199 Felton Spencer .15 .40
200 John Stockton .30 .75
201 Greg Anthony .15 .40
202 Anthony Avent .15 .40
203 Blue Edwards .15 .40
204 Chris King .15 .40
205 Lawrence Moten .15 .40
206 Vancouver Grizzlies Logo .15 .40
207 Eric Murdock .15 .40
208 Bryant Reeves .15 .40
209 Gerald Wilkins .15 .40
210 B.J. Armstrong .15 .40
211 Jerome Kersey .15 .40
212 Donyell Marshall .15 .40
213 Chris Mullin .25 .60
214 Golden State Warriors Logo .15 .40
215 Rony Seikaly .15 .40
216 Joe Smith .20 .50
217 Latrell Sprewell .25 .60
218 Kevin Willis .15 .40
219 Brent Barry .20 .50
220 Terry Dehere .15 .40
221 Lamond Murray .15 .40
222 Eric Piatkowski .20 .50
223 Pooh Richardson .15 .40
224 Los Angeles Clippers Logo .15 .40
225 Rodney Rogers .15 .40
226 Malik Sealy .15 .40
227 Loy Vaught .15 .40
228 Elden Campbell .15 .40
229 Cedric Ceballos .15 .40
230 Vlade Divac .25 .60
231 Eddie Jones .25 .60
232 George Lynch .15 .40
233 Los Angeles Lakers Logo .15 .40
234 Anthony Peeler .15 .40
235 Sedale Threatt .15 .40
236 Nick Van Exel .25 .60
237 Charles Barkley .40 1.00
238 Michael Finley .30 .75
239 A.C. Green .20 .50
240 Kevin Johnson .25 .60
241 Danny Manning .20 .50
242 Elliot Perry .15 .40
243 Phoenix Suns Logo .15 .40
244 Wayman Tisdale .15 .40
245 Wesley Person .15 .40
246 Chris Dudley .15 .40
247 Harvey Grant .15 .40
248 Aaron McKie .15 .40
249 Clifford Robinson .15 .40
250 Portland Trail Blazers Logo .15 .40
251 James Robinson .15 .40
252 Arvydas Sabonis .20 .50
253 Rod Strickland .15 .40
254 Buck Williams .15 .40
255 Tyus Edney .15 .40
256 Kevin Gamble .15 .40
257 Brian Grant .20 .50
258 Sarunas Marciulionis .15 .40
259 Sacramento Kings Logo .15 .40
260 Billy Owens .15 .40
261 Olden Polynice .15 .40
262 Mitch Richmond .25 .60
263 Michael Smith .15 .40
264 Vincent Askew .15 .40
265 Hersey Hawkins .15 .40
266 Ervin Johnson .15 .40
267 Shawn Kemp .25 .60
268 Nate McMillan .15 .40
269 Seattle Supersonics Logo .15 .40
270 Gary Payton .25 .60
271 Sam Perkins .15 .40
272 Detlef Schrempf .25 .60
273 Mahmoud Abdul-Rauf LL .15 .40
274 Tim Legler LL .15 .40
275 Anthony Mason LL .15 .40
276 Gheorghe Muresan LL .15 .40
277 Dikembe Mutombo LL .25 .60
278 Gary Payton LL .25 .60
279 Dennis Rodman LL .50 1.25
280 John Stockton LL .30 .75
281 Michael Finley .30 .75
282 Kevin Garnett .60 1.50
283 Antonio McDyess .25 .60
284 Bryant Reeves .15 .40
285 Arvydas Sabonis .20 .50
286 Joe Smith .20 .50
287 Jerry Stackhouse .30 .75
288 Damon Stoudamire .20 .50

1998-99 Panini Stickers

COMPLETE SET (156) 250.00 500.00
1 NBA Logo 1.25 3.00
2 Dana Barros 1.25 3.00
3 Ron Mercer 1.50 4.00
4 Kenny Anderson 1.50 4.00
5 Antoine Walker 2.00 5.00
6 Walter McCarty 1.25 3.00
7 Tim Hardaway 2.00 5.00
8 Alonzo Mourning 4.00 10.00
9 Jamal Mashburn 1.50 4.00
10 Dan Majerle 2.00 5.00
11 P.J. Brown 1.25 3.00
12 Jayson Williams 1.25 3.00
13 Sam Cassell 1.50 4.00
14 Kendall Gill 1.25 3.00
15 Keith Van Horn 2.00 5.00
16 Kerry Kittles 1.25 3.00
17 Patrick Ewing 4.00 10.00
18 Latrell Sprewell 2.00 5.00
19 Larry Johnson 2.00 5.00
20 Marcus Camby 1.50 4.00
21 Allan Houston 1.50 4.00
22 Anfernee Hardaway 4.00 10.00
23 Nick Anderson 1.25 3.00
24 Derek Strong 1.25 3.00
25 Bo Outlaw 1.25 3.00
26 Horace Grant 1.50 4.00
27 Theo Ratliff 1.50 4.00
28 Allen Iverson 4.00 10.00
29 Tim Thomas 2.00 5.00
30 Eric Snow
31 Scott Williams 1.25 3.00
32 Juwan Howard 1.50 4.00
33 Mitch Richmond 2.00 5.00
34 Tracy Murray 1.25 3.00
35 Rod Strickland 1.25 3.00
36 Calbert Cheaney 1.25 3.00
37 Dikembe Mutombo 2.00 5.00
38 Mookie Blaylock 1.25 3.00
39 Tyrone Corbin 1.25 3.00
40 Steve Smith 1.50 4.00
41 Alan Henderson 1.25 3.00
42 Anthony Mason 1.25 3.00
43 Derrick Coleman 1.50 4.00
44 David Wesley 1.25 3.00
45 Glen Rice 2.00 5.00
46 Bobby Phills 1.25 3.00
47 Ron Harper 1.50 4.00
48 Toni Kukoc 2.00 5.00
49 Mark Bryant 1.25 3.00
50 Brent Barry 1.50 4.00
51 Andrew Lang 1.25 3.00
52 Shawn Kemp 4.00 10.00
53 Wesley Person 1.25 3.00
54 Derek Anderson 1.25 3.00
55 Brevin Knight 1.25 3.00
56 Zydrunas Ilgauskas 2.00 5.00
57 Grant Hill 4.00 10.00
58 Jerry Stackhouse 2.00 5.00
59 Joe Dumars 2.00 5.00
60 Christian Laettner 1.50 4.00
61 Bison Dele 1.25 3.00
62 Rik Smits 1.50 4.00
63 Jalen Rose 1.50 4.00
64 Mark Jackson 1.50 4.00
65 Reggie Miller 4.00 10.00
66 Chris Mullin 2.00 5.00
67 Tyrone Hill 1.25 3.00
68 Glenn Robinson 1.50 4.00
69 Armon Gilliam 1.25 3.00
70 Terrell Brandon 1.25 3.00
71 Ray Allen 4.00 10.00
72 Reggie Slater 1.25 3.00
73 John Wallace 1.25 3.00
74 Doug Christie 1.25 3.00
75 Charles Oakley 1.50 4.00
76 Tracy McGrady 4.00 10.00
77 Shawn Bradley 1.25 3.00
78 Michael Finley 2.00 5.00
79 A.C. Green 1.50 4.00
80 Chris Anstey 1.25 3.00
81 Hot Rod Williams 1.25 3.00
82 Nick Van Exel 1.50 4.00
83 Bryant Stith 1.25 3.00
84 Eric Williams 1.25 3.00
85 Chauncey Billups 2.50 6.00
86 Antonio McDyess 1.50 4.00
87 Charles Barkley 4.00 10.00
88 Scottie Pippen 4.00 10.00
89 Hakeem Olajuwon 4.00 10.00
90 Matt Maloney 1.25 3.00
91 Rodrick Rhodes 1.25 3.00
92 Kevin Garnett 3.00 8.00
93 Sam Mitchell 1.25 3.00
94 Malik Sealy 1.25 3.00
95 Stephon Marbury 2.50 6.00
96 Anthony Peeler 1.25 3.00
97 David Robinson 4.00 10.00
98 Sean Elliott 2.00 5.00
99 Tim Duncan 4.00 10.00
100 Avery Johnson 1.50 4.00
101 Steve Kerr 1.50 4.00
102 Karl Malone 4.00 10.00
103 John Stockton 4.00 10.00
104 Howard Eisley 1.25 3.00
105 Bryon Russell 1.25 3.00
106 Jeff Hornacek 1.50 4.00
107 Bryant Reeves 1.25 3.00
108 Shareef Abdur-Rahim 2.00 5.00
109 Sam Mack 1.25 3.00
110 Tony Massenburg 1.25 3.00
111 Michael Smith 1.25 3.00
112 John Starks 1.50 4.00
113 Terry Cummings 1.50 4.00
114 Erick Dampier 1.25 3.00
115 Chris Mills 1.25 3.00
116 Donyell Marshall 1.25 3.00
117 Rodney Rogers 1.25 3.00
118 Darrick Martin 1.25 3.00
119 Lorenzen Wright 1.25 3.00
120 Lamond Murray 1.25 3.00
121 Pooh Richardson 1.25 3.00
122 Shaquille O'Neal 5.00 12.00
123 Robert Horry 1.50 4.00
124 Eddie Jones 2.00 5.00
125 Kobe Bryant 8.00 20.00
126 Rick Fox 1.25 3.00
127 Jason Kidd 4.00 10.00
128 Rex Chapman 1.25 3.00
129 Clifford Robinson 1.25 3.00
130 Tom Gugliotta 1.25 3.00
131 Danny Manning 1.50 4.00
132 Isaiah Rider 1.50 4.00
133 Damon Stoudamire 1.50 4.00
134 Stacey Augmon 1.50 4.00
135 Rasheed Wallace 2.00 5.00
136 Arvydas Sabonis 1.50 4.00
137 Chris Webber 4.00 10.00
138 Terry Dehere 1.25 3.00
139 Tariq Abdul-Wahad 1.25 3.00
140 Vlade Divac 2.00 5.00
141 Corliss Williamson 1.25 3.00
142 Vin Baker 1.50 4.00
143 Hersey Hawkins 1.25 3.00
144 Dale Ellis 1.25 3.00
145 Detlef Schrempf 2.00 5.00
146 Gary Payton 2.00 5.00
147 Tim Duncan 4.00 10.00
148 Rod Strickland 1.25 3.00
149 Dikembe Mutombo 2.00 5.00
150 Avery Johnson 1.50 4.00
151 Shaquille O'Neal 5.00 12.00
152 Michael Olowokandi 2.50 6.00
153 Mike Bibby 3.00 8.00
154 Raef Lafrentz 2.50 6.00
155 Robert Traylor 2.00 5.00
156 Vince Carter 10.00 25.00

1999-00 Panini Stickers

COMPLETE SET (210) 400.00 800.00
1 NBA Logo 1.50 4.00
2 Boston Celtics Logo 1.50 4.00
3 Kenny Anderson 2.00 5.00
4 Dana Barros 1.50 4.00
5 Calbert Cheaney 1.50 4.00
6 Paul Pierce 5.00 12.00

7 Vitaly Potapenko 1.50 4.00
8 Antoine Walker 2.50 6.00
9 P.J. Brown 1.50 4.00
10 Tim Hardaway 2.50 6.00
11 Miami Heat Logo 1.50 4.00
12 Voshon Lenard 1.50 4.00
13 Dan Majerle 2.50 6.00
14 Jamal Mashburn 2.00 5.00
15 Alonzo Mourning 5.00 12.00
16 New Jersey Nets Logo 1.50 4.00
17 Scott Burrell 1.50 4.00
18 Kendall Gill 1.50 4.00
19 Kerry Kittles 1.50 4.00
20 Stephon Marbury 2.00 5.00
21 Keith Van Horn 2.00 5.00
22 Jayson Williams 1.50 4.00
23 Marcus Camby 2.00 5.00
24 Patrick Ewing 5.00 12.00
25 New York Knicks Logo 1.50 4.00
26 Allan Houston 2.00 5.00
27 Larry Johnson 2.50 6.00
28 Latrell Sprewell 2.50 6.00
29 Charlie Ward 1.50 4.00
30 Orlando Magic Logo 1.50 4.00
31 Tariq Abdul-Wahad 1.50 4.00
32 Darrell Armstrong 1.50 4.00
33 Michael Doleac 1.50 4.00
34 Chris Gatling 1.50 4.00
35 Matt Harpring 1.50 4.00
36 Charles Outlaw 1.50 4.00
37 Matt Geiger 1.50 4.00
38 Larry Hughes 2.00 5.00
39 Philadelphia 76ers Logo 1.50 4.00
40 Allen Iverson 5.00 12.00
41 George Lynch 1.50 4.00
42 Billy Owens 1.50 4.00
43 Theo Ratliff 2.00 5.00
44 Washington Wizards Logo 1.50 4.00
45 Isaac Austin 1.50 4.00
46 Juwan Howard 2.00 5.00
47 Mitch Richmond 2.50 6.00
48 Rod Strickland 1.50 4.00
49 Chris Whitney 1.50 4.00
50 Lorenzo Williams 1.50 4.00
51 Bimbo Coles 1.50 4.00
52 LaPhonso Ellis 1.50 4.00
53 Atlanta Hawks Logo 1.50 4.00
54 Alan Henderson 1.50 4.00
55 Jim Jackson 1.50 4.00
56 Dikembe Mutombo 2.50 6.00
57 Isaiah Rider 2.00 5.00
58 Charlotte Hornets Logo 1.50 4.00
59 Elden Campbell 1.50 4.00
60 Derrick Coleman 2.00 5.00
61 Eddie Jones 2.50 6.00
62 Anthony Mason 1.50 4.00
63 Brad Miller 2.00 5.00
64 David Wesley 1.50 4.00
65 B.J. Armstrong 1.50 4.00
66 Randy Brown 1.50 4.00
67 Chicago Bulls Logo 1.50 4.00
68 Kornell David 2.00 5.00
69 Hersey Hawkins 1.50 4.00
70 Toni Kukoc 2.50 6.00
71 Dickey Simpkins 1.50 4.00
72 Cleveland Cavaliers Logo 1.50 4.00
73 Danny Ferry 1.50 4.00
74 Cedric Henderson 1.50 4.00
75 Zydrunas Ilgauskas 2.00 5.00
76 Shawn Kemp 5.00 12.00
77 Brevin Knight 1.50 4.00
78 Wesley Person 1.50 4.00
79 Jud Buechler 1.50 4.00
80 Grant Hill 5.00 12.00
81 Detroit Pistons Logo 1.50 4.00
82 Lindsey Hunter 1.50 4.00
83 Christian Laettner 2.00 5.00
84 Jerry Stackhouse 2.50 6.00
85 Jerome Williams 1.50 4.00
86 Indiana Pacers Logo 1.50 4.00
87 Dale Davis 1.50 4.00
88 Mark Jackson 2.00 5.00
89 Reggie Miller 5.00 12.00
90 Sam Perkins 1.50 4.00
91 Jalen Rose 2.00 5.00
92 Rik Smits 2.50 6.00
93 Ray Allen 5.00 12.00
94 Sam Cassell 2.00 5.00
95 Milwaukee Bucks Logo 1.50 4.00
96 Dale Ellis 1.50 4.00
97 Danny Manning 2.00 5.00
98 Glenn Robinson 2.00 5.00
99 Tim Thomas 2.00 5.00
100 Toronto Raptors Logo 1.50 4.00
101 Vince Carter 5.00 12.00
102 Doug Christie 2.00 5.00
103 Dell Curry 1.50 4.00
104 Antonio Davis 1.50 4.00
105 Tracy McGrady 5.00 12.00
106 Kevin Willis 1.50 4.00
107 Shawn Bradley 1.50 4.00
108 Cedric Ceballos 1.50 4.00
109 Dallas Mavericks Logo 1.50 4.00
110 Michael Finley 2.50 6.00
111 Dirk Nowitzki 5.00 12.00
112 Robert Pack 1.50 4.00
113 Hubert Davis 1.50 4.00
114 Denver Nuggets Logo 1.50 4.00
115 Cory Alexander 1.50 4.00
116 Chauncey Billups 2.50 6.00
117 Raef LaFrentz 2.00 5.00
118 Antonio McDyess 2.00 5.00
119 Ron Mercer 2.00 5.00
120 Nick Van Exel 2.00 5.00
121 Cuttino Mobley 1.50 4.00
122 Hakeem Olajuwon 5.00 12.00
123 Houston Rockets Logo 1.50 4.00
124 Charles Barkley 5.00 12.00
125 Shandon Anderson 1.50 4.00
126 Walt Williams 1.50 4.00
127 Matt Bullard 1.50 4.00
128 Minnesota Timberwolves Logo 1.50 4.00
129 Terrell Brandon 1.50 4.00
130 Kevin Garnett 4.00 10.00
131 Radoslav Nesterovic 2.50 6.00
132 Anthony Peeler 1.50 4.00
133 Malik Sealy 1.50 4.00
134 Joe Smith 2.00 5.00
135 Tim Duncan 5.00 12.00
136 Mario Elie 1.50 4.00
137 San Antonio Spurs Logo 1.50 4.00
138 Terry Porter 1.50 4.00
139 Avery Johnson 2.00 5.00
140 David Robinson 5.00 12.00
141 Malik Rose 1.50 4.00
142 Utah Jazz logo 1.50 4.00
143 Howard Eisley 1.50 4.00
144 Karl Malone 5.00 12.00
145 Greg Ostertag 1.50 4.00
146 Bryon Russell 1.50 4.00
147 Jeff Hornacek 2.00 5.00
148 John Stockton 5.00 12.00
149 Shareef Abdur-Rahim 2.00 5.00
150 Mike Bibby 2.50 6.00
151 Vancouver Grizzlies Logo 1.50 4.00
152 Othella Harrington 1.50 4.00
153 Felipe Lopez 1.50 4.00
154 Bryant Reeves 1.50 4.00
155 Dennis Scott 1.50 4.00
156 Golden State Warriors Logo 1.50 4.00
157 Mookie Blaylock 1.50 4.00
158 Antawn Jamison 2.50 6.00
159 Donyell Marshall 1.50 4.00
160 Chris Mills 1.50 4.00
161 John Starks 2.00 5.00
162 Terry Cummings 2.00 5.00
163 Derek Anderson 1.50 4.00
164 Tyrone Nesby 2.00 5.00
165 Los Angeles Clippers Logo 1.50 4.00
166 Michael Olowokandi 1.50 4.00
167 Eric Piatkowski 2.00 5.00
168 Brian Skinner 1.50 4.00
169 Maurice Taylor 1.50 4.00
170 Los Angeles Lakers Logo 1.50 4.00
171 Kobe Bryant 10.00 25.00
172 Derek Fisher 2.50 6.00
173 Rick Fox 1.50 4.00
174 Robert Horry 2.00 5.00
175 A.C. Green 2.00 5.00
176 Glen Rice 2.50 6.00
177 Tom Gugliotta 1.50 4.00
178 Anfernee Hardaway 5.00 12.00
179 Phoenix Suns Logo 1.50 4.00
180 Jason Kidd 5.00 12.00
181 Luc Longley 2.00 5.00
182 Clifford Robinson 1.50 4.00
183 Rodney Rogers 1.50 4.00
184 Portland Trail Blazers Logo 1.50 4.00
185 Scottie Pippen 5.00 12.00
186 Arvydas Sabonis 2.00 5.00
187 Detlef Schrempf 2.00 5.00
188 Steve Smith 2.00 5.00
189 Damon Stoudamire 2.00 5.00
190 Rasheed Wallace 2.50 6.00
191 Nick Anderson 1.50 4.00
192 Vlade Divac 2.50 6.00
193 Sacramento Kings Logo 1.50 4.00
194 Peja Stojakovic 2.50 6.00
195 Chris Webber 5.00 12.00
196 Jason Williams 3.00 8.00
197 Corliss Williamson 1.50 4.00
198 Seattle Supersonics Logo 1.50 4.00
199 Vin Baker 2.00 5.00
200 Brent Barry 2.00 5.00
201 Greg Foster 1.50 4.00
202 Horace Grant 2.00 5.00
203 Vernon Maxwell 1.50 4.00
204 Gary Payton 2.50 6.00
205 Elton Brand 6.00 15.00
206 Steve Francis 6.00 15.00
207 Baron Davis 6.00 15.00
208 Lamar Odom 6.00 15.00
209 Jonathan Bender 2.50 6.00
210 Wally Szczerbiak 5.00 12.00

2009-10 Panini Stickers

COMPLETE SET (384) 30.00 80.00
1 Boston Celtics Logo .10 .25
2 Kevin Garnett .25 .60
3 Paul Pierce .15 .40
4 Rajon Rondo .15 .40
5 Lester Hudson .10 .25
6 Ray Allen .15 .40
7 Kendrick Perkins .10 .25
8 Eddie House .10 .25
9 Glen Davis .10 .25
10 Rasheed Wallace .15 .40
11 Robert Parish .15 .40
12 New Jersey Nets Logo .10 .25
13 Devin Harris .10 .25
14 Brook Lopez .12 .30
15 Yi Jianlian .12 .30
16 Terrence Williams .10 .25
17 Bobby Simmons .10 .25
18 New Jersey Nets Records .10 .25
19 Jarvis Hayes .10 .25
20 Tony Battie .10 .25
21 Rafer Alston .10 .25
22 Courtney Lee .12 .30
23 New York Knicks Logo .10 .25
24 Al Harrington .12 .30
25 Danilo Gallinari .12 .30
26 Chris Duhon .10 .25
27 Jordan Hill .12 .30
28 Wilson Chandler .12 .30
29 Willis Reed .15 .40
30 Nate Robinson .10 .25
31 David Lee .10 .25
32 Jared Jeffries .10 .25
33 Darko Milicic .10 .25
34 Philadelphia 76ers Logo .10 .25
35 Andre Iguodala .12 .30
36 Thaddeus Young .10 .25
37 Samuel Dalembert .10 .25
38 Jrue Holiday .20 .50
39 Elton Brand .15 .40
40 Billy Cunningham .15 .40
41 Louis Williams .12 .30
42 Willie Green .10 .25
43 Jason Kapono .10 .25
44 Primoz Brezec .10 .25
45 Toronto Raptors Logo .10 .25
46 Chris Bosh .15 .40
47 Andrea Bargnani .12 .30
48 Jose Calderon .10 .25
49 DeMar DeRozan .40 1.00
50 Rasho Nesterovic .10 .25
51 Toronto Raptors Records .10 .25
52 Marco Belinelli .10 .25
53 Jarrett Jack .12 .30
54 Antoine Wright .10 .25
55 Hedo Turkoglu .12 .30
56 Chicago Bulls Logo .10 .25
57 Derrick Rose .25 .60
58 Luol Deng .12 .30
59 John Salmons .12 .30
60 James Johnson .12 .30
61 Brad Miller .12 .30
62 Chicago Bulls Records .10 .25
63 Joakim Noah .12 .30
64 Tyrus Thomas .10 .25
65 Jannero Pargo .10 .25
66 Kirk Hinrich .12 .30
67 Cleveland Cavaliers Logo .10 .25
68 LeBron James .60 1.50
69 Mo Williams .12 .30
70 Delonte West .10 .25
71 Danny Green .20 .50
72 Daniel Gibson .12 .30
73 Cleveland Cavaliers Records .10 .25
74 Anthony Parker .10 .25
75 Shaquille O'Neal .30 .75
76 Anderson Varejao .10 .25
77 Zydrunas Ilgauskas .12 .30
78 Detroit Pistons Logo .10 .25
79 Tayshaun Prince .12 .30
80 Richard Hamilton .12 .30
81 Rodney Stuckey .10 .25
82 Austin Daye .10 .25
83 Ben Gordon .12 .30
84 Isiah Thomas .15 .40
85 Will Bynum .10 .25
86 Kwame Brown .10 .25
87 Charlie Villanueva .10 .25
88 Ben Wallace .12 .30
89 Indiana Pacers Logo .10 .25
90 Danny Granger .12 .30
91 Mike Dunleavy .10 .25
92 T.J. Ford .10 .25
93 Tyler Hansbrough .12 .30
94 Jeff Foster .10 .25
95 Indiana Pacers Records .10 .25
96 Earl Watson .10 .25
97 Dahntay Jones .10 .25
98 Troy Murphy .10 .25
99 Brandon Rush .10 .25
100 Milwaukee Bucks Logo .10 .25
101 Andrew Bogut .12 .30
102 Michael Redd .12 .30
103 Francisco Elson .10 .25
104 Brandon Jennings .15 .40
105 Charlie Bell .10 .25
106 Luke Ridnour .12 .30
107 Luc Mbah A Moute .10 .25
108 Hakim Warrick .12 .30
109 Ersan Ilyasova .10 .25
110 Oscar Robertson .15 .40
111 Atlanta Hawks Logo .10 .25
112 Joe Johnson .12 .30
113 Josh Smith .12 .30
114 Mike Bibby .12 .30
115 Jeff Teague .15 .40
116 Al Horford .15 .40
117 Bob Pettit .15 .40
118 Maurice Evans .10 .25
119 Zaza Pachulia .10 .25
120 Marvin Williams .12 .30
121 Jamal Crawford .15 .40
122 Charlotte Bobcats Logo .10 .25
123 Boris Diaw .12 .30
124 Gerald Wallace .12 .30
125 Raja Bell .12 .30
126 Gerald Henderson .12 .30
127 DeSagana Diop .10 .25
128 Charlotte Bobcats Records .10 .25
129 D.J. Augustin .10 .25
130 Vladimir Radmanovic .10 .25
131 Tyson Chandler .12 .30
132 Raymond Felton .12 .30
133 Miami Heat Logo .10 .25
134 Dwyane Wade .25 .60
135 Mario Chalmers .12 .30
136 Michael Beasley .10 .25
137 Chris Quinn .10 .25
138 Udonis Haslem .10 .25
139 Miami Heat Records .10 .25
140 Daequan Cook .10 .25
141 Joel Anthony .15 .40
142 Quentin Richardson .12 .30
143 Jermaine O'Neal .12 .30
144 Orlando Magic Logo .10 .25
145 Dwight Howard .12 .30
146 Rashard Lewis .12 .30
147 Jameer Nelson .10 .25
148 Mickael Pietrus .10 .25
149 J.J. Redick .15 .40
150 Orlando Magic Records .10 .25
151 Anthony Johnson .10 .25
152 Vince Carter .20 .50
153 Ryan Anderson .12 .30
154 Matt Barnes .10 .25
155 Washington Wizards Logo .10 .25
156 Antawn Jamison .12 .30
157 Gilbert Arenas .12 .30
158 Caron Butler .12 .30
159 Nick Young .12 .30
160 Andray Blatche .10 .25
161 Elvin Hayes .15 .40
162 Mike James .10 .25
163 Mike Miller .12 .30
164 Randy Foye .10 .25
165 Fabricio Oberto .10 .25
166 Andre Iguodala MIN .12 .30
167 Joe Johnson MIN .12 .30
168 O.J. Mayo MIN .10 .25
169 Anthony Morrow 3PT .10 .25
170 Jameer Nelson 3PT .10 .25
171 Troy Murphy 3PT .10 .25
172 Chris Paul STEAL .20 .50
173 Dwyane Wade STEAL .25 .60
174 Jason Kidd STEAL .15 .40
175 David Lee DD .10 .25
176 Dwight Howard DD .12 .30
177 Chris Paul DD .20 .50
178 Terry Cummings PTT .12 .30
179 Blake Griffin PTT .60 1.50
180 Walt Frazier PTT .15 .40
181 Jordan Hill PTT .12 .30
182 Pau Gasol PTT .15 .40
183 Marc Gasol PTT .15 .40
184 Kevin Durant PTT .40 1.00
185 James Harden PTT .75 2.00
186 Mitch Richmond PTT .15 .40
187 Omri Casspi PTT .12 .30
188 Chris Mullin PTT .15 .40
189 Stephen Curry PTT 12.00 30.00
190 Alvan Adams PTT .10 .25
191 Taylor Griffin PTT .10 .25
192 Jose Calderon FT .10 .25
193 Ray Allen FT .15 .40
194 Steve Nash FT .15 .40
195 Dwight Howard BL .12 .30
196 Chris Andersen BL .12 .30
197 Marcus Camby BL .10 .25
198 Chris Paul AST .20 .50
199 Deron Williams AST .12 .30
200 Steve Nash AST .15 .40
201 Dwight Howard REB .12 .30
202 David Lee REB .10 .25
203 Troy Murphy REB .10 .25
204 Denver Nuggets Logo .10 .25
205 Carmelo Anthony .20 .50
206 Chauncey Billups .15 .40
207 J.R. Smith .12 .30
208 Ty Lawson .15 .40
209 Nene .12 .30
210 Denver Nuggets Records .10 .25
211 Kenyon Martin .12 .30
212 Arron Afflalo .10 .25
213 Chris Andersen .12 .30
214 Joey Graham .10 .25
215 Minnesota Timberwolves Logo .10 .25
216 Al Jefferson .12 .30
217 Ryan Gomes .10 .25
218 Kevin Love .15 .40
219 Jonny Flynn UER .10 .25
220 Ryan Hollins .10 .25
221 Minnesota Timberwolves Records .10 .25
222 Damien Wilkins .10 .25
223 Corey Brewer .10 .25
224 Ramon Sessions .12 .30
225 Sasha Pavlovic .10 .25
226 Oklahoma City Thunder Logo .10 .25
227 Kevin Durant .40 1.00
228 Jeff Green .12 .30
229 Russell Westbrook .40 1.00
230 James Harden .75 2.00
231 Nenad Krstic .10 .25
232 Oklahoma City Thunder Records .10 .25
233 Thabo Sefolosha .10 .25
234 Shaun Livingston .10 .25
235 Kevin Ollie .10 .25
236 Kyle Weaver .10 .25
237 Portland Trail Blazers Logo .10 .25
238 Brandon Roy .15 .40
239 LaMarcus Aldridge .15 .40
240 Travis Outlaw .12 .30
241 Jeff Pendergraph .10 .25
242 Steve Blake .10 .25
243 Bill Walton .15 .40
244 Rudy Fernandez .10 .25
245 Greg Oden .12 .30
246 Joel Przybilla .10 .25
247 Andre Miller .12 .30
248 Utah Jazz Logo .10 .25
249 Deron Williams .12 .30
250 Carlos Boozer .12 .30
251 Mehmet Okur .10 .25
252 Eric Maynor .10 .25
253 Ronnie Brewer .12 .30
254 Karl Malone .20 .50
255 Andrei Kirilenko .12 .30
256 C.J. Miles .12 .30
257 Kyle Korver .12 .30
258 Paul Millsap .12 .30
259 Golden State Warriors Logo .10 .25
260 Stephen Jackson .12 .30
261 Monta Ellis .12 .30
262 Corey Maggette .12 .30
263 Stephen Curry 12.00 30.00
264 Kelenna Azubuike .10 .25
265 Rick Barry .12 .30
266 Andris Biedrins .10 .25
267 Anthony Morrow .10 .25
268 Ronny Turiaf .10 .25
269 C.J. Watson .10 .25
270 Los Angeles Clippers Logo .10 .25
271 Eric Gordon .12 .30
272 Al Thornton .12 .30
273 Chris Kaman .12 .30
274 Blake Griffin .60 1.50
275 Marcus Camby .10 .25
276 Los Angeles Clippers Records .10 .25
277 Rasual Butler .10 .25
278 Baron Davis .12 .30
279 Sebastian Telfair .10 .25
280 Craig Smith .10 .25
281 Los Angeles Lakers Logo .10 .25
282 Kobe Bryant .60 1.50
283 Pau Gasol .15 .40
284 Andrew Bynum .10 .25
285 Adam Morrison .10 .25
286 Lamar Odom .12 .30
287 Kareem Abdul-Jabbar .25 .60
288 Derek Fisher .12 .30
289 Sasha Vujacic .10 .25
290 Jordan Farmar .10 .25
291 Ron Artest .15 .40
292 Phoenix Suns Logo .10 .25
293 Steve Nash .15 .40
294 Jason Richardson .15 .40
295 Amare Stoudemire .12 .30
296 Earl Clark .12 .30
297 Leandro Barbosa .12 .30
298 Phoenix Suns Records .10 .25
299 Channing Frye .12 .30
300 Grant Hill .20 .50
301 Jared Dudley .10 .25
302 Goran Dragic .30 .75
303 Sacramento Kings Logo .10 .25
304 Kevin Martin .12 .30
305 Andres Nocioni .10 .25
306 Francisco Garcia .10 .25
307 Tyreke Evans .12 .30
308 Spencer Hawes .10 .25
309 Sacramento Kings Records .10 .25
310 Jason Thompson .10 .25
311 Beno Udrih .10 .25
312 Sean May .10 .25
313 Sergio Rodriguez .10 .25
314 Dallas Mavericks Logo .10 .25
315 Dirk Nowitzki .20 .50
316 Jason Kidd .15 .40
317 Josh Howard .12 .30
318 Rodrigue Beaubois .10 .25
319 Jason Terry .12 .30
320 Dallas Mavericks Records .10 .25
321 Jose Barea .20 .50
322 Erick Dampier .10 .25
323 Shawn Marion .12 .30
324 Tim Thomas .10 .25
325 Houston Rockets Logo .10 .25
326 Yao Ming .20 .50
327 Tracy McGrady .15 .40
328 Luis Scola .12 .30
329 Jermaine Taylor .10 .25
330 Aaron Brooks .10 .25
331 Clyde Drexler .20 .50
332 Shane Battier .15 .40
333 Carl Landry .10 .25
334 Kyle Lowry .12 .30
335 Trevor Ariza .10 .25
336 Memphis Grizzlies Logo .10 .25
337 O.J. Mayo .10 .25
338 Rudy Gay .15 .40
339 Marc Gasol .15 .40
340 Hasheem Thabeet .10 .25
341 Mike Conley Jr. .12 .30
342 Memphis Grizzlies Records .10 .25
343 Darrell Arthur .12 .30
344 Marko Jaric .10 .25
345 Zach Randolph .12 .30
346 Steven Hunter .10 .25
347 New Orleans Hornets Logo .10 .25
348 Chris Paul .20 .50
349 David West .12 .30
350 Peja Stojakovic .15 .40
351 Darren Collison .15 .40
352 Ike Diogu .10 .25
353 New Orleans Hornets Records .10 .25
354 James Posey .10 .25
355 Emeka Okafor .12 .30
356 Hilton Armstrong .10 .25
357 Devin Brown .10 .25
358 San Antonio Spurs Logo .10 .25
359 Tony Parker .15 .40
360 Tim Duncan .25 .60
361 Manu Ginobili .15 .40
362 DeJuan Blair .12 .30
363 Roger Mason .10 .25
364 George Gervin .15 .40
365 Matt Bonner .10 .25
366 Michael Finley .15 .40
367 Richard Jefferson .12 .30
368 Antonio McDyess .12 .30
369 Kobe Bryant PTS .60 1.50
370 Dwyane Wade PTS .25 .60
371 LeBron James PTS .60 1.50
372 Shaquille O'Neal FG .30 .75
373 Nene FG .12 .30
374 Andris Biedrins FG .10 .25
375 Dwyane Wade SCO .25 .60
376 LeBron James SCO .60 1.50
377 Kobe Bryant SCO .60 1.50
378 LeBron James PRA .60 1.50
379 Dwyane Wade PRA .25 .60
380 Chris Paul PRA .20 .50
381 LeBron James MVP .60 1.50
382 Kobe Bryant FIN MVP .60 1.50
383 Jason Terry 6th Man .12 .30
384 Derrick Rose ROY .25 .60

2010-11 Panini Stickers

COMPLETE SET (378) 25.00 60.00
1 NBA Logo .08 .30
2 2011 All-Star Game Logo .08 .25
3 2011 Playoffs Logo .08 .25
4 2011 Finals Logo .08 .25
5 Western Conference Logo .08 .25
6 Eastern Conference Logo .08 .25
7 Boston Celtics Logo .08 .25
8 Paul Pierce .15 .40
9 Ray Allen .15 .40
10 Shaquille O'Neal .30 .75
11 Rajon Rondo .15 .40
12 Rasheed Wallace .15 .40
13 Jermaine O'Neal .12 .30
14 Nate Robinson .10 .25
15 Boston Celtics Leaders .08 .25
16 Glen Davis .10 .25
17 Kevin Garnett .25 .60
18 New Jersey Nets Logo .08 .25
19 Brook Lopez .12 .30
20 Travis Outlaw .12 .30
21 Jordan Farmar .10 .25
22 Devin Harris .10 .25
23 Anthony Morrow .10 .25
24 Kris Humphries .10 .25
25 Troy Murphy .10 .25
26 Terrence Williams .10 .25
27 Johan Petro .10 .25
28 New York Knicks Logo .08 .25
29 Amare Stoudemire .12 .30
30 Danilo Gallinari .12 .30
31 Kelenna Azubuike .10 .25
32 Wilson Chandler .12 .30
33 Bill Walker .10 .25
34 Ronny Turiaf .10 .25
35 Toney Douglas .10 .25
36 Raymond Felton .12 .30
37 Anthony Randolph .10 .25
38 Philadelphia 76ers Logo .08 .25
39 Andre Iguodala .12 .30
40 Louis Williams .12 .30
41 Thaddeus Young .10 .25
42 Elton Brand .15 .40
43 Jodie Meeks .15 .40
44 Marreese Speights .10 .25
45 Jrue Holiday .15 .40
46 Spencer Hawes .10 .25
47 Andres Nocioni .10 .25
48 Toronto Raptors Logo .08 .25
49 Andrea Bargnani .12 .30
50 Leandro Barbosa .12 .30
51 Amir Johnson .10 .25
52 Jarrett Jack .12 .30
53 Jose Calderon .10 .25
54 DeMar DeRozan .15 .40
55 Sonny Weems .10 .25
56 Julian Wright .10 .25
57 Marcus Banks .10 .25
58 Chicago Bulls Logo .08 .25
59 Derrick Rose .20 .50
60 Carlos Boozer .12 .30
61 Luol Deng .12 .30
62 Chicago Bulls Leaders .08 .25
63 Joakim Noah .12 .30
64 Ronnie Brewer .12 .30
65 Flip Murray .10 .25
66 Kyle Korver .12 .30
67 Jannero Pargo .10 .25
68 Taj Gibson .12 .30
69 Cleveland Cavaliers Logo .08 .25
70 Antawn Jamison .12 .30
71 J.J. Hickson .10 .25
72 Mo Williams .12 .30
73 Jamario Moon .10 .25
74 Anthony Parker .10 .25
75 Ryan Hollins .10 .25
76 Ramon Sessions .12 .30
77 Cleveland Cavaliers Leaders .08 .25
78 Daniel Gibson .12 .30
79 Anderson Varejao .10 .25
80 Detroit Pistons Logo .08 .25
81 Richard Hamilton .12 .30
82 Rodney Stuckey .12 .30
83 Tayshaun Prince .12 .30
84 Jonas Jerebko .10 .25
85 Ben Gordon .12 .30
86 Chris Wilcox .10 .25
87 DaJuan Summers .10 .25
88 Ben Wallace .12 .30
89 Austin Daye .10 .25
90 Indiana Pacers Logo .08 .25
91 Danny Granger .12 .30
92 Roy Hibbert .12 .30
93 T.J. Ford .10 .25
94 Darren Collison .12 .30
95 Dahntay Jones .10 .25
96 Brandon Rush .10 .25
97 A.J. Price .10 .25
98 Mike Dunleavy .10 .25
99 Tyler Hansbrough .12 .30
100 Milwaukee Bucks Logo .08 .25
101 Brandon Jennings .10 .25
102 Corey Maggette .12 .30
103 Andrew Bogut .12 .30
104 Carlos Delfino .10 .25
105 John Salmons .12 .30
106 Drew Gooden .12 .30
107 Chris Douglas-Roberts .10 .25
108 Milwaukee Bucks Leaders .08 .25
109 Luc Mbah a Moute .10 .25
110 Ersan Ilyasova .12 .30
111 Atlanta Hawks Logo .08 .25
112 Joe Johnson .12 .30
113 Josh Smith .12 .30
114 Mike Bibby .12 .30
115 Jamal Crawford .15 .40
116 Al Horford .12 .30
117 Maurice Evans .10 .25
118 Jeff Teague .12 .30
119 Marvin Williams .12 .30
120 Zaza Pachulia .10 .25
121 Charlotte Bobcats Logo .08 .25
122 Stephen Jackson .12 .30
123 Gerald Wallace .12 .30
124 Boris Diaw .12 .30
125 Charlotte Bobcats Leaders .08 .25
126 Nazr Mohammed .10 .25
127 D.J. Augustin .10 .25
128 Shaun Livingston .10 .25
129 Erick Dampier .10 .25
130 Tyrus Thomas .10 .25
131 Gerald Henderson .10 .25
132 Miami Heat Logo .08 .25
133 Dwyane Wade .25 .60
134 LeBron James .75 2.00
135 Chris Bosh .15 .40
136 Udonis Haslem .10 .25
137 Zydrunas Ilgauskas .12 .30
138 Mike Miller .12 .30
139 Carlos Arroyo .10 .25
140 Mario Chalmers .12 .30
141 Joel Anthony .10 .25
142 Orlando Magic Logo .08 .25
143 Dwight Howard .12 .30
144 Quentin Richardson .12 .30
145 Vince Carter .20 .50
146 Rashard Lewis .12 .30
147 Jameer Nelson .10 .25
148 Ryan Anderson .12 .30
149 J.J. Redick .15 .40
150 Orlando Magic Leaders .08 .25
151 Marcin Gortat .12 .30
152 Mickael Pietrus .10 .25
153 Washington Wizards Logo .08 .25
154 Gilbert Arenas .12 .30
155 Yi Jianlian .12 .30
156 Andray Blatche .10 .25
157 Josh Howard .12 .30
158 Al Thornton .10 .25
159 Kirk Hinrich .12 .30
160 Nick Young .12 .30
161 Fabricio Oberto .10 .25
162 JaVale McGee .12 .30
163 Dallas Mavericks Logo .08 .25
164 Dirk Nowitzki .20 .50
165 Jason Kidd .15 .40
166 Caron Butler .12 .30
167 Jason Terry .12 .30
168 DeShawn Stevenson .10 .25
169 Shawn Marion .12 .30
170 Brendan Haywood .10 .25
171 Dallas Mavericks Leaders .08 .25
172 Rodrigue Beaubois .10 .25
173 Tyson Chandler .12 .30
174 Houston Rockets Logo .08 .25
175 Aaron Brooks .10 .25
176 Kevin Martin .12 .30
177 Yao Ming .20 .50
178 Houston Rockets Leaders .08 .25
179 Shane Battier .12 .30
180 Kyle Lowry .12 .30
181 Chase Budinger .10 .25
182 Chuck Hayes .10 .25
183 Brad Miller .12 .30
184 Luis Scola .12 .30
185 Memphis Grizzlies Logo .08 .25
186 O.J. Mayo .10 .25
187 Mike Conley Jr. .15 .40
188 Rudy Gay .15 .40
189 Memphis Grizzlies Leaders .08 .25
190 Zach Randolph .12 .30
191 Sam Young .10 .25
192 Hasheem Thabeet .10 .25
193 Marc Gasol .15 .40
194 Darrell Arthur .10 .25
195 Hamed Haddadi .10 .25
196 New Orleans Hornets Logo .08 .25
197 Chris Paul .20 .50
198 Peja Stojakovic .15 .40
199 Trevor Ariza .10 .25
200 Emeka Okafor .12 .30
201 David West .12 .30
202 Marcus Thornton .10 .25
203 Aaron Gray .10 .25
204 Darius Songaila .10 .25
205 Marco Belinelli .10 .25
206 San Antonio Spurs Logo .08 .25
207 Tim Duncan .25 .60
208 Manu Ginobili .15 .40
209 Tony Parker .15 .40
210 San Antonio Spurs Leaders .08 .25
211 Richard Jefferson .12 .30
212 DeJuan Blair .10 .25
213 Matt Bonner .10 .25
214 Tiago Splitter .15 .40
215 Antonio McDyess .12 .30
216 George Hill .12 .30
217 Denver Nuggets Logo .08 .25
218 Carmelo Anthony .20 .50
219 Chauncey Billups .15 .40
220 Chris Andersen .12 .30
221 Arron Afflalo .10 .25
222 Ty Lawson .10 .25
223 Kenyon Martin .12 .30
224 Al Harrington .12 .30
225 Denver Nuggets Leaders .08 .25
226 J.R. Smith .12 .30
227 Nene .12 .30
228 Minnesota Timberwolves Logo .08 .25
229 Kevin Love .15 .40
230 Sebastian Telfair .10 .25
231 Corey Brewer .10 .25
232 Jonny Flynn .10 .25
233 Michael Beasley .10 .25
234 Kosta Koufos .10 .25
235 Luke Ridnour .12 .30
236 Martell Webster .12 .30
237 Darko Milicic .10 .25
238 Oklahoma City Thunder Logo .08 .25
239 Kevin Durant .40 1.00
240 Russell Westbrook .40 1.00
241 Jeff Green .12 .30
242 James Harden .25 .60
243 Serge Ibaka .12 .30
244 Nenad Krstic .10 .25
245 Nick Collison .12 .30
246 Oklahoma City Thunder Leaders .08 .25
247 Eric Maynor .10 .25
248 Thabo Sefolosha .10 .25
249 Portland Trail Blazers Logo .08 .25
250 LaMarcus Aldridge .15 .40
251 Andre Miller .12 .30
252 Jerryd Bayless .12 .30
253 Dante Cunningham .10 .25
254 Nicolas Batum .12 .30
255 Marcus Camby .10 .25
256 Brandon Roy .15 .40
257 Greg Oden .12 .30
258 Rudy Fernandez .10 .25
259 Utah Jazz Logo .08 .25
260 Deron Williams .12 .30
261 Al Jefferson .12 .30
262 Mehmet Okur .10 .25
263 Utah Jazz Leaders .08 .25
264 C.J. Miles .12 .30
265 Andrei Kirilenko .12 .30
266 Raja Bell .12 .30
267 Sundiata Gaines .10 .25
268 Paul Millsap .12 .30
269 Ronnie Price .10 .25
270 Golden State Warriors Logo .08 .25
271 Monta Ellis .12 .30
272 Stephen Curry .60 1.50
273 Andris Biedrins .10 .25
274 Golden State Warriors Leaders .08 .25
275 Dorell Wright .10 .25
276 Reggie Williams .15 .40
277 David Lee .10 .25
278 Charlie Bell .10 .25
279 Dan Gadzuric .10 .25
280 Vladimir Radmanovic .10 .25
281 Los Angeles Clippers Logo .08 .25
282 Chris Kaman .12 .30
283 Eric Gordon .12 .30
284 Baron Davis .12 .30
285 Rasual Butler .10 .25
286 Craig Smith .10 .25
287 Randy Foye .10 .25
288 Ryan Gomes .10 .25
289 Brian Cook .10 .25
290 Blake Griffin .15 .40
291 Los Angeles Lakers Logo .08 .25
292 Kobe Bryant .60 1.50
293 Ron Artest .15 .40
294 Pau Gasol .15 .40
295 Los Angeles Lakers Leaders .08 .25
296 Derek Fisher .12 .30
297 Lamar Odom .12 .30
298 Andrew Bynum .10 .25
299 Steve Blake .10 .25
300 Luke Walton .10 .25
301 Sasha Vujacic .10 .25
302 Phoenix Suns Logo .08 .25
303 Steve Nash .15 .40
304 Goran Dragic .12 .30
305 Hedo Turkoglu .12 .30
306 Phoenix Suns Leaders .08 .25
307 Jared Dudley .10 .25
308 Channing Frye .12 .30
309 Grant Hill .20 .50
310 Jason Richardson .15 .40
311 Robin Lopez .10 .25
312 Hakim Warrick .12 .30
313 Sacramento Kings Logo .08 .25
314 Tyreke Evans .10 .25
315 Carl Landry .10 .25
316 Beno Udrih .10 .25
317 Jason Thompson .10 .25
318 Omri Casspi .10 .25
319 Donte Greene .10 .25
320 Francisco Garcia .10 .25
321 Antoine Wright .10 .25
322 Samuel Dalembert .10 .25
323 Kobe Bryant 2000 .60 1.50
324 Kobe Bryant 2000 .60 1.50
325 Kobe Bryant 2001 .60 1.50
326 Kobe Bryant 2001 .60 1.50
327 Kobe Bryant 2002 .60 1.50
328 Kobe Bryant 2002 .60 1.50
329 Kobe Bryant 2004 .60 1.50
330 Kobe Bryant 2008 .60 1.50
331 Kobe Bryant 2009 .60 1.50
332 Kobe Bryant 2009 .60 1.50
333 Kobe Bryant 2010 .60 1.50
334 Kobe Bryant 2010 .60 1.50
335 Kobe Bryant 2010 .60 1.50
336 NBA Europe 2010 .08 .25
337 NBA Europe 2010 .08 .25
338 NBA Europe 2010 .08 .25
339 NBA Europe 2010 .08 .25
340 NBA London 2011 .08 .25
341 Noche Latina 2010 .08 .25
342 Noche Latina 2010 .08 .25
343 NBA Mexico 2010 .08 .25
344 NBA China 2010 .08 .25
345 NBA China 2010 .08 .25
346 NBA China 2010 .08 .25
347 NBA without borders .08 .25
348 NBA without borders .08 .25
349 John Wall .75 2.00
350 Evan Turner .12 .30
351 Derrick Favors .20 .50
352 Wesley Johnson .10 .25
353 DeMarcus Cousins .50 1.25
354 Ekpe Udoh .10 .25
355 Greg Monroe .20 .50
356 Al-Farouq Aminu .15 .40
357 Gordon Hayward .25 .60
358 Paul George .50 1.25
359 Cole Aldrich .12 .30
360 Xavier Henry .10 .25
361 Ed Davis .10 .25
362 Patrick Patterson .12 .30
363 Larry Sanders .10 .25
364 Luke Babbitt .12 .30
365 Eric Bledsoe .20 .50
366 Avery Bradley .20 .50
367 James Anderson .10 .25
368 Craig Brackins .10 .25
369 Elliot Williams .10 .25
370 Trevor Booker .12 .30
371 Damion James .10 .25
372 Dominique Jones .10 .25
373 LeBron James MVP .75 2.00
374 Tyreke Evans ROY .10 .25
375 Jamal Crawford 6th Man .15 .40
376 Kobe Bryant FIN MVP .60 1.50
377 Dwyane Wade AS MVP .25 .60
378 Dwight Howard DEF POY .12 .30

2012-13 Panini Stickers

COMPLETE SET (360) 20.00 50.00
1 Paul Pierce .15 .40
2 Rajon Rondo .15 .40
3 Kevin Garnett .25 .60
4 Avery Bradley .12 .30
5 Brandon Bass .10 .25
6 Jason Terry .12 .30
7 Jeff Green .12 .30
8 Chris Wilcox .10 .25
9 Deron Williams .12 .30
10 Brook Lopez .12 .30
11 Gerald Wallace .12 .30
12 MarShon Brooks .12 .30
13 Kris Humphries .10 .25
14 C.J. Watson .10 .25
15 Joe Johnson .12 .30
16 Reggie Evans .10 .25
17 Carmelo Anthony .20 .50
18 Amare Stoudemire .12 .30
19 Tyson Chandler .12 .30
20 J.R. Smith .12 .30
21 Jason Kidd .15 .40
22 Marcus Camby .12 .30
23 Raymond Felton .12 .30
24 Iman Shumpert .15 .40
25 Jrue Holiday .15 .40
26 Evan Turner .10 .25
27 Andrew Bynum .10 .25
28 Thaddeus Young .10 .25
29 Lavoy Allen .10 .25
30 Spencer Hawes .10 .25
31 Dorell Wright .10 .25
32 Nick Young .12 .30
33 Andrea Bargnani .12 .30

34 DeMar DeRozan .15 .40
35 Jose Calderon .10 .25
36 Ed Davis .10 .25
37 Amir Johnson .10 .25
38 Linas Kleiza .10 .25
39 Landry Fields .10 .25
40 Kyle Lowry .12 .30
41 Derrick Rose .20 .50
42 Luol Deng .12 .30
43 Joakim Noah .12 .30
44 Carlos Boozer .12 .30
45 Marco Belinelli .10 .25
46 Kirk Hinrich .12 .30
47 Richard Hamilton .12 .30
48 Taj Gibson .12 .30
49 Kyrie Irving .75 2.00
50 Tristan Thompson .15 .40
51 Alonzo Gee .10 .25
52 Daniel Gibson .12 .30
53 Anderson Varejao .10 .25
54 Samardo Samuels .10 .25
55 C.J. Miles .12 .30
56 Omri Casspi .10 .25
57 Greg Monroe .12 .30
58 Brandon Knight .15 .40
59 Tayshaun Prince .12 .30
60 Jason Maxiell .10 .25
61 Corey Maggette .12 .30
62 Rodney Stuckey .12 .30
63 Jonas Jerebko .10 .25
64 Austin Daye .10 .25
65 Roy Hibbert .12 .30
66 Danny Granger .12 .30
67 David West .12 .30
68 Paul George .20 .50
69 Tyler Hansbrough .12 .30
70 George Hill .12 .30
71 D.J. Augustin .10 .25
72 Gerald Green .12 .30
73 Brandon Jennings .10 .25
74 Monta Ellis .12 .30
75 Ersan Ilyasova .10 .25
76 Luc Mbah A Moute .10 .25
77 Drew Gooden .12 .30
78 Samuel Dalembert .10 .25
79 Ekpe Udoh .10 .25
80 Mike Dunleavy .10 .25
81 Al Horford .12 .30
82 Josh Smith .12 .30
83 Jeff Teague .12 .30
84 Zaza Pachulia .10 .25
85 Kyle Korver .12 .30
86 Louis Williams .12 .30
87 Anthony Morrow .10 .25
88 Devin Harris .10 .25
89 Kemba Walker .30 .75
90 Gerald Henderson .10 .25
91 Bismack Biyombo .10 .25
92 Ramon Sessions .12 .30
93 B.J. Mullens .10 .25
94 Ben Gordon .12 .30
95 Reggie Williams .12 .30
96 Tyrus Thomas .10 .25
97 LeBron James .60 1.50
98 Dwyane Wade .25 .60
99 Chris Bosh .15 .40
100 Udonis Haslem .10 .25
101 Mario Chalmers .12 .30
102 Shane Battier .12 .30
103 Norris Cole .10 .25
104 Ray Allen .15 .40
105 Jameer Nelson .10 .25
106 Glen Davis .10 .25
107 Hedo Turkoglu .12 .30
108 J.J. Redick .15 .40
109 Nikola Vucevic .15 .40
110 Gustavo Ayon .10 .25
111 Arron Afflalo .12 .30
112 Al Harrington .12 .30
113 John Wall .20 .50
114 Nene .12 .30
115 Jordan Crawford .10 .25
116 Trevor Ariza .10 .25
117 Trevor Booker .10 .25
118 Kevin Seraphin .10 .25
119 Emeka Okafor .12 .30
120 Chris Singleton .10 .25
121 Dirk Nowitzki .20 .50
122 Shawn Marion .12 .30
123 Vince Carter .20 .50
124 Rodrigue Beaubois .10 .25
125 Darren Collison .12 .30
126 Chris Kaman .12 .30
127 Elton Brand .15 .40
128 O.J. Mayo .10 .25
129 Kevin Martin .12 .30
130 Chandler Parsons .15 .40
131 Patrick Patterson .10 .25
132 Jeremy Lin .15 .40
133 Shaun Livingston .10 .25
134 Omer Asik .12 .30
135 Gary Forbes .10 .25
136 Carlos Delfino .10 .25
137 Rudy Gay .15 .40
138 Marc Gasol .15 .40
139 Mike Conley .12 .30
140 Zach Randolph .12 .30
141 Marreese Speights .10 .25
142 Tony Allen .10 .25
143 Darrell Arthur .10 .25
144 Jerryd Bayless .12 .30
145 Eric Gordon .12 .30
146 Jason Smith .10 .25
147 Ryan Anderson .12 .30
148 Al-Farouq Aminu .12 .30
149 Greivis Vasquez .12 .30
150 Xavier Henry .10 .25
151 Lance Thomas .10 .25
152 Robin Lopez .10 .25
153 Tim Duncan .25 .60
154 Tony Parker .15 .40
155 Manu Ginobili .15 .40
156 Gary Neal .12 .30
157 Kawhi Leonard .75 2.00
158 Tiago Splitter .12 .30
159 Matt Bonner .10 .25
160 Stephen Jackson .12 .30
161 Ty Lawson .10 .25
162 Danilo Gallinari .10 .25
163 Wilson Chandler .12 .30
164 Kenneth Faried .15 .40
165 Andre Miller .12 .30
166 Andre Iguodala .12 .30
167 Timofey Mozgov .10 .25
168 JaVale McGee .12 .30
169 Kevin Love .15 .40
170 Ricky Rubio .15 .40
171 Nikola Pekovic .10 .25
172 Derrick Williams .10 .25
173 Andrei Kirilenko .12 .30
174 J.J. Barea .12 .30
175 Luke Ridnour .12 .30
176 Brandon Roy .15 .40
177 Kevin Durant .40 1.00
178 Russell Westbrook .40 1.00
179 James Harden .25 .60
180 Serge Ibaka .12 .30
181 Thabo Sefolosha .10 .25
182 Nick Collison .12 .30
183 Kendrick Perkins .10 .25
184 Daequan Cook .10 .25
185 LaMarcus Aldridge .15 .40
186 Nicolas Batum .12 .30
187 J.J. Hickson .10 .25
188 Nolan Smith .10 .25
189 Luke Babbitt .10 .25
190 Wesley Matthews .10 .25
191 Ronnie Price .10 .25
192 Elliot Williams .10 .25
193 Paul Millsap .15 .40
194 Al Jefferson .12 .30
195 Gordon Hayward .15 .40
196 Derrick Favors .12 .30
197 Alec Burks .15 .40
198 Enes Kanter .12 .30
199 Mo Williams .12 .30
200 Marvin Williams .12 .30
201 David Lee .10 .25
202 Stephen Curry .60 1.50
203 Klay Thompson .60 1.50
204 Carl Landry .10 .25
205 Charles Jenkins .10 .25
206 Jarrett Jack .12 .30
207 Brandon Rush .10 .25
208 Andrew Bogut .12 .30
209 Chris Paul .20 .50
210 Blake Griffin .15 .40
211 DeAndre Jordan .15 .40
212 Caron Butler .12 .30
213 Grant Hill .20 .50
214 Eric Bledsoe .12 .30
215 Chauncey Billups .15 .40
216 Lamar Odom .12 .30
217 Kobe Bryant .60 1.50
218 Pau Gasol .15 .40
219 Steve Nash .15 .40
220 Dwight Howard .12 .30
221 Metta World Peace .15 .40
222 Steve Blake .10 .25
223 Jordan Hill .10 .25
224 Antawn Jamison .12 .30
225 Marcin Gortat .12 .30
226 Jared Dudley .10 .25
227 Channing Frye .12 .30
228 Luis Scola .12 .30
229 Markieff Morris .15 .40
230 Wesley Johnson .12 .30
231 Goran Dragic .12 .30
232 Michael Beasley .10 .25
233 Tyreke Evans .10 .25
234 DeMarcus Cousins .15 .40
235 Isaiah Thomas .25 .60
236 Marcus Thornton .10 .25
237 Jimmer Fredette .10 .25
238 Jason Thompson .10 .25
239 Aaron Brooks .10 .25
240 Chuck Hayes .10 .25
241 Anthony Davis .75 2.00
242 Michael Kidd-Gilchrist .15 .40
243 Bradley Beal .25 .60
244 Dion Waiters .15 .40
245 Thomas Robinson .12 .30
246 Damian Lillard .60 1.50
247 Harrison Barnes .25 .60
248 Terrence Ross .15 .40
249 Andre Drummond .25 .60
250 Austin Rivers .15 .40
251 Miami Heat NBA Champs .60 1.50
Dwyane Wade
LeBron James
252 LeBron James MVP .60 1.50
253 LeBron James .60 1.50
Kevin Durant Finals
254 Oklahoma City Thunder West Champs .40
1.00
255 Miami Heat East Champs .15 .40
Chris Bosh
256 Kobe Bryant .60 1.50
LeBron James ASG
257 Kevin Durant ASG .40 1.00
258 Blake Griffin ASG .15 .40
259 2012 All-Star Game .20 .50
260 Deron Williams ASG .12 .30
261 Kevin Love ASG .15 .40
262 LeBron James MVP .60 1.50
263 Kyrie Irving ROY .75 2.00
264 James Harden 6th Man .25 .60
265 Tyson Chandler D-POY .12 .30
266 Ryan Anderson MIP .12 .30
A1 NBA Logo FOIL .15 .40
A2 NBA Trophy Logo FOIL .15 .40
A3 Eastern Conference Logo FOIL .15 .40
A4 Western Conference Logo FOIL .15 .40
A5 Boston Celtics Logo FOIL .15 .40
A6 Brooklyn Nets Logo FOIL .15 .40
A7 New York Knicks Logo FOIL .15 .40
A8 Philadelphia 76ers Logo FOIL .15 .40
A9 Toronto Raptors Logo FOIL .15 .40
A10 Chicago Bulls Logo FOIL .15 .40
A11 Cleveland Cavaliers Logo FOIL .15 .40
A12 Detroit Pistons Logo FOIL .15 .40
A13 Indiana Pacers Logo FOIL .15 .40
A14 Milwaukee Bucks Logo FOIL .15 .40
A15 Atlanta Hawks Logo FOIL .15 .40
A16 Charlotte Bobcats Logo FOIL .15 .40
A17 Miami Heat Logo FOIL .15 .40
A18 Orlando Magic Logo FOIL .15 .40
A19 Washington Wizards Logo FOIL .15 .40
A20 Dallas Mavericks Logo FOIL .15 .40
A21 Houston Rockets Logo FOIL .15 .40
A22 Memphis Grizzlies Logo FOIL .15 .40
A23 New Orleans Hornets Logo FOIL .15 .40
A24 San Antonio Spurs Logo FOIL .15 .40
A25 Denver Nuggets Logo FOIL .15 .40
A26 Minnesota Timberwolves Logo FOIL.15 .40
A27 Oklahoma City Thunder Logo FOIL.15 .40
A28 Portland Trail Blazers Logo FOIL .15 .40
A29 Utah Jazz Logo FOIL .15 .40
A30 Golden State Warriors Logo FOIL .15 .40
A31 Los Angeles Clippers Logo FOIL .15 .40
A32 Los Angeles Lakers Logo FOIL .15 .40
A33 Phoenix Suns Logo FOIL .15 .40
A34 Sacramento Kings Logo FOIL .15 .40
A35 Paul Pierce FOIL .25 .60
A36 Rajon Rondo FOIL .25 .60
A37 Deron Williams FOIL .20 .50
A38 Brook Lopez FOIL .20 .50
A39 Carmelo Anthony FOIL .30 .75
A40 Amare Stoudemire FOIL .20 .50
A41 Jrue Holiday FOIL .25 .60
A42 Evan Turner FOIL .15 .40
A43 Andrea Bargnani FOIL .20 .50
A44 DeMar DeRozan FOIL .25 .60
A45 Derrick Rose FOIL .30 .75
A46 Luol Deng FOIL .20 .50
A47 Kyrie Irving FOIL 1.25 3.00
A48 Tristan Thompson FOIL .25 .60
A49 Greg Monroe FOIL .20 .50
A50 Brandon Knight FOIL .25 .60
A51 Roy Hibbert FOIL .20 .50
A52 Danny Granger FOIL .20 .50
A53 Brandon Jennings FOIL .15 .40
A54 Monta Ellis FOIL .20 .50
A55 Al Horford FOIL .20 .50
A56 Josh Smith FOIL .20 .50
A57 Kemba Walker FOIL .50 1.25
A58 Gerald Henderson FOIL .15 .40
A59 LeBron James FOIL 1.00 2.50
A60 Dwyane Wade FOIL .40 1.00
A61 Jameer Nelson FOIL .15 .40
A62 Glen Davis FOIL .15 .40
A63 John Wall FOIL .30 .75
A64 Nene FOIL .20 .50
A65 Dirk Nowitzki FOIL .30 .75
A66 Shawn Marion FOIL .20 .50
A67 Kevin Martin FOIL .20 .50
A68 Jeremy Lin FOIL .25 .60
A69 Rudy Gay FOIL .25 .60
A70 Marc Gasol FOIL .25 .60
A71 Eric Gordon FOIL .20 .50
A72 Anthony David FOIL 1.25 3.00
A73 Tim Duncan FOIL .40 1.00
A74 Tony Parker FOIL .25 .60
A75 Ty Lawson FOIL .15 .40
A76 Danilo Gallinari FOIL .15 .40
A77 Kevin Love FOIL .25 .60
A78 Ricky Rubio FOIL .25 .60
A79 Kevin Durant FOIL .60 1.50
A80 Russell Westbrook FOIL .60 1.50
A81 LaMarcus Aldridge FOIL .25 .60
A82 Nicolas Batum FOIL .20 .50
A83 Paul Millsap FOIL .25 .60
A84 Al Jefferson FOIL .20 .50
A85 David Lee FOIL .15 .40
A86 Stephen Curry FOIL 1.00 2.50
A87 Chris Paul FOIL .30 .75
A88 Blake Griffin FOIL .25 .60
A89 Kobe Bryant FOIL 1.00 2.50
A90 Steve Nash FOIL .25 .60
A91 Marcin Gortat FOIL .20 .50
A92 Goran Dragic FOIL .20 .50
A93 Tyreke Evans FOIL .15 .40
A94 DeMarcus Cousins FOIL .25 .60

2013-14 Panini Stickers

COMPLETE SET (363) 20.00 50.00
1 NBA Logo .20 .50
2 NBA Logo .20 .50
3 NBA Champions .20 .50
4 NBA Champions .20 .50
5 Brandon Bass .10 .25
6 Jeff Green .12 .30
7 Rajon Rondo .15 .40
8 Jared Sullinger .10 .25
9 Gerald Wallace .12 .30
10 Keith Bogans .10 .25
11 Avery Bradley .12 .30
12 MarShon Brooks .12 .30
13 Rajon Rondo .15 .40
14 Jeff Green .12 .30
15 Brook Lopez .12 .30
16 Andray Blatche .10 .25
17 Brook Lopez .12 .30
18 Kevin Garnett .25 .60
19 Reggie Evans .10 .25
20 Andrei Kirilenko .12 .30
21 Paul Pierce .15 .40
22 Joe Johnson .12 .30
23 Deron Williams .12 .30
24 Deron Williams .12 .30
25 Tyson Chandler .12 .30
26 Andrea Bargnani .12 .30
27 Carmelo Anthony .20 .50
28 Amar'e Stoudemire .12 .30
29 Carmelo Anthony .20 .50
30 Metta World Peace .15 .40
31 Iman Shumpert .10 .25
32 Raymond Felton .12 .30
33 J.R. Smith .12 .30
34 Tyson Chandler .12 .30
35 Kwame Brown .10 .25
36 LaVoy Allen .10 .25
37 Evan Turner .10 .25
38 Spencer Hawes .10 .25
39 Arnett Moultrie .10 .25
40 Thaddeus Young .10 .25
41 Evan Turner .10 .25
42 Michael Carter-Williams .15 .40
43 Jason Richardson .15 .40
44 Thaddeus Young .10 .25
45 Jonas Valanciunas .12 .30
46 Tyler Hansbrough .12 .30
47 Rudy Gay .15 .40
48 Amir Johnson .10 .25
49 Landry Fields .10 .25
50 Rudy Gay .15 .40
51 DeMar DeRozan .15 .40
52 Kyle Lowry .12 .30
53 Terrence Ross .12 .30
54 DeMar DeRozan .15 .40
55 Joakim Noah .12 .30
56 Carlos Boozer .12 .30
57 Derrick Rose .20 .50
58 Luol Deng .12 .30
59 Mike Dunleavy .10 .25
60 Taj Gibson .12 .30
61 Jimmy Butler .15 .40
62 Kirk Hinrich .12 .30
63 Derrick Rose .20 .50
64 Joakim Noah .12 .30
65 Andrew Bynum .10 .25
66 Anderson Varejao .10 .25
67 Kyrie Irving .30 .75
68 Tyler Zeller .12 .30
69 Tristan Thompson .12 .30
70 Kyrie Irving .30 .75
71 Jarrett Jack .12 .30
72 C.J. Miles .12 .30
73 Dion Waiters .12 .30
74 Dion Waiters .12 .30
75 Andre Drummond .15 .40
76 Greg Monroe .12 .30
77 Greg Monroe .12 .30
78 Jonas Jerebko .10 .25
79 Josh Smith .12 .30
80 Chauncey Billups .15 .40
81 Brandon Jennings .10 .25
82 Kyle Singler .10 .25
83 Rodney Stuckey .12 .30
84 Andre Drummond .15 .40
85 Roy Hibbert .12 .30
86 Chris Copeland .10 .25
87 Paul George .20 .50
88 Danny Granger .12 .30
89 Luis Scola .12 .30
90 David West .12 .30
91 Paul George .20 .50
92 George Hill .12 .30
93 Lance Stephenson .12 .30
94 Roy Hibbert .12 .30
95 Larry Sanders .10 .25
96 Ekpe Udoh .10 .25
97 Larry Sanders .10 .25
98 Zaza Pachulia .10 .25
99 John Henson .12 .30
100 Ersan Ilyasova .10 .25
101 Brandon Knight .12 .30
102 O.J. Mayo .10 .25
103 Luke Ridnour .12 .30
104 Ersan Ilyasova .10 .25
105 Al Horford .12 .30
106 Elton Brand .15 .40
107 Al Horford .12 .30
108 DeMarre Carroll .10 .25
109 Paul Millsap .15 .40
110 Kyle Korver .12 .30
111 John Jenkins .10 .25
112 Jeff Teague .12 .30
113 Louis Williams .12 .30
114 Louis Williams .12 .30
115 Bismack Biyombo .10 .25
116 Al Jefferson .12 .30
117 Kemba Walker .15 .40
118 Jeff Adrien .10 .25
119 Michael Kidd-Gilchrist .15 .40
120 Jeff Taylor .10 .25
121 Gerald Henderson .10 .25
122 Ramon Sessions .12 .30
123 Kemba Walker .15 .40
124 Michael Kidd-Gilchrist .15 .40
125 Chris Bosh .15 .40
126 Chris Andersen .12 .30
127 LeBron James .60 1.50
128 Udonis Haslem .10 .25
129 LeBron James .60 1.50
130 Ray Allen .15 .40
131 Mario Chalmers .12 .30
132 Norris Cole .10 .25
133 Dwyane Wade .25 .60
134 Dwyane Wade .25 .60
135 Nikola Vucevic .12 .30
136 Glen Davis .10 .25
137 Nikola Vucevic .12 .30
138 Maurice Harkless .10 .25
139 Tobias Harris .12 .30
140 Andrew Nicholson .10 .25
141 Hedo Turkoglu .12 .30
142 Arron Afflalo .10 .25
143 Jameer Nelson .10 .25
144 Tobias Harris .12 .30
145 Emeka Okafor .12 .30
146 Kevin Seraphin .10 .25
147 John Wall .20 .50
148 Trevor Ariza .10 .25
149 Trevor Booker .10 .25
150 Nene .12 .30
151 Martell Webster .10 .25
152 Bradley Beal .15 .40
153 John Wall .20 .50
154 Bradley Beal .15 .40
155 Brandan Wright .10 .25
156 Jae Crowder .12 .30
157 Dirk Nowitzki .20 .50
158 Shawn Marion .12 .30
159 Dirk Nowitzki .20 .50
160 Vince Carter .20 .50
161 Jose Calderon .10 .25
162 Wayne Ellington .10 .25
163 Monta Ellis .12 .30
164 Shawn Marion .12 .30
165 Omer Asik .12 .30
166 Dwight Howard .12 .30
167 James Harden .25 .60
168 Donatas Motiejunas .12 .30
169 Chandler Parsons .12 .30
170 Francisco Garcia .10 .25
171 Patrick Beverley .10 .25
172 James Harden .25 .60
173 Jeremy Lin .15 .40
174 Jeremy Lin .15 .40
175 Marc Gasol .15 .40
176 Kosta Koufos .10 .25
177 Marc Gasol .15 .40
178 Ed Davis .10 .25
179 Quincy Pondexter .10 .25
180 Tayshaun Prince .12 .30
181 Zach Randolph .12 .30
182 Tony Allen .10 .25
183 Mike Conley .12 .30
184 Zach Randolph .12 .30
185 Anthony Davis .30 .75
186 Jason Smith .10 .25
187 Anthony Davis .30 .75
188 Al-Farouq Aminu .12 .30
189 Ryan Anderson .12 .30
190 Tyreke Evans .10 .25
191 Eric Gordon .12 .30
192 Jrue Holiday .15 .40
193 Brian Roberts .10 .25
194 Ryan Anderson .12 .30
195 Tiago Splitter .12 .30
196 Tim Duncan .25 .60
197 Tim Duncan .25 .60
198 Kawhi Leonard .25 .60
199 Danny Green .12 .30
200 Marco Belinelli .10 .25
201 Manu Ginobili .15 .40
202 Cory Joseph .10 .25
203 Tony Parker .15 .40
204 Tony Parker .15 .40
205 JaVale McGee .12 .30
206 J.J. Hickson .10 .25
207 Ty Lawson .10 .25
208 Wilson Chandler .12 .30
209 Kenneth Faried .12 .30
210 Danilo Gallinari .10 .25
211 Randy Foye .10 .25
212 Ty Lawson .10 .25
213 Andre Miller .12 .30
214 Danilo Gallinari .10 .25
215 Nikola Pekovic .10 .25
216 Kevin Love .15 .40
217 Kevin Love .15 .40
218 Chase Budinger .10 .25
219 Derrick Williams .10 .25
220 Jose Barea .12 .30
221 Kevin Martin .12 .30
222 Ricky Rubio .15 .40
223 Alexy Shved .10 .25
224 Ricky Rubio .15 .40
225 Kendrick Perkins .10 .25
226 Nick Collison .12 .30
227 Kevin Durant .40 1.00
228 Serge Ibaka .12 .30
229 Kevin Durant .40 1.00
230 Jeremy Lamb .10 .25
231 Reggie Jackson .12 .30
232 Thabo Sefolosha .10 .25
233 Russell Westbrook .40 1.00
234 Russell Westbrook .40 1.00
235 Meyers Leonard .10 .25
236 Robin Lopez .10 .25
237 LaMarcus Aldridge .15 .40
238 LaMarcus Aldridge .15 .40
239 Victor Claver .10 .25
240 Thomas Robinson .10 .25
241 Nicolas Batum .12 .30
242 Damian Lillard .30 .75
243 Wesley Matthews .10 .25
244 Damian Lillard .30 .75
245 Enes Kanter .10 .25
246 Derrick Favors .12 .30
247 Gordon Hayward .15 .40
248 Jeremy Evans .10 .25
249 Marvin Williams .12 .30
250 Gordon Hayward .15 .40
251 Brandon Rush .10 .25
252 Alec Burks .10 .25
253 John Lucas III .10 .25
254 Derrick Favors .12 .30
255 Andrew Bogut .12 .30
256 Festus Ezeli .10 .25
257 Stephen Curry .60 1.50
258 David Lee .10 .25
259 Harrison Barnes .12 .30
260 Draymond Green .20 .50
261 Andre Iguodala .12 .30
262 Stephen Curry .60 1.50
263 Klay Thompson .20 .50
264 David Lee .10 .25
265 Ryan Hollins .10 .25
266 DeAndre Jordan .15 .40
267 Chris Paul .20 .50
268 Matt Barnes .10 .25
269 Blake Griffin .15 .40
270 Darren Collison .12 .30
271 Jamal Crawford .15 .40
272 Chris Paul .20 .50
273 J.J. Redick .15 .40
274 Blake Griffin .15 .40
275 Jordan Hill .10 .25
276 Chris Kaman .12 .30
277 Kobe Bryant .60 1.50
278 Pau Gasol .15 .40
279 Wesley Johnson .12 .30
280 Nick Young .15 .40
281 Steve Blake .10 .25
282 Kobe Bryant .60 1.50
283 Steve Nash .15 .40
284 Pau Gasol .15 .40
285 Marcin Gortat .12 .30
286 Michael Beasley .10 .25
287 Marcin Gortat .12 .30
288 Caron Butler .12 .30
289 Markieff Morris .10 .25
290 Marcus Morris .10 .25
291 Eric Bledsoe .12 .30
292 Goran Dragic .12 .30
293 Kendall Marshall .12 .30
294 Goran Dragic .12 .30
295 DeMarcus Cousins .15 .40
296 Patrick Patterson .10 .25
297 DeMarcus Cousins .15 .40
298 Jason Thompson .10 .25
299 John Salmons .12 .30
300 Jimmer Fredette .10 .25
301 Isaiah Thomas .15 .40
302 Marcus Thornton .10 .25
303 Greivis Vasquez .12 .30
304 Isaiah Thomas .15 .40
305 Carmelo Anthony .20 .50
306 Dwight Howard .12 .30
307 DeAndre Jordan .15 .40
308 Kevin Durant .40 1.00
309 Rajon Rondo .15 .40
310 Jose Calderon .10 .25
311 Chris Paul .20 .50
312 Serge Ibaka .12 .30
313 Zach Randolph .12 .30
314 David Lee .10 .25
315 Kobe Bryant .60 1.50
316 Marc Gasol .15 .40
317 Tim Duncan .25 .60
318 Danilo Gallinari .10 .25
319 Dirk Nowitzki .20 .50
320 Andrew Bogut .12 .30
321 Tony Parker .15 .40
322 Steve Nash .15 .40
323 Kevin Durant .40 1.00
324 Anderson Varejao .10 .25
325 All-Star Game .20 .50
326 All-Star Game .20 .50
327 All-Star Game .20 .50
328 All-Star Game .20 .50
329 All-Star Game .20 .50
330 Rising Star Challenge .20 .50
331 Rising Star Challenge .20 .50
332 Terrence Ross .12 .30
333 Kyrie Irving .30 .75
334 Chris Paul .20 .50
335 All-Star Game .20 .50
336 Anthony Bennett .12 .30
337 Victor Oladipo .20 .50
338 Otto Porter .15 .40
339 Cody Zeller .12 .30
340 Alex Len .12 .30
341 Nerlens Noel .20 .50
342 Ben McLemore .12 .30
343 Kentavious Caldwell-Pope .15 .40
344 Trey Burke .12 .30
345 C.J. McCollum .25 .60
346 Damian Lillard .30 .75
347 Anthony Davis .30 .75
348 Bradley Beal .15 .40
349 Harrison Barnes .12 .30
350 Michael Kidd-Gilchrist .15 .40
351 Dion Waiters .12 .30
352 Terrence Ross .12 .30
353 Andre Drummond .15 .40
354 Tyler Zeller .12 .30
355 John Henson .12 .30
356 Festus Ezeli .10 .25
357 Jared Sullinger .10 .25
358 LeBron James .60 1.50
359 Marc Gasol .15 .40
360 Damian Lillard .30 .75
361 J.R. Smith .12 .30
362 Paul George .20 .50
363 LeBron James .60 1.50

2014-15 Panini Stickers

COMPLETE SET (470) 20.00 50.00
1 Panini Knight Logo .10 .25
2 NBA Logo .10 .25
3 Rajon Rondo FOIL .25 .60
4 Jeff Green FOIL .20 .50
5 Celtics Home Jersey .10 .25
6 Celtics Road Jersey .10 .25
7 Rajon Rondo .15 .40
8 Jeff Green .12 .30
9 Avery Bradley .12 .30
10 Brandon Bass .10 .25
11 Celtics Logo .10 .25
12 Jared Sullinger .10 .25
13 Kelly Olynyk .10 .25
14 Tyler Zeller .12 .30
15 Marcus Smart .15 .40
16 Joe Johnson FOIL .20 .50
17 Deron Williams FOIL .20 .50
18 Nets Home Jersey .10 .25
19 Nets Road Jersey .10 .25
20 Joe Johnson .12 .30
21 Deron Williams .12 .30
22 Kevin Garnett .25 .60
23 Mason Plumlee .12 .30
24 Nets Logo .10 .25
25 Alan Anderson .10 .25
26 Brook Lopez .12 .30
27 Andrei Kirilenko .12 .30
28 Mirza Teletovic .10 .25
29 Carmelo Anthony FOIL .30 .75
30 Tim Hardaway Jr. FOIL .15 .40
31 Knicks Home Jersey .10 .25
32 Knicks Road Jersey .10 .25
33 Carmelo Anthony .20 .50
34 Tim Hardaway Jr. .10 .25
35 Amar'e Stoudemire .15 .40
36 J.R. Smith .12 .30
37 Knicks Logo .10 .25
38 Andrea Bargnani .12 .30
39 Pablo Prigioni .10 .25
40 Jose Calderon .10 .25
41 Iman Shumpert .10 .25
42 M.Carter-Williams FOIL .15 .40
43 Tony Wroten FOIL .15 .40
44 76ers Home Jersey .10 .25
45 76ers Road Jersey .10 .25
46 Michael Carter-Williams .10 .25
47 Alexey Shved .10 .25
48 Nerlens Noel .12 .30
49 Henry Sims .10 .25
50 76ers Logo .10 .25
51 Tony Wroten .10 .25
52 Joel Embiid .50 1.25
53 Jason Richardson .15 .40
54 Hollis Thompson .12 .30
55 DeMar DeRozan FOIL .25 .60
56 Kyle Lowry FOIL .20 .50
57 Raptors Home Jersey .10 .25
58 Raptors Road Jersey .10 .25
59 DeMar DeRozan .15 .40
60 Kyle Lowry .12 .30
61 Greivis Vasquez .12 .30
62 Jonas Valanciunas .12 .30
63 Raptors Logo .10 .25
64 Terrence Ross .12 .30
65 Amir Johnson .10 .25
66 Patrick Patterson .10 .25
67 Louis Williams .12 .30
68 Derrick Rose FOIL .30 .75
69 Joakim Noah FOIL .20 .50
70 Bulls Home Jersey .10 .25
71 Bulls Road Jersey .10 .25
72 Derrick Rose .20 .50
73 Joakim Noah .12 .30
74 Pau Gasol .15 .40
75 Tony Snell .10 .25
76 Bulls Logo .10 .25
77 Kirk Hinrich .12 .30
78 Jimmy Butler .15 .40
79 Taj Gibson .12 .30
80 Mike Dunleavy .10 .25
81 Kyrie Irving FOIL .50 1.25
82 LeBron James FOIL 1.00 2.50
83 Cavaliers Home Jersey .10 .25
84 Cavaliers Road Jersey .10 .25
85 Kyrie Irving .30 .75
86 LeBron James .60 1.50
87 Dion Waiters .12 .30
88 Tristan Thompson .12 .30
89 Cavaliers Logo .10 .25
90 Shawn Marion .12 .30
91 Kevin Love .15 .40
92 Anderson Varejao .10 .25
93 Matt Dellavedova .12 .30
94 Andre Drummond FOIL .25 .60
95 Greg Monroe FOIL .20 .50
96 Pistons Home Jersey .10 .25
97 Pistons Road Jersey .10 .25
98 Greg Monroe .12 .30
99 Andre Drummond .15 .40
100 Brandon Jennings .10 .25
101 Josh Smith .12 .30
102 Pistons Logo .10 .25
103 Kyle Singler .10 .25
104 Kentavious Caldwell-Pope .10 .25
105 Jonas Jerebko .10 .25
106 Luigi Datome .10 .25
107 Roy Hibbert FOIL .20 .50
108 David West FOIL .20 .50
109 Pacers Home Jersey .10 .25
110 Pacers Road Jersey .10 .25
111 Paul George .20 .50
112 David West .12 .30
113 Roy Hibbert .12 .30
114 Luis Scola .12 .30
115 Pacers Logo .10 .25
116 Rodney Stuckey .12 .30
117 C.J. Watson .10 .25
118 George Hill .12 .30
119 Ian Mahinmi .10 .25
120 Jabari Parker FOIL .40 1.00
121 G.Antetokounmpo FOIL .50 1.25
122 Bucks Home Jersey .10 .25
123 Bucks Road Jersey .10 .25
124 Jabari Parker .25 .60
125 Giannis Antetokounmpo .30 .75
126 Brandon Knight .12 .30
127 Larry Sanders .10 .25
128 Bucks Logo .10 .25
129 Ersan Ilyasova .10 .25
130 John Henson .12 .30
131 Nate Wolters .12 .30
132 Zaza Pachulia .10 .25
133 Jeff Teague FOIL .20 .50
134 Paul Millsap FOIL .25 .60
135 Hawks Home Jersey .10 .25
136 Hawks Road Jersey .10 .25
137 Jeff Teague .12 .30
138 Paul Millsap .15 .40
139 Al Horford .12 .30
140 Dennis Schroder .12 .30
141 Hawks Logo .10 .25
142 Elton Brand .15 .40
143 Kyle Korver .12 .30
144 Pero Antic .10 .25
145 DeMarre Carroll .10 .25
146 Al Jefferson FOIL .20 .50
147 Kemba Walker FOIL .25 .60
148 Hornets Home Jersey .10 .25
149 Hornets Road Jersey .10 .25
150 Al Jefferson .12 .30
151 Kemba Walker .15 .40
152 Michael Kidd-Gilchrist .12 .30
153 Gerald Henderson .10 .25
154 Hornets Logo .10 .25
155 Bismack Biyombo .10 .25
156 Cody Zeller .10 .25
157 Lance Stephenson .12 .30
158 Noah Vonleh .12 .30
159 Chris Bosh FOIL .25 .60
160 Dwyane Wade FOIL .40 1.00
161 Heat Home Jersey .10 .25
162 Heat Road Jersey .10 .25
163 Chris Bosh .15 .40
164 Dwyane Wade .25 .60
165 Mario Chalmers .12 .30
166 Udonis Haslem .10 .25
167 Heat Logo .10 .25
168 Josh McRoberts .10 .25
169 Chris Andersen .12 .30
170 Luol Deng .12 .30
171 Norris Cole .10 .25
172 Nikola Vucevic FOIL .20 .50
173 Victor Oladipo FOIL .20 .50
174 Magic Home Jersey .10 .25
175 Magic Road Jersey .10 .25
176 Nikola Vucevic .12 .30
177 Victor Oladipo .12 .30
178 Tobias Harris .12 .30
179 Aaron Gordon .25 .60
180 Magic Logo .10 .25
181 Maurice Harkless .10 .25
182 Channing Frye .12 .30
183 Elfrid Payton .15 .40
184 Evan Fournier .10 .25
185 John Wall FOIL .30 .75
186 Bradley Beal FOIL .25 .60
187 Wizards Home Jersey .10 .25
188 Wizards Road Jersey .10 .25
189 John Wall .20 .50
190 Bradley Beal .15 .40
191 Nene .12 .30
192 Paul Pierce .15 .40
193 Wizards Logo .10 .25
194 Otto Porter .12 .30
195 Marcin Gortat .12 .30
196 Martell Webster .10 .25
197 Andre Miller .12 .30
198 Dirk Nowitzki FOIL .30 .75
199 Monta Ellis FOIL .20 .50
200 Mavericks Home Jersey .10 .25
201 Mavericks Road Jersey .10 .25
202 Dirk Nowitzki .20 .50
203 Monta Ellis .12 .30
204 Tyson Chandler .12 .30
205 Devin Harris .10 .25
206 Mavericks Logo .10 .25
207 Raymond Felton .12 .30
208 Jae Crowder .10 .25
209 Jameer Nelson .10 .25
210 Chandler Parsons .12 .30
211 Dwight Howard FOIL .20 .50
212 James Harden FOIL .40 1.00
213 Rockets Home Jersey .10 .25
214 Rockets Road Jersey .10 .25
215 Dwight Howard .12 .30
216 James Harden .25 .60
217 Trevor Ariza .10 .25
218 Donatas Motiejunas .10 .25
219 Rockets Logo .10 .25
220 Patrick Beverley .10 .25
221 Terrence Jones .12 .30
222 Troy Daniels .10 .25
223 Robert Covington .10 .25
224 Marc Gasol FOIL .25 .60
225 Zach Randolph FOIL .20 .50
226 Grizzlies Home Jersey .10 .25
227 Grizzlies Road Jersey .10 .25
228 Marc Gasol .15 .40
229 Zach Randolph .12 .30
230 Tayshaun Prince .12 .30
231 Mike Conley .12 .30
232 Grizzlies Logo .10 .25
233 Vince Carter .20 .50
234 Tony Allen .10 .25
235 Courtney Lee .12 .30
236 Kosta Koufos .10 .25
237 Anthony Davis FOIL .50 1.25
238 Jrue Holiday FOIL .20 .50
239 Pelicans Home Jersey .10 .25
240 Pelicans Road Jersey .10 .25
241 Jrue Holiday .12 .30
242 Anthony Davis .30 .75
243 Eric Gordon .12 .30
244 Jeff Withey .10 .25
245 Pelicans Logo .10 .25
246 Ryan Anderson .10 .25
247 Omer Asik .12 .30
248 Austin Rivers .12 .30
249 Tyreke Evans .10 .25
250 Tim Duncan FOIL .40 1.00
251 Kawhi Leonard FOIL .40 1.00
252 Spurs Home Jersey .10 .25
253 Spurs Road Jersey .10 .25
254 Tim Duncan .25 .60
255 Kawhi Leonard .25 .60
256 Tony Parker .15 .40
257 Manu Ginobili .15 .40
258 Spurs Logo .10 .25
259 Patty Mills .15 .40
260 Tiago Splitter .12 .30
261 Boris Diaw .12 .30
262 Marco Belinelli .10 .25
263 Ty Lawson FOIL .15 .40
264 Danilo Gallinari FOIL .15 .40
265 Nuggets Home Jersey .10 .25
266 Nuggets Road Jersey .10 .25
267 Ty Lawson .10 .25
268 Danilo Gallinari .10 .25
269 Wilson Chandler .12 .30
270 Kenneth Faried .12 .30
271 Nuggets Logo .10 .25
272 Arron Afflalo .10 .25
273 JaVale McGee .12 .30
274 J.J. Hickson .10 .25
275 Timofey Mozgov .10 .25
276 Ricky Rubio FOIL .25 .60
277 Kevin Martin FOIL .20 .50
278 Timberwolves Home Jersey .10 .25
279 Timberwolves Road Jersey .10 .25
280 Andrew Wiggins .50 1.25
281 Ricky Rubio .15 .40
282 Nikola Pekovic .10 .25
283 Corey Brewer .10 .25
284 Timberwolves Logo .10 .25
285 Gorgui Dieng .10 .25
286 Jose Barea .12 .30
287 Thaddeus Young .10 .25
288 Kevin Martin .12 .30
289 Kevin Durant FOIL .60 1.50
290 Russell Westbrook FOIL .60 1.50
291 Thunder Home Jersey .10 .25
292 Thunder Road Jersey .10 .25
293 Kevin Durant .40 1.00
294 Russell Westbrook .40 1.00
295 Reggie Jackson .10 .25
296 Serge Ibaka .12 .30
297 Thunder Logo .10 .25
298 Jeremy Lamb .10 .25
299 Nick Collison .12 .30
300 Kendrick Perkins .10 .25
301 Steven Adams .12 .30
302 Damian Lillard FOIL .50 1.25
303 LaMarcus Aldridge FOIL .25 .60
304 Trail Blazers Home Jersey .10 .25
305 Trail Blazers Road Jersey .10 .25
306 Damian Lillard .30 .75

307 LaMarcus Aldridge .15 .40
308 Dorell Wright .10 .25
309 Robin Lopez .10 .25
310 Trail Blazers Logo .10 .25
311 Nicolas Batum .12 .30
312 Thomas Robinson .10 .25
313 Wesley Matthews .10 .25
314 C.J. McCollum .15 .40
315 Gordon Hayward FOIL .25 .60
316 Trey Burke FOIL .15 .40
317 Jazz Home Jersey .10 .25
318 Jazz Road Jersey .10 .25
319 Gordon Hayward .15 .40
320 Trey Burke .10 .25
321 Derrick Favors .12 .30
322 Alec Burks .10 .25
323 Jazz Logo .10 .25
324 Enes Kanter .10 .25
325 Rudy Gobert .15 .40
326 Jeremy Evans .10 .25
327 Dante Exum .15 .40
328 Stephen Curry FOIL 1.00 2.50
329 Klay Thompson FOIL .30 .75
330 Warriors Home Jersey .10 .25
331 Warriors Road Jersey .10 .25
332 Stephen Curry .60 1.50
333 Klay Thompson .20 .50
334 David Lee .10 .25
335 Andre Iguodala .12 .30
336 Warriors Logo .10 .25
337 Draymond Green .20 .50
338 Harrison Barnes .12 .30
339 Shaun Livingston .10 .25
340 Andrew Bogut .12 .30
341 Chris Paul FOIL .30 .75
342 Blake Griffin FOIL .25 .60
343 Clippers Home Jersey .10 .25
344 Clippers Road Jersey .10 .25
345 Chris Paul .20 .50
346 Blake Griffin .15 .40
347 J.J. Redick .15 .40
348 Spencer Hawes .10 .25
349 Clippers Logo .10 .25
350 DeAndre Jordan .15 .40
351 Matt Barnes .10 .25
352 Glen Davis .10 .25
353 Jamal Crawford .15 .40
354 Kobe Bryant FOIL 1.00 2.50
355 Nick Young FOIL .20 .50
356 Lakers Home Jersey .10 .25
357 Lakers Road Jersey .10 .25
358 Kobe Bryant .60 1.50
359 Nick Young .12 .30
360 Steve Nash .15 .40
361 Jeremy Lin .15 .40
362 Lakers Logo .10 .25
363 Carlos Boozer .12 .30
364 Jordan Hill .10 .25
365 Ryan Kelly .10 .25
366 Julius Randle .25 .60
367 Isaiah Thomas FOIL .25 .60
368 Goran Dragic FOIL .20 .50
369 Suns Home Jersey .10 .25
370 Suns Road Jersey .10 .25
371 Eric Bledsoe .12 .30
372 Goran Dragic .12 .30
373 Isaiah Thomas .15 .40
374 Gerald Green .12 .30
375 Suns Logo .10 .25
376 Marcus Morris .10 .25
377 Markieff Morris .10 .25
378 Miles Plumlee .10 .25
379 T.J. Warren .15 .40
380 Rudy Gay FOIL .25 .60
381 DeMarcus Cousins FOIL .25 .60
382 Kings Home Jersey .10 .25
383 Kings Road Jersey .10 .25
384 Rudy Gay .15 .40
385 DeMarcus Cousins .15 .40
386 Ben McLemore .10 .25
387 Ray McCallum .10 .25
388 Kings Logo .10 .25
389 Darren Collison .12 .30
390 Derrick Williams .10 .25
391 Jason Thompson .10 .25
392 Nik Stauskas .12 .30
393 Manu Ginobili .15 .40
394 Matt Dellavedova .12 .30
395 Mirza Teletovic .10 .25
396 Nene .12 .30
397 Serge Ibaka .12 .30
398 Tony Parker .15 .40
399 Dennis Schroder .12 .30
400 Andrea Bargnani .12 .30
401 Jose Barea .12 .30
402 Goran Dragic .12 .30
403 Victor Claver .10 .25
404 Enes Kanter .10 .25
405 Global Games - Manchester .10 .25
406 Global Games - Manila .10 .25
407 Global Games - Rio de Janeiro .10 .25
408 Global Games - Taipei .10 .25
409 Global Games - Shanghai .10 .25
410 Global Games - Beijing .10 .25
411 Global Games - Istanbul .10 .25
412 Global Games - London .10 .25
413 Christmas Day Games Logo .10 .25
414 Bulls .10 .25
Nets
415 Thunder .10 .25
Knicks
416 Heat .10 .25
Lakers
417 Rockets .10 .25
Spurs
418 Clippers .10 .25
Warriors
419 Kyrie Irving .30 .75
All-Star Game MVP
420 John Wall .20 .50
Dunk Contest
421 Rising Stars Challenge .10 .25
422 Andre Drummond .15 .40
Rising Stars Challenge MVP
423 Trey Burke .10 .25
Skills Challenge Team
424 Damian Lillard .30 .75
Skills Challenge Team
425 Marco Belinelli .10 .25
{3-Point Shooting Contest
426 All-Star Game Logo .10 .25
427 Paul George AS .20 .50
428 Carmelo Anthony AS .20 .50
429 LeBron James AS .60 1.50
430 Stephen Curry AS .60 1.50
431 Kevin Durant AS .40 1.00
432 James Harden AS .25 .60
433 Chris Paul AS .20 .50
434 Western Conference First Round .10 .25
435 Western Conference First Round .10 .25
436 Western Conference Second Round.10 .25
437 Western Conference Finals .10 .25
438 Eastern Conference First Round .10 .25
439 Eastern Conference First Round .10 .25
440 Eastern Conference First Round .10 .25
441 Eastern Conference Finals .10 .25
442 NBA Finals Game 1 .10 .25
443 NBA Finals Game 2 .10 .25
444 NBA Finals Game 3 .10 .25
445 NBA Finals Game 4 .10 .25
446 NBA Finals Game 5 .10 .25
447 NBA Champions .10 .25
448 NBA Champions .10 .25
449 Kawhi Leonard .25 .60
NBA Finals MVP
450 Alonzo Mourning HOF .20 .50
451 Nolan Richardson HOF .15 .40
452 Mitch Richmond HOF .15 .40
453 Gary Williams HOF .15 .40
454 Hall of Fame Logo .10 .25
455 David Stern HOF .15 .40
456 Doug McDermott .15 .40
457 Zach LaVine .25 .60
458 Rodney Hood .15 .40
459 Shabazz Napier .12 .30
460 P.J. Hairston .10 .25
461 James Young .10 .25
462 Gary Harris .15 .40
463 Kevin Durant .40 1.00
MVP
464 Michael Carter-Williams .10 .25
Rookie of the Year
465 Joakim Noah .12 .30
Defensive Player of the Year
466 Jamal Crawford .15 .40
Sixth Man of the Year
467 Goran Dragic .12 .30
Most Improved Player of the Year
468 Luol Deng .12 .30
Kennedy Citizenship Award
469 Mike Conley .12 .30
NBA Sportsmanship Award
470 Shane Battier .12 .30
Twyman-Stokes Teammate of the Year

2015-16 Panini Stickers

COMPLETE SET (483) 20.00 50.00
1 Dirk Nowitzki .20 .50
Highest-scoring international player
2 Panini Knight Logo .10 .25
3 NBA Logo .10 .25
4 Kobe Bryant .60 1.50
#3 on All-Time scoring list
5 Klay Thompson .20 .50
Record for points in a quarter
6 Kyrie Irving .30 .75
NBA-best 57 points in one game
7 Russell Westbrook .40 1.00
Registers 11 triple-doubles
8 Anthony Davis .30 .75
Historic Statline
9 Avery Bradley FOIL .20 .50
10 Boston Celtics .10 .25
Home Jersey
11 Boston Celtics .10 .25
Away Jersey
12 Marcus Smart FOIL .20 .50
13 Marcus Smart .12 .30
14 Boston Celtics Logo .10 .25
15 Avery Bradley .12 .30
16 Jared Sullinger .10 .25
17 Evan Turner .12 .30
18 Tyler Zeller .12 .30
19 Kelly Olynyk .10 .25
20 Isaiah Thomas .15 .40
21 Terry Rozier .12 .30
22 Brook Lopez FOIL .20 .50
23 Brooklyn Nets .10 .25
Home Jersey
24 Brooklyn Nets .10 .25
Away Jersey
25 Joe Johnson FOIL .20 .50
26 Joe Johnson .12 .30
27 Brooklyn Nets Logo .10 .25
28 Brook Lopez .12 .30
29 Bojan Bogdanovic .10 .25
30 Shane Larkin .10 .25
31 Thaddeus Young .10 .25
32 Jarrett Jack .12 .30
33 Thomas Robinson .10 .25
34 Markel Brown .10 .25
35 Carmelo Anthony FOIL .30 .75
36 New York Knicks .10 .25
Home Jersey
37 New York Knicks .10 .25
Away Jersey
38 Kristaps Porzingis FOIL .60 1.50
39 Carmelo Anthony .20 .50
40 New York Knicks Logo .10 .25
41 Kristaps Porzingis .40 1.00
42 Cleanthony Early .10 .25
43 Langston Galloway .10 .25
44 Robin Lopez .10 .25
45 Jose Calderon .10 .25
46 Arron Afflalo .10 .25
47 Derrick Williams .10 .25
48 Tony Wroten FOIL .15 .40
49 Philadelphia 76ers .10 .25
Home Jersey
50 Philadelphia 76ers .10 .25
Away Jersey
51 Nerlens Noel FOIL .20 .50
52 Nerlens Noel .12 .30
53 Philadelphia 76ers Logo .10 .25
54 Tony Wroten .10 .25
55 Robert Covington .10 .25
56 Isaiah Canaan .12 .30
57 Jahlil Okafor .20 .50
58 Jerami Grant .10 .25
59 Joel Embiid .25 .60
60 JaKarr Sampson .10 .25
61 DeMar DeRozan FOIL .25 .60
62 Toronto Raptors .10 .25
Home Jersey
63 Toronto Raptors .10 .25
Away Jersey
64 Kyle Lowry FOIL .20 .50
65 DeMar DeRozan .15 .40
66 Toronto Raptors Logo .10 .25
67 Kyle Lowry .12 .30
68 Jonas Valanciunas .12 .30
69 Terrence Ross .12 .30
70 DeMarre Carroll .10 .25
71 Patrick Patterson .10 .25
72 Bruno Caboclo .10 .25
73 James Johnson .10 .25
74 Derrick Rose FOIL .30 .75
75 Chicago Bulls .10 .25
Home Jersey
76 Chicago Bulls .10 .25
Away Jersey
77 Jimmy Butler FOIL .25 .60
78 Derrick Rose .20 .50
79 Chicago Bulls Logo .10 .25
80 Pau Gasol .15 .40
81 Jimmy Butler .15 .40
82 Joakim Noah .12 .30
83 Taj Gibson .12 .30
84 Nikola Mirotic .12 .30
85 Doug McDermott .12 .30
86 Tony Snell .10 .25
87 LeBron James FOIL 1.00 2.50
88 Cleveland Cavaliers .10 .25
Home Jersey
89 Cleveland Cavaliers .10 .25
Away Jersey
90 Kyrie Irving FOIL .50 1.25
91 LeBron James .60 1.50
92 Cleveland Cavaliers Logo .10 .25
93 Kyrie Irving .30 .75
94 Iman Shumpert .10 .25
95 Timofey Mozgov .10 .25
96 Tristan Thompson .12 .30
97 Kevin Love .15 .40
98 Matthew Dellavedova .12 .30
99 J.R. Smith .12 .30
100 Andre Drummond FOIL .25 .60
101 Detroit Pistons .10 .25
Home Jersey
102 Detroit Pistons .10 .25
Away Jersey
103 Brandon Jennings FOIL .15 .40
104 Andre Drummond .15 .40
105 Detroit Pistons Logo .10 .25
106 Brandon Jennings .10 .25
107 Kentavious Caldwell-Pope .12 .30
108 Reggie Jackson .12 .30
109 Stanley Johnson .12 .30
110 Spencer Dinwiddie .10 .25
111 Jodie Meeks .12 .30
112 Marcus Morris .10 .25
113 Paul George FOIL .30 .75
114 Indiana Pacers .10 .25
Home Jersey
115 Indiana Pacers .10 .25
Away Jersey
116 George Hill FOIL .20 .50
117 Paul George .20 .50
118 Indiana Pacers Logo .10 .25
119 George Hill .12 .30
120 C.J. Miles .12 .30
121 Rodney Stuckey .12 .30
122 Solomon Hill .10 .25
123 Myles Turner .15 .40
124 Monta Ellis .12 .30
125 Joe Young .12 .30
126 Giannis Antetokounmpo FOIL .50 1.25
127 Milwaukee Bucks .10 .25
Home Jersey
128 Milwaukee Bucks .10 .25
Away Jersey
129 Jabari Parker FOIL .30 .75
130 Giannis Antetokounmpo .30 .75
131 Milwaukee Bucks Logo .10 .25
132 Jabari Parker .20 .50
133 Michael Carter-Williams .10 .25
134 Khris Middleton .12 .30
135 Greg Monroe .12 .30
136 O.J. Mayo .10 .25
137 Tyler Ennis .10 .25
138 John Henson .12 .30
139 Al Horford .12 .30
140 Atlanta Hawks .10 .25
Home Jersey
141 Atlanta Hawks .10 .25
Away Jersey
142 Jeff Teague .12 .30
143 Al Horford .12 .30
144 Atlanta Hawks Logo .10 .25
145 Jeff Teague .12 .30
146 Kyle Korver .12 .30
147 Paul Millsap .15 .40
148 Dennis Schroder .12 .30
149 Thabo Sefolosha .10 .25
150 Tiago Splitter .12 .30
151 Tim Hardaway Jr. .10 .25
152 Kemba Walker .15 .40
153 Charlotte Hornets .10 .25
Home Jersey
154 Charlotte Hornets .10 .25
Away Jersey
155 Al Jefferson .12 .30
156 Kemba Walker .15 .40
157 Charlotte Hornets Logo .10 .25
158 Al Jefferson .12 .30
159 Michael Kidd-Gilchrist .12 .30
160 Nicolas Batum .12 .30
161 Marvin Williams .12 .30
162 Frank Kaminsky .15 .40
163 Jeremy Lin .15 .40
164 Cody Zeller .10 .25
165 Chris Bosh .15 .40
166 Miami Heat .10 .25
Home Jersey
167 Miami Heat .10 .25
Away Jersey
168 Dwyane Wade .25 .60
169 Dwyane Wade .25 .60
170 Miami Heat Logo .10 .25
171 Chris Bosh .15 .40
172 Luol Deng .12 .30
173 Goran Dragic .12 .30
174 Hassan Whiteside .12 .30
175 Justise Winslow .15 .40
176 Chris Andersen .12 .30
177 Mario Chalmers .12 .30
178 Victor Oladipo .12 .30
179 Orlando Magic .10 .25
Home Jersey
180 Orlando Magic .10 .25
Away Jersey
181 Nikola Vucevic .12 .30
182 Victor Oladipo .12 .30
183 Orlando Magic Logo .10 .25
184 Nikola Vucevic .12 .30
185 Elfrid Payton .12 .30
186 Tobias Harris .12 .30
187 Mario Hezonja .12 .30
188 Aaron Gordon .12 .30
189 Channing Frye .12 .30
190 Evan Fournier .12 .30
191 John Wall .20 .50
192 Washington Wizards .10 .25
Home Jersey
193 Washington Wizards .10 .25
Away Jersey
194 Bradley Beal .15 .40
195 John Wall .20 .50
196 Washington Wizards Logo .10 .25
197 Bradley Beal .15 .40
198 Marcin Gortat .12 .30
199 Martell Webster .10 .25
200 Nene .12 .30
201 Otto Porter Jr. .12 .30
202 Kris Humphries .10 .25
203 Ramon Sessions .12 .30
204 Chandler Parsons .12 .30
205 Dallas Mavericks .10 .25
Home Jersey
206 Dallas Mavericks .10 .25
Away Jersey
207 Dirk Nowitzki .20 .50
208 Dirk Nowitzki .20 .50
209 Dallas Mavericks Logo .10 .25
210 Chandler Parsons .12 .30
211 Wesley Matthews .10 .25
212 J.J. Barea .12 .30
213 Devin Harris .10 .25
214 Deron Williams .12 .30
215 Justin Anderson .12 .30
216 Charlie Villanueva .10 .25
217 James Harden .25 .60
218 Houston Rockets .10 .25
Home Jersey
219 Houston Rockets .10 .25
Away Jersey
220 Dwight Howard .12 .30
221 James Harden .25 .60
222 Houston Rockets Logo .10 .25
223 Dwight Howard .12 .30
224 Trevor Ariza .10 .25
225 Sam Dekker .12 .30
226 Patrick Beverley .10 .25
227 Donatas Motiejunas .10 .25
228 Corey Brewer .10 .25
229 Terrence Jones .12 .30
230 Mike Conley .15 .40
231 Memphis Grizzlies .10 .25
Home Jersey
232 Memphis Grizzlies .10 .25
Away Jersey
233 Zach Randolph .12 .30
234 Zach Randolph .12 .30
235 Memphis Grizzlies Logo .10 .25
236 Mike Conley .15 .40
237 Marc Gasol .15 .40
238 Tony Allen .10 .25
239 Courtney Lee .12 .30
240 Jeff Green .12 .30
241 Jordan Adams .10 .25
242 Vince Carter .20 .50
243 Anthony Davis .30 .75
244 New Orleans Pelicans .10 .25
Home Jersey
245 New Orleans Pelicans .10 .25
Away Jersey
246 Tyreke Evans .10 .25
247 Anthony Davis .30 .75
248 New Orleans Pelicans Logo .10 .25
249 Tyreke Evans .10 .25
250 Jrue Holiday .12 .30
251 Eric Gordon .12 .30
252 Alexis Ajinca .10 .25
253 Omer Asik .12 .30
254 Ryan Anderson .12 .30
255 Quincy Pondexter .10 .25
256 Tony Parker .15 .40
257 San Antonio Spurs .10 .25
Home Jersey
258 San Antonio Spurs .10 .25
Away Jersey
259 Kwahi Leonard .40 1.00
260 Kwahi Leonard .40 1.00
261 San Antonio Spurs Logo .10 .25
262 Tim Duncan .25 .60
263 Tony Parker .15 .40
264 Manu Ginobili .15 .40
265 Lamarcus Aldridge .15 .40
266 Danny Green .12 .30
267 Kyle Anderson .10 .25
268 Boris Diaw .12 .30
269 Kenneth Faried .12 .30
270 Denver Nuggets .10 .25
Home Jersey
271 Denver Nuggets .10 .25
Away Jersey
272 Emmanuel Mudiay .15 .40
273 Kenneth Faried .12 .30
274 Denver Nuggets Logo .10 .25
275 Danilo Gallinari .12 .30
276 Randy Foye .10 .25
277 Emmanuel Mudiay .15 .40
278 Jusuf Nurkic .10 .25
279 Wilson Chandler .12 .30
280 Gary Harris .12 .30
281 J.J. Hickson .10 .25
282 Andrew Wiggins .25 .60
283 Minnesota Timberwolves .10 .25
Home Jersey
284 Minnesota Timberwolves .10 .25
Away Jersey
285 Ricky Rubio .15 .40
286 Andrew Wiggins .25 .60
287 Minnesota Timberwolves Logo .10 .25
288 Ricky Rubio .15 .40
289 Kevin Garnett .25 .60
290 Zach LaVine .15 .40
291 Kevin Martin .12 .30
292 Karl-Anthony Towns .75 2.00
293 Shabazz Muhammad .12 .30
294 Anthony Bennett .10 .25
295 Kevin Durant .40 1.00
296 Oklahoma City Thunder .10 .25
Home Jersey
297 Oklahoma City Thunder .10 .25
Away Jersey
298 Russell Westbrook .40 1.00
299 Kevin Durant .40 1.00
300 Oklahoma City Thunder Logo .10 .25
301 Russell Westbrook .40 1.00
302 Serge Ibaka .12 .30
303 Enes Kanter .10 .25
304 Dion Waiters .12 .30
305 Anthony Morrow .10 .25
306 Steven Adams .12 .30
307 Mitch McGary .10 .25
308 Damian Lillard .30 .75
309 Portland Trail Blazers .10 .25
Home Jersey
310 Portland Trail Blazers .10 .25
Away Jersey
311 C.J. McCollum .15 .40
312 Damian Lillard .30 .75
313 Portland Trail Blazers Logo .10 .25
314 Gerald Henderson .10 .25
315 C.J. McCollum .15 .40
316 Meyers Leonard .10 .25
317 Noah Vonleh .10 .25
318 Ed Davis .10 .25
319 Al-Farouq Aminu .12 .30
320 Allen Crabbe .10 .25
321 Derrick Favors .12 .30
322 Utah Jazz .10 .25
Home Jersey
323 Utah Jazz .10 .25
Away Jersey
324 Gordon Hayward .15 .40
325 Gordon Hayward .15 .40
326 Utah Jazz Logo .10 .25
327 Derrick Favors .12 .30
328 Rudy Gobert .15 .40
329 Trey Burke .10 .25
330 Dante Exum .12 .30
331 Alec Burks .10 .25
332 Rodney Hood .12 .30
333 Joe Ingles .10 .25
334 Stephen Curry .60 1.50
335 Golden State Warriors .10 .25
Home Jersey
336 Golden State Warriors .10 .25
Away Jersey
337 Klay Thompson .20 .50
338 Stephen Curry .60 1.50
339 Golden State Warriors Logo .10 .25
340 Klay Thompson .20 .50
341 Harrison Barnes .12 .30
342 Andre Iguodala .12 .30
343 Draymond Green .20 .50
344 Andrew Bogut .12 .30
345 Shaun Livingston .10 .25
346 Leandro Barbosa .10 .25
347 Chris Paul .20 .50
348 Los Angeles Clippers .10 .25
Home Jersey
349 Los Angeles Clippers .10 .25
Away Jersey
350 Blake Griffin .15 .40
351 Chris Paul .20 .50
352 Los Angeles Clippers Logo .10 .25
353 Blake Griffin .15 .40
354 DeAndre Jordan .15 .40
355 J.J. Redick .15 .40
356 Jamal Crawford .15 .40
357 Lance Stephenson .12 .30
358 Paul Pierce .15 .40
359 Josh Smith .12 .30
360 Kobe Bryant .60 1.50
361 Los Angeles Lakers .10 .25
Home Jersey
362 Los Angeles Lakers .10 .25
Away Jersey
363 Julius Randle .15 .40
364 Kobe Bryant .60 1.50
365 Los Angeles Lakers Logo .10 .25
366 Julius Randle .15 .40
367 Jordan Clarkson .15 .40
368 D'Angelo Russell .40 1.00
369 Lou Williams .12 .30
370 Roy Hibbert .12 .30
371 Nick Young .12 .30
372 Ryan Kelly .10 .25
373 Eric Bledsoe .12 .30
374 Phoenix Suns .10 .25
Home Jersey
375 Phoenix Suns .10 .25
Away Jersey
376 Brandon Knight .12 .30
377 Eric Bledsoe .12 .30
378 Phoenix Suns Logo .10 .25
379 Brandon Knight .12 .30
380 Alex Len .10 .25
381 Tyson Chandler .12 .30
382 T.J. Warren .12 .30
383 Archie Goodwin .10 .25
384 Markieff Morris .10 .25
385 P.J. Tucker .10 .25
386 DeMarcus Cousins .15 .40
387 Sacramento Kings .10 .25
Home Jersey
388 Sacramento Kings .10 .25
Away Jersey
389 Rudy Gay .15 .40
390 DeMarcus Cousins .15 .40
391 Sacramento Kings Logo .10 .25
392 Rudy Gay .15 .40
393 Rajon Rondo .15 .40
394 Darren Collison .12 .30
395 Willie Cauley-Stein .15 .40
396 Ben McLemore .10 .25
397 Marc Belinelli .10 .25
398 Omri Casspi .10 .25
399 Trey Lyles .15 .40
400 Devin Booker .50 1.25
401 Cameron Payne .12 .30
402 Kelly Oubre Jr. .12 .30
403 Rashad Vaughn .10 .25
404 Jerian Grant .10 .25
405 Bobby Portis .15 .40
406 Rondae Hollis-Jefferson .12 .30
407 Tyus Jones .15 .40
408 All-Star Game FOIL .10 .25
409 Zach LaVine .15 .40
410 Zach LaVine .15 .40
411 Russell Westbrook .40 1.00
412 Stephen Curry .60 1.50
413 Stephen Curry .60 1.50
414 2016 All-Star Toronto FOIL .10 .25
415 Patrick Beverley .10 .25
416 Patrick Beverley .10 .25
417 LaMarcus Aldridge .15 .40
418 Stephen Curry .60 1.50
419 Tim Duncan .25 .60
420 Kevin Durant .40 1.00
421 James Harden .25 .60
422 Damian Lillard .30 .75
423 Dirk Nowitzki .20 .50
424 Chris Paul .20 .50
425 Klay Thompson .20 .50
426 Carmelo Anthony .20 .50
427 Jimmy Butler .15 .40
428 Pau Gasol .15 .40
429 Al Horford .12 .30
430 Kyrie Irving .30 .75
431 LeBron James .60 1.50
432 Kyle Lowry .12 .30
433 Jeff Teague .12 .30
434 John Wall .20 .50
435 Warriors v Pelicans .10 .25
436 Trail Blazers v Grizzles .10 .25
437 Clippers v Spurs .10 .25
438 Rockets v Mavericks .10 .25
439 Warriors v Grizzlies .10 .25
440 Clippers v Rockets .10 .25
441 Warriors v Rockets .10 .25
442 Hawks v Nets .10 .25
443 Raptors v Wizards .10 .25
444 Bulls v Bucks .10 .25
445 Cavaliers v Celtics .10 .25
446 Hawks v Wizards .10 .25
447 Bulls v Cavaliers .10 .25
448 Hawks v Cavaliers .10 .25
449 The Finals .10 .25
Game 1
450 The Finals .10 .25
Game 2
451 The Finals .10 .25
Game 3
452 The Finals .10 .25
Game 4
453 The Finals .10 .25
Game 5
454 The Finals .10 .25
Game 6
455 Warriors Team .10 .25
456 Warriors Team .10 .25
457 Andre Iguodala MVP .12 .30
458 Warriors Champsionship Logo .10 .25
459 Warriors Champsionship Logo .10 .25
460 Larry O'Brien Trophy .15 .40
461 Stephen Curry MVP .60 1.50
462 Andrew Wiggins ROY .25 .60
463 Kawhi Leonard DPOY .25 .60
464 Lou Williams .12 .30
6th Man
465 Jimmy Butler .15 .40
Most Improved
466 Joakim Noah .12 .30
Citizenship Award
467 Kyle Korver .12 .30
Sportsmanship Award
468 Basketball HOF .10 .25
469 John Calipari .15 .40
470 Louie Dampier .15 .40
471 Spencer Haywood .10 .25
472 Tommy Heinsohn .15 .40
473 Dikembe Mutombo .15 .40
474 Jo Jo White .12 .30
475 Kobe Bryant Championship 1 .60 1.50
476 Kobe Bryant Championship 2 .60 1.50
477 Kobe Bryant Championship 3 .60 1.50
478 Kobe Bryant Championship 4 .60 1.50
479 Kobe Bryant Championship 5 .60 1.50
480 Kobe Bryant Photo 1 .60 1.50
481 Kobe Bryant Photo 2 .60 1.50
482 Kobe Bryant Photo 3 .60 1.50
483 Kobe Bryant Photo 4 .60 1.50

1987-88 Panini Spanish Stickers

The 1987-88 Panini Spanish Supersport Sticker set consists of 161 stickers, each measuring approximately 2 1/8" by 3". The stickers were designed to be placed in an album measuring approximately 9 1/8" by 10 3/4". The sticker fronts display color photos of athletes from several countries and representing various sports. Among the sports represented are Basketball (1-42), Track and Field (43-84), Soccer (85-126), Motor Sports (127-140), Bicyling (141-147), and Tennis (148-161).

COMPLETE SET (161) 200.00 400.00
1 Larry Bird 15.00 40.00
2 Kareem Abdul-Jabbar 10.00 25.00
3 Earvin Magic Johnson 15.00 40.00
4 Michael Jordan 50.00 120.00
5 Isiah Thomas 8.00 20.00
6 Stephen Baeck .20 .50
7 Tony Balogun .20 .50
8 Alexandr Belostenni .20 .50
9 Karl Brown .20 .50
10 Fanis Christodoulou .20 .50
11 Danko Cvjeticanin .20 .50
12 Sandro Dell'Agnello .20 .50
13 Vlade Divac 3.00 8.00
14 Nikos Filippou .20 .50
15 Nikos Gallis 1.25 3.00
16 Valeri Goborov .20 .50
17 Andrea Gracis .20 .50
18 Henning Harnisch .20 .50
19 Colin Irish .20 .50
20 Pertram Koch .20 .50
21 Jens Kujawa .20 .50
22 Rimas Kurtinaitis .75 2.00
23 Bob McAdoo 4.00 10.00
24 Walter Magnifico 8.00 20.00
25 Sharunas Marchulenis 2.00 5.00
26 Sven Meyer .20 .50
27 Igor Miglinieks .20 .50
28 Jacques Monclar .20 .50
29 Frederic Monetti .20 .50
30 Stephane Ostrowski .75 2.00
31 Drazen Petrovic 10.00 25.00
32 Dino Radja 1.50 4.00
33 Zoran Radovic .40 1.00
34 Antonello Riva 1.50 4.00
35 Oscar Schmidt 6.00 15.00
36 Christian Soule .20 .50
37 Titt Sokk .20 .50
38 Francesco Vescovi .20 .50
39 Georges Vestris .20 .50
40 Alexander Volkov 1.50 4.00
41 Stojan Vrankovic 1.25 3.00
42 Panagiotis Yiannakis .20 .50

1990-91 Panini Stickers Greek

COMPLETE SET (180) 600.00 1200.00
1 Magic Johnson 4.00 10.00
2 Mychal Thompson 1.00 2.50
3 Vlade Divac 1.50 4.00
4 Byron Scott 1.00 2.50
5 James Worthy 2.00 5.00
6 A.C. Green 1.00 2.50
7 Jerome Kersey 1.00 2.50
8 Clyde Drexler 4.00 10.00
9 Buck Williams 1.00 2.50
10 Kevin Duckworth 1.00 2.50
11 Terry Porter 1.00 2.50
12 Cliff Robinson 1.50 4.00
13 Tom Chambers 1.00 2.50
14 Dan Majerle 1.50 4.00
15 Mark West 1.00 2.50
16 Kevin Johnson 1.50 4.00
17 Jeff Hornacek 1.50 4.00
18 Kurt Rambis 1.00 2.50
19 Nate McMillan 1.00 2.50
20 Shawn Kemp 5.00 12.00
21 Dale Ellis 1.00 2.50
22 Michael Cage 1.00 2.50
23 Xavier McDaniel 1.00 2.50
24 Derrick McKey 1.00 2.50
25 Manute Bol 1.00 2.50
26 Chris Mullin 2.00 5.00
27 Terry Teagle 1.00 2.50
28 Tim Hardaway 2.00 5.00
29 Sarunas Marciulionis 1.00 2.50
30 Mitch Richmond 4.00 10.00
31 Gary Grant 1.00 2.50
32 Danny Manning 1.50 4.00
33 Benoit Benjamin 1.00 2.50
34 Ron Harper 1.50 4.00
35 Ken Norman 1.00 2.50
36 Charles Smith 1.00 2.50
37 Harold Pressley 1.00 2.50
38 Antoine Carr 1.00 2.50
39 Danny Ainge 1.50 4.00
40 Wayman Tisdale 1.00 2.50
41 Ralph Sampson 1.00 2.50
42 Vinny Del Negro 1.00 2.50
43 David Robinson 5.00 12.00
44 Sean Elliott 2.00 5.00
45 Terry Cummings 1.50 4.00
46 Willie Anderson 1.00 2.50
47 Rod Strickland 1.50 4.00
48 Frank Brickowski 1.00 2.50
49 Karl Malone 6.00 15.00
50 Darrell Griffith 1.00 2.50
51 John Stockton 6.00 15.00
52 Blue Edwards 1.00 2.50
53 Mark Eaton 1.00 2.50
54 Thurl Bailey 1.00 2.50
55 Rolando Blackman 1.00 2.50
56 Sam Perkins 1.00 2.50
57 James Donaldson 1.00 2.50
58 Herb Williams 1.00 2.50
59 Roy Tarpley 1.00 2.50
60 Derek Harper 1.00 2.50
61 Michael Adams 1.00 2.50
62 Blair Rasmussen 1.00 2.50
63 Jerome Lane 1.00 2.50
64 Walter Davis 1.00 2.50
65 Todd Lichti 1.00 2.50
66 Joe Barry Carroll 1.00 2.50
67 Vernon Maxwell 1.00 2.50
68 Otis Thorpe 1.00 2.50
69 Hakeem Olajuwon 4.00 10.00
70 Buck Johnson 1.00 2.50
71 Eric (Sleepy) Floyd 1.00 2.50
72 Mitchell Wiggins 1.00 2.50
73 Tony Campbell 1.00 2.50
74 Tod Murphy 1.00 2.50
75 Tyrone Corbin 1.00 2.50
76 Sam Mitchell 1.00 2.50
77 Randy Breuer 1.00 2.50
78 Pooh Richardson 1.00 2.50
79 Rex Chapman 1.50 4.00
80 Dell Curry 1.00 2.50
81 Muggsy Bogues 1.50 4.00
82 J.R. Reid 1.00 2.50
83 Armon Gilliam 1.00 2.50
84 Kelly Tripucka 1.00 2.50
85 Dennis Rodman 5.00 12.00
86 Joe Dumars 2.00 5.00
87 Isiah Thomas 2.00 5.00
88 Bill Laimbeer 1.50 4.00
89 Vinnie Johnson 1.00 2.50
90 James Edwards 1.00 2.50
91 Michael Jordan 150.00 300.00
92 Stacey King 1.00 2.50
93 Scottie Pippen 6.00 15.00
94 John Paxson 1.00 2.50
95 Horace Grant 1.00 2.50
96 Craig Hodges 1.00 2.50
97 Brad Lohaus 1.00 2.50
98 Jack Sikma 1.00 2.50
99 Ricky Pierce 1.00 2.50
100 Greg Anderson 1.00 2.50
101 Alvin Robertson 1.00 2.50
102 Jay Humphries 1.00 2.50
103 Mark Price 1.50 4.00
104 Winston Bennett 1.00 2.50
105 Brad Daugherty 1.00 2.50
106 Craig Ehlo 1.00 2.50
107 Larry Nance 1.00 2.50
108 Hot Rod Williams 1.00 2.50
109 Rik Smits 1.50 4.00
110 Chuck Person 1.00 2.50
111 Reggie Miller 4.00 10.00
112 LaSalle Thompson 1.00 2.50
113 Detlef Schrempf 1.50 4.00
114 Vern Fleming 1.00 2.50
115 Moses Malone 1.50 4.00
116 Doc Rivers 1.50 4.00
117 Dominique Wilkins 2.50 6.00
118 Spud Webb 1.50 4.00
119 Kevin Willis 1.00 2.50
120 Kenny Smith 1.00 2.50
121 Otis Smith 1.00 2.50
122 Sidney Green 1.00 2.50
123 Nick Anderson 1.00 2.50
124 Scott Skiles 1.00 2.50
125 Jerry Reynolds 1.00 2.50
126 Terry Catledge 1.00 2.50
127 Charles Barkley 4.00 10.00
128 Ron Anderson 1.00 2.50
129 Hersey Hawkins 1.00 2.50
130 Mike Gminski 1.00 2.50
131 Johnny Dawkins 1.00 2.50
132 Rick Mahorn 1.00 2.50
133 Michael Smith 1.00 2.50
134 Reggie Lewis 1.00 2.50
135 Larry Bird 10.00 25.00
136 Kevin McHale 2.00 5.00
137 Joe Kleine 1.00 2.50
138 Robert Parish 1.50 4.00
139 Maurice Cheeks 1.00 2.50
140 Patrick Ewing 4.00 10.00
141 Charles Oakley 1.50 4.00
142 Gerald Wilkins 1.00 2.50
143 Kenny Walker 1.50 4.00
144 Mark Jackson 1.00 2.50
145 Mark Alarie 1.00 2.50
146 John Williams 1.00 2.50
147 Darrell Walker 1.00 2.50
148 Bernard King 1.00 2.50
149 Harvey Grant 1.00 2.50
150 Ledell Eackles 1.00 2.50
151 Glen Rice 5.00 12.00
152 Kevin Edwards 1.00 2.50
153 Tellis Frank 1.00 2.50
154 Rony Seikaly 1.00 2.50
155 Billy Thompson 1.00 2.50
156 Sherman Douglas 1.00 2.50
157 Roy Hinson 1.00 2.50
158 Chris Morris 1.00 2.50
159 Lester Conner 1.00 2.50
160 Sam Bowie 1.00 2.50
161 Purvis Short 1.00 2.50
162 Mookie Blaylock 1.50 4.00
A John Stockton AS 2.50 6.00
B Magic Johnson AS 2.50 6.00
C A.C. Green AS 1.00 2.50
D Hakeem Olajuwon AS 2.50 6.00
E James Worthy AS 1.50 4.00
F Isiah Thomas AS 1.25 3.00
G Michael Jordan AS 150.00 300.00
H Larry Bird AS 4.00 10.00
I Patrick Ewing AS 2.50 6.00
J Charles Barkley AS 2.50 6.00
K Michael Jordan 150.00 300.00
L Larry Bird 4.00 10.00
M Hakeem Olajuwon 2.50 6.00
N NBA Finals 1.00 2.50
O NBA Finals 1.00 2.50
P NBA Finals 1.00 2.50
Q NBA Finals 1.00 2.50
R NBA Finals 1.00 2.50

1988-89 Panini Stickers Spanish

The 1989 (covering the 1988-89 season) Panini Spanish basketball set consists of 292 stickers, each measuring approximately 2" by 2 5/8". The sticker album measures approximately 9" by 12". The fronts display color action player photos enclosed by white borders. The stickers are numbered on the back and arranged alphabetically according to teams within the Atlantic and Central Divisions of the Western Conference, and the Midwest and Pacific Divisions of the Eastern Conference. The set closes with several topical subsets: All Star Game (253-258), East All Stars (259-271), West All Stars (272-284), and 1989 Stars NBA (285-292).

COMPLETE SET (292) 250.00 450.00
1 NBA Official .40 1.00
2 NBA Official .40 1.00
3 Boston Celtics Logo .40 1.00
4 Jimmy Rodgers CO .40 1.00
5 Dennis Johnson 1.50 4.00
6 Brian Shaw .75 2.00
7 Danny Ainge 1.25 3.00
8 Larry Bird 12.50 30.00
9 Kevin McHale 3.00 8.00

10 Robert Parish 1.50 4.00
11 Robert Parish IA .75 2.00
12 Celtics Jersey .40 1.00
13 Charlotte Hornets .40 1.00
14 Dick Harter CO .40 1.00
15 Rex Chapman 2.00 5.00
16 Muggsy Bogues 2.00 5.00
17 Kelly Tripucka .40 1.00
18 Robert Reid .40 1.00
19 Kurt Rambis .75 2.00
20 Dave Hoppen .40 1.00
21 Muggsy Bogues IA .75 2.00
22 Hornets Jersey .40 1.00
23 New Jersey Nets Logo .40 1.00
24 Willis Reed CO .75 2.00
25 John Bagley .40 1.00
26 Dennis Hopson .40 1.00
27 Mike McGee .40 1.00
28 Roy Hinson .40 1.00
29 Buck Williams .75 2.00
30 Joe Barry Carroll .40 1.00
31 Roy Hinson IA .40 1.00
32 Nets Jersey .40 1.00
33 New York Knicks Logo .40 1.00
34 Rick Pitino CO 1.25 3.00
35 Mark Jackson 3.00 8.00
36 Trent Tucker .40 1.00
37 Johnny Newman .40 1.00
38 Gerald Wilkins .40 1.00
39 Charles Oakley .40 1.00
40 Patrick Ewing 5.00 12.00
41 Gerald Wilkins IA .40 1.00
42 Knicks Jersey .40 1.00
43 Philadelphia 76ers .40 1.00
44 Jim Lynam CO .40 1.00
45 Maurice Cheeks 1.25 3.00
46 Hersey Hawkins 1.50 4.00
47 Ron Anderson .40 1.00
48 Charles Barkley 8.00 20.00
49 Cliff Robinson .40 1.00
50 Mike Gminski .75 2.00
51 Hersey Hawkins IA .75 2.00
52 76ers Jersey .40 1.00
53 Washington Bullets .40 1.00
54 Wes Unseld CO .75 2.00
55 Jeff Malone .75 2.00
56 Darrell Walker .40 1.00
57 Bernard King .75 2.00
58 Terry Catledge .40 1.00
59 John Williams .40 1.00
60 Dave Feitl .40 1.00
61 Jeff Malone IA .40 1.00
62 Bullets Jersey .40 1.00
63 Atlanta Hawks Logo .40 1.00
64 Mike Fratello CO .40 1.00
65 Doc Rivers 1.25 3.00
66 Spud Webb 1.00 2.50
67 Reggie Theus .75 2.00
68 Dominique Wilkins 5.00 12.00
69 Kevin Willis .75 2.00
70 Moses Malone 2.00 5.00
71 Reggie Theus IA .40 1.00
72 Hawks Jersey .40 1.00
73 Chicago Bulls Logo .40 1.00
74 Doug Collins CO 1.00 2.50
75 Craig Hodges .40 1.00
76 Michael Jordan 30.00 80.00
77 Scottie Pippen 15.00 40.00
78 Horace Grant 3.00 8.00
79 Brad Sellers .40 1.00
80 Bill Cartwright .75 2.00
81 Brad Sellers IA .40 1.00
82 Bulls Jersey .40 1.00
83 Cleveland Cavaliers .40 1.00
84 Lenny Wilkens CO .75 2.00
85 Mark Price 1.50 4.00
86 Ron Harper 1.50 4.00
87 Hot Rod Williams .40 1.00
88 Mike Sanders .40 1.00
89 Larry Nance .75 2.00
90 Brad Daugherty .75 2.00
91 Mike Sanders IA .40 1.00
92 Cavaliers Jersey .40 1.00
93 Detroit Pistons Logo .40 1.00
94 Chuck Daly CO 1.50 4.00
95 Isiah Thomas 4.00 10.00
96 Joe Dumars 3.00 8.00
97 Dennis Rodman 8.00 20.00
98 Adrian Dantley 1.25 3.00
99 John Salley .75 2.00
100 Bill Laimbeer 1.25 3.00
101 Dennis Rodman IA 5.00 12.00
102 Pistons Jersey .40 1.00
103 Indiana Pacers Logo .40 1.00
104 Dick Versace CO .60 1.50
105 Vern Fleming .40 1.00
106 Reggie Miller 10.00 25.00
107 Chuck Person .75 2.00
108 Herb Williams .40 1.00
109 Steve Stipanovich .40 1.00
110 Rik Smits 2.00 5.00
111 Chuck Person IA .40 1.00
112 Pacers Jersey .40 1.00
113 Milwaukee Bucks Logo .40 1.00
114 Del Harris CO .40 1.00
115 Sidney Moncrief 1.25 3.00
116 Jay Humphries .40 1.00
117 Paul Pressey .40 1.00
118 Ricky Pierce .75 2.00
119 Terry Cummings .75 2.00
120 Jack Sikma .75 2.00
121 Jay Humphries IA .40 1.00
122 Bucks Jersey .40 1.00
123 Mavericks Logo .40 1.00
124 John MacLeod CO .40 1.00
125 Derek Harper .75 2.00
126 Rolando Blackman 1.00 2.50
127 Detlef Schrempf 1.50 4.00
128 Mark Aguirre .75 2.00
129 Sam Perkins .75 2.00
130 James Donaldson .40 1.00
131 Sam Perkins IA .60 1.50
132 Mavericks Jersey .40 1.00
133 Denver Nuggets Logo .40 1.00
134 Doug Moe CO .40 1.00
135 Walter Davis .75 2.00
136 Michael Adams .40 1.00
137 Fat Lever .75 2.00
138 Alex English 1.25 3.00
139 Wayne Cooper .40 1.00
140 Danny Schayes .40 1.00
141 Fat Lever IA .40 1.00
142 Nuggets Jersey .40 1.00
143 Houston Rockets Logo .40 1.00
144 Don Chaney CO .40 1.00
145 Sleepy Floyd .40 1.00
146 Mike Woodson .40 1.00
147 Purvis Short .40 1.00
148 Buck Johnson .40 1.00
149 Otis Thorpe .75 2.00
150 Hakeem Olajuwon 5.00 12.00
151 Otis Thorpe IA .40 1.00
152 Rockets Jersey .40 1.00
153 Miami Heat Logo .40 1.00
154 Ron Rothstein CO .75 2.00
155 Jon Sundvold .40 1.00
156 Kevin Edwards .40 1.00
157 Grant Long .75 2.00
158 Billy Thompson .75 2.00
159 Dwayne Washington .40 1.00
160 Rony Seikaly 1.25 3.00
161 Rony Seikaly IA .40 1.00
162 Heat Jersey .40 1.00
163 San Antonio Spurs .40 1.00
164 Larry Brown CO 2.00 5.00
165 Johnny Dawkins .75 2.00
166 Alvin Robertson .40 1.00
167 Willie Anderson .40 1.00
168 Albert King .40 1.00
169 Greg Anderson .40 1.00
170 Frank Brickowski .40 1.00
171 Willie Anderson IA .40 1.00
172 Spurs Jersey .40 1.00
173 Utah Jazz Logo .40 1.00
174 Jerry Sloan CO 3.00 8.00
175 John Stockton 8.00 20.00
176 Darrell Griffith .75 2.00
177 Marc Iavaroni .40 1.00
178 Thurl Bailey .40 1.00
179 Karl Malone 8.00 20.00
180 Mark Eaton .75 2.00
181 Thurl Bailey IA .40 1.00
182 Jazz Jersey .40 1.00
183 Golden State Warriors .40 1.00
184 Don Nelson CO .75 2.00
185 Mitch Richmond 6.00 15.00
186 Winston Garland .40 1.00
187 Larry Smith .40 1.00
188 Chris Mullin 2.50 6.00
189 Ralph Sampson .75 2.00
190 Manute Bol .75 2.00
191 Ralph Sampson IA .40 1.00
192 Warriors Jersey .40 1.00
193 Los Angeles Clippers .40 1.00
194 Don Casey CO .40 1.00
195 Gary Grant .40 1.00
196 Quintin Dailey .40 1.00
197 Norm Nixon .75 2.00
198 Ken Norman .40 1.00
199 Danny Manning 1.50 4.00
200 Benoit Benjamin .40 1.00
201 Ken Norman IA .40 1.00
202 Clippers Jersey .40 1.00
203 Los Angeles Lakers .40 1.00
204 Pat Riley CO 1.50 4.00
205 Magic Johnson 10.00 25.00
206 Byron Scott 1.25 3.00
207 James Worthy 2.50 6.00
208 A.C. Green 1.50 4.00
209 Mychal Thompson .75 2.00
210 Kareem Abdul-Jabbar 6.00 15.00
211 Byron Scott IA .75 2.00
212 Lakers Jersey .40 1.00
213 Phoenix Suns Logo .40 1.00
214 Cotton Fitzsimmons CO .75 2.00
215 Kevin Johnson 2.00 5.00
216 Dan Majerle 2.00 5.00
217 Eddie Johnson .40 1.00
218 Armon Gilliam .40 1.00
219 Tom Chambers 1.25 3.00
220 Mark West .40 1.00
221 Kevin Johnson IA .75 2.00
222 Suns Jersey .40 1.00
223 Portland Trail .40 1.00
224 Mike Schuler CO .40 1.00
225 Terry Porter .75 2.00
226 Clyde Drexler 6.00 15.00
227 Jerome Kersey .40 1.00
228 Kiki Vandeweghe 1.25 3.00
229 Steve Johnson .40 1.00
230 Kevin Duckworth .40 1.00
231 Jerome Kersey IA .40 1.00
232 Trail Blazers Jersey .40 1.00
233 Sacramento Kings Logo .40 1.00
234 Jerry Reynolds CO .40 1.00
235 Kenny Smith .75 2.00
236 Rodney McCray .40 1.00
237 Derek Smith .75 2.00
238 Ed Pinckney .40 1.00
239 Jim Petersen .40 1.00
240 LaSalle Thompson .40 1.00
241 Kenny Smith IA .40 1.00
242 Kings Jersey .40 1.00
243 Seattle Supersonics .40 1.00
244 Bernie Bickerstaff CO .40 1.00
245 Nate McMillan .75 2.00
246 Dale Ellis .75 2.00
247 Xavier McDaniel .40 1.00
248 Derrick McKey .40 1.00
249 Michael Cage .40 1.00
250 Alton Lister .40 1.00
251 Xavier McDaniel IA .40 1.00
252 Supersonics Jersey .40 1.00
253 AS Puzzle 1.25 3.00
Patrick Ewing
Hakeem Olajuwon
254 AS Puzzle 1.25 3.00
Karl Malone
255 AS Puzzle .40 1.00
256 AS Puzzle .40 1.00
257 AS Puzzle .40 1.00
Fat Lever
258 AS Puzzle .40 1.00
259 Lenny Wilkens CO AS .75 2.00
260 Isiah Thomas AS 1.50 4.00
261 Michael Jordan AS 10.00 25.00
262 Dominique Wilkins AS 2.50 6.00
263 Charles Barkley AS 4.00 10.00
264 Moses Malone AS 1.25 3.00
265 Mark Jackson AS 1.25 3.00
266 Mark Price AS .75 2.00
267 Larry Nance AS .75 2.00
268 Terry Cummings AS .75 2.00
269 Kevin McHale AS 1.25 3.00
270 Brad Daugherty AS .40 1.00
271 Patrick Ewing AS 2.00 5.00
272 Pat Riley CO AS 1.25 3.00
273 John Stockton AS 5.00 12.00
274 Dale Ellis AS .40 1.00
275 Alex English AS .75 2.00
276 Karl Malone AS 4.00 10.00
277 Hakeem Olajuwon AS 3.00 8.00
278 Kareem Abdul-Jabbar AS 3.00 8.00
279 Clyde Drexler AS 3.00 8.00
280 Chris Mullin AS 1.25 3.00
281 James Worthy AS 1.50 4.00
282 Tom Chambers AS .75 2.00
283 Kevin Duckworth AS .40 1.00
284 Mark Eaton AS .40 1.00
285 Michael Jordan AW 15.00 40.00
286 Mark Jackson AW 1.25 3.00
287 Charles Barkley AW 3.00 8.00
288 Jack Sikma AW .40 1.00
289 Michael Cage AW .40 1.00
290 Mark Eaton AW .40 1.00
291 John Stockton AW 4.00 10.00
292 Doug Moe CO AW .40 1.00
XX Album 6.00 15.00
Dominique Wilkins
Larry Bird

1989-90 Panini Stickers Spanish

The 1989-90 Panini Spanish Basketball set consists of 272 stickers, each measuring approximately 2 1/8" by 3". The stickers were designed to be placed in an album measuring approximately 9" by 11 7/8". The sticker fronts display color player photos and are arranged according to teams within the Atlantic and Central Divisions of the Eastern Conference, and the Midwest and Pacific Divisions of the Western Conference. The set closes with the topical subset: NBA All Stars (244-267), the NBA logo (268) and four Puzzle Cards (269-272).

COMPLETE SET (272) 125.00 275.00
1 Boston Celtics Logo .40 1.00
2 Dennis Johnson .75 2.00
3 Reggie Lewis .75 2.00
4 Kelvin Upshaw .40 1.00
5 Kevin Gamble .40 1.00
6 Larry Bird 8.00 20.00
7 Ed Pinckney .40 1.00
8 Kevin McHale 2.00 5.00
9 Robert Parish .75 2.00
10 Miami Heat Logo .40 1.00
11 Jon Sundvold .40 1.00
12 Rory Sparrow .40 1.00
13 Dwayne Washington .40 1.00
14 Billy Thompson .40 1.00
15 Grant Long .40 1.00
16 Kevin Edwards .40 1.00
17 Pat Cummings .40 1.00
18 Rony Seikaly .40 1.00
19 New Jersey Nets Logo .40 1.00
20 Dennis Hopson .40 1.00
21 Lester Conner .40 1.00
22 Chris Morris .40 1.00
23 Charles Shackleford .40 1.00
24 Purvis Short .40 1.00
25 Roy Hinson .40 1.00
26 Sam Bowie .60 1.50
27 Joe Barry Carroll .40 1.00
28 New York Knicks Logo .40 1.00
29 Mark Jackson 1.00 2.50
30 Rod Strickland .75 2.00
31 Gerald Wilkins .40 1.00
32 Trent Tucker .40 1.00
33 Johnny Newman .40 1.00
34 Kenny Walker .40 1.00
35 Charles Oakley .60 1.50
36 Patrick Ewing 3.00 8.00
37 Philadelphia 76ers Logo .40 1.00
38 Scott Brooks .40 1.00
39 Johnny Dawkins .40 1.00
40 Hersey Hawkins .75 2.00
41 Derek Smith .75 2.00
42 Ron Anderson .40 1.00
43 Charles Barkley 5.00 12.00
44 Rick Mahorn .40 1.00
45 Mike Gminski .40 1.00
46 Washington Bullets Logo .40 1.00
47 Steve Colter .40 1.00
48 Jeff Malone .40 1.00
49 Ledell Eackles .40 1.00
50 Darrell Walker .40 1.00
51 Bernard King .75 2.00
52 Charles Jones .40 1.00
53 Mark Alarie .40 1.00
54 Harvey Grant .40 1.00
55 Atlanta Hawks Logo .40 1.00
56 Anthony Webb .75 2.00
57 Glenn Rivers .75 2.00
58 John Battle .40 1.00
59 Dominique Wilkins 3.00 8.00
60 Cliff Levingston .40 1.00
61 Jon Koncak .40 1.00
62 Antoine Carr .40 1.00
63 Moses Malone 1.25 3.00
64 Chicago Bulls Logo .75 2.00
65 Craig Hodges .40 1.00
66 John Paxson .75 2.00
67 Michael Jordan 20.00 50.00
68 Scottie Pippen 6.00 15.00
69 Charles Davis .40 1.00
70 Horace Grant 1.00 2.50
71 Will Perdue .40 1.00
72 Bill Cartwright .75 2.00
73 Cleveland Cavaliers Logo .40 1.00
74 Mark Price .75 2.00
75 Craig Ehlo .60 1.50
76 Chris Dudley .40 1.00
77 Randolph Keys .40 1.00
78 Larry Nance .75 2.00
79 John Williams .40 1.00
80 Paul Mokeski .40 1.00
81 Wayne Rollins .40 1.00
82 Pistons .40 1.00
83 Isiah Thomas 2.50 6.00
84 Vinnie Johnson .60 1.50
85 Joe Dumars 1.25 3.00
86 Mark Aguirre .60 1.50
87 Dennis Rodman 4.00 10.00
88 John Salley .75 2.00
89 James Edwards .40 1.00
90 Bill Laimbeer .75 2.00
91 Indiana Pacers Logo .40 1.00
92 Reggie Miller 4.00 10.00
93 Vern Fleming .40 1.00
94 Randy Wittman .40 1.00
95 Chuck Person .40 1.00
96 Mike Sanders .40 1.00
97 Rickey Green .40 1.00
98 Lasalle Thompson .40 1.00
99 Rik Smits .75 2.00
100 Milwaukee Bucks Logo .40 1.00
101 Jay Humphries .40 1.00
102 Ricky Pierce .40 1.00
103 Paul Pressey .40 1.00
104 Alvin Robertson .40 1.00
105 Tony Brown .40 1.00
106 Fred Roberts .40 1.00
107 Randy Breuer .40 1.00
108 Jack Sikma .60 1.50
109 Orlando Magic Logo .40 1.00
110 Sam Vincent .40 1.00
111 Reggie Theus .75 2.00
112 Scott Skiles .75 2.00
113 Otis Smith .40 1.00
114 Sidney Green .40 1.00
115 Nick Anderson 1.25 3.00
116 Terry Catledge .40 1.00
117 Mark Acres .40 1.00
118 Hornets .40 1.00
119 Muggsy Bogues 1.00 2.50
120 Dell Curry .40 1.00
121 Rex Chapman .75 2.00
122 Kelly Tripucka .40 1.00
123 Jerry Sichting .40 1.00
124 Brian Rowsom .40 1.00
125 J.R. Reid .40 1.00
126 Stuart Gray .40 1.00
127 Dallas Mavericks Logo .40 1.00
128 Brad Davis .40 1.00
129 Derek Harper .75 2.00
130 Rolando Blackman .75 2.00
131 Adrian Dantley .75 2.00
132 Herb Williams .40 1.00
133 Bill Wennington .40 1.00
134 Sam Perkins .75 2.00
135 James Donaldson .40 1.00
136 Denver Nuggets Logo .40 1.00
137 Walter Davis .75 2.00
138 Michael Adams .40 1.00
139 Lafayette Lever .40 1.00
140 Alex English .75 2.00
141 Todd Lichti .40 1.00
142 Jerome Lane .40 1.00
143 Tim Kempton .40 1.00
144 Blair Rasmussen .40 1.00
145 Houston Rockets Logo .40 1.00
146 Eric Floyd .40 1.00
147 Mike Woodson .40 1.00
148 Derrick Chievous .40 1.00
149 John Lucas .50 1.25
150 Buck Johnson .40 1.00
151 Otis Thorpe .40 1.00
152 Larry Smith .40 1.00
153 Akeem Olajuwon 5.00 12.00
154 Minnesota T'wolves Logo .40 1.00
155 Pooh Richardson .40 1.00
156 Sidney Lowe .40 1.00
157 Doug West .40 1.00
158 Adrian Branch .75 2.00
159 Tony Campbell .40 1.00
160 David Rivers .40 1.00
161 Steve Johnson .40 1.00
162 Brad Lohaus .40 1.00
163 San Antonio Spurs Logo .40 1.00
164 Maurice Cheeks .75 2.00
165 Vernon Maxwell .40 1.00
166 Zarko Paspalj .40 1.00
167 Sean Elliott 2.00 5.00
168 Terry Cummings .75 2.00
169 Frank Brickowski .40 1.00
170 Willie Anderson .40 1.00
171 David Robinson 10.00 25.00
172 Utah Jazz Logo .40 1.00
173 John Stockton 6.00 15.00
174 Darrell Griffith .60 1.50
175 Bobby Hansen .40 1.00
176 Karl Malone 6.00 15.00
177 Mike Brown .40 1.00
178 Thurl Bailey .40 1.00
179 Eric Leckner .40 1.00
180 Mark Eaton .40 1.00
181 Golden State Warrior Logo .40 1.00
182 Winston Garland .40 1.00
183 Mitch Richmond 2.00 5.00
184 Sarunas Marciulionis .75 2.00
185 Terry Teagle .40 1.00
186 Chris Mullin 1.50 4.00
187 Rod Higgins .40 1.00
188 Uwe Blab .40 1.00
189 Manute Bol .40 1.00
190 Los Angeles Clippers Logo .40 1.00
191 Gary Grant .40 1.00
192 Ron Harper .75 2.00
193 Ken Norman .40 1.00
194 Charles Smith .40 1.00
195 Danny Manning .75 2.00
196 Joe Wolf .40 1.00
197 Benoit Benjamin .40 1.00
198 Ken Bannister .40 1.00
199 Los Angeles Lakers Logo .40 1.00
200 Earvin Johnson 8.00 20.00
201 Byron Scott .75 2.00
202 Michael Cooper .75 2.00
203 Orlando Woolridge .40 1.00
204 James Worthy 1.50 4.00
205 A.C. Green .75 2.00
206 Vlade Divac 2.50 6.00
207 Mychal Thompson .40 1.00
208 Phoenix Suns Logo .40 1.00
209 Kevin Johnson .75 2.00
210 Jeff Hornacek 1.50 4.00
211 Greg Grant .40 1.00
212 Dan Majerle .75 2.00
213 Tim Perry .40 1.00
214 Eddie Johnson .40 1.00
215 Tom Chambers .75 2.00
216 Andrew Lang .40 1.00
217 Portland Trail Blazers Logo .40 1.00
218 Clyde Drexler 5.00 12.00
219 Terry Porter .75 2.00
220 Drazen Petrovic 3.00 8.00
221 Jerome Kersey .40 1.00
222 Mark Bryant .40 1.00
223 Danny Young .40 1.00
224 Wayne Cooper .40 1.00
225 Kevin Duckworth .40 1.00
226 Sacramento Kings Logo .40 1.00
227 Danny Ainge 1.25 3.00
228 Michael Jackson .40 1.00
229 Vinny Del Negro .40 1.00
230 Kenny Smith .75 2.00
231 Harold Pressley .40 1.00
232 Rodney McCray .40 1.00
233 Wayman Tisdale .40 1.00
234 Greg Kite .40 1.00
235 Seattle Supersonics Logo .40 1.00
236 Sedale Threatt .40 1.00
237 Avery Johnson 1.25 3.00
238 Nate McMillan .60 1.50
239 Dale Ellis .40 1.00
240 Xavier McDaniel .40 1.00
241 Derrick McKey .40 1.00
242 Michael Cage .40 1.00
243 Olden Polynice .40 1.00
244 Charles Barkley 3.00 8.00
245 Larry Bird 4.00 10.00
246 Tom Chambers .75 2.00
247 Adrian Dantley .40 1.00
248 Clyde Drexler 3.00 8.00
249 Joe Dumars .75 2.00
250 Dale Ellis .40 1.00
251 Patrick Ewing 1.50 4.00
252 A.C. Green .75 2.00
253 Earvin Johnson 4.00 10.00
254 Michael Jordan 12.50 30.00
255 Bill Laimbeer .75 2.00
256 Jeff Malone .40 1.00
257 Karl Malone 3.00 8.00
258 Moses Malone .75 2.00
259 Xavier McDaniel .40 1.00
260 Akeem Olajuwon 2.50 6.00
261 Robert Parish .75 2.00
262 Mark Price .75 2.00
263 Jack Sikma .40 1.00
264 John Stockton 4.00 10.00
265 Isiah Thomas 2.00 5.00
266 Dominique Wilkins 2.50 6.00
267 James Worthy 1.25 3.00
268 NBA Logo .40 1.00
269 Puzzle Card .40 1.00
270 Puzzle Card .40 1.00
271 Puzzle Card .40 1.00
272 Puzzle Card .40 1.00

1990-91 Panini Stickers Spanish

COMPLETE SET (217) 150.00 300.00
1 NBA Logo .40 1.00
2 Boston Celtics Logo .40 1.00
3 Reggie Lewis .60 1.50
4 Larry Bird 6.00 15.00
5 Michael Smith .40 1.00
6 Kevin McHale 2.00 5.00
7 Joe Kleine .40 1.00
8 Robert Parish 1.25 3.00
9 Miami Heat Logo .40 1.00
10 Sherman Douglas .40 1.00
11 Kevin Edwards .40 1.00
12 Glen Rice 2.00 5.00
13 Billy Thompson 1.25 3.00
14 Telfis Frank .60 1.50
15 Rony Seikaly .40 1.00
16 New Jersey Nets Logo .40 1.00
17 Mookie Blaylock .75 2.00
18 Lester Conner .40 1.00
19 Purvis Short .40 1.00
20 Chris Morris .40 1.00
21 Roy Hinson .40 1.00
22 Sam Bowie .60 1.50
23 New York Knicks Logo .40 1.00
24 Maurice Cheeks .75 2.00
25 Mark Jackson 1.25 3.00
26 Gerald Wilkins .40 1.00
27 Kenny Walker .40 1.00
28 Charles Oakley .40 1.00
29 Patrick Ewing 4.00 10.00
30 Philadelphia 76ers Logo .40 1.00
31 Johnny Dawkins .40 1.00
32 Hersey Hawkins .60 1.50
33 Ron Anderson .40 1.00
34 Charles Barkley 5.00 12.00
35 Rick Mahorn .40 1.00
36 Mike Gminski .40 1.00
37 Washington Bullets Logo .40 1.00
38 Ledell Eackles .40 1.00
39 Darrell Walker .40 1.00
40 Bernard King .75 2.00
41 John Williams .40 1.00
42 Mark Alarie .60 1.50
43 Harvey Grant .40 1.00
44 Atlanta Hawks Logo .40 1.00
45 Anthony Webb .75 2.00
46 Doc Rivers .75 2.00
47 Kenny Smith .75 2.00
48 Dominique Wilkins 4.00 10.00
49 Kevin Willis .75 2.00
50 Moses Malone 1.25 3.00
51 Charlotte Hornets Logo .40 1.00
52 Muggsy Bogues .75 2.00
53 Rex Chapman .75 2.00
54 Dell Curry .75 2.00
55 Kelly Tripucka .40 1.00
56 Armon Gilliam .40 1.00
57 J.R. Reid .40 1.00
58 Chicago Bulls Logo .40 1.00
59 Craig Hodges .40 1.00
60 John Paxson .75 2.00
61 Michael Jordan 20.00 50.00
62 Scottie Pippen 6.00 15.00
63 Horace Grant 1.00 2.50
64 Stacey King .40 1.00
65 Cleveland Cavaliers Logo .40 1.00
66 Mark Price .75 2.00
67 Craig Ehlo .60 1.50
68 Winston Bennett .40 1.00
69 John Williams .40 1.00
70 Larry Nance .75 2.00
71 Brad Daugherty .40 1.00
72 Detroit Pistons Logo .40 1.00
73 Isiah Thomas 4.00 10.00
74 Joe Dumars 2.50 6.00
75 Vinnie Johnson .75 2.00
76 Dennis Rodman 4.00 10.00
77 Bill Laimbeer .75 2.00
78 James Edwards .40 1.00
79 Indiana Pacers Logo .40 1.00
80 Vern Fleming .40 1.00
81 Reggie Miller 5.00 12.00
82 Chuck Person .40 1.00
83 LaSalle Thompson .40 1.00
84 Detlef Schrempf .75 2.00
85 Rik Smits .75 2.00
86 Milwaukee Bucks Logo .40 1.00
87 Alvin Robertson .40 1.00
88 Jay Humphries .40 1.00
89 Ricky Pierce .40 1.00
90 Brad Lohaus .40 1.00
91 Jack Sikma .60 1.50
92 Greg Anderson .40 1.00
93 Dallas Mavericks Logo .40 1.00
94 Derek Harper .75 2.00
95 Rolando Blackman .75 2.00
96 Brad Davis .60 1.50
97 Roy Tarpley .40 1.00
98 Herb Williams .40 1.00
99 James Donaldson .40 1.00
100 Denver Nuggets Logo .40 1.00
101 Michael Adams .40 1.00
102 Walter Davis .75 2.00
103 Todd Lichti .40 1.00
104 Jerome Lane .40 1.00
105 Blair Rasmussen .40 1.00
106 Joe Barry Carroll .40 1.00
107 Houston Rockets Logo .40 1.00
108 Eric Floyd .40 1.00
109 Mitchell Wiggins .40 1.00
110 Vernon Maxwell .40 1.00
111 Otis Thorpe .60 1.50
112 Buck Johnson .40 1.00
113 Hakeem Olajuwon 5.00 12.00
114 Minnesota T-wolves Logo .40 1.00
115 Pooh Richardson .40 1.00
116 Tony Campbell .40 1.00
117 Tyrone Corbin .40 1.00
118 Sam Mitchell .60 1.50
119 Tod Murphy .40 1.00
120 Randy Breuer .40 1.00
121 Orlando Magic Logo .40 1.00
122 Scott Skiles .75 2.00
123 Otis Smith .40 1.00
124 Terry Catledge .40 1.00
125 Jerry Reynolds .40 1.00
126 Nick Anderson .75 2.00
127 Sidney Green .40 1.00
128 San Antonio Spurs Logo .40 1.00
129 Rod Strickland .60 1.50
130 Willie Anderson .40 1.00
131 Sean Elliott 1.25 3.00
132 Terry Cummings .75 2.00
133 Frank Brickowski .40 1.00
134 David Robinson 6.00 15.00
135 Utah Jazz Logo .40 1.00
136 John Stockton 6.00 15.00
137 Darrell Griffith .40 1.00
138 Theodore Edwards .40 1.00
139 Karl Malone 6.00 15.00
140 Thurl Bailey .40 1.00
141 Mark Eaton .40 1.00
142 Golden St. Warriors Logo .40 1.00
143 Tim Hardaway 2.00 5.00
144 Mitch Richmond 2.00 5.00
145 Chris Mullin 2.00 5.00
146 Sarunas Marciulionis .75 2.00
147 Terry Teagle .40 1.00
148 Manute Bol .40 1.00
149 L.A. Clippers Logo .40 1.00
150 Gary Grant .40 1.00
151 Ron Harper .75 2.00
152 Ken Norman .40 1.00
153 Charles Smith .40 1.00
154 Danny Manning .75 2.00
155 Benoit Benjamin .40 1.00
156 L.A. Lakers Logo .40 1.00
157 Magic Johnson 6.00 15.00
158 Byron Scott 1.00 2.50
159 James Worthy 2.00 5.00
160 A.C. Green 1.00 2.50
161 Vlade Divac .75 2.00
162 Mychal Thompson .60 1.50
163 Phoenix Suns Logo .40 1.00
164 Kevin Johnson .75 2.00
165 Jeff Hornacek .75 2.00
166 Dan Majerle .75 2.00
167 Tom Chambers .75 2.00
168 Kurt Rambis .75 2.00
169 Mark West .40 1.00
170 Portland Trailblazers Logo .40 1.00
171 Terry Porter .75 2.00
172 Clyde Drexler 5.00 12.00
173 Jerome Kersey .40 1.00
174 Cliff Robinson 1.25 3.00
175 Buck Williams .75 2.00
176 Kevin Duckworth .40 1.00
177 Sacramento Kings Logo .40 1.00
178 Vinny Del Negro .60 1.50
179 Danny Ainge 1.25 3.00
180 Wayman Tisdale .60 1.50
181 Antoine Carr .40 1.00
182 Greg Kite .40 1.00
183 Ralph Sampson .75 2.00
184 Seattle Sonics Logo .40 1.00
185 Nate McMillan .60 1.50
186 Dale Ellis .60 1.50
187 Xavier McDaniel .60 1.50
188 Shawn Kemp 2.00 5.00
189 Derrick McKey .40 1.00
190 Michael Cage .40 1.00
191 Dennis Rodman AW 1.00 2.50
192 Dennis Rodman AW 1.00 2.50
193 Darrell Walker AW .40 1.00
194 Darrell Walker AW .40 1.00
195 Ricky Pierce AW .40 1.00
196 Ricky Pierce AW .40 1.00
197 Isiah Thomas AW 1.00 2.50
198 Isiah Thomas AW 1.00 2.50
199 David Robinson AW 1.50 4.00
200 David Robinson AW 1.50 4.00
201 Magic Johnson AW 1.50 4.00
202 Magic Johnson AW 1.50 4.00
203 Larry Bird AW 2.00 5.00
204 Larry Bird AW 2.00 5.00
205 Michael Jordan AW 4.00 10.00
206 Michael Jordan AW 4.00 10.00
207 Hakeem Olajuwon AW 1.25 3.00
208 Hakeem Olajuwon AW 1.25 3.00
209 Puzzle Card #1 .40 1.00
210 Puzzle Card #2 .40 1.00
211 Puzzle Card #3 .40 1.00
212 Puzzle Card #4 .40 1.00
213 Puzzle Card #5 .40 1.00
214 Puzzle Card #6 .40 1.00
215 Puzzle Card #7 .40 1.00
216 Puzzle Card #8 .40 1.00
217 Puzzle Card #9 .40 1.00

2011 Panini Team Colors National Convention

TC5 Derrick Rose 2.00 5.00
TC6 Joakim Noah 1.25 3.00

2009-10 Panini Threads

COMP.SET w/o RCs (100) 15.00 30.00
RC STATED PRINT RUN 126 TO 700 SETS
ASTERISK CARDS FROM PANINI UPDATE
1 LeBron James 1.50 4.00
2 Dwyane Wade .60 1.50
3 Chris Paul .50 1.25
4 Kobe Bryant 1.50 4.00
5 Dirk Nowitzki .50 1.25
6 Dwight Howard .30 .75
7 Al Jefferson .30 .75
8 Chris Bosh .40 1.00
9 Kevin Durant 1.00 2.50
10 Danny Granger .30 .75
11 Tim Duncan .60 1.50
12 Antawn Jamison .30 .75
13 Deron Williams .30 .75
14 Carmelo Anthony .50 1.25
15 Zach Randolph .30 .75
16 Brandon Roy .40 1.00
17 Stephen Jackson .30 .75
18 Pau Gasol .40 1.00
19 Tony Parker .40 1.00
20 David West .30 .75
21 Devin Harris .25 .60
22 Joe Johnson .30 .75
23 Amare Stoudemire .30 .75
24 Yao Ming .50 1.25
25 Caron Butler .30 .75
26 Kevin Martin .30 .75
27 Vince Carter .50 1.25
28 David Lee .25 .60
29 Andre Iguodala .30 .75
30 Paul Pierce .40 1.00
31 Carlos Boozer .30 .75
32 Troy Murphy .25 .60
33 Steve Nash .40 1.00
34 Shaquille O'Neal .75 2.00
35 Al Harrington .30 .75
36 Ben Gordon .30 .75
37 LaMarcus Aldridge .40 1.00
38 Gilbert Arenas .30 .75
39 Andre Miller .30 .75
40 Chauncey Billups .40 1.00
41 Gerald Wallace .30 .75
42 Jamal Crawford .40 1.00
43 Michael Redd .30 .75
44 Derrick Rose .60 1.50
45 Monta Ellis .30 .75
46 Hedo Turkoglu .30 .75
47 Kevin Garnett .60 1.50
48 Richard Jefferson .30 .75
49 Mehmet Okur .25 .60
50 Baron Davis .30 .75
51 Rudy Gay .40 1.00
52 Rashard Lewis .30 .75
53 Corey Maggette .30 .75
54 Richard Hamilton .30 .75
55 John Salmons .30 .75
56 Ron Artest .40 1.00
57 Jameer Nelson .25 .60
58 Russell Westbrook 1.00 2.50
59 Allen Iverson .50 1.25
60 O.J. Mayo .25 .60
61 Rajon Rondo .40 1.00
62 Jason Terry .30 .75
63 Mo Williams .30 .75
64 Josh Smith .30 .75
65 Jeff Green .30 .75
66 Nate Robinson .25 .60
67 Andris Biedrins .25 .60
68 Tracy McGrady .40 1.00
69 Raymond Felton .30 .75
70 Josh Howard .30 .75
71 Charlie Villanueva .25 .60
72 Jose Calderon .25 .60
73 Ray Allen .40 1.00
74 Andrew Bogut .30 .75
75 Emeka Okafor .30 .75
76 Paul Millsap .30 .75
77 Jason Kidd .40 1.00
78 Elton Brand .40 1.00
79 Nene .30 .75
80 T.J. Ford .25 .60
81 Andrew Bynum .25 .60
82 Randy Foye .25 .60
83 Manu Ginobili .40 1.00
84 Marcus Camby .25 .60
85 Shawn Marion .30 .75
86 Al Thornton .30 .75
87 Mike Bibby .30 .75
88 Jason Richardson .40 1.00
89 Al Horford .40 1.00
90 Tayshaun Prince .30 .75
91 Luis Scola .30 .75
92 Brad Miller .30 .75
93 Boris Diaw .30 .75
94 Brook Lopez .30 .75
95 Lamar Odom .30 .75
96 Luol Deng .30 .75
97 Andrea Bargnani .30 .75
98 Jermaine O'Neal .30 .75
99 Rasheed Wallace .40 1.00
100 Michael Beasley .25 .60
101 Blake Griffin/640 AU RC 40.00 100.00
102 Hasheem Thabeet/315 AU RC 4.00 10.00
103 James Harden/660 AU RC 60.00 150.00
104 Tyreke Evans/150 AU RC 30.00 80.00
105 R.Beaubois/640 AU RC 6.00 15.00
106 Jonny Flynn/625 AU RC 4.00 10.00
107 Stephen Curry/625 AU RC 200.00 400.00
108 Jordan Hill/700 AU RC 5.00 12.00
109 Derrick Brown/150 AU RC 12.00 30.00
110 B.Jennings/640 AU RC 6.00 15.00
111 T.Williams/160 AU RC 4.00 10.00
112 G.Henderson/630 AU RC 5.00 12.00
113 T.Hansbrough/650 AU RC 10.00 25.00
114 Earl Clark/625 AU RC 5.00 12.00
115 Austin Daye/700 AU RC 4.00 10.00
116 James Johnson/630 AU RC 5.00 12.00
117 Jrue Holiday/630 AU RC 8.00 20.00
118 Ty Lawson/330 AU RC 6.00 15.00
119 Jeff Teague/660 AU RC 6.00 15.00
120 Eric Maynor/126 AU RC 15.00 40.00
121 Darren Collison/160 AU RC 6.00 15.00
122 Dante Cunningham/650 AU RC 4.00 10.00
123 Omri Casspi/660 AU RC 5.00 12.00
124 B.J. Mullens/630 AU RC 4.00 10.00
125 Taj Gibson/330 AU RC 6.00 15.00
126 DeMarre Carroll/630 AU RC 5.00 12.00
127 Wayne Ellington/630 AU RC 6.00 15.00
128 Toney Douglas/630 AU RC 4.00 10.00
129 Jeff Pendergraph/660 AU RC 4.00 10.00
130 DaJuan Summers/630 AU RC 4.00 10.00
131 Sam Young/365 AU RC 4.00 10.00
132 DeJuan Blair/625 AU RC 5.00 12.00
133 Jodie Meeks/625 AU RC 6.00 15.00
134 Chase Budinger/640 AU RC 5.00 12.00
135 Taylor Griffin/640 AU RC 4.00 10.00
136 DeMar DeRozan/700 RC* 12.00 30.00
137 Jonas Jerebko/700 RC* 6.00 15.00
138 Wesley Matthews/683 RC* 6.00 15.00
139 Marcus Thornton/696 RC* 5.00 12.00
140 Jermaine Taylor/696 RC* 4.00 10.00

2009-10 Panini Threads Century Proof Gold

*GOLD: 1.5X TO 4X BASE HI
STATED PRINT RUN 99 SER.#'d SETS

2009-10 Panini Threads Century Proof Orange

*ORANGE: .5X TO 1.25X BASE HI
RANDOM INSERTS IN RETAIL PACKS

2009-10 Panini Threads Century Proof Platinum

*PLATINUM: 3X TO 8X BASE HI
STATED PRINT RUN 25 SER.#'d SETS

2009-10 Panini Threads Century Proof Silver

*SILVER: .75X TO 2X BASE HI
STATED PRINT RUN 249 SER.#'d SETS

2009-10 Panini Threads ABA Legends

COMPLETE SET (10) 6.00 15.00
RANDOM INSERTS IN PACKS
*PROOF: .75X TO 2X BASE HI
PRINT RUN 100 SER.#'d SETS
1 Dan Issel 1.25 3.00
2 Rick Barry 1.25 3.00
3 Artis Gilmore 1.25 3.00
4 George Gervin 1.50 4.00
5 David Thompson 1.25 3.00
6 Louie Dampier 1.50 4.00
7 Moses Malone 1.50 4.00
8 Connie Hawkins 1.50 4.00
9 George McGinnis 1.00 2.50
10 Billy Cunningham 1.50 4.00

2009-10 Panini Threads ABA Legends Autographs

STATED PRINT RUN 25 SER.#'d SETS
1 Dan Issel 10.00 25.00
2 Rick Barry 20.00 40.00
3 Artis Gilmore 20.00 40.00
4 George Gervin 25.00 50.00
5 David Thompson 15.00 30.00
8 Connie Hawkins 25.00 50.00
9 George McGinnis 8.00 20.00

2009-10 Panini Threads Century Collection Materials

STATED PRINT RUN 100 TO 250 SER.#'d SETS
1 Dwight Howard/250 2.50 6.00
2 Tim Duncan/100 5.00 12.00
3 Kobe Bryant/250 8.00 20.00
4 Tracy McGrady/250 3.00 8.00
6 Mike Bibby/250 2.50 6.00
9 Jason Kidd/250 3.00 8.00
10 LaMarcus Aldridge/250 3.00 8.00
11 Michael Beasley/250 2.00 5.00
12 Andre Iguodala/250 2.50 6.00
13 Elton Brand/250 3.00 8.00
14 LeBron James/100 10.00 25.00
17 Chris Paul/250 4.00 10.00
19 Dwyane Wade/250 5.00 12.00

2009-10 Panini Threads Century Collection Materials Prime
*PRIME: .75X TO 2X BASE HI
STATED PRINT RUN 5 TO 25 SER.#'d SETS
SOME UNPRICED DUE TO SCARCITY
8 Dirk Nowitzki/20 8.00 20.00
15 Amare Stoudemire/25 5.00 12.00
18 Gilbert Arenas/25 5.00 12.00
20 Tony Parker/20 6.00 15.00

2009-10 Panini Threads Century Stars
COMPLETE SET (25) 15.00 30.00
RANDOM INSERTS IN PACKS
*PROOF: .6X TO 1.5X BASE HI
PROOF PRINT RUN 100 SER.#'d SETS
1 Joe Johnson .60 1.50
2 Kevin Garnett 1.25 3.00
3 LeBron James 3.00 8.00
4 Jason Kidd .75 2.00
5 Carmelo Anthony 1.00 2.50
6 Yao Ming 1.00 2.50
7 Baron Davis .60 1.50
8 Kobe Bryant 3.00 8.00
9 Chris Paul 1.00 2.50
10 Kevin Durant 2.00 5.00
11 Vince Carter 1.00 2.50
12 Grant Hill 1.00 2.50
13 Tony Parker .75 2.00
14 Carlos Boozer .60 1.50
15 Antawn Jamison .60 1.50
16 Derrick Rose 1.25 3.00
17 Richard Hamilton .60 1.50
18 Danny Granger .60 1.50
19 Dwyane Wade 1.25 3.00
20 Andrew Bogut .60 1.50
21 Devin Harris .50 1.25
22 Nate Robinson .50 1.25
23 Elton Brand .75 2.00
24 Brandon Roy .75 2.00
25 Chris Bosh .75 2.00

2009-10 Panini Threads Century Stars Autographs
STATED PRINT RUN 10 TO 50 SER.#'d SETS
SOME UNPRICED DUE TO SCARCITY
4 Jason Kidd/25 15.00 40.00
8 Kobe Bryant/50 75.00 150.00
13 Tony Parker/25 15.00 40.00
18 Danny Granger/25 8.00 20.00

2009-10 Panini Threads Century Stars Materials
STATED PRINT RUN 100 TO 250 SER.#'d SETS
2 Kevin Garnett/250 5.00 12.00
3 LeBron James/100 10.00 25.00
4 Jason Kidd/250 3.00 8.00
6 Yao Ming/250 4.00 10.00
8 Kobe Bryant/250 8.00 20.00
9 Chris Paul/250 4.00 10.00
10 Kevin Durant/250 6.00 15.00
14 Carlos Boozer/250 2.50 6.00
19 Dwyane Wade/250 5.00 12.00
20 Andrew Bogut/250 2.50 6.00
22 Nate Robinson/250 2.00 5.00
23 Elton Brand/250 3.00 8.00
25 Chris Bosh/250 3.00 8.00

2009-10 Panini Threads Century Stars Materials Prime
*PRIME: .75X TO 2X BASE HI
STATED PRINT RUN 3 TO 25 SER.#'d SETS
SOME UNPRICED DUE TO SCARCITY
10 Kevin Durant/25 15.00 40.00
21 Devin Harris/25 4.00 10.00

2009-10 Panini Threads Generations
COMPLETE SET (15) 10.00 25.00
RANDOM INSERTS IN PACKS
*PROOF: 1X TO 2.5X BASE HI
PROOF PRINT RUN 100 SER.#'d SETS
1 J.West/K.Bryant 3.00 8.00
2 M.Redd/O.Robertson .75 2.00
3 C.Mullin/S.Jackson .75 2.00
4 C.Anthony/D.Thompson 1.00 2.50
5 B.Gordon/I.Thomas .75 2.00
6 K.Johnson/S.Nash .75 2.00
7 J.Hill/W.Reed .75 2.00
8 S.Curry/T.Hardaway 8.00 20.00
9 A.Dantley/D.Williams .60 1.50
10 D.Granger/J.Rose .75 2.00
11 P.Gasol/V.Divac .75 2.00
12 K.Durant/X.McDaniel 2.00 5.00
13 J.Havlicek/L.Bird 2.00 5.00
14 A.English/C.Billups .75 2.00
15 C.Hawkins/R.Artest .75 2.00

2009-10 Panini Threads Generations Autographs
STATED PRINT RUN 25 TO 50 SER.#'d SETS
1 J.West/K.Bryant/25 150.00 300.00
7 J.Hill/W.Reed/50 10.00 25.00
8 S.Curry/T.Hardaway/50 200.00 400.00

2009-10 Panini Threads Generations Materials
STATED PRINT RUN 100 SER.#'d SETS
UNPRICED PRIME PRINT RUN 10 SER.#'d SETS
1 J.West/K.Bryant 15.00 30.00
3 C.Mullin/S.Jackson 4.00 10.00

2009-10 Panini Threads Jerseys
STATED PRINT RUN 25 TO 100 SER.#'d SETS
1 LeBron James/100 8.00 20.00
2 Dwyane Wade/100 4.00 10.00
3 Chris Paul/100 4.00 10.00
4 Kobe Bryant/100 8.00 20.00
5 Dirk Nowitzki/100 4.00 10.00
6 Dwight Howard/100 2.50 6.00
8 Chris Bosh/100 3.00 8.00
9 Kevin Durant/100 8.00 20.00
11 Tim Duncan/100 5.00 12.00
13 Deron Williams/100 2.50 6.00
16 Brandon Roy/100 3.00 8.00
17 Stephen Jackson/100 2.50 6.00
18 Pau Gasol/100 3.00 8.00
19 Tony Parker/100 3.00 8.00
20 David West/100 2.50 6.00
24 Yao Ming/100 4.00 10.00
28 David Lee/100 2.00 5.00
29 Andre Iguodala/100 2.50 6.00
30 Paul Pierce/100 3.00 8.00
31 Carlos Boozer/100 2.50 6.00
37 LaMarcus Aldridge/100 3.00 8.00
38 Gilbert Arenas/100 2.50 6.00
41 Gerald Wallace/100 2.50 6.00
44 Derrick Rose/100 8.00 20.00
47 Kevin Garnett/100 5.00 12.00
60 O.J. Mayo/100 2.00 5.00
61 Rajon Rondo/100 3.00 8.00
62 Jason Terry/100 2.50 6.00
66 Nate Robinson/100 2.00 5.00
68 Tracy McGrady/100 3.00 8.00
70 Josh Howard/100 2.50 6.00
72 Jose Calderon/100 2.00 5.00
73 Ray Allen/100 3.00 8.00
74 Andrew Bogut/100 2.50 6.00
76 Paul Millsap/100 2.50 6.00
77 Jason Kidd/100 3.00 8.00
78 Elton Brand/100 3.00 8.00
79 Nene/100 2.50 6.00
81 Andrew Bynum/100 2.00 5.00
83 Manu Ginobili/25 3.00 8.00
87 Mike Bibby/100 2.50 6.00
90 Tayshaun Prince/100 2.50 6.00
97 Andrea Bargnani/100 2.50 6.00
98 Jermaine O'Neal/100 2.50 6.00
100 Michael Beasley/100 2.00 5.00

2009-10 Panini Threads Jerseys Prime
*PRIME: .75X TO 2X BASE HI
STATED PRINT RUNS 5 TO 25 SER.#'d SETS
SOME UNPRICED DUE TO SCARCITY
1 LeBron James/25 20.00 50.00
2 Dwyane Wade/25 10.00 25.00
12 Antawn Jamison/25 5.00 12.00
22 Joe Johnson/25 5.00 12.00
23 Amare Stoudemire/25 5.00 12.00
26 Kevin Martin/20 5.00 12.00
35 Al Harrington/25 5.00 12.00
43 Michael Redd/25 5.00 12.00
49 Mehmet Okur/25 4.00 10.00
52 Rashard Lewis/25 5.00 12.00
64 Josh Smith/25 5.00 12.00

2009-10 Panini Threads Kobe Bryant Letters
STATED PRINT RUN 240 SER.#'d SETS
1 Kobe Bryant 75.00 150.00

2009-10 Panini Threads Legends
COMPLETE SET (15) 8.00 20.00
RANDOM INSERTS IN PACKS
*PROOF: .6X TO 1.5X BASE HI
PROOF PRINT RUN 100 SER.#'d SETS
1 Magic Johnson 3.00 8.00
2 Willis Reed 1.25 3.00
3 Kareem Abdul-Jabbar 2.00 5.00
4 John Havlicek 1.25 3.00
5 Isiah Thomas 1.25 3.00
6 Slick Watts .75 2.00
7 David Thompson 1.00 2.50
8 Jerry West 1.50 4.00
9 Danny Ainge 1.25 3.00
10 Alex English 1.00 2.50
11 Hal Greer 1.00 2.50
12 Artis Gilmore 1.00 2.50
13 Walt Frazier 1.25 3.00
14 Chris Mullin 1.25 3.00
15 Tom Heinsohn 1.25 3.00

2009-10 Panini Threads Legends Autographs
STATED PRINT RUN 25 SER.#'d SETS
2 Willis Reed 10.00 25.00
4 John Havlicek 20.00 40.00
7 David Thompson 20.00 40.00
8 Jerry West 25.00 50.00
10 Alex English 10.00 25.00
12 Artis Gilmore 10.00 25.00
13 Walt Frazier 10.00 25.00
14 Chris Mullin 15.00 30.00

2009-10 Panini Threads Legends Materials
STATED PRINT RUN 50 TO 100 SER.#'d SETS
*PRIME: .6X TO 1.5X BASE HI
PRIME PRINT RUN 10 TO 25 SETS
SOME PRIME UNPRICED DUE TO SCARCITY
1 Magic Johnson/100 6.00 15.00
3 Kareem Abdul-Jabbar/100 6.00 15.00
5 Isiah Thomas/100 5.00 12.00
8 Jerry West/50 8.00 20.00
9 Danny Ainge/100 5.00 12.00
10 Alex English/100 4.00 10.00
12 Artis Gilmore/100 4.00 10.00
13 Walt Frazier/50 6.00 15.00
14 Chris Mullin/100 5.00 12.00
15 Tom Heinsohn/100 5.00 12.00

2009-10 Panini Threads Rookie Collection Materials
STATED PRINT RUN 250 SER.#'d SETS
*PRIME: .75X TO 2X BASE HI
PRIME PRINT RUN 25 SER.#'d SETS
1 Blake Griffin 10.00 25.00
2 Hasheem Thabeet 1.50 4.00
3 James Harden 12.00 30.00
4 Tyreke Evans 2.00 5.00
5 Jonny Flynn 1.50 4.00
6 Stephen Curry 50.00 120.00
7 Jordan Hill 2.00 5.00
8 DeMar DeRozan 6.00 15.00
9 Brandon Jennings 2.50 6.00
10 Terrence Williams 1.50 4.00
11 Gerald Henderson 2.00 5.00
12 Tyler Hansbrough 2.00 5.00
13 Earl Clark 2.00 5.00
14 Austin Daye 1.50 4.00
15 James Johnson 2.00 5.00
16 Jrue Holiday 3.00 8.00
17 Ty Lawson 2.50 6.00
18 Jeff Teague 2.50 6.00
19 Eric Maynor 1.50 4.00
20 Darren Collison 2.50 6.00
21 Omri Casspi 2.00 5.00
22 B.J. Mullens 1.50 4.00
23 Rodrigue Beaubois 1.50 4.00
24 Taj Gibson 2.50 6.00
25 DeMarre Carroll 2.00 5.00
26 Wayne Ellington 2.50 6.00
27 Toney Douglas 1.50 4.00
28 Jeff Pendergraph 1.50 4.00
29 DaJuan Summers 1.50 4.00
30 Sam Young 1.50 4.00
31 DeJuan Blair 2.00 5.00
32 Jodie Meeks 2.50 6.00
33 Chase Budinger 2.00 5.00
34 Taylor Griffin 1.50 4.00
35 Jermaine Taylor 1.50 4.00

2009-10 Panini Threads Rookie Collection Materials Signatures
STATED PRINT RUN 50 SER.#'d SETS
1 Blake Griffin 100.00 200.00
2 Hasheem Thabeet 5.00 12.00
4 Tyreke Evans 6.00 15.00
5 Jonny Flynn 5.00 12.00
6 Stephen Curry 300.00 600.00
7 Jordan Hill 6.00 15.00
9 Brandon Jennings 8.00 20.00
10 Terrence Williams 5.00 12.00
11 Gerald Henderson 6.00 15.00
12 Tyler Hansbrough 6.00 15.00
13 Earl Clark 6.00 15.00
14 Austin Daye 5.00 12.00
15 James Johnson 6.00 15.00
16 Jrue Holiday 10.00 25.00
17 Ty Lawson 8.00 20.00
18 Jeff Teague 8.00 20.00
21 Omri Casspi 6.00 15.00
22 B.J. Mullens 5.00 12.00
23 Rodrigue Beaubois 5.00 12.00
25 DeMarre Carroll 6.00 15.00
27 Toney Douglas 5.00 12.00
28 Jeff Pendergraph 5.00 12.00
29 DaJuan Summers 5.00 12.00
30 Sam Young 5.00 12.00
31 DeJuan Blair 6.00 15.00
32 Jodie Meeks 8.00 20.00
33 Chase Budinger 6.00 15.00
34 Taylor Griffin 5.00 12.00
35 Jermaine Taylor 5.00 12.00

2009-10 Panini Threads Rookie Collection Materials Prime Signatures
*PRIME: .5X TO 1.25X HI COLUMN
STATED PRINT RUN 25 SER.#'d SETS
1 Blake Griffin 125.00 300.00
6 Stephen Curry 400.00 800.00

2009-10 Panini Threads Rookie Preview Jerseys
STATED PRINT RUN 100 SER.#'d SETS
INSERTED INTO RETAIL PACKS
1 Blake Griffin 10.00 25.00
2 Hasheem Thabeet 1.50 4.00
3 James Harden 12.00 30.00
4 Tyreke Evans 2.00 5.00
5 Jonny Flynn 1.50 4.00
6 Stephen Curry 60.00 150.00
7 Jordan Hill 2.00 5.00
8 DeMar DeRozan 6.00 15.00
9 Brandon Jennings 2.50 6.00
10 Terrence Williams 1.50 4.00
11 Gerald Henderson 2.00 5.00
12 Tyler Hansbrough 2.00 5.00
13 Earl Clark 2.00 5.00
14 Austin Daye 1.50 4.00
15 James Johnson 2.00 5.00
16 Jrue Holiday 3.00 8.00
17 Ty Lawson 2.50 6.00
18 Jeff Teague 2.50 6.00
19 Eric Maynor 1.50 4.00
20 Darren Collison 2.50 6.00
21 Omri Casspi 2.00 5.00
22 B.J. Mullens 1.50 4.00
23 Rodrigue Beaubois 1.50 4.00
24 Taj Gibson 2.50 6.00
25 DeMarre Carroll 2.00 5.00
26 Wayne Ellington 2.50 6.00
27 Toney Douglas 1.50 4.00
28 Jeff Pendergraph 1.50 4.00
29 DaJuan Summers 1.50 4.00
30 Sam Young 1.50 4.00
31 DeJuan Blair 2.00 5.00
32 Chase Budinger 2.00 5.00
33 Jermaine Taylor 1.50 4.00

2009-10 Panini Threads Rookie Preview Jerseys Autographs
STATED PRINT RUN 50 SER.#'d SETS
INSERTED INTO RETAIL PACKS
1 Blake Griffin 40.00 100.00
2 Hasheem Thabeet 4.00 10.00
4 Tyreke Evans 5.00 12.00
5 Jonny Flynn 4.00 10.00
6 Stephen Curry 300.00 600.00
7 Jordan Hill 5.00 12.00
9 Brandon Jennings 6.00 15.00
10 Terrence Williams 4.00 10.00
11 Gerald Henderson 5.00 12.00
12 Tyler Hansbrough 5.00 12.00
13 Earl Clark 5.00 12.00
14 Austin Daye 4.00 10.00
15 James Johnson 5.00 12.00
16 Jrue Holiday 8.00 20.00
17 Ty Lawson 6.00 15.00
18 Jeff Teague 6.00 15.00
21 Omri Casspi 5.00 12.00
22 B.J. Mullens 4.00 10.00
23 Rodrigue Beaubois 4.00 10.00
25 DeMarre Carroll 5.00 12.00
27 Toney Douglas 4.00 10.00
28 Jeff Pendergraph 4.00 10.00
29 DaJuan Summers 4.00 10.00
30 Sam Young 4.00 10.00
31 DeJuan Blair 5.00 12.00
32 Chase Budinger 5.00 12.00
33 Jermaine Taylor 4.00 10.00

2009-10 Panini Threads Silver Signatures
STATED PRINT RUN 10 TO 99 SER.#'d SETS
SOME UNPRICED DUE TO SCARCITY
4 Kobe Bryant/99 60.00 150.00
5 Dirk Nowitzki/25 40.00 100.00
10 Danny Granger/99 6.00 15.00
19 Tony Parker/50 8.00 20.00
21 Devin Harris/50 6.00 15.00
28 David Lee/50 5.00 12.00
29 Andre Iguodala/50 5.00 12.00
71 Charlie Villanueva/50 5.00 12.00
77 Jason Kidd/25 8.00 20.00
87 Mike Bibby/50 5.00 12.00

2009-10 Panini Threads Team Threads Away
COMPLETE SET (50) 25.00 50.00
HOME VERSION: .4X TO 1X AWAY
1 Joe Johnson .75 2.00
2 Mike Bibby .75 2.00
3 Paul Pierce 1.00 2.50
4 Rajon Rondo 1.00 2.50
5 Gerald Wallace .75 2.00
6 Joakim Noah .75 2.00
7 LeBron James 4.00 10.00
8 Shaquille O'Neal 2.00 5.00
9 Dirk Nowitzki 1.25 3.00
10 Shawn Marion .75 2.00
11 Carmelo Anthony 1.25 3.00
12 Ben Gordon .75 2.00
13 Richard Hamilton .75 2.00
14 Stephen Jackson .75 2.00
15 Tracy McGrady 1.00 2.50
16 Danny Granger .75 2.00
17 Baron Davis .75 2.00
18 Marcus Camby .60 1.50
19 Kobe Bryant 4.00 10.00
20 Ron Artest 1.00 2.50
21 O.J. Mayo .60 1.50
22 Dwyane Wade 1.50 4.00
23 Jermaine O'Neal .75 2.00
24 Andrew Bogut .75 2.00
25 Michael Redd .75 2.00
26 Kevin Love 1.00 2.50
27 Devin Harris .60 1.50
28 Rafer Alston .60 1.50
29 Chris Paul 1.25 3.00
30 Peja Stojakovic 1.00 2.50
31 David Lee .60 1.50
32 Nate Robinson .60 1.50
33 Kevin Durant 2.50 6.00
34 Dwight Howard .75 2.00
35 Vince Carter 1.25 3.00
36 Andre Iguodala .75 2.00
37 Elton Brand 1.00 2.50
38 Amare Stoudemire .75 2.00
39 Steve Nash 1.00 2.50
40 Brandon Roy 1.00 2.50
41 LaMarcus Aldridge 1.00 2.50
42 Kevin Martin .75 2.00
43 Tim Duncan 1.50 4.00
44 Tony Parker 1.00 2.50
45 Chris Bosh 1.00 2.50
46 Hedo Turkoglu .75 2.00
47 Deron Williams .75 2.00
48 Carlos Boozer .75 2.00
49 Antawn Jamison .75 2.00
50 Gilbert Arenas .75 2.00

2009-10 Panini Threads Team Threads Away Autographs
STATED PRINT RUN 5 TO 25 SER.#'d SETS
*HOME VERSION: .4X TO 1X AWAY
ASTERISK CARDS FROM PANINI UPDATE
2 Mike Bibby/25 30.00 60.00
4 Rajon Rondo/25 30.00 80.00
16 Danny Granger/25* 8.00 20.00
19 Kobe Bryant/25 125.00 250.00
23 Jermaine O'Neal/25 8.00 20.00
26 Kevin Love/25 25.00 50.00
27 Devin Harris/25 8.00 20.00
36 Andre Iguodala/25 8.00 20.00
37 Elton Brand/25 8.00 20.00
44 Tony Parker/25 30.00 80.00
45 Chris Bosh/25* 8.00 20.00
47 Deron Williams/25* 25.00 60.00
48 Carlos Boozer/25 15.00 40.00

2009-10 Panini Threads Triple Threat
COMPLETE SET 6.00 15.00
RANDOM INSERTS IN PACKS
*PROOF: .6X TO 1.5X BASE HI
PROOF PRINT RUN 100 SER.#'d SETS
1 LeBron James 3.00 8.00
2 Chris Paul 1.00 2.50
3 Jason Kidd .75 2.00
4 Kobe Bryant 3.00 8.00
5 Andre Miller .60 1.50
6 Rajon Rondo .75 2.00
7 Pau Gasol .75 2.00
8 Tracy McGrady .75 2.00
9 Dwight Howard .60 1.50
10 Russell Westbrook 2.00 5.00

2009-10 Panini Threads Triple Threat Autographs
STATED PRINT RUN 50 SER.#'d SETS
3 Jason Kidd 12.00 30.00
4 Kobe Bryant 100.00 200.00

2009-10 Panini Threads Triple Threat Materials
STATED PRINT RUN 90 TO 100 SER.#'d SETS
1 LeBron James/90 10.00 25.00
2 Chris Paul/100 4.00 10.00
3 Jason Kidd/100 3.00 8.00
4 Kobe Bryant/100 8.00 20.00
6 Rajon Rondo/100 3.00 8.00
7 Pau Gasol/95 3.00 8.00
8 Tracy McGrady/100 3.00 8.00
9 Dwight Howard/100 2.50 6.00

2009-10 Panini Threads Triple Threat Materials Prime
*PRIME: .75X TO 2X BASE HI
STATED PRINT RUN 5 TO 25 SER.#'d SETS
SOME UNPRICED DUE TO SCARCITY
4 Kobe Bryant/25 20.00 50.00

2010-11 Panini Threads
COMP.SET w/o RCs (100) 15.00 30.00
ROOKIE PRINT RUN 399 SER.#'d SETS
EXCH.EXPIRATION 5/24/2012
1 Al-Farouq Aminu AU RC 5.00 12.00
2 Andy Rautins AU RC 3.00 8.00
3 Willie Warren AU RC 3.00 8.00
4 Cole Aldrich AU RC 4.00 10.00
5 Craig Brackins AU RC 3.00 8.00
6 Da'Sean Butler AU RC 5.00 12.00
7 Damion James AU RC 3.00 8.00
8 Daniel Orton AU RC 3.00 8.00
9 DeMarcus Cousins AU RC 15.00 40.00
10 Derrick Favors AU RC 5.00 12.00
11 Devin Ebanks AU RC 3.00 8.00
12 Dexter Pittman AU RC 3.00 8.00
13 Dominique Jones AU RC 3.00 8.00
14 Ed Davis AU RC 3.00 8.00
15 Ekpe Udoh AU RC 3.00 8.00
16 Elliot Williams AU RC 3.00 8.00
17 Eric Bledsoe AU RC 6.00 15.00
18 Evan Turner AU RC 4.00 10.00
19 Gani Lawal AU RC 3.00 8.00
20 Gordon Hayward AU RC 15.00 40.00
21 Greg Monroe AU RC 6.00 15.00
22 Greivis Vasquez AU RC 4.00 10.00
23 Hassan Whiteside AU RC 10.00 25.00
24 James Anderson AU RC 3.00 8.00
25 John Wall AU RC 30.00 80.00
26 Xavier Henry AU RC 3.00 8.00
27 Lance Stephenson AU RC 5.00 12.00
28 Larry Sanders AU RC 3.00 8.00
29 Lazar Hayward AU RC 3.00 8.00
30 Luke Babbitt AU RC 4.00 10.00
31 Luke Harangody AU RC 3.00 8.00
32 Patrick Patterson AU RC 4.00 10.00
33 Paul George AU RC 40.00 100.00
34 Quincy Pondexter AU RC 3.00 8.00
35 Stanley Robinson AU RC 3.00 8.00
36 Keith Gallon AU RC 3.00 8.00
37 Trevor Booker AU RC 4.00 10.00
38 Wesley Johnson AU RC 3.00 8.00
39 Andrew Bogut .30 .75
40 John Salmons .30 .75
41 Brandon Jennings .25 .60
42 Michael Beasley .25 .60
43 Martell Webster .30 .75
44 Kevin Love .40 1.00
45 Brook Lopez .30 .75
46 Troy Murphy .25 .60
47 Devin Harris .25 .60
48 Chris Paul .50 1.25
49 David West .30 .75
50 Marcus Thornton .25 .60
51 Amare Stoudemire .30 .75
52 Anthony Randolph .25 .60
53 Danilo Gallinari .30 .75
54 Raymond Felton .30 .75
55 Kevin Durant 1.00 2.50
56 Russell Westbrook 1.00 2.50
57 Jeff Green .30 .75
58 Dwight Howard .30 .75
59 Vince Carter .50 1.25
60 Rashard Lewis .30 .75
61 J.J. Redick .40 1.00
62 Andre Iguodala .30 .75
63 Allen Iverson .50 1.25
64 Elton Brand .40 1.00
65 Steve Nash .40 1.00
66 Robin Lopez .25 .60
67 Channing Frye .30 .75
68 LaMarcus Aldridge .40 1.00
69 Brandon Roy .40 1.00
70 Andre Miller .30 .75
71 Greg Oden .30 .75
72 Tyreke Evans .25 .60
73 Samuel Dalembert .25 .60
74 Carl Landry .25 .60
75 Tim Duncan .60 1.50
76 Tony Parker .40 1.00
77 Manu Ginobili .40 1.00
78 Richard Jefferson .30 .75
79 Andrea Bargnani .30 .75
80 Jose Calderon .25 .60
81 Leandro Barbosa .30 .75
82 Deron Williams .30 .75
83 Al Jefferson .30 .75
84 Paul Millsap .30 .75
85 Al Thornton .25 .60
86 Kirk Hinrich .30 .75
87 Josh Howard .30 .75
88 Joe Johnson .30 .75
89 Josh Smith .30 .75
90 Al Horford .30 .75
91 Jamal Crawford .40 1.00
92 Paul Pierce .40 1.00
93 Rajon Rondo .40 1.00
94 Kevin Garnett .60 1.50
95 Shaquille O'Neal .75 2.00
96 Stephen Jackson .30 .75
97 Gerald Wallace .30 .75
98 Gerald Henderson .25 .60
99 Carlos Boozer .30 .75
100 Derrick Rose .50 1.25
101 Luol Deng .30 .75
102 Joakim Noah .30 .75
103 Antawn Jamison .30 .75
104 Daniel Gibson .30 .75
105 Mo Williams .30 .75
106 Dirk Nowitzki .50 1.25
107 Jason Kidd .40 1.00
108 Jason Terry .30 .75
109 Carmelo Anthony .50 1.25
110 Chauncey Billups .40 1.00
111 Al Harrington .30 .75
112 Nene .30 .75
113 Ben Gordon .30 .75
114 Richard Hamilton .30 .75
115 Tracy McGrady .40 1.00
116 Monta Ellis .30 .75
117 Stephen Curry 1.50 4.00
118 David Lee .25 .60
119 Shane Battier .30 .75
120 Kevin Martin .30 .75
121 Luis Scola .30 .75
122 Yao Ming .50 1.25
123 Danny Granger .30 .75
124 Mike Dunleavy .25 .60
125 Tyler Hansbrough .30 .75
126 Baron Davis .30 .75
127 Eric Gordon .30 .75
128 Chris Kaman .30 .75
129 Kobe Bryant 1.50 4.00
130 Derek Fisher .30 .75
131 Pau Gasol .40 1.00
132 Lamar Odom .30 .75
133 Rudy Gay .40 1.00
134 Marc Gasol .40 1.00
135 Zach Randolph .30 .75
136 Chris Bosh .40 1.00
137 Dwyane Wade .60 1.50
138 LeBron James 2.00 5.00

2010-11 Panini Threads Century Proof Gold
*GOLD: 1.5X TO 4X BASE HI
STATED PRINT RUN 99 SER.#'d SETS

2010-11 Panini Threads Century Proof Orange
*ORANGE: 1X TO 2.5X BASE HI
STATED PRINT RUN 199 SER.#'d SETS
INSERTED IN RETAIL PACKS ONLY

2010-11 Panini Threads Century Proof Platinum
*PLATINUM: 3X TO 8X BASE HI
STATED PRINT RUN 25 SER.#'d SETS

2010-11 Panini Threads Century Proof Silver
*SILVER: 1X TO 2.5X BASE HI
STATED PRINT RUN 199 SER.#'d SETS

2010-11 Panini Threads All-Time Big Men
COMPLETE SET (25) 12.50 25.00
RANDOM INSERTS IN PACKS
*PROOF: .75X TO 2X BASE HI
PROOF: STATED PRINT RUN 99 SER.#'d SETS
1 Bill Russell 1.50 4.00
2 Kareem Abdul-Jabbar 1.50 4.00
3 Bill Walton 1.00 2.50
4 Artis Gilmore .75 2.00
5 Hakeem Olajuwon 1.25 3.00
6 Patrick Ewing 1.25 3.00
7 Walt Bellamy .75 2.00
8 Wes Unseld 1.00 2.50
9 Dolph Schayes 1.00 2.50
10 Elvin Hayes 1.00 2.50
11 Karl Malone 1.25 3.00
12 Wayne Embry .60 1.50
13 Alonzo Mourning 1.25 3.00
14 Arnie Risen 1.00 2.50
15 Bill Cartwright .75 2.00
16 Bob Lanier .75 2.00
17 Clyde Lovellette 1.00 2.50
18 Wilt Chamberlain 2.00 5.00
19 Dave Cowens .60 1.50
20 David Robinson 1.50 4.00
21 Moses Malone 1.00 2.50
22 Nate Thurmond .75 2.00
23 Mark Eaton .60 1.50
24 George Mikan 2.00 5.00
25 Robert Parish 1.00 2.50

2010-11 Panini Threads All-Time Big Men Autographs
STATED PRINT RUN 10 TO 49 SER.#'d SETS
SOME UNPRICED DUE TO SCARCITY
1 Bill Russell/25 50.00 120.00
2 Kareem Abdul-Jabbar/25 40.00 80.00
3 Bill Walton/25 10.00 25.00
4 Artis Gilmore/49 6.00 15.00
5 Hakeem Olajuwon/25 20.00 50.00
7 Walt Bellamy/49 6.00 15.00
8 Wes Unseld/49 6.00 15.00
9 Dolph Schayes/49 6.00 15.00
13 Alonzo Mourning/25 15.00 40.00
14 Arnie Risen/49 6.00 15.00
15 Bill Cartwright/49 6.00 15.00
16 Bob Lanier/25 6.00 15.00
17 Clyde Lovellette/25 6.00 15.00
22 Nate Thurmond/25 10.00 25.00
25 Robert Parish/49 6.00 15.00

2010-11 Panini Threads All-Time Big Men Materials
STATED PRINT RUN 399 SER.#'d SETS
5 Hakeem Olajuwon 4.00 10.00
6 Patrick Ewing 4.00 10.00
11 Karl Malone 4.00 10.00
13 Alonzo Mourning 4.00 10.00
23 Mark Eaton 2.00 5.00

2010-11 Panini Threads All-Time Big Men Materials Prime
*PRIME: .75X TO 2X BASE HI
STATED PRINT RUN 50 SER.#'d SETS
2 Kareem Abdul-Jabbar 12.00 30.00
6 Patrick Ewing 12.00 30.00
11 Karl Malone 10.00 25.00
16 Bob Lanier 5.00 12.00
19 Dave Cowens 4.00 10.00
25 Robert Parish 6.00 15.00

2010-11 Panini Threads Century Collection Materials
STATED PRINT RUN 399 SER.#'d SETS
*PRIME: .75X TO 2X BASE HI
PRIME STATED PRINT RUN 50 SER.#'d SETS
1 Ben Gordon 2.50 6.00
2 Yi Jianlian 2.50 6.00
3 Wayne Ellington 2.50 6.00
4 Tyler Hansbrough 2.50 6.00
5 Trevor Ariza 2.00 5.00
6 Thaddeus Young 2.00 5.00
7 Terrence Williams 2.00 5.00
8 Samuel Dalembert 2.00 5.00
9 Ron Artest 3.00 8.00
10 Rodrigue Beaubois 2.00 5.00
11 Luis Scola 2.50 6.00
12 Josh Howard 2.50 6.00
13 Jonny Flynn 2.00 5.00
14 Joakim Noah 2.50 6.00
15 James Harden 5.00 12.00
16 J.J. Barea 2.50 6.00
17 Elton Brand 3.00 8.00
18 Earl Clark 2.00 5.00
19 DeMarre Carroll 2.50 6.00
20 David West 2.50 6.00
21 Brandon Jennings 2.00 5.00
22 Andre Iguodala 2.50 6.00
23 Stephen Curry 12.00 30.00
24 Michael Redd 2.50 6.00
25 James Johnson 2.00 5.00

2010-11 Panini Threads Century Legends
COMPLETE SET (15) 7.50 15.00
RANDOM INSERTS IN PACKS
*PROOF: .6X TO 1.5X BASE HI
PROOF: STATED PRINT RUN 99 SER.#'d SETS
1 Adrian Dantley 1.00 2.50
2 Bob Dandridge .75 2.00
3 Calvin Murphy 1.00 2.50
4 Frank Ramsey 1.25 3.00
5 Gary Payton 1.25 3.00
6 Jerry Lucas 1.25 3.00
7 Jerry Sloan 1.25 3.00
8 Jo Jo White 1.00 2.50
9 Kelly Tripucka .75 2.00
10 Robert Horry 1.25 3.00
11 Sam Perkins .75 2.00
12 Scottie Pippen 2.50 6.00
13 Spencer Haywood 1.25 3.00
14 Toni Kukoc 1.25 3.00
15 World B. Free 1.00 2.50

2010-11 Panini Threads Century Legends Autographs
STATED PRINT RUN 10 TO 50 SER.#'d SETS
SOME UNPRICED DUE TO SCARCITY
1 Adrian Dantley/25 5.00 12.00
2 Bob Dandridge/50 8.00 20.00
4 Frank Ramsey/50 8.00 20.00
9 Kelly Tripucka/25 8.00 20.00
10 Robert Horry/50 20.00 50.00
14 Toni Kukoc/50 20.00 50.00

2010-11 Panini Threads Century Legends Materials
STATED PRINT RUN 399 SER.#'d SETS
5 Gary Payton 3.00 8.00
11 Sam Perkins 2.00 5.00
12 Scottie Pippen 6.00 15.00
14 Toni Kukoc 3.00 8.00

2010-11 Panini Threads Century Legends Materials Prime
*PRIME: .75X TO 2X BASE HI
STATED PRINT RUN 50 SER.#'d SETS
12 Scottie Pippen 25.00 60.00

2010-11 Panini Threads Century Stars
COMPLETE SET (25) 10.00 20.00
RANDOM INSERTS IN PACKS
*PROOF: .6X TO 1.5X BASE HI
PROOF STATED PRINT RUN 99 SER.#'d SETS
1 Al Jefferson .60 1.50
2 Allen Iverson 1.00 2.50
3 Amare Stoudemire .60 1.50
4 Andrea Bargnani .60 1.50
5 Anthony Randolph .50 1.25
6 Carlos Boozer .60 1.50
7 Caron Butler .60 1.50
8 Chauncey Billups .75 2.00
9 Chris Bosh .75 2.00
10 Chris Kaman .60 1.50
11 Chris Paul 1.00 2.50
12 Derrick Rose 1.00 2.50
13 Dirk Nowitzki 1.00 2.50
14 Dwight Howard .60 1.50
15 Dwyane Wade 1.25 3.00
16 Joe Johnson .60 1.50
17 Kevin Durant 2.00 5.00
18 Kevin Garnett 1.25 3.00
19 LeBron James 4.00 10.00
20 Paul Pierce .75 2.00
21 Rudy Gay .75 2.00
22 Russell Westbrook 2.00 5.00
23 Shaquille O'Neal 1.50 4.00
24 Steve Nash .75 2.00
25 Tim Duncan 1.25 3.00

2010-11 Panini Threads Century Stars Autographs
STATED PRINT RUN 5 TO 25 SER.#'d SETS
SOME UNPRICED DUE TO SCARCITY
4 Andrea Bargnani/25 5.00 12.00
5 Anthony Randolph/25 5.00 12.00
8 Chauncey Billups/25 5.00 12.00
9 Chris Bosh/25 15.00 40.00
22 Russell Westbrook/25 50.00 120.00

2010-11 Panini Threads Century Stars Materials
STATED PRINT RUN 99 TO 399 SER.#'d SETS
1 Al Jefferson/399 2.50 6.00
2 Allen Iverson/99 4.00 10.00
4 Andrea Bargnani/399 2.50 6.00
6 Carlos Boozer/399 2.50 6.00
7 Caron Butler/399 2.50 6.00
8 Chauncey Billups/399 3.00 8.00
13 Dirk Nowitzki/399 4.00 10.00
14 Dwight Howard/399 2.50 6.00
15 Dwyane Wade/399 5.00 12.00
20 Paul Pierce/399 3.00 8.00
23 Shaquille O'Neal/399 6.00 15.00
25 Tim Duncan/399 5.00 12.00

2010-11 Panini Threads Century Stars Materials Prime
*PRIME: .75X TO 2X BASE HI
STATED PRINT RUN 50 SER.#'d SETS
2 Allen Iverson 12.00 30.00
12 Derrick Rose 8.00 20.00
24 Steve Nash 6.00 15.00

2010-11 Panini Threads Jerseys
STATED PRINT RUN 99 TO 399 SER.#'d SETS
39 Andrew Bogut/299 2.00 5.00
41 Brandon Jennings/399 1.50 4.00
42 Michael Beasley/399 1.50 4.00
44 Kevin Love/399 2.50 6.00
47 Devin Harris/299 1.50 4.00
48 Chris Paul/399 3.00 8.00
49 David West/399 2.00 5.00
52 Anthony Randolph/399 1.50 4.00
54 Raymond Felton/399 2.00 5.00
58 Dwight Howard/399 2.00 5.00
59 Vince Carter/399 3.00 8.00
60 Rashard Lewis/399 2.00 5.00
61 J.J. Redick/399 2.50 6.00
62 Andre Iguodala/399 2.00 5.00
63 Allen Iverson/99 3.00 8.00
64 Elton Brand/399 2.50 6.00
65 Steve Nash/399 2.50 6.00
66 Robin Lopez/399 1.50 4.00
67 Channing Frye/399 2.00 5.00
68 LaMarcus Aldridge/399 2.50 6.00
69 Brandon Roy/399 2.50 6.00
70 Andre Miller/399 2.00 5.00
71 Greg Oden/399 2.00 5.00
73 Samuel Dalembert/399 1.50 4.00
75 Tim Duncan/399 4.00 10.00
76 Tony Parker/399 2.50 6.00
77 Manu Ginobili/399 2.50 6.00
78 Richard Jefferson/399 2.00 5.00
79 Andrea Bargnani/399 2.00 5.00
80 Jose Calderon/399 1.50 4.00
81 Leandro Barbosa/399 2.00 5.00
82 Deron Williams/399 2.00 5.00
83 Al Jefferson/399 2.00 5.00
86 Kirk Hinrich/299 2.00 5.00
90 Al Horford/399 2.00 5.00
92 Paul Pierce/399 2.50 6.00
95 Shaquille O'Neal/399 5.00 12.00
96 Stephen Jackson/399 2.00 5.00
98 Gerald Henderson/349 1.50 4.00
99 Carlos Boozer/399 2.00 5.00
102 Joakim Noah/399 2.00 5.00
103 Antawn Jamison/399 2.00 5.00
106 Dirk Nowitzki/399 3.00 8.00
108 Jason Terry/399 2.00 5.00
110 Chauncey Billups/399 2.50 6.00
112 Nene/399 2.00 5.00
113 Ben Gordon/399 2.00 5.00
115 Tracy McGrady/399 2.50 6.00
117 Stephen Curry/199 10.00 25.00
119 Shane Battier/399 2.00 5.00
120 Kevin Martin/399 2.00 5.00
121 Luis Scola/399 2.00 5.00
124 Mike Dunleavy/99 1.50 4.00
125 Tyler Hansbrough/399 2.00 5.00
129 Kobe Bryant/399 8.00 20.00
130 Derek Fisher/399 2.00 5.00
131 Pau Gasol/399 2.50 6.00
132 Lamar Odom/399 2.00 5.00
137 Dwyane Wade/399 4.00 10.00

2010-11 Panini Threads Jerseys Prime
*PRIME: .75X TO 2X BASE HI
STATED PRINT RUN 25 TO 50 SER.#'d SETS
63 Allen Iverson/50 10.00 25.00
65 Steve Nash/50 8.00 20.00
100 Derrick Rose/50 6.00 15.00

2010-11 Panini Threads Rookie Collection Materials
STATED PRINT RUN 399 SER.#'d SETS
*PRIME: .75X TO 2X BASE HI
PRIME STATED PRINT RUN 50 SER.#'d SETS
1 John Wall 15.00 40.00
2 Evan Turner 1.50 4.00
3 Derrick Favors 2.50 6.00
4 Wesley Johnson 1.25 3.00
5 DeMarcus Cousins 6.00 15.00
6 Ekpe Udoh 1.25 3.00
7 Greg Monroe 2.50 6.00
8 Al-Farouq Aminu 2.00 5.00
9 Gordon Hayward 3.00 8.00
10 Paul George 6.00 15.00
11 Cole Aldrich 1.50 4.00
12 Xavier Henry 1.25 3.00
13 Patrick Patterson 1.50 4.00
14 Larry Sanders 1.25 3.00
15 Luke Babbitt 1.50 4.00
16 Eric Bledsoe 2.50 6.00
17 Avery Bradley 2.50 6.00
18 James Anderson 1.25 3.00
19 Craig Brackins 1.25 3.00
20 Elliot Williams 1.25 3.00
21 Trevor Booker 1.50 4.00
22 Damion James 1.25 3.00
23 Dominique Jones 1.25 3.00
24 Quincy Pondexter 1.25 3.00
25 Jordan Crawford 1.50 4.00
26 Greivis Vasquez 1.50 4.00
27 Daniel Orton 1.25 3.00
28 Lazar Hayward 1.25 3.00
29 Dexter Pittman 1.25 3.00
30 Hassan Whiteside 4.00 10.00
31 Andy Rautins 1.25 3.00
32 Lance Stephenson 2.00 5.00
33 Da'Sean Butler 2.00 5.00
34 Devin Ebanks 1.25 3.00
35 Gani Lawal 1.25 3.00

2010-11 Panini Threads Rookie Collection Materials Signatures
STATED PRINT RUN 50 SER.#'d SETS
*SIG.PRIME: .75X TO 2X HI
SIG.PRIME PRINT RUN 25 SER.#'d SETS
1 John Wall 40.00 100.00
2 Evan Turner 5.00 12.00
3 Derrick Favors 8.00 20.00
4 Wesley Johnson 4.00 10.00
5 DeMarcus Cousins 20.00 50.00
6 Ekpe Udoh 4.00 10.00
7 Greg Monroe 8.00 20.00
8 Al-Farouq Aminu 6.00 15.00
9 Gordon Hayward 10.00 25.00
10 Paul George 75.00 200.00
11 Cole Aldrich 5.00 12.00
12 Xavier Henry 4.00 10.00
13 Patrick Patterson 5.00 12.00
14 Larry Sanders 4.00 10.00
15 Luke Babbitt 5.00 12.00
16 Eric Bledsoe 8.00 20.00
17 Avery Bradley 8.00 20.00
18 James Anderson 4.00 10.00

19 Craig Brackins 4.00 10.00
20 Elliot Williams 4.00 10.00
21 Trevor Booker 5.00 12.00
22 Damion James 4.00 10.00
23 Dominique Jones 4.00 10.00
24 Quincy Pondexter 4.00 10.00
25 Jordan Crawford 5.00 12.00
26 Greivis Vasquez 5.00 12.00
27 Daniel Orton 4.00 10.00
28 Lazar Hayward 4.00 10.00
29 Dexter Pittman 4.00 10.00
30 Hassan Whiteside 20.00 50.00
31 Andy Rautins 4.00 10.00
32 Lance Stephenson 6.00 15.00
33 Da'Sean Butler 6.00 15.00
34 Devin Ebanks 4.00 10.00
35 Gani Lawal 4.00 10.00

2010-11 Panini Threads Rookie Team Threads Away

COMPLETE SET (40) 20.00 40.00
RANDOM INSERTS IN PACKS
*HOME VERSION: .4X TO 1X BASE HI
HOME VERSION RANDOM INSERTS IN PACKS
1 Al-Farouq Aminu .75 2.00
2 Andy Rautins .50 1.25
3 Avery Bradley 1.00 2.50
4 Cole Aldrich .60 1.50
5 Craig Brackins .50 1.25
6 Darington Hobson .50 1.25
7 Damion James .50 1.25
8 Daniel Orton .50 1.25
9 DeMarcus Cousins 2.50 6.00
10 Derrick Favors 1.00 2.50
11 Brian Zoubek .50 1.25
12 Jeremy Lin 5.00 12.00
13 Dominique Jones .50 1.25
14 Ed Davis .50 1.25
15 Ekpe Udoh .50 1.25
16 Elliot Williams .50 1.25
17 Eric Bledsoe 1.00 2.50
18 Evan Turner .60 1.50
19 Gani Lawal .50 1.25
20 Gordon Hayward 1.25 3.00
21 Greg Monroe 1.00 2.50
22 Greivis Vasquez .60 1.50
23 Hassan Whiteside 1.50 4.00
24 James Anderson .50 1.25
25 John Wall 4.00 10.00
26 Jordan Crawford .60 1.50
27 Lance Stephenson .75 2.00
28 Larry Sanders .50 1.25
29 Lazar Hayward .50 1.25
30 Luke Babbitt .60 1.50
31 Luke Harangody .50 1.25
32 Patrick Patterson .60 1.50
33 Paul George 2.50 6.00
34 Quincy Pondexter .50 1.25
35 Stanley Robinson .50 1.25
36 Keith Gallon .50 1.25
37 Trevor Booker .60 1.50
38 Wesley Johnson .50 1.25
39 Willie Warren .50 1.25
40 Xavier Henry .50 1.25

2010-11 Panini Threads Rookie Team Threads Home Autographs

STATED PRINT RUN 77 TO 99 SER.#'d SETS
1 Al-Farouq Aminu/97 6.00 15.00
2 Andy Rautins/99 4.00 10.00
3 Avery Bradley/97 8.00 20.00
4 Cole Aldrich/99 5.00 12.00
5 Craig Brackins/99 4.00 10.00
6 Darington Hobson/99 4.00 10.00
7 Damion James/99 4.00 10.00
8 Daniel Orton/99 4.00 10.00
9 DeMarcus Cousins/99 25.00 60.00
10 Derrick Favors/99 6.00 15.00
11 Brian Zoubek/99 EXCH 4.00 10.00
12 Jeremy Lin/99 75.00 200.00
13 Dominique Jones/99 4.00 10.00
14 Ed Davis/99 4.00 10.00
15 Ekpe Udoh/99 4.00 10.00
16 Elliot Williams/99 4.00 10.00
17 Eric Bledsoe/99 8.00 20.00
18 Evan Turner/99 5.00 12.00
19 Gani Lawal/99 4.00 10.00
20 Gordon Hayward/99 10.00 25.00
21 Greg Monroe/99 12.00 30.00
22 Greivis Vasquez/99 5.00 12.00
23 Hassan Whiteside/99 12.00 30.00
24 James Anderson/99 4.00 10.00
25 John Wall/99 30.00 80.00
26 Jordan Crawford/99 5.00 12.00
27 Lance Stephenson/99 6.00 15.00
28 Larry Sanders/99 4.00 10.00
29 Lazar Hayward/99 4.00 10.00
30 Luke Babbitt/99 5.00 12.00
31 Luke Harangody/77 4.00 10.00
32 Patrick Patterson/99 5.00 12.00
33 Paul George/99 75.00 200.00
34 Quincy Pondexter/99 4.00 10.00
35 Stanley Robinson/99 EXCH 4.00 10.00
36 Keith Gallon/99 4.00 10.00
37 Trevor Booker/99 5.00 12.00
38 Wesley Johnson/99 4.00 10.00
39 Willie Warren/99 4.00 10.00
40 Xavier Henry/99 4.00 10.00

2010-11 Panini Threads Silver Signatures

STATED PRINT RUN 9 TO 49 SER.#'d SETS
SOME UNPRICED DUE TO SCARCITY
39 Andrew Bogut/24 5.00 12.00
41 Brandon Jennings/24 4.00 10.00
42 Michael Beasley/24 4.00 10.00
44 Kevin Love/24 12.00 30.00
45 Brook Lopez/24 5.00 12.00
47 Devin Harris/24 4.00 10.00
50 Marcus Thornton/49 4.00 10.00
51 Amare Stoudemire/24 5.00 12.00
52 Anthony Randolph/24 4.00 10.00
56 Russell Westbrook/49 50.00 120.00
59 Vince Carter/24 15.00 40.00
61 J.J. Redick/24 10.00 25.00
65 Steve Nash/24 30.00 80.00
66 Robin Lopez/49 4.00 10.00
67 Channing Frye/49 4.00 10.00
68 LaMarcus Aldridge/24 8.00 20.00
69 Brandon Roy/24 8.00 20.00
72 Tyreke Evans/49 4.00 10.00
73 Samuel Dalembert/49 4.00 10.00
74 Carl Landry/49 4.00 10.00
76 Tony Parker/24 8.00 20.00
79 Andrea Bargnani/24 5.00 12.00
82 Deron Williams/24 5.00 12.00
87 Josh Howard/24 4.00 10.00
93 Rajon Rondo/24 8.00 20.00
95 Shaquille O'Neal/24 60.00 120.00
98 Gerald Henderson/49 4.00 10.00
100 Derrick Rose/24 50.00 120.00
101 Luol Deng/24 5.00 12.00
105 Mo Williams/24 5.00 12.00
107 Jason Kidd/24 12.00 30.00
110 Chauncey Billups/24 5.00 12.00
114 Richard Hamilton/24 5.00 12.00
117 Stephen Curry/24 75.00 200.00
125 Tyler Hansbrough/49 5.00 12.00
128 Chris Kaman/24 4.00 10.00
129 Kobe Bryant/24 100.00 250.00
130 Derek Fisher/24 5.00 12.00
131 Pau Gasol/24 12.00 30.00
132 Lamar Odom/24 10.00 25.00
134 Marc Gasol/24 10.00 25.00
135 Zach Randolph/24 5.00 12.00
136 Chris Bosh/24 15.00 40.00

2010-11 Panini Threads Team Threads Away

COMPLETE SET (50) 30.00 60.00
RANDOM INSERTS IN PACKS
*HOME VERSION: .4X TO 1X BASE HI
HOME VERSION RANDOM INSERTS IN PACKS
1 Josh Smith .75 2.00
2 Al Horford .75 2.00
3 Shaquille O'Neal 2.00 5.00
4 Kevin Garnett 1.50 4.00
5 Stephen Jackson .75 2.00
6 Derrick Rose 1.25 3.00
7 Carlos Boozer .75 2.00
8 Antawn Jamison .75 2.00
9 Dirk Nowitzki 1.25 3.00
10 Jason Kidd 1.00 2.50
11 Chauncey Billups 1.00 2.50
12 Chris Andersen .75 2.00
13 Tracy McGrady 1.00 2.50
14 Tayshaun Prince .75 2.00
15 Monta Ellis .75 2.00
16 David Lee .60 1.50
17 Yao Ming 1.25 3.00
18 Kevin Martin .75 2.00
19 Darren Collison .75 2.00
20 Randy Foye .60 1.50
21 Eric Gordon .75 2.00
22 Kobe Bryant 4.00 10.00
23 Pau Gasol 1.00 2.50
24 Marc Gasol 1.00 2.50
25 Zach Randolph .75 2.00
26 LeBron James 5.00 12.00
27 Chris Bosh 1.00 2.50
28 Brandon Jennings .60 1.50
29 John Salmons .75 2.00
30 Michael Beasley .60 1.50
31 Brook Lopez .75 2.00
32 Troy Murphy .60 1.50
33 Chris Paul 1.25 3.00
34 David West .75 2.00
35 Amare Stoudemire .75 2.00
36 Anthony Randolph .60 1.50
37 Kevin Durant 2.50 6.00
38 Russell Westbrook 2.50 6.00
39 Dwight Howard .75 2.00
40 Andre Iguodala .75 2.00
41 Steve Nash 1.00 2.50
42 Andre Miller .75 2.00
43 Tyreke Evans .60 1.50
44 Richard Jefferson .75 2.00
45 Andrea Bargnani .75 2.00
46 Leandro Barbosa .75 2.00
47 Deron Williams .75 2.00
48 Al Jefferson .75 2.00
49 Al Thornton .60 1.50
50 Kirk Hinrich .75 2.00

2010-11 Panini Threads Team Threads Away Autographs

STATED PRINT RUN 10 TO 99 SER.#'d SETS
*HOME VERSION: .4X TO 1X BASE HI
HOME PRINT RUN 10 TO 99 SER.#'d SETS
SOME UNPRICED DUE TO SCARCITY
2 Al Horford/49 5.00 12.00
3 Shaquille O'Neal/15 75.00 150.00
10 Jason Kidd/25 12.00 30.00
12 Chris Andersen/25 20.00 50.00
19 Darren Collison/49 5.00 12.00
20 Randy Foye/49 5.00 12.00
22 Kobe Bryant/99 100.00 200.00
24 Marc Gasol/25 12.00 30.00
25 Zach Randolph/49 12.00 30.00
28 Brandon Jennings/49 12.00 30.00
38 Russell Westbrook/49 25.00 60.00
40 Andre Iguodala/25 8.00 20.00
43 Tyreke Evans/49 12.00 30.00
47 Deron Williams/25 15.00 40.00
49 Al Thornton/49 5.00 12.00

2010-11 Panini Threads Triple Threat

COMPLETE SET (10) 7.50 15.00
RANDOM INSERTS IN PACKS
*PROOF: .6X TO 1.5X BASE HI
PROOF STATED PRINT RUN 99 SER.#'d SETS
1 Jason Kidd .75 2.00
2 Deron Williams .60 1.50
3 Andre Iguodala .60 1.50
4 Russell Westbrook 2.00 5.00
5 LeBron James 4.00 10.00
6 Carlos Boozer .60 1.50
7 Rajon Rondo .75 2.00
8 Kobe Bryant 3.00 8.00
9 Brandon Roy .75 2.00
10 Steve Nash .75 2.00

2010-11 Panini Threads Triple Threat Autographs

STATED PRINT RUN 5 TO 50 SER.#'d SETS
SOME UNPRICED DUE TO SCARCITY
1 Jason Kidd/15 25.00 60.00
4 Russell Westbrook/50 40.00 100.00
7 Rajon Rondo/15 12.00 30.00
8 Kobe Bryant/50 100.00 200.00
9 Brandon Roy/50 8.00 20.00

2010-11 Panini Threads Triple Threat Materials

STATED PRINT RUN 399 SER.#'d SETS
2 Deron Williams 2.50 6.00
3 Andre Iguodala 2.50 6.00
6 Carlos Boozer 2.50 6.00
8 Kobe Bryant 6.00 15.00
9 Brandon Roy 3.00 8.00

2010-11 Panini Threads Triple Threat Materials Prime

*PRIME: .75X TO 2X BASE HI
STATED PRINT RUN 50 SER.#'d SETS
10 Steve Nash 8.00 20.00

2012-13 Panini Threads

COMP.SET w/o RCs (150) 12.00 30.00
UNPRICED PLATINUM PRINT RUN 10 SETS
1 Al Horford .30 .75
2 Jeff Teague .30 .75
3 Josh Smith .30 .75
4 Joe Johnson .30 .75
5 Kirk Hinrich .30 .75
6 Paul Pierce .40 1.00
7 Ray Allen .40 1.00
8 Rajon Rondo .40 1.00
9 Kevin Garnett .60 1.50
10 Avery Bradley .30 .75
11 Brandon Bass .25 .60
12 D.J. Augustin .25 .60
13 Gerald Henderson .25 .60
14 Corey Maggette .30 .75
15 Derrick Rose .50 1.25
16 Carlos Boozer .30 .75
17 Luol Deng .30 .75
18 Joakim Noah .30 .75
19 Richard Hamilton .30 .75
20 John Lucas III .25 .60
21 Anderson Varejao .25 .60
22 Antawn Jamison .30 .75
23 Omri Casspi .25 .60
24 Dirk Nowitzki .50 1.25
25 Jason Terry .30 .75
26 Shawn Marion .30 .75
27 Jason Kidd .40 1.00
28 Vince Carter .50 1.25
29 Delonte West .25 .60
30 Ty Lawson .25 .60
31 Danilo Gallinari .25 .60
32 Andre Miller .30 .75
33 JaVale McGee .30 .75
34 Arron Afflalo .30 .75
35 Al Harrington .30 .75
36 Greg Monroe .30 .75
37 Rodney Stuckey .30 .75
38 Tayshaun Prince .30 .75
39 Ben Gordon .30 .75
40 Jason Maxiell .25 .60
41 Stephen Curry 1.50 4.00
42 Andrew Bogut .30 .75
43 David Lee .25 .60
44 Nate Robinson .25 .60
45 Dorell Wright .25 .60
46 Brandon Rush .25 .60
47 Kevin Martin .30 .75
48 Luis Scola .30 .75
49 Kyle Lowry .30 .75
50 Goran Dragic .30 .75
51 Courtney Lee .30 .75
52 Danny Granger .30 .75
53 David West .30 .75
54 George Hill .30 .75
55 Roy Hibbert .30 .75
56 Paul George .50 1.25
57 Darren Collison .30 .75
58 Chris Paul .50 1.25
59 Blake Griffin .40 1.00
60 Nick Young .30 .75
61 Caron Butler .30 .75
62 Mo Williams .30 .75
63 DeAndre Jordan .40 1.00
64 Kobe Bryant 1.50 4.00
65 Andrew Bynum .25 .60
66 Pau Gasol .40 1.00
67 Ramon Sessions .30 .75
68 Devin Ebanks .25 .60
69 Metta World Peace .40 1.00
70 Rudy Gay .40 1.00
71 Zach Randolph .30 .75
72 O.J. Mayo .25 .60
73 Marc Gasol .40 1.00
74 Marreese Speights .25 .60
75 Mike Conley .30 .75
76 LeBron James 1.50 4.00
77 Chris Bosh .40 1.00
78 Dwyane Wade .60 1.50
79 Mario Chalmers .30 .75
80 Shane Battier .30 .75
81 Mike Miller .30 .75
82 Monta Ellis .30 .75
83 Brandon Jennings .25 .60
84 Ersan Ilyasova .25 .60
85 Drew Gooden .30 .75
86 Luc Mbah a Moute .25 .60
87 Kevin Love .40 1.00
88 Ricky Rubio .40 1.00
89 Nikola Pekovic .25 .60
90 Luke Ridnour .30 .75
91 Michael Beasley .25 .60
92 Wesley Johnson .30 .75
93 Eric Gordon .30 .75
94 Jarrett Jack .30 .75
95 Chris Kaman .30 .75
96 Marco Belinelli .25 .60
97 Greivis Vasquez .30 .75
98 Kevin Durant 1.00 2.50
99 Russell Westbrook 1.00 2.50
100 James Harden .60 1.50
101 Serge Ibaka .30 .75
102 Kendrick Perkins .25 .60
103 Derek Fisher .30 .75
104 Dwight Howard .30 .75
105 Jameer Nelson .25 .60
106 J.J. Redick .40 1.00
107 Glen Davis .25 .60
108 Jason Richardson .40 1.00
109 Ryan Anderson .30 .75
110 Andre Iguodala .30 .75
111 Evan Turner .25 .60
112 Louis Williams .30 .75
113 Jrue Holiday .40 1.00
114 Elton Brand .40 1.00
115 Thaddeus Young .25 .60
116 Steve Nash .40 1.00
117 Grant Hill .50 1.25
118 Jared Dudley .25 .60
119 Marcin Gortat .30 .75
120 Channing Frye .30 .75
121 Shannon Brown .25 .60
122 Tyreke Evans .25 .60
123 DeMarcus Cousins .40 1.00
124 Marcus Thornton .25 .60
125 Terrence Williams .25 .60
126 Jason Thompson .25 .60
127 Tim Duncan .60 1.50
128 Tony Parker .40 1.00
129 Manu Ginobili .40 1.00
130 Stephen Jackson .30 .75
131 Danny Green .30 .75
132 Gary Neal .30 .75
133 Andrea Bargnani .30 .75
134 DeMar DeRozan .40 1.00
135 Jose Calderon .25 .60
136 Jerryd Bayless .30 .75
137 Linas Kleiza .25 .60
138 Ed Davis .25 .60
139 Al Jefferson .30 .75
140 Devin Harris .25 .60
141 Paul Millsap .40 1.00
142 Derrick Favors .30 .75
143 Gordon Hayward .40 1.00
144 DeMarre Carroll .25 .60
145 Josh Howard .30 .75
146 John Wall .50 1.25
147 Jordan Crawford .25 .60
148 Nene .30 .75
149 Cartier Martin RC .40 1.00
150 Trevor Booker .25 .60
151 Kyrie Irving AU RC 50.00 120.00
152 Derrick Williams AU RC 2.50 6.00
153 Enes Kanter AU RC 3.00 8.00
154 Tristan Thompson AU RC 4.00 10.00
155 Jan Vesely AU RC 2.50 6.00
156 Bismack Biyombo AU RC 2.50 6.00
157 Brandon Knight AU RC 4.00 10.00
158 Kemba Walker AU RC 15.00 40.00
159 Klay Thompson AU RC 40.00 100.00
160 Alec Burks AU RC 4.00 10.00
161 Markieff Morris AU RC 4.00 10.00
162 Marcus Morris AU RC 3.00 8.00
163 Kawhi Leonard AU RC 60.00 150.00
164 Nikola Vucevic AU RC 4.00 10.00
165 Iman Shumpert AU RC 4.00 10.00
166 Chris Singleton AU RC 2.50 6.00
167 Tobias Harris AU RC 4.00 10.00
168 Nolan Smith AU RC 2.50 6.00
169 Kenneth Faried AU RC 4.00 10.00
170 Reggie Jackson AU RC 4.00 10.00
171 MarShon Brooks AU RC 3.00 8.00
172 Jordan Hamilton AU RC 2.50 6.00
173 JaJuan Johnson AU RC 2.50 6.00
174 Norris Cole AU RC 2.50 6.00
175 Cory Joseph AU RC 2.50 6.00
176 Jimmy Butler AU RC 20.00 50.00
177 Justin Harper AU RC 2.50 6.00
178 Shelvin Mack AU RC 3.00 8.00
179 Tyler Honeycutt AU RC 2.50 6.00
180 Jordan Williams AU RC 3.00 8.00
181 Trey Thompkins AU RC 2.50 6.00
182 Chandler Parsons AU RC 4.00 10.00
183 Jeremy Tyler AU RC 2.50 6.00
184 Jon Leuer AU RC 3.00 8.00
185 Darius Morris AU RC 2.50 6.00
186 Malcolm Lee AU RC 2.50 6.00
187 Charles Jenkins AU RC 2.50 6.00
189 Andrew Goudelock AU RC 2.50 6.00
190 Travis Leslie AU RC 2.50 6.00
192 Josh Selby AU RC 2.50 6.00
193 Lavoy Allen AU RC 2.50 6.00
195 DeAndre Liggins AU RC 3.00 8.00
196 E'Twaun Moore AU RC 2.50 6.00
197 Isaiah Thomas AU RC 20.00 50.00
198 Ivan Johnson AU RC 2.50 6.00
199 Greg Stiemsma AU RC 2.50 6.00
200 Lance Thomas AU RC 2.50 6.00
201 Anthony Davis AU RC 75.00 150.00
202 M.Kidd-Gilchrist AU RC 4.00 10.00
203 Bradley Beal AU RC 15.00 40.00
204 Dion Waiters AU RC 4.00 10.00
205 Thomas Robinson AU RC 3.00 8.00
206 Robbie Hummel AU RC 2.50 6.00
207 Harrison Barnes AU RC 6.00 15.00
208 Terrence Ross AU RC 4.00 10.00
209 Andre Drummond AU RC 10.00 25.00
210 Austin Rivers AU RC 4.00 10.00
211 Meyers Leonard AU RC 3.00 8.00
212 Jeremy Lamb AU RC 4.00 10.00
213 Kendall Marshall AU RC 2.50 6.00
214 John Henson AU RC 4.00 10.00
215 Moe Harkless AU RC 4.00 10.00
216 Royce White AU RC 2.50 6.00
217 Tyler Zeller AU RC 3.00 8.00
218 Terrence Jones AU RC 3.00 8.00
219 Andrew Nicholson AU RC 2.50 6.00
220 Evan Fournier AU RC 4.00 10.00
221 Jared Sullinger AU RC 3.00 8.00
222 Fab Melo AU RC 2.50 6.00
223 John Jenkins AU RC 2.50 6.00
224 Jared Cunningham AU RC 2.50 6.00
225 Tony Wroten AU RC 3.00 8.00
226 Miles Plumlee AU RC 2.50 6.00
227 Arnett Moultrie AU RC 2.50 6.00
228 Perry Jones AU RC 2.50 6.00
229 Marquis Teague AU RC 2.50 6.00
230 Festus Ezeli AU RC 3.00 8.00
231 Jeff Taylor AU RC 2.50 6.00
232 Robert Sacre AU RC 2.50 6.00
233 Bernard James AU RC 2.50 6.00
234 Jae Crowder AU RC 6.00 15.00
235 Draymond Green AU RC 12.00 30.00
236 Orlando Johnson AU RC 2.50 6.00
237 Quincy Acy AU RC 2.50 6.00
238 Quincy Miller AU RC 2.50 6.00
240 Will Barton AU RC 3.00 8.00
241 Tyshawn Taylor AU RC 2.50 6.00
242 Doron Lamb AU RC 2.50 6.00
243 Mike Scott AU RC 2.50 6.00
244 Kim English AU RC 2.50 6.00
246 Darius Miller AU RC 2.50 6.00
247 Kevin Murphy AU RC 2.50 6.00
248 Kyle O'Quinn AU RC 2.50 6.00
249 Kris Joseph AU RC 2.50 6.00
250 T.Shengelia AU RC EXCH 2.50 6.00

2012-13 Panini Threads Century Proof Gold

*GOLD: 4X TO 10X BASE HI
STATED PRINT RUN 25 SER.#'d SETS

2012-13 Panini Threads Century Proof Red

*RED: .75X TO 2X BASE HI
RANDOM INSERTS IN RETAIL PACKS

2012-13 Panini Threads Century Proof Silver

*SILVER: 1.5X TO 4X BASE HI
STATED PRINT RUN 99 SER.#'d SETS

2012-13 Panini Threads Authentic Threads

RANDOM INSERTS IN PACKS
1 Ray Allen 3.00 8.00
2 Tim Duncan 5.00 12.00
3 LeBron James 12.00 30.00
4 Jason Kidd 3.00 8.00
5 Anderson Varejao 2.00 5.00
6 Antawn Jamison 2.50 6.00
7 Andre Iguodala 2.50 6.00
8 Jameer Nelson 2.00 5.00
9 Marc Gasol 3.00 8.00
10 Kevin Martin 2.50 6.00
11 Nick Collison 2.50 6.00
12 Jamal Crawford 3.00 8.00
13 Joe Johnson 2.50 6.00
14 Tyrus Thomas 2.00 5.00
15 Jordan Crawford 2.00 5.00
16 George Hill 2.50 6.00
17 Tayshaun Prince 2.50 6.00
18 Taj Gibson 2.50 6.00
19 Luol Deng 2.50 6.00
20 Manu Ginobili 3.00 8.00
21 O.J. Mayo 2.00 5.00
22 Dirk Nowitzki 4.00 10.00
23 John Salmons 2.50 6.00
24 Channing Frye 2.50 6.00
25 Devin Harris 2.00 5.00
26 Pau Gasol 3.00 8.00
27 Randy Foye 2.00 5.00
28 Caron Butler 2.50 6.00
29 Josh Smith 2.50 6.00
30 David Lee 2.00 5.00
31 DeMar DeRozan 3.00 8.00
32 Jose Calderon 2.00 5.00
33 Evan Turner 2.00 5.00
34 Thaddeus Young 2.00 5.00
35 Landry Fields 2.00 5.00
36 Amare Stoudemire 2.50 6.00
37 Brook Lopez 2.50 6.00
38 Kris Humphries 2.00 5.00
39 Deron Williams 2.50 6.00
40 J.J. Redick 3.00 8.00
41 Glen Davis 2.00 5.00
42 LaMarcus Aldridge 3.00 8.00
43 James Harden 5.00 12.00
44 Anthony Mason 2.50 6.00
45 Luke Ridnour 2.50 6.00
46 Wayne Ellington 2.00 5.00
47 Tony Parker 3.00 8.00
48 Derrick Rose 4.00 10.00
49 D.J. Augustin 2.00 5.00
50 Kevin Durant 8.00 20.00
51 Al Jefferson 2.50 6.00
52 Josh Howard 2.50 6.00
53 Drew Gooden 2.50 6.00
54 Udonis Haslem 2.00 5.00
55 Chris Kaman 2.50 6.00
56 Emeka Okafor 2.50 6.00
57 Rajon Rondo 3.00 8.00
58 Kevin Garnett 5.00 12.00
59 Kenny Anderson 2.50 6.00
60 John Wall 4.00 10.00
61 Joakim Noah 2.50 6.00
62 Jrue Holiday 3.00 8.00
63 Mike Conley 2.50 6.00
64 David West 2.50 6.00
65 Elton Brand 3.00 8.00
66 Chase Budinger 2.00 5.00
67 Andrew Bynum 2.00 5.00
68 Dwight Howard 2.50 6.00
69 Rudy Fernandez 2.00 5.00
70 Al Horford 2.50 6.00
71 Brandon Knight 2.00 5.00
72 Kyrie Irving 10.00 25.00
73 Derrick Williams 1.25 3.00
74 MarShon Brooks 1.50 4.00
75 Markieff Morris 2.00 5.00

2012-13 Panini Threads Authentic Threads Prime

*PRIME: 1X TO 2.5X BASE HI
STATED PRINT RUN ONE TO 25 SER.#'d SETS
SOME UNPRICED DUE TO SCARCITY
20 Manu Ginobili/25 10.00 25.00
48 Derrick Rose/25 30.00 80.00

2012-13 Panini Threads Century Greats

COMPLETE SET (25) 12.00 30.00
RANDOM INSERTS IN PACKS
1 Larry Bird 2.00 5.00
2 Moses Malone .75 2.00
3 Shaquille O'Neal 1.50 4.00
4 Patrick Ewing 1.00 2.50
5 Bill Sharman .75 2.00
6 Bill Russell 1.25 3.00
7 John Havlicek 1.00 2.50
8 Hakeem Olajuwon 1.00 2.50
9 Kareem Abdul-Jabbar 1.25 3.00
10 Wilt Chamberlain 1.50 4.00
11 Julius Erving 1.25 3.00
12 Scottie Pippen 1.50 4.00
13 Magic Johnson 2.00 5.00
14 Jerry West 1.00 2.50
15 David Robinson 1.25 3.00
16 Isiah Thomas .75 2.00
17 James Worthy 1.00 2.50
18 Nate Archibald .60 1.50
19 Elvin Hayes .75 2.00
20 Clyde Drexler 1.00 2.50
21 Elgin Baylor .75 2.00
22 Oscar Robertson 1.00 2.50
23 Walt Frazier .75 2.00
24 Bill Walton .75 2.00
25 K.C. Jones .75 2.00

2012-13 Panini Threads Century Stars

RANDOM INSERTS IN PACKS
1 Chris Paul 5.00 12.00
2 Tim Duncan 6.00 15.00
3 Kevin Garnett 6.00 15.00
4 Kobe Bryant 15.00 40.00
5 Dirk Nowitzki 5.00 12.00
6 Blake Griffin 4.00 10.00
7 Kevin Durant 10.00 25.00
8 Dwight Howard 3.00 8.00
9 Steve Nash 4.00 10.00
10 LeBron James 15.00 40.00
11 Paul Pierce 4.00 10.00
12 Tony Parker 4.00 10.00
13 Dwyane Wade 6.00 15.00
14 Derrick Rose 5.00 12.00
15 Carmelo Anthony 5.00 12.00
16 Josh Smith 3.00 8.00
17 Amare Stoudemire 3.00 8.00
18 Kevin Martin 3.00 8.00
19 Carlos Boozer 3.00 8.00
20 Zach Randolph 3.00 8.00
21 Tyreke Evans 2.50 6.00
22 Kevin Love 4.00 10.00
23 Russell Westbrook 10.00 25.00
24 LaMarcus Aldridge 4.00 10.00
25 Deron Williams 3.00 8.00

2012-13 Panini Threads Floor Generals

COMPLETE SET (20) 8.00 20.00
RANDOM INSERTS IN PACKS
1 Rajon Rondo .75 2.00
2 Derrick Rose 1.00 2.50
3 John Wall 1.00 2.50
4 Deron Williams .60 1.50
5 Steve Nash .75 2.00
6 Russell Westbrook 2.00 5.00
7 Chris Paul 1.00 2.50
8 Stephen Curry 3.00 8.00
9 Ty Lawson .50 1.25
10 Raymond Felton .60 1.50
11 Tony Parker .75 2.00
12 Dwyane Wade 1.25 3.00
13 Brandon Jennings .50 1.25
14 Jrue Holiday .75 2.00
15 Jason Kidd 1.00 2.50
16 Ramon Sessions .60 1.50
17 Ricky Rubio .75 2.00
18 Kyrie Irving 2.50 6.00
19 Devin Harris .50 1.25
20 Jeremy Lin .75 2.00

2012-13 Panini Threads High Flyers

COMPLETE SET (30) 10.00 25.00
RANDOM INSERTS IN PACKS
1 Blake Griffin .75 2.00
2 LeBron James 3.00 8.00
3 Rudy Gay .75 2.00
4 Derrick Rose 1.00 2.50
5 Russell Westbrook 2.00 5.00
6 JaVale McGee .60 1.50
7 Josh Smith .60 1.50
8 Dwyane Wade 1.25 3.00
9 Dwight Howard .60 1.50
10 DeMar DeRozan .75 2.00
11 Kevin Durant 2.00 5.00
12 Jeremy Evans .50 1.25
13 DeAndre Jordan .75 2.00
14 J.R. Smith .60 1.50
15 Alonzo Gee .50 1.25
16 Kenneth Faried .75 2.00
17 Paul George 1.00 2.50
18 John Wall 1.00 2.50
19 Andre Iguodala .60 1.50
20 Gerald Green .60 1.50
21 Vince Carter 1.00 2.50
22 Tracy McGrady .75 2.00
23 Nate Robinson .50 1.25
24 Jason Richardson .75 2.00
25 Kobe Bryant 3.00 8.00
26 Gerald Wallace .60 1.50
27 Shannon Brown .50 1.25
28 Terrence Williams .50 1.25
29 Serge Ibaka .60 1.50
30 Amare Stoudemire .60 1.50

2012-13 Panini Threads Inside Presence

COMPLETE SET (25) 8.00 20.00
RANDOM INSERTS IN PACKS
1 Tim Duncan 1.25 3.00
2 Andrew Bynum .50 1.25
3 Kevin Love .75 2.00
4 Dwight Howard .60 1.50
5 Pau Gasol .75 2.00
6 Blake Griffin .75 2.00
7 Brook Lopez .60 1.50
8 Al Jefferson .60 1.50
9 DeMarcus Cousins .75 2.00
10 Kevin Garnett 1.25 3.00
11 Greg Monroe .60 1.50
12 Marc Gasol .75 2.00
13 Nikola Pekovic .50 1.25
14 Chris Kaman .60 1.50
15 Roy Hibbert .60 1.50
16 Al Horford .60 1.50
17 Andrew Bogut .60 1.50
18 Tyson Chandler .60 1.50
19 LaMarcus Aldridge .75 2.00
20 JaVale McGee .60 1.50
21 DeAndre Jordan .75 2.00
22 Joakim Noah .60 1.50
23 Nene .60 1.50
24 Marcin Gortat .60 1.50
25 Tristan Thompson .75 2.00

2012-13 Panini Threads Private Signings

RANDOM INSERTS IN PACKS
1 Deron Williams 50.00 125.00
2 Antawn Jamison 6.00 15.00
3 Tyson Chandler 10.00 25.00
4 Monta Ellis 8.00 20.00

2012-13 Panini Threads Rookie Team Threads

COMPLETE SET (22) 10.00 25.00
RANDOM INSERTS IN PACKS
1 Kemba Walker 1.50 4.00
2 Kenneth Faried .75 2.00
4 Kawhi Leonard 4.00 10.00
5 Ivan Johnson .50 1.25
6 Bismack Biyombo .50 1.25
7 Chris Singleton .50 1.25
8 Marcus Morris .60 1.50
9 Reggie Jackson .75 2.00
10 Enes Kanter .60 1.50
11 Lavoy Allen .50 1.25
12 Damian Lillard 3.00 8.00
13 Terrence Ross .75 2.00
14 Meyers Leonard .60 1.50
15 John Henson .75 2.00
16 Royce White .50 1.25
17 Tyler Zeller .60 1.50
18 Terrence Jones .60 1.50
19 Andrew Nicholson .50 1.25
20 Fab Melo .50 1.25
21 Evan Fournier .75 2.00
22 John Jenkins .50 1.25
23 Marquis Teague .50 1.25

2012-13 Panini Threads Rookie Team Threads Autographs

RANDOM INSERTS IN PACKS
1 Kyrie Irving 60.00 150.00
2 Brandon Knight 5.00 12.00
3 Isaiah Thomas 20.00 50.00
5 Klay Thompson 40.00 100.00
6 Iman Shumpert 5.00 12.00
7 Chandler Parsons 5.00 12.00
8 Derrick Williams 3.00 8.00
9 Tristan Thompson 12.00 30.00
10 Kawhi Leonard 50.00 120.00
11 Jimmer Fredette 3.00 8.00
12 Markieff Morris 5.00 12.00
13 Norris Cole 3.00 8.00
14 Thomas Robinson 4.00 10.00
15 Harrison Barnes 15.00 40.00
16 Austin Rivers 10.00 25.00
17 Anthony Davis 75.00 150.00
18 Bradley Beal 12.00 30.00
19 Michael Kidd-Gilchrist 5.00 12.00
20 Jeremy Lamb 5.00 12.00
21 Kendall Marshall 3.00 8.00
22 Jared Sullinger 4.00 10.00
23 Andre Drummond 20.00 50.00
24 Perry Jones 3.00 8.00
25 Dion Waiters 10.00 25.00

2012-13 Panini Threads Signage

RANDOM INSERTS IN PACKS
1 Willis Reed 8.00 20.00
2 DeMarcus Cousins 12.00 30.00
3 Artis Gilmore 6.00 15.00
4 Stephen Curry 100.00 250.00
5 Kobe Bryant 75.00 150.00
6 Andrew Bynum 5.00 12.00
7 Bill Walton 5.00 12.00
8 Blake Griffin 20.00 50.00
9 Steve Nash 20.00 50.00
10 Grant Hill 30.00 80.00
11 Larry Bird 40.00 100.00
12 Michael Finley 5.00 12.00
13 Kevin Durant 75.00 200.00
14 Dave Cowens 6.00 15.00
15 Tom Chambers 5.00 12.00
16 Wesley Matthews 5.00 12.00
17 Kevin Love 12.00 30.00
18 Magic Johnson 40.00 100.00
19 Chris Mullin 10.00 25.00
20 World B. Free 5.00 12.00
21 James Worthy 10.00 25.00
22 Trevor Booker EXCH 5.00 12.00
23 Joe Dumars 6.00 15.00
24 David Robinson 15.00 40.00
25 Jrue Holiday 5.00 12.00
26 Elvin Hayes 6.00 15.00
27 Cedric Ceballos 5.00 12.00
28 Lenny Wilkens 10.00 25.00
29 Josh Smith 5.00 12.00
30 Monta Ellis 5.00 12.00
31 Rolando Blackman 5.00 12.00
32 Roy Hibbert 5.00 12.00
33 Clyde Lovellette 6.00 15.00
34 Ben Gordon 5.00 12.00
35 Tayshaun Prince 5.00 12.00
36 Sean Elliott 8.00 20.00
37 Robert Parish 5.00 12.00
38 Carlos Boozer 5.00 12.00
39 Jamal Mashburn 8.00 20.00
40 Allan Houston EXCH 8.00 20.00
41 Brook Lopez 5.00 12.00
42 Tim Hardaway 6.00 15.00
43 Andre Iguodala 5.00 12.00
44 Zach Randolph 5.00 12.00
45 Mike Conley 5.00 12.00
46 Kyle Lowry 5.00 12.00
47 Kurt Rambis 8.00 20.00
48 Jason Kidd 15.00 40.00
49 Tyson Chandler EXCH 6.00 15.00
50 Dolph Schayes 5.00 12.00

2012-13 Panini Threads Talented Twosomes

COMPLETE SET (14) 8.00 20.00
RANDOM INSERTS IN PACKS
1 K.Durant/R.Westbrook 2.00 5.00
2 L.Deng/C.Boozer .60 1.50
3 L.James/D.Wade 3.00 8.00
4 P.Pierce/R.Rondo .75 2.00
5 K.Bryant/P.Gasol 3.00 8.00
6 T.Evans/D.Cousins .75 2.00
7 T.Lawson/A.Miller .60 1.50
8 Z.Randolph/M.Gasol .75 2.00
9 T.Parker/T.Duncan 1.25 3.00
10 C.Anthony/A.Stoudemire 1.00 2.50
11 S.Curry/D.Lee 3.00 8.00
12 R.Gay/M.Conley .60 1.50
13 A.Jefferson/P.Millsap .75 2.00
14 B.Knight/G.Monroe .75 2.00

2012-13 Panini Threads Team Threads

COMPLETE SET (25) 12.00 30.00
RANDOM INSERTS IN PACKS
1 Metta World Peace 1.00 2.50
2 Kevin Garnett 1.50 4.00
3 Dwight Howard .75 2.00
4 LeBron James 4.00 10.00
5 Louis Williams .75 2.00
6 Manu Ginobili 1.00 2.50
7 Jason Terry .75 2.00
8 Carmelo Anthony 1.25 3.00
9 Kevin Love 1.00 2.50
10 George Hill .75 2.00
11 Jeff Teague .75 2.00
12 Serge Ibaka .75 2.00
13 Paul Pierce 1.00 2.50
14 Ricky Rubio 1.00 2.50
15 Marcin Gortat .75 2.00
16 Jeremy Lin 1.00 2.50
17 Marc Gasol 1.00 2.50
18 Ersan Ilyasova .60 1.50
19 Nicolas Batum .75 2.00
20 Nick Young .75 2.00
21 Gordon Hayward 1.00 2.50
22 Brandon Rush .60 1.50
23 David West .75 2.00
24 Luis Scola .75 2.00
25 Luol Deng .75 2.00

2012-13 Panini Threads Team Threads Autographs

RANDOM INSERTS IN PACKS
1 James Harden 50.00 120.00
2 Kobe Bryant 100.00 200.00
3 Kevin Durant 100.00 200.00
4 Kevin Love 20.00 50.00
6 Stephen Curry 200.00 400.00
7 Chris Paul EXCH 25.00 60.00
8 Tony Parker 12.00 30.00
10 Marcus Thornton 6.00 15.00
11 Vince Carter 20.00 50.00
12 JaVale McGee 6.00 15.00
13 Derrick Favors 6.00 15.00
15 Darren Collison 6.00 15.00
16 Andrew Bogut 15.00 40.00
17 Evan Turner 6.00 15.00
18 Landry Fields 6.00 15.00
19 Ray Allen 50.00 120.00
21 Danilo Gallinari 8.00 20.00
23 Greg Monroe 6.00 15.00
24 Eric Gordon 8.00 20.00
25 Kevin Martin 6.00 15.00

2012-13 Panini Threads Triple Threat Materials

RANDOM INSERTS IN PACKS
1 Lopez/Big Al/Dwight 2.00 5.00
2 Martin/DeRzn/Granger 2.50 6.00
3 Gasol/Horford/Barg 2.50 6.00
4 Dragic/Barea/Gordon 2.00 5.00
5 Duncan/Gasol/Scola 4.00 10.00
6 Lawson/Rondo/DWill 2.50 6.00
7 Harden/Wstbrk/Durant 6.00 15.00
8 Gasol/Kobe/Bynum 10.00 25.00
9 Lee/Griffin/Cousins 2.50 6.00
10 Zach/Boozer/Amare 2.00 5.00
11 Pierce/Gay/Granger 2.50 6.00
12 Butler/Iguodala/Deng 2.00 5.00
13 Harden/Mayo/Conley 4.00 10.00
14 Carter/Dirk/Pierce 3.00 8.00
15 Rip/Manu/Gordon 2.50 6.00
16 Turner/Fields/Hywrd 2.50 6.00
17 Augustin/Hedo/Zach 2.00 5.00
18 Rose/Williams/Paul 3.00 8.00
19 Bosh/Wade/LeBron 10.00 25.00
20 Brooks/Redick/Wright 2.50 6.00
21 Dwight/O'Neal/Gasol 2.50 6.00
22 Brand/Kaman/Hawes 2.50 6.00
23 Okafor/Davis/Haywd 2.00 5.00
24 Felton/Conley/Miller 2.00 5.00
25 Nelson/Harris/Davis 2.00 5.00

2012-13 Panini Threads Triple Threat Materials Prime

*PRIME: 1.25X TO 3X BASE HI
STATED PRINT RUN 10 TO 25 SER.#'d SETS

2013 Panini Threads 2011 Draft All-Star Game

COMPLETE SET (6) 10.00 25.00
1 Kyrie Irving 8.00 20.00
2 Derrick Williams 1.50 4.00
3 Brandon Knight 2.00 5.00
4 Kenneth Faried 2.00 5.00
5 Kemba Walker 2.00 5.00
6 Klay Thompson 2.50 6.00

2013 Panini Threads 2012 Draft All-Star Game

COMPLETE SET (6) 8.00 20.00
1 Anthony Davis 5.00 12.00
2 Michael Kidd-Gilchrist 2.50 6.00
3 Thomas Robinson .75 2.00
4 Harrison Barnes 2.50 6.00
5 Austin Rivers 2.00 5.00
6 Jared Sullinger 2.00 5.00

2014-15 Panini Threads

1 Al Horford .50 1.25
2 Al Jefferson .50 1.25
3 Alec Burks .40 1.00
4 Alonzo Mourning .75 2.00
5 Amar'e Stoudemire .60 1.50
6 Amir Johnson .40 1.00
7 Anderson Varejao .40 1.00
8 Andre Drummond .60 1.50
9 Andrew Bogut .50 1.25
10 Anthony Davis 1.25 3.00
11 Anthony Morrow .40 1.00
12 Arron Afflalo .40 1.00
13 Artis Gilmore .50 1.25
14 Austin Rivers .50 1.25
15 Avery Bradley .50 1.25
16 Ben McLemore .40 1.00
17 Bernard King .50 1.25
18 Blake Griffin .60 1.50
19 Bradley Beal .60 1.50
20 Brandon Jennings .40 1.00
21 Brandon Knight .50 1.25
22 Brook Lopez .50 1.25
23 Carlos Boozer .50 1.25
24 Carmelo Anthony .75 2.00
25 Caron Butler .50 1.25
26 Chandler Parsons .50 1.25
27 Channing Frye .50 1.25
28 Chris Andersen .50 1.25
29 Chris Bosh .60 1.50
30 Chris Mullin .60 1.50
31 Chris Paul .75 2.00
32 Cody Zeller .40 1.00
33 Corey Brewer .40 1.00
34 Courtney Lee .50 1.25
35 Damian Lillard 1.25 3.00
36 Danilo Gallinari .40 1.00
37 Danny Green .50 1.25
38 Darren Collison .50 1.25
39 David Lee .40 1.00
40 David Robinson 1.00 2.50
41 David West .50 1.25
42 DeAndre Jordan .60 1.50
43 DeMar DeRozan .60 1.50
44 DeMarcus Cousins .60 1.50
45 DeMarre Carroll .40 1.00
46 Dennis Schroder .50 1.25
47 Deron Williams .50 1.25
48 Derrick Favors .50 1.25
49 Derrick Rose .75 2.00
50 Devin Harris .40 1.00
51 Dirk Nowitzki .75 2.00
52 Dominique Wilkins .75 2.00
53 Donatas Motiejunas .40 1.00
54 Draymond Green .75 2.00
55 Dwight Howard .50 1.25
56 Dwyane Wade 1.00 2.50
57 Enes Kanter .40 1.00
58 Eric Bledsoe .50 1.25
59 Eric Gordon .50 1.25
60 Ersan Ilyasova .40 1.00
61 Evan Fournier .40 1.00
62 Evan Turner .40 1.00
63 Gary Payton .60 1.50
64 Giannis Antetokounmpo 1.25 3.00
65 Glen Rice .50 1.25
66 Goran Dragic .50 1.25
67 Gordon Hayward .60 1.50
68 Gorgui Dieng .40 1.00
69 Greg Monroe .50 1.25
70 Hakeem Olajuwon .75 2.00
71 Harrison Barnes .50 1.25
72 Henry Sims RC .40 1.00
73 Hollis Thompson .50 1.25
74 Iman Shumpert .40 1.00
75 Isaiah Thomas .60 1.50
76 Jamal Crawford .60 1.50
77 Jameer Nelson .40 1.00
78 James Harden 1.00 2.50
79 Jared Sullinger .40 1.00
80 Jarrett Jack .50 1.25
81 Jason Thompson .40 1.00
82 Jeff Green .50 1.25
83 Jeff Teague .50 1.25
84 Jeremy Lin .60 1.50
85 Jimmy Butler .60 1.50
86 J.J. Redick .60 1.50
87 Joakim Noah .50 1.25
88 Joe Dumars .60 1.50
89 Joe Johnson .50 1.25
90 John Stockton 1.00 2.50
91 John Wall .75 2.00
92 Jonas Valanciunas .50 1.25
93 Jordan Hill .40 1.00
94 Jose Calderon .40 1.00
95 Josh Smith .50 1.25
96 Jrue Holiday .50 1.25
97 Julius Erving 1.00 2.50
98 Kareem Abdul-Jabbar 1.00 2.50
99 Karl Malone .75 2.00
100 Kawhi Leonard 1.00 2.50
101 Kelly Olynyk .40 1.00
102 Kemba Walker .60 1.50
103 Kenneth Faried .50 1.25
104 Kentavious Caldwell-Pope .40 1.00
105 Kevin Durant 1.50 4.00
106 Kevin Garnett 1.00 2.50
107 Kevin Love .60 1.50
108 Kevin McHale .60 1.50
109 Kirk Hinrich .50 1.25
110 Klay Thompson .75 2.00
111 Kobe Bryant 2.50 6.00
112 Kyle Korver .50 1.25
113 Kyle Lowry .50 1.25
114 Kyrie Irving 1.25 3.00
115 LaMarcus Aldridge .60 1.50
116 Lance Stephenson .50 1.25
117 Larry Bird 1.50 4.00
118 Larry Sanders .40 1.00
119 LeBron James 2.50 6.00
120 Luc Mbah a Moute .40 1.00
121 Luis Scola .50 1.25
122 Luol Deng .50 1.25
123 Magic Johnson 1.50 4.00
124 Manu Ginobili .60 1.50
125 Marc Gasol .60 1.50
126 Marcin Gortat .50 1.25
127 Marcus Morris .40 1.00
128 Mario Chalmers .50 1.25
129 Markieff Morris .40 1.00
130 Marvin Williams .50 1.25
131 Matt Barnes .40 1.00
132 Maurice Harkless .40 1.00
133 Michael Carter-Williams .40 1.00
134 Michael Kidd-Gilchrist .50 1.25
135 Mike Conley .50 1.25
136 Mike Dunleavy .40 1.00
137 Miles Plumlee .40 1.00
138 Mirza Teletovic .40 1.00
139 Mo Williams .50 1.25
140 Monta Ellis .50 1.25
141 Nene .50 1.25
142 Nerlens Noel .50 1.25
143 Nick Young .50 1.25
144 Nicolas Batum .50 1.25
145 Nikola Pekovic .40 1.00
146 Nikola Vucevic .50 1.25
147 Norris Cole .40 1.00
148 O.J. Mayo .40 1.00
149 Omer Asik .50 1.25
150 Omri Casspi .40 1.00
151 Otto Porter .50 1.25
152 Patrick Beverley .40 1.00
153 Patrick Patterson .40 1.00
154 Pau Gasol .60 1.50
155 Paul George .75 2.00
156 Paul Millsap .60 1.50
157 Paul Pierce .60 1.50
158 Rajon Rondo .60 1.50
159 Reggie Jackson .40 1.00
160 Ricky Rubio .60 1.50
161 Robin Lopez .40 1.00
162 Rodney Stuckey .50 1.25
163 Roy Hibbert .50 1.25
164 Rudy Gay .60 1.50
165 Rudy Gobert .60 1.50
166 Russell Westbrook 1.50 4.00
167 Shane Larkin .40 1.00
168 Scottie Pippen 1.25 3.00
169 Serge Ibaka .50 1.25
170 Shaquille O'Neal 1.25 3.00
171 Shawn Marion .50 1.25
172 Solomon Hill .40 1.00
173 Stephen Curry 2.50 6.00
174 Steve Blake .40 1.00
175 Steven Adams .50 1.25
176 Terrence Jones .50 1.25
177 Terrence Ross .50 1.25
178 Thaddeus Young .40 1.00
179 Tiago Splitter .50 1.25
180 Tim Duncan 1.00 2.50
181 Tim Hardaway Jr. .40 1.00
182 Timofey Mozgov .40 1.00
183 Tobias Harris .50 1.25
184 Tony Allen .40 1.00
185 Tony Parker .60 1.50
186 Trevor Ariza .40 1.00
187 Tony Wroten .40 1.00
188 Trey Burke .40 1.00
189 Tristan Thompson .50 1.25
190 Ty Lawson .40 1.00
191 Tyreke Evans .40 1.00
192 Tyson Chandler .50 1.25
193 Victor Oladipo .50 1.25
194 Vince Carter .75 2.00
195 Walt Frazier .60 1.50
196 Wesley Johnson .50 1.25
197 Wesley Matthews .40 1.00
198 Wilson Chandler .50 1.25
199 Zach Randolph .50 1.25
200 Zaza Pachulia .40 1.00
201 Andrew Wiggins TT RC 12.00 30.00
202 Jabari Parker TT RC 3.00 8.00
203 Damjan Rudez TT RC 1.25 3.00
204 Bojan Bogdanovic TT RC 1.50 4.00
205 Elfrid Payton TT RC 2.00 5.00
206 P.J. Hairston TT RC 1.25 3.00
207 Jordan Adams TT RC 1.25 3.00
208 Julius Randle TT RC 3.00 8.00
209 Dante Exum TT RC 2.00 5.00
210 Doug McDermott TT RC 2.00 5.00
211 Zach LaVine TT RC 3.00 8.00
212 Nikola Mirotic TT RC 2.50 6.00
213 Cleanthony Early TT RC 1.25 3.00
214 Glenn Robinson III TT RC 1.25 3.00
215 K.J. McDaniels TT RC 1.50 4.00
216 Marcus Smart TT RC 2.00 5.00
217 Rodney Hood TT RC 2.00 5.00
218 Jordan Clarkson TT RC 2.00 5.00
219 James Young TT RC 1.25 3.00
220 Aaron Gordon TT RC 3.00 8.00
221 Gary Harris TT RC 2.00 5.00
222 Adreian Payne TT RC 1.50 4.00
223 Jusuf Nurkic TT RC 2.00 5.00
224 Kostas Papanikolaou TT RC 1.25 3.00
225 Noah Vonleh TT RC 1.50 4.00
226 Cory Jefferson TT RC 1.25 3.00
227 Shabazz Napier TT RC 1.50 4.00
228 Nik Stauskas TT RC 1.50 4.00
229 James Ennis TT RC 1.25 3.00
230 Kyle Anderson TT RC 2.00 5.00
231 Joel Embiid TT RC 6.00 15.00
232 Tyler Ennis TT RC 1.25 3.00
233 Nick Johnson TT RC 1.25 3.00
234 T.J. Warren TT RC 2.00 5.00
235 Joe Ingles TT RC 1.25 3.00
236 Jerami Grant TT RC 1.25 3.00
237 Joe Harris TT RC 1.25 3.00
238 Erick Green TT RC 1.25 3.00
239 Markel Brown TT RC 1.25 3.00
240 Tarik Black TT RC 1.25 3.00
241 Joel Embiid LTHR RC 8.00 20.00
242 Aaron Gordon LTHR RC 4.00 10.00
243 Bojan Bogdanovic LTHR RC 2.00 5.00
244 Jordan Adams LTHR RC 1.50 4.00
245 Zach LaVine LTHR RC 4.00 10.00
246 Dante Exum LTHR RC 2.50 6.00
247 Glenn Robinson III LTHR RC 1.50 4.00
248 Jabari Parker LTHR RC 4.00 10.00
249 Rodney Hood LTHR RC 2.50 6.00
250 Damjan Rudez LTHR RC 1.50 4.00
251 Joe Ingles LTHR RC 1.50 4.00
252 Elfrid Payton LTHR RC 2.50 6.00
253 Andrew Wiggins LTHR RC 8.00 20.00
254 Damien Inglis LTHR RC 1.50 4.00
255 Tarik Black LTHR RC 1.50 4.00
256 Joe Harris LTHR RC 1.50 4.00
257 P.J. Hairston LTHR RC 1.50 4.00
258 K.J. McDaniels LTHR RC 2.00 5.00
259 Kostas Papanikolaou LTHR RC 1.50 4.00
260 T.J. Warren LTHR RC 2.50 6.00
261 Marcus Smart LTHR RC 2.50 6.00
262 Jarnell Stokes LTHR RC 1.50 4.00
263 Russ Smith LTHR RC 1.50 4.00
264 Cleanthony Early LTHR RC 1.50 4.00
265 Clint Capela LTHR RC 2.00 5.00
266 C.J. Wilcox LTHR RC 1.50 4.00
267 Doug McDermott LTHR RC 2.50 6.00
268 Tyler Ennis LTHR RC 1.50 4.00
269 Nikola Mirotic LTHR RC 3.00 8.00
270 James Ennis LTHR RC 1.50 4.00
271 Cory Jefferson LTHR RC 1.50 4.00
272 James Young LTHR RC 1.50 4.00
273 Shabazz Napier LTHR RC 2.00 5.00
274 Jusuf Nurkic LTHR RC 2.50 6.00
275 Adreian Payne LTHR RC 2.00 5.00
276 Jordan Clarkson LTHR RC 2.50 6.00
277 Nik Stauskas LTHR RC 2.00 5.00
278 Gary Harris LTHR RC 2.50 6.00
279 Nick Johnson LTHR RC 1.50 4.00
280 Devyn Marble LTHR RC 1.50 4.00
281 Kyle Anderson LTHR RC 2.50 6.00
282 Noah Vonleh LTHR RC 2.00 5.00
283 Cameron Bairstow LTHR RC 1.50 4.00
284 Julius Randle LTHR RC 4.00 10.00
285 Erick Green LTHR RC 1.50 4.00
286 Joel Embiid ETCH RC 5.00 12.00
287 Aaron Gordon ETCH RC 2.50 6.00
288 Bojan Bogdanovic ETCH RC 1.25 3.00
289 Jordan Adams ETCH RC 1.00 2.50
290 Zach LaVine ETCH RC 2.50 6.00
291 Dante Exum ETCH RC 1.50 4.00
292 Glenn Robinson III ETCH RC 1.00 2.50
293 Jabari Parker ETCH RC 2.50 6.00
294 Rodney Hood ETCH RC 1.50 4.00
295 Damjan Rudez ETCH RC 1.00 2.50
296 Joe Ingles ETCH RC 1.00 2.50
297 Elfrid Payton ETCH RC 1.50 4.00
298 Andrew Wiggins ETCH RC 10.00 25.00
299 Damien Inglis ETCH RC 1.00 2.50
300 Tarik Black ETCH RC 1.00 2.50
301 Joe Harris ETCH RC 1.00 2.50
302 P.J. Hairston ETCH RC 1.00 2.50
303 K.J. McDaniels ETCH RC 1.25 3.00
304 Kostas Papanikolaou ETCH RC 1.00 2.50
305 T.J. Warren ETCH RC 1.50 4.00
306 Marcus Smart ETCH RC 1.50 4.00
307 Jarnell Stokes ETCH RC 1.00 2.50
308 Russ Smith ETCH RC 1.00 2.50
309 Cleanthony Early ETCH RC 1.00 2.50
310 Clint Capela ETCH RC 1.25 3.00
311 C.J. Wilcox ETCH RC 1.00 2.50
312 Doug McDermott ETCH RC 1.50 4.00
313 Tyler Ennis ETCH RC 1.00 2.50
314 Nikola Mirotic ETCH RC 2.00 5.00
315 James Ennis ETCH RC 1.00 2.50
316 Cory Jefferson ETCH RC 1.00 2.50
317 James Young ETCH RC 1.00 2.50
318 Shabazz Napier ETCH RC 1.25 3.00
319 Jusuf Nurkic ETCH RC 1.50 4.00
320 Adreian Payne ETCH RC 1.25 3.00
321 Jordan Clarkson ETCH RC 1.50 4.00
322 Nik Stauskas ETCH RC 1.25 3.00
323 Gary Harris ETCH RC 1.50 4.00
324 Nick Johnson ETCH RC 1.00 2.50
325 Devyn Marble ETCH RC 1.00 2.50
326 Kyle Anderson ETCH RC 1.50 4.00
327 Noah Vonleh ETCH RC 1.25 3.00
328 Cameron Bairstow ETCH RC 1.00 2.50
329 Julius Randle ETCH RC 2.50 6.00
330 Erick Green ETCH RC 1.00 2.50
331 Joel Embiid WOOD RC 6.00 15.00
332 Aaron Gordon WOOD RC 3.00 8.00
333 Bojan Bogdanovic WOOD RC 1.50 4.00
334 Jordan Adams WOOD RC 1.25 3.00
335 Zach LaVine WOOD RC 3.00 8.00
336 Dante Exum WOOD RC 2.00 5.00
337 Glenn Robinson III WOOD RC 1.25 3.00
338 Jabari Parker WOOD RC 3.00 8.00
339 Rodney Hood WOOD RC 2.00 5.00
340 Damjan Rudez WOOD RC 1.25 3.00
341 Joe Ingles WOOD RC 1.25 3.00
342 Elfrid Payton WOOD RC 2.00 5.00
343 Andrew Wiggins WOOD RC 4.00 10.00
344 Damien Inglis WOOD RC 1.25 3.00
345 Tarik Black WOOD RC 1.25 3.00
346 Joe Harris WOOD RC 1.25 3.00
347 P.J. Hairston WOOD RC 1.25 3.00
348 K.J. McDaniels WOOD RC 1.50 4.00
349 Kostas Papanikolaou WOOD RC 1.25 3.00
350 T.J. Warren WOOD RC 2.00 5.00
351 Marcus Smart WOOD RC 2.00 5.00
352 Jarnell Stokes WOOD RC 1.25 3.00
353 Russ Smith WOOD RC 1.25 3.00
354 Cleanthony Early WOOD RC 1.25 3.00
355 Clint Capela WOOD RC 1.50 4.00
356 C.J. Wilcox WOOD RC 1.25 3.00
357 Doug McDermott WOOD RC 2.00 5.00
358 Tyler Ennis WOOD RC 1.25 3.00
359 Nikola Mirotic WOOD RC 2.50 6.00
360 James Ennis WOOD RC 1.25 3.00
361 Cory Jefferson WOOD RC 1.25 3.00
362 James Young WOOD RC 1.25 3.00
363 Shabazz Napier WOOD RC 1.50 4.00
364 Jusuf Nurkic WOOD RC 2.00 5.00
365 Adreian Payne WOOD RC 1.50 4.00
366 Jordan Clarkson WOOD RC 2.00 5.00
367 Nik Stauskas WOOD RC 1.50 4.00
368 Gary Harris WOOD RC 2.00 5.00
369 Nick Johnson WOOD RC 1.25 3.00
370 Devyn Marble WOOD RC 1.25 3.00
371 Kyle Anderson WOOD RC 2.00 5.00
372 Noah Vonleh WOOD RC 1.50 4.00
373 Cameron Bairstow WOOD RC 1.25 3.00
374 Julius Randle WOOD RC 3.00 8.00
375 Erick Green WOOD RC 1.25 3.00

2014-15 Panini Threads Century Proof Gold

*VETS: .6X TO 1.5X BASE HI
RANDOM INSERTS IN PACKS
STATED PRINT RUN 25 SER.#'d SETS

2014-15 Panini Threads Century Proof Red

*VETS: .5X TO 1.2X BASE HI
RANDOM INSERTS IN PACKS
STATED PRINT RUN 199 SER.#'d SETS

2014-15 Panini Threads ABA Legends

RANDOM INSERTS IN PACKS
1 Louie Dampier 2.00 5.00
2 Artis Gilmore 1.50 4.00
3 Billy Paultz 2.00 5.00
4 Julius Erving 3.00 8.00
5 Charlie Scott 1.50 4.00
6 Freddie Lewis 1.25 3.00
7 Jimmy Jones 1.25 3.00
8 Ron Boone 1.25 3.00
9 George Gervin 2.00 5.00
10 Dan Issel 1.50 4.00

2014-15 Panini Threads Authentic Threads

RANDOM INSERTS IN PACKS
STATED PRINT RUN B/WN 78-199 COPIES PER
*PRIME: 1.5X TO 4X BASE HI
1 Al Horford/199 3.00 8.00
2 Jae Crowder/199 1.25 3.00
3 Derrick Favors/199 1.50 4.00
4 Carmelo Anthony/199 2.50 6.00
5 Harrison Barnes/199 1.50 4.00
6 Jimmy Butler/199 2.00 5.00
7 Andre Drummond/199 2.00 5.00
8 Jared Sullinger/199 1.25 3.00
9 Danny Green/199 1.50 4.00
10 Kevin Durant/199 5.00 12.00
11 Chris Paul/199 2.50 6.00
12 John Wall/199 2.50 6.00
13 DeAndre Jordan/199 2.00 5.00
14 Klay Thompson/78 2.50 6.00
15 Chris Andersen/199 1.50 4.00
16 Goran Dragic/199 1.50 4.00
17 Kirk Hinrich/199 1.50 4.00
18 Draymond Green/199 2.50 6.00
19 Jrue Holiday/199 1.50 4.00
20 Bradley Beal/199 2.00 5.00
21 Dwight Howard/199 1.50 4.00
22 Stephen Curry/199 8.00 20.00
23 Dirk Nowitzki/199 2.50 6.00
24 Kawhi Leonard/199 3.00 8.00
25 Marc Gasol/199 2.00 5.00
26 Joakim Noah/199 1.50 4.00
27 Iman Shumpert/199 1.25 3.00
28 DeMarcus Cousins/199 2.00 5.00
29 Ersan Ilyasova/199 1.25 3.00
30 Anderson Varejao/199 1.25 3.00
31 Dwyane Wade/199 3.00 8.00
32 Jeff Teague/199 1.50 4.00
33 David Lee/199 1.25 3.00
34 Kenneth Faried/199 1.50 4.00
35 James Harden/199 3.00 8.00
36 Norris Cole/199 1.25 3.00
37 Kobe Bryant/199 8.00 20.00
38 Greg Monroe/199 1.50 4.00
39 Deron Williams/199 1.50 4.00
40 Chris Bosh/199 2.00 5.00

2014-15 Panini Threads Century Greats

RANDOM INSERTS IN PACKS
*RED: .5X TO 1.2X BASE HI
1 Larry Bird 3.00 8.00
2 Magic Johnson 3.00 8.00
3 Julius Erving 2.00 5.00
4 Scottie Pippen 2.50 6.00
5 John Stockton 2.00 5.00
6 Moses Malone 1.25 3.00
7 Dominique Wilkins 1.50 4.00
8 David Robinson 2.00 5.00
9 Bill Russell 2.00 5.00
10 Kareem Abdul-Jabbar 2.00 5.00
11 Oscar Robertson 1.50 4.00
12 Karl Malone 1.50 4.00
13 Wilt Chamberlain 2.50 6.00
14 Hakeem Olajuwon 1.50 4.00
15 Jerry West 1.50 4.00
16 Gary Payton 1.25 3.00
17 Clyde Drexler 1.50 4.00
18 John Havlicek 1.50 4.00
19 Chet Walker 1.00 2.50
20 George Mikan 2.50 6.00

2014-15 Panini Threads Century Greats Century Proof Gold

*GOLD: .6X TO 1.5X BASE HI
RANDOM INSERTS IN PACKS
STATED PRINT RUN 25 SER.#'d SETS
13 Wilt Chamberlain 10.00 25.00

2014-15 Panini Threads Century Greats Threads

RANDOM INSERTS IN PACKS
STATED PRINT RUN 199 SER.#'d SETS
*PRIME: 1.2X TO 3X BASE HI
1 Yao Ming 4.00 10.00
2 Larry Johnson 4.00 10.00
3 Kareem Abdul-Jabbar 5.00 12.00
4 Scottie Pippen 6.00 15.00
5 Kevin McHale 3.00 8.00
6 Magic Johnson 6.00 15.00
7 Jason Kidd 3.00 8.00
8 John Stockton 5.00 12.00
9 Shaquille O'Neal 6.00 15.00
10 Hakeem Olajuwon 4.00 10.00
11 Karl Malone 4.00 10.00
12 Robert Parish 3.00 8.00
13 Grant Hill 4.00 10.00
14 Julius Erving 5.00 12.00
15 Patrick Ewing 4.00 10.00
16 David Robinson 5.00 12.00
17 Joe Dumars 3.00 8.00
18 Moses Malone 3.00 8.00
19 Larry Bird 8.00 20.00
20 Tracy McGrady 3.00 8.00
21 Alex English 2.50 6.00
22 Gary Payton 3.00 8.00
23 Dikembe Mutombo 3.00 8.00
24 Alonzo Mourning 4.00 10.00
25 Tim Hardaway 3.00 8.00
26 Clyde Drexler 4.00 10.00
27 Chris Mullin 3.00 8.00
28 Allen Iverson 4.00 10.00
29 Mitch Richmond 3.00 8.00
30 Artis Gilmore 2.50 6.00

2014-15 Panini Threads Debut Threads

RANDOM INSERTS IN PACKS
STATED PRINT RUN 199 SER.#'d SETS
1 Julius Randle 3.00 8.00
2 Cory Jefferson 1.25 3.00
3 Jarnell Stokes 1.25 3.00
4 Andrew Wiggins 15.00 40.00
5 Noah Vonleh 1.50 4.00
6 James Ennis 1.25 3.00
7 Marcus Smart 2.00 5.00
8 Elfrid Payton 2.00 5.00
9 Kyle Anderson 2.00 5.00
10 Markel Brown 1.25 3.00
11 T.J. Warren 2.00 5.00
12 Rodney Hood 2.00 5.00
13 Joel Embiid 6.00 15.00
14 Tyler Ennis 1.25 3.00
15 K.J. McDaniels 1.50 4.00
16 Jabari Parker 3.00 8.00
17 Nik Stauskas 1.50 4.00
18 Doug McDermott 2.00 5.00
19 P.J. Hairston 1.25 3.00
20 Glenn Robinson III 1.25 3.00
21 Adreian Payne 1.50 4.00
22 C.J. Wilcox 1.25 3.00
23 Joe Harris 3.00 8.00
24 Dante Exum 2.00 5.00
25 Shabazz Napier 1.50 4.00
26 Cleanthony Early 1.25 3.00
27 Damien Inglis 1.25 3.00
28 Zach LaVine 3.00 8.00
29 James Young 3.00 8.00
30 Russ Smith 1.25 3.00
31 Aaron Gordon 3.00 8.00
32 Gary Harris 2.00 5.00
33 Jordan Adams 1.25 3.00
34 Johnny O'Bryant 1.25 3.00
35 Jerami Grant 1.25 3.00
36 Mitch McGary 1.25 3.00
37 Bruno Caboclo 1.50 4.00

2014-15 Panini Threads Floor Generals

RANDOM INSERTS IN PACKS
*RED: .6X TO 1.5X BASE HI
*GOLD: .8X TO 2X BASE HI
1 Elfrid Payton 1.25 3.00
2 Rajon Rondo 1.25 3.00
3 Patrick Beverley .75 2.00
4 Tony Parker 1.25 3.00
5 Mike Conley 1.00 2.50
6 Ricky Rubio 1.25 3.00
7 Russell Westbrook 3.00 8.00
8 Brandon Knight 1.00 2.50
9 Mario Chalmers 1.00 2.50
10 George Hill 1.00 2.50
11 Michael Carter-Williams .75 2.00
12 Goran Dragic 1.00 2.50
13 Damian Lillard 2.50 6.00
14 Trey Burke .75 2.00
15 Stephen Curry 3.00 8.00
16 John Wall 1.50 4.00
17 Kyrie Irving 2.50 6.00
18 Derrick Rose 1.50 4.00
19 Chris Paul 1.50 4.00
20 Jeff Teague 1.00 2.50

2014-15 Panini Threads Freshman Pairs Jerseys

RANDOM INSERTS IN PACKS
STATED PRINT RUN 199 SER.#'d SETS
1 A.Wiggins/J.Parker 8.00 20.00
2 D.Exum/J.Embiid 8.00 20.00
3 A.Wiggins/J.Embiid 8.00 20.00
4 D.Exum/A.Wiggins 8.00 20.00
5 J.Parker/D.Exum 4.00 10.00
6 A.Gordon/E.Payton 4.00 10.00
7 M.McGary/N.Stauskas 2.00 5.00
8 A.Wiggins/Z.LaVine 8.00 20.00
9 A.Gordon/J.Parker 4.00 10.00
10 B.Caboclo/D.Exum 2.50 6.00
11 R.Smith/S.Napier 2.00 5.00
12 Z.LaVine/A.Gordon 4.00 10.00
13 D.Inglis/D.Exum 2.50 6.00
14 R.Hood/J.Parker 4.00 10.00
15 T.Ennis/P.Hairston 1.50 4.00
16 M.Smart/M.Brown 2.50 6.00
17 J.Young/J.Stokes 1.50 4.00
18 R.Hood/R.Smith 2.50 6.00
19 D.McDermott/N.Stauskas 2.50 6.00
20 J.Young/J.Randle 4.00 10.00
21 K.Anderson/Z.LaVine 4.00 10.00
22 A.Payne/G.Harris 2.50 6.00

2014-15 Panini Threads Freshman Pairs Jerseys Prime

*PRIME: .6X TO 1.5X BASE HI
RANDOM INSERTS IN PACKS
STATED PRINT RUN 25 SER.#'d SETS
4 Dante Exum 30.00 80.00
Andrew Wiggins

2014-15 Panini Threads High Flyers

RANDOM INSERTS IN PACKS
*RED: .5X TO 1.2X BASE HI
1 Blake Griffin 1.25 3.00
2 Terrence Ross .75 2.00
3 Kenneth Faried .75 2.00
4 LeBron James 4.00 10.00
5 Gerald Green .75 2.00
6 Russell Westbrook 2.50 6.00
7 DeAndre Jordan 1.00 2.50
8 Aaron Gordon 1.50 4.00
9 DeMar DeRozan 1.00 2.50
10 Zach LaVine 1.50 4.00
11 Anthony Davis 2.00 5.00
12 Kobe Bryant 4.00 10.00
13 Kevin Durant 2.50 6.00
14 Josh Smith .75 2.00
15 Paul George 1.25 3.00
16 Andrew Wiggins 3.00 8.00
17 James Harden 1.50 4.00
18 John Wall 1.25 3.00
19 Rudy Gay 1.00 2.50
20 Serge Ibaka .75 2.00

2014-15 Panini Threads Rookie Jumbo Materials

RANDOM INSERTS IN PACKS
STATED PRINT RUN 199 SER.#'d SETS
1 Andrew Wiggins 12.00 30.00
2 Jabari Parker 6.00 15.00
3 Joel Embiid 12.00 30.00
4 Aaron Gordon 6.00 15.00
5 Dante Exum 4.00 10.00
6 Marcus Smart 4.00 10.00
7 Julius Randle 6.00 15.00
8 Nik Stauskas 3.00 8.00
9 Noah Vonleh 3.00 8.00
10 Elfrid Payton 4.00 10.00
11 Doug McDermott 4.00 10.00
12 Zach LaVine 6.00 15.00
13 T.J. Warren 4.00 10.00
14 Adreian Payne 3.00 8.00
15 James Young 2.50 6.00
16 Tyler Ennis 2.50 6.00
17 Gary Harris 4.00 10.00
18 Bruno Caboclo 3.00 8.00
19 Mitch McGary 2.50 6.00
20 Jordan Adams 2.50 6.00
21 Rodney Hood 4.00 10.00
22 Shabazz Napier 3.00 8.00
23 P.J. Hairston 2.50 6.00
24 C.J. Wilcox 2.50 6.00
25 Kyle Anderson 4.00 10.00
26 Jarnell Stokes 2.50 6.00
27 Spencer Dinwiddie 3.00 8.00
28 Glenn Robinson III 2.50 6.00
29 Russ Smith 2.50 6.00
30 Cory Jefferson 2.50 6.00

2014-15 Panini Threads Rookie Jumbo Materials Prime

*PRIME: .6X TO 1.5X BASE HI
RANDOM INSERTS IN PACKS
STATED PRINT RUN 25 SER.#'d SETS
1 Andrew Wiggins 30.00 80.00

2014-15 Panini Threads Rookie Signage

RANDOM INSERTS IN PACKS
1 Damjan Rudez 3.00 8.00
2 Joe Harris 3.00 8.00
3 Andrew Wiggins 60.00 150.00
4 Lucas Nogueira 3.00 8.00
5 Aaron Gordon 8.00 20.00
6 T.J. Warren 4.00 10.00
7 Jabari Parker 15.00 40.00
8 Joel Embiid 20.00 50.00
9 Tyler Ennis 3.00 8.00
10 Damien Inglis 3.00 8.00
11 Rodney Hood 5.00 12.00
12 Zach LaVine 10.00 25.00
13 Elfrid Payton 5.00 12.00
14 Johnny O'Bryant 3.00 8.00
15 K.J. McDaniels 4.00 10.00
16 Jerami Grant 3.00 8.00
17 James Ennis 3.00 8.00
18 Erick Green 3.00 8.00
19 Shabazz Napier 4.00 10.00
20 P.J. Hairston 3.00 8.00
21 Nik Stauskas 4.00 10.00
22 C.J. Wilcox 3.00 8.00
23 Adreian Payne 4.00 10.00
24 Mitch McGary 3.00 8.00
25 Noah Vonleh 4.00 10.00
26 Marcus Smart 5.00 12.00
27 Jusuf Nurkic 5.00 12.00
28 Doug McDermott 5.00 12.00
29 Julius Randle 12.00 30.00
30 Gary Harris 5.00 12.00

2014-15 Panini Threads Rookie Threads

RANDOM INSERTS IN PACKS
1 Julius Randle 5.00 12.00
2 Cory Jefferson 2.00 5.00
3 Jarnell Stokes 2.00 5.00
4 Andrew Wiggins 10.00 25.00
5 Noah Vonleh 2.50 6.00
6 James Ennis 2.00 5.00
7 Marcus Smart 3.00 8.00
8 Elfrid Payton 3.00 8.00
9 Kyle Anderson 3.00 8.00
10 Markel Brown 2.00 5.00
11 T.J. Warren 3.00 8.00
12 Rodney Hood 3.00 8.00
13 Joel Embiid 10.00 25.00
14 Tyler Ennis 2.00 5.00
15 K.J. McDaniels 2.50 6.00
16 Jabari Parker 4.00 10.00
17 Nik Stauskas 2.50 6.00
18 Doug McDermott 3.00 8.00
19 P.J. Hairston 2.00 5.00
20 Glenn Robinson III 2.00 5.00
21 Adreian Payne 2.50 6.00
22 Mitch McGary 2.00 5.00
23 Joe Harris 2.00 5.00
24 Dante Exum 3.00 8.00
25 Shabazz Napier 2.50 6.00
26 Cleanthony Early 2.00 5.00
27 Bruno Caboclo 2.50 6.00
28 Zach LaVine 5.00 12.00
29 James Young 2.00 5.00
30 Russ Smith 2.00 5.00
31 Aaron Gordon 5.00 12.00
32 Gary Harris 3.00 8.00
33 Jordan Adams 2.00 5.00
34 Julius Randle 5.00 12.00
35 Cory Jefferson 2.00 5.00
36 Jarnell Stokes 2.00 5.00
37 Andrew Wiggins 4.00 10.00
38 Noah Vonleh 2.50 6.00
39 James Ennis 2.00 5.00
40 Marcus Smart 3.00 8.00
41 Elfrid Payton 3.00 8.00
42 Kyle Anderson 3.00 8.00
43 Markel Brown 2.00 5.00
44 T.J. Warren 3.00 8.00
45 Rodney Hood 3.00 8.00
46 Joel Embiid 10.00 25.00
47 Tyler Ennis 2.00 5.00
48 K.J. McDaniels 2.50 6.00
49 Jabari Parker 5.00 12.00
50 Nik Stauskas 2.50 6.00
51 Doug McDermott 3.00 8.00
52 P.J. Hairston 2.00 5.00
53 Glenn Robinson III 2.00 5.00
54 Adreian Payne 2.50 6.00
55 Mitch McGary 2.00 5.00
56 Joe Harris 2.00 5.00
57 Dante Exum 3.00 8.00
58 Shabazz Napier 2.50 6.00
59 Cleanthony Early 2.00 5.00
60 Bruno Caboclo 2.50 6.00
61 Zach LaVine 5.00 12.00
62 James Young 2.00 5.00
63 Russ Smith 2.00 5.00
64 Aaron Gordon 5.00 12.00
65 Gary Harris 3.00 8.00
66 Jordan Adams 2.00 5.00
67 Julius Randle 5.00 12.00
68 Cory Jefferson 2.00 5.00
69 Jarnell Stokes 2.00 5.00
70 Andrew Wiggins 5.00 12.00
71 Noah Vonleh 2.50 6.00
72 James Ennis 2.00 5.00
73 Marcus Smart 3.00 8.00
74 Elfrid Payton 3.00 8.00
75 Kyle Anderson 3.00 8.00
76 Markel Brown 2.00 5.00
77 T.J. Warren 3.00 8.00
78 Rodney Hood 3.00 8.00
79 Joel Embiid 10.00 25.00
80 Tyler Ennis 2.00 5.00
81 K.J. McDaniels 2.50 6.00
82 Jabari Parker 5.00 12.00
83 Nik Stauskas 2.50 6.00
84 Doug McDermott 3.00 8.00
85 P.J. Hairston 2.00 5.00
86 Glenn Robinson III 2.00 5.00
87 Adreian Payne 2.50 6.00
88 Mitch McGary 2.00 5.00
89 Joe Harris 2.00 5.00
90 Dante Exum 3.00 8.00
91 Shabazz Napier 2.50 6.00
92 Cleanthony Early 2.00 5.00
93 Bruno Caboclo 2.50 6.00
94 Zach LaVine 5.00 12.00
95 James Young 2.00 5.00
96 Russ Smith 2.00 5.00
97 Aaron Gordon 5.00 12.00
98 Gary Harris 3.00 8.00
99 Jordan Adams 2.00 5.00
100 Andrew Wiggins 10.00 25.00

2014-15 Panini Threads Rookie Threads Signatures

RANDOM INSERTS IN PACKS
STATED PRINT RUN B/WN 149-249 COPIES PER
1 Andrew Wiggins/149 60.00 150.00
2 Jabari Parker/149 25.00 60.00
3 Joel Embiid/149 40.00 100.00
4 Dante Exum/149 5.00 12.00
5 Rodney Hood/249 5.00 12.00
6 Glenn Robinson III/249 3.00 8.00
7 T.J. Warren/249 5.00 12.00
8 Marcus Smart/149 5.00 12.00
9 Nik Stauskas/249 4.00 10.00
10 Zach LaVine/249 12.00 30.00
11 Spencer Dinwiddie/249 4.00 10.00
12 Kyle Anderson/249 5.00 12.00
13 Damien Inglis/249 3.00 8.00
15 Tyler Ennis/149 3.00 8.00
16 Aaron Gordon/149 8.00 20.00
17 Doug McDermott/249 5.00 12.00
18 Adreian Payne/249 4.00 10.00
19 Gary Harris/249 5.00 12.00
20 Jordan Adams/249 3.00 8.00
23 Joe Harris/249 6.00 15.00
24 Markel Brown/249 3.00 8.00
25 Mitch McGary/249 6.00 15.00
27 Elfrid Payton/249 12.00 30.00
28 James Ennis/249 3.00 8.00
29 Shabazz Napier/249 4.00 10.00
30 James Young/249 3.00 8.00
31 Jerami Grant/249 3.00 8.00
32 Julius Randle/149 15.00 40.00
33 K.J. McDaniels/249 4.00 10.00

2014-15 Panini Threads Rookie Threads Signatures Prime

*PRIME: .8X TO 2X BASE HI
RANDOM INSERTS IN PACKS
STATED PRINT RUN 25 SER.#'d SETS

2014-15 Panini Threads Rookie View Autographs

RANDOM INSERTS IN PACKS
1 Russ Smith 3.00 8.00
2 Markel Brown 3.00 8.00
3 Cory Jefferson 3.00 8.00
4 K.J. McDaniels 4.00 10.00
6 Jarnell Stokes 3.00 8.00
7 Joe Harris 3.00 8.00
8 Cleanthony Early 3.00 8.00
9 P.J. Hairston 3.00 8.00
10 Jerami Grant 3.00 8.00
11 Rodney Hood 5.00 12.00
12 Kyle Anderson 5.00 12.00
13 Aaron Gordon 8.00 20.00
14 Noah Vonleh 4.00 10.00
16 Nik Stauskas 4.00 10.00
17 Elfrid Payton 5.00 12.00
18 Jabari Parker 15.00 40.00
19 Julius Randle 5.00 12.00
20 Andrew Wiggins 30.00 80.00
21 Joel Embiid 50.00 120.00
22 Bruno Caboclo 4.00 10.00
23 Spencer Dinwiddie 4.00 10.00
25 T.J. Warren 5.00 12.00
26 James Young 3.00 8.00
27 Doug McDermott 12.00 30.00
28 Gary Harris 5.00 12.00
29 Shabazz Napier 4.00 10.00
33 Marcus Smart 8.00 20.00
34 Zach LaVine 10.00 25.00
35 Adreian Payne 4.00 10.00
36 C.J. Wilcox 3.00 8.00

2014-15 Panini Threads Signage

RANDOM INSERTS IN PACKS
STATED PRINT RUN B/WN 49-199 COPIES PER
1 Roy Hibbert/99 4.00 10.00
2 Kyle Korver/99 4.00 10.00
3 Lance Stephenson/199 4.00 10.00
5 Steve Blake/199 3.00 8.00
6 Henry Sims/199 3.00 8.00
7 Josh Smith/49 4.00 10.00
9 Brook Lopez/49 4.00 10.00
10 James Jones/199 3.00 8.00
11 Andrew Nicholson/199 3.00 8.00
13 Trey Burke/49 3.00 8.00
14 Mike Muscala/199 3.00 8.00
16 Ben McLemore/49 3.00 8.00
17 Nerlens Noel/49 4.00 10.00
18 Carl Landry/99 3.00 8.00
19 Troy Daniels/199 3.00 8.00
20 Jason Terry/49 4.00 10.00
21 Dennis Schroder/199 4.00 10.00
22 Maurice Harkless/199 3.00 8.00
23 Kobe Bryant/49 50.00 120.00
24 Kevin Durant/49 40.00 100.00
25 Solomon Hill/199 3.00 8.00
26 Kevin Love/49 10.00 25.00
27 C.J. McCollum/49 5.00 12.00
28 Manu Ginobili/49 15.00 40.00
29 Paul George/49 12.00 30.00
30 Dwyane Wade/49 25.00 60.00
31 Carmelo Anthony/49 15.00 40.00
32 Anthony Bennett/49 3.00 8.00
33 Luis Scola/99 4.00 10.00
34 Jrue Holiday/99 4.00 10.00
35 Kevin Martin/49 4.00 10.00
36 Adrian Dantley/199 4.00 10.00
37 Hal Greer/49 4.00 10.00
38 Kareem Abdul-Jabbar/49 20.00 50.00
39 Rick Barry/49 4.00 10.00
40 Dominique Wilkins/49 8.00 20.00
42 Gary Payton/49 5.00 12.00
43 Clyde Drexler/49 10.00 25.00
44 James Worthy/49 12.00 30.00
45 Dan Issel/199 4.00 10.00
46 George Gervin/49 10.00 25.00
47 Jerry West/49 20.00 50.00
48 Julius Erving/49 20.00 50.00
49 David Robinson/49 12.00 30.00
50 Chris Mullin/49 10.00 25.00

2014-15 Panini Threads Talented Twosomes

RANDOM INSERTS IN PACKS
1 E.Bledsoe/G.Dragic .75 2.00
2 L.Aldridge/D.Lillard 2.50 6.00
3 K.Durant/R.Westbrook 2.50 6.00
4 K.Thompson/S.Curry 4.00 10.00
5 B.Griffin/C.Paul 1.25 3.00
6 B.Beal/J.Wall 1.25 3.00
7 M.Ellis/D.Nowitzki 1.25 3.00
8 K.Lowry/D.DeRozan 1.00 2.50
9 M.Ginobili/T.Parker 1.00 2.50
10 C.Bosh/D.Wade 1.50 4.00
11 K.Irving/L.James 4.00 10.00
12 R.Rubio/A.Wiggins 3.00 8.00
13 C.Anthony/T.Hardaway Jr. 1.25 3.00
14 Z.Randolph/M.Conley .75 2.00
15 D.Howard/J.Harden 1.50 4.00

2014-15 Panini Threads Team Threads

1 Jeff Teague 1.50 4.00
2 Al Jefferson 1.50 4.00
3 Kyrie Irving 4.00 10.00
4 Brandon Jennings 1.25 3.00
5 Paul George 2.50 6.00
6 Kobe Bryant 8.00 20.00
7 Luol Deng 1.50 4.00
8 Jrue Holiday 1.50 4.00
9 Victor Oladipo 1.50 4.00
10 LaMarcus Aldridge 2.00 5.00
11 DeMar DeRozan 2.00 5.00
12 Paul Millsap 2.00 5.00
13 Lance Stephenson 1.50 4.00
14 LeBron James 8.00 20.00
15 Andre Drummond 2.00 5.00
16 Roy Hibbert 1.50 4.00
17 Marc Gasol 2.00 5.00
18 Giannis Antetokounmpo 4.00 10.00
19 Carmelo Anthony 2.50 6.00
20 Nerlens Noel 1.50 4.00
21 DeMarcus Cousins 2.00 5.00
22 Kyle Lowry 1.50 4.00
23 Rajon Rondo 2.00 5.00
24 Derrick Rose 8.00 20.00
25 Dirk Nowitzki 2.50 6.00
26 Klay Thompson 2.50 6.00
27 Blake Griffin 2.00 5.00
28 Zach Randolph 1.50 4.00
29 Brandon Knight 1.50 4.00
30 Tim Hardaway Jr. 1.25 3.00
31 Goran Dragic 1.50 4.00
32 Kawhi Leonard 3.00 8.00
33 Gordon Hayward 2.00 5.00
34 Avery Bradley 1.50 4.00
35 Joakim Noah 1.50 4.00
36 Chandler Parsons 1.50 4.00
37 Stephen Curry 8.00 20.00
38 Chris Paul 2.50 6.00
39 Chris Bosh 2.00 5.00
40 Ricky Rubio 2.00 5.00
41 Kevin Durant 5.00 12.00
42 Eric Bledsoe 1.50 4.00
43 Tim Duncan 3.00 8.00
44 John Wall 6.00 15.00
45 Deron Williams 1.50 4.00
46 Pau Gasol 2.00 5.00
47 Ty Lawson 1.25 3.00

48 Dwight Howard 1.50 4.00
49 DeAndre Jordan 2.00 5.00
50 Dwyane Wade 3.00 8.00
51 Anthony Davis 4.00 10.00
52 Russell Westbrook 5.00 12.00
53 Damian Lillard 4.00 10.00
54 Tony Parker 2.00 5.00
55 Bradley Beal 2.00 5.00
56 Kevin Garnett 3.00 8.00
57 Kevin Love 2.00 5.00
58 Kenneth Faried 1.50 4.00
59 James Harden 3.00 8.00
60 Jeremy Lin 2.00 5.00

2014-15 Panini Threads Threads Signatures

RANDOM INSERTS IN PACKS
STATED PRINT RUN B/WN 15-99 COPIES PER
NO PRICING ON QTY 15 OR LESS
1 Kobe Bryant/35 100.00 200.00
2 Kevin Durant/35 50.00 120.00
3 Kyrie Irving/35 40.00 100.00
4 Deron Williams/35 4.00 10.00
5 Otto Porter/35 4.00 10.00
6 Cody Zeller/35 3.00 8.00
7 Michael Carter-Williams/99 3.00 8.00
8 Victor Oladipo/35
9 Tobias Harris/99 4.00 10.00
10 Al Horford/35 4.00 10.00
11 Bradley Beal/99 8.00 20.00
12 Ryan Kelly/99 3.00 8.00
13 Taj Gibson/99 4.00 10.00
14 Carmelo Anthony/35 20.00 50.00
15 Paul George/15
16 Jeff Green/99
17 Tiago Splitter/75 4.00 10.00
18 Jared Dudley/99 3.00 8.00
19 Andre Iguodala/99 4.00 10.00
20 Steve Nash/35 12.00 30.00
21 J.R. Smith/99 4.00 10.00
22 Chris Bosh/35 5.00 12.00
23 Brandon Knight/99 4.00 10.00
24 Andre Drummond/99 5.00 12.00
25 Josh Smith/35
26 Kevin Martin/99 4.00 10.00
27 Caron Butler/99
28 Anthony Bennett/35 3.00 8.00
29 Tristan Thompson/99 4.00 10.00
30 Udonis Haslem/99 3.00 8.00
31 Jodie Meeks/99 4.00 10.00
32 Kyle Korver/99 4.00 10.00
33 Derrick Favors/99 4.00 10.00
34 Gordon Hayward/75 6.00 15.00
35 Luis Scola/99 4.00 10.00
36 Jordan Hill/99 3.00 8.00
37 James Jones/99 3.00 8.00
38 Brook Lopez/99 4.00 10.00
39 Ryan Anderson/99 3.00 8.00
40 Alan Anderson/99 3.00 8.00
41 Maurice Harkless/99 3.00 8.00
42 Gerald Wallace/99 4.00 10.00
43 Austin Rivers/99 4.00 10.00
44 Draymond Green/99 12.00 30.00
45 Enes Kanter/99 3.00 8.00
46 Corey Brewer/99 3.00 8.00
47 Greg Monroe/65 4.00 10.00
48 Nick Young/99 4.00 10.00
49 Tony Snell/75 3.00 8.00
50 Nick Collison/99 4.00 10.00
51 Chris Andersen/35
52 Tony Allen/65 3.00 8.00
53 J.J. Redick/65 5.00 12.00
54 Nikola Pekovic/75 3.00 8.00
55 Danny Green/99 4.00 10.00
56 Michael Kidd-Gilchrist/35 4.00 10.00
57 Mason Plumlee/99 4.00 10.00
58 Gorgui Dieng/99 3.00 8.00
59 Timofey Mozgov/99 3.00 8.00
60 Kentavious Caldwell-Pope/99 3.00 8.00
61 Alex Len/35 3.00 8.00
62 Trey Burke/99 3.00 8.00
63 Andrea Bargnani/99 4.00 10.00
64 Brandon Bass/99 3.00 8.00
65 George Hill/99 4.00 10.00

2014-15 Panini Threads Threads Signatures Prime

*PRIME: .5X TO 1.2X BASE HI
RANDOM INSERTS IN PACKS
STATED PRINT RUN 25 SER.#'d SETS
LACK OF PRICING DUE TO MARKET INFO

2014-15 Panini Threads View Autographs

RANDOM INSERTS IN PACKS
2 Brandon Jennings 5.00 12.00
3 Caron Butler 3.00 8.00
4 Chris Bosh 8.00 20.00
7 John Wall 20.00 50.00
8 Larry Sanders 3.00 8.00
9 Pau Gasol 20.00 50.00
10 Samuel Dalembert 4.00 10.00
11 Steve Nash 15.00 40.00
12 Xavier Henry 4.00 10.00
13 DeMarcus Cousins 10.00 25.00
14 Boris Diaw 4.00 10.00

2014-15 Panini Threads Voices of the Game Autographs

RANDOM INSERTS IN PACKS
STATED PRINT RUN B/WN 49-499 COPIES PER
1 Craig Sager/499 30.00 80.00
2 Rick Kamla/499 2.50 6.00
3 Ernie Johnson/499 10.00 25.00
4 Kenny Smith/99 4.00 10.00
5 Bob Knight/49 30.00 80.00
6 Steve Smith/299 4.00 10.00
7 Clark Kellogg/499 3.00 8.00
8 Walt Frazier/99 8.00 20.00
9 Chris Webber/49 30.00 80.00
10 Dick Vitale/99 20.00 50.00
11 Phil Chenier/349 3.00 8.00
12 Ron Boone/299 3.00 8.00
13 Mychal Thompson/349 3.00 8.00
14 Shaquille O'Neal/49 40.00 100.00
15 Michael Cage/349 3.00 8.00
16 Jon McGlocklin/199 4.00 10.00
17 Doug Collins/199 10.00 25.00
18 Grant Hill/49 15.00 40.00
19 Sidney Moncrief/349 2.50 6.00
20 Brent Barry/99 4.00 10.00

2015-16 Panini Threads

COMP.SET w/o RCs (150) 20.00 50.00
1 Ricky Rubio .40 1.00
2 Goran Dragic .30 .75
3 Joe Johnson .30 .75
4 Evan Fournier .30 .75
5 Pau Gasol .40 1.00
6 Zaza Pachulia .25 .60
7 DeMar DeRozan .40 1.00
8 Andre Iguodala .30 .75
9 Brook Lopez .30 .75
10 Julius Randle .40 1.00
11 Kevin Garnett .60 1.50
12 Dwyane Wade .60 1.50
13 Gary Harris .30 .75
14 Tobias Harris .30 .75
15 Jimmy Butler .40 1.00
16 Deron Williams .30 .75
17 Kyle Lowry .30 .75
18 Klay Thompson .50 1.25
19 Thaddeus Young .25 .60
20 Kobe Bryant 1.50 4.00
21 Kevin Martin .30 .75
22 Hassan Whiteside .30 .75
23 Will Barton .25 .60
24 Elfrid Payton .30 .75
25 Nikola Mirotic .30 .75
26 Wesley Matthews .25 .60
27 Jonas Valanciunas .30 .75
28 Draymond Green .50 1.25
29 Bojan Bogdanovic .25 .60
30 Roy Hibbert .30 .75
31 Zach LaVine .40 1.00
32 Luol Deng .30 .75
33 Jameer Nelson .25 .60
34 Nikola Vucevic .30 .75
35 Doug McDermott .30 .75
36 Chandler Parsons .30 .75
37 DeMarre Carroll .25 .60
38 Festus Ezeli .25 .60
39 Jarrett Jack .30 .75
40 Lou Williams .30 .75
41 Gordon Hayward .40 1.00
42 Nicolas Batum .30 .75
43 LeBron James 1.50 4.00
44 Tim Duncan .60 1.50
45 George Hill .30 .75
46 Mike Conley .40 1.00
47 Luis Scola .30 .75
48 Blake Griffin .40 1.00
49 Nerlens Noel .30 .75
50 Ben McLemore .25 .60
51 Rudy Gobert .40 1.00
52 Marvin Williams .30 .75
53 Kevin Love .40 1.00
54 Tony Parker .40 1.00
55 Paul George .50 1.25
56 Zach Randolph .30 .75
57 Jae Crowder .25 .60
58 DeAndre Jordan .40 1.00
59 Tony Wroten .25 .60
60 DeMarcus Cousins .40 1.00
61 Derrick Favors .30 .75
62 Kemba Walker .40 1.00
63 Kyrie Irving .75 2.00
64 Manu Ginobili .40 1.00
65 Monta Ellis .30 .75
66 Marc Gasol .40 1.00
67 Isaiah Thomas .40 1.00
68 J.J. Redick .40 1.00
69 Nik Stauskas .25 .60
70 Rajon Rondo .40 1.00
71 Rodney Hood .30 .75
72 Al Jefferson .30 .75
73 Mo Williams .30 .75
74 Kawhi Leonard .60 1.50
75 Rodney Stuckey .30 .75
76 Courtney Lee .30 .75
77 Avery Bradley .30 .75
78 Chris Paul .50 1.25
79 Jerami Grant .25 .60
80 Rudy Gay .40 1.00
81 Alec Burks .25 .60
82 Jeremy Lin .40 1.00
83 Timofey Mozgov .25 .60
84 LaMarcus Aldridge .40 1.00
85 Jordan Hill .25 .60
86 Jeff Green .30 .75
87 Jared Sullinger .25 .60
88 Paul Pierce .40 1.00
89 Isaiah Canaan .30 .75
90 Darren Collison .30 .75
91 Damian Lillard .75 2.00
92 John Wall .50 1.25
93 Marcus Morris .25 .60
94 Dwight Howard .30 .75
95 Khris Middleton .30 .75
96 Eric Gordon .30 .75
97 Marcus Smart .30 .75
98 Brandon Knight .30 .75
99 Russell Westbrook 1.00 2.50
100 Paul Millsap .40 1.00
101 C.J. McCollum .40 1.00
102 Otto Porter .30 .75
103 Kentavious Caldwell-Pope .30 .75
104 James Harden .60 1.50
105 Greg Monroe .30 .75
106 Anthony Davis .75 2.00
107 Carmelo Anthony .50 1.25
108 Eric Bledsoe .30 .75
109 Kevin Durant 1.00 2.50
110 Al Horford .30 .75
111 Mason Plumlee .30 .75
112 Bradley Beal .40 1.00
113 Andre Drummond .40 1.00
114 Ty Lawson .25 .60
115 Giannis Antetokounmpo .75 2.00
116 Ryan Anderson .30 .75
117 Langston Galloway .25 .60
118 Markieff Morris .25 .60
119 Serge Ibaka .30 .75
120 Jeff Teague .30 .75
121 Meyers Leonard .25 .60
122 Marcin Gortat .30 .75
123 Reggie Jackson .30 .75
124 Trevor Ariza .25 .60
125 Michael Carter-Williams .25 .60
126 Jrue Holiday .30 .75
127 Robin Lopez .25 .60
128 Tyson Chandler .30 .75
129 Enes Kanter .25 .60
130 Kent Bazemore .30 .75
131 Al-Farouq Aminu .30 .75
132 Nene .30 .75
133 Brandon Jennings .25 .60
134 Corey Brewer .25 .60
135 Jabari Parker .50 1.25
136 Tyreke Evans .25 .60
137 Jose Calderon .25 .60
138 T.J. Warren .30 .75
139 Dion Waiters .30 .75
140 Kyle Korver .30 .75
141 Danilo Gallinari .30 .75
142 Victor Oladipo .30 .75
143 Derrick Rose .50 1.25
144 Dirk Nowitzki .50 1.25
145 Stephen Curry 1.50 4.00
146 Kenneth Faried .30 .75
147 Sasha Vujacic .25 .60
148 Jordan Clarkson .40 1.00
149 Andrew Wiggins .60 1.50
150 Chris Bosh .40 1.00
151 R.J. Hunter RC .50 1.25
152 Frank Kaminsky RC .75 2.00
153 Salah Mejri RC .50 1.25
154 Josh Richardson RC .75 2.00
155 Terry Rozier RC .60 1.50
156 Kristaps Porzingis RC 2.00 5.00
157 Cliff Alexander RC .50 1.25
158 Anthony Brown RC .50 1.25
159 Myles Turner RC .75 2.00
160 Luis Montero RC .50 1.25
161 Rashad Vaughn RC .50 1.25
162 Jahlil Okafor RC 1.00 2.50
163 Sam Dekker RC .60 1.50
164 Justin Anderson RC .60 1.50
165 Trey Lyles RC .75 2.00
166 Larry Nance Jr. RC .75 2.00
167 Cristiano Felicio RC .60 1.50
168 Boban Marjanovic RC .60 1.50
169 Nemanja Bjelica RC .60 1.50
170 D'Angelo Russell RC 2.00 5.00
171 Raul Neto RC .50 1.25
172 Jerian Grant RC .50 1.25
173 Sasha Kaun RC .50 1.25
174 Justise Winslow RC .75 2.00
175 Tyus Jones RC .75 2.00
176 Marcelo Huertas RC .60 1.50
177 Rakeem Christmas RC .50 1.25
178 Bobby Portis RC .75 2.00
179 Nikola Jokic RC 1.00 2.50
180 Delon Wright RC .60 1.50
181 Richaun Holmes RC .60 1.50
182 Jordan Mickey RC .50 1.25
183 Stanley Johnson RC .60 1.50
184 Karl-Anthony Towns RC 4.00 10.00
185 Willie Cauley-Stein RC .75 2.00
186 Mario Hezonja RC .60 1.50
187 Aaron Harrison RC .60 1.50
188 Cameron Payne RC .60 1.50
189 Norman Powell RC .60 1.50
190 Devin Booker RC 2.50 6.00
191 Rondae Hollis-Jefferson RC .60 1.50
192 Joe Young RC .60 1.50
193 T.J. McConnell RC .60 1.50
194 Kelly Oubre Jr. RC .60 1.50
195 Jonathon Simmons RC .75 2.00
196 Montrezl Harrell RC .60 1.50
197 Darrun Hilliard RC .50 1.25
198 Walter Tavares RC .50 1.25
199 Pat Connaughton RC .50 1.25
200 Emmanuel Mudiay RC .75 2.00
201 Boban Marjanovic LTHR .75 2.00
202 Myles Turner LTHR 1.00 2.50
203 Jarell Martin LTHR RC .75 2.00
204 Pat Connaughton LTHR .60 1.50
205 Montrezl Harrell LTHR .75 2.00
206 Cameron Payne LTHR .75 2.00
207 Willie Cauley-Stein LTHR 1.00 2.50
208 Emmanuel Mudiay LTHR 1.00 2.50
209 Jonathon Simmons LTHR 1.00 2.50
210 Jahlil Okafor LTHR 1.25 3.00
211 Kevon Looney LTHR RC .75 2.00
212 Mario Hezonja LTHR .75 2.00
213 Karl-Anthony Towns LTHR 5.00 12.00
214 Rakeem Christmas LTHR .60 1.50
215 Tyus Jones LTHR 1.00 2.50
216 Larry Nance Jr. LTHR 1.00 2.50
217 Justin Anderson LTHR .75 2.00
218 Bobby Portis LTHR 1.00 2.50
219 Marcelo Huertas LTHR .75 2.00
220 Norman Powell LTHR .75 2.00
221 Justise Winslow LTHR 1.00 2.50
222 Trey Lyles LTHR 1.00 2.50
223 Sam Dekker LTHR .75 2.00
224 Terry Rozier LTHR .75 2.00
225 Frank Kaminsky LTHR 1.00 2.50
226 T.J. McConnell LTHR .75 2.00
227 Rondae Hollis-Jefferson LTHR .75 2.00
228 Kristaps Porzingis LTHR 2.50 6.00
229 Josh Richardson LTHR 1.00 2.50
230 Chris McCullough LTHR RC .60 1.50
231 R.J. Hunter LTHR .60 1.50
232 Joe Young LTHR .75 2.00
233 Devin Booker LTHR 3.00 8.00
234 Jordan Mickey LTHR .60 1.50
235 Delon Wright LTHR .75 2.00
236 Jerian Grant LTHR .60 1.50
237 D'Angelo Russell LTHR 2.50 6.00
238 Stanley Johnson LTHR .75 2.00
239 Richaun Holmes LTHR .75 2.00
240 Kelly Oubre Jr. LTHR .75 2.00
241 Nikola Jokic LTHR 1.25 3.00
242 Raul Neto LTHR .60 1.50
243 Nemanja Bjelica LTHR .75 2.00
244 Rashad Vaughn LTHR .60 1.50
245 Anthony Brown LTHR .60 1.50
246 Boban Marjanovic WOOD 1.25 3.00
247 Myles Turner WOOD 1.50 4.00
248 Jarell Martin WOOD 1.25 3.00
249 Pat Connaughton WOOD 1.00 2.50
250 Montrezl Harrell WOOD 1.25 3.00
251 Cameron Payne WOOD 1.25 3.00
252 Willie Cauley-Stein WOOD 1.50 4.00
253 Emmanuel Mudiay WOOD 1.50 4.00
254 Jonathon Simmons WOOD 1.50 4.00
255 Jahlil Okafor WOOD 2.00 5.00
256 Kevon Looney WOOD RC 1.25 3.00
257 Mario Hezonja WOOD 1.25 3.00
258 Karl-Anthony Towns WOOD 8.00 20.00
259 Rakeem Christmas WOOD 1.00 2.50
260 Tyus Jones WOOD 1.50 4.00
261 Larry Nance Jr. WOOD 1.50 4.00
262 Justin Anderson WOOD 1.25 3.00
263 Bobby Portis WOOD 1.50 4.00
264 Marcelo Huertas WOOD 1.25 3.00
265 Norman Powell WOOD 1.25 3.00
266 Justise Winslow WOOD 1.50 4.00
267 Trey Lyles WOOD 1.50 4.00
268 Sam Dekker WOOD 1.25 3.00
269 Terry Rozier WOOD 1.25 3.00
270 Frank Kaminsky WOOD 1.50 4.00
271 T.J. McConnell WOOD 1.25 3.00
272 Rondae Hollis-Jefferson WOOD 1.25 3.00
273 Kristaps Porzingis WOOD 4.00 10.00
274 Josh Richardson WOOD 1.50 4.00
275 Chris McCullough WOOD 1.00 2.50
276 R.J. Hunter WOOD 1.00 2.50
277 Joe Young WOOD 1.25 3.00
278 Devin Booker WOOD 5.00 12.00
279 Jordan Mickey WOOD 1.00 2.50
280 Delon Wright WOOD 1.25 3.00
281 Jerian Grant WOOD 1.00 2.50
282 D'Angelo Russell WOOD 4.00 10.00
283 Stanley Johnson WOOD 1.25 3.00
284 Richaun Holmes WOOD 1.25 3.00
285 Kelly Oubre Jr. WOOD 1.25 3.00
286 Nikola Jokic WOOD 2.00 5.00
287 Raul Neto WOOD 1.00 2.50
288 Nemanja Bjelica WOOD 1.25 3.00
289 Rashad Vaughn WOOD 1.00 2.50
290 Anthony Brown WOOD 1.00 2.50
291 Boban Marjanovic ETCH .75 2.00
292 Myles Turner ETCH 1.00 2.50
293 Jarell Martin ETCH .75 2.00
294 Pat Connaughton ETCH .60 1.50
295 Montrezl Harrell ETCH .75 2.00
296 Cameron Payne ETCH .75 2.00
297 Willie Cauley-Stein ETCH 1.00 2.50
298 Emmanuel Mudiay ETCH 1.00 2.50
299 Jonathon Simmons ETCH 1.00 2.50
300 Jahlil Okafor ETCH 1.25 3.00
301 Kevon Looney ETCH RC .75 2.00
302 Mario Hezonja ETCH .75 2.00
303 Karl-Anthony Towns ETCH 5.00 12.00
304 Rakeem Christmas ETCH .60 1.50
305 Tyus Jones ETCH 1.00 2.50
306 Larry Nance Jr. ETCH 1.00 2.50
307 Justin Anderson ETCH .75 2.00
308 Bobby Portis ETCH 1.00 2.50
309 Marcelo Huertas ETCH .75 2.00
310 Norman Powell ETCH .75 2.00
311 Justise Winslow ETCH 1.00 2.50
312 Trey Lyles ETCH 1.00 2.50
313 Sam Dekker ETCH .75 2.00
314 Terry Rozier ETCH .75 2.00
315 Frank Kaminsky ETCH 1.00 2.50
316 T.J. McConnell ETCH .75 2.00
317 Rondae Hollis-Jefferson ETCH .75 2.00
318 Kristaps Porzingis ETCH 2.50 6.00
319 Josh Richardson ETCH 1.00 2.50
320 Chris McCullough ETCH .60 1.50
321 R.J. Hunter ETCH .60 1.50
322 Joe Young ETCH .75 2.00
323 Devin Booker ETCH 3.00 8.00
324 Jordan Mickey ETCH .60 1.50
325 Delon Wright ETCH .75 2.00
326 Jerian Grant ETCH .60 1.50
327 D'Angelo Russell ETCH 2.50 6.00
328 Stanley Johnson ETCH .75 2.00
329 Richaun Holmes ETCH .75 2.00
330 Kelly Oubre Jr. ETCH .75 2.00
331 Nikola Jokic ETCH 1.25 3.00
332 Raul Neto ETCH .60 1.50
333 Nemanja Bjelica ETCH .75 2.00
334 Rashad Vaughn ETCH .60 1.50
335 Anthony Brown ETCH .60 1.50

2015-16 Panini Threads Century Proof Gold

*RED 1-150: 2.5X TO 6X BASIC
RANDOM INSERTS IN PACKS
1-150 PRINT RUN 25 SER.#'d SETS
151-200 PRINT RUN 10 SER.#'d SETS
NO 151-200 PRICING DUE TO SCARCITY

2015-16 Panini Threads Century Proof Red

*RED 1-150: .6X TO 1.5X BASIC
*RED 151-200: .6X TO 1.5X BASIC
RANDOM INSERTS IN PACKS
STATED PRINT RUN 99 SER.#'d SETS

2015-16 Panini Threads Authentic Threads

RANDOM INSERTS IN PACKS
STATED PRINT RUN 99-199 SER.#'d SETS
2 Kevin Garnett/199 4.00 10.00
3 Mike Bibby/199 2.00 5.00
4 Tony Parker/199 2.50 6.00
5 Kyrie Irving/99 5.00 12.00
6 Jared Sullinger/199 1.50 4.00
7 Dwight Howard/99 2.00 5.00
8 Markieff Morris/199 1.50 4.00
9 Bobby Jackson/199 1.50 4.00
10 Carmelo Anthony/99 3.00 8.00
11 Joe Smith/199 2.00 5.00
12 LaMarcus Aldridge/199 2.50 6.00
13 Rick Fox/199 2.00 5.00
14 Anthony Davis/99 5.00 12.00
15 Avery Bradley/99 2.00 5.00
16 Joakim Noah/99 2.00 5.00
18 Mo Williams/199 2.00 5.00
20 Brad Daugherty/199 2.00 5.00
21 Keith Van Horn/199 2.00 5.00
22 Russell Westbrook/199 6.00 15.00
23 Kobe Bryant/199 10.00 25.00
24 Doug McDermott/99 2.00 5.00
25 Stephen Curry/99 10.00 25.00
26 Kelly Olynyk/99 1.50 4.00
27 John Wall/99 3.00 8.00
28 Serge Ibaka/99 2.00 5.00
29 Brent Barry/199 1.50 4.00
30 DeMarcus Cousins/199 2.50 6.00
32 Tim Duncan/199 4.00 10.00
33 Kevin Durant/199 6.00 15.00
34 Eric Gordon/199 2.00 5.00
35 James Harden/99 4.00 10.00
36 Kentavious Caldwell-Pope/199 2.00 5.00
37 LeBron James/199 10.00 25.00
38 T.J. Warren/199 2.00 5.00
40 Kawhi Leonard/199 4.00 10.00

2015-16 Panini Threads Century Collection Materials

RANDOM INSERTS IN PACKS
STATED PRINT RUN 57-75 SER.#'d SETS
1 Cazzie Russell/75 2.50 6.00
2 Larry Johnson/75 4.00 10.00
3 David Robinson/75 5.00 12.00
4 Michael Redd/75 2.50 6.00
6 Ray Allen/75 3.00 8.00
7 Isiah Thomas/75 3.00 8.00
8 Shaquille O'Neal/75 6.00 15.00
10 Karl Malone/75 4.00 10.00
11 Charles Oakley/75 2.50 6.00
13 Dennis Rodman/75 6.00 15.00
14 Patrick Ewing/75 4.00 10.00
15 Gary Payton/75 3.00 8.00
16 Richard Hamilton/75 2.50 6.00
17 Jamal Mashburn/75 3.00 8.00
18 Steve Kerr/57 2.50 6.00
19 Alonzo Mourning/75 4.00 10.00
20 Kenny Smith/75 2.50 6.00
21 Clifford Robinson/75 2.00 5.00
22 Manute Bol/75 3.00 8.00
23 Doc Rivers/75 3.00 8.00
24 Grant Hill/75 4.00 10.00
25 Mike Bibby/75 2.50 6.00
26 Scottie Pippen/75 6.00 15.00
27 John Starks/75 2.50 6.00
28 Toni Kukoc/75 3.00 8.00
29 Alvan Adams/75 2.00 5.00
30 Kevin Duckworth/75 2.00 5.00
31 Danny Manning/75 2.50 6.00
32 Mark Aguirre/75 2.50 6.00
33 Dominique Wilkins/75 4.00 10.00
34 Ralph Sampson/75 2.50 6.00
35 Hakeem Olajuwon/75 4.00 10.00
36 Shane Battier/75 2.50 6.00
37 John Stockton/75 5.00 12.00
38 World B. Free/75 2.50 6.00
39 Ben Wallace/75 2.50 6.00
40 Larry Bird/75 8.00 20.00

2015-16 Panini Threads Century Greats

RANDOM INSERTS IN PACKS
*RED/99: .75X TO 2X BASIC
*GOLD/25: 1.2X TO 3X BASIC
1 Karl Malone .75 2.00
2 Bill Russell 1.00 2.50
3 Wilt Chamberlain 1.25 3.00
4 Elgin Baylor .60 1.50
5 John Havlicek .75 2.00
6 Patrick Ewing .75 2.00
7 Elvin Hayes .60 1.50
8 David Robinson 1.00 2.50
9 Shaquille O'Neal 1.25 3.00
10 Hakeem Olajuwon .75 2.00
11 Jerry West .75 2.00
12 Isiah Thomas .60 1.50
13 Bob Cousy 1.00 2.50
14 Julius Erving 1.00 2.50
15 Larry Bird 1.50 4.00
16 Clyde Drexler .75 2.00
17 Magic Johnson 1.50 4.00
18 John Stockton 1.00 2.50
19 Kareem Abdul-Jabbar 1.00 2.50
20 Oscar Robertson .75 2.00

2015-16 Panini Threads Century Greats Threads

RANDOM INSERTS IN PACKS
STATED PRINT RUN 170-199 SER.#'d SETS
1 Scottie Pippen/199 5.00 12.00
2 Adrian Dantley/199 2.00 5.00
3 Clifford Robinson/199 1.50 4.00
4 Mark Aguirre/199 2.00 5.00
5 Ralph Sampson/199 2.00 5.00
6 Alonzo Mourning/199 3.00 8.00
7 Kenny Smith/199 2.00 5.00
8 Gary Payton/199 2.50 6.00
9 Toni Kukoc/199 2.50 6.00
10 Isiah Thomas/199 2.50 6.00
11 Larry Bird/199 6.00 15.00
12 Ben Wallace/199 2.00 5.00
13 Michael Redd/199 2.00 5.00
14 Danny Manning/199 2.00 5.00
15 Ray Allen/199 2.50 6.00
16 Dennis Rodman/199 5.00 12.00
17 Shaquille O'Neal/199 5.00 12.00
18 Grant Hill/199 3.00 8.00
19 Clyde Drexler/199 3.00 8.00
20 John Stockton/199 4.00 10.00
21 Larry Johnson/199 3.00 8.00
22 Charles Oakley/199 2.00 5.00
23 David Robinson/199 4.00 10.00
24 Patrick Ewing/199 3.00 8.00
25 Richard Hamilton/199 2.00 5.00
26 Doc Rivers/199 2.50 6.00
27 Steve Kerr/170 2.50 6.00
28 Hakeem Olajuwon/199 3.00 8.00
29 Karl Malone/199 3.00 8.00
30 World B. Free/199 2.00 5.00

2015-16 Panini Threads Century Signatures

RANDOM INSERTS IN PACKS
PRINT RUNS B/WN 25-199 COPIES PER
1 Sam Bowie/199 2.50 6.00
2 Oscar Robertson/25 25.00 60.00
3 Cuttino Mobley/199 2.50 6.00
4 Wes Unseld/199 4.00 10.00
5 Larry Nance/199 3.00 8.00
6 Calvin Murphy/170 3.00 8.00
7 Terry Cummings/199 3.00 8.00
8 Kareem Abdul-Jabbar/25
9 Wayne Embry/199 2.50 6.00
10 Julius Erving/25 30.00 80.00
11 Ron Harper/199 4.00 10.00
12 Anfernee Hardaway/111 10.00 25.00
13 Theo Ratliff/199 2.50 6.00
14 Bernard King/149 3.00 8.00
15 Raef LaFrentz/199 2.50 6.00
16 Dikembe Mutombo/199 4.00 10.00
17 Billy Paultz/199 4.00 10.00
18 Magic Johnson/25 25.00 60.00
19 Tony Delk/199 2.50 6.00
20 John Stockton/25 15.00 40.00
21 Antoine Carr/199 2.50 6.00
22 Larry Brown/199 8.00 20.00
23 Will Perdue/199 2.50 6.00
24 Frank Ramsey/199 8.00 20.00
25 Eddie Jones/199 3.00 8.00
26 Scott Brooks/199 2.50 6.00
27 Paul Westphal/199 4.00 10.00
28 Larry Bird/25 40.00 100.00
29 Kenny Anderson/199 3.00 8.00
30 Karl Malone/25

2015-16 Panini Threads Century Stars

RANDOM INSERTS IN PACKS
1 Kobe Bryant 20.00 50.00
2 Tim Duncan 8.00 20.00
3 Andrew Wiggins 8.00 20.00
4 LeBron James 25.00 60.00
5 Carmelo Anthony 6.00 15.00
6 Anthony Davis 10.00 25.00
7 Kyrie Irving 10.00 25.00
8 James Harden 8.00 20.00
9 Dirk Nowitzki 6.00 15.00
10 Russell Westbrook 12.00 30.00
11 Derrick Rose 6.00 15.00
12 John Wall 6.00 15.00
13 Kevin Garnett 8.00 20.00
14 Kevin Durant 12.00 30.00
15 Dwight Howard 4.00 10.00
16 Stephen Curry 25.00 60.00
17 Damian Lillard 10.00 25.00
18 Chris Paul 6.00 15.00
19 Dwyane Wade 8.00 20.00
20 Blake Griffin 5.00 12.00

2015-16 Panini Threads Debut Threads

RANDOM INSERTS IN PACKS
STATED PRINT RUN 199 SER.#'d SETS
1 Justin Anderson 1.50 4.00
2 Rondae Hollis-Jefferson 1.50 4.00
3 Jordan Mickey 1.25 3.00
4 Myles Turner 2.00 5.00
5 D'Angelo Russell 4.00 10.00
6 Delon Wright 1.50 4.00
7 R.J. Hunter 1.25 3.00
8 Stanley Johnson 1.50 4.00
9 Devin Booker 4.00 10.00
10 Kelly Oubre Jr. 1.50 4.00
11 Mario Hezonja 1.50 4.00
12 Emmanuel Mudiay 2.00 5.00
13 Cameron Payne 1.50 4.00
14 Terry Rozier 1.50 4.00
15 Bobby Portis 2.00 5.00
16 Kristaps Porzingis 5.00 12.00
17 Justise Winslow 2.00 5.00
18 Montrezl Harrell 1.50 4.00
20 Jerian Grant 1.25 3.00
21 Frank Kaminsky 2.00 5.00
22 Chris McCullough 1.25 3.00
23 Sam Dekker 1.50 4.00
24 Richaun Holmes 1.50 4.00
25 Willie Cauley-Stein 2.00 5.00
26 Tyus Jones 2.00 5.00
27 Anthony Brown 1.25 3.00
28 Trey Lyles 2.00 5.00
29 Karl-Anthony Towns 6.00 15.00
30 Jahlil Okafor 3.00 8.00

2015-16 Panini Threads Floor Generals

RANDOM INSERTS IN PACKS
*RED/99: .75X TO 2X BASIC
*GOLD/25: 1.2X TO 3X BASIC
1 Jason Kidd .60 1.50
2 LeBron James 2.50 6.00
3 Allen Iverson .75 2.00
4 Kyrie Irving 1.25 3.00
5 Russell Westbrook 1.50 4.00
6 Kyle Lowry .50 1.25
7 Tony Parker .60 1.50
8 Jeff Teague .50 1.25
9 John Stockton 1.00 2.50
10 Pete Maravich 1.00 2.50
11 Chris Paul .75 2.00
12 James Harden 1.00 2.50
13 Steve Nash .60 1.50
14 Damian Lillard 1.25 3.00
15 Isiah Thomas .60 1.50
16 Michael Carter-Williams .40 1.00
17 Stephen Curry 2.50 6.00
18 Ty Lawson .40 1.00
19 Gary Payton .60 1.50
20 John Wall .75 2.00

2015-16 Panini Threads Hardwood Pioneers

RANDOM INSERTS IN PACKS
*RED/49: .75X TO 2X BASIC
*GOLD/25: 1.2X TO 3X BASIC
1 Bob Pettit .60 1.50
2 Bob Cousy 1.00 2.50
3 Elgin Baylor .60 1.50
4 Wilt Chamberlain 1.25 3.00
5 Lenny Wilkens .60 1.50
6 Clyde Lovellette .60 1.50
7 Bill Russell 1.00 2.50
8 George Mikan 1.25 3.00
9 Oscar Robertson .75 2.00
10 Sam Jones .60 1.50

2015-16 Panini Threads High Flyers

RANDOM INSERTS IN PACKS
*RED/99: .75X TO 2X BASIC
*GOLD/25: 1.2X TO 3X BASIC
1 DeAndre Jordan .60 1.50
2 Kobe Bryant 2.50 6.00
3 Russell Westbrook 1.50 4.00
4 Dwight Howard .50 1.25
5 Kenny Walker .40 1.00
6 Julius Erving 1.00 2.50
7 Clyde Drexler .75 2.00
8 Blake Griffin .60 1.50
9 Scottie Pippen 1.25 3.00
10 Zach LaVine .60 1.50
11 Dee Brown .40 1.00
12 Spud Webb .50 1.25
13 Darrell Griffith .40 1.00
14 Larry Nance .50 1.25
15 Shaquille O'Neal 1.25 3.00
16 Dominique Wilkins .75 2.00
17 Tracy McGrady .60 1.50
18 LeBron James 2.50 6.00
19 Victor Oladipo .50 1.25
20 Shawn Kemp 1.00 2.50

2015-16 Panini Threads Precision Players

RANDOM INSERTS IN PACKS
*RED/99: .75X TO 2X BASIC
*GOLD/25: 1.2X TO 3X BASIC
1 Kyrie Irving 1.25 3.00
2 Klay Thompson .75 2.00
3 Damian Lillard 1.25 3.00
4 Anthony Davis 1.25 3.00
5 Kevin Love .60 1.50
6 LaMarcus Aldridge .60 1.50
7 DeMar DeRozan .60 1.50
8 Al Horford .50 1.25
9 Bradley Beal .60 1.50
10 Kawhi Leonard 1.00 2.50
11 Tobias Harris .50 1.25
12 Tim Duncan 1.00 2.50
13 Chris Paul .75 2.00
14 Dirk Nowitzki .75 2.00
15 Jimmy Butler .60 1.50
16 Blake Griffin .60 1.50
17 Pau Gasol .60 1.50
18 Wesley Matthews .40 1.00
19 Andrew Wiggins 1.00 2.50
20 Chandler Parsons .50 1.25

2015-16 Panini Threads Rookie Signage

RANDOM INSERTS IN PACKS
1 Kelly Oubre Jr. 3.00 8.00
2 Justise Winslow 4.00 10.00
3 Rondae Hollis-Jefferson 3.00 8.00
4 Stanley Johnson 3.00 8.00
5 Kevon Looney 3.00 8.00
6 Myles Turner 10.00 25.00
7 Larry Nance Jr. 4.00 10.00
8 Karl-Anthony Towns 60.00 150.00
9 Rashad Vaughn 2.50 6.00
10 Emmanuel Mudiay 6.00 15.00
11 Terry Rozier 3.00 8.00
12 Willie Cauley-Stein 10.00 25.00
13 Justin Anderson 3.00 8.00
14 Frank Kaminsky 5.00 12.00
15 Nemanja Bjelica 3.00 8.00
16 Trey Lyles 5.00 12.00
17 Raul Neto 2.50 6.00
18 D'Angelo Russell 15.00 40.00
19 Delon Wright 3.00 8.00
20 Kristaps Porzingis 40.00 100.00
21 Sam Dekker 3.00 8.00
22 Tyus Jones 4.00 10.00
23 Bobby Portis 4.00 10.00
24 Devin Booker 20.00 50.00
25 Nikola Jokic 20.00 50.00
26 Jerian Grant 2.50 6.00
27 Darrun Hilliard 2.50 6.00
28 Jahlil Okafor 12.00 30.00
29 Cameron Payne 3.00 8.00

2015-16 Panini Threads Rookie Team Threads

RANDOM INSERTS IN PACKS
1 Devin Booker 5.00 12.00
2 Raul Neto 1.00 2.50
3 Rashad Vaughn 1.00 2.50
4 Norman Powell 1.25 3.00
5 Karl-Anthony Towns 20.00 50.00
6 Justin Anderson 1.25 3.00
7 Mario Hezonja 1.25 3.00
8 Larry Nance Jr. 1.50 4.00
9 Frank Kaminsky 1.50 4.00
10 Jordan Mickey 1.00 2.50
11 Cameron Payne 1.25 3.00
12 Nikola Jokic 4.00 10.00
13 Sam Dekker 1.25 3.00
14 Boban Marjanovic 1.25 3.00
15 D'Angelo Russell 4.00 10.00
16 Bobby Portis 1.50 4.00
17 Willie Cauley-Stein 1.50 4.00
18 R.J. Hunter 1.00 2.50
19 Justise Winslow 1.50 4.00
20 Anthony Brown 1.00 2.50
21 Kelly Oubre Jr. 1.25 3.00
22 Marcelo Huertas 1.25 3.00
23 Jonathon Simmons 1.50 4.00
24 Jerian Grant 1.00 2.50
25 Jahlil Okafor 2.00 5.00
26 Rondae Hollis-Jefferson 1.25 3.00
27 Emmanuel Mudiay 1.50 4.00
28 Chris McCullough 1.00 2.50
29 Myles Turner 1.50 4.00
30 Nemanja Bjelica 1.25 3.00
31 Terry Rozier 1.25 3.00
32 Richaun Holmes 1.25 3.00
33 Delon Wright 1.25 3.00
34 Pat Connaughton 1.00 2.50
35 Kristaps Porzingis 4.00 10.00
36 Tyus Jones 1.50 4.00
37 Stanley Johnson 1.25 3.00
38 Montrezl Harrell 1.25 3.00
39 Trey Lyles 1.50 4.00
40 T.J. McConnell 1.25 3.00

2015-16 Panini Threads Rookie Threads

RANDOM INSERTS IN PACKS
*PRIME/25: 2X TO 5X BASIC
1 Karl-Anthony Towns 6.00 15.00
2 Karl-Anthony Towns 6.00 15.00
3 Karl-Anthony Towns 6.00 15.00
4 Karl-Anthony Towns 6.00 15.00
5 Karl-Anthony Towns 6.00 15.00
6 D'Angelo Russell 4.00 10.00
7 D'Angelo Russell 4.00 10.00
8 D'Angelo Russell 4.00 10.00
9 D'Angelo Russell 4.00 10.00
10 D'Angelo Russell 4.00 10.00
11 Jahlil Okafor 2.50 6.00
12 Jahlil Okafor 2.50 6.00
13 Jahlil Okafor 2.50 6.00
14 Jahlil Okafor 2.50 6.00
15 Jahlil Okafor 2.50 6.00
16 Kristaps Porzingis 5.00 12.00
17 Kristaps Porzingis 5.00 12.00
18 Kristaps Porzingis 5.00 12.00
19 Kristaps Porzingis 5.00 12.00
20 Kristaps Porzingis 5.00 12.00
21 Mario Hezonja 1.50 4.00
22 Mario Hezonja 1.50 4.00
23 Mario Hezonja 1.50 4.00
24 Mario Hezonja 1.50 4.00
25 Mario Hezonja 1.50 4.00
26 Willie Cauley-Stein 2.00 5.00
27 Willie Cauley-Stein 2.00 5.00
28 Willie Cauley-Stein 2.00 5.00
29 Willie Cauley-Stein 2.00 5.00
30 Willie Cauley-Stein 2.00 5.00
31 Emmanuel Mudiay 2.00 5.00
32 Emmanuel Mudiay 2.00 5.00
33 Emmanuel Mudiay 2.00 5.00
34 Emmanuel Mudiay 2.00 5.00
35 Emmanuel Mudiay 2.00 5.00
36 Stanley Johnson 1.50 4.00
37 Stanley Johnson 1.50 4.00
38 Stanley Johnson 1.50 4.00
39 Stanley Johnson 1.50 4.00
40 Stanley Johnson 1.50 4.00
41 Frank Kaminsky 2.00 5.00
42 Frank Kaminsky 2.00 5.00
43 Frank Kaminsky 2.00 5.00
44 Frank Kaminsky 2.00 5.00
45 Frank Kaminsky 2.00 5.00
46 Justise Winslow 2.00 5.00
47 Justise Winslow 2.00 5.00
48 Justise Winslow 2.00 5.00
49 Justise Winslow 2.00 5.00
50 Justise Winslow 2.00 5.00
51 Myles Turner 2.00 5.00
52 Myles Turner 2.00 5.00
53 Myles Turner 2.00 5.00
54 Myles Turner 2.00 5.00
55 Myles Turner 2.00 5.00
56 Trey Lyles 2.00 5.00
57 Trey Lyles 2.00 5.00
58 Trey Lyles 2.00 5.00
59 Trey Lyles 2.00 5.00
60 Trey Lyles 2.00 5.00
61 Devin Booker 4.00 10.00
62 Devin Booker 4.00 10.00
63 Devin Booker 4.00 10.00
64 Devin Booker 4.00 10.00
65 Devin Booker 4.00 10.00
66 Cameron Payne 1.50 4.00
67 Cameron Payne 1.50 4.00
68 Cameron Payne 1.50 4.00
69 Cameron Payne 1.50 4.00
70 Cameron Payne 1.50 4.00
71 Kelly Oubre Jr. 1.50 4.00
72 Kelly Oubre Jr. 1.50 4.00
73 Kelly Oubre Jr. 1.50 4.00
74 Kelly Oubre Jr. 1.50 4.00
75 Kelly Oubre Jr. 1.50 4.00
76 Terry Rozier 1.50 4.00
77 Terry Rozier 1.50 4.00
78 Terry Rozier 1.50 4.00
79 Terry Rozier 1.50 4.00
80 Terry Rozier 1.50 4.00
86 Sam Dekker 1.50 4.00
87 Sam Dekker 1.50 4.00
88 Sam Dekker 1.50 4.00
89 Sam Dekker 1.50 4.00
90 Sam Dekker 1.50 4.00
91 Jerian Grant 1.25 3.00
92 Jerian Grant 1.25 3.00
93 Jerian Grant 1.25 3.00
94 Jerian Grant 1.25 3.00
95 Jerian Grant 1.25 3.00
96 Delon Wright 1.50 4.00
97 Delon Wright 1.50 4.00
98 Delon Wright 1.50 4.00
99 Delon Wright 1.50 4.00
100 Delon Wright 1.50 4.00

2015-16 Panini Threads Rookie Threads Signatures

RANDOM INSERTS IN PACKS
PRINT RUNS B/WN 99-199 COPIES PER
1 Karl-Anthony Towns/199 60.00 150.00
2 D'Angelo Russell/199 15.00 40.00
3 Jahlil Okafor/199 12.00 30.00
4 Emmanuel Mudiay/199 8.00 20.00
5 Kristaps Porzingis/99 30.00 80.00
7 Justise Winslow/199 10.00 25.00
8 Willie Cauley-Stein/199 10.00 25.00
9 Tyus Jones/199 5.00 12.00
10 Stanley Johnson/199 4.00 10.00
11 Frank Kaminsky/199 5.00 12.00
12 Devin Booker/199 25.00 60.00
13 Myles Turner/199 10.00 25.00
14 Trey Lyles/199 5.00 12.00
15 Jerian Grant/199 3.00 8.00
17 Delon Wright/199 4.00 10.00
18 Cameron Payne/199 4.00 10.00
19 Kelly Oubre Jr./199 4.00 10.00
20 Terry Rozier/199 4.00 10.00
21 Sam Dekker/199 4.00 10.00
22 Rondae Hollis-Jefferson/199 4.00 10.00
23 Justin Anderson/199 4.00 10.00

24 Bobby Portis/199 5.00 12.00
25 Kevon Looney/199 4.00 10.00
26 R.J. Hunter/199 3.00 8.00
27 Jarell Martin/199 4.00 10.00
28 Anthony Brown/199 3.00 8.00
29 Chris McCullough/199 3.00 8.00
30 Montrezl Harrell/199 4.00 10.00
31 Jordan Mickey/199 3.00 8.00
32 Walter Tavares/199 3.00 8.00
34 Pat Connaughton/199 3.00 8.00

2015-16 Panini Threads Rookie Threads Signatures Prime

*PRIME/25: .6X TO 1.5X BASIC
RANDOM INSERTS IN PACKS
PRINT RUNS B/WN 15-25 COPIES PER
NO PRIICNG ON QTY 15
35 Joe Young/25 15.00 40.00

2015-16 Panini Threads Signage

RANDOM INSERTS IN PACKS
PRINT RUNS B/WN 15-199 COPIES PER
NO PRICING ON QTY 15
1 Trey Burke/199 2.50 6.00
2 Elgin Baylor/49
3 Rodney Stuckey/199 3.00 8.00
4 Cody Zeller/199 2.50 6.00
5 Tom Gugliotta/199 2.50 6.00
6 Derrick Williams/99 2.50 6.00
7 Jeff Malone/199 2.50 6.00
9 Artis Gilmore/99 3.00 8.00
11 Kevin Willis/199 2.50 6.00
12 Anfernee Hardaway/49 10.00 25.00
13 Bob McAdoo/199 5.00 12.00
14 Richard Hamilton/49
15 Cedric Maxwell/199 2.50 6.00
16 Julius Randle/99 10.00 25.00
17 Sam Bowie/199 2.50 6.00
19 Chris Mullin/99 6.00 15.00
21 Chase Budinger/199 2.50 6.00
22 Anthony Bennett/199 2.50 6.00
23 Steve Novak/199 2.50 6.00
24 Otto Porter/99 3.00 8.00
25 Jason Smith/199 2.50 6.00
26 Ben McLemore/99
27 Tony Delk/199 2.50 6.00
29 Kentavious Caldwell-Pope/99 3.00 8.00
31 Courtney Lee/199 3.00 8.00
32 Gary Payton/49 8.00 20.00
33 Jusuf Nurkic/199 2.50 6.00
34 Alex Len/99 2.50 6.00
35 Ron Harper/199 4.00 10.00
36 Nerlens Noel/99 3.00 8.00
37 Glenn Robinson III/199 2.50 6.00
39 Tayshaun Prince/99 3.00 8.00
41 Wayne Embry/199 2.50 6.00
42 Michael Kidd-Gilchrist/49
43 C.J. Watson/199
44 Bob Lanier/83 8.00 20.00
45 Cuttino Mobley/199 2.50 6.00
46 Andre Drummond/99 4.00 10.00
47 Antoine Carr/199 2.50 6.00
49 C.J. McCollum/199 6.00 15.00

2015-16 Panini Threads Team Threads

RANDOM INSERTS IN PACKS
1 DeMar DeRozan 1.50 4.00
2 Dwyane Wade 2.50 6.00
3 James Harden 2.50 6.00
4 Brook Lopez 1.25 3.00
5 Tim Duncan 2.50 6.00
6 Andre Iguodala 1.25 3.00
7 Kevin Love 1.50 4.00
8 Rudy Gay 1.50 4.00
9 Andrew Wiggins 2.50 6.00
10 Kyrie Irving 3.00 8.00
11 Derrick Rose 2.00 5.00
12 Gordon Hayward 1.50 4.00
13 Chris Paul 2.00 5.00
14 Rudy Gobert 1.50 4.00
15 LaMarcus Aldridge 1.50 4.00
16 Kyle Korver 1.25 3.00
17 Jimmy Butler 1.50 4.00
18 Tony Parker 1.50 4.00
19 Ricky Rubio 1.50 4.00
20 Damian Lillard 3.00 8.00
21 LeBron James 6.00 15.00
22 Eric Bledsoe 1.25 3.00
23 Russell Westbrook 4.00 10.00
24 Pau Gasol 1.50 4.00
25 John Wall 2.00 5.00
26 Al Jefferson 1.25 3.00
27 Dwight Howard 1.25 3.00
28 Kobe Bryant 6.00 15.00
29 Kenneth Faried 1.25 3.00
30 Klay Thompson 2.00 5.00
31 Kevin Durant 4.00 10.00
32 Kyle Lowry 1.25 3.00
33 Blake Griffin 1.50 4.00
34 Jeff Teague 1.25 3.00
35 DeMarcus Cousins 1.50 4.00
36 Greg Monroe 1.25 3.00
37 Paul George 2.00 5.00
38 Paul Pierce 1.50 4.00
39 Monta Ellis 1.25 3.00
40 Mike Conley 1.50 4.00
41 Anthony Davis 3.00 8.00
42 Andre Drummond 1.50 4.00
43 Marc Gasol 1.50 4.00
44 Goran Dragic 1.25 3.00
45 Carmelo Anthony 2.00 5.00
46 Zach Randolph 1.25 3.00
47 Al Horford 1.25 3.00
48 Tyreke Evans 1.00 2.50
49 Chandler Parsons 1.25 3.00
50 Stephen Curry 15.00 40.00
51 Dirk Nowitzki 2.00 5.00
52 Tyson Chandler 1.25 3.00
53 Kawhi Leonard 2.50 6.00
54 Joakim Noah 1.25 3.00
55 Draymond Green 2.00 5.00
56 Danny Green 1.25 3.00
57 Chris Bosh 1.50 4.00
58 Jabari Parker 2.00 5.00
59 Bradley Beal 1.50 4.00
60 DeAndre Jordan 1.50 4.00

2015-16 Panini Threads Threads Signatures

RANDOM INSERTS IN PACKS
PRINT RUNS B/WN 17-49 COPIES PER
*PRIME/25: .6X TO 1.5X BASIC
1 Trey Burke/35 3.00 8.00
2 John Wall/25 15.00 40.00
3 World B. Free/35
4 Marcus Smart/39 4.00 10.00
6 Zach Randolph/35
7 Rafer Alston/49 3.00 8.00
8 Kobe Bryant/25
9 Tyson Chandler/35
10 Anthony Davis/25 30.00 80.00
11 Goran Dragic/35
12 Chris Webber/25 40.00 100.00
13 Mike Conley/35 5.00 12.00
14 Harrison Barnes/35 8.00 20.00
16 Jrue Holiday/35 4.00 10.00
17 Brad Daugherty/49
18 Chris Paul/25 25.00 60.00
19 Josh Smith/35 4.00 10.00
20 Blake Griffin/25 15.00 40.00
22 Jabari Parker/25
24 Richard Hamilton/35
25 Jusuf Nurkic/49 3.00 8.00
26 Tyreke Evans/35
27 Reggie Jackson/49
28 Dwyane Wade/25 40.00 100.00
29 Al Horford/35 4.00 10.00
30 Dwight Howard/17
31 Andrea Bargnani/35 4.00 10.00
33 Wesley Matthews/49 3.00 8.00
34 Otto Porter/35 4.00 10.00
35 Timofey Mozgov/49 3.00 8.00
36 Ben McLemore/35 3.00 8.00
37 Donatas Motiejunas/49 3.00 8.00
38 Carmelo Anthony/20 15.00 40.00
39 Steve Kerr/35 10.00 25.00
40 Kyrie Irving/25 12.00 30.00
41 Brandon Knight/35 4.00 10.00
42 Andrew Wiggins/25 20.00 50.00
43 Nik Stauskas/49
44 Chris Andersen/35 4.00 10.00
45 Cody Zeller/35 3.00 8.00
47 Isaiah Canaan/49 4.00 10.00
48 Kevin Durant/25 50.00 120.00
49 C.J. McCollum/35 8.00 20.00
51 Danilo Gallinari/35 4.00 10.00
52 Kevin Love/35 10.00 25.00
53 DeMarre Carroll/49 3.00 8.00
54 Joe Johnson/35
55 Matthew Dellavedova/49 12.00 30.00
56 Andre Drummond/35 6.00 15.00
57 Jordan Clarkson/49 5.00 12.00
58 Allen Iverson/25 50.00 120.00
59 Michael Carter-Williams/35
60 Pau Gasol/25 10.00 25.00
61 Danny Manning/35
62 Victor Oladipo/35 4.00 10.00
63 T.J. Warren/49
64 Julius Randle/35 8.00 20.00
65 Tim Hardaway Jr./49 3.00 8.00

2015-16 Panini Threads Triple Threat Materials

RANDOM INSERTS IN PACKS
STATED PRINT RUN 199 SER.#'d SETS
1 Nicolas Batum 2.00 5.00
2 Carmelo Anthony 3.00 8.00
3 Tim Duncan 4.00 10.00
4 Aaron Gordon 2.00 5.00
5 Kawhi Leonard 4.00 10.00
6 Andrew Wiggins 4.00 10.00
7 Dante Exum 2.00 5.00
8 Brook Lopez 2.00 5.00
9 Iman Shumpert 1.50 4.00
10 Kevin Durant 6.00 15.00
11 Rajon Rondo 2.50 6.00
12 Clyde Drexler 3.00 8.00
13 Tony Parker 2.50 6.00
14 LeBron James 20.00 50.00
15 Bradley Beal 2.50 6.00
16 Kobe Bryant 10.00 25.00
17 David West 2.50 6.00
18 Chris Andersen 2.00 5.00
19 John Henson 2.00 5.00
20 LaMarcus Aldridge 2.50 6.00
21 Terrence Ross 2.00 5.00
22 Damian Lillard 5.00 12.00
23 Trey Burke 1.50 4.00
24 Russell Westbrook 6.00 15.00
25 C.J. McCollum 2.50 6.00
26 Brandon Jennings 1.50 4.00
27 George Hill 2.00 5.00
28 Eric Bledsoe 2.00 5.00
29 Marcus Smart 2.00 5.00
30 Manu Ginobili 2.50 6.00

2015-16 Panini Threads Voices of the Game Autographs

RANDOM INSERTS IN PACKS
PRINT RUNS B/WN 10-199 COPIES PER
NO PRICING ON QTY 10
1 Bob Knight/49 15.00 40.00
3 Chris Webber/49 25.00 60.00
4 Kenny Smith/115 3.00 8.00
5 Steve Kerr/99 10.00 25.00
6 Doug Collins/199 4.00 10.00
7 Jalen Rose/199 4.00 10.00
8 Avery Johnson/199 3.00 8.00
9 Rick Fox/199 3.00 8.00
10 Grant Hill/49 25.00 60.00

2016-17 Panini Threads

COMP.SET w/o RCs (150) 20.00 50.00
1 Paul George .40 1.00
2 Marcus Smart .25 .60
3 Andrew Wiggins .50 1.25
4 Jimmy Butler .30 .75
5 DeAndre Jordan .30 .75
6 Jeremy Lin .30 .75
7 Rudy Gay .30 .75
8 Harrison Barnes .25 .60
9 Ersan Ilyasova .20 .50
10 Tony Snell .20 .50
11 Al Horford .25 .60
12 James Harden .50 1.25
13 Andre Drummond .30 .75
14 Evan Fournier .25 .60
15 Gordon Hayward .30 .75
16 Dion Waiters .25 .60
17 Will Barton .20 .50
18 Marc Gasol .30 .75
19 Robin Lopez .20 .50
20 Ricky Rubio .30 .75
21 Rudy Gobert .30 .75
22 Cody Zeller .20 .50
23 Trevor Booker .20 .50
24 Andre Roberson .20 .50
25 Dirk Nowitzki .40 1.00
26 JaMychal Green .20 .50
27 Nicolas Batum .25 .60
28 Justise Winslow .25 .60
29 Trey Lyles .25 .60
30 Mike Conley .25 .60
31 D'Angelo Russell .40 1.00
32 Bojan Bogdanovic .20 .50
33 Enes Kanter .20 .50
34 Marcin Gortat .25 .60
35 Greg Monroe .25 .60
36 J.R. Smith .25 .60
37 Joakim Noah .25 .60
38 Solomon Hill .20 .50
39 Tim Hardaway Jr. .20 .50
40 Hassan Whiteside .25 .60
41 Jae Crowder .25 .60
42 Avery Bradley .25 .60
43 Dennis Schroder .25 .60
44 Thaddeus Young .20 .50
45 Kentavious Caldwell-Pope .25 .60
46 Maurice Harkless .20 .50
47 Klay Thompson .40 1.00
48 Serge Ibaka .25 .60
49 C.J. McCollum .25 .60
50 Kevin Durant .75 2.00
51 Paul Millsap .30 .75
52 Bradley Beal .30 .75
53 Danny Green .25 .60
54 Emmanuel Mudiay .25 .60
55 Tyler Johnson .20 .50
56 Ty Lawson .20 .50
57 Jusuf Nurkic .20 .50
58 Victor Oladipo .25 .60
59 Joel Embiid .50 1.25
60 Anthony Davis .60 1.50
61 Tony Parker .30 .75
62 Blake Griffin .30 .75
63 DeMarcus Cousins .30 .75
64 LeBron James 1.25 3.00
65 Elfrid Payton .25 .60
66 Luol Deng .25 .60
67 Terrence Ross .25 .60
68 Marvin Williams .25 .60
69 Steven Adams .25 .60
70 Stephen Curry 1.25 3.00
71 Robert Covington .20 .50
72 Taj Gibson .25 .60
73 Kristaps Porzingis .60 1.50
74 Derrick Rose .40 1.00
75 Wilson Chandler .25 .60
76 Zach LaVine .30 .75
77 Reggie Jackson .25 .60
78 Kevin Love .30 .75
79 Jrue Holiday .25 .60
80 E'Twaun Moore .20 .50
81 Pau Gasol .30 .75
82 Derrick Favors .25 .60
83 Rodney Hood .25 .60
84 Karl-Anthony Towns .75 2.00
85 Chris Paul .40 1.00
86 Kyle Lowry .25 .60
87 Nikola Vucevic .25 .60
88 Nick Young .25 .60
89 Gorgui Dieng .20 .50
90 Marcus Morris .20 .50
91 Clint Capela .20 .50
92 Tristan Thompson .25 .60
93 Arron Afflalo .20 .50
94 DeMar DeRozan .30 .75
95 Carmelo Anthony .40 1.00
96 Allen Crabbe .20 .50
97 Luc Mbah a Moute .20 .50
98 Dwyane Wade .50 1.25
99 Darren Collison .25 .60
100 Myles Turner .25 .60
101 Mason Plumlee .25 .60
102 Tim Frazier .20 .50
103 Brandon Knight .25 .60
104 John Wall .40 1.00
105 Kemba Walker .30 .75
106 Markieff Morris .20 .50
107 Eric Bledsoe .25 .60
108 Michael Kidd-Gilchrist .25 .60
109 Jabari Parker .40 1.00
110 Ryan Anderson .25 .60
111 Vince Carter .40 1.00
112 Jonas Valanciunas .25 .60
113 Matthew Dellavedova .25 .60
114 Lou Williams .25 .60
115 Devin Booker .50 1.25
116 Damian Lillard .60 1.50
117 Monta Ellis .25 .60
118 Tobias Harris .25 .60
119 Jeff Teague .25 .60
120 LaMarcus Aldridge .30 .75
121 Giannis Antetokounmpo .60 1.50
122 Draymond Green .40 1.00
123 Jahlil Okafor .25 .60
124 Danilo Gallinari .25 .60
125 Brook Lopez .25 .60
126 Kyrie Irving .60 1.50
127 Dwight Howard .25 .60
128 Russell Westbrook .75 2.00
129 Sean Kilpatrick .20 .50
130 Wesley Matthews .20 .50
131 T.J. Warren .25 .60
132 Patrick Beverley .20 .50
133 Tyson Chandler .25 .60
134 Brandon Jennings .20 .50
135 Trevor Ariza .20 .50
136 J.J. Barea .25 .60
137 Kawhi Leonard .50 1.25
138 Otto Porter .25 .60
139 Deron Williams .25 .60
140 Jordan Clarkson .25 .60
141 Tony Allen .20 .50
142 Isaiah Thomas .30 .75
143 Sergio Rodriguez .20 .50
144 Kyle Korver .25 .60
145 Andre Iguodala .25 .60
146 Goran Dragic .25 .60
147 Aaron Gordon .25 .60
148 Cory Joseph .20 .50
149 Rajon Rondo .30 .75
150 J.J. Redick .30 .75
151 Domantas Sabonis RC .60 1.50
152 Henry Ellenson RC .50 1.25
153 Willy Hernangomez RC .50 1.25
154 DeAndre' Bembry RC .40 1.00
155 Damian Jones RC .40 1.00
156 Ben Simmons RC 2.50 6.00
157 Malcolm Brogdon RC 1.00 2.50
158 Buddy Hield RC 1.00 2.50
159 A.J. Hammons RC .40 1.00
160 Taurean Prince RC .60 1.50
161 Malcolm Delaney RC .50 1.25
162 Malik Beasley RC .40 1.00
163 Mindaugas Kuzminskas RC .50 1.25
164 Brice Johnson RC .40 1.00
165 Deyonta Davis RC .40 1.00
166 Brandon Ingram RC 2.50 6.00
167 Diamond Stone RC .40 1.00
168 Jamal Murray RC 1.25 3.00
169 Kay Felder RC .40 1.00
170 Georgios Papagiannis RC .40 1.00
171 Yogi Ferrell RC .50 1.25
172 Caris LeVert RC .50 1.25
173 Davis Bertans RC .60 1.50
174 Pascal Siakam RC .40 1.00
175 Ivica Zubac RC .60 1.50
176 Jaylen Brown RC 1.50 4.00
177 Stephen Zimmerman RC .40 1.00
178 Marquese Chriss RC 1.00 2.50
179 Dario Saric RC 1.25 3.00
180 Denzel Valentine RC .50 1.25
181 Tomas Satoransky RC .40 1.00
182 Malachi Richardson RC .50 1.25
183 Ron Baker RC .50 1.25
184 Skal Labissiere RC .60 1.50
185 Cheick Diallo RC .40 1.00
186 Dragan Bender RC .50 1.25
187 Isaiah Whitehead RC .40 1.00
188 Jakob Poeltl RC .50 1.25
189 Rodney McGruder RC .50 1.25
190 Juan Hernangomez RC .50 1.25
191 Patrick McCaw RC .75 2.00
192 T. Luwawu-Cabarrot RC .75 2.00
193 Chinanu Onuaku RC .40 1.00
194 Dejounte Murray RC .75 2.00
195 Tyler Ulis RC 1.25 3.00
196 Kris Dunn RC 1.25 3.00
197 Demetrius Jackson RC .40 1.00
198 Thon Maker RC 1.25 3.00
199 Dorian Finney-Smith RC .50 1.25
200 Wade Baldwin IV RC .40 1.00
201 Deyonta Davis LTHR .50 1.25
202 Patrick McCaw LTHR 1.00 2.50
203 Georgios Papagiannis LTHR .50 1.25
204 Kris Dunn LTHR 1.50 4.00
205 Jaylen Brown LTHR 2.00 5.00
206 Denzel Valentine LTHR .60 1.50
207 Domantas Sabonis LTHR .75 2.00
208 Skal Labissiere LTHR .75 2.00
209 Ben Simmons LTHR 6.00 15.00
210 Isaiah Whitehead LTHR .50 1.25
211 Brandon Ingram LTHR 3.00 8.00
212 Dejounte Murray LTHR 1.00 2.50
213 Caris LeVert LTHR .60 1.50
214 Demetrius Jackson LTHR .50 1.25
215 Marquese Chriss LTHR 1.25 3.00
216 Tomas Satoransky LTHR .50 1.25
217 Henry Ellenson LTHR .60 1.50
218 Cheick Diallo LTHR .50 1.25
219 Malcolm Brogdon LTHR 1.25 3.00
220 Jakob Poeltl LTHR .60 1.50
221 Jamal Murray LTHR 1.50 4.00
222 Tyler Ulis LTHR 1.50 4.00
223 Ivica Zubac LTHR .75 2.00
224 Thon Maker LTHR 1.50 4.00
225 Dario Saric LTHR 1.50 4.00
226 Malachi Richardson LTHR .60 1.50
227 Damian Jones LTHR .50 1.25
228 Dragan Bender LTHR .60 1.50
229 Buddy Hield LTHR 1.25 3.00
230 Juan Hernangomez LTHR .60 1.50
231 Damian Jones WOOD .75 2.00
232 Domantas Sabonis WOOD 1.25 3.00
233 Isaiah Whitehead WOOD .75 2.00
234 Marquese Chriss WOOD 2.00 5.00
235 Jamal Murray WOOD 2.50 6.00
236 Deyonta Davis WOOD .75 2.00
237 Thon Maker WOOD 2.50 6.00
238 Kris Dunn WOOD 2.50 6.00
239 Dragan Bender WOOD 1.00 2.50
240 Skal Labissiere WOOD 1.25 3.00
241 Brandon Ingram WOOD 5.00 12.00
242 Malcolm Brogdon WOOD 2.00 5.00
243 Tyler Ulis WOOD 2.50 6.00
244 Patrick McCaw WOOD 1.50 4.00
245 Dario Saric WOOD 2.50 6.00
246 Jaylen Brown WOOD 3.00 8.00
247 Buddy Hield WOOD 2.00 5.00
248 Ben Simmons WOOD 10.00 25.00
249 Dejounte Murray WOOD 1.50 4.00
250 Jakob Poeltl WOOD 1.00 2.50
251 Ivica Zubac WOOD 1.25 3.00
252 Georgios Papagiannis WOOD .75 2.00
253 Malachi Richardson WOOD 1.00 2.50
254 Denzel Valentine WOOD 1.00 2.50
255 Domantas Sabonis ETCH .75 2.00
256 Henry Ellenson ETCH .60 1.50
257 Damian Jones ETCH .50 1.25
258 Ben Simmons ETCH 6.00 15.00
259 Malcolm Brogdon ETCH 1.25 3.00
260 Buddy Hield ETCH 1.25 3.00
261 A.J. Hammons ETCH .50 1.25
262 Brice Johnson ETCH .50 1.25
263 Deyonta Davis ETCH .50 1.25
264 Brandon Ingram ETCH 3.00 8.00
265 Diamond Stone ETCH .50 1.25
266 Jamal Murray ETCH 1.50 4.00
267 Georgios Papagiannis ETCH .50 1.25
268 Caris LeVert ETCH .60 1.50
269 Ivica Zubac ETCH .75 2.00
270 Jaylen Brown ETCH 2.00 5.00
271 Marquese Chriss ETCH 1.25 3.00
272 Dario Saric ETCH 1.50 4.00
273 Denzel Valentine ETCH .60 1.50
274 Tomas Satoransky ETCH .50 1.25
275 Malachi Richardson ETCH .60 1.50
276 Skal Labissiere ETCH .75 2.00
277 Cheick Diallo ETCH .50 1.25
278 Dragan Bender ETCH .60 1.50
279 Isaiah Whitehead ETCH .50 1.25
280 Jakob Poeltl ETCH .60 1.50
281 Juan Hernangomez ETCH .60 1.50
282 Patrick McCaw ETCH 1.00 2.50
283 Dejounte Murray ETCH 1.00 2.50
284 Tyler Ulis ETCH 1.50 4.00
285 Kris Dunn ETCH 1.50 4.00
286 Demetrius Jackson ETCH .50 1.25
287 Thon Maker ETCH 1.50 4.00

2016-17 Panini Threads Century Proof Dazzle

*DAZZLE: 1.2X TO 3X BASIC
*DAZZLE RC: .6X TO 1.5X BASIC RC
RANDOM INSERTS IN PACKS
156 Ben Simmons 25.00 60.00

2016-17 Panini Threads Century Proof Dazzle Orange

*ORANGE: 4X TO 10X BASIC
*ORANGE RC: 2X TO 5X BASIC RC
RANDOM INSERTS IN PACKS
STATED PRINT RUN 25 SER.#'d SETS
156 Ben Simmons 60.00 150.00

2016-17 Panini Threads Century Proof Holo

*HOLO: 1.5X TO 4X BASIC
*HOLO RC: 1X TO 2.5X BASIC RC
RANDOM INSERTS IN PACKS
156 Ben Simmons 30.00 80.00

2016-17 Panini Threads Century Proof Red

*RED: 1X TO 2.5X BASIC
*RED: .5X TO 1.2X BASIC RC
RANDOM INSERTS IN PACKS
STATED PRINT RUN 199 SER.#'d SETS
156 Ben Simmons 10.00 25.00

2016-17 Panini Threads Authentic Threads

RANDOM INSERTS IN PACKS
1 Karl-Anthony Towns 4.00 10.00
2 Jeff Teague 2.50 6.00
3 LeBron James 10.00 25.00
4 DeMar DeRozan 3.00 8.00
5 Marc Gasol 3.00 8.00
6 Blake Griffin 3.00 8.00
7 Dwyane Wade 4.00 10.00
8 Draymond Green 4.00 10.00
9 Eric Gordon 2.50 6.00
10 Kawhi Leonard 5.00 12.00
11 James Harden 4.00 10.00
12 Damian Lillard 4.00 10.00
13 DeMarcus Cousins 3.00 8.00
14 Anthony Davis 4.00 10.00
15 Dennis Schroder 2.50 6.00
16 D'Angelo Russell 4.00 10.00
17 Kyle Lowry 2.50 6.00
18 Kyrie Irving 5.00 12.00
19 Andre Drummond 3.00 8.00
20 Devin Booker 4.00 10.00
21 Kevin Love 3.00 8.00
22 Andrew Wiggins 4.00 10.00
23 DeAndre Jordan 3.00 8.00
24 Emmanuel Mudiay 2.50 6.00
25 Ricky Rubio 3.00 8.00
26 John Wall 4.00 10.00
27 Goran Dragic 2.50 6.00
28 Dirk Nowitzki 4.00 10.00
29 Serge Ibaka 2.50 6.00
30 Brook Lopez 2.50 6.00
31 Kemba Walker 3.00 8.00
32 Derrick Rose 4.00 10.00
33 Elfrid Payton 2.50 6.00
34 Dwight Howard 2.50 6.00
35 Bradley Beal 3.00 8.00
36 Eric Bledsoe 2.50 6.00
37 Harrison Barnes 2.50 6.00
38 Danilo Gallinari 2.50 6.00
39 Chris Paul 4.00 10.00
40 Carmelo Anthony 4.00 10.00

2016-17 Panini Threads Autographs

RANDOM INSERTS IN PACKS
1 Trey Lyles
2 Mike Muscala 2.50 6.00
3 James Ennis
4 Cody Zeller 2.50 6.00
5 C.J. McCollum
6 Justin Hamilton
7 Ian Clark 2.50 6.00
8 Josh Huestis
9 Larry Nance Jr. 3.00 8.00
10 Sean Kilpatrick 2.50 6.00
11 Mario Hezonja
12 Richaun Holmes 2.50 6.00
13 Dwight Powell
14 E'Twaun Moore
15 Maurice Harkless 2.50 6.00
16 Victor Oladipo 3.00 8.00
17 Kyle O'Quinn 2.50 6.00
18 Justin Anderson 3.00 8.00
19 Kobe Bryant 60.00 150.00
20 Michael Carter-Williams 2.50 6.00
21 Langston Galloway
22 Jordan McRae
23 Kevin Love
24 Kevin Durant 75.00 200.00
25 Jeremy Lin 15.00 40.00
26 Zach LaVine
27 Karl-Anthony Towns 15.00 40.00
28 Carmelo Anthony
29 Kyrie Irving 30.00 80.00
30 Anthony Davis

2016-17 Panini Threads Automatic

RANDOM INSERTS IN PACKS
1 Steve Nash 3.00 8.00
2 Giannis Antetokounmpo 6.00 15.00
3 Carmelo Anthony 4.00 10.00
4 Russell Westbrook 8.00 20.00
5 Kyle Lowry 2.50 6.00
6 Damian Lillard 6.00 15.00
7 Dirk Nowitzki 4.00 10.00
8 DeMar DeRozan 3.00 8.00
9 Kobe Bryant 12.00 30.00
10 Jimmy Butler 3.00 8.00
11 Kyrie Irving 6.00 15.00
12 Steve Kerr 3.00 8.00
13 John Wall 4.00 10.00
14 James Harden 5.00 12.00
15 C.J. McCollum 2.50 6.00
16 Kevin Durant 8.00 20.00
17 Ray Allen 3.00 8.00
18 Stephen Curry 12.00 30.00
19 Larry Bird 8.00 20.00
20 Klay Thompson 4.00 10.00

2016-17 Panini Threads Board of Directors

RANDOM INSERTS IN PACKS
*DAZZLE: .75X TO 2X BASIC
*RED: .6X TO 1.5X BASIC
*HOLO: 1X TO 2.5X BASIC
*ORANGE/25: 2X TO 5X BASIC
1 Marcin Gortat .40 1.00
2 Hassan Whiteside .40 1.00
3 Hakeem Olajuwon .60 1.50
4 DeAndre Jordan .50 1.25
5 Dennis Rodman 1.00 2.50
6 Anthony Davis 1.00 2.50
7 Wilt Chamberlain 1.00 2.50
8 Dwight Howard .40 1.00
9 Bill Russell .75 2.00
10 Karl-Anthony Towns 1.25 3.00
11 Karl Malone .60 1.50
12 Andre Drummond .50 1.25
13 Shaquille O'Neal 1.25 3.00
14 Rudy Gobert .50 1.25
15 Patrick Ewing .60 1.50

2016-17 Panini Threads Bringing Down the House

RANDOM INSERTS IN PACKS
1 John Wall 3.00 8.00
2 Julius Erving 4.00 10.00
3 Damian Lillard 5.00 12.00
4 Shaquille O'Neal 6.00 15.00
5 Russell Westbrook 6.00 15.00
6 Zach LaVine 2.50 6.00
7 Giannis Antetokounmpo 5.00 12.00
8 Anthony Davis 5.00 12.00
9 DeMar DeRozan 2.50 6.00
10 Dwight Howard 2.00 5.00
11 Shawn Kemp 4.00 10.00
12 Dominique Wilkins 3.00 8.00
13 Kevin Durant 6.00 15.00
14 Kobe Bryant 10.00 25.00
15 Derrick Rose 3.00 8.00

2016-17 Panini Threads Century Collection Materials

RANDOM INSERTS IN PACKS
STATED PRINT RUN 99 SER.#'d SETS
1 Jamal Mashburn 3.00 8.00
2 Tracy McGrady 3.00 8.00
3 Kevin McHale 3.00 8.00
4 Scottie Pippen 6.00 15.00
5 Joe Dumars 3.00 8.00
6 Robert Parish 3.00 8.00
7 Kiki Vandeweghe 2.50 6.00
8 Kareem Abdul-Jabbar 5.00 12.00
9 Gary Payton 3.00 8.00
10 Chris Mullin 3.00 8.00
11 Grant Hill 4.00 10.00
12 Clyde Drexler 4.00 10.00
13 Shaquille O'Neal 4.00 10.00
14 Brent Barry 2.00 5.00
15 Alonzo Mourning 10.00 25.00
16 Alex English 2.50 6.00
17 Karl Malone 4.00 10.00
18 Anfernee Hardaway 5.00 12.00
19 Jason Kidd 3.00 8.00
20 John Stockton 5.00 12.00
21 Nick Van Exel 3.00 8.00
22 Michael Finley 3.00 8.00
23 Patrick Ewing 4.00 10.00
24 Kobe Bryant 10.00 25.00
25 Hakeem Olajuwon 4.00 10.00
26 Larry Johnson 4.00 10.00
27 David Robinson 4.00 10.00
28 Allen Iverson 4.00 10.00
29 Larry Bird 10.00 25.00
30 Tim Duncan 4.00 10.00

2016-17 Panini Threads Century Stars

RANDOM INSERTS IN PACKS
1 Stephen Curry 20.00 50.00
2 LeBron James 40.00 100.00
3 Russell Westbrook 12.00 30.00
4 Kyrie Irving 10.00 25.00
5 Kevin Durant 12.00 30.00
6 Ben Simmons 40.00 100.00
7 Brandon Ingram 20.00 50.00
8 Jaylen Brown 12.00 30.00
9 Kris Dunn 10.00 25.00
10 Buddy Hield 8.00 20.00

2016-17 Panini Threads Debut Threads

RANDOM INSERTS IN PACKS
*PRIME/25: .75X TO 2X BASIC
1 Isaiah Whitehead 2.00 5.00
2 Pascal Siakam 2.00 5.00
3 Henry Ellenson 2.50 6.00
4 Kris Dunn 4.00 10.00
5 Marquese Chriss 4.00 10.00
6 Ivica Zubac 3.00 8.00
7 Jakob Poeltl 2.50 6.00
8 Jamal Murray 4.00 10.00
9 Kay Felder 2.00 5.00
10 Caris LeVert 2.50 6.00
11 Damian Jones 2.00 5.00
12 Tyler Ulis 4.00 10.00
13 Diamond Stone 2.00 5.00
14 Brandon Ingram 5.00 12.00
15 Thon Maker 4.00 10.00
16 Skal Labissiere 3.00 8.00
17 Denzel Valentine 2.50 6.00
18 Malachi Richardson 2.50 6.00
19 A.J. Hammons 2.00 5.00
20 Dragan Bender 2.50 6.00
21 Deyonta Davis 2.00 5.00
22 Jaylen Brown 5.00 12.00
23 Demetrius Jackson 2.00 5.00
24 Cheick Diallo 2.00 5.00
25 Brice Johnson 2.00 5.00
26 Buddy Hield 4.00 10.00
27 Juan Hernangomez 2.50 6.00
28 Patrick McCaw 4.00 10.00
29 Malcolm Brogdon 4.00 10.00
30 Stephen Zimmerman 2.00 5.00

2016-17 Panini Threads Floor Generals

RANDOM INSERTS IN PACKS
*DAZZLE: .75X TO 2X BASIC
*RED: .6X TO 1.5X BASIC
*HOLO: 1X TO 2.5X BASIC
*ORANGE/25: 2X TO 5X BASIC
1 James Harden .75 2.00
2 Ricky Rubio .50 1.25
3 Chris Paul .60 1.50
4 Kyrie Irving 1.00 2.50
5 Damian Lillard 1.00 2.50
6 Stephen Curry 2.00 5.00
7 Mark Jackson .40 1.00
8 Anfernee Hardaway 1.25 3.00
9 John Stockton .75 2.00
10 Jason Kidd .50 1.25
11 Russell Westbrook 1.25 3.00
12 Steve Francis .40 1.00
13 John Wall .60 1.50
14 Gary Payton .50 1.25
15 Rajon Rondo .50 1.25

2016-17 Panini Threads Front-Row Seat

RANDOM INSERTS IN PACKS
*DAZZLE: .75X TO 2X BASIC
*RED: .6X TO 1.5X BASIC
*HOLO: 1X TO 2.5X BASIC
*ORANGE/25: 2X TO 5X BASIC
1 Dwyane Wade .75 2.00
2 Paul George .60 1.50
3 Carmelo Anthony .60 1.50
4 Kawhi Leonard .75 2.00
5 Damian Lillard 1.00 2.50
6 Stephen Curry 2.00 5.00
7 Al Horford .40 1.00
8 Paul Millsap .50 1.25
9 Kevin Love .50 1.25
10 DeMarcus Cousins .50 1.25
11 Mike Conley .40 1.00
12 Anthony Davis 1.00 2.50
13 Karl-Anthony Towns 1.25 3.00
14 Russell Westbrook 1.25 3.00
15 DeAndre Jordan .50 1.25
16 Kevin Durant 1.25 3.00
17 John Wall .60 1.50
18 Kyle Lowry .40 1.00
19 Andre Drummond .50 1.25
20 LaMarcus Aldridge .50 1.25
21 Kyrie Irving 1.00 2.50
22 James Harden .75 2.00
23 Marc Gasol .50 1.25
24 Chris Paul .60 1.50
25 Klay Thompson .60 1.50
26 LeBron James 2.00 5.00
27 Jimmy Butler .50 1.25
28 Draymond Green .60 1.50
29 Gordon Hayward .50 1.25
30 Blake Griffin .50 1.25

2016-17 Panini Threads Hardwood Pioneers

RANDOM INSERTS IN PACKS
*DAZZLE: .75X TO 2X BASIC
*RED: .6X TO 1.5X BASIC
*HOLO: 1X TO 2.5X BASIC
*ORANGE/25: 2X TO 5X BASIC
1 Dave DeBusschere .50 1.25
2 Wilt Chamberlain 1.00 2.50
3 Elgin Baylor .50 1.25
4 Oscar Robertson .60 1.50
5 Larry Bird 1.25 3.00
6 Elvin Hayes .50 1.25
7 Jerry West .60 1.50
8 Lenny Wilkens .50 1.25
9 Earl Monroe .50 1.25
10 Bill Russell .75 2.00
11 Kareem Abdul-Jabbar .75 2.00
12 Magic Johnson 1.25 3.00
13 John Havlicek .60 1.50
14 Gail Goodrich .40 1.00
15 Julius Erving .75 2.00

2016-17 Panini Threads High Octane

RANDOM INSERTS IN PACKS
*DAZZLE: .75X TO 2X BASIC
*RED: .6X TO 1.5X BASIC
*HOLO: 1X TO 2.5X BASIC
*ORANGE/25: 2X TO 5X BASIC
1 Allen Iverson .60 1.50
2 Derrick Rose .60 1.50
3 Spud Webb .40 1.00
4 Russell Westbrook 1.25 3.00
5 Manu Ginobili .50 1.25
6 Avery Bradley .40 1.00
7 Clyde Drexler .60 1.50
8 Elfrid Payton .40 1.00
9 Isiah Thomas .50 1.25
10 Dennis Schroder .40 1.00
11 Muggsy Bogues .40 1.00
12 Eric Bledsoe .40 1.00
13 Isaiah Thomas .50 1.25
14 Dwyane Wade .75 2.00
15 Chris Paul .60 1.50
16 Jeff Teague .40 1.00
17 Kenny Smith .40 1.00
18 Victor Oladipo .40 1.00
19 Nate Archibald .40 1.00
20 Kyrie Irving 1.00 2.50
21 James Harden .75 2.00
22 John Wall .60 1.50
23 Damon Stoudamire .40 1.00
24 Tony Parker .50 1.25
25 Rajon Rondo .50 1.25

2016-17 Panini Threads Materials

RANDOM INSERTS IN PACKS
1 Joakim Noah 2.50 6.00
2 Adreian Payne 2.00 5.00
3 Karl-Anthony Towns 4.00 10.00
4 Al-Farouq Aminu 2.50 6.00
5 Jusuf Nurkic 2.00 5.00
6 Dante Exum 2.50 6.00
7 Rajon Rondo 3.00 8.00
8 Jeff Teague 2.50 6.00
9 LeBron James 10.00 25.00
10 Andrew Bogut 2.50 6.00
11 DeMar DeRozan 3.00 8.00
12 Marc Gasol 3.00 8.00
13 Blake Griffin 3.00 8.00
14 Dwyane Wade 4.00 10.00
15 Draymond Green 4.00 10.00
16 Eric Gordon 2.50 6.00
17 Andre Iguodala 2.50 6.00
18 Kawhi Leonard 5.00 12.00
19 James Harden 4.00 10.00
20 Deron Williams 2.50 6.00
21 Brandon Knight 2.50 6.00
22 Damian Lillard 4.00 10.00
23 DeMarcus Cousins 3.00 8.00
24 Bojan Bogdanovic 2.00 5.00
25 Anthony Davis 4.00 10.00
26 Dennis Schroder 2.50 6.00
27 D'Angelo Russell 4.00 10.00
28 Kyle Lowry 2.50 6.00
29 Derrick Favors 2.50 6.00
30 Aaron Gordon 2.50 6.00
31 Kyrie Irving 5.00 12.00
32 Andre Drummond 3.00 8.00
33 Devin Booker 4.00 10.00
34 Greg Monroe 2.50 6.00
35 Kevin Love 3.00 8.00
36 Jrue Holiday 2.50 6.00
37 Brandon Jennings 2.00 5.00
38 Ben McLemore 2.00 5.00
39 Jonas Valanciunas 2.50 6.00
40 Al Horford 2.50 6.00
41 Andrew Wiggins 4.00 10.00
42 Dwight Powell 2.00 5.00
43 DeAndre Jordan 3.00 8.00
44 Emmanuel Mudiay 2.50 6.00
45 Marcin Gortat 2.50 6.00
46 Ricky Rubio 3.00 8.00
47 John Wall 4.00 10.00
48 DeMarre Carroll 2.00 5.00
49 Goran Dragic 2.50 6.00
50 Al Jefferson 2.50 6.00
51 Dirk Nowitzki 4.00 10.00
52 Serge Ibaka 2.50 6.00
53 J.J. Barea 2.50 6.00
54 Brook Lopez 2.50 6.00
55 Kemba Walker 3.00 8.00
56 Derrick Rose 4.00 10.00
57 Elfrid Payton 2.50 6.00
58 Dwight Howard 2.50 6.00
59 Bradley Beal 3.00 8.00
60 Eric Bledsoe 2.50 6.00
61 Jeremy Lamb 2.00 5.00
62 Harrison Barnes 2.50 6.00
63 Justin Anderson 2.50 6.00
64 C.J. McCollum 2.50 6.00
65 Danilo Gallinari 2.50 6.00
66 Chris Paul 4.00 10.00
67 Darren Collison 2.50 6.00
68 Devin Harris 2.00 5.00
69 Michael Kidd-Gilchrist 2.50 6.00
70 Carmelo Anthony 4.00 10.00

2016-17 Panini Threads NBA Legends Ink

RANDOM INSERTS IN PACKS
PRINT RUNS B/WN 10-99 COPIES PER
NO PRICING ON QTY 10
1 Kobe Bryant/99 60.00 150.00
2 Vin Baker/99 3.00 8.00
3 Bill Willoughby/99
4 Magic Johnson/99 20.00 50.00
5 Spud Webb/99 4.00 10.00
6 Walter Berry/99 3.00 8.00
7 Dan Issel/99
8 Tom Gugliotta/99
9 World B. Free/99
10 Elvin Hayes/59 5.00 12.00
11 Bob Dandridge/99
12 Sidney Moncrief/99
13 Zydrunas Ilgauskas/99 4.00 10.00
14 Kenny Anderson/49
15 Dennis Scott/49
16 Shane Battier/69
17 Vinny Del Negro/99 4.00 10.00
18 Dennis Rodman/99 30.00 80.00
19 Vernon Maxwell/49
20 Rashard Lewis/99
21 Kurt Rambis/49
22 Juwan Howard/99 4.00 10.00
23 Kevin Willis/99
24 Ron Harper/99 5.00 12.00
25 Raef LaFrentz/99 3.00 8.00
26 Larry Nance/99 4.00 10.00
27 Scottie Pippen/49 40.00 100.00
29 Avery Johnson/99 4.00 10.00
30 Kendall Gill/99

2016-17 Panini Threads Rookie Signage

RANDOM INSERTS IN PACKS
PRINT RUNS B/WN 199-299 COPIES PER

1 Brandon Ingram/199 30.00 80.00
2 Jaylen Brown/199 20.00 50.00
3 Kris Dunn/199 10.00 25.00
4 Buddy Hield/299 15.00 40.00
6 Jamal Murray/199 20.00 50.00
8 Kay Felder/199 3.00 8.00
9 Marquese Chriss/199 8.00 20.00
10 Dragan Bender/199 6.00 15.00
11 Malcolm Brogdon/199 15.00 40.00
12 Denzel Valentine/299 4.00 10.00
13 Taurean Prince/299 5.00 12.00
14 DeAndre' Bembry/299 3.00 8.00
15 Brice Johnson/199
16 Wade Baldwin IV/199
17 Malachi Richardson/199 4.00 10.00
18 Juan Hernangomez/199 10.00 25.00
19 Ivica Zubac/299 6.00 15.00
20 Cheick Diallo/299
22 Henry Ellenson/199 4.00 10.00
23 Georges Niang/199 3.00 8.00
24 Jakob Poeltl/199 4.00 10.00
25 Pascal Siakam/199
26 Domantas Sabonis/199 8.00 20.00
27 Dario Saric/199 10.00 25.00
28 Damian Jones/199 3.00 8.00
29 Skal Labissiere/199 12.00 30.00
30 Diamond Stone/299 3.00 8.00
31 Paul Zipser/199 5.00 12.00
32 Demetrius Jackson/299 3.00 8.00
33 Deyonta Davis/299 3.00 8.00
34 Malik Beasley/199 3.00 8.00
35 Georgios Papagiannis/299 3.00 8.00
36 Mindaugas Kuzminskas/299 4.00 10.00
37 Thon Maker/299 12.00 30.00
38 Jake Layman/299 4.00 10.00
39 Michael Gbinije/299 3.00 8.00
40 T. Luwawu-Cabarrot/299 6.00 15.00

2016-17 Panini Threads Signage

RANDOM INSERTS IN PACKS
PRINT RUNS B/WN 49-99 COPIES PER
1 C.J. McCollum/99 6.00 15.00
2 Victor Oladipo/99
3 Trey Lyles/99 4.00 10.00
4 Jason Terry/99 4.00 10.00
5 Norman Powell/99
6 Jeremy Lin/49 10.00 25.00
7 Zach LaVine/99 5.00 12.00
8 Justise Winslow/49
9 Tristan Thompson/49 4.00 10.00
10 Rondae Hollis-Jefferson/99 3.00 8.00
11 Kevin Durant/99 75.00 150.00
12 Kyrie Irving/99 25.00 60.00
13 Blake Griffin/49
14 Jabari Parker/75
15 Andrew Wiggins/99 10.00 25.00
16 Isaiah Thomas/49 12.00 30.00
17 Karl-Anthony Towns/99 25.00 60.00
18 Carmelo Anthony/49
19 Kristaps Porzingis/99 15.00 40.00
20 Kobe Bryant/99 60.00 150.00
21 Marc Gasol/49
22 Myles Turner/75
23 Devin Booker/49 20.00 50.00
24 John Wall/49 10.00 25.00
25 Andre Drummond/99 5.00 12.00
26 Anthony Davis/49 25.00 60.00
27 J.J. Barea/99 20.00 50.00
28 Sean Kilpatrick/99
29 Al Horford/49
30 E'Twaun Moore/99 3.00 8.00

2016-17 Panini Threads Swingmen

RANDOM INSERTS IN PACKS
1 LeBron James 20.00 50.00
2 Gordon Hayward 5.00 12.00
3 Nicolas Batum 4.00 10.00
4 Larry Bird 12.00 30.00
5 Klay Thompson 6.00 15.00
6 Julius Erving 8.00 20.00
7 Andre Iguodala 4.00 10.00
8 Andrew Wiggins 8.00 20.00
9 Kevin Durant 12.00 30.00
10 Otto Porter 4.00 10.00
11 Paul George 6.00 15.00
12 Kobe Bryant 20.00 50.00
13 Carmelo Anthony 6.00 15.00
14 Jerry West 6.00 15.00
15 Giannis Antetokounmpo 10.00 25.00
16 Scottie Pippen 10.00 25.00
17 DeMar DeRozan 5.00 12.00
18 Tobias Harris 4.00 10.00
19 Kawhi Leonard 8.00 20.00
20 Harrison Barnes 4.00 10.00

2016-17 Panini Threads Team Threads Die Cuts

RANDOM INSERTS IN PACKS
1 Dwyane Wade 2.50 6.00
2 Kyrie Irving 3.00 8.00
3 Isaiah Thomas 1.50 4.00
4 Avery Bradley 1.25 3.00
5 Blake Griffin 1.50 4.00
6 Justise Winslow 1.25 3.00
7 Carmelo Anthony 2.00 5.00
8 Kristaps Porzingis 3.00 8.00
9 Jordan Clarkson 1.25 3.00
10 Jeremy Lin 1.50 4.00
11 Anthony Davis 3.00 8.00
12 Jrue Holiday 1.25 3.00
13 DeMar DeRozan 1.50 4.00
14 Ryan Anderson 1.25 3.00
15 Devin Booker 2.50 6.00
16 Andrew Wiggins 2.50 6.00
17 Karl-Anthony Towns 4.00 10.00
18 Stephen Curry 10.00 25.00
19 Kevin Durant 8.00 20.00
20 John Wall 2.00 5.00
21 Joel Embiid 2.50 6.00
22 Robert Covington 1.00 2.50
23 Giannis Antetokounmpo 3.00 8.00
24 Jabari Parker 2.00 5.00
25 Jimmy Butler 1.50 4.00
26 LeBron James 6.00 15.00
27 Chris Paul 2.00 5.00
28 Marc Gasol 1.50 4.00
29 Mike Conley 1.25 3.00
30 Dwight Howard 1.25 3.00
31 Dennis Schroder 1.25 3.00
32 Goran Dragic 1.25 3.00
33 Frank Kaminsky 1.25 3.00
34 Kemba Walker 1.50 4.00
35 Gordon Hayward 1.50 4.00
36 Rodney Hood 1.25 3.00
37 DeMarcus Cousins 1.50 4.00
38 Rudy Gay 1.50 4.00
39 Aaron Gordon 1.25 3.00
40 Serge Ibaka 1.25 3.00
41 Deron Williams 1.25 3.00
42 Dirk Nowitzki 2.00 5.00
43 Brook Lopez 1.25 3.00
44 Danilo Gallinari 1.25 3.00
45 Nikola Jokic 1.50 4.00
46 Paul George 2.00 5.00
47 Jeff Teague 1.25 3.00
48 Reggie Jackson 1.25 3.00
49 Andre Drummond 1.50 4.00
50 Kyle Lowry 1.25 3.00
51 James Harden 2.50 6.00
52 Kawhi Leonard 2.50 6.00
53 LaMarcus Aldridge 1.50 4.00
54 Eric Bledsoe 1.25 3.00
55 Russell Westbrook 4.00 10.00
56 Steven Adams 1.25 3.00
57 Damian Lillard 3.00 8.00
58 C.J. McCollum 1.25 3.00
59 Markieff Morris 1.00 2.50
60 D'Angelo Russell 2.00 5.00

2016-17 Panini Threads Team Threads Die Cuts Autographs

RANDOM INSERTS IN PACKS
STATED PRINT RUN 99 SER.#'d SETS
1 Dwyane Wade 30.00 80.00
2 Kyrie Irving 50.00 120.00
3 Isaiah Thomas 30.00 80.00
4 Avery Bradley 10.00 25.00
5 Blake Griffin 25.00 60.00
6 Justise Winslow 20.00 50.00
7 Carmelo Anthony
8 Kristaps Porzingis 30.00 80.00
9 Jordan Clarkson 4.00 10.00
10 Jeremy Lin 30.00 80.00
11 Anthony Davis 40.00 100.00
12 Jrue Holiday 8.00 20.00
13 DeMar DeRozan
14 Ryan Anderson 4.00 10.00
15 Devin Booker 50.00 120.00
16 Andrew Wiggins 25.00 60.00
17 Karl-Anthony Towns 40.00 100.00
18 Stephen Curry 300.00 500.00
19 Kevin Durant 150.00 400.00
20 John Wall

2016-17 Panini Threads Team Threads Rookie Die Cuts

RANDOM INSERTS IN PACKS
1 Brandon Ingram 6.00 15.00
2 Jaylen Brown 4.00 10.00
3 Kris Dunn 3.00 8.00
4 Buddy Hield 2.50 6.00
5 Patrick McCaw 2.00 5.00
6 Jamal Murray 3.00 8.00
7 Tyler Ulis 3.00 8.00
8 Kay Felder 1.00 2.50
9 Marquese Chriss 2.50 6.00
10 Dragan Bender 1.25 3.00
11 Malcolm Brogdon 2.50 6.00
12 Denzel Valentine 1.25 3.00
13 Taurean Prince 1.50 4.00
14 DeAndre' Bembry 1.00 2.50
15 Brice Johnson 1.00 2.50
16 Wade Baldwin IV 1.00 2.50
17 Malachi Richardson 1.25 3.00
18 Juan Hernangomez 1.25 3.00
19 Ivica Zubac 1.50 4.00
20 Cheick Diallo 1.00 2.50
21 Jakob Poeltl 1.25 3.00
22 Pascal Siakam 1.00 2.50
23 Domantas Sabonis 1.50 4.00
24 Dario Saric 3.00 8.00
25 Damian Jones 1.00 2.50
26 Skal Labissiere 1.50 4.00
27 Demetrius Jackson 1.00 2.50
28 Deyonta Davis 1.00 2.50
29 Malik Beasley 1.00 2.50
30 Tomas Satoransky 1.00 2.50
31 Thon Maker 3.00 8.00
32 Chinanu Onuaku 1.00 2.50
33 Dorian Finney-Smith 1.25 3.00
34 Caris LeVert 1.25 3.00
35 Henry Ellenson 1.25 3.00
36 Georges Niang 1.00 2.50
37 Diamond Stone 1.00 2.50
38 Paul Zipser 1.50 4.00
39 Georgios Papagiannis 1.00 2.50
40 Ben Simmons 20.00 50.00

2016-17 Panini Threads Team Threads Rookie Die Cuts Autographs

RANDOM INSERTS IN PACKS
STATED PRINT RUN 199 SER.#'d SETS
1 Brandon Ingram 50.00 120.00
2 Jaylen Brown 40.00 100.00
3 Kris Dunn 20.00 50.00
4 Buddy Hield 30.00 80.00
5 Patrick McCaw 15.00 40.00
6 Jamal Murray
7 Tyler Ulis
8 Kay Felder
9 Marquese Chriss
10 Dragan Bender 12.00 30.00
11 Malcolm Brogdon 15.00 40.00
12 Denzel Valentine 4.00 10.00
13 Taurean Prince
14 DeAndre' Bembry 3.00 8.00
15 Brice Johnson
16 Wade Baldwin IV 3.00 8.00
17 Malachi Richardson 8.00 20.00
18 Juan Hernangomez 10.00 25.00
19 Ivica Zubac 25.00 60.00
20 Cheick Diallo 8.00 20.00
21 Jakob Poeltl
22 Pascal Siakam 3.00 8.00
23 Domantas Sabonis 12.00 30.00
24 Dario Saric 25.00 60.00
25 Damian Jones 3.00 8.00
26 Skal Labissiere 12.00 30.00
27 Demetrius Jackson
28 Deyonta Davis 3.00 8.00
29 Malik Beasley
30 Tomas Satoransky 8.00 20.00
31 Thon Maker 20.00 50.00
32 Chinanu Onuaku 3.00 8.00
33 Dorian Finney-Smith 4.00 10.00

2016-17 Panini Threads The Rooks

RANDOM INSERTS IN PACKS
1 Skal Labissiere 5.00 12.00
2 Taurean Prince 5.00 12.00
3 Jakob Poeltl 4.00 10.00
4 Deyonta Davis 3.00 8.00
5 Dejounte Murray 6.00 15.00
6 Jamal Murray 10.00 25.00
7 Pascal Siakam 3.00 8.00
8 Domantas Sabonis 5.00 12.00
9 Dario Saric 10.00 25.00
10 Ben Simmons 25.00 60.00
11 Cheick Diallo 3.00 8.00
12 Malik Beasley 3.00 8.00
13 Juan Hernangomez 4.00 10.00
14 Brandon Ingram 20.00 50.00
15 Tyler Ulis 10.00 25.00
16 Georgios Papagiannis 3.00 8.00
17 Ivica Zubac 5.00 12.00
18 Henry Ellenson 4.00 10.00
19 Denzel Valentine 4.00 10.00
20 Malcolm Brogdon 8.00 20.00
21 Dragan Bender 4.00 10.00
22 Brice Johnson 3.00 8.00
23 Patrick McCaw 6.00 15.00
24 Diamond Stone 3.00 8.00
25 Kris Dunn 10.00 25.00
26 Caris LeVert 4.00 10.00
27 Jaylen Brown 12.00 30.00
28 Damian Jones 3.00 8.00
29 Malachi Richardson 4.00 10.00
30 Buddy Hield 8.00 20.00
31 Isaiah Whitehead 3.00 8.00
32 Stephen Zimmerman 3.00 8.00
33 Timothe Luwawu-Cabarrot 6.00 15.00
34 Marquese Chriss 8.00 20.00
35 Thon Maker 10.00 25.00

2013-14 Panini Titanium

1 Jrue Holiday .50 1.25
2 Gerald Wallace .40 1.00
3 Nikola Vucevic .40 1.00
4 Deron Williams .40 1.00
5 Luol Deng .40 1.00
6 Channing Frye .40 1.00
7 Damian Lillard 1.00 2.50
8 Manu Ginobili .50 1.25
9 Dirk Nowitzki .60 1.50
10 Tim Duncan .75 2.00
11 Greivis Vasquez .40 1.00
12 Dion Waiters .40 1.00
13 Dwight Howard .40 1.00
14 Evan Turner .30 .75
15 Kyrie Irving 1.00 2.50
16 Gerald Henderson .30 .75
17 Chris Bosh .50 1.25
18 Paul George .60 1.50
19 Arron Afflalo .30 .75
20 James Harden .75 2.00
21 Chris Paul .60 1.50
22 Zach Randolph .40 1.00
23 Carmelo Anthony .60 1.50
24 Derrick Favors .40 1.00
25 Brandon Knight .40 1.00
26 Josh Smith .40 1.00
27 Kemba Walker .50 1.25
28 Amar'e Stoudemire .40 1.00
29 Jameer Nelson .30 .75
30 Al Horford .40 1.00
31 Kobe Bryant 2.00 5.00
32 Rudy Gay .50 1.25
33 John Wall .60 1.50
34 Danny Granger .40 1.00
35 Jeff Green .40 1.00
36 Ricky Rubio .50 1.25
37 Rajon Rondo .50 1.25
38 Roy Hibbert .40 1.00
39 Kevin Martin .40 1.00
40 Eric Bledsoe .40 1.00
41 Jeremy Lin .50 1.25
42 Kevin Garnett .75 2.00
43 Carl Landry .30 .75
44 Blake Griffin .50 1.25
45 Enes Kanter .30 .75
46 Al Jefferson .40 1.00
47 Paul Millsap .50 1.25
48 Steve Novak
49 Dwyane Wade .75 2.00
50 Anthony Davis 1.00 2.50
51 Andre Drummond .50 1.25
52 Joakim Noah .40 1.00
53 Serge Ibaka .40 1.00
54 Jason Richardson .50 1.25
55 DeMarcus Cousins .50 1.25
56 Nicolas Batum .40 1.00
57 Paul Pierce .50 1.25
58 LeBron James 2.00 5.00
59 DeMar DeRozan .50 1.25
60 LaMarcus Aldridge .50 1.25
61 J.J. Redick .50 1.25
62 Gordon Hayward .50 1.25
63 Bradley Beal .50 1.25
64 Tyson Chandler .40 1.00
65 Mike Conley .40 1.00
66 Harrison Barnes .40 1.00
67 Thaddeus Young .30 .75
68 Shawn Marion .40 1.00
69 Jeff Teague .40 1.00
70 Kevin Love .50 1.25
71 Carlos Boozer .40 1.00
72 O.J. Mayo .30 .75
73 DeAndre Jordan .50 1.25
74 Andre Miller .40 1.00
75 Steve Nash .50 1.25
76 Klay Thompson .60 1.50
77 Anderson Varejao .30 .75
78 Pau Gasol .50 1.25
79 Kenneth Faried .40 1.00
80 Brandon Jennings .30 .75
81 Russell Westbrook 1.25 3.00
82 Tyreke Evans .30 .75
83 Vince Carter .60 1.50
84 Marcin Gortat .40 1.00
85 Jimmer Fredette .30 .75
86 Monta Ellis .40 1.00
87 Nikola Pekovic .30 .75
88 George Hill .40 1.00
89 Derrick Rose .60 1.50
90 Goran Dragic .40 1.00
91 Andrew Bogut .40 1.00
92 Mario Chalmers .40 1.00
93 Larry Sanders .30 .75
94 Joe Johnson .40 1.00
95 Stephen Curry 2.00 5.00
96 J.R. Smith .40 1.00
97 Tony Parker .50 1.25
98 Marc Gasol .50 1.25
99 Kevin Durant 1.25 3.00
100 Ty Lawson .30 .75

2013-14 Panini Titanium Draft Position

*JSY NUM p/r 15-19: .75X TO 2X RET RC
*JSY NUM p/r 15-19: 1.5X TO 4X RET VET
*JSY NUM p/r 20-25: .6X TO 1.5X RET RC
*JSY NUM p/r 20-25: 1.2X TO 3X RET VET
*JSY NUM p/r 26-36: .5X TO 1.2X RET RC
*JSY NUM p/r 26-36: 1X TO 2.5X RET VET
*JSY NUM p/r 37-49: .4X TO 1X RET RC
*JSY NUM p/r 56-60: .5X TO 1.2X RET VET
PRINT RUNS B/WN 1-60 COPIES PER
NO PRICING ON QTY 14 OR LESS

2013-14 Panini Titanium Draft Year

*DRAFT YR: .5X TO 1.2X BASIC RETAIL
PRINT RUNS B/WN 1-99 COPIES PER
NO PRICING ON QTY 13 OR LESS

2013-14 Panini Titanium Electric Endorsements

PRINT RUNS B/WN 25-299 COPIES PER
EXCHANGE DEADLINE 8/26/2015
1 Kobe Bryant/75 75.00 150.00
2 Harrison Barnes/99 8.00 20.00
3 Carlos Delfino/299 3.00 8.00
4 Blake Griffin/25 25.00 60.00
5 Mark Jackson/99 4.00 10.00
6 Isaiah Thomas/299 12.00 30.00
7 Luc Mbah a Moute/299 3.00 8.00
8 Kevin Durant/75 60.00 150.00
9 Sean Elliott/299 5.00 12.00
10 Anfernee Hardaway/49 40.00 100.00
11 Eddie Jones/149 4.00 10.00
12 Kyrie Irving/49 50.00 120.00
13 Kawhi Leonard/249 40.00 100.00
14 Jarrett Jack/99 4.00 10.00
15 MarShon Brooks/199 4.00 10.00
16 Tony Parker/49 30.00 80.00
17 Grant Hill/49 40.00 100.00
18 Stephen Curry/49 75.00 200.00
19 Michael Finley/49 8.00 20.00
20 Kenny Walker/249 3.00 8.00

2013-14 Panini Titanium Jersey Number

*JSY NUM p/r 15-19: .75X TO 2X RET RC
*JSY NUM p/r 15-19: 1.5X TO 4X RET VET
*JSY NUM p/r 20-25: .6X TO 1.5X RET RC
*JSY NUM p/r 20-25: 1.2X TO 3X RET VET
*JSY NUM p/r 26-36: .5X TO 1.2X RET RC
*JSY NUM p/r 26-36: 1X TO 2.5X RET VET
*JSY NUM p/r 37-49: .4X TO 1X RET RC
*JSY NUM p/r 37-49: .75X TO 2X RET VET
*JSY NUM p/r 50-100: .5X TO 1.2X RET VET
PRINT RUNS B/WN 1-100 COPIES PER
NO PRICING ON QTY 14 OR LESS
115 G.Antetokounmpo/34 40.00 100.00
172 Kevin Durant/35 30.00 80.00

2013-14 Panini Titanium Titanum 22

*TITAN 22 1-100: 8X TO 20X BASIC RET.
*TITAN 22 101-1142: .6X TO 1.5X BASIC RET.
*TITAN 22 143-200: 1.2X TO 3X BASIC RET.
STATED PRINT RUN 22 SER.#'d SETS

2013-14 Panini Titanium Atomic Numbers

STATED PRINT RUN 99 SER.#'d SETS
1 Bernard King 2.00 5.00
2 Clyde Drexler 3.00 8.00
3 Danny Ainge 2.50 6.00
4 Dave DeBusschere 2.50 6.00
5 Elgin Baylor 2.50 6.00
6 George Karl 2.50 6.00
7 Jamaal Franklin 1.50 4.00
8 Jay Williams 1.50 4.00
9 Otto Porter 2.50 6.00
10 Rolando Blackman 2.00 5.00
11 Isaiah Thomas 2.50 6.00
12 Taj Gibson 2.00 5.00
13 Tiago Splitter 2.00 5.00
14 Moses Malone 2.50 6.00
15 Tom Chambers 2.00 5.00
16 Miles Plumlee 1.50 4.00
17 Jim Jackson 1.50 4.00
18 Matt Barnes 1.50 4.00
19 Larry Nance 2.00 5.00
20 John Salley 1.50 4.00
21 John Drew 2.50 6.00
22 Rod Higgins 2.50 6.00

2013-14 Panini Titanium Conductors

STATED PRINT RUN 49 SER.#'d SETS
1 Jrue Holiday 3.00 8.00
2 Steve Nash 3.00 8.00
3 Raymond Felton 2.50 6.00
4 Deron Williams 2.50 6.00
5 Chris Paul 4.00 10.00
6 Stephen Curry 12.00 30.00
7 Tony Parker 3.00 8.00
8 Jeremy Lin 3.00 8.00
9 Jose Calderon 2.00 5.00
10 Russell Westbrook 8.00 20.00
11 Mario Chalmers 2.50 6.00
12 Damian Lillard 6.00 15.00
13 Rajon Rondo 3.00 8.00
14 John Wall 4.00 10.00
15 Kyrie Irving 6.00 15.00
16 Mike Conley 2.50 6.00
17 Ty Lawson 2.00 5.00
18 Ricky Rubio 3.00 8.00
19 Pete Maravich 5.00 12.00
20 John Stockton 5.00 12.00
21 Jason Kidd 3.00 8.00
22 Mark Jackson 2.50 6.00
23 Magic Johnson 8.00 20.00
24 Isiah Thomas 3.00 8.00
25 Gary Payton 3.00 8.00
26 Tim Hardaway 3.00 8.00
27 Oscar Robertson 4.00 10.00
28 Bob Cousy 5.00 12.00

2013-14 Panini Titanium Double Double Jerseys

PRINT RUNS B/WN 149-279 COPIES PER
1 Amar'e Stoudemire/279 3.00 8.00
2 Taj Gibson/279 3.00 8.00
3 JaVale McGee/279 3.00 8.00
4 Deron Williams/279 3.00 8.00
5 Jeremy Lin/279 4.00 10.00
6 LeBron James/279 12.00 30.00
7 Samuel Dalembert/279 2.50 6.00
8 Tyson Chandler/279 3.00 8.00
9 Andre Iguodala/279 3.00 8.00
10 Caron Butler/279 3.00 8.00
11 Kobe Bryant/279 10.00 25.00
12 Joakim Noah/279 3.00 8.00
13 Damian Lillard/279 8.00 20.00
14 Andrew Bynum/279 2.50 6.00
15 Chris Kaman/279 3.00 8.00
16 Brandon Jennings/279 2.50 6.00
17 Goran Dragic/279 3.00 8.00
18 Kenneth Faried/249 3.00 8.00
19 Michael Beasley/279 2.50 6.00
20 Tim Duncan/279 5.00 12.00
21 Paul Pierce/279 4.00 10.00
22 Elton Brand/279 4.00 10.00
23 Carmelo Anthony/279 5.00 12.00
24 Kevin Garnett/279 6.00 15.00
25 Jimmer Fredette/279 2.50 6.00
26 Klay Thompson/279 6.00 15.00
27 Blake Griffin/279 4.00 10.00
28 Dwight Howard/279 3.00 8.00
29 O.J. Mayo/279 2.50 6.00
30 Russell Westbrook/279 5.00 12.00
31 Omer Asik/279 3.00 8.00
32 Zach Randolph/279 3.00 8.00
33 Arron Afflalo/279 2.50 6.00
34 John Wall/279 5.00 12.00
35 Derrick Rose/279 5.00 12.00
36 Udonis Haslem/279 2.50 6.00
37 Greg Monroe/279 3.00 8.00
38 Kevin Love/279 4.00 10.00
39 Rajon Rondo/249 4.00 10.00
40 Ty Lawson/279 2.50 6.00
41 Nick Young/279 4.00 10.00
42 Rodney Stuckey/229 3.00 8.00
43 Evan Turner/279 2.50 6.00
44 Anthony Davis/279 8.00 20.00
45 Dwyane Wade/279 6.00 15.00
46 DeMar DeRozan/279 4.00 10.00
47 Chris Paul/249 5.00 12.00
48 Kevin Durant/279 10.00 25.00
49 Xavier Henry/149 5.00 12.00
50 Tony Parker/249 4.00 10.00

2013-14 Panini Titanium Double Double Jerseys Prime

*PRIME: .75X TO 2X BASIC
PRINT RUNS B/WN 3-25 COPIES PER
NO PRICING ON QTY 10 OR LESS

2013-14 Panini Titanium Draft Day Autographs

EXCHANGE DEADLINE 8/26/2015
1 Ben McLemore 4.00 10.00
2 Otto Porter 10.00 25.00
3 Michael Carter-Williams 5.00 12.00
4 Victor Oladipo 6.00 15.00
5 C.J. McCollum 12.00 30.00
6 Shabazz Muhammad 4.00 10.00
7 Rudy Gobert 8.00 20.00
8 Shane Larkin 3.00 8.00
9 Tony Mitchell
10 Mason Plumlee 5.00 12.00
11 Trey Burke 4.00 10.00
12 Alex Len 4.00 10.00
13 Anthony Bennett 4.00 10.00
14 Sergey Karasev EXCH 3.00 8.00
15 Andre Roberson 3.00 8.00
16 Ricky Ledo 3.00 8.00
17 Giannis Antetokounmpo 60.00 150.00
18 Gorgui Dieng
19 Allen Crabbe
20 Steven Adams 5.00 12.00

2013-14 Panini Titanium Elements Jerseys

*PRIME/15-25: 1X TO 2.5X BASIC
1 Carmelo Anthony 3.00 8.00
2 Grant Hill 3.00 8.00
3 Marcin Gortat 2.00 5.00
4 Ryan Anderson 2.00 5.00
5 Tristan Thompson 2.00 5.00
6 Magic Johnson 6.00 15.00
7 Paul Pierce 2.50 6.00
8 Rasheed Wallace 2.50 6.00
9 Kobe Bryant 10.00 25.00
10 Brandon Jennings 1.50 4.00
11 Joe Johnson 2.00 5.00
12 Blake Griffin 2.50 6.00
13 Alex English 2.00 5.00
14 Danny Green 2.00 5.00
15 J.J. Barea 2.00 5.00
16 Thabo Sefolosha 1.50 4.00
17 LaMarcus Aldridge 2.50 6.00
18 Nene 2.00 5.00
19 Thaddeus Young 1.50 4.00
20 Kevin Martin 2.00 5.00
21 Serge Ibaka 2.00 5.00
22 Metta World Peace 2.50 6.00
23 Kevin Durant 6.00 15.00
24 Jared Sullinger 1.50 4.00
25 Dirk Nowitzki 3.00 8.00
26 Jrue Holiday 2.50 6.00
27 Al Horford 2.00 5.00
28 Bradley Beal 2.50 6.00
29 Kyle Lowry 2.00 5.00
30 Chandler Parsons 2.00 5.00
31 Kenneth Faried 2.00 5.00
32 LeBron James 10.00 25.00
33 Michael Kidd-Gilchrist 2.50 6.00
34 Shaquille O'Neal 5.00 12.00
35 Tracy McGrady 2.50 6.00
36 Raymond Felton 2.00 5.00
37 Luol Deng 2.00 5.00
38 Kawhi Leonard 4.00 10.00
39 Carlos Boozer 2.00 5.00
40 David Lee 1.50 4.00
41 Spencer Hawes 1.50 4.00
42 Amar'e Stoudemire 2.00 5.00
43 Chris Paul 3.00 8.00
44 Deron Williams 2.00 5.00
45 Jason Richardson 2.50 6.00
46 Kemba Walker 2.50 6.00
47 Norris Cole 1.50 4.00
48 Robert Parish 2.50 6.00
49 Will Bynum 1.50 4.00
50 Klay Thompson 3.00 8.00
51 Rajon Rondo 2.50 6.00
52 Nate Robinson 1.50 4.00
53 John Wall 3.00 8.00
54 Iman Shumpert 1.50 4.00
55 Darren Collison 2.00 5.00
56 Bismack Biyombo 1.50 4.00
57 Clyde Drexler 3.00 8.00
58 Kenyon Martin 2.00 5.00
59 Dwyane Wade 4.00 10.00
60 Joakim Noah 2.00 5.00
61 Kevin McHale 2.50 6.00
62 Michael Beasley 1.50 4.00
63 Damian Lillard 5.00 12.00
64 Ty Lawson 1.50 4.00
65 Mike Miller 2.00 5.00
66 Kevin Love 2.50 6.00
67 James Harden 4.00 10.00
68 Andre Miller 2.00 5.00
69 Brook Lopez 2.00 5.00
70 DeAndre Jordan 2.50 6.00
71 Bill Laimbeer 2.00 5.00
72 Greivis Vasquez 2.00 5.00
73 Jameer Nelson 1.50 4.00
74 Pau Gasol 2.50 6.00
75 Tim Duncan 4.00 10.00

2013-14 Panini Titanium Enshrinement Ink

PRINT RUNS B/WN 25-199 COPIES PER
EXCHANGE DEADLINE 8/26/2015
1 Joe Dumars/25
2 Nate Archibald/25 8.00 20.00
3 Earl Monroe/25 20.00 50.00
4 John Stockton/25
5 Chris Mullin/149 10.00 25.00
6 Alex English/199 4.00 10.00
7 Bailey Howell/199 5.00 12.00
8 Gail Goodrich/25 4.00 10.00
9 Nate Thurmond/25
10 Bob Lanier/25 4.00 10.00
11 Kareem Abdul-Jabbar/49 30.00 60.00
12 Robert Parish/25
14 Jamaal Wilkes/199 5.00 12.00
15 Wes Unseld/25 20.00 50.00
16 Larry Bird/49 60.00 120.00
17 Gary Payton/49 5.00 12.00
18 Ralph Sampson/25 15.00 40.00
19 Artis Gilmore/25 8.00 20.00
20 Jerry West/25 30.00 80.00
21 Bob McAdoo/199 10.00 25.00
22 Isiah Thomas/25
23 Jerry Lucas/25 12.00 30.00
24 Adrian Dantley/199
25 Elgin Baylor/25 20.00 50.00
26 Scottie Pippen/49 75.00 150.00
27 David Thompson/199 4.00 10.00
28 Magic Johnson/49 30.00 80.00
29 Karl Malone/49 30.00 80.00
30 Connie Hawkins/199 5.00 12.00

2013-14 Panini Titanium Fundamentals

STATED PRINT RUN 199 SER.#'d SETS
1 Tim Duncan 2.50 6.00
2 Carmelo Anthony 2.00 5.00
3 Deron Williams 1.25 3.00
4 Kyle Lowry 1.25 3.00
5 Greivis Vasquez 1.25 3.00
6 Steve Nash 1.50 4.00
7 Klay Thompson 2.00 5.00
8 Tony Parker 1.50 4.00
9 Dennis Rodman 3.00 8.00
10 Magic Johnson 4.00 10.00
11 Tayshaun Prince 1.25 3.00
12 James Harden 2.50 6.00
13 Kemba Walker 1.50 4.00
14 Goran Dragic 1.25 3.00
15 J.J. Hickson 1.00 2.50
16 Dirk Nowitzki 2.00 5.00
17 Andre Miller 1.25 3.00
18 Chris Paul 2.00 5.00
19 John Stockton 2.50 6.00
20 Hakeem Olajuwon 2.00 5.00
21 Shane Battier 1.25 3.00
22 Kyrie Irving 3.00 8.00
23 Tyreke Evans 1.00 2.50
24 Ricky Rubio 1.50 4.00
25 Kevin Garnett 2.50 6.00
26 Steve Novak 1.00 2.50
27 Ray Allen 1.50 4.00
28 Andre Iguodala 1.25 3.00
29 Karl Malone 2.00 5.00
30 David Robinson 2.50 6.00
31 LeBron James 6.00 15.00
32 Stephen Curry 6.00 15.00
33 Ryan Anderson 1.25 3.00
34 Gordon Hayward 1.50 4.00
35 DeMarcus Cousins 1.50 4.00
36 Kevin Martin 1.25 3.00
37 Chauncey Billups 1.50 4.00
38 Antawn Jamison 1.25 3.00
39 Kareem Abdul-Jabbar 2.50 6.00
40 George Mikan 3.00 8.00
41 Kobe Bryant 6.00 15.00
42 LaMarcus Aldridge 1.50 4.00
43 Ty Lawson 1.00 2.50
44 Damian Lillard 3.00 8.00
45 Jose Calderon 1.00 2.50
46 Jimmer Fredette 1.00 2.50
47 Pau Gasol 1.50 4.00
48 Kyle Korver 1.25 3.00
49 Larry Bird 4.00 10.00
50 Oscar Robertson 2.00 5.00

2013-14 Panini Titanium Game Gear Duals

PRINT RUNS B/WN 49-155 COPIES PER
1 A.Bradley/R.Rondo/125 4.00 10.00
2 K.Walker/M.Gilchrist/155 4.00 10.00
3 D.Nowitzki/J.Kidd/155 5.00 12.00
4 B.Griffin/C.Paul/125 5.00 12.00
5 D.Wade/L.James/155 15.00 40.00
6 E.Udoh/E.Ilyasova/155 2.50 6.00
7 K.Garnett/P.Pierce/155 6.00 15.00
8 K.Durant/R.Westbrook/155 10.00 25.00
9 E.Turner/T.Young/155 2.50 6.00
10 D.Lillard/K.Irving/155 8.00 20.00
11 D.Howard/J.Harden/155 6.00 15.00
12 G.Hill/P.George/155 5.00 12.00
13 A.Horford/J.Teague/125 3.00 8.00
14 K.Bryant/P.Gasol/155 15.00 40.00
15 C.Bosh/U.Haslem/155 4.00 10.00
16 K.Love/K.Martin/155 4.00 10.00
17 D.Waiters/K.Irving/155 8.00 20.00
18 N.Vucevic/V.Oladipo/155 6.00 15.00
19 E.Bledsoe/G.Dragic/155 3.00 8.00
20 I.Thomas/J.Fredette/155 4.00 10.00
21 A.Davis/A.Rivers/155 8.00 20.00
22 C.Anthony/T.Chandler/155 5.00 12.00
23 D.Rose/J.Noah/155 5.00 12.00
24 M.Gasol/Z.Randolph/155 4.00 10.00
25 N.Cole/R.Allen/155 4.00 10.00
26 H.Barnes/S.Curry/155 15.00 40.00
27 K.Faried/T.Lawson/125 3.00 8.00
28 C.Anthony/M.Williams/155 8.00 20.00
29 D.Howard/H.Olajuwon/79 5.00 12.00
30 C.Paul/D.Williams/125
31 M.Morris/M.Morris/155
32 D.Nowitzki/K.Love/155 5.00 12.00
33 A.Bennett/L.Johnson/155 5.00 12.00
34 M.Johnson/S.Nash/49 10.00 25.00
35 K.Jabbar/T.Duncan/49 6.00 15.00
36 T.Splitter/T.Duncan/155 6.00 15.00
37 A.Johnson/D.DeRozan/155 4.00 10.00
38 B.Beal/J.Wall/155 5.00 12.00
39 J.Butler/T.Gibson/155 4.00 10.00
40 P.Ewing/T.Chandler/79 6.00 15.00
41 J.Noah/S.Pippen/125 8.00 20.00
42 G.Payton/R.Westbrook/49 10.00 25.00
43 I.Thomas/I.Thomas/79 4.00 10.00
44 J.Lin/Y.Ming/79 5.00 12.00
45 D.Brown/D.Wilkins/49 6.00 15.00
46 M.Ginobili/T.Parker/125 6.00 15.00
47 D.Favors/G.Hayward/155 4.00 10.00
48 D.Williams/J.Terry/155
49 F.Lever/T.Lawson/155 2.50 6.00
50 J.Worthy/K.Bryant/49 10.00 25.00

2013-14 Panini Titanium Game Gear Duals Prime

*PRIME: .75X TO 2X BASIC
PRINT RUNS B/WN 2-25 COPIES PER
NO PRICING ON QTY 10 OR LESS
5 D.Wade/L.James/25 100.00 200.00
28 Anthony/Carter-Williams/15 20.00 50.00
33 A.Bennett/L.Johnson/25 10.00 25.00
40 P.Ewing/T.Chandler/25 20.00 50.00
41 J.Noah/S.Pippen/25 40.00 100.00

2013-14 Panini Titanium Gamers

1 Tracy McGrady
2 Grant Hill 5.00 12.00
3 LeBron James
4 Steve Nash 4.00 10.00
5 Jason Kidd 4.00 10.00
6 Paul Pierce 4.00 10.00
7 Rasheed Wallace 4.00 10.00
8 Deron Williams 3.00 8.00
9 Blake Griffin 4.00 10.00
10 Clyde Drexler 5.00 12.00
11 Dwight Howard 3.00 8.00
12 Allen Iverson 5.00 12.00
13 Ray Allen 4.00 10.00
14 Tim Duncan 6.00 15.00
15 Shaquille O'Neal 8.00 20.00
16 Eric Gordon 3.00 8.00
17 Kevin Durant 8.00 20.00
18 Pau Gasol 4.00 10.00
19 Dwyane Wade 6.00 15.00
20 Dirk Nowitzki 5.00 12.00
21 Joakim Noah 3.00 8.00
22 Al Horford 3.00 8.00
23 Kobe Bryant 8.00 20.00
24 Carmelo Anthony 5.00 12.00
25 Kyrie Irving 8.00 20.00

2013-14 Panini Titanium Gamers Prime

*PRIME: .75X TO 2X BASIC
PRINT RUNS B/WN 2-25 COPIES PER
NO PRICING ON QTY 10 OR LESS
MANY NOT PRICED DUE TO LACK OF INFO
1 Tracy McGrady/25 20.00 50.00
2 Grant Hill/25 50.00 100.00
7 Rasheed Wallace/25 40.00 80.00
10 Clyde Drexler/25 40.00 80.00
14 Tim Duncan/25 30.00 60.00
19 Dwyane Wade/25 12.00 30.00
21 Joakim Noah/25 12.00 30.00
23 Kobe Bryant/25 50.00 100.00

2013-14 Panini Titanium Luster

STATED PRINT RUN 99 SER.#'d SETS
1 Kobe Bryant 10.00 25.00
2 James Harden 4.00 10.00
3 Steve Nash 2.50 6.00
4 Jeremy Lin 2.50 6.00
5 LeBron James 10.00 25.00
6 Deron Williams 2.00 5.00
7 Derrick Rose 3.00 8.00
8 Carmelo Anthony 3.00 8.00
9 Kyrie Irving 5.00 12.00
10 Chandler Parsons 2.00 5.00
11 Blake Griffin 2.50 6.00
12 Damian Lillard 5.00 12.00
13 Ricky Rubio 2.50 6.00
14 Stephen Curry 10.00 25.00
15 Kevin Durant 6.00 15.00
16 Vince Carter 3.00 8.00
17 Jeff Teague 2.00 5.00
18 Rajon Rondo 2.50 6.00
19 John Wall 3.00 8.00
20 Chris Paul 3.00 8.00
21 Brandon Jennings 1.50 4.00
22 Paul George 3.00 8.00
23 Tyreke Evans 1.50 4.00
24 Shawn Marion 2.00 5.00
25 Chris Bosh 2.50 6.00

2013-14 Panini Titanium Metallic Marks

PRINT RUNS B/WN 25-299 COPIES PER
EXCHANGE DEADLINE 8/26/2015
1 Kevin Durant/99 EXCH 60.00 150.00
2 Danilo Gallinari/25 3.00 8.00
3 Detlef Schrempf/299 6.00 15.00
4 Stephen Curry/25 50.00 120.00
5 David Thompson/299 4.00 10.00
6 Kyrie Irving/49 60.00 150.00
7 Kurt Rambis/299 3.00 8.00
8 Raymond Felton/25
9 Muggsy Bogues/299 6.00 15.00
10 Blake Griffin/49 12.00 30.00
11 Marcin Gortat/99 4.00 10.00
12 Reggie Theus/299 6.00 15.00
13 Tony Parker/25 20.00 50.00
14 Kobe Bryant/49 100.00 200.00
15 Klay Thompson/25
16 Andrei Kirilenko/25
17 J.R. Smith/25
18 Scottie Pippen/49
19 Monta Ellis/25 EXCH 4.00 10.00
20 Byron Mullens/299 3.00 8.00
21 Greivis Vasquez/249 8.00 20.00
22 John Starks/299 4.00 10.00
23 Cedric Ceballos/299 6.00 15.00
24 Kent Bazemore/299 4.00 10.00
25 Michael Cage/299 3.00 8.00

2013-14 Panini Titanium New Wave Signatures

1 Anthony Davis 40.00 100.00
2 Jared Sullinger 3.00 8.00
3 Derrick Williams
4 Alec Burks 3.00 8.00
5 MarShon Brooks 4.00 10.00
6 Kyle Lowry 4.00 10.00
7 Danilo Gallinari 3.00 8.00
8 Jeff Ayres 3.00 8.00
9 Greg Monroe 4.00 10.00
10 Daniel Orton 3.00 8.00
11 Bradley Beal
12 Jared Cunningham 3.00 8.00
13 Enes Kanter 3.00 8.00
14 Kawhi Leonard 40.00 100.00
15 Norris Cole 3.00 8.00
16 Stephen Jackson 4.00 10.00
17 Jrue Holiday
18 Tyshawn Taylor 3.00 8.00
19 Al-Farouq Aminu 4.00 10.00
20 Landry Fields 3.00 8.00
21 Eric Gordon 4.00 10.00
22 Patrick Beverley 3.00 8.00
23 Tristan Thompson
24 Nikola Vucevic
25 Dorell Wright 3.00 8.00
26 Terrence Ross 4.00 10.00
27 Gerald Henderson 3.00 8.00
28 Hollis Thompson 4.00 10.00
29 Gordon Hayward 5.00 12.00
30 Lance Stephenson 4.00 10.00
31 Harrison Barnes 4.00 10.00
32 Festus Ezeli 3.00 8.00
33 Jan Vesely 3.00 8.00
34 Iman Shumpert 3.00 8.00
35 Henry Sims 5.00 12.00
36 Austin Rivers 4.00 10.00
37 Tyreke Evans 3.00 8.00
38 Ersan Ilyasova 3.00 8.00
39 Patrick Patterson
40 Ish Smith 3.00 8.00
41 Andre Drummond 8.00 20.00
42 Draymond Green 12.00 30.00
43 Robbie Hummel 3.00 8.00
44 Tobias Harris 4.00 10.00
45 Andre Iguodala 6.00 15.00
46 Blake Griffin EXCH 20.00 50.00
47 Nick Young 5.00 12.00
48 E'Twaun Moore 3.00 8.00
49 James Anderson 3.00 8.00
50 Derrick Favors 4.00 10.00
51 Meyers Leonard 3.00 8.00
52 Quincy Miller
53 Kemba Walker
54 Kenneth Faried
55 Chandler Parsons EXCH 4.00 10.00
56 James Harden 30.00 80.00
57 Ty Lawson
58 D.J. Augustin 3.00 8.00
59 Andrea Bargnani 4.00 10.00
60 Robert Sacre
61 DeMarre Carroll 3.00 8.00
62 Khris Middleton
63 Jimmer Fredette
64 Greg Smith 3.00 8.00
65 Jon Leuer 3.00 8.00
66 Stephen Curry 75.00 200.00
67 Alexey Shved
68 Diante Garrett 3.00 8.00

69 Greivis Vasquez
70 Michael Kidd-Gilchrist
71 Maurice Harkless 3.00 8.00
72 Kyrie Irving 30.00 80.00
73 Klay Thompson
74 Reggie Jackson 4.00 10.00
75 Jason Smith
76 Nikola Pekovic 3.00 8.00
77 Perry Jones 3.00 8.00
78 Kent Bazemore 4.00 10.00
79 Courtney Lee
80 Alan Anderson 3.00 8.00

2013-14 Panini Titanium Reserve Signatures

PRINT RUNS B/WN 25-299 COPIES PER
EXCHANGE DEADLINE 8/26/2015
1 Kobe Bryant/49 EXCH 100.00 200.00
2 Tyson Chandler/25
3 Mario Chalmers/99 4.00 10.00
4 Eddie Jones/199 4.00 10.00
5 Nikola Vucevic/225 EXCH 4.00 10.00
6 Norm Nixon/299 5.00 12.00
7 Larry Johnson/199 10.00 25.00
8 Kyrie Irving/49 30.00 80.00
9 Anthony Davis/49 40.00 100.00
10 DeAndre Jordan/25
11 MarShon Brooks/249 4.00 10.00
12 Isiah Thomas/25 20.00 50.00
13 Karl Malone/49 50.00 100.00
14 Xavier Henry/299 3.00 8.00
15 Mitch Richmond/249 5.00 12.00
16 Jerryd Bayless/299 4.00 10.00
17 Kevin Durant/49 60.00 150.00
18 Bismack Biyombo/299 3.00 8.00
19 Jerry Lucas/49 12.00 30.00
20 Grant Hill/49 30.00 60.00
21 Kendall Gill/299 6.00 15.00
22 Dee Brown/299 6.00 15.00
23 Horace Grant/49 8.00 20.00
24 Dorell Wright/299 3.00 8.00
25 Keith Van Horn/249 4.00 10.00

2013-14 Panini Titanium Retail

101-200 PRINT RUN 149 COPIES PER
1 Jrue Holiday .30 .75
2 Gerald Wallace .25 .60
3 Nikola Vucevic .25 .60
4 Deron Williams .25 .60
5 Luol Deng .25 .60
6 Channing Frye .25 .60
7 Damian Lillard .60 1.50
8 Manu Ginobili .30 .75
9 Dirk Nowitzki .40 1.00
10 Tim Duncan .50 1.25
11 Greivis Vasquez .25 .60
12 Dion Waiters .25 .60
13 Dwight Howard .25 .60
14 Evan Turner .20 .50
15 Kyrie Irving .60 1.50
16 Gerald Henderson .20 .50
17 Chris Bosh .30 .75
18 Paul George .40 1.00
19 Arron Afflalo .20 .50
20 James Harden .50 1.25
21 Chris Paul .40 1.00
22 Zach Randolph .25 .60
23 Carmelo Anthony .40 1.00
24 Derrick Favors .25 .60
25 Brandon Knight .25 .60
26 Josh Smith .25 .60
27 Kemba Walker .30 .75
28 Amar'e Stoudemire .25 .60
29 Jameer Nelson .20 .50
30 Al Horford .25 .60
31 Kobe Bryant 1.25 3.00
32 Rudy Gay .30 .75
33 John Wall .40 1.00
34 Danny Granger .25 .60
35 Jeff Green .25 .60
36 Ricky Rubio .30 .75
37 Rajon Rondo .30 .75
38 Roy Hibbert .25 .60
39 Kevin Martin .25 .60
40 Eric Bledsoe .25 .60
41 Jeremy Lin .30 .75
42 Kevin Garnett .50 1.25
43 Carl Landry
44 Blake Griffin .30 .75
45 Enes Kanter .20 .50
46 Al Jefferson .25 .60
47 Paul Millsap .30 .75
48 Steve Novak .20 .50
49 Dwyane Wade .50 1.25
50 Anthony Davis .60 1.50
51 Andre Drummond .30 .75
52 Joakim Noah .25 .60
53 Serge Ibaka .25 .60
54 Jason Richardson .30 .75
55 DeMarcus Cousins .30 .75
56 Nicolas Batum .25 .60
57 Paul Pierce .30 .75
58 LeBron James 1.25 3.00
59 DeMar DeRozan .30 .75
60 LaMarcus Aldridge .30 .75
61 J.J. Redick .30 .75
62 Gordon Hayward .30 .75
63 Bradley Beal .30 .75
64 Tyson Chandler .25 .60
65 Mike Conley .25 .60
66 Harrison Barnes .25 .60
67 Thaddeus Young .20 .50
68 Shawn Marion .25 .60
69 Jeff Teague .25 .60
70 Kevin Love .30 .75
71 Carlos Boozer .25 .60
72 O.J. Mayo .20 .50
73 DeAndre Jordan .30 .75
74 Andre Miller .25 .60
75 Steve Nash .30 .75
76 Klay Thompson .40 1.00
77 Anderson Varejao .20 .50
78 Pau Gasol .30 .75
79 Kenneth Faried .25 .60
80 Brandon Jennings .20 .50
81 Russell Westbrook .75 2.00
82 Tyreke Evans .20 .50
83 Vince Carter .40 1.00
84 Marcin Gortat .25 .60
85 Jimmer Fredette .20 .50
86 Monta Ellis .25 .60
87 Nikola Pekovic .20 .50
88 George Hill .25 .60
89 Derrick Rose .40 1.00
90 Goran Dragic .25 .60
91 Andrew Bogut .25 .60
92 Mario Chalmers .25 .60
93 Larry Sanders .20 .50
94 Joe Johnson .25 .60
95 Stephen Curry 1.25 3.00
96 J.R. Smith .25 .60
97 Tony Parker .30 .75
98 Marc Gasol .30 .75
99 Kevin Durant .75 2.00
100 Ty Lawson .20 .50
101 Anthony Bennett RC 3.00 8.00
102 Victor Oladipo RC 5.00 12.00
103 Otto Porter RC 4.00 10.00
104 Cody Zeller RC 3.00 8.00
105 Alex Len RC 3.00 8.00
106 Nerlens Noel RC 5.00 12.00
107 Ben McLemore RC 3.00 8.00
108 Kentavious Caldwell-Pope RC 4.00 10.00
109 Trey Burke RC 3.00 8.00
110 C.J. McCollum RC 6.00 15.00
111 M.Carter-Williams RC 4.00 10.00
112 Steven Adams RC 4.00 10.00
113 Kelly Olynyk RC 3.00 8.00
114 Shabazz Muhammad RC 3.00 8.00
115 G.Antetokounmpo RC 30.00 80.00
116 Dennis Schroder RC 4.00 10.00
117 Shane Larkin RC 2.50 6.00
118 Sergey Karasev RC 2.50 6.00
119 Tony Snell RC 3.00 8.00
120 Gorgui Dieng RC 3.00 8.00
121 Mason Plumlee RC 4.00 10.00
122 Solomon Hill RC 2.50 6.00
123 Tim Hardaway Jr. RC 4.00 10.00
124 Reggie Bullock RC 3.00 8.00
125 Andre Roberson RC 2.50 6.00
126 Rudy Gobert RC 5.00 12.00
127 Archie Goodwin RC 3.00 8.00
128 Nemanja Nedovic RC 2.50 6.00
129 Allen Crabbe RC 3.00 8.00
130 Carrick Felix RC 2.50 6.00
131 Isaiah Canaan RC 2.50 6.00
132 Glen Rice Jr. RC 2.50 6.00
133 Ray McCallum RC 2.50 6.00
134 Tony Mitchell RC 2.50 6.00
135 Nate Wolters RC 3.00 8.00
136 Jeff Withey RC 2.50 6.00
137 Jamaal Franklin RC 2.50 6.00
138 Ricky Ledo RC 2.50 6.00
139 Erik Murphy RC 2.50 6.00
140 Ryan Kelly RC 2.50 6.00
141 Peyton Siva RC 2.50 6.00
142 Vitor Faverani RC 2.50 6.00
143 Kobe Bryant 8.00 20.00
144 James Harden 3.00 8.00
145 Steve Nash 2.00 5.00
146 Dwight Howard 1.50 4.00
147 LeBron James 8.00 20.00
148 Deron Williams 1.50 4.00
149 Derrick Rose 2.50 6.00
150 Anthony Davis 4.00 10.00
151 Kyrie Irving 4.00 10.00
152 Dwyane Wade 3.00 8.00
153 Kevin Garnett 3.00 8.00
154 Carmelo Anthony 2.50 6.00
155 Kenneth Faried 1.50 4.00
156 Tim Duncan 3.00 8.00
157 Blake Griffin 2.00 5.00
158 Paul Pierce 2.00 5.00
159 Damian Lillard 4.00 10.00
160 Rajon Rondo 2.00 5.00
161 Tony Parker 2.00 5.00
162 Chris Paul 2.50 6.00
163 DeMarcus Cousins 2.00 5.00
164 Tyson Chandler 1.50 4.00
165 Brandon Jennings 1.25 3.00
166 Kawhi Leonard 3.00 8.00
167 Paul George 2.50 6.00
168 Russell Westbrook 5.00 12.00
169 John Wall 2.50 6.00
170 Dirk Nowitzki 2.50 6.00
171 Larry Sanders 1.25 3.00
172 Kevin Durant 5.00 12.00
173 Joakim Noah 1.50 4.00
174 Zach Randolph 1.50 4.00
175 Vince Carter 2.50 6.00
176 Kevin Love 2.00 5.00
177 Stephen Curry 8.00 20.00
178 Marcin Gortat 1.50 4.00
179 Manu Ginobili 2.00 5.00
180 Ricky Rubio 2.00 5.00
181 Isiah Thomas 2.00 5.00
182 Dominique Wilkins 2.50 6.00
183 Kevin McHale 2.00 5.00
184 Hakeem Olajuwon 2.50 6.00
185 David Robinson 3.00 8.00
186 Julius Erving 3.00 8.00
187 Bill Russell 3.00 8.00
188 Magic Johnson 5.00 12.00
189 Larry Bird 5.00 12.00
190 Wilt Chamberlain 4.00 10.00
191 Karl Malone 2.50 6.00
192 Anfernee Hardaway 5.00 12.00
193 Oscar Robertson 2.50 6.00
194 Jason Kidd 2.00 5.00
195 Grant Hill 2.50 6.00
196 Kareem Abdul-Jabbar 3.00 8.00
197 Pete Maravich 3.00 8.00
198 Shaquille O'Neal 4.00 10.00
199 Scottie Pippen 4.00 10.00
200 Gary Payton 2.00 5.00

2013-14 Panini Titanium Rookie Jerseys

PRINT RUNS B/WN 85-325 COPIES PER
ALL VERSIONS EQUALLY PRICED
1 Anthony Bennett/325 2.50 6.00
2 Victor Oladipo/325 6.00 15.00
3 Otto Porter/325 3.00 8.00
4 Cody Zeller/325 2.50 6.00
5 Alex Len/325 2.50 6.00
6 Nerlens Noel/325 4.00 10.00
7 Ben McLemore/325 2.50 6.00
8 Kentavious Caldwell-Pope/325 3.00 8.00
9 Trey Burke/325 2.50 6.00
10 C.J. McCollum/325 5.00 12.00
11 M.Carter-Williams/325 3.00 8.00
12 Steven Adams/325 3.00 8.00
13 Kelly Olynyk/325 2.50 6.00
14 Shabazz Muhammad/325 2.50 6.00
15 G.Antetokounmpo/325 25.00 60.00
16 Shane Larkin/325 2.00 5.00
17 Tony Snell/325 2.50 6.00
18 Mason Plumlee/325 3.00 8.00
19 Tim Hardaway Jr./325 3.00 8.00
20 Glen Rice Jr./325 2.00 5.00
21 Anthony Bennett/325 2.50 6.00
22 Victor Oladipo/325 6.00 15.00
23 Otto Porter/325 3.00 8.00
24 Cody Zeller/325 2.50 6.00
25 Alex Len/325 2.50 6.00
26 Nerlens Noel/325 4.00 10.00
27 Ben McLemore/325 2.50 6.00
28 Kentavious Caldwell-Pope/325 3.00 8.00
29 Trey Burke/325 2.50 6.00
30 C.J. McCollum/325 5.00 12.00
31 Michael Carter-Williams/325 3.00 8.00
32 Steven Adams/325 3.00 8.00
33 Kelly Olynyk/325 2.50 6.00
34 Shabazz Muhammad/325 2.50 6.00
35 G.Antetokounmpo/325 25.00 60.00
36 Shane Larkin/325 2.00 5.00
37 Tony Snell/325 2.50 6.00
38 Mason Plumlee/325 3.00 8.00
39 Tim Hardaway Jr./325 3.00 8.00
40 Glen Rice Jr./325 2.00 5.00
41 Anthony Bennett/325 2.50 6.00
42 Victor Oladipo/325 6.00 15.00
43 Otto Porter/325 3.00 8.00
44 Cody Zeller/325 2.50 6.00
45 Alex Len/325 2.50 6.00
46 Nerlens Noel/325 4.00 10.00
47 Ben McLemore/325 2.50 6.00
48 Kentavious Caldwell-Pope/325 3.00 8.00
49 Trey Burke/325 2.50 6.00
50 C.J. McCollum/325 5.00 12.00
51 Michael Carter-Williams/325 3.00 8.00
52 Steven Adams/325 3.00 8.00
53 Kelly Olynyk/325 2.50 6.00
54 Shabazz Muhammad/325 2.50 6.00
55 G.Antetokounmpo/325 25.00 60.00
56 Shane Larkin/325 2.00 5.00
57 Tony Snell/325 2.50 6.00
58 Mason Plumlee/325 3.00 8.00
59 Tim Hardaway Jr./325 3.00 8.00
60 Glen Rice Jr./325 2.00 5.00
61 Anthony Bennett/325 2.50 6.00
62 Victor Oladipo/325 6.00 15.00
63 Otto Porter/325 3.00 8.00
64 Cody Zeller/325 2.50 6.00
65 Alex Len/325 2.50 6.00
66 Nerlens Noel/325 4.00 10.00
67 Ben McLemore/325 2.50 6.00
68 Kentavious Caldwell-Pope/325 3.00 8.00
69 Trey Burke/325 2.50 6.00
70 C.J. McCollum/325 5.00 12.00
71 Michael Carter-Williams/325 3.00 8.00
72 Steven Adams/325 3.00 8.00
73 Kelly Olynyk/325 2.50 6.00
74 Shabazz Muhammad/325 2.50 6.00
75 G.Antetokounmpo/325 25.00 60.00
76 Shane Larkin/325 2.00 5.00
77 Tony Snell/325 2.50 6.00
78 Mason Plumlee/325 3.00 8.00
79 Tim Hardaway Jr./325 3.00 8.00
80 Glen Rice Jr./325 2.00 5.00
81 Anthony Bennett/85 3.00 8.00
82 Victor Oladipo/85 8.00 20.00
83 Otto Porter/85 4.00 10.00
84 Cody Zeller/85 3.00 8.00
85 Alex Len/85 3.00 8.00
86 Nerlens Noel/85 5.00 12.00
87 Ben McLemore/85 3.00 8.00
88 Kentavious Caldwell-Pope/85 4.00 10.00
89 Trey Burke/85 3.00 8.00
90 C.J. McCollum/85 6.00 15.00
91 M.Carter-Williams/85 4.00 10.00
92 Steven Adams/85 4.00 10.00
93 Kelly Olynyk/85 3.00 8.00
94 Shabazz Muhammad/85 3.00 8.00
95 G.Antetokounmpo/85 30.00 80.00
96 Shane Larkin/85 2.50 6.00
97 Tony Snell/85 3.00 8.00
98 Mason Plumlee/85 4.00 10.00
99 Tim Hardaway Jr./85 4.00 10.00
100 Glen Rice Jr./85 2.50 6.00

2013-14 Panini Titanium Strength

STATED PRINT RUN 99 SER.#'d SETS
1 Anthony Davis 5.00 12.00
2 Josh Smith 2.00 5.00
3 Kobe Bryant 10.00 25.00
4 Paul Pierce 2.50 6.00
5 Tim Duncan 4.00 10.00
6 Pau Gasol 2.50 6.00
7 Dwight Howard 2.00 5.00
8 Kevin Durant 6.00 15.00
9 Zach Randolph 2.00 5.00
10 Serge Ibaka 2.00 5.00
11 Chris Bosh 2.50 6.00
12 Anderson Varejao 1.50 4.00
13 Marc Gasol 2.50 6.00
14 Tyson Chandler 2.00 5.00
15 LeBron James 10.00 25.00
16 DeMarcus Cousins 2.50 6.00
17 Blake Griffin 2.50 6.00
18 Kenneth Faried 2.00 5.00
19 Dwyane Wade 4.00 10.00
20 Kevin Garnett 4.00 10.00
21 Carmelo Anthony 3.00 8.00
22 Dirk Nowitzki 3.00 8.00
23 Joakim Noah 2.00 5.00
24 Metta World Peace 2.50 6.00
25 Nate Robinson 1.50 4.00

2013-14 Panini Titanium Team Titans

STATED PRINT RUN 149 SER.#'d SETS
1 A.Drummond/G.Monroe 2.00 5.00
2 D.Waiters/K.Irving 4.00 10.00
3 E.Bledsoe/G.Dragic 1.50 4.00
4 D.Wade/L.James 8.00 20.00
5 K.Bryant/P.Gasol 8.00 20.00
6 B.Griffin/C.Paul 2.50 6.00
7 K.Thompson/S.Curry 8.00 20.00
8 B.Beal/J.Wall 2.50 6.00
9 D.Lillard/L.Aldridge 4.00 10.00
10 B.Lopez/D.Williams 1.50 4.00
11 K.Love/R.Rubio 2.00 5.00
12 K.Durant/R.Westbrook 5.00 12.00
13 C.Anthony/T.Chandler 2.50 6.00
14 D.Howard/J.Harden 3.00 8.00
15 P.George/R.Hibbert 2.50 6.00
16 D.Nowitzki/S.Marion 2.50 6.00
17 T.Duncan/T.Parker 3.00 8.00
18 K.Faried/T.Lawson 1.50 4.00
19 E.Turner/T.Young 1.25 3.00
20 D.Rose/J.Noah 2.50 6.00
21 D.DeRozan/K.Lowry 2.00 5.00
22 D.Favors/G.Hayward 2.00 5.00
23 M.Conley/Z.Randolph 1.50 4.00
24 A.Bradley/R.Rondo 2.00 5.00
25 A.Davis/J.Holiday 4.00 10.00

2013-14 Panini Titanium Titanic Threads Jumbo

PRINT RUNS B/WN 99-299 COPIES PER
1 Al Horford/299 3.00 8.00
2 Andrew Bynum/299 2.50 6.00
3 Chauncey Billups/299 4.00 10.00
4 Deron Williams/299 3.00 8.00
5 Jamal Crawford/299 4.00 10.00
6 Kareem Abdul-Jabbar/99 8.00 20.00
7 Larry Johnson/299 5.00 12.00
8 Robert Parish/99 4.00 10.00
9 Tracy McGrady/99 4.00 10.00
10 Zach Randolph/99 3.00 8.00
11 Alex English/99 3.00 8.00
12 Anfernee Hardaway/99 12.00 30.00
13 Chris Bosh/299 4.00 10.00
14 Kevin Martin/299 3.00 8.00
15 James Harden/299 6.00 15.00
16 Karl Malone/299 5.00 12.00
17 LeBron James/299 12.00 30.00
18 Russell Westbrook/299 10.00 25.00
19 James Worthy/99 5.00 12.00
20 Isiah Thomas/99 4.00 10.00
21 Al-Farouq Aminu/198 3.00 8.00
22 Antawn Jamison/299 3.00 8.00
23 Dirk Nowitzki/299 5.00 12.00
24 Chris Paul/299 5.00 12.00
25 Jason Kidd/299 4.00 10.00
26 Brandon Bass/299 2.50 6.00
27 Magic Johnson/99 10.00 25.00
28 Scottie Pippen/99 8.00 20.00
29 Jeff Green/299 3.00 8.00
30 Shane Battier/299 3.00 8.00
31 Alonzo Mourning/99 15.00 40.00
32 Anthony Davis/99 8.00 20.00
33 Clyde Drexler/99 10.00 25.00
34 Dominique Wilkins/99
35 Vinnie Johnson/99 4.00 10.00
36 Kenneth Faried/299 3.00 8.00
37 Metta World Peace/299 4.00 10.00
38 Shaquille O'Neal/99 8.00 20.00
39 Tyson Chandler/299 3.00 8.00
40 Nate Robinson/299 2.50 6.00
41 Andray Blatche/299 2.50 6.00
42 Bill Laimbeer/99 3.00 8.00
43 Damian Lillard/99 8.00 20.00
44 Dwight Howard/299 3.00 8.00
45 Mike Miller/299 3.00 8.00
46 Jeremy Lin/299 4.00 10.00
47 Patrick Ewing/99 5.00 12.00
48 Stephen Curry/299 8.00 20.00
49 Jayson Williams/299 2.50 6.00
50 Tayshaun Prince/99 3.00 8.00
51 Andre Iguodala/299 3.00 8.00
52 Nate Wolters/299 3.00 8.00
53 Danilo Gallinari/299 2.50 6.00
54 Dwyane Wade/99 6.00 15.00
55 Jermaine O'Neal/299 3.00 8.00
56 Kevin Garnett/299 6.00 15.00
57 Pau Gasol/299 4.00 10.00
58 Moses Malone/99 4.00 10.00
59 Luol Deng/299 3.00 8.00
60 Kevin Durant/299 8.00 20.00
61 Andre Miller/299 3.00 8.00
62 Jodie Meeks/299 3.00 8.00
63 David Robinson/99 6.00 15.00
64 Fat Lever/299 3.00 8.00
65 Joakim Noah/299 3.00 8.00
66 Kevin McHale/99 4.00 10.00
67 Paul Pierce/299 4.00 10.00
68 Steve Nash/299 4.00 10.00
69 Raymond Felton/299 3.00 8.00
70 Jason Terry/299 3.00 8.00
71 Carlos Boozer/299 3.00 8.00
72 Andrei Kirilenko/99 3.00 8.00
73 DeMar DeRozan/299 4.00 10.00
74 Gary Payton/99 4.00 10.00
75 Joe Dumars/299 4.00 10.00
76 Kevin Love/299 4.00 10.00
77 Rajon Rondo/299 4.00 10.00
78 Taj Gibson/299 3.00 8.00
79 Victor Oladipo/299 5.00 12.00
80 G.Antetokounmpo/299 5.00 12.00
81 Amar'e Stoudemire/99 3.00 8.00
82 DeMarcus Cousins/299 4.00 10.00
83 Carmelo Anthony/299 5.00 12.00
84 Gerald Wallace/99 3.00 8.00
85 John Wall/99 5.00 12.00
86 Kobe Bryant/299 12.00 30.00
87 Ray Allen/299 6.00 15.00
88 Tim Duncan/299 6.00 15.00
89 Mario Chalmers/299 3.00 8.00
90 Larry Bird/99 12.00 30.00
91 Ben McLemore/299 5.00 12.00
92 Caron Butler/299 3.00 8.00
93 Channing Frye/99 3.00 8.00
94 Grant Hill/299 5.00 12.00
95 John Stockton/99 6.00 15.00
96 Kyrie Irving/99 8.00 20.00
97 Kendrick Perkins/299 2.50 6.00
98 Tony Parker/99 4.00 10.00
99 Anthony Bennett/299 3.00 8.00
100 M.Carter-Williams/299 8.00 20.00

2013-14 Panini Titanium Titans

STATED PRINT RUN 199 SER.#'d SETS
1 Kevin Garnett 2.50 6.00
2 Tim Duncan 2.50 6.00
3 Dirk Nowitzki 2.00 5.00
4 Kobe Bryant 6.00 15.00
5 LeBron James 10.00 25.00
6 Paul Pierce 1.50 4.00
7 Steve Nash 1.50 4.00
8 Dwyane Wade 2.50 6.00
9 Vince Carter 2.00 5.00
10 Dwight Howard 1.25 3.00
11 Chris Paul 2.00 5.00
12 Blake Griffin 1.50 4.00
13 Kyrie Irving 3.00 8.00
14 Anthony Davis 3.00 8.00
15 Tony Parker 1.50 4.00
16 Carmelo Anthony 2.00 5.00
17 Kevin Durant 4.00 10.00
18 James Harden 2.50 6.00
19 Russell Westbrook 4.00 10.00
20 Stephen Curry 6.00 15.00
21 Marc Gasol 1.50 4.00
22 Kenneth Faried 1.25 3.00
23 Joakim Noah 1.25 3.00
24 Ray Allen 1.50 4.00
25 Damian Lillard 3.00 8.00

2014-15 Paramount

COMPLETE SET (100)
SP's RANDOMLY INSERTED
1 Tony Parker .75 2.00
2 Kobe Bryant 3.00 8.00
3 Damian Lillard 1.50 4.00
4 Kevin Durant 2.00 5.00
5 Paul George 1.00 2.50
6 Dirk Nowitzki 1.00 2.50
7 Anthony Davis 1.50 4.00
8 Russell Westbrook 2.00 5.00
9 James Harden 1.25 3.00
10 Blake Griffin .75 2.00
11 Stephen Curry 2.00 5.00
12 LeBron James 4.00 10.00
13 Derrick Rose 1.00 2.50
14 Kyrie Irving 1.50 4.00
15 Rajon Rondo .75 2.00
16 Dwyane Wade 1.25 3.00
17 Carmelo Anthony 1.00 2.50
18 Tim Duncan 1.25 3.00
19 Kevin Love .75 2.00
20 Chris Paul 1.00 2.50
21 Magic Johnson 2.00 5.00
22 Larry Bird 2.00 5.00
23 Scottie Pippen 1.50 4.00
24 Allen Iverson 1.00 2.50
25 Chris Webber .75 2.00
26 Andrew Wiggins RC 8.00 20.00
27 Jabari Parker RC 2.50 6.00
28 Joel Embiid RC 5.00 12.00
29 Aaron Gordon RC 2.50 6.00
30 Dante Exum RC 1.50 4.00
31 Marcus Smart RC 1.50 4.00
32 Julius Randle RC 2.50 6.00
33 Nik Stauskas RC 1.25 3.00
34 Noah Vonleh RC 1.25 3.00
35 Elfrid Payton RC 1.50 4.00
36 Doug McDermott RC 1.50 4.00
37 Zach LaVine RC 2.50 6.00
38 T.J. Warren RC 1.50 4.00
39 Adreian Payne RC 1.25 3.00
40 Cleanthony Early RC 1.00 2.50
41 James Young RC 1.00 2.50
42 Tyler Ennis RC 1.00 2.50
43 Gary Harris RC 1.50 4.00
44 Bruno Caboclo RC 1.25 3.00
45 Mitch McGary RC 1.00 2.50
46 Jordan Adams RC 1.00 2.50
47 Shabazz Napier RC 1.25 3.00
48 Rodney Hood RC 1.50 4.00
49 Glenn Robinson III RC 1.00 2.50
50 P.J. Hairston RC 1.00 2.50
51 Tony Parker SP 5.00 12.00
52 Kobe Bryant SP 20.00 50.00
53 Damian Lillard SP 10.00 25.00
54 Kevin Durant SP 12.00 30.00
55 Paul George SP 6.00 15.00
56 Dirk Nowitzki SP 6.00 15.00
57 Anthony Davis SP 10.00 25.00
58 Russell Westbrook SP 12.00 30.00
59 James Harden SP 8.00 20.00
60 Blake Griffin SP 5.00 12.00
61 Stephen Curry SP 20.00 50.00
62 LeBron James SP 20.00 50.00
63 Derrick Rose SP 6.00 15.00
64 Kyrie Irving SP 10.00 25.00
65 Rajon Rondo SP 5.00 12.00
66 Dwyane Wade SP 8.00 20.00
67 Carmelo Anthony SP 6.00 15.00
68 Tim Duncan SP 8.00 20.00
69 Kevin Love SP 5.00 12.00
70 Chris Paul SP 6.00 15.00
71 Magic Johnson SP 12.00 30.00
72 Larry Bird SP 12.00 30.00
73 Scottie Pippen SP 10.00 25.00
74 Allen Iverson SP 6.00 15.00
75 Chris Webber SP 5.00 12.00
76 Andrew Wiggins SP 125.00 250.00
77 Jabari Parker SP 8.00 20.00
78 Joel Embiid SP 15.00 40.00
79 Aaron Gordon SP 8.00 20.00
80 Dante Exum SP 5.00 12.00
81 Marcus Smart SP 5.00 12.00
82 Julius Randle SP 8.00 20.00
83 Nik Stauskas SP 4.00 10.00
84 Noah Vonleh SP 4.00 10.00
85 Elfrid Payton SP 5.00 12.00
86 Doug McDermott SP 5.00 12.00
87 Zach LaVine SP 8.00 20.00
88 T.J. Warren SP 5.00 12.00
89 Adreian Payne SP 4.00 10.00
90 Cleanthony Early SP 3.00 8.00
91 James Young SP 3.00 8.00
92 Tyler Ennis SP 3.00 8.00
93 Gary Harris SP 5.00 12.00
94 Bruno Caboclo SP 4.00 10.00
95 Mitch McGary SP 3.00 8.00
96 Jordan Adams SP 3.00 8.00
97 Shabazz Napier SP 4.00 10.00
98 Rodney Hood SP 5.00 12.00
99 Glenn Robinson III SP 3.00 8.00
100 P.J. Hairston SP 3.00 8.00

2014-15 Paramount Blue

*BLUE VETS: 4X TO 10X BASE HI
*BLUE RK: 2X TO 5X BASE HI
STATED PRINT RUN 25 SER.#'d SETS
18 Tim Duncan 10.00 25.00
26 Andrew Wiggins 75.00 150.00
27 Jabari Parker 40.00 100.00

2014-15 Paramount Bronze

*GOLD VETS: 2X TO 5X BASE HI
*GOLD RK: 1X TO 2.5X BASE HI
STATED PRINT RUN 50 SER.#'d SETS

2014-15 Paramount Next Day Autographs

STATED PRINT RUN B/WN 49-110 COPIES PER
EXCHANGE DEADLINE 7/7/2016
NDAG Aaron Gordon/100 10.00 25.00
NDAP Adreian Payne/100 5.00 12.00
NDAW Andrew Wiggins/100 150.00 250.00
NDBC Bruno Caboclo/100 5.00 12.00
NDCE Cleanthony Early/100 4.00 10.00
NDCJ Cory Jefferson/100 4.00 10.00
NDCW C.J. Wilcox/100 4.00 10.00
NDDI Damien Inglis/100 4.00 10.00
NDDM Doug McDermott/100 6.00 15.00
NDEP Elfrid Payton/100 15.00 40.00
NDGH Gary Harris/105 6.00 15.00
NDGR Glenn Robinson III/100 4.00 10.00
NDJA Jordan Adams/100 4.00 10.00
NDJE Joel Embiid/49 200.00 500.00
NDJG Jerami Grant/100 4.00 10.00
NDJH Joe Harris/100 4.00 10.00
NDJO Johnny O'Bryant/85 4.00 10.00
NDJP Jabari Parker/110 60.00 150.00
NDJR Julius Randle/100 20.00 50.00
NDJS Jarnell Stokes/101 4.00 10.00
NDJY James Young/100 4.00 10.00
NDKA Kyle Anderson/100 6.00 15.00
NDKM K.J. McDaniels/100 5.00 12.00
NDMB Markel Brown/100 4.00 10.00
NDMM Mitch McGary/101 4.00 10.00
NDMS Marcus Smart/100 20.00 50.00
NDNS Nik Stauskas/100 5.00 12.00
NDNV Noah Vonleh/100 5.00 12.00
NDPH P.J. Hairston/100 4.00 10.00
NDRH Rodney Hood/100 6.00 15.00
NDRS Russ Smith/98 4.00 10.00
NDSD Spencer Dinwiddie/100 5.00 12.00
NDSN Shabazz Napier/100 5.00 12.00
NDTA Thanasis Antetokounmpo/97 4.00 10.00
NDTE Tyler Ennis/97 4.00 10.00
NDTW T.J. Warren/94 15.00 40.00
NDZL Zach LaVine/100 30.00 80.00

2014-15 Paramount Past and Present Jerseys

STATED PRINT RUN B/WN 20-40 COPIES PER
1 Paul Millsap/20 4.00 10.00
2 LeBron James/40 15.00 40.00
3 Monta Ellis/40 3.00 8.00
4 Kevin Garnett/40 3.00 8.00
5 James Harden/40 10.00 25.00
6 Chris Andersen/25 3.00 8.00
7 Dwight Howard/40 3.00 8.00
12 David Lee/20 2.50 6.00
14 Steve Nash/40 4.00 10.00
15 Carmelo Anthony/40 5.00 12.00
16 Chris Paul/40 5.00 12.00
18 Chris Bosh/40 4.00 10.00
19 Eric Bledsoe/40 3.00 8.00

2014-15 Paramount Past and Present Jerseys Prime

*PRIME: 1X TO 2.5X BASE HI
STATED PRINT RUN B/WN 15-25 COPIES PER
1 Paul Millsap/15 25.00 60.00
2 LeBron James/20 100.00 200.00
4 Kevin Garnett/25 20.00 50.00
6 Chris Andersen/15 15.00 40.00
7 Dwight Howard/20 25.00 60.00
15 Carmelo Anthony/25 15.00 40.00

2014-15 Paramount Penmanship Autographs

STATED PRINT RUN B/WN 35-99 COPIES PER
EXCHANGE DEADLINE 7/7/2016
1 Kobe Bryant/35 50.00 120.00
2 Karl Malone/35 40.00 100.00
3 Magic Johnson/35 30.00 80.00
4 Larry Bird/35 30.00 80.00
5 John Stockton/35 20.00 50.00
6 Kevin Durant/35 50.00 120.00
7 Kareem Abdul-Jabbar/35 30.00 80.00
8 Anthony Davis/35 40.00 100.00
9 Kyrie Irving/35 30.00 80.00
10 Steve Nash/49 15.00 40.00
11 Jason Kidd/49 15.00 40.00
12 Kevin Love/49 15.00 40.00
13 Tony Parker/49 15.00 40.00
14 Stephen Curry/49 125.00 300.00
15 Grant Hill/49 25.00 60.00
16 Anthony Bennett/49 4.00 10.00
17 Victor Oladipo/49 8.00 20.00
18 DeMarcus Cousins/49 12.00 30.00
19 Ben McLemore/49 4.00 10.00
21 Tyson Chandler/49 5.00 12.00
22 C.J. McCollum/49 6.00 15.00
23 Harrison Barnes/49 10.00 25.00
24 Andre Drummond/49 10.00 25.00
25 LaMarcus Aldridge/49 12.00 30.00
26 Artis Gilmore/49 5.00 12.00
27 M.Carter-Williams/49 4.00 10.00
29 Jason Terry/49 5.00 12.00
30 Dolph Schayes/49 6.00 15.00
31 Danny Manning/49 5.00 12.00
32 Kenny Smith/49 5.00 12.00
33 Kyle Korver/49 6.00 15.00
34 Luis Scola/49 5.00 12.00
36 Danny Green/99 5.00 12.00
37 Tiago Splitter/99 5.00 12.00
38 Allan Houston/99 5.00 12.00
39 Thabo Sefolosha/99 4.00 10.00
40 Jeff Green/99 5.00 12.00
41 Nick Young/99 5.00 12.00
43 Iman Shumpert/99 4.00 10.00
44 Jason Thompson/99 4.00 10.00
45 Kyle Lowry/99 5.00 12.00
46 Alex English/99 5.00 12.00
47 Kevin Willis/99 4.00 10.00
48 Kurt Rambis/99 4.00 10.00
49 Robert Horry/99 5.00 12.00
50 Sam Perkins/99 4.00 10.00
51 D.J. Augustin/99 4.00 10.00
52 Enes Kanter/99 4.00 10.00
53 John Starks/99 5.00 12.00
54 Isaiah Thomas/99 20.00 50.00
55 Mark Price/99 6.00 15.00
56 Dee Brown/99 4.00 10.00
57 Cazzie Russell/99 5.00 12.00
58 Eddie Jones/99 5.00 12.00
59 Jo Jo White/99 5.00 12.00
60 Steve Blake/99 4.00 10.00

2014-15 Paramount Penmanship Autographs Blue

*BLUE: .6X TO 1.5X BASE HI
STATED PRINT RUN 25 SER.#'d SETS
EXCHANGE DEADLINE 7/7/2016
2 Karl Malone 40.00 100.00

2014-15 Paramount Penmanship Rookie Autographs

*BLUE: .6X TO 1.5X BASE HI
STATED PRINT RUN 99 SER.#'d SETS
EXCHANGE DEADLINE 7/7/2016
1 Andrew Wiggins 50.00 120.00
2 Jabari Parker 30.00 80.00
3 Joel Embiid 40.00 100.00
4 Aaron Gordon 10.00 25.00
5 Dante Exum 8.00 20.00
6 Marcus Smart 6.00 15.00
7 Julius Randle 12.00 30.00
8 Nik Stauskas 6.00 15.00
9 Noah Vonleh 5.00 12.00
10 Elfrid Payton 6.00 15.00
11 Doug McDermott 6.00 15.00
12 Zach LaVine 20.00 50.00
13 T.J. Warren 5.00 12.00
14 Adreian Payne 5.00 12.00
15 James Young 4.00 10.00
16 Tyler Ennis 4.00 10.00
17 Gary Harris 6.00 15.00
18 Bruno Caboclo 5.00 12.00
19 Mitch McGary 4.00 10.00
20 Jordan Adams 4.00 10.00
22 Shabazz Napier 5.00 12.00
24 C.J. Wilcox 4.00 10.00
25 Kyle Anderson 5.00 12.00
26 Jusuf Nurkic 6.00 15.00
27 Joe Harris 4.00 10.00
29 Jarnell Stokes 4.00 10.00
30 Spencer Dinwiddie 5.00 12.00
31 Glenn Robinson III 4.00 10.00
33 Russ Smith 4.00 10.00
34 Dwight Powell 4.00 10.00
36 Cory Jefferson 4.00 10.00
37 Johnny O'Bryant 4.00 10.00
38 Damjan Rudez 4.00 10.00
39 Damien Inglis 4.00 10.00
40 Jordan Clarkson 6.00 15.00

2014-15 Paramount Rookie Impressions Autographs

STATED PRINT RUN 49 SER.#'d SETS
EXCHANGE DEADLINE 7/7/2016
1 Aaron Gordon 12.00 30.00
2 Adreian Payne 6.00 15.00
3 Andrew Wiggins 50.00 120.00
4 Bruno Caboclo 6.00 15.00
5 C.J. Wilcox 5.00 12.00
6 Cleanthony Early 5.00 12.00
7 Cory Jefferson 5.00 12.00
8 Damien Inglis 5.00 12.00
9 Doug McDermott 8.00 20.00
10 Elfrid Payton 8.00 20.00
11 Gary Harris 8.00 20.00
12 Glenn Robinson III 5.00 12.00
13 Jabari Parker 15.00 40.00
14 James Young 5.00 12.00
15 Jarnell Stokes 5.00 12.00
16 Jerami Grant 5.00 12.00
17 Joe Harris 5.00 12.00
18 Joel Embiid 40.00 100.00
19 Johnny O'Bryant 5.00 12.00
20 Jordan Adams 5.00 12.00
21 Julius Randle 12.00 30.00
22 K.J. McDaniels 6.00 15.00
23 Kyle Anderson 8.00 20.00
24 Marcus Smart 8.00 20.00
25 Markel Brown 5.00 12.00
26 Mitch McGary 5.00 12.00
27 Nik Stauskas 6.00 15.00
28 Noah Vonleh 6.00 15.00
29 Rodney Hood 8.00 20.00
30 Russ Smith 5.00 12.00
31 Shabazz Napier 6.00 15.00
32 Spencer Dinwiddie 6.00 15.00
33 T.J. Warren 8.00 20.00
34 Tyler Ennis 5.00 12.00
35 Zach LaVine 20.00 50.00

2014-15 Paramount Rookie Jumbo Jerseys

STATED PRINT RUN 49 SER.#'d SETS
*PRIME: 1X TO 2.5X BASE HI
1 Damien Inglis 2.50 6.00
2 Markel Brown 2.50 6.00
3 Gary Harris 6.00 15.00
4 P.J. Hairston 2.50 6.00
5 James Young 2.50 6.00
6 Spencer Dinwiddie 3.00 8.00
7 Aaron Gordon 2.50 6.00
8 Joel Embiid 12.00 30.00
9 C.J. Wilcox 2.50 6.00
10 K.J. McDaniels 3.00 8.00
11 Dante Exum 4.00 10.00
12 Mitch McGary 2.50 6.00
13 Glenn Robinson III 2.50 6.00
14 Rodney Hood 4.00 10.00
15 Jarnell Stokes 2.50 6.00
16 T.J. Warren 4.00 10.00
17 Adreian Payne 3.00 8.00
18 Johnny O'Bryant 2.50 6.00
19 Cleanthony Early 2.50 6.00
20 Kyle Anderson 4.00 10.00
21 Doug McDermott 4.00 10.00
22 Nik Stauskas 3.00 8.00
23 Jabari Parker 6.00 15.00
24 Russ Smith 2.50 6.00
25 Jerami Grant 2.50 6.00
26 Tyler Ennis 2.50 6.00
27 Andrew Wiggins 12.00 30.00
28 Jordan Adams 2.50 6.00
29 Cory Jefferson 2.50 6.00
30 Marcus Smart 4.00 10.00
31 Elfrid Payton 4.00 10.00
32 Noah Vonleh 3.00 8.00
33 James Ennis 2.50 6.00
34 Joe Harris 2.50 6.00
35 Shabazz Napier 3.00 8.00
36 Zach LaVine 6.00 15.00
37 Bruno Caboclo 3.00 8.00
38 Julius Randle 6.00 15.00

2014-15 Paramount Rookies Home and Away Jerseys

STATED PRINT RUN 40 SER.#'d SETS
1 Andrew Wiggins 12.00 30.00
2 Glenn Robinson III 2.50 6.00
3 Elfrid Payton 4.00 10.00
5 Aaron Gordon 6.00 15.00
6 Damien Inglis 2.50 6.00
8 James Young 2.50 6.00
9 Russ Smith 2.50 6.00
10 K.J. McDaniels 3.00 8.00
12 Rodney Hood 4.00 10.00
13 Noah Vonleh 3.00 8.00
14 Adreian Payne 3.00 8.00
15 Zach LaVine 6.00 15.00
16 Markel Brown 2.50 6.00
17 Doug McDermott 4.00 10.00
18 Spencer Dinwiddie 3.00 8.00
19 Jerami Grant 2.50 6.00
20 Dante Exum 4.00 10.00
21 Cory Jefferson 2.50 6.00
22 Jarnell Stokes 2.50 6.00
23 James Ennis 2.50 6.00
25 Bruno Caboclo 3.00 8.00
26 Gary Harris 4.00 10.00
28 Joel Embiid 12.00 30.00
30 Mitch McGary 2.50 6.00
31 Marcus Smart 4.00 10.00
32 T.J. Warren 4.00 10.00
33 Joe Harris 2.50 6.00
34 Cleanthony Early 2.50 6.00
35 Julius Randle 6.00 15.00
36 P.J. Hairston 2.50 6.00
37 Jabari Parker 6.00 15.00
38 C.J. Wilcox 2.50 6.00

2014-15 Paramount Rookies Home and Away Jerseys Prime

*PRIME: .8X TO 2X BASE HI
STATED PRINT RUN 25 SER.#'d SETS

1968-70 Partridge Meats

These black and white (with some red trim and text) photo-like cards feature players from all three Cincinnati major league sports teams of that time: Cincinnati Reds baseball (BB1-BB20), Cincinnati Bengals football (FB1-FB5), and Cincinnati Royals basketball (BK1-BK2). The cards measure approximately 4" by 5" or 3-3/4" by 5-1/2" and were issued over a period of years. The cards are blank backed and a "Mr. Whopper" card was also issued in honor of the 7'-3" company spokesperson. The Tom Rhoads football card was only recently discovered, in 2012, adding to the prevailing thought that these cards were issued over a period of years since its format matches some of the baseball cards and not the other four more well-known football cards in the set. Joe Morgan was also recently added to the checklist indicating that more cards could turn up in the future. This card follows the same format as Gullett, May, Perez, and Tolan (all measuring 3-3/4" by 5-1/2") missing the team's logo on the cap, missing the team's nickname in the text, and missing the company's slogan below the image. Some collectors believe this style to be consistent with a 1972 release.

1968-70 Partridge Meats

COMPLETE SET (14) 400.00 800.00
BK1 Adrian Smith SP 30.00 60.00
BK2 Tom Van Arsdale SP 30.00 60.00

1977-78 Pepsi All-Stars

This set of eight photos was sponsored by Pepsi. The borderless color player photos measure approximately 8" by 10" and are printed on thick cardboard stock. All the photos depict players either shooting or dunking the ball. The Pepsi logo and the player's name appear in the upper right corner. In blue print the back presents various statistics. The photos are unnumbered and are checklisted below in alphabetical order.
COMPLETE SET (8) 350.00 550.00
1 Rick Barry 15.00 40.00
2 Dave Cowens 15.00 40.00
3 Julius Erving 40.00 75.00
4 Kareem Abdul-Jabbar 40.00 75.00
5 Pete Maravich 150.00 300.00
6 Bob McAdoo 20.00 50.00
7 David Thompson 15.00 40.00
8 Bill Walton 40.00 75.00

1992 Philadelphia Daily News

This nine-card set, which is aptly subtitled "Great Moments in Philadelphia Sports," was sponsored by the Philadelphia Daily News. The fronts of the standard-size cards have red borders and feature miniature reproductions of newspaper front pages with famous headlines and memorable photos. Each card captures a great moment in the history of Philadelphia sports. Sports represented are baseball, (cards 1 and 7-8) hockey, (2) basketball, (3-4) football, (5-6) and boxing (9). The backs are printed in gray, black and white and provide text relating to the event commemorated on the card.

COMPLETE SET (9) 1.40 3.50
3 V .10 .25
Villanova wins NCAA Championship
4 Hoopla .10 .25
Sixers win NBA Championship

1981-82 Philip Morris

This 18-card standard-size set was included in the Champions of American Sport program and features major stars from a variety of sports. The program was issued in conjunction with a traveling exhibition organized by the National Portrait Gallery and the Smithsonian Institution and sponsored by Philip Morris and Miller Brewing Company. The cards are either reproductions of works of art (paintings) or famous photographs of the time. The cards are frequently found with a perforated edge on at least one side. The cards were actually obtained from two perforated pages in the program. There is no notation anywhere on the cards indicating the manufacturer or sponsor.

COMPLETE SET (18) 40.00 100.00
14 Bill Russell 6.00 15.00

1974-75 Picture Buttons

These 11 buttons were issued in 1974, and feature many of the superstar calliber players of the time. Please note that each button was done in full color.

COMPLETE SET (11) 300.00 600.00
1 Kareem Abdul-Jabbar 50.00 100.00
2 Bill Bradley 40.00 80.00
3 Dave DeBusschere 25.00 50.00
4 Walt Frazier 40.00 80.00
5 John Havlicek 50.00 100.00
6 Bob Lanier 25.00 50.00
7 Jerry Lucas 12.50 25.00
8 Pete Maravich 75.00 125.00
9 Willis Reed 40.00 80.00
10 Jerry West 50.00 100.00
11 JoJo White 12.50 25.00

1997 Pinnacle Inside WNBA

The 1997 Pinnacle Inside set was issued in one series totalling 82 cards and honors the first women playing in the WNBA. The set was distributed in cans containing ten cards each with a suggested retail price of $2.99. The fronts feature color action player photos with player information on the backs. The set contains the topical subsets: Hoops Scoops (57-72), and Style & Grace (73-80). Scheduled release date is October, 1997.

COMPLETE SET (81) 12.00 30.00
1 Lisa Leslie RC 2.50 6.00
2 Cynthia Cooper RC 4.00 10.00
3 Rebecca Lobo RC 1.25 3.00
4 Michele Timms RC 1.25 3.00
5 Ruthie Bolton-Holifield RC 1.00 2.50
6 Michelle Edwards RC .40 1.00
7 Vicky Bullett RC .30 .75
8 Tammi Reiss RC .30 .75
9 Penny Toler RC .30 .75
10 Tia Jackson RC .20 .50
11 Rhonda Mapp RC .25 .60
12 Elena Baranova RC .60 1.50
13 Tina Thompson RC 2.50 6.00
14 Merlakia Jones RC .30 .75
15 Tora Suber RC .30 .75
16 Sophia Witherspoon RC .30 .75
17 Tajama Abraham RC .20 .50
18 Jessie Hicks RC .20 .50
19 Tina Nicholson RC .20 .50
20 Tiffany Woosley RC .25 .60
21 Chantel Tremitiere RC .20 .50
22 Daedra Charles RC .20 .50
23 Nancy Lieberman-Cline RC .75 2.00
24 Denique Graves RC .20 .50
25 Toni Foster RC .30 .75
26 Sheryl Swoopes RC 2.50 6.00
27 Kym Hampton RC .30 .75
28 Sharon Manning RC .20 .50
29 Janice Lawrence Braxton RC .20 .50
30 Sue Wicks RC .30 .75
31 Lady Hardmon RC .20 .50
32 Jamila Wideman RC .30 .75
33 Bridgette Gordon RC .20 .50
34 Lynette Woodard RC .50 1.25
35 Kim Perrot RC .75 2.00
36 Teresa Weatherspoon RC 1.50 4.00
37 Andrea Stinson RC .50 1.25
38 Janeth Arcain RC .20 .50
39 Pamela McGee RC .30 .75
40 Tamecka Dixon RC .30 .75
41 Wendy Palmer RC .60 1.50
42 Umeki Webb RC .20 .50
43 Isabelle Fijalkowski RC .20 .50
44 Jennifer Gillom RC .60 1.50
45 Latasha Byears RC .30 .75
46 Haixia Zheng RC .20 .50
47 Kisha Ford RC .20 .50
48 Eva Nemcova RC .40 1.00
49 Penny Moore RC .30 .75
50 Mwadi Mabika RC .20 .50
51 Kim Williams RC .20 .50
52 Wanda Guyton RC .20 .50
53 Vickie Johnson RC .30 .75
54 Deborah Carter RC .20 .50
55 Bridget Pettis RC .20 .50
56 Andrea Congreaves RC .20 .50
57 Haixia Zheng HS .10 .25
58 Tammi Reiss HS .15 .40
59 Jennifer Gillom HS .30 .75
60 Bridgette Gordon HS .10 .25
61 Janice Lawrence Braxton HS .10 .25
62 Cynthia Cooper HS 2.00 5.00
63 Teresa Weatherspoon HS .75 2.00
64 Elena Baranova HS .30 .75
65 N. Lieberman-Cline HS .40 1.00
66 Andrea Congreaves HS .10 .25
67 Sophia Witherspoon HS .15 .40
68 Vicky Bullett HS .15 .40
69 R.Bolton-Holifield HS .50 1.25
70 Tina Thompson HS 1.25 3.00
71 Lynette Woodard HS .25 .60
72 Jamila Wideman HS .15 .40
73 Lisa Leslie SG 1.25 3.00
74 Wendy Palmer SG .30 .75
75 Michele Timms SG .60 1.50
76 R.Bolton-Holifield SG .50 1.25
77 Andrea Stinson SG .25 .60
78 Lynette Woodard SG .25 .60
79 Cynthia Cooper SG 2.00 5.00
80 Rebecca Lobo SG .60 1.50
81 Checklist .20 .50

1997 Pinnacle Inside WNBA Court Collection

COMPLETE SET (81) 40.00 100.00
*COURT: 1.25X TO 3X HI COLUMN
STATED ODDS 1:7

1997 Pinnacle Inside WNBA Executive Collection

*EXEC: 4X TO 10X BASE CARD HI
STATED ODDS 1:47

1997 Pinnacle Inside WNBA Cans

This set of 17 cans feature color action photos of the stars of the league's inaugural season along with their team's logo. Two player cans per team were issued. Each can contained ten cards. A special WNBA can was also distributed. Prices below refer to opened cans.

COMPLETE SET (17) 10.00 25.00
1 Andrea Stinson .50 1.25
2 Vicky Bullett .30 .75
3 Lynette Woodard .50 1.25
4 Michelle Edwards .40 1.00
5 Cynthia Cooper 4.00 10.00
6 Tina Thompson 2.50 6.00
7 Lisa Leslie 2.50 6.00
8 Jamila Wideman .30 .75
9 Teresa Weatherspoon 1.50 4.00
10 Rebecca Lobo 1.25 3.00
11 Michele Timms 1.25 3.00
12 Bridget Pettis .20 .50
13 Bridgette Gordon .20 .50
14 Ruthie Bolton-Holifield 1.00 2.50
15 Wendy Palmer .60 1.50
16 Elena Baranova .60 1.50
17 WNBA League .40 1.00

1997 Pinnacle Inside WNBA My Town

Randomly inserted in cans at the rate of one in 19, this eight-card set features color photos of franchise players printed on a holographic foil card stock with a micro-etched backdrop of the player's team city.

COMPLETE SET (8) 12.00 30.00
1 Lisa Leslie 5.00 12.00
2 Lady Hardmon .40 1.00
3 Michele Timms 2.50 6.00
4 Ruthie Bolton-Holifield 2.00 5.00
5 Andrea Stinson 1.00 2.50
6 Michelle Edwards .75 2.00
7 Cynthia Cooper 8.00 20.00
8 Rebecca Lobo 2.50 6.00

1997 Pinnacle Inside WNBA Team Development

Randomly inserted in cans at the rate of one in 19, this eight-card set features color photos of the WNBA first round draft picks printed on an all-foil card stock with foil stamped treatments.

COMPLETE SET (8) 10.00 25.00
1 Tina Thompson 8.00 20.00
2 Pamela McGee 1.00 2.50
3 Jamila Wideman 1.00 2.50
4 Eva Nemcova 1.25 3.00
5 Tammi Reiss 1.00 2.50
6 Sue Wicks 1.00 2.50
7 Tora Suber 1.00 2.50
8 Toni Foster 1.00 2.50

1998 Pinnacle WNBA

The 1998 Pinnacle WNBA set was issued in one series totalling 85 cards. Each pack came with 10 cards with a suggested retail price of $2.49. This was the second year that Pinnacle distributed the only cards for the WNBA. The card fronts carried either an action or posed player shot, and their statistics from the first year of the WNBA.

COMPLETE SET (85) 10.00 25.00
1 Rhonda Blades RC .30 .75
2 Lisa Leslie 1.25 3.00
3 Jennifer Gillom .50 1.25
4 Ruthie Bolton-Holifield .75 2.00
5 Wendy Palmer .50 1.25
6 Sophia Witherspoon .30 .75
7 Eva Nemcova .30 .75
8 Andrea Stinson .50 1.25
9 Heidi Burge RC .30 .75
10 Cynthia Cooper 1.50 4.00
11 Christy Smith RC .30 .75
12 Penny Moore .30 .75
13 Penny Toler .30 .75
14 Bridget Pettis .20 .50
15 Tora Suber .30 .75
16 Elena Baranova .50 1.25
17 Rebecca Lobo .75 2.00
18 Isabelle Fijalkowski .20 .50
19 Vicky Bullett .30 .75
20 Tina Thompson .75 2.00
21 Andrea Kuklova RC .30 .75
22 Rita Williams RC .40 1.00
23 Tamecka Dixon .30 .75
24 Michele Timms .75 2.00
25 Bridgette Gordon .20 .50
26 Tammi Reiss .30 .75
27 Kym Hampton .30 .75
28 Janice Braxton .20 .50
29 Rhonda Mapp .25 .60
30 Janeth Arcain .20 .50
31 Lynette Woodard .50 1.25
32 Tammy Jackson RC .30 .75
33 Haixia Zheng .20 .50
34 Toni Foster .30 .75
35 Chantel Tremitiere .20 .50
36 Vickie Johnson .30 .75
37 Michelle Edwards .40 1.00
38 Wanda Guyton .20 .50
39 Kim Perrot .60 1.50
40 Sheryl Swoopes 1.25 3.00
41 Merlakia Jones .30 .75
42 Teresa Weatherspoon .75 2.00
43 Kim Williams .20 .50
44 Lady Hardmon .20 .50
45 Latasha Byears .30 .75
46 Umeki Webb .20 .50
47 Pamela McGee .30 .75
48 Nikki McCray RC 1.25 3.00
49 Cindy Brown RC .75 2.00
50 Tiffany Woosley .25 .60
51 Andrea Congreaves .20 .50
52 Jamila Wideman .30 .75
53 Mwadi Mabika .20 .50
54 Murriel Page RC .50 1.25
55 Mikiko Hagiwara RC .30 .75
56 Linda Burgess RC .30 .75
57 Olympia Scott RC .30 .75
58 Dena Head RC .30 .75
59 Quacy Barnes RC .30 .75
60 Suzie McConnell-Serio RC 1.00 2.50
61 Trena Trice RC .30 .75
62 Rushia Brown RC .30 .75
63 Kisha Ford .20 .50
64 Sharon Manning .20 .50
65 Tangela Smith RC .30 .75
66 Jim Lewis CO .20 .50
67 Nancy Lieberman-Cline CO .75 2.00
68 Van Chancellor CO .30 .75
69 Denise Taylor CO .30 .75
70 Heidi VanDerveer CO .30 .75
71 Marynell Meadors CO .20 .50
72 Linda Hill-MacDonald CO .20 .50
73 Nancy Darsch CO .30 .75
74 Cheryl Miller CO 1.25 3.00
75 Julie Rousseau CO .30 .75
76 Rebecca Lobo P .40 1.00
77 Jennifer Gillom P .25 .60
78 Janeth Arcain P .10 .25
79 Rhonda Mapp P .12 .30
80 Cynthia Cooper P .75 2.00
81 Tina Thompson P .40 1.00
82 Kym Hampton P .15 .40
83 Cynthia Cooper P .75 2.00
84 Checklist .20 .50
85 Checklist .20 .50
S66 Sheryl Swoopes PROMO .75 2.00

1998 Pinnacle WNBA Court Collection

*COURT: 1.25X TO 3X BASE CARD HI
STATED ODDS 1:3

1998 Pinnacle WNBA Arena Collection

*ARENA: 4X TO 10X BASE CARD HI
STATED ODDS 1:19

1998 Pinnacle WNBA Coast to Coast

Randomly inserted in packs at a rate of one in 9, this 10-card set features players who can take it from one end of the court to another. The card fronts feature a player photo against silver foil with "Coast 2 Coast" running along the bottom of the card. The card backs feature commentary.

COMPLETE SET (10) 10.00 25.00
1 Lynette Woodard 1.00 2.50
2 Nikki McCray 2.50 6.00
3 Lisa Leslie 2.50 6.00
4 Andrea Stinson 1.00 2.50
5 Eva Nemcova .60 1.50
6 Cynthia Cooper 3.00 8.00
7 Teresa Weatherspoon 1.50 4.00
8 Wendy Palmer 1.00 2.50
9 Ruthie Bolton-Holifield 1.50 4.00
10 Michele Timms 1.50 4.00

1998 Pinnacle WNBA Number Ones

Randomly inserted into packs at a rate of one in 19, this 9-card set features number one draft picks. The card fronts are on silver foil with "Number 1 Ones" across the bottom. Card backs feature a black and white background of the card front with a brief commentary on the player.

COMPLETE SET (9) 8.00 20.00
1 Malgorzata Dydek 2.50 6.00
2 Ticha Penicheiro 3.00 8.00
3 Murriel Page 1.50 4.00
4 Korie Hlede 2.00 5.00
5 Allison Feaster 1.50 4.00
6 Cindy Blodgett 2.00 5.00
7 Tracy Reid 1.25 3.00
8 Alicia Thompson 1.00 2.50
9 Nyree Roberts 1.00 2.50

1998 Pinnacle WNBA Planet Pinnacle

Randomly inserted into packs at a rate of one in 9, this 10-card set features international players. The card fronts feature a posed player shot in a black and red "swirl" against silver foil. Card backs contain a facial shot with commentary.

COMPLETE SET (10) 12.00 30.00
1 Korie Hlede 2.50 6.00
2 Eva Nemcova 1.25 3.00
3 Haixia Zheng .75 2.00
4 Michele Timms 3.00 8.00
5 Ticha Penicheiro 4.00 10.00
6 Elena Baranova 2.00 5.00
7 Rebecca Lobo 3.00 8.00
8 Isabelle Fijalkowski .75 2.00
9 Andrea Congreaves .75 2.00
10 Sheryl Swoopes 5.00 12.00

2013-14 Pinnacle

COMPLETE SET (300) 30.00 80.00
1 C.J. McCollum RC .60 1.50
2 Allen Crabbe RC .30 .75
3 Victor Oladipo RC .50 1.25
4 Ian Clark RC .30 .75
5 G.Antetokounmpo RC 3.00 8.00
6 Reggie Bullock RC .30 .75
7 Luigi Datome RC .25 .60
8 Ricky Ledo RC .25 .60
9 Erik Murphy RC .25 .60
10 Kelly Olynyk RC .30 .75
11 Jeff Withey RC .25 .60
12 Archie Goodwin RC .30 .75
13 Steven Adams RC .40 1.00
14 Dwight Buycks RC .25 .60
15 Elias Harris RC .30 .75
16 Isaiah Canaan RC .25 .60
17 Robert Covington RC .25 .60
18 Sergey Karasev RC .25 .60
19 Cody Zeller RC .30 .75
20 Pero Antic RC .25 .60
21 Ben McLemore RC .30 .75
22 Alex Len RC .30 .75
23 Ognjen Kuzmic RC .25 .60
24 Gorgui Dieng RC .30 .75
25 Jamaal Franklin RC .25 .60
26 Nemanja Nedovic RC .25 .60
27 Kentavious Caldwell-Pope RC .40 1.00
28 Carrick Felix RC .25 .60
29 Mason Plumlee RC .40 1.00
30 Miroslav Raduljica RC .25 .60
31 Glen Rice Jr. RC .25 .60
32 Nerlens Noel RC .50 1.25
33 Andre Roberson RC .25 .60
34 Shabazz Muhammad RC .30 .75
35 Ryan Kelly RC .25 .60
36 Tony Mitchell RC .25 .60
37 Gal Mekel RC .25 .60
38 Anthony Bennett RC .30 .75
39 Vitor Faverani RC .25 .60
40 Dennis Schroder RC .40 1.00
41 Trey Burke RC .30 .75
42 M.Carter-Williams RC .40 1.00
43 Tim Hardaway Jr. RC .40 1.00
44 Nate Wolters RC .30 .75
45 Solomon Hill RC .25 .60
46 Otto Porter RC .40 1.00
47 Shane Larkin RC .25 .60
48 Tony Snell RC .30 .75
49 Phil Pressey RC .25 .60
50 Ray McCallum RC .25 .60
51 Josh Smith .25 .60
52 Andrei Kirilenko .25 .60
53 Chauncey Billups .30 .75
54 Mike Conley .25 .60
55 Kawhi Leonard .50 1.25
56 Marcus Morris .20 .50
57 Serge Ibaka .25 .60
58 Tayshaun Prince .25 .60
59 Will Bynum .20 .50
60 Bradley Beal .30 .75
61 Jared Sullinger .20 .50
62 Taj Gibson .25 .60
63 Draymond Green .40 1.00
64 Ray Allen .30 .75
65 Carl Landry .20 .50
66 Evan Turner .20 .50
67 Anthony Davis .60 1.50
68 Tony Allen .20 .50
69 Ty Lawson .20 .50
70 Emeka Okafor .25 .60
71 Marquis Teague .20 .50
72 Paul Pierce .30 .75
73 Jonas Jerebko .20 .50
74 Marc Gasol .30 .75
75 Damian Lillard .60 1.50
76 Andrew Nicholson .20 .50
77 J.R. Smith .25 .60
78 Zach Randolph .25 .60
79 Rodney Stuckey .25 .60
80 Eric Maynor .20 .50
81 Jamal Crawford .30 .75
82 Mike Dunleavy .20 .50
83 David Lee .20 .50
84 Udonis Haslem .20 .50
85 Robin Lopez .20 .50
86 Jeremy Lamb .20 .50
87 Tyreke Evans .20 .50
88 Tony Wroten .20 .50
89 Dirk Nowitzki .40 1.00
90 John Wall .40 1.00
91 Louis Williams .25 .60
92 Ramon Sessions .25 .60
93 Brandon Knight .25 .60
94 Kosta Koufos .20 .50
95 Manu Ginobili .30 .75
96 Luis Scola .25 .60
97 Thabo Sefolosha .20 .50
98 Nick Young .30 .75
99 Evan Fournier .25 .60
100 Alec Burks .20 .50
101 Kyle Korver .25 .60
102 Kirk Hinrich .25 .60
103 Andrew Bogut .25 .60
104 Norris Cole .20 .50
105 DeMarcus Cousins .30 .75
106 Jason Richardson .30 .75
107 Pablo Prigioni .20 .50
108 Kobe Bryant 1.25 3.00
109 Jae Crowder .25 .60
110 Derrick Favors .25 .60
111 John Jenkins .20 .50
112 Michael Kidd-Gilchrist .30 .75
113 Andre Drummond .30 .75
114 Blake Griffin .30 .75
115 Joel Freeland .20 .50
116 E'Twaun Moore .20 .50
117 Austin Rivers .25 .60
118 Pau Gasol .30 .75
119 J.J. Hickson .20 .50
120 Enes Kanter .20 .50
121 Jeff Teague .25 .60
122 Joakim Noah .25 .60
123 Andre Iguodala .25 .60
124 LeBron James 1.25 3.00
125 Victor Claver .20 .50
126 Kendrick Perkins .20 .50
127 Alexey Shved .20 .50
128 Steve Blake .20 .50
129 Monta Ellis .25 .60
130 Gordon Hayward .30 .75
131 Elton Brand .30 .75
132 Kemba Walker .30 .75
133 Stephen Curry 1.25 3.00
134 Larry Sanders .20 .50
135 Tiago Splitter .25 .60
136 Marcin Gortat .25 .60
137 Amar'e Stoudemire .25 .60
138 Robert Sacre .20 .50
139 JaVale McGee .25 .60
140 John Lucas III .20 .50
141 Al Horford .25 .60
142 Jimmy Butler .30 .75
143 Jeremy Lin .30 .75
144 Mario Chalmers .25 .60
145 Greivis Vasquez .25 .60
146 Spencer Hawes .20 .50
147 Carmelo Anthony .40 1.00
148 Steve Nash .30 .75
149 Samuel Dalembert .20 .50
150 Amir Johnson .20 .50
151 Rajon Rondo .30 .75
152 Bismack Biyombo .20 .50
153 Klay Thompson .40 1.00
154 O.J. Mayo .20 .50
155 LaMarcus Aldridge .30 .75
156 Jameer Nelson .20 .50
157 Eric Gordon .25 .60
158 Chris Paul .40 1.00
159 Jordan Hamilton .20 .50
160 D.J. Augustin .20 .50
161 MarShon Brooks .25 .60
162 Derrick Rose .40 1.00
163 James Harden .50 1.25
164 Dwyane Wade .50 1.25
165 Will Barton .20 .50
166 Kevin Durant .75 2.00
167 Corey Brewer .20 .50
168 David West .25 .60
169 Shawn Marion .25 .60
170 DeMar DeRozan .30 .75
171 Kris Humphries .20 .50
172 Al Jefferson .25 .60
173 Kent Bazemore .25 .60
174 John Henson .25 .60
175 Tim Duncan .50 1.25
176 P.J. Tucker .20 .50
177 Andrea Bargnani .25 .60
178 DeAndre Jordan .30 .75
179 Kenneth Faried .25 .60
180 Jonas Valanciunas .25 .60
181 Jeff Green .25 .60
182 Tyler Zeller .25 .60
183 Dwight Howard .25 .60
184 Ersan Ilyasova .20 .50
185 Isaiah Thomas .30 .75
186 Thaddeus Young .20 .50
187 Raymond Felton .25 .60
188 George Hill .25 .60
189 Vince Carter .40 1.00
190 Kyle Lowry .25 .60
191 Brandon Bass .20 .50
192 Luol Deng .25 .60
193 Harrison Barnes .25 .60
194 Ricky Rubio .30 .75
195 Meyers Leonard .20 .50
196 Nikola Vucevic .25 .60
197 Jrue Holiday .30 .75
198 J.J. Redick .30 .75
199 Nate Robinson .20 .50
200 Landry Fields .20 .50
201 Avery Bradley .25 .60
202 Tristan Thompson .25 .60
203 Chandler Parsons .25 .60
204 Chris Andersen .25 .60
205 Eric Bledsoe .25 .60
206 Ronnie Brewer .25 .60
207 Derrick Williams .20 .50
208 Danny Granger .25 .60
209 Chris Kaman .25 .60
210 Rudy Gay .30 .75
211 Kevin Garnett .50 1.25
212 Jarrett Jack .25 .60
213 Aaron Brooks .20 .50
214 Kevin Martin .25 .60
215 Tony Parker .30 .75
216 Markieff Morris .20 .50
217 Iman Shumpert .20 .50
218 Jared Dudley .20 .50
219 Randy Foye .20 .50
220 Terrence Ross .25 .60
221 Joe Johnson .25 .60
222 Kyrie Irving .60 1.50
223 Roy Hibbert .25 .60
224 Nikola Pekovic .20 .50
225 Jimmer Fredette .20 .50
226 Lavoy Allen .20 .50
227 Al-Farouq Aminu .25 .60
228 Chris Copeland .20 .50
229 Anderson Varejao .20 .50
230 Boris Diaw .25 .60
231 Jason Terry .25 .60
232 Earl Clark .20 .50
233 Paul George .40 1.00
234 Brandon Jennings .20 .50
235 Nicolas Batum .25 .60
236 Tobias Harris .25 .60
237 Ryan Anderson .25 .60
238 Matt Barnes .20 .50
239 Timofey Mozgov .20 .50
240 Danny Green .25 .60
241 Deron Williams .25 .60
242 C.J. Miles .25 .60
243 Lance Stephenson .25 .60
244 Chris Bosh .30 .75
245 Goran Dragic .25 .60
246 Russell Westbrook .75 2.00
247 Kevin Love .30 .75
248 Ryan Hollins .20 .50
249 Andrew Bynum .20 .50
250 Brook Lopez .25 .60
251 Dikembe Mutombo .30 .75
252 Dan Issel .25 .60
253 Magic Johnson .75 2.00
254 Oscar Robertson .40 1.00
255 Wilt Chamberlain .60 1.50
256 Shawn Kemp .50 1.25
257 Gheorghe Muresan .20 .50
258 David Robinson .50 1.25
259 Patrick Ewing .40 1.00
260 Jason Williams .25 .60
261 Yao Ming .40 1.00
262 Michael Finley .30 .75
263 Dominique Wilkins .40 1.00
264 Mark Price .30 .75
265 George McGinnis .20 .50
266 Christian Laettner .25 .60
267 Julius Erving .50 1.25
268 Nate Thurmond .25 .60
269 Manute Bol .30 .75
270 Clyde Drexler .40 1.00
271 George Mikan .60 1.50
272 Bob Lanier .25 .60
273 Larry Bird .75 2.00
274 Isiah Thomas .30 .75
275 Elgin Baylor .30 .75
276 Anfernee Hardaway .75 2.00
277 World B. Free .25 .60
278 Karl Malone .40 1.00
279 Walt Frazier .30 .75
280 Bill Walton .30 .75
281 David Thompson .25 .60
282 Bill Russell .50 1.25
283 Rolando Blackman .25 .60
284 Alonzo Mourning .40 1.00
285 George Gervin .30 .75
286 John Stockton .50 1.25
287 Tom Chambers .25 .60
288 Eddie Jones .25 .60
289 Larry Nance .25 .60
290 Scottie Pippen .60 1.50
291 Nate Archibald .25 .60
292 Jason Kidd .30 .75
293 Spud Webb .25 .60
294 Gary Payton .30 .75
295 Shaquille O'Neal .60 1.50
296 Drazen Petrovic .30 .75
297 Kareem Abdul-Jabbar .50 1.25
298 Dennis Rodman .60 1.50
299 Rick Barry .25 .60
300 Hakeem Olajuwon .40 1.00

2013-14 Pinnacle Artist's Proofs

*AP 1-50: 1X TO 2.5X BASIC
*AP 51-300: 1.2X TO 3X BASIC

2013-14 Pinnacle Artist's Proofs Blue

*AP BLUE 1-50: .6X TO 1.5X BASIC
*AP BLUE 51-300: .6X TO 1.5X BASIC

2013-14 Pinnacle Artist's Proofs Green

*AP GREEN 1-50: X TO X BASIC
*AP GREEN 51-300: X TO X BASIC
STATED PRINT RUN 25 SER.#'d SETS

2013-14 Pinnacle Artist's Proofs Red

*AP RED 1-50: .6X TO 1.5X BASIC
*AP RED 51-300: .6X TO 1.5X BASIC

2013-14 Pinnacle Autographs

EXCHANGE DEADLINE 7/15/2015
1 Kyrie Irving 40.00 80.00
2 Al Horford 3.00 8.00
3 Alan Anderson 2.50 6.00
4 Alex Len 3.00 8.00
5 Al-Farouq Aminu 3.00 8.00
6 Allan Houston
7 Allen Crabbe 3.00 8.00
8 Andre Drummond 4.00 10.00
9 Andre Miller 3.00 8.00
10 Andre Roberson 2.50 6.00
11 Andrei Kirilenko 3.00 8.00
12 Andrew Bogut 15.00 40.00
13 Anfernee Hardaway 30.00 80.00
14 Antawn Jamison
15 Anthony Bennett 3.00 8.00
16 Anthony Davis 30.00 80.00
17 Anthony Mason
18 Archie Goodwin 3.00 8.00
19 Artis Gilmore 3.00 8.00
20 Bailey Howell 4.00 10.00
21 Ben Gordon
22 Ben McLemore 3.00 8.00
23 Bill Cartwright 3.00 8.00
24 Bill Sharman 4.00 10.00
25 Blake Griffin
26 Bob Dandridge 2.50 6.00
27 Bobby Jackson 2.50 6.00
28 Brent Barry 2.50 6.00
29 Brook Lopez
30 Bruce Bowen 2.50 6.00
31 Bryon Russell 2.50 6.00
32 Ian Clark 3.00 8.00
33 C.J. McCollum 25.00 60.00
34 C.J. Miles 3.00 8.00
35 Calvin Murphy
36 Campy Russell 2.50 6.00
37 Carl Landry
38 Caron Butler 3.00 8.00
39 Cazzie Russell 3.00 8.00
40 Cedric Maxwell
41 Chase Budinger
42 Chris Kaman 3.00 8.00
43 Chris Mullin 10.00 25.00
44 Chris Whitney 2.50 6.00
45 Clyde Drexler 20.00 50.00
46 Cody Zeller 3.00 8.00
47 Connie Hawkins
48 Corey Brewer 2.50 6.00
49 Courtney Lee
50 D.J. Augustin
51 Dale Davis 2.50 6.00
52 Damon Jones 2.50 6.00
53 Dan Majerle
54 Danny Manning
55 Darrell Walker 4.00 10.00
56 David Robinson 15.00 40.00
57 David Thompson
58 Dennis Schroder 4.00 10.00
59 Derek Anderson 2.50 6.00
60 Deron Williams
61 Derrick Coleman 4.00 10.00
62 Derrick Favors 3.00 8.00
63 Doc Rivers
64 Dominique Wilkins 6.00 15.00
65 Draymond Green 8.00 20.00
66 Dwight Howard 6.00 15.00
67 Dwyane Wade
68 Earl Clark 2.50 6.00
69 Earl Monroe
70 Eric Maynor
71 Erik Murphy 2.50 6.00
72 Ersan Ilyasova
73 Fat Lever 3.00 8.00
74 Gary Payton 12.00 30.00
75 George Hill
76 Giannis Antetokounmpo 60.00 150.00
77 Glen Rice Jr. 2.50 6.00
78 Gorgui Dieng 3.00 8.00
79 Grant Hill 20.00 50.00
80 Carrick Felix 2.50 6.00
81 Greg Anthony 2.50 6.00
82 Greg Ostertag 5.00 12.00
83 Hakeem Olajuwon
84 Harrison Barnes
85 Harvey Grant
86 Horace Grant 4.00 10.00
87 Isaiah Canaan 2.50 6.00
88 Isiah Thomas
89 Jamaal Franklin 2.50 6.00
90 Jalen Rose 4.00 10.00
91 Ish Smith 2.50 6.00
92 Jan Vesely
93 Jared Dudley 2.50 6.00
94 Jared Jeffries
95 Jarrett Jack 3.00 8.00
96 Jason Kidd 15.00 40.00
97 Jeff Malone 2.50 6.00
98 Jeff Ayres 2.50 6.00
99 Jeff Taylor 2.50 6.00
100 Jeff Withey 2.50 6.00
101 Jimmer Fredette 2.50 6.00
102 Jo Jo White 3.00 8.00
103 John Henson
104 John Lucas 4.00 10.00
105 John Salley 8.00 20.00
106 Jon Leuer
107 Jonas Jerebko 2.50 6.00
108 Josh Harrellson
109 Josh Smith
110 K.C. Jones
111 Kareem Abdul-Jabbar 25.00 60.00
112 Kawhi Leonard 40.00 100.00
113 Kelly Olynyk 3.00 8.00
114 Kenny Walker 2.50 6.00
115 Kentavious Caldwell-Pope
116 Kevin Durant 60.00 150.00
117 Kevin Willis 6.00 15.00
118 Khris Middleton 3.00 8.00
119 Kobe Bryant 60.00 150.00
120 Kurt Rambis 2.50 6.00
121 Jayson Williams 2.50 6.00
122 Kyle Lowry
123 Dennis Rodman 20.00 50.00
124 Lamond Murray
125 Lance Stephenson 3.00 8.00
126 Larry Bird 30.00 60.00
127 Lavoy Allen
128 Leonard Robinson 2.50 6.00
129 Lindsey Hunter 2.50 6.00
130 Luc Longley 3.00 8.00
131 Magic Johnson
132 Nick Collison 3.00 8.00
133 Marcus Thornton
134 Mark Jackson
135 MarShon Brooks 3.00 8.00
136 Marvin Williams
137 Mason Plumlee 4.00 10.00
138 Maurice Harkless
139 Michael Cage 2.50 6.00
140 Michael Carter-Williams 4.00 10.00
141 Michael Finley
142 Micheal Ray Richardson
143 Mike Conley
144 Mitch Richmond 10.00 25.00
145 Muggsy Bogues 3.00 8.00
146 Nate Archibald 10.00 25.00
147 Nate Wolters 3.00 8.00
148 Nemanja Nedovic 2.50 6.00
149 Nerlens Noel 5.00 12.00
150 Nick Anderson 4.00 10.00
151 Nick Young 4.00 10.00
152 Nikola Pekovic
153 Nikola Vucevic 3.00 8.00
154 Hollis Thompson 3.00 8.00
155 Otto Porter 10.00 25.00
156 Peja Stojakovic 8.00 20.00
157 Peyton Siva 2.50 6.00
158 Ray McCallum 2.50 6.00
159 Phil Pressey 2.50 6.00
160 Reggie Jackson
161 Richard Jefferson
162 Rick Fox
163 Ricky Ledo 2.50 6.00
164 Robbie Hummel 2.50 6.00
165 Rod Strickland
166 Roy Hibbert
167 Rudy Gobert 12.00 30.00
168 Ryan Kelly 3.00 8.00
169 Sam Jones 8.00 20.00
170 Scott Skiles
171 Scottie Pippen 50.00 120.00
172 Shelvin Mack 2.50 6.00
173 Shabazz Muhammad 3.00 8.00
174 Shane Larkin 2.50 6.00
175 Sidney Moncrief 5.00 12.00
176 Sleepy Floyd 2.50 6.00
177 Solomon Hill 2.50 6.00
178 Steve Kerr 4.00 10.00
179 Tayshaun Prince 3.00 8.00
180 Terry Porter 2.50 6.00
181 Tim Hardaway Jr. 4.00 10.00
182 Satch Sanders 4.00 10.00
183 Tom Gugliotta
184 Toni Kukoc 10.00 25.00
185 Tracy McGrady 15.00 40.00
186 Gal Mekel 2.50 6.00
187 Tony Snell 3.00 8.00
188 Travis Best
189 Trey Burke 3.00 8.00
190 Victor Oladipo 12.00 30.00
191 Vin Baker 2.50 6.00
192 Vince Carter 15.00 40.00
193 Vinny Del Negro
194 Vlade Divac
195 Walt Bellamy 3.00 8.00
196 Wes Unseld 4.00 10.00
197 World B. Free
198 Xavier Henry
199 Zach Randolph
200 Zydrunas Ilgauskas

2013-14 Pinnacle Awaiting the Call

COMPLETE SET (15) 8.00 20.00
1 Jason Kidd .60 1.50
2 Grant Hill .75 2.00
3 Kobe Bryant 2.50 6.00
4 Tim Duncan 1.00 2.50
5 Shaquille O'Neal 1.25 3.00
6 Dwyane Wade 1.00 2.50
7 Kevin Garnett 1.00 2.50
8 LeBron James 2.50 6.00
9 Paul Pierce .60 1.50
10 Ray Allen .60 1.50
11 Tony Parker .60 1.50
12 Steve Nash .60 1.50
13 Chris Bosh .60 1.50
14 Chris Paul .75 2.00
15 Vince Carter .75 2.00

2013-14 Pinnacle Awaiting the Call Artist's Proofs

*AP: .6X TO 1.5X BASIC

2013-14 Pinnacle Awaiting the Call Artist's Proofs Green

*AP GREEN: 1.5X TO 4X BASIC
STATED PRINT RUN 25 SER.#'d SETS

2013-14 Pinnacle Awaiting the Call Die Cuts

*DIE CUT: 1X TO 2.5X BASIC
STATED PRINT RUN 99 SER.#'d SETS

2013-14 Pinnacle Behind the Numbers

COMPLETE SET (20) 8.00 20.00
1 Tim Duncan 1.00 2.50
2 Kyrie Irving 1.25 3.00
3 Kobe Bryant 2.50 6.00
4 Kevin Durant 1.50 4.00
5 Blake Griffin .60 1.50
6 Damian Lillard 1.25 3.00
7 LeBron James 2.50 6.00
8 Chris Paul .75 2.00
9 Ricky Rubio .60 1.50
10 Stephen Curry 2.50 6.00
11 Rajon Rondo .60 1.50
12 Dwight Howard .50 1.25
13 Carmelo Anthony .75 2.00
14 Derrick Rose .75 2.00
15 Dirk Nowitzki .75 2.00
16 Patrick Ewing .75 2.00
17 Dennis Rodman 1.25 3.00
18 Larry Bird 1.50 4.00
19 Magic Johnson 1.50 4.00
20 Shaquille O'Neal 1.25 3.00

2013-14 Pinnacle Behind the Numbers Artist's Proofs

*AP: .6X TO 1.5X BASIC

2013-14 Pinnacle Behind the Numbers Artist's Proofs Green

*AP GREEN: 1.5X TO 4X BASIC
STATED PRINT RUN 25 SER.#'d SETS

2013-14 Pinnacle Behind the Numbers Die Cuts

*DIE CUT: 1X TO 2.5X BASIC
STATED PRINT RUN 99 SER.#'d SETS

2013-14 Pinnacle Big Bang

COMPLETE SET (20) 6.00 15.00
1 Andre Drummond .60 1.50
2 Anderson Varejao .40 1.00
3 Tyson Chandler .50 1.25
4 Joakim Noah .50 1.25
5 Al Horford .50 1.25
6 DeAndre Jordan .60 1.50
7 Marcin Gortat .50 1.25
8 Nikola Vucevic .50 1.25
9 Kevin Love .60 1.50
10 Enes Kanter .40 1.00
11 Dwight Howard .50 1.25
12 Al Jefferson .50 1.25
13 Marc Gasol .60 1.50
14 Udonis Haslem .40 1.00
15 Tim Duncan 1.00 2.50
16 David Lee .40 1.00
17 Pau Gasol .60 1.50
18 Roy Hibbert .50 1.25
19 Jonas Valanciunas .50 1.25
20 Serge Ibaka .50 1.25

2013-14 Pinnacle Big Bang Artist's Proofs

*AP: .6X TO 1.5X BASIC

2013-14 Pinnacle Big Bang Artist's Proofs Green

*AP GREEN: 1.5X TO 4X BASIC
STATED PRINT RUN 25 SER.#'d SETS

2013-14 Pinnacle Big Bang Die Cuts

*DIE CUT: 1X TO 2.5X BASIC
STATED PRINT RUN 99 SER.#'d SETS

2013-14 Pinnacle Clear Vision 1st Quarter

1 Kobe Bryant 5.00 12.00

2 Serge Ibaka 1.00 2.50
3 Paul George 1.50 4.00
4 Brandon Knight 1.00 2.50
5 Joakim Noah 1.00 2.50
6 Avery Bradley 1.00 2.50
7 Tony Parker 1.25 3.00
8 Marcin Gortat 1.00 2.50
9 Carmelo Anthony 1.50 4.00
10 Dwyane Wade 2.00 5.00
11 Manu Ginobili 1.25 3.00
12 George Hill 1.00 2.50
13 Andre Drummond 1.25 3.00
14 Jimmy Butler 1.25 3.00
15 Jeff Teague 1.00 2.50
16 Tim Duncan 2.00 5.00
17 Eric Bledsoe 1.00 2.50
18 Eric Gordon 1.00 2.50
19 Chris Bosh 1.25 3.00
20 Larry Sanders .75 2.00
21 Jeremy Lin 1.25 3.00
22 Ty Lawson 1.00 2.50
23 Derrick Rose 1.50 4.00
24 Al Horford 1.00 2.50
25 Kawhi Leonard 2.00 5.00
26 Thaddeus Young .75 2.00
27 Anthony Davis 2.50 6.00
28 Zach Randolph 1.00 2.50
29 J.J. Redick 1.25 3.00
30 James Harden 2.00 5.00
31 Kenneth Faried 1.00 2.50
32 Michael Kidd-Gilchrist 1.25 3.00
33 John Wall 1.50 4.00
34 Jimmer Fredette .75 2.00
35 Evan Turner .75 2.00
36 Ricky Rubio 1.25 3.00
37 Mike Conley 1.00 2.50
38 Amar'e Stoudemire 1.00 2.50
39 Dwight Howard 1.00 2.50
40 Vince Carter 1.50 4.00
41 Kemba Walker 1.25 3.00
42 Bradley Beal 1.25 3.00
43 Isaiah Thomas 1.25 3.00
44 Tobias Harris 1.00 2.50
45 Kevin Love 1.25 3.00
46 Pau Gasol 1.25 3.00
47 Nicolas Batum 1.00 2.50
48 Stephen Curry 5.00 12.00
49 Shawn Marion 1.00 2.50
50 Paul Pierce 1.25 3.00
51 Gordon Hayward 1.25 3.00
52 DeMarcus Cousins 1.25 3.00
53 Nikola Vucevic 1.00 2.50
54 John Henson 1.00 2.50
55 Steve Nash 1.25 3.00
56 Jared Sullinger .75 2.00
57 Harrison Barnes 1.00 2.50
58 Dirk Nowitzki 1.50 4.00
59 Kris Humphries .75 2.00
60 Derrick Favors 1.00 2.50
61 LaMarcus Aldridge 1.25 3.00
62 Russell Westbrook 3.00 8.00
63 Ersan Ilyasova .75 2.00
64 Chris Paul 1.50 4.00
65 JaVale McGee 1.00 2.50
66 David Lee .75 2.00
67 Anderson Varejao .75 2.00
68 Deron Williams 1.00 2.50
69 Jonas Valanciunas 1.00 2.50
70 Damian Lillard 2.50 6.00
71 Kevin Durant 3.00 8.00
72 LeBron James 5.00 12.00
73 Blake Griffin 1.25 3.00
74 Chandler Parsons 1.00 2.50
75 Greg Monroe 1.00 2.50
76 Kyrie Irving 2.50 6.00
77 Rajon Rondo 1.25 3.00
78 DeMar DeRozan 1.25 3.00
79 Goran Dragic 1.00 2.50
80 Tyson Chandler 1.00 2.50
81 Magic Johnson 3.00 8.00
82 Larry Bird 3.00 8.00
83 David Robinson 2.00 5.00
84 Hakeem Olajuwon 1.50 4.00
85 Pete Maravich 2.00 5.00
86 Wilt Chamberlain 2.50 6.00
87 Shaquille O'Neal 2.50 6.00
88 George Gervin 1.25 3.00
89 Anfernee Hardaway 3.00 8.00
90 Karl Malone 1.50 4.00
91 Scottie Pippen 2.50 6.00
92 Gary Payton 1.25 3.00
93 Earl Monroe 1.25 3.00
94 Kareem Abdul-Jabbar 2.00 5.00
95 Shawn Kemp 1.00 2.50
96 Isiah Thomas 2.00 5.00
97 Dennis Rodman 2.50 6.00
98 Grant Hill 1.50 4.00
99 Jason Kidd 1.25 3.00
100 John Stockton 2.00 5.00

2013-14 Pinnacle Clear Vision 2nd Quarter
*2ND QTR: 1X TO 2.5X BASIC
STATED PRINT RUN 36 SER.#'d SETS

2013-14 Pinnacle Clear Vision 3rd Quarter
*3RD QTR: 1.5X TO 4X BASIC
STATED PRINT RUN 24 SER.#'d SETS

2013-14 Pinnacle Essence of the Game Autographs
PRINT RUNS B/WN 25-199 COPIES PER
EXCHANGE DEADLINE 7/15/2015
1 D.J. Augustin/199 4.00 10.00
2 Andre Miller/99
3 Ersan Ilyasova/199
4 Andray Blatche/199 4.00 10.00
5 Jordan Crawford/199 4.00 10.00
6 Ronnie Brewer/179
7 Tyreke Evans/49
8 John Lucas/199 6.00 15.00
9 Darrell Griffith/199 4.00 10.00
10 Steve Smith/199 6.00 15.00
11 Nicolas Batum/199 EXCH 12.00 30.00
12 Allan Houston/99
13 Kenneth Faried/99
14 Kyrie Irving/99 30.00 80.00
15 Goran Dragic/99 12.00 30.00
16 Marcin Gortat/99 15.00 40.00
17 B.J. Armstrong/99 8.00 20.00
18 Greivis Vasquez/199 5.00 12.00
19 Blake Griffin/99
20 Maurice Harkless/199 4.00 10.00
21 Tiago Splitter/149
22 Norm Nixon/199
23 Reggie Theus/199 5.00 12.00
24 Kevin Martin/49
25 Andrew Bogut/99 10.00 25.00
26 Derrick Favors/49
27 J.J. Redick/99 6.00 15.00
28 Jared Dudley/25
29 Zydrunas Ilgauskas/199 5.00 12.00
30 Mike Conley/99
31 Ty Lawson/49 4.00 10.00
32 Nick Van Exel/49 8.00 20.00
33 Spud Webb/199
34 Andre Drummond/49 6.00 15.00
35 Kawhi Leonard/99 50.00 120.00
36 Iman Shumpert/199
37 Nikola Pekovic/199 4.00 10.00
38 Steve Blake/199 4.00 10.00
39 Jimmer Fredette/149
40 Steve Francis/49 12.00 30.00
41 Charles Oakley/199 6.00 15.00
42 Zach Randolph/49
43 Chuck Person/99 8.00 20.00
44 Kobe Bryant/99 100.00 200.00
45 Kevin Durant/99 60.00 150.00
46 Chase Budinger/149 4.00 10.00
47 Monta Ellis/49 5.00 12.00
48 Ramon Sessions/199
49 Shannon Brown/199
50 DeMarcus Cousins/25 10.00 25.00

2013-14 Pinnacle Jamfest
COMPLETE SET (20) 8.00 20.00
1 Terrence Ross .50 1.25
2 Paul George .75 2.00
3 Harrison Barnes .50 1.25
4 Kenneth Faried .50 1.25
5 Blake Griffin .60 1.50
6 DeMar DeRozan .60 1.50
7 DeAndre Jordan .60 1.50
8 J.R. Smith .50 1.25
9 LeBron James 2.50 6.00
10 Kevin Durant 1.50 4.00
11 Kobe Bryant 2.50 6.00
12 Amar'e Stoudemire .50 1.25
13 Vince Carter .75 2.00
14 James Harden 1.00 2.50
15 Dwyane Wade 1.00 2.50
16 Dominique Wilkins .75 2.00
17 Clyde Drexler .75 2.00
18 Julius Erving 1.00 2.50
19 Larry Nance .50 1.25
20 Darryl Dawkins .40 1.00

2013-14 Pinnacle Jamfest Artist's Proofs
*AP: .6X TO 1.5X BASIC

2013-14 Pinnacle Jamfest Artist's Proofs Green
*AP GREEN: 1.5X TO 4X BASIC
STATED PRINT RUN 25 SER.#'d SETS

2013-14 Pinnacle Jamfest Die Cuts
*DIE CUT: 1X TO 2.5X BASIC
STATED PRINT RUN 99 SER.#'d SETS

2013-14 Pinnacle Museum Collection
*MUSEUM 1-50: 1.5X TO 4X BASIC
*MUSEUM 51-300: 2X TO 5X BASIC

2013-14 Pinnacle Performers Jerseys
1 Tim Duncan 4.00 10.00
2 Monta Ellis 2.00 5.00
3 Michael Kidd-Gilchrist 2.50 6.00
4 Mo Williams 2.00 5.00
5 J.R. Smith
6 Nick Young 4.00 10.00
7 Matt Barnes
8 Pablo Prigioni 1.50 4.00
9 Dirk Nowitzki 3.00 8.00
10 Kobe Bryant 8.00 20.00
11 Kevin Durant 6.00 15.00
12 Dwight Howard 2.00 5.00
13 Tony Parker 2.50 6.00
14 Kevin Love 2.50 6.00
15 Russell Westbrook
16 Rajon Rondo
17 Raymond Felton 2.00 5.00
18 Amar'e Stoudemire
19 Ryan Anderson
20 Stephen Curry 10.00 25.00
21 Steve Nash 2.50 6.00
22 Ty Lawson 1.50 4.00
23 Ben Gordon 2.00 5.00
24 Kyrie Irving 5.00 12.00
25 Chris Bosh 2.50 6.00
26 Kawhi Leonard 4.00 10.00
27 Zach Randolph 2.00 5.00
28 LeBron James 10.00 25.00
29 Andre Drummond 2.50 6.00
30 Kenneth Faried 2.00 5.00
31 Brandan Wright 1.50 4.00
32 Carl Landry 1.50 4.00
33 Carlos Delfino
34 Carmelo Anthony 3.00 8.00
35 Anthony Davis 5.00 12.00
36 Al Jefferson 2.00 5.00
37 Dwyane Wade 4.00 10.00
38 Danny Green 2.00 5.00
39 DeAndre Jordan 2.50 6.00
40 DeMar DeRozan 2.50 6.00
41 Deron Williams 2.00 5.00
42 Derrick Favors 2.00 5.00
43 Derrick Rose 2.50 6.00
44 Dion Waiters 2.00 5.00
45 Ersan Ilyasova 1.50 4.00
46 Jason Terry 2.00 5.00
47 Gerald Henderson 1.50 4.00
48 Glen Davis 1.50 4.00
49 Gordon Hayward 2.50 6.00
50 Jason Richardson 2.50 6.00
51 Paul Pierce 2.50 6.00
52 Andrew Bynum
53 MarShon Brooks 2.00 5.00
54 LaMarcus Aldridge 2.50 6.00
55 Kevin Garnett 4.00 10.00
56 Evan Fournier 2.00 5.00
57 Roy Hibbert 2.00 5.00
58 Blake Griffin 2.50 6.00
59 Channing Frye
60 Omer Asik 2.00 5.00
61 David Lee 1.50 4.00
62 Rodney Stuckey
63 Kirk Hinrich 2.00 5.00
64 Joakim Noah 2.00 5.00
65 Avery Bradley 2.00 5.00

2013-14 Pinnacle Performers Jerseys Prime
*PRIME: 1.2X TO 3X BASIC
PRINT RUN B/WN 1-25 COPIES PER
NO PRICING ON QTY 10 OR LESS

2013-14 Pinnacle Pinnacle of Success Autographs
PRINT RUNS B/WN 25-199 COPIES PER
EXCHANGE DEADLINE 7/15/2015
1 Stephen Curry/99 60.00 150.00
2 Jason Terry/99 5.00 12.00
3 Joakim Noah/99
4 John Havlicek/25
5 Ralph Sampson/99 5.00 12.00
6 Toni Kukoc/199 6.00 15.00
7 Scottie Pippen/49
8 Steve Kerr/99 10.00 25.00
9 Sean Elliott/199 6.00 15.00
10 Elvin Hayes/99 6.00 15.00
11 Michael Finley/99 12.00 30.00
12 Rick Mahorn/199 4.00 10.00
13 Mark Jackson/99 5.00 12.00
14 Kobe Bryant/99 100.00 200.00
15 Kevin Durant/49 60.00 150.00
16 Chris Bosh/49 10.00 25.00
17 Tony Parker/49 40.00 100.00
18 Hakeem Olajuwon/49 15.00 40.00
19 Steve Nash/25
20 Gail Goodrich/99 6.00 15.00
21 Jerry West/49
22 Walt Bellamy/99
23 Mario Chalmers/99 EXCH 5.00 12.00
24 Chris Andersen/49 40.00 80.00
25 Tom Heinsohn/199 20.00 50.00
26 Sidney Moncrief/199 4.00 10.00
27 Spencer Haywood/199 4.00 10.00
28 Horace Grant/99 12.00 30.00
29 Kyrie Irving/99 30.00 80.00
30 Norris Cole/199 4.00 10.00
31 Byron Scott/99 5.00 12.00
32 Julius Erving/49 50.00 100.00
33 Larry Bird/49 40.00 80.00
34 Magic Johnson/49 EXCH 40.00 80.00
35 Tyson Chandler/99 5.00 12.00
36 Glen Rice/99
37 Grant Hill/99 25.00 60.00
38 Bill Laimbeer/199 5.00 12.00
39 Bill Walton/99 6.00 15.00
40 Jack Sikma/199 5.00 12.00
41 A.C. Green/199 6.00 15.00
42 Robert Horry/199 12.00 30.00
43 Anderson Varejao/99 4.00 10.00
44 Kyle Lowry/199 5.00 12.00
45 Jonas Valanciunas/199 5.00 12.00
46 Kenny Smith/99 5.00 12.00
47 Jrue Holiday/99 6.00 15.00
48 Vlade Divac/199 6.00 15.00
49 Bob Dandridge/199 6.00 15.00
50 Bill Cartwright/199 5.00 12.00

2013-14 Pinnacle Position Powers
1 Pete Maravich 1.00 2.50
2 Magic Johnson 1.50 4.00
3 John Stockton 1.00 2.50
4 Mark Jackson .50 1.25
5 Kobe Bryant 2.50 6.00
6 Clyde Drexler .75 2.00
7 George Gervin .60 1.50
8 Allen Iverson .75 2.00
9 LeBron James 2.50 6.00
10 Larry Bird 1.50 4.00
11 Julius Erving 1.00 2.50
12 Scottie Pippen 1.25 3.00
13 Karl Malone .75 2.00
14 Tim Duncan 1.00 2.50
15 Dirk Nowitzki .75 2.00
16 Dennis Rodman 1.25 3.00
17 Shaquille O'Neal 1.25 3.00
18 Bill Russell 1.00 2.50
19 Kareem Abdul-Jabbar 1.00 2.50
20 Wilt Chamberlain 1.25 3.00

2013-14 Pinnacle Position Powers Artist's Proofs
*AP: .6X TO 1.5X BASIC

2013-14 Pinnacle Position Powers Artist's Proofs Green
*AP GREEN: 1.5X TO 4X BASIC
STATED PRINT RUN 25 SER.#'d SETS

2013-14 Pinnacle Position Powers Die Cuts
*DIE CUT: 1X TO 2.5X BASIC
STATED PRINT RUN 99 SER.#'d SETS

2013-14 Pinnacle Scoring Kings
COMPLETE SET (15) 8.00 20.00
1 Kareem Abdul-Jabbar 1.00 2.50
2 Karl Malone .75 2.00
3 Kobe Bryant 2.50 6.00
4 Wilt Chamberlain 1.25 3.00
5 Julius Erving 1.00 2.50
6 Moses Malone .60 1.50
7 Shaquille O'Neal 1.25 3.00
8 Dan Issel .50 1.25
9 Elvin Hayes .60 1.50
10 Hakeem Olajuwon .75 2.00
11 Oscar Robertson .75 2.00
12 Dominique Wilkins .75 2.00
13 George Gervin .60 1.50
14 John Havlicek .75 2.00
15 Alex English .60 1.50

2013-14 Pinnacle Scoring Kings Artist's Proofs
*AP: .6X TO 1.5X BASIC

2013-14 Pinnacle Scoring Kings Artist's Proofs Green
*AP GREEN: 1.5X TO 4X BASIC
STATED PRINT RUN 25 SER.#'d SETS

2013-14 Pinnacle Scoring Kings Die Cuts
*DIE CUT: 1X TO 2.5X BASIC
STATED PRINT RUN 99 SER.#'d SETS

2013-14 Pinnacle Team 2020
1 Anthony Bennett .50 1.25
2 Kyrie Irving 1.25 3.00
3 Brandon Knight .50 1.25
4 Bradley Beal .60 1.50
5 Harrison Barnes .50 1.25
6 Draymond Green .75 2.00
7 John Wall .75 2.00
8 Kawhi Leonard 1.00 2.50
9 Anthony Davis 1.25 3.00
10 Otto Porter .60 1.50
11 Dennis Schroder .60 1.50
12 Nerlens Noel .75 2.00
13 Trey Burke .60 1.50
14 Jimmy Butler .60 1.50
15 Chandler Parsons .50 1.25
16 Dion Waiters .50 1.25
17 Nikola Vucevic .50 1.25
18 Blake Griffin .60 1.50
19 Shane Larkin .40 1.00
20 Norris Cole .40 1.00
21 Tobias Harris .50 1.25
22 Shabazz Muhammad .50 1.25
23 Michael Carter-Williams .60 1.50
24 Andre Drummond .60 1.50
25 Damian Lillard 1.25 3.00
26 Victor Oladipo .75 2.00
27 Klay Thompson .75 2.00
28 Ben McLemore .60 1.50
29 Cody Zeller .50 1.25
30 C.J. McCollum 1.00 2.50

2013-14 Pinnacle Team 2020 Artist's Proofs
*AP: .6X TO 1.5X BASIC

2013-14 Pinnacle Team 2020 Artist's Proofs Green
*AP GREEN: 1.5X TO 4X BASIC
STATED PRINT RUN 25 SER.#'d SETS

2013-14 Pinnacle Team 2020 Die Cuts
*DIE CUT: 1X TO 2.5X BASIC
STATED PRINT RUN 99 SER.#'d SETS

2013-14 Pinnacle Team Pinnacle
COMPLETE SET (20) 8.00 20.00
1 K.Durant/D.Wade 1.50 4.00
2 R.Westbrook/T.Parker 1.50 4.00
3 L.James/K.Bryant 2.50 6.00
4 B.Griffin/A.Davis 1.25 3.00
5 C.Paul/D.Rose .75 2.00
6 C.Anthony/K.Durant 1.50 4.00
7 D.Lillard/K.Irving 1.25 3.00
8 H.Barnes/V.Carter .75 2.00
9 B.Beal/C.Parsons .60 1.50
10 P.Gasol/M.Gasol .60 1.50
11 O.Mayo/D.DeRozan .60 1.50
12 R.Rondo/J.Wall .75 2.00
13 R.Rubio/D.Williams .60 1.50
14 D.Nowitzki/K.Love .75 2.00
15 D.Howard/R.Hibbert .50 1.25
16 P.George/P.Pierce .75 2.00
17 K.Garnett/T.Duncan 1.00 2.50
18 K.Bryant/K.Durant 2.50 6.00
19 L.James/K.Durant 2.50 6.00
20 K.Irving/K.Bryant 2.50 6.00

2013-14 Pinnacle Team Pinnacle Artist's Proofs
*AP: .6X TO 1.5X BASIC

2013-14 Pinnacle Team Pinnacle Artist's Proofs Green
*AP GREEN: 1.5X TO 4X BASIC
STATED PRINT RUN 25 SER.#'d SETS

2013-14 Pinnacle Team Pinnacle Die Cuts
*DIE CUT: 1X TO 2.5X BASIC
STATED PRINT RUN 99 SER.#'d SETS

2013-14 Pinnacle The Naturals
COMPLETE SET (20) 8.00 20.00
1 LeBron James 2.50 6.00
2 Kobe Bryant 2.50 6.00
3 Blake Griffin .60 1.50
4 Kyrie Irving 1.25 3.00
5 Anthony Davis 1.25 3.00
6 Harrison Barnes .50 1.25
7 Tim Duncan 1.00 2.50
8 Yao Ming 1.00 2.50
9 Shaquille O'Neal 1.25 3.00
10 Patrick Ewing .75 2.00
11 David Robinson 1.00 2.50
12 Allen Iverson .75 2.00
13 Derrick Rose .75 2.00
14 Kevin Durant 1.50 4.00
15 Paul Pierce .75 2.00
16 Kevin Garnett 1.00 2.50
17 Grant Hill .60 1.50
18 Jason Kidd .60 1.50
19 Ray Allen .60 1.50
20 Carmelo Anthony .75 2.00

2013-14 Pinnacle The Naturals Artist's Proofs
*AP: .6X TO 1.5X BASIC

2013-14 Pinnacle The Naturals Artist's Proofs Green
*AP GREEN: 1.5X TO 4X BASIC
STATED PRINT RUN 25 SER.#'d SETS

2013-14 Pinnacle The Naturals Die Cuts
*DIE CUT: 1X TO 2.5X BASIC
STATED PRINT RUN 99 SER.#'d SETS

2013-14 Pinnacle Upstarts Jerseys
1 Anthony Bennett
2 Victor Oladipo 2.50 6.00
3 Otto Porter 2.50 6.00
4 Nerlens Noel
5 Ben McLemore 2.00 5.00
6 Kentavious Caldwell-Pope 2.50 6.00
7 Trey Burke 2.00 5.00
8 Michael Carter-Williams 2.50 6.00
9 Steven Adams 2.50 6.00
10 Kelly Olynyk 2.00 5.00
11 Shabazz Muhammad
12 Giannis Antetokounmpo 8.00 20.00
13 Tony Snell 2.00 5.00
14 Shane Larkin 1.50 4.00
15 Mason Plumlee 2.50 6.00
16 Tim Hardaway Jr. 2.50 6.00
17 Andre Roberson 1.50 4.00
18 Archie Goodwin 2.00 5.00
19 Glen Rice Jr. 1.50 4.00
20 Nate Wolters 2.00 5.00
21 Jeff Withey 1.50 4.00
22 Dennis Schroder 2.50 6.00
23 Jamaal Franklin 1.50 4.00
24 Erik Murphy 1.50 4.00
25 Peyton Siva
26 Ryan Kelly 1.50 4.00
27 Isaiah Canaan 1.50 4.00
28 Alex Len
29 C.J. McCollum 4.00 10.00
30 Cody Zeller 2.00 5.00
31 Solomon Hill 1.50 4.00
32 Reggie Bullock 2.00 5.00
33 Allen Crabbe 2.00 5.00
34 Tony Mitchell 1.50 4.00
35 Ricky Ledo 1.50 4.00

2013-14 Pinnacle Upstarts Jerseys Prime
*BLUE PRIME: 1.2X TO 3X BASIC
STATED PRINT RUN 25 SER.#'d SETS

2013-14 Pinnacle Z-Team
COMPLETE SET (20) 8.00 20.00
1 Kobe Bryant 2.50 6.00
2 LeBron James 2.50 6.00
3 Anthony Davis 1.25 3.00
4 Kyrie Irving 1.25 3.00
5 Kevin Durant 1.50 4.00
6 Carmelo Anthony .75 2.00
7 Derrick Rose .75 2.00
8 John Wall .75 2.00
9 James Harden 1.00 2.50
10 Chris Paul .75 2.00
11 Paul George .75 2.00
12 Rajon Rondo .60 1.50
13 Kawhi Leonard 1.00 2.50
14 Kenneth Faried .50 1.25
15 Damian Lillard 1.25 3.00
16 Ricky Rubio .60 1.50
17 Brandon Knight .50 1.25
18 Blake Griffin .60 1.50
19 Dirk Nowitzki .75 2.00
20 Stephen Curry 2.50 6.00

2013-14 Pinnacle Z-Team Artist's Proofs
*AP: .6X TO 1.5X BASIC

2013-14 Pinnacle Z-Team Artist's Proofs Green
*AP GREEN: 1.5X TO 4X BASIC
STATED PRINT RUN 25 SER.#'d SETS

2013-14 Pinnacle Z-Team Die Cuts
*DIE CUT: 1X TO 2.5X BASIC
STATED PRINT RUN 99 SER.#'d SETS

1968-69 Pipers Minnesota Team Issue
Each of these team-issued photos measure approximately 4 1/4" by 5 1/2" and feature black and white player portraits. The player's name is listed below the photo. The backs are blank. The photos are unnumbered and listed below alphabetically.
COMPLETE SET (10) 35.00 75.00
1 Frank Card 2.00 5.00
2 Connie Hawkins 15.00 40.00
3 Art Heyman 3.00 8.00
4 Arvesta Kelly 2.50 6.00
5 Mike Lewis 2.50 6.00
6 George Sutor 2.00 5.00
7 Steve Vacendak 2.00 5.00
8 Chico Vaughn 2.00 5.00
9 Tom Washington 3.00 8.00
10 Charlie Williams 3.00 8.00

1990-91 Pistons Star
This 14-card standard-size set was produced by Star Company and sponsored by Home Respiratory Health Care, Inc., and the HRHC logo appears on the top of each card back. The front features a color action photo of the player, on a royal blue background that washes out in the middle of the card. In white lettering the player's name, team, and position appear below the picture. In blue lettering the back presents biographical and statistical information in a horizontal format.
COMPLETE SET (14) 1.50 4.00
1 Mark Aguirre .20 .50
2 William Bedford .08 .25
3 Joe Dumars .40 1.00
4 James Edwards .08 .25
5 David Greenwood .08 .25
6 Scott Hastings .08 .25
7 Gerald Henderson .08 .25
8 Vinnie Johnson .20 .50
9 Bill Laimbeer .40 1.00
10 Dennis Rodman .60 1.50
11 John Salley .08 .25
12 Isiah Thomas .40 1.00
13 Chuck Daly CO .20 .50
14 Maia A. Porche PRES .08 .25

1977-78 Pistons Team Issue
These blank-backed black and white photos, which measure 8" by 10" feature members of the 1977-78 Detroit Pistons. Since these photos are unnumbered, we have sequenced them in alphabetical order.
COMPLETE SET (11) 20.00 35.00
1 Roger Brown 1.25 3.00
2 M.L. Carr 3.00 8.00
3 Leon Douglas 1.25 3.00
4 Al Eberhard 1.25 3.00
5 Chris Ford 2.50 6.00
6 Larry Jones 1.25 3.00
7 Al Menendez 1.25 3.00
8 Eric Money 1.25 3.00
9 Willie Norwood 1.25 3.00
10 Howard Porter 1.50 4.00
11 Ralph Simpson 1.50 4.00

1978-79 Pistons Team Issue
These 8" by 10" blank-backed black and white photos feature members of the 1978-79 Detroit Pistons. Since these photos are unnumbered, we have sequenced them in alphabetical order.
COMPLETE SET (13) 20.00 35.00
1 M.L. Carr 1.00 2.50
2 Leon Douglas .75 2.00
3 Chris Ford 1.50 4.00
4 Gus Gerard .75 2.00
5 Bubbles Hawkins .75 2.00
6 Bob Lanier 3.00 8.00
7 John Long .75 2.00
8 Ben Poquette .75 2.00
9 Kevin Porter 1.00 2.50
10 Terry Tyler .75 2.00
11 Dick Vitale CO 5.00 10.00
12 Al Menendez ACO .75 2.00
Mike Abdenor TR
13 Mike Brunker ACO .75 2.00
Richie Adubato ACO

1990-91 Pistons Unocal
This 16-card standard-size set was produced by Hoops for UNOCAL 76 to commemorate the Piston's back to back championship seasons. A photo album to hold the cards was available for 2.76 at all participating UNOCAL 76 filling stations. Beginning on December 1, 1990 and continuing through the end of March, one card was given away each week with a fuel purchase at participating stations. The cards feature color action player photos on white card stock. A blue banner is draped along the top of the picture, and it reads "89-90 Back to Back World Champions." A Lawrence O'Brien trophy is superimposed at the middle of the banner. Player information and the team name are given in a reddish-orange stripe below the picture. On a blue background, the backs have a head shot of the player in the upper left corner, biographical information, and statistics for the player's NBA career. The cards are unnumbered.
COMPLETE SET (16) 3.00 8.00
1 Mark Aguirre .30 .75
2 Chuck Daly CO .60 1.50
3 Joe Dumars .60 1.50
4 James Edwards .20 .50
5 Vinnie Johnson .30 .75
6 Vinnie Johnson .30 .75
(The Shot)
7 Bill Laimbeer .30 .75
8 Lawrence O'Brien .20 .50
Trophy
9 Dennis Rodman .75 2.00
10 John Salley .20 .50
11 Isiah Thomas .75 2.00
12 Isiah Thomas MVP .75 2.00
13 Celebration Card .20 .50
14 Team Photo .50 1.25
15 Two Championship Rings .20 .50
16 1990 World Champions .20 .50

1991-92 Pistons Unocal
This 16-card standard size set marks the second straight year that Hoops has produced a set for UNOCAL 76. The production run was reported to be 2.5 million cards or roughly 157,000 sets. The cards were distributed two per week with a fill up as part of a promotion that began November 28 and ran through March 1992. In addition, 125,000 vinyl photo albums were produced, and collectors who purchased one for 2.76 at participating UNOCAL filling stations received a redemption card that could be exchanged for a complete set. The fronts feature color action player photos framed in yellow on a blue card face. The upper left and lower right corners of the pictures are cut out. On various color panels, the backs carry a color head shot, biography, career summary, and complete statistics. The cards are unnumbered and checklisted below in alphabetical order, with the multi-player cards listed at the end.
COMPLETE SET (16) 3.00 8.00
1 Mark Aguirre .30 .75
2 Dave Bing .40 1.00
3 Chuck Daly CO .30 .75
4 Joe Dumars .60 1.50
5 Joe Dumars .60 1.50
1991 Pistons MVP
6 Bill Laimbeer .30 .75
7 Bill Laimbeer .30 .75
All-Time Leading Rebounder
8 Dennis Rodman .60 1.50
9 John Salley .20 .50
10 Isiah Thomas .75 2.00
11 Isiah Thomas .75 2.00
All-Time Leading Scorer
12 Darrell Walker .20 .50
13 Orlando Woolridge .20 .50
14 Team Photo .50 1.25
1989 World Champs
15 Mark Aguirre .30 .75
Joe Dumars
Bill Laimbeer
Dennis Rodman
Isiah Thomas
Chuck Daly CO
16 Brad Sellers .20 .50
Bob McCann
Charles Thomas
William Bedford
Lance Blanks

2007-08 Pistons Upper Deck
COMPLETE SET (5) 1.25 3.00
1 Richard Hamilton .30 .75
2 Chauncey Billups .40 1.00
3 Tayshaun Prince .30 .75
4 Rasheed Wallace .40 1.00
5 Chris Webber .40 1.00

2008 Playoff Contenders
This set was released on February 4, 2009. The base set consists of 130 cards.
COMP.SET w/o AU's (50) 8.00 20.00
COMMON CARD (1-50) .25 .60
COMMON AU (51-130) 3.00 8.00
OVERALL AUTO ODDS 5 PER BOX
EXCHANGE DEADLINE 8/4/2010
78 D.Rose AU/88 * 150.00 300.00
103 M.Beasley AU/88 * 30.00 60.00
112 O.Mayo AU/88 * 40.00 80.00

2008 Playoff Contenders Playoff Ticket
COMMON CARD (51-130) 1.00 2.50
OVERALL INSERT ODDS 1:3

2009-10 Playoff Contenders
COMP.SET w/o SPs (100) 25.00 50.00
AU RC APPROX.ODDS FOUR PER BOX
UNPRICED CHAMP.TIX PRINT RUN ONE SET
1 Kevin Garnett .75 2.00
2 Paul Pierce .50 1.25
3 Rajon Rondo .50 1.25
4 Dirk Nowitzki .60 1.50
5 Jason Terry .40 1.00
6 Josh Howard .40 1.00
7 Shawn Marion .40 1.00
8 Brook Lopez .40 1.00
9 Devin Harris .30 .75
10 Yi Jianlian .40 1.00
11 Luis Scola .40 1.00
12 Tracy McGrady .50 1.25
13 Trevor Ariza .30 .75
14 Danilo Gallinari .40 1.00
15 Darko Milicic .30 .75
16 David Lee .30 .75
17 Nate Robinson .30 .75
18 Allen Iverson .60 1.50
19 Marc Gasol .50 1.25
20 O.J. Mayo .40 1.00
21 Zach Randolph .40 1.00
22 Andre Iguodala .40 1.00
23 Elton Brand .50 1.25
24 Thaddeus Young .40 1.00
25 Chris Paul .60 1.50
26 David West .40 1.00
27 Peja Stojakovic .50 1.25
28 Andrea Bargnani .40 1.00
29 Chris Bosh .50 1.25
30 Jarrett Jack .30 .75
31 Jose Calderon .30 .75
32 Michael Finley .50 1.25
33 Richard Jefferson .30 .75
34 Tim Duncan .75 2.00
35 Tony Parker .50 1.25
36 Derrick Rose .75 2.00
37 Joakim Noah .40 1.00
38 Tyrus Thomas .30 .75
39 Carmelo Anthony .60 1.50
40 Chauncey Billups .50 1.25
41 J.R. Smith .40 1.00
42 Nene .40 1.00
43 LeBron James 2.00 5.00
44 Shaquille O'Neal 1.00 2.50
45 Zydrunas Ilgauskas .40 1.00
46 Al Jefferson .40 1.00
47 Kevin Love .50 1.25
48 Ryan Gomes .30 .75
49 Ben Gordon .40 1.00
50 Richard Hamilton .40 1.00
51 Tayshaun Prince .40 1.00
52 Andre Miller .40 1.00
53 Brandon Roy .50 1.25
54 LaMarcus Aldridge .50 1.25
55 Rudy Fernandez .30 .75
56 Danny Granger .40 1.00
57 T.J. Ford .30 .75
58 Troy Murphy .30 .75
59 Jeff Green .40 1.00
60 Kevin Durant 1.25 3.00
61 Russell Westbrook 1.25 3.00
62 Andrew Bogut .40 1.00
63 Kurt Thomas .30 .75
64 Michael Redd .40 1.00
65 Andrei Kirilenko .40 1.00
66 Deron Williams .40 1.00
67 Mehmet Okur .30 .75
68 Joe Johnson .40 1.00
69 Josh Smith .40 1.00
70 Mike Bibby .40 1.00
71 Anthony Randolph .30 .75
72 Corey Maggette .40 1.00
73 Stephen Jackson .40 1.00
74 Boris Diaw .40 1.00
75 D.J. Augustin .30 .75
76 Gerald Wallace .40 1.00
77 Raja Bell .40 1.00
78 Al Thornton .40 1.00
79 Baron Davis .40 1.00
80 Chris Kaman .40 1.00
81 Eric Gordon .40 1.00
82 Daequan Cook .30 .75
83 Dwyane Wade .75 2.00
84 Jermaine O'Neal .40 1.00
85 Andrew Bynum .30 .75
86 Kobe Bryant 2.00 5.00
87 Pau Gasol .50 1.25
88 Ron Artest .50 1.25
89 Dwight Howard .40 1.00
90 Jameer Nelson .40 1.00
91 Vince Carter .60 1.50
92 Amare Stoudemire .50 1.25
93 Grant Hill .60 1.50
94 Steve Nash .50 1.25
95 Antawn Jamison .40 1.00
96 Caron Butler .40 1.00
97 Gilbert Arenas .40 1.00
98 Andres Nocioni .30 .75
99 Kevin Martin .40 1.00
100 Sean May .30 .75
101 Blake Griffin SP AU RC 50.00 120.00
102 Hasheem Thabeet SP AU RC 4.00 10.00
103 James Harden SP AU RC 100.00 250.00
104 Tyreke Evans SP AU RC 5.00 12.00
105 Jonny Flynn SP AU RC 4.00 10.00
106 Stephen Curry SP AU RC 400.00 800.00
107 Jordan Hill SP AU RC 5.00 12.00
108 Brandon Jennings SP AU RC 6.00 15.00
109 T.Williams SP AU RC 4.00 10.00
110 G.Henderson AU RC 5.00 12.00
111 Tyler Hansbrough SP AU RC 5.00 12.00
112 Earl Clark SP AU RC 4.00 10.00
113 Austin Daye AU RC 4.00 10.00
114 James Johnson AU RC 5.00 12.00
115 Jrue Holiday AU RC 8.00 20.00
116 Ty Lawson AU RC 6.00 15.00
117 Jeff Teague AU RC 6.00 15.00
118 Eric Maynor AU RC 4.00 10.00
119 Darren Collison AU RC 6.00 15.00
120 Omri Casspi AU RC 5.00 12.00
121 B.J. Mullens AU RC 4.00 10.00
122 Rodrigue Beaubois AU RC 4.00 10.00
123 Taj Gibson AU RC 6.00 15.00
124 DeMarre Carroll AU RC 5.00 12.00
125 Wayne Ellington AU RC 6.00 15.00
126 Toney Douglas AU RC 4.00 10.00
127 J.Pendergraph AU RC 4.00 10.00
128 Jermaine Taylor AU RC 4.00 10.00
129 D.Cunningham SP AU RC 4.00 10.00
130 DaJuan Summers AU RC 4.00 10.00
131 Sam Young AU RC 4.00 10.00
132 DeJuan Blair AU RC 6.00 15.00
133 Jodie Meeks AU RC 6.00 15.00
134 Chase Budinger AU RC 5.00 12.00
135 Taylor Griffin AU RC 4.00 10.00
136 Kareem Abdul-Jabbar 2.00 5.00
137 Isiah Thomas 1.25 3.00
138 Bernard King 1.25 3.00
139 Danny Manning 1.00 2.50
140 Larry Bird 3.00 8.00
141 Artis Gilmore 1.00 2.50
142 Jalen Rose 1.25 3.00
143 John Havlicek 1.25 3.00
144 A.C. Green 1.25 3.00
145 Spencer Haywood .75 2.00
146 Hal Greer 1.00 2.50
147 Oscar Robertson 1.25 3.00
148 World B. Free 1.00 2.50
149 Sidney Moncrief .75 2.00
150 Maurice Cheeks 1.25 3.00

2009-10 Playoff Contenders Classic Tickets Signatures
STATED PRINT RUN 25 SER.#'d SETS
136 Kareem Abdul-Jabbar 20.00 50.00
137 Isiah Thomas 15.00 40.00
138 Bernard King 10.00 25.00
139 Danny Manning 10.00 25.00
140 Larry Bird 60.00 120.00
141 Artis Gilmore 10.00 25.00
142 Jalen Rose 15.00 40.00
143 John Havlicek 25.00 50.00
144 A.C. Green 10.00 25.00
145 Spencer Haywood 10.00 25.00
146 Hal Greer 10.00 25.00
147 Oscar Robertson 50.00 120.00
149 Sidney Moncrief 10.00 25.00
150 Maurice Cheeks 10.00 25.00

2009-10 Playoff Contenders Playoff Tickets
STATED PRINT RUN 5 TO 50 SER.#'d SETS
MOST UNPRICED DUE TO SCARCITY
86 Kobe Bryant/50 100.00 200.00

2009-10 Playoff Contenders Award Contenders
COMPLETE SET (20) 8.00 20.00
RANDOM INSERTS IN PACKS
*BLACK: 1X TO 2.5X BASE HI
BLACK PRINT RUN 50 SER.#'d SETS
*GOLD: .75X TO 2X BASE HI
GOLD PRINT RUN 100 SER.#'d SETS
1 Kobe Bryant 3.00 8.00
2 Danny Granger .60 1.50
3 Al Harrington .60 1.50
4 Ben Gordon .60 1.50
5 Carmelo Anthony 1.00 2.50
6 Chris Bosh .75 2.00
7 Dirk Nowitzki 1.00 2.50
8 Dwyane Wade 1.25 3.00
9 Kevin Love .75 2.00
10 LeBron James 3.00 8.00
11 Tony Parker .75 2.00
12 Michael Redd .60 1.50
13 Ray Allen .75 2.00
14 Tim Duncan 1.25 3.00
15 Tracy McGrady .75 2.00
16 Deron Williams .60 1.50
17 Dwight Howard .60 1.50
18 Paul Pierce .75 2.00
19 Chris Paul 1.00 2.50
20 Chauncey Billups .75 2.00

2009-10 Playoff Contenders Award Contenders Autographs
STATED PRINT RUN 5 TO 50 SER.#'d SETS
MOST UNPRICED DUE TO SCARCITY
1 Kobe Bryant/50 75.00 150.00

2009-10 Playoff Contenders Draft Class

COMPLETE SET (25) 10.00 25.00
RANDOM INSERTS IN PACKS
*BLACK: .75X TO 2X BASE HI
BLACK PRINT RUN 50 SER.#'d SETS
*GOLD: .6X TO 1.5X BASE HI
GOLD PRINT RUN 100 SER.#'d SETS
UNPRICED AUTO PRINT RUN 10 SETS
1 Andrea Bargnani 1.00 2.50
2 Adam Morrison .75 2.00
3 J.J. Redick 1.25 3.00
4 Jordan Farmar .75 2.00
5 Daniel Gibson 1.00 2.50
6 Greg Oden 1.00 2.50
7 Kevin Durant 3.00 8.00
8 Al Horford 1.25 3.00
9 Mike Conley Jr. 1.00 2.50
10 Yi Jianlian 1.00 2.50
11 Joakim Noah 1.00 2.50
12 Acie Law .75 2.00
13 Thaddeus Young .75 2.00
14 Al Thornton 1.00 2.50
15 Aaron Brooks .75 2.00
16 Ramon Sessions 1.00 2.50
17 Derrick Rose 2.00 5.00
18 Michael Beasley .75 2.00
19 Russell Westbrook 3.00 8.00
20 Danilo Gallinari 1.00 2.50
21 Eric Gordon 1.00 2.50
22 D.J. Augustin .75 2.00
23 Brook Lopez 1.00 2.50
24 Anthony Randolph .75 2.00
25 Paul Millsap 1.00 2.50

2009-10 Playoff Contenders Draft Tandems

COMPLETE SET (20) 15.00 30.00
RANDOM INSERTS IN PACKS
*BLACK: .6X TO 1.5X BASE HI
BLACK PRINT RUN 50 SER.#'d SETS
*GOLD: .5X TO 1.25X BASE HI
GOLD PRINT RUN 100 SER.#'d SETS
UNPRICED AUTO PRINT RUN 10 SETS
1 H.Thabeet/M.Beasley .75 2.00
2 A.Bargnani/T.Duncan 2.00 5.00
3 C.Bosh/C.Paul 1.50 4.00
4 K.Love/R.Felton 1.25 3.00
5 E.Gordon/R.Foye 1.00 2.50
6 C.Kaman/Y.Jianlian 1.00 2.50
7 A.Stoudemire/J.Noah 1.00 2.50
8 J.Worthy/L.Johnson 1.50 4.00
9 A.Mourning/S.Bradley 1.50 4.00
10 D.Mutombo/G.Rice 1.25 3.00
11 M.Richmond/S.Moncrief 1.25 3.00
12 C.Brewer/K.Hinrich 1.00 2.50
13 A.Bynum/P.Pierce 1.25 3.00
14 D.Harper/R.Horry 1.00 2.50
15 J.Rose/K.Malone 1.50 4.00
16 D.Majerle/T.Hardaway 1.25 3.00
17 B.Griffin/M.Johnson 5.00 12.00
18 D.Williams/J.Harden 6.00 15.00
19 C.Mullin/S.Curry 10.00 25.00
20 D.Schrempf/J.Hill 1.25 3.00

2009-10 Playoff Contenders Legendary Contenders

COMPLETE SET (20) 10.00 25.00
RANDOM INSERTS IN PACKS
*BLACK: .75X TO 2X BASE HI
BLACK PRINT RUN 50 SER.#'d SETS
*GOLD: .6X TO 1.5X BASE HI
GOLD PRINT RUN 100 SER.#'d SETS
UNPRICED AUTO PRINT RUN 10 SETS
1 Willis Reed 1.50 4.00
2 Shawn Bradley 1.00 2.50
3 Jeff Hornacek 1.25 3.00
5 Dolph Schayes 1.50 4.00
6 Bill Laimbeer 1.25 3.00
7 Kenny Walker 1.00 2.50
8 Connie Hawkins 1.50 4.00
9 Clyde Drexler 2.00 5.00
10 Rony Seikaly 1.00 2.50
11 Larry Johnson 1.50 4.00
12 Cedric Ceballos 1.00 2.50
14 Kurt Rambis 1.00 2.50
15 Joe Dumars 1.50 4.00
16 Bobby Wanzer 1.00 2.50
17 Dan Majerle 1.25 3.00
18 George McGinnis 1.00 2.50
19 Gheorghe Muresan 1.00 2.50

2009-10 Playoff Contenders Lottery Winners

COMPLETE SET (30) 15.00 30.00
RANDOM INSERTS IN PACKS
*BLACK: 1X TO 2.5X BASE HI
BLACK PRINT RUN 50 SER.#'d SETS
*GOLD: .75X TO 2X BASE HI
GOLD PRINT RUN 100 SER.#'d SETS
UNPRICED AUTO PRINT RUN 5 TO 10 SETS
1 LeBron James 3.00 8.00
2 Allen Iverson 1.00 2.50
3 Tim Duncan 1.25 3.00
4 Yao Ming 1.00 2.50
5 Derrick Rose 1.25 3.00
6 Kevin Garnett 1.25 3.00
7 Blake Griffin 3.00 8.00
8 Jason Kidd .75 2.00
9 Carmelo Anthony 1.00 2.50
10 Deron Williams .60 1.50
11 Chris Paul 1.00 2.50
12 Rudy Gay .75 2.00
13 Brandon Roy .75 2.00
14 LaMarcus Aldridge .75 2.00
15 Andrea Bargnani .60 1.50
16 Andre Iguodala .60 1.50
17 Chris Bosh .75 2.00
18 Jeff Green .60 1.50
19 Dwyane Wade 1.25 3.00
20 Chris Kaman .60 1.50
21 Paul Pierce .75 2.00
22 Andrew Bynum .50 1.25
23 Kevin Durant 2.00 5.00
24 Joakim Noah .60 1.50
25 Al Thornton .60 1.50
26 Charlie Villanueva .50 1.25
27 Emeka Okafor .60 1.50
28 Michael Beasley .50 1.25
29 Mike Bibby .60 1.50
30 Shane Battier .75 2.00

2009-10 Playoff Contenders One-Two Punch

COMPLETE SET (25) 15.00 30.00
RANDOM INSERTS IN PACKS
*BLACK: .6X TO 1.5X BASE HI
BLACK PRINT RUN 50 SER.#'d SETS
*GOLD: .5X TO 1.25X BASE HI
GOLD PRINT RUN 100 SER.#'d SETS
UNPRICED AUTO PRINT RUN 5 TO 10 SETS
1 B.Roy/G.Oden 1.50 4.00
2 J.Green/K.Durant 4.00 10.00
3 C.Bosh/H.Turkoglu 1.50 4.00
4 E.Brand/T.Young 1.50 4.00
5 A.Randolph/R.Bell 1.25 3.00
6 S.Jackson/R.Felton 1.25 3.00
7 D.Nowitzki/J.Howard 2.00 5.00
8 B.Gordon/C.Villanueva 1.25 3.00
9 S.Battier/T.Ariza 1.50 4.00
10 C.Kaman/M.Camby 1.25 3.00
11 L.Odom/P.Gasol 1.50 4.00
12 D.Harris/R.Alston 1.00 2.50
13 D.West/P.Stojakovic 1.50 4.00
14 C.Billups/J.Smith 1.50 4.00
15 A.Jefferson/K.Love 1.50 4.00
16 C.Boozer/D.Williams 1.25 3.00
17 O.Mayo/R.Gay 1.50 4.00
18 R.Rondo/R.Allen 1.50 4.00
19 L.Barbosa/S.Nash 1.50 4.00
20 A.Horford/M.Bibby 1.50 4.00
21 D.Rose/J.Noah 2.50 6.00
22 A.Varejao/S.O'Neal 3.00 8.00
23 R.Hamilton/T.Prince 1.25 3.00
24 D.Granger/T.Murphy 1.25 3.00
25 M.Beasley/U.Haslem 1.00 2.50

2009-10 Playoff Contenders Perennial Contenders

COMPLETE SET (20) 10.00 25.00
RANDOM INSERTS IN PACKS
*BLACK: .75X TO 2X BASE HI
BLACK PRINT RUN 50 SER.#'d SETS
*GOLD: .6X TO 1.5X BASE HI
GOLD PRINT RUN 100 SER.#'d SETS
1 Rasheed Wallace 1.00 2.50
2 Joakim Noah .75 2.00
3 Shaquille O'Neal 2.00 5.00
4 Jason Terry .75 2.00
5 Chauncey Billups 1.00 2.50
6 Tayshaun Prince .75 2.00
7 Tracy McGrady 1.00 2.50
8 Kobe Bryant 4.00 10.00
9 Nate Robinson .60 1.50
10 Vince Carter 1.25 3.00
11 Grant Hill 1.25 3.00
12 Greg Oden .75 2.00
13 Tony Parker 1.00 2.50
14 Carlos Boozer .75 2.00
15 Ron Artest 1.00 2.50
16 Paul Pierce 1.00 2.50
17 Deron Williams .75 2.00
18 Ben Wallace .75 2.00
19 LeBron James 4.00 10.00
20 Andre Iguodala .75 2.00

2009-10 Playoff Contenders Perennial Contenders Autographs

STATED PRINT RUN 5 TO 50 SER.#'d SETS
SOME UNPRICED DUE TO SCARCITY
8 Kobe Bryant/50 100.00 200.00

2009-10 Playoff Contenders Rookie of the Year Contenders

COMPLETE SET (15) 10.00 25.00
RANDOM INSERTS IN PACKS
*BLACK: 1.25X TO 3X BASE HI
BLACK PRINT RUN 50 SER.#'d SETS
*GOLD: .75X TO 2X BASE HI
GOLD PRINT RUN 100 SER.#'d SETS
1 Blake Griffin 4.00 10.00
2 DeJuan Blair .75 2.00
3 Omri Casspi .75 2.00
4 Chase Budinger .75 2.00
5 Hasheem Thabeet .60 1.50
6 James Harden 5.00 12.00
7 Brandon Jennings 1.00 2.50
8 Jonny Flynn .60 1.50
9 Jordan Hill .75 2.00
10 Stephen Curry 25.00 60.00
11 Terrence Williams .60 1.50
12 Ty Lawson 1.00 2.50
13 Tyler Hansbrough .75 2.00
14 Tyreke Evans .75 2.00
15 Taj Gibson 1.00 2.50

2009-10 Playoff Contenders Rookie of the Year Contenders Autographs

STATED PRINT RUN 25 SER.#'d SETS
1 Blake Griffin 50.00 100.00
2 DeJuan Blair 6.00 15.00
3 Omri Casspi 6.00 15.00
4 Chase Budinger 6.00 15.00
5 Hasheem Thabeet 5.00 12.00
6 James Harden 50.00 125.00
7 Brandon Jennings 8.00 20.00
8 Jonny Flynn 5.00 12.00
9 Jordan Hill 6.00 15.00
10 Stephen Curry 500.00 1000.00
11 Terrence Williams 5.00 12.00
12 Ty Lawson 8.00 20.00
13 Tyler Hansbrough 6.00 15.00
14 Tyreke Evans 6.00 15.00
15 Taj Gibson 8.00 20.00

2009-10 Playoff Contenders Round Numbers

COMPLETE SET (25) 20.00 40.00
RANDOM INSERTS IN PACKS
*BLACK: .6X TO 1.5X BASE HI
BLACK PRINT RUN 50 SER.#'d SETS
*GOLD: .5X TO 1.25X BASE HI
GOLD PRINT RUN 100 SER.#'d SETS
1 M.Redd/R.Sessions 1.00 2.50
2 L.Aldridge/T.Duncan 2.00 5.00
3 C.Bosh/P.Gasol 1.25 3.00
4 B.Gordon/V.Carter 1.50 4.00
5 R.Lewis/T.Ariza 1.00 2.50
6 C.Anthony/P.Pierce 1.50 4.00
7 D.Howard/G.Oden 1.00 2.50
8 K.Garnett/T.Hansbrough 2.00 5.00
9 B.Griffin/K.Bryant 5.00 12.00
10 C.Boozer/P.Millsap 1.00 2.50
11 O.Mayo/T.Williams .75 2.00
12 B.Jennings/C.Paul 1.50 4.00
13 S.Nash/T.Lawson 1.25 3.00
14 D.Wade/S.Curry 15.00 40.00
15 M.Ellis/S.Jackson 1.00 2.50
16 B.Roy/J.Flynn .75 2.00
17 J.Kidd/T.Evans 1.25 3.00
18 D.Rose/J.Harden 6.00 15.00
19 A.Bogut/H.Thabeet 1.00 2.50
20 M.Ginobili/M.Williams 1.25 3.00
21 D.Williams/G.Henderson 1.00 2.50
22 J.Hill/K.Durant 3.00 8.00
23 A.Bargnani/D.Nowitzki 1.50 4.00
24 A.Stoudemire/E.Brand 1.25 3.00
25 G.Arenas/M.Chalmers 1.00 2.50

2009-10 Playoff Contenders Round Numbers Autographs

STATED PRINT RUN 10 TO 25 SER.#'d SETS
SOME UNPRICED DUE TO SCARCITY
9 B.Griffin/K.Bryant/25 200.00 400.00

2010-11 Playoff Contenders Patches

COMP.SET w/o RCs (100) 15.00 40.00
EXCH.EXPIRATION 8/16/2010
UNPRICED CHAMP.TICK.PRINT RUN ONE SET
1 Kobe Bryant 2.00 5.00
2 Pau Gasol .50 1.25
3 Sasha Vujacic .30 .75
4 Lamar Odom .40 1.00
5 Blake Griffin .50 1.25
6 Baron Davis .40 1.00
7 Eric Gordon .40 1.00
8 Stephen Curry 2.00 5.00
9 Monta Ellis .40 1.00
10 David Lee .30 .75
11 Channing Frye .40 1.00
12 Steve Nash .50 1.25
13 Robin Lopez .30 .75
14 Samuel Dalembert .30 .75
15 Tyreke Evans .30 .75
16 Carl Landry .30 .75
17 Carmelo Anthony .60 1.50
18 Chauncey Billups .50 1.25
19 Al Harrington .40 1.00
20 Chris Andersen .40 1.00
21 LaMarcus Aldridge .50 1.25
22 Marcus Camby .30 .75
23 Brandon Roy .50 1.25
24 Al Jefferson .40 1.00
25 Deron Williams .40 1.00
26 Andrei Kirilenko .40 1.00
27 Kevin Durant 1.25 3.00
28 Jeff Green .40 1.00
29 Russell Westbrook 1.25 3.00
30 James Harden .75 2.00
31 Jonny Flynn .30 .75
32 Anthony Tolliver .30 .75
33 Kevin Love .50 1.25
34 Caron Butler .40 1.00
35 Brendan Haywood .30 .75
36 Dirk Nowitzki .60 1.50
37 Jason Kidd .50 1.25
38 Aaron Brooks .30 .75
39 Kevin Martin .40 1.00
40 Yao Ming .60 1.50
41 DeJuan Blair .30 .75
42 Richard Jefferson .40 1.00
43 Tony Parker .50 1.25
44 Tim Duncan .75 2.00
45 Trevor Ariza .30 .75
46 Chris Paul .60 1.50
47 David West .40 1.00
48 Mike Conley Jr. .50 1.25
49 Marc Gasol .50 1.25
50 Zach Randolph .40 1.00
51 O.J. Mayo .30 .75
52 Rajon Rondo .50 1.25
53 Shaquille O'Neal 1.00 2.50
54 Paul Pierce .50 1.25
55 Kevin Garnett .75 2.00
56 Brook Lopez .40 1.00
57 Terrence Williams .30 .75
58 Devin Harris .30 .75
59 Toney Douglas .30 .75
60 Amare Stoudemire .40 1.00
61 Danilo Gallinari .40 1.00
62 Jrue Holiday .50 1.25
63 Elton Brand .50 1.25
64 Andre Iguodala .40 1.00
65 DeMar DeRozan .50 1.25
66 Andrea Bargnani .40 1.00
67 Leandro Barbosa .40 1.00
68 Joakim Noah .40 1.00
69 Derrick Rose .60 1.50
70 Carlos Boozer .40 1.00
71 Taj Gibson .40 1.00
72 Tayshaun Prince .40 1.00
73 Ben Gordon .40 1.00
74 Tracy McGrady .50 1.25
75 Daniel Gibson .40 1.00
76 Antawn Jamison .40 1.00
77 Ramon Sessions .40 1.00
78 Darren Collison .40 1.00
79 Tyler Hansbrough .40 1.00
80 Danny Granger .40 1.00
81 Andrew Bogut .40 1.00
82 Brandon Jennings .30 .75
83 John Salmons .40 1.00
84 Jamal Crawford .50 1.25
85 Joe Johnson .40 1.00
86 Josh Smith .40 1.00
87 Al Horford .40 1.00
88 Stephen Jackson .40 1.00
89 Gerald Henderson .30 .75
90 Gerald Wallace .40 1.00
91 Dwyane Wade .75 2.00
92 Chris Bosh .50 1.25
93 LeBron James 2.50 6.00
94 Mike Miller .40 1.00
95 Dwight Howard .40 1.00
96 Vince Carter .60 1.50
97 Jameer Nelson .30 .75
98 Al Thornton .30 .75
99 JaVale McGee .40 1.00
100 Andray Blatche .30 .75
101 John Wall AU RC 30.00 80.00
102 Evan Turner AU RC 3.00 8.00
103 Derrick Favors AU RC 5.00 12.00
104 Wesley Johnson AU RC 2.50 6.00
105 DeMarcus Cousins AU RC 30.00 80.00
106 Ekpe Udoh AU RC 2.50 6.00
107 Greg Monroe AU RC 5.00 12.00
108 Al-Farouq Aminu AU RC 4.00 10.00
109 Gordon Hayward AU RC 15.00 40.00
110 Paul George AU RC 30.00 80.00
111 Cole Aldrich AU RC 3.00 8.00
112 Xavier Henry AU RC 2.50 6.00
113 Ed Davis AU RC 2.50 6.00
114 Patrick Patterson AU RC 3.00 8.00
115 Larry Sanders AU RC 2.50 6.00
116 Luke Babbitt AU RC 3.00 8.00
117 Eric Bledsoe AU RC 5.00 12.00
118 Avery Bradley AU RC 5.00 12.00
119 James Anderson AU RC 2.50 6.00
120 Gary Neal AU RC 4.00 10.00
121 Elliot Williams AU RC 2.50 6.00
122 Trevor Booker AU RC 3.00 8.00
123 Damion James AU RC 2.50 6.00
124 Dominique Jones AU RC 2.50 6.00
125 Quincy Pondexter AU RC 2.50 6.00
126 Jordan Crawford AU RC 3.00 8.00
127 Greivis Vasquez AU RC 3.00 8.00
128 Daniel Orton AU RC 2.50 6.00
129 Lazar Hayward AU RC 2.50 6.00
130 Dexter Pittman AU RC 2.50 6.00
131 Hassan Whiteside AU RC 12.00 30.00
132 Lance Stephenson AU RC 4.00 10.00
133 Gary Forbes AU RC 2.50 6.00
134 Devin Ebanks AU RC 2.50 6.00
135 Gani Lawal AU RC 2.50 6.00
136 Luke Harangody AU RC 2.50 6.00
137 Willie Warren AU RC 2.50 6.00
138 Terrico White AU RC 2.50 6.00
139 Jeremy Evans AU RC 5.00 12.00
140 Timofey Mozgov AU RC 4.00 10.00
141 Jeremy Lin AU RC 30.00 80.00
142 Sherron Collins AU RC 2.50 6.00
143 Armon Johnson AU RC 2.50 6.00
144 Tiago Splitter AU RC 4.00 10.00
145 Landry Fields AU RC 3.00 8.00
146 Andy Rautins AU RC 2.50 6.00
147 Kevin Seraphin AU RC 2.50 6.00
148 Solomon Alabi AU RC 2.50 6.00
149 Derrick Caracter AU RC 2.50 6.00
150 Omer Asik AU RC 4.00 10.00
151 John Wall AU SP 40.00 100.00
152 Evan Turner AU SP 4.00 10.00
153 Derrick Favors AU SP 6.00 15.00
154 Wesley Johnson AU SP 3.00 8.00
155 DeMarcus Cousins AU SP 25.00 60.00
156 Ekpe Udoh AU SP 3.00 8.00
157 Greg Monroe AU SP 6.00 15.00
158 Al-Farouq Aminu AU SP 5.00 12.00
159 Gordon Hayward AU SP 15.00 40.00
160 Paul George AU SP 50.00 120.00
161 Cole Aldrich AU SP 4.00 10.00
162 Xavier Henry AU SP 3.00 8.00
163 Ed Davis AU SP 3.00 8.00
164 Patrick Patterson AU SP 4.00 10.00
165 Larry Sanders AU SP 3.00 8.00
166 Luke Babbitt AU SP 4.00 10.00
167 Eric Bledsoe AU SP 6.00 15.00
168 Avery Bradley AU SP 8.00 20.00
169 James Anderson AU SP 3.00 8.00
170 Gary Neal AU SP 5.00 12.00
171 Elliot Williams AU SP 3.00 8.00
172 Trevor Booker AU SP 4.00 10.00
173 Damion James AU SP 3.00 8.00
174 Dominique Jones AU SP 3.00 8.00
175 Quincy Pondexter AU SP 3.00 8.00
176 Jordan Crawford AU SP 4.00 10.00
177 Greivis Vasquez AU SP 4.00 10.00
178 Daniel Orton AU SP 3.00 8.00
179 Lazar Hayward AU SP 3.00 8.00
180 Dexter Pittman AU SP 3.00 8.00
181 Hassan Whiteside AU SP 10.00 25.00
182 Lance Stephenson AU SP 5.00 12.00
183 Gary Forbes AU SP 3.00 8.00
184 Devin Ebanks AU SP 3.00 8.00
185 Gani Lawal AU SP 3.00 8.00
186 Luke Harangody AU SP 3.00 8.00
187 Willie Warren AU SP 3.00 8.00
188 Terrico White AU SP 3.00 8.00
189 Jeremy Evans AU SP 3.00 8.00
190 Timofey Mozgov AU SP 5.00 12.00
191 Jeremy Lin AU SP 40.00 80.00
192 Sherron Collins AU SP 3.00 8.00
193 Armon Johnson AU SP 3.00 8.00
194 Tiago Splitter AU SP 5.00 12.00
195 Landry Fields AU SP 4.00 10.00
196 Andy Rautins AU SP 3.00 8.00
197 Kevin Seraphin AU SP 3.00 8.00
198 Solomon Alabi AU SP 3.00 8.00
199 Derrick Caracter AU SP 3.00 8.00
200 Omer Asik AU SP 6.00 15.00

2010-11 Playoff Contenders Patches Die Cuts Black

*DC BLACK: 2X TO 5X BASE HI
STATED PRINT RUN 49 SER.#'d SETS

2010-11 Playoff Contenders Patches Die Cuts Gold

*DC GOLD: 1.5X TO 4X BASE HI
STATED PRINT RUN 99 SER.#'d SETS

2010-11 Playoff Contenders Patches Die Cuts Silver

*DC SILVER: 1X TO 2.5X BASE HI
STATED PRINT RUN 299 SER.#'d SETS

2010-11 Playoff Contenders Patches One-Two Punch

COMPLETE SET (25) 20.00 40.00
RANDOM INSERTS IN PACKS
*DC BLACK: 1.25X TO 3X BASE HI
DC BLACK PRINT RUN 49 SER.#'d SETS
*DC GOLD: 1X TO 2.5X BASE HI
DC GOLD PRINT RUN 99 SER.#'d SETS
*DC SILVER: .6X TO 1.5X BASE HI
DC SILVER PRINT RUN 299 SER.#'d SETS
1 R.Rondo/S.O'Neal 1.50 4.00
2 R.Allen/P.Pierce .75 2.00
3 R.Rondo/K.Garnett 1.25 3.00
4 D.Rose/J.Noah 1.00 2.50
5 B.Jennings/A.Bogut .60 1.50
6 S.Curry/M.Ellis 3.00 8.00
7 K.Durant/R.Westbrook 2.00 5.00
8 J.Kidd/D.Nowitzki 1.00 2.50
9 T.Douglas/A.Stoudemire .60 1.50
10 L.James/D.Wade 4.00 10.00
11 C.Bosh/L.James 4.00 10.00
12 B.Griffin/B.Davis .75 2.00
13 B.Gordon/B.Wallace .60 1.50
14 C.Anthony/Nene 1.00 2.50
15 D.Harris/B.Lopez .60 1.50
16 J.Johnson/A.Horford .60 1.50
17 J.Nelson/D.Howard .60 1.50
18 T.Evans/C.Landry .50 1.25
19 J.Flynn/M.Beasley .50 1.25
20 J.Holiday/E.Brand .75 2.00
21 C.Paul/E.Okafor 1.00 2.50
22 O.J. Mayo/M.Gasol .75 2.00
23 K.Bryant/P.Gasol 3.00 8.00
24 K.Bryant/D.Fisher 3.00 8.00
25 S.Nash/C.Frye .75 2.00

2010-11 Playoff Contenders Patches Place in History

COMPLETE SET (25) 12.50 30.00
RANDOM INSERTS IN PACKS
*DC BLACK: 1.25X TO 3X BASE HI
DC BLACK PRINT RUN 49 SER.#'d SETS
*DC GOLD: 1X TO 2.5X BASE HI
DC GOLD PRINT RUN 99 SER.#'d SETS
*DC SILVER: .6X TO 1.5X BASE HI
DC SILVER PRINT RUN 299 SER.#'d SETS
1 James Harden 1.25 3.00
2 Brook Lopez .60 1.50
3 Joakim Noah .60 1.50
4 J.J. Redick .75 2.00
5 Andrew Bogut .60 1.50
6 Andre Iguodala .60 1.50
7 Carmelo Anthony 1.00 2.50
8 Amare Stoudemire .60 1.50
9 Pau Gasol .75 2.00
10 Hedo Turkoglu .60 1.50
11 Shawn Marion .60 1.50
12 Dirk Nowitzki 1.00 2.50
13 Chauncey Billups .75 2.00
14 Kobe Bryant 3.00 8.00
15 Kevin Garnett 1.25 3.00
16 Jason Kidd .75 2.00
17 Shawn Bradley .50 1.25
18 Shaquille O'Neal 1.50 4.00
19 Larry Johnson 1.00 2.50
20 Gary Payton .75 2.00
21 Sean Elliott .75 2.00
22 Hersey Hawkins .50 1.25
23 Scottie Pippen 1.50 4.00
24 Walter Berry .50 1.25
25 Chris Mullin .75 2.00

2010-11 Playoff Contenders Patches Place in History Autographs Gold

STATED PRINT RUN 10 TO 49 SER.#'d SETS
SOME UNPRICED DUE TO SCARCITY
UNPRICED BLACK PRINT RUN 5 TO 10 SETS
1 James Harden/49 40.00 100.00
2 Brook Lopez/49 6.00 15.00
3 Joakim Noah/49 8.00 20.00
4 J.J. Redick/49 6.00 15.00
5 Andrew Bogut/49 8.00 20.00
6 Andre Iguodala/49 6.00 15.00
8 Amare Stoudemire/49 10.00 25.00
9 Pau Gasol/49 20.00 50.00
12 Dirk Nowitzki/49 50.00 125.00
13 Chauncey Billups/49 8.00 20.00
14 Kobe Bryant/49 125.00 225.00
16 Jason Kidd/49 12.00 30.00
19 Larry Johnson/15 50.00 120.00
20 Gary Payton/49 10.00 25.00
21 Sean Elliott/15 12.00 30.00
22 Hersey Hawkins/49 6.00 15.00
23 Scottie Pippen/49 50.00 120.00
24 Walter Berry/49 6.00 15.00
25 Chris Mullin/49 12.50 30.00

2010-11 Playoff Contenders Patches Rookie of the Year Contenders

COMPLETE SET (15) 10.00 25.00
RANDOM INSERTS IN PACKS
*DC BLACK: 1.25X TO 3X BASE HI
DC BLACK PRINT RUN 49 SER.#'d SETS
*DC GOLD: 1X TO 2.5X BASE HI
DC GOLD PRINT RUN 99 SER.#'d SETS
*DC SILVER: .6X TO 1.5X BASE HI
DC SILVER PRINT RUN 299 SER.#'d SETS
1 John Wall 4.00 10.00
2 Blake Griffin .75 2.00
3 Evan Turner .60 1.50
4 Wesley Johnson .50 1.25
5 Derrick Favors 1.00 2.50
6 DeMarcus Cousins 2.50 6.00
7 Gordon Hayward 1.25 3.00
8 Cole Aldrich .60 1.50
9 Ekpe Udoh .50 1.25
10 Ed Davis .50 1.25
11 Xavier Henry .50 1.25
12 Greg Monroe 1.00 2.50
13 James Anderson .50 1.25
14 Patrick Patterson .60 1.50
15 Al-Farouq Aminu .75 2.00

2010-11 Playoff Contenders Patches Rookie of the Year Contenders Autographs Gold

STATED PRINT RUN 49 SER.#'d SETS
UNPRICED BLACK PRINT RUN 10 SER.#'d SETS
1 John Wall 50.00 120.00
2 Blake Griffin 20.00 50.00
3 Evan Turner 6.00 15.00
4 Wesley Johnson 5.00 12.00
5 Derrick Favors 10.00 25.00
6 DeMarcus Cousins 25.00 60.00
7 Gordon Hayward 12.00 30.00
8 Cole Aldrich 6.00 15.00
9 Ekpe Udoh 5.00 12.00
10 Ed Davis 5.00 12.00
11 Xavier Henry 5.00 12.00
12 Greg Monroe 10.00 25.00
13 James Anderson 5.00 12.00
14 Patrick Patterson 6.00 15.00
15 Al-Farouq Aminu 8.00 20.00

2010-11 Playoff Contenders Patches Starting Blocks

COMPLETE SET (30) 20.00 40.00
RANDOM INSERTS IN PACKS
*DC BLACK: 1.25X TO 3X BASE HI
DC BLACK PRINT RUN 49 SER.#'d SETS
*DC GOLD: 1X TO 2.5X BASE HI
DC GOLD PRINT RUN 99 SER.#'d SETS
*DC SILVER: .6X TO 1.5X BASE HI
DC SILVER PRINT RUN 299 SER.#'d SETS
1 T.Evans/D.Cousins 2.50 6.00
2 S.Curry/E.Udoh 3.00 8.00
3 M.Speights/E.Turner .60 1.50
4 B.Lopez/D.Favors 1.00 2.50
5 A.Daye/G.Monroe 1.00 2.50
6 B.Jennings/L.Sanders .50 1.25
7 D.Carroll/X.Henry .60 1.50
8 D.Rose/T.Gibson 1.00 2.50
9 J.McGee/J.Wall 4.00 10.00
10 J.Flynn/W.Johnson .50 1.25
11 D.DeRozan/E.Davis .75 2.00
12 D.Gallinari/T.Douglas .60 1.50
13 J.Evans/G.Hayward 1.25 3.00
14 B.Lopez/D.James .60 1.50
15 E.Gordon/B.Griffin .75 2.00
16 D.J. Augustin/G.Henderson .50 1.25
17 T.Young/J.Holiday .75 2.00
18 J.Noah/J.Johnson .60 1.50
19 T.Hansbrough/P.George 2.50 6.00
20 T.Evans/O.Casspi .50 1.25
21 T.Gibson/J.Johnson .60 1.50
22 B.Griffin/A.Aminu .75 2.00
23 A.Brooks/P.Patterson .60 1.50
24 R.Stuckey/G.Monroe 1.00 2.50
25 J.Noah/D.Rose 1.00 2.50
26 H.Whiteside/T.Evans 1.50 4.00
27 A.Horford/J.Crawford .60 1.50
28 A.Bargnani/D.DeRozan .75 2.00
29 R.Rondo/A.Bradley 1.00 2.50
30 R.Gay/G.Vasquez .75 2.00

2010-11 Playoff Contenders Patches Starting Blocks Autographs Gold

STATED PRINT RUN 25 TO 49 SER.#'d SETS
UNPRICED BLACK PRINT RUN 10 SER.#'d SETS
1 T.Evans/D.Cousins/49 15.00 40.00
2 S.Curry/E.Udoh/49 75.00 200.00
4 B.Lopez/D.Favors/49 15.00 40.00
5 A.Daye/G.Monroe/49 6.00 15.00
6 B.Jennings/L.Sanders/49 15.00 40.00
7 D.Carroll/X.Henry/49 6.00 15.00
8 D.Rose/T.Gibson/49 60.00 120.00
9 J.McGee/J.Wall/49 50.00 125.00
10 J.Flynn/W.Johnson/49 10.00 25.00
11 D.DeRozan/E.Davis/49 15.00 40.00
12 D.Gallinari/T.Douglas/25 6.00 15.00
13 J.Evans/G.Hayward/49 12.50 30.00
14 B.Lopez/D.James/49 6.00 15.00
15 E.Gordon/B.Griffin/49 15.00 40.00
16 D.J. Augustin/G.Henderson/49 6.00 15.00
18 J.Noah/J.Johnson/49 8.00 20.00
19 T.Hansbrough/P.George/49 15.00 40.00
20 T.Evans/O.Casspi/49 12.50 30.00
21 T.Gibson/J.Johnson/49 8.00 20.00
22 B.Griffin/A.Aminu/49 50.00 125.00
23 A.Brooks/P.Patterson/49 12.50 30.00
25 J.Noah/D.Rose/49 60.00 150.00
26 H.Whiteside/T.Evans/49 10.00 25.00
27 A.Horford/J.Crawford/49 6.00 15.00
28 A.Bargnani/D.DeRozan/49 10.00 25.00
29 R.Rondo/A.Bradley/49 6.00 15.00

2009-10 Playoff National Treasures

COMP.SET w/o RCs (185) 500.00 700.00
1-185 PRINT RUN 99 SER.#'d SETS
186-200 RC PRINT RUN 99 SER.#'d SETS
UNPRICED PLATINUM PRINT RUN 1 TO 5 SETS
UNPRICED SILVER PRINT RUN 10 SETS
1 Kobe Bryant 12.00 30.00
2 LeBron James 12.00 30.00
3 Dwight Howard 2.50 6.00
4 Derrick Rose 5.00 12.00
5 Dwyane Wade 5.00 12.00
6 Kevin Garnett 5.00 12.00
7 Chris Paul 4.00 10.00
8 Paul Pierce 3.00 8.00
9 Shaquille O'Neal 6.00 15.00
10 Pau Gasol 3.00 8.00
11 Carmelo Anthony 4.00 10.00
12 Steve Nash 3.00 8.00
13 David Lee 2.00 5.00
14 Allen Iverson 4.00 10.00
15 Kevin Durant 8.00 20.00
16 Monta Ellis 2.50 6.00
17 Dirk Nowitzki 4.00 10.00
18 Chris Bosh 3.00 8.00
19 Brandon Roy 3.00 8.00
20 Amare Stoudemire 2.50 6.00
21 Joe Johnson 2.50 6.00
22 Zach Randolph 2.50 6.00
23 Carlos Boozer 2.50 6.00
24 Rudy Gay 3.00 8.00
25 Stephen Jackson 2.50 6.00
26 Corey Maggette 2.50 6.00
27 Brook Lopez 2.50 6.00
28 Aaron Brooks 2.00 5.00
29 Rodney Stuckey 2.00 5.00
30 Chris Kaman 2.50 6.00
31 O.J. Mayo 2.00 5.00
32 Tim Duncan 5.00 12.00
33 Al Jefferson 2.50 6.00
34 Andre Iguodala 2.50 6.00
35 Deron Williams 2.50 6.00
36 David West 2.50 6.00
37 Mo Williams 2.50 6.00
38 Gerald Wallace 2.50 6.00
39 Andrea Bargnani 2.50 6.00
40 Antawn Jamison 2.50 6.00
41 Luol Deng 2.50 6.00
42 Al Harrington 2.50 6.00
43 Jamal Crawford 3.00 8.00
44 Jason Terry 2.50 6.00
45 Baron Davis 2.50 6.00
46 Russell Westbrook 8.00 20.00
47 Michael Beasley 2.00 5.00
48 Caron Butler 2.50 6.00
49 Carl Landry 2.00 5.00
50 LaMarcus Aldridge 3.00 8.00
51 Ray Allen 3.00 8.00
52 Trevor Ariza 2.00 5.00
53 Tony Parker 3.00 8.00
54 Chauncey Billups 3.00 8.00
55 Luis Scola 2.50 6.00
56 Josh Smith 2.50 6.00
57 Andrew Bynum 2.00 5.00
58 Marc Gasol 3.00 8.00
59 Jason Richardson 3.00 8.00
60 Jeff Green 2.50 6.00
61 Danny Granger 2.50 6.00
62 Nene 2.50 6.00
63 Vince Carter 4.00 10.00
64 Charlie Villanueva 2.00 5.00
65 Rajon Rondo 3.00 8.00
66 Eric Gordon 2.50 6.00
67 Elton Brand 3.00 8.00
68 D.J. Augustin 2.00 5.00
69 Derek Fisher 2.50 6.00
70 Devin Harris 2.00 5.00
71 Emeka Okafor 2.50 6.00
72 Jason Kidd 3.00 8.00
73 Jermaine O'Neal 2.50 6.00
74 Josh Howard 2.50 6.00
75 Kevin Love 3.00 8.00
76 Lamar Odom 2.50 6.00
77 Mike Bibby 2.50 6.00
78 Randy Foye 2.00 5.00
79 Richard Hamilton 2.50 6.00
80 Ron Artest 3.00 8.00
81 Ronnie Brewer 2.50 6.00
82 Rudy Fernandez 2.00 5.00
83 Ryan Gomes 2.00 5.00
84 Shane Battier 3.00 8.00
85 T.J. Ford 2.00 5.00
86 Ben Gordon 2.50 6.00
87 Rashard Lewis 2.50 6.00
88 Shawn Marion 2.50 6.00
89 Troy Murphy 2.00 5.00
90 Chris Duhon 2.00 5.00
91 Raymond Felton 2.50 6.00
92 Andre Miller 2.50 6.00
93 Jarrett Jack 2.50 6.00
94 Mike Conley Jr. 2.50 6.00
95 Kendrick Perkins 2.00 5.00
96 Chris Andersen 2.50 6.00
97 Greg Oden 2.50 6.00
98 Danilo Gallinari 2.50 6.00
99 Yi Jianlian 2.50 6.00
100 Wilson Chandler 2.50 6.00
101 Ed Macauley LEG 3.00 8.00
102 Bob Cousy LEG 5.00 12.00
103 Bob Pettit LEG 3.00 8.00
104 Dolph Schayes LEG 3.00 8.00
105 Bill Russell LEG 5.00 12.00
106 Bill Sharman LEG 3.00 8.00
107 Elgin Baylor LEG 3.00 8.00
108 Cliff Hagan LEG 2.50 6.00
109 Jerry Lucas LEG 3.00 8.00
110 Oscar Robertson LEG 3.00 8.00
111 Jerry West LEG 4.00 10.00
112 Hal Greer LEG 2.50 6.00
113 Slater Martin LEG 3.00 8.00
114 Frank Ramsey LEG 3.00 8.00
115 Willis Reed LEG 3.00 8.00
116 Jack Twyman LEG 3.00 8.00
117 John Havlicek LEG 3.00 8.00
118 Sam Jones LEG 4.00 10.00
119 Nate Thurmond LEG 2.50 6.00
120 Billy Cunningham LEG 3.00 8.00
121 Tom Heinsohn LEG 3.00 8.00
122 Rick Barry LEG 2.50 6.00
123 Walt Frazier LEG 3.00 8.00
124 Bobby Wanzer LEG 2.00 5.00
125 Clyde Lovellette LEG 3.00 8.00
126 Wes Unseld LEG 3.00 8.00
127 K.C. Jones LEG 3.00 8.00
128 Lenny Wilkens LEG 3.00 8.00
129 Elvin Hayes LEG 3.00 8.00
130 Earl Monroe LEG 3.00 8.00
131 Nate Archibald LEG 2.50 6.00
132 Dave Cowens LEG 2.00 5.00
133 Harry Gallatin LEG 3.00 8.00
134 Connie Hawkins LEG 3.00 8.00
135 Bob Lanier LEG 2.50 6.00
136 Walt Bellamy LEG 2.50 6.00
137 Dan Issel LEG 2.50 6.00
138 Bill Walton LEG 3.00 8.00
139 Kareem Abdul-Jabbar LEG 5.00 12.00
140 Vern Mikkelsen LEG 3.00 8.00
141 George Gervin LEG 3.00 8.00
142 Gail Goodrich LEG 2.50 6.00
143 David Thompson LEG 2.50 6.00
144 Alex English LEG 2.50 6.00
145 Bailey Howell LEG 3.00 8.00
146 Larry Bird LEG 8.00 20.00
147 Marques Haynes LEG 3.00 8.00
148 Arnie Risen LEG 3.00 8.00
149 Kevin McHale LEG 3.00 8.00
150 Bob McAdoo LEG 2.50 6.00
151 Isiah Thomas LEG 3.00 8.00
152 Magic Johnson LEG 8.00 20.00
153 Robert Parish LEG 3.00 8.00
154 James Worthy LEG 4.00 10.00
155 Clyde Drexler LEG 4.00 10.00
156 Lynette Woodard LEG 3.00 8.00
157 Jalen Rose LEG 3.00 8.00
158 Joe Dumars LEG 3.00 8.00
159 Dominique Wilkins LEG 4.00 10.00
160 Adrian Dantley LEG 2.50 6.00
161 Patrick Ewing LEG 4.00 10.00
162 Hakeem Olajuwon LEG 4.00 10.00
163 David Robinson LEG 5.00 12.00
164 John Stockton LEG 5.00 12.00
165 John Kundla LEG 3.00 8.00
166 Earl Lloyd LEG 3.00 8.00
167 Alonzo Mourning LEG 4.00 10.00
168 Bernard King LEG 2.50 6.00
169 Bill Laimbeer LEG 2.50 6.00
170 Scottie Pippen LEG 6.00 15.00
171 Chris Mullin LEG 3.00 8.00
172 Danny Manning LEG 2.50 6.00
173 Dennis Rodman LEG 6.00 15.00
174 Detlef Schrempf LEG 3.00 8.00
175 Dikembe Mutombo LEG 3.00 8.00
176 George McGinnis LEG 2.00 5.00
177 Jeff Hornacek LEG 2.50 6.00
178 Sidney Moncrief LEG 2.00 5.00
179 Pat Riley LEG 3.00 8.00
180 Tom Gola LEG 3.00 8.00
181 Calvin Murphy LEG 2.50 6.00
182 Nancy Lieberman LEG 4.00 10.00
183 Meadowlark Lemon LEG 3.00 8.00
184 Geese Ausbie LEG 3.00 8.00
185 Curly Neal LEG 3.00 8.00
186 Jonas Jerebko RC 8.00 20.00
187 Marcus Thornton RC 6.00 15.00
188 Wesley Matthews RC 15.00 40.00
189 Serge Ibaka RC 8.00 20.00
190 A.J. Price RC 5.00 12.00
191 Jon Brockman RC 5.00 12.00
192 Dante Cunningham RC 5.00 12.00
193 Derrick Brown RC 5.00 12.00
194 Sundiata Gaines RC 5.00 12.00
195 Marcus Landry RC 5.00 12.00
196 Lester Hudson RC 5.00 12.00
197 Danny Green RC 10.00 25.00
198 David Andersen RC 5.00 12.00
199 DeMar DeRozan 12.00 30.00
200 Ricky Rubio RC 12.00 30.00
201 Blake Griffin JSY AU RC 1000.00 1500.00
202 Hasheem Thabeet JSY AU RC 12.00 30.00
203 Jms Harden JSY AU RC 1500.00 2000.00
204 Tyreke Evans JSY AU RC 100.00 200.00
205 Jonny Flynn JSY AU RC 12.00 30.00
206 Stph Curry JSY AU RC 10000.00 15000.00
207 Jordan Hill JSY AU RC 15.00 40.00
208 D. DeRozan JSY AU RC 400.00 800.00
209 B.Jennings JSY AU RC 25.00 60.00
210 T.Williams JSY AU RC 12.00 30.00
211 G.Henderson JSY AU RC 15.00 40.00
212 T.Hansbrough JSY AU RC 15.00 40.00
213 Earl Clark JSY AU RC 15.00 40.00
214 Austin Daye JSY AU RC 12.00 30.00
215 James Johnson JSY AU RC 25.00 60.00
216 Jrue Holiday JSY AU RC 75.00 150.00
217 Ty Lawson JSY AU RC 20.00 50.00
218 Jeff Teague JSY AU RC 20.00 50.00
219 Eric Maynor JSY AU RC 12.00 30.00
220 D.Collison JSY AU RC 15.00 40.00
221 Omri Casspi JSY AU RC 15.00 40.00
222 B.J. Mullens JSY AU RC 12.00 30.00
223 R.Beaubois JSY AU RC 12.00 30.00
224 Taj Gibson JSY AU RC 20.00 50.00
225 DeMarre Carroll JSY AU RC 15.00 40.00
226 Wayne Ellington JSY AU RC 12.00 30.00
227 Toney Douglas JSY AU RC 12.00 30.00
228 Jeff Pendergraph JSY AU RC 12.00 30.00
229 Jermaine Taylor JSY AU RC 12.00 30.00
230 DaJuan Summers JSY AU RC 12.00 30.00
231 Sam Young JSY AU RC 12.00 30.00
232 DeJuan Blair JSY AU RC 12.00 30.00
233 Jodie Meeks JSY AU RC 20.00 50.00
234 Chase Budinger JSY AU RC 15.00 40.00
235 Taylor Griffin JSY AU RC 12.00 30.00
236 Tyreke Evans JSY AU/97 15.00 40.00
237 Darren Collison JSY AU 20.00 50.00
238 Hasheem Thabeet JSY AU 12.00 30.00

2009-10 Playoff National Treasures Century Gold

1-200 UNPRICED PRINT RUN 5 SETS
201-238 PRINT RUN 25 SER.#'d SETS
201 Blake Griffin JSY AU 1500.00 2500.00
202 Hasheem Thabeet JSY AU 15.00 40.00
203 James Harden JSY AU 2500.00 3000.00
204 Tyreke Evans JSY AU 125.00 300.00
205 Jonny Flynn JSY AU 15.00 40.00
206 S.Curry JSY AU 15000.00 20000.00
207 Jordan Hill JSY AU 20.00 50.00
208 DeMar DeRozan JSY AU 300.00 600.00
209 Brandon Jennings JSY AU 30.00 80.00
210 Terrence Williams JSY AU 15.00 40.00
211 Gerald Henderson JSY AU 20.00 50.00
212 Tyler Hansbrough JSY AU 20.00 50.00
213 Earl Clark JSY AU 20.00 50.00
214 Austin Daye JSY AU 15.00 40.00
215 James Johnson JSY AU 20.00 50.00
216 Jrue Holiday JSY AU 125.00 300.00
217 Ty Lawson JSY AU 25.00 60.00
218 Jeff Teague JSY AU 50.00 100.00
219 Eric Maynor JSY AU 15.00 40.00
220 Darren Collison JSY AU 25.00 60.00
221 Omri Casspi JSY AU 30.00 80.00
222 B.J. Mullens JSY AU 12.00 30.00
223 Rodrigue Beaubois JSY AU 15.00 40.00
224 Taj Gibson JSY AU 25.00 60.00
225 DeMarre Carroll JSY AU 20.00 50.00
226 Wayne Ellington JSY AU 15.00 40.00

227 Toney Douglas JSY AU 15.00 40.00
228 Jeff Pendergraph JSY AU 15.00 40.00
229 Jermaine Taylor JSY AU 15.00 40.00
230 DaJuan Summers JSY AU 15.00 40.00
231 Sam Young JSY AU 15.00 40.00
232 DeJuan Blair JSY AU 15.00 40.00
233 Jodie Meeks JSY AU 25.00 60.00
234 Chase Budinger JSY AU 20.00 50.00
235 Taylor Griffin JSY AU 15.00 40.00
236 Tyreke Evans JSY AU 40.00 100.00
237 Darren Collison JSY AU 25.00 60.00
238 Hasheem Thabeet JSY AU 15.00 40.00

2009-10 Playoff National Treasures 25th Anniversary Team

COMPLETE SET (10) 25.00 50.00
STATED PRINT RUN 25 SER.#'d SETS
1 Dolph Schayes 3.00 8.00
2 Bob Pettit 3.00 8.00
3 Bill Russell 5.00 12.00
4 George Mikan 6.00 15.00
5 Bob Cousy 5.00 12.00
6 Bill Sharman 3.00 8.00
7 Sam Jones 4.00 10.00
8 Paul Arizin 3.00 8.00
9 Bob Davies 3.00 8.00
10 Red Auerbach 4.00 10.00

2009-10 Playoff National Treasures 25th Anniversary Team Signatures

STATED PRINT RUN 5 TO 25 SER.#'d SETS
SOME UNPRICED DUE TO SCARCITY
1 Dolph Schayes/25 8.00 20.00
2 Bob Pettit/25 12.00 30.00
6 Bill Sharman/25 10.00 25.00

2009-10 Playoff National Treasures 35th Anniversary Team

COMPLETE SET (10) 30.00 80.00
STATED PRINT RUN 35 SER.#'d SETS
1 Kareem Abdul-Jabbar 6.00 15.00
2 Elgin Baylor 4.00 10.00
3 Bob Cousy 6.00 15.00
4 John Havlicek 4.00 10.00
5 George Mikan 8.00 20.00
6 Bob Pettit 4.00 10.00
7 Oscar Robertson 4.00 10.00
8 Bill Russell 6.00 15.00
9 Jerry West 5.00 12.00
10 Wilt Chamberlain 8.00 20.00

2009-10 Playoff National Treasures 35th Anniversary Team Signatures

STATED PRINT RUN 5 TO 25 SER.#'d SETS
SOME UNPRICED DUE TO SCARCITY
1 Kareem Abdul-Jabbar/25 50.00 100.00
9 Jerry West/25 30.00 80.00

2009-10 Playoff National Treasures All Decade Materials

STATED PRINT RUN 10 TO 99 SER.#'d SETS
SOME UNPRICED DUE TO SCARCITY
1 George Mikan/99 12.50 30.00
8 Kareem Abdul-Jabbar/25 8.00 20.00
12 Scottie Pippen/49 10.00 25.00
13 Shaquille O'Neal/49 8.00 20.00
14 Kobe Bryant/99 12.00 30.00
16 Dirk Nowitzki/99 5.00 12.00
17 Tim Duncan/99 6.00 15.00
18 Kevin Garnett/99 6.00 15.00
19 Tracy McGrady/99 4.00 10.00
20 Steve Nash/49 8.00 20.00

2009-10 Playoff National Treasures All Decade Materials Prime

*PRIME: .6X TO 1.5X HI COLUMN
STATED PRINT RUN 5 TO 25 SER.#'d SETS
SOME UNPRICED DUE TO SCARCITY
10 Magic Johnson/25 15.00 40.00
11 Dominique Wilkins/25 8.00 20.00
14 Kobe Bryant/25 25.00 60.00

2009-10 Playoff National Treasures All Decade Materials Signatures

STATED PRINT RUN ONE TO 25 SER.#'d SETS
SOME UNPRICED DUE TO SCARCITY
UNPRICED PRIME PRINT RUN ONE TO 10 SETS
14 Kobe Bryant/25 125.00 250.00

2009-10 Playoff National Treasures All Decade Signatures

STATED PRINT RUN 3 TO 25 SER.#'d SETS
SOME UNPRICED DUE TO SCARCITY
UNPRICED COMBO PRINT RUN FIVE SETS
UNPRICED QUAD PRINT RUN FIVE SETS
UNPRICED TRIO PRINT RUN 3 TO 5 SETS
14 Kobe Bryant/25 125.00 225.00

2009-10 Playoff National Treasures All NBA

STATED PRINT RUN 25 SER.#'d SETS
1 Karl Malone 6.00 15.00
2 Elgin Baylor 5.00 12.00
3 Jerry West 8.00 20.00
4 Kareem Abdul-Jabbar 8.00 20.00
5 Bob Cousy 8.00 20.00
6 Bob Pettit 5.00 12.00
7 Magic Johnson 12.00 30.00
8 Larry Bird 12.00 30.00
9 Oscar Robertson 5.00 12.00
10 Dolph Schayes 5.00 12.00
11 Hakeem Olajuwon 6.00 15.00
12 Kobe Bryant 15.00 40.00
13 George Gervin 5.00 12.00
14 Rick Barry 4.00 10.00
15 Bill Sharman 5.00 12.00
16 David Robinson 8.00 20.00
17 John Havlicek 5.00 12.00
18 Walt Frazier 5.00 12.00
19 Ed Macauley 5.00 12.00
20 Elvin Hayes 5.00 12.00
21 Isiah Thomas 5.00 12.00
22 Jerry Lucas 5.00 12.00
23 Nate Archibald 4.00 10.00
24 Scottie Pippen 10.00 25.00
25 Bill Russell 8.00 20.00

2009-10 Playoff National Treasures All NBA Materials

STATED PRINT RUN 10 TO 99 SER.#'d SETS
SOME UNPRICED DUE TO SCARCITY
1 Karl Malone/99 5.00 12.00
4 Kareem Abdul-Jabbar/25 10.00 25.00
11 Hakeem Olajuwon/99 5.00 12.00
12 Kobe Bryant/99 10.00 25.00
24 Scottie Pippen/49 10.00 25.00

2009-10 Playoff National Treasures All NBA Materials Prime

STATED PRINT RUN 5 TO 25 SER.#'d SETS
SOME UNPRICED DUE TO SCARCITY
1 Karl Malone/25 15.00 30.00
7 Magic Johnson/25 15.00 40.00
11 Hakeem Olajuwon/25 10.00 25.00
12 Kobe Bryant/25 25.00 60.00

2009-10 Playoff National Treasures All NBA Materials Signatures

STATED PRINT RUN ONE TO 25 SER.#'d SETS
SOME UNPRICED DUE TO SCARCITY
UNPRICED PRIME PRINT RUN ONE TO 10 SETS
12 Kobe Bryant/25 125.00 250.00

2009-10 Playoff National Treasures All NBA Signatures

STATED PRINT RUN 4 TO 49 SER.#'d SETS
SOME UNPRICED DUE TO SCARCITY
10 Dolph Schayes/25 8.00 20.00
11 Hakeem Olajuwon/25 20.00 40.00
12 Kobe Bryant/25 125.00 225.00
14 Rick Barry/25
15 Bill Sharman/25 10.00 25.00
18 Walt Frazier/25 12.00 30.00
23 Nate Archibald/49 8.00 20.00

2009-10 Playoff National Treasures Biography Materials

STATED PRINT RUN 49 TO 99 SER.#'d SETS
1 Kobe Bryant/99 10.00 25.00
2 LeBron James/49 10.00 25.00
3 Kevin Durant/49 12.00 30.00
4 Dirk Nowitzki/99 5.00 12.00
5 Dwyane Wade/99 6.00 15.00
6 Carmelo Anthony/99 5.00 12.00
7 Chris Bosh/49 4.00 10.00
8 Dwight Howard/99 3.00 8.00
9 Tim Duncan/99 6.00 15.00
10 Shaquille O'Neal/49 8.00 20.00

2009-10 Playoff National Treasures Biography Materials Prime

*PRIME: .6X TO 1.5X HI COLUMN
STATED PRINT RUN ONE TO 25 SER.#'d SETS
SOME UNPRICED DUE TO SCARCITY
1 Kobe Bryant/25 30.00 80.00

2009-10 Playoff National Treasures Biography Materials Autographs

STATED PRINT RUN 3 TO 25 SER.#'d SETS
SOME UNPRICED DUE TO SCARCITY
UNPRICED PRIME PRINT RUN ONE TO 10 SETS
1 Kobe Bryant/25 125.00 250.00

2009-10 Playoff National Treasures Century Materials

STATED PRINT RUN ONE TO 99 SER.#'d SETS
SOME UNPRICED DUE TO SCARCITY
UNPRICED NBA LOGO PRINT RUN 1 TO 2 SETS
UNPRICED NBA TAGS PRINT RUN 1 TO 4 SETS
UNPRICED TEAM LOGO PRINT RUN 1 TO 5 SETS
1 Kobe Bryant/99 12.00 30.00
2 LeBron James/49 12.00 30.00
3 Dwight Howard/99 3.00 8.00
4 Derrick Rose/99 6.00 15.00
5 Dwyane Wade/99 6.00 15.00
6 Kevin Garnett/99 6.00 15.00
7 Chris Paul/99 5.00 12.00
8 Paul Pierce/99 4.00 10.00
9 Shaquille O'Neal/49 8.00 20.00
10 Pau Gasol/99 4.00 10.00
11 Carmelo Anthony/99 5.00 12.00
12 Steve Nash/49 4.00 10.00
13 David Lee/49 2.50 6.00
14 Allen Iverson/99 5.00 12.00
15 Kevin Durant/49 10.00 25.00
16 Monta Ellis/49 3.00 8.00
17 Dirk Nowitzki/99 5.00 12.00
18 Chris Bosh/49 4.00 10.00
19 Brandon Roy/49 4.00 10.00
20 Amare Stoudemire/99 3.00 8.00
21 Joe Johnson/99 3.00 8.00
23 Carlos Boozer/99 3.00 8.00
24 Rudy Gay/99 4.00 10.00
26 Corey Maggette/99 3.00 8.00
27 Brook Lopez/99 3.00 8.00
29 Rodney Stuckey/99 2.50 6.00
30 Chris Kaman/49 3.00 8.00
31 O.J. Mayo/99 2.50 6.00
32 Tim Duncan/99 6.00 15.00
33 Al Jefferson/99 3.00 8.00
34 Andre Iguodala/99 3.00 8.00
35 Deron Williams/25 5.00 12.00
36 David West/99 3.00 8.00
38 Gerald Wallace/99 3.00 8.00
39 Andrea Bargnani/99 3.00 8.00
40 Antawn Jamison/49 3.00 8.00
41 Luol Deng/99 3.00 8.00
44 Jason Terry/99 3.00 8.00
45 Baron Davis/99 3.00 8.00
46 Russell Westbrook/99 10.00 25.00
47 Michael Beasley/99 2.50 6.00
48 Caron Butler/49 3.00 8.00
49 Carl Landry/99 2.50 6.00
50 LaMarcus Aldridge/99 4.00 10.00
51 Ray Allen/99 4.00 10.00
52 Trevor Ariza/99 2.50 6.00
53 Tony Parker/99 4.00 10.00
54 Chauncey Billups/25 4.00 10.00
55 Luis Scola/99 3.00 8.00
56 Josh Smith/99 3.00 8.00
58 Marc Gasol/99 4.00 10.00
59 Jason Richardson/99 4.00 10.00
60 Jeff Green/99 3.00 8.00
61 Danny Granger/99 3.00 8.00
62 Nene/99 3.00 8.00
63 Vince Carter/99 5.00 12.00
65 Rajon Rondo/99 4.00 10.00
66 Eric Gordon/99 3.00 8.00
67 Elton Brand/99 4.00 10.00
68 D.J. Augustin/99 2.50 6.00
69 Derek Fisher/49 6.00 15.00
70 Devin Harris/99 2.50 6.00
71 Emeka Okafor/49 3.00 8.00
73 Jermaine O'Neal/99 3.00 8.00
75 Kevin Love/99 4.00 10.00
76 Lamar Odom/99 3.00 8.00
77 Mike Bibby/99 3.00 8.00
78 Randy Foye/99 2.50 6.00
79 Richard Hamilton/99 3.00 8.00
80 Ron Artest/99 4.00 10.00
82 Rudy Fernandez/99 2.50 6.00
84 Shane Battier/99 4.00 10.00
85 T.J. Ford/99 2.50 6.00
86 Ben Gordon/99 3.00 8.00
87 Rashard Lewis/99 3.00 8.00
88 Shawn Marion/99 3.00 8.00
89 Troy Murphy/99 2.50 6.00
90 Chris Duhon/99 2.50 6.00
91 Raymond Felton/99 3.00 8.00
92 Andre Miller/99 3.00 8.00
94 Mike Conley Jr./99 3.00 8.00
96 Chris Andersen/99 3.00 8.00
97 Greg Oden/99 3.00 8.00
99 Yi Jianlian/99 3.00 8.00
100 Wilson Chandler/99 3.00 8.00
121 Tom Heinsohn/25 4.00 10.00
130 Earl Monroe/25 4.00 10.00
132 Dave Cowens/49 2.50 6.00
135 Bob Lanier/99 5.00 12.00
139 Kareem Abdul-Jabbar/25 8.00 20.00
144 Alex English/25 6.00 15.00
149 Kevin McHale/99 4.00 10.00
153 Robert Parish/49 4.00 10.00
155 Clyde Drexler/25 8.00 20.00
158 Joe Dumars/25 6.00 15.00
161 Patrick Ewing/99 6.00 15.00
162 Hakeem Olajuwon/99 5.00 12.00
167 Alonzo Mourning/99 6.00 15.00
168 Bernard King/99 6.00 15.00
170 Scottie Pippen/49 8.00 20.00
171 Chris Mullin/99 4.00 10.00
172 Danny Manning/99 3.00 8.00
174 Detlef Schrempf/99 6.00 15.00
175 Dikembe Mutombo/99 5.00 12.00
177 Jeff Hornacek/99 3.00 8.00
193 Derrick Brown/25 2.50 6.00

2009-10 Playoff National Treasures Century Materials Prime

*PRIME: .75X TO 2X BASE HI
STATED PRINT RUN ONE TO 25 SER.#'d SETS
SOME UNPRICED DUE TO SCARCITY
4 Derrick Rose/25 12.00 30.00
14 Allen Iverson/25 20.00 40.00
121 Tom Heinsohn/15 10.00 25.00
137 Dan Issel/25 6.00 15.00
144 Alex English/25 8.00 20.00
152 Magic Johnson/25 25.00 60.00
158 Joe Dumars/25 8.00 20.00
159 Dominique Wilkins/25 10.00 25.00
160 Adrian Dantley/25 6.00 15.00
161 Patrick Ewing/25 15.00 40.00
164 John Stockton/25 10.00 25.00
168 Bernard King/25 8.00 20.00
171 Chris Mullin/25 12.50 30.00

2009-10 Playoff National Treasures Century Materials Signatures

STATED PRINT RUN ONE TO 99 SER.#'d SETS
SOME UNPRICED DUE TO SCARCITY
UNPRICED LOGO SIG.PRINT RUN ONE SET
UNPRICED TAG SIG.PRINT RUN ONE SET
UNPRICED TEAM SIG.PRINT RUN 1 TO 5 SETS
1 Kobe Bryant/25 125.00 225.00
14 Allen Iverson/25 75.00 150.00
19 Brandon Roy/25 12.50 30.00
20 Amare Stoudemire/25 8.00 20.00
30 Chris Kaman/49 8.00 20.00
34 Andre Iguodala/49 8.00 20.00
35 Deron Williams/25 12.50 30.00
39 Andrea Bargnani/49 8.00 20.00
45 Baron Davis/99 8.00 20.00
49 Carl Landry/99 8.00 20.00
53 Tony Parker/25 15.00 40.00
54 Chauncey Billups/25 8.00 20.00
57 Andrew Bynum/25 15.00 40.00
68 D.J. Augustin/99 8.00 20.00
71 Emeka Okafor/49 8.00 20.00
85 T.J. Ford/25 8.00 20.00
96 Chris Andersen/99 12.00 30.00
132 Dave Cowens/49 10.00 25.00
144 Alex English/28 8.00 20.00
168 Bernard King/99 8.00 20.00
171 Chris Mullin/49 20.00 40.00
172 Danny Manning/49 12.50 30.00
174 Detlef Schrempf/99 8.00 20.00

2009-10 Playoff National Treasures Century Materials Prime Signatures

STATED PRINT RUN ONE TO 25 SER.#'d SETS
SOME UNPRICED DUE TO SCARCITY
30 Chris Kaman/25 10.00 25.00
34 Andre Iguodala/25 10.00 25.00
49 Carl Landry/25 10.00 25.00
96 Chris Andersen/25 30.00 60.00
132 Dave Cowens/25 15.00 30.00
168 Bernard King/25 10.00 25.00
171 Chris Mullin/25 30.00 80.00
172 Danny Manning/25 15.00 40.00
193 Derrick Brown/25 10.00 25.00

2009-10 Playoff National Treasures Century Signatures

STATED PRINT RUN 5 TO 99 SER.#'d SETS
SOME UNPRICED DUE TO SCARCITY
ASTERISK CARDS FROM PANINI UPDATE
UNPRICED PLAT.SIG PRINT RUN ONE SET
1 Kobe Bryant/25* 125.00 250.00
28 Aaron Brooks/25 6.00 15.00
30 Chris Kaman/25 6.00 15.00
34 Andre Iguodala/25 6.00 15.00
39 Andrea Bargnani/25 6.00 15.00
45 Baron Davis/25 6.00 15.00
46 Russell Westbrook/25 75.00 200.00
47 Michael Beasley/25 6.00 15.00
52 Trevor Ariza/25 6.00 15.00
54 Chauncey Billups/25 8.00 20.00
64 Charlie Villanueva/25 6.00 15.00
68 D.J. Augustin/25 6.00 15.00
70 Devin Harris/25 6.00 15.00
71 Emeka Okafor/25 6.00 15.00
73 Jermaine O'Neal/25 6.00 15.00
74 Josh Howard/25 6.00 15.00
75 Kevin Love/25 20.00 50.00
77 Mike Bibby/25 6.00 15.00
78 Randy Foye/25 5.00 12.00
79 Richard Hamilton/25 6.00 15.00
80 Ron Artest/25 12.00 30.00
81 Ronnie Brewer/25 6.00 15.00
84 Shane Battier/25 8.00 20.00
85 T.J. Ford/25 6.00 15.00
96 Chris Andersen/25 6.00 15.00
104 Dolph Schayes/25 12.00 30.00
108 Cliff Hagan/25 6.00 15.00
112 Hal Greer/25 6.00 15.00
114 Frank Ramsey/25 12.00 30.00
115 Willis Reed/25 10.00 25.00
119 Nate Thurmond/25 10.00 25.00
123 Walt Frazier/25 12.50 30.00
124 Bobby Wanzer/25 10.00 25.00
126 Wes Unseld/25 15.00 40.00
128 Lenny Wilkens/25 10.00 25.00
129 Elvin Hayes/25 15.00 30.00
131 Nate Archibald/25 10.00 25.00
132 Dave Cowens/25 10.00 25.00
133 Harry Gallatin/25 10.00 25.00
137 Dan Issel/17 8.00 20.00
141 George Gervin/25 10.00 25.00
142 Gail Goodrich/25 10.00 25.00
143 David Thompson/25 10.00 25.00
145 Bailey Howell/25 10.00 25.00
147 Marques Haynes/25 12.00 30.00
148 Arnie Risen/25 10.00 25.00
150 Bob McAdoo/25 15.00 30.00
153 Robert Parish/25 15.00 30.00
154 James Worthy/25 30.00 60.00
155 Clyde Drexler/25 20.00 50.00
162 Hakeem Olajuwon/25 25.00 60.00
168 Bernard King/25 10.00 25.00
169 Bill Laimbeer/15 12.50 30.00
171 Chris Mullin/25 15.00 40.00
172 Danny Manning/25 10.00 25.00
174 Detlef Schrempf/25 20.00 50.00
175 Dikembe Mutombo/25 12.00 30.00
176 George McGinnis/25 10.00 25.00
177 Jeff Hornacek/25 10.00 25.00
178 Sidney Moncrief/25 8.00 20.00
179 Pat Riley/25 15.00 40.00
181 Calvin Murphy/25 8.00 20.00
182 Nancy Lieberman/25 8.00 20.00
183 Meadowlark Lemon/25 15.00 40.00
186 Jonas Jerebko/99 6.00 15.00
187 Marcus Thornton/99 5.00 12.00
188 Wesley Matthews/99 6.00 15.00
189 Serge Ibaka/99 6.00 15.00
190 A.J. Price/99 4.00 10.00
191 Jon Brockman/99 4.00 10.00
192 Dante Cunningham/99 4.00 10.00
193 Derrick Brown/99 4.00 10.00
194 Sundiata Gaines/99 4.00 10.00
195 Marcus Landry/99 4.00 10.00
196 Lester Hudson/99 4.00 10.00
197 Danny Green/99 8.00 20.00
198 David Andersen/99 4.00 10.00
199 DeMar DeRozan/99 15.00 40.00
200 Ricky Rubio/99 60.00 150.00

2009-10 Playoff National Treasures Champions

COMPLETE SET (10) 40.00 80.00
STATED PRINT RUN 25 SER.#'d SETS
1 John Kundla 5.00 12.00
2 Vern Mikkelsen 5.00 12.00
3 Earl Lloyd 5.00 12.00
4 Dolph Schayes 5.00 12.00
5 Arnie Risen 5.00 12.00
6 Bobby Wanzer 3.00 8.00
7 Clyde Drexler 6.00 15.00
8 Chauncey Billups 5.00 12.00
9 Shaquille O'Neal 10.00 25.00
10 Tony Parker 5.00 12.00

2009-10 Playoff National Treasures Champions Signature Combos

STATED PRINT RUN 5 TO 25 SER.#'d SETS
SOME UNPRICED DUE TO SCARCITY
UNPRICED QUAD PRINT RUN 5 SER.#'d SETS
3 D.Cowens/J.Havlicek/25 30.00 80.00
4 E.Hayes/W.Unseld/25 25.00 50.00

2009-10 Playoff National Treasures Champions Signatures

STATED PRINT RUN 5 TO 99 SER.#'d SETS
SOME UNPRICED DUE TO SCARCITY
4 Dolph Schayes/25 10.00 25.00
6 Bobby Wanzer/99 6.00 15.00
7 Clyde Drexler/25 20.00 40.00
10 Tony Parker/15 12.00 30.00

2009-10 Playoff National Treasures Colossal Materials

STATED PRINT RUN 5 TO 99 SER.#'d SETS
SOME UNPRICED DUE TO SCARCITY
UNPRICED LOGO PRINT RUNS ONE TO 5 SETS
1 Kobe Bryant/99 12.00 30.00
2 Blake Griffin/25 12.00 30.00
3 Kevin Durant/49 10.00 25.00
4 James Harden/25 15.00 40.00
5 Dirk Nowitzki/99 5.00 12.00
6 Tyreke Evans/25 2.50 6.00
7 Carmelo Anthony/49 5.00 12.00
8 Jonny Flynn/25 2.00 5.00
9 Chris Bosh/25 5.00 12.00
10 Stephen Curry/25 60.00 150.00
11 David Lee/25 2.50 6.00
12 DeMar DeRozan/25 8.00 20.00
14 Brandon Jennings/25 3.00 8.00
15 Steve Nash/49 10.00 25.00
16 Terrence Williams/25 2.00 5.00
18 Omri Casspi/25 2.50 6.00
19 Andre Iguodala/99 3.00 8.00
20 Darren Collison/25 3.00 8.00
22 Taj Gibson/25 3.00 8.00
23 Russell Westbrook/99 10.00 25.00
24 Ty Lawson/25 3.00 8.00
25 Danny Granger/99 3.00 8.00
26 DeJuan Blair/25 2.50 6.00
27 Ray Allen/99 4.00 10.00
28 Chase Budinger/25 2.50 6.00
29 Rajon Rondo/99 4.00 10.00
30 Sam Young/25 2.00 5.00
32 Jrue Holiday/25 4.00 10.00
33 LeBron James/49 15.00 40.00
34 Tyler Hansbrough/25 2.50 6.00
35 Dwyane Wade/99 6.00 15.00
36 Amare Stoudemire/99 3.00 8.00
37 Derrick Rose/99 6.00 15.00
38 Dwight Howard/99 3.00 8.00
40 Tim Duncan/99 6.00 15.00
41 Brandon Roy/49 4.00 10.00
42 Chris Paul/49 5.00 12.00
43 Pau Gasol/99 4.00 10.00
44 Shaquille O'Neal/49 8.00 20.00
45 Josh Smith/99 3.00 8.00
47 Paul Pierce/99 4.00 10.00
48 Eric Gordon/99 3.00 8.00
49 Tony Parker/99 4.00 10.00
50 Kevin Garnett/25 6.00 15.00

2009-10 Playoff National Treasures Colossal Materials Prime

STATED PRINT RUN ONE TO 25 SER.#'d SETS
MOST UNPRICED DUE TO SCARCITY
UNPRICED JSY NO.PRIME PRINT RUN 1 TO 10 SETS
1 Kobe Bryant/25 40.00 100.00

2009-10 Playoff National Treasures Colossal Materials Jersey Numbers

SY NUMB: SAME VALUE AS BASE
STATED PRINT RUN 10 TO 99 SER.#'d SETS
SOME UNPRICED DUE TO SCARCITY
23 Russell Westbrook/25 8.00 20.00
27 Ray Allen/25 8.00 20.00
43 Pau Gasol/25 10.00 25.00
47 Paul Pierce/99 4.00 10.00

2009-10 Playoff National Treasures Colossal Materials Signatures

STATED PRINT RUN 3 TO 49 SER.#'d SETS
SOME UNPRICED DUE TO SCARCITY
*JSY NUMBER: .4X TO 1X HI COLUMN
JSY NUMBER PRINT RUN 4 TO 49 SETS
1 Kobe Bryant/25 125.00 250.00
4 James Harden/49 50.00 120.00
6 Tyreke Evans/49 20.00 50.00
8 Jonny Flynn/49 4.00 10.00
9 Chris Bosh/25 15.00 40.00
10 Stephen Curry/49 300.00 600.00
12 DeMar DeRozan/49 15.00 40.00
14 Brandon Jennings/49 6.00 15.00
16 Terrence Williams/49 4.00 10.00
18 Omri Casspi/49 5.00 12.00
19 Andre Iguodala/49 6.00 15.00
20 Darren Collison/49 6.00 15.00
24 Ty Lawson/49 12.00 30.00
26 DeJuan Blair/49 5.00 12.00
28 Chase Budinger/49 5.00 12.00
30 Sam Young/49 4.00 10.00
32 Jrue Holiday/49 15.00 40.00
34 Tyler Hansbrough/49 5.00 12.00
41 Brandon Roy/25 12.50 30.00
49 Tony Parker/15 15.00 40.00

2009-10 Playoff National Treasures Colossal Materials Prime Signatures

STATED PRINT RUN ONE TO 25 SER.#'d SETS
SOME UNPRICED DUE TO SCARCITY
*JSY NUMBER: .4X TO 1X HI COLUMN
JSY NUMBER PRINT RUN ONE TO 25 SETS
12 DeMar DeRozan/25 30.00 80.00
14 Brandon Jennings/25 15.00 40.00
26 DeJuan Blair/25 12.00 30.00
32 Jrue Holiday/25 20.00 50.00

2009-10 Playoff National Treasures NBA Gear Dual

STATED PRINT RUN 10 TO 99 SER.#'d SETS
SOME UNPRICED DUE TO SCARCITY
TAGS NOT PRICED DUE TO SCARCITY
1 Kobe Bryant/99 15.00 30.00
2 LeBron James/49 15.00 30.00
3 Blake Griffin/25 12.00 30.00
5 James Harden/25 15.00 40.00
6 Dwyane Wade/99 5.00 12.00
7 Tyreke Evans/25 2.50 6.00
8 Carmelo Anthony/49 4.00 10.00
9 Jonny Flynn/25 2.00 5.00
10 Chris Paul/99 4.00 10.00
11 Stephen Curry/25 150.00 400.00
12 Dwight Howard/99 2.50 6.00
13 DeMar DeRozan/25 8.00 20.00
14 Earl Clark/25 2.50 6.00
15 Brandon Jennings/25 3.00 8.00
16 Gerald Henderson/25 2.50 6.00
17 Terrence Williams/25 2.00 5.00
18 Toney Douglas/25 2.00 5.00
19 Omri Casspi/25 2.50 6.00
20 Wayne Ellington/25 3.00 8.00
21 Darren Collison/25 3.00 8.00
22 Austin Daye/25 2.00 5.00
23 Taj Gibson/25 3.00 8.00
24 Jeff Teague/25 3.00 8.00
25 Ty Lawson/25 3.00 8.00
26 Eric Maynor/25 2.00 5.00
27 DeJuan Blair/25 2.50 6.00
28 James Johnson/25 2.50 6.00
29 Chase Budinger/25 2.50 6.00
30 Jordan Hill/25 2.50 6.00
31 Sam Young/25 2.00 5.00
32 Hasheem Thabeet/25 2.00 5.00
33 Jrue Holiday/25 4.00 10.00
34 Rodrigue Beaubois/25 2.00 5.00
35 Tyler Hansbrough/25 2.50 6.00

2009-10 Playoff National Treasures NBA Gear Dual Prime

*PRIME: .5X TO 1.25X BASE HI
STATED PRINT RUN 5 TO 49 SER.#'d SETS
SOME UNPRICED DUE TO SCARCITY
1 Kobe Bryant/49 40.00 80.00
8 Carmelo Anthony/25 10.00 25.00
10 Chris Paul/20 10.00 25.00
29 Chase Budinger/25 8.00 20.00

2009-10 Playoff National Treasures NBA Gear Dual Signatures

STATED PRINT RUN 3 TO 30 SER.#'d SETS
SOME UNPRICED DUE TO SCARCITY
*PRIME: .5X TO 1.25X HI COLUMN
PRIME PRINT RUN 3 TO 49 SETS
1 Kobe Bryant/25 125.00 250.00
3 Blake Griffin/25 100.00 200.00
5 James Harden/30 100.00 250.00
7 Tyreke Evans/30 20.00 50.00
9 Jonny Flynn/30 4.00 10.00
11 Stephen Curry/30 300.00 600.00
13 DeMar DeRozan/30 15.00 40.00
14 Earl Clark/30 5.00 12.00
15 Brandon Jennings/30 15.00 40.00
16 Gerald Henderson/30 5.00 12.00
17 Terrence Williams/30 4.00 10.00
18 Toney Douglas/30 4.00 10.00
19 Omri Casspi/30 5.00 12.00
20 Wayne Ellington/30 6.00 15.00
21 Darren Collison/30 6.00 15.00
22 Austin Daye/30 4.00 10.00
23 Taj Gibson/30 6.00 15.00
24 Jeff Teague/30 6.00 15.00
25 Ty Lawson/30 6.00 15.00
26 Eric Maynor/25 4.00 10.00
27 DeJuan Blair/30 5.00 12.00
28 James Johnson/30 5.00 12.00
29 Chase Budinger/30 5.00 12.00
30 Jordan Hill/30 5.00 12.00
31 Sam Young/30 4.00 10.00
32 Hasheem Thabeet/30 4.00 10.00
33 Jrue Holiday/30 8.00 20.00
34 Rodrigue Beaubois/30 4.00 10.00
35 Tyler Hansbrough/30 5.00 12.00

2009-10 Playoff National Treasures NBA Gear Trios

STATED PRINT RUN 10 TO 99 SER.#'d SETS
SOME UNPRICED DUE TO SCARCITY
1 Kobe Bryant/99 15.00 30.00
2 LeBron James/49 12.00 30.00
3 Blake Griffin/25 30.00 80.00
5 James Harden/25 20.00 50.00
6 Dwyane Wade/99 6.00 15.00
7 Tyreke Evans/25 3.00 8.00
8 Carmelo Anthony/49 6.00 15.00
9 Jonny Flynn/25 2.50 6.00
10 Chris Paul/99 5.00 12.00
11 Stephen Curry/25 200.00 400.00
12 Dwight Howard/99 3.00 8.00
13 DeMar DeRozan/25 10.00 25.00
14 Earl Clark/25 3.00 8.00
15 Brandon Jennings/25 4.00 10.00
16 Gerald Henderson/25 3.00 8.00
17 Terrence Williams/25 2.50 6.00
18 Toney Douglas/25 2.50 6.00
19 Omri Casspi/25 3.00 8.00
20 Wayne Ellington/25 4.00 10.00
21 Darren Collison/25 4.00 10.00
22 Austin Daye/25 2.50 6.00
23 Taj Gibson/25 4.00 10.00
24 Jeff Teague/25 4.00 10.00
25 Ty Lawson/25 4.00 10.00
26 Eric Maynor/25 2.50 6.00
27 DeJuan Blair/25 3.00 8.00
28 James Johnson/25 3.00 8.00
29 Chase Budinger/25 3.00 8.00
30 Jordan Hill/25 3.00 8.00
31 Sam Young/25 2.50 6.00
32 Hasheem Thabeet/25 2.50 6.00
33 Jrue Holiday/25 5.00 12.00
34 Rodrigue Beaubois/25 2.50 6.00
35 Tyler Hansbrough/25 3.00 8.00

2009-10 Playoff National Treasures NBA Gear Trios Prime

*PRIME: .5X TO 1.25X BASE HI
STATED PRINT RUN 5 TO 49 SER.#'d SETS
SOME UNPRICED DUE TO SCARCITY
1 Kobe Bryant/49 40.00 75.00
8 Carmelo Anthony/49 12.00 30.00
10 Chris Paul/49 12.00 30.00

2009-10 Playoff National Treasures NBA Gear Trios Signatures

STATED PRINT RUN 3 TO 30 SER.#'d SETS
SOME UNPRICED DUE TO SCARCITY
*PRIME: .6X TO 1.5X HI COLUMN
PRIME PRINT RUN 3 TO 49 SETS
1 Kobe Bryant/25 150.00 300.00
5 James Harden/30 50.00 120.00
7 Tyreke Evans/30 10.00 25.00
9 Jonny Flynn/30 4.00 10.00
11 Stephen Curry/30 300.00 600.00
13 DeMar DeRozan/30 15.00 40.00
14 Earl Clark/30 5.00 12.00
15 Brandon Jennings/30 6.00 15.00
16 Gerald Henderson/30 5.00 12.00
17 Terrence Williams/30 4.00 10.00
18 Toney Douglas/30 4.00 10.00
19 Omri Casspi/30 5.00 12.00
20 Wayne Ellington/30 6.00 15.00
21 Darren Collison/30 6.00 15.00
22 Austin Daye/30 4.00 10.00
23 Taj Gibson/30 10.00 25.00
24 Jeff Teague/30 6.00 15.00
25 Ty Lawson/30 6.00 15.00
26 Eric Maynor/25 4.00 10.00
27 DeJuan Blair/30 5.00 12.00
28 James Johnson/30 5.00 12.00
29 Chase Budinger/30 5.00 12.00
30 Jordan Hill/30 5.00 12.00
31 Sam Young/30 4.00 10.00
32 Hasheem Thabeet/30 4.00 10.00
33 Jrue Holiday/30 15.00 40.00
34 Rodrigue Beaubois/30 4.00 10.00
35 Tyler Hansbrough/30 5.00 12.00

2009-10 Playoff National Treasures NBA Greatest

COMPLETE SET (30) 125.00 250.00
PRINT RUN 25 SER.#'d SETS
1 Kareem Abdul-Jabbar 8.00 20.00
2 Nate Archibald 4.00 10.00
3 Rick Barry 4.00 10.00
4 Larry Bird 12.00 30.00
5 Bob Cousy 8.00 20.00
6 Dave Cowens 3.00 8.00
7 Clyde Drexler 6.00 15.00
8 Walt Frazier 5.00 12.00
9 George Gervin 5.00 12.00
10 Hal Greer 4.00 10.00
11 John Havlicek 5.00 12.00
12 Elvin Hayes 5.00 12.00
13 Magic Johnson 12.00 30.00
14 Kevin McHale 5.00 12.00
15 George Mikan 10.00 25.00
16 Earl Monroe 5.00 12.00
17 Shaquille O'Neal 10.00 25.00
18 Robert Parish 5.00 12.00
19 Scottie Pippen 10.00 25.00
20 Willis Reed 5.00 12.00
21 Oscar Robertson 5.00 12.00
22 Bill Russell 8.00 20.00
23 Dolph Schayes 5.00 12.00
24 Isiah Thomas 5.00 12.00
25 Nate Thurmond 4.00 10.00
26 Wes Unseld 5.00 12.00
27 Bill Walton 5.00 12.00
28 Jerry West 6.00 15.00
29 Lenny Wilkens 5.00 12.00
30 James Worthy 6.00 15.00

2009-10 Playoff National Treasures NBA Greatest Materials

STATED PRINT RUN 10 TO 99 SER.#'d SETS
SOME UNPRICED DUE TO SCARCITY
1 Kareem Abdul-Jabbar/25 10.00 25.00
6 Dave Cowens/99 4.00 10.00
7 Clyde Drexler/25 12.00 30.00
14 Kevin McHale/99 6.00 15.00
15 George Mikan/99 12.00 30.00
16 Earl Monroe/25 10.00 25.00
17 Shaquille O'Neal/49 10.00 25.00
18 Robert Parish/49 6.00 15.00
19 Scottie Pippen/49 10.00 25.00

2009-10 Playoff National Treasures NBA Greatest Materials Prime

*PRIME: .6X TO 1.5X HI COLUMN
STATED PRINT RUN 5 TO 25 SER.#'d SETS
SOME UNPRICED DUE TO SCARCITY
13 Magic Johnson/25 15.00 40.00

2009-10 Playoff National Treasures NBA Greatest Materials Signatures

STATED PRINT RUN ONE TO 49 SER.#'d SETS
SOME UNPRICED DUE TO SCARCITY
6 Dave Cowens/49 10.00 25.00
7 Clyde Drexler/49 25.00 50.00

2009-10 Playoff National Treasures NBA Greatest Materials Prime Signatures

STATED PRINT RUN ONE TO 25 SER.#'d SETS
SOME UNPRICED DUE TO SCARCITY
6 Dave Cowens/25 20.00 50.00

2009-10 Playoff National Treasures NBA Greatest Signature Combos

STATED PRINT RUN 5 TO 99 SER.#'d SETS
SOME UNPRICED DUE TO SCARCITY
1 B.Pettit/L.Wilkens/25 25.00 50.00
4 E.Hayes/W.Unseld/25 25.00 60.00
5 B.Walton/C.Drexler/99

2009-10 Playoff National Treasures NBA Greatest Signature Quads

STATED PRINT RUN 3 TO 15 SER.#'d SETS
SOME UNPRICED DUE TO SCARCITY
2 McH/Parish/Wltn/Bird/15 150.00 300.00

2009-10 Playoff National Treasures NBA Greatest Signatures

STATED PRINT RUN 3 TO 25 SER.#'d SETS
SOME UNPRICED DUE TO SCARCITY
UNPRICED TRIO SIG PRINT RUN 5 SER.#'d SETS
2 Nate Archibald/25 12.00 30.00
6 Dave Cowens/25 12.00 30.00
7 Clyde Drexler/25 25.00 50.00
8 Walt Frazier/25 12.00 30.00
10 Hal Greer/25 12.00 30.00
18 Robert Parish/25 12.00 30.00
20 Willis Reed/25 12.00 30.00
23 Dolph Schayes/25 12.00 30.00
25 Nate Thurmond/25 15.00 40.00
26 Wes Unseld/25 20.00 40.00
27 Bill Walton/25 12.00 30.00
30 James Worthy/25 30.00 60.00

2009-10 Playoff National Treasures Notable Nicknames

STATED PRINT RUN 10 TO 99 SER.#'d SETS
SOME UNPRICED DUE TO SCARCITY
BC Billy Cunningham/55 60.00 150.00
BW Bill Walton/99 15.00 40.00
CD Clyde Drexler/25 125.00 225.00
DC Dave Cowens/99 25.00 60.00
DW Dominique Wilkins/25 150.00 250.00
EH Elvin Hayes/25 100.00 200.00
EM Earl Monroe/99 90.00 150.00
FR Frank Ramsey/49 30.00 80.00
GG George Gervin/99 15.00 40.00
HG Harry Gallatin/49 25.00 60.00
JH John Havlicek/49 75.00 150.00
LB Larry Bird/25 350.00 700.00
NT Nate Thurmond/25 75.00 150.00
OR Oscar Robertson/25 150.00 350.00
WR Willis Reed/99 30.00 60.00
JWE Jerry West/25 150.00 300.00
KB1 Kobe Bryant Mamba/99 700.00 1200.00
KB2 Kobe Bryant MVP/35 700.00 1200.00

2009-10 Playoff National Treasures Pen Pals

STATED PRINT RUN 50 SER.#'d SETS
1 Blake Griffin 90.00 150.00
2 Hasheem Thabeet 4.00 10.00
3 James Harden 100.00 250.00
4 Jordan Hill 5.00 12.00
5 Stephen Curry 300.00 600.00
6 Tyler Hansbrough 5.00 12.00
7 Tyreke Evans 12.00 30.00
8 B.Griffin/H.Thabeet 60.00 150.00
9 B.Griffin/T.Hansbrough 50.00 100.00
10 D.Collison/J.Holiday 15.00 40.00
11 D.Blair/S.Young 10.00 25.00
12 E.Clark/T.Williams 10.00 25.00
13 J.Harden/J.Hill 30.00 80.00
14 J.Johnson/J.Teague 10.00 25.00
15 C.Budinger/J.Hill 12.50 30.00
16 T.Lawson/T.Hansbrough 25.00 60.00
17 Blair/Thabeet/Flynn 8.00 20.00

2009-10 Playoff National Treasures Signature Patches College

STATED PRINT RUN 25 TO 77 SER.#'d SETS
UNPRICED NBA LOGO PRINT RUN 5 TO 10 SETS
UNPRICED NBA LOGOMAN PRINT RUN ONE SET
2 Carmelo Anthony/27 30.00 80.00
3 Bill Walton/77 15.00 40.00
4 Dominique Wilkins/25 15.00 40.00
7 Dave Cowens/27 15.00 40.00
8 Oscar Robertson/27 40.00 100.00
9 David Thompson/27 12.50 30.00
10 Rick Barry/26 12.50 30.00
13 Isiah Thomas/27 15.00 40.00
15 Jerry West/26 40.00 80.00
17 John Havlicek/28 30.00 60.00
19 Kareem Abdul-Jabbar/27 40.00 80.00
25 Magic Johnson/27 40.00 100.00

2009-10 Playoff National Treasures Signature Patches NBA Team

STATED PRINT RUN 49 TO 100 SER.#'d SETS
1 Bill Russell/49 60.00 120.00
2 Carmelo Anthony/53 25.00 60.00
3 Bill Walton/50 10.00 25.00
5 Bob Cousy/54 35.00 70.00
6 Nate Thurmond/53 10.00 25.00
7 Dave Cowens/52 12.00 30.00
8 Oscar Robertson/53 40.00 100.00
9 David Thompson/51 10.00 25.00
10 Rick Barry/51 10.00 25.00
11 Dennis Rodman/53 25.00 60.00
12 Robert Parish/49 12.00 30.00
13 Isiah Thomas/53 12.50 30.00
14 Scottie Pippen/53 100.00 200.00
15 Jerry West/54 30.00 80.00
17 John Havlicek/52 25.00 60.00
18 Steve Nash/25 50.00 100.00
19 Kareem Abdul-Jabbar/54 40.00 80.00
23 Larry Bird/49 60.00 150.00
24 Kobe Bryant/100 100.00 200.00
25 Magic Johnson/51 50.00 120.00

2009-10 Playoff National Treasures Souvenir Cuts

STATED PRINT RUN ONE TO 25 SER.#'d SETS
SOME UNPRICED DUE TO SCARCITY
1 George Mikan/15 125.00 250.00
6 Andy Phillip/25 75.00 200.00
7 Paul Arizin/25 25.00 60.00

2009-10 Playoff National Treasures Timeline Materials Custom Names

STATED PRINT RUN 10 TO 99 SER.#'d SETS
SOME UNPRICED DUE TO SCARCITY
*NICKNAMES: .4X TO 1X BASE HI
1 Kobe Bryant/99 12.00 30.00
2 LeBron James/49 12.00 30.00
3 Tyreke Evans/49 2.50 6.00
4 Brandon Jennings/49 3.00 8.00
5 Stephen Curry/49 150.00 400.00
6 Jonny Flynn/49 2.00 5.00
7 Taj Gibson/49 3.00 8.00
9 Ty Lawson/49 3.00 8.00
10 Shaquille O'Neal/49 8.00 20.00
11 DeJuan Blair/49 2.50 6.00
12 Dirk Nowitzki/99 5.00 12.00
14 Dwyane Wade/99 6.00 15.00
15 Derrick Rose/99 6.00 15.00
16 Carmelo Anthony/49 5.00 12.00
17 David Lee/25 2.50 6.00
18 Chris Bosh/25 4.00 10.00
19 Brook Lopez/99 3.00 8.00
20 Dwight Howard/99 3.00 8.00
21 Joe Johnson/99 3.00 8.00
22 Tim Duncan/99 6.00 15.00
23 James Harden/49 40.00 80.00
24 Steve Nash/25 8.00 20.00
25 Darren Collison/49 3.00 8.00
27 Omri Casspi/49 2.50 6.00
28 Chris Paul/99 5.00 12.00
29 Blake Griffin/49 12.00 30.00
30 Pau Gasol/99 4.00 10.00

2009-10 Playoff National Treasures Timeline Materials Custom Names Prime

*PRIME: .6X TO 1.5X HI COLUMN
STATED PRINT RUN 3 TO 25 SER.#'d SETS
SOME UNPRICED DUE TO SCARCITY
*NICKNAMES: .4X TO 1X BASE HI
1 Kobe Bryant/25 25.00 60.00
29 Blake Griffin/25 40.00 100.00

2009-10 Playoff National Treasures Timeline Materials Custom Names Signatures

STATED PRINT RUN 3 TO 30 SER.#'d SETS
SOME UNPRICED DUE TO SCARCITY
*NICKNAMES: .4X TO 1X BASE HI
1 Kobe Bryant/25 125.00 250.00
3 Tyreke Evans/30 6.00 15.00
4 Brandon Jennings/30 8.00 20.00
5 Stephen Curry/30 800.00 1200.00
6 Jonny Flynn/30 5.00 12.00
7 Taj Gibson/30 8.00 20.00
9 Ty Lawson/30 8.00 20.00
11 DeJuan Blair/30 6.00 15.00
17 David Lee/25 15.00 30.00
18 Chris Bosh/25 20.00 50.00
23 James Harden/30 50.00 120.00
25 Darren Collison/30 8.00 20.00
27 Omri Casspi/30 6.00 15.00
29 Blake Griffin/30 175.00 350.00

2009-10 Playoff National Treasures Timeline Materials Custom Names Prime Signatures

STATED PRINT RUN ONE TO 25 SER.#'d SETS
SOME UNPRICED DUE TO SCARCITY
*NICKNAMES: .4X TO 1X BASE HI
4 Brandon Jennings/25 25.00 60.00
5 Stephen Curry/25 800.00 1200.00
6 Jonny Flynn/25 6.00 15.00
7 Taj Gibson/25 10.00 25.00
11 DeJuan Blair/25 8.00 20.00
23 James Harden/25 125.00 250.00

2010-11 Playoff National Treasures

1-185 PRINT RUN 99 SER.#'d SETS
JSY AU RC PRINT RUN 71 TO 99 SETS
UNPRICED RC BLACK PRINT RUN ONE SET
UNPRICED SILVER PRINT RUN 10 SETS
UNPRICED PLAT.PRINT RUN ONE TO 5 SETS
1 Josh Smith 3.00 8.00
2 Al Horford 3.00 8.00
3 Jamal Crawford 4.00 10.00
4 Joe Johnson 3.00 8.00
5 Kevin Garnett 6.00 15.00
6 Shaquille O'Neal 8.00 20.00
7 Rajon Rondo 4.00 10.00
8 Ray Allen 4.00 10.00
9 Paul Pierce 4.00 10.00
10 D.J. Augustin 2.50 6.00
11 Stephen Jackson 3.00 8.00
12 Joakim Noah 3.00 8.00
13 Derrick Rose 5.00 12.00
14 Luol Deng 3.00 8.00
15 Carlos Boozer 3.00 8.00
16 Antawn Jamison 3.00 8.00
17 Baron Davis 3.00 8.00
18 Dirk Nowitzki 5.00 12.00
19 Tyson Chandler 3.00 8.00
20 Jason Kidd 4.00 10.00
21 Shawn Marion 3.00 8.00
22 Raymond Felton 3.00 8.00
23 Nene 3.00 8.00
24 Danilo Gallinari 3.00 8.00
25 Ty Lawson 2.50 6.00
26 Tayshaun Prince 3.00 8.00
27 Rodney Stuckey 3.00 8.00
28 Ben Gordon 3.00 8.00
29 Richard Hamilton 3.00 8.00
30 Monta Ellis 3.00 8.00
31 David Lee 2.50 6.00
32 Stephen Curry 15.00 40.00
33 Kevin Martin 3.00 8.00
34 Luis Scola 3.00 8.00
35 Kyle Lowry 3.00 8.00
36 Danny Granger 3.00 8.00
37 Roy Hibbert 3.00 8.00
38 Darren Collison 3.00 8.00
39 Eric Gordon 3.00 8.00
40 Blake Griffin 4.00 10.00
41 Mo Williams 3.00 8.00
42 Kobe Bryant 15.00 40.00
43 Derek Fisher 3.00 8.00
44 Andrew Bynum 2.50 6.00
45 Lamar Odom 3.00 8.00
46 Pau Gasol 4.00 10.00
47 O.J. Mayo 2.50 6.00
48 Rudy Gay 4.00 10.00
49 Mike Conley Jr. 4.00 10.00
50 Zach Randolph 3.00 8.00
51 Dwyane Wade 6.00 15.00
52 Chris Bosh 4.00 10.00
53 Mike Bibby 3.00 8.00
54 LeBron James 12.00 30.00
55 Andrew Bogut 3.00 8.00
56 Brandon Jennings 2.50 6.00
57 John Salmons 3.00 8.00
58 Kevin Love 4.00 10.00
59 Michael Beasley 2.50 6.00
60 Anthony Morrow 2.50 6.00
61 Brook Lopez 3.00 8.00
62 Deron Williams 3.00 8.00
63 Chris Paul 5.00 12.00
64 David West 3.00 8.00
65 Emeka Okafor 3.00 8.00
66 Trevor Ariza 2.50 6.00
67 Amare Stoudemire 3.00 8.00
68 Carmelo Anthony 5.00 12.00
69 Chauncey Billups 4.00 10.00
70 James Harden 6.00 15.00
71 Kevin Durant 10.00 25.00
72 Russell Westbrook 10.00 25.00
73 Dwight Howard 3.00 8.00
74 Jameer Nelson 2.50 6.00
75 Jason Richardson 4.00 10.00
76 Andre Iguodala 3.00 8.00
77 Elton Brand 4.00 10.00
78 Jrue Holiday 4.00 10.00
79 Grant Hill 6.00 15.00
80 Steve Nash 4.00 10.00
81 Vince Carter 5.00 12.00
82 Brandon Roy 4.00 10.00
83 Gerald Wallace 3.00 8.00
84 LaMarcus Aldridge 4.00 10.00
85 Wesley Matthews 2.50 6.00
86 Marcus Thornton 2.50 6.00
87 Tyreke Evans 2.50 6.00
88 Manu Ginobili 4.00 10.00
89 Richard Jefferson 3.00 8.00
90 Tim Duncan 6.00 15.00
91 Tony Parker 4.00 10.00
92 Andrea Bargnani 3.00 8.00
93 DeMar DeRozan 4.00 10.00
94 Leandro Barbosa 3.00 8.00
95 Al Jefferson 3.00 8.00
96 Devin Harris 2.50 6.00
97 Paul Millsap 3.00 8.00
98 Andray Blatche 2.50 6.00
99 Nick Young 3.00 8.00
100 Rashard Lewis 3.00 8.00
101 Julius Erving 6.00 15.00
102 Bill Russell 6.00 15.00
103 Oscar Robertson 5.00 12.00
104 Dave Bing 4.00 10.00
105 Elvin Hayes 4.00 10.00
106 Wilt Chamberlain 8.00 20.00
107 Larry Bird 10.00 25.00
108 Karl Malone 5.00 12.00
109 Jerry Sloan 4.00 10.00
110 Pete Maravich 6.00 15.00
111 Bill Walton 4.00 10.00
112 Scottie Pippen 8.00 20.00
113 Henry Bibby 2.50 6.00
114 Dominique Wilkins 5.00 12.00
115 Kareem Abdul-Jabbar 6.00 15.00
116 Kiki Vandeweghe 3.00 8.00
117 Norm Nixon 2.50 6.00
118 Anfernee Hardaway 10.00 25.00
119 David Robinson 6.00 15.00
120 Kevin McHale 4.00 10.00
121 Dolph Schayes 4.00 10.00
122 Danny Schayes 4.00 10.00
123 Walt Frazier 4.00 10.00
124 Tim Hardaway 4.00 10.00
125 Magic Johnson 10.00 25.00
126 Clyde Drexler 5.00 12.00
127 Dale Ellis 2.50 6.00
128 Bailey Howell 4.00 10.00
129 Mark Price 4.00 10.00
130 Alonzo Mourning 5.00 12.00
131 Byron Scott 3.00 8.00
132 Chris Mullin 4.00 10.00
133 John Salley 2.50 6.00
134 Jerry West 5.00 12.00
135 Dennis Scott 2.50 6.00
136 Walter Berry 2.50 6.00
137 Wes Unseld 4.00 10.00
138 John Stockton 6.00 15.00
139 K.C. Jones 4.00 10.00
140 Rex Chapman 4.00 10.00
141 Patrick Ewing 6.00 15.00
142 Tom Chambers 3.00 8.00
143 Dell Curry 2.50 6.00
144 Hakeem Olajuwon 5.00 12.00
145 Danny Ainge 4.00 10.00
146 Rickey Green 4.00 10.00
147 Dave DeBusschere 4.00 10.00
148 Vlade Divac 4.00 10.00
149 Mark Eaton 2.50 6.00
150 Shawn Kemp 8.00 20.00
151 Jamal Mashburn 4.00 10.00
152 Sam Jones 4.00 10.00
153 Xavier McDaniel 2.50 6.00
154 Elgin Baylor 4.00 10.00
155 David Thompson 3.00 8.00
156 George Gervin 4.00 10.00
157 Albert King 4.00 10.00
158 Isiah Thomas 4.00 10.00
159 Willis Reed 4.00 10.00
160 Walt Bellamy 3.00 8.00
161 Bob Cousy 6.00 15.00
162 Gary Payton 4.00 10.00
163 Jalen Rose 4.00 10.00
164 Chris Webber 4.00 10.00
165 Sean Elliott 4.00 10.00
166 Steve Kerr 4.00 10.00
167 Christian Laettner 3.00 8.00
168 Dan Issel 3.00 8.00
169 Sidney Wicks 4.00 10.00
170 Dan Majerle 3.00 8.00
171 Rick Barry 3.00 8.00
172 George Mikan 8.00 20.00
173 Dikembe Mutombo 4.00 10.00
174 Gail Goodrich 3.00 8.00
175 Darryl Dawkins 2.50 6.00
176 Doc Rivers 4.00 10.00
177 Mitch Richmond 4.00 10.00
178 John Paxson 3.00 8.00
179 John Havlicek 5.00 12.00
180 Moses Malone 4.00 10.00
181 Glen Rice 3.00 8.00
182 Buck Williams 2.50 6.00
183 Ron Harper 4.00 10.00
184 Bob Love 4.00 10.00
185 Dave Cowens 2.50 6.00
186 Devin Ebanks RC 3.00 8.00
187 Craig Brackins RC 3.00 8.00
188 Kevin Seraphin RC 3.00 8.00
189 Omer Asik RC 6.00 15.00
190 Gary Forbes RC 3.00 8.00
191 Semih Erden RC 3.00 8.00
192 Nikola Pekovic RC 12.00 30.00
193 Manny Harris RC 5.00 12.00
194 Jeremy Lin RC 25.00 60.00
195 Jeremy Evans RC 3.00 8.00
196 Eugene Jeter RC 5.00 12.00
197 Samardo Samuels RC 3.00 8.00
198 Ishmael Smith RC 5.00 12.00
199 Armon Johnson RC 3.00 8.00
200 Derrick Caracter RC 3.00 8.00
201 John Wall JSY AU/99 RC 800.00 1200.00
202 Evan Turner JSY AU/99 RC 20.00 50.00
203 D.Favors JSY AU/99 RC 50.00 120.00
204 W.Johnson JSY AU/99 RC 15.00 40.00
205 D.Cousins JSY AU/99 RC 500.00 800.00
206 Ekpe Udoh JSY AU/99 RC 15.00 40.00
207 G.Monroe JSY AU/99 RC 60.00 150.00
208 A.Aminu JSY AU/99 RC 25.00 60.00
209 G.Hayward JSY AU/99 RC 400.00 800.00
210 P.George JSY AU/99 RC 1500.00 2000.00
211 Cole Aldrich JSY AU/99 RC 15.00 40.00
212 Xavier Henry JSY AU/99 RC 15.00 40.00
213 Ed Davis JSY AU/75 RC 15.00 40.00
214 P.Patterson JSY AU/99 RC 20.00 50.00
215 Larry Sanders JSY AU/71 RC 60.00 120.00
216 Luke Babbitt JSY AU/99 RC 20.00 50.00
217 E.Bledsoe JSY AU/86 RC 100.00 250.00
218 A.Bradley JSY AU/99 RC 75.00 200.00
219 J.Anderson JSY AU/99 RC 15.00 40.00
220 Elliot Williams JSY AU/99 RC 15.00 40.00
221 Trevor Booker JSY AU/99 RC 15.00 40.00
222 Damion James JSY AU/99 RC 15.00 40.00
223 D.Jones JSY AU/99 RC 15.00 40.00
224 Q.Pondexter JSY AU/99 RC 15.00 40.00
225 J.Crawford JSY AU/99 RC 20.00 50.00
226 G.Vasquez JSY AU/99 RC 20.00 50.00
227 Daniel Orton JSY AU/99 RC 15.00 40.00
228 L.Hayward JSY AU/99 RC 15.00 40.00
229 H.Whiteside JSY AU/99 RC 200.00 400.00
230 Terrico White JSY AU/99 RC 15.00 40.00
231 Andy Rautins JSY AU/99 RC 15.00 40.00
232 L.Stphnsn JSY AU/99 RC 40.00 100.00
233 L.Harangody JSY AU/99 RC 15.00 40.00
234 Willie Warren JSY AU/99 RC 15.00 40.00
235 Gani Lawal JSY AU/99 RC 15.00 40.00
236 Dexter Pittman JSY AU/99 RC 15.00 40.00
237 T.Mozgov JSY AU/99 RC 25.00 60.00
238 Landry Fields JSY AU/99 RC 20.00 50.00
239 Gary Neal JSY AU/99 RC 25.00 60.00

2010-11 Playoff National Treasures Century Gold

UNPRICED 1-200 PRINT RUN 5 SETS
JSY AU STATED PRINT RUN 25 SETS
201 John Wall JSY AU 1500.00 2500.00
202 Evan Turner JSY AU 40.00 100.00
203 Derrick Favors JSY AU 125.00 300.00
204 Wesley Johnson JSY AU 30.00 80.00
205 D. Cousins JSY AU 600.00 1000.00
206 Ekpe Udoh JSY AU 30.00 80.00
207 Greg Monroe JSY AU 125.00 300.00
208 Al-Farouq Aminu JSY AU 50.00 125.00
209 Gordon Hayward JSY AU 500.00 1000.00
210 Paul George JSY AU 3000.00 4000.00
211 Cole Aldrich JSY AU 30.00 80.00
212 Xavier Henry JSY AU 30.00 80.00
213 Ed Davis JSY AU 30.00 80.00
214 Patrick Patterson JSY AU 40.00 100.00
215 Larry Sanders JSY AU 30.00 80.00
216 Luke Babbitt JSY AU 40.00 100.00
217 Eric Bledsoe JSY AU 175.00 350.00
218 Avery Bradley JSY AU 150.00 400.00
219 James Anderson JSY AU 30.00 80.00
220 Elliot Williams JSY AU 30.00 80.00
221 Trevor Booker JSY AU 40.00 100.00
222 Damion James JSY AU 30.00 80.00
223 Dominique Jones JSY AU 30.00 80.00
224 Quincy Pondexter JSY AU 30.00 80.00
225 Jordan Crawford JSY AU 40.00 100.00
226 Greivis Vasquez JSY AU 40.00 100.00
227 Daniel Orton JSY AU 30.00 80.00
228 Lazar Hayward JSY AU 30.00 80.00
229 Hassan Whiteside JSY AU 400.00 800.00
230 Terrico White JSY AU 30.00 80.00
231 Andy Rautins JSY AU 30.00 80.00
232 Lance Stephenson JSY AU 100.00 250.00
233 Luke Harangody JSY AU 30.00 80.00
234 Willie Warren JSY AU 30.00 80.00
235 Gani Lawal JSY AU 30.00 80.00
236 Dexter Pittman JSY AU 30.00 80.00
237 Timofey Mozgov JSY AU 50.00 125.00
238 Landry Fields JSY AU 40.00 100.00
239 Gary Neal JSY AU 50.00 125.00

2010-11 Playoff National Treasures ABA Legends

STATED PRINT RUN 25 SER.#'d SETS
1 Julius Erving 10.00 25.00
2 Rick Barry 5.00 12.00
3 Moses Malone 6.00 15.00
4 Billy Cunningham 6.00 15.00
5 George Gervin 6.00 15.00
6 Dan Issel 5.00 12.00
7 Connie Hawkins 6.00 15.00
8 Artis Gilmore 5.00 12.00
9 George McGinnis 4.00 10.00
10 Wilt Chamberlain 10.00 25.00

2010-11 Playoff National Treasures ABA Legends Signatures

STATED PRINT RUN 10 TO 99 SER.#'d SETS
SOME UNPRICED DUE TO SCARCITY
2 Rick Barry/99 12.00 30.00
4 Billy Cunningham/99 60.00 150.00
5 George Gervin/25 20.00 50.00
6 Dan Issel/25 20.00 50.00
7 Connie Hawkins/99 12.00 30.00
8 Artis Gilmore/99 12.00 30.00
9 George McGinnis/99 30.00 80.00

2010-11 Playoff National Treasures All Decade

STATED PRINT RUN 25 SER.#'d SETS
1 George Mikan 8.00 20.00
2 Bill Russell 6.00 15.00
3 Elgin Baylor 4.00 10.00
4 Jerry West 6.00 15.00
5 Sam Jones 4.00 10.00
6 Kareem Abdul-Jabbar 6.00 15.00
7 George Gervin 4.00 10.00
8 John Havlicek 5.00 12.00
9 Magic Johnson 10.00 25.00
10 Larry Bird 10.00 25.00
11 Julius Erving 6.00 15.00
12 Kevin McHale 4.00 10.00
13 Dominique Wilkins 5.00 12.00
14 David Robinson 6.00 15.00
15 Clyde Drexler 8.00 20.00
16 Gary Payton 4.00 10.00
17 LeBron James 15.00 40.00
18 Kobe Bryant 12.00 30.00
19 Paul Pierce 3.00 8.00
20 Dirk Nowitzki 4.00 10.00

2010-11 Playoff National Treasures All Decade Materials

STATED PRINT RUN ONE TO 99 SER.#'d SETS
SOME UNPRICED DUE TO SCARCITY
1 George Mikan/25 12.50 30.00
3 Elgin Baylor/49 4.00 10.00
5 Sam Jones/49 4.00 10.00
6 Kareem Abdul-Jabbar/99 8.00 20.00
7 George Gervin/49 4.00 10.00
10 Larry Bird/49 10.00 25.00
11 Julius Erving/49 6.00 15.00
12 Kevin McHale/99 4.00 10.00
13 Dominique Wilkins/25 8.00 20.00
14 David Robinson/99 6.00 15.00
15 Clyde Drexler/99 5.00 12.00
16 Gary Payton/99 4.00 10.00
17 LeBron James/99 15.00 40.00
18 Kobe Bryant/99 12.00 30.00
19 Paul Pierce/99 4.00 10.00
20 Dirk Nowitzki/99 5.00 12.00

2010-11 Playoff National Treasures All Decade Materials Prime

*PRIME: .75X TO 2X BASE HI
STATED PRINT RUN ONE TO 25 SER.#'d SETS
SOME UNPRICED DUE TO SCARCITY
11 Julius Erving/25 12.00 30.00
16 Gary Payton/25 12.00 30.00

2010-11 Playoff National Treasures All Decade Materials Signatures

STATED PRINT RUN 5 TO 25 SER.#'d SETS
SOME UNPRICED DUE TO SCARCITY
UNPRICED PRIME PRINT RUN ONE TO 10 SETS
3 Elgin Baylor/25 15.00 40.00
5 Sam Jones/25 15.00 40.00
7 George Gervin/25 15.00 40.00
13 Dominique Wilkins/25 15.00 40.00
14 David Robinson/25 30.00 80.00
15 Clyde Drexler/25 20.00 50.00
16 Gary Payton/25 15.00 40.00
18 Kobe Bryant/25 125.00 250.00
19 Paul Pierce/25 20.00 50.00

2010-11 Playoff National Treasures All Decade Signatures

STATED PRINT RUN 10 TO 25 SER.#'d SETS
SOME UNPRICED DUE TO SCARCITY
UNPRICED COMBO PRINT RUN 5 SETS
UNPRICED QUAD PRINT RUN 5 SETS
UNPRICED TRIO PRINT RUN 5 SETS
3 Elgin Baylor/25 15.00 40.00
5 Sam Jones/25 12.00 30.00
7 George Gervin/25 15.00 40.00
8 John Havlicek/25 15.00 40.00
12 Kevin McHale/25 25.00 60.00
13 Dominique Wilkins/25 8.00 20.00
14 David Robinson/25 30.00 80.00
15 Clyde Drexler/25 25.00 60.00
16 Gary Payton/25 12.00 30.00
18 Kobe Bryant/25 100.00 200.00
19 Paul Pierce/25 15.00 40.00

2010-11 Playoff National Treasures All NBA

STATED PRINT RUN 25 SER.#'d SETS
1 George Mikan 6.00 15.00
2 Bill Walton 3.00 8.00
3 Chris Mullin 3.00 8.00
4 Clyde Drexler 8.00 20.00
5 Connie Hawkins 3.00 8.00
6 Dominique Wilkins 4.00 10.00
7 Earl Monroe 5.00 12.00
8 Gail Goodrich 2.50 6.00
9 Harry Gallatin 3.00 8.00
10 John Stockton 6.00 15.00
11 Moses Malone 3.00 8.00
12 Patrick Ewing 8.00 20.00
13 Sidney Moncrief 2.00 5.00
14 Spencer Haywood 3.00 8.00
15 Tim Hardaway 3.00 8.00
16 Wes Unseld 3.00 8.00
17 Willis Reed 3.00 8.00
18 Alonzo Mourning 6.00 15.00
19 Bernard King 2.50 6.00
20 Julius Erving 5.00 12.00
21 Kevin McHale 3.00 8.00
22 Kevin Durant 8.00 20.00
23 Kobe Bryant 12.00 30.00
24 Kevin Garnett 5.00 12.00
25 Steve Nash 3.00 8.00

2010-11 Playoff National Treasures All NBA Materials

STATED PRINT RUN 25 TO 99 SER.#'d SETS
1 George Mikan/25 12.50 30.00
3 Chris Mullin/49 4.00 10.00
4 Clyde Drexler/99 5.00 12.00
6 Dominique Wilkins/25 8.00 20.00
7 Earl Monroe/99 4.00 10.00
10 John Stockton/99 6.00 15.00
12 Patrick Ewing/99 8.00 20.00
15 Tim Hardaway/49 4.00 10.00
18 Alonzo Mourning/49 6.00 15.00
19 Bernard King/49 3.00 8.00
20 Julius Erving/49 6.00 15.00
21 Kevin McHale/99 4.00 10.00
22 Kevin Durant/49 12.00 30.00
23 Kobe Bryant/99 10.00 25.00
24 Kevin Garnett/99 6.00 15.00
25 Steve Nash/99 4.00 10.00

2010-11 Playoff National Treasures All NBA Materials Prime

*PRIME: .75X TO 2X BASE HI
STATED PRINT RUN ONE TO 25 SER.#'d SETS
SOME UNPRICED DUE TO SCARCITY
7 Earl Monroe/25 12.00 30.00
12 Patrick Ewing/25 25.00 60.00
18 Alonzo Mourning/25 25.00 60.00
20 Julius Erving/25 20.00 50.00
22 Kevin Durant/25 25.00 60.00
23 Kobe Bryant/25 25.00 60.00
24 Kevin Garnett/25 12.00 30.00
25 Steve Nash/25 10.00 25.00

2010-11 Playoff National Treasures All NBA Materials Signatures

STATED PRINT RUN 5 TO 25 SER.#'d SETS
SOME UNPRICED DUE TO SCARCITY
UNPRICED PRIME PRINT RUN 5 TO 10 SETS
3 Chris Mullin/25 15.00 40.00
4 Clyde Drexler/25 25.00 60.00
6 Dominique Wilkins/25 20.00 50.00
7 Earl Monroe/25 12.00 30.00
15 Tim Hardaway/25 12.00 30.00
19 Bernard King/25 8.00 20.00
23 Kobe Bryant/25 125.00 225.00

2010-11 Playoff National Treasures All NBA Signatures

STATED PRINT RUN 10 TO 99 SER.#'d SETS
SOME UNPRICED DUE TO SCARCITY
3 Chris Mullin/49 10.00 25.00
5 Connie Hawkins/99 10.00 25.00
6 Dominique Wilkins/49 12.00 30.00
7 Earl Monroe/25 12.00 30.00
8 Gail Goodrich/99 6.00 15.00
9 Harry Gallatin/99 6.00 15.00
13 Sidney Moncrief/99 6.00 15.00
14 Spencer Haywood/99 6.00 15.00
15 Tim Hardaway/99 6.00 15.00
16 Wes Unseld/99 6.00 15.00
17 Willis Reed/49 10.00 25.00
19 Bernard King/99 6.00 15.00
21 Kevin McHale/25 25.00 60.00
23 Kobe Bryant/99 100.00 200.00
25 Steve Nash/25 30.00 80.00

2010-11 Playoff National Treasures Biography Materials

ATED PRINT RUN 25 TO 99 SER.#'d SETS
1 Kevin Durant/49 10.00 25.00
2 Kobe Bryant/99 12.00 30.00
3 Blake Griffin/25 4.00 10.00
4 LeBron James/99 12.00 30.00
5 Dirk Nowitzki/99 5.00 12.00
6 Derrick Rose/99 5.00 12.00
7 Chris Paul/99 5.00 12.00
8 Zach Randolph/99 3.00 8.00
9 Steve Nash/99 4.00 10.00
10 Tyreke Evans/99 2.50 6.00
11 Al Jefferson/99 3.00 8.00
12 Tony Parker/49 4.00 10.00
13 Stephen Curry/25 15.00 40.00
14 Joakim Noah/99 3.00 8.00
15 Dwight Howard/49 3.00 8.00
16 Kevin Martin/99 3.00 8.00
17 Monta Ellis/99 3.00 8.00
18 Kevin Garnett/99 6.00 15.00
19 Kevin Love/99 4.00 10.00
20 Russell Westbrook/99 10.00 25.00

2010-11 Playoff National Treasures Biography Materials Prime

*PRIME: .75X TO 2X BASE HI
STATED PRINT RUN 5 TO 25 SER.#'d SETS
SOME UNPRICED DUE TO SCARCITY
9 Steve Nash/25 10.00 25.00

2010-11 Playoff National Treasures Biography Materials Autographs

STATED PRINT RUN 10 TO 25 SER.#'d SETS
SOME UNPRICED DUE TO SCARCITY
UNPRICED PRIME PRINT RUN 5 TO 10 SETS
2 Kobe Bryant/25 125.00 250.00
8 Zach Randolph/25 12.00 30.00
10 Tyreke Evans/20 15.00 40.00
11 Al Jefferson/25 8.00 20.00
12 Tony Parker/25 15.00 40.00
13 Stephen Curry/25 50.00 120.00
14 Joakim Noah/25 12.00 30.00
16 Kevin Martin/25 8.00 20.00
17 Monta Ellis/25 10.00 25.00
19 Kevin Love/25 20.00 50.00
20 Russell Westbrook/25 60.00 150.00

2010-11 Playoff National Treasures Century Materials

STATED PRINT RUN ONE TO 99 SER.#'d SETS
SOME UNPRICED DUE TO SCARCITY
UNPRICED LOGO PRINT RUN ONE SET
UNPRICED LOGO SIG PRINT RUN ONE SET
UNPRICED TAG PRINT RUN ONE SET
UNPRICED TAG SIG PRINT RUN ONE SET
1 Josh Smith/25 4.00 10.00
2 Al Horford/25 4.00 10.00
4 Joe Johnson/25 4.00 10.00
5 Kevin Garnett/25 8.00 20.00
6 Shaquille O'Neal/25 10.00 25.00
7 Rajon Rondo/25 5.00 12.00
8 Ray Allen/49 5.00 12.00
9 Paul Pierce/25 5.00 12.00
10 D.J. Augustin/25 3.00 8.00
11 Stephen Jackson/25 4.00 10.00
12 Joakim Noah/25 4.00 10.00
13 Derrick Rose/25 12.00 30.00
14 Luol Deng/25 4.00 10.00
15 Carlos Boozer/25 4.00 10.00
16 Antawn Jamison/25 4.00 10.00
18 Dirk Nowitzki/25 6.00 15.00
19 Tyson Chandler/25 4.00 10.00
20 Jason Kidd/25 5.00 12.00
21 Shawn Marion/25 4.00 10.00
23 Nene/25 4.00 10.00
24 Danilo Gallinari/49 4.00 10.00
25 Ty Lawson/49 3.00 8.00
26 Tayshaun Prince/25 4.00 10.00
27 Rodney Stuckey/15 4.00 10.00
28 Ben Gordon/25 4.00 10.00
29 Richard Hamilton/49 4.00 10.00
30 Monta Ellis/49 4.00 10.00
31 David Lee/25 3.00 8.00
32 Stephen Curry/25 25.00 60.00
33 Kevin Martin/49 4.00 10.00
34 Luis Scola/49 4.00 10.00
35 Kyle Lowry/49 4.00 10.00
36 Danny Granger/49 4.00 10.00
37 Roy Hibbert/49 4.00 10.00
38 Darren Collison/49 4.00 10.00
39 Eric Gordon/25 4.00 10.00
40 Blake Griffin/49 5.00 12.00
41 Mo Williams/25 4.00 10.00
42 Kobe Bryant/25 15.00 40.00
43 Derek Fisher/25 4.00 10.00
44 Andrew Bynum/99 3.00 8.00
45 Lamar Odom/99 4.00 10.00
46 Pau Gasol/99 5.00 12.00
47 O.J. Mayo/25 3.00 8.00
48 Rudy Gay/25 5.00 12.00
49 Mike Conley Jr./25 5.00 12.00
50 Zach Randolph/25 4.00 10.00
51 Dwyane Wade/25 4.00 10.00
52 Chris Bosh/49 5.00 12.00
54 LeBron James/99 12.00 30.00
55 Andrew Bogut/49 4.00 10.00
56 Brandon Jennings/49 3.00 8.00
57 John Salmons/25 4.00 10.00
58 Kevin Love/25 5.00 12.00
59 Michael Beasley/25 3.00 8.00
60 Anthony Morrow/25 3.00 8.00
61 Brook Lopez/25 4.00 10.00
63 Chris Paul/25 6.00 15.00
64 David West/25 4.00 10.00
65 Emeka Okafor/25 4.00 10.00
66 Trevor Ariza/49 3.00 8.00
67 Amare Stoudemire/25 4.00 10.00
68 Carmelo Anthony/25 6.00 15.00
69 Chauncey Billups/49 5.00 12.00
70 James Harden/25 8.00 20.00
71 Kevin Durant/49 10.00 25.00
72 Russell Westbrook/49 12.00 30.00
73 Dwight Howard/25 4.00 10.00
74 Jameer Nelson/25 3.00 8.00
75 Jason Richardson/25 5.00 12.00
76 Andre Iguodala/49 4.00 10.00
77 Elton Brand/99 5.00 12.00
78 Jrue Holiday/49 5.00 12.00
79 Grant Hill/99 8.00 20.00
80 Steve Nash/99 5.00 12.00
81 Vince Carter/99 6.00 15.00
82 Brandon Roy/99 5.00 12.00
84 LaMarcus Aldridge/99 5.00 12.00
85 Wesley Matthews/99 3.00 8.00
87 Tyreke Evans/99 3.00 8.00
88 Manu Ginobili/99 5.00 12.00
89 Richard Jefferson/99 4.00 10.00
90 Tim Duncan/99 8.00 20.00
91 Tony Parker/49 5.00 12.00
92 Andrea Bargnani/99 4.00 10.00
93 DeMar DeRozan/99 5.00 12.00
94 Leandro Barbosa/99 4.00 10.00
95 Al Jefferson/99 4.00 10.00
96 Devin Harris/99 3.00 8.00
97 Paul Millsap/99 4.00 10.00
99 Nick Young/99 4.00 10.00
101 Julius Erving/49 6.00 15.00
106 Wilt Chamberlain/25 30.00 80.00
107 Larry Bird/49 10.00 25.00
108 Karl Malone/99 5.00 12.00
112 Scottie Pippen/99 8.00 20.00
114 Dominique Wilkins/25 8.00 20.00
115 Kareem Abdul-Jabbar/25 6.00 15.00
116 Kiki Vandeweghe/99 3.00 8.00
118 Anfernee Hardaway/99 8.00 20.00
119 David Robinson/49 6.00 15.00
120 Kevin McHale/49 4.00 10.00
126 Clyde Drexler/49 6.00 15.00
128 Bailey Howell/99 4.00 10.00
129 Mark Price/99 4.00 10.00
130 Alonzo Mourning/49 6.00 15.00
132 Chris Mullin/49 4.00 10.00
135 Dennis Scott/99 2.50 6.00
138 John Stockton/99 6.00 15.00
141 Patrick Ewing/99 8.00 20.00
142 Tom Chambers/25 3.00 8.00
144 Hakeem Olajuwon/99 5.00 12.00
149 Mark Eaton/49 2.50 6.00
152 Sam Jones/49 4.00 10.00
154 Elgin Baylor/99 5.00 12.00
156 George Gervin/49 4.00 10.00
163 Jalen Rose/99 4.00 10.00
164 Chris Webber/99 4.00 10.00
170 Dan Majerle/99 3.00 8.00
172 George Mikan/25 12.00 30.00
173 Dikembe Mutombo/99 5.00 12.00
181 Glen Rice/99 3.00 8.00
183 Ron Harper/99 4.00 10.00
186 Devin Ebanks/99 3.00 8.00
187 Craig Brackins/99 3.00 8.00
188 Kevin Seraphin/99 3.00 8.00
194 Jeremy Lin/99 30.00 80.00

2010-11 Playoff National Treasures Century Materials Prime

*PRIME: 1.25X TO 3X BASE HI
STATED PRINT RUN ONE TO 25 SER.#'d SETS
SOME UNPRICED DUE TO SCARCITY
13 Derrick Rose/25 50.00 125.00
42 Kobe Bryant/25 75.00 150.00
112 Scottie Pippen/25 40.00 100.00
130 Alonzo Mourning/25 20.00 50.00
164 Chris Webber/25 12.00 30.00

2010-11 Playoff National Treasures Century Materials Prime Signatures

STATED PRINT RUN ONE TO 25 SER.#'d SETS
SOME UNPRICED DUE TO SCARCITY
2 Al Horford/25 12.00 30.00
4 Joe Johnson/25 15.00 40.00
10 D.J. Augustin/25 12.00 30.00
11 Stephen Jackson/25 12.00 30.00
12 Joakim Noah/25 25.00 60.00
16 Antawn Jamison/25 12.00 30.00
20 Jason Kidd/25 40.00 100.00
25 Ty Lawson/25 40.00 100.00
30 Monta Ellis/25 25.00 60.00
31 David Lee/25 12.00 30.00
33 Kevin Martin/25 12.00 30.00
36 Danny Granger/25 12.00 30.00
37 Roy Hibbert/25 20.00 50.00
38 Darren Collison/25 15.00 40.00
42 Kobe Bryant/25 175.00 325.00
44 Andrew Bynum/25 30.00 80.00
48 Rudy Gay/25 15.00 40.00
49 Mike Conley Jr./25 12.00 30.00
50 Zach Randolph/25 12.00 30.00
61 Brook Lopez/25 15.00 40.00
70 James Harden/25 30.00 80.00
72 Russell Westbrook/20 100.00 250.00
74 Jameer Nelson/25 15.00 40.00
78 Jrue Holiday/25 15.00 40.00
79 Grant Hill/25 50.00 120.00
81 Vince Carter/25 50.00 125.00
82 Brandon Roy/25 20.00 50.00
84 LaMarcus Aldridge/25 15.00 40.00
87 Tyreke Evans/15 20.00 50.00
91 Tony Parker/25 25.00 60.00
92 Andrea Bargnani/25 12.00 30.00
93 DeMar DeRozan/25 20.00 50.00
96 Devin Harris/25 12.00 30.00
116 Kiki Vandeweghe/25 12.00 30.00
128 Bailey Howell/25 15.00 40.00
129 Mark Price/25 60.00 150.00
142 Tom Chambers/15 15.00 40.00
144 Hakeem Olajuwon/25 30.00 80.00
168 Dan Issel/25 12.00 30.00
170 Dan Majerle/25 15.00 40.00
173 Dikembe Mutombo/25 30.00 80.00
181 Glen Rice/25 15.00 40.00
183 Ron Harper/25 25.00 60.00
186 Devin Ebanks/25 12.00 30.00
194 Jeremy Lin/25 1800.00 3000.00

2010-11 Playoff National Treasures Century Materials Signatures

STATED PRINT RUN ONE TO 99 SER.#'d SETS
SOME UNPRICED DUE TO SCARCITY
1 Josh Smith/25 8.00 20.00
2 Al Horford/25 8.00 20.00
4 Joe Johnson/25 8.00 20.00
7 Rajon Rondo/49 25.00 60.00
8 Ray Allen/25 25.00 60.00
9 Paul Pierce/25 20.00 50.00
10 D.J. Augustin/99 8.00 20.00
11 Stephen Jackson/99 8.00 20.00
12 Joakim Noah/25 15.00 40.00
16 Antawn Jamison/99 8.00 20.00
19 Tyson Chandler/35 8.00 20.00
20 Jason Kidd/25 25.00 60.00
24 Danilo Gallinari/25 10.00 25.00
25 Ty Lawson/99 10.00 25.00
28 Ben Gordon/25 8.00 20.00
30 Monta Ellis/99 12.00 30.00
31 David Lee/49 10.00 25.00
32 Stephen Curry/25 75.00 150.00
33 Kevin Martin/99 8.00 20.00
36 Danny Granger/25 8.00 20.00
37 Roy Hibbert/99 8.00 20.00
38 Darren Collison/49 8.00 20.00
41 Mo Williams/99 8.00 20.00
42 Kobe Bryant/99 100.00 200.00
43 Derek Fisher/49 10.00 25.00
44 Andrew Bynum/49 10.00 25.00
48 Rudy Gay/99 8.00 20.00
49 Mike Conley Jr./99 8.00 20.00
50 Zach Randolph/99 8.00 20.00
55 Andrew Bogut/25 8.00 20.00
56 Brandon Jennings/25 8.00 20.00
58 Kevin Love/25 15.00 40.00
61 Brook Lopez/25 8.00 20.00
65 Emeka Okafor/25 8.00 20.00
66 Trevor Ariza/49 8.00 20.00
69 Chauncey Billups/25 12.00 30.00
70 James Harden/49 15.00 40.00
72 Russell Westbrook/49 40.00 100.00
74 Jameer Nelson/99 8.00 20.00
76 Andre Iguodala/49 8.00 20.00
78 Jrue Holiday/49 10.00 25.00
79 Grant Hill/25 40.00 100.00
81 Vince Carter/25 25.00 60.00
82 Brandon Roy/25 12.00 30.00
84 LaMarcus Aldridge/49 8.00 20.00
85 Wesley Matthews/99 8.00 20.00
87 Tyreke Evans/49 8.00 20.00
91 Tony Parker/25 12.00 30.00
92 Andrea Bargnani/49 8.00 20.00
93 DeMar DeRozan/25 12.00 30.00
95 Al Jefferson/25 8.00 20.00
96 Devin Harris/25 8.00 20.00
114 Dominique Wilkins/25 15.00 40.00
116 Kiki Vandeweghe/99 8.00 20.00
119 David Robinson/25 20.00 50.00
126 Clyde Drexler/25 25.00 60.00
128 Bailey Howell/99 8.00 20.00
129 Mark Price/49 10.00 25.00
132 Chris Mullin/49 12.00 30.00
142 Tom Chambers/49 8.00 20.00
144 Hakeem Olajuwon/25 25.00 60.00
152 Sam Jones/49 12.00 30.00
154 Elgin Baylor/25 15.00 40.00
163 Jalen Rose/99 8.00 20.00
170 Dan Majerle/99 6.00 15.00
173 Dikembe Mutombo/25 12.00 30.00
181 Glen Rice/49 10.00 25.00
183 Ron Harper/99 8.00 20.00
186 Devin Ebanks/99 8.00 20.00
187 Craig Brackins/99 8.00 20.00
194 Jeremy Lin/99 175.00 350.00

2010-11 Playoff National Treasures Century Signatures

STATED PRINT RUN ONE TO 99 SER.#'d SETS
SOME UNPRICED DUE TO SCARCITY
UNPRICED PLATINUM PRINT RUN ONE SET
1 Josh Smith/25 6.00 15.00
2 Al Horford/25 6.00 15.00
4 Joe Johnson/25 6.00 15.00
7 Rajon Rondo/49 8.00 20.00
8 Ray Allen/25 25.00 60.00
9 Paul Pierce/25 15.00 40.00
10 D.J. Augustin/99 6.00 15.00
11 Stephen Jackson/99 6.00 15.00
12 Joakim Noah/25 6.00 15.00
16 Antawn Jamison/99 6.00 15.00
17 Baron Davis/25 8.00 20.00
19 Tyson Chandler/20 6.00 15.00
20 Jason Kidd/25 12.00 30.00
22 Raymond Felton/99 6.00 15.00
24 Danilo Gallinari/25 10.00 25.00
25 Ty Lawson/99 6.00 15.00
28 Ben Gordon/25 6.00 15.00
30 Monta Ellis/49 10.00 25.00
31 David Lee/25 6.00 15.00
32 Stephen Curry/49 60.00 150.00
33 Kevin Martin/99 6.00 15.00
36 Danny Granger/25 6.00 15.00
37 Roy Hibbert/99 8.00 20.00
38 Darren Collison/25 6.00 15.00
41 Mo Williams/99 6.00 15.00
42 Kobe Bryant/99 100.00 200.00
43 Derek Fisher/49 8.00 20.00
44 Andrew Bynum/25 12.00 30.00
48 Rudy Gay/99 6.00 15.00
49 Mike Conley Jr./99 6.00 15.00
50 Zach Randolph/49 8.00 20.00
52 Chris Bosh/25 12.00 30.00
53 Mike Bibby/99 6.00 15.00
55 Andrew Bogut/25 15.00 40.00
56 Brandon Jennings/25 8.00 20.00
58 Kevin Love/25 15.00 40.00
61 Brook Lopez/49 6.00 15.00
62 Deron Williams/25 8.00 20.00
65 Emeka Okafor/25 6.00 15.00
66 Trevor Ariza/49 6.00 15.00
69 Chauncey Billups/25 12.00 30.00
70 James Harden/49 15.00 40.00
72 Russell Westbrook/49 40.00 100.00
74 Jameer Nelson/49 6.00 15.00
76 Andre Iguodala/49 8.00 20.00
78 Jrue Holiday/49 6.00 15.00
79 Grant Hill/25 100.00 200.00
80 Steve Nash/25 30.00 70.00
81 Vince Carter/25 15.00 40.00
82 Brandon Roy/25 10.00 25.00
84 LaMarcus Aldridge/25 8.00 20.00
85 Wesley Matthews/99 6.00 15.00
87 Tyreke Evans/49 6.00 15.00
91 Tony Parker/49 10.00 25.00
92 Andrea Bargnani/49 6.00 15.00
93 DeMar DeRozan/25 15.00 40.00
95 Al Jefferson/25 6.00 15.00
96 Devin Harris/99 6.00 15.00
103 Oscar Robertson/25 50.00 120.00
105 Elvin Hayes/49 8.00 20.00
111 Bill Walton/25 10.00 25.00
114 Dominique Wilkins/25 12.00 30.00
116 Kiki Vandeweghe/99 6.00 15.00
120 Kevin McHale/25 10.00 25.00
121 Dolph Schayes/49 6.00 15.00
123 Walt Frazier/49 10.00 25.00
124 Tim Hardaway/75 6.00 15.00
127 Dale Ellis/99 6.00 15.00
128 Bailey Howell/99 6.00 15.00
129 Mark Price/99 6.00 15.00
131 Byron Scott/99 8.00 20.00
132 Chris Mullin/49 10.00 25.00
136 Walter Berry/99 6.00 15.00
137 Wes Unseld/99 6.00 15.00
139 K.C. Jones/20 8.00 20.00
142 Tom Chambers/99 6.00 15.00
143 Dell Curry/99 6.00 15.00
144 Hakeem Olajuwon/25 20.00 50.00
148 Vlade Divac/99 6.00 15.00
149 Mark Eaton/99 6.00 15.00
151 Jamal Mashburn/99 6.00 15.00
152 Sam Jones/49 8.00 20.00
153 Xavier McDaniel/99 6.00 15.00
154 Elgin Baylor/25 15.00 40.00
155 David Thompson/99 6.00 15.00
156 George Gervin/25 10.00 25.00
158 Isiah Thomas/49 12.00 30.00
159 Willis Reed/49 8.00 20.00
160 Walt Bellamy/50 6.00 15.00
162 Gary Payton/25 10.00 25.00
163 Jalen Rose/49 10.00 25.00
165 Sean Elliott/25 12.00 30.00
167 Christian Laettner/49 6.00 15.00
168 Dan Issel/25 6.00 15.00
170 Dan Majerle/99 6.00 15.00
171 Rick Barry/99 8.00 20.00
173 Dikembe Mutombo/49 10.00 25.00
174 Gail Goodrich/99 6.00 15.00
175 Darryl Dawkins/99 6.00 15.00
176 Doc Rivers/49 10.00 25.00
179 John Havlicek/15 15.00 40.00
181 Glen Rice/49 12.00 30.00
183 Ron Harper/99 8.00 20.00
184 Bob Love/99 6.00 15.00
185 Dave Cowens/25 6.00 15.00
186 Devin Ebanks/15 6.00 15.00
187 Craig Brackins/99 5.00 12.00
189 Omer Asik/99 5.00 12.00
190 Gary Forbes/99 5.00 12.00
191 Semih Erden/99 5.00 12.00
192 Nikola Pekovic/99 10.00 25.00
194 Jeremy Lin/99 100.00 250.00
195 Jeremy Evans/99 5.00 12.00
196 Eugene Jeter/99 8.00 20.00
198 Ishmael Smith/49 8.00 20.00
200 Derrick Caracter/99 5.00 12.00

2010-11 Playoff National Treasures Champions

STATED PRINT RUN 25 SER.#'d SETS
1 Bill Russell 6.00 15.00
2 Kareem Abdul-Jabbar 6.00 15.00
3 Oscar Robertson 6.00 15.00
4 David Robinson 6.00 15.00
5 John Havlicek 5.00 12.00
6 Rick Barry 3.00 8.00
7 Hakeem Olajuwon 5.00 12.00
8 Dennis Rodman 8.00 20.00
9 Isiah Thomas 4.00 10.00
10 Robert Horry 4.00 10.00

2010-11 Playoff National Treasures Champions Signatures

STATED PRINT RUN 10 TO 25 SER.#'d SETS
SOME UNPRICED DUE TO SCARCITY
3 Oscar Robertson/25 100.00 200.00
5 John Havlicek/25 20.00 50.00
6 Rick Barry/25 15.00 40.00
7 Hakeem Olajuwon/25 30.00 80.00
8 Dennis Rodman/25 40.00 80.00
9 Isiah Thomas/25 15.00 40.00
10 Robert Horry/25 40.00 100.00

2010-11 Playoff National Treasures Champions Signatures Combos
STATED PRINT RUN 2 TO 20 SER.#'d SETS
UNPRICED QUAD PRINT RUN 2 TO 5 SETS
2 D.Rodman/B.Laimbeer/20 25.00 60.00
7 Pierce/Rondo/15 50.00 125.00
9 E.Hayes/W.Unseld/20 20.00 50.00
10 T.Parker/R.Horry/20 20.00 50.00

2010-11 Playoff National Treasures Colossal Materials
STATED PRINT RUN 5 TO 99 SER.#'d SETS
SOME UNPRICED DUE TO SCARCITY
UNPRICED PRIME PRINT RUN ONE TO 10 SETS
UNPRICED LOGO PRINT RUN ONE TO 5 SETS
UNPRICED LOGO SIG PRINT RUN ONE TO 5 SETS
1 Kevin Durant/49 8.00 20.00
2 Al Horford/99 3.00 8.00
3 Al Jefferson/99 3.00 8.00
4 Alex English/99 3.00 8.00
5 Pau Gasol/99 4.00 10.00
6 Larry Bird/25 10.00 25.00
7 Brook Lopez/49 3.00 8.00
8 John Wall/99 10.00 25.00
9 James Harden/99 6.00 15.00
10 Gary Payton/49 4.00 10.00
11 Patrick Ewing/99 8.00 20.00
12 Ray Allen/49 4.00 10.00
13 DeMarcus Cousins/99 6.00 15.00
14 Derrick Rose/99 5.00 12.00
15 Landry Fields/99 1.50 4.00
16 Kevin Love/99 4.00 10.00
17 Dikembe Mutombo/99 4.00 10.00
18 Kobe Bryant/99 12.00 30.00
19 Evan Turner/99 1.50 4.00
20 Stephen Curry/25 15.00 40.00
21 Tyreke Evans/99 2.50 6.00
22 Wesley Johnson/99 1.25 3.00
23 Rajon Rondo/99 6.00 15.00
24 Blake Griffin/25 4.00 10.00
25 Hakeem Olajuwon/49 6.00 15.00
26 Dwight Howard/49 3.00 8.00
28 Gordon Hayward/99 3.00 8.00
29 Jalen Rose/49 4.00 10.00
30 Jonny Flynn/99 2.50 6.00
31 Bill Laimbeer/99 3.00 8.00
32 Andrew Bogut/49 3.00 8.00
33 Brandon Jennings/49 2.50 6.00
34 Caron Butler/49 3.00 8.00
35 Clyde Drexler/49 8.00 20.00
36 Cole Aldrich/99 1.50 4.00
37 Detlef Schrempf/99 8.00 20.00
38 Eric Bledsoe/99 2.50 6.00
39 Robert Horry/25 6.00 15.00
40 Tim Duncan/99 6.00 15.00
41 Toni Kukoc/45 6.00 15.00
42 Xavier McDaniel/49 2.50 6.00
43 Kelly Tripucka/49 2.50 6.00
44 Luke Babbitt/99 1.50 4.00
46 Robert Parish/20 5.00 12.00
48 Chris Bosh/25 5.00 12.00
49 Xavier Henry/99 1.25 3.00
50 Paul George/99 10.00 25.00

2010-11 Playoff National Treasures Colossal Materials Prime Signatures
STATED PRINT RUN ONE TO 25 SER.#'d SETS
SOME UNPRICED DUE TO SCARCITY
2 Al Horford/25 10.00 25.00
4 Alex English/25 15.00 40.00
8 John Wall/25 100.00 200.00
18 Kobe Bryant/25 300.00 600.00
19 Evan Turner/25 30.00 80.00
25 Hakeem Olajuwon/25 75.00 150.00
28 Gordon Hayward/25 25.00 60.00
45 Mark Price/25 75.00 150.00
46 Robert Parish/25 12.50 30.00
50 Paul George/25 200.00 400.00

2010-11 Playoff National Treasures Colossal Materials Signatures
STATED PRINT RUN ONE TO 49 SER.#'d SETS
SOME UNPRICED DUE TO SCARCITY
2 Al Horford/25 6.00 15.00
3 Al Jefferson/25 6.00 15.00
4 Alex English/49 6.00 15.00
9 James Harden/20 25.00 60.00
13 DeMarcus Cousins/25 20.00 50.00
15 Landry Fields/49 5.00 12.00
16 Kevin Love/15 15.00 40.00
17 Dikembe Mutombo/25 20.00 50.00
18 Kobe Bryant/20 125.00 225.00
19 Evan Turner/49 5.00 12.00
21 Tyreke Evans/25 10.00 25.00
22 Wesley Johnson/49 4.00 10.00
28 Gordon Hayward/49 10.00 25.00
30 Jonny Flynn/25 6.00 15.00
31 Bill Laimbeer/49 5.00 12.00
32 Andrew Bogut/25 12.00 30.00
33 Brandon Jennings/25 15.00 40.00
34 Caron Butler/23 6.00 15.00
36 Cole Aldrich/49 5.00 12.00
37 Detlef Schrempf/49 10.00 25.00
38 Eric Bledsoe/49 8.00 20.00
41 Toni Kukoc/20 25.00 60.00
42 Xavier McDaniel/20 10.00 25.00
44 Luke Babbitt/49 5.00 12.00
46 Robert Parish/25 10.00 25.00
49 Xavier Henry/49 4.00 10.00
50 Paul George/49 40.00 100.00

2010-11 Playoff National Treasures Colossal Materials Jersey Numbers
STATED PRINT RUN 5 TO 99 SER.#'d SETS
SOME UNPRICED DUE TO SCARCITY
UNPRICED PRIME PRINT RUN ONE TO 10 SETS
1 Kevin Durant/99 10.00 25.00
2 Al Horford/99 3.00 8.00
3 Al Jefferson/99 3.00 8.00
4 Alex English/99 3.00 8.00
5 Pau Gasol/99 4.00 10.00
6 Larry Bird/25 10.00 25.00
7 Brook Lopez/49 3.00 8.00
8 John Wall/99 10.00 25.00
9 James Harden/40 6.00 15.00
10 Gary Payton/49 4.00 10.00
11 Patrick Ewing/99 8.00 20.00
12 Ray Allen/49 4.00 10.00
13 DeMarcus Cousins/99 6.00 15.00
14 Derrick Rose/99 5.00 12.00
15 Landry Fields/99 1.50 4.00
16 Kevin Love/20 6.00 15.00
17 Dikembe Mutombo/99 4.00 10.00
18 Kobe Bryant/49 12.50 30.00
19 Evan Turner/99 1.50 4.00
20 Stephen Curry/25 15.00 40.00
21 Tyreke Evans/99 2.50 6.00
22 Wesley Johnson/99 1.25 3.00
23 Rajon Rondo/99 6.00 15.00
24 Blake Griffin/25 12.00 30.00
25 Hakeem Olajuwon/49 6.00 15.00
26 Dwight Howard/49 3.00 8.00
28 Gordon Hayward/99 3.00 8.00
29 Jalen Rose/49 4.00 10.00
30 Jonny Flynn/99 2.50 6.00
31 Bill Laimbeer/99 3.00 8.00
32 Andrew Bogut/99 3.00 8.00
33 Brandon Jennings/49 2.50 6.00
34 Caron Butler/49 3.00 8.00
35 Clyde Drexler/49 8.00 20.00
36 Cole Aldrich/99 1.50 4.00
37 Detlef Schrempf/99 8.00 20.00
38 Eric Bledsoe/99 2.50 6.00
39 Robert Horry/25 6.00 15.00
40 Tim Duncan/99 6.00 15.00
41 Toni Kukoc/49 6.00 15.00
42 Xavier McDaniel/49 2.50 6.00
43 Kelly Tripucka/99 2.50 6.00
44 Luke Babbitt/99 1.50 4.00
46 Robert Parish/35 4.00 10.00
48 Chris Bosh/25 5.00 12.00
49 Xavier Henry/99 1.25 3.00
50 Paul George/99 6.00 15.00

2010-11 Playoff National Treasures Colossal Materials Jersey Numbers Prime Signatures
STATED PRINT RUN ONE TO 25 SER.#'d SETS
SOME UNPRICED DUE TO SCARCITY
2 Al Horford/25 10.00 25.00
4 Alex English/25 12.00 30.00
9 James Harden/25 25.00 60.00
15 Landry Fields/25 8.00 20.00
19 Evan Turner/25 12.00 30.00
21 Tyreke Evans/15 20.00 50.00
25 Hakeem Olajuwon/15 50.00 100.00
28 Gordon Hayward/25 25.00 60.00
31 Bill Laimbeer/25 15.00 40.00
36 Cole Aldrich/25 8.00 20.00
42 Xavier McDaniel/25 10.00 25.00
43 Kelly Tripucka/20 10.00 25.00
44 Luke Babbitt/25 8.00 20.00
45 Mark Price/15 40.00 100.00
49 Xavier Henry/25 6.00 15.00
50 Paul George/25 30.00 80.00

2010-11 Playoff National Treasures Colossal Materials Jersey Numbers Signatures
STATED PRINT RUN 2 TO 49 SER.#'d SETS
SOME UNPRICED DUE TO SCARCITY
2 Al Horford/25 6.00 15.00
3 Al Jefferson/25 6.00 15.00
4 Alex English/49 6.00 15.00
7 Brook Lopez/25 6.00 15.00
8 John Wall/15 75.00 200.00
9 James Harden/15 25.00 60.00
12 Ray Allen/20 30.00 80.00
13 DeMarcus Cousins/25 20.00 50.00
15 Landry Fields/49 5.00 12.00
17 Dikembe Mutombo/25 25.00 60.00
19 Evan Turner/49 12.00 30.00
22 Wesley Johnson/49 4.00 10.00
28 Gordon Hayward/49 10.00 25.00
29 Jalen Rose/15 30.00 80.00
31 Bill Laimbeer/15 12.00 30.00
32 Andrew Bogut/25 12.00 30.00
33 Brandon Jennings/25 12.00 30.00
34 Caron Butler/25 6.00 15.00
36 Cole Aldrich/49 5.00 12.00
37 Detlef Schrempf/49 10.00 25.00
38 Eric Bledsoe/49 8.00 20.00
41 Toni Kukoc/15 25.00 60.00
42 Xavier McDaniel/49 6.00 15.00
43 Kelly Tripucka/18 6.00 15.00
44 Luke Babbitt/49 5.00 12.00
45 Mark Price/20 40.00 100.00
46 Robert Parish/15 10.00 25.00
49 Xavier Henry/49 4.00 10.00
50 Paul George/49 50.00 120.00

2010-11 Playoff National Treasures Hall of Fame
STATED PRINT RUN 25 SER.#'d SETS
1 Clyde Drexler 8.00 20.00
2 Jerry West 6.00 15.00
3 Larry Bird 12.00 30.00
4 Wes Unseld 5.00 12.00
5 Chris Mullin 5.00 12.00
6 Julius Erving 8.00 20.00
7 Rick Barry 4.00 10.00
8 Oscar Robertson 6.00 15.00
9 Artis Gilmore 4.00 10.00
10 Isiah Thomas 5.00 12.00
11 James Worthy 6.00 15.00
12 Moses Malone 5.00 12.00
13 Dominique Wilkins 6.00 15.00
14 Kareem Abdul-Jabbar 8.00 20.00
15 Dan Issel 4.00 10.00
16 Elgin Baylor 5.00 12.00
17 Robert Parish 5.00 12.00
18 John Stockton 8.00 20.00
19 David Robinson 8.00 20.00
20 Kevin McHale 5.00 12.00
21 Earl Monroe 5.00 12.00
22 Scottie Pippen 12.00 30.00
23 Joe Dumars 5.00 12.00
24 George Mikan 10.00 25.00
25 Bill Russell 8.00 20.00
26 George Gervin 5.00 12.00
27 Dennis Rodman 10.00 25.00
28 Karl Malone 6.00 15.00
29 John Havlicek 6.00 15.00
30 Magic Johnson 12.00 30.00

2010-11 Playoff National Treasures Hall of Fame Materials
STATED PRINT RUN ONE TO 99 SER.#'d SETS
SOME UNPRICED DUE TO SCARCITY
1 Clyde Drexler/25 8.00 20.00
3 Larry Bird/49 10.00 25.00
5 Chris Mullin/49 5.00 12.00
6 Julius Erving/49 6.00 15.00
11 James Worthy/99 6.00 15.00
12 Moses Malone/99 4.00 10.00
13 Dominique Wilkins/25 8.00 20.00
14 Kareem Abdul-Jabbar/99 6.00 15.00
16 Elgin Baylor/49 6.00 15.00
17 Robert Parish/99 4.00 10.00
18 John Stockton/99 6.00 15.00
19 David Robinson/49 6.00 15.00
20 Kevin McHale/99 4.00 10.00
21 Earl Monroe/99 4.00 10.00
22 Scottie Pippen/99 8.00 20.00
23 Joe Dumars/99 4.00 10.00
24 George Mikan/25 12.00 30.00
26 George Gervin/49 4.00 10.00
28 Karl Malone/99 5.00 12.00

2010-11 Playoff National Treasures Hall of Fame Materials Prime
*PRIME: 1X TO 2.5X BASE HI
STATED PRINT RUN ONE TO 25 SER.#'d SETS
SOME UNPRICED DUE TO SCARCITY
15 Dan Issel/25 8.00 20.00
22 Scottie Pippen/25 40.00 100.00
23 Joe Dumars/25 10.00 25.00
28 Karl Malone/25 15.00 40.00

2010-11 Playoff National Treasures Hall of Fame Materials Prime Signatures
STATED PRINT RUN ONE TO 25 SER.#'d SETS
SOME UNPRICED DUE TO SCARCITY
5 Chris Mullin/25 30.00 80.00
9 Artis Gilmore/25 20.00 50.00
10 Isiah Thomas/25 25.00 60.00
11 James Worthy/25 25.00 60.00
15 Dan Issel/25 50.00 120.00
17 Robert Parish/25 15.00 40.00
21 Earl Monroe/25 20.00 50.00
23 Joe Dumars/25 25.00 60.00

2010-11 Playoff National Treasures Hall of Fame Materials Signatures
STATED PRINT RUN ONE TO 49 SER.#'d SETS
SOME UNPRICED DUE TO SCARCITY
1 Clyde Drexler/25 25.00 60.00
5 Chris Mullin/49 12.00 30.00
11 James Worthy/25 25.00 60.00
13 Dominique Wilkins/25 20.00 50.00
16 Elgin Baylor/25 60.00 150.00
17 Robert Parish/25 12.00 30.00
19 David Robinson/25 25.00 60.00
21 Earl Monroe/25 12.00 30.00
23 Joe Dumars/49 12.00 30.00

2010-11 Playoff National Treasures Hall of Fame Signatures
STATED PRINT RUN 10 TO 25 SER.#'d SETS
SOME UNPRICED DUE TO SCARCITY
3 Larry Bird/25 75.00 150.00
4 Wes Unseld/25 25.00 60.00
5 Chris Mullin/25 20.00 50.00
7 Rick Barry/25 10.00 25.00
8 Oscar Robertson/25 100.00 200.00
9 Artis Gilmore/25 10.00 25.00
10 Isiah Thomas/25 15.00 40.00
11 James Worthy/25 15.00 40.00
13 Dominique Wilkins/25 25.00 60.00
15 Dan Issel/25 10.00 25.00
16 Elgin Baylor/25 20.00 50.00
17 Robert Parish/25 10.00 25.00
20 Kevin McHale/25 30.00 80.00
21 Earl Monroe/25 10.00 25.00
23 Joe Dumars/25 10.00 25.00
26 George Gervin/25 12.00 30.00
27 Dennis Rodman/25 25.00 60.00
29 John Havlicek/25 40.00 100.00

2010-11 Playoff National Treasures Hall of Fame Signatures Combos
STATED PRINT RUN 10 TO 50 SER.#'d SETS
SOME UNPRICED DUE TO SCARCITY
UNPRICED QUAD PRINT RUN 5 SETS
UNPRICED TRIO PRINT RUN 5 SETS
3 J.Havlicek/J.West/25 40.00 100.00
4 Lovellette/Schayes/50 10.00 25.00
5 R.Parish/Olajuwon/25 35.00 70.00

2010-11 Playoff National Treasures NBA Gear Dual
STATED PRINT RUN 25 TO 99 SER.#'d SETS
UNPRICED TAG PRINT RUN ONE TO 5 SETS
UNPRICED TAG SIG PRINT RUN ONE TO 5 SETS
1 John Wall/99 12.00 30.00
2 Joakim Noah/99 4.00 10.00
3 Blake Griffin/25 10.00 25.00
4 Tyreke Evans/50 3.00 8.00
5 LeBron James/99 12.00 30.00
6 Evan Turner/99 2.00 5.00
7 Kobe Bryant/99 12.00 30.00
8 DeMarcus Cousins/99 8.00 20.00
9 Kevin Durant/49 10.00 25.00
10 Landry Fields/99 2.00 5.00
11 Stephen Curry/25 20.00 50.00
12 Greg Monroe/99 3.00 8.00
13 Andrew Bogut/49 4.00 10.00
14 Gordon Hayward/99 4.00 10.00
15 Brandon Jennings/99 3.00 8.00
16 Wesley Johnson/99 1.50 4.00
17 LaMarcus Aldridge/99 5.00 12.00
18 Al-Farouq Aminu/99 2.50 6.00
19 Dirk Nowitzki/99 6.00 15.00
20 Paul George/99 12.00 30.00
21 Josh Smith/99 4.00 10.00
22 Xavier Henry/99 1.50 4.00
23 Avery Bradley/99 3.00 8.00
24 Larry Sanders/99 1.50 4.00
25 Cole Aldrich/99 2.00 5.00
26 Luke Babbitt/99 2.00 5.00
27 Greivis Vasquez/99 2.00 5.00
28 Eric Bledsoe/99 3.00 8.00
29 James Anderson/99 1.50 4.00
30 Patrick Patterson/99 2.00 5.00
31 Elliot Williams/99 1.50 4.00
32 Ed Davis/99 1.50 4.00
33 Damion James/99 1.50 4.00
34 Daniel Orton/99 1.50 4.00
35 Lazar Hayward/99 1.50 4.00

2010-11 Playoff National Treasures NBA Gear Dual Prime
*PRIME STARS: .6X TO 1.5X BASE HI
*PRIME ROOKIES: .75X TO 2X BASE HI
STATED PRINT RUN ONE TO 49 SER.#'d SETS
SOME UNPRICED DUE TO SCARCITY
7 Kobe Bryant/49 40.00 70.00

2010-11 Playoff National Treasures NBA Gear Dual Prime Signatures
STATED PRINT RUN ONE TO 49 SER.#'d SETS
SOME UNPRICED DUE TO SCARCITY
6 Evan Turner/49 10.00 25.00
7 Kobe Bryant/49 125.00 250.00
10 Landry Fields/49 6.00 15.00
12 Greg Monroe/49 10.00 25.00
14 Gordon Hayward/49 12.00 30.00
20 Paul George/25 25.00 60.00
23 Avery Bradley/25 10.00 25.00
24 Larry Sanders/25 5.00 12.00
25 Cole Aldrich/49 6.00 15.00
29 James Anderson/49 5.00 12.00
30 Patrick Patterson/49 6.00 15.00
31 Elliot Williams/25 5.00 12.00
33 Damion James/49 5.00 12.00
34 Daniel Orton/49 5.00 12.00
35 Lazar Hayward/49 5.00 12.00

2010-11 Playoff National Treasures NBA Gear Dual Signatures
STATED PRINT RUN 5 TO 30 SER.#'d SETS
SOME UNPRICED DUE TO SCARCITY
4 Tyreke Evans/30 12.00 30.00
6 Evan Turner/30 12.00 30.00
7 Kobe Bryant/30 100.00 200.00
8 DeMarcus Cousins/30 20.00 50.00
10 Landry Fields/30 5.00 12.00
11 Stephen Curry/25 150.00 400.00
12 Greg Monroe/30 8.00 20.00
14 Gordon Hayward/30 12.00 30.00
15 Brandon Jennings/30 8.00 20.00
16 Wesley Johnson/30 4.00 10.00
18 Al-Farouq Aminu/30 6.00 15.00
20 Paul George/30 40.00 80.00
22 Xavier Henry/30 15.00 40.00
23 Avery Bradley/30 8.00 20.00
24 Larry Sanders/30 4.00 10.00
25 Cole Aldrich/30 5.00 12.00
26 Luke Babbitt/30 5.00 12.00
27 Greivis Vasquez/30 5.00 12.00
28 Eric Bledsoe/30 25.00 60.00
29 James Anderson/30 4.00 10.00
30 Patrick Patterson/30 5.00 12.00
31 Elliot Williams/30 4.00 10.00
32 Ed Davis/30 4.00 10.00
33 Damion James/30 4.00 10.00
34 Daniel Orton/30 4.00 10.00
35 Lazar Hayward/30 4.00 10.00

2010-11 Playoff National Treasures NBA Gear Trios
STATED PRINT RUN 25 TO 99 SER.#'d SETS
1 John Wall/99 15.00 40.00
2 Joakim Noah/99 5.00 12.00
3 Blake Griffin/25 6.00 15.00
4 Tyreke Evans/99 4.00 10.00
5 LeBron James/99 15.00 40.00
6 Evan Turner/99 2.50 6.00
7 Kobe Bryant/99 15.00 40.00
8 DeMarcus Cousins/99 10.00 25.00
9 Kevin Durant/49 10.00 25.00
10 Landry Fields/99 2.50 6.00
11 Stephen Curry/25 25.00 60.00
12 Greg Monroe/99 4.00 10.00
13 Andrew Bogut/49 5.00 12.00
14 Gordon Hayward/99 5.00 12.00
15 Brandon Jennings/49 4.00 10.00
16 Wesley Johnson/99 2.00 5.00
17 LaMarcus Aldridge/99 6.00 15.00
18 Al-Farouq Aminu/99 3.00 8.00
19 Dirk Nowitzki/99 8.00 20.00
20 Paul George/99 12.00 30.00
21 Josh Smith/99 5.00 12.00
22 Xavier Henry/99 2.00 5.00
23 Avery Bradley/99 4.00 10.00
24 Larry Sanders/99 2.00 5.00
25 Cole Aldrich/99 2.50 6.00
26 Luke Babbitt/99 2.50 6.00
27 Greivis Vasquez/99 2.50 6.00
28 Eric Bledsoe/99 4.00 10.00
29 James Anderson/99 2.00 5.00
30 Patrick Patterson/99 2.50 6.00
31 Elliot Williams/99 2.00 5.00
32 Ed Davis/99 2.00 5.00
33 Damion James/99 2.00 5.00
34 Daniel Orton/99 2.00 5.00
35 Lazar Hayward/99 2.00 5.00

2010-11 Playoff National Treasures NBA Gear Trios Prime
*PRIME: .6X TO 1.5X BASE HI
STATED PRINT RUN ONE TO 49 SER.#'d SETS
SOME UNPRICED DUE TO SCARCITY
1 John Wall/49 30.00 80.00
7 Kobe Bryant/49 40.00 100.00

2010-11 Playoff National Treasures NBA Gear Trios Prime Signatures
STATED PRINT RUN ONE TO 49 SER.#'d SETS
SOME UNPRICED DUE TO SCARCITY
4 Tyreke Evans/25 25.00 60.00
6 Evan Turner/49 20.00 50.00
10 Landry Fields/49 6.00 15.00
12 Greg Monroe/49 10.00 25.00
14 Gordon Hayward/49 12.00 30.00
20 Paul George/25 30.00 80.00
24 Larry Sanders/25 15.00 40.00
25 Cole Aldrich/49 10.00 25.00
27 Greivis Vasquez/25 25.00 60.00
29 James Anderson/49 5.00 12.00
30 Patrick Patterson/49 6.00 15.00
33 Damion James/49 5.00 12.00
34 Daniel Orton/49 5.00 12.00
35 Lazar Hayward/49 5.00 12.00

2010-11 Playoff National Treasures NBA Gear Trios Signatures
STATED PRINT RUN 5 TO 30 SER.#'d SETS
SOME UNPRICED DUE TO SCARCITY
4 Tyreke Evans/30 12.00 30.00
6 Evan Turner/30 12.00 30.00
7 Kobe Bryant/30 100.00 200.00
8 DeMarcus Cousins/30 20.00 50.00
10 Landry Fields/30 5.00 12.00
11 Stephen Curry/25 20.00 50.00
12 Greg Monroe/30 8.00 20.00
14 Gordon Hayward/30 10.00 25.00
15 Brandon Jennings/30 12.00 30.00
16 Wesley Johnson/30 4.00 10.00
18 Al-Farouq Aminu/30 6.00 15.00
20 Paul George/30 60.00 120.00
22 Xavier Henry/30 10.00 25.00
23 Avery Bradley/30 8.00 20.00
24 Larry Sanders/30 4.00 10.00
25 Cole Aldrich/30 5.00 12.00
26 Luke Babbitt/30 5.00 12.00
27 Greivis Vasquez/30 5.00 12.00
28 Eric Bledsoe/30 20.00 50.00
29 James Anderson/30 4.00 10.00
30 Patrick Patterson/30 5.00 12.00
31 Elliot Williams/30 4.00 10.00
32 Ed Davis/30 4.00 10.00
33 Damion James/30 4.00 10.00
34 Daniel Orton/30 4.00 10.00
35 Lazar Hayward/30 4.00 10.00

2010-11 Playoff National Treasures Notable Nicknames
STATED PRINT RUN 10 TO 99 SER.#'d SETS
SOME UNPRICED DUE TO SCARCITY
1 David Robinson/25 125.00 250.00
2 Isiah Thomas/49 40.00 100.00
3 Gary Payton/49 40.00 100.00
4 Dennis Rodman/25 100.00 200.00
6 Jason Terry/49 EXCH 30.00 80.00
7 Hakeem Olajuwon/25 75.00 150.00
8 Magic Johnson/10
9 Earl Monroe/25 25.00 60.00
10 Robert Parish/99 12.00 30.00
12 Darryl Dawkins/99 15.00 40.00
13 Larry Johnson/99 25.00 60.00
14 Dan Majerle/99 25.00 60.00
15 James Worthy/25 50.00 120.00
16 David Thompson/99 10.00 25.00
17 Vince Carter/35 75.00 200.00
18 Chris Andersen/99 150.00 300.00
19 Kevin Johnson/49 40.00 100.00
20 LaMarcus Aldridge/25 40.00 100.00
21 Dan Issel/49 15.00 40.00

2010-11 Playoff National Treasures Pen Pals
STATED PRINT RUN 5 TO 25 SER.#'d SETS
SOME UNPRICED DUE TO SCARCITY
1 C.Brackins/Pondexter/25 8.00 20.00
2 J.Wall/E.Turner/25 30.00 60.00
3 W.Johnson/G.Hayward/25 10.00 25.00
4 C.Aldrich/X.Henry/25 8.00 20.00
5 E.Bledsoe/A.Aminu/25 12.00 30.00
6 P.George/L.Babbitt/25 10.00 25.00
7 E.Turner/X.Henry/25 15.00 40.00
8 D.Favors/D.James/25 12.00 30.00
9 Wall/Turner/Favors/15 125.00 250.00
10 Johnson/Cousins/Udoh/15 15.00 40.00
11 Monroe/Aminu/Hayward/15 12.00 30.00
12 Johnson/Monroe/Jones/15 15.00 40.00
13 Cousins/Aldrich/Orton/15 20.00 50.00
14 Brackins/James/Udoh/15 15.00 40.00

2010-11 Playoff National Treasures Private Signings
STATED PRINT RUN 25 TO 99 SER.#'d SETS
1 Dennis Rodman/25 50.00 120.00
2 Elvin Hayes/99 8.00 20.00
3 Dominique Wilkins/49 15.00 40.00
4 Nate Archibald/99 10.00 25.00
5 Rick Barry/99 10.00 25.00

2010-11 Playoff National Treasures Signature Patches NBA Team
STATED PRINT RUN 10 TO 99 SER.#'d SETS
SOME UNPRICED DUE TO SCARCITY
UNPRICED LOGO PRINT RUN 5 TO 10 SETS
1 Stephen Curry/99 75.00 150.00
2 John Wall/25 125.00 250.00
3 Chris Bosh/25 15.00 40.00
5 Kobe Bryant/49 100.00 200.00
7 Blake Griffin/25 50.00 120.00
9 Jason Terry/49 EXCH 12.50 30.00
10 Jalen Rose/99 6.00 15.00
12 Russell Westbrook/25 60.00 150.00
15 Bill Walton/49 10.00 25.00
16 Elvin Hayes/49 8.00 20.00
17 Kevin Durant/25 125.00 225.00
18 Kevin Love/25 20.00 50.00
21 Adrian Dantley/99 6.00 15.00
22 Earl Monroe/99 12.50 30.00
23 John Havlicek/49 15.00 40.00
25 Joe Dumars/49 10.00 25.00

2010-11 Playoff National Treasures Souvenir Cuts
STATED PRINT RUN ONE TO 30 SER.#'d SETS
SOME UNPRICED DUE TO SCARCITY
7 Paul Arizin/15 30.00 80.00
8 Paul Endacott/30 30.00 80.00
9 Al Cervi/25 25.00 60.00

2010-11 Playoff National Treasures Springfield Bound
STATED PRINT RUN 25 SER.#'d SETS
1 Kobe Bryant 30.00 80.00
2 Shaquille O'Neal 15.00 40.00
3 Jason Kidd 8.00 20.00
4 Steve Nash 8.00 20.00
5 Paul Pierce 8.00 20.00
6 Tim Duncan 12.00 30.00
7 LeBron James 30.00 80.00
8 Ray Allen 8.00 20.00
9 Dirk Nowitzki 10.00 25.00
10 Kevin Garnett 12.00 30.00

2010-11 Playoff National Treasures Springfield Bound Signatures
STATED PRINT RUN 25 SER.#'d SETS
1 Kobe Bryant 125.00 250.00
3 Jason Kidd 25.00 60.00
4 Steve Nash 30.00 80.00
5 Paul Pierce 25.00 60.00
8 Ray Allen 30.00 80.00

2010-11 Playoff National Treasures Timeline Materials Custom Names
STATED PRINT RUN 25 TO 99 SER.#'d SETS
1 Kobe Bryant/99 10.00 25.00
2 Kevin Garnett/49 8.00 20.00
3 Stephen Jackson/99 4.00 10.00
4 Alonzo Mourning/49 8.00 20.00
5 Amare Stoudemire/99 4.00 10.00
6 Andrew Bogut/49 4.00 10.00
7 DeMar DeRozan/99 5.00 12.00
8 Jodie Meeks/99 5.00 12.00
9 Kevin Durant/49 10.00 25.00
10 Paul Pierce/99 5.00 12.00
11 Toney Douglas/99 3.00 8.00
12 Jonny Flynn/99 3.00 8.00
13 Mark Price/99 5.00 12.00
14 Brandon Jennings/49 3.00 8.00
15 Carlos Boozer/99 4.00 10.00
16 DeJuan Blair/99 3.00 8.00
17 Derek Fisher/99 4.00 10.00
18 James Harden/99 8.00 20.00
19 James Jones/99 3.00 8.00
20 Jrue Holiday/99 5.00 12.00
21 LeBron James/99 10.00 25.00
22 Chris Paul/99 6.00 15.00
23 Kevin Love/99 5.00 12.00
24 Lamar Odom/99 4.00 10.00
25 LaMarcus Aldridge/99 5.00 12.00
26 Rajon Rondo/99 5.00 12.00
27 Russell Westbrook/99 12.00 30.00
28 Stephen Curry/25 20.00 50.00
29 Wesley Matthews/99 3.00 8.00
30 Dwight Howard/99 4.00 10.00

2010-11 Playoff National Treasures Timeline Materials Custom Names Prime
*PRIME: .6X TO 1.5X BASE HI
STATED PRINT RUN 5 TO 25 SER.#'d SETS
SOME UNPRICED DUE TO SCARCITY
1 Kobe Bryant/25 25.00 60.00
4 Alonzo Mourning/25 20.00 50.00
9 Kevin Durant/25 30.00 80.00
13 Mark Price/24 10.00 25.00

2010-11 Playoff National Treasures Timeline Materials Custom Names Prime Signatures
STATED PRINT RUN 5 TO 25 SER.#'d SETS
SOME UNPRICED DUE TO SCARCITY
1 Kobe Bryant/25 125.00 250.00
3 Stephen Jackson/20 15.00 40.00
7 DeMar DeRozan/25 20.00 50.00
9 Kevin Durant/25 100.00 200.00
10 Paul Pierce/25 30.00 80.00
11 Toney Douglas/25 10.00 25.00
12 Jonny Flynn/25 10.00 25.00
13 Mark Price/17 20.00 50.00
18 James Harden/23 30.00 80.00
20 Jrue Holiday/23 12.00 30.00
25 LaMarcus Aldridge/16 40.00 100.00

2010-11 Playoff National Treasures Timeline Materials Custom Names Signatures
STATED PRINT RUN 10 TO 30 SER.#'d SETS
SOME UNPRICED DUE TO SCARCITY
1 Kobe Bryant/30 100.00 200.00
3 Stephen Jackson/30 6.00 15.00
7 DeMar DeRozan/30 12.00 30.00
8 Jodie Meeks/30 6.00 15.00
10 Paul Pierce/30 15.00 40.00
11 Toney Douglas/30 6.00 15.00
12 Jonny Flynn/30 6.00 15.00
13 Mark Price/30 10.00 25.00
14 Brandon Jennings/30 10.00 25.00
16 DeJuan Blair/30 8.00 20.00
17 Derek Fisher/30 10.00 25.00
18 James Harden/30 20.00 50.00
20 Jrue Holiday/30 8.00 20.00
23 Kevin Love/30 15.00 40.00
25 LaMarcus Aldridge/30 15.00 40.00
26 Rajon Rondo/30 20.00 50.00
27 Russell Westbrook/30 50.00 120.00
28 Stephen Curry/25 75.00 150.00
29 Wesley Matthews/30 6.00 15.00

2010-11 Playoff National Treasures Timeline Materials Custom Team Nicknames
STATED PRINT RUN 10 TO 99 SER.#'d SETS
SOME UNPRICED DUE TO SCARCITY
1 Kobe Bryant/99 10.00 25.00
2 Kevin Garnett/49 8.00 20.00
3 Stephen Jackson/99 4.00 10.00
4 Alonzo Mourning/49 8.00 20.00
5 Amare Stoudemire/99 4.00 10.00
6 Andrew Bogut/49 4.00 10.00
7 DeMar DeRozan/99 5.00 12.00
9 Kevin Durant/49 10.00 25.00
10 Paul Pierce/99 5.00 12.00
11 Toney Douglas/49 3.00 8.00
12 Jonny Flynn/99 3.00 8.00
14 Brandon Jennings/99 3.00 8.00
15 Carlos Boozer/99 4.00 10.00
16 DeJuan Blair/99 3.00 8.00
17 Derek Fisher/25 4.00 10.00
18 James Harden/99 8.00 20.00
19 James Jones/99 3.00 8.00
20 Jrue Holiday/99 5.00 12.00
21 LeBron James/99 10.00 25.00
22 Chris Paul/99 6.00 15.00
23 Kevin Love/99 5.00 12.00
24 Lamar Odom/99 4.00 10.00
25 LaMarcus Aldridge/99 5.00 12.00
26 Rajon Rondo/99 5.00 12.00
27 Russell Westbrook/99 12.00 30.00
28 Stephen Curry/25 20.00 50.00
29 Wesley Matthews/99 3.00 8.00
30 Dwight Howard/99 4.00 10.00
31 Jodie Meeks/99 5.00 12.00

2010-11 Playoff National Treasures Timeline Materials Custom Team Nicknames Prime
*PRIME: .6X TO 1.5X BASE HI
STATED PRINT RUN 2 TO 25 SER.#'d SETS
SOME UNPRICED DUE TO SCARCITY
1 Kobe Bryant/25 25.00 60.00
4 Alonzo Mourning/25 15.00 40.00

2010-11 Playoff National Treasures Timeline Materials Custom Team Nicknames Prime Signatures
STATED PRINT RUN 5 TO 25 SER.#'d SETS
SOME UNPRICED DUE TO SCARCITY
1 Kobe Bryant/23 175.00 350.00
7 DeMar DeRozan/25 20.00 50.00
11 Toney Douglas/17 10.00 25.00
13 Mark Price/20 30.00 80.00
18 James Harden/15 30.00 80.00
25 LaMarcus Aldridge/15 20.00 50.00

2010-11 Playoff National Treasures Timeline Materials Custom Team Nicknames Signatures
STATED PRINT RUN 5 TO 30 SER.#'d SETS
SOME UNPRICED DUE TO SCARCITY
1 Kobe Bryant/30 100.00 200.00
3 Stephen Jackson/30 6.00 15.00
7 DeMar DeRozan/30 12.00 30.00
8 Jodie Meeks/30 6.00 15.00
11 Toney Douglas/30 6.00 15.00
12 Jonny Flynn/30 6.00 15.00
14 Brandon Jennings/30 10.00 25.00
16 DeJuan Blair/30 8.00 20.00
17 Derek Fisher/30 10.00 25.00
18 James Harden/30 30.00 60.00
20 Jrue Holiday/30 8.00 20.00
23 Kevin Love/30 15.00 40.00
25 LaMarcus Aldridge/30 8.00 20.00
27 Russell Westbrook/30 50.00 120.00
28 Stephen Curry/25 100.00 200.00
29 Wesley Matthews/30 6.00 15.00

2013 Pop Century
COMMON CARD 3.00 8.00
*SILVER/25: .5X TO 1.2X BASIC CARDS
*BLUE/10: UNPRICED DUE TO SCARCITY
*RED/5: UNPRICED DUE TO SCARCITY
*GOLD/1: UNPRICED DUE TO SCARCITY
*P.P.BLACK/1: UNPRICED DUE TO SCARCITY
*P.P.CYAN/1: UNPRICED DUE TO SCARCITY
*P.P.MAGENTA/1: UNPRICED DUE TO SCARCITY
*P.P.YELLOW/1: UNPRICED DUE TO SCARCITY
BADR2 Dennis Rodman 8.00 20.00

2013 Pop Century Co-Stars Autographs
COMMON CARD 6.00 15.00
*SILVER/25: .5X TO 1.2X BASIC CARDS
*BLUE/10: UNPRICED DUE TO SCARCITY
*RED/5: UNPRICED DUE TO SCARCITY
*GOLD/1: UNPRICED DUE TO SCARCITY
*P.P.BLACK/1: UNPRICED DUE TO SCARCITY
*P.P.CYAN/1: UNPRICED DUE TO SCARCITY
*P.P.MAGENTA/1: UNPRICED DUE TO SCARCITY
*P.P.YELLOW/1: UNPRICED DUE TO SCARCITY
CS15 D.Snider/D.Rodman 12.00 30.00

2013 Pop Century Keeping It Real Autographs
COMMON CARD 3.00 8.00
*SILVER/25: .5X TO 1.2X BASIC CARDS
*BLUE/10: UNPRICED DUE TO SCARCITY
*RED/5: UNPRICED DUE TO SCARCITY
*GOLD/1: UNPRICED DUE TO SCARCITY
*P.P.BLACK/1: UNPRICED DUE TO SCARCITY
*P.P.CYAN/1: UNPRICED DUE TO SCARCITY
*P.P.MAGENTA/1: UNPRICED DUE TO SCARCITY
*P.P.YELLOW/1: UNPRICED DUE TO SCARCITY
KRDR2 Dennis Rodman 6.00 15.00

2015 Pop Century
COMMON CARD 5.00 12.00
*SILVER/25: UNPRICED DUE TO SCARCITY
*PURPLE/15: UNPRICED DUE TO SCARCITY
*BLUE/10: UNPRICED DUE TO SCARCITY
*RED/5: UNPRICED DUE TO SCARCITY
*GOLD/1: UNPRICED DUE TO SCARCITY
*P.P.BLACK/1: UNPRICED DUE TO SCARCITY
*P.P.CYAN/1: UNPRICED DUE TO SCARCITY
*P.P.MAGENTA/1: UNPRICED DUE TO SCARCITY
*P.P.YELLOW/1: UNPRICED DUE TO SCARCITY
BADR1 Dennis Rodman 6.00 15.00

1977-78 Post Auerbach Tips
These 12 cereal-box cards measure approximately 7 3/16" by 1 3/16" and were available (they formed the back panel of the cereal box) on 15-ounce (cards 1-6) and 20-ounce (cards 7-12) boxes of Post Raisin Bran and Post Grape Nuts. The blank-backed cards feature "NBA" Tips from legendary Boston Celtics coach Red Auerbach. A drawing of him accompanies his description of each line-illustrated play. The cards are numbered on the front.
COMPLETE SET (12) 60.00 120.00
COMMON TIP (1-12) 6.00 12.00

1960 Post Cereal
These large cards measure approximately 7" by 8 3/4". The 1960 Post Cereal Sports Stars set contains nine cards depicting current baseball, football and basketball players. Each card comprised the entire back of a Grape Nuts Flakes Box and is blank backed. The color player photos are set on a colored background surrounded by a wooden frame design, and they are unnumbered (assigned numbers below for reference according to sport). The catalog designation is F278-26.
COMPLETE SET (9) 3000.00 5000.00
BK1 Bob Cousy 200.00 400.00
BK2 Bob Pettit 150.00 300.00

1995 Post Honeycomb Posters
Inserted in specially marked Post Honeycomb Cereal boxes, this set of three posters measures 11" by 17" when unfolded. It carries a color action player photo against a computerized color player portrait. The player's first name in block lettering appears across the top, while his facsimile signature is printed towards the bottom. Instant winners could receive a personally autographed basketball player poster of the player depicted on the poster. The back has the official rules and a note about whether the poster is an instant winner. The posters are unnumbered and checklisted below in alphabetical order.
COMPLETE SET (3) 2.00 5.00
1 Patrick Ewing .75 2.00
2 Shawn Kemp .75 2.00
3 Alonzo Mourning .75 2.00

2006-07 Press Pass Legends
Issued in early February 2007, Press Pass Legends features some of the NBA's greatest legends, current players and rookies on a thick card stock with silver foil highlights. An interesting note about the Press Pass Legends product is that it includes the first-ever cut signature of Pete Maravich (serially numbered to five). Card numbers 1-18 showcase the year's rookies and cards 19-70 showcase retired legends and coaches, all in their college uniforms. Also found randomly in the product are exchanges for full-sized basketball autographed by Elton Brand, Richard Hamilton and Lamar Odom. Press Pass hit the market in 18-pack boxes of five cards each and carried an original suggested retail price of $9.00 per pack.
COMPLETE SET (70) 20.00 50.00
UNPRICED PLATINUM PRINT RUN ONE SET
UNPRICED PRESS PLATE PRINT RUN ONE SET
1 Ronnie Brewer .60 1.50
2 J.J. Redick .75 2.00
3 Shelden Williams .50 1.25
4 Adam Morrison .60 1.50
5 Rajon Rondo 1.00 2.50
6 Tyrus Thomas .50 1.25
7 Rodney Carney .40 1.00
8 Shawne Williams .40 1.00
9 Maurice Ager .40 1.00
10 Shannon Brown .40 1.00
11 Cedric Simmons .40 1.00
12 Mardy Collins .40 1.00
13 LaMarcus Aldridge 1.50 4.00
14 Hilton Armstrong .40 1.00
15 Rudy Gay .75 2.00
16 Marcus Williams .40 1.00
17 Randy Foye .60 1.50
18 Brandon Roy .60 1.50
19 Sidney Moncrief .40 1.00
20 Nate Thurmond .60 1.50
21 Larry Nance .50 1.25
22 Sue Bird 2.00 5.00
23 Diana Taurasi 2.00 5.00
24 Jay Bilas .60 1.50
25 Sleepy Floyd .40 1.00
26 Dominique Wilkins .75 2.00
27 Clyde Drexler .75 2.00
27B Clyde Drexler Color 1.00 2.50
28 Elvin Hayes .60 1.50
28B Elvin Hayes Color .75 2.00
29 Hakeem Olajuwon .75 2.00
30 Steve Alford .60 1.50
31 Calbert Cheaney .60 1.50
32 Scott May .60 1.50
33 Isiah Thomas .60 1.50
34 Larry Bird 1.50 4.00
34B Larry Bird 2.00 5.00
35 Connie Hawkins .60 1.50
36 Danny Manning .50 1.25
36B Danny Manning Color .60 1.50
37 Jo Jo White .50 1.25
38 Rex Chapman .60 1.50
39 Dan Issel .50 1.25
40 Pat Riley .75 2.00
41 Pete Maravich 1.00 2.50
42 Wes Unseld .60 1.50
43 Rick Barry .50 1.25
44 Lou Hudson .60 1.50
45 David Robinson 1.00 2.50
46 Spud Webb .50 1.25
47 David Thompson .50 1.25
48 Brad Daugherty .50 1.25
49 Bob McAdoo .50 1.25
50 Sam Perkins .40 1.00
51 Kenny Smith .50 1.25
52 Bill Laimbeer .50 1.25
53 Adrian Dantley .50 1.25
54 John Havlicek .60 1.50
55 A.C. Green .60 1.50
56 Bill Russell 1.25 3.00
57 Walt Frazier .60 1.50
58 Mark Jackson .50 1.25
59 Bernard King .50 1.25
60 Henry Bibby .40 1.00
61 Bill Walton .60 1.50
61B Bill Walton Color .75 2.00
62 Stacey Augmon .40 1.00
63 Reggie Theus .50 1.25
64 Ralph Sampson .50 1.25
65 Jerry West .75 2.00
66 Dean Smith .60 1.50
67 Digger Phelps .60 1.50
68 John Wooden .60 1.50

69 Jerry Tarkanian .60 1.50
70 Larry Bird CL 1.25 3.00
NNO Elton Brand Ball 15.00 40.00
NNO Rip Hamilton Ball 12.50 30.00
NNO Lamar Odom Ball 15.00 40.00

2006-07 Press Pass Legends Bronze
*BRONZE: .5X TO 1.25X BASE HI
PRINT RUN 899 SER.#'d SETS

2006-07 Press Pass Legends Emerald
*EMERALD: 2X TO 5X BASE HI
PRINT RUN 25 SER.#'d SETS

2006-07 Press Pass Legends Gold
*GOLD: 1X TO 2.5X BASE HI
PRINT RUN 99 SER.#'d SETS

2006-07 Press Pass Legends Silver
*SILVER: .6X TO 1.5X BASE HI
PRINT RUN 499 SER.#'d SETS

2006-07 Press Pass Legends Alumni Association
COMPLETE SET (10) 10.00 25.00
STATED ODDS 1:9
1 S.Moncrief/R.Brewer 1.50 4.00
2 J.Bilas/J.J.Redick 2.50 6.00
3 C.Drexler/E.Hayes 2.00 5.00
4 I.Thomas/S.Alford 2.50 6.00
5 J.White/D.Manning 1.50 4.00
6 P.Riley/D.Issel 1.50 4.00
7 P.Maravich/Ty.Thomas 6.00 15.00
8 B.McAdoo/S.Perkins 1.50 4.00
9 A.Dantley/B.Laimbeer 1.50 4.00
10 D.Turasi/S.Bird 3.00 8.00

2006-07 Press Pass Legends Alumni Association Autographs
INT RUN 50 SER.#'d SETS
1 S.Moncrief/R.Brewer 15.00 40.00
2 J.Bilas/J.J.Redick 20.00 40.00
3 C.Drexler/E.Hayes 20.00 50.00
4 I.Thomas/S.Alford 25.00 60.00
5 J.White/D.Manning 25.00 60.00
6 P.Riley/D.Issel 25.00 60.00
9 A.Dantley/B.Laimbeer 25.00 60.00

2006-07 Press Pass Legends Center Court Cuts
NDOM INSERTS IN PACKS
2 Bill Russell/75 100.00 160.00
2B Bill Russell Red 100.00 200.00

2006-07 Press Pass Legends Legendary Legacy
COMPLETE SET (10) 8.00 20.00
STATED ODDS 1:9
1 Clyde Drexler 1.00 2.50
2 Steve Alford .75 2.00
3 Isiah Thomas .75 2.00
4 Larry Bird 2.00 5.00
5 Danny Manning .60 1.50
6 Pat Riley 1.00 2.50
7 Sam Perkins .50 1.25
8 Bill Walton .75 2.00
9 Jerry West 1.00 2.50
10 Pete Maravich 1.25 3.00

2006-07 Press Pass Legends Legendary Legacy Autographs
INT RUN LISTED IN CL BELOW
2 Steve Alford/155 6.00 15.00
3 Isiah Thomas/75 15.00 40.00
4 Larry Bird/50 90.00 180.00
5 Danny Manning/50 15.00 40.00
6 Pat Riley/125 20.00 50.00
7 Sam Perkins/400 6.00 15.00
8 Bill Walton/50 10.00 25.00
9 Jerry West/175 25.00 60.00

2006-07 Press Pass Legends Legendary Legacy Autographs Platinum
PRINT RUNS LISTED IN CL BELOW
SOME UNPRICED DUE TO SCARCITY
2 Steve Alford/25 20.00 50.00
3 Isiah Thomas/25 20.00 50.00
4 Larry Bird/18 100.00 200.00
5 Danny Manning/25 30.00 60.00
6 Pat Riley/25 30.00 80.00
7 Sam Perkins/25 15.00 40.00
9 Jerry West/25 50.00 120.00

2006-07 Press Pass Legends Naismith Award Winners
MPLETE SET (10) 8.00 20.00
STATED ODDS 1:9
1 Pete Maravich 1.25 3.00
2 Bill Walton .75 2.00
3 David Thompson .60 1.50
4 Scott May .75 2.00
5 Larry Bird 2.00 5.00
6 Ralph Sampson .60 1.50
7 David Robinson 1.25 3.00
8 Danny Manning .60 1.50
9 Calbert Cheaney .75 2.00
10 J.J. Redick 1.00 2.50

2006-07 Press Pass Legends Naismith Award Winners Autographs
PRINT RUNS LISTED IN CL BELOW
2 Bill Walton/75 10.00 25.00
3 David Thompson/275 10.00 25.00
3F D.Thompson Red/20 12.00 30.00
4 Scott May/400 5.00 12.00
4A Scott May Red/34 6.00 15.00
6 Ralph Sampson/400 6.00 15.00
6B Ralph Sampson Red 8.00 20.00
7 David Robinson/50 30.00 80.00
8 Danny Manning/100 12.50 30.00
8B D.Manning Red/49 15.00 40.00
9 Calbert Cheaney/400 5.00 12.00
10 J.J. Redick/275 10.00 25.00
10A J.J. Redick Go Duke/24 12.00 30.00

2006-07 Press Pass Legends Naismith Award Winners Autographs Platinum
PRINT RUNS LISTED IN CL BELOW
SOME UNPRICED DUE TO SCARCITY
2 Bill Walton 15.00 40.00
3 David Thompson 15.00 40.00
5 Larry Bird 100.00 200.00
7 David Robinson 60.00 150.00
8 Danny Manning 20.00 50.00
9 Calbert Cheaney 8.00 20.00

2006-07 Press Pass Legends Saturday Swatches
APPROXIMATE ODDS ONE PER BOX
*PRIME: .6X TO 1.25X BASE HI
PRIME PRINT RUN 50 SER.#'d SETS
1 Ronnie Brewer 3.00 8.00
2 David Lee 2.00 5.00
3 Rodney Carney 2.00 5.00
4 Shannon Brown 2.00 5.00
5 Danny Granger 2.50 6.00
6 Sean May 2.00 5.00
7 LaMarcus Aldridge 6.00 15.00
8 Rudy Gay 4.00 10.00
9 Kyle Lowry 4.00 10.00
10 Chris Paul 4.00 10.00
11 Brandon Roy 3.00 8.00

2006-07 Press Pass Legends Signatures
PROXIMATELY TWO TO THREE PER BOX
1 LaMarcus Aldridge 8.00 20.00
2 L.Aldridge Red/25 8.00 20.00
3 Steve Alford 6.00 15.00
5 Alford Red 1987 Champs/25 15.00 40.00
6 Hilton Armstrong 2.50 6.00
9 Stacey Augmon 4.00 10.00
11 Rick Barry 10.00 25.00
12 R.Barry Go Canes/24 20.00 50.00
13 Rick Barry Red/30 12.50 30.00
14 Henry Bibby 4.00 10.00
19 Henry Bibby Red/22 6.00 15.00
20 Jay Bilas 4.00 10.00
21 Bilas 21 1986 37-3/51 10.00 25.00
51 Larry Bird 40.00 100.00
53 Ronnie Brewer 4.00 10.00
55 Calbert Cheaney 4.00 10.00
59 Adrian Dantley 6.00 15.00
60 Brad Daugherty 4.00 10.00
61 Daugherty Go Heels/35 8.00 20.00
62 Daugherty Red Go Heels/24 10.00 25.00
63 Clyde Drexler 12.50 30.00
64 Eric Sleepy Floyd 4.00 10.00
66 Eric Sleepy Floyd/16 10.00 25.00
67 Eric Sleepy Floyd Red/54 8.00 20.00
68 Randy Foye 4.00 10.00
69 R.Foye Foyeboy/25 10.00 25.00
70 Randy Foye Red/24 10.00 25.00
71 Walt Frazier 8.00 20.00
75 Rudy Gay 5.00 12.00
78 A.C. Green 4.00 10.00
79 A.C. Green 45/80 6.00 15.00
80 A.C. Green Red/25 8.00 20.00
83 John Havlicek 12.50 30.00
86 Connie Hawkins 8.00 20.00
87 C.Hawkins Go Hawkeyes/24 20.00 50.00
89 Elvin Hayes 4.00 10.00
90 Elvin Hayes Red/25 8.00 20.00
91 Hayes Red The Big E/25 15.00 40.00
92 Lou Hudson 4.00 10.00
93 Lou Hudson Red/28 10.00 25.00
94 Dan Issel 4.00 10.00
97 Bernard King 6.00 15.00
98 Bill Laimbeer 6.00 15.00
99 B.Laimbeer 1978 Final 4/25 20.00 50.00
100 B.Laimbeer Red/25 20.00 50.00
101 Danny Manning 12.00 30.00
104 Scott May Red 4.00 10.00
105 Sidney Moncrief 4.00 10.00
107 Moncrief Go Hogs/22 12.50 30.00
108 Moncrief Red/30 8.00 20.00
109 Adam Morrison 8.00 20.00
110 A.Morrison Go Zags/37 15.00 30.00
112 Larry Nance 4.00 10.00
114 Larry Nance Red/32 6.00 15.00
116 Hakeem Olajuwon 15.00 40.00
117 Sam Perkins 8.00 20.00
118 Digger Phelps 8.00 20.00
119 D.Phelps Go Irish/25 10.00 25.00
121 J.J. Redick 12.50 30.00
122 Pat Riley 12.50 30.00
123 David Robinson 30.00 75.00
124 D.Robinson Red/24 75.00 150.00
125 Rajon Rondo 6.00 15.00
126 Brandon Roy 4.00 10.00
128 Brandon Roy Red/25 15.00 40.00
129 Ralph Sampson 6.00 15.00
130 R.Sampson Red/86 8.00 20.00
131 Kenny Smith 8.00 20.00
132 Kenny Smith Jet/20 12.50 30.00
134 Kenny Smith Red/69 8.00 20.00
135 K.Smith Red Jet/26 8.00 20.00
136 Dean Smith 75.00 150.00
138 Jerry Tarkanian 10.00 25.00
142 Tarkanian Red/23 15.00 40.00
143 Diana Taurasi 8.00 20.00
145 Reggie Theus 4.00 10.00
148 Isiah Thomas 10.00 25.00
150 Tyrus Thomas 3.00 8.00
151 Thomas T-Time Gx Tgrs/25 10.00 25.00
153 David Thompson 10.00 25.00
161 Nate Thurmond 4.00 10.00
162 N.Thurmond Red/25 10.00 25.00
165 Wes Unseld 4.00 10.00
168 Bill Walton 8.00 20.00
169 Bill Walton Red/17 15.00 40.00
170 Spud Webb 5.00 12.00
171 Jerry West 20.00 50.00
175 Jo Jo White 6.00 15.00
176 Jo Jo White Red/24 12.50 30.00
178 Dominique Wilkins 15.00 40.00
179 D.Wilkins Red/24 25.00 60.00
181 Shelden Williams 3.00 8.00
185 John Wooden 75.00 150.00
186 John Wooden UCLA/25 75.00 150.00

2007-08 Press Pass Legends
Released in October 2007, Press Pass legends boasts a 70 card base set that features retired NBA legends, current NBA players and current NBA rookie players. The base cards feature a white backdrop along with a mix of color and black and white photos for certain players. Legends was packed out in boxes that contain three mini-boxes each and each mini-box contains six packs of five cards per. The original suggested retail price per pack was $8.99.
COMPLETE SET (70) 20.00 40.00
UNPRICED PLATINUM PRINT RUN ONE SET
UNPRICED PRESS PLATES PRINT RUN ONE SET
1 Jared Dudley .60 1.50
2 Jason Smith .60 1.50
3 Josh McRoberts .60 1.50
4 Taurean Green .50 1.25
5 Javaris Crittenton .50 1.25
6 Glen Davis .60 1.50
7 Nick Fazekas .50 1.25
8 Aaron Gray .50 1.25
9 Morris Almond .50 1.25
10 Acie Law .50 1.25
11 Aaron Afflalo .75 2.00
12 Brandan Wright .75 2.00
13 Nick Young 1.00 2.50
14 Gabe Pruitt .50 1.25
15 Spencer Hawes .60 1.50
16 Sean Elliott .75 2.00
17 Lafette Lever .60 1.50
18 Byron Scott .60 1.50
19 Robert Parish .75 2.00
20 Scottie Pippen 1.25 3.00
21 Dan Majerle .60 1.50
22 Tree Rollins .50 1.25
23 Sue Bird 2.50 6.00
24 Jay Bilas .75 2.00
25 Bobby Hurley .75 2.00
26 George Gervin .75 2.00
27 Dominique Wilkins 1.00 2.50
28 Kenny Anderson .60 1.50
29 Willis Reed .75 2.00
30 Larry Bird 2.00 5.00
31 Artis Gilmore .60 1.50
32 JoJo White .60 1.50
33 Rolando Blackman .60 1.50
34 Dan Issel .60 1.50
35 Pete Maravich 1.25 3.00
36 Joe Dumars .75 2.00
37 Hal Greer .60 1.50
38 Rick Barry .60 1.50
39 Glen Rice .60 1.50
40 David Robinson 1.25 3.00
41 Michael Cooper .60 1.50
42 Calvin Murphy .60 1.50
43 John Paxson .60 1.50
44 John Havlicek .75 2.00
45 Jerry Lucas .75 2.00
46 A.C. Green .75 2.00
47 Lenny Wilkens .75 2.00
48 Bill Russell 1.25 3.00
49 Elgin Baylor .75 2.00
50 Alex English .60 1.50
51 Dick McGuire .75 2.00
52 Sherman Douglas .75 2.00
53 Henry Bibby .50 1.25
54 Bill Walton .75 2.00
55 Kiki Vandeweghe .60 1.50
56 Phil Ford .75 2.00
57 George Karl .75 2.00
58 Sam Perkins .50 1.25
59 Kenny Smith .60 1.50
60 James Worthy 1.00 2.50
61 Stacey Augmon .50 1.25
62 Larry Johnson .75 2.00
63 Jerry Tarkanian .75 2.00
64 Gus Williams .50 1.25
65 Nate Archibald .60 1.50
66 Muggsy Bogues .60 1.50
67 Detlef Schrempf .75 2.00
68 Earl Monroe .75 2.00
69 Jerry West 1.00 2.50
70 Tarkanian/L.Johnson/S.Augmon .75 2.00

2007-08 Press Pass Legends Bronze
*BRONZE: .5X TO 1.25X BASE HI
BRONZE PRINT RUN 899 SER.#'d SETS

2007-08 Press Pass Legends Emerald
*EMERALD: 2.5X TO 6X BASE HI
PRINT RUN 25 SER.#'d SETS

2007-08 Press Pass Legends Gold
*GOLD: 1.25X TO 3X BASE HI
GOLD PRINT RUN 99 SER.#'d SETS

2007-08 Press Pass Legends Silver
*SILVER: .6X TO 1.5X BASE HI
PRINT RUN 499 SER.#'d SETS

2007-08 Press Pass Legends All-American
COMPLETE SET (11) 8.00 20.00
STATED ODDS 1:9
1 Sean Elliott .75 2.00
2 Larry Bird 2.00 5.00
3 Glen Davis .60 1.50
4 Pete Maravich 1.25 3.00
5 David Robinson 1.25 3.00
6 John Paxson .60 1.50
7 Acie Law .50 1.25
8 Aaron Afflalo .75 2.00
9 James Worthy 1.00 2.50
10 Larry Johnson .75 2.00
11 Nick Fazekas .50 1.25

2007-08 Press Pass Legends All-American Autographs
INT RUNS LISTED IN CHECKLIST
UNPRICED PLATINUM PRINT RUN 25 SETS
EXCH EXPIRATION DATE 10/1/08
1 Sean Elliott/258 6.00 15.00
2 Larry Bird/50 40.00 80.00
3 Glen Davis/255 5.00 12.00
6 John Paxson/236 8.00 20.00
6A John Paxson Red/23 20.00 40.00
7 Acie Law/245 6.00 15.00
8 Aaron Afflalo/232 5.00 12.00
9 James Worthy/25 30.00 60.00
10 Larry Johnson 25.00 50.00
11 Nick Fazekas 4.00 10.00
11A Nick Fazekas Red/31 5.00 12.00

2007-08 Press Pass Legends Alumni Association
COMPLETE SET (10) 10.00 25.00
STATED ODDS 1:9
1 L.Lever/B.Scott 2.50 6.00
2 B.Hurley/J.McRoberts 4.00 10.00
3 K.Anderson/J.Crittenton 2.00 5.00
4 P.Maravich/G.Davis 4.00 10.00
5 J.Lucas/J.Havlicek 2.00 5.00
6 H.Bibby/K.Vandeweghe 2.00 5.00
7 J.Worthy/B.Wright 2.50 6.00
8 L.Johnson/S.Augmon 2.00 5.00
9 N.Young/G.Williams 2.00 5.00
10 D.Schrempf/S.Hawes 2.00 5.00

2007-08 Press Pass Legends Alumni Association Autographs
PRINT RUNS LISTED IN CHECKLIST
1 L.Lever/B.Scott/50 15.00 30.00
2 B.Hurley/J.McRoberts/48 15.00 30.00
3 K.Anderson/J.Crittenton/45 10.00 25.00
6 H.Bibby/K.Vandeweghe 10.00 25.00
7 J.Worthy/B.Wright 12.00 30.00
8 L.Johnson/S.Augmon 25.00 50.00
9 N.Young/G.Williams/46 10.00 25.00
SBDT S.Bird/D.Taurasi/25 35.00 75.00

2007-08 Press Pass Legends Center Court Cuts
PRINT RUNS LISTED IN CHECKLIST
2 Bill Russell/53 40.00 100.00
2A Bill Russell Red/13 100.00 200.00
2B Bill Russell Red #6/19 100.00 200.00

2007-08 Press Pass Legends Legendary Legacy
COMPLETE SET (10) 8.00 20.00
STATED ODDS 1:9
1 Robert Parish 1.00 2.50
2 Scottie Pippen 1.50 4.00
3 Willis Reed 1.00 2.50
4 Larry Bird 2.50 6.00
5 Joe Dumars 1.00 2.50
6 David Robinson 1.50 4.00
7 Elgin Baylor 1.00 2.50
8 James Worthy 1.25 3.00
9 Nate Archibald .75 2.00
10 Earl Monroe 1.00 2.50

2007-08 Press Pass Legends Legendary Legacy Marks
INT RUNS LISTED IN CHECKLIST
UNPRICED PLATINUM PRINT RUN ONE TO 25 SETS
1 Robert Parish Red/265 8.00 20.00
2 Scottie Pippen/35 60.00 150.00
2A Scottie Pippen Red/50 60.00 150.00
3 Willis Reed/100 8.00 20.00
4 Larry Bird/50 40.00 80.00
5 Joe Dumars/25 8.00 20.00
7 Elgin Baylor/129 15.00 30.00
8 James Worthy/50 20.00 40.00
9 Nate Archibald/24 8.00 20.00
10 Earl Monroe/42 10.00 25.00
10B Earl Monroe Red/50 10.00 25.00

2007-08 Press Pass Legends Select Swatches
PROXIMATELY 1:18 PACKS
*PREMIUM: .5X TO 1.25X BASE HI
PREMIUM PRINT RUN 50 SER.#'d SETS
PATCH PRINT RUN 10 SER.#'d SETS
1 Rudy Gay 3.00 8.00
2 Nick Fazekas 2.00 5.00
3 LaMarcus Aldridge 4.00 10.00
4 Acie Law 2.00 5.00
5 Brandan Wright 3.00 8.00
6 Nick Young 4.00 10.00
7 Brandon Roy 3.00 8.00

2007-08 Press Pass Legends Signatures
APPROXIMATELY FOUR PER BOX
EXCHANGE EXPIRATION 10/1/08
4 Morris Almond 4.00 10.00
5 Morris Almond Go Rice/25 6.00 15.00
6 Kenny Anderson 5.00 12.00
7 Kenny Anderson Red/48 6.00 15.00
9 Nate Archibald 5.00 12.00
10 Nate Archibald Red/25 15.00 30.00
11 Stacey Augmon 4.00 10.00
13 Stacey Augmon Red/68 6.00 15.00
14 Rick Barry 6.00 15.00
15 Rick Barry Go Canes/35 15.00 30.00
16 Rick Barry Red/40 15.00 30.00
17 Elgin Baylor 15.00 30.00
18 Henry Bibby 4.00 10.00
22 Jay Bilas 5.00 12.00
23 J.Bilas ESPN Duke 21/39 6.00 15.00
34 Jay Bilas Red/62 10.00 25.00
35 Larry Bird 40.00 80.00
36 Sue Bird 8.00 20.00
38 Sue Bird Red 15.00 30.00
39 Rolando Blackman 6.00 15.00
40 R.Blackman Ro Silk/38 20.00 40.00
41 Rolando Blackman Red/25 25.00 50.00
42 Muggsy Bogues 6.00 15.00
43 M.Bogues Go Deacs/26 25.00 50.00
44 Muggsy Bogues Red/52 10.00 25.00
46 Michael Cooper 4.00 10.00
49 Michael Cooper Red 6.00 15.00
51 Javaris Crittenton 4.00 10.00
52 Javaris Crittenton Red/158 5.00 12.00
53 Glen Davis 6.00 15.00
54 Sherman Douglas 4.00 10.00
56 Sherman Douglas Red/82 5.00 12.00
57 Jared Dudley 4.00 10.00
58 Joe Dumars 6.00 15.00
59 Sean Elliott 5.00 12.00
62 Alex English 4.00 10.00
64 Alex English Red 6.00 15.00
69 Phil Ford 10.00 25.00
72 George Gervin 6.00 15.00
74 George Gervin Red/45 10.00 25.00
75 Artis Gilmore 5.00 12.00
76 Artis Gilmore A-Train/199 10.00 25.00
78 Artis Gilmore Red/186 6.00 15.00
79 A.Gilmore Red A-Train/74 10.00 25.00
81 Aaron Gray 4.00 10.00
84 Hal Greer 6.00 15.00
85 Hal Greer Go Herd/25 15.00 30.00
86 Hal Greer Red/50 10.00 25.00
87 Spencer Hawes 4.00 10.00
91 Spencer Hawes Red/50 5.00 12.00
92 Bobby Hurley 6.00 15.00
94 Bobby Hurley Red/46 15.00 30.00
95 Dan Issel 6.00 15.00
96 Dan Issel The Horse/25 30.00 60.00
98 Larry Johnson 8.00 20.00
99 George Karl 6.00 15.00
103 George Karl Red/57 8.00 20.00
104 Lafayette Lever 4.00 10.00
105 Lafayette Lever Fat/25 25.00 50.00
106 L.Lever Red Fat/50 15.00 30.00
107 Jerry Lucas 10.00 25.00
108 Jerry Lucas Go Bucks/25 30.00 60.00
109 Jerry Lucas Red/50 15.00 30.00
110 Dan Majerle 8.00 20.00
111 Dan Majerle Thunder/25 40.00 80.00
112 Dan Majerle Red/50 25.00 40.00
113 Dick McGuire 6.00 15.00
114 Dick McGuire Red/50 8.00 20.00
115 D.McGuire Red Tricky/25 15.00 30.00
116 Earl Monroe 8.00 20.00
117 Calvin Murphy 4.00 10.00
118 Calvin Murphy Red/50 6.00 15.00
120 Robert Parish 8.00 20.00
121 John Paxson 6.00 15.00
123 John Paxson Go Irish/14 20.00 40.00
125 Sam Perkins Smooth 6.00 15.00
127 Scottie Pippen 75.00 150.00
129 Willis Reed Go Tigers/25 20.00 50.00
130 Willis Reed Red/25 25.00 50.00
131 Glen Rice 41 5.00 12.00
133 David Robinson 25.00 50.00
137 Tree Rollins 4.00 10.00
140 Tree Rollins Red/46 5.00 12.00
141 Detlef Schrempf 6.00 15.00
142 D.Schrempf Go Huskies/25 25.00 50.00
144 Byron Scott 4.00 10.00
146 Byron Scott Red/100 15.00 30.00
147 Jason Smith 4.00 10.00
150 Jerry Tarkanian 12.00 30.00
154 Jerry Tarkanian Red/50 10.00 25.00
155 Lenny Wilkens 4.00 10.00
156 Lenny Wilkens Lefty/25 15.00 30.00
157 Lenny Wilkens Red/50 15.00 30.00
158 Dominique Wilkins 12.00 30.00
160 Dominique Wilkins Red/77 30.00 60.00
162 D.Wilk Red Hum.Hi.Film/23 15.00 40.00
163 Gus Williams 4.00 10.00
165 Gus Williams Red/50 5.00 12.00
166 James Worthy 25.00 50.00
167 Brandan Wright 10.00 25.00
168 Nick Young 6.00 15.00
169 Josh McRoberts 6.00 15.00

2007-08 Press Pass Legends Student and Teacher Signatures
RANDOM INSERTS IN PACKS
SAJT S.Augmon/J.Tarkanian 25.00 60.00
SAJT L.Johnson/J.Tarkanian 30.00 80.00

2008-09 Press Pass Legends
COMPLETE SET (70) 12.00 30.00
UNPRICED PLATE PRINT RUN ONE SET
UNPRICED PLATINUM PRINT RUN ONE SET
1 Jerryd Bayless .50 1.25
2 Sonny Weems .40 1.00
3 Trent Plaisted .40 1.00
4 DeVon Hardin .40 1.00
5 Marreese Speights .50 1.25
6 Patrick Ewing Jr. .40 1.00
7 Roy Hibbert .60 1.50
8 Eric Gordon 1.00 2.50
9 D.J. White .50 1.25
10 Danilo Gallinari 1.00 2.50
11 Mario Chalmers .60 1.50
12 Darnell Jackson .40 1.00
13 Brandon Rush .50 1.25
14 Michael Beasley .60 1.50
15 Anthony Randolph .40 1.00
16 Joey Dorsey .40 1.00
17 Chris Douglas-Roberts .40 1.00
18 Derrick Rose 2.50 6.00
19 J.J. Hickson .50 1.25
20 J.R. Giddens .40 1.00
21 Kosta Koufos .50 1.25
22 Malik Hairston .40 1.00
23 Bryce Taylor .60 1.50
24 Brook Lopez .75 2.00
25 Robin Lopez .60 1.50
26 Chris Lofton .60 1.50
27 Candace Parker 1.50 4.00
28 D.J. Augustin .50 1.25
29 DeAndre Jordan .75 2.00
30 Kevin Love 2.00 5.00
31 Russell Westbrook 5.00 12.00
32 O.J. Mayo .60 1.50
33 Shan Foster .40 1.00
34 Courtney Lee .50 1.25
35 Sean Elliott .60 1.50
36 Sidney Moncrief .40 1.00
37 Corliss Williamson .40 1.00
38 Larry Nance .50 1.25
39 Bobby Hurley .60 1.50
40 Sleepy Floyd .40 1.00
41 Clyde Drexler .75 2.00
42 Calbert Cheaney .40 1.00
43 Larry Bird 1.50 4.00
44 Danny Manning .50 1.25
45 Rolando Blackman .50 1.25
46 Cliff Hagan .50 1.25
47 Darrell Griffith .40 1.00
48 Bailey Howell .60 1.50
49 David Robinson 1.00 2.50
50 Sidney Lowe .60 1.50
51 Michael Cooper .50 1.25
52 Calvin Murphy .50 1.25
53 Willis Reed .60 1.50
54 Brad Daugherty .50 1.25
55 Nate Archibald .50 1.25
56 James Worthy .60 1.50
57 Jerry Lucas .60 1.50
58 Elgin Baylor .60 1.50
59 Mark Jackson .50 1.25
60 Ernie Grunfeld .60 1.50
61 Bernard King .50 1.25
62 Henry Bibby .40 1.00
63 Gail Goodrich .50 1.25
64 Bill Walton .60 1.50
65 John Wooden .75 2.00
66 Stacey Augmon .40 1.00
67 Jerry Tarkanian .60 1.50
68 Gus Williams .40 1.00
69 Jerry West .75 2.00
70 UCLA CL .75 2.00

2008-09 Press Pass Legends Bronze
*BRONZE: .5X TO 1.25X BASE HI
BRONZE PRINT RUN 750 SER.#'d SETS

2008-09 Press Pass Legends Emerald
*EMERALD: 2X TO 5X BASE HI
EMERALD PRINT RUN 25 SETS

2008-09 Press Pass Legends Gold
*GOLD: .75X TO 2X BASE HI
GOLD PRINT RUN 99 SETS

2008-09 Press Pass Legends Silver
*SILVER: .6X TO 1.5X BASE HI
SILVER PRINT RUN 199 SETS

2008-09 Press Pass Legends All-American
COMPLETE SET (10) 10.00 25.00
STATED ODDS 1:9
1 Sidney Moncrief .60 1.50
2 Bobby Hurley 1.00 2.50
3 Larry Bird 2.50 6.00
4 Brandon Rush .75 2.00
5 Michael Beasley 1.00 2.50
6 Brad Daugherty .75 2.00
7 Derrick Rose 4.00 10.00
8 Candace Parker 2.50 6.00
9 D.J. Augustin .75 2.00
10 Kevin Love 3.00 8.00

2008-09 Press Pass Legends All-American Autographs
STATED PRINT RUN 30 TO 271 SER.#'d SETS
1 Sidney Moncrief/271 4.00 10.00
2 Bobby Hurley/195 10.00 25.00
3 Larry Bird/50 40.00 80.00
4 Brandon Rush/159 4.00 10.00
5 Michael Beasley/160 12.50 30.00
6 Brad Daugherty/210 4.00 10.00
7 Derrick Rose/165 30.00 80.00
8 Candace Parker/46 40.00 80.00
9 D.J. Augustin/105 6.00 15.00
10 Kevin Love/78 20.00 50.00
AACC Calbert Cheaney/266 4.00 10.00
AACW Corliss Williamson/165 4.00 10.00
AADG Darrell Griffith/270 4.00 10.00
AADM Danny Manning/169 8.00 20.00
AADR David Robinson/30 30.00 80.00

2008-09 Press Pass Legends All-American Autographs Platinum
STATED PRINT RUN ONE TO 25 SETS
SOME UNPRICED DUE TO SCARCITY
7 Derrick Rose/25 50.00 120.00
8 Candace Parker/25 40.00 100.00
9 D.J. Augustin/25 10.00 25.00
10 Kevin Love/25 25.00 60.00
AADM Danny Manning/25 10.00 25.00
AADR David Robinson/25 30.00 80.00

2008-09 Press Pass Legends Alumni Association
COMPLETE SET (10) 6.00 15.00
STATED ODDS 1:9
1 S.Elliott/J.Bayless 1.50 4.00
2 S.Moncrief/C.Williamson 1.25 3.00
3 C.Cheaney/E.Gordon 1.50 4.00
4 D.Manning/B.Rush 1.50 4.00
5 J.Lucas/K.Koufos 1.25 3.00
7 G.Goodrich/R.Westbrook 2.00 5.00
6 B.Walton/K.Love 2.00 5.00
8 E.Grunfield/B.King 1.50 4.00
9 R.Blackman/M.Beasley 2.00 5.00
10 G.Williams/O.Mayo 1.50 4.00

2008-09 Press Pass Legends Alumni Association Autographs
STATED PRINT RUN 38 TO 50 SER.#'d SETS
1 S.Elliott/J.Bayless/50 20.00 40.00
2 Moncrief/Williamson/49 10.00 25.00
3 Cheaney/E.Gordon/50 10.00 25.00
4 Manning/B.Rush/50 15.00 40.00
5 J.Lucas/Koufos/50 10.00 25.00
7 Goodrich/Westbrook/50 60.00 150.00
6 B.Walton/K.Love/50 25.00 50.00
9 Blackman/Beasley/49 20.00 50.00
10 G.Williams/Mayo/50 15.00 40.00
AABLRL B.Lopez/R.Lopez/38 20.00 40.00
AAJWBD Worthy/Daugherty/50 20.00 50.00
AAMCJG M.Cooper/Giddens/50 10.00 25.00
AASFRH S.Floyd/Hibbert/50 20.00 40.00

2008-09 Press Pass Legends Legendary Legacy
COMPLETE SET (10) 5.00 12.00
STATED ODDS 1:9
1 Clyde Drexler 1.25 3.00
2 Bobby Hurley 1.00 2.50
3 Larry Bird 2.50 6.00
4 Danny Manning .75 2.00
5 Bailey Howell 1.00 2.50
6 David Robinson 1.50 4.00
7 Calvin Murphy .75 2.00
8 Jerry Lucas 1.00 2.50
9 Gail Goodrich .75 2.00
10 Bill Walton 1.00 2.50

2008-09 Press Pass Legends Legendary Legacy Autographs
STATED PRINT RUN ONE TO 259 SETS
SOME UNPRICED DUE TO SCARCITY
1 Clyde Drexler/98 20.00 50.00
2 Bobby Hurley/200 10.00 25.00
3 Larry Bird/50 40.00 100.00
4 Danny Manning/146 8.00 20.00
5 Bailey Howell/213 5.00 12.00
6 David Robinson/30 40.00 100.00
7 Calvin Murphy/255 5.00 12.00
8 Jerry Lucas/100 6.00 15.00
9 Gail Goodrich/160 5.00 12.00
10 Bill Walton/50 6.00 15.00
10B Bill Walton Red/25* 15.00 40.00
LLBD Brad Daugherty/210 5.00 12.00
LLCW Corliss Williamson/165 5.00 12.00
LLDG Darrell Griffith/259 5.00 12.00
LLJW Jerry West/102 20.00 50.00
LLJW2 Jerry West Red/26* 50.00 100.00
LLJWO James Worthy/50 20.00 50.00

2008-09 Press Pass Legends Legendary Legacy Autographs Platinum
STATED PRINT RUN 4 TO 25 SETS
SOME UNPRICED DUE TO SCARCITY
1 Clyde Drexler 30.00 80.00
2 Bobby Hurley 12.50 30.00
3 Larry Bird 50.00 120.00
4 Danny Manning 10.00 25.00
5 Bailey Howell 10.00 25.00
6 David Robinson 50.00 100.00
7 Calvin Murphy 10.00 25.00
8 Jerry Lucas 10.00 25.00
9 Gail Goodrich/25 10.00 25.00
10 Bill Walton 15.00 40.00
LLBD Brad Daugherty 10.00 25.00
LLJW Jerry West 20.00 50.00
LLJWO James Worthy 25.00 60.00
LLJWO1 J.Worthy Big Game/25* 40.00 80.00

2008-09 Press Pass Legends Select Signatures
APPROX.THREE AU's PER MINI BOX
AR Anthony Randolph 4.00 10.00
AR1 A.Randolph Red/46* 5.00 12.00
BD Brad Daugherty 4.00 10.00
BH Bailey Howell 6.00 15.00
BH1 B.Howell Go Dawgs/25* 10.00 25.00
BH2 B.Howell Red/46* 8.00 20.00
BHU Bobby Hurley 10.00 25.00
BHU1 B.Hurley Go Duke/25* 75.00 150.00
BHU2 B.Hurley Red/46* 12.00 30.00
BK Bernard King 6.00 15.00
BK1 B.King Go Vols/18* 25.00 60.00
BK2 B.King Red/50* 8.00 20.00
BL Brook Lopez 8.00 20.00
BL2 B.Lopez Red/25* 8.00 20.00
BR Brandon Rush 4.00 10.00
BW Bill Walton 8.00 20.00
CC Calbert Cheaney 4.00 10.00
CC1 C.Cheaney Go Big Red/25* 6.00 15.00
CC2 C.Cheaney Red/50* 5.00 12.00
CD Clyde Drexler 15.00 40.00
CD1 C.Drexler The Glide/25* 60.00 120.00
CD2 C.Drexler Red/50* 10.00 25.00
CDR Chris Douglas-Roberts 4.00 10.00
CDR2 C.Douglas-Roberts Red/50* 5.00 12.00
CH Cliff Hagan 4.00 10.00
CH2 Cliff Hagen Red/51* 5.00 12.00
CL Courtney Lee 6.00 15.00
CM Calvin Murphy 4.00 10.00
CM1 Calvin Murphy Murph/25* 5.00 12.00
CM2 C.Murphy Red/49* 5.00 12.00
CP Candace Parker Red 30.00 80.00
CP1 C.Parker Blue Go Vols/2* 30.00 80.00
CW Corliss Williamson 4.00 10.00
CW1 C.Williamson Big Nasty/15* 8.00 20.00
DA D.J. Augustin 6.00 15.00
DG Darrell Griffith 4.00 10.00
DG2 D.Griffith Red/48* 6.00 15.00
DGA Danilo Gallinari 6.00 15.00
DGA2 D.Gallinari Red/13* 10.00 25.00
DJ DeAndre Jordan 8.00 20.00
DM Danny Manning 8.00 20.00
DM1 D.Manning Red/58* 10.00 25.00
DR David Robinson 20.00 40.00
DRO Derrick Rose 20.00 50.00
DRO1 D.Rose D.Pooh Rose/25* 40.00 100.00
DRO2 Derrick Rose Red/50* 50.00 100.00
DW D.J. White 4.00 10.00
DW1 D.White Red Go IU/25* 10.00 25.00
EB Elgin Baylor 10.00 25.00
EB1 E.Baylor Go Chieftains/25* 25.00 60.00
EB2 E.Baylor Red/50* 15.00 40.00
EG Eric Gordon 8.00 20.00
EG2 E.Gordon Red/46* 10.00 25.00
EGR Ernie Grunfeld 8.00 20.00
EGR1 E.Grunfeld Red/50* 10.00 25.00
GG Gail Goodrich 5.00 12.00
GW Gus Williams 4.00 10.00
GW2 G.Williams Red/125* 6.00 15.00
HB Henry Bibby 4.00 10.00
JB Jerryd Bayless 5.00 12.00
JB2 J.Bayless Red/50* 8.00 20.00
JD Joey Dorsey 4.00 10.00
JD1 J.Dorsey Red Hulk/47* 6.00 15.00
JG J.R. Giddens 4.00 10.00
JG1 J.Giddens Red/54* 5.00 12.00
JL Jerry Lucas 6.00 15.00
JT Jerry Tarkanian 6.00 15.00
JT1 Jerry Tarkanian Red/50* 8.00 20.00
JW Jerry West 25.00 50.00
JWD John Wooden 40.00 80.00
JWO James Worthy 15.00 30.00
JWO1 J.Worthy Red/59* 15.00 40.00
KK Kosta Koufos 4.00 10.00
KK2 Kosta Koufos Red/54* 6.00 15.00
KL Kevin Love Red 20.00 50.00
LB Larry Bird 30.00 60.00
LN Larry Nance 4.00 10.00
MB Michael Beasley 5.00 12.00
MB2 M.Beasley 27/30* 25.00 50.00
MB3 M. Beasley Red/25* 15.00 40.00
MC Michael Cooper 6.00 15.00
MJ Mark Jackson 5.00 12.00
MS Marreese Speights 4.00 10.00
OM O.J. Mayo 8.00 20.00
OM1 O.J. Mayo Red/39* 10.00 25.00
OM2 O.Mayo Red Juice/50* 20.00 40.00
RB Rolando Blackman 4.00 10.00
RB1 R.Blackman Go K-State/25* 10.00 25.00
RB2 Rolando Blackman Red/49* 6.00 15.00
RH Roy Hibbert 5.00 12.00
RL Robin Lopez 5.00 12.00
RL2 R.Lopez Red/48* 6.00 15.00
RW Russell Westbrook 60.00 150.00
RW2 R.Westbrook Red/25 75.00 200.00
SA Stacey Augmon 4.00 10.00
SA1 S.Augmon Plasticman/25* 15.00 30.00
SA2 S.Augmon Red/50* 6.00 15.00
SE Sean Elliott 4.00 10.00
SE1 S.Elliott Red/50* 8.00 20.00
SF Sleepy Floyd 4.00 10.00
SL Sidney Lowe 4.00 10.00
SM Sidney Moncrief 4.00 10.00
SM1 S.Moncrief Super Sid/35* 30.00 60.00

2008-09 Press Pass Legends Select Swatches
RANDOM INSERTS IN PACKS
UNPRICED PATCH PRINT RUN 10 SETS
*PLATINUM: .6X TO 1.5X BASE
PLATINUM PRINT RUN 50 SER. #'d SETS
SSWAR Anthony Randolph 2.50 6.00
SSWBL Brook Lopez 2.50 6.00
SSWBR Brandon Rush 2.50 6.00
SSWDA D.J. Augustin 2.50 6.00
SSWDR Derrick Rose 4.00 10.00
SSWJD Joey Dorsey 2.50 6.00
SSWRH Roy Hibbert 2.00 5.00
SSWRL Robin Lopez 2.50 6.00
SSWRW Russell Westbrook 8.00 20.00

2008-09 Press Pass Legends Student and Teacher Signatures
PRINT RUN 25 SER.#'d SETS
STBWJW Walton/Wooden 100.00 200.00
STGGJW Goodrich/Wooden 60.00 150.00
STHBJW Bibby/Wooden 75.00 150.00

2012 Press Pass Legends Hall of Fame Blue
LGJW James Worthy/2*

2012 Press Pass Legends Hall of Fame Blue Red Ink
STATED PRINT RUN 2-35
LGJW James Worthy/33* 12.00 30.00

2012 Press Pass Legends Hall of Fame Red
STATED PRINT RUN 1-50
EXCH DEADLINE 12/31/2013
LGJW James Worthy/35 12.00 30.00

2012 Press Pass Legends Hall of Fame Champions Blue
STATED PRINT RUN 19-35
CHJW James Worthy/35 15.00 40.00

2012 Press Pass Legends Hall of Fame Champions Purple
STATED PRINT RUN 8-25
CHJW James Worthy/25 15.00 40.00

2009-10 Prestige
MP.SET w/o RCs (150) 10.00 25.00
UNPRICED BLACK PRINT RUN 10 SETS
1 Joe Johnson .30 .75
2 Josh Smith .30 .75
3 Mike Bibby .30 .75
4 Jamal Crawford .40 1.00
5 Kevin Garnett .60 1.50
6 Paul Pierce .40 1.00
7 Ray Allen .40 1.00
8 Rajon Rondo .40 1.00
9 Gerald Wallace .30 .75
10 Boris Diaw .30 .75
11 Emeka Okafor .30 .75
12 Ben Gordon .30 .75
13 John Salmons .30 .75
14 Derrick Rose .60 1.50
15 Luol Deng .30 .75
16 LeBron James 1.50 4.00
17 Mo Williams .30 .75
18 Zydrunas Ilgauskas .30 .75
19 Delonte West .25 .60
20 Shaquille O'Neal .75 2.00
21 Dirk Nowitzki .50 1.25
22 Jason Terry .30 .75
23 Josh Howard .30 .75
24 Jason Kidd .40 1.00
25 Carmelo Anthony .50 1.25
26 Chauncey Billups .40 1.00
27 Nene .30 .75
28 Richard Hamilton .30 .75
29 Allen Iverson .50 1.25
30 Tayshaun Prince .30 .75
31 Rasheed Wallace .40 1.00
32 Stephen Jackson .30 .75
33 Corey Maggette .30 .75
34 Yao Ming .50 1.25
35 Tracy McGrady .40 1.00
36 Ron Artest .40 1.00
37 Luis Scola .30 .75
38 Danny Granger .30 .75
39 T.J. Ford .25 .60
40 Mike Dunleavy .25 .60
41 Marquis Daniels .25 .60
42 Zach Randolph .30 .75
43 Al Thornton .30 .75
44 Eric Gordon .30 .75
45 Baron Davis .30 .75
46 Kobe Bryant 1.50 4.00
47 Pau Gasol .40 1.00
48 Lamar Odom .30 .75
49 Derek Fisher .30 .75
50 O.J. Mayo .25 .60
51 Rudy Gay .40 1.00
52 Marc Gasol .40 1.00
53 Dwyane Wade .60 1.50
54 Jermaine O'Neal .30 .75
55 Michael Beasley .25 .60
56 Udonis Haslem .25 .60
57 Michael Redd .30 .75
58 Charlie Villanueva .25 .60
59 Al Jefferson .30 .75
60 Ryan Gomes .25 .60
61 Kevin Love .40 1.00
62 Devin Harris .25 .60
63 Brook Lopez .30 .75
64 Yi Jianlian .30 .75
65 Chris Paul .50 1.25
66 David West .30 .75
67 Peja Stojakovic .40 1.00

68 Rasual Butler .25 .60
69 Al Harrington .30 .75
70 Nate Robinson .25 .60
71 David Lee .25 .60
72 Larry Hughes .30 .75
73 Kevin Durant 1.00 2.50
74 Jeff Green .30 .75
75 Russell Westbrook 1.00 2.50
76 Dwight Howard .30 .75
77 Rashard Lewis .30 .75
78 Hedo Turkoglu .30 .75
79 Jameer Nelson .25 .60
80 Vince Carter .50 1.25
81 Andre Iguodala .30 .75
82 Andre Miller .30 .75
83 Thaddeus Young .25 .60
84 Elton Brand .40 1.00
85 Amare Stoudemire .30 .75
86 Steve Nash .40 1.00
87 Jason Richardson .40 1.00
88 Brandon Roy .40 1.00
89 LaMarcus Aldridge .40 1.00
90 Greg Oden .30 .75
91 Kevin Martin .30 .75
92 Andres Nocioni .25 .60
93 Jason Thompson .25 .60
94 Tony Parker .40 1.00
95 Tim Duncan .60 1.50
96 Manu Ginobili .40 1.00
97 Michael Finley .40 1.00
98 Richard Jefferson .30 .75
99 Chris Bosh .40 1.00
100 Andrea Bargnani .30 .75
101 Shawn Marion .30 .75
102 Deron Williams .30 .75
103 Mehmet Okur .25 .60
104 Carlos Boozer .30 .75
105 Ronnie Brewer .30 .75
106 Antawn Jamison .30 .75
107 Caron Butler .30 .75
108 Nick Young .30 .75
109 Andray Blatche .25 .60
110 Randy Foye .25 .60
111 Kareem Abdul-Jabbar 1.00 2.50
112 Bob Dandridge .40 1.00
113 Alvan Adams .40 1.00
114 A.C. Green .60 1.50
115 Dave Bing .60 1.50
116 Larry Bird 1.50 4.00
117 Nate Thurmond .50 1.25
118 Michael Cooper .50 1.25
119 Bob Cousy 1.00 2.50
120 Adrian Dantley .50 1.25
121 Darryl Dawkins .40 1.00
122 Clyde Drexler .75 2.00
123 Elvin Hayes .60 1.50
124 Walt Frazier .60 1.50
125 World B. Free .50 1.25
126 George Gervin .60 1.50
127 Gail Goodrich .50 1.25
128 Tim Hardaway .60 1.50
129 Connie Hawkins .60 1.50
130 K.C. Jones .60 1.50
131 Bernard King .50 1.25
132 Bob Lanier .50 1.25
133 Dan Majerle .50 1.25
134 Karl Malone .75 2.00
135 Sam Perkins .40 1.00
136 Slick Watts .40 1.00
137 Bob McAdoo .50 1.25
138 Xavier McDaniel .40 1.00
139 Sidney Moncrief .40 1.00
140 Robert Parish .60 1.50
141 Oscar Robertson .60 1.50
142 Paul Silas .60 1.50
143 Moses Malone .60 1.50
144 Dennis Rodman 1.25 3.00
145 Bill Russell 1.00 2.50
146 Bill Bradley .75 2.00
147 Bill Walton .60 1.50
148 Spud Webb .50 1.25
149 Cedric Ceballos .40 1.00
150 Jerry West .75 2.00
151 Blake Griffin RC 4.00 10.00
152 Hasheem Thabeet RC .60 1.50
153 James Harden RC 5.00 12.00
154 Tyreke Evans RC .75 2.00
155 Blake Griffin College RC 4.00 10.00
156 Jonny Flynn RC .60 1.50
157 Stephen Curry RC 10.00 25.00
158 Jordan Hill RC .75 2.00
159 DeMar DeRozan RC 2.50 6.00
160 Brandon Jennings SP 15.00 30.00
161 Terrence Williams RC .60 1.50
162 Gerald Henderson RC .75 2.00
163 Tyler Hansbrough SP 10.00 25.00
164 Earl Clark RC .75 2.00
165 Austin Daye RC .60 1.50
166 James Johnson RC .75 2.00
167 Jrue Holiday RC 1.25 3.00
168 Ty Lawson RC 1.00 2.50
169 Jeff Teague RC 1.00 2.50
170 Eric Maynor RC .60 1.50
171 Darren Collison RC 1.00 2.50
172 Hasheem Thabeet UConn RC .60 1.50
173 Omri Casspi RC .75 2.00
174 B.J. Mullens RC .60 1.50
175 Rodrigue Beaubois RC .60 1.50
176 Taj Gibson SP 8.00 20.00
177 DeMarre Carroll SP 6.00 15.00
178 Wayne Ellington RC 1.00 2.50
179 Toney Douglas RC .60 1.50
180 Tyreke Evans Memphis RC .75 2.00
181 Jeff Pendergraph RC .60 1.50
182 Jermaine Taylor RC .60 1.50
183 Dante Cunningham RC .60 1.50
184 DaJuan Summers RC .60 1.50
185 Sam Young RC .60 1.50
186 DeJuan Blair RC .75 2.00
187 Jon Brockman RC .60 1.50
188 Derrick Brown RC .60 1.50
189 Jodie Meeks RC 1.00 2.50
190 Jonas Jerebko SP 5.00 12.00
191 Marcus Thornton RC .75 2.00
192 Chase Budinger RC .75 2.00
193 Goran Suton RC .60 1.50
194 Danny Green RC 1.25 3.00
195 Taylor Griffin RC .60 1.50
196 A.J. Price RC .60 1.50
197 Jrue Holiday UCLA RC 1.25 3.00
198 Lester Hudson RC .60 1.50
199 Jack McClinton RC .60 1.50
200 Patrick Beverley RC 1.00 2.50
201 Blake Griffin RC 4.00 10.00
202 Hasheem Thabeet RC .60 1.50
203 James Harden RC 5.00 12.00
204 Tyreke Evans RC .75 2.00
205 Jordan Hill Arizona SP 8.00 20.00
206 Jonny Flynn RC .60 1.50
207 Stephen Curry RC 10.00 25.00
208 Jordan Hill RC .75 2.00
209 DeMar DeRozan RC 2.50 6.00
210 Brandon Jennings RC 1.00 2.50
211 Terrence Williams RC .60 1.50
212 Gerald Henderson RC .75 2.00
213 Tyler Hansbrough RC .75 2.00
214 Earl Clark RC .75 2.00
215 Austin Daye RC .60 1.50
216 James Johnson RC .75 2.00
217 Jrue Holiday RC 1.25 3.00
218 Ty Lawson SP 8.00 20.00
219 Jeff Teague RC 1.00 2.50
220 Eric Maynor SP 6.00 15.00
221 Darren Collison RC 1.00 2.50
222 Tyler Hansbrough RC .75 2.00
223 Omri Casspi RC .75 2.00
224 B.J. Mullens RC .60 1.50
225 Rodrigue Beaubois RC .60 1.50
226 Taj Gibson RC 1.00 2.50
227 DeMarre Carroll RC .75 2.00
228 Wayne Ellington RC 1.00 2.50
229 Toney Douglas RC .60 1.50
230 Stephen Curry Davidson RC 10.00 25.00
231 Jeff Pendergraph RC .60 1.50
232 Jermaine Taylor RC .60 1.50
233 Dante Cunningham SP 5.00 12.00
234 DaJuan Summers RC .60 1.50
235 Sam Young RC .60 1.50
236 DeJuan Blair RC .75 2.00
237 Jon Brockman RC .60 1.50
238 Derrick Brown RC .60 1.50
239 Jodie Meeks RC 1.00 2.50
240 Jonas Jerebko RC 1.00 2.50
241 Marcus Thornton RC .75 2.00
242 Chase Budinger RC .75 2.00
243 Goran Suton RC .60 1.50
244 Danny Green RC 1.25 3.00
245 Taylor Griffin RC .60 1.50
246 A.J. Price RC .60 1.50
247 James Johnson Wake SP 6.00 15.00
248 Lester Hudson RC .60 1.50
249 Jack McClinton RC .60 1.50
250 Patrick Beverley RC 1.00 2.50
251 Wesley Matthews RC* 1.00 2.50
252 Patrick Mills RC* 2.00 5.00
253 Serge Ibaka RC* 1.00 2.50
254 Marcus Landry RC* .60 1.50
255 Sundiata Gaines RC* .60 1.50
251A Wesley Matthews AU* 5.00 12.00
252A Patrick Mills AU* 12.00 30.00
253A Serge Ibaka AU* 5.00 12.00
254A Marcus Landry AU* 3.00 8.00
255A Sundiata Gaines AU* 3.00 8.00

2009-10 Prestige Bonus Shots Black Signatures

STATED PRINT RUN 25 TO 250 SER.#'d SETS
ASTERISK CARDS FROM PANINI UPDATE
46 Kobe Bryant/25 90.00 150.00
120 Adrian Dantley/100 5.00 12.00
124 Walt Frazier/100 6.00 15.00
129 Connie Hawkins/100 6.00 15.00
137 Bob McAdoo/50 15.00 30.00
139 Sidney Moncrief/100 4.00 10.00
141 Oscar Robertson/50 20.00 50.00
145 Bill Russell/50 40.00 100.00
147 Bill Walton/50 6.00 15.00
151 Blake Griffin/25 100.00 250.00
153 James Harden/25 50.00 120.00
154 Tyreke Evans/25 20.00 50.00
155 Blake Griffin/25 100.00 250.00
157 Stephen Curry/25 700.00 1000.00
158 Jordan Hill/25 5.00 12.00
160 Brandon Jennings/25 6.00 15.00
161 Terrence Williams/25 4.00 10.00
162 Gerald Henderson/25 5.00 12.00
163 Tyler Hansbrough/25 5.00 12.00
164 Earl Clark/25 5.00 12.00
166 James Johnson/25 5.00 12.00
167 Jrue Holiday/25 15.00 40.00
169 Jeff Teague/25 6.00 15.00
171 Darren Collison/50 6.00 15.00
173 Omri Casspi/50 5.00 12.00
174 B.J. Mullens/50 4.00 10.00
175 Rodrigue Beaubois/50 4.00 10.00
176 Taj Gibson/50 6.00 15.00
177 DeMarre Carroll/50 5.00 12.00
179 Toney Douglas/50 4.00 10.00
180 Tyreke Evans/50 5.00 12.00
182 Jermaine Taylor/100 4.00 10.00
183 Dante Cunningham/100 4.00 10.00
186 DeJuan Blair/100 5.00 12.00
188 Derrick Brown/100 4.00 10.00
189 Jodie Meeks/100 6.00 15.00
191 Marcus Thornton/100 5.00 12.00
192 Chase Budinger/100 5.00 12.00
193 Goran Suton/100 4.00 10.00
194 Danny Green/100 20.00 50.00
197 Jrue Holiday/25 15.00 40.00
199 Jack McClinton/100 4.00 10.00
201 Blake Griffin/25 30.00 80.00
202 Hasheem Thabeet/25 4.00 10.00
203 James Harden/25 50.00 120.00
204 Tyreke Evans/25 12.00 30.00
205 Jordan Hill/25 5.00 12.00
207 Stephen Curry/25 700.00 1000.00
208 Jordan Hill/25 5.00 12.00
210 Brandon Jennings/25 6.00 15.00
211 Terrence Williams/25 4.00 10.00
212 Gerald Henderson/25 5.00 12.00
213 Tyler Hansbrough/25 5.00 12.00
214 Earl Clark/25 5.00 12.00
216 James Johnson/25 5.00 12.00
217 Jrue Holiday/25 15.00 40.00
219 Jeff Teague/25 6.00 15.00
221 Darren Collison/50 6.00 15.00
222 Tyler Hansbrough/25 5.00 12.00
223 Omri Casspi/50 5.00 12.00
224 B.J. Mullens/50 4.00 10.00
225 Rodrigue Beaubois/50 4.00 10.00
226 Taj Gibson/50 6.00 15.00
227 DeMarre Carroll/50 5.00 12.00
229 Toney Douglas/50 4.00 10.00
230 Stephen Curry/50 700.00 1000.00
232 Jermaine Taylor/100 4.00 10.00
233 Dante Cunningham/100 4.00 10.00
236 DeJuan Blair/100 5.00 12.00
238 Derrick Brown/100 4.00 10.00
239 Jodie Meeks/100 6.00 15.00
241 Marcus Thornton/100 5.00 12.00
242 Chase Budinger/100 5.00 12.00
243 Goran Suton/100 4.00 10.00
244 Danny Green/100 20.00 50.00
246 A.J. Price/100 4.00 10.00
247 James Johnson/50 5.00 12.00
249 Jack McClinton/100 4.00 10.00
251 Wesley Matthews/250* 6.00 15.00
252 Patrick Mills/250* 12.00 30.00
253 Serge Ibaka/250* 6.00 15.00
254 Marcus Landry/250* 4.00 10.00
255 Sundiata Gaines/250* 4.00 10.00

2009-10 Prestige Bonus Shots Green

*GREEN 1-150: 3X TO 8X BASE HI
*GREEN 151-250: 1.5X TO 4X BASE HI
STATED PRINT RUN 25 SER.#'d SETS
SP CARDS SAME VALUE AS NON SP
29 Allen Iverson 6.00 15.00
157 Stephen Curry 60.00 150.00
207 Stephen Curry 60.00 150.00
230 Stephen Curry 60.00 150.00

2009-10 Prestige Bonus Shots Orange

*ORANGE 1-150: .75X TO 2X BASE HI
*ORANGE 151-250: .6X TO 1.5X BASE HI
STATED PRINT RUN 300 SER.#'d SETS
SP CARDS SAME VALUE AS NON SP
157 Stephen Curry 25.00 60.00
207 Stephen Curry 25.00 60.00
230 Stephen Curry 25.00 60.00

2009-10 Prestige Draft Picks Light Blue

*BLUE: .4X TO 1X BASE HI
PRINT RUN 999 SER.#'d SETS
SP CARDS SAME VALUE AS NON SP

2009-10 Prestige Draft Picks Light Blue Autographs

STATED PRINT RUN 50 TO 699 SER.#'d SETS
151 Blake Griffin/50 75.00 200.00
153 James Harden/100 30.00 80.00
154 Tyreke Evans/50 3.00 8.00
155 Blake Griffin/50 75.00 200.00
157 Stephen Curry/100 500.00 700.00
158 Jordan Hill/50 3.00 8.00
160 Brandon Jennings/100 4.00 10.00
161 Terrence Williams/100 2.50 6.00
162 Gerald Henderson/50 6.00 15.00
163 Tyler Hansbrough/100 3.00 8.00
164 Earl Clark/100 3.00 8.00
165 Austin Daye/100 2.50 6.00
166 James Johnson/50 3.00 8.00
167 Jrue Holiday/100 5.00 12.00
169 Jeff Teague/100 4.00 10.00
171 Darren Collison/399 4.00 10.00
173 Omri Casspi/499 3.00 8.00
174 B.J. Mullens/499 2.50 6.00
175 Rodrigue Beaubois/499 2.50 6.00
176 Taj Gibson/499 4.00 10.00
177 DeMarre Carroll/499 3.00 8.00
179 Toney Douglas/399 2.50 6.00
180 Tyreke Evans/50 15.00 40.00
181 Jeff Pendergraph/399 2.50 6.00
182 Jermaine Taylor/699 2.50 6.00
183 Dante Cunningham/699 2.50 6.00
186 DeJuan Blair/699 3.00 8.00
188 Derrick Brown/699 2.50 6.00
189 Jodie Meeks/699 4.00 10.00
191 Marcus Thornton/699 3.00 8.00
192 Chase Budinger/699 3.00 8.00
193 Goran Suton/499 2.50 6.00
194 Danny Green/499 5.00 12.00
196 A.J. Price/699 2.50 6.00
197 Jrue Holiday/100 5.00 12.00
199 Jack McClinton/699 2.50 6.00
201 Blake Griffin/50 40.00 100.00
203 James Harden/100 30.00 80.00
204 Tyreke Evans/50 3.00 8.00
205 Jordan Hill/50 3.00 8.00
207 Stephen Curry/100 400.00 600.00
208 Jordan Hill/50 3.00 8.00
210 Brandon Jennings/100 4.00 10.00
211 Terrence Williams/100 2.50 6.00
212 Gerald Henderson/50 6.00 15.00
213 Tyler Hansbrough/100 3.00 8.00
214 Earl Clark/100 3.00 8.00
215 Austin Daye/100 2.50 6.00
216 James Johnson/50 3.00 8.00
217 Jrue Holiday/100 5.00 12.00
219 Jeff Teague/100 4.00 10.00
221 Darren Collison/399 4.00 10.00
222 Tyler Hansbrough/100 3.00 8.00
223 Omri Casspi/499 3.00 8.00
224 B.J. Mullens/499 2.50 6.00
225 Rodrigue Beaubois/499 2.50 6.00
226 Taj Gibson/499 4.00 10.00
227 DeMarre Carroll/499 3.00 8.00
229 Toney Douglas/399 2.50 6.00
230 Stephen Curry/100 500.00 800.00
231 Jeff Pendergraph/100 2.50 6.00
232 Jermaine Taylor/699 2.50 6.00
233 Dante Cunningham/699 2.50 6.00
236 DeJuan Blair/699 3.00 8.00
238 Derrick Brown/699 2.50 6.00
239 Jodie Meeks/699 4.00 10.00
241 Marcus Thornton/699 3.00 8.00
242 Chase Budinger/699 3.00 8.00
243 Goran Suton/499 2.50 6.00
244 Danny Green/499 5.00 12.00
246 A.J. Price/699 2.50 6.00
247 James Johnson/50 3.00 8.00
249 Jack McClinton/699 2.50 6.00

2009-10 Prestige Connections

COMPLETE SET (10) 10.00 25.00
RANDOM INSERTS IN PACKS
1 L.Walton/J.Hill .75 2.00
2 Y.Ming/S.Yue 1.25 3.00
3 Y.Ming/Y.Jianlian 1.25 3.00
4 M.Gasol/P.Gasol 1.00 2.50
5 J.Posey/D.West .75 2.00
6 J.Johnson/J.Teague 1.00 2.50
7 J.Holiday/D.Collison 1.25 3.00
8 B.Griffin/T.Hansbrough 5.00 12.00
9 D.Curry/S.Curry 8.00 20.00
10 S.Jackson/J.Smith .75 2.00

2009-10 Prestige Connections Materials

PRINT RUN 250 SER.#'d SETS
UNPRICED PRIME PRINT RUN 10 SETS
6 J.Johnson/J.Teague 4.00 10.00
7 J.Holiday/D.Collison 5.00 12.00
8 B.Griffin/T.Hansbrough 15.00 40.00

2009-10 Prestige Franchise Favorites

COMPLETE SET (19) 8.00 20.00
RANDOM INSERT IN PACKS
1 Amare Stoudemire .60 1.50
2 Carmelo Anthony 1.00 2.50
3 Chris Bosh .75 2.00
4 Chris Paul 1.00 2.50
5 Deron Williams .60 1.50
6 Dirk Nowitzki 1.00 2.50
7 Dwight Howard .60 1.50
8 Dwyane Wade 1.25 3.00
9 Kobe Bryant 3.00 8.00
10 LeBron James 3.00 8.00
11 Paul Pierce .75 2.00
12 Tim Duncan 1.25 3.00
13 Yao Ming 1.00 2.50
14 Danny Granger .60 1.50
15 Michael Redd .60 1.50
16 Ben Gordon .60 1.50
17 Gilbert Arenas .60 1.50
18 Kevin Durant 2.00 5.00
19 Brandon Roy .75 2.00

2009-10 Prestige Hardcourt Heroes

COMPLETE SET (20) 6.00 15.00
RANDOM INSERT IN PACKS
1 Joe Johnson .50 1.25
2 Rajon Rondo .60 1.50
3 Ben Gordon .50 1.25
4 LeBron James 2.50 6.00
5 Josh Howard .50 1.25
6 Carmelo Anthony .75 2.00
7 Yao Ming .75 2.00
8 Danny Granger .50 1.25
9 Baron Davis .50 1.25
10 Pau Gasol .60 1.50
11 Jermaine O'Neal .50 1.25
12 Michael Redd .50 1.25
13 Devin Harris .40 1.00
14 David Lee .40 1.00
15 Kevin Durant 1.50 4.00
16 Amare Stoudemire .50 1.25
17 Brandon Roy .60 1.50
18 Tony Parker .60 1.50
19 Chris Bosh .60 1.50
20 Carlos Boozer .50 1.25
BG Blake Griffin PROMO 5.00 12.00
JH Jordan Hill PROMO 1.00 2.50

2009-10 Prestige Hardcourt Heroes Materials

STATED PRINT RUN 250 SER.#'d SETS
UNPRICED PRIME PRINT RUN 10 SER.#'d SETS
1 Joe Johnson 2.50 6.00
5 Josh Howard 2.50 6.00
7 Yao Ming 4.00 10.00
11 Jermaine O'Neal 2.50 6.00
14 David Lee 2.00 5.00
17 Brandon Roy 3.00 8.00
19 Chris Bosh 3.00 8.00
20 Carlos Boozer 2.50 6.00

2009-10 Prestige Inside the Numbers

COMPLETE SET (10) 4.00 10.00
RANDOM INSERT IN PACKS
1 Derrick Rose 1.25 3.00
2 Tim Duncan 1.25 3.00
3 Kobe Bryant 3.00 8.00
4 Richard Hamilton .60 1.50
5 T.J. Ford .50 1.25
6 Gilbert Arenas .60 1.50
7 Deron Williams .60 1.50
8 Marcus Camby .50 1.25
9 Chauncey Billups .75 2.00
10 O.J. Mayo .50 1.25

2009-10 Prestige Inside the Numbers Materials

STATED PRINT RUN 100 TO 250 SER.#'d SETS
UNPRICED PRIME PRINT RUN 10 SER.#'d SETS
2 Tim Duncan/150 5.00 12.00
3 Kobe Bryant/100 10.00 25.00
7 Deron Williams/250 2.50 6.00
10 O.J. Mayo/100 2.00 5.00

2009-10 Prestige Inside the Numbers Signatures

STATED PRINT RUN 25 SER.#'d SETS
3 Kobe Bryant 100.00 225.00

2009-10 Prestige NBA Draft Class

COMPLETE SET (34) 25.00 50.00
RANDOM INSERT IN PACKS
1 Blake Griffin 5.00 12.00
2 Hasheem Thabeet .75 2.00
3 James Harden 6.00 15.00
4 Tyreke Evans 1.00 2.50
5 Rodrigue Beaubois .75 2.00
6 Jonny Flynn .75 2.00
7 Stephen Curry 12.00 30.00
8 Jordan Hill 1.00 2.50
9 DeMar DeRozan 3.00 8.00
10 Brandon Jennings 1.25 3.00
11 Terrence Williams .75 2.00
12 Gerald Henderson 1.00 2.50
13 Tyler Hansbrough 1.00 2.50
14 Earl Clark 1.00 2.50
15 Austin Daye .75 2.00
16 James Johnson 1.00 2.50
17 Jrue Holiday 1.50 4.00
18 Ty Lawson 1.25 3.00
19 Jeff Teague 1.25 3.00
20 Eric Maynor .75 2.00
21 Darren Collison 1.25 3.00
23 Omri Casspi 1.00 2.50
24 B.J. Mullens .75 2.00
25 Taj Gibson 1.25 3.00
26 DeMarre Carroll 1.00 2.50
27 Wayne Ellington 1.25 3.00
28 Toney Douglas .75 2.00
29 Jeff Pendergraph .75 2.00
30 DaJuan Summers .75 2.00
31 Sam Young .75 2.00
32 DeJuan Blair 1.00 2.50
33 Jodie Meeks 1.25 3.00
34 Chase Budinger 1.00 2.50
35 Taylor Griffin .75 2.00
36 Patrick Mills 2.50 6.00

2009-10 Prestige NBA Draft Class Autographs

RANDOM INSERTS IN PACKS
1 Blake Griffin 30.00 80.00
2 Hasheem Thabeet 3.00 8.00
3 James Harden 75.00 200.00
4 Tyreke Evans 4.00 10.00
5 Rodrigue Beaubois 3.00 8.00
6 Jonny Flynn 3.00 8.00
7 Stephen Curry 300.00 600.00
8 Jordan Hill 4.00 10.00
10 Brandon Jennings 5.00 12.00
11 Terrence Williams 3.00 8.00
12 Gerald Henderson 4.00 10.00
13 Tyler Hansbrough 4.00 10.00
14 Earl Clark 4.00 10.00
15 Austin Daye 3.00 8.00
16 James Johnson 4.00 10.00
17 Jrue Holiday 6.00 15.00
18 Ty Lawson 5.00 12.00
19 Jeff Teague 5.00 12.00
20 Eric Maynor 3.00 8.00
21 Darren Collison 5.00 12.00
23 Omri Casspi 4.00 10.00
24 B.J. Mullens 3.00 8.00
25 Taj Gibson 5.00 12.00
26 DeMarre Carroll 4.00 10.00
27 Wayne Ellington 5.00 12.00
28 Toney Douglas 3.00 8.00
29 Jeff Pendergraph 3.00 8.00
30 DaJuan Summers/249 3.00 8.00
31 Sam Young 3.00 8.00
32 DeJuan Blair 4.00 10.00
33 Jodie Meeks 5.00 12.00
34 Chase Budinger 4.00 10.00
35 Taylor Griffin 3.00 8.00

2009-10 Prestige NBA Draft Class Autographs Logos

STATED PRINT RUN 124 TO 125 SER.#'d SETS
1 Blake Griffin 100.00 200.00
2 Hasheem Thabeet/124 4.00 10.00
3 James Harden 100.00 250.00
4 Tyreke Evans 5.00 12.00
5 Rodrigue Beaubois 4.00 10.00
6 Jonny Flynn 4.00 10.00
7 Stephen Curry 400.00 800.00
8 Jordan Hill 5.00 12.00
10 Brandon Jennings 6.00 15.00
11 Terrence Williams/124 4.00 10.00
12 Gerald Henderson 5.00 12.00
13 Tyler Hansbrough 5.00 12.00
14 Earl Clark/124 5.00 12.00
15 Austin Daye 4.00 10.00
16 James Johnson 5.00 12.00
17 Jrue Holiday/124 8.00 20.00
18 Ty Lawson 12.00 30.00
19 Jeff Teague 6.00 15.00
20 Eric Maynor 4.00 10.00
21 Darren Collison 6.00 15.00
23 Omri Casspi 5.00 12.00
24 B.J. Mullens 4.00 10.00
25 Taj Gibson 6.00 15.00
26 DeMarre Carroll 5.00 12.00
27 Wayne Ellington 6.00 15.00
28 Toney Douglas 4.00 10.00
29 Jeff Pendergraph 4.00 10.00
30 DaJuan Summers 4.00 10.00
31 Sam Young 4.00 10.00
32 DeJuan Blair 5.00 12.00
33 Jodie Meeks 6.00 15.00
34 Chase Budinger 5.00 12.00
35 Taylor Griffin 4.00 10.00

2009-10 Prestige NBA Draft Class Autographs Logos College

STATED PRINT RUN 93 TO 100 SER.#'d SETS
UNPRICED DRAFT LOGO PRINT RUN 10 SETS
1 Blake Griffin/99 75.00 150.00
2 Hasheem Thabeet/100 5.00 12.00
3 James Harden/100 50.00 120.00
4 Tyreke Evans/100 6.00 15.00
5 Rodrigue Beaubois/100 5.00 12.00
6 Jonny Flynn/100 5.00 12.00
7 Stephen Curry/100 400.00 800.00
8 Jordan Hill/100 6.00 15.00
10 Brandon Jennings/100 8.00 20.00
11 Terrence Williams/100 5.00 12.00
12 Gerald Henderson/100 6.00 15.00
13 Tyler Hansbrough/100 20.00 50.00
14 Earl Clark/100 6.00 15.00
15 Austin Daye/100 5.00 12.00
16 James Johnson/100 6.00 15.00
17 Jrue Holiday/100 10.00 25.00
18 Ty Lawson/98 8.00 20.00
19 Jeff Teague/100 8.00 20.00
21 Darren Collison/100 8.00 20.00
23 Omri Casspi/100 6.00 15.00
24 B.J. Mullens/100 5.00 12.00
25 Taj Gibson/100 8.00 20.00
26 DeMarre Carroll/100 6.00 15.00
27 Wayne Ellington/100 8.00 20.00
28 Toney Douglas/93 5.00 12.00
29 Jeff Pendergraph/100 5.00 12.00
30 DaJuan Summers/100 5.00 12.00
31 Sam Young/98 5.00 12.00
32 DeJuan Blair/100 6.00 15.00
33 Jodie Meeks/99 15.00 40.00
34 Chase Budinger/99 6.00 15.00
35 Taylor Griffin/100 5.00 12.00

2009-10 Prestige Old School

COMPLETE SET (18) 10.00 25.00
RANDOM INSERTS IN PACKS
1 Connie Hawkins 1.50 4.00
2 Bob McAdoo 1.25 3.00
3 Dan Issel 1.25 3.00
4 Kevin McHale 1.50 4.00
5 David Thompson 1.25 3.00
6 Bill Bradley 2.00 5.00
7 Ralph Sampson 1.25 3.00
8 Kenny Walker 1.00 2.50
9 Bryant Reeves 1.00 2.50
10 Dave Cowens 1.00 2.50
11 Joe Dumars 1.50 4.00
12 Oscar Robertson 1.50 4.00
13 Mark Aguirre 1.25 3.00
14 Chris Mullin 1.50 4.00
15 Al Attles 1.50 4.00
16 Walt Frazier 1.50 4.00
17 Dell Curry 1.00 2.50
18 Bill Walton 1.50 4.00

2009-10 Prestige Old School Materials

COMPLETE SET (2) 6.00 15.00
STATED PRINT RUN 250 SER.#'d SETS
4 Kevin McHale 4.00 10.00
14 Chris Mullin 4.00 10.00

2009-10 Prestige Old School Signatures

STATED PRINT RUN 50 TO 100 SER.#'d SETS
ASTERISK CARDS FROM PANINI UPDATE
1 Connie Hawkins*/100 12.50 30.00
2 Bob McAdoo/100 20.00 40.00
3 Dan Issel/100 10.00 25.00
4 Kevin McHale*/100 25.00 60.00
5 David Thompson/100 8.00 20.00
8 Kenny Walker*/100 15.00 40.00
10 Dave Cowens/99 8.00 20.00
12 Oscar Robertson/50 50.00 100.00
14 Chris Mullin*/100 15.00 40.00
15 Al Attles/100 10.00 25.00
16 Walt Frazier*/100 8.00 20.00
17 Dell Curry/96 8.00 20.00
18 Bill Walton/82 15.00 40.00

2009-10 Prestige Playmakers

COMPLETE SET (18) 6.00 15.00
RANDOM INSERT IN PACKS
1 Rajon Rondo .75 2.00
2 Mike Bibby .60 1.50
3 D.J. Augustin .50 1.25
4 Chauncey Billups .75 2.00
5 Danny Granger .60 1.50
6 Shane Battier .75 2.00
7 Derek Fisher .60 1.50
8 Kevin Love .75 2.00
9 David West .60 1.50
10 Nate Robinson .50 1.25
11 Russell Westbrook 2.00 5.00
12 Jameer Nelson .50 1.25
13 Brandon Roy .75 2.00
14 Deron Williams .60 1.50
15 Jason Terry .60 1.50
16 Tayshaun Prince .60 1.50
17 Michael Redd .60 1.50
18 Devin Harris .50 1.25

2009-10 Prestige Playmakers Materials

STATED PRINT RUN 250 SER.#'d SETS
2 Mike Bibby 2.50 6.00
6 Shane Battier 3.00 8.00
10 Nate Robinson 2.00 5.00
13 Brandon Roy 3.00 8.00
14 Deron Williams 2.50 6.00
15 Jason Terry 2.50 6.00

2009-10 Prestige Playmakers Signatures

STATED PRINT RUN 50 TO 100 SER.#'d SETS
ASTERISK CARDS FROM PANINI UPDATE
2 Mike Bibby/100 5.00 12.00
8 Kevin Love/50 15.00 40.00
11 Russell Westbrook/100 50.00 120.00
13 Brandon Roy*/57 10.00 25.00
14 Deron Williams*/100 8.00 20.00
18 Devin Harris*/100 5.00 12.00

2009-10 Prestige Preferred Materials

STATED PRINT RUN 150 TO 250 SETS
UNPRICED PATCH PRINT RUN 10 SER.#'d SETS
1 Brandon Roy/250 3.00 8.00
2 Jermaine O'Neal/250 2.50 6.00
4 LaMarcus Aldridge/250 3.00 8.00
5 David Lee/250 2.00 5.00
6 Joe Johnson/250 2.50 6.00
7 Elton Brand/250 3.00 8.00
8 Dirk Nowitzki/250 4.00 10.00
9 Tracy McGrady/250 3.00 8.00
10 Tim Duncan/150 5.00 12.00

2009-10 Prestige Prestigious Picks Green

STATED PRINT RUN 500 SER.#'d SETS
*BLACK: 1X TO 2.5X BASE HI
BLACK PRINT RUN 25 SER.#'d SETS
*GOLD: .5X TO 1.25X BASE HI
GOLD PRINT RUN 100 SER.#'d SETS
UNPRICED PLATINUM PRINT RUN 10 SETS
1 Blake Griffin 6.00 15.00
2 Hasheem Thabeet 1.00 2.50
3 James Harden 8.00 20.00
4 Tyreke Evans 1.25 3.00
5 Jonny Flynn 1.00 2.50
6 Stephen Curry 40.00 100.00
7 Jordan Hill 1.25 3.00
8 DeMar DeRozan 4.00 10.00
9 Brandon Jennings 1.50 4.00
10 Terrence Williams 1.00 2.50
11 Gerald Henderson 1.25 3.00
12 Tyler Hansbrough 1.25 3.00
13 Earl Clark 1.25 3.00
14 Austin Daye 1.00 2.50
15 James Johnson 1.25 3.00
16 Jrue Holiday 2.00 5.00
17 Ty Lawson 1.50 4.00
18 Jeff Teague 1.50 4.00
19 Eric Maynor 1.00 2.50
20 Darren Collison 1.50 4.00
21 Omri Casspi 1.25 3.00
22 B.J. Mullens 1.00 2.50
23 Rodrigue Beaubois 1.00 2.50
24 Taj Gibson 1.50 4.00
25 DeMarre Carroll 1.25 3.00
26 Wayne Ellington 1.50 4.00
27 Toney Douglas 1.00 2.50
28 Jeff Pendergraph 1.00 2.50
29 Jeff Pendergraph 1.00 2.50
30 DaJuan Summers 1.00 2.50
31 Sam Young 1.00 2.50
32 DeJuan Blair 1.25 3.00
33 Jodie Meeks 1.50 4.00
34 Chase Budinger 1.25 3.00
35 Taylor Griffin 1.00 2.50
36 Blake Griffin 6.00 15.00
37 Hasheem Thabeet 1.00 2.50
38 Jordan Hill 1.25 3.00
39 Tyler Hansbrough 1.25 3.00
40 Jonny Flynn 1.00 2.50
41 James Harden 8.00 20.00
42 DeMar DeRozan 4.00 10.00
43 Gerald Henderson 1.25 3.00
44 Jrue Holiday 2.00 5.00
45 B.J. Mullens 1.00 2.50
46 Darren Collison 1.50 4.00
47 Chase Budinger 1.25 3.00
48 Wayne Ellington 1.50 4.00
49 Jodie Meeks 1.50 4.00
50 Tyreke Evans 1.25 3.00

2009-10 Prestige Prestigious Picks Signatures Black

STATED PRINT RUN 50 TO 100 SER.#'d SETS
1 Blake Griffin/100 30.00 80.00
3 James Harden/50 50.00 120.00
4 Tyreke Evans/50 5.00 12.00
6 Stephen Curry/50 500.00 700.00
7 Jordan Hill/50 5.00 12.00
9 Brandon Jennings/50 6.00 15.00
10 Terrence Williams/50 4.00 10.00
11 Gerald Henderson/50 5.00 12.00
12 Tyler Hansbrough/50 5.00 12.00
13 Earl Clark/50 5.00 12.00
14 Austin Daye/50 4.00 10.00
15 James Johnson/50 5.00 12.00
16 Jrue Holiday/50 8.00 20.00
18 Jeff Teague/50 6.00 15.00
20 Darren Collison/50 6.00 15.00
21 Omri Casspi/50 5.00 12.00
22 B.J. Mullens/50 4.00 10.00
23 Rodrigue Beaubois/50 4.00 10.00
24 Taj Gibson/50 6.00 15.00
25 DeMarre Carroll/50 5.00 12.00
27 Toney Douglas/50 4.00 10.00
28 Jeff Pendergraph/50 4.00 10.00
29 Jeff Pendergraph/50 4.00 10.00
32 DeJuan Blair/50 5.00 12.00
33 Jodie Meeks/50 6.00 15.00
34 Chase Budinger/50 5.00 12.00
36 Blake Griffin/100 40.00 80.00
38 Jordan Hill/50 5.00 12.00
39 Tyler Hansbrough/50 5.00 12.00
41 James Harden/50 50.00 120.00
43 Gerald Henderson/50 5.00 12.00
44 Jrue Holiday/50 8.00 20.00
45 B.J. Mullens/50 4.00 10.00
46 Darren Collison/50 6.00 15.00
47 Chase Budinger/50 5.00 12.00
49 Jodie Meeks/50 6.00 15.00
50 Tyreke Evans/50 5.00 12.00

2009-10 Prestige Prestigious Picks Materials Blue

RANDOM INSERTS IN PACKS
*BLACK: 1.25X TO 3X BASE HI
BLACK PRINT RUN 25 SER.#'d SETS
*GOLD: .6X TO 1.5X BASE HI
GOLD PRINT RUN 50 SER.#'d SETS
*GREEN: .5X TO 1.25X BASE HI
GREEN PRINT RUN 100 SER.#'d SETS
*PLATINUM PATCH: 1.5X TO 4X BASE HI
PLATINUM PRINT RUN 25 SER.#'d SETS
1 Blake Griffin 10.00 25.00
2 Hasheem Thabeet 1.00 2.50
3 James Harden 8.00 20.00
4 Tyreke Evans 1.25 3.00
5 Jonny Flynn 1.00 2.50
6 Stephen Curry 40.00 100.00
7 Jordan Hill 1.25 3.00
8 DeMar DeRozan 4.00 10.00
9 Brandon Jennings 1.50 4.00
10 Terrence Williams 1.00 2.50
11 Gerald Henderson 1.25 3.00
12 Tyler Hansbrough 1.25 3.00
13 Earl Clark 1.25 3.00
14 Austin Daye 1.00 2.50
15 James Johnson 1.25 3.00
16 Jrue Holiday 2.00 5.00
17 Ty Lawson 1.50 4.00
18 Jeff Teague 1.50 4.00
19 Eric Maynor 1.00 2.50
20 Darren Collison 1.50 4.00
21 Omri Casspi 1.25 3.00
22 B.J. Mullens 1.00 2.50
23 Rodrigue Beaubois 1.00 2.50
24 Taj Gibson 1.50 4.00
25 DeMarre Carroll 1.25 3.00
26 Wayne Ellington 1.50 4.00
27 Toney Douglas 1.00 2.50
29 Jeff Pendergraph 1.00 2.50
30 DaJuan Summers 1.00 2.50
31 Sam Young 1.00 2.50
32 DeJuan Blair 1.25 3.00
33 Jodie Meeks 1.50 4.00
34 Chase Budinger 1.25 3.00
35 Taylor Griffin 1.00 2.50
38 Jordan Hill 1.25 3.00
46 Darren Collison 1.50 4.00
47 Chase Budinger 1.25 3.00
49 Jodie Meeks 1.50 4.00
50 Tyreke Evans 1.25 3.00

2009-10 Prestige Prestigious Pros Black Signatures

STATED PRINT RUN 25 SER.#'d SETS
1 Kobe Bryant 100.00 200.00

2009-10 Prestige Prestigious Pros Green

STATED PRINT RUN 500 SER.#'d SETS
*BLACK: 1.25X TO 3X BASE HI
BLACK PRINT RUN 25 SER.#'d SETS
*GOLD: 1X TO 2.5X BASE HI
GOLD PRINT RUN 100 SER.#'d SETS
UNPRICED PLATINUM PRINT RUN 10 SETS
1 Kobe Bryant 3.00 8.00
2 LeBron James 3.00 8.00
3 Dwyane Wade 1.25 3.00
4 Chris Paul 1.00 2.50
5 Kevin Garnett 1.25 3.00
6 Josh Howard .60 1.50
7 Gilbert Arenas .60 1.50
8 Steve Nash .75 2.00
9 Dirk Nowitzki 1.00 2.50
10 Danny Granger .60 1.50
11 Yao Ming 1.00 2.50
12 Joe Johnson .60 1.50
13 Carmelo Anthony 1.00 2.50
14 Richard Hamilton .60 1.50
15 Stephen Jackson .60 1.50
16 Zach Randolph .60 1.50
17 Rudy Gay .75 2.00
18 Michael Redd .60 1.50
19 Al Jefferson .60 1.50
20 Emeka Okafor .60 1.50
21 Devin Harris .50 1.25
22 Tracy McGrady .75 2.00
23 Ben Gordon .60 1.50
24 Al Harrington .60 1.50
25 Kevin Durant 2.00 5.00
26 Dwight Howard .60 1.50
27 Andre Iguodala .60 1.50
28 Brandon Roy .75 2.00
29 Paul Pierce .75 2.00
30 Jamal Crawford .75 2.00
31 Kevin Martin .60 1.50
32 Tim Duncan 1.25 3.00
33 Allen Iverson 1.00 2.50
34 Chris Bosh .75 2.00
35 Deron Williams .60 1.50
36 Mo Williams .60 1.50
37 Antawn Jamison .60 1.50
38 Vince Carter 1.00 2.50
39 Ron Artest .75 2.00
40 Amare Stoudemire .60 1.50
41 O.J. Mayo .50 1.25
42 Shawn Marion .60 1.50
43 Chauncey Billups .75 2.00
44 Tony Parker .75 2.00
45 LaMarcus Aldridge .75 2.00
46 Ray Allen .75 2.00
47 Pau Gasol .75 2.00
48 Derrick Rose 1.25 3.00
49 Russell Westbrook 2.00 5.00
50 Richard Jefferson .60 1.50

2009-10 Prestige Prestigious Pros Materials Black

*BLACK: 1.25X TO 3X BASE HI
BLACK PRINT RUN 25 SER.#'d SETS
1A Kobe Bryant AU/25 90.00 150.00

2009-10 Prestige Prestigious Pros Materials Blue

STATED PRINT RUN 150 TO 250 SER.#'d SETS
UNPRICED PLAT.PRINT RUN 10 TO 25 SETS
1 Kobe Bryant/200 10.00 25.00
4 Chris Paul/250 4.00 10.00
5 Kevin Garnett/250 5.00 12.00
6 Josh Howard/250 2.50 6.00
9 Dirk Nowitzki/250 4.00 10.00
11 Yao Ming/250 4.00 10.00
12 Joe Johnson/250 2.50 6.00
19 Al Jefferson/250 2.50 6.00
22 Tracy McGrady/250 3.00 8.00
24 Al Harrington/250 2.50 6.00
26 Dwight Howard/250 2.50 6.00
27 Andre Iguodala/250 2.50 6.00
28 Brandon Roy/250 3.00 8.00
31 Kevin Martin/250 2.50 6.00
32 Tim Duncan/150 5.00 12.00
34 Chris Bosh/250 3.00 8.00
35 Deron Williams/250 2.50 6.00
41 O.J. Mayo/150 2.00 5.00
45 LaMarcus Aldridge/250 3.00 8.00

2009-10 Prestige Prestigious Pros Materials Gold

*GOLD: .6X TO 1.5X BASE HI
GOLD PRINT RUN 50 SER.#'d SETS
1A Kobe Bryant AU/50 75.00 150.00

2009-10 Prestige Prestigious Pros Materials Green

*GREEN: .5X TO 1.25X BASE HI
GREEN PRINT RUN 100 SER.#'d SETS
1A Kobe Bryant AU/100 100.00 200.00

2009-10 Prestige Stars of the NBA

COMPLETE SET (20) 15.00 30.00
RANDOM INSERT IN PACKS
1 LeBron James 3.00 8.00
2 Kobe Bryant 3.00 8.00
3 Dwyane Wade 1.25 3.00
4 Dirk Nowitzki 1.00 2.50
5 Dwight Howard .60 1.50
6 Chris Paul 1.00 2.50
7 Shaquille O'Neal 1.50 4.00

8 Kevin Durant 2.00 5.00
9 Danny Granger .60 1.50
10 Kevin Garnett 1.25 3.00
11 Allen Iverson 1.00 2.50
12 Carmelo Anthony 1.00 2.50
13 Yao Ming 1.00 2.50
14 O.J. Mayo .50 1.25
15 Vince Carter 1.00 2.50
16 Tim Duncan 1.25 3.00
17 Chris Bosh .75 2.00
18 Deron Williams .60 1.50
19 Gilbert Arenas .60 1.50
20 Ben Gordon .60 1.50

2009-10 Prestige Stars of the NBA Materials

STATED PRINT RUN 100 TO 250 SER.#'d SETS
UNPRICED PATCH PRINT RUN 10 SER.#'d SETS
2 Kobe Bryant/100 12.50 30.00
4 Dirk Nowitzki/250 4.00 10.00
5 Dwight Howard/250 2.50 6.00
6 Chris Paul/250 4.00 10.00
10 Kevin Garnett/250 5.00 12.00
13 Yao Ming/250 4.00 10.00
14 O.J. Mayo/250 2.00 5.00
16 Tim Duncan/150 5.00 12.00
17 Chris Bosh/250 3.00 8.00
18 Deron Williams/250 2.50 6.00

2009-10 Prestige Stat Stars

COMPLETE SET (20) 10.00 25.00
RANDOM INSERT IN PACKS
1 O.J. Mayo .50 1.25
2 Kevin Love .75 2.00
3 Derrick Rose 1.25 3.00
4 Kevin Durant 2.00 5.00
5 Luis Scola .60 1.50
6 Ramon Sessions .60 1.50
7 Dwyane Wade 1.25 3.00
8 LeBron James 3.00 8.00
9 Kobe Bryant 3.00 8.00
10 Dirk Nowitzki 1.00 2.50
11 Dwight Howard .60 1.50
12 Troy Murphy .50 1.25
13 Tim Duncan 1.25 3.00
14 Yao Ming 1.00 2.50
15 Chris Paul 1.00 2.50
16 Deron Williams .60 1.50
17 Jose Calderon .50 1.25
18 Ray Allen .75 2.00
19 Shaquille O'Neal 1.50 4.00
20 Rashard Lewis .60 1.50

2009-10 Prestige Stat Stars Materials

STATED PRINT RUN 150 TO 250 SER.#'d SETS
UNPRICED PRIME PRINT RUN 10 SER.#'d SETS
1 O.J. Mayo/200 2.00 5.00
5 Luis Scola/250 2.50 6.00
9 Kobe Bryant/150 12.50 30.00
10 Dirk Nowitzki/250 4.00 10.00
11 Dwight Howard/250 2.50 6.00
13 Tim Duncan/150 5.00 12.00
14 Yao Ming/250 4.00 10.00
15 Chris Paul/250 4.00 10.00
16 Deron Williams/250 2.50 6.00
17 Jose Calderon/250 2.00 5.00

2009-10 Prestige Super Sophs

COMPLETE SET (9) 6.00 15.00
RANDOM INSERTS IN PACKS
1 Derrick Rose 2.00 5.00
2 Marc Gasol 1.25 3.00
3 Russell Westbrook 3.00 8.00
4 Rudy Fernandez .75 2.00
5 O.J. Mayo .75 2.00
6 Danilo Gallinari 1.00 2.50
7 Michael Beasley .75 2.00
8 Eric Gordon 1.00 2.50
9 Brook Lopez 1.00 2.50

2009-10 Prestige Super Sophs Signatures

STATED PRINT RUN 57 TO 100 SETS
3 Russell Westbrook/57* 60.00 150.00
8 Eric Gordon/100* 8.00 20.00

2009-10 Prestige True Colors

COMPLETE SET (10) 4.00 10.00
RANDOM INSERT IN PACKS
1 Kobe Bryant 3.00 8.00
2 Tim Duncan 1.25 3.00
3 Paul Pierce .75 2.00
4 Zydrunas Ilgauskas .60 1.50
5 Dirk Nowitzki 1.00 2.50
6 Jeff Foster .50 1.25
7 Michael Redd .60 1.50
8 Samuel Dalembert .50 1.25
9 Andrei Kirilenko .60 1.50
10 Brendan Haywood .50 1.25

2009-10 Prestige True Colors Materials

STATED PRINT RUN 50 TO 250 SER.#'d SETS
UNPRICED PRIMARY PRINT RUN 10 SETS
1 Kobe Bryant/50 15.00 40.00
2 Tim Duncan/150 5.00 12.00
4 Zydrunas Ilgauskas/250 2.50 6.00
5 Dirk Nowitzki/250 4.00 10.00
6 Jeff Foster/250 2.00 5.00
8 Samuel Dalembert/250 2.00 5.00
9 Andrei Kirilenko/250 2.50 6.00

2009-10 Prestige True Colors Signatures

STATED PRINT RUN 25 SER.#'d SETS
1 Kobe Bryant 100.00 200.00

2010-11 Prestige

COMPLETE SET (250) 60.00 150.00
ASTERISK CARDS INSERTED IN SEASON UPDATE
UNPRICED BONUS BLACK PRINT RUN 10 SETS
1 Al Horford .30 .75
2 Jamal Crawford .40 1.00
3 Josh Smith .30 .75
4 Mike Bibby .30 .75
5 Glen Davis .25 .60
6 Kendrick Perkins .25 .60
7 Kevin Garnett .60 1.50
8 Rajon Rondo .40 1.00
9 Boris Diaw .30 .75
10 D.J. Augustin .25 .60
11 Gerald Wallace .30 .75
12 Stephen Jackson .30 .75
13 Derrick Rose .50 1.25
14 Joakim Noah .30 .75
15 Luol Deng .30 .75
16 Taj Gibson .30 .75
17 Anderson Varejao .25 .60
18 Antawn Jamison .30 .75
19 Anthony Parker .25 .60
20 LeBron James 2.00 5.00
21 Caron Butler .30 .75
22 Dirk Nowitzki .50 1.25
23 Jason Kidd .40 1.00
24 Shawn Marion .30 .75
25 Carmelo Anthony .50 1.25
26 Chauncey Billups .40 1.00
27 J.R. Smith .30 .75
28 Nene .30 .75
29 Ben Gordon .30 .75
30 Richard Hamilton .30 .75
31 Rodney Stuckey .30 .75
32 Tayshaun Prince .30 .75
33 Andris Biedrins .25 .60
34 Anthony Randolph .25 .60
35 Monta Ellis .30 .75
36 Stephen Curry 1.50 4.00
37 Aaron Brooks .25 .60
38 Kevin Martin .30 .75
39 Shane Battier .30 .75
40 Trevor Ariza .25 .60
41 Dahntay Jones .25 .60
42 Danny Granger .30 .75
43 T.J. Ford .25 .60
44 Troy Murphy .25 .60
45 Baron Davis .30 .75
46 Blake Griffin .40 1.00
47 Chris Kaman .30 .75
48 Eric Gordon .30 .75
49 Kobe Bryant 1.50 4.00
50 Lamar Odom .30 .75
51 Pau Gasol .40 1.00
52 Ron Artest .40 1.00
53 Marc Gasol .40 1.00
54 Mike Conley Jr. .40 1.00
55 O.J. Mayo .25 .60
56 Zach Randolph .30 .75
57 Dwyane Wade .60 1.50
58 James Jones .25 .60
59 Jermaine O'Neal .30 .75
60 Michael Beasley .25 .60
61 Andrew Bogut .30 .75
62 Brandon Jennings .25 .60
63 Ersan Ilyasova .30 .75
64 Luc Mbah a Moute .25 .60
65 Al Jefferson .30 .75
66 Corey Brewer .25 .60
67 Kevin Love .40 1.00
68 Ramon Sessions .30 .75
69 Brook Lopez .30 .75
70 Courtney Lee .30 .75
71 Devin Harris .25 .60
72 Yi Jianlian .30 .75
73 Chris Paul .50 1.25
74 David West .30 .75
75 Emeka Okafor .30 .75
76 Marcus Thornton .25 .60
77 Danilo Gallinari .30 .75
78 David Lee .25 .60
79 Toney Douglas .25 .60
80 Wilson Chandler .30 .75
81 James Harden .60 1.50
82 Jeff Green .30 .75
83 Kevin Durant 1.00 2.50
84 Russell Westbrook 1.00 2.50
85 Dwight Howard .30 .75
86 Jameer Nelson .25 .60
87 Rashard Lewis .30 .75
88 Vince Carter .50 1.25
89 Andre Iguodala .30 .75
90 Elton Brand .40 1.00
91 Louis Williams .30 .75
92 Thaddeus Young .25 .60
93 Amare Stoudemire .30 .75
94 Jason Richardson .40 1.00
95 Leandro Barbosa .30 .75
96 Steve Nash .40 1.00
97 Andre Miller .30 .75
98 Brandon Roy .40 1.00
99 Greg Oden .30 .75
100 LaMarcus Aldridge .40 1.00
101 Beno Udrih .25 .60
102 Carl Landry .25 .60
103 Jason Thompson .25 .60
104 Tyreke Evans .25 .60
105 George Hill .30 .75
106 Manu Ginobili .40 1.00
107 Tim Duncan .60 1.50
108 Tony Parker .40 1.00
109 Andrea Bargnani .30 .75
110 Chris Bosh .40 1.00
111 Hedo Turkoglu .30 .75
112 Jarrett Jack .30 .75
113 Andrei Kirilenko .30 .75
114 Deron Williams .30 .75
115 Mehmet Okur .25 .60
116 Paul Millsap .30 .75
117 Al Thornton .25 .60
118 Andray Blatche .25 .60
119 JaVale McGee .30 .75
120 Nick Young .30 .75
121 Alvan Adams .25 .60
122 Charles Oakley .40 1.00
123 Chris Webber .40 1.00
124 Connie Hawkins .40 1.00
125 Dell Curry .25 .60
126 Gary Payton .40 1.00
127 Gheorghe Muresan .25 .60
128 Hal Greer .30 .75
129 Jalen Rose .40 1.00
130 Jamal Mashburn .40 1.00
131 James Worthy .50 1.25
132 Joe Dumars .40 1.00
133 John Stockton .60 1.50
134 K.C. Jones .40 1.00
135 Kelly Tripucka .25 .60
136 Kurt Rambis .25 .60
137 Larry Bird 1.00 2.50
138 Larry Johnson .50 1.25
139 Magic Johnson 1.00 2.50
140 Maurice Cheeks .25 .60
141 Michael Cooper .30 .75
142 Mike Dunleavy, Sr. .40 1.00
143 Moses Malone .40 1.00
144 Muggsy Bogues .30 .75
145 Nate Thurmond .30 .75
146 Pete Maravich .60 1.50
147 Quinn Buckner .40 1.00
148 Rolando Blackman .30 .75
149 Sidney Moncrief .25 .60
150 Toni Kukoc .40 1.00
151 John Wall RC 6.00 15.00
152 Evan Turner RC 1.00 2.50
153 Derrick Favors RC 1.50 4.00
154 Wesley Johnson RC .75 2.00
155 DeMarcus Cousins RC 4.00 10.00
156 Ekpe Udoh RC .75 2.00
157 Greg Monroe RC 1.50 4.00
158 Al-Farouq Aminu RC 1.25 3.00
159 Gordon Hayward RC 2.00 5.00
160 Paul George RC 4.00 10.00
161 Cole Aldrich RC 1.00 2.50
162 Xavier Henry RC .75 2.00
163 Ed Davis RC .75 2.00
164 Patrick Patterson RC 1.00 2.50
165 Larry Sanders RC .75 2.00
166 Luke Babbitt RC 1.00 2.50
167 Kevin Seraphin RC .75 2.00
168 Eric Bledsoe RC 1.50 4.00
169 Avery Bradley RC 1.50 4.00
170 James Anderson RC .75 2.00
171 Craig Brackins RC .75 2.00
172 Elliot Williams RC .75 2.00
173 Trevor Booker RC 1.00 2.50
174 Damion James RC .75 2.00
175 Dominique Jones RC .75 2.00
176 Quincy Pondexter RC .75 2.00
177 Jordan Crawford RC 1.00 2.50
178 Greivis Vasquez RC 1.00 2.50
179 Daniel Orton RC .75 2.00
180 Lazar Hayward RC .75 2.00
181 Tibor Pleiss RC 1.25 3.00
182 Dexter Pittman RC .75 2.00
183 Hassan Whiteside RC 2.50 6.00
184 Armon Johnson RC .75 2.00
185 Brian Zoubek RC .75 2.00
186 Terrico White RC .75 2.00
187 Jeremy Lin RC 8.00 20.00
188 Andy Rautins RC .75 2.00
189 Landry Fields RC 1.00 2.50
190 Lance Stephenson RC 1.25 3.00
191 Jarvis Varnado RC .75 2.00
192 Da'Sean Butler RC 1.25 3.00
193 Devin Ebanks RC .75 2.00
194 Wesley Johnson RC .75 2.00
195 Terrico White RC .75 2.00
196 Gani Lawal RC .75 2.00
197 Keith Gallon RC .75 2.00
198 Lance Stephenson RC 1.25 3.00
199 John Wall RC 6.00 15.00
200 Solomon Alabi RC .75 2.00
201 Devin Ebanks RC .75 2.00
202 Luke Harangody RC .75 2.00
203 Hassan Whiteside RC 2.50 6.00
204 Willie Warren RC .75 2.00
205 Andy Rautins RC .75 2.00
206 Evan Turner RC 1.00 2.50
207 Keith Gallon RC .75 2.00
208 Derrick Caracter RC .75 2.00
209 Stanley Robinson RC .75 2.00
210 Jeremy Lin RC 8.00 20.00
211 John Wall RC 6.00 15.00
212 Evan Turner RC 1.00 2.50
213 Derrick Favors RC 1.50 4.00
214 Wesley Johnson RC .75 2.00
215 DeMarcus Cousins RC 4.00 10.00
216 Ekpe Udoh RC .75 2.00
217 Greg Monroe RC 1.50 4.00
218 Al-Farouq Aminu RC 1.25 3.00
219 Gordon Hayward RC 2.00 5.00
220 Paul George RC 4.00 10.00
221 Cole Aldrich RC 1.00 2.50
222 Xavier Henry RC .75 2.00
223 Ed Davis RC .75 2.00
224 Patrick Patterson RC 1.00 2.50
225 Larry Sanders RC .75 2.00
226 Luke Babbitt RC 1.00 2.50
227 Eric Bledsoe RC 1.50 4.00
228 Avery Bradley RC 1.50 4.00
229 James Anderson RC .75 2.00
230 Craig Brackins RC .75 2.00
231 Elliot Williams RC .75 2.00
232 Trevor Booker RC 1.00 2.50
233 Damion James RC .75 2.00
234 Dominique Jones RC .75 2.00
235 Quincy Pondexter RC .75 2.00
236 Jordan Crawford RC 1.00 2.50
237 Greivis Vasquez RC 1.00 2.50
238 Daniel Orton RC .75 2.00
239 Lazar Hayward RC .75 2.00
240 Dexter Pittman RC .75 2.00
241 Da'Sean Butler RC 1.25 3.00
242 Luke Harangody RC .75 2.00
243 Willie Warren RC .75 2.00
244 Gani Lawal RC .75 2.00
245 Stanley Robinson RC .75 2.00
246 Gary Neal RC* 1.25 3.00
247 Gary Forbes RC* .75 2.00
248 Omer Asik RC* 1.50 4.00
249 Semih Erden RC* .75 2.00
250 Timofey Mozgov RC* 1.25 3.00

2010-11 Prestige Bonus Shots Gold

*GOLD 1-150: .75X TO 2X BASE HI
*GOLD 151-245: .5X TO 1.25X BASE HI
GOLD PRINT RUN 249 SER.#'d SETS

2010-11 Prestige Bonus Shots Green

*GREEN 1-150: 4X TO 10X BASE HI
*GREEN 151-245: 1.5X TO 4X BASE HI
GREEN PRINT RUN 25 SER.#'d SETS
187 Jeremy Lin 50.00 125.00
210 Jeremy Lin 50.00 125.00

2010-11 Prestige Bonus Shots Orange

*ORANGE 1-150: .6X TO 1.5X BASE HI
*ORANGE 151-245: .4X TO 1X BASE HI
STATED PRINT RUN 499 SER.#'d SETS
RANDOM INSERTS IN RETAIL PACKS

2010-11 Prestige Bonus Shots Purple

*PURPLE 1-150: 2X TO 5X BASE HI
*PURPLE 151-245: 1X TO 2.5X BASE HI
PURPLE PRINT RUN 49 SER.#'d SETS

2010-11 Prestige Bonus Shots Black Signatures

STATED PRINT RUN 25 TO 99 SER.#'d SETS
ASTERISK CARDS INSERTED IN SEASON UPDATE
16 Taj Gibson/25 5.00 12.00
30 Richard Hamilton/50 6.00 15.00
37 Aaron Brooks/99 5.00 12.00
43 T.J. Ford/25 5.00 12.00
46 Blake Griffin/99 20.00 50.00
49 Kobe Bryant/49 75.00 200.00
52 Ron Artest/50 15.00 40.00
59 Jermaine O'Neal/50 5.00 12.00
60 Michael Beasley/25 10.00 25.00
67 Kevin Love/25 12.00 30.00
71 Devin Harris/25 5.00 12.00
75 Emeka Okafor/50 5.00 12.00
76 Marcus Thornton/99 5.00 12.00
79 Toney Douglas/99 5.00 12.00
81 James Harden/99 20.00 50.00
89 Andre Iguodala/50 5.00 12.00
93 Amare Stoudemire/25 15.00 40.00
98 Brandon Roy/50 8.00 20.00
102 Carl Landry/50 5.00 12.00
104 Tyreke Evans/99 4.00 10.00
121 Alvan Adams/50 5.00 12.00
126 Gary Payton/25 20.00 40.00
128 Hal Greer/50 5.00 12.00
145 Nate Thurmond/25 8.00 20.00
149 Sidney Moncrief/50 5.00 12.00
151 John Wall/99 30.00 80.00
152 Evan Turner/25 5.00 12.00
153 Derrick Favors/99 8.00 20.00
154 Wesley Johnson/99 4.00 10.00
155 DeMarcus Cousins/99 25.00 60.00
156 Ekpe Udoh/99 4.00 10.00
158 Al-Farouq Aminu/99 6.00 15.00
161 Cole Aldrich/99 5.00 12.00
162 Xavier Henry/99 4.00 10.00
163 Ed Davis/99 4.00 10.00
164 Patrick Patterson/99 5.00 12.00
166 Luke Babbitt/99 5.00 12.00
167 Kevin Seraphin/25 4.00 10.00
168 Eric Bledsoe/99 8.00 20.00
169 Avery Bradley/99 8.00 20.00
170 James Anderson/99 4.00 10.00
171 Craig Brackins/25 4.00 10.00
175 Dominique Jones/25 4.00 10.00
176 Quincy Pondexter/99 4.00 10.00
177 Jordan Crawford/99 5.00 12.00
179 Daniel Orton/99 4.00 10.00
180 Lazar Hayward/99 4.00 10.00
184 Armon Johnson/99 4.00 10.00
186 Terrico White/99 4.00 10.00
187 Jeremy Lin/99 60.00 150.00
188 Andy Rautins/99 4.00 10.00
189 Landry Fields/99 5.00 12.00
190 Lance Stephenson/99 6.00 15.00
192 Da'Sean Butler/99 6.00 15.00
194 Wesley Johnson/99 4.00 10.00
195 Terrico White/99 4.00 10.00
196 Gani Lawal/99 4.00 10.00
197 Keith Gallon/99 4.00 10.00
198 Lance Stephenson/99 6.00 15.00
199 John Wall/99 30.00 80.00
200 Solomon Alabi/99 4.00 10.00
202 Luke Harangody/99 4.00 10.00
205 Andy Rautins/99 4.00 10.00
206 Evan Turner/25 5.00 12.00
207 Keith Gallon/99 4.00 10.00
210 Jeremy Lin/99 60.00 150.00
211 John Wall/99 30.00 80.00
212 Evan Turner/25 5.00 12.00
213 Derrick Favors/99 8.00 20.00
214 Wesley Johnson/99 4.00 10.00
215 DeMarcus Cousins/99 25.00 60.00
216 Ekpe Udoh/99 4.00 10.00
218 Al-Farouq Aminu/99 6.00 15.00
221 Cole Aldrich/99 5.00 12.00
222 Xavier Henry/99 4.00 10.00
223 Ed Davis/99 4.00 10.00
224 Patrick Patterson/99 5.00 12.00
226 Luke Babbitt/99 5.00 12.00
227 Eric Bledsoe/99 8.00 20.00
228 Avery Bradley/99 8.00 20.00
229 James Anderson/99 4.00 10.00
230 Craig Brackins/25 4.00 10.00
234 Dominique Jones/25 4.00 10.00
235 Quincy Pondexter/99 4.00 10.00
236 Jordan Crawford/99 5.00 12.00
238 Daniel Orton/99 4.00 10.00
239 Lazar Hayward/99 4.00 10.00
241 Da'Sean Butler/99 6.00 15.00
242 Luke Harangody/99 4.00 10.00
244 Gani Lawal/99 4.00 10.00
246 Gary Neal/99* 6.00 15.00
247 Gary Forbes/99* 4.00 10.00
248 Omer Asik/99* 8.00 20.00
249 Semih Erden/99* 4.00 10.00
250 Timofey Mozgov/99* 6.00 15.00

2010-11 Prestige Draft Picks Light Blue

*LIGHT BLUE: .3X TO .8X BASE HI
STATED PRINT RUN 999 SER.#'d SETS

2010-11 Prestige Draft Picks Rights Autographs

STATED PRINT RUN 25 TO 199 SER.#'d SETS
ASTERISK CARDS INSERTED IN SEASON UPDATE
151 John Wall/99 30.00 80.00
152 Evan Turner/25 5.00 12.00
153 Derrick Favors/199 6.00 15.00
154 Wesley Johnson/99 3.00 8.00
155 DeMarcus Cousins/199 15.00 40.00
156 Ekpe Udoh/199 3.00 8.00
158 Al-Farouq Aminu/199 5.00 12.00
161 Cole Aldrich/199 4.00 10.00
162 Xavier Henry/199 3.00 8.00
163 Ed Davis/199 3.00 8.00
164 Patrick Patterson/99 4.00 10.00
166 Luke Babbitt/199 4.00 10.00
167 Kevin Seraphin/25 3.00 8.00
168 Eric Bledsoe/199 6.00 15.00
169 Avery Bradley/199 6.00 15.00
170 James Anderson/199 3.00 8.00
171 Craig Brackins/25 3.00 8.00
175 Dominique Jones/25 10.00 25.00
176 Quincy Pondexter/199 3.00 8.00
177 Jordan Crawford/199 4.00 10.00
179 Daniel Orton/199 3.00 8.00
180 Lazar Hayward/199 3.00 8.00
182 Dexter Pittman/49 3.00 8.00
184 Armon Johnson/199 3.00 8.00
186 Terrico White/199 3.00 8.00
187 Jeremy Lin/199 50.00 125.00
188 Andy Rautins/199 3.00 8.00
189 Landry Fields/199 4.00 10.00
190 Lance Stephenson/199 5.00 12.00
192 Da'Sean Butler/199 5.00 12.00
194 Wesley Johnson/99 3.00 8.00
195 Terrico White/199 3.00 8.00
196 Gani Lawal/199 3.00 8.00
197 Keith Gallon/99 3.00 8.00
198 Lance Stephenson/199 5.00 12.00
199 John Wall/99 40.00 100.00
200 Solomon Alabi/199 3.00 8.00
202 Luke Harangody/99 3.00 8.00
205 Andy Rautins/199 3.00 8.00
206 Evan Turner/25 4.00 10.00
207 Keith Gallon/99 3.00 8.00
210 Jeremy Lin/199 30.00 80.00
211 John Wall/99 30.00 60.00
212 Evan Turner/25 15.00 40.00
213 Derrick Favors/199 6.00 15.00
214 Wesley Johnson/99 3.00 8.00
215 DeMarcus Cousins/199 15.00 40.00
216 Ekpe Udoh/199 3.00 8.00
218 Al-Farouq Aminu/199 5.00 12.00
221 Cole Aldrich/199 4.00 10.00
222 Xavier Henry/199 3.00 8.00
223 Ed Davis/199 3.00 8.00
224 Patrick Patterson/99 4.00 10.00
226 Luke Babbitt/199 4.00 10.00
227 Eric Bledsoe/199 6.00 15.00
228 Avery Bradley/199 6.00 15.00
229 James Anderson/199 3.00 8.00
230 Craig Brackins/25 3.00 8.00
234 Dominique Jones/25 10.00 25.00
235 Quincy Pondexter/199 3.00 8.00
236 Jordan Crawford/199 4.00 10.00
238 Daniel Orton/199 3.00 8.00
239 Lazar Hayward/199 3.00 8.00
240 Dexter Pittman/49 3.00 8.00
244 Gani Lawal/199 3.00 8.00
246 Gary Neal/199* 5.00 12.00
247 Gary Forbes/199* 3.00 8.00
248 Omer Asik/199* 6.00 15.00
249 Semih Erden/199* 3.00 8.00
250 Timofey Mozgov/199* 5.00 12.00

2010-11 Prestige Franchise Favorites

COMPLETE SET (30) 15.00 30.00
RANDOM INSERTS IN PACKS
1 Ray Allen .60 1.50
2 Brook Lopez .50 1.25
3 Al Harrington .50 1.25
4 Allen Iverson .75 2.00
5 Andrea Bargnani .50 1.25
6 Luol Deng .50 1.25
7 Antawn Jamison .50 1.25
8 Tayshaun Prince .50 1.25
9 Danny Granger .50 1.25
10 Brandon Jennings .40 1.00
11 Joe Johnson .50 1.25
12 Stephen Jackson .50 1.25
13 Dwyane Wade 1.00 2.50
14 Dwight Howard .50 1.25
15 Al Thornton .40 1.00
16 Dirk Nowitzki .75 2.00
17 Kevin Martin .50 1.25
18 Zach Randolph .50 1.25
19 Chris Paul .75 2.00
20 Tim Duncan 1.00 2.50
21 Carmelo Anthony .75 2.00
22 Kevin Love .60 1.50
23 LaMarcus Aldridge .60 1.50
24 Kevin Durant 1.50 4.00
25 Deron Williams .50 1.25
26 Monta Ellis .50 1.25
27 Baron Davis .50 1.25
28 Kobe Bryant 2.50 6.00
29 Steve Nash .60 1.50
30 Tyreke Evans .40 1.00

2010-11 Prestige Franchise Favorites Materials

STATED PRINT RUN 50 TO 249 SER.#'d SETS
*PRIME: .75X TO 2X BASE HI
PRIME PRINT RUN 5 TO 49 SER.#'d SETS
1 Ray Allen/149 3.00 8.00
2 Brook Lopez/249 2.50 6.00
4 Allen Iverson/199 4.00 10.00
5 Andrea Bargnani/249 2.50 6.00
6 Luol Deng/249 2.50 6.00
8 Tayshaun Prince/249 2.50 6.00
9 Danny Granger/249 2.50 6.00
10 Brandon Jennings/249 2.00 5.00
11 Joe Johnson/249 2.50 6.00
13 Dwyane Wade/249 5.00 12.00
14 Dwight Howard/249 2.50 6.00
16 Dirk Nowitzki/249 4.00 10.00
17 Kevin Martin/249 2.50 6.00
19 Chris Paul/249 4.00 10.00
20 Tim Duncan/249 5.00 12.00
21 Carmelo Anthony/249 4.00 10.00
22 Kevin Love/249 3.00 8.00
23 LaMarcus Aldridge/249 3.00 8.00
24 Kevin Durant/50 8.00 20.00
25 Deron Williams/249 2.50 6.00
27 Baron Davis/249 2.50 6.00
28 Kobe Bryant/249 8.00 20.00
29 Steve Nash/249 3.00 8.00
30 Tyreke Evans/249 2.00 5.00

2010-11 Prestige Franchise Favorites Signatures

STATED PRINT RUN 10 TO 49 SER.#'d SETS
SOME UNPRICED DUE TO SCARCITY
10 Brandon Jennings/25 15.00 40.00
22 Kevin Love/25 12.00 30.00
25 Deron Williams/25 10.00 25.00
27 Baron Davis/49 6.00 15.00
28 Kobe Bryant/49 75.00 150.00
30 Tyreke Evans/49 10.00 25.00

2010-11 Prestige Hardcourt Heroes

COMPLETE SET (20) 10.00 25.00
RANDOM INSERTS IN PACKS
1 LeBron James 3.00 8.00
2 Kevin Durant 1.50 4.00
3 David Lee .40 1.00
4 Chris Bosh .60 1.50
5 Pau Gasol .60 1.50
6 Dwight Howard .50 1.25
7 Chris Paul .75 2.00
8 Carlos Boozer .50 1.25
9 Dirk Nowitzki .75 2.00
10 Dwyane Wade 1.00 2.50
11 Marc Gasol .60 1.50
12 Amare Stoudemire .50 1.25
13 Tim Duncan 1.00 2.50
14 Carmelo Anthony .75 2.00
15 Kobe Bryant 2.50 6.00
16 Deron Williams .50 1.25
17 Gerald Wallace .50 1.25
18 Josh Smith .50 1.25
19 Steve Nash .60 1.50
20 Brook Lopez .50 1.25

2010-11 Prestige Hardcourt Heroes Materials

STATED PRINT RUN 50 TO 249 SER.#'d SETS
*PRIME: .75X TO 2X BASE HI
PRIME PRINT RUN 10 TO 49 SER.#'d SETS
1 LeBron James/50 10.00 25.00
2 Kevin Durant/50 8.00 20.00
4 Chris Bosh/249 3.00 8.00
5 Pau Gasol/249 3.00 8.00
6 Dwight Howard/249 2.50 6.00
7 Chris Paul/249 4.00 10.00
8 Carlos Boozer/249 2.50 6.00
9 Dirk Nowitzki/249 4.00 10.00
10 Dwyane Wade/249 5.00 12.00
11 Marc Gasol/249 3.00 8.00
12 Amare Stoudemire/249 2.50 6.00
13 Tim Duncan/249 5.00 12.00
14 Carmelo Anthony/249 4.00 10.00
15 Kobe Bryant/249 8.00 20.00
16 Deron Williams/249 2.50 6.00
17 Gerald Wallace/249 2.50 6.00
18 Josh Smith/249 2.50 6.00
19 Steve Nash/249 3.00 8.00
20 Brook Lopez/249 2.50 6.00

2010-11 Prestige Hardcourt Heroes Signatures

STATED PRINT RUN 10 TO 25 SER.#'d SETS
12 Amare Stoudemire/25 15.00 40.00
15 Kobe Bryant/25 100.00 200.00
16 Deron Williams/25 5.00 12.00

2010-11 Prestige Inside the Numbers

COMPLETE SET (10) 4.00 10.00
RANDOM INSERTS IN PACKS
1 Danny Granger .50 1.25
2 Dwyane Wade 1.00 2.50
3 Dwight Howard .50 1.25
4 Chris Bosh .60 1.50
5 Carmelo Anthony .75 2.00
6 Aaron Brooks .40 1.00
7 Dirk Nowitzki .75 2.00
8 Stephen Jackson .50 1.25
9 David West .50 1.25
10 Zach Randolph .50 1.25

2010-11 Prestige Inside the Numbers Materials

STATED PRINT RUN 149 TO 249 SER.#'d SETS
*PRIME: .75X TO 2X BASE HI
PRIME PRINT RUN 25 TO 49 SER.#'d SETS
1 Danny Granger/149 2.50 6.00
2 Dwyane Wade/249 5.00 12.00
3 Dwight Howard/249 2.50 6.00
4 Chris Bosh/249 3.00 8.00
5 Carmelo Anthony/249 4.00 10.00
7 Dirk Nowitzki/249 4.00 10.00
9 David West/249 2.50 6.00

2010-11 Prestige Inside the Numbers Signatures

STATED PRINT RUN 25 SER.#'d SETS
INSERTED IN PACKS OF SEASON UPDATE
1 Danny Granger* 6.00 15.00

2010-11 Prestige NBA Draft Class

COMPLETE SET (40) 40.00 80.00
STATED PRINT RUN 499 SER.#'d SETS
1 John Wall 6.00 15.00
2 Evan Turner 1.00 2.50
3 Derrick Favors 1.50 4.00
4 Wesley Johnson .75 2.00
5 DeMarcus Cousins 4.00 10.00
6 Ekpe Udoh .75 2.00
7 Greg Monroe 1.50 4.00
8 Al-Farouq Aminu 1.25 3.00
9 Gordon Hayward 2.00 5.00
10 Paul George 4.00 10.00
11 Cole Aldrich 1.00 2.50
12 Xavier Henry .75 2.00
13 Ed Davis .75 2.00
14 Patrick Patterson 1.00 2.50
15 Larry Sanders .75 2.00
16 Luke Babbitt 1.00 2.50
17 Kevin Seraphin .75 2.00
18 Eric Bledsoe 1.50 4.00
19 Avery Bradley 1.50 4.00
20 James Anderson .75 2.00
21 Craig Brackins .75 2.00
22 Elliot Williams .75 2.00
23 Trevor Booker 1.00 2.50
24 Damion James .75 2.00
25 Dominique Jones .75 2.00
26 Quincy Pondexter .75 2.00
27 Jordan Crawford 1.00 2.50
28 Greivis Vasquez 1.00 2.50
29 Daniel Orton .75 2.00
30 Lazar Hayward .75 2.00
31 Dexter Pittman .75 2.00
32 Da'Sean Butler 1.25 3.00
33 Luke Harangody .75 2.00
34 Willie Warren .75 2.00
35 Gani Lawal .75 2.00
36 Hassan Whiteside 2.50 6.00
37 Andy Rautins .75 2.00
38 Lance Stephenson 1.25 3.00
39 Devin Ebanks .75 2.00
40 Keith Gallon .75 2.00

2010-11 Prestige NBA Draft Class Draft Logo Signatures

STATED PRINT RUN 199 TO 499 SER.#'d SETS
LOGOMAN PRINT RUN 10 SER.#'d SETS
LOGOMAN UNPRICED DUE TO SCARCITY
1 John Wall/199 20.00 50.00
2 Evan Turner/199 3.00 8.00
3 Derrick Favors/199 5.00 12.00
4 Wesley Johnson/299 2.50 6.00
5 DeMarcus Cousins/299 12.00 30.00
6 Ekpe Udoh/299 2.50 6.00
7 Greg Monroe/299 5.00 12.00
8 Al-Farouq Aminu/299 4.00 10.00
9 Gordon Hayward/299 6.00 15.00
10 Paul George/299 50.00 100.00
11 Cole Aldrich/299 3.00 8.00
12 Xavier Henry/299 2.50 6.00
13 Ed Davis/299 2.50 6.00
14 Patrick Patterson/299 3.00 8.00
15 Larry Sanders/399 2.50 6.00
16 Luke Babbitt/399 3.00 8.00
17 Kevin Seraphin/399 2.50 6.00
18 Eric Bledsoe/399 5.00 12.00
19 Avery Bradley/396 5.00 12.00
20 James Anderson/399 2.50 6.00
21 Craig Brackins/399 2.50 6.00
22 Elliot Williams/399 2.50 6.00
23 Trevor Booker/399 3.00 8.00
24 Damion James/499 2.50 6.00
25 Dominique Jones/499 2.50 6.00
26 Quincy Pondexter/399 2.50 6.00
27 Jordan Crawford/499 3.00 8.00
28 Greivis Vasquez/499 3.00 8.00
29 Daniel Orton/499 2.50 6.00
30 Lazar Hayward/499 2.50 6.00
31 Dexter Pittman/499 2.50 6.00
32 Da'Sean Butler/499 4.00 10.00
33 Luke Harangody/499 2.50 6.00
34 Willie Warren/399 2.50 6.00
35 Gani Lawal/399 2.50 6.00
36 Hassan Whiteside/399 8.00 20.00
37 Andy Rautins/499 2.50 6.00
38 Lance Stephenson/499 12.00 30.00
39 Devin Ebanks/499 2.50 6.00
40 Keith Gallon/499 2.50 6.00

2010-11 Prestige NBA Draft Class Signatures

STATED PRINT RUN 263 TO 299 SER.#'d SETS
1 John Wall/283 25.00 60.00
2 Evan Turner/299 4.00 10.00
3 Derrick Favors/295 6.00 15.00
4 Wesley Johnson/299 3.00 8.00
5 DeMarcus Cousins/299 10.00 25.00
6 Ekpe Udoh/299 3.00 8.00
7 Greg Monroe/299 6.00 15.00
8 Al-Farouq Aminu/296 5.00 12.00
9 Gordon Hayward/299 8.00 20.00
10 Paul George/299 30.00 80.00
11 Cole Aldrich/299 4.00 10.00
12 Xavier Henry/292 3.00 8.00
13 Ed Davis/299 3.00 8.00
14 Patrick Patterson/299 4.00 10.00
15 Larry Sanders/299 3.00 8.00
16 Luke Babbitt/299 4.00 10.00
17 Kevin Seraphin/299 3.00 8.00
18 Eric Bledsoe/297 6.00 15.00
19 Avery Bradley/298 6.00 15.00
20 James Anderson/299 3.00 8.00
21 Craig Brackins/299 3.00 8.00
22 Elliot Williams/299 3.00 8.00
23 Trevor Booker/294 4.00 10.00
24 Damion James/299 3.00 8.00
25 Dominique Jones/299 3.00 8.00
26 Quincy Pondexter/299 3.00 8.00
27 Jordan Crawford/299 4.00 10.00
28 Greivis Vasquez/299 4.00 10.00
29 Daniel Orton/299 3.00 8.00
30 Lazar Hayward/299 3.00 8.00
31 Dexter Pittman/299 3.00 8.00
32 Da'Sean Butler/299 5.00 12.00
33 Luke Harangody/284 3.00 8.00
34 Willie Warren/292 3.00 8.00
35 Gani Lawal/299 3.00 8.00
36 Hassan Whiteside/263 10.00 25.00
37 Andy Rautins/299 3.00 8.00
38 Lance Stephenson/299 4.00 10.00
39 Devin Ebanks/299 3.00 8.00
40 Keith Gallon/299 3.00 8.00

2010-11 Prestige Old School

COMPLETE SET (20) 15.00 30.00
RANDOM INSERTS IN PACKS
1 Earl Monroe 1.25 3.00
2 George Gervin 1.25 3.00
3 Paul Westphal 1.25 3.00
4 Elgin Baylor 1.25 3.00
5 Doc Rivers 1.25 3.00
6 Gail Goodrich 1.00 2.50
7 Gary Payton 1.25 3.00
8 Isiah Thomas 1.25 3.00
9 Jeff Hornacek 1.00 2.50
10 Kelly Tripucka .75 2.00
11 Maurice Cheeks .75 2.00
12 Nate Archibald 1.00 2.50
13 Rick Barry 1.00 2.50
14 Sidney Moncrief .75 2.00
15 Campy Russell .75 2.00
16 Vlade Divac 1.25 3.00
17 Alonzo Mourning 1.50 4.00
18 Sean Elliott 1.25 3.00
19 Cedric Maxwell 1.25 3.00
20 Rolando Blackman 1.00 2.50

2010-11 Prestige Old School Materials

STATED PRINT RUN 25 TO 249 SER.#'d SETS
*PRIME: .75X TO 2X BASE HI
PRIME PRINT RUN 25 TO 49 SER.#'d SETS
1 Earl Monroe/25 6.00 15.00
7 Gary Payton/249 4.00 10.00
9 Jeff Hornacek/149 3.00 8.00
10 Kelly Tripucka/249 2.50 6.00
11 Maurice Cheeks/249 2.50 6.00
17 Alonzo Mourning/249 5.00 12.00
20 Rolando Blackman/249 3.00 8.00

2010-11 Prestige Old School Signatures

STATED PRINT RUN 49 SER.#'d SETS
ASTERISK CARDS INSERTED IN SEASON UPDATE
1 Earl Monroe* 8.00 20.00
2 George Gervin 8.00 20.00
3 Paul Westphal* 8.00 20.00
4 Elgin Baylor* 10.00 25.00
5 Doc Rivers* 10.00 25.00
6 Gail Goodrich 8.00 20.00
7 Gary Payton* 10.00 25.00
8 Isiah Thomas* 12.00 30.00
9 Jeff Hornacek 8.00 20.00
12 Nate Archibald 8.00 20.00
13 Rick Barry 8.00 20.00
14 Sidney Moncrief* 8.00 20.00
15 Campy Russell* 8.00 20.00
16 Vlade Divac* 15.00 40.00
18 Sean Elliott* 15.00 40.00
19 Cedric Maxwell* 8.00 20.00

2010-11 Prestige Playmakers

COMPLETE SET (20) 15.00 30.00
RANDOM INSERTS IN PACKS
1 Steve Nash .75 2.00
2 Chris Paul 1.00 2.50
3 Devin Harris .50 1.25
4 Jose Calderon .50 1.25
5 Stephen Curry 3.00 8.00
6 Tony Parker .75 2.00
7 Baron Davis .60 1.50
8 Andre Iguodala .60 1.50
9 Chris Duhon .50 1.25
10 Mike Conley Jr. .75 2.00
11 Raymond Felton .60 1.50
12 Jason Kidd .75 2.00
13 Brandon Jennings .50 1.25
14 Derrick Rose 1.00 2.50
15 Jameer Nelson .50 1.25
16 LeBron James 4.00 10.00
17 Andre Miller .60 1.50
18 Tyreke Evans .50 1.25
19 Darren Collison .60 1.50
20 Jonny Flynn .50 1.25

2010-11 Prestige Playmakers Materials

STATED PRINT RUN 50 TO 249 SER.#'d SETS
*PRIME: .75X TO 2X HI
PRIME PRINT RUN 5 TO 49 SER.#'d SETS
1 Steve Nash/249 3.00 8.00
2 Chris Paul/249 4.00 10.00
3 Devin Harris/249 2.00 5.00
4 Jose Calderon/249 2.00 5.00
5 Stephen Curry/249 12.00 30.00
6 Tony Parker/249 3.00 8.00
7 Baron Davis/249 2.50 6.00
8 Andre Iguodala/249 2.50 6.00
9 Chris Duhon/249 2.00 5.00
10 Mike Conley Jr./100 3.00 8.00
11 Raymond Felton/249 2.50 6.00
12 Jason Kidd/249 3.00 8.00
13 Brandon Jennings/249 2.00 5.00
14 Derrick Rose/149 4.00 10.00
15 Jameer Nelson/249 2.00 5.00
16 LeBron James/50 10.00 25.00
17 Andre Miller/249 2.50 6.00
18 Tyreke Evans/249 2.00 5.00
19 Darren Collison/249 2.50 6.00
20 Jonny Flynn/249 2.00 5.00

2010-11 Prestige Playmakers Signatures

STATED PRINT RUN 10 TO 49 SETS
INSERTED IN PACKS OF SEASON UPDATE
1 Steve Nash/25 30.00 80.00
3 Devin Harris/25 6.00 15.00
5 Stephen Curry/49 15.00 40.00
6 Tony Parker/42 15.00 40.00
13 Brandon Jennings/25 10.00 25.00

2010-11 Prestige Preferred Materials

COMPLETE SET (9) 20.00 40.00
STATED PRINT RUN 199 TO 249 SER.#'d SETS
MAT.SIG.PRINT RUN 10 TO 15 SETS
MAT.SIG.UNPRICED DUE TO SCARCITY
2 Allen Iverson/199 5.00 12.00
3 Jason Kidd/249 3.00 8.00
4 Devin Harris/249 2.00 5.00
5 Chris Bosh/249 3.00 8.00
6 Richard Hamilton/249 2.50 6.00
7 Amare Stoudemire/249 2.50 6.00
8 Russell Westbrook/99 8.00 20.00
9 Al Jefferson/249 2.50 6.00
10 Andrea Bargnani/249 2.50 6.00

2010-11 Prestige Preferred Materials Patches

*PATCH: .75X TO 2X BASE HI
STATED PRINT RUN 25 SER.#'d SETS
PATCH SIG.PRINT RUN 5 TO 10 SER.#'d SETS
PATCH SIG.UNPRICED DUE TO SCARCITY
1 Rajon Rondo/25 10.00 25.00

2010-11 Prestige Preferred Materials Signatures

STATED PRINT RUN 10 TO 15 SER.#'d SETS
SOME UNPRICED DUE TO SCARCITY

2010-11 Prestige Preferred Materials Signatures

4 Devin Harris/15 8.00 20.00
5 Chris Bosh/15 12.00 30.00
6 Richard Hamilton/15 8.00 20.00
7 Amare Stoudemire/15 15.00 40.00
10 Andrea Bargnani/15 8.00 20.00

2010-11 Prestige Preferred Signatures

STATED PRINT RUN 10 TO 40 SER.#'d SETS
SOME UNPRICED DUE TO SCARCITY
4 Devin Harris/25 6.00 15.00
7 Amare Stoudemire/40 8.00 20.00
10 Andrea Bargnani/35 6.00 15.00

2010-11 Prestige Prestigious Picks Green

COMPLETE SET (35) 40.00 80.00
STATED PRINT RUN 499 SER.#'d SETS
*BLACK: 1.25X TO 3X BASE HI
BLACK PRINT RUN 25 SER.#'d SETS
*GOLD: .6X TO 1.5X BASE HI
GOLD PRINT RUN 99 SER.#'d SETS
*ORANGE: .6X TO 1.5X BASE HI
ORANGE PRINT RUN 299 SER.#'d SETS
UNPRICED PLATINUM PRINT RUN 10 SETS
1 John Wall 6.00 15.00
2 Evan Turner 1.00 2.50
3 Derrick Favors 1.50 4.00
4 Wesley Johnson .75 2.00
5 DeMarcus Cousins 4.00 10.00
6 Ekpe Udoh .75 2.00
7 Greg Monroe 1.50 4.00
8 Al-Farouq Aminu 1.25 3.00
9 Gordon Hayward 2.00 5.00
10 Paul George 4.00 10.00
11 Cole Aldrich 1.00 2.50
12 Xavier Henry .75 2.00
13 Ed Davis .75 2.00
14 Patrick Patterson 1.00 2.50
15 Larry Sanders .75 2.00
16 Luke Babbitt 1.00 2.50
17 Eric Bledsoe 1.50 4.00
18 Avery Bradley 1.50 4.00
19 James Anderson .75 2.00
20 Craig Brackins .75 2.00
21 Elliot Williams .75 2.00
22 Trevor Booker 1.00 2.50
23 Damion James .75 2.00
24 Dominique Jones .75 2.00
25 Quincy Pondexter .75 2.00
26 Jordan Crawford 1.00 2.50
27 Greivis Vasquez 1.00 2.50
28 Daniel Orton .75 2.00
29 Lazar Hayward .75 2.00
30 Dexter Pittman .75 2.00
31 Da'Sean Butler 1.25 3.00
32 Luke Harangody .75 2.00
33 Willie Warren .75 2.00
34 Gani Lawal .75 2.00
35 Stanley Robinson .75 2.00

2010-11 Prestige Prestigious Picks Materials Green

STATED PRINT RUN 499 SER.#'d SETS
*BLACK: .6X TO 1.5X BASE HI
BLACK PRINT RUN 25 SER.#'d SETS
*GOLD: .5X TO 1.25X BASE HI
GOLD PRINT RUN 99 SER.#'d SETS
UNPRICED PLATINUM PRINT RUN 10 SETS
1 John Wall 10.00 25.00
2 Evan Turner 1.50 4.00
3 Derrick Favors 2.50 6.00
4 Wesley Johnson 1.25 3.00
5 DeMarcus Cousins 6.00 15.00
6 Ekpe Udoh 1.25 3.00
7 Greg Monroe 2.50 6.00
8 Al-Farouq Aminu 2.00 5.00
9 Gordon Hayward 3.00 8.00
10 Paul George 6.00 15.00
11 Cole Aldrich 1.50 4.00
12 Xavier Henry 1.25 3.00
13 Ed Davis 1.25 3.00
14 Patrick Patterson 1.50 4.00
15 Larry Sanders 1.25 3.00
16 Luke Babbitt 1.50 4.00
17 Eric Bledsoe 2.50 6.00
18 Avery Bradley 2.50 6.00
19 James Anderson 1.25 3.00
20 Craig Brackins 1.25 3.00
21 Elliot Williams 1.25 3.00
22 Trevor Booker 1.50 4.00
23 Damion James 1.25 3.00
24 Dominique Jones 1.25 3.00
25 Quincy Pondexter 1.25 3.00
26 Jordan Crawford 1.50 4.00
27 Greivis Vasquez 1.50 4.00
28 Daniel Orton 1.25 3.00
29 Lazar Hayward 1.25 3.00
30 Dexter Pittman 1.25 3.00
31 Da'Sean Butler 2.00 5.00
32 Luke Harangody 1.25 3.00
33 Willie Warren 1.25 3.00
34 Gani Lawal 1.25 3.00

2010-11 Prestige Prestigious Picks Signatures Black

STATED PRINT RUN 25 TO 249 SER.#'d SETS
1 John Wall/49 40.00 100.00
2 Evan Turner/25 12.00 30.00
3 Derrick Favors/249 5.00 12.00
4 Wesley Johnson/249 2.50 6.00
5 DeMarcus Cousins/249 12.00 30.00
6 Ekpe Udoh/249 2.50 6.00
8 Al-Farouq Aminu/249 4.00 10.00
11 Cole Aldrich/249 3.00 8.00
12 Xavier Henry/249 2.50 6.00
13 Ed Davis/249 2.50 6.00
14 Patrick Patterson/149 3.00 8.00
16 Luke Babbitt/249 3.00 8.00
17 Eric Bledsoe/249 5.00 12.00
18 Avery Bradley/249 5.00 12.00
19 James Anderson/249 2.50 6.00
24 Dominique Jones/25 8.00 20.00
25 Quincy Pondexter/249 2.50 6.00
26 Jordan Crawford/249 3.00 8.00
28 Daniel Orton/249 2.50 6.00
29 Lazar Hayward/249 2.50 6.00
30 Dexter Pittman/49 2.50 6.00
31 Da'Sean Butler/49 5.00 12.00
32 Luke Harangody/99 2.50 6.00
34 Gani Lawal/249 2.50 6.00

2010-11 Prestige Prestigious Pros Green

COMPLETE SET (65) 40.00 80.00
STATED PRINT RUN 499 SER.#'d SETS
*BLACK: 1.25X TO 3X BASE HI
BLACK PRINT RUN 25 SER.#'d SETS
*GOLD: .5X TO 1.25X BASE HI
GOLD PRINT RUN 99 SER.#'d SETS
*ORANGE: .6X TO 1.5X BASE HI
ORANGE PRINT RUN 299 SER.#'d SETS
UNPRICED PLATINUM PRINT RUN 10 SETS
1 Ray Allen 1.00 2.50
2 Glen Davis .60 1.50
3 Kevin Garnett 1.50 4.00
4 Yi Jianlian .75 2.00
5 Terrence Williams .60 1.50
6 Bill Walker .60 1.50
7 Chris Duhon .60 1.50
8 Elton Brand 1.00 2.50
9 Thaddeus Young .60 1.50
10 Hedo Turkoglu .75 2.00
11 Jose Calderon .60 1.50
12 Joakim Noah .75 2.00
13 Kirk Hinrich .75 2.00
14 Shaquille O'Neal 2.00 5.00
15 Zydrunas Ilgauskas .75 2.00
16 LeBron James 5.00 12.00
17 Richard Hamilton .75 2.00
18 Rodney Stuckey .75 2.00
19 Mike Dunleavy .60 1.50
20 Troy Murphy .60 1.50
21 Andrew Bogut .75 2.00
22 Michael Redd .75 2.00
23 Al Horford .75 2.00
24 Mike Bibby .75 2.00
25 D.J. Augustin .60 1.50
26 Tyson Chandler .75 2.00
27 Carlos Arroyo .60 1.50
28 Mario Chalmers .75 2.00
29 Dwyane Wade 1.50 4.00
30 Marcin Gortat .75 2.00
31 Mickael Pietrus .60 1.50
32 Randy Foye .60 1.50
33 Nick Young .75 2.00
34 Shawn Marion .75 2.00
35 Caron Butler .75 2.00
36 Shane Battier .75 2.00
37 Luis Scola .75 2.00
38 Marc Gasol 1.00 2.50
39 O.J. Mayo .60 1.50
40 David West .75 2.00
41 Peja Stojakovic 1.00 2.50
42 Richard Jefferson .75 2.00
43 Tim Duncan 1.50 4.00
44 Arron Afflalo .60 1.50
45 J.R. Smith .75 2.00
46 Kevin Love 1.00 2.50
47 Al Jefferson .75 2.00
48 Greg Oden .75 2.00
49 Rudy Fernandez .60 1.50
50 Russell Westbrook 2.50 6.00
51 Jeff Green .75 2.00
52 Andrei Kirilenko .75 2.00
53 Carlos Boozer .75 2.00
54 Andris Biedrins .60 1.50
55 Anthony Randolph .60 1.50
56 Baron Davis .75 2.00
57 Chris Kaman .75 2.00
58 Derek Fisher .75 2.00
59 Ron Artest 1.00 2.50
60 Kobe Bryant 4.00 10.00
61 Leandro Barbosa .75 2.00
62 Grant Hill 1.25 3.00
63 Channing Frye .75 2.00
64 Omri Casspi .60 1.50
65 Tyreke Evans .60 1.50

2010-11 Prestige Prestigious Pros Materials Black

*BLACK: .6X TO 1.5X BASE HI
STATED PRINT RUN 10 TO 25 SER.#'d SETS

2010-11 Prestige Prestigious Pros Materials Gold

*GOLD: .5X TO 1.25X BASE HI
STATED PRINT RUN 25 TO 99 SER.#'d SETS

2010-11 Prestige Prestigious Pros Materials Green

STATED PRINT RUN 50 TO 499 SER.#'d SETS
BLACK PRINT RUN 10 TO 25 SER.#'d SETS
GOLD PRINT RUN 25 TO 99 SER.#'d SETS
PLATINUM PRINT RUN 5 TO 25 SETS
1 Ray Allen/199 3.00 8.00
2 Glen Davis 2.00 5.00
3 Kevin Garnett 5.00 12.00
5 Terrence Williams 2.00 5.00
6 Bill Walker 2.00 5.00
7 Chris Duhon 2.00 5.00
8 Elton Brand 3.00 8.00
9 Thaddeus Young 2.00 5.00
10 Hedo Turkoglu 2.50 6.00
11 Jose Calderon 2.00 5.00
12 Joakim Noah 2.50 6.00
13 Kirk Hinrich 2.50 6.00
14 Shaquille O'Neal 6.00 15.00
15 Zydrunas Ilgauskas 2.50 6.00
16 LeBron James/50 10.00 25.00
17 Richard Hamilton 2.50 6.00
18 Rodney Stuckey 2.50 6.00
19 Mike Dunleavy 2.00 5.00
20 Troy Murphy 2.00 5.00
21 Andrew Bogut 2.50 6.00
22 Michael Redd 2.50 6.00
23 Al Horford 2.50 6.00
24 Mike Bibby 2.50 6.00
25 D.J. Augustin 2.00 5.00
27 Carlos Arroyo 2.00 5.00
28 Mario Chalmers 2.50 6.00
29 Dwyane Wade 5.00 12.00
30 Marcin Gortat 2.50 6.00
31 Mickael Pietrus 2.00 5.00
32 Randy Foye 2.00 5.00
33 Nick Young 2.50 6.00
34 Shawn Marion 2.50 6.00
35 Caron Butler 2.50 6.00
36 Shane Battier 2.50 6.00
37 Luis Scola 2.50 6.00
38 Marc Gasol 3.00 8.00
39 O.J. Mayo 2.00 5.00
40 David West 2.50 6.00
41 Peja Stojakovic 3.00 8.00
42 Richard Jefferson 2.50 6.00
43 Tim Duncan 5.00 12.00
44 Arron Afflalo 2.00 5.00
45 J.R. Smith 2.50 6.00
46 Kevin Love 3.00 8.00
47 Al Jefferson 2.50 6.00
48 Greg Oden 2.50 6.00
49 Rudy Fernandez 2.00 5.00
50 Russell Westbrook/99 8.00 20.00
51 Jeff Green 2.50 6.00
52 Andrei Kirilenko 2.50 6.00
53 Carlos Boozer 2.50 6.00
54 Andris Biedrins 2.00 5.00
55 Anthony Randolph 2.00 5.00
56 Baron Davis 2.50 6.00
57 Chris Kaman 2.50 6.00
58 Derek Fisher 2.50 6.00
59 Ron Artest 3.00 8.00
60 Kobe Bryant 8.00 20.00
61 Leandro Barbosa 2.50 6.00
62 Grant Hill 6.00 15.00
63 Channing Frye 2.50 6.00
64 Omri Casspi 2.00 5.00
65 Tyreke Evans 2.00 5.00

2010-11 Prestige Prestigious Pros Materials Patches Platinum

*PATCH: .75X TO 2X BASE HI
STATED PRINT RUN 5 TO 25 SER.#'d SETS

2010-11 Prestige Prestigious Pros Signatures Black

STATED PRINT RUN 24 TO 49 SER.#'d SETS
5 Terrence Williams/49 5.00 12.00
25 D.J. Augustin/49 5.00 12.00
32 Randy Foye/49 5.00 12.00
36 Shane Battier/49 5.00 12.00
46 Kevin Love/25 8.00 20.00
56 Baron Davis/49 6.00 15.00
57 Chris Kaman/24 5.00 12.00
59 Ron Artest/25 12.50 30.00
60 Kobe Bryant/49 100.00 200.00
64 Omri Casspi/49 5.00 12.00
65 Tyreke Evans/49 10.00 25.00

2010-11 Prestige Stars of the NBA

COMPLETE SET (14) 15.00 30.00
RANDOM INSERTS IN PACKS
1 Rajon Rondo 1.00 2.50
2 Joe Johnson .75 2.00
3 Amare Stoudemire .75 2.00
4 Tyreke Evans .60 1.50
5 Paul Pierce 1.00 2.50
6 Russell Westbrook 2.50 6.00
7 Kobe Bryant 4.00 10.00
8 Derrick Rose 1.25 3.00
9 Monta Ellis .75 2.00
10 David Lee .60 1.50
11 Caron Butler .75 2.00
12 LeBron James 5.00 12.00
13 Pau Gasol 1.00 2.50
14 Chauncey Billups 1.00 2.50
15 Kevin Martin .75 2.00

2010-11 Prestige Stars of the NBA Materials

STATED PRINT RUN 50 TO 249 SER.#'d SETS
2 Joe Johnson/249 2.50 6.00
3 Amare Stoudemire/249 2.50 6.00
4 Tyreke Evans/249 2.00 5.00
5 Paul Pierce/249 3.00 8.00
6 Russell Westbrook/99 8.00 20.00
7 Kobe Bryant/249 8.00 20.00
8 Derrick Rose/149 4.00 10.00
11 Caron Butler/249 2.50 6.00
12 LeBron James/50 8.00 20.00
13 Pau Gasol/249 3.00 8.00
14 Chauncey Billups/249 3.00 8.00
15 Kevin Martin/249 2.50 6.00

2010-11 Prestige Stars of the NBA Materials Prime

*PRIME: .75X TO 2X HI
STATED PRINT RUN 5 TO 49 SER.#'d SETS
SOME UNPRICED DUE TO SCARCITY

2010-11 Prestige Stars of the NBA Signatures

STATED PRINT RUN 10 TO 25 SER.#'d SETS
SOME UNPRICED DUE TO SCARCITY
3 Amare Stoudemire/25 15.00 40.00
4 Tyreke Evans/25 12.00 30.00
7 Kobe Bryant/25 100.00 200.00

2010-11 Prestige Stat Stars

COMPLETE SET (25) 20.00 40.00
RANDOM INSERTS IN PACKS
1 Kevin Durant 2.00 5.00
2 LeBron James 4.00 10.00
3 Carmelo Anthony 1.00 2.50
4 Kobe Bryant 3.00 8.00
5 Dwyane Wade 1.25 3.00
6 Monta Ellis .60 1.50
7 Dirk Nowitzki 1.00 2.50
8 Dwight Howard .60 1.50
9 Marcus Camby .50 1.25
10 Zach Randolph .60 1.50
11 David Lee .50 1.25
12 Pau Gasol .75 2.00
13 Carlos Boozer .60 1.50
14 Steve Nash .75 2.00
15 Chris Paul 1.00 2.50
16 Deron Williams .60 1.50
17 Rajon Rondo .75 2.00
18 Jason Kidd .75 2.00
19 Baron Davis .60 1.50
20 Andrew Bogut .60 1.50
21 Josh Smith .60 1.50
22 Brendan Haywood .50 1.25
23 Chris Andersen .60 1.50
24 Samuel Dalembert .50 1.25
25 Brook Lopez .60 1.50

2010-11 Prestige Stat Stars Materials

STATED PRINT RUN 50 TO 249 SER.#'d SETS
*PRIME: .75X TO 2X HI
PRIME PRINT RUN 10 TO 49 SER.#'d SETS
1 Kevin Durant/50 8.00 20.00
2 LeBron James/50 10.00 25.00
3 Carmelo Anthony/249 4.00 10.00
4 Kobe Bryant/249 8.00 20.00
5 Dwyane Wade/249 5.00 12.00
7 Dirk Nowitzki/249 4.00 10.00
8 Dwight Howard/249 2.50 6.00
9 Marcus Camby/249 2.00 5.00
12 Pau Gasol/249 3.00 8.00
13 Carlos Boozer/249 2.50 6.00
14 Steve Nash/249 3.00 8.00
15 Chris Paul/249 4.00 10.00
16 Deron Williams/249 2.50 6.00
18 Jason Kidd/249 3.00 8.00
19 Baron Davis/249 2.50 6.00
20 Andrew Bogut/249 2.50 6.00
21 Josh Smith/249 2.50 6.00
22 Brendan Haywood/249 2.00 5.00
23 Chris Andersen/249 2.50 6.00
24 Samuel Dalembert/249 2.00 5.00
25 Brook Lopez/249 2.50 6.00

2010-11 Prestige Stat Stars Signatures

STATED PRINT RUN 10 TO 25 SER.#'d SETS
SOME UNPRICED DUE TO SCARCITY
4 Kobe Bryant/25 100.00 200.00
16 Deron Williams/25 12.00 30.00
19 Baron Davis/25 10.00 25.00

2010-11 Prestige Super Sophs

COMPLETE SET (5) 4.00 10.00
RANDOM INSERTS IN PACKS
1 Tyreke Evans .60 1.50
2 Brandon Jennings .60 1.50
3 Stephen Curry 4.00 10.00
4 Darren Collison .75 2.00
5 DeJuan Blair .60 1.50

2010-11 Prestige Super Sophs Materials

STATED PRINT RUN 249 SER.#'d SETS
*PRIME: .75X TO 2X HI
PRIME PRINT RUN 5 TO 49 SER.#'d SETS
1 Tyreke Evans/249 2.00 5.00
2 Brandon Jennings/249 2.00 5.00
3 Stephen Curry/249 12.00 30.00
4 Darren Collison/249 2.50 6.00
5 DeJuan Blair/249 2.00 5.00

2010-11 Prestige Super Sophs Signatures

STATED PRINT RUN 25 SER.#'d SETS
INSERTED IN PACKS OF SEASON UPDATE
2 Brandon Jennings/25 10.00 25.00
3 Stephen Curry/25

2010-11 Prestige True Colors

RANDOM INSERTS IN PACKS
1 Kobe Bryant 3.00 8.00
2 Tim Duncan 1.25 3.00
3 Paul Pierce .75 2.00
4 Dirk Nowitzki 1.00 2.50
5 Tony Parker .75 2.00

2010-11 Prestige True Colors Materials

STATED PRINT RUN 249 SER.#'d SETS
*PRIME: .75X TO 2X HI
PRIME PRINT RUN 10 TO 49 SER.#'d SETS
1 Kobe Bryant/249 8.00 20.00
2 Tim Duncan/249 5.00 12.00
3 Paul Pierce/249 3.00 8.00
4 Dirk Nowitzki/249 4.00 10.00
5 Tony Parker/249 3.00 8.00

2010-11 Prestige True Colors Signatures

STATED PRINT RUN 25 SER.#'d SETS
ASTERISK CARDS INSERTED IN SEASON UPDATE
1 Kobe Bryant/25 100.00 200.00
5 Tony Parker/25* 15.00 40.00

2012-13 Prestige

ROOKIES INSERTED ONE PER PACK
UNPRICED BLACK PRINT RUN 10 SETS
1 LaMarcus Aldridge .40 1.00
2 Ray Allen .40 1.00
3 Al-Farouq Aminu .30 .75
4 JaVale McGee .30 .75
5 Ryan Anderson .30 .75
6 Carmelo Anthony .50 1.25
7 Trevor Ariza .25 .60
8 D.J. Augustin .25 .60
9 J.J. Barea .30 .75
10 Andrea Bargnani .30 .75
11 Nicolas Batum .30 .75
12 Michael Beasley .25 .60
13 Rodrigue Beaubois .25 .60
14 DeJuan Blair .25 .60
15 Andrew Bogut .30 .75
16 Trevor Booker .25 .60
17 Carlos Boozer .30 .75
18 Chris Bosh .40 1.00
19 Avery Bradley .30 .75
20 Elton Brand .40 1.00
21 Kobe Bryant 1.50 4.00
22 Andrew Bynum .25 .60
23 Jose Calderon .25 .60
24 Vince Carter .50 1.25
25 Mario Chalmers .30 .75
26 Tyson Chandler .30 .75
27 Darren Collison .30 .75
28 Mike Conley .30 .75
29 DeMarcus Cousins .40 1.00
30 Jamal Crawford .40 1.00
31 Jordan Crawford .25 .60
32 Stephen Curry 1.50 4.00
33 Ed Davis .25 .60
34 Glen Davis .25 .60
35 Boris Diaw .30 .75
36 Luol Deng .30 .75
37 DeMar DeRozan .40 1.00
38 Goran Dragic .30 .75
39 Jared Dudley .25 .60
40 Tim Duncan .60 1.50
41 Kevin Durant 1.00 2.50
42 Devin Ebanks .25 .60
43 Monta Ellis .30 .75
44 Tyreke Evans .25 .60
45 Raymond Felton .30 .75
46 Landry Fields .25 .60
47 Channing Frye .30 .75
48 Danilo Gallinari .25 .60
49 Kevin Garnett .60 1.50
50 Marc Gasol .40 1.00
51 Pau Gasol .40 1.00
52 Rudy Gay .40 1.00
53 Paul George .50 1.25
54 Taj Gibson .30 .75
55 Manu Ginobili .40 1.00
56 Drew Gooden .30 .75
57 Ben Gordon .30 .75
58 Eric Gordon .30 .75
59 Marcin Gortat .30 .75
60 Danny Granger .30 .75
61 Blake Griffin .40 1.00
62 Tyler Hansbrough .30 .75
63 James Harden .60 1.50
64 Al Harrington .30 .75
65 Gordon Hayward .40 1.00
66 Gerald Henderson .25 .60
67 Roy Hibbert .30 .75
68 George Hill .30 .75
69 Grant Hill .50 1.25
70 Jrue Holiday .40 1.00
71 Al Horford .30 .75
72 Dwight Howard .30 .75
73 Kris Humphries .25 .60
74 Serge Ibaka .30 .75
75 Andre Iguodala .30 .75
76 Ersan Ilyasova .25 .60
77 Jarrett Jack .30 .75
78 Stephen Jackson .30 .75
79 LeBron James 1.50 4.00
80 Antawn Jamison .30 .75
81 Al Jefferson .30 .75
82 Brandon Jennings .25 .60
83 Joe Johnson .30 .75
84 DeAndre Jordan .40 1.00
85 Chris Kaman .30 .75
86 Jason Kidd .40 1.00
87 Carl Landry .25 .60
88 Ty Lawson .25 .60
89 Courtney Lee .30 .75
90 David Lee .25 .60
91 Jeremy Lin .40 1.00
92 Brook Lopez .30 .75
93 Kevin Love .40 1.00
94 Kyle Lowry .30 .75
95 Corey Maggette .30 .75
96 Shawn Marion .30 .75
97 Kevin Martin .30 .75
98 Wesley Matthews .25 .60
99 O.J. Mayo .25 .60
100 Andre Miller .30 .75
101 Paul Millsap .40 1.00
102 Greg Monroe .30 .75
103 Steve Nash .40 1.00
104 Jameer Nelson .25 .60
105 Nene .30 .75
106 Steve Novak .25 .60
107 Joakim Noah .30 .75
108 Dirk Nowitzki .50 1.25
109 Emeka Okafor .30 .75
110 Tony Parker .40 1.00
111 Chris Paul .50 1.25
112 Tayshaun Prince .30 .75
113 Zach Randolph .30 .75
114 Jason Richardson .40 1.00
115 Luke Ridnour .30 .75
116 Nate Robinson .25 .60
117 Rajon Rondo .40 1.00
118 Derrick Rose .50 1.25
119 Ricky Rubio .40 1.00
120 Luis Scola .30 .75
121 Ramon Sessions .30 .75
122 J.R. Smith .30 .75
123 Josh Smith .30 .75
124 Marreese Speights .25 .60
125 Amare Stoudemire .30 .75
126 Rodney Stuckey .30 .75
127 Jeff Teague .30 .75
128 Jason Terry .30 .75
129 Jason Thompson .25 .60
130 Marcus Thornton .25 .60
131 Hedo Turkoglu .30 .75
132 Evan Turner .25 .60
133 Ekpe Udoh .25 .60
134 Anderson Varejao .25 .60
135 Dwyane Wade .60 1.50
136 John Wall .50 1.25
137 Gerald Wallace .30 .75
138 David West .30 .75
139 Delonte West .25 .60
140 Russell Westbrook 1.00 2.50
141 Deron Williams .30 .75
142 Louis Williams .30 .75
143 Mo Williams .30 .75
144 Metta World Peace .40 1.00
145 Dorell Wright .25 .60
146 Nick Young .30 .75
147 Richard Hamilton .30 .75
148 Thaddeus Young .25 .60
149 Kirk Hinrich .30 .75
150 Paul Pierce .40 1.00
151 Kyrie Irving RC 4.00 10.00
152 Derrick Williams RC .50 1.25
153 Brandon Knight RC .75 2.00
154 MarShon Brooks RC .60 1.50
155 Klay Thompson RC 3.00 8.00
156 Kemba Walker RC 1.50 4.00
157 Isaiah Thomas RC 1.25 3.00
158 Kenneth Faried RC .75 2.00
159 Iman Shumpert RC .75 2.00
160 Chandler Parsons RC .75 2.00
161 Tristan Thompson RC .75 2.00
162 Kawhi Leonard RC 4.00 10.00
163 Jimmer Fredette RC .50 1.25
164 Vernon Macklin RC .60 1.50
165 Markieff Morris RC .75 2.00
166 Alec Burks RC .75 2.00
167 Norris Cole RC .50 1.25
168 Ivan Johnson RC .50 1.25
169 Jeremy Pargo RC .50 1.25
170 Gustavo Ayon RC .50 1.25
171 Charles Jenkins RC .50 1.25
172 Nikola Vucevic RC .75 2.00
173 Donald Sloan RC .50 1.25
174 Bismack Biyombo RC .50 1.25
175 Tobias Harris RC .75 2.00
176 Jeremy Tyler RC .50 1.25
177 Jon Leuer RC .60 1.50
178 Jan Vesely RC .50 1.25
179 Chris Singleton RC .50 1.25
180 Enes Kanter RC .60 1.50
181 Jordan Williams RC .60 1.50
182 Jordan Hamilton RC .50 1.25
183 Josh Harrellson RC .50 1.25
184 Andrew Goudelock RC .50 1.25
185 Lavoy Allen RC .50 1.25
186 Lance Thomas RC .50 1.25
187 Cory Higgins RC .50 1.25
188 Nolan Smith RC .50 1.25
189 Marcus Morris RC .60 1.50
190 Trey Thompkins RC .50 1.25
191 Elliot Williams .25 .60
192 Terrel Harris RC .50 1.25
193 Shelvin Mack RC .60 1.50
194 JaJuan Johnson RC .50 1.25
195 Reggie Jackson RC .75 2.00
196 Greg Stiemsma RC .50 1.25
197 E'Twaun Moore RC .50 1.25
198 Josh Selby RC .50 1.25
199 Jimmy Butler RC 2.50 6.00
200 Cory Joseph RC .50 1.25
201 Anthony Davis RC 4.00 10.00
202 Austin Rivers RC .75 2.00
203 Jeremy Lamb RC .75 2.00
204 Michael Kidd-Gilchrist RC .75 2.00
205 Terrence Ross RC .75 2.00
206 Andre Drummond RC 1.25 3.00
207 Thomas Robinson RC .60 1.50
208 Kendall Marshall RC .50 1.25
209 Terrence Jones RC .60 1.50
210 Meyers Leonard RC .60 1.50
211 Harrison Barnes RC 1.25 3.00
212 Bradley Beal RC 1.25 3.00
213 Dion Waiters RC .75 2.00
214 Damian Lillard RC 3.00 8.00
215 John Henson RC .75 2.00
216 Moe Harkless RC .75 2.00
217 Royce White RC .50 1.25
218 Tyler Zeller RC .60 1.50
219 Andrew Nicholson RC .50 1.25
220 Evan Fournier RC .75 2.00
221 Jared Sullinger RC .60 1.50
222 Fab Melo RC .50 1.25
223 Tony Wroten RC .60 1.50
224 Perry Jones RC .50 1.25
225 Miles Plumlee RC .50 1.25
226 Jared Cunningham RC .50 1.25
227 John Jenkins RC .50 1.25
228 Marquis Teague RC .50 1.25
229 Festus Ezeli RC .60 1.50
230 Arnett Moultrie RC .50 1.25
231 Bernard James RC .50 1.25
232 Orlando Johnson RC .50 1.25
233 Jeff Taylor RC .50 1.25
234 Quincy Acy RC .50 1.25
235 Justin Harper RC .50 1.25
236 Jae Crowder RC .60 1.50
237 Draymond Green RC 2.50 6.00
238 Quincy Miller RC .50 1.25
239 Khris Middleton RC .75 2.00
240 Will Barton RC .60 1.50
241 Kim English RC .50 1.25
242 Darius Miller RC .50 1.25
243 Doron Lamb RC .50 1.25
244 Mike Scott RC .50 1.25
245 Justin Hamilton RC .60 1.50
246 Tornike Shengelia RC .50 1.25
247 Kyle O'Quinn RC .50 1.25
248 Robert Sacre RC .50 1.25
249 Tyshawn Taylor RC .50 1.25
250 Kris Joseph RC .50 1.25

2012-13 Prestige Bonus Shots Gold

*GOLD: 1X TO 2.5X BASE HI
STATED PRINT RUN 249 SER.#'d SETS

2012-13 Prestige All-Stars East

COMPLETE SET (14) 20.00 50.00
RANDOM INSERTS IN RETAIL PACKS
1 Dwyane Wade 2.50 6.00
2 Derrick Rose 2.00 5.00
3 Dwight Howard 1.25 3.00
4 LeBron James 6.00 15.00
5 Carmelo Anthony 2.00 5.00
6 Chris Bosh 1.50 4.00
7 Luol Deng 1.25 3.00
8 Roy Hibbert 1.25 3.00
9 Andre Iguodala 1.25 3.00
10 Rajon Rondo 1.50 4.00
11 Paul Pierce 1.50 4.00
12 Deron Williams 1.25 3.00
13 Tom Thibodeau 1.50 4.00
14 Team Photo 4.00 10.00

2012-13 Prestige All-Stars West

COMPLETE SET (14) 20.00 50.00
RANDOM INSERTS IN RETAIL PACKS
1 Kobe Bryant 6.00 15.00
2 Chris Paul 2.00 5.00
3 Andrew Bynum 1.00 2.50
4 Blake Griffin 1.50 4.00
5 Kevin Durant 4.00 10.00
6 LaMarcus Aldridge 1.50 4.00
7 Marc Gasol 1.50 4.00
8 Kevin Love 1.50 4.00
9 Steve Nash 1.50 4.00
10 Dirk Nowitzki 2.00 5.00
11 Tony Parker 1.50 4.00
12 Russell Westbrook 4.00 10.00
13 Scott Brooks 1.00 2.50
14 Team Photo 4.00 10.00

2012-13 Prestige Connections

COMPLETE SET (25) 12.00 30.00
RANDOM INSERTS IN PACKS
1 A.Davis/M.Kidd-Gilchrist 3.00 8.00
2 Marc.Morris/Mark.Morris .60 1.50
3 R.Westbrook/K.Love 1.50 4.00
4 J.Holiday/D.Collison .60 1.50
5 V.Carter/A.Jamison .75 2.00
6 J.Terry/M.Ginobili .60 1.50
7 L.Aldridge/K.Durant 1.50 4.00
8 J.Wall/R.Rondo .75 2.00
9 C.Paul/B.Griffin .75 2.00
10 D.DeRozan/T.Gibson .60 1.50
11 O.J. Mayo/N.Young .50 1.25
12 T.Parker/N.Batum .60 1.50
13 M.Gasol/P.Gasol .60 1.50
14 E.Turner/M.Conley .50 1.25
15 D.Rose/T.Evans .75 2.00
16 T.Chandler/D.Howard .50 1.25
17 S.Nash/D.Nowitzki .75 2.00
18 D.Fisher/K.Bryant 2.50 6.00
19 J.Noah/A.Horford .50 1.25
20 D.Wade/L.James 2.50 6.00
21 R.Gay/R.Allen .60 1.50
22 R.Hamilton/B.Gordon .50 1.25
23 S.Marion/A.Stoudemire .50 1.25
24 K.Malone/J.Stockton 1.00 2.50
25 M.Johnson/L.Bird 2.50 6.00

2012-13 Prestige Distinctive Ink

RANDOM INSERTS IN PACKS
1 Kevin Durant 150.00 300.00
2 Kobe Bryant 75.00 150.00
3 Gordon Hayward 6.00 15.00
4 O.J. Mayo EXCH 10.00 25.00
5 Danilo Gallinari 6.00 15.00
6 Marcin Gortat 10.00 25.00
7 Monta Ellis 10.00 25.00
8 Stephen Jackson 8.00 20.00
9 Andrew Bogut 8.00 20.00
10 Danny Granger EXCH 8.00 20.00

2012-13 Prestige Franchise Favorites

COMPLETE SET (25) 10.00 25.00
RANDOM INSERTS IN PACKS
1 Kevin Durant 1.50 4.00
2 Kevin Martin .50 1.25
3 Al Horford .50 1.25
4 Stephen Curry 2.50 6.00
5 Dirk Nowitzki .75 2.00
6 LeBron James 2.50 6.00
7 Paul Pierce .60 1.50
8 Deron Williams .50 1.25
9 Dwight Howard .50 1.25
10 Kobe Bryant 2.50 6.00
11 Blake Griffin .60 1.50
12 Ricky Rubio .60 1.50
13 Joakim Noah .50 1.25
14 Danny Granger .50 1.25
15 Manu Ginobili .60 1.50
16 Tayshaun Prince .50 1.25
17 Marc Gasol .60 1.50
18 Carmelo Anthony .75 2.00
19 Kyrie Irving 2.50 6.00
20 John Wall .75 2.00
21 DeMar DeRozan .60 1.50
22 Andre Iguodala .50 1.25
23 Tony Parker .60 1.50
24 Kevin Love .60 1.50
25 Ty Lawson .40 1.00

2012-13 Prestige Hardcourt Heroes

COMPLETE SET (25) 10.00 25.00
RANDOM INSERTS IN PACKS
1 Rajon Rondo .60 1.50
2 Carmelo Anthony .75 2.00
3 Kevin Durant 1.50 4.00
4 Kobe Bryant 2.50 6.00
5 LeBron James 2.50 6.00
6 Dirk Nowitzki .75 2.00
7 Kevin Love .60 1.50
8 Dwyane Wade 1.00 2.50
9 Derrick Rose .75 2.00
10 Dwight Howard .50 1.25
11 Tim Duncan 1.00 2.50
12 LaMarcus Aldridge .60 1.50
13 Blake Griffin .60 1.50
14 Steve Nash .60 1.50
15 Josh Smith .50 1.25
16 Andrew Bynum .40 1.00
17 Tyreke Evans .40 1.00
18 Russell Westbrook 1.50 4.00
19 Chris Paul .75 2.00
20 Brandon Jennings .40 1.00
21 John Wall .75 2.00
22 Kevin Garnett 1.00 2.50
23 Al Jefferson .50 1.25
24 Rudy Gay .60 1.50
25 Monta Ellis .50 1.25

2012-13 Prestige Inside the Numbers Materials

RANDOM INSERTS IN PACKS
1 Kevin Durant 6.00 15.00
2 Kobe Bryant 10.00 25.00
3 Tyson Chandler 2.00 5.00
4 Rajon Rondo 4.00 10.00
5 Ricky Rubio 8.00 20.00
6 Joe Johnson 2.00 5.00
7 Chris Paul 3.00 8.00
8 Steve Nash 2.50 6.00
9 Serge Ibaka 2.00 5.00
10 Dwight Howard 2.00 5.00
11 Mike Conley 2.00 5.00
12 Kevin Love 2.50 6.00
13 Andrew Bynum 1.50 4.00
14 DeAndre Jordan 2.50 6.00
15 Josh Smith 2.00 5.00
16 DeMarcus Cousins 2.50 6.00
17 Blake Griffin 2.50 6.00
18 LeBron James 10.00 25.00
19 Russell Westbrook 6.00 15.00
20 Carmelo Anthony 3.00 8.00
21 Derrick Rose 10.00 25.00
22 Dwyane Wade 4.00 10.00
23 Jose Calderon 1.50 4.00
24 Deron Williams 2.00 5.00
25 John Wall 3.00 8.00
26 Jason Kidd 2.50 6.00
27 Paul Pierce 2.50 6.00
28 LaMarcus Aldridge 2.50 6.00
29 Marcus Camby 2.00 5.00
30 Metta World Peace 2.50 6.00
31 David Lee 1.50 4.00
32 Kyrie Irving 12.00 30.00
33 Stephen Curry 10.00 25.00
34 Tony Parker 2.50 6.00
35 Luol Deng 2.00 5.00
36 Marc Gasol 2.50 6.00
37 Manu Ginobili 2.50 6.00
38 Ryan Anderson 2.00 5.00
39 Kevin Garnett 4.00 10.00
40 Andre Miller 2.00 5.00
41 James Harden 4.00 10.00
42 Antawn Jamison 2.00 5.00
43 Tim Duncan 4.00 10.00
44 Dirk Nowitzki 3.00 8.00
45 Jordan Crawford 1.50 4.00
46 Greg Monroe 2.00 5.00
47 Kenneth Faried 2.50 6.00
48 Baron Davis 2.00 5.00
49 Ty Lawson 1.50 4.00
50 Amare Stoudemire 2.00 5.00

2012-13 Prestige Inside the Numbers Materials Prime

*PRIME: 1.25X TO 3X BASE HI
STATED PRINT RUN 25 SER.#'d SETS
5 Ricky Rubio 40.00 100.00
21 Derrick Rose 10.00 25.00
23 Jose Calderon 10.00 25.00
26 Jason Kidd 10.00 25.00
27 Paul Pierce 12.00 30.00
37 Manu Ginobili 12.00 30.00
47 Kenneth Faried 40.00 100.00

2012-13 Prestige Old School Signatures

STATED PRINT RUN 25 TO 99 SETS
1 Rick Barry/49 15.00 40.00
2 Walt Bellamy/99 6.00 15.00
3 Tom Chambers/99 6.00 15.00
4 Bob Lanier/49 10.00 25.00
5 Spud Webb/99 EXCH 8.00 20.00
6 Kenny Anderson/99 6.00 15.00
7 Rod Strickland/99 6.00 15.00
8 Steve Smith/99 8.00 20.00
9 Vlade Divac/99 EXCH 6.00 15.00
10 Adrian Dantley/99 6.00 15.00
11 Buck Williams/99 6.00 15.00
12 Sidney Moncrief/99 6.00 15.00
13 Reggie Theus/99 6.00 15.00
14 Eddie Johnson/99 8.00 20.00
15 Kevin Willis/99 6.00 15.00
16 Larry Johnson/99 EXCH 6.00 15.00
17 Detlef Schrempf/99 10.00 25.00
18 Fat Lever/99 6.00 15.00
19 Kenny Walker/99 12.00 30.00
21 Dikembe Mutombo/49 10.00 25.00
22 Sam Perkins/99 EXCH 6.00 15.00
23 Cedric Ceballos/99 EXCH 12.00 30.00
24 Dan Majerle/99 8.00 20.00
25 Terry Porter/99 8.00 20.00
26 Jamal Mashburn/99 6.00 15.00
27 Danny Manning/49 8.00 20.00
28 Mitch Richmond/99 12.00 30.00
29 Glen Rice/49 10.00 25.00
30 Chris Mullin/99 8.00 20.00
31 Steve Kerr/49 12.00 30.00
32 Joe Dumars/49 8.00 20.00
33 John Stockton/25 100.00 175.00
34 Rex Chapman/99 8.00 20.00
35 Kurt Rambis/99 6.00 15.00
36 Robert Parish/49 8.00 20.00
37 Maurice Cheeks/99 6.00 15.00

2012-13 Prestige Playmakers

RANDOM INSERTS IN PACKS
1 Kobe Bryant 40.00 100.00
2 LeBron James 30.00 80.00
3 Kevin Durant 40.00 100.00
4 Blake Griffin 10.00 25.00
5 Derrick Rose 25.00 60.00
6 Kevin Love 10.00 25.00
7 Dwight Howard 8.00 20.00
8 Deron Williams 8.00 20.00
9 Dirk Nowitzki 12.00 30.00
10 Dwyane Wade 15.00 40.00
11 LaMarcus Aldridge 10.00 25.00
12 Tony Parker 10.00 25.00
13 David Lee 6.00 15.00
14 Russell Westbrook 25.00 60.00
15 Josh Smith 8.00 20.00
16 Rudy Gay 10.00 25.00
17 Brandon Jennings 6.00 15.00
18 Carmelo Anthony 12.00 30.00
19 Al Jefferson 8.00 20.00
20 Chris Paul 12.00 30.00
21 Rajon Rondo 10.00 25.00
22 John Wall 12.00 30.00
23 Joe Johnson 8.00 20.00
24 Paul Pierce 10.00 25.00
25 Danny Granger 8.00 20.00

2012-13 Prestige Prestigious Picks Signatures

RANDOM INSERTS IN PACKS
1 Kyrie Irving 40.00 100.00
2 Derrick Williams 2.50 6.00
3 Enes Kanter 3.00 8.00
4 Tristan Thompson 4.00 10.00
5 Jan Vesely 2.50 6.00
6 Bismack Biyombo 2.50 6.00
7 Brandon Knight 4.00 10.00
8 Kemba Walker 8.00 20.00
9 Jimmer Fredette 2.50 6.00
10 Klay Thompson 25.00 60.00
11 Alec Burks 4.00 10.00
12 Markieff Morris 4.00 10.00
13 Marcus Morris 3.00 8.00

14 Kawhi Leonard 60.00 150.00
15 Nikola Vucevic 4.00 10.00
16 Iman Shumpert 4.00 10.00
17 Chris Singleton 2.50 6.00
18 Tobias Harris 4.00 10.00
19 Nolan Smith 2.50 6.00
20 Kenneth Faried 4.00 10.00
21 Reggie Jackson 4.00 10.00
22 MarShon Brooks 3.00 8.00
23 Jordan Hamilton 2.50 6.00
24 JaJuan Johnson 2.50 6.00
25 Norris Cole 2.50 6.00
26 Cory Joseph 2.50 6.00
27 Jimmy Butler 20.00 50.00
28 Shelvin Mack 3.00 8.00
29 Tyler Honeycutt 2.50 6.00
30 Jordan Williams 3.00 8.00
31 Trey Thompkins 2.50 6.00
32 Chandler Parsons 4.00 10.00
33 Jeremy Tyler 2.50 6.00
34 Jon Leuer 3.00 8.00
35 Darius Morris 2.50 6.00
36 Malcolm Lee 2.50 6.00
37 Charles Jenkins 2.50 6.00
38 Josh Harrellson 2.50 6.00
39 Andrew Goudelock 2.50 6.00
40 Josh Selby 2.50 6.00
41 Isaiah Thomas 15.00 40.00
42 Lavoy Allen 2.50 6.00
43 E'Twaun Moore 2.50 6.00
44 Courtney Fortson 2.50 6.00
45 Anthony Davis 75.00 200.00
46 Michael Kidd-Gilchrist 4.00 10.00
47 Bradley Beal 12.00 30.00
48 Dion Waiters 4.00 10.00
49 Thomas Robinson 3.00 8.00
51 Harrison Barnes 8.00 20.00
52 Terrence Ross 4.00 10.00
53 Andre Drummond 6.00 15.00
54 Austin Rivers 4.00 10.00
55 Meyers Leonard 3.00 8.00
56 Jeremy Lamb 4.00 10.00
57 Kendall Marshall 2.50 6.00
58 John Henson 4.00 10.00
59 Moe Harkless 4.00 10.00
60 Royce White 2.50 6.00
61 Tyler Zeller 3.00 8.00
62 Terrence Jones 3.00 8.00
63 Andrew Nicholson 2.50 6.00
64 Evan Fournier 4.00 10.00
65 Jared Sullinger 3.00 8.00
66 Fab Melo 2.50 6.00
67 John Jenkins 2.50 6.00
68 Jared Cunningham 2.50 6.00
69 Tony Wroten 3.00 8.00
70 Miles Plumlee 2.50 6.00
71 Arnett Moultrie 2.50 6.00
72 Perry Jones 2.50 6.00
73 Marquis Teague 2.50 6.00
74 Festus Ezeli 3.00 8.00
75 Bernard James 2.50 6.00

2012-13 Prestige Prestigious Pros Signatures

RANDOM INSERTS IN PACKS
1 Derrick Rose
2 Kevin Durant EXCH
3 Kobe Bryant 75.00 150.00
4 Blake Griffin 30.00 80.00
5 Andrea Bargnani 4.00 10.00
6 Stephen Curry 100.00 200.00
7 Tyreke Evans EXCH 4.00 10.00
8 Raymond Felton EXCH 4.00 10.00
9 Jeff Teague 4.00 10.00
10 Devin Ebanks 4.00 10.00
11 George Hill 4.00 10.00
12 Mike Conley 4.00 10.00
13 Al Horford 4.00 10.00
14 Paul Millsap EXCH 6.00 15.00
15 Stephen Jackson 6.00 15.00
16 Ty Lawson
17 Marcus Thornton 4.00 10.00
18 Marcin Gortat EXCH 8.00 20.00
19 Brook Lopez 4.00 10.00
20 Jordan Crawford 4.00 10.00
21 Zach Randolph 6.00 15.00
23 Luol Deng 4.00 10.00
24 Kevin Love 15.00 40.00
25 Derek Fisher 5.00 12.00

2012-13 Prestige Stars of the NBA

COMPLETE SET (25) 8.00 20.00
RANDOM INSERTS IN PACKS
1 Russell Westbrook 1.50 4.00
2 Pau Gasol .60 1.50
3 Greg Monroe .50 1.25
4 DeMarcus Cousins .60 1.50
5 Chris Bosh .60 1.50
6 Joe Johnson .50 1.25
7 Elton Brand .60 1.50
8 Shawn Marion .50 1.25
9 LeBron James 2.50 6.00
10 Louis Williams .50 1.25
11 Tyson Chandler .50 1.25
12 David Lee .40 1.00
13 Rudy Gay .60 1.50
14 Dirk Nowitzki .75 2.00
15 James Harden 1.00 2.50
16 Kevin Martin .50 1.25
17 Marcus Thornton .40 1.00
18 Chris Paul .75 2.00
19 Brook Lopez .50 1.25
20 Andrew Bogut .50 1.25
21 Ty Lawson .40 1.00
22 Raymond Felton .50 1.25
23 Carlos Boozer .50 1.25
24 Ray Allen .60 1.50
25 Amare Stoudemire .50 1.25

2012-13 Prestige True Colors Materials

RANDOM INSERTS IN PACKS
1 Deron Williams 2.00 5.00
2 Jason Kidd 2.50 6.00
3 Andre Iguodala 2.00 5.00
4 Ricky Rubio 5.00 12.00
5 Danny Granger 2.00 5.00
6 Ryan Anderson 2.00 5.00
7 Paul Millsap 2.50 6.00
8 LeBron James 10.00 25.00
9 Kevin Garnett 4.00 10.00
10 Dwight Howard 2.00 5.00
11 Ty Lawson 1.50 4.00
12 Al Horford 2.00 5.00
13 Steve Nash 2.50 6.00
14 DeMarcus Cousins 2.50 6.00
15 Carmelo Anthony 3.00 8.00
16 Ray Allen 2.50 6.00
17 Tim Duncan 4.00 10.00
18 Eric Gordon 2.00 5.00
19 Kyrie Irving 10.00 25.00
20 Andrea Bargnani 2.00 5.00
21 Russell Westbrook 6.00 15.00
22 Brandon Jennings 1.50 4.00
23 Baron Davis 2.00 5.00
24 Luol Deng 2.00 5.00
25 Stephen Curry 6.00 15.00
26 Kevin Durant 6.00 15.00
27 Jrue Holiday 2.50 6.00
28 Andrew Bynum 1.50 4.00
29 Luis Scola 2.00 5.00
30 Brandon Knight 2.00 5.00
31 Klay Thompson 8.00 20.00
32 Tristan Thompson 2.00 5.00
33 Jordan Crawford 1.50 4.00
34 Drew Gooden 2.00 5.00
35 Danilo Gallinari 1.50 4.00
36 Michael Beasley 1.50 4.00
37 David West 2.00 5.00
38 Raymond Felton 2.00 5.00
39 Kemba Walker 4.00 10.00
40 Kawhi Leonard 5.00 12.00
41 Josh Smith 2.00 5.00
42 Anderson Varejao 1.50 4.00
43 O.J. Mayo 1.50 4.00
44 Mario Chalmers 2.00 5.00
45 Glen Davis 1.50 4.00
46 Mo Williams 2.00 5.00
47 Joakim Noah 2.00 5.00
48 Jared Dudley 2.00 5.00
49 Brook Lopez 2.00 5.00
50 Chris Kaman 2.00 5.00

2012-13 Prestige True Colors Materials Prime

*PRIME: 1.25X TO 3X BASE HI
STATED PRINT RUN 25 SER.#'d SETS
8 LeBron James 40.00 100.00
15 Carmelo Anthony 12.00 30.00
16 Ray Allen 10.00 25.00

2013-14 Prestige

COMPLETE SET (200) 20.00 50.00
1 Kendrick Perkins .25 .60
2 Austin Rivers .30 .75
3 Andre Iguodala .30 .75
4 Dwight Howard .30 .75
5 Paul George .50 1.25
6 Omer Asik .30 .75
7 Kyle Singler .25 .60
8 Anderson Varejao .25 .60
9 Kemba Walker .40 1.00
10 Nene .30 .75
11 Evan Turner .25 .60
12 Nicolas Batum .30 .75
13 Kevin Durant 1.00 2.50
14 Greivis Vasquez .30 .75
15 Chris Bosh .40 1.00
16 Tony Wroten .25 .60
17 Jeff Green .30 .75
18 David Lee .25 .60
19 JaVale McGee .30 .75
20 Derrick Favors .30 .75
21 Michael Kidd-Gilchrist .40 1.00
22 Jeff Teague .30 .75
23 Jason Richardson .40 1.00
24 Wesley Matthews .25 .60
25 Andre Miller .30 .75
26 Ryan Anderson .30 .75
27 Dwyane Wade .60 1.50
28 Andrew Bogut .30 .75
29 Eric Bledsoe .30 .75
30 Al Jefferson .30 .75
31 Kenneth Faried .30 .75
32 Tristan Thompson .30 .75
33 Ramon Sessions .30 .75
34 Josh Smith .30 .75
35 Jrue Holiday .40 1.00
36 DeMarcus Cousins .40 1.00
37 Reggie Jackson .30 .75
38 Terrence Ross .30 .75
39 LeBron James 1.50 4.00
40 Bradley Beal .40 1.00
41 Danny Granger .30 .75
42 Harrison Barnes .30 .75
43 Andrew Bynum .25 .60
44 Tyler Zeller .30 .75
45 Brook Lopez .30 .75
46 Louis Williams .30 .75
47 Thaddeus Young .25 .60
48 Isaiah Thomas .40 1.00
49 Russell Westbrook 1.00 2.50
50 Jonas Valanciunas .30 .75
51 Chauncey Billups .40 1.00
52 Metta World Peace .40 1.00
53 David West .30 .75
54 Kent Bazemore .30 .75
55 Ty Lawson .25 .60
56 Derrick Rose .50 1.25
57 Deron Williams .30 .75
58 Andrew Nicholson .25 .60
59 Goran Dragic .30 .75
60 Emeka Okafor .30 .75
61 Serge Ibaka .30 .75
62 Andrei Kirilenko .30 .75
63 Ray Allen .40 1.00
64 Pau Gasol .40 1.00
65 George Hill .30 .75
66 Klay Thompson .50 1.25
67 Wilson Chandler .30 .75
68 Jimmy Butler .40 1.00
69 Gerald Wallace .30 .75
70 Gordon Hayward .40 1.00
71 Danilo Gallinari .25 .60
72 Tyreke Evans .25 .60
73 Amar'e Stoudemire .30 .75
74 Kevin Love .40 1.00
75 Shane Battier .30 .75
76 Steve Blake .25 .60
77 DeAndre Jordan .40 1.00
78 Richard Jefferson .30 .75
79 Chris Kaman .30 .75
80 John Wall .50 1.25
81 Joe Johnson .30 .75
82 Derek Fisher .30 .75
83 Marcin Gortat .30 .75
84 Kawhi Leonard .60 1.50
85 Carmelo Anthony .50 1.25
86 Ricky Rubio .40 1.00
87 Udonis Haslem .25 .60
88 Steve Nash .40 1.00
89 Roy Hibbert .30 .75
90 Paul Millsap .40 1.00
91 Enes Kanter .25 .60
92 Kirk Hinrich .30 .75
93 Avery Bradley .30 .75
94 Jameer Nelson .25 .60
95 Marcus Morris .25 .60
96 Manu Ginobili .40 1.00
97 Ersan Ilyasova .25 .60
98 Nikola Pekovic .25 .60
99 Marc Gasol .40 1.00
100 DeMar DeRozan .40 1.00
101 Greg Oden .30 .75
102 Brandon Rush .25 .60
103 Dirk Nowitzki .50 1.25
104 Luol Deng .30 .75
105 Jared Sullinger .25 .60
106 Maurice Harkless .25 .60
107 Markieff Morris .25 .60
108 Tiago Splitter .30 .75
109 J.R. Smith .30 .75
110 Brandon Jennings .25 .60
111 Mike Conley .30 .75
112 Chris Paul .50 1.25
113 Chandler Parsons .30 .75
114 Andre Drummond .40 1.00
115 O.J. Mayo .25 .60
116 Nate Robinson .25 .60
117 Kevin Garnett .60 1.50
118 Nikola Vucevic .30 .75
119 Kendall Marshall .30 .75
120 Tim Duncan .60 1.50
121 Tyson Chandler .30 .75
122 J.J. Redick .40 1.00
123 Tayshaun Prince .30 .75
124 Larry Sanders .25 .60
125 James Harden .60 1.50
126 Brandon Knight .30 .75
127 Shawn Marion .30 .75
128 Taj Gibson .30 .75
129 Paul Pierce .40 1.00
130 Tobias Harris .30 .75
131 Damian Lillard .75 2.00
132 Tony Parker .40 1.00
133 Al-Farouq Aminu .30 .75
134 John Henson .30 .75
135 Tony Allen .25 .60
136 Jamal Crawford .40 1.00
137 Jeremy Lin .40 1.00
138 Rudy Gay .40 1.00
139 Vince Carter .50 1.25
140 Byron Mullens .25 .60
141 Rajon Rondo .40 1.00
142 Steve Novak .25 .60
143 LaMarcus Aldridge .40 1.00
144 Amir Johnson .25 .60
145 Anthony Davis .75 2.00
146 Monta Ellis .30 .75
147 J.J. Hickson .25 .60
148 Greg Monroe .30 .75
149 Thomas Robinson .25 .60
150 Zach Randolph .30 .75
151 Al Horford .30 .75
152 Kyrie Irving .75 2.00
153 Draymond Green .50 1.25
154 Kobe Bryant 1.50 4.00
155 Alexey Shved .25 .60
156 Jimmer Fredette .25 .60
157 Arron Afflalo .25 .60
158 Joakim Noah .30 .75
159 Stephen Curry 1.50 4.00
160 Blake Griffin .40 1.00
161 Anthony Bennett RC .60 1.50
162 Victor Oladipo RC 1.00 2.50
163 Otto Porter RC .75 2.00
164 Cody Zeller RC .60 1.50
165 Alex Len RC .60 1.50
166 Nerlens Noel RC 1.00 2.50
167 Ben McLemore RC .60 1.50
168 Kentavious Caldwell-Pope RC .75 2.00
169 Trey Burke RC .60 1.50
170 C.J. McCollum RC 1.25 3.00
171 M.Carter-Williams RC .75 2.00
172 Steven Adams RC .75 2.00
173 Kelly Olynyk RC .60 1.50
174 Shabazz Muhammad RC .60 1.50
175 G.Antetokounmpo RC 6.00 15.00
176 Carrick Felix RC .50 1.25
177 Dennis Schroeder RC .75 2.00
178 Shane Larkin RC .50 1.25
179 Sergey Karasev RC .50 1.25
180 Tony Snell RC .60 1.50
181 Gorgui Dieng RC .60 1.50
182 Mason Plumlee RC .75 2.00
183 Solomon Hill RC .50 1.25
184 Tim Hardaway Jr. RC .75 2.00
185 Reggie Bullock RC .60 1.50
186 Andre Roberson RC .50 1.25
187 Archie Goodwin RC .60 1.50
188 Ricky Ledo RC .50 1.25
189 Phil Pressey RC .50 1.25
190 Jamaal Franklin RC .50 1.25
191 Peyton Siva RC .50 1.25
192 Glen Rice Jr. RC .50 1.25
193 Ray McCallum RC .50 1.25
194 Elias Harris RC .60 1.50
195 C.J. Leslie RC .50 1.25
196 Tony Mitchell RC .50 1.25
197 Ryan Kelly RC .50 1.25
198 Ian Clark RC .60 1.50
199 Allen Crabbe RC .60 1.50
200 Erik Murphy RC .50 1.25

2013-14 Prestige Bonus Shots Blue

*BLUE 1-160: 1X TO 2.5X BASIC
*BLUE 161-200: 1X TO 2.5X BASIC

2013-14 Prestige Bonus Shots Red

*RED 1-160: 1X TO 2.5X BASIC
*RED 161-200: 1X TO 2.5X BASIC

2013-14 Prestige Bonus Shots Silver

*SILVER 1-160: 1X TO 2.5X BASIC
*SILVER 161-200: 1X TO 2.5X BASIC

2013-14 Prestige Bonus Shots Autographs

EXCHANGE DEADLINE 5/6/2015
1 Kenyon Martin 4.00 10.00
2 DeSagana Diop 3.00 8.00
3 Ricky Davis 4.00 10.00
4 Greg Stiemsma 3.00 8.00
5 P.J. Tucker 3.00 8.00
6 John Lucas III 3.00 8.00
7 Nicolas Batum 4.00 10.00
8 Marcus Thornton 3.00 8.00
9 Ish Smith 3.00 8.00
10 Kyle O'Quinn 3.00 8.00
11 DeAndre Liggins 3.00 8.00
12 Luc Longley 4.00 10.00
13 Marquis Daniels 3.00 8.00
14 C.J. Miles 4.00 10.00
15 Jon Leuer 3.00 8.00
16 Jeff Taylor 3.00 8.00
17 Keith Bogans 3.00 8.00
18 Khris Middleton 4.00 10.00
19 Earl Clark 3.00 8.00
20 Anthony Mason 4.00 10.00
21 Antoine Walker 4.00 10.00
22 Antonio Davis 3.00 8.00
23 Bonzi Wells 3.00 8.00
24 Brandon Rush 3.00 8.00
25 Bruce Bowen 3.00 8.00
26 Byron Scott 4.00 10.00
27 Cedric Maxwell 3.00 8.00
28 Dahntay Jones 3.00 8.00
29 Darrell Griffith 3.00 8.00
30 John Paxson 4.00 10.00
31 Kenny Anderson 4.00 10.00
32 Luc Mbah a Moute 3.00 8.00
33 Mark Price 5.00 12.00
34 Maurice Cheeks 3.00 8.00
35 Terry Porter 3.00 8.00
36 Walt Williams 3.00 8.00
37 Xavier McDaniel 3.00 8.00
38 Corey Brewer 3.00 8.00
39 Zydrunas Ilgauskas 4.00 10.00
40 Ekpe Udoh 3.00 8.00
41 Goran Dragic 4.00 10.00
42 James Johnson 3.00 8.00
43 Jan Vesely 3.00 8.00
44 Jerryd Bayless 4.00 10.00
45 Nikola Pekovic 3.00 8.00
46 Rolando Blackman 4.00 10.00
47 Danny Green 4.00 10.00
48 Gerald Henderson 3.00 8.00
49 Alvan Adams 3.00 8.00
50 Chris Mullin 5.00 12.00
51 Dan Majerle 4.00 10.00
52 Derrick Coleman 5.00 12.00
53 Chris Bosh 5.00 12.00
54 James Worthy 6.00 15.00
55 Shane Battier
56 Tyreke Evans 3.00 8.00
57 Joe Johnson
58 Walt Frazier 5.00 12.00
59 Artis Gilmore 4.00 10.00
60 Brent Barry 3.00 8.00
61 Nick Van Exel 5.00 12.00
62 Michael Finley 5.00 12.00
63 Harrison Barnes 10.00 25.00
64 Jordan Hill 3.00 8.00
65 Steve Francis 4.00 10.00
66 Robert Parish 5.00 12.00
67 Peja Stojakovic
68 Kelly Tripucka
69 Jason Terry 4.00 10.00
70 Danilo Gallinari 3.00 8.00
71 Charlie Villanueva 3.00 8.00
72 Brandon Knight 4.00 10.00
73 Bill Walton
74 Andrei Kirilenko
75 Devin Harris
76 Richard Jefferson 4.00 10.00
77 Steve Novak 3.00 8.00
78 Kris Humphries
79 John Henson 4.00 10.00
80 Anderson Varejao 3.00 8.00
81 Dikembe Mutombo 5.00 12.00
82 Eric Gordon 4.00 10.00
83 Carl Landry 3.00 8.00
84 Kyle Korver 4.00 10.00
85 Kendrick Perkins 3.00 8.00
86 B.J. Armstrong 5.00 12.00
87 Andrew Bogut
88 Marcin Gortat 4.00 10.00
89 Robert Horry 4.00 10.00
90 Kyrie Irving EXCH 30.00 80.00
91 Boris Diaw 4.00 10.00
92 Xavier Henry 3.00 8.00
93 Dave Cowens 3.00 8.00
94 Will Perdue 3.00 8.00
95 Kevin Durant 60.00 120.00
96 Spencer Haywood 3.00 8.00
97 Sleepy Floyd 3.00 8.00
98 Rodney Stuckey 4.00 10.00
99 Kobe Bryant 75.00 150.00
100 Michael Cage 3.00 8.00

2013-14 Prestige Bonus Shots Autographs Blue

*BLUE: .4X TO 1X BASE HI
PRINT RUNS B/WN 5-99 COPIES PER
EXCHANGE DEADLINE 5/6/2015

2013-14 Prestige Bonus Shots Autographs Red

*RED: X TO X BASE HI
PRINT RUNS B/WN 5-99 COPIES PER
NO PRICING DUE TO LACK OF M ARKET INFO
EXCHANGE DEADLINE 5/6/2015

2013-14 Prestige Bonus Shots Materials

1 Jared Sullinger 2.00 5.00
2 Paul Pierce 3.00 8.00
3 Brandon Bass 2.00 5.00
4 Larry Bird 10.00 25.00
5 Rajon Rondo 3.00 8.00
6 Reggie Lewis 8.00 20.00
7 Avery Bradley 2.50 6.00
8 Dee Brown 2.00 5.00
9 Zaza Pachulia 2.00 5.00
10 Jeff Teague 2.50 6.00
11 John Jenkins 2.00 5.00
12 Gerald Wallace 2.50 6.00
13 Nene 2.50 6.00
14 Brook Lopez 2.50 6.00
15 Michael Kidd-Gilchrist 3.00 8.00
16 Kemba Walker 3.00 8.00
17 Gerald Henderson 2.00 5.00
18 Tyrus Thomas 2.00 5.00
19 Richard Hamilton 2.50 6.00
20 Luol Deng 2.50 6.00
21 Joakim Noah 2.50 6.00
22 Tristan Thompson 2.50 6.00
23 Tyler Zeller 2.50 6.00
24 Dirk Nowitzki 4.00 10.00
25 Tim Duncan 5.00 12.00
26 Manu Ginobili 3.00 8.00
27 Tony Parker 3.00 8.00
28 Kenneth Faried 2.50 6.00
29 Jordan Hamilton 2.00 5.00
30 Alex English 2.50 6.00
31 Jalen Rose 3.00 8.00
32 Kyle Singler 2.00 5.00
33 Andre Drummond 3.00 8.00
34 Rick Mahorn 2.00 5.00
35 Isiah Thomas 3.00 8.00
36 Klay Thompson 4.00 10.00
37 Harrison Barnes 2.50 6.00
38 Carl Landry 2.00 5.00
39 Jeremy Lin 3.00 8.00
40 Carlos Delfino 2.00 5.00
41 Orlando Johnson 2.00 5.00
42 Danny Granger 2.50 6.00
43 David West 2.50 6.00
44 Danny Manning 2.50 6.00
45 Caron Butler 2.50 6.00
46 Lamar Odom 2.50 6.00
47 Eric Bledsoe 2.50 6.00
48 Chris Paul 4.00 10.00
49 Blake Griffin 3.00 8.00
50 Kobe Bryant 10.00 25.00
51 Pau Gasol 3.00 8.00
52 Metta World Peace 3.00 8.00
53 Zach Randolph 2.50 6.00
54 Marc Gasol 3.00 8.00
55 LeBron James 10.00 25.00
56 Joel Anthony 2.00 5.00
57 John Henson 2.50 6.00
58 Luc Mbah a Moute 2.00 5.00
59 Monta Ellis 2.50 6.00
60 Drew Gooden 2.50 6.00
61 Kevin Love 3.00 8.00
62 Austin Rivers 2.50 6.00
63 Anthony Davis 6.00 15.00
64 Darius Miller 2.00 5.00
65 Amar'e Stoudemire 2.50 6.00
66 Carmelo Anthony 4.00 10.00
67 Tyson Chandler 2.50 6.00
68 Pablo Prigioni 2.00 5.00
69 Andrew Nicholson 2.00 5.00
70 Hedo Turkoglu 2.50 6.00
71 Glen Davis 2.00 5.00
72 Jameer Nelson 2.00 5.00
73 Evan Turner 2.00 5.00
74 Jrue Holiday 3.00 8.00
75 Jason Richardson 3.00 8.00
76 Nick Young 3.00 8.00
77 Kendall Marshall 2.50 6.00
78 Channing Frye 2.50 6.00
79 Damian Lillard 6.00 15.00
80 LaMarcus Aldridge 3.00 8.00
81 Isaiah Thomas 3.00 8.00
82 Jonas Valanciunas 2.50 6.00
83 DeMar DeRozan 3.00 8.00
84 Al Jefferson 2.50 6.00
85 John Wall 4.00 10.00
86 Anthony Bennett 2.50 6.00
87 Victor Oladipo 4.00 10.00
88 Otto Porter 3.00 8.00
89 Nerlens Noel 4.00 10.00
90 Ben McLemore 2.50 6.00
91 Kentavious Caldwell-Pope 3.00 8.00
92 Trey Burke 2.50 6.00
93 Michael Carter-Williams 3.00 8.00
94 Steven Adams 3.00 8.00
95 Kelly Olynyk 2.50 6.00
96 Shabazz Muhammad 2.50 6.00
97 Tony Snell 2.50 6.00
98 Mason Plumlee 3.00 8.00
99 Tim Hardaway Jr. 3.00 8.00
100 Glen Rice Jr. 2.00 5.00

2013-14 Prestige Bonus Shots Materials Prime

*PRIME: .75X TO 2X BASE HI
PRINT RUNS B/WN 10-25 COPIES PER

2013-14 Prestige Connections

1 C.Bosh/A.Mourning .75 2.00
2 D.Lee/R.Barry .50 1.25
3 H.Olajuwon/D.Howard .75 2.00
4 B.King/C.Anthony .75 2.00
5 D.Robinson/T.Duncan 1.00 2.50
6 D.Williams/P.Pierce .60 1.50
7 B.Walton/B.Griffin .60 1.50
8 B.Lanier/G.Monroe .50 1.25
9 R.Westbrook/G.Payton 1.50 4.00
10 K.Johnson/G.Dragic .60 1.50
11 J.Harden/C.Drexler 1.00 2.50
12 D.Rose/S.Pippen 1.25 3.00
13 B.Lopez/D.Dawkins .50 1.25
14 D.Nowitzki/M.Aguirre .75 2.00
15 K.Faried/A.English .50 1.25
16 K.Bryant/M.Johnson 2.50 6.00
17 R.Rondo/N.Archibald .60 1.50
18 A.Horford/D.Wilkins .75 2.00
19 R.Parish/J.Sullinger .60 1.50
20 M.Ginobili/S.Elliott .60 1.50

2013-14 Prestige Distinctive Ink

PRINT RUNS B/WN 15-99 COPIES PER
2013-14 Prestige Bonus Shots Autographs
1 Derrick Williams/50 4.00 10.00
2 Kendall Marshall/99 5.00 12.00
3 Karl Malone/25 30.00 80.00
4 Chris Bosh/15 12.00 30.00
5 Tiago Splitter/99 5.00 12.00
6 Larry Bird/50 50.00 100.00
7 Magic Johnson/50 30.00 60.00
8 David Robinson/15
9 Dwight Howard/15 20.00 50.00
10 Raymond Felton/15
11 Kobe Bryant/99 60.00 150.00
12 David West/99 5.00 12.00
13 Antawn Jamison/99 5.00 12.00
14 Chris Andersen/25
15 Kevin Durant/75 40.00 100.00
16 Rajon Rondo/25 15.00 40.00
17 Chris Kaman/25
18 Kevin Love/15
19 Kyrie Irving/50 EXCH 30.00 80.00
20 Norris Cole/99 4.00 10.00
21 Tyson Chandler/50 5.00 12.00
22 Jeff Teague/99 5.00 12.00
23 Nicolas Batum/99 5.00 12.00
24 Jarrett Jack/99 5.00 12.00
25 J.J. Redick/99 6.00 15.00
26 Jeff Green/99 5.00 12.00
27 Scottie Pippen/50 50.00 120.00
28 Kareem Abdul-Jabbar/25
29 Gary Payton/50 15.00 40.00
30 Tyreke Evans/25 4.00 10.00
31 Zach Randolph/15
32 Steve Francis/50 5.00 12.00
33 Isiah Thomas/50 6.00 15.00
34 Rick Fox/50 12.00 30.00
35 Grant Hill/15 25.00 60.00
36 Nate Archibald/25 5.00 12.00
37 J.R. Smith/99 5.00 12.00
38 Horace Grant/99 10.00 25.00
39 David Thompson/99 5.00 12.00
40 Tom Chambers/99 4.00 10.00

2013-14 Prestige Franchise Favorites

1 Al Horford .50 1.25
2 Rajon Rondo .60 1.50
3 Brook Lopez .50 1.25
4 Kemba Walker .60 1.50
5 Derrick Rose .75 2.00
6 Kyrie Irving 1.25 3.00
7 Dirk Nowitzki .75 2.00
8 Kenneth Faried .50 1.25
9 Greg Monroe .50 1.25
10 Stephen Curry 2.50 6.00
11 James Harden 1.00 2.50
12 Roy Hibbert .50 1.25
13 Chris Paul .75 2.00
14 Kobe Bryant 2.50 6.00
15 Marc Gasol .60 1.50
16 LeBron James 2.50 6.00
17 Larry Sanders .40 1.00
18 Kevin Love .60 1.50
19 Anthony Davis 1.25 3.00
20 Carmelo Anthony .75 2.00
21 Kevin Durant 1.50 4.00
22 Jameer Nelson .40 1.00
23 Evan Turner .40 1.00
24 Marcin Gortat .50 1.25
25 LaMarcus Aldridge .60 1.50
26 Isaiah Thomas .60 1.50
27 Tim Duncan 1.00 2.50
28 DeMar DeRozan .60 1.50
29 Gordon Hayward .60 1.50
30 John Wall .75 2.00

2013-14 Prestige Hardcourt Heroes

1 Carmelo Anthony .75 2.00
2 Kobe Bryant 2.50 6.00
3 Kevin Durant 1.50 4.00
4 Monta Ellis .50 1.25
5 Rudy Gay .60 1.50
6 Blake Griffin .60 1.50
7 James Harden 1.00 2.50
8 LeBron James 2.50 6.00
9 Al Jefferson .50 1.25
10 David Lee .40 1.00
11 Damian Lillard 1.25 3.00
12 Dirk Nowitzki .75 2.00
13 Tony Parker .60 1.50
14 Chris Paul .75 2.00
15 Paul Pierce .60 1.50
16 Zach Randolph .50 1.25
17 Rajon Rondo .60 1.50
18 Dwyane Wade 1.00 2.50
19 Russell Westbrook 1.50 4.00
20 Deron Williams .50 1.25

2013-14 Prestige NBA Materials

1 Jrue Holiday 3.00 8.00
2 LeBron James 10.00 25.00
3 Deron Williams 2.50 6.00
4 Russell Westbrook 8.00 20.00
5 Al Horford 2.50 6.00
6 Kyrie Irving 6.00 15.00
7 Paul Pierce 3.00 8.00
8 Dirk Nowitzki 4.00 10.00
9 Ben Gordon 2.50 6.00
10 Devin Harris 2.00 5.00
11 Tim Duncan 5.00 12.00
12 Shane Battier 2.50 6.00
13 Monta Ellis 2.50 6.00
14 Terrence Ross 2.50 6.00
15 Anthony Davis 6.00 15.00
16 Austin Rivers 2.50 6.00
17 Thabo Sefolosha 2.00 5.00
18 Thaddeus Young 2.00 5.00
19 DeMar DeRozan 3.00 8.00
20 Thomas Robinson 2.00 5.00
21 Manu Ginobili 3.00 8.00
22 Drew Gooden 2.50 6.00
23 Kendall Marshall 2.50 6.00
24 Blake Griffin 3.00 8.00
25 Al Jefferson 2.50 6.00

2013-14 Prestige NBA Materials Prime

*PRIME: .75X TO 2X BASE HI
PRINT RUNS B/WN 12-25 COPIES PER
NO PRICING ON QTY 12

2013-14 Prestige Old School Signatures

PRINT RUNS B/WN 10-99 COPIES PER
NO PRICING ON QTY 10
EXCHANGE DEADLINE 5/6/2015
1 Allan Houston/49 10.00 25.00
2 World B. Free/50 5.00 12.00
3 Spencer Haywood/99 4.00 10.00
4 Elgin Baylor/10
5 Wes Unseld/25 6.00 15.00
6 Scottie Pippen/50 75.00 150.00
7 Connie Hawkins/99 6.00 15.00
8 Michael Cooper/99 5.00 12.00
9 A.C. Green/99 6.00 15.00
10 Larry Nance/99 5.00 12.00
11 Dominique Wilkins/75 10.00 25.00
12 Bob Dandridge/99 4.00 10.00
13 George Gervin/50 6.00 15.00
14 Jo Jo White/99 5.00 12.00
15 Bailey Howell/99 6.00 15.00
16 Slick Watts/99 4.00 10.00
17 George McGinnis/99 4.00 10.00
18 Lenny Wilkens/50 6.00 15.00
19 Hal Greer/50 5.00 12.00
20 Darryl Dawkins/99 4.00 10.00
21 Len Elmore/99 4.00 10.00
22 Nate Thurmond/25 5.00 12.00
23 Rory Sparrow/99 4.00 10.00
24 Herb Williams/99 4.00 10.00
25 Otis Birdsong/99 5.00 12.00
26 Gail Goodrich/50 5.00 12.00
27 Bill Sharman/10
28 Artis Gilmore/25
29 Campy Russell/99 4.00 10.00
30 Gus Williams/99 4.00 10.00
31 Satch Sanders/99 6.00 15.00
32 Bill Laimbeer/99 5.00 12.00
33 John Lucas/99 6.00 15.00
34 Dean Meminger/99 8.00 20.00
35 Reggie Theus/99 5.00 12.00
36 Sidney Moncrief/99 4.00 10.00
37 Elvin Hayes/10
38 James Worthy/25 10.00 25.00
39 John Havlicek/10
40 Hot Rod Williams/99 4.00 10.00
41 Bill Walton/99 6.00 15.00
42 Ralph Sampson/25
43 Rick Barry/10
44 Dave Stallworth/99 6.00 15.00
45 Bob Lanier/25
46 Buck Williams/99 4.00 10.00
47 Henry Bibby/99 4.00 10.00
48 Paul Westphal/99 6.00 15.00
49 Mel Daniels/99 6.00 15.00
50 Bobby Jones/99 5.00 12.00
51 Mark Aguirre/99 5.00 12.00
52 Dolph Schayes/10
53 Willis Reed/25
54 Sam Jones/25 10.00 25.00
55 Dennis Rodman/25 12.00 30.00
56 Harry Gallatin/99 6.00 15.00
57 Calvin Murphy/10
58 Danny Manning/10
59 Hakeem Olajuwon/75 15.00 40.00
60 Bernard King/99 5.00 12.00

2013-14 Prestige Playmakers

1 James Harden 6.00 15.00
2 Stephen Curry 15.00 40.00
3 Kobe Bryant 20.00 50.00
4 Carmelo Anthony 5.00 12.00
5 Tim Duncan 6.00 15.00
6 Kevin Durant 10.00 25.00
7 Blake Griffin 4.00 10.00
8 Dwight Howard 3.00 8.00
9 LaMarcus Aldridge 4.00 10.00
10 Kyrie Irving 8.00 20.00
11 LeBron James 20.00 50.00
12 Damian Lillard 8.00 20.00
13 Kevin Love 4.00 10.00
14 Steve Nash 4.00 10.00
15 Tony Parker 4.00 10.00
16 Chris Paul 5.00 12.00
17 Rajon Rondo 4.00 10.00
18 Derrick Rose 5.00 12.00
19 Dwyane Wade 6.00 15.00
20 Russell Westbrook 10.00 25.00
21 Ricky Rubio 4.00 10.00
22 John Wall 5.00 12.00
23 Blake Griffin 4.00 10.00
24 Dirk Nowitzki 5.00 12.00
25 Paul George 5.00 12.00

2013-14 Prestige Prestigious Picks

1 Anthony Bennett 2.00 5.00
2 Victor Oladipo 3.00 8.00
3 Otto Porter 2.50 6.00
4 Cody Zeller 2.00 5.00
5 Alex Len 2.00 5.00
6 Nerlens Noel 3.00 8.00
7 Ben McLemore 2.00 5.00
8 Kentavious Caldwell-Pope 2.50 6.00
9 Trey Burke 2.00 5.00
10 C.J. McCollum 4.00 10.00
11 Michael Carter-Williams 2.50 6.00
12 Steven Adams 2.50 6.00
13 Kelly Olynyk 2.00 5.00
14 Shabazz Muhammad 2.00 5.00
15 Shane Larkin 1.50 4.00
16 Tim Hardaway Jr. 2.50 6.00
17 Glen Rice Jr. 1.50 4.00
18 Mason Plumlee 2.50 6.00
19 Dennis Schroeder 2.50 6.00
20 Sergey Karasev 1.50 4.00
21 Reggie Bullock 2.00 5.00
22 Tony Mitchell 1.50 4.00
23 Archie Goodwin 2.00 5.00
24 Rudy Gobert 3.00 8.00
25 Tony Snell 2.00 5.00

2013-14 Prestige Prestigious Pioneers

1 Kareem Abdul-Jabbar 1.00 2.50
2 Al Attles .60 1.50
3 Elgin Baylor .60 1.50
4 Wilt Chamberlain 1.25 3.00
5 Bob Cousy 1.00 2.50
6 Walt Frazier .60 1.50
7 Artis Gilmore .50 1.25
8 John Havlicek .75 2.00
9 Clyde Lovellette .60 1.50
10 Pete Maravich 1.00 2.50
11 George Mikan 1.25 3.00
12 Vern Mikkelsen .60 1.50
13 Bob Pettit .60 1.50
14 Willis Reed .60 1.50
15 Oscar Robertson .75 2.00
16 Bill Russell 1.00 2.50
17 Dolph Schayes .60 1.50
18 Wes Unseld
19 Jerry West .75 2.00
20 Lenny Wilkens .60 1.50

2013-14 Prestige Prestigious Posts

COMPLETE SET (10) 6.00 15.00
1 Andrew Bogut 1.00 2.50
2 Chris Bosh 1.25 3.00
3 Tyson Chandler 1.00 2.50
4 DeMarcus Cousins 1.25 3.00
5 Tim Duncan 2.00 5.00
6 Marc Gasol 1.25 3.00
7 Roy Hibbert 1.00 2.50
8 Dwight Howard 1.00 2.50
9 Brook Lopez 1.00 2.50
10 Joakim Noah 1.00 2.50

2013-14 Prestige Prestigious Premieres Signatures

EXCHANGE DEADLINE 5/6/2015
1 Nate Wolters 4.00 10.00
2 Erik Murphy 3.00 8.00
3 C.J. Leslie 3.00 8.00
4 Kelly Olynyk 4.00 10.00
5 Anthony Bennett 4.00 10.00
6 Trey Burke 4.00 10.00
7 Jeff Withey 3.00 8.00
8 Phil Pressey 3.00 8.00
9 Peyton Siva 3.00 8.00
10 Shabazz Muhammad 4.00 10.00
11 Victor Oladipo 6.00 15.00
12 C.J. McCollum 15.00 40.00
13 Grant Jerrett 3.00 8.00
14 Archie Goodwin 4.00 10.00
15 Mason Plumlee 5.00 12.00
16 Giannis Antetokounmpo 75.00 200.00
17 Otto Porter 5.00 12.00
18 Michael Carter-Williams 5.00 12.00
19 Jamaal Franklin 3.00 8.00
20 Elias Harris 4.00 10.00
21 Solomon Hill 3.00 8.00
22 Carrick Felix 3.00 8.00
23 Cody Zeller 4.00 10.00
24 Steven Adams 5.00 12.00
25 Ian Clark 4.00 10.00
26 Allen Crabbe 4.00 10.00
27 Tim Hardaway Jr. 5.00 12.00
28 Dennis Schroeder 5.00 12.00
29 Alex Len 4.00 10.00
30 Ben McLemore 4.00 10.00
31 Tony Snell 4.00 10.00
32 Glen Rice Jr. 3.00 8.00
33 Reggie Bullock 4.00 10.00
34 Shane Larkin 3.00 8.00
35 Nerlens Noel 6.00 15.00
36 Kentavious Caldwell-Pope 5.00 12.00
37 Ryan Kelly 3.00 8.00
38 Tony Mitchell 3.00 8.00
39 Andre Roberson 3.00 8.00
40 Isaiah Canaan 3.00 8.00

2013-14 Prestige Prestigious Pros

1 LaMarcus Aldridge 2.00 5.00
2 Carmelo Anthony 2.50 6.00
3 Bradley Beal 2.00 5.00
4 Carlos Boozer 1.50 4.00
5 Chris Bosh 2.00 5.00
6 Kobe Bryant 10.00 25.00
7 Mike Conley 1.50 4.00
8 DeMarcus Cousins 2.00 5.00
9 Jamal Crawford 2.00 5.00
10 Anthony Davis 4.00 10.00
11 Luol Deng 1.50 4.00
12 DeMar DeRozan 2.00 5.00
13 Goran Dragic 1.50 4.00
14 Kevin Durant 5.00 12.00
15 Monta Ellis 1.50 4.00
16 Tyreke Evans 1.25 3.00
17 Marc Gasol 2.00 5.00
18 Rudy Gay 2.00 5.00
19 Paul George 2.50 6.00
20 Manu Ginobili 2.00 5.00
21 Ben Gordon 1.50 4.00
22 Blake Griffin 2.00 5.00
23 Jameer Nelson 1.25 3.00
24 Gordon Hayward 2.00 5.00
25 Jrue Holiday 2.00 5.00
26 Dwight Howard 1.50 4.00
27 Serge Ibaka 1.50 4.00
28 Kyrie Irving 4.00 10.00
29 LeBron James 10.00 25.00
30 Al Jefferson 1.50 4.00
31 Brandon Jennings 1.25 3.00
32 Joe Johnson 1.50 4.00
33 Ty Lawson 1.25 3.00
34 David Lee 1.25 3.00
35 Damian Lillard 4.00 10.00
36 Brook Lopez 1.50 4.00
37 Joakim Noah 1.50 4.00
38 Chandler Parsons 1.50 4.00
39 Chris Paul 2.50 6.00
40 Paul Pierce 2.00 5.00

41 Zach Randolph 1.50 4.00
42 J.R. Smith 1.50 4.00
43 Josh Smith 1.50 4.00
44 Klay Thompson 2.50 6.00
45 Dwyane Wade 3.00 8.00
46 Kemba Walker 2.00 5.00
47 John Wall 2.50 6.00
48 David West 1.50 4.00
49 Russell Westbrook 5.00 12.00
50 Deron Williams 1.50 4.00

2013-14 Prestige Stars of the NBA Signatures

PRINT RUNS B/WN 10-99 COPIES PER
NO PRICING ON QTY 10
EXCHANGE DEADLINE 5/6/2015
1 Dwight Howard/25 30.00 60.00
2 J.R. Smith/25 5.00 12.00
3 Tyson Chandler/25 5.00 12.00
4 Kevin Love/25 20.00 50.00
5 Eric Gordon/25
6 Josh Smith/25
7 Deron Williams/25 5.00 12.00
8 Dwyane Wade/25 90.00 150.00
9 Tyreke Evans/25 4.00 10.00
10 Rajon Rondo/25 15.00 40.00
11 Connie Hawkins/99 6.00 15.00
12 Chris Bosh/15
13 O.J. Mayo/25
14 Metta World Peace/25
15 Norris Cole/99 6.00 15.00
16 Harrison Barnes/50 5.00 12.00
17 Dan Issel/99 5.00 12.00
18 Rolando Blackman/99 5.00 12.00
19 Raymond Felton/15
20 Ryan Anderson/99 5.00 12.00
21 J.J. Redick/25 30.00 60.00
22 Goran Dragic/25
23 Kobe Bryant/50 90.00 150.00
24 Kevin Durant/50 40.00 100.00
25 Kyrie Irving/50 50.00 120.00
26 David West/99 5.00 12.00
27 Danny Green/99 5.00 12.00
28 Joe Johnson/10
29 Antawn Jamison/99 5.00 12.00
30 Nick Young/99 6.00 15.00
31 Marcin Gortat/25 12.00 30.00
32 LaMarcus Aldridge/10
33 Vince Carter/10
34 DeMarcus Cousins/10
35 Ty Lawson/25 4.00 10.00
36 John Lucas/99 6.00 15.00
37 MarShon Brooks/49 6.00 15.00
38 Andre Drummond/25 20.00 50.00
39 Isaiah Thomas/99 12.00 30.00
40 Bradley Beal/25 12.00 30.00
41 Kawhi Leonard/25 30.00 80.00
42 Reggie Theus/99 5.00 12.00
43 Blake Griffin/50 40.00 80.00
44 Nikola Vucevic/99 5.00 12.00
45 Jeff Green/25 5.00 12.00
46 Danilo Gallinari/25 4.00 10.00
47 Andrea Bargnani/25
48 Bill Laimbeer/99 5.00 12.00
49 Andre Miller/25 5.00 12.00
50 Kendrick Perkins/25
51 Kevin Martin/10
52 Jason Terry/10
53 Mark Aguirre/99 5.00 12.00
54 Anderson Varejao/25
55 Taj Gibson/99 5.00 12.00
56 Joakim Noah/10
57 Steve Nash/25 15.00 40.00
58 James Harden/25 EXCH 30.00 80.00
59 Monta Ellis/25 EXCH 5.00 12.00
60 David Robinson/25

2013-14 Prestige True Colors Materials

1 Joe Johnson 2.50 6.00
2 Tristan Thompson 2.50 6.00
3 Kyle Singler 2.00 5.00
4 David West 2.50 6.00
5 Buck Williams 2.00 5.00
6 Russell Westbrook 8.00 20.00
7 Jeff Teague 2.50 6.00
8 Gerald Wallace 2.50 6.00
9 Kyrie Irving 6.00 15.00
10 Grant Hill 4.00 10.00
11 Danny Granger 2.50 6.00
12 Steve Novak 2.00 5.00
13 Kevin Durant 6.00 15.00
14 Kendall Marshall 2.50 6.00
15 DeShawn Stevenson 2.00 5.00
16 Dirk Nowitzki 4.00 10.00
17 Andre Drummond 3.00 8.00
18 Ronny Turiaf 2.00 5.00
19 Karl Malone 4.00 10.00
20 Nick Anderson 3.00 8.00
21 Monta Ellis 2.50 6.00
22 Fat Lever 2.50 6.00
23 Jae Crowder 2.50 6.00
24 Klay Thompson 4.00 10.00
25 Ron Harper 3.00 8.00
26 Patrick Ewing 4.00 10.00
27 Glen Davis 2.00 5.00
28 Jason Richardson 3.00 8.00
29 Danny Ainge 3.00 8.00
30 Kenneth Faried 2.50 6.00
31 Harrison Barnes 2.50 6.00
32 Eric Bledsoe 2.50 6.00
33 Raymond Felton 2.50 6.00
34 Arron Afflalo 2.00 5.00
35 Ersan Ilyasova 2.00 5.00
36 Larry Bird 8.00 20.00
37 Andre Miller 2.50 6.00
38 Draymond Green 4.00 10.00
39 DeAndre Jordan 3.00 8.00
40 J.R. Smith 2.50 6.00
41 Marcin Gortat 2.50 6.00
42 Luc Mbah a Moute 2.00 5.00
43 Michael Kidd-Gilchrist 3.00 8.00
44 Alex English 2.50 6.00
45 Carl Landry 2.00 5.00
46 Danny Manning 2.50 6.00
47 Carmelo Anthony 4.00 10.00
48 Goran Dragic 2.50 6.00
49 D.J. Augustin 2.00 5.00
50 Taj Gibson 2.50 6.00
51 Andre Iguodala 2.50 6.00
52 John Lucas 3.00 8.00
53 Chris Paul 4.00 10.00
54 Amar'e Stoudemire 2.50 6.00
55 Michael Beasley 2.00 5.00
56 Thaddeus Young 2.00 5.00
57 Carlos Boozer 2.50 6.00
58 Rodney Stuckey 2.50 6.00
59 Carlos Delfino 2.00 5.00
60 Blake Griffin 3.00 8.00
61 Lance Thomas 2.00 5.00
62 Omer Asik 2.50 6.00
63 Evan Turner 2.00 5.00
64 Zydrunas Ilgauskas 2.50 6.00
65 Bob Lanier 2.50 6.00
66 Brent Barry 2.00 5.00
67 Shaquille O'Neal 6.00 15.00
68 Austin Rivers 2.50 6.00
69 Zaza Pachulia 2.00 5.00
70 Lavoy Allen 2.00 5.00
71 Tyler Zeller 2.50 6.00
72 Rick Mahorn 2.00 5.00
73 Roy Hibbert 2.50 6.00
74 Cazzie Russell 2.50 6.00
75 Anthony Davis 6.00 15.00

2013-14 Prestige True Colors Materials Prime

*PRIME: .75X TO 2X BASE HI
PRINT RUNS B/WN 5-25 COPIES PER
NO PRICING ON QTY 10 OR LESS

2014-15 Prestige

COMPLETE SET (200) 40.00 80.00
1 Ricky Rubio .40 1.00
2 Jamal Crawford .40 1.00
3 Tiago Splitter .30 .75
4 Al Horford .30 .75
5 Jordan Hill .25 .60
6 Ben McLemore .25 .60
7 Kyle Lowry .30 .75
8 Corey Brewer .25 .60
9 Nerlens Noel .30 .75
10 Enes Kanter .25 .60
11 Robin Lopez .25 .60
12 Jameer Nelson .25 .60
13 Tim Duncan .60 1.50
14 Al Jefferson .30 .75
15 Jose Calderon .25 .60
16 Blake Griffin .40 1.00
17 Kyrie Irving .75 2.00
18 Damian Lillard .75 2.00
19 Nick Collison .30 .75
20 Eric Bledsoe .30 .75
21 Roy Hibbert .30 .75
22 James Harden .60 1.50
23 Tim Hardaway Jr. .25 .60
24 Alex Len .25 .60
25 Josh Smith .30 .75
26 Bradley Beal .40 1.00
27 LaMarcus Aldridge .40 1.00
28 Danilo Gallinari .25 .60
29 Nick Young .30 .75
30 Eric Gordon .30 .75
31 Rudy Gay .40 1.00
32 Jared Sullinger .25 .60
33 Al-Farouq Aminu .25 .60
34 Tobias Harris .30 .75
35 Jrue Holiday .30 .75
36 Brandon Bass .25 .60
37 Lance Stephenson .30 .75
38 David Lee .25 .60
39 Nicolas Batum .30 .75
40 Ersan Ilyasova .25 .60
41 Russell Westbrook 1.00 2.50
42 Jason Thompson .25 .60
43 Tony Parker .40 1.00
44 Amar'e Stoudemire .40 1.00
45 Kawhi Leonard .60 1.50
46 Brandon Jennings .25 .60
47 LeBron James 1.50 4.00
48 David West .30 .75
49 Nikola Pekovic .25 .60
50 George Hill .30 .75
51 Ryan Anderson .25 .60
52 Jason Terry .30 .75
53 Tony Snell .25 .60
54 Amir Johnson .25 .60
55 Kelly Olynyk .25 .60
56 Brandon Knight .30 .75
57 Luol Deng .30 .75
58 DeAndre Jordan .40 1.00
59 Nikola Vucevic .30 .75
60 Gerald Green .30 .75
61 Serge Ibaka .30 .75
62 JaVale McGee .30 .75
63 Tony Wroten .25 .60
64 Anderson Varejao .25 .60
65 Kemba Walker .40 1.00
66 Brook Lopez .30 .75
67 Manu Ginobili .40 1.00
68 DeMar DeRozan .40 1.00
69 Norris Cole .25 .60
70 Gerald Henderson .25 .60
71 Shawn Marion .30 .75
72 Jeff Green .30 .75
73 Trey Burke .25 .60
74 Andre Drummond .40 1.00
75 Kenneth Faried .30 .75
76 C.J. McCollum .40 1.00
77 Marc Gasol .40 1.00
78 O.J. Mayo .25 .60
79 Dennis Schroder .30 .75
80 Giannis Antetokounmpo .75 2.00
81 Stephen Curry 1.50 4.00
82 Jeff Teague .30 .75
83 Tristan Thompson .30 .75
84 Andre Iguodala .30 .75
85 Kentavious Caldwell-Pope .25 .60
86 Carlos Boozer .30 .75
87 Marcin Gortat .30 .75
88 Deron Williams .30 .75
89 Otto Porter .30 .75
90 Goran Dragic .30 .75
91 Steve Nash .40 1.00
92 Jeremy Lin .40 1.00
93 Ty Lawson .25 .60
94 Andrew Bogut .30 .75
95 Kevin Durant 1.00 2.50
96 Carmelo Anthony .50 1.25
97 Marco Belinelli .25 .60
98 Derrick Favors .30 .75
99 Pau Gasol .40 1.00
100 Gordon Hayward .40 1.00
101 Steven Adams .30 .75
102 Jimmy Butler .40 1.00
103 Tyreke Evans .25 .60
104 Anthony Bennett .25 .60
105 Kevin Garnett .60 1.50
106 Caron Butler .30 .75
107 Mason Plumlee .30 .75
108 Derrick Rose .50 1.25
109 Paul George .50 1.25
110 Taj Gibson .30 .75
111 Gorgui Dieng .25 .60
112 Joakim Noah .30 .75
113 Tyson Chandler .30 .75
114 Anthony Davis .75 2.00
115 Kevin Love .40 1.00
116 Chandler Parsons .30 .75
117 Matt Barnes .25 .60
118 Dion Waiters .30 .75
119 Paul Millsap .40 1.00
120 Greg Monroe .30 .75
121 Tayshaun Prince .30 .75
122 Jodie Meeks .30 .75
123 Victor Oladipo .30 .75
124 Archie Goodwin .25 .60
125 Klay Thompson .50 1.25
126 Channing Frye .30 .75
127 Michael Carter-Williams .25 .60
128 Dirk Nowitzki .50 1.25
129 Paul Pierce .40 1.00
130 Harrison Barnes .30 .75
131 Terrence Jones .30 .75
132 Joe Johnson .30 .75
133 Vince Carter .50 1.25
134 Arron Afflalo .25 .60
135 Kevin Martin .30 .75
136 Chris Bosh .40 1.00
137 Mike Conley .30 .75
138 Dwight Howard .30 .75
139 Rajon Rondo .40 1.00
140 Isaiah Thomas .40 1.00
141 Terrence Ross .30 .75
142 John Wall .50 1.25
143 Wesley Matthews .25 .60
144 Avery Bradley .30 .75
145 Kobe Bryant 1.50 4.00
146 Chris Paul .50 1.25
147 Monta Ellis .30 .75
148 DeMarcus Cousins .40 1.00
149 Randy Foye .25 .60
150 J.J. Redick .40 1.00
151 Thaddeus Young .25 .60
152 Jonas Valanciunas .30 .75
153 Zach Randolph .30 .75
154 Michael Kidd-Gilchrist .30 .75
155 Kyle Korver .30 .75
156 Cody Zeller .25 .60
157 Nene .30 .75
158 Dwyane Wade .60 1.50
159 J.R. Smith .30 .75
160 Michael Beasley .25 .60
161 Andrew Wiggins RC 2.50 6.00
162 Jabari Parker RC 1.25 3.00
163 Joel Embiid RC 2.50 6.00
164 Aaron Gordon RC 1.25 3.00
165 Dante Exum RC .75 2.00
166 Marcus Smart RC .75 2.00
167 Julius Randle RC 1.25 3.00
168 Nik Stauskas RC .60 1.50
169 Noah Vonleh RC .60 1.50
170 Elfrid Payton RC .75 2.00
171 Doug McDermott RC .75 2.00
172 Zach LaVine RC 1.25 3.00
173 T.J. Warren RC .75 2.00
174 Adreian Payne RC .60 1.50
175 James Young RC .50 1.25
176 Tyler Ennis RC .50 1.25
177 Gary Harris RC .75 2.00
178 Mitch McGary RC .50 1.25
179 Jordan Adams RC .50 1.25
180 Rodney Hood RC .75 2.00
181 Shabazz Napier RC .60 1.50
182 P.J. Hairston RC .50 1.25
183 C.J. Wilcox RC .50 1.25
184 Josh Huestis RC .50 1.25
185 Kyle Anderson RC .75 2.00
186 Damien Inglis RC .50 1.25
187 K.J. McDaniels RC .60 1.50
188 Joe Harris RC .50 1.25
189 Cleanthony Early RC .50 1.25
190 Jarnell Stokes RC .50 1.25
191 Johnny O'Bryant RC .50 1.25
192 Erick Green RC .50 1.25
193 Spencer Dinwiddie RC .60 1.50
194 Jerami Grant RC .50 1.25
195 Jordan Clarkson RC .75 2.00
196 Russ Smith RC .50 1.25
197 Thanasis Antetokounmpo RC .50 1.25
198 Jordan McRae RC .50 1.25
199 Xavier Thames RC .50 1.25
200 Cory Jefferson RC .50 1.25

2014-15 Prestige Bonus Shots Blue

*VETS: 1.2X TO 3X BASE HI
*ROOKIES: 1.5X TO 4X BASE HI
RANDOM INSERTS IN PACKS
STATED PRINT RUN 99 SER.#'d SETS

2014-15 Prestige Bonus Shots Orange Die Cuts

*VETS: 2.5X TO 6X BASE HI
*ROOKIES: 3X TO 8X BASE HI
RANDOM INSERTS IN PACKS
STATED PRINT RUN 25 SER.#'d SETS

2014-15 Prestige Bonus Shots Purple

*VETS: 1.5X TO 4X BASE HI
*ROOKIES: 2X TO 5X BASE HI
RANDOM INSERTS IN PACKS
STATED PRINT RUN 49 SER.#'d SETS

2014-15 Prestige Bonus Shots Red

*VETS: 1X TO 2.5X BASE HI
*ROOKIES: 1.2X TO 3X BASE HI
RANDOM INSERTS IN PACKS
STATED PRINT RUN 199 SER.#'d SETS

2014-15 Prestige Bonus Shots Autographs

RANDOM INSERTS IN PACKS
PRINT RUNS B/WN 10-99 COPIES PER
NO PRICING ON QTY 10
*BLUE/25: .5X TO 1.2X BASE HI
*RED/49: .4X TO 1X BASE HI
*RED/25: .5X TO 1.2X BASE HI
1 Glen Rice Jr./49
3 Gorgui Dieng/49 4.00 10.00
9 Terry Porter/49 4.00 10.00
11 Arnett Moultrie/99
13 Tim Hardaway Jr./49 4.00 10.00
19 Thaddeus Young/49
21 Khris Middleton/49 5.00 12.00
23 Rudy Gobert/99 6.00 15.00
29 Horace Grant/49 6.00 15.00
31 Tony Snell/49 4.00 10.00
33 Luigi Datome/99 4.00 10.00
39 Isaiah Thomas/49 12.00 30.00
41 Reggie Bullock/99
43 Carrick Felix/99
49 Rick Mahorn/49 4.00 10.00
51 Nemanja Nedovic/99
53 Solomon Hill/99 4.00 10.00
59 Amir Johnson/49
61 Gal Mekel/49 4.00 10.00
63 Isaiah Canaan/99 5.00 12.00
67 Marvin Williams/49 5.00 12.00
69 Spencer Hawes/49
71 P.J. Tucker/99 4.00 10.00
73 Ray McCallum/49
77 Brandan Wright/49 4.00 10.00
79 Sean Elliott/49 6.00 15.00
81 Hollis Thompson/99
83 Ryan Kelly/49 4.00 10.00
87 Bismack Biyombo/49
89 Mark Aguirre/49 5.00 12.00
91 Dennis Schroder/49 5.00 12.00
93 Phil Pressey/99 4.00 10.00
97 Steven Adams/49 5.00 12.00
99 Greg Buckner/49

2014-15 Prestige Connections

RANDOM INSERTS IN PACKS
1 D.Williams/J.Kidd .60 1.50
2 D.Robinson/T.Duncan 1.00 2.50
3 B.Cousy/R.Rondo 1.00 2.50
4 A.Iverson/M.Carter-Williams .75 2.00
5 B.Walton/L.Aldridge .60 1.50
6 T.Lawson/F.Lever .40 1.00
7 A.Gilmore/J.Noah .50 1.25
8 M.Price/K.Irving 1.25 3.00
9 A.Drummond/B.Laimbeer .60 1.50
10 B.Griffin/B.McAdoo .60 1.50
11 R.Barry/K.Thompson .75 2.00
12 E.Baylor/K.Bryant 2.50 6.00
13 A.Mourning/A.Davis 1.25 3.00
14 M.Malone/D.Howard .60 1.50
15 T.Porter/D.Lillard 1.25 3.00
16 L.James/O.Robertson 2.50 6.00
17 D.Wade/J.Dumars 1.00 2.50
18 C.Andersen/D.Rodman 1.25 3.00
19 K.Durant/G.Gervin 1.50 4.00
20 L.Bird/C.Anthony 1.50 4.00

2014-15 Prestige Franchise Favorites

RANDOM INSERTS IN PACKS
1 Al Horford .50 1.25
2 Rajon Rondo .60 1.50
3 Deron Williams .50 1.25
4 Gerald Henderson .40 1.00
5 Derrick Rose .75 2.00
6 LeBron James 2.50 6.00
7 Dirk Nowitzki .75 2.00
8 Ty Lawson .40 1.00
9 Greg Monroe .50 1.25
10 Stephen Curry 2.50 6.00
11 James Harden 1.00 2.50
12 Paul George .75 2.00
13 Blake Griffin .60 1.50
14 Kobe Bryant 2.50 6.00
15 Mike Conley .50 1.25
16 Dwyane Wade 1.00 2.50
17 Ersan Ilyasova .40 1.00
18 Ricky Rubio .60 1.50
19 Anthony Davis 1.25 3.00
20 Carmelo Anthony .75 2.00
21 Kevin Durant 1.50 4.00
22 Nikola Vucevic .50 1.25
23 Michael Carter-Williams .40 1.00
24 Goran Dragic .50 1.25
25 LaMarcus Aldridge .60 1.50
26 DeMarcus Cousins .60 1.50
27 Tim Duncan 1.00 2.50
28 DeMar DeRozan .60 1.50
29 Gordon Hayward .60 1.50
30 John Wall .75 2.00

2014-15 Prestige Hardcourt Heroes

RANDOM INSERTS IN PACKS
1 Joe Johnson .50 1.25
2 Chris Bosh .60 1.50
3 Dirk Nowitzki .75 2.00
4 Damian Lillard 1.25 3.00
5 Vince Carter .75 2.00
6 LeBron James 2.50 6.00
7 Russell Westbrook 1.50 4.00
8 Stephen Curry 2.50 6.00
9 Kevin Durant 1.50 4.00
10 Jeff Green .50 1.25
11 Kobe Bryant 2.50 6.00
12 Carmelo Anthony .75 2.00
13 Anthony Davis 1.25 3.00
14 Chris Paul .75 2.00
15 Dwyane Wade 1.00 2.50
16 Kevin Love .60 1.50
17 Manu Ginobili .60 1.50
18 Klay Thompson .75 2.00
19 Tim Duncan 1.00 2.50
20 Kyrie Irving 1.25 3.00

2014-15 Prestige Mystery Rookies

RANDOM INSERTS IN PACKS
1 Andrew Wiggins 10.00 25.00
2 Dante Exum 3.00 8.00
3 Marcus Smart 3.00 8.00
4 T.J. Warren 3.00 8.00
5 James Young 2.00 5.00
6 Jabari Parker 5.00 12.00
7 Jerami Grant 2.00 5.00
8 Nick Johnson 2.00 5.00
9 Glenn Robinson III 2.00 5.00
10 Joe Harris 2.00 5.00
11 Jordan Adams 2.00 5.00
12 Aaron Gordon 5.00 12.00
13 Julius Randle 5.00 12.00
14 Zach LaVine 5.00 12.00
15 Gary Harris 3.00 8.00
16 Kyle Anderson 3.00 8.00
17 Markel Brown 2.00 5.00
18 Bruno Caboclo 2.50 6.00
19 Semaj Christon 2.00 5.00
20 Damien Inglis 2.00 5.00
21 Russ Smith 2.00 5.00
22 Joel Embiid 10.00 25.00
23 Nik Stauskas 2.50 6.00
24 Doug McDermott 3.00 8.00
25 Rodney Hood 3.00 8.00
26 Cleanthony Early 2.00 5.00
27 Jordan Clarkson 3.00 8.00
28 Mitch McGary 2.00 5.00
29 Thanasis Antetokounmpo 2.00 5.00
30 Jarnell Stokes 2.00 5.00
31 Adreian Payne 2.50 6.00
32 Tyler Ennis 2.00 5.00
33 Noah Vonleh 2.50 6.00
34 Elfrid Payton 3.00 8.00
35 Shabazz Napier 2.50 6.00
36 P.J. Hairston 2.00 5.00
37 Cory Jefferson 2.00 5.00
38 Xavier Thames 2.00 5.00
39 Lamar Patterson 2.00 5.00
40 Jordan McRae 2.00 5.00

2014-15 Prestige NBA Materials

RANDOM INSERTS IN PACKS
STATED PRINT RUN 99 SER.#'d SETS
*PURPLE/199: .4X TO 1X BASIC
1 Andray Blatche 2.00 5.00
2 Andre Iguodala 2.50 6.00
3 Brandon Bass 2.00 5.00
4 Carlos Boozer 2.50 6.00
5 Chris Bosh 3.00 8.00
6 David Lee 2.00 5.00
7 DeAndre Jordan 3.00 8.00
8 Harrison Barnes 2.50 6.00
9 J.R. Smith 2.50 6.00
10 Jamal Crawford 3.00 8.00
11 Jimmy Butler 3.00 8.00
12 Joe Johnson 2.50 6.00
13 Jordan Hill 2.00 5.00
14 Kevin Garnett 5.00 12.00
15 Kevin Love 3.00 8.00
16 Mario Chalmers 2.50 6.00
17 Nick Collison 2.50 6.00
18 Pau Gasol 3.00 8.00
19 Paul Pierce 2.00 5.00
20 Raymond Felton 2.50 6.00
21 Serge Ibaka 2.50 6.00
22 Taj Gibson 2.50 6.00
23 Steven Adams 2.50 6.00
24 Tony Snell 2.00 5.00
25 Tyson Chandler 2.50 6.00

2014-15 Prestige Prestigious Pioneers

RANDOM INSERTS IN PACKS
1 George Mikan 1.25 3.00
2 Bob Pettit .60 1.50
3 Bob Cousy 1.00 2.50
4 Dolph Schayes .60 1.50
5 Bill Russell 1.00 2.50
6 Elgin Baylor .60 1.50
7 Bill Sharman .60 1.50
8 Wilt Chamberlain 1.25 3.00
9 Oscar Robertson .75 2.00
10 Jerry West .75 2.00
11 Willis Reed .60 1.50
12 Hal Greer .50 1.25
13 John Havlicek .75 2.00
14 Pete Maravich 1.00 2.50
15 Rick Barry .50 1.25
16 Julius Erving 1.00 2.50
17 Kareem Abdul-Jabbar 1.00 2.50
18 Larry Bird 1.50 4.00
19 Magic Johnson 1.50 4.00
20 Dominique Wilkins .75 2.00

2014-15 Prestige Prestigious Posts

RANDOM INSERTS IN PACKS
1 DeAndre Jordan 1.00 2.50
2 Andre Drummond 1.00 2.50
3 Kevin Love 1.00 2.50
4 Joakim Noah .75 2.00
5 Dwight Howard .75 2.00
6 Tim Duncan 1.50 4.00
7 Anthony Davis 2.00 5.00
8 Blake Griffin 1.00 2.50
9 Marcin Gortat .75 2.00
10 LaMarcus Aldridge 1.00 2.50

2014-15 Prestige Prestigious Premieres Signatures

RANDOM INSERTS IN PACKS
PPAG Aaron Gordon 10.00 25.00
PPAP Adreian Payne 5.00 12.00
PPAW Andrew Wiggins 50.00 120.00
PPBC Bruno Caboclo 5.00 12.00
PPCE Cleanthony Early 4.00 10.00
PPCJ Cory Jefferson 4.00 10.00
PPCW C.J. Wilcox 4.00 10.00
PPDD Doug McDermott 4.00 10.00
PPDE Dante Exum 6.00 15.00
PPEP Elfrid Payton 6.00 15.00
PPGH Gary Harris 6.00 15.00
PPGR Glenn Robinson III 4.00 10.00
PPJA Jordan Adams 4.00 10.00
PPJE Joel Embiid 40.00 100.00
PPJP Jabari Parker 12.00 30.00
PPJR Julius Randle 10.00 25.00
PPJS Jarnell Stokes 4.00 10.00
PPJY James Young 4.00 10.00
PPKA Kyle Anderson 4.00 10.00
PPMM Mitch McGary 4.00 10.00
PPMS Marcus Smart 6.00 15.00
PPNS Nik Stauskas 5.00 12.00
PPNV Noah Vonleh 5.00 12.00
PPRH Rodney Hood 6.00 15.00
PPRS Russ Smith 4.00 10.00
PPSN Shabazz Napier 5.00 12.00
PPSP Spencer Dinwiddie 5.00 12.00
PPTA Thanasis Antetokounmpo 4.00 10.00
PPTE Tyler Ennis 4.00 10.00
PPTJ T.J. Warren 6.00 15.00
PPZL Zach LaVine 12.00 30.00

2014-15 Prestige True Colors Materials

RANDOM INSERTS IN PACKS
*PURPLE/49-199: .5X TO 1.2X BASIC
*PRIME/25: .75X TO 2X BASIC
1 Jimmy Butler/75 3.00 8.00
2 Ty Lawson/75 2.00 5.00
3 Kevin Love/75 3.00 8.00
4 Kenneth Faried/75 2.50 6.00
5 Al Horford/75 2.50 6.00
6 Pau Gasol/75 3.00 8.00
7 DeMarcus Cousins/75 3.00 8.00
8 Russell Westbrook/75 8.00 20.00
9 James Harden/75 5.00 12.00
10 Tim Duncan/75 5.00 12.00
11 Jrue Holiday/75 2.50 6.00
12 Tyson Chandler/75 2.50 6.00
13 Kevin Durant/75 8.00 20.00
14 Kobe Bryant/75 12.00 30.00
15 Blake Griffin/75 3.00 8.00
16 Ricky Rubio/75 3.00 8.00
17 Dirk Nowitzki/75 4.00 10.00
18 Steve Nash/75 3.00 8.00
19 Jeff Teague/75 2.50 6.00
20 Tony Parker/75 3.00 8.00
21 M.Carter-Williams/75 2.00 5.00
22 Zach Randolph/75 2.50 6.00
23 LeBron James/75 12.00 30.00
24 Kyrie Irving/75 6.00 15.00
25 Carmelo Anthony/75 4.00 10.00
26 David Robinson/49 5.00 12.00
27 Patrick Ewing/49 4.00 10.00
28 Dikembe Mutombo/49 3.00 8.00
29 Gary Payton/49 3.00 8.00
30 Julius Erving/49 5.00 12.00
31 Hakeem Olajuwon/49 4.00 10.00
32 Scottie Pippen/49 6.00 15.00
33 Shaquille O'Neal/49 6.00 15.00
34 Clyde Drexler/49 4.00 10.00
35 Zydrunas Ilgauskas/49 2.50 6.00
36 Joe Dumars/49 3.00 8.00
37 Aaron Gordon/99 5.00 12.00
38 Gary Harris/99 3.00 8.00
39 James Ennis/99 2.00 5.00
40 Elfrid Payton/99 3.00 8.00
41 Julius Randle/99 5.00 12.00
42 Mitch McGary/99 2.00 5.00
43 Noah Vonleh/99 2.50 6.00
44 Shabazz Napier/99 2.50 6.00
45 Tyler Ennis/99 2.00 5.00
46 P.J. Hairston/99 2.00 5.00
47 Joe Harris/99 2.00 5.00
48 Adreian Payne/99 2.50 6.00
49 Glenn Robinson III/99 2.00 5.00
51 Doug McDermott/99 3.00 8.00
52 Kyle Anderson/99 3.00 8.00
53 Johnny O'Bryant/99 2.00 5.00
54 Rodney Hood/99 3.00 8.00
55 Spencer Dinwiddie/99 2.50 6.00
56 Thanasis Antetokounmpo/99 2.00 5.00
57 Cleanthony Early/99 2.00 5.00
58 Markel Brown/99 2.00 5.00
59 Cory Jefferson/99 2.00 5.00
60 Andrew Wiggins/99 6.00 15.00
61 Jabari Parker/99 5.00 12.00
62 Jordan Adams/99 2.00 5.00
63 Damien Inglis/99 2.00 5.00
64 Marcus Smart/99 3.00 8.00
65 Nik Stauskas/99 2.50 6.00
66 Russ Smith/99 2.00 5.00
67 T.J. Warren/99 3.00 8.00
68 Zach LaVine/99 5.00 12.00
69 Jarnell Stokes/99 2.00 5.00
70 Jerami Grant/99 2.00 5.00
71 K.J. McDaniels/99 2.50 6.00
72 C.J. Wilcox/99 2.00 5.00
73 James Young/99 2.00 5.00
74 Joel Embiid/99 10.00 25.00
75 Bruno Caboclo/99 2.50 6.00

2014-15 Prestige Plus

1 Ricky Rubio .50 1.25
2 Jamal Crawford .50 1.25
3 Tiago Splitter .40 1.00
4 Al Horford .40 1.00
5 Jordan Hill .30 .75
6 Ben McLemore .30 .75
7 Kyle Lowry .40 1.00
8 Corey Brewer .30 .75
9 Nerlens Noel .40 1.00
10 Enes Kanter .30 .75
11 Robin Lopez .30 .75
12 Jameer Nelson .30 .75
13 Tim Duncan .75 2.00
14 Al Jefferson .40 1.00
15 Jose Calderon .30 .75
16 Blake Griffin .50 1.25
17 Kyrie Irving 1.00 2.50
18 Damian Lillard 1.00 2.50
19 Nick Collison .40 1.00
20 Eric Bledsoe .40 1.00
21 Roy Hibbert .40 1.00
22 James Harden .75 2.00
23 Tim Hardaway Jr. .30 .75
24 Alex Len .30 .75
25 Josh Smith .40 1.00
26 Bradley Beal .50 1.25
27 LaMarcus Aldridge .50 1.25
28 Danilo Gallinari .30 .75
29 Nick Young .40 1.00
30 Eric Gordon .40 1.00
31 Rudy Gay .50 1.25
32 Jared Sullinger .30 .75
33 Al-Farouq Aminu .30 .75
34 Tobias Harris .40 1.00
35 Jrue Holiday .40 1.00
36 Brandon Bass .30 .75
37 Lance Stephenson .40 1.00
38 David Lee .30 .75
39 Nicolas Batum .40 1.00
40 Ersan Ilyasova .30 .75
41 Russell Westbrook 1.25 3.00
42 Jason Thompson .30 .75
43 Tony Parker .50 1.25
44 Amar'e Stoudemire .50 1.25
45 Kawhi Leonard .75 2.00
46 Brandon Jennings .30 .75
47 LeBron James 2.00 5.00
48 David West .40 1.00
49 Nikola Pekovic .30 .75
50 George Hill .40 1.00
51 Ryan Anderson .30 .75
52 Jason Terry .40 1.00
53 Tony Snell .30 .75
54 Amir Johnson .30 .75
55 Kelly Olynyk .30 .75
56 Brandon Knight .40 1.00
57 Luol Deng .40 1.00
58 DeAndre Jordan .50 1.25
59 Nikola Vucevic .40 1.00
60 Gerald Green .40 1.00
61 Serge Ibaka .40 1.00
62 JaVale McGee .40 1.00
63 Tony Wroten .30 .75
64 Anderson Varejao .30 .75
65 Kemba Walker .50 1.25
66 Brook Lopez .40 1.00
67 Manu Ginobili .50 1.25
68 DeMar DeRozan .50 1.25
69 Norris Cole .30 .75
70 Gerald Henderson .30 .75
71 Shawn Marion .40 1.00
72 Jeff Green .40 1.00
73 Trey Burke .30 .75
74 Andre Drummond .50 1.25
75 Kenneth Faried .40 1.00
76 C.J. McCollum .50 1.25
77 Marc Gasol .50 1.25
78 O.J. Mayo .30 .75
79 Dennis Schroder .40 1.00
80 Giannis Antetokounmpo 1.00 2.50
81 Stephen Curry 2.00 5.00
82 Jeff Teague .40 1.00
83 Tristan Thompson .40 1.00
84 Andre Iguodala .40 1.00
85 Kentavious Caldwell-Pope .30 .75
86 Carlos Boozer .40 1.00
87 Marcin Gortat .40 1.00
88 Deron Williams .40 1.00
89 Otto Porter .40 1.00
90 Goran Dragic .40 1.00
91 Steve Nash .50 1.25
92 Jeremy Lin .50 1.25
93 Ty Lawson .30 .75
94 Andrew Bogut .40 1.00
95 Kevin Durant 1.25 3.00
96 Carmelo Anthony .60 1.50
97 Marco Belinelli .30 .75
98 Derrick Favors .40 1.00
99 Pau Gasol .50 1.25
100 Gordon Hayward .50 1.25
101 Steven Adams .40 1.00
102 Jimmy Butler .50 1.25
103 Tyreke Evans .30 .75
104 Anthony Bennett .30 .75
105 Kevin Garnett .75 2.00
106 Caron Butler .40 1.00
107 Mason Plumlee .40 1.00
108 Derrick Rose .60 1.50
109 Paul George .60 1.50
110 Taj Gibson .40 1.00
111 Gorgui Dieng .30 .75
112 Joakim Noah .40 1.00
113 Tyson Chandler .40 1.00
114 Anthony Davis 1.00 2.50
115 Kevin Love .50 1.25
116 Chandler Parsons .40 1.00
117 Matt Barnes .30 .75
118 Dion Waiters .40 1.00
119 Paul Millsap .50 1.25
120 Greg Monroe .40 1.00
121 Tayshaun Prince .40 1.00
122 Jodie Meeks .40 1.00
123 Victor Oladipo .40 1.00
124 Archie Goodwin .30 .75
125 Klay Thompson .60 1.50
126 Channing Frye .40 1.00
127 Michael Carter-Williams .30 .75
128 Dirk Nowitzki .60 1.50
129 Paul Pierce .50 1.25
130 Harrison Barnes .40 1.00
131 Terrence Jones .40 1.00
132 Joe Johnson .40 1.00
133 Vince Carter .60 1.50
134 Arron Afflalo .30 .75
135 Kevin Martin .40 1.00
136 Chris Bosh .50 1.25
137 Mike Conley .40 1.00
138 Dwight Howard .40 1.00
139 Rajon Rondo .50 1.25
140 Isaiah Thomas .50 1.25
141 Terrence Ross .40 1.00
142 John Wall .60 1.50
143 Wesley Matthews .30 .75
144 Avery Bradley .40 1.00
145 Kobe Bryant 2.00 5.00
146 Chris Paul .60 1.50
147 Monta Ellis .40 1.00
148 DeMarcus Cousins .50 1.25
149 Randy Foye .30 .75
150 J.J. Redick .50 1.25
151 Thaddeus Young .30 .75
152 Jonas Valanciunas .40 1.00
153 Zach Randolph .40 1.00
154 Michael Kidd-Gilchrist .40 1.00
155 Kyle Korver .40 1.00
156 Cody Zeller .30 .75
157 Nene .40 1.00
158 Dwyane Wade .75 2.00
159 J.R. Smith .40 1.00
160 Michael Beasley .30 .75
161 Andrew Wiggins RC 3.00 8.00
162 Jabari Parker RC 1.50 4.00
163 Joel Embiid RC 3.00 8.00
164 Aaron Gordon RC 1.50 4.00
165 Dante Exum RC 1.00 2.50
166 Marcus Smart RC 1.00 2.50
167 Julius Randle RC 1.50 4.00
168 Nik Stauskas RC .75 2.00
169 Noah Vonleh RC .75 2.00
170 Elfrid Payton RC 1.00 2.50
171 Doug McDermott RC 1.00 2.50
172 Zach LaVine RC 1.50 4.00
173 T.J. Warren RC 1.00 2.50
174 Adreian Payne RC .75 2.00
175 James Young RC .60 1.50
176 Tyler Ennis RC .60 1.50
177 Gary Harris RC 1.00 2.50
178 Mitch McGary RC .60 1.50
179 Jordan Adams RC .60 1.50
180 Rodney Hood RC 1.00 2.50
181 Shabazz Napier RC .75 2.00
182 P.J. Hairston RC .60 1.50
183 C.J. Wilcox RC .60 1.50
184 Josh Huestis RC .60 1.50
185 Kyle Anderson RC 1.00 2.50
186 Damien Inglis RC .60 1.50
187 K.J. McDaniels RC .75 2.00
188 Joe Harris RC .60 1.50
189 Cleanthony Early RC .60 1.50
190 Jarnell Stokes RC .60 1.50
191 Johnny O'Bryant RC .60 1.50
192 Erick Green RC .60 1.50
193 Spencer Dinwiddie RC .75 2.00
194 Jerami Grant RC .60 1.50
195 Jordan Clarkson RC 1.00 2.50
196 Russ Smith RC .60 1.50
197 Thanasis Antetokounmpo RC .60 1.50
198 Jordan McRae RC .60 1.50
199 Xavier Thames RC .60 1.50
200 Cory Jefferson RC .60 1.50

2014-15 Prestige Plus Bonus Shots Blue

*VETS: 1X TO 2.5X BASE HI
*ROOKIES: 1.2X TO 3X BASE HI
RANDOM INSERTS IN PACKS
STATED PRINT RUN 99 SER.#'d SETS

2014-15 Prestige Plus Bonus Shots Orange Die Cuts

*VETS: 2X TO 5X BASE HI
*ROOKIES: 2.5X TO 6X BASE HI
RANDOM INSERTS IN PACKS
STATED PRINT RUN 25 SER.#'d SETS

2014-15 Prestige Plus Bonus Shots Purple

*VETS: 1.2X TO 3X BASE HI
*ROOKIES: 1.5X TO 4X BASE HI
STATED PRINT RUN 49 SER.#'d SETS

2014-15 Prestige Plus Bonus Shots Red

*VETS: .75X TO 2X BASE HI
*ROOKIES: 1X TO 2.5X BASE HI
RANDOM INSERTS IN PACKS
STATED PRINT RUN 199 SER.#'d SETS

2014-15 Prestige Plus Bonus Shots Autographs

*RED/49: .4X TO 1X BASE HI
*BLUE/25: .5X TO 1.2X BASE HI
STATED PRINT RUN 10-99
NO PRICING ON QTY 10 OR LESS
1 Glen Rice Jr./99 4.00 10.00
2 Dolph Schayes/25
3 Gorgui Dieng/99 4.00 10.00
5 Chuck Person/25
7 David Thompson/25
9 Terry Porter/99
11 Arnett Moultrie/99 4.00 10.00
12 Bill Sharman/25
13 Tim Hardaway Jr./99 4.00 10.00
15 Danny Green/25
17 Glen Rice/25 5.00 12.00
19 Thaddeus Young/99
21 Khris Middleton/99
23 Rudy Gobert/99
25 Chet Walker/25
27 Enes Kanter/25 4.00 10.00
29 Horace Grant/99 6.00 15.00
31 Tony Snell/99
33 Luigi Datome/99
35 Devin Harris/25
37 Harry Gallatin/25 6.00 15.00
39 Isaiah Thomas/99 12.00 30.00
41 Reggie Bullock/99
43 Carrick Felix/99
45 Greg Anthony/25 4.00 10.00
47 Cedric Maxwell/25 4.00 10.00
49 Rick Mahorn/99
51 Nemanja Nedovic/99
53 Solomon Hill/99
55 C.J. Watson/25
57 Marcin Gortat/25 20.00 50.00
59 Amir Johnson/99 4.00 10.00
61 Gal Mekel/99
63 Isaiah Canaan/99
64 Richard Jefferson/25
65 Kevin Willis/25
67 Marvin Williams/99
69 Spencer Hawes/99
71 P.J. Tucker/99
73 Ray McCallum/99

74 Mike Conley/25
75 Dan Majerle/25 5.00 12.00
77 Brandan Wright/99
79 Sean Elliott/99 6.00 15.00
81 Hollis Thompson/99 5.00 12.00
83 Ryan Kelly/99
84 Allan Houston/25
85 Kurt Rambis/25
87 Bismack Biyombo/99 4.00 10.00
89 Mark Aguirre/99
91 Dennis Schroder/99 5.00 12.00
92 Bradley Beal/25
93 Phil Pressey/99
94 Ryan Anderson/25 4.00 10.00
95 Adrian Dantley/25
97 Steven Adams/99 5.00 12.00
99 Greg Buckner/99 4.00 10.00

2014-15 Prestige Plus Connections

RANDOM INSERTS IN PACKS
1 D.Williams/J.Kidd .75 2.00
2 D.Robinson/T.Duncan 1.25 3.00
3 B.Cousy/R.Rondo 1.25 3.00
4 A.Iverson/M.Carter-Williams 1.00 2.50
5 B.Walton/L.Aldridge .75 2.00
6 T.Lawson/F.Lever .50 1.25
7 A.Gilmore/J.Noah .60 1.50
8 M.Price/K.Irving 1.50 4.00
9 A.Drummond/B.Laimbeer .75 2.00
10 B.Griffin/B.McAdoo .75 2.00
11 R.Barry/K.Thompson 1.00 2.50
12 E.Baylor/K.Bryant 3.00 8.00
13 A.Mourning/A.Davis 1.50 4.00
14 M.Malone/D.Howard .75 2.00
15 T.Porter/D.Lillard 1.50 4.00
16 L.James/O.Robertson 3.00 8.00
17 D.Wade/J.Dumars 1.25 3.00
18 C.Andersen/D.Rodman 1.50 4.00
19 K.Durant/G.Gervin 2.00 5.00
20 L.Bird/C.Anthony 2.00 5.00

2014-15 Prestige Plus Franchise Favorites

RANDOM INSERTS IN PACKS
1 Al Horford .60 1.50
2 Rajon Rondo .75 2.00
3 Deron Williams .60 1.50
4 Gerald Henderson .50 1.25
5 Derrick Rose 1.00 2.50
6 LeBron James 3.00 8.00
7 Dirk Nowitzki 1.00 2.50
8 Ty Lawson .50 1.25
9 Greg Monroe .60 1.50
10 Stephen Curry 3.00 8.00
11 James Harden 1.25 3.00
12 Paul George 1.00 2.50
13 Blake Griffin .75 2.00
14 Kobe Bryant 3.00 8.00
15 Mike Conley .60 1.50
16 Dwyane Wade 1.25 3.00
17 Ersan Ilyasova .50 1.25
18 Ricky Rubio .75 2.00
19 Anthony Davis 1.50 4.00
20 Carmelo Anthony 1.00 2.50
21 Kevin Durant 2.00 5.00
22 Nikola Vucevic .60 1.50
23 Michael Carter-Williams .50 1.25
24 Goran Dragic .60 1.50
25 LaMarcus Aldridge .75 2.00
26 DeMarcus Cousins .75 2.00
27 Tim Duncan 1.25 3.00
28 DeMar DeRozan .75 2.00
29 Gordon Hayward .75 2.00
30 John Wall 1.00 2.50

2014-15 Prestige Plus Hardcourt Heroes

RANDOM INSERTS IN PACKS
1 Joe Johnson .60 1.50
2 Chris Bosh .75 2.00
3 Dirk Nowitzki 1.00 2.50
4 Damian Lillard 1.50 4.00
5 Vince Carter 1.00 2.50
6 LeBron James 3.00 8.00
7 Russell Westbrook 2.00 5.00
8 Stephen Curry 3.00 8.00
9 Kevin Durant 2.00 5.00
10 Jeff Green .60 1.50
11 Kobe Bryant 3.00 8.00
12 Carmelo Anthony 1.00 2.50
13 Anthony Davis 1.50 4.00
14 Chris Paul 1.00 2.50
15 Dwyane Wade 1.25 3.00
16 Kevin Love .75 2.00
17 Manu Ginobili .75 2.00
18 Klay Thompson 1.00 2.50
19 Tim Duncan 1.25 3.00
20 Kyrie Irving 1.50 4.00

2014-15 Prestige Plus NBA Materials

RANDOM INSERTS IN PACKS
PRINT RUN B/WN 99-199 COPIES PER
1 Andray Blatche/99 2.00 5.00
2 Andre Iguodala/99 2.50 6.00
3 Brandon Bass/99 2.00 5.00
4 Carlos Boozer/99 2.50 6.00
5 Chris Bosh/99 3.00 8.00
6 David Lee/99 2.00 5.00
7 DeAndre Jordan/99 3.00 8.00
8 Harrison Barnes/99 2.50 6.00
9 J.R. Smith/99 2.50 6.00
10 Jamal Crawford/99 3.00 8.00
11 Jimmy Butler/99 3.00 8.00
12 Joe Johnson/99 2.50 6.00
13 Jordan Hill/99 2.00 5.00
14 Kevin Garnett/99 5.00 12.00
15 Kevin Love/199 3.00 8.00
16 Mario Chalmers/99 2.50 6.00
17 Nick Collison/99 2.50 6.00
18 Pau Gasol/199 3.00 8.00
19 Paul Pierce/99 3.00 8.00
20 Raymond Felton/199 2.50 6.00
21 Serge Ibaka/99 2.50 6.00
22 Taj Gibson/99 2.50 6.00
23 Steven Adams/99 2.50 6.00
24 Tony Snell/99 2.00 5.00
25 Tyson Chandler/199 2.50 6.00

2014-15 Prestige Plus Playmakers

RANDOM INSERTS IN PACKS
1 Kevin Durant 12.00 30.00
2 LeBron James 75.00 150.00
3 Kevin Love 5.00 12.00
4 Anthony Davis 10.00 25.00
5 DeMarcus Cousins 5.00 12.00
6 Chris Paul 6.00 15.00
7 Carmelo Anthony 6.00 15.00
8 Stephen Curry 20.00 50.00
9 Blake Griffin 5.00 12.00
10 Dirk Nowitzki 6.00 15.00
11 James Harden 8.00 20.00
12 Andre Drummond 5.00 12.00
13 Al Jefferson 4.00 10.00
14 LaMarcus Aldridge 5.00 12.00
15 Goran Dragic 4.00 10.00
16 Tim Duncan 8.00 20.00
17 Dwight Howard 8.00 20.00
18 Isaiah Thomas 5.00 12.00
19 Paul George 6.00 15.00
20 Kyrie Irving 15.00 40.00
21 Kyle Lowry 4.00 10.00
22 Mike Conley 4.00 10.00
23 Joakim Noah 4.00 10.00
24 Kenneth Faried 4.00 10.00
25 Paul Millsap 5.00 12.00

2014-15 Prestige Plus Prestigious Pioneers

RANDOM INSERTS IN PACKS
1 George Mikan 1.50 4.00
2 Bob Pettit .75 2.00
3 Bob Cousy 1.25 3.00
4 Dolph Schayes .75 2.00
5 Bill Russell 1.25 3.00
6 Elgin Baylor .75 2.00
7 Bill Sharman .75 2.00
8 Wilt Chamberlain 1.50 4.00
9 Oscar Robertson 1.00 2.50
10 Jerry West 1.00 2.50
11 Willis Reed .75 2.00
12 Hal Greer .60 1.50
13 John Havlicek 1.00 2.50
14 Pete Maravich 1.25 3.00
15 Rick Barry .60 1.50
16 Julius Erving 1.25 3.00
17 Kareem Abdul-Jabbar 1.25 3.00
18 Larry Bird 2.00 5.00
19 Magic Johnson 2.00 5.00
20 Dominique Wilkins 1.00 2.50

2014-15 Prestige Plus Prestigious Posts

RANDOM INSERTS IN PACKS
1 DeAndre Jordan 1.25 3.00
2 Andre Drummond 1.25 3.00
3 Kevin Love 1.25 3.00
4 Joakim Noah 1.00 2.50
5 Dwight Howard 1.00 2.50
6 Tim Duncan 2.00 5.00
7 Anthony Davis 2.50 6.00
8 Blake Griffin 1.25 3.00
9 Marcin Gortat 1.00 2.50
10 LaMarcus Aldridge 1.25 3.00

2014-15 Prestige Plus Prestigious Premieres Signatures

PPAG Aaron Gordon 10.00 25.00
PPAP Adreian Payne 8.00 20.00
PPAW Andrew Wiggins 100.00 200.00
PPBC Bruno Caboclo 4.00 10.00
PPCE Cleanthony Early 3.00 8.00
PPCJ Cory Jefferson 3.00 8.00
PPCW C.J. Wilcox 3.00 8.00
PPDD Doug McDermott 5.00 12.00
PPDE Dante Exum 5.00 12.00
PPEP Elfrid Payton 15.00 40.00
PPGH Gary Harris 5.00 12.00
PPGR Glenn Robinson III 3.00 8.00
PPJA Jordan Adams 3.00 8.00
PPJE Joel Embiid 20.00 50.00
PPJN Jusuf Nurkic
PPJP Jabari Parker 40.00 100.00
PPJR Julius Randle 20.00 50.00
PPJS Jarnell Stokes 3.00 8.00
PPJY James Young 3.00 8.00
PPKA Kyle Anderson 8.00 20.00
PPMM Mitch McGary 3.00 8.00
PPMS Marcus Smart 25.00 60.00
PPNS Nik Stauskas 4.00 10.00
PPNV Noah Vonleh 8.00 20.00
PPRH Rodney Hood 5.00 12.00
PPRS Russ Smith 3.00 8.00
PPSN Shabazz Napier 4.00 10.00
PPSP Spencer Dinwiddie 4.00 10.00
PPTA Thanasis Antetokounmpo 3.00 8.00
PPTE Tyler Ennis 3.00 8.00
PPTJ T.J. Warren 5.00 12.00
PPZL Zach LaVine 10.00 25.00

2014-15 Prestige Plus Prestigious Pros

RANDOM INSERTS IN PACKS
1 Kobe Bryant 8.00 20.00
2 Anthony Davis 4.00 10.00
3 DeMarcus Cousins 2.00 5.00
4 Monta Ellis 1.50 4.00
5 Tim Duncan 3.00 8.00
6 Chris Paul 2.50 6.00
7 Victor Oladipo 1.50 4.00
8 Josh Smith 1.50 4.00
9 Manu Ginobili 2.00 5.00
10 Rajon Rondo 2.00 5.00
11 Paul Pierce 2.00 5.00
12 Mike Conley 1.50 4.00
13 Ricky Rubio 2.00 5.00
14 Tristan Thompson 1.50 4.00
15 DeAndre Jordan 2.00 5.00
16 Paul George 2.50 6.00
17 Stephen Curry 8.00 20.00
18 Kevin Durant 5.00 12.00
19 Isaiah Thomas 2.00 5.00
20 Jonas Valanciunas 1.50 4.00
21 Ty Lawson 1.25 3.00
22 Michael Carter-Williams 1.25 3.00
23 Chris Bosh 2.00 5.00
24 Derrick Rose 2.50 6.00
25 Al Horford 1.50 4.00
26 Gerald Green 1.50 4.00
27 LaMarcus Aldridge 2.00 5.00
28 John Wall 2.50 6.00
29 Jameer Nelson 1.25 3.00
30 Marcin Gortat 1.50 4.00
31 Kevin Garnett 3.00 8.00
32 Trevor Ariza 1.25 3.00
33 Klay Thompson 2.50 6.00
34 Taj Gibson 1.50 4.00
35 Kemba Walker 2.00 5.00
36 Kenneth Faried 1.50 4.00
37 Joakim Noah 1.50 4.00
38 Al Jefferson 1.50 4.00
39 Carmelo Anthony 2.50 6.00
40 Damian Lillard 4.00 10.00
41 Serge Ibaka 1.50 4.00
42 Kyle Lowry 1.50 4.00
43 Jimmy Butler 2.00 5.00
44 Andrew Bogut 1.50 4.00
45 Steve Nash 2.00 5.00
46 Nicolas Batum 1.50 4.00
47 Marc Gasol 2.00 5.00
48 Blake Griffin 2.00 5.00
49 Kevin Love 2.00 5.00
50 Rudy Gay 2.00 5.00
51 Andre Drummond 2.00 5.00
52 Paul Millsap 2.00 5.00
53 Trey Burke 1.25 3.00
54 Roy Hibbert 1.50 4.00
55 Tony Parker 2.00 5.00
56 Lance Stephenson 1.50 4.00
57 Jeff Green 1.50 4.00
58 Vince Carter 2.50 6.00
59 Pau Gasol 2.00 5.00
60 Kyle Korver 1.50 4.00
61 Mario Chalmers 1.50 4.00
62 Thaddeus Young 1.25 3.00
63 Jeff Teague 1.50 4.00
64 Brandon Jennings 1.25 3.00
65 Robin Lopez 1.25 3.00
66 Derrick Favors 1.50 4.00
67 Greg Monroe 1.50 4.00
68 Zach Randolph 1.50 4.00
69 Dwight Howard 1.50 4.00
70 Goran Dragic 1.50 4.00
71 Dirk Nowitzki 2.50 6.00
72 DeMar DeRozan 2.00 5.00
73 James Harden 3.00 8.00
74 LeBron James 8.00 20.00
75 Kyrie Irving 4.00 10.00

2014-15 Prestige Plus True Colors Materials

RANDOM INSERTS IN PACKS
STATED PRINT RUN 99-199
*PRIME/25: .75X TO 2X BASE HI
1 Jimmy Butler/199 3.00 8.00
2 Ty Lawson/199 2.00 5.00
3 Kevin Love/199 3.00 8.00
4 Kenneth Faried/199 2.50 6.00
5 Al Horford/199 2.50 6.00
6 Pau Gasol/199 3.00 8.00
7 DeMarcus Cousins/199 3.00 8.00
8 Russell Westbrook/199 8.00 20.00
9 James Harden/199 5.00 12.00
10 Tim Duncan/199 5.00 12.00
11 Jrue Holiday/199 2.50 6.00
12 Tyson Chandler/199 2.50 6.00
13 Kevin Durant/199 8.00 20.00
14 Kobe Bryant/199 10.00 25.00
15 Blake Griffin/199 3.00 8.00
16 Ricky Rubio/199 3.00 8.00
17 Dirk Nowitzki/199 4.00 10.00
18 Steve Nash/199 3.00 8.00
19 Jeff Teague/199 2.50 6.00
20 Tony Parker/199 3.00 8.00
21 M.Carter-Williams/199 2.00 5.00
22 Zach Randolph/199 2.50 6.00
23 LeBron James/199 12.00 30.00
24 Kyrie Irving/199 6.00 15.00
25 Carmelo Anthony/199 4.00 10.00
26 David Robinson/99 5.00 12.00
27 Patrick Ewing/199 4.00 10.00
28 Dikembe Mutombo/199 3.00 8.00
29 Gary Payton/199 3.00 8.00
30 Julius Erving/199 5.00 12.00
31 Hakeem Olajuwon/99 4.00 10.00
32 Scottie Pippen/199 6.00 15.00
33 Shaquille O'Neal/99 6.00 15.00
34 Clyde Drexler/199 4.00 10.00
35 Zydrunas Ilgauskas/99 2.50 6.00
36 Joe Dumars/99 3.00 8.00
37 Aaron Gordon/199 5.00 12.00
38 Gary Harris/199 3.00 8.00
39 James Ennis/199 8.00 20.00
40 Elfrid Payton/199 3.00 8.00
41 Julius Randle/199 5.00 12.00
42 Mitch McGary/199 2.00 5.00
43 Noah Vonleh/199 2.50 6.00
44 Shabazz Napier/199 2.50 6.00
45 Tyler Ennis/199 2.00 5.00
46 P.J. Hairston/199 2.00 5.00
47 Joe Harris/199 2.00 5.00
48 Adreian Payne/199 2.50 6.00
49 Glenn Robinson III/199 2.00 5.00
51 Doug McDermott/199 3.00 8.00
52 Kyle Anderson/199 3.00 8.00
53 Johnny O'Bryant/199 2.00 5.00
54 Rodney Hood/199 3.00 8.00
55 Spencer Dinwiddie/199 2.50 6.00
56 Thanasis Antetokounmpo/199 2.00 5.00
57 Cleanthony Early/199 2.00 5.00
58 Markel Brown/199 2.00 5.00
59 Cory Jefferson/199 2.00 5.00
60 Andrew Wiggins/199 10.00 25.00
61 Jabari Parker/199 5.00 12.00
62 Jordan Adams/199 2.00 5.00
63 Damien Inglis/199 2.00 5.00
64 Marcus Smart/199 3.00 8.00
65 Nik Stauskas/199 2.50 6.00
66 Russ Smith/199 2.00 5.00
67 T.J. Warren/199 3.00 8.00
68 Zach LaVine/199 5.00 12.00
69 Jarnell Stokes/199 2.00 5.00
70 Jerami Grant/199 2.00 5.00
71 K.J. McDaniels/199 2.50 6.00
72 C.J. Wilcox/199 2.00 5.00
73 James Young/199 2.00 5.00
74 Joel Embiid/199 10.00 25.00
75 Bruno Caboclo/199 2.50 6.00

2014-15 Prestige Premium

COMPLETE SET (200) 50.00 100.00
1 Ricky Rubio .75 2.00
2 Jamal Crawford .75 2.00
3 Tiago Splitter .60 1.50
4 Al Horford .60 1.50
5 Jordan Hill .50 1.25
6 Ben McLemore .50 1.25
7 Kyle Lowry .60 1.50
8 Corey Brewer .50 1.25
9 Nerlens Noel .60 1.50
10 Enes Kanter .50 1.25
11 Robin Lopez .50 1.25
12 Jameer Nelson .50 1.25
13 Tim Duncan 1.25 3.00
14 Al Jefferson .60 1.50
15 Jose Calderon .50 1.25
16 Blake Griffin .75 2.00
17 Kyrie Irving 1.50 4.00
18 Damian Lillard 1.50 4.00
19 Nick Collison .60 1.50
20 Eric Bledsoe .60 1.50
21 Roy Hibbert .60 1.50
22 James Harden 1.25 3.00
23 Tim Hardaway Jr. .50 1.25
24 Alex Len .50 1.25
25 Josh Smith .60 1.50
26 Bradley Beal .75 2.00
27 LaMarcus Aldridge .75 2.00
28 Danilo Gallinari .50 1.25
29 Nick Young .60 1.50
30 Eric Gordon .60 1.50
31 Rudy Gay .75 2.00
32 Jared Sullinger .50 1.25
33 Al-Farouq Aminu .50 1.25
34 Tobias Harris .60 1.50
35 Jrue Holiday .60 1.50
36 Brandon Bass .50 1.25
37 Lance Stephenson .60 1.50
38 David Lee .50 1.25
39 Nicolas Batum .60 1.50
40 Ersan Ilyasova .50 1.25
41 Russell Westbrook 2.00 5.00
42 Jason Thompson .50 1.25
43 Tony Parker .75 2.00
44 Amar'e Stoudemire .75 2.00
45 Kawhi Leonard 1.25 3.00
46 Brandon Jennings .50 1.25
47 LeBron James 3.00 8.00
48 David West .60 1.50
49 Nikola Pekovic .50 1.25
50 George Hill .60 1.50
51 Ryan Anderson .50 1.25
52 Jason Terry .60 1.50
53 Tony Snell .50 1.25
54 Amir Johnson .50 1.25
55 Kelly Olynyk .50 1.25
56 Brandon Knight .60 1.50
57 Luol Deng .60 1.50
58 DeAndre Jordan .75 2.00
59 Nikola Vucevic .60 1.50
60 Gerald Green .60 1.50
61 Serge Ibaka .60 1.50
62 JaVale McGee .60 1.50
63 Tony Wroten .50 1.25
64 Anderson Varejao .50 1.25
65 Kemba Walker .75 2.00
66 Brook Lopez .60 1.50
67 Manu Ginobili .75 2.00
68 DeMar DeRozan .75 2.00
69 Norris Cole .50 1.25
70 Gerald Henderson .50 1.25
71 Shawn Marion .60 1.50
72 Jeff Green .60 1.50
73 Trey Burke .50 1.25
74 Andre Drummond .75 2.00
75 Kenneth Faried .60 1.50
76 C.J. McCollum .75 2.00
77 Marc Gasol .75 2.00
78 O.J. Mayo .50 1.25
79 Dennis Schroder .60 1.50
80 Giannis Antetokounmpo 1.50 4.00
81 Stephen Curry 3.00 8.00
82 Jeff Teague .60 1.50
83 Tristan Thompson .60 1.50
84 Andre Iguodala .60 1.50
85 Kentavious Caldwell-Pope .50 1.25
86 Carlos Boozer .60 1.50
87 Marcin Gortat .60 1.50
88 Deron Williams .60 1.50
89 Otto Porter .60 1.50
90 Goran Dragic .60 1.50
91 Steve Nash .75 2.00
92 Jeremy Lin .75 2.00
93 Ty Lawson .50 1.25
94 Andrew Bogut .60 1.50
95 Kevin Durant 2.00 5.00
96 Carmelo Anthony 1.00 2.50
97 Marco Belinelli .50 1.25
98 Derrick Favors .60 1.50
99 Pau Gasol .75 2.00
100 Gordon Hayward .75 2.00
101 Steven Adams .60 1.50
102 Jimmy Butler .75 2.00
103 Tyreke Evans .50 1.25
104 Anthony Bennett .50 1.25
105 Kevin Garnett 1.25 3.00
106 Caron Butler .60 1.50
107 Mason Plumlee .60 1.50
108 Derrick Rose 1.00 2.50
109 Paul George 1.00 2.50
110 Taj Gibson .60 1.50
111 Gorgui Dieng .50 1.25
112 Joakim Noah .60 1.50
113 Tyson Chandler .60 1.50
114 Anthony Davis 1.50 4.00
115 Kevin Love .75 2.00
116 Chandler Parsons .60 1.50
117 Matt Barnes .50 1.25
118 Dion Waiters .60 1.50
119 Paul Millsap .75 2.00
120 Greg Monroe .60 1.50
121 Tayshaun Prince .60 1.50
122 Jodie Meeks .60 1.50
123 Victor Oladipo .60 1.50
124 Archie Goodwin .50 1.25
125 Klay Thompson 1.00 2.50
126 Channing Frye .60 1.50
127 Michael Carter-Williams .50 1.25
128 Dirk Nowitzki 1.00 2.50
129 Paul Pierce .75 2.00
130 Harrison Barnes .60 1.50
131 Terrence Jones .60 1.50
132 Joe Johnson .60 1.50
133 Vince Carter 1.00 2.50
134 Arron Afflalo .50 1.25
135 Kevin Martin .60 1.50
136 Chris Bosh .75 2.00
137 Mike Conley .60 1.50
138 Dwight Howard .60 1.50
139 Rajon Rondo .75 2.00
140 Isaiah Thomas .75 2.00
141 Terrence Ross .60 1.50
142 John Wall 1.00 2.50
143 Wesley Matthews .50 1.25
144 Avery Bradley .60 1.50
145 Kobe Bryant 3.00 8.00
146 Chris Paul 1.00 2.50
147 Monta Ellis .60 1.50
148 DeMarcus Cousins .75 2.00
149 Randy Foye .50 1.25
150 J.J. Redick .75 2.00
151 Thaddeus Young .50 1.25
152 Jonas Valanciunas .60 1.50
153 Zach Randolph .60 1.50
154 Michael Kidd-Gilchrist .60 1.50
155 Kyle Korver .60 1.50
156 Cody Zeller .50 1.25
157 Nene .60 1.50
158 Dwyane Wade 1.25 3.00
159 J.R. Smith .60 1.50
160 Michael Beasley .50 1.25
161 Andrew Wiggins RC 5.00 12.00
162 Jabari Parker RC 2.50 6.00
163 Joel Embiid RC 5.00 12.00
164 Aaron Gordon RC 2.50 6.00
165 Dante Exum RC 1.50 4.00
166 Marcus Smart RC 1.50 4.00
167 Julius Randle RC 2.50 6.00
168 Nik Stauskas RC 1.25 3.00
169 Noah Vonleh RC 1.25 3.00
170 Elfrid Payton RC 1.50 4.00
171 Doug McDermott RC 1.50 4.00
172 Zach LaVine RC 2.50 6.00
173 T.J. Warren RC 1.50 4.00
174 Adreian Payne RC 1.25 3.00
175 James Young RC 1.00 2.50
176 Tyler Ennis RC 1.00 2.50
177 Gary Harris RC 1.50 4.00
178 Mitch McGary RC 1.00 2.50
179 Jordan Adams RC 1.00 2.50
180 Rodney Hood RC 1.50 4.00
181 Shabazz Napier RC 1.25 3.00
182 P.J. Hairston RC 1.00 2.50
183 C.J. Wilcox RC 1.00 2.50
184 Bruno Caboclo RC 1.25 3.00
185 Kyle Anderson RC 1.50 4.00
186 Damien Inglis RC 1.00 2.50
187 K.J. McDaniels RC 1.25 3.00
188 Joe Harris RC 1.00 2.50
189 Cleanthony Early RC 1.00 2.50
190 Jarnell Stokes RC 1.00 2.50
191 Johnny O'Bryant RC 1.00 2.50
192 Erick Green RC 1.00 2.50
193 Spencer Dinwiddie RC 1.25 3.00
194 Jerami Grant RC 1.00 2.50
195 Jordan Clarkson RC 1.50 4.00
196 Russ Smith RC 1.00 2.50
197 Thanasis Antetokounmpo RC 1.00 2.50
198 Jordan McRae RC 1.00 2.50
199 Xavier Thames RC 1.00 2.50
200 Cory Jefferson RC 1.00 2.50

2014-15 Prestige Premium Bonus Shots Blue

*VETS: .6X TO 1.5X BASE HI
*ROOKIES: .75X TO 2X BASE HI
RANDOM INSERTS IN PACKS
STATED PRINT RUN 99 SER.#'d SETS

2014-15 Prestige Premium Bonus Shots Orange Die Cuts

*VETS: 1.2X TO 3X BASE HI
*ROOKIES: 1.5X TO 4X BASE HI
RANDOM INSERTS IN PACKS
STATED PRINT RUN 25 SER.#'d SETS

2014-15 Prestige Premium Bonus Shots Purple

*VETS: .8X TO 2X BASE HI
*ROOKIES: 1X TO 2.5X BASE HI
RANDOM INSERTS IN PACKS
STATED PRINT RUN 49 SER.#'d SETS

2014-15 Prestige Premium Bonus Shots Red

*VETS: .5X TO 1.2X BASE HI
*ROOKIES: .6X TO 1.5X BASE HI
RANDOM INSERTS IN PACKS
STATED PRINT RUN 199 SER.#'d SETS

2014-15 Prestige Premium Bonus Shots Autographs

PRINT RUNS B/WN 15-199 COPIES PER
NO PRICING ON QTY 15 OR LESS
*BLUE/75: .4X TO 1X BASIC
*BLUE/25: .5X TO 1.2 BASIC
*ORANGE/49: .4X TO 1X BASIC
*RED/49-99: .4X TO 1X BASIC
*RED/25: .5X TO 1.2X BASIC
1 Glen Rice Jr./199
2 Dolph Schayes/25
3 Gorgui Dieng/199
4 Kelly Tripucka/25
5 Chuck Person/49
6 Dwyane Wade/15
7 David Thompson/49 5.00 12.00
8 Hakeem Olajuwon/15 12.00 30.00
9 Terry Porter/149
10 Anfernee Hardaway/25 15.00 40.00
11 Arnett Moultrie/199 4.00 10.00
12 Bill Sharman/25 12.00 30.00
13 Tim Hardaway Jr./199 4.00 10.00
14 Nate Archibald/25
15 Danny Green/49 5.00 12.00
16 John Stockton/15
17 Glen Rice/49 5.00 12.00
18 Ray Allen/15
19 Thaddeus Young/149
20 Nerlens Noel/99 5.00 12.00
21 Khris Middleton/199
22 Jared Sullinger/25
23 Rudy Gobert/199 8.00 20.00
24 Jason Terry/25
25 Chet Walker/49
26 Paul George/15
27 Enes Kanter/49
28 Vince Carter/15
29 Horace Grant/149 6.00 15.00
30 Kentavious Caldwell-Pope/99 4.00 10.00
31 Tony Snell/199 4.00 10.00
32 Elvin Hayes/49 6.00 15.00
33 Luigi Datome/199 4.00 10.00
34 Andrei Kirilenko/25
35 Devin Harris/49
36 Carmelo Anthony/15
37 Harry Gallatin/49
38 Anthony Bennett/99
39 Isaiah Thomas/149
40 Michael Finley/49
41 Reggie Bullock/199
42 Gail Goodrich/49 6.00 15.00
43 Carrick Felix/199
44 Steve Kerr/25 8.00 20.00
45 Greg Anthony/49
46 Dirk Nowitzki/15
47 Cedric Maxwell/49
48 Gary Payton/15
49 Rick Mahorn/149
50 Nick Van Exel/25 6.00 15.00
51 Nemanja Nedovic/199
52 Peja Stojakovic/49
53 Solomon Hill/199 4.00 10.00
54 Joe Dumars/25
55 C.J. Watson/49
56 John Havlicek/15
57 Marcin Gortat/49 15.00 40.00
58 Clyde Drexler/49 12.00 30.00
59 Amir Johnson/149
60 C.J. McCollum/99 6.00 15.00
61 Gal Mekel/199 4.00 10.00
62 Kenny Smith/25
63 Isaiah Canaan/199 5.00 12.00
64 Richard Jefferson/49
65 Kevin Willis/49
66 Anthony Davis/49 40.00 100.00
67 Marvin Williams/149
68 Victor Oladipo/99 5.00 12.00
69 Spencer Hawes/149
70 M.Carter-Williams/99 4.00 10.00
71 P.J. Tucker/199 4.00 10.00
72 Nate Thurmond/25
73 Ray McCallum/199 4.00 10.00
74 Mike Conley/49
75 Dan Majerle/49 5.00 12.00
76 John Wall/15
77 Brandan Wright/149
78 Cody Zeller/99 4.00 10.00
79 Sean Elliott/149 6.00 15.00
80 Trey Burke/99 4.00 10.00
81 Hollis Thompson/199 5.00 12.00
82 Robert Parish/25 6.00 15.00
83 Ryan Kelly/199 4.00 10.00
84 Allan Houston/49
85 Kurt Rambis/49 4.00 10.00
86 Elgin Baylor/49
87 Bismack Biyombo/149
88 Otto Porter/99 5.00 12.00
89 Mark Aguirre/149
90 Walt Bellamy/75
91 Dennis Schroder/199 5.00 12.00
92 Bradley Beal/25 6.00 15.00
93 Phil Pressey/199 4.00 10.00
94 Ryan Anderson/49
95 Adrian Dantley/49
96 Jason Kidd/49 15.00 40.00
97 Steven Adams/149 5.00 12.00
98 Alex Len/99
99 Greg Buckner/149 4.00 10.00
100 Danny Manning/49

2014-15 Prestige Premium Bonus Shots Materials

RANDOM INSERTS IN PACKS
PRINT RUNS B/WN 49-99 COPIES PER
*ORANGE/25: .6 TO 1.5X BASIC
1 J.J. Redick/75 3.00 8.00
2 Stephen Curry/99 12.00 30.00
3 Joe Johnson/75 2.50 6.00
4 Trey Burke/75 2.00 5.00
5 Kevin Durant/99 5.00 12.00
6 Al Horford/75 2.50 6.00
7 Manu Ginobili/75 3.00 8.00
8 Chris Andersen/75 2.50 6.00
9 Pau Gasol/99 3.00 8.00
10 Dikembe Mutombo/99 3.00 8.00
11 Isaiah Thomas/75 3.00 8.00
12 Steve Nash/99 3.00 8.00
13 Tristan Thompson/75 2.50 6.00
14 John Wall/99 4.00 10.00
15 Kyrie Irving/99 6.00 15.00
16 Alex English/75 2.50 6.00
17 Marc Gasol/99 3.00 8.00
18 Chris Paul/99 4.00 10.00
19 Paul George/75 4.00 10.00
20 Dirk Nowitzki/99 4.00 10.00
21 James Harden/99 5.00 12.00
22 Steven Adams/75 2.50 6.00
23 Jose Calderon/75 2.00 5.00
24 Ty Lawson/75 2.00 5.00
25 Kobe Bryant/99 12.00 30.00
26 Allen Iverson/99 4.00 10.00
27 Damian Lillard/99 6.00 15.00
28 M.Carter-Williams/75 4.00 10.00
29 Paul Pierce/75 3.00 8.00
30 Dominique Wilkins/75 4.00 10.00
31 Jason Kidd/75 3.00 8.00
32 Taj Gibson/75 2.50 6.00
33 Josh Smith/75 2.50 6.00
34 Tyreke Evans/75 2.00 5.00
35 Kevin Garnett/99 5.00 12.00
36 Larry Johnson/75 4.00 10.00
37 David Lee/75 2.00 5.00
38 Michael Kidd-Gilchrist/75 2.50 6.00
39 Ray Allen/75 3.00 8.00
40 Dwight Howard/99 2.50 6.00
41 Jeff Green/75 2.50 6.00
42 Tayshaun Prince/75 2.50 6.00
43 Jrue Holiday/75 2.50 6.00
44 Tyson Chandler/75 2.50 6.00
45 Kevin Love/99 3.00 8.00
46 Anthony Davis/99 6.00 15.00
47 Mike Conley/75 2.50 6.00
48 DeAndre Jordan/75 3.00 8.00
49 Ricky Rubio/75 3.00 8.00
50 Goran Dragic/75 2.50 6.00
51 Jeff Teague/75 2.50 6.00
52 Terrence Ross/75 2.50 6.00
53 Kareem Abdul-Jabbar/49 5.00 12.00
54 Victor Oladipo/75 2.50 6.00
55 Kevin McHale/75 3.00 8.00
56 Monta Ellis/75 2.50 6.00
57 Avery Bradley/75 2.50 6.00
58 DeMar DeRozan/99 3.00 8.00
59 Russell Westbrook/99 8.00 20.00
60 Grant Hill/75 4.00 10.00
61 Jeremy Lin/75 3.00 8.00
62 Thaddeus Young/75 2.00 5.00
63 Karl Malone/49 4.00 10.00
64 Zach Randolph/75 2.50 6.00
65 Klay Thompson/75 8.00 20.00
66 Ben McLemore/75 2.00 5.00
67 Nikola Vucevic/75 2.50 6.00
68 DeMarcus Cousins/75 3.00 8.00
69 Ryan Anderson/75 2.00 5.00
70 Greg Monroe/75 2.50 6.00
71 Jimmy Butler/75 3.00 8.00
72 Tim Duncan/99 5.00 12.00
73 Dion Waiters/75 2.50 6.00
74 Kawhi Leonard/75 5.00 12.00
75 LaMarcus Aldridge/75 3.00 8.00
76 Blake Griffin/99 3.00 8.00
77 Norris Cole/75 2.00 5.00
78 Dennis Schroder/99 2.50 6.00
79 Serge Ibaka/75 2.50 6.00
80 Harrison Barnes/75 2.50 6.00
81 Joakim Noah/99 2.50 6.00
82 Tony Parker/99 3.00 8.00
83 Kemba Walker/75 3.00 8.00
84 Shawn Kemp/75 5.00 12.00
85 Lance Stephenson/75 2.50 6.00
86 Brandon Jennings/75 2.00 5.00
87 Otto Porter/75 2.50 6.00
88 Deron Williams/75 2.50 6.00
89 Shaquille O'Neal/49 6.00 15.00
90 Iman Shumpert/75 2.00 5.00
91 Joe Dumars/75 3.00 8.00
92 Tim Hardaway Jr./75 2.00 5.00
93 Kenneth Faried/75 2.50 6.00
94 Hakeem Olajuwon/75 4.00 10.00
95 LeBron James/99 12.00 30.00
96 Carmelo Anthony/99 4.00 10.00
97 Derrick Rose/75 4.00 10.00
98 Patrick Ewing/49 4.00 10.00
99 Shawn Marion/75 2.50 6.00
100 Michael Finley/75 3.00 8.00

2014-15 Prestige Premium Connections

RANDOM INSERTS IN PACKS
1 D.Williams/J.Kidd .75 2.00
2 D.Robinson/T.Duncan 1.25 3.00
3 B.Cousy/R.Rondo 1.25 3.00
4 A.Iverson/M.Carter-Williams 1.00 2.50
5 B.Walton/L.Aldridge .75 2.00
6 T.Lawson/F.Lever .50 1.25
7 A.Gilmore/J.Noah .60 1.50
8 M.Price/K.Irving 1.50 4.00
9 A.Drummond/B.Laimbeer .75 2.00
10 B.Griffin/B.McAdoo .75 2.00
11 R.Barry/K.Thompson 1.00 2.50
12 E.Baylor/K.Bryant 3.00 8.00
13 A.Mourning/A.Davis 1.50 4.00
14 M.Malone/D.Howard .75 2.00
15 T.Porter/D.Lillard 1.50 4.00
16 L.James/O.Robertson 3.00 8.00
17 D.Wade/J.Dumars 1.25 3.00
18 C.Andersen/D.Rodman 1.50 4.00
19 K.Durant/G.Gervin 2.00 5.00
20 L.Bird/C.Anthony 2.00 5.00

2014-15 Prestige Premium Distinctive Ink

RANDOM INSERTS IN PACKS.
PRINT RUNS B/WN 10-175 COPIES PER
NO PRICING ON QTY 10
2 Khris Middleton/175
3 Kobe Bryant/25 100.00 200.00
4 Robert Parish/25
8 Tyler Zeller/175 5.00 12.00
10 Spencer Hawes/175 4.00 10.00
11 Bill Walton/25 12.00 30.00
12 Tony Snell/175 4.00 10.00
13 Kevin Durant/25
14 Marcin Gortat/49
16 Jason Thompson/149 4.00 10.00
20 Rick Mahorn/175 4.00 10.00
21 Ralph Sampson/25
22 Dennis Schroder/175
23 Blake Griffin/25
24 Chase Budinger/49
26 Mark Aguirre/149
28 Brandan Wright/175
30 Tim Hardaway Jr./175 4.00 10.00
31 Avery Johnson/25
32 Nate Wolters/175 5.00 12.00
33 Anthony Davis/25 60.00 120.00
34 Horace Grant/49
36 C.J. Watson/175
38 Jordan Crawford/175 5.00 12.00
40 Alan Anderson/175 4.00 10.00

2014-15 Prestige Premium Franchise Favorites

RANDOM INSERTS IN PACKS
1 Al Horford .60 1.50
2 Rajon Rondo .75 2.00
3 Deron Williams .60 1.50
4 Gerald Henderson .50 1.25
5 Derrick Rose 1.00 2.50
6 LeBron James 3.00 8.00
7 Dirk Nowitzki 1.00 2.50
8 Ty Lawson .50 1.25
9 Greg Monroe .60 1.50
10 Stephen Curry 3.00 8.00
11 James Harden 1.25 3.00
12 Paul George 1.00 2.50
13 Blake Griffin .75 2.00
14 Kobe Bryant 3.00 8.00
15 Mike Conley .60 1.50
16 Dwyane Wade 1.25 3.00
17 Ersan Ilyasova .50 1.25
18 Ricky Rubio .75 2.00
19 Anthony Davis 1.50 4.00
20 Carmelo Anthony 1.00 2.50
21 Kevin Durant 2.00 5.00
22 Nikola Vucevic .60 1.50
23 Michael Carter-Williams .50 1.25
24 Goran Dragic .60 1.50
25 LaMarcus Aldridge .75 2.00
26 DeMarcus Cousins .75 2.00
27 Tim Duncan 1.25 3.00
28 DeMar DeRozan .75 2.00
29 Gordon Hayward .75 2.00
30 John Wall 1.00 2.50

2014-15 Prestige Premium Hardcourt Heroes

RANDOM INSERTS IN PACKS
1 Joe Johnson .60 1.50
2 Chris Bosh .75 2.00
3 Dirk Nowitzki 1.00 2.50
4 Damian Lillard 1.50 4.00
5 Vince Carter 1.00 2.50
6 LeBron James 3.00 8.00
7 Russell Westbrook 2.00 5.00
8 Stephen Curry 3.00 8.00
9 Kevin Durant 2.00 5.00
10 Jeff Green .60 1.50
11 Kobe Bryant 3.00 8.00
12 Carmelo Anthony 1.00 2.50
13 Anthony Davis 1.50 4.00
14 Chris Paul 1.00 2.50
15 Dwyane Wade 1.25 3.00
16 Kevin Love .75 2.00
17 Manu Ginobili .75 2.00
18 Klay Thompson 1.00 2.50
19 Tim Duncan 1.25 3.00
20 Kyrie Irving 1.50 4.00

2014-15 Prestige Premium Old School Signatures

RANDOM INSERTS IN PACKS
PRINT RUNS B/WN 15-175 COPIES PER
NO PRICING ON QTY 15 OR LESS
2 Dick Van Arsdale/175 5.00 12.00
4 Steve Mix/175
6 Cedric Ceballos/175 8.00 20.00
7 Nate Archibald/25
8 Horace Grant/149 8.00 20.00
10 Dan Issel/175 5.00 12.00
12 Bill Willoughby/175
13 Scott Wedman/175
15 John Thompson/25
16 Bobby Jones/175
17 Ralph Sampson/25
18 David Thompson/149 5.00 12.00
20 Tim Hardaway/175
22 Campy Russell/175
23 George Karl/25 6.00 15.00
24 Micheal Ray Richardson/175 5.00 12.00
25 Dolph Schayes/25
26 Bob Dandridge/175 6.00 12.00
27 Glen Rice/49
28 Cazzie Russell/149
30 Rick Mahorn/175 4.00 10.00
32 John Salley/175 4.00 10.00
33 Bill Walton/25
34 Maurice Cheeks/175
35 George Gervin/25 12.00 30.00
36 Gary Trent/175
37 Wayne Embry/149 10.00 25.00
38 Mark Aguirre/149
40 Jack Sikma/175 5.00 12.00
41 Michael Curry/175
43 Isiah Thomas/25
44 Jim Jackson/175 4.00 10.00
45 Nate Thurmond/25
46 Eddie Johnson/175 4.00 10.00
47 John Lucas/144 6.00 15.00
50 Mark Landsberger/175
52 Terry Porter/175 4.00 10.00
53 World B. Free/25
54 Tom Van Arsdale/175 5.00 12.00
55 Joe Dumars/25 6.00 15.00
56 Harvey Grant/175 4.00 10.00
57 George McGinnis/149 4.00 10.00
58 Adrian Smith/175 5.00 12.00
60 Doug Collins/175 6.00 15.00

2014-15 Prestige Premium Playmakers

RANDOM INSERTS IN PACKS
1 Kevin Durant 15.00 40.00
2 LeBron James 75.00 150.00
3 Kevin Love 6.00 15.00
4 Anthony Davis 15.00 40.00
5 DeMarcus Cousins 15.00 40.00
6 Chris Paul 8.00 20.00
7 Carmelo Anthony 8.00 20.00
8 Stephen Curry 25.00 60.00
9 Blake Griffin 6.00 15.00
10 Dirk Nowitzki 8.00 20.00
11 James Harden 10.00 25.00
12 Andre Drummond 6.00 15.00
13 Al Jefferson 5.00 12.00
14 LaMarcus Aldridge 6.00 15.00
15 Goran Dragic 5.00 12.00

16 Tim Duncan 10.00 25.00
17 Dwight Howard 5.00 12.00
18 Isaiah Thomas 6.00 15.00
19 Paul George 8.00 20.00
20 Kyrie Irving 20.00 50.00
21 Kyle Lowry 5.00 12.00
22 Mike Conley 5.00 12.00
23 Joakim Noah 5.00 12.00
24 Kenneth Faried 5.00 12.00
25 Paul Millsap 6.00 15.00

2014-15 Prestige Premium Preeminent Ink

RANDOM INSERTS IN PACKS
PRINT RUNS B/WN 10-175 COPIES PER
NO PRICING DUE TO SCARCITY
1 Danny Green/49
5 Dee Brown/175 4.00 10.00
8 Kobe Bryant/25
10 Kyrie Irving/25 25.00 60.00
13 Reggie Jackson/149 4.00 10.00
14 Thaddeus Young/175 4.00 10.00
18 Kevin Durant/25 30.00 80.00
21 JaVale McGee/49 5.00 12.00
23 Wesley Matthews/175 4.00 10.00
24 Tim Hardaway Jr./175 4.00 10.00
28 Blake Griffin/25 20.00 50.00
31 Terrence Ross/149
37 Anthony Davis/25 75.00 150.00
38 Marcin Gortat/49 15.00 40.00
40 Isaiah Thomas/175

2014-15 Prestige Premium Prestigious Pioneers

RANDOM INSERTS IN PACKS
1 George Mikan 1.50 4.00
2 Bob Pettit .75 2.00
3 Bob Cousy 1.25 3.00
4 Dolph Schayes .75 2.00
5 Bill Russell 1.25 3.00
6 Elgin Baylor .75 2.00
7 Bill Sharman .75 2.00
8 Wilt Chamberlain 1.50 4.00
9 Oscar Robertson 1.00 2.50
10 Jerry West 1.00 2.50
11 Willis Reed .75 2.00
12 Hal Greer .60 1.50
13 John Havlicek 1.00 2.50
14 Pete Maravich 1.25 3.00
15 Rick Barry .60 1.50
16 Julius Erving 1.25 3.00
17 Kareem Abdul-Jabbar 1.25 3.00
18 Larry Bird 2.00 5.00
19 Magic Johnson 2.00 5.00
20 Dominique Wilkins 1.00 2.50

2014-15 Prestige Premium Prestigious Posts

RANDOM INSERTS IN PACKS
1 DeAndre Jordan 1.25 3.00
2 Andre Drummond 1.25 3.00
3 Kevin Love 1.25 3.00
4 Joakim Noah 1.00 2.50
5 Dwight Howard 1.00 2.50
6 Tim Duncan 2.00 5.00
7 Anthony Davis 2.50 6.00
8 Blake Griffin 1.25 3.00
9 Marcin Gortat 1.00 2.50
10 LaMarcus Aldridge 1.25 3.00

2014-15 Prestige Premium Prestigious Premieres Signatures

RANDOM INSERTS IN PACKS
PPAG Aaron Gordon 6.00 15.00
PPAP Adreian Payne 4.00 10.00
PPAW Andrew Wiggins 100.00 200.00
PPBC Bruno Caboclo 4.00 10.00
PPCE Cleanthony Early 3.00 8.00
PPCJ Cory Jefferson 3.00 8.00
PPCW C.J. Wilcox 3.00 8.00
PPDD Doug McDermott 5.00 12.00
PPDE Dante Exum 5.00 12.00
PPEP Elfrid Payton 5.00 12.00
PPGH Gary Harris 5.00 12.00
PPGR Glenn Robinson III 3.00 8.00
PPJA Jordan Adams 3.00 8.00
PPJE Joel Embiid 20.00 50.00
PPJP Jabari Parker 40.00 100.00
PPJR Julius Randle 8.00 20.00
PPJS Jarnell Stokes 3.00 8.00
PPJY James Young 3.00 8.00
PPKA Kyle Anderson 8.00 20.00
PPMM Mitch McGary 3.00 8.00
PPMS Marcus Smart 5.00 12.00
PPNS Nik Stauskas 4.00 10.00
PPNV Noah Vonleh 8.00 20.00
PPRH Rodney Hood 5.00 12.00
PPRS Russ Smith 3.00 8.00
PPSN Shabazz Napier 5.00 12.00
PPSP Spencer Dinwiddie 4.00 10.00
PPTA Thanasis Antetokounmpo 3.00 8.00
PPTE Tyler Ennis 3.00 8.00
PPTJ T.J. Warren 5.00 12.00
PPZL Zach LaVine 12.00 30.00

2014-15 Prestige Premium Prestigious Pros

RANDOM INSERTS IN PACKS
1 Kobe Bryant 8.00 20.00
2 Anthony Davis 4.00 10.00
3 DeMarcus Cousins 2.00 5.00
4 Monta Ellis 1.50 4.00
5 Tim Duncan 3.00 8.00
6 Chris Paul 2.50 6.00
7 Victor Oladipo 1.50 4.00
8 Josh Smith 1.50 4.00
9 Manu Ginobili 2.00 5.00
10 Rajon Rondo 2.00 5.00
11 Paul Pierce 2.00 5.00
12 Mike Conley 1.50 4.00
13 Ricky Rubio 2.00 5.00
14 Tristan Thompson 1.50 4.00
15 DeAndre Jordan 2.00 5.00
16 Paul George 2.50 6.00
17 Stephen Curry 8.00 20.00
18 Kevin Durant 5.00 12.00
19 Isaiah Thomas 2.00 5.00
20 Jonas Valanciunas 1.50 4.00
21 Ty Lawson 1.25 3.00
22 Michael Carter-Williams 1.25 3.00
23 Chris Bosh 2.00 5.00
24 Derrick Rose 2.50 6.00
25 Al Horford 1.50 4.00
26 Gerald Green 1.50 4.00
27 LaMarcus Aldridge 2.00 5.00
28 John Wall 2.50 6.00
29 Jameer Nelson 1.25 3.00
30 Marcin Gortat 1.50 4.00
31 Kevin Garnett 3.00 8.00
32 Trevor Ariza 1.25 3.00
33 Klay Thompson 2.50 6.00
34 Taj Gibson 1.50 4.00
35 Kemba Walker 2.00 5.00
36 Kenneth Faried 1.50 4.00
37 Joakim Noah 1.50 4.00
38 Al Jefferson 1.50 4.00
39 Carmelo Anthony 2.50 6.00
40 Damian Lillard 4.00 10.00
41 Serge Ibaka 1.50 4.00
42 Kyle Lowry 1.50 4.00
43 Jimmy Butler 2.00 5.00
44 Andrew Bogut 1.50 4.00
45 Steve Nash 2.00 5.00
46 Nicolas Batum 1.50 4.00
47 Marc Gasol 2.00 5.00
48 Blake Griffin 2.00 5.00
49 Kevin Love 2.00 5.00
50 Rudy Gay 2.00 5.00
51 Andre Drummond 2.00 5.00
52 Paul Millsap 2.00 5.00
53 Trey Burke 1.25 3.00
54 Roy Hibbert 1.50 4.00
55 Tony Parker 2.00 5.00
56 Lance Stephenson 1.50 4.00
57 Jeff Green 1.50 4.00
58 Vince Carter 2.50 6.00
59 Pau Gasol 2.00 5.00
60 Kyle Korver 1.50 4.00
61 Mario Chalmers 1.50 4.00
62 Thaddeus Young 1.25 3.00
63 Jeff Teague 1.50 4.00
64 Brandon Jennings 1.25 3.00
65 Robin Lopez 1.25 3.00
66 Derrick Favors 1.50 4.00
67 Greg Monroe 1.50 4.00
68 Zach Randolph 1.50 4.00
69 Dwight Howard 1.50 4.00
70 Goran Dragic 1.50 4.00
71 Dirk Nowitzki 2.50 6.00
72 DeMar DeRozan 2.00 5.00
73 James Harden 3.00 8.00
74 LeBron James 15.00 40.00
75 Kyrie Irving 4.00 10.00

2014-15 Prestige Premium Stars of the NBA Signatures

RANDOM INSERTS IN PACKS
PRINT RUNS B/WN 10-175 COPIES PER
NO PRICING ON QTY 10
1 Kobe Bryant/25
8 Jo Jo White/149
10 John Salley/175 4.00 10.00
11 Tristan Thompson/25 5.00 12.00
12 Kevin Durant/25 75.00 150.00
14 Marcin Gortat/49 5.00 12.00
16 Reggie Jackson/149
18 Kevin Willis/149 4.00 10.00
20 Tim Hardaway/175
21 Blake Griffin/25 30.00 80.00
22 Andrea Bargnani/25 5.00 12.00
24 Allan Houston/49 10.00 25.00
27 Nikola Vucevic/149 5.00 12.00
28 Isaiah Thomas/175 6.00 15.00
30 Eddie Jones/175 5.00 12.00
32 Nate Thurmond/25 15.00 40.00
34 Terrence Ross/149 5.00 12.00
36 Doug Collins/149
40 Maurice Cheeks/175
45 David Thompson/149 5.00 12.00
47 Mahmoud Abdul-Rauf/175 12.00 30.00
49 Antoine Walker/175 5.00 12.00
51 World B. Free/25
55 Adrian Dantley/149 5.00 12.00
57 Dan Issel/175 5.00 12.00
59 Bob Dandridge/175 4.00 10.00

2015-16 Prestige

1 J.R. Smith .30 .75
2 Luol Deng .30 .75
3 Tristan Thompson .30 .75
4 Chris Paul .50 1.25
5 Jeremy Lin .40 1.00
6 Josh Smith .30 .75
7 Thaddeus Young .25 .60
8 Kevin Garnett .60 1.50
9 Henry Sims .25 .60
10 Kevin Love .40 1.00
11 Khris Middleton .30 .75
12 Matthew Dellavedova .30 .75
13 Al Jefferson .30 .75
14 Matt Barnes .25 .60
15 Jordan Hill .25 .60
16 Corey Brewer .25 .60
17 Tony Wroten .25 .60
18 Jameer Nelson .25 .60
19 Kosta Koufos .25 .60
20 Brandon Bass .25 .60
21 Michael Carter-Williams .25 .60
22 Avery Bradley .30 .75
23 Gerald Henderson .25 .60
24 Spencer Hawes .25 .60
25 Carlos Boozer .30 .75
26 Tim Duncan .60 1.50
27 David West .40 1.00
28 Nerlens Noel .30 .75
29 LaMarcus Aldridge .40 1.00
30 Giannis Antetokounmpo .75 2.00
31 DeAndre Jordan .40 1.00
32 Marcus Smart .30 .75
33 Joe Ingles .25 .60
34 Tobias Harris .30 .75
35 Tony Allen .25 .60
36 Kawhi Leonard .60 1.50
37 C.J. Watson .25 .60
38 Hollis Thompson .25 .60
39 Wesley Matthews .25 .60
40 Zaza Pachulia .25 .60
41 Marc Gasol .40 1.00
42 Tyler Zeller .30 .75
43 Derrick Williams .25 .60
44 Courtney Lee .30 .75
45 Monta Ellis .30 .75
46 Manu Ginobili .40 1.00
47 Luis Scola .30 .75
48 Robert Covington .25 .60
49 Arron Afflalo .25 .60
50 Derrick Rose .50 1.25
51 Jeff Green .30 .75
52 Jared Sullinger .25 .60
53 Andre Miller .30 .75
54 Vince Carter .50 1.25
55 Al-Farouq Aminu .30 .75
56 Danny Green .30 .75
57 Roy Hibbert .30 .75
58 Nicolas Batum .30 .75
59 Nikola Mirotic .30 .75
60 Robin Lopez .25 .60
61 DeMarre Carroll .25 .60
62 Evan Turner .30 .75
63 Shane Larkin .25 .60
64 Zach Randolph .30 .75
65 Rajon Rondo .40 1.00
66 Brandon Knight .30 .75
67 Omer Asik .30 .75
68 Chris Kaman .30 .75
69 Mike Dunleavy .25 .60
70 Paul Millsap .40 1.00
71 Pau Gasol .40 1.00
72 Blake Griffin .40 1.00
73 Andrea Bargnani .30 .75
74 Mike Conley .40 1.00
75 Tyson Chandler .30 .75
76 Gerald Green .30 .75
77 Eric Gordon .30 .75
78 Damian Lillard .75 2.00
79 Aaron Brooks .25 .60
80 Goran Dragic .30 .75
81 Jimmy Butler .40 1.00
82 J.J. Redick .40 1.00
83 Jason Smith .25 .60
84 Al Horford .30 .75
85 Alan Anderson .25 .60
86 Dion Waiters .30 .75
87 Greg Monroe .30 .75
88 Jabari Parker .50 1.25
89 LeBron James 1.50 4.00
90 Joakim Noah .30 .75
91 Dwyane Wade .60 1.50
92 Jamal Crawford .40 1.00
93 Wesley Johnson .30 .75
94 Kyle Korver .30 .75
95 Brook Lopez .30 .75
96 Kevin Durant 1.00 2.50
97 Amir Johnson .25 .60
98 Ersan Ilyasova .25 .60
99 Timofey Mozgov .25 .60
100 Kyrie Irving .75 2.00
101 Nikola Vucevic .30 .75
102 Enes Kanter .25 .60
103 Jusuf Nurkic .25 .60
104 Harrison Barnes .30 .75
105 Thabo Sefolosha .25 .60
106 Jrue Holiday .30 .75
107 Michael Kidd-Gilchrist .30 .75
108 Greivis Vasquez .30 .75
109 Jason Thompson .25 .60
110 Boris Diaw .30 .75
111 Elfrid Payton .30 .75
112 Steven Adams .30 .75
113 Ty Lawson .25 .60
114 Draymond Green .50 1.25
115 Jeff Teague .30 .75
116 Norris Cole .25 .60
117 Alec Burks .25 .60
118 Kyle Lowry .30 .75
119 Darren Collison .30 .75
120 Tiago Splitter .30 .75
121 Victor Oladipo .30 .75
122 Andrew Wiggins .60 1.50
123 Kenneth Faried .30 .75
124 Stephen Curry 1.50 4.00
125 Hassan Whiteside .30 .75
126 Ryan Anderson .30 .75
127 Derrick Favors .30 .75
128 Jonas Valanciunas .30 .75
129 Tim Hardaway Jr. .25 .60
130 Tony Parker .40 1.00
131 Devin Harris .25 .60
132 Gorgui Dieng .25 .60
133 Danilo Gallinari .30 .75
134 Klay Thompson .50 1.25
135 Chris Andersen .30 .75
136 Tyreke Evans .25 .60
137 Rudy Gobert .40 1.00
138 Patrick Patterson .25 .60
139 Carmelo Anthony .50 1.25
140 Marcus Morris .25 .60
141 Chandler Parsons .30 .75
142 Ricky Rubio .40 1.00
143 Wilson Chandler .30 .75
144 Bradley Beal .40 1.00
145 Mario Chalmers .30 .75
146 Andre Drummond .40 1.00
147 Trey Burke .25 .60
148 DeMar DeRozan .40 1.00
149 Langston Galloway .25 .60
150 Markieff Morris .25 .60
151 Dirk Nowitzki .50 1.25
152 Nikola Pekovic .25 .60
153 Gary Harris .30 .75
154 Nene .30 .75
155 Chris Bosh .40 1.00
156 Jodie Meeks .30 .75
157 Dante Exum .30 .75
158 Trevor Ariza .25 .60
159 Nick Young .30 .75
160 P.J. Tucker .25 .60
161 Bojan Bogdanovic .25 .60
162 Kevin Martin .30 .75
163 Solomon Hill .25 .60
164 John Wall .50 1.25
165 Lance Stephenson .30 .75
166 Brandon Jennings .25 .60
167 Gordon Hayward .40 1.00
168 Donatas Motiejunas .25 .60
169 Jordan Clarkson .40 1.00
170 Eric Bledsoe .30 .75
171 Joe Johnson .30 .75
172 Zach LaVine .40 1.00
173 Paul George .50 1.25
174 Marcin Gortat .30 .75
175 Kemba Walker .40 1.00
176 Caron Butler .30 .75
177 Ben McLemore .25 .60
178 Dwight Howard .30 .75
179 Kobe Bryant 1.50 4.00
180 Reggie Jackson .30 .75
181 Deron Williams .30 .75
182 Andrew Bogut .30 .75
183 George Hill .30 .75
184 Otto Porter .30 .75
185 Marvin Williams .30 .75
186 Kentavious Caldwell-Pope .30 .75
187 DeMarcus Cousins .40 1.00
188 James Harden .60 1.50
189 Aaron Gordon .30 .75
190 Russell Westbrook 1.00 2.50
191 Jarrett Jack .30 .75
192 Andre Iguodala .30 .75
193 Anthony Davis .75 2.00
194 Paul Pierce .40 1.00
195 Cody Zeller .25 .60
196 Terrence Ross .30 .75
197 Rudy Gay .40 1.00
198 Patrick Beverley .25 .60
199 Channing Frye .30 .75
200 Serge Ibaka .30 .75
201 Stanley Johnson RC .60 1.50
202 Jordan Mickey RC .50 1.25
203 Jerian Grant RC .50 1.25
204 Darrun Hilliard RC .50 1.25
205 Rashad Vaughn RC .50 1.25
206 Andrew Harrison RC .75 2.00
207 Karl-Anthony Towns RC 4.00 10.00
208 Rondae Hollis-Jefferson RC .60 1.50
209 Kristaps Porzingis RC 2.00 5.00
210 R.J. Hunter RC .50 1.25
211 Frank Kaminsky RC .75 2.00
212 Larry Nance Jr. RC .75 2.00
213 Trey Lyles RC .75 2.00
214 Pat Connaughton RC .50 1.25
215 Kelly Oubre Jr. RC .60 1.50
216 Tyus Jones RC .75 2.00
217 D'Angelo Russell RC 2.00 5.00
218 Bobby Portis RC .75 2.00
219 Mario Hezonja RC .60 1.50
220 Anthony Brown RC .50 1.25
221 Devin Booker RC 2.50 6.00
222 Montrezl Harrell RC .60 1.50
223 Cameron Payne RC .60 1.50
224 Rakeem Christmas RC .50 1.25
225 Sam Dekker RC .60 1.50
226 Kevon Looney RC .60 1.50
227 Jahlil Okafor RC 1.00 2.50
228 Justin Anderson RC .60 1.50
229 Justise Winslow RC .75 2.00
230 Pierre Jackson RC .50 1.25
231 Myles Turner RC .75 2.00
232 Walter Tavares RC .50 1.25
233 Delon Wright RC .60 1.50
234 Joe Young RC .60 1.50
235 Terry Rozier RC .60 1.50
236 Norman Powell RC .60 1.50
237 Emmanuel Mudiay RC .75 2.00
238 Jarell Martin RC .60 1.50
239 Willie Cauley-Stein RC .75 2.00
240 Chris McCullough RC .50 1.25

2015-16 Prestige Bonus Shots Blue

*BLUE: 1.2X TO 3X BASIC
*BLUE RC: 1.2X TO 3X BASIC
RANDOM INSERTS IN PACKS
STATED PRINT RUN 99 SER.#'d SETS
207 Karl-Anthony Towns 20.00 50.00

2015-16 Prestige Bonus Shots Light Blue

*LT.BLUE VET: .5X TO 1.2X BASIC
*LT.BLUE RC: .5X TO 1.2X BASIC
RANDOM INSERTS IN PACKS

2015-16 Prestige Bonus Shots Orange Die Cuts

*ORANGE: 1X TO 2.5X BASIC
*ORANGE RC: 1X TO 2.5X BASIC
RANDOM INSERTS IN PACKS
STATED PRINT RUN 149 SER.#'d SETS

2015-16 Prestige Bonus Shots Purple

*PURPLE: 1.5X TO 4X BASIC
*PURPLE RC: 1.5X TO 4X BASIC
RANDOM INSERTS IN PACKS
STATED PRINT RUN 49 SER.#'d SETS
207 Karl-Anthony Towns 25.00 60.00

2015-16 Prestige Bonus Shots Red

*RED: .75X TO 2X BASIC
*RED RC: .75X TO 2X BASIC
RANDOM INSERTS IN PACKS
STATED PRINT RUN 199 SER.#'d SETS

2015-16 Prestige Acetate Rookies

RANDOM INSERTS IN PACKS
1 Pierre Jackson .75 2.00
2 Stanley Johnson 1.00 2.50
3 Rakeem Christmas .75 2.00
4 Emmanuel Mudiay 1.25 3.00
5 Kevon Looney 1.00 2.50
6 Darrun Hilliard .75 2.00
7 Bobby Portis 1.25 3.00
8 Sam Dekker 1.00 2.50
9 Branden Dawson .75 2.00
10 Trey Lyles 1.25 3.00
11 Joe Young 1.00 2.50
12 Willie Cauley-Stein 1.25 3.00
13 Walter Tavares .75 2.00
14 Jahlil Okafor 1.50 4.00
15 Larry Nance Jr. 1.25 3.00
16 Nikola Jokic 1.50 4.00
17 Justin Anderson 1.00 2.50
18 Tyus Jones 1.25 3.00
19 Jonathon Simmons 1.25 3.00
20 Jerian Grant .75 2.00
21 Norman Powell 1.00 2.50
22 Justise Winslow 1.25 3.00
23 Montrezl Harrell 1.00 2.50
24 D'Angelo Russell 3.00 8.00
25 Anthony Brown .75 2.00
26 Cliff Alexander .75 2.00
27 Rondae Hollis-Jefferson 1.00 2.50
28 Cameron Payne 1.00 2.50
29 Tyler Harvey .75 2.00
30 Myles Turner 1.25 3.00
31 Richaun Holmes 1.00 2.50
32 Mario Hezonja 1.00 2.50
33 Jordan Mickey .75 2.00
34 Karl-Anthony Towns 6.00 15.00
35 R.J. Hunter .75 2.00
36 Josh Huestis .75 2.00
37 Kelly Oubre Jr. 1.00 2.50
38 Rashad Vaughn .75 2.00
39 Aaron Harrison 1.00 2.50
40 Devin Booker 4.00 10.00
41 Dakari Johnson .75 2.00
42 Kristaps Porzingis 3.00 8.00
43 Chris McCullough .75 2.00
44 Josh Richardson 1.25 3.00
45 Jarell Martin 1.00 2.50
46 Ryan Boatright 1.00 2.50
47 Terry Rozier 1.00 2.50
48 Delon Wright 1.00 2.50
49 Andrew Harrison 1.25 3.00
50 Frank Kaminsky 1.25 3.00

2015-16 Prestige Bonus Shots Autographs

RANDOM INSERTS IN PACKS
PRINT RUNS B/WN 10-49 COPIES PER
NO PRICING ON QTY 10
EXCHANGE DEADLINE 4/19/2017
1 Robert Covington/49 4.00 10.00
2 Lorenzo Brown/49 4.00 10.00
3 Grant Jerrett/49
4 Ian Clark/49 4.00 10.00
6 Ray McCallum/49
7 Dwight Powell/49 4.00 10.00
9 James Ennis/49 4.00 10.00
10 Cameron Bairstow/49 4.00 10.00
11 Reggie Bullock/49 4.00 10.00
13 Mike Muscala/49 4.00 10.00
18 Antonio McDyess/49 5.00 12.00
20 Devyn Marble/49
25 Jordan Clarkson/49
26 Joe Harris/25
27 Matthew Dellavedova/49
28 Damien Inglis/49
29 Carl Landry/25
30 Erick Green/49
31 Bob Dandridge/49
32 Darrell Griffith/49
33 Phil Pressey/49
34 Ricky Pierce/49
35 James Michael McAdoo/49 4.00 10.00
36 Jabari Brown/49 5.00 12.00
37 Eddie Jones/49 5.00 12.00
38 Steve Novak/25
39 Andre Roberson/49
40 Donatas Motiejunas/49
41 Jerami Grant/49
42 Kyle O'Quinn/49
43 Isaiah Canaan/49 5.00 12.00
44 Terry Cummings/49
45 Jamal Mashburn/49
47 Allen Crabbe/49
48 Kevin Willis/49
50 Hollis Thompson/49 4.00 10.00
51 Jarnell Stokes/49
52 James Johnson/49
53 C.J. Miles/49
54 Chuck Person/25 6.00 15.00
55 John Salley/49 4.00 10.00
56 Kurt Rambis/25 5.00 12.00
57 John Lucas/25
58 Jeff Malone/49 4.00 10.00
59 Brian Roberts/49
61 Kenny Walker/25 5.00 12.00
62 Bobby Jones/49
63 Kenny Anderson/49
64 Alan Anderson/25
65 Mason Plumlee/49 5.00 12.00
67 Cuttino Mobley/25
68 Bojan Bogdanovic/49 4.00 10.00
69 Charles Oakley/49 5.00 12.00
70 Glenn Robinson III/49 4.00 10.00
71 Maurice Harkless/25
72 Scott Skiles/49
73 Satch Sanders/25 10.00 25.00
77 Johnny O'Bryant/49
78 Mario Elie/25
79 Larry Nance/25 6.00 15.00
80 Quincy Acy/49
81 Scott Brooks/25 5.00 12.00
82 Mark Price/49 6.00 15.00
83 Keith Van Horn/25 6.00 15.00
84 Rik Smits/49
85 Maurice Cheeks/25 5.00 12.00
86 Chase Budinger/25
87 Walter Davis/25
88 Ryan Kelly/49
89 Jason Smith/25
90 Nikola Mirotic/25 6.00 15.00
91 Norm Nixon/25
93 Cazzie Russell/25
94 Vin Baker/25
95 Kendall Gill/25
97 Bill Cartwright/25
98 Tom Chambers/25
99 Theo Ratliff/25
100 Will Perdue/25 5.00 12.00

2015-16 Prestige Brilliant Beginnings

RANDOM INSERTS IN PACKS
*STARBURST: .6X TO 1.5X BASIC
1 Rajon Rondo .60 1.50
2 Tyreke Evans .40 1.00
3 Larry Bird 1.50 4.00
4 Tim Duncan 1.00 2.50
5 Alonzo Mourning .75 2.00
6 David Robinson 1.00 2.50
7 Steve Nash .60 1.50
8 Kobe Bryant 2.50 6.00
9 Tracy McGrady .60 1.50
10 Chris Paul .75 2.00
11 Chris Andersen .50 1.25
12 Dwight Howard .50 1.25
13 Magic Johnson 1.50 4.00
14 Ray Allen .60 1.50
15 Kevin Garnett 1.00 2.50
16 Allen Iverson .75 2.00
17 Dikembe Mutombo .60 1.50
18 Kevin Durant 1.50 4.00
19 James Harden 1.00 2.50
20 Shawn Kemp 1.00 2.50
21 J.R. Smith .50 1.25
22 Carmelo Anthony .75 2.00
23 Karl Malone .75 2.00
24 Chris Webber .60 1.50
25 Hakeem Olajuwon .75 2.00
26 Dwyane Wade 1.00 2.50
27 Tony Parker .60 1.50
28 Kyrie Irving 1.25 3.00
29 Deron Williams .50 1.25
30 LeBron James 2.50 6.00
31 Pau Gasol .60 1.50
32 Baron Davis .50 1.25
33 John Stockton 1.00 2.50
34 Latrell Sprewell .50 1.25
35 Paul Pierce .60 1.50
36 Chris Bosh .60 1.50
37 Grant Hill .75 2.00
38 Anthony Davis 1.25 3.00
39 Joakim Noah .50 1.25
40 Kevin Love .60 1.50
41 Joe Johnson .50 1.25
42 Vince Carter .75 2.00
43 Dirk Nowitzki .75 2.00
44 Shaquille O'Neal 1.25 3.00
45 Jason Kidd .60 1.50
46 Anfernee Hardaway 1.50 4.00
47 Manu Ginobili .60 1.50
48 John Wall .75 2.00
49 Blake Griffin .60 1.50
50 Stephen Curry 2.50 6.00

2015-16 Prestige Distinctive Ink

RANDOM INSERTS IN PACKS
PRINT RUNS B/WN 21-199 COPIES PER
EXCHANGE DEADLINE 4/19/2017
1 James Worthy/49 8.00 20.00
2 Michael Carter-Williams/49
3 Kobe Bryant/25
4 Steve Novak/149 3.00 8.00
5 Chris Webber/25
6 Julius Randle/49 6.00 15.00
7 Mike Muscala/199 3.00 8.00
8 Robert Covington/199 3.00 8.00
9 Jo Jo White/149 4.00 10.00
10 Victor Oladipo/49 5.00 12.00
11 Vlade Divac/149 5.00 12.00
12 Kentavious Caldwell-Pope/49
13 Kevin Durant/25
14 Andre Roberson/199 3.00 8.00
15 Andrew Wiggins/49 25.00 60.00
16 Kevin Willis/149 3.00 8.00
17 Walter Davis/149 3.00 8.00
18 C.J. McCollum/49 6.00 15.00
19 Walt Frazier/49 6.00 15.00
20 Ben McLemore/49 4.00 10.00
21 Danny Manning/149 4.00 10.00
22 Nerlens Noel/49 6.00 15.00
23 Kyrie Irving/25
24 Donatas Motiejunas/199 3.00 8.00
25 Jabari Parker/25
26 Michael Kidd-Gilchrist/49 5.00 12.00
27 Nikola Mirotic/99 5.00 12.00
28 Otto Porter/49 5.00 12.00
29 Paul Westphal/149 5.00 12.00
30 Alex Len/49
31 Jamaal Wilkes/149 5.00 12.00
32 Jordan Clarkson/199 5.00 12.00
33 Carmelo Anthony/21 15.00 40.00
34 Jerami Grant/199 3.00 8.00
35 Ricky Rubio/49 6.00 15.00
36 Noah Vonleh/49 4.00 10.00
37 Norm Nixon/149 3.00 8.00
38 Trey Burke/49 4.00 10.00
39 Christian Laettner/49 5.00 12.00
40 Anthony Bennett/49 4.00 10.00
41 Dolph Schayes/149 5.00 12.00
42 Ricky Pierce/199
43 Allen Iverson/25 50.00 120.00
44 Terry Cummings/149 4.00 10.00
45 Enes Kanter/149 3.00 8.00
46 Mason Plumlee/199 4.00 10.00
47 Gary Payton/49 6.00 15.00
48 Shabazz Muhammad/149 4.00 10.00
49 Clyde Drexler/49 10.00 25.00
50 Cody Zeller/49 4.00 10.00

2015-16 Prestige Franchise Favorites

RANDOM INSERTS IN PACKS
*CRYSTAL/99: 1.2X TO 3X
*CHECK/125: 1.2X TO 3X
1 Hakeem Olajuwon .75 2.00
2 John Stockton 1.00 2.50
3 Blake Griffin .60 1.50
4 Joe Dumars .60 1.50
5 Kyrie Irving 1.25 3.00
6 Jerry West .75 2.00
7 Kevin Durant 1.50 4.00
8 Tim Duncan 1.00 2.50
9 Isiah Thomas .60 1.50
10 Dirk Nowitzki .75 2.00
11 Patrick Ewing .75 2.00
12 Bill Russell 1.00 2.50
13 Anthony Davis 1.25 3.00
14 David Robinson 1.00 2.50
15 LeBron James 2.50 6.00
16 Larry Bird 1.50 4.00
17 Russell Westbrook 1.50 4.00
18 Kobe Bryant 2.50 6.00
19 Julius Erving 1.00 2.50
20 Dwyane Wade 1.00 2.50

2015-16 Prestige Freshman Fabrics

RANDOM INSERTS IN PACKS
*PRIME/25: .75X TO 2X BASIC
1 Karl-Anthony Towns 8.00 20.00
2 D'Angelo Russell 4.00 10.00
3 Jahlil Okafor 4.00 10.00
4 Kristaps Porzingis 8.00 20.00
5 Myles Turner 2.50 6.00
6 Willie Cauley-Stein 2.50 6.00
7 Emmanuel Mudiay 2.50 6.00
8 Stanley Johnson 2.00 5.00
9 Frank Kaminsky 2.50 6.00
10 Justise Winslow 2.50 6.00

2015-16 Prestige Freshman Fabrics Jumbo

RANDOM INSERTS IN PACKS
*PRIME/25: .75X TO 2X BASIC
1 Karl-Anthony Towns 8.00 20.00
2 D'Angelo Russell 6.00 15.00
3 Jahlil Okafor 3.00 8.00
4 Kristaps Porzingis 6.00 15.00
5 Montrezl Harrell 2.00 5.00
6 Willie Cauley-Stein 2.50 6.00
7 Emmanuel Mudiay 2.50 6.00
8 Stanley Johnson 2.00 5.00
9 Frank Kaminsky 2.50 6.00
10 Justise Winslow 2.50 6.00
11 Myles Turner 2.50 6.00
12 Trey Lyles 2.50 6.00
13 Devin Booker 8.00 20.00
14 Cameron Payne 2.00 5.00
15 Kelly Oubre Jr. 2.00 5.00
16 Terry Rozier 2.00 5.00
17 R.J. Hunter 1.50 4.00
18 Sam Dekker 2.00 5.00
19 Jerian Grant 1.50 4.00
20 Delon Wright 2.00 5.00
21 Justin Anderson 2.00 5.00
22 Bobby Portis 2.50 6.00
23 Rondae Hollis-Jefferson 2.00 5.00
24 Tyus Jones 2.50 6.00
25 Kevon Looney 2.00 5.00

2015-16 Prestige Freshman Flashback Jumbo Materials

RANDOM INSERTS IN PACKS
*PRIME/25: 1X TO 2.5X BASIC
1 Andre Drummond 2.50 6.00
2 Anthony Davis 5.00 12.00
3 Bradley Beal 2.50 6.00
4 Tristan Thompson 2.00 5.00
5 Enes Kanter 1.50 4.00
6 Harrison Barnes 2.00 5.00
7 Iman Shumpert 1.50 4.00
8 Jimmy Butler 2.50 6.00
9 Kawhi Leonard 4.00 10.00
10 Kemba Walker 2.50 6.00
11 Kenneth Faried 2.00 5.00
12 Klay Thompson 3.00 8.00
13 Kyrie Irving 5.00 12.00
14 Nikola Vucevic 2.00 5.00
15 Tobias Harris 2.00 5.00

2015-16 Prestige NBA Materials

RANDOM INSERTS IN PACKS
*PRIME/25: .75X TO 2X BASIC
1 Carmelo Anthony 3.00 8.00
2 Chris Bosh 2.50 6.00
3 Clyde Drexler 3.00 8.00
4 David Robinson 4.00 10.00
5 Dikembe Mutombo 2.50 6.00
6 Grant Hill 3.00 8.00
7 Jared Sullinger 1.50 4.00
8 Joakim Noah 2.00 5.00
9 Kevin Love 2.50 6.00
10 Larry Bird 8.00 20.00
11 Patrick Ewing 3.00 8.00
12 Shaquille O'Neal 5.00 12.00
13 Victor Oladipo 2.00 5.00
14 Kyrie Irving 5.00 12.00
15 John Wall 3.00 8.00
16 Derrick Rose 3.00 8.00
17 Marcus Smart 2.00 5.00
18 Andre Drummond 2.50 6.00
19 Stephen Curry 10.00 25.00
20 Blake Griffin 2.50 6.00
21 Damian Lillard 5.00 12.00
22 Kyle Lowry 2.00 5.00
23 Trey Burke 1.50 4.00
24 DeMar DeRozan 2.50 6.00
25 Dwyane Wade 4.00 10.00

2015-16 Prestige NBA Passport Signatures

RANDOM INSERTS IN PACKS
STATED PRINT RUN 99 SER.#'d SETS
EXCHANGE DEADLINE 4/19/2017
1 Karl-Anthony Towns 125.00 250.00
2 D'Angelo Russell 60.00 150.00
3 Jahlil Okafor 30.00 80.00
4 Emmanuel Mudiay 30.00 80.00
5 Kristaps Porzingis 100.00 250.00
6 Mario Hezonja 20.00 50.00
7 Justise Winslow 25.00 60.00
8 Willie Cauley-Stein 20.00 50.00
9 Stanley Johnson 8.00 20.00
10 Frank Kaminsky 6.00 15.00
11 Devin Booker 100.00 250.00
12 Myles Turner 20.00 50.00
13 Jerian Grant 4.00 10.00
14 Trey Lyles 6.00 15.00
15 Cameron Payne 12.00 30.00
16 Delon Wright 5.00 12.00
17 Rashad Vaughn 4.00 10.00
18 Kelly Oubre Jr. 5.00 12.00
19 Sam Dekker 10.00 25.00
20 Terry Rozier 5.00 12.00
21 Rondae Hollis-Jefferson 5.00 12.00
22 Bobby Portis 10.00 25.00
23 Justin Anderson 5.00 12.00
24 Jarell Martin 5.00 12.00
25 R.J. Hunter 4.00 10.00
26 Anthony Brown 4.00 10.00
28 Chris McCullough 4.00 10.00
29 Jordan Mickey 4.00 10.00
30 Larry Nance Jr. 15.00 40.00
31 Montrezl Harrell 5.00 12.00
32 Dakari Johnson 4.00 10.00
33 Darrun Hilliard 4.00 10.00
34 Pat Connaughton 4.00 10.00
35 Rakeem Christmas 4.00 10.00
36 Richaun Holmes 5.00 12.00
38 Andrew Harrison 6.00 15.00
40 Joe Young 5.00 12.00
42 Tyler Harvey 4.00 10.00
43 Branden Dawson 4.00 10.00
44 Tyus Jones 15.00 40.00
46 Aaron Harrison 8.00 20.00
48 Josh Richardson 10.00 25.00
49 Walter Tavares 4.00 10.00

2015-16 Prestige Old School Signatures

RANDOM INSERTS IN PACKS
PRINT RUNS B/WN 20-199 COPIES PER
EXCHANGE DEADLINE 4/19/2017
1 Jeff Malone/199 3.00 8.00
2 Theo Ratliff/199 3.00 8.00
3 Cliff Hagan/49
4 Gary Payton/49 10.00 25.00
5 Larry Brown/49 6.00 15.00
6 Shaquille O'Neal/20
7 Keith Van Horn/199 4.00 10.00
8 Hakeem Olajuwon/49 12.00 30.00
9 Ricky Pierce/199 3.00 8.00
10 Cazzie Russell/199 4.00 10.00
11 John Lucas/199 5.00 12.00
12 Will Perdue/199 3.00 8.00
13 Charles Oakley/199 4.00 10.00
14 Fat Lever/199 4.00 10.00
15 Artis Gilmore/49
16 Magic Johnson/25 30.00 80.00
17 Maurice Cheeks/199 3.00 8.00
18 Kevin McHale/49 10.00 25.00
19 Terry Cummings/199 4.00 10.00
20 Vin Baker/199 3.00 8.00
21 Kenny Walker/199 3.00 8.00
22 Billy Paultz/199 5.00 12.00
23 Scott Skiles/199 4.00 10.00
24 Avery Johnson/49 5.00 12.00
25 Mario Elie/199 3.00 8.00
26 Julius Erving/25 40.00 100.00
27 Walter Davis/199 3.00 8.00
28 Tracy McGrady/49 12.00 30.00
29 Kevin Willis/199 3.00 8.00
30 Kendall Gill/199 3.00 8.00
31 Bobby Jones/199 4.00 10.00
32 Brad Daugherty/199 4.00 10.00
33 Satch Sanders/199 8.00 20.00
34 Bob Dandridge/199 3.00 8.00
35 Larry Nance/199 4.00 10.00
36 John Stockton/25 20.00 50.00
37 Norm Nixon/199 3.00 8.00
38 Clyde Drexler/49 10.00 25.00
39 Chuck Person/199 4.00 10.00
40 Bill Cartwright/199 4.00 10.00
41 Kenny Anderson/199 4.00 10.00
42 Tom Gugliotta/199 3.00 8.00
43 Robert Parish/49 6.00 15.00
44 Cedric Maxwell/199 3.00 8.00
45 Rik Smits/199 4.00 10.00
46 David Robinson/49 20.00 50.00
47 Bernard King/49
48 Grant Hill/49 10.00 25.00
49 Kurt Rambis/199 3.00 8.00
50 Tom Chambers/199 4.00 10.00

2015-16 Prestige Playmakers

RANDOM INSERTS IN PACKS
*LT.BLUE/99: .75X TO 2X BASIC
*BRONZE/49: 1X TO 2.5X BASIC
1 Klay Thompson .75 2.00
2 Andrew Wiggins 1.00 2.50
3 LeBron James 2.50 6.00
4 Carmelo Anthony .75 2.00
5 Russell Westbrook 1.50 4.00
6 Stephen Curry 2.50 6.00
7 Damian Lillard 1.25 3.00
8 James Harden 1.00 2.50
9 Derrick Rose .75 2.00
10 Kawhi Leonard 1.00 2.50
11 Dwight Howard .50 1.25
12 Kobe Bryant 2.50 6.00
13 Anthony Davis 1.25 3.00
14 Manu Ginobili .60 1.50
15 Chris Bosh .60 1.50
16 Tony Parker .60 1.50
17 DeMar DeRozan .60 1.50
18 John Wall .75 2.00
19 Dirk Nowitzki .75 2.00
20 Kevin Durant 1.50 4.00
21 Dwyane Wade 1.00 2.50
22 Kyrie Irving 1.25 3.00
23 Blake Griffin .60 1.50
24 Bradley Beal .60 1.50
25 Chris Paul .75 2.00

2015-16 Prestige Preeminent Ink

RANDOM INSERTS IN PACKS
PRINT RUNS B/WN 20-149 COPIES PER
EXCHANGE DEADLINE 4/19/2017
1 Michael Carter-Williams/49 4.00 10.00
2 Tom Gugliotta/149
3 Alex Len/49 4.00 10.00
4 Satch Sanders/149 5.00 12.00
5 Michael Kidd-Gilchrist/49 5.00 12.00
6 Karl Malone/25 20.00 50.00
7 Chris Webber/49 50.00 120.00
8 Allen Iverson/25 40.00 100.00
9 Carl Landry/149 3.00 8.00
10 Bill Russell/20 50.00 120.00
11 Kentavious Caldwell-Pope/49 5.00 12.00
12 Cedric Maxwell/149 3.00 8.00
13 Otto Porter/49 5.00 12.00
14 Chase Budinger/149 3.00 8.00
15 Kevin Love/49 6.00 15.00
16 John Stockton/25 20.00 50.00
17 Kyrie Irving/49
18 Carmelo Anthony/20

19 Shabazz Muhammad/49 5.00 12.00
20 Kobe Bryant/25
21 Ben McLemore/49 4.00 10.00
22 Kurt Rambis/149 3.00 8.00
23 Cody Zeller/49 4.00 10.00
24 Chuck Person/149 4.00 10.00
25 Clyde Drexler/49 15.00 40.00
26 Julius Erving/25 25.00 60.00
27 Anthony Davis/49 30.00 80.00
28 Chris Paul/30 20.00 50.00
29 Trey Burke/49 4.00 10.00
30 Alan Anderson/149 3.00 8.00
31 Nerlens Noel/49 5.00 12.00
32 John Lucas/149 5.00 12.00
33 Victor Oladipo/49 5.00 12.00
34 Rik Smits/149 4.00 10.00
35 Dennis Rodman/49 15.00 40.00
36 Magic Johnson/25 30.00 80.00
37 Oscar Robertson/25 30.00 80.00
38 Kevin Durant/25 50.00 120.00
39 Noah Vonleh/49 4.00 10.00
40 Dorell Wright/149 3.00 8.00
41 Julius Randle/49 10.00 25.00
42 Kenny Walker/149 3.00 8.00
43 Anthony Bennett/49
44 Nikola Mirotic/99 5.00 12.00
45 Tracy McGrady/49 12.00 30.00
46 Larry Bird/25 30.00 80.00
47 Jerry West/25
48 Shaquille O'Neal/20
49 C.J. McCollum/49 6.00 15.00
50 Maurice Harkless/149 3.00 8.00

2015-16 Prestige Prestigious Passers

RANDOM INSERTS IN PACKS
*CRYSTAL/99: 1.2X TO 3X
*CHECK/125: 1.2X TO 3X
1 Chris Paul .75 2.00
2 John Wall .75 2.00
3 Damian Lillard 1.25 3.00
4 Russell Westbrook 1.50 4.00
5 LeBron James 2.50 6.00
6 Stephen Curry 2.50 6.00
7 Tony Parker .60 1.50
8 Kyrie Irving 1.25 3.00
9 Magic Johnson 1.50 4.00
10 John Stockton 1.00 2.50
11 Isiah Thomas .60 1.50
12 Jason Kidd .60 1.50
13 Steve Nash .60 1.50
14 Ty Lawson .40 1.00
15 Tim Hardaway .60 1.50

2015-16 Prestige Prestigious Picks

RANDOM INSERTS IN PACKS
*LT.BLUE/99: 1X TO 2.5X BASIC
*BRONZE/49: 1.2X TO 3X BASIC
1 Chris McCullough .40 1.00
2 Kelly Oubre Jr. .50 1.25
3 Delon Wright .50 1.25
4 Mario Hezonja .50 1.25
5 Jahlil Okafor .75 2.00
6 Rakeem Christmas .40 1.00
7 Justin Anderson .50 1.25
8 Sam Dekker .50 1.25
9 Anthony Brown .40 1.00
10 Trey Lyles .60 1.50
11 Dakari Johnson .40 1.00
12 Kevon Looney .50 1.25
13 Devin Booker 2.00 5.00
14 Montrezl Harrell .50 1.25
15 Jarell Martin .50 1.25
16 Rashad Vaughn .40 1.00
17 Justise Winslow .60 1.50
18 Stanley Johnson .50 1.25
19 Bobby Portis .60 1.50
20 Willie Cauley-Stein .60 1.50
21 D'Angelo Russell 1.50 4.00
22 Kristaps Porzingis 1.50 4.00
23 Emmanuel Mudiay .60 1.50
24 Myles Turner .60 1.50
25 Jerian Grant .40 1.00
26 Rondae Hollis-Jefferson .50 1.25
27 Karl-Anthony Towns 3.00 8.00
28 Terry Rozier .50 1.25
29 Cameron Payne .50 1.25
30 Tyus Jones .60 1.50
31 Darrun Hilliard .40 1.00
32 Larry Nance Jr. .60 1.50
33 R.J. Hunter .40 1.00
34 Frank Kaminsky .60 1.50
35 Jordan Mickey .40 1.00

2015-16 Prestige Prestigious Premieres Signatures

RANDOM INSERTS IN PACKS
STATED PRINT RUN 299 SER.#'d SETS
*CHECK/25: .6X TO 1.5X BASIC
EXCHANGE DEADLINE 4/19/2017
1 Karl-Anthony Towns 75.00 200.00
2 D'Angelo Russell 20.00 50.00
3 Jahlil Okafor 6.00 15.00
4 Emmanuel Mudiay 5.00 12.00
5 Kristaps Porzingis 30.00 80.00
6 Mario Hezonja 4.00 10.00
7 Justise Winslow 5.00 12.00
8 Willie Cauley-Stein 8.00 20.00
9 Stanley Johnson 4.00 10.00
10 Frank Kaminsky 5.00 12.00
11 Devin Booker 40.00 100.00
12 Myles Turner 10.00 25.00
13 Jerian Grant 3.00 8.00
14 Trey Lyles 5.00 12.00
15 Cameron Payne 4.00 10.00
16 Delon Wright 4.00 10.00
17 Rashad Vaughn 3.00 8.00
18 Kelly Oubre Jr. 4.00 10.00
19 Sam Dekker 4.00 10.00
20 Terry Rozier 4.00 10.00
21 Rondae Hollis-Jefferson 4.00 10.00
22 Bobby Portis 5.00 12.00
23 Justin Anderson 4.00 10.00
24 Jarell Martin 4.00 10.00
25 R.J. Hunter 3.00 8.00
26 Anthony Brown 3.00 8.00
28 Chris McCullough 3.00 8.00
29 Jordan Mickey 3.00 8.00
30 Larry Nance Jr. 5.00 12.00
31 Montrezl Harrell 4.00 10.00
32 Dakari Johnson 3.00 8.00
33 Darrun Hilliard 3.00 8.00
34 Pat Connaughton 3.00 8.00
35 Rakeem Christmas 3.00 8.00
36 Richaun Holmes 4.00 10.00
38 Andrew Harrison 5.00 12.00
40 Joe Young 4.00 10.00
42 Tyler Harvey 3.00 8.00
43 Branden Dawson 3.00 8.00
44 Tyus Jones 8.00 20.00
46 Aaron Harrison 4.00 10.00
48 Josh Richardson 5.00 12.00
49 Walter Tavares 3.00 8.00

2015-16 Prestige Prestigious Pros

RANDOM INSERTS IN PACKS
*LT.BLUE/99: .75X TO 2X BASIC
*BRONZE/49: 1X TO 2.5X BASIC
1 Kenneth Faried .50 1.25
2 Russell Westbrook 1.50 4.00
3 Marc Gasol .60 1.50
4 Kobe Bryant 2.50 6.00
5 Paul Millsap .60 1.50
6 John Wall .75 2.00
7 Manu Ginobili .60 1.50
8 LeBron James 2.50 6.00
9 Dwight Howard .50 1.25
10 Carmelo Anthony .75 2.00
11 Chris Bosh .60 1.50
12 Tony Parker .60 1.50
13 Al Horford .50 1.25
14 Dirk Nowitzki .75 2.00
15 Kyle Lowry .50 1.25
16 Kyrie Irving 1.25 3.00
17 Bradley Beal .60 1.50
18 Kevin Durant 1.50 4.00
19 Goran Dragic .50 1.25
20 Stephen Curry 2.50 6.00
21 Kawhi Leonard 1.00 2.50
22 Kevin Love .60 1.50
23 Klay Thompson .75 2.00
24 Joakim Noah .50 1.25
25 Eric Bledsoe .50 1.25
26 Tim Duncan 1.00 2.50
27 Mike Conley .60 1.50
28 Chris Paul .75 2.00
29 DeMarcus Cousins .60 1.50
30 Blake Griffin .60 1.50
31 Andre Drummond .60 1.50
32 James Harden 1.00 2.50
33 Rudy Gay .60 1.50
34 Damian Lillard 1.25 3.00
35 Zach Randolph .50 1.25
36 Dwyane Wade 1.00 2.50
37 Andrew Wiggins 1.00 2.50
38 Anthony Davis 1.25 3.00
39 DeMar DeRozan .60 1.50
40 Derrick Rose .75 2.00

2015-16 Prestige Stars of the NBA Signatures

RANDOM INSERTS IN PACKS
PRINT RUNS B/WN 25-149 COPIES PER
EXCHANGE DEADLINE 4/19/2017
1 Shaquille O'Neal/25 50.00 120.00
2 Gary Payton/49
3 Allen Iverson/25 60.00 150.00
4 Rajon Rondo/49
5 Chris Webber/25 60.00 150.00
6 Hakeem Olajuwon/25 20.00 50.00
7 Paul George/25 25.00 60.00
8 Nerlens Noel/49 6.00 15.00
9 Alonzo Mourning/25 20.00 50.00
10 Artis Gilmore/49 5.00 12.00
11 Blake Griffin/25 15.00 40.00
12 Walt Frazier/49 6.00 15.00
13 Dennis Rodman/25 20.00 50.00
14 Roy Hibbert/149 4.00 10.00
15 Jerry West/25 20.00 50.00
16 John Stockton/25 20.00 50.00
17 Kyrie Irving/49
18 Nick Van Exel/49 40.00 100.00
19 Kareem Abdul-Jabbar/25 30.00 80.00
20 Nikola Mirotic/99 5.00 12.00
21 Julius Erving/25 40.00 100.00
22 Clyde Drexler/25 15.00 40.00
23 Oscar Robertson/25 25.00 60.00
24 Peja Stojakovic/49 10.00 25.00
25 Kevin Durant/25
26 Trey Burke/49
27 Chris Paul/28 30.00 80.00
28 Charles Oakley/149 4.00 10.00
29 Earl Monroe/25
30 Bernard King/49 5.00 12.00
31 Jabari Parker/25 10.00 25.00
32 James Worthy/49 10.00 25.00
33 Anfernee Hardaway/49 20.00 50.00
34 Harrison Barnes/49 10.00 25.00
35 Ricky Rubio/25 8.00 20.00
36 Victor Oladipo/49 5.00 12.00
37 Yao Ming/25 15.00 40.00
38 Damon Stoudamire/149 4.00 10.00
39 Andrew Wiggins/49 30.00 80.00
40 Vin Baker/149 3.00 8.00
41 David Robinson/25 12.00 30.00
42 Vlade Divac/149 5.00 12.00
43 Wes Unseld/49 6.00 15.00
44 Grant Hill/49
45 Kobe Bryant/25
46 Michael Carter-Williams/49
47 Magic Johnson/25 25.00 60.00
48 Robert Parish/149 5.00 12.00
49 Carmelo Anthony/25 20.00 50.00
50 Brandon Knight/149 4.00 10.00

2015-16 Prestige Stat Stars

RANDOM INSERTS IN PACKS
*CRYSTAL/99: 1.2X TO 3X
*CHECK/125: 1.2X TO 3X
1 Dwight Howard .50 1.25
2 Wilt Chamberlain 1.25 3.00
3 Tim Duncan 1.00 2.50
4 Magic Johnson 1.50 4.00
5 Bill Russell 1.00 2.50
6 Stephen Curry 2.50 6.00
7 Russell Westbrook 1.50 4.00
8 Larry Brown .60 1.50
9 Kevin Durant 1.50 4.00
10 Kawhi Leonard 1.00 2.50
11 Steve Nash .60 1.50
12 John Stockton 1.00 2.50
13 Allen Iverson .75 2.00
14 Steve Kerr .60 1.50
15 Julius Erving 1.00 2.50
16 DeAndre Jordan .60 1.50
17 Dikembe Mutombo .60 1.50
18 Chris Paul .75 2.00
19 Kobe Bryant 2.50 6.00
20 Anthony Davis 1.25 3.00
21 John Wall .75 2.00
22 Dennis Rodman 1.25 3.00
23 Jerry West .75 2.00
24 LeBron James 2.50 6.00
25 Artis Gilmore .50 1.25

2015-16 Prestige True Colors Materials

RANDOM INSERTS IN PACKS
*PRIME/25: 1X TO 2.5X BASIC
1 Allen Iverson 4.00 10.00
2 Chris Andersen 1.50 4.00
3 Clifford Robinson 1.25 3.00
4 Danny Manning 1.50 4.00
5 DeMarcus Cousins 2.00 5.00
6 Dirk Nowitzki 2.50 6.00
7 Hakeem Olajuwon 2.50 6.00
8 Jimmy Butler 2.00 5.00
9 Kenny Anderson 1.50 4.00
10 Kobe Bryant 8.00 20.00
11 Nikola Vucevic 1.50 4.00
12 Ray Allen 2.00 5.00
13 Tim Duncan 3.00 8.00
14 Kevin Durant 5.00 12.00
15 Anthony Davis 4.00 10.00
16 Andrew Wiggins 3.00 8.00
17 LeBron James 8.00 20.00
18 Chandler Parsons 1.50 4.00
19 Brandon Jennings 1.25 3.00
20 James Harden 3.00 8.00
21 Chris Paul 2.50 6.00
22 Tony Parker 2.00 5.00
23 Bradley Beal 2.00 5.00
24 Aaron Gordon 1.50 4.00
25 Elfrid Payton 1.50 4.00

2016-17 Prestige

COMPLETE SET (200) 20.00 50.00
1 Kenneth Faried .30 .75
2 Jose Calderon .25 .60
3 Isaiah Thomas .40 1.00
4 Anthony Davis .75 2.00
5 Paul George .50 1.25
6 Nick Collison .30 .75
7 Stephen Curry 1.50 4.00
8 Andrew Wiggins .60 1.50
9 Kent Bazemore .30 .75
10 Aaron Gordon .30 .75
11 Chandler Parsons .30 .75
12 Eric Bledsoe .30 .75
13 Andre Drummond .40 1.00
14 Evan Turner .25 .60
15 Giannis Antetokounmpo .75 2.00
16 Jeremy Lin .40 1.00
17 Dante Exum .30 .75
18 Nene .30 .75
19 DeMarcus Cousins .40 1.00
20 J.J. Redick .40 1.00
21 David Lee .25 .60
22 Dwight Howard .30 .75
23 DeMar DeRozan .40 1.00
24 Matthew Dellavedova .30 .75
25 Julius Randle .40 1.00
26 Trevor Ariza .25 .60
27 Kevin Durant 1.00 2.50
28 Elfrid Payton .30 .75
29 Eric Gordon .30 .75
30 Jeremy Lamb .25 .60
31 Enes Kanter .25 .60
32 Wesley Matthews .25 .60
33 Willie Cauley-Stein .30 .75
34 Dwyane Wade .60 1.50
35 Nik Stauskas .25 .60
36 Josh McRoberts .25 .60
37 J.R. Smith .30 .75
38 Zach Randolph .30 .75
39 Mason Plumlee .30 .75
40 Emmanuel Mudiay .30 .75
41 Paul Pierce .40 1.00
42 Kyle Lowry .30 .75
43 Kelly Olynyk .25 .60
44 Devin Booker .60 1.50
45 Kentavious Caldwell-Pope .30 .75
46 Jared Sullinger .25 .60
47 Dennis Schroder .30 .75
48 Tyreke Evans .25 .60
49 Monta Ellis .30 .75
50 Kawhi Leonard .60 1.50
51 Jameer Nelson .25 .60
52 Cory Joseph .25 .60
53 Danilo Gallinari .30 .75
54 Dion Waiters .30 .75
55 Jahlil Okafor .30 .75
56 Brook Lopez .30 .75
57 Serge Ibaka .30 .75
58 Jordan Clarkson .30 .75
59 Klay Thompson .50 1.25
60 Karl-Anthony Towns 1.00 2.50
61 Roy Hibbert .30 .75
62 Russell Westbrook 1.00 2.50
63 Ryan Anderson .30 .75
64 Derrick Favors .30 .75
65 Greg Monroe .30 .75
66 Jimmy Butler .40 1.00
67 Marc Gasol .40 1.00
68 Ty Lawson .25 .60
69 Deron Williams .30 .75
70 Tony Parker .40 1.00
71 Jordan Hill .25 .60
72 Paul Millsap .40 1.00
73 C.J. McCollum .30 .75
74 Al Jefferson .30 .75
75 Jonas Valanciunas .30 .75
76 Iman Shumpert .25 .60
77 Jabari Parker .50 1.25
78 Gordon Hayward .40 1.00
79 Reggie Jackson .30 .75
80 Matt Barnes .25 .60
81 Marcus Smart .30 .75
82 Jrue Holiday .30 .75
83 Chris Paul .50 1.25
84 Andrew Bogut .30 .75
85 Omri Casspi .25 .60
86 Patrick Beverley .25 .60
87 Rajon Rondo .40 1.00
88 Justise Winslow .30 .75
89 Joakim Noah .30 .75
90 Luis Scola .30 .75
91 Damian Lillard .75 2.00
92 Jusuf Nurkic .25 .60
93 Mike Conley .30 .75
94 Tyson Chandler .30 .75
95 Kemba Walker .40 1.00
96 Victor Oladipo .30 .75
97 Andre Iguodala .30 .75
98 Nerlens Noel .30 .75
99 Kevin Love .40 1.00
100 Nikola Vucevic .30 .75
101 Harrison Barnes .30 .75
102 Kristaps Porzingis .75 2.00
103 Zach LaVine .40 1.00
104 Kyle Korver .30 .75
105 Justin Anderson .30 .75
106 Tony Snell .25 .60
107 Stanley Johnson .25 .60
108 Pau Gasol .40 1.00
109 Al Horford .30 .75
110 Joe Johnson .30 .75
111 Myles Turner .30 .75
112 Kyrie Irving .75 2.00
113 Omer Asik .30 .75
114 Marvin Williams .30 .75
115 Langston Galloway .25 .60
116 Hassan Whiteside .30 .75
117 Jerryd Bayless .30 .75
118 Anthony Bennett .25 .60
119 Derrick Rose .50 1.25
120 JaVale McGee .30 .75
121 DeAndre Jordan .40 1.00
122 LaMarcus Aldridge .40 1.00
123 Nikola Mirotic .30 .75
124 Rudy Gay .40 1.00
125 Carmelo Anthony .50 1.25
126 Luol Deng .30 .75
127 Arron Afflalo .25 .60
128 Avery Bradley .30 .75
129 Brandon Knight .30 .75
130 Jeff Teague .30 .75
131 Trey Lyles .30 .75
132 Tobias Harris .30 .75
133 Draymond Green .50 1.25
134 Al-Farouq Aminu .30 .75
135 Dirk Nowitzki .50 1.25
136 Goran Dragic .30 .75
137 Joel Embiid .60 1.50
138 D'Angelo Russell .50 1.25
139 Jodie Meeks .30 .75
140 Robin Lopez .25 .60
141 Steven Adams .30 .75
142 Vince Carter .50 1.25
143 Brandon Jennings .25 .60
144 Rondae Hollis-Jefferson .25 .60
145 E'Twaun Moore .25 .60
146 James Harden .60 1.50
147 Ricky Rubio .40 1.00
148 LeBron James 1.50 4.00
149 Blake Griffin .40 1.00
150 Cody Zeller .25 .60
151 Ben Simmons RC 3.00 8.00
152 Brandon Ingram RC 3.00 8.00
153 Jaylen Brown RC 2.00 5.00
154 Dragan Bender RC .60 1.50
155 Kris Dunn RC 1.50 4.00
156 Buddy Hield RC 1.25 3.00
157 Jamal Murray RC 1.50 4.00
158 Marquese Chriss RC 1.25 3.00
159 Jakob Poeltl RC .60 1.50
160 Thon Maker RC 1.50 4.00
161 Domantas Sabonis RC .75 2.00
162 Taurean Prince RC .75 2.00
163 Georgios Papagiannis RC .50 1.25
164 Denzel Valentine RC .60 1.50
165 Juan Hernangomez RC .60 1.50
166 Wade Baldwin IV RC .50 1.25
167 Henry Ellenson RC .60 1.50
168 Malik Beasley RC .50 1.25
169 Caris LeVert RC .60 1.50
170 DeAndre' Bembry RC .50 1.25
171 Malachi Richardson RC .60 1.50
172 Timothe Luwawu-Cabarrot RC 1.00 2.50
173 Brice Johnson RC .50 1.25
174 Pascal Siakam RC .50 1.25
175 Skal Labissiere RC .75 2.00
176 Dejounte Murray RC 1.00 2.50
177 Damian Jones RC .50 1.25
178 Deyonta Davis RC .50 1.25
179 Ivica Zubac RC .75 2.00
180 Cheick Diallo RC .50 1.25
181 Tyler Ulis RC 1.50 4.00
182 Malcolm Brogdon RC 1.25 3.00
183 Chinanu Onuaku RC .50 1.25
184 Patrick McCaw RC 1.00 2.50
185 Diamond Stone RC .50 1.25
186 Stephen Zimmerman RC .50 1.25
187 Isaiah Whitehead RC .50 1.25
188 Demetrius Jackson RC .50 1.25
189 A.J. Hammons RC .50 1.25
190 Kay Felder RC .50 1.25
191 Jake Layman RC .60 1.50
192 Georges Niang RC .50 1.25
193 Joel Bolomboy RC .50 1.25
194 Sheldon McClellan RC .50 1.25
195 Tim Quarterman RC .50 1.25
196 Tomas Satoransky RC .50 1.25
197 Mindaugas Kuzminskas RC .60 1.50
198 Ron Baker RC .60 1.50
199 Marshall Plumlee RC .50 1.25
200 Dario Saric RC 1.50 4.00

2016-17 Prestige Bonus Shots Red

*RED: 1.5X TO 4X BASIC
*RED RC: .75X TO 2X BASIC
RANDOM INSERTS IN PACKS
STATED PRINT RUN 75 SER.#'d SETS
151 Ben Simmons 20.00 50.00

2016-17 Prestige Crystal

*CRYSTAL: 2X TO 5X BASIC
*CRYSTAL RC: 1X TO 2.5X BASIC
RANDOM INSERTS IN PACKS
151 Ben Simmons 30.00 80.00

2016-17 Prestige Horizon

*HORIZON: 1.2X TO 3X BASIC
*HORIZON RC: .6X TO 1.5X BASIC
RANDOM INSERTS IN PACKS
151 Ben Simmons 15.00 40.00

2016-17 Prestige Metallized

*METALIZED: 2.5X TO 6X BASIC
*METALIZED RC: 1.2X TO 3X BASIC
RANDON INSERTS IN PACKS
151 Ben Simmons 25.00 60.00

2016-17 Prestige Rain

*RAIN: 1X TO 2.5X BASIC
*RAIN RC: .5X TO 1.2X BASIC
RANDOM INSERTS IN PACKS
151 Ben Simmons 10.00 25.00

2016-17 Prestige Acetate Rookies

RANDOM INSERTS IN PACKS
1 Brandon Ingram 4.00 10.00
2 Ben Simmons 6.00 15.00
3 Dario Saric 2.00 5.00
4 Marquese Chriss 1.50 4.00
5 Dragan Bender .75 2.00
6 Patrick McCaw 1.25 3.00
7 Kris Dunn 2.00 5.00
8 Jaylen Brown 2.50 6.00
9 Thon Maker 2.00 5.00
10 Wade Baldwin IV .60 1.50
11 Denzel Valentine .75 2.00
12 Tyler Ulis 2.00 5.00
13 Kay Felder .60 1.50
14 Taurean Prince 1.00 2.50
15 Brice Johnson .60 1.50
16 Buddy Hield 1.50 4.00
17 Jamal Murray 2.00 5.00
18 Domantas Sabonis 1.00 2.50
19 Henry Ellenson .75 2.00
20 Malcolm Brogdon 1.50 4.00
21 Pascal Siakam .60 1.50
22 Jakob Poeltl .75 2.00
23 Diamond Stone .60 1.50
24 Ivica Zubac 1.00 2.50
25 Jake Layman .75 2.00

2016-17 Prestige Acetate Veterans

RANDOM INSERTS IN PACKS
1 LeBron James 4.00 10.00
2 Giannis Antetokounmpo 2.00 5.00
3 Stephen Curry 4.00 10.00
4 Kevin Durant 2.50 6.00
5 Kyrie Irving 2.00 5.00
6 John Wall 1.25 3.00
7 Damian Lillard 2.00 5.00
8 Russell Westbrook 2.50 6.00
9 James Harden 1.50 4.00
10 Paul George 1.25 3.00
11 Karl-Anthony Towns 2.50 6.00
12 Jimmy Butler 1.00 2.50
13 Dwyane Wade 1.50 4.00
14 Blake Griffin 1.00 2.50
15 D'Angelo Russell 1.25 3.00
16 Carmelo Anthony 1.25 3.00
17 Kristaps Porzingis 2.00 5.00
18 DeMarcus Cousins 1.00 2.50
19 DeMar DeRozan 1.00 2.50
20 Anthony Davis 2.00 5.00
21 Kawhi Leonard 1.50 4.00
22 Devin Booker 1.50 4.00
23 Andrew Wiggins 1.50 4.00
24 Joel Embiid 1.50 4.00
25 Chris Paul 1.25 3.00

2016-17 Prestige All-Time Greats

COMPLETE SET (20) 15.00 40.00
RANDOM INSERTS IN PACKS
*RAIN: .6X TO 1.5X BASIC
*HORIZON: .75X TO 2X BASIC
*CRYSTAL: 1.2X TO 3X BASIC
1 Patrick Ewing .75 2.00
2 Dominique Wilkins .75 2.00
3 Mitch Richmond .60 1.50
4 Ray Allen .60 1.50
5 Robert Parish .60 1.50
6 Joe Dumars .60 1.50
7 Magic Johnson 1.50 4.00
8 Ralph Sampson .50 1.25
9 Julius Erving 1.00 2.50
10 Bill Walton .60 1.50
11 Shaquille O'Neal 1.50 4.00
12 Tracy McGrady .60 1.50
13 Allen Iverson .75 2.00
14 Scottie Pippen 1.25 3.00
15 Alonzo Mourning .75 2.00
16 Isiah Thomas .60 1.50
17 Bill Russell 1.00 2.50
18 Steve Nash .60 1.50
19 Walt Frazier .60 1.50
20 Jason Kidd .60 1.50

2016-17 Prestige Bonus Shots Signatures

RANDOM INSERTS IN PACKS
1 Mike Muscala 3.00 8.00
2 Cody Zeller
3 C.J. McCollum 4.00 10.00
4 E'Twaun Moore
5 Justin Hamilton 3.00 8.00
6 Ian Clark 5.00 12.00
7 James Ennis 3.00 8.00
8 Josh Huestis
9 Dwight Powell
10 Victor Oladipo 4.00 10.00
11 Maurice Harkless 12.00 30.00
12 Steve Novak 3.00 8.00
13 Walter Tavares 3.00 8.00
14 Michael Carter-Williams
15 Reggie Bullock
16 Langston Galloway
17 Noah Vonleh 3.00 8.00
18 Troy Daniels 3.00 8.00
19 Jason Smith
20 Allen Crabbe
21 Kevon Looney
22 Alan Anderson 3.00 8.00
23 Aaron Harrison 3.00 8.00
24 Jordan Clarkson
25 Jeff Withey 3.00 8.00
26 Jordan McRae 3.00 8.00
27 C.J. Miles 4.00 10.00
28 T.J. McConnell
29 Jason Terry 6.00 15.00
30 Alex Len
31 James Johnson
32 Hollis Thompson
33 Isaiah Canaan 5.00 12.00
34 Jason Terry 6.00 15.00
35 Deron Williams
36 Glenn Robinson III 3.00 8.00
37 Norman Powell
38 Brian Roberts
39 Michael Kidd-Gilchrist
40 P.J. Tucker•
41 Tyler Ennis
42 Tristan Thompson
43 Rondae Hollis-Jefferson 3.00 8.00
44 Rashad Vaughn 3.00 8.00
45 Terrence Jones
46 Dante Exum
47 Ed Davis 3.00 8.00
48 Alec Burks
49 Justin Holiday
50 Bill Willoughby 3.00 8.00
51 Vin Baker 3.00 8.00
52 Chris Herren
53 Zydrunas Ilgauskas
54 Brian Grant
55 Bob Dandridge 3.00 8.00
56 Charlie Bell 3.00 8.00
57 Tony Campbell 3.00 8.00
58 Jim Chones 3.00 8.00
59 Shawn Kemp
60 Chucky Brown 3.00 8.00
61 Mark Price
62 Harvey Grant 3.00 8.00
63 Rick Fox
64 Jim Jackson 3.00 8.00
65 Jeff Malone
66 Shane Battier
67 Sean Elliott 5.00 12.00
68 Jonathan Bender 3.00 8.00
69 Jared Jeffries
70 Gary Trent
71 Cedric Ceballos 5.00 12.00
72 Dale Ellis 3.00 8.00
73 Chris Whitney 3.00 8.00
74 Kevin Willis 3.00 8.00
75 Vinny Del Negro 4.00 10.00
76 Kenny Walker 5.00 12.00
77 Jamal Mashburn 5.00 12.00
78 Bo Kimble 3.00 8.00
79 Ron Boone 3.00 8.00
80 Dell Curry 5.00 12.00
81 Tree Rollins 3.00 8.00
82 Damon Jones 3.00 8.00
83 Lamond Murray 3.00 8.00
84 Bobby Jones
85 Dan Majerle
86 Mark Landsberger 3.00 8.00
87 Dan Issel
88 Mario Elie 6.00 15.00
89 Junior Bridgeman
90 Denzel Valentine 4.00 10.00
91 Taurean Prince 6.00 15.00
92 Juan Hernangomez 6.00 15.00
93 Chinanu Onuaku
94 Jake Layman 4.00 10.00
95 Damian Jones 3.00 8.00
96 Georgios Papagiannis 3.00 8.00
97 Domantas Sabonis 5.00 12.00
98 Wade Baldwin IV 3.00 8.00
99 Michael Gbinije 3.00 8.00
100 Demetrius Jackson 3.00 8.00

2016-17 Prestige Distinctive Ink

RANDOM INSERTS IN PACKS
PRINT RUNS B/WN 75-199 COPIES PER
1 C.J. McCollum/149 6.00 15.00
2 Victor Oladipo/75 4.00 10.00
3 Dwight Powell/199 2.50 6.00
4 Michael Carter-Williams/199 2.50 6.00
5 Jordan Clarkson/199 3.00 8.00
6 Jeremy Lin/75 30.00 80.00
7 Jabari Parker/75
8 Allen Crabbe/199 2.50 6.00
9 Kevin Love/75
10 Dwyane Wade/75 15.00 40.00
11 Kyrie Irving/75 30.00 80.00
12 Dirk Nowitzki/75 50.00 120.00
13 D'Angelo Russell/75 15.00 40.00
14 Bobby Portis/199
15 Marc Gasol/75 12.00 30.00
16 Blake Griffin/75 15.00 40.00
17 Carmelo Anthony/75 12.00 30.00
18 Shawn Kemp/199 25.00 60.00
19 Scottie Pippen/75 30.00 80.00
20 Rick Fox/199 3.00 8.00
21 Dan Majerle/199 3.00 8.00
22 Adrian Dantley/199 3.00 8.00
23 Karl Malone/75 20.00 50.00
24 Yao Ming/75 30.00 80.00
25 Artis Gilmore/75 4.00 10.00

2016-17 Prestige Franchise Favorites

COMPLETE SET (15) 10.00 25.00
RANDOM INSERTS IN PACKS
*RAIN: .6X TO 1.5X BASIC
*HORIZON: .75X TO 2X BASIC
*CRYSTAL: 1.2X TO 3X BASIC
1 Dirk Nowitzki .75 2.00
2 Jimmy Butler .60 1.50
3 Kyrie Irving 1.25 3.00
4 Blake Griffin .60 1.50
5 Mike Conley .50 1.25
6 Paul Millsap .60 1.50
7 Kemba Walker .60 1.50
8 DeMarcus Cousins .60 1.50
9 Carmelo Anthony .75 2.00
10 Tony Parker .60 1.50
11 Klay Thompson .75 2.00
12 Kyle Lowry .50 1.25
13 Anthony Davis 1.25 3.00
14 Gordon Hayward .60 1.50
15 Andre Drummond .60 1.50

2016-17 Prestige Freshman Fabrics Jumbo

RANDOM INSERTS IN PACKS
STATED PRINT RUN 99 SER. #'d SETS
1 A.J. Hammons 1.50 4.00
2 Brandon Ingram 6.00 15.00
3 Brice Johnson 1.50 4.00
4 Buddy Hield 4.00 10.00
5 Caris LeVert 2.00 5.00
6 Cheick Diallo 1.50 4.00
7 Chinanu Onuaku 1.50 4.00
8 Damian Jones 1.50 4.00
9 Dario Saric 10.00 25.00
10 Demetrius Jackson 1.50 4.00
11 Denzel Valentine 2.00 5.00
12 Deyonta Davis 1.50 4.00
13 Diamond Stone 1.50 4.00
14 Domantas Sabonis 2.50 6.00
15 Dragan Bender 2.00 5.00
16 Georges Niang 1.50 4.00
17 Georgios Papagiannis 1.50 4.00
18 Henry Ellenson 2.00 5.00
19 Isaiah Whitehead 1.50 4.00
20 Ivica Zubac 2.50 6.00
21 Jakob Poeltl 2.00 5.00
22 Jamal Murray 4.00 10.00
23 Jaylen Brown 5.00 12.00
24 Juan Hernangomez 2.00 5.00
25 Kay Felder 1.50 4.00
26 Kris Dunn 4.00 10.00
27 Malachi Richardson 2.00 5.00
28 Malcolm Brogdon 4.00 10.00
29 Malik Beasley 1.50 4.00
30 Marquese Chriss 4.00 10.00
31 Pascal Siakam 1.50 4.00
32 Patrick McCaw 3.00 8.00
33 Skal Labissiere 2.50 6.00
34 Stephen Zimmerman 1.50 4.00
35 Thon Maker 4.00 10.00
36 Timothe Luwawu-Cabarrot 3.00 8.00
37 Tyler Ulis 5.00 12.00
38 Wade Baldwin IV 1.50 4.00
39 Taurean Prince 2.50 6.00

2016-17 Prestige Hardcourt Heroes

COMPLETE SET (15) 6.00 15.00
RANDOM INSERTS IN PACKS
*RAINBOW/25: 1X TO 2.5X BASIC
1 Kyrie Irving 1.25 3.00
2 Dwyane Wade 1.00 2.50
3 Kevin Durant 1.50 4.00
4 Blake Griffin .60 1.50
5 Andrew Wiggins 1.00 2.50
6 Eric Bledsoe .50 1.25
7 Bradley Beal .60 1.50
8 Paul Millsap .60 1.50
9 Al Horford .50 1.25
10 Kawhi Leonard 1.00 2.50
11 Kyle Lowry .50 1.25
12 Rudy Gay .60 1.50
13 Derrick Rose .75 2.00
14 Jordan Clarkson .50 1.25
15 Goran Dragic .50 1.25

2016-17 Prestige Highlight Reel

COMPLETE SET (10) 10.00 25.00
RANDOM INSERTS IN PACKS
*RAIN: .6X TO 1.5X BASIC
*HORIZON: .75X TO 2X BASIC
*CRYSTAL: 1.2X TO 3X BASIC
1 Anthony Davis 1.25 3.00
2 Aaron Gordon .50 1.25
3 Kevin Durant 1.50 4.00
4 Russell Westbrook 1.50 4.00
5 Damian Lillard 1.25 3.00
6 James Harden 1.00 2.50
7 Dwyane Wade 1.00 2.50
8 Myles Turner .50 1.25
9 Brandon Ingram 2.50 6.00
10 Joel Embiid 1.00 2.50

2016-17 Prestige Inside the Numbers

RANDOM INSERTS IN PACKS
*RAIN: .6X TO 1.5X BASIC
*HORIZON: .75X TO 2X BASIC
*CRYSTAL: 1.2X TO 3X BASIC
1 Stephen Curry 2.50 6.00
2 James Harden 1.00 2.50
3 Kevin Durant 1.50 4.00
4 DeMarcus Cousins .60 1.50
5 LeBron James 2.50 6.00
6 Damian Lillard 1.25 3.00
7 Anthony Davis 1.25 3.00
8 Russell Westbrook 1.50 4.00
9 DeMar DeRozan .60 1.50
10 Paul George .75 2.00
11 Andre Drummond .60 1.50
12 DeAndre Jordan .60 1.50
13 Hassan Whiteside .50 1.25
14 Dwight Howard .50 1.25
15 Pau Gasol .60 1.50
16 Rajon Rondo .60 1.50
17 John Wall .75 2.00
18 Chris Paul .75 2.00
19 Ricky Rubio .60 1.50
20 Kyle Lowry .50 1.25

2016-17 Prestige Jerseys

RANDOM INSERTS IN PACKS
STATED PRINT RUN 199 SER. #'d SETS
*PRIME/25: 1X TO 2.5X BASIC
1 Andrew Wiggins 4.00 10.00
2 Bradley Beal 2.50 6.00
3 Carmelo Anthony 3.00 8.00
4 David Robinson 4.00 10.00
5 DeMarre Carroll 1.50 4.00
6 Jimmy Butler 2.50 6.00
7 Deron Williams 2.00 5.00
8 Dirk Nowitzki 3.00 8.00
9 Doug McDermott 2.00 5.00
10 Draymond Green 3.00 8.00
11 Dwyane Wade 4.00 10.00
12 Elfrid Payton 2.00 5.00
13 Elton Brand 2.50 6.00
14 Emmanuel Mudiay 2.00 5.00
15 Enes Kanter 1.50 4.00
16 Frank Kaminsky 2.00 5.00
17 George Hill 2.00 5.00
18 Goran Dragic 2.00 5.00
19 Hassan Whiteside 2.00 5.00
20 J.J. Redick 2.50 6.00
21 Jahlil Okafor 2.00 5.00
22 John Stockton 4.00 10.00
23 Kemba Walker 2.50 6.00
24 Kevin Durant 6.00 15.00
25 Kevin Love 2.50 6.00
26 LeBron James 10.00 25.00
27 Manu Ginobili 2.50 6.00
28 Mason Plumlee 2.00 5.00
29 Myles Turner 2.00 5.00
30 Paul George 3.00 8.00

2016-17 Prestige NBA Passport Signatures

RANDOM INSERTS IN PACKS
PRINT RUNS B/WN 99-199 COPIES PER
1 Brandon Ingram/99 50.00 120.00
2 Denzel Valentine/99 8.00 20.00
3 Taurean Prince/99 6.00 15.00
4 Juan Hernangomez/149 8.00 20.00
5 Wade Baldwin IV/99 8.00 20.00
6 Malcolm Brogdon/149 12.00 30.00
7 Brice Johnson/149 2.50 6.00
8 DeAndre' Bembry/149 2.50 6.00
9 Kay Felder/149 2.50 6.00
10 Jaylen Brown/99 30.00 80.00
11 Kris Dunn/99 15.00 40.00
12 Thon Maker/99 25.00 60.00
13 Jamal Murray/99 30.00 80.00
14 Buddy Hield/99 20.00 50.00
15 Jakob Poeltl/99 4.00 10.00
16 Marquese Chriss/99 20.00 50.00
17 Henry Ellenson/99 6.00 15.00
18 Dragan Bender/99 12.00 30.00
19 Patrick McCaw/149 12.00 30.00
20 Tyler Ulis/99 20.00 50.00
21 Chinanu Onuaku/149 2.50 6.00
22 Domantas Sabonis/99 10.00 25.00
23 Cheick Diallo/149 2.50 6.00
24 Timothe Luwawu-Cabarrot/99 6.00 15.00
25 Malik Beasley/149 2.50 6.00

2016-17 Prestige Old School Signatures

RANDOM INSERTS IN PACKS
PRINT RUNS B/WN 49-199 COPIES PER
1 Karl Malone/49 25.00 60.00
2 Jo Jo White/199 8.00 20.00
3 A.C. Green/199 4.00 10.00
4 Adrian Dantley/199 3.00 8.00
5 Alex English/199 3.00 8.00
6 Spud Webb/199 3.00 8.00
7 Shawn Kemp/49 40.00 100.00
8 Kenny Walker/49 8.00 20.00
9 Dan Issel/49 4.00 10.00
10 Scottie Pippen/49 40.00 100.00
11 Kurt Rambis/199 2.50 6.00
12 John Stockton/199 20.00 50.00
13 Kobe Bryant/49 75.00 200.00
14 Tom Heinsohn/99 12.00 30.00
15 Kiki Vandeweghe/49
16 Dan Majerle/99 4.00 10.00
17 Rick Barry/199 3.00 8.00
18 Rudy Tomjanovich/49 6.00 15.00
19 Vlade Divac/49 5.00 12.00
20 Christian Laettner/49

2016-17 Prestige Playmakers

RANDOM INSERTS IN PACKS
1 Kyrie Irving 10.00 25.00
2 Chris Paul 6.00 15.00
3 John Wall 6.00 15.00
4 DeMar DeRozan 5.00 12.00
5 LeBron James 30.00 80.00
6 Russell Westbrook 12.00 30.00
7 James Harden 8.00 20.00
8 Goran Dragic 4.00 10.00
9 Ty Lawson 3.00 8.00
10 Jeff Teague 4.00 10.00
11 Stephen Curry 20.00 50.00
12 Deron Williams 4.00 10.00
13 Kristaps Porzingis 10.00 25.00
14 Karl-Anthony Towns 12.00 30.00
15 Tony Parker 5.00 12.00
16 Kevin Durant 12.00 30.00
17 Jimmy Butler 5.00 12.00
18 Kawhi Leonard 8.00 20.00
19 Anthony Davis 10.00 25.00
20 Paul George 6.00 15.00
21 DeMarcus Cousins 5.00 12.00
22 Damian Lillard 10.00 25.00
23 Mike Conley 4.00 10.00
24 DeAndre Jordan 5.00 12.00
25 Giannis Antetokounmpo 10.00 25.00
26 Dirk Nowitzki 6.00 15.00
27 Blake Griffin 5.00 12.00
28 C.J. McCollum 4.00 10.00
29 Isaiah Thomas 5.00 12.00
30 Andre Drummond 5.00 12.00

2016-17 Prestige Preeminent Ink

RANDOM INSERTS IN PACKS
PRINT RUNS B/WN 49-199 COPIES PER
1 Bill Willoughby/199
2 Vin Baker/199 3.00 8.00
3 Zydrunas Ilgauskas/199 4.00 10.00
4 Brian Grant/199 3.00 8.00

Card	Low	High
5 Bob Dandridge/199	3.00	8.00
6 Jim Chones/199	3.00	8.00
7 Chucky Brown/199	3.00	8.00
8 Mark Price/199	5.00	12.00
9 Rick Fox/99	3.00	8.00
10 Jim Jackson/199	3.00	8.00
11 Jeff Malone/99	2.50	6.00
12 Kevin Willis/99	2.50	6.00
13 Luol Deng/99	3.00	8.00
14 Zach Randolph/99		
15 Paul Millsap/99	4.00	10.00
16 Nikola Vucevic/99		
17 Danilo Gallinari/99	3.00	8.00
18 Avery Bradley/99	3.00	8.00
19 Zaza Pachulia/99	12.00	30.00
20 Jae Crowder/99	6.00	15.00
21 Tony Allen/99	2.50	6.00
22 Nicolas Batum/99	3.00	8.00
23 Kent Bazemore/99		
24 Dwight Powell/199		
25 Hassan Whiteside/99		
26 Al Horford/99	12.00	30.00
27 Andrew Wiggins/49	20.00	50.00
28 Kevin Love/49	10.00	25.00
29 Nikola Jokic/199		
30 Kristaps Porzingis/99	20.00	50.00
31 Karl-Anthony Towns/49	30.00	80.00
32 Devin Booker/99	20.00	50.00
33 Justise Winslow/99	3.00	8.00
34 C.J. McCollum/99	6.00	15.00
35 Myles Turner/99		
36 Draymond Green/99	10.00	25.00
37 Zach LaVine/99	6.00	15.00
38 Kenneth Faried/99	3.00	8.00
39 DeMar DeRozan/49		
40 Dirk Nowitzki/49	60.00	150.00

2016-17 Prestige Prestigious Passers

Card	Low	High
COMPLETE SET (10)	10.00	25.00
RANDOM INSERTS IN PACKS		
*RAIN: .6X TO 1.5X BASIC		
*HORIZON: .75X TO 2X BASIC		
*CRYSTAL: 1.2X TO 3X BASIC		
1 Rajon Rondo	.60	1.50
2 Russell Westbrook	1.50	4.00
3 John Wall	.75	2.00
4 Chris Paul	.75	2.00
5 Ricky Rubio	.60	1.50
6 James Harden	1.00	2.50
7 Draymond Green	.75	2.00
8 Damian Lillard	1.25	3.00
9 LeBron James	2.50	6.00
10 Stephen Curry	2.50	6.00

2016-17 Prestige Prestigious Picks

Card	Low	High
RANDOM INSERTS IN PACKS		
1 Ben Simmons	25.00	60.00
2 Brandon Ingram	25.00	60.00
3 Jaylen Brown	15.00	40.00
4 Dragan Bender	5.00	12.00
5 Kris Dunn	12.00	30.00
6 Buddy Hield	10.00	25.00
7 Jamal Murray	12.00	30.00
8 Marquese Chriss	10.00	25.00
9 Jakob Poeltl	5.00	12.00
10 Thon Maker	12.00	30.00
11 Domantas Sabonis	6.00	15.00
12 Taurean Prince	6.00	15.00
13 Georgios Papagiannis	4.00	10.00
14 Denzel Valentine	5.00	12.00
15 Juan Hernangomez	5.00	12.00
16 Wade Baldwin IV	4.00	10.00
17 Henry Ellenson	5.00	12.00
18 Malik Beasley	4.00	10.00
19 Caris LeVert	5.00	12.00
20 DeAndre' Bembry	4.00	10.00
21 Malachi Richardson	5.00	12.00
22 Timothe Luwawu-Cabarrot	8.00	20.00
23 Brice Johnson	4.00	10.00
24 Pascal Siakam	4.00	10.00
25 Skal Labissiere	6.00	15.00
26 Dejounte Murray	8.00	20.00
27 Damian Jones	4.00	10.00
28 Deyonta Davis	4.00	10.00
29 Ivica Zubac	6.00	15.00
30 Cheick Diallo	4.00	10.00
31 Tyler Ulis	12.00	30.00
32 Malcolm Brogdon	10.00	25.00
33 Chinanu Onuaku	4.00	10.00
34 Patrick McCaw	8.00	20.00
35 Diamond Stone	4.00	10.00
36 Stephen Zimmerman	4.00	10.00
37 Isaiah Whitehead	4.00	10.00
38 Demetrius Jackson	4.00	10.00
39 A.J. Hammons	4.00	10.00
40 Kay Felder	4.00	10.00

2016-17 Prestige Prestigious Pioneers

Card	Low	High
COMPLETE SET (20)	10.00	25.00
RANDOM INSERTS IN PACKS		
*RAINBOW: 1X TO 2.5X BASIC		
1 Julius Erving	1.00	2.50
2 Shaquille O'Neal	1.50	4.00
3 Allen Iverson	.75	2.00
4 Oscar Robertson	.75	2.00
5 Hakeem Olajuwon	.75	2.00
6 Jerry West	.75	2.00
7 Latrell Sprewell	.50	1.25
8 Dennis Rodman	1.25	3.00
9 Bill Russell	1.00	2.50
10 James Worthy	.75	2.00
11 Larry Bird	1.50	4.00
12 David Robinson	1.00	2.50
13 Yao Ming	.75	2.00
14 George Gervin	.60	1.50
15 Karl Malone	.75	2.00
16 John Stockton	1.00	2.50
17 Isiah Thomas	.60	1.50
18 Chris Webber	.60	1.50
19 Grant Hill	.75	2.00
20 Shawn Kemp	1.00	2.50

2016-17 Prestige Prestigious Premieres Signatures

Card	Low	High
RANDOM INSERTS IN PACKS		
1 Denzel Valentine	6.00	15.00
2 Taurean Prince	5.00	12.00
3 Juan Hernangomez	5.00	12.00
4 Chinanu Onuaku	3.00	8.00
5 Jake Layman	4.00	10.00
6 Damian Jones	3.00	8.00
7 Georgios Papagiannis	3.00	8.00
8 Domantas Sabonis	5.00	12.00
9 Wade Baldwin IV	3.00	8.00
10 Michael Gbinije	3.00	8.00
11 Demetrius Jackson	3.00	8.00
12 Malcolm Brogdon	12.00	30.00
13 Ivica Zubac	8.00	20.00
14 Deyonta Davis	3.00	8.00
15 Brice Johnson	3.00	8.00
16 DeAndre' Bembry	3.00	8.00
17 Pascal Siakam	3.00	8.00
18 Cheick Diallo	3.00	8.00
19 Timothe Luwawu-Cabarrot	6.00	15.00
20 Kay Felder	3.00	8.00
21 Jaylen Brown	20.00	50.00
22 Thon Maker	10.00	25.00
23 Mindaugas Kuzminskas	4.00	10.00
24 Malik Beasley	3.00	8.00
25 Jamal Murray	15.00	40.00
26 Buddy Hield	12.00	30.00
27 Kris Dunn	10.00	25.00
28 Jakob Poeltl	4.00	10.00
29 Marquese Chriss	6.00	15.00
30 Henry Ellenson	4.00	10.00
31 Dragan Bender	4.00	10.00
32 Georges Niang	3.00	8.00
33 A.J. Hammons	3.00	8.00
34 Patrick McCaw	10.00	25.00
35 Diamond Stone	3.00	8.00
36 Tyler Ulis	10.00	25.00
37 Ron Baker	10.00	25.00
38 Caris LeVert	4.00	10.00
39 Brandon Ingram	30.00	80.00
40 Malachi Richardson	4.00	10.00
41 Dejounte Murray		
42 Dario Saric	10.00	25.00
43 Joel Bolomboy	3.00	8.00
44 Kyle Wiltjer	3.00	8.00
45 Willy Hernangomez	6.00	15.00
46 Sheldon McClellan	3.00	8.00
47 Paul Zipser	5.00	12.00
48 Marshall Plumlee	3.00	8.00
49 Tim Quarterman	3.00	8.00
50 Fred VanVleet	6.00	15.00

2016-17 Prestige Prestigious Pros

Card	Low	High
RANDOM INSERTS IN PACKS		
1 Paul Millsap	3.00	8.00
2 Al Horford	2.50	6.00
3 Brook Lopez	2.50	6.00
4 Kemba Walker	3.00	8.00
5 Jimmy Butler	3.00	8.00
6 LeBron James	20.00	50.00
7 Dirk Nowitzki	4.00	10.00
8 Kenneth Faried	2.50	6.00
9 Andre Drummond	3.00	8.00
10 Stephen Curry	12.00	30.00
11 James Harden	5.00	12.00
12 Paul George	4.00	10.00
13 Chris Paul	4.00	10.00
14 D'Angelo Russell	4.00	10.00
15 Marc Gasol	3.00	8.00
16 Justise Winslow	2.50	6.00
17 Giannis Antetokounmpo	6.00	15.00
18 Karl-Anthony Towns	8.00	20.00
19 Anthony Davis	6.00	15.00
20 Carmelo Anthony	4.00	10.00
21 Russell Westbrook	8.00	20.00
22 Nikola Vucevic	2.50	6.00
23 Jahlil Okafor	2.50	6.00
24 Eric Bledsoe	2.50	6.00
25 Damian Lillard	6.00	15.00
26 DeMarcus Cousins	3.00	8.00
27 Kawhi Leonard	5.00	12.00
28 DeMar DeRozan	3.00	8.00
29 Gordon Hayward	3.00	8.00
30 John Wall	4.00	10.00

2016-17 Prestige Reminiscent

Card	Low	High
COMPLETE SET (15)	10.00	25.00
RANDOM INSERTS IN PACKS		
*RAINBOW: 1X TO 2.5X BASIC		
1 Durant/Ingram	2.50	6.00
2 Brown/Butler	1.50	4.00
3 Nikola Mirotic	.50	1.25
Dragan Bender		
4 Dunn/Wall	1.25	3.00
5 Beal/Hield	1.00	2.50
6 Thompson/Murray	1.25	3.00
7 Chriss/Williams	1.00	2.50
8 Andrew Bogut	.50	1.25
Jakob Poeltl		
9 Porzingis/Maker	1.25	3.00
10 Domantas Sabonis	.60	1.50
Greg Monroe		
11 Evan Turner	.50	1.25
Denzel Valentine		
12 Murray/Barton	.75	2.00
13 DeMarre Carroll	.60	1.50
Taurean Prince		
14 Simmons/Griffin	2.50	6.00
15 Henry Ellenson	.60	1.50
Kevin Love		

2016-17 Prestige Rookie Class

Card	Low	High
COMPLETE SET (25)	20.00	50.00
RANDOM INSERTS IN PACKS		
*RAIN: .6X TO 1.5X BASIC		
*HORIZON: .75X TO 2X BASIC		
*CRYSTAL: 1.2X TO 3X BASIC		
1 Brandon Ingram	2.50	6.00
2 Jaylen Brown	1.50	4.00
3 Kris Dunn	1.25	3.00
4 Dragan Bender	.50	1.25
5 Marquese Chriss	1.00	2.50
6 Buddy Hield	1.00	2.50
7 Jamal Murray	1.25	3.00
8 Jakob Poeltl	.50	1.25
9 Thon Maker	1.25	3.00
10 Denzel Valentine	.50	1.25
11 Domantas Sabonis	.60	1.50
12 Dejounte Murray	.75	2.00
13 Juan Hernangomez	.50	1.25
14 Taurean Prince	.60	1.50
15 Henry Ellenson	.50	1.25
16 Caris LeVert	.50	1.25
17 Timothe Luwawu-Cabarrot	.75	2.00
18 Brice Johnson	.40	1.00
19 Wade Baldwin IV	.40	1.00
20 Georgios Papagiannis	.40	1.00
21 Dario Saric	1.25	3.00
22 Malik Beasley	.40	1.00
23 DeAndre' Bembry	.40	1.00
24 Malachi Richardson	.50	1.25
25 Pascal Siakam	.40	1.00

2016-17 Prestige Stars of the NBA Signatures

Card	Low	High
RANDOM INSERTS IN PACKS		
PRINT RUNS B/WN 49-199 COPIES PER		
1 Stephen Curry/49	150.00	300.00
2 Dennis Schroder/199	3.00	8.00
3 Kristaps Porzingis/199	20.00	50.00
4 John Wall/49	15.00	40.00
5 DeMar DeRozan/199		
6 Paul George/49	25.00	60.00
7 Jonas Valanciunas/199	3.00	8.00
8 Isaiah Thomas/199	12.00	30.00
9 E'Twaun Moore/199	2.50	6.00
10 Will Barton/199	2.50	6.00
11 Anthony Davis/49	30.00	80.00
12 Myles Turner/199	6.00	15.00
13 Jabari Parker/49	12.00	30.00
14 Tobias Harris/199	3.00	8.00
15 D'Angelo Russell/49		
16 Tony Parker/99	12.00	30.00
17 Kyrie Irving/49	25.00	60.00
18 Devin Booker/199	20.00	50.00
19 Pau Gasol/49	20.00	50.00
20 Gordon Hayward/199	6.00	15.00
21 Michael Carter-Williams/199	2.50	6.00
22 Jae Crowder/199	6.00	15.00
23 Matthew Dellavedova/199	5.00	12.00
24 Kyle Lowry/49		
25 Thaddeus Young/99	3.00	8.00
26 Victor Oladipo/49	4.00	10.00
27 Karl-Anthony Towns/49	30.00	80.00
28 Seth Curry/199	10.00	25.00
29 Jordan Clarkson/99	8.00	20.00
30 Dirk Nowitzki/49	60.00	150.00
31 Elfrid Payton/49	4.00	10.00
32 LaMarcus Aldridge/49	10.00	25.00
33 Mike Muscala/199	2.50	6.00
34 Blake Griffin/49	12.00	30.00
35 Eric Bledsoe/49		
36 C.J. McCollum/199	8.00	20.00
37 Draymond Green/49	15.00	40.00
38 Goran Dragic/199	3.00	8.00
39 Carmelo Anthony/49	15.00	40.00
40 Kevin Durant/49	60.00	150.00

2016-17 Prestige Stat Stars

Card	Low	High
COMPLETE SET (20)	6.00	15.00
RANDOM INSERTS IN PACKS		
*RAINBOW: 1X TO 2.5X BASIC		
1 DeMarcus Cousins	.60	1.50
2 Giannis Antetokounmpo	1.25	3.00
3 Jimmy Butler	.60	1.50
4 Karl-Anthony Towns	1.50	4.00
5 LeBron James	2.50	6.00
6 Isaiah Thomas	.60	1.50
7 Chris Paul	.75	2.00
8 Marc Gasol	.60	1.50
9 Stephen Curry	2.50	6.00
10 Hassan Whiteside	.50	1.25
11 Kemba Walker	.60	1.50
12 Carmelo Anthony	.75	2.00
13 Damian Lillard	1.25	3.00
14 Jeremy Lin	.60	1.50
15 John Wall	.75	2.00
16 Paul George	.75	2.00
17 Anthony Davis	1.25	3.00
18 DeMar DeRozan	.60	1.50
19 James Harden	1.00	2.50
20 Russell Westbrook	1.50	4.00

2016-17 Prestige Teamwork

Card	Low	High
COMPLETE SET (30)	10.00	25.00
RANDOM INSERTS IN PACKS		
*RAINBOW/25: 1X TO 2.5X BASIC		
1 Okafor/Embiid	1.00	2.50
2 Parker/Antetokounmpo	1.25	3.00
3 Wade/Butler	1.00	2.50
4 Irving/James	2.50	6.00
5 Isaiah Thomas	.60	1.50
Al Horford		
6 Griffin/Paul	.75	2.00
7 Marc Gasol	.60	1.50
Mike Conley		
8 Dennis Schroder	.60	1.50
Paul Millsap		
9 Hassan Whiteside	.50	1.25
Justise Winslow		
10 Kemba Walker	.60	1.50
Nicolas Batum		
11 Gordon Hayward	.60	1.50
Rodney Hood		
12 Rudy Gay	.60	1.50
DeMarcus Cousins		
13 Rose/Anthony	.75	2.00
14 Russell/Clarkson	.75	2.00
15 Aaron Gordon	.50	1.25
Elfrid Payton		
16 Williams/Nowitzki	.75	2.00
17 Jeremy Lin	.60	1.50
Brook Lopez		
18 Danilo Gallinari	.50	1.25
Emmanuel Mudiay		
19 Teague/George	.75	2.00
20 Davis/Evans	1.25	3.00
21 Andre Drummond	.60	1.50
Reggie Jackson		
22 DeMar DeRozan	.60	1.50
Kyle Lowry		
23 Harden/Anderson	1.00	2.50
24 Leonard/Aldridge	1.00	2.50
25 Bledsoe/Booker	1.00	2.50
26 Westbrook/Adams	1.50	4.00
27 Towns/Wiggins	1.50	4.00
28 McCollum/Lillard	1.25	3.00
29 Curry/Durant	2.50	6.00
30 Beal/Wall	.75	2.00

2016-17 Prestige True Colors Materials

Card	Low	High
RANDOM INSERTS IN PACKS		
STATED PRINT RUN 199 SER. #'d SETS		
*PRIME/25: 1X TO 2.5X BASIC		
1 Aaron Gordon	2.50	6.00
2 Al Horford	2.50	6.00
3 Allen Iverson	6.00	15.00
4 Manu Ginobili	3.00	8.00
5 Andrew Wiggins	5.00	12.00
6 Kevin Love	3.00	8.00
7 Bojan Bogdanovic	2.00	5.00
8 Bradley Beal	3.00	8.00
9 Brook Lopez	2.50	6.00
10 C.J. McCollum	2.50	6.00
11 Carmelo Anthony	4.00	10.00
12 Dan Issel	2.50	6.00
13 Danny Manning	2.50	6.00
14 DeAndre Jordan	3.00	8.00
15 Deron Williams	2.50	6.00
17 Gorgui Dieng	2.00	5.00
18 Grant Hill	4.00	10.00
19 Jamal Crawford	3.00	8.00
20 Jeff Teague	2.50	6.00
21 Jimmy Butler	3.00	8.00
22 Justise Winslow	2.50	6.00
23 Jusuf Nurkic	2.00	5.00
24 Karl Malone	4.00	10.00
25 Karl-Anthony Towns	8.00	20.00
26 Kawhi Leonard	5.00	12.00
27 Kyrie Irving	6.00	15.00
28 Stephen Curry	12.00	30.00
29 Klay Thompson	4.00	10.00
30 Kyle Lowry	2.50	6.00
31 Michael Kidd-Gilchrist	2.50	6.00

1980-81 Pride New Orleans WBL

This 11-card set features the 1980-81 New Orleans Pride of the Women's Basketball League. It's believed that 13 cards actually exist, but we only have 11 cards that have been verified at this point in time. According to the backs, these cards were available at Dome Souvenir Stands or at the Pride office. Inside white borders, the fronts display blue-tinted posed action shots. The player's uniform number and autograph are printed on the picture. In blue print on a white background, the backs carry biography, player profile, and a "Trade 'em and win!" contest.

Card	Low	High
COMPLETE SET (11)	50.00	100.00
1 Kathy Andrykowski	4.00	10.00
2 Sybil Blalock	4.00	10.00
3 Cindy Brogden	7.50	15.00
4 Vicky Chapman	4.00	10.00
5 Beverly Crusoe	4.00	10.00
6 Sharon Farrah	4.00	10.00
7 Eileen Feeney	4.00	10.00
8 Augusta Forest	4.00	10.00
9 Bertha Hardy	4.00	10.00
10 Sue Peters	4.00	10.00
11 Heidi Wayment	4.00	10.00

2008 Prime Cuts Playoff Contenders Autographs

Card	Low	High
OVERALL AU/MEM ODDS 4 PER BOX		
EXCHANGE DEADLINE 6/26/2010		
23 O.J. Mayo	30.00	60.00
24 Michael Beasley	15.00	40.00
25 Derrick Rose	150.00	300.00

1985 Prism/Jewel Stickers

These gaudy metallic stickers measure different sizes but most are approximately 2 11/16" by 4". The front features a colorful drawn picture of the player, with the player's name in block lettering, and a facsimile autograph. The picture has rounded corners and a silver border. The backs are blank. The stickers are unnumbered and are checklisted below in alphabetical order by subject.

Card	Low	High
COMPLETE SET (14)	500.00	1000.00
1 Kareem Abdul-Jabbar	20.00	40.00
2 Larry Bird	40.00	100.00
3 Bird vs. Worthy	30.00	60.00
4 Julius Erving	30.00	60.00
5 Patrick Ewing	30.00	60.00
6 Magic Johnson	30.00	65.00
7 Michael Jordan	800.00	1200.00
8 Moses Malone	6.00	15.00
9 Malone vs. Jabbar	8.00	20.00
10 Sidney Moncrief	4.00	10.00
11 Ralph Sampson	4.00	10.00
12 Isiah Thomas	8.00	20.00
13 Kelly Tripucka	4.00	10.00
14 Buck Williams	4.00	10.00

1989-90 ProCards CBA

The 1989-90 ProCards CBA basketball set contains 207 standard-size cards. The cards were distributed in individual sealed team bags. Reportedly 2,000 sets were produced and distributed. The individual team sets reportedly originally retailed for approximately 3.00 each. The fronts feature posed or action color player photos on a light tan background. Overlaying the upper left corner of the picture is a white circle (representing a basketball), with the CBA logo on it. Just below the circle a basketball rim and net are drawn. The player's name, position, and team are given in black lettering in the lower right corner of the card face. On a gray background with black borders and lettering the horizontally oriented backs present biographical and statistical information. The team logo appears in the cut-out section at the upper right corner. The cards are numbered on the back and arranged according to teams as follows: Sioux Falls SkyForce (1-13), Wichita Falls Texans (14-25), Rapid City Thrillers (26-37), Quad City Thunder (38-50), Pensacola Tornados (51-60), Omaha Racers (61-74, 206-7), Columbus Horizon (75-86), Rockford Lightning (87-100), Albany Patroons (101-114), Santa Barbara Islanders (115-127), Grand Rapids Hoops (128-140), Tulsa Fast Breakers (141-153), LaCrosse Catbirds (154-165), Topeka Sizzlers (166-178), Cedar Rapids Silver Bullets (179-192), and San Jose Jammers (193-205). The set features the first professional cards of Chris Childs, Mario Elie and John Starks.

Card	Low	High
COMPLETE SET (207)	50.00	120.00
1 Sioux Falls Checklist	.30	.75
2 Ben Wilson	.30	.75
3 Leonard Harris	.40	1.00
4 Laurent Crawford	.30	.75
5 Steve Grayer	.50	1.25
6 Jim Lampley	.30	.75
7 Eric Brown	.30	.75
8 Dennis Nutt	.50	1.25
9 Ralph Lewis	.30	.75
10 Lashun McDaniel	.30	.75
11 Leo Parent	.30	.75
12 Ron Ekker	.30	.75
13 Terry Gould	.30	.75
14 Wichita Falls CL	.30	.75
15 Mark Peterson	.30	.75
16 Greg Van Soelen	.30	.75
17 Maurice Selvin	.30	.75
18 Michael Tait	.40	1.00
19 Deon Hunter	.40	1.00
20 Randy Henry	.30	.75
21 Kenny McClary	.40	1.00
22 Earl Walker	.30	.75
23 Jeff Hodge	.30	.75
24 Martin Nessley	.50	1.25
25 On Court Staff	.30	.75
26 Rapid City Checklist	.30	.75
27 Daren Queenan	.40	1.00
28 Carey Scurry	.30	.75
29 Keith Smart	1.25	3.00
30 Jim Thomas	.50	1.25
31 Pearl Washington	.75	2.00
32 Chris Childs	2.00	5.00
33 Jarvis Basnight	.50	1.25
34 Dwight Boyd	.30	.75
35 Raymond Brown	.40	1.00
36 Sylvester Gray	.40	1.00
37 Eric Musselman CO	1.25	3.00
38 Quad City Checklist	.30	.75
39 Kenny Gattison	1.25	3.00
40 Lafester Rhodes	.30	.75
41 Perry Young	.40	1.00
42 Wiley Brown	.40	1.00
43 Jose Slaughter	.75	2.00
44 Gerald Greene	.40	1.00
45 Lloyd Daniels	1.50	4.00
46 Bill Jones	.30	.75
47 Sean Couch	.30	.75
48 Marty Eggleston	.40	1.00
49 Mauro Panaggio CO	.40	1.00
50 Dan Panaggio CO	.30	.75
51 Pensacola Checklist	.30	.75
52 Joe Mullaney CO	1.00	2.50
53 Mark Wade	.30	.75
54 Larry Houzer	.30	.75
55 Clifford Lett	.30	.75
56 Tony Dawson	.40	1.00
57 Johnathan Edwards	.30	.75
58 Jim Farmer	.60	1.50
59 Dwayne Taylor	.30	.75
60 Bob McCann	.40	1.00
61 Omaha Checklist	.30	.75
62 Silks Rodie	.30	.75
63 Racers Front Office	.30	.75
64 Rodie-Team Mascot	.30	.75
65 Tim Price	.30	.75
66 Barry Glanzer	.30	.75
67 Greg Wiltjer	.40	1.00
68 Ron Kellogg	.30	.75
69 Tat Hunter	.30	.75
70 Reginald Turner	.30	.75
71 Jerry Adams	.30	.75
72 Roland Gray	.30	.75
73 Tim Legler	1.25	3.00
74 Corey Gaines	.60	1.50
75 Columbus Checklist	.30	.75
76 Gary Youmans	.30	.75
77 Kelvin Ransey	.75	2.00
78 Chip Engelland	1.50	4.00
79 Brian Martin	.30	.75
80 Ray Hall	.30	.75
81 Jay Burson	.40	1.00
82 Bill Martin	.60	1.50
83 Eric Mudd	.30	.75
84 Tom Schafer	.30	.75
85 Steve Harris	.40	1.00
86 Eric Newsome	.30	.75
87 Rockford Checklist	.30	.75
88 Charley Rosen	1.50	4.00
89 Tom Hart	.30	.75
90 Team Picture	.30	.75
91 Brent Carmichael	.30	.75
92 Fred Cofield	.40	1.00
93 Darren Guest	.30	.75
94 Bobby Parks	.30	.75
95 Elston Turner	.60	1.50
96 Adrian McKinnon	.30	.75
97 Gary Massey	.30	.75
98 Tim Dillon	.40	1.00
99 Herb Blunt	.30	.75
100 Greg Grissom	.30	.75
101 Albany Checklist	.30	.75
102 Leroy Witherspoon	.30	.75
103 Vincent Askew	2.00	5.00
104 Clinton Smith	.30	.75
105 Andre Patterson	.40	1.00
106 Jim Ferrer	.30	.75
107 Willie Glass	.60	1.50
108 Darryl Joe	.30	.75
109 Mario Elie	2.50	6.00
110 Dave Popson	.75	2.00
111 Danny Pearson	.30	.75
112 Doc Nunnally	.30	.75
113 Gene Espeland	.30	.75
114 Gerald Oliver CO	.30	.75
115 Santa Barbara CL	.30	.75
116 Luther Burks	.40	1.00
117 Brian Christensen	.30	.75
118 Kevin Francewar	.30	.75
119 Leon Wood	1.25	3.00
120 Derrick Gervin	.75	2.00
121 Larry Spriggs	.75	2.00
122 Michael Phelps	.40	1.00
123 Mike Ratliff	.30	.75
124 Steffond Johnson	.40	1.00
125 Mitch McMullen	.30	.75
126 Sonny Allen	.30	.75
127 Don Ford	.60	1.50
128 Grand Rapids CL	.30	.75
129 Lorenzo Sutton	.30	.75
130 Willie Simmons	.40	1.00
131 Kenny Fields	.40	1.00
132 Winston Crite	.30	.75
133 Eric McLaughlin	.30	.75
134 Tony Brown	.40	1.00
135 Ricky Wilson	.40	1.00
136 Milt Newton	.40	1.00
137 Albert Springs	.30	.75
138 Herbert Crook	.40	1.00
139 Mike Mashak ACO	.30	.75
140 Jim Sleeper	.30	.75
141 Tulsa Checklist	.30	.75
142 Terry Faggins	.30	.75
143 Ozell Jones	.40	1.00
144 Brian Rahilly	.30	.75
145 Duane Washington	.60	1.50
146 Ron Spivey	.30	.75
147 Henry Bibby CO	.60	1.50
148 Al Gipson	.40	1.00
149 Greg Jones	.30	.75
150 Andre Moore	.60	1.50
151 Tracy Moore	.60	1.50
152 Steve Bontranger	.30	.75
153 Bubby Breaker Mascot	.30	.75
154 LaCrosse Checklist	.30	.75
155 Mike Williams	.30	.75
156 Vince Hamilton	.40	1.00
157 John Harris	.30	.75
158 Tony White	.30	.75
159 Todd Alexander	.30	.75
160 Richard Johnson	.30	.75
161 Leo Rautins	1.00	2.50
162 Dwayne McClain	1.00	2.50
163 Carlos Clark	1.00	2.50
164 Vada Martin	.30	.75
165 Flip Saunders	1.50	4.00
166 Topeka Checklist	.30	.75
167 Cedric Hunter	.30	.75
168 Elfrem Jackson	.30	.75
169 Glen Clem	.30	.75
170 Mike Richmond	.30	.75
171 Jim Rowinski	.30	.75
172 Craig Jackson	.30	.75
173 Tony Mack	.30	.75
174 Hubert Henderson	.30	.75
175 Kevin Nixon	.30	.75
176 Haywoode Workman	1.25	3.00
177 Porter Cutrell	.30	.75
178 Mike Riley	.30	.75
179 Cedar Rapids CL	.30	.75
180 Bullet Bear	.30	.75
181 George Whittaker	.30	.75
182 Tom Domako	.30	.75
183 Al Lorenzen	.30	.75
184 Darryl Johnson	.40	1.00
185 Mel Braxton	.30	.75
186 Orlando Graham	.30	.75
187 Reggie Owens	.30	.75
188 John Starks	6.00	15.00
189 Kenny Drummond	.30	.75
190 Mark Plansky	.30	.75
191 Anthony Blakley	.40	1.00
192 Everette Stephens	.75	2.00
193 San Jose Checklist	.30	.75
194 Cory Russell	.30	.75
195 Jim Ellis	.30	.75
196 Butch Hays	.60	1.50
197 Mike Doktorczyk	.30	.75
198 Scooter Barry	1.50	4.00
199 Monroe Douglass	.30	.75
200 Scott Fisher	.40	1.00
201 David Boone	.30	.75
202 Jervis Cole	.30	.75
203 Freddie Banks	.30	.75
204 Richard Morton	.30	.75
205 Dan Williams	.30	.75
206 Mike Thibault CO	.30	.75
207 Omaha Coaches	.30	.75
Omaha Racers		

1990-91 ProCards CBA

The 1990-91 ProCards CBA basketball set contains 203 standard-size cards. The individual team sets reportedly originally retailed for approximately 3.00 each. The color player photos on the fronts are framed by a filmstrip design in red on a white card face. The horizontally oriented backs are printed in black on light purple and feature biographical as well as statistical information. The cards are checklisted below according to teams as follows: Omaha Racers (1-16), Cedar Rapids Silver Bullets (17-29), Pensacola Tornados (30-44), Rockford Lightning (45-59), Lacrosse Catbirds (60-71), Rapid City Thrillers (72-81), Sioux Falls Skyforce (82-96), Oklahoma City Cavalry (97-107), Tulsa Fast Breakers (108-118), Wichita Falls Texans (119-134), Quad City Thunder (135-148), Albany Patroons (149-162), Grand Rapids Hoops (163-171), Columbus Horizon (172-183), Yakima Sun Kings (184-192), and San Jose Jammers (193-203). The set contains the first professional card of Anthony Mason.

Card	Low	High
COMPLETE SET (203)	40.00	100.00
1 Jim Les	.75	2.00
2 Ron Moore	.25	.60
3 Rod Mason	.25	.60
4 Paul Weakly	.25	.60
5 Brian Howard	.40	1.00
6 Pat Bolden	.25	.60
7 Mike Thibault CO	.30	.75
8 Tim Legler	1.00	2.50
9 Cedric Hunter	.30	.75
10 Mark Peterson	.25	.60
11 Greg Wiltjer	.40	1.00
12 The Idelman's	.25	.60
13 The Silks and Rodie	.25	.60
14 Basketball Staff	.25	.60
15 Front Office Staff	.25	.60
16 Omaha Checklist	.25	.60
17 Calvin Duncan	.25	.60
18 Pat Durham	.40	1.00
19 Steve Grayer	.40	1.00
20 Roy Marble	.60	1.50
21 Tony Martin	.30	.75
22 Shawn McDaniel	.25	.60
23 Peter Thibeaux	.25	.60
24 Clarence Thompson	.25	.60
25 Demone Webster	.25	.60
26 A.J. Wynder	.40	1.00
27 Steve Kahl	.25	.60
28 Steve Bontranger	.25	.60
29 Cedar Rapids CL	.25	.60
30 Skeeter Henry	.40	1.00
31 Eugene McDowell	.25	.60
32 Bruce Wheatley	.25	.60
33 Mark Wade	.30	.75
34 Cheyenne Gibson	.25	.60
35 Clifford Lett	.30	.75
36 Larry Houzer	.25	.60
37 Tony Dawson	.25	.60
38 Richard Hollis	.30	.75
39 Ed Leonard and	.25	.60
Joe Corona		
40 Front Office Staff	.25	.60
41 Torry the Tornado	.25	.60
42 Fred Bryan	.25	.60
43 Jim Goodman	.25	.60
44 Pensacola Checklist	.25	.60
45 Joe Fredrick	.25	.60
46 Everette Stephens	.60	1.50
47 Mario Donaldson	.25	.60
48 Dan Godfread	.25	.60
49 Haakon Austefjord	.25	.60
50 Gary Massey	.25	.60
51 Chris Childs	1.25	3.00
52 Gerry Wright	.25	.60
53 Marty Conlon	1.00	2.50
54 Tony Costner	.25	.60
55 Steve Hayes CO	.50	1.25
56 Tom Hart	.25	.60
57 Paul Kulick	.25	.60
58 Rockford Team Photo	.25	.60
59 Rockford Checklist	.25	.60
60 Mike Williams	.25	.60
61 Brian Rahilly	.25	.60
62 Bill Martin	.40	1.00
63 Vince Hamilton	.30	.75
64 Dwayne McClain	.75	2.00
65 Bart Kofoed	.40	1.00
66 Dominic Pressley	.30	.75
67 Herb Dixon	.25	.60
68 Todd Mitchell	.30	.75
69 Ben Mitchell	.25	.60
70 Flip Saunders	1.25	3.00
71 LaCrosse Checklist	.25	.60
72 Keith Smart	1.00	2.50
73 Stevie Thompson	.75	2.00
74 Brian Rowsom	.40	1.00
75 Tony Martin	.30	.75
76 Joe Ward	.25	.60
77 Fennis Dembo	.40	1.00
78 Glenn Puddy	.25	.60
79 Lanard Copeland	.60	1.50
80 Carl Brown	.25	.60
81 Rapid City Checklist	.25	.60
82 Dennis Nutt	.40	1.00
83 Leonard Harris	.30	.75
84 Tharon Mayes	.30	.75
85 Melvin McCants	.40	1.00
86 Tracy Mitchell	.30	.75
87 Ken Redfield	.30	.75
88 Frank Ross	.25	.60
89 Michael Phelps	.30	.75
90 Brian Christensen	.25	.60
91 Kevin McKenna	.60	1.50
92 Steve Raab	.25	.60
93 Clay Moser	.25	.60
94 Tony Khing	.25	.60
95 Little Dude	.25	.60
96 Sioux Falls Checklist	.25	.60
97 Perry Young	.40	1.00
98 Ozell Jones	.40	1.00
99 Willie Simmons	.25	.60
100 Alvin Heggs	.25	.60
101 Kelsey Weems	.30	.75
102 Anthony Frederick	.30	.75
103 Royce Jeffries	.25	.60
104 Darryl McDonald	.60	1.50
105 Sgt. Slammer	.25	.60
106 Charley Rosen	1.25	3.00
107 Oklahoma City CL	.25	.60
108 Keith Wilson	.25	.60
109 James Carter	.25	.60
110 Tracy Moore	.40	1.00
111 Mark Plansky	.30	.75
112 Charles Bradley	.25	.60
113 Leroy Combs	.25	.60
114 Anthony Mason	4.00	10.00
115 Gary Voce	.40	1.00
116 Jim Lampley	.30	.75
117 Henry Bibby CO	.60	1.50
118 Tulsa Checklist	.25	.60
119 Texans Logo	.25	.60
120 Ennis Whatley	.75	2.00
121 Mike Mitchell	.40	1.00
122 Derrick Taylor	.30	.75
123 Kenny Atkinson	.25	.60
124 Jaren Jackson	.50	1.25
125 Cedric Ball	.25	.60
126 Chris Munk	.25	.60
127 Mark Becker	.25	.60
128 Rodney Blake	.25	.60
129 Kurt Portmann	.25	.60
130 Henry James	.40	1.00
131 John Treloar ACO	.25	.60
132 Dave Whitney ACO	.25	.60
133 Mike Davis ACO	.50	1.25
134 Wichita Falls CL	.25	.60
135 Milt Wagner	1.00	2.50
136 Phil Henderson	.60	1.50
137 Tony Harris	.25	.60
138 Steve Bardo	.40	1.00
139 A.J. Wynder	.40	1.00
140 Joel DeBortoli	.40	1.00
141 Tim Anderson	.25	.60
142 Ron Draper	.25	.60
143 Barry Sumpter	.30	.75
144 Demone Webster	.25	.60
145 Thunderbird Dance Team	.25	.60
146 Mauro Panaggio CO	.40	1.00
147 Dan Panaggio CO	.25	.60
148 Quad City Checklist	.25	.60
149 Albert King	.40	1.00
150 Keith Smith	.25	.60
151 Mario Elie	2.00	5.00
152 Albert Springs	.25	.60
153 Jeff Fryer	.25	.60
154 Clinton Smith	.25	.60
155 Vincent Askew	1.50	4.00
156 Paul Graham	.75	2.00
157 Ben McDonald	.60	1.50
158 Willie McDuffie	.25	.60
159 George Karl CO	2.50	6.00
160 Terry Stotts	1.00	2.50
161 Doc Nunnally	.25	.60
162 Albany Checklist	.25	.60
163 Reggie Fox	.25	.60
164 Sedric Toney	.30	.75
165 Ron Draper	.25	.60
166 Alex Austin	.25	.60
167 Robert Brickey	.40	1.00
168 Ricky Blanton	.40	1.00
169 Stan Kimbrough	.25	.60
170 Ron Cavenall	.25	.60
171 Grand Rapids CL	.25	.60
172 Darren Henrie	.25	.60
173 Duane Washington	.50	1.25
174 Barry Stevens	.25	.60
175 Craig Neal	.25	.60
176 Ron Spivey	.25	.60
177 Kerry Hammonds	.25	.60
178 Brian Martin	.25	.60
179 Jerome Henderson	.25	.60
180 John McIntyre	.25	.60
181 Chris Childs	1.25	3.00
182 The Jacobson's	.25	.60
183 Columbus Checklist	.25	.60
184 Luther Burks	.25	.60
185 Lee Campbell	.25	.60
186 Corey Gaines	.40	1.00
187 Mike Higgins	.25	.60
188 Ron Kellogg	.25	.60
189 Bart Kofoed	.40	1.00
190 Jim Rowinski	.25	.60
191 Riley Smith	.25	.60
192 Yakima Checklist	.25	.60
193 Mike Yoest	.25	.60
194 Freddie Banks	.30	.75
195 Scooter Barry	1.25	3.00
196 Richard Morton	.25	.60
197 Kelby Stuckey	.25	.60
198 Jervis Cole	.25	.60
199 Kenny McClary	.30	.75
200 Joe Wallace	.25	.60
201 Mark Tillmon	.30	.75
202 Greg Butler	.30	.75
203 San Jose Checklist	.25	.60

1991-92 ProCards CBA

The 1991-92 ProCards CBA basketball set contains 206 standard-size cards. The individual team sets reportedly originally retailed for approximately 3.00 each. The fronts feature a mix of posed and action color player photos, bordered in silver. Two stripes that shade from pink to white accent the pictures on the left and bottom; the CBA logo appears in a circle at their intersection. On a gray background with black borders and lettering, the backs present biographical and statistical information. Seven teams found sponsors that listed their business on the card back, of which four were sports card shops. The cards are numbered on the back and checklisted below according to teams as follows: Bakersfield Jammers (1-11, 72), Wichita Texans (12-24), Rockford Lightning (25-35), Quad City Thunder (36-48), Oklahoma City Cavalry (49-60), Rapid City Thrillers (61-71), Fort Wayne Fury (73-85), Yakima Sun Kings (86-97), Grand Rapids Hoops (98-109), Sioux Falls Skyforce (110-121, 206), Tri-City Chinook (122-135), Columbus Horizon (136-147), LaCrosse Catbirds (148-159), Albany Patroons (160-171), Tulsa Zone (172-183), Omaha Racers (184-195), and Birmingham Bandits (196-205).

Card	Low	High
COMPLETE SET (206)	30.00	80.00
1 Chris Childs	1.25	3.00
2 Mark Tillmon	.30	.75
3 Greg Butler	.30	.75
4 Keith Hill	.20	.50
5 Jean Derouillere	.20	.50
6 Levy Middlebrooks	.20	.50
7 Tank Collins	.20	.50
8 Sam Williams	.20	.50
9 Herman Kull CO	.20	.50
10 Don Ford ACO	.40	1.00
11 Charles Charlesworth TR	.20	.50
12 Calvin Oldham	.20	.50
13 Larty Smith	.20	.50
14 Trent Jackson	.20	.50
15 Rob Rose	.40	1.00
16 Walter Bond	.40	1.00
17 Jeff Majerle	.40	1.00
18 Brad Baldridge	.20	.50
19 Kurt Portman	.20	.50
20 Cedric Jenkins	.30	.75
21 John Treloar CO	.20	.50
22 Mike Davis ACO	.60	1.50
23 Dave Whitney ACO	.20	.50

24 Wichita Falls CL .20 .50
25 Tim Dillon .20 .50
26 Kenny Miller .20 .50
27 Stevie Wise .20 .50
28 Dan Godfread .20 .50
29 Mario Donaldson .20 .50
30 Steve Berger .20 .50
31 Corey Beasley .20 .50
32 Danny Jones .20 .50
33 Lanny Van Eman CO .20 .50
34 Tony Morocco ACO .20 .50
35 Rockford CL .20 .50
36 Bobby Martin .40 1.00
37 Dwight Moody .30 .75
38 Tim Anderson .20 .50
39 A.J. Wynder .40 1.00
40 Keith Robinson .30 .75
41 Steve Scheffler .60 1.50
42 Anthony Bowie 1.00 2.50
43 Tony Harris .40 1.00
44 Barry Mitchell .30 .75
45 Tom Sheehey .20 .50
46 Dan Panaggio CO .20 .50
47 Mike Mashak ACO .20 .50
48 Quad City CL .20 .50
49 Bernard Thompson .40 1.00
50 Daryll Walker .20 .50
51 Darryl Kennedy .30 .75
52 Stevie Thompson .40 1.00
53 Kelsey Weems .30 .75
54 Steve Burtt .40 1.00
55 Junie Lewis .20 .50
56 Chris Harris .20 .50
57 Jeff Hodge .20 .50
58 Demone Webster .20 .50
59 Henry Bibby CO .50 1.25
60 Oklahoma City CL .20 .50
61 Jarvis Basnight .30 .75
62 Ed Horton .30 .75
63 Stanley Brundy .20 .50
64 Irving Thomas .30 .75
65 Nate Johnston .20 .50
66 Keith Smart .75 2.00
67 Larry Robinson .20 .50
68 Michael Anderson .20 .50
69 Eric Musselman CO .60 1.50
70 Duane Ticknor ACO .20 .50
71 Rapid City CL .20 .50
72 Bakersfield CL .20 .50
73 Lyndon Jones .30 .75
74 Warren Bradley .20 .50
75 Anthony Corbitt .20 .50
76 Tony Karasek .20 .50
77 Mark Peterson .20 .50
78 Dan Palombizio .40 1.00
79 Ricky Hall .20 .50
80 John Cooper .40 1.00
81 Carl Thomas .30 .75
82 Travis Williams .20 .50
83 Gerald Oliver CO .20 .50
84 Kevin Kacer TR .50 1.25
Terry Stotts ACO
Dave Carrington ACO
Walter Jordan ACO
85 Fort Wayne CL .20 .50
86 Ronn McMahon .20 .50
87 Sean Tyson .20 .50
88 McKinley Singleton .20 .50
89 Teo Alibegovic .20 .50
90 Joey Johnson .20 .50
91 Riley Smith .20 .50
92 Alex Austin .20 .50
93 Dennis Williams .20 .50
94 Luther Burks .20 .50
95 Bill Klucas CO .20 .50
96 Jack Miller ACO .20 .50
97 Yakima CL .20 .50
98 Roy Fisher .40 1.00
99 Reggie Isaac .20 .50
100 Reggie Jordan .40 1.00
101 Cedric Lewis .40 1.00
102 Jeff Martin .40 1.00
103 Dyron Nix .50 1.25
104 Walter Watts .20 .50
105 Gary Waites .20 .50
106 Gerald Paddio .40 1.00
107 Bruce Stewart CO .20 .50
108 Jeff Burkhamer ACO .20 .50
109 Grand Rapids CL .20 .50
110 Petur Gudmundsson .75 2.00
111 Ralph Lewis .20 .50
112 John Smith .20 .50
113 Tony Farmer .30 .75
114 Matt Roe .40 1.00
115 Darryl McDonald .60 1.50
116 Corey Gaines .40 1.00
117 Richard Rellford .30 .75
118 Ken Redfield .30 .75
119 Chuckie White .20 .50
120 Kevin McKenna CO .50 1.25
121 Clay Moser ACO .20 .50
122 Donald Royal 1.50 4.00
123 Wayne Tinkle .20 .50
124 Jim Usevitch .20 .50
125 Eric Dunn .20 .50
126 Jeffty Connelly .20 .50
127 Alan Pollard .20 .50
128 Clifford Scales .30 .75
129 Harold Wright .20 .50
130 Willie Simms .20 .50
131 Michael Holton .40 1.00
132 Terrill Hall .20 .50
133 Calvin Duncan .20 .50
Guard
Assistant CO
134 Steve Hayes CO .50 1.25
135 Yakima CL .20 .50
136 Duane Washington .50 1.25
137 Kermit Holmes .20 .50
138 Mike Goodson .20 .50
139 Byron Dinkins .40 1.00
140 Leonard Harris .30 .75
141 Louis Banks .20 .50
142 James Bradley .20 .50
143 Jeff King .20 .50
144 Ron Spivey .20 .50
145 Orlando Graham .20 .50
146 Vincent Chickerella CO .20 .50
147 Columbus CL .20 .50
148 Daron Hoges .20 .50
149 Von McDade .20 .50
150 Byron Irvin .40 1.00
151 Patrick Tompkins .20 .50
152 Brian Rahilly .20 .50
153 Kenny Battle .40 1.00
154 Jaren Jackson .40 1.00
155 Troy Truvillion .20 .50
156 Mark Davis .40 1.00
157 Vince Hamilton .25 .60
158 Don Zierden ACO .20 .50
and Mike McCollow ACO
159 LaCrosse CL .20 .50
160 Derrick Chievous .40 1.00
161 Jeff Sanders .40 1.00
162 Marc Brown .20 .50
163 Johnnie Hilliad .20 .50
164 Jerry Johnson .20 .50
165 Dave Popson .40 1.00
166 Derrick Rowland .20 .50
167 Jose Slaughter .50 1.25
168 Steve Wright .20 .50
169 Charley Rosen CO 1.00 2.50
170 Lowes Moore ACO .30 .75
171 Albany CL .20 .50
172 Jasper Hooks .20 .50
173 Tracy Moore .30 .75
174 Keith Wilson .20 .50
175 Shawn McDaniel .20 .50
176 Sam Johnson .20 .50
177 Jeff Fryer .20 .50
178 A.C. Carver .20 .50
179 Jawann Oldham .60 1.50
180 Lefty Moore .20 .50
181 Anthony Blakley .40 1.00
182 Steve Bontranger CO .20 .50
183 Tulsa CL .20 .50
184 Cedric Hunter .30 .75
185 Ronnie Grandison .30 .75
186 Ricky Jones .40 1.00
187 Tim Legler .75 2.00
188 Chip Engelland 1.25 3.00
189 Brian Howard .40 1.00
190 Greg Wiltjer .20 .50
191 Rod Mason .20 .50
192 Roland Gray .20 .50
193 Tat Hunter .20 .50
194 Mike Thibault CO .30 .75
195 Omaha CL .20 .50
196 Chris Collier .20 .50
197 Skeeter Henry .30 .75
198 Emmett Smith .20 .50
199 Anthony Houston .20 .50
200 Michael Cutright .30 .75
201 Michael Ansley .60 1.50
202 Eugene McDowell .20 .50
203 Eric Johnson .20 .50
204 Mo McHone CO .30 .75
205 Birmingham CL .20 .50
206 Sioux Falls CL .20 .50

1987 Pro Basketball Reading Kit

This NBA reading kit was released in 1987. The set features 40-pages (measuring 8 1/2"x14 1/4") of reading material and pictures of star NBA players. Please note that this reading kit was produced using full-color pages.

COMPLETE SET (40) 75.00 135.00
1 Ralph Sampson 1.50 4.00
Hakeem Olajuwon
2 Cheryl Miller 1.50 4.00
3 Paul Arizin 1.00 2.50
4 Walt Frazier 1.25 3.00
5 Joe Fulks 1.00 2.50
6 Manute Bol .75 2.00
7 Referees .75 2.00
8 Bob Pettit 1.25 3.00
9 Patrick Ewing 2.00 5.00
10 Bob Pettit 1.25 3.00
11 Charles Barkley 2.50 6.00
12 Maurice Stokes 1.00 2.50
13 Madison Square Garden .75 2.00
14 Artis Gilmore 1.00 2.50
15 Dr. James Naismith .75 2.00
16 George Mikan 1.25 3.00
17 ABA .75 2.00
18 Spud Webb .75 2.00
19 John Havlicek 1.25 3.00
20 Bob Cousy 2.00 5.00
21 Moses Malone 1.50 4.00
22 Eddie Gottlieb .75 2.00
23 Jerry West 2.50 6.00
24 Dave DeBusschere 1.25 3.00
25 Magic Johnson 3.00 8.00
26 Hall of Fame .75 2.00
27 Minneapolis Lakers .75 2.00
28 Kareem Abdul-Jabbar 3.00 8.00
29 Dolph Schayes 1.00 2.50
30 Elgin Baylor 1.25 3.00
31 Julius Erving 4.00 10.00
32 Jerry Krause .75 2.00
33 Wilt Chamberlain 4.00 10.00
34 Michael Jordan 6.00 15.00
35 Bill Sharman 1.00 2.50
36 Larry Bird 4.00 10.00
37 Bill Russell 3.00 8.00
38 Philadelphia 76ers .75 2.00
39 Oscar Robertson 2.50 6.00
40 Bill Walton 2.00 5.00

1993 Pro Line Live LPs

These 20 limited-print, foil-stamped standard-size cards spotlight top young NFL talent along with three top NBA draft picks. The cards were randomly inserted throughout 1993 Classic Pro Line packs on an average of four per point of purchase box. Each card front features a color player action shot that is borderless on three sides. The right side is edged by a team-colored stripe that carries the player's name in gold foil. The gold-foil limited print seal, which carries the words "One of 40,000," appears at the lower right. In its top half, the back carries another player action shot, followed below by career highlights in a team-colored area at the bottom. The cards are numbered on the back with an "LP" prefix.

COMPLETE SET (20) 6.00 15.00
LP1 Chris Webber .75 2.00
LP2 Shaquille O'Neal 1.50 4.00
LP3 Jamal Mashburn .10 .30

1994 Pro Mags Promos

Produced by Chris Martin Enterprises, Inc., this set 3-card promotional set consists of collectible magnets, each measuring 2 1/8" by 3 3/8". The fronts feature a color player cutout superposed on a gray-streaked background. The player's first name is printed at one of the lower corners. The team logo rounds out the front.

COMPLETE SET (3) 4.00 10.00
1 Shaquille O'Neal UER 2.00 5.00
name spelled O'Neil
2 Grant Hill 2.00 5.00
3 Jason Kidd 2.00 5.00

1994 Pro Mags

Produced by Chris Martin Enterprises, Inc., this set consists of 135 collectible magnets, each measuring 2 1/8" by 3 3/8". The magnets were sold five to a blister pack. A checklist card (printed on glossy paper) and a free team magnet were included in each blister pack. The fronts feature a color player cutout superposed on a gray-streaked background. The player's first name is printed at one of the lower corners, with his last name printed vertically in team color-coded shadow lettering. The team logo rounds out the front. The cards are grouped alphabetically within teams and checklisted below alphabetically according to teams.

COMPLETE SET (135) 40.00 100.00
1 Stacey Augmon .50 1.25
2 Mookie Blaylock .40 1.00
3 Doug Edwards .40 1.00
4 Adam Keefe .40 1.00
5 Danny Manning .50 1.25
6 Dee Brown .40 1.00
7 Sherman Douglas .40 1.00
8 Rick Fox .40 1.00
9 Xavier McDaniel .40 1.00
10 Robert Parish .60 1.50
11 Muggsy Bogues .50 1.25
12 Dell Curry .40 1.00
13 Hersey Hawkins .40 1.00
14 Larry Johnson .60 1.50
15 Alonzo Mourning 1.25 3.00
16 B.J. Armstrong .40 1.00
17 Horace Grant .50 1.25
18 Toni Kukoc .75 2.00
19 John Paxson .50 1.25
20 Scottie Pippen 2.00 5.00
21 Brad Daugherty .50 1.25
22 John Williams .40 1.00
23 Chris Mills .40 1.00
24 Larry Nance .50 1.25
25 Gerald Wilkins .40 1.00
26 Doug Smith .40 1.00
27 Jim Jackson .40 1.00
28 Popeye Jones .40 1.00
29 Jamal Mashburn .60 1.50
30 Randy White .40 1.00
31 Mahmoud Abdul-Rauf .40 1.00
32 LaPhonso Ellis .40 1.00
33 Dikembe Mutombo .60 1.50
34 Reggie Williams .40 1.00
35 Rodney Rogers .40 1.00
36 Joe Dumars .60 1.50
37 Sean Elliott .60 1.50
38 Allan Houston .60 1.50
39 Lindsey Hunter .40 1.00
40 Terry Mills .40 1.00
41 Tim Hardaway .60 1.50
42 Chris Mullin .75 2.00
43 Billy Owens .40 1.00
44 Latrell Sprewell .75 2.00
45 Chris Webber 2.50 6.00
46 Robert Horry .60 1.50
47 Vernon Maxwell .40 1.00
48 Hakeem Olajuwon .75 2.00
49 Kenny Smith .50 1.25
50 Otis Thorpe .40 1.00
51 Dale Davis .40 1.00
52 Reggie Miller 1.25 3.00
53 Pooh Richardson .40 1.00
54 Rik Smits .50 1.25
55 LaSalle Thompson .40 1.00
56 Dominique Wilkins .75 2.00
57 Ron Harper .50 1.25
58 Mark Jackson .50 1.25
59 Stanley Roberts .40 1.00
60 Loy Vaught .40 1.00
61 Sam Bowie .40 1.00
62 Vlade Divac .60 1.50
63 George Lynch .40 1.00
64 Anthony Peeler .40 1.00
65 James Worthy .75 2.00
66 Harold Miner .40 1.00
67 Glen Rice .60 1.50
68 Rony Seikaly .50 1.25
69 Brian Shaw .40 1.00
70 Steve Smith .50 1.25
71 Vin Baker .60 1.50
72 Theodore Edwards .40 1.00
73 Todd Day .40 1.00
74 Eric Murdock .40 1.00
75 Jon Barry .40 1.00
76 Thurl Bailey .40 1.00
77 Christian Laettner .50 1.25
78 Chuck Person .50 1.25
79 Doug West .40 1.00
80 Micheal Williams .40 1.00
81 Derrick Coleman .50 1.25
82 Rick Mahorn .40 1.00
83 Johnny Newman .40 1.00
84 Kenny Anderson .50 1.25
85 Rex Walters .40 1.00
86 Greg Anthony .40 1.00
87 Rolando Blackman .50 1.25
88 Patrick Ewing .75 2.00
89 Charles Oakley .50 1.25
90 John Starks .50 1.25
91 Nick Anderson .40 1.00
92 Anfernee Hardaway 1.00 2.50
93 Donald Royal .40 1.00
94 Dennis Scott .40 1.00
95 Scott Skiles .40 1.00
96 Dana Barros .40 1.00
97 Shawn Bradley .40 1.00
98 Johnny Dawkins .40 1.00
99 Tim Perry .40 1.00
100 Clarence Weatherspoon .40 1.00
101 Charles Barkley 1.50 4.00
102 Cedric Ceballos .40 1.00
103 Malcolm Mackey .40 1.00
104 Dan Majerle .60 1.50
105 Danny Ainge .60 1.50
106 Clyde Drexler .75 2.00
107 Jerome Kersey .40 1.00
108 Rod Strickland .40 1.00
109 Buck Williams .40 1.00
110 Clifford Robinson .40 1.00
111 Mitch Richmond .60 1.50
112 Lionel Simmons .40 1.00
113 Wayman Tisdale .40 1.00
114 Walt Williams .40 1.00
115 Spud Webb .60 1.50
116 Dale Ellis .40 1.00
117 J.R. Reid .40 1.00
118 David Robinson 1.00 2.50
119 Dennis Rodman 1.50 4.00
120 Vinny Del Negro .40 1.00
121 Kendall Gill .40 1.00
122 Ervin Johnson .40 1.00
123 Shawn Kemp .75 2.00
124 Gary Payton .60 1.50
125 Sam Perkins .40 1.00
126 Karl Malone 1.50 4.00
127 Tyrone Corbin .40 1.00
128 Jeff Hornacek .50 1.25
129 Felton Spencer .40 1.00
130 John Stockton 2.00 5.00
131 Michael Adams .40 1.00
132 Calbert Cheaney .40 1.00
133 Tom Gugliotta .40 1.00
134 Don MacLean .40 1.00
135 Pervis Ellison .40 1.00

1994-95 Pro Mags Rookie Showcase

Produced by Chris Martin Enterprises, Inc., this set of 12 magnets was sold in a cello-wrapped and individually-numbered cardboard sleeve. The sleeve carries a checklist on its back panel and unfolds to reveal the magnets. The magnets measure 2 1/8" by 3 3/8" and have rounded corners. Inside black borders, the fronts display two color player photos, one superposed on the other. The words "Rookie Showcase" are printed above, while the player's name is stamped in gold foil below. The magnets are numbered in the upper left corner.

COMPLETE SET (12) 10.00 25.00
1 Tony Dumas .60 1.50
2 Brian Grant 1.00 2.50
3 Juwan Howard 1.00 2.50
4 Donyell Marshall .60 1.50
5 Eric Mobley .40 1.00
6 Eric Montross .50 1.25
7 Carlos Rogers .50 1.25
8 Jalen Rose 1.50 4.00
9 Charlie Ward .60 1.50
10 Grant Hill 3.00 8.00
11 Glenn Robinson 1.25 3.00
12 Jason Kidd 3.00 8.00

1995 Pro Mags

Produced by Chris Martin Enterprises, this 145-magnet set measures approximately 2 1/4" by 3 1/2". These magnets have rounded corners and were sold in packs of five. Each pack included a checklist, printed as a card rather than a magnet. The fronts feature color action player photos with the player's name printed vertically in gold foil along one side. The NBA and team logos are at the bottom. The magnets are checklisted alphabetically according to teams.

COMPLETE SET (145) 60.00 150.00
1 Stacey Augmon .60 1.50
2 Mookie Blaylock .50 1.25
3 Ken Norman .50 1.25
4 Steve Smith .60 1.50
5 Grant Long .50 1.25
6 Eric Williams .75 2.00
7 Eric Montross .50 1.25
8 Sherman Douglas .50 1.25
9 Dee Brown .50 1.25
10 Dino Radja .50 1.25
11 Larry Johnson .75 2.00
12 Alonzo Mourning 1.00 2.50
13 Muggsy Bogues .60 1.50
14 Scott Burrell .50 1.25
15 Kendall Gill .50 1.25
16 Dennis Rodman 1.50 4.00
17 Scottie Pippen 1.25 3.00
18 Ron Harper .60 1.50
19 Toni Kukoc .75 2.00
20 Dickey Simpkins .50 1.25
21 Danny Ferry .50 1.25
22 Tyrone Hill .50 1.25
23 Michael Cage .50 1.25
24 Chris Mills .50 1.25
25 Terrell Brandon .50 1.25
26 Jason Kidd 1.25 3.00
27 Jamal Mashburn .75 2.00
28 Tony Dumas .50 1.25
29 Roy Tarpley .50 1.25
30 Jim Jackson .50 1.25
31 Dikembe Mutombo .75 2.00
32 Jalen Rose 1.00 2.50
33 Robert Pack .50 1.25
34 Antonio McDyess 1.00 2.50
35 Reggie Williams .50 1.25
36 Grant Hill 1.25 3.00
37 Joe Dumars .75 2.00
38 Lindsey Hunter .50 1.25
39 Allan Houston .60 1.50
40 Terry Mills .50 1.25
41 Tim Hardaway .75 2.00
42 Chris Mullin .75 2.00
43 Joe Smith 1.00 2.50
44 Latrell Sprewell .75 2.00
45 Donyell Marshall .50 1.25
46 Hakeem Olajuwon 1.00 2.50
47 Robert Horry .60 1.50
48 Sam Cassell .75 2.00
49 Kenny Smith .60 1.50
50 Clyde Drexler 1.00 2.50
51 Reggie Miller 1.00 2.50
52 Mark Jackson .75 2.00
53 Rik Smits .60 1.50
54 Dale Davis .50 1.25
55 Derrick McKey .50 1.25
56 Loy Vaught .50 1.25
57 Terry Dehere .50 1.25
58 Lamond Murray .50 1.25
59 Eric Piatkowski .60 1.50
60 Pooh Richardson .50 1.25
61 Vlade Divac .75 2.00
62 Anthony Peeler .50 1.25
63 Nick Van Exel .75 2.00
64 Cedric Ceballos .50 1.25
65 Eddie Jones 1.00 2.50
66 Sasha Danilovic .75 2.00
67 Glen Rice .75 2.00
68 Khalid Reeves .50 1.25
69 Billy Owens .50 1.25
70 Kevin Willis .50 1.25
71 Glenn Robinson .60 1.50
72 Vin Baker .60 1.50
73 Todd Day .50 1.25
74 Eric Mobley .50 1.25
75 Jon Barry .50 1.25
76 Isaiah Rider .75 2.00
77 Christian Laettner .60 1.50
78 Kevin Garnett 6.00 15.00
79 Doug West .50 1.25
80 Sean Rooks .50 1.25
81 Derrick Coleman .60 1.50
82 Rick Mahorn .50 1.25
83 Rex Walters .50 1.25
84 Kenny Anderson .60 1.50
85 Ed O'Bannon .75 2.00
86 Patrick Ewing 1.00 2.50
87 John Starks .60 1.50
88 Charles Oakley .60 1.50
89 Anthony Mason .50 1.25
90 Derek Harper .60 1.50
91 Anfernee Hardaway 1.25 3.00
92 Brian Shaw .50 1.25
93 Shaquille O'Neal 2.00 5.00
94 Brooks Thompson .50 1.25
95 Horace Grant .60 1.50
96 Tim Perry .50 1.25
97 Sharone Wright .50 1.25
98 Jerry Stackhouse 2.50 6.00
99 Clarence Weatherspoon .50 1.25
100 Vernon Maxwell .50 1.25
101 Charles Barkley 1.25 3.00
102 Danny Manning .60 1.50
103 Michael Finley 2.50 6.00
104 Kevin Johnson .75 2.00
105 Wayman Tisdale .50 1.25
106 Randolph Childress .75 2.00
107 Gary Trent .75 2.00
108 James Robinson .50 1.25
109 Buck Williams .50 1.25
110 Clifford Robinson .50 1.25
111 Corliss Williamson .75 2.00
112 Bobby Hurley .50 1.25
113 Brian Grant .60 1.50
114 Mitch Richmond .75 2.00
115 Walt Williams .50 1.25
116 David Robinson 1.25 3.00
117 Will Perdue .50 1.25
118 Chuck Person .50 1.25
119 Sean Elliott .75 2.00
120 Vinny Del Negro .50 1.25
121 Ervin Johnson .50 1.25
122 Shawn Kemp .75 2.00
123 Sam Perkins .50 1.25
124 Detlef Schrempf .75 2.00
125 Gary Payton .75 2.00
126 Karl Malone 1.00 2.50
127 John Stockton 1.00 2.50
128 Felton Spencer .50 1.25
129 Jeff Hornacek .60 1.50
130 Adam Keefe .50 1.25
131 Chris Webber 1.00 2.50
132 Juwan Howard .75 2.00
133 Calbert Cheaney .50 1.25
134 Rasheed Wallace 2.50 6.00
135 Gheorghe Muresan .50 1.25
136 Ed Pinckney .50 1.25
137 Tony Massenburg .50 1.25
138 Damon Stoudamire 2.00 5.00
139 Acie Earl .50 1.25
140 Alvin Robertson .50 1.25
141 Greg Anthony .50 1.25
142 Benoit Benjamin .50 1.25
143 Antonio Harvey .50 1.25
144 Byron Scott .75 2.00
145 Bryant Reeves .75 2.00

1995-96 Pro Mags Die Cuts

These 27 magnets were produced by Chris Martin Enterprises. Each magnet measures approximately 3 1/2" by 3 1/2". The front features a color action player cut-out with the team name, team logo and player's last name on a white background cut in the shape of the team logo and player's name. The player's first name is printed in small gold foil letters over his last name along with the words "Die-Cut Magnets" above. Actually, there are two known variations. One has "Die-Cut Magnets" written above the name and the player's first name printed larger, the other has "Die-Cut Magnets" in the bottom left corner in gold foil and smaller type on the player's first name. The magnets are unnumbered and checklisted below in alphabetical order.

COMPLETE SET (27) 12.00 30.00
1 Charles Barkley 2.00 5.00
2 Patrick Ewing 1.50 4.00
3 Anfernee Hardaway 1.50 4.00
4 Tim Hardaway 1.25 3.00
5 Grant Hill 1.50 4.00
6 Larry Johnson 1.25 3.00
7 Magic Johnson 3.00 8.00
8 Shawn Kemp 1.25 3.00
9 Jason Kidd 1.50 4.00
10 Karl Malone 1.50 4.00
11 Jamal Mashburn 1.25 3.00
12 Reggie Miller 1.50 4.00
13 Shaquille O'Neal 2.00 5.00
14 Hakeem Olajuwon 1.25 3.00
15 Scottie Pippen 2.00 5.00
16 Mitch Richmond 1.25 3.00
17 Isaiah Rider .75 2.00
18 David Robinson 1.50 4.00
19 Glenn Robinson 1.25 3.00
20 Dennis Rodman 2.50 6.00
21 Jerry Stackhouse 1.50 4.00
22 John Stockton 2.00 5.00
23 Damon Stoudamire 1.25 3.00
24 Nick Van Exel 1.25 3.00
25 Chris Webber 1.50 4.00

1995 Pro Mags Lost In Space

Produced by Chris Martin Enterprises, this 6-magnet set measures approximately 2 1/4" by 3 1/2". These magnets have rounded corners and were randomly included with the regular packs. The fronts feature color action player photos against a gold foil background with the player's name printed vertically in gold foil along one side. The NBA and team logos are at the bottom

COMPLETE SET (6) 8.00 20.00
LIS1 Anfernee Hardaway 3.00 8.00
LIS2 Antonio McDyess 1.25 3.00
LIS3 Isaiah Rider 2.00 5.00
LIS4 Ed O'Bannon 1.00 2.50
LIS5 Latrell Sprewell 2.00 5.00
LIS6 Robert Pack 1.25 3.00

1995 Pro Mags USA Basketball

Produced by Chris Martin Enterprises, this 10-magnet set features the first ten players chosen for the Dream Team. The magnets measure approximately 2 1/4" by 3 1/2", have rounded corners and were sold in packs of three. The fronts feature a color action player cut-out over a red, white, and blue screened background with the words "USA Basketball". Both the player's name running vertically along the side and a facsimile autograph across the bottom are printed in gold foil. Die cut magnets of each player were also produced, using the same action photos as in the regular magnets. These die cuts are valued at 2X the values listed below.

COMPLETE SET (10) 8.00 20.00
1 Hakeem Olajuwon 1.25 3.00
2 Glenn Robinson .75 2.00
3 Karl Malone 1.25 3.00
4 Shaquille O'Neal 2.50 6.00
5 Reggie Miller 1.25 3.00
6 David Robinson 1.50 4.00
7 John Stockton 1.25 3.00
8 Anfernee Hardaway 1.50 4.00
9 Scottie Pippen 1.50 4.00
10 Grant Hill 1.50 4.00

1997-98 Pro Mags Heroes of the Locker Room

This 20-card set was released by Crown Pro to various stores across the U.S.. These magnets are not numbered and listed below in alphabetical order. Since this was designed to be a 20 card set, obviously this list is incomplete so all additions are appreciated.

COMPLETE SET 15.00 30.00
1 Kobe Bryant 5.00 12.00
2 Tim Duncan 3.00 8.00
3 Grant Hill 1.50 4.00
4 Kevin Garnett 1.50 4.00
5 Karl Malone 1.25 3.00
6 Keith Van Horn 1.50 4.00

1992 Pro Set Club

This nine-card standard-size set illustrates the fundamentals of playing basketball. On the fronts, the color action shots of youngsters illustrate the fundamental aspect of the game featured on the card. A special Pro Set Club logo and a lavender bar cut across the bottom of the picture. Within aqua borders, the horizontal backs have an extended caption as well as a question-and-answer trivia feature. The cards are numbered on the back.

COMPLETE SET (9) 2.00 5.00
COMMON CARD (1-9) .15 .40
9 Basketball 1.00 2.50
Pro Player
(David Robinson)

1991 Pro Set Pro Files

These cards measure the standard size. The fronts have full-bleed color photos, with facsimile autographs inscribed across the bottom of the pictures. Reportedly only 150 of each were produced and approximately 100 of each were handed out as part of a contest on the Pro Files TV show. Each week viewers were invited to send in their names and addresses to a Pro Set post office box. All subjects in the set made appearances on the TV show. The show was hosted by Craig James and Tim Brant and was aired on Saturday nights in Dallas and sponsored by Pro Set. The cards were subtitled "Signature Series". The cards are unnumbered and are listed in alphabetical order by subject in the checklist below. All of the cards were facsimile autographed except for Anne Smith who signed all of her cards personally.

COMPLETE SET (13) 120.00 300.00
3 James Donaldson 4.00 10.00
6 Larry Johnson 8.00 20.00
13 Herb Williams 4.00 10.00

1991-92 Pro Set Prototypes

These standard-size cards were samples produced by Pro Set with the hopes of obtaining an NBA license. The fronts feature full-bleed color action photos, with the player's name and team name printed in two team color-coded bars that overlay the bottom of the picture. These bars intersect a circle displaying the team logo at the lower right corner. The horizontal backs carry biography, statistical (college and pro) information, and career highlights on the left portion, with a blank slot for a player photo on the right portion. The information is "dummy"; for example, Jordan's card back carries some player information on Glen Rice. The words "Prototype For Review Only" are printed on a turquoise triangle at the upper right corner. The cards are numbered "000" on the back and checklisted below in alphabetical order.

1 Tom Chambers 40.00 80.00
2 Patrick Ewing 75.00 200.00
3 Magic Johnson 100.00 250.00
4 Michael Jordan 300.00 600.00
5 Karl Malone 80.00 200.00

1996 Pro Stamps

Produced by Chris Martin Enterprises, this 12-sheet set of stamps features NBA Players against a stamp background. Each sheet contains 12 stamps. The backs of the sheets contain a checklist by team and an offer to "Practice With The Pros". The sheets are numbered in the upper left of the front. The stamps are priced in sheet form. A Pro Stamp Collector Album was also available in special retail boxes. It is priced at the bottom and is not considered part of the set.

COMPLETE SET (12) 15.00 40.00
1 Brooks Thompson 2.00 5.00
Larry Johnson
Robert Pack
Mitch Richmond
Stacey Augmon
Terry Dehere
Charles Barkley
Bryant Reeves
Derek Harper
Corliss Williamson
Rex Walters
Tyrone Hill
2 Horace Grant 1.50 4.00
Derrick McKey
Antonio McDyess
Brian Grant
Mookie Blaylock
Loy Vaught
Gary Payton
Benoit Benjamin
Anthony Mason
Joe Smith
Rick Mahorn
Randolph Childress
3 Ervin Johnson 1.50 4.00
Dale Davis
Reggie Williams
Bobby Hurley
Ken Norman
Clifford Robinson
Detlef Schrempf
Antonio Harvey
Charles Oakley
Latrell Sprewell
Derrick Coleman
Gary Trent
4 Shawn Kemp 1.50 4.00
Rik Smits
Patrick Ewing
Corliss Williamson
Steve Smith
Buck Williams
Sam Perkins
Greg Anthony
John Starks
Rony Seiklay
Grant Long
James Robinson
5 Hakeem Olajuwon 2.50 6.00
Cedric Ceballos
Jason Kidd
Glen Rice
Glenn Robinson
Alvin Robertson
Toni Kukoc
David Robinson
Calbert Cheaney
Grant Hill
Isaiah Rider
Danny Ferry
6 Robert Horry 1.50 4.00
Nick Van Exel
Jamal Mashburn
Sasha Danilovic
Vin Baker
Ed Pinckney
Ron Harper
Will Perdue
Juwan Howard
Joe Dumars
Dino Radja
Sean Rooks
7 Sam Cassell 2.00 5.00
Anthony Peeler
Tony Dumas
Charles Barkley
Khalid Reeves
Damon Stoudamire
Scottie Pippen
Chuck Person
Chris Webber
Lindsey Hunter
Dee Brown
Doug West
8 Kenny Smith 2.00 5.00
Vlade Divac
Roy Tarpley
Anfernee Hardaway
Billy Owens
Tony Massenburg
Dennis Rodman
Sean Elliott
Adam Keefe
Rasheed Wallace
Sherman Douglas
Kevin Garnett
9 Clyde Drexler 2.00 5.00
Kendall Gill
Eddie Jones
Jerry Stackhouse
Kevin Willis
Acie Earl
Wayman Tisdale
Dickey Simpkins
Jeff Hornacek
Gheorghe Muresan
Eric Montross
Christian Laettner
10 Anfernee Hardaway 2.00 5.00
Scott Burrell
Jim Jackson
Sharone Wright
Todd Day
Pooh Richardson
Kevin Johnson
Vinny Del Negro
Felton Spencer
Allan Houston
Eric Williams
Tyrone Hill
11 Brian Shaw 2.00 5.00
Muggsy Bogues
Dikembe Mutombo
Tim Perry
Hakeem Olajuwon
Eric Piatkowski
Michael Finley
Reggie Miller
John Stockton
Terry Mills
Ed O'Bannon
Michael Cage
12 Dennis Scott 2.00 5.00
Alonzo Mourning
Jalen Rose
Walt Williams
Eric Murdock
Lamond Murray
Danny Manning
Mark Jackson
Karl Malone
Tim Hardaway
Kenny Anderson
Chris Mills
NNO Collector's Album 1.25 3.00

1991 Pro Stars Posters

These three posters were folded, cello wrapped, and inserted in Pro Stars cereal boxes. Through an offer on the side panel of the box, the collector could receive another poster by sending in three Pro Stars UPC symbols and 1.00 for postage and handling. In the cello packs, the posters measure approximately 4 1/2" by 4"; they unfold to a narrow poster that measures approximately 4 1/2" by 24". On a background of blue, purple, and bright yellow stars, a cartoon drawing portrays the athlete in an action pose. At the bottom of each poster appears a player profile in English and French. The backsides of all three posters combine to form a composite poster featuring all three players. The posters are unnumbered and listed below alphabetically.

COMPLETE SET (3) 4.00 10.00
2 Michael Jordan 2.00 5.00

1993-94 Quad City Thunder CBA

Released by the Quad City Thunder, this 13-card set features the 1993-94 CBA Champions on a card stock that has blue and red borders.

COMPLETE SET (13) 1.25 3.00
1 Mike Bell .15 .40
2 Gary Collier .15 .40
3 Tate George .20 .50
4 Bill Jones .15 .40
5 Randolph Keys .20 .50
6 Richard Manning .15 .40
7 Kevin Pritchard .20 .50
8 LaBradford Smith .15 .40
9 Maurice Stokes .30 .75
10 Barry Sumpter .15 .40
11 Shon Tarver .15 .40
12 Thunder Coaches .15 .40
13 Team Picture .15 .40

1979-80 Quaker Iron-Ons

This 10-card set was sponsored by the Quaker Company and was offically licensed by the NBA. Each iron-on measures 4 3/8" by 6 1/8". Card fronts contain a head shot of the player with directions for the iron-on. The backs are blank.

COMPLETE SET (9) 125.00 250.00
1 Kareem Abdul-Jabbar 20.00 40.00
2 Rick Barry 10.00 25.00
3 Julius Erving 25.00 50.00
4 George Gervin 15.00 40.00
5 Elvin Hayes 10.00 20.00
6 Maurice Lucas 5.00 12.00
7 Pete Maravich 45.00 90.00
8 David Thompson 10.00 20.00
9 Paul Westphal 6.00 12.00

1987 Quaker Sports Illustrated Mini Posters

These 7" x 11" mini posters were inserted in boxes of Quaker Chewy Granola Bars. The front contains a full-color player action shot, and says "A Sports Illustrated Poster" in the bottom right corner. The back has an offer to send in four UPC seals in exchange for one of 192 2' x 3' posters listed on the back. The player list is made of mostly baseball, basketball and football but includes ten other categories including surfing, U.S. ski team, Golf and racquetball to name a few. A complete checklist of mini posters is still somewhat questionable. This list includes only the basketball posters known to exist. Any further information that expands on this checklist would be appreciated. The posters are unnumbered and listed below in alphabetical order.

COMPLETE SET (7) 60.00 150.00
1 Larry Bird 12.50 30.00
2 Julius Erving 6.00 15.00
3 Magic Johnson 10.00 25.00
4 Michael Jordan 25.00 60.00
5 Hakeem Olajuwon 8.00 20.00
6 Spud Webb 4.00 10.00
7 Dominique Wilkins 5.00 12.00

1954 Quaker Sports Oddities

This 27-card set features strange moments in sports and was issued as an insert inside Quaker Puffed Rice cereal boxes. Fronts of the cards are drawings depicting the person or the event. In a stripe at the top of the card face appear the words "Sports Oddities." Two colorful drawings fill the remaining space: the left half is a portrait, while the right half is action-oriented. A variety of sports are included. The cards measure approximately 2 1/4" by 3 1/2" and have rounded corners. The last line on the back of each card declares, "It's Odd but True." A person could also buy the complete set for fifteen cents and two box tops from Quaker Puffed Wheat or Quaker Rice. If a collector did send in their material to Quaker Oats the set came back in a specially marked box with the cards in cellophane

wrapping. Sets in original wrapping are valued at 1.25x to 1.5X the high column listings in our checklist.
COMPLETE SET (27) 125.00 250.00
5 Harold(Bunny) Levitt 15.00 30.00
12 Dartmouth College BK 7.50 15.00
23 Harlem Globetrotters 20.00 40.00
24 Everett Dean BK 12.50 25.00

1961-64 Rawlings

These photos were released during the 1960's by Rawlings to promote their products. Please note that these photos were done in black and white, and have blank backs.
COMPLETE SET (7) 125.00 250.00
1 Richie Guerin 10.00 25.00
2 Cliff Hagan 17.50 35.00
3 John Havlicek 40.00 70.00
4 Gus Johnson 10.00 25.00
5 Bob Pettit 40.00 70.00
6 Frank Ramsey 10.00 25.00
7 Len Wilkens 25.00 60.00

1995 Real Action Pop-Ups

COMPLETE SET (7) 2.50 6.00
4 Pooh Richardson .40 1.00

1992-93 Reebok Shawn Kemp

Sponsored by Reebok and Olympic Sports, this 7-card set spotlights Shawn Kemp. The first three cards of the set were distributed individually at shoe stores in the Seattle area. The last four cards were available only on a perforated strip; after separation, the cards measure the standard size. The first three cards are much more difficult to obtain than the four-card strip. The fronts feature color action player photos framed by green borders. The player's name is printed vertically in yellow block lettering in the left border. In green and blue print on white, the backs present biography, statistics and sponsor logos. The cards are numbered "X of 7."
COMPLETE SET (7) 15.00 30.00
COMMON CARD (1-3) 3.00 8.00
COMMON CARD (4-7) 1.25 3.00

1998 Reebok Rebecca Lobo Postcard

This postcard features WNBA superstar Rebecca Lobo. The card was distributed by "Go Card" to participating Tower Records stores. The photo is of Rebecca Lobo holding up a Reebok shoe.
1 Rebecca Lobo 1.25 3.00

2005-06 Reflections

Released in late October, this 150-card set features veterans on cards 1-100 and rookies sequentially numbered to 1499 on cards 101-150. All cards are printed on holofoil board and players are set against a background that showcases the featured player's team name. Reflections was packaged in 12-pack boxes where packs contained four cards and carried a suggested retail price of $9.99.
COMP.SET w/o RC's (100) 20.00 50.00
RC PRINT RUN 1499 SER.#'d SETS
UNPRICED BLACK PRINT RUN ONE SET
UNPRICED GOLD PRINT RUN 5 SETS
1 Al Harrington .50 1.25
2 Josh Smith .50 1.25
3 Josh Childress .50 1.25
4 Joe Johnson .50 1.25
5 Paul Pierce .60 1.50
6 Antoine Walker .50 1.25
7 Gary Payton .60 1.50
8 Al Jefferson .50 1.25
9 Emeka Okafor .50 1.25
10 Primoz Brezec .40 1.00
11 Gerald Wallace .50 1.25
12 Michael Jordan 5.00 12.00
13 Ben Gordon .50 1.25
14 Luol Deng .50 1.25
15 Kirk Hinrich .50 1.25
16 LeBron James 2.50 6.00
17 Dajuan Wagner .40 1.00
18 Drew Gooden .50 1.25
19 Larry Hughes .50 1.25
20 Dirk Nowitzki 1.00 2.50
21 Jason Terry .50 1.25
22 Michael Finley .60 1.50
23 Jerry Stackhouse .50 1.25
24 Andre Miller .50 1.25
25 Carmelo Anthony 1.25 3.00
26 Kenyon Martin .50 1.25
27 Earl Boykins .40 1.00
28 Rasheed Wallace .60 1.50
29 Ben Wallace .50 1.25
30 Richard Hamilton .50 1.25
31 Chauncey Billups .60 1.50
32 Baron Davis .50 1.25
33 Derek Fisher .50 1.25
34 Jason Richardson .60 1.50
35 Tracy McGrady .75 2.00
36 Yao Ming .75 2.00
37 Juwan Howard .50 1.25
38 Jermaine O'Neal .50 1.25
39 Ron Artest .60 1.50
40 Jamaal Tinsley .40 1.00
41 Corey Maggette .50 1.25
42 Elton Brand .60 1.50
43 Shaun Livingston .40 1.00
44 Kobe Bryant 2.50 6.00
45 Brian Cook .40 1.00
46 Lamar Odom .50 1.25
47 Mike Miller .50 1.25
48 Pau Gasol .60 1.50
49 Shane Battier .50 1.25
50 Shaquille O'Neal 1.25 3.00
51 Dwyane Wade 1.00 2.50
52 Udonis Haslem .40 1.00
53 Joe Smith .50 1.25
54 Michael Redd .50 1.25
55 Desmond Mason .40 1.00
56 Kevin Garnett 1.00 2.50
57 Wally Szczerbiak .50 1.25
58 Sam Cassell .50 1.25
59 Vince Carter 1.00 2.50
60 Jason Kidd 1.00 2.50
61 Richard Jefferson .50 1.25
62 Jamaal Magloire .40 1.00
63 J.R. Smith .50 1.25
64 Bostjan Nachbar .40 1.00
65 Allan Houston .50 1.25
66 Stephon Marbury .50 1.25
67 Jamal Crawford .60 1.50
68 Dwight Howard .50 1.25
69 Grant Hill .75 2.00
70 Jameer Nelson .40 1.00
71 Steve Francis .50 1.25
72 Allen Iverson 1.00 2.50
73 Andre Iguodala .50 1.25
74 Chris Webber .60 1.50
75 Samuel Dalembert .40 1.00
76 Amare Stoudemire .50 1.25
77 Steve Nash .75 2.00
78 Quentin Richardson .50 1.25
79 Shawn Marion .50 1.25
80 Damon Stoudamire .50 1.25
81 Zach Randolph .50 1.25
82 Sebastian Telfair .50 1.25
83 Peja Stojakovic .60 1.50
84 Mike Bibby .60 1.50
85 Cuttino Mobley .40 1.00
86 Manu Ginobili .60 1.50
87 Tim Duncan 1.00 2.50
88 Tony Parker .60 1.50
89 Ray Allen .60 1.50
90 Rashard Lewis .60 1.50
91 Luke Ridnour .50 1.25
92 Ronald Murray .40 1.00
93 Chris Bosh .60 1.50
94 Morris Peterson .40 1.00
95 Rafael Araujo .40 1.00
96 Andrei Kirilenko .50 1.25
97 Raul Lopez .40 1.00
98 Carlos Boozer .50 1.25
99 Antawn Jamison .50 1.25
100 Gilbert Arenas .50 1.25
101 Travis Diener RC 1.00 2.50
102 Julius Hodge RC 1.00 2.50
103 David Lee RC 1.50 4.00
104 Sarunas Jasikevicius RC 1.50 4.00
105 Jason Maxiell RC 1.25 3.00
106 Luther Head RC 1.25 3.00
107 Amir Johnson RC 1.50 4.00
108 Linas Kleiza RC 1.00 2.50
109 Uros Slokar RC 1.50 4.00
110 Andray Blatche RC 1.50 4.00
111 Sean May RC 1.00 2.50
112 Alex Acker RC 1.00 2.50
113 Nate Robinson RC 1.50 4.00
114 Brandon Bass RC 1.25 3.00
115 Ike Diogu RC 1.00 2.50
116 Daniel Ewing RC 1.25 3.00
117 Salim Stoudamire RC 1.25 3.00
118 Dijon Thompson RC 1.00 2.50
119 Danny Granger RC 2.00 5.00
120 Chris Taft RC 1.25 3.00
121 Louis Williams RC 1.50 4.00
122 Channing Frye RC 1.50 4.00
123 Francisco Garcia RC 1.25 3.00
124 Ryan Gomes RC 1.25 3.00
125 Von Wafer RC 1.00 2.50
126 Jarrett Jack RC 1.50 4.00
127 Lawrence Roberts RC 1.00 2.50
128 Ricky Sanchez RC 1.50 4.00
129 C.J. Miles RC 1.50 4.00
130 Ersan Ilyasova RC 1.50 4.00
131 Robert Whaley RC 1.00 2.50
132 Monta Ellis RC 2.00 5.00
133 Bracey Wright RC 1.00 2.50
134 Johan Petro RC 1.00 2.50
135 Will Bynum RC 1.25 3.00
136 Andrew Bynum RC 1.25 3.00
137 Martynas Andriuskevicius RC 1.00 2.50
138 Charlie Villanueva RC 1.50 4.00
139 Antoine Wright RC 1.25 3.00
140 Joey Graham RC 1.25 3.00
141 Wayne Simien RC 1.00 2.50
142 Hakim Warrick RC 1.25 3.00
143 Gerald Green RC 1.50 4.00
144 Marvin Williams RC 1.50 4.00
145 Deron Williams RC 2.00 5.00
146 Rashad McCants RC 1.25 3.00
147 Martell Webster RC 1.25 3.00
148 Raymond Felton RC 1.50 4.00
149 Chris Paul RC 6.00 15.00
150 Andrew Bogut RC 2.00 5.00

2005-06 Reflections Blue

*BLUE VETS: 2X TO 5X BASE HI
*BLUE RCs: 1.5X TO 4X BASE HI
PRINT RUN 50 SER.#'d SETS
RC PLAYERS HAVE AUTOGRAPHS
NOT ALL RCs WERE PRODUCED
12 Michael Jordan 300.00 600.00
149 Chris Paul AU 40.00 100.00

2005-06 Reflections Green

*GREEN VETS: 3X TO 8X BASE HI
*GREEN RCs: 1.25X TO 3X BASE HI
PRINT RUN 25 SER.#'d SETS
RC PLAYERS HAVE PATCH SWATCH
NOT ALL RCs WERE PRODUCED
12 Michael Jordan 400.00 800.00

2005-06 Reflections Purple

*PURPLE VETS: .6X TO 1.5X BASE HI
1-100 PURPLE STATED ODDS 1:3
*PURPLE RCs: .6X TO 1.5X BASE HI
PURPLE RC PRINT RUN 250 SER.#'d SETS
12 Michael Jordan 20.00 50.00

2005-06 Reflections Red

*RED VETS: 1X TO 2.5X BASE HI
PRINT RUN 100 SER.#'d SETS
RC PLAYERS HAVE JSY SWATCH
NOT ALL RC's WERE PRODUCED
12 Michael Jordan 100.00 250.00
44 Kobe Bryant 10.00 25.00

2005-06 Reflections Compare and Contrast Autographs

Randomly seeded in packs, this 40-card set is horizontally designed and showcases two players and their autographs, one on the front and one on the back. Each card is sequentially numbered to 30 copies.
PRINT RUN 30 SER.#'d SETS
AB Andriuskevicius/Bogut 20.00 50.00
AK A.Miller/K.Hinrich 12.00 30.00
AT T.Ariza/D.Thompson 12.50 30.00
BH C.Billups/R.Hamilton 25.00 50.00
BT A.Bogut/C.Taft 20.00 50.00
CO J.Childress/L.Odom 12.50 30.00
DF B.Davis/D.Fisher 12.50 30.00
EF D.Ewing/R.Felton 12.50 30.00
FL C.Frye/D.Lee 12.50 30.00
FP R.Felton/C.Paul 40.00 100.00
GG D.Granger/J.Graham 20.00 40.00
GS B.Gordon/J.R.Smith 25.00 50.00
GW G.Green/M.Webster 12.50 30.00
IC I.Diogu/C.Frye 25.00 60.00
IJ A.Iguodala/R.Jefferson 25.00 50.00
JA A.Jamison/G.Arenas 12.50 30.00
JJ R.Jefferson/A.Jamison 12.50 30.00
JM L.James/T.McGrady 150.00 300.00
LJ M.Jordan/L.James 600.00 1000.00
LT S.Livingston/S.Telfair 12.50 30.00
MF R.McCants/R.Felton 30.00 60.00
MH Y.Ming/D.Howard 30.00 60.00
MK S.Marbury/J.Kidd 20.00 50.00
MM B.Miller/J.Magloire 12.50 30.00
NB S.Nash/M.Bibby 50.00 100.00
NT J.Nelson/S.Telfair 12.50 30.00
PW C.Paul/D.Williams 100.00 200.00
RC M.Redd/J.Crawford 12.50 30.00
SF S.Stoudamire/C.Frye 25.00 60.00
SS D.Stoudamire/S.Stoud 12.50 30.00
VW C.Villanueva/H.Warrick 30.00 60.00
WH D.Williams/L.Head 75.00 150.00
WM Mv.Williams/S.May 20.00 40.00
WV Mv.Williams/C.Villanueva 30.00 60.00
WW A.Wright/M.Webster 12.50 30.00

2005-06 Reflections Compare and Contrast Jerseys

Randomly seeded in packs, this 40-card set is a horizontally designed and places a player and a jersey swatch on each side of the card and is serially numbered to 100 copies.
PRINT RUN 100 SER.#'d SETS
AJ A.Houston/J.Crawford 4.00 10.00
AL R.Allen/R.Lewis 5.00 12.00
AR S.Abdur-Rahim/Z.Randolph 4.00 10.00
BC C.Butler/B.Cook 4.00 10.00
BJ K.Bryant/M.Jordan 40.00 80.00
BM C.Bosh/D.Marshall 4.00 10.00
BN E.Boykins/Nene 4.00 10.00
BT A.Bogut/C.Taft 5.00 12.00
BW P.Brezec/G.Wallace 4.00 10.00
FM R.Felton/R.McCants 8.00 20.00
FR D.Fisher/J.Richardson 4.00 10.00
GP M.Ginobili/T.Parker 10.00 25.00
GS F.Garcia/S.Stoudamire 4.00 10.00
GW G.Green/M.Webster 4.00 10.00
HC A.Harrington/J.Childress 4.00 10.00
HT D.Harris/S.Telfair 4.00 10.00
JJ M.Jordan/L.James 40.00 80.00
LB R.Lopez/C.Boozer 4.00 10.00
MC B.Miller/E.Curry 4.00 10.00
MR D.Miles/Z.Randolph 4.00 10.00
MS M.Miller/S.Swift 4.00 10.00
OA J.O'Neal/R.Artest 4.00 10.00
OH S.O'Neal/U.Haslem 10.00 25.00
PF C.Paul/R.Felton 12.50 30.00
PR M.Peterson/J.Rose 4.00 10.00
RA J.Rose/R.Araujo 4.00 10.00
SC W.Szczerbiak/S.Cassell 4.00 10.00
SF S.Stoudamire/C.Frye 4.00 10.00
SH J.Stackhouse/D.Harris 4.00 10.00
SK Joe Smith/T.Kukoc 5.00 12.00
SM W.Simien/S.May 4.00 10.00
TJ J.Tinsley/S.Jackson 4.00 10.00
WG D.Williams/F.Garcia 6.00 15.00
WI D.Wagner/Z.Ilgauskas 4.00 10.00
WK C.Webber/K.Korver 8.00 20.00
WM Mv.Williams/S.May 4.00 10.00
WV H.Warrick/C.Villanueva 4.00 10.00
WW Mv.Williams/H.Warrick 4.00 10.00

2005-06 Reflections Compare and Contrast Quad Jerseys

Randomly seeded in packs and limited to 10 serially numbered copies, this 28-card set places two players and their jerseys on each side of the card.
PRINT RUN 50 SER.#'d SETS
UNPRICED AUTO PRINT RUN 10 SETS
ADHC Arenas/Dixon/Houstn/Crwfrd 8.00 20.00
ALRM Allen/Lewis/Redd/Mason 8.00 20.00
BBPW Kobe/Butler/Payton/Walker 15.00 40.00
BMIG Brand/Magg/Ilgaus/Gooden 6.00 15.00
BNLB Boykins/Nene/Lopez/Boozer 6.00 15.00
FHMH Francis/Hill/Marb/Hou 8.00 20.00
FSFH Fizer/JoSmith/Francis/Hill 12.50 30.00
GPBH Manu/Parker/Billups/Rip 12.50 30.00
GSWH Garnett/Szcz/Sheed/Rip 12.50 30.00
HCVA Hinrich/Curry/Vexel/A-Rahim 6.00 15.00
HCWJ Hrngtn/Chldrss/Walker/BigAl 6.00 15.00
JASF SJcksn/Artest/Stack/Finley 6.00 15.00
JGKJ LeBron/Gooden/Kidd/R-Jeff 15.00 40.00
JJBA MJ/LeBron/Kobe/Melo 100.00 200.00
JMSM JoJhnsn/Marion/Bassy/Miles 6.00 15.00
KDPA Korver/Dalmb/MPete/Araujo 8.00 20.00
LBBC Lvngstn/Brand/Butler/Cook 6.00 15.00
MFMW May/Felton/McCants/Williams 10.00 25.00
MJMM Marion/Jhnsn/Miller/Cuttino 8.00 20.00
MNBW K-Mart/Nene/Brezec/G.Wallace 6.00 15.00
PFHW Pietrus/Fish/Ju.Howard/Wesley 8.00 20.00
RPWC J-Rich/Mo-Pete/Webb/Crwfrd 12.00 30.00
TFMM Jet/Finley/A.Miller/K-Mart 10.00 25.00

2005-06 Reflections Compare and Contrast Octa Jerseys

Limited to 25 serially numbered copy per, this eleven-card set places eight players along with their jerseys, four per side, on each card.
PRINT RUN 25 SER.#'d SETS
UNPRICED AUTO PRINT RUN ONE SET
2 AI/AJ/DS/BU/DH/SL/JN/DW 15.00 40.00
3 DH/BG/LD/JS/AB/MW/CP/DW 20.00 50.00
4 KB/LO/CB/VD/MB/PS/BM/CM 60.00 120.00
5 LJ/DG/ZI/DW/KH/LD/TC/EC 60.00 120.00
6 TD/TP/MG/BU/DN/MF/JT/JS 15.00 40.00
7 RA/RL/LR/RM/AM/KM/N/EB 25.00 60.00
9 GA/JH/AJ/JD/JO/RA/JT/SJ 10.00 25.00
10 PP/AW/GP/AJ/SD/AI/KK/CW 15.00 40.00
11 CB/JR/RA/DM/MR/DM/TK/MF 25.00 60.00
12 TM/YM/DW/JH/PG/SB/SS/MM 40.00 80.00

2005-06 Reflections Fabrics

Inserted in packs at the rate of one in six, this 42-card set is horizontally designed with a player photo on the left and a square swatch of jersey on the right.
STATED ODDS 1:6
*FABRIC BLUE/50: .6X TO 1.5X BASE HI
*FABRIC GREEN/25: .75X TO 2X BASE HI
*FABRIC RED/100: .5X TO 1.25X BASE HI
UNPRICED AUTO PRINT RUN ONE SET
UNPRICED GOLD PRINT RUN 5 SETS
AH Al Harrington 2.00 5.00
AJ Antawn Jamison 2.00 5.00
AK Andrei Kirilenko 2.00 5.00
AM Andre Miller 2.00 5.00
AR Carlos Arroyo 1.50 4.00
AS Amare Stoudemire 2.00 5.00
BD Baron Davis 2.00 5.00
BG Ben Gordon 2.00 5.00
BW Ben Wallace 2.00 5.00
CA Carmelo Anthony 5.00 12.00
CB Chauncey Billups SP 2.50 6.00
CM Corey Maggette 2.00 5.00
DH Dwight Howard 2.00 5.00
DM Desmond Mason SP 2.00 5.00
DN Dirk Nowitzki 4.00 10.00
GA Gilbert Arenas 2.00 5.00
GP Gary Payton 2.50 6.00
JC Jamal Crawford 2.50 6.00
JK Jason Kidd 4.00 10.00
JN Jameer Nelson SP 1.50 4.00
JR J.R. Smith 2.00 5.00
JS Josh Smith 2.00 5.00
KB Kobe Bryant 8.00 20.00
KG Kevin Garnett 4.00 10.00
KK Kyle Korver 2.00 5.00
LD Luol Deng 2.00 5.00
LJ LeBron James 15.00 40.00
LO Lamar Odom 2.00 5.00
MB Mike Bibby 2.50 6.00
MJ Michael Jordan SP 40.00 100.00
MR Michael Redd SP 2.00 5.00
PG Pau Gasol 2.50 6.00
PP Paul Pierce 2.50 6.00
PS Peja Stojakovic 2.50 6.00
RJ Richard Jefferson 2.00 5.00
SB Shane Battier 2.00 5.00
SM Stephon Marbury 2.00 5.00
SN Steve Nash 3.00 8.00
SO Shaquille O'Neal 5.00 12.00
TD Tim Duncan 4.00 10.00
TM Tracy McGrady 3.00 8.00
YM Yao Ming 3.00 8.00

2005-06 Reflections Fabrics Dual Swatch

Inserted in packs, this 42-card set parallels the design of the Fabrics set with two swatches of memorabilia and sequential numbering to 50.
*DUAL SWATCH: .6X TO 1.5X BASE FAB HI
PRINT RUN 50 SER.#'d SETS
*BLUE: .75X TO 2X BASE FAB HI
BLUE PRINT RUN 25 SER.#'d SETS
UNPRICED AUTO PRINT RUN ONE SET
UNPRICED GOLD PRINT RUN 5 SETS
UNPRICED GREEN PRINT RUN 10 SETS

2005-06 Reflections Fabrics Triple Swatch

*TRIPLE SWATCH: 1.25X TO 3X BASE FAB HI
PRINT RUN 25 SER.#'d SETS
*BLUE: 1.5X TO 4X BASE FAB HI
BLUE PRINT RUN 20 SER.#'d SETS
UNPRICED AUTO PRINT RUN ONE SET
UNPRICED GOLD PRINT RUN 5 SETS
UNPRICED GREEN PRINT RUN 10 SETS

2005-06 Reflections Signatures

Inserted in packs at the rate of one in 34, this 71-card set features a player photo along the top, a centered autograph sticker and on some cards, sequential numbering to 35. See checklist for details.
STATED ODDS 1:34
SP's/PRINT RUNS LISTED IN CHECKLIST
UNPRICED BLACK PRINT RUN ONE SET
UNPRICED GOLD PRINT RUN 5 SETS
AA Alex Acker 2.00 5.00
AH Al Harrington 3.00 8.00
AI Andre Iguodala/35 10.00 25.00
AJ Antawn Jamison SP 4.00 10.00
AM Andre Miller SP 4.00 10.00
AN Martynas Andriuskevicius 2.00 5.00
AR Carlos Arroyo 8.00 20.00
BG Ben Gordon/35 8.00 20.00
BU Beno Udrih 3.00 8.00
BW Ben Wallace/35 10.00 25.00
CA Carmelo Anthony/35 15.00 40.00
CD Chris Duhon 3.00 8.00
CK Chris Kaman SP 3.00 8.00
CM Corey Maggette SP 3.00 8.00
CW Chris Wilcox SP 3.00 8.00
DA David Harrison 3.00 8.00
DF Derek Fisher 4.00 10.00
DH Dwight Howard/35 15.00 40.00
DM Desmond Mason 3.00 8.00
DS Damon Stoudamire SP 4.00 10.00
DW Dorell Wright 3.00 8.00
FG Francisco Garcia 2.50 6.00
GP Gary Payton/35 10.00 25.00
GR Danny Granger 4.00 10.00
HW Hakim Warrick 2.50 6.00
JA Jalen Rose 4.00 10.00
JG Joey Graham 2.50 6.00
JH Josh Howard SP 3.00 8.00
JJ Jarrett Jack 3.00 8.00
JK Jason Kidd/35 12.50 30.00
JM Jamaal Magloire 3.00 8.00
JN Jameer Nelson SP 3.00 8.00
JO Amir Johnson 3.00 8.00
JP Johan Petro 2.00 5.00
JS Jerry Stackhouse SP 6.00 15.00
JU Julius Hodge 2.00 5.00
JV Jackson Vroman 3.00 8.00
KA Kareem Rush 3.00 8.00
KH Kirk Hinrich/35 10.00 25.00
KM Kevin Martin 3.00 8.00
LH Luther Head 2.50 6.00
LJ LeBron James/35 100.00 250.00
LK Linas Kleiza 2.00 5.00
LU Luke Jackson 3.00 8.00
MD Marquis Daniels SP 3.00 8.00
MJ Michael Jordan/35 800.00 1200.00
MP Morris Peterson 3.00 8.00
MW Maurice Williams 3.00 8.00
NR Nate Robinson SP 8.00 20.00
PA Pavel Podkolzin 3.00 8.00
PB Primoz Brezec 3.00 8.00
PP Paul Pierce/35 10.00 25.00
PS Pape Sow 3.00 8.00
RA Rafael Araujo 3.00 8.00
RM Ronald Murray 3.00 8.00
SB Shane Battier 3.00 8.00
SM Stephon Marbury/35 10.00 25.00
SN Steve Nash/35 25.00 60.00
SS Salim Stoudamire 2.50 6.00
SV Sasha Vujacic 3.00 8.00
TA Tony Allen 3.00 8.00
TK Toni Kukoc 3.00 8.00
TM Tracy McGrady/35 15.00 40.00
TR Trevor Ariza 3.00 8.00
UH Udonis Haslem 4.00 10.00
VK Viktor Khryapa 3.00 8.00
WS Wayne Simien SP 2.00 5.00
YM Yao Ming/35 25.00 60.00

2005-06 Reflections Signatures Blue

Inserted in packs, this 95-card set parallels the Signatures set on blue foil and is enhanced with sequential numbering to either 50 or 15. See checklist for details.
*BLUE: .6X TO 1.5X BASE HI
PRINT RUN 15 TO 50 SER.#'d SETS
SP/15 NOT PRICED DUE TO SCARCITY
AB Andrew Bogut/50 20.00 50.00
BY Andrew Bynum/50 25.00 60.00
CF Channing Frye/50 10.00 25.00
CP Chris Paul/50 20.00 50.00
CV Charlie Villanueva/50 8.00 20.00
GA Gilbert Arenas/50 8.00 20.00
GG Gerald Green/50 8.00 20.00
JC Josh Childress/50 5.00 12.00
JR J.R. Smith/50 6.00 15.00
JW Jason Williams/50 20.00 50.00
LO Lamar Odom/50 8.00 20.00
MA Marvin Williams/50 8.00 20.00
MB Mike Bibby/50 6.00 15.00
MC Rashad McCants/50 4.00 10.00
PG Pau Gasol/50 10.00 25.00
QR Quentin Richardson/50 5.00 12.00
RF Raymond Felton/50 12.00 30.00
RH Richard Hamilton/50 10.00 25.00
RJ Richard Jefferson/50 5.00 12.00
SL Shaun Livingston/50 5.00 12.00
WE Martell Webster/50 5.00 12.00
WI Deron Williams/50 25.00 60.00

2005-06 Reflections Signatures Green

Inserted in packs, this 95-card set parallels the Signatures set on green foil and is enhanced with sequential numbering to either 25 or 10. See checklist for details.
*GREEN: .75X TO 2X BASE HI
PRINT RUN 10 TO 25 SER.#'d SETS
SP/10 NOT PRICED DUE TO SCARCITY
AB Andrew Bogut/25 25.00 60.00
BY Andrew Bynum/25 30.00 80.00
CF Channing Frye/25 12.50 30.00
CP Chris Paul/25 50.00 120.00
CV Charlie Villanueva/25 10.00 25.00
GA Gilbert Arenas/25 10.00 25.00
GG Gerald Green/25 10.00 25.00
JC Josh Childress/25 6.00 15.00
JR J.R. Smith/25 8.00 20.00
JW Jason Williams/25 40.00 100.00
LO Lamar Odom/25 10.00 25.00
MA Marvin Williams/25 10.00 25.00
MB Mike Bibby/25 8.00 20.00
MC Rashad McCants/25 5.00 12.00
PG Pau Gasol/25 12.50 30.00
QR Quentin Richardson/25 6.00 15.00
RF Raymond Felton/25 15.00 40.00
RH Richard Hamilton/25 12.50 30.00
RJ Richard Jefferson/25 6.00 15.00
SE Sean May/25 6.00 15.00
SL Shaun Livingston/25 6.00 15.00
WE Martell Webster/25 6.00 15.00
WI Deron Williams/25 30.00 80.00

2005-06 Reflections Signatures Red

Inserted in packs, this 95-card set parallels the Signatures set on red foil and is enhanced with sequential numbering to either 100 or 25. See checklist for details.
*RED: .5X TO 1.25X BASE HI
PRINT RUN 25 TO 100 SER.#'d SETS
BY Andrew Bynum/100 15.00 40.00
CV Charlie Villanueva/100 6.00 15.00
GG Gerald Green/100 6.00 15.00
JC Josh Childress/100 4.00 10.00
JR J.R. Smith/100 5.00 12.00
JW Jason Williams/100 25.00 60.00
MB Mike Bibby/100 5.00 12.00
MC Rashad McCants/100 3.00 8.00
QR Quentin Richardson/100 4.00 10.00
RH Richard Hamilton/100 8.00 20.00
RJ Richard Jefferson/100 4.00 10.00
SE Sean May/100 4.00 10.00

2006-07 Reflections

Released in early September 2006, Reflections features a 149-card base set where cards 1-100 picture NBA veterans and cards 101-149 picture NBA rookies where cards 101-110 are serially numbered to 150 and cards 111-125 are serially numbered to 799 and cards 126-149 are serially numbered to 399. All cards are printed on a thick foil-board card stock.
COMP.SET w/o SP's 25.00 60.00
111-125 RC PRINT RUN 799 SER.#'d SETS
126-149 RC PRINT RUN 399 SER.#'d SETS
UNPRICED BLACK PRINT RUN ONE SET
1 Josh Childress .50 1.25
2 Joe Johnson .50 1.25
3 Marvin Williams .50 1.25
4 Dan Dickau .40 1.00
5 Paul Pierce .60 1.50
6 Wally Szczerbiak .50 1.25
7 Raymond Felton .50 1.25
8 Emeka Okafor .50 1.25
9 Kareem Rush .40 1.00
10 Gerald Wallace .50 1.25
11 Tyson Chandler .50 1.25
12 Luol Deng .50 1.25
13 Ben Gordon .50 1.25
14 Michael Jordan 5.00 12.00
15 Larry Hughes .50 1.25
16 Zydrunas Ilgauskas .50 1.25
17 LeBron James 2.50 6.00
18 Donyell Marshall .40 1.00
19 Marquis Daniels .40 1.00
20 Josh Howard .50 1.25
21 Dirk Nowitzki 1.00 2.50
22 Jason Terry .50 1.25
23 Carmelo Anthony .75 2.00
24 Earl Boykins .40 1.00
25 Marcus Camby .50 1.25
26 Kenyon Martin .50 1.25
27 Chauncey Billups .60 1.50
28 Richard Hamilton .50 1.25
29 Rasheed Wallace .60 1.50
30 Baron Davis .50 1.25
31 Ike Diogu .40 1.00
32 Mike Dunleavy .50 1.25
33 Troy Murphy .40 1.00
34 Luther Head .50 1.25
35 Tracy McGrady .75 2.00
36 Yao Ming .75 2.00
37 Jermaine O'Neal .50 1.25
38 Peja Stojakovic .60 1.50
39 Jamaal Tinsley .40 1.00
40 Chris Kaman .50 1.25
41 Sam Cassell .50 1.25
42 Shaun Livingston .40 1.00
43 Cuttino Mobley .40 1.00
44 Kobe Bryant 2.50 6.00
45 Devean George .40 1.00
46 Lamar Odom .50 1.25
47 Pau Gasol .60 1.50
48 Bobby Jackson .40 1.00
49 Mike Miller .50 1.25
50 Shaquille O'Neal 1.25 3.00
51 Dwyane Wade 1.00 2.50
52 Jason Williams .50 1.25
53 Andrew Bogut .50 1.25
54 T.J. Ford .40 1.00
55 Michael Redd .50 1.25
56 Ricky Davis .50 1.25
57 Kevin Garnett 1.00 2.50
58 Troy Hudson .40 1.00
59 Vince Carter .75 2.00
60 Jason Collins .40 1.00
61 Richard Jefferson .50 1.25
62 Jason Kidd 1.00 2.50
63 Desmond Mason .40 1.00
64 Chris Paul .75 2.00
65 J.R. Smith .50 1.25
66 Steve Francis .50 1.25
67 Channing Frye .50 1.25
68 Stephon Marbury .50 1.25
69 Dwight Howard .50 1.25
70 Darko Milicic .40 1.00
71 Jameer Nelson .40 1.00
72 Andre Iguodala .50 1.25
73 Allen Iverson .75 2.00
74 Chris Webber .60 1.50
75 Boris Diaw .50 1.25
76 Shawn Marion .50 1.25
77 Steve Nash .75 2.00
78 Amare Stoudemire .50 1.25
79 Juan Dixon .40 1.00
80 Darius Miles .40 1.00
81 Sebastian Telfair .40 1.00
82 Ron Artest .60 1.50
83 Mike Bibby .60 1.50
84 Brad Miller .50 1.25
85 Tim Duncan 1.00 2.50
86 Manu Ginobili .60 1.50
87 Robert Horry .50 1.25
88 Tony Parker .60 1.50
89 Ray Allen .60 1.50
90 Rashard Lewis .60 1.50
91 Luke Ridnour .50 1.25
92 Chris Bosh .60 1.50
93 Joey Graham .40 1.00
94 Charlie Villanueva .40 1.00
95 Carlos Boozer .50 1.25
96 Andrei Kirilenko .50 1.25
97 Deron Williams .50 1.25
98 Gilbert Arenas .50 1.25
99 Caron Butler .50 1.25
100 Antawn Jamison .50 1.25
101 Adam Morrison RC 2.50 6.00
102 Tyrus Thomas RC 2.00 5.00
103 Rudy Gay RC 3.00 8.00
104 Andrea Bargnani RC 2.50 6.00
105 LaMarcus Aldridge RC 6.00 15.00
106 Brandon Roy RC 2.50 6.00
107 Randy Foye RC 2.50 6.00
108 Marcus Williams RC 1.50 4.00
109 Rodney Carney RC 1.50 4.00
110 Shelden Williams RC 2.00 5.00
111 Patrick O'Bryant RC 1.00 2.50
112 Cedric Simmons RC 1.00 2.50
113 Jordan Farmar RC 1.50 4.00
114 J.J. Redick RC 2.00 5.00
115 Tarence Kinsey RC 1.00 2.50
116 Kevin Pittsnogle RC 1.25 3.00
117 Ronnie Brewer RC 1.50 4.00
118 Shawne Williams RC 1.00 2.50
119 Allan Ray RC 1.00 2.50
120 Shannon Brown RC 1.00 2.50
121 Kyle Lowry RC 2.00 5.00
122 Mardy Collins RC 1.00 2.50
123 Hilton Armstrong RC 1.00 2.50
124 Maurice Ager RC 1.00 2.50
125 Quincy Douby RC 1.00 2.50
126 Rajon Rondo RC 3.00 8.00
127 Mike Gansey RC 1.25 3.00
128 Joel Freeland RC 1.25 3.00
129 Josh Boone RC 1.25 3.00
130 Saer Sene RC 1.25 3.00
131 Denham Brown RC 1.25 3.00
132 Renaldo Balkman RC 1.50 4.00
133 Will Blalock RC 1.25 3.00
134 David Noel RC 1.25 3.00
135 Steve Novak RC 1.50 4.00
136 Solomon Jones RC 1.25 3.00
137 Dee Brown RC 1.25 3.00
138 Hassan Adams RC 1.25 3.00
139 Bobby Jones RC 1.25 3.00
140 Thabo Sefolosha RC 2.00 5.00
141 James White RC 1.25 3.00
142 Paul Davis RC 1.25 3.00
143 P.J. Tucker RC 1.50 4.00
144 Ryan Hollins RC 1.50 4.00
145 Damir Markota RC 1.25 3.00
146 Leon Powe RC 1.50 4.00
147 James Augustine RC 1.25 3.00
148 Alexander Johnson RC 1.25 3.00
149 Daniel Gibson RC 1.50 4.00

2006-07 Reflections Blue

*1-100 BLUE: 2X TO 5X BASE HI
*101-110 BLUE RC: .75X TO 2X BASE HI
*111-125 BLUE RC: 1.25X TO 3X BASE HI
*126-149 BLUE RC: 1X TO 2.5X BASE HI
BLUE PRINT RUN 49 SER.#'d SETS

2006-07 Reflections Copper

*1-100 COPPER: 1.5X TO 4X BASE HI
*101-110 COPPER RC: .5X TO 1.25X BASE HI
*111-125 COPPER RC: .75X TO 2X BASE HI
*126-149 COPPER RC: .6X TO 1.5X BASE HI
COPPER PRINT RUN 99 SER.#'d SETS

2006-07 Reflections Dual Fabric

APPROXIMATE ODDS 1:12
*GOLD FABRIC: .4X TO 1X BASE HI
GOLD PRINT RUN 100 SER.#'d SETS
*COPPER FABRIC: .5X TO 1.25X BASE HI
COPPER PRINT RUN 50 SER.#'d SETS
*PATCH BLUE: 1.25X TO 3X BASE HI
PAT.BLUE PRINT RUN 15 SER.#'d SETS
UNPRICED AUTO PATCH PRINT RUN ONE SET
AH R.Allen/R.Hamilton 4.00 10.00
AI G.Arenas/A.Iguodala 4.00 10.00
AN R.Araujo/N.Hilario 4.00 10.00
AW C.Anthony/H.Warrick 5.00 12.00
BC C.Butler/B.Gordon 4.00 10.00
BD C.Boozer/L.Deng 4.00 10.00
BG B.Bowen/M.Ginobili 4.00 10.00
BH E.Brand/D.Howard 5.00 12.00
BM K.Bryant/T.McGrady 10.00 25.00
CB T.Chandler/K.Brown 4.00 10.00
CR E.Curry/Z.Randolph 4.00 10.00
DM R.Davis/R.McCants 4.00 10.00
DP T.Duncan/T.Parker 6.00 15.00
DR B.Davis/J.Richardson 4.00 10.00
DS M.Dunleavy/P.Stojakovic 4.00 10.00
FR S.Francis/N.Robinson 4.00 10.00
FV C.Frye/C.Villanueva 4.00 10.00
FW R.Felton/D.Williams 5.00 12.00
GC D.George/B.Cook 4.00 10.00
GJ K.Garnett/R.Jefferson 5.00 12.00
HB M.Bibby/K.Hinrich 4.00 10.00
HH J.Howard/D.Harris 4.00 10.00
HR J.Howard/J.Rose 4.00 10.00
JH E.Jones/L.Hughes 4.00 10.00
JJ M.Jordan/L.James 100.00 200.00
JW J.Johnson/M.Williams 4.00 10.00
KH J.Kidd/G.Hill 10.00 25.00
KW C.Webber/K.Korver 4.00 10.00
LF F.Jones/L.Jackson 4.00 10.00
LO R.Lewis/E.Okafor 4.00 10.00
MG D.Mason/J.Graham 4.00 10.00
MI D.Mutombo/Z.Ilgauskas 4.00 10.00
MK J.McInnis/N.Krstic 4.00 10.00
MM C.Maggette/C.Mobley 4.00 10.00
MN S.Nash/S.Marion 5.00 12.00
NS S.Nash/A.Stoudemire 5.00 12.00
NT J.Nelson/S.Telfair 4.00 10.00
NU B.Nachbar/B.Udrih 4.00 10.00
OW J.Williams/S.O'Neal 8.00 20.00
PJ P.Pierce/A.Jamison 4.00 10.00
RB M.Redd/A.Bogut 4.00 10.00
SJ W.Szczerbiak/A.Jefferson 4.00 10.00
SM S.Swift/D.Milicic 4.00 10.00
TO J.Tinsley/J.O'Neal 4.00 10.00
WB B.Wallace/C.Bosh 4.00 10.00
WC J.Williams/S.Cassell 4.00 10.00
WK C.Webber/A.Kirilenko 4.00 10.00
WN R.Wallace/D.Nowitzki 5.00 12.00
WP A.Walker/T.Prince 4.00 10.00

2006-07 Reflections Mirror Image Dual Auto Jersey

PRINT RUN 25 SER.#'d SETS
UNPRICED PATCH PRINT RUN 10 SETS
AB R.Artest/B.Bowen 12.50 30.00
BD B.Davis/C.Billups 12.50 30.00
BH D.Howard/A.Bogut 25.00 60.00
BO E.Brand/E.Okafor 12.50 30.00
BP M.Bibby/C.Paul 50.00 100.00
GB K.Garnett/C.Bosh 25.00 60.00
JJ M.Jordan/L.James 450.00 750.00
NK S.Nash/J.Kidd 60.00 120.00
TR S.Telfair/N.Robinson 12.50 30.00

2006-07 Reflections Mirror Image Dual Jersey

PRINT RUN 100 SER.#'d SETS
*PATCHES: .75X TO 2X BASE HI
PATCH PRINT RUN 50 SER.#'d SETS
AB R.Artest/B.Bowen 4.00 10.00
BD B.Davis/C.Billups 4.00 10.00
BH D.Howard/A.Bogut 6.00 15.00
BO E.Brand/E.Okafor 4.00 10.00
BP M.Bibby/C.Paul 5.00 12.00
BS K.Brown/S.Swift 4.00 10.00
CI V.Carter/A.Iguodala 5.00 12.00
CS J.Childress/J.Smith 4.00 10.00
DB T.Duncan/E.Brand 5.00 12.00
DH L.Hughes/M.Daniels 4.00 10.00
FM S.Francis/S.Marbury 4.00 10.00
FV C.Frye/C.Villanueva 4.00 10.00
GB K.Garnett/C.Bosh 5.00 12.00
HB K.Bryant/R.Hamilton 8.00 20.00
HD R.Hamilton/R.Davis 4.00 10.00
HM G.Hill/T.McGrady 10.00 25.00
JA L.James/C.Anthony 20.00 40.00
JH K.Hinrich/S.Jasikevicius 4.00 10.00
JJ M.Jordan/L.James 50.00 120.00
JR A.Jamison/J.Richardson 4.00 10.00
KM A.Kirilenko/D.Milicic 4.00 10.00
MH S.Marion/D.Howard 5.00 12.00
MO J.Magloire/J.O'Neal 4.00 10.00
MP A.Miller/T.Parker 4.00 10.00
NG D.Nowitzki/P.Gasol 6.00 15.00
NK S.Nash/J.Kidd 10.00 25.00
OM Y.Ming/S.O'Neal 10.00 25.00
PR P.Pierce/J.Richardson 4.00 10.00
RG M.Redd/B.Gordon 4.00 10.00
RJ Q.Richardson/J.Johnson 4.00 10.00
SG W.Szczerbiak/M.Ginobili 4.00 10.00
SO A.Stoudemire/J.O'Neal 4.00 10.00
TM J.Tinsley/J.McInnis 4.00 10.00
TR S.Telfair/N.Robinson 4.00 10.00
WO C.Webber/L.Odom 5.00 12.00

2006-07 Reflections Signature Copper

*COPPER: .75X TO 2X SILVER HI
STATED PRINT RUN 10-20 SER.#'d SETS
SOME UNPRICED DUE TO SCARCITY

2006-07 Reflections Signature Gold

*GOLD: .5X TO 1.25X SILVER HI
STATED PRINT RUN 25 TO 50 SER.#'d SETS
MJ Michael Jordan/25 500.00 800.00

2006-07 Reflections Signature Silver

APPROXIMATE ODDS 1:12
UNPRICED BLACK PRINT RUN ONE SET
UNPRICED BLUE PRINT RUN 5 SETS
AB Andrea Bargnani 8.00 20.00
AD Hassan Adams 2.50 6.00
AI Andre Iguodala 5.00 12.00
AJ Al Jefferson 4.00 10.00
BA Brent Barry 4.00 10.00
BB Bruce Bowen 4.00 10.00
BD Baron Davis 5.00 12.00
BJ Bobby Jackson 4.00 10.00
BM Brad Miller 4.00 10.00
BN Denham Brown 2.50 6.00
BR Brandon Roy 10.00 25.00
BS Bobby Simmons 4.00 10.00
CA Carmelo Anthony 15.00 40.00
CB Chauncey Billups 6.00 15.00
CD Chris Duhon 4.00 10.00
CH Chris Bosh 8.00 20.00
CM Cuttino Mobley 4.00 10.00
CP Chris Paul 20.00 50.00
CS Cedric Simmons 2.50 6.00
DA Marquis Daniels 4.00 10.00
DB Dee Brown 2.50 6.00
DE Daniel Ewing 4.00 10.00
DG Daniel Gibson 3.00 8.00
DH Dwight Howard 10.00 25.00
DN David Noel 2.50 6.00
EB Elton Brand 5.00 12.00
EO Emeka Okafor 4.00 10.00
FR Raymond Felton 6.00 15.00
HA Hilton Armstrong 2.50 6.00
HO Hakeem Olajuwon 10.00 25.00
ID Ike Diogu 4.00 10.00
JB Josh Boone 2.50 6.00
JJ Joe Johnson 5.00 12.00
JS Bobby Jones 2.50 6.00
JT Jarrett Jack 4.00 10.00
JW James White 2.50 6.00
KG Kevin Garnett 20.00 50.00
KL Kyle Lowry 5.00 12.00
LA LaMarcus Aldridge 12.00 30.00
LJ LeBron James 100.00 200.00
LO Lamar Odom 4.00 10.00
LR Luke Ridnour 4.00 10.00
MA Maurice Ager 2.50 6.00
MB Mike Bibby 6.00 15.00
MC Mardy Collins 2.50 6.00
MR Michael Redd 5.00 12.00
MW Marcus Williams 2.50 6.00
NO Steve Novak 3.00 8.00
NR Nate Robinson 5.00 12.00
PD Paul Davis 2.50 6.00
PO Patrick O'Bryant 2.50 6.00
PP Paul Pierce 8.00 20.00
PS Peja Stojakovic 6.00 15.00
PT P.J. Tucker 3.00 8.00
QD Quincy Douby 2.50 6.00
RA Ron Artest 4.00 10.00

RB Ronnie Brewer 4.00 10.00
RC Rodney Carney 2.50 6.00
RF Randy Foye 8.00 20.00
RG Rudy Gay 8.00 20.00
RJ Richard Jefferson 4.00 10.00
RM Rashad McCants 4.00 10.00
RR Rajon Rondo 20.00 50.00
RT Ronny Turiaf 8.00 20.00
RY Ryan Hollins 3.00 8.00
SJ Solomon Jones 2.50 6.00
SN Steve Nash 25.00 60.00
SW Shelden Williams 3.00 8.00
TT Tyrus Thomas 6.00 15.00
VC Vince Carter 30.00 80.00
WI Shawne Williams 2.50 6.00
WM Marvin Williams 3.00 8.00
WS Wayne Simien 4.00 10.00

2006-07 Reflections Triple Fabric Gold

PRINT RUN 100 SER.#'d SETS
*COPPER: .5X TO 1.25X BASE HI
COPPER PRINT RUN 50 SER.#'d SETS
*PATCHES: 1X TO 2.5X BASE HI
PATCH PRINT RUN 15 SER.#'d SETS
UNPRICED AUTO PRINT RUN ONE SET
AB Andray Blatche 2.50 6.00
AI Andre Iguodala 3.00 8.00
AJ Al Jefferson 3.00 8.00
AK Andrei Kirilenko 3.00 8.00
AS Amare Stoudemire 3.00 8.00
AW Antoine Walker 3.00 8.00
BH Brendan Haywood 2.50 6.00
BR Kwame Brown 2.50 6.00
BW Ben Wallace 3.00 8.00
CA Carmelo Anthony 5.00 12.00
CM Corey Maggette 3.00 8.00
DG Danny Granger 3.00 8.00
DH Devin Harris 2.50 6.00
DN Dirk Nowitzki 8.00 20.00
EB Elton Brand 4.00 10.00
GA Gilbert Arenas 3.00 8.00
GE Devean George 2.50 6.00
GO Drew Gooden 3.00 8.00
JH Josh Howard 3.00 8.00
JK Jason Kidd 6.00 15.00
JM Jamaal Magloire 2.50 6.00
JR Jason Richardson 4.00 10.00
JS J.R. Smith 3.00 8.00
KB Kobe Bryant 15.00 40.00
KG Kevin Garnett 6.00 15.00
KH Kirk Hinrich 3.00 8.00
LD Luol Deng 3.00 8.00
LH Larry Hughes 3.00 8.00
LJ LeBron James 25.00 60.00
MB Mike Bibby 4.00 10.00
MC Jeff McInnis 2.50 6.00
MD Mike Dunleavy 3.00 8.00
MG Manu Ginobili 4.00 10.00
MJ Michael Jordan 50.00 120.00
MW Martell Webster 3.00 8.00
PG Pau Gasol 4.00 10.00
PS Peja Stojakovic 4.00 10.00
RD Ricky Davis 3.00 8.00
RF Raymond Felton 3.00 8.00
RJ Richard Jefferson 3.00 8.00
RL Rashard Lewis 4.00 10.00
RM Rashad McCants 2.50 6.00
RS Robert Swift 2.50 6.00
SC Sam Cassell 3.00 8.00
SO Shaquille O'Neal 8.00 20.00
TD Tim Duncan 6.00 15.00
TM Tracy McGrady 5.00 12.00
VC Vince Carter 5.00 12.00
WS Wally Szczerbiak 3.00 8.00
YM Yao Ming 5.00 12.00

1987-88 Rockford Lightning CBA

Produced for the Lightning by the Rockford Litho Centre, this 10-card set features black and white photos on a blue and red card design with player biographies and an advertisement for Gary's Dugout Sports Cards store on the back.

COMPLETE SET (10) 1.50 4.00
COMMON CARD (1-10) .15 .40
1 Fred Cofield .30 .75
2 Bruce Douglas .15 .40
3 John Fox .15 .40
4 Carl Henry .30 .75
5 Jim Lampley .15 .40
6 Pete Myers .30 .75
7 Richard Rellford .15 .40
8 Charley Rosen CO .40 1.00
9 John Schweitz .30 .75
10 David Wood .50 1.25

2001 Rockers Fleer WNBA

Produced by Fleer, this sheet was given away to the first 5000 fans at the last game of the 2001 season at Gund Arena. Cards feature perforated edges, as they were released in the form of a sheet, white borders, and a colored frame around the card to match the team's colors.

COMPLETE SET (9) 4.00 10.00
1 Eva Nemcova 1.25 3.00
2 Ann Wauters 1.25 3.00
3 Merlakia Jones .40 1.00
4 Mery Andrade .40 1.00
5 Cleveland Rockers .40 1.00
6 Rushia Brown .40 1.00
7 Helen Darling .40 1.00
8 Vicky Hall .40 1.00
9 Chasity Melvin .40 1.00

1971-72 Rockets Carnation Milk

Issued on the side of Carnation Milk cartons, the side panels were used to picture members of the 1971-72 Houston Rockets. Since these were unnumbered, the cards are sequenced in alphabetical order.

COMPLETE SET 300.00 600.00
1 Dick Cunningham 30.00 60.00
2 Dick Gibbs 30.00 60.00
3 Elvin Hayes 75.00 150.00
4 Stu Lantz 50.00 100.00
5 Cliff Meely 30.00 60.00
6 Calvin Murphy 50.00 100.00
7 Mike Newlin 40.00 75.00
8 Rudy Tomjanovich 60.00 120.00

1969-70 Rockets Coca-Cola

Measuring 8 1/2" by 11", this 9-card set features members from the 1969-70 San Diego Rockets. The fronts feature color close-up shots, with the player's name, weight, age and college. The team logo is located in the lower left corner, with a Coca-Cola logo in the lower right. The backs feature text, the Coca-Cola logo and "Rockets Cage Club", and are not numbered. The photos are listed below in alphabetical order.

COMPLETE SET (9) 75.00 150.00
1 Rick Adelman 8.00 20.00
2 Jim Barnett 5.00 10.00
3 John Block 5.00 10.00
4 Elvin Hayes 12.50 25.00
5 Toby Kimball 5.00 10.00
6 Stu Lantz 8.00 20.00
7 Pat Riley 15.00 40.00
8 John Trapp 5.00 10.00
9 Art Williams 5.00 10.00

1971-72 Rockets Denver Team Issue

Each of these team-issued photos measure approximately 8" by 10" and feature black and white player portraits. The player's name is listed below the photo. Each sheet contains eight photos. The backs are blank. The photos are unnumbered and listed below alphabetically.

COMPLETE SET (2) 15.00 30.00
1 Byron Beck 7.50 15.00
Art Becker
Julian Hammond
Marv Roberts
Ralph Simpson
Dwight Waller
Chuck Williams
Steve Wilson
2 Stan Albeck ACO 10.00 20.00
Larry Brown
Alex Hannum CO
Julius Keye
Del Klone GM
Dave Robisch
Al Smith
Lloyd Williams TR

1968-69 Rockets Jack in the Box

This 14-card set of San Diego Rockets was sponsored by Jack-in-the-Box and available at their restaurants in the greater San Diego area. There is evidence that this set was substantially reissued the following year with cards of Bobby Smith and Bernie Williams replacing the cards of Harry Barnes and Henry Finkel. Bobby Smith's only season with the San Diego Rockets was 1969-70 and Harry Barnes' only season with the San Diego Rockets was 1968-69. The cards only measure approximately 2" by 3" and have the appearance of wallet-size photos. The fronts have posed color head and shoulders shots, with the player's name, team name, team logo, and sponsor's logo below the picture. The backs are blank. The cards are unnumbered and are checklisted below in alphabetical order. The two cards in the set that are more difficult to find are marked by SP in the checklist below. The set features the first professional cards of Rick Adelman, Elvin Hayes, and Pat Riley among others.

COMPLETE SET (14) 50.00 90.00
1 Rick Adelman 2.50 6.00
2 Harry Barnes SP 20.00 50.00
3 Jim Barnett .75 2.00
4 John Block .60 1.50
5 Henry Finkel SP 20.00 50.00
6 Elvin Hayes 3.00 8.00
7 Toby Kimball .60 1.50
8 Don Kojis .60 1.50
9 Stu Lantz 1.25 3.00
10 Pat Riley 4.00 10.00
11 Bobby Smith 1.50 4.00
12 John Trapp .60 1.50
13 Art Williams .60 1.50
14 Bernie Williams 1.00 2.50

1978-79 Rockets Photos

This six card oversized glossy set was released during the 1978-79 season, and features such Rockets stars as Rudy Tomjanovich and Moses Malone. Please note that these black and white cards measure 8"x10", and have blank backs.

COMPLETE SET 15.00 30.00
1 Rick Barry 3.00 8.00
2 Alonzo Bradley 1.00 2.50
3 Jacky Dorsey 1.00 2.50
4 Mike Dunleavy 1.50 4.00
5 Moses Malone 2.50 6.00
6 Calvin Murphy 2.00 5.00
7 Mike Newlin 1.25 3.00
8 Jackie Robinson 1.00 2.50
9 Rudy Tomjanovich 2.00 5.00
10 Slick Watts 1.25 3.00

1975-76 Rockets Team Issue

This 8"x10" set was produced for the Houston Rockets during the 1975-76 season. The set features eight cards of the team's players and coaches Please note that the card of Tom Nissalke was done as a 5"x7" card.

COMPLETE SET (8) 12.50 25.00
1 John Johnson 1.50 4.00
2 Kevin Kunnert 1.25 3.00
3 Mike Newlin 1.50 4.00
4 Ed Ratleff 1.25 3.00
5 Ron Riley 1.25 3.00
6 Rudy White 1.25 3.00
7 Dave Wohl 1.25 3.00
8 Tom Nissalke CO 1.25 3.00

1977-78 Rockets Team Issue

These eight photos featured members of the 1976-77 Houston Rockets. Since they are unnumbered we have sequenced them in alphabetical order.

COMPLETE SET 10.00 20.00
1 John Johnson 1.50 4.00
2 Kevin Kunnert 1.25 3.00
3 Mike Newlin 1.50 4.00
4 Tom Nissalke CO 1.25 3.00
5 Ed Ratleff 1.25 3.00
6 Ron Riley 1.25 3.00
7 Rudy White 1.25 3.00
8 Dave Wohl 1.50 4.00

1990-91 Rockets Team Issue

Each of these Houston Rockets team-issued photos measure approximately 6" by 9" and feature a close-up color player portrait bordered in white. A facsimile autograph and the uniform number accent the front. The backs are blank. The photos are unnumbered and listed below alphabetically.

COMPLETE SET (5) 4.00 10.00
1 Dave Jamerson .30 .75
2 Buck Johnson .30 .75
3 Hakeem Olajuwon 3.00 8.00
4 Otis Thorpe .60 1.50
5 David Wood .30 .75

1971-72 Rockets Team Photo

his black and white press photo, measuring 7 3/4" x 10", was issued for the Houston Rockets' first NBA season. The photo is made up of twelve pictures divided up into three rows. Each individual shot is a close-up of each player. The Houston Rockets' debut logo appears at the bottom middle.

1 Team Photo 6.00 12.00
Curtis Perry
Elvin Hayes
Dick Cunningham
John Egan
Dick Gibbs
Rudy Tomjanovich
Mike Newlin
Jim Davis
Cliff Meely
Calvin Murphy
Stu Lantz
John Vallely

2008-09 Rockets Upper Deck

COMPLETE SET (14) 2.50 6.00
1 Yao Ming .40 1.00
2 Tracy McGrady .30 .75
3 Shane Battier .25 .60
4 Rafer Alston .20 .50
5 Luis Scola .25 .60
6 Chuck Hayes .20 .50
7 Steve Francis .30 .75
8 Luther Head .20 .50
9 Carl Landry .20 .50
10 Dikembe Mutombo .30 .75
11 Ron Artest .30 .75
12 Joey Dorsey .20 .50
13 Rick Adelman CO .20 .50
14 Hakeem Olajuwon .40 1.00

2009-10 Rookies and Stars

COMP.SET w/o SPs (115) 12.50 30.00
AU RC PRINT RUNS LISTED IN CHECKLIST
ASTERISK CARDS FROM PANINI UPDATE
1 Josh Smith .30 .75
2 Joe Johnson .30 .75
3 Mike Bibby .30 .75
4 Paul Pierce .40 1.00
5 Ray Allen .40 1.00
6 Rajon Rondo .40 1.00
7 Kevin Garnett .60 1.50
8 Gerald Wallace .30 .75
9 Boris Diaw .30 .75
10 Raja Bell .30 .75
11 Derrick Rose .60 1.50
12 John Salmons .30 .75
13 Kirk Hinrich .30 .75
14 LeBron James 1.50 4.00
15 Shaquille O'Neal .75 2.00
16 Mo Williams .30 .75
17 Dirk Nowitzki .50 1.25
18 Josh Howard .30 .75
19 Jason Kidd .40 1.00
20 Jason Terry .30 .75
21 Shawn Marion .30 .75
22 Carmelo Anthony .50 1.25
23 Chauncey Billups .40 1.00
24 J.R. Smith .30 .75
25 Richard Hamilton .30 .75
26 Tayshaun Prince .30 .75
27 Allen Iverson .50 1.25
28 Stephen Jackson .30 .75
29 Corey Maggette .30 .75
30 Monta Ellis .30 .75
31 Yao Ming .50 1.25
32 Tracy McGrady .40 1.00
33 Trevor Ariza .25 .60
34 Danny Granger .30 .75
35 Mike Dunleavy .25 .60
36 T.J. Ford .25 .60
37 Al Thornton .30 .75
38 Eric Gordon .30 .75
39 Kobe Bryant 1.50 4.00
40 Pau Gasol .40 1.00
41 Ron Artest .40 1.00
42 Andrew Bynum .25 .60
43 Rudy Gay .40 1.00
44 O.J. Mayo .25 .60
45 Mike Conley Jr. .30 .75
46 Zach Randolph .30 .75
47 Dwyane Wade .60 1.50
48 Michael Beasley .25 .60
49 Jermaine O'Neal .30 .75
50 Udonis Haslem .25 .60
51 Michael Redd .30 .75
52 Ramon Sessions .30 .75
53 Andrew Bogut .30 .75
54 Al Jefferson .30 .75
55 Ryan Gomes .25 .60
56 Kevin Love .40 1.00
57 Devin Harris .25 .60
58 Brook Lopez .30 .75
59 Rafer Alston .25 .60
60 Chris Paul .50 1.25
61 David West .30 .75
62 Peja Stojakovic .40 1.00
63 Al Harrington .30 .75
64 Nate Robinson .25 .60
65 Wilson Chandler .30 .75
66 Kevin Durant 1.00 2.50
67 Jeff Green .30 .75
68 Russell Westbrook 1.00 2.50
69 Dwight Howard .30 .75
70 Rashard Lewis .30 .75
71 Jameer Nelson .25 .60
72 Vince Carter .50 1.25
73 Andre Iguodala .30 .75
74 Elton Brand .40 1.00
75 Thaddeus Young .25 .60
76 Amare Stoudemire .30 .75
77 Steve Nash .40 1.00
78 Leandro Barbosa .30 .75
79 Channing Frye .30 .75
80 Brandon Roy .40 1.00
81 LaMarcus Aldridge .40 1.00
82 Greg Oden .30 .75
83 Kevin Martin .30 .75
84 Andres Nocioni .25 .60
85 Spencer Hawes .25 .60
86 Tony Parker .40 1.00
87 Tim Duncan .60 1.50
88 Manu Ginobili .40 1.00
89 Richard Jefferson .30 .75
90 Chris Bosh .40 1.00
91 Hedo Turkoglu .30 .75
92 Andrea Bargnani .30 .75
93 Deron Williams .30 .75
94 Carlos Boozer .30 .75
95 Andrei Kirilenko .30 .75
96 Ronnie Brewer .30 .75
97 Antawn Jamison .30 .75
98 Gilbert Arenas .30 .75
99 Caron Butler .30 .75
100 Randy Foye .25 .60
101 Kareem Abdul-Jabbar .60 1.50
102 Elvin Hayes .40 1.00
103 Karl Malone .50 1.25
104 Arnie Risen .40 1.00
105 Jalen Rose .40 1.00
106 Dave DeBusschere .40 1.00
107 Artis Gilmore .30 .75
108 Nate Archibald .30 .75
109 Mark Eaton .25 .60
110 Darryl Dawkins .25 .60
111 Spencer Haywood .25 .60
112 Bill Cartwright .30 .75
113 Moses Malone .40 1.00
114 Magic Johnson 1.00 2.50
115 Sleepy Floyd .25 .60
116 Dante Cunningham RC .50 1.25
117 Jon Brockman RC .50 1.25
118 Jonas Jerebko RC .75 2.00
119 Derrick Brown RC .50 1.25
120 Dionte Christmas RC .50 1.25
121 Marcus Thornton RC .60 1.50
122 Danny Green RC 1.00 2.50
123 Goran Suton RC .50 1.25
124 Jack McClinton RC .50 1.25
125 A.J. Price RC .50 1.25
126 Serge Ibaka RC .75 2.00
127 DeMar DeRozan RC 2.00 5.00
128 Chris Hunter RC .50 1.25
129 Lester Hudson RC .50 1.25
130 David Andersen RC .50 1.25
131 Blake Griffin AU/449 RC 25.00 60.00
132 H.Thabeet AU/449 RC 4.00 10.00
133 James Harden AU/449 RC 50.00 120.00
134 Tyreke Evans AU/379 RC 5.00 12.00
135 Jonny Flynn AU/449 RC 4.00 10.00
136 Stephen Curry AU/449 RC 250.00 400.00
137 Jordan Hill AU/449 RC 5.00 12.00
138 Dante Cunningham AU/437 RC 4.00 10.00
139 B.Jennings AU/379 RC 6.00 15.00
140 T.Williams AU/356 RC 4.00 10.00
141 Gerald Henderson AU/449 RC 5.00 12.00
142 T.Hansbrough AU/449 RC 5.00 12.00
143 Earl Clark AU/449 RC 5.00 12.00
144 Austin Daye AU/369 RC 4.00 10.00
145 James Johnson AU/449 RC 5.00 12.00
146 Jrue Holiday AU/449 RC 8.00 20.00
147 Ty Lawson AU/369 RC 6.00 15.00
148 Jeff Teague AU/449 RC 6.00 15.00
149 Eric Maynor AU/369 RC 4.00 10.00
150 Darren Collison AU/347 RC 6.00 15.00
151 Omri Casspi AU/449 RC 5.00 12.00
152 B.J. Mullens AU/379 RC 4.00 10.00
153 R.Beaubois AU/390 RC 4.00 10.00
154 Taj Gibson AU/369 RC 6.00 15.00
155 DeMarre Carroll AU/449 RC 5.00 12.00
156 Wayne Ellington AU/416 RC 6.00 15.00
157 Toney Douglas AU/379 RC 4.00 10.00
158 Jermaine Taylor AU/449 RC 4.00 10.00
159 Jeff Pendergraph AU/449 RC 4.00 10.00
160 DaJuan Summers AU/378 RC 4.00 10.00
161 Sam Young AU/369 RC 4.00 10.00
162 DeJuan Blair AU/449 RC 5.00 12.00
163 Chase Budinger AU/369 RC 5.00 12.00
164 Jodie Meeks AU/449 RC 6.00 15.00
165 Taylor Griffin AU/380 RC 4.00 10.00
166 D.Derozan AU/499 RC* 30.00 80.00
167 W.Matthews AU/499 RC* 6.00 15.00
168 Serge Ibaka AU/499 RC* 6.00 15.00
169 M.Thornton AU/499 RC* 5.00 12.00
170 J.Jerebko AU/499 RC* 6.00 15.00

2009-10 Rookies and Stars Gold

*GOLD 1-115: 1X TO 2.5X BASE HI
*GOLD 116-130: .75X TO 2X BASE HI
*GOLD 131-165: .6X TO 1.5X BASE HI
GOLD 1-130 PRINT RUN 500 SER.#'d SETS
GOLD 131-165 PRINT RUN 25 SER.#'d SETS
136 Stephen Curry AU 800.00 1200.00

2009-10 Rookies and Stars Gold Holofoil

*GOLD STARS: 2X TO 5X BASE HI
*GOLD RCs: 1.25X TO 3X BASE HI
STATED PRINT RUN 250 SER.#'d SETS

2009-10 Rookies and Stars Current NBA Team Patches Signatures

STATED PRINT RUN 199 SER.#'d SETS
1 Kobe Bryant 100.00 200.00

2009-10 Rookies and Stars Dress for Success Materials

STATED PRINT RUN 299 SER.#'d SETS
*PRIME: 1X TO 2.5X BASE HI
PRIME PRINT RUN 50 SER.#'d SETS
1 Blake Griffin 8.00 20.00
2 Hasheem Thabeet 1.25 3.00
3 James Harden 10.00 25.00
4 Tyreke Evans 1.50 4.00
5 Jonny Flynn 1.25 3.00
6 Stephen Curry 25.00 100.00
7 Jordan Hill 1.50 4.00
8 DeMar DeRozan 5.00 12.00
9 Brandon Jennings 2.00 5.00
10 Terrence Williams 1.25 3.00
11 Gerald Henderson 1.50 4.00
12 Tyler Hansbrough 1.50 4.00
13 Earl Clark 1.50 4.00
14 Austin Daye 1.25 3.00
15 James Johnson 1.50 4.00
16 Jrue Holiday 2.50 6.00
17 Ty Lawson 2.00 5.00
18 Jeff Teague 2.00 5.00
19 Eric Maynor 1.25 3.00
20 Darren Collison 2.00 5.00
21 Omri Casspi 1.50 4.00
22 B.J. Mullens 1.25 3.00
23 Rodrigue Beaubois 1.25 3.00
24 Taj Gibson 2.00 5.00
25 DeMarre Carroll 1.50 4.00
26 Wayne Ellington 2.00 5.00
27 Toney Douglas 1.25 3.00
28 Jermaine Taylor 1.25 3.00
29 Jeff Pendergraph 1.25 3.00
30 DaJuan Summers 1.25 3.00
31 Sam Young 1.25 3.00
32 DeJuan Blair 1.50 4.00
33 Chase Budinger 1.50 4.00
34 Jodie Meeks 2.00 5.00
35 Taylor Griffin 1.25 3.00

2009-10 Rookies and Stars Dress for Success Materials Signatures

STATED PRINT RUN 25 SER.#'d SETS
UNPRICED PRIME SIG PRINT RUN 10 SETS
1 Blake Griffin 150.00 300.00
2 Hasheem Thabeet 4.00 10.00
3 James Harden 50.00 120.00
4 Tyreke Evans 20.00 50.00
5 Jonny Flynn 4.00 10.00
6 Stephen Curry 500.00 1000.00
7 Jordan Hill 5.00 12.00
9 Brandon Jennings 6.00 15.00
10 Terrence Williams 4.00 10.00
11 Gerald Henderson 5.00 12.00
12 Tyler Hansbrough 5.00 12.00
13 Earl Clark 5.00 12.00
14 Austin Daye 4.00 10.00
15 James Johnson 5.00 12.00
16 Jrue Holiday 8.00 20.00
18 Jeff Teague 6.00 15.00
21 Omri Casspi 5.00 12.00
22 B.J. Mullens 4.00 10.00
23 Rodrigue Beaubois 4.00 10.00
25 DeMarre Carroll 5.00 12.00
26 Wayne Ellington 6.00 15.00
27 Toney Douglas 4.00 10.00
28 Jermaine Taylor 4.00 10.00
29 Jeff Pendergraph 4.00 10.00
30 DaJuan Summers 4.00 10.00
32 DeJuan Blair 5.00 12.00
33 Chase Budinger 5.00 12.00
34 Jodie Meeks 6.00 15.00
35 Taylor Griffin 4.00 10.00

2009-10 Rookies and Stars Freshman Orientation Materials

STATED PRINT RUN 299 SER.#'d SETS
*PRIME: 1X TO 2.5X BASE HI
PRIME PRINT RUN 50 SER.#'d SETS
1 Blake Griffin 8.00 20.00
2 Hasheem Thabeet 1.25 3.00
3 James Harden 10.00 25.00
4 Tyreke Evans 1.50 4.00
5 Jonny Flynn 1.25 3.00
6 Stephen Curry 40.00 100.00
7 Jordan Hill 1.50 4.00
8 DeMar DeRozan 5.00 12.00
9 Brandon Jennings 2.00 5.00
10 Terrence Williams 1.25 3.00
11 Gerald Henderson 1.50 4.00
12 Tyler Hansbrough 1.50 4.00
13 Earl Clark 1.50 4.00
14 Austin Daye 1.25 3.00
15 James Johnson 1.50 4.00
16 Jrue Holiday 2.50 6.00
17 Ty Lawson 2.00 5.00
18 Jeff Teague 2.00 5.00
19 Eric Maynor 1.25 3.00
20 Darren Collison 2.00 5.00
21 Omri Casspi 1.50 4.00
22 B.J. Mullens 1.25 3.00
23 Rodrigue Beaubois 1.25 3.00
24 Taj Gibson 2.00 5.00
25 DeMarre Carroll 1.50 4.00
26 Wayne Ellington 2.00 5.00
27 Toney Douglas 1.25 3.00
28 Jermaine Taylor 1.25 3.00
29 Jeff Pendergraph 1.25 3.00
30 DaJuan Summers 1.25 3.00
31 Sam Young 1.25 3.00
32 DeJuan Blair 1.50 4.00
33 Chase Budinger 1.50 4.00
34 Jodie Meeks 2.00 5.00
35 Taylor Griffin 1.25 3.00

2009-10 Rookies and Stars Freshman Orientation Materials Signatures

STATED PRINT RUN 25 SER.#'d SETS
UNPRICED PRIME SIG PRINT RUN 10 SETS
1 Blake Griffin 75.00 150.00
2 Hasheem Thabeet 4.00 10.00
3 James Harden 50.00 120.00
4 Tyreke Evans 10.00 25.00
5 Jonny Flynn 4.00 10.00
6 Stephen Curry 800.00 1200.00
7 Jordan Hill 5.00 12.00
9 Brandon Jennings 20.00 50.00
10 Terrence Williams 4.00 10.00
11 Gerald Henderson 5.00 12.00
12 Tyler Hansbrough 5.00 12.00
13 Earl Clark 5.00 12.00
14 Austin Daye 4.00 10.00
15 James Johnson 5.00 12.00
16 Jrue Holiday 8.00 20.00
18 Jeff Teague 6.00 15.00
21 Omri Casspi 5.00 12.00
22 B.J. Mullens 4.00 10.00
23 Rodrigue Beaubois 4.00 10.00
24 Taj Gibson 6.00 15.00
25 DeMarre Carroll 5.00 12.00
26 Wayne Ellington 6.00 15.00
27 Toney Douglas 4.00 10.00
28 Jermaine Taylor 4.00 10.00
29 Jeff Pendergraph 4.00 10.00
30 DaJuan Summers 4.00 10.00
32 DeJuan Blair 5.00 12.00
33 Chase Budinger 5.00 12.00
34 Jodie Meeks 6.00 15.00
35 Taylor Griffin 4.00 10.00

2009-10 Rookies and Stars Gold Materials

STATED PRINT RUN 99 TO 250 SER.#'d SETS
1 Josh Smith/250 2.50 6.00
3 Mike Bibby/250 2.50 6.00
13 Kirk Hinrich/250 2.50 6.00
14 LeBron James/250 8.00 20.00
17 Dirk Nowitzki/99 4.00 10.00
18 Josh Howard/250 2.50 6.00
19 Jason Kidd/250 3.00 8.00
20 Jason Terry/250 2.50 6.00
22 Carmelo Anthony/250 4.00 10.00
26 Tayshaun Prince/250 2.50 6.00
28 Stephen Jackson/250 2.50 6.00
31 Yao Ming/250 4.00 10.00
32 Tracy McGrady/250 3.00 8.00
39 Kobe Bryant/99 8.00 20.00
42 Andrew Bynum/250 2.00 5.00
45 Mike Conley Jr./250 2.50 6.00
47 Dwyane Wade/250 5.00 12.00
48 Michael Beasley/250 2.00 5.00
49 Jermaine O'Neal/100 2.50 6.00
50 Udonis Haslem/250 2.00 5.00
51 Michael Redd/250 2.50 6.00
53 Andrew Bogut/250 2.50 6.00
54 Al Jefferson/250 2.50 6.00
56 Kevin Love/250 3.00 8.00
57 Devin Harris/199 2.00 5.00
62 Peja Stojakovic/250 3.00 8.00
63 Al Harrington/250 2.50 6.00
66 Kevin Durant/250 6.00 15.00
69 Dwight Howard/250 2.50 6.00
70 Rashard Lewis/250 2.50 6.00
73 Andre Iguodala/250 2.50 6.00
74 Elton Brand/250 3.00 8.00
75 Thaddeus Young/250 2.00 5.00
76 Amare Stoudemire/250 2.50 6.00
77 Steve Nash/250 3.00 8.00
80 Brandon Roy/250 3.00 8.00
81 LaMarcus Aldridge/250 3.00 8.00
82 Greg Oden/250 2.50 6.00
84 Andres Nocioni/250 2.00 5.00
86 Tony Parker/250 3.00 8.00
87 Tim Duncan/250 5.00 12.00
88 Manu Ginobili/250 3.00 8.00
92 Andrea Bargnani/250 2.50 6.00
93 Deron Williams/250 2.50 6.00
94 Carlos Boozer/250 2.50 6.00
95 Andrei Kirilenko/250 2.50 6.00
127 DeMar DeRozan/250 8.00 20.00

2009-10 Rookies and Stars Gold Stars

COMPLETE SET (15) 8.00 20.00
RANDOM INSERTS IN PACKS
*BLACK: .75X TO 2X BASE HI
BLACK PRINT RUN 100 SER.#'d SETS
*GOLD: .5X TO 1.25X BASE HI
GOLD PRINT RUN 500 SER.#'d SETS
*HOLOFOIL: .6X TO 1.5X BASE HI
HOLO PRINT RUN 250 SER.#'d SETS
1 Dwyane Wade 1.25 3.00
2 Kobe Bryant 3.00 8.00
3 LeBron James 3.00 8.00
4 Dirk Nowitzki 1.00 2.50
5 Danny Granger .60 1.50
6 Kevin Durant 2.00 5.00
7 Chris Paul 1.00 2.50
8 Carmelo Anthony 1.00 2.50
9 Chris Bosh .75 2.00
10 Brandon Roy .75 2.00
11 Joe Johnson .60 1.50
12 Devin Harris .50 1.25
13 Deron Williams .60 1.50
14 Dwight Howard .60 1.50
15 Paul Pierce .75 2.00

2009-10 Rookies and Stars Gold Stars Materials

RANDOM INSERTS IN PACKS
*PRIME: 1X TO 2.5X BASE HI
PRIME PRINT RUN 10 TO 50 SER.#'d SETS
1 Dwyane Wade 4.00 10.00
2 Kobe Bryant 8.00 20.00
3 LeBron James 8.00 20.00
4 Dirk Nowitzki 3.00 8.00
6 Kevin Durant 6.00 15.00
7 Chris Paul 3.00 8.00
8 Carmelo Anthony 3.00 8.00
9 Chris Bosh 2.50 6.00
10 Brandon Roy 2.50 6.00
11 Joe Johnson 2.00 5.00
12 Devin Harris 1.50 4.00
13 Deron Williams 2.00 5.00
14 Dwight Howard 2.00 5.00

2009-10 Rookies and Stars Gold Stars Signatures

STATED PRINT RUN 10 TO 25 SER.#'d SETS
SOME UNPRICED DUE TO SCARCITY
2 Kobe Bryant/25 100.00 200.00

2009-10 Rookies and Stars Moments in Time

COMPLETE SET (15) 15.00 30.00
RANDOM INSERTS IN PACKS
*BLACK: .75X TO 2X BASE HI
BLACK PRINT RUN 100 SER.#'d SETS
*GOLD: .5X TO 1.25X BASE HI
GOLD PRINT RUN 500 SER.#'d SETS
*HOLOFOIL: .6X TO 1.5X BASE HI
HOLO PRINT RUN 250 SER.#'d SETS
1 Bob Pettit 1.00 2.50
2 Wilt Chamberlain 2.00 5.00
3 John Havlicek 1.00 2.50
4 Bill Russell 1.50 4.00
5 Willis Reed 1.00 2.50
6 Jerry West 1.25 3.00
7 Bill Walton 1.00 2.50
8 Darryl Dawkins .60 1.50
9 Magic Johnson 2.50 6.00
10 Spud Webb .75 2.00
11 Larry Bird 2.50 6.00
12 Kareem Abdul-Jabbar 1.50 4.00
13 Shaquille O'Neal 2.00 5.00
14 LeBron James 4.00 10.00
15 Kobe Bryant 4.00 10.00

2009-10 Rookies and Stars Prime Cuts

STATED PRINT RUN 25 TO 50 SER.#'d SETS
1 Mike Bibby/50 5.00 12.00
2 Dirk Nowitzki/50 8.00 20.00
3 Tracy McGrady/25 6.00 15.00
4 Elton Brand/50 6.00 15.00
5 Brandon Roy/50 6.00 15.00
6 Michael Beasley/50 4.00 10.00
7 Andre Iguodala/50 5.00 12.00
8 Amare Stoudemire/50 5.00 12.00
9 Andrea Bargnani/50 5.00 12.00
10 Manu Ginobili/50 6.00 15.00
11 Nate Robinson/50 4.00 10.00
12 Al Jefferson/50 5.00 12.00
13 O.J. Mayo/50 4.00 10.00
14 Tony Parker/50 6.00 15.00
15 Carlos Boozer/50 5.00 12.00

2009-10 Rookies and Stars Prime Cuts Signatures

STATED PRINT RUN 25 SER.#'d SETS
1 Mike Bibby 10.00 25.00
2 Dirk Nowitzki 100.00 200.00
6 Michael Beasley 15.00 40.00
15 Carlos Boozer 10.00 25.00

2009-10 Rookies and Stars Retired NBA Team Patches Signatures

STATED PRINT RUN 99 TO 394 SER.#'d SETS
1 Willis Reed/99 10.00 25.00
2 Elvin Hayes/99 8.00 20.00
3 Sidney Moncrief/199 6.00 15.00
4 Danny Manning/199 6.00 15.00
5 Bill Laimbeer/199 6.00 15.00
6 Dan Majerle/99 6.00 15.00
7 Bob Cousy/199 15.00 40.00
8 Earl Monroe/99 12.50 30.00
9 Darryl Dawkins/99 10.00 25.00
10 Adrian Dantley/99 6.00 15.00
11 Byron Scott/199 10.00 25.00
12 Nate Thurmond/199 8.00 20.00
13 Cazzie Russell/199 6.00 15.00
14 Tim Hardaway/199 6.00 15.00
15 Kurt Rambis/99 12.50 30.00
16 Rick Barry/199 8.00 20.00
17 Manute Bol/199 30.00 60.00
18 Artis Gilmore/199 8.00 20.00
19 Spencer Haywood/394 6.00 15.00

2009-10 Rookies and Stars Sharp Shooters

COMPLETE SET (15) 6.00 15.00
RANDOM INSERTS IN PACKS
*BLACK: .75X TO 2X BASE HI
BLACK PRINT RUN 100 SER.#'d SETS
*GOLD: .5X TO 1.25X BASE HI
GOLD PRINT RUN 500 SER.#'d SETS
*HOLOFOIL: .6X TO 1.5X BASE HI
HOLO PRINT RUN 250 SER.#'d SETS
UNPRICED SIG.PRINT RUN 10 SETS
1 Anthony Morrow .75 2.00
2 D.J. Augustin .75 2.00
3 Jameer Nelson .75 2.00
4 Jason Kapono .75 2.00
5 Kelenna Azubuike .75 2.00
6 Kevin Durant 3.00 8.00
7 Mehmet Okur .75 2.00
8 Mo Williams 1.00 2.50
9 Steve Nash 1.25 3.00
10 Troy Murphy .75 2.00
11 Chauncey Billups 1.25 3.00
12 David West 1.00 2.50
13 Dirk Nowitzki 2.00 5.00
14 Manu Ginobili 1.25 3.00
15 Ray Allen 1.25 3.00

2009-10 Rookies and Stars Sharp Shooters Materials

RANDOM INSERTS IN PACKS
*PRIME: .75X TO 2X BASE HI
PRIME PRINT RUN 50 SER.#'d SETS
6 Kevin Durant 8.00 20.00
9 Steve Nash 3.00 8.00
13 Dirk Nowitzki 4.00 10.00
14 Manu Ginobili 3.00 8.00

2009-10 Rookies and Stars Signatures

STATED PRINT RUN 25 TO 250 SER.#'d SETS
3 Mike Bibby/50 6.00 15.00
17 Dirk Nowitzki/25 50.00 120.00
19 Jason Kidd/25 10.00 25.00
39 Kobe Bryant/25 100.00 225.00
42 Andrew Bynum/25 10.00 25.00
48 Michael Beasley/25 12.00 30.00
56 Kevin Love/25 15.00 40.00
73 Andre Iguodala/25 6.00 15.00
94 Carlos Boozer/50 6.00 15.00
102 Elvin Hayes/25 6.00 15.00
104 Arnie Risen/25 6.00 15.00
107 Artis Gilmore/50 6.00 15.00
108 Nate Archibald/25 12.50 30.00
111 Spencer Haywood/25 8.00 20.00
115 Sleepy Floyd/25 8.00 20.00
117 Jon Brockman/250 3.00 8.00
121 Marcus Thornton/250 4.00 10.00
122 Danny Green/250 6.00 15.00
123 Goran Suton/250 3.00 8.00
124 Jack McClinton/250 3.00 8.00
125 A.J. Price/250 3.00 8.00
129 Lester Hudson/250 3.00 8.00

2009-10 Rookies and Stars Stardom

COMPLETE SET (15) 8.00 20.00
RANDOM INSERTS IN PACKS
*BLACK: .75X TO 2X BASE HI
BLACK PRINT RUN 100 SER.#'d SETS
*GOLD: .5X TO 1.25X BASE HI
GOLD PRINT RUN 500 SER.#'d SETS
*HOLOFOIL: .6X TO 1.5X BASE HI
HOLO PRINT RUN 250 SER.#'d SETS
1 Mike Bibby .75 2.00
2 Rajon Rondo 1.00 2.50
3 Raja Bell .75 2.00
4 Kirk Hinrich .75 2.00
5 Shaquille O'Neal 2.00 5.00
6 Jason Terry .75 2.00
7 Chauncey Billups 1.00 2.50
8 Baron Davis .75 2.00
9 Kobe Bryant 4.00 10.00
10 O.J. Mayo .60 1.50
11 Jermaine O'Neal .75 2.00
12 Elton Brand 1.00 2.50
13 Greg Oden .75 2.00
14 Tim Duncan 1.50 4.00
15 Hedo Turkoglu .75 2.00

2009-10 Rookies and Stars Stardom Materials

RANDOM INSERTS IN PACKS
1 Mike Bibby 2.00 5.00
4 Kirk Hinrich 2.00 5.00
6 Jason Terry 2.00 5.00
9 Kobe Bryant 8.00 20.00
11 Jermaine O'Neal 2.00 5.00
12 Elton Brand 2.50 6.00
13 Greg Oden 2.00 5.00
14 Tim Duncan 4.00 10.00

2009-10 Rookies and Stars Stardom Signatures

STATED PRINT RUN 50 SER.#'d SETS
1 Mike Bibby 8.00 20.00
9 Kobe Bryant 100.00 200.00

2009-10 Rookies and Stars Statistical Standouts Materials

STATED PRINT RUN 99 TO 299 SER.#'d SETS
*PRIME: .75X TO 2X BASE HI
PRIME PRINT RUN 10 TO 50 SER.#'d SETS
SOME PRIME UNPRICED DUE TO SCARCITY
1 Chris Paul/299 4.00 10.00
2 Dirk Nowitzki/299 4.00 10.00
3 Dwyane Wade/299 5.00 12.00
4 Kobe Bryant/99 10.00 25.00
5 LeBron James/299 8.00 20.00
6 Al Jefferson/299 2.50 6.00
8 Dwight Howard/299 2.50 6.00
9 Stephen Jackson/299 2.50 6.00
11 Devin Harris/299 2.00 5.00
12 Joe Johnson/299 2.50 6.00
13 Pau Gasol/299 3.00 8.00
14 Tony Parker/299 3.00 8.00
15 Kevin Martin/299 2.50 6.00

2009-10 Rookies and Stars Statistical Standouts Materials Signatures

STATED PRINT RUN 25 SER.#'d SETS
UNPRICED PRIME SIG PRINT RUN 10 SETS
2 Dirk Nowitzki 50.00 120.00
4 Kobe Bryant 125.00 225.00

2009-10 Rookies and Stars Studio Combo Rookies

COMPLETE SET (10) 10.00 25.00
RANDOM INSERTS IN PACKS
*BLACK: .75X TO 2X BASE HI
BLACK PRINT RUN 100 SER.#'d SETS
*GOLD: .5X TO 1.25X BASE HI
GOLD PRINT RUN 500 SER.#'d SETS
*HOLOFOIL: .6X TO 1.5X BASE HI
HOLO PRINT RUN 250 SER.#'d SETS
1 B.Griffin/T.Griffin 3.00 8.00
2 C.Budinger/J.Hill .60 1.50
3 D.DeRozan/T.Gibson 2.00 5.00
4 T.Lawson/T.Hansbrough .75 2.00
5 J.Johnson/J.Teague .75 2.00
6 D.Collison/J.Holiday 1.00 2.50
7 J.Harden/J.Pendergraph 5.00 12.00
8 D.Blair/H.Thabeet .60 1.50
9 S.Curry/T.Evans 8.00 20.00
10 B.Griffin/T.Hansbrough 3.00 8.00

2009-10 Rookies and Stars Studio Combo Rookies Materials

STATED PRINT RUN 299 SER.#'d SETS
*PRIME: 1X TO 2.5X BASE HI
PRIME PRINT RUN 50 SER.#'d SETS
1 B.Griffin/T.Griffin 6.00 15.00
2 C.Budinger/J.Hill 2.00 5.00
3 D.DeRozan/T.Gibson 4.00 10.00
4 T.Lawson/T.Hansbrough 1.50 4.00
5 J.Johnson/J.Teague 1.50 4.00
6 D.Collison/J.Holiday 2.00 5.00
7 J.Harden/J.Pendergraph 8.00 20.00
8 D.Blair/H.Thabeet 1.25 3.00
9 S.Curry/T.Evans 15.00 40.00
10 B.Griffin/T.Hansbrough 6.00 15.00

2009-10 Rookies and Stars Studio Combo Rookies Signatures

STATED PRINT RUN 50 SER.#'d SETS
1 B.Griffin/T.Griffin 25.00 60.00
2 C.Budinger/J.Hill 10.00 25.00
4 T.Lawson/T.Hansbrough 20.00 50.00
5 J.Johnson/J.Teague 10.00 25.00
6 D.Collison/J.Holiday 15.00 40.00
7 J.Harden/J.Pendergraph 15.00 40.00
8 D.Blair/H.Thabeet 12.50 30.00
9 S.Curry/T.Evans 200.00 400.00
10 B.Griffin/T.Hansbrough 50.00 120.00

2009-10 Rookies and Stars Team Leaders

COMPLETE SET (30) 20.00 40.00
RANDOM INSERTS IN PACKS
*BLACK: .75X TO 2X BASE HI
BLACK PRINT RUN 100 SER.#'d SETS
*GOLD: .5X TO 1.25X BASE HI
GOLD PRINT RUN 500 SER.#'d SETS
*HOLOFOIL: .6X TO 1.5X BASE HI
HOLO PRINT RUN 250 SER.#'d SETS
1 Atlanta Hawks .75 2.00
2 Boston Celtics 1.25 3.00
3 Charlotte Bobcats .60 1.50
4 Chicago Bulls 1.25 3.00
5 Cleveland Cavaliers 3.00 8.00
6 Dallas Mavericks 1.00 2.50
7 Denver Nuggets 1.00 2.50
8 Detroit Pistons .60 1.50
9 Golden State Warriors .75 2.00
10 Houston Rockets 1.00 2.50
11 Indiana Pacers .60 1.50
12 Los Angeles Clippers .60 1.50
13 Los Angeles Lakers 3.00 8.00
14 Memphis Grizzlies .75 2.00
15 Miami Heat 1.25 3.00
16 Milwaukee Bucks .60 1.50
17 Minnesota Timberwolves .60 1.50
18 New Jersey Nets .60 1.50
19 New Orleans Hornets 1.00 2.50
20 New York Knicks .75 2.00
21 Oklahoma City Thunder 2.00 5.00
22 Orlando Magic .60 1.50
23 Philadelphia 76ers .60 1.50
24 Phoenix Suns 1.50 4.00
25 Portland Trail Blazers .75 2.00
26 Sacramento Kings .60 1.50
27 San Antonio Spurs 1.25 3.00
28 Toronto Raptors .75 2.00
29 Utah Jazz .60 1.50
30 Washington Wizards .60 1.50

2010-11 Rookies and Stars

COMP.SET w/o RCs (115) 12.50 30.00
AU RC PRINT RUNS LISTED IN CHECKLIST
ASTERISK CARDS INSERTED IN SEASON UPDATE
EXCH EXPIRATION 5/10/12
1 Ray Allen .40 1.00
2 Paul Pierce .40 1.00
3 Rajon Rondo .40 1.00
4 Kevin Garnett .60 1.50
5 Brook Lopez .30 .75
6 Devin Harris .25 .60
7 Troy Murphy .25 .60
8 Amare Stoudemire .30 .75
9 Anthony Randolph .25 .60
10 Danilo Gallinari .30 .75
11 Andre Iguodala .30 .75
12 Elton Brand .40 1.00
13 Thaddeus Young .25 .60
14 Andrea Bargnani .30 .75
15 Leandro Barbosa .30 .75
16 Jose Calderon .25 .60
17 Carlos Boozer .30 .75
18 Derrick Rose .50 1.25
19 Joakim Noah .30 .75
20 Luol Deng .30 .75
21 Antawn Jamison .30 .75
22 Mo Williams .30 .75
23 Daniel Gibson .30 .75
24 Ben Gordon .30 .75
25 Richard Hamilton .30 .75
26 Tayshaun Prince .30 .75
27 Danny Granger .30 .75
28 Tyler Hansbrough .30 .75
29 Mike Dunleavy .25 .60
30 Andrew Bogut .30 .75
31 Brandon Jennings .25 .60
32 John Salmons .30 .75
33 Joe Johnson .30 .75
34 Josh Smith .30 .75
35 Al Horford .30 .75
36 Jamal Crawford .40 1.00
37 Gerald Henderson .25 .60
38 Stephen Jackson .30 .75
39 Gerald Wallace .30 .75
40 LeBron James 2.00 5.00
41 Dwyane Wade .60 1.50
42 Chris Bosh .40 1.00
43 Dwight Howard .30 .75
44 Vince Carter .50 1.25
45 J.J. Redick .40 1.00
46 Josh Howard .30 .75
47 Al Thornton .25 .60
48 Gilbert Arenas .30 .75
49 Kirk Hinrich .30 .75
50 Dirk Nowitzki .50 1.25
51 Jason Kidd .40 1.00
52 Shawn Marion .30 .75
53 Caron Butler .30 .75
54 Kevin Martin .30 .75
55 Shane Battier .30 .75
56 Luis Scola .30 .75
57 Yao Ming .50 1.25
58 Marc Gasol .40 1.00
59 Rudy Gay .40 1.00
60 Zach Randolph .30 .75
61 Chris Paul .50 1.25
62 Emeka Okafor .30 .75
63 David West .30 .75
64 Tim Duncan .60 1.50
65 Tony Parker .40 1.00
66 Richard Jefferson .30 .75
67 Carmelo Anthony .50 1.25
68 Chauncey Billups .40 1.00
69 Chris Andersen .30 .75
70 Nene .30 .75
71 Kevin Love .40 1.00
72 Michael Beasley .25 .60
73 Jonny Flynn .25 .60
74 Brandon Roy .40 1.00
75 Rudy Fernandez .25 .60
76 Greg Oden .30 .75
77 Kevin Durant 1.00 2.50
78 Russell Westbrook 1.00 2.50
79 Jeff Green .30 .75
80 Deron Williams .30 .75
81 Al Jefferson .30 .75
82 Andrei Kirilenko .30 .75
83 Paul Millsap .30 .75
84 David Lee .25 .60
85 Monta Ellis .30 .75
86 Stephen Curry 4.00 10.00
87 Eric Gordon .30 .75
88 Chris Kaman .30 .75
89 Baron Davis .30 .75
90 Kobe Bryant 1.50 4.00
91 Pau Gasol .40 1.00
92 Lamar Odom .30 .75
93 Ron Artest .40 1.00
94 Steve Nash .40 1.00
95 Hedo Turkoglu .30 .75
96 Channing Frye .30 .75
97 Grant Hill .50 1.25
98 Tyreke Evans .25 .60
99 Samuel Dalembert .25 .60
100 Carl Landry .25 .60
101 Rolando Blackman .30 .75
102 Joe Dumars .40 1.00
103 Wayne Embry .25 .60
104 Walt Frazier .40 1.00
105 Gail Goodrich .30 .75
106 John Havlicek .50 1.25
107 Rod Hundley .40 1.00
108 Phil Jackson .50 1.25
109 K.C. Jones .40 1.00
110 Clyde Lovellette .40 1.00
111 Jerry Lucas .40 1.00
112 Nate McMillan .40 1.00
113 Willis Reed .40 1.00
114 Paul Silas .40 1.00
115 Jerry West .50 1.25
116 Armon Johnson RC .50 1.25
117 Sherron Collins RC .50 1.25
118 Terrico White RC .50 1.25
119 Darington Hobson RC .50 1.25
120 Landry Fields RC .60 1.50
121 Tony Gaffney RC .50 1.25
122 Ben Uzoh RC .50 1.25
123 Ishmael Smith RC .75 2.00
124 Tweety Carter RC .50 1.25
125 Tiago Splitter RC .75 2.00
126 Solomon Alabi RC .50 1.25
127 Magnum Rolle RC .50 1.25
128 Pape Sy RC .50 1.25
129 Jeremy Lin RC 3.00 8.00
130 Derrick Caracter RC .50 1.25
131 J.Crawford AU/443 RC 3.00 8.00
132 Luke Harangody AU/460 RC 2.50 6.00
133 Avery Bradley AU/449 RC 5.00 12.00
134 Kevin Seraphin AU/499 RC 2.50 6.00
135 Dominique Jones AU/453 RC 2.50 6.00
136 Greg Monroe AU/454 RC 5.00 12.00
137 Ekpe Udoh AU/457 RC 2.50 6.00
138 P.Patterson AU/455 RC 3.00 8.00
139 L.Stephenson AU/457 RC 4.00 10.00
140 Paul George AU/455 RC 30.00 80.00
141 Eric Bledsoe AU/499 RC 5.00 12.00
142 Willie Warren AU/456 RC 2.50 6.00
143 Al-Farouq Aminu AU/499 RC 4.00 10.00
144 Devin Ebanks AU/455 RC 2.50 6.00
145 Xavier Henry AU/455 RC 2.50 6.00
146 Greivis Vasquez AU/455 RC 3.00 8.00
147 Dexter Pittman AU/455 RC 2.50 6.00
148 Da'Sean Butler AU/455 RC 4.00 10.00
149 Keith Gallon AU/455 RC 2.50 6.00
150 Larry Sanders AU/455 RC 2.50 6.00
151 Lazar Hayward AU/455 RC 2.50 6.00
152 Wes.Johnson AU/452 RC 2.50 6.00
153 Derrick Favors AU/458 RC 5.00 12.00
154 Damion James AU/454 RC 2.50 6.00
155 Craig Brackins AU/455 RC 2.50 6.00
156 Q.Pondexter AU/461 RC 2.50 6.00
157 Andy Rautins AU/499 RC 2.50 6.00
158 Cole Aldrich AU/450 RC 3.00 8.00
159 Daniel Orton AU/449 RC 2.50 6.00
160 Evan Turner AU/455 RC 3.00 8.00
161 Gani Lawal AU/457 RC 2.50 6.00
162 Elliot Williams AU/461 RC 2.50 6.00
163 Luke Babbitt AU/454 RC 3.00 8.00
164 D.Cousins AU/454 RC 20.00 50.00
165 H. Whiteside AU/458 RC 8.00 20.00
166 J.Anderson AU/459 RC 2.50 6.00
167 Ed Davis AU/455 RC 2.50 6.00
168 G.Hayward AU/455 RC 6.00 15.00
169 Trevor Booker AU/456 RC 3.00 8.00
170 John Wall AU/454 RC 25.00 60.00
171 Landry Fields AU/499* 3.00 8.00
172 Gary Neal AU/499 RC* 4.00 10.00
173 Omer Asik AU/499 RC* 5.00 12.00
174 Semih Erden AU/411 RC* 2.50 6.00
175 Gary Forbes AU/499 RC* 2.50 6.00

2010-11 Rookies and Stars Gold

*GOLD STARS: 1X TO 2.5X BASE HI
*GOLD 116-130: .6X TO 1.5X BASE HI
*GOLD 131-175: .75X TO 2X BASE HI
GOLD 1-130 PRINT RUN 499 SER.#'d SETS
GOLD 131-175 PRINT RUN 25 SER.#'d SETS
ASTERISK CARDS INSERTED IN SEASON UPDATE

2010-11 Rookies and Stars Gold Holofoil

*HOLO STARS: 2X TO 5X BASE HI
*HOLO RCs: 1.25X TO 3X BASE HI
STATED PRINT RUN 199 SER.#'d SETS

2010-11 Rookies and Stars Gold Materials

STATED PRINT RUN 25 TO 299 SER.#'d SETS
1 Ray Allen/50 3.00 8.00
2 Paul Pierce/299 3.00 8.00
3 Rajon Rondo/299 3.00 8.00
4 Kevin Garnett/50 5.00 12.00
6 Devin Harris/299 2.00 5.00
11 Andre Iguodala/299 2.50 6.00
12 Elton Brand/299 3.00 8.00
13 Thaddeus Young/299 2.00 5.00
14 Andrea Bargnani/299 2.50 6.00
15 Leandro Barbosa/299 2.50 6.00
18 Derrick Rose/50 4.00 10.00
19 Joakim Noah/299 2.50 6.00
20 Luol Deng/50 2.50 6.00
21 Antawn Jamison/299 2.50 6.00
24 Ben Gordon/299 2.50 6.00
26 Tayshaun Prince/299 2.50 6.00
28 Tyler Hansbrough/299 2.50 6.00
29 Mike Dunleavy/99 2.00 5.00
30 Andrew Bogut/100 2.50 6.00
31 Brandon Jennings/299 2.00 5.00
33 Joe Johnson/54 2.50 6.00
37 Gerald Henderson/299 2.00 5.00
38 Stephen Jackson/299 2.50 6.00
39 Gerald Wallace/99 2.50 6.00
41 Dwyane Wade/199 5.00 12.00
43 Dwight Howard/299 2.50 6.00
44 Vince Carter/299 4.00 10.00
45 J.J. Redick/299 3.00 8.00
46 Josh Howard/299 2.50 6.00
48 Gilbert Arenas/299 2.50 6.00
49 Kirk Hinrich/299 2.50 6.00
51 Jason Kidd/50 3.00 8.00
52 Shawn Marion/299 2.50 6.00
53 Caron Butler/299 2.50 6.00
54 Kevin Martin/299 2.50 6.00
55 Shane Battier/299 2.50 6.00
56 Luis Scola/199 2.50 6.00
58 Marc Gasol/99 3.00 8.00
59 Rudy Gay/99 3.00 8.00
61 Chris Paul/299 4.00 10.00
62 Emeka Okafor/299 2.50 6.00
63 David West/299 2.50 6.00
64 Tim Duncan/299 5.00 12.00
65 Tony Parker/299 3.00 8.00
66 Richard Jefferson/299 2.50 6.00
67 Carmelo Anthony/25 4.00 10.00
68 Chauncey Billups/299 3.00 8.00
70 Nene/299 2.50 6.00
71 Kevin Love/299 3.00 8.00
72 Michael Beasley/299 2.00 5.00
73 Jonny Flynn/299 2.00 5.00
74 Brandon Roy/299 3.00 8.00
75 Rudy Fernandez/299 2.00 5.00
76 Greg Oden/299 2.50 6.00
78 Russell Westbrook/299 8.00 20.00
80 Deron Williams/299 2.50 6.00
81 Al Jefferson/299 2.50 6.00
82 Andrei Kirilenko/299 2.50 6.00
86 Stephen Curry/299 12.00 30.00
87 Eric Gordon/99 2.50 6.00
88 Chris Kaman/150 2.50 6.00
89 Baron Davis/100 2.50 6.00
91 Pau Gasol/299 3.00 8.00
92 Lamar Odom/299 2.50 6.00
93 Ron Artest/299 3.00 8.00
94 Steve Nash/299 3.00 8.00
95 Hedo Turkoglu/299 2.50 6.00
96 Channing Frye/299 2.50 6.00
99 Samuel Dalembert/299 2.00 5.00
101 Rolando Blackman/50 2.50 6.00
102 Joe Dumars/99 3.00 8.00
118 Terrico White/299 2.00 5.00
129 Jeremy Lin/299 12.00 30.00

2010-11 Rookies and Stars Dress for Success Materials

STATED PRINT RUN 15 TO 299 SER.#'d SETS
*PRIME: .75X TO 2X BASE HI
PRIME PRINT RUN 10 TO 49 SER.#'d SETS
1 John Wall/299 8.00 20.00
2 Andre Miller/299 2.50 6.00
3 Evan Turner/299 1.50 4.00
4 Wesley Johnson/299 1.25 3.00
5 Andris Biedrins/299 2.00 5.00
6 Derrick Favors/299 2.50 6.00
7 Ekpe Udoh/299 1.25 3.00
8 Emeka Okafor/299 2.50 6.00
9 Eric Gordon/99 2.50 6.00
10 Caron Butler/299 2.50 6.00
11 Gani Lawal/299 1.25 3.00
12 Gerald Henderson/299 2.00 5.00
13 Goran Dragic/199 2.50 6.00
14 Gordon Hayward/299 3.00 8.00
15 Greg Monroe/299 2.50 6.00
16 Greg Oden/299 2.50 6.00
17 Greivis Vasquez/299 1.50 4.00
18 Hassan Whiteside/299 4.00 10.00
19 J.J. Barea/299 4.00 10.00
20 J.J. Redick/299 3.00 8.00
21 J.R. Smith/299 2.50 6.00
22 James Anderson/299 1.25 3.00
23 Jeff Green/15 2.50 6.00
24 Dwight Howard/299 2.50 6.00
25 Jose Calderon/299 2.00 5.00
26 Lance Stephenson/299 2.00 5.00
27 Marcus Camby/299 2.00 5.00
28 Mike Dunleavy/99 2.00 5.00
29 DeMarcus Cousins/299 6.00 15.00
30 Joakim Noah/299 2.50 6.00
31 Xavier Henry/299 1.25 3.00
32 Nene/299 2.50 6.00
33 Al-Farouq Aminu/299 2.00 5.00
34 Larry Sanders/299 1.25 3.00
35 Paul George/299 6.00 15.00

2010-11 Rookies and Stars Dress for Success Materials Signatures

STATED PRINT RUN 5 TO 25 SER.#'d SETS
PRIME SIG.PRINT RUN 10 SER.#'d SETS
PRIME SIG.UNPRICED DUE TO SCARCITY
1 John Wall/25 50.00 100.00
2 Andre Miller/25 6.00 15.00
3 Evan Turner/25 15.00 40.00
4 Wesley Johnson/25 4.00 10.00
6 Derrick Favors/25 20.00 50.00
7 Ekpe Udoh/25 4.00 10.00
9 Eric Gordon/25 8.00 20.00
11 Gani Lawal/25 4.00 10.00
12 Gerald Henderson/25 6.00 15.00
13 Goran Dragic/25 15.00 40.00
14 Gordon Hayward/25 10.00 25.00
15 Greg Monroe/25 15.00 40.00
17 Greivis Vasquez/25 5.00 12.00
18 Hassan Whiteside/25 12.00 30.00
19 J.J. Barea/25 20.00 50.00
21 J.R. Smith/25 6.00 15.00
22 James Anderson/25 4.00 10.00
26 Lance Stephenson/25 6.00 15.00
27 Marcus Camby/25 6.00 15.00
28 Mike Dunleavy/25 6.00 15.00
29 DeMarcus Cousins/25 25.00 60.00
31 Xavier Henry/25 4.00 10.00
33 Al-Farouq Aminu/25 6.00 15.00
34 Larry Sanders/25 4.00 10.00
35 Paul George/25 75.00 150.00

2010-11 Rookies and Stars Freshman Orientation Double Materials

STATED PRINT RUN 399 SER.#'d SETS
*PRIME: 1X TO 2.5X BASE HI
PRIME: PRINT RUN 25 TO 49 SER.#'d SETS
1 John Wall 10.00 25.00
2 Evan Turner 1.50 4.00
3 Derrick Favors 2.50 6.00
4 Wesley Johnson 1.25 3.00
5 DeMarcus Cousins 6.00 15.00
6 Ekpe Udoh 1.25 3.00
7 Greg Monroe 2.50 6.00
8 Al-Farouq Aminu 2.00 5.00
9 Gordon Hayward 3.00 8.00
10 Paul George 6.00 15.00
11 Cole Aldrich 1.50 4.00
12 Xavier Henry 1.25 3.00
13 Patrick Patterson 1.50 4.00
14 Larry Sanders 1.25 3.00
15 Luke Babbitt 1.50 4.00
16 Eric Bledsoe 2.50 6.00
17 Avery Bradley 2.50 6.00
18 James Anderson 1.25 3.00
19 Craig Brackins 1.25 3.00
20 Elliot Williams 1.25 3.00
21 Trevor Booker 1.50 4.00
22 Damion James 1.25 3.00
23 Dominique Jones 1.25 3.00
24 Quincy Pondexter 1.25 3.00
25 Jordan Crawford 1.50 4.00
26 Greivis Vasquez 1.50 4.00
27 Daniel Orton 1.25 3.00
28 Lazar Hayward 1.25 3.00
29 Dexter Pittman 1.25 3.00
30 Hassan Whiteside 4.00 10.00
31 Lance Stephenson 2.00 5.00
32 Da'Sean Butler 2.00 5.00
33 Devin Ebanks 1.25 3.00
34 Gani Lawal 1.25 3.00
35 Luke Harangody 1.25 3.00

2010-11 Rookies and Stars Freshman Orientation Double Materials Signatures

STATED PRINT RUN 49 SER.#'d SETS
PRIME SIG.PRINT RUN 10 SER.#'d SETS
PRIME SIG.UNPRICED DUE TO SCARCITY
1 John Wall 50.00 125.00
2 Evan Turner 12.00 30.00
3 Derrick Favors 6.00 15.00
4 Wesley Johnson 3.00 8.00
5 DeMarcus Cousins 15.00 40.00
6 Ekpe Udoh 3.00 8.00
7 Greg Monroe 6.00 15.00
8 Al-Farouq Aminu 5.00 12.00
9 Gordon Hayward 8.00 20.00
10 Paul George 15.00 40.00
11 Cole Aldrich 4.00 10.00
12 Xavier Henry 6.00 15.00
13 Patrick Patterson 10.00 25.00
14 Larry Sanders 3.00 8.00
15 Luke Babbitt 6.00 15.00
16 Eric Bledsoe 6.00 15.00
17 Avery Bradley 6.00 15.00
18 James Anderson 3.00 8.00
19 Craig Brackins 3.00 8.00
20 Elliot Williams 3.00 8.00
21 Trevor Booker 4.00 10.00
22 Damion James 3.00 8.00
23 Dominique Jones 3.00 8.00
24 Quincy Pondexter 3.00 8.00
25 Jordan Crawford 4.00 10.00
26 Greivis Vasquez 4.00 10.00
27 Daniel Orton 3.00 8.00
28 Lazar Hayward EXCH 3.00 8.00
29 Dexter Pittman 3.00 8.00
30 Hassan Whiteside 10.00 25.00
31 Lance Stephenson 5.00 12.00
32 Da'Sean Butler 5.00 12.00
33 Devin Ebanks 10.00 25.00
34 Gani Lawal 3.00 8.00
35 Luke Harangody 3.00 8.00

2010-11 Rookies and Stars Game Garb Materials

STATED PRINT RUN 10 TO 49 SER.#'d SETS
1 Al Horford/49 5.00 12.00
2 Ben Gordon/49 5.00 12.00
3 Brook Lopez/49 5.00 12.00
4 Caron Butler/25 5.00 12.00
5 Chris Kaman/25 5.00 12.00
6 Danny Granger/15 5.00 12.00
7 Eric Gordon/25 5.00 12.00
8 Grant Hill/49 20.00 50.00
9 Luol Deng/15 5.00 12.00
11 Nene/49 5.00 12.00
12 Paul Pierce/49 6.00 15.00
13 Steve Nash/25 8.00 20.00
14 Tim Duncan/49 10.00 25.00
15 Vince Carter/49 8.00 20.00

2010-11 Rookies and Stars Game Garb Materials Signatures

STATED PRINT RUN 5 TO 49 SER.#'d SETS
SOME UNPRICED DUE TO SCARCITY
1 Al Horford/25 8.00 20.00
2 Ben Gordon/25 8.00 20.00
5 Chris Kaman/49 8.00 20.00
7 Eric Gordon/25 10.00 25.00

2010-11 Rookies and Stars Moments in Time

COMPLETE SET (15) 7.50 15.00
RANDOM INSERTS IN PACKS
*BLACK: .75X TO 2X BASE HI
BLACK PRINT RUN 99 SER.#'d SETS
*GOLD: .5X TO 1.25X BASE HI
GOLD PRINT RUN 499 SER.#'d SETS
*HOLO: .6X TO 1.5X BASE HI
HOLO PRINT RUN 199 SER.#'d SETS
1 Bob Cousy 1.25 3.00
2 Elgin Baylor .75 2.00
3 Jerry West 1.00 2.50
4 John Havlicek 1.00 2.50
5 George Gervin .75 2.00
6 Kareem Abdul-Jabbar 1.25 3.00
7 Larry Bird 2.00 5.00
8 Magic Johnson 2.00 5.00
9 92 USA Men's Olympic 2.50 6.00
10 A.C. Green .75 2.00
11 John Stockton 1.25 3.00
12 Karl Malone 1.00 2.50
13 LeBron James 4.00 10.00
14 Kobe Bryant 3.00 8.00
15 Tyreke Evans .50 1.25

2010-11 Rookies and Stars Prime Cuts

STATED PRINT RUN 25 TO 50 SER.#'d SETS
1 Allen Iverson/50 12.00 30.00
2 Alonzo Mourning/50 12.00 30.00
3 Andre Iguodala/50 8.00 20.00
4 Carmelo Anthony/50 12.00 30.00
5 Chris Paul/50 12.00 30.00
6 Clyde Drexler/50 12.00 30.00
7 Dirk Nowitzki/50 12.00 30.00
8 Dwight Howard/50 8.00 20.00
9 Dwyane Wade/25 15.00 40.00
10 Gary Payton/50 10.00 25.00
11 John Stockton/50 15.00 40.00
12 Kareem Abdul-Jabbar/50 15.00 40.00
13 Karl Malone/50 12.00 30.00
14 Magic Johnson/50 20.00 50.00
15 Vince Carter/50 12.00 30.00

2010-11 Rookies and Stars Retired NBA Team Patches Signatures

STATED PRINT RUN 54 TO 99 SER.#'d SETS
1 Bill Cartwright/99 15.00 40.00
2 Bob Dandridge/99 8.00 20.00
3 Chris Ford/99 10.00 25.00
4 Dennis Rodman/99 20.00 50.00
5 G.Muresan/99 EXCH 8.00 20.00
6 Kelly Tripucka/99 6.00 15.00
7 Kevin Johnson/99 EXCH 20.00 50.00
8 Maurice Cheeks/99 6.00 15.00
9 Dominique Wilkins/54 12.50 30.00
10 Xavier McDaniel/99 6.00 15.00

2010-11 Rookies and Stars Sharp Shooters

COMPLETE SET (15) 5.00 12.00
RANDOM INSERTS IN PACKS
*BLACK: .75X TO 2X BASE HI
BLACK: STATED PRINT RUN 99 SER.#'d SETS
*GOLD: .5X TO 1.25X BASE HI
GOLD: STATED PRINT RUN 499 SER.#'d SETS
*HOLO: .6X TO 1.5X BASE HI
HOLO STATED PRINT RUN 199 SER.#'d SETS
1 Dwight Howard .75 2.00
2 Kendrick Perkins .60 1.50
3 Nene .75 2.00
4 Marc Gasol 1.00 2.50
5 Andrew Bynum .60 1.50
6 Carlos Boozer .75 2.00
7 Amare Stoudemire .75 2.00
8 Al Horford .75 2.00
9 David Lee .60 1.50
10 Paul Millsap .75 2.00
11 Pau Gasol 1.00 2.50
12 Kevin Garnett 1.50 4.00
13 Chris Bosh 1.00 2.50
14 Tim Duncan 1.50 4.00
15 Rajon Rondo 1.00 2.50

2010-11 Rookies and Stars Sharp Shooters Materials

STATED PRINT RUN 99 SER.#'d SETS
*PRIME: .75X TO 2X BASE HI
PRIME PRINT RUN ONE TO 49 SER.#'d SETS
SOME PRIME UNPRICED DUE TO SCARCITY
1 Dwight Howard 2.50 6.00
3 Nene 2.50 6.00
4 Marc Gasol 3.00 8.00
5 Andrew Bynum 2.00 5.00
8 Al Horford 2.50 6.00
11 Pau Gasol 3.00 8.00
12 Kevin Garnett 5.00 12.00
14 Tim Duncan 5.00 12.00
15 Rajon Rondo 3.00 8.00

2010-11 Rookies and Stars Sharp Shooters Signatures

STATED PRINT RUN 10 TO 49 SER.#'d SETS
SOME UNPRICED DUE TO SCARCITY
4 Marc Gasol/25 12.00 30.00
5 Andrew Bynum/49 8.00 20.00
6 Carlos Boozer/49 6.00 15.00
7 Amare Stoudemire/15 25.00 60.00
8 Al Horford/49 6.00 15.00
9 David Lee/49 6.00 15.00
11 Pau Gasol/15 15.00 40.00
15 Rajon Rondo/15 25.00 60.00

2010-11 Rookies and Stars Signatures

STATED PRINT RUN 5 TO 49 SER.#'d SETS
SOME UNPRICED DUE TO SCARCITY
8 Amare Stoudemire/15 30.00 80.00
11 Andre Iguodala/25 4.00 10.00
14 Andrea Bargnani/49 6.00 15.00
28 Tyler Hansbrough/99 4.00 10.00
37 Gerald Henderson/149 4.00 10.00
46 Josh Howard/99 4.00 10.00
51 Jason Kidd/25 12.00 30.00
55 Shane Battier/49 4.00 10.00
62 Emeka Okafor/25 4.00 10.00
73 Jonny Flynn/199 4.00 10.00
86 Stephen Curry/49 75.00 150.00
89 Baron Davis/25 6.00 15.00
90 Kobe Bryant/99 50.00 120.00
93 Ron Artest/25 10.00 25.00
98 Tyreke Evans/99 10.00 25.00
100 Carl Landry/99 4.00 10.00
105 Gail Goodrich/49 6.00 15.00
106 John Havlicek/25 15.00 40.00
116 Armon Johnson/99 2.50 6.00
118 Terrico White/299 2.50 6.00
120 Landry Fields/349 3.00 8.00
126 Solomon Alabi/350 2.50 6.00
129 Jeremy Lin/499 30.00 80.00

2010-11 Rookies and Stars Stardom

COMPLETE SET (15) 10.00 20.00
RANDOM INSERTS IN PACKS
*BLACK: .75X TO 2X BASE HI
BLACK STATED PRINT RUN 99 SER.#'d SETS
*GOLD: .5X TO 1.25X BASE HI
GOLD STATED PRINT RUN 499 SER.#'d SETS
*HOLO: .6X TO 1.5X BASE HI
HOLO STATED PRINT RUN 199 SER.#'d SETS
1 Kobe Bryant 3.00 8.00
2 LeBron James 4.00 10.00
3 Dirk Nowitzki 1.00 2.50
4 Dwight Howard .60 1.50
5 Paul Pierce .75 2.00
6 Chris Paul 1.00 2.50
7 Chris Bosh .75 2.00
8 Kevin Durant 2.00 5.00
9 Tyreke Evans .50 1.25
10 Steve Nash .75 2.00
11 Deron Williams .60 1.50
12 Derrick Rose 1.00 2.50
13 Dwyane Wade 1.25 3.00
14 Brandon Jennings .50 1.25
15 Carlos Boozer .60 1.50

2010-11 Rookies and Stars Stardom Materials

STATED PRINT RUN 50 TO 99 SER.#'d SETS
1 Kobe Bryant/99 8.00 20.00
3 Dirk Nowitzki/99 4.00 10.00
4 Dwight Howard/99 2.50 6.00
5 Paul Pierce/99 3.00 8.00
6 Chris Paul/99 4.00 10.00
10 Steve Nash/99 3.00 8.00
11 Deron Williams/99 2.50 6.00
12 Derrick Rose/50 4.00 10.00
13 Dwyane Wade/99 5.00 12.00
14 Brandon Jennings/99 2.00 5.00

2010-11 Rookies and Stars Stardom Signatures

STATED PRINT RUN 49 SER.#'d SETS
1 Kobe Bryant 100.00 200.00
9 Tyreke Evans 12.50 30.00
14 Brandon Jennings 10.00 25.00

2010-11 Rookies and Stars Statistical Standouts Materials

STATED PRINT RUN 25 TO 199 SER.#'d SETS
*PRIME: .75X TO 2X BASE HI
PRIME PRINT RUN 5 TO 49 SER.#'d SETS
SOME PRIME UNPRICED DUE TO SCARCITY
2 Carmelo Anthony/25 4.00 10.00
3 Kobe Bryant/199 8.00 20.00
4 Dirk Nowitzki/199 4.00 10.00
6 Joe Johnson/199 2.50 6.00
7 Steve Nash/199 3.00 8.00
8 Deron Williams/199 2.50 6.00
9 Rajon Rondo/199 3.00 8.00
10 Jason Kidd/149 3.00 8.00
11 Dwight Howard/199 2.50 6.00
12 Marcus Camby/199 2.00 5.00
13 Andrew Bogut/100 2.50 6.00
14 Josh Smith/25 2.50 6.00
15 Chris Andersen/199 2.50 6.00

2010-11 Rookies and Stars Statistical Standouts Materials Signatures

STATED PRINT RUN 10 TO 25 SER.#'d SETS
UNPRICED PRIME PRINT RUN 5 TO 10 SETS
3 Kobe Bryant/25 100.00 200.00
6 Joe Johnson/25 10.00 25.00
8 Deron Williams/25 12.00 30.00
9 Rajon Rondo/25 20.00 50.00
10 Jason Kidd/25 20.00 50.00
12 Marcus Camby/25 10.00 25.00
15 Chris Andersen/25 20.00 50.00

2010-11 Rookies and Stars Studio Combo Rookies

COMPLETE SET (10) 7.50 15.00
RANDOM INSERTS IN PACKS
*BLACK: .75X TO 2X BASE HI
BLACK PRINT RUN 99 SER.#'d SETS
*GOLD: .5X TO 1.25X BASE HI
GOLD PRINT RUN 499 SER.#'d SETS
*HOLO: .6X TO 1.5X BASE HI
HOLO PRINT RUN 199 SER.#'d SETS
1 E.Turner/J.Wall 3.00 8.00
2 W.Johnson/D.Favors 1.50 4.00
3 E.Udoh/D.Cousins 1.50 4.00
4 G.Monroe/A.Aminu 1.00 2.50
5 G.Hayward/P.George 1.50 4.00
6 J.Wall/D.Cousins 4.00 10.00
7 C.Aldrich/X.Henry 1.00 2.50
8 E.Bledsoe/P.Patterson 1.50 4.00
9 D.Ebanks/D.Butler 1.00 2.50
10 J.Wall/D.Orton 2.50 6.00

2010-11 Rookies and Stars Studio Combo Rookies Materials

STATED PRINT RUN 399 SER.#'d SETS
*PRIME: .75X TO 2X BASE HI
PRIME PRINT RUN 49 SER.#'d SETS
1 E.Turner/J.Wall 8.00 20.00
2 W.Johnson/D.Favors 6.00 15.00
3 E.Udoh/D.Cousins 4.00 10.00
4 G.Monroe/A.Aminu 3.00 8.00
5 G.Hayward/P.George 4.00 10.00
6 J.Wall/D.Cousins 10.00 25.00
7 C.Aldrich/X.Henry 3.00 8.00
8 E.Bledsoe/P.Patterson 5.00 12.00
9 D.Ebanks/D.Butler 3.00 8.00
10 J.Wall/D.Orton 8.00 20.00

2010-11 Rookies and Stars Studio Combo Rookies Signatures

STATED PRINT RUN 49 SER.#'d SETS
1 E.Turner/J.Wall 30.00 60.00
2 W.Johnson/D.Favors 15.00 40.00
3 E.Udoh/D.Cousins 10.00 25.00
4 G.Monroe/A.Aminu 10.00 25.00
5 G.Hayward/P.George 20.00 50.00
6 J.Wall/D.Cousins 40.00 100.00
7 C.Aldrich/X.Henry 10.00 25.00
8 E.Bledsoe/P.Patterson 10.00 25.00
9 D.Ebanks/D.Butler 10.00 25.00
10 J.Wall/D.Orton 30.00 60.00

2010-11 Rookies and Stars Superstars

COMPLETE SET (15) 7.50 15.00
RANDOM INSERTS IN PACKS
*BLACK: .75X TO 2X BASE HI
BLACK STATED PRINT RUN 99 SER.#'d SETS
*GOLD: .5X TO 1.25X BASE HI
GOLD STATED PRINT RUN 499 SER.#'d SETS
*HOLO: .6X TO 1.5X BASE HI
HOLO STATED PRINT RUN 199 SER.#'d SETS
1 Kobe Bryant 3.00 8.00
2 LeBron James 4.00 10.00
3 Dwight Howard .60 1.50
4 Dwyane Wade 1.25 3.00
5 Kevin Durant 2.00 5.00
6 Steve Nash .75 2.00
7 Dirk Nowitzki 1.00 2.50
8 Andrew Bogut .60 1.50
9 Deron Williams .60 1.50
10 Carmelo Anthony 1.00 2.50
11 Rajon Rondo .75 2.00
12 Brandon Roy .75 2.00
13 Tim Duncan 1.25 3.00
14 Josh Smith .60 1.50
15 Chris Bosh .75 2.00

2010-11 Rookies and Stars Superstars Materials

STATED PRINT RUN 25 TO 299 SER.#'d SETS
*PRIME: .75X TO 2X BASE HI
PRIME STATED PRINT RUN 5 TO 49 SETS
SOME PRIME UNPRICED DUE TO SCARCITY
1 Kobe Bryant/299 8.00 20.00
3 Dwight Howard/299 2.50 6.00
4 Dwyane Wade/299 5.00 12.00
6 Steve Nash/299 3.00 8.00
7 Dirk Nowitzki/299 4.00 10.00
8 Andrew Bogut/100 2.50 6.00
9 Deron Williams/299 2.50 6.00
10 Carmelo Anthony/25 4.00 10.00
11 Rajon Rondo/299 3.00 8.00
12 Brandon Roy/299 3.00 8.00
13 Tim Duncan/299 5.00 12.00
14 Josh Smith/25 2.50 6.00

2010-11 Rookies and Stars Superstars Signatures

STATED PRINT RUN 5 TO 49 SER.#'d SETS
SOME UNPRICED DUE TO SCARCITY
1 Kobe Bryant/49 100.00 200.00
9 Deron Williams/25 12.50 30.00
11 Rajon Rondo/15 25.00 60.00
12 Brandon Roy/49 8.00 20.00

2010-11 Rookies and Stars Team Leaders

COMPLETE SET (30) 12.50 25.00
RANDOM INSERTS IN PACKS
*BLACK: .75X TO 2X BASE HI
BLACK STATED PRINT RUN 99 SER.#'d SETS
*GOLD: .5X TO 1.25X BASE HI
GOLD STATED PRINT RUN 499 SER.#'d SETS
*HOLO: .6X TO 1.5X BASE HI
HOLO STATED PRINT RUN 199 SER.#'d SETS
1 Horford/Johnson/Smith .60 1.50
2 Garnett/Pierce/Rondo 1.25 3.00
3 Wallace/Jackson/Diaw .60 1.50
4 Boozer/Deng /Rose 1.00 2.50
5 Varejao/Williams/Jamison .60 1.50
6 Butler/Kidd/Nowitzki 1.00 2.50
7 Anthony/Billups/Nene 1.00 2.50
8 Hamilton/Prince/Gordon .60 1.50
9 Ellis/Lee/Curry 3.00 8.00
10 Martin/Brooks/Scola .60 1.50
11 Dunleavy/Ford/Granger .60 1.50
12 Davis/Gordon/Kaman .60 1.50
13 Gasol/Odom/Bryant 3.00 8.00
14 Gasol/Mayo/Randolph .75 2.00
15 Wade/James/Bosh 4.00 10.00
16 Jennings/Salmons/Bogut .60 1.50
17 Love/Beasley/Webster .75 2.00
18 Murphy/Harris/Lopez .60 1.50
19 Paul/West/Ariza 1.00 2.50
20 Gallinari/Stoud/Randolph .60 1.50
21 Durant/Green/Westbrook 2.00 5.00
22 Howard/Lewis/Carter 1.00 2.50
23 Iguodala/Young/Brand .75 2.00
24 Nash/Richardson/Frye .75 2.00
25 Roy/Aldridge/Miller .75 2.00
26 Dalembert/Landry/Evans .50 1.25
27 Duncan/Ginobili/Parker 1.25 3.00
28 Bargnani/Calderon/Barbosa .60 1.50
29 Jefferson/Kirilenko/Williams .60 1.50
30 Howard/Thornton/Arenas .60 1.50

2010-11 Rookies and Stars Kids Foot Locker

This promotion was offered in late 2010 through early 2011 at participating Kids Foot Locker stores. With every $20 purchase, you received one six-card pack.

COMPLETE SET (6) 6.00 15.00
1 Kobe Bryant 2.50 6.00
2 Wesley Johnson .40 1.00
3 Rajon Rondo .60 1.50
4 Derrick Rose .75 2.00
5 Evan Turner .50 1.25
6 John Wall 3.00 8.00

2009-10 Rookies and Stars Longevity

COMP.SET w/o SPs (115) 15.00 30.00
1 Josh Smith .30 .75
2 Joe Johnson .30 .75
3 Mike Bibby .30 .75
4 Paul Pierce .40 1.00
5 Ray Allen .40 1.00
6 Rajon Rondo .40 1.00
7 Kevin Garnett .60 1.50
8 Gerald Wallace .30 .75
9 Boris Diaw .30 .75
10 Raja Bell .30 .75
11 Derrick Rose .60 1.50
12 John Salmons .30 .75
13 Kirk Hinrich .30 .75
14 LeBron James 1.50 4.00
15 Shaquille O'Neal .75 2.00
16 Mo Williams .30 .75
17 Dirk Nowitzki .50 1.25
18 Josh Howard .30 .75
19 Jason Kidd .40 1.00
20 Jason Terry .30 .75
21 Shawn Marion .30 .75
22 Carmelo Anthony .50 1.25
23 Chauncey Billups .40 1.00
24 J.R. Smith .30 .75
25 Richard Hamilton .30 .75
26 Tayshaun Prince .30 .75
27 Allen Iverson .50 1.25
28 Stephen Jackson .30 .75
29 Corey Maggette .30 .75
30 Monta Ellis .30 .75
31 Yao Ming .50 1.25
32 Tracy McGrady .40 1.00
33 Trevor Ariza .25 .60
34 Danny Granger .30 .75
35 Mike Dunleavy .25 .60
36 T.J. Ford .25 .60
37 Al Thornton .30 .75
38 Eric Gordon .30 .75
39 Kobe Bryant 1.50 4.00
40 Pau Gasol .40 1.00
41 Ron Artest .40 1.00
42 Andrew Bynum .25 .60
43 Rudy Gay .40 1.00
44 O.J. Mayo .25 .60
45 Mike Conley Jr. .30 .75
46 Zach Randolph .30 .75
47 Dwyane Wade .60 1.50
48 Michael Beasley .25 .60
49 Jermaine O'Neal .30 .75
50 Udonis Haslem .25 .60
51 Michael Redd .30 .75
52 Ramon Sessions .30 .75
53 Andrew Bogut .30 .75
54 Al Jefferson .30 .75
55 Ryan Gomes .25 .60
56 Kevin Love .40 1.00
57 Devin Harris .25 .60
58 Brook Lopez .30 .75
59 Rafer Alston .25 .60
60 Chris Paul .50 1.25
61 David West .30 .75
62 Peja Stojakovic .40 1.00
63 Al Harrington .30 .75
64 Nate Robinson .25 .60
65 Wilson Chandler .30 .75
66 Kevin Durant 1.00 2.50
67 Jeff Green .30 .75
68 Russell Westbrook 1.00 2.50
69 Dwight Howard .30 .75
70 Rashard Lewis .30 .75
71 Jameer Nelson .25 .60
72 Vince Carter .50 1.25
73 Andre Iguodala .30 .75
74 Elton Brand .40 1.00
75 Thaddeus Young .25 .60
76 Amare Stoudemire .30 .75
77 Steve Nash .40 1.00
78 Leandro Barbosa .30 .75
79 Channing Frye .30 .75
80 Brandon Roy .40 1.00
81 LaMarcus Aldridge .40 1.00
82 Greg Oden .30 .75
83 Kevin Martin .30 .75
84 Andres Nocioni .25 .60
85 Spencer Hawes .25 .60
86 Tony Parker .40 1.00
87 Tim Duncan .60 1.50
88 Manu Ginobili .40 1.00
89 Richard Jefferson .30 .75
90 Chris Bosh .40 1.00
91 Hedo Turkoglu .30 .75
92 Andrea Bargnani .30 .75
93 Deron Williams .30 .75
94 Carlos Boozer .30 .75
95 Andrei Kirilenko .30 .75
96 Ronnie Brewer .30 .75
97 Antawn Jamison .30 .75

98 Gilbert Arenas .30 .75
99 Caron Butler .30 .75
100 Randy Foye .25 .60
101 Kareem Abdul-Jabbar .60 1.50
102 Elvin Hayes .40 1.00
103 Karl Malone .50 1.25
104 Arnie Risen .40 1.00
105 Jalen Rose .40 1.00
106 Dave DeBusschere .40 1.00
107 Artis Gilmore .30 .75
108 Nate Archibald .30 .75
109 Mark Eaton .25 .60
110 Darryl Dawkins .25 .60
111 Spencer Haywood .25 .60
112 Bill Cartwright .30 .75
113 Moses Malone .40 1.00
114 Magic Johnson 1.00 2.50
115 Sleepy Floyd .25 .60
116 Dante Cunningham RC .40 1.00
117 Jon Brockman RC .40 1.00
118 Jonas Jerebko RC .60 1.50
119 Derrick Brown RC .40 1.00
120 Dionte Christmas RC .40 1.00
121 Marcus Thornton RC .50 1.25
122 Danny Green RC .75 2.00
123 Goran Suton RC .40 1.00
124 Jack McClinton RC .40 1.00
125 A.J. Price RC .40 1.00
126 Serge Ibaka RC .60 1.50
127 DeMar DeRozan RC 1.50 4.00
128 Chris Hunter RC .40 1.00
129 Lester Hudson RC .40 1.00
130 David Andersen RC .40 1.00

2009-10 Rookies and Stars Longevity Ruby

*1-130 RUBY: 2X TO 5X BASE HI
1-130 RUBY PRINT RUN 250 SER.#'d SETS
131-164 PRINT RUN 43 TO 49 SER.#'d SETS
131 Blake Griffin AU 100.00 250.00
132 Hasheem Thabeet AU 5.00 12.00
133 James Harden AU 60.00 150.00
134 Tyreke Evans AU 6.00 15.00
135 Jonny Flynn AU 5.00 12.00
136 Stephen Curry AU 800.00 1200.00
137 Jordan Hill AU 6.00 15.00
139 Brandon Jennings AU 8.00 20.00
140 Terrence Williams AU 5.00 12.00
141 Gerald Henderson AU 6.00 15.00
142 Tyler Hansbrough AU 6.00 15.00
143 Earl Clark AU 6.00 15.00
144 Austin Daye AU 5.00 12.00
145 James Johnson AU/43 6.00 15.00
146 Jrue Holiday AU 10.00 25.00
147 Ty Lawson AU 5.00 12.00
148 Jeff Teague AU 8.00 20.00
149 Eric Maynor AU 5.00 12.00
150 Darren Collison AU 8.00 20.00
151 Omri Casspi AU 6.00 15.00
152 B.J. Mullens AU 5.00 12.00
153 Rodrigue Beaubois AU 5.00 12.00
154 Taj Gibson AU 8.00 20.00
155 DeMarre Carroll AU 6.00 15.00
156 Wayne Ellington AU 8.00 20.00
157 Toney Douglas AU 5.00 12.00
158 Jermaine Taylor AU 5.00 12.00
159 Jeff Pendergraph AU 5.00 12.00
160 DaJuan Summers AU 5.00 12.00
161 Sam Young AU 5.00 12.00
162 DeJuan Blair AU/48 6.00 15.00
163 Chase Budinger AU 6.00 15.00
164 Jodie Meeks AU 8.00 20.00
165 Taylor Griffin AU 5.00 12.00

2009-10 Rookies and Stars Longevity Dress for Success Materials Jerseys

STATED PRINT RUN 299 SER.#'d SETS
1 Blake Griffin 8.00 20.00
2 Hasheem Thabeet 1.25 3.00
3 James Harden 10.00 25.00
4 Tyreke Evans 1.50 4.00
5 Jonny Flynn 1.25 3.00
6 Stephen Curry 25.00 60.00
7 Jordan Hill 1.50 4.00
8 DeMar DeRozan 5.00 12.00
9 Brandon Jennings 2.00 5.00
10 Terrence Williams 1.25 3.00
11 Gerald Henderson 1.50 4.00
12 Tyler Hansbrough 1.50 4.00
13 Earl Clark 1.50 4.00
14 Austin Daye 1.25 3.00
15 James Johnson 1.50 4.00
16 Jrue Holiday 2.50 6.00
17 Ty Lawson 2.00 5.00
18 Jeff Teague 2.00 5.00
19 Eric Maynor 1.25 3.00
20 Darren Collison 2.00 5.00
21 Omri Casspi 1.50 4.00
22 B.J. Mullens 1.25 3.00
23 Rodrigue Beaubois 1.25 3.00
24 Taj Gibson 2.00 5.00
25 DeMarre Carroll 1.50 4.00
26 Wayne Ellington 2.00 5.00
27 Toney Douglas 1.25 3.00
28 Jermaine Taylor 1.25 3.00
29 Jeff Pendergraph 1.25 3.00
30 DaJuan Summers 1.25 3.00
31 Sam Young 1.25 3.00
32 DeJuan Blair 1.50 4.00
33 Chase Budinger 1.50 4.00
34 Jodie Meeks 2.00 5.00
35 Taylor Griffin 1.25 3.00

2009-10 Rookies and Stars Longevity Freshman Orientation Materials Jerseys

STATED PRINT RUN 299 SER.#'d SETS
1 Blake Griffin 8.00 20.00
2 Hasheem Thabeet 1.25 3.00
3 James Harden 10.00 25.00
4 Tyreke Evans 1.50 4.00
5 Jonny Flynn 1.25 3.00
6 Stephen Curry 40.00 100.00
7 Jordan Hill 1.50 4.00
8 DeMar DeRozan 5.00 12.00
9 Brandon Jennings 2.00 5.00
10 Terrence Williams 1.25 3.00
11 Gerald Henderson 1.50 4.00
12 Tyler Hansbrough 1.50 4.00
13 Earl Clark 1.50 4.00
14 Austin Daye 1.25 3.00
15 James Johnson 1.50 4.00
16 Jrue Holiday 2.50 6.00
17 Ty Lawson 2.00 5.00
18 Jeff Teague 2.00 5.00
19 Eric Maynor 1.25 3.00
20 Darren Collison 2.00 5.00
21 Omri Casspi 1.50 4.00
22 B.J. Mullens 1.25 3.00
23 Rodrigue Beaubois 1.25 3.00
24 Taj Gibson 2.00 5.00
25 DeMarre Carroll 1.50 4.00
26 Wayne Ellington 2.00 5.00
27 Toney Douglas 1.25 3.00
28 Jermaine Taylor 1.25 3.00
29 Jeff Pendergraph 1.25 3.00
30 DaJuan Summers 1.25 3.00
31 Sam Young 1.25 3.00
32 DeJuan Blair 1.50 4.00
33 Chase Budinger 1.50 4.00
34 Jodie Meeks 2.00 5.00
35 Taylor Griffin 1.25 3.00

2009-10 Rookies and Stars Longevity Materials Ruby

STATED PRINT RUN 99 TO 250 SER.#'d SETS
*SAPPHIRE: .6X TO 1.5X BASE HI
SAPPHIRE PRINT RUN 25 SER.#'d SETS
1 Josh Smith/250 2.50 6.00
3 Mike Bibby/250 2.50 6.00
13 Kirk Hinrich/250 2.50 6.00
14 LeBron James/250 8.00 20.00
17 Dirk Nowitzki/250 4.00 10.00
18 Josh Howard/250 2.50 6.00
19 Jason Kidd/250 3.00 8.00
20 Jason Terry/250 2.50 6.00
22 Carmelo Anthony/250 4.00 10.00
26 Tayshaun Prince/250 2.50 6.00
31 Yao Ming/250 4.00 10.00
32 Tracy McGrady/250 3.00 8.00
39 Kobe Bryant/99 10.00 25.00
40 Pau Gasol/250 3.00 8.00
42 Andrew Bynum/250 2.00 5.00
44 O.J. Mayo/250 2.00 5.00
45 Mike Conley Jr./250 2.50 6.00
47 Dwyane Wade/250 5.00 12.00
49 Jermaine O'Neal/150 2.50 6.00
50 Udonis Haslem/250 2.00 5.00
51 Michael Redd/250 2.50 6.00
53 Andrew Bogut/250 2.50 6.00
54 Al Jefferson/250 2.50 6.00
56 Kevin Love/250 3.00 8.00
57 Devin Harris/150 2.00 5.00
60 Chris Paul/250 4.00 10.00
62 Peja Stojakovic/250 3.00 8.00
63 Al Harrington/250 2.50 6.00
64 Nate Robinson/250 2.00 5.00
66 Kevin Durant/150 8.00 20.00
69 Dwight Howard/250 2.50 6.00
70 Rashard Lewis/250 2.50 6.00
73 Andre Iguodala/250 2.50 6.00
74 Elton Brand/250 3.00 8.00
75 Thaddeus Young/250 2.00 5.00
76 Amare Stoudemire/250 2.50 6.00
77 Steve Nash/150 3.00 8.00
80 Brandon Roy/250 3.00 8.00
81 LaMarcus Aldridge/250 3.00 8.00
82 Greg Oden/250 2.50 6.00
83 Kevin Martin/250 2.50 6.00
84 Andres Nocioni/250 2.00 5.00
86 Tony Parker/250 3.00 8.00
87 Tim Duncan/250 5.00 12.00
88 Manu Ginobili/250 3.00 8.00
90 Chris Bosh/250 3.00 8.00
92 Andrea Bargnani/250 2.50 6.00
93 Deron Williams/250 2.50 6.00
94 Carlos Boozer/250 2.50 6.00
95 Andrei Kirilenko/250 2.50 6.00
101 Kareem Abdul-Jabbar/250 5.00 12.00
102 Elvin Hayes/250 3.00 8.00
103 Karl Malone/250 4.00 10.00
113 Moses Malone/150 3.00 8.00
115 Sleepy Floyd/250 2.00 5.00
127 DeMar DeRozan/250 8.00 20.00

2009-10 Rookies and Stars Longevity Signatures

STATED PRINT RUN 10 TO 999 SER.#'d SETS
SOME UNPRICED DUE TO SCARCITY
3 Mike Bibby/25 6.00 15.00
19 Jason Kidd/25 10.00 25.00
39 Kobe Bryant/25 100.00 225.00
42 Andrew Bynum/100 8.00 20.00
56 Kevin Love/25 15.00 40.00
102 Elvin Hayes/25 10.00 25.00
104 Arnie Risen/25 6.00 15.00
107 Artis Gilmore/50 6.00 15.00
108 Nate Archibald/25 15.00 30.00
111 Spencer Haywood/25 8.00 20.00
117 Jon Brockman/874 2.00 5.00
121 Marcus Thornton/374 2.50 6.00
122 Danny Green/874 4.00 10.00
123 Goran Suton/773 2.00 5.00
124 Jack McClinton/474 2.00 5.00
125 A.J. Price/474 2.00 5.00
129 Lester Hudson/999 2.00 5.00

2010-11 Rookies and Stars Longevity

COMP.SET w/o RCs (115) 12.50 30.00
EXCH EXPIRATION 5/10/12
1 Ray Allen .40 1.00
2 Paul Pierce .40 1.00
3 Rajon Rondo .40 1.00
4 Kevin Garnett .60 1.50
5 Brook Lopez .30 .75
6 Devin Harris .25 .60
7 Troy Murphy .25 .60
8 Amare Stoudemire .30 .75
9 Anthony Randolph .25 .60
10 Danilo Gallinari .30 .75
11 Andre Iguodala .30 .75
12 Elton Brand .40 1.00
13 Thaddeus Young .25 .60
14 Andrea Bargnani .30 .75
15 Leandro Barbosa .30 .75
16 Jose Calderon .25 .60
17 Carlos Boozer .30 .75
18 Derrick Rose .50 1.25
19 Joakim Noah .30 .75
20 Luol Deng .30 .75
21 Antawn Jamison .30 .75
22 Mo Williams .30 .75
23 Daniel Gibson .30 .75
24 Ben Gordon .30 .75
25 Richard Hamilton .30 .75
26 Tayshaun Prince .30 .75
27 Danny Granger .30 .75
28 Tyler Hansbrough .30 .75
29 Mike Dunleavy .25 .60
30 Andrew Bogut .30 .75
31 Brandon Jennings .25 .60
32 John Salmons .30 .75
33 Joe Johnson .30 .75
34 Josh Smith .30 .75
35 Al Horford .30 .75
36 Jamal Crawford .40 1.00
37 Gerald Henderson .25 .60
38 Stephen Jackson .30 .75
39 Gerald Wallace .30 .75
40 LeBron James 2.00 5.00
41 Dwyane Wade .60 1.50
42 Chris Bosh .40 1.00
43 Dwight Howard .30 .75
44 Vince Carter .50 1.25
45 J.J. Redick .40 1.00
46 Josh Howard .30 .75
47 Al Thornton .25 .60
48 Gilbert Arenas .30 .75
49 Kirk Hinrich .30 .75
50 Dirk Nowitzki .50 1.25
51 Jason Kidd .40 1.00
52 Shawn Marion .30 .75
53 Caron Butler .30 .75
54 Kevin Martin .30 .75
55 Shane Battier .30 .75
56 Luis Scola .30 .75
57 Yao Ming .50 1.25
58 Marc Gasol .40 1.00
59 Rudy Gay .40 1.00
60 Zach Randolph .30 .75
61 Chris Paul .50 1.25
62 Emeka Okafor .30 .75
63 David West .30 .75
64 Tim Duncan .60 1.50
65 Tony Parker .40 1.00
66 Richard Jefferson .30 .75
67 Carmelo Anthony .50 1.25
68 Chauncey Billups .40 1.00
69 Chris Andersen .30 .75
70 Nene .30 .75
71 Kevin Love .40 1.00
72 Michael Beasley .25 .60
73 Jonny Flynn .25 .60
74 Brandon Roy .40 1.00
75 Rudy Fernandez .25 .60
76 Greg Oden .30 .75
77 Kevin Durant 1.00 2.50
78 Russell Westbrook 1.00 2.50
79 Jeff Green .30 .75
80 Deron Williams .30 .75
81 Al Jefferson .30 .75
82 Andrei Kirilenko .30 .75
83 Paul Millsap .30 .75
84 David Lee .25 .60
85 Monta Ellis .30 .75
86 Stephen Curry 4.00 10.00
87 Eric Gordon .30 .75
88 Chris Kaman .30 .75
89 Baron Davis .30 .75
90 Kobe Bryant 1.50 4.00
91 Pau Gasol .40 1.00
92 Lamar Odom .30 .75
93 Ron Artest .40 1.00
94 Steve Nash .40 1.00
95 Hedo Turkoglu .30 .75
96 Channing Frye .30 .75
97 Grant Hill .50 1.25
98 Tyreke Evans .25 .60
99 Samuel Dalembert .25 .60
100 Carl Landry .25 .60
101 Rolando Blackman .30 .75
102 Joe Dumars .40 1.00
103 Wayne Embry .25 .60
104 Walt Frazier .40 1.00
105 Gail Goodrich .30 .75
106 John Havlicek .50 1.25
107 Rod Hundley .40 1.00
108 Phil Jackson .50 1.25
109 K.C. Jones .40 1.00
110 Clyde Lovellette .40 1.00
111 Jerry Lucas .40 1.00
112 Nate McMillan .40 1.00
113 Willis Reed .40 1.00
114 Paul Silas .40 1.00
115 Jerry West .50 1.25
116 Armon Johnson RC .40 1.00
117 Sherron Collins RC .40 1.00
118 Terrico White RC .40 1.00
119 Darington Hobson RC .40 1.00
120 Landry Fields RC .50 1.25
121 Tony Gaffney RC .40 1.00
122 Ben Uzoh RC .40 1.00
123 Ishmael Smith RC .60 1.50
124 Tweety Carter RC .40 1.00
125 Tiago Splitter RC .60 1.50
126 Solomon Alabi RC .40 1.00
127 Magnum Rolle RC .40 1.00
128 Pape Sy RC .40 1.00
129 Jeremy Lin RC 6.00 15.00
130 Derrick Caracter RC .40 1.00

2010-11 Rookies and Stars Longevity Ruby

*RUBY 1-130: 2X TO 5X BASE HI
1-130 RUBY PRINT RUN 250 SER.#'d SETS
131-170 PRINT RUN 5 TO 49 SER.#'d SETS
131 Jordan Crawford AU/49 5.00 12.00
132 Luke Harangody AU/49 4.00 10.00
133 Avery Bradley AU/49 8.00 20.00
134 Kevin Seraphin AU/49 4.00 10.00
135 Dominique Jones AU/49 4.00 10.00
136 Greg Monroe AU/49 8.00 20.00
137 Ekpe Udoh AU/49 4.00 10.00
138 Patrick Patterson AU/49 5.00 12.00
139 Lance Stephenson AU/49 6.00 15.00
140 Paul George AU/49 50.00 120.00
141 Eric Bledsoe AU/49 8.00 20.00
142 Willie Warren AU/49 4.00 10.00
144 Devin Ebanks AU/49 4.00 10.00
145 Xavier Henry AU/49 4.00 10.00
146 Greivis Vasquez AU/49 5.00 12.00
147 Dexter Pittman AU/49 4.00 10.00
148 Da'Sean Butler AU/49 6.00 15.00
149 Keith Gallon AU/49 4.00 10.00
150 Larry Sanders AU/49 4.00 10.00
151 Lazar Hayward AU/49 4.00 10.00
152 Wesley Johnson AU/49 4.00 10.00
153 Derrick Favors AU/49 8.00 20.00
154 Damion James AU/49 4.00 10.00
155 Craig Brackins AU/49 4.00 10.00
156 Quincy Pondexter AU/49 4.00 10.00
157 Andy Rautins AU/49 4.00 10.00
158 Cole Aldrich AU/49 5.00 12.00
159 Daniel Orton AU/49 4.00 10.00
160 Evan Turner AU/49 5.00 12.00
161 Gani Lawal AU/49 4.00 10.00
162 Elliot Williams AU/49 4.00 10.00
163 Luke Babbitt AU/49 5.00 12.00
164 DeMarcus Cousins AU/49 50.00 120.00
165 Hassan Whiteside AU/49 12.00 30.00
166 James Anderson AU/49 4.00 10.00
167 Ed Davis AU/49 4.00 10.00
168 Gordon Hayward AU/49 10.00 25.00
169 Trevor Booker AU/49 5.00 12.00
170 John Wall AU/49 30.00 80.00

2010-11 Rookies and Stars Longevity Sapphire

*SAPPHIRE 1-130: 3X TO 8X BASE HI
1-130 PRINT RUN 25 SER.#'d SETS
UNPRICED 131-170 AU PRINT RUN ONE SET
129 Jeremy Lin 12.00 30.00

2010-11 Rookies and Stars Longevity Dress for Success Materials

STATED PRINT RUN 99 TO 299 SER.#'d SETS
1 John Wall/299 10.00 25.00
2 Andre Miller/299 2.50 6.00
3 Evan Turner/299 1.50 4.00
4 Wesley Johnson/299 1.25 3.00
5 Andris Biedrins/299 2.00 5.00
6 Derrick Favors/299 2.50 6.00
7 Ekpe Udoh/299 1.25 3.00
8 Emeka Okafor/299 2.50 6.00
9 Eric Gordon/99 2.50 6.00
10 Evan Turner/299 1.50 4.00
11 Gani Lawal/299 1.25 3.00
12 Gerald Henderson/299 2.00 5.00
13 Goran Dragic/199 2.50 6.00
14 Gordon Hayward/299 3.00 8.00
15 Greg Monroe/299 2.50 6.00
16 Greg Oden/299 2.50 6.00
17 Greivis Vasquez/299 1.50 4.00
18 Hassan Whiteside/299 4.00 10.00
19 J.J. Barea/299 2.50 6.00
20 J.J. Redick/299 3.00 8.00
21 J.R. Smith/299 2.50 6.00
22 James Anderson/299 1.25 3.00
24 Dwight Howard/299 2.50 6.00
25 Jose Calderon/299 2.00 5.00
26 Lance Stephenson/299 2.00 5.00
27 Marcus Camby/299 2.00 5.00
28 Mike Dunleavy/199 2.00 5.00
29 DeMarcus Cousins/299 6.00 15.00
30 Wesley Johnson/299 1.25 3.00
31 Xavier Henry/299 1.25 3.00
32 Derrick Favors/299 2.50 6.00
33 Al-Farouq Aminu/299 2.00 5.00
34 Larry Sanders/299 1.25 3.00
35 Paul George/299 6.00 15.00

2010-11 Rookies and Stars Longevity Freshman Orientation Materials

STATED PRINT RUN 299 SER.#'d SETS
1 John Wall 10.00 25.00
2 Evan Turner 1.50 4.00
3 Derrick Favors 2.50 6.00
4 Wesley Johnson 1.25 3.00
5 DeMarcus Cousins 6.00 15.00
6 Ekpe Udoh 1.25 3.00
7 Greg Monroe 2.50 6.00
8 Al-Farouq Aminu 2.00 5.00
9 Gordon Hayward 3.00 8.00
10 Paul George 8.00 20.00
11 Cole Aldrich 1.50 4.00
12 Xavier Henry 1.25 3.00
13 Patrick Patterson 1.50 4.00
14 Larry Sanders 1.25 3.00
15 Luke Babbitt 1.50 4.00
16 Eric Bledsoe 2.50 6.00
17 Avery Bradley 2.50 6.00
18 James Anderson 1.25 3.00
19 Craig Brackins 1.25 3.00
20 Elliot Williams 1.25 3.00
21 Trevor Booker 1.50 4.00
22 Damion James 1.25 3.00
23 Dominique Jones 1.25 3.00
24 Quincy Pondexter 1.25 3.00
25 Jordan Crawford 1.50 4.00
26 Greivis Vasquez 1.50 4.00
27 Daniel Orton 1.25 3.00
28 Lazar Hayward 1.25 3.00
29 Dexter Pittman 1.25 3.00
30 Hassan Whiteside 4.00 10.00
31 Lance Stephenson 2.00 5.00
32 Da'Sean Butler 2.00 5.00
33 Devin Ebanks 1.25 3.00
34 Gani Lawal 1.25 3.00
35 Luke Harangody 1.25 3.00

2010-11 Rookies and Stars Longevity Materials Sapphire

STATED PRINT RUN 25 SER.#'d SETS
1 Ray Allen 5.00 12.00
2 Paul Pierce 5.00 12.00
3 Rajon Rondo 5.00 12.00
4 Kevin Garnett 8.00 20.00
6 Devin Harris 3.00 8.00
11 Andre Iguodala 4.00 10.00
12 Elton Brand 5.00 12.00
13 Thaddeus Young 3.00 8.00
15 Leandro Barbosa 4.00 10.00
16 Jose Calderon 3.00 8.00
18 Derrick Rose 6.00 15.00
19 Joakim Noah 4.00 10.00
20 Luol Deng 4.00 10.00
21 Antawn Jamison 4.00 10.00
24 Ben Gordon 4.00 10.00
26 Tayshaun Prince 4.00 10.00
28 Tyler Hansbrough 4.00 10.00
29 Mike Dunleavy 3.00 8.00
30 Andrew Bogut 4.00 10.00
31 Brandon Jennings 3.00 8.00
33 Joe Johnson 4.00 10.00
34 Josh Smith 4.00 10.00
35 Al Horford 4.00 10.00
37 Gerald Henderson 3.00 8.00
38 Stephen Jackson 4.00 10.00
39 Gerald Wallace 4.00 10.00
41 Dwyane Wade 8.00 20.00
43 Dwight Howard 4.00 10.00
44 Vince Carter 6.00 15.00
45 J.J. Redick 5.00 12.00
46 Josh Howard 4.00 10.00
48 Gilbert Arenas 4.00 10.00
49 Kirk Hinrich 4.00 10.00
50 Dirk Nowitzki 6.00 15.00
51 Jason Kidd 5.00 12.00
52 Shawn Marion 4.00 10.00
53 Caron Butler 4.00 10.00
54 Kevin Martin 4.00 10.00
55 Shane Battier 4.00 10.00
56 Luis Scola 4.00 10.00
58 Marc Gasol 5.00 12.00
59 Rudy Gay 5.00 12.00
61 Chris Paul 6.00 15.00
62 Emeka Okafor 4.00 10.00
63 David West 4.00 10.00
64 Tim Duncan 8.00 20.00
65 Tony Parker 5.00 12.00
66 Richard Jefferson 4.00 10.00
67 Carmelo Anthony 6.00 15.00
68 Chauncey Billups 5.00 12.00
69 Chris Andersen 4.00 10.00
70 Nene 4.00 10.00
71 Kevin Love 5.00 12.00
72 Michael Beasley 3.00 8.00
73 Jonny Flynn 3.00 8.00
74 Brandon Roy 5.00 12.00
75 Rudy Fernandez 3.00 8.00
76 Greg Oden 4.00 10.00
78 Russell Westbrook 12.00 30.00
80 Deron Williams 4.00 10.00
82 Andrei Kirilenko 4.00 10.00
86 Stephen Curry 25.00 60.00
88 Chris Kaman 4.00 10.00
89 Baron Davis 4.00 10.00
90 Kobe Bryant 15.00 40.00
91 Pau Gasol 5.00 12.00
92 Lamar Odom 4.00 10.00
93 Ron Artest 5.00 12.00
94 Steve Nash 5.00 12.00
95 Hedo Turkoglu 4.00 10.00
96 Channing Frye 4.00 10.00
97 Grant Hill 10.00 25.00
99 Samuel Dalembert 3.00 8.00
101 Rolando Blackman 4.00 10.00
102 Joe Dumars 5.00 12.00
118 Terrico White 3.00 8.00
129 Jeremy Lin 100.00 200.00

2010-11 Rookies and Stars Longevity Signatures

STATED PRINT RUN 5 TO 799 SER.#'d SETS
SOME UNPRICED DUE TO SCARCITY
8 Amare Stoudemire/15 25.00 60.00
11 Andre Iguodala/25 4.00 10.00
14 Andrea Bargnani/49 5.00 12.00
28 Tyler Hansbrough/99 4.00 10.00
37 Gerald Henderson/149 4.00 10.00
46 Josh Howard/99 4.00 10.00
51 Jason Kidd/25 12.50 30.00
62 Emeka Okafor/25 4.00 10.00
73 Jonny Flynn/199 4.00 10.00
86 Stephen Curry/49 15.00 40.00
89 Baron Davis/20 6.00 15.00
90 Kobe Bryant/49 75.00 150.00
93 Ron Artest/25 12.50 30.00
98 Tyreke Evans/99 10.00 25.00
100 Carl Landry/99 4.00 10.00
105 Gail Goodrich/49 5.00 12.00
106 John Havlicek/25 15.00 40.00
116 Armon Johnson/149 2.50 6.00
117 Sherron Collins/799 2.50 6.00
118 Terrico White/299 2.50 6.00
119 Darington Hobson/799 2.50 6.00
120 Landry Fields/349 3.00 8.00
121 Tony Gaffney/799 2.50 6.00
123 Ishmael Smith/799 4.00 10.00
124 Tweety Carter/499 2.50 6.00
125 Tiago Splitter/799 3.00 8.00
126 Solomon Alabi/350 2.50 6.00
127 Magnum Rolle/799 2.50 6.00
128 Pape Sy/799 2.50 6.00
129 Jeremy Lin/599 40.00 100.00
130 Derrick Caracter/799 2.50 6.00

1978-79 Royal Crown Cola

This set was sponsored by RC Cola, and its logo appears at the top of the card face. The cards were supposedly primarily issued in the southern New England area. The cards were intended to be placed in six-packs of Royal Crown Cola, one per six-pack. The cards measure 3" by 6". The front features a black-and-white head shot framed by a basketball hoop net on red and blue panels. The backs carry a mail-in offer to purchase a Spalding basketball for $6.99. The cards are unnumbered and are checklisted below in alphabetical order. The cards were apparently only licensed by the NBA Players Association since there are no team logos or team markings anywhere on the cards. The set features early professional cards of Walter Davis and Bernard King. Variations of Nate Archibald, Julius Erving, and Walt Frazier cards are reported. They measure 2 1/4" by 9 1/2", have the mail-in offer beneath the picture, and are blank-backed. They are also distinguished by a NBA Players logo, a 1978 MSA (Michael Schlecter Associates) copyright. and a 1978 RC Cola Co. copyright at the bottom.

COMPLETE SET 1500.00 3000.00
1 Kareem Abdul-Jabbar 150.00 300.00
2 Nate Archibald 50.00 100.00
3 Rick Barry 50.00 100.00
4 Jim Chones 25.00 50.00
5 Doug Collins 40.00 80.00
6 Dave Cowens 50.00 100.00
7 Adrian Dantley 45.00 90.00
8 Walter Davis 45.00 85.00
9 John Drew 20.00 45.00
10 Julius Erving 175.00 350.00
11 Walt Frazier 50.00 100.00
12 George Gervin 60.00 120.00
13 Artis Gilmore 45.00 90.00
14 Elvin Hayes 45.00 90.00
15 Dan Issel 45.00 90.00
16 Marques Johnson 35.00 70.00
17 Mickey Johnson 20.00 45.00
18 Bernard King 50.00 100.00
19 Bob Lanier 50.00 100.00
20 Maurice Lucas 35.00 65.00
21 Pete Maravich 300.00 475.00
22 Bob McAdoo 45.00 90.00
23 George McGinnis 30.00 60.00
24 Eric Money 25.00 45.00
25 Earl Monroe 45.00 90.00
26 Calvin Murphy 35.00 75.00
27 Robert Parish 60.00 120.00
28 Billy Paultz 25.00 45.00
29 Jack Sikma 35.00 65.00
30 Ricky Sobers 25.00 45.00
31 David Thompson 60.00 120.00
32 Rudy Tomjanovich 45.00 90.00
33 Wes Unseld 45.00 90.00
34 Norm Van Lier 30.00 60.00
35 Bill Walton 75.00 150.00
36 Marvin Webster 25.00 45.00
37 Scott Wedman 25.00 45.00
38 Paul Westphal 40.00 75.00
39 Jo Jo White 35.00 70.00
40 John Williamson 25.00 45.00
41 Brian Winters 40.00 80.00

1979-80 Royal Crown Cola Cans

The 1979 Royal Crown Cola Cans contain 35 standard-sized cans. The cans were made from steel, and thus are susceptible to rust if they have been in a moisture filled environment. The players head is in an oval picture shaped like a basketball and contains a short biographies below the picture. Each can is numbered "X" of 35. Cans opened from the bottom command up to a 25% premium over the prices listed below.

COMPLETE SET (35) 225.00 450.00
1 Dave Cowens 7.50 15.00
2 Nate Archibald 5.00 10.00
3 Artis Gilmore 7.50 15.00
4 David Thompson 7.50 15.00
5 Bob Lanier 5.00 10.00
6 Rick Barry 10.00 20.00
7 Rudy Tomjanovich 5.00 10.00
8 Kareem Abdul-Jabbar 20.00 40.00
9 Brian Winters 2.00 5.00
10 Bernard King 3.00 8.00
11 Pete Maravich 25.00 50.00
12 Bob McAdoo 5.00 10.00
13 Doug Collins 5.00 10.00
14 George McGinnis 5.00 10.00
15 Walter Davis 2.00 5.00
16 Paul Westphal 5.00 10.00
17 Robert Parish 7.50 15.00
18 Bill Walton 12.50 25.00
19 George Gervin 12.50 25.00
20 Elvin Hayes 7.50 15.00
21 Norm Van Lier 2.00 5.00
22 Dan Issel 7.50 15.00
23 Julius Erving 20.00 40.00
24 Jim Chones 2.00 5.00
25 Jo Jo White 3.00 8.00
26 Calvin Murphy 6.00 12.00
27 Earl Monroe 7.50 15.00
28 Billy Paultz 2.00 5.00
29 John Drew 2.00 5.00
30 John Williamson 2.00 5.00
31 Jack Sikma 3.00 8.00
32 Scott Wedman 2.00 5.00
33 Ricky Sobers 2.00 5.00
34 Maurice Lucas 3.00 8.00
35 Marvin Webster 2.00 5.00

1952 Royal Desserts

The 1952 Royal Desserts Stars of Basketball set contains eight horizontally oriented cards. The cards formed the backs of Royal Desserts packages of the period; consequently many cards are found with uneven edges stemming from the method of cutting the cards off the box. Each card has its number and the statement "Royal Stars of Basketball" in a red rectangle at the top. The cards measure approximately 2 5/8" by 3 1/4". The cards fronts have a stripe at the top and are divided into halves. The left half has a light-blue tinted head shot of the player and a facsimile autograph, while the right half has career summary. The blue tinted picture contains a facsimile autograph of the player. An album was presumably available as it is advertised on the card. The catalog designation for this scarce set is F219-2. The key card in the set is George Mikan.

COMPLETE SET (8) 7000.00 9500.00
1 Fred Schaus 350.00 700.00
2 Dick McGuire 400.00 850.00
3 Jack Nichols 250.00 500.00
4 Frank Brian 250.00 500.00
5 Joe Fulks 700.00 1200.00
6 George Mikan 3000.00 4000.00
7 Jim Pollard 700.00 1200.00
8 Buddy Jeanette 400.00 800.00

1970-71 Royals Cincinnati Team Issue

Measuring 8 1/2" by 11", this 12-photo set features members of the 1970-71 Cincinnati Royals. The fronts feature three photos - one drawing, one head shot and one in-action shot, with the player's name in the lower left and the team name in the lower right. The player's facsimile autograph is located on the in-action shot. The photos are black and white. The backs are black and listed below in alphabetical order.

COMPLETE SET (12) 50.00 100.00
1 Nate Archibald 8.00 20.00
2 Bob Arnzen 2.00 5.00
3 Moe Barr 2.00 5.00
4 Bob Cousy 12.50 25.00
5 Johnny Green 3.00 8.00
6 Greg Hyder 2.00 5.00
7 Darrall Imhoff 3.00 8.00
8 Sam Lacey 3.00 8.00
9 Charlie Paulk 2.00 5.00
10 Flynn Robinson 3.00 8.00
11 Tom Van Arsdale 3.00 8.00
12 Norm Van Lier 5.00 10.00

1972 7-11 Cups

Distributed through 7-11 in 1972, these cups feature color portraits of NBA players. They also feature a facsimile autograph and the player's name and team underneath the photo. The "back" side of the cup features statistics and a brief summary on the player. It also contains the 7-11 and NBA Players Association logos. The cups are not numbered and listed below in alphabetical order.

COMPLETE SET 300.00 600.00
1 Kareem Abdul-Jabbar 20.00 40.00
2 Mahdi Abdul-Rahman 5.00 10.00
3 Nate Archibald 8.00 20.00
4 Rick Barry 8.00 20.00
5 Dave Bing 6.00 15.00
6 Austin Carr 5.00 10.00
7 Wilt Chamberlain 25.00 50.00
8 Dave DeBusschere 8.00 20.00
9 Walt Frazier 10.00 20.00
10 Gail Goodrich 6.00 15.00
11 Hal Greer 6.00 15.00
12 Happy Hairston 5.00 10.00
13 John Havlicek 10.00 25.00
14 Connie Hawkins 8.00 20.00
15 Elvin Hayes 10.00 20.00
16 Spencer Haywood 5.00 10.00
17 Lou Hudson 5.00 10.00
18 John Johnson 5.00 10.00
19 Don Kojis 5.00 10.00
20 Bob Lanier 7.50 15.00
21 Kevin Loughery 5.00 10.00
22 Jerry Lucas 6.00 15.00
23 Pete Maravich 50.00 100.00
24 Jack Marin 5.00 10.00
25 Jim McMillian 5.00 10.00
26 Jeff Mullins 5.00 10.00
27 Geoff Petrie 5.00 10.00
28 Willis Reed 8.00 20.00
29 Oscar Robertson 15.00 30.00
30 Paul Silas 6.00 15.00
31 Jerry Sloan 8.00 20.00
32 Elmore Smith 5.00 10.00
33 Nate Thurmond 6.00 15.00
34 Wes Unseld 6.00 15.00
35 Dick Van Arsdale 6.00 12.00
36 Tom Van Arsdale 6.00 12.00
37 Chet Walker 6.00 12.00
38 John Warren 5.00 10.00
39 Jerry West 25.00 50.00
40 Jo Jo White 6.00 15.00

1981 7-Up Jumbos

These thin-stock cards, measuring approximately 5 1/4" x 8 1/2", were given away at 7-Up point-of-purchase displays. With the slogan "Feelin' 7-Up", the cards were produced highlighting the cola's different sports spokesmen of that time. The fronts contain a full-bleed color posed player photograph and a facsimile autograph. The backs have a green border, and some highlights of the player inside a white box. The cards were first available during the 1980-81 basketball season, and therefore Magic Johnson's card is one of his earliest professional pieces. Ann Meyers, another basketball great in her own right, is also represented in the set. Any other additions to this checklist would be greatly appreciated. The cards are unnumbered and checklisted below in alphabetical order.

COMPLETE SET (7) 30.00 75.00
3 Magic Johnson BK 10.00 25.00
5 Ann Meyers BK 6.00 15.00

1976-77 76ers Canada Dry Cans

The 1976-77 Canada Dry Philadelphia 76ers Cans team issue contains at least 14 standard-sized cans which paid tribute to the "Team of the Year 1976-77". Under this caption, the cans contain a 76ers logo and a black and white headshot of the player with the name, uniform number and position below the picture.There is no number given other than the jersey number, thus the set is listed below alphabetically. Cans opened from the bottom command up to a 25% premium over the prices below.The checklist below is thought to be incomplete--any additional input on this series would be appreciated.

COMPLETE SET (14) 37.50 75.00
1 Henry Bibby 2.50 6.00
2 Joe Bryant 2.50 6.00
3 Harvey Catchings 1.50 4.00
4 Darryl Dawkins 5.00 10.00
5 Al Domenico TR 1.50 4.00
6 Mike Dunleavy 3.00 8.00
7 Julius Erving 15.00 30.00
8 Lloyd Free 2.50 6.00
9 Terry Furlow 1.50 4.00
10 Caldwell Jones 2.50 6.00
11 George McGinnis 5.00 10.00
12 Jack McMahon ACO 1.50 4.00
13 Steve Mix 1.50 4.00
14 Gene Shue CO 3.00 8.00

2001-02 76ers Fleer

Released in conjunction with Fleer, this 6-cards set was issued as a team sheet and given away at a Sixers game during the 2001-02 season.

COMPLETE SET (6) 2.00 5.00
NNO Allen Iverson 1.00 2.50
NNO Aaron McKie .30 .75
NNO Team Photo .40 1.00
NNO Eric Snow .30 .75
NNO Larry Brown CO .40 1.00
NNO Dikembe Mutombo .50 1.25

2001-02 76ers Fleer NBA All-Star Jam Session

Issued to fans via a wrapper redemption program at the 2001-02 All-Star Weekend show, Feb 8th-10th, this set was limited to just 7,600 total and was available only at the Fleer booth. The card numbers were not known at press time, so they've been listed in alphabetical order for convenience.

COMPLETE SET (6) 3.00 8.00
1 Speedy Claxton .50 1.25
2 Derrick Coleman .60 1.50
3 Allen Iverson 1.50 4.00
4 Aaron McKie .50 1.25
5 Dikembe Mutombo .75 2.00
6 Eric Snow .50 1.25

1989-90 76ers Kodak

This team photo album was jointly sponsored by Jack's Cameras and Kodak. The photo album consists of three sheets, each measuring approximately 8" by 11" and joined together to form one continuous sheet. The first sheet features a team photo of the Philadelphia 76ers. While the second sheet presents two rows of five cards each, the third sheet presents six additional player cards, with the remaining four slots filled in by coupons redeemable at Jack's Cameras. After perforation, the cards measure 2 3/16" by 3 3/4". The card front features a color action player photo, with a red border on white card stock. The player's name and position are given below the picture, and the 76ers logo is sandwiched between the sponsors' logos. The backs have the Philadelphia 76ers logo in blue and red print. The cards are presented in the album in alphabetical order, with coaches at the end, and we have checklisted them below accordingly. The set features an early professional card of Hersey Hawkins.

COMPLETE SET (16) 6.00 15.00
1 Ron Anderson .20 .50
2 Charles Barkley 3.00 8.00
3 Scott Brooks .40 1.00
4 Lanard Copeland .20 .50
5 Johnny Dawkins .40 1.00
6 Mike Gminski .40 1.00
7 Hersey Hawkins .75 2.00
8 Rick Mahorn .30 .75
9 Kurt Nimphius .20 .50
10 Kenny Payne .20 .50
11 Derek Smith .40 1.00
12 Bob Thornton .20 .50
13 Big Shot (Team Mascot) .20 .50
14 Jim Lynam CO .20 .50
15 Fred Carter ACO .20 .50
16 Buzz Braman ACO .75 2.00

1975-76 76ers McDonald's Standups

The 1975-76 McDonalds Philadelphia 76ers set contains six blank-backed cards measuring approximately 3 3/4" by 7". The cards were produced by Johnny Pro Enterprises. The cards are die cut, allowing the player pictures to be punched out and displayed. Johnny Pro Enterprises originally sold the sets directly to consumers for $1.25 postpaid. The cards are unnumbered and checklisted below in alphabetical order.

COMPLETE SET (6) 6.00 15.00
1 Fred Carter 1.25 3.00
2 Harvey Catchings 1.25 3.00
3 Doug Collins 3.00 8.00
4 Billy Cunningham 3.00 8.00
5 George McGinnis 2.00 5.00
6 Steve Mix 1.25 3.00

1979-80 76ers Stand-ups

This set was released during the 1979-80 season, and features twelve of the 76er's top players. These full-color player figures were produced on very thick stock, and stand about ten inches tall. Please note that these stand-ups are not numbered and are listed below in alphabetical order.

COMPLETE SET (12) 60.00 120.00
1 Henry Bibby 3.00 8.00
2 Joe Bryant 3.00 8.00
3 Harvey Catchings 2.50 6.00
4 Doug Collins 7.50 15.00
5 Darryl Dawkins 6.00 12.00
6 Mike Dunleavy 5.00 12.00
7 Julius Erving 30.00 55.00
8 Lloyd Free 5.00 10.00
9 Terry Furlow 2.50 6.00
10 Caldwell Jones 2.50 6.00
11 George McGinnis 5.00 10.00
12 Steve Mix 2.50 6.00

1969-70 76ers Team Issue

Each of these team-issued photos measure approximately 5 3/4" by 7 1/4" and feature black and white player portraits. The player's name is listed below the photo. The backs are blank. The photos are unnumbered and listed below alphabetically.

COMPLETE SET (11) 25.00 50.00
1 Archie Clark 2.00 5.00
2 Bill Cunningham 5.00 10.00
3 Hal Greer 3.00 8.00
4 Matt Guokas 2.50 6.00
5 Fred Hetzel 1.25 3.00
6 Darrall Imhoff 1.25 3.00
7 Luke Jackson 2.00 5.00
8 Wally Jones 2.00 5.00
9 Bud Ogden 1.25 3.00
10 Jack Ramsay CO 2.50 6.00
11 George Wilson 1.25 3.00

1970-71 76ers Team Issue

Measuring 5 1/2" by 7", this 13-photo set was issued for the 1970-71 season. The front photos feature a black and white posed shot with the player's name and team directly underneath. The backs are blank, unnumbered, and listed below in alphabetical order.

COMPLETE SET (13) 20.00 40.00
1 Dennis Awtrey 1.00 2.50
2 Archie Clark 1.50 4.00
3 Billy Cunningham 3.00 8.00
4 Connie Dierking 1.25 3.00
5 Fred Foster 1.00 2.50

6 Hal Greer 2.00 5.00
7 Al Henry 1.00 2.50
8 Bailey Howell 1.25 3.00
9 Luke Jackson 1.25 3.00
10 Wally Jones 1.50 4.00
11 Bud Ogden 1.00 2.50
12 Jack Ramsay CO 2.00 5.00
13 Jim Washington 1.25 3.00

1976-77 76ers Team Issue Black and White

This 8"x10" set was produced for the Philadelphia 76ers during the 1976-77 season. The set features 12 black and white cards of the team's players and coaches.

COMPLETE SET (12) 15.00 30.00
1 Henry Bibby 1.50 4.00
2 Joe Bryant 1.50 4.00
3 Fred Carter 1.25 3.00
4 Harvey Catchings 1.25 3.00
5 Lloyd Free 2.00 5.00
6 Steve Mix 1.25 3.00
7 Coniel Norman 1.25 3.00
8 F. Eugene Dixon Jr. PRES 1.25 3.00
9 Al Domenico TR 1.25 3.00
10 Jack McMahon CO 1.25 3.00
11 Gene Shue CO 1.50 4.00
12 Pat Williams VP 1.25 3.00

1976-77 76ers Team Issue Color

These 12 color blank-backed photos, which measure 4 3/4" by 6 1/2" feature members of the Eastern Conference Champions Philadelphia 76ers. These photos were sold in a 12-pack.

COMPLETE SET (12) 20.00 50.00
1 Henry Bibby 1.25 3.00
2 Joe Bryant 1.50 4.00
3 Harvey Catchings .75 2.00
4 Doug Collins 3.00 8.00
5 Darryl Dawkins 2.50 6.00
6 Mike Dunleavy 2.00 5.00
7 Julius Erving 12.00 30.00
8 Lloyd Free 2.00 5.00
9 Terry Furlow .75 2.00
10 Caldwell Jones 1.25 3.00
11 George McGinnis 1.50 4.00
12 Steve Mix .75 2.00

1948-1950 Safe-T-Card

Cards from this set were issued in the Washington D.C. area in the late 1940s and early 1950s. Each card was printed in either black or red and features an artist's rendering of a famous area athlete or personality from a variety of sports. The card backs feature an ad for Jim Gibbons Cartoon-A-Quiz television show along with an ad from a local business. The player's facsimile autograph and team or sport affiliation is included on the fronts.

4 Red Auerbach 50.00 100.00
25 Bob Feerick BK 15.00 30.00
36 Kleggie Hermsen BK 15.00 30.00

1997 Scholastic Ultimate NBA Postcards

These 30 postcards were issued in a Scholastic book entitled "The Ultimate NBA Postcard Book" with an SRP of $7.99. Each postcard is perforated at the top and measures approximately 5 3/4" x 6 1/3". Fronts include a color action shot inside a color border. The player's name is written in block letters on the photo, the player's team is printed at the bottom next to a team logo, and player position is written vertically on the right side. Backs include some "vital statistics" and a small biography. The rest follows the format of a basic postcard. The cards are unnumbered and listed below in alphabetical order.

COMPLETE SET (30) 6.00 15.00
1 Greg Anthony .20 .50
2 Vin Baker .20 .50
3 Shawn Bradley .20 .50
4 Terrell Brandon .20 .50
5 Elden Campbell .20 .50
6 Sam Cassell .30 .75
7 Joe Dumars .40 1.00
8 Patrick Ewing .40 1.00
9 Kevin Garnett 1.50 4.00
10 Kevin Johnson .30 .75
11 Shawn Kemp .25 .60
12 Toni Kukoc .30 .75
13 Karl Malone .60 1.50
14 Jamal Mashburn .30 .75
15 Antonio McDyess .30 .75
16 Alonzo Mourning .40 1.00
17 Dino Radja .20 .50
18 Glen Rice .20 .50
19 Mitch Richmond .30 .75
20 David Robinson .40 1.00
21 Arvydas Sabonis .30 .75
22 Dennis Scott .20 .50
23 Joe Smith .25 .60
24 Steve Smith .30 .75
25 Rik Smits .20 .50
26 John Starks .20 .50
27 Damon Stoudamire .30 .75
28 Loy Vaught .20 .50
29 Clarence Weatherspoon .20 .50
30 Chris Webber .75 2.00

2012 Score Hot Rookies Toronto Fall Expo

CRACKED ICE/25: 1.5X TO 4X BASE HI
19 Kyrie Irving 6.00 15.00
20 Anthony Davis 6.00 15.00
21 Tristan Thompson 2.00 5.00
22 Terrence Ross 1.50 4.00

1995 Score Board Phone Card Promo

NNO Shaquille O'Neal 4.00 10.00
Hakeem Olajuwon

2012-13 Select

COMP.SET w/o AUs (150) 15.00 40.00
AU SER.#'d B/WN 149-449 COPIES PER
JSY AU SER.#'d 149-399 COPIES PER
EXCHANGE DEADLINE 10/03/2014
1 Al Horford .30 .75
2 Anthony Morrow .25 .60
3 Jeff Teague .30 .75
4 Josh Smith .30 .75
5 Brook Lopez .30 .75
6 Deron Williams .30 .75
7 Gerald Wallace .30 .75
8 Joe Johnson .30 .75
9 Kris Humphries .25 .60
10 Brandon Bass .25 .60
11 Courtney Lee .30 .75
12 Jason Terry .30 .75
13 Jeff Green .30 .75
14 Kevin Garnett .60 1.50
15 Paul Pierce .40 1.00
16 Rajon Rondo .40 1.00
17 Ben Gordon .30 .75
18 Gerald Henderson .25 .60
19 Carlos Boozer .30 .75
20 Derrick Rose .50 1.25
21 Joakim Noah .30 .75
22 Luol Deng .30 .75
23 Nate Robinson .25 .60
24 Taj Gibson .30 .75
25 Anderson Varejao .25 .60
26 Darren Collison .30 .75
27 Dirk Nowitzki .50 1.25
28 O.J. Mayo .25 .60
29 Vince Carter .50 1.25
30 Andre Iguodala .30 .75
31 Danilo Gallinari .25 .60
32 JaVale McGee .30 .75
33 Ty Lawson .25 .60
34 Wilson Chandler .30 .75
35 Greg Monroe .30 .75
36 Rodney Stuckey .30 .75
37 Andrew Bogut .30 .75
38 David Lee .25 .60
39 Stephen Curry 1.50 4.00
40 James Harden .60 1.50
41 Jeremy Lin .40 1.00
42 Danny Granger .30 .75
43 David West .30 .75
44 Paul George .50 1.25
45 Roy Hibbert .30 .75
46 Blake Griffin .40 1.00
47 Chauncey Billups .40 1.00
48 Chris Paul .50 1.25
49 DeAndre Jordan .40 1.00
50 Eric Bledsoe .30 .75
51 Grant Hill .50 1.25
52 Antawn Jamison .30 .75
53 Dwight Howard .30 .75
54 Kobe Bryant 1.50 4.00
55 Metta World Peace .40 1.00
56 Pau Gasol .40 1.00
57 Steve Blake .25 .60
58 Steve Nash .40 1.00
59 Marc Gasol .40 1.00
60 Marreese Speights .25 .60
61 Mike Conley .30 .75
62 Rudy Gay .40 1.00
63 Zach Randolph .30 .75
64 Chris Bosh .40 1.00
65 Dwyane Wade .60 1.50
66 LeBron James 1.50 4.00
67 Mario Chalmers .30 .75
68 Ray Allen .40 1.00
69 Shane Battier .30 .75
70 Brandon Jennings .25 .60
71 Ersan Ilyasova .25 .60
72 Monta Ellis .30 .75
73 Andrei Kirilenko .30 .75
74 Brandon Roy .40 1.00
75 Kevin Love .40 1.00
76 Ricky Rubio .40 1.00
77 Eric Gordon .30 .75
78 Ryan Anderson .30 .75
79 Amar'e Stoudemire .30 .75
80 Carmelo Anthony .50 1.25
81 Jason Kidd .40 1.00
82 J.R. Smith .30 .75
83 Marcus Camby .30 .75
84 Raymond Felton .30 .75
85 Tyson Chandler .30 .75
86 Kendrick Perkins .25 .60
87 Kevin Martin .30 .75
88 Kevin Durant 1.00 2.50
89 Russell Westbrook 1.00 2.50
90 Serge Ibaka .30 .75
91 Arron Afflalo .30 .75
92 Glen Davis .25 .60
93 Jameer Nelson .25 .60
94 Andrew Bynum .25 .60
95 Evan Turner .25 .60
96 Jason Richardson .40 1.00
97 Jrue Holiday .40 1.00
98 Nick Young .30 .75
99 Goran Dragic .30 .75
100 Marcin Gortat .30 .75
101 Michael Beasley .25 .60
102 LaMarcus Aldridge .40 1.00
103 Nicolas Batum .30 .75
104 Wesley Matthews .25 .60
105 DeMarcus Cousins .40 1.00
106 Marcus Thornton .25 .60
107 Tyreke Evans .25 .60
108 DeJuan Blair .25 .60
109 Manu Ginobili .40 1.00
110 Tim Duncan .60 1.50
111 Tony Parker .40 1.00
112 Andrea Bargnani .30 .75
113 DeMar DeRozan .40 1.00
114 Kyle Lowry .30 .75
115 Al Jefferson .30 .75
116 Derrick Favors .30 .75
117 Gordon Hayward .40 1.00
118 Mo Williams .30 .75
119 John Wall .50 1.25
120 Nene .30 .75
121 Danny Ainge .40 1.00
122 Nate Archibald .30 .75
123 Elgin Baylor .40 1.00
124 Walt Bellamy .30 .75
125 Wilt Chamberlain .75 2.00
126 Darryl Dawkins .25 .60
127 Vlade Divac .40 1.00
128 Julius Erving .60 1.50
129 Patrick Ewing .50 1.25
130 Walt Frazier .40 1.00
131 Horace Grant .40 1.00
132 Anfernee Hardaway 1.00 2.50
133 John Havlicek .50 1.25
134 Dennis Johnson .30 .75
135 Magic Johnson 1.00 2.50
136 Bernard King .30 .75
137 Toni Kukoc .40 1.00
138 Jerry Lucas .40 1.00
139 Moses Malone .40 1.00
140 Kevin McHale .40 1.00
141 Earl Monroe .40 1.00
142 Shaquille O'Neal .75 2.00
143 Willis Reed .40 1.00
144 Bill Russell .60 1.50
145 Rik Smits .40 1.00
146 John Starks .30 .75
147 Isiah Thomas .40 1.00
148 David Thompson .30 .75
149 Spud Webb .30 .75
150 Damian Lillard RC 3.00 8.00
151 Kyrie Irving AU/149 RC 50.00 100.00
152 Anthony Davis AU/149 RC 125.00 250.00
153 Derrick Williams AU/149 RC 3.00 8.00
154 M.Kidd-Gilchrist AU/149 RC 5.00 12.00
155 Enes Kanter AU/199 RC 4.00 10.00
156 Bradley Beal AU/149 RC 15.00 40.00
157 Tristan Thompson AU/149 5.00 12.00
158 Dion Waiters AU/149 5.00 12.00
159 Jonas Valanciunas AU/149 5.00 12.00
160 Thomas Robinson AU/149 RC 4.00 10.00
161 Jan Vesely AU/199 3.00 8.00
162 Bismack Biyombo AU/399 RC 3.00 8.00
163 Harrison Barnes AU/149 RC 12.00 30.00
164 Brandon Knight AU/149 RC 5.00 12.00
165 Terrence Ross AU/149 5.00 12.00
166 Kemba Walker AU/149 RC 12.00 30.00
167 A. Drummond AU/149 RC 15.00 40.00
168 Jimmer Fredette AU/149 3.00 8.00
169 Austin Rivers AU/149 RC 5.00 12.00
170 Klay Thompson AU/149 50.00 120.00
171 Meyers Leonard AU/149 4.00 10.00
172 Alec Burks AU/299 RC 5.00 12.00
173 Jeremy Lamb AU/149 5.00 12.00
174 Markieff Morris AU/299 RC 5.00 12.00
175 Kendall Marshall AU/199 3.00 8.00
176 Marcus Morris AU/299 RC 4.00 10.00
177 John Henson AU/149 5.00 12.00
178 Kawhi Leonard AU/199 75.00 200.00
179 Maurice Harkless AU/299 RC 5.00 12.00
180 Nikola Vucevic AU/399 RC 5.00 12.00
181 Royce White AU/299 RC 3.00 8.00
182 Iman Shumpert AU/199 RC 5.00 12.00
183 Tyler Zeller AU/199 4.00 10.00
184 Chris Singleton AU/399 RC 3.00 8.00
185 Terrence Jones AU/199 4.00 10.00
186 Tobias Harris AU/299 RC 5.00 12.00
187 A.Nicholson AU/299 RC 3.00 8.00
188 Donatas Motiejunas AU/299 RC 4.00 10.00
189 Evan Fournier AU/299 RC 5.00 12.00
190 Nolan Smith AU/299 RC 3.00 8.00
191 Jared Sullinger AU/149 RC 4.00 10.00
192 Kenneth Faried AU/199 5.00 12.00
193 Fab Melo AU/199 RC 3.00 8.00
194 Reggie Jackson AU/399 RC 5.00 12.00
195 John Jenkins AU/399 RC 3.00 8.00
196 MarShon Brooks AU/399 RC 4.00 10.00
197 Jared Cunningham AU/399 RC 3.00 8.00
198 Jordan Hamilton AU/449 RC 3.00 8.00
199 Tony Wroten AU/199 4.00 10.00
200 Miles Plumlee AU/399 RC 3.00 8.00
201 Norris Cole AU/199 3.00 8.00
202 Arnett Moultrie AU/399 RC 3.00 8.00
203 Perry Jones AU/399 RC 3.00 8.00
204 Cory Joseph AU/449 RC 3.00 8.00
205 Marquis Teague AU/399 RC 3.00 8.00
206 Jimmy Butler AU/399 RC 15.00 40.00
207 Festus Ezeli AU/399 RC 4.00 10.00
208 E'Twaun Moore AU/399 RC 3.00 8.00
209 DeAndre Liggins AU/449 RC 4.00 10.00
210 Kyle Singler AU/449 RC 3.00 8.00
211 Chandler Parsons AU/299 RC 5.00 12.00
212 Quincy Acy AU/449 RC 3.00 8.00
213 Tyler Honeycutt AU/449 RC 3.00 8.00
214 Bernard James AU/449 RC 3.00 8.00
215 Charles Jenkins AU/349 3.00 8.00
216 Jae Crowder AU/449 RC 4.00 10.00
217 Darius Morris AU/449 RC 3.00 8.00
218 D. Green AU/449 RC 25.00 60.00
219 Malcolm Lee AU/449 RC 3.00 8.00
220 Orlando Johnson AU/449 RC 3.00 8.00
221 Jon Leuer AU/349 RC 4.00 10.00
222 Will Barton AU/449 RC 4.00 10.00
223 Tyshawn Taylor AU/449 RC 3.00 8.00
224 Julyan Stone AU/449 RC 3.00 8.00
225 Doron Lamb AU/449 RC 3.00 8.00
226 Kim English AU/449 RC 3.00 8.00
227 Mike Scott AU/449 RC 3.00 8.00
228 Kevin Murphy AU/449 RC 3.00 8.00
229 Kyle O'Quinn AU/449 RC 3.00 8.00
230 Lavoy Allen AU/399 RC 3.00 8.00
231 Tornike Shengelia AU/449 RC 3.00 8.00
232 Darius Miller AU/449 RC 3.00 8.00
233 Isaiah Thomas AU/449 RC 20.00 50.00
234 Trey Thompkins AU/449 RC 3.00 8.00
235 Robert Sacre AU/449 RC 3.00 8.00
236 Kyrie Irving JSY AU/149 RC 50.00 100.00
237 D.Williams JSY AU/149 RC 3.00 8.00
238 Enes Kanter JSY AU/199 RC 4.00 10.00
239 T.Thompson JSY AU/199 RC 5.00 12.00
240 J.Valanciunas JSY AU/199 RC 5.00 12.00
241 Jan Vesely JSY AU/249 RC 3.00 8.00
242 Bismack Biyombo JSY AU/299 3.00 8.00
243 Brandon Knight JSY AU/149 RC 5.00 12.00
244 K. Walker JSY AU/149 RC 10.00 25.00
245 J.Fredette JSY AU/199 RC 3.00 8.00
246 K. Thompson JSY AU/199 RC 60.00 150.00
247 Alec Burks JSY AU/299 RC 5.00 12.00
248 Markieff Morris JSY AU/299 RC 5.00 12.00
249 Marcus Morris JSY AU/299 RC 4.00 10.00
250 K. Leonard JSY AU/249 RC 75.00 200.00
251 N.Vucevic JSY AU/399 RC 5.00 12.00
252 Iman Shumpert JSY AU/199 RC 5.00 12.00
253 Chris Singleton JSY AU/399 RC 3.00 8.00
254 Tobias Harris JSY AU/299 RC 5.00 12.00
255 Nolan Smith JSY AU/299 RC 3.00 8.00
256 Kenneth Faried JSY AU/249 RC 5.00 12.00
257 Reggie Jackson JSY AU/399 RC 5.00 12.00
258 M.Brooks JSY AU/399 RC 4.00 10.00
259 Jordan Hamilton JSY AU/399 3.00 8.00
260 Norris Cole JSY AU/249 RC 3.00 8.00
261 Cory Joseph JSY AU/399 3.00 8.00
262 J. Butler JSY AU/399 RC 25.00 60.00
263 Kyle Singler JSY AU/399 3.00 8.00
264 Trey Thompkins JSY AU/399 3.00 8.00
265 C.Parsons JSY AU/299 RC 5.00 12.00
266 Lavoy Allen JSY AU/399 RC 3.00 8.00
267 Isaiah Thomas JSY AU/399 30.00 80.00
268 Tyler Honeycutt JSY AU/399 3.00 8.00
269 Malcolm Lee JSY AU/399 3.00 8.00
270 A. Davis JSY AU/149 RC 125.00 250.00
271 Kidd-Gilchrist JSY AU/149 RC 5.00 12.00
272 B. Beal JSY AU/149 RC 20.00 50.00
273 T.Robinson JSY AU/149 RC 4.00 10.00
274 Dion Waiters JSY AU/199 RC 5.00 12.00
275 H.Barnes JSY AU/149 RC 8.00 20.00
276 Terrence Ross JSY AU/199 RC 5.00 12.00
277 A.Drummond JSY AU/149 RC 20.00 50.00
278 Austin Rivers JSY AU/149 RC 5.00 12.00
279 M.Leonard JSY AU/199 RC 4.00 10.00
280 Jeremy Lamb JSY AU/199 RC 5.00 12.00
281 Kendall Marshall JSY AU/249 RC 3.00 8.00
282 John Henson JSY AU/199 RC 5.00 12.00
283 Royce White JSY AU/299 RC 3.00 8.00
284 Tyler Zeller JSY AU/249 RC 4.00 10.00
285 Terrence Jones JSY AU/249 RC 4.00 10.00
286 A.Nicholson JSY AU/299 RC 3.00 8.00
287 Evan Fournier JSY AU/299 RC 5.00 12.00
288 Jared Sullinger JSY AU/149 RC 4.00 10.00
289 Tony Wroten JSY AU/249 RC 4.00 10.00
290 Miles Plumlee JSY AU/399 RC 3.00 8.00
291 Arnett Moultrie JSY AU/399 RC 3.00 8.00
292 Perry Jones JSY AU/399 RC 3.00 8.00
293 M.Teague JSY AU/399 RC 3.00 8.00
294 Festus Ezeli JSY AU/399 RC 4.00 10.00
296 Bernard James JSY AU/399 3.00 8.00
297 Jae Crowder JSY AU/399 4.00 10.00
298 D. Green JSY AU/399 25.00 60.00
299 Orlando Johnson JSY AU/399 3.00 8.00
300 Quincy Miller JSY AU/399 RC 3.00 8.00
301 Quincy Acy JSY AU/399 3.00 8.00
302 Khris Middleton JSY AU/399 RC 5.00 12.00
303 Kyle O'Quinn JSY AU/399 3.00 8.00
304 Tyshawn Taylor JSY AU/399 3.00 8.00
305 Doron Lamb JSY AU/399 3.00 8.00
306 Kris Joseph JSY AU/399 RC 3.00 8.00
307 Kim English JSY AU/399 3.00 8.00
308 Robert Sacre JSY AU/399 3.00 8.00
309 Kevin Murphy JSY AU/399 3.00 8.00
310 Fab Melo JSY AU/249 RC 3.00 8.00
311 D. Lillard JSY AU/49 RC 200.00 300.00

2012-13 Select Prizms

*PRIZM: 1.5X TO 4X BASIC
*PRIZM AU: .5X TO 1.2X BASIC
*PRIZM JSY AU: .5X TO 1.2X BASIC
AU SER.#'d B/WN 99-199 COPIES PER
JSY AU SER.#'d 99-199 COPIES PER
EXCHANGE DEADLINE 10/03/2014
54 Kobe Bryant 8.00 20.00
152 Anthony Davis AU/99 200.00 400.00
156 Bradley Beal AU/99 25.00 60.00

2012-13 Select All-Star Selections

1 Kevin Durant 2.50 6.00
2 LeBron James 4.00 10.00
3 Dwight Howard .75 2.00
4 Kobe Bryant 4.00 10.00
5 James Harden 1.50 4.00
6 Dirk Nowitzki 1.25 3.00
7 Dwyane Wade 1.50 4.00
8 Chris Paul 1.25 3.00
9 Kevin Garnett 1.50 4.00
10 Tim Duncan 1.50 4.00
11 Grant Hill 1.25 3.00
12 Shaquille O'Neal 2.00 5.00
13 George Gervin 1.00 2.50
14 David Thompson .75 2.00
15 Chris Webber 1.00 2.50
16 Allen Iverson 1.25 3.00
17 Gary Payton 1.00 2.50
18 Karl Malone 1.25 3.00
19 Dominique Wilkins 1.25 3.00
20 Hakeem Olajuwon 1.25 3.00
21 David Robinson 1.50 4.00
22 Larry Bird 2.50 6.00
23 Julius Erving 1.50 4.00
24 Magic Johnson 2.50 6.00
25 Clyde Drexler 1.25 3.00

2012-13 Select Hall Selections

1 Larry Bird 2.50 6.00
2 Kareem Abdul-Jabbar 1.50 4.00
3 Elgin Baylor 1.00 2.50
4 Wilt Chamberlain 2.00 5.00
5 Patrick Ewing 1.25 3.00
6 John Stockton 1.50 4.00
7 David Robinson 1.50 4.00
8 Hakeem Olajuwon 1.25 3.00
9 Scottie Pippen 2.00 5.00
10 Bill Russell 1.50 4.00
11 Dennis Rodman 2.00 5.00
12 Pete Maravich 1.50 4.00
13 Julius Erving 1.50 4.00
14 Karl Malone 1.25 3.00
15 Jerry West 1.25 3.00
16 Oscar Robertson 1.25 3.00
17 George Mikan 2.00 5.00
18 Clyde Drexler 1.25 3.00
19 Bill Walton 1.00 2.50
20 James Worthy 1.25 3.00
21 Moses Malone 1.00 2.50
22 Don Nelson 1.00 2.50
23 Wes Unseld 1.00 2.50
24 Drazen Petrovic 1.00 2.50
25 Dave Cowens .60 1.50

2012-13 Select Hot Rookies

1 Anthony Davis 6.00 15.00
2 Dion Waiters 1.25 3.00
3 Damian Lillard 5.00 12.00
4 Michael Kidd-Gilchrist 1.25 3.00
5 Thomas Robinson 1.00 2.50
6 Austin Rivers 1.25 3.00
7 Bradley Beal 2.00 5.00
8 Jonas Valanciunas 1.25 3.00
9 Harrison Barnes 2.00 5.00
10 Jae Crowder 1.00 2.50
11 Tyler Zeller 1.00 2.50
12 Andre Drummond 2.00 5.00
13 Kyle Singler .75 2.00
14 Meyers Leonard 1.00 2.50
15 Maurice Harkless 1.25 3.00
16 Jared Sullinger 1.00 2.50
17 John Henson 1.25 3.00
18 Festus Ezeli 1.00 2.50
19 Tornike Shengelia
20 Perry Jones .75 2.00
21 Mirza Teletovic 1.00 2.50
22 Kendall Marshall .75 2.00
23 Miles Plumlee .75 2.00
24 Draymond Green 4.00 10.00
25 Bernard James .75 2.00
26 Pablo Prigioni .75 2.00
27 Darius Miller .75 2.00
28 Terrence Jones 1.00 2.50
29 Fab Melo .75 2.00
30 Alexey Shved .75 2.00
31 Kyrie Irving 6.00 15.00
32 Kemba Walker 2.50 6.00
33 Kenneth Faried 1.25 3.00
34 Kawhi Leonard 6.00 15.00
35 Klay Thompson 5.00 12.00
36 E'Twaun Moore .75 2.00
37 Chandler Parsons 1.25 3.00
38 Isaiah Thomas 1.50 4.00
39 Brandon Knight 1.25 3.00
40 Nikola Vucevic 1.25 3.00
41 MarShon Brooks 1.00 2.50
42 Derrick Williams .75 2.00
43 Jimmer Fredette .75 2.00
44 Norris Cole .75 2.00
45 Enes Kanter 1.00 2.50
46 Marcus Morris 1.00 2.50
47 Tristan Thompson 1.25 3.00
48 Tobias Harris 1.50 4.00
49 Markieff Morris 1.25 3.00
50 Lavoy Allen .75 2.00

2012-13 Select Hot Stars

1 Kobe Bryant 4.00 10.00
2 Kevin Durant 2.50 6.00
3 Dwyane Wade 1.50 4.00
4 Dwight Howard .75 2.00
5 LeBron James 4.00 10.00
6 Paul Pierce 1.00 2.50
7 Kyrie Irving 5.00 12.00
8 Blake Griffin 1.00 2.50
9 Kevin Love 1.00 2.50
10 Carmelo Anthony 1.25 3.00
11 Deron Williams .75 2.00
12 James Harden 1.50 4.00
13 Russell Westbrook 2.50 6.00
14 Tim Duncan 1.50 4.00
15 Chris Paul 1.25 3.00
16 Rajon Rondo 1.00 2.50
17 Kevin Garnett 1.50 4.00
18 Kemba Walker 2.00 5.00
19 Chris Bosh 1.00 2.50
20 Derrick Rose 1.25 3.00
21 Dirk Nowitzki 1.25 3.00
22 Stephen Curry 4.00 10.00
23 Jeremy Lin 1.00 2.50
24 Steve Nash 1.00 2.50
25 Marc Gasol 1.00 2.50

2012-13 Select In-Flight Selections

1 Blake Griffin 1.00 2.50
2 Anthony Davis 5.00 12.00
3 LeBron James 4.00 10.00
4 Rajon Rondo 1.00 2.50
5 Derrick Rose 1.25 3.00
6 Kobe Bryant 4.00 10.00
7 Chris Paul 1.25 3.00
8 O.J. Mayo .60 1.50
9 Dwyane Wade 1.50 4.00
10 Serge Ibaka .75 2.00
11 Andre Iguodala .75 2.00
12 Harrison Barnes 1.50 4.00
13 Paul George 1.25 3.00
14 Thomas Robinson .75 2.00
15 Tyson Chandler .75 2.00
16 Vince Carter 1.25 3.00
17 Dion Waiters 1.00 2.50
18 Jason Terry .75 2.00
19 Tyreke Evans .60 1.50
20 Kevin Durant 2.50 6.00
21 Kevin Love 1.00 2.50
22 Michael Kidd-Gilchrist 1.00 2.50
23 Jeremy Lin 1.00 2.50
24 Kawhi Leonard 5.00 12.00
25 Ricky Rubio 1.00 2.50

2012-13 Select Select Stars Jersey Autographs

PRINT RUNS B/WN 20-199 COPIES PER
NO DEROZAN PRICING DUE TO SCARCITY
EXCHANGE DEADLINE 10/03/2014
1 Kevin Durant/199 50.00 120.00
2 Kobe Bryant/199 100.00 200.00
3 Blake Griffin/199 15.00 40.00
4 Zach Randolph/299 5.00 12.00
5 Joakim Noah/299 5.00 12.00
6 David Lee/299 EXCH 4.00 10.00
7 DeMarcus Cousins/299 10.00 25.00
9 J.J. Redick/299 6.00 15.00
10 Marcus Thornton/299 4.00 10.00
11 Andre Iguodala/299 5.00 12.00
12 Carlos Boozer/299 EXCH 5.00 12.00
13 Derrick Favors/299 5.00 12.00
14 Kevin Love/199 20.00 50.00
15 Kirk Hinrich/299 EXCH 5.00 12.00
16 LaMarcus Aldridge/199 8.00 20.00
17 Brook Lopez/199 5.00 12.00
18 Rashard Lewis/299 5.00 12.00
19 Stephen Curry/125 100.00 250.00
20 Stephen Jackson/199 5.00 12.00
21 Taj Gibson/199 5.00 12.00
22 Tayshaun Prince/199 EXCH 5.00 12.00
24 Tony Allen/199 4.00 10.00
25 Ty Lawson/299 4.00 10.00

2012-13 Select Select Stars Jersey Autographs Prizms

*PRIZMS: .5X TO 1.2X BASIC
PRINT RUNS B/WN 15-99 COPIES PER
NO DEROZAN PRICING DUE TO SCARCITY
EXCHANGE DEADLINE 10/03/2014
1 Kevin Durant/49 200.00 300.00
2 Kobe Bryant/99 100.00 200.00

2012-13 Select White Hot Rookies

1 Anthony Davis 8.00 20.00
2 Dion Waiters 1.50 4.00
3 Damian Lillard 6.00 15.00
4 Michael Kidd-Gilchrist 1.50 4.00
5 Thomas Robinson 1.25 3.00
6 Austin Rivers 1.50 4.00
7 Bradley Beal 2.50 6.00
8 Jonas Valanciunas 1.50 4.00
9 Harrison Barnes 2.50 6.00
10 Jae Crowder 1.25 3.00
11 Tyler Zeller 1.25 3.00
12 Andre Drummond 2.50 6.00
13 Kyle Singler 1.00 2.50
14 Meyers Leonard 1.25 3.00
15 Maurice Harkless 1.50 4.00
16 Jared Sullinger 1.25 3.00
17 John Henson 1.50 4.00
18 Festus Ezeli 1.25 3.00
19 Tornike Shengelia 1.00 2.50
20 Perry Jones 1.00 2.50
21 Mirza Teletovic 1.25 3.00
22 Kendall Marshall 1.00 2.50
23 Miles Plumlee 1.00 2.50
24 Draymond Green 5.00 12.00
25 Bernard James 1.00 2.50
26 Pablo Prigioni 1.00 2.50
27 Darius Miller 1.00 2.50
28 Terrence Jones 1.25 3.00
29 Fab Melo 1.00 2.50
30 Alexey Shved 1.00 2.50
31 Kyrie Irving 8.00 20.00
32 Kemba Walker 3.00 8.00
33 Kenneth Faried 1.50 4.00
34 Kawhi Leonard 8.00 20.00
35 Klay Thompson 6.00 15.00
36 E'Twaun Moore 1.00 2.50
37 Chandler Parsons 1.50 4.00
38 Isaiah Thomas 2.00 5.00
39 Brandon Knight 1.50 4.00
40 Nikola Vucevic 1.50 4.00
41 MarShon Brooks 1.25 3.00
42 Derrick Williams 1.00 2.50
43 Jimmer Fredette 1.00 2.50
44 Norris Cole 1.00 2.50
45 Enes Kanter 1.25 3.00
46 Marcus Morris 1.25 3.00
47 Tristan Thompson 1.50 4.00
48 Tobias Harris
49 Markieff Morris 1.50 4.00
50 Lavoy Allen 1.00 2.50

2012-13 Select White Hot Stars

1 Kobe Bryant 5.00 12.00
2 Kevin Durant 3.00 8.00
3 Dwyane Wade 2.00 5.00
4 Dwight Howard 1.00 2.50
5 LeBron James 5.00 12.00
6 Paul Pierce 1.25 3.00
7 Kyrie Irving 6.00 15.00
8 Blake Griffin 1.25 3.00
9 Kevin Love 1.25 3.00
10 Carmelo Anthony 1.50 4.00
11 Deron Williams 1.00 2.50
12 James Harden 2.00 5.00
13 Russell Westbrook 3.00 8.00
14 Tim Duncan 2.00 5.00
15 Chris Paul 1.50 4.00
16 Rajon Rondo 1.25 3.00
17 Kevin Garnett 2.00 5.00
18 Kemba Walker 2.50 6.00
19 Chris Bosh 1.25 3.00
20 Derrick Rose 1.50 4.00
21 Dirk Nowitzki 1.50 4.00
22 Stephen Curry 5.00 12.00
23 Jeremy Lin 1.25 3.00
24 Steve Nash 1.25 3.00
25 Marc Gasol 1.25 3.00

2013-14 Select

COMPLETE SET (200) 20.00 50.00
1 Ersan Ilyasova .20 .50
2 James Harden .50 1.25
3 Danny Granger .25 .60
4 Goran Dragic .25 .60
5 Manu Ginobili .30 .75
6 Taj Gibson .25 .60
7 Gerald Wallace .25 .60
8 DeMarcus Cousins .30 .75
9 Klay Thompson .40 1.00
10 Joakim Noah .25 .60
11 Kendrick Perkins .20 .50
12 J.J. Redick .30 .75
13 Jordan Hill .20 .50
14 Al-Farouq Aminu .25 .60
15 Rajon Rondo .30 .75
16 Tyler Hansbrough .25 .60
17 Brook Lopez .25 .60
18 Eric Bledsoe .25 .60
19 Jeremy Lin .30 .75
20 Shawn Marion .25 .60
21 Jimmy Butler .30 .75
22 Zach Randolph .25 .60
23 Shane Battier .25 .60
24 LeBron James 1.25 3.00
25 Terrence Jones .25 .60
26 Tristan Thompson .25 .60
27 Carlos Boozer .25 .60
28 Thabo Sefolosha .20 .50
29 Chris Paul .40 1.00
30 Josh Smith .25 .60
31 Tiago Splitter .25 .60
32 Larry Sanders .20 .50
33 Kobe Bryant 1.25 3.00
34 Paul George .40 1.00
35 David Lee .20 .50
36 Kawhi Leonard .50 1.25
37 Jose Calderon .20 .50
38 Eric Gordon .25 .60
39 Mike Conley .25 .60
40 Harrison Barnes .25 .60
41 Jan Vesely .20 .50
42 Jrue Holiday .30 .75
43 Nick Young .30 .75
44 Vince Carter .40 1.00
45 Marc Gasol .30 .75
46 Gerald Green .25 .60
47 Rodney Stuckey .25 .60
48 Michael Beasley .20 .50
49 Mario Chalmers .25 .60
50 George Hill .25 .60
51 Marcus Thornton .20 .50
52 Arron Afflalo .20 .50
53 Evan Turner .20 .50
54 Gerald Henderson .20 .50
55 Nicolas Batum .25 .60
56 Greivis Vasquez .25 .60
57 Dwight Howard .25 .60
58 Chris Kaman .25 .60
59 Ricky Rubio .30 .75
60 Blake Griffin .30 .75
61 Nikola Vucevic .25 .60
62 Damian Lillard .60 1.50
63 Thomas Robinson .20 .50
64 Kyle Lowry .25 .60
65 John Wall .40 1.00
66 Greg Monroe .25 .60
67 Jamal Crawford .30 .75
68 Lance Stephenson .25 .60
69 Tyson Chandler .25 .60
70 John Henson .25 .60
71 Anthony Davis .60 1.50
72 Tony Parker .30 .75
73 DeMar DeRozan .30 .75
74 Jason Richardson .30 .75
75 Kevin Garnett .50 1.25
76 Spencer Hawes .20 .50
77 Tony Allen .20 .50
78 Andrew Bogut .25 .60
79 Glen Davis .20 .50
80 Tyreke Evans .20 .50
81 Dwyane Wade .50 1.25
82 Derrick Favors .25 .60
83 Marcin Gortat .25 .60
84 Iman Shumpert .20 .50
85 Ty Lawson .20 .50
86 Stephen Curry 1.25 3.00
87 Chris Bosh .30 .75
88 J.J. Hickson .20 .50
89 Marcus Morris .20 .50
90 Thaddeus Young .20 .50
91 Roy Hibbert .25 .60
92 Paul Millsap .30 .75
93 Jimmer Fredette .20 .50
94 O.J. Mayo .20 .50
95 Luis Scola .25 .60
96 Jameer Nelson .20 .50
97 Kevin Martin .25 .60
98 Kyrie Irving .60 1.50
99 Isaiah Thomas .30 .75
100 Wesley Matthews .20 .50
101 Brandon Jennings .20 .50
102 Al Jefferson .25 .60
103 Danilo Gallinari .20 .50
104 Tayshaun Prince .25 .60
105 Raymond Felton .25 .60
106 Khris Middleton .25 .60
107 Amare Stoudemire .25 .60
108 Miles Plumlee .20 .50
109 Tim Duncan .50 1.25
110 Jonas Valanciunas .25 .60
111 Anderson Varejao .20 .50
112 Andrei Kirilenko .25 .60
113 Steve Nash .30 .75
114 David West .25 .60
115 Rudy Gay .30 .75
116 J.R. Smith .25 .60
117 Serge Ibaka .25 .60
118 Deron Williams .25 .60
119 Marvin Williams .25 .60
120 Trevor Ariza .20 .50
121 Andray Blatche .20 .50
122 Carmelo Anthony .40 1.00
123 J.J. Barea .25 .60
124 Andre Drummond .30 .75
125 Avery Bradley .25 .60
126 Pau Gasol .30 .75
127 Markieff Morris .20 .50
128 Al Horford .25 .60
129 Martell Webster .20 .50
130 Joe Johnson .25 .60
131 Jeff Green .25 .60
132 Derrick Rose .40 1.00
133 Russell Westbrook .75 2.00
134 Kirk Hinrich .25 .60
135 Bradley Beal .30 .75
136 Kevin Durant .75 2.00
137 LaMarcus Aldridge .30 .75
138 Kemba Walker .30 .75
139 Jeff Teague .25 .60
140 Monta Ellis .25 .60
141 Kenneth Faried .25 .60
142 Dirk Nowitzki .40 1.00
143 Nikola Pekovic .20 .50
144 Brandon Bass .20 .50
145 Michael Kidd-Gilchrist .30 .75
146 Kevin Love .30 .75
147 Danny Green .25 .60
148 Dion Waiters .25 .60
149 Kris Humphries .20 .50
150 Chandler Parsons .25 .60
151 Luol Deng .25 .60
152 Andre Iguodala .25 .60
153 Enes Kanter .20 .50
154 Kyle Korver .25 .60
155 Richard Jefferson .25 .60
156 Ray Allen .30 .75
157 Gordon Hayward .30 .75
158 JaVale McGee .25 .60
159 Paul Pierce .30 .75
160 DeAndre Jordan .30 .75
161 Gorgui Dieng RC .40 1.00
162 Dwight Buycks RC .30 .75
163 Shane Larkin RC .30 .75
164 Dennis Schroder RC .50 1.25
165 Vitor Faverani RC .30 .75
166 Kentavious Caldwell-Pope RC .50 1.25
167 Phil Pressey RC .30 .75
168 Nate Wolters RC .40 1.00
169 Tony Snell RC .40 1.00
170 Solomon Hill RC .30 .75
171 Lorenzo Brown RC .30 .75
172 Sergey Karasev RC .30 .75
173 Tony Mitchell RC .30 .75
174 Nerlens Noel RC .60 1.50
175 Victor Oladipo RC .60 1.50
176 Brandon Davies RC .30 .75
177 Archie Goodwin RC .40 1.00
178 G.Antetokounmpo RC 5.00 12.00
179 Reggie Bullock RC .40 1.00
180 Trey Burke RC .40 1.00
181 Luigi Datome RC .30 .75
182 C.J. McCollum RC .75 2.00
183 Shabazz Muhammad RC .40 1.00
184 Kelly Olynyk RC .40 1.00
185 Cody Zeller RC .40 1.00
186 Tim Hardaway Jr. RC .50 1.25
187 Anthony Bennett RC .40 1.00
188 Gal Mekel RC .30 .75
189 Matthew Dellavedova RC .50 1.25
190 M.Carter-Williams RC .50 1.25
191 Peyton Siva RC .30 .75
192 Otto Porter RC .50 1.25
193 Alex Len RC .40 1.00
194 Glen Rice Jr. RC .30 .75
195 Steven Adams RC .50 1.25
196 Ben McLemore RC .40 1.00
197 Mason Plumlee RC .50 1.25
198 Nemanja Nedovic RC .30 .75
199 Rudy Gobert RC .60 1.50
200 Pero Antic RC .30 .75

2013-14 Select Prizms

*PRIZMS: 2X TO 5X BASIC
*PRIZMS RC: 1.2X TO 3X BASIC
178 Giannis Antetokounmpo 25.00 60.00

2013-14 Select Prizms Blue

*PRIZMS BLUE: 6X TO 15X BASIC
*PRIZMS BLUE RC: 4X TO 10X BASIC
STATED PRINT RUN 49 SER.#'d SETS
24 LeBron James 25.00 60.00
33 Kobe Bryant 25.00 60.00
178 Giannis Antetokounmpo 50.00 120.00

2013-14 Select Prizms Purple

*PRIZMS PURPLE: 5X TO 12X BASIC
*PRIZMS PURPLE RC: 3X TO 8X BASIC
STATED PRINT RUN 99 SER.#'d SETS
174 Nerlens Noel 25.00 60.00
175 Victor Oladipo 20.00 50.00
178 Giannis Antetokounmpo 40.00 100.00

2013-14 Select Clutch

1 Dirk Nowitzki 1.25 3.00
2 Ray Allen 1.00 2.50
3 Kobe Bryant 4.00 10.00
4 Robert Horry .75 2.00
5 Chauncey Billups 1.00 2.50
6 LeBron James 4.00 10.00
7 Kevin Durant 2.50 6.00
8 Larry Bird 2.50 6.00
9 Dwyane Wade 1.50 4.00
10 Paul Pierce 1.00 2.50
11 Damian Lillard 2.00 5.00
12 Vinnie Johnson 1.00 2.50
13 Jerry West 1.25 3.00
14 Steve Kerr 1.00 2.50
15 Magic Johnson 2.50 6.00

2013-14 Select Clutch Prizms

*PRIZMS: .75X TO 2X BASIC
6 LeBron James 10.00 25.00

2013-14 Select Clutch Prizms Blue

*PRIZMS BLUE: 2X TO 5X BASIC
STATED PRINT RUN 49 SER.#'d SETS

2013-14 Select Clutch Prizms Purple

*PRIZMS PURPLE: 1.5X TO 4X BASIC
STATED PRINT RUN 99 SER.#'d SETS

2013-14 Select Draft Selections

1 Anthony Bennett .75 2.00
2 Victor Oladipo 1.25 3.00
3 Otto Porter 1.00 2.50
4 Cody Zeller .75 2.00
5 Alex Len .75 2.00
6 Nerlens Noel 1.25 3.00
7 Ben McLemore .75 2.00
8 Kentavious Caldwell-Pope 1.00 2.50
9 Trey Burke .75 2.00
10 C.J. McCollum 1.50 4.00
11 Michael Carter-Williams 1.00 2.50
12 Steven Adams 1.00 2.50
13 Kelly Olynyk .75 2.00
14 Shabazz Muhammad .75 2.00
15 Giannis Antetokounmpo 8.00 20.00
16 Shane Larkin .60 1.50
17 Sergey Karasev .60 1.50
18 Tony Snell .75 2.00
19 Gorgui Dieng .75 2.00
20 Mason Plumlee 1.00 2.50
21 Solomon Hill .60 1.50
22 Tim Hardaway Jr. 1.00 2.50
23 Rudy Gobert 1.25 3.00
24 Archie Goodwin .75 2.00
25 Nate Wolters .75 2.00

2013-14 Select Draft Selections Prizms

*PRIZMS: .75X TO 2X BASIC

2013-14 Select Draft Selections Prizms Blue

*PRIZMS BLUE: 2X TO 5X BASIC
STATED PRINT RUN 49 SER.#'d SETS

2013-14 Select Draft Selections Prizms Purple
*PRIZMS PURPLE: 1.5X TO 4X BASIC
STATED PRINT RUN 99 SER.#'d SETS

2013-14 Select Franchise Signatures
EXCHANGE DEADLINE 12/25/2015
4 Udonis Haslem 3.00 8.00
5 Bob Dandridge 3.00 8.00
6 Jack Sikma 4.00 10.00
10 Kyrie Irving EXCH 60.00 120.00
11 Anthony Davis 50.00 120.00
14 Gerald Henderson 3.00 8.00
15 Bruce Bowen 3.00 8.00
16 Zydrunas Ilgauskas 4.00 10.00
25 Michael Cooper 4.00 10.00

2013-14 Select Franchise Signatures Blue
*BLUE: .5X TO 1.2X PURPLE
PRINT RUNS B/WN 20-49 COPIES PER
EXCHANGE DEADLINE 12/25/2015
10 Kyrie Irving/20 EXCH 50.00 120.00
14 Gerald Henderson/49 5.00 12.00
15 Bruce Bowen/49 10.00 25.00
20 Kobe Bryant/20 125.00 250.00
23 Shaquille O'Neal/20 100.00 250.00

2013-14 Select Franchise Signatures Purple
*PURPLE: .5X TO 1.2X BASIC
PRINT RUNS B/WN 30-60 COPIES PER
EXCHANGE DEADLINE 12/25/2015
1 Kyle Lowry/60 5.00 12.00
2 Kevin Love/30
3 Serge Ibaka/30
7 Allan Houston/49 5.00 12.00
8 Isiah Thomas/30
9 John Havlicek/30
12 Bradley Beal/30 30.00 60.00
13 Roy Hibbert/30
17 Michael Finley/30 6.00 15.00
19 Kevin Durant/30
20 Kobe Bryant/30
21 Tony Parker/30 25.00 60.00
22 Jared Sullinger/30
23 Shaquille O'Neal/30 75.00 150.00
24 Goran Dragic/30
25 Michael Cooper/60

2013-14 Select Hall Selections Signatures
EXCHANGE DEADLINE 12/25/2015
9 Bob McAdoo 4.00 10.00
21 Dan Issel 4.00 10.00

2013-14 Select Hall Selections Signatures Prizms Blue
*BLUE: .5X TO 1.2X PURPLE
STATED PRINT RUN 20 SER.#'d SETS
EXCHANGE DEADLINE 12/25/2015
4 Gail Goodrich 12.00 30.00
7 Karl Malone 60.00 120.00
15 Kevin McHale 10.00 25.00
19 Jerry Lucas 12.00 30.00
20 Bernard King 10.00 25.00
23 Nate Thurmond 8.00 20.00

2013-14 Select Hall Selections Signatures Prizms Purple
*PURPLE: .6X TO 1.5X BASIC
STATED PRINT RUN 30 SER.#'d SETS
EXCHANGE DEADLINE 12/25/2015
1 Chris Mullin 8.00 20.00
2 Dolph Schayes
3 Robert Parish 8.00 20.00
4 Gail Goodrich
5 Hakeem Olajuwon
6 Magic Johnson 50.00 100.00
7 Karl Malone 30.00 80.00
8 Scottie Pippen
10 Adrian Dantley 6.00 15.00
11 Clyde Drexler 40.00 80.00
12 Joe Dumars 10.00 25.00
13 Ralph Sampson 6.00 15.00
14 James Worthy 15.00 40.00
15 Kevin McHale 15.00 40.00
16 Kareem Abdul-Jabbar 40.00 100.00
17 Larry Bird 50.00 100.00
18 David Robinson 25.00 60.00
19 Jerry Lucas
20 Bernard King
22 Nate Archibald 6.00 15.00
23 Nate Thurmond
24 Dennis Rodman 20.00 50.00
25 Julius Erving 40.00 80.00

2013-14 Select Jersey Autographs
EXCHANGE DEADLINE 12/25/2015
2 Eddie Johnson
12 Buck Williams 4.00 10.00
16 Kobe Bryant 75.00 150.00
21 Dee Brown 4.00 10.00
22 Rory Sparrow 4.00 10.00
30 Steve Mix 4.00 10.00
33 John Wall 20.00 50.00
34 Steve Smith 5.00 12.00
36 Nick Collison 5.00 12.00
37 Anthony Mason
38 Scottie Pippen 50.00 120.00
39 Charles Oakley 6.00 15.00

2013-14 Select Jersey Autographs Blue
*BLUE: .5X TO 1.2X PURPLE
PRINT RUNS B/WN 20-49 COPIES PER
EXCHANGE DEADLINE 12/25/2015
5 Tracy McGrady/20 30.00 60.00
16 Kobe Bryant/20 100.00 200.00
25 Kevin Durant/20 75.00 150.00
28 Josh Smith/20 8.00 20.00
38 Scottie Pippen/20 50.00 120.00
40 James Worthy/20 20.00 50.00

2013-14 Select Jersey Autographs Purple
*PURPLE: .5X TO 1.2X BASIC
PRINT RUNS B/WN 30-99 COPIES PER
EXCHANGE DEADLINE 12/25/2015
1 Derrick Favors/30
2 Eddie Johnson/99 5.00 12.00
3 Kenny Sky Walker/49 5.00 12.00
4 Kyrie Irving/30
5 Tracy McGrady/30 15.00 40.00
6 Kenneth Faried/30
7 Al Horford/30 6.00 15.00
8 Deron Williams/30 6.00 15.00
9 Harrison Barnes/30
10 Steve Nash/30 20.00 50.00
11 Enes Kanter/30
12 Buck Williams/99 10.00 25.00
13 Kevin Willis/49 5.00 12.00
14 Shaquille O'Neal/30
15 James Harden/30 20.00 50.00
17 Stephen Curry/30
18 Andre Drummond/30 8.00 20.00
19 Andre Iguodala/30
20 Goran Dragic/30 6.00 15.00
21 Dee Brown/99 5.00 12.00
23 Jalen Rose/30 8.00 20.00
24 Ralph Sampson/30 6.00 15.00
25 Kevin Durant/30 75.00 150.00
26 Kevin Love/30 20.00 50.00
27 Bradley Beal/30 15.00 40.00
28 Josh Smith/30
29 Mike Conley/30 6.00 15.00
31 Karl Malone/30
32 Alex English/49 6.00 15.00
35 Tom Chambers/49 6.00 15.00
38 Scottie Pippen/30 50.00 120.00
40 James Worthy/30 20.00 50.00

2013-14 Select Red Hot
1 J.R. Smith .75 2.00
2 DeMarcus Cousins 1.00 2.50
3 Kobe Bryant 4.00 10.00
4 Victor Oladipo 1.25 3.00
5 Jeff Teague .75 2.00
6 Russell Westbrook 2.50 6.00
7 Shawn Marion .75 2.00
8 Harrison Barnes .75 2.00
9 Chris Paul 1.25 3.00
10 Ricky Rubio 1.00 2.50
11 Jameer Nelson .60 1.50
12 Tony Parker 1.00 2.50
13 Kevin Durant 2.50 6.00
14 Nate Wolters .75 2.00
15 Paul Millsap 1.00 2.50
16 Joakim Noah .75 2.00
17 Monta Ellis .75 2.00
18 Klay Thompson 1.25 3.00
19 Zach Randolph .75 2.00
20 Kevin Love 1.00 2.50
21 Thaddeus Young .60 1.50
22 Tim Duncan 1.50 4.00
23 Kyrie Irving 2.00 5.00
24 Ben McLemore .75 2.00
25 Rajon Rondo 1.00 2.50
26 Derrick Rose 1.25 3.00
27 Kenneth Faried .75 2.00
28 James Harden 1.50 4.00
29 Dwyane Wade 1.50 4.00
30 Tyreke Evans .60 1.50
31 Eric Bledsoe .75 2.00
32 Derrick Favors .75 2.00
33 Damian Lillard 2.00 5.00
34 Giannis Antetokounmpo 8.00 20.00
35 Paul Pierce 1.00 2.50
36 Anderson Varejao .60 1.50
37 Dirk Nowitzki 1.25 3.00
38 Roy Hibbert .75 2.00
39 LeBron James 4.00 10.00
40 Anthony Davis 2.00 5.00
41 Nicolas Batum .75 2.00
42 Marcin Gortat .75 2.00
43 Michael Carter-Williams 1.00 2.50
44 Trey Burke .75 2.00
45 Brook Lopez .75 2.00
46 Dion Waiters .75 2.00
47 Brandon Jennings .60 1.50
48 Paul George 1.25 3.00
49 O.J. Mayo .60 1.50
50 Amare Stoudemire .75 2.00

2013-14 Select Red Hot Prizms
*PRIZMS: 3X TO 8X BASIC
STATED PRINT RUN 25 SER.#'d SETS
34 Giannis Antetokounmpo 75.00 200.00

2013-14 Select Red Hot Prizms Blue
*BLUE: X TO X BASIC
STATED PRINT RUN 49 SER.#'d SETS
3 Kobe Bryant 25.00 60.00
34 Giannis Antetokounmpo 60.00 150.00
39 LeBron James 25.00 60.00

2013-14 Select Red Hot Prizms Purple
*PURPLE: 1.5X TO 4X BASIC
STATED PRINT RUN 99 SER.#'d SETS
3 Kobe Bryant 20.00 50.00

2013-14 Select Rookie Jersey Autographs
EXCHANGE DEADLINE 12/25/2015
1 Giannis Antetokounmpo 75.00 200.00
2 Mason Plumlee 5.00 12.00
3 Glen Rice Jr. 3.00 8.00
4 Erik Murphy 3.00 8.00
5 Victor Oladipo 6.00 15.00
6 Luigi Datome 3.00 8.00
7 Otto Porter 5.00 12.00
8 Nerlens Noel 6.00 15.00
9 Trey Burke 4.00 10.00
10 Steven Adams 5.00 12.00
11 Shane Larkin 3.00 8.00
12 Tim Hardaway Jr. 5.00 12.00
13 Nate Wolters 4.00 10.00
14 Ricky Ledo 3.00 8.00
15 Matthew Dellavedova 5.00 12.00
16 Rudy Gobert 8.00 20.00
17 Cody Zeller 4.00 10.00
18 Ben McLemore 4.00 10.00
19 C.J. McCollum 12.00 30.00
20 Kelly Olynyk 4.00 10.00
21 Tony Snell 4.00 10.00
22 Archie Goodwin 4.00 10.00
23 Tony Mitchell 3.00 8.00
24 Gal Mekel 3.00 8.00
25 Peyton Siva 3.00 8.00
26 Anthony Bennett 4.00 10.00
27 Alex Len 4.00 10.00
28 Kentavious Caldwell-Pope 5.00 12.00
29 Michael Carter-Williams 5.00 12.00
30 Shabazz Muhammad 4.00 10.00

2013-14 Select Rookie Jersey Autographs Blue
*BLUE: .6X TO 1.5X BASIC
PRINT RUNS B/WN 35-49 COPIES PER
EXCHANGE DEADLINE 12/25/2015

2013-14 Select Rookie Jersey Autographs Purple
*PURPLE: .5X TO 1.2X BASIC
PRINT RUNS B/WN 60-99 COPIES PER
EXCHANGE DEADLINE 12/25/2015

2013-14 Select Signatures
EXCHANGE DEADLINE 12/25/2015
1 Marcin Gortat 6.00 15.00
3 John Lucas 5.00 12.00
4 Cazzie Russell 4.00 10.00
8 P.J. Tucker 3.00 8.00
9 Kobe Bryant 75.00 150.00
10 Nick Collison 4.00 10.00
11 Brandon Bass 3.00 8.00
13 George McGinnis 3.00 8.00
14 Fat Lever 4.00 10.00
17 Derrick Coleman 5.00 12.00
18 Kevin Durant 50.00 120.00
19 Patrick Beverley 3.00 8.00
20 Jan Vesely 3.00 8.00
21 Roy Hibbert 4.00 10.00
23 Jay Williams 3.00 8.00
24 Theo Ratliff 3.00 8.00
27 Vin Baker 3.00 8.00
29 Jon Leuer 3.00 8.00
30 Tobias Harris 4.00 10.00
33 Clifford Robinson 3.00 8.00
34 B.J. Armstrong 5.00 12.00
38 Ramon Sessions 4.00 10.00
39 Nando De Colo 4.00 10.00
40 Taj Gibson 4.00 10.00
43 Gus Williams 3.00 8.00
48 Brian Roberts 3.00 8.00
49 Greg Oden 4.00 10.00
50 Enes Kanter 3.00 8.00

2013-14 Select Signatures Blue
*BLUE: .5X TO 1.2X PURPLE
PRINT RUNS B/WN 15-49 COPIES PER
NO PRICING ON QTY 15 OR LESS
EXCHANGE DEADLINE 12/25/2015
5 Jason Kidd/20 40.00 80.00
15 Julius Erving/20 50.00 100.00
37 Magic Johnson/20 30.00 60.00

2013-14 Select Signatures Purple
*PURPLE: .5X TO 1.2X BASIC
PRINT RUNS B/WN 25-99 COPIES PER
EXCHANGE DEADLINE 12/25/2015
1 Marcin Gortat/99 10.00 25.00
2 Steve Nash/25
5 Jason Kidd/25
6 Gail Goodrich/25 5.00 12.00
7 Byron Scott/25
12 Kevin Love/25 25.00 60.00
13 George McGinnis/25 20.00 50.00
14 Fat Lever/99 10.00 25.00
15 Julius Erving/25
16 George Gervin/25 12.00 30.00
22 Al Horford/25
25 Earl Monroe/25 8.00 20.00
26 Peja Stojakovic/25 12.00 30.00
28 Kyrie Irving/25
32 Andre Iguodala/25 12.00 30.00
35 Kevin McHale/25
36 Steve Francis/25
37 Magic Johnson/25 50.00 100.00
40 Taj Gibson/25 10.00 25.00
41 Bradley Beal/25
42 Andre Drummond/25
44 Danny Manning/25
45 Hakeem Olajuwon/25 30.00 60.00
46 Kenny Smith/25
47 John Stockton/25

2013-14 Select Skills
1 Kemba Walker 1.00 2.50
2 John Wall 1.25 3.00
3 Dwight Howard .75 2.00
4 Tim Duncan 1.50 4.00
5 Damian Lillard 2.00 5.00
6 Stephen Curry 4.00 10.00
7 Blake Griffin 1.00 2.50
8 Rajon Rondo 1.00 2.50
9 DeMar DeRozan 1.00 2.50
10 Greg Monroe .75 2.00
11 LeBron James 4.00 10.00
12 Dirk Nowitzki 1.25 3.00
13 Marc Gasol 1.00 2.50
14 Kenneth Faried .75 2.00
15 Kevin Durant 2.50 6.00
16 Chris Paul 1.25 3.00
17 DeMarcus Cousins 1.00 2.50
18 Paul Pierce 1.00 2.50
19 Derrick Rose 1.25 3.00
20 Paul George 1.25 3.00
21 Dwyane Wade 1.50 4.00
22 James Harden 1.50 4.00
23 Anthony Davis 2.00 5.00
24 Kevin Love 1.00 2.50
25 Russell Westbrook 2.50 6.00
26 Kobe Bryant 4.00 10.00
27 LaMarcus Aldridge 1.00 2.50
28 Carmelo Anthony 1.25 3.00
29 Kyrie Irving 2.00 5.00
30 Kyle Korver .75 2.00

2013-14 Select Skills Prizms
*PRIZMS: .75X TO 2X BASIC

2013-14 Select Skills Prizms Blue
*BLUE: 2X TO 5X BASIC
STATED PRINT RUN 49 SER.#'d SETS
11 LeBron James 25.00 60.00

2013-14 Select Skills Prizms Purple
*PURPLE: 1.5X TO 4X BASIC
STATED PRINT RUN 99 SER.#'d SETS
11 LeBron James 20.00 50.00
15 Kevin Durant 20.00 50.00
26 Kobe Bryant 20.00 50.00

2013-14 Select Sky High
1 Blake Griffin 1.00 2.50
2 Nate Robinson .60 1.50
3 Vince Carter 1.25 3.00
4 Jason Richardson 1.00 2.50
5 Dwight Howard .75 2.00
6 Kevin Durant 2.50 6.00
7 Kobe Bryant 4.00 10.00
8 LeBron James 4.00 10.00
9 Terrence Ross .75 2.00
10 Gerald Green .75 2.00

2013-14 Select Sky High Prizms
*PRIZMS: .75X TO 2X BASIC

2013-14 Select Sky High Prizms Blue
*BLUE: 2X TO 5X BASIC
STATED PRINT RUN 49 SER.#'d SETS
7 Kobe Bryant 25.00 60.00

2013-14 Select Sky High Prizms Purple
*PURPLE: 1.5X TO 4X BASIC
STATED PRINT RUN 99 SER.#'d SETS

2013-14 Select Stars
1 Kyrie Irving 2.00 5.00
2 Anthony Davis 2.00 5.00
3 Kobe Bryant 4.00 10.00
4 Kevin Love 1.00 2.50
5 Dirk Nowitzki 1.25 3.00
6 Damian Lillard 2.00 5.00
7 Carmelo Anthony 1.25 3.00
8 Tim Duncan 1.50 4.00
9 Paul George 1.25 3.00
10 Kevin Durant 2.50 6.00

2013-14 Select Stars Prizms
*PRIZMS: .75X TO 2X BASIC

2013-14 Select Stars Prizms Blue
*BLUE: 2X TO 5X BASIC
STATED PRINT RUN 49 SER.#'d SETS
3 Kobe Bryant 25.00 60.00

2013-14 Select Stars Prizms Purple
*PURPLE: 1.5X TO 4X BASIC
STATED PRINT RUN 99 SER.#'d SETS

2013-14 Select Swatches
2 James Jones 2.00 5.00
3 Amare Stoudemire 2.50 6.00
4 Robert Parish 3.00 8.00
5 Michael Beasley 2.00 5.00
6 Raymond Felton 2.50 6.00
7 LeBron James 10.00 25.00
8 Al Horford 2.50 6.00
9 Kemba Walker 3.00 8.00
10 Klay Thompson 4.00 10.00
11 Dikembe Mutombo 3.00 8.00
12 Patrick Ewing 8.00 20.00
14 Alex English 2.50 6.00
15 DeJuan Blair 2.00 5.00
16 Kyrie Irving 6.00 15.00
17 Dwyane Wade 5.00 12.00
18 Kevin Garnett 5.00 12.00
19 Jimmy Butler 3.00 8.00
20 Anthony Davis 6.00 15.00
21 Bill Laimbeer 2.50 6.00
22 Norris Cole 2.00 5.00
23 DeMarcus Cousins 3.00 8.00
24 Clyde Drexler 4.00 10.00
25 MarShon Brooks 2.50 6.00
26 Dirk Nowitzki 4.00 10.00
27 Kevin Love 3.00 8.00
28 Paul Pierce 3.00 8.00
29 Andre Drummond 3.00 8.00
30 Jrue Holiday 3.00 8.00
31 Jayson Williams 2.00 5.00
32 Jermaine O'Neal 2.50 6.00
33 Joe Dumars 3.00 8.00
34 Shaquille O'Neal 6.00 15.00
35 Tayshaun Prince 2.50 6.00
36 Kenneth Faried 2.50 6.00
37 Ricky Rubio 4.00 10.00
38 Monta Ellis 2.50 6.00
39 Brandon Jennings 2.00 5.00
40 Joakim Noah 2.50 6.00
41 Bob Lanier 2.50 6.00
42 Chris Mullin 3.00 8.00
43 Scottie Pippen 6.00 15.00
44 Walter Berry 2.00 5.00
45 Boris Diaw 2.50 6.00
46 James Harden 5.00 12.00
47 Carmelo Anthony 4.00 10.00
48 Stephen Curry 6.00 15.00
49 Josh Smith 2.50 6.00
50 Anderson Varejao 2.00 5.00
51 Bernard King 2.50 6.00
52 Grant Hill 4.00 10.00
53 Karl Malone 4.00 10.00
54 Ray Allen 5.00 12.00
55 Tobias Harris 2.50 6.00
56 Dwight Howard 2.50 6.00
57 Kevin Durant 6.00 15.00
58 O.J. Mayo 2.00 5.00
59 Harrison Barnes 2.50 6.00
60 Jeremy Lin 3.00 8.00
61 Anfernee Hardaway 8.00 20.00
62 Larry Johnson 4.00 10.00
65 Tyson Chandler 2.50 6.00
66 Paul George 4.00 10.00
67 Russell Westbrook 8.00 20.00
68 Bradley Beal 3.00 8.00
69 Andre Iguodala 2.50 6.00
70 Tony Parker 3.00 8.00
74 Nate Robinson 2.00 5.00
75 Derrick Favors 2.50 6.00
76 Blake Griffin 3.00 8.00
78 Deron Williams 2.50 6.00
79 David Lee 2.00 5.00
81 Jose Calderon 2.00 5.00
84 Udonis Haslem 2.00 5.00
85 Caron Butler 2.50 6.00
87 Tim Duncan 5.00 12.00
88 Al Jefferson 2.50 6.00
90 Xavier McDaniel 2.00 5.00
92 Tracy McGrady 3.00 8.00
94 Danilo Gallinari 2.00 5.00
95 Steve Novak 2.00 5.00
96 Kobe Bryant 8.00 20.00
97 John Wall 4.00 10.00
98 Michael Kidd-Gilchrist 3.00 8.00
99 Pau Gasol 3.00 8.00
100 DeMar DeRozan 3.00 8.00

2013-14 Select Swatches Prizms
*PRIZMS: .75X TO 2X BASIC
STATED PRINT RUN 25 SER.#'d SETS

2013-14 Select Swatches Prizms Blue
*PRIZMS BLUE: .6X TO 1.5X BASIC
PRINT RUNS B/WN 35-49 COPIES PER

2013-14 Select Swatches Prizms Purple
*PRIZMS PURPLE: .5X TO 1.2X BASIC
PRINT RUNS B/WN 60-99 COPIES PER
1 Kelly Tripucka 3.00 8.00
13 Hakeem Olajuwon 5.00 12.00
15 DeJuan Blair 2.50 6.00
63 John Stockton 10.00 25.00
71 Reggie Lewis 12.00 30.00
72 David Robinson 5.00 12.00
77 Damian Lillard 6.00 15.00
80 Marc Gasol 4.00 10.00
83 Kevin McHale
86 Chris Paul 5.00 12.00
89 Steve Nash 4.00 10.00
91 Paul Westphal 4.00 10.00
96 Kobe Bryant 20.00 50.00

2013-14 Select Top Selections Jersey Autographs
EXCHANGE DEADLINE 12/25/2015
1 Charles Oakley 5.00 12.00
2 Cedric Maxwell 3.00 8.00
3 Bill Cartwright 4.00 10.00
15 Kevin Durant 40.00 100.00
18 Kobe Bryant
24 Kenyon Martin 4.00 10.00
29 Larry Johnson 10.00 25.00

2013-14 Select Top Selections Jersey Autographs Prizms Blue
*PRIZMS BLUE: .5X TO 1.2X PURPLE
PRINT RUNS B/WN 15-49 COPIES PER
NO PRICING ON QTY 15
EXCHANGE DEADLINE 12/25/2015
5 Chris Bosh/20 15.00 40.00
20 Robert Parish/20 15.00 40.00
21 Magic Johnson/20 40.00 80.00
26 Bradley Beal/20 20.00 50.00

2013-14 Select Top Selections Jersey Autographs Prizms Purple
*PRIZMS PURPLE: .5X TO 1.2X BASIC
PRINT RUNS B/WN 20-99 COPIES PER
EXCHANGE DEADLINE 12/25/2015
3 Bill Cartwright/99 5.00 12.00
4 Dikembe Mutombo/30 6.00 15.00
5 Chris Bosh/30
6 Kevin Love/30 20.00 50.00
7 Harrison Barnes/30 5.00 12.00
8 James Harden/30
9 Kareem Abdul-Jabbar/30 30.00 80.00
10 Fred Brown/99 4.00 10.00
11 Larry Bird/30 30.00 80.00
12 Sidney Moncrief/79 4.00 10.00
13 David Robinson/30 20.00 50.00
14 Grant Hill/30 30.00 60.00
16 Kawhi Leonard/75 50.00 120.00
17 LaMarcus Aldridge/30 15.00 40.00
18 Kobe Bryant/30 125.00 250.00
19 Bob Lanier/20
20 Robert Parish/30
21 Magic Johnson/30
22 John Wall/30
23 Dan Majerle/99 5.00 12.00
24 Kenyon Martin/99 5.00 12.00
25 Kyrie Irving/30 50.00 100.00
26 Bradley Beal/30
27 Kelly Tripucka/30 4.00 10.00
28 Cazzie Russell/99 5.00 12.00
30 Bernard King/30 5.00 12.00

2013-14 Select White Hot
1 LeBron James 4.00 10.00
2 Kemba Walker 1.00 2.50
3 Ty Lawson .60 1.50
4 Jeremy Lin 1.00 2.50
5 Chris Bosh 1.00 2.50
6 Jrue Holiday 1.00 2.50
7 Nikola Vucevic .75 2.00
8 Rudy Gay 1.00 2.50
9 Kyrie Irving 2.00 5.00
10 Victor Oladipo 1.25 3.00
11 Al Horford .75 2.00
12 Luol Deng .75 2.00
13 Andre Drummond 1.00 2.50
14 Blake Griffin 1.00 2.50
15 Larry Sanders .60 1.50
16 Tyson Chandler .75 2.00
17 Evan Turner .60 1.50
18 Manu Ginobili 1.00 2.50
19 Kobe Bryant 4.00 10.00
20 Anthony Bennett .75 2.00
21 Kevin Garnett 1.50 4.00
22 Carlos Boozer .75 2.00
23 Andre Iguodala .75 2.00
24 DeAndre Jordan 1.00 2.50
25 Ersan Ilyasova .60 1.50
26 Carmelo Anthony 1.25 3.00
27 Goran Dragic .75 2.00
28 DeMar DeRozan 1.00 2.50
29 Kevin Durant 2.50 6.00
30 C.J. McCollum 1.50 4.00
31 Deron Williams .75 2.00
32 Vince Carter 1.25 3.00
33 Stephen Curry 4.00 10.00
34 Marc Gasol 1.00 2.50
35 Nikola Pekovic .60 1.50
36 Serge Ibaka .75 2.00
37 LaMarcus Aldridge 1.00 2.50
38 Bradley Beal 1.00 2.50
39 Damian Lillard 2.00 5.00
40 Nerlens Noel 1.25 3.00
41 Al Jefferson .75 2.00
42 Dirk Nowitzki 1.25 3.00
43 Dwight Howard .75 2.00
44 Mike Conley .75 2.00
45 Kevin Martin .75 2.00
46 Russell Westbrook 2.50 6.00
47 Isaiah Thomas 1.00 2.50
48 John Wall 1.25 3.00
49 Michael Carter-Williams 1.00 2.50
50 Steven Adams 1.00 2.50

2013-14 Select White Hot Prizms
*PRIZMS: 3X TO 8X BASIC
STATED PRINT RUN 25 SER.#'d SETS

2013-14 Select White Hot Prizms Blue
*BLUE: 2X TO 5X BASIC
STATED PRINT RUN 49 SER.#'d SETS
1 LeBron James 25.00 60.00
19 Kobe Bryant 25.00 60.00

2013-14 Select White Hot Prizms Purple
*PURPLE: 1.5X TO 4X BASIC
STATED PRINT RUN 99 SER.#'d SETS

2013-14 Select Young Bloods
1 James Harden 1.50 4.00
2 Kemba Walker 1.00 2.50
3 Michael Carter-Williams 1.00 2.50
4 Anthony Davis 2.00 5.00
5 Victor Oladipo 1.25 3.00
6 Damian Lillard 2.00 5.00
7 Kenneth Faried .75 2.00
8 Kyrie Irving 2.00 5.00
9 Jimmy Butler 1.00 2.50
10 Cody Zeller .75 2.00

2013-14 Select Young Bloods Prizms
*PRIZMS: .75X TO 2X BASIC

2013-14 Select Young Bloods Prizms Blue
*BLUE: 2X TO 5X BASIC
STATED PRINT RUN 49 SER.#'d SETS

2013-14 Select Young Bloods Prizms Purple
*PURPLE: 1.5X TO 4X BASIC
STATED PRINT RUN 99 SER.#'d SETS

2014-15 Select
RANDOM INSERTS IN PACKS
1 Stephen Curry CON 1.25 3.00
2 Dwyane Wade CON .50 1.25
3 Victor Oladipo CON .25 .60
4 Larry Sanders CON .20 .50
5 Marcin Gortat CON .25 .60
6 LaMarcus Aldridge CON .30 .75
7 Serge Ibaka CON .25 .60
8 Roy Hibbert CON .25 .60
9 Klay Thompson CON .40 1.00
10 Chris Bosh CON .30 .75
11 Nikola Vucevic CON .25 .60
12 Ersan Ilyasova CON .20 .50
13 Tim Duncan CON .50 1.25
14 Damian Lillard CON .60 1.50
15 Anthony Davis CON .60 1.50
16 Deron Williams CON .25 .60
17 Andre Iguodala CON .25 .60
18 Luol Deng CON .25 .60
19 Goran Dragic CON .25 .60
20 Kobe Bryant CON 1.25 3.00
21 Tony Parker CON .30 .75
22 Al Jefferson CON .25 .60
23 Jrue Holiday CON .25 .60
24 Kevin Garnett CON .50 1.25
25 Derrick Rose CON .40 1.00
26 James Harden CON .50 1.25
27 Miles Plumlee CON .20 .50
28 Nick Young CON .25 .60
29 Patty Mills CON .30 .75
30 Michael Kidd-Gilchrist CON .25 .60
31 Tyreke Evans CON .20 .50
32 Ricky Rubio CON .30 .75
33 Joakim Noah CON .25 .60
34 Dwight Howard CON .25 .60
35 Isaiah Thomas CON .30 .75
36 Jeremy Lin CON .30 .75
37 Rudy Gay CON .30 .75
38 Chris Paul CON .40 1.00
39 Brandon Jennings CON .20 .50
40 Al Horford CON .25 .60
41 Pau Gasol CON .30 .75
42 Terrence Jones CON .25 .60
43 Markieff Morris CON .20 .50
44 DeMar DeRozan CON .30 .75
45 Ben McLemore CON .20 .50
46 Blake Griffin CON .30 .75
47 Andre Drummond CON .30 .75
48 Michael Carter-Williams CON .20 .50
49 Jimmy Butler CON .30 .75
50 Trevor Ariza CON .20 .50
51 Gordon Hayward CON .30 .75
52 Kyle Lowry CON .25 .60
53 Darren Collison CON .25 .60
54 Ty Lawson CON .20 .50
55 Josh Smith CON .25 .60
56 Nerlens Noel CON .25 .60
57 LeBron James CON 1.25 3.00
58 Dirk Nowitzki CON .40 1.00
59 Trey Burke CON .20 .50
60 Terrence Ross CON .25 .60
61 Vince Carter CON .40 1.00
62 Kenneth Faried CON .25 .60
63 Carmelo Anthony CON .40 1.00
64 Rajon Rondo CON .30 .75
65 Kyrie Irving CON .60 1.50
66 Chandler Parsons CON .25 .60
67 Derrick Favors CON .25 .60
68 Bradley Beal CON .30 .75
69 Zach Randolph CON .25 .60
70 Kevin Durant CON .75 2.00
71 Jose Calderon CON .20 .50
72 Jeff Teague CON .25 .60
73 Kevin Love CON .30 .75
74 Monta Ellis CON .25 .60
75 Giannis Antetokounmpo CON .60 1.50
76 John Wall CON .40 1.00
77 Mike Conley CON .25 .60
78 Russell Westbrook CON .75 2.00
79 Paul George CON .40 1.00
80 Wesley Matthews CON .20 .50
81 Bruno Caboclo CON RC .25 .60
82 P.J. Hairston CON RC .20 .50
83 Marcus Smart CON RC .30 .75
84 Zach LaVine CON RC .50 1.25
85 Nik Stauskas CON RC .25 .60
86 Elfrid Payton CON RC .30 .75
87 Dante Exum CON RC .30 .75
88 James Young CON RC .20 .50
89 Julius Randle CON RC .50 1.25
90 Joel Embiid CON RC 1.00 2.50
91 Aaron Gordon CON RC .50 1.25
92 Adreian Payne CON RC .25 .60
93 Gary Harris CON RC .30 .75
94 Doug McDermott CON RC .30 .75
95 Shabazz Napier CON RC .25 .60
96 Cleanthony Early CON RC .20 .50
97 T.J. Warren CON RC .30 .75
98 Mitch McGary CON RC .20 .50
99 Jabari Parker CON RC .50 1.25
100 Andrew Wiggins CON RC 4.00 10.00
101 Kobe Bryant PRE 4.00 10.00
102 Russell Westbrook PRE 2.50 6.00
103 Mirza Teletovic PRE .60 1.50
104 Reggie Jackson PRE .60 1.50
105 Danilo Gallinari PRE .60 1.50
106 Hollis Thompson PRE .75 2.00
107 Derrick Rose PRE 1.25 3.00
108 Kevin Durant PRE 2.50 6.00
109 Paul Pierce PRE 1.00 2.50
110 Tim Hardaway Jr. PRE .60 1.50
111 Tony Snell PRE .60 1.50
112 Tayshaun Prince PRE .75 2.00
113 Stephen Curry PRE 4.00 10.00
114 Carmelo Anthony PRE 1.25 3.00
115 DeMarcus Cousins PRE 1.00 2.50
116 Eric Gordon PRE .75 2.00
117 Paul Millsap PRE 1.00 2.50
118 Shareef Abdur-Rahim PRE .75 2.00
119 LeBron James PRE 4.00 10.00
120 Andrew Wiggins PRE 3.00 8.00
121 Avery Bradley PRE .75 2.00
122 J.J. Redick PRE 1.00 2.50
123 Kyle Korver PRE .75 2.00
124 Danny Granger PRE .75 2.00
125 Kyrie Irving PRE 2.00 5.00
126 Marcus Smart PRE 1.00 2.50
127 Robin Lopez PRE .60 1.50
128 Kelly Olynyk PRE .60 1.50
129 Otto Porter PRE .75 2.00
130 David West PRE .75 2.00
131 James Harden PRE 1.50 4.00
132 Dante Exum PRE 1.00 2.50
133 Amar'e Stoudemire PRE 1.00 2.50
134 Tony Wroten PRE .60 1.50
135 Jonas Valanciunas PRE .75 2.00
136 Chris Copeland PRE .60 1.50
137 Tony Parker PRE 1.00 2.50
138 James Young PRE .60 1.50
139 Andrea Bargnani PRE .75 2.00
140 Jodie Meeks PRE .75 2.00
141 Jae Crowder PRE .60 1.50
142 Mason Plumlee PRE .75 2.00
143 Damian Lillard PRE 2.00 5.00
144 Jabari Parker PRE 1.50 4.00
145 Marco Belinelli PRE .60 1.50
146 Tobias Harris PRE .75 2.00
147 Shawn Marion PRE .75 2.00
148 Jarrett Jack PRE .75 2.00
149 Chris Paul PRE 1.25 3.00
150 Julius Randle PRE 1.50 4.00
151 Gerald Green PRE .75 2.00
152 Norris Cole PRE .60 1.50
153 C.J. McCollum PRE 1.00 2.50
154 Tyson Chandler PRE .75 2.00
155 Blake Griffin PRE 1.00 2.50
156 Zach LaVine PRE 1.50 4.00
157 Tiago Splitter PRE .75 2.00
158 JaVale McGee PRE .75 2.00
159 Draymond Green PRE 1.25 3.00
160 Gerald Henderson PRE .60 1.50
161 Wes Unseld PRE 1.00 2.50
162 Chris Webber PRE 1.00 2.50
163 Nate Thurmond PRE .75 2.00
164 Larry Johnson PRE 1.25 3.00
165 Allen Iverson PRE 1.25 3.00
166 Julius Erving PRE 1.50 4.00
167 Baron Davis PRE .75 2.00
168 Magic Johnson PRE 2.50 6.00
169 Karl Malone PRE 1.25 3.00
170 Hakeem Olajuwon PRE 1.25 3.00
171 Sam Perkins PRE .60 1.50
172 Bill Bradley PRE 1.25 3.00
173 Tim Hardaway PRE 1.00 2.50
174 Shaquille O'Neal PRE 2.00 5.00
175 Pete Maravich PRE 1.50 4.00
176 Alonzo Mourning PRE 1.25 3.00
177 Scottie Pippen PRE 2.00 5.00
178 Isiah Thomas PRE 1.00 2.50
179 Bob Lanier PRE .75 2.00
180 Jalen Rose PRE 1.00 2.50
181 Jerome Williams PRE .60 1.50
182 Doug Collins PRE 1.00 2.50
183 George Gervin PRE 1.00 2.50
184 Wilt Chamberlain PRE 2.00 5.00
185 Bojan Bogdanovic PRE .75 2.00
186 Jusuf Nurkic PRE 1.00 2.50
187 Clint Capela PRE .75 2.00
188 Markel Brown PRE .60 1.50
189 Johnny O'Bryant PRE .60 1.50
190 Damien Inglis PRE .60 1.50
191 Lucas Nogueira PRE .60 1.50
192 Rodney Hood PRE 1.00 2.50
193 Noah Vonleh PRE .75 2.00
194 Cameron Bairstow PRE .60 1.50
195 Russ Smith PRE .60 1.50
196 Jarnell Stokes PRE .60 1.50
197 Spencer Dinwiddie PRE .75 2.00
198 Tyler Ennis PRE .60 1.50
199 Kyle Anderson PRE 1.00 2.50
200 Glenn Robinson III PRE .60 1.50
201 Larry Bird COU 3.00 8.00
202 David Robinson COU 2.00 5.00
203 Clyde Drexler COU 1.50 4.00
204 John Stockton COU 2.00 5.00
205 Chris Mullin COU 1.25 3.00
206 Scottie Pippen COU 2.50 6.00
207 Magic Johnson COU 3.00 8.00
208 Christian Laettner COU 1.00 2.50
209 Kobe Bryant COU 5.00 12.00
210 Derrick Rose COU 1.50 4.00
211 Stephen Curry COU 5.00 12.00
212 LeBron James COU 5.00 12.00
213 Kyrie Irving COU 2.50 6.00
214 James Harden COU 2.00 5.00
215 Kevin Durant COU 3.00 8.00
216 Klay Thompson COU 1.50 4.00
217 Anthony Davis COU 2.50 6.00
218 Rudy Gay COU 1.25 3.00
219 Kenneth Faried COU 1.00 2.50
220 Mason Plumlee COU 1.00 2.50
221 Tyson Chandler COU 1.00 2.50
222 Chris Paul COU 1.50 4.00
223 Kevin Love COU 1.25 3.00
224 Carmelo Anthony COU 1.50 4.00
225 Russell Westbrook COU 3.00 8.00
226 Karl Malone COU 1.50 4.00
227 Anfernee Hardaway COU 3.00 8.00
228 Grant Hill COU 1.50 4.00
229 Gary Payton COU 1.25 3.00
230 Jason Kidd COU 1.25 3.00
231 Shaquille O'Neal COU 2.50 6.00
232 Dwight Howard COU 1.00 2.50
233 Chris Bosh COU 1.25 3.00
234 Deron Williams COU 1.00 2.50
235 Ray Allen COU 1.25 3.00
236 Andre Drummond COU 1.25 3.00
237 Allen Iverson COU 1.50 4.00
238 Vince Carter COU 1.50 4.00
239 Tim Hardaway COU 1.25 3.00
240 Hakeem Olajuwon COU 1.50 4.00
241 Shawn Kemp COU 2.00 5.00
242 Dikembe Mutombo COU 1.25 3.00
243 Manute Bol COU 1.25 3.00
244 Nate Archibald COU 1.00 2.50
245 Dennis Rodman COU 2.50 6.00
246 Kareem Abdul-Jabbar COU 2.00 5.00
247 Mark Jackson COU 1.00 2.50
248 Bill Russell COU 2.00 5.00
249 Oscar Robertson COU 1.50 4.00
250 Bob Cousy COU 2.00 5.00
251 Moses Malone COU 1.25 3.00
252 Latrell Sprewell COU 1.00 2.50
253 Dave DeBusschere COU 1.25 3.00
254 Jerry West COU 1.50 4.00
255 Vlade Divac COU 1.25 3.00
256 Dion Waiters COU 1.00 2.50
257 Greg Monroe COU 1.00 2.50
258 Bradley Beal COU 1.25 3.00
259 Chris Andersen COU 1.00 2.50
260 Steven Adams COU 1.00 2.50
261 J.R. Smith COU 1.00 2.50
262 Kevin Martin COU 1.00 2.50
263 John Henson COU 1.00 2.50
264 Marc Gasol COU 1.25 3.00
265 Manu Ginobili COU 1.25 3.00
266 Steve Nash COU 1.25 3.00
267 Kemba Walker COU 1.25 3.00
268 Jamal Crawford COU 1.25 3.00
269 Brook Lopez COU 1.00 2.50
270 Tony Parker COU 1.25 3.00
271 Damian Lillard COU 2.50 6.00
272 John Wall COU 1.50 4.00
273 DeMarcus Cousins COU 1.25 3.00
274 Lance Stephenson COU 1.00 2.50
275 Dennis Schroder COU 1.00 2.50
276 Taj Gibson COU 1.00 2.50
277 Joe Johnson COU 1.00 2.50
278 Nicolas Batum COU 1.00 2.50
279 Eric Bledsoe COU 1.00 2.50
280 Omer Asik COU 1.00 2.50
281 Cory Jefferson COU .75 2.00
282 Zach LaVine COU 2.00 5.00
283 Adreian Payne COU 1.00 2.50
284 T.J. Warren COU 1.25 3.00
285 Gary Harris COU 1.25 3.00
286 Rodney Hood COU 1.25 3.00
287 Nik Stauskas COU 1.00 2.50
288 Bruno Caboclo COU 1.00 2.50
289 Elfrid Payton COU 1.25 3.00
290 Jordan Adams COU .75 2.00
291 James Ennis COU .75 2.00
292 Aaron Gordon COU 2.00 5.00
293 Jabari Parker COU 2.00 5.00
294 Andrew Wiggins COU 10.00 25.00
295 Doug McDermott COU 1.25 3.00
296 Julius Randle COU 2.00 5.00
297 Dante Exum COU 1.25 3.00
298 Marcus Smart COU 1.25 3.00
299 C.J. Wilcox COU .75 2.00
300 Damjan Rudez COU .75 2.00

2014-15 Select Concourse Prizms Blue
*CON BLUE: 1.25X TO 3X BASE HI
RANDOM INSERTS IN PACKS
STATED PRINT RUN 249 SER.#'d SETS
100 Andrew Wiggins 10.00 25.00

2014-15 Select Concourse Prizms Orange
*CON. RED: 2.5X TO 6X BASE HI
RANDOM INSERTS IN PACKS
STATED PRINT RUN 60 SER.#'d SETS
84 Zach LaVine 10.00 25.00
90 Joel Embiid 15.00 40.00
100 Andrew Wiggins 15.00 40.00

2014-15 Select Concourse Prizms Red
*CON. RED: 2X TO 5X BASE HI
RANDOM INSERTS IN PACKS
STATED PRINT RUN 149 SER.#'d SETS
99 Jabari Parker 12.00 30.00
100 Andrew Wiggins 12.00 30.00

2014-15 Select Courtside Prizms Copper
*COUR.COPPER: 1X TO 2.5X BASE HI
RANDOM INSERTS IN PACKS
STATED PRINT RUN 49 SER.#'d SETS
209 Kobe Bryant 30.00 80.00
212 LeBron James 25.00 60.00
215 Kevin Durant 12.00 30.00
294 Andrew Wiggins 20.00 50.00

2014-15 Select Premier Prizms Light Blue Die Cut
*PRE.LIGHT BLUE: .8X TO 2X BASE HI
RANDOM INSERTS IN PACKS
STATED PRINT RUN 199 SER.#'d SETS

2014-15 Select Premier Prizms Light Purple Die Cut
*PRE.LIGHT PURP: 1X TO 2.5X BASE HI
RANDOM INSERTS IN PACKS
STATED PRINT RUN 99 SER.#'d SETS
107 Derrick Rose 15.00 40.00
125 Kyrie Irving 8.00 20.00
162 Chris Webber 10.00 25.00

2014-15 Select Premier Prizms Tie Dye Die Cut
*PRE.TIE DYE: 6X TO 15X BASE HI
RANDOM INSERTS IN PACKS
STATED PRINT RUN 25 SER.#'d SETS
121 Avery Bradley 6.00 15.00
162 Chris Webber 40.00 100.00
175 Pete Maravich 15.00 40.00
184 Wilt Chamberlain 20.00 50.00

2014-15 Select Prizms Blue and Silver
*CON.BLUE SILV: 1.25X TO 3X BASE HI
*PRE.BLUE SILV: .8X TO 2X BASE HI
*COUR.BLUE SILV: .8X TO 2X BASE HI
RANDOM INSERTS IN PACKS
100 Andrew Wiggins CON 15.00 40.00
294 Andrew Wiggins COU 20.00 50.00

2014-15 Select Prizms Silver
*CON.SILVER: 1X TO 2.5X BASE HI
*PRE.SILVER: .6X TO 1.5X BASE HI
*COUR.SILVER: .6X TO 1.5X BASE HI
RANDOM INSERTS IN PACKS
282 Zach LaVine COU 15.00 40.00
294 Andrew Wiggins COU 20.00 50.00

2014-15 Select Prizms Tie Dye
*CON.TIE DYE: 12X TO 30X BASE HI
*PRE.TIE DYE: 4X TO 10X BASE HI
*COUR.TIE DYE: 3X TO 8X BASE HI
RANDOM INSERTS IN PACKS
STATED PRINT RUN 25 SER.#'d SETS
20 Kobe Bryant CON 30.00 80.00
25 Derrick Rose CON 25.00 60.00
57 LeBron James CON 75.00 150.00
78 Russell Westbrook CON 15.00 40.00
100 Andrew Wiggins CON 75.00 150.00
159 Draymond Green PRE 10.00 25.00
209 Kobe Bryant COU 125.00 250.00
211 Stephen Curry COU 100.00 250.00
226 Karl Malone COU 20.00 50.00
230 Jason Kidd COU 25.00 60.00
235 Ray Allen COU 30.00 80.00
237 Allen Iverson COU 30.00 80.00
238 Vince Carter COU 20.00 50.00
242 Dikembe Mutombo COU 20.00 50.00
266 Steve Nash COU 25.00 60.00

2014-15 Select City to City Jerseys
RANDOM INSERTS IN PACKS
STATED PRINT RUN 199 SER.#'d SETS
1 Shaquille O'Neal 6.00 15.00
2 LeBron James 15.00 40.00
3 Tracy McGrady 3.00 8.00
4 Vince Carter 4.00 10.00
5 Dwight Howard 2.50 6.00
6 Steve Nash 3.00 8.00
7 Carmelo Anthony 4.00 10.00
8 Monta Ellis 2.50 6.00
9 Chris Bosh 3.00 8.00
10 Ray Allen 3.00 8.00
11 Chris Andersen 2.50 6.00
12 Chris Paul 4.00 10.00
13 Grant Hill 4.00 10.00
14 Paul Pierce 3.00 8.00
15 Kevin Garnett 5.00 12.00
16 Jason Kidd 3.00 8.00
17 Clyde Drexler 4.00 10.00
18 Scottie Pippen 4.00 10.00
19 Amar'e Stoudemire 3.00 8.00
20 Deron Williams 2.50 6.00
21 Larry Johnson 4.00 10.00
22 Marcin Gortat 2.50 6.00
23 Alonzo Mourning 4.00 10.00
24 Dikembe Mutombo 3.00 8.00
25 Joe Johnson 2.50 6.00

2014-15 Select City to City Jerseys Prizms Copper
*COPPER: .5X TO 1.2X BASE HI
RANDOM INSERTS IN PACKS
STATED PRINT RUN 49 SER.#'d SETS
24 Dikembe Mutombo 12.00 30.00

2014-15 Select City to City Jerseys Prizms Tie Dye
*TIE DYE: 2X TO 5X BASE HI
RANDOM INSERTS IN PACKS
STATED PRINT RUN 25 SER.#'d SETS
1 Shaquille O'Neal 30.00 80.00
3 Tracy McGrady 25.00 60.00
4 Vince Carter 30.00 80.00
10 Ray Allen 30.00 80.00
11 Chris Andersen 25.00 60.00
13 Grant Hill 40.00 100.00
16 Jason Kidd 25.00 60.00
24 Dikembe Mutombo 25.00 60.00

2014-15 Select Die Cut Autographs
RANDOM INSERTS IN PACKS
STATED PRINT RUN B/WN 25-99 COPIES PER
1 Jeff Green/40 5.00 12.00
3 Nerlens Noel/25 15.00 40.00
4 Kevin Martin/25 12.00 30.00
5 John Stockton/25 30.00 80.00
6 Walt Frazier/25 10.00 25.00
7 Joe Dumars/25 10.00 25.00
8 Alex English/40 5.00 12.00
10 Karl Malone/25 25.00 60.00
11 Tracy McGrady/25 25.00 60.00
12 Allen Iverson/25 50.00 120.00
13 Clyde Drexler/25 8.00 20.00
14 Grant Hill/25 25.00 60.00
16 Chris Mullin/25 10.00 25.00
17 Toni Kukoc/40 12.00 30.00
18 Muggsy Bogues/99 5.00 12.00
19 Carmelo Anthony/25 25.00 60.00
20 M.Carter-Williams/25 15.00 40.00
22 Tristan Thompson/25 5.00 12.00
24 Stephen Curry/25 75.00 200.00
25 Troy Daniels/99 4.00 10.00
26 Al Horford/25 5.00 12.00
27 Chris Bosh/25 10.00 25.00
31 Gorgui Dieng/99 4.00 10.00
32 Eric Gordon/25 5.00 12.00
33 Jrue Holiday/40 5.00 12.00
34 P.J. Tucker/99 4.00 10.00
35 Marvin Williams/99 5.00 12.00
36 Marcin Gortat/40 5.00 12.00
37 Bradley Beal/25 6.00 15.00
38 Lance Stephenson/40 5.00 12.00
39 Hakeem Olajuwon/25 15.00 40.00
42 Kurt Rambis/40 4.00 10.00
43 Vlade Divac/99 6.00 15.00
44 Spud Webb/99 5.00 12.00
45 Dikembe Mutombo/40 15.00 40.00
46 John Starks/99 5.00 12.00
47 Jason Kidd/25 20.00 50.00
48 Eddie Jones/99 5.00 12.00
49 Luc Longley/99 5.00 12.00
50 Bruce Bowen/99 4.00 10.00
51 Robert Horry/40 5.00 12.00
52 Michael Cooper/40 5.00 12.00
55 Matthew Dellavedova/99 12.00 30.00
56 John Wall/25 30.00 80.00
57 Danilo Gallinari/25 4.00 10.00
58 Austin Rivers/25 5.00 12.00
60 Zach Randolph/25 12.00 30.00
61 Marcus Smart/99 6.00 15.00
62 Andrew Wiggins/99 60.00 150.00
63 Kyle Anderson/99 6.00 15.00
64 Zach LaVine/99 20.00 50.00
65 Nik Stauskas/99 5.00 12.00
66 Elfrid Payton/99 6.00 15.00
67 T.J. Warren/99 6.00 15.00
68 Rodney Hood/99 6.00 15.00
69 Dante Exum/99 12.00 30.00
70 Mitch McGary/99 4.00 10.00
71 Lucas Nogueira/99 4.00 10.00
72 James Young/99 4.00 10.00
73 P.J. Hairston/99 4.00 10.00
74 Julius Randle/99 12.00 30.00
75 Jabari Parker/99 30.00 80.00
76 Gary Harris/99 6.00 15.00
77 Joe Harris/99 4.00 10.00
78 Shabazz Napier/99 5.00 12.00
79 Noah Vonleh/99 5.00 12.00
81 Jordan Clarkson/99 20.00 50.00
82 Joel Embiid/99 40.00 100.00
83 Aaron Gordon/99 10.00 25.00
84 Jusuf Nurkic/99 6.00 15.00
85 Doug McDermott/99 6.00 15.00
86 Russ Smith/99 4.00 10.00
87 Cameron Bairstow/99 4.00 10.00
88 Jarnell Stokes/99 4.00 10.00
89 James Ennis/99 4.00 10.00
90 Adreian Payne/99 5.00 12.00
92 C.J. Wilcox/99 4.00 10.00
93 Cleanthony Early/99 4.00 10.00
94 Devyn Marble/99 4.00 10.00
96 Damien Inglis/99 4.00 10.00
97 Jerami Grant/99 4.00 10.00
98 Nikola Mirotic/99 4.00 10.00
99 Jordan Adams/99 4.00 10.00

2014-15 Select Double Team Jerseys
RANDOM INSERTS IN PACKS
STATED PRINT RUN 149 SER.#'d SETS
1 K.Durant/R.Westbrook 6.00 15.00
3 K.Love/L.James 12.00 30.00
4 K.Irving/L.James 12.00 30.00
5 D.Williams/J.Johnson 2.50 6.00
6 A.Stoudemire/C.Anthony 4.00 10.00
7 J.Butler/J.Noah 6.00 15.00
8 A.Drummond/G.Monroe 3.00 8.00
9 P.George/R.Hibbert 4.00 10.00
10 A.Horford/K.Korver 2.50 6.00
11 K.Walker/M.Kidd-Gilchrist 3.00 8.00
12 C.Andersen/C.Bosh 3.00 8.00
13 D.Wade/L.Deng 3.00 8.00
14 B.Beal/J.Wall 4.00 10.00
15 M.Gortat/Nene 2.50 6.00
16 D.Nowitzki/T.Chandler 4.00 10.00
17 M.Ellis/R.Rondo 3.00 8.00
18 D.Howard/J.Harden 5.00 12.00
19 M.Gasol/Z.Randolph 3.00 8.00
20 A.Davis/T.Evans 4.00 10.00
21 T.Duncan/T.Parker 5.00 12.00
22 D.Green/K.Leonard 3.00 8.00
23 A.Afflalo/K.Faried 2.50 6.00
24 D.Lillard/L.Aldridge 6.00 15.00
25 K.Thompson/S.Curry 12.00 30.00
26 A.Bogut/D.Lee 2.50 6.00
27 B.Griffin/C.Paul 4.00 10.00
28 J.Lin/K.Bryant 6.00 15.00
29 E.Bledsoe/G.Dragic 2.50 6.00
30 B.McLemore/D.Cousins 3.00 8.00

2014-15 Select Double Team Jerseys Prizms Copper
*COPPER: .5X TO 1.2X BASE HI
RANDOM INSERTS IN PACKS
STATED PRINT RUN 49 SER.#'d SETS
15 Marcin Gortat 8.00 20.00
Nene
20 Anthony Davis 5.00 12.00
Tyreke Evans

2014-15 Select Double Team Jerseys Prizms Tie Dye
*TIE DYE: 1.2X TO 3X BASE HI
RANDOM INSERTS IN PACKS
STATED PRINT RUN 25 SER.#'d SETS
12 Chris Andersen 12.00 30.00
Chris Bosh
13 Dwyane Wade 50.00 120.00
Luol Deng
14 Bradley Beal 12.00 30.00
John Wall
16 Dirk Nowitzki 15.00 40.00
Tyson Chandler
25 Klay Thompson 40.00 100.00
Stephen Curry
26 Andrew Bogut 20.00 50.00
David Lee
28 Jeremy Lin 40.00 100.00
Kobe Bryant
29 Eric Bledsoe 12.00 30.00
Goran Dragic

2014-15 Select Fame Game Autographs
RANDOM INSERTS IN PACKS
STATED PRINT RUN B/WN 60-199 COPIES PER
1 Larry Bird/60 40.00 100.00
2 John Stockton/60 20.00 50.00
3 Magic Johnson/60 30.00 80.00
4 Jerry West/60 15.00 40.00
5 Elgin Baylor/60 5.00 12.00
7 Dominique Wilkins/60 6.00 15.00
8 James Worthy/60 10.00 25.00
9 Rick Barry/60 8.00 20.00
10 Walt Frazier/60 8.00 20.00
11 Robert Parish/149 5.00 12.00
12 George Gervin/149 5.00 12.00
13 Dolph Schayes/99 5.00 12.00
14 Joe Dumars/149 5.00 12.00
15 Nate Thurmond/149 4.00 10.00
17 Isiah Thomas/149 8.00 20.00
18 Alex English/199 4.00 10.00
19 Dan Issel/149 4.00 10.00
20 Sarunas Marciulionis/199 5.00 12.00

2014-15 Select Fame Game Autographs Prizms Copper
*COPPER: .6X TO 1.5X BASE HI
RANDOM INSERTS IN PACKS
STATED PRINT RUN 49 SER.#'d SETS
9 Rick Barry 6.00 15.00
12 George Gervin 10.00 25.00

2014-15 Select Jersey Autographs
RANDOM INSERTS IN PACKS
STATED PRINT RUN B/WN 35-199 COPIES PER
3 Trey Burke/35 3.00 8.00
4 Robert Sacre/199 3.00 8.00
5 Bradley Beal/35 5.00 12.00
6 Andre Iguodala/35 10.00 25.00
7 Tristan Thompson/35 4.00 10.00
8 Andrea Bargnani/35 4.00 10.00
9 Brook Lopez/35 4.00 10.00
10 Rodney Stuckey/40 4.00 10.00
11 Zach Randolph/35 4.00 10.00
12 Danny Green/35 4.00 10.00
13 Patty Mills/199 10.00 25.00
14 Andre Drummond/35 8.00 20.00
16 Ty Lawson/35 3.00 8.00
17 Luigi Datome/199 3.00 8.00
18 Stephen Curry/35 150.00 300.00
20 Shane Battier/35 4.00 10.00
21 Gordon Hayward/99 5.00 12.00
22 Hal Greer/35 4.00 10.00
24 John Stockton/35 25.00 60.00
25 Cedric Maxwell/199 3.00 8.00
27 Fred Brown/199 3.00 8.00
28 Ryan Anderson/35 3.00 8.00
30 Doug Collins/199 3.00 8.00
32 Larry Johnson/35 6.00 15.00
33 Michael Kidd-Gilchrist/35 4.00 10.00
34 Clyde Drexler/35 12.00 30.00
35 Kiki Vandeweghe/199 4.00 10.00
36 Dan Majerle/99 4.00 10.00
37 Tiago Splitter/35 4.00 10.00
38 Jonas Valanciunas/99 4.00 10.00
40 Chris Bosh/35 10.00 25.00
41 Andre Miller/35 4.00 10.00
42 Kelly Olynyk/199 3.00 8.00
43 Kyle Singler/199 3.00 8.00
44 Thaddeus Young/199 3.00 8.00
45 Carmelo Anthony/35 20.00 50.00
46 Jose Calderon/35 6.00 15.00
47 Jason Terry/35 4.00 10.00
49 Luol Deng/125 4.00 10.00
50 Dennis Schroder/199 4.00 10.00
51 Kyle Korver/35 4.00 10.00
52 C.J. McCollum/35 15.00 40.00
53 DeMarre Carroll/199 3.00 8.00
54 Jeff Green/35 4.00 10.00
55 George Hill/35 4.00 10.00
57 Perry Jones/199 3.00 8.00
60 Anthony Davis/35 50.00 120.00
62 Tayshaun Prince/35 15.00 40.00
63 Kevin Love/35 12.00 30.00
64 J.J. Redick/35 10.00 25.00
66 Walter Berry/199 3.00 8.00
67 Alex Len/35 3.00 8.00
68 Ben McLemore/35 3.00 8.00
69 Carl Landry/35 3.00 8.00

2014-15 Select Jersey Autographs Prizms Tie Dye
*TIE DYE: 1.5X TO 4X BASE HI
RANDOM INSERTS IN PACKS
STATED PRINT RUN 25 SER.#'d SETS
1 Al Horford/25 15.00 40.00
6 Andre Iguodala/25 20.00 50.00
13 Patty Mills/25 20.00 50.00
16 Ty Lawson/25 20.00 50.00
18 Stephen Curry/25 150.00 300.00
20 Shane Battier/25 4.00 10.00
26 Artis Gilmore/25 15.00 40.00
50 Dennis Schroder/25 20.00 50.00
60 Anthony Davis/25 100.00 250.00
61 Chris Kaman/25 15.00 40.00
63 Kevin Love/25 30.00 80.00
64 J.J. Redick/25 30.00 80.00
67 Alex Len/25 12.00 30.00

2014-15 Select On Hallowed Ground Jerseys
RANDOM INSERTS IN PACKS
STATED PRINT RUN 149 SER.#'d SETS
*COPPER: .5X TO 1.2X BASE HI
1 Kareem Abdul-Jabbar 6.00 15.00
2 Dennis Rodman 5.00 12.00
3 Patrick Ewing 5.00 12.00
4 Gary Payton 4.00 10.00
5 Magic Johnson 6.00 15.00
6 Alex English 3.00 8.00
7 Kevin McHale 4.00 10.00
8 Clyde Drexler 5.00 12.00
9 Robert Parish 4.00 10.00
10 Larry Bird 6.00 15.00
11 Hakeem Olajuwon 5.00 12.00
12 Karl Malone 5.00 12.00
13 David Robinson 5.00 12.00
14 John Stockton 4.00 10.00
15 Alonzo Mourning 5.00 12.00

2014-15 Select On Hallowed Ground Jerseys Prizms Tie Dye
*TIE DYE: .8X TO 2X BASE HI
RANDOM INSERTS IN PACKS
STATED PRINT RUN 25 SER.#'d SETS
1 Kareem Abdul-Jabbar 15.00 40.00
11 Hakeem Olajuwon 30.00 80.00
12 Karl Malone 12.00 30.00

2014-15 Select Rookie Jersey Autographs
RANDOM INSERTS IN PACKS
STATED PRINT RUN 199 SER.#'d SETS
1 Andrew Wiggins 40.00 100.00
2 Jabari Parker 20.00 50.00
3 Joel Embiid 40.00 100.00
4 Markel Brown 3.00 8.00
5 T.J. Warren 5.00 12.00
6 James Ennis 3.00 8.00
7 Gary Harris 5.00 12.00
8 Adreian Payne 4.00 10.00
9 Marcus Smart 5.00 12.00
10 Kyle Anderson 5.00 12.00
11 Russ Smith 3.00 8.00
12 Noah Vonleh 4.00 10.00
13 Zach LaVine 15.00 40.00
14 C.J. Wilcox 3.00 8.00
15 Tyler Ennis 3.00 8.00
16 Doug McDermott 5.00 12.00
17 Spencer Dinwiddie 4.00 10.00
18 Damien Inglis 3.00 8.00
19 P.J. Hairston 3.00 8.00
20 K.J. McDaniels 4.00 10.00
21 James Young 3.00 8.00
22 Bruno Caboclo 4.00 10.00
23 Mitch McGary 3.00 8.00
24 Nik Stauskas 4.00 10.00
25 Aaron Gordon 8.00 20.00
26 Elfrid Payton 5.00 12.00
27 Shabazz Napier 4.00 10.00
28 Dante Exum 5.00 12.00
29 Rodney Hood 5.00 12.00
30 Johnny O'Bryant 3.00 8.00

2014-15 Select Rookie Jersey Autographs Prizms Orange
*ORANGE: .5X TO 1.2X BASE HI
RANDOM INSERTS IN PACKS
STATED PRINT RUN 49 SER.#'d SETS
28 Dante Exum 15.00 40.00

2014-15 Select Rookie Jersey Autographs Prizms Tie Dye
*TIE DYE: .8X TO 2X BASE HI
RANDOM INSERTS IN PACKS
STATED PRINT RUN 25 SER.#'d SETS
3 Joel Embiid 125.00 400.00
5 T.J. Warren 15.00 40.00
7 Gary Harris 15.00 40.00
11 Russ Smith 12.00 30.00
13 Zach LaVine 75.00 200.00
25 Aaron Gordon 30.00 80.00
26 Elfrid Payton 75.00 150.00
28 Dante Exum 30.00 80.00

2014-15 Select Rookie Signatures
RANDOM INSERTS IN PACKS
STATED PRINT RUN 275 SER.#'d SETS
RSAG Aaron Gordon 12.00 30.00
RSAP Adreian Payne 4.00 10.00
RSAW Andrew Wiggins 60.00 150.00
RSBB Bojan Bogdanovic 3.00 8.00
RSCB Cameron Bairstow 3.00 8.00
RSCE Cleanthony Early 3.00 8.00
RSCJ Cory Jefferson 3.00 8.00
RSDE Dante Exum 5.00 12.00
RSDM Doug McDermott 5.00 12.00
RSDR Damjan Rudez 3.00 8.00
RSEP Elfrid Payton 5.00 12.00
RSGH Gary Harris 3.00 8.00
RSGR Glenn Robinson III 3.00 8.00
RSJC Jordan Clarkson 12.00 30.00
RSJE Joel Embiid 60.00 150.00
RSJP Jabari Parker 20.00 50.00
RSJR Julius Randle 15.00 40.00
RSJY James Young 3.00 8.00
RSMB Markel Brown 3.00 8.00
RSMM Mitch McGary 3.00 8.00
RSMS Marcus Smart 5.00 12.00
RSNS Nik Stauskas 3.00 8.00
RSNV Noah Vonleh 4.00 10.00
RSRH Rodney Hood 5.00 12.00
RSSN Shabazz Napier 4.00 10.00
RSTE Tyler Ennis 3.00 8.00
RSTW T.J. Warren 5.00 12.00
RSZD Zoran Dragic 3.00 8.00
RSZL Zach LaVine 15.00 40.00

2014-15 Select Rookie Signatures Prizms Copper
*COPPER: .6X TO 1.5X BASE HI
RANDOM INSERTS IN PACKS
STATED PRINT RUN 49 SER.#'d SETS

2014-15 Select Rookie Swatches
RANDOM INSERTS IN PACKS
STATED PRINT RUN 199 SER.#'d SETS
*PURPLE: .5X TO 1.2X BASE HI
1 Jabari Parker 5.00 12.00
2 Aaron Gordon 3.00 8.00
3 Russ Smith 2.00 5.00
4 Bruno Caboclo 2.50 6.00
5 Joel Embiid 4.00 10.00
6 Andrew Wiggins 10.00 25.00
7 K.J. McDaniels 2.50 6.00
8 Cleanthony Early 2.00 5.00
9 Nik Stauskas 2.50 6.00
10 Dante Exum 3.00 8.00
12 Doug McDermott 3.00 8.00
14 Rodney Hood 3.00 8.00
15 Marcus Smart 3.00 8.00
16 Shabazz Napier 4.00 10.00
18 T.J. Warren 3.00 8.00
19 Julius Randle 5.00 12.00
20 Tyler Ennis 2.00 5.00
21 Zach LaVine 5.00 12.00
22 Noah Vonleh 2.50 6.00
23 Damien Inglis 2.00 5.00
24 Elfrid Payton 3.00 8.00
25 Spencer Dinwiddie 2.50 6.00
26 Mitch McGary 2.00 5.00
27 Adreian Payne 2.50 6.00
28 Kyle Anderson 2.00 5.00
29 James Ennis 2.00 5.00

2014-15 Select Rookie Swatches Prizms Orange
*ORANGE: .6X TO 1.5X BASE HI
RANDOM INSERTS IN PACKS
STATED PRINT RUN 60 SER.#'d SETS

2014-15 Select Rookie Swatches Prizms Tie Dye
*TIE DYE: 1X TO 2.5X BASE HI
RANDOM INSERTS IN PACKS
STATED PRINT RUN 25 SER.#'d SETS
5 Joel Embiid 30.00 80.00
6 Andrew Wiggins 150.00 300.00
14 Rodney Hood 8.00 20.00
19 Julius Randle 20.00 50.00
21 Zach LaVine 20.00 50.00
24 Elfrid Payton 30.00 80.00
26 Mitch McGary 10.00 25.00

2014-15 Select Signatures
STATED PRINT RUN B/WN 60-99 COPIES PER
STATED PRINT RUN B/WN 149-199 COPIES PER
RANDOM INSERTS IN PACKS
1 Kobe Bryant/60 75.00 150.00
2 Shaquille O'Neal/60 75.00 150.00
3 Kevin Durant/60 60.00 120.00
4 Julius Erving/60 40.00 100.00
5 Karl Malone/60 25.00 60.00
6 John Wall/60 20.00 50.00
7 Anthony Davis/60 75.00 150.00
8 Kyrie Irving/60 40.00 100.00
9 Reggie Jackson/199 4.00 10.00
10 Jason Kidd/60 10.00 25.00
11 Ray Allen/60 20.00 50.00
12 Tracy McGrady/60 15.00 40.00
13 Kevin Love/60 15.00 40.00
14 Vince Carter/60 15.00 40.00
15 Anthony Bennett/60 5.00 12.00
16 Grant Hill/60 12.00 30.00
17 Tony Parker/60 15.00 40.00
18 Victor Oladipo/60 6.00 15.00
19 Rick Fox/99 5.00 12.00
20 Ben McLemore/75 5.00 12.00
23 Artis Gilmore/75 6.00 15.00
24 Andre Drummond/75 8.00 20.00
25 Bradley Beal/75 8.00 20.00
26 Harrison Barnes/75 6.00 15.00
27 Patty Mills/199 8.00 20.00
28 C.J. McCollum/149 4.00 10.00
29 Michael Carter-Williams/149 2.50 6.00
30 Trey Burke/149 2.50 6.00
31 Allan Houston/149 3.00 8.00
32 Dick Van Arsdale/199 3.00 8.00
33 Jared Sullinger/149 2.50 6.00
34 Kevin Martin/149 3.00 8.00
35 Scott Brooks/149 2.50 6.00
36 Tiago Splitter/199 3.00 8.00
37 Kurt Rambis/199 2.50 6.00
38 Tom Chambers/199 3.00 8.00
39 Toni Kukoc/199 6.00 15.00
41 Kendall Gill/199 2.50 6.00
42 Mahmoud Abdul-Rauf/199 2.50 6.00
43 Muggsy Bogues/199 4.00 10.00
44 Mark Price/199 4.00 10.00
45 Scott Skiles/199 3.00 8.00
46 Spud Webb/199 5.00 12.00
47 Tim Hardaway/199 4.00 10.00
48 Rudy Tomjanovich/199 3.00 8.00
49 Kelly Olynyk/199 2.50 6.00

2014-15 Select Signatures Prizms Copper
*COPPER: 1X TO 2.5X BASE p/r 149-199
*COPPER: .5X TO 1.2X BASE p/r60-99
RANDOM INSERTS IN PACKS
STATED PRINT RUN 49 SER.#'d SETS
34 Kevin Martin 5.00 12.00
44 Mark Price 10.00 25.00
46 Spud Webb 8.00 20.00

2014-15 Select Sparks Jerseys
RANDOM INSERTS IN PACKS
STATED PRINT RUN B/WN 40-149 COPIES PER
1 Manu Ginobili/149 2.50 6.00
2 Chris Paul/149 2.50 6.00
3 Klay Thompson/149 5.00 12.00
4 James Harden/149 6.00 15.00
6 Eric Gordon/149 2.50 6.00
7 Monta Ellis/149 3.00 8.00
8 LeBron James/149 12.00 30.00
10 Kyrie Irving/149 6.00 15.00
11 Patty Mills/149 10.00 25.00
12 Ty Lawson/149 2.50 6.00
13 Russell Westbrook/149 10.00 25.00
14 John Wall/149 5.00 12.00
15 Avery Bradley/149 3.00 8.00
16 Damian Lillard/149 6.00 15.00
17 Jeff Teague/149 3.00 8.00
18 Kawhi Leonard/149 6.00 15.00
19 Stephen Curry/149 10.00 25.00
20 Jose Calderon/40 2.50 6.00
21 Michael Carter-Williams/149 2.50 6.00
22 Deron Williams/149 2.50 6.00
23 Rajon Rondo/149 4.00 10.00
24 Goran Dragic/149 3.00 8.00
25 Reggie Jackson/149 2.50 6.00
29 Jeff Green/149 3.00 8.00
30 Tony Parker/149 4.00 10.00

2014-15 Select Sparks Jerseys Prizms Copper
*COPPER: .5X TO 1.2X BASE HI
RANDOM INSERTS IN PACKS
STATED PRINT RUN B/WN 10-49 COPIES PER
NO PRICING ON QTY 10 OR LESS
1 Manu Ginobili/49 5.00 12.00
2 Chris Paul/49 5.00 12.00
9 Kemba Walker/49 3.00 8.00
19 Stephen Curry/49 15.00 40.00
26 Gordon Hayward/49 3.00 8.00
27 Mario Chalmers/49 4.00 10.00

2014-15 Select Sparks Jerseys Prizms Tie Dye
*TIE DYE: .6X TO 1.5X BASE HI
RANDOM INSERTS IN PACKS
STATED PRINT RUN 25 SER.#'d SETS
1 Manu Ginobili/25 10.00 25.00
3 Klay Thompson/25 12.00 30.00
8 LeBron James/25 125.00 250.00
18 Kawhi Leonard/25 30.00 80.00
19 Stephen Curry/25 30.00 80.00
30 Tony Parker/25 10.00 25.00

2014-15 Select Swatches
RANDOM INSERTS IN PACKS
STATED PRINT RUN 75 SER.#'d SETS
1 Alex Len 2.00 5.00
2 Dan Majerle 2.50 6.00
3 Deron Williams 2.50 6.00
4 Bill Laimbeer 2.50 6.00
5 Greg Monroe 2.50 6.00
6 Bradley Beal 3.00 8.00
7 DeMar DeRozan 3.00 8.00
8 Hakeem Olajuwon 4.00 10.00
9 Allen Iverson 4.00 10.00
10 Kyrie Irving 6.00 15.00
11 Danny Manning 2.50 6.00
12 Bismack Biyombo 2.00 5.00
13 Jason Kidd 3.00 8.00
14 DeMarcus Cousins 3.00 8.00
15 Amar'e Stoudemire 3.00 8.00
16 Magic Johnson 5.00 12.00
17 David Lee 2.00 5.00
18 Chris Andersen 2.50 6.00
19 Dwight Howard 2.50 6.00
20 Julius Erving 5.00 12.00
21 Blake Griffin 3.00 8.00
22 Clifford Robinson 2.00 5.00
23 Harrison Barnes 2.50 6.00
24 Kobe Bryant 8.00 20.00
25 Enes Kanter 2.00 5.00
26 Chris Paul 4.00 10.00
27 Eric Bledsoe 2.50 6.00
28 Al Horford 2.50 6.00
29 Dwyane Wade 5.00 12.00
30 Danny Green 2.50 6.00
31 Bobby Jackson 2.00 5.00
32 Gary Payton 3.00 8.00
33 Dennis Rodman 5.00 12.00
34 Andrew Bogut 2.50 6.00
35 Kevin Durant 6.00 15.00
36 Dikembe Mutombo 3.00 8.00
37 Anfernee Hardaway 5.00 12.00
38 Jeff Green 2.50 6.00
39 Carmelo Anthony 4.00 10.00
40 Ersan Ilyasova 2.00 5.00
41 Adrian Dantley 2.50 6.00
42 Dirk Nowitzki 4.00 10.00
43 Joakim Noah 2.50 6.00
44 Brandon Knight 2.50 6.00
45 DeAndre Jordan 3.00 8.00
46 John Stockton 5.00 12.00
47 Andre Drummond 3.00 8.00
48 David West 2.50 6.00
49 Larry Bird 8.00 20.00
50 Ben Wallace 3.00 8.00
51 LeBron James 12.00 30.00
52 Damian Lillard 5.00 12.00
53 J.J. Redick 3.00 8.00
54 Aaron Brooks 2.00 5.00
55 J.R. Smith 2.50 6.00
56 Chris Mullin 3.00 8.00
57 James Harden 5.00 12.00
58 Anthony Davis 6.00 15.00
59 Iman Shumpert 2.00 5.00
60 Clyde Drexler 4.00 10.00
61 Gerald Green 2.50 6.00
62 Alex English 2.50 6.00
63 Grant Hill 4.00 10.00
64 David Robinson 5.00 12.00
65 Gordon Hayward 3.00 8.00
66 Kawhi Leonard 5.00 12.00
67 Draymond Green 4.00 10.00
68 Chris Bosh 3.00 8.00
69 Dion Waiters 2.50 6.00
70 Al Jefferson 2.50 6.00

2014-15 Select Swatches Prizms Purple
*PURPLE: .5X TO 1.2X BASE HI
RANDOM INSERTS IN PACKS
STATED PRINT RUN 75 SER.#'d SETS
56 Chris Mullin 3.00 8.00

2014-15 Select Swatches Prizms Tie Dye
*TIE DYE: 1X TO 2.5X BASE HI
RANDOM INSERTS IN PACKS
STATED PRINT RUN B/WN 10-25 COPIES PER
NO PRICING ON QTY 10 OR LESS
LACK OF PRICING DUE TO MARKET INFO
1 Alex Len/25 10.00 25.00
6 Bradley Beal/25 12.00 30.00
8 Hakeem Olajuwon/25 25.00 60.00
9 Allen Iverson/25 30.00 80.00
14 DeMarcus Cousins/25 10.00 25.00
18 Chris Andersen/25 12.00 30.00
19 Dwight Howard/25 12.00 30.00
24 Kobe Bryant/25 75.00 150.00
32 Gary Payton/25 10.00 25.00
33 Dennis Rodman/25 30.00 80.00
35 Kevin Durant/25 30.00 80.00
37 Anfernee Hardaway/25 30.00 80.00
42 Dirk Nowitzki/25 15.00 40.00
43 Joakim Noah/25 15.00 40.00
46 John Stockton/25 25.00 60.00
51 LeBron James/25 40.00 100.00
52 Damian Lillard/25 25.00 60.00
57 James Harden/25 12.00 30.00
62 Alex English/25 5.00 12.00
63 Grant Hill/25 40.00 100.00
66 Kawhi Leonard/25 20.00 50.00
68 Chris Bosh/25 15.00 40.00

2015-16 Select
1 Andrew Wiggins CON .50 1.25
2 Bojan Bogdanovic CON .20 .50
3 Dennis Schroder CON .25 .60
4 Frank Kaminsky CON RC .50 1.25
5 James Young CON .20 .50
6 Jusuf Nurkic CON .20 .50
7 Kobe Bryant CON 1.25 3.00
8 Myles Turner CON RC .50 1.25
9 Reggie Jackson CON .25 .60
10 Terrence Ross CON .25 .60
11 Aaron Harrison CON RC .40 1.00
12 Brook Lopez CON .25 .60
13 Deron Williams CON .25 .60
14 Gary Harris CON .25 .60
15 Jarell Martin CON RC .40 1.00
16 Karl-Anthony Towns CON RC 2.50 6.00
17 Kristaps Porzingis CON RC 1.25 3.00
18 Nemanja Bjelica CON RC .40 1.00
19 Robin Lopez CON .20 .50
20 Terry Rozier CON RC .40 1.00
21 Alec Burks CON .20 .50
22 Carmelo Anthony CON .40 1.00
23 Derrick Rose CON .40 1.00
24 Goran Dragic CON .25 .60
25 Jeff Teague CON .25 .60
26 Kawhi Leonard CON .50 1.25
27 Kyle Lowry CON .25 .60
28 Nicolas Batum CON .25 .60
29 Rodney Stuckey CON .25 .60
30 Tim Duncan CON .50 1.25
31 Alex Len CON .20 .50
32 Chris Paul CON .40 1.00
33 Dirk Nowitzki CON .40 1.00
34 Gordon Hayward CON .30 .75
35 Jerian Grant CON RC .30 .75
36 Oscar Robertson CON .40 1.00
37 Kyrie Irving CON .60 1.50
38 Nik Stauskas CON .20 .50
39 Rondae Hollis-Jefferson CON RC .40 1.00
40 Trey Burke CON .20 .50
41 Al-Farouq Aminu CON .25 .60
42 Corey Brewer CON .20 .50
43 Dwyane Wade CON .50 1.25
44 Ian Mahinmi CON .20 .50
45 Jimmy Butler CON .30 .75
46 Kemba Walker CON .30 .75
47 LeBron James CON 1.25 3.00
48 Nikola Mirotic CON .25 .60
49 Rudy Gay CON .30 .75
50 Tyreke Evans CON .20 .50
51 Amare Stoudemire CON .25 .60
52 Damian Lillard CON .60 1.50
53 Elfrid Payton CON .25 .60
54 J.J. Barea CON .25 .60
55 John Wall CON .40 1.00
56 Kenneth Faried CON .25 .60
57 Manu Ginobili CON .30 .75
58 Nikola Vucevic CON .25 .60
59 Russell Westbrook CON .75 2.00
60 Victor Oladipo CON .25 .60
61 Andre Iguodala CON .25 .60
62 D'Angelo Russell CON RC 1.25 3.00
63 Emmanuel Mudiay CON RC .50 1.25
64 Jabari Parker CON .40 1.00
65 Jordan Clarkson CON .30 .75
66 Kevin Durant CON .75 2.00
67 Marc Gasol CON .30 .75
68 Noah Vonleh CON .20 .50
69 Kelly Oubre Jr. CON RC .40 1.00
70 Walter Tavares CON RC .30 .75
71 Anthony Davis CON .60 1.50
72 Darrun Hilliard CON RC .30 .75
73 Eric Bledsoe CON .25 .60
74 Jahlil Okafor CON RC .60 1.50
75 Josh Smith CON .25 .60
76 Kevin Love CON .30 .75
77 Marcus Smart CON .25 .60
78 Omer Asik CON .25 .60
79 Serge Ibaka CON .25 .60
80 Willie Cauley-Stein CON RC .50 1.25
81 Arron Afflalo CON .20 .50
82 Delon Wright CON RC .40 1.00
83 Ersan Ilyasova CON .20 .50
84 JaKarr Sampson CON .20 .50
85 Justin Anderson CON RC .40 1.00
86 Kevon Looney CON RC .40 1.00
87 Mario Hezonja CON RC .40 1.00
88 Otto Porter CON .25 .60
89 Stanley Johnson CON RC .40 1.00
90 Zach LaVine CON .30 .75
91 Blake Griffin CON .30 .75
92 DeMarcus Cousins CON .30 .75
93 Evan Turner CON .25 .60
94 James Harden CON .50 1.25
95 Justise Winslow CON RC .50 1.25
96 Klay Thompson CON .40 1.00
97 Montrezl Harrell CON RC .40 1.00
98 Paul George CON .40 1.00
99 Stephen Curry CON 1.25 3.00
100 Zach Randolph CON .25 .60
101 Anthony Davis PRE 1.50 4.00
102 Cameron Payne PRE RC 1.00 2.50
103 Derrick Rose PRE 1.00 2.50
104 Greg Monroe PRE .60 1.50
105 Jerian Grant PRE .75 2.00
106 Jrue Holiday PRE .60 1.50
107 Kyrie Irving PRE 1.50 4.00
108 Montrezl Harrell PRE 1.00 2.50
109 Raul Neto PRE RC .75 2.00
110 Tim Duncan PRE 1.25 3.00
111 Aaron Gordon PRE .60 1.50
112 Carmelo Anthony PRE 1.00 2.50
113 Duje Dukan PRE RC .75 2.00
114 Harrison Barnes PRE .60 1.50
115 Joakim Noah PRE .60 1.50
116 Julius Randle PRE .75 2.00
117 LaMarcus Aldridge PRE .75 2.00
118 Nerlens Noel PRE .60 1.50
119 Reggie Jackson PRE .60 1.50
120 Tim Hardaway Jr. PRE .50 1.25
121 Al Jefferson PRE .60 1.50
122 Chris Andersen PRE .60 1.50
123 Dwight Howard PRE .60 1.50
124 Hassan Whiteside PRE .60 1.50
125 Joe Ingles PRE .50 1.25
126 Justise Winslow PRE 1.25 3.00
127 Lance Thomas PRE .50 1.25
128 Nikola Jokic PRE RC 1.50 4.00
129 R.J. Hunter PRE RC .75 2.00
130 Tony Parker PRE .75 2.00
131 Andre Drummond PRE .75 2.00
132 Chris McCullough PRE RC .75 2.00
133 Dwyane Wade PRE 1.25 3.00
134 Isaiah Thomas PRE .75 2.00
135 Joe Johnson PRE .60 1.50
136 Karl-Anthony Towns PRE 6.00 15.00
137 Larry Nance Jr. PRE RC 1.25 3.00
138 Norman Powell PRE RC 1.00 2.50
139 Robert Covington PRE .50 1.25
140 Trey Lyles PRE .75 2.00
141 Andrew Wiggins PRE 1.25 3.00
142 Chris Paul PRE 1.00 2.50
143 Elfrid Payton PRE .60 1.50
144 J.J. Hickson PRE .50 1.25
145 Joe Young PRE RC 1.00 2.50
146 Kelly Oubre Jr. PRE 1.00 2.50
147 LeBron James PRE 3.00 8.00
148 Pat Connaughton PRE RC .75 2.00
149 Rudy Gobert PRE .75 2.00
150 Ty Lawson PRE .50 1.25
151 Blake Griffin PRE .75 2.00
152 Damian Lillard PRE 1.50 4.00
153 Emmanuel Mudiay PRE 1.25 3.00
154 Jabari Parker PRE 1.00 2.50
155 John Wall PRE 1.00 2.50
156 Kevin Durant PRE 2.00 5.00
157 Marco Belinelli PRE .50 1.25
158 Pau Gasol PRE .75 2.00
159 Russell Westbrook PRE 2.00 5.00
160 Tyson Chandler PRE .60 1.50
161 Bobby Portis PRE RC 1.25 3.00
162 D'Angelo Russell PRE 3.00 8.00
163 Eric Bledsoe PRE .60 1.50
164 Jahlil Okafor PRE 1.50 4.00
165 Jonathon Simmons PRE RC 1.25 3.00
166 Kevin Garnett PRE 1.25 3.00
167 Matthew Dellavedova PRE .60 1.50
168 Paul Pierce PRE .75 2.00
169 Sam Dekker PRE RC 1.00 2.50
170 Tyus Jones PRE RC 1.25 3.00
171 Bradley Beal PRE .75 2.00
172 DeMar DeRozan PRE .75 2.00
173 Evan Fournier PRE .60 1.50
174 James Harden PRE 1.25 3.00
175 Jordan Hill PRE .50 1.25
176 Klay Thompson PRE 1.00 2.50
177 Maurice Harkless PRE .50 1.25
178 Avery Bradley PRE .60 1.50
179 Stephen Curry PRE 3.00 8.00
180 Walter Tavares PRE .75 2.00
181 Branden Dawson PRE RC .75 2.00
182 DeMarre Carroll PRE .50 1.25
183 Frank Kaminsky PRE 1.25 3.00
184 Jeff Green PRE .60 1.50
185 Jordan Mickey PRE RC .75 2.00
186 Kobe Bryant PRE 3.00 8.00
187 Mike Conley PRE .75 2.00
188 Rajon Rondo PRE .75 2.00
189 T.J. Warren PRE .60 1.50
190 Wesley Matthews PRE .50 1.25
191 Brandon Knight PRE .60 1.50
192 Deron Williams PRE .60 1.50
193 Giannis Antetokounmpo PRE 1.50 4.00
194 Jeremy Lin PRE .75 2.00
195 Josh Richardson PRE RC 1.25 3.00
196 Kristaps Porzingis PRE 3.00 8.00
197 Monta Ellis PRE .60 1.50
198 Rashad Vaughn PRE RC .75 2.00
199 Tiago Splitter PRE .60 1.50
200 Willie Cauley-Stein PRE 1.25 3.00
201 Bradley Beal COU 1.00 2.50
202 Cameron Payne COU 1.25 3.00
203 Devin Booker COU RC 5.00 12.00
204 Jerian Grant COU 1.00 2.50
205 Kemba Walker COU 1.00 2.50
206 Marc Gasol COU 1.00 2.50
207 Paul George COU 1.25 3.00
208 Stanley Johnson COU 1.25 3.00
209 Allen Crabbe COU .60 1.50
210 Chandler Parsons COU .75 2.00
211 Draymond Green COU 1.25 3.00
212 Jimmy Butler COU 1.00 2.50
213 Kenneth Faried COU .75 2.00
214 Marcin Gortat COU .75 2.00
215 Raul Neto COU 1.00 2.50
216 T.J. Warren COU .75 2.00
217 Andrew Wiggins COU 1.50 4.00
218 Damian Lillard COU 2.00 5.00
219 Elfrid Payton COU .75 2.00
220 Joe Young COU 1.25 3.00
221 Kentavious Caldwell-Pope COU .75 2.00
222 Marcus Smart COU .75 2.00
223 Rakeem Christmas COU RC 1.00 2.50
224 Thabo Sefolosha COU .60 1.50
225 Anthony Brown COU RC 1.00 2.50
226 D'Angelo Russell COU 4.00 10.00
227 Emmanuel Mudiay COU 1.50 4.00
228 Jonas Valanciunas COU .75 2.00
229 Khris Middleton COU .75 2.00

230 Mario Hezonja COU 1.25 3.00
231 Rashad Vaughn COU 1.00 2.50
232 Tobias Harris COU .75 2.00
233 Austin Rivers COU .75 2.00
234 Danilo Gallinari COU .75 2.00
235 Enes Kanter COU .60 1.50
236 Jordan Clarkson COU 1.00 2.50
237 Klay Thompson COU 1.25 3.00
238 Michael Carter-Williams COU .60 1.50
239 Reggie Jackson COU .75 2.00
240 Trey Lyles COU 1.00 2.50
241 Ben McLemore COU .60 1.50
242 Darren Collison COU .75 2.00
243 Eric Gordon COU .75 2.00
244 Jrue Holiday COU .75 2.00
245 Kristaps Porzingis COU 4.00 10.00
246 Myles Turner COU 1.50 4.00
247 R.J. Hunter COU 1.00 2.50
248 Tristan Thompson COU .75 2.00
249 Bojan Bogdanovic COU .60 1.50
250 DeAndre Jordan COU 1.00 2.50
251 George Hill COU .75 2.00
252 Justin Anderson COU 1.25 3.00
253 Kyle Korver COU .75 2.00
254 Nemanja Bjelica COU 1.25 3.00
255 Rondae Hollis-Jefferson COU 1.25 3.00
256 Tyus Jones COU 1.50 4.00
257 Brandon Jennings COU .60 1.50
258 Delon Wright COU 1.25 3.00
259 Giannis Antetokounmpo COU 2.00 5.00
260 Justise Winslow COU 1.50 4.00
261 Kyle Lowry COU .75 2.00
262 Nene COU .75 2.00
263 Rudy Gobert COU 1.00 2.50
264 Victor Oladipo COU .75 2.00
265 Brandon Knight COU .75 2.00
266 DeMarcus Cousins COU 1.00 2.50
267 Jahlil Okafor COU 2.00 5.00
268 Karl-Anthony Towns COU 8.00 20.00
269 Kyrie Irving COU 2.00 5.00
270 Nikola Mirotic COU .75 2.00
271 Sam Dekker COU 1.25 3.00
272 Zach LaVine COU 1.00 2.50
273 C.J. McCollum COU 1.00 2.50
274 Derrick Rose COU 1.25 3.00
275 Jeremy Lamb COU .60 1.50
276 Kawhi Leonard COU 1.50 4.00
277 Langston Galloway COU .60 1.50
278 Norman Powell COU 1.25 3.00
279 Shane Larkin COU .60 1.50
280 Zach Randolph COU .75 2.00
281 Anthony Davis COU 2.00 5.00
282 Chris Andersen COU .75 2.00
283 Dirk Nowitzki COU 1.25 3.00
284 James Harden COU 1.50 4.00
285 Kevin Love COU 1.00 2.50
286 Russell Westbrook COU 2.50 6.00
287 Tony Parker COU 1.00 2.50
288 Blake Griffin COU 1.00 2.50
289 Chris Bosh COU 1.00 2.50
290 Dwight Howard COU .75 2.00
291 Jeremy Lin COU 1.00 2.50
292 Kobe Bryant COU 4.00 10.00
293 Stephen Curry COU 4.00 10.00
294 Vince Carter COU 1.25 3.00
295 Carmelo Anthony COU 1.25 3.00
296 Chris Paul COU 1.25 3.00
297 Dwyane Wade COU 1.50 4.00
298 Kevin Durant COU 2.50 6.00
299 Tim Duncan COU 1.50 4.00
300 LeBron James COU 4.00 10.00

2015-16 Select Concourse Prizms Blue
*BLUE: 1.2X TO 3X BASIC
*BLUE RC: .75X TO 2X BASIC RC
RANDOM INSERTS IN PACKS
STATED PRINT RUN 249 SER.#'d SETS
16 Karl-Anthony Towns 15.00 40.00
17 Kristaps Porzingis 6.00 15.00

2015-16 Select Concourse Prizms Orange
*ORANGE: 3X TO 8X BASIC
*ORANGE RC: 2X TO 5X BASIC RC
RANDOM INSERTS IN PACKS
STATED PRINT RUN 60 SER.#'d SETS
16 Karl-Anthony Towns 30.00 80.00
17 Kristaps Porzingis 15.00 40.00
62 D'Angelo Russell 12.00 30.00

2015-16 Select Concourse Prizms Pink
*PINK: 8X TO 20X BASIC
*PINK RC: 5X TO 12X BASIC RC
STATED PRINT RUN 20 SER.#'d SETS
16 Karl-Anthony Towns 50.00 120.00
17 Kristaps Porzingis 40.00 100.00
62 D'Angelo Russell 30.00 80.00

2015-16 Select Concourse Prizms Red
*RED: 1.2X TO 3X BASIC
*RED RC: .75X TO 2X BASIC RC
RANDOM INSERTS IN PACKS
STATED PRINT RUN 149 SER.#'d SETS
16 Karl-Anthony Towns 15.00 40.00
17 Kristaps Porzingis 6.00 15.00

2015-16 Select Courtside Prizms Copper
*COPPER: 1X TO 2.5X BASIC
*COPPER RC: .6X TO 1.5X BASIC RC
RANDOM INSERTS IN PACKS
STATED PRINT RUN 49 SER.#'d SETS
268 Karl-Anthony Towns 20.00 50.00

2015-16 Select Premier Prizms Light Blue Die Cut
*LT.BLUE: .75X TO 2X BASIC
*LT.BLUE RC: .5X TO 1.2X BASIC RC
RANDOM INSERTS IN PACKS
STATED PRINT RUN 199 SER.#'d SETS
136 Karl-Anthony Towns 10.00 25.00
179 Stephen Curry 10.00 25.00
196 Kristaps Porzingis 10.00 25.00

2015-16 Select Premier Prizms Purple Die Cut
*PURPLE: 1X TO 2.5X BASIC
*PURPLE RC: .6X TO 1.5X BASIC RC
RANDOM INSERTS IN PACKS
STATED PRINT RUN 99 SER.#'d SETS
136 Karl-Anthony Towns 12.00 30.00
179 Stephen Curry 12.00 30.00
196 Kristaps Porzingis 12.00 30.00

2015-16 Select Prizms Silver
*SILVER 1-100: 1.5X TO 4X BASIC
*SILVER 1-100: 1X TO 2.5X BASIC RC
*SILVER 101-200: .6X TO 1.5X BASIC
*SILVER 101-200: .4X TO 1X BASIC RC
*SILVER 201-300: .6X TO 1.5X BASIC
*SILVER 201-300: .4X TO 1X BASIC RC
RANDOM INSERTS IN PACKS

2015-16 Select Prizms Tie Dye
*TIE DYE 1-100: 8X TO 20X BASIC
*TIE DYE 1-100: 5X TO 12X BASIC RC
*TIE DYE 101-200: 3X TO 8X BASIC
*TIE DYE 101-200: 2X TO 5X BASIC RC
*TIE DYE 201-300: 2.5X TO 6X BASIC
*TIE DYE 201-300: 1.5X TO 4X BASIC RC
RANDOM INSERTS IN PACKS
STATED PRINT RUN 25 SER.#'d SETS
1 Andrew Wiggins CON 30.00 80.00
7 Kobe Bryant CON 50.00 120.00
8 Myles Turner CON 25.00 60.00
16 Karl-Anthony Towns CON 125.00 300.00
17 Kristaps Porzingis CON 75.00 200.00
26 Kawhi Leonard CON 20.00 50.00
30 Tim Duncan CON 20.00 50.00
45 Jimmy Butler CON 12.00 30.00
47 LeBron James CON 60.00 150.00
74 Jahlil Okafor CON 25.00 60.00
90 Zach LaVine CON 20.00 50.00
95 Justise Winslow CON 30.00 80.00
98 Paul George CON 15.00 40.00
99 Stephen Curry CON 60.00 150.00
110 Tim Duncan PRE 20.00 50.00
112 Carmelo Anthony PRE 25.00 60.00
126 Justise Winslow PRE 30.00 80.00
136 Karl-Anthony Towns PRE 125.00 300.00
141 Andrew Wiggins PRE 30.00 80.00
147 LeBron James PRE 60.00 150.00
164 Jahlil Okafor PRE 25.00 60.00
165 Jonathon Simmons PRE 12.00 30.00
179 Stephen Curry PRE 60.00 150.00
186 Kobe Bryant PRE 50.00 120.00
193 G. Antetokounmpo PRE 15.00 40.00
196 Kristaps Porzingis PRE 75.00 200.00
203 Devin Booker COU 50.00 120.00
207 Paul George COU 15.00 40.00
212 Jimmy Butler COU 12.00 30.00
217 Andrew Wiggins COU 30.00 80.00
246 Myles Turner COU 25.00 60.00
259 G. Antetokounmpo COU 15.00 40.00
260 Justise Winslow COU 30.00 80.00
267 Jahlil Okafor COU 25.00 60.00
268 Karl-Anthony Towns COU 125.00 300.00
272 Zach LaVine COU 20.00 50.00
276 Kawhi Leonard COU 20.00 50.00
292 Kobe Bryant COU 50.00 120.00
295 Carmelo Anthony COU 25.00 60.00
299 Tim Duncan COU 20.00 50.00
300 LeBron James COU 60.00 150.00

2015-16 Select Prizms Tri Color
*TRI CLR 1-100: 1.5X TO 4X BASIC
*TRI CLR 1-100: 1X TO 2.5X BASIC RC
*TRI CLR 101-200: .6X TO 1.5X BASIC
*TRI CLR 101-200: .4X TO 1X BASIC RC
RANDOM INSERTS IN PACKS

2015-16 Select City to City Jerseys
RANDOM INSERTS IN PACKS
PRINT RUNS B/WN 35-149 COPIES PER
1 Clyde Drexler/49 4.00 10.00
2 LeBron James/149 10.00 25.00
3 Dan Majerle/49 2.50 6.00
4 Nick Young/149 2.50 6.00
5 Jalen Rose/149 3.00 8.00
6 Shaquille O'Neal/49 5.00 12.00
7 Karl Malone/49 4.00 10.00
8 Toni Kukoc/149 3.00 8.00
9 Adrian Dantley/99 2.50 6.00
10 Kevin Garnett/149 4.00 10.00
11 Boris Diaw/149 2.50 6.00
12 Luol Deng/149 2.50 6.00
13 Danilo Gallinari/149 2.50 6.00
14 Ray Allen/99 3.00 8.00
15 Jason Kidd/99 3.00 8.00
16 Tobias Harris/149 2.50 6.00
17 Kelly Tripucka/35 2.00 5.00
18 Wilson Chandler/49 2.50 6.00
19 Al Jefferson/49 2.50 6.00
20 Larry Johnson/149 4.00 10.00
21 Nikola Vucevic/149 2.50 6.00
22 Mark Jackson/99 2.50 6.00
23 Eric Gordon/149 2.50 6.00
24 Raymond Felton/149 2.50 6.00
25 Jrue Holiday/149 2.50 6.00

2015-16 Select City to City Jerseys Prizms Tie Dye
*TIE DYE: 1X TO 2.5X BASIC
RANDOM INSERTS IN PACKS
STATED PRINT RUN 25 SER.#'d SETS
1 Clyde Drexler 20.00 50.00
2 LeBron James 60.00 150.00
6 Shaquille O'Neal 25.00 60.00
7 Karl Malone 20.00 50.00
8 Toni Kukoc 15.00 40.00
10 Kevin Garnett 20.00 50.00
14 Ray Allen 25.00 60.00
15 Jason Kidd 20.00 50.00
20 Larry Johnson 20.00 50.00

2015-16 Select Die Cut Autographs
RANDOM INSERTS IN PACKS
PRINT RUNS B/WN 25-60 COPIES PER
EXCHANGE DEADLINE 9/9/2017
1 Chris Andersen/25 10.00 25.00
2 Reggie Jackson/60 6.00 15.00
3 Jrue Holiday/25 5.00 12.00
4 Jordan Clarkson/60 5.00 12.00
5 Ben McLemore/25 4.00 10.00
6 Ray McCallum/60 3.00 8.00
7 Tyler Ennis/60 3.00 8.00
8 Victor Oladipo/25 5.00 12.00
9 Mike Conley/60 5.00 12.00
10 Harrison Barnes/25 5.00 12.00
11 Thabo Sefolosha/60 3.00 8.00
12 Ryan Anderson/60 4.00 10.00
13 Jason Terry/60 4.00 10.00
14 Shabazz Muhammad/60 4.00 10.00
15 Donatas Motiejunas/60 3.00 8.00
16 Julius Randle/25 10.00 25.00
17 Ed Davis/60 3.00 8.00
18 Josh Smith/25 5.00 12.00
19 Goran Dragic/60 4.00 10.00
20 T.J. Warren/60 4.00 10.00
21 Steven Adams/60 10.00 25.00
22 Brandon Knight/60 4.00 10.00
23 Andre Drummond/25 6.00 15.00
24 Trey Burke/60 3.00 8.00
25 Andrew Bogut/60 5.00 12.00
26 Langston Galloway/60 3.00 8.00
27 Zach Randolph/25 5.00 12.00
28 C.J. McCollum/60 5.00 12.00
29 Michael Carter-Williams/60 8.00 20.00
30 Kevin Martin/25 5.00 12.00
31 Khris Middleton/60 4.00 10.00
32 Alec Burks/60 3.00 8.00
33 Chris Paul/25 20.00 50.00
34 DeMarre Carroll/60 3.00 8.00
35 Brandon Bass/60 3.00 8.00
36 Kentavious Caldwell-Pope/25 5.00 12.00
37 Jusuf Nurkic/60 3.00 8.00
38 Kevin Love/25 12.00 30.00
39 Chris Bosh/25 10.00 25.00
40 Dwyane Wade/25 40.00 100.00
41 Otto Porter/25 5.00 12.00
42 Tony Allen/60 3.00 8.00
43 Oscar Robertson/25 30.00 80.00
44 Chris Mullin/60 10.00 25.00
45 Kareem Abdul-Jabbar/25 25.00 60.00
46 John Stockton/25 20.00 50.00
47 Connie Hawkins/60 8.00 20.00
48 Dennis Rodman/25 15.00 40.00
49 Tracy McGrady/25 15.00 40.00
50 Antonio McDyess/60 4.00 10.00
51 Steve Francis/60 8.00 20.00
52 Yao Ming/25 20.00 50.00
53 Anfernee Hardaway/25 20.00 50.00
54 Rick Barry/25 5.00 12.00
55 Jerry Lucas/60 5.00 12.00
56 Bill Walton/60 5.00 12.00
57 Alex English/60 4.00 10.00
58 Artis Gilmore/25 5.00 12.00
59 Ralph Sampson/60 4.00 10.00
60 Wes Unseld/25 8.00 20.00

2015-16 Select Die Cut Rookie Autographs
RANDOM INSERTS IN PACKS
STATED PRINT RUN 60 SER.#'d SETS
EXCHANGE DEADLINE 9/9/2017
1 Karl-Anthony Towns 125.00 250.00
2 D'Angelo Russell 30.00 80.00
3 Jahlil Okafor 25.00 60.00
4 Emmanuel Mudiay 10.00 25.00
5 Kristaps Porzingis 90.00 150.00
6 Mario Hezonja 5.00 12.00
7 Justise Winslow 12.00 30.00
8 Willie Cauley-Stein 6.00 15.00
9 Stanley Johnson 10.00 25.00
10 Tyus Jones 6.00 15.00
11 Frank Kaminsky 8.00 20.00
12 Devin Booker 60.00 150.00
13 Myles Turner 20.00 50.00
14 Jerian Grant 4.00 10.00
15 Trey Lyles 8.00 20.00
16 Cameron Payne 5.00 12.00
17 Delon Wright 5.00 12.00
18 Rashad Vaughn 4.00 10.00
19 Kelly Oubre Jr. 6.00 15.00
20 Sam Dekker 5.00 12.00
21 Terry Rozier 6.00 15.00
22 Rondae Hollis-Jefferson 5.00 12.00
23 Bobby Portis 10.00 25.00
24 Justin Anderson 5.00 12.00
25 Kevon Looney 5.00 12.00
26 Jarell Martin 5.00 12.00
27 R.J. Hunter 4.00 10.00
28 Josh Huestis 4.00 10.00
29 Norman Powell 5.00 12.00
30 Jordan Mickey 4.00 10.00
31 Branden Dawson 4.00 10.00
32 Duje Dukan 4.00 10.00
33 Walter Tavares 4.00 10.00
34 Larry Nance Jr. 6.00 15.00
35 Jonathon Simmons 10.00 25.00
36 Aaron Harrison 5.00 12.00
37 Montrezl Harrell 5.00 12.00
38 Nikola Jokic 40.00 100.00
39 Raul Neto 4.00 10.00
40 Pat Connaughton 4.00 10.00

2015-16 Select Rookie Jersey Autographs
RANDOM INSERTS IN PACKS
STATED PRINT RUN 125 SER.#'d SETS
EXCHANGE DEADLINE 9/9/2017
*COPPER/49: .5X TO 1.2X BASIC
1 Karl-Anthony Towns 100.00 250.00
2 D'Angelo Russell 30.00 80.00
3 Jahlil Okafor 6.00 15.00
4 Emmanuel Mudiay 12.00 30.00
5 Kristaps Porzingis 40.00 100.00
6 Mario Hezonja 4.00 10.00
7 Justise Winslow 10.00 25.00
8 Willie Cauley-Stein 15.00 40.00
9 Stanley Johnson 4.00 10.00
10 Tyus Jones 8.00 20.00
11 Frank Kaminsky 6.00 15.00
12 Devin Booker 40.00 100.00
13 Myles Turner 15.00 40.00
14 Jerian Grant 3.00 8.00
15 Trey Lyles 5.00 12.00
16 Cameron Payne 4.00 10.00
17 Delon Wright 4.00 10.00
19 Kelly Oubre Jr. 4.00 10.00
20 Sam Dekker 4.00 10.00
21 Terry Rozier 4.00 10.00
22 Rondae Hollis-Jefferson 4.00 10.00
23 Bobby Portis 5.00 12.00
24 Justin Anderson 4.00 10.00
25 Kevon Looney 4.00 10.00
26 Jarell Martin 4.00 10.00
27 R.J. Hunter 3.00 8.00
28 Anthony Brown 3.00 8.00
29 Chris McCullough 3.00 8.00
30 Jordan Mickey 3.00 8.00
31 Josh Huestis 3.00 8.00
32 Montrezl Harrell 4.00 10.00
33 Richaun Holmes 4.00 10.00

2015-16 Select Rookie Jersey Autographs Prizms Tie Dye
*TIE DYE: 2X TO 5X BASIC
RANDOM INSERTS IN PACKS
STATED PRINT RUN 25 SER.#'d SETS
EXCHANGE DEADLINE 9/9/2017
1 Karl-Anthony Towns 800.00 1200.00

2015-16 Select Rookie Signatures
RANDOM INSERTS IN PACKS
STATED PRINT RUN 199 SER.#'d SETS
EXCHANGE DEADLINE 9/9/2017
*COPPER/49: .5X TO 1.2X BASIC
RSSD Sam Dekker 4.00 10.00
RSFK Frank Kaminsky 5.00 12.00
RSKO Kelly Oubre Jr. 4.00 10.00
RSRH Rondae Hollis-Jefferson 4.00 10.00
RSBP Bobby Portis 5.00 12.00
RSJO Jahlil Okafor 10.00 25.00
RSKL Kevon Looney 4.00 10.00
RSAB Anthony Brown 3.00 8.00
RSRN Raul Neto 3.00 8.00
RSCP Cameron Payne 4.00 10.00
RSJM Jarell Martin 4.00 10.00
RSKP Kristaps Porzingis 60.00 150.00
RSJS Jonathon Simmons 15.00 40.00
RSJR Josh Richardson 5.00 12.00
RSJG Jerian Grant 3.00 8.00
RSMH Mario Hezonja 4.00 10.00
RSTR Terry Rozier 4.00 10.00
RSTM T.J. McConnell 4.00 10.00
RSDR D'Angelo Russell 20.00 50.00
RSJK Jordan Mickey 3.00 8.00
RSLN Larry Nance Jr. 5.00 12.00
RSDL Delon Wright 4.00 10.00
RSJA Justin Anderson 4.00 10.00
RSMT Myles Turner 15.00 40.00
RSWT Walter Tavares 3.00 8.00
RSNP Norman Powell 4.00 10.00
RSDB Devin Booker 40.00 100.00
RSJW Justise Winslow 8.00 20.00
RSWC Willie Cauley-Stein 10.00 25.00
RSEM Emmanuel Mudiay 8.00 20.00
RSKT Karl-Anthony Towns 150.00 300.00
RSRV Rashad Vaughn 3.00 8.00
RSNB Nemanja Bjelica 4.00 10.00
RSDD Duje Dukan 3.00 8.00
RSDH Darrun Hilliard 3.00 8.00
RSNJ Nikola Jokic 30.00 80.00

2015-16 Select Rookie Swatches
RANDOM INSERTS IN PACKS
STATED PRINT RUN 149 COPIES PER
*PURPLE/99: .4X TO 1X BASIC
*ORANGE/60 .4X TO 1X BASIC
1 Jahlil Okafor 4.00 10.00
2 Mario Hezonja 2.50 6.00
3 Justise Winslow 3.00 8.00
4 Frank Kaminsky 3.00 8.00
5 Karl-Anthony Towns 15.00 40.00
6 Jerian Grant 2.00 5.00
7 Delon Wright 2.50 6.00
8 Willie Cauley-Stein 3.00 8.00
10 D'Angelo Russell 8.00 20.00
11 Kelly Oubre Jr. 2.50 6.00
12 Terry Rozier 2.50 6.00
13 Stanley Johnson 2.50 6.00
14 Sam Dekker 2.50 6.00
15 Jordan Mickey 2.00 5.00
16 Emmanuel Mudiay 3.00 8.00
17 Chris McCullough 2.00 5.00
18 Kevon Looney 2.50 6.00
19 Tyus Jones 3.00 8.00
20 Devin Booker 10.00 25.00
21 Rondae Hollis-Jefferson 2.50 6.00
22 Kristaps Porzingis 10.00 25.00
23 Myles Turner 3.00 8.00
24 Trey Lyles 3.00 8.00
25 Bobby Portis 3.00 8.00
26 Justin Anderson 2.50 6.00
27 Cameron Payne 2.50 6.00
28 Jarell Martin 2.50 6.00
29 R.J. Hunter 2.00 5.00
30 Anthony Brown 2.00 5.00

2015-16 Select Rookie Swatches Prizms Tie Dye
*TIE DYE: 1X TO 2.5X BASIC
RANDOM INSERTS IN PACKS
STATED PRINT RUN 25 SER.#'d SETS
1 Jahlil Okafor 20.00 50.00
5 Karl-Anthony Towns 100.00 200.00
10 D'Angelo Russell 25.00 60.00
20 Devin Booker 40.00 100.00
23 Myles Turner 20.00 50.00

2015-16 Select Signatures
RANDOM INSERTS IN PACKS
PRINT RUNS B/WN 99-149 COPIES PER
EXCHANGE DEADLINE 9/9/2017
*COPPER/49: .5X TO 1.2X BASIC
1 Kobe Bryant/99 90.00 150.00
2 Clyde Drexler/99 12.00 30.00
3 Bill Walton/149 5.00 12.00
4 Zach LaVine/149 12.00 30.00
5 Gary Harris/149 4.00 10.00
6 Mo Williams/149 4.00 10.00
7 Kevin Durant/99 40.00 100.00
8 Jason Kidd/99 10.00 25.00
9 Robert Parish/149 5.00 12.00
10 Doug McDermott/149 4.00 10.00
11 Elfrid Payton/149 4.00 10.00
12 Blake Griffin/99 15.00 40.00
13 Chris Paul/99 20.00 50.00
14 Kevin Love/99 10.00 25.00
15 Mark Jackson/149 4.00 10.00
16 Carmelo Anthony/99 20.00 50.00
17 Kenny Anderson/149 4.00 10.00
18 T.J. Warren/149 4.00 10.00
19 Julius Erving/99 30.00 80.00
20 Tracy McGrady/99 12.00 30.00
21 Dikembe Mutombo/149 10.00 25.00
23 Victor Oladipo/99 4.00 10.00
24 Mike Conley/149 5.00 12.00
25 Karl Malone/99 20.00 50.00
26 Anfernee Hardaway/99 15.00 40.00
27 Marcin Gortat/149 4.00 10.00
28 Tony Allen/149 3.00 8.00
29 Bojan Bogdanovic/149 3.00 8.00
30 Gary Neal/149 4.00 10.00
31 Anthony Davis/99 40.00 100.00
32 Gary Payton/99 8.00 20.00
33 Allan Houston/149 4.00 10.00
34 Cuttino Mobley/149 3.00 8.00
35 Langston Galloway/149 3.00 8.00
36 Dwyane Wade/99 20.00 50.00
37 Alonzo Mourning/99 6.00 15.00
38 Kenneth Faried/149 4.00 10.00
39 Danny Green/149 4.00 10.00
40 Antoine Carr/149 3.00 8.00
41 Chris Bosh/99 5.00 12.00
42 Nene/149 4.00 10.00
43 Timofey Mozgov/149 3.00 8.00
44 Andre Drummond/99 8.00 20.00
46 Thaddeus Young/149 3.00 8.00
47 Jonas Valanciunas/149 4.00 10.00
48 Joe Ingles/149 3.00 8.00
49 John Wall/99 15.00 40.00
50 J.R. Smith/149 8.00 20.00
51 Sonny Weems/149 3.00 8.00
52 Marcus Smart/99 4.00 10.00
53 Mason Plumlee/149 4.00 10.00
54 Tony Parker/99 12.00 30.00
56 Andrew Wiggins/99 40.00 100.00
57 Julius Randle/99 10.00 25.00
58 Tim Hardaway Jr./149 3.00 8.00
59 Tarik Black/149 3.00 8.00
60 Gordon Hayward/149 5.00 12.00

2015-16 Select Sparks Jerseys
RANDOM INSERTS IN PACKS
PRINT RUNS B/WN 49-99 COPIES PER
1 John Stockton/49 4.00 10.00
2 Stephen Curry/99 12.00 30.00
3 Gary Payton/99 3.00 8.00
4 Derrick Rose/99 5.00 12.00
5 DeMar DeRozan/99 3.00 8.00
6 Paul George/49 4.00 10.00
7 Carmelo Anthony/99 4.00 10.00
8 Kobe Bryant/99 8.00 20.00
9 Tony Parker/99 3.00 8.00
10 Kyrie Irving/99 5.00 12.00
11 Jimmy Butler/99 3.00 8.00
12 LeBron James/99 10.00 25.00
13 Elfrid Payton/99 2.50 6.00
14 Russell Westbrook/99 4.00 10.00
15 Damian Lillard/99 5.00 12.00
16 Manu Ginobili/99 3.00 8.00
17 Allen Iverson/49 4.00 10.00
18 Kevin Durant/99 6.00 15.00
19 John Wall/99 4.00 10.00
20 Anthony Davis/99 6.00 15.00
21 Jason Kidd/99 3.00 8.00
22 James Harden/99 5.00 12.00
23 Dwyane Wade/99 5.00 12.00
24 Ricky Rubio/99 3.00 8.00
25 Chris Paul/99 4.00 10.00

2015-16 Select Sparks Jerseys Prizms Tie Dye
*TIE DYE: 1X TO 2.5X BASIC
RANDOM INSERTS IN PACKS
PRINT RUNS B/WN 15-25 COPIES PER
1 John Stockton/25 20.00 50.00
2 Stephen Curry/15 60.00 150.00
3 Gary Payton/25 15.00 40.00
4 Derrick Rose/25 25.00 60.00
7 Carmelo Anthony/15 15.00 40.00
8 Kobe Bryant/25 50.00 120.00
12 LeBron James/25 60.00 150.00
14 Russell Westbrook/25 20.00 50.00
17 Allen Iverson/25 20.00 50.00
18 Kevin Durant/25 20.00 50.00
22 James Harden/25 12.00 30.00

2015-16 Select Swatches
RANDOM INSERTS IN PACKS
PRINT RUNS B/WN 60-149 COPIES PER
*PURPLE/49-99: .4X TO 1X BASIC
*ORANGE/49-60: .4X TO 1X BASIC
*ORANGE/35: .5X TO 1.2X BASIC
1 John Wall/99 4.00 10.00
2 Manu Ginobili/60 3.00 8.00
3 Kevin Durant/60 5.00 12.00
4 Zach LaVine/60 3.00 8.00
5 Chris Bosh/149 3.00 8.00
6 Paul George/60 4.00 10.00
7 Rodney Hood/99 2.50 6.00
8 Kevin Love/60 3.00 8.00
9 Marcin Gortat/99 2.50 6.00
10 Dirk Nowitzki/149 4.00 10.00
11 Bradley Beal/99 3.00 8.00
12 Kawhi Leonard/149 5.00 12.00
13 Tobias Harris/149 2.50 6.00
14 Ricky Rubio/99 3.00 8.00
15 Vince Carter/99 4.00 10.00
16 James Harden/60 5.00 12.00
17 Brandon Jennings/99 2.00 5.00
18 Joakim Noah/149 2.50 6.00
19 Nene/149 2.50 6.00
20 Tim Hardaway Jr./60 2.00 5.00
21 Gordon Hayward/99 3.00 8.00
22 DeMarcus Cousins/149 3.00 8.00
23 Russell Westbrook/149 8.00 20.00
24 Eric Gordon/99 2.50 6.00
25 Mike Conley/60 3.00 8.00
26 Dwight Howard/60 2.50 6.00
27 Metta World Peace/149 2.00 5.00
28 Jimmy Butler/99 3.00 8.00
29 Terrence Ross/60 2.50 6.00
30 Kenneth Faried/99 2.50 6.00
31 Kyle Lowry/99 2.50 6.00
32 Damian Lillard/149 5.00 12.00
33 Langston Galloway/149 2.00 5.00
34 Andrew Wiggins/99 5.00 12.00
35 Marc Gasol/149 3.00 8.00
36 Stephen Curry/99 20.00 50.00
37 Kevin Garnett/149 5.00 12.00
38 Derrick Rose/99 5.00 12.00
39 Jose Calderon/149 2.00 5.00
40 Chandler Parsons/99 2.50 6.00
41 DeMar DeRozan/60 3.00 8.00
42 Eric Bledsoe/149 2.50 6.00
43 Carmelo Anthony/60 4.00 10.00
44 Giannis Antetokounmpo/60 6.00 15.00
45 DeAndre Jordan/149 3.00 8.00
46 Klay Thompson/60 4.00 10.00
47 Marcus Smart/99 2.50 6.00
48 Kemba Walker/99 3.00 8.00
49 T.J. Warren/99 2.50 6.00
50 LeBron James/60 10.00 25.00
51 Tony Parker/99 3.00 8.00
52 Nerlens Noel/99 2.50 6.00
53 Ryan Anderson/60 2.50 6.00
54 Mario Chalmers/149 2.50 6.00
55 Chris Paul/99 4.00 10.00
56 Harrison Barnes/99 2.50 6.00
57 Avery Bradley/99 2.50 6.00
58 Dennis Schroder/99 2.50 6.00
59 Alex Len/149 2.00 5.00
60 Kobe Bryant/149 12.00 30.00
61 Tim Duncan/99 5.00 12.00
62 Victor Oladipo/149 2.50 6.00
63 Tyreke Evans/99 2.00 5.00
64 Dwyane Wade/60 5.00 12.00
65 Blake Griffin/99 4.00 10.00
66 Draymond Green/99 4.00 10.00
67 Kyrie Irving/99 6.00 15.00
68 Al Horford/149 2.50 6.00
69 Ian Mahinmi/149 2.00 5.00
70 Jared Sullinger/149 2.00 5.00

2015-16 Select Swatches Prizms Tie Dye
*TIE DYE/15-25: 1X TO 2.5X BASIC
RANDOM INSERTS IN PACKS
PRINT RUNS B/WN 5-25 COPIES PER
NO PRICING ON QTY 5
3 Kevin Durant/25 25.00 60.00
4 Zach LaVine/25 25.00 60.00
5 Chris Bosh/25 20.00 50.00
6 Paul George/25 20.00 50.00
12 Kawhi Leonard/25 20.00 50.00
28 Jimmy Butler/25 20.00 50.00
34 Andrew Wiggins/25 20.00 50.00
36 Stephen Curry/15 125.00 250.00
37 Kevin Garnett/25 15.00 40.00
38 Derrick Rose/25 20.00 50.00
46 Klay Thompson/25 25.00 60.00
50 LeBron James/18 100.00 200.00
55 Chris Paul/25 20.00 50.00
60 Kobe Bryant/25 90.00 150.00
61 Tim Duncan/25 20.00 50.00
64 Dwyane Wade/25 20.00 50.00
65 Blake Griffin/25 15.00 40.00

2015-16 Select Throwback Memorabilia
RANDOM INSERTS IN PACKS
PRINT RUNS B/WN 35-149 COPIES PER
1 Kevin Garnett/149 5.00 12.00
2 J.J. Barea/149 2.50 6.00
3 Danilo Gallinari/149 2.50 6.00
4 Richard Jefferson/49 2.50 6.00
5 Devin Harris/49 2.00 5.00
6 Timofey Mozgov/149 2.00 5.00
7 Iman Shumpert/149 2.00 5.00
8 Jeff Green/49 2.50 6.00
9 Al Jefferson/49 2.50 6.00
10 Kevin Martin/149 2.50 6.00
11 Brandon Knight/149 2.50 6.00
12 Pau Gasol/149 3.00 8.00
13 Zaza Pachulia/149 2.00 5.00
14 Robert Covington/149 2.00 5.00
15 Dion Waiters/149 2.50 6.00
16 Tobias Harris/149 2.50 6.00
17 Isaiah Thomas/149 3.00 8.00
18 Jeremy Lin/149 3.00 8.00
19 Amare Stoudemire/149 2.50 6.00
20 LeBron James/149 10.00 25.00
21 Chandler Parsons/149 2.50 6.00
22 Paul Millsap/149 3.00 8.00
23 Darren Collison/149 2.50 6.00
24 Rudy Gay/149 3.00 8.00
25 Evan Turner/149 2.50 6.00
26 Trevor Ariza/149 2.00 5.00
27 J.R. Smith/149 2.50 6.00
28 Jodie Meeks/149 2.50 6.00
29 Andre Miller/149 2.50 6.00
30 Lou Williams/149 2.50 6.00
31 Channing Frye/149 2.50 6.00
32 Paul Pierce/149 3.00 8.00
33 DeJuan Blair/149 2.00 5.00
34 Thabo Sefolosha/149 2.00 5.00
35 Gerald Green/149 2.50 6.00
36 Tyson Chandler/149 2.50 6.00
37 Jamal Crawford/49 3.00 8.00
38 Boris Diaw/149 2.50 6.00
39 Anthony Bennett/149 2.00 5.00
40 Matt Barnes/149 2.00 5.00
41 Corey Brewer/149 2.00 5.00
42 Raymond Felton/149 2.50 6.00
43 DeMarre Carroll/122 2.00 5.00
44 Thaddeus Young/149 2.00 5.00
45 Mike Dunleavy/149 2.00 5.00
46 Vince Carter/149 4.00 10.00
47 Jarrett Jack/149 2.50 6.00
48 Kevin Love/149 3.00 8.00
49 Arron Afflalo/149 2.00 5.00
50 Mo Williams/149 2.50 6.00

2015-16 Select Throwback Memorabilia Prizms Tie Dye
*TIE DYE: 1X TO 2.5X BASIC
RANDOM INSERTS IN PACKS
PRINT RUNS B/WN 14-25 COPIES PER
20 LeBron James/25 60.00 150.00
46 Vince Carter/25 20.00 50.00

2016-17 Select
1 Buddy Hield RC .75 2.00
2 Dwight Howard .25 .60
3 Harrison Barnes .25 .60
4 Jamal Murray RC 1.00 2.50
5 Kyle Lowry .25 .60
6 Kyrie Irving .60 1.50
7 Randy Foye .20 .50
8 Rashad Vaughn .20 .50
9 Zaza Pachulia .20 .50
10 Al Jefferson .25 .60
11 Cheick Diallo RC .30 .75
12 Dion Waiters .25 .60
13 Gorgui Dieng .20 .50
14 Jabari Parker .40 1.00
15 Kyle Anderson .20 .50
16 Langston Galloway .20 .50
17 Paul George .40 1.00
18 Reggie Bullock .20 .50
19 Willy Hernangomez RC .40 1.00
20 Trey Lyles .25 .60
21 Patrick Beverley .20 .50
22 Deyonta Davis .20 .50
23 Georges Niang RC .30 .75
24 Jae Crowder .25 .60
25 Kris Dunn RC 1.00 2.50
26 Dirk Nowitzki .40 1.00
27 Pau Gasol .30 .75
28 Reggie Jackson .25 .60
29 Willie Cauley-Stein .25 .60
30 Alex Abrines RC .50 1.25
31 Chris Andersen .25 .60
32 Derrick Rose .40 1.00
33 Jaylen Brown RC 1.25 3.00
34 Kenneth Faried .25 .60
35 Klay Thompson .40 1.00
36 Lou Williams .25 .60
37 Patty Mills .30 .75
38 Robert Covington .20 .50
39 Wade Baldwin IV RC .30 .75
40 Alex Len .20 .50
41 David West .25 .60
42 Deron Williams .25 .60
43 Gary Harris .25 .60
44 Ish Smith .20 .50
45 Khris Middleton .25 .60
46 Luol Deng .25 .60
47 Omri Casspi .20 .50
48 Rudy Gobert .30 .75
49 Jrue Holiday .25 .60
50 Andrew Wiggins .50 1.25
51 Damian Lillard .60 1.50
52 Dennis Schroder .25 .60
53 Evan Fournier .25 .60
54 James Harden .50 1.25
55 Kevon Looney .25 .60
56 Malik Beasley RC .30 .75
57 Norman Powell .20 .50
58 Russell Westbrook .75 2.00
59 Tyler Ulis RC 1.00 2.50
60 Ben Simmons RC 2.00 5.00
61 D'Angelo Russell .40 1.00
62 DeMar DeRozan .30 .75
63 Eric Bledsoe .25 .60
64 JaMychal Green .20 .50
65 Kevin Love .30 .75
66 Marcelo Huertas .20 .50
67 Nene .25 .60
68 Ryan Anderson .25 .60
69 Corey Brewer .20 .50
70 Blake Griffin .30 .75
71 Brook Lopez .25 .60
72 Darren Collison .25 .60
73 Emmanuel Mudiay .25 .60
74 Mike Muscala .20 .50
75 Kemba Walker .30 .75
76 Marco Belinelli .20 .50
77 Monta Ellis .25 .60
78 Serge Ibaka .25 .60
79 Tomas Satoransky RC .30 .75
80 Bojan Bogdanovic .20 .50
81 Brice Johnson RC .30 .75
82 Dario Saric RC 1.00 2.50
83 Luis Scola .25 .60
84 Jeremy Lamb .20 .50
85 Kelly Olynyk .20 .50
86 Mario Hezonja .20 .50
87 Maurice Harkless .20 .50
88 Stephen Curry 1.25 3.00
89 Tobias Harris .25 .60
90 Bradley Beal .30 .75
91 Brandon Ingram RC 2.00 5.00
92 Danilo Gallinari .25 .60
93 Dwyane Wade .50 1.25
94 Jonathon Simmons .30 .75
95 Justise Winslow .25 .60
96 Marquese Chriss RC .75 2.00
97 Marshall Plumlee .20 .50
98 Steven Adams .25 .60
99 Taurean Prince RC .50 1.25
100 Jonas Valanciunas .25 .60
101 Brandon Ingram 2.50 6.00
102 Brandon Jennings .40 1.00
103 Isaiah Thomas .60 1.50
104 Ian Mahinmi .40 1.00
105 Kent Bazemore .50 1.25
106 Kentavious Caldwell-Pope .50 1.25
107 Nikola Vucevic .50 1.25
108 Noah Vonleh .40 1.00
109 Thon Maker RC 2.00 5.00
110 Bobby Portis .40 1.00
111 Thaddeus Young .40 1.00
112 Brandon Knight .50 1.25
113 Henry Ellenson RC .75 2.00
114 Ivica Zubac RC 1.00 2.50
115 Kelly Oubre Jr. .40 1.00
116 Kevin Durant 1.50 4.00
117 Nikola Mirotic .50 1.25
118 Pascal Siakam RC .60 1.50
119 T. Luwawu-Cabarrot RC 1.25 3.00
120 Boban Marjanovic .40 1.00
121 Thabo Sefolosha .40 1.00
122 Buddy Hield 1.00 2.50
123 Hassan Whiteside .50 1.25
124 J.J. Redick .60 1.50
125 Karl-Anthony Towns 1.50 4.00
126 Kris Dunn 1.25 3.00
127 Myles Turner .50 1.25
128 Patrick McCaw RC 1.25 3.00
129 Tony Parker .60 1.50
130 Bismack Biyombo .40 1.00
131 Dirk Nowitzki .75 2.00
132 Caris LeVert RC .75 2.00
133 Greg Monroe .50 1.25
134 Jahlil Okafor .50 1.25
135 Juan Hernangomez RC .75 2.00
136 Kyle Korver .50 1.25
137 Monta Ellis .50 1.25
138 Paul Pierce .60 1.50
139 Trevor Ariza .40 1.00
140 Taj Gibson .50 1.25
141 Ben Simmons 3.00 8.00
142 Carmelo Anthony .75 2.00
143 Georgios Papagiannis RC .60 1.50
144 Jake Layman RC .75 2.00
145 Josh Richardson .40 1.00
146 LaMarcus Aldridge .60 1.50
147 Mirza Teletovic .40 1.00
148 Rajon Rondo .60 1.50
149 Trevor Booker .40 1.00
150 Austin Rivers .50 1.25
151 T.J. McConnell .40 1.00
152 Chris Paul .75 2.00
153 George Hill .50 1.25
154 James Ennis .40 1.00
155 Jonas Valanciunas .50 1.25
156 Damian Lillard 1.25 3.00
157 Mindaugas Kuzminskas RC .75 2.00
158 Ramon Sessions .50 1.25
159 Tyler Johnson .40 1.00
160 Arron Afflalo .40 1.00
161 Stephen Curry 2.50 6.00
162 Clint Capela .40 1.00
163 Ersan Ilyasova .40 1.00
164 DeMarre Carroll .40 1.00
165 Jordan Clarkson .50 1.25
166 Mike Dunleavy .40 1.00
167 Pau Gasol .60 1.50
168 Richard Jefferson .50 1.25
169 Victor Oladipo .50 1.25
170 Anthony Davis 1.25 3.00
171 Sheldon McClellan RC .60 1.50
172 DeMarcus Cousins .60 1.50
173 Eric Gordon .50 1.25
174 Jaylen Brown 1.50 4.00
175 John Wall .75 2.00
176 Malik Beasley .40 1.00
177 Mike Conley .50 1.25
178 Ricky Rubio .60 1.50
179 Vince Carter .75 2.00
180 Shabazz Muhammad .50 1.25
181 Allen Crabbe .40 1.00
182 Demetrius Jackson RC .60 1.50
183 Dwight Powell .40 1.00
184 Jeff Teague .50 1.25
185 Tyson Chandler .50 1.25
186 Marc Gasol .60 1.50
187 Michael Kidd-Gilchrist .50 1.25
188 Rodney Hood .50 1.25
189 Wayne Ellington .40 1.00
190 A.J. Hammons RC .60 1.50
191 Al Horford .50 1.25
192 Seth Curry .60 1.50
193 Dion Waiters .50 1.25
194 Domantas Sabonis RC 1.00 2.50
195 Joakim Noah .50 1.25
196 Joe Johnson .50 1.25
197 Markieff Morris .40 1.00
198 Matthew Dellavedova .50 1.25
199 Rodney Stuckey .40 1.00
200 Wesley Matthews .40 1.00
201 Anthony Davis 1.50 4.00
202 Damian Lillard 1.50 4.00
203 DeMarcus Cousins .75 2.00
204 Georges Niang .50 1.25
205 Giannis Antetokounmpo 1.50 4.00
206 James Harden 1.25 3.00
207 Kevin Durant 2.00 5.00
208 Marcus Smart .60 1.50
209 Zach LaVine .75 2.00
210 Chris Paul 1.00 2.50
211 Aaron Gordon .60 1.50
212 D'Angelo Russell 1.00 2.50
213 Dennis Schroder .60 1.50
214 Frank Kaminsky .60 1.50
215 Goran Dragic .60 1.50
216 Jeremy Lin .75 2.00
217 Kris Dunn 1.50 4.00
218 Marvin Williams .60 1.50
219 Tristan Thompson .60 1.50
220 Sam Dekker .60 1.50
221 Andre Drummond .75 2.00
222 Dante Exum .60 1.50
223 Denzel Valentine RC 1.00 2.50
224 Evan Turner .50 1.25
225 Gordon Hayward .75 2.00
226 Jimmy Butler .75 2.00
227 Kristaps Porzingis 1.50 4.00
228 Michael Gbinije RC .75 2.00
229 Timofey Mozgov .50 1.25
230 Chandler Parsons .60 1.50
231 Andrew Wiggins 1.25 3.00
232 Dario Saric 1.50 4.00
233 Derrick Favors .60 1.50
234 Evan Fournier .60 1.50
235 Will Barton .50 1.25
236 Joel Embiid 1.25 3.00
237 Kyrie Irving 2.00 5.00
238 Myles Turner .60 1.50
239 T.J. Warren .60 1.50
240 Carmelo Anthony 1.00 2.50
241 Avery Bradley .60 1.50
242 DeAndre' Bembry RC .75 2.00
243 Derrick Rose 1.00 2.50
244 Elfrid Payton .60 1.50
245 Iman Shumpert .50 1.25
246 John Wall 1.00 2.50
247 Malachi Richardson RC 1.00 2.50
248 Nicolas Batum .60 1.50
249 Stephen Zimmerman RC .75 2.00
250 Cameron Payne .50 1.25

251 Ben Simmons 4.00 10.00
252 DeAndre Jordan .75 2.00
253 Devin Booker 1.25 3.00
254 Draymond Green 1.25 3.00
255 Isaiah Whitehead RC .75 2.00
256 Julius Randle .75 2.00
257 Manu Ginobili .75 2.00
258 Nikola Jokic .75 2.00
259 Stanley Johnson .50 1.25
260 C.J. McCollum .60 1.50
261 Blake Griffin .75 2.00
262 Dejounte Murray RC 1.50 4.00
263 Diamond Stone RC .75 2.00
264 Dragan Bender RC 1.00 2.50
265 Jakob Poeltl RC 1.00 2.50
266 Justise Winslow .60 1.50
267 Marcin Gortat .60 1.50
268 Rondae Hollis-Jefferson .50 1.25
269 Solomon Hill .50 1.25
270 Buddy Hield 1.25 3.00
271 Bobby Portis .50 1.25
272 DeMar DeRozan .75 2.00
273 Domantas Sabonis .75 2.00
274 Doug McDermott .60 1.50
275 Jamal Murray 1.50 4.00
276 Karl-Anthony Towns 2.00 5.00
277 Marcus Morris .50 1.25
278 Sergio Rodriguez .50 1.25
279 Skal Labissiere RC 1.25 3.00
280 Brandon Ingram 3.00 8.00
281 Thon Maker 1.50 4.00
282 Zach Randolph .60 1.50
283 Ryan Anderson .60 1.50
284 Russell Westbrook 2.00 5.00
285 Cory Joseph .50 1.25
286 LeBron James 3.00 8.00
287 Andre Iguodala .60 1.50
288 Kawhi Leonard 1.25 3.00
289 LeBron James 3.00 8.00
290 LeBron James 3.00 8.00
291 Dirk Nowitzki 1.00 2.50
292 Kobe Bryant 3.00 8.00
293 Kobe Bryant 3.00 8.00
294 Paul Pierce .75 2.00
295 Tony Parker .75 2.00
296 Dwyane Wade 1.25 3.00
297 Chauncey Billups .75 2.00
298 Shaquille O'Neal 2.00 5.00
299 Shaquille O'Neal 2.00 5.00
300 Shaquille O'Neal 2.00 5.00

2016-17 Select Prizms Blue

*PRIZMS BLUE: 1.2X TO 3X BASIC
*PRIZMS BLUE RC: .75X TO 2X BASIC RC
RANDOM INSERTS IN PACKS
STATED PRINT RUN 299 SER.#'d SETS
60 Ben Simmons 25.00 60.00

2016-17 Select Prizms Copper

*PRIZMS COPPER: 1X TO 2.5X BASIC
*PRIZMS COPPER RC: .6X TO 1.5X BASIC RC
RANDOM INSERTS IN PACKS
STATED PRINT RUN 49 SER.#'d SETS
217 Kris Dunn 8.00 20.00
232 Dario Saric 30.00 80.00
251 Ben Simmons 125.00 300.00
270 Buddy Hield 6.00 15.00
275 Jamal Murray 10.00 25.00
279 Skal Labissiere 12.00 30.00
280 Brandon Ingram 30.00 80.00
281 Thon Maker 20.00 50.00
286 LeBron James 50.00 120.00
287 Andre Iguodala 10.00 25.00
288 Kawhi Leonard 12.00 30.00
289 LeBron James 20.00 50.00
290 LeBron James 20.00 50.00
291 Dirk Nowitzki 20.00 50.00
292 Kobe Bryant 20.00 50.00
293 Kobe Bryant 20.00 50.00
294 Paul Pierce 12.00 30.00
295 Tony Parker 15.00 40.00
296 Dwyane Wade 20.00 50.00
297 Chauncey Billups 6.00 15.00
298 Shaquille O'Neal 10.00 25.00
299 Shaquille O'Neal 10.00 25.00
300 Shaquille O'Neal 10.00 25.00

2016-17 Select Prizms Light Blue Die-Cut

*PRIZMS LT.BLUE: 1.2X TO 3X BASIC
*PRIZMS LT.BLUE RC: .75X TO 2X BASIC RC
RANDOM INSERTS IN PACKS
STATED PRINT RUN 199 SER.#'d SETS
141 Ben Simmons 30.00 80.00

2016-17 Select Prizms Maroon

*PRIZMS MARN: 1.5X TO 4X BASIC
*PRIZMS MARN RC: 1X TO 2.5X BASIC RC
RANDOM INSERTS IN PACKS
STATED PRINT RUN 175 SER.#'d SETS
60 Ben Simmons 30.00 80.00

2016-17 Select Prizms Neon Yellow Die-Cut

*PRIZMS YLLW: 2X TO 5X BASIC
*PRIZMS YLLW RC: 1.2X TO 3X BASIC RC
RANDOM INSERTS IN PACKS
STATED PRINT RUN 75 SER.#'d SETS
122 Buddy Hield 10.00 25.00
126 Kris Dunn 12.00 30.00
141 Ben Simmons 60.00 150.00
161 Stephen Curry 20.00 50.00

2016-17 Select Prizms Orange

*PRIZMS ORNGE: 2.5X TO 6X BASIC
*PRIZMS ORNGE RC: 1.5X TO 4X BASIC RC
RANDOM INSERTS IN PACKS
STATED PRINT RUN 60 SER.#'d SETS
4 Jamal Murray 8.00 20.00
33 Jaylen Brown 12.00 30.00
59 Tyler Ulis 12.00 30.00
60 Ben Simmons 75.00 200.00
82 Dario Saric 10.00 25.00
91 Brandon Ingram 15.00 40.00
96 Marquese Chriss 10.00 25.00

2016-17 Select Prizms Purple Die-Cut

*PRIZMS PURPLE: 1X TO 2.5X BASIC
*PRIZMS PURPLE RC: .6X TO 1.5X BASIC RC
RANDOM INSERTS IN PACKS
STATED PRINT RUN 99 SER.#'d SETS
122 Buddy Hield 5.00 12.00
141 Ben Simmons 40.00 100.00

2016-17 Select Prizms Silver

*SILVER 1-100: 1.X TO 3X BASIC
*SILVER 1-100 RC: .75X TO 2X BASIC RC
*SILVER 101-200: .6X TO 1.5X BASIC
*SILVER 101-200 RC: .4X TO 1X BASIC RC
*SILVER 201-300: .6X TO 1.5X BASIC
*SILVER 201-300 RC: .4X TO 1X BASIC RC
RANDOM INSERTS IN PACKS
60 Ben Simmons 20.00 50.00
141 Ben Simmons 20.00 50.00
251 Ben Simmons 40.00 100.00

2016-17 Select Prizms Tie-Dye

*PRIZM TD 1-100: 8X TO 20X BASIC
*PRIZM TD 1-100 RC: 5X TO 12X BASIC RC
*PRIZM TD 101-200: 4X TO 10X BASIC
*PRIZM TD 101-200 RC: 2.5X TO 6X BASIC RC
*PRIZM TD 201-300: 3X TO 8X BASIC
*PRIZM TD 201-300 RC: 2X TO 5X BASIC RC
RANDOM INSERTS IN PACKS
STATED PRINT RUN 25 SER.#'d SETS
1 Buddy Hield 25.00 60.00
4 Jamal Murray 50.00 120.00
6 Kyrie Irving 20.00 50.00
19 Willy Hernangomez 15.00 40.00
25 Kris Dunn 25.00 60.00
33 Jaylen Brown 60.00 150.00
59 Tyler Ulis 25.00 60.00
60 Ben Simmons 300.00 600.00
82 Dario Saric 40.00 100.00
88 Stephen Curry 40.00 100.00
91 Brandon Ingram 60.00 150.00
96 Marquese Chriss 30.00 80.00
101 Brandon Ingram 60.00 150.00
109 Thon Maker 40.00 100.00
114 Ivica Zubac 25.00 60.00
116 Kevin Durant 50.00 120.00
122 Buddy Hield 25.00 60.00
126 Kris Dunn 25.00 60.00
135 Juan Hernangomez 20.00 50.00
141 Ben Simmons 300.00 600.00
161 Stephen Curry 40.00 100.00
170 Anthony Davis 30.00 80.00
201 Anthony Davis 30.00 80.00
205 Giannis Antetokounmpo 20.00 50.00
207 Kevin Durant 50.00 120.00
216 Jeremy Lin 20.00 50.00
217 Kris Dunn 25.00 60.00
232 Dario Saric 40.00 100.00
237 Kyrie Irving 25.00 60.00
251 Ben Simmons 300.00 600.00
270 Buddy Hield 20.00 50.00
275 Jamal Murray 60.00 150.00
279 Skal Labissiere 50.00 120.00
280 Brandon Ingram 60.00 150.00
281 Thon Maker 40.00 100.00
286 LeBron James 150.00 300.00
287 Andre Iguodala 40.00 100.00
288 Kawhi Leonard 50.00 120.00
289 LeBron James 125.00 250.00
290 LeBron James 125.00 250.00
291 Dirk Nowitzki 75.00 200.00
292 Kobe Bryant 150.00 250.00
293 Kobe Bryant 150.00 250.00
294 Paul Pierce 50.00 150.00
295 Tony Parker 75.00 200.00
296 Dwyane Wade 100.00 250.00
297 Chauncey Billups 40.00 100.00
298 Shaquille O'Neal 60.00 150.00
299 Shaquille O'Neal 60.00 150.00
300 Shaquille O'Neal 60.00 150.00

2016-17 Select Prizms Tri-Color

*TRICLR 1-100: 1.2X TO 3X BASIC
*TRICLR 1-100 RC: .75X TO 2X BASIC RC
*TRICLR 101-200: .6X TO 1.5X BASIC
*TRICLR 101-200 RC: .4X TO 1X BASIC RC
RANDOM INSERTS IN PACKS
60 Ben Simmons 20.00 50.00
141 Ben Simmons 20.00 50.00

2016-17 Select Prizms White

*PRIZMS WHITE: 1.5X TO 4X BASIC
*PRIZMS WHITE RC: 1X TO 2.5X BASIC RC
RANDOM INSERTS IN PACKS
STATED PRINT RUN 149 SER.#'d SETS
4 Jamal Murray 5.00 12.00
60 Ben Simmons 50.00 120.00
91 Brandon Ingram 12.00 30.00
96 Marquese Chriss 6.00 15.00

2016-17 Select Die-Cut Autographs

RANDOM INSERTS IN PACKS
PRINT RUNS B/WN 49-99 COPIES PER
*PLSR p/r 49-60: .4X TO 1X p/r 49-60
*PLSR p/r 49-60: .5X TO 1.2X p/r 75-99
*PLSR p/r 35: .5X TO 1.2X p/r 49-60
*PLSR p/r 35: .6X TO 1.5X p/r 75-99
*SCPE p/r 49: .4X TO 1X p/r 49-60
*SCPE p/r 49: .5X TO 1.2X p/r 75-99
*SCPE p/r 25: .6X TO 1.5X p/r 49-60
*SCPE p/r 25: .75X TO 2X p/r 75-99
1 Michael Carter-Williams/60 3.00 8.00
2 Shawn Kemp/99 20.00 50.00
3 Scottie Pippen/49 40.00 100.00
4 Jim Jackson/99
5 Yao Ming/49 25.00 60.00
6 Glen Rice/99 3.00 8.00
7 Jeff Hornacek/99 3.00 8.00
8 Kevon Looney/99
9 Sean Elliott/99 6.00 15.00
10 Dirk Nowitzki/49 60.00 150.00
11 Artis Gilmore/60 4.00 10.00
12 Rick Barry/49
13 D'Angelo Russell/49 15.00 40.00
14 Dennis Rodman/49 20.00 50.00
15 Toni Kukoc/99 10.00 25.00
16 Bernard King/60 4.00 10.00
17 Chauncey Billups/75 4.00 10.00
18 Louie Dampier/75 6.00 15.00
19 Vince Carter/49 12.00 30.00
20 Carmelo Anthony/49
21 Adrian Dantley/99 3.00 8.00
22 Dwyane Wade/49 25.00 60.00
23 Jordan Clarkson/99 3.00 8.00
24 Rick Fox/99
25 Cedric Ceballos/99 2.50 6.00
26 Kobe Bryant/60 100.00 250.00
27 Tristan Thompson/99 3.00 8.00
28 Tyler Ennis/99 2.50 6.00
29 Michael Kidd-Gilchrist/49
30 Dante Exum/49 4.00 10.00
31 Latrell Sprewell/99 5.00 12.00
32 David Robinson/49 15.00 40.00
33 Spud Webb/99 5.00 12.00
34 Jalen Rose/99 4.00 10.00
35 Victor Oladipo/99 5.00 12.00
36 Gary Harris/75 3.00 8.00
37 Chris Paul/49 20.00 50.00
38 Shaquille O'Neal/49 30.00 80.00
39 Kevin Durant/49 75.00 200.00
40 Anthony Davis/49 30.00 80.00
41 Anthony Bennett/49 3.00 8.00
42 Cody Zeller/49 3.00 8.00
43 Alex Len/49 3.00 8.00
44 Dan Majerle/99 5.00 12.00
45 Jamal Mashburn/99 5.00 12.00
46 Deron Williams/49 4.00 10.00
47 Reggie Jackson/99 3.00 8.00
48 Horace Grant/99 4.00 10.00
49 Michael Finley/99 5.00 12.00
50 Bob Lanier/49 4.00 10.00
51 Jamaal Wilkes/99 4.00 10.00
52 Brian Grant/99 2.50 6.00
53 David Thompson/75 3.00 8.00
54 Michael Cooper/99 3.00 8.00
55 Kyrie Irving/49 40.00 100.00
56 Kevin Love/49 10.00 25.00
57 Karl Malone/49 20.00 50.00
58 Calvin Murphy/99 3.00 8.00
59 Jeremy Lin/49 30.00 80.00

2016-17 Select Die-Cut Rookie Autographs

RANDOM INSERTS IN PACKS
STATED PRINTED RUN 199 SER.#'d SETS
*SCOPE/49: .5X TO 1.2X BASIC
1 Domantas Sabonis 4.00 10.00
2 Pascal Siakam 2.50 6.00
3 Malcolm Brogdon 15.00 40.00
4 Jakob Poeltl 3.00 8.00
5 Henry Ellenson 3.00 8.00
6 Wade Baldwin IV 2.50 6.00
7 Ivica Zubac 12.00 30.00
8 Timothe Luwawu-Cabarrot 6.00 15.00
9 Thon Maker 20.00 50.00
10 Jamal Murray 15.00 40.00
11 Buddy Hield 12.00 30.00
12 Cheick Diallo 2.50 6.00
13 Kris Dunn 12.00 30.00
14 Marquese Chriss 10.00 25.00
15 Malik Beasley 2.50 6.00
16 Dragan Bender 8.00 20.00
17 Georges Niang 4.00 10.00
19 Deyonta Davis 2.50 6.00
20 DeAndre' Bembry 2.50 6.00
21 Denzel Valentine 8.00 20.00
22 Damian Jones 2.50 6.00
23 Brice Johnson 2.50 6.00
25 Marshall Plumlee 2.50 6.00
26 Ron Baker 3.00 8.00
27 Brandon Ingram 30.00 80.00
28 Jake Layman 3.00 8.00
29 Jaylen Brown 15.00 40.00
30 Willy Hernangomez 8.00 20.00
31 Paul Zipser 4.00 10.00
32 A.J. Hammons 2.50 6.00
33 Michael Gbinije 2.50 6.00
34 Mindaugas Kuzminskas 3.00 8.00
35 Sean Kilpatrick 2.50 6.00
36 Georgios Papagiannis 2.50 6.00
37 Kay Felder 2.50 6.00
38 Juan Hernangomez 5.00 12.00
39 Demetrius Jackson 2.50 6.00
40 Dorian Finney-Smith 3.00 8.00

2016-17 Select Die-Cut Rookie Autographs Pulsar

*PULSAR: .4X TO 1X BASIC
RANDOM INSERTS IN PACKS
STATED PRINT RUN 99 SER.#'d SETS
18 Patrick McCaw 12.00 30.00

2016-17 Select Duets Memorabilia

RANDOM INSERTS IN PACKS
STATED PRINT RUN 149 SER.#'d SETS
1 James/Irving 15.00 40.00
2 Thompson/Curry 15.00 40.00
3 DeMar DeRozan 3.00 8.00
Kyle Lowry
4 Paul/Griffin 4.00 10.00
5 Wiggins/LaVine 5.00 12.00
6 Anthony/Porzingis 5.00 12.00
7 Beal/Wall 4.00 10.00
9 DeMarcus Cousins 3.00 8.00
Rudy Gay
10 Leonard/Aldridge 5.00 12.00
11 Kemba Walker 3.00 8.00
Michael Kidd-Gilchrist
13 Williams/Nowitzki
14 Andre Drummond 3.00 8.00
Kentavious Caldwell-Pope
15 Russell/Clarkson 4.00 10.00
16 Marc Gasol 3.00 8.00
Mike Conley
17 Hassan Whiteside 2.50 6.00
Justise Winslow
18 Monroe/Giannis 5.00 12.00
20 Aaron Gordon 2.50 6.00
Nikola Vucevic
21 MCollum/Lillard 6.00 15.00
23 Bledsoe/Booker 5.00 12.00
24 Thomas/Smart 6.00 15.00

2016-17 Select Duets Memorabilia Prizms Copper

*COPPER: .5X TO 1.2X BASIC
RANDOM INSERTS IN PACKS
STATED PRINT RUN 49 SER.#'d SETS
13 Williams/Nowitzki 8.00 20.00
19 Westbrook/Adams 15.00 40.00
25 Harden/Beverley 8.00 20.00

2016-17 Select Duets Memorabilia Prizms Purple

*PURPLE: .4X TO 1X BASIC
RANDOM INSERTS IN PACKS
PRINT RUNS B/WN 78-99 COPIES PER
13 Williams/Nowitzki 6.00 15.00
19 Westbrook/Adams 12.00 30.00
25 Harden/Beverley/78 6.00 15.00

2016-17 Select Duets Memorabilia Prizms Tie-Dye

*TIEDYE: .75X TO 2X BASIC
RANDOM INSERTS IN PACKS
PRINT RUNS B/WN 10-25 COPIES PER
NO PRICING ON QTY 10
10 Leonard/Aldridge 20.00 50.00
19 Westbrook/Adams 60.00 150.00
24 Thomas/Smart 25.00 60.00

2016-17 Select In Flight Signatures

RANDOM INSERTS IN PACKS
STATED PRINT RUN 99 SER.#'d SETS
*ORANGE/60: .5X TO 1.2X BASIC
*TIEDYE/25: .75X TO 2X BASIC
2 Kobe Bryant 100.00 250.00
4 Clyde Drexler 15.00 40.00
5 Ray Allen 20.00 50.00
6 Norman Powell 2.50 6.00
7 Shawn Kemp 25.00 60.00
8 Spud Webb 5.00 12.00
10 Kyrie Irving 30.00 80.00
12 Carmelo Anthony 12.00 30.00
13 Jordan Clarkson 3.00 8.00
14 Justise Winslow 3.00 8.00
15 Zach LaVine 10.00 25.00
16 Grant Hill 12.00 30.00
17 Latrell Sprewell 10.00 25.00
19 Reggie Jackson 3.00 8.00
20 Evan Fournier 3.00 8.00

2016-17 Select Rookie Signatures

RANDOM INSERTS IN PACKS
STATED PRINT RUN 299 SER.#'d SETS
*ORANGE/60: .5X TO 1.2X BASIC
*TIEDYE/25: .75X TO 2X BASIC
1 Brandon Ingram 30.00 80.00
2 Jaylen Brown 25.00 60.00
3 Buddy Hield 12.00 30.00
4 Kris Dunn 12.00 30.00
5 Jamal Murray 15.00 40.00
6 Marquese Chriss 15.00 40.00
7 Jakob Poeltl 3.00 8.00
8 Thon Maker 8.00 20.00
9 Domantas Sabonis 4.00 10.00
10 Dario Saric 12.00 30.00
12 Denzel Valentine 6.00 15.00
13 Taurean Prince 4.00 10.00
14 Skal Labissiere 10.00 25.00
15 Caris LeVert 6.00 15.00
16 Damian Jones 2.50 6.00
17 Demetrius Jackson 2.50 6.00
18 Henry Ellenson 3.00 8.00
19 Wade Baldwin IV 2.50 6.00
20 Juan Hernangomez 5.00 12.00
21 Timothe Luwawu-Cabarrot 6.00 15.00
24 Malik Beasley 2.50 6.00
25 Mindaugas Kuzminskas 3.00 8.00
27 DeAndre' Bembry 2.50 6.00
29 Malachi Richardson 3.00 8.00
30 Pascal Siakam 2.50 6.00
31 Tomas Satoransky 2.50 6.00
32 Ivica Zubac 12.00 30.00
33 Malcolm Brogdon 15.00 40.00
35 Georges Niang 4.00 10.00
36 Jake Layman 3.00 8.00
37 Kay Felder 2.50 6.00
38 Paul Zipser 6.00 15.00
39 Stephen Zimmerman 2.50 6.00
40 Marshall Plumlee 2.50 6.00

2016-17 Select Rookie Swatches

RANDOM INSERTS IN PACKS
*PURPLE/99: .5X TO 1.2X BASIC
*ORANGE/60: .5X TO 1.2X BASIC
*TIEDYE/25: 1X TO 2.5X BASIC
1 A.J. Hammons 1.50 4.00
2 Brandon Ingram 5.00 12.00
3 Brice Johnson 1.50 4.00
4 Buddy Hield 4.00 10.00
5 Caris LeVert 2.00 5.00
6 Cheick Diallo 1.50 4.00
7 Chinanu Onuaku 1.50 4.00
8 Damian Jones 1.50 4.00
9 Dejounte Murray 3.00 8.00
10 Demetrius Jackson 1.50 4.00
11 Denzel Valentine 2.00 5.00
12 Deyonta Davis 1.50 4.00
13 Dragan Bender 2.00 5.00
15 Georgios Papagiannis 1.50 4.00
16 Henry Ellenson 2.00 5.00
17 Isaiah Whitehead 1.50 4.00
18 Ivica Zubac 2.50 6.00
19 Jakob Poeltl 2.00 5.00
20 Jamal Murray 5.00 12.00
21 Jaylen Brown 5.00 12.00
22 Juan Hernangomez 2.00 5.00
23 Kay Felder 1.50 4.00
24 Kris Dunn 4.00 10.00
25 Malachi Richardson 2.00 5.00
26 Malcolm Brogdon 4.00 10.00
27 Malik Beasley 1.50 4.00
28 Marquese Chriss 4.00 10.00
29 Pascal Siakam 1.50 4.00
30 Patrick McCaw 3.00 8.00
31 Skal Labissiere 2.50 6.00
32 Stephen Zimmerman 1.50 4.00
33 Thon Maker 4.00 10.00
34 Timothe Luwawu-Cabarrot 3.00 8.00
35 Tyler Ulis 5.00 12.00
36 Wade Baldwin IV 1.50 4.00

2016-17 Select Signatures

RANDOM INSERTS IN PACKS
PRINT RUNS B/WN 99-149 COPIES PER
*ORANGE/60: .5X TO 1.2X BASIC
*TIEDYE/25: .75X TO 2X BASIC
1 Jeremy Lin/99 25.00 60.00
2 Reggie Jackson/149 3.00 8.00
3 Andrew Wiggins/99 20.00 50.00
4 John Starks/149 5.00 12.00
5 Kevin Durant/99 60.00 150.00
6 Ricky Rubio/99 10.00 25.00
7 Karl-Anthony Towns/99 30.00 80.00
8 Kyrie Irving/99 30.00 80.00
9 Kent Bazemore/149 3.00 8.00
10 Dennis Rodman/99 15.00 40.00
11 Anthony Davis/99 30.00 80.00
13 Jamal Mashburn/149 5.00 12.00
14 Dwyane Wade/99 20.00 50.00
15 Luol Deng/149 3.00 8.00
16 Evan Fournier/149 3.00 8.00
17 Marcelo Huertas/149 2.50 6.00
18 Sean Elliott/149 4.00 10.00
19 Allen Iverson/99 50.00 120.00
20 Marc Gasol/99 10.00 25.00
21 Festus Ezeli/149 2.50 6.00
22 Kobe Bryant/99 100.00 250.00
23 Shawn Kemp/149 15.00 40.00
26 Kevin Love/99 10.00 25.00
27 Langston Galloway/149 2.50 6.00
28 Jae Crowder/149 3.00 8.00
29 Clint Capela/149 2.50 6.00
31 Goran Dragic/99 3.00 8.00
32 Nicolas Batum/149 3.00 8.00
33 Kenneth Faried/99 3.00 8.00
34 Kristaps Porzingis/99 20.00 50.00
35 Justise Winslow/99 3.00 8.00
36 Jordan Clarkson/99 3.00 8.00
37 Tobias Harris/99 3.00 8.00
38 Boban Marjanovic/149 2.50 6.00
39 Nikola Jokic/149 12.00 30.00
40 Tony Parker/99 10.00 25.00

2016-17 Select Sparks Memorabilia

RANDOM INSERTS IN PACKS
STATED PRINT RUN 199 SER.#'d SETS
*PURPLE/99: .4X TO 1X BASIC
1 Nikola Mirotic 2.50 6.00
2 J.R. Smith 2.50 6.00
3 Patrick Beverley 2.00 5.00
6 Devin Harris 2.00 5.00
7 Jamal Crawford 3.00 8.00
8 Jeff Green 2.50 6.00
9 Iman Shumpert 2.00 5.00
10 Shabazz Muhammad 2.50 6.00
12 Dante Exum 2.50 6.00
13 Otto Porter 2.50 6.00
18 Justin Anderson 2.50 6.00
19 Doug McDermott 2.50 6.00
20 Eric Gordon 2.50 6.00
22 Matthew Dellavedova 2.50 6.00
23 Chris McCullough 2.00 5.00
24 Brandon Knight 2.50 6.00
25 Marcus Smart 2.50 6.00

2016-17 Select Sparks Memorabilia Prizms Copper

*COPPER: .5X TO 1.2X BASIC
RANDOM INSERTS IN PACKS
STATED PRINT RUN 49 SER.#'d SETS
17 Leandro Barbosa 2.50 6.00

2016-17 Select Sparks Memorabilia Prizms Tie-Dye

*TIEDYE: .75X TO 2X BASIC
RANDOM INSERTS IN PACKS
PRINT RUNS B/WN 5-25 COPIES PER
NO PRICING ON QTY 5
4 T.J. Warren/25 5.00 12.00
7 Jamal Crawford/25 100.00 250.00
17 Leandro Barbosa/25 4.00 10.00
21 Rondae Hollis-Jefferson/25 4.00 10.00

2016-17 Select Swatches

RANDOM INSERTS IN PACKS
1 Cody Zeller 1.50 4.00
2 Jimmy Butler 2.50 6.00
3 Tyler Zeller 2.00 5.00
4 Bojan Bogdanovic 1.50 4.00
5 Marcus Morris 1.50 4.00
6 Doug McDermott 2.00 5.00
7 Kyle Korver 2.00 5.00
8 Frank Kaminsky 2.00 5.00
9 Nikola Mirotic 2.00 5.00
10 Derrick Rose 3.00 8.00
11 LeBron James 10.00 25.00
12 Thabo Sefolosha 1.50 4.00
13 Michael Kidd-Gilchrist 2.00 5.00
14 Terry Rozier 2.00 5.00
15 Brook Lopez 2.00 5.00
16 Tony Parker 2.50 6.00
17 Kyrie Irving 6.00 15.00
18 Kentavious Caldwell-Pope 2.00 5.00
19 Kevin Love 2.50 6.00
20 Trevor Ariza 1.50 4.00
21 James Harden 4.00 10.00
23 Deron Williams 2.00 5.00
24 Nicolas Batum 2.00 5.00
25 DeMarre Carroll 1.50 4.00
26 Danny Green 2.00 5.00
27 Carmelo Anthony 4.00 10.00
28 George Hill 2.00 5.00
29 Monta Ellis 2.00 5.00
30 Dirk Nowitzki 4.00 10.00
31 Bradley Beal 2.50 6.00
32 Jamal Crawford 2.50 6.00
33 J.J. Redick 2.50 6.00
34 Jahlil Okafor 2.00 5.00
36 Russell Westbrook 6.00 15.00
37 Udonis Haslem 1.50 4.00
39 Rudy Gay 2.50 6.00
40 Rudy Gobert 2.50 6.00
41 Marc Gasol 2.50 6.00
42 Adreian Payne 1.50 4.00
43 Derrick Favors 2.00 5.00
44 Mike Conley 2.00 5.00
45 John Henson 2.00 5.00
46 Stephen Curry 12.00 30.00
47 Karl-Anthony Towns 5.00 12.00
48 Joakim Noah 2.00 5.00
49 Damian Lillard 4.00 10.00
50 Kyle Lowry 2.00 5.00
51 Ricky Rubio 2.50 6.00
52 Zach LaVine 2.50 6.00
53 Omer Asik 2.00 5.00
54 Myles Turner 2.00 5.00
55 Joe Johnson 2.00 5.00
57 Kevin Durant 6.00 15.00
58 Serge Ibaka 2.00 5.00
59 Rodney Hood 2.00 5.00
60 Manu Ginobili 2.50 6.00
61 Khris Middleton 2.00 5.00
62 Kawhi Leonard 4.00 10.00
63 Jonas Valanciunas 2.00 5.00
64 Kristaps Porzingis 4.00 10.00

2016-17 Select Swatches Prizms Orange

*ORANGE: .5X TO 1.2X BASIC
RANDOM INSERTS IN PACKS
STATED PRINT RUN 60 SER.#'d SETS
35 Roy Hibbert 2.50 6.00
38 Zach Randolph 2.50 6.00

2016-17 Select Swatches Prizms Purple

*PURPLE: .5X TO 1.2X BASIC
RANDOM INSERTS IN PACKS
STATED PRINT RUN 99 SER.#'d SETS
38 Zach Randolph 2.50 6.00

2016-17 Select Swatches Prizms Tie-Dye

*TIEDYE: 1X TO 2.5X BASIC
RANDOM INSERTS IN PACKS
STATED PRINT RUN 25 SER.#'d SETS
2 Jimmy Butler 15.00 40.00
11 LeBron James 60.00 150.00
22 Terrence Ross 5.00 12.00
32 Jamal Crawford 100.00 250.00
35 Roy Hibbert 5.00 12.00
36 Russell Westbrook 25.00 60.00
38 Zach Randolph 5.00 12.00
46 Stephen Curry 60.00 150.00
64 Kristaps Porzingis 20.00 50.00

2016-17 Select Throwback Memorabilia

RANDOM INSERTS IN PACKS
PRINT RUNS B/WN 50-199 COPIES PER
2 Luol Deng/199 2.50 6.00
3 Michael Beasley/199 2.00 5.00
4 David West/199 2.50 6.00
7 D.J. Augustin/199 2.00 5.00
8 Chandler Parsons/199 2.50 6.00
9 Paul Pierce/199 3.00 8.00
12 Monta Ellis/199 2.50 6.00
13 Iman Shumpert/199 2.00 5.00
14 Jrue Holiday/199 2.50 6.00
15 Jose Calderon/199 2.00 5.00
17 Leandro Barbosa/199 2.00 5.00
18 Michael Carter-Williams/199 2.00 5.00
19 LeBron James/85 10.00 25.00
20 Arron Afflalo/199 2.00 5.00
21 Derrick Williams/199 2.00 5.00
22 Michael Beasley/50 2.00 5.00
23 Eric Gordon/122 2.50 6.00
24 Isaiah Canaan/199 2.50 6.00
25 Jerryd Bayless/199 2.50 6.00
28 Nene/199 2.50 6.00
30 Vince Carter/199 4.00 10.00
31 David West/199 2.50 6.00
32 Vince Carter/199 4.00 10.00
33 Evan Fournier/199 2.50 6.00
34 Channing Frye/199 2.50 6.00
36 Jameer Nelson/199 2.00 5.00
38 Anthony Bennett/199 2.00 5.00
39 Evan Turner/199 2.00 5.00
41 Nicolas Batum/199 2.50 6.00
42 Miles Plumlee/199 2.00 5.00
43 Derrick Rose/199 4.00 10.00
45 Gerald Green/199 2.50 6.00
46 Vince Carter/199 4.00 10.00
47 Isaiah Thomas/199 3.00 8.00
48 Marcus Morris/199 2.00 5.00
49 Deron Williams/199 2.50 6.00

2016-17 Select Throwback Memorabilia Prizms Copper

*COPPER: .5X TO 1.2X BASIC
RANDOM INSERTS IN PACKS
PRINT RUNS B/WN 48-49 COPIES PER
6 Isaiah Thomas/49 4.00 10.00

2016-17 Select Throwback Memorabilia Prizms Purple

*PURPLE: .4X TO 1X BASIC
RANDOM INSERTS IN PACKS
STATED PRINT RUN 99 SER.#'d SETS
6 Isaiah Thomas 3.00 8.00
26 Tyson Chandler 2.50 6.00

2016-17 Select Throwback Memorabilia Prizms Tie-Dye

*TIEDYE: .75X TO 2X BASIC
RANDOM INSERTS IN PACKS
PRINT RUNS B/WN 21-25 COPIES PER
6 Isaiah Thomas/25 6.00 15.00
19 LeBron James/25 60.00 150.00

1990-91 SkyBox Prototypes

This ten-card set of prototypes was issued singly as well as in a complete sheet. The cards were mailed out to prospective dealers and members of the media to show the unique new design of the inaugural SkyBox issue. The cards are distinguishable by the presence of a red diagonal "prototype" line cutting across the upper left corner of the front. The cards are standard size, 2 1/2" by 3 1/2" and are numbered on the back.

COMPLETE SET (10) 30.00 80.00
41 Michael Jordan 15.00 40.00
91 Dennis Rodman 4.00 10.00
138 Magic Johnson 6.00 15.00
151 Rony Seikaly 1.00 2.50
162 Ricky Pierce 1.00 2.50
173 Pooh Richardson 1.00 2.50
224 Kevin Johnson 1.50 4.00
233 Clyde Drexler 4.00 10.00
260 David Robinson 5.00 12.00
282 Karl Malone 6.00 15.00
NNO SkyBox Logo 2.00 5.00
Distributed at 1990 National Convention

1990-91 SkyBox

This 1990-91 set marks SkyBox's entry into the basketball card market. The complete set contains 423 standard-size cards featuring NBA players. The set was released in two series of 300 and 123 cards, respectively. Foil packs for each series contained 15 cards. However, the second series packs contained a mix of players from both series. The second series cards replaced 123 cards from the first series, which then became short-prints compared to other cards in the first series. The front features an action shot of the player on a computer-generated background of various color schemes. The player's name appears in a black stripe at the bottom with the team logo superimposed at the left lower corner. The photo is bordered in gold. The back presents head shots of the player with gold borders on white background. Player statistics are given in a box below the photo. The cards are checklisted below alphabetically according to team. Subsets are Coaches (301-327), Team Checklists (328-354), Lottery Picks (355-365), Updates (366-420), and Checklists (421-423). Rookie Cards of note included in the set are Nick Anderson, Mookie Blaylock, Derrick Coleman, Vlade Divac, Sean Elliott, Danny Ferry, Kendall Gill, Tim Hardaway, Chris Jackson, Avery Johnson, Shawn Kemp, Gary Payton, Drazen Petrovic, Glen Rice, Clifford Robinson and Dennis Scott. First series single prints (SP) are noted below.

COMPLETE SET (423) 10.00 20.00
COMPLETE SERIES 1 (300) 6.00 12.00
COMPLETE SERIES 2 (123) 4.00 8.00
1 John Battle .02 .10
2 Duane Ferrell SP RC .08 .25
3 Jon Koncak .02 .10
4 Cliff Levingston SP .08 .25
5 John Long SP .08 .25
6 Moses Malone .08 .25
7 Doc Rivers .02 .10
8 Kenny Smith SP .08 .25
9 Alexander Volkov RC .02 .10
10 Spud Webb .02 .10
11 Dominique Wilkins .08 .25
12 Kevin Willis .02 .10
13 John Bagley .02 .10
14 Larry Bird .40 1.00
15 Kevin Gamble .02 .10
16 Dennis Johnson SP .08 .25
17 Joe Kleine .02 .10
18 Reggie Lewis .02 .10
19 Kevin McHale .02 .10
20 Robert Parish .02 .10
21 Jim Paxson SP .08 .25
22 Ed Pinckney .02 .10
23 Brian Shaw .08 .25
24 Michael Smith .02 .10
25 Richard Anderson SP .08 .25
26 Muggsy Bogues .02 .10
27 Rex Chapman .08 .25
28 Dell Curry .02 .10
29 Armon Gilliam .02 .10
30 Michael Holton SP .08 .25
31 Dave Hoppen .02 .10
32 J.R. Reid RC .02 .10
33 Robert Reid SP .08 .25
34 Brian Rowsom SP .08 .25
35 Kelly Tripucka .02 .10
36 Micheal Williams SP UER .08 .25
37 B.J. Armstrong RC .02 .10
38 Bill Cartwright .02 .10
39 Horace Grant .02 .10
40 Craig Hodges .02 .10
41 Michael Jordan 1.25 3.00
42 Stacey King RC .02 .10
43 Ed Nealy SP .02 .10
44 John Paxson .02 .10
45 Will Perdue .02 .10
46 Scottie Pippen .40 1.00
47 Jeff Sanders SP RC .08 .25
48 Winston Bennett .02 .10
49 Chucky Brown RC .02 .10
50 Brad Daugherty .02 .10
51 Craig Ehlo .02 .10
52 Steve Kerr .08 .25
53 Paul Mokeski SP .08 .25
54 John Morton .02 .10
55 Larry Nance .02 .10
56 Mark Price .02 .10
57 Tree Rollins SP .08 .25
58 Hot Rod Williams .02 .10
59 Steve Alford .02 .10
60 Rolando Blackman .02 .10
61 Adrian Dantley SP .08 .25
62 Brad Davis .02 .10
63 James Donaldson .02 .10
64 Derek Harper .02 .10
65 Anthony Jones SP .08 .25
66 Sam Perkins SP .08 .25
67 Roy Tarpley .02 .10
68 Bill Wennington SP .08 .25
69 Randy White RC .02 .10
70 Herb Williams .02 .10
71 Michael Adams .02 .10
72 Joe Barry Carroll SP .08 .25
73 Walter Davis .02 .10
74 Alex English SP .08 .25
75 Bill Hanzlik .02 .10
76 Tim Kempton SP .08 .25
77 Jerome Lane .02 .10
78 Lafayette Lever SP .08 .25
79 Todd Lichti RC .02 .10
80 Blair Rasmussen .02 .10
81 Danny Schayes SP .08 .25
82 Mark Aguirre .02 .10
83 William Bedford RC .02 .10
84 Joe Dumars .08 .25
85 James Edwards .02 .10
86 David Greenwood SP .08 .25
87 Scott Hastings .02 .10
88 Gerald Henderson SP .08 .25
89 Vinnie Johnson .02 .10
90 Bill Laimbeer .02 .10
91 Dennis Rodman .25 .60
91B Dennis Rodman Left .40 1.00
92 John Salley .02 .10
93 Isiah Thomas .08 .25
94 Manute Bol SP .08 .25
95 Tim Hardaway RC .60 1.50
96 Rod Higgins .02 .10
97 Sarunas Marciulionis RC .02 .10
98 Chris Mullin .08 .25
99 Jim Petersen .02 .10
100 Mitch Richmond .10 .30
101 Mike Smrek .02 .10
102 Terry Teagle SP .08 .25
103 Tom Tolbert RC .02 .10
104 Kelvin Upshaw SP .08 .25
105 Anthony Bowie SP RC .08 .25
106 Adrian Caldwell .02 .10
107 Eric(Sleepy) Floyd .02 .10
108 Buck Johnson .02 .10
109 Vernon Maxwell .02 .10
110 Hakeem Olajuwon .15 .40
111 Larry Smith .02 .10
112A Otis Thorpe ERR .60 1.50
112B Otis Thorpe COR .02 .10
113A M. Wiggins SP ERR .60 1.50
113B M. Wiggins SP COR .08 .25
114 Vern Fleming .02 .10
115 Rickey Green SP .08 .25
116 George McCloud RC .08 .25
117 Reggie Miller .10 .30
118A Dyron Nix SP ERR .60 1.50
118B Dyron Nix SP COR .08 .25
119 Chuck Person .02 .10
120 Mike Sanders .02 .10
121 Detlef Schrempf .02 .10
122 Rik Smits .08 .25
123 LaSalle Thompson .02 .10
124 Benoit Benjamin .02 .10
125 Winston Garland .02 .10
126 Tom Garrick .02 .10
127 Gary Grant .02 .10
128 Ron Harper .02 .10
129 Danny Manning .02 .10
130 Jeff Martin .02 .10
131 Ken Norman .02 .10
132 Charles Smith .02 .10
133 Joe Wolf SP .08 .25
134 Michael Cooper SP .08 .25
135 Vlade Divac RC .25 .60
136 Larry Drew .02 .10
137 A.C. Green .02 .10
138 Magic Johnson .30 .75
139 Mark McNamara SP .08 .25
140 Byron Scott .02 .10
141 Mychal Thompson .02 .10
142 Orlando Woolridge SP .08 .25
143 James Worthy .08 .25
144 Terry Davis RC .02 .10
145 Sherman Douglas RC .02 .10
146 Kevin Edwards .02 .10
147 Tellis Frank SP .08 .25
148 Scott Haffner SP .08 .25
149 Grant Long .02 .10
150 Glen Rice RC .40 1.00
151 Rony Seikaly .02 .10
152 Rory Sparrow SP .08 .25
153 Jon Sundvold .02 .10
154 Billy Thompson .02 .10
155 Greg Anderson .02 .10
156 Ben Coleman SP .08 .25
157 Jeff Grayer RC .02 .10
158 Jay Humphries .02 .10
159 Frank Kornet .02 .10
160 Larry Krystkowiak .02 .10
161 Brad Lohaus .02 .10
162 Ricky Pierce .02 .10
163 Paul Pressey SP .08 .25
164 Fred Roberts .02 .10
165 Alvin Robertson .02 .10
166 Jack Sikma .02 .10
167 Randy Breuer .02 .10
168 Tony Campbell .02 .10
169 Tyrone Corbin .02 .10
170 Sidney Lowe SP .08 .25
171 Sam Mitchell RC .02 .10
172 Tod Murphy .02 .10
173 Pooh Richardson RC .02 .10
174 Donald Royal SP RC .08 .25
175 Brad Sellers SP .08 .25
176 Mookie Blaylock RC .15 .40
177 Sam Bowie .02 .10
178 Lester Conner .02 .10
179 Derrick Gervin .02 .10
180 Jack Haley RC .02 .10
181 Roy Hinson .02 .10
182 Dennis Hopson SP .08 .25
183 Chris Morris .02 .10
184 Pete Myers SP RC .08 .25
185 Purvis Short SP .08 .25
186 Maurice Cheeks .02 .10
187 Patrick Ewing .08 .25
188 Stuart Gray .02 .10
189 Mark Jackson .02 .10
190 Johnny Newman SP .08 .25
191 Charles Oakley .02 .10
192 Brian Quinnett .02 .10
193 Trent Tucker .02 .10
194 Kiki Vandeweghe .02 .10
195 Kenny Walker .02 .10
196 Eddie Lee Wilkins .02 .10
197 Gerald Wilkins .02 .10
198 Mark Acres .02 .10
199 Nick Anderson RC .15 .40
200 Michael Ansley .02 .10
201 Terry Catledge .02 .10

202 Dave Corzine SP .08 .25
203 Sidney Green SP .08 .25
204 Jerry Reynolds .02 .10
205 Scott Skiles .02 .10
206 Otis Smith .02 .10
207 Reggie Theus SP .08 .25
208 Jeff Turner .02 .10
209 Sam Vincent .02 .10
210 Ron Anderson .02 .10
211 Charles Barkley .15 .40
212 Scott Brooks SP .08 .25
213 Lanard Copeland SP .08 .25
214 Johnny Dawkins .02 .10
215 Mike Gminski .02 .10
216 Hersey Hawkins .02 .10
217 Rick Mahorn .02 .10
218 Derek Smith SP .08 .25
219 Bob Thornton .02 .10
220 Tom Chambers .02 .10
221 Greg Grant SP RC .08 .25
222 Jeff Hornacek .02 .10
223 Eddie Johnson .02 .10
224A Kevin Johnson Lower .08 .25
224B Kevin Johnson Upper .08 .25
225 Andrew Lang RC .08 .25
226 Dan Majerle .08 .25
227 Mike McGee SP .08 .25
228 Tim Perry .02 .10
229 Kurt Rambis .02 .10
230 Mark West .02 .10
231 Mark Bryant .02 .10
232 Wayne Cooper .02 .10
233 Clyde Drexler .08 .25
234 Kevin Duckworth .02 .10
235 Byron Irvin SP .08 .25
236 Jerome Kersey .02 .10
237 Drazen Petrovic RC .10 .30
238 Terry Porter .02 .10
239 Clifford Robinson RC .15 .40
240 Buck Williams .02 .10
241 Danny Young .02 .10
242 Danny Ainge SP .08 .25
243 Randy Allen SP .08 .25
244A Antoine Carr SP .08 .25
244B Antoine Carr .02 .10
245 Vinny Del Negro SP .08 .25
246 Pervis Ellison SP RC .08 .25
247 Greg Kite SP .08 .25
248 Rodney McCray SP .08 .25
249 Harold Pressley SP .08 .25
250 Ralph Sampson .02 .10
251 Wayman Tisdale .02 .10
252 Willie Anderson .02 .10
253 Uwe Blab SP .08 .25
254 Frank Brickowski SP .08 .25
255 Terry Cummings .02 .10
256 Sean Elliott RC .20 .50
257 Caldwell Jones SP .08 .25
258 Johnny Moore SP .08 .25
259 Zarko Paspalj SP .08 .25
260 David Robinson .30 .75
261 Rod Strickland .08 .25
262 David Wingate SP .08 .25
263 Dana Barros RC .08 .25
264 Michael Cage .02 .10
265 Quintin Dailey .02 .10
266 Dale Ellis .02 .10
267 Steve Johnson SP .08 .25
268 Shawn Kemp RC 1.00 2.50
269 Xavier McDaniel .02 .10
270 Derrick McKey .02 .10
271A Nate McMillan SP ERR .08 .25
271B Nate McMillan COR .02 .10
272 Olden Polynice .02 .10
273 Sedale Threatt .02 .10
274 Thurl Bailey .02 .10
275 Mike Brown .02 .10
276 Mark Eaton .02 .10
277 Blue Edwards RC .02 .10
278 Darrell Griffith .02 .10
279 Bobby Hansen SP .08 .25
280 Eric Johnson .02 .10
281 Eric Leckner SP .08 .25
282 Karl Malone .15 .40
283 Delaney Rudd .02 .10
284 John Stockton .10 .30
285 Mark Alarie .02 .10
286 Steve Colter SP .08 .25
287 Ledell Eackles SP .08 .25
288 Harvey Grant .02 .10
289 Tom Hammonds RC .02 .10
290 Charles Jones RC .02 .10
291 Bernard King .02 .10
292 Jeff Malone SP .08 .25
293 Darrell Walker .02 .10
294 John Williams .02 .10
295 Checklist 1 SP .08 .25
296 Checklist 2 SP .08 .25
297 Checklist 3 SP .08 .25
298 Checklist 4 SP .08 .25
299 Checklist 5 SP .08 .25
300 Danny Ferry SP RC .20 .50
301 Bob Weiss CO .02 .10
302 Chris Ford CO .02 .10
303 Gene Littles CO .02 .10
304 Phil Jackson CO .10 .30
305 Lenny Wilkens CO .10 .30
306 Richie Adubato CO .02 .10
307 Paul Westhead CO .02 .10
308 Chuck Daly CO .10 .30
309 Don Nelson CO .10 .30
310 Don Chaney CO .02 .10
311 Dick Versace CO .02 .10
312 Mike Schuler CO .02 .10
313 Mike Dunleavy CO .02 .10
314 Ron Rothstein CO .02 .10
315 Del Harris CO .02 .10
316 Bill Musselman CO .02 .10
317 Bill Fitch CO .02 .10
318 Stu Jackson CO .02 .10
319 Matt Guokas CO .02 .10
320 Jim Lynam CO .02 .10
321 Cotton Fitzsimmons CO .02 .10
322 Rick Adelman CO .02 .10
323 Dick Motta CO .02 .10
324 Larry Brown CO .02 .10
325 K.C. Jones CO .10 .30
326 Jerry Sloan CO .10 .30
327 Wes Unseld CO .02 .10
328 Atlanta Hawks TC .02 .10
329 Boston Celtics TC .02 .10
330 Charlotte Hornets TC .02 .10
331 Chicago Bulls TC .10 .30
332 Cleveland Cavaliers TC .02 .10
333 Dallas Mavericks TC .02 .10
334 Denver Nuggets TC .02 .10
335 Detroit Pistons TC .02 .10
336 Golden State Warriors TC .02 .10
337 Houston Rockets TC .02 .10
338 Indiana Pacers TC .02 .10
339 Los Angeles Clippers TC .02 .10
340 Los Angeles Lakers TC .02 .10
341 Miami Heat TC .02 .10
342 Milwaukee Bucks TC .02 .10
343 Minnesota Timberwolves TC .02 .10
344 New Jersey Nets TC .02 .10
345 New York Knicks TC .02 .10
346 Orlando Magic TC .02 .10
347 Philadelphia 76ers TC .02 .10
348 Phoenix Suns TC .02 .10
349 Portland Trail Blazers TC .02 .10
350 Sacramento Kings TC .02 .10
351 San Antonio Spurs TC .02 .10
352 Seattle SuperSonics TC .02 .10
353 Utah Jazz TC .02 .10
354 Washington Bullets TC .02 .10
355 Rumeal Robinson RC .02 .10
356 Kendall Gill RC .50 1.25
357 Chris Jackson RC .25 .60
358 Tyrone Hill RC .20 .50
359 Bo Kimble RC .02 .10
360 Willie Burton RC .02 .10
361 Felton Spencer RC .10 .30
362 Derrick Coleman RC .50 1.25
363 Dennis Scott RC .30 .75
364 Lionel Simmons RC .10 .30
365 Gary Payton RC 2.00 5.00
366 Tim McCormick .02 .10
367 Sidney Moncrief .02 .10
368 Kenny Gattison RC .02 .10
369 Randolph Keys .02 .10
370 Johnny Newman .02 .10
371 Dennis Hopson .02 .10
372 Cliff Levingston .02 .10
373 Derrick Chievous .02 .10
374 Danny Ferry .10 .30
375 Alex English .02 .10
376 Lafayette Lever .02 .10
377 Rodney McCray .02 .10
378 T.R. Dunn .02 .10
379 Corey Gaines .02 .10
380 Avery Johnson RC .30 .75
381 Joe Wolf .02 .10
382 Orlando Woolridge .02 .10
383 Tree Rollins .02 .10
384 Steve Johnson .02 .10
385 Kenny Smith .02 .10
386 Mike Woodson .02 .10
387 Greg Dreiling RC .02 .10
388 Micheal Williams .10 .30
389 Randy Wittman .02 .10
390 Ken Bannister .02 .10
391 Sam Perkins .10 .30
392 Terry Teagle .02 .10
393 Milt Wagner .02 .10
394 Frank Brickowski .02 .10
395 Danny Schayes .02 .10
396 Scott Brooks .02 .10
397 Doug West RC .10 .30
398 Chris Dudley RC .02 .10
399 Reggie Theus .10 .30
400 Greg Grant .02 .10
401 Greg Kite .02 .10
402 Mark McNamara .02 .10
403 Manute Bol .02 .10
404 Rickey Green .02 .10
405 Kenny Battle RC .02 .10
406 Ed Nealy .02 .10
407 Danny Ainge .10 .30
408 Steve Colter .02 .10
409 Bobby Hansen .02 .10
410 Eric Leckner .02 .10
411 Rory Sparrow .02 .10
412 Bill Wennington .02 .10
413 Sidney Green .02 .10
414 David Greenwood .02 .10
415 Paul Pressey .02 .10
416 Reggie Williams .02 .10
417 Dave Corzine .02 .10
418 Jeff Malone .02 .10
419 Pervis Ellison .02 .10
420 Byron Irvin .02 .10
421 Checklist 1 .02 .10
422 Checklist 2 .02 .10
423 Checklist 3 .02 .10
NNO SkyBox Salutes the NBA 2.50 6.00

1991-92 SkyBox Prototypes

Cards from this 20-card standard-size set of prototypes were mailed out to prospective dealers and members of the media to show the new design of the 1991-92 SkyBox issue. The cards are distinguishable by the presence of a black diagonal "prototype" line cutting across the upper left corner of the back. Dennis Rodman and Chris Mullin are supposed to be the two toughest as they were reportedly withdrawn early.

COMPLETE SET (20) 25.00 60.00
24 Rex Chapman 1.00 2.50
86 Dennis Rodman SP 6.00 15.00
95 Chris Mullin SP 3.00 8.00
97 Mitch Richmond 2.50 6.00
114 Reggie Miller 3.00 8.00
130 Charles Smith 1.00 2.50
137 Magic Johnson 5.00 12.00
143 James Worthy 1.50 4.00
173 Pooh Richardson 1.00 2.50
189 Patrick Ewing 2.50 6.00
205 Dennis Scott 1.00 2.50
211 Charles Barkley 4.00 10.00
216 Hersey Hawkins 1.00 2.50
223 Tom Chambers 1.00 2.50
237 Clyde Drexler 2.50 6.00
238 Kevin Duckworth 1.00 2.50
240 Terry Porter 1.00 2.50
242 Buck Williams 1.00 2.50
268 Ricky Pierce 1.00 2.50
294 Bernard King 1.00 2.50

1991-92 SkyBox

The complete 1991-92 SkyBox basketball set contains 659 standard-size cards. The set was released in two series of 350 and 309 cards, respectively. This year SkyBox did not package both first and second series cards in second series packs. The cards were available in 15-card fin-sealed foil packs that feature four different mail-in offers on the back, or 62-card blister packs that contain two (of four) SkyBox logo cards not available in the 15-card foil packs. The fronts feature color action player photos overlaying multi-colored computer-generated geometric shapes and stripes. The pictures are borderless and the card face is white. The player's name appears in different color lettering at the bottom of each card, with the team logo in the lower right corner. In a trapezoid shape, the backs have non-action color player photos. At the bottom biographical and statistical information appear inside a color-striped diagonal. The cards are numbered and checklisted below alphabetically within team order. Subsets are Stats (298-307), Best Single Game Performance (308-312), NBA All-Star Weekend Highlights (313-317), NBA All-Rookie Team (318-322), GQ's "NBA All-Star Style Team" (323-327), Centennial Highlights (328-332), Great Moments from the NBA Finals (333-337), Stay in School (338-344), Checklists (345-350), Team Logos (351-377), Coaches (378-404), Game Frames (405-431), Sixth Man (432-458), Teamwork (459-485), Rising Stars (486-512), Lottery Picks (513-523), Centennial (524-529), 1992 USA Basketball Team (530-546), 1988 USA Basketball Team (547-556), 1984 USA Basketball Team (557-563), The Magic of SkyBox (564-571), SkyBox Salutes (572-576), Skymasters (577-588), Shooting Stars (589-602), Small School Sensations (603-609), NBA Stay in School (610-614), Player Updates (615-653), and Checklists (654-659). As part of a promotion with Cheerios, four SkyBox cards from the basic set were inserted into specially marked 10-ounce and 15-ounce cereal boxes. These cereal boxes appeared on store shelves in December 1991 and January 1992, and they depicted images of SkyBox cards on the front, back, and side panels. An unnumbered gold foil-stamped 1992 USA Basketball Team photo card was randomly inserted into second series foil packs, while the blister packs featured two-card sets of NBA MVPs from the same team for consecutive years. As a mail-in offer a limited Clyde Drexler Olympic card was sent to the first 10,000 respondents in return for ten SkyBox wrappers and 1.00 for postage and handling. Rookie Cards of note include Kenny Anderson, Stacey Augmon, Terrell Brandon, Larry Johnson, Dikembe Mutombo, Steve Smith and John Starks.

COMPLETE SET (659) 30.00 60.00
COMPLETE SERIES 1 (350) 10.00 20.00
COMPLETE SERIES 2 (309) 20.00 40.00
1 John Battle .02 .10
2 Duane Ferrell .02 .10
3 Jon Koncak .02 .10
4 Moses Malone .15 .40
5 Tim McCormick .02 .10
6 Sidney Moncrief .02 .10
7 Doc Rivers .07 .20
8 Rumeal Robinson UER .02 .10
9 Spud Webb .07 .20
10 Dominique Wilkins .15 .40
11 Kevin Willis .02 .10
12 Larry Bird .60 1.50
13 Dee Brown .02 .10
14 Kevin Gamble .02 .10
15 Joe Kleine .02 .10
16 Reggie Lewis .07 .20
17 Kevin McHale .07 .20
18 Robert Parish .07 .20
19 Ed Pinckney .02 .10
20 Brian Shaw .02 .10
21 Michael Smith .02 .10
22 Stojko Vrankovic .02 .10
23 Muggsy Bogues .07 .20
24 Rex Chapman .07 .20
25 Dell Curry .02 .10
26 Kenny Gattison .02 .10
27 Kendall Gill .07 .20
28 Mike Gminski .02 .10
29 Randolph Keys .02 .10
30 Eric Leckner .02 .10
31 Johnny Newman .02 .10
32 J.R. Reid .02 .10
33 Kelly Tripucka .02 .10
34 B.J. Armstrong .02 .10
35 Bill Cartwright .02 .10
36 Horace Grant .07 .20
37 Craig Hodges .02 .10
38 Dennis Hopson .02 .10
39 Michael Jordan 2.00 5.00
40 Stacey King .02 .10
41 Cliff Levingston .02 .10
42 John Paxson .02 .10
43 Will Perdue .02 .10
44 Scottie Pippen .50 1.25
45 Winston Bennett .02 .10
46 Chucky Brown .02 .10
47 Brad Daugherty .02 .10
48 Craig Ehlo .02 .10
49 Danny Ferry .02 .10
50 Steve Kerr .07 .20
51 John Morton .02 .10
52 Larry Nance .07 .20
53 Mark Price .02 .10
54 Darnell Valentine .02 .10
55 John Williams .02 .10
56 Steve Alford .02 .10
57 Rolando Blackman .02 .10
58 Brad Davis .02 .10
59 James Donaldson .02 .10
60 Derek Harper .07 .20
61 Fat Lever .02 .10
62 Rodney McCray .02 .10
63 Roy Tarpley .02 .10
64 Kelvin Upshaw .02 .10
65 Randy White .02 .10
66 Herb Williams .02 .10
67 Michael Adams .02 .10
68 Greg Anderson .02 .10
69 Anthony Cook .02 .10
70 Chris Jackson .02 .10
71 Jerome Lane .02 .10
72 Marcus Liberty .02 .10
73 Todd Lichti .02 .10
74 Blair Rasmussen .02 .10
75 Reggie Williams .02 .10
76 Joe Wolf .02 .10
77 Orlando Woolridge .02 .10
78 Mark Aguirre .02 .10
79 William Bedford .02 .10
80 Lance Blanks .02 .10
81 Joe Dumars .15 .40
82 James Edwards .02 .10
83 Scott Hastings .02 .10
84 Vinnie Johnson .02 .10
85 Bill Laimbeer .07 .20
86 Dennis Rodman .30 .75
87 John Salley .02 .10
88 Isiah Thomas .15 .40
89 Mario Elie RC .15 .40
90 Tim Hardaway .25 .60
91 Rod Higgins .02 .10
92 Tyrone Hill .07 .20
93 Les Jepsen .02 .10
94 Alton Lister .02 .10
95 Sarunas Marciulionis .02 .10
96 Chris Mullin .15 .40
97 Jim Petersen .02 .10
98 Mitch Richmond .15 .40
99 Tom Tolbert .02 .10
100 Adrian Caldwell .02 .10
101 Eric(Sleepy) Floyd .02 .10
102 Dave Jamerson .02 .10
103 Buck Johnson .02 .10
104 Vernon Maxwell .02 .10
105 Hakeem Olajuwon .25 .60
106 Kenny Smith .02 .10
107 Larry Smith .02 .10
108 Otis Thorpe .07 .20
109 Kennard Winchester RC .02 .10
110 David Wood RC .02 .10
111 Greg Dreiling .02 .10
112 Vern Fleming .02 .10
113 George McCloud .02 .10
114 Reggie Miller .15 .40
115 Chuck Person .02 .10
116 Mike Sanders .02 .10
117 Detlef Schrempf .07 .20
118 Rik Smits .07 .20
119 LaSalle Thompson .02 .10
120 Kenny Williams .02 .10
121 Micheal Williams .02 .10
122 Ken Bannister .02 .10
123 Winston Garland .02 .10
124 Gary Grant .02 .10
125 Ron Harper .07 .20
126 Bo Kimble .02 .10
127 Danny Manning .07 .20
128 Jeff Martin .02 .10
129 Ken Norman .02 .10
130 Olden Polynice .02 .10
131 Charles Smith .02 .10
132 Loy Vaught .02 .10
133 Elden Campbell .07 .20
134 Vlade Divac .07 .20
135 Larry Drew .02 .10
136 A.C. Green .07 .20
137 Magic Johnson .50 1.25
138 Sam Perkins .07 .20
139 Byron Scott .07 .20
140 Tony Smith .02 .10
141 Terry Teagle .02 .10
142 Mychal Thompson .02 .10
143 James Worthy .15 .40
144 Willie Burton .02 .10
145 Bimbo Coles .02 .10
146 Terry Davis .02 .10
147 Sherman Douglas .02 .10
148 Kevin Edwards .02 .10
149 Alec Kessler .02 .10
150 Grant Long .02 .10
151 Glen Rice .15 .40
152 Rony Seikaly .02 .10
153 Jon Sundvold .02 .10
154 Billy Thompson .02 .10
155 Frank Brickowski .02 .10
156 Lester Conner .02 .10
157 Jeff Grayer .02 .10
158 Jay Humphries .02 .10
159 Larry Krystkowiak .02 .10
160 Brad Lohaus .02 .10
161 Dale Ellis .07 .20
162 Fred Roberts .02 .10
163 Alvin Robertson .02 .10
164 Danny Schayes .02 .10
165 Jack Sikma .02 .10
166 Randy Breuer .02 .10
167 Scott Brooks .02 .10
168 Tony Campbell .02 .10
169 Tyrone Corbin .02 .10
170 Gerald Glass .02 .10
171 Sam Mitchell .02 .10
172 Tod Murphy .02 .10
173 Pooh Richardson .02 .10
174 Felton Spencer .02 .10
175 Bob Thornton .02 .10
176 Doug West .02 .10
177 Mookie Blaylock .07 .20
178 Sam Bowie .02 .10
179 Jud Buechler .02 .10
180 Derrick Coleman .07 .20
181 Chris Dudley .02 .10
182 Tate George .02 .10
183 Jack Haley .02 .10
184 Terry Mills RC .15 .40
185 Chris Morris .02 .10
186 Drazen Petrovic .07 .20
187 Reggie Theus .07 .20
188 Maurice Cheeks .02 .10
189 Patrick Ewing .15 .40
190 Mark Jackson .07 .20
191 Jerrod Mustaf .02 .10
192 Charles Oakley .07 .20
193 Brian Quinnett .02 .10
194 John Starks RC .15 .40
195 Trent Tucker .02 .10
196 Kiki Vandeweghe .02 .10
197 Kenny Walker .02 .10
198 Gerald Wilkins .02 .10
199 Mark Acres .02 .10
200 Nick Anderson .07 .20
201 Michael Ansley .02 .10
202 Terry Catledge .02 .10
203 Greg Kite .02 .10
204 Jerry Reynolds .02 .10
205 Dennis Scott .07 .20
206 Scott Skiles .02 .10
207 Otis Smith .02 .10
208 Jeff Turner .02 .10
209 Sam Vincent .02 .10
210 Ron Anderson .02 .10
211 Charles Barkley .25 .60
212 Manute Bol .02 .10
213 Johnny Dawkins .02 .10
214 Armon Gilliam .02 .10
215 Rickey Green .02 .10
216 Hersey Hawkins .07 .20
217 Rick Mahorn .02 .10
218 Brian Oliver .02 .10
219 Andre Turner .02 .10
220 Jayson Williams .15 .40
221 Joe Barry Carroll .02 .10
222 Cedric Ceballos .07 .20
223 Tom Chambers .02 .10
224 Jeff Hornacek .07 .20
225 Kevin Johnson .15 .40
226 Negele Knight .02 .10
227 Andrew Lang .02 .10
228 Dan Majerle .07 .20
229 Xavier McDaniel .02 .10
230 Kurt Rambis .02 .10
231 Mark West .02 .10
232 Alaa Abdelnaby .02 .10
233 Danny Ainge .07 .20
234 Mark Bryant .02 .10
235 Wayne Cooper .02 .10
236 Walter Davis .02 .10
237 Clyde Drexler .15 .40
238 Kevin Duckworth .02 .10
239 Jerome Kersey .02 .10
240 Terry Porter .02 .10
241 Clifford Robinson .07 .20
242 Buck Williams .02 .10
243 Anthony Bonner .02 .10
244 Antoine Carr .02 .10
245 Duane Causwell .02 .10
246 Bobby Hansen .02 .10
247 Jim Les RC .02 .10
248 Travis Mays .02 .10
249 Ralph Sampson .02 .10
250 Lionel Simmons .02 .10
251 Rory Sparrow .02 .10
252 Wayman Tisdale .02 .10
253 Bill Wennington .02 .10
254 Willie Anderson .02 .10
255 Terry Cummings .02 .10
256 Sean Elliott .07 .20
257 Sidney Green .02 .10
258 David Greenwood .02 .10
259 Avery Johnson .07 .20
260 Paul Pressey .02 .10
261 David Robinson .30 .75
262 Dwayne Schintzius .02 .10
263 Rod Strickland .15 .40
264 David Wingate .02 .10
265 Dana Barros .02 .10
266 Benoit Benjamin .02 .10
267 Michael Cage .02 .10
268 Quintin Dailey .02 .10
269 Ricky Pierce .02 .10
270 Eddie Johnson .07 .20
271 Shawn Kemp .40 1.00
272 Derrick McKey .02 .10
273 Nate McMillan .02 .10
274 Gary Payton .40 1.00
275 Sedale Threatt .02 .10
276 Thurl Bailey .02 .10
277 Mike Brown .02 .10
278 Tony Brown .02 .10
279 Mark Eaton .02 .10
280 Blue Edwards .02 .10
281 Darrell Griffith .02 .10
282 Jeff Malone .02 .10
283 Karl Malone .25 .60
284 Delaney Rudd .02 .10
285 John Stockton .15 .40
286 Andy Toolson .02 .10
287 Mark Alarie .02 .10
288 Ledell Eackles .02 .10
289 Pervis Ellison .02 .10
290 A.J. English .02 .10
291 Harvey Grant .02 .10
292 Tom Hammonds .02 .10
293 Charles Jones .02 .10
294 Bernard King .02 .10
295 Darrell Walker .02 .10
296 John Williams .02 .10
297 Haywoode Workman RC .07 .20
298 Muggsy Bogues .02 .10
299 Lester Conner .02 .10
300 Michael Adams .02 .10
301 Chris Mullin Minutes .07 .20
302 Otis Thorpe .02 .10
303 Rich/Hard/Mullin TRIO .15 .40
304 Darrell Walker .02 .10
305 Jerome Lane .02 .10
306 John Stockton Assists .07 .20
307 Michael Jordan Points 1.00 2.50
308 Michael Adams .02 .10
309 L.Smith/J.Lane .02 .10
310 Scott Skiles .02 .10
311 H.Olajuwon/D.Robinson .15 .40
312 Alvin Robertson .02 .10
313 Stay In School Jam .02 .10
314 Craig Hodges 3P .02 .10
315 Dee Brown SD .02 .10
316 Charles Barkley AS-MVP .15 .40
317 Behind the Scenes .15 .40
318 Derrick Coleman ART .02 .10
319 Lionel Simmons ART .02 .10
320 Dennis Scott ART .02 .10
321 Kendall Gill ART .02 .10
322 Dee Brown ART .02 .10
323 Magic Johnson GQ .25 .60
324 Hakeem Olajuwon GQ .15 .40
325 K.Willis/D.Wilkins GQ .07 .20
326 K.Willis/D.Wilkins GQ .07 .20
327 Gerald Wilkins GQ .02 .10
328 Centennial Logo Card .02 .10
329 Old-Fashioned Ball .02 .10
330 Women Take the Court .02 .10
331 The Peach Basket .02 .10
332 Dr. James Naismith .07 .20
333 M.Johnson/M.Jordan FIN .75 2.00
334 Michael Jordan FIN 1.00 2.50
335 Vlade Divac FIN .02 .10
336 John Paxson FIN .02 .10
337 Bulls Team/M.Jordan .50 1.25
338 Language Arts .02 .10
339 Mathematics .02 .10
340 Vocational Education .02 .10
341 Social Studies .02 .10
342 Physical Education .02 .10
343 Art .02 .10
344 Science .02 .10
345 Checklist 1 (1-60) .02 .10
346 Checklist 2 (61-120) .02 .10
347 Checklist 3 (121-180) .02 .10
348 Checklist 4 (181-244) .02 .10
349 Checklist 5 (245-305) .02 .10
350 Checklist 6 (306-350) .02 .10
351 Atlanta Hawks TL .02 .10
352 Boston Celtics TL .02 .10
353 Charlotte Hornets TL .02 .10
354 Chicago Bulls TL .02 .10
355 Cleveland Cavaliers TL .02 .10
356 Dallas Mavericks TL .02 .10
357 Denver Nuggets TL .02 .10
358 Detroit Pistons TL .02 .10
359 Golden State Warriors TL .02 .10
360 Houston Rockets TL .02 .10
361 Indiana Pacers TL .02 .10
362 Los Angeles Clippers TL .02 .10
363 Los Angeles Lakers TL .02 .10
364 Miami Heat TL .02 .10
365 Milwaukee Bucks TL .02 .10
366 Minnesota Timberwolves TL .02 .10
367 New Jersey Nets TL .02 .10
368 New York Knicks TL .02 .10
369 Orlando Magic TL .02 .10
370 Philadelphia 76ers TL .02 .10
371 Phoenix Suns TL .02 .10
372 Portland Trail Blazers TL .02 .10
373 Sacramento Kings TL .02 .10
374 San Antonio Spurs TL .02 .10
375 Seattle Supersonics TL .02 .10
376 Utah Jazz TL .02 .10
377 Washington Bullets TL .02 .10
378 Bob Weiss CO .02 .10
379 Chris Ford CO .02 .10
380 Allan Bristow CO .02 .10
381 Phil Jackson CO .07 .20
382 Lenny Wilkens CO .07 .20
383 Richie Adubato CO .02 .10
384 Paul Westhead CO .02 .10
385 Chuck Daly CO .07 .20
386 Don Nelson CO .07 .20
387 Don Chaney CO .02 .10
388 Bob Hill CO RC .02 .10
389 Mike Schuler CO .02 .10
390 Mike Dunleavy CO .02 .10
391 Kevin Loughery CO .02 .10
392 Del Harris CO .02 .10
393 Jimmy Rodgers CO .02 .10
394 Bill Fitch CO .02 .10
395 Pat Riley CO .07 .20
396 Matt Guokas CO .02 .10
397 Jim Lynam CO .02 .10
398 Cotton Fitzsimmons CO .02 .10
399 Rick Adelman CO .02 .10
400 Dick Motta CO .02 .10
401 Larry Brown CO .02 .10
402 K.C. Jones CO .07 .20
403 Jerry Sloan CO .07 .20
404 Wes Unseld CO .07 .20
405 Mo Cheeks GF .02 .10
406 Dee Brown GF .02 .10
407 Rex Chapman GF .02 .10
408 Michael Jordan GF 1.00 2.50
409 John Williams GF .02 .10
410 James Donaldson GF .02 .10
411 Dikembe Mutombo GF .15 .40
412 Isiah Thomas GF .07 .20
413 Tim Hardaway GF .15 .40
414 Hakeem Olajuwon GF .15 .40
415 Detlef Schrempf GF .02 .10
416 Danny Manning GF .02 .10
417 Magic Johnson GF .25 .60
418 Bimbo Coles GF .02 .10
419 Alvin Robertson GF .02 .10
420 Sam Mitchell GF .02 .10
421 Sam Bowie GF .02 .10
422 Mark Jackson GF .02 .10
423 Orlando Magic GF .02 .10
424 Charles Barkley GF .15 .40
425 Dan Majerle GF .02 .10
426 Robert Pack GF .02 .10
427 Wayman Tisdale GF .02 .10
428 David Robinson GF .15 .40
429 Nate McMillan GF .02 .10
430 Karl Malone GF .15 .40
431 Michael Adams GF .02 .10
432 Duane Ferrell SM .02 .10
433 Kevin McHale SM .02 .10
434 Dell Curry SM .02 .10
435 B.J. Armstrong SM .02 .10
436 John Williams SM .02 .10
437 Brad Davis SM .02 .10
438 Marcus Liberty SM .02 .10
439 Mark Aguirre SM .02 .10
440 Rod Higgins SM .02 .10
441 Eric (Sleepy) Floyd SM .02 .10
442 Detlef Schrempf SM .02 .10
443 Loy Vaught SM .02 .10
444 Terry Teagle SM .02 .10
445 Kevin Edwards SM .02 .10
446 Dale Ellis SM .02 .10
447 Tod Murphy SM .02 .10
448 Chris Dudley SM .02 .10
449 Mark Jackson SM .02 .10
450 Jerry Reynolds SM .02 .10
451 Ron Anderson SM .02 .10
452 Dan Majerle SM .02 .10
453 Danny Ainge SM .02 .10
454 Jim Les SM .02 .10
455 Paul Pressey SM .02 .10
456 Ricky Pierce SM .02 .10
457 Mike Brown SM .02 .10
458 Ledell Eackles SM .02 .10
459 D.Wilkins/Willis TW .07 .20
460 L.Bird/R.Parish TW .15 .40
461 R.Chapman/Gill TW .02 .10
462 M.Jordan/S.Pippen TW .60 1.50
463 C.Ehlo/M.Price TW .02 .10
464 D.Harper/R.Blackman TW .02 .10
465 R.Williams/C.Jackson TW .02 .10
466 I.Thomas/B.Laimbeer TW .07 .20
467 T.Hard/C.Mullin TW .07 .20
468 V.Maxwell/K.Smith TW .02 .10
469 D.Schrempf/R.Miller TW .07 .20
470 C.Smith/D.Manning TW .02 .10
471 M.Johnson/J.Worthy TW .15 .40
472 G.Rice/R.Seikaly TW .15 .40
473 J.Hump/A.Robertson TW .02 .10
474 T.Campbell/P.Rich TW .02 .10
475 D.Coleman/S.Bowie TW .02 .10
476 P.Ewing/C.Oakley TW .07 .20
477 D.Scott/S.Skiles TW .02 .10
478 C.Barkley/H.Hawkins TW .15 .40
479 K.Johnson/T.Chambers TW .07 .20
480 C.Drexler/T.Porter TW .15 .40
481 L.Simmons/W.Tisdale TW .02 .10
482 T.Cummings/S.Elliott TW .02 .10
483 E.Johnson/R.Pierce TW .02 .10
484 K.Malone/J.Stockton TW .15 .40
485 H.Grant/B.King TW .02 .10
486 Rumeal Robinson RS .02 .10
487 Dee Brown RS .02 .10
488 Kendall Gill RS .02 .10
489 B.J. Armstrong RS .02 .10
490 Danny Ferry RS .02 .10
491 Randy White RS .02 .10
492 Chris Jackson RS .02 .10
493 Lance Blanks RS .02 .10
494 Tim Hardaway RS .15 .40
495 Vernon Maxwell RS .02 .10
496 Micheal Williams RS .02 .10
497 Charles Smith RS .02 .10
498 Vlade Divac RS .02 .10
499 Willie Burton RS .02 .10
500 Jeff Grayer RS .02 .10
501 Pooh Richardson RS .02 .10
502 Derrick Coleman RS .02 .10
503 John Starks RS .07 .20
504 Dennis Scott RS .02 .10
505 Hersey Hawkins RS .02 .10
506 Negele Knight RS .02 .10
507 Clifford Robinson RS .02 .10
508 Lionel Simmons RS .02 .10
509 David Robinson RS .15 .40
510 Gary Payton RS .20 .50
511 Blue Edwards RS .02 .10
512 Harvey Grant RS .02 .10
513 Larry Johnson RC .60 1.50
514 Kenny Anderson RC .30 .75
515 Billy Owens RC .15 .40
516 Dikembe Mutombo RC .60 1.50
517 Steve Smith RC .60 1.50
518 Doug Smith RC .02 .10
519 Luc Longley RC .15 .40
520 Mark Macon RC .02 .10
521 Stacey Augmon RC .15 .40
522 Brian Williams RC .15 .40
523 Terrell Brandon RC .50 1.25
524 The Ball .02 .10
525 The Basket .02 .10
526 The 24-second Shot .02 .10
527 The Game Program .02 .10
528 The Championship Gift .02 .10
529 Championship Trophy .02 .10
530 Charles Barkley USA .50 1.25
531 Larry Bird USA 1.25 3.00
532 Patrick Ewing USA .30 .75
533 Magic Johnson USA 1.00 2.50
534 Michael Jordan USA 3.00 8.00
535 Karl Malone USA .50 1.25
536 Chris Mullin USA .15 .40
537 Scottie Pippen USA 1.00 2.50
538 David Robinson USA .60 1.50
539 John Stockton USA .30 .75
540 Chuck Daly CO USA .15 .40
541 P.J.Carlesimo CO USA RC .07 .20
542 M.Krzyzewski CO USA RC .30 .75
543 Lenny Wilkens CO USA .07 .20
544 Team USA 1 1.00 2.50
545 Team USA 2 1.00 2.50
546 Team USA 3 1.00 2.50
547 Willie Anderson USA .02 .10
548 Stacey Augmon USA .15 .40
549 Bimbo Coles USA .02 .10
550 Jeff Grayer USA .02 .10
551 Hersey Hawkins USA .02 .10
552 Dan Majerle USA .02 .10
553 Danny Manning USA .02 .10
554 J.R. Reid USA .02 .10
555 Mitch Richmond USA .30 .75
556 Charles Smith USA .02 .10
557 Vern Fleming USA .02 .10
558 Joe Kleine USA .02 .10
559 Jon Koncak USA .02 .10
560 Sam Perkins USA .02 .10
561 Alvin Robertson USA .02 .10
562 Wayman Tisdale USA .02 .10
563 Jeff Turner USA .02 .10
564 Tony Campbell MAG .02 .10
565 Joe Dumars MAG .07 .20
566 Horace Grant MAG .02 .10
567 Reggie Lewis MAG .02 .10
568 Hakeem Olajuwon MAG .15 .40
569 Sam Perkins MAG .02 .10
570 Chuck Person MAG .02 .10
571 Buck Williams MAG .02 .10
572 Michael Jordan SAL 1.00 2.50
573 Bernard King SAL .02 .10
574 Moses Malone SAL .07 .20
575 Robert Parish SAL .02 .10
576 Pat Riley CO SAL .07 .20
577 Dee Brown SM .02 .10
578 Rex Chapman SM .02 .10
579 Clyde Drexler SM .07 .20
580 Blue Edwards SM .02 .10
581 Ron Harper SM .02 .10
582 Kevin Johnson SM .07 .20
583 Michael Jordan SM 1.00 2.50
584 Shawn Kemp SM .30 .75
585 Xavier McDaniel SM .02 .10
586 Scottie Pippen SM .25 .60
587 Kenny Smith SM .02 .10
588 Dominique Wilkins SM .07 .20
589 Michael Adams SS .02 .10
590 Danny Ainge SS .02 .10
591 Larry Bird SS .30 .75
592 Dale Ellis SS .02 .10
593 Hersey Hawkins SS .02 .10
594 Jeff Hornacek SS .02 .10
595 Jeff Malone SS .02 .10
596 Reggie Miller SS .07 .20
597 Chris Mullin SS .07 .20
598 John Paxson SS .02 .10
599 Drazen Petrovic SS .02 .10
600 Ricky Pierce SS .02 .10
601 Mark Price SS .02 .10
602 Dennis Scott SS .02 .10
603 Manute Bol SMALL .02 .10
604 Jerome Kersey SMALL .02 .10
605 Charles Oakley SMALL .02 .10
606 Scottie Pippen SMALL .25 .60
607 Terry Porter SMALL .02 .10
608 Dennis Rodman SMALL .15 .40
609 Sedale Threatt SMALL .02 .10
610 Business .02 .10
611 Engineering .02 .10
612 Law .02 .10
613 Liberal Arts .02 .10
614 Medicine .02 .10
615 Maurice Cheeks .02 .10
616 Travis Mays .02 .10
617 Blair Rasmussen .02 .10
618 Alexander Volkov .02 .10
619 Rickey Green .02 .10
620 Bobby Hansen .02 .10
621 John Battle .02 .10
622 Terry Davis .02 .10
623 Walter Davis .02 .10
624 Winston Garland .02 .10
625 Scott Hastings .02 .10
626 Brad Sellers .02 .10
627 Darrell Walker .02 .10
628 Orlando Woolridge .02 .10
629 Tony Brown .02 .10
630 James Edwards .02 .10
631 Doc Rivers .07 .20
632 Jack Haley .02 .10
633 Sedale Threatt .02 .10
634 Moses Malone .15 .40
635 Thurl Bailey .02 .10
636 Rafael Addison RC .02 .10
637 Tim McCormick .02 .10
638 Xavier McDaniel .02 .10
639 Charles Shackleford .02 .10
640 Mitchell Wiggins .02 .10
641 Jerrod Mustaf .02 .10
642 Dennis Hopson .02 .10
643 Les Jepsen .02 .10
644 Mitch Richmond .15 .40
645 Dwayne Schintzius .02 .10
646 Spud Webb .07 .20
647 Jud Buechler .02 .10
648 Antoine Carr .02 .10
649 Tyrone Corbin .02 .10
650 Michael Adams .02 .10
651 Ralph Sampson .02 .10
652 Andre Turner .02 .10
653 David Wingate .02 .10
654 Checklist S .02 .10
655 Checklist K .02 .10
656 Checklist Y .02 .10
657 Checklist B .02 .10
658 Checklist O .02 .10
659 Checklist X .02 .10
NNO Clyde Drexler USA 20.00 50.00
NNO Team USA Card 6.00 12.00

1991-92 SkyBox Blister Inserts

The first four inserts were featured in series one blister packs, while the last two were inserted in series two blister packs. The cards measure the standard size. The first four have logos on their front and comments on the back. The last two are double-sided cards and display most valuable players from the same team for two consecutive years. The cards are numbered on the back with Roman numerals.

COMPLETE SET (6) 1.00 2.50
ONE CARD PER BLISTER PACK
1 USA Basketball .08 .25
2 Stay in School .08 .25
3 Orlando All-Star .08 .25
4 Inside Stuff .08 .25
5 M.Johnson/J.Worthy .40 1.00
6 J.Dumars/I.Thomas .20 .50

1992-93 SkyBox

The complete 1992-93 SkyBox basketball set contains 413 standard-size cards. The set was released in two series of 327 and 86 cards, respectively. Both series foil packs contained 12 cards each with 36 packs to a box. Suggested retail price was 1.15 per pack. Reported production quantities were approximately 15,000 20-box cases for the first series and 15,000 20-

box cases for the second series. The new front design features computer-generated screens of color blended with full-bleed color action photos. The backs carry full-bleed non-action close-up photos overlaid by a column displaying complete statistics and a color stripe with a personal "bio-bit." Cards of second series rookies have a gold seal in the other lower corner. In addition, the second series Draft Pick rookie cards were printed in shorter supply than the other cards in the second series set. First series cards are checklisted below alphabetically according team order. Subsets are Coaches (255-281), Team Tix (282-308), 1992 NBA All-Star Weekend Highlights (309-313), 1992 NBA Finals (314-318), 1992 NBA All-Rookie Team (319), and Public Service (230-321). The set concludes with checklist cards (322-327). The cards are numbered on the back. Special gold-foil stamped cards of Magic Johnson and David Robinson, some personally autographed, were randomly inserted in first series foil packs. Versions of these Johnson and Robinson cards with sparkling silver foil were also produced and one of each accompanied the first 7,500 cases ordered exclusively by hobby accounts. According to SkyBox approximately one of every 36 packs contained either a Magic Johnson or David Robinson SP card. The "Head of the Class" mail-away card features the first six 1992 NBA draft picks. The card was made available to the first 20,000 fans through a mail-in offer for three wrappers from each series of 1992-93 SkyBox cards plus 3.25 for postage and handling. The horizontal front features three color, cut-out player photos against a black background. Three wide vertical stripes in shades of red and violet run behind the players. A gold bar near the bottom carries the phrase "Head of the Class 1992 Top NBA Draft Picks." The back features three player photos similar to the ones on the front. The background design is the same except the wide stripes are green, orange, and blue. A white bar at the lower right corner carries the serial number and production run (20,000). Rookie Cards of note include Tom Gugliotta, Robert Horry, Christian Laettner, Alonzo Mourning, Shaquille O'Neal, Latrell Sprewell and Clarence Weatherspoon.

COMPLETE SET (413) 15.00 40.00
COMPLETE SERIES 1 (327) 10.00 25.00
COMPLETE SERIES 2 (86) 6.00 15.00
1 Stacey Augmon .08 .25
2 Maurice Cheeks .02 .10
3 Duane Ferrell .02 .10
4 Paul Graham .02 .10
5 Jon Koncak .02 .10
6 Blair Rasmussen .02 .10
7 Rumeal Robinson .02 .10
8 Dominique Wilkins .20 .50
9 Kevin Willis .02 .10
10 Larry Bird .75 2.00
11 Dee Brown .02 .10
12 Sherman Douglas .02 .10
13 Rick Fox .08 .25
14 Kevin Gamble .02 .10
15 Reggie Lewis .08 .25
16 Kevin McHale .20 .50
17 Robert Parish .08 .25
18 Ed Pinckney .02 .10
19 Muggsy Bogues .08 .25
20 Dell Curry .02 .10
21 Kenny Gattison .02 .10
22 Kendall Gill .08 .25
23 Mike Gminski .02 .10
24 Tom Hammonds .02 .10
25 Larry Johnson .25 .60
26 Johnny Newman .02 .10
27 J.R. Reid .02 .10
28 B.J. Armstrong .02 .10
29 Bill Cartwright .02 .10
30 Horace Grant .08 .25
31 Michael Jordan 2.50 6.00
32 Stacey King .02 .10
33 John Paxson .02 .10
34 Will Perdue .02 .10
35 Scottie Pippen .60 1.50
36 Scott Williams .02 .10
37 John Battle .02 .10
38 Terrell Brandon .20 .50
39 Brad Daugherty .02 .10
40 Craig Ehlo .02 .10
41 Danny Ferry .02 .10
42 Henry James .02 .10
43 Larry Nance .02 .10
44 Mark Price .02 .10
45 Mike Sanders .02 .10
46 Hot Rod Williams .02 .10
47 Rolando Blackman .02 .10
48 Terry Davis .02 .10
49 Derek Harper .08 .25
50 Donald Hodge .02 .10
51 Mike Iuzzolino .02 .10
52 Fat Lever .02 .10
53 Rodney McCray .02 .10
54 Doug Smith .02 .10
55 Randy White .02 .10
56 Herb Williams .02 .10
57 Greg Anderson .02 .10
58 Walter Davis .02 .10
59 Winston Garland .02 .10
60 Chris Jackson .02 .10
61 Marcus Liberty .02 .10
62 Todd Lichti .02 .10
63 Mark Macon .02 .10
64 Dikembe Mutombo .25 .60
65 Reggie Williams .02 .10
66 Mark Aguirre .02 .10
67 William Bedford .02 .10
68 Lance Blanks .02 .10
69 Joe Dumars .20 .50
70 Bill Laimbeer .08 .25
71 Dennis Rodman .40 1.00
72 John Salley .02 .10
73 Isiah Thomas .20 .50
74 Darrell Walker .02 .10
75 Orlando Woolridge .02 .10
76 Victor Alexander .02 .10
77 Mario Elie .08 .25
78 Chris Gatling .02 .10
79 Tim Hardaway .25 .60
80 Tyrone Hill .02 .10
81 Alton Lister .02 .10
82 Sarunas Marciulionis .02 .10
83 Chris Mullin .20 .50
84 Billy Owens .08 .25
85 Matt Bullard .02 .10
86 Sleepy Floyd .02 .10
87 Avery Johnson .02 .10
88 Buck Johnson .02 .10
89 Vernon Maxwell .02 .10
90 Hakeem Olajuwon .30 .75
91 Kenny Smith .02 .10
92 Larry Smith .02 .10
93 Otis Thorpe .08 .25
94 Dale Davis .02 .10
95 Vern Fleming .02 .10
96 George McCloud .02 .10
97 Reggie Miller .20 .50
98 Chuck Person .02 .10
99 Detlef Schrempf .08 .25
100 Rik Smits .08 .25
101 LaSalle Thompson .02 .10
102 Micheal Williams .02 .10
103 James Edwards .02 .10
104 Gary Grant .02 .10
105 Ron Harper .08 .25
106 Bo Kimble .02 .10
107 Danny Manning .08 .25
108 Ken Norman .02 .10
109 Olden Polynice .02 .10
110 Doc Rivers .08 .25
111 Charles Smith .02 .10
112 Loy Vaught .02 .10
113 Elden Campbell .08 .25
114 Vlade Divac .08 .25
115 A.C. Green .08 .25
116 Jack Haley .02 .10
117 Sam Perkins .08 .25
118 Byron Scott .08 .25
119 Tony Smith .02 .10
120 Sedale Threatt .02 .10
121 James Worthy .20 .50
122 Keith Askins .02 .10
123 Willie Burton .02 .10
124 Bimbo Coles .02 .10
125 Kevin Edwards .02 .10
126 Alec Kessler .02 .10
127 Grant Long .02 .10
128 Glen Rice .20 .50
129 Rony Seikaly .02 .10
130 Brian Shaw .02 .10
131 Steve Smith .25 .60
132 Frank Brickowski .02 .10
133 Dale Ellis .02 .10
134 Jeff Grayer .02 .10
135 Jay Humphries .02 .10
136 Larry Krystkowiak .02 .10
137 Moses Malone .20 .50
*138 Fred Roberts .02 .10
139 Alvin Robertson .02 .10
140 Danny Schayes .02 .10
141 Thurl Bailey .02 .10
142 Scott Brooks .02 .10
143 Tony Campbell .02 .10
144 Gerald Glass .02 .10
145 Luc Longley .08 .25
146 Sam Mitchell .02 .10
147 Pooh Richardson .02 .10
148 Felton Spencer .02 .10
149 Doug West .02 .10
150 Rafael Addison .02 .10
151 Kenny Anderson .20 .50
152 Mookie Blaylock .08 .25
153 Sam Bowie .02 .10
154 Derrick Coleman .08 .25
155 Chris Dudley .02 .10
156 Tate George .02 .10
157 Terry Mills .02 .10
158 Chris Morris .02 .10
159 Drazen Petrovic .02 .10
160 Greg Anthony .02 .10
161 Patrick Ewing .20 .50
162 Mark Jackson .08 .25
163 Anthony Mason .20 .50
164 Tim McCormick .02 .10
165 Xavier McDaniel .02 .10
166 Charles Oakley .08 .25
167 John Starks .08 .25
168 Gerald Wilkins .02 .10
169 Nick Anderson .08 .25
170 Terry Catledge .02 .10
171 Jerry Reynolds .02 .10
172 Stanley Roberts .02 .10
173 Dennis Scott .08 .25
174 Scott Skiles .02 .10
175 Jeff Turner .02 .10
176 Sam Vincent .02 .10
177 Brian Williams .02 .10
178 Ron Anderson .02 .10
179 Charles Barkley .30 .75
180 Manute Bol .02 .10
181 Johnny Dawkins .02 .10
182 Armon Gilliam .02 .10
183 Greg Grant .02 .10
184 Hersey Hawkins .08 .25
185 Brian Oliver .02 .10
186 Charles Shackleford .02 .10
187 Jayson Williams .08 .25
188 Cedric Ceballos .08 .25
189 Tom Chambers .02 .10
190 Jeff Hornacek .08 .25
191 Kevin Johnson .20 .50
192 Negele Knight .02 .10
193 Andrew Lang .02 .10
194 Dan Majerle .08 .25
195 Jerrod Mustaf .02 .10
196 Tim Perry .02 .10
197 Mark West .02 .10
198 Alaa Abdelnaby .02 .10
199 Danny Ainge .08 .25
200 Mark Bryant .02 .10
201 Clyde Drexler .20 .50
202 Kevin Duckworth .02 .10
203 Jerome Kersey .02 .10
204 Robert Pack .02 .10
205 Terry Porter .02 .10
206 Clifford Robinson .08 .25
207 Buck Williams .08 .25
208 Anthony Bonner .02 .10
209 Randy Brown .02 .10
210 Duane Causwell .02 .10
211 Pete Chilcutt .02 .10
212 Dennis Hopson .02 .10
213 Jim Les .02 .10
214 Mitch Richmond .20 .50
215 Lionel Simmons .02 .10
216 Wayman Tisdale .02 .10
217 Spud Webb .08 .25
218 Willie Anderson .02 .10
219 Antoine Carr .02 .10
220 Terry Cummings .08 .25
221 Sean Elliott .08 .25
222 Sidney Green .02 .10
223 Vinnie Johnson .02 .10
224 David Robinson .30 .75
225 Rod Strickland .20 .50
226 Greg Sutton .02 .10
227 Dana Barros .02 .10
228 Benoit Benjamin .02 .10
229 Michael Cage .02 .10
230 Eddie Johnson .02 .10
231 Shawn Kemp .40 1.00
232 Derrick McKey .02 .10
233 Nate McMillan .02 .10
234 Gary Payton .40 1.00
235 Ricky Pierce .02 .10
236 David Benoit .02 .10
237 Mike Brown .02 .10
238 Tyrone Corbin .02 .10
239 Mark Eaton .02 .10
240 Blue Edwards .02 .10
241 Jeff Malone .02 .10
242 Karl Malone .30 .75
243 Eric Murdock .02 .10
244 John Stockton .20 .50
245 Michael Adams .02 .10
246 Rex Chapman .02 .10
247 Ledell Eackles .02 .10
248 Pervis Ellison .02 .10
249 A.J. English .02 .10
250 Harvey Grant .02 .10
251 Charles Jones .02 .10
252 Bernard King .02 .10
253 LaBradford Smith .02 .10
254 Larry Stewart .02 .10
255 Bob Weiss CO .02 .10
256 Chris Ford CO .02 .10
257 Allan Bristow CO .02 .10
258 Phil Jackson CO .08 .25
259 Lenny Wilkens CO .08 .25
260 Richie Adubato CO .02 .10
261 Dan Issel CO .02 .10
262 Ron Rothstein CO .02 .10
263 Don Nelson CO .08 .25
264 Rudy Tomjanovich CO .08 .25
265 Bob Hill CO .02 .10
266 Larry Brown CO .08 .25
267 Randy Pfund CO RC .02 .10
268 Kevin Loughery CO .02 .10
269 Mike Dunleavy CO .02 .10
270 Jimmy Rodgers CO .02 .10
271 Chuck Daly CO .08 .25
272 Pat Riley CO .08 .25
273 Matt Guokas CO .02 .10
274 Doug Moe CO .02 .10
275 Paul Westphal CO .02 .10
276 Rick Adelman CO .02 .10
277 Garry St. Jean CO RC .02 .10
278 Jerry Tarkanian CO RC .02 .10
279 George Karl CO .08 .25
280 Jerry Sloan CO .08 .25
281 Wes Unseld CO .08 .25
282 Dominique Wilkins TT .08 .25
283 Reggie Lewis TT .02 .10
284 Kendall Gill TT .02 .10
285 Horace Grant TT .02 .10
286 Brad Daugherty TT .02 .10
287 Derek Harper TT .02 .10
288 Chris Jackson TT .02 .10
289 Isiah Thomas TT .08 .25
290 Chris Mullin TT .08 .25
291 Kenny Smith TT .02 .10
292 Reggie Miller TT .08 .25
293 Ron Harper TT .02 .10
294 Vlade Divac TT .02 .10
295 Glen Rice TT .08 .25
296 Moses Malone TT .08 .25
297 Doug West TT .02 .10
298 Derrick Coleman TT .02 .10
299 Patrick Ewing TT .08 .25
300 Scott Skiles TT .02 .10
301 Hersey Hawkins TT .02 .10
302 Kevin Johnson TT .08 .25
303 Clifford Robinson TT .02 .10
304 Spud Webb TT .02 .10
305 David Robinson TT COR .20 .50
305A Dav.Robinson TT ERR 299 .20 .50
306 Shawn Kemp TT .20 .50
307 John Stockton TT .08 .25
308 Pervis Ellison TT .02 .10
309 Craig Hodges AS .02 .10
310 Magic Johnson AS MVP .30 .75
311 Cedric Ceballos AS SD .02 .10
312 D.Rodman/Group AS .20 .50
313 K.Malone/Group AS .20 .50
314 Michael Jordan MVP 1.25 3.00
315 Clyde Drexler FIN .08 .25
316 Danny Ainge PO .08 .25
317 Scottie Pippen FIN .30 .75
318 M.Jordan CHAMP .20 .50
319 L.Johnson/D.Mut. ART .20 .50
320 NBA Stay in School .02 .10
321 Boys and Girls .02 .10
322 Checklist 1 .02 .10
323 Checklist 2 .02 .10
324 Checklist 3 .02 .10
325 Checklist 4 .02 .10
326 Checklist 5 .02 .10
327 Checklist 6 .02 .10
328 Adam Keefe SP RC .02 .10
329 Sean Rooks SP RC .02 .10
330 Xavier McDaniel .02 .10
331 Kiki Vandeweghe .02 .10
332 Alonzo Mourning SP RC 1.25 3.00
333 Rodney McCray .02 .10
334 Gerald Wilkins .02 .10
335 Tony Bennett SP RC .02 .10
336 LaPhonso Ellis SP RC .20 .50
337 Bryant Stith SP RC .20 .50
338 Isaiah Morris SP RC .02 .10
339 Olden Polynice .02 .10
340 Jeff Grayer .02 .10
341 Byron Houston SP RC .02 .10
342 Latrell Sprewell SP RC 1.50 4.00
343 Scott Brooks .02 .10
344 Frank Johnson .02 .10
345 Robert Horry SP RC .20 .50
346 David Wood .02 .10
347 Sam Mitchell .02 .10
348 Pooh Richardson .02 .10
349 Malik Sealy SP RC .20 .50
350 Morlon Wiley .02 .10
351 Mark Jackson .08 .25
352 Stanley Roberts .02 .10
353 Elmore Spencer SP RC .02 .10
354 John Williams .02 .10
355 Randy Woods SP RC .02 .10
356 James Edwards .02 .10
357 Jeff Sanders .02 .10
358 Magic Johnson .60 1.50
359 Anthony Peeler SP RC .20 .50
360 Harold Miner SP RC .20 .50
361 John Salley .02 .10
362 Alaa Abdelnaby .02 .10
363 Todd Day SP RC .20 .50
364 Blue Edwards .02 .10
365 Lee Mayberry SP RC .02 .10
366 Eric Murdock .02 .10
367 Mookie Blaylock .08 .25
368 Anthony Avent RC .02 .10
369 Christian Laettner SP RC .40 1.00
370 Chuck Person .02 .10
371 Chris Smith SP RC .20 .50
372 Micheal Williams .02 .10
373 Rolando Blackman .02 .10
374 Tony Campbell UER .02 .10
375 Hubert Davis SP RC .20 .50
376 Travis Mays .02 .10
377 Doc Rivers .08 .25
378 Charles Smith .02 .10
379 Rumeal Robinson .02 .10
380 Vinny Del Negro .02 .10
381 Steve Kerr .08 .25
382 Shaquille O'Neal SP RC 3.00 8.00
383 Donald Royal .02 .10
384 Jeff Hornacek .08 .25
385 Andrew Lang .02 .10
386 Tim Perry UER .02 .10
387 C.Weatherspoon SP RC .20 .50
388 Danny Ainge .08 .25
389 Charles Barkley .30 .75
390 Tim Kempton .02 .10
391 Oliver Miller SP RC .20 .50
392 Dave Johnson SP RC .20 .50
393 Tracy Murray SP RC .20 .50
394 Rod Strickland .20 .50
395 Marty Conlon .02 .10
396 Walt Williams SP RC .20 .50
397 Lloyd Daniels RC .02 .10
398 Dale Ellis .02 .10
399 Dave Hoppen .02 .10
400 Larry Smith .02 .10
401 Doug Overton .02 .10
402 Isaac Austin RC .08 .25
403 Jay Humphries .02 .10
404 Larry Krystkowiak .02 .10
405 Tom Gugliotta SP RC .60 1.50
406 Buck Johnson .02 .10
407 Don MacLean SP RC .20 .50
408 Marlon Maxey SP RC .20 .50
409 Corey Williams SP RC .20 .50
410 D.Majerle OLY .08 .25
411 Checklist 1 .02 .10
412 Checklist 2 .02 .10
413 Checklist 3 .02 .10
NNO Admiral Comes Prep Silver 1.50 4.00
NNO Magic Never Ends Silver 2.50 6.00
NNO David Robinson AU 60.00 150.00
NNO Admiral Comes Prep Gold 1.50 4.00
NNO Magic Johnson AU 75.00 200.00
NNO Head of the Class 10.00 25.00
NNO Magic Never Ends Gold 2.50 6.00

1992-93 SkyBox Draft Picks

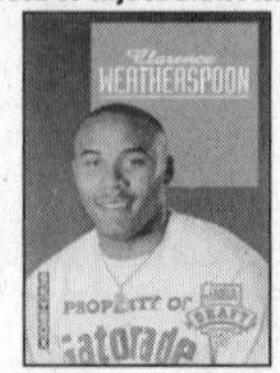

This 25-card standard-size insert set showcases the first round picks from the 1992 NBA Draft. The cards were randomly inserted into 12-card (both series) foil packs. According to SkyBox, approximately one out of every eight packs contained a Draft Pick card. The card numbering (1-27) reflects the actual order in which each player was selected. Six players (2, 10-11, 15-16, 18) available by the first series cut-off date were issued in first series foil packs, while the rest of the first round picks who signed NBA contracts were issued in second series packs. DP4 and DP17, intended for Jim Jackson and Doug Christie respectively, were not issued with this set because neither player signed a professional contract in time to be included in the second series. They were issued in 1993-94 first series packs. The fronts display an opaque metallic gold rectangle set off from the player. On a gradated gold background, the backs present player profiles. A white rectangle that runs vertically the length of the card contains statistics. The team logo is superimposed on this rectangle. The cards are numbered on the back with a "DP" prefix.

COMPLETE SET (25) 8.00 20.00
COMPLETE SERIES 1 (6) 2.00 5.00
COMPLETE SERIES 2 (19) 6.00 15.00
SER.1/2 STATED ODDS 1:8
DP1 Shaquille O'Neal 5.00 12.00
DP2 Alonzo Mourning 1.50 4.00
DP3 Christian Laettner .50 1.25
DP5 LaPhonso Ellis .40 1.00
DP6 Tom Gugliotta .75 2.00
DP7 Walt Williams .30 .75
DP8 Todd Day .30 .75
DP9 Clarence Weatherspoon .30 .75
DP10 Adam Keefe .15 .40
DP11 Robert Horry .50 1.25
DP12 Harold Miner .30 .75
DP13 Bryant Stith .30 .75
DP14 Malik Sealy .30 .75
DP15 Anthony Peeler .30 .75
DP16 Randy Woods .15 .40
DP18 Tracy Murray .30 .75
DP19 Don MacLean .15 .40
DP20 Hubert Davis .30 .75
DP21 Jon Barry .30 .75
DP22 Oliver Miller .30 .75
DP23 Lee Mayberry .15 .40
DP24 Latrell Sprewell 2.50 6.00
DP25 Elmore Spencer .15 .40
DP26 Dave Johnson .15 .40
DP27 Byron Houston .15 .40

1992-93 SkyBox Olympic Team

Each card in this 12-card standard-size set features an action photo of a team member and his complete statistics from the Olympic Games. According to SkyBox, the cards were randomly inserted into 12-card first series foil packs at a rate of approximately one per six. The backs tell the story of U.S. Men's Olympic Team, from scrimmage in Monte Carlo to the medal ceremony in Barcelona. The cards are numbered on the back with a "USA" prefix.

COMPLETE SET (12) 12.00 30.00
SER.1 STATED ODDS 1:6
USA1 Clyde Drexler .60 1.50
USA2 Chris Mullin .60 1.50
USA3 John Stockton .60 1.50
USA4 Karl Malone 1.00 2.50
USA5 Scottie Pippen 2.00 5.00
USA6 Larry Bird 2.50 6.00
USA7 Charles Barkley 1.00 2.50
USA8 Patrick Ewing .60 1.50
USA9 Christian Laettner 1.25 3.00
USA10 David Robinson 1.00 2.50
USA11 Michael Jordan 5.00 12.00
USA12 Magic Johnson 2.00 5.00

1992-93 SkyBox David Robinson

This ten-card standard-size insert set provides a look at Robinson at various stages of his life. Included are photos from his childhood, indulging in hobbies, with his family at the Naval Academy and his present day super stardom. The first five cards were randomly inserted in first series 12-card foil packs, while the second five were found in second series packs. According to SkyBox, approximately one of every eight packs contains a David Robinson insert card. The cards feature a different design than the regular issue cards. The fronts display color photos tilted slightly to the left with a special seal overlaying the upper left corner. The surrounding card face shows two colors.

COMPLETE SET (10) 2.00 4.00
COMPLETE SERIES 1 (5) 1.00 2.00
COMPLETE SERIES 2 (5) 1.00 2.00
COMMON D.ROB. (R1-R10) .20 .50
SER.1/2 STATED ODDS 1:8

1992-93 SkyBox School Ties

Randomly inserted in 1992-93 SkyBox second series 12-card foil packs at a reported rate of one per four, this 18-card standard-size set consists of six different three-card "School Ties" interlocking cards. When the three cards in each puzzle are placed together, they create a montage of active NBA players from one particular college. The fronts feature several color player photos that have team color-coded picture frames. The team logo appears in a team color-coded banner that is superimposed across the bottom of the picture. The backs have brightly colored backgrounds and display information about the college, the players, and a checklist of the players on the three-card puzzle. The cards are numbered on the back with an "ST" prefix.

COMPLETE SET (18) 7.50 15.00
SER.2 STATED ODDS 1:4
ST1 P.Ewing/A.Mourning 1.00 2.50
ST2 D.Mutombo/S.Floyd .20 .50
ST3 R.Williams/D.Wingate .08 .25
ST4 K.Anderson/D.Ferrell .20 .50
ST5 Hammonds/J.Barry/M.Price .08 .25
ST6 J.Salley/D.Scott .20 .50
ST7 R.Addison/D.Johnson .08 .25
ST8 Owens/Coleman/Seikaly .20 .50
ST9 S.Douglas/D.Schayes .08 .25
ST10 N.Anderson/K.Gill .20 .50
ST11 D.Harper/E.Johnson .08 .25
ST12 M.Liberty/K.Norman .08 .25
ST13 G.Anthony/S.Augmon .20 .50
ST14 Gilliam/L.Johnson/Green .20 .50
ST15 E.Spencer/G.Paddio .08 .25
ST16 Worthy/Jordan/Perkins 4.00 10.00
ST17 Reid/Chilcu/Daugherty/Fox .08 .25
ST18 Davis/Smith/Williams .20 .50

1992-93 SkyBox Thunder and Lightning

Randomly inserted into second series 12-card foil packs at a reported rate of one per 40 packs, each card in this nine-card standard-size set features a pair of teammates. There is a photo on each side. The catchword on the front is "Thunder", referring to a dominant power player, while "Lightning" on the back captures the speed of a guard. The cards are highlighted by a litho-foil printing which gives a foil-look to the graphics around the basketball. The cards have color action player photos against a dark background, with computer enhancement around the ball and player. On the front, the power player's name appears at the bottom and is underlined by a thin yellow stripe. The word "Thunder" appears below the stripe. On the horizontal backs, the speed player's name is displayed in the upper right with the same yellow underline, but the word Lightning" appears below it. The cards are numbered on the back with a "TL" prefix.

COMPLETE SET (9) 15.00 40.00
SER.2 STATED ODDS 1:40
TL1 D.Mutombo/M.Macon 1.50 4.00
TL2 B.Williams/C.Drexler 1.50 4.00
TL3 C.Barkley/K.Johnson 3.00 8.00
TL4 P.Ellison/M.Adams .60 1.50
TL5 L.Johnson/M.Bogues 1.50 4.00
TL6 B.Daugherty/M.Price .60 1.50
TL7 S.Kemp/G.Payton 6.00 15.00
TL8 K.Malone/J.Stockton 5.00 12.00
TL9 B.Owens/T.Hardaway 2.00 5.00

2008-09 SkyBox

This set was released on February 17, 2009. The base set consists of 230 cards. Cards 1-200 feature veterans, and cards 201-230 are rookies. Rookies were inserted at a rate of one in three and the Close Ups subset was inserted at one in 1.25.

COMPLETE SET (230) 40.00 80.00
APPROXIMATE CLOSE ODDS 1:1.25
1 Mike Bibby .25 .60
2 Acie Law .25 .60
3 Al Horford .30 .75
4 Joe Johnson .25 .60
5 Josh Smith .25 .60
6 Marvin Williams .25 .60
7 Ray Allen .30 .75
8 Glen Davis .20 .50
9 Kevin Garnett .50 1.25
10 Paul Pierce .30 .75
11 Leon Powe .20 .50
12 Rajon Rondo .30 .75
13 Raymond Felton .25 .60
14 Adam Morrison .20 .50
15 Emeka Okafor .25 .60
16 Boris Diaw .25 .60
17 Gerald Wallace .25 .60
18 Luol Deng .25 .60
19 Ben Gordon .25 .60
20 Kirk Hinrich .25 .60
21 Joakim Noah .25 .60
22 Andres Nocioni .20 .50
23 Tyrus Thomas .20 .50
24 Daniel Gibson .25 .60
25 Zydrunas Ilgauskas .25 .60
26 LeBron James 1.25 3.00
27 Anderson Varejao .20 .50
28 Ben Wallace .25 .60
29 Jose Barea .40 1.00
30 Josh Howard .25 .60
31 Jason Kidd .30 .75
32 Dirk Nowitzki .40 1.00
33 Jason Terry .25 .60
34 Carmelo Anthony .40 1.00
35 Shaun Livingston .20 .50
36 Chauncey Billups .30 .75
37 Kenyon Martin .25 .60
38 J.R. Smith .25 .60
39 Allen Iverson .40 1.00
40 Richard Hamilton .25 .60
41 Jason Maxiell .20 .50
42 Tayshaun Prince .25 .60
43 Rodney Stuckey .25 .60
44 Rasheed Wallace .30 .75
45 Kelenna Azubuike .20 .50
46 Matt Barnes .20 .50
47 Corey Maggette .25 .60
48 Monta Ellis .25 .60
49 Jamal Crawford .30 .75
50 Stephen Jackson .25 .60
51 Shane Battier .25 .60
52 Luther Head .20 .50
53 Carl Landry .20 .50
54 Tracy McGrady .30 .75
55 Yao Ming .40 1.00
56 Luis Scola .25 .60
57 Mike Dunleavy .25 .60
58 Danny Granger .25 .60
59 Troy Murphy .20 .50
60 T.J. Ford .20 .50
61 Jamaal Tinsley .20 .50
62 Elton Brand .30 .75
63 Chris Kaman .25 .60
64 Ricky Davis .25 .60
65 Baron Davis .25 .60
66 Zach Randolph .25 .60
67 Al Thornton .25 .60
68 Kobe Bryant 1.25 3.00
69 Andrew Bynum .20 .50
70 Jordan Farmar .20 .50
71 Pau Gasol .30 .75
72 Lamar Odom .25 .60
73 Sasha Vujacic .20 .50
74 Mike Conley Jr. .25 .60
75 Rudy Gay .30 .75
76 Kyle Lowry .30 .75
77 Mike Miller .25 .60
78 Hakim Warrick .25 .60
79 Daequan Cook .20 .50
80 Marcus Camby .20 .50
81 Udonis Haslem .20 .50
82 Shawn Marion .25 .60
83 Alonzo Mourning .40 1.00
84 Dwyane Wade .50 1.25
85 Andrew Bogut .25 .60
86 Richard Jefferson .25 .60
87 Desmond Mason .20 .50
88 Michael Redd .25 .60
89 Ramon Sessions .25 .60
90 Mo Williams .25 .60
91 Corey Brewer .25 .60
92 Randy Foye .30 .75
93 Al Jefferson .25 .60
94 Rashad McCants .20 .50
95 Sebastian Telfair .20 .50
96 Josh Boone .20 .50
97 Vince Carter .40 1.00
98 Devin Harris .20 .50
99 Yi Jianlian .30 .75
100 Keyon Dooling .20 .50
101 Sean Williams .25 .60
102 Tyson Chandler .25 .60
103 Chris Paul .40 1.00
104 Morris Peterson .20 .50
105 Peja Stojakovic .30 .75
106 David West .25 .60
107 Julian Wright .25 .60
108 Al Harrington .25 .60
109 Eddy Curry .20 .50
110 David Lee .20 .50
111 Stephon Marbury .25 .60
112 Cuttino Mobley .20 .50
113 Quentin Richardson .25 .60
114 Keith Bogans .20 .50
115 Maurice Evans .20 .50
116 Dwight Howard .25 .60
117 Rashard Lewis .25 .60
118 Jameer Nelson .20 .50
119 Hedo Turkoglu .25 .60
120 Samuel Dalembert .20 .50
121 Reggie Evans .20 .50
122 Willie Green .20 .50
123 Andre Iguodala .25 .60
124 Andre Miller .25 .60
125 Thaddeus Young .25 .60
126 Leandro Barbosa .25 .60
127 Jason Richardson .30 .75
128 Grant Hill .40 1.00
129 Steve Nash .30 .75
130 Shaquille O'Neal .60 1.50
131 Amare Stoudemire .25 .60
132 LaMarcus Aldridge .30 .75
133 Steve Blake .20 .50
134 Greg Oden .25 .60
135 Brandon Roy .30 .75
136 Martell Webster .25 .60
137 Beno Udrih .20 .50
138 Ron Artest .30 .75
139 Francisco Garcia .20 .50
140 Kevin Martin .25 .60
141 Brad Miller .25 .60
142 Brent Barry .20 .50
143 Bruce Bowen .20 .50
144 Tim Duncan .50 1.25
145 Michael Finley .30 .75
146 Manu Ginobili .30 .75
147 Tony Parker .30 .75
148 Nick Collison .25 .60
149 Kevin Durant .75 2.00
150 Jeff Green .25 .60
151 Earl Watson .20 .50
152 Chris Wilcox .20 .50
153 Damien Wilkins .20 .50
154 Andrea Bargnani .25 .60
155 Chris Bosh .30 .75
156 Jose Calderon .20 .50
157 Jermaine O'Neal .25 .60
158 Jamario Moon .20 .50
159 Anthony Parker .20 .50
160 Carlos Boozer .25 .60
161 Ronnie Brewer .25 .60
162 Andrei Kirilenko .25 .60
163 Kyle Korver .25 .60
164 Mehmet Okur .20 .50
165 Deron Williams .25 .60
166 Gilbert Arenas .25 .60
167 Caron Butler .25 .60
168 Antawn Jamison .25 .60
169 DeShawn Stevenson .20 .50
170 Nick Young .25 .60
171 Al Horford CU .40 1.00
172 Joe Johnson CU .30 .75
173 Kevin Garnett CU .60 1.50
174 Paul Pierce CU .40 1.00
175 Larry Johnson CU .40 1.00
176 Michael Jordan CU 3.00 8.00
177 LeBron James CU 1.50 4.00
178 Ben Wallace CU .30 .75
179 Dirk Nowitzki CU .50 1.25
180 Carmelo Anthony CU .50 1.25
181 Allen Iverson CU .50 1.25
182 Isiah Thomas CU .40 1.00
183 Monta Ellis CU .30 .75
184 Magic Johnson CU 1.00 2.50
185 Kobe Bryant CU 1.50 4.00
186 Dwyane Wade CU .60 1.50
187 Oscar Robertson CU .40 1.00
188 Vince Carter CU .50 1.25
189 Chris Paul CU .50 1.25
190 Patrick Ewing CU .50 1.25
191 Dwight Howard CU .30 .75
192 Julius Erving CU .60 1.50
193 Steve Nash CU .40 1.00
194 Shaquille O'Neal CU .75 2.00
195 Brandon Roy CU .40 1.00
196 Tim Duncan CU .60 1.50
197 Kevin Durant CU 1.00 2.50
198 Chris Bosh CU .40 1.00
199 Deron Williams CU .30 .75
200 Gilbert Arenas CU .30 .75
201 Derrick Rose RC 4.00 10.00
202 Michael Beasley RC 1.00 2.50
203 O.J. Mayo RC 1.00 2.50
204 Russell Westbrook RC 25.00 60.00
205 Kevin Love RC 3.00 8.00
206 Danilo Gallinari RC 1.50 4.00
207 Eric Gordon RC 1.50 4.00
208 Joe Alexander RC .60 1.50
209 D.J. Augustin RC .75 2.00
210 Brook Lopez RC 1.25 3.00
211 Jerryd Bayless RC .75 2.00
212 Jason Thompson RC .60 1.50
213 Brandon Rush RC .75 2.00
214 Robin Lopez RC 1.00 2.50
215 Roy Hibbert RC 1.00 2.50
216 Alexis Ajinca RC .60 1.50
217 George Hill RC 1.00 2.50
218 Donte Greene RC .60 1.50
219 J.J. Hickson RC .75 2.00
220 D.J. White RC .75 2.00
221 Mario Chalmers RC 1.00 2.50
222 Mike Taylor RC .60 1.50
223 Kosta Koufos RC .75 2.00
224 Kyle Weaver RC .60 1.50
225 Rudy Fernandez RC .75 2.00
226 Nicolas Batum RC 1.25 3.00
227 Luc Richard Mbah A Moute RC .75 2.00
228 Marc Gasol RC 2.00 5.00
229 Darnell Jackson RC .60 1.50
230 Richard Hendrix RC .60 1.50

2008-09 SkyBox Ruby

*VETS 1-170: 12X TO 30X BASE HI
*SUBSET 171-200: 10X TO 25X BASE HI
*ROOKIES 201-230: 4X TO 10X BASE HI
STATED PRINT RUN 50 SER.#'d SETS
29 Jose Barea 15.00 40.00
39 Allen Iverson 20.00 50.00
68 Kobe Bryant 60.00 150.00
84 Dwyane Wade 25.00 60.00
128 Grant Hill 25.00 60.00
149 Kevin Durant 50.00 125.00
176 Michael Jordan CU 125.00 250.00
177 LeBron James CU 100.00 175.00
181 Allen Iverson CU 20.00 50.00
185 Kobe Bryant CU 60.00 150.00
186 Dwyane Wade CU 25.00 60.00
197 Kevin Durant CU 50.00 125.00
204 Russell Westbrook 150.00 400.00
226 Nicolas Batum 25.00 60.00

2008-09 SkyBox Emerald Rookie Autographs

COMBINED AUTO ODDS 1:12
202 Michael Beasley 40.00 100.00
203 O.J. Mayo 40.00 100.00
204 Russell Westbrook 175.00 350.00
205 Kevin Love 150.00 300.00
207 Eric Gordon 30.00 80.00
208 Joe Alexander 5.00 12.00
210 Brook Lopez 15.00 40.00
212 Jason Thompson 5.00 12.00
213 Brandon Rush 6.00 15.00
214 Robin Lopez 8.00 20.00
215 Roy Hibbert 8.00 20.00
216 Alexis Ajinca 5.00 12.00
217 George Hill 8.00 20.00
218 Donte Greene 5.00 12.00
219 J.J. Hickson 20.00 50.00
220 D.J. White 6.00 15.00
221 Mario Chalmers 8.00 20.00
222 Mike Taylor 5.00 12.00
224 Kyle Weaver 5.00 12.00
226 Nicolas Batum 30.00 80.00
227 Luc Richard Mbah A Moute 6.00 15.00
229 Darnell Jackson 5.00 12.00
230 Richard Hendrix 5.00 12.00

2008-09 SkyBox Fresh Ink

COMBINED AUTO ODDS 1:12
FICD Chris Duhon 4.00 10.00
FICM Chris Mihm 4.00 10.00
FICW C.J. Watson 4.00 10.00
FIGP Gabe Pruitt 4.00 10.00
FIJF Jordan Farmar 4.00 10.00
FIKD Kevin Durant 50.00 100.00
FIKG Kevin Garnett 40.00 80.00
FIMA Morris Almond 4.00 10.00
FIMW Mario West 4.00 10.00
FIRR Rajon Rondo 10.00 25.00
FISV Sasha Vujacic 4.00 10.00
FIWM Mo Williams 5.00 12.00

2008-09 SkyBox Larger Than Life

COMBINED MEM.ODDS 1:4
*RETAIL GREEN: .4X TO 1X HI COLUMN
*PATCHES: 1.25X TO 3X HI COLUMN
PATCH PRINT RUN 25 SER.#'d SETS
LLAS Amare Stoudemire 1.50 4.00
LLCA Carmelo Anthony 2.50 6.00
LLDN Dirk Nowitzki 2.50 6.00
LLDW Deron Williams 1.50 4.00
LLEB Elton Brand 2.00 5.00
LLGA Gilbert Arenas 1.50 4.00
LLJJ Joe Johnson 1.50 4.00
LLKB Kobe Bryant 8.00 20.00
LLKG Kevin Garnett 3.00 8.00
LLLJ LeBron James 8.00 20.00
LLME Monta Ellis 1.50 4.00
LLMG Manu Ginobili 2.00 5.00
LLPP Paul Pierce 2.00 5.00
LLRA Ray Allen 2.00 5.00
LLRH Richard Hamilton 2.00 5.00
LLSM Shawn Marion 1.50 4.00
LLSN Steve Nash 2.00 5.00
LLSO Shaquille O'Neal 4.00 10.00
LLTD Tim Duncan 3.00 8.00
LLVC Vince Carter 2.50 6.00

2008-09 SkyBox Metal Universe

COMPLETE SET (100) 75.00 150.00
APPROXIMATE ODDS 1:2
1 Kevin Garnett 2.00 5.00
2 LeBron James 5.00 12.00
3 Dwight Howard 1.00 2.50
4 Kobe Bryant 5.00 12.00
5 Carmelo Anthony 1.50 4.00
6 Tim Duncan 2.00 5.00
7 Yao Ming 1.50 4.00
8 Dwyane Wade 2.00 5.00
9 Dirk Nowitzki 1.50 4.00
10 Jason Kidd 1.25 3.00
11 Allen Iverson 1.50 4.00
12 Tracy McGrady 1.25 3.00
13 Steve Nash 1.25 3.00
14 Ray Allen 1.25 3.00
15 Amare Stoudemire 1.00 2.50
16 Vince Carter 1.50 4.00
17 Shaquille O'Neal 2.50 6.00
18 Chris Bosh 1.25 3.00
19 Gilbert Arenas 1.00 2.50
20 Chauncey Billups 1.25 3.00
21 Paul Pierce 1.25 3.00
22 Chris Paul 1.50 4.00
23 Michael Jordan 40.00 100.00
24 Carlos Boozer 1.00 2.50
25 Manu Ginobili 1.25 3.00
26 Shawn Marion 1.00 2.50
27 Tony Parker 1.25 3.00
28 Baron Davis 1.00 2.50
29 Shane Battier 1.00 2.50
30 Kevin Durant 3.00 8.00
31 Yi Jianlian 1.25 3.00
32 Luis Scola 1.00 2.50
33 Josh Howard 1.00 2.50
34 Marcus Camby .75 2.00
35 Grant Hill 1.50 4.00
36 Michael Redd 1.00 2.50
37 Caron Butler 1.00 2.50
38 Richard Hamilton 1.00 2.50
39 Rasheed Wallace 1.25 3.00

40 Hedo Turkoglu 1.00 2.50
41 Jason Terry 1.00 2.50
42 Tyson Chandler 1.00 2.50
43 Andrew Bogut 1.00 2.50
44 Tayshaun Prince 1.00 2.50
45 Ben Wallace 1.00 2.50
46 Joe Johnson 1.00 2.50
47 T.J. Ford .75 2.00
48 Rashard Lewis 1.00 2.50
49 Jermaine O'Neal 1.00 2.50
50 LaMarcus Aldridge 1.25 3.00
51 Pau Gasol 1.25 3.00
52 Chris Kaman 1.00 2.50
53 Emeka Okafor 1.00 2.50
54 Eddy Curry .75 2.00
55 Al Horford 1.25 3.00
56 Josh Smith 1.00 2.50
57 Gerald Wallace 1.00 2.50
58 Ben Gordon 1.00 2.50
59 Monta Ellis 1.00 2.50
60 Elton Brand 1.25 3.00
61 Rudy Gay 1.25 3.00
62 Al Jefferson 1.00 2.50
63 David West 1.00 2.50
64 Jamal Crawford 1.25 3.00
65 Andre Iguodala 1.00 2.50
66 Brandon Roy 1.25 3.00
67 Greg Oden 1.00 2.50
68 Kevin Martin 1.00 2.50
69 Jamario Moon .75 2.00
70 Deron Williams 1.00 2.50
71 Derrick Rose 5.00 12.00
72 Michael Beasley 1.25 3.00
73 O.J. Mayo 1.25 3.00
74 Russell Westbrook 10.00 25.00
75 Kevin Love 6.00 15.00
76 Danilo Gallinari 2.00 5.00
77 Eric Gordon 2.00 5.00
78 Joe Alexander .75 2.00
79 D.J. Augustin 1.00 2.50
80 Brook Lopez 1.50 4.00
81 Jerryd Bayless 1.00 2.50
82 Jason Thompson .75 2.00
83 Brandon Rush 1.00 2.50
84 Anthony Randolph .75 2.00
85 Robin Lopez 1.25 3.00
86 Marreese Speights 1.00 2.50
87 Roy Hibbert 1.25 3.00
88 Javale McGee 1.50 4.00
89 J.J. Hickson 1.00 2.50
90 Alexis Ajinca .75 2.00
91 Ryan Anderson 1.00 2.50
92 Courtney Lee 1.00 2.50
93 Kosta Koufos 1.00 2.50
94 Nicolas Batum 1.50 4.00
95 George Hill 1.25 3.00
96 D.J. White 1.00 2.50
97 J.R. Giddens .75 2.00
98 Luc Richard Mbah A Moute 1.00 2.50
99 Marc Gasol 2.50 6.00
100 Rudy Fernandez 1.00 2.50

2008-09 SkyBox Metal Universe Precious Metal Gems Red

*STARS: 6X TO 15X BASE HI
*ROOKIES: 3X TO 8X BASE HI
STATED PRINT RUN 40 SER.#'d SETS
CARDS SERIALLY #'d TO 50
FIRST TEN #'s ARE GREEN
GREEN UNPRICED DUE TO SCARCITY
4 Kobe Bryant 150.00 400.00
8 Dwyane Wade 75.00 150.00
10 Jason Kidd 40.00 100.00
11 Allen Iverson 40.00 100.00
13 Steve Nash 30.00 80.00
23 Michael Jordan 900.00 1500.00
74 Russell Westbrook 250.00 450.00
75 Kevin Love 100.00 250.00
94 Nicolas Batum 30.00 80.00
99 Marc Gasol 30.00 80.00

2008-09 SkyBox One on One Dual Memorabilia

COMBINED MEM ODDS 1:4
OOAH R.Hamilton/R.Allen 3.00 8.00
OOAJ G.Arenas/L.James 6.00 15.00
OOBA C.Anthony/K.Bryant 8.00 20.00
OOBB A.Bynum/C.Boozer 3.00 8.00
OOBG K.Garnett/K.Bryant 6.00 15.00
OOBH M.Bibby/K.Hinrich 3.00 8.00
OOBM K.Martin/E.Brand 3.00 8.00
OOBO S.O'Neal/K.Bryant 8.00 20.00
OOBP T.Parker/C.Billups 3.00 8.00
OOCI A.Iguodala/V.Carter 3.00 8.00
OODG P.Gasol/T.Duncan 4.00 10.00
OODM T.Duncan/Y.Ming 3.00 8.00
OOGW K.Garnett/R.Wallace 4.00 10.00
OOHB C.Bosh/D.Howard 3.00 8.00
OOHG M.Ginobili/R.Hamilton 3.00 8.00
OOJA C.Anthony/L.James 8.00 20.00
OOKC J.Kidd/V.Carter 4.00 10.00
OOMH S.Marion/J.Howard 3.00 8.00
OOMM C.Maggette/S.Marbury 3.00 8.00
OOMO Y.Ming/S.O'Neal 4.00 10.00
OOMW D.Williams/T.McGrady 3.00 8.00
OONG P.Gasol/D.Nowitzki 4.00 10.00
OONP S.Nash/T.Parker 4.00 10.00
OOPF J.Farmar/T.Parker 3.00 8.00
OOPJ P.Pierce/L.James 6.00 15.00
OOPP P.Pierce/T.Prince 3.00 8.00
OOPW C.Paul/D.Williams 4.00 10.00
OORR J.Richardson/Z.Randolph 3.00 8.00
OOSH D.Howard/A.Stoudemire 4.00 10.00
OOWR B.Roy/D.Williams 3.00 8.00

2008-09 SkyBox Paraph Signatures

COMBINED AUTOGRAPH ODDS 1:12
PSAM Alonzo Mourning 30.00 60.00
PSAT Alando Tucker 4.00 10.00
PSDH Dwight Howard 15.00 40.00
PSJK Jason Kidd 20.00 40.00
PSJN Joakim Noah 4.00 10.00
PSKD Michael Jordan 300.00 550.00
PSLA LaMarcus Aldridge 4.00 10.00
PSPP Paul Pierce 15.00 40.00
PSRJ Richard Jefferson 4.00 10.00
PSTP Tayshaun Prince 4.00 10.00

2008-09 SkyBox Rookie Prevue

COMBINED MEM ODDS 1:4
*RETAIL GREEN: .4X TO 1X HI COLUMN
UNPRICED PATCH PRINT RUN 10 SETS
RPAR Anthony Randolph 1.00 2.50
RPBL Brook Lopez 2.00 5.00
RPDA D.J. Augustin 1.25 3.00
RPDJ DeAndre Jordan 2.00 5.00
RPDR Derrick Rose 4.00 10.00
RPEG Eric Gordon 2.50 6.00
RPGH George Hill 1.50 4.00
RPJA Joe Alexander 1.00 2.50
RPJB Jerryd Bayless 1.25 3.00
RPJH J.J. Hickson 1.25 3.00
RPJT Jason Thompson 1.00 2.50
RPKK Kosta Koufos 1.25 3.00
RPKL Kevin Love 4.00 10.00
RPKW Kyle Weaver 1.00 2.50
RPMB Michael Beasley 1.50 4.00
RPMC Mario Chalmers 1.50 4.00
RPOM O.J. Mayo 1.50 4.00
RPRL Robin Lopez 1.50 4.00
RPSW Sonny Weems 1.00 2.50
RPWS Walter Sharpe 1.00 2.50

2008-09 SkyBox Signature Set Dual

STATED PRINT RUN 23 TO 25 SER.#'d SETS
SSAW Anderson/S.Williams/25 10.00 25.00
SSBW C.Watson/Belinelli/25 6.00 15.00
SSDG K.Durant/J.Green/25 50.00 125.00
SSFD R.Felton/J.Dudley/25 8.00 20.00
SSFR B.Roy/Fernandez/25 25.00 50.00
SSGA R.Gay/D.Arthur/25 8.00 20.00
SSGN B.Gordon/J.Noah/25 8.00 20.00
SSJB A.Jefferson/Brewer/25 8.00 20.00
SSJJ L.James/M.Jordan/23 600.00 1000.00
SSJS Sessions/R.Jefferson/25 6.00 15.00
SSKJ D.Jordan/C.Kaman/25 8.00 20.00
SSPG K.Garnett/P.Pierce/25 100.00 200.00
SSPS T.Prince/Stuckey/25 10.00 25.00
SSSB J.Smith/R.Balkman/25 6.00 15.00
SSSW J.Smith/M.Speights/25 8.00 20.00
SSTS Tucker/Singletary/25 6.00 15.00
SSWC Chandler/D.West/25 8.00 20.00
SSWH M.Williams/Horford/25 8.00 20.00
SSWV S.Vujacic/L.Walton/25 10.00 25.00

2008-09 SkyBox Standouts

COMBINED MEM ODDS 1:4
*RETAIL GREEN: .4X TO 1X HI COLUMN
*PATCHES: .75X TO 2X HI COLUMN
PATCH PRINT RUN 25 SER.#'d SETS
SOAB Andrew Bynum 2.00 5.00
SOAK Andrei Kirilenko 2.50 6.00
SOBU Beno Udrih 2.00 5.00
SOCK Chris Kaman 2.50 6.00
SODW Deron Williams 2.50 6.00
SOFO Randy Foye 3.00 8.00
SOJC Jarron Collins 2.00 5.00
SOJH Josh Howard 2.50 6.00
SOJR Jason Richardson 3.00 8.00
SOLD Luol Deng 2.50 6.00
SOLH Luther Head 2.00 5.00
SOLR Luke Ridnour 2.50 6.00
SOME Monta Ellis 2.50 6.00
SOPD Paul Davis 2.00 5.00
SORF Raymond Felton 2.50 6.00
SORG Rudy Gay 3.00 8.00
SOSD Samuel Dalembert 2.00 5.00
SOSS Stromile Swift 2.00 5.00
SOUH Udonis Haslem 2.00 5.00
SOZR Zach Randolph 2.50 6.00

1999-00 SkyBox APEX

Replacing the Thunder brand, this was the premiere year for the APEX brand. The set contained 163 cards, featuring 150 veterans and 13 rookies. The cards came eight to a pack with a suggested retail price of $2.69. The rookie cards were inserted at one in 13 packs. Two checklists were also included and inserted at one in six. 50 serial numbered cards were also included that could be redeemed for a Keith Van Horn autographed jersey.

COMPLETE SET (163) 60.00 120.00
COMPLETE SET w/o RC (150) 10.00 25.00
151-163 STATED ODDS 1:13
UNPRICED XTREME PRINT RUN ONE SET
1 Paul Pierce .40 1.00
2 Stephon Marbury .25 .60
3 Chris Webber .30 .75
4 Kobe Bryant 1.25 3.00
5 David Robinson .50 1.25
6 Gary Payton .30 .75
7 Kornel David RC .25 .60
8 Glenn Robinson .25 .60
9 Nick Van Exel .25 .60
10 Jelani McCoy .20 .50
11 Charles Oakley .25 .60
12 Michael Finley .30 .75
13 Steve Smith .25 .60
14 Arvydas Sabonis .25 .60
15 Cuttino Mobley .20 .50
16 Eric Piatkowski .25 .60
17 Bobby Jackson .20 .50
18 Keith Van Horn .25 .60
19 Shaquille O'Neal .75 2.00
20 Karl Malone .40 1.00
21 Allan Houston .25 .60
22 Ron Mercer .25 .60
23 Vince Carter .60 1.50
24 Lindsey Hunter .20 .50
25 Scottie Pippen .50 1.25
26 Wesley Person .20 .50
27 Vitaly Potapenko .20 .50
28 Glen Rice .30 .75
29 Tyrone Nesby RC .25 .60
30 Detlef Schrempf .25 .60
31 Clifford Robinson .20 .50
32 Joe Smith .25 .60
33 P.J. Brown .20 .50
34 Christian Laettner .25 .60
35 Avery Johnson .25 .60
36 Kevin Garnett .50 1.25
37 Jason Kidd .50 1.25
38 Kenny Anderson .25 .60
39 Shawn Kemp .30 .75
40 Bison Dele .20 .50
41 Rodney Rogers .20 .50
42 Jamal Mashburn .25 .60
43 Grant Hill .40 1.00
44 Larry Johnson .30 .75
45 Darrell Armstrong .20 .50
46 Shandon Anderson .20 .50
47 Kendall Gill .20 .50
48 Jason Williams .40 1.00
49 Tom Gugliotta .20 .50
50 Ray Allen .30 .75
51 Sam Mitchell .20 .50
52 Brent Barry .25 .60
53 Antawn Jamison .30 .75
54 Chris Mullin .30 .75
55 Alan Henderson .20 .50
56 Derek Anderson .20 .50
57 Tim Thomas .25 .60
58 Anfernee Hardaway .50 1.25
59 Pat Garrity .20 .50
60 Corliss Williamson .20 .50
61 Gary Trent .20 .50
62 Greg Ostertag .20 .50
63 Vin Baker .25 .60
64 LaPhonso Ellis .20 .50
65 Brevin Knight .20 .50
66 Rick Fox .20 .50
67 Bryant Reeves .20 .50
68 Mark Jackson .25 .60
69 John Starks .25 .60
70 Robert Traylor .20 .50
71 Maurice Taylor .20 .50
72 Hersey Hawkins .20 .50
73 Zydrunas Ilgauskas .25 .60
74 Charles Barkley .50 1.25
75 Isaac Austin .20 .50
76 Mike Bibby .30 .75
77 Michael Olowokandi .20 .50
78 Brian Grant .20 .50
79 Felipe Lopez .20 .50
80 Chris Crawford .20 .50
81 Dee Brown .20 .50
82 Antoine Walker .30 .75
83 Vlade Divac .30 .75
84 Rod Strickland .20 .50
85 Dickey Simpkins .20 .50
86 Donyell Marshall .20 .50
87 Larry Hughes .25 .60
88 Rasheed Wallace .30 .75
89 Erick Dampier .20 .50
90 Kerry Kittles .20 .50
91 Mitch Richmond .30 .75
92 Isaiah Rider .25 .60
93 Bobby Phills .20 .50
94 Dirk Nowitzki .60 1.50
95 Cedric Henderson .20 .50
96 Howard Eisley .20 .50
97 Toni Kukoc .30 .75
98 Jalen Rose .25 .60
99 Michael Doleac .20 .50
100 Matt Geiger .20 .50
101 Bryon Russell .20 .50
102 Alvin Williams .20 .50
103 Shawn Bradley .20 .50
104 Latrell Sprewell .30 .75
105 Vernon Maxwell .20 .50
106 Tim Hardaway .30 .75
107 Peja Stojakovic .30 .75
108 Tracy Murray .20 .50
109 Theo Ratliff .25 .60
110 Dikembe Mutombo .30 .75
111 Alonzo Mourning .40 1.00
112 Raef LaFrentz .25 .60
113 Marcus Camby .25 .60
114 Eddie Jones .30 .75
115 Chauncey Billups .30 .75
116 Jayson Williams .20 .50
117 Anthony Mason .20 .50
118 Tracy McGrady .50 1.25
119 John Stockton .40 1.00
120 Matt Harpring .20 .50
121 Mario Elie .20 .50
122 Juwan Howard .25 .60
123 Antonio McDyess .25 .60
124 Ricky Davis .30 .75
125 Reggie Miller .30 .75
126 Allen Iverson .60 1.50
127 Terrell Brandon .20 .50
128 Hakeem Olajuwon .40 1.00
129 Damon Stoudamire .25 .60
130 Randy Brown .20 .50
131 Cedric Ceballos .20 .50
132 Jerry Stackhouse .30 .75
133 Michael Dickerson .20 .50
134 Rik Smits .30 .75
135 Cherokee Parks .20 .50
136 Tim Duncan .60 1.50
137 Shareef Abdur-Rahim .25 .60
138 Derek Fisher .30 .75
139 Bo Outlaw .20 .50
140 Eric Snow .25 .60
141 Jaren Jackson .20 .50
142 Tony Battie .25 .60
143 Derrick Coleman .25 .60
144 Corey Benjamin .20 .50
145 Steve Nash .50 1.25
146 Mookie Blaylock .20 .50
147 Voshon Lenard .20 .50
148 Vinny Del Negro .20 .50
149 Jeff Hornacek .25 .60
150 Patrick Ewing .40 1.00
151 Elton Brand RC 1.50 4.00
152 Steve Francis RC 1.50 4.00
153 Baron Davis RC 1.50 4.00
154 Lamar Odom RC 1.50 4.00
155 Jonathan Bender RC .60 1.50
156 Wally Szczerbiak RC 1.25 3.00
157 Richard Hamilton RC 1.25 3.00
158 Andre Miller RC 1.25 3.00
159 Shawn Marion RC 1.25 3.00
160 Jason Terry RC 1.00 2.50
161 Trajan Langdon RC .60 1.50
162 A.Radojevic RC .40 1.00
163 Corey Maggette RC 1.00 2.50
P2 Stephon Marbury PROMO 1.00 2.50
NNO K.Van Horn AU JSY/50 30.00 80.00

1999-00 SkyBox APEX Xtra

*STARS: 25X TO 60X BASE CARD HI
*RCs: 3X TO 8X BASE HI
STATED PRINT RUN 50 SERIAL #'d SETS
4 Kobe Bryant 200.00 400.00
125 Reggie Miller 25.00 60.00

1999-00 SkyBox APEX Allies

Randomly inserted in packs at one in six, this 15-card set features two superstar teammates on the same card.

COMPLETE SET (15) 5.00 12.00
STATED ODDS 1:6 HOB/RET
1 K.Bryant/S.O'Neal 2.00 5.00
2 K.Van Horn/S.Marbury .40 1.00
3 J.Stockton/K.Malone .60 1.50
4 M.Bibby/S.Abdur-Rahim .50 1.25
5 A.Iverson/L.Hughes 1.00 2.50
6 M.Olowokandi/M.Taylor .30 .75
7 V.Carter/T.McGrady 1.00 2.50
8 G.Hill/J.Stackhouse .60 1.50
9 J.Williams/C.Webber .60 1.50
10 T.Duncan/D.Robinson 1.00 2.50
11 J.Kidd/T.Gugliotta .75 2.00
12 V.Baker/G.Payton .50 1.25
13 A. Mourning/T. Hardaway .60 1.50
14 S.Kemp/B.Knight .50 1.25
15 A.McDyess/R.LaFrentz .40 1.00

1999-00 SkyBox APEX Cutting Edge

Randomly inserted in packs at one in 24, this 15-card set features players on the cutting edge of superstardom. The cards are die cut.

COMPLETE SET (15) 15.00 30.00
STATED ODDS 1:24 HOB/RET
*PLUS: 1.25X TO 3X HI COLUMN
PLUS: STATED ODDS 1:240 HOB/RET
*WARP TEK: 15X TO 40X VALUE
WARP TEK: PRINT RUN 25 SERIAL #'d SETS
1 Allen Iverson 2.00 5.00
2 Paul Pierce 1.25 3.00
3 Vince Carter 2.00 5.00
4 Jason Williams 1.25 3.00
5 Kobe Bryant 8.00 20.00
6 Kevin Garnett 1.50 4.00
7 Stephon Marbury .75 2.00
8 Jason Kidd 1.50 4.00
9 Tim Duncan 2.00 5.00
10 Mike Bibby 1.00 2.50
11 Marcus Camby .75 2.00
12 Michael Olowokandi .60 1.50
13 Antawn Jamison 1.00 2.50
14 Keith Van Horn .75 2.00
15 Raef LaFrentz .75 2.00

1999-00 SkyBox APEX First Impressions

Randomly inserted in packs at one in 12, this 20-card set features the top rookies from the 1999-2000 season. The cards feature embossing and holofoil.

COMPLETE SET (20) 10.00 25.00
STATED ODDS 1:12 HOB/RET
1 Jonathan Bender .50 1.25
2 Steve Francis 1.25 3.00
3 Ron Artest 1.00 2.50
4 Baron Davis 1.25 3.00
5 Shawn Marion 1.00 2.50
6 Jason Terry .75 2.00
7 Elton Brand 1.25 3.00
8 Kenny Thomas .50 1.25
9 Trajan Langdon .50 1.25
10 Aleksandar Radojevic .30 .75
11 Corey Maggette .75 2.00
12 Jeff Foster .50 1.25
13 Scott Padgett .40 1.00
14 Lamar Odom 1.25 3.00
15 William Avery .40 1.00
16 Andre Miller 1.00 2.50
17 Wally Szczerbiak 1.00 2.50
18 Richard Hamilton 1.00 2.50
19 James Posey .50 1.25
20 Jumaine Jones .40 1.00

1999-00 SkyBox APEX Jam Session

Randomly inserted in packs at one in 96, this 15-card set features the NBA's top stars and aerial artists. The cards feature a die cut design with holofoil stamping on plastic stock.

COMPLETE SET (15) 40.00 80.00
STATED ODDS 1:96 HOB/RET
1 Stephon Marbury 2.00 5.00
2 Paul Pierce 3.00 8.00
3 Kobe Bryant 20.00 50.00
4 Keith Van Horn 2.00 5.00
5 Shaquille O'Neal 6.00 15.00
6 Anfernee Hardaway 4.00 10.00
7 Grant Hill 3.00 8.00
8 Antonio McDyess 2.00 5.00
9 Kevin Garnett 4.00 10.00
10 Tracy McGrady 4.00 10.00
11 Shareef Abdur-Rahim 2.00 5.00
12 Shawn Kemp 2.50 6.00
13 Antoine Walker 2.50 6.00
14 Eddie Jones 2.50 6.00
15 Vin Baker 2.00 5.00

1999-00 SkyBox APEX Net Shredders

Randomly inserted in packs, this 10-card set features a piece of a game-used net in a card. The nets were obtained from Toronto, Philadelphia, Milwaukee, Sacramento and San Antonio.

RANDOM INSERTS IN HOBBY PACKS
1 Vince Carter 30.00 80.00
2 Tracy McGrady 25.00 60.00
3 Allen Iverson 30.00 80.00
4 Larry Hughes 12.00 30.00
5 Glenn Robinson 12.00 30.00
6 Ray Allen 15.00 40.00
7 Jason Williams 20.00 50.00
8 Chris Webber 15.00 40.00
9 Tim Duncan 25.00 60.00
10 David Robinson 25.00 60.00

1999-00 SkyBox APEX Lamar Odom

This one standard-sized card was sent to dealers to announce Fleer/SkyBox's signing of Lamar Odom as a spokesman. The cards are done in the style of 1999-00 SkyBox APEX. The cards are serially numbered out of 2000. Card backs are not numbered.

NNO Lamar Odom 3.00 8.00

2003-04 SkyBox Autographics

Released in late February 2004, this 90-card set places full-color player photos on a tan background with the words "Skybox Autographics" across the middle of the card. Card numbers 1-45 showcase veteran players and cards 46-90 feature rookies and are sequentially numbered to 1500. Autographics was packaged in four pack boxes where packs contained five cards and no suggested retail price was published.

COMP.SET w/o SP's (45) 12.50 30.00
46-90 RC PRINT RUN 1500 SER.#'d SETS
1 Vince Carter .60 1.50
2 Kobe Bryant 1.50 4.00
3 Tony Parker .40 1.00
4 Richard Hamilton .30 .75
5 Jamal Mashburn .30 .75
6 Paul Pierce .40 1.00
7 Allan Houston .30 .75
8 Carlos Boozer .30 .75
9 Michael Redd .40 1.00
10 Chris Webber .40 1.00
11 Yao Ming .75 2.00
12 Tracy McGrady .50 1.25
13 Zach Randolph .30 .75
14 Ben Wallace .30 .75
15 Kenyon Martin .30 .75
16 Ray Allen .40 1.00
17 Jermaine O'Neal .30 .75
18 Bonzi Wells .25 .60
19 Ron Artest .40 1.00
20 Peja Stojakovic .40 1.00
21 Dirk Nowitzki .60 1.50
22 Desmond Mason .30 .75
23 Morris Peterson .25 .60
24 Eddy Curry .25 .60
25 Kevin Garnett .60 1.50
26 Rashard Lewis .40 1.00
27 Jason Richardson .40 1.00
28 Amare Stoudemire .50 1.25
29 Steve Francis .30 .75
30 Allen Iverson .60 1.50
31 Jason Terry .30 .75
32 Pau Gasol .40 1.00
33 Manu Ginobili .50 1.25
34 Reggie Miller .40 1.00
35 Cuttino Mobley .25 .60
36 Mike Bibby .40 1.00
37 Mike Dunleavy .30 .75
38 Jason Kidd .60 1.50
39 Shareef Abdur-Rahim .30 .75
40 Elton Brand .40 1.00
41 Kwame Brown .25 .60
42 Shaquille O'Neal 1.00 2.50
43 Tim Duncan .60 1.50
44 Nene .30 .75
45 Baron Davis .30 .75
46 Boris Diaw RC 1.50 4.00
47 Luke Walton RC 1.50 4.00
48 Willie Green RC 1.00 2.50
49 Marcus Banks RC 1.00 2.50
50 Dahntay Jones RC 1.25 3.00
51 Leandro Barbosa RC 1.50 4.00
52 Josh Howard RC 1.50 4.00
53 Ndudi Ebi RC 1.00 2.50
54 Chris Bosh RC 2.50 6.00
55 Carmelo Anthony RC 5.00 12.00
56 Zoran Planinic RC 1.00 2.50
57 Aleksandar Pavlovic RC 1.25 3.00
58 Marquis Daniels RC 1.25 3.00
59 Keith McLeod RC 1.00 2.50
60 Ben Handlogten RC 1.00 2.50
61 Francisco Elson RC 1.00 2.50
62 David West RC 1.50 4.00
63 Maurice Williams RC 1.50 4.00
64 Brian Cook RC 1.00 2.50
65 Keith Bogans RC 1.00 2.50
66 Kendrick Perkins RC 1.25 3.00
67 Troy Bell RC 1.00 2.50
68 Kyle Korver RC 2.00 5.00
69 Mickael Pietrus RC 1.25 3.00
70 Maciej Lampe RC 1.00 2.50
71 Steve Blake RC 1.25 3.00
72 Chris Kaman RC 1.50 4.00
73 Curtis Borchardt 1.50 4.00
74 Kirk Hinrich RC 1.50 4.00
75 Dwyane Wade RC 5.00 12.00
76 Zarko Cabarkapa RC 1.00 2.50
77 LeBron James RC 60.00 150.00
78 Jerome Beasley RC 1.00 2.50
79 Nick Collison RC 1.25 3.00
80 Linton Johnson RC 1.00 2.50
81 Udonis Haslem RC 1.25 3.00
82 Travis Outlaw RC 1.25 3.00
83 Jason Kapono RC 1.00 2.50
84 T.J. Ford RC 1.25 3.00
85 Luke Ridnour RC 1.25 3.00
86 Darko Milicic RC 1.25 3.00
87 Mike Sweetney RC 1.00 2.50
88 Jarvis Hayes RC 1.00 2.50
89 Josh Moore RC 1.00 2.50
90 Reece Gaines RC 1.00 2.50

2003-04 SkyBox Autographics Insignia Purple

*PURPLE STARS: 6X TO 15X BASE HI
*PURPLE RCs: 2X TO 5X BASE HI

2003-04 SkyBox Autographics Insignia Silver

*SILVER SINGLES: 2.5X TO 6X BASE HI
*SILVER RCs: 1X TO 2X BASE HI
SILVER PRINT RUN 150 SER.#'d SETS
77 LeBron James 150.00 400.00

2003-04 SkyBox Autographics Autoclassics

Randomly inserted in packs at the rate of one in 12, this 15-card set features a horizontal design and black and white player photos set against a red white and blue background.

COMPLETE SET (15) 10.00 25.00
STATED ODDS 1:12
1 Vince Carter 1.25 3.00
2 Shawn Marion .60 1.50
3 Tracy McGrady 1.00 2.50
4 David Robinson 1.25 3.00
5 Paul Pierce .75 2.00
6 Carmelo Anthony 2.50 6.00
7 Stephon Marbury .60 1.50
8 Jason Richardson .75 2.00
9 Steve Francis .60 1.50
10 Chris Bosh 1.25 3.00
11 Dirk Nowitzki 1.25 3.00
12 Allen Iverson 1.25 3.00
13 Yao Ming 1.50 4.00
14 Shaquille O'Neal 2.00 5.00
15 Tim Duncan 1.25 3.00

2003-04 SkyBox Autographics Autoclassics Memorabilia

Randomly seeded in packs, this 15-card set parallels the base Autoclassics set enhanced with a swatch of game worn memorabilia and sequential numbering to 45. Several other versions of this set were produced: Gold versions are sequentially numbered to five, Signature versions are sequentially numbered to 25 and a one of one signature version.

PRINT RUN 45 SER.#'d SETS
AI Allen Iverson 12.00 30.00
CA Carmelo Anthony 12.00 30.00
CB Chris Bosh 10.00 25.00
DN Dirk Nowitzki 12.00 30.00
DR David Robinson 12.00 30.00
JR Jason Richardson 8.00 20.00
PP Paul Pierce 8.00 20.00
SF Steve Francis 6.00 15.00
SM Shawn Marion 6.00 15.00
SM Stephon Marbury 6.00 15.00
SO Shaquille O'Neal 20.00 50.00
TD Tim Duncan 12.00 30.00
TM Tracy McGrady 10.00 25.00
VC Vince Carter 12.00 30.00
YM Yao Ming 15.00 40.00

2003-04 SkyBox Autographics Autoclassics Signatures

Randomly inserted, this six-card set parallels the design of the base Autoclassics set enhanced with a cut signature and is sequentially numbered to 25.

PRINT RUN 25 SER.#'d SETS
UNPRICED GOLD PRINT RUN ONE SET
CA Carmelo Anthony 100.00 200.00
SM Shawn Marion 12.50 30.00
VC Vince Carter 20.00 50.00

2003-04 SkyBox Autographics Autographs

Randomly inserted, this 41-card set places full color player photos along with an embedded cut signature on a blue background with blue borders. Each card is sequentially numbered.

PRINT RUNS LISTED BELOW
AM Aaron McKie/300 2.50 6.00
AP Aleksandar Pavlovic/300 3.00 8.00
AW Antoine Walker/200 5.00 12.00
BD Boris Diaw/300 4.00 10.00
BM Brad Miller/250 3.00 8.00
CA Carmelo Anthony 20.00 50.00
DJ Dahntay Jones/450 3.00 8.00
DW1 Dwyane Wade/200 15.00 40.00
DW2 David West/350 4.00 10.00
DW3 Dajuan Wagner/200 4.00 10.00
JD Juan Dixon/300 4.00 10.00
JH Josh Howard/200 4.00 10.00
JK Jason Kapono/400 2.50 6.00
KK Kyle Korver/400 5.00 12.00
KR Kareem Rush/300 4.00 10.00
LR Luke Ridnour/500 3.00 8.00
LW Luke Walton/400 4.00 10.00
MB Marcus Banks/400 2.50 6.00
MG Manu Ginobili/200 12.00 30.00
MP Mickael Pietrus/300 3.00 8.00
NH Nene/250 4.00 10.00
PP Paul Pierce/200 6.00 15.00
PS Peja Stojakovic/200 6.00 15.00
RM Ronald Murray/250 4.00 10.00
SA Shareef Abdur-Rahim/250 4.00 10.00
SC Speedy Claxton/300 4.00 10.00
SM Shawn Marion/150 5.00 12.00
TC Tyson Chandler/400 5.00 12.00
TH Travis Hansen/400 2.50 6.00
TM Tracy McGrady/200 10.00 25.00
TP1 Tayshaun Prince/200 3.00 8.00
TP2 Tony Parker/200 8.00 20.00
UH Udonis Haslem/300 3.00 8.00
VC Vince Carter/600 8.00 20.00
WZ Wang Zhizhi/300 15.00 40.00
ZC Zarko Cabarkapa/300 2.50 6.00
ZP Zoran Planinic/300 2.50 6.00

2003-04 SkyBox Autographics Autographs Gold

*GOLD: .75X TO 2X BASE AU HI
PRINT RUN 50 SER.#'d SETS

2003-04 SkyBox Autographics Autographs Silver

*SILVER: .5X TO 1.25X BASE HI
PRINT RUN 150 SER.#'d SETS
SM Shawn Marion 5.00 12.00

2003-04 SkyBox Autographics Autographs on Location

Randomly seeded, this six card set parallels the base Autographs set enhanced with the words, "Autographs on Location" and is sequentially numbered to 99.

PRINT RUN 99 SER.#'d SETS
AW Antoine Walker 8.00 20.00
CA Carmelo Anthony 30.00 80.00
DW Dwyane Wade 40.00 100.00
PP Paul Pierce 15.00 40.00
TM Tracy McGrady 15.00 40.00
VC Vince Carter 10.00 25.00

2003-04 SkyBox Autographics Autographs Jerseys

Randomly inserted in packs, this seven card set parallels the design of the base Autographs set enhanced with a swatch of a game worn jersey and each card is sequentially numbered to 125.

PRINT RUN 125 SER.#'d SETS
CA Carmelo Anthony 40.00 80.00
MP Mickael Pietrus 6.00 15.00
TM Tracy McGrady 15.00 40.00
TP Tayshaun Prince 6.00 15.00
TP Tony Parker 10.00 25.00

2003-04 SkyBox Autographics Autographs Patches

PRINT RUN 25 SER.#'d SETS
CA Carmelo Anthony 100.00 200.00
TM Tracy McGrady 30.00 80.00
TP Tayshaun Prince 12.50 30.00

2003-04 SkyBox Autographics Jerseygraphics

Randomly inserted in packs, this 60-card set features a horizontal design with a close-up photo of the player's face along with a square-shaped swatch of game worn jersey. The borders on the card are blue, and each card is sequentially numbered to 350. Silver and Gold versions were also inserted. Silver is sequentially numbered to 150 and Gold to 50.

PRINT RUN 100 TO 350 SER.#'d SETS
*GOLD: .6X TO 1.5X BASE HI
GOLD PRINT RUN 50 SER.#'d SETS
AI Allen Iverson/350 4.00 10.00
AK Andrei Kirilenko/350 2.50 6.00
AS Amare Stoudemire/350 3.00 8.00
BD Baron Davis/350 2.00 5.00
BW1 Bonzi Wells/350 2.00 5.00
BW2 Ben Wallace/350 2.00 5.00
CA Carmelo Anthony/350 8.00 20.00
CB Chris Bosh/350 4.00 10.00
CK Chris Kaman/350 2.50 6.00
CW Chris Webber/220 2.50 6.00
DN Dirk Nowitzki/260 4.00 10.00
DW1 Dwyane Wade/350 8.00 20.00
DW2 David West/350 2.50 6.00
DW3 Dajuan Wagner/350 2.00 5.00
EB Elton Brand/350 2.50 6.00
EC Eddy Curry/350 1.50 4.00
GA Gilbert Arenas/350 2.00 5.00
GP Gary Payton/350 2.50 6.00
GR Glenn Robinson/350 2.00 5.00
JH Jarvis Hayes/350 1.50 4.00
JK Jason Kidd/350 4.00 10.00
JO Jermaine O'Neal/350 2.00 5.00
JR Jason Richardson/350 2.50 6.00
JS Jerry Stackhouse/350 2.00 5.00
KB Kwame Brown/350 2.00 5.00
KG Kevin Garnett/350 4.00 10.00
KM1 Karl Malone/350 3.00 8.00
KM2 Kenyon Martin/350 2.00 5.00
LS Latrell Sprewell/350 2.00 5.00
MB Marcus Banks/200 1.50 4.00
MB Mike Bibby/350 2.50 6.00
MD Mike Dunleavy/350 2.00 5.00
MF Michael Finley/160 2.50 6.00
MG Manu Ginobili/350 3.00 8.00
MP1 Mickael Pietrus/200 2.00 5.00
MP2 Morris Peterson/350 1.50 4.00
MR Michael Redd/350 2.50 6.00
MS Mike Sweetney/350 1.50 4.00
NH Nene/350 2.00 5.00
PG Pau Gasol/350 2.50 6.00
PP Paul Pierce/350 2.50 6.00
PS Peja Stojakovic/300 2.50 6.00
RA Ray Allen/350 2.50 6.00
RG Reece Gaines/350 1.50 4.00
RH Richard Hamilton/350 2.00 5.00
RM Reggie Miller/350 2.50 6.00
SA Shareef Abdur-Rahim/350 2.00 5.00
SF Steve Francis/350 2.00 5.00
SM1 Stephon Marbury/350 2.00 5.00
SM2 Shawn Marion/350 2.00 5.00
SO Shaquille O'Neal/350 6.00 15.00
SP Scottie Pippen/100 8.00 20.00
TC Tyson Chandler/350 2.00 5.00
TD Tim Duncan/350 4.00 10.00
TM Tracy McGrady/350 3.00 8.00
TO Travis Outlaw/350 2.00 5.00
TP1 Tayshaun Prince/350 2.00 5.00
TP2 Tony Parker/350 2.50 6.00
VC Vince Carter/350 4.00 10.00
YM Yao Ming/350 5.00 12.00

2003-04 SkyBox Autographics Jerseygraphics Silver

*SILVER: .5X TO 1.25X BASE JSY HI
PRINT RUN 150 SER.#'d SETS
SP Scottie Pippen 8.00 20.00

2003-04 SkyBox Autographics Rookies Affirmed

Inserted at the rate of one in four, this 15-card set features a horizontal design and pairs a rookie player with a veteran player. The background is gray and the player photos appear in black and white.

COMPLETE SET (15) 10.00 25.00
STATED ODDS 1:4
1 C.Anthony/T.McGrady 1.50 4.00
2 C.Bosh/V.Carter .75 2.00
3 D.West/J.Mashburn .50 1.25
4 T.Bell/P.Gasol .50 1.25
5 M.Pietrus/J.Richardson .50 1.25
6 D.Wade/J.Stackhouse 1.50 4.00
7 U.Haslem/S.Marbury .40 1.00
8 J.Hayes/R.Murray .30 .75
9 R.Gaines/T.Parker .50 1.25
10 M.Banks/P.Pierce .50 1.25
11 K.Hinrich/S.Nash .60 1.50
12 L.James/K.Bryant 12.00 30.00
13 C.Kaman/Y.Ming 1.00 2.50
14 T.Ford/A.Iverson .75 2.00
15 D.Milicic/D.Nowitzki .75 2.00

2003-04 SkyBox Autographics Rookies Affirmed Game-Used

Randomly seeded, this 10-card set parallels the base Rookies Affirmed set enhanced with a swatch of game-worn memorabilia from each of the two players and sequential numbering to 500.

PRINT RUN 500 SER.#'d SETS
*PATCH: 1X TO 2.5X BASE HI
PATCH PRINT RUN 50 SER.#'d SETS
CATM C.Anthony/T.McGrady 8.00 20.00
CBVC C.Bosh/V.Carter 6.00 15.00
DWAS D.West/J.Mashburn 4.00 10.00
DWRL D.Wade/J.Stackhouse 8.00 20.00
JHRM J.Hayes/R.Murray 4.00 10.00
MBPP M.Banks/P.Pierce 4.00 10.00
MPJR M.Pietrus/J.Richardson 4.00 10.00
RGTP R.Gaines/T.Parker 4.00 10.00
TBPG T.Bell/P.Gasol 4.00 10.00
UHBW U.Haslem/S.Marbury 4.00 10.00

2003-04 SkyBox Autographics Rookies Affirmed Game-Used Autographs

Randomly inserted and sequentially numbered to 50, this version of the Rookies Affirmed set boasts both memorabilia swatches and player autographs.

PRINT RUN 50 SER.#'d SETS
CATM C.Anthony/T.McGrady 75.00 150.00
DWRL D.Wade/J.Stackhouse 75.00 150.00
MBPP M.Banks/P.Pierce 15.00 40.00

2004-05 SkyBox Autographics

Releasaed in June 2005, Autographics boasts a 105-card checklist featuring 60 veteran players and 105 rookies serially numbered to 750. The base cards have tan backgrounds with accent team color along the top and a facsimile signature in silver foil tewards the bottom. The rookies are similar but do not feature a facsimile autograph. Skybox Autographics was offered in both Hobby and Retail formats where both were packaged in five card packs, but Hobby boxes contained 12 packs and retail, 24.

COMP.SET w/o SP's (60) 15.00 40.00
61-105 RC PRINT RUN 750 SER.#'d SETS
1 Dwyane Wade .60 1.50
2 Derek Fisher .30 .75
3 Latrell Sprewell .30 .75
4 Peja Stojakovic .40 1.00
5 LeBron James 2.50 6.00
6 Elton Brand .40 1.00
7 Allan Houston .30 .75
8 Chris Bosh .40 1.00
9 Carmelo Anthony .75 2.00
10 Shaquille O'Neal 1.00 2.50
11 Steve Nash .50 1.25
12 Antawn Jamison .30 .75
13 Darko Milicic .25 .60
14 Michael Redd .30 .75
15 Shawn Marion .30 .75
16 Dirk Nowitzki .60 1.50
17 Kobe Bryant 1.50 4.00
18 Steve Francis .30 .75
19 Carlos Boozer .30 .75
20 Karl Malone .50 1.25
21 T.J. Ford .25 .60
22 Darius Miles .25 .60
23 Paul Pierce .40 1.00
24 Jermaine O'Neal .30 .75
25 Baron Davis .30 .75
26 Tony Parker .40 1.00
27 Kirk Hinrich .30 .75
28 Chris Kaman .30 .75
29 Stephon Marbury .30 .75
30 Rashard Lewis .40 1.00
31 Ben Wallace .30 .75
32 Antoine Walker .40 1.00
33 Amare Stoudemire .30 .75
34 Gary Payton .40 1.00
35 Yao Ming .75 2.00
36 Richard Jefferson .30 .75
37 Tim Duncan .60 1.50
38 Drew Gooden .25 .60
39 Lamar Odom .30 .75
40 Grant Hill .50 1.25
41 Vince Carter .60 1.50
42 Michael Finley .40 1.00
43 Jason Williams .30 .75
44 Samuel Dalembert .25 .60
45 Andrei Kirilenko .30 .75
46 Jason Kapono .25 .60
47 Reggie Miller .40 1.00
48 Jamaal Magloire .25 .60
49 Ray Allen .40 1.00
50 Kenyon Martin .30 .75
51 Pau Gasol .40 1.00
52 Allen Iverson .60 1.50
53 Gilbert Arenas .30 .75
54 Jason Richardson .40 1.00
55 Kevin Garnett .60 1.50
56 Zach Randolph .30 .75
57 Al Harrington .30 .75
58 Tracy McGrady .50 1.25
59 Jason Kidd .60 1.50
60 Chris Webber .40 1.00
61 Andris Biedrins RC 1.00 2.50
62 Robert Swift RC 1.00 2.50
63 Pavel Podkolzin RC 1.00 2.50
64 Kevin Martin RC 2.00 5.00
65 Beno Udrih RC 1.25 3.00
66 David Harrison RC 1.00 2.50

67 Andre Emmett RC 1.00 2.50
68 Emeka Okafor RC 1.25 3.00
69 Dwight Howard RC 3.00 8.00
70 Ben Gordon RC 1.50 4.00
71 Shaun Livingston RC 1.50 4.00
72 Devin Harris RC 1.25 3.00
73 Josh Childress RC 1.25 3.00
74 Luol Deng RC 1.50 4.00
75 Rafael Araujo RC 1.00 2.50
76 Andre Iguodala RC 2.00 5.00
77 Luke Jackson RC 1.00 2.50
78 Sebastian Telfair RC 1.25 3.00
79 Kris Humphries RC 1.50 4.00
80 Al Jefferson RC 2.00 5.00
81 Kirk Snyder RC 1.00 2.50
82 Josh Smith RC 1.50 4.00
83 J.R. Smith RC 1.50 4.00
84 Dorell Wright RC 1.50 4.00
85 Jameer Nelson RC 1.50 4.00
86 Delonte West RC 1.50 4.00
87 Tony Allen RC 1.50 4.00
88 Sasha Vujacic RC 1.50 4.00
89 Andres Nocioni RC 1.50 4.00
90 Royal Ivey RC 1.25 3.00
91 Trevor Ariza RC 1.50 4.00
92 Chris Duhon RC 1.50 4.00
93 John Edwards RC 1.00 2.50
94 Jackson Vroman RC 1.00 2.50
95 Quinton Ross 1.00 2.50
96 Erik Daniels RC 1.25 3.00
97 Anderson Varejao RC 1.25 3.00
98 Lionel Chalmers RC 1.50 4.00
99 Carlos Delfino 1.00 2.50
100 Jared Reiner RC 1.50 4.00
101 Bernard Robinson RC 1.25 3.00
102 Peter John Ramos RC 1.00 2.50
103 D.J. Mbenga RC 1.25 3.00
104 Mario Kasun RC 1.25 3.00
105 Nenad Krstic RC 1.50 4.00

2004-05 SkyBox Autographics Insignia

*1-60 INSIGNIA: 2.5X TO 6X BASE HI
*61-105 INSIGNIA: .5X TO 1.25X BASE HI
PRINT RUN 150 SER.#'d SETS

2004-05 SkyBox Autographics Insignia 25

*1-60 INSIGNIA: 6X TO 15X BASE HI
*61-105 INSIGNIA: 1.5X TO 4X BASE HI
PRINT RUN 25 SER.#'d SETS

2004-05 SkyBox Autographics Autographs Jerseys

Randomly inserted in packs at the rate of one in 20, this 31-card set features a horizontal design with player photos on the left, a square swatch of jersey on the right and a cut signature below it. Some players were issued and individually numbered, so they are listed in the checklist with print runs. Several different parallels were issued and break down as follows: the 100 set is serially numbered to 100, the 30 set is serially numbered to 30, Embossed is serially numbered to 65 and Embossed 8 is serially numbered to eight.

STATED ODDS 1:20
*AU JSY 100: .5X TO 1.25X BASE AU JSY HI
BASE SER.#'d VER. DO NOT HAVE 100 AU
*AU JSY 30: .6X TO 1.5X BASE AU JSY HI
*EMBOSS: .5X TO 1.25X BASE AU JSY HI
*#'d VER.EMBOSS SAME VALUE AS BASE
EMBOSSED PRINT RUN 65 SER.#'d SETS
AJ Antawn Jamison/76 4.00 10.00
AK Andrei Kirilenko 4.00 10.00
BD Baron Davis/24 10.00 25.00
BD Boris Diaw 4.00 10.00
BW Ben Wallace 12.50 30.00
CA Carlos Arroyo 3.00 8.00
CB Carlos Boozer/29 8.00 20.00
CD Chris Duhon/47 5.00 12.00
CD Carlos Delfino 3.00 8.00
DH David Harrison 3.00 8.00
DW David West 4.00 10.00
JD Juan Dixon 3.00 8.00
JH Josh Howard 5.00 12.00
LW Luke Walton 3.00 8.00
MD Mike Dunleavy/20 4.00 10.00
MP Mickael Pietrus 4.00 10.00
NC Nick Collison/53 4.00 10.00
PS Peja Stojakovic/53 15.00 30.00
QR Quinton Ross 3.00 8.00
RH Richard Hamilton/90 10.00 25.00
TO Travis Outlaw 4.00 10.00
VC Vince Carter 12.50 30.00

2004-05 SkyBox Autographics Autographs Patches

Randomly inserted, this 31-card set parallels the base Autographs Jerseys set enhanced with patch swatches and sequential numbering to 75.

PRINT RUN 75 SER.#'d SETS
PATCHES 10 UNPRICED DUE TO SCARCITY
*AU EMBOSSED: .4X TO 1X BASE HI
AU EMBOSS PRINT RUN 50 SER.#'d SETS
AU EMBOSS 5 UNPRICED DUE TO SCARCITY
AK Andrei Kirilenko 15.00 40.00
AV Anderson Varejao 10.00 25.00
AW Antoine Walker 15.00 40.00
BD Boris Diaw 12.50 30.00
BW Ben Wallace 15.00 40.00
CA Carlos Arroyo 20.00 50.00
CB Carlos Boozer 10.00 25.00
GA Gilbert Arenas 10.00 25.00
JD Juan Dixon 10.00 25.00
LW Luke Walton 10.00 25.00
MD Mike Dunleavy 10.00 25.00
MP Mickael Pietrus 10.00 25.00
NC Nick Collison 10.00 25.00
QR Quinton Ross 10.00 25.00
RH Richard Hamilton 20.00 50.00

2004-05 SkyBox Autographics Future Signs

Inserted in Hobby packs at the rate of one in six and Retail at the rate of one in 12, this 20-card set places player portrait photos on the top in colors that match their team color's highlights wih tan and white borders.

COMPLETE SET (20) 10.00 25.00
STATED ODDS 1:6 H, 1:12 R
1 Andris Biedrins .40 1.00
2 Robert Swift .40 1.00
3 Pavel Podkolzin .40 1.00
4 Ben Gordon .60 1.50
5 Shaun Livingston .60 1.50
6 Devin Harris .50 1.25
7 Josh Childress .50 1.25
8 Luol Deng .60 1.50
9 Rafael Araujo .40 1.00
10 Luke Jackson .40 1.00
11 Sebastian Telfair .50 1.25
12 Kris Humphries .60 1.50
13 Al Jefferson .75 2.00
14 Kirk Snyder .40 1.00
15 Josh Smith .60 1.50
16 J.R. Smith .60 1.50
17 Dorell Wright .60 1.50
18 Jameer Nelson .60 1.50
19 Delonte West .60 1.50
20 Tony Allen .60 1.50

2004-05 SkyBox Autographics Future Signs Autographs

Randomly seeded in packs at the rate of one in 19, this 16-card set parallels the desing of the Future Signs set enhanced with a player autograph along the bottom of the card.

STATED ODDS 1:19
*AUTO 100: .5X TO 1.25X BASE AU HI
*AUTO 50: .75X TO 2X BASE AU HI
*AUTO EMBOSS: .6X TO 1.5X BASE AU HI
AU EMBOSS PRINT RUN 85 SER.#'d SETS
*AUTO EMBOSS 20: 1X TO 2.5X BASE HI
AB Andris Biedrins 2.50 6.00
AJ Al Jefferson 5.00 12.00
BG Ben Gordon 4.00 10.00
DW Dorell Wright 4.00 10.00
DW2 Delonte West 4.00 10.00
JC Josh Childress 3.00 8.00
JS2 J.R. Smith 4.00 10.00
KH Kris Humphries 4.00 10.00
KS Kirk Snyder 2.50 6.00
LD Luol Deng 4.00 10.00
PP Pavel Podkolzin 2.50 6.00
RA Rafael Araujo 2.50 6.00

2004-05 SkyBox Autographics Future Signs Autographs Patches

PRINT RUN 70 SER.#'d SETS
JS2 J.R. Smith 10.00 25.00
KH Kris Humphries 10.00 25.00
RA Rafael Araujo 6.00 15.00

2004-05 SkyBox Autographics Jerseygraphics

Randomly inserted in Retail packs at the rate of one in 40, this 17-card set features a horizontal design that places player photos on the left and jersey swatches on the right towards the top.

STATED ODDS 1:40 RETAIL
AI Allen Iverson 4.00 10.00
AS Amare Stoudemire 2.00 5.00
BD Boris Diaw 2.00 5.00
CA Carmelo Anthony 5.00 12.00
CB Chris Bosh 2.50 6.00
DN Dirk Nowitzki 4.00 10.00
DW Dajuan Wagner 2.00 5.00
JD Juan Dixon 2.00 5.00
JO Jermaine O'Neal 2.00 5.00
KB Kevin Garnett 4.00 10.00
MD Mike Dunleavy 2.00 5.00
MG Manu Ginobili 3.00 8.00
MJ Marko Jaric 2.00 5.00
MS Mike Sweetney 2.00 5.00
SF Steve Francis 2.00 5.00
SM Stephon Marbury 2.00 5.00
VC Vince Carter 4.00 10.00

2004-05 SkyBox Autographics Master Collection

PRINT RUN 25 SER.#'d SETS
BW Ben Wallace 15.00 40.00
CB Charles Barkley 300.00 600.00
CB2 Carlos Boozer 15.00 40.00
DW Dwyane Wade 100.00 200.00
EB Elton Brand 15.00 40.00
GP Gary Payton 25.00 60.00
LD Luol Deng 30.00 80.00
PS Peja Stojakovic 20.00 50.00
SM Shawn Marion 15.00 40.00
TP Tony Parker 15.00 40.00
VC Vince Carter 30.00 80.00

2004-05 SkyBox Autographics Signature Moves

Inserted in Hobby packs at the rate of one in 12 and Retail at the rate of one in 24, this 10-card set has white borders along the top, full-color player action photos in the middle and is highlighted with irridescent foil.

COMPLETE SET (10) 8.00 20.00
STATED ODDS 1:12 H, 1:24 R
1 Allen Iverson 1.00 2.50
2 LeBron James 4.00 10.00
3 Carmelo Anthony 1.25 3.00
4 Shaquille O'Neal 1.50 4.00
5 Kobe Bryant 2.50 6.00
6 Vince Carter 1.00 2.50
7 Tracy McGrady .75 2.00
8 Jason Kidd 1.00 2.50
9 Kevin Garnett 1.00 2.50
10 Tim Duncan 1.00 2.50

1990-91 SkyBox Broadcasters

These four standard-size cards were issued to the respective NBC announcers to hand out as business cards. Production quantities remain unknown. The cards have the same design as the 1990-91 SkyBox regular issue, with computer-generated backgrounds, gold borders, and photos on both sides. The backs also have biographical information on the announcers. The cards are unnumbered and checklisted below in alphabetical order.

COMPLETE SET (4) 100.00 250.00
1 Bob Costas 40.00 100.00
2 Julie Moran 20.00 40.00
(Michael Jordan on back)
3 Ahmad Rashad 15.00 30.00
4 Pat Riley 40.00 100.00

1991-92 SkyBox Canadian Minis

This set of 50 mini-trading cards was a sports promotion in Canada involving SkyBox and Hostess/Frito Lay. The miniature cards measure 1 1/4" by 1 3/4,". One card was inserted into each specially marked bag of Hostess/Frito Lay products, including Doritos, Ruffles, Cheetos, O'Ryans, and Hostess. It was claimed that nine out of every ten bags contained a card, and in the event that the consumer purchased a bag without a card, a card could be obtained without charge through a mail-in offer. The promotion ran January 20 through March, and was supported by colorful displays at more than 75,000 locations in Canada as well as televisions ads. The card design was identical to the regular issue, with the exception that the backs feature bilingual information.

COMPLETE SET (50) 8.00 20.00
1 Kevin Willis .08 .25
2 Larry Bird 1.00 2.50
3 Kevin McHale .30 .75
4 Robert Parish .20 .50
5 Kendall Gill .20 .50
6 J.R. Reid .08 .25
7 Michael Jordan 2.50 6.00
8 Scottie Pippen .75 2.00
9 Brad Daugherty .08 .25
10 Larry Nance .20 .50
11 Rolando Blackman .20 .50
12 Derek Harper .20 .50
13 Chris Jackson .08 .25
14 Jerome Lane .08 .25
15 Joe Dumars .40 1.00
16 Dennis Rodman .60 1.50
17 Tim Hardaway .40 1.00
18 Chris Mullin .40 1.00
19 Hakeem Olajuwon .60 1.50
20 Otis Thorpe .20 .50
21 Reggie Miller .60 1.50
22 Detlef Schrempf .20 .50
23 Danny Manning .20 .50
24 Charles Smith .08 .25
25 Magic Johnson .75 2.00
26 James Worthy .40 1.00
27 Sherman Douglas .08 .25
28 Rony Seikaly .08 .25
29 Alvin Robertson .08 .25
30 Tony Campbell .08 .25
31 Derrick Coleman .20 .50
32 Charles Oakley .20 .50
33 Dennis Scott .08 .25
34 Scott Skiles .20 .50
35 Charles Barkley .60 1.50
36 Hersey Hawkins .20 .50
37 Jeff Hornacek .30 .75
38 Kevin Johnson .30 .75
39 Clyde Drexler .60 1.50
40 Terry Porter .08 .25
41 Wayman Tisdale .08 .25
42 Terry Cummings .08 .25
43 David Robinson .75 2.00
44 Shawn Kemp .30 .75
45 Ricky Pierce .08 .25
46 Karl Malone .75 2.00
47 John Stockton .75 2.00
48 Harvey Grant .08 .25
49 Bernard King .30 .75
50 Checklist Card .08 .25

1999-00 SkyBox Dominion

The premier release of Dominion replaces the SkyBox Thunder brand. The set was released in one series as a 220-card set with 175 base cards, 20 rookies and two subsets: 3 for All and World Tour. The cards feature a color action shot of the player against a black and white background.

COMPLETE SET (220) 15.00 40.00
1 Jason Williams .25 .60
2 Isaiah Rider .15 .40
3 Tim Hardaway .20 .50
4 Isaac Austin .12 .30
5 Joe Smith .15 .40
6 Mitch Richmond .20 .50
7 Sam Mitchell .12 .30
8 Terrell Brandon .12 .30
9 Grant Long .12 .30
10 Shaquille O'Neal .50 1.25
11 Derrick Coleman .15 .40
12 Rod Strickland .12 .30
13 J.R. Reid .12 .30
14 Tyrone Corbin .12 .30
15 Jeff Hornacek .15 .40
16 Malik Rose .12 .30
17 Terry Davis .12 .30
18 Theo Ratliff .15 .40
19 Kevin Willis .12 .30
20 Raef LaFrentz .15 .40
21 Othella Harrington .12 .30
22 Marcus Camby .15 .40
23 Keon Clark .12 .30
24 Robert Pack .12 .30
25 Sam Mack .12 .30
26 Shawn Kemp .20 .50
27 Nick Anderson .12 .30
28 Bill Wennington .12 .30
29 Steve Smith .15 .40
30 Kobe Bryant .75 2.00
31 Bobby Phills .12 .30
32 Cedric Ceballos .12 .30
33 Derek Fisher .20 .50
34 Doug Christie .15 .40
35 Danny Manning .15 .40
36 Eric Murdock .12 .30
37 Glen Rice .20 .50
38 Dikembe Mutombo .20 .50
39 Jason Kidd .30 .75
40 Cedric Henderson .12 .30
41 Rasheed Wallace .20 .50
42 Tim Duncan .40 1.00
43 John Stockton .25 .60
44 Dell Curry .12 .30
45 Muggsy Bogues .15 .40
46 Danny Fortson .12 .30
47 Charles Oakley .15 .40
48 Elden Campbell .12 .30
49 Tony Massenburg .12 .30
50 Kevin Garnett .30 .75
51 Cherokee Parks .12 .30
52 LaPhonso Ellis .12 .30
53 Sam Cassell .15 .40
54 Shawn Bradley .12 .30
55 David Robinson .30 .75
56 Juwan Howard .15 .40
57 Lindsey Hunter .12 .30
58 Mark Jackson .15 .40
59 Olden Polynice .12 .30
60 Tracy McGrady .30 .75
61 Michael Finley .20 .50
62 Matt Geiger .12 .30
63 Maurice Taylor .12 .30
64 Rex Chapman .12 .30
65 Chris Mullin .20 .50
66 Ray Allen .20 .50
67 Bison Dele .12 .30
68 Dickey Simpkins .12 .30
69 Alvin Williams .12 .30
70 Grant Hill .25 .60
71 Mark Bryant .12 .30
72 Adam Keefe .12 .30
73 Alan Henderson .12 .30
74 Eric Snow .15 .40
75 Matt Harpring .12 .30
76 Jalen Rose .15 .40
77 Derek Harper .15 .40
78 Kerry Kittles .12 .30
79 Tony Battie .15 .40
80 Larry Hughes .15 .40
81 Arvydas Sabonis .15 .40
82 Allan Houston .15 .40
83 Tom Gugliotta .12 .30
84 Reggie Miller .20 .50
85 Dejuan Wheat .12 .30
86 Pat Garrity .12 .30
87 Karl Malone .25 .60
88 Sam Perkins .12 .30
89 Michael Olowokandi .12 .30
90 Anfernee Hardaway .30 .75
91 Bryant Reeves .12 .30
92 Gary Trent .12 .30
93 George Lynch .12 .30
94 Scottie Pippen .30 .75
95 Jerry Stackhouse .20 .50
96 Kendall Gill .12 .30
97 Vin Baker .15 .40
98 Dale Davis .12 .30
99 Charles Barkley .30 .75
100 Allen Iverson .40 1.00
101 Keith Van Horn .15 .40
102 Andrew DeClercq .12 .30
103 Michael Doleac .12 .30
104 Chauncey Billups .20 .50
105 Chris Mills .12 .30
106 Lamond Murray .12 .30
107 Glenn Robinson .15 .40
108 Brian Grant .12 .30
109 Christian Laettner .15 .40
110 Antawn Jamison .20 .50
111 Erick Dampier .12 .30
112 Vernon Maxwell .12 .30
113 Kenny Anderson .15 .40
114 Clarence Weatherspoon .12 .30
115 Corliss Williamson .12 .30
116 Paul Pierce .25 .60
117 Clifford Robinson .12 .30
118 Damon Stoudamire .15 .40
119 Dana Barros .12 .30
120 Stephon Marbury .15 .40
120B Stephon Marbury PROMO .60 1.50
121 Latrell Sprewell .20 .50
122 Tyronn Lue .12 .30
123 Walt Williams .12 .30
124 P.J. Brown .12 .30
125 Gary Payton .20 .50
126 Nick Van Exel .15 .40
127 Bryant Stith .12 .30
128 Eric Piatkowski .15 .40
129 Tyrone Nesby RC .15 .40
130 Ron Mercer .15 .40
131 Hersey Hawkins .12 .30
132 Vlade Divac .20 .50
133 Darrick Martin .12 .30
134 Avery Johnson .15 .40
135 Jaren Jackson .12 .30
136 Brevin Knight .12 .30
137 Wesley Person .12 .30
138 Derek Anderson .12 .30
139 Tim Thomas .15 .40
140 Antonio McDyess .15 .40
141 A.C. Green .15 .40
142 Chris Webber .20 .50
143 Scott Burrell .12 .30
144 John Starks .15 .40
145 Howard Eisley .12 .30
146 Mike Bibby .20 .50
147 Toni Kukoc .20 .50
148 Eddie Jones .20 .50
149 Otis Thorpe .12 .30
150 Shareef Abdur-Rahim .15 .40
151 Calbert Cheaney .12 .30
152 Cuttino Mobley .12 .30
153 Michael Dickerson .12 .30
154 Sean Elliott .20 .50
155 Terry Porter .12 .30
156 Dean Garrett .12 .30
157 Charlie Ward .12 .30
158 Larry Johnson .20 .50
159 Dan Majerle .20 .50
160 Jayson Williams .12 .30
161 Anthony Peeler .12 .30
162 Ron Harper .12 .30
163 Darrell Armstrong .12 .30
164 Kurt Thomas .12 .30
165 Brent Barry .15 .40
166 Lawrence Funderburke .12 .30
167 Terry Cummings .15 .40
168 Jamal Mashburn .15 .40
169 Robert Traylor .12 .30
170 Greg Ostertag .12 .30
171 Brad Miller .15 .40
172 Mario Elie .12 .30
173 Antoine Walker .20 .50
174 Ricky Davis .20 .50
175 Vince Carter .40 1.00
176 Hakeem Olajuwon WT .25 .60
177 Luc Longley WT .15 .40
178 Tim Duncan WT .40 1.00
179 Rick Fox WT .12 .30
180 Zydrunas Ilgauskas WT .15 .40
181 Toni Kukoc WT .20 .50
182 Felipe Lopez WT .12 .30
183 Dikembe Mutombo WT .20 .50
184 Steve Nash WT .30 .75
185 Dirk Nowitzki WT .40 1.00
186 Vitaly Potapenko WT .12 .30
187 Detlef Schrempf WT .15 .40
188 Rik Smits WT .20 .50
189 Vladimir Stepania WT .12 .30
190 Peja Stojakovic WT .20 .50
191 Donyell Marshall 3FA .12 .30
192 Shareef Abdur-Rahim 3FA .15 .40
193 Michael Dickerson 3FA .12 .30
194 Damon Stoudamire 3FA .15 .40
195 Allen Iverson 3FA .40 1.00
196 Grant Hill 3FA .25 .60
197 Scottie Pippen 3FA .30 .75
198 Bryon Russell 3FA .12 .30
199 Alonzo Mourning 3FA .25 .60
200 Patrick Ewing 3FA .25 .60
201 Ron Artest RC .40 1.00
202 William Avery RC .15 .40
203 Lamar Odom RC .50 1.25
204 Baron Davis RC .50 1.25
205 John Celestand RC .12 .30
206 Jumaine Jones RC .15 .40
207 Andre Miller RC .40 1.00
208 Elton Brand RC .50 1.25
209 James Posey RC .20 .50
210 Jason Terry RC .30 .75
211 Kenny Thomas RC .20 .50
212 Steve Francis RC .50 1.25
213 Wally Szczerbiak RC .40 1.00
214 Richard Hamilton RC .40 1.00
215 Jonathan Bender RC .20 .50
216 Shawn Marion RC .40 1.00
217 A.Radojevic RC .12 .30
218 Tim James RC .12 .30
219 Trajan Langdon RC .20 .50
220 Corey Maggette RC .30 .75

1999-00 SkyBox Dominion 2 Point Play

Randomly inserted in packs at one in nine, this 10-card set features two players who are similar in their games.

COMPLETE SET (10) 5.00 12.00
STATED ODDS 1:9
*PLUS: .75X TO 2X HI COLUMN
PLUS: STATED ODDS 1:90
*WARP TEK: 12X TO 30X HI COLUMN
WARP TEK: STATED ODDS 1:900
1 K.Van Horn/G.Hill .60 1.50
2 P.Pierce/S.Pippen .75 2.00
3 T.Duncan/K.Garnett 1.00 2.50
4 K.Bryant/V.Carter 2.00 5.00
5 S.O'Neal/M.Olowokandi 1.25 3.00
6 C.Webber/S.Kemp .50 1.25
7 J.Williams/A.Iverson 1.00 2.50
8 S.Marbury/A.Hardaway .75 2.00
9 J.Kidd/M.Bibby .75 2.00
10 S.Abdur-Rahim/A.McDyess .40 1.00

1999-00 SkyBox Dominion Game Day 2K

Randomly inserted in packs at one in three, this 20-card set focuses on young players destined to lead the NBA into the next century. The cards are featured on silver foil.

COMPLETE SET (20) 4.00 10.00
STATED ODDS 1:3
*PLUS: 1.5X TO 4X HI COLUMN
PLUS: STATED ODDS 1:30
1 Vince Carter .60 1.50
2 Kobe Bryant 1.25 3.00
3 Dirk Nowitzki .60 1.50
4 Cuttino Mobley .20 .50
5 Kevin Garnett .50 1.25
6 Stephon Marbury .25 .60
7 Shaquille O'Neal .75 2.00
8 Keith Van Horn .25 .60
9 Paul Pierce .40 1.00
10 Jason Williams .40 1.00
11 Mike Bibby .30 .75
12 Michael Dickerson .20 .50
13 Antawn Jamison .30 .75
14 Raef LaFrentz .25 .60
15 Tyrone Nesby .25 .60
16 Ron Mercer .25 .60
17 Tracy McGrady .50 1.25
18 Larry Hughes .25 .60
19 Robert Traylor .20 .50
20 Michael Doleac .20 .50

1999-00 SkyBox Dominion Game Day 2K Warp Tek

*WARP TEK: 8X TO 20X VALUE
STATED ODDS 1:300
2 Kobe Bryant 40.00 100.00

1999-00 SkyBox Dominion Hats Off

Randomly inserted in packs, this 14-card set features top players from the 1999 NBA Draft and the hats they wore on Draft Day. Each hat was cut up and a piece from it is mounted on each card. Each card is serially numbered and listed below.

PRINT RUNS LISTED BELOW
1 Elton Brand/135 10.00 25.00
2 Steve Francis/170 10.00 25.00
3 Baron Davis/170 10.00 25.00
4 Wally Szczerbiak/140 8.00 20.00
5 Richard Hamilton/150 8.00 20.00
6 Andre Miller/140 8.00 20.00
7 Shawn Marion/150 8.00 20.00
8 Jason Terry/170 6.00 15.00
9 A.Radojevic/135 2.50 6.00
10 William Avery/185 3.00 8.00
11 Ron Artest/140 8.00 20.00
12 James Posey/170 4.00 10.00
13 Tim James/140 2.50 6.00
14 Jumaine Jones/135 3.00 8.00

1999-00 SkyBox Dominion Sky's the Limit

Randomly inserted in packs at one in 24, this 15-card set features talented NBA players who are head and shoulders above the rest of the league. The cards feature silver foil on the front.

COMPLETE SET (15) 12.50 30.00
STATED ODDS 1:24
*PLUS: 1.5X TO 4X HI COLUMN
PLUS: STATED ODDS 1:240
*WARP TEK: 15X TO 40X VALUE
WARP TEK: PRINT RUN 25 SERIAL #'d SETS
1 Kevin Garnett 1.50 4.00
2 Jason Williams 1.25 3.00
3 Grant Hill 1.25 3.00
4 Keith Van Horn .75 2.00
5 Allen Iverson 2.00 5.00
6 Ron Mercer .75 2.00
7 Anfernee Hardaway 1.50 4.00
8 Kobe Bryant 4.00 10.00
9 Shareef Abdur-Rahim .75 2.00
10 Jason Kidd 1.50 4.00
11 Shaquille O'Neal 2.50 6.00
12 Stephon Marbury .75 2.00
13 Paul Pierce 1.25 3.00
14 Tim Duncan 2.00 5.00
15 Vince Carter 2.00 5.00

2000 SkyBox Dominion WNBA

Released for the first time in 2000, this 156-card set features players from the WNBA. Each pack carried 10 cards. Cards featured an action shot of each player against a white background. The player's name and team were in silver foil. The base set contained 104 regular player cards, 22 Expansion Draft cards and 30 Smooth Moves cards.

COMPLETE SET (156) 10.00 25.00
SUBSET CARDS HALF VALUE OF BASE CARDS
1 Cynthia Cooper 1.25 3.00
2 Sue Wicks .30 .75
3 Clarisse Machanguana RC .20 .50
4 Adrienne Goodson .20 .50
5 Astou Ndiaye RC .60 1.50
6 Crystal Robinson .20 .50
7 Tora Suber .30 .75
8 Lady Hardmon .20 .50
9 Maria Stepanova .20 .50
10 Mwadi Mabika .20 .50
11 Rebecca Lobo .60 1.50
12 Ticha Penicheiro .50 1.25
13 Vicky Bullett .30 .75
14 Adia Barnes .20 .50
15 Andrea Stinson .40 1.00
16 Sheryl Swoopes 1.25 3.00
17 Heather Owen RC .20 .50
18 Andrea Congreaves .20 .50
19 Brandy Reed .30 .75
20 Dawn Staley .50 1.25
21 Jennifer Rizzotti RC 1.00 2.50
22 Latasha Byears .30 .75
23 Merlakia Jones .30 .75
24 Niesa Johnson RC .20 .50
25 Rushia Brown .20 .50
26 Taj McWilliams RC .30 .75
27 Wendy Palmer .50 1.25
28 Krystyna Lara RC .30 .75
29 Andrea Lloyd Curry RC .30 .75
30 Carla McGhee .20 .50
31 DeLisha Milton .20 .50
32 Katie Smith .60 1.50
33 Mery Andrade .20 .50
34 Nikki McCray .50 1.25
35 Ruthie Bolton-Holifield .60 1.50
36 Tamecka Dixon .30 .75
37 Tracy Henderson RC .20 .50
38 Yolanda Griffith .60 1.50
39 LaTonya Johnson .20 .50
40 Coquese Washington .20 .50
41 Chamique Holdsclaw 1.25 3.00
42 Dominique Canty RC .60 1.50
43 Kedra Holland-Corn RC .30 .75
44 Michele Timms .60 1.50
45 Nykesha Sales .30 .75
46 Shalonda Enis RC .20 .50
47 Tamika Whitmore RC .30 .75
48 Tracy Reid .30 .75
49 Kate Starbird .30 .75
50 Amanda Wilson RC .60 1.50
51 Sonia Chase RC .30 .75
52 Elaine Powell .20 .50
53 Michelle Edwards .40 1.00
54 Olympia Scott-Richardson .20 .50
55 Shannon Johnson .20 .50
56 Tammy Jackson .20 .50
57 Ukari Figgs .20 .50
58 Linda Burgess .20 .50
59 Angie Braziel RC .40 1.00
60 Tricia Bader RC .20 .50
61 Adrienne Johnson .30 .75
62 Chasity Melvin RC .20 .50
63 Korie Hlede .30 .75
64 Michelle Griffiths .20 .50
65 Penny Moore .30 .75
66 Sheri Sam .20 .50
67 Tangela Smith .20 .50
68 Val Whiting .20 .50
69 Angie Potthoff .20 .50
70 Cindy Brown .30 .75
71 Kristin Folkl .30 .75
72 Lisa Leslie 1.00 2.50
73 Monica Lamb .20 .50
74 Teresa Weatherspoon .75 2.00
75 Valerie Still RC .60 1.50
76 Tonya Edwards .20 .50
77 Heather Quella RC .30 .75
78 Cass Bauer RC .50 1.25
79 Bridget Pettis .20 .50
80 Cindy Blodgett .30 .75
81 Janeth Arcain .20 .50
82 Kym Hampton .30 .75
83 Margo Dydek .40 1.00
84 Murriel Page .25 .60
85 Sonja Tate .20 .50
86 Vickie Johnson .30 .75
87 Eva Nemcova .30 .75
88 Charlotte Smith .20 .50
89 Venus Lacy RC .20 .50
90 Polina Tzekova RC .20 .50
91 Dalma Ivanyi RC .20 .50
92 Allison Feaster .25 .60
93 Becky Hammon RC 2.50 6.00
94 Amaya Valdemoro RC .30 .75
95 Jennifer Gillom .50 1.25
96 La'Keshia Frett RC .20 .50
97 Markita Aldridge RC .20 .50
98 Natalie Williams .40 1.00
99 Rhonda Mapp .25 .60
100 Suzie McConnell-Serio .40 1.00
101 Tina Thompson .60 1.50
102 Wanda Guyton .20 .50
103 Lisa Harrison RC .50 1.25
104 Andrea Nagy RC .50 1.25
105 Edna Campbell ED .25 .60
106 Nina Bjedov ED RC .20 .50
107 Sonja Henning ED RC .30 .75
108 Toni Foster ED .30 .75
109 Angela Aycock ED RC .30 .75
110 Charmin Smith ED RC .50 1.25
111 Chantel Tremitiere ED .20 .50
112 Gordana Grubin ED RC .20 .50
113 Kara Wolters ED .25 .60
114 Rita Williams ED .25 .60
115 Stephanie McCarty ED .40 1.00
116 Monica Maxwell ED RC .20 .50
117 Debbie Black ED .30 .75
118 Elena Baranova ED .50 1.25
119 Sharon Manning ED .20 .50
120 Molly Goodenbour ED RC .20 .50
121 Alisa Burras ED RC .30 .75
122 Mila Nikolich ED RC .20 .50
123 Jamila Wideman ED .30 .75
124 Michele VanGorp ED .25 .60
125 Sophia Witherspoon ED .30 .75
126 Tari Phillips ED .20 .50
127 Sheri Sam SM .10 .25
128 Mwadi Mabika SM .10 .25
129 Murriel Page SM .12 .30
130 Latasha Byears SM .15 .40
131 Dominique Canty SM .30 .75
132 Crystal Robinson SM .10 .25
133 Cynthia Cooper SM .60 1.50
134 Ruthie Bolton-Holifield SM .30 .75
135 Cindy Brown SM .15 .40
136 Kristin Folkl SM .15 .40
137 Jennifer Gillom SM .25 .60
138 Adrienne Goodson SM .10 .25
139 Vickie Johnson SM .15 .40
140 Merlakia Jones SM .15 .40
141 Rebecca Lobo SM .30 .75
142 Nikki McCray SM .25 .60
143 Suzie McConnell-Serio SM .20 .50
144 DeLisha Milton SM .10 .25
145 Eva Nemcova SM .15 .40
146 Wendy Palmer SM .25 .60
147 Brandy Reed SM .15 .40
148 Nykesha Sales SM .15 .40
149 Andrea Stinson SM .20 .50
150 Michele Timms SM .30 .75
151 Valerie Still SM .30 .75
152 Andrea Nagy SM .25 .60
153 Tonya Edwards SM .10 .25
154 Taj McWilliams SM .15 .40
155 Kedra Holland-Corn SM .15 .40
156 Maria Stepanova SM .10 .25

2000 SkyBox Dominion WNBA Extra

COMPLETE SET (156) 75.00 150.00
*EXTRA: 1.5X TO 4X BASE CARD HI
STATED ODDS 1:3

2000 SkyBox Dominion WNBA All-WNBA

Randomly inserted in packs at one in 18, this 10-card set features players from the All-WNBA First and Second Teams from 1999. Card backs carry an "AW" prefix.

COMPLETE SET (10) 12.50 30.00
AW1 Sheryl Swoopes 4.00 10.00
AW2 Natalie Williams 1.25 3.00
AW3 Yolanda Griffith 2.00 5.00
AW4 Cynthia Cooper 4.00 10.00
AW5 Ticha Penicheiro 1.50 4.00
AW6 Chamique Holdsclaw 4.00 10.00
AW7 Tina Thompson 2.00 5.00
AW8 Lisa Leslie 3.00 8.00
AW9 Teresa Weatherspoon 2.50 6.00
AW10 Shannon Johnson .60 1.50

2000 SkyBox Dominion WNBA Autographics

Randomly inserted in packs at one in 144, this 12-card set features autographs of top WNBA players. Card backs are not numbered and listed below in alphabetical order.

STATED ODDS 1:144
NNO CARDS LISTED BELOW ALPHABETICALLY
1 Ruthie Bolton-Holifield 4.00 10.00
2 Cynthia Cooper 8.00 20.00
3 Jennifer Gillom 3.00 8.00
4 Yolanda Griffith 4.00 10.00
5 Kedra Holland-Corn 2.00 5.00
6 Lisa Leslie 6.00 15.00
7 Taj McWilliams 2.00 5.00
8 Ticha Penicheiro 3.00 8.00
9 Crystal Robinson 1.25 3.00
10 Andrea Stinson 2.50 6.00
11 Sue Wicks 2.00 5.00
12 Kate Starbird 2.00 5.00

2000 SkyBox Dominion WNBA Girls Rock

Randomly inserted in packs at one in 35, this 10-card set features key players in the WNBA on a die cut foilboard background. Card backs carry a "GR" prefix.

COMPLETE SET (10) 15.00 40.00
GR1 Sheryl Swoopes 5.00 12.00
GR2 Chamique Holdsclaw 5.00 12.00
GR3 Dawn Staley 2.00 5.00
GR4 Katie Smith 2.50 6.00
GR5 Yolanda Griffith 2.50 6.00
GR6 Ticha Penicheiro 2.00 5.00
GR7 Teresa Weatherspoon 3.00 8.00
GR8 Natalie Williams 1.50 4.00
GR9 Lisa Leslie 4.00 10.00
GR10 Cynthia Cooper 5.00 12.00

2000 SkyBox Dominion WNBA Supreme Court

Randomly inserted in packs at one in 12, this 20-card set features the best all-around players in the WNBA. Card backs carry a "SC" prefix.

COMPLETE SET (20) 12.50 30.00
SC1 Dawn Staley 1.50 4.00
SC2 Merlakia Jones 1.00 2.50
SC3 Eva Nemcova 1.00 2.50
SC4 Suzie McConnell-Serio 1.25 3.00
SC5 Cynthia Cooper 4.00 10.00
SC6 Brandy Reed 1.00 2.50
SC7 Katie Smith 2.00 5.00
SC8 Vickie Johnson 1.00 2.50
SC9 Rebecca Lobo 2.00 5.00
SC10 Shannon Johnson .60 1.50
SC11 Nykesha Sales 1.00 2.50
SC12 Jennifer Gillom 1.50 4.00
SC13 Nikki McCray 1.50 4.00
SC14 Michele Timms 2.00 5.00
SC15 Tina Thompson 2.00 5.00
SC16 Ruthie Bolton-Holifield 2.00 5.00
SC17 Wendy Palmer 1.50 4.00
SC18 DeLisha Milton .60 1.50
SC19 Andrea Stinson 1.25 3.00
SC20 Adrienne Goodson .60 1.50

2000 SkyBox Dominion WNBA The Cooper Collection

Randomly inserted in packs at one in six, this eight-card set features different shots of league MVP Cynthia Cooper. Card backs carry a "CC" prefix.

COMPLETE SET (8) 4.00 10.00
COMMON CARD (CC1-CC8) .75 2.00

1995-96 SkyBox Expansion Debut

Produced by SkyBox, this two-card set commemorates the debut of the Toronto Raptors and Vancover Grizzlies. Both card fronts carry a red background with the expansion team's logo. Card backs contain a photo of Grant Hill with his commentary on the new teams. The cards are not numbered and listed below in alphabetical order.

COMPLETE SET (2) 2.00 5.00
1 Toronto Raptors 1.25 3.00
Grant Hill
2 Vancover Grizzlies 1.25 3.00
Grant Hill

2004-05 SkyBox Fresh Ink

Issued in February 2005, the Fresh Ink set consists of 120 cards divided up into 90 veteran players and 30 rookies serially numbered to 499. All base cards have wood court borders along the top and bottom where the veteran players have accent colors set to match team colors. Fresh Ink was offered in both Hobby and Retail formats where both were packaged in five card packs while boxes for Hobby contained 18 packs and boxes for Retail contained 24.

COMP.SET w/o SP's (90) 15.00 40.00
RC PRINT RUN 499 SER.#'d SETS
UNPRICED PARALLEL ONE EXISTS
1 T.J. Ford .20 .50
2 Pau Gasol .30 .75
3 Kirk Hinrich .25 .60
4 Shawn Marion .25 .60
5 Darius Miles .20 .50
6 Dirk Nowitzki .50 1.25
7 Paul Pierce .30 .75
8 Theron Smith .20 .50
9 Rasheed Wallace .30 .75
10 Kobe Bryant 1.25 3.00
11 Kevin Garnett .50 1.25
12 Steve Nash .40 1.00
13 Gilbert Arenas .25 .60
14 Udonis Haslem .20 .50
15 Ben Wallace .25 .60
16 Ray Allen .30 .75
17 Elton Brand .30 .75
18 Caron Butler .25 .60
19 Drew Gooden .20 .50
20 Richard Hamilton .25 .60
21 Grant Hill .40 1.00
22 Jason Kapono .20 .50
23 Tony Parker .30 .75
24 Jalen Rose .25 .60
25 Amare Stoudemire .25 .60
26 Gerald Wallace .25 .60
27 Jason Williams .25 .60
28 LeBron James 2.00 5.00
29 Jamal Crawford .30 .75
30 Earl Boykins .20 .50
31 Michael Finley .30 .75
32 Chris Kaman .25 .60
33 Stephon Marbury .25 .60
34 Shaquille O'Neal .75 2.00
35 Antoine Walker .30 .75
36 Ron Artest .30 .75
37 Samuel Dalembert .20 .50
38 Reece Gaines .20 .50
39 Rashard Lewis .30 .75
40 Desmond Mason .25 .60
41 Jason Richardson .30 .75
42 Wally Szczerbiak .25 .60
43 Bonzi Wells .20 .50
44 Tim Duncan .50 1.25
45 Lamar Odom .25 .60
46 Jermaine O'Neal .25 .60
47 Mickael Pietrus .25 .60
48 Zach Randolph .25 .60
49 Joe Smith .25 .60
50 Allan Houston .25 .60
51 Carmelo Anthony .60 1.50
52 Manu Ginobili .40 1.00
53 Tyronn Lue .20 .50
54 Tayshaun Prince .25 .60
55 Luke Ridnour .25 .60
56 Peja Stojakovic .30 .75
57 Dwyane Wade .50 1.25
58 David West .25 .60
59 Allen Iverson .50 1.25
60 Richard Jefferson .25 .60
61 Andrei Kirilenko .25 .60
62 Latrell Sprewell .25 .60
63 Jason Kidd .50 1.25
64 Baron Davis .25 .60

65 Al Harrington .25 .60
66 Jarvis Hayes .20 .50
67 Gary Payton .30 .75
68 Chris Webber .30 .75
69 Vince Carter .50 1.25
70 Eric Williams .20 .50
71 Nene .25 .60
72 Chris Bosh .30 .75
73 Sam Cassell .25 .60
74 Mike Dunleavy .25 .60
75 Steve Francis .25 .60
76 Antawn Jamison .25 .60
77 Joe Johnson .25 .60
78 Corey Maggette .25 .60
79 Jamaal Magloire .20 .50
80 Kenyon Martin .25 .60
81 Reggie Miller .30 .75
82 Yao Ming .60 1.50
83 Dajuan Wagner .20 .50
84 Willie Green .20 .50
85 Shareef Abdur-Rahim .25 .60
86 Tracy McGrady .40 1.00
87 Carlos Arroyo .20 .50
88 Michael Redd .25 .60
89 Alonzo Mourning .40 1.00
90 Mike Bibby .30 .75
91 Luke Jackson RC 1.00 2.50
92 Matt Freije RC 1.25 3.00
93 Kevin Martin RC 2.00 5.00
94 Josh Smith RC 1.50 4.00
95 Kris Humphries RC 1.50 4.00
96 Trevor Ariza RC 1.50 4.00
97 Shaun Livingston RC 1.50 4.00
98 Pavel Podkolzin RC 1.00 2.50
99 Kirk Snyder RC 1.00 2.50
100 Beno Udrih RC 1.25 3.00
101 Tony Allen RC 1.50 4.00
102 Chris Duhon RC 1.50 4.00
103 Josh Childress RC 1.25 3.00
104 David Harrison RC 1.00 2.50
105 Al Jefferson RC 2.00 5.00
106 Rafael Araujo RC 1.00 2.50
107 Andre Emmett RC 1.00 2.50
108 Devin Harris RC 1.25 3.00
109 Andre Iguodala RC 2.00 5.00
110 Emeka Okafor RC 1.25 3.00
111 Dorell Wright RC 1.50 4.00
112 Luol Deng RC 1.50 4.00
113 Dwight Howard RC 3.00 8.00
114 J.R. Smith RC 1.50 4.00
115 Sasha Vujacic RC 1.50 4.00
116 Jameer Nelson RC 1.50 4.00
117 Robert Swift RC 1.00 2.50
118 Sebastian Telfair RC 1.25 3.00
119 Andris Biedrins RC 1.00 2.50
120 Ben Gordon RC 1.50 4.00

2004-05 SkyBox Fresh Ink 50

*50 SINGLES: 3X TO 8X BASE HI
*50 RC's: 1.25X TO 3X BASE HI
PRINT RUN 50 SER.#'d SETS

2004-05 SkyBox Fresh Ink Autographs

PRINT RUN 199 SER.#'d SETS
*AUTO 99: .5X TO 1.25X BASE AU HI
*AUTO 25: .75X TO 2X BASE AU HI
*RED AUTO: .4X TO 1X BASE AU HI
RED AUTO: RANDOM INSERTS IN RETAIL PACKS
N Nene 5.00 12.00
AJ Al Jefferson 6.00 15.00
AK Andrei Kirilenko 8.00 20.00
AV Anderson Varejao 4.00 10.00
BG Ben Gordon 5.00 12.00
BW Ben Wallace 8.00 20.00
CA Carmelo Anthony 15.00 30.00
CB Carlos Boozer 5.00 12.00
CB Chris Bosh 10.00 25.00
CD Carlos Delfino 5.00 12.00
CD2 Chris Duhon 5.00 12.00
DH Devin Harris 4.00 10.00
DH David Harrison 3.00 8.00
DW Dwyane Wade 30.00 80.00
DW David West 5.00 12.00
GA Gilbert Arenas 8.00 20.00
JC Josh Childress 4.00 10.00
JR Jason Richardson 5.00 12.00
JS Jerry Stackhouse 6.00 15.00
JS2 Josh Smith 5.00 12.00
KH2 K.Humphries Gophers 6.00 15.00
KM Kenyon Martin 8.00 20.00
KS Kirk Snyder 3.00 8.00
LC Lionel Chalmers 5.00 12.00
LD Luol Deng 5.00 12.00
LJ Luke Jackson 3.00 8.00
MB2 Matt Bonner 5.00 12.00
MP Mickael Pietrus 5.00 12.00
MS Mike Sweetney 5.00 12.00
NC Nick Collison 5.00 12.00
QR Quinton Ross 5.00 12.00
RH Richard Hamilton 8.00 20.00
RS Robert Swift 3.00 8.00
TA2 Tony Allen OK State 10.00 25.00
TO Travis Outlaw 5.00 12.00
VC Vince Carter 12.50 30.00

2004-05 SkyBox Fresh Ink Five on Five

Inserted in Hobby packs at the rate of one in 432, this 10-card set features a horizontal design with five small black and white headshots from a single team on one side and five from another rival team on the other.
STATED ODDS 1:432
6 Kings/Trailblazers 6.00 15.00
8 Suns/Jazz 8.00 20.00

2004-05 SkyBox Fresh Ink Five on Five Jerseys

PRINT RUN 199 SER.#'d SETS
1 Spurs/Mavericks 12.00 30.00
2 Pistons/Pacers 12.00 30.00
3 Timberwolves/Nuggets 12.00 30.00
4 Nets/Heat 12.00 30.00
5 Celtics/Knicks 12.00 30.00
6 Kings/Trailblazers 12.00 30.00
7 76ers/Wizards 12.00 30.00
9 Bucks/Hornets 12.00 30.00

2004-05 SkyBox Fresh Ink Game Breakers

Randomly inserted in Hobby packs at the rate of one in 18 and Retail at the rate of one in 24, this 15-card set features two players on each card side by side.
COMPLETE SET (15) 30.00 80.00
STATED ODDS 1:18 H, 1:24 R
1 K.Garnett/T.Duncan 3.00 8.00
2 S.O'Neal/A.Mourning 2.50 6.00
3 S.Marbury/J.Kidd 2.50 6.00
4 L.Bird/M.Johnson 8.00 20.00
5 P.Pierce/A.Walker 2.50 6.00
6 L.James/K.Bryant 5.00 12.00
7 D.Nowitzki/S.Nash 3.00 8.00
8 I.Thomas/M.Cooper 4.00 10.00
9 C.Anthony/D.Wade 3.00 8.00
10 P.Gasol/A.Kirilenko 2.50 6.00
11 R.Miller/B.Davis 2.50 6.00
12 C.Barkley/S.Pippen 8.00 20.00
13 V.Carter/A.Jamison 2.50 6.00
14 T.McGrady/S.Francis 2.50 6.00
15 D.West/J.Nelson 2.00 5.00

2004-05 SkyBox Fresh Ink Game Breakers Jerseys

PRINT RUN 199 SER.#'d SETS
*PATCHES: .75X TO 2X BASE HI
PATCH PRINT RUN 49 SER.#'d SETS
1 K.Garnett/T.Duncan 10.00 25.00
5 P.Pierce/A.Walker 6.00 15.00
7 D.Nowitzki/S.Nash 6.00 15.00
9 C.Anthony/D.Wade 8.00 20.00
10 P.Gasol/A.Kirilenko 6.00 15.00
11 R.Miller/B.Davis 6.00 15.00
13 V.Carter/A.Jamison 6.00 15.00
14 T.McGrady/S.Francis 6.00 15.00
15 D.West/J.Nelson 6.00 15.00

2004-05 SkyBox Fresh Ink Property Of

Inserted in Hobby packs at the rate of one in three and Retail packs at the rate of one in six, this 30-card set places players on a gray background set to look like the "Property of" sweat shirts teams use during training camp.
COMPLETE SET (30) 12.00 30.00
STATED ODDS 1:3 H, 1:6 R
1 Josh Childress .50 1.25
2 Kevin McHale .75 2.00
3 Emeka Okafor .50 1.25
4 Ben Gordon .60 1.50
5 LeBron James 4.00 10.00
6 Michael Finley .60 1.50
7 Carmelo Anthony 1.25 3.00
8 Ben Wallace .50 1.25
9 Rick Barry .50 1.25
10 Yao Ming 1.25 3.00
11 Jermaine O'Neal .50 1.25
12 Elton Brand .60 1.50
13 Kobe Bryant 2.50 6.00
14 Jason Williams .50 1.25
15 Dwyane Wade 1.00 2.50
16 Michael Redd .50 1.25
17 Latrell Sprewell .50 1.25
18 Richard Jefferson .50 1.25
19 Baron Davis .50 1.25
20 Walt Frazier .60 1.50
21 Dwight Howard 1.25 3.00
22 Allen Iverson 1.00 2.50
23 Kevin Johnson .60 1.50
24 Clyde Drexler .75 2.00
25 Peja Stojakovic .60 1.50
26 Manu Ginobili .75 2.00
27 Ray Allen .60 1.50
28 Chris Bosh .60 1.50
29 Andrei Kirilenko .50 1.25
30 Elvin Hayes .60 1.50

2004-05 SkyBox Fresh Ink Property Of Jerseys

PRINT RUN 199 SER.#'d SETS
*PATCHES: .75X TO 2X BASE HI
PATCH PRINT RUN 99 SER.#'d SETS
1 Josh Childress 2.50 6.00
6 Michael Finley 3.00 8.00
7 Carmelo Anthony 6.00 15.00
8 Ben Wallace 2.50 6.00
10 Yao Ming 6.00 15.00
11 Jermaine O'Neal 2.50 6.00
12 Elton Brand 3.00 8.00
14 Jason Williams 2.50 6.00
15 Dwyane Wade 8.00 20.00
16 Michael Redd 2.50 6.00
17 Latrell Sprewell 2.50 6.00
18 Richard Jefferson 2.50 6.00
19 Baron Davis 2.50 6.00
21 Dwight Howard 8.00 20.00
22 Allen Iverson 5.00 12.00
25 Peja Stojakovic 3.00 8.00
26 Manu Ginobili 4.00 10.00
27 Ray Allen 3.00 8.00
29 Andrei Kirilenko 2.50 6.00

2004-05 SkyBox Fresh Ink Teammate Tandems

Inserted in Hobby packs at the rate of one in 108 and Retail packs at the rate of one in 360, this 10-card set features two players from the same team and their head shots side by side.
COMPLETE SET (10) 20.00 50.00
STATED ODDS 1:108 H, 1:360 R
1 Y.Ming/T.McGrady 4.00 10.00
2 S.O'Neal/D.Wade 5.00 12.00
3 M.Finley/D.Nowitzki 4.00 10.00
4 R.Hamilton/B.Wallace 3.00 8.00
5 T.Ford/M.Redd 3.00 8.00
6 K.Garnett/L.Sprewell 4.00 10.00
7 R.Jefferson/J.Kidd 4.00 10.00
8 C.Bosh/J.Rose 3.00 8.00
9 M.Pietrus/J.Richardson 3.00 8.00
10 T.Duncan/T.Parker 4.00 10.00

2004-05 SkyBox Fresh Ink Teammate Tandems Jerseys

PRINT RUN 199 SER.#'d SETS
*RETAIL: .4X TO 1X HI COLUMN
RETAIL STATED ODDS 1:24 PACKS
*PATCHES: 1X TO 2.5X BASE HI
PATCH PRINT RUN 49 SER.#'d SETS
PATCH 10 NOT PRICED DUE TO SCARCITY
1 Y.Ming/T.McGrady 6.00 15.00
3 M.Finley/D.Nowitzki 8.00 20.00
4 R.Hamilton/B.Wallace 5.00 12.00
5 T.Ford/M.Redd 5.00 12.00
6 K.Garnett/L.Sprewell 6.00 15.00
7 R.Jefferson/J.Kidd 5.00 12.00
9 M.Pietrus/J.Richardson 5.00 12.00
10 T.Duncan/T.Parker 6.00 15.00

1999-00 SkyBox Impact

The 1999-00 SkyBox Impact set was released in May,2000 as a 200-card set. Each pack contained 10-cards and carried a suggested retail price of .99. In addition, a Vince Carter Slam Dunk card was added to the set near the end of production, the card is serial numbered to 2000. There were also 15 hand-numbered autographed versions of this card which were inserted into packs.
COMPLETE SET (200) 12.50 30.00
V.CARTER COMM: PRINT RUN #'d TO 2000
V.CARTER AU: PRINT RUN #'d TO 15
BOTH CARTERS RANDOM INS.IN PACKS
1 Tim Duncan .30 .75
2 Doug Christie .12 .30
3 Mark Jackson .12 .30
4 Paul Pierce .20 .50
5 James Posey RC .15 .40
6 Steve Smith .12 .30
7 Charlie Ward .10 .25
8 Elton Brand RC .40 1.00
9 Howard Eisley .10 .25
10 Grant Hill .20 .50
11 Christian Laettner .12 .30
12 Corey Maggette RC .25 .60
13 Scot Pollard .10 .25
14 Robert Traylor .10 .25
15 Nick Anderson .10 .25
16 Pat Garrity .10 .25
17 Hersey Hawkins .10 .25
18 Troy Hudson .15 .40
19 Charles Oakley .12 .30
20 Gary Payton .15 .40
21 Rik Smits .15 .40
22 Muggsy Bogues .12 .30
23 Dale Davis .10 .25
24 Larry Johnson .15 .40
25 Antonio McDyess .12 .30
26 Alonzo Mourning .20 .50
27 Scottie Pippen .25 .60
28 Rod Strickland .10 .25
29 Antoine Walker .15 .40
30 Allen Iverson .30 .75
31 Sam Cassell .12 .30
32 Mookie Blaylock .10 .25
33 Jim Jackson .10 .25
34 Brevin Knight .10 .25
35 Anthony Peeler .10 .25
36 Bryon Russell .10 .25
37 Maurice Taylor .10 .25
38 Elden Campbell .10 .25
39 Austin Croshere .10 .25
40 Keith Van Horn .12 .30
41 Raef LaFrentz .12 .30
42 Jamal Mashburn .12 .30
43 Jermaine O'Neal .12 .30
44 Glenn Robinson .12 .30
45 Mitch Richmond .15 .40
46 Keon Clark .10 .25
47 Derrick Coleman .12 .30
48 Patrick Ewing .20 .50
49 Brian Grant .10 .25
50 Kobe Bryant .60 1.50
51 Dan Majerle .15 .40
52 Ruben Patterson .10 .25
53 Walt Williams .10 .25
54 Chris Childs .10 .25
55 Baron Davis RC .40 1.00
56 Richard Hamilton RC .30 .75
57 Voshon Lenard .10 .25
58 Vernon Maxwell .10 .25
59 Hakeem Olajuwon .20 .50
60 Jason Williams .20 .50
61 Gary Trent .10 .25
62 Kenny Anderson .12 .30
63 Shawn Bradley .10 .25
64 Obinna Ekezie RC .12 .30
65 Tom Gugliotta .10 .25
66 Ron Harper .10 .25
67 Corey Benjamin .10 .25
68 Donyell Marshall .10 .25
69 David Robinson .25 .60
70 Stephon Marbury .12 .30
71 Marcus Camby .12 .30
72 Horace Grant .12 .30
73 Tim Hardaway .15 .40
74 Greg Foster .10 .25
75 Cuttino Mobley .10 .25
76 Rodney Buford RC .15 .40
77 Clifford Robinson .10 .25
78 Isaac Austin .10 .25
79 Robert Pack .10 .25
80 Eddie Jones .15 .40
81 Shawn Marion RC .30 .75
82 Anthony Mason .10 .25
83 Oliver Miller .10 .25
84 Dirk Nowitzki .30 .75
85 Jayson Williams .10 .25
86 Brent Barry .12 .30
87 P.J. Brown .10 .25
88 Kelvin Cato .10 .25
89 Jim McIlvaine .10 .25
90 Steve Francis RC .40 1.00
91 Bryant Reeves .10 .25
92 Jerry Stackhouse .15 .40
93 Allan Houston .12 .30
94 Kevin Garnett .25 .60
95 Karl Malone .20 .50
96 David Wesley .10 .25
97 Eddie Robinson RC .15 .40
98 Ben Wallace .12 .30
99 Chris Webber .15 .40
100 Lamar Odom RC .40 1.00
101 Shandon Anderson .10 .25
102 Terrell Brandon .10 .25
103 Jeff Hornacek .12 .30
104 Terry Mills .10 .25
105 Tyrone Nesby RC .12 .30
106 Bo Outlaw .10 .25
107 Peja Stojakovic .15 .40
108 Ron Artest RC .30 .75
109 Tony Battie .12 .30
110 Cedric Ceballos .10 .25
111 Anfernee Hardaway .25 .60
112 Othella Harrington .10 .25
113 Dennis Rodman .30 .75
114 Loy Vaught .10 .25
115 Malik Rose .10 .25
116 Vin Baker .12 .30
117 Charles Barkley .25 .60
118 Michael Finley .15 .40
119 Adrian Griffin RC .15 .40
120 Jason Kidd .25 .60
121 Gheorghe Muresan .10 .25
122 Cherokee Parks .10 .25
123 Glen Rice .15 .40
124 Bimbo Coles .10 .25
125 Andrew DeClercq .10 .25
126 Matt Geiger .10 .25
127 Bobby Jackson .10 .25
128 Michael Olowokandi .10 .25
129 Greg Ostertag .10 .25
130 Tracy McGrady .25 .60
131 Rodney Rogers .10 .25
132 Juwan Howard .12 .30
133 Terry Cummings .12 .30
134 Mario Elie .10 .25
135 Trajan Langdon RC .15 .40
136 George Lynch .10 .25
137 Roshown McLeod .10 .25
138 Joe Smith .12 .30
139 John Stockton .20 .50
140 Ray Allen .15 .40
141 Vince Carter .30 .75
142 Al Harrington .15 .40
143 Ron Mercer .12 .30
144 Vitaly Potapenko .10 .25
145 Arvydas Sabonis .12 .30
146 Latrell Sprewell .15 .40
147 Aaron Williams .10 .25
148 Shareef Abdur-Rahim .12 .30
149 Vonteego Cummings RC .10 .25
150 Shaquille O'Neal .40 1.00
151 Derek Fisher .15 .40
152 Todd MacCulloch RC .15 .40
153 Andre Miller RC .30 .75
154 Dikembe Mutombo .15 .40
155 Ervin Johnson .10 .25
156 Michael Dickerson .10 .25
157 A.C. Green .12 .30
158 Kevin Willis .10 .25
159 Kerry Kittles .10 .25
160 Damon Stoudamire .12 .30
161 Eric Snow .12 .30
162 Bob Sura .10 .25
163 Jason Terry RC .25 .60
164 Derek Anderson .10 .25
165 Randy Brown .10 .25
166 Vlade Divac .15 .40
167 Chris Gatling .10 .25
168 Lindsey Hunter .10 .25
169 Tim Thomas .12 .30
170 Antawn Jamison .15 .40
171 Alan Henderson .10 .25
172 Larry Hughes .12 .30
173 Shawn Kemp .15 .40
174 Radoslav Nesterovic RC .15 .40
175 Scott Padgett .12 .30
176 Brian Skinner .10 .25
177 Jerome Williams .10 .25
178 Corliss Williamson .10 .25
179 Sean Elliott .15 .40
180 Wally Szczerbiak RC .30 .75
181 Toni Kukoc .15 .40
182 Chucky Atkins RC .15 .40
183 Jalen Rose .12 .30
184 Nick Van Exel .12 .30
185 Rasheed Wallace .15 .40
186 Avery Johnson .12 .30
187 Jamie Feick RC .12 .30
188 Adonal Foyle .10 .25
189 Devean George RC .15 .40
190 Mike Bibby .15 .40
191 Lamond Murray .10 .25
192 Billy Owens .10 .25
193 Isaiah Rider .12 .30
194 Darrell Armstrong .10 .25
195 Antonio Davis .10 .25
196 Dale Ellis .10 .25
197 Tim Young RC .15 .40
198 Roy Rogers .10 .25
199 Terry Porter .10 .25
200 Reggie Miller .15 .40
P141 Vince Carter PROMO .60 1.50
NNO V.Carter COMM 5.00 12.00

1999-00 SkyBox Impact Rewind '99

Inserted one per pack, this 40-card set highlights moments from the 1998-99 NBA season. Card backs carry a "RN" prefix.
COMPLETE SET (40) 6.00 15.00
ONE PER PACK
RN1 Tim Duncan .50 1.25
RN2 David Robinson .40 1.00
RN3 Sean Elliott .25 .60
RN4 Mario Elie .15 .40
RN5 Avery Johnson .20 .50
RN6 Malik Rose .15 .40
RN7 Jaren Jackson .15 .40
RN8 Tim Duncan .50 1.25
RN9 Gerald King .15 .40
RN10 Jerome Kersey .15 .40
RN11 Steve Kerr .20 .50
RN12 Antonio Daniels .15 .40
RN13 Karl Malone .30 .75
RN14 Vince Carter .50 1.25
RN15 Karl Malone .30 .75
RN16 Tim Duncan .50 1.25
RN17 Alonzo Mourning .30 .75
RN18 Allen Iverson .50 1.25
RN19 Jason Kidd .40 1.00
RN20 Chris Webber .25 .60
RN21 Grant Hill .30 .75
RN22 Shaquille O'Neal .60 1.50
RN23 Gary Payton .25 .60
RN24 Tim Hardaway .25 .60
RN25 Kevin Garnett .40 1.00
RN26 Antonio McDyess .20 .50
RN27 Hakeem Olajuwon .30 .75
RN28 Kobe Bryant 1.00 2.50
RN29 John Stockton .30 .75
RN30 Vince Carter .50 1.25
RN31 Paul Pierce .30 .75
RN32 Jason Williams .30 .75
RN33 Mike Bibby .25 .60
RN34 Matt Harpring .15 .40
RN35 Michael Dickerson .15 .40
RN36 Cuttino Mobley .15 .40
RN37 Michael Doleac .15 .40
RN38 Michael Olowokandi .15 .40
RN39 Antawn Jamison .25 .60
RN40 Vince Carter .50 1.25

1999-00 SkyBox Impact Tattoos

Randomly inserted into packs at 1:4, this 29-card set features temporary tattoos of all the current NBA teams.
COMMON CARD (1-29) .40 1.00
2 Boston Celtics .75 2.00
4 Chicago Bulls .75 2.00
8 Detroit Pistons .50 1.25
13 Los Angeles Lakers .75 2.00
18 New York Knicks .75 2.00
24 San Antonio Spurs .50 1.25

1991 SkyBox Magic Johnson Video

This standard-size card was enclosed in cellophane and included as an insert with the "Magic Johnson - Always Showtime" VHS video tape. The front features a cut-out action shot of Johnson superimposed on the familiar SkyBox bright colored computer-generated geometric background. In a horizontal format
NNO Magic Johnson 6.00 15.00

2003-04 SkyBox LE

Released in early March 2004, Skybox LE consists of 160 cards divided up as follows: cards 1-110 are veterans and 111-160 are rookies sequentially numbered to 399. Some of the cards are randomly numbered to 99. Base cards have full-color player action photography with white borders and die cut edges (retail versions are not die cut). Skybox LE was packaged in 18-pack boxes where packs contained three cards and carried a suggested retail price of $3.99.
COMP.SET w/o SP's (110) 12.50 30.00
PRINT RUN 399 SER.#'d SETS
1 Jason Terry .25 .60
2 Antoine Walker .30 .75
3 Paul Pierce .30 .75
4 Eddy Curry .20 .50
5 Ricky Davis .25 .60
6 Jamal Crawford .30 .75
7 Raef LaFrentz .20 .50
8 Darius Miles .20 .50
9 Ray Allen .30 .75
10 Sam Cassell .25 .60
11 Andre Miller .25 .60
12 Dirk Nowitzki .50 1.25
13 Zach Randolph .25 .60
14 Tim Duncan .50 1.25
15 Gary Payton .30 .75
16 Ben Wallace .25 .60
17 Michael Finley .30 .75
18 David Wesley .20 .50
19 Nick Van Exel .25 .60
20 Marcus Camby .25 .60
21 Gilbert Arenas .25 .60
22 Marcus Haislip .20 .50
23 Cuttino Mobley .20 .50
24 Tayshaun Prince .25 .60
25 Chris Webber .30 .75
26 Reggie Miller .30 .75
27 Chauncey Billups .30 .75
28 Quentin Richardson .25 .60
29 Mike Dunleavy .25 .60
30 Karl Malone .40 1.00
31 Yao Ming .60 1.50
32 Tyson Chandler .25 .60
33 Jason Williams .25 .60
34 Eddie Griffin .20 .50
35 Eddie Jones .25 .60
36 Jamaal Tinsley .20 .50
37 Michael Redd .30 .75
38 Elton Brand .30 .75
39 Rashard Lewis .30 .75
40 Vince Carter .50 1.25
41 Wally Szczerbiak .25 .60
42 Chris Wilcox .20 .50
43 Kenyon Martin .25 .60
44 Shaquille O'Neal .75 2.00
45 Baron Davis .25 .60
46 Pau Gasol .30 .75
47 Dikembe Mutombo .30 .75
48 Shane Battier .25 .60
40 Drew Gooden .25 .60
50 Lamar Odom .25 .60
51 Glenn Robinson .25 .60
52 Tim Thomas .20 .50
53 Shawn Marion .25 .60
54 Kevin Garnett .50 1.25
55 Stephon Marbury .25 .60
56 Rasheed Wallace .30 .75
57 Troy Hudson .20 .50
58 Mike Bibby .30 .75
59 Jason Kidd .50 1.25
60 Tony Parker .30 .75
61 Andrei Kirilenko .30 .75
62 Manu Ginobili .40 1.00
63 Kerry Kittles .20 .50
64 Brent Barry .20 .50
65 Allan Houston .25 .60
66 Morris Peterson .20 .50
67 Tracy McGrady .40 1.00
68 Matt Harpring .20 .50
69 Erick Dampier .20 .50
70 Jerry Stackhouse .25 .60
71 John Salmons .25 .60
72 Stephen Jackson .25 .60
73 Scottie Pippen .50 1.25
74 Dajuan Wagner .20 .50
75 Keon Clark .20 .50
76 Carlos Boozer .25 .60
77 Steve Nash .40 1.00
78 Nene .25 .60
79 Keith Van Horn .25 .60
80 Earl Boykins .20 .50
81 Richard Hamilton .25 .60
82 Jason Richardson .30 .75
83 Steve Francis .25 .60
84 Jermaine O'Neal .25 .60
85 Ron Artest .30 .75
86 Corey Maggette .25 .60
87 Kwame Brown .20 .50
88 Kobe Bryant 1.25 3.00
89 Mike Miller .25 .60
90 Caron Butler .25 .60
91 Desmond Mason .25 .60
92 Latrell Sprewell .25 .60
93 Richard Jefferson .25 .60
94 Jamal Mashburn .25 .60
95 Troy Murphy .20 .50
96 Peja Stojakovic .30 .75
97 Allen Iverson .50 1.25
98 Amare Stoudemire .40 1.00
99 Rasho Nesterovic .20 .50
100 Bonzi Wells .20 .50
101 Bobby Jackson .20 .50
102 Anfernee Hardaway .50 1.25
103 Larry Hughes .25 .60
104 Shareef Abdur-Rahim .25 .60
105 Hedo Turkoglu .25 .60
106 Alvin Williams .20 .50
107 Qyntel Woods .20 .50
108 Brad Miller .25 .60
109 Jalen Rose .25 .60
110 Antonio Davis .20 .50
111 David West RC 2.50 6.00
112 Boris Diaw RC 2.50 6.00
113 Travis Hansen RC 1.50 4.00
114 Marcus Banks RC 1.50 4.00
115 Kendrick Perkins RC 2.00 5.00
116 Darius Songaila 1.50 4.00
117 Kirk Hinrich/99 RC 8.00 20.00
118 LeBron James/99 RC 300.00 600.00
119 Jason Kapono RC 1.50 4.00
120 Josh Howard RC 2.50 6.00
121 Marquis Daniels RC 2.00 5.00
122 Carmelo Anthony/99 RC 50.00 100.00
123 Darko Milicic/99 RC 6.00 15.00
124 Zaur Pachulia RC 2.50 6.00
125 Mickael Pietrus RC 2.00 5.00
126 Ben Handlogten RC 1.50 4.00
127 James Jones RC 1.50 4.00
128 Chris Kaman RC 2.50 6.00
129 Josh Moore RC 1.50 4.00
130 Brian Cook RC 1.50 4.00
131 Luke Walton RC 2.50 6.00
132 Troy Bell RC 1.50 4.00
133 Dahntay Jones RC 2.00 5.00
134 Dwyane Wade/99 RC 30.00 80.00
135 Udonis Haslem RC 2.00 5.00
136 T.J. Ford/99 RC 6.00 15.00
137 Ndudi Ebi RC 1.50 4.00
138 Zoran Planinic RC 1.50 4.00
139 Raul Lopez 2.50 6.00
140 Francisco Elson RC 1.50 4.00
141 Mike Sweetney RC 1.50 4.00
142 Maciej Lampe RC 1.50 4.00
143 Slavko Vranes RC 1.50 4.00
144 Keith Bogans/99 RC 5.00 12.00
145 Reece Gaines RC 1.50 4.00
146 Willie Green RC 1.50 4.00
147 Kyle Korver RC 3.00 8.00
148 Zarko Cabarkapa RC 1.50 4.00
149 Leandro Barbosa RC 2.50 6.00
150 Travis Outlaw RC 2.00 5.00
151 Curtis Borchardt 2.50 6.00
152 Alex Garcia RC 1.50 4.00
153 Richie Frahm RC 2.50 6.00
154 Nick Collison RC 2.00 5.00
155 Luke Ridnour/99 RC 6.00 15.00
156 Chris Bosh/99 RC 12.00 30.00
157 Aleksandar Pavlovic RC 2.00 5.00
158 Maurice Williams RC 2.50 6.00
159 Jarvis Hayes/99 RC 5.00 12.00
160 Steve Blake RC 2.00 5.00

2003-04 SkyBox LE Retail

COMPLETE SET (160) 30.00 60.00
*VETS: SAME PRICE AS HOBBY
111 David West RC .75 2.00
112 Boris Diaw RC .75 2.00
113 Travis Hansen RC .50 1.25
114 Marcus Banks RC .50 1.25
115 Kendrick Perkins RC .60 1.50
116 Darius Songaila .50 1.25
117 Kirk Hinrich RC .75 2.00
118 LeBron James RC 8.00 20.00
119 Jason Kapono RC .50 1.25
120 Josh Howard RC .75 2.00
121 Marquis Daniels RC .60 1.50
122 Carmelo Anthony RC 2.50 6.00
123 Darko Milicic RC .60 1.50
124 Zaur Pachulia RC .75 2.00
125 Mickael Pietrus RC .60 1.50
126 Ben Handlogten RC .50 1.25
127 James Jones RC .50 1.25
128 Chris Kaman RC .75 2.00
129 Josh Moore RC .50 1.25
130 Brian Cook RC .50 1.25
131 Luke Walton RC .75 2.00
132 Troy Bell RC .50 1.25
133 Dahntay Jones RC .60 1.50
134 Dwyane Wade RC 2.50 6.00
135 Udonis Haslem RC .60 1.50
136 T.J. Ford RC .60 1.50
137 Ndudi Ebi RC .50 1.25
138 Zoran Planinic RC .50 1.25
139 Raul Lopez .75 2.00
140 Francisco Elson RC .50 1.25
141 Mike Sweetney RC .50 1.25
142 Maciej Lampe RC .50 1.25
143 Slavko Vranes RC .50 1.25
144 Keith Bogans RC .50 1.25
145 Reece Gaines RC .50 1.25
146 Willie Green RC .50 1.25
147 Kyle Korver RC 1.00 2.50
148 Zarko Cabarkapa RC .50 1.25
149 Leandro Barbosa RC .75 2.00
150 Travis Outlaw RC .60 1.50
151 Curtis Borchardt .75 2.00
152 Alex Garcia RC .50 1.25
153 Richie Frahm RC .75 2.00
154 Nick Collison RC .60 1.50
155 Luke Ridnour RC .60 1.50
156 Chris Bosh RC 1.25 3.00
157 Aleksandar Pavlovic RC .60 1.50
158 Maurice Williams RC .75 2.00
159 Jarvis Hayes RC .50 1.25
160 Steve Blake RC .60 1.50

2003-04 SkyBox LE Artist Proofs

*AP SINGLES: 5X TO 12X BASE HI
*AP RCs: .75X TO 2X BASE HI
*AP RCs/99: .25X TO .6X BASE HI
PRINT RUN 50 SER.#'d SETS

2003-04 SkyBox LE Gold Proofs

*GOLD SINGLES: 4X TO 10X BASE HI
*GOLD RC's: .6X TO 1.5X BASE HI
*GOLD RC's/99: .2X TO .5X BASE HI
PRINT RUN 150 SER.#'d SETS

2003-04 SkyBox LE Photographer Proofs

*PP SINGLES: 8X TO 20X BASE HI
*PP RCs: 1X TO 2.5 BASE HI
*PP RCs/99: .4X TO 1X BASE HI
PHOTO.PROOF PRINT RUN 25 SER.#'d SETS

2003-04 SkyBox LE Championship MettLE

Randomly seeded in packs, this eight-card set features players from America's Team USA Olympic squad. Each card, except for Larry Brown, has a full-color photo and a swatch of game-worn memorabilia. A parallel version of this set was also produced and is sequentially numbered to 10.
STATED PRINT RUN 99 SER.#'d SETS
LARRY BROWN DOES NOT HAVE JSY
RGAI Allen Iverson 12.00 30.00
RGJK Jason Kidd 10.00 25.00
RGJO Jermaine O'Neal 5.00 12.00
RGLB Larry Brown 3.00 8.00
RGMB Mike Bibby 6.00 15.00
RGRA Ray Allen 6.00 15.00
RGTD Tim Duncan 10.00 25.00
RGTM Tracy McGrady 8.00 20.00

2003-04 SkyBox LE History of the Draft Autographs

Randomly inserted in packs, this three-card set features a full-color player action photo with an embedded cut signature. No odds or print run was given for this set.
RANDOM INSERTS IN PACKS
UNPRICED PARALLEL/10 EXISTS
1 Vince Carter 15.00 40.00
2 Manu Ginobili 12.50 30.00

2003-04 SkyBox LE History of the Draft Autographs 99

Randomly seeded, this six-card set parallels the base HOD Autographs set enhanced with sequential numbering to 99.
PRINT RUN 99 SER.#'d SETS
*AUTO 50: .5X TO 1.25X AUTO 99
1 Vince Carter 12.00 30.00
2 Manu Ginobili 15.00 40.00
3 Shawn Marion 8.00 20.00
4 Paul Pierce 15.00 30.00
6 Tracy McGrady 10.00 25.00

2003-04 SkyBox LE History of the Draft The 90s

Randomly inserted in packs, this 40-card set utilizes a similar design to the HOD Autographs cards enhanced with a swatch of game used memorabilia and sequential numbering to the last two digits of the year each player was drafted. A version numbered to 50 and one numbered to 10 were also produced.
CARDS #'d TO PLAYER'S DRAFT YEAR
*PAR.50 SINGLES: .6X TO 1.5X BASE JSY HI
HDAI Allen Iverson/96 5.00 12.00
HDAJ Antawn Jamison/98 2.50 6.00
HDAW Antoine Walker/96 3.00 8.00
HDBD Baron Davis/99 2.50 6.00
HDBW Bonzi Wells/98 2.00 5.00
HDCM Corey Maggette/99 2.50 6.00
HDCW Chris Webber/93 3.00 8.00
HDDN Dirk Nowitzki/98 5.00 12.00
HDEB Elton Brand/99 3.00 8.00
HDGP Gary Payton/90 3.00 8.00
HDGR Glenn Robinson/94 2.50 6.00
HDJK Jason Kidd/94 5.00 12.00
HDJM Jamal Mashburn/93 2.50 6.00
HDJO Jermaine O'Neal/96 2.50 6.00
HDJR Jalen Rose/94 2.50 6.00
HDJS Jerry Stackhouse/95 2.50 6.00
HDJT Jason Terry/99 2.50 6.00
HDKG Kevin Garnett/95 5.00 12.00
HDKV Keith Van Horn/97 2.50 6.00
HDLO Lamar Odom/99 2.50 6.00
HDLS Latrell Sprewell/92 2.50 6.00
HDMB Mike Bibby/98 3.00 8.00
HDMF Michael Finley/95 3.00 8.00
HDMG Manu Ginobili/99 4.00 10.00
HDPP Paul Pierce/98 3.00 8.00
HDPS Peja Stojakovic/96 3.00 8.00
HDRA Ray Allen/96 3.00 8.00
HDRD Ricky Davis/98 2.50 6.00
HDRH Richard Hamilton/99 2.50 6.00
HDRL Rashard Lewis/98 3.00 8.00
HDRW Rasheed Wallace/95 3.00 8.00
HDSA Shareef Abdur-Rahim/96 2.50 6.00
HDSF Steve Francis/99 2.50 6.00
HDSM Shawn Marion/99 2.50 6.00
HDSM Stephon Marbury/96 2.50 6.00
HDSN Steve Nash/96 4.00 10.00
HDSO Shaquille O'Neal/92 8.00 20.00
HDTD Tim Duncan/97 5.00 12.00
HDTM Tracy McGrady/97 4.00 10.00
HDVC Vince Carter/98 5.00 12.00

2003-04 SkyBox LE Jersey Proofs

Randomly inserted in packs, this 50-card set uses the design from the base Skybox LE set enhanced with a square swatch of game used memorabilia. Each card is sequentially numbered to 399. Two parallel versions of this set were also issued: one sequentially numbered to 50 and one numbered to 10.
PRINT RUN 399 SER.#'d SETS
*PAR.50 SINGLES: .6X TO 1.5X BASE JSY HI
3 Paul Pierce 2.50 6.00
4 Eddy Curry 1.50 4.00
9 Ray Allen 2.50 6.00
12 Dirk Nowitzki 4.00 10.00
14 Tim Duncan 4.00 10.00
16 Ben Wallace 2.00 5.00
24 Tayshaun Prince 2.00 5.00
25 Chris Webber 2.50 6.00
26 Reggie Miller 2.50 6.00
29 Mike Dunleavy 2.00 5.00
30 Karl Malone 3.00 8.00
31 Yao Ming 5.00 12.00
32 Tyson Chandler 2.00 5.00
37 Michael Redd 2.50 6.00
38 Elton Brand 2.50 6.00
40 Drew Gooden 2.00 5.00
43 Kenyon Martin 2.00 5.00
44 Shaquille O'Neal 6.00 15.00
45 Baron Davis 2.00 5.00
46 Pau Gasol 2.50 6.00
48 Shane Battier 2.00 5.00
50 Lamar Odom 2.00 5.00
53 Shawn Marion 2.00 5.00
54 Kevin Garnett 4.00 10.00
55 Stephon Marbury 2.00 5.00
56 Rasheed Wallace 2.50 6.00
58 Mike Bibby 2.50 6.00
59 Jason Kidd 4.00 10.00
60 Tony Parker 2.50 6.00
61 Andrei Kirilenko 2.50 6.00
67 Tracy McGrady 3.00 8.00
70 Jerry Stackhouse 2.00 5.00
73 Scottie Pippen 6.00 15.00
77 Steve Nash 3.00 8.00
78 Nene 2.00 5.00
81 Richard Hamilton 2.00 5.00
82 Jason Richardson 2.50 6.00
83 Steve Francis 2.00 5.00
84 Jermaine O'Neal 2.00 5.00
87 Kwame Brown 2.00 5.00
90 Caron Butler 2.00 5.00
92 Latrell Sprewell 2.00 5.00
93 Richard Jefferson 2.00 5.00
96 Peja Stojakovic 2.50 6.00
97 Allen Iverson 4.00 10.00
98 Amare Stoudemire 3.00 8.00
100 Bonzi Wells 2.00 5.00
104 Shareef Abdur-Rahim 2.00 5.00
109 Jalen Rose 2.00 5.00

2003-04 SkyBox LE League Leaders

Inserted in packs at the rate of one in 18, this nine-card set focuses on NBA stat leaders. Each card has a full-color player action photo with white borders along the right and bottom of the card. A one of one parallel version was also inserted into packs.
COMPLETE SET (9) 5.00 12.00
STATED ODDS 1:18
1 Tracy McGrady .75 2.00
2 Ben Wallace .50 1.25
3 Jason Kidd 1.00 2.50
4 Allen Iverson 1.00 2.50
5 Eddy Curry .40 1.00
6 Kevin Garnett 1.00 2.50
7 Caron Butler .50 1.25
8 Amare Stoudemire .75 2.00
9 Yao Ming 1.25 3.00

2003-04 SkyBox LE League Leaders Game-Used

Randomly inserted in packs, this nine-card set parallels the design of the base League Leaders set enhanced with a square swatch of game-used memorabilia in the lower left-hand corner of the card. Each card is sequentially numbered to 75. Two parallel versions of this set were also inserted, one is sequentially numbered to 50 and the other is numbered to 10.
PRINT RUN 75 SER.#'d SETS
*PAR.50 SINGLES: .5X TO 1.25X BASE JSY HI
LLAI Allen Iverson 5.00 12.00
LLAS Amare Stoudemire 4.00 10.00
LLBW Ben Wallace 2.50 6.00
LLCB Caron Butler 2.50 6.00
LLEC Eddy Curry 2.00 5.00
LLJK Jason Kidd 5.00 12.00
LLKG Kevin Garnett 5.00 12.00
LLTM Tracy McGrady 4.00 10.00
LLYM Yao Ming 6.00 15.00

2003-04 SkyBox LE Rare Form

Inserted in packs at the rate of one in 288, this 10-card set features rounded die-cut tops and bottoms, gray borders, an irridescent finish and full-color player action photography. An Executive Proof version of this set was printed as well and these cards are numbered one of one.

STATED ODDS 1:288
1 Vince Carter 5.00 12.00
2 Carmelo Anthony 10.00 25.00
3 Dwyane Wade 10.00 25.00
4 Dajuan Wagner 2.00 5.00
5 Tony Parker 3.00 8.00
6 Caron Butler 2.50 6.00
7 Tyson Chandler 2.50 6.00
8 Chris Bosh 5.00 12.00
9 Jason Richardson 3.00 8.00
10 Jerry Stackhouse 2.50 6.00

2003-04 SkyBox LE Rare Form Autographs

Randomly inserted in packs at the overall odds of one in 18 for all autograph cards, this 19-card set parallels the design for the base Rare Form insert set enhanced with an embedded cut signature. The following cards were not released: 10, 12, 14, 16 and 18. Print runs are listed next to the player.

OVERALL AUTOGRAPH ODDS 1:18
1 Vince Carter/259 12.50 30.00
2 Carmelo Anthony/190 25.00 60.00
3 Tony Parker/260 10.00 25.00
5 Tyson Chandler 4.00 10.00
6 Troy Bell/350 2.50 6.00
7 Boris Diaw/275 4.00 10.00
8 Mickael Pietrus/290 3.00 8.00
9 Josh Howard/880 4.00 10.00
13 Travis Outlaw 3.00 8.00
15 Brian Cook/490 2.50 6.00
17 Dahntay Jones/350 3.00 8.00
19 Zaur Pachulia/790 4.00 10.00
20 Kendrick Perkins/395 3.00 8.00
21 Tayshaun Prince/100 5.00 12.00
22 Mike Sweetney/130 2.50 6.00
23 Maurice Williams/425 4.00 10.00
24 Travis Hansen/330 2.50 6.00

2003-04 SkyBox LE Rare Form Autographs 150

Randomly seeded, this 24-card set parallels the base Rare Form Autographs set enhanced with sequential numbering to 150.

PRINT RUN 150 SER.#'d SETS
*AU 50 SINGLES: .5X TO 1.25X AU 150 HI
UNPRICED AUTO SERIAL #'d TO 10 EXIST
1 Vince Carter 15.00 40.00
2 Carmelo Anthony 30.00 80.00
3 Tony Parker 12.50 30.00
4 Caron Butler 5.00 12.00
5 Tyson Chandler 5.00 12.00
6 Troy Bell 3.00 8.00
7 Boris Diaw 5.00 12.00
8 Mickael Pietrus 4.00 10.00
9 Josh Howard 5.00 12.00
10 David West 5.00 12.00
11 Luke Walton 5.00 12.00
13 Travis Outlaw 4.00 10.00
15 Brian Cook 3.00 8.00
17 Dahntay Jones 4.00 10.00
19 Zaur Pachulia 5.00 12.00
20 Kendrick Perkins 4.00 10.00
21 Tayshaun Prince 5.00 12.00
22 Mike Sweetney 3.00 8.00
23 Maurice Williams 5.00 12.00
24 Travis Hansen 3.00 8.00

2003-04 SkyBox LE Rare Form Game-Used

Randomly inserted in packs, this 10-card set parallels the Rare Form insert set design enhanced with a swatch of Game-Used memorabilia and sequential numbering to 99. Two parallel sets were also inserted into packs, a version numbered to 50 and one numbered to 10.

PRINT RUN 99 SER.#'d SETS
*PAR.50 SINGLES: .5X TO 1.25X BASE JSY HI
RFCA Carmelo Anthony 10.00 25.00
RFCB Chris Bosh 5.00 12.00
RFCB Caron Butler 2.50 6.00
RFDW Dwyane Wade 10.00 25.00
RFDW Dajuan Wagner 2.00 5.00
RFJR Jason Richardson 3.00 8.00
RFJS Jerry Stackhouse 2.50 6.00
RFTC Tyson Chandler 2.50 6.00
RFTP Tony Parker 3.00 8.00
RFVC Vince Carter 5.00 12.00

2003-04 SkyBox LE Sky's the Limit

Randomly seeded in packs at the rate of one in six, this 20-card set places full-color player action photos against a white and blue background. An Executive Proof version of this set was issued also. Each card is numbered one of one.

COMPLETE SET (20) 10.00 25.00
STATED ODDS 1:6
1 Baron Davis .40 1.00
2 Dirk Nowitzki .75 2.00
3 Tayshaun Prince .40 1.00
4 Caron Butler .40 1.00
5 Steve Nash .60 1.50
6 Shawn Marion .40 1.00
7 Scottie Pippen .75 2.00
8 Kobe Bryant 2.00 5.00
9 Tony Parker .50 1.25
10 Amare Stoudemire .60 1.50
11 Jason Richardson .50 1.25
12 Manu Ginobili .60 1.50
13 Drew Gooden .40 1.00
14 Paul Pierce .50 1.25
15 Yao Ming 1.00 2.50
16 LeBron James 6.00 15.00
17 Darko Milicic .40 1.00
18 Carmelo Anthony 1.50 4.00
19 Chris Bosh .75 2.00
20 Dwyane Wade 1.50 4.00

2003-04 SkyBox LE Sky's the Limit Game-Used

Randomly inserted, this 17-card set parallels the Sky's the Limit insert set enhanced with a swatch of Game-Used memorabilia. Each card is sequentially numbered to 99. Two parallel sets were also produced, one sequentially numbered to 50 and the other numbered to 10.

PRINT RUN 99 SER.#'d SETS
*PAR.50 SINGLES: .5X TO 1.25X BASE JSY HI
SLBD Baron Davis 2.50 6.00
SLCA Carmelo Anthony 10.00 25.00
SLCB Caron Butler 2.50 6.00
SLCB Chris Bosh 5.00 12.00
SLDG Drew Gooden 2.50 6.00
SLDN Dirk Nowitzki 5.00 12.00
SLDW Dwyane Wade 10.00 25.00
SLJR Jason Richardson 3.00 8.00
SLMG Manu Ginobili 4.00 10.00
SLPP Paul Pierce 3.00 8.00
SLSM Shawn Marion 2.50 6.00
SLSN Steve Nash 4.00 10.00
SLSP Scottie Pippen 8.00 20.00
SLTD Amare Stoudemire 4.00 10.00
SLTP Tayshaun Prince 2.50 6.00
SLTP Tony Parker 3.00 8.00
SLYM Yao Ming 6.00 15.00

2004-05 SkyBox LE

Released in January of 2005, this 125-card set features 75 veterans and 50 rookies. The rookie cards are numbered randomly to either 499 or 99, the ones numbered to 99 are denoted as such in the checklist. Both Hobby and Retail versions of this set were offered where Hobby cards are die cut and retail are not. Hobby and Retail were both packaged in 16-pack boxes, but Hobby packs contained three cards and retail contained five.

COMP.SET w/o SP's (75) 20.00 40.00
1 Tony Parker .30 .75
2 Vince Carter .50 1.25
3 Al Harrington .25 .60
4 Dwyane Wade .50 1.25
5 Latrell Sprewell .25 .60
6 Michael Finley .30 .75
7 Caron Butler .25 .60
8 Zach Randolph .25 .60
9 Peja Stojakovic .30 .75
10 Eddy Curry .20 .50
11 Allen Iverson .50 1.25
12 Kirk Hinrich .25 .60
13 Jason Williams .25 .60
14 Hedo Turkoglu .25 .60
15 Manu Ginobili .40 1.00
16 Eddie House .20 .50
17 Reggie Miller .30 .75
18 Steve Francis .25 .60
19 LeBron James 2.00 5.00
20 Dirk Nowitzki .50 1.25
21 Stephon Marbury .25 .60
22 Ray Allen .30 .75
23 Carmelo Anthony .60 1.50
24 Lamar Odom .25 .60
25 Jamaal Magloire .20 .50
26 Shareef Abdur-Rahim .25 .60
27 Chris Webber .30 .75
28 Jason Richardson .30 .75
29 Richard Jefferson .25 .60
30 Richard Hamilton .25 .60
31 Alonzo Mourning .40 1.00
32 Chris Bosh .30 .75
33 Mike Dunleavy .25 .60
34 Andrei Kirilenko .25 .60
35 Tracy McGrady .40 1.00
36 T.J. Ford .20 .50
37 Jason Kidd .50 1.25
38 Carlos Arroyo .20 .50
39 Rasheed Wallace .30 .75
40 Gilbert Arenas .25 .60
41 Kenyon Martin .25 .60
42 Tim Duncan .50 1.25
43 Yao Ming .60 1.50
44 Carlos Boozer .25 .60
45 Michael Redd .25 .60
46 Larry Hughes .25 .60
47 Antoine Walker .30 .75
48 Kevin Garnett .50 1.25
49 Willie Green .20 .50
50 Tyson Chandler .25 .60
51 Elton Brand .30 .75
52 Allan Houston .25 .60
53 Shawn Marion .25 .60
54 Ricky Davis .25 .60
55 Shaquille O'Neal .75 2.00
56 Steve Nash .40 1.00
57 Jarvis Hayes .20 .50
58 Zydrunas Ilgauskas .25 .60
59 Corey Maggette .25 .60
60 Ben Wallace .25 .60
61 Darius Miles .20 .50
62 Drew Gooden .20 .50
63 Pau Gasol .30 .75
64 Jamal Crawford .30 .75
65 Gary Payton .30 .75
66 Jermaine O'Neal .25 .60
67 Jason Kapono .20 .50
68 Marquis Daniels .20 .50
69 Kobe Bryant 1.25 3.00
70 Baron Davis .25 .60
71 Mike Bibby .30 .75
72 Rashard Lewis .30 .75
73 Paul Pierce .30 .75
74 Sam Cassell .25 .60
75 Amare Stoudemire .25 .60
76 Dwight Howard/99 RC 8.00 20.00
77 Emeka Okafor/99 RC 3.00 8.00
78 Ben Gordon/99 RC 4.00 10.00
79 Shaun Livingston/99 RC 4.00 10.00
80 Devin Harris/99 RC 3.00 8.00
81 Josh Childress/99 RC 3.00 8.00
82 Luol Deng/99 RC 4.00 10.00
83 Rafael Araujo/99 RC 2.50 6.00
84 Andre Iguodala/99 RC 5.00 12.00
85 Luke Jackson/99 RC 2.50 6.00
86 Andris Biedrins/99 RC 2.50 6.00
87 Robert Swift RC 1.25 3.00
88 Sebastian Telfair/99 RC 3.00 8.00
89 Kris Humphries RC 2.00 5.00
90 Al Jefferson RC 2.50 6.00
91 Kirk Snyder RC 1.25 3.00
92 Josh Smith/99 RC 4.00 10.00
93 J.R. Smith/99 RC 4.00 10.00
94 Dorell Wright RC 2.00 5.00
95 Jameer Nelson/99 RC 4.00 10.00
96 Pavel Podkolzin RC 1.25 3.00
97 Nenad Krstic RC 2.00 5.00
98 Andres Nocioni/99 RC 4.00 10.00
99 Delonte West RC 2.00 5.00
100 Tony Allen RC 2.00 5.00
101 Kevin Martin RC 2.50 6.00
102 Sasha Vujacic/99 RC 4.00 10.00
103 Beno Udrih RC 1.50 4.00
104 David Harrison RC 1.25 3.00
105 Anderson Varejao/99 RC 3.00 8.00
106 Jackson Vroman RC 1.25 3.00
107 Peter John Ramos RC 1.25 3.00
108 Lionel Chalmers RC 2.00 5.00
109 Donta Smith RC 1.25 3.00
110 Andre Emmett RC 1.25 3.00
111 Antonio Burks RC 1.50 4.00
112 Royal Ivey RC 1.50 4.00
113 Chris Duhon/99 RC 4.00 10.00
114 Erik Daniels RC 1.50 4.00
115 Justin Reed RC 1.25 3.00
116 Horace Jenkins RC 2.00 5.00
117 D.J. Mbenga RC 1.50 4.00
118 Trevor Ariza RC 2.00 5.00
119 Tim Pickett RC 2.00 5.00
120 Bernard Robinson RC 1.50 4.00
121 Ibrahim Kutluay RC 2.00 5.00
122 Romain Sato RC 1.25 3.00
123 Luis Flores RC 1.50 4.00
124 Damien Wilkins RC 1.50 4.00
125 Yuta Tabuse/99 RC 4.00 10.00

2004-05 SkyBox LE Retail

COMPLETE SET (125) 20.00 50.00
*VETS: SAME PRICE AS HOBBY
76 Dwight Howard RC 1.50 4.00
77 Emeka Okafor RC .60 1.50
78 Ben Gordon RC .75 2.00
79 Shaun Livingston RC .75 2.00
80 Devin Harris RC .60 1.50
81 Josh Childress RC .60 1.50
82 Luol Deng RC .75 2.00
83 Rafael Araujo RC .50 1.25
84 Andre Iguodala RC 1.00 2.50
85 Luke Jackson RC .50 1.25
86 Andris Biedrins RC .50 1.25
87 Robert Swift RC .50 1.25
88 Sebastian Telfair RC .60 1.50
89 Kris Humphries RC .75 2.00
90 Al Jefferson RC 1.00 2.50
91 Kirk Snyder RC .50 1.25
92 Josh Smith RC .75 2.00
93 J.R. Smith RC .75 2.00
94 Dorell Wright RC .75 2.00
95 Jameer Nelson RC .75 2.00
96 Pavel Podkolzin RC .50 1.25
97 Nenad Krstic RC .75 2.00
98 Andres Nocioni RC .75 2.00
99 Delonte West RC .75 2.00
100 Tony Allen RC .75 2.00
101 Kevin Martin RC 1.00 2.50
102 Sasha Vujacic RC .75 2.00
103 Beno Udrih RC .60 1.50
104 David Harrison RC .50 1.25
105 Anderson Varejao RC .60 1.50
106 Jackson Vroman RC .50 1.25
107 Peter John Ramos RC .50 1.25
108 Lionel Chalmers RC .75 2.00
109 Donta Smith RC .50 1.25
110 Andre Emmett RC .50 1.25
111 Antonio Burks RC .60 1.50
112 Royal Ivey RC .60 1.50
113 Chris Duhon RC .75 2.00
114 Erik Daniels RC .60 1.50
115 Justin Reed RC .50 1.25
116 Horace Jenkins RC .75 2.00
117 D.J. Mbenga RC .60 1.50
118 Trevor Ariza RC .75 2.00
119 Tim Pickett RC .75 2.00
120 Bernard Robinson RC .60 1.50
121 Ibrahim Kutluay RC .75 2.00
122 Romain Sato RC .50 1.25
123 Luis Flores RC .60 1.50
124 Damien Wilkins RC .60 1.50
125 Yuta Tabuse RC .75 2.00

2004-05 SkyBox LE 150

*LE 150 1-75 SINGLES: 2X TO 5X BASE HI
*LE 150 RC/499 SINGLES: .6X TO 1.5X BASE HI

2004-05 SkyBox LE 50

*LE 50 1-75 STARS: 3X TO 8X BASE HI
*LE 50 RCs/99: .5X TO 1.25X BASE HI
*LE 50 RCs/499: 1X TO 2.5X BASE HI

2004-05 SkyBox LE 35

*1-75 SINGLES: 4X TO 10X BASE HI
*RCs/99: .6X TO 1.5X BASE HI
*RCs/499: 1.25X TO 3X BASE HI

2004-05 SkyBox LE Jersey Proofs

STATED ODDS 1:60
*JSY 99 SINGLES: .5X TO 1.25X BASE JSY HI
*PATCH SINGLES: 1X TO 2.5X BASE JSY HI
PATCH PRINT RUN 50 SER.#'d SETS
1 Tony Parker 2.50 6.00
2 Vince Carter 4.00 10.00
3 Al Harrington 2.00 5.00
4 Dwyane Wade 4.00 10.00
5 Latrell Sprewell 2.00 5.00
7 Caron Butler 2.00 5.00
8 Zach Randolph 2.00 5.00
9 Peja Stojakovic 2.50 6.00
10 Eddy Curry 1.50 4.00
11 Allen Iverson 4.00 10.00
12 Kirk Hinrich 2.00 5.00
13 Jason Williams 2.00 5.00
15 Manu Ginobili 3.00 8.00
17 Reggie Miller 2.50 6.00
18 Steve Francis 2.00 5.00
21 Stephon Marbury 2.00 5.00
22 Ray Allen 2.50 6.00
23 Carmelo Anthony 5.00 12.00
24 Lamar Odom 2.00 5.00
26 Shareef Abdur-Rahim 2.00 5.00
28 Jason Richardson 2.50 6.00
32 Chris Bosh 2.50 6.00
33 Mike Dunleavy 2.00 5.00
34 Andrei Kirilenko 2.00 5.00
35 Tracy McGrady 3.00 8.00
36 T.J. Ford 1.50 4.00
39 Rasheed Wallace 2.50 6.00
40 Gilbert Arenas 2.00 5.00
42 Tim Duncan 4.00 10.00
43 Yao Ming 5.00 12.00
44 Carlos Boozer 2.00 5.00
46 Larry Hughes 2.00 5.00
48 Kevin Garnett 4.00 10.00
50 Tyson Chandler 2.00 5.00
51 Elton Brand 2.50 6.00
52 Allan Houston 2.00 5.00
53 Shawn Marion 2.00 5.00
55 Shaquille O'Neal 6.00 15.00
56 Steve Nash 3.00 8.00
59 Corey Maggette 2.00 5.00
60 Ben Wallace 2.00 5.00
61 Darius Miles 2.00 5.00
63 Pau Gasol 2.50 6.00
65 Gary Payton 2.50 6.00
71 Mike Bibby 2.50 6.00
72 Rashard Lewis 2.50 6.00
73 Paul Pierce 2.50 6.00
75 Amare Stoudemire 2.00 5.00

2004-05 SkyBox LE Future Legends

Inserted in packs at the rate of one in 12, this 24-card set is horizontally designed with a player photo on the right and a top/bottom cut design with team colors featured on each. A one of one numbered version of this set was inserted also.

COMPLETE SET (24) 20.00 50.00
STATED ODDS 1:12
1 Dwight Howard 2.00 5.00
2 Jameer Nelson 1.00 2.50
3 Shaun Livingston 1.00 2.50
4 Sebastian Telfair .75 2.00
5 Ben Gordon 1.00 2.50
6 Luol Deng 1.00 2.50
7 Josh Childress .75 2.00
8 Josh Smith 1.00 2.50
9 Andre Iguodala 1.25 3.00
10 J.R. Smith 1.00 2.50
11 Kris Humphries 1.00 2.50
12 Kirk Snyder .60 1.50
13 Devin Harris .75 2.00
14 Pavel Podkolzin .60 1.50
15 Rafael Araujo .60 1.50
16 Robert Swift .60 1.50
17 Andris Biedrins .60 1.50
18 Luke Jackson .60 1.50
19 Chris Duhon 1.00 2.50
20 Dorell Wright 1.00 2.50
21 Tony Allen 1.00 2.50
22 Delonte West 1.00 2.50
23 Yuta Tabuse 1.00 2.50
24 Emeka Okafor .75 2.00

2004-05 SkyBox LE Future Legends Jerseys

Randomly inserted in packs, this 21-card set parallels the design of the base Future Legends insert set enhanced with a swatch of jersey and sequential numbering to 75. Several other versions of this set were also issued and break down as follows: Patches serial numbered to 25, Patches Dual serial numbered to 10, Patches Dual one of ones, Patches Autographs serial numbered to 25 and Patches Dual Autographs numbered as one of ones.

PRINT RUN 75 SER.#'d SETS
*JERSEY 50 SINGLES: .5X TO 1.25X BASE HI
*PATCH: 1X TO 2.5X BASE HI
PATCH PRINT RUN 25 SER.#'d SETS
AB Andris Biedrins 1.50 4.00
AI Andre Iguodala 3.00 8.00
AJ Al Jefferson 3.00 8.00
BG Ben Gordon 2.50 6.00
DH Dwight Howard 5.00 12.00
DH2 Devin Harris 2.00 5.00
DW Dorell Wright 2.50 6.00
DW2 Delonte West 2.50 6.00
FL Sasha Vujacic 2.50 6.00
JC Josh Childress 2.00 5.00
JN Jameer Nelson 2.50 6.00
JS Josh Smith 2.50 6.00
JS J.R. Smith 2.50 6.00
KH Kris Humphries 2.50 6.00
KS Kirk Snyder 1.50 4.00
LD Luol Deng 2.50 6.00
LJ Luke Jackson 1.50 4.00
RA Rafael Araujo 1.50 4.00
SL Shaun Livingston 2.50 6.00
ST Sebastian Telfair 2.00 5.00
TA Tony Allen 2.50 6.00
YT Yuta Tabuse 2.50 6.00

2004-05 SkyBox LE Future Legends of the Draft Patches Autographs

Randomly inserted in packs, this 17-card set parallels the design of the base Draft Jerseys set enhanced with patch swatches and autographs. Each card is serially numbered to 25.

PRINT RUN 25 SER.#'d SETS
UNPRICED PATCH DUAL PRINT RUN ONE SET
AB Andris Biedrins 5.00 12.00
AJ Al Jefferson 10.00 25.00
BG Ben Gordon 20.00 50.00
DH2 Devin Harris 6.00 15.00
JS Josh Smith 8.00 20.00
JS J.R. Smith 8.00 20.00
KH Kris Humphries 8.00 20.00
KS Kirk Snyder 5.00 12.00
LJ Luke Jackson 5.00 12.00
RA Rafael Araujo 5.00 12.00
ST Sebastian Telfair 6.00 15.00
YT Yuta Tabuse 8.00 20.00

2004-05 SkyBox LE Legends of the Draft

Inserted in Hobby packs at the rate of one in four and Retail packs at the rate of one in eight, this 20-card set features retired greats on a horizontally designed card with a small head shot in the upper right corner, white backgrounds for the top and brown backgrounds for the bottom. A one of one serial numbered version of this set was also produced.

COMPLETE SET (20) 15.00 40.00
STATED ODDS 1:4 H, 1:8 R
1 Oscar Robertson 1.25 3.00
2 Walt Bellamy 1.00 2.50
3 Elgin Baylor 1.25 3.00
4 Cazzie Russell 1.00 2.50
5 Bob Lanier 1.00 2.50
6 Kevin McHale 1.50 4.00
7 Bill Walton 1.25 3.00
8 John Havlicek 1.25 3.00
9 Robert Parish 1.25 3.00
10 Isiah Thomas 1.25 3.00
11 Walt Frazier 1.25 3.00
12 George Gervin 1.25 3.00
13 Nate Archibald 1.00 2.50
14 Bob Cousy 2.00 5.00
15 Rick Barry 1.00 2.50
16 Earl Monroe 1.25 3.00
17 Willis Reed 1.25 3.00
18 Darryl Dawkins .75 2.00
19 Wes Unseld 1.25 3.00
20 Pat Riley 1.50 4.00

2004-05 SkyBox LE Legends of the Draft Jerseys

Seeded randomly in packs, this 40-card set parallels the look of the Legends of the draft but replaces retired players with action players, adds a jersey from a game and sequential numbering to 50. Several other versions of this set were inserted, one serial numbered to 25, a Dual set serial numbered to 10 and a one of one version. Patch Autograph versions for single players were inserted an serial numbered to 25 and a one of one Patch Autograph Dual set was produced as well.

PRINT RUN 50 SER.#'d SETS
*PATCH: .6X TO 1.5X BASE HI
PATCH PRINT RUN 25 SER.#'d SETS
AH Anfernee Hardaway 10.00 25.00
AI Allen Iverson 6.00 15.00
AK Andrei Kirilenko 3.00 8.00
AS Amare Stoudemire 3.00 8.00
AW Antoine Walker 4.00 10.00
BD Baron Davis 3.00 8.00
CA Carmelo Anthony 8.00 20.00
CM Corey Maggette 3.00 8.00
CW Chris Webber 4.00 10.00
DN Dirk Nowitzki 6.00 15.00
DW Dwyane Wade 6.00 15.00
EB Elton Brand 4.00 10.00
JK Jason Kidd 6.00 15.00
JO Jermaine O'Neal 3.00 8.00
JR Jason Richardson 4.00 10.00
KM Kenyon Martin 3.00 8.00
LO Lamar Odom 3.00 8.00
MB Mike Bibby 4.00 10.00
PG Pau Gasol 4.00 10.00
PP Paul Pierce 4.00 10.00
RA Ray Allen 4.00 10.00
RH Richard Hamilton 3.00 8.00
RM Reggie Miller 4.00 10.00
RW Rasheed Wallace 4.00 10.00
SF Steve Francis 3.00 8.00
SM Stephon Marbury 3.00 8.00
SM2 Shawn Marion 3.00 8.00
SO Shaquille O'Neal 10.00 25.00
SP Scottie Pippen 20.00 50.00
TD Tim Duncan 6.00 15.00
TP Tony Parker 4.00 10.00
TW Tracy McGrady 5.00 12.00
VC Vince Carter 6.00 15.00
YM Yao Ming 8.00 20.00

2004-05 SkyBox LE Legends of the Draft Jerseys Year

Randomly inserted in packs, this 40-card set parallels the base Legends of the Draft Jerseys insert enhanced with serial numbering to the year each player was drafted.

JSY #'d TO PLAYER DRAFT YEAR
AI Allen Iverson/96 5.00 12.00
AK Andrei Kirilenko/99 2.50 6.00
AS Amare Stoudemire/102 2.50 6.00
AW Antoine Walker/96 3.00 8.00
BD Baron Davis/99 2.50 6.00
CA Carmelo Anthony/103 6.00 15.00
CM Corey Maggette/99 2.50 6.00
CW Chris Webber/93 3.00 8.00
DN Dirk Nowitzki/98 5.00 12.00
DW Dwyane Wade/103 5.00 12.00
EB Elton Brand/99 3.00 8.00
JK Jason Kidd/94 5.00 12.00
JO Jermaine O'Neal/96 2.50 6.00
JR Jason Richardson/101 3.00 8.00
JS Jerry Stackhouse/95 2.50 6.00
KG Kevin Garnett/95 5.00 12.00
KM Kenyon Martin/100 2.50 6.00
LO Lamar Odom/99 2.50 6.00
MB Mike Bibby/98 3.00 8.00
PG Pau Gasol/101 3.00 8.00
PJ Peja Stojakovic/96 3.00 8.00
PP Paul Pierce/98 3.00 8.00
RA Ray Allen/96 3.00 8.00
RH Richard Hamilton/99 2.50 6.00
RM Reggie Miller/87 3.00 8.00
RW Rasheed Wallace/95 3.00 8.00
SF Steve Francis/99 2.50 6.00
SM2 Shawn Marion/99 2.50 6.00
SN Steve Nash/96 4.00 10.00
SP Scottie Pippen/87 15.00 40.00
TD Tim Duncan/97 5.00 12.00
TP Tony Parker/101 3.00 8.00
TW Tracy McGrady/97 4.00 10.00
VC Vince Carter/98 5.00 12.00
YM Yao Ming/102

2004-05 SkyBox LE Legends of the Draft Patches Autographs

Randomly inserted in packs, this 40-card set parallels the base Legends of the Draft Jerseys insert enhanced with patches and player autographs. Each card is sequentially numbered to 25.

PRINT RUN 25 SER.#'d SETS
BD Baron Davis 15.00 40.00
CA Carmelo Anthony 30.00 80.00
CM Corey Maggette 12.00 30.00
DW Dwyane Wade 100.00 200.00
EB Elton Brand 12.00 30.00
JK Jason Kidd 30.00 80.00
JS Jerry Stackhouse 20.00 50.00
KM Kenyon Martin 20.00 50.00
RJ Richard Jefferson 12.00 30.00
SM Stephon Marbury 20.00 50.00
TM Tracy McGrady 25.00 60.00
VC Vince Carter 30.00 80.00

2004-05 SkyBox LE Rare Form

Inserted in Retail packs at the rate of one in 576, this 10-card set is die cut in the middle and places a player on the top half of a card accented by his team's colors. A one of one verson of this set was also inserted.

COMPLETE SET (10) 60.00 150.00
STATED ODDS 1:576 RETAIL
1 Shaquille O'Neal 10.00 25.00
2 Dwyane Wade 6.00 15.00
3 Carmelo Anthony 8.00 20.00
4 Kenyon Martin 3.00 8.00
5 Allen Iverson 6.00 15.00
6 Vince Carter 6.00 15.00
7 Kevin Garnett 6.00 15.00
8 Tim Duncan 6.00 15.00
9 LeBron James 25.00 60.00
10 Kobe Bryant 15.00 40.00

2004-05 SkyBox LE Rare Form Jerseys

Randomly inserted in packs, this 10-card set parallels the design of the base Rare Form insert set enhanced with a swatch of game worn jersey and sequential numbering to 50. Several other versions of this set were inserted and break down as follows: Jersey Numbers are serially numbered to featured player's jersey numger, Patches contain a patch swatch and are sequentially numbered to 25, Patches Dual feature two players and patches and are sequentially numbered to 10, and Patch Dual one of one's exist.

PRINT RUN 50 SER.#'d SETS
AI Allen Iverson 6.00 15.00
AS Amare Stoudemire 3.00 8.00
CA Carmelo Anthony 8.00 20.00
DW Dwyane Wade 6.00 15.00
KG Kevin Garnett 6.00 15.00
KM Kenyon Martin 3.00 8.00
SN Steve Nash 5.00 12.00
SO Shaquille O'Neal 10.00 25.00
TD Tim Duncan 6.00 15.00
VC Vince Carter 6.00 15.00

2004-05 SkyBox LE Rare Form Jerseys Numbers

STATED PRINT RUN 3 TO 32 SETS
SOME UNPRICED DUE TO SCARCITY
AS Amare Stoudemire/32 4.00 10.00
KG Kevin Garnett/21 8.00 20.00
SO Shaquille O'Neal/32 12.00 30.00
VC Vince Carter/15 12.00 30.00

2004-05 SkyBox LE Sky's the Limit Jerseys

PRINT RUN 99 SER.#'d SETS
*JSY 50 SINGLES: .5X TO 1.25X BASE JSY
PATCH PRINT RUN 25 SER.#'d SETS
AI Allen Iverson 5.00 12.00
AI2 Andre Iguodala 4.00 10.00
BD Baron Davis 2.50 6.00
BG Ben Gordon 3.00 8.00
DH Dwight Howard 6.00 15.00
DH Devin Harris 2.50 6.00
DN Dirk Nowitzki 5.00 12.00
DW Dwyane Wade 5.00 12.00
DW2 Dorell Wright 3.00 8.00
EB Elton Brand 3.00 8.00
JK Jason Kidd 5.00 12.00
JN Jameer Nelson 3.00 8.00
JS J.R. Smith 3.00 8.00
KH Kirk Hinrich 2.50 6.00
RJ Richard Jefferson 2.50 6.00
SF Steve Francis 2.50 6.00
SL Shaun Livingston 3.00 8.00
ST Sebastian Telfair 2.50 6.00
TM Tracy McGrady 4.00 10.00
YM Yao Ming 6.00 15.00

1991-92 SkyBox Mark and See Minis

Published by Golden Book (Western Publishing Company Inc.) and SkyBox, this 14-card set was featured on perforated sheets inserted in two 5 1/2" by 8" USA Basketball "Mark and See" booklets (numbered 22381 and 22382). Each booklet came with a special marker, and answers to the multiple-choice questions was revealed by coloring in the blank spaces provided for answers. The first ten cards are perforated, measure approximately 2 1/4" by 2 3/4", and are printed on thin card stock. The fronts are identical to the regular 1991-92 SkyBox II cards, displaying a posed color shot of the player against a computer-generated background consisting of stars and stripes. The words "Barcelona '92" are printed along the left edge. The player's name is at the bottom. In contrast to the regular issue cards, the backs are black-and-white and show a player photo in a flag-shaped icon. A player quote about the Olympic games is featured. Included in the first booklet is a 7 1/4" by 3 1/2" panel that could be cut into three cards, each numbered and measuring approximately 2 3/8" by 3 3/8". It displays the entire team in front of a background showing the words "Barcelona '92" in large red letters above a row of gold stars against a sky scene. The second booklet also featured a 7 1/4" by 3 1/2" panel with a team photo, but it was not numbered and not designed to be cut into smaller player cards. Each card has the complete team listed with the featured players marked by an asterisk.

COMPLETE SET (14) 20.00 50.00
530 Charles Barkley 2.50 6.00
531 Larry Bird 4.00 10.00
532 Patrick Ewing 1.50 4.00
533 Magic Johnson 1.50 4.00
534 Michael Jordan 10.00 25.00
535 Karl Malone 3.00 8.00
536 Chris Mullin 1.50 4.00
537 Scottie Pippen 2.50 6.00
538 David Robinson 2.50 6.00
539 John Stockton 3.00 8.00
544 Team USA Card 1 .75 2.00
545 Team USA Card 2 2.50 6.00
546 Team USA Card 3 1.25 3.00
NNO Team Photo 1.50 4.00

1993 SkyBox Milestone Promos

These two standard-size promo cards were issued to promote the forthcoming 100-card SkyBox Milestone (The Dakota Universe) set, which features characters from Milestone Media, the multicultural-themed imprint distributed by DC Comics. Inside a turquoise frame and a black-and-brown outer border, the fronts feature cartoon-like caricatures of NBA players, each is portrayed wearing futuristic body armor. On a beige panel, the horizontal backs contain an advertisement for the forthcoming card issue. The cards are unnumbered and checklisted below in alphabetical order.

COMPLETE SET (2) 2.50 6.00
1 Magic (Magic Johnson) 1.50 4.00
2 The Admiral (David Robinson 1.50 4.00

1998-99 SkyBox Molten Metal

This was the first year for the Molten Metal set. The set was issued in 6-card packs with a suggested retail price of $4.99. The set was one series only, containing 150 cards. The set was broken up into 3 different subsets - cards 1-100 was the Metal Smiths subset, cards 101-130 was the Heavy Metal subset and cards 131-150 was the Supernatural subset. The Metal Smiths subset cards were inserted at four per pack, the Heavy Metal subset cards were inserted one per pack and the Supernatural subset cards were inserted one in two packs.

COMPLETE SET (150) 20.00 50.00
CARDS 1-100 INSERTED 4:1 PACKS
CARDS 101-130 INSERTED 1:1 PACKS
CARDS 131-150 INSERTED 1:2 PACKS
1 Maurice Taylor .10 .25
2 Bison Dele .10 .25
3 Anthony Mason .10 .25
4 John Starks .12 .30
5 Anthony Johnson .10 .25
6 Calbert Cheaney .10 .25
7 Roshown McLeod RC .30 .75
8 Jalen Rose .12 .30
9 Kelvin Cato .10 .25
10 Walter McCarty .10 .25
11 Isaac Austin .10 .25
12 Arvydas Sabonis .12 .30
13 David Wesley .10 .25
14 Jim Jackson .10 .25
15 Elden Campbell .10 .25
16 Michael Doleac RC .40 1.00
17 Chris Webber .15 .40
18 Mitch Richmond .15 .40
19 Johnny Newman .10 .25
20 Jayson Williams .10 .25
21 George Lynch .10 .25
22 Ron Harper .12 .30
23 Donyell Marshall .10 .25
24 Derek Fisher .15 .40
25 Matt Harpring RC .50 1.25
26 Jason Williams RC 1.25 3.00
27 Toni Kukoc .15 .40
28 Clarence Weatherspoon .10 .25
29 Eddie Jones .15 .40
30 Bo Outlaw .10 .25
31 Zydrunas Ilgauskas .15 .40
32 Michael Dickerson RC .50 1.25
33 Tyronn Lue RC .50 1.25
34 Theo Ratliff .12 .30
35 Dirk Nowitzki RC 3.00 8.00
36 Robert Traylor RC .50 1.25
37 Gary Trent .10 .25
38 Wesley Person .10 .25
39 Bryce Drew RC .30 .75
40 P.J. Brown .10 .25
41 Joe Smith .12 .30
42 Avery Johnson .12 .30
43 Chris Anstey .10 .25
44 Mario Elie .10 .25
45 Voshon Lenard .10 .25
46 Rex Chapman .10 .25
47 Hersey Hawkins .10 .25
48 Shawn Bradley .10 .25
49 Matt Maloney .10 .25
50 Dan Majerle .15 .40
51 Pat Garrity RC .40 1.00
52 Sam Perkins .10 .25
53 Mookie Blaylock .10 .25
54 Al Harrington RC .75 2.00
55 Clifford Robinson .10 .25
56 Alan Henderson .10 .25
57 Chris Mullin .15 .40
58 Dennis Scott .10 .25
59 A.C. Green .12 .30
60 Tyrone Hill .10 .25
61 Chauncey Billups .20 .50
62 Michael Finley .15 .40
63 Terrell Brandon .10 .25
64 Detlef Schrempf .15 .40
65 Bonzi Wells RC .50 1.25
66 Larry Johnson .15 .40
67 Bryant Reeves .10 .25
68 Raef LaFrentz RC .60 1.50
69 Kendall Gill .10 .25
70 Bryon Russell .10 .25
71 Bobby Phills .10 .25
72 Tony Delk .10 .25
73 Lorenzen Wright .10 .25
74 Keon Clark RC .50 1.25
75 Billy Owens .10 .25
76 Tracy Murray .10 .25
77 Bobby Jackson .10 .25
78 Sam Cassell .12 .30
79 Corliss Williamson .10 .25
80 Jeff Hornacek .12 .30
81 LaPhonso Ellis .10 .25
82 Sam Mitchell .10 .25
83 Sean Elliott .15 .40
84 John Wallace .10 .25
85 Dikembe Mutombo .15 .40
86 Rik Smits .12 .30
87 Isaiah Rider .12 .30
88 Joe Dumars .15 .40
89 Allan Houston .12 .30
90 Sam Mack .10 .25
91 Paul Pierce RC 2.00 5.00
92 Lamond Murray .10 .25
93 Rasheed Wallace .15 .40
94 Danny Fortson .10 .25
95 Cherokee Parks .10 .25
96 Antonio Daniels .10 .25
97 Shandon Anderson .10 .25
98 Ricky Davis RC .75 2.00
99 Rodney Rogers .10 .25
100 Tariq Abdul-Wahad .10 .25
101 Glenn Robinson .20 .50
102 Ron Mercer .20 .50
103 Alonzo Mourning .30 .75
104 Marcus Camby .20 .50
105 Steve Smith .20 .50
106 Tim Hardaway .25 .60
107 Rod Strickland .15 .40
108 Reggie Miller .30 .75
109 Juwan Howard .20 .50
110 Hakeem Olajuwon .30 .75
111 John Stockton .30 .75
112 Antonio McDyess .20 .50
113 Charles Barkley .40 1.00
114 Karl Malone .30 .75
115 Jerry Stackhouse .25 .60
116 Tracy McGrady .40 1.00
117 Brevin Knight .15 .40
118 Gary Payton .25 .60
119 Derek Anderson .15 .40
120 Glen Rice .25 .60
121 David Robinson .40 1.00
122 Vin Baker .20 .50
123 Tom Gugliotta .15 .40
124 Patrick Ewing .30 .75
125 Ray Allen .30 .75
126 Anfernee Hardaway .40 1.00
127 Jason Kidd .40 1.00
128 Kenny Anderson .20 .50
129 Kerry Kittles .15 .40
130 Tim Thomas .25 .60
131 Shareef Abdur-Rahim .40 1.00
132 Mike Bibby RC 1.25 3.00
133 Kobe Bryant 1.50 4.00
134 Vince Carter RC 4.00 10.00
135 Tim Duncan .75 2.00
136 Kevin Garnett .60 1.50
137 Grant Hill .60 1.50
138 Larry Hughes RC 1.50 4.00
139 Allen Iverson .75 2.00
140 Antawn Jamison RC 1.25 3.00
141 Michael Jordan 3.00 8.00
142 Shawn Kemp .40 1.00
143 Stephon Marbury .50 1.25
144 Michael Olowokandi RC 1.00 2.50
145 Shaquille O'Neal 1.00 2.50
146 Scottie Pippen .60 1.50
147 Dennis Rodman .75 2.00
148 Damon Stoudamire .30 .75
149 Keith Van Horn .40 1.00
150 Antoine Walker .40 1.00

1998-99 SkyBox Molten Metal Xplosion

COMPLETE SET (150) 175.00 350.00
*1-100 STARS/RCs: 1X TO 2.5X BASE HI
1-100 STATED ODDS 1:2.5
*101-130 STARS: 2.5X TO 6X BASE HI
101-130 STATED ODDS 1:18
*131-150 STARS: 5X TO 12X BASE HI
*131-150 RCs: 1.5X TO 4X BASE HI
131-150 STATED ODDS 1:60
134 Vince Carter 20.00 50.00
147 Dennis Rodman 12.00 30.00

1998-99 SkyBox Molten Metal Fusion

1-30 STATED ODDS 1:16
31-50: PRINT RUN 40 SERIAL #'d SETS
36/37/39/41-43: PRINT RUN 250 #'d SETS
1 Glenn Robinson 2.50 6.00
2 Ron Mercer 2.50 6.00
3 Alonzo Mourning 4.00 10.00
4 Marcus Camby 2.50 6.00
5 Steve Smith 2.50 6.00
6 Tim Hardaway 3.00 8.00
7 Rod Strickland 2.00 5.00
8 Reggie Miller 4.00 10.00
9 Juwan Howard 2.50 6.00
10 Hakeem Olajuwon 4.00 10.00
11 John Stockton 4.00 10.00
12 Antonio McDyess 2.50 6.00
13 Charles Barkley 5.00 12.00
14 Karl Malone 4.00 10.00
15 Jerry Stackhouse 3.00 8.00
16 Tracy McGrady 5.00 12.00
17 Brevin Knight 2.00 5.00
18 Gary Payton 3.00 8.00
19 Derek Anderson 2.00 5.00
20 Glen Rice 3.00 8.00
21 David Robinson 5.00 12.00
22 Vin Baker 2.50 6.00
23 Tom Gugliotta 2.00 5.00
24 Patrick Ewing 4.00 10.00
25 Ray Allen 4.00 10.00
26 Anfernee Hardaway 5.00 12.00
27 Jason Kidd 5.00 12.00
28 Kenny Anderson 2.50 6.00
29 Kerry Kittles 2.00 5.00

30 Tim Thomas 3.00 8.00
31 Shareef Abdur-Rahim 50.00 125.00
32 Mike Bibby 40.00 100.00
33 Kobe Bryant 200.00 500.00
34 Vince Carter 125.00 300.00
35 Tim Duncan 100.00 250.00
36 Kevin Garnett 25.00 60.00
37 Grant Hill 25.00 60.00
38 Larry Hughes 50.00 125.00
39 Allen Iverson 40.00 100.00
40 Antawn Jamison 40.00 100.00
41 Michael Jordan 600.00 1200.00
42 Shawn Kemp 15.00 40.00
43 Stephon Marbury 20.00 50.00
44 Michael Olowokandi 30.00 80.00
45 Shaquille O'Neal 125.00 300.00
46 Scottie Pippen 80.00 200.00
47 Dennis Rodman 125.00 300.00
48 Damon Stoudamire 40.00 100.00
49 Keith Van Horn 50.00 125.00
50 Antoine Walker 50.00 125.00

1998-99 SkyBox Molten Metal Fusion Titanium

1-30 STATED ODDS 1:96
31-50: PRINT RUN 250 SERIAL #'d SETS
36/37/39/41-43: PRINT RUN 40 #'d SETS
1 Glenn Robinson 5.00 12.00
2 Ron Mercer 5.00 12.00
3 Alonzo Mourning 8.00 20.00
4 Marcus Camby 5.00 12.00
5 Steve Smith 5.00 12.00
6 Tim Hardaway 6.00 15.00
7 Rod Strickland 4.00 10.00
8 Reggie Miller 8.00 20.00
9 Juwan Howard 5.00 12.00
10 Hakeem Olajuwon 8.00 20.00
11 John Stockton 8.00 20.00
12 Antonio McDyess 5.00 12.00
13 Charles Barkley 10.00 25.00
14 Karl Malone 8.00 20.00
15 Jerry Stackhouse 6.00 15.00
16 Tracy McGrady 10.00 25.00
17 Brevin Knight 4.00 10.00
18 Gary Payton 6.00 15.00
19 Derek Anderson 4.00 10.00
20 Glen Rice 6.00 15.00
21 David Robinson 12.00 30.00
22 Vin Baker 5.00 12.00
23 Tom Gugliotta 4.00 10.00
24 Patrick Ewing 8.00 20.00
25 Ray Allen 8.00 20.00
26 Anfernee Hardaway 10.00 25.00
27 Jason Kidd 10.00 25.00
28 Kenny Anderson 5.00 12.00
29 Kerry Kittles 4.00 10.00
30 Tim Thomas 6.00 15.00
31 Shareef Abdur-Rahim 15.00 40.00
32 Mike Bibby 12.00 30.00
33 Kobe Bryant 125.00 250.00
34 Vince Carter 40.00 100.00
35 Tim Duncan 75.00 200.00
36 Kevin Garnett 250.00 500.00
37 Grant Hill 80.00 200.00
38 Larry Hughes 15.00 40.00
39 Allen Iverson 125.00 300.00
40 Antawn Jamison 12.00 30.00
41 Michael Jordan 1500.00 2500.00
42 Shawn Kemp 50.00 125.00
43 Stephon Marbury 60.00 150.00
44 Michael Olowokandi 10.00 25.00
45 Shaquille O'Neal 40.00 100.00
46 Scottie Pippen 30.00 80.00
47 Dennis Rodman 50.00 125.00
48 Damon Stoudamire 12.00 30.00
49 Keith Van Horn 15.00 40.00
50 Antoine Walker 15.00 40.00

1992-93 SkyBox Nestle

Collectors could obtain two standard-size cards in multi-packs of Nestle Crunch Minis, Nestle Crunch bars, Raisinets, Baby Ruth, and Butterfinger. A special binder to hold the cards was also available through a mail-in offer. These cards are identical to 1992-93 SkyBox series I cards, with the exception that they have no card numbers on them. They are checklisted below in alphabetical order.

COMPLETE SET (50) 60.00 150.00
1 Michael Adams .75 2.00
2 Rolando Blackman 1.00 2.50
3 Manute Bol 1.25 3.00
4 Dee Brown .75 2.00
5 Tony Campbell .75 2.00
6 Derrick Coleman 1.25 3.00
7 Brad Daugherty .75 2.00
8 Clyde Drexler 3.00 8.00
9 Joe Dumars 2.00 5.00
10 Sean Elliott 2.00 5.00
11 Pervis Ellison .75 2.00
12 Kendall Gill 1.25 3.00
13 Tim Hardaway 2.00 5.00
14 Derek Harper 1.25 3.00
15 Hersey Hawkins 1.25 3.00
16 Chris Jackson 1.00 2.50
17 Mark Jackson 1.50 4.00
18 Kevin Johnson 1.50 4.00
19 Shawn Kemp 3.00 8.00
20 Reggie Lewis 1.25 3.00
21 Dan Majerle 1.50 4.00
22 Karl Malone 4.00 10.00
23 Danny Manning 1.25 3.00
24 Reggie Miller 4.00 10.00
25 Chris Mullin 2.50 6.00
26 Dikembe Mutombo 1.50 4.00
27 Charles Oakley 1.25 3.00
28 John Paxson 1.25 3.00
29 Sam Perkins 1.25 3.00
30 Drazen Petrovic 3.00 8.00
31 Ricky Pierce .75 2.00
32 Scottie Pippen 5.00 12.00
33 Terry Porter .75 2.00
34 Mark Price 1.25 3.00
35 J.R. Reid .75 2.00
36 Glen Rice 2.50 6.00
37 Alvin Robertson .75 2.00
38 David Robinson 4.00 10.00
39 Dennis Rodman 4.00 10.00
40 Detlef Schrempf 1.25 3.00
41 Dennis Scott 1.25 3.00
42 Rony Seikaly .75 2.00
43 Scott Skiles 1.25 3.00
44 Charles Smith .75 2.00
45 Kenny Smith .75 2.00
46 John Stockton 5.00 12.00
47 Otis Thorpe 1.25 3.00
48 Wayman Tisdale .75 2.00
49 Dominique Wilkins 3.00 8.00
50 James Worthy 2.50 6.00

1993-94 SkyBox Premium Promos

This six-card standard-size promo set was issued to promote the scheduled November 1993 release of SkyBox I and its inserts. The fronts feature full-bleed color action photos. Cards 1, 3 and 6 below represent the regular issue, and each has a white stripe down one side the card front containing the player's name, position, and team. The SkyBox Premium foil stamp logo appears on the front. The back features a close-up player photo on the top half, and the player's stats and biography on the back. Card 2 below represents the All-Rookie Team inserts and has a black band down the right side of the front containing the player's name and position with the All-Rookie Team logo. The back has a brief biography on a white card face. Card 4 below represents the Showdown Series and has a black foil band stamped along the bottom of the two-player photo on the front, which has the players' names in gold along with the Showdown Series logo. The horizontal back has narrow-cropped close-up photos of each player along the left and right edges with comparative stats between. Card 5 below represents the Center Stage inserts and has the player's name in prismatic silver lettering at the top of front photo and a brief biography on the back. The cards are unnumbered and checklisted below in alphabetical order.

COMPLETE SET (6) 5.00 12.00
1 Michael Jordan 4.00 10.00
2 Christian Laettner .40 1.00
3 Dan Majerle .50 1.25
4 Alonzo Mourning .75 2.00
Patrick Ewing
5 Shaquille O'Neal 2.00 5.00
6 David Robinson .75 2.00

1993-94 SkyBox Premium

The 1993-94 SkyBox basketball set contains 341 standard-size cards that were issued in series of 191 and 150 respectively. Cards were issued in 12-card packs with 36 packs per box. The cards feature full-bleed color action photos with a wide white stripe down one side of the front containing the player's name, position, and team. The SkyBox Premium foil stamp logo appears superimposed on the front. The backs display a second player close-up shot on the top half, and the player's statistics and scouting report on the bottom half. The cards are numbered on the back and grouped alphabetically within team order. Subsets are Playoff Performances (4-21), Changing Faces (292-318), and Costacos Brothers Poster Cards (319-338). Rookie Cards of note include Vin Baker, Anfernee Hardaway, Allan Houston, Jamal Mashburn, Nick Van Exel and Chris Webber. The odds of finding a Head of the Class Exchange card are one in 360 first series packs. It was redeemable for a Head of the Class card featuring the top six 1993 draft picks. The redemption date was April 15, 1994.

COMPLETE SET (341) 12.00 30.00
COMPLETE SERIES 1 (191) 6.00 15.00
COMPLETE SERIES 2 (150) 6.00 15.00
DP4/DP17: SER.1 STATED ODDS 1:36
HOC EXCH: SER.1 STATED ODDS 1:360
1 Checklist .10 .25
2 Checklist .10 .25
3 Checklist .10 .25
4 Larry Johnson PO .15 .40
5 Alonzo Mourning PO .25 .60
6 Hakeem Olajuwon PO .20 .50
7 Brad Daugherty PO .12 .30
8 Oliver Miller PO .10 .25
9 David Robinson PO .25 .60
10 Patrick Ewing PO .20 .50
11 Ricky Pierce PO .10 .25
12 Sam Perkins PO .10 .25
13 John Starks PO .12 .30
14 Michael Jordan PO 1.25 3.00
15 Dan Majerle PO .15 .40
16 Scottie Pippen PO .30 .75
17 Shawn Kemp PO .20 .50
18 Charles Barkley PO .25 .60
19 Horace Grant PO .12 .30
20 K.Johnson/M.Jordan PO .25 .60
21 John Paxson PO .12 .30
22 David Robinson IS .25 .60
23 NBA On NBC .10 .25
24 Stacey Augmon .12 .30
25 Mookie Blaylock .10 .25
26 Craig Ehlo .10 .25
27 Adam Keefe .10 .25
28 Dominique Wilkins .20 .50
29 Kevin Willis .10 .25
30 Dee Brown .10 .25
31 Sherman Douglas .10 .25
32 Rick Fox .10 .25
33 Kevin Gamble .10 .25
34 Xavier McDaniel .10 .25
35 Robert Parish .15 .40
36 Muggsy Bogues .12 .30
37 Dell Curry .10 .25
38 Kendall Gill .10 .25
39 Larry Johnson .15 .40
40 Alonzo Mourning .25 .60
41 Johnny Newman .10 .25
42 B.J. Armstrong .10 .25
43 Bill Cartwright .12 .30
44 Horace Grant .12 .30
45 Michael Jordan 1.25 3.00
46 John Paxson .12 .30
47 Scottie Pippen .30 .75
48 Scott Williams .10 .25
49 Terrell Brandon .12 .30
50 Brad Daugherty .12 .30
51 Larry Nance .12 .30
52 Mark Price .15 .40
53 Gerald Wilkins .10 .25
54 John Williams .10 .25
55 Terry Davis .10 .25
56 Derek Harper .12 .30
57 Jim Jackson .12 .30
58 Sean Rooks .10 .25
59 Doug Smith .10 .25
60 Mahmoud Abdul-Rauf .10 .25
61 LaPhonso Ellis .10 .25
62 Mark Macon .10 .25
63 Dikembe Mutombo .15 .40
64 Bryant Stith .10 .25
65 Reggie Williams .10 .25
66 Joe Dumars .15 .40
67 Bill Laimbeer .12 .30
68 Terry Mills .10 .25
69 Alvin Robertson .10 .25
70 Dennis Rodman .30 .75
71 Isiah Thomas .15 .40
72 Victor Alexander .10 .25
73 Tim Hardaway .15 .40
74 Tyrone Hill .10 .25
75 Sarunas Marciulionis .10 .25
76 Chris Mullin .15 .40
77 Billy Owens .10 .25
78 Latrell Sprewell .25 .60
79 Robert Horry .15 .40
80 Vernon Maxwell .10 .25
81 Hakeem Olajuwon .20 .50
82 Kenny Smith .12 .30
83 Otis Thorpe .10 .25
84 Dale Davis .10 .25
85 Reggie Miller .20 .50
86 Pooh Richardson .10 .25
87 Detlef Schrempf .15 .40
88 Malik Sealy .10 .25
89 Rik Smits .12 .30
90 Ron Harper .12 .30
91 Mark Jackson .12 .30
92 Danny Manning .12 .30
93 Stanley Roberts .10 .25
94 Loy Vaught .10 .25
95 Randy Woods .10 .25
96 Sam Bowie .10 .25
97 Doug Christie .10 .25
98 Vlade Divac .15 .40
99 Anthony Peeler .10 .25
100 Sedale Threatt .10 .25
101 James Worthy .20 .50
102 Grant Long .10 .25
103 Harold Miner .10 .25
104 Glen Rice .15 .40
105 John Salley .10 .25
106 Rony Seikaly .10 .25
107 Steve Smith .12 .30
108 Anthony Avent .10 .25
109 Jon Barry .10 .25
110 Frank Brickowski .10 .25
111 Blue Edwards .10 .25
112 Todd Day .10 .25
113 Lee Mayberry .10 .25
114 Eric Murdock .10 .25
115 Thurl Bailey .10 .25
116 Christian Laettner .12 .30
117 Chuck Person .12 .30
118 Doug West .10 .25
119 Micheal Williams .10 .25
120 Kenny Anderson .12 .30
121 Benoit Benjamin .10 .25
122 Derrick Coleman .12 .30
123 Chris Morris .10 .25
124 Rumeal Robinson .10 .25
125 Rolando Blackman .12 .30
126 Patrick Ewing .20 .50
127 Anthony Mason .10 .25
128 Charles Oakley .12 .30
129 Doc Rivers .12 .30
130 Charles Smith .10 .25
131 John Starks .12 .30
132 Nick Anderson .10 .25
133 Shaquille O'Neal .60 1.50
134 Donald Royal .10 .25
135 Dennis Scott .10 .25
136 Scott Skiles .10 .25
137 Brian Williams .10 .25
138 Johnny Dawkins .10 .25
139 Hersey Hawkins .10 .25
140 Jeff Hornacek .12 .30
141 Andrew Lang .10 .25
142 Tim Perry .10 .25
143 Clarence Weatherspoon .10 .25
144 Danny Ainge .15 .40
145 Charles Barkley .25 .60
146 Cedric Ceballos .12 .30
147 Kevin Johnson .15 .40
148 Oliver Miller .10 .25
149 Dan Majerle .15 .40
150 Clyde Drexler .20 .50
151 Harvey Grant .10 .25
152 Jerome Kersey .10 .25
153 Terry Porter .10 .25
154 Clifford Robinson .10 .25
155 Rod Strickland .10 .25
156 Buck Williams .10 .25
157 Mitch Richmond .15 .40
158 Lionel Simmons .10 .25
159 Wayman Tisdale .10 .25
160 Spud Webb .12 .30
161 Walt Williams .10 .25
162 Antoine Carr .10 .25
163 Lloyd Daniels .10 .25
164 Sean Elliott .15 .40
165 Dale Ellis .10 .25
166 Avery Johnson .12 .30
167 J.R. Reid .10 .25
168 David Robinson .25 .60
169 Shawn Kemp .20 .50
170 Derrick McKey .10 .25
171 Nate McMillan .10 .25
172 Gary Payton .20 .50
173 Sam Perkins .10 .25
174 Ricky Pierce .10 .25
175 Tyrone Corbin .10 .25
176 Jay Humphries .10 .25
177 Jeff Malone .10 .25
178 Karl Malone .20 .50
179 John Stockton .20 .50
180 Michael Adams .10 .25
181 Kevin Duckworth .10 .25
182 Pervis Ellison .10 .25
183 Tom Gugliotta .12 .30
184 Don MacLean .10 .25
185 Brent Price .10 .25
186 George Lynch RC .20 .50
187 Rex Walters RC .20 .50
188 Shawn Bradley RC .20 .50
189 Ervin Johnson RC .20 .50
190 Luther Wright RC .20 .50
191 Calbert Cheaney RC .20 .50
192 Craig Ehlo .10 .25
193 Duane Ferrell .10 .25
194 Paul Graham .10 .25
195 Andrew Lang .10 .25
196 Chris Corchiani .10 .25
197 Acie Earl RC .20 .50
198 Dino Radja RC .20 .50
199 Ed Pinckney .10 .25
200 Tony Bennett .10 .25
201 Scott Burrell RC .20 .50
202 Kenny Gattison .10 .25
203 Hersey Hawkins .10 .25
204 Eddie Johnson .10 .25
205 Corie Blount RC .20 .50
206 Steve Kerr .12 .30
207 Toni Kukoc RC .50 1.25
208 Pete Myers .10 .25
209 Danny Ferry .10 .25
210 Tyrone Hill .10 .25
211 Gerald Madkins RC .20 .50
212 Chris Mills RC .20 .50
213 Lucious Harris RC .20 .50
214 Popeye Jones RC .20 .50
215 Jamal Mashburn RC .30 .75
216 Darnell Mee RC .20 .50
217 Rodney Rogers RC .20 .50
218 Brian Williams .10 .25
219 Greg Anderson .10 .25
220 Sean Elliott .15 .40
221 Allan Houston RC .40 1.00
222 Lindsey Hunter RC .20 .50
223 Chris Gatling .10 .25
224 Josh Grant RC .20 .50
225 Keith Jennings .10 .25
226 Avery Johnson .12 .30
227 Chris Webber RC 1.00 2.50
228 Sam Cassell RC .40 1.00
229 Mario Elie .10 .25
230 Richard Petruska RC .20 .50
231 Eric Riley RC .20 .50
232 Antonio Davis RC .25 .60
233 Scott Haskin RC .20 .50
234 Derrick McKey .10 .25
235 Mark Aguirre .12 .30
236 Terry Dehere RC .20 .50
237 Gary Grant .10 .25
238 Randy Woods .10 .25
239 Sam Bowie .10 .25
240 Elden Campbell .10 .25
241 Nick Van Exel RC .40 1.00
242 Manute Bol .10 .25
243 Brian Shaw .10 .25
244 Vin Baker RC .30 .75
245 Brad Lohaus .10 .25
246 Ken Norman .10 .25
247 Derek Strong RC .20 .50
248 Danny Schayes .10 .25
249 Mike Brown .10 .25
250 Luc Longley .12 .30
251 Isaiah Rider RC .30 .75
252 Kevin Edwards .10 .25
253 Armon Gilliam .10 .25
254 Greg Anthony .10 .25
255 Anthony Bonner .10 .25
256 Tony Campbell .10 .25
257 Hubert Davis .10 .25
258 Litterial Green .10 .25
259 Anfernee Hardaway RC 1.00 2.50
260 Larry Krystkowiak .10 .25
261 Todd Lichti .10 .25
262 Dana Barros .10 .25
263 Greg Graham RC .20 .50
264 Warren Kidd RC .20 .50
265 Moses Malone .15 .40
266 A.C. Green .12 .30
267 Joe Kleine .10 .25
268 Malcolm Mackey RC .20 .50
269 Mark Bryant .10 .25
270 Chris Dudley .10 .25
271 Harvey Grant .10 .25
272 James Robinson RC .20 .50
273 Duane Causwell .10 .25
274 Bobby Hurley RC .20 .50
275 Jim Les .10 .25
276 Willie Anderson .10 .25
277 Terry Cummings .12 .30
278 Vinny Del Negro .10 .25
279 Sleepy Floyd .10 .25
280 Dennis Rodman .30 .75
281 Vincent Askew .10 .25
282 Kendall Gill .10 .25
283 Steve Scheffler .10 .25
284 Detlef Schrempf .15 .40
285 David Benoit .10 .25
286 Tom Chambers .12 .30
287 Felton Spencer .10 .25
288 Rex Chapman .10 .25
289 Kevin Duckworth .10 .25
290 Gheorghe Muresan RC .20 .50
291 Kenny Walker .10 .25
292 A.Lang/C.Ehlo CF .10 .25
293 D.Radja/A.Earl CF .10 .25
294 E.Johnson/H.Hawkins CF .10 .25
295 T.Kukoc/C.Blount CF .25 .60
296 T.Hill/C.Mills CF .10 .25
297 J.Mashburn/P.Jones CF .15 .40
298 D.Mee/R.Rogers CF .10 .25
299 L.Hunter/A.Houston CF .20 .50
300 C.Webber/A.Johnson CF .50 1.25
301 S.Cassell/M.Elie CF .20 .50
302 D.McKey/A.Davis CF .12 .30
303 T.Dehere/M.Aguirre CF .10 .25
304 N.Van Exel/G.Lynch CF .20 .50
305 H.Miner/S.Smith CF .12 .30
306 K.Norman/V.Baker CF .15 .40
307 M.Brown/I.Rider CF .15 .40
308 K.Edwards/R.Walters CF .10 .25
309 H.Davis/A.Bonner CF .10 .25
310 A.Hardaway/Kryst CF .50 1.25
311 M.Malone/S.Bradley CF .10 .25
312 J.Kleine/A.C. Green CF .12 .30
313 H.Grant/C.Dudley CF .10 .25
314 B.Hurley/M.Richmond CF .10 .25
315 S.Floyd/D.Rodman CF .30 .75
316 K.Gill/D.Schrempf CF .15 .40
317 F.Spencer/L.Wright CF .10 .25
318 C.Cheaney/Duckworth CF .10 .25
319 Karl Malone PC .20 .50
320 Alonzo Mourning PC .25 .60
321 Scottie Pippen PC .30 .75
322 Mark Price PC .15 .40
323 LaPhonso Ellis PC .10 .25
324 Joe Dumars PC .15 .40
325 Chris Mullin PC .15 .40
326 Ron Harper PC .12 .30
327 Glen Rice PC .15 .40
328 Christian Laettner PC .12 .30
329 Kenny Anderson PC .12 .30
330 John Starks PC .12 .30
331 Shaquille O'Neal PC .60 1.50
332 Charles Barkley PC .25 .60
333 Clifford Robinson PC .10 .25
334 Clyde Drexler PC .20 .50
335 Mitch Richmond PC .15 .40
336 David Robinson PC .25 .60
337 Shawn Kemp PC .20 .50
338 John Stockton PC .20 .50
339 Checklist 4 .10 .25
340 Checklist 5 .10 .25
341 Checklist 6 .10 .25
DP4 Jim Jackson 1992 .40 1.00
DP17 Doug Christie 1992 .15 .40
NNO Expired HOC Exchange .60 1.50
NNO Head of Class Card 12.00 30.00

1993-94 SkyBox Premium All-Rookies

Randomly inserted in first series 12-card packs at a rate of one in 36, this standard-size five-card set features top rookies from the 1992-93 season. The design features borderless fronts with color action player cutouts set against metallic game-crowd backgrounds. The player's name appears in gold-foil lettering at the upper left. The white back carries a color player head shot along with career highlights.

COMPLETE SET (5) 4.00 10.00
SER.1 STATED ODDS 1:36
AR1 Shaquille O'Neal 3.00 8.00
AR2 Alonzo Mourning 1.00 2.50
AR3 Christian Laettner .50 1.25
AR4 Tom Gugliotta .50 1.25
AR5 LaPhonso Ellis .40 1.00

1993-94 SkyBox Premium Center Stage

Randomly inserted in first series packs at a rate of one in 12, this 9-card standard-size set showcases some of the best players in the NBA. Card fronts feature are borderless fronts with color action player cutouts placed against black backgrounds. The player's name is centered at the top in prismatic silver-foil lettering. The white back features a color action player cutout and player biography.

COMPLETE SET (9) 8.00 20.00
SER.1 STATED ODDS 1:12
CS1 Michael Jordan 5.00 12.00
CS2 Shaquille O'Neal 2.50 6.00
CS3 Charles Barkley 1.00 2.50
CS4 John Starks .50 1.25
CS5 Larry Johnson .60 1.50
CS6 Hakeem Olajuwon .75 2.00
CS7 Kenny Anderson .50 1.25
CS8 Mahmoud Abdul-Rauf .40 1.00
CS9 Clifford Robinson .40 1.00

1993-94 SkyBox Premium Draft Picks

These 26 standard-size cards were random inserts in both first series (Nos. 2, 6-8, 12, 15) and second series (the other 20) 12-card packs. The odds of finding one of these cards are one in every 12 packs. Card No. 26 was scheduled to be LSU center Geert Hammink. Hammink decided to play in Europe and his card was pulled. The fronts feature a color player action cutout set off to one side and superposed upon a ghosted posed color player photo. The player's name, the team that drafted him, and his draft pick number appear at the top. The white back carries the player's name, career highlights, and pre-NBA statistics. The cards are numbered on the back with a "DP" prefix. The set is sequenced in draft order.

COMPLETE SET (26) 12.00 30.00
COMPLETE SERIES 1 (9) 3.00 8.00
COMPLETE SERIES 2 (17) 10.00 25.00
SER.1/2 STATED ODDS 1:12
DP1 Chris Webber 3.00 8.00
DP2 Shawn Bradley .50 1.25
DP3 Anfernee Hardaway 3.00 8.00
DP4 Jamal Mashburn .75 2.00
DP5 Isaiah Rider .75 2.00
DP6 Calbert Cheaney .50 1.25
DP7 Bobby Hurley .50 1.25
DP8 Vin Baker .75 2.00
DP9 Rodney Rogers .50 1.25
DP10 Lindsey Hunter .50 1.25
DP11 Allan Houston 1.00 2.50
DP12 George Lynch .50 1.25
DP13 Terry Dehere .50 1.25
DP14 Scott Haskin .50 1.25
DP15 Doug Edwards .50 1.25
DP16 Rex Walters .50 1.25
DP17 Greg Graham .50 1.25
DP18 Luther Wright .50 1.25
DP19 Acie Earl .50 1.25
DP20 Scott Burrell .50 1.25
DP21 James Robinson .50 1.25
DP22 Chris Mills .50 1.25
DP23 Ervin Johnson .50 1.25
DP24 Sam Cassell 1.00 2.50
DP25 Corie Blount .50 1.25
DP27 Malcolm Mackey .50 1.25

1993-94 SkyBox Premium Dynamic Dunks

These nine standard-size cards were random inserts in second series 12-card packs. The odds of finding one of these cards are one in every 36 packs. The horizontal fronts feature color dunking-action player cutouts superposed upon borderless black and gold metallic backgrounds. The player's name appears in gold lettering at the bottom right. The horizontal black back carries another color dunking-action player photo. The player's name and a comment on his dunking style appear in white lettering beneath the photo. The set is sequenced in alphabetical order.

COMPLETE SET (9) 8.00 20.00
SER.2 STATED ODDS 1:36
D1 Nick Anderson .40 1.00
D2 Charles Barkley 1.00 2.50
D3 Robert Horry .60 1.50
D4 Michael Jordan 5.00 12.00
D5 Shawn Kemp .75 2.00
D6 Anthony Mason .40 1.00
D7 Alonzo Mourning 1.00 2.50
D8 Hakeem Olajuwon .75 2.00
D9 Dominique Wilkins .75 2.00

1993-94 SkyBox Premium Shaq Talk

The 1993-94 SkyBox Shaq Talk set consists of 10 cards that were randomly inserted in first (cards 1-5) and second series (6-10) 12-card packs. The odds of finding one of these cards are reportedly one in every 36 packs. The standard size cards spotlight Shaquille O'Neal. The fronts feature cut-out action shots of Shaq over a ghosted background. The set title is superimposed across the top of the card in red lettering. The white backs have a ghosted SkyBox Premium logo. At the top is a quote from Shaquille regarding game strategy and below is player critique by a basketball analyst. The cards are numbered on the back with a "Shaq Talk" prefix.

COMPLETE SET (10) 12.50 30.00
COMPLETE SERIES 1 (5) 6.00 15.00
COMPLETE SERIES 2 (5) 6.00 15.00
COMMON SHAQ (1-10) 2.00 5.00
SER.1/2 STATED ODDS 1:36

1993-94 SkyBox Premium Showdown Series

These 12 standard-size cards were random inserts in first (cards 1-6) and second series (7-12) 12-card packs. The odds of finding one of these cards are one in every six packs. Each front features a borderless color action photo of the two players involved in the "Showdown." Both players' names appear, one vs. the other, in gold lettering within a metallic black stripe near the bottom. The horizontal white back carries a color player close-up for each player on each side. The players' names appear beneath each photo. Comparative statistics fill in the area between the two player photos.

COMPLETE SET (12) 2.00 5.00
COMPLETE SERIES 1 (6) 1.00 2.50
COMPLETE SERIES 2 (6) 1.00 2.50
SER.1/2 STATED ODDS 1:6
SS1 A.Mourning/P.Ewing .15 .40
SS2 S.O'Neal/P.Ewing .40 1.00
SS3 A.Mourning/S.O'Neal .40 1.00
SS4 H.Olajuwon/D.Mutombo .12 .30
SS5 D.Robinson/H.Olajuwon .15 .40
SS6 D.Robinson/D.Mutombo .15 .40
SS7 S.Kemp/K.Malone .12 .30
SS8 L.Johnson/C.Barkley .15 .40
SS9 D.Wilkins/S.Pippen .20 .50
SS10 R.Miller/J.Dumars .12 .30
SS11 C.Drexler/M.Jordan .75 2.00
SS12 M.Johnson/L.Bird .30 .75

1993-94 SkyBox Premium Thunder and Lightning

Randomly inserted in second series packs at a rate of one in 12 packs, this standard-size nine-card set features players pictured on both sides. On one side a guard would be featured and a forward or center on the other side. Borderless on either side, the color action player cutouts set against metallic backgrounds.

COMPLETE SET (9) 3.00 8.00
SER.2 STATED ODDS 1:12
TL1 J.Mashburn/J.Jackson .40 1.00
TL2 H.Miner/S.Smith .20 .50
TL3 I.Rider/M.Williams .40 1.00
TL4 D.Coleman/K.Anderson .20 .50
TL5 P.Ewing/J.Starks .30 .75
TL6 S.O'Neal/A.Hardaway 2.50 6.00
TL7 S.Bradley/J.Hornacek .25 .60
TL8 W.Williams/B.Hurley .25 .60
TL9 D.Rodman/D.Robinson .50 1.25

1993-94 SkyBox Premium USA Tip-Off

The 13-card 1993-94 SkyBox USA Tip-Off set could be only acquired by sending in the USA Exchange card. The USA Exchange cards were randomly inserted in SkyBox series two packs. The Tip-Off redemption expiration was 6/15/94. It should be noted that Michael Jordan is not part of the set. Card fronts and backs feature studio photos of players in their USA Basketball uniforms.

COMPLETE SET (14) 10.00 25.00
EXCH.CARD: SER.2 STATED ODDS 1:240
1 S.Smith/M.Johnson 1.50 4.00
2 L.Johnson/C.Barkley 1.00 2.50
3 P.Ewing/A.Mourning 1.00 2.50
4 S.Kemp/K.Malone .75 2.00
5 C.Mullin/D.Majerle .60 1.50
6 J.Stockton/M.Price .75 2.00
7 C.Laettner/D.Coleman .50 1.25
8 D.Wilkins/C.Drexler .75 2.00
9 J.Dumars/S.Pippen 1.25 3.00
10 D.Robinson/S.O'Neal 2.50 6.00
11 R.Miller/L.Bird 2.00 5.00
12 Tim Hardaway .60 1.50
13 Isiah Thomas .60 1.50
NNO Expired USA Exchange .60 1.50

1993-94 SkyBox Premium USA Tip-Off Gold

*GOLD: 1X TO 2.5X BASIC

1994-95 SkyBox Premium Promo Sheet

Measuring 7" by 10 1/2", this promo sheet was inserted in Sports Cards magazine to promote the 1994-95 SkyBox second series cards. The perforated sheet features six cards. The cards are priced individually due to numerous sheets torn apart.

COMPLETE SET (6) .75 2.00
255 Glenn Robinson .40 1.00
295 Scott Skiles .08 .25
R3 Jamal Mashburn .15 .40
DP12 Khalid Reeves .08 .25
SF14 Danny Manning .15 .40
SU21 Isaiah Rider .15 .40

1994-95 SkyBox Premium

The 350 standard-size cards that comprise the 1994-95 SkyBox set were issued in two separate series of 200 and 150 cards respectively. Cards were distributed in 12-card hobby and retail packs with a suggested retail price of $1.99 each. Unlike first series packs, each second series pack contained an insert card. Card fronts feature full-bleed action photos with the player's name running down the upper-left corner. The cards are grouped alphabetically within teams and checklisted below alphabetically according to teams. Subsets are NBA on NBC (176-185), Dynamic Duals (186-197), USA Basketball (198), Checklists (298-300), SkySlams (301-313), SkyShots (314-325), SkySwats (326-338), and SkyPilots (339-350). Every first series pack contained an Action and Drama Instant Win game card, offering the chance to play one-on-one with Magic Johnson, or receive a number of other prizes including autographed Hakeem Olajuwon or David Robinson jerseys, a dual autographed Olajuwon/Robinson card or an exclusive Magic Johnson exchange card available only through this promotion. A special three-card panel featuring Johnson, Olajuwon and Robinson was available by mailing in forty first series wrappers before the June 30th, 1995 deadline. Also, three Master Series Preview Press Sheet Exchange cards were randomly seeded into one in every 360 first series packs. The cards were redeemable for 50-card uncut press sheets of SkyBox's new super-premium Emotion cards. The expiration date for the Emotion Press Sheets was March 1, 1995. As a final note, approximately one in every 360 first series retail packs contained an unannounced Hakeem Olajuwon Gold "stealth" card. Approximately one in every 360 second series retail packs contained an unannounced Grant Hill Gold "stealth" card. A standard-size promo card featuring Hakeem Olajuwon was issued to preview the set; a 3 1/2" by 5" jumbo version, distinguished by a gold foil autograph, was issued as a chiptopper in retail boxes. Three 5" by 7" jumbo featuring Grant Hill were also issued as a chiptoppers. Series 1 Sam's retail boxes contained a jumbo Grant Hill Hoops rookie card, Series 2 retail boxes contained a jumbo Grant Hill SkyBox rookie card and Series 2 vintage retail boxes contained a jumbo replica of his Slammin' Universe card. Rookie Cards in this set include Grant Hill, Jason Kidd and Glenn Robinson.

COMPLETE SET (350) 15.00 30.00
COMPLETE SERIES 1 (200) 7.50 15.00
COMPLETE SERIES 2 (150) 7.50 15.00
EMOTION SHEETS A/B/C EXP: 3/1/95
THIRD PRIZE GAME CARD EXP: 6/30/95
OLAJ.GLD: SER.1 STATED ODDS 1:360 RET
DUAL AU: SER.2 STATED ODDS 1:15,000
GHO: SER.2 STATED ODDS 1:360 RETAIL
1 Stacey Augmon .12 .30
2 Mookie Blaylock .10 .25
3 Doug Edwards .10 .25
4 Craig Ehlo .10 .25
5 Adam Keefe .10 .25
6 Danny Manning .12 .30
7 Kevin Willis .10 .25
8 Dee Brown .10 .25
9 Sherman Douglas .10 .25
10 Acie Earl .10 .25
11 Kevin Gamble .10 .25
12 Xavier McDaniel .10 .25
13 Dino Radja .10 .25
14 Muggsy Bogues .12 .30
15 Scott Burrell .10 .25
16 Dell Curry .10 .25
17 LeRon Ellis .10 .25
18 Hersey Hawkins .10 .25
19 Larry Johnson .15 .40
20 Alonzo Mourning .20 .50
21 B.J. Armstrong .10 .25
22 Corie Blount .10 .25
23 Horace Grant .12 .30
24 Toni Kukoc .20 .50
25 Luc Longley .12 .30
26 Scottie Pippen .30 .75
27 Scott Williams .10 .25
28 Terrell Brandon .10 .25
29 Brad Daugherty .12 .30
30 Tyrone Hill .10 .25
31 Chris Mills .10 .25
32 Bobby Phills .10 .25
33 Mark Price .15 .40
34 Gerald Wilkins .10 .25
35 Lucious Harris .10 .25
36 Jim Jackson .10 .25
37 Popeye Jones .10 .25
38 Jamal Mashburn .15 .40
39 Sean Rooks .10 .25
40 Mahmoud Abdul-Rauf .10 .25
41 LaPhonso Ellis .10 .25
42 Dikembe Mutombo .15 .40
43 Robert Pack .10 .25
44 Rodney Rogers .10 .25
45 Bryant Stith .10 .25
46 Reggie Williams .10 .25
47 Joe Dumars .15 .40
48 Sean Elliott .15 .40
49 Allan Houston .15 .40
50 Lindsey Hunter .10 .25
51 Terry Mills .10 .25
52 Victor Alexander .10 .25
53 Tim Hardaway .15 .40
54 Chris Mullin .15 .40
55 Billy Owens .10 .25
56 Latrell Sprewell .20 .50
57 Chris Webber .25 .60
58 Sam Cassell .15 .40
59 Carl Herrera .10 .25
60 Robert Horry .15 .40
61 Vernon Maxwell .10 .25
62 Hakeem Olajuwon .20 .50
63 Kenny Smith .12 .30
64 Otis Thorpe .10 .25
65 Antonio Davis .10 .25
66 Dale Davis .10 .25
67 Derrick McKey .10 .25
68 Reggie Miller .20 .50
69 Pooh Richardson .10 .25
70 Rik Smits .12 .30
71 Haywoode Workman .10 .25
72 Terry Dehere .10 .25
73 Harold Ellis .10 .25
74 Ron Harper .12 .30
75 Mark Jackson .12 .30
76 Loy Vaught .10 .25
77 Dominique Wilkins .20 .50
78 Elden Campbell .10 .25
79 Doug Christie .10 .25
80 Vlade Divac .15 .40
81 George Lynch .10 .25
82 Anthony Peeler .10 .25
83 Sedale Threatt .10 .25
84 Nick Van Exel .15 .40
85 Harold Miner .10 .25
86 Glen Rice .15 .40
87 John Salley .10 .25
88 Rony Seikaly .10 .25
89 Brian Shaw .10 .25
90 Steve Smith .12 .30
91 Vin Baker .15 .40
92 Jon Barry .10 .25
93 Todd Day .10 .25
94 Blue Edwards .10 .25
95 Lee Mayberry .10 .25
96 Eric Murdock .10 .25
97 Mike Brown .10 .25
98 Stacey King .10 .25
99 Christian Laettner .12 .30
100 Isaiah Rider .15 .40
101 Doug West .10 .25
102 Micheal Williams .10 .25
103 Kenny Anderson .12 .30
104 P.J. Brown .10 .25
105 Derrick Coleman .12 .30
106 Kevin Edwards .10 .25
107 Chris Morris .10 .25
108 Rex Walters .10 .25
109 Hubert Davis .10 .25
110 Patrick Ewing .20 .50
111 Derek Harper .12 .30
112 Anthony Mason .10 .25
113 Charles Oakley .12 .30
114 Charles Smith .10 .25
115 John Starks .12 .30
116 Nick Anderson .10 .25
117 Anfernee Hardaway .25 .60
118 Shaquille O'Neal .40 1.00
119 Donald Royal .10 .25
120 Dennis Scott .10 .25
121 Scott Skiles .10 .25
122 Dana Barros .10 .25
123 Shawn Bradley .10 .25
124 Johnny Dawkins .10 .25
125 Greg Graham .10 .25
126 Clarence Weatherspoon .10 .25
127 Danny Ainge .15 .40
128 Charles Barkley .25 .60
129 Cedric Ceballos .10 .25
130 A.C. Green .12 .30
131 Kevin Johnson .15 .40
132 Dan Majerle .15 .40
133 Oliver Miller .10 .25
134 Clyde Drexler .20 .50
135 Harvey Grant .10 .25
136 Tracy Murray .10 .25
137 Terry Porter .10 .25
138 Clifford Robinson .10 .25
139 James Robinson .10 .25
140 Rod Strickland .10 .25
141 Bobby Hurley .10 .25
142 Olden Polynice .10 .25
143 Mitch Richmond .15 .40
144 Lionel Simmons .10 .25
145 Wayman Tisdale .10 .25
146 Spud Webb .12 .30
147 Walt Williams .10 .25
148 Willie Anderson .10 .25
149 Vinny Del Negro .10 .25
150 Dale Ellis .10 .25
151 J.R. Reid .10 .25
152 David Robinson .25 .60
153 Dennis Rodman .30 .75
154 Kendall Gill .10 .25
155 Shawn Kemp .15 .40
156 Nate McMillan .10 .25
157 Gary Payton .15 .40
158 Sam Perkins .10 .25
159 Ricky Pierce .10 .25
160 Detlef Schrempf .15 .40
161 David Benoit .10 .25
162 Tyrone Corbin .10 .25
163 Jeff Hornacek .12 .30
164 Jay Humphries .10 .25
165 Karl Malone .20 .50
166 Bryon Russell .10 .25
167 Felton Spencer .10 .25
168 John Stockton .20 .50
169 Michael Adams .10 .25
170 Rex Chapman .10 .25
171 Calbert Cheaney .10 .25
172 Pervis Ellison .10 .25
173 Tom Gugliotta .10 .25
174 Don MacLean .10 .25
175 Gheorghe Muresan .10 .25
176 Charles Barkley NBC .25 .60
177 Charles Oakley NBC .12 .30
178 Hakeem Olajuwon NBC .20 .50
179 Dikembe Mutombo NBC .15 .40
180 Scottie Pippen NBC .30 .75
181 Sam Cassell NBC .15 .40
182 Karl Malone NBC .20 .50
183 Reggie Miller PO .20 .50
184 Patrick Ewing NBC .20 .50
185 Vernon Maxwell NBC .10 .25

186 A.Hardaway/S.Smith DD .25 .60
187 S.O'Neal/C.Webber DD .40 1.00
188 R.Rogers/J.Mashburn DD .15 .40
189 T.Kukoc/D.Radja DD .20 .50
190 L.Hunter/K.Anderson DD .12 .30
191 L.Sprewell/J.Jackson DD .20 .50
192 C.Weatherspoon/V.Baker DD .15 .40
193 C.Cheaney/C.Mills DD .10 .25
194 I.Rider/R.Horry DD .15 .40
195 S.Cassell/Van Exel DD .15 .40
196 G.Muresan/S.Bradley DD .10 .25
197 L.Ellis/T.Gugliotta DD .10 .25
198 USA Basketball Card .10 .25
199 Checklist .10 .25
200 Checklist .10 .25
201 Sergei Bazarevich RC .15 .40
202 Tyrone Corbin .10 .25
203 Grant Long .10 .25
204 Ken Norman .10 .25
205 Steve Smith .12 .30
206 Blue Edwards .10 .25
207 Greg Minor RC .15 .40
208 Eric Montross RC .12 .30
209 Dominique Wilkins .20 .50
210 Michael Adams .10 .25
211 Kenny Gattison .10 .25
212 Darrin Hancock .12 .30
213 Robert Parish .15 .40
214 Ron Harper .12 .30
215 Steve Kerr .12 .30
216 Will Perdue .10 .25
217 Dickey Simpkins RC .12 .30
218 John Battle .10 .25
219 Michael Cage .10 .25
220 Tony Dumas RC .15 .40
221 Jason Kidd RC .75 2.00
222 Roy Tarpley .10 .25
223 Dale Ellis .10 .25
224 Jalen Rose RC .40 1.00
225 Bill Curley RC .10 .25
226 Grant Hill RC .75 2.00
227 Oliver Miller .10 .25
228 Mark West .10 .25
229 Tom Gugliotta .10 .25
230 Ricky Pierce .10 .25
231 Carlos Rogers RC .12 .30
232 Clifford Rozier RC .10 .25
233 Rony Seikaly .10 .25
234 Tim Breaux .10 .25
235 Duane Ferrell .10 .25
236 Mark Jackson .12 .30
237 Byron Scott .12 .30
238 John Williams .10 .25
239 Lamond Murray RC .15 .40
240 Eric Piatkowski RC .20 .50
241 Pooh Richardson .10 .25
242 Malik Sealy .10 .25
243 Cedric Ceballos .10 .25
244 Eddie Jones RC .50 1.25
245 Anthony Miller RC .15 .40
246 Tony Smith .10 .25
247 Kevin Gamble .10 .25
248 Brad Lohaus .10 .25
249 Billy Owens .10 .25
250 Khalid Reeves RC .12 .30
251 Kevin Willis .10 .25
252 Eric Mobley RC .10 .25
253 Johnny Newman .10 .25
254 Ed Pinckney .10 .25
255 Glenn Robinson RC .30 .75
256 Howard Eisley .15 .40
257 Donyell Marshall RC .15 .40
258 Yinka Dare RC .10 .25
259 Sean Higgins .10 .25
260 Jayson Williams .10 .25
261 Charlie Ward RC .15 .40
262 Monty Williams RC .12 .30
263 Horace Grant .12 .30
264 Brian Shaw .10 .25
265 Brooks Thompson RC .12 .30
266 Derrick Alston RC .10 .25
267 B.J. Tyler RC .10 .25
268 Scott Williams .10 .25
269 Sharone Wright RC .12 .30
270 Antonio Lang RC .15 .40
271 Danny Manning .12 .30
272 Wesley Person RC .15 .40
273 Trevor Ruffin RC .10 .25
274 Wayman Tisdale .10 .25
275 Jerome Kersey .10 .25
276 Aaron McKie RC .15 .40
277 Frank Brickowski .10 .25
278 Brian Grant RC .25 .60
279 Michael Smith RC .10 .25
280 Terry Cummings .12 .30
281 Sean Elliott .15 .40
282 Avery Johnson .12 .30
283 Moses Malone .15 .40
284 Chuck Person .12 .30
285 Vincent Askew .10 .25
286 Bill Cartwright .12 .30
287 Sarunas Marciulionis .10 .25
288 Dontonio Wingfield RC .15 .40
289 Jay Humphries .10 .25
290 Adam Keefe .10 .25
291 Jamie Watson RC .10 .25
292 Kevin Duckworth .10 .25
293 Juwan Howard RC .25 .60
294 Jim McIlvaine RC .12 .30
295 Scott Skiles .10 .25
296 Anthony Tucker RC .10 .25
297 Chris Webber .25 .60
298 Checklist 201-265 .10 .25
299 Checklist 266-345 .10 .25
300 Checklist 346-350/Inserts .10 .25
301 Vin Baker SSL .15 .40
302 Charles Barkley SSL .25 .60
303 Derrick Coleman SSL .12 .30
304 Clyde Drexler SSL .20 .50
305 LaPhonso Ellis SSL .10 .25
306 Larry Johnson SSL .15 .40
307 Shawn Kemp SSL .15 .40
308 Karl Malone SSL .20 .50
309 Jamal Mashburn SSL .15 .40
310 Scottie Pippen SSL .30 .75
311 Dominique Wilkins SSL .20 .50
312 Walt Williams SSL .10 .25
313 Sharone Wright SSL .07 .20
314 B.J. Armstrong SSH .10 .25
315 Joe Dumars SSH .15 .40
316 Tony Dumas SSH .10 .25
317 Tim Hardaway SSH .15 .40
318 Toni Kukoc SSH .20 .50
319 Danny Manning SSH .12 .30
320 Reggie Miller SSH .20 .50
321 Chris Mullin SSH .15 .40
322 Wesley Person SSH .10 .25
323 John Starks SSH .12 .30
324 John Stockton SSH .20 .50
325 Clarence Weatherspoon SSH .10 .25
326 Shawn Bradley SSW .10 .25
327 Vlade Divac SSW .15 .40
328 Patrick Ewing SSW .20 .50
329 Christian Laettner SSW .12 .30
330 Eric Montross SSW .07 .20
331 Gheorghe Muresan SSW .10 .25
332 Dikembe Mutombo SSW .15 .40
333 Hakeem Olajuwon SSW .20 .50
334 Robert Parish SSW .15 .40
335 David Robinson SSW .25 .60
336 Dennis Rodman SSW .30 .75
337 Rony Seikaly SSW .10 .25
338 Rik Smits SSW .12 .30
339 Kenny Anderson SPI .12 .30
340 Dee Brown SPI .10 .25
341 Bobby Hurley SPI .10 .25
342 Kevin Johnson SPI .15 .40
343 Jason Kidd SPI .50 1.25
344 Gary Payton SPI .15 .40
345 Mark Price SPI .15 .40
346 Khalid Reeves SPI .07 .20
347 Jalen Rose SPI .25 .60
348 Latrell Sprewell SPI .20 .50
349 B.J. Tyler SPI .05 .15
350 Charlie Ward SPI .10 .25
PR Hakeem Olajuwon PROMO .40 1.00
PR Hakeem Olajuwon JUMBO PROMO .40 1.00
GHO Grant Hill Gold 5.00 12.00
NNO Grant Hill Hoops JUMBO 2.50 6.00
NNO Grant Hill SkyBox JUMBO 2.50 6.00
NNO H.Olajuwon Gold 4.00 10.00
NNO Grant Hill Slammin' Univ. JUMBO 2.50 6.00
NNO Emotion Sheet A 15.00 30.00
NNO Emotion Sheet B 15.00 30.00
NNO Emotion Exchange A Expired .40 1.00
NNO Emotion Exchange B Expired .40 1.00
NNO Emotion Exchange C Expired .40 1.00
NNO 3rd Prize Game Card Expired .08 .25
NNO H.Olajuwon/D.Robinson AU 150.00 300.00
NNO Magic Johnson Exchange Card 2.00 5.00
NNO 3 Card Panel Exchange 1.50 4.00
Magic Johnson
Hakeem Olajuwon
David Robinson

1994-95 SkyBox Premium Center Stage

Randomly inserted in all first series packs at a rate of one in 72, cards from this nine-card standard-size set feature a selection of the game's top stars. Card fronts feature full-color player photos over etched-foil backgrounds.

COMPLETE SET (9) 20.00 50.00
SER.1 STATED ODDS 1:72
CS1 Hakeem Olajuwon 2.50 6.00
CS2 Shaquille O'Neal 6.00 15.00
CS3 Anfernee Hardaway 3.00 8.00
CS4 Chris Webber 3.00 8.00
CS5 Scottie Pippen 4.00 10.00
CS6 David Robinson 3.00 8.00
CS7 Latrell Sprewell 2.50 6.00
CS8 Charles Barkley 3.00 8.00
CS9 Alonzo Mourning 2.50 6.00

1994-95 SkyBox Premium Draft Picks

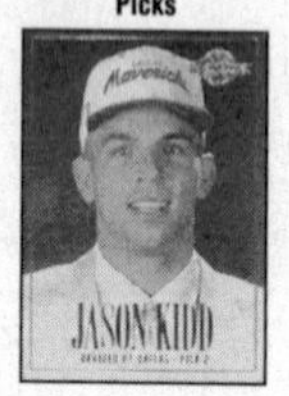

These 27 standard-size cards were random inserts in both first series (Nos. 2, 9, 10, 14 and 23) and second series (the other 22) packs. The first series cards were randomly seeded into one in every 45 packs. The second series cards were randomly seeded into one in every 18 packs. The set features all twenty-seven first round draft selections from the 1994 NBA draft. The foil card fronts feature a head shot of each player. The cards are numbered with a "DP" prefix. The set is sequenced in draft order.

COMPLETE SET (27) 15.00 40.00
COMPLETE SERIES 1 (5) 8.00 20.00
COMPLETE SERIES 2 (22) 10.00 25.00
SER.1 ODDS 1:45; SER.2 ODDS 1:18
DP1 Glenn Robinson 1.25 3.00
DP2 Jason Kidd 3.00 8.00
DP3 Grant Hill 3.00 8.00
DP4 Donyell Marshall .60 1.50
DP5 Juwan Howard 1.00 2.50
DP6 Sharone Wright .50 1.25
DP7 Lamond Murray .60 1.50
DP8 Brian Grant 1.00 2.50
DP9 Eric Montross .50 1.25
DP10 Eddie Jones 2.00 5.00
DP11 Carlos Rogers .50 1.25
DP12 Khalid Reeves .50 1.25
DP13 Jalen Rose 1.50 4.00
DP14 Yinka Dare .40 1.00
DP15 Eric Piatkowski .75 2.00
DP16 Clifford Rozier .40 1.00
DP17 Aaron McKie .60 1.50
DP18 Eric Mobley .40 1.00
DP19 Tony Dumas .60 1.50
DP20 B.J. Tyler .40 1.00
DP21 Dickey Simpkins .50 1.25
DP22 Bill Curley .40 1.00
DP23 Wesley Person .60 1.50
DP24 Monty Williams .50 1.25
DP25 Greg Minor .60 1.50
DP26 Charlie Ward .60 1.50
DP27 Brooks Thompson .50 1.25

1994-95 SkyBox Premium Grant Hill

Randomly inserted exclusively into one in every 36 second series hobby packs, cards from this 5-card standard-size set highlight the Detroit rookie, and SkyBox spokesperson, in various action shots. Full-color photos are set against a psychedelic background.

COMPLETE SET (5) 10.00 25.00
COMMON HILL (GH1-GH5) 3.00 8.00
SER.2 STATED ODDS 1:36 HOBBY

1994-95 SkyBox Premium Head of the Class

This 6-card standard-size set was available exclusively by mailing in the SkyBox Head of the Class exchange card before the June 15th, 1995 deadline. The Head of the Class exchange card was randomly inserted into one in every 480 first series packs. SkyBox selected six top rookies from the 1994-95 NBA season to be featured in the set. Card fronts feature a full-color player photo against a computer generated textured background. The set is sequenced in alphabetical order.

COMPLETE SET (6) 8.00 20.00
EXCH.CARD: SER.1 STATED ODDS 1:480
1 Grant Hill 4.00 10.00
2 Juwan Howard 1.25 3.00
3 Jason Kidd 4.00 10.00
4 Donyell Marshall .75 2.00
5 Glenn Robinson 1.50 4.00
6 Sharone Wright .60 1.50
NNO Checklist Card .40 1.00
NNO HOC Exchange Card Expired .75 2.00

1994-95 SkyBox Premium Ragin' Rookies Promos

These standard-size promo cards were issued to preview the 1994-95 SkyBox Premium series. All the cards belong to the Ragin' Rookies insert set. The fronts display full-bleed color action photos with frayed white edges. Across the top of the photo, the player's last name appears in red foil beneath "Ragin' Rookies" in white. The horizontal backs have a player profile on the left portion and a second color player photo on the right. The top left corner is cut off to mark the promotional nature of these cards. The cards are numbered on the back.

COMPLETE SET (7) 1.50 4.00
RR8 Lindsey Hunter .30 .75
RR10 Sam Cassell .50 1.25
RR13 Nick Van Exel .50 1.25
RR15 Vin Baker .50 1.25
RR16 Isaiah Rider .50 1.25
RR19 Shawn Bradley .30 .75
RR23 Bryon Russell .30 .75

1994-95 SkyBox Premium Ragin' Rookies

Randomly inserted into all first series packs at a rate of one in five, cards from this 24-card set feature a selection of the top rookies from the 1993 NBA draft. Full-color action photos feature a scratched border design.

COMPLETE SET (24) 10.00 25.00
SER.1 STATED ODDS 1:5
RR1 Dino Radja .60 1.50
RR2 Corie Blount .60 1.50
RR3 Toni Kukoc 1.25 3.00
RR4 Chris Mills .60 1.50
RR5 Jamal Mashburn 1.00 2.50
RR6 Rodney Rogers .60 1.50
RR7 Allan Houston 1.00 2.50
RR8 Lindsey Hunter .60 1.50
RR9 Chris Webber 1.50 4.00
RR10 Sam Cassell 1.00 2.50
RR11 Antonio Davis .60 1.50
RR12 Terry Dehere .60 1.50
RR13 Nick Van Exel 1.00 2.50
RR14 George Lynch .60 1.50
RR15 Vin Baker 1.00 2.50
RR16 Isaiah Rider 1.00 2.50
RR17 P.J. Brown .60 1.50
RR18 Anfernee Hardaway 1.50 4.00
RR19 Shawn Bradley .60 1.50
RR20 James Robinson .60 1.50
RR21 Bobby Hurley .60 1.50
RR22 Ervin Johnson .60 1.50
RR23 Bryon Russell .60 1.50
RR24 Calbert Cheaney .60 1.50

1994-95 SkyBox Premium Revolution

Randomly inserted into second series packs at a rate of one in 72, cards from this 10-card standard-size set feature a selection of NBA stars. The horizontal fronts feature full-color player photos against etched-foil backgrounds featuring team colors. The set is sequenced in alphabetical order.

COMPLETE SET (10) 20.00 50.00
SER.2 STATED ODDS 1:72
R1 Patrick Ewing 2.50 6.00
R2 Grant Hill 5.00 12.00
R3 Jamal Mashburn 2.00 5.00
R4 Alonzo Mourning 2.50 6.00
R5 Dikembe Mutombo 2.00 5.00
R6 Shaquille O'Neal 5.00 12.00
R7 Scottie Pippen 4.00 10.00
R8 Glenn Robinson 2.00 5.00
R9 Latrell Sprewell 2.50 6.00
R10 Chris Webber 3.00 8.00

1994-95 SkyBox Premium SkyTech Force

Randomly inserted into second series packs at a rate of one in two, cards from this 30-card standard-size set feature a selection of the NBA's top stars. Card fronts feature foil backgrounds. The player's name is in gold foil on the bottom while the words "SkyTech Force" is printed vertically on the right. The backs contain some career information as well as a color action photo. The cards are numbered in the upper right with an "SF" prefix and are sequenced in alphabetical order.

COMPLETE SET (30) 4.00 10.00
SER.2 STATED ODDS 1:2
SF1 Kenny Anderson .20 .50
SF2 B.J. Armstrong .15 .40
SF3 Charles Barkley .40 1.00
SF4 Shawn Bradley .15 .40
SF5 LaPhonso Ellis .15 .40
SF6 Anfernee Hardaway .40 1.00
SF7 Bobby Hurley .15 .40
SF8 Kevin Johnson .25 .60
SF9 Larry Johnson .25 .60
SF10 Shawn Kemp .25 .60
SF11 Jason Kidd 1.25 3.00
SF12 Christian Laettner .20 .50
SF13 Karl Malone .30 .75
SF14 Danny Manning .20 .50
SF15 Chris Mills .15 .40
SF16 Chris Mullin .25 .60
SF17 Lamond Murray .25 .60
SF18 Charles Oakley .20 .50
SF19 Hakeem Olajuwon .30 .75
SF20 Gary Payton .25 .60
SF21 Mark Price .25 .60
SF22 Dino Radja .15 .40
SF23 Mitch Richmond .25 .60
SF24 Clifford Robinson .15 .40
SF25 David Robinson .40 1.00
SF26 Dennis Rodman .50 1.25
SF27 Dickey Simpkins .20 .50
SF28 John Starks .20 .50
SF29 John Stockton .30 .75
SF30 Charlie Ward .25 .60

1994-95 SkyBox Premium Slammin' Universe

Randomly inserted into second series packs at a rate of one in two, cards from this 30-card standard-size set feature a selection of the NBA's top dunkers. The horizontal card fronts feature full-color player action shots against a foil "galaxy" background. The cards are numbered with a "SU" prefix and are sequenced in alphabetical order.

COMPLETE SET (30) 4.00 10.00
SER.2 STATED ODDS 1:2
SU1 Vin Baker .25 .60
SU2 Dee Brown .15 .40
SU3 Derrick Coleman .20 .50
SU4 Clyde Drexler .30 .75
SU5 Joe Dumars .25 .60
SU6 Tony Dumas .25 .60
SU7 Patrick Ewing .30 .75
SU8 Horace Grant .20 .50
SU9 Tom Gugliotta .15 .40
SU10 Grant Hill 1.25 3.00
SU11 Jim Jackson .15 .40
SU12 Toni Kukoc .30 .75
SU13 Donyell Marshall .25 .60
SU14 Jamal Mashburn .25 .60
SU15 Reggie Miller .30 .75
SU16 Eric Montross .20 .50
SU17 Alonzo Mourning .30 .75
SU18 Dikembe Mutombo .25 .60
SU19 Shaquille O'Neal .60 1.50
SU20 Glen Rice .25 .60
SU21 Isaiah Rider .25 .60
SU22 Glenn Robinson .50 1.25
SU23 Jalen Rose .60 1.50
SU24 Detlef Schrempf .25 .60
SU25 Steve Smith .20 .50
SU26 Latrell Sprewell .30 .75
SU27 Rod Strickland .15 .40
SU28 B.J. Tyler .15 .40
SU29 Nick Van Exel .25 .60
SU30 Dominique Wilkins .30 .75

1995-96 SkyBox Premium Promo Sheet

Measuring 8" by 10 1/2", this promo sheet was issued to preview the second series of the 1995-96 SkyBox set. The perforated sheet consists of eight cards, with an advertisement in the center of the sheet. The cards are identical their regular issue counterparts including the card numbers. The cards are priced individually due to numerous sheets torn apart.

COMPLETE SET (8) 3.00 8.00
153 Dana Barros .30 .75
182 Alonzo Mourning .60 1.50
229 Brent Barry .40 1.00
235 Jerry Stackhouse .75 2.00
255 Tim Hardaway .50 1.25
283 Grant Hill .75 2.00
285 Clyde Drexler .60 1.50
HH13 Michael Finley .75 2.00
S7 Anfernee Hardaway .40 1.00

1995-96 SkyBox Premium

The 1995-96 SkyBox set was issued in two series of 150 and 151 standard-size cards, for a total of 301. The cards were issued in 12-card regular packs at a suggested retail price of $1.99, and jumbo packs of 20 were sold at $3.99. Full-bleed fronts feature a full-color action player cutout against a one-color background of either blue, cyan, yellow or magenta. A computer-generated flame streaks out from the basketball the player is holding. Backs feature a one-color player action shot in a vertical strip on the right side of the cards and a full color close-up shot at the bottom left. The top right features a player biography and career stats. The set is arranged and checklisted below alphabetically according to teams by city. Subsets are Front and Center (125-133), Turning Point (134-142), Expansion Teams (143-148), Rookies (219-248), Honor Roll (249-298) and Checklists (299-300). Key Rookie Cards include Michael Finley, Kevin Garnett, Antonio McDyess, Joe Smith, Jerry Stackhouse and Damon Stoudamire. A 5" by 7" jumbo featuring Grant Hill (card #226) was issued as a chiptopper in retail boxes. In addition, parallel lenticular versions of the Grant Hill and Jerry Stackhouse Meltdown inserts were available through a second series wrapper offer. Both cards are unnumbered and feature nifty moving backgrounds in which a steel wall turns to goo as fireworks explode. Collectors had to send in two wrappers along with a check or money order for $9.99 per card before the December 31st, 1996 deadline.

COMPLETE SET (301) 17.50 35.00
COMPLETE SERIES 1 (150) 7.50 15.00
COMPLETE SERIES 2 (151) 10.00 20.00
SUBSET SAME VALUE AS BASE CARDS
MELTDOWN WRAPPER EXCH.EXP: 12/31/96
1 Stacey Augmon .15 .40
2 Mookie Blaylock .12 .30
3 Grant Long .12 .30
4 Steve Smith .15 .40
5 Dee Brown .12 .30
6 Sherman Douglas .12 .30
7 Eric Montross .12 .30
8 Dino Radja .12 .30
9 Dominique Wilkins .25 .60
10 Muggsy Bogues .15 .40
11 Scott Burrell .12 .30
12 Dell Curry .12 .30
13 Larry Johnson .20 .50
14 Alonzo Mourning .25 .60
15 Michael Jordan UER 1.50 4.00
16 Steve Kerr .15 .40
17 Toni Kukoc .20 .50
18 Scottie Pippen .30 .75
19 Terrell Brandon .12 .30
20 Tyrone Hill .12 .30
21 Chris Mills .12 .30
22 Mark Price .20 .50
23 John Williams .12 .30
24 Tony Dumas .12 .30
25 Jim Jackson .12 .30
26 Popeye Jones .12 .30
27 Jason Kidd .30 .75
28 Jamal Mashburn .20 .50
29 LaPhonso Ellis .12 .30
30 Dikembe Mutombo .20 .50
31 Robert Pack .12 .30
32 Jalen Rose .25 .60
33 Bryant Stith .12 .30
34 Joe Dumars .20 .50
35 Grant Hill .30 .75
36 Allan Houston .15 .40
37 Lindsey Hunter .12 .30
38 Chris Gatling .12 .30
39 Tim Hardaway .20 .50
40 Donyell Marshall .12 .30
41 Chris Mullin .20 .50
42 Carlos Rogers .12 .30
43 Latrell Sprewell .20 .50
44 Sam Cassell .20 .50
45 Clyde Drexler .25 .60
46 Robert Horry .15 .40
47 Hakeem Olajuwon .25 .60
48 Kenny Smith .15 .40
49 Dale Davis .12 .30
50 Mark Jackson .15 .40
51 Reggie Miller .25 .60
52 Rik Smits .15 .40
53 Lamond Murray .12 .30
54 Eric Piatkowski .15 .40
55 Pooh Richardson .12 .30
56 Rodney Rogers .12 .30
57 Loy Vaught .12 .30
58 Elden Campbell .12 .30
59 Cedric Ceballos .12 .30
60 Vlade Divac .20 .50
61 Eddie Jones .20 .50
62 Anthony Peeler .12 .30
63 Nick Van Exel .20 .50
64 Bimbo Coles .12 .30
65 Billy Owens .12 .30
66 Khalid Reeves .12 .30
67 Glen Rice .20 .50
68 Kevin Willis .12 .30
69 Vin Baker .15 .40
70 Todd Day .12 .30
71 Eric Murdock .12 .30
72 Glenn Robinson .15 .40
73 Tom Gugliotta .12 .30
74 Christian Laettner .15 .40
75 Isaiah Rider .20 .50
76 Doug West .12 .30
77 Kenny Anderson .15 .40
78 P.J. Brown .12 .30
79 Derrick Coleman .15 .40
80 Armon Gilliam .12 .30
81 Patrick Ewing .25 .60
82 Derek Harper .15 .40
83 Anthony Mason .12 .30
84 Charles Oakley .15 .40
85 John Starks .15 .40
86 Nick Anderson .12 .30
87 Horace Grant .15 .40
88 Anfernee Hardaway .30 .75
89 Shaquille O'Neal .50 1.25
90 Dana Barros .12 .30
91 Shawn Bradley .12 .30
92 Clarence Weatherspoon .12 .30
93 Sharone Wright .12 .30
94 Charles Barkley .30 .75
95 Kevin Johnson .20 .50
96 Dan Majerle .20 .50
97 Danny Manning .15 .40
98 Wesley Person .12 .30
99 Clifford Robinson .12 .30
100 Rod Strickland .12 .30
101 Otis Thorpe .12 .30
102 Buck Williams .12 .30
103 Brian Grant .15 .40
104 Olden Polynice .12 .30
105 Mitch Richmond .20 .50
106 Walt Williams .12 .30
107 Vinny Del Negro .12 .30
108 Sean Elliott .20 .50
109 Avery Johnson .15 .40
110 David Robinson .30 .75
111 Dennis Rodman .40 1.00
112 Shawn Kemp .20 .50
113 Gary Payton .20 .50
114 Sam Perkins .12 .30
115 Detlef Schrempf .20 .50
116 David Benoit .12 .30
117 Jeff Hornacek .15 .40
118 Karl Malone .25 .60
119 John Stockton .25 .60
120 Calbert Cheaney .12 .30
121 Juwan Howard .20 .50
122 Don MacLean .12 .30
123 Gheorghe Muresan .12 .30
124 Chris Webber .25 .60
125 Robert Horry FC .15 .40
126 Mark Jackson FC .15 .40
127 Steve Smith FC .15 .40
128 Lamond Murray FC .12 .30
129 Christian Laettner FC .15 .40
130 Kenny Anderson FC .15 .40
131 Anthony Mason FC .12 .30
132 Kevin Johnson FC .20 .50
133 Jeff Hornacek FC .15 .40
134 Larry Johnson TP .20 .50
135 Popeye Jones TP .12 .30
136 Allan Houston TP .15 .40
137 Chris Gatling TP .12 .30
138 Sam Cassell TP .20 .50
139 Anthony Peeler TP .12 .30
140 Vin Baker TP .15 .40
141 Dana Barros TP .12 .30
142 Gheorghe Muresan TP .12 .30
143 Toronto Raptors .12 .30
144 Vancouver Grizzlies .12 .30
145 G.Rice/M.Bogues EXP .20 .50
146 N.Anderson/C.Laettner EXP .15 .40
147 John Salley TF .12 .30
148 Greg Anthony TF .12 .30
149 Checklist #1 .12 .30
150 Checklist #2 .12 .30
151 Craig Ehlo .12 .30
152 Spud Webb .15 .40
153 Dana Barros .12 .30
154 Rick Fox .12 .30
155 Kendall Gill .12 .30
156 Khalid Reeves .12 .30
157 Glen Rice .20 .50
158 Luc Longley .15 .40
159 Dennis Rodman .40 1.00
160 Dickey Simpkins .12 .30
161 Danny Ferry .12 .30
162 Dan Majerle .20 .50
163 Bobby Phills .12 .30
164 Lucious Harris .12 .30
165 George McCloud .12 .30
166 Mahmoud Abdul-Rauf .12 .30
167 Don MacLean .12 .30
168 Reggie Williams .12 .30
169 Terry Mills .12 .30
170 Otis Thorpe .12 .30
171 B.J. Armstrong .12 .30
172 Rony Seikaly .12 .30
173 Chucky Brown .12 .30
174 Mario Elie .12 .30
175 Antonio Davis .12 .30
176 Ricky Pierce .12 .30
177 Terry Dehere .12 .30
178 Rodney Rogers .12 .30
179 Malik Sealy .12 .30
180 Brian Williams .12 .30
181 Sedale Threatt .12 .30
182 Alonzo Mourning .25 .60
183 Lee Mayberry .12 .30
184 Sean Rooks .12 .30
185 Shawn Bradley .12 .30
186 Kevin Edwards .12 .30
187 Hubert Davis .12 .30
188 Charles Smith .12 .30
189 Charlie Ward .12 .30
190 Dennis Scott .12 .30
191 Brian Shaw .12 .30
192 Derrick Coleman .15 .40
193 Richard Dumas .12 .30
194 Vernon Maxwell .12 .30
195 A.C. Green .15 .40
196 Elliot Perry .12 .30
197 John Williams .12 .30
198 Aaron McKie .12 .30
199 Bobby Hurley .12 .30
200 Michael Smith UER .12 .30
201 J.R. Reid .12 .30
202 Hersey Hawkins .12 .30
203 Willie Anderson .12 .30
204 Oliver Miller .12 .30
205 Tracy Murray .12 .30
206 Alvin Robertson .12 .30
207 Carlos Rogers UER .12 .30
208 John Salley .12 .30
209 Zan Tabak .12 .30
210 Adam Keefe .12 .30
211 Chris Morris .12 .30
212 Greg Anthony .12 .30
213 Blue Edwards .12 .30
214 Kenny Gattison .12 .30
215 Antonio Harvey .12 .30
216 Chris King .12 .30
217 Byron Scott .15 .40
218 Robert Pack .12 .30
219 Alan Henderson RC .20 .50
220 Eric Williams RC .20 .50
221 George Zidek RC .15 .40
222 Jason Caffey RC .20 .50
223 Bob Sura RC .15 .40
224 Cherokee Parks RC .15 .40
225 Antonio McDyess RC .25 .60
226 Theo Ratliff RC .30 .75
227 Joe Smith RC .25 .60
228 Travis Best RC .20 .50
229 Brent Barry RC .30 .75
230 Sasha Danilovic RC .20 .50
231 Kurt Thomas RC .20 .50
232 Shawn Respert RC .15 .40
233 Kevin Garnett RC 1.50 4.00
234 Ed O'Bannon RC .15 .40
235 Jerry Stackhouse RC .60 1.50
236 Michael Finley RC .60 1.50
237 Mario Bennett RC .15 .40
238 Randolph Childress RC .15 .40
239 Arvydas Sabonis RC .40 1.00
240 Gary Trent RC .20 .50
241 Tyus Edney RC .20 .50
242 Corliss Williamson RC .20 .50
243 Cory Alexander RC .20 .50
244 Damon Stoudamire RC .50 1.25
245 Greg Ostertag RC .20 .50
246 Lawrence Moten RC .20 .50
247 Bryant Reeves RC .15 .40
248 Rasheed Wallace RC .60 1.50
249 Muggsy Bogues HR .15 .40
250 Dell Curry HR .12 .30
251 Scottie Pippen HR .30 .75
252 Danny Ferry HR .12 .30
253 Mahmoud Abdul-Rauf HR .12 .30
254 Joe Dumars HR .20 .50
255 Tim Hardaway HR .20 .50
256 Chris Mullin HR .20 .50
257 Hakeem Olajuwon HR .25 .60
258 Kenny Smith HR .15 .40
259 Reggie Miller HR .25 .60
260 Rik Smits HR .15 .40
261 Vlade Divac HR .20 .50
262 Doug West HR .12 .30
263 Patrick Ewing HR .25 .60
264 Charles Oakley HR .15 .40
265 Nick Anderson HR .12 .30
266 Dennis Scott HR .12 .30
267 Jeff Turner HR .12 .30
268 Charles Barkley HR .30 .75
269 Kevin Johnson HR .20 .50
270 Clifford Robinson HR .12 .30
271 Buck Williams HR .12 .30
272 Lionel Simmons HR .12 .30
273 David Robinson HR .30 .75
274 Gary Payton HR .20 .50
275 Karl Malone HR .25 .60
276 John Stockton HR .25 .60
277 Steve Smith ELE .15 .40
278 Michael Jordan ELE 1.50 4.00
279 Jim Jackson ELE .12 .30
280 Jason Kidd ELE .30 .75
281 Jamal Mashburn ELE .20 .50
282 Dikembe Mutombo ELE .20 .50
283 Grant Hill ELE .30 .75
284 Tim Hardaway ELE .20 .50
285 Clyde Drexler ELE .25 .60
286 Cedric Ceballos ELE .12 .30
287 Gary Payton ELE .20 .50
288 Billy Owens ELE .12 .30
289 Vin Baker ELE .15 .40
290 Glenn Robinson ELE .15 .40
291 Kenny Anderson ELE .15 .40
292 Anfernee Hardaway ELE .30 .75
293 Shaquille O'Neal ELE .50 1.25
294 Charles Barkley ELE .30 .75
295 Rod Strickland ELE .12 .30
296 Mitch Richmond ELE .20 .50
297 Juwan Howard ELE .20 .50
298 Chris Webber ELE .25 .60
299 Checklist #1 .12 .30
300 Checklist #2 .12 .30
301 Magic Johnson .50 1.25
PR Grant Hill JUMBO 2.50 6.00
NNO G.Hill Meltdown 10.00 25.00
NNO J.Stackhouse Meltdown 12.50 30.00

1995-96 SkyBox Premium Atomic

Randomly inserted in all series one packs at a rate of one in four regular packs and one in three jumbo packs, this 15-card standard-size set highlights the play of the NBA's power men. Borderless fronts have etched foil backgrounds with a full-color action player cutout. An atomic symbol surrounds the ball the player is holding and the player's name, team and position are stamped in gold foil at the middle left of the card. Skybox's "Atomic" logo is printed at the bottom left. Backs are numbered with the prefix "A" and have a faded, one color action shot of the player and continues with the basketball as the center of an atomic symbol. Player biography and an inset color photo are set against red bars on the bottom half of the card.

COMPLETE SET (15) 2.50 6.00
SER.1 STATED ODDS 1:4 HOBBY/RETAIL
A1 Eric Montross .25 .60
A2 Charles Oakley .30 .75
A3 Rik Smits .30 .75
A4 Vlade Divac .40 1.00
A5 Buck Williams .25 .60
A6 Vin Baker .30 .75
A7 Glenn Robinson .30 .75
A8 Isaiah Rider .40 1.00
A9 Derrick Coleman .30 .75
A10 Clarence Weatherspoon .25 .60
A11 Sharone Wright .25 .60
A12 Brian Grant .30 .75
A13 Jim Jackson .25 .60
A14 Clyde Drexler .50 1.25
A15 Anfernee Hardaway .60 1.50

1995-96 SkyBox Premium Close-Ups

A short player history is the focus of this nine-card standard-size set that features both established players and up-and-coming rookies. The cards were randomly inserted in all series one packs at a rate of one in nine regular packs and one in six jumbo packs. They were also inserted one per special series one Wal-Mart retail pack. Borderless fronts feature an extreme color close-up of the player's face set against an etched foil background. The player's first name is stamped in gold foil script against his last name which is printed larger and in full block letters. The SkyBox logo and "Close-Up" are stamped in gold foil at the bottom left of the card. The backs feature a stretched one-color player photo on the right side of the card. The left side has the player's name, team logo and a short player history printed in black type. The set is sequenced in alphabetical order by team.

COMPLETE SET (9) 10.00 20.00
SER.1 STATED ODDS 1:9 RETAIL
ONE PER SPECIAL SER.1 RETAIL PACK
C1 Scottie Pippen 2.00 5.00
C2 Grant Hill 2.00 5.00
C3 Clyde Drexler 1.50 4.00
C4 Nick Van Exel 1.25 3.00
C5 Tom Gugliotta .75 2.00
C6 Patrick Ewing 1.50 4.00
C7 Charles Barkley 2.00 5.00
C8 Karl Malone 1.50 4.00
C9 Juwan Howard 1.25 3.00

1995-96 SkyBox Premium Dynamic

Randomly inserted at a rate of one in four series one regular packs and one in three series one jumbo packs, this 12-card standard-size set features the most intense NBA players. Fronts feature a full-color action player photo handling a ball that is exploding. The player is set against a bright red etched foil background with the "Dynamic" logo scrawled at an angle across the bottom. The player's name is printed on the bottom right of the card. Full-bleed, one-color backs are numbered with the prefix "D" and picture the player in an action shot and a full color close-up inset. The player's name is printed in white caps and a player profile is printed in black type on tilted red bars. The set is sequenced in alphabetical team order.

COMPLETE SET (12) 2.50 6.00
SER.1 STATED ODDS 1:4 HOBBY/RETAIL
D1 Larry Johnson .40 1.00
D2 Alonzo Mourning .50 1.25
D3 Dikembe Mutombo .40 1.00
D4 Jalen Rose .50 1.25
D5 Grant Hill .60 1.50
D6 Latrell Sprewell .40 1.00
D7 Reggie Miller .50 1.25
D8 John Starks .30 .75
D9 Calbert Cheaney .25 .60
D10 Dennis Rodman .75 2.00
D11 Detlef Schrempf .40 1.00
D12 Chris Webber .50 1.25

1995-96 SkyBox Premium High Hopes

Randomly inserted in all second series packs at a rate of one in 18, this 20-card set focuses on the hot young stars of the NBA. Borderless fronts feature the player in a full-color action cutout, with "High Hopes" spelled out in red and yellow spark and flame block letters on a black background. The player's name is printed in gold foil at the bottom. Backs have another full-color action cutout set against a back blackground with a player profile printed in white type. "High Hopes" is printed vertically on the right side.

COMPLETE SET (20) 15.00 40.00
SER.2 STATED ODDS 1:18 H/R, 1:12 JUM
HH1 Alan Henderson .75 2.00
HH2 Eric Williams .75 2.00
HH3 George Zidek .60 1.50
HH4 Bob Sura .60 1.50
HH5 Cherokee Parks .60 1.50
HH6 Antonio McDyess 1.00 2.50
HH7 Joe Smith 1.00 2.50
HH8 Brent Barry 1.25 3.00
HH9 Shawn Respert .60 1.50
HH10 Kevin Garnett 6.00 15.00
HH11 Ed O'Bannon .60 1.50
HH12 Jerry Stackhouse 2.50 6.00
HH13 Michael Finley 2.50 6.00
HH14 Arvydas Sabonis 1.50 4.00
HH15 Gary Trent .75 2.00
HH16 Tyus Edney .75 2.00
HH17 Damon Stoudamire 2.00 5.00
HH18 Greg Ostertag .75 2.00
HH19 Bryant Reeves .60 1.50
HH20 Rasheed Wallace 2.50 6.00

1995-96 SkyBox Premium Hot Sparks

Randomly inserted in second series hobby packs only at a rate of one in 12, this 10-card set notes the players who make things happen in the NBA. Fronts have a full-color action cutout with the player's name printed vertically in gold foil on the right side. A mauve computerized image serves as a background. A similar but darker background appears on the back with another full-color action cutout and a player profile printed in white type.

COMPLETE SET (11) 8.00 20.00
SER.2 STATED ODDS 1:12 HOBBY
HS1 Mookie Blaylock .60 1.50
HS2 Jason Kidd 1.50 4.00
HS3 Tim Hardaway 1.00 2.50
HS4 Nick Van Exel 1.00 2.50
HS5 Kenny Anderson .75 2.00
HS6 Anfernee Hardaway 1.50 4.00
HS7 Rod Strickland .60 1.50
HS8 Gary Payton 1.00 2.50
HS9 Damon Stoudamire 1.50 4.00
HS10 John Stockton 1.25 3.00
HS11 Magic Johnson 2.50 6.00

1995-96 SkyBox Premium Kinetic

Randomly inserted in all first series at a rate of one in four (and one in three jumbo), cards from this 9-card standard-size set highlight the NBA's speed demons. Full-bleed fronts have swirling color swoops and surround a full-color player cutout set against an etched foil background. Player's name and team name are printed in silver foil at the bottom. Borderless backs feature a one-color player cutout and continues with the swoosh patterns. A full-color head shot is inset with a white border and a player profile is printed in black type on gold bars.

COMPLETE SET (9)	1.25	3.00
SER.1 STATED ODDS 1:4 HOBBY/RETAIL		
K1 Mookie Blaylock	.25	.60
K2 Tim Hardaway	.40	1.00
K3 Lamond Murray UER	.25	.60
K4 Stacey Augmon	.30	.75
K5 Nick Van Exel	.40	1.00
K6 Khalid Reeves	.25	.60
K7 Kenny Anderson	.30	.75
K8 Rod Strickland	.25	.60
K9 Gary Payton	.40	1.00

1995-96 SkyBox Premium Larger Than Life

Randomly inserted in first series regular and jumbo packs at a rate of one in 48 and one in 36 respectively, this 10-card standard-size set showcases those players who have established themselves in the NBA. A sunburst design is etched into gold foil and serves as a background for the fronts which include a full-color action player cutout. The "Larger Than Life" logo is printed diagonally and upwards from the bottom right and tapers up to the SkyBox logo. The player's first name is printed in lower case black type just above his last name which appears in all caps red type. Backs continue with the sunburst pattern on the gold type. A player profile is printed in black type on the right side and a full-color action cutout appears on the left side. The set is sequenced in alphabetical team order.

COMPLETE SET (10)	15.00	40.00
SER.1 STATED ODDS 1:48 HOBBY/RETAIL		
L1 Michael Jordan	15.00	40.00
L2 Jason Kidd	2.00	5.00
L3 Grant Hill	2.00	5.00
L4 Hakeem Olajuwon	1.50	4.00
L5 Glenn Robinson	1.00	2.50
L6 Patrick Ewing	1.50	4.00
L7 Shaquille O'Neal	3.00	8.00
L8 Charles Barkley	2.00	5.00
L9 David Robinson	2.00	5.00
L10 John Stockton	1.50	4.00

1995-96 SkyBox Premium Lottery Exchange

Hobbyists received this 13-card set after collecting the three separate Lottery Exchange cards randomly inserted into first series packs (each card was seeded at a rate of 1:40 packs). The expiration date for exchanging the cards was June 15th, 1996. The set consists of the first thirteen players selected in the 1995 NBA draft. Card fronts feature a full-color player action cutout set against a murky colored background.

COMPLETE SET (13)	15.00	40.00
ONE SET PER THREE EXCH.CARDS BY MAIL		
EXCH.CARDS: SER.1 STATED ODDS 1:40		
1 Joe Smith	1.00	2.50
2 Antonio McDyess	1.00	2.50
3 Jerry Stackhouse	2.50	6.00
4 Rasheed Wallace	2.50	6.00
5 Kevin Garnett	4.00	10.00
6 Bryant Reeves	.60	1.50
7 Damon Stoudamire	2.00	5.00
8 Shawn Respert	.60	1.50
9 Ed O'Bannon	.60	1.50
10 Kurt Thomas	.75	2.00
11 Gary Trent	.75	2.00
12 Cherokee Parks	.60	1.50
13 Corliss Williamson	.75	2.00
NNO Exchange Card 1	.40	1.00
NNO Exchange Card 2	.40	1.00
NNO Exchange Card 3	.40	1.00

1995-96 SkyBox Premium Meltdown

Randomly inserted in second series regular packs at a rate of one in 54 and jumbo packs at a rate of one in 42, this 10-card set is a tribute to the league's hottest scorers. Borderless fronts have a foil finish with an image of green and blue melting metal. A full-color player cutout appears on the front with his name and team printed on the bottom. Blue metal showers down in a cascade on the back with a full-color action cutout and a player profile printed in white type.

COMPLETE SET (10)	40.00	100.00
SER.2 STATED ODDS 1:54 H/R, 1:42 JUM		
M1 Michael Jordan	30.00	80.00
M2 Dan Majerle	1.50	4.00
M3 Jason Kidd	2.50	6.00
M4 Antonio McDyess	2.00	5.00
M5 Grant Hill	2.50	6.00
M6 Joe Smith	2.00	5.00
M7 Hakeem Olajuwon	2.00	5.00
M8 Shaquille O'Neal	4.00	10.00
M9 Jerry Stackhouse	5.00	12.00
M10 David Robinson	2.50	6.00

1995-96 SkyBox Premium Rookie Prevue

Randomly inserted in first series packs at a rate of one in nine, this 20-card standard-size set focuses on the hot rookies of 1994-95. The borderless fronts include a full-color action player cutout on the right. The player's last name is printed in gold foil across the top with his first name in smaller type underneath the last name. The background is a red and gold sunburst pattern with "Rookie Prevue" in bold block letters on the bottom left. Backs also carry the "Rookie Prevue" logo at the bottom left and a player action cutout on the right. The background continues the red and gold sunburst design and the player's name and a short profile is printed in black type on the upper left side of the back. The set is sequenced in dratt order.

COMPLETE SET (20)	20.00	50.00
SER.1 STATED ODDS 1:9 HOBBY/RETAIL		
RP1 Joe Smith	1.25	3.00
RP2 Antonio McDyess	1.25	3.00
RP3 Jerry Stackhouse	3.00	8.00
RP4 Rasheed Wallace	3.00	8.00
RP5 Bryant Reeves	.75	2.00
RP6 Damon Stoudamire	2.50	6.00
RP7 Shawn Respert	.75	2.00
RP8 Ed O'Bannon	.75	2.00
RP9 Kurt Thomas	1.00	2.50
RP10 Gary Trent	1.00	2.50
RP11 Cherokee Parks	.75	2.00
RP12 Corliss Williamson	1.00	2.50
RP13 Eric Williams	1.00	2.50
RP14 Brent Barry	1.50	4.00
RP15 Alan Henderson	1.00	2.50
RP16 Bob Sura	.75	2.00
RP17 Theo Ratliff	1.50	4.00
RP18 Randolph Childress	.75	2.00
RP19 Michael Finley	3.00	8.00
RP20 George Zidek	.75	2.00

1995-96 SkyBox Premium Standouts

Randomly inserted in first series packs at a rate of one in 18 regular packs and one in 36 jumbo packs, this 12-card standard-size set spotlights the play of the NBA's hot rookies. The fronts feature the player in a full-color action cutout set against a metallic copper foil. The player stands on top of a circular "Skybox Standouts" logo and his name is stamped in gold foil at the upper right corner. A full-color action player cutout appears on the back and is set against the "Standouts" logo. A player profile appears on the top left of the card and the player's name and team are printed in a reverse type process on a strip of light blue across the bottom.

COMPLETE SET (12)	15.00	30.00
SER.1 STATED ODDS 1:18 H/R, 1:36 JUM		
S1 Alonzo Mourning	2.50	6.00
S2 Scottie Pippen	3.00	8.00
S3 Danny Manning	1.50	4.00
S4 Jamal Mashburn	2.00	5.00
S5 Latrell Sprewell	2.00	5.00
S6 Reggie Miller	2.50	6.00
S7 Anfernee Hardaway	3.00	8.00
S8 Brian Grant	1.50	4.00
S9 Shawn Kemp	2.00	5.00
S10 Clifford Robinson	1.25	3.00
S11 Joe Dumars	2.00	5.00
S12 Chris Webber	2.50	6.00

1995-96 SkyBox Premium Standouts Hobby

Randomly inserted exclusivelt into first series hobby packs at a rate of one in 18, this six-card set is a tribute to the league's best. Borderless fronts have gold foil paper and the player's name is stamped in the upper right in a lighter gold foil. A full-color action player cutout appears and stand directly on a circular pattern that reads "Skybox Standouts." Backs have another full-color action cutout with a player profile, the Skybox medallion and a granite-like strip with the player's name and team etched inside.

COMPLETE SET (6)	20.00	50.00
SER.1 STATED ODDS 1:18 HOBBY		
SH1 Michael Jordan	12.00	30.00
SH2 Jason Kidd	4.00	10.00
SH3 Hakeem Olajuwon	3.00	8.00
SH4 Eddie Jones	2.50	6.00
SH5 Shaquille O'Neal	6.00	15.00
SH6 Grant Hill	4.00	10.00

1995-96 SkyBox Premium USA Basketball

Randomly inserted in second series retail packs at a rate of one in 12 and one in every second series jumbo pack and one per series two special retail pack, this set features the first ten players selected to the 1996 USA men's basketball team. Card fronts feature full-color action cutouts of Team USA members pictured in their Olympic togs set against a gray background of a globe.

COMPLETE SET (10)	8.00	20.00
SER.2 STATED ODDS 1:12 RETAIL		
ONE PER SPECIAL SER.2 RETAIL PACK		
U1 Anfernee Hardaway	1.25	3.00
U2 Grant Hill	1.25	3.00
U3 Karl Malone	1.00	2.50
U4 Reggie Miller	1.00	2.50
U5 Scottie Pippen	1.25	3.00
U6 Hakeem Olajuwon	1.00	2.50
U7 Shaquille O'Neal	2.00	5.00
U8 David Robinson	1.25	3.00
U9 Glenn Robinson	.60	1.50
U10 John Stockton	1.00	2.50

1996-97 SkyBox Premium

The 1996-97 Skybox set was issued with a total of 281 cards. The set was issued in two series with series one totaling 131 cards and series two totaling 150. The 12-card packs retail for $2.99 each. The cards are grouped alphabetically within teams. Rookie cards that were available in the first series included Shareef Abdur-Rahim, Kobe Bryant, Marcus Camby, Allen Iverson, Stephon Marbury and Antoine Walker. A Jerry Stackhouse promo was released before the set that is identical to the regular issue card except it does not have a card number on the back. It is listed below at the end of the set.

COMPLETE SET (281)	20.00	35.00
COMPLETE SERIES 1 (131)	12.50	25.00
COMPLETE SERIES 2 (150)	7.50	15.00
PM/DT SUBSET CARDS SAME VALUE AS BASE		
1 Mookie Blaylock	.12	.30
2 Alan Henderson	.12	.30
3 Christian Laettner	.15	.40
4 Dikembe Mutombo	.20	.50
5 Steve Smith	.15	.40
6 Dana Barros	.12	.30
7 Rick Fox	.12	.30
8 Dino Radja	.12	.30
9 Antoine Walker RC	.40	1.00
10 Eric Williams	.12	.30
11 Dell Curry	.12	.30
12 Tony Delk RC	.25	.60
13 Matt Geiger	.12	.30
14 Glen Rice	.20	.50
15 Ron Harper	.15	.40
16 Michael Jordan	1.50	4.00
17 Toni Kukoc	.20	.50
18 Scottie Pippen	.30	.75
19 Dennis Rodman	.40	1.00
20 Terrell Brandon	.12	.30
21 Danny Ferry	.12	.30
22 Chris Mills	.12	.30
23 Bobby Phills	.12	.30
24 Vitaly Potapenko RC	.20	.50
25 Jim Jackson	.12	.30
26 Jason Kidd	.30	.75
27 Jamal Mashburn	.15	.40
28 George McCloud	.12	.30
29 Samaki Walker RC	.20	.50
30 LaPhonso Ellis	.12	.30
31 Antonio McDyess	.20	.50
32 Bryant Stith	.12	.30
33 Joe Dumars	.20	.50
34 Grant Hill	.30	.75
35 Lindsey Hunter	.12	.30
36 Theo Ratliff	.12	.30
37 Otis Thorpe	.12	.30
38 Todd Fuller RC	.15	.40
39 Chris Mullin	.20	.50
40 Joe Smith	.15	.40
41 Latrell Sprewell	.20	.50
42 Charles Barkley	.30	.75
43 Clyde Drexler	.25	.60
44 Mario Elie	.12	.30
45 Hakeem Olajuwon	.25	.60
46 Erick Dampier RC	.25	.60
47 Dale Davis	.12	.30
48 Derrick McKey	.12	.30
49 Reggie Miller	.25	.60
50 Rik Smits	.15	.40
51 Brent Barry	.15	.40
52 Rodney Rogers	.12	.30
53 Loy Vaught	.12	.30
54 Lorenzen Wright RC	.20	.50
55 Kobe Bryant RC	4.00	10.00
56 Cedric Ceballos	.12	.30
57 Eddie Jones	.20	.50
58 Shaquille O'Neal	.50	1.25
59 Nick Van Exel	.20	.50
60 Tim Hardaway	.20	.50
61 Alonzo Mourning	.25	.60
62 Kurt Thomas	.12	.30
63 Ray Allen RC	1.00	2.50
64 Vin Baker	.15	.40
65 Shawn Respert	.12	.30
66 Glenn Robinson	.15	.40
67 Kevin Garnett	.50	1.25
68 Tom Gugliotta	.12	.30
69 Stephon Marbury RC	.60	1.50
70 Sam Mitchell	.12	.30
71 Shawn Bradley	.12	.30
72 Kendall Gill	.12	.30
73 Kerry Kittles RC	.25	.60
74 Ed O'Bannon	.12	.30
75 Patrick Ewing	.25	.60
76 Larry Johnson	.20	.50
77 Charles Oakley	.15	.40
78 John Starks	.15	.40
79 John Wallace RC	.25	.60
80 Nick Anderson	.12	.30
81 Horace Grant	.15	.40
82 Anfernee Hardaway	.30	.75
83 Dennis Scott	.12	.30
84 Derrick Coleman	.15	.40
85 Allen Iverson RC	1.25	3.00
86 Jerry Stackhouse	.25	.60
87 Clarence Weatherspoon	.12	.30
88 Michael Finley	.25	.60
89 Robert Horry	.15	.40
90 Kevin Johnson	.20	.50
91 Steve Nash RC	1.25	3.00
92 Wesley Person	.12	.30
93 Aaron McKie	.12	.30
94 Jermaine O'Neal RC	.40	1.00
95 Clifford Robinson	.12	.30
96 Arvydas Sabonis	.15	.40
97 Gary Trent	.12	.30
98 Tyus Edney	.12	.30
99 Brian Grant	.15	.40
100 Mitch Richmond	.20	.50
101 Billy Owens	.12	.30
102 Corliss Williamson	.12	.30
103 Vinny Del Negro	.12	.30
104 Sean Elliott	.20	.50
105 Avery Johnson	.15	.40
106 Chuck Person	.15	.40
107 David Robinson	.30	.75
108 Hersey Hawkins	.12	.30
109 Shawn Kemp	.20	.50
110 Gary Payton	.20	.50
111 Sam Perkins	.12	.30
112 Detlef Schrempf	.20	.50
113 Marcus Camby RC	.40	1.00
114 Carlos Rogers	.12	.30
115 Damon Stoudamire	.15	.40
116 Zan Tabak	.12	.30
117 Antoine Carr	.12	.30
118 Jeff Hornacek	.15	.40
119 Karl Malone	.25	.60
120 Chris Morris	.12	.30
121 John Stockton	.25	.60
122 Shareef Abdur-Rahim RC	.40	1.00
123 Greg Anthony	.12	.30
124 Bryant Reeves	.12	.30
125 Roy Rogers RC	.20	.50
126 Calbert Cheaney	.12	.30
127 Juwan Howard	.15	.40
128 Gheorghe Muresan	.12	.30
129 Chris Webber	.25	.60
130 Checklist	.12	.30
131 Checklist	.12	.30
132 Jon Barry	.12	.30
133 Christian Laettner	.15	.40
134 Dikembe Mutombo	.20	.50
135 Dee Brown	.12	.30
136 Todd Day	.12	.30
137 David Wesley	.12	.30
138 Vlade Divac	.20	.50
139 Anthony Goldwire	.12	.30
140 Anthony Mason	.12	.30
141 Jason Caffey	.12	.30
142 Luc Longley	.15	.40
143 Tyrone Hill	.12	.30
144 Antonio Lang	.12	.30
145 Sam Cassell	.15	.40
146 Chris Gatling	.12	.30
147 Eric Montross	.12	.30
148 Ervin Johnson	.12	.30
149 Sarunas Marciulionis	.12	.30
150 Stacey Augmon	.15	.40
151 Grant Long	.12	.30
152 Terry Mills	.12	.30
153 Kenny Smith	.15	.40
154 B.J. Armstrong	.12	.30
155 Bimbo Coles	.12	.30
156 Charles Barkley	.30	.75
157 Brent Price	.12	.30
158 Duane Ferrell	.12	.30
159 Jalen Rose	.15	.40
160 Terry Dehere	.12	.30
161 Bo Outlaw	.12	.30
162 Corie Blount	.12	.30
163 Shaquille O'Neal	.50	1.25
164 Rumeal Robinson	.12	.30
165 P.J. Brown	.12	.30
166 Ronnie Grandison	.12	.30
167 Sherman Douglas	.12	.30
168 Johnny Newman	.12	.30
169 James Robinson	.12	.30
170 Doug West	.12	.30
171 Robert Pack	.12	.30
172 Khalid Reeves	.12	.30
173 Chris Childs	.12	.30
174 Allan Houston	.15	.40
175 Charlie Ward	.12	.30
176 Darrell Armstrong RC	.40	1.00
177 Gerald Wilkins	.12	.30
178 Lucious Harris	.12	.30
179 Robert Horry	.15	.40
180 Danny Manning	.15	.40
181 Kenny Anderson	.15	.40
182 Isaiah Rider	.15	.40
183 Rasheed Wallace	.25	.60
184 Mahmoud Abdul-Rauf	.12	.30
185 Cory Alexander	.12	.30
186 Vernon Maxwell	.12	.30
187 Dominique Wilkins	.25	.60
188 Nate McMillan	.12	.30
189 Larry Stewart	.12	.30
190 Doug Christie	.12	.30
191 Hubert Davis	.12	.30
192 Walt Williams	.12	.30
193 Adam Keefe	.12	.30
194 Greg Ostertag	.12	.30
195 John Stockton	.25	.60
196 George Lynch	.12	.30
197 Lee Mayberry	.12	.30
198 Tracy Murray	.12	.30
199 Rod Strickland	.12	.30
200 Shareef Abdur-Rahim ROO	.20	.50
201 Ray Allen ROO	.50	1.25
202 Shandon Anderson ROO RC	.20	.50
203 Kobe Bryant ROO	2.50	6.00
204 Marcus Camby ROO	.20	.50
205 Erick Dampier ROO	.12	.30
206 Emanual Davis ROO RC	.25	.60
207 Tony Delk ROO	.12	.30
208 Brian Evans ROO RC	.25	.60
209 Derek Fisher ROO RC	.30	.75
210 Todd Fuller ROO	.07	.20
211 Dean Garrett ROO RC	.25	.60
212 Reggie Geary ROO RC	.25	.60
213 Darvin Ham ROO RC	.25	.60
214 Othella Harrington ROO RC	.25	.60
215 Shane Heal ROO RC	.25	.60
216 Allen Iverson ROO	.60	1.50
217 Dontae' Jones ROO RC	.25	.60
218 Kerry Kittles ROO	.12	.30
219 Priest Lauderdale ROO RC	.15	.40
220 Randy Livingston ROO RC	.25	.60
221 Matt Maloney ROO RC	.20	.50
222 Stephon Marbury ROO	.30	.75
223 Walter McCarty ROO RC	.25	.60
224 Amal McCaskill ROO RC	.25	.60
225 Jeff McInnis ROO RC	.25	.60
226 Martin Muursepp ROO RC	.15	.40
227 Steve Nash ROO	.40	1.00
228 Ruben Nembhard ROO RC	.25	.60
229 Jermaine O'Neal ROO	.20	.50
230 Vitaly Potapenko ROO	.10	.25
231 Virginius Praskevicius ROO RC	.25	.60
232 Roy Rogers ROO	.10	.25
233 Malik Rose ROO RC	.30	.75
234 Antoine Walker ROO	.20	.50
235 Samaki Walker ROO	.10	.25
236 Ben Wallace ROO RC	1.25	3.00
237 John Wallace ROO	.12	.30
238 Jerome Williams ROO RC	.20	.50
239 Lorenzen Wright ROO	.10	.25
240 Sam Cassell PM	.15	.40
241 Anfernee Hardaway PM	.30	.75
242 Tim Hardaway PM	.20	.50
243 Grant Hill PM	.30	.75
244 Allan Houston PM	.15	.40
245 Juwan Howard PM	.15	.40
246 Kevin Johnson PM	.20	.50
247 Michael Jordan PM	1.50	4.00
248 Jason Kidd PM	.30	.75
249 Karl Malone PM	.25	.60
250 Reggie Miller PM	.25	.60
251 Gary Payton PM	.20	.50
252 Wesley Person PM	.12	.30
253 Glen Rice PM	.20	.50
254 David Robinson PM	.30	.75
255 Steve Smith PM	.15	.40
256 Latrell Sprewell PM	.20	.50
257 Jerry Stackhouse PM	.25	.60
258 Rod Strickland PM	.12	.30
259 Nick Van Exel PM	.20	.50
260 Charles Barkley DT	.30	.75
261 Dale Davis DT	.12	.30
262 Patrick Ewing DT	.25	.60
263 Michael Finley DT	.25	.60
264 Chris Gatling DT	.12	.30
265 Armon Gilliam DT	.12	.30
266 Tyrone Hill DT	.12	.30
267 Robert Horry DT	.15	.40
268 Mark Jackson DT	.15	.40
269 Shawn Kemp DT	.20	.50
270 Jamal Mashburn DT	.15	.40
271 Anthony Mason DT	.12	.30
272 Alonzo Mourning DT	.25	.60
273 Dikembe Mutombo DT	.20	.50
274 Shaquille O'Neal DT	.50	1.25
275 Isaiah Rider DT	.15	.40
276 Dennis Rodman DT	.40	1.00
277 Damon Stoudamire DT	.15	.40
278 Chris Webber DT	.25	.60
279 Jayson Williams DT	.12	.30
280 Checklist (132-239)	.12	.30
281 Checklist (240-281/inserts)	.12	.30
NNO Jerry Stackhouse PROMO	.75	2.00

1996-97 SkyBox Premium Rubies

*STARS: 12.5X TO 30X BASE CARD HI		
*RCs: 8X TO 20X BASE HI		
*PM/DT SUBSET: 8X TO 20X BASE HI		
ONE PER SER.1/2 HOBBY BOX		
16 Michael Jordan	150.00	400.00
18 Scottie Pippen	12.00	30.00
55 Kobe Bryant	300.00	450.00
59 Nick Van Exel	8.00	20.00
85 Allen Iverson	15.00	40.00
203 Kobe Bryant ROO	100.00	200.00
216 Allen Iverson ROO	20.00	50.00
227 Steve Nash ROO	10.00	25.00
247 Michael Jordan PM	75.00	150.00

1996-97 SkyBox Premium Autographics

Randomly inserted in the following 1996-97 products: Hoops series one and two, SkyBox series one and two, SkyBox Z-Force series one and two and SkyBox EX2000 all at a rate of one in 72, this set features autographs of some of the top stars in the NBA. Card design is identical for each issue and several players had their cards seeded into more than one of the aforementioned products. Card fronts feature a background in the particular player's team colors and an action shot of the player. Most of the cards were autographed vertically along the left side. Card backs are black with a spotlight photo, the player's name and career statistics. The first 100 cards of each player were autographed in blue ink and the remaining number were in black. A couple exceptions include Hakeem Olajuwon and Scottie Pippen, who autographed all of their cards in blue ink only. Also, Kevin Garnett autographed two-thirds of his cards in blue and the rest in black. The cards below are not numbered and are listed alphabetically. As far as set value, the set is considered complete with the Kevin Garnett Black, Hakeem Olajuwon Blue and the Scottie Pippen Blue. Both Olajuwon and Pippen are also listed under the Blue set. Recently, some news of counterfeits have surfaced. The focal cards being reproduced include the Grant Hill, Kevin Garnett and Scottie Pippen. These cards feature no chipping on the edges, a lighter color of black on the back, a fuzzy copyright line and, in general, a poor autograph. These do, however, have the SkyBox logo stamped on the card.

STATED ODDS 1:72 FLEER/SKYBOX PROD.		
SET INCLUDES #'s 22A, 61 AND 68		
CARDS LISTED BELOW ALPHABETICALLY		
BEWARE COUNTERFEITS		
1 Ray Allen	50.00	100.00
2 Kenny Anderson	5.00	12.00
3 Nick Anderson	10.00	25.00
4 B.J. Armstrong	6.00	15.00
5 Vincent Askew	5.00	12.00
6 Dana Barros	5.00	12.00
7 Brent Barry	5.00	12.00
8 Travis Best	5.00	12.00
9 Muggsy Bogues	6.00	15.00
10 P.J. Brown	5.00	12.00
11 Randy Brown	6.00	15.00
12 Marcus Camby	20.00	50.00
13 Chris Childs	5.00	12.00
14 Dell Curry	5.00	12.00
15 Andrew DeClercq	5.00	12.00
16 Tony Delk	8.00	20.00
17 Sherman Douglas	5.00	12.00
18 Clyde Drexler	50.00	100.00
19 Tyus Edney	5.00	12.00
20 Michael Finley	6.00	15.00
21 Rick Fox	6.00	15.00
22 Kevin Garnett	100.00	250.00
23 Matt Geiger	5.00	12.00
24 Kendall Gill	5.00	12.00
25 Brian Grant	5.00	12.00
26 Tim Hardaway	10.00	25.00
27 Grant Hill	60.00	150.00
28 Tyrone Hill	5.00	12.00
29 Allan Houston	5.00	12.00
30 Juwan Howard	30.00	80.00
31 Zydrunas Ilgauskas	6.00	15.00
32 Jim Jackson	5.00	12.00
33 Mark Jackson	5.00	12.00
34 Eddie Jones	15.00	40.00
35 Adam Keefe	5.00	12.00
36 Steve Kerr	12.00	30.00
37 Kerry Kittles	8.00	20.00
38 Toni Kukoc	15.00	40.00
39 Andrew Lang	5.00	12.00
40 Voshon Lenard	5.00	12.00
41 Grant Long	5.00	12.00
42 Luc Longley	8.00	20.00
43 George Lynch	5.00	12.00
44 Don MacLean	5.00	12.00
45 Stephon Marbury	20.00	50.00
46 Lee Mayberry	5.00	12.00
47 Walter McCarty	5.00	12.00
48 George McCloud	75.00	200.00
49 Antonio McDyess	15.00	40.00
50 Nate McMillan	5.00	12.00
51 Chris Mills	5.00	12.00
52 Sam Mitchell	5.00	12.00
53 Eric Montross	5.00	12.00
54 Chris Morris	5.00	12.00
55 Lawrence Moten	5.00	12.00
56 Alonzo Mourning	100.00	250.00
57 Gheorghe Muresan	6.00	15.00
58 Steve Nash	200.00	400.00
59 Ed O'Bannon	5.00	12.00
60 Charles Oakley	10.00	25.00
62 Greg Ostertag	5.00	12.00
63 Billy Owens	5.00	12.00
64 Sam Perkins	5.00	12.00
65 Chuck Person	5.00	12.00
66 Wesley Person	5.00	12.00
67 Bobby Phills	5.00	12.00
69 Theo Ratliff	5.00	12.00
70 Glen Rice	5.00	12.00
71 Rodney Rogers	5.00	12.00
72 Byron Scott	5.00	12.00
73 Dennis Scott	5.00	12.00
74 Joe Smith	10.00	25.00
75 Kenny Smith	6.00	15.00
76 Rik Smits	5.00	12.00
77 Eric Snow	5.00	12.00
78 Latrell Sprewell	6.00	15.00
79 Jerry Stackhouse	6.00	15.00
80 John Starks	5.00	12.00
81 Bryant Stith	5.00	12.00
82 Damon Stoudamire	75.00	200.00
83 Rod Strickland	50.00	120.00
84 Bob Sura	5.00	12.00
85 Zan Tabak	5.00	12.00
86 Loy Vaught	6.00	15.00
87 Antoine Walker	25.00	60.00
88 Samaki Walker	6.00	15.00
89 John Wallace	6.00	15.00
90 Bill Wennington	6.00	15.00
91 David Wesley	5.00	12.00
92 Doug West	5.00	12.00
93 Monty Williams	5.00	12.00
94 Joe Wolf	5.00	12.00
95 Sharone Wright	5.00	12.00

1996-97 SkyBox Premium Autographics Blue

*BLUE: .75X TO 2X VALUE		
ALL OLAJUWON CARDS SIGNED IN BLUE		
ALL PIPPEN CARDS SIGNED IN BLUE		
GARNETT BLUE CARDS 2:1 VERSUS BLACK		
NO JOHN WALLACE BLUE AU's EXIST		
18 Clyde Drexler	100.00	250.00
22 Kevin Garnett	100.00	250.00
34 Eddie Jones	40.00	100.00
36 Steve Kerr	15.00	40.00
45 Stephon Marbury	50.00	120.00
58 Steve Nash	400.00	800.00
61 Hakeem Olajuwon	75.00	200.00
68 Scottie Pippen	125.00	250.00
82 Damon Stoudamire	100.00	250.00

1996-97 SkyBox Premium Close-Ups

Randomly inserted in all series one packs at a rate of one in 24, this 9-card set features a die cut design and gives collectors a close-up view of players in action with a crystal ball in the background.

COMPLETE SET (9)	8.00	20.00
SER.1 STATED ODDS 1:24 HOBBY/RETAIL		
CU1 Anfernee Hardaway	2.00	5.00
CU2 Grant Hill	2.00	5.00
CU3 Juwan Howard	1.00	2.50
CU4 Jason Kidd	2.00	5.00
CU5 Shawn Kemp	1.25	3.00
CU6 Alonzo Mourning	1.50	4.00
CU7 Hakeem Olajuwon	1.50	4.00
CU8 Jerry Stackhouse	1.50	4.00
CU9 Damon Stoudamire	1.00	2.50

1996-97 SkyBox Premium Emerald Autographs

Loosely inserted one in 20 hobby boxes as exchange cards, this 5-card set features autographed base cards. Each card contains green "emerald" foil rather than the standard gold foil. Most of the redemption autographs were returned signed in black ink, however, Marcus Camby redemptions were available in both blue and black ink. The expiration date was February 1, 1998.

SER.2 STATED ODDS 1:20 HOBBY BOXES		
E1 Ray Allen	30.00	80.00
E2 Marcus Camby	10.00	25.00
E3 Grant Hill	100.00	200.00
E4 Kerry Kittles	6.00	15.00
E5 Jerry Stackhouse	10.00	25.00
NNO Expired Trade Cards	.40	1.00

1996-97 SkyBox Premium Golden Touch

Randomly inserted in all series two packs at a rate of one in 240, this set focuses on veterans and rookies who can make just about any shot on the court. Cards carry a heavily die cut design.

COMPLETE SET (10)	200.00	500.00
SER.2 STATED ODDS 1:240 HOBBY/RETAIL		
1 Vin Baker	6.00	15.00
2 Terrell Brandon	5.00	12.00
3 Allan Houston	6.00	15.00
4 Allen Iverson	20.00	50.00
5 Michael Jordan	200.00	400.00
6 Shawn Kemp	10.00	25.00
7 Karl Malone	10.00	25.00
8 Stephon Marbury	8.00	20.00
9 Latrell Sprewell	8.00	20.00
10 Damon Stoudamire	6.00	15.00

1996-97 SkyBox Premium Intimidators

Randomly inserted in all series two packs at a rate of one in 8, this 20-card set focuses on players who can intimidate on the court. Card fronts feature the player's name and team written vertically around the shot of the player.

COMPLETE SET (20)	12.00	30.00
SER.2 STATED ODDS 1:8 HOBBY/RETAIL		
1 Shareef Abdur-Rahim	1.00	2.50
2 Charles Barkley	1.50	4.00
3 Marcus Camby	1.00	2.50
4 Elden Campbell	.60	1.50
5 Derrick Coleman	.75	2.00
6 Patrick Ewing	1.25	3.00
7 Michael Finley	1.25	3.00
8 Kevin Garnett	2.50	6.00
9 Jim Jackson	.60	1.50
10 Anthony Mason	.60	1.50
11 Antonio McDyess	1.00	2.50
12 Alonzo Mourning	1.25	3.00
13 Gheorghe Muresan	.60	1.50
14 Dikembe Mutombo	1.00	2.50
15 Shaquille O'Neal	2.50	6.00
16 Isaiah Rider	.75	2.00
17 Clifford Robinson	.60	1.50
18 David Robinson	1.50	4.00
19 Dennis Rodman	2.00	5.00
20 Clarence Weatherspoon	.60	1.50

1996-97 SkyBox Premium Larger Than Life

Randomly inserted in series one hobby packs only at a rate of one in 180, this 18-card set features cards that are presented in 4-color image action photos horizontally. The images are set against a background featuring the player's portrait in the shadow. The player's names are gold foil stamped. Card backs feature a "B" prefix.

COMPLETE SET (18)	200.00	500.00
SER.1 STATED ODDS 1:180 HOBBY		
B1 Shareef Abdur-Rahim	5.00	12.00
B2 Marcus Camby	5.00	12.00
B3 Kevin Garnett	15.00	40.00
B4 Anfernee Hardaway	15.00	40.00
B5 Grant Hill	10.00	25.00
B6 Allen Iverson	15.00	40.00
B7 Michael Jordan	125.00	300.00
B8 Shawn Kemp	6.00	15.00
B9 Stephon Marbury	8.00	20.00
B10 Jamal Mashburn	5.00	12.00
B11 Antonio McDyess	6.00	15.00
B12 Alonzo Mourning	8.00	20.00
B13 Dikembe Mutombo	6.00	15.00
B14 Hakeem Olajuwon	8.00	20.00
B15 Shaquille O'Neal	15.00	40.00
B16 Dennis Rodman	12.00	30.00
B17 Jerry Stackhouse	8.00	20.00
B18 Damon Stoudamire	5.00	12.00

1996-97 SkyBox Premium Net Set

Randomly inserted in series two hobby packs only at a rate of one in 48, this 20-card set focuses on the league's superstars.

COMPLETE SET (20)	60.00	150.00
SER.2 STATED ODDS 1:48 HOBBY		
1 Vin Baker	1.50	4.00
2 Clyde Drexler	2.50	6.00
3 Patrick Ewing	2.50	6.00
4 Anfernee Hardaway	3.00	8.00
5 Grant Hill	3.00	8.00
6 Juwan Howard	1.50	4.00
7 Allen Iverson	10.00	25.00
8 Michael Jordan	30.00	80.00
9 Shawn Kemp	2.00	5.00
10 Jason Kidd	3.00	8.00
11 Karl Malone	2.50	6.00
12 Stephon Marbury	5.00	12.00
13 Alonzo Mourning	2.50	6.00
14 Hakeem Olajuwon	2.50	6.00
15 Shaquille O'Neal	5.00	12.00
16 Scottie Pippen	5.00	12.00
17 David Robinson	3.00	8.00
18 Joe Smith	1.50	4.00
19 Damon Stoudamire	1.50	4.00
20 Chris Webber	2.50	6.00

1996-97 SkyBox Premium New Edition

Randomly inserted in series two retail packs only at a rate of one in 36, this 10-card set focuses on rookies featuring a die cut design that looks similar to the front of a video game machine.

COMPLETE SET (10)	30.00	60.00
SER.2 STATED ODDS 1:36 RETAIL		
1 Shareef Abdur-Rahim	1.50	4.00
2 Ray Allen	4.00	10.00
3 Kobe Bryant	15.00	40.00
4 Marcus Camby	1.50	4.00
5 Allen Iverson	8.00	20.00
6 Kerry Kittles	1.00	2.50
7 Matt Maloney	.75	2.00
8 Stephon Marbury	2.50	6.00
9 Steve Nash	5.00	12.00
10 Samaki Walker	.75	2.00

1996-97 SkyBox Premium Rookie Prevue

Randomly inserted in series one packs at a rate of one in 54, this 18-card set focuses on the top 18 players from the 1996 NBA Draft. Card fronts feature a foil background. Card backs are numbered with a "R" prefix.

COMPLETE SET (18)	15.00	40.00
SER.1 STATED ODDS 1:54 HOBBY/RETAIL		
R1 Shareef Abdur-Rahim	2.00	5.00
R2 Ray Allen	5.00	12.00
R3 Kobe Bryant	10.00	25.00
R4 Marcus Camby	2.00	5.00
R5 Erick Dampier	1.25	3.00
R6 Tony Delk	1.25	3.00
R7 Brian Evans	1.25	3.00
R8 Todd Fuller	.75	2.00
R9 Allen Iverson	6.00	15.00
R10 Kerry Kittles	1.25	3.00
R11 Stephon Marbury	3.00	8.00
R12 Steve Nash	6.00	15.00
R13 Vitaly Potapenko	1.00	2.50
R14 Roy Rogers	1.00	2.50
R15 Antoine Walker	2.00	5.00
R16 Samaki Walker	1.00	2.50
R17 John Wallace	1.25	3.00
R18 Lorenzen Wright	1.00	2.50

1996-97 SkyBox Premium Standouts

Randomly inserted in series one retail packs only at a rate of one in 180, this 9-card set features laser cut photos of standout NBA players which are silhouetted over a foil background which contains a giant basketball net graphic. Card backs are numbered with a "SO" prefix.

COMPLETE SET (9)	50.00	120.00
SER.1 STATED ODDS 1:180 RETAIL		
SO1 Grant Hill	10.00	25.00
SO2 Juwan Howard	5.00	12.00
SO3 Jason Kidd	10.00	25.00
SO4 Reggie Miller	8.00	20.00
SO5 Shaquille O'Neal	12.00	30.00
SO6 Gary Payton	6.00	15.00
SO7 Scottie Pippen	10.00	25.00
SO8 Mitch Richmond	6.00	15.00
SO9 Joe Smith	5.00	12.00

1996-97 SkyBox Premium Thunder and Lightning

andomly inserted in all series two packs at a rate of one in 144, this 10-card multi-player set focuses on some of the NBA's most deadly combinations. The "outside" card contains the first player while the second player is contained inside the first one.

COMPLETE SET (10)	25.00	60.00
SER.2 STATED ODDS 1:144 HOBBY/RETAIL		
1 M.Jordan/S.Pippen	15.00	40.00
2 K.Johnson/D.Manning	2.00	5.00
3 G.Hill/J.Dumars	3.00	8.00
4 L.Sprewell/J.Smith	2.00	5.00
5 C.Barkley/H.Olajuwon	3.00	8.00
6 V.Baker/G.Robinson	1.50	4.00
7 P.Ewing/L.Johnson	2.50	6.00
8 S.Kemp/G.Payton	2.00	5.00
9 K.Malone/J.Stockton	2.50	6.00
10 J.Howard/C.Webber	2.50	6.00

1996-97 SkyBox Premium Triple Threats

The first nine cards were randomly inserted into first series packs at roughly one per pack. The bonus Triple Threat cards were randomly inserted in first series packs at a rate of one in 240, and feature three members from the NBA Champion Chicago Bulls. These cards differed from the first nine by the use of a metallic background. All card backs were numbered with a "TT" prefix.

COMPLETE SET (9)	1.50	4.00
SPs: SER.1 STATED ODDS 1:720 HOB/RET		
*RUBY: 10X TO 25X BASE HI		
SPs DO NOT HAVE RUBY PARALLEL		
TT1 Chris Mullin	.40	1.00
TT2 Joe Smith	.30	.75
TT3 Latrell Sprewell	.40	1.00
TT4 Avery Johnson	.30	.75
TT5 Sean Elliott	.40	1.00
TT6 David Robinson	.60	1.50
TT7 John Stockton	.50	1.25
TT8 Karl Malone	.50	1.25
TT9 Jeff Hornacek	.30	.75
TT10 Dennis Rodman SP	3.00	8.00
TT11 Michael Jordan SP	12.00	30.00
TT12 Scottie Pippen SP	2.50	6.00

1997-98 SkyBox Premium

This 250-card set features borderless color action player images printed on 20 pt. stock with holographic foil stamping and was distributed in eight-card packs with a suggested retail price of $2.59. The backs carry information about the player and career statistics. The second series contained the subset "Team SkyBox" that was inserted into packs at a rate of one in four.

COMPLETE SET (250)	50.00	90.00
COMPLETE SERIES 1 (125)	12.50	25.00
COMPLETE SERIES 2 (125)	40.00	70.00
TS SUBSET 1:4 HOB/RET		
1 Grant Hill	.40	1.00
2 Matt Maloney	.15	.40
3 Vinny Del Negro	.15	.40
4 Kevin Willis	.15	.40
5 Mark Jackson	.20	.50
6 Ray Allen	.30	.75
7 Derrick Coleman	.20	.50
8 Isaiah Rider	.20	.50
9 Rod Strickland	.15	.40
10 Danny Ferry	.15	.40
11 Antonio Davis	.15	.40
12 Glenn Robinson	.20	.50
13 Cedric Ceballos	.15	.40
14 Sean Elliott	.25	.60
15 Walt Williams	.15	.40
16 Glen Rice	.25	.60
17 Clyde Drexler	.30	.75
18 Sherman Douglas	.15	.40
19 Othella Harrington	.15	.40
20 John Stockton	.30	.75
21 Priest Lauderdale	.15	.40
22 Khalid Reeves	.15	.40
23 Kobe Bryant	1.25	3.00
24 Vin Baker UER	.20	.50
25 Steve Nash	.50	1.25
26 Jeff Hornacek	.20	.50
27 Tyrone Corbin	.15	.40
28 Charles Barkley	.40	1.00
29 Michael Jordan	2.00	5.00
30 Latrell Sprewell	.25	.60
31 Anfernee Hardaway	.40	1.00
32 Steve Kerr	.20	.50
33 Joe Smith	.20	.50
34 Jermaine O'Neal	.20	.50
35 Ron Mercer RC	.30	.75
36 Antonio McDyess	.20	.50
37 Patrick Ewing	.30	.75
38 Avery Johnson	.20	.50
39 Toni Kukoc	.25	.60
40 Sam Perkins	.15	.40
41 Voshon Lenard	.15	.40
42 Detlef Schrempf	.25	.60
43 Horace Grant	.20	.50
44 Luc Longley	.20	.50
45 Todd Fuller	.15	.40
46 Tim Hardaway	.25	.60
47 Nick Anderson	.15	.40
48 Scottie Pippen	.40	1.00
49 Lindsey Hunter	.15	.40
50 Shawn Kemp	.25	.60

51 Larry Johnson .25 .60
52 Shawn Bradley .15 .40
53 Martin Muursepp .15 .40
54 Jamal Mashburn .20 .50
55 John Starks .20 .50
56 Rony Seikaly .15 .40
57 Gary Payton .25 .60
58 Juwan Howard .20 .50
59 Vitaly Potapenko .15 .40
60 Reggie Miller .30 .75
61 Alonzo Mourning .30 .75
62 Roy Rogers .15 .40
63 Antoine Walker .25 .60
64 Joe Dumars .25 .60
65 Allan Houston .20 .50
66 Hersey Hawkins .15 .40
67 Dell Curry .15 .40
68 Tony Delk .15 .40
69 Mookie Blaylock .15 .40
70 Derek Harper .20 .50
71 Loy Vaught .15 .40
72 Tom Gugliotta .15 .40
73 Mitch Richmond .25 .60
74 Dikembe Mutombo .25 .60
75 Tony Battie RC .25 .60
76 Derek Fisher .25 .60
77 Jason Kidd .40 1.00
78 Shareef Abdur-Rahim .25 .60
79 Tracy McGrady RC 1.00 2.50
80 Anthony Mason .15 .40
81 Mario Elie .15 .40
82 Karl Malone .30 .75
83 Mark Price .25 .60
84 Steve Smith .20 .50
85 LaPhonso Ellis .15 .40
86 Robert Horry .20 .50
87 Wesley Person .15 .40
88 Marcus Camby .25 .60
89 Antonio Daniels RC .25 .60
90 Eddie Jones .25 .60
91 Gary Trent .15 .40
92 Danny Fortson RC .25 .60
93 Chris Childs .15 .40
94 David Robinson .40 1.00
95 Bryant Reeves .15 .40
96 Chris Webber .25 .60
97 P.J. Brown .15 .40
98 Tyrone Hill .15 .40
99 Dale Davis .15 .40
100 Allen Iverson .50 1.25
101 Jerry Stackhouse .25 .60
102 Arvydas Sabonis .20 .50
103 Damon Stoudamire .20 .50
104 Tim Thomas RC .30 .75
105 Christian Laettner .20 .50
106 Robert Pack .15 .40
107 Lorenzen Wright .15 .40
108 Olden Polynice .15 .40
109 Terrell Brandon .15 .40
110 Theo Ratliff .20 .50
111 Kevin Garnett .40 1.00
112 Tim Duncan RC 1.25 3.00
113 Bryon Russell .15 .40
114 Chauncey Billups RC .75 2.00
115 Dale Ellis .15 .40
116 Shaquille O'Neal .60 1.50
117 Keith Van Horn RC .40 1.00
118 Kenny Anderson .20 .50
119 Dennis Rodman .50 1.25
120 Hakeem Olajuwon .30 .75
121 Stephon Marbury .30 .75
122 Kendall Gill .15 .40
123 Kerry Kittles .15 .40
124 Checklist .15 .40
125 Checklist .15 .40
126 Anthony Johnson RC .25 .60
127 Chris Anstey RC .15 .40
128 Dean Garrett .15 .40
129 Rik Smits .20 .50
130 Tracy Murray .15 .40
131 Charles O'Bannon RC .25 .60
132 Eldridge Recasner .15 .40
133 Johnny Taylor RC .20 .50
134 Priest Lauderdale .15 .40
135 Rod Strickland .15 .40
136 Alan Henderson .15 .40
137 Austin Croshere RC .20 .50
138 Buck Williams .15 .40
139 Clifford Robinson .15 .40
140 Darrell Armstrong .15 .40
141 Dennis Scott .15 .40
142 Carl Herrera .15 .40
143 Maurice Taylor RC .25 .60
144 Chris Gatling .15 .40
145 Alvin Williams RC .25 .60
146 Antonio McDyess .20 .50
147 Chauncey Billups .40 1.00
148 George McCloud .15 .40
149 George Lynch .15 .40
150 John Thomas RC .15 .40
151 Jayson Williams .15 .40
152 Otis Thorpe .15 .40
153 Serge Zwikker RC .25 .60
154 Chris Crawford RC .25 .60
155 Muggsy Bogues .20 .50
156 Mark Jackson .20 .50
157 Dontonio Wingfield .15 .40
158 Rodrick Rhodes RC .20 .50
159 Sam Cassell .20 .50
160 Hubert Davis .15 .40
161 Clarence Weatherspoon .15 .40
162 Eddie Johnson .15 .40
163 Jacque Vaughn RC .20 .50
164 Mark Price .25 .60
165 Terry Dehere .15 .40
166 Travis Knight .15 .40
167 Charles Smith RC .20 .50
168 David Wesley .15 .40
169 David Wingate .15 .40
170 Todd Day .15 .40
171 Adonal Foyle RC .20 .50
172 Chris Mills .15 .40
173 Paul Grant RC .15 .40
174 Adam Keefe .15 .40
175 Erick Dampier UER .15 .40
176 Ervin Johnson .15 .40
177 Lamond Murray .15 .40
178 Vlade Divac .25 .60
179 Bobby Phills .15 .40
180 Brian Williams .15 .40
181 Chris Dudley .15 .40
182 Tyrone Hill .15 .40
183 Donyell Marshall .15 .40
184 Kevin Gamble .15 .40
185 Scot Pollard RC .25 .60
186 Cherokee Parks .15 .40
187 Terry Mills .15 .40
188 Glen Rice .25 .60
189 Shawn Respert .15 .40
190 Terrell Brandon .15 .40
191 Keith Closs RC .25 .60
192 Tariq Abdul-Wahad RC .20 .50
193 Wesley Person .15 .40
194 Chuck Person .20 .50
195 Derek Anderson RC .25 .60
196 Jon Barry .15 .40
197 Chris Mullin .25 .60
198 Ed Gray RC .20 .50
199 Charlie Ward .15 .40
200 Kelvin Cato RC .20 .50
201 Michael Finley .25 .60
202 Rick Fox .15 .40
203 Scott Burrell .15 .40
204 Vin Baker .20 .50
205 Eric Snow .15 .40
206 Isaac Austin .15 .40
207 Keith Booth RC .20 .50
208 Brian Grant .15 .40
209 Chris Webber .25 .60
210 Eric Williams .15 .40
211 Jim Jackson .15 .40
212 Anthony Parker RC .25 .60
213 Brevin Knight RC .25 .60
214 Cory Alexander .15 .40
215 James Robinson .15 .40
216 Bobby Jackson RC .30 .75
217 Bo Outlaw .15 .40
218 God Shammgod RC .25 .60
219 James Cotton RC .25 .60
220 Jud Buechler .15 .40
221 Shandon Anderson .15 .40
222 Kevin Johnson .25 .60
223 Chris Morris .15 .40
224 Shareef Abdur-Rahim TS .50 1.25
225 Ray Allen TS .60 1.50
226 Kobe Bryant TS 2.50 6.00
227 Marcus Camby TS .50 1.25
228 Antonio Daniels TS .50 1.25
229 Tim Duncan TS 2.50 6.00
230 Kevin Garnett TS .75 2.00
231 Anfernee Hardaway TS .75 2.00
232 Grant Hill TS .75 2.00
233 Allen Iverson TS 1.00 2.50
234 Bobby Jackson TS .60 1.50
235 Michael Jordan TS 4.00 10.00
236 Shawn Kemp TS .50 1.25
237 Karl Malone TS .60 1.50
238 Stephon Marbury TS .60 1.50
239 Hakeem Olajuwon TS .60 1.50
240 Shaquille O'Neal TS 1.25 3.00
241 Gary Payton TS .50 1.25
242 Scottie Pippen TS .75 2.00
243 David Robinson TS .75 2.00
244 Dennis Rodman TS 1.00 2.50
245 Jerry Stackhouse TS .50 1.25
246 Damon Stoudamire TS .40 1.00
247 Keith Van Horn TS .75 2.00
248 Antoine Walker TS .50 1.25
249 Grant Hill CL .40 1.00
250 Hakeem Olajuwon CL .30 .75
NNO A.Iverson Shoe Bronze .50 1.25
NNO A.Iverson Shoe Ruby 5.00 12.00
NNO A.Iverson Shoe Gold 1.50 4.00
NNO A.Iverson Shoe Silver .75 2.00
NNO A.Iverson Shoe Emerald 12.50 30.00

1997-98 SkyBox Premium Star Rubies

*STARS: 100X TO 200X BASE CARD HI
*RCs: 50X TO 100X BASE HI
*TS: SAME VALUE AS BASE RUBY
STATED PRINT RUN 50 SERIAL #'d SETS
1 Grant Hill 150.00 300.00
6 Ray Allen 150.00 400.00
17 Clyde Drexler 125.00 250.00
20 John Stockton 300.00 600.00
23 Kobe Bryant 2500.00 4000.00
25 Steve Nash 300.00 600.00
28 Charles Barkley 150.00 300.00
29 Michael Jordan 6000.00 8000.00
30 Latrell Sprewell 75.00 150.00
31 Anfernee Hardaway 500.00 1000.00
32 Steve Kerr 75.00 200.00
37 Patrick Ewing 80.00 200.00
46 Tim Hardaway 75.00 150.00
48 Scottie Pippen 600.00 1200.00
50 Shawn Kemp 75.00 150.00
51 Larry Johnson 60.00 150.00
57 Gary Payton 200.00 500.00
60 Reggie Miller 125.00 250.00
72 Tom Gugliotta 60.00 150.00
77 Jason Kidd 125.00 250.00
79 Tracy McGrady 400.00 800.00
82 Karl Malone 125.00 250.00
90 Eddie Jones 100.00 200.00
94 David Robinson 150.00 300.00
96 Chris Webber 400.00 800.00
100 Allen Iverson 200.00 400.00
101 Jerry Stackhouse 75.00 200.00
111 Kevin Garnett 175.00 350.00
112 Tim Duncan 1500.00 2500.00
116 Shaquille O'Neal 250.00 500.00
117 Keith Van Horn 75.00 200.00
119 Dennis Rodman 400.00 800.00
120 Hakeem Olajuwon 125.00 250.00
147 Chauncey Billups 125.00 300.00
209 Chris Webber 100.00 200.00

1997-98 SkyBox Premium And One

This 10-card set was randomly inserted in series one packs at a rate of one in 96. These cards were inserted inside the 1997-98 Skybox Premium And One Wrappers.

COMPLETE SET (10) 20.00 50.00
SER.1 STATED ODDS 1:96 HOB/RET
1 Shawn Kemp 1.50 4.00
2 Hakeem Olajuwon 2.00 5.00
3 Charles Barkley 2.50 6.00
4 Antoine Walker 1.50 4.00
5 Dennis Rodman 3.00 8.00
6 Tim Duncan 8.00 20.00
7 Marcus Camby 1.50 4.00
8 Keith Van Horn 2.50 6.00
9 Shareef Abdur-Rahim 1.50 4.00
10 Michael Jordan 12.00 30.00

1997-98 SkyBox Premium And One Wrappers

*WRAPPERS: .4X TO 1X BASIC

1997-98 SkyBox Premium Autographics

Randomly inserted in packs of all Fleer/SkyBox products, this set features autographs of some of the NBA's best players. For Hoops 1, these were inserted at a rate of one in 240 hobby and retail packs. For Hoops 2, these were inserted at a rate of one in 144 hobby and retail. For Metal and Metal Championship, these cards were inserted one in 120 hobby and retail. For SkyBox Premium 1 and 2, these cards were inserted one in 72 packs. For SkyBox E-X2001, these cards were inserted one in 60 packs. For SkyBox Z-Force 1 and 2, these cards were inserted one in 120 packs. Both Tracy McGrady and Rasheed Wallace only have Century Marks cards - no regular ones. Those cards are included in the set price, but are priced in the Century Mark set. The cards are not numbered and listed below alphabetically.

ALL MCGRADY CARDS ARE CEN.MARKS
ALL R.WALLACE CARDS ARE CEN.MARKS
STATED ODDS 1:240 HOOPS 1; 1:144 HOOPS 2
STATED ODDS 1:96 METAL; 1:72 MET.CHAMP
STATED ODDS 1:72 SKYBOX; 1:60 E-X
STATED ODDS 1:120 Z-FORCE 1,2
CARDS LISTED BELOW ALPHABETICALLY
1 Shareef Abdur-Rahim 10.00 25.00
2 Cory Alexander 3.00 8.00
3 Kenny Anderson 5.00 12.00
4 Nick Anderson 4.00 10.00
5 Stacey Augmon 6.00 15.00
6 Isaac Austin 3.00 8.00
7 Vin Baker 8.00 20.00
8 Charles Barkley 700.00 1300.00
9 Dana Barros 4.00 10.00
10 Brent Barry 4.00 10.00
11 Tony Battie 5.00 12.00
12 Travis Best 4.00 10.00
13 Corie Blount 3.00 8.00
14 P.J. Brown 4.00 10.00
15 Randy Brown 5.00 12.00
16 Jud Buechler 4.00 10.00
17 Marcus Camby 8.00 20.00
18 Elden Campbell 5.00 12.00
19 Chris Carr 4.00 10.00
20 Kelvin Cato 5.00 12.00
21 Duane Causwell 4.00 10.00
22 Rex Chapman 4.00 10.00
23 Calbert Cheaney 4.00 10.00
24 Randolph Childress 4.00 10.00
25 Derrick Coleman 6.00 15.00
26 Austin Croshere 5.00 12.00
27 Dell Curry 4.00 10.00
28 Ben Davis 8.00 20.00
29 Mark Davis 4.00 10.00
30 Andrew DeClercq 3.00 8.00
31 Tony Delk 4.00 10.00
32 Vlade Divac 8.00 25.00
33 Clyde Drexler 30.00 80.00
34 Joe Dumars 6.00 15.00
35 Howard Eisley 4.00 10.00
36 Danny Ferry 4.00 10.00
37 Michael Finley 6.00 15.00
38 Derek Fisher 5.00 12.00
39 Danny Fortson 8.00 20.00
40 Todd Fuller 4.00 10.00
41 Chris Gatling 4.00 10.00
42 Matt Geiger 4.00 10.00
43 Brian Grant 4.00 10.00
44 Tom Gugliotta 6.00 15.00
45 Tim Hardaway 15.00 40.00
46 Ron Harper 20.00 50.00
47 Othella Harrington 4.00 10.00
48 Grant Hill 75.00 200.00
49 Tyrone Hill 4.00 10.00
50 Allan Houston 5.00 12.00
51 Juwan Howard 10.00 25.00
52 Lindsey Hunter 8.00 20.00
53 Bobby Hurley 4.00 10.00
54 Jim Jackson 5.00 12.00
55 Avery Johnson 4.00 10.00
56 Eddie Johnson 4.00 10.00
57 Ervin Johnson 4.00 10.00
58 Larry Johnson 15.00 40.00
59 Popeye Jones 4.00 10.00
60 Adam Keefe 4.00 10.00
61 Steve Kerr 8.00 20.00
62 Kerry Kittles 10.00 25.00
63 Brevin Knight 5.00 12.00
64 Travis Knight 4.00 10.00
65 George Lynch 4.00 10.00
66 Don MacLean 4.00 10.00
67 Stephon Marbury 20.00 50.00
68 Donny Marshall 5.00 12.00
69 Walter McCarty 5.00 12.00
70 Antonio McDyess 8.00 20.00
72 Ron Mercer 6.00 15.00
73 Reggie Miller 75.00 200.00
74 Chris Mills 4.00 10.00
75 Sam Mitchell 5.00 12.00
76 Chris Morris 3.00 8.00
77 Alonzo Mourning 40.00 100.00
78 Chris Mullin 12.00 30.00
79 Dikembe Mutombo 20.00 50.00
80 Anthony Parker 5.00 12.00
81 Sam Perkins 5.00 12.00
82 Elliot Perry 4.00 10.00
83 Bobby Phills 6.00 15.00
84 Eric Piatkowski 4.00 10.00
85 Scottie Pippen 125.00 300.00
86 Vitaly Potapenko 4.00 10.00
87 Brent Price 4.00 10.00
88 Theo Ratliff 4.00 10.00
89 Glen Rice 10.00 25.00
90 Glenn Robinson 6.00 15.00
91 Dennis Rodman 150.00 300.00
92 Roy Rogers 4.00 10.00
93 Malik Rose 4.00 10.00
94 Joe Smith 10.00 25.00
95 Tony Smith 3.00 8.00
96 Eric Snow 5.00 12.00
97 Jerry Stackhouse Pistons 12.00 30.00
98 Jerry Stackhouse Sixers 12.00 30.00
99 John Starks 15.00 40.00
100 Bryant Stith 4.00 10.00
101 Erick Strickland 4.00 10.00
102 Rod Strickland 15.00 40.00
103 Nick Van Exel 15.00 40.00
104 Keith Van Horn 10.00 25.00
105 David Vaughn 3.00 8.00
106 Jacque Vaughn 4.00 10.00
107 Antoine Walker 6.00 15.00
109 Clarence Weatherspoon 4.00 10.00
110 David Wesley 4.00 10.00
111 Dominique Wilkins 15.00 40.00
112 Gerald Wilkins 4.00 10.00
113 Eric Williams 4.00 10.00
114 John Williams 4.00 10.00
115 Lorenzo Williams 3.00 8.00
116 Monty Williams 3.00 8.00
117 Scott Williams 4.00 10.00
118 Walt Williams 4.00 10.00
119 Lorenzen Wright 4.00 10.00

1997-98 SkyBox Premium Autographics Century Marks

*CENTURY MARKS: 1.25X TO 3X VALUE
STATED PRINT RUN 100 HAND #'d SETS
1 Shareef Abdur-Rahim 40.00 100.00
8 Charles Barkley 1000.00 1600.00
33 Clyde Drexler 60.00 150.00
46 Ron Harper 100.00 250.00
48 Grant Hill 500.00 850.00
50 Allan Houston 90.00 175.00
61 Steve Kerr 100.00 250.00
62 Kerry Kittles 25.00 60.00
67 Stephon Marbury 200.00 300.00
71 Tracy McGrady 600.00 1000.00
73 Reggie Miller 200.00 400.00
77 Alonzo Mourning 100.00 200.00
85 Scottie Pippen 600.00 1000.00
90 Glenn Robinson 25.00 60.00
91 Dennis Rodman 500.00 1000.00
102 Rod Strickland 30.00 80.00
107 Antoine Walker 40.00 100.00
108 Rasheed Wallace 450.00 750.00

1997-98 SkyBox Premium Competitive Advantage

Randomly inserted into series two packs at a rate of one in 96, this 15-card set features some of the best players on die cut, matte finished cards. The cards feature a background of Mount Olympus. Card backs are numbered with a "CA" prefix.

COMPLETE SET (15) 300.00 600.00
SER.2 STATED ODDS 1:96 HOB/RET
CA1 Allen Iverson 10.00 25.00
CA2 Kobe Bryant 25.00 60.00
CA3 Michael Jordan 150.00 400.00
CA4 Shaquille O'Neal 12.00 30.00
CA5 Stephon Marbury 6.00 15.00
CA6 Shareef Abdur-Rahim 5.00 12.00
CA7 Marcus Camby 5.00 12.00
CA8 Kevin Garnett 8.00 20.00
CA9 Dennis Rodman 10.00 25.00
CA10 Anfernee Hardaway 8.00 20.00
CA11 Ray Allen 6.00 15.00
CA12 Scottie Pippen 8.00 20.00
CA13 Shawn Kemp 5.00 12.00
CA14 Hakeem Olajuwon 6.00 15.00
CA15 John Stockton 6.00 15.00

1997-98 SkyBox Premium Golden Touch

Randomly inserted into series two packs at a rate of one in 360, this 15-card die cut set features some of the NBA's biggest superstars on embossed satin gold-foil. Card backs are numbered with a "GT" prefix.

SER.2 STATED ODDS 1:360 HOB/RET
GT1 Michael Jordan 600.00 1000.00
GT2 Allen Iverson 100.00 250.00
GT3 Kobe Bryant 150.00 400.00
GT4 Shaquille O'Neal 75.00 200.00
GT5 Stephon Marbury 30.00 80.00
GT6 Marcus Camby 8.00 20.00
GT7 Anfernee Hardaway 125.00 300.00
GT8 Kevin Garnett 60.00 150.00
GT9 Shareef Abdur-Rahim 30.00 80.00
GT10 Dennis Rodman 75.00 200.00
GT11 Grant Hill 30.00 80.00
GT12 Kerry Kittles 30.00 80.00
GT13 Antoine Walker 30.00 80.00
GT14 Scottie Pippen 75.00 200.00
GT15 Damon Stoudamire 12.00 30.00

1997-98 SkyBox Premium Jam Pack

Randomly inserted into series two packs at a rate of one in 18, this 15-card set features stars on the rise on 100% holofoil cardboard. The fronts feature a scenic background that has the players "walking on water". Card backs carry a "JP" prefix.

COMPLETE SET (15) 20.00 40.00
SER.2 STATED ODDS 1:18 HOB/RET
JP1 Ray Allen 2.50 6.00
JP2 Damon Stoudamire 1.50 4.00
JP3 Shawn Kemp 2.00 5.00
JP4 Hakeem Olajuwon 2.50 6.00
JP5 Jerry Stackhouse 2.00 5.00
JP6 John Wallace 1.25 3.00
JP7 Juwan Howard 1.50 4.00
JP8 David Robinson 3.00 8.00
JP9 Gary Payton 2.00 5.00
JP10 Joe Smith 1.50 4.00
JP11 Charles Barkley 3.00 8.00
JP12 Terrell Brandon 1.25 3.00
JP13 Vin Baker 1.50 4.00
JP14 Antonio McDyess 1.50 4.00
JP15 Tim Duncan 4.00 10.00

1997-98 SkyBox Premium Next Game

Randomly inserted in series one packs at the rate of one in six, this 15-card set features color photos of the 1997-98 season's top NBA rookies. The backs carry player information.

COMPLETE SET (15) 5.00 12.00
SER.1 STATED ODDS 1:6 HOB/RET
1 Derek Anderson .30 .75
2 Tony Battie .30 .75
3 Chauncey Billups 1.00 2.50
4 Kelvin Cato .25 .60
5 Austin Croshere .25 .60
6 Antonio Daniels .30 .75
7 Tim Duncan 1.50 4.00
8 Danny Fortson .30 .75
9 Adonal Foyle .25 .60
10 Tracy McGrady 1.25 3.00
11 Ron Mercer .40 1.00
12 Olivier Saint-Jean .25 .60
13 Maurice Taylor .30 .75
14 Tim Thomas .40 1.00
15 Keith Van Horn .50 1.25

1997-98 SkyBox Premium Premium Players

Randomly inserted in series one packs at the rate of one in 192, this 15-card set features letter box photography in the backsground and a player highlighted in the foreground with silver rainbow foil and team colors.

COMPLETE SET (15) 300.00 700.00
SER 1 STATED ODDS 1:192 HOB/RET
1 Michael Jordan 200.00 500.00
2 Allen Iverson 10.00 25.00
3 Kobe Bryant 30.00 80.00
4 Shaquille O'Neal 12.00 30.00
5 Stephon Marbury 6.00 15.00
6 Marcus Camby 5.00 12.00
7 Anfernee Hardaway 10.00 25.00
8 Kevin Garnett 12.00 30.00
9 Shareef Abdur-Rahim 5.00 12.00
10 Dennis Rodman 12.00 30.00
11 Ray Allen 6.00 15.00
12 Grant Hill 8.00 20.00
13 Kerry Kittles 5.00 12.00
14 Karl Malone 6.00 15.00
15 Scottie Pippen 12.00 30.00

1997-98 SkyBox Premium Reebok Chase Bronze

Inserted one per series one pack, this 15-card set is a partial parallel version of the regular set in three tiers of scarcity (bronze, silver and gold). Allen Iverson also has a special embossed foil card. Please refer to the basic SkyBox set for those values. Card backs carry one of three colors: bronze, gold or silver. The bronze is the base set and is priced below. Please refer to the multipliers in the header to ascertain values for the cards.

COMPLETE SET (15) 2.00 5.00
*GOLD: 12.5X TO 3X BRONZE
*SILVER: .5X TO 1.25X BRONZE
ONE PER SER.1 PACK
3 Vinny Del Negro .15 .40
5 Mark Jackson .20 .50
12 Glenn Robinson .20 .50
13 Cedric Ceballos .15 .40
17 Clyde Drexler .30 .75
38 Avery Johnson .20 .50
41 Voshon Lenard .15 .40
50 Shawn Kemp .25 .60
81 Mario Elie .15 .40
84 Steve Smith .20 .50
98 Tyrone Hill .15 .40
100 Allen Iverson .50 1.25
106 Robert Pack .15 .40
116 Shaquille O'Neal .60 1.50
118 Kenny Anderson .20 .50

1997-98 SkyBox Premium Rock 'n Fire

Randomly inserted in series one packs at the rate of one in 18, this 10-card set is reversible and featues a color action photo of a rising basketball star on one side and his portrait on the other with silver foil highlights. The card slides into a frame which carries more player information.

COMPLETE SET (10) 20.00 50.00
SER 1 STATED ODDS 1:18 HOB/RET
1 Allen Iverson 3.00 8.00
2 Kobe Bryant 8.00 20.00
3 Shaquille O'Neal 4.00 10.00
4 Stephon Marbury 2.00 5.00
5 Marcus Camby 1.50 4.00
6 Anfernee Hardaway 2.50 6.00
7 Kevin Garnett 2.50 6.00
8 Shareef Abdur-Rahim 1.50 4.00
9 Damon Stoudamire 1.25 3.00
10 Grant Hill 2.50 6.00

1997-98 SkyBox Premium Silky Smooth

Randomly inserted in series one packs at the rate of one in 360, this 10-card set features a glossy color action player photo with silver and gold holofoil and viewed through a matte coated, laser-cut net which can be opened to expose the card.

COMPLETE SET (10) 300.00 600.00
SER.1 STATED ODDS 1:360 HOB/RET
1 Michael Jordan 150.00 400.00
2 Allen Iverson 15.00 40.00
3 Kobe Bryant 30.00 80.00
4 Shaquille O'Neal 15.00 40.00
5 Stephon Marbury 6.00 15.00
6 Gary Payton 8.00 20.00
7 Anfernee Hardaway 12.00 30.00
8 Kevin Garnett 8.00 20.00
9 Scottie Pippen 8.00 20.00
10 Grant Hill 8.00 20.00

1997-98 SkyBox Premium Star Search

Randomly inserted into series two packs at a rate of one in six, this 15-card set features the top prospects from the 1997 Draft Class. The card fronts, when closed, feature a small photo of the player in front of a curtain. The fronts can be opened to "raise the curtain" on these players to reveal an action shot. Card backs are numbered with a "SS" prefix.

COMPLETE SET (15) 5.00 12.00
SER.2 STATED ODDS 1:6 HOB/RET
SS1 Tim Duncan 1.50 4.00
SS2 Tony Battie .30 .75
SS3 Keith Van Horn .50 1.25
SS4 Antonio Daniels .30 .75
SS5 Chauncey Billups 1.00 2.50
SS6 Ron Mercer .40 1.00
SS7 Tracy McGrady 1.25 3.00
SS8 Danny Fortson .30 .75
SS9 Brevin Knight .30 .75
SS10 Derek Anderson .30 .75
SS11 Bobby Jackson .40 1.00
SS12 Jacque Vaughn .25 .60
SS13 Tim Thomas .40 1.00
SS14 Austin Croshere .25 .60
SS15 Kelvin Cato .25 .60

1997-98 SkyBox Premium Thunder and Lightning

Randomly inserted into series two packs at a rate of one in 192, this 15-card set features a combination of rainbow holofoil and phosphorescent pigmentation to highlight a collection of stars who use their physical prowess to the team's advantage. Unlike past years, which featured two players, this only features one. One side features the player as "thunder" in his home uniform while the flip side shows him as "lightning" in his away uniform. Card backs are numbered with a "TL" prefix.

COMPLETE SET (15) 300.00 600.00
SER.2 STATED ODDS 1:192 HOB/RET
TL1 Stephon Marbury 8.00 20.00
TL2 Shareef Abdur-Rahim 6.00 15.00
TL3 Shaquille O'Neal 20.00 50.00
TL4 Scottie Pippen 20.00 50.00
TL5 Michael Jordan 125.00 300.00
TL6 Marcus Camby 6.00 15.00
TL7 Kobe Bryant 40.00 100.00
TL8 Kevin Garnett 10.00 25.00
TL9 Kerry Kittles 4.00 10.00
TL10 Grant Hill 15.00 40.00
TL11 Dennis Rodman 15.00 40.00
TL12 Damon Stoudamire 5.00 12.00
TL13 Antoine Walker 6.00 15.00
TL14 Anfernee Hardaway 15.00 40.00
TL15 Allen Iverson 15.00 40.00

1998-99 SkyBox Premium

The 1998-99 SkyBox Premium set was issued with a total of 266 standard size cards. The 8-card packs were released in two series and retailedl for $2.69 each. The fronts feature color game-action photography on ultra thick 20-pt. stock. The cards also carry holographic foil stamping. The rookie subset cards were inserted at a rate of one in four series two packs.

COMPLETE SET (265) 60.00 120.00
COMPLETE SET w/o SP (225) 20.00 40.00
COMPLETE SERIES 1 (125) 12.50 25.00
COMPLETE SERIES 2 (140) 50.00 100.00
RC STATED ODDS 1:4 PACKS
1 Tim Duncan .50 1.25
2 Voshon Lenard .15 .40
3 John Starks .20 .50
4 Juwan Howard .20 .50
5 Michael Finley .25 .60
6 Bobby Jackson .15 .40
7 Glenn Robinson .20 .50
8 Antonio McDyess .20 .50
9 Eric Williams .15 .40
10 Zydrunas Ilgauskas .25 .60
11 Terrell Brandon .15 .40
12 Shandon Anderson .15 .40
13 Rod Strickland .15 .40
14 Dennis Rodman .50 1.25
15 Clarence Weatherspoon .15 .40
16 P.J. Brown .15 .40
17 Anfernee Hardaway .40 1.00
18 Dikembe Mutombo .25 .60
19 Patrick Ewing .30 .75
20 Scottie Pippen .40 1.00
21 Shaquille O'Neal .60 1.50
22 Donyell Marshall .15 .40
23 Michael Jordan 2.00 5.00
24 Mark Price .25 .60
25 Jim Jackson .15 .40
26 Isaiah Rider .20 .50
27 Eddie Jones .25 .60
28 Detlef Schrempf .25 .60
29 Corliss Williamson .15 .40
30 Bo Outlaw .15 .40
31 Allen Iverson .50 1.25
32 Luc Longley .20 .50
33 Theo Ratliff .20 .50
34 Antoine Walker .25 .60
35 Lamond Murray .15 .40
36 Avery Johnson .20 .50
37 John Stockton .30 .75
38 David Wesley .15 .40
39 Elden Campbell .15 .40
40 Grant Hill .40 1.00
41 Sam Cassell .20 .50
42 Tracy McGrady .40 1.00
43 Glen Rice .25 .60
44 Kobe Bryant 1.00 2.50
45 John Wallace .15 .40
46 Bobby Phills .15 .40
47 Jerry Stackhouse .25 .60
48 Stephon Marbury .30 .75
49 Jeff Hornacek .20 .50
50 Tom Gugliotta .15 .40
51 Joe Dumars .25 .60
52 Johnny Newman .15 .40
53 Kevin Garnett .40 1.00
54 Dennis Scott .15 .40
55 Anthony Mason .15 .40
56 Rodney Rogers .15 .40
57 Bryon Russell .15 .40
58 Maurice Taylor .15 .40
59 Mookie Blaylock .15 .40
60 Shawn Bradley .15 .40
61 Matt Maloney .15 .40
62 Karl Malone .30 .75
63 Larry Johnson .25 .60
64 Calbert Cheaney .15 .40
65 Steve Smith .20 .50
66 Toni Kukoc .25 .60
67 Reggie Miller .30 .75
68 Jayson Williams .15 .40
69 Gary Payton .25 .60
70 Sean Elliott .25 .60
71 Charles Barkley .40 1.00
72 Tim Hardaway .25 .60
73 Rasheed Wallace .25 .60
74 Tariq Abdul-Wahad .15 .40
75 Kenny Anderson .20 .50
76 Chris Mullin .25 .60
77 Keith Van Horn .25 .60
78 Hersey Hawkins .15 .40
79 Ron Mercer .20 .50
80 Rik Smits .20 .50
81 David Robinson .40 1.00
82 Derek Anderson .15 .40
83 Danny Fortson .15 .40
84 Jason Kidd .40 1.00
85 Chauncey Billups .30 .75
86 Chris Anstey .15 .40
87 Hakeem Olajuwon .30 .75
88 Bryant Reeves .15 .40
89 Anthony Johnson .15 .40
90 Shawn Kemp .25 .60
91 Brevin Knight .15 .40
92 Ray Allen .30 .75
93 Tim Thomas .25 .60
94 Jalen Rose .20 .50
95 Kerry Kittles .15 .40
96 Vin Baker .20 .50
97 Shareef Abdur-Rahim .25 .60
98 Alonzo Mourning .30 .75
99 Joe Smith .20 .50
100 Damon Stoudamire .20 .50
101 Alan Henderson .15 .40
102 Walter McCarty .15 .40
103 Vlade Divac .25 .60
104 Wesley Person .15 .40
105 A.C. Green .20 .50
106 Malik Sealy .15 .40
107 Carl Thomas .15 .40
108 Brent Price .15 .40
109 Mark Jackson .20 .50
110 Lorenzen Wright .15 .40
111 Derek Fisher .25 .60
112 Michael Smith .15 .40
113 Tyrone Hill .15 .40
114 Cherokee Parks .15 .40
115 Kendall Gill .15 .40
116 Darrell Armstrong .15 .40
117 Derrick Coleman .20 .50
118 Rex Chapman .15 .40
119 Arvydas Sabonis .20 .50
120 Billy Owens .15 .40
121 Sam Perkins .15 .40
122 Gary Trent .15 .40
123 Sam Mack .15 .40
124 Tracy Murray .15 .40
125 Allan Houston .20 .50
126 Mitch Richmond .25 .60
127 Carl Herrera .15 .40
128 Ron Harper .20 .50
129 Gary Trent .15 .40
130 Chris Webber .25 .60
131 Antonio Daniels .15 .40
132 Charles Oakley .20 .50
133 Marcus Camby .20 .50
134 Tony Battie .20 .50
135 Otis Thorpe .15 .40
136 Dale Davis .15 .40
137 Chuck Person .20 .50
138 Ervin Johnson .15 .40
139 Jamal Mashburn .20 .50
140 Brian Grant .15 .40
141 Chris Mills .15 .40
142 Doug Christie .15 .40
143 George McCloud .15 .40
144 Todd Fuller .15 .40
145 Jerome Williams .15 .40
146 Chauncey Billups .30 .75
147 Dean Garrett .15 .40
148 Robert Pack .15 .40
149 Clarence Weatherspoon .15 .40
150 Tim Legler .15 .40
151 Bob Sura .15 .40
152 B.J. Armstrong .15 .40
153 Charlie Ward .15 .40
154 Rony Seikaly .15 .40
155 Chris Carr .15 .40
156 Eldridge Recasner .15 .40
157 Michael Stewart .15 .40
158 Jim McIlvaine .15 .40
159 Adam Keefe .15 .40
160 Antonio Davis .15 .40
161 Lawrence Funderburke .15 .40
162 Greg Ostertag .15 .40
163 Dan Majerle .25 .60
164 Dale Ellis .15 .40
165 Greg Anthony .15 .40
166 Chris Whitney .15 .40
167 Eric Piatkowski .20 .50
168 Tom Gugliotta .15 .40
169 Luc Longley .20 .50
170 Antonio McDyess .20 .50
171 George Lynch .15 .40
172 Dell Curry .15 .40
173 Johnny Newman .15 .40
174 Christian Laettner .20 .50
175 Steve Kerr .20 .50
176 Popeye Jones .15 .40
177 Brent Barry .20 .50
178 Billy Owens .15 .40
179 Cherokee Parks .15 .40
180 Derek Harper .20 .50
181 Howard Eisley .15 .40
182 Matt Geiger .15 .40
183 Darrick Martin .15 .40
184 Isaac Austin .15 .40
185 Dennis Scott .15 .40
186 Derrick Coleman .20 .50
187 Sam Perkins .15 .40
188 Latrell Sprewell .25 .60
189 Jud Buechler .15 .40
190 Jason Caffey .15 .40
191 Vlade Divac .25 .60
192 Travis Best .15 .40
193 Loy Vaught .15 .40
194 Mario Elie .15 .40
195 Ed Gray .15 .40
196 Joe Smith .20 .50
197 John Starks .20 .50
198 Anthony Johnson .15 .40
199 Kurt Thomas .15 .40
200 Chris Dudley .15 .40
201 Shareef Abdur-Rahim NF .25 .60
202 Ray Allen NF .30 .75
203 Vin Baker NF .20 .50
204 Charles Barkley NF .40 1.00
205 Kobe Bryant NF 1.00 2.50
206 Tim Duncan NF .50 1.25
207 Anfernee Hardaway NF .40 1.00
208 Grant Hill NF .40 1.00
209 Allen Iverson NF .50 1.25
210 Jason Kidd NF .40 1.00
211 Shawn Kemp NF .25 .60
212 Shaquille O'Neal NF .60 1.50
213 Kerry Kittles NF .15 .40
214 Karl Malone NF .30 .75
215 Stephon Marbury NF .30 .75
216 Ron Mercer NF .20 .50
217 Reggie Miller NF .30 .75
218 Kevin Garnett NF .40 1.00
219 Gary Payton NF .25 .60
220 Scottie Pippen NF .40 1.00
221 David Robinson NF .40 1.00
222 Hakeem Olajuwon NF .30 .75
223 Damon Stoudamire NF .20 .50
224 Keith Van Horn NF .25 .60
225 Antoine Walker NF .25 .60
226 Cory Carr RC .60 1.50
227 Cuttino Mobley RC 1.50 4.00
228 Miles Simon RC .75 2.00
229 J.R. Henderson RC .75 2.00
230 Jason Williams RC 2.00 5.00
231 Felipe Lopez RC .50 1.25
232 Shammond Williams RC .75 2.00
233 Ricky Davis RC 1.25 3.00
234 Vince Carter RC 4.00 10.00
235 Antawn Jamison RC 1.25 3.00
236 Ryan Stack RC .75 2.00
237 Nazr Mohammed RC .75 2.00
238 Sam Jacobson RC .60 1.50
239 Larry Hughes RC 1.50 4.00
240 Ruben Patterson RC .75 2.00
241 Al Harrington RC 1.25 3.00
242 Ansu Sesay RC .75 2.00
243 Vladimir Stepania RC .75 2.00
244 Matt Harpring RC .75 2.00
245 Andrae Patterson RC .60 1.50
246 Pat Garrity RC .60 1.50
247 Bonzi Wells RC .75 2.00
248 Bryce Drew RC .50 1.25
249 Toby Bailey RC .75 2.00
250 Michael Doleac RC .60 1.50
251 Michael Dickerson RC .75 2.00
252 Peja Stojakovic RC 2.00 5.00
253 Robert Traylor RC .75 2.00
254 Tyronn Lue RC .75 2.00
255 Dirk Nowitzki RC 5.00 12.00
256 Raef LaFrentz RC 1.00 2.50
257 Jelani McCoy RC .75 2.00
258 Michael Olowokandi RC 1.00 2.50
259 Brian Skinner RC .75 2.00
260 Keon Clark RC .75 2.00
261 Roshown McLeod RC .50 1.25
262 Mike Bibby RC 1.25 3.00
263 Paul Pierce RC 3.00 8.00
264 Tyson Wheeler RC .75 2.00
265 Corey Benjamin RC .50 1.25

1998-99 SkyBox Premium Star Rubies

*STARS: 50X TO 120X BASE CARD HI
*RCs: 8X TO 20X BASE HI
VETS: STATED PRINT RUN 50 SERIAL #'d SETS
RC's: STATED PRINT RUN 25 SERIAL #'d SETS
M.JORDAN #266 RUBY DOES NOT EXIST
1 Tim Duncan 80.00 200.00
14 Dennis Rodman 150.00 400.00
17 Anfernee Hardaway 300.00 600.00
20 Scottie Pippen 200.00 400.00
21 Shaquille O'Neal 300.00 500.00
23 Michael Jordan 4000.00 6000.00
27 Eddie Jones 75.00 150.00
31 Allen Iverson 80.00 200.00
40 Grant Hill 125.00 300.00
42 Tracy McGrady 80.00 200.00
44 Kobe Bryant 1500.00 2500.00
53 Kevin Garnett 125.00 250.00
63 Larry Johnson 75.00 200.00
67 Reggie Miller 50.00 120.00
71 Charles Barkley 300.00 500.00
84 Jason Kidd 150.00 300.00
87 Hakeem Olajuwon 125.00 250.00
90 Shawn Kemp 100.00 200.00
92 Ray Allen 50.00 120.00
98 Alonzo Mourning 125.00 250.00
188 Latrell Sprewell 50.00 120.00
202 Ray Allen NF 50.00 120.00
204 Charles Barkley NF 200.00 400.00
205 Kobe Bryant NF 750.00 1500.00
206 Tim Duncan NF 80.00 200.00
207 Anfernee Hardaway NF 100.00 200.00
208 Grant Hill NF 100.00 250.00
209 Allen Iverson NF 80.00 200.00
210 Jason Kidd NF 150.00 300.00
211 Shawn Kemp NF 100.00 200.00
212 Shaquille O'Neal NF 150.00 300.00

217 Reggie Miller NF 50.00 120.00
218 Kevin Garnett NF 125.00 250.00
220 Scottie Pippen NF 200.00 400.00
222 Hakeem Olajuwon NF 50.00 120.00
230 Jason Williams 50.00 120.00
234 Vince Carter 600.00 1000.00
252 Peja Stojakovic 50.00 120.00
255 Dirk Nowitzki 600.00 1000.00
262 Mike Bibby 50.00 120.00
263 Paul Pierce 300.00 600.00

1998-99 SkyBox Premium 3D's

Randomly inserted in series one packs at a rate of one in 96, this 15-card insert features color action photography on a special patterned holographic laminant.

COMPLETE SET (15) 400.00 800.00
SER.1 STATED ODDS 1:96
1 Kobe Bryant 75.00 200.00
2 Anfernee Hardaway 20.00 50.00
3 Allen Iverson 40.00 100.00
4 Michael Jordan 200.00 500.00
5 Stephon Marbury 12.00 30.00
6 Ron Mercer 4.00 10.00
7 Shareef Abdur-Rahim 5.00 12.00
8 Tim Duncan 30.00 80.00
9 Damon Stoudamire 10.00 25.00
10 Kevin Garnett 20.00 50.00
11 Grant Hill 20.00 50.00
12 Scottie Pippen 20.00 50.00
13 Keith Van Horn 5.00 12.00
14 Dennis Rodman 20.00 50.00
15 Shaquille O'Neal 20.00 50.00

1998-99 SkyBox Premium Autographics

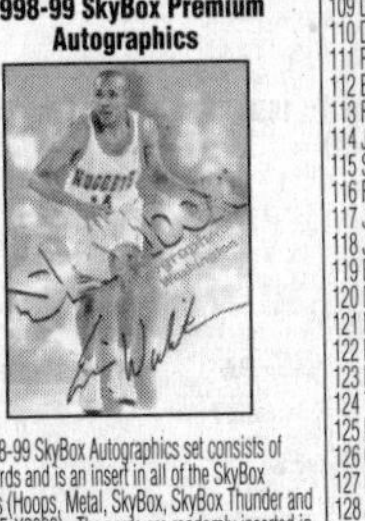

The 1998-99 SkyBox Autographics set consists of many cards and is an insert in all of the SkyBox products (Hoops, Metal, SkyBox, SkyBox Thunder and SkyBox E-X2002). The cards are randomly inserted in packs at a rate of 1:18 for E-X Century, 1:144 for Hoops, 1:68 for Metal, 1:24 for SkyBox Molten Metal, 1:68 for SkyBox Premium series one, 1:24 for SkyBox Premium series two and 1:112 for SkyBox Thunder 1. Allen Iverson signed equal amounts of both black and blue ink cards. The rookies Autographics were originally available via redemption, but were also inserted into packs "live" in later releases. The redemption date for those cards was June 1, 1999. The set is unnumbered and checklisted below in alphabetical order.

STATED ODDS 1:18 E-X; 1:144 HOOPS
STATED ODDS 1:68 METAL; 1:24 MOLTEN
STATED ODDS 1:68 SKYBOX 1; 1:24 SKYBOX 2
STATED ODDS 1:112 THUNDER
IVERSON SIGNED EQUAL BLACK/BLUE
1 Tariq Abdul-Wahad 5.00 12.00
2 Shareef Abdur-Rahim 8.00 20.00
3 Cory Alexander 4.00 10.00
4 Ray Allen 20.00 50.00
5 Kenny Anderson 6.00 15.00
6 Nick Anderson 5.00 12.00
7 Chris Anstey 4.00 10.00
8 Isaac Austin 4.00 10.00
9 Vin Baker 10.00 25.00
10 Dana Barros 4.00 10.00
11 Tony Battie 4.00 10.00
12 Corey Benjamin 4.00 10.00
13 Travis Best 4.00 10.00
14 Mike Bibby 5.00 12.00
15 Chauncey Billups 10.00 25.00
16 Corie Blount 4.00 10.00
17 Terrell Brandon 6.00 15.00
18 P.J. Brown 4.00 10.00
19 Scott Burrell 5.00 12.00
20 Jason Caffey 4.00 10.00
21 Marcus Camby 4.00 10.00
22 Elden Campbell 8.00 20.00
23 Chris Carr 4.00 10.00
24 Cory Carr 4.00 10.00
25 Vince Carter 50.00 120.00
26 Kelvin Cato 4.00 10.00
27 Calbert Cheaney 4.00 10.00
28 Keith Closs 4.00 10.00
29 Antonio Daniels 4.00 10.00
30 Dale Davis 8.00 20.00
31 Ricky Davis 10.00 25.00
32 Andrew DeClercq 4.00 10.00
33 Tony Delk 5.00 12.00
34 Michael Dickerson 6.00 15.00
35 Michael Doleac 5.00 12.00
36 Bryce Drew 4.00 10.00
37 Tim Duncan 500.00 800.00
38 Howard Eisley 4.00 10.00
39 Danny Ferry 5.00 12.00
40 Derek Fisher 6.00 15.00
41 Danny Fortson 4.00 10.00
42 Adonal Foyle 4.00 10.00
43 Todd Fuller 4.00 10.00
44 Kevin Garnett 150.00 300.00
45 Pat Garrity 5.00 12.00
46 Brian Grant 5.00 12.00
47 Tom Gugliotta 6.00 15.00
48 Tom Hammonds 4.00 10.00
49 Tim Hardaway 12.50 30.00
50 Matt Harpring 6.00 15.00
51 Othella Harrington 4.00 10.00
52 Hersey Hawkins 8.00 20.00
53 Cedric Henderson 4.00 10.00
54 Grant Hill 250.00 500.00
55 Tyrone Hill 4.00 10.00
56 Allan Houston 20.00 50.00
57 Juwan Howard 10.00 25.00
58 Larry Hughes 10.00 25.00
59 Zydrunas Ilgauskas 15.00 30.00
60 Allen Iverson 175.00 350.00
61 Bobby Jackson 4.00 10.00
62 Antawn Jamison 8.00 20.00
63 Anthony Johnson 4.00 10.00
64 Ervin Johnson 4.00 10.00
65 Larry Johnson 12.00 30.00
66 Eddie Jones 20.00 50.00
67 Adam Keefe 4.00 10.00
68 Shawn Kemp 50.00 120.00
69 Steve Kerr 8.00 20.00
70 Jason Kidd 50.00 120.00
71 Kerry Kittles 6.00 15.00
72 Brevin Knight 5.00 12.00
73 Raef LaFrentz 6.00 15.00
74 Felipe Lopez 4.00 10.00
75 George Lynch 4.00 10.00
76 Karl Malone 250.00 450.00
77 Danny Manning 10.00 25.00
78 Stephon Marbury 20.00 50.00
79 Donyell Marshall 5.00 12.00
80 Tony Massenburg 4.00 10.00
81 Walter McCarty 4.00 10.00
82 Jelani McCoy 4.00 10.00
83 Antonio McDyess 8.00 20.00
84 Tracy McGrady 15.00 40.00
85 Ron Mercer 6.00 15.00
86 Sam Mitchell 4.00 10.00
87 Nazr Mohammed 5.00 12.00
88 Alonzo Mourning 25.00 60.00
89 Chris Mullin 10.00 25.00
90 Dikembe Mutombo 12.00 30.00
91 Hakeem Olajuwon 50.00 120.00
92 Michael Olowokandi 6.00 15.00
93 Elliot Perry 4.00 10.00
94 Bobby Phills 4.00 10.00
95 Eric Piatkowski 4.00 10.00
96 Scottie Pippen 150.00 300.00
97 Scot Pollard 5.00 12.00
98 Vitaly Potapenko 4.00 10.00
99 Brent Price 4.00 10.00
100 Theo Ratliff 5.00 12.00
101 Eldridge Recasner 4.00 10.00
102 Bryant Reeves 5.00 12.00
103 Glen Rice 8.00 20.00
104 Chris Robinson 4.00 10.00
105 David Robinson 100.00 175.00
106 Glenn Robinson 5.00 12.00
107 Dennis Rodman 250.00 500.00
108 Bryon Russell 5.00 12.00
109 Danny Schayes 4.00 10.00
110 Detlef Schrempf 10.00 25.00
111 Rony Seikaly 5.00 12.00
112 Brian Skinner 4.00 10.00
113 Reggie Slater 4.00 10.00
114 Joe Smith 6.00 15.00
115 Steve Smith 8.00 20.00
116 Rik Smits 6.00 15.00
117 Jerry Stackhouse 12.00 30.00
118 John Starks 5.00 12.00
119 Bryant Stith 4.00 10.00
120 Damon Stoudamire 8.00 20.00
121 Mark Strickland 4.00 10.00
122 Rod Strickland 6.00 15.00
123 Bob Sura 4.00 10.00
124 Tim Thomas 5.00 12.00
125 Robert Traylor 5.00 12.00
126 Gary Trent 4.00 10.00
127 Keith Van Horn 6.00 15.00
128 Jacque Vaughn 4.00 10.00
129 Antoine Walker 6.00 15.00
130 Eric Washington 4.00 10.00
131 Clarence Weatherspoon 4.00 10.00
132 Bonzi Wells 8.00 20.00
133 David Wesley 4.00 10.00
134 Eric Williams 4.00 10.00
135 Jason Williams 30.00 80.00
136 Jayson Williams 4.00 10.00
137 Monty Williams 4.00 10.00
138 Walt Williams 4.00 10.00
139 Lorenzen Wright 4.00 10.00

1998-99 SkyBox Premium Autographics Blue

*BLUE: .75X TO 2X VALUE
STATED PRINT RUN 50 SERIAL #'d SETS
25 Vince Carter 250.00 500.00
37 Tim Duncan 1000.00 1500.00
44 Kevin Garnett 300.00 600.00
56 Allan Houston 40.00 100.00
60 Allen Iverson 200.00 500.00
65 Larry Johnson 60.00 150.00
70 Jason Kidd 150.00 400.00
76 Karl Malone 400.00 800.00
84 Tracy McGrady 125.00 300.00
91 Hakeem Olajuwon 150.00 300.00
96 Scottie Pippen 500.00 1000.00
107 Dennis Rodman 1000.00 2000.00

1998-99 SkyBox Premium B.P.O.

Randomly inserted in series two packs at one in six, this 15-card set features the game's brightest young stars. Card fronts feature gold-foil stamping against a black background.

COMPLETE SET (15) 5.00 12.00
SER.2 STATED ODDS 1:6 HOB/RET
1 Ron Mercer .30 .75
2 Shareef Abdur-Rahim .40 1.00
3 Stephon Marbury .50 1.25
4 Tim Thomas .40 1.00
5 Tim Duncan .75 2.00
6 Mike Bibby .60 1.50
7 Ray Allen .50 1.25
8 Shawn Kemp .40 1.00
9 Vince Carter 2.00 5.00
10 Antoine Walker .40 1.00
11 Raef LaFrentz .50 1.25
12 Damon Stoudamire .30 .75
13 Keith Van Horn .40 1.00
14 Kerry Kittles .25 .60
15 Allen Iverson .75 2.00

1998-99 SkyBox Premium Fresh Faces

Randomly inserted in series two packs at a rate of one in 36, this 10-card set focuses on the rookie class from the 1998-99 season.

COMPLETE SET (10) 10.00 25.00
SER.2 STATED ODDS 1:36 HOB/RET
1 Mike Bibby 1.00 2.50
2 Vince Carter 3.00 8.00
3 Al Harrington 1.00 2.50
4 Larry Hughes 1.25 3.00
5 Antawn Jamison 1.00 2.50
6 Raef LaFrentz .75 2.00
7 Michael Olowokandi .75 2.00
8 Paul Pierce 2.50 6.00
9 Robert Traylor .60 1.50
10 Bonzi Wells .60 1.50

1998-99 SkyBox Premium Intimidation Nation

Randomly inserted in series one packs at a rate of one in 360, this 10-card insert set offers gold rainbow holo-foil stamping and features close-up color player photos.

COMPLETE SET (10) 600.00 1000.00
SER.1 STATED ODDS 1:360
1 Shaquille O'Neal 30.00 80.00
2 Kobe Bryant 125.00 250.00
3 Kevin Garnett 30.00 80.00
4 Grant Hill 20.00 50.00
5 Shawn Kemp 15.00 40.00
6 Keith Van Horn 12.00 30.00
7 Antoine Walker 12.00 30.00
8 Michael Jordan 400.00 800.00
9 Gary Payton 12.00 30.00
10 Tim Duncan 30.00 80.00

1998-99 SkyBox Premium Just Cookin'

Randomly inserted in series one packs at a rate of one in 12, this 10-card set features some of the game's top rookies from 1998 on silver holographic foil.

COMPLETE SET (10) 2.50 6.00
SER.1 STATED ODDS 1:12
1 Maurice Taylor .40 1.00
2 Brevin Knight .40 1.00
3 Tim Thomas .60 1.50
4 Chauncey Billups .75 2.00
5 Chris Anstey .40 1.00
6 Tracy McGrady 1.00 2.50
7 Zydrunas Ilgauskas .60 1.50
8 Antonio Daniels .40 1.00
9 Bobby Jackson .40 1.00
10 Derek Anderson .40 1.00

1998-99 SkyBox Premium Mod Squad

Randomly inserted in series two packs at one in 18, this 16-card set features player's in off the court settings. The cards feature a silver and black foil background.

COMPLETE SET (16) 15.00 40.00
SER.2 STATED ODDS 1:18 HOB/RET
1 Tim Thomas .75 2.00
2 Shaquille O'Neal 2.00 5.00
3 Scottie Pippen 1.25 3.00
4 Kobe Bryant 3.00 8.00
5 Kevin Garnett 1.25 3.00
6 Grant Hill 1.25 3.00
7 Anfernee Hardaway 1.25 3.00
8 Antoine Walker .75 2.00
9 Stephon Marbury 1.00 2.50
10 Kerry Kittles .50 1.25
11 Allen Iverson 1.50 4.00
12 Gary Payton .75 2.00
13 Damon Stoudamire .60 1.50
14 Marcus Camby .60 1.50
15 Shareef Abdur-Rahim .75 2.00
16 Michael Jordan 6.00 15.00

1998-99 SkyBox Premium Net Set

Randomly inserted into series one packs at one in 36, this 15-card set features some of the biggest names in the game on etched silver rainbow foilboard.

COMPLETE SET (15) 25.00 50.00
SER.1 STATED ODDS 1:36
1 Ron Mercer 1.50 4.00
2 Shawn Kemp 2.00 5.00
3 Brevin Knight 1.25 3.00
4 Maurice Taylor 1.25 3.00
5 Ray Allen 2.50 6.00
6 Dennis Rodman 4.00 10.00
7 Kerry Kittles 1.25 3.00
8 Tim Thomas 2.00 5.00
9 Gary Payton 2.00 5.00
10 Marcus Camby 1.50 4.00
11 Karl Malone 2.50 6.00
12 Juwan Howard 1.50 4.00
13 Zydrunas Ilgauskas 2.00 5.00
14 Scottie Pippen 3.00 8.00
15 Anfernee Hardaway 3.00 8.00

1998-99 SkyBox Premium Slam Funk

Randomly inserted in series two packs at one in 360, this 10-card set highlights players who play above the rim. These plastic cards feature rainbow holo-lamination.

COMPLETE SET (10) 100.00 200.00
SER.2 STATED ODDS 1:360 HOB/RET
1 Kobe Bryant 75.00 200.00
2 Kevin Garnett 25.00 60.00
3 Grant Hill 15.00 40.00
4 Shaquille O'Neal 25.00 60.00
5 Michael Olowokandi 4.00 10.00
6 Tim Duncan 25.00 60.00
7 Antawn Jamison 5.00 12.00
8 Keith Van Horn 8.00 20.00
9 Ron Mercer 6.00 15.00
10 Scottie Pippen 12.00 30.00

1998-99 SkyBox Premium Smooth

Randomly inserted in series one packs at a rate of one 6, this 15-card insert set features color action photos surrounded by a solid black background with silver rainbow holofoil stamping.

COMPLETE SET (15) 3.00 8.00
SER.1 STATED ODDS 1:6
1 Stephon Marbury .50 1.25
2 Shareef Abdur-Rahim .40 1.00
3 Keith Van Horn .40 1.00
4 Marcus Camby .30 .75
5 Ray Allen .50 1.25
6 Allen Iverson .75 2.00
7 Kerry Kittles .25 .60
8 Tim Thomas .40 1.00
9 Damon Stoudamire .30 .75
10 Antoine Walker .40 1.00
11 Brevin Knight .25 .60
12 Zydrunas Ilgauskas .40 1.00
13 Ron Mercer .30 .75
14 Maurice Taylor .25 .60
15 Tim Duncan .75 2.00

1998-99 SkyBox Premium Soul of the Game

Randomly inserted in series one packs at a rate of one in 18, this 15-card insert set offers a color action photo on a rainbow foil background that appears to change colors.

COMPLETE SET (15) 150.00 400.00
SER.1 STATED ODDS 1:18
1 Michael Jordan 75.00 200.00
2 Antoine Walker 1.25 3.00
3 Scottie Pippen 10.00 25.00
4 Grant Hill 2.00 5.00
5 Dennis Rodman 15.00 40.00
6 Kobe Bryant 15.00 40.00
7 Kevin Garnett 10.00 25.00
8 Shaquille O'Neal 10.00 25.00
9 Stephon Marbury 1.50 4.00
10 Kerry Kittles .75 2.00
11 Anfernee Hardaway 8.00 20.00
12 Allen Iverson 10.00 25.00
13 Damon Stoudamire 1.00 2.50
14 Marcus Camby 1.00 2.50
15 Shareef Abdur-Rahim 1.25 3.00

1998-99 SkyBox Premium That's Jam

Randomly inserted in series two packs at one in 96, this 15-card set features offensive superstars on a clear plastic background.

COMPLETE SET (15) 100.00 250.00
SER.2 STATED ODDS 1:96 HOB/RET
1 Tim Duncan 6.00 15.00
2 Stephon Marbury 4.00 10.00
3 Shareef Abdur-Rahim 3.00 8.00
4 Shaquille O'Neal 15.00 40.00
5 Ron Mercer 2.50 6.00
6 Scottie Pippen 6.00 15.00
7 Antawn Jamison 2.50 6.00
8 Anfernee Hardaway 10.00 25.00
9 Damon Stoudamire 2.50 6.00
10 Allen Iverson 15.00 40.00
11 Keith Van Horn 3.00 8.00
12 Grant Hill 5.00 12.00
13 Kevin Garnett 8.00 20.00
14 Kobe Bryant 30.00 80.00
15 Antoine Walker 3.00 8.00

1999-00 SkyBox Premium

Released in one series, this 150-card set was released in eight-card packs that carried a suggested retail price of $2.69. There were two versions of the 25-card rookie subset: the regular rookie cards, which were portrait cards and not inserted and special action shots, which were inserted at one in eight.

COMPLETE SET (150) 40.00 100.00
COMPLETE SET w/o SP (125) 12.50 30.00
101-125 SP's STATED ODDS 1:8
1 Vince Carter .60 1.50
2 Nick Anderson .20 .50
3 Isaiah Rider .25 .60
4 Mitch Richmond .30 .75
5 Danny Fortson .20 .50
6 Kenny Anderson .25 .60
7 Reggie Miller .30 .75
8 Tracy McGrady .50 1.25
9 Steve Nash .50 1.25
10 Robert Traylor .20 .50
11 Tom Gugliotta .20 .50
12 Steve Smith .25 .60
13 Jalen Rose .25 .60
14 Kerry Kittles .20 .50
15 Nick Van Exel .25 .60
16 Raef LaFrentz .25 .60
17 Damon Stoudamire .25 .60
18 Gary Trent .20 .50
19 Jayson Williams .20 .50
20 Brian Grant .20 .50
21 Rod Strickland .20 .50
22 Larry Hughes .25 .60
23 Derek Anderson .20 .50
24 Hakeem Olajuwon .40 1.00
25 Ray Allen .30 .75
26 Gary Payton .30 .75
27 Michael Finley .30 .75
28 Keith Van Horn .25 .60
29 Clifford Robinson .20 .50
30 Shawn Kemp .30 .75
31 Glenn Robinson .25 .60
32 Theo Ratliff .25 .60
33 Lindsey Hunter .20 .50
34 Chris Webber .30 .75
35 Grant Hill .40 1.00
36 Vlade Divac .30 .75
37 Paul Pierce .40 1.00
38 Tyrone Nesby RC .25 .60
39 Larry Johnson .30 .75
40 Bryon Russell .20 .50
41 Antoine Walker .30 .75
42 Michael Olowokandi .20 .50
43 John Stockton .40 1.00
44 Elden Campbell .20 .50
45 Christian Laettner .25 .60
46 Maurice Taylor .20 .50
47 Shareef Abdur-Rahim .25 .60
48 Ricky Davis .30 .75
49 Jerry Stackhouse .30 .75
50 Kobe Bryant 1.25 3.00
51 Jason Williams .40 1.00
52 Mike Bibby .30 .75
53 Eddie Jones .30 .75
54 Antawn Jamison .30 .75
55 Shaquille O'Neal .75 2.00
56 Tim Duncan .60 1.50
57 Cherokee Parks .20 .50
58 Antonio McDyess .25 .60
59 Rasheed Wallace .30 .75
60 Anthony Mason .20 .50
61 Chris Mills .20 .50
62 Glen Rice .30 .75
63 Latrell Sprewell .30 .75
64 Darrell Armstrong .20 .50
65 Sean Elliott .30 .75
66 Juwan Howard .25 .60
67 Brent Barry .25 .60
68 John Starks .25 .60
69 Tim Hardaway .30 .75
70 Marcus Camby .25 .60
71 Anfernee Hardaway .50 1.25
72 Avery Johnson .25 .60
73 Tariq Abdul-Wahad .20 .50
74 Charles Barkley .50 1.25
75 Stephon Marbury .25 .60
76 Jamal Mashburn .25 .60
77 Matt Harpring .20 .50
78 David Robinson .50 1.25
79 Cedric Ceballos .20 .50
80 Terrell Brandon .20 .50
81 Jason Kidd .50 1.25
82 Toni Kukoc .30 .75
83 Michael Dickerson .20 .50
84 Alonzo Mourning .40 1.00
85 Kevin Garnett .50 1.25
86 Matt Geiger .20 .50
87 Vin Baker .25 .60
88 Dikembe Mutombo .30 .75
89 Hersey Hawkins .20 .50
90 Joe Smith .25 .60
91 Charles Oakley .25 .60
92 Ron Mercer .25 .60
93 Rik Smits .30 .75
94 Patrick Ewing .40 1.00
95 Karl Malone .40 1.00
96 Scottie Pippen .50 1.25
97 Zydrunas Ilgauskas .25 .60
98 Sam Cassell .25 .60
99 Detlef Schrempf .25 .60
100 Allen Iverson .60 1.50
101 Elton Brand RC .75 2.00
101A Elton Brand SP 2.00 5.00
102 Steve Francis RC .75 2.00
102A Steve Francis SP 2.00 5.00
103 Baron Davis RC .75 2.00
103A Baron Davis SP 2.00 5.00
104 Lamar Odom RC .75 2.00
104A Lamar Odom SP 2.00 5.00
105 Jonathan Bender RC .30 .75
105A Jonathan Bender SP .75 2.00
106 Wally Szczerbiak RC .60 1.50
106A Wally Szczerbiak SP 1.50 4.00
107 Richard Hamilton RC .60 1.50
107A Richard Hamilton SP 1.50 4.00
108 Andre Miller RC .60 1.50
108A Andre Miller SP 1.50 4.00
109 Shawn Marion RC .60 1.50
109A Shawn Marion SP 1.50 4.00
110 Jason Terry RC .50 1.25
110A Jason Terry SP 1.25 3.00
111 Trajan Langdon RC .30 .75
111A Trajan Langdon SP .75 2.00
112 A.Radojevic RC .20 .50
112A A.Radojevic SP .50 1.25
113 Corey Maggette RC .50 1.25
113A Corey Maggette SP 1.25 3.00
114 William Avery RC .25 .60
114A William Avery SP .60 1.50
115 Vonteego Cummings RC .20 .50
115A Vonteego Cummings SP .50 1.25
116 Ron Artest RC .60 1.50
116A Ron Artest SP 1.50 4.00
117 Cal Bowdler RC .20 .50
117A Cal Bowdler SP .50 1.25
118 James Posey RC .30 .75
118A James Posey SP .75 2.00
119 Quincy Lewis RC .20 .50
119A Quincy Lewis SP .50 1.25
120 Dion Glover RC .25 .60
120A Dion Glover SP .60 1.50
121 Jeff Foster RC .30 .75
121A Jeff Foster SP .75 2.00
122 Kenny Thomas RC .30 .75
122A Kenny Thomas SP .75 2.00
123 Devean George RC .30 .75
123A Devean George SP .75 2.00
124 Scott Padgett RC .25 .60
124A Scott Padgett SP .60 1.50
125 Tim James RC .20 .50
125A Tim James SP .50 1.25

1999-00 SkyBox Premium Star Rubies

*STARS: 30X TO 80X HI COLUMN
*RCs: 12X TO 30X HI
*SPs: 8X TO 20X HI
STARS/RC's: PRINT RUN 45 SERIAL #'d SETS
SPs: PRINT RUN 25 SERIAL #'d SETS
24 Hakeem Olajuwon 40.00 100.00
30 Shawn Kemp 125.00 300.00
35 Grant Hill 75.00 200.00
50 Kobe Bryant 250.00 500.00
55 Shaquille O'Neal 150.00 300.00
56 Tim Duncan 200.00 500.00
71 Anfernee Hardaway 50.00 125.00
78 David Robinson 50.00 125.00
84 Alonzo Mourning 150.00 300.00
85 Kevin Garnett 175.00 350.00
96 Scottie Pippen 100.00 200.00

1999-00 SkyBox Premium Autographics

Randomly inserted in all of the SkyBox products, this 113-card set features autographs of the top NBA stars and rookies. The cards are not numbered and listed below in alphabetical order. The cards were inserted in all products at one in 68, except Hoops Decade, which was inserted at one in 144, Metal, which was inserted at one in 96 and SkyBox Impact, which was inserted at one in 288.

STATED ODDS 1:68/1:144 HOO DECADE
STATED ODDS 1:96 METAL
STATED ODDS 1:288 IMPACT
1 Cory Alexander 2.00 5.00
2 Ray Allen 60.00 150.00
3 Darrell Armstrong 3.00 8.00
4 Ron Artest 3.00 8.00
5 William Avery 2.50 6.00
6 Charles Barkley 800.00 1200.00
7 Dana Barros 2.00 5.00
8 Corey Benjamin 2.00 5.00
9 Travis Best 3.00 8.00
10 Mike Bibby 10.00 25.00
11 Calvin Booth 3.00 8.00
12 Cal Bowdler 2.00 5.00
13 Bruce Bowen 6.00 15.00
14 P.J. Brown 3.00 8.00
15 Jud Buechler 3.00 8.00
16 Marcus Camby 8.00 20.00
17 Elden Campbell 4.00 10.00
18 Cory Carr 2.00 5.00
19 Vince Carter 25.00 60.00
20 John Celestand 2.00 5.00
21 Dell Curry 3.00 8.00
22 Baron Davis 6.00 15.00
23 Andrew DeClercq 2.00 5.00
24 Tony Delk 4.00 10.00
25 Michael Dickerson 3.00 8.00
26 Michael Doleac 2.00 5.00
27 Bryce Drew 2.00 5.00
28 Obinna Ekezie 2.50 6.00
29 Evan Eschmeyer 4.00 10.00
30 Michael Finley 10.00 25.00
31 Greg Foster 2.00 5.00
32 Jeff Foster 3.00 8.00
33 Steve Francis 10.00 25.00
34 Todd Fuller 2.00 5.00
35 Lawrence Funderburke 3.00 8.00
36 Dean Garrett 3.00 8.00
37 Pat Garrity 3.00 8.00
38 Devean George 4.00 10.00
39 Kendall Gill 5.00 12.00
40 Dion Glover 2.50 6.00
41 Brian Grant 3.00 8.00
42 Paul Grant 2.00 5.00
43 Tom Gugliotta 8.00 20.00
44 Richard Hamilton 6.00 15.00
45 Tim Hardaway 10.00 25.00
46 Matt Harpring 2.00 5.00
47 Al Harrington 3.00 8.00
48 Othella Harrington 2.00 5.00
49 Troy Hudson 3.00 8.00
50 Larry Hughes 8.00 20.00
51 Tim James 2.00 5.00
52 Antawn Jamison 6.00 15.00
53 Anthony Johnson 3.00 8.00
54 Avery Johnson 6.00 15.00
55 Ervin Johnson 2.00 5.00
56 Eddie Jones 6.00 15.00
57 Jumaine Jones 2.50 6.00
58 Adam Keefe 2.00 5.00
59 Shawn Kemp 50.00 120.00
60 Kerry Kittles 6.00 15.00
61 Raef LaFrentz 5.00 12.00
62 Trajan Langdon 5.00 12.00
63 Quincy Lewis 2.00 5.00
64 Felipe Lopez 3.00 8.00
65 Tyronn Lue 3.00 8.00
66 George Lynch 3.00 8.00
67 Sam Mack 2.00 5.00
68 Stephon Marbury 12.00 30.00
69 Shawn Marion 8.00 20.00
70 Tony Massenburg 2.00 5.00
71 Jelani McCoy 2.00 5.00
72 Antonio McDyess 8.00 20.00
73 Tracy McGrady 20.00 50.00
74 Roshown McLeod 2.00 5.00
75 Brad Miller 5.00 12.00
76 Sam Mitchell 3.00 8.00
77 Nazr Mohammed 6.00 15.00
78 Alonzo Mourning 50.00 120.00
79 Tyrone Nesby 2.50 6.00
80 Shaquille O'Neal 125.00 250.00
81 Lamar Odom 12.00 30.00
82 Hakeem Olajuwon 30.00 80.00
83 Michael Olowokandi 2.00 5.00
84 Andrae Patterson 2.00 5.00
85 Eric Piatkowski 2.50 6.00
86 Scottie Pippen 75.00 150.00
87 Scot Pollard 2.00 5.00
88 James Posey 6.00 15.00
89 Brent Price 2.00 5.00
90 Aleksandar Radojevic 3.00 8.00
91 Theo Ratliff 3.00 8.00
92 J.R. Reid 2.00 5.00
93 David Robinson 75.00 200.00
94 Glenn Robinson 3.00 8.00
95 Jalen Rose 8.00 20.00
96 Michael Ruffin 2.50 6.00
97 Wally Szczerbiak 6.00 15.00
98 Joe Smith 8.00 20.00
99 Jerry Stackhouse 8.00 20.00
100 John Starks 8.00 20.00
101 Vladimir Stepania 3.00 8.00
102 Damon Stoudamire 6.00 15.00
103 Maurice Taylor 3.00 8.00
104 Jason Terry 8.00 20.00
105 Kenny Thomas 3.00 8.00
106 Robert Traylor 3.00 8.00
107 Gary Trent 2.00 5.00
108 Antoine Walker 10.00 25.00
109 Chris Webber 500.00 800.00
110 David Wesley 3.00 8.00
111 Aaron Williams 2.00 5.00
112 Jerome Williams 2.00 5.00
113 Haywoode Workman 3.00 8.00
115 Scott Padgett 2.50 6.00

1999-00 SkyBox Premium Autographics Blue

*BLUE: .75X TO 2X VALUE
STATED PRINT RUN 50 SERIAL #'d SETS
3 Darrell Armstrong 10.00 25.00
6 Charles Barkley 1800.00 2200.00
17 Elden Campbell 10.00 25.00
19 Vince Carter 200.00 400.00
22 Baron Davis 40.00 100.00
73 Tracy McGrady 60.00 120.00
78 Alonzo Mourning 80.00 200.00
81 Lamar Odom 50.00 120.00
97 Wally Szczerbiak 20.00 50.00

1999-00 SkyBox Premium Back for More

Randomly inserted in packs at one in six, this 15-card set focuses on the sensational sophomores for the 1999-00 class.

COMPLETE SET (15) 5.00 12.00
STATED ODDS 1:6 HOB/RET
1 Mike Bibby .75 2.00
2 Tyrone Nesby .60 1.50
3 Ricky Davis .75 2.00
4 Michael Dickerson .50 1.25
5 Michael Doleac .50 1.25
6 Antawn Jamison .75 2.00
7 Larry Hughes .60 1.50
8 Matt Harpring .50 1.25
9 Peja Stojakovic .75 2.00
10 Raef LaFrentz .60 1.50
11 Michael Olowokandi .50 1.25
12 Robert Traylor .50 1.25
13 Paul Pierce 1.00 2.50
14 Kornel David .60 1.50
15 Jason Williams 1.00 2.50

1999-00 SkyBox Premium Club Vertical

Randomly inserted in packs, this 10-card set focuses on aerial artists on die cut and embossed red-foil cards. The cards are serially numbered to 100.

STATED PRINT RUN 100 SERIAL #'d SETS
1 Vince Carter 40.00 100.00
2 Tim Duncan 75.00 200.00
3 Shaquille O'Neal 125.00 300.00
4 Paul Pierce 25.00 60.00
5 Kobe Bryant 400.00 800.00
6 Kevin Garnett 60.00 150.00
7 Keith Van Horn 15.00 40.00
8 Jason Williams 25.00 60.00
9 Grant Hill 60.00 150.00
10 Allen Iverson 60.00 150.00

1999-00 SkyBox Premium Genuine Coverage

Randomly inserted in packs, this six-card set features swatches of game-used jerseys from top NBA stars. The cards are serially numbered and each is listed after the player's name.

STATED PRINT RUN 275 TO 450 SETS
1 Kobe Bryant/340 25.00 60.00
2 Vince Carter/355 12.00 30.00
3 Patrick Ewing/450 10.00 25.00
4 Grant Hill/370 25.00 60.00
5 Allen Iverson/275 12.00 30.00
6 Alonzo Mourning/360 15.00 40.00

1999-00 SkyBox Premium Good Stuff

Randomly inserted in packs at one in 36, this 10-card set features superstar veterans on fuscia-foil stamped silver foil.

COMPLETE SET (10) 10.00 25.00
STATED ODDS 1:36 HOB/RET
*PARALLEL: 8X TO 20X HI COLUMN
PARALLEL: PRINT RUN 99 SERIAL #'d SETS
1 Kobe Bryant 6.00 15.00
2 Vince Carter 2.00 5.00
3 Jason Williams 1.25 3.00
4 Paul Pierce 1.25 3.00
5 Tim Duncan 2.00 5.00
6 Kevin Garnett 1.50 4.00
7 Grant Hill 1.25 3.00
8 Keith Van Horn .75 2.00
9 Allen Iverson 2.00 5.00
10 Shaquille O'Neal 2.50 6.00

1999-00 SkyBox Premium Majestic

Randomly inserted in packs at one in 12, this 15-card set features some of the games most stylish stars. The cards feature matte-varnished finish.

COMPLETE SET (15) 6.00 15.00
STATED ODDS 1:12 HOB/RET
1 Antawn Jamison .60 1.50
2 Jason Kidd 1.00 2.50
3 Ron Mercer .50 1.25
4 Shawn Kemp .60 1.50
5 Stephon Marbury .50 1.25
6 Shaquille O'Neal 1.50 4.00
7 Larry Hughes .50 1.25
8 Kevin Garnett 1.00 2.50
9 Antoine Walker .60 1.50
10 Keith Van Horn .50 1.25
11 Anfernee Hardaway 1.00 2.50
12 Tim Duncan 1.25 3.00
13 Scottie Pippen 1.00 2.50
14 Shareef Abdur-Rahim .50 1.25
15 Chris Webber .60 1.50

1999-00 SkyBox Premium Prime Time Rookies

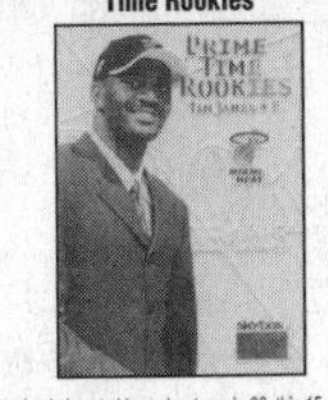

Randomly inserted in packs at one in 96, this 15-card set features some of the leagues top rookies on plastic cards with silver and clear patterned holo-foil stamping. Card backs carry a "PT" prefix.

COMPLETE SET (15) 25.00 60.00
STATED ODDS 1:96 HOB/RET
PT1 Elton Brand 4.00 10.00
PT2 Steve Francis 4.00 10.00
PT3 Baron Davis 4.00 10.00
PT4 Lamar Odom 4.00 10.00
PT5 Jonathan Bender 1.50 4.00
PT6 Wally Szczerbiak 3.00 8.00
PT7 Richard Hamilton 3.00 8.00
PT8 Andre Miller 3.00 8.00
PT9 Shawn Marion 3.00 8.00
PT10 Jason Terry 2.50 6.00
PT11 Trajan Langdon 1.50 4.00
PT12 Dion Glover 1.25 3.00
PT13 Corey Maggette 2.50 6.00
PT14 William Avery 1.25 3.00
PT15 Tim James 1.00 2.50

1999-00 SkyBox Premium Prime Time Rookies Autographs

STATED PRINT RUN 25 SERIAL #'d SETS
PT1 Elton Brand 40.00 100.00
PT2 Steve Francis 40.00 100.00
PT3 Baron Davis 40.00 100.00
PT4 Lamar Odom 40.00 100.00
PT5 Jonathan Bender 15.00 40.00
PT6 Wally Szczerbiak 30.00 80.00
PT7 Richard Hamilton 30.00 80.00
PT8 Andre Miller 30.00 80.00
PT9 Shawn Marion 30.00 80.00
PT10 Jason Terry 20.00 50.00
PT11 Trajan Langdon 15.00 40.00
PT12 Dion Glover 12.00 30.00
PT13 Corey Maggette 25.00 60.00
PT14 William Avery 12.00 30.00
PT15 Tim James 10.00 25.00

2004-05 SkyBox Premium

Released in May 2005, Skybox Premium consists of a 100-card set divided up into 75 veteran players and 25 rookies serially numbered to 999. Base cards have mostly white in the background with a centered black and white photo offset by a full-color player action photo. Skybox Premium was offered in both Hobby and Retail formats where both were released in five card packs but Hobby boxes contained 12 packs and Retail contained 24.

COMP.SET w/o SP's (75) 15.00 40.00
76-100 RC PRINT RUN 999 SER.#'d SETS
1 Dwyane Wade .60 1.50
2 Rashard Lewis .40 1.00
3 Jermaine O'Neal .30 .75
4 Ben Wallace .30 .75
5 Steve Francis .30 .75
6 Lamar Odom .30 .75
7 Jason Richardson .40 1.00
8 Jarvis Hayes .25 .60
9 Carmelo Anthony .75 2.00
10 Tony Parker .40 1.00
11 Eddy Curry .25 .60
12 Nene .30 .75
13 Kevin Garnett .60 1.50
14 Darius Miles .25 .60
15 Elton Brand .40 1.00
16 Zach Randolph .30 .75
17 Mike Dunleavy .30 .75
18 Dajuan Wagner .25 .60
19 Steve Nash .50 1.25
20 Ron Artest .40 1.00
21 Ricky Davis .30 .75
22 Antawn Jamison .30 .75
23 Jamal Mashburn .30 .75
24 T.J. Ford .25 .60
25 Amare Stoudemire .30 .75
26 Jason Kapono .25 .60
27 Shawn Marion .30 .75
28 Corliss Williamson .25 .60
29 Reggie Miller .40 1.00
30 Desmond Mason .30 .75
31 Pau Gasol .40 1.00
32 Baron Davis .30 .75
33 Allen Iverson .60 1.50
34 Darko Milicic .25 .60
35 Ray Allen .40 1.00
36 Jason Williams .30 .75
37 Michael Redd .30 .75
38 Yao Ming .75 2.00
39 Antoine Walker .40 1.00
40 Jason Terry .30 .75
41 Sam Cassell .30 .75
42 Richard Jefferson .30 .75
43 Manu Ginobili .50 1.25
44 Dirk Nowitzki .60 1.50
45 Peja Stojakovic .40 1.00
46 Samuel Dalembert .25 .60
47 Latrell Sprewell .30 .75
48 Gerald Wallace .30 .75
49 Andrei Kirilenko .30 .75
50 Nick Van Exel .30 .75
51 Jalen Rose .30 .75
52 Shaquille O'Neal 1.00 2.50
53 Shareef Abdur-Rahim .30 .75
54 Tracy McGrady .50 1.25
55 Rasheed Wallace .40 1.00
56 Cuttino Mobley .25 .60
57 Jason Kidd .60 1.50
58 Chris Webber .40 1.00
59 Paul Pierce .40 1.00
60 Mike Bibby .40 1.00
61 Allan Houston .30 .75
62 Kobe Bryant 1.50 4.00
63 Kenyon Martin .30 .75
64 LeBron James 2.50 6.00
65 Tim Duncan .60 1.50
66 Stephon Marbury .30 .75
67 Kirk Hinrich .30 .75
68 Chris Bosh .40 1.00
69 Corey Maggette .30 .75
70 Vince Carter .60 1.50
71 Caron Butler .30 .75
72 Stephen Jackson .30 .75
73 Carlos Boozer .30 .75
74 Michael Finley .40 1.00
75 Jamal Crawford .40 1.00
76 Dwight Howard RC 3.00 8.00

77 Emeka Okafor RC 1.25 3.00
78 Ben Gordon RC 1.50 4.00
79 Shaun Livingston RC 1.50 4.00
80 Devin Harris RC 1.25 3.00
81 Josh Childress RC 1.25 3.00
82 Luol Deng RC 1.50 4.00
83 Rafael Araujo RC 1.00 2.50
84 Andre Iguodala RC 2.00 5.00
85 Luke Jackson RC 1.00 2.50
86 Andris Biedrins RC 1.00 2.50
87 Robert Swift RC 1.00 2.50
88 Sebastian Telfair RC 1.25 3.00
89 Kris Humphries RC 1.50 4.00
90 Al Jefferson RC 2.00 5.00
91 Kirk Snyder RC 1.00 2.50
92 Josh Smith RC 1.50 4.00
93 J.R. Smith RC 1.50 4.00
94 Dorell Wright RC 1.50 4.00
95 Jameer Nelson RC 1.50 4.00
96 Bernard Robinson RC 1.25 3.00
97 Andre Emmett RC 1.00 2.50
98 Delonte West RC 1.50 4.00
99 Tony Allen RC 1.50 4.00
100 Kevin Martin RC 2.00 5.00

2004-05 SkyBox Premium Ruby

*1-75 RUBY: 2.5X TO 6X BASE HI
*76-100 RUBY RC's: 1X TO 2.5X BASE HI
PRINT RUN 75 SER.#'d SETS
64 LeBron James 50.00 120.00

2004-05 SkyBox Premium Autographs

Limted to 100 copies, this 30-card set parallels the look of the base Skybox Premium set but is enhanced with authentic player autographs. A die cut version was also inserted in sets, and no odds were given for these.

PRINT RUN 100 SER.#'d SETS
*DIE CUTS: .4X TO 1X BASE AU HI
DIE CUTS: RANDOM INSERTS IN PACKS
6 Lamar Odom 6.00 15.00
12 Nene 6.00 15.00
22 Antawn Jamison 6.00 15.00
49 Andrei Kirilenko 6.00 15.00
70 Vince Carter 15.00 40.00
78 Ben Gordon 6.00 15.00
82 Luol Deng 6.00 15.00
83 Rafael Araujo 4.00 10.00
85 Luke Jackson 4.00 10.00
86 Andris Biedrins 4.00 10.00
87 Robert Swift 4.00 10.00
89 Kris Humphries 6.00 15.00
91 Kirk Snyder 4.00 10.00
93 J.R. Smith 6.00 15.00
94 Dorell Wright 6.00 15.00
97 Andre Emmett 4.00 10.00
98 Delonte West 6.00 15.00

2004-05 SkyBox Premium Hometown Shout Outs

Inserted in packs, this 12-card set features a horizontal design with full-color player photos set against black and white backgrounds. Each card is sequentially numbered, and print runs appear in the checklist.
COMPLETE SET (12) 10.00 25.00
PRINT RUNS LISTED IN CHECKLIST
1 Carmelo Anthony/410 1.50 4.00
2 Dwyane Wade/708 1.25 3.00
3 Rasheed Wallace/215 .75 2.00
4 Allen Iverson/757 1.25 3.00
5 Paul Pierce/510 .75 2.00
6 Richard Jefferson/602 .60 1.50
7 Tim Duncan/340 1.25 3.00
8 Michael Redd/614 .60 1.50
9 Elton Brand/914 .75 2.00
10 LeBron James/330 5.00 12.00
11 Vince Carter/386 1.25 3.00
12 Kobe Bryant/610 3.00 8.00

2004-05 SkyBox Premium Hometown Shout Outs Autographs

Randomly seeded in packs, this 15-card set parallels the design of the base Hometown Shout Outs set enhanced with player autographs. Each card is sequentially numbered and print runs appear in the checklist.
PRINT RUNS LISTED IN CHECKLIST
CA Carmelo Anthony/25 30.00 80.00
CA Carlos Arroyo/250 15.00 40.00
CD Carlos Delfino/250 4.00 10.00
DH David Harrison/250 4.00 10.00
DW Dwyane Wade/50 20.00 50.00
HS Ha Seung-Jin/240 4.00 10.00
JJ Joe Johnson/250 5.00 12.00
NC Nick Collison/150 4.00 10.00
PP Paul Pierce 6.00 15.00
RJ Richard Jefferson/75 6.00 15.00
VC Vince Carter 15.00 40.00

2004-05 SkyBox Premium Hometown Shout Outs Jerseys

Randomly seeded in Hobby packs overall at one in six and Retail packs overall at one in 48, this 10-card set parallels the design of the base Hometown Shout Outs set enhanced with player jersey swatches. A Patch version serially numbered to 15 was also issued and contains premium jersey patch swatches.
OVERALL GAME USED ODDS 1:6 H, 1:48 R
*JERSEY 75 SINGLES: .6X TO 1.5X BASE HI
AI Allen Iverson 4.00 10.00
CA Carmelo Anthony 5.00 12.00
DW Dwyane Wade 4.00 10.00
EB Elton Brand 2.50 6.00
MR Michael Redd 2.00 5.00
PP Paul Pierce 2.50 6.00
RJ Richard Jefferson 2.00 5.00
RW Rasheed Wallace 2.50 6.00
TD Tim Duncan 4.00 10.00
VC Vince Carter 4.00 10.00

2004-05 SkyBox Premium Parquet Performers

Inserted in Hobby packs at the rate of one in 12, this 15-card set is horizontally designed and showcases great players from the past. Each card features a piece of Floor from the original Boston Garden.
STATED ODDS 1:12
1 Danny Ainge 6.00 15.00
2 Nate Archibald 6.00 15.00
3 Larry Bird 12.50 30.00
4 Kevin McHale 6.00 15.00
5 K.C. Jones 6.00 15.00
7 Pete Maravich 20.00 50.00
8 Jo Jo White 12.00 30.00
9 Robert Parish 10.00 25.00
10 John Havlicek 6.00 15.00
11 Bob Cousy 40.00 100.00
12 Tom Heinsohn 6.00 15.00
13 Dave Cowens 6.00 15.00
14 Bill Sharman 6.00 15.00
15 Sam Jones 6.00 15.00

2004-05 SkyBox Premium Parquet Performers Autographs

Inserted in Hobby packs at the rate of one in 144, this 13-card set parallels the base Parquet Performers set but is autographed. Many of these cards were never issued due to the shut-down of Fleer/Skybox International in the summer of 2005.
STATED ODDS 1:144
BC Bob Cousy 15.00 40.00
BS Bill Sharman 12.00 30.00
DA Danny Ainge 20.00 50.00
DC Dave Cowens 20.00 50.00
KM Kevin McHale 75.00 150.00
NA Nate Archibald 15.00 40.00
RP Robert Parish 15.00 40.00
SJ Sam Jones 12.00 30.00
TH Tom Heinsohn 15.00 40.00

2004-05 SkyBox Premium Performers

Seeded in both Hobby and Retail packs at the rate of one in six, this 20-card set is horizontally designed with a tan background to represent the wood floor of a basketball court and player photos in the top right.
COMPLETE SET (20) 10.00 25.00
STATED ODDS 1:6
1 Tracy McGrady .60 1.50
2 Kenyon Martin .40 1.00
3 Chris Webber .50 1.25
4 Kevin Garnett .75 2.00
5 Shaquille O'Neal 1.25 3.00
6 Allen Iverson .75 2.00
7 Steve Francis .40 1.00
8 Manu Ginobili .60 1.50
9 Paul Pierce .50 1.25
10 Ben Wallace .40 1.00
11 Carmelo Anthony 1.00 2.50
12 Peja Stojakovic .50 1.25
13 Richard Hamilton .40 1.00
14 Stephon Marbury .40 1.00
15 Vince Carter .75 2.00
16 Kobe Bryant 2.00 5.00
17 LeBron James 3.00 8.00
18 Dirk Nowitzki .75 2.00
19 Jermaine O'Neal .40 1.00
20 Dwyane Wade .75 2.00

2004-05 SkyBox Premium Performers Autographs

Randomly inserted in packs, this 11-card set parallels the design of the base Premium Performers set enhanced with player autographs and sequential numbering. Print runs are listed in the checklist.
PRINT RUNS LISTED IN CHECKLIST
BW Ben Wallace/25 15.00 40.00
CA Carmelo Anthony/25 30.00 80.00
DW Dwyane Wade/50 40.00 100.00
JO Jermaine O'Neal/50 12.00 30.00
KM Kenyon Martin/50 8.00 20.00
MG Manu Ginobili/41 20.00 50.00
PS Peja Stojakovic/100 8.00 20.00
RH Richard Hamilton/78 8.00 20.00
SM Stephon Marbury/50 8.00 20.00
TM Tracy McGrady/43 20.00 50.00
VC Vince Carter 15.00 40.00

2004-05 SkyBox Premium Performers Jerseys

Inserted in Hobby packs at one in six overall and Retal packs at one in 48 overall, this 18-card set parallels the design of the base Premium Performers set enhanced with a swatch of jersey. A Patch version serially numbered to 15 was also inserted.
OVERALL GAME USED ODDS 1:6 H, 1:48 R
*JERSEY 75 SINGLES: .5X TO 1.25X BASE HI
AI Allen Iverson 4.00 10.00
BW Ben Wallace 2.00 5.00
CA Carmelo Anthony 5.00 12.00
CW Chris Webber 2.50 6.00
DN Dirk Nowitzki 4.00 10.00
DW Dwyane Wade 4.00 10.00
JO Jermaine O'Neal 2.00 5.00
KG Kevin Garnett 4.00 10.00
KM Kenyon Martin 2.00 5.00
MG Manu Ginobili 3.00 8.00
PP Paul Pierce 2.50 6.00
PS Peja Stojakovic 2.50 6.00
RH Richard Hamilton 2.00 5.00
SF Steve Francis 2.00 5.00
SM Stephon Marbury 2.00 5.00
SO Shaquille O'Neal 6.00 15.00
TM Tracy McGrady 3.00 8.00
VC Vince Carter 4.00 10.00

2004-05 SkyBox Premium Proven Performers

Inserted in both Hobby and Retail packs at the rate of one in 24, this 15-card set is horizontally designed with black backgrounds on the top, gray on the bottom and black and white photos of retired legends.
COMPLETE SET (15) 15.00 40.00
STATED ODDS 1:24
1 Nate Archibald 1.50 4.00
2 Darryl Dawkins 1.25 3.00
3 Walt Frazier 2.00 5.00
4 George Gervin 2.00 5.00
5 John Havlicek 2.00 5.00
6 Robert Parish 2.00 5.00
7 Isiah Thomas 2.00 5.00
8 Earl Monroe 2.00 5.00
9 Oscar Robertson 2.00 5.00
10 Charles Barkley 3.00 8.00
11 Dave Bing 2.00 5.00
12 Magic Johnson 5.00 12.00
13 Bob Cousy 3.00 8.00
14 Bernard King 1.50 4.00
15 Kevin McHale 2.50 6.00

2004-05 SkyBox Premium Proven Performers Autographs

Randomly inserted in packs, this set parallels the base Proven Performers set enhanced with authentic player autographs. Most of these cards were never released due to Fleer/Skybox International closing down in the summer of 2005.
PRINT RUNS LISTED IN CHECKLIST
EM Earl Monroe 10.00 25.00
EM2 Earl Monroe JSY 12.00 30.00
GG George Gervin/100 12.00 30.00
MJ Magic Johnson/25 50.00 120.00
NA Nate Archibald 10.00 25.00
RP Robert Parish 12.00 30.00
WF Walt Frazier 10.00 25.00
WF2 Walt Frazier JSY 15.00 40.00

2004-05 SkyBox Premium Proven Performers Jerseys

Inserted in Hobby packs at one in six overall and Retail packs at one in 48 overall, this set parallels the base Proven Performers set enhanced with swatches of jersey. A Patch version numbered to 15 was also inserted.
OVERALL GAME USED ODDS 1:6 H, 1:48 R
CB Charles Barkley 12.00 30.00
IT Isiah Thomas 6.00 15.00
KM Kevin McHale 6.00 15.00
RP Robert Parish 6.00 15.00

2004-05 SkyBox Premium Proven Performers Jerseys 75

*75 SINGLES: .5X TO 1.25X BASE JSY HI
PRINT RUN 75 SER.#'d SETS
CB Charles Barkley 25.00 60.00

1994 SkyBox Premium Blue Chips Prototypes

Issued in a cello pack, this three-card standard-size (2 1/2" by 3 1/2") set previewed the forthcoming 90-card set that captured scenes from the motion picture "Blue Chips." During the film's opening weekend, February 18-20, 1994, moviegoers at 500 select theaters across the country received these prototype packs. The first card presented an offer to receive a Blue Chips SP card for 6.99. The other two cards displayed full-bleed color shots on their fronts in addition to the movie title and card subtitle. On a background consisting of a ghosted and differently cropped front photo, the backs provide a caption to the photo. The cards are stamped "Prototype" in red and are unnumbered.
COMPLETE SET (3) 1.50 4.00
1 Title card (Mail-in offer) .20 .50
2 Pete Pep Talk 1 (Nick Nolte and team) .40 1.00
3 A Few Tips (Nick Nolte and Shaquille O'Neal) 1.50 4.00

1994 SkyBox Premium Blue Chips

This 90-card standard-size set is based on Paramount Pictures' film, Blue Chips, starring Nick Nolte, NBA stars Shaquille O'Neal and Anfernee Hardaway, former Indiana University star Matt Nover, as well as several other (former and current) players and coaches from college and pro basketball. During the film's opening weekend, Feb. 18-20, the first 1,000 moviegoers received three-card sample packs at each of 500 select theaters across the country. Each sample contained two randomly chosen cards from the 90-card series and an advertisement card. It is reported that a 90-card factory set also exists. The fronts display full-bleed color shots in addition to the movie title and card subtitle. On a background consisting of a ghosted and differently cropped front photo, the backs provide a caption to the photo. The set is subdivided as follows: Story Cards (1-49), Character Cards (50-65), Action Cards (66-72), Behind-the-Scenes (73-88), and Checklists (89-90).
COMPLETE SET (90) 3.00 8.00
1 Pete Pep Talk 1 .05 .15
2 Thousands Cheer .05 .15
3 Stacking Hands .05 .15
4 Two More Points .05 .15
5 You're Outta Here .05 .15
6 Pete Punts .05 .15
7 Q and A .05 .15
8 Pete's Nemesis .05 .15
9 Sympathetic Ear (Bob Cousy listening to Nick Nolte) .15 .40
10 Pete's Dolphin Tank .05 .15
11 Film at 11 .05 .15
12 Gotta Have Heart .05 .15
13 Pete Pep Talk 2 .05 .15
14 Another Game, Another Loss .05 .15
15 Scouting at St. Joe's .05 .15
16 At Home With Butch (Hardaway at home with mother) .20 .50
17 Let's Make A Deal .05 .15
18 Uncle Phil's Big Score .05 .15
19 The First Sighting .05 .15
20 The First Dunk (O'Neal slam dunking) .20 .50
21 Hiring the Tutor (O'Neal introduced to Mary McDonnell) .20 .50
22 A Tutor with Class .05 .15
23 Hometown Parade (Matt Nover) .08 .25
24 Back Home in Indiana .05 .15
25 The Hard Sell (Nolte recruiting Matt Nover) .05 .15
26 Varsity vs. Blue Chips .05 .15
27 Ed Smells Something .05 .15
28 Unfinished Business .05 .15
29 On Campus (Shaquille O'Neal Penny Hardaway Matt Nover girl watching) .20 .50
30 News Crew (O'Neal with microphone in hand) .20 .50
31 Rick's on the Air .08 .25
32 Secret is Revealed .05 .15
33 Unhappy Seeing Happy .05 .15
34 Butch at Practice (Hardaway kneeling, basketball in hand) .20 .50
35 A Few Tips (Nolte coaching O'Neal in practice) .20 .50
36 More Preparation .05 .15
37 Two Old Friends (Nick Nolte Bob Cousy) .20 .50
38 Pete Challenges Tony .05 .15
39 We want Indiana (O'Neal in huddle) .20 .50
40 Taking the Lead (O'Neal shooting) .20 .50
41 Job Well Done (O'Neal on bench) .20 .50
42 On the Move (O'Neal establishing position) .20 .50
43 Fans Go Wild .05 .15
44 The Celebration (O'Neal and Hardaway celebrating) .20 .50
45 Victory Returns .05 .15
46 Ed's Full-Court Press .05 .15
47 Happy's Last Hurrah .05 .15
48 No Longer the Coach .05 .15
49 Always the Teacher .05 .15
50 Coach Bell .05 .15
51 Pete's Assistants .05 .15
52 Vic Roker (Bob Cousy) .15 .40
53 Happy Kuykendall .05 .15
54 Uncle Phil .05 .15
55 Jenny Bell .05 .15
56 Butch McRae (Anfernee Hardaway) .20 .50
57 Neon Bodeaux (Shaquille O'Neal) .20 .50
58 Billy Friedkin (Movie Director) .05 .15
59 Tony .05 .15
60 The Dolphin Girl .05 .15
61 Team 1 .05 .15
62 Team 2 .05 .15
63 Lavada McRae .05 .15
64 Ed Axelby .05 .15
65 Ricky Roe (Matt Nover) .08 .25
66 Under the Hoop (O'Neal playing defense) .20 .50
67 Precision Pass (Hardaway passing) .20 .50
68 Up and In .05 .15
69 Foul .05 .15
70 Out of My Way (O'Neal establishing position) .20 .50
71 Taking a Breather (O'Neal taking breather during timeout) .20 .50
72 Neon at the Line (O'Neal shooting free throw) .20 .50
73 Give Neon the Ball .20 .50
74 Mary McDonnell .05 .15
75 Standing Tall (O'Neal holding net) .20 .50
76 Nick and Rob (Nolte and Cousy conversing on campus) .15 .40
77 Roll Camera (O'Neal joking during filming) .20 .50
78 Nick Nolte and the Crew .05 .15
79 Pre-school with Shaq (O'Neal with pre-school kids) .20 .50
80 Piling On .05 .15
81 Mary Up in Arms (Mary McDonnell in O'Neal's arms) .20 .50
82 Five Blue-Chippers Penny Hardaway Shaquille O'Neal Matt Nover Nick Nolte William Friedkin .20 .50
83 The Exorcist (O'Neal making face) .20 .50
84 Checking the Stats (O'Neal reading sports magazine) .20 .50
85 Anfernee's Tricks (Hardaway holding two basketballs) .20 .50
86 The Legendary .05 .15
87 Shaq at Practice (O'Neal holding ball over head) .20 .50
88 Shaq Rehearses (O'Neal posed with basketball in hand) .20 .50
89 Checklist A .05 .15
90 Checklist B .05 .15

1994 SkyBox Premium Blue Chips Foil

Each of the blue chippers, O'Neal, Hardaway, and Nover, is featured on two different foil cards in a bonus insert set randomly inserted in eight-card packs. Reportedly 12,500 of each of the six cards were printed, with each individually numbered ("X of 12,500"). Finally, an SP foil card of O'Neal making the game-winning dunk was available only by mail for 6.99 until 6/1/94 or while supplies lasted. These foil cards utilize the same technology as the "Shaq Talk" insert in the 1993-94 SkyBox Premium series. The cards are numbered on the back with an "F" prefix.
COMPLETE SET (7) 20.00 50.00
F1 Getting to Know Butch McRae Anfernee Hardaway 5.00 12.00
F2 Butch Up Close Anfernee Hardaway 5.00 12.00
F3 Getting to Know Neon Shaquille O'Neal 5.00 12.00
F4 Neon Takes Charge Shaquille O'Neal 5.00 12.00
F5 Getting to Know Ricky Roe, Matt Nover 1.50 4.00
F6 Ricky on the Line Matt Nover 1.50 4.00
SP Neon's game-winner (O'Neal Mail-away) 5.00 12.00

1993-94 SkyBox Premium Pepsi Shaq Attaq

A cover card and four cards featuring horizontal fronts with full-bleed glossy color stills from Shaquille O'Neal's Pepsi commercial were distributed in 5-card cello packs. At the bottom of each photo, the Pepsi logo and "Shaq Attaq" in gold lettering appear. The horizontal back displays a white-bordered still on the left with the Pepsi logo in its upper left. On the right, "SHAQ" appears in gold lettering, with a brief statement about him beneath. The SkyBox logo at the bottom rounds out the card. The cards are numbered on the back.
COMPLETE SET (5) 6.00 15.00
COMMON CARD (1-4) 2.50 6.00
5 Cover Card .40 1.00

1993-94 SkyBox Schick

Issued in three-card packs inserted in Schick products, the 1993-94 Schick/SkyBox Premium set contains 52 cards that measure the standard size (2 1/2" by 3 1/2"). The fronts feature full-bleed color action photos with a wide white stripe down one side of the card front containing the player's name, position, and team. The SkyBox Premium foil stamp logo appears superimposed on the front. The backs display a second player close-up shot on the top half, and the player's statistics and scouting report on the bottom half. The cards are unnumbered and checklisted below in alphabetical order. The Shawn Bradley card is believed to be a short-print.
COMPLETE SET (52) 60.00 150.00
1 Kenny Anderson 1.25 3.00
2 Greg Anthony 1.00 2.50
3 Vin Baker 2.50 6.00
4 Stacey Augmon 1.25 3.00
5 Corie Blount 1.50 4.00
6 Shawn Bradley 1.50 4.00
7 Terrell Brandon 1.25 3.00
8 P.J. Brown 1.50 4.00
9 Scott Burrell 1.50 4.00
10 Sam Cassell 3.00 8.00
11 Calbert Cheaney 1.50 4.00
12 Doug Christie 1.00 2.50
13 Lloyd Daniels 1.00 2.50
14 Hubert Davis 1.00 2.50
15 Todd Day 1.00 2.50
16 Terry Dehere 1.50 4.00
17 Acie Earl 1.50 4.00
18 LaPhonso Ellis 1.00 2.50
19 Tom Gugliotta 1.25 3.00
20 Anfernee Hardaway 8.00 20.00
21 Scott Haskin 1.50 4.00
22 Robert Horry 1.50 4.00
23 Allan Houston 3.00 8.00
24 Lindsey Hunter 1.50 4.00
25 Bobby Hurley 1.50 4.00
26 Jim Jackson 1.25 3.00
27 Ervin Johnson 1.50 4.00
28 Adam Keefe 1.00 2.50
29 Toni Kukoc 4.00 10.00
30 Christian Laettner 1.25 3.00
31 Malcolm Mackey 1.50 4.00
32 Jamal Mashburn 2.50 6.00
33 Oliver Miller 1.00 2.50
34 Chris Mills 1.50 4.00
35 Harold Miner 1.00 2.50
36 Alonzo Mourning 2.50 6.00
37 Tracy Murray 1.00 2.50
38 Shaquille O'Neal 6.00 15.00
39 Anthony Peeler 1.00 2.50
40 Dino Radja 1.50 4.00
41 Isaiah Rider 2.50 6.00
42 James Robinson 1.50 4.00
43 Rodney Rogers 1.50 4.00
44 Malik Sealy 1.00 2.50
45 Steve Smith 1.25 3.00
46 Elmore Spencer 1.00 2.50
47 Latrell Sprewell 2.50 6.00
48 Rex Walters 1.50 4.00
49 Clarence Weatherspoon 1.00 2.50
50 Chris Webber 8.00 20.00
51 Walt Williams 1.00 2.50
52 Luther Wright 1.50 4.00

1993-94 SkyBox Sportslook Promo

This standard-size promo card was offered in the Sportslook magazine. The front displays a full-bleed color player photo with a vertical white bar on the left carrying the player's name in silver lettering. The back has a color player close-up shot on the top portion and a player profile with stats below. The card is unnumbered.
RR8 Magic Johnson 1.25 3.00

1993 SkyBox Story-of-a-Game

This three-card standard-size set was inserted into dual video cassette packs of California-based Strand Home Video's "The Story of a Game." A 32-page basketball booklet was also included in the video pack. Each UV-coated card features off-court full-bleed color photos of David Robinson on the front. The video's logo appears in the upper right, and the SkyBox logo is displayed in the lower left. The backs of the cards have a gray stripe at the top that contains the title and distributor of the video, and a narrow blank pinkish stripe at the bottom. Between these, covering the major portion of the back, are positive statements made by Robinson about the video printed in black over a purplish field that has the video's title in large white upper case lettering.
COMPLETE SET (3) 4.00 10.00
COMMON CARD (1-3) 1.50 4.00

1998-99 SkyBox Thunder

The 1998-99 SkyBox Thunder set consists of 125 standard size cards. The 8-card packs retail for a suggested price of $1.59. The fronts feature a new design with a color image of the player against a contemporary background. The base set is tiered with cards 1-50 coming 4 per pack, cards 51-100 coming 3 per pack and cards 101-125 coming one per pack.
COMPLETE SET (127) 10.00 25.00
CARDS 1-50 INSERTED 4:1
CARDS 51-100 INSERTED 3:1
CARDS 101-125 INSERTED 1:1
1 Kerry Kittles .12 .30
2 Larry Johnson .20 .50
3 Hakeem Olajuwon .25 .60
4 Glenn Robinson .15 .40
5 Alonzo Mourning .25 .60
6 Reggie Miller .25 .60
7 Toni Kukoc .20 .50
8 Corliss Williamson .12 .30
9 Nick Van Exel .15 .40
10 Mookie Blaylock .12 .30
11 Michael Smith .12 .30
12 Avery Johnson .15 .40
13 Brian Williams .12 .30
14 Doug Christie .12 .30
15 Danny Fortson .12 .30
16 Michael Stewart .12 .30
17 Anthony Peeler .12 .30
18 Cedric Henderson .12 .30
19 Lamond Murray .12 .30
20 Walt Williams .12 .30
21 Samaki Walker .12 .30
22 David Wesley .12 .30
23 Maurice Taylor .12 .30
24 Todd Fuller .12 .30
25 Jeff Hornacek .15 .40
26 Danny Manning .15 .40
27 Detlef Schrempf .20 .50
28 Nick Anderson .12 .30
29 Ron Harper .15 .40
30 Brian Shaw .12 .30
31 Bryant Stith .12 .30
32 Chris Whitney .12 .30
33 Patrick Ewing .25 .60
34 Travis Knight .12 .30
35 Tracy McGrady .30 .75
36 Dan Majerle .20 .50
37 Dale Davis .12 .30
38 Kelvin Cato .12 .30
39 Zydrunas Ilgauskas .20 .50
40 Sean Elliott .20 .50
41 Tony Delk .12 .30
42 Bobby Phills .12 .30
43 Clifford Robinson .12 .30
44 Shawn Bradley .12 .30
45 Aaron McKie .12 .30
46 Mark Jackson .15 .40
47 P.J. Brown .12 .30
48 Armon Gilliam .12 .30
49 Ed Gray .12 .30
50 Olden Polynice .12 .30
51 Kendall Gill .12 .30
52 Bryon Russell .12 .30
53 Dale Ellis .12 .30
54 Mark Price .20 .50
55 Donyell Marshall .12 .30
56 John Starks .15 .40
57 Jerome Williams .12 .30
58 Rodney Rogers .12 .30
59 Michael Finley .20 .50
60 Marcus Camby .15 .40
61 Chris Anstey .12 .30
62 Rodrick Rhodes .12 .30
63 Derek Anderson .12 .30
64 Jermaine O'Neal .20 .50
65 Glen Rice .20 .50
66 Bryant Reeves .12 .30
67 Jalen Rose .15 .40
68 Calbert Cheaney .12 .30
69 Steve Smith .15 .40
70 Shandon Anderson .12 .30
71 Tony Battie .15 .40
72 Kenny Anderson .15 .40
73 Tim Hardaway .20 .50
74 Antonio Daniels .12 .30
75 Charles Barkley .30 .75
76 Chauncey Billups .25 .60
77 Lindsey Hunter .12 .30
78 Terrell Brandon .12 .30
79 Anthony Mason .12 .30
80 Elden Campbell .12 .30
81 Rasheed Wallace .20 .50
82 Erick Dampier .12 .30
83 Tracy Murray .12 .30
84 Sam Cassell .15 .40
85 Bobby Jackson .12 .30
86 Horace Grant .15 .40
87 Brent Price .12 .30
88 Allan Houston .15 .40
89 Brevin Knight .12 .30
90 Steve Nash .30 .75
91 Lorenzen Wright .12 .30
92 Hubert Davis .12 .30
93 Walter McCarty .12 .30
94 Jamal Mashburn .15 .40
95 Dikembe Mutombo .20 .50
96 Chris Carr .12 .30
97 Tariq Abdul-Wahad .12 .30
98 Chris Mullin .20 .50
99 Charlie Ward .12 .30
100 Tim Thomas .20 .50
101 Tim Duncan .40 1.00
102 Antoine Walker .20 .50
103 Stephon Marbury .25 .60
104 Ray Allen .25 .60
105 Shawn Kemp .20 .50
106 Michael Jordan 1.50 4.00
107 Gary Payton .20 .50
108 Kobe Bryant .75 2.00
109 Karl Malone .25 .60
110 Kevin Garnett .30 .75
111 Jason Kidd .30 .75
112 Dennis Rodman .40 1.00
113 Grant Hill .30 .75
114 Keith Van Horn .20 .50
115 Shareef Abdur-Rahim .20 .50
116 Ron Mercer .15 .40
117 Allen Iverson .40 1.00
118 Shaquille O'Neal .50 1.25
119 Anfernee Hardaway .30 .75
120 Scottie Pippen .30 .75
121 David Robinson .30 .75
122 Vin Baker .15 .40
123 John Stockton .25 .60
124 Eddie Jones .20 .50
125 Juwan Howard .15 .40
126 Checklist .12 .30
127 Checklist .12 .30
NNO Grant Hill SAMPLE .75 2.00

1998-99 SkyBox Thunder Rave

*STARS: 30X TO 80X BASE CARD HI
STATED PRINT RUN 150 SERIAL #'d SETS
106 Michael Jordan 500.00 1000.00
108 Kobe Bryant 400.00 800.00
112 Dennis Rodman 40.00 100.00
118 Shaquille O'Neal 60.00 150.00

1998-99 SkyBox Thunder Super Rave

*STARS: 120X TO 300X BASE CARD HI
STATED PRINT RUN 25 SERIAL #'d SETS
3 Hakeem Olajuwon 100.00 250.00
6 Reggie Miller 125.00 300.00
35 Tracy McGrady 125.00 300.00
75 Charles Barkley 125.00 300.00
101 Tim Duncan 200.00 500.00
105 Shawn Kemp 125.00 300.00
106 Michael Jordan 4000.00 7000.00
108 Kobe Bryant 2000.00 3500.00
110 Kevin Garnett 200.00 500.00
111 Jason Kidd 125.00 300.00
112 Dennis Rodman 200.00 500.00
113 Grant Hill 125.00 300.00
117 Allen Iverson 150.00 400.00
118 Shaquille O'Neal 300.00 800.00
119 Anfernee Hardaway 125.00 300.00
120 Scottie Pippen 200.00 500.00

1998-99 SkyBox Thunder Boss

The 1998-99 SkyBox Thunder Boss set consists of 20 cards and is an insert to the 1998-99 SkyBox Thunder base set. The cards are randomly inserted in packs at a rate of one in 16. The fronts feature full color action photos of the twenty of the NBA's best players on sculpted embossed cards.
COMPLETE SET (20) 15.00 30.00
STATED ODDS 1:16 HOB/RET
1 Shareef Abdur-Rahim .75 2.00
2 Vin Baker .60 1.50
3 Tim Duncan 1.50 4.00
4 Kevin Garnett 1.25 3.00
5 Tim Hardaway .75 2.00
6 Grant Hill 1.25 3.00
7 Michael Jordan 8.00 20.00
8 Shawn Kemp .75 2.00
9 Jason Kidd 1.25 3.00
10 Karl Malone 1.00 2.50
11 Stephon Marbury 1.00 2.50
12 Ron Mercer .60 1.50
13 Shaquille O'Neal 2.00 5.00
14 Gary Payton .75 2.00
15 Scottie Pippen 1.25 3.00
16 Glenn Robinson .60 1.50
17 John Stockton 1.00 2.50
18 Damon Stoudamire .60 1.50
19 Keith Van Horn .75 2.00
20 Antoine Walker .75 2.00

1998-99 SkyBox Thunder Bringin' It

The 1998-99 SkyBox Thunder Bringin' It set consists of 10 cards and is an insert to the 1998-99 SkyBox Thunder base set. The cards are randomly inserted in packs at a rate of one in 8. The fold-out fronts are silver foil-stamped and provide statistics from ten of the league's most outstanding players.
COMPLETE SET (10) 3.00 8.00
STATED ODDS 1:8 HOB/RET
1 Charles Barkley .60 1.50
2 Anfernee Hardaway .60 1.50
3 Eddie Jones .40 1.00
4 Karl Malone .50 1.25
5 Hakeem Olajuwon .50 1.25
6 Shaquille O'Neal 1.00 2.50
7 Scottie Pippen .60 1.50
8 Glen Rice .40 1.00
9 David Robinson .60 1.50
10 Dennis Rodman .75 2.00

1998-99 SkyBox Thunder Flight School

The 1998-99 SkyBox Thunder Flight School set consists of 12 cards and is an insert to the 1998-99 SkyBox Thunder base set. The cards are randomly inserted in hobby packs only at a rate of one in 96. The fronts feature full color action photos complete with "binocular" design.
COMPLETE SET (12) 40.00 100.00
STATED ODDS 1:96 HOBBY
1 Ray Allen 2.00 5.00
2 Kobe Bryant 6.00 15.00
3 Michael Finley 1.50 4.00
4 Kevin Garnett 2.50 6.00
5 Anfernee Hardaway 2.50 6.00
6 Grant Hill 2.50 6.00
7 Allen Iverson 3.00 8.00
8 Eddie Jones 1.50 4.00
9 Michael Jordan 30.00 80.00
10 Shawn Kemp 1.50 4.00
11 Antonio McDyess 1.25 3.00
12 Ron Mercer 1.25 3.00

1998-99 SkyBox Thunder Lift Off

The 1998-99 SkyBox Thunder Lift Off set consists of 10 cards and is an insert to the 1998-99 SkyBox Thunder base set. The cards are randomly inserted in packs at a rate of one in 56. The fronts feature black and white full bleed photos of first and second year standouts "shooting" their teams into the future. Each star is featured on hyperplaid diffraction film-laminated stock.
COMPLETE SET (10) 15.00 40.00
STATED ODDS 1:56 HOB/RET 1.50 4.00
1 Shareef Abdur-Rahim 1.50 4.00
2 Ray Allen 2.00 5.00
3 Kobe Bryant 6.00 15.00
4 Tim Duncan 3.00 8.00
5 Allen Iverson 3.00 8.00
6 Kerry Kittles 1.00 2.50
7 Stephon Marbury 2.00 5.00
8 Ron Mercer 1.25 3.00
9 Keith Van Horn 1.50 4.00
10 Antoine Walker 1.50 4.00

1998-99 SkyBox Thunder Noyz Boyz

The 1998-99 SkyBox Thunder Noyz Boyz set consists of 15 cards and is an insert to the 1998-99 SkyBox Thunder base set. The cards are randomly inserted in packs at a rate of one in 300. The fronts feature color photos of 15 of the NBA's most electric players. The cards are die-cut, foil-stamped and printed on "illusion" stock with material finish.
COMPLETE SET (15) 2000.00 4000.00
STATED ODDS 1:300 HOB/RET
1 Shareef Abdur-Rahim 15.00 40.00
2 Ray Allen 40.00 100.00
3 Kobe Bryant 150.00 400.00
4 Tim Duncan 125.00 300.00
5 Kevin Garnett 75.00 200.00
6 Anfernee Hardaway 60.00 150.00
7 Grant Hill 50.00 120.00
8 Allen Iverson 60.00 150.00
9 Michael Jordan 1200.00 2000.00
10 Stephon Marbury 40.00 100.00
11 Shaquille O'Neal 60.00 150.00
12 Scottie Pippen 60.00 150.00
13 Dennis Rodman 75.00 200.00
14 Keith Van Horn 15.00 40.00
15 Antoine Walker 15.00 40.00

1992 SkyBox USA

The 1992 SkyBox USA basketball set contains 110 cards which were distributed in foil-wrap packs. The set includes nine cards of each of the first ten NBA players named to the team, two cards of each coach, and two checklist cards. The set concludes with a "Magic On" subset, representing Johnson's thoughts on his teammates. The wax packs included randomly inserted cards autographed by Magic Johnson and David Robinson as well as a plastic trading card featuring a team photo. However, the autographed cards were not certified. The standard-size cards feature on the fronts full-bleed glossy color action shots, with the player's name and the card's subtitle printed across the top of the picture. On the upper portion, the backs feature a color close-up photo, while the lower portion presents statistics or summarizes the player's professional career.
COMPLETE SET (110) 12.50 25.00
1 Charles Barkley NBA Update .10 .30
2 Charles Barkley NBA Rookie .10 .30
3 Charles Barkley Game Strategy .10 .30
4 Charles Barkley NBA Best Game .10 .30
5 Charles Barkley Off the Court .10 .30
6 Charles Barkley NBA Playoffs .10 .30
7 Charles Barkley NBA All-Star Record .10 .30
8 Charles Barkley NBA Shooting .10 .30
9 Charles Barkley NBA Rebounds .10 .30
10 Larry Bird NBA Update .20 .50
11 Larry Bird NBA Rookie .20 .50
12 Larry Bird Game Strategy .20 .50
13 Larry Bird NBA Best Game .20 .50
14 Larry Bird Off the Court .20 .50
15 Larry Bird NBA Playoffs .20 .50
16 Larry Bird NBA All-Star Record .20 .50
17 Larry Bird NBA Shooting .20 .50
18 Larry Bird NBA Rebounds .20 .50
19 Patrick Ewing NBA Update .08 .25
20 Patrick Ewing NBA Rookie .08 .25
21 Patrick Ewing Game Strategy .08 .25
22 Patrick Ewing NBA Best Game .08 .25
23 Patrick Ewing Off the Court .08 .25
24 Patrick Ewing NBA Playoffs .08 .25
25 Patrick Ewing NBA All-Star Record .08 .25
26 Patrick Ewing NBA Shooting .08 .25
27 Patrick Ewing NBA Rebounds .08 .25
28 Magic Johnson NBA Update .20 .50
29 Magic Johnson NBA Rookie .20 .50
30 Magic Johnson Game Strategy .20 .50
31 Magic Johnson NBA Best Game .20 .50

32 Magic Johnson Off the Court .20 .50
33 Magic Johnson NBA Playoffs .20 .50
34 Magic Johnson NBA All-Star Record .20 .50
35 Magic Johnson NBA Shooting .20 .50
36 Magic Johnson NBA Assists .20 .50
37 Michael Jordan NBA Update .60 1.50
38 Michael Jordan NBA Rookie .60 1.50
39 Michael Jordan Game Strategy .60 1.50
40 Michael Jordan NBA Best Game .60 1.50
41 Michael Jordan Off the Court .60 1.50
42 Michael Jordan NBA Playoffs .60 1.50
43 Michael Jordan NBA All-Star Record .60 1.50
44 Michael Jordan NBA Shooting .60 1.50
45 Michael Jordan NBA All-Time Records .60 1.50
46 Karl Malone NBA Update .08 .25
47 Karl Malone NBA Rookie .08 .25
48 Karl Malone Game Strategy .08 .25
49 Karl Malone NBA Best Game .08 .25
50 Karl Malone Off the Court .08 .25
51 Karl Malone NBA Playoffs .08 .25
52 Karl Malone NBA All-Star Record .08 .25
53 Karl Malone NBA Shooting .08 .25
54 Karl Malone NBA Rebounds .08 .25
55 Chris Mullin NBA Update .08 .25
56 Chris Mullin NBA Rookie .08 .25
57 Chris Mullin Game Strategy .08 .25
58 Chris Mullin NBA Best Game .08 .25
59 Chris Mullin Off the Court .08 .25
60 Chris Mullin NBA Playoffs .08 .25
61 Chris Mullin NBA All-Star Record .08 .25
62 Chris Mullin NBA Shooting .08 .25
63 Chris Mullin NBA Minutes .08 .25
64 Scottie Pippen NBA Update .15 .40
65 Scottie Pippen NBA Rookie .15 .40
66 Scottie Pippen Game Strategy .15 .40
67 Scottie Pippen NBA Best Game .15 .40
68 Scottie Pippen Off the Court .15 .40
69 Scottie Pippen NBA Playoffs .15 .40
70 Scottie Pippen NBA All-Star Record .15 .40
71 Scottie Pippen NBA Shooting .15 .40
72 Scottie Pippen NBA Steals and Blocks .15 .40
73 David Robinson NBA Update .10 .30
74 David Robinson NBA Rookie .10 .30
75 David Robinson Game Strategy .10 .30
76 David Robinson NBA Best Game .10 .30
77 David Robinson Off the Court .10 .30
78 David Robinson NBA Playoffs .10 .30
79 David Robinson NBA All-Star .10 .30
80 David Robinson NBA Shooting .10 .30
81 David Robinson NBA All-Around .10 .30
82 John Stockton NBA Update .08 .25
83 John Stockton NBA Rookie .08 .25
84 John Stockton Game Strategy .08 .25
85 John Stockton NBA Best Game .08 .25
86 John Stockton Off the Court .08 .25
87 John Stockton NBA Playoffs .08 .25
88 John Stockton NBA All-Star Record .08 .25
89 John Stockton NBA Shooting .08 .25
90 John Stockton NBA Assists .08 .25
91 P.J. Carlesimo CO College Coaching .08 .25
92 P.J. Carlesimo CO NCAA Coaching Record .08 .25
93 Chuck Daly CO NBA Coaching .08 .25
94 Chuck Daly CO NCAA Coaching Record .08 .25
95 Mike Krzyzewski CO College Coaching .10 .30
96 Mike Krzyzewski CO College Coaching Record .10 .30
97 Lenny Wilkens CO NBA Coaching .08 .25
98 Lenny Wilkens CO NBA Coaching Record .08 .25
99 Checklist 1-54 .08 .25
100 Checklist 55-110 .08 .25
101 Magic on Barkley .10 .30
102 Magic on Bird .20 .50
103 Magic on Ewing .08 .25
104 Magic on Magic .20 .50
105 Magic on Jordan .60 1.50
106 Magic on Malone .08 .25
107 Magic on Mullin .08 .25
108 Magic on Pippen .15 .40
109 Magic on Robinson .10 .30
110 Magic on Stockton .08 .25
NNO Plastic Team Card 4.00 10.00

1994 SkyBox USA Prototypes

These eight prototypes were issued to showcase the design of the 1994 SkyBox USA set, which was issued in June 1994. Except for the Dumars and Kemp cards, the front features a borderless color shot of the player in his Team USA uniform posed in front of a portion of the American flag. The fronts of the Dumars and Kemp cards are borderless action shots. The player's name appears in silver foil within a red stripe near the bottom, along with the USA logo. The backs are of several different designs, since the cards represent different subsets, but generally they have a red, white, and blue design. The prototypes are not marked as such and are unnumbered and checklisted below in alphabetical order.

COMPLETE SET (8) 1.25 3.00
1 Derrick Coleman .20 .50
2 Joe Dumars .25 .60
3 Magic Johnson .60 1.50
4 Larry Johnson .25 .60
5 Shawn Kemp .25 .60
6 Alonzo Mourning .30 .75
7 Isiah Thomas .25 .60
8 Dominique Wilkins .30 .75

1994 SkyBox USA

These 89 standard-size cards honor the '94 Team USA players. Cards were issued in 10-card packs with 24 packs per box. The borderless fronts feature color posed and action player shots. The player's name appears in silver-foil lettering within a red stripe near the bottom. Each player has a subset of six cards, the backs of which carry information about each player's international experience, NBA rookie year, best game, NBA update, trademark move, and comments on the player by Magic Johnson. In addition, a T-shirt exchange card (one in 300 packs) was available with this product. The offer was valid through October 31, 1994. The On the Court exchange card was redeemable for a a set featuring action from the 1994 Olympic games.

COMPLETE SET (89) 6.00 15.00
1 Alonzo Mourning .20 .50
2 Alonzo Mourning .20 .50
3 Alonzo Mourning .20 .50
4 Alonzo Mourning .20 .50
5 Alonzo Mourning .20 .50
6 Alonzo Mourning .20 .50
7 Larry Johnson .15 .40
8 Larry Johnson .15 .40
9 Larry Johnson .15 .40
10 Larry Johnson .15 .40
11 Larry Johnson .15 .40
12 Larry Johnson .15 .40
13 Shawn Kemp .15 .40
14 Shawn Kemp .15 .40
15 Shawn Kemp .15 .40
16 Shawn Kemp .15 .40
17 Shawn Kemp .15 .40
18 Shawn Kemp .15 .40
19 Mark Price .15 .40
20 Mark Price .15 .40
21 Mark Price .15 .40
22 Mark Price .15 .40
23 Mark Price .15 .40
24 Mark Price .15 .40
25 Steve Smith .12 .30
26 Steve Smith .12 .30
27 Steve Smith .12 .30
28 Steve Smith .12 .30
29 Steve Smith .12 .30
30 Steve Smith .12 .30
31 Dominique Wilkins .20 .50
32 Dominique Wilkins .20 .50
33 Dominique Wilkins .20 .50
34 Dominique Wilkins .20 .50
35 Dominique Wilkins .20 .50
36 Dominique Wilkins .20 .50
37 Derrick Coleman .12 .30
38 Derrick Coleman .12 .30
39 Derrick Coleman .12 .30
40 Derrick Coleman .12 .30
41 Derrick Coleman .12 .30
42 Derrick Coleman .12 .30
43 Isiah Thomas .15 .40
44 Isiah Thomas .15 .40
45 Isiah Thomas .15 .40
46 Isiah Thomas .15 .40
47 Isiah Thomas .15 .40
48 Isiah Thomas .15 .40
49 Joe Dumars .15 .40
50 Joe Dumars .15 .40
51 Joe Dumars .15 .40
52 Joe Dumars .15 .40
53 Joe Dumars .15 .40
54 Joe Dumars .15 .40
55 Dan Majerle .15 .40
56 Dan Majerle .15 .40
57 Dan Majerle .15 .40
58 Dan Majerle .15 .40
59 Dan Majerle .15 .40
60 Dan Majerle .15 .40
61 Tim Hardaway .15 .40
62 Tim Hardaway .15 .40
63 Tim Hardaway .15 .40
64 Tim Hardaway .15 .40
65 Tim Hardaway .15 .40
66 Tim Hardaway .15 .40
67 Shaquille O'Neal .40 1.00
68 Shaquille O'Neal .40 1.00
69 Shaquille O'Neal .40 1.00
70 Shaquille O'Neal .40 1.00
71 Shaquille O'Neal .40 1.00
72 Shaquille O'Neal .40 1.00
73 Reggie Miller .20 .50
74 Reggie Miller .20 .50
75 Reggie Miller .20 .50
76 Reggie Miller .20 .50
77 Reggie Miller .20 .50
78 Reggie Miller .20 .50
79 Don Chaney CO .15 .40
80 Pete Gillen CO .15 .40
81 Rick Majerus CO .15 .40
82 Don Nelson CO .15 .40
83 '94 USA Team .15 .40
84 International Rules Time .15 .40
85 International Rules Court Dimensions .15 .40
86 International Rules Rules .15 .40
87 Magic Johnson Passing the Torch .40 1.00
88 David Robinson Passing the Torch .25 .60
89 Checklist .08 .25
NNO Expired T-Shirt Exch. .08 .25

1994 SkyBox USA Gold

Randomly inserted at a rate of 1 in 4 packs, this parallel set features standard-size cards that differ from their '94 SkyBox USA counterparts only by the embossed gold-foil highlights. The cards are numbered on the back. Please refer to the multiplier provided below (coupled with the prices of the corresponding regular issue cards) to ascertain value.

COMPLETE SET (89) 25.00 60.00
*GOLD: 1.25X TO 3X HI COLUMN

1994 SkyBox USA Autographs

These scarce chase cards were inserted in SkyBox USA packs at a rate of about two per case. Each player signed his "Trademark Move" card from the regular issue set. These are the only seven players known to have signed cards for this product. The signatures are in gold paint, and the cards are embossed with the SkyBox seal to distinguish them from any cards signed after the product's release.

COMPLETE SET (7) 300.00 600.00
11A Larry Johnson 25.00 60.00
17A Shawn Kemp 50.00 125.00
35A Dominique Wilkins 40.00 100.00
47A Isiah Thomas 50.00 125.00
53A Joe Dumars 40.00 100.00
59A Dan Majerle 40.00 100.00
65A Tim Hardaway 30.00 80.00

1994 SkyBox USA Dream Play

Randomly inserted in packs at a rate of one in 35, these 13 standard-size cards feature on their borderless fronts posed action color cutouts of the players in their Team USA uniforms set on a dark play diagram background. The player's name appears in prismatic silver-foil lettering at the top. The white back carries play diagrams and descriptions.

COMPLETE SET (13) 4.00 10.00
DP1 Alonzo Mourning .60 1.50
DP2 Larry Johnson .50 1.25
DP3 Shawn Kemp .50 1.25
DP4 Mark Price .50 1.25
DP5 Steve Smith .40 1.00
DP6 Dominique Wilkins .60 1.50
DP7 Derrick Coleman .40 1.00
DP8 Isiah Thomas .50 1.25
DP9 Joe Dumars .50 1.25
DP10 Dan Majerle .50 1.25
DP11 Tim Hardaway .50 1.25
DP12 Shaquille O'Neal 1.25 3.00
DP13 Reggie Miller .60 1.50

1994 SkyBox USA Kevin Johnson

This 14-card standard-size set was issued through a wrapper redemption program. The collector received a complete set in exchange for nine wrappers. The offer expired October 31, 1994. The first six cards have the player's name in silver foil lettering, while the next six have the player's name and SkyBox logo in gold foil. The final two cards represent the Dream Play and Portrait insert sets. The silver and gold cards are distingushed in the listing below by "S" and "G" prefixes respectively.

COMPLETE SET (14) 10.00 25.00
90G Kevin Johnson International .75 2.00
90S Kevin Johnson International .20 .50
91G Kevin Johnson NBA Rookie .75 2.00
91S Kevin Johnson NBA Rookie .20 .50
92G Kevin Johnson Best Game .75 2.00
92S Kevin Johnson Best Game .20 .50
93G Kevin Johnson NBA Update .75 2.00
93S Kevin Johnson NBA Update .20 .50
94G Kevin Johnson Trademark Move .75 2.00
94S Kevin Johnson Trademark Move .20 .50
95G Kevin Johnson Magic on Johnson .75 2.00
95S Kevin Johnson Magic on Johnson .20 .50
DP14 Kevin Johnson Dream Play 1.25 3.00
PT14 Kevin Johnson Portrait 5.00 12.00

1994 SkyBox USA On The Court

This 14 card standard-size set was available exclusively by exchanging the SkyBox USA On the Court trade card before the November 15th, 1994 deadline. The trade card was randomly inserted into one in every 300 SkyBox USA packs. Each member of Dream Team II is represented in this set. The set is called as "On the Court" as all photos were all taken in Toronto during the World Championships in 1994.

COMPLETE SET (14) 6.00 15.00
1 Isiah Thomas .75 2.00
2 Tim Hardaway .75 2.00
3 Reggie Miller 1.00 2.50
4 Steve Smith .60 1.50
5 Joe Dumars .75 2.00
6 Shawn Kemp .75 2.00
7 Mark Price .75 2.00
8 Dan Majerle .75 2.00
9 Kevin Johnson .75 2.00
10 Derrick Coleman .60 1.50
11 Alonzo Mourning 1.00 2.50
12 Dominique Wilkins 1.00 2.50
13 Larry Johnson .75 2.00
14 Shaquille O'Neal 2.00 5.00
NNO Exp.On The Court Exch. .20 .50

1994 SkyBox USA Portraits

Randomly inserted at a rate of one in 100 packs, these 13 standard-size cards feature embossed gold foil-bordered fronts with posed color portraits of the players in their Team USA uniforms. The player's name appears in embossed lettering within the gold-foil lower margin. The red, white, and blue back carries a quote from the player.

COMPLETE SET (13) 40.00 80.00
PT1 Alonzo Mourning 6.00 15.00
PT2 Larry Johnson 5.00 12.00
PT3 Shawn Kemp 5.00 12.00
PT4 Mark Price 5.00 12.00
PT5 Steve Smith 4.00 10.00
PT6 Dominique Wilkins 6.00 15.00
PT7 Derrick Coleman 4.00 10.00
PT8 Isiah Thomas 5.00 12.00
PT9 Joe Dumars 5.00 12.00
PT10 Dan Majerle 5.00 12.00
PT11 Tim Hardaway 5.00 12.00
PT12 Shaquille O'Neal 12.00 30.00
PT13 Reggie Miller 6.00 15.00

1996 SkyBox USA

The 1996 SkyBox USA set, featuring members of Dream Team 3, was issued in one series totalling 60 cards. The 6-card packs retailed for $1.99 each. The set features the topical subsets: Grant's Slant (1-10), Brag Book (11-20), Playing for Pride (21-30), Contribution (31-50), Coaches (51-54) and Awesome Duos (55-59). Card fronts feature an Olympic ring background with an action shot of the player.

COMPLETE SET (60) 5.00 12.00
1 Anfernee Hardaway GS .25 .60
2 Grant Hill GS .25 .60
3 Karl Malone GS .20 .50
4 Reggie Miller GS .20 .50
5 Scottie Pippen GS .25 .60
6 Hakeem Olajuwon GS .20 .50
7 Shaquille O'Neal GS .40 1.00
8 David Robinson GS .25 .60
9 Glenn Robinson GS .12 .30
10 John Stockton GS .20 .50
11 Anfernee Hardaway .25 .60
12 Grant Hill .25 .60
13 Karl Malone .20 .50
14 Reggie Miller .20 .50
15 Scottie Pippen .25 .60
16 Hakeem Olajuwon .20 .50
17 Shaquille O'Neal .40 1.00
18 David Robinson .25 .60
19 Glenn Robinson .12 .30
20 John Stockton .20 .50
21 Anfernee Hardaway .25 .60
22 Grant Hill .25 .60
23 Karl Malone .20 .50
24 Reggie Miller .20 .50
25 Scottie Pippen .25 .60
26 Hakeem Olajuwon .20 .50
27 Shaquille O'Neal .40 1.00
28 David Robinson .25 .60
29 Glenn Robinson .12 .30
30 John Stockton .20 .50
31 Anfernee Hardaway .25 .60
32 Grant Hill .25 .60
33 Karl Malone .20 .50
34 Reggie Miller .20 .50
35 Scottie Pippen .25 .60
36 Hakeem Olajuwon .20 .50
37 Shaquille O'Neal .40 1.00
38 David Robinson .25 .60
39 Glenn Robinson .12 .30
40 John Stockton .20 .50
41 Anfernee Hardaway .25 .60
42 Grant Hill .25 .60
43 Karl Malone .20 .50
44 Reggie Miller .20 .50
45 Scottie Pippen .25 .60
46 Hakeem Olajuwon .20 .50
47 Shaquille O'Neal .40 1.00
48 David Robinson .25 .60
49 Glenn Robinson .12 .30
50 John Stockton .20 .50
51 Lenny Wilkens CO .15 .40
52 Bobby Cremins .15 .40
53 Clem Haskins .15 .40
54 Jerry Sloan .15 .40
55 Shaquille O'Neal Anfernee Hardaway AD .30 .75
56 Karl Malone John Stockton AD .15 .40
57 David Robinson Hakeem Olajuwon AD .15 .40
58 Scottie Pippen Grant Hill AD .15 .40
59 Reggie Miller Glenn Robinson AD .15 .40
60 Checklist .08 .25
NNO Grant Hill Promo Sheet 1.25 3.00

1996 SkyBox USA Bronze

Randomly inserted in hobby and retail packs at a rate of one in 12, this set features the first ten players selected to the 1996 USA men's basketball team. Card fronts feature foil printing and UV coating.

COMPLETE SET (10) 8.00 20.00
*SPARKLE: .5X TO 1.25X VALUE
SPARKLE: STATED ODDS 1:18 HOBBY
B1 Anfernee Hardaway 1.50 4.00
B2 Grant Hill 1.50 4.00
B3 Karl Malone 1.25 3.00
B4 Reggie Miller 1.25 3.00
B5 Scottie Pippen 1.50 4.00
B6 Hakeem Olajuwon 1.25 3.00
B7 Shaquille O'Neal 2.50 6.00
B8 David Robinson 1.50 4.00
B9 Glenn Robinson .75 2.00
B10 John Stockton 1.25 3.00

1996 SkyBox USA Gold

COMPLETE SET (10) 40.00 100.00
*SPARKLE: .5X TO 1.25X VALUE
SPARKLE: STATED ODDS 1:180 HOBBY
G1 Anfernee Hardaway 8.00 20.00
G2 Grant Hill 8.00 20.00
G3 Karl Malone 6.00 15.00
G4 Reggie Miller 6.00 15.00
G5 Scottie Pippen 8.00 20.00
G6 Hakeem Olajuwon 6.00 15.00
G7 Shaquille O'Neal 12.00 30.00
G8 David Robinson 8.00 20.00
G9 Glenn Robinson 4.00 10.00
G10 John Stockton 6.00 15.00

1996 SkyBox USA Quads

Randomly inserted in packs at a rate of one in 3, this 15-card set features the first ten players selected to the 1996 USA men's basketball team. The standard-sized cards actually feature four preforated mini quadrant cards. These mini cards are replicas of the basic issue cards. Each of the original ten members of the team have their own quads. In addtion, the final five quads are based on the following themes: Power, Versatility, Passing, Defense and Scoring.

COMPLETE SET (15) 5.00 12.00
Q1 Anfernee Hardaway .75 2.00
Q2 Grant Hill .75 2.00
Q3 Karl Malone .60 1.50
Q4 Reggie Miller .60 1.50
Q5 Scottie Pippen .75 2.00
Q6 Hakeem Olajuwon .60 1.50
Q7 Shaquille O'Neal 1.25 3.00
Q8 David Robinson .75 2.00
Q9 Glenn Robinson .40 1.00
Q10 John Stockton .60 1.50
Q11 Power Quad .40 1.00
Q12 Versatility Quad .40 1.00
Q13 Passing Quad .40 1.00
Q14 Defensive Quad .40 1.00
Q15 Scorers Quad .40 1.00

1996 SkyBox USA Silver

COMPLETE SET (10) 20.00 50.00
*SPARKLE: .5X TO 1.25X VALUE
SPARKLE: STATED ODDS 1:72 HOBBY
S1 Anfernee Hardaway 4.00 10.00
S2 Grant Hill 4.00 10.00
S3 Karl Malone 3.00 8.00
S4 Reggie Miller 3.00 8.00
S5 Scottie Pippen 4.00 10.00
S6 Hakeem Olajuwon 3.00 8.00
S7 Shaquille O'Neal 6.00 15.00
S8 David Robinson 4.00 10.00
S9 Glenn Robinson 2.00 5.00
S10 John Stockton 3.00 8.00

1996 SkyBox USA Wrapper Exchange

This 25-card set was available via a wrapper exchange program. Sets could be obtained by sending in 10 wrappers along with $3 for postage and handling before the December 31, 1996 deadline. The set contains cards for Charles Barkley and Mitch Richmond, two \late additions to the team, and has all of the subset and insert cards that they would have had if they were in the basic set.

COMPLETE SET (25) 5.00 12.00
61 Charles Barkley GS .25 .60
62 Mitch Richmond GS .15 .40
63 Charles Barkley BB .25 .60
64 Mitch Richmond BB .15 .40
65 Charles Barkley PP .25 .60
66 Mitch Richmond PP .15 .40
67 Charles Barkley CON .25 .60
68 Mitch Richmond CON .15 .40
69 Charles Barkley CON .25 .60
70 Mitch Richmond CON .15 .40
71 Charles Barkley Mitch Richmond AD .15 .40
B11 Charles Barkley Bronze .60 1.50
B12 Mitch Richmond Bronze .40 1.00
G11 Charles Barkley Gold 1.50 4.00
G12 Mitch Richmond Gold 1.00 2.50
Q16 Charles Barkley Quad 1.00 2.50
Q17 Mitch Richmond Quad .60 1.50
S11 Charles Barkley Silver 1.00 2.50
S12 Mitch Richmond Silver .60 1.50
BS11 Charles Barkley Bronze Sparkle .60 1.50
BS12 Mitch Richmond Bronze Sparkle .40 1.00
GS11 Charles Barkley Gold Sparkle 1.50 4.00
GS12 Mitch Richmond Gold Sparkle 1.00 2.50
SS11 Charles Barkley Silver Sparkle 1.00 2.50
SS12 Mitch Richmond Silver Sparkle .60 1.50

1996 SkyBox USA Texaco

This 14-card set was available in 3-card packs through a joint promotion between Texaco and Fleer/SkyBox. Packs could be obtained with a 8-gallon fill-up (one) or for $.89 per pack. The card fronts have a gray background with a full player shot. The player's name is in red foil on the card front.

COMPLETE SET (14) 2.50 6.00
1 Charles Barkley .50 1.25
2 Anfernee Hardaway .50 1.25
3 Grant Hill .50 1.25
4 Karl Malone .40 1.00
5 Reggie Miller .40 1.00
6 Hakeem Olajuwon .40 1:00
7 Shaquille O'Neal .75 2.00
8 Scottie Pippen .50 1.25
9 Mitch Richmond .30 .75
10 David Robinson .50 1.25
11 Glenn Robinson .25 .60
12 John Stockton .40 1.00
13 Lenny Wilkens CO .30 .75
14 Team Card .30 .75

1991 Smokey's Larry Johnson

This seven-card set was sponsored by Smokey's Sportscards, Inc. (Las Vegas, Nevada) in honor of Larry Johnson, the 1990-91 NCAA Player of the Year. Set production was limited to 49,500, and the unique set number appears on a cardboard picture frame that accompanies the seven cards. The standard-size cards have high gloss color action photos on the front, with gold borders on a black card face. Johnson's name is written in aqua and white lettering at the bottom of the card. Inside a gold border, the glossy backs have a black marble design. A color mugshot of Johnson appears at the top of each back, and an extended caption to the card appears in a pale green rectangle. The promo card was distributed at the 1991 National Convention and at the FanFest in Toronto as a Smokey's advertisement. A total of 72,000 cards were printed, with each bearing a unique serial number on the back.

COMPLETE SET (7) 2.00 5.00
COMMON CARD (1-7) .40 1.00
PR Larry Johnson PROMO .50 1.25

2001 Sol Fleer WNBA

This set was produced by Fleer and handed out at the August 10th Sol's game to the first 5000 ticket-holders. Cards feature perforated edges, as they were released in the form of a sheet, white borders, and a colored frame around the card to match the team's colors.

COMPLETE SET (9) 4.00 10.00
1 Debbie Black .40 1.00
2 Katrina Colleton .40 1.00
3 Tracy Reid .40 1.00
4 Kisha Ford .40 1.00
5 Kristen Rasmussen .40 1.00
6 Sandy Brondello 1.50 4.00
7 Marlies Askamp .40 1.00
8 Ron Rothstein .40 1.00
9 Sheri Sam .40 1.00

1994-95 SP

The complete 1994-95 SP set (issued by Upper Deck) consists of 165-card standard size cards issued in eight-card packs (suggested retail price $3.99). Boxes were distributed exclusively to hobby dealers. The set features full-bleed fronts with color action photos. There is a gold strip down the left side with the player name while the team name is at the bottom. The backs feature another color action photo with the statistics at the bottom and a gold hologram at the bottom left. The only subset is Premier Prospects (1-30) which highlights rookies. Unlike the regular player cards, these rookie-focused cards have a full-bleed gold foil background with a silver foil pyramid at the bottom with the player's name in it. The backs have a vertical color player photo on the right and statistics on the left. After the Premier Prospects subset, the cards are grouped alphabetically within teams. Two parallel Michael Jordan cards (red and silver), both numbered MJ1, were randomly inserted into packs. The cards feature feature photos from Jordan's return with the words "He's Back March 19, 1995" in red foil. The red version was inserted at a ratio of one in every 30 packs. The silver version was inserted at a ratio of one in every 192 packs. Rookie Cards of note in this set include Grant Hill, Juwan Howard, Eddie Jones, Jason Kidd and Glenn Robinson.

COMPLETE SET (165) 15.00 30.00
MJ1R: STATED ODDS 1:30
MJ1S: STATED ODDS 1:192
1 Glenn Robinson FOIL RC .60 1.50
2 Jason Kidd FOIL RC 2.00 5.00
3 Grant Hill FOIL RC 2.00 5.00
4 Donyell Marshall FOIL RC .30 .75
5 Juwan Howard FOIL RC .50 1.25
6 Sharone Wright FOIL RC .25 .60
7 Lamond Murray FOIL RC .30 .75
8 Brian Grant FOIL RC .50 1.25
9 Eric Montross FOIL RC .25 .60
10 Eddie Jones FOIL RC 1.00 2.50
11 Carlos Rogers FOIL RC .25 .60
12 Khalid Reeves FOIL RC .25 .60
13 Jalen Rose FOIL RC .75 2.00
14 Eric Piatkowski FOIL RC .40 1.00
15 Clifford Rozier FOIL RC .20 .50
16 Aaron McKie FOIL RC .30 .75
17 Eric Mobley FOIL RC .20 .50
18 Tony Dumas FOIL RC .30 .75
19 B.J. Tyler FOIL RC .20 .50
20 Dickey Simpkins FOIL RC .25 .60
21 Bill Curley FOIL RC .20 .50
22 Wesley Person FOIL RC .30 .75
23 Monty Williams FOIL RC .25 .60
24 Greg Minor FOIL RC .30 .75
25 Charlie Ward FOIL RC .30 .75
26 Brooks Thompson FOIL RC .25 .60
27 Trevor Ruffin FOIL RC .20 .50
28 Derrick Alston FOIL RC .20 .50
29 Michael Smith FOIL RC .20 .50
30 Dontonio Wingfield FOIL RC .30 .75
31 Stacey Augmon .15 .40
32 Steve Smith .15 .40
33 Mookie Blaylock .12 .30
34 Grant Long .12 .30
35 Ken Norman .12 .30
36 Dominique Wilkins .25 .60
37 Dino Radja .12 .30
38 Dee Brown .12 .30
39 David Wesley .12 .30
40 Rick Fox .12 .30
41 Alonzo Mourning .25 .60
42 Larry Johnson .20 .50
43 Hersey Hawkins .12 .30
44 Scott Burrell .12 .30
45 Muggsy Bogues .15 .40
46 Scottie Pippen .40 1.00
47 Toni Kukoc .25 .60
48 B.J. Armstrong .12 .30
49 Will Perdue .12 .30
50 Ron Harper .15 .40
51 Mark Price .20 .50
52 Tyrone Hill .12 .30
53 Chris Mills .12 .30
54 John Williams .12 .30
55 Bobby Phills .12 .30
56 Jim Jackson .12 .30
57 Jamal Mashburn .20 .50
58 Popeye Jones .12 .30
59 Roy Tarpley .12 .30
60 Lorenzo Williams .12 .30
61 Mahmoud Abdul-Rauf .12 .30
62 Rodney Rogers .12 .30
63 Bryant Stith .12 .30
64 Dikembe Mutombo .20 .50
65 Robert Pack .12 .30
66 Joe Dumars .20 .50
67 Terry Mills .12 .30
68 Oliver Miller .12 .30
69 Lindsey Hunter .12 .30
70 Mark West .12 .30
71 Latrell Sprewell .25 .60
72 Tim Hardaway .20 .50
73 Ricky Pierce .12 .30
74 Rony Seikaly .12 .30
75 Tom Gugliotta .12 .30
76 Hakeem Olajuwon .25 .60
77 Clyde Drexler .25 .60
78 Vernon Maxwell .12 .30
79 Robert Horry .20 .50
80 Sam Cassell .20 .50
81 Reggie Miller .25 .60
82 Rik Smits .15 .40
83 Derrick McKey .12 .30
84 Mark Jackson .15 .40
85 Dale Davis .12 .30
86 Loy Vaught .12 .30
87 Terry Dehere .12 .30
88 Malik Sealy .12 .30
89 Pooh Richardson .12 .30
90 Tony Massenburg .12 .30
91 Cedric Ceballos .12 .30
92 Nick Van Exel .20 .50
93 George Lynch .12 .30
94 Vlade Divac .20 .50
95 Elden Campbell .12 .30
96 Glen Rice .20 .50
97 Kevin Willis .12 .30
98 Billy Owens .12 .30
99 Bimbo Coles .12 .30
100 Harold Miner .12 .30
101 Vin Baker .20 .50
102 Todd Day .12 .30
103 Marty Conlon .12 .30
104 Lee Mayberry .12 .30
105 Eric Murdock .12 .30
106 Isaiah Rider .20 .50
107 Doug West .12 .30
108 Christian Laettner .15 .40
109 Sean Rooks .12 .30
110 Stacey King .12 .30
111 Derrick Coleman .15 .40
112 Kenny Anderson .15 .40
113 Chris Morris .12 .30
114 Armon Gilliam .12 .30
115 Benoit Benjamin .12 .30
116 Patrick Ewing .25 .60
117 Charles Oakley .15 .40
118 John Starks .15 .40
119 Derek Harper .15 .40
120 Charles Smith .12 .30
121 Shaquille O'Neal .50 1.25
122 Anfernee Hardaway .30 .75
123 Nick Anderson .12 .30
124 Horace Grant .15 .40
125 Donald Royal .12 .30
126 Clarence Weatherspoon .12 .30
127 Dana Barros .12 .30
128 Jeff Malone .12 .30
129 Willie Burton .12 .30
130 Shawn Bradley .12 .30
131 Charles Barkley .30 .75
132 Kevin Johnson .20 .50
133 Danny Manning .15 .40
134 Dan Majerle .20 .50
135 A.C. Green .15 .40
136 Otis Thorpe .12 .30
137 Clifford Robinson .12 .30
138 Rod Strickland .12 .30
139 Buck Williams .12 .30
140 James Robinson .12 .30
141 Mitch Richmond .20 .50
142 Walt Williams .12 .30
143 Olden Polynice .12 .30
144 Spud Webb .15 .40
145 Duane Causwell .12 .30
146 David Robinson .30 .75
147 Dennis Rodman .40 1.00
148 Sean Elliott .20 .50
149 Avery Johnson .15 .40
150 J.R. Reid .12 .30
151 Shawn Kemp .20 .50
152 Gary Payton .20 .50
153 Detlef Schrempf .20 .50
154 Nate McMillan .12 .30
155 Kendall Gill .12 .30
156 Karl Malone .25 .60
157 John Stockton .25 .60
158 Jeff Hornacek .15 .40
159 Felton Spencer .12 .30
160 David Benoit .12 .30
161 Chris Webber .30 .75
162 Rex Chapman .12 .30
163 Don MacLean .12 .30
164 Calbert Cheaney .12 .30
165 Scott Skiles .12 .30
P23 M.Jordan Promo 4.00 10.00
MJ1R M.Jordan Red 2.50 6.00
MJ1S M.Jordan Silver 8.00 20.00

1994-95 SP Die Cuts

COMPLETE SET (165) 20.00 50.00
*STARS: 1X TO 2.5X BASE CARD HI
*RCs: .75X TO 2X BASE HI
ONE PER PACK

1994-95 SP Holoviews

Cards from this 36-card standard size set were randomly inserted in packs at a rate of one in five. The set features a mixture of NBA stars coupled with a wide selection of 1994-95 rookies. The fronts feature color action photos with a hologram of company spokesperson Shawn Kemp on the left with the player's name in silver just to the right. In addition, a holographic head shot of each player is placed in the lower left corner. The backs have a black and white photo on the right and player information on the left.

COMPLETE SET (36) 12.00 30.00
STATED ODDS 1:5
*DIE CUTS: 1X TO 2.5X HI COLUMN
DIE CUTS: STATED ODDS 1:75
PC1 Eric Montross .40 1.00
PC2 Dominique Wilkins 1.00 2.50
PC3 Larry Johnson .75 2.00
PC4 Dickey Simpkins .40 1.00
PC5 Jalen Rose 1.25 3.00
PC6 Latrell Sprewell 1.00 2.50
PC7 Carlos Rogers .40 1.00
PC8 Lamond Murray .50 1.25
PC9 Eddie Jones 1.50 4.00
PC10 Cedric Ceballos .50 1.25
PC11 Khalid Reeves .40 1.00
PC12 Glenn Robinson 1.00 2.50
PC13 Christian Laettner .60 1.50
PC14 Derrick Coleman .60 1.50
PC15 Vin Baker .50 1.25
PC16 Donyell Marshall .50 1.25
PC17 Kenny Anderson .60 1.50
PC18 Sharone Wright .40 1.00
PC19 Wesley Person .50 1.25
PC20 Brian Grant .75 2.00
PC21 Mitch Richmond .75 2.00
PC22 Shawn Kemp .75 2.00
PC23 Gary Payton .75 2.00
PC24 Juwan Howard .75 2.00
PC25 Stacey Augmon .60 1.50
PC26 Aaron McKie .50 1.25
PC27 Clifford Rozier .30 .75
PC28 Eric Piatkowski .60 1.50
PC29 Shaquille O'Neal 3.00 8.00
PC30 Charlie Ward .50 1.25
PC31 Monty Williams .40 1.00
PC32 Jason Kidd 2.50 6.00
PC33 Bill Curley .30 .75
PC34 Grant Hill 2.50 6.00
PC35 Jamal Mashburn .75 2.00
PC36 Nick Van Exel .75 2.00

1995 SP

This 150-card set is the inaugural SP brand issue from Upper Deck. The set is made up of seven sub-sets: Cup Contenders (1-30), Drivers (31-74), Cars (75-116), Premier Prospects (117-120), Owners (121-135) and Crew Chiefs (136-150). The product came seven cards per pack, 32 packs per box and six boxes per case. The original suggested retail price per pack was $3.99 and the product was available only through hobby outlets. At the time it was announced that SP Racing was the lowest produced SP product across the 5 major sports that have that brand. Also, SP was delayed a month from its original release date so that it could include a special Comebacks Hologram insert card of Ernie Irvan and Michael Jordan. The Comebacks card could be found one per 192 packs.

COMPLETE SET (150) 10.00 25.00
CB1 E.Irvan Michael Jordan 8.00 20.00

1995-96 SP

The 1995-96 Upper Deck SP set was issued in one series totalling 167 cards. The 8-card packs, distributed exclusively to hobby outlets, retailed for $4.19 each. The first 147 cards are grouped by team alphabetically by city. The set ends with the rookie-based subset Premier Prospects (148-167) which feature a totally different design to the basic cards. Card stock thickness was upgraded from the previous year. A special Hakeem Olajuwon Commemorative card (celebrating his achievement of becoming only the ninth player in NBA history to score 20,000 points and grab 10,000 rebounds) was randomly seeded into 1 in every 359 packs. Rookie Cards of note in this set include Michael Finley, Kevin Garnett, Antonio McDyess, Jerry Stackhouse and Damon Stoudamire.

COMPLETE SET (167) 12.00 30.00
C1: STATED ODDS 1:359
1 Stacey Augmon .20 .50
2 Mookie Blaylock .15 .40
3 Andrew Lang .15 .40
4 Steve Smith .20 .50
5 Spud Webb .20 .50
6 Dana Barros .15 .40
7 Dee Brown .15 .40
8 Todd Day .15 .40
9 Rick Fox .15 .40
10 Eric Montross .15 .40
11 Dino Radja .15 .40
12 Kenny Anderson .20 .50
13 Scott Burrell .15 .40
14 Dell Curry .15 .40
15 Matt Geiger .15 .40
16 Larry Johnson .25 .60
17 Glen Rice .25 .60
18 Steve Kerr .20 .50
19 Toni Kukoc .25 .60
20 Luc Longley .20 .50
21 Scottie Pippen .40 1.00
22 Dennis Rodman .50 1.25
23 Michael Jordan 2.00 5.00
24 Terrell Brandon .15 .40
25 Michael Cage .15 .40
26 Danny Ferry .15 .40
27 Chris Mills .15 .40
28 Bobby Phills .15 .40
29 Tony Dumas .15 .40
30 Jim Jackson .15 .40
31 Popeye Jones .15 .40
32 Jason Kidd .40 1.00
33 Jamal Mashburn .25 .60
34 Mahmoud Abdul-Rauf .15 .40
35 LaPhonso Ellis .15 .40
36 Dikembe Mutombo .25 .60
37 Jalen Rose .30 .75
38 Bryant Stith .15 .40
39 Joe Dumars .25 .60
40 Grant Hill .40 1.00
41 Lindsey Hunter .15 .40
42 Allan Houston .20 .50
43 Otis Thorpe .15 .40
44 B.J. Armstrong .15 .40
45 Tim Hardaway .25 .60
46 Chris Mullin .25 .60
47 Latrell Sprewell .25 .60
48 Rony Seikaly .15 .40
49 Sam Cassell .25 .60
50 Clyde Drexler .30 .75
51 Robert Horry .20 .50
52 Hakeem Olajuwon .30 .75
53 Kenny Smith .20 .50
54 Dale Davis .15 .40
55 Derrick McKey .15 .40
56 Reggie Miller .30 .75
57 Ricky Pierce .15 .40
58 Rik Smits .20 .50
59 Lamond Murray .15 .40
60 Rodney Rogers .15 .40
61 Malik Sealy .15 .40
62 Loy Vaught .15 .40
63 Brian Williams .15 .40
64 Elden Campbell .15 .40
65 Cedric Ceballos .15 .40
66 Magic Johnson .60 1.50
67 Eddie Jones .25 .60
68 Nick Van Exel .25 .60
69 Bimbo Coles .15 .40
70 Alonzo Mourning .30 .75
71 Billy Owens .15 .40
72 Kevin Willis .15 .40
73 Vin Baker .20 .50
74 Benoit Benjamin .15 .40
75 Sherman Douglas .15 .40
76 Lee Mayberry .15 .40
77 Glenn Robinson .20 .50
78 Tom Gugliotta .15 .40
79 Christian Laettner .20 .50
80 Sam Mitchell .15 .40
81 Terry Porter .15 .40
82 Isaiah Rider .25 .60
83 Shawn Bradley .15 .40
84 P.J. Brown .15 .40
85 Kendall Gill .15 .40
86 Armon Gilliam .15 .40
87 Jayson Williams .15 .40
88 Patrick Ewing .30 .75
89 Derek Harper .20 .50
90 Anthony Mason .15 .40
91 Charles Oakley .20 .50
92 John Starks .20 .50
93 Nick Anderson .15 .40
94 Horace Grant .20 .50
95 Anfernee Hardaway .40 1.00
96 Shaquille O'Neal .60 1.50
97 Dennis Scott .15 .40
98 Derrick Coleman .20 .50
99 Vernon Maxwell .15 .40
100 Trevor Ruffin .15 .40
101 Clarence Weatherspoon .15 .40
102 Sharone Wright .15 .40
103 Charles Barkley .40 1.00
104 A.C. Green .20 .50
105 Kevin Johnson .25 .60
106 Wesley Person .15 .40
107 John Williams .15 .40
108 Chris Dudley .15 .40
109 Harvey Grant .15 .40
110 Aaron McKie .15 .40
111 Clifford Robinson .15 .40
112 Rod Strickland .15 .40
113 Brian Grant .20 .50
114 Sarunas Marciulionis .15 .40
115 Olden Polynice .15 .40
116 Mitch Richmond .25 .60
117 Walt Williams .15 .40
118 Vinny Del Negro .15 .40
119 Sean Elliott .25 .60
120 Avery Johnson .20 .50
121 Chuck Person .20 .50
122 David Robinson .40 1.00
123 Hersey Hawkins .15 .40
124 Shawn Kemp .25 .60
125 Gary Payton .25 .60
126 Sam Perkins .15 .40
127 Detlef Schrempf .25 .60
128 Oliver Miller .15 .40
129 Tracy Murray .15 .40
130 Ed Pinckney .15 .40
131 Alvin Robertson .15 .40
132 Zan Tabak .15 .40
133 Jeff Hornacek .20 .50
134 Adam Keefe .15 .40
135 Karl Malone .30 .75
136 Chris Morris .15 .40
137 John Stockton .30 .75
138 Greg Anthony .15 .40
139 Blue Edwards .15 .40
140 Kenny Gattison .15 .40
141 Chris King .15 .40
142 Byron Scott .20 .50
143 Calbert Cheaney .15 .40
144 Juwan Howard .25 .60
145 Gheorghe Muresan .15 .40
146 Robert Pack .15 .40
147 Chris Webber .30 .75
148 Alan Henderson RC .25 .60
149 Eric Williams RC .25 .60
150 George Zidek RC .20 .50
151 Bob Sura RC .20 .50
152 Antonio McDyess RC .30 .75
153 Theo Ratliff RC .40 1.00
154 Joe Smith RC .30 .75
155 Brent Barry RC .40 1.00
156 Sasha Danilovic RC .25 .60
157 Kurt Thomas RC .25 .60
158 Shawn Respert RC .20 .50
159 Kevin Garnett RC 5.00 12.00
160 Ed O'Bannon RC .20 .50
161 Jerry Stackhouse RC 1.50 4.00
162 Michael Finley RC .75 2.00
163 Arvydas Sabonis RC .50 1.25
164 Cory Alexander RC .25 .60
165 Damon Stoudamire RC .60 1.50
166 Bryant Reeves RC .20 .50
167 Rasheed Wallace RC .75 2.00
C1 H.Olajuwon Comm. 5.00 12.00
P23 Michael Jordan PROMO 4.00 10.00

1995-96 SP All-Stars

Randomly inserted in packs at a rate of one in five, this 30-card set features the 24 players from the 1996 NBA All-Star game in addition to six potential future All-Star athletes. Each card features a double die-cut design and silver foil stamping.

COMPLETE SET (30) 15.00 40.00
STATED ODDS 1:5
*GOLD: 2.5X TO 6X HI COLUMN
GOLD: STATED ODDS 1:61
AS1 Anfernee Hardaway 1.00 2.50
AS2 Michael Jordan 6.00 15.00
AS3 Grant Hill 1.00 2.50
AS4 Scottie Pippen 1.00 2.50
AS5 Shaquille O'Neal 1.50 4.00
AS6 Vin Baker .50 1.25
AS7 Terrell Brandon .40 1.00
AS8 Patrick Ewing .75 2.00
AS9 Juwan Howard .60 1.50
AS10 Reggie Miller .75 2.00
AS11 Alonzo Mourning .75 2.00
AS12 Glen Rice .60 1.50
AS13 Clyde Drexler .75 2.00
AS14 Jason Kidd 1.00 2.50
AS15 Charles Barkley 1.00 2.50
AS16 Shawn Kemp .60 1.50
AS17 Hakeem Olajuwon .75 2.00
AS18 Sean Elliott .60 1.50
AS19 Karl Malone .75 2.00
AS20 Dikembe Mutombo .60 1.50
AS21 Gary Payton .60 1.50
AS22 Mitch Richmond .60 1.50
AS23 David Robinson 1.00 2.50
AS24 John Stockton .75 2.00
AS25 Jerry Stackhouse 1.00 2.50
AS26 Damon Stoudamire .75 2.00
AS27 Rasheed Wallace 1.00 2.50
AS28 Kevin Garnett 2.50 6.00
AS29 Antonio McDyess .40 1.00
AS30 Joe Smith .40 1.00

1995-96 SP Holoviews

Randomly inserted in packs at a rate of one in seven, this 40-card set features a selection of youngsters and veteran stars from all 29 teams. Each card utilizes the special Holoview technology and features four holographic head shot images in the background.

COMPLETE SET (40) 40.00 100.00
STATED ODDS 1:7
PC1 Mookie Blaylock 1.00 2.50
PC2 Eric Williams .75 2.00
PC3 Larry Johnson 1.50 4.00
PC4 George Zidek .60 1.50
PC5 Michael Jordan 15.00 40.00
PC6 Bob Sura .60 1.50
PC7 Jason Kidd 2.50 6.00
PC8 Cherokee Parks .60 1.50
PC9 Antonio McDyess 1.00 2.50
PC10 Grant Hill 2.50 6.00
PC11 Theo Ratliff 1.25 3.00
PC12 Joe Smith 1.00 2.50
PC13 Latrell Sprewell 1.50 4.00
PC14 Hakeem Olajuwon 2.00 5.00
PC15 Travis Best .75 2.00
PC16 Brent Barry 1.25 3.00
PC17 Nick Van Exel 1.50 4.00
PC18 Kurt Thomas .75 2.00
PC19 Shawn Respert .60 1.50
PC20 Glenn Robinson 1.25 3.00
PC21 Christian Laettner 1.25 3.00
PC22 Ed O'Bannon .60 1.50
PC23 Patrick Ewing 2.00 5.00
PC24 Anfernee Hardaway 2.50 6.00
PC25 Shaquille O'Neal 4.00 10.00
PC26 Jerry Stackhouse 2.50 6.00
PC27 Mario Bennett .60 1.50
PC28 Michael Finley 2.50 6.00
PC29 Randolph Childress .60 1.50
PC30 Brian Grant 1.25 3.00
PC31 Mitch Richmond 1.50 4.00
PC32 Cory Alexander .75 2.00
PC33 David Robinson 2.50 6.00
PC34 Sherrell Ford .60 1.50
PC35 Shawn Kemp 1.50 4.00
PC36 Damon Stoudamire 2.00 5.00
PC37 Greg Ostertag .75 2.00
PC38 Bryant Reeves .60 1.50
PC39 Juwan Howard 1.50 4.00
PC40 Rasheed Wallace 2.50 6.00

1995-96 SP Holoviews Die Cuts

*DIE CUTS: 1.5X TO 4X HI COLUMN
STATED ODDS 1:76
PC13 Latrell Sprewell 8.00 20.00

1995-96 SP Jordan Collection

Randomly inserted at a rate of one in every 29 packs, these four cards cards continue the collection of Michael Jordan commemorative cards issued across all of Upper Deck's various 1995-96 brands.

COMPLETE SET (4) 12.00 30.00
COMMON CARD (JC17-JC20) 4.00 10.00
RANDOM INSERT IN PACKS

1996-97 SP

The 1996-97 SP set was issued in one series totalling 146 cards. The set contains the topical subset Premier Prospects (127-146). Cards were issued in 8-card packs with a suggested retail price of $3.99. Card fronts feature a player shot with his name running horizontally across the bottom and the player's team running vertically across the side.

COMPLETE SET (146) 17.50 35.00
RC's CONDITION SENSITIVE
1 Mookie Blaylock .15 .40
2 Christian Laettner .20 .50
3 Dikembe Mutombo .25 .60
4 Steve Smith .20 .50
5 Dana Barros .15 .40
6 Rick Fox .15 .40
7 Dino Radja .15 .40
8 Eric Williams .15 .40
9 Dell Curry .15 .40
10 Vlade Divac .25 .60
11 Anthony Mason .15 .40
12 Glen Rice .25 .60
13 Scottie Pippen .40 1.00
14 Toni Kukoc .25 .60
15 Luc Longley .20 .50
16 Michael Jordan 2.00 5.00
17 Dennis Rodman .50 1.25
18 Terrell Brandon .15 .40
19 Tyrone Hill .15 .40
20 Bobby Phills .15 .40
21 Bob Sura .15 .40
22 Chris Gatling .15 .40
23 Jim Jackson .15 .40
24 Sam Cassell .20 .50
25 Jamal Mashburn .20 .50
26 Dale Ellis .15 .40
27 LaPhonso Ellis .15 .40
28 Mark Jackson .20 .50
29 Antonio McDyess .25 .60
30 Bryant Stith .15 .40
31 Joe Dumars .25 .60
32 Grant Hill .40 1.00
33 Lindsey Hunter .15 .40
34 Otis Thorpe .15 .40
35 Chris Mullin .25 .60
36 Mark Price .25 .60
37 Joe Smith .20 .50
38 Latrell Sprewell .25 .60
39 Charles Barkley .40 1.00
40 Clyde Drexler .30 .75
41 Mario Elie .15 .40
42 Hakeem Olajuwon .30 .75
43 Travis Best .15 .40
44 Dale Davis .15 .40
45 Reggie Miller .30 .75
46 Rik Smits .20 .50
47 Pooh Richardson .15 .40
48 Rodney Rogers .15 .40
49 Malik Sealy .15 .40
50 Loy Vaught .15 .40
51 Elden Campbell .15 .40
52 Robert Horry .20 .50
53 Eddie Jones .25 .60
54 Shaquille O'Neal .60 1.50
55 Nick Van Exel .25 .60
56 Sasha Danilovic .15 .40
57 Tim Hardaway .25 .60
58 Dan Majerle .25 .60
59 Alonzo Mourning .30 .75
60 Vin Baker .20 .50
61 Sherman Douglas .15 .40
62 Armon Gilliam .15 .40
63 Glenn Robinson .20 .50
64 Kevin Garnett .60 1.50
65 Tom Gugliotta .15 .40
66 Terry Porter .15 .40
67 Doug West .15 .40
68 Shawn Bradley .15 .40
69 Kendall Gill .15 .40
70 Robert Pack .15 .40
71 Jayson Williams .15 .40
72 Chris Childs .15 .40
73 Patrick Ewing .30 .75
74 Allan Houston .20 .50
75 Larry Johnson .25 .60
76 John Starks .20 .50
77 Nick Anderson .15 .40
78 Horace Grant .20 .50
79 Anfernee Hardaway .40 1.00
80 Dennis Scott .15 .40
81 Derrick Coleman .20 .50
82 Mark Davis .15 .40
83 Jerry Stackhouse .30 .75
84 Clarence Weatherspoon .15 .40
85 Cedric Ceballos .15 .40
86 Kevin Johnson .25 .60
87 Jason Kidd .40 1.00
88 Danny Manning .20 .50
89 Wesley Person .15 .40
90 Kenny Anderson .20 .50
91 Isaiah Rider .20 .50
92 Clifford Robinson .15 .40
93 Arvydas Sabonis .20 .50
94 Rasheed Wallace .30 .75
95 Mahmoud Abdul-Rauf .15 .40
96 Brian Grant .20 .50
97 Olden Polynice .15 .40
98 Mitch Richmond .25 .60
99 Corliss Williamson .15 .40
100 Sean Elliott .25 .60
101 Avery Johnson .20 .50
102 David Robinson .40 1.00
103 Dominique Wilkins .30 .75
104 Hersey Hawkins .15 .40
105 Jim McIlvaine .15 .40
106 Shawn Kemp .25 .60
107 Gary Payton .25 .60
108 Detlef Schrempf .25 .60
109 Doug Christie .15 .40
110 Popeye Jones .15 .40
111 Damon Stoudamire .20 .50
112 Walt Williams .15 .40
113 Jeff Hornacek .20 .50
114 Karl Malone .30 .75
115 Greg Ostertag .15 .40
116 Bryon Russell .15 .40
117 John Stockton .30 .75
118 Greg Anthony .15 .40
119 Blue Edwards .15 .40
120 Anthony Peeler .15 .40
121 Bryant Reeves .15 .40
122 Calbert Cheaney .15 .40
123 Juwan Howard .20 .50
124 Gheorghe Muresan .15 .40
125 Rod Strickland .15 .40
126 Chris Webber .30 .75
127 Antoine Walker RC .60 1.50
128 Tony Delk RC .40 1.00
129 Vitaly Potapenko RC .30 .75
130 Samaki Walker RC .30 .75
131 Todd Fuller RC .25 .60
132 Erick Dampier RC .40 1.00
133 Lorenzen Wright RC .30 .75
134 Kobe Bryant RC 6.00 15.00
135 Derek Fisher RC .50 1.25
136 Ray Allen RC 2.00 5.00
137 Stephon Marbury RC 1.00 2.50
138 Kerry Kittles RC .40 1.00
139 Walter McCarty RC .40 1.00
140 John Wallace RC .40 1.00
141 Allen Iverson RC 2.50 6.00
142 Steve Nash RC 3.00 8.00
143 Jermaine O'Neal RC .60 1.50
144 Marcus Camby RC .60 1.50
145 Shareef Abdur-Rahim RC .60 1.50
146 Roy Rogers RC .30 .75
S16 Michael Jordan Sample 2.50 6.00

1996-97 SP Game Film

Randomly inserted in packs at a rate of one in 120, this 10-card set uses slide photography and video film to capture the moves of each particular player. Card backs contain a "GF" prefix.

COMPLETE SET (10) 75.00 200.00
STATED ODDS 1:120
GF1 Michael Jordan 40.00 100.00
GF2 Kevin Garnett 10.00 25.00
GF3 Charles Barkley 6.00 15.00
GF4 Anfernee Hardaway 6.00 15.00
GF5 Shaquille O'Neal 12.00 30.00
GF6 Jim Jackson 2.50 6.00
GF7 Dennis Rodman 8.00 20.00
GF8 Alonzo Mourning 5.00 12.00
GF9 Grant Hill 6.00 15.00
GF10 Shawn Kemp 5.00 12.00

1996-97 SP Holoviews

Randomly inserted in packs at a rate of one in 10, this 40-card set features the top NBA players with Holoview technology. Unlike past years, there is no die-cut parallel. Card backs are numbered with a "PC" prefix.

COMPLETE SET (40) 75.00 150.00
STATED ODDS 1:10
PC1 Mookie Blaylock 1.00 2.50
PC2 Antoine Walker 1.50 4.00
PC3 Eric Williams 1.00 2.50
PC4 Tony Delk 1.00 2.50
PC5 Michael Jordan 25.00 60.00
PC6 Dennis Rodman 3.00 8.00
PC7 Vitaly Potapenko .75 2.00
PC8 Bob Sura 1.00 2.50
PC9 Jamal Mashburn 1.25 3.00
PC10 Antonio McDyess 1.50 4.00
PC11 Grant Hill 2.50 6.00
PC12 Joe Smith 1.25 3.00
PC13 Latrell Sprewell 1.50 4.00
PC14 Charles Barkley 2.50 6.00
PC15 Hakeem Olajuwon 2.00 5.00
PC16 Erick Dampier 1.00 2.50
PC17 Lorenzen Wright .75 2.00
PC18 Kobe Bryant 30.00 80.00
PC19 Shaquille O'Neal 4.00 10.00
PC20 Alonzo Mourning 2.00 5.00
PC21 Ray Allen 4.00 10.00
PC22 Kevin Garnett 4.00 10.00
PC23 Stephon Marbury 2.50 6.00
PC24 Kerry Kittles 1.00 2.50
PC25 Walter McCarty 1.00 2.50
PC26 John Wallace 1.00 2.50
PC27 Anfernee Hardaway 2.50 6.00
PC28 Allen Iverson 5.00 12.00
PC29 Jerry Stackhouse 2.00 5.00
PC30 Steve Nash 5.00 12.00
PC31 Jermaine O'Neal 1.50 4.00
PC32 Brian Grant 1.25 3.00
PC33 Mitch Richmond 1.50 4.00
PC34 David Robinson 2.50 6.00
PC35 Shawn Kemp 1.50 4.00
PC36 Marcus Camby 1.50 4.00
PC37 Damon Stoudamire 1.25 3.00
PC38 John Stockton 2.00 5.00
PC39 Shareef Abdur-Rahim 1.50 4.00
PC40 Juwan Howard 1.25 3.00

1996-97 SP Inside Info

Inserted as a chiptopper at one per box, this 17-card set features several action and portrait photos of the players. In addition, each card has a special slide-out portion containing more information. The basic set contains 16 cards and the 17th is for Michael Jordan commemorating his 25,000 point.

COMPLETE SET (17) 50.00 120.00
ONE PER BOX
*GOLD: 1.5X TO 4X HI COLUMN
GOLD: RANDOM INSERTS IN BOXES
IN1 Charles Barkley 4.00 10.00
IN2 Kevin Garnett 6.00 15.00
IN3 Anfernee Hardaway 4.00 10.00
IN4 Grant Hill 4.00 10.00
IN5 Allen Iverson 6.00 15.00
IN6 Jason Kidd 4.00 10.00
IN7 Shawn Kemp 2.50 6.00
IN8 Antonio McDyess 2.50 6.00
IN9 Dikembe Mutombo 2.50 6.00
IN10 Shaquille O'Neal 6.00 15.00
IN11 Hakeem Olajuwon 3.00 8.00
IN12 Dennis Rodman 5.00 12.00
IN13 Jerry Stackhouse 3.00 8.00
IN14 John Stockton 4.00 10.00
IN15 Damon Stoudamire 2.00 5.00
IN16 Chris Webber 3.00 8.00
IN17 Michael Jordan 25K 20.00 50.00

1996-97 SP Rookie Jumbos

Released in special retail outlets, this 20-card set featured 5" by 7" cards of the rookie subset from 96-97 SP. The set originally carried a retail price of $19.99.

COMPLETE SET (20) 12.00 30.00
1 Antoine Walker 1.00 2.50
2 Tony Delk .60 1.50
3 Vitaly Potapenko .50 1.25
4 Samaki Walker .50 1.25
5 Todd Fuller .40 1.00
6 Erick Dampier .60 1.50
7 Lorenzen Wright .50 1.25
8 Kobe Bryant 12.50 30.00
9 Derek Fisher .75 2.00
10 Ray Allen 2.50 6.00
11 Stephon Marbury 1.50 4.00
12 Kerry Kittles .60 1.50
13 Walter McCarty .60 1.50
14 John Wallace .60 1.50
15 Allen Iverson 3.00 8.00
16 Steve Nash 3.00 8.00
17 Jermaine O'Neal 1.00 2.50
18 Marcus Camby 1.00 2.50
19 Shareef Abdur-Rahim 1.00 2.50
20 Roy Rogers .50 1.25

1996-97 SP SPx Force

Randomly inserted in packs at a rate of one in 360, this 5-card set features the holoview technology of four players per card divided into particular themes: Scoring, Rebounding, Playmakers, Defenders and All-Around Talents. In addition, the All-Around Talents card also came in four different autographed versions, with each player individually signing 100 cards. Each of the autographed cards are sequentially numbered.

STATED ODDS 1:360
F1 MJ/Stack/Mitch/Spree 30.00 80.00
F2 Kemp/Rod/Barkley/Juwan 15.00 40.00
F3 Blay/VanX/Marbury/Stoud 10.00 25.00
F4 Camby/Damp/Penny/McD 10.00 25.00
F5 MJ/Penny/Kemp/Stoud 40.00 100.00
A1 Anfernee Hardaway AU 125.00 250.00
A2 Michael Jordan AU 1200.00 2200.00
A3 Shawn Kemp AU 175.00 350.00
A4 Damon Stoudamire AU 75.00 150.00

2012 SP

COMP.SET w/o SP's (50) 8.00 20.00
51-80 STATED ODDS 1:4
61 Michael Jordan PS 3.00 8.00

2012 SP Blue

*BLUE: .5X TO 1.2X BASIC CARDS
*BLUE PS (51-80): 1.5X TO 4X BASIC CARDS
STATED ODDS 1:2 RETAIL
PS (51-80) STATED ODDS 1:48 RETAIL

2014 SP

COMP.SET w/o SPs (50) 8.00 20.00
*1-50 RETAIL: .4X TO 1X SP AUTH.
*51-75 AM RETAIL: .4X TO 1X SP AUTH.

2014 SP Blue

*1-50 BLUE: .6X TO 1.5X SP AUTHENTIC
1-50 STATED ODDS 1:3
*1-50 BLUE: .6X TO 1.5X SP AUTHENTIC
51-68 STATED ODDS 1:33
*1-50 BLUE: .6X TO 1.5X SP AUTHENTIC
69-75 STATED ODDS 1:86

1997-98 SP Authentic

This is the first year that the brand name SP has changed over to SP Authentic, due to the heavy inclusion of autographs and memorabilia. The set size is 176 cards that were issued in five-card packs which carried a suggested retail price of $4.99.

COMPLETE SET (176) 60.00 120.00
RCs CONDITION SENSITIVE !
1 Steve Smith .30 .75
2 Dikembe Mutombo .40 1.00
3 Christian Laettner .30 .75
4 Mookie Blaylock .25 .60
5 Alan Henderson .25 .60
6 Antoine Walker .40 1.00
7 Ron Mercer RC 1.00 2.50
8 Walter McCarty .25 .60
9 Kenny Anderson .30 .75
10 Travis Knight .25 .60
11 Dana Barros .25 .60
12 Glen Rice .40 1.00
13 Vlade Divac .40 1.00
14 Dell Curry .25 .60
15 David Wesley .25 .60
16 Bobby Phills .25 .60
17 Anthony Mason .25 .60
18 Toni Kukoc .40 1.00
19 Dennis Rodman .75 2.00
20 Ron Harper .30 .75
21 Steve Kerr .30 .75
22 Scottie Pippen .60 1.50
23 Michael Jordan 3.00 8.00
24 Shawn Kemp .40 1.00
25 Wesley Person .25 .60
26 Derek Anderson RC .75 2.00
27 Zydrunas Ilgauskas .40 1.00
28 Brevin Knight RC .75 2.00
29 Michael Finley .40 1.00
30 Shawn Bradley .25 .60
31 A.C. Green .30 .75
32 Hubert Davis .25 .60
33 Dennis Scott .25 .60
34 Tony Battie RC .75 2.00
35 Bobby Jackson RC 1.00 2.50
36 LaPhonso Ellis .25 .60
37 Bryant Stith .25 .60
38 Dean Garrett .25 .60
39 Danny Fortson RC .75 2.00
40 Grant Hill .60 1.50
41 Brian Williams .25 .60
42 Lindsey Hunter .25 .60
43 Malik Sealy .25 .60
44 Jerry Stackhouse .40 1.00
45 Muggsy Bogues .30 .75
46 Joe Smith .30 .75
47 Donyell Marshall .25 .60
48 Erick Dampier .25 .60
49 Bimbo Coles .25 .60
50 Charles Barkley .60 1.50
51 Hakeem Olajuwon .50 1.25
52 Clyde Drexler .50 1.25
53 Kevin Willis .25 .60
54 Mario Elie .25 .60
55 Reggie Miller .50 1.25
56 Rik Smits .30 .75
57 Chris Mullin .40 1.00
58 Antonio Davis .25 .60
59 Dale Davis .25 .60
60 Mark Jackson .30 .75
61 Brent Barry .30 .75
62 Loy Vaught .25 .60
63 Rodney Rogers .25 .60
64 Lamond Murray .25 .60
65 Maurice Taylor RC .75 2.00
66 Shaquille O'Neal 1.00 2.50
67 Eddie Jones .40 1.00
68 Kobe Bryant 2.00 5.00
69 Nick Van Exel .30 .75
70 Robert Horry .30 .75
71 Tim Hardaway .40 1.00
72 Jamal Mashburn .30 .75
73 Alonzo Mourning .50 1.25
74 Isaac Austin .25 .60
75 P.J. Brown .25 .60
76 Ray Allen .50 1.25
77 Glenn Robinson .30 .75
78 Ervin Johnson .25 .60
79 Terrell Brandon .25 .60
80 Tyrone Hill .25 .60
81 Stephon Marbury .50 1.25
82 Kevin Garnett .60 1.50
83 Tom Gugliotta .25 .60
84 Chris Carr .25 .60
85 Cherokee Parks .25 .60
86 Sam Cassell .30 .75
87 Chris Gatling .25 .60
88 Kendall Gill .25 .60
89 Keith Van Horn RC 1.25 3.00
90 Jayson Williams .25 .60
91 Kerry Kittles .25 .60
92 Patrick Ewing .50 1.25
93 Larry Johnson .40 1.00
94 Chris Childs .25 .60
95 John Starks .30 .75
96 Charles Oakley .30 .75
97 Allan Houston .30 .75
98 Mark Price .40 1.00
99 Anfernee Hardaway .60 1.50
100 Rony Seikaly .25 .60
101 Horace Grant .30 .75
102 Bo Outlaw .25 .60
103 Clarence Weatherspoon .25 .60
104 Allen Iverson .75 2.00
105 Jim Jackson .25 .60
106 Theo Ratliff .30 .75
107 Tim Thomas RC 1.00 2.50
108 Danny Manning .30 .75
109 Jason Kidd .60 1.50
110 Kevin Johnson .40 1.00
111 Rex Chapman .25 .60
112 Clifford Robinson .25 .60
113 Antonio McDyess .30 .75
114 Damon Stoudamire .30 .75
115 Isaiah Rider .30 .75
116 Arvydas Sabonis .30 .75
117 Rasheed Wallace .40 1.00
118 Brian Grant .25 .60
119 Gary Trent .25 .60
120 Mitch Richmond .40 1.00
121 Corliss Williamson .25 .60
122 Lawrence Funderburke RC .75 2.00
123 Olden Polynice .25 .60
124 Billy Owens .25 .60
125 Avery Johnson .30 .75
126 Sean Elliott .40 1.00
127 David Robinson .60 1.50
128 Tim Duncan RC ! 7.50 15.00
129 Jaren Jackson .25 .60
130 Detlef Schrempf .40 1.00
131 Gary Payton .40 1.00
132 Vin Baker .30 .75
133 Hersey Hawkins .25 .60
134 Dale Ellis .25 .60
135 Sam Perkins .25 .60
136 Marcus Camby .40 1.00
137 John Wallace .25 .60
138 Doug Christie .25 .60
139 Chauncey Billups RC 4.00 10.00
140 Walt Williams .25 .60
141 Karl Malone .50 1.25
142 Bryon Russell .25 .60
143 Jeff Hornacek .30 .75
144 Greg Ostertag .25 .60
145 John Stockton .50 1.25
146 Shandon Anderson .25 .60
147 Shareef Abdur-Rahim .40 1.00
148 Bryant Reeves .25 .60
149 Antonio Daniels RC .75 2.00
150 Otis Thorpe .25 .60
151 Blue Edwards .25 .60
152 Chris Webber .40 1.00
153 Juwan Howard .30 .75
154 Rod Strickland .25 .60
155 Calbert Cheaney .25 .60
156 Tracy Murray .25 .60
157 Chauncey Billups FW 1.25 3.00
158 Ed Gray FW RC .75 2.00
159 Tony Battie FW .40 1.00
160 Keith Van Horn FW .60 1.50
161 Cedric Henderson FW RC .75 2.00
162 Kelvin Cato FW RC .60 1.50
163 Tariq Abdul-Wahad FW RC .60 1.50
164 Derek Anderson FW .40 1.00
165 Tim Duncan FW 2.00 5.00
166 Tracy McGrady FW RC 6.00 15.00
167 Ron Mercer FW .50 1.25
168 Bobby Jackson FW .50 1.25
169 Antonio Daniels FW .40 1.00
170 Zydrunas Ilgauskas FW .40 1.00
171 Maurice Taylor FW .40 1.00
172 Tim Thomas FW .50 1.25
173 Brevin Knight FW .40 1.00
174 Lawrence Funderburke FW .40 1.00
175 Jacque Vaughn FW RC .60 1.50
176 Danny Fortson FW .40 1.00
SPA23 Michael Jordan PROMO 3.00 8.00

1997-98 SP Authentic Authentics

Randomly inserted into packs at an overall rate of one in 288, this 20-card set features redemption cards for various pieces of memorabilia (both signed and unsigned) from Michael Jordan, Anfernee Hardaway and Shawn Kemp. The cards are not numbered and are listed below in alphabetical order by player.

OVERALL STATED ODDS 1:288
A1 Jordan/AU Game/23 1200.00 2000.00
J1 Jordan/Game/100 150.00 300.00
J2 Michael Jordan 150.00 300.00
J3 Michael Jordan 150.00 300.00
J4 Michael Jordan 150.00 300.00
J5 Michael Jordan 150.00 300.00
AH1 Hard/AU Blk.Jsy/100 200.00 350.00
AH2 Hard/AU Blue Jsy/190 125.00 250.00
AH3 Hard/AU SI Cover/300 25.00 50.00
AH4 Hard/8x10 Photo/300 15.00 30.00
MJ1 Jordan/AU Jersey/50 1000.00 2000.00
MJ2 Jordan/AU 16x20/100 450.00 700.00
MJ3 Jordan/2-card/500 35.00 60.00
MJ4 Jordan/8x10/400 35.00 60.00
MJ5 Jordan/Gold Card/250 15.00 40.00
MJ7 Jordan/Poster/200 30.00 80.00
NNO SP Uncut Sheet/200 90.00 150.00
SK1 Kemp/AU Jersey/35 300.00 500.00
SK2 Kemp/AU Photo/104 40.00 80.00
SK3 Kemp/AU Mini-ball/100 40.00 80.00

1997-98 SP Authentic BuyBack

Randomly inserted into packs at a rate of one in 309 packs, this 36-card set features 15 different player autographs on past SP issued cards and/or inserts. Each card is different in regards to how many each player signed and those numbers have been provided by Upper Deck.

STATED ODDS 1:309 PACKS
CARDS NUMBERED BELOW ALPHABETICALLY
PRINT RUNS PROVIDED BY UD
1 S.Abdur-Rahim 96-7/192 20.00 50.00
2 Vin Baker 94-5/17 12.50 30.00
3 Vin Baker 95-6/71 12.50 30.00
4 Vin Baker 95-6AS/83 12.50 30.00
5 Clyde Drexler 94-5/141 30.00 80.00
6 Clyde Drexler 95-6/200 30.00 80.00
7 Clyde Drexler 96-7/63 30.00
8 A.Hardaway 94-5/77 40.00 100.00
9 A.Hardaway 95-6/100 40.00 100.00
10 A.Hardaway 96-7/31 100.00 200.00
11 Tim Hardaway 94-5/126 30.00 80.00
12 Tim Hardaway 95-6/84 30.00 80.00
13 Tim Hardaway 96-7/43 20.00 50.00
14 Juwan Howard 94-5/50 15.00 40.00
15 Juwan Howard 95-6/300 12.50 30.00
16 Juwan Howard 95-6AS/50 12.50 30.00
17 Juwan Howard 96-7/33 12.50 30.00
18 Eddie Jones 94-5/50 25.00 60.00
19 Eddie Jones 95-6/87 20.00 50.00
20 Eddie Jones 96-7/18 20.00 50.00
21 M.Jordan 94-5MJ1R/55 1000.00 2000.00
22 Jason Kidd 94-5/50 75.00 150.00
23 Jason Kidd 95-6/300 50.00 100.00
24 Jason Kidd 95-6AS/43 50.00 100.00
25 Jason Kidd 96-7/43 50.00 100.00
26 Kerry Kittles 96-7/201 12.50 30.00
27 Karl Malone 94-5/187 60.00 120.00
28 Karl Malone 95-6/36 60.00 120.00
29 Glen Rice 95-6AS78 12.50 30.00
30 Glen Rice 96-7/47 12.50 30.00
31 Mitch Richmond 94-5/95 12.50 30.00
32 Mitch Richmond 95-6/83 12.50 30.00
33 Mitch Richmond 96-7/39 12.50 30.00
34 D.Stoudamire 95-6/35 30.00 80.00
35 D.Stoudamire 96-7/36 25.00 60.00
36 Antoine Walker 96-7/132 15.00 40.00

1997-98 SP Authentic Premium Portraits

Randomly inserted into packs at a rate of one in 1,528, this seven-card set features an autograph from some of the top stars in the NBA. Card backs are numbered with the player's initials.

STATED ODDS 1:1,528
DP Damon Stoudamire 25.00 60.00
EP Eddie Jones 40.00 100.00
JP Jason Kidd 100.00 200.00
KP Kerry Kittles 15.00 40.00
MP Dikembe Mutombo 30.00 80.00
RP Glen Rice 25.00 60.00
TP Tim Hardaway 15.00 40.00

1997-98 SP Authentic Profiles 1

Randomly inserted into packs at a rate of one in three, this 40-card set profiles some of the leagues best players. Card backs are numbered with a "P" prefix.

COMPLETE SET (40) 30.00 60.00
STATED ODDS 1:3
*PRO.2: 1.25X TO 3X HI COLUMN
PRO.2: STATED ODDS 1:12
P1 Michael Jordan 4.00 10.00
P2 Glen Rice .50 1.25
P3 Brent Barry .40 1.00
P4 LaPhonso Ellis .30 .75
P5 Allen Iverson 1.00 2.50
P6 Dikembe Mutombo .50 1.25
P7 Charles Barkley .75 2.00
P8 Antoine Walker .50 1.25
P9 Karl Malone .60 1.50
P10 Jason Kidd .75 2.00
P11 Gary Payton .50 1.25
P12 Kevin Garnett .75 2.00
P13 Keith Van Horn .40 1.00
P14 Glenn Robinson .40 1.00
P15 Michael Finley .50 1.25
P16 Hakeem Olajuwon .60 1.50
P17 Chris Webber .50 1.25
P18 Mitch Richmond .50 1.25
P19 Marcus Camby .50 1.25
P20 Tim Hardaway .50 1.25
P21 Shawn Kemp .50 1.25
P22 Reggie Miller .60 1.50

P23 Shaquille O'Neal 1.25 3.00
P24 Chauncey Billups .75 2.00
P25 Grant Hill .75 2.00
P26 Shareef Abdur-Rahim .50 1.25
P27 David Robinson .75 2.00
P28 Scottie Pippen .75 2.00
P29 Juwan Howard .40 1.00
P30 Anfernee Hardaway .75 2.00
P31 Jerry Stackhouse .50 1.25
P32 Kobe Bryant 2.50 6.00
P33 Patrick Ewing .60 1.50
P34 Alonzo Mourning .60 1.50
P35 John Stockton .60 1.50
P36 Kenny Anderson .40 1.00
P37 Tim Duncan 1.25 3.00
P38 Stephon Marbury .60 1.50
P39 Dennis Rodman 1.00 2.50
P40 Joe Smith .40 1.00

1997-98 SP Authentic Profiles 3

*STARS: 12X TO 30X VALUE
*RCs: 10X TO 25X VALUE
STATED PRINT RUN 100 SERIAL #'d SETS
P1 Michael Jordan 800.00 1600.00
P9 Karl Malone 50.00 120.00
P11 Gary Payton 40.00 100.00
P12 Kevin Garnett 100.00 250.00
P16 Hakeem Olajuwon 100.00 250.00
P23 Shaquille O'Neal 40.00 100.00
P25 Grant Hill 50.00 120.00
P27 David Robinson 50.00 125.00
P28 Scottie Pippen 125.00 300.00
P30 Anfernee Hardaway 75.00 150.00
P31 Jerry Stackhouse 20.00 50.00
P32 Kobe Bryant 300.00 550.00
P33 Patrick Ewing 60.00 150.00
P34 Alonzo Mourning 60.00 150.00
P37 Tim Duncan 200.00 500.00
P39 Dennis Rodman 100.00 200.00

1997-98 SP Authentic Sign of the Times

Randomly inserted into packs at a rate of one in 42, this 22-card set features autographs of several different NBA players. Card backs are numbered with the player's initials.

STATED ODDS 1:42
AH Allan Houston 10.00 25.00
AJ Avery Johnson 8.00 20.00
BB Brent Barry 6.00 15.00
BW Brian Williams 12.00 30.00
CM Chris Mullin 10.00 25.00
DM Dikembe Mutombo 10.00 25.00
DS Damon Stoudamire 6.00 15.00
EJ Eddie Jones 15.00 40.00
GM Gheorghe Muresan 6.00 15.00
GP Gary Payton 15.00 40.00
GR Glen Rice 8.00 20.00
HW Juwan Howard 8.00 20.00
KJ Kevin Johnson 20.00 50.00
KK Kerry Kittles 5.00 12.00
LH Lindsey Hunter 5.00 12.00
MB Mookie Blaylock 5.00 12.00
MR Mitch Richmond 10.00 25.00
SC Sam Cassell 6.00 15.00
SE Sean Elliott 6.00 15.00
TE Terrell Brandon 5.00 12.00
TG Tom Gugliotta 5.00 12.00
TH Tim Hardaway 10.00 25.00
VB Vin Baker 5.00 12.00

1997-98 SP Authentic Sign of the Times Stars and Rookies

Randomly inserted into packs at a rate of one in 113, this 12-card set features autographs of some of the top stars and rookies from 1997-98. Card backs are numbered with the player's initials.

STATED ODDS 1:113
AW Antoine Walker 8.00 20.00
CD Clyde Drexler 75.00 200.00
CH Chauncey Billups 10.00 25.00
JK Jason Kidd 40.00 100.00
JS John Stockton TRADE 25.00 50.00
KM Karl Malone 40.00 80.00
KV Keith Van Horn 6.00 15.00
MJ Michael Jordan 10000.00 15000.00
RO Ron Mercer 5.00 12.00

SA Shareef Abdur-Rahim 6.00 15.00
TB Tony Battie 5.00 12.00

1998-99 SP Authentic

The 1998-99 SP Authentic set contained 120 cards and was released in five-card packs with a suggested retail price of $4.99. The set also featured short-printed rookie F/X cards featuring the top 30 rookies. Each of the rookie cards were serially numbered to 3500.

COMPLETE SET w/o RC (90) 20.00 40.00
RC PRINT RUN 3500 SERIAL #'d SETS
1 Michael Jordan 1.25 3.00
2 Michael Jordan 1.25 3.00
3 Michael Jordan 1.25 3.00
4 Michael Jordan 1.25 3.00
5 Michael Jordan 1.25 3.00
6 Michael Jordan 1.25 3.00
7 Michael Jordan 1.25 3.00
8 Michael Jordan 1.25 3.00
9 Michael Jordan 1.25 3.00
10 Michael Jordan 1.25 3.00
11 Steve Smith .25 .60
12 Dikembe Mutombo .30 .75
13 Alan Henderson .20 .50
14 Antoine Walker .30 .75
15 Ron Mercer .25 .60
16 Kenny Anderson .25 .60
17 Derrick Coleman .25 .60
18 David Wesley .20 .50
19 Glen Rice .30 .75
20 Toni Kukoc .30 .75
21 Ron Harper .25 .60
22 Brent Barry .25 .60
23 Shawn Kemp .30 .75
24 Zydrunas Ilgauskas .30 .75
25 Brevin Knight .20 .50
26 Michael Finley .30 .75
27 Steve Nash .50 1.25
28 Cedric Ceballos .20 .50
29 Antonio McDyess .25 .60
30 Nick Van Exel .25 .60
31 Grant Hill .50 1.25
32 Jerry Stackhouse .30 .75
33 Bison Dele .20 .50
34 John Starks .25 .60
35 Chris Mills .20 .50
36 Hakeem Olajuwon .40 1.00
37 Charles Barkley .50 1.25
38 Scottie Pippen .50 1.25
39 Reggie Miller .40 1.00
40 Chris Mullin .30 .75
41 Rik Smits .25 .60
42 Lamond Murray .20 .50
43 Maurice Taylor .20 .50
44 Kobe Bryant 1.25 3.00
45 Dennis Rodman .60 1.50
46 Shaquille O'Neal .75 2.00
47 Alonzo Mourning .40 1.00
48 Tim Hardaway .30 .75
49 Jamal Mashburn .25 .60
50 Ray Allen .40 1.00
51 Glenn Robinson .25 .60
52 Terrell Brandon .20 .50
53 Kevin Garnett .50 1.25
54 Stephon Marbury .40 1.00
55 Joe Smith .25 .60
56 Keith Van Horn .30 .75
57 Kendall Gill .20 .50
58 Jayson Williams .20 .50
59 Patrick Ewing .40 1.00
60 Allan Houston .25 .60
61 Larry Johnson .30 .75
62 Anfernee Hardaway .50 1.25
63 Horace Grant .25 .60
64 Allen Iverson .60 1.50
65 Tim Thomas .30 .75
66 Jason Kidd .50 1.25
67 Tom Gugliotta .20 .50
68 Rex Chapman .20 .50
69 Damon Stoudamire .25 .60
70 Isaiah Rider .25 .60
71 Rasheed Wallace .30 .75
72 Chris Webber .30 .75
73 Vlade Divac .30 .75
74 Corliss Williamson .20 .50
75 Tim Duncan .60 1.50
76 David Robinson .50 1.25
77 Sean Elliott .30 .75
78 Detlef Schrempf .30 .75
79 Vin Baker .25 .60
80 Gary Payton .30 .75
81 Doug Christie .20 .50
82 Tracy McGrady .50 1.25
83 Karl Malone .40 1.00
84 John Stockton .40 1.00
85 Jeff Hornacek .25 .60
86 Shareef Abdur-Rahim .30 .75
87 Bryant Reeves .20 .50
88 Juwan Howard .25 .60
89 Mitch Richmond .30 .75
90 Rod Strickland .20 .50
91 Michael Olowokandi RC 3.00 8.00
92 Mike Bibby RC 4.00 10.00
93 Raef LaFrentz RC 3.00 8.00
94 Antawn Jamison RC 4.00 10.00
95 Vince Carter RC 75.00 200.00
96 Robert Traylor RC 2.50 6.00
97 Jason Williams RC 8.00 20.00
98 Larry Hughes RC 8.00 20.00
99 Dirk Nowitzki RC 75.00 200.00
100 Paul Pierce RC 25.00 60.00
101 Bonzi Wells RC 2.50 6.00
102 Michael Doleac RC 2.00 5.00
103 Keon Clark RC 2.50 6.00
104 Michael Dickerson RC 2.50 6.00
105 Matt Harpring RC 2.50 6.00
106 Bryce Drew RC 1.50 4.00
107 Pat Garrity RC 2.00 5.00
108 Roshown McLeod RC 1.50 4.00
109 Ricky Davis RC 4.00 10.00
110 Brian Skinner RC 2.50 6.00
111 Tyronn Lue RC 2.50 6.00
112 Felipe Lopez RC 1.50 4.00
113 Al Harrington RC 6.00 15.00
114 Sam Jacobson RC 2.00 5.00
115 Cory Carr RC 2.00 5.00
116 Corey Benjamin RC 1.50 4.00
117 Nazr Mohammed RC 2.50 6.00
118 Rashard Lewis RC 8.00 20.00
119 Peja Stojakovic RC 8.00 20.00
120 Andrae Patterson RC 2.00 5.00
23P Michael Jordan PROMO 2.50 6.00

1998-99 SP Authentic Authentics

Randomly inserted in packs at one in 864, this 27-card set features memorabilia redemption cards. Each card appears in different quantities and could be redeemed for special pieces of memorabilia. Card backs carry a "T" prefix. Only one of each card was available for the game-worn authentics (T18-T27). These cards are, therefore, not priced.

STATED ODDS 1:864
T18-T27 NOT PRICED DUE TO SCARCITY
T1 L.Bird Ball/10 400.00 600.00
T2 J.Erving/SI Cover/25 125.00 250.00
T3 A.Hard/SI Cover/200 25.00 50.00
T4 A.Hard/8x10/200 25.00 50.00
T5 T.Hard/Mini-ball/125 20.00 40.00
T6 T.Hard/8x10/150 12.50 25.00
T7 T.Hard/8x10/75 20.00 40.00
T8 J.Howard/Mini-ball/150 12.50 25.00
T9 E.Jones/Mini-ball/50 20.00 40.00
T10 E.Jones/8x10/100 15.00 30.00
T11 M.Jordan/Blk.Jersey/23 1500.00 2500.00
T12 M.Jordan/Wht.Jersey/23 1500.00 2500.00
T13 S.Kemp/8x10/150 20.00 40.00
T14 S.Kemp/Jersey/30 200.00 400.00
T15 G.Payton/SI Cover/75 50.00 100.00
T16 S.Pippen/Ball/25 150.00 300.00
T17 Forum Floor Pieces/23 125.00 250.00

1998-99 SP Authentic First Class

Randomly inserted in packs at one in seven, this 30-card set features the NBA's hottest stars featured on a unique die cut design. Card backs carry a "FC" prefix.

COMPLETE SET (30) 15.00 40.00
STATED ODDS 1:7
FC1 Michael Jordan 6.00 15.00
FC2 Dikembe Mutombo .50 1.25
FC3 Antoine Walker .50 1.25
FC4 Glen Rice .50 1.25
FC5 Toni Kukoc .50 1.25
FC6 Shawn Kemp .50 1.25
FC7 Michael Finley .50 1.25
FC8 Raef LaFrentz .60 1.50
FC9 Grant Hill .75 2.00
FC10 Antawn Jamison .75 2.00
FC11 Scottie Pippen .75 2.00
FC12 Reggie Miller .60 1.50
FC13 Michael Olowokandi .60 1.50
FC14 Kobe Bryant 2.00 5.00
FC15 Tim Hardaway .50 1.25
FC16 Ray Allen .60 1.50
FC17 Kevin Garnett .75 2.00
FC18 Keith Van Horn .50 1.25
FC19 Allan Houston .40 1.00
FC20 Anfernee Hardaway .75 2.00
FC21 Allen Iverson 1.00 2.50
FC22 Jason Kidd .75 2.00
FC23 Damon Stoudamire .40 1.00
FC24 Jason Williams 1.25 3.00
FC25 Tim Duncan 1.00 2.50
FC26 Gary Payton .50 1.25
FC27 Vince Carter 2.50 6.00
FC28 Karl Malone .60 1.50
FC29 Mike Bibby .75 2.00
FC30 Mitch Richmond .50 1.25

1998-99 SP Authentic MICHAEL

Randomly inserted in packs at one in 144, this 15-card set features Michael Jordan on Ionix technology. Card backs carry a "M" prefix.

COMPLETE SET (15) 150.00 300.00
COMMON CARD (M1-15) 12.00 30.00
STATED ODDS 1:144

1998-99 SP Authentic NBA 2K

Randomly inserted in packs at one in 23, this 20-card set looks at the future of the NBA, highlighting the stars of tomorrow. Card backs carry a "2K" prefix.

COMPLETE SET (20) 25.00 60.00
STATED ODDS 1:23
2K1 Michael Olowokandi 1.25 3.00
2K2 Mike Bibby 1.50 4.00
2K3 Raef LaFrentz 1.25 3.00
2K4 Antawn Jamison 1.50 4.00
2K5 Vince Carter 5.00 12.00
2K6 Robert Traylor 1.00 2.50
2K7 Jason Williams 2.50 6.00
2K8 Larry Hughes 2.00 5.00
2K9 Dirk Nowitzki 6.00 15.00
2K10 Paul Pierce 4.00 10.00
2K11 Cuttino Mobley 2.00 5.00
2K12 Michael Doleac .75 2.00
2K13 Corey Benjamin .60 1.50
2K14 Michael Dickerson 1.00 2.50
2K15 Allen Iverson 2.00 5.00
2K16 Kobe Bryant 4.00 10.00
2K17 Tim Duncan 2.00 5.00
2K18 Keith Van Horn 1.00 2.50
2K19 Kevin Garnett 1.50 4.00
2K20 Grant Hill 1.50 4.00

1998-99 SP Authentic Sign of the Times Bronze

Randomly inserted in packs at one in 23, this 45-card set features autographs of NBA players. The cards are numbered by initials.

STATED ODDS 1:23
AM Antonio McDyess 6.00 15.00
AV Avery Johnson 5.00 12.00
BE Blue Edwards 5.00 12.00
BG Brian Grant 5.00 12.00
BK Brevin Knight 5.00 12.00
BL Mookie Blaylock 5.00 12.00
BP Bobby Phills 5.00 12.00
BR Bryon Russell 6.00 15.00
CB Chauncey Billups 6.00 15.00
CC Chris Carr 5.00 12.00
CH Calbert Cheaney 5.00 12.00
DA Derek Anderson 6.00 15.00
DC Doug Christie 6.00 15.00
DK Derek Fisher 6.00 15.00
DM Donyell Marshall 5.00 12.00
DN Danny Manning 5.00 12.00
DT Detlef Schrempf 10.00 25.00
DV David Wesley 5.00 12.00
ED Erick Dampier 5.00 12.00
EG Ed Gray 5.00 12.00
GR Glen Rice 6.00 15.00
HG Horace Grant 8.00 20.00
HW Juwan Howard 6.00 15.00
JH Jeff Hornacek 10.00 25.00
JR Jalen Rose 5.00 12.00
JW Jerome Williams 5.00 12.00
JY Jayson Williams 5.00 12.00
KA Kenny Anderson 5.00 12.00
LH Lindsey Hunter 5.00 12.00
LJ Larry Johnson 12.00 30.00
MG Tracy McGrady 20.00 50.00
MI Michael Finley 6.00 15.00
MK Mark Jackson 5.00 12.00
NA Nick Anderson 5.00 12.00
OH Othella Harrington 5.00 12.00
PJ P.J. Brown 5.00 12.00
RH Ron Harper 20.00 50.00
RR Rodrick Rhodes 5.00 12.00
SE Sean Elliott 6.00 15.00
TB Terrell Brandon 6.00 15.00
TK Toni Kukoc 10.00 25.00
TQ Tariq Abdul-Wahad 5.00 12.00
TR Theo Ratliff 5.00 12.00
TY Maurice Taylor 5.00 12.00
WM Walter McCarty 5.00 12.00

1998-99 SP Authentic Sign of the Times Gold

Randomly inserted in packs at one in 864, this 4-card set features a super-rare die cut autograph of NBA players. Card backs are numbered by the player's initials.

STATED ODDS 1:864
AI Allen Iverson 350.00 450.00
AW Antoine Walker 15.00 40.00
MJ Michael Jordan 2000.00 4000.00
TH Tim Hardaway 25.00 60.00

1998-99 SP Authentic Sign of the Times Silver

Randomly inserted in packs at one in 115, this 13-card set features autographs of NBA players. Card backs carry the player's initials.

STATED ODDS 1:115
AJ Antawn Jamison 8.00 20.00
DR Dennis Rodman 60.00 120.00
HO Hakeem Olajuwon 25.00 60.00
LR Larry Hughes 12.00 30.00
MB Mike Bibby 8.00 20.00
MO Michael Olowokandi 5.00 12.00
MT Dikembe Mutombo 8.00 20.00
PN Anfernee Hardaway 60.00 120.00
RL Raef LaFrentz 5.00 12.00
RM Ron Mercer 5.00 12.00
RT Robert Traylor 5.00 12.00
SH Shawn Kemp 30.00 80.00
VC Vince Carter 75.00 200.00

1999-00 SP Authentic

Released in May 2000, the 1999-00 SP Authentic product contained 135 cards, offered in five-card packs with a suggested retail price of $4.99. The base set contained 90 veterans and 45 rookies. The rookie subset was serially numbered to 1500.

COMPLETE SET (135) 200.00 400.00
COMPLETE SET w/o RC (90) 15.00 40.00
91-135 PRINT RUN 1500 SERIAL #'d SETS
1 Dikembe Mutombo .40 1.00
2 Jim Jackson .25 .60
3 Alan Henderson .25 .60
4 Antoine Walker .40 1.00
5 Paul Pierce .50 1.25
6 Kenny Anderson .30 .75
7 Eddie Jones .40 1.00
8 Derrick Coleman .30 .75
9 Anthony Mason .25 .60
10 Chris Carr .25 .60
11 Hersey Hawkins .25 .60
12 B.J. Armstrong .25 .60
13 Shawn Kemp .40 1.00
14 Bob Sura .25 .60
15 Lamond Murray .25 .60
16 Michael Finley .40 1.00
17 Cedric Ceballos .25 .60
18 Dirk Nowitzki .75 2.00
19 Erick Strickland .25 .60
20 Antonio McDyess .30 .75
21 Nick Van Exel .30 .75
22 Grant Hill .50 1.25
23 Jerry Stackhouse .40 1.00
24 Lindsey Hunter .25 .60
25 Christian Laettner .30 .75
26 Antawn Jamison .40 1.00
27 Chris Mills .25 .60
28 Larry Hughes .30 .75
29 Charles Barkley .60 1.50
30 Hakeem Olajuwon .50 1.25
31 Cuttino Mobley .25 .60
32 Reggie Miller .40 1.00
33 Jalen Rose .30 .75
34 Rik Smits .40 1.00
35 Maurice Taylor .25 .60
36 Derek Anderson .25 .60
37 Tyrone Nesby RC .30 .75
38 Kobe Bryant 1.50 4.00
39 Shaquille O'Neal 1.00 2.50
40 Glen Rice .40 1.00
41 Tim Hardaway .40 1.00
42 Alonzo Mourning .50 1.25
43 Jamal Mashburn .30 .75
44 Ray Allen .40 1.00
45 Sam Cassell .30 .75
46 Glenn Robinson .30 .75
47 Kevin Garnett .60 1.50
48 Terrell Brandon .25 .60
49 Joe Smith .30 .75
50 Stephon Marbury .30 .75
51 Keith Van Horn .30 .75
52 Jamie Feick RC .30 .75
53 Kerry Kittles .25 .60
54 Allan Houston .30 .75
55 Latrell Sprewell .40 1.00
56 Patrick Ewing .50 1.25
57 Darrell Armstrong .25 .60
58 Ron Mercer .30 .75
59 Michael Doleac .25 .60
60 Allen Iverson .75 2.00
61 Toni Kukoc .40 1.00
62 Eric Snow .30 .75
63 Anfernee Hardaway .60 1.50
64 Jason Kidd .60 1.50
65 Tom Gugliotta .25 .60
66 Scottie Pippen .60 1.50
67 Steve Smith .30 .75
68 Damon Stoudamire .30 .75
69 Jason Williams .50 1.25
70 Peja Stojakovic .40 1.00
71 Chris Webber .40 1.00
72 Vlade Divac .40 1.00
73 Tim Duncan .75 2.00
74 David Robinson .60 1.50
75 Avery Johnson .30 .75
76 Gary Payton .40 1.00
77 Vin Baker .30 .75
78 Vernon Maxwell .25 .60
79 Vince Carter .75 2.00
80 Tracy McGrady .60 1.50
81 Doug Christie .30 .75
82 Karl Malone .50 1.25
83 John Stockton .50 1.25
84 Jeff Hornacek .30 .75
85 Mike Bibby .40 1.00
86 Shareef Abdur-Rahim .30 .75
87 Othella Harrington .25 .60
88 Mitch Richmond .40 1.00
89 Juwan Howard .30 .75
90 Rod Strickland .25 .60
91 Elton Brand RC 8.00 20.00
92 Steve Francis RC 8.00 20.00
93 Baron Davis RC 12.00 30.00
94 Lamar Odom RC 8.00 20.00
95 Jonathan Bender RC 3.00 8.00
96 Wally Szczerbiak RC 6.00 15.00
97 Richard Hamilton RC 6.00 15.00
98 Andre Miller RC 6.00 15.00
99 Shawn Marion RC 6.00 15.00
100 Jason Terry RC 5.00 12.00
101 Trajan Langdon RC 3.00 8.00
102 A.Radojevic RC 2.00 5.00
103 Corey Maggette RC 10.00 25.00
104 William Avery RC 2.50 6.00
105 Ron Artest RC 6.00 15.00
106 James Posey RC 3.00 8.00
107 Quincy Lewis RC 2.00 5.00
108 Dion Glover RC 2.50 6.00
109 Kenny Thomas RC 3.00 8.00
110 Devean George RC 3.00 8.00
111 Tim James RC 2.00 5.00
112 Vonteego Cummings RC 2.00 5.00
113 Jumaine Jones RC 2.50 6.00
114 Scott Padgett RC 2.50 6.00
115 Adrian Griffin RC 3.00 8.00
116 Anthony Carter RC 2.50 6.00
117 Todd MacCulloch RC 3.00 8.00
118 Chucky Atkins RC 3.00 8.00
119 Obinna Ekezie RC 2.50 6.00
120 Eddie Robinson RC 3.00 8.00
121 Michael Ruffin RC 2.50 6.00
122 Laron Profit RC 2.50 6.00
123 Cal Bowdler RC 2.00 5.00
124 Chris Herren RC 2.50 6.00
125 Milt Palacio RC 3.00 8.00
126 Jeff Foster RC 3.00 8.00
127 Ryan Bowen RC 3.00 8.00
128 Tim Young RC 3.00 8.00
129 Derrick Dial RC 3.00 8.00
130 Greg Buckner RC 3.00 8.00
131 Rodney Buford RC 3.00 8.00
132 Evan Eschmeyer RC 2.50 6.00
133 Jermaine Jackson RC 3.00 8.00
134 John Celestand RC 2.00 5.00
135 Ryan Robertson RC 2.00 5.00
KG Kevin Garnett PROMO .60 1.50

1999-00 SP Authentic Athletic

Randomly inserted in packs at one in 12, this 12-card set featured players best known for their head-turning athletic moves. Card backs carry an "A" prefix.

COMPLETE SET (12) 8.00 20.00
STATED ODDS 1:12
A1 Grant Hill .75 2.00
A2 Shareef Abdur-Rahim .50 1.25
A3 Jason Kidd 1.00 2.50
A4 Vince Carter 1.25 3.00
A5 Steve Francis 1.50 4.00
A6 Scottie Pippen 1.00 2.50
A7 Paul Pierce .75 2.00
A8 Kobe Bryant 2.50 6.00
A9 Stephon Marbury .50 1.25
A10 Michael Finley .60 1.50
A11 Eddie Jones .60 1.50
A12 Kevin Garnett 1.00 2.50

1999-00 SP Authentic Authentics

Randomly inserted in packs at one in 15000, this 10-card set features memorabilia redemption cards good for an autographed authentic jersey of the featured athlete. Only 100 total cards were available - ten cards per player.

1999-00 SP Authentic BuyBack

Randomly inserted in packs at one in 288, this 120-card set features previous SP/SP Authentic cards bought back by Upper Deck, autographed by the players. Print runs for each card are listed below. The cards are listed in alphabetical order. Some of the tougher cards are unpriced, but are listed below for checklisting purposes.

STATED ODDS 1:288
PRINT RUNS LISTED BELOW
LOWER PRINT RUNS UNPRICED
2 M.Bibby 98-9SPA2K/42 20.00 50.00
3A K.Bryant Redemption 40.00 100.00
8 K.Bryant 98-9SPA/132 150.00 300.00
9 K.Garnett 95-6SP/21 100.00 200.00
11 K.Garnett 96-7SP/21 100.00 200.00
15 K.Garnett 98-9SPA/NNO 50.00 100.00
18 B.Grant 94-5SP/NNO 6.00 15.00
22 B.Grant 95-6SP/NNO 6.00 15.00
25 B.Grant 96-7SP/16 15.00 40.00
26 B.Grant 97-8SPA/16 15.00 40.00
27 T.Gugliotta 94-5SP/24 10.00 25.00
29 T.Gugliotta 95-6SP/24 10.00 25.00
30 T.Gugliotta 96-7SP/24 10.00 25.00
32 T.Gugliotta 98-9SPA/110 6.00 15.00
33 A.Hard 94-5SP/30 100.00 200.00
35 A.Hard 95-6SP/30 100.00 200.00
40 A.Hard 98-9SPA/32 100.00 200.00
43 L.Hughes 98-9SPA2K/90 12.00 30.00
44 M.Jackson 94-5SP/NNO 6.00 15.00
48 A.Jmsn 98-9SPAFC/NNO 6.00 15.00
50 E.Jones 94-5SP/NNO 30.00 80.00
52 E.Jones 95-6SP/NNO 10.00 25.00
54 E.Jones 96-7SP/NNO 10.00 25.00
60 B.Knight 97-8SPA/24 10.00 25.00
61 B.Knight 98-9SPA/NNO 6.00 15.00
63 R.LaFrentz 98-9SPAFC/NNO 6.00 15.00
64 R.LaFrentz 98-9SPA2K/NNO 6.00 15.00
65 K.Malone 94-5SP/NNO 30.00 75.00
74 J.O'Neal 96-7SP/170 40.00 100.00
77 G.Rice 94-5SP/41 15.00 40.00
79 G.Rice 95-6SP/NNO 8.00 20.00
82 G.Rice 96-7SP/41 15.00 40.00
85 G.Rice 98-9SPA/NNO 8.00 20.00
87 J.Rose 94-5SP/100 25.00 60.00
88 J.Rose 95-6SP/120 12.50 30.00
89 J.Stack 95-6SP/NNO 25.00 60.00
94 J.Stack 96-7SP/16 40.00 100.00
96 J.Stack 97-8SPA/25 40.00 100.00
97 J.Stack 98-9SPA/NNO 12.50 30.00
98 D.Stoud 95-6SP/NNO 10.00 25.00
100 D.Stoud 95-6SPHo/35 25.00 60.00
102 D.Stoud 96-7SP/31 25.00 60.00
105 D.Stoud 98-9SPA/NNO 10.00 25.00
108 M.Taylor 97-8SPA/20 12.50 30.00
109 M.Taylor 98-9SPA/NNO 6.00 15.00
111 R.Traylor 98-9SPA2K/NNO 6.00 15.00
112 A.Walker 96-7SP/NNO 15.00 40.00
114 A.Walker 97-8SPA/19 25.00 60.00
115 A.Walker 98-9SPA/NNO 12.50 30.00
117 Jay.Will 95-6SP/NNO 6.00 15.00
118 Jay.Will 96-7SP/33 8.00 20.00
120 Jay.Will 98-9SPA/NNO 6.00 15.00

1999-00 SP Authentic First Class

Randomly inserted in packs at one in 12, this 12-card set featured the more talented players in the NBA. The cards carry a "FC" prefix.

COMPLETE SET (12) 6.00 15.00
STATED ODDS 1:12
FC1 Kevin Garnett 1.00 2.50
FC2 Kobe Bryant 2.50 6.00
FC3 Gary Payton .60 1.50
FC4 Tim Hardaway .60 1.50
FC5 Antonio McDyess .50 1.25
FC6 Allan Houston .50 1.25
FC7 Jason Kidd 1.00 2.50
FC8 Reggie Miller .60 1.50
FC9 Jason Williams .75 2.00
FC10 Allen Iverson 1.25 3.00
FC11 David Robinson 1.00 2.50
FC12 Shaquille O'Neal 1.50 4.00

1999-00 SP Authentic Maximum Force

Randomly inserted in packs at one in four, this 15-card set highlighted the stars who make a strong impact on the game. Card backs carry a "M" prefix.

COMPLETE SET (15) 4.00 10.00
STATED ODDS 1:4
M1 Karl Malone .50 1.25
M2 Antawn Jamison .40 1.00
M3 Shareef Abdur-Rahim .30 .75
M4 Tim Duncan .75 2.00
M5 Allen Iverson .75 2.00
M6 Michael Finley .40 1.00
M7 Kevin Garnett .60 1.50
M8 Kobe Bryant 1.50 4.00
M9 Gary Payton .40 1.00
M10 Keith Van Horn .30 .75
M11 Chris Webber .40 1.00
M12 Glenn Robinson .30 .75
M13 Alonzo Mourning .50 1.25
M14 Antoine Walker .40 1.00
M15 Antonio McDyess .30 .75

1999-00 SP Authentic Premier Powers

Randomly inserted in packs at one in 72, this nine-card set captured the sheer domination of some of the NBA's most irresistible forces. Card backs carry a "P" prefix.

COMPLETE SET (9) 20.00 50.00
STATED ODDS 1:72
P1 Kobe Bryant 6.00 15.00
P2 Kevin Garnett 2.50 6.00
P3 Tim Duncan 3.00 8.00
P4 Elton Brand 4.00 10.00
P5 Vince Carter 3.00 8.00
P6 Lamar Odom 4.00 10.00
P7 Grant Hill 2.00 5.00
P8 Shaquille O'Neal 4.00 10.00
P9 Allen Iverson 3.00 8.00

1999-00 SP Authentic Sign of the Times

Randomly inserted in packs at one in 23, this 58-card set features autographs from NBA stars and rookies. Card backs are numbered by the players initials.

STATED ODDS 1:23
AC Anthony Carter 4.00 10.00
AD Antonio Davis 4.00 10.00
AG Adrian Griffin 4.00 10.00
AH Al Harrington 4.00 10.00
AJ Antawn Jamison 5.00 12.00
AL Alan Henderson 4.00 10.00
AM Andre Miller 4.00 10.00
AN Anfernee Hardaway 60.00 150.00
AW Antoine Walker 5.00 12.00
BD Baron Davis 6.00 15.00
BG Brian Grant 4.00 10.00
BR Brevin Knight 4.00 10.00
BW Bonzi Wells 4.00 10.00
CA Chucky Atkins 4.00 10.00
CM Corey Maggette 4.00 10.00
CR Austin Croshere 4.00 10.00
CT Cuttino Mobley 4.00 10.00
DA Darrell Armstrong 4.00 10.00
DG Dion Glover 4.00 10.00
DN Dirk Nowitzki 60.00 150.00
DS Damon Stoudamire 5.00 12.00
EJ Eddie Jones 10.00 25.00
GR Glen Rice 6.00 15.00
JB Jonathan Bender 4.00 10.00
JO Jermaine O'Neal 4.00 10.00
JP James Posey 4.00 10.00
JR Jalen Rose 8.00 20.00
JS Jerry Stackhouse 6.00 15.00
JT Jason Terry 5.00 12.00
JY Jayson Williams 4.00 10.00
KB Kobe Bryant 125.00 250.00
KG Kevin Garnett 50.00 100.00
KM Karl Malone 75.00 150.00
LH Larry Hughes 8.00 20.00
LM Lamond Murray 4.00 10.00
MB Mike Bibby 4.00 10.00
MD Antonio McDyess 8.00 20.00
ME Mario Elie 8.00 20.00
MI Michael Dickerson 4.00 10.00
MJ Michael Jordan 900.00 1400.00
MK Mark Jackson 4.00 10.00
MT Maurice Taylor 4.00 10.00
QL Quincy Lewis 4.00 10.00
RA Ron Artest 8.00 20.00
RH Richard Hamilton 5.00 12.00
RL Raef LaFrentz 4.00 10.00
RP Ruben Patterson 4.00 10.00
RT Robert Traylor 4.00 10.00
SF Steve Francis 6.00 15.00
SH Shawn Marion 5.00 12.00
SM Sam Mack 4.00 10.00
SU Bob Sura 4.00 10.00
TG Tom Gugliotta 4.00 10.00
TL Trajan Langdon 4.00 10.00
TN Tyrone Nesby 4.00 10.00
TR Tracy McGrady 15.00 40.00
WA William Avery 4.00 10.00
WS Wally Szczerbiak 4.00 10.00

1999-00 SP Authentic Sign of the Times Gold

*GOLD: 1.5X TO 4X BASE AUTO
STATED PRINT RUN 25 SERIAL #'d SETS
KB Kobe Bryant 300.00 600.00
KM Karl Malone 250.00 500.00
ME Mario Elie 20.00 50.00

1999-00 SP Authentic Supremacy

Randomly inserted in packs at one in 24, this nine-card set features the "go-to guys" when the game is on the line. Card backs carry a "S" prefix.

COMPLETE SET (9) 8.00 20.00
STATED ODDS 1:24
S1 Vince Carter 1.50 4.00
S2 Shaquille O'Neal 2.00 5.00
S3 Tim Duncan 1.50 4.00
S4 Kevin Garnett 1.25 3.00
S5 Jason Williams 1.00 2.50
S6 Stephon Marbury .60 1.50
S7 Gary Payton .75 2.00
S8 Kobe Bryant 3.00 8.00
S9 Grant Hill 1.00 2.50

2000-01 SP Authentic

The 2000-01 SP Authentic product released in June, 2001 and featured a 136-card base set that was broken into tiers as follows: Base Veterans (1-90), and Rookies (91-136) that were serial numbered to either 500, 1250, or 2000 (please see print runs below). Each pack contained five cards and carried a suggested retail price of $4.99.

COMP.SET w/o SP's (90) 10.00 25.00
1 Jason Terry .40 1.00
2 Alan Henderson .25 .60
3 Lorenzen Wright .25 .60
4 Paul Pierce .40 1.00
5 Antoine Walker .30 .75
6 Bryant Stith .25 .60
7 Jamal Mashburn .30 .75
8 Baron Davis .40 1.00
9 David Wesley .25 .60
10 Elton Brand .40 1.00
11 Ron Artest .40 1.00
12 Ron Mercer .25 .60
13 Andre Miller .30 .75
14 Lamond Murray .25 .60
15 Jim Jackson .25 .60
16 Michael Finley .40 1.00
17 Dirk Nowitzki .60 1.50
18 Steve Nash .60 1.50
19 Antonio McDyess .30 .75
20 Nick Van Exel .30 .75
21 Raef LaFrentz .25 .60
22 Jerry Stackhouse .30 .75
23 Chucky Atkins .25 .60
24 Joe Smith .30 .75
25 Antawn Jamison .40 1.00
26 Larry Hughes .30 .75
27 Mookie Blaylock .25 .60
28 Steve Francis .30 .75
29 Hakeem Olajuwon .50 1.25
30 Cuttino Mobley .25 .60
31 Reggie Miller .40 1.00
32 Jermaine O'Neal .30 .75
33 Jalen Rose .30 .75
34 Travis Best .25 .60
35 Lamar Odom .30 .75
36 Corey Maggette .30 .75
37 Eric Piatkowski .25 .60
38 Shaquille O'Neal 1.00 2.50
39 Kobe Bryant 1.50 4.00
40 Isaiah Rider .30 .75
41 Horace Grant .30 .75
42 Eddie Jones .40 1.00
43 Brian Grant .25 .60
44 Tim Hardaway .40 1.00
45 Ray Allen .40 1.00
46 Glenn Robinson .30 .75
47 Sam Cassell .30 .75
48 Kevin Garnett .60 1.50
49 Terrell Brandon .25 .60
50 Chauncey Billups .40 1.00
51 Wally Szczerbiak .30 .75
52 Stephon Marbury .30 .75
53 Keith Van Horn .30 .75
54 Aaron Williams .25 .60
55 Latrell Sprewell .30 .75
56 Allan Houston .30 .75
57 Glen Rice .30 .75
58 Tracy McGrady .60 1.50
59 Grant Hill .50 1.25
60 Darrell Armstrong .25 .60
61 Allen Iverson .75 2.00
62 Dikembe Mutombo .40 1.00
63 Aaron McKie .25 .60
64 Jason Kidd .60 1.50
65 Clifford Robinson .25 .60
66 Shawn Marion .30 .75
67 Damon Stoudamire .30 .75
68 Steve Smith .30 .75
69 Rasheed Wallace .40 1.00
70 Chris Webber .40 1.00
71 Jason Williams .40 1.00
72 Peja Stojakovic .40 1.00
73 Tim Duncan .75 2.00
74 David Robinson .60 1.50
75 Derek Anderson .25 .60
76 Gary Payton .40 1.00
77 Rashard Lewis .40 1.00
78 Patrick Ewing .50 1.25
79 Vince Carter .75 2.00
80 Charles Oakley .30 .75
81 Antonio Davis .25 .60
82 Karl Malone .50 1.25
83 John Stockton .50 1.25
84 John Starks .30 .75
85 Shareef Abdur-Rahim .30 .75
86 Mike Bibby .40 1.00
87 Michael Dickerson .25 .60
88 Richard Hamilton .30 .75
89 Mitch Richmond .30 .75
90 Christian Laettner .30 .75
91 Kenyon Martin AU/500 RC 12.00 30.00
92 Stromile Swift AU/500 RC 5.00 12.00
93 Darius Miles AU/500 RC 6.00 15.00
94 Marcus Fizer/1250 RC 2.50 6.00
95 Mike Miller AU/500 RC 8.00 20.00
96 DerMarr Johnson AU/500 RC 4.00 10.00
97 Chris Mihm/1250 RC 2.00 5.00
98 Jamal Crawford/1250 RC 6.00 15.00
99 Joel Przybilla/2000 RC 1.50 4.00
100 Keyon Dooling/1250 RC 2.50 6.00
101 Jerome Moiso/1250 RC 1.50 4.00
102 Etan Thomas/2000 RC 2.00 5.00
103 Courtney Alexander/1250 RC 2.00 5.00
104 Mateen Cleaves/1250 RC 2.00 5.00
105 Jason Collier/2000 RC 2.00 5.00
106 Hedo Turkoglu/1250 RC 4.00 10.00
107 Desmond Mason/1250 RC 3.00 8.00
108 Q.Richardson/1250 RC 2.50 6.00
109 Jamaal Magloire/1250 RC 2.50 6.00
110 Speedy Claxton/2000 RC 2.00 5.00
111 M.Peterson AU/500 RC 5.00 12.00
112 Donnell Harvey/2000 RC 1.50 4.00
113 D.Stevenson/1250 RC 2.50 6.00
114 Jake Tsakalidis/2000 RC 1.25 3.00
115 S.Samake/2000 RC 1.25 3.00
116 Erick Barkley/2000 RC 1.25 3.00
117 Mark Madsen/2000 RC 2.00 5.00
118 A.J. Guyton/1250 RC 1.50 4.00
119 O.Oyedeji/2000 RC 1.25 3.00
120 Eddie House/1250 RC 2.00 5.00
121 Eduardo Najera/2000 RC 2.00 5.00
122 Lavor Postell/2000 RC 1.25 3.00
123 Hanno Mottola/1250 RC 1.50 4.00
124 Ira Newble/2000 RC 1.50 4.00
125 Chris Porter/1250 RC 1.50 4.00
126 R.Wolkowyski/2000 RC 1.25 3.00
127 Pepe Sanchez/2000 RC 2.00 5.00
128 S.Jackson/1250 RC 4.00 10.00
129 Marc Jackson/1250 RC 2.00 5.00
130 Dragan Tarlac/2000 RC 1.25 3.00
131 Lee Nailon/2000 2.00 5.00
132 Mike Penberthy/1250 RC 2.50 6.00
133 Mark Blount/2000 RC 2.00 5.00
134 Dan Langhi/2000 RC 1.25 3.00
135 Daniel Santiago/2000 RC 2.00 5.00
136 Wang Zhizhi AU/500 RC 25.00 60.00
S1 Kobe Bryant PROMO 1.00 2.50

2000-01 SP Authentic Athletic

Randomly inserted into packs at one in 24, this 7-card insert features some of the most athletic players in the NBA. Card backs carry an "A" prefix.

COMPLETE SET (7) 5.00 12.00
STATED ODDS 1:24
A1 Allen Iverson 1.25 3.00
A2 Elton Brand .60 1.50
A3 Antonio McDyess .50 1.25
A4 Vince Carter 1.25 3.00
A5 Kobe Bryant 2.50 6.00
A6 Grant Hill .75 2.00
A7 Kevin Garnett 1.00 2.50

2000-01 SP Authentic BuyBack

Randomly inserted in packs at one in 2500, this insert set features previous SP/SP Authentic cards bought back by Upper Deck, and autographed by the players. Print runs for each card are listed below. The cards are listed in alphabetical order. Some of the tougher cards are unpriced, but are listed below for checklisting purposes. Each card was acompanied by a certificate of authenticity from Upper Deck, and all of the UDA holograms carry an "AAA" prefix to the numbering.

STATED ODDS 1:2500
MOST AU's NOT PRICED DUE TO SCARCITY
20 K.Garnett 95-6SP/21 150.00 300.00
45 T.Hardaway 98-9SPA/40 15.00 40.00
47 T.Hardaway 99-0SPA/17 20.00 50.00
61 M.Jordan 94-5SP/23 750.00 1500.00
84 T.McGrady 98-9SPA/20 75.00 150.00
85 T.McGrady 99-0SPA/27 50.00 100.00
105 J.Stack 95-6SP/22 40.00 100.00
110 A.Walker 96-7SP/24 30.00 80.00

2000-01 SP Authentic First Class

Randomly inserted into packs at one in 24, this 7-card insert features players that are first class citizens on and off the court. Card backs carry a "FC" prefix.

COMPLETE SET (7) 6.00 15.00
STATED ODDS 1:24
FC1 Shareef Abdur-Rahim .50 1.25
FC2 Kevin Garnett 1.00 2.50
FC3 Baron Davis .60 1.50
FC4 Shaquille O'Neal 1.50 4.00
FC5 Rashard Lewis .60 1.50
FC6 Paul Pierce .60 1.50
FC7 Kobe Bryant 2.50 6.00

2000-01 SP Authentic Premier Powers

Randomly inserted into packs at one in 24, this 7-card insert features some of the most overpowering players in the NBA. Card backs carry an "P" prefix.

COMPLETE SET (7) 6.00 15.00
STATED ODDS 1:24
P1 Chris Webber .60 1.50
P2 Allen Iverson 1.25 3.00
P3 Kobe Bryant 2.50 6.00
P4 Rasheed Wallace .60 1.50
P5 Tracy McGrady 1.00 2.50
P6 Kevin Garnett 1.00 2.50
P7 Tim Duncan 1.25 3.00

2000-01 SP Authentic Sign of the Times

Randomly inserted in packs at one in 23, this 48-card set features autographs from NBA stars and rookies. Card backs are numbered by the players initials. Please note that a few of the players packed out as exchange cards, and must be redeemed no later that 01/18/02.

STATED ODDS 1:23
AC Austin Croshere 2.50 6.00
AJ Antawn Jamison 4.00 10.00
AM Antonio McDyess 4.00 10.00
AR Darrell Armstrong 4.00 10.00
AW Antoine Walker 6.00 15.00
CA Courtney Alexander 3.00 8.00
CM Chris Mihm 3.00 8.00
DA Darius Miles 4.00 10.00
DE Desmond Mason 5.00 12.00
DH Donnell Harvey 3.00 8.00
DJ DerMarr Johnson 3.00 8.00
DN Dirk Nowitzki 60.00 150.00
DS DeShawn Stevenson 4.00 10.00
EB Erick Barkley 2.50 6.00
EJ Eddie Jones 5.00 12.00
ET Etan Thomas 4.00 10.00
FI Marcus Fizer 4.00 10.00
GP Gary Payton 12.00 30.00
JA Jamaal Magloire 4.00 10.00
JB Jonathan Bender 4.00 10.00
JC Jamal Crawford 5.00 12.00
JM Jerome Moiso 2.50 6.00
JO Jermaine O'Neal 6.00 15.00
JP Joel Przybilla 3.00 8.00
JR Jalen Rose 4.00 10.00
JS Jerry Stackhouse 6.00 15.00
KB Kobe Bryant SP 75.00 200.00
KG Kevin Garnett SP 40.00 80.00
KM Kenyon Martin 6.00 15.00
MA Corey Maggette 3.00 8.00
MB Mike Bibby 6.00 15.00
MC Mateen Cleaves 3.00 8.00
MF Michael Finley 8.00 20.00
MK Mike Miller 6.00 15.00
MM Mark Madsen 4.00 10.00
MN Mamadou N'Diaye 2.50 6.00
MP Morris Peterson 4.00 10.00
MP Mike Penberthy 4.00 10.00
QR Quentin Richardson 4.00 10.00
RH Richard Hamilton 6.00 15.00
RM Reggie Miller 50.00 125.00
SC Speedy Claxton 4.00 10.00
SF Steve Francis 5.00 12.00
SJ Stephen Jackson 10.00 25.00
SM Shawn Marion 5.00 12.00
SS Stromile Swift 4.00 10.00
TM Tracy McGrady 12.00 30.00
TT Tim Thomas 4.00 10.00

2000-01 SP Authentic Sign of the Times Platinum

Randomly inserted in packs at one in 287, this 28-card set features autographs from NBA stars and rookies. Card backs are numbered by the players initials. Please note that a few of the players packed out as exchange cards, and must be redeemed no later that 01/18/02. Also be aware that there were only 200 serial-numbered sets produced unless noted below.

*PLATINUM: .6X TO 1.5X BASIC SIGN
STATED ODDS 1:287
PRINT RUN 200 SETS UNLESS NOTED
KG Kevin Garnett/21 150.00 300.00
MJ Michael Jordan/23 1000.00 2000.00

2000-01 SP Authentic Sign of the Times Double

Randomly inserted into packs at one in 287, this 18-card insert set features dual-player autographs from both NBA veterans and rookies. Please note that a few of the cards packed out as exchange cards, and must be redeemed no later that 01/18/02.

STATED ODDS 1:287
CADH C.Alexander/D.Harvey 5.00 12.00
DADS D.Miles/D.Stevenson 6.00 15.00
DAQR D.Miles/Q.Richardson 8.00 20.00
FIJC M.Fizer/J.Crawford 6.00 15.00
JCDS J.Crawford/D.Stevenson 6.00 15.00
KBKG K.Bryant/K.Garnett 125.00 250.00
KBKM K.Bryant/K.Martin 80.00 160.00
KBSF K.Bryant/S.Francis 80.00 200.00
KBTM K.Bryant/T.McGrady 100.00 200.00
KGKM K.Garnett/K.Martin 50.00 120.00
KMDA K.Martin/D.Miles 10.00 25.00
KMDJ K.Martin/D.Johnson 6.00 15.00
KMFI K.Martin/M.Fizer 5.00 12.00
KMSJ K.Martin/S.Jackson 8.00 20.00
KMSS K.Martin/S.Swift 6.00 15.00
MCMP M.Cleaves/M.Peterson 6.00 15.00

MJDR M.Jordan/J.Erving 600.00 1000.00
MJKB M.Jordan/K.Bryant 600.00 1000.00

2000-01 SP Authentic Sign of the Times Triple

Randomly inserted into packs, this 6-card insert set features three player autographs from both NBA veterans and rookies. Please note that a few of the cards packed out as exchange cards, and must be redeemed no later that 01/18/02. Also be aware that there were only 25 serial numbered sets produced.

STATED PRINT RUN 25 SERIAL #'d SETS
DRMGLB Erving/Magic/Bird 300.00 600.00
KBKGKM Kobe/Garnett/Martin 200.00 400.00
KBMJKG Kobe/Jordan/Garnett 1000.00 2000.00
KBMJMG Kobe/Jordan/Magic 1200.00 2200.00
KMSJMJ Martin/S.Jcksn/M.Jcksn 40.00 100.00
KMSSDA Martin/Swift/Miles 40.00 100.00

2000-01 SP Authentic Special Forces

Randomly inserted into packs at one in 24, this 7-card insert features some of the best shooters in the NBA. Card backs carry an "SF" prefix.

COMPLETE SET (7) 5.00 12.00
STATED ODDS 1:24
SF1 Kobe Bryant 2.50 6.00
SF2 Steve Francis .50 1.25
SF3 Eddie Jones .60 1.50
SF4 Shaquille O'Neal 1.50 4.00
SF5 Stephon Marbury .50 1.25
SF6 Lamar Odom .50 1.25
SF7 Kevin Garnett 1.00 2.50

2000-01 SP Authentic Spectacular

Randomly inserted into packs at one in 24, this 7-card insert features players that have a knack for getting on the nightly highlight reels. Card backs carry an "SP" prefix.

COMPLETE SET (7) 5.00 12.00
STATED ODDS 1:24
SP1 Kobe Bryant 2.50 6.00
SP2 Chris Webber .60 1.50
SP3 Latrell Sprewell .50 1.25
SP4 Vince Carter 1.25 3.00
SP5 Rashard Lewis .60 1.50
SP6 Tim Duncan 1.25 3.00
SP7 Karl Malone .75 2.00

2000-01 SP Authentic Supremacy

Randomly inserted in packs at one in 24, this 7-card set features the "go-to guys" when the game is on the line. Card backs carry a "S" prefix.

COMPLETE SET (7) 6.00 15.00
STATED ODDS 1:24
S1 Shaquille O'Neal 1.50 4.00
S2 Tim Duncan 1.25 3.00
S3 Kevin Garnett 1.00 2.50
S4 Allen Iverson 1.25 3.00
S5 Kobe Bryant 2.50 6.00
S6 Vince Carter 1.25 3.00
S7 Jason Kidd 1.00 2.50

2001-02 SP Authentic

Released in early May 2002, SP Authentic boasts a 165-card set divided up into 90 base cards, 50 rookie cards, numbers 91-140, and 15 Spectaculars, numbers 141-165, which are sequentially numbered to 1000. Veteran cards feature full color player action photos are set against a colored background centered on an all-white embossed card stock. The rookie cards are divided up as follows: card numbers 91-106 are sequentially numbered to 1600 and have gray scale portraits of the player, orange highlights, and a piece of film with a picture from a game. Card numbers 107-115 are sequentially numbered to 550 and share the same design. Card numbers 116-131 are sequentially numbered to 1525 and also feature the same design with green highlights instead of yellow, and have authentic player autographs instead of a film cell. Card numbers 132-140 are sequentaily numbered to 700 and are also autographed. SP Authentic was packaged in 24-pack boxes with packs containing five cards and carried a suggested retail price of $4.99.

COMP.SET w/o SP's (90) 20.00 40.00
91-106 PRINT RUN 1600 SER.#'d SETS
107-115 PRINT RUN 550 SER.#'d SETS
116-131 PRINT RUN 1525 SER.#'d SETS
132-140 PRINT RUN 700 SER.#'d SETS
141-159 PRINT RUN 2000 SER.#'d SETS
160-165 PRINT RUN 1000 SER.#'d SETS
1 Shareef Abdur-Rahim .30 .75
2 Jason Terry .40 1.00
3 Dion Glover .25 .60
4 Paul Pierce .40 1.00
5 Antoine Walker .30 .75
6 Kenny Anderson .30 .75
7 Baron Davis .40 1.00
8 David Wesley .25 .60
9 Jamal Mashburn .30 .75
10 Jalen Rose .30 .75
11 Fred Hoiberg .25 .60
12 Marcus Fizer .25 .60
13 Andre Miller .30 .75
14 Lamond Murray .25 .60
15 Chris Mihm .25 .60
16 Dirk Nowitzki .60 1.50
17 Steve Nash .60 1.50
18 Michael Finley .40 1.00
19 Nick Van Exel .30 .75
20 Antonio McDyess .30 .75
21 Juwan Howard .30 .75
22 James Posey .25 .60
23 Jerry Stackhouse .30 .75
24 Clifford Robinson .25 .60
25 Ben Wallace .30 .75
26 Antawn Jamison .40 1.00
27 Larry Hughes .30 .75
28 Danny Fortson .25 .60
29 Steve Francis .30 .75
30 Cuttino Mobley .25 .60
31 Reggie Miller .40 1.00
32 Al Harrington .30 .75
33 Jermaine O'Neal .30 .75
34 Darius Miles .25 .60
35 Elton Brand .40 1.00
36 Lamar Odom .30 .75
37 Corey Maggette .30 .75
38 Kobe Bryant 1.50 4.00
39 Shaquille O'Neal 1.00 2.50
40 Rick Fox .25 .60
41 Lindsey Hunter .25 .60
42 Stromile Swift .25 .60
43 Michael Dickerson .25 .60
44 Jason Williams .30 .75
45 Alonzo Mourning .50 1.25
46 Eddie Jones .30 .75
47 Anthony Carter .25 .60
48 Ray Allen .40 1.00
49 Glenn Robinson .30 .75
50 Sam Cassell .30 .75
51 Kevin Garnett .60 1.50
52 Terrell Brandon .25 .60
53 Wally Szczerbiak .30 .75
54 Joe Smith .30 .75
55 Jason Kidd .60 1.50
56 Kenyon Martin .40 1.00
57 Mark Jackson .30 .75
58 Allan Houston .30 .75
59 Latrell Sprewell .30 .75
60 Marcus Camby .30 .75
61 Tracy McGrady .60 1.50
62 Grant Hill .50 1.25
63 Mike Miller .30 .75
64 Allen Iverson .75 2.00
65 Dikembe Mutombo .40 1.00
66 Aaron McKie .25 .60
67 Stephon Marbury .30 .75
68 Shawn Marion .30 .75
69 Anfernee Hardaway .60 1.50
70 Rasheed Wallace .40 1.00
71 Bonzi Wells .25 .60
72 Derek Anderson .25 .60
73 Chris Webber .40 1.00
74 Mike Bibby .40 1.00
75 Peja Stojakovic .40 1.00
76 Tim Duncan .75 2.00
77 David Robinson .60 1.50
78 Antonio Daniels .25 .60
79 Gary Payton .40 1.00
80 Rashard Lewis .40 1.00
81 Desmond Mason .30 .75
82 Vince Carter .60 1.50
83 Morris Peterson .25 .60
84 Antonio Davis .25 .60
85 Karl Malone .50 1.25
86 John Stockton .50 1.25
87 Donyell Marshall .25 .60
88 Richard Hamilton .30 .75
89 Courtney Alexander .25 .60
90 Michael Jordan 6.00 15.00
91 Tierre Brown RC 2.00 5.00
92 Damone Brown RC 1.25 3.00
93 Michael Bradley RC 1.25 3.00
94 Kedrick Brown RC 1.25 3.00
95 Alton Ford RC 2.00 5.00
96 Jason Collins RC 1.50 4.00
97 Antonis Fotsis RC 1.25 3.00
98 Mengke Bateer RC 2.00 5.00
99 Trenton Hassell RC 1.50 4.00
100 Jamison Brewer RC 2.00 5.00
101 Bobby Simmons RC 2.00 5.00
102 Mike James RC 2.00 5.00
103 Oscar Torres RC 2.00 5.00
104 Brandon Armstrong RC 1.25 3.00
105 Will Solomon RC 2.00 5.00
106 Vladimir Radmanovic RC 2.00 5.00
107 Kirk Haston RC 2.00 5.00
108 Gerald Wallace RC 4.00 10.00
109 Andrei Kirilenko RC 5.00 12.00
110 Joseph Forte RC 2.00 5.00
111 Brendan Haywood RC 3.00 8.00
112 Zach Randolph RC 5.00 12.00
113 DeSagana Diop RC 2.50 6.00
114 Shane Battier RC 6.00 15.00
115 Pau Gasol RC 10.00 25.00
116 Alvin Jones AU RC 2.50 6.00
117 Zeljko Rebraca AU RC 3.00 8.00
118 Kenny Satterfield AU RC 2.00 5.00
119 Jarron Collins AU RC 3.00 8.00
120 Ruben Boumtje-Boumtje AU RC 3.00 8.00
121 Loren Woods AU RC 2.00 5.00
122 Earl Watson AU RC 3.00 8.00
123 Jeff Trepagnier AU RC 2.00 5.00
124 Brian Scalabrine AU RC 3.00 8.00
125 Terence Morris AU RC 3.00 8.00
126 Gilbert Arenas AU RC 8.00 20.00
127 S.Dalembert AU RC 3.00 8.00
128 Jeryl Sasser AU RC 2.00 5.00
129 Rodney White AU RC 2.00 5.00
130 Eddie Griffin AU RC 2.50 6.00
131 Tyson Chandler AU RC 5.00 12.00
132 Steven Hunter AU RC 3.00 8.00
133 Troy Murphy AU RC 4.00 10.00
134 Richard Jefferson AU RC 6.00 15.00
135 Joe Johnson AU RC 5.00 12.00
136 Eddy Curry AU RC 4.00 10.00
137 J.Richardson AU RC 5.00 12.00
138 Tony Parker AU RC 30.00 80.00
139 Jamaal Tinsley AU RC 4.00 10.00
140 Kwame Brown AU RC 4.00 10.00
141 Paul Pierce SPEC 1.25 3.00
142 Tim Duncan SPEC 2.50 6.00
143 Stephon Marbury SPEC 1.00 2.50
144 Shareef Abdur-Rahim SPEC 1.00 2.50
145 Ray Allen SPEC 1.25 3.00
146 Bonzi Wells SPEC .75 2.00
147 Kenyon Martin SPEC 1.25 3.00
148 Darius Miles SPEC .75 2.00
149 Baron Davis SPEC 1.25 3.00
150 Dirk Nowitzki SPEC 2.00 5.00
151 Antoine Walker SPEC 1.00 2.50
152 Mike Miller SPEC 1.00 2.50
153 Shawn Marion SPEC 1.00 2.50
154 Jason Kidd SPEC 2.00 5.00
155 Elton Brand SPEC 1.25 3.00
156 Antawn Jamison SPEC 1.25 3.00
157 Rashard Lewis SPEC 1.25 3.00
158 Steve Francis SPEC 1.00 2.50
159 Tracy McGrady SPEC 2.00 5.00
160 Kobe Bryant SPEC 6.00 15.00
161 Allen Iverson SPEC 3.00 8.00
162 Vince Carter SPEC 2.50 6.00
163 Shaquille O'Neal SPEC 4.00 10.00
164 Kevin Garnett SPEC 2.50 6.00
165 Michael Jordan SPEC 12.00 30.00
PROMO Michael Jordan PROMO 4.00 10.00

2001-02 SP Authentic Dual Signatures

Randomly inserted in packs, this six card set features two autographs from NBA superstars on each card. Small square portrait photos appear of each of the featured players where a signing box is left next to them for authentic player autographs. Each card is squentially numbered to 50.

PRINT RUN 50 SER.#'d SETS
DR/LB J.Erving/L.Bird 150.00 300.00
KB/MG K.Bryant/M.Johnson 200.00 400.00
MG/LB M.Johnson/L.Bird 150.00 300.00
MJ/DR M.Jordan/J.Erving 500.00 1000.00
MJ/KB M.Jordan/K.Bryant 600.00 1200.00
TC/EC T.Chandler/E.Curry 10.00 25.00

2001-02 SP Authentic Rookie Authentics

Randomly seeded in packs, this 23-card set is designed horizontally with full color player photos on the left and a large square jersey swatch on the right. Each card is sequentially numbered to 1275.

PRINT RUN 1275 SER.#'d SETS
RAAK Andrei Kirilenko 3.00 8.00
RABA Brandon Armstrong 1.25 3.00
RAEC Eddy Curry 2.00 5.00
RAEG Eddie Griffin 1.50 4.00
RAGW Gerald Wallace 2.50 6.00
RAJA Jarron Collins 2.00 5.00
RAJC Jason Collins 1.50 4.00
RAJF Joseph Forte 1.25 3.00
RAJJ Joe Johnson 2.50 6.00
RAJR Jason Richardson 2.50 6.00
RAJS Jeryl Sasser 1.25 3.00
RAKB Kedrick Brown 1.25 3.00
RAKW Kwame Brown 2.00 5.00
RAMB Michael Bradley 1.25 3.00
RARJ Richard Jefferson 3.00 8.00
RARW Rodney White 1.25 3.00
RASD Samuel Dalembert 2.00 5.00
RASH Steven Hunter 1.50 4.00
RATC Tyson Chandler 3.00 8.00
RATH Trenton Hassell 1.50 4.00
RATM Terence Morris 2.00 5.00
RATP Tony Parker 10.00 25.00
RAVR Vladimir Radmanovic 2.00 5.00

2001-02 SP Authentic Signatures

Randomly seeded in packs, this 24-card set is horizontally designed with full color player action photos on the right side and a white strip on the bottom third of the card where player autographs appear. Each card is squentially numbered to 390.

PRINT RUN 390 SER.#'d SETS
UNPRICED TRIPLE AUTO PRINT RUN 10 SETS
AJ Alvin Jones 3.00 8.00
DJ DerMarr Johnson 4.00 10.00
EG Eddie Griffin 3.00 8.00
GA Gilbert Arenas 8.00 20.00
GW Gerald Wallace 5.00 12.00
JC Jason Collins 8.00 20.00
JJ Joe Johnson 5.00 12.00
JR Jason Richardson 5.00 12.00
JS Jeryl Sasser 2.50 6.00
JT Jamaal Tinsley 4.00 10.00
KM Kenyon Martin 6.00 15.00
KS Kenny Satterfield 2.50 6.00
KW Kwame Brown 4.00 10.00
LW Loren Woods 2.50 6.00
MM Mike Miller 5.00 12.00
MP Morris Peterson 4.00 10.00
QR Quentin Richardson 3.00 8.00
RJ Richard Jefferson 6.00 15.00
RW Rodney White 2.50 6.00
SH Steven Hunter 3.00 8.00
TC Tyson Chandler 6.00 15.00
TM Troy Murphy 4.00 10.00
TP Tony Parker 30.00 80.00
VR Vladimir Radmanovic 4.00 10.00

2001-02 SP Authentic Star Signatures

Randomly inserted in packs, this six card set utilizes the same design as the Star Signatures with cards sequentially numbered to 75.

PRINT RUN 75 SER.#'d SETS
DMS Darius Miles 15.00 30.00
JKS Jason Kidd 25.00 60.00
KBS Kobe Bryant 150.00 300.00
KGS Kevin Garnett 40.00 100.00
MJS Michael Jordan 400.00 800.00
SAS Shareef Abdur-Rahim 15.00 30.00

2001-02 SP Authentic Superstar Authentics

Randomly seeded in packs, this seven card set is designed horizontally with full color player photos on the left and a large square jersey swatch on the right. Each card is sequentially numbered to 200.

PRINT RUN 200 SER.#'d SETS
SAAI Allen Iverson 10.00 25.00
SACW Chris Webber 8.00 20.00
SAJK Jason Kidd 8.00 20.00
SAKB Kobe Bryant 12.00 30.00
SAKG Kevin Garnett 8.00 20.00
SAMJ Michael Jordan 30.00 80.00
SATM Tracy McGrady 8.00 20.00

2002-03 SP Authentic

Released in April 2003, SP Authentic was issued as a 203-card set divided up as follows: Veteran cards 1-100, SP Specials veterans card numbers 101-142 (sequentially numbered to 2000), Autographed Rookies card numbers 143-174 (sequentially numbered to 1500), and Rookie cards numbers 175-203 (sequentially numbered to 1500). Several veteran players also had autographed versions of their base cards inserted into the product. These cards are denoted as "A" versions and are not included in the base set price or card count. Base cards have white borders and a white background with gray hatch marks along the left and right side of the card. SP Authentic was packaged in 24-pack boxes where packs contained five cards and carried a suggested retail price of $4.99.

COMP.SET w/o SP's (100) 15.00 40.00
101-142 PRINT RUN 2000 SER.#'d SETS
143-174 PRINT RUN 1500 SER.#'d SETS
175-203 PRINT RUN 1500 SER.#'d SETS
1 Glenn Robinson .30 .75
2 Shareef Abdur-Rahim .30 .75
3 Jason Terry .30 .75
4 Theo Ratliff .25 .60
5 Paul Pierce .40 1.00
5A Paul Pierce AU 15.00 40.00
6 Antoine Walker .30 .75
6A Antoine Walker AU 8.00 20.00
7 Tony Delk .25 .60
8 Vin Baker .30 .75
9 Jalen Rose .30 .75
10 Eddy Curry .25 .60
11 Tyson Chandler .40 1.00
11A Tyson Chandler AU 5.00 12.00
12 Marcus Fizer .25 .60
12A Marcus Fizer AU 5.00 12.00
13 Darius Miles .25 .60
14 Zydrunas Ilgauskas .30 .75
15 Dirk Nowitzki .60 1.50
16 Michael Finley .40 1.00
17 Steve Nash .50 1.25
18 Raef LaFrentz .25 .60
19 Juwan Howard .30 .75
20 Rodney White .25 .60
21 Ben Wallace .30 .75
22 Richard Hamilton .30 .75
23 Chauncey Billups .40 1.00
24 Chucky Atkins .25 .60
25 Jason Richardson .40 1.00
26 Antawn Jamison .40 1.00
27 Gilbert Arenas .40 1.00
28 Steve Francis .30 .75
29 Cuttino Mobley .25 .60
30 Jermaine O'Neal .30 .75
30A Jermaine O'Neal AU 8.00 20.00
31 Jamaal Tinsley .25 .60
32 Reggie Miller .40 1.00
33 Ron Artest .40 1.00
34 Elton Brand .40 1.00
35 Andre Miller .30 .75
36 Michael Olowokandi .25 .60
37 Kobe Bryant 1.50 4.00
38 Shaquille O'Neal 1.00 2.50
39 Robert Horry .30 .75
40 Derek Fisher .30 .75
41 Pau Gasol .50 1.25
42 Shane Battier .40 1.00
43 Eddie Jones .30 .75
44 Brian Grant .25 .60
45 Malik Allen .25 .60
46 Gary Payton .40 1.00
47 Sam Cassell .30 .75
48 Kevin Garnett .60 1.50
49 Wally Szczerbiak .30 .75
50 Troy Hudson .25 .60
51 Radoslav Nesterovic .25 .60
52 Jason Kidd .60 1.50
53 Richard Jefferson .40 1.00
54 Kenyon Martin .30 .75
54A Kenyon Martin AU 8.00 20.00
55 Kerry Kittles .25 .60
56 Baron Davis .30 .75
57 Jamal Mashburn .30 .75
58 David Wesley .25 .60
59 P.J. Brown .25 .60
60 Jamaal Magloire .25 .60
60A Jamaal Magloire AU 5.00 12.00
61 Allan Houston .30 .75
62 Kurt Thomas .25 .60
63 Latrell Sprewell .30 .75
64 Clarence Weatherspoon .25 .60
65 Tracy McGrady .60 1.50
66 Grant Hill .50 1.25
67 Mike Miller .30 .75
67A Mike Miller AU 8.00 20.00
68 Allen Iverson .60 1.50
69 Keith Van Horn .30 .75
70 Stephon Marbury .30 .75
71 Shawn Marion .30 .75
72 Anfernee Hardaway .60 1.50
73 Rasheed Wallace .40 1.00
74 Derek Anderson .25 .60
75 Scottie Pippen .60 1.50
76 Bonzi Wells .25 .60
77 Chris Webber .40 1.00
78 Mike Bibby .40 1.00
78A Mike Bibby AU 6.00 15.00
79 Peja Stojakovic .40 1.00
80 Hedo Turkoglu .30 .75
81 Vlade Divac .30 .75
82 Tim Duncan .75 2.00
83 David Robinson .60 1.50
84 Tony Parker .50 1.25
85 Steve Smith .30 .75
86 Ray Allen .40 1.00
87 Rashard Lewis .40 1.00
88 Brent Barry .25 .60
89 Elden Campbell .25 .60
90 Vince Carter .60 1.50
91 Morris Peterson .25 .60
92 Antonio Davis .25 .60
93 Alvin Williams .25 .60
94 Karl Malone .50 1.25
95 John Stockton .50 1.25
96 Andrei Kirilenko .40 1.00
97 DeShawn Stevenson .25 .60
97A DeShawn Stevenson AU 5.00 12.00
98 Jerry Stackhouse .30 .75
99 Michael Jordan 3.00 8.00
100 Kwame Brown .25 .60
101 Kobe Bryant SPEC 4.00 10.00
102 Allen Iverson SPEC 1.50 4.00
103 Pau Gasol SPEC 1.25 3.00
104 Antoine Walker SPEC .75 2.00
105 Jermaine O'Neal SPEC .75 2.00
106 Ray Allen SPEC 1.00 2.50
107 Baron Davis SPEC .75 2.00
108 Tim Duncan SPEC 2.00 5.00
109 Rashard Lewis SPEC 1.00 2.50
110 Michael Jordan SPEC 10.00 25.00
111 Stephon Marbury SPEC .75 2.00
112 Shareef Abdur-Rahim SPEC .75 2.00
113 Vince Carter SPEC 1.50 4.00
114 Allan Houston SPEC .75 2.00
115 Dirk Nowitzki SPEC 1.50 4.00
116 Grant Hill SPEC 1.25 3.00
117 Mike Bibby SPEC 1.00 2.50
118 Derek Anderson SPEC .60 1.50
119 Shaquille O'Neal SPEC 2.50 6.00
120 Steve Francis SPEC .75 2.00
121 Richard Jefferson SPEC 1.00 2.50
122 Ben Wallace SPEC .75 2.00
123 Jason Kidd SPEC 1.50 4.00
124 Jalen Rose SPEC .75 2.00
125 Paul Pierce SPEC 1.00 2.50
126 Michael Finley SPEC 1.00 2.50
127 Jamal Mashburn SPEC .75 2.00
128 Elton Brand SPEC 1.00 2.50
129 Rasheed Wallace SPEC 1.00 2.50
130 Gary Payton SPEC 1.00 2.50
131 Tracy McGrady SPEC 1.50 4.00
132 Richard Hamilton SPEC .75 2.00
133 Chris Webber SPEC 1.00 2.50
134 Karl Malone SPEC 1.25 3.00
135 Darius Miles SPEC .60 1.50
136 Shawn Marion SPEC .75 2.00
137 Kevin Garnett SPEC 1.50 4.00
138 Eddie Jones SPEC .75 2.00
139 Jason Richardson SPEC 1.00 2.50
140 Glenn Robinson SPEC .75 2.00
141 Jerry Stackhouse SPEC .75 2.00
142 Shane Battier SPEC 1.00 2.50
143 Yao Ming AU RC 40.00 100.00
144 Jay Williams AU RC 3.00 8.00
145 Drew Gooden AU RC 3.00 8.00
146 N.Tskitishvili AU RC 2.00 5.00
147 DaJuan Wagner AU RC 2.50 6.00
148 Nene Hilario AU RC 3.00 8.00
149 Chris Wilcox AU RC 2.50 6.00
150 Amare Stoudemire AU RC 6.00 15.00
151 Caron Butler AU RC 6.00 15.00
152 Jared Jeffries AU RC 2.50 6.00
153 Melvin Ely AU RC 2.50 6.00
154 Marcus Haislip AU RC 2.50 6.00
155 Fred Jones AU RC 2.50 6.00
156 Bostjan Nachbar AU RC 2.50 6.00
157 Jiri Welsch AU RC 2.50 6.00
158 Juan Dixon AU RC 3.00 8.00
159 Curtis Borchardt AU RC 2.00 5.00
160 Ryan Humphrey AU RC 2.50 6.00
161 Kareem Rush AU RC 2.50 6.00
162 Qyntel Woods AU RC 2.50 6.00
163 Casey Jacobsen AU RC 2.50 6.00
164 Tayshaun Prince AU RC 5.00 12.00
165 Frank Williams AU RC 2.00 5.00
166 John Salmons AU RC 3.00 8.00
167 Chris Jefferies AU RC 2.00 5.00
168 Dan Dickau AU RC 2.50 6.00
169 Carlos Boozer AU RC 3.00 8.00
170 Marko Jaric AU 3.00 8.00
171 Sam Clancy AU RC 2.50 6.00
172 Manu Ginobili AU RC 30.00 80.00
173 V.Yarbrough AU RC 2.00 5.00
174 Gordan Giricek AU RC 3.00 8.00
175 Predrag Savovic RC 1.25 3.00
176 Mike Dunleavy RC 1.50 4.00
177 Tamar Slay RC 1.00 2.50
178 Rasual Butler RC 1.50 4.00
179 Reggie Evans RC 1.50 4.00
180 Igor Rakocevic RC 1.00 2.50
181 Juaquin Hawkins RC 1.00 2.50
182 J.R. Bremer RC 1.00 2.50
183 Cezary Trybanski RC 1.50 4.00
184 Junior Harrington RC 1.00 2.50
185 Efthimios Rentzias RC 1.00 2.50
186 Smush Parker RC 1.50 4.00
187 Jamal Sampson RC 1.50 4.00
188 Roger Mason RC 1.25 3.00
189 Robert Archibald RC 1.00 2.50
190 Mehmet Okur RC 1.50 4.00
191 Dan Gadzuric RC 1.25 3.00
192 Pat Burke RC 1.00 2.50
193 Lonny Baxter RC 1.00 2.50
194 Tito Maddox RC 1.00 2.50
195 Jannero Pargo RC 1.00 2.50
196 Ronald Murray RC 1.50 4.00
197 Mike Wilks RC 1.50 4.00
198 Mike Batiste RC 1.00 2.50
199 Chris Owens RC 1.00 2.50
200 Raul Lopez RC 1.50 4.00
201 Antoine Rigaudeau RC 1.50 4.00
202 Ken Johnson 1.50 4.00
203 Maceo Baston RC 1.50 4.00
NNO Michael Jordan PROMO 2.00 5.00

2002-03 SP Authentic Limited

*1-100 STARS: 3X TO 8X BASE CARD HI
*1-100 AU's: .75X TO 2X BASE CARD HI
*101-142 SPEC: 1.25X TO 3X BASE CARD HI
1-142 PRINT RUN 100 SER.#'d SETS
*RCs: 1.5X TO 4X BASE CARD HI
143-203 RC PRINT RUN 50 SER.#'d SETS
150 Amare Stoudemire AU 60.00 150.00
151 Caron Butler AU 40.00 100.00

2002-03 SP Authentic Dual Excellence Signatures

Randomly inserted in packs, this six-card set features two players and two player autographs on each card. Small square portrait photos of the players appear on the top and the bottom of the card, next to which is an authentic player autograph. Each card is sequentially numbered to 25.

PRINT RUN 25 SER.#'d SETS
JEKA J.Erving/K.Abdul-Jabbar 150.00 300.00
KBJK K.Bryant/J.Kidd 175.00 350.00
KBMB K.Bryant/M.Bibby 125.00 250.00
MJLB M.Jordan/L.Bird 500.00 1000.00

2002-03 SP Authentic Marks of Distinction

Randomly inserted in packs, this 10-card set features both current and retired NBA players. Full color player portraits are bordered with gold and set on a card with gray and white borders. Each card is autographed and sequentially numbered to 50.

PRINT RUN 50 SER.#'d SETS
BRM Bill Russell 150.00 300.00
DRM Julius Erving 75.00 200.00
JKM Jason Kidd 75.00 150.00
JRM Jason Richardson 12.00 30.00
JWM Jay Williams 12.00 30.00
KAM Kareem Abdul-Jabbar 75.00 150.00
KBM Kobe Bryant 200.00 400.00
KGM Kevin Garnett 60.00 150.00
LBM Larry Bird 50.00 120.00
MJM Michael Jordan 400.00 800.00

2002-03 SP Authentic SP Dual Signatures

Randomly inserted at the rate of one Dual or Single Signature per box, this 12-card set places one player photo on the top next to his signature and the same on the bottom. All cards have gold foil highlights.

ONE SINGLE SIG OR DUAL SIG PER BOX
ASCJ A.Stoudemire/C.Jacobsen 10.00 25.00
CWME C.Wilcox/M.Ely 6.00 15.00
DRKA J.Erving/Kareem SP 100.00 250.00
DWCB D.Wagner/C.Boozer 6.00 15.00
EGMJ M.Ginobili/M.Jaric 15.00 40.00
JJJD J.Dixon/J.Jeffries 6.00 15.00
JKKM J.Kidd/K.Marton 20.00 50.00
JWTC JayWill/Chandler SP 15.00 40.00
KBKA Bryant/Kareem SP 200.00 400.00
MJKB Jordan/Bryant SP 700.00 1200.00
PPAW P.Pierce/A.Walker 15.00 40.00
YMJW Y.Ming/J.Williams 25.00 60.00

2002-03 SP Authentic SP Signatures

Randomly inserted in packs at the rate of one single or one dual signature per box, this 40-card set places full-color player portraits in the lower left hand corner set against a gray-scale action photo in the background. All cards contain authentic player autographs.

ONE SINGLE SIG OR DUAL SIG PER BOX
AW Antoine Walker 5.00 12.00
BN Bostjan Nachbar 2.50 6.00
CA Carlos Boozer 3.00 8.00
CB Chauncey Billups 6.00 15.00
CU Curtis Borchardt 2.00 5.00
CW Chris Wilcox 2.50 6.00
DD Dan Dickau 2.50 6.00
DG Dan Gadzuric 2.50 6.00
DR Julius Erving SP 50.00 120.00
DS DeShawn Stevenson 3.00 8.00
DW DaJuan Wagner 2.50 6.00
EG Manu Ginobili 15.00 40.00
ET Etan Thomas 3.00 8.00
FW Frank Williams 2.00 5.00
GW Gerald Wallace 6.00 15.00
JD Juan Dixon 3.00 8.00
JK Jason Kidd 15.00 40.00
JM Jamaal Magloire 3.00 8.00
JO Jermaine O'Neal 4.00 10.00
JR Jason Richardson 4.00 10.00
JS John Salmons 3.00 8.00
JW Jay Williams 6.00 15.00
KA Kareem Abdul-Jabbar 25.00 60.00
KB Kobe Bryant SP 125.00 250.00
KG Kevin Garnett SP 40.00 100.00
KM Kenyon Martin 6.00 15.00
KR Kareem Rush 2.50 6.00
LB Larry Bird 100.00 200.00
MB Mike Bibby 5.00 12.00
MF Marcus Fizer 3.00 8.00
MJ Michael Jordan SP 600.00 1000.00
MM Mike Miller 5.00 12.00
MO Jerome Moiso 4.00 10.00
PP Paul Pierce 10.00 25.00
PS Peja Stojakovic 6.00 15.00
SC Sam Clancy 2.50 6.00
SM Shawn Marion SP 8.00 20.00
TC Tyson Chandler 5.00 12.00
WE Jiri Welsch 2.50 6.00
YM Yao Ming 20.00 50.00

2002-03 SP Authentic Beckett.com Samples

SAMPLES: .75X TO 2X BASE HI

2003-04 SP Authentic

Released in March 2004, this 189-card set is divided up as follows: cards 1-90 are base veteran cards with framed oval full-color player photos; 91-132 and 144 are spectaculars cards sequentially numbered to 3999 with full-color player photos set on an "S" shaped wave background; 133-147 are rookie players sequentially numbered to 999; 148-153 are rookie players sequentially numbered to 500; and 154-189 are autographed rookie cards sequentially numbered to 1250. SP Authentic was packed in 24-pack boxes of five cards each and carried a suggested retail price of $4.99.

COMP.SET w/o SP's (90) 15.00 40.00
154-189 PRINT RUN 1250 SER.#'d SETS
HASLEM ON 138 NO RC AND 188 AU RC
1 Shareef Abdur-Rahim .30 .75
2 Theo Ratliff .25 .60
3 Jason Terry .30 .75
4 Raef LaFrentz .25 .60
5 Vin Baker .25 .60
6 Paul Pierce .40 1.00
7 Antonio Davis .25 .60
8 Scottie Pippen .60 1.50
9 Tyson Chandler .30 .75
10 Dajuan Wagner .25 .60
11 Carlos Boozer .30 .75
12 Zydrunas Ilgauskas .30 .75
13 Dirk Nowitzki .60 1.50
14 Antoine Walker .40 1.00
15 Steve Nash .50 1.25
16 Michael Finley .40 1.00
17 Earl Boykins .25 .60
18 Andre Miller .30 .75
19 Nene .30 .75
20 Chauncey Billups .40 1.00
21 Richard Hamilton .30 .75
22 Ben Wallace .30 .75
23 Clifford Robinson .25 .60
24 Jason Richardson .40 1.00
25 Nick Van Exel .30 .75
26 Yao Ming .75 2.00
27 Cuttino Mobley .25 .60
28 Steve Francis .30 .75
29 Jermaine O'Neal .30 .75
30 Reggie Miller .40 1.00
31 Ron Artest .40 1.00
32 Elton Brand .40 1.00
33 Corey Maggette .30 .75
34 Quentin Richardson .30 .75
35 Kobe Bryant 1.50 4.00
36 Karl Malone .50 1.25
37 Gary Payton .40 1.00
38 Shaquille O'Neal 1.00 2.50
39 Pau Gasol .40 1.00
40 Bonzi Wells .25 .60
41 Mike Miller .30 .75
42 Lamar Odom .30 .75
43 Eddie Jones .30 .75
44 Caron Butler .30 .75
45 Toni Kukoc .40 1.00
46 Desmond Mason .30 .75
47 Michael Redd .40 1.00
48 Latrell Sprewell .30 .75
49 Kevin Garnett .60 1.50
50 Sam Cassell .30 .75
51 Richard Jefferson .30 .75
52 Kenyon Martin .30 .75
53 Jason Kidd .60 1.50
54 Jamal Mashburn .30 .75
55 Baron Davis .30 .75
56 David Wesley .25 .60
57 Allan Houston .30 .75
58 Stephon Marbury .30 .75
59 Keith Van Horn .30 .75
60 Gordan Giricek .25 .60
61 Drew Gooden .30 .75
62 Tracy McGrady .50 1.25
63 Glenn Robinson .30 .75
64 Allen Iverson .60 1.50
65 Eric Snow .25 .60
66 Amare Stoudemire .50 1.25
67 Antonio McDyess .30 .75
68 Shawn Marion .30 .75
69 Zach Randolph .30 .75
70 Damon Stoudamire .30 .75
71 Rasheed Wallace .40 1.00
72 Peja Stojakovic .40 1.00
73 Chris Webber .40 1.00
74 Mike Bibby .40 1.00
75 Brad Miller .30 .75
76 Tony Parker .40 1.00
77 Tim Duncan .60 1.50
78 Manu Ginobili .50 1.25
79 Vladimir Radmanovic .25 .60
80 Ray Allen .40 1.00
81 Rashard Lewis .40 1.00
82 Morris Peterson .25 .60
83 Vince Carter .60 1.50
84 Jalen Rose .30 .75
85 Andrei Kirilenko .40 1.00
86 Matt Harpring .25 .60
87 Carlos Arroyo .30 .75
88 Gilbert Arenas .30 .75
89 Larry Hughes .30 .75
90 Jerry Stackhouse .30 .75
91 Kobe Bryant SPEC 4.00 10.00
92 Jason Kidd SPEC 1.50 4.00
93 Rasheed Wallace SPEC 1.00 2.50
94 Jalen Rose SPEC .75 2.00
95 Tim Duncan SPEC 1.50 4.00
96 Shareef Abdur-Rahim SPEC .75 2.00
97 Baron Davis SPEC .75 2.00
98 Pau Gasol SPEC 1.00 2.50
99 Allen Iverson SPEC 1.50 4.00
100 Yao Ming SPEC 2.00 5.00
101 Gary Payton SPEC 1.00 2.50
102 Ray Allen SPEC 1.00 2.50
103 Tracy McGrady SPEC 1.25 3.00
104 Amare Stoudemire SPEC 1.25 3.00
105 Tony Parker SPEC 1.00 2.50
106 Stephon Marbury SPEC .75 2.00
107 Richard Hamilton SPEC .75 2.00
108 Chris Webber SPEC 1.00 2.50
109 Elton Brand SPEC 1.00 2.50
110 Jerry Stackhouse SPEC .75 2.00
111 Andre Miller SPEC .75 2.00
112 Kevin Garnett SPEC 1.50 4.00
113 Jason Richardson SPEC 1.00 2.50
114 Allan Houston SPEC .75 2.00
115 Dajuan Wagner SPEC .60 1.50
116 Richard Jefferson SPEC .75 2.00
117 Shaquille O'Neal SPEC 2.50 6.00
118 Latrell Sprewell SPEC .75 2.00
119 Rashard Lewis SPEC 1.00 2.50
120 Steve Nash SPEC 1.25 3.00
121 Desmond Mason SPEC .75 2.00
122 Mike Bibby SPEC 1.00 2.50
123 Shawn Marion SPEC .75 2.00
124 Vince Carter SPEC 1.50 4.00
125 Caron Butler SPEC .75 2.00
126 Gilbert Arenas SPEC .75 2.00
127 Dirk Nowitzki SPEC 1.50 4.00
128 Paul Pierce SPEC 1.00 2.50
129 Jermaine O'Neal SPEC .75 2.00
130 Andrei Kirilenko SPEC 1.00 2.50
131 Michael Jordan SPEC 8.00 20.00
132 Steve Francis SPEC .75 2.00
133 T.J. Ford RC 2.00 5.00
134 Kirk Hinrich RC 2.50 6.00
135 Nick Collison RC 2.00 5.00
136 Maurice Carter RC 2.50 6.00
137 Francisco Elson RC 1.50 4.00
138 Udonis Haslem 2.00 5.00
139 Jon Stefansson RC 1.50 4.00
140 Richie Frahm RC 2.50 6.00
141 Ronald Dupree RC 1.50 4.00
142 Josh Moore RC 1.50 4.00
143 Alex Garcia RC 1.50 4.00
144 Zach Randolph SPEC .75 2.00
145 Ben Handlogten RC 1.50 4.00
146 Devin Brown RC 1.50 4.00
147 Marquis Daniels RC 2.00 5.00
148 LeBron James AU RC 4000.00 5000.00
149 Darko Milicic AU RC 5.00 12.00
150 Carmelo Anthony AU RC 50.00 120.00
151 Chris Bosh AU RC 20.00 50.00
152 Dwyane Wade AU RC 75.00 200.00
153 Jarvis Hayes AU RC 4.00 10.00
154 Mickael Pietrus AU RC 3.00 8.00
155 Chris Kaman AU RC 4.00 10.00
156 Dahntay Jones AU RC 3.00 8.00
157 Marcus Banks AU RC 2.50 6.00
158 Luke Ridnour AU RC 3.00 8.00
159 Reece Gaines AU RC 2.50 6.00
160 Troy Bell AU RC 2.50 6.00
161 Mike Sweetney AU RC 2.50 6.00
162 David West AU RC 4.00 10.00
163 Aleksandar Pavlovic AU RC 3.00 8.00
164 Steve Blake AU RC 3.00 8.00
165 Boris Diaw AU RC 4.00 10.00
166 Zoran Planinic AU RC 2.50 6.00
167 Travis Outlaw AU RC 3.00 8.00
168 Brian Cook AU RC 2.50 6.00
169 Jerome Beasley AU RC 2.50 6.00
170 Ndudi Ebi AU RC 2.50 6.00
171 Kendrick Perkins AU RC 3.00 8.00
172 Leandro Barbosa AU RC 4.00 10.00
173 Josh Howard AU RC 4.00 10.00
174 Maciej Lampe AU RC 2.50 6.00
175 Jason Kapono AU RC 2.50 6.00
176 Luke Walton AU RC 4.00 10.00
177 Slavko Vranes AU RC 2.50 6.00
178 Zarko Cabarkapa AU RC 2.50 6.00
179 Zaur Pachulia AU RC 4.00 10.00
180 Maurice Williams AU RC 4.00 10.00
181 Brandon Hunter AU RC 2.50 6.00
182 Keith Bogans AU RC 2.50 6.00
183 Travis Hansen AU RC 2.50 6.00
184 Theron Smith AU RC 2.50 6.00
185 Willie Green AU RC 2.50 6.00
186 James Jones AU RC 2.50 6.00
187 Kyle Korver AU RC 5.00 12.00
188 Udonis Haslem AU RC 3.00 8.00
189 James Lang AU RC 2.50 6.00

2003-04 SP Authentic Limited

*1-90 SINGLES: 2X TO 5X BASE HI
*91-132 SPEC: .75X TO 2X BASE HI
*133-147 RCs: .75X TO 2X BASE HI
1-147 PRINT RUN 100 SER.#'d SETS
148-153 PRINT RUN 50 SER.#'d SETS
*154-189 AU RCs: .6X TO 1.5X BASE HI
154-189 PRINT RUN 100 SER.#'d SETS
35 Kobe Bryant 12.00 30.00
91 Kobe Bryant SPEC 12.00 30.00
148 LeBron James AU 4000.00 6000.00

2003-04 SP Authentic Limited Extra

*1-90 SINGLES: 6X TO 15X BASE HI
*91-132 SPEC: 2.5X TO 6X BASE HI
*133-147 RCs: 1.25X TO 3X BASE HI
1-147 PRINT RUN 25 SER.#'d SETS
*154-189 AU RCs: 1X TO 2.5X BASE HI
154-189 PRINT RUN 25 SER.#'d SETS
35 Kobe Bryant 40.00 100.00
131 Michael Jordan SPEC 75.00 150.00
180 Maurice Williams AU 30.00 80.00

2003-04 SP Authentic Signatures

Inserted in packs with all other autographs at the overall odds of one in 24, this 59-card set utilizes a horizontal design with full-color player action photos on the right and authentic player autographs on the left.

ALL SIG STATED ODDS 1:24
ADA Antonio McDyess 5.00 12.00
AJA Antawn Jamison 5.00 12.00
AMJ Andre Miller 4.00 10.00
CAA Corey Maggette 4.00 10.00
CBA Chauncey Billups 8.00 20.00
CHA Chris Bosh 12.00 30.00
CKA Chris Kaman 4.00 10.00
COA Carlos Boozer 4.00 10.00
CYA Carmelo Anthony SP 25.00 60.00
DAA Darius Miles 4.00 10.00
DEA Desmond Mason 4.00 10.00
DJA Dahntay Jones 3.00 8.00
DMA Darko Milicic 3.00 8.00
DRA David Robinson 15.00 40.00
DWA Dajuan Wagner 4.00 10.00
DYA Dwyane Wade 60.00 150.00
ECA Eddy Curry 4.00 10.00
EGA Manu Ginobili 20.00 50.00
GAA Gilbert Arenas 8.00 20.00
GGA Gordan Giricek 4.00 10.00
GPA Gary Payton 25.00 60.00
GWA Gerald Wallace 4.00 10.00
JAA Jarvis Hayes 2.50 6.00
JEA Julius Erving 30.00 80.00
JHA Josh Howard 4.00 10.00
JKA Jason Kidd 12.00 30.00
JOA Jason Kapono 2.50 6.00
JRA Jason Richardson SP 6.00 15.00
JSA Jerry Stackhouse 5.00 12.00
KBA Kobe Bryant SP 100.00 200.00
KGA Kevin Garnett SP 30.00 80.00
KKA Kyle Korver 5.00 12.00
KOA Keith Bogans 2.50 6.00
LBA Larry Bird 60.00 120.00
LJA LeBron James SP 500.00 1000.00
LOA Lamar Odom 6.00 15.00
LWA Luke Walton 4.00 10.00
MAA Marcus Banks 2.50 6.00
MBA Mike Bibby 4.00 10.00
MJA Michael Jordan SP 350.00 700.00
MOA Morris Peterson 4.00 10.00
MPA Mickael Pietrus 3.00 8.00
MSA Mike Sweetney 2.50 6.00
MWA Maurice Williams 4.00 10.00
NEA Ndudi Ebi 2.50 6.00
PEA Patrick Ewing 125.00 250.00
PPA Paul Pierce 12.00 30.00
PSA Peja Stojakovic 15.00 40.00
RHA Richard Hamilton 6.00 15.00
SAA Shareef Abdur-Rahim 4.00 10.00
SBA Shane Battier 4.00 10.00

SMA Shawn Marion 6.00 15.00
SVA Slavko Vranes 2.50 6.00
TBA Troy Bell 2.50 6.00
TMA Tracy McGrady 15.00 40.00
TPA Tony Parker 15.00 40.00
YMA Yao Ming 15.00 40.00
ZOA Alonzo Mourning 10.00 25.00
ZPA Zoran Planinic 2.50 6.00

2003-04 SP Authentic Signatures Dual

Inserted in packs at the rate of one in 288, this 29-card set pairs players where one is on the top and one is on the bottom and their signatures. Small portrait photos appear on the right while the autographs appear on the left.

STATED ODDS 1:288
AKA S.Abdur-R/J.Kidd 12.00 30.00
ASA G.Arenas/J.Stackhouse 8.00 20.00
BBA T.Bell/S.Battier 8.00 20.00
BMA L.Bird/A.Mourning SP 175.00 325.00
BRA B.Barry/L.Ridnour 4.00 10.00
BSA M.Bibby/P.Stojakovic 15.00 30.00
CRA E.Curry/J.Rose 8.00 20.00
CWA B.Cook/L.Walton 4.00 10.00
ESA J.Erving/A.Stoudemire SP 50.00 100.00
GBA K.Garnett/K.Bryant SP 150.00 300.00
HAD R.Hamilton/C.Billups 12.00 30.00
HPA B.Hunter/P.Pierce 8.00 20.00
JAA L.James/C.Anthony SP 600.00 1000.00
JJA M.Jordan/L.James SP 1200.00 1800.00
KJA J.Kidd/R.Jefferson SP 20.00 50.00
MDA S.Marion/L.Barbosa 8.00 20.00
MGA T.McGrady/R.Gaines SP 15.00 40.00
MIA D.Milicic/C.Billups SP 8.00 20.00
MLA A.McDyess/M.Lampe 8.00 20.00
MSA A.Miller/R.Gaines 8.00 20.00
NAA Nene/C.Anthony SP 30.00 80.00
OPA T.Outlaw/K.Perkins 8.00 20.00
OWA L.Odom/D.Wade 30.00 60.00
PBA M.Peterson/C.Bosh 8.00 20.00
PGA T.Parker/M.Ginobili 20.00 50.00
PKA G.Payton/K.Bryant SP 125.00 250.00
RPA J.Richardson/M.Pietrus 8.00 20.00
SRA J.Stockton/D.Robinson 60.00 150.00
WMA D.Wagner/D.Miles 8.00 20.00

2003-04 SP Authentic Signatures Triple

Randomly inserted, the design of this set is very similar to the Dual Signatures insert with one more player added. There are nine cards in the set and each card is sequentially numbered to 15.

PRINT RUN 15 SER.#'d SETS
AMN Carmelo/A.Miller/Nene 75.00 150.00
HPW Hayes/Pietrus/West 40.00 100.00
JJB LeBron/MJ/Kobe 2000.00 3500.00
KPB Kidd/Parker/Banks 100.00 200.00
MBK Darko/Bosh/Kaman 50.00 120.00
MRP McGrady/J.Rich/Pierce 100.00 200.00
PBJ Payton/Kobe/Magic 250.00 500.00
SMB Amare/Marion/Barb 50.00 125.00

2003-04 SP Authentic SPGU Authentic Fabrics Dual

Randomly inserted in packs, this 12-card set features a horizontal design with two players, one on each of the left and right side of the card with two swatches of jersey in the center. Each card is sequentially numbered to 50.

PRINT RUN 50 SER.#'d SETS
UNPRICED QUAD PRINT RUN 10 SETS
AMJ C.Anthony/A.Miller 20.00 40.00
BGJ T.Bell/P.Gasol 6.00 15.00
BOJ K.Bryant/L.Walton 12.00 30.00
GMJ R.Gaines/T.McGrady 8.00 20.00
HSJ J.Hayes/J.Stackhouse 6.00 15.00
HTJ T.Hansen/J.Terry 6.00 15.00
KBJ C.Kaman/E.Brand 6.00 15.00
MSJ D.Milicic/A.Stoudemire 8.00 20.00
PRJ M.Pietrus/J.Richardson 6.00 15.00
SHJ M.Sweetney/A.Houston 6.00 15.00
WBJ D.Wade/C.Butler 25.00 60.00

2003-04 SP Authentic SPGU Authentic Fabrics Triple

Randomly inserted, this 12-card set places three players and three swatches of game used fabric on a card where each is sequentially numbered to 25.

PRINT RUN 25 SER.#'d SETS
CCP Chandler/Curry/Pip 50.00 120.00
DMW B.Davis/Mash/West 12.50 30.00
GSE KG/Sprewell/Ebi 20.00 50.00
JJM LeBron/MJ/McGrady 200.00 400.00
JMW LeBron/Darko/Wade 150.00 300.00
MBJ M.Miller/Battier/Jones 12.50 30.00
MML McDyess/Marion/Lampe 12.50 30.00
MRK D.Mason/Redd/Kukoc 30.00 80.00
POB Payton/Shaq/Kobe 75.00 150.00
VRP Van Exel/J-Rich/Pietrus 12.50 30.00

2003-04 SP Authentic SPGU Rookie Authentic Fabrics

Randomly inserted, this 30-card set uses the same design as SP Game Used Authentic Fabrics with the SP Authentic logo appearing on the card instead. Full-color player photos appear on the right while a square swatch of memorabilia appears on the left. A Patch version was also issued, and these cards are sequentially numbered to 50.

PRINT RUN 150 SER.#'d SETS
APJ Aleksandar Pavlovic 3.00 8.00
BDJ Boris Diaw 4.00 10.00
CHJ Chris Bosh 6.00 15.00
CKJ Chris Kaman 4.00 10.00
CYJ Carmelo Anthony 12.00 30.00
DEJ David West 4.00 10.00
DJJ Dahntay Jones 3.00 8.00
DMJ Darko Milicic 3.00 8.00
DYJ Dwyane Wade 20.00 50.00
JHJ Jarvis Hayes 2.50 6.00
JKJ Jason Kapono 2.50 6.00
JOJ Josh Howard 4.00 10.00
KOJ Keith Bogans 2.50 6.00
KPJ Kendrick Perkins 3.00 8.00
KPJ Zoran Planinic 2.50 6.00
LBJ Leandro Barbosa 4.00 10.00
LJJ LeBron James 100.00 200.00
LRJ Luke Ridnour 3.00 8.00
LWJ Luke Walton 4.00 10.00
MAJ Marcus Banks 2.50 6.00
MIJ Mike Sweetney 2.50 6.00
MLJ Maciej Lampe 2.50 6.00
MPJ Mickael Pietrus 3.00 8.00
NEJ Ndudi Ebi 2.50 6.00
RGJ Reece Gaines 2.50 6.00
SBJ Steve Blake 3.00 8.00
TBJ Troy Bell 2.50 6.00
THJ Travis Hansen 2.50 6.00
TOJ Travis Outlaw 3.00 8.00
ZCJ Zarko Cabarkapa 2.50 6.00

2003-04 SP Authentic SPGU Rookie Authentic Patches

This 30-card set is a parallel insert to the SPGU Rookie Authentic Fabrics set enhanced with premium patch memorabilia swatches and sequential numbering to 50.

*PATCHES: 1X TO 2.5X BASE FAB HI
PRINT RUN 50 SER.#'d SETS
LJP LeBron James 150.00 400.00

2003-04 SP Authentic SPGU Rookie Exclusive Autographs Update

Randomly seeded in packs, this seven card set utilizes the design from the SP Game Used Rookie Exclusive Autographs set with the SP Authentic logo prominently displayed. Each card is sequentially numbered to 100. Please note that upon release, card number R49 was not issued.

PRINT RUN 100 SER.#'d SETS
R43 Mike Sweetney 5.00 12.00
R44 Francisco Elson 5.00 12.00
R45 Marquis Daniels 6.00 15.00
R46 Theron Smith 5.00 12.00
R47 Willie Green 5.00 12.00
R48 Udonis Haslem 6.00 15.00
R50 James Jones 5.00 12.00

2004-05 SP Authentic

Issued in March, SP Authentic consists of a 186-card set with 90 veteran cards, 40 Essentials subset cards (91-130) sequentially numbered to 2999, 10 rookie cards (131-140) sequentially numbered to 999, 39 autographed rookie cards (141-145, 147-180) sequentially numbered to 1499, six different autographed versions of card 146 (all sequentially numbered to 10) and six autographed rookie cards sequentially numbered to 999 (181-186) SP Authentic was packaged in 24-pack boxes where packs contained five cards and carried a SRP of $4.99.

COMP.SET w/o SP's (90)
91-130 ESS PRINT RUN 2999 SER.#'d SETS
131-140 RC PRINT RUN 999 SER.#'d SETS
141-180 RC PRINT RUN 1499 SER.#'d SETS
SIX AU VERSIONS FOR CARD #146
181-186 RC PRINT RUN 999 SER.#'d SETS
1 Al Harrington .30 .75
2 Antoine Walker .40 1.00
3 Tony Delk .25 .60
4 Gary Payton .40 1.00
5 Mark Blount .25 .60
6 Paul Pierce .40 1.00
7 Kareem Rush .25 .60
8 Gerald Wallace .30 .75
9 Jason Kapono .25 .60
10 Eddy Curry .25 .60
11 Kirk Hinrich .30 .75
12 Tyson Chandler .30 .75
13 Drew Gooden .25 .60
14 LeBron James 2.50 6.00
15 Zydrunas Ilgauskas .30 .75
16 Dirk Nowitzki .60 1.50
17 Jason Terry .30 .75
18 Michael Finley .40 1.00
19 Carmelo Anthony .75 2.00
20 Kenyon Martin .30 .75
21 Andre Miller .30 .75
22 Ben Wallace .30 .75
23 Chauncey Billups .40 1.00
24 Rasheed Wallace .40 1.00
25 Derek Fisher .30 .75
26 Jason Richardson .40 1.00
27 Speedy Claxton .25 .60
28 Juwan Howard .30 .75
29 Tracy McGrady .50 1.25
30 Yao Ming .75 2.00
31 Jermaine O'Neal .30 .75
32 Reggie Miller .40 1.00
33 Fred Jones .25 .60
34 Corey Maggette .30 .75
35 Elton Brand .40 1.00
36 Kerry Kittles .25 .60
37 Caron Butler .30 .75
38 Kobe Bryant 1.50 4.00
39 Lamar Odom .30 .75
40 Bonzi Wells .25 .60
41 Jason Williams .30 .75
42 Pau Gasol .40 1.00
43 Dwyane Wade .60 1.50
44 Eddie Jones .30 .75
45 Shaquille O'Neal 1.00 2.50
46 Desmond Mason .30 .75
47 Keith Van Horn .30 .75
48 Michael Redd .30 .75
49 Kevin Garnett .60 1.50
50 Latrell Sprewell .30 .75
51 Sam Cassell .30 .75
52 Vince Carter .60 1.50
53 Jason Kidd .60 1.50
54 Richard Jefferson .30 .75
55 Baron Davis .30 .75
56 Jamaal Magloire .25 .60
57 P.J. Brown .25 .60
58 Allan Houston .30 .75
59 Jamal Crawford .40 1.00
60 Stephon Marbury .30 .75
61 Hedo Turkoglu .30 .75
62 Grant Hill .50 1.25
63 Steve Francis .30 .75
64 Allen Iverson .60 1.50
65 Glenn Robinson .30 .75
66 Kyle Korver .30 .75
67 Amare Stoudemire .30 .75
68 Shawn Marion .30 .75
69 Steve Nash .50 1.25
70 Darius Miles .25 .60
71 Shareef Abdur-Rahim .30 .75
72 Zach Randolph .30 .75
73 Chris Webber .40 1.00
74 Mike Bibby .40 1.00
75 Peja Stojakovic .40 1.00
76 Manu Ginobili .50 1.25
77 Tim Duncan .60 1.50
78 Tony Parker .40 1.00
79 Rashard Lewis .40 1.00
80 Ray Allen .40 1.00
81 Ronald Murray .25 .60
82 Donyell Marshall .25 .60
83 Jalen Rose .30 .75
84 Chris Bosh .40 1.00
85 Andrei Kirilenko .30 .75
86 Carlos Boozer .30 .75
87 Matt Harpring .25 .60
88 Antawn Jamison .30 .75
89 Gilbert Arenas .30 .75
90 Larry Hughes .30 .75
91 Bill Russell ESS 2.00 5.00
92 Larry Bird ESS 3.00 8.00
93 Paul Pierce ESS 1.25 3.00
94 Michael Jordan ESS 10.00 25.00
95 LeBron James ESS 8.00 20.00
96 Dirk Nowitzki ESS 2.00 5.00
97 Carmelo Anthony ESS 2.50 6.00
98 Ben Wallace ESS 1.00 2.50
99 Isiah Thomas ESS 1.25 3.00
100 Tracy McGrady ESS 1.50 4.00
101 Yao Ming ESS 2.50 6.00
102 Jermaine O'Neal ESS 1.00 2.50
103 Reggie Miller ESS 1.25 3.00
104 Elton Brand ESS 1.25 3.00
105 Kareem Abdul-Jabbar ESS 2.00 5.00
106 Kobe Bryant ESS 5.00 12.00
107 Magic Johnson ESS 3.00 8.00
108 Wilt Chamberlain ESS 2.50 6.00
109 Pau Gasol ESS 1.25 3.00
110 Dwyane Wade ESS 2.00 5.00
111 Shaquille O'Neal ESS 3.00 8.00
112 Michael Redd ESS 1.00 2.50
113 Oscar Robertson ESS 1.25 3.00
114 Kevin Garnett ESS 2.00 5.00
115 Sam Cassell ESS 1.00 2.50
116 Jason Kidd ESS 2.00 5.00
117 Baron Davis ESS 1.00 2.50
118 Stephon Marbury ESS 1.00 2.50
119 Steve Francis ESS 1.00 2.50
120 Allen Iverson ESS 2.00 5.00
121 Julius Erving ESS 2.00 5.00
122 Amare Stoudemire ESS 1.00 2.50
123 Shawn Marion ESS 1.00 2.50
124 Chris Webber ESS 1.25 3.00
125 Peja Stojakovic ESS 1.25 3.00
126 Tim Duncan ESS 2.00 5.00
127 Ray Allen ESS 1.25 3.00
128 Vince Carter ESS 2.00 5.00
129 Andrei Kirilenko ESS 1.00 2.50
130 John Stockton ESS 2.00 5.00
131 Emeka Okafor RC 1.50 4.00
132 Mario Kasun RC 1.50 4.00
133 Andre Barrett RC 2.00 5.00
134 Ha Seung-Jin RC 2.00 5.00
135 Horace Jenkins RC 2.00 5.00
136 Tony Bobbitt RC 2.00 5.00
137 Luis Flores RC 1.50 4.00
138 John Edwards RC 1.25 3.00
139 Beno Udrih RC 1.50 4.00
140 Erik Daniels RC 1.50 4.00
141 Nenad Krstic AU RC 4.00 10.00
142 Yuta Tabuse AU RC 4.00 10.00
143 Pape Sow AU RC 3.00 8.00
144 Andres Nocioni AU RC 4.00 10.00
145 Bernard Robinson AU RC 3.00 8.00
147 Trevor Ariza AU RC 4.00 10.00
148 Damien Wilkins AU RC 3.00 8.00
149 Justin Reed AU RC 2.50 6.00
150 Chris Duhon AU RC 4.00 10.00
151 Royal Ivey AU RC 3.00 8.00
152 Antonio Burks AU RC 3.00 8.00
153 Andre Emmett AU RC 2.50 6.00
154 Donta Smith AU RC 2.50 6.00
155 Lionel Chalmers AU RC 4.00 10.00
156 P.J. Ramos AU RC 2.50 6.00
157 Jackson Vroman AU RC 2.50 6.00
158 Anderson Varejao AU RC 3.00 8.00
159 David Harrison AU RC 2.50 6.00
160 D.J. Mbenga AU RC 3.00 8.00
161 Sasha Vujacic AU RC 4.00 10.00
162 Kevin Martin AU RC 5.00 12.00
163 Tony Allen AU RC 4.00 10.00
164 Delonte West AU RC 4.00 10.00
165 Romain Sato AU RC 2.50 6.00
166 Viktor Khryapa AU RC 2.50 6.00
167 Pavel Podkolzin AU RC 2.50 6.00
168 Jameer Nelson AU RC 4.00 10.00
169 Dorell Wright AU RC 4.00 10.00
170 J.R. Smith AU RC 4.00 10.00
171 Josh Smith AU RC 4.00 10.00
172 Kirk Snyder AU RC 2.50 6.00
173 Al Jefferson AU RC 5.00 12.00
174 Kris Humphries AU RC 4.00 10.00
175 Sebastian Telfair AU RC 3.00 8.00
176 Robert Swift AU RC 2.50 6.00
177 Andris Biedrins AU RC 2.50 6.00
178 Luke Jackson AU RC 2.50 6.00
179 Andre Iguodala AU RC 10.00 25.00
180 Rafael Araujo AU RC 2.50 6.00
181 Luol Deng AU RC 6.00 15.00
182 Josh Childress AU RC 5.00 12.00
183 Devin Harris AU RC 5.00 12.00
184 Shaun Livingston AU RC 8.00 20.00
185 Ben Gordon AU RC 6.00 15.00
186 Dwight Howard AU RC 20.00 50.00

2004-05 SP Authentic Limited

*1-90: 2.5X TO 6X BASE HI
*91-130 ESS: .75X TO 2X BASE HI
*131-140 RC: 1X TO 2.5X BASE HI
*141-180 AU RC: .6X TO 1.5X BASE HI
*181-186 AU RC: .5X TO 1.25X BASE HI
STATED PRINT RUN 100 SER.#'d SETS

2004-05 SP Authentic Limited Extra

*1-90: 6X TO 15X BASE HI
*91-130 ESS: 2X TO 5X BASE HI
*131-140 RC: 1.25X TO 3X BASE HI
*141-180 AU RC: 1X TO 2.5X BASE HI
*181-186 AU RC: .6X TO 1.5X BASE HI
STATED PRINT RUN 25 SER.#'d SETS
CARD 146 NOT ISSUED
142 Yuta Tabuse AU 10.00 25.00
173 Al Jefferson AU 40.00 100.00
181 Luol Deng AU 40.00 100.00
185 Ben Gordon AU 40.00 100.00

2004-05 SP Authentic Fabrics Dual

Randomly inserted, this 25-card set places two players, top and bottom, along with a swatch of jersey and sequential numbering to 100. Triple player versions sequentially numbered to 25 and Quadruple player versions numbered to ten were also randomly seeded in packs.

PRINT RUN 100 SER.#'d SETS
UNPRICED QUAD PRINT RUN 10 SER.#'d SETS
AH T.Ariza/A.Houston 3.00 8.00
AM R.Araujo/D.Marshall 2.00 5.00
BJ K.Bryant/L.James 20.00 50.00
BO C.Butler/L.Odom 2.50 6.00
BS A.Biedrins/K.Snyder 2.00 5.00
CW J.Childress/A.Walker 3.00 8.00
DB L.Deng/E.Brand 3.00 8.00
DP C.Duhon/S.Pippen 5.00 12.00
HB K.Humphries/C.Boozer 3.00 8.00
HF D.Howard/S.Francis 6.00 15.00
HO D.Harrison/J.O'Neal 2.50 6.00
HS D.Harris/J.Stackhouse 2.50 6.00
HW R.Hamilton/R.Wallace 3.00 8.00
IR A.Iguodala/G.Robinson 4.00 10.00
JA A.Jamison/G.Arenas 2.50 6.00
JJ L.James/M.Jordan 60.00 150.00
JP A.Jefferson/G.Payton 4.00 10.00
KB A.Kirilenko/C.Boozer 2.50 6.00
KJ N.Krstic/R.Jefferson 3.00 8.00
LM S.Livingston/C.Maggette 3.00 8.00
MM K.Martin/A.Miller 2.50 6.00
MW K.Martin/C.Webber 3.00 8.00
SM J.R.Smith/J.Mashburn 3.00 8.00
SR H.Seung-Jin/Z.Randolph 3.00 8.00
TM S.Telfair/D.Miles 2.50 6.00

2004-05 SP Authentic Fabrics Triple

Inserted randomly, this seven card set features three player head shots and three player jerseys along with sequential numbering to 25.

PRINT RUN 25 SER.#'d SETS
BSA Bird/Peja/Ray Allen 30.00 80.00
GBR Gordon/Kobe/O.Robertson 15.00 40.00
JAJ Jordan/Carmelo/LeBron 80.00 200.00
JBJ Jordan/Kobe/LeBron 100.00 200.00
JSC Magic/Stockton/Cousy 40.00 100.00
JSG LeBron/Amare/Gasol 15.00 40.00
NFT Dirk/Finley/J.Terry 15.00 40.00
OMT J.O'Neal/R.Miller/Tinsley 15.00 40.00
ROO Admiral/Hakeem/Shaq 40.00 100.00

2004-05 SP Authentic Fabrics Patches

Inserted in packs, this 42-card set parallels the design of the Authentic Fabrics insert set enhanced with a swatch of game-worn patch. Each card is sequentially numbered to 50.

PRINT RUN 50 SER.#'d SETS
AI Andre Iguodala 8.00 20.00
AJ Al Jefferson 8.00 20.00
AK Andrei Kirilenko 5.00 12.00
AR Rafael Araujo 4.00 10.00
AS Amare Stoudemire 5.00 12.00
BD Baron Davis 5.00 12.00
BG Ben Gordon 6.00 15.00
BI Andris Biedrins 4.00 10.00
CA Carmelo Anthony 12.00 30.00
DE Devin Harris 5.00 12.00
DH Dwight Howard 12.00 30.00
DN Dirk Nowitzki 10.00 25.00
DW Dorell Wright 6.00 15.00
JC Josh Childress 5.00 12.00
JE Julius Erving 15.00 40.00
JK Jason Kidd 10.00 25.00
JN Jameer Nelson 6.00 15.00
JR J.R. Smith 6.00 15.00
JS Josh Smith 6.00 15.00
KB Kobe Bryant 25.00 60.00
KG Kevin Garnett 10.00 25.00
KH Kris Humphries 6.00 15.00
KS Kirk Snyder 4.00 10.00
LB Larry Bird 30.00 80.00
LD Luol Deng 6.00 15.00
LJ LeBron James 40.00 100.00
LU Luke Jackson 4.00 10.00
MA Magic Johnson 30.00 80.00
MJ Michael Jordan 125.00 250.00
PP Paul Pierce 10.00 25.00
PS Peja Stojakovic 6.00 15.00
RA Ray Allen 12.00 30.00
SH Shawn Marion 5.00 12.00
SL Shaun Livingston 6.00 15.00
SM Stephon Marbury 5.00 12.00
SO Shaquille O'Neal 40.00 80.00
ST Sebastian Telfair 5.00 12.00
TD Tim Duncan 10.00 25.00
TM Tracy McGrady 8.00 20.00
TP Tony Parker 6.00 15.00
YM Yao Ming 12.00 30.00
YT Anderson Varejao

2004-05 SP Authentic Fabrics Autographs

Limited to 50 copies, this set places players on a background set to match team colors, a swatch of jersey in the lower right corner and an authentic player autograph.

PRINT RUN 50 SER.#'d SETS
AI Andre Iguodala 10.00 25.00
AJ Al Jefferson 25.00 60.00
AK Andrei Kirilenko 8.00 20.00
AR Rafael Araujo 5.00 12.00
AS Amare Stoudemire 30.00 80.00
BD Baron Davis 8.00 20.00
BG Ben Gordon 25.00 60.00
BI Andris Biedrins 5.00 12.00
BW Ben Wallace 15.00 40.00
CA Carmelo Anthony 30.00 80.00
DE Devin Harris 6.00 15.00
DH Dwight Howard 40.00 100.00
DW Dorell Wright 8.00 20.00
JC Josh Childress 6.00 15.00
JE Julius Erving 60.00 150.00
JK Jason Kidd 20.00 50.00
JN Jameer Nelson 12.00 30.00
JR J.R. Smith 25.00 60.00
JS Josh Smith 25.00 60.00
JW Jason Williams 40.00 100.00
KB Kobe Bryant 150.00 400.00
KG Kevin Garnett 40.00 100.00
KH Kris Humphries 8.00 20.00
KS Kirk Snyder 5.00 12.00
LB Larry Bird 100.00 200.00
LD Luol Deng 25.00 60.00
LJ LeBron James 150.00 300.00
LU Luke Jackson 5.00 12.00
MA Magic Johnson 75.00 150.00
MJ Michael Jordan 400.00 700.00
PG Pau Gasol 12.00 30.00
PP Paul Pierce 25.00 60.00
PS Peja Stojakovic 12.00 30.00
RA Ray Allen 40.00 100.00
SH Shawn Marion 12.00 30.00
SL Shaun Livingston 8.00 20.00
SM Stephon Marbury 15.00 40.00
ST Sebastian Telfair 6.00 15.00
TM Tracy McGrady 30.00 80.00
YM Yao Ming 30.00 80.00

2004-05 SP Authentic Fabrics Rookies

Inserted in packs at the combined rate of all memorabilia cards at one in 24, this 42-card set parallels the design of the Authentic Fabrics insert set but focuses on rookie players.

COMBINED ODDS FOR MEMORABILIA 1:24
AB Antonio Burks SP 2.00 5.00
AE Andre Emmett 1.50 4.00
AI Andre Iguodala 3.00 8.00
AJ Al Jefferson 3.00 8.00
AV Anderson Varejao 2.00 5.00
BG Ben Gordon 2.50 6.00
BI Andris Biedrins 1.50 4.00
BR Bernard Robinson 2.00 5.00
CD Chris Duhon 2.50 6.00
DA David Harrison 1.50 4.00
DE Devin Harris 2.00 5.00
DH Dwight Howard 5.00 12.00
DS Donta Smith 1.50 4.00
DW Dorell Wright 2.50 6.00
HS Ha Seung-Jin 2.50 6.00
JC Josh Childress 2.00 5.00
JN Jameer Nelson 2.50 6.00
JR J.R. Smith 2.50 6.00
JS Josh Smith SP 3.00 8.00
JV Jackson Vroman 1.50 4.00
KH Kris Humphries 2.50 6.00
KM Kevin Martin 3.00 8.00
KS Kirk Snyder 1.50 4.00
LC Lionel Chalmers 2.50 6.00
LD Luol Deng 2.50 6.00
LU Luke Jackson 1.50 4.00
MF Matt Freije 2.00 5.00
NK Nenad Krstic 2.50 6.00
PR Peter John Ramos 1.50 4.00
RA Rafael Araujo 1.50 4.00
RS Robert Swift SP 1.50 4.00
SL Shaun Livingston 2.50 6.00
ST Sebastian Telfair 2.00 5.00
SV Sasha Vujacic 2.50 6.00
TA Tony Allen 2.50 6.00
TR Trevor Ariza 2.50 6.00
WE Delonte West 2.50 6.00

2004-05 SP Authentic Signatures

Inserted at a combined rate for all autographed cards at one in 24, this 97-card set employs a horizontal design where player photos appear on the left and an autograph appears on the right.

ALL SIGNATURE STATED ODDS 1:24
SINGLE AND DUAL COMBINED ODDS 1:288
AB Antonio Burks 3.00 8.00
AE Andre Emmett 2.50 6.00
AH Al Harrington 3.00 8.00
AI Andre Iguodala 8.00 20.00
AJ Antawn Jamison 5.00 12.00
AK Andrei Kirilenko 4.00 10.00
AL Al Jefferson 10.00 25.00
AM Andre Miller 4.00 10.00
AN Antonio McDyess 5.00 12.00
AR Rafael Araujo 2.50 6.00
AS Amare Stoudemire 6.00 15.00
AV Anderson Varejao 3.00 8.00
AY Carlos Arroyo 15.00 40.00
BD Baron Davis 5.00 12.00
BE Ben Wallace 15.00 40.00
BG Ben Gordon 10.00 25.00
BI Andris Biedrins 2.50 6.00
BK Bernard King 8.00 20.00
BO Carlos Boozer 4.00 10.00
BR Bill Russell 60.00 150.00
BU Beno Udrih 3.00 8.00
BW Bill Walton 4.00 10.00
CA Carmelo Anthony 20.00 50.00
CD Chris Duhon 4.00 10.00
CH Chauncey Billups 6.00 15.00
CL Clyde Drexler 15.00 40.00
CM Corey Maggette 4.00 10.00
CR Jamal Crawford 4.00 10.00
DE Devin Harris 3.00 8.00
DF Derek Fisher 5.00 12.00
DH Dwight Howard 12.00 30.00
DM Desmond Mason 4.00 10.00
DR David Robinson 30.00 60.00
DS Donta Smith 2.50 6.00
DW Dorell Wright 4.00 10.00
GA Gilbert Arenas 6.00 15.00
GP Gary Payton 8.00 20.00
HA David Harrison 2.50 6.00
HO Hakeem Olajuwon 20.00 50.00
JA Jason Richardson 4.00 10.00
JC Josh Childress 3.00 8.00
JE Julius Erving 40.00 100.00
JH Josh Howard 4.00 10.00
JK Jason Kidd 15.00 40.00
JN Jameer Nelson 4.00 10.00
JO John Stockton 50.00 120.00
JR J.R. Smith 8.00 20.00
JS Josh Smith 8.00 20.00
JV Jackson Vroman 2.50 6.00
JW Jason Williams 30.00 80.00
KB Kobe Bryant 100.00 200.00
KE Kevin Martin 5.00 12.00
KG Kevin Garnett 25.00 60.00
KH Kris Humphries 4.00 10.00
KI Kirk Hinrich 10.00 25.00
KS Kirk Snyder 2.50 6.00
LB Larry Bird 50.00 120.00
LC Lionel Chalmers 4.00 10.00
LD Luol Deng 4.00 10.00
LJ LeBron James 150.00 300.00
LO Lamar Odom 5.00 12.00
LU Luke Jackson 2.50 6.00
MA Magic Johnson 75.00 150.00
MB Mike Bibby 4.00 10.00
MD Marquis Daniels 4.00 10.00
MJ Michael Jordan 300.00 600.00
MR Michael Redd 4.00 10.00
NK Nenad Krstic 4.00 10.00
NO Andres Nocioni 4.00 10.00
PA Pavel Podkolzin 2.50 6.00
PE Peter John Ramos 2.50 6.00
PG Pau Gasol 10.00 25.00
PP Paul Pierce 25.00 60.00
PR Pat Riley 12.00 30.00
PS Peja Stojakovic 5.00 12.00
RH Richard Hamilton 6.00 15.00
RI Royal Ivey 3.00 8.00
RJ Richard Jefferson 4.00 10.00
RN Dennis Rodman 50.00 120.00
RO Jalen Rose 6.00 15.00
RS Robert Swift 2.50 6.00
RY Ray Allen 15.00 40.00
SA Shareef Abdur-Rahim 4.00 10.00
SC Sam Cassell 4.00 10.00
SH Shawn Marion 6.00 15.00
SM Stephon Marbury 8.00 20.00
ST Sebastian Telfair 3.00 8.00
SV Sasha Vujacic 4.00 10.00
TA Tony Allen 2.50 6.00
TM Tracy McGrady 15.00 40.00
TP Tony Parker 12.00 30.00
WE Delonte West 4.00 10.00
WF Walt Frazier 10.00 25.00
WR Willis Reed 10.00 25.00
YM Yao Ming 30.00 80.00
ZR Zach Randolph 4.00 10.00

2004-05 SP Authentic Signatures Dual

Inserted at the rate of one in 288, this 74-card set utilizes some of the design aspects of the Signatures insert but places two players and two autographs on each card front. Triple player versions sequentially numbered to 15 and Quadruple player versions sequentially numbered to ten were also inserted.

SINGLE AND DUAL COMBINED ODDS 1:288
UNPRICED TRIPLE PRINT RUN 15 SETS
UNPRICED QUAD PRINT RUN 10 SETS
AB C.Arroyo/C.Boozer 6.00 15.00
AJ T.Allen/A.Jefferson 10.00 25.00
AM C.Anthony/A.Miller SP 15.00 40.00
AR S.Abdur-R/Z.Randolph 6.00 15.00
AT S.Abdur-Rahim/S.Telfair 6.00 15.00
BB B.Wallace/C.Billups 8.00 20.00
BJ L.Bird/M.Johnson 150.00 300.00
BO K.Bryant/L.Odom SP 125.00 300.00
CA J.Crawford/T.Ariza 8.00 20.00
CB S.Cassell/M.Bibby 8.00 20.00
CL Chalmers/Livingston 8.00 20.00
CS J.Childress/D.Smith 6.00 15.00
CT C.Anthony/T.McGrady 50.00 100.00
DH L.Deng/K.Hinrich 8.00 20.00
DJ D.Howard/J.R.Smith 15.00 40.00
DM B.Davis/J.Magloire 6.00 15.00
DS B.Davis/J.R.Smith 8.00 20.00
EB A.Emmett/A.Burks 6.00 15.00
GC Garnett/Cassell SP 30.00 80.00
GD B.Gordon/L.Deng 8.00 20.00
GH B.Gordon/R.Hamilton 8.00 20.00
GM K.Garnett/T.McGrady 50.00 100.00
HD D.Harris/M.Daniels 6.00 15.00
HG D.Howard/B.Gordon 75.00 200.00
HJ D.Harris/J.Stackhouse 6.00 15.00
HN D.Howard/J.Nelson 25.00 60.00
HR H.Olajuwon/D.Robinson 100.00 200.00
HS A.Harrington/Josh Smith 8.00 20.00
IS A.Iguodala/J.R.Smith 10.00 25.00
JA A.Jamison/G.Arenas 6.00 15.00
JC J.Stockton/C.Arroyo 75.00 150.00
JJ M.Jordan/L.James 400.00 800.00
JK R.Jefferson/N.Krstic 8.00 20.00
JW A.Jefferson/D.West 10.00 25.00
KD K.Garnett/D.Howard 75.00 150.00
KH Kirilenko/Humphries 8.00 20.00
KJ J.Kidd/R.Jefferson 12.00 30.00
KK J.Kidd/N.Krstic 12.00 30.00
KR B.King/W.Reed 30.00 80.00
LC L.James/C.Anthony 200.00 400.00
LK L.James/K.Bryant 350.00 650.00
LL L.James/L.Jackson 100.00 250.00
MB K.Martin/M.Bibby 10.00 25.00
MC S.Marbury/J.Crawford 8.00 20.00
MJ M.Daniels/J.Howard 8.00 20.00
ML C.Maggette/S.Livingston 8.00 20.00
MM T.McGrady/Y.Ming 75.00 150.00
MP A.Miller/T.Parker 8.00 20.00
NW J.Nelson/DelWest 8.00 20.00
OR L.Odom/K.Rush 6.00 15.00
PH Podkolzin/Harris 6.00 15.00
PM G.Payton/S.Marbury 30.00 80.00
PU T.Parker/B.Udrih 8.00 20.00
RB J.Richardson/A.Biedrins 8.00 20.00
RD R.Swift/Dam.Wilkins 6.00 15.00
RF J.Richardson/D.Fisher 8.00 20.00
RL R.Allen/L.Ridnour 8.00 20.00
RM M.Redd/D.Mason SP 6.00 15.00
RO B.Russell/H.Olajuwon 100.00 200.00
SA J.Stockton/A.Kirilenko 100.00 200.00
SB P.Stojakovic/M.Bibby SP 8.00 20.00
SD Stoudemire/Deng 8.00 20.00
SH Snyder/Humphries 8.00 20.00
SK J.Stockton/J.Kidd 100.00 200.00
SM A.Stoudemire/S.Marion SP 50.00 100.00
SW J.R.Smith/D.Wright 8.00 20.00
TN S.Telfair/J.Nelson 8.00 20.00
WB J.Williams/S.Battier 6.00 15.00

2005-06 SP Authentic

Released in January 2006, SP Authentic consists of 157 cards where cards 1-90 feature veteran players, cards 91-132 feature rookie autograph cards serially numbered to 1299 and cards 133-157 feature rookies serially numbered to 999. Base cards have white backgrounds with color accents set to match team colors. SP Authentic was packaged in 24-pack boxes of five cards each and upon release, carried a $4.99 SRP.

COMP.SET w/o SP's (90) 15.00 40.00
91-132 PRINT RUN 1299 SER.#'d SETS
133-157 PRINT RUN 999 SER.#'d SETS
1 Boris Diaw .30 .75
2 Josh Childress .30 .75
3 Josh Smith .30 .75
4 Antoine Walker .30 .75
5 Al Jefferson .30 .75
6 Paul Pierce .40 1.00
7 Kareem Rush .25 .60
8 Emeka Okafor .30 .75
9 Gerald Wallace .30 .75
10 Ben Gordon .30 .75
11 Kirk Hinrich .30 .75
12 Michael Jordan 3.00 8.00
13 Drew Gooden .30 .75
14 LeBron James 1.50 4.00
15 Luke Jackson .25 .60
16 Dirk Nowitzki .60 1.50
17 Jason Terry .30 .75
18 Josh Howard .40 1.00
19 Nene Hilario .30 .75
20 Carmelo Anthony .75 2.00
21 Kenyon Martin .30 .75
22 Ben Wallace .30 .75
23 Chauncey Billups .40 1.00
24 Rasheed Wallace .40 1.00
25 Baron Davis .30 .75
26 Jason Richardson .40 1.00
27 Mike Dunleavy .30 .75
28 David Wesley .25 .60
29 Tracy McGrady .50 1.25
30 Yao Ming .50 1.25
31 Jamaal Tinsley .25 .60
32 Jermaine O'Neal .30 .75
33 Fred Jones .25 .60
34 Corey Maggette .30 .75
35 Elton Brand .40 1.00
36 Shaun Livingston .25 .60
37 Caron Butler .30 .75
38 Kobe Bryant 1.50 4.00
39 Wilt Chamberlain .75 2.00
40 Jason Williams .30 .75
41 Pau Gasol .40 1.00
42 Shane Battier .30 .75
43 Udonis Haslem .25 .60
44 Dwyane Wade .60 1.50
45 Shaquille O'Neal .75 2.00
46 Desmond Mason .25 .60
47 T.J. Ford .25 .60
48 Michael Redd .30 .75
49 Kevin Garnett .60 1.50
50 Wally Szczerbiak .30 .75
51 Ndudi Ebi .25 .60
52 Jason Kidd .60 1.50
53 Richard Jefferson .30 .75
54 Vince Carter .60 1.50
55 Lee Nailon .25 .60
56 J.R. Smith .30 .75
57 Jamaal Magloire .25 .60
58 Jamal Crawford .40 1.00
59 Stephon Marbury .30 .75
60 Quentin Richardson .30 .75
61 Dwight Howard .30 .75
62 Grant Hill .50 1.25
63 Steve Francis .30 .75
64 Allen Iverson .60 1.50
65 Andre Iguodala .30 .75
66 Chris Webber .40 1.00
67 Amare Stoudemire .30 .75
68 Shawn Marion .30 .75
69 Steve Nash .50 1.25
70 Sebastian Telfair .30 .75
71 Darius Miles .25 .60
72 Zach Randolph .30 .75
73 Brad Miller .30 .75
74 Mike Bibby .40 1.00
75 Peja Stojakovic .40 1.00
76 Manu Ginobili .40 1.00
77 Tim Duncan .60 1.50
78 Tony Parker .40 1.00
79 Luke Ridnour .30 .75
80 Rashard Lewis .40 1.00
81 Ray Allen .40 1.00
82 Chris Bosh .40 1.00
83 Morris Peterson .25 .60
84 Jalen Rose .40 1.00
85 Andrei Kirilenko .30 .75
86 Carlos Boozer .30 .75
87 John Stockton .75 2.00
88 Antawn Jamison .30 .75
89 Gilbert Arenas .30 .75
90 Brendan Haywood .25 .60
91 Andrew Bogut AU RC 6.00 15.00
92 Marvin Williams AU RC 5.00 12.00
93 Deron Williams AU RC 6.00 15.00
94 Chris Paul AU RC 40.00 100.00
95 Raymond Felton AU RC 5.00 12.00
96 Martell Webster AU RC 4.00 10.00
97 Charlie Villanueva AU RC 5.00 12.00
98 Channing Frye AU RC 5.00 12.00
99 Brandon Bass AU RC 8.00 20.00
100 Travis Diener AU RC 3.00 8.00
101 Andray Blatche AU RC 5.00 12.00
102 Monta Ellis AU RC 6.00 15.00
103 Sean May AU RC 3.00 8.00
104 Rashad McCants AU RC 4.00 10.00
105 Antoine Wright AU RC 4.00 10.00
106 Joey Graham AU RC 4.00 10.00
107 Danny Granger AU RC 6.00 15.00
108 Gerald Green AU RC 5.00 12.00
109 Hakim Warrick AU RC 4.00 10.00
110 Julius Hodge AU RC 3.00 8.00
111 Sarunas Jasikevicius AU RC 5.00 12.00
112 M.Andriuskevicius AU RC 3.00 8.00
113 Francisco Garcia AU RC 4.00 10.00
114 Luther Head AU RC 4.00 10.00
115 Nate Robinson AU RC 5.00 12.00
116 Jason Maxiell AU RC 4.00 10.00
117 Wayne Simien AU RC 3.00 8.00
118 David Lee AU RC 5.00 12.00
119 Daniel Ewing AU RC 4.00 10.00
120 Louis Williams AU RC 5.00 12.00
121 Salim Stoudamire AU RC 4.00 10.00
122 Jarrett Jack AU RC 5.00 12.00
123 Andrew Bynum AU RC 4.00 10.00
124 C.J. Miles AU RC 5.00 12.00
125 Ersan Ilyasova AU RC 5.00 12.00
126 Will Bynum AU RC 4.00 10.00
127 Lawrence Roberts AU RC 3.00 8.00
128 Dijon Thompson AU RC 3.00 8.00
129 Johan Petro AU RC 3.00 8.00
130 Bracey Wright AU RC 3.00 8.00
131 Ike Diogu AU RC 3.00 8.00
132 Ryan Gomes AU RC 4.00 10.00
133 Ronnie Price RC 1.50 4.00
134 Alan Anderson RC 1.25 3.00
135 Esteban Batista RC 1.25 3.00
136 Linas Kleiza RC 1.25 3.00
137 Eddie Basden RC 1.25 3.00
138 Josh Powell RC 1.50 4.00
139 Kevin Burleson RC 2.00 5.00
140 Von Wafer RC 1.25 3.00
141 Rawle Marshall RC 1.25 3.00
142 Gerald Fitch RC 1.25 3.00
143 Robert Whaley RC 1.25 3.00
144 Orien Greene RC 1.50 4.00
145 Fabricio Oberto RC 1.50 4.00
146 Amir Johnson RC 2.00 5.00
147 Shavlik Randolph RC 1.50 4.00
148 Arvydas Macijauskas RC 1.25 3.00
149 Alex Acker RC 1.25 3.00
150 James Singleton RC 1.25 3.00
151 Anthony Roberson RC 1.50 4.00
152 Earl Barron RC 1.50 4.00
153 Dwayne Jones RC 1.25 3.00
154 Sean Banks RC 1.25 3.00
155 Sharrod Ford RC 1.25 3.00
156 Andre Owens RC 1.25 3.00
157 Donell Taylor RC 1.25 3.00

2005-06 SP Authentic Limited Extra Autographs

PRINT RUN 9 TO 25 SER.#'d SETS
SOME UNPRICED DUE TO SCARCITY
5 Al Jefferson/25 8.00 20.00
9 Gerald Wallace/25 8.00 20.00
14 LeBron James/25 300.00 600.00
29 Tracy McGrady/25 40.00 100.00
30 Yao Ming/25 40.00 100.00
65 Andre Iguodala/25 8.00 20.00
70 Sebastian Telfair/25 8.00 20.00
82 Chris Bosh/25 25.00 60.00
84 Jalen Rose/25 8.00 20.00
88 Antawn Jamison/25 8.00 20.00

2005-06 SP Authentic Limited Extra Patches

ATCH: 8X TO 20X BASE HI
PRINT RUN 25 SER.#'d SETS
38 Kobe Bryant 30.00 80.00
39 Wilt Chamberlain 100.00 200.00
47 Oscar Robertson 60.00 120.00
62 Grant Hill 12.50 30.00
66 Chris Webber 12.50 30.00
76 Manu Ginobili 12.50 30.00
87 John Stockton 50.00 100.00

2005-06 SP Authentic Limited Extra Rookie Autographs

INT RUN 25 SER.#'d SETS
91 Andrew Bogut JSY 15.00 40.00
92 Marvin Williams JSY 12.00 30.00
93 Deron Williams JSY 40.00 100.00
94 Chris Paul JSY 250.00 500.00
95 Raymond Felton JSY 12.00 30.00
96 Martell Webster JSY 10.00 25.00
97 Charlie Villanueva JSY 12.00 30.00
98 Channing Frye JSY 12.00 30.00
99 Brandon Bass JSY 10.00 25.00
100 Travis Diener JSY 8.00 20.00
101 Andray Blatche JSY 12.00 30.00
102 Monta Ellis JSY 15.00 40.00
103 Sean May JSY 8.00 20.00
104 Rashad McCants JSY 10.00 25.00
105 Antoine Wright JSY 10.00 25.00
106 Joey Graham JSY 10.00 25.00
107 Danny Granger JSY 15.00 40.00

108 Gerald Green JSY 12.00 30.00
109 Hakim Warrick JSY 10.00 25.00
110 Julius Hodge JSY 8.00 20.00
111 Sarunas Jasikevicius JSY 12.00 30.00
112 Martynas Andriuskevicius JSY 8.00 20.00
113 Francisco Garcia JSY 10.00 25.00
114 Luther Head JSY 10.00 25.00
115 Nate Robinson JSY 12.00 30.00
116 Jason Maxiell JSY 10.00 25.00
117 Wayne Simien JSY 8.00 20.00
118 David Lee JSY 12.00 30.00
119 Daniel Ewing JSY 10.00 25.00
120 Louis Williams JSY 12.00 30.00
121 Salim Stoudamire JSY 10.00 25.00
122 Jarrett Jack JSY 12.00 30.00
123 Andrew Bynum JSY 10.00 25.00
124 C.J. Miles JSY 12.00 30.00
125 Ersan Ilyasova JSY 12.00 30.00
126 Will Bynum 8.00 20.00
127 Lawrence Roberts 6.00 15.00
128 Dijon Thompson 6.00 15.00
129 Johan Petro 6.00 15.00
130 Bracey Wright 6.00 15.00
131 Ike Diogu 6.00 15.00
132 Ryan Gomes 8.00 20.00

2005-06 SP Authentic Limited Rookie Autographs

PRINT RUN 100 SER.#'d SETS
91 Andrew Bogut 10.00 25.00
92 Marvin Williams 8.00 20.00
93 Deron Williams 15.00 40.00
94 Chris Paul 60.00 150.00
95 Raymond Felton 8.00 20.00
96 Martell Webster 6.00 15.00
97 Charlie Villanueva 8.00 20.00
98 Channing Frye 8.00 20.00
99 Brandon Bass 6.00 15.00
100 Travis Diener 5.00 12.00
101 Andray Blatche 8.00 20.00
102 Monta Ellis 15.00 40.00
103 Sean May 5.00 12.00
104 Rashad McCants 6.00 15.00
105 Antoine Wright 6.00 15.00
106 Joey Graham 6.00 15.00
107 Danny Granger 10.00 25.00
108 Gerald Green 8.00 20.00
109 Hakim Warrick 6.00 15.00
110 Julius Hodge 5.00 12.00
111 Sarunas Jasikevicius 8.00 20.00
112 Martynas Andriuskevicius 5.00 12.00
113 Francisco Garcia 6.00 15.00
114 Luther Head 6.00 15.00
115 Nate Robinson 8.00 20.00
116 Jason Maxiell 6.00 15.00
117 Wayne Simien 5.00 12.00
118 David Lee 8.00 20.00
119 Daniel Ewing 6.00 15.00
120 Louis Williams 8.00 20.00
121 Salim Stoudamire 6.00 15.00
122 Jarrett Jack 8.00 20.00
123 Andrew Bynum 30.00 80.00
124 C.J. Miles 8.00 20.00
125 Ersan Ilyasova 8.00 20.00
126 Will Bynum 6.00 15.00
127 Lawrence Roberts 5.00 12.00
128 Dijon Thompson 5.00 12.00
129 Johan Petro 5.00 12.00
130 Bracey Wright 5.00 12.00
131 Ike Diogu 5.00 12.00
132 Ryan Gomes 6.00 15.00

2005-06 SP Authentic Limited Rookie Patches

PRINT RUN 100 SER.#'d SETS
SER #'s 1/1299 THROUGH 100/1299
91 Andrew Bogut 30.00 80.00
92 Marvin Williams 8.00 20.00
93 Deron Williams 100.00 200.00
94 Chris Paul 150.00 400.00
95 Raymond Felton 8.00 20.00
96 Martell Webster 6.00 15.00
97 Charlie Villanueva 8.00 20.00
98 Channing Frye 8.00 20.00
99 Brandon Bass 6.00 15.00
100 Travis Diener 5.00 12.00
101 Andray Blatche 8.00 20.00
102 Monta Ellis 50.00 120.00
103 Sean May 5.00 12.00
104 Rashad McCants 6.00 15.00
105 Antoine Wright 6.00 15.00
106 Joey Graham 6.00 15.00
107 Danny Granger 10.00 25.00
108 Gerald Green 8.00 20.00
109 Hakim Warrick 6.00 15.00
110 Julius Hodge 5.00 12.00
111 Sarunas Jasikevicius 8.00 20.00
112 Martynas Andriuskevicius 5.00 12.00
113 Francisco Garcia 6.00 15.00
114 Luther Head 6.00 15.00
115 Nate Robinson 8.00 20.00
116 Jason Maxiell 6.00 15.00
117 Wayne Simien 5.00 12.00
118 David Lee 8.00 20.00
119 Daniel Ewing 6.00 15.00
120 Louis Williams 8.00 20.00
121 Salim Stoudamire 6.00 15.00
122 Jarrett Jack 8.00 20.00
123 Andrew Bynum 6.00 15.00
124 C.J. Miles 8.00 20.00

2005-06 SP Authentic Limited Rookies

*LIMITED: 1X TO 2.5X BASE HI
PRINT RUN 100 SER.#'d SETS
*EXTRA: 1.5X TO 4X BASE HI
EXTRA PRINT RUN 25 SER.#'d SETS

2005-06 SP Authentic Limited Warm Ups

PRINT RUN 100 SER.#'d SETS
3 Josh Smith 2.50 6.00
4 Antoine Walker 2.50 6.00
7 Kareem Rush 2.00 5.00
13 Drew Gooden 2.50 6.00
15 Luke Jackson 2.00 5.00
16 Dirk Nowitzki 5.00 12.00
17 Jason Terry 2.50 6.00
18 Josh Howard 3.00 8.00
19 Nene Hilario 2.50 6.00
21 Kenyon Martin 2.50 6.00
24 Rasheed Wallace 3.00 8.00
26 Jason Richardson 3.00 8.00
27 Mike Dunleavy 2.50 6.00
28 David Wesley 2.00 5.00
31 Jamaal Tinsley 2.00 5.00
32 Jermaine O'Neal 2.50 6.00
33 Fred Jones 2.00 5.00
34 Corey Maggette 2.50 6.00
35 Elton Brand 3.00 8.00
36 Shaun Livingston 2.00 5.00
37 Caron Butler 2.50 6.00
38 Kobe Bryant 12.50 30.00
39 Wilt Chamberlain 20.00 50.00
40 Jason Williams 2.50 6.00
43 Udonis Haslem 2.00 5.00
45 Shaquille O'Neal 6.00 15.00
46 Desmond Mason 2.00 5.00
50 Wally Szczerbiak 2.50 6.00
51 Ndudi Ebi 2.00 5.00
53 Richard Jefferson 2.50 6.00
55 Lee Nailon 2.00 5.00
58 Jamal Crawford 3.00 8.00
60 Quentin Richardson 2.50 6.00
62 Grant Hill 4.00 10.00
63 Steve Francis 2.50 6.00
66 Chris Webber 3.00 8.00
67 Amare Stoudemire 2.50 6.00
71 Darius Miles 2.00 5.00
72 Zach Randolph 2.50 6.00
73 Brad Miller 2.50 6.00
74 Mike Bibby 3.00 8.00
75 Peja Stojakovic 3.00 8.00
76 Manu Ginobili 3.00 8.00
77 Tim Duncan 5.00 12.00
78 Tony Parker 3.00 8.00
79 Luke Ridnour 2.50 6.00
80 Rashard Lewis 3.00 8.00
81 Ray Allen 3.00 8.00
83 Morris Peterson 2.00 5.00
86 Carlos Boozer 2.50 6.00
87 John Stockton 6.00 15.00
89 Gilbert Arenas 2.50 6.00
90 Brendan Haywood 2.00 5.00

2005-06 SP Authentic Limited Warm Ups Autographs

INT RUN 100 SER.#'d SETS
2 Josh Childress 6.00 15.00
5 Al Jefferson 8.00 20.00
6 Paul Pierce 15.00 40.00
9 Gerald Wallace 6.00 15.00
10 Ben Gordon 10.00 25.00
12 Michael Jordan 300.00 600.00
14 LeBron James 250.00 500.00
20 Carmelo Anthony 15.00 50.00
22 Ben Wallace 10.00 25.00
23 Chauncey Billups 6.00 15.00
25 Baron Davis 6.00 15.00
29 Tracy McGrady 20.00 50.00
30 Yao Ming 20.00 50.00
41 Pau Gasol 10.00 25.00
49 Kevin Garnett 25.00 60.00
52 Jason Kidd 15.00 40.00
56 J.R. Smith 6.00 15.00
57 Jamaal Magloire 6.00 15.00
59 Stephon Marbury 6.00 15.00
61 Dwight Howard 25.00 60.00
65 Andre Iguodala 6.00 15.00
69 Steve Nash 30.00 80.00
70 Sebastian Telfair 6.00 15.00
82 Chris Bosh 12.50 30.00
84 Jalen Rose 6.00 15.00
85 Andrei Kirilenko 6.00 15.00
88 Antawn Jamison 6.00 15.00

2005-06 SP Authentic Sensational Sigs

Inserted in packs randomly, this 42-card set features both veterans and rookies where player photos appear on the right, a team-uniform colored border appears on the left and an autograph appears centered along the bottom.
RANDOM INSERTS IN PACKS
AB Andray Blatche 4.00 10.00
AL Al Jefferson 3.00 8.00
AN Martynas Andriuskevicius 2.50 6.00
AW Antoine Wright 3.00 8.00
BB Brandon Bass 3.00 8.00
BK Bernard King 6.00 15.00
CJ C.J. Miles 4.00 10.00
CM Cuttino Mobley 4.00 10.00
CT Chris Taft 3.00 8.00
CV Charlie Villanueva 4.00 10.00
CW Chris Wilcox 2.50 6.00
DE Daniel Ewing 3.00 8.00
DT Dijon Thompson 2.50 6.00
EI Ersan Ilyasova 4.00 10.00
GG Gerald Green 4.00 10.00
GW Gerald Wallace 3.00 8.00
HW Hakim Warrick 3.00 8.00
ID Ike Diogu 2.50 6.00
JA Jason Maxiell 3.00 8.00
JH Julius Hodge 2.50 6.00
KK Kyle Korver 5.00 12.00
LJ LeBron James SP 400.00 800.00
LR Lawrence Roberts 2.50 6.00
LW Louis Williams 4.00 10.00
MA Martell Webster 3.00 8.00
MD Marquis Daniels 4.00 10.00
ME Monta Ellis 5.00 12.00
MJ Michael Jordan SP 700.00 1200.00
MW Maurice Williams 4.00 10.00
RF Raymond Felton 4.00 10.00
RG Ryan Gomes 3.00 8.00
RM Rashad McCants 3.00 8.00
SB Shane Battier 4.00 10.00
SJ Sarunas Jasikevicius 4.00 10.00
SM Sean May 2.50 6.00
TA Tony Allen 4.00 10.00
UH Udonis Haslem 2.50 6.00
WB Will Bynum 3.00 8.00

2005-06 SP Authentic Sign of the Times All-Stars

Found randomly seeded in packs, this 24-card set is horizontally designed with player images on the left, the set name in gold foil on right side at the top and an autograph at the bottom. Each card is serially numbered to 50.
PRINT RUN 50 SER.#'d SETS
AJ Antawn Jamison 6.00 15.00
AK Andrei Kirilenko 6.00 15.00
AM Antonio McDyess 6.00 15.00
BL Bill Laimbeer 15.00 40.00
BM Brad Miller 6.00 15.00
GA Gilbert Arenas 6.00 15.00
GP Gary Payton 15.00 40.00
GR Glenn Robinson 10.00 25.00
JK Jason Kidd 15.00 40.00
JM Jamaal Magloire 6.00 15.00
KG Kevin Garnett 25.00 60.00
LJ LeBron James 200.00 400.00
PP Paul Pierce 12.50 30.00
SA Shareef Abdur-Rahim 6.00 15.00
SC Sam Cassell 6.00 15.00
SM Stephon Marbury 8.00 20.00
SN Steve Nash 40.00 100.00
ST Jerry Stackhouse 12.00 30.00
TM Tracy McGrady 40.00 100.00
WA Ben Wallace 12.50 30.00
YM Yao Ming 20.00 50.00

2005-06 SP Authentic Sign of the Times Dual

Randomly inserted, this 24-card set places two players, their photos and their autographs on horizontally designed cards that utilize team jersey colors and gold foil highlights. Each card is serially numbered to 50.
PRINT RUN 50 SER.#'d SETS
UNPRICED TRIPLE PRINT RUN 15 SETS
BF A.Bogut/C.Frye 15.00 40.00
BH C.Bosh/D.Howard 30.00 80.00
BW A.Bogut/M.Williams 12.50 30.00
CB C.Billups/B.Wallace 20.00 50.00
FL C.Frye/D.Lee 12.50 30.00
FM R.Felton/S.May 12.50 30.00
GB F.Garcia/M.Bibby 12.50 30.00
GJ D.Granger/S.Jasikevivius 12.50 30.00
GM G.Green/T.McGrady 20.00 50.00
GW P.Gasol/H.Warrick 12.50 30.00
HK J.Hodge/L.Kleiza 12.50 30.00
HR L.Head/N.Robinson 12.50 30.00
JG A.Jefferson/G.Green 12.50 30.00
JH L.James/D.Howard 150.00 300.00
JJ L.James/M.Jordan 700.00 1000.00
MO Y.Ming/H.Olajuwon 25.00 60.00
NL C.Neal/M.Lemon 40.00 80.00
PW C.Paul/D.Williams 50.00 120.00
VG C.Villanueva/J.Graham 12.50 30.00
WB M.Webster/A.Bynum 20.00 50.00
WJ M.Webster/J.Jack 12.50 30.00
WP M.Williams/C.Paul 40.00 100.00
WS M.Williams/S.Stoudamire 12.50 30.00

2005-06 SP Authentic Sign of the Times Legends

Found randomly seeded in packs, this 23-card set is horizontally designed with player images on the left, the set name in gold foil on right side at the top and an autograph at the bottom. Each card is serially numbered to 25.
PRINT RUN 25 SER.#'d SETS
BK Bob Knight 30.00 80.00
BR Bill Russell 100.00 250.00
BW Bill Walton 20.00 50.00
DR Dennis Rodman 75.00 150.00
EH Elvin Hayes 15.00 40.00
GG George Gervin 15.00 40.00
HO Hakeem Olajuwon 20.00 50.00
IT Isiah Thomas 15.00 40.00
JE Julius Erving 20.00 50.00
JH John Stockton 100.00 200.00
JW John Wooden 75.00 150.00
KA Kareem Abdul-Jabbar 50.00 120.00
LB Larry Bird 100.00 200.00
LW Lenny Wilkens 15.00 40.00
LY Larry Brown 20.00 50.00
MA Magic Johnson 75.00 150.00
MJ Michael Jordan 500.00 1000.00
PR Pat Riley 15.00 40.00
RP Robert Parish 15.00 40.00
SP Scottie Pippen 150.00 300.00
WF Walt Frazier 15.00 40.00
WR Willis Reed 15.00 40.00

2005-06 SP Authentic Sign of the Times Rookies

Found randomly seeded in packs, this 25-card set is horizontally designed with player images on the left, the set name in gold foil on right side at the top and an autograph at the bottom. Each card is serially numbered to 100.
PRINT RUN 100 SER.#'d SETS
AB Andrew Bogut 8.00 20.00
AN Andrew Bynum 5.00 12.00
CF Channing Frye 6.00 15.00
CP Chris Paul 50.00 120.00
CV Charlie Villanueva 6.00 15.00
DG Danny Granger 8.00 20.00
DT Dijon Thompson 4.00 10.00
DW Deron Williams 8.00 20.00
FG Francisco Garcia 5.00 12.00
GE Gerald Green 6.00 15.00
HW Hakim Warrick 5.00 12.00
ID Ike Diogu 4.00 10.00
JA Jason Maxiell 5.00 12.00
JG Joey Graham 5.00 12.00
JJ Jarrett Jack 6.00 15.00
JP Johan Petro 4.00 10.00
JU Julius Hodge 4.00 10.00
LH Luther Head 5.00 12.00
MW Marvin Williams 6.00 15.00
NR Nate Robinson 6.00 15.00
RF Raymond Felton 6.00 15.00
RM Rashad McCants 5.00 12.00
SE Sean May 4.00 10.00
SS Salim Stoudamire 5.00 12.00
WE Martell Webster 5.00 12.00

2005-06 SP Authentic Sign of the Times Veterans

Found randomly seeded in packs, this 25-card set is horizontally designed with player images on the left, the set name in gold foil on right side at the top and an autograph at the bottom. Each card is serially numbered to 75.
PRINT RUN 75 SER.#'d SETS
AH Al Harrington 6.00 15.00
AL Al Jefferson 6.00 15.00
CA Carlos Boozer 6.00 15.00
CB Chauncey Billups 10.00 25.00
CH Chris Bosh 10.00 25.00
CM Cuttino Mobley 6.00 15.00
DH Dwight Howard 15.00 40.00
DS Damon Stoudamire 6.00 15.00
GW Gerald Wallace 6.00 15.00
JC Josh Childress 6.00 15.00
JN Jameer Nelson 6.00 15.00
JR Jalen Rose 8.00 20.00
KH Kirk Hinrich 6.00 15.00
KK Kyle Korver 6.00 15.00
LO Lamar Odom 8.00 20.00
MD Marquis Daniels 6.00 15.00
MP Morris Peterson 6.00 15.00
PG Pau Gasol 10.00 25.00
RH Richard Hamilton 10.00 25.00
RJ Richard Jefferson 6.00 15.00
SB Shane Battier 6.00 15.00
SI J.R. Smith 6.00 15.00
TA Trevor Ariza 6.00 15.00
UH Udonis Haslem 6.00 15.00

2006-07 SP Authentic

Issued in late April 2007, SP Authentic boasts a clean design with a white background and pictures veteran players on card numbers 1-90, rookies serially numbered to 199 on cards 91-100, autograph rookies serially numbered to 999 on cards 101-122 and autograph rookies serially numbered to 299 on cards 124-132. All rookie autographs are signed directly on-card. SP Authentic is packaged in 24-pack boxes of five cards each and carried an initial suggested retail price of $4.99 per pack.
COMP.SET w/o SP's (100) 15.00 35.00
101-122 AU RC PRINT RUN 999 SER.#'d SETS
123-132 AU RC PRINT RUN 299 SER.#'d SETS
1 Joe Johnson .30 .75
2 Marvin Williams .30 .75
3 Josh Childress .30 .75
4 Paul Pierce .40 1.00
5 Sebastian Telfair .25 .60
6 Gerald Green .30 .75
7 Emeka Okafor .30 .75
8 Raymond Felton .30 .75
9 Gerald Wallace .30 .75
10 Ben Wallace .30 .75
11 Ben Gordon .30 .75
12 Kirk Hinrich .30 .75
13 LeBron James 1.50 4.00
14 Zydrunas Ilgauskas .30 .75
15 Drew Gooden .30 .75
16 Jason Terry .30 .75
17 Dirk Nowitzki .60 1.50
18 Devin Harris .25 .60
19 Carmelo Anthony .50 1.25
20 Kenyon Martin .30 .75
21 Andre Miller .30 .75
22 Chauncey Billups .40 1.00
23 Richard Hamilton .30 .75
24 Rasheed Wallace .40 1.00
25 Jason Richardson .40 1.00
26 Baron Davis .30 .75
27 Troy Murphy .25 .60
28 Tracy McGrady .50 1.25
29 Yao Ming .50 1.25
30 Shane Battier .30 .75
31 Jermaine O'Neal .30 .75
32 Sarunas Jasikevicius .30 .75
33 Al Harrington .30 .75
34 Elton Brand .40 1.00
35 Sam Cassell .30 .75
36 Chris Kaman .30 .75
37 Kobe Bryant 1.50 4.00
38 Lamar Odom .30 .75
39 Vladimir Radmanovic .25 .60
40 Pau Gasol .40 1.00
41 Hakim Warrick .30 .75
42 Damon Stoudamire .30 .75
43 Shaquille O'Neal .75 2.00
44 Dwyane Wade .60 1.50
45 Alonzo Mourning .50 1.25
46 Andrew Bogut .30 .75
47 Charlie Villanueva .25 .60
48 Michael Redd .30 .75
49 Kevin Garnett .60 1.50
50 Ricky Davis .30 .75
51 Rashad McCants .25 .60
52 Vince Carter .50 1.25
53 Jason Kidd .60 1.50
54 Richard Jefferson .30 .75
55 Chris Paul .50 1.25
56 Peja Stojakovic .40 1.00
57 Tyson Chandler .30 .75
58 Stephon Marbury .30 .75
59 Channing Frye .30 .75
60 Nate Robinson .25 .60
61 Grant Hill .50 1.25
62 Dwight Howard .30 .75
63 Jameer Nelson .25 .60
64 Allen Iverson .50 1.25
65 Andre Iguodala .30 .75
66 Kyle Korver .30 .75
67 Steve Nash .50 1.25
68 Amare Stoudemire .30 .75
69 Shawn Marion .30 .75
70 Jamaal Magloire .25 .60
71 Martell Webster .30 .75
72 Jarrett Jack .30 .75
73 Mike Bibby .40 1.00
74 Ron Artest .40 1.00
75 Brad Miller .30 .75
76 Tony Parker .40 1.00
77 Tim Duncan .60 1.50
78 Manu Ginobili .40 1.00
79 Ray Allen .40 1.00
80 Rashard Lewis .40 1.00
81 Luke Ridnour .30 .75
82 Chris Bosh .40 1.00
83 T.J. Ford .25 .60
84 Joey Graham .25 .60
85 Carlos Boozer .30 .75
86 Andrei Kirilenko .30 .75
87 Deron Williams .30 .75
88 Gilbert Arenas .30 .75
89 Antawn Jamison .30 .75
90 Andray Blatche .25 .60
91 Adam Morrison RC 2.00 5.00
92 Alexander Johnson RC 1.25 3.00
93 J.J. Redick RC 2.50 6.00
94 Vassilis Spanoulis RC 1.25 3.00
95 Jorge Garbajosa RC 1.50 4.00
96 Leon Powe RC 1.50 4.00
97 Chris Quinn RC 1.25 3.00
98 Tarence Kinsey RC 1.25 3.00
99 Yakhouba Diawara RC 1.25 3.00
100 Robert Hite RC 1.25 3.00
101 Thabo Sefolosha AU RC 6.00 15.00
102 Ronnie Brewer AU RC 6.00 15.00
103 Cedric Simmons AU RC 4.00 10.00
104 Dee Brown AU RC 4.00 10.00
105 Craig Smith AU RC 5.00 12.00
106 Rodney Carney AU RC 4.00 10.00
107 Pops Mensah-Bonsu AU RC 4.00 10.00
108 Shawne Williams AU RC 4.00 10.00
109 Quincy Douby AU RC 4.00 10.00
110 Renaldo Balkman AU RC 5.00 12.00
111 Rajon Rondo AU RC 12.00 30.00
112 Marcus Williams AU RC 4.00 10.00
113 Josh Boone AU RC 4.00 10.00
114 Kyle Lowry AU RC 8.00 20.00
115 Shannon Brown AU RC 4.00 10.00
116 Jordan Farmar AU RC 6.00 15.00
117 Sergio Rodriguez AU RC 6.00 15.00
118 Maurice Ager AU RC 4.00 10.00
119 Mardy Collins AU RC 4.00 10.00
120 James White AU RC 4.00 10.00
121 Steve Novak AU RC 5.00 12.00
122 Solomon Jones AU RC 4.00 10.00
123 Andrea Bargnani AU RC 8.00 20.00
124 L.Aldridge AU RC 30.00 80.00
125 Tyrus Thomas AU RC 6.00 15.00
126 Shelden Williams AU RC 6.00 15.00
127 Brandon Roy AU RC 8.00 20.00
128 Randy Foye AU RC 8.00 20.00
129 Rudy Gay AU RC 10.00 25.00
130 Patrick O'Bryant AU RC 5.00 12.00
131 Saer Sene AU RC 5.00 12.00
132 Hilton Armstrong AU RC 5.00 12.00

2006-07 SP Authentic Gold

*1-90 GOLD: 4X TO 10X BASE HI
*91-100 GOLD RCs: 1X TO 2.5X BASE HI
*101-122 GOLD AU RCs: 1X TO 2.5X BASE HI
*123-132 GOLD AU RCs: .75X TO 2X BASE HI
GOLD PRINT RUN 25 SER.#'d SETS
124 LaMarcus Aldridge AU 40.00 100.00
127 Brandon Roy AU 40.00 100.00
129 Rudy Gay AU 40.00 100.00

2006-07 SP Authentic Autographed Jerseys

PRINT RUN 50 SER.#'d SETS
AI Andre Iguodala 6.00 15.00
AJ Al Jefferson 8.00 20.00
AM Alonzo Mourning 40.00 80.00
AR Allan Ray 5.00 12.00
BD Baron Davis 10.00 25.00
BG Ben Gordon 10.00 25.00
BI Chauncey Billups 6.00 15.00
CB Chris Bosh 12.00 30.00
CM Corey Maggette 5.00 12.00
CP Chris Paul 25.00 60.00
CS Craig Smith 5.00 12.00
DI Boris Diaw 5.00 12.00
DN David Noel 5.00 12.00
DW Deron Williams 12.00 30.00
JK Jason Kidd 15.00 40.00
JS J.R. Smith 5.00 12.00
KD Keyon Dooling 5.00 12.00
KH Kirk Hinrich 10.00 25.00
KK Kyle Korver 5.00 12.00
LB Leandro Barbosa 6.00 15.00
LH Larry Hughes 6.00 15.00
LR Luke Ridnour 5.00 12.00
MA Maurice Ager 5.00 12.00
MB Mike Bibby 6.00 15.00
MD Marquis Daniels 5.00 12.00
MJ Mike James 5.00 12.00
QD Quincy Douby 5.00 12.00
RB Raja Bell 12.50 30.00
RF Raymond Felton 6.00 15.00
RJ Richard Jefferson 5.00 12.00
RM Rashad McCants 5.00 12.00
SM Sean May 5.00 12.00
TC Tyson Chandler 5.00 12.00
TF T.J. Ford 5.00 12.00
TP Tayshaun Prince 6.00 15.00

2006-07 SP Authentic Autographed Jerseys Dual

PRINT RUN 25 SER.#'d SETS
DBD M.Bibby/Q.Douby 12.00 30.00
DBH C.Billups/R.Hamilton 12.00 30.00
DCP C.Paul/T.Chandler 20.00 40.00
DCR M.Collins/Q.Richardson 8.00 20.00
DDH C.Duhon/K.Hinrich 12.00 30.00
DDO B.Davis/P.O'Bryant 8.00 20.00
DFB C.Frye/R.Balkman 8.00 20.00
DHB L.Hughes/S.Brown 8.00 20.00
DKI K.Korver/A.Iguodala 12.00 30.00
DKJ J.Kidd/R.Jefferson 25.00 60.00
DNM D.Noel/R.McCants 8.00 20.00

2006-07 SP Authentic Autographed Jerseys Triple

PRINT RUN 15 SER.#'d SETS
UNPRICED QUAD PRINT RUN 5 SETS
CFR Collins/Frye/Richardson 20.00 50.00
HBP Billups/Hamilton/Prince 20.00 50.00
JEJ Jordan/James/Erving 750.00 1000.00
MMD McGrady/Ming/Drexler 100.00 200.00
NDP Paul/Nash/Davis 100.00 200.00

2006-07 SP Authentic Chirography

APPROXIMATE ODDS 1:30
*GOLD: .6X TO 1.5X BASE HI
PRINT RUN 25 SER.#'d SETS
AI Andre Iguodala 6.00 15.00
BE Charlie Bell 4.00 10.00
BG Ben Gordon 6.00 15.00
BM Brad Miller 4.00 10.00
BO Chris Bosh 12.00 30.00
BR Brandon Roy 10.00 25.00
CB Chauncey Billups 5.00 12.00
CM Corey Maggette 4.00 10.00
DG Danny Granger 4.00 10.00
DM Damir Markota 4.00 10.00
DW Deron Williams 10.00 25.00
FG Francisco Garcia 4.00 10.00
GG Gerald Green 4.00 10.00
HW Hakim Warrick 4.00 10.00
IU Ime Udoka 4.00 10.00
JA Antawn Jamison 5.00 12.00
JG Joey Graham 4.00 10.00
JJ Jarrett Jack 4.00 10.00
JK Jason Kapono 4.00 10.00
JS J.R. Smith 5.00 12.00
KI Jason Kidd 10.00 25.00
KK Kyle Korver 4.00 10.00
LA LaMarcus Aldridge 12.00 30.00
LB Leandro Barbosa 4.00 10.00
LR Luke Ridnour 4.00 10.00
MI Mile Ilic 4.00 10.00
MW Martell Webster 4.00 10.00
NO Steve Novak 5.00 12.00
NR Nate Robinson 6.00 15.00
PA Paul Millsap 5.00 12.00
PM Pops Mensah-Bonsu 4.00 10.00
QR Quentin Richardson 4.00 10.00
RB Raja Bell 8.00 20.00
RH Ryan Hollins 4.00 10.00
RJ Richard Jefferson 4.00 10.00
RM Rashad McCants 4.00 10.00
RR Rajon Rondo 12.00 30.00
RT Ronny Turiaf 5.00 12.00
SA Shareef Abdur-Rahim 4.00 10.00
SB Shannon Brown 5.00 12.00
SJ Solomon Jones 4.00 10.00
SK Steve Kerr 6.00 15.00
SM Sean May 4.00 10.00
SN Steve Nash 25.00 60.00
SR Sergio Rodriguez 4.00 10.00
SW Shawne Williams 4.00 10.00
TC Tyson Chandler 5.00 12.00
TF T.J. Ford 4.00 10.00
TM Tracy McGrady 10.00 25.00
TP Tayshaun Prince 5.00 12.00
TS Thabo Sefolosha 6.00 15.00
TT Tyrus Thomas 6.00 15.00
VC Vince Carter 12.00 30.00
WI Shelden Williams 4.00 10.00

2006-07 SP Authentic Fabrics

APPROXIMATE ODDS 1:24
AB Andrew Bogut 2.00 5.00
AI Andre Iguodala 2.00 5.00
AJ Antawn Jamison 2.00 5.00
AM Alonzo Mourning 3.00 8.00
AW Antoine Walker 2.00 5.00
BL Bill Laimbeer 2.00 5.00
BW Ben Wallace 2.00 5.00
CA Carmelo Anthony 3.00 8.00
CB Chauncey Billups 2.50 6.00
CM Corey Maggette 2.00 5.00
CP Chris Paul 3.00 8.00
DM Darko Milicic 2.00 5.00
DN Dirk Nowitzki 4.00 10.00
DR David Robinson 4.00 10.00
GG George Gervin 2.50 6.00
GP Gary Payton 2.50 6.00
HO Hakeem Olajuwon 3.00 8.00
JC Josh Childress 2.00 5.00
JK Jason Kidd 4.00 10.00
KA Kareem Abdul-Jabbar 8.00 20.00
KB Kobe Bryant 8.00 20.00
KH Kirk Hinrich 2.00 5.00
LH Larry Hughes 2.00 5.00
LJ LeBron James 10.00 25.00
LO Lamar Odom 2.00 5.00
MA Donyell Marshall 2.00 5.00
MJ Michael Jordan 20.00 50.00
MW Marvin Williams 2.00 5.00
NR Nate Robinson 1.50 4.00
PP Paul Pierce 2.50 6.00
RW Rasheed Wallace 2.50 6.00
SE Sean Elliott 2.50 6.00
SO Shaquille O'Neal 5.00 12.00
TC Tyson Chandler 2.00 5.00
TM Tracy McGrady 3.00 8.00
TP Tayshaun Prince 2.00 5.00
VC Vince Carter 3.00 8.00
WF Walt Frazier 2.50 6.00
YM Yao Ming 3.00 8.00
ZI Zydrunas Ilgauskas 2.00 5.00

2006-07 SP Authentic Fabrics Dual

PRINT RUN 100 SER.#'d SETS
BI K.Bryant/A.Iverson 15.00 40.00
DR D.Robinson/T.Duncan 12.50 30.00
GM K.Garnett/R.McCants 5.00 12.00
GW P.Gasol/H.Warrick 5.00 12.00
JJ M.Jordan/L.James 50.00 120.00
JP C.Paul/L.James 12.00 30.00
KC V.Carter/J.Kidd 10.00 25.00
MA C.Anthony/K.Martin 5.00 12.00
MF S.Marbury/W.Frazier 5.00 12.00
MJ T.McGrady/L.James 15.00 40.00
MM M.Jordan/M.Johnson 40.00 100.00
NH D.Nowitzki/D.Harris 5.00 12.00
NS S.Nash/A.Stoudemire 8.00 20.00
PB L.Bird/P.Pierce 20.00 40.00

2006-07 SP Authentic Fabrics Triple

PRINT RUN 50 SER.#'d SETS
BOF Bryant/Odom/Farmar 15.00 40.00
DMO O'Neal/Ming/Duncan 15.00 40.00
GFR Foye/Gay/Redick 10.00 25.00
JEB Jordan/Bird/Erving 60.00 150.00
MMN McGrady/Ming/Novak 12.50 30.00
NMS Nash/Stoudemire/Marion 15.00 40.00

2006-07 SP Authentic Fabrics Quad

PRINT RUN 25 SER.#'d SETS
ARSA Aldridge/Roy/Arm/Simmons 25.00 60.00
IGJB James/Ilgausk/Gden/Brown 30.00 80.00
KCJW Jefferson/Carter/Kidd/Williams 20.00 50.00
WHGT Gordon/Hinrich/Wallace/Thomas 20.00 50.00
WWMO Shaq/Walker/JWill/Zo 30.00 80.00

2006-07 SP Authentic Rookie Autographed Patches

PRINT RUN 30 SER.#'d SETS
UNPRICED LOGO PRINT RUN ONE SET
AB Andrea Bargnani 50.00 100.00
BJ Bobby Jones 8.00 20.00
BR Brandon Roy 100.00 200.00
HA Hilton Armstrong 8.00 20.00
JB Josh Boone 8.00 20.00
JF Jordan Farmar 12.00 30.00
JG Jorge Garbajosa 10.00 25.00
JW James White 8.00 20.00
LA LaMarcus Aldridge 60.00 150.00
MA Maurice Ager 8.00 20.00
MW Marcus Williams 8.00 20.00
PD Paul Davis 8.00 20.00
PO Patrick O'Bryant 8.00 20.00
PT P.J. Tucker 10.00 25.00
RB Ronnie Brewer 12.00 30.00
RC Rodney Carney 8.00 20.00
RF Randy Foye 12.00 30.00
RG Rudy Gay 12.00 30.00
RR Rajon Rondo 150.00 300.00
SB Shannon Brown 8.00 20.00
SN Steve Novak 10.00 25.00
SS Saer Sene 8.00 20.00
SW Shelden Williams 10.00 25.00
WI Shawne Williams 8.00 20.00

2006-07 SP Authentic Rookie Exclusives Jerseys

APPROXIMATE ODDS 1:30
*PATCH: 1.5X TO 4X BASE HI
PATCH PRINT RUN 25 SER.#'d SETS
AB Andrea Bargnani 2.50 6.00
AR Allan Ray 1.50 4.00
BR Brandon Roy 2.50 6.00
CS Cedric Simmons 1.50 4.00
DE Dee Brown 1.50 4.00
DN David Noel 1.50 4.00
JB Josh Boone 1.50 4.00
JF Jordan Farmar 2.50 6.00
JG Jorge Garbajosa 2.00 5.00
JW James White 1.50 4.00
MA Maurice Ager 1.50 4.00
MC Mardy Collins 1.50 4.00
MW Marcus Williams 1.50 4.00
PD Paul Davis 1.50 4.00
PO Patrick O'Bryant 1.50 4.00
QD Quincy Douby 1.50 4.00
RB Renaldo Balkman 2.00 5.00
RC Rodney Carney 1.50 4.00
RF Randy Foye 2.50 6.00
RG Rudy Gay 3.00 8.00
RO Ronnie Brewer 2.50 6.00
RR Rajon Rondo 8.00 20.00
SB Shannon Brown 1.50 4.00
SJ Solomon Jones 1.50 4.00
SM Craig Smith 2.00 5.00
SN Steve Novak 2.00 5.00
SS Saer Sene 1.50 4.00
TS Thabo Sefolosha 2.50 6.00
TT Tyrus Thomas 2.00 5.00
WI Shawne Williams 1.50 4.00

2006-07 SP Authentic Rookie Exclusives Jerseys Autographs

PRINT RUN 60 SER.#'d SETS
AB Andrea Bargnani 8.00 20.00
BR Brandon Roy 20.00 50.00
DE Dee Brown 5.00 12.00
DN David Noel 5.00 12.00
JB Josh Boone 5.00 12.00
JF Jordan Farmar 8.00 20.00
JG Jorge Garbajosa 6.00 15.00
JW James White 5.00 12.00
MA Maurice Ager 5.00 12.00
MC Mardy Collins 5.00 12.00
MW Marcus Williams 5.00 12.00
PD Paul Davis 5.00 12.00
PO Patrick O'Bryant 5.00 12.00
QD Quincy Douby 5.00 12.00
RB Renaldo Balkman 6.00 15.00
RC Rodney Carney 5.00 12.00
RF Randy Foye 8.00 20.00
RG Rudy Gay 10.00 25.00
RO Ronnie Brewer 8.00 20.00
RR Rajon Rondo 30.00 80.00
SB Shannon Brown 5.00 12.00
SJ Solomon Jones 5.00 12.00
SM Craig Smith 6.00 15.00
SN Steve Novak 6.00 15.00
SS Saer Sene 5.00 12.00
TS Thabo Sefolosha 8.00 20.00
TT Tyrus Thomas 6.00 15.00
WI Shawne Williams 5.00 12.00

2006-07 SP Authentic Sign of the Times All-Stars

PRINT RUN 50 SER.#'d SETS
AD Adrian Dantley 6.00 15.00
AJ Antawn Jamison 6.00 15.00
BD Baron Davis 6.00 15.00
BL Bill Laimbeer 15.00 40.00
BM Brad Miller 6.00 15.00
CB Chris Bosh 10.00 25.00
CD Clyde Drexler 15.00 40.00
CH Connie Hawkins 8.00 20.00
DA Brad Daugherty 6.00 15.00
DR David Robinson 40.00 80.00
JK Jason Kidd 20.00 50.00
JM Jamaal Magloire 6.00 15.00
MR Michael Ray Richardson 6.00 15.00
PP Paul Pierce 15.00 40.00
PS Peja Stojakovic 6.00 15.00
RH Richard Hamilton 8.00 20.00
RO Dennis Rodman 30.00 80.00
SE Sean Elliott 12.50 30.00
SN Steve Nash 50.00 100.00
TM Tracy McGrady 15.00 40.00
VC Vince Carter 40.00 100.00
YM Yao Ming 15.00 40.00

2006-07 SP Authentic Sign of the Times Legends

PRINT RUN 25 SER.#'d SETS
BK Bernard King 8.00 20.00
BW Bill Walton 20.00 50.00
CM Cedric Maxwell 8.00 20.00
FR World B. Free 10.00 25.00
HO Hakeem Olajuwon 20.00 40.00
JE Julius Erving 50.00 100.00
LB Larry Bird 60.00 120.00
MA Magic Johnson 60.00 120.00
ME Mark Eaton 8.00 20.00
MJ Michael Jordan 300.00 600.00
NA Nate Archibald 8.00 20.00
PW Paul Westphal 8.00 20.00
SP Sam Perkins 8.00 20.00
TC Tom Chambers 8.00 20.00
WF Walt Frazier 15.00 40.00

2006-07 SP Authentic Sign of the Times Rookies

PRINT RUN 100 SER.#'d SETS
AB Andrea Bargnani 12.00 30.00
AR Allan Ray 2.50 6.00
BR Brandon Roy 12.00 30.00
CS Cedric Simmons 2.50 6.00
HA Hassan Adams 2.50 6.00
HI Hilton Armstrong 2.50 6.00
JB Josh Boone 2.50 6.00
KL Kyle Lowry 5.00 12.00
LA LaMarcus Aldridge 15.00 40.00
MC Mardy Collins 2.50 6.00
PM Pops Mensah-Bonsu 2.50 6.00
PO Patrick O'Bryant 2.50 6.00
QD Quincy Douby 2.50 6.00
RB Renaldo Balkman 3.00 8.00
RC Rodney Carney 2.50 6.00
RF Randy Foye 4.00 10.00
RG Rudy Gay 5.00 12.00
RH Ryan Hollins 3.00 8.00
RR Rajon Rondo 25.00 60.00
SB Shannon Brown 2.50 6.00
SS Saer Sene 2.50 6.00
SW Shelden Williams 3.00 8.00
TS Thabo Sefolosha 4.00 10.00
TT Tyrus Thomas 3.00 8.00
WB Will Blalock 2.50 6.00

2006-07 SP Authentic Sign of the Times Veterans

PRINT RUN 75 SER.#'d SETS
BG Ben Gordon 12.00 30.00
BM Brad Miller 4.00 10.00
BO Chris Bosh 12.00 30.00
CB Chauncey Billups 6.00 15.00
CM Corey Maggette 4.00 10.00
DG Danny Granger 4.00 10.00
DS DeShawn Stevenson 4.00 10.00
DW Deron Williams 10.00 25.00
GG Gerald Green 4.00 10.00
HW Hakim Warrick 4.00 10.00
JJ Jarrett Jack 4.00 10.00
KH Kirk Hinrich 12.00 30.00
LB Leandro Barbosa 4.00 10.00
MJ Mike James 4.00 10.00
MW Marvin Williams 4.00 10.00
RB Raja Bell 8.00 20.00
RJ Richard Jefferson 4.00 10.00
TF T.J. Ford 4.00 10.00

2006-07 SP Authentic Sign of the Times Dual

PRINT RUN 100 SER.#'d SETS
UNLESS LISTED IN CHECKLIST
UNPRICED QUAD PRINT RUN 5 SETS
UNPRICED TRIPLE PRINT RUN 10 SETS
SDAB Bargnani/Aldridge/15 12.00 30.00
SDAM Ager/Mnsh-Bsu/15 12.00 30.00
SDAR A.Ray/R.Rondo/15 30.00 80.00
SDBA H.Adams/J.Boone 10.00 25.00
SDBB D.Brown/R.Brewer 10.00 25.00
SDBF C.Bosh/T.J. Ford 20.00 40.00
SDCN R.Carney/S.Novak 10.00 25.00
SDFB C.Frye/R.Balkman 10.00 25.00
SDGB D.Gibson/S.Brown 10.00 25.00
SDHA J.Augustine/Hollins/15 12.00 30.00
SDHB R.Hamilton/Billups/15 12.00 30.00
SDHG B.Gordon/K.Hinrich 20.00 50.00
SDIJ A.Iguodala/B.Jones 20.00 40.00
SDJJ M.Jordan/L.James 600.00 1200.00
SDKD B.Davis/J.Kidd 20.00 40.00
SDKN J.Kidd/S.Nash/15 40.00 100.00
SDMA Carmelo/McGrady/15 60.00 150.00
SDMD B.Miller/P.Davis/15 10.00 25.00
SDOH R.Felton/E.Okafor 15.00 30.00
SDPB W.Blalock/T.Prince/15 10.00 25.00
SDPJ P.Pierce/R.Jefferson 25.00 50.00
SDRJ Rondo/Jefferson/15 30.00 80.00
SDRK K.Korver/Q.Rich/15 15.00 40.00
SDRR B.Roy/S.Rdrgz/15 30.00 80.00
SDSA C.Simmons/H.Armstrong 10.00 25.00
SDSJ D.Stevenson/A.Jamison/15 10.00 25.00
SDTS T.Sefolosha/T.Thomas/15 10.00 25.00
SDWA D.West/T.Allen/15 10.00 25.00
SDWG H.Warrick/R.Gay/15 15.00 40.00
SDWJ S.Williams/S.Jones/15 10.00 25.00
SDWR B.Wallace/D.Rodman/15 60.00 120.00
SDWW S.Williams/J.White 10.00 25.00

2007-08 SP Authentic

Released in February 2008, SP Authentic features a

153-card set where cards 1-100 picture veteran players, cards 101-106 picture rookie players and are sequentially numbered to 299, cards 107-113 picture rookie players along with authentic autographs and sequential numbering to 999, cards 114-117 picture rookie players along with authentic autographs and sequential numbering to 299, cards 118 and 119 picture rookie players with authentic autographs and sequential numbering to 999 and cards 122-153 picture rookie players with both premium patch swatches and authentic autographs along with sequential numbering to either 599, 399 or 299. SP Authentic is packaged in 24-pack boxes of five cards each and carried an intial suggested retail price of $4.99.

COMP.SET w/o SP's (100) 25.00 50.00
UNPRICED DIE CUT PRINT RUN 10 SETS
1 Brandon Roy .50 1.25
2 Channing Frye .40 1.00
3 Jarrett Jack .40 1.00
4 LaMarcus Aldridge .60 1.50
5 Delonte West .30 .75
6 Johan Petro .30 .75
7 Nick Collison .40 1.00
8 Joe Johnson .40 1.00
9 Josh Smith .40 1.00
10 Marvin Williams .40 1.00
11 Hakim Warrick .40 1.00
12 Pau Gasol .50 1.25
13 Rudy Gay .50 1.25
14 Al Jefferson .40 1.00
15 Paul Pierce .50 1.25
16 Ray Allen .50 1.25
17 Andrew Bogut .40 1.00
18 Charlie Villanueva .30 .75
19 Maurice Williams .40 1.00
20 Michael Redd .40 1.00
21 Kevin Garnett .75 2.00
22 Randy Foye .50 1.25
23 Ricky Davis .40 1.00
24 Emeka Okafor .40 1.00
25 Gerald Wallace .40 1.00
26 Jason Richardson .50 1.25
27 David Lee .30 .75
28 Eddy Curry .30 .75
29 Stephon Marbury .40 1.00
30 Zach Randolph .40 1.00
31 Brad Miller .40 1.00
32 Kevin Martin .40 1.00
33 Mike Bibby .50 1.25
34 Ron Artest .50 1.25
35 Jamaal Tinsley .30 .75
36 Jermaine O'Neal .40 1.00
37 Mike Dunleavy .40 1.00
38 Andre Iguodala .40 1.00
39 Andre Miller .40 1.00
40 Rodney Carney .30 .75
41 Chris Paul .60 1.50
42 David West .40 1.00
43 Tyson Chandler .40 1.00
44 Corey Maggette .40 1.00
45 Cuttino Mobley .40 1.00
46 Elton Brand .50 1.25
47 Darko Milicic .30 .75
48 Dwight Howard .40 1.00
49 Hedo Turkoglu .40 1.00
50 Rashard Lewis .40 1.00
51 Antawn Jamison .40 1.00
52 Caron Butler .40 1.00
53 Gilbert Arenas .40 1.00
54 Jason Kidd .50 1.25
55 Richard Jefferson .40 1.00
56 Vince Carter .60 1.50
57 Baron Davis .40 1.00
58 Monta Ellis .40 1.00
59 Stephen Jackson .40 1.00
60 Jordan Farmar .30 .75
61 Kobe Bryant 2.00 5.00
62 Lamar Odom .40 1.00
63 Alonzo Mourning .60 1.50
64 Dwyane Wade .75 2.00
65 Shaquille O'Neal 1.00 2.50
66 Allen Iverson .60 1.50
67 Carmelo Anthony .60 1.50
68 Marcus Camby .30 .75
69 Andrea Bargnani .50 1.25
70 Chris Bosh .50 1.25
71 Jose Calderon .30 .75
72 T.J. Ford .30 .75
73 Ben Gordon .40 1.00
74 Ben Wallace .40 1.00
75 Kirk Hinrich .40 1.00
76 Luol Deng .40 1.00
77 Larry Hughes .40 1.00
78 LeBron James 2.00 5.00
79 Zydrunas Ilgauskas .40 1.00
80 Andrei Kirilenko .40 1.00
81 Carlos Boozer .40 1.00
82 Deron Williams .40 1.00
83 Mehmet Okur .30 .75
84 Luther Head .40 1.00
85 Tracy McGrady .50 1.25
86 Yao Ming .60 1.50
87 Chauncey Billups .50 1.25
88 Rasheed Wallace .50 1.25
89 Richard Hamilton .40 1.00
90 Tayshaun Prince .40 1.00
91 Manu Ginobili .50 1.25
92 Tim Duncan .75 2.00
93 Tony Parker .50 1.25
94 Amare Stoudemire .40 1.00
95 Grant Hill .60 1.50
96 Shawn Marion .40 1.00
97 Steve Nash .60 1.50
98 Dirk Nowitzki .60 1.50
99 Jason Terry .40 1.00
100 Josh Howard .40 1.00
101 Greg Oden/299 RC 4.00 10.00
102 Yi Jianlian/299 RC 5.00 12.00
103 Brandan Wright/299 RC 4.00 10.00
104 Thaddeus Young/299 RC 4.00 10.00
105 Nick Young/299 RC 5.00 12.00
106 Jamario Moon/299 RC 3.00 8.00
106B Guillermo Diaz/299 4.00 10.00
107 Marco Belinelli AU/999 RC 5.00 12.00
108 Darryl Watkins AU/999 RC 3.00 8.00
109 Oleksiy Pecherov AU/999 RC 5.00 12.00
110 Juan Carlos Navarro AU/999 RC 4.00 10.00
111 JamesOn Curry AU/999 RC 3.00 8.00
112 Demetris Nichols AU/999 RC 3.00 8.00
113 Herbert Hill AU/999 RC 3.00 8.00
114 Coby Karl/299 RC 2.50 6.00
115 Darius Washington/299 4.00 10.00
116 Glen Davis AU/999 RC 4.00 10.00
117 Cheikh Samb/299 RC 2.50 6.00
118 Ramon Sessions AU/999 RC 5.00 12.00
119 Luis Scola AU/999 RC 6.00 15.00
122 Spencer Hawes JSY AU/599 RC 5.00 12.00
123 Acie Law JSY AU/599 RC 4.00 10.00
124 Julian Wright JSY AU/599 RC 4.00 10.00
125 Al Thornton JSY AU/599 RC 5.00 12.00
126 R.Stuckey JSY AU/599 RC 5.00 12.00
127 Sean Williams JSY AU/599 RC 4.00 10.00
128 J.Crittenton JSY AU/599 RC 4.00 10.00
129 Jason Smith JSY AU/599 RC 5.00 12.00
130 D.Cook JSY AU/599 RC 5.00 12.00
131 Jared Dudley JSY AU/599 RC 5.00 12.00
132 W.Chandler JSY AU/599 RC 5.00 12.00
133 Morris Almond JSY AU/599 RC 4.00 10.00
134 Arron Afflalo JSY AU/599 RC 6.00 15.00
135 Alando Tucker JSY AU/599 RC 4.00 10.00
136 Carl Landry JSY AU/599 RC 4.00 10.00
137 Gabe Pruitt JSY AU/599 RC 4.00 10.00
138 Aaron Brooks/299 RC 3.00 8.00
139 Nick Fazekas JSY AU/599 RC 4.00 10.00
140 J.Davidson JSY AU/599 RC 4.00 10.00
141 J.McRoberts JSY AU/599 RC 5.00 12.00
142 Glen Davis/299 RC 3.00 8.00
143 Adam Haluska JSY AU/599 RC 4.00 10.00
147 D.McGuire JSY AU/599 RC 4.00 10.00
148 Aaron Gray JSY AU/599 RC 4.00 10.00
149 Taurean Green JSY AU/599 RC 4.00 10.00
150 D.J. Strawberry JSY AU/599 RC 4.00 10.00
151 Chris Richard JSY AU/399 RC 4.00 10.00
152 K.Durant JSY AU/299 RC 800.00 1200.00
153 Al Horford JSY AU/299 RC 15.00 40.00
154 M.Conley Jr. JSY AU/299 RC 12.00 30.00
155 Jeff Green JSY AU/299 RC 10.00 25.00
156 Corey Brewer JSY AU/299 RC 12.00 30.00
157 J.Noah JSY AU/299 RC 30.00 80.00

2007-08 SP Authentic By The Number Career Points

PRINT RUN 75 SER.#'d SETS
*JERSEY NUMB: .5X TO 1.25X BASE HI
JSY NUM PRINT RUN 25 SER.#'d SETS
*RC YEAR SAME VALUE AS POINTS
RC YEAR PRINT RUN 50 SER.#'d SETS
EXCH EXPIRE DATE 1/28/10
BNAD Adrian Dantley 8.00 20.00
BNAH Al Harrington 8.00 20.00
BNAJ Al Jefferson 8.00 20.00
BNAU James Augustine 8.00 20.00
BNBA Leandro Barbosa 8.00 20.00
BNBD Baron Davis 15.00 30.00
BNBJ Bobby Jackson 8.00 20.00
BNBM Brad Miller 8.00 20.00
BNBR Brandon Roy 20.00 40.00
BNBW Bill Walton 15.00 30.00
BNCA Carmelo Anthony 20.00 50.00
BNCH Tom Chambers 8.00 20.00
BNDA Brad Daugherty 8.00 20.00
BNDG Daniel Gibson 10.00 25.00
BNDH Dwight Howard 20.00 50.00
BNDM Donyell Marshall 8.00 20.00
BNDW Deron Williams 15.00 40.00
BNHA Hilton Armstrong 8.00 20.00
BNHO Hakeem Olajuwon 20.00 40.00
BNJA Antawn Jamison 15.00 30.00
BNJJ Jarrett Jack 8.00 20.00
BNJO Michael Jordan/23 400.00 600.00
BNJW Jamaal Wilkes 8.00 20.00
BNKB Kobe Bryant/24 200.00 400.00
BNKH Kirk Hinrich 8.00 20.00
BNLA LaMarcus Aldridge 15.00 40.00
BNLB Larry Bird 75.00 150.00
BNLJ LeBron James 150.00 325.00
BNMJ Magic Johnson 75.00 150.00
BNPE Morris Peterson 8.00 20.00
BNPM Paul Millsap 8.00 20.00
BNPP Paul Pierce 15.00 30.00
BNQR Quentin Richardson 8.00 20.00
BNRB Rick Barry 12.00 30.00
BNRG Rudy Gay 8.00 20.00
BNRR Rajon Rondo 25.00 60.00
BNSA Shareef Abdur-Rahim 10.00 25.00
BNSH Spencer Haywood 8.00 20.00
BNSK Steve Kerr 10.00 25.00
BNSM Sidney Moncrief 8.00 20.00
BNSP Sam Perkins 8.00 20.00
BNTC Terry Cummings 8.00 20.00
BNTP Tayshaun Prince 10.00 25.00
BNTT Tyrus Thomas 10.00 25.00
BNTY Tyson Chandler 8.00 20.00
BNVC Vince Carter 20.00 40.00
BNWF Walt Frazier 15.00 40.00
BNYM Yao Ming 20.00 50.00

2007-08 SP Authentic Chirography

RANDOM INSERTS IN PACKS
EXCH.EXPIRE DATE 1/28/10
CRAD Adrian Dantley 6.00 15.00
CRAJ Antawn Jamison 4.00 10.00
CRAM Alonzo Mourning 20.00 40.00
CRBD Baron Davis 6.00 15.00
CRCM Chris Mihm 4.00 10.00
CRDR Dennis Rodman 20.00 50.00
CRDW Deron Williams 10.00 25.00
CRFG Francisco Garcia 4.00 10.00
CRGI Artis Gilmore 6.00 15.00
CRJO Magic Johnson 40.00 100.00
CRLJ LeBron James 125.00 250.00
CRRO Brandon Roy 10.00 25.00
CRRP Robert Parish 6.00 15.00
CRSA Shareef Abdur-Rahim 4.00 10.00
CRSP Sam Perkins 6.00 15.00
CRTP Tayshaun Prince 6.00 15.00
CRWE Jerry West 40.00 100.00
CRWF Walt Frazier 15.00 40.00

2007-08 SP Authentic Chirography Gold

STATED PRINT RUN 5 TO 25 SER.#'d SETS
EXCHANGE EXPIRATION 1/28/10
CRAB Andrea Bargnani 8.00 20.00
CRAD Adrian Dantley 15.00 30.00
CRAM Alonzo Mourning 60.00 120.00
CRBD Baron Davis 15.00 40.00
CRBJ Bobby Jackson 8.00 20.00
CRBW Bill Walton 15.00 40.00
CRCD Chuck Daly 50.00 120.00
CRCH Connie Hawkins 20.00 40.00
CRDA Brad Daugherty 15.00 30.00
CRDG Daniel Gibson 15.00 30.00
CRDN Don Nelson 20.00 40.00
CRDR Dennis Rodman 25.00 60.00
CRDT David Thompson 15.00 30.00
CRDW Deron Williams 20.00 50.00
CRFG Francisco Garcia 8.00 20.00
CRHO Hakeem Olajuwon 25.00 50.00
CRJK Jason Kidd 20.00 40.00
CRJO Magic Johnson 60.00 120.00
CRJW Jamaal Wilkes 10.00 25.00
CRLB Leandro Barbosa 15.00 30.00
CRMB Mike Bibby 8.00 20.00
CRMI Andre Miller 8.00 20.00
CRMP Mark Price 20.00 50.00
CRPA Tony Parker 20.00 40.00
CRPP Paul Pierce 25.00 50.00
CRRB Rick Barry 8.00 20.00
CRRO Brandon Roy 25.00 60.00
CRRP Robert Parish 20.00 50.00
CRSB Shannon Brown 12.00 30.00
CRSN Steve Nash 50.00 100.00
CRSP Sam Perkins 15.00 30.00
CRST John Stockton 40.00 80.00
CRTC Tom Chambers 8.00 20.00
CRTY Tyson Chandler 15.00 30.00
CRWA Don Slick Watts 8.00 20.00
CRWE Jerry West 60.00 150.00
CRWF Walt Frazier 20.00 50.00

2007-08 SP Authentic Destination Stardom

COMPLETE SET (30) 20.00 40.00
RANDOM INSERTS IN PACKS
DS1 Kevin Durant 8.00 20.00
DS2 Al Horford 1.00 2.50
DS3 Mike Conley Jr. 1.00 2.50
DS4 Jeff Green .75 2.00
DS5 Corey Brewer .75 2.00
DS6 Joakim Noah .75 2.00
DS7 Spencer Hawes .60 1.50
DS8 Acie Law .50 1.25
DS9 Julian Wright .50 1.25
DS10 Al Thornton .60 1.50
DS11 Rodney Stuckey .60 1.50
DS12 Sean Williams .50 1.25
DS13 Marco Belinelli .75 2.00
DS14 Javaris Crittenton .50 1.25
DS15 Jason Smith .60 1.50
DS16 Daequan Cook .60 1.50
DS17 Jared Dudley .60 1.50
DS18 Wilson Chandler .60 1.50
DS19 Morris Almond .50 1.25
DS20 Arron Afflalo .75 2.00
DS21 Alando Tucker .50 1.25
DS22 Glen Davis .60 1.50
DS23 Carl Landry .50 1.25
DS24 Gabe Pruitt .50 1.25
DS25 Luis Scola 1.00 2.50
DS26 Nick Fazekas .50 1.25
DS27 Jermareo Davidson .50 1.25
DS28 Josh McRoberts .60 1.50
DS29 Kyrylo Fesenko .50 1.25
DS30 Aaron Gray .50 1.25

2007-08 SP Authentic Profiles

COMPLETE SET (60) 25.00 50.00
RANDOM INSERTS IN PACKS
AP1 Acie Law .60 1.50
AP2 Al Horford 1.25 3.00
AP3 Al Thornton .75 2.00
AP4 Arron Afflalo 1.00 2.50
AP5 Corey Brewer 1.00 2.50
AP6 Daequan Cook .75 2.00
AP7 Jared Dudley .75 2.00
AP8 Jason Smith .75 2.00
AP9 Javaris Crittenton .60 1.50
AP10 Jeff Green 1.00 2.50
AP11 Joakim Noah 1.00 2.50
AP12 Julian Wright .60 1.50
AP13 Kevin Durant 10.00 25.00
AP14 Marco Belinelli 1.00 2.50
AP15 Mike Conley Jr. 1.25 3.00
AP16 Morris Almond .60 1.50
AP17 Rodney Stuckey .75 2.00
AP18 Sean Williams .60 1.50
AP19 Spencer Hawes .75 2.00
AP20 Wilson Chandler .75 2.00
AP21 Allen Iverson 1.25 3.00
AP22 Carlos Boozer .75 2.00
AP23 Carmelo Anthony 1.25 3.00
AP24 Chauncey Billups 1.00 2.50
AP25 Chris Bosh 1.00 2.50
AP26 Dirk Nowitzki 1.25 3.00
AP27 Dwyane Wade 1.50 4.00
AP28 Gilbert Arenas .75 2.00
AP29 Jason Kidd 1.00 2.50
AP30 Kevin Garnett 1.50 4.00
AP31 Kobe Bryant 4.00 10.00
AP32 LeBron James 4.00 10.00
AP33 Ray Allen 1.00 2.50
AP34 Shaquille O'Neal 2.00 5.00
AP35 Steve Nash 1.25 3.00
AP36 Tim Duncan 1.50 4.00
AP37 Tony Parker 1.00 2.50
AP38 Tracy McGrady 1.00 2.50
AP39 Vince Carter 1.25 3.00
AP40 Yao Ming 1.25 3.00
AP41 Adrian Dantley .75 2.00
AP42 Bill Walton 1.00 2.50
AP43 Chris Mullin 1.00 2.50
AP44 David Robinson 1.50 4.00
AP45 Elvin Hayes 1.00 2.50
AP46 George Gervin 1.00 2.50
AP47 Hakeem Olajuwon 1.25 3.00
AP48 Jerry West 1.25 3.00
AP49 John Stockton 1.50 4.00
AP50 Julius Erving 1.50 4.00
AP51 Kareem Abdul-Jabbar 1.50 4.00
AP52 Karl Malone 1.25 3.00
AP53 Larry Bird 2.50 6.00
AP54 Magic Johnson 2.50 6.00
AP55 Michael Jordan 8.00 20.00
AP56 Moses Malone 1.00 2.50
AP57 Oscar Robertson 1.00 2.50
AP58 Rick Barry .75 2.00
AP59 Robert Parish 1.00 2.50
AP60 Wilt Chamberlain 2.00 5.00

2007-08 SP Authentic Recruiting Class 2007

STATED PRINT RUN 60 TO 75 SER.#'d SETS
*CITY NAME: SAME VALUE AS BASE
CITY NAME STATED PRINT RUN 50 SETS
UNPRICED DRAFT POS.PRINT RUN 15 SETS
*TEAM NAME: .5X TO 1.25X BASE HI
TEAM NAME STATED PRINT RUN 25 SETS
EXCH EXPIRE DATE 1/28/10
RCAA Arron Afflalo/75 6.00 15.00
RCAB Aaron Brooks/75 5.00 12.00
RCAH Al Horford/75 10.00 25.00
RCAL Acie Law/75 4.00 10.00
RCAT Al Thornton/75 5.00 12.00
RCCB Corey Brewer/75 6.00 15.00
RCCL Carl Landry/75 4.00 10.00
RCDC Daequan Cook/75 5.00 12.00
RCDM Dominic McGuire/75 4.00 10.00
RCDU Jared Dudley/75 5.00 12.00
RCGD Glen Davis/75 5.00 12.00
RCGP Gabe Pruitt/75 4.00 10.00
RCJC Javaris Crittenton/75 4.00 10.00
RCJD Jermareo Davidson/75 4.00 10.00
RCJG Jeff Green/75 6.00 15.00
RCJM Josh McRoberts/75 5.00 12.00
RCJN Joakim Noah/75 30.00 80.00
RCJS Jason Smith/75 5.00 12.00
RCJW Julian Wright/75 4.00 10.00
RCKD Kevin Durant/60 150.00 300.00
RCMA Morris Almond/75 4.00 10.00
RCMB Marco Belinelli/75 6.00 15.00
RCMC Mike Conley Jr./75 8.00 20.00
RCNF Nick Fazekas/75 4.00 10.00
RCRS Rodney Stuckey/75 5.00 12.00
RCSH Spencer Hawes/75 5.00 12.00
RCSW Sean Williams/75 4.00 10.00
RCTG Taurean Green/75 4.00 10.00
RCTU Alando Tucker/75 4.00 10.00
RCWC Wilson Chandler/75 5.00 12.00

2007-08 SP Authentic Sign of the Times Dual

PRINT RUN 16 TO 50 SER.#'d SETS
UNPRICED TRIPLE PRINT RUN 10 SETS
UNPRICED QUAD PRINT RUN 5 SETS
UNPRICED SIXES PRINT RUN 5 SETS
EXCH EXPIRE DATE 1/28/10
STAR L.Aldridge/B.Roy 25.00 50.00
STAW D.Williams/J.Augustine 10.00 25.00
STBD P.Davis/S.Brown 8.00 20.00
STBG M.Bibby/F.Garcia 10.00 25.00
STDB B.Diaw/L.Barbosa 10.00 25.00
STDG K.Durant/J.Green 100.00 250.00
STDM M.Jordan/D.Rodman 300.00 550.00
STFB T.Ford/J.Boone 10.00 25.00
STGC R.Gay/M.Conley Jr. 10.00 25.00
STGM D.Marshall/D.Gibson 8.00 20.00
STGN A.Gray/J.Noah 15.00 30.00
STGR R.Rondo/D.Gibson 10.00 25.00
STHM A.Harrington/P.Millsap 8.00 20.00
STJA S.Jones/J.Augustine 8.00 20.00
STJC A.Jefferson/R.Carney 15.00 40.00
STJR M.Johnson/P.Riley 50.00 100.00
STJS A.Jamison/D.Stevenson 8.00 20.00
STLA M.Ager/K.Lowry 8.00 20.00
STMD C.Mihm/P.Davis 8.00 20.00
STMG H.Greer/A.Miller 8.00 20.00
STMN S.May/D.Noel/31 8.00 20.00
STMP P.Millsap/L.Powe 8.00 20.00
STMS M.Ager/S.Brown 8.00 20.00
STMT A.Mourning/T.Thomas 12.00 30.00
STOS H.Olajuwon/R.Sampson 25.00 50.00
STPD T.Prince/A.Dantley 15.00 30.00
STPJ T.Prince/L.James 100.00 225.00
STPW T.Parker/D.Williams 15.00 40.00
STRP R.Rondo/H.Armstrong 20.00 40.00
STSA C.Simmons/H.Armstrong 8.00 20.00
STSJ S.May/J.Dudley 8.00 20.00
STWA B.Walton/L.Aldridge 15.00 30.00
STWD D.Wilkins/Y.Diawara 8.00 20.00
STWJ S.Williams/S.Jones 8.00 20.00
STWP B.Walton/R.Parish 15.00 40.00

2008-09 SP Authentic

This set was released on February 3, 2009. The base set consists of 141 cards.

COMP.SET w/o SP's (100) 25.00 50.00
UNPRICED DIE CUT PRINT RUN 10 SETS
UNPRICED RC LOGOMAN PRINT RUN ONE SET
1 Dwyane Wade .75 2.00
2 Alonzo Mourning .60 1.50
3 Daequan Cook .30 .75
4 Kevin Durant 1.25 3.00
5 Jeff Green .40 1.00
6 Chris Wilcox .30 .75
7 Al Jefferson .40 1.00
8 Corey Brewer .40 1.00
9 Randy Foye .50 1.25
10 Rudy Gay .50 1.25
11 Mike Conley Jr. .40 1.00
12 Mike Miller .40 1.00
13 Jamal Crawford .50 1.25
14 Eddy Curry .30 .75
15 Quentin Richardson .40 1.00
16 Stephon Marbury .40 1.00
17 Chris Kaman .40 1.00
18 Marcus Camby .30 .75
19 Baron Davis .40 1.00
20 Michael Redd .40 1.00
21 Richard Jefferson .40 1.00
22 Mo Williams .40 1.00
23 Emeka Okafor .40 1.00
24 Gerald Wallace .40 1.00
25 Jason Richardson .50 1.25
26 Joakim Noah .40 1.00
27 Luol Deng .40 1.00
28 Ben Gordon .40 1.00
29 Michael Jordan 4.00 10.00
30 Vince Carter .60 1.50
31 Yi Jianlian .50 1.25
32 Devin Harris .30 .75
33 T.J. Ford .30 .75
34 Danny Granger .40 1.00
35 Mike Dunleavy .40 1.00
36 Ron Artest .50 1.25
37 Kevin Martin .40 1.00
38 Brad Miller .40 1.00
39 Brandon Roy .50 1.25
40 LaMarcus Aldridge .50 1.25
41 Greg Oden .40 1.00
42 Corey Maggette .40 1.00
43 Al Harrington .40 1.00
44 Monta Ellis .40 1.00
45 Al Horford .50 1.25
46 Joe Johnson .40 1.00
47 Josh Smith .40 1.00
48 Mike Bibby .40 1.00
49 Andre Iguodala .40 1.00
50 Andre Miller .40 1.00
51 Thaddeus Young .40 1.00
52 Chris Bosh .50 1.25
53 Jermaine O'Neal .40 1.00
54 Jose Calderon .30 .75
55 Antawn Jamison .40 1.00
56 Caron Butler .40 1.00
57 Gilbert Arenas .40 1.00
58 LeBron James 2.00 5.00
59 Daniel Gibson .40 1.00
60 Anderson Varejao .30 .75
61 Allen Iverson .60 1.50
62 Carmelo Anthony .60 1.50
63 Elton Brand .50 1.25
64 Jason Kidd .50 1.25
65 Dirk Nowitzki .60 1.50
66 Josh Howard .40 1.00
67 Dwight Howard .40 1.00
68 Hedo Turkoglu .40 1.00
69 Rashard Lewis .40 1.00
70 Deron Williams .40 1.00
71 Carlos Boozer .40 1.00
72 Andrei Kirilenko .40 1.00
73 Ronnie Brewer .40 1.00
74 Shaquille O'Neal 1.00 2.50
75 Steve Nash .50 1.25
76 Amare Stoudemire .40 1.00
77 Leandro Barbosa .40 1.00
78 Yao Ming .60 1.50
79 Tracy McGrady .50 1.25
80 Shane Battier .40 1.00
81 Luis Scola .40 1.00
82 Tim Duncan .75 2.00
83 Tony Parker .50 1.25
84 Manu Ginobili .50 1.25
85 Chris Paul .60 1.50
86 David West .40 1.00
87 Tyson Chandler .40 1.00
88 Peja Stojakovic .50 1.25
89 Kobe Bryant 2.00 5.00
90 Pau Gasol .50 1.25
91 Lamar Odom .40 1.00
92 Andrew Bynum .30 .75
93 Chauncey Billups .50 1.25
94 Richard Hamilton .40 1.00
95 Rasheed Wallace .50 1.25
96 Tayshaun Prince .40 1.00
97 Kevin Garnett .75 2.00
98 Paul Pierce .50 1.25
99 Ray Allen .50 1.25
100 Rajon Rondo .50 1.25
101 Alexis Ajinca AU/199 RC 5.00 12.00
102 Joe Alexander JSY AU/499 RC 5.00 12.00
103 R.Anderson JSY AU/499 RC 6.00 15.00
104 Darrell Arthur JSY AU/499 RC 6.00 15.00
105 D.J. Augustin JSY AU/299 RC 6.00 15.00
106 J.Bayless JSY AU/299 RC 6.00 15.00
107 M.Beasley JSY AU/299 RC 8.00 20.00
108 M.Chalmers JSY AU/499 RC 8.00 20.00
109 Joe Crawford AU/199 RC 5.00 12.00
110 Joey Dorsey JSY AU/499 RC 5.00 12.00
111 C.D-Roberts JSY AU/499 RC 5.00 12.00
112 Patrick Ewing Jr. JSY AU/499 RC 5.00 12.00
113 Danilo Gallinari AU/199 RC 12.00 30.00
114 J.R. Giddens JSY AU/499 RC 5.00 12.00
115 Eric Gordon JSY AU/299 RC 12.00 30.00
116 Donte Greene JSY AU/499 RC 5.00 12.00
117 Malik Hairston AU/199 RC 5.00 12.00
118 Roy Hibbert JSY AU/499 RC 8.00 20.00
119 J.J. Hickson JSY AU/499 RC 6.00 15.00
120 George Hill JSY AU/499 RC 8.00 20.00
121 D.Jordan JSY AU/499 RC 20.00 50.00
122 Kosta Koufos JSY AU/499 RC 6.00 15.00
123 Courtney Lee JSY AU/499 RC 6.00 15.00
124 Brook Lopez JSY AU/299 RC 10.00 25.00
125 Robin Lopez JSY AU/499 RC 8.00 20.00
126 Kevin Love JSY AU/299 RC 60.00 150.00
127 O.J. Mayo JSY AU/299 RC 8.00 20.00
128 J.McGee JSY AU/499 RC 10.00 25.00
129 A.Randolph JSY AU/499 RC 5.00 12.00
130 D.Rose JSY AU/299 RC 125.00 300.00
131 Brandon Rush JSY AU/299 RC 6.00 15.00
132 Walter Sharpe JSY AU/499 RC 5.00 12.00
133 Sean Singletary AU/199 RC 5.00 12.00
134 M.Speights JSY AU/499 RC 6.00 15.00
135 Mike Taylor AU/199 RC 5.00 12.00
136 J.Thompson JSY AU/499 RC 5.00 12.00
137 Kyle Weaver JSY AU/499 RC 5.00 12.00
138 Sonny Weems JSY AU/499 RC 5.00 12.00
139 R.Westbrook JSY AU/299 RC 300.00 600.00
140 D.J. White JSY AU/499 RC 6.00 15.00
147 R.Fernandez JSY AU/499 RC 6.00 15.00

2008-09 SP Authentic Chirography

COMBINED AUTO ODDS 1:12
CAD Adrian Dantley 5.00 12.00
CAE Alex English 5.00 12.00
CAG Artis Gilmore 5.00 12.00
CBD Brad Daugherty 5.00 12.00
CBL Bob Lanier 5.00 12.00
CBS Bill Sharman 8.00 20.00
CBW Buck Williams 5.00 12.00
CDD Darryl Dawkins 6.00 15.00
CDR Dennis Rodman 20.00 50.00
CDT David Thompson 6.00 15.00
CDW Don Watts 5.00 12.00
CGG George Gervin 8.00 20.00
CGM George McGinnis 5.00 12.00
CGO Gail Goodrich 10.00 25.00
CGR Glen Rice 15.00 30.00
CJE Julius Erving 40.00 100.00
CJH John Havlicek 30.00 80.00
CJS John Salley 6.00 15.00
CLB Larry Bird 50.00 100.00
CMC Maurice Cheeks 5.00 12.00
CMJ Michael Jordan 350.00 550.00
CNT Nate Thurmond 6.00 15.00
CRB Rick Barry 8.00 20.00
CRO David Robinson 40.00 80.00
CRP Robert Parish 10.00 25.00
CSJ Sam Jones 12.00 30.00
CSK Steve Kerr 8.00 20.00
CTH Tom Heinsohn 15.00 40.00
CTS Tom Sanders 8.00 20.00
CVD Vlade Divac 15.00 40.00
CWF Walt Frazier 12.00 30.00
CWI Dominique Wilkins 15.00 30.00
CXM Xavier McDaniel 6.00 15.00

2008-09 SP Authentic Destination Stardom

COMPLETE SET (30) 15.00 40.00
STATED ODDS 1:3
DS1 Derrick Rose 3.00 8.00
DS2 Michael Beasley .75 2.00
DS3 O.J. Mayo .75 2.00
DS4 Russell Westbrook 6.00 15.00
DS5 Kevin Love 2.50 6.00
DS6 Danilo Gallinari 1.25 3.00
DS7 Eric Gordon 1.25 3.00
DS8 Joe Alexander .50 1.25
DS9 D.J. Augustin .60 1.50
DS10 Brook Lopez 1.00 2.50
DS11 Jerryd Bayless .60 1.50
DS12 Jason Thompson .50 1.25
DS13 Brandon Rush .60 1.50
DS14 Anthony Randolph .50 1.25
DS15 Robin Lopez .75 2.00
DS16 Marreese Speights .60 1.50
DS17 Roy Hibbert .75 2.00
DS18 Javale McGee 1.00 2.50
DS19 J.J. Hickson .60 1.50
DS20 Alexis Ajinca .50 1.25
DS21 Courtney Lee .60 1.50
DS22 D.J. White .60 1.50
DS23 J.R. Giddens .50 1.25
DS24 Joey Dorsey .50 1.25
DS25 Sonny Weems .50 1.25
DS26 Mario Chalmers .75 2.00
DS27 Sun Yue 1.00 2.50
DS28 Rudy Fernandez .60 1.50
DS29 Marc Gasol 1.50 4.00
DS30 Hamed Haddadi .75 2.00

2008-09 SP Authentic Limited Memorabilia

NDOM INSERTS IN PACKS
SPLAD Darrell Arthur 2.00 5.00
SPLAR Anthony Randolph 1.50 4.00
SPLBL Brook Lopez 3.00 8.00
SPLBR Brandon Rush 2.00 5.00
SPLCD Chris Douglas-Roberts 1.50 4.00
SPLDA D.J. Augustin 2.00 5.00
SPLDG Donte Greene 1.50 4.00
SPLDJ DeAndre Jordan 3.00 8.00
SPLDR Derrick Rose 15.00 40.00
SPLEG Eric Gordon 4.00 10.00
SPLGH George Hill 2.50 6.00
SPLJA Joe Alexander 1.50 4.00
SPLJB Jerryd Bayless 2.00 5.00
SPLJD Joey Dorsey 1.50 4.00
SPLJG J.R. Giddens 1.50 4.00
SPLJH J.J. Hickson 2.00 5.00
SPLJM Javale McGee 3.00 8.00
SPLJT Jason Thompson 1.50 4.00
SPLKK Kosta Koufos 2.00 5.00
SPLKL Kevin Love 8.00 20.00
SPLKW Kyle Weaver 1.50 4.00
SPLMB Michael Beasley 2.50 6.00
SPLMC Mario Chalmers 2.50 6.00
SPLMS Marreese Speights 2.00 5.00
SPLOM O.J. Mayo 2.50 6.00
SPLRA Ryan Anderson 2.00 5.00
SPLRF Rudy Fernandez 2.00 5.00
SPLRL Robin Lopez 2.50 6.00
SPLSW Sonny Weems 1.50 4.00
SPLWS Walter Sharpe 1.50 4.00

2008-09 SP Authentic Profiles

COMPLETE SET (60) 30.00 60.00
STATED ODDS 1:3
AP1 Charles Oakley .75 2.00
AP2 Dominique Wilkins 1.00 2.50
AP3 James Worthy .75 2.00
AP4 Joe Dumars .75 2.00
AP5 Julius Erving 1.25 3.00
AP6 Kareem Abdul-Jabbar 1.25 3.00
AP7 Larry Bird 2.00 5.00
AP8 Larry Johnson .75 2.00
AP9 Magic Johnson 2.00 5.00
AP10 Michael Jordan 6.00 15.00
AP11 Muggsy Bogues .60 1.50
AP12 Oscar Robertson .75 2.00
AP13 Rick Mahorn .50 1.25
AP14 Spud Webb .60 1.50
AP15 Vlade Divac .75 2.00
AP16 Al Horford .75 2.00
AP17 Amare Stoudemire .60 1.50
AP18 Carlos Boozer .60 1.50
AP19 Chris Bosh .75 2.00
AP20 David West .60 1.50
AP21 Dirk Nowitzki 1.00 2.50
AP22 Dwight Howard .60 1.50
AP23 Kevin Garnett 1.25 3.00
AP24 LeBron James 3.00 8.00
AP25 Pau Gasol .75 2.00
AP26 Rasheed Wallace .75 2.00
AP27 Shaquille O'Neal 1.50 4.00
AP28 Shawn Marion .60 1.50
AP29 Tim Duncan 1.25 3.00
AP30 Yao Ming 1.00 2.50
AP31 Allen Iverson 1.00 2.50
AP32 Baron Davis .60 1.50
AP33 Carmelo Anthony 1.00 2.50
AP34 Chauncey Billups .75 2.00
AP35 Chris Paul 1.00 2.50
AP36 Deron Williams .60 1.50
AP37 Dwyane Wade 1.25 3.00
AP38 Joe Johnson .60 1.50
AP39 Kevin Durant 2.00 5.00
AP40 Kobe Bryant 3.00 8.00
AP41 Paul Pierce .75 2.00
AP42 Steve Nash .75 2.00
AP43 Tony Parker .75 2.00
AP44 Tracy McGrady .75 2.00
AP45 Vince Carter 1.00 2.50
AP46 Derrick Rose 3.00 8.00
AP47 Michael Beasley .75 2.00
AP48 O.J. Mayo .75 2.00
AP49 Russell Westbrook 6.00 15.00
AP50 Kevin Love 2.50 6.00
AP51 Danilo Gallinari 1.25 3.00
AP52 Sun Yue 1.00 2.50
AP53 Jason Thompson .50 1.25
AP54 Eric Gordon 1.25 3.00
AP55 Rudy Fernandez .60 1.50
AP56 Marc Gasol 1.50 4.00
AP57 D.J. Augustin .60 1.50
AP58 Jerryd Bayless .60 1.50
AP59 Luc Richard Mbah A Moute .60 1.50
AP60 Hamed Haddadi .75 2.00

2008-09 SP Authentic Recruiting Class City Name

TOTAL PRINT RUNS LISTED
RCCBL Brook Lopez/13 30.00 80.00
RCCBW Bill Walker/26 25.00 50.00
RCCDA Darrell Arthur/34 20.00 40.00
RCCDG Danilo Gallinari/13 30.00 80.00
RCCDJ D.J. Augustin/16 30.00 60.00
RCCDR Derrick Rose/23 300.00 600.00
RCCDW D.J. White/38 12.00 30.00
RCCEG Eric Gordon/17 30.00 60.00
RCCGH George Hill/40 25.00 50.00
RCCJA Joe Alexander/24 12.00 30.00
RCCJB Jerryd Bayless/20 25.00 60.00
RCCJC Joe Crawford/34 12.00 30.00
RCCJG J.R. Giddens/26 20.00 50.00
RCCJH J.J. Hickson/36 30.00 60.00
RCCJM Javale McGee/31 25.00 60.00
RCCJT Jason Thompson/25 25.00 50.00
RCCKL Kevin Love/48 75.00 150.00
RCCMB Michael Beasley/17 50.00 120.00
RCCMS Marreese Speights/30 20.00 50.00
RCCOM O.J. Mayo/35 50.00 120.00
RCCPE Patrick Ewing Jr./37 12.00 30.00
RCCRA Ryan Anderson/29 20.00 40.00
RCCRH Roy Hibbert/37 25.00 50.00
RCCRL Robin Lopez/27 12.00 30.00
RCCRW Russell Westbrook/19 175.00 350.00
RCCSS Sean Singletary/27 12.00 30.00
RCCWS Walter Sharpe/14 12.00 30.00

2008-09 SP Authentic Recruiting Class Full Name

TOTAL PRINT RUNS LISTED
RCNAR Anthony Randolph/75 12.00 30.00
RCNBR Brandon Rush/66 12.00 30.00
RCNBW Bill Walker/80 12.00 30.00
RCNDA Darrell Arthur/78 12.00 30.00
RCNDJ D.J. Augustin/80 20.00 50.00
RCNDR Derrick Rose/66 150.00 400.00
RCNDW D.J. White/77 12.00 30.00
RCNGH George Hill/80 12.00 30.00
RCNJA Joe Alexander/72 12.00 30.00
RCNJB Jerryd Bayless/65 15.00 40.00
RCNJC Joe Crawford/77 12.00 30.00
RCNJG J.R. Giddens/81 12.00 30.00
RCNJM Javale McGee/77 15.00 40.00
RCNJT Jason Thompson/65 15.00 40.00
RCNKL Kevin Love/18 100.00 250.00
RCNMB Michael Beasley/70 30.00 80.00
RCNMS Marreese Speights/80 12.00 30.00
RCNOM O.J. Mayo/30 50.00 120.00
RCNPE Patrick Ewing Jr./84 12.00 30.00
RCNRA Ryan Anderson/84 12.00 30.00
RCNRH Roy Hibbert/70 20.00 40.00
RCNRL Robin Lopez/80 12.00 30.00
RCNRW Russell Westbrook/64 50.00 100.00
RCNSS Sean Singletary/84 12.00 30.00
RCNWS Walter Sharpe/84 12.00 30.00

2008-09 SP Authentic Sign of the Times Dual

PRINT RUN 50 SER.#'d SETS
UNPRICED QUAD PRINT RUN 5 SETS
UNPRICED TRIPLE PRINT RUN 10 SETS
SDAR L.Aldridge/B.Roy 15.00 40.00
SDBB S.Battier/R.Brewer 8.00 20.00
SDBW M.Belinelli/C.Watson 6.00 15.00
SDCC Conley Jr./Conley Sr. 8.00 20.00
SDCO E.Okafor/T.Chandler 6.00 15.00
SDDG K.Durant/J.Green 40.00 100.00
SDFF R.Felton/R.Foye 6.00 15.00
SDGC R.Gay/M.Conley 6.00 15.00
SDGH A.Horford/K.Garnett 25.00 50.00
SDHA W.Herrmann/A.Afflalo 6.00 15.00
SDHM A.Horford/J.Moon 8.00 20.00
SDIS R.Stuckey/A.Iguodala 10.00 25.00
SDJS J.Boone/S.Williams 6.00 15.00
SDJW R.Jefferson/M.Williams 6.00 15.00
SDKB C.Billups/J.Kidd 15.00 30.00
SDKJ C.Kaman/A.Jefferson 6.00 15.00
SDKK C.Karl/G.Karl 6.00 15.00
SDMI A.Iguodala/A.Miller 6.00 15.00
SDOB L.Odom/C.Boozer 8.00 20.00
SDPA R.Allen/P.Pierce 40.00 80.00
SDPH T.Price/D.Howard 20.00 40.00
SDPP T.Parker/C.Paul 35.00 75.00
SDSB A.Bynum/A.Stoudemire 12.50 30.00
SDSV J.Smith/S.Vujacic 6.00 15.00
SDTS A.Thornton/L.Scola 8.00 20.00
SDVR S.Vujacic/R.Rondo 15.00 40.00
SDWG D.West/R.Gay 10.00 25.00
SDWL L.Walton/C.Landry 6.00 15.00

2008-09 SP Authentic Varsity Letters Legends City Name

TOTAL PRINT RUNS LISTED
SOME UNPRICED DUE TO SCARCITY
VLBD Brad Daugherty/18* 15.00 40.00
VLBL Bob Lanier/14* 30.00 60.00
VLBR Bill Russell/13* 125.00 250.00
VLDR Dennis Rodman/12* 200.00 400.00
VLDW Don Watts/13* 15.00 40.00
VLMP Mark Price/18* 150.00 300.00
VLRB Rick Barry/19* 40.00 80.00
VLRM Rick Mahorn/14* 25.00 60.00
VLRO David Robinson/15* 100.00 200.00
VLSJ Sam Jones/13* 50.00 120.00
VLTC Tom Chambers/11* 25.00 50.00

2008-09 SP Authentic Varsity Letters Legends Full Name

TOTAL PRINT RUNS LISTED
VLBD Brad Daugherty/39* 10.00 25.00
VLBL Bob Lanier/18* 20.00 40.00
VLBR Bill Russell/22* 125.00 250.00
VLDR Dennis Rodman/24* 25.00 60.00
VLDW Don Watts/39* 12.00 30.00
VLGR Glen Rice/24* 75.00 150.00
VLLJ Larry Johnson/24* 100.00 200.00
VLMB Muggsy Bogues/36* 60.00 150.00
VLMJ Michael Jordan/26* 900.00 1500.00
VLMP Mark Price/36* 125.00 250.00
VLRB Rick Barry/27* 30.00 60.00
VLRO David Robinson/26* 75.00 150.00
VLSJ Sam Jones/24* 60.00 120.00
VLTC Tom Chambers/33* 15.00 40.00

2008-09 SP Authentic Varsity Letters Veterans City Name

TOTAL PRINT RUNS LISTED
SOME UNPRICED DUE TO SCARCITY
VVAB Andrew Bogut/14* 15.00 30.00
VVAH Al Horford/39* 15.00 30.00
VVAM Alonzo Mourning/27* 100.00 200.00
VVAT Alando Tucker/48* 15.00 30.00
VVBG Ben Gordon/23* 25.00 50.00
VVCK Chris Kaman/17* 15.00 30.00
VVCL Carl Landry/14* 25.00 60.00
VVCP Chris Paul/10* 150.00 300.00
VVDC Daequan Cook/42* 15.00 30.00
VVDH Dwight Howard/22* 50.00 120.00
VVJA Antawn Jamison/17* 30.00 60.00
VVJF Jordan Farmar/28* 15.00 30.00
VVKB Kobe Bryant/16* 300.00 500.00
VVKD Kevin Durant/19* 150.00 300.00
VVKG Kevin Garnett/13* 75.00 150.00
VVLJ LeBron James/18* 350.00 600.00
VVLW Luke Walton/28* 15.00 30.00
VVMC Mike Conley Jr./16* 20.00 50.00
VVMW Mario West/32* 15.00 30.00
VVQR Quentin Richardson/42* 15.00 30.00
VVRJ Richard Jefferson/29* 15.00 30.00
VVRS Ramon Sessions/39* 15.00 30.00
VVST Rodney Stuckey/21* 20.00 50.00
VVSV Sasha Vujacic/44* 20.00 40.00

2008-09 SP Authentic Varsity Letters Veterans Full Name

TOTAL PRINT RUN LISTED
VVAH Al Horford/81* 6.00 15.00
VVAM Alonzo Mourning/56* 75.00 150.00
VVAT Alando Tucker/84* 6.00 15.00
VVBD Baron Davis/60* 6.00 15.00
VVBG Ben Gordon/63* 20.00 40.00
VVBY Andrew Bynum/55* 15.00 40.00
VVCK Chris Kaman/60* 6.00 15.00
VVCL Carl Landry/90* 15.00 30.00
VVCP Chris Paul/54* 50.00 100.00
VVDC Daequan Cook/88* 6.00 15.00
VVDH Dwight Howard/60* 30.00 80.00
VVDW David West/72* 6.00 15.00
VVJA Antawn Jamison/65* 15.00 30.00
VVJF Jordan Farmar/84* 20.00 40.00
VVKB Kobe Bryant/20* 300.00 500.00
VVKD Kevin Durant/22* 200.00 350.00
VVKG Kevin Garnett/24* 75.00 150.00
VVLJ LeBron James/22* 300.00 500.00
VVLW Luke Walton/80* 6.00 15.00
VVMC Mike Conley Jr./60* 15.00 40.00
VVMW Mario West/72* 6.00 15.00
VVQR Quentin Richardson/85* 6.00 15.00
VVRJ Richard Jefferson/80* 6.00 15.00
VVRS Ramon Sessions/91* 6.00 15.00
VVST Rodney Stuckey/78* 12.00 30.00
VVSV Sasha Vujacic/84* 6.00 15.00

2008-09 SP Authentic Vital Signs

COMBINED AUTO ODDS 1:12
VSAH Al Horford 4.00 10.00
VSBG Ben Gordon 6.00 15.00
VSDF Derek Fisher 8.00 20.00
VSDH Dwight Howard 15.00 30.00
VSDL David Lee 4.00 10.00
VSDW David West 6.00 15.00
VSJB Josh Boone 4.00 10.00
VSJG Jeff Green 5.00 12.00
VSKB Kobe Bryant 125.00 250.00
VSKD Kevin Durant 60.00 150.00
VSKG Kevin Garnett 50.00 100.00
VSLJ LeBron James 200.00 350.00
VSLW Luke Walton 4.00 10.00
VSRF Rudy Fernandez 8.00 20.00
VSRG Rudy Gay 4.00 10.00
VSRS Rodney Stuckey 4.00 10.00
VSSE Ramon Sessions 5.00 12.00
VSTC Tyson Chandler 4.00 10.00

2010-11 SP Authentic

Released in May, 2011, the 2010-11 SP Authentic set was issued in six-card packs with 24 packs per box. The base issue cards are complete at a 100-card set and the autographs are complete at a 42-card set. For the autographs, most players had their last names used, although #203, #209, #221 and #240 used the word "Rookie" to spell out their Lettermen individual sets. To obtain the full print runs on the autographs take the number of letters in their last name (or "Rookie" for the numbers listed above) and multiply that by the serial-numbering on the actual card.

COMP.SET w/o RCs (100) 8.00 20.00
AU PRINT RUN 149 TO 299 SER.#'d SETS
MOST AU PRINT RUNS BASED ON LAST NAME
TOTAL PRINT RUN LISTED WITH ASTERISK
1 Michael Jordan 2.50 6.00
2 Jerry West .40 1.00
3 Bill Walton .30 .75
4 Bill Russell .50 1.25

5 David Robinson .50 1.25
6 Hakeem Olajuwon .40 1.00
7 Alonzo Mourning .40 1.00
8 Christian Laettner .25 .60
9 Magic Johnson .75 2.00
10 George Gervin .30 .75
11 Clyde Drexler .40 1.00
12 Dominique Wilkins .40 1.00
13 John Stockton .50 1.25
14 Larry Bird .75 2.00
15 James Worthy .40 1.00
16 Julius Erving .50 1.25
17 Bruce Bowen .20 .50
18 Phil Ford .30 .75
19 Bobby Jones .25 .60
20 B.J. Armstrong .30 .75
21 Rick Barry .25 .60
22 Elgin Baylor .30 .75
23 LeBron James 1.50 4.00
24 Jim Jackson .20 .50
25 Larry Brown .30 .75
26 Bill Cartwright .25 .60
27 Cynthia Cooper .40 1.00
28 Walter Davis .20 .50
29 Adrian Dantley .25 .60
30 Brad Daugherty .25 .60
31 Hubert Davis .20 .50
32 Vlade Divac .30 .75
33 Rick Fox .25 .60
34 Walt Frazier .30 .75
35 Gail Goodrich .25 .60
36 Darrell Griffith .20 .50
37 Anfernee Hardaway .75 2.00
38 James Harden .50 1.25
39 Robert Horry .30 .75
40 John Havlicek .40 1.00
41 Steve Alford .30 .75
42 Rod Hundley .30 .75
43 Lauren Jackson .40 1.00
44 Mark Jackson .25 .60
45 Avery Johnson .25 .60
46 Larry Johnson .40 1.00
47 Rex Walters .20 .50
48 Shawn Kemp .50 1.25
49 Toni Kukoc .30 .75
50 Bill Laimbeer .25 .60
51 Lonnie Shelton .20 .50
52 Freddie Lewis .30 .75
53 George Lynch .30 .75
54 Danny Manning .25 .60
55 Sam Perkins .20 .50
56 Greg Anthony .20 .50
57 Bill Sharman .30 .75
58 Candace Parker .75 2.00
59 Terry Porter .20 .50
60 Glen Rice .25 .60
61 Micheal Ray Richardson .25 .60
62 Mateen Cleaves .20 .50
63 Dennis Rodman .60 1.50
64 Derrick Rose .40 1.00
65 Pat Riley .30 .75
66 Calbert Cheaney .30 .75
67 Cazzie Russell .25 .60
68 Bobby Hurley .30 .75
69 Jack Sikma .25 .60
70 Sam Cassell .25 .60
71 Jerry Sloan .30 .75
72 Kenny Smith .25 .60
73 J.R. Reid .20 .50
74 Tim Hardaway .30 .75
75 David Thompson .25 .60
76 Reggie Theus .30 .75
77 Rudy Tomjanovich .25 .60
78 Chet Walker .25 .60
79 Russell Westbrook .75 2.00
80 Marion Jones .40 1.00
81 Steve Fisher .40 1.00
82 Tom Izzo .30 .75
83 Roy Williams .60 1.50
84 Bill Self .40 1.00
85 Jim Boeheim .40 1.00
86 Gary Williams .40 1.00
87 Mike Montgomery .30 .75
88 Jim Calhoun .40 1.00
89 Billy Donovan .30 .75
90 Mark Few .30 .75
91 Ben Howland .30 .75
92 Thad Matta .30 .75
93 Bruce Pearl .30 .75
94 Bob Huggins .30 .75
95 Bo Ryan .30 .75
96 Tubby Smith .30 .75
97 Sean Miller .30 .75
98 Rick Majerus .30 .75
99 Jay Wright .30 .75
100 Jamie Dixon .30 .75
201 Hassan Whiteside AU/2691* 15.00 40.00
202 Terrico White AU/1495* 6.00 15.00
203 Andy Rautins AU/1794* 6.00 15.00
204 Derrick Favors AU/894* 12.00 30.00
205 Al-Farouq Aminu AU/745* 6.00 15.00
206 Cole Aldrich AU/1043* 10.00 25.00
207 D.Cousins AU/1043* 20.00 50.00
208 Ed Davis AU/745* 3.00 8.00
209 H.N'Diaye AU/1794* 5.00 12.00
210 Greg Monroe AU/894* 15.00 40.00
211 Brian Zoubek AU/894* 8.00 20.00
212 Manny Harris AU/1794* 5.00 12.00
213 Damion James AU/745* 3.00 8.00
214 S.Robinson AU/1192* 3.00 8.00
215 Armon Johnson AU/2093* 3.00 8.00
216 Craig Brackins AU/2093* 3.00 8.00
217 Gani Lawal AU/1495* 3.00 8.00
218 Luke Babbitt AU/2093* 4.00 10.00
219 D.Jones AU/1495* 3.00 8.00
220 Xavier Henry AU/745* 3.00 8.00
221 Solomon Alabi AU/1794* 3.00 8.00
222 J.Crawford AU/2392* 4.00 10.00
223 Eric Bledsoe AU/1043* 20.00 50.00
224 Jerome Jordan AU/894* 5.00 12.00
225 J.Anderson AU/2392* 3.00 8.00
226 Dexter Pittman AU/2093* 3.00 8.00
227 Da'Sean Butler AU/894* 8.00 20.00
228 Trevor Booker AU/1794* 6.00 15.00
229 Ekpe Udoh AU/596* 3.00 8.00
230 Sherron Collins AU/2093* 3.00 8.00
231 Deon Thompson AU/1192* 5.00 12.00
232 Gordon Hayward AU/1043* 25.00 60.00
233 Scottie Reynolds AU/1192* 5.00 12.00
234 J.Varnado AU/1043* EXCH 3.00 8.00
235 Q.Pondexter AU/2691* 8.00 20.00
236 Luke Harangody AU/2691* 3.00 8.00
237 Paul George AU/894* 30.00 80.00
238 Greivis Vasquez AU/2093* 6.00 15.00
239 Aubrey Coleman AU/1043* 5.00 12.00
240 Lazar Hayward AU/1794* 3.00 8.00
241 Elliot Williams AU/2392* 3.00 8.00
242 Devin Ebanks AU/1794* 3.00 8.00

2010-11 SP Authentic By The Letter Legend Last Name

This autograph set was randomly inserted into packs and features the Lettermen style. To obtain the complete print run, take the actual serial-numbering on the card and multiply that by the player's last name. The only exceptions appear to be for Jim Jackson and Robert Horry, which should spell out "Legend".

STATED PRINT RUN 30 TO 149 SER.#'d SETS
MOST PRINT RUNS BASED ON LAST NAME
TOTAL PRINT RUN LISTED WITH ASTERISK
LAJ Avery Johnson/525* 10.00 25.00
LAM Alonzo Mourning/240* 50.00 125.00
LBC Bill Cartwright/300* 10.00 25.00
LBJ B.J. Armstrong/1341* 10.00 25.00
LBL Bill Laimbeer/1192* 10.00 25.00
LBS Bill Sharman/210* 15.00 40.00
LBW Bill Walton/180* 15.00 40.00
LCA Sam Cassell/1043* 10.00 25.00
LCC Cynthia Cooper/180* 10.00 25.00
LCL Christian Laettner/600* 10.00 25.00
LCP Candace Parker/894* 20.00 50.00
LCW Chet Walker/450* 10.00 25.00
LDA Danny Manning/210* 30.00 80.00
LDR Derrick Rose/596* 75.00 150.00
LDT David Thompson/240* 10.00 25.00
LEB Elgin Baylor/180* 15.00 40.00
LGG Gail Goodrich/240* 15.00 40.00
LHO Hakeem Olajuwon/240* 30.00 80.00
LJE Julius Erving/180* 50.00 120.00
LJH James Harden/180* 20.00 50.00
LJJ Jim Jackson/894* 10.00 25.00
LJR J.R. Reid/596* 10.00 25.00
LJS Jerry Sloan/375* 10.00 25.00
LKS Kenny Smith/150* 10.00 25.00
LLB Larry Bird/120* 50.00 120.00
LLJ LeBron James/150* 175.00 350.00
LMJ Michael Jordan/180* 300.00 600.00
LRF Rick Fox/90* 20.00 50.00
LRI Glen Rice/120* 30.00 80.00
LRO David Robinson/240* 60.00 150.00
LRU Bill Russell/210* 75.00 150.00
LRW R.Westbrook/1341* 40.00 100.00
LRY Robert Horry/894* 15.00 40.00
LSA Steve Alford/894* 10.00 25.00
LSC Sidney Crosby/180* 150.00 300.00
LTP Terry Porter/450* 12.00 30.00

2010-11 SP Authentic Chirography

STATED ODDS 1:128 PACKS
CAH Anfernee Hardaway 50.00 120.00
CCP Candace Parker 10.00 25.00
CDE DeMarcus Cousins 20.00 50.00
CDF Derrick Favors 15.00 40.00
CHR Robert Horry 10.00 25.00
CJJ Jim Jackson 8.00 20.00
CRF Rick Fox 8.00 20.00

2010-11 SP Authentic Holo F/X

COMPLETE SET (42) 30.00 80.00
STATED ODDS 1:6 PACKS
1 Derrick Rose 1.25 3.00
2 Walt Frazier 1.00 2.50
3 Christian Laettner .75 2.00
4 Robert Horry 1.00 2.50
5 Anfernee Hardaway 2.50 6.00
6 Julius Erving 1.50 4.00
7 Larry Bird 2.50 6.00
8 Jim Jackson .60 1.50
9 Elgin Baylor 1.00 2.50
10 Tim Hardaway 1.00 2.50
11 Dennis Rodman 2.00 5.00
12 Kenny Smith .75 2.00
13 Jerry West 1.25 3.00
14 Bill Russell 1.50 4.00
15 Xavier Henry .60 1.50
16 Greg Anthony .60 1.50
17 Magic Johnson 2.50 6.00
18 George Gervin 1.00 2.50
19 Hakeem Olajuwon 1.25 3.00
20 David Robinson 1.50 4.00
21 LeBron James 5.00 12.00
22 Ed Davis .60 1.50
23 Michael Jordan 8.00 20.00
24 Greg Monroe 1.25 3.00
25 Bill Walton 1.00 2.50
26 Cazzie Russell .75 2.00
27 Alonzo Mourning 1.25 3.00
28 Rick Fox .75 2.00
29 Candace Parker 2.50 6.00
30 Danny Manning .75 2.00
31 Clyde Drexler 1.25 3.00
32 Derrick Favors 1.25 3.00
33 Al-Farouq Aminu 1.00 2.50
34 DeMarcus Cousins 3.00 8.00
35 Larry Johnson 1.25 3.00
36 James Worthy 1.25 3.00
37 David Thompson .75 2.00
38 Jim Boeheim 1.25 3.00
39 Bill Self 1.00 2.50
40 Roy Williams 2.00 5.00
41 Ben Howland 1.00 2.50
42 Tom Izzo 1.00 2.50

2010-11 SP Authentic Holo F/X Die Cuts

*HOLO DC: 2X TO 5X BASE HI
STATED ODDS 1:144 PACKS
11 Dennis Rodman 12.50 30.00
21 LeBron James 50.00 120.00
23 Michael Jordan 100.00 200.00
27 Alonzo Mourning 15.00 40.00

2010-11 SP Authentic Jordan Brand Classic

RANDOM INSERTS IN PACKS
JCDA Ed Davis 1.25 3.00
JCDE Devin Ebanks 1.25 3.00
JCEB Devin Ebanks 1.25 3.00
JCED Ed Davis 1.25 3.00
JCGM Greg Monroe 2.50 6.00
JCMG Greg Monroe 2.50 6.00
JCMO Greg Monroe 2.50 6.00

2010-11 SP Authentic Michael Jordan Supreme Court Floor

This 40-card insert set features an oversized swatch of North Carolina floor. The set was broken up into four tiers (which are also written on the back of each card) which feature "Common" for cards 1-10, "Uncommon" for 11-20, "Rare" for 21-30 and "Ultra Rare" for 31-40. The common versions feature a light blue color, the uncommon feature a red color, the rare feature a black color and the ultra rare feature a brown color. The cards were inserted at an overall rate of 1:48 packs.

COMMON FLOOR (1-10) 12.00 30.00
UNCOMMON FLOOR (11-20) 15.00 40.00
RARE FLOOR (21-30) 20.00 50.00
ULTRA RARE FLOOR (31-40) 40.00 100.00
COMBINED ODDS 1:48 PACKS
UNPRICED AUTO PRINT RUN 5 SETS

2010-11 SP Authentic Sign of the Times

The Julius Erving card in this set was released in the 2012-13 SP Authentic product.

STATED ODDS 1:128 PACKS
UNPRICED DUAL PRINT RUN 10 SETS
UNPRICED QUAD PRINT RUN 2 TO 5 SETS
UNPRICED TRIPLE PRINT RUN 8 SETS
SAD Adrian Dantley 3.00 8.00
SBC Bobby Cremins 3.00 8.00
SBD Billy Donovan 12.00 30.00
SBH Bob Huggins 15.00 40.00
SBW Bill Walton 15.00 40.00
SCB Craig Brackins 3.00 8.00
SDM Danny Manning 8.00 20.00
SDR Derrick Rose 30.00 80.00
SDW Donald Williams 3.00 8.00
SEB Elgin Baylor 8.00 20.00
SFL Freddie Lewis 3.00 8.00
SGE George Gervin 10.00 25.00
SGL Gani Lawal 3.00 8.00
SHA John Havlicek 40.00 100.00
SJA James Anderson 3.00 8.00
SJD Jamie Dixon 10.00 25.00
SJE Julius Erving 75.00 150.00
SJO Magic Johnson 25.00 60.00
SJS Jack Sikma 3.00 8.00
SLB Larry Bird 60.00 150.00
SLE LeBron James 150.00 400.00
SLJ LeBron James 150.00 400.00
SMC Michael Cooper 3.00 8.00
SMF Mark Few 12.00 30.00
SMI Michael Jordan 300.00 600.00
SMJ Michael Jordan 300.00 600.00
SMM Mike Montgomery 3.00 8.00
SMR Micheal Ray Richardson 3.00 8.00
SRM Rick Majerus 4.00 10.00
SRW*Russell Westbrook 75.00 200.00
SRX Rex Walters 3.00 8.00
SSC Sam Cassell 3.00 8.00
SSK Shawn Kemp 30.00 60.00
SSP Sam Perkins 6.00 15.00
STB Trevor Booker 3.00 8.00
STK Toni Kukoc 12.00 30.00
STS Tubby Smith 3.00 8.00
SWE Bruce Weber 4.00 10.00
SWF Walt Frazier 10.00 25.00

2011-12 SP Authentic

COMPLETE SET (100) 40.00 100.00
1 Michael Jordan 2.00 5.00
2 LeBron James 1.25 3.00
3 Grant Hill .40 1.00
4 Walt Frazier .30 .75
5 Anfernee Hardaway .75 2.00
6 Alonzo Mourning .40 1.00
7 Julius Erving .50 1.25
8 David Robinson .50 1.25
9 Russell Westbrook .75 2.00
10 Magic Johnson .75 2.00
11 Derrick Rose .40 1.00
12 Hakeem Olajuwon .40 1.00
13 Clyde Drexler .40 1.00
14 James Worthy .40 1.00
15 Larry Bird .75 2.00
16 Tristan Thompson .40 1.00
17 Jimmer Fredette .20 .50
18 Alec Burks .30 .75
19 Bismack Biyombo .30 .75
20 Justin Harper .25 .60
21 Demetri McCamey .25 .60
22 Nolan Smith .20 .50
23 Klay Thompson 1.00 2.50
24 Nikola Vucevic .30 .75
25 JaJuan Johnson .20 .50
26 Reggie Jackson .30 .75
27 Kawhi Leonard 2.50 6.00
28 Tobias Harris .30 .75
29 MarShon Brooks .25 .60
30 Tyler Honeycutt .25 .60
31 Marcus Morris .25 .60
32 Markieff Morris .30 .75
33 Norris Cole .30 .75
34 Cory Joseph .25 .60
35 Shelvin Mack .20 .50
36 Jordan Williams .20 .50
37 Chandler Parsons .30 .75
38 Chris Singleton .20 .50
39 Jonas Valanciunas .40 1.00
40 Donatas Motiejunas .25 .60
41 Jon Leuer .25 .60
42 Malcolm Lee .25 .60
43 Charles Jenkins .25 .60
44 Travis Leslie .25 .60
45 Josh Selby .25 .60
46 Keith Benson .25 .60
47 E'Twaun Moore .40 1.00
48 Matt Howard .30 .75
49 Scotty Hopson .20 .50
50 Durrell Summers .20 .50
51 LeBron James FX 2.50 6.00
52 Michael Jordan FX 5.00 12.00
53 Alonzo Mourning FX .75 2.00
54 Larry Johnson FX .75 2.00
55 Magic Johnson FX 1.50 4.00
56 Clyde Drexler FX .75 2.00
57 Hakeem Olajuwon FX .75 2.00
58 John Havlicek FX .75 2.00
59 David Robinson FX 1.00 2.50
60 Julius Erving FX 1.00 2.50
61 Mark Jackson FX .50 1.25
62 Adrian Dantley FX .50 1.25
63 Dennis Rodman FX 1.25 3.00
64 Danny Manning FX 1.00 2.50
65 Gail Goodrich FX .50 1.25
66 Anfernee Hardaway FX 1.50 4.00
67 Glen Rice FX .50 1.25
68 Hal Greer FX .50 1.25
69 Derrick Rose FX .75 2.00
70 Grant Hill FX 1.00 2.50
71 Russell Westbrook FX 1.50 4.00
72 Bill Laimbeer FX .50 1.25
73 Walt Frazier FX .60 1.50
74 Bill Russell FX 1.00 2.50
75 James Worthy FX .75 2.00
76 Rick Barry FX .50 1.25
77 Jerry West FX .75 2.00
78 Larry Bird FX 1.50 4.00
79 Bill Walton FX .60 1.50
80 Elgin Baylor FX .60 1.50
81 David Thompson FX .50 1.25
82 Tim Hardaway FX .60 1.50
83 Jack Sikma FX .50 1.25
84 Chet Walker FX .50 1.25
85 Tristan Thompson FX 1.00 2.50
86 Jonas Valanciunas FX 1.00 2.50
87 Jimmer Fredette FX .50 1.25
88 Kawhi Leonard FX 6.00 15.00
89 Bismack Biyombo FX .75 2.00
90 Klay Thompson FX 15.00 40.00
91 Alec Burks FX .75 2.00
92 Markieff Morris FX .75 2.00
93 Marcus Morris FX .60 1.50
94 Nikola Vucevic FX .75 2.00
95 Chris Singleton FX .50 1.25
96 Tobias Harris FX .75 2.00
97 Nolan Smith FX .50 1.25
98 Reggie Jackson FX .75 2.00
99 JaJuan Johnson FX .50 1.25
100 Cory Joseph FX .60 1.50

2011-12 SP Authentic Autographs

RANDOM INSERTS IN PACKS
FB FX PRINT RUN 3 TO 50 SER.#'d SETS
SOME FB FX UNPRICED DUE TO SCARCITY
1 Michael Jordan 250.00 500.00
2 LeBron James 125.00 250.00
3 Grant Hill 100.00 200.00
4 Walt Frazier 12.00 30.00
5 Anfernee Hardaway 40.00 100.00
6 Alonzo Mourning 30.00 80.00
7 Julius Erving 40.00 100.00
8 David Robinson 30.00 80.00
9 Russell Westbrook 50.00 120.00
10 Magic Johnson 50.00 120.00
11 Derrick Rose 75.00 150.00
12 Hakeem Olajuwon 30.00 80.00
13 Clyde Drexler 40.00 100.00
14 James Worthy 15.00 40.00
15 Larry Bird 50.00 125.00
16 Tristan Thompson 6.00 15.00
17 Jimmer Fredette 4.00 10.00
18 Alec Burks 6.00 15.00
19 Bismack Biyombo 6.00 15.00
20 Justin Harper 5.00 12.00
21 Demetri McCamey 5.00 12.00
22 Nolan Smith 4.00 10.00
23 Klay Thompson 30.00 80.00
24 Nikola Vucevic 6.00 15.00
25 JaJuan Johnson 4.00 10.00
26 Reggie Jackson 6.00 15.00
27 Kawhi Leonard 75.00 200.00
28 Tobias Harris 6.00 15.00
29 MarShon Brooks 5.00 12.00
30 Tyler Honeycutt 5.00 12.00
31 Marcus Morris 5.00 12.00
32 Markieff Morris 6.00 15.00
33 Norris Cole 6.00 15.00
34 Cory Joseph 5.00 12.00
35 Shelvin Mack 4.00 10.00
36 Jordan Williams 4.00 10.00
37 Chandler Parsons 6.00 15.00
38 Chris Singleton 4.00 10.00
39 Jonas Valanciunas 8.00 20.00
41 Jon Leuer 5.00 12.00
42 Malcolm Lee 5.00 12.00
43 Charles Jenkins 5.00 12.00
44 Travis Leslie 5.00 12.00
45 Josh Selby 5.00 12.00
46 Keith Benson 5.00 12.00
47 E'Twaun Moore 8.00 20.00
48 Matt Howard 6.00 15.00
49 Scotty Hopson 4.00 10.00
50 Durrell Summers 4.00 10.00
62 Adrian Dantley FX/50 6.00 15.00
72 Bill Laimbeer FX/50 6.00 15.00
82 Tim Hardaway FX/50 8.00 20.00
83 Jack Sikma FX/50 6.00 15.00
84 Chet Walker FX/50 6.00 15.00
85 Tristan Thompson FX/50 8.00 20.00
86 Jonas Valanciunas FX/50 12.00 30.00
87 Jimmer Fredette FX/50 6.00 15.00
88 Kawhi Leonard FX/50 100.00 250.00
89 Bismack Biyombo FX/50 10.00 25.00
90 Klay Thompson FX/50 100.00 200.00
91 Alec Burks FX/50 10.00 25.00
92 Markieff Morris FX/50 10.00 25.00
93 Marcus Morris FX/50 8.00 20.00
95 Chris Singleton FX/50 6.00 15.00
96 Tobias Harris FX/50 12.00 30.00
97 Nolan Smith FX/50 6.00 15.00
98 Reggie Jackson FX/50 10.00 25.00
99 JaJuan Johnson FX/50 6.00 15.00
100 Cory Joseph FX/50 8.00 20.00

2011-12 SP Authentic Autographs Gold

STATED PRINT RUN 3 TO 25 SER.#'d SETS
SOME UNPRICED DUE TO SCARCITY
22 Nolan Smith/25 20.00 50.00
28 Tobias Harris/25 25.00 60.00
29 MarShon Brooks/25 40.00 100.00
33 Norris Cole/25 40.00 100.00

2011-12 SP Authentic By The Letter

The Anfernee Hardaway, Magic Johnson and Walt Frazier cards in this set were released in the 2012-13 SP Authentic product. The Mark Few card was issued in 2013-14 SP Authentic.

STATED PRINT RUN 5 TO 100 SER.#'d SETS
TOTAL PRINT RUN LISTED WITH ASTERISK
BLAH Anfernee Hardaway/35* 40.00 80.00
BLAM Alonzo Mourning/50* 40.00 100.00
BLBD Billy Donovan/210* 10.00 25.00
BLBL Bill Laimbeer/675* 6.00 15.00
BLBR Bill Russell/15* 100.00 200.00
BLCD Clyde Drexler/35* 40.00 100.00
BLCL Christian Laettner/400* 12.00 30.00
BLDM Danny Manning/150* 8.00 20.00
BLDR Derrick Rose/35* 60.00 120.00
BLDT David Thompson/175* 10.00 25.00
BLGA Greg Anthony/400* 6.00 15.00
BLGG Gail Goodrich/40* 12.00 30.00
BLGH Grant Hill/60* 50.00 120.00
BLHO Hakeem Olajuwon/35* 40.00 100.00
BLJE Julius Erving/25* 50.00 120.00
BLJW Jay Wright/135* 8.00 20.00
BLLB Larry Bird/60* 75.00 150.00
BLLJ LeBron James/345* 125.00 250.00
BLMB Mike Brey/225* 6.00 15.00
BLMF Mark Few/245* 12.00 30.00
BLMG Magic Johnson/65* 60.00 120.00
BLMJ Michael Jordan/299* 250.00 400.00
BLRB Rick Barry/50* 20.00 50.00
BLRO David Robinson/20* 60.00 150.00
BLRW Russell Westbrook/300* 60.00 150.00
BLRY Bo Ryan/225* 20.00 50.00
BLSF Steve Fisher/200* 6.00 15.00
BLTH Tim Hardaway/400* 10.00 25.00
BLWA Bill Walton/40* 20.00 50.00
BLWE Jerry West/60* 50.00 125.00
BLWF Walt Frazier/80* 12.00 30.00
BLAD1 Adrian Dantley D,N/50* 6.00 15.00
BLAD2 A.Dantley A,E,M,O,R,T/350* 6.00 15.00
BLBC1 B.Cartwright A,C,N,R,S/225* 6.00 15.00
BLBC2 B.Cartwright F,O,I/150* 6.00 15.00
BLBH1 Ben Howland U/15* 8.00 20.00
BLBH2 B.Howland A,C,L/90* 6.00 15.00
BLCR1 Cazzie Russell M/25* 8.00 20.00
BLCR2 C.Russell A,C,G,H,I,N/350* 6.00 15.00
BLCW1 Chet Walker B,Y/20* 6.00 15.00
BLCW2 C.Walker A,D,E,L,R/125* 6.00 15.00
BLDG1 Darrell Griffith V/25* 8.00 20.00
BLDG2 D.Griffith E,I,L,O,S,U/675* 6.00 15.00
BLEB1 Elgin Baylor E,T/100* 12.00 30.00
BLEB2 Elgin Baylor A,L,S/225* 12.00 30.00
BLFL1 Freddie Lewis/100* 6.00 15.00
BLFL2 F.Lewis A,E,I,N,O,R,S,T/550* 6.00 15.00
BLGR1 Glen Rice/25* 6.00 15.00
BLGR2 G.Rice A,C,G,H,I,N/525* 6.00 15.00
BLGW1 Gary Williams M,Y/30* 25.00 60.00
BLGW2 G.Williams A,D,L,N,R/150* 12.00 30.00
BLJC1 Jim Calhoun N/50* 15.00 40.00
BLJC2 J.Calhoun C,O,U/150* 6.00 15.00
BLJD1 Jamie Dixon P,T/30* 6.00 15.00
BLJD2 J.Dixon B,G,H,I,R,S,U/245* 6.00 15.00
BLJJ1 J.Jackson H,I,O/400* 6.00 15.00
BLJJ2 J.Jackson A,E,S,T/250* 8.00 20.00
BLJR1 J.R. Reid C,N/30* 10.00 25.00
BLJR2 J.Reid A,H,I,L,O,R,T/150* 10.00 25.00
BLLS1 L.Shelton A,E,T/250* 6.00 15.00
BLLS2 L.Shelton G,N,O,R,S/450* 6.00 15.00
BLRH1 Robert Horry B/50* 6.00 15.00
BLRH2 R.Horry A,L,M/600* 6.00 15.00
BLSC1 Sam Cassell A,E,T/125* 6.00 15.00
BLSC2 S.Cassell D,I,L,O,R,S/450* 6.00 15.00
BLSC3 Sam Cassell F/100* 6.00 15.00
BLTM1 Thad Matta O/40* 12.50 30.00
BLTM2 T.Matta A,E,H,I,S,T/245* 8.00 20.00
BLTS1 Tubby Smith M/10* 8.00 20.00
BLTS2 Tubby Smith N/30* 8.00 20.00
BLTS3 T.Smith A,E,I,O,S,T/150* 6.00 15.00

2011-12 SP Authentic College Pride Autographs

The Lonnie Shelton, Magic Johnson, Dennis Rodman and Roy Williams cards in this set were issued in the 2012-13 SP Authentic product. The Tom Izzo card was issued in 2013-14 SP Authentic.

STATED PRINT RUN 5 TO 40 SER.#'d SETS
SOME UNPRICED DUE TO SCARCITY
UNPRICED PARALLEL PRINT RUN 3 TO 10 SETS
CJAL Solomon Alabi/40 6.00 15.00
CJBA B.J. Armstrong/40 20.00 50.00
CJBD Billy Donovan/40 15.00 40.00
CJBH Ben Howland/40 8.00 20.00
CJBL Bill Laimbeer/40 8.00 20.00
CJBS Bill Self/40 30.00 80.00
CJBW Bill Walton/40 15.00 40.00
CJCL Christian Laettner/40 15.00 40.00
CJCR Cazzie Russell/40 10.00 25.00
CJDC DeMarcus Cousins/40 30.00 80.00
CJDM Danny Manning/40 20.00 50.00
CJDT David Thompson/40 12.50 30.00
CJEB Elgin Baylor/40 6.00 15.00
CJFL Freddie Lewis/40 6.00 15.00
CJGR Glen Rice/40 12.00 30.00
CJHU Bobby Hurley/40 30.00 80.00
CJJB Jim Boeheim/40 40.00 100.00
CJJO Michael Jordan/40 300.00 600.00
CJKS Kenny Smith/40 6.00 15.00
CJLJ LeBron James/40 100.00 200.00
CJLS Lonnie Shelton/40 8.00 20.00
CJLU Luke Babbitt/40 6.00 15.00
CJRT Reggie Theus/40 10.00 25.00
CJRU Russell Westbrook/40 50.00 120.00
CJSA Steve Alford/40 15.00 40.00
CJSC Sam Cassell/40 6.00 15.00
CJSH Bill Sharman/40 8.00 20.00
CJTH Tim Hardaway/40 15.00 40.00
CJTI T.Izzo/40 25.00 60.00
CJTS Tubby Smith/40 6.00 15.00
CJWR Jay Wright/40 12.50 30.00

2011-12 SP Authentic Home Court Signatures

Some of the Brad Daugherty, Bob McAdoo, Clyde Drexler, Lebron James, Michael Jordan and Walt Frazier cards in this set were issued in the 2012-13 SP Authentic product. The Shelden Williams card was issued in 2013-14 SP Authentic.

RANDOM INSERTS IN PACKS
HCAD Adrian Dantley 4.00 10.00
HCAH Anfernee Hardaway 50.00 120.00
HCAM Alonzo Mourning 12.00 30.00
HCBC Bill Cartwright 4.00 10.00
HCBD Brad Daugherty 4.00 10.00
HCBH Bobby Hurley 4.00 10.00
HCBL Bill Laimbeer 4.00 10.00
HCBM Bob McAdoo 4.00 10.00
HCBR Bill Russell 75.00 150.00
HCBW Bill Walton 10.00 25.00
HCCD Clyde Drexler 10.00 25.00
HCCL Christian Laettner 8.00 20.00
HCCR Cazzie Russell 4.00 10.00
HCDG Darrell Griffith 4.00 10.00
HCDM Danny Manning 4.00 10.00
HCDR David Robinson 40.00 100.00
HCDT David Thompson 12.00 30.00
HCEB Elgin Baylor 8.00 20.00
HCGH Grant Hill 75.00 200.00
HCGO Gail Goodrich 10.00 25.00
HCGR Glen Rice 4.00 10.00
HCHO Hakeem Olajuwon 15.00 40.00
HCJA Jim Jackson 8.00 20.00
HCJE Julius Erving 50.00 120.00
HCJH John Havlicek 20.00 50.00
HCJJ JaJuan Johnson 4.00 10.00
HCJW James Worthy 20.00 50.00
HCLB Larry Bird 125.00 225.00
HCLJ LeBron James 150.00 250.00
HCLO Brook Lopez 4.00 10.00
HCMA Magic Johnson 40.00 100.00
HCMJ Michael Jordan 200.00 500.00
HCNS Nolan Smith 8.00 20.00
HCRB Rick Barry 4.00 10.00
HCRF Rick Fox 4.00 10.00
HCRH Robert Horry 4.00 10.00
HCRT Reggie Theus 4.00 10.00
HCSC Sam Cassell 4.00 10.00
HCSM Kenny Smith 4.00 10.00
HCSP Sam Perkins 4.00 10.00
HCSW S.Williams 4.00 10.00
HCTO Rudy Tomjanovich 10.00 25.00
HCWE Jerry West 50.00 125.00
HCWF Walt Frazier 4.00 10.00

2011-12 SP Authentic Jordan Brand Classic

RANDOM INSERTS IN PACKS
JCHO Scotty Hopson 1.00 2.50
JCLE Malcolm Lee 1.25 3.00
JCML Malcolm Lee 1.25 3.00
JCSH Scotty Hopson 1.00 2.50
JBCCJ Cory Joseph 1.25 3.00
JBCSE Josh Selby 1.25 3.00
JBCTH Tobias Harris 1.50 4.00
JBCTT Tristan Thompson 2.00 5.00

2011-12 SP Authentic Jordan Brand Classic Autographs

RANDOM INSERTS IN PACKS
JBCCJ Cory Joseph 6.00 15.00
JBCSE Josh Selby 6.00 15.00
JBCTH Tobias Harris 10.00 25.00
JBCTT Tristan Thompson 10.00 25.00

2011-12 SP Authentic North Carolina Floor

RANDOM INSERTS IN PACKS
UNCBD Brad Daugherty 4.00 10.00
UNCBP Buzz Peterson 4.00 10.00
UNCJO Michael Jordan 10.00 25.00
UNCJR J.R. Reid 4.00 10.00
UNCJW James Worthy 5.00 12.00
UNCKS Kenny Smith 4.00 10.00
UNCMI Michael Jordan 10.00 25.00
UNCMJ Michael Jordan 10.00 25.00
UNCPE Sam Perkins 4.00 10.00
UNCRE J.R. Reid 4.00 10.00
UNCSM Kenny Smith 4.00 10.00
UNCSP Sam Perkins 4.00 10.00
UNCWF Joe Wolf 4.00 10.00
UNCWO James Worthy 5.00 12.00

2011-12 SP Authentic North Carolina Floor Autographs

STATED PRINT RUN 10 TO 75 SER.#'d SETS
SOME UNPRICED DUE TO SCARCITY
UNCBD Brad Daugherty/75 10.00 25.00
UNCBP Buzz Peterson/75 10.00 25.00
UNCJO Michael Jordan/23 400.00 600.00
UNCJR J.R. Reid/75 10.00 25.00
UNCMI Michael Jordan/23 400.00 600.00
UNCMJ Michael Jordan/23 400.00 600.00
UNCPE Sam Perkins/75 12.00 30.00
UNCRE J.R. Reid/75 10.00 25.00
UNCSP Sam Perkins/75 10.00 25.00
UNCWF Joe Wolf/75 10.00 25.00

2011-12 SP Authentic Sign of the Times Dual

MMON CARD 8.00 20.00
STATED PRINT RUN ONE TO 30 SETS
SOME UNPRICED DUE TO SCARCITY
UNPRICED QUAD PRINT RUN 4 SETS
S2LD A.Dantley/Laimbeer/30 8.00 20.00
S2PD S.Perkins/Daugherty/30 12.00 30.00
S2SP S.Perkins/K.Smith/30 12.00 30.00

2011-12 SP Authentic Sign of the Times Triple

STATED PRINT RUN ONE TO 25 SETS
SOME UNPRICED DUE TO SCARCITY
S3BCH Calhoun/Donvn/Hwlnd/25 12.00 30.00
S3SPD Smith/Daugherty/Perkins/25 15.00 40.00

2012 SP Authentic

COMP. SET w/o SP's (50) 8.00 20.00
51-80 STATED ODDS 1:2.5
EXCHANGE DEADLINE 9/4/2014
61 Michael Jordan PS 3.00 8.00

2012 SP Authentic Limited Parade of Stars Autographs

STATED PRINT RUN 10-25
NO PRICING ON CARDS #'d UNDER 25
EXCHANGE DEADLINE 9/4/2014
61 Michael Jordan/25 600.00 1000.00

2012 SP Authentic Sign of the Times

OUP A ODDS 1:2,714
GROUP B ODDS 1:1,403
GROUP C ODDS 1:424
GROUP D ODDS 1:275
GROUP E ODDS 1:31
GROUP F ODDS 1:28
EXCHANGE DEADLINE 9/5/2014
STMJ Michael Jordan A 300.00 550.00

2012 SP Authentic Sign of the Times Duals

GROUP A ODDS 1:53,664
GROUP B ODDS 1:6,240
GROUP C ODDS 1:2,199
GROUP D ODDS 1:596
GROUP E ODDS 1:539
EXCHANGE DEADLINE 9/4/2014
ST2TM T.Woods/M.Jordan B

2012-13 SP Authentic

COMPLETE SET (100) 30.00 60.00
COMP.SET w/o FB (50) 6.00 15.00
FLASHBACK ODDS 1:4
1 Michael Jordan 2.00 5.00
2 Dominique Wilkins .30 .75
3 Larry Bird .60 1.50
4 Magic Johnson .60 1.50
5 David Robinson .40 1.00
6 Hakeem Olajuwon .30 .75
7 Allen Iverson .30 .75
8 Anfernee Hardaway .60 1.50
9 Dennis Rodman .50 1.25
10 Isiah Thomas .25 .60
11 Bill Russell .40 1.00
12 Larry Johnson .30 .75
13 Julius Erving .40 1.00
14 Ray Allen .25 .60
15 Gary Payton .25 .60
16 Karl Malone .30 .75
17 LeBron James 1.00 2.50
18 Jason Kidd .25 .60
19 Chris Paul .30 .75
20 Grant Hill .30 .75
21 Meyers Leonard .20 .50
22 Jeremy Lamb .25 .60
23 Kendall Marshall .15 .40
24 Moe Harkless .25 .60
25 Tyler Zeller .20 .50
26 Andrew Nicholson .15 .40
27 Evan Fournier .25 .60
28 Jared Cunningham .15 .40
29 Miles Plumlee .15 .40
30 Arnett Moultrie .15 .40
31 Bernard James .15 .40
32 Jae Crowder .20 .50
33 Draymond Green .75 2.00
34 Quincy Acy .15 .40
35 Khris Middleton .25 .60
36 Will Barton .20 .50
37 Tyshawn Taylor .15 .40
38 Darius Miller .15 .40
39 Kevin Murphy .15 .40
40 Kris Joseph .15 .40
41 Darius Johnson-Odom .15 .40
42 Robbie Hummel .15 .40
43 Robert Sacre .15 .40
44 William Buford .15 .40
45 John Shurna .15 .40
46 Wesley Witherspoon .15 .40
47 Ricardo Ratliffe .15 .40
48 Tomas Satoransky .15 .40
49 Justin Hamilton .20 .50
50 JaMychal Green .15 .40
51 Alonzo Mourning FB .75 2.00
52 Anfernee Hardaway FB 1.50 4.00
53 Bill Russell FB 1.00 2.50
54 Chris Paul FB .75 2.00
55 Clyde Drexler FB .75 2.00
56 David Robinson FB 1.00 2.50
57 Dominique Wilkins FB .75 2.00
58 Grant Hill FB .75 2.00
59 Hakeem Olajuwon FB .75 2.00
60 Cheryl Miller FB .60 1.50
61 Jason Kidd FB .60 1.50
62 Julius Erving FB 1.00 2.50
63 Larry Bird FB 1.50 4.00
64 Larry Johnson FB .75 2.00
65 LeBron James FB 2.50 6.00
66 Magic Johnson FB 1.50 4.00
67 Michael Jordan FB 5.00 12.00
68 Bernard King FB .50 1.25
69 Derrick Coleman FB .60 1.50
70 Gary Payton FB .60 1.50
71 Karl Malone FB .75 2.00
72 Eddie Jones FB .50 1.25
73 Spud Webb FB .50 1.25
74 Antoine Walker FB .50 1.25
75 Ray Allen FB .60 1.50
76 Jeff Hornacek FB .50 1.25
77 John Havlicek FB .75 2.00
78 Allen Iverson FB .75 2.00
79 Connie Hawkins FB .60 1.50
80 Dennis Rodman FB 1.25 3.00
81 Muggsy Bogues FB .50 1.25
82 Isiah Thomas FB .60 1.50
83 Walt Frazier FB .60 1.50
84 Jamal Mashburn FB .60 1.50
85 Bill Walton FB .60 1.50
86 Meyers Leonard FB .50 1.25
87 Jeremy Lamb FB .60 1.50
88 Kendall Marshall FB .40 1.00
89 Moe Harkless FB .60 1.50
90 Tyler Zeller FB .50 1.25
91 Evan Fournier FB .60 1.50
92 Jared Cunningham FB .40 1.00
93 Miles Plumlee FB .40 1.00
94 Arnett Moultrie FB .40 1.00
95 Bernard James FB .40 1.00
96 Draymond Green FB 2.00 5.00
97 Darius Johnson-Odom FB .40 1.00
98 Darius Miller FB .40 1.00
99 Tyshawn Taylor FB .40 1.00
100 Andrew Nicholson FB .40 1.00

2012-13 SP Authentic Autographs

GROUP A ODDS 1:2228 HOBBY
GROUP B ODDS 1:1574 HOBBY
GROUP C ODDS 1:217 HOBBY
GROUP D ODDS 1:101 HOBBY
GROUP E ODDS 1:51 HOBBY
GROUP A FX ODDS 1:3009 HOBBY
GROUP B FX ODDS 1:2217 HOBBY
GROUP C FX ODDS 1:759 HOBBY
GROUP D FX ODDS 1:290 HOBBY
NO GROUP A PRICING DUE TO SCARCITY
1 Michael Jordan A 200.00 400.00
2 Dominique Wilkins A 6.00 15.00
6 Hakeem Olajuwon A 12.00 30.00
7 Allen Iverson A 25.00 60.00
13 Julius Erving B 20.00 50.00
16 Karl Malone B 15.00 40.00
17 LeBron James A 150.00 300.00
19 Chris Paul C EXCH 20.00 50.00
20 Grant Hill B 12.00 30.00
21 Meyers Leonard B 5.00 12.00
23 Kendall Marshall C 6.00 15.00
24 Moe Harkless C 4.00 10.00
25 Tyler Zeller C 4.00 10.00
26 Andrew Nicholson C 4.00 10.00
27 Evan Fournier C 5.00 12.00
28 Jared Cunningham E 4.00 10.00
29 Miles Plumlee E 4.00 10.00
30 Arnett Moultrie E 4.00 10.00
31 Bernard James E 4.00 10.00
32 Jae Crowder D 4.00 10.00
33 Draymond Green E 15.00 40.00
34 Quincy Acy E 4.00 10.00
35 Khris Middleton D 4.00 10.00
36 Will Barton E 4.00 10.00
37 Tyshawn Taylor C 6.00 15.00
38 Darius Miller D 4.00 10.00
39 Kevin Murphy E 4.00 10.00
40 Kris Joseph E 4.00 10.00
41 Darius Johnson-Odom E 4.00 10.00
42 Robbie Hummel D 4.00 10.00
43 Robert Sacre D 4.00 10.00
44 William Buford D 4.00 10.00
46 Wesley Witherspoon D 4.00 10.00
48 Tomas Satoransky D 4.00 10.00
49 Justin Hamilton E 4.00 10.00
50 JaMychal Green D 4.00 10.00
53 Bill Russell FX B 60.00 120.00
54 Chris Paul FX C EXCH 15.00 40.00
60 Cheryl Miller FX B 8.00 20.00
66 Magic Johnson FX A 40.00 80.00
67 Michael Jordan FX B 300.00 500.00
73 Spud Webb FX C 6.00 15.00
76 Jeff Hornacek FX B 10.00 25.00
79 Connie Hawkins FX B 6.00 15.00
80 Dennis Rodman FX A 12.00 30.00
81 Muggsy Bogues FX C 6.00 15.00
82 Isiah Thomas FX B 12.00 30.00
83 Walt Frazier FX B 6.00 15.00
84 Jamal Mashburn FX B 8.00 20.00
86 Meyers Leonard FX C 5.00 12.00
88 Kendall Marshall FX C 6.00 15.00
89 Moe Harkless FX D 4.00 10.00
90 Tyler Zeller FX C 6.00 15.00
91 Evan Fournier FX D 5.00 12.00
92 Jared Cunningham FX D 4.00 10.00
93 Miles Plumlee FX D 4.00 10.00
94 Arnett Moultrie FX D 4.00 10.00
95 Bernard James FX C 4.00 10.00
96 Draymond Green FX D 15.00 40.00
97 Darius Johnson-Odom FX D 4.00 10.00
98 Darius Miller FX D 4.00 10.00
99 Tyshawn Taylor FX D 6.00 15.00
100 Andrew Nicholson FX D 4.00 10.00

2012-13 SP Authentic Autographs Gold

PRINT RUNS B/WN 5-30 COPIES PER
NO PRICING ON QTY OF 5 DUE TO SCARCITY
EXCHANGE DEADLINE 4/23/2015
21 Meyers Leonard/30 10.00 25.00
23 Kendall Marshall/30 15.00 40.00
24 Moe Harkless/30 20.00 50.00
25 Tyler Zeller/30 6.00 15.00
26 Andrew Nicholson/30 8.00 20.00
27 Evan Fournier/30 10.00 25.00
28 Jared Cunningham/30 6.00 15.00
29 Miles Plumlee/30 8.00 20.00
30 Arnett Moultrie/30 8.00 20.00
31 Bernard James/30 6.00 15.00
32 Jae Crowder/30 10.00 25.00
33 Draymond Green/30 30.00 80.00
34 Quincy Acy/30 6.00 15.00
35 Khris Middleton/30 6.00 15.00
36 Will Barton/30 6.00 15.00
37 Tyshawn Taylor/30 10.00 25.00
38 Darius Miller/30 10.00 25.00
39 Kevin Murphy/30 6.00 15.00
40 Kris Joseph/30 10.00 25.00
41 Darius Johnson-Odom/30 8.00 20.00
42 Robbie Hummel/30 8.00 20.00
43 Robert Sacre/30
44 William Buford/30 8.00 20.00

46 Wesley Witherspoon/30
48 Tomas Satoransky/30 8.00 20.00
49 Justin Hamilton/30
50 JaMychal Green/30 6.00 15.00

2012-13 SP Authentic By The Letter Signatures

COMMON CARD 6.00 15.00
SERIAL NUMBERS B/WN 3-100 COPIES PER
TOTAL PRINT RUNS B/WN 9-700 COPIES PER
NO PRICING ON TOTAL 21 OR LESS
EXCHANGE DEADLINE 4/23/2015
AD Adrian Dantley/90* 10.00 25.00
AG A.C. Green/550* 6.00 15.00
AH Anfernee Hardaway/35* 75.00 150.00
AI Allen Iverson/30* 100.00 200.00
AL Allan Houston/450* 8.00 20.00
AM Alonzo Mourning/30* 40.00 80.00
AW Antoine Walker/600* 8.00 20.00
BD Brad Daugherty/650* 6.00 15.00
BH Bobby Hurley/400* 8.00 20.00
BK Bernard King/675* 8.00 20.00
BL Bill Laimbeer/675* 6.00 15.00
BM Bob McAdoo/650* 6.00 15.00
BO Muggsy Bogues/250* 6.00 15.00
CH Connie Hawkins/350* 6.00 15.00
CL Christian Laettner/400* 20.00 50.00
CO Derrick Coleman/400* 6.00 15.00
CP Chris Paul/30* 30.00 60.00
DC Dave Cowens/36* 8.00 20.00
DM Danny Manning/150* 10.00 25.00
DR David Robinson/20* 25.00 60.00
DW Dominique Wilkins/70* 20.00 50.00
EJ Eddie Jones/600* 8.00 20.00
FL Fat Lever/600* 6.00 15.00
GP Gary Payton/33* 40.00 80.00
GR Glen Rice/400* 6.00 15.00
HG Hal Greer/80* 6.00 15.00
HM Harold Miner/300* 8.00 20.00
HO Hakeem Olajuwon/35* 30.00 60.00
JH Jeff Hornacek/450* 8.00 20.00
JJ Jim Jackson/675* 10.00 25.00
JK Jason Kidd/30* 50.00 100.00
JO Magic Johnson/39* 75.00 150.00
KM Karl Malone/39* 75.00 150.00
LA Larry Bird/36* 75.00 150.00
LB LeBron James/75* 200.00 300.00
LH Lou Hudson/675* 6.00 15.00
MA Mark A. Jackson/175* 6.00 15.00
MB Mookie Blaylock/600* 6.00 15.00
MC Michael Cooper/675* 6.00 15.00
MJ Michael Jordan/299* 200.00 400.00
MP Mark Price/55* 25.00 60.00
MR M.Ray Richardson/700* 6.00 15.00
MW1 Mark West/350* 6.00 15.00
MW2 Mark West/150* 10.00 25.00
MW3 Mark West/200* 10.00 25.00
NV Nick Van Exel/500* 10.00 25.00
RA Ray Allen/25* 60.00 120.00
RM Reggie Miller/40* 100.00 200.00
RO Dennis Rodman/33* 50.00 100.00
RT Reggie Theus/400* 6.00 15.00
SB Shawn Bradley/225* 6.00 15.00
SE Sean Elliott/700* 8.00 20.00
SH Spencer Haywood/700* 6.00 15.00
SW Spud Webb/525* 6.00 15.00
TH Tim Hardaway/400* 6.00 15.00
VN Vinny Del Negro/525* 6.00 15.00
WF Walt Frazier/400* 10.00 25.00

2012-13 SP Authentic Canvas Collection

STATED ODDS 1:8
*GOLD: 1.5X TO 4X BASIC
STATED GOLD ODDS 1:72
CC1 Alonzo Mourning .75 2.00
CC2 Anfernee Hardaway 1.50 4.00
CC3 Bill Russell 1.00 2.50
CC4 Clyde Drexler .75 2.00
CC5 David Robinson 1.00 2.50
CC6 Dominique Wilkins .75 2.00
CC7 Hakeem Olajuwon .75 2.00
CC8 Sean Elliott .60 1.50
CC9 Julius Erving 1.00 2.50
CC10 Larry Bird 1.50 4.00
CC11 Larry Johnson .75 2.00
CC12 Magic Johnson 1.50 4.00
CC13 Michael Jordan 5.00 12.00
CC14 Dennis Rodman 1.25 3.00
CC15 Walt Frazier .60 1.50
CC16 John Havlicek .75 2.00
CC17 Isiah Thomas .60 1.50
CC18 Tim Hardaway .60 1.50
CC19 Bill Walton .60 1.50
CC20 Shawn Bradley .40 1.00
CC21 Bob McAdoo .50 1.25
CC22 Gary Payton .60 1.50
CC23 Rod Strickland .40 1.00
CC24 Karl Malone .75 2.00
CC25 Allen Iverson .75 2.00
CC26 Antoine Walker .50 1.25
CC27 Derrick Coleman .60 1.50
CC28 Vinny Del Negro .40 1.00
CC29 Mookie Blaylock .40 1.00
CC30 Cheryl Miller .60 1.50
CC31 Ray Allen .60 1.50
CC32 Jason Kidd .60 1.50
CC33 LeBron James 2.50 6.00
CC34 Chris Paul .75 2.00
CC35 Grant Hill .75 2.00
CC36 Meyers Leonard .50 1.25
CC37 Jeremy Lamb 1.00 2.50
CC38 Kendall Marshall .40 1.00
CC39 Moe Harkless .60 1.50
CC40 Tyler Zeller .50 1.25
CC41 Andrew Nicholson .40 1.00
CC42 Evan Fournier .60 1.50
CC43 Jared Cunningham .40 1.00
CC44 Miles Plumlee .40 1.00
CC45 Arnett Moultrie .40 1.00

2012-13 SP Authentic Canvas Collection Autographs

GROUP A ODDS 1:8301
GROUP B ODDS 1:3024
GROUP C ODDS 1:1160
GROUP D ODDS 1:706
GROUP E ODDS 1:154
NO GROUP A-B PRICING DUE TO SCARCITY
EXCHANGE DEADLINE 4/23/2015
CC1 Alonzo Mourning B 75.00 150.00
CC6 Dominique Wilkins E 6.00 15.00
CC7 Hakeem Olajuwon C 6.00 15.00
CC8 Sean Elliott E 4.00 10.00
CC18 Tim Hardaway D 4.00 10.00
CC21 Bob McAdoo D 10.00 25.00
CC23 Rod Strickland E 4.00 10.00
CC26 Antoine Walker C 8.00 20.00
CC34 Chris Paul C 20.00 50.00
CC35 Grant Hill C 20.00 50.00
CC36 Meyers Leonard D 6.00 15.00
CC38 Kendall Marshall D 6.00 15.00
CC39 Moe Harkless E 4.00 10.00
CC40 Tyler Zeller E 6.00 15.00
CC41 Andrew Nicholson E 4.00 10.00
CC42 Evan Fournier E 4.00 10.00
CC43 Jared Cunningham E 4.00 10.00
CC44 Miles Plumlee E 4.00 10.00
CC45 Arnett Moultrie E 4.00 10.00

2012-13 SP Authentic College Pride Autographs

PRINT RUNS B/WN 10-75 COPIES PER
NO PRICING ON QTY 10
EXCHANGE DEADLINE 4/23/2015
BD Brad Daugherty/75 6.00 15.00
BK Bernard King/75 12.00 30.00
BM Bob McAdoo/75 10.00 25.00
CW Chet Walker/75 6.00 15.00
HG Hal Greer/75 6.00 15.00
HM Harold Miner/75 6.00 15.00
JJ Jim Jackson/75 6.00 15.00
JO Michael Jordan/23 250.00 400.00
LJ LeBron James/23 150.00 300.00
MB Mookie Blaylock/75 10.00 25.00
MC Michael Cooper/75 8.00 20.00
MP Mark Price/75 10.00 25.00
MR Micheal Ray Richardson/75 6.00 15.00
RH Robert Horry/75 8.00 20.00
SB Shawn Bradley/75 8.00 20.00
SW Spud Webb/75 6.00 15.00
WF Walt Frazier/75 8.00 20.00

2012-13 SP Authentic Final Floor Dual Signatures

GROUP A ODDS 1:7697
GROUP B ODDS 1: 2861
NO GROUP A PRICING DUE TO SCARCITY
EXCHANGE DEADLINE 4/23/2015
HH G.Hill/B.Hurley B 30.00 80.00
HL G.Hill/C.Laettner B 40.00 80.00
WN Bill Walton/Swen Nater A 12.00 30.00

2012-13 SP Authentic Final Floor Signatures

GROUP A ODDS 1:42,336
GROUP B ODDS 1:3849
GROUP C ODDS 1:420
NO GROUP A PRICING DUE TO SCARCITY
EXCHANGE DEADLINE 4/23/2015
AR Antoine Walker C 6.00 15.00
CD Clyde Drexler C 6.00 15.00
CL Clyde Lovellette C 10.00 25.00
CM Cheryl Miller C 6.00 15.00
DM Danny Manning C 8.00 20.00
DT David Thompson C 10.00 25.00
GH Grant Hill B
GR Glen Rice C 6.00 15.00
HO Hakeem Olajuwon B 25.00 60.00
JO Michael Jordan B 300.00 500.00
LJ Larry Johnson B 40.00 80.00
MB Mookie Blaylock C 10.00 25.00
MJ Magic Johnson A
SN Swen Nater B 10.00 25.00

2012-13 SP Authentic Home Court Signatures

GROUP A ODDS 1:3334
GROUP B ODDS 1:2447
GROUP C ODDS 1:1411
GROUP D ODDS 1:295
GROUP E ODDS 1:161
NO GROUP A PRICING DUE TO SCARCITY
EXCHANGE DEADLINE 4/23/2015
AH Anfernee Hardaway B 30.00 80.00
AM Alonzo Mourning B 15.00 40.00
AW Antoine Walker D 6.00 15.00
BK Bernard King D 8.00 20.00
BO Muggsy Bogues D 6.00 15.00
CD Clyde Drexler A 15.00 40.00
DR Dennis Rodman B 15.00 40.00
DW Dominique Wilkins B 12.00 30.00
GH Grant Hill B 25.00 60.00
GP Gary Payton A 20.00 50.00
HM Harold Miner E 6.00 15.00
IT Isiah Thomas C 10.00 25.00
JA LeBron James D 125.00 250.00
JM Jamal Mashburn C 6.00 15.00
JO Michael Jordan E 250.00 400.00
LB Larry Bird A 75.00 150.00
LH Lou Hudson D 6.00 15.00
LS Lonnie Shelton E 6.00 15.00
MB Mookie Blaylock E 6.00 15.00
MI Michael Jordan E 200.00 400.00
MR Micheal Ray Richardson C 10.00 25.00
NV Nick Van Exel E 6.00 15.00
RA Ray Allen B
RM Reggie Miller B 90.00 150.00
SB Shawn Bradley E 6.00 15.00
SE Sean Elliott E 6.00 15.00
SH Spencer Haywood D 6.00 15.00
SW Spud Webb D 6.00 15.00
TH Tim Hardaway E 6.00 15.00
VN V.Del Negro 6.00 15.00

2012-13 SP Authentic Jordan Brand Classic Jerseys 09

BU William Buford 2.50 6.00
GR JaMychal Green 2.50 6.00
JG JaMychal Green 2.50 6.00
WB William Buford 2.50 6.00
WE Wesley Witherspoon 3.00 8.00
WI Wesley Witherspoon 3.00 8.00

2012-13 SP Authentic Jordan Brand Classic Jerseys 13

BA Will Barton 2.50 6.00
KM Kendall Marshall 2.50 6.00
MA Kendall Marshall 2.50 6.00
WB Will Barton 2.50 6.00

2012-13 SP Authentic Jordan Brand Classic Jerseys 13 Autographs

GROUP A ODDS 1:8467
GROUP B ODDS 1: 2822
BA Will Barton B 6.00 15.00
KM Kendall Marshall A 12.00 30.00
MA Kendall Marshall A 12.00 30.00
WB Will Barton B 6.00 15.00

2012-13 SP Authentic Nicknames Signatures

GROUP A ODDS 1:211,680 HOBBY
GROUP B ODDS 1:10,326 HOBBY
GROUP C ODDS 1:4704 HOBBY
GROUP D ODDS 1:3681 HOBBY
GROUP E ODDS 1:1291 HOBBY
NO A-D PRICING DUE TO SCARCITY
EXCHANGE DEADLINE 4/23/2015
AG A.C. Green E 10.00 25.00
BR Bryant Reeves E 8.00 20.00
CH Connie Hawkins E 6.00 15.00
DR David Robinson The Admiral C 25.00 60.00
DT David Thompson Skywalker D 10.00 25.00
HM Harold Miner E 15.00 40.00
HO Hakeem Olajuwon The Dream B 25.00 60.00
JM Jamal Mashburn E 12.00 30.00
RA Ray Allen Ray Ray C 50.00 120.00
WF Walt Frazier Clyde D 10.00 25.00

2012-13 SP Authentic Sign of the Times

COMMON CARD 4.00 10.00
GROUP A ODDS 1:4923
GROUP B ODDS 1:4234
GROUP C ODDS 1:1058
GROUP D ODDS 1:736
GROUP E ODDS 1:97
NO GROUP A-B PRICING DUE TO SCARCITY
EXCHANGE DEADLINE 4/23/2015
BD Brad Daugherty E 4.00 10.00
BK Bernard King C 6.00 15.00
BL Bill Laimbeer E 4.00 10.00
BM Bob McAdoo E 8.00 20.00
BO Muggsy Bogues E 6.00 15.00
EJ Eddie Jones D 5.00 12.00
HM Harold Miner E 8.00 20.00
HO Jeff Hornacek C 6.00 15.00
IT Isiah Thomas A 12.00 30.00
JJ Jim Jackson D 5.00 12.00
LB Larry Bird A 25.00 60.00
LS Lonnie Shelton E 4.00 10.00
MB Mookie Blaylock B 10.00 25.00
MC Michael Cooper D 4.00 10.00
MW Mark West E 4.00 10.00
NV Nick Van Exel E 3.00 8.00
PR Pooh Richardson E 4.00 10.00
SB Shawn Bradley E 4.00 10.00
SE Sean Elliott E 4.00 10.00
SH Spencer Haywood E 4.00 10.00
SW Spud Webb C 4.00 10.00
TH Tim Hardaway E 5.00 12.00
TK Toni Kukoc C 6.00 15.00

2013-14 SP Authentic

F/X ODDS 1:4 HOBBY
1 Dominique Wilkins .40 1.00
2 Karl Malone .40 1.00
3 Allen Iverson .40 1.00
4 Grant Hill .40 1.00
5 Isiah Thomas .30 .75
6 Reggie Miller .30 .75
7 Glenn Robinson .25 .60
8 David Robinson .50 1.25
9 Anfernee Hardaway .75 2.00
10 Larry Bird .75 2.00
11 Magic Johnson .75 2.00
12 Julius Erving .50 1.25
13 Chris Paul .40 1.00
14 LeBron James 1.25 3.00
15 Michael Jordan 2.50 6.00
16 Jay Williams .20 .50
17 Keith Smart .30 .75
18 Paul George .40 1.00
19 Rajon Rondo .30 .75
20 Joe Smith .25 .60
21 Archie Goodwin .50 1.25
22 Sergey Karasev .40 1.00
23 Tony Snell .50 1.25
24 Solomon Hill .40 1.00
25 Ryan Kelly .40 1.00
26 Seth Curry 1.25 3.00
27 Andre Roberson .40 1.00
28 Shane Larkin .40 1.00
29 Lucas Nogueira .40 1.00
30 Livio Jean-Charles .40 1.00
31 Isaiah Canaan .40 1.00
32 Tim Hardaway Jr. .60 1.50
33 Nemanja Nedovic .40 1.00
34 Mason Plumlee .60 1.50
35 Grant Jerrett .40 1.00
36 Giannis Antetokounmpo 5.00 12.00
37 Ricardo Ledo .40 1.00
38 Dennis Schroeder .60 1.50
39 Erick Green .50 1.25
40 Deshaun Thomas .40 1.00
41 Mike Muscala .60 1.50
42 C.J. Leslie .40 1.00
43 Lorenzo Brown .40 1.00
44 Reggie Bullock .50 1.25
45 Peyton Siva .40 1.00
46 Skylar Diggins 1.25 3.00
47 Allen Crabbe .50 1.25
48 Jamaal Franklin .40 1.00
49 Rudy Gobert .75 2.00
50 Pierre Jackson .40 1.00
51 Dominique Wilkins F/X .60 1.50
52 Karl Malone F/X .60 1.50
53 Bill Walton F/X .50 1.25
54 Allen Iverson F/X .60 1.50
55 Grant Hill F/X .60 1.50
56 Hakeem Olajuwon F/X .60 1.50
57 Isiah Thomas F/X .50 1.25
58 Dennis Rodman F/X 1.00 2.50
59 Reggie Miller F/X .50 1.25
60 Rajon Rondo F/X .50 1.25
61 David Robinson F/X .75 2.00
62 Larry Johnson F/X .60 1.50
63 Alonzo Mourning F/X .60 1.50
64 Anfernee Hardaway F/X 1.25 3.00
65 Kenny Anderson F/X .40 1.00
66 Larry Bird F/X 1.25 3.00
67 Magic Johnson F/X 1.25 3.00
68 Julius Erving F/X .75 2.00
69 Chris Paul F/X .60 1.50
70 Jason Kidd F/X .50 1.25
71 LeBron James F/X 2.00 5.00
72 Michael Jordan F/X 4.00 10.00
73 Jay Williams F/X .30 .75
74 Keith Smart F/X .50 1.25
75 Donyell Marshall F/X .30 .75
76 Glenn Robinson F/X .40 1.00
77 Allan Houston F/X .40 1.00
78 Paul George F/X .60 1.50
79 Joe Smith F/X .40 1.00
80 Jerry Lucas F/X .50 1.25
81 Micheal Ray Richardson F/X .40 1.00
82 John Havlicek F/X .60 1.50
83 Terrell Brandon F/X .30 .75
84 Cheryl Miller F/X .50 1.25
85 Glen Rice F/X .40 1.00
86 Mason Plumlee F/X 1.00 2.50
87 Shane Larkin F/X .60 1.50
88 Lucas Nogueira F/X .60 1.50
89 Dennis Schroeder F/X 1.00 2.50
90 Tim Hardaway Jr. F/X 1.00 2.50
91 G.Antetokounmpo F/X 8.00 20.00
92 Andre Roberson F/X .60 1.50
93 Archie Goodwin F/X .75 2.00
94 Livio Jean-Charles F/X .60 1.50
95 Sergey Karasev F/X .60 1.50
96 Skylar Diggins F/X 2.00 5.00
97 Reggie Bullock F/X .75 2.00
98 Solomon Hill F/X .60 1.50
99 Tony Snell F/X .75 2.00
100 Allen Crabbe F/X .75 2.00

2013-14 SP Authentic Rookie Film F/X

STATED ODDS 1:72 HOBBY
51 Dominique Wilkins 2.50 6.00
52 Karl Malone 2.50 6.00
53 Bill Walton 2.00 5.00
54 Allen Iverson 5.00 12.00
55 Grant Hill 6.00 15.00
56 Hakeem Olajuwon 6.00 15.00
57 Isiah Thomas 2.00 5.00
58 Dennis Rodman 4.00 10.00
59 Reggie Miller 2.00 5.00
60 Rajon Rondo 2.00 5.00
61 David Robinson 8.00 20.00
62 Larry Johnson 2.50 6.00
63 Alonzo Mourning 8.00 20.00
64 Anfernee Hardaway 8.00 20.00
65 Kenny Anderson 1.50 4.00
66 Larry Bird 8.00 20.00
67 Magic Johnson 8.00 20.00
68 Julius Erving 8.00 20.00
69 Chris Paul 2.50 6.00
70 Jason Kidd 2.00 5.00
71 LeBron James 10.00 25.00
72 Michael Jordan 25.00 60.00
73 Jay Williams 1.25 3.00
74 Keith Smart 2.00 5.00
75 Donyell Marshall 1.25 3.00
76 Glenn Robinson 1.50 4.00
77 Allan Houston 1.50 4.00
78 Paul George 2.50 6.00
79 Joe Smith 1.50 4.00
80 Jerry Lucas 2.00 5.00
81 Micheal Ray Richardson 1.50 4.00
82 John Havlicek 5.00 12.00
83 Terrell Brandon 1.25 3.00
84 Cheryl Miller 2.00 5.00
85 Glen Rice 1.50 4.00
86 Mason Plumlee 2.00 5.00
87 Shane Larkin 1.25 3.00
88 Lucas Nogueira 1.25 3.00
89 Dennis Schroeder 2.00 5.00
90 Tim Hardaway Jr. 8.00 20.00
91 Giannis Antetokounmpo 10.00 40.00
92 Andre Roberson 1.25 3.00
93 Archie Goodwin 1.50 4.00
94 Livio Jean-Charles 1.25 3.00
95 Sergey Karasev 1.25 3.00
96 Skylar Diggins 4.00 10.00
97 Reggie Bullock 1.50 4.00
98 Solomon Hill 1.25 3.00
99 Tony Snell 1.50 4.00
100 Allen Crabbe 1.50 4.00

2013-14 SP Authentic Rookie FX Film Autographs

GROUP A ODDS 1:4050 HOBBY
GROUP B ODDS 1:360 HOBBY
NO GROUP A PRICING AVAILABLE
EXCHANGE DEADLINE 3/13/2016
65 Kenny Anderson B
73 Jay Williams B 10.00 25.00
74 Keith Smart B 6.00 15.00
75 Donyell Marshall B
76 Glenn Robinson B
79 Joe Smith B 5.00 12.00
81 Micheal Ray Richardson B 8.00 20.00
86 Mason Plumlee B 6.00 15.00
87 Shane Larkin B
88 Lucas Nogueira B
90 Tim Hardaway Jr. B
91 Giannis Antetokounmpo B 40.00 100.00
93 Archie Goodwin B 10.00 25.00
94 Livio Jean-Charles B 4.00 10.00
96 Skylar Diggins B 12.00 30.00
97 Reggie Bullock B 10.00 25.00
98 Solomon Hill B 10.00 25.00

2013-14 SP Authentic Autographs

GROUP A ODDS 1:2642 HOBBY
GROUP B ODDS 1:1960 HOBBY
GROUP C ODDS 1:31 HOBBY
F/X GROUP A ODDS 1:1215 HOBBY
F/X GROUP B ODDS 1:124 HOBBY
EXCHANGE DEADLINE 3/13/2016
1 Dominique Wilkins A
2 Karl Malone A
4 Grant Hill A
5 Isiah Thomas A
7 Glenn Robinson B 5.00 12.00
8 David Robinson A 30.00 60.00
9 Anfernee Hardaway B 12.00 30.00
10 Larry Bird A 60.00 120.00
11 Magic Johnson A
12 Julius Erving A
14 LeBron James A
15 Michael Jordan B 300.00 400.00
16 Jay Williams C 4.00 10.00
17 Keith Smart A
18 Paul George A 50.00 100.00
19 Rajon Rondo A 15.00 40.00
20 Joe Smith C 5.00 12.00
21 Archie Goodwin C 5.00 12.00
23 Tony Snell C 5.00 12.00
24 Solomon Hill C 4.00 10.00
25 Ryan Kelly C 4.00 10.00
26 Seth Curry C 20.00 50.00
27 Andre Roberson C 4.00 10.00
28 Shane Larkin C 4.00 10.00
29 Lucas Nogueira C 4.00 10.00
30 Livio Jean-Charles C 4.00 10.00
31 Isaiah Canaan C 4.00 10.00
32 Tim Hardaway Jr. C 8.00 20.00
33 Nemanja Nedovic C 4.00 10.00
34 Mason Plumlee C 6.00 15.00
35 Grant Jerrett C 4.00 10.00
36 Giannis Antetokounmpo C 30.00 80.00
39 Erick Green C 5.00 12.00
40 Deshaun Thomas C 4.00 10.00
41 Mike Muscala C 6.00 15.00
43 Lorenzo Brown C 4.00 10.00
44 Reggie Bullock C 5.00 12.00
45 Peyton Siva C 6.00 15.00
46 Skylar Diggins C 10.00 25.00
47 Allen Crabbe C 5.00 12.00
48 Jamaal Franklin C 4.00 10.00
49 Rudy Gobert C 12.00 30.00
50 Pierre Jackson C 4.00 10.00
51 Dominique Wilkins F/X A
52 Karl Malone F/X A
53 Bill Walton F/X A 8.00 20.00
54 Allen Iverson F/X A
55 Grant Hill F/X A 15.00 40.00
56 Hakeem Olajuwon F/X A 20.00 50.00
57 Isiah Thomas F/X A 10.00 25.00
58 Dennis Rodman F/X A 15.00 40.00
60 Rajon Rondo F/X A 10.00 25.00
61 David Robinson F/X A 8.00 20.00
62 Larry Johnson F/X A 12.00 30.00
63 Alonzo Mourning F/X A 20.00 50.00
64 Anfernee Hardaway F/X A 20.00 50.00
65 Kenny Anderson F/X B 5.00 12.00
66 Larry Bird F/X A
67 Magic Johnson F/X A 30.00 80.00
68 Julius Erving F/X A 30.00 60.00
70 Jason Kidd F/X A 12.00 30.00
71 LeBron James F/X A
72 Michael Jordan F/X A
73 Jay Williams F/X B 4.00 10.00
74 Keith Smart F/X B 6.00 15.00
75 Donyell Marshall F/X B 4.00 10.00
76 Glenn Robinson F/X B 5.00 12.00
77 Allan Houston F/X A 8.00 20.00
78 Paul George F/X A
79 Joe Smith F/X B 5.00 12.00
80 Jerry Lucas F/X A
81 Micheal Ray Richardson F/X B 5.00 12.00
82 John Havlicek F/X A
84 Cheryl Miller F/X A 6.00 15.00
85 Glen Rice F/X A
86 Mason Plumlee F/X B 6.00 15.00
87 Shane Larkin F/X B 4.00 10.00
88 Lucas Nogueira F/X B
90 Tim Hardaway Jr. F/X B 10.00 25.00
91 G.Antetokounmpo F/X B 30.00 80.00
93 Archie Goodwin F/X B 5.00 12.00
94 Livio Jean-Charles F/X B 4.00 10.00
96 Skylar Diggins F/X B 12.00 30.00
97 Reggie Bullock F/X B 5.00 12.00
98 Solomon Hill F/X B 4.00 10.00

2013-14 SP Authentic By the Letter Signatures

OVERALL ODDS ONE PER BOX
SERIAL NUMBERS B/WN 3-75 PER
TOTAL PRINT RUNS B/WN 9-455 PER
EXCHANGE DEADLINE 3/13/2016
BLAC A.C. Green/385* 8.00 20.00
BLAE Alex English/455* 6.00 15.00
BLAH Allan Houston/315* 12.00 30.00
BLAM Alonzo Mourning/30* 75.00 150.00
BLAW Antoine Walker/400* 10.00 25.00
BLBD Brad Daugherty/455* 6.00 15.00
BLBL Bill Laimbeer/450* 6.00 15.00
BLBR Bryant Reeves/455* 6.00 15.00
BLBU Buck Williams/400* 8.00 20.00
BLBW Bill Walton/40* 10.00 25.00
BLCC Calbert Cheaney/420* 10.00 25.00
BLCL Christian Laettner/40* 20.00 50.00
BLCM Cheryl Miller/105* 6.00 15.00
BLCW Corliss Williamson/400* 6.00 15.00
BLDB Drew Barry/110* 6.00 15.00
BLDC Dave Cowens/180* 6.00 15.00
BLDR David Robinson/40* 30.00 60.00
BLDW Dominique Wilkins/70* 15.00 40.00
BLGH Grant Hill/40* 40.00 100.00
BLGL Glenn Robinson/450* 6.00 15.00
BLGR Glen Rice/80* 10.00 25.00
BLHA Anfernee Hardaway/21* 50.00 100.00
BLHO Hakeem Olajuwon/21*
BLIT Isiah Thomas/35* 30.00 60.00
BLJE Julius Erving/15* 60.00 120.00
BLJK Jason Kidd/30* 50.00 100.00
BLJL Jerry Lucas/135* 15.00 40.00
BLJM Jamal Mashburn/400* 10.00 25.00
BLJO Magic Johnson/39* 50.00 100.00
BLJS Joe Smith/400* 8.00 20.00
BLJW Jay Williams/200* 12.00 30.00
BLKA Kenny Anderson/385* 6.00 15.00
BLKG Kendall Gill/400* 10.00 25.00
BLKK Kerry Kittles/450* 10.00 25.00
BLKM Karl Malone/39* 30.00 60.00
BLKS Keith Smart/420* 10.00 25.00
BLLA Larry Johnson/20* 50.00 100.00
BLLB Larry Bird/36* 50.00 100.00
BLLE LaPhonso Ellis/450* 6.00 15.00
BLLJ LeBron James/150* 150.00 250.00
BLMA Donyell Marshall/375* 6.00 15.00
BLMJ Michael Jordan/299* 250.00 500.00
BLOB Otis Birdsong/420* 6.00 15.00
BLPG Paul George/110* 25.00 60.00
BLRH Robert Horry/350* 6.00 15.00
BLRM Ron Mercer/400* 6.00 15.00
BLRO Dennis Rodman/36* 40.00 80.00
BLRR Rajon Rondo/80* 50.00 100.00
BLRS Rod Strickland/450* 6.00 15.00
BLRU Bill Russell/9*
BLSB Shawn Bradley/420* 8.00 20.00
BLSC Detlef Schrempf/350* 12.00 30.00
BLSE Sean Elliott/420* 8.00 20.00
BLSN Swen Nater/300* 6.00 15.00
BLSP Sam Perkins/455* 6.00 15.00
BLTB Terrell Brandon/450* 6.00 15.00
BLTG Tony Gwynn/60* 40.00 80.00
BLTH Tim Hardaway/140* 6.00 15.00

2013-14 SP Authentic Canvas

CC1 Dominique Wilkins .60 1.50
CC2 Karl Malone .60 1.50
CC3 Allen Iverson .60 1.50
CC4 Grant Hill .60 1.50
CC5 Hakeem Olajuwon .60 1.50
CC6 Isiah Thomas .50 1.25
CC7 Dennis Rodman 1.00 2.50
CC8 Reggie Miller .50 1.25
CC9 Paul George .60 1.50
CC10 David Robinson .75 2.00
CC11 Anfernee Hardaway 1.25 3.00
CC12 Larry Bird 1.00 2.50
CC13 Magic Johnson 1.25 3.00
CC14 Julius Erving .75 2.00
CC15 Chris Paul .60 1.50
CC16 Derrick Coleman .50 1.25
CC17 LeBron James 2.00 5.00
CC18 Michael Jordan 4.00 10.00
CC19 Larry Johnson .60 1.50
CC20 Jay Williams .30 .75
CC21 Glenn Robinson .40 1.00
CC22 Jerry Lucas .50 1.25
CC23 Dave Cowens .30 .75
CC24 Joe Smith .40 1.00
CC25 John Havlicek .60 1.50
CC26 Kenny Anderson .40 1.00
CC27 Glen Rice .40 1.00
CC28 Cheryl Miller .50 1.25
CC29 Rajon Rondo .50 1.25
CC30 Alonzo Mourning .60 1.50
CC31 Archie Goodwin .40 1.00
CC32 Sergey Karasev .30 .75
CC33 Tony Snell .40 1.00
CC34 Peyton Siva .30 .75
CC35 Ryan Kelly .30 .75
CC36 Seth Curry 1.00 2.50
CC37 Erick Green .40 1.00
CC38 Shane Larkin .30 .75
CC39 Lucas Nogueira .30 .75
CC40 Solomon Hill .30 .75
CC41 Isaiah Canaan .30 .75
CC42 Tim Hardaway Jr. .50 1.25
CC43 Andre Roberson .30 .75
CC44 Mason Plumlee .50 1.25
CC45 Livio Jean-Charles .30 .75
CC46 Giannis Antetokounmpo 4.00 10.00
CC47 Deshaun Thomas .30 .75
CC48 Dennis Schroeder .50 1.25
CC49 Nemanja Nedovic .30 .75
CC50 Lorenzo Brown .30 .75
CC51 Grant Jerrett .30 .75
CC52 C.J. Leslie .30 .75
CC53 Reggie Bullock .40 1.00
CC54 Mike Muscala .50 1.25
CC55 Ricardo Ledo .30 .75
CC56 Skylar Diggins 1.00 2.50
CC57 Allen Crabbe .40 1.00
CC58 Jamaal Franklin .30 .75
CC59 Rudy Gobert .60 1.50
CC60 Pierre Jackson .30 .75

2013-14 SP Authentic Canvas Autographs

GROUP A ODDS 1:2000 HOBBY
GROUP B ODDS 1:1333 HOBBY
GROUP C ODDS 1:80 HOBBY
EXCHANGE DEADLINE 3/13/2016
CC1 Dominique Wilkins A
CC2 Karl Malone A 30.00 60.00
CC3 Allen Iverson A
CC4 Grant Hill A
CC5 Hakeem Olajuwon A
CC6 Isiah Thomas B 10.00 25.00
CC7 Dennis Rodman A
CC9 Paul George A
CC10 David Robinson A 20.00 50.00
CC11 Anfernee Hardaway A 20.00 50.00
CC12 Larry Bird A
CC13 Magic Johnson A
CC14 Julius Erving A
CC17 LeBron James B 150.00 250.00
CC18 Michael Jordan B
CC19 Larry Johnson A
CC20 Jay Williams C 10.00 25.00
CC21 Glenn Robinson C 5.00 12.00
CC22 Jerry Lucas C 6.00 15.00
CC23 Dave Cowens B 4.00 10.00
CC24 Joe Smith C 5.00 12.00
CC26 Kenny Anderson C 5.00 12.00
CC27 Glen Rice C 5.00 12.00
CC28 Cheryl Miller A
CC29 Rajon Rondo A 12.00 30.00
CC30 Alonzo Mourning A
CC31 Archie Goodwin C 5.00 12.00
CC34 Peyton Siva C 4.00 10.00
CC35 Ryan Kelly C 4.00 10.00
CC36 Seth Curry C 30.00 80.00
CC37 Erick Green C 5.00 12.00
CC38 Shane Larkin C 4.00 10.00
CC39 Lucas Nogueira C 4.00 10.00
CC40 Solomon Hill C 4.00 10.00
CC41 Isaiah Canaan C 4.00 10.00
CC42 Tim Hardaway Jr. C 15.00 40.00
CC43 Andre Roberson C 4.00 10.00
CC44 Mason Plumlee C 6.00 15.00
CC45 Livio Jean-Charles C 4.00 10.00
CC46 Giannis Antetokounmpo C 50.00 120.00
CC47 Deshaun Thomas C 4.00 10.00
CC49 Nemanja Nedovic C 4.00 10.00
CC50 Lorenzo Brown C 4.00 10.00
CC51 Grant Jerrett C 4.00 10.00
CC53 Reggie Bullock C 5.00 12.00
CC54 Mike Muscala C 6.00 15.00
CC56 Skylar Diggins B 8.00 20.00
CC57 Allen Crabbe C
CC58 Jamaal Franklin C 4.00 10.00
CC59 Rudy Gobert B
CC60 Pierre Jackson C 4.00 10.00

2013-14 SP Authentic LeBron James Supreme Court

COMMON ODDS 1:44 HOBBY
UNCOMMON ODDS 1:216 HOBBY
RARE ODDS 1:432 HOBBY
AUTOS RANDOMLY INSERTED
EXCHANGE DEADLINE 3/13/2016
SC1 LeBron James C 10.00 25.00
SC2 LeBron James C 10.00 25.00
SC3 LeBron James C 10.00 25.00
SC4 LeBron James C 10.00 25.00
SC5 LeBron James C 10.00 25.00
SC6 LeBron James U 10.00 25.00
SC7 LeBron James U 10.00 25.00
SC8 LeBron James U 10.00 25.00
SC9 LeBron James U 10.00 25.00
SC10 LeBron James U 10.00 25.00
SC11 LeBron James R 12.00 30.00
SC12 LeBron James R 12.00 30.00
SC13 LeBron James R 12.00 30.00
SC14 LeBron James R 12.00 30.00
SC15 LeBron James R 12.00 30.00
SC16 LeBron James AU/10 200.00 300.00
SC17 LeBron James AU/10 200.00 300.00
SC18 LeBron James AU/10 200.00 300.00
SC19 LeBron James AU/10 200.00 300.00
SC20 LeBron James AU/10 200.00 300.00

2013-14 SP Authentic On Court Authentics

STATED ODDS 1:72 HOBBY
OCAAH Allan Houston 2.50 6.00
OCABL Bill Laimbeer 2.50 6.00
OCABW Bill Walton 3.00 8.00
OCACL Christian Laettner 6.00 15.00
OCACP Chris Paul 4.00 10.00
OCADC Derrick Coleman 3.00 8.00
OCADM Danny Manning 2.50 6.00
OCADW Dominique Wilkins 4.00 10.00
OCAEH Elvin Hayes 3.00 8.00
OCAGH Grant Hill 6.00 15.00
OCAHO Hakeem Olajuwon 6.00 15.00
OCAIT Isiah Thomas 3.00 8.00
OCAJE Julius Erving 8.00 20.00
OCAJK Jason Kidd 3.00 8.00
OCAJO Michael Jordan 15.00 40.00
OCAJS Joe Smith 6.00 15.00
OCAKM Karl Malone 4.00 10.00
OCAKS Keith Smart 3.00 8.00
OCALA Larry Johnson 4.00 10.00
OCALB Larry Bird 8.00 20.00
OCALJ LeBron James 12.00 30.00
OCAMI Michael Jordan 25.00 60.00
OCAMJ Magic Johnson 8.00 20.00
OCAMR Micheal Ray Richardson 2.50 6.00
OCAPG Paul George 4.00 10.00
OCARH Robert Horry 2.50 6.00
OCARR Rajon Rondo 10.00 25.00
OCASB Shawn Bradley 2.00 5.00

2013-14 SP Authentic On Court Authentics Signatures

GROUP A ODDS 1:10,128 HOBBY
GROUP B ODDS 1:4535 HOBBY
GROUP C ODDS 1:616 HOBBY
EXCHANGE DEADLINE 3/13/2016
OCASBW Bill Walton C 6.00 15.00
OCASCL Christian Laettner C 12.00 30.00
OCASDW Dominique Wilkins B
OCASGH Grant Hill A
OCASHO Hakeem Olajuwon A
OCASIT Isiah Thomas C 12.00 30.00
OCASJK Jason Kidd A
OCASJO Michael Jordan B 300.00 500.00
OCASKM Karl Malone A
OCASLA Larry Johnson A
OCASLB Larry Bird A
OCASLJ LeBron James B EXCH
OCASSB Shawn Bradley C 4.00 10.00

2013-14 SP Authentic Sign of the Times

GROUP A ODDS 1:2267 HOBBY
GROUP B ODDS 1:646 HOBBY
GROUP C ODDS 1:69 HOBBY
EXCHANGE DEADLINE 3/13/2016
SAH Allan Houston B
SAI Allen Iverson A
SAW Antoine Walker B 5.00 12.00
SBD Brad Daugherty C 5.00 12.00
SBL Bill Laimbeer C 5.00 12.00
SBO Muggsy Bogues C 5.00 12.00
SBW Bill Walton A
SCC Calbert Cheaney C 4.00 10.00
SCL Christian Laettner B 5.00 12.00
SCM Cheryl Miller A
SDB Drew Barry C 4.00 10.00
SDO Donyell Marshall C 4.00 10.00
SDR David Robinson A
SDS Detlef Schrempf C 6.00 15.00
SDW Dominique Wilkins A
SEH Elvin Hayes B 6.00 15.00
SEJ Eddie Jones C 5.00 12.00
SEL Sean Elliott C 6.00 15.00
SGH Grant Hill A
SGR Glenn Robinson C 5.00 12.00
SHA Anfernee Hardaway A
SHM Harold Miner C 4.00 10.00
SJE Julius Erving A
SJH James Harden A
SJK Jason Kidd A
SJL Jerry Lucas B 6.00 15.00
SJM Jamal Mashburn B 6.00 15.00
SJO Michael Jordan A
SJS Joe Smith C 5.00 12.00
SJW Jay Williams B
SKA Kenny Anderson C 5.00 12.00
SKG Kendall Gill C 8.00 20.00
SKK Kerry Kittles C 4.00 10.00
SKM Karl Malone A
SKS Keith Smart C 6.00 15.00
SLB Larry Bird A
SLJ LeBron James A EXCH
SLS Lonnie Shelton C 4.00 10.00
SMA Danny Manning A 20.00 50.00
SMJ Magic Johnson A 30.00 60.00
SOB Otis Birdsong C 5.00 12.00
SPG Paul George A
SRH Robert Horry B 5.00 12.00
SRR Rajon Rondo A
SRS Rod Strickland C 4.00 10.00
SSB Shawn Bradley C 4.00 10.00
STH Tim Hardaway B
STK Toni Kukoc A
STR Theo Ratliff C 4.00 10.00

2013-14 SP Authentic Sign of the Times Dual

GROUP A ODDS 1:10,128 HOBBY
GROUP B ODDS 1:5840 HOBBY
GROUP C ODDS 1:1380 HOBBY
NO A-B PRICING DUE TO SCARCITY
EXCHANGE DEADLINE 3/13/2016
S2BR B.Reeves/S.Bradley C 6.00 15.00
S2GC R.Gobert/L.Charles C 15.00 40.00
S2GS G.Jerrett/S.Hill C 6.00 15.00
S2MW J.Mashburn/A.Walker C 20.00 50.00
S2PK M.Plumlee/R.Kelly C 10.00 25.00
S2SR J.Smith/G.Robinson C 20.00 50.00
S2TT T.Hardaway/T.Hardaway Jr. C 20.00 50.00
S2WM A.Walker/R.Mercer C
S2WN B.Walton/S.Nater C

2014 SP Authentic

COMP.SET w/o SP's (50) 6.00 15.00
51-68 STATED ODDS 1:4
69-75 STATED ODDS 1:9
23 Michael Jordan 1.25 3.00
69 T.Woods/M.Jordan AM 3.00 8.00

2014 SP Authentic Green

*GREEN/99: 6X TO 15X BASIC CARDS

2014 SP Authentic Limited Autographs

STATED PRINT RUN 10-100
23 Michael Jordan/10

2014 SP Authentic Sign of the Times

GROUP A ODDS 1:8,123
GROUP B ODDS 1:1,408
GROUP C ODDS 1:1,067
GROUP D ODDS 1:413
GROUP E ODDS 1:353
GROUP F ODDS 1:64
GROUP G ODDS 1:55
GROUP H ODDS 1:35
SOTTMJ Michael Jordan A

2014-15 SP Authentic

STATED PRINT RUN B/WN 175-475 COPIES PER
RANDOM INSERTS IN PACKS
1 Alex English .30 .75
2 Alonzo Mourning .50 1.25
3 Anfernee Hardaway 1.00 2.50
4 Antonio McDyess .30 .75
5 Bill Russell .60 1.50
6 Bill Walton .40 1.00
7 Brad Daugherty .30 .75
8 Lonnie Shelton .25 .60
9 Byron Scott .30 .75
10 Tracy McGrady .40 1.00
11 Christian Laettner .30 .75
12 Danny Manning .30 .75
13 David Robinson .60 1.50
14 Bo Kimble .25 .60
15 Allan Houston .30 .75
16 Fat Lever .30 .75
17 Doc Rivers .40 1.00
18 Buck Williams .25 .60
19 Eric Piatkowski .25 .60
20 Grant Hill .50 1.25
21 Chauncey Billups .40 1.00
22 Dave Cowens .25 .60
23 Elvin Hayes .40 1.00
24 James Harden .60 1.50
25 James Worthy .50 1.25
26 Jerry West .50 1.25
27 John Stockton .60 1.50
28 Julius Erving .60 1.50
29 Harold Miner .25 .60
30 Jerry Lucas .40 1.00
31 Bo Outlaw .25 .60
32 Larry Bird 1.00 2.50
33 Nick Van Exel .40 1.00
34 LeBron James 1.50 4.00
35 Magic Johnson 1.00 2.50
36 Michael Jordan 2.00 5.00
37 Micheal Ray Richardson .30 .75
38 John Salley .25 .60
39 Shaquille O'Neal .75 2.00
40 Jay Williams .25 .60
41 Pervis Ellison .25 .60
42 Reggie Theus .30 .75
43 Donyell Marshall .25 .60
44 Robert Horry .30 .75
45 Stephen Curry 1.50 4.00
46 Larry Johnson .50 1.25
47 Sleepy Floyd .25 .60
48 Yao Ming .50 1.25
49 Vinny Del Negro .30 .75
50 Kendall Gill .25 .60
51 Keith Smart AM 1.50 4.00
52 Bill Russell AM 2.50 6.00

53 Bill Walton AM 1.50 4.00
54 Sam Perkins AM 1.00 2.50
55 Christian Laettner AM 1.25 3.00
56 Danny Manning AM 1.25 3.00
57 David Robinson AM 2.50 6.00
58 Grant Hill AM 2.00 5.00
59 Glen Rice AM 1.25 3.00
60 Shaquille O'Neal AM 3.00 8.00
61 James Worthy AM 2.00 5.00
62 Jerry West AM 2.00 5.00
63 Julius Erving AM 2.50 6.00
64 Larry Bird AM 4.00 10.00
65 Yao Ming AM 2.00 5.00
66 LeBron James AM 6.00 15.00
67 Magic Johnson AM 4.00 10.00
68 Michael Jordan AM 12.00 30.00
69 Pervis Ellison AM 1.00 2.50
70 Corliss Williamson AM 1.00 2.50
71 M.Johnson/L.Bird AM 4.00 10.00
72 M.Jordan/J.Worthy AM 12.00 30.00
73 D.Daniels/S.Napier AM 1.25 3.00
74 S.Napier/J.Young AM 1.25 3.00
75 G.Hill/C.Laettner AM 2.00 5.00
76 Jordan Adams AU/475 3.00 8.00
77 Joe Harris AU/475 3.00 8.00
78 Spencer Dinwiddie AU/475 4.00 10.00
79 Mitch McGary AU/475
80 Dwight Powell AU/475 3.00 8.00
81 Clint Capela AU/475 4.00 10.00
82 P.J. Hairston AU/475 6.00 15.00
83 Dario Saric AU/475 15.00 40.00
84 Alessandro Gentile AU/475 3.00 8.00
85 Thanasis Antetokounmpo AU/475 3.00 8.00
86 Zach LaVine AU/475 10.00 40.00
87 Josh Huestis AU/475 3.00 8.00
88 Doug McDermott AU/475 5.00 12.00
89 Nikola Mirotic AU/475 6.00 15.00
90 Jusuf Nurkic AU/475 5.00 12.00
91 James Young AU/475 3.00 8.00
92 C.J. Wilcox AU/475 3.00 8.00
93 Jordan Clarkson AU/475 5.00 12.00
94 DeAndre Daniels AU/475 6.00 15.00
95 Adreian Payne AU/475 4.00 10.00
96 Rodney Hood AU/475 6.00 15.00
97 Cleanthony Early AU/475 3.00 8.00
98 Shabazz Napier AU/475 8.00 20.00
99 Glenn Robinson III AU/475 3.00 8.00
100 James Michael McAdoo AU/475 4.00 10.00
101 Elfrid Payton AU/175 5.00 12.00
102 Nik Stauskas AU/175
103 T.J. Warren AU/175 10.00 25.00
104 Gary Harris AU/175 5.00 12.00
105 Aaron Gordon AU/175 8.00 20.00

2014-15 SP Authentic Authentic Moments Autographs

RANDOM INSERTS IN PACKS
LACK OF PRICING DUE TO MARKET INFO
51 Keith Smart 5.00 12.00
53 Bill Walton 20.00 50.00
54 Sam Perkins 3.00 8.00
55 Christian Laettner 12.00 30.00
56 Danny Manning 4.00 10.00
58 Grant Hill 25.00 60.00
65 Yao Ming 15.00 40.00
66 LeBron James 150.00 300.00
69 Pervis Ellison 3.00 8.00
75 G.Hill/C.Laettner 20.00 50.00

2014-15 SP Authentic Autographs Emerald

RANDOM INSERTS IN PACKS
STATED PRINT RUN B/WN 5-75 COPIES PER
NO PRICING ON QTY 5 OR LESS
1 Alex English/75 6.00 15.00
6 Bill Walton/75 4.00 10.00
7 Brad Daugherty/75
12 Danny Manning/75 12.00 30.00
14 Bo Kimble/75 2.50 6.00
15 Allan Houston/75
16 Fat Lever/75 3.00 8.00
17 Doc Rivers/75 4.00 10.00
22 Dave Cowens/75 2.50 6.00
37 Micheal Ray Richardson/75 3.00 8.00
41 Pervis Ellison/75 2.50 6.00
43 Donyell Marshall/75 2.50 6.00
49 Vinny Del Negro/75 3.00 8.00
50 Kendall Gill/75 8.00 20.00

2014-15 SP Authentic Chirography

RANDOM INSERTS IN PACKS
STATED PRINT RUN B/WN 3-75 COPIES PER
NO PRICING ON QTY 10 OR LESS
CEP Eric Piatkowski/75 4.00 10.00
CKG Kendall Gill/75 6.00 15.00
CMJ Michael Jordan/23 300.00 400.00

2014-15 SP Authentic Limited Autographs

PRINT RUNS B/WN 5-75 COPIES PER
NO PRICING ON QTY 10 OR LESS
1 Alex English AU/75 6.00 15.00
4 Antonio McDyess AU/75 6.00 15.00
7 Brad Daugherty AU/75 6.00 15.00
8 Lonnie Shelton AU/75 5.00 12.00
14 Bo Kimble AU/75 5.00 12.00
15 Allan Houston AU/75 6.00 15.00
16 Fat Lever AU/75 6.00 15.00
18 Buck Williams AU/75 5.00 12.00
19 Eric Piatkowski AU/75 5.00 12.00
29 Harold Miner AU/75 5.00 12.00
31 Bo Outlaw AU/75 5.00 12.00
33 Nick Van Exel AU/75 8.00 20.00
37 Micheal Ray Richardson AU/75 6.00 15.00
38 John Salley AU/75 5.00 12.00
40 Jay Williams AU/75 5.00 12.00
42 Reggie Theus AU/75 6.00 15.00
43 Donyell Marshall AU/75 5.00 12.00
47 Sleepy Floyd AU/75 5.00 12.00
50 Kendall Gill AU/75 5.00 12.00
51 Keith Smart AM AU C
52 Bill Russell AM AU A
53 Bill Walton AM AU C
54 Sam Perkins AM AU F
55 Christian Laettner AM AU E
56 Danny Manning AM AU D
57 David Robinson AM AU A
58 Grant Hill AM AU B
59 Glen Rice AM AU B
60 Shaquille O'Neal AM AU A
61 James Worthy AM AU A
62 Jerry West AM AU A
63 Julius Erving AM AU A
65 Yao Ming AM AU D
66 LeBron James AM AU D
67 Magic Johnson AM AU A
68 Michael Jordan AM AU E
69 Pervis Ellison AM AU F
70 Corliss Williamson AM AU C
71 Magic Johnson
Larry Bird AM AU A
72 Michael Jordan
James Worthy AM AU A
73 DeAndre Daniels
Shabazz Napier AM AU C
74 James Young
Shabazz Napier AM AU B
75 Grant Hill
Christian Laettner AM AU B

2014-15 SP Authentic Limited Patch Autographs

RANDOM INSERTS IN PACKS
STATED PRINT RUN B/WN 25-50 COPIES PER
77 Joe Harris/50 4.00 10.00
78 Spencer Dinwiddie/50 10.00 25.00
80 Dwight Powell/50 4.00 10.00
81 Clint Capela/50 15.00 40.00
82 P.J. Hairston/50 4.00 10.00
85 Thanasis Antetokounmpo/50 4.00 10.00
86 Nikola Mirotic/50 12.00 30.00
87 Josh Huestis/50 4.00 10.00
88 Doug McDermott/50 15.00 40.00
89 Zach LaVine/50 20.00 50.00
91 James Young/50 4.00 10.00
93 Jordan Clarkson/50 40.00 100.00
95 Adreian Payne/50 5.00 12.00
96 Rodney Hood/50 20.00 50.00
98 Shabazz Napier/50 12.00 30.00
99 Glenn Robinson III/50 25.00 60.00
101 Elfrid Payton/25 50.00 120.00
102 Nik Stauskas/25 12.00 30.00
103 T.J. Warren/25 20.00 50.00
104 Gary Harris/25 20.00 50.00
105 Aaron Gordon/25 30.00 80.00

2014-15 SP Authentic Marks of Distinction

RANDOM INSERTS IN PACKS
STATED PRINT RUN B/WN 3-50 COPIES PER
NO PRICING ON QTY 3 OR LESS
MDBW Bill Walton/50 6.00 15.00
MDLJ LeBron James/23 EXCH 200.00 400.00

2014-15 SP Authentic Rookie Chirography

RANDOM INSERTS IN PACKS
STATED PRINT RUN B/WN 10-99 COPIES PER
NO PRICING ON QTY 10 OR LESS
RCCW C.J. Wilcox/99 3.00 8.00
RCJA Jordan Adams/99 3.00 8.00

2014-15 SP Authentic Rookie Extended

RANDOM INSERTS IN PACKS
R1 Clint Capela 1.25 3.00
R2 P.J. Hairston 1.00 2.50
R3 Dario Saric 2.50 6.00
R4 DeAndre Daniels 1.00 2.50
R5 Glenn Robinson III 1.00 2.50
R6 Shabazz Napier 1.25 3.00
R7 Cleanthony Early 1.00 2.50
R8 Rodney Hood 1.50 4.00
R9 Jordan Adams 1.00 2.50
R10 Jusuf Nurkic 1.50 4.00
R11 Thanasis Antetokounmpo 1.00 2.50
R12 Josh Huestis 1.00 2.50
R13 Doug McDermott 1.50 4.00
R14 Zach LaVine 2.50 6.00
R15 Mitch McGary 1.00 2.50
R16 James Young 1.00 2.50
R17 Nikola Mirotic 2.00 5.00
R18 C.J. Wilcox 1.00 2.50
R19 Joe Harris 1.00 2.50
R20 Adreian Payne 1.25 3.00
R21 T.J. Warren 1.50 4.00
R22 Gary Harris 1.50 4.00
R23 Nik Stauskas 1.25 3.00
R24 Elfrid Payton 1.50 4.00
R25 Aaron Gordon 2.50 6.00

2014-15 SP Authentic Rookie Extended Autographs Emerald

RANDOM INSERTS IN PACKS
STATED PRINT RUN 25-225 COPIES PER
R1 Clint Capela/225 4.00 10.00
R2 P.J. Hairston/225 6.00 15.00
R3 Dario Saric/225 10.00 25.00
R6 Shabazz Napier/225 4.00 10.00
R7 Cleanthony Early/225 3.00 8.00
R8 Rodney Hood/225 5.00 12.00
R9 Jordan Adams/225 3.00 8.00
R10 Jusuf Nurkic/225 5.00 12.00
R11 Thanasis Antetokounmpo/225 3.00 8.00
R12 Josh Huestis/225 3.00 8.00
R13 Doug McDermott/225 5.00 12.00
R14 Zach LaVine/225 10.00 25.00
R16 James Young/225 3.00 8.00
R17 Nikola Mirotic/225 20.00 50.00
R18 C.J. Wilcox/225 3.00 8.00
R19 Joe Harris/225 3.00 8.00
R20 Adreian Payne/225 4.00 10.00
R21 T.J. Warren/150 8.00 20.00
R22 Gary Harris/150 5.00 12.00
R23 Nik Stauskas/150 5.00 12.00
R24 Elfrid Payton/25 12.00 30.00
R25 Aaron Gordon/25 12.00 30.00

2014-15 SP Authentic Rookie Extended Autographs Red

*RED: 1X TO 2.5X EMERALD HI
RANDOM INSERTS IN PACKS
STATED PRINT RUN B/WN 5-50 COPIES PER
NO PRICING ON QTY 10 OR LESS
R15 Mitch McGary/50 8.00 20.00

2014-15 SP Authentic Sign of the Times

RANDOM INSERTS IN PACKS
SOTAE Alex English 3.00 8.00
SOTAH Anfernee Hardaway 12.00 30.00
SOTAM Antonio McDyess 3.00 8.00
SOTAP Adreian Payne 5.00 12.00
SOTBD Brad Daugherty 3.00 8.00
SOTBW Bill Walton 12.00 30.00
SOTCB Chauncey Billups 4.00 10.00
SOTCE Cleanthony Early 4.00 10.00
SOTCW C.J. Wilcox 2.50 6.00
SOTGH Grant Hill 12.00 30.00
SOTGO Aaron Gordon 6.00 15.00
SOTHA Gary Harris 4.00 10.00
SOTJM James Michael McAdoo 3.00 8.00
SOTKG Kendall Gill 5.00 12.00
SOTKS Keith Smart 4.00 10.00
SOTMM Mitch McGary 2.50 6.00
SOTMR Micheal Ray Richardson 3.00 8.00
SOTNS Nik Stauskas 3.00 8.00
SOTPE Pervis Ellison 3.00 8.00
SOTPY Patric Young 2.50 6.00
SOTRT Reggie Theus 3.00 8.00
SOTSC Stephen Curry 50.00 120.00
SOTSF Sleepy Floyd 2.50 6.00
SOTSN Shabazz Napier 3.00 8.00
SOTYM Yao Ming 15.00 40.00

2014-15 SP Authentic Sign of the Times Triple

RANDOM INSERTS IN PACKS
STATED PRINT RUN B/WN 3-20 COPIES PER
NO PRICING ON QTY 3 OR LESS
SOT3HHM Mourning/Hardaway/Hill/20 40.00 100.00

2007-08 SP Authentic Retail

The Retail version of SP Authentic differs from the Hobby version in that the cards display the "SP" logo rather than the full "SP Authentic" logo, and the rookie cards are not autographed or serially numbered.
COMPLETE SET (153) 30.00 80.00
*VETS: .25X TO .6X HOBBY SP
101 Greg Oden RC 1.25 3.00
102 Yi Jianlian RC 1.50 4.00
103 Brandan Wright RC 1.25 3.00
104 Thaddeus Young RC 1.25 3.00
105 Nick Young RC 1.50 4.00
106 Jamario Moon RC 1.00 2.50
106B Guillermo Diaz 1.25 3.00
107 Marco Belinelli RC 1.25 3.00
108 Darryl Watkins RC .75 2.00
109 Oleksiy Pecherov RC 1.25 3.00
110 Juan Carlos Navarro RC 1.00 2.50
111 JamesOn Curry RC .75 2.00
112 Demetris Nichols RC .75 2.00
113 Herbert Hill RC .75 2.00
114 Coby Karl RC .75 2.00
115 Darius Washington 1.25 3.00
116 Louis Amundson RC .75 2.00
117 Cheikh Samb RC .75 2.00
118 Ramon Sessions RC 1.25 3.00
119 Luis Scola RC 1.50 4.00
122 Spencer Hawes RC 1.00 2.50
123 Acie Law RC .75 2.00
124 Julian Wright RC .75 2.00
125 Al Thornton RC 1.00 2.50
126 Rodney Stuckey RC 1.00 2.50
127 Sean Williams RC .75 2.00
128 Javaris Crittenton RC .75 2.00
129 Jason Smith RC 1.00 2.50
130 Daequan Cook RC 1.00 2.50
131 Jared Dudley RC 1.00 2.50
132 Wilson Chandler RC 1.00 2.50
133 Morris Almond RC .75 2.00
134 Arron Afflalo RC 1.25 3.00
135 Alando Tucker RC .75 2.00
136 Carl Landry RC .75 2.00
137 Gabe Pruitt RC .75 2.00
138 Aaron Brooks RC 1.00 2.50
139 Nick Fazekas RC .75 2.00
140 Jermareo Davidson RC .75 2.00
141 Josh McRoberts RC 1.00 2.50
142 Glen Davis RC 1.00 2.50
143 Adam Haluska RC .75 2.00
147 Dominic McGuire RC .75 2.00
148 Aaron Gray RC .75 2.00
149 Taurean Green RC .75 2.00
150 D.J. Strawberry RC .75 2.00
151 Chris Richard RC .75 2.00
152 Kevin Durant RC 12.00 30.00
153 Al Horford RC 1.50 4.00
154 Mike Conley Jr. RC 1.50 4.00
155 Jeff Green RC 1.25 3.00
156 Corey Brewer RC 1.25 3.00
157 Joakim Noah RC 1.25 3.00

2007-08 SP Authentic Retail Rookie Autographs

PRINT RUNS LISTED IN CHECKLIST
UNPRICED LOGO PRINT RUN ONE SET
UNPRICED PARALLEL PRINT RUN 10 SETS
INSERTED INTO RETAIL SP PACKS
122 Spencer Hawes/599 5.00 12.00
123 Acie Law/100 4.00 10.00
124 Julian Wright/100 4.00 10.00
125 Al Thornton/599 5.00 12.00
126 Rodney Stuckey/599 5.00 12.00
127 Sean Williams/100 4.00 10.00
128 Javaris Crittenton/100 4.00 10.00
129 Jason Smith/100 5.00 12.00
130 Daequan Cook/100 5.00 12.00
131 Jared Dudley/100 5.00 12.00
132 Wilson Chandler/599 5.00 12.00
133 Morris Almond/100 4.00 10.00
134 Arron Afflalo/599 6.00 15.00
135 Alando Tucker/100 4.00 10.00
136 Carl Landry/100 4.00 10.00
137 Gabe Pruitt/100 4.00 10.00
138 Aaron Brooks/599 5.00 12.00
139 Nick Fazekas/599 4.00 10.00
140 Jermareo Davidson/100 4.00 10.00
141 Josh McRoberts/599 5.00 12.00
142 Glen Davis/599 5.00 12.00
143 Adam Haluska/599 4.00 10.00
147 Dominic McGuire/100 4.00 10.00
148 Aaron Gray/100 4.00 10.00
149 Taurean Green/599 4.00 10.00
150 D.J. Strawberry/599 4.00 10.00
151 Chris Richard/100 4.00 10.00
152 Kevin Durant/399 500.00 1000.00
153 Al Horford/399 8.00 20.00
154 Mike Conley Jr./100 8.00 20.00
155 Jeff Green/399 6.00 15.00
156 Corey Brewer/100 6.00 15.00
157 Joakim Noah/100 6.00 15.00

2008-09 SP Authentic Retail

COMP.SET w/o RCs (100) 10.00 25.00
*VETS: .25X TO .6X BASE HOBBY
101 Alexis Ajinca AU RC 4.00 10.00
102 Joe Alexander AU RC 4.00 10.00
103 Ryan Anderson AU RC 5.00 12.00
104 Darrell Arthur AU RC 5.00 12.00
106 Jerryd Bayless AU RC 5.00 12.00
107 Michael Beasley AU RC 6.00 15.00
108 Mario Chalmers AU RC 6.00 15.00
109 Joe Crawford AU RC 4.00 10.00
110 Joey Dorsey AU RC 4.00 10.00
112 Patrick Ewing Jr. AU RC 4.00 10.00
113 Danilo Gallinari AU RC 10.00 25.00
114 J.R. Giddens AU RC 4.00 10.00
115 Eric Gordon AU RC 10.00 25.00
116 Donte Greene AU RC 4.00 10.00
118 Roy Hibbert AU RC 6.00 15.00
119 J.J. Hickson AU RC 5.00 12.00
121 DeAndre Jordan AU RC 15.00 40.00
122 Kosta Koufos AU RC 5.00 12.00
123 Courtney Lee AU RC 5.00 12.00
125 Robin Lopez AU RC 6.00 15.00
126 Kevin Love AU RC 20.00 50.00
127 O.J. Mayo AU RC 6.00 15.00
128 Javale McGee AU RC 8.00 20.00
129 Anthony Randolph AU RC 4.00 10.00
130 Derrick Rose AU RC 150.00 300.00
131 Brandon Rush AU RC 5.00 12.00
132 Walter Sharpe AU RC 4.00 10.00
133 Sean Singletary AU RC 4.00 10.00
134 Marreese Speights AU RC 5.00 12.00
135 Mike Taylor AU RC 4.00 10.00
136 Jason Thompson AU RC 4.00 10.00
137 Kyle Weaver AU RC 4.00 10.00
138 Sonny Weems AU RC 4.00 10.00
139 Russell Westbrook AU RC 250.00 500.00
140 D.J. White AU RC 5.00 12.00
147 Rudy Fernandez AU RC 5.00 12.00

1994-95 SP Championship

The premier edition of the 1994-95 SP Championship series (made by Upper Deck) consists of 135 standard size cards issued in six-card foil packs, each with a suggested retail price of $2.99. SP Championship cards were shipped exclusively to retail outlets. Card fronts feature full-bleed, color action photos with a foil SP Championship logo. The player's name runs up the side of the card in small gold foil print. Team name is contained in a foil oval. After a Road to the Finals (1-27) subset, the cards are grouped alphabetically within team order. Rookie Cards of note in this set include Grant Hill, Juwan Howard, Eddie Jones, Jason Kidd and Glenn Robinson.
COMPLETE SET (135) 15.00 30.00
1 Mookie Blaylock RF .10 .25
2 Dominique Wilkins RF .20 .50
3 Alonzo Mourning RF .20 .50
4 Michael Jordan RF 1.50 4.00
5 Mark Price RF .15 .40
6 Jamal Mashburn RF .15 .40
7 Dikembe Mutombo RF .15 .40
8 Grant Hill RF .40 1.00
9 Latrell Sprewell RF .20 .50
10 Hakeem Olajuwon RF .20 .50
11 Reggie Miller RF .20 .50
12 Loy Vaught RF .10 .25
13 Nick Van Exel RF .15 .40
14 Glen Rice RF .15 .40
15 Glenn Robinson RF .15 .40
16 Isaiah Rider RF .15 .40
17 Kenny Anderson RF .12 .30
18 Patrick Ewing RF .20 .50
19 Shaquille O'Neal RF .40 1.00
20 Dana Barros RF .10 .25
21 Charles Barkley RF .25 .60
22 Clifford Robinson RF .10 .25
23 Mitch Richmond RF .15 .40
24 David Robinson RF .25 .60
25 Shawn Kemp RF .15 .40
26 Karl Malone RF .20 .50
27 Chris Webber RF .25 .60
28 Stacey Augmon .12 .30
29 Mookie Blaylock .10 .25
30 Grant Long .10 .25
31 Steve Smith .12 .30
32 Dee Brown .10 .25
33 Eric Montross RC .12 .30
34 Dino Radja .10 .25
35 Dominique Wilkins .20 .50
36 Muggsy Bogues .12 .30
37 Scott Burrell .10 .25
38 Larry Johnson .15 .40
39 Alonzo Mourning .20 .50
40 B.J. Armstrong .10 .25
41 Michael Jordan 3.00 8.00
42 Toni Kukoc .20 .50
43 Scottie Pippen .30 .75
44 Tyrone Hill .10 .25
45 Chris Mills .10 .25
46 Mark Price .15 .40
47 John Williams .10 .25
48 Jim Jackson .10 .25
49 Jason Kidd RC .75 2.00
50 Jamal Mashburn .15 .40
51 Roy Tarpley .10 .25
52 Mahmoud Abdul-Rauf .10 .25
53 Dikembe Mutombo .15 .40
54 Rodney Rogers .10 .25
55 Bryant Stith .10 .25
56 Joe Dumars .15 .40
57 Grant Hill RC .75 2.00
58 Lindsey Hunter .10 .25
59 Terry Mills .10 .25
60 Tim Hardaway .15 .40
61 Donyell Marshall RC .15 .40
62 Chris Mullin .15 .40
63 Latrell Sprewell .20 .50
64 Sam Cassell .15 .40
65 Clyde Drexler .20 .50
66 Vernon Maxwell .10 .25
67 Hakeem Olajuwon .20 .50
68 Dale Davis .10 .25
69 Mark Jackson .12 .30
70 Reggie Miller .20 .50
71 Rik Smits .12 .30
72 Terry Dehere .10 .25
73 Lamond Murray RC .15 .40
74 Pooh Richardson .10 .25
75 Loy Vaught .10 .25
76 Cedric Ceballos .10 .25
77 Vlade Divac .15 .40
78 Eddie Jones RC .50 1.25
79 Nick Van Exel .15 .40
80 Bimbo Coles .10 .25
81 Billy Owens .10 .25
82 Glen Rice .15 .40
83 Kevin Willis .10 .25
84 Vin Baker .15 .40
85 Marty Conlon .10 .25
86 Eric Murdock .10 .25
87 Glenn Robinson RC .30 .75
88 Tom Gugliotta .10 .25
89 Christian Laettner .12 .30
90 Isaiah Rider .15 .40
91 Doug West .10 .25
92 Kenny Anderson .12 .30
93 Benoit Benjamin .10 .25
94 Derrick Coleman .12 .30
95 Armon Gilliam .10 .25
96 Patrick Ewing .20 .50
97 Derek Harper .12 .30
98 Charles Oakley .12 .30
99 John Starks .12 .30
100 Nick Anderson .10 .25
101 Horace Grant .12 .30
102 Anfernee Hardaway .25 .60
103 Shaquille O'Neal .40 1.00
104 Dana Barros .10 .25
105 Shawn Bradley .10 .25
106 Clarence Weatherspoon .10 .25
107 Sharone Wright RC .12 .30
108 Charles Barkley .25 .60
109 Kevin Johnson .15 .40
110 Dan Majerle .15 .40
111 Wesley Person RC .15 .40
112 Terry Porter .10 .25
113 Clifford Robinson .10 .25
114 Rod Strickland .10 .25
115 Buck Williams .10 .25
116 Brian Grant RC .25 .60
117 Mitch Richmond .15 .40
118 Spud Webb .12 .30
119 Walt Williams .10 .25
120 Vinny Del Negro .10 .25
121 Sean Elliott .15 .40
122 David Robinson .25 .60
123 Dennis Rodman .30 .75
124 Kendall Gill .10 .25
125 Shawn Kemp .15 .40
126 Gary Payton .15 .40
127 Detlef Schrempf .15 .40
128 David Benoit .10 .25
129 Jeff Hornacek .12 .30
130 Karl Malone .20 .50
131 John Stockton .20 .50
132 Rex Chapman .10 .25
133 Calbert Cheaney .10 .25
134 Juwan Howard RC .25 .60
135 Chris Webber .25 .60

1994-95 SP Championship Die Cuts

COMPLETE SET (135) 30.00 60.00
*DIE CUT: 1X TO 2.5X BASE CARD HI

1994-95 SP Championship Future Playoff Heroes

Randomly inserted at a rate of 1 in every 40 packs, this 10-card standard-size set spotlights up-and-coming NBA stars who figure to be Playoff Heroes in the coming years. Unlike, the glossy regular issue cards, these inserts feature a throwback design element incorporating basic cardboard-style backgrounds against glossy color player action photos. The set is sequenced in alphabetical order.
COMPLETE SET (10) 15.00 40.00
STATED ODDS 1:40
*DIE CUTS: 2.5X TO 6X HI COLUMN
DIE CUTS: STATED ODDS 1:300
F1 Brian Grant 1.25 3.00
F2 Anfernee Hardaway 2.50 6.00
F3 Grant Hill 4.00 10.00
F4 Eddie Jones 2.50 6.00
F5 Jamal Mashburn 1.50 4.00
F6 Shaquille O'Neal 4.00 10.00
F7 Isaiah Rider 1.50 4.00
F8 Glenn Robinson 1.50 4.00
F9 Latrell Sprewell 2.00 5.00
F10 Chris Webber 2.50 6.00

1994-95 SP Championship Playoff Heroes

Randomly inserted at a rate of one in every 15 packs, this 10-card standard size set features active NBA Playoff performers. Unlike, the glossy regular issue cards, these inserts feature a throwback design element incorporating basic cardboard-style backgrounds against glossy color player action photos. A number of cards slipped through production with scuffed logos on front. In addition, some others also had "Future Playoff Heroes" logos rather than the regular "Playoff Heroes" logos. None of these variations trade for a premium. The set is sequenced in alphabetical order.
COMPLETE SET (10) 10.00 25.00
STATED ODDS 1:15
*DIE CUTS: 2X TO 5X HI COLUMN
DIE CUTS: STATED ODDS 1:225
P1 Charles Barkley 1.25 3.00
P2 Michael Jordan 6.00 15.00
P3 Shawn Kemp .75 2.00
P4 Moses Malone .75 2.00
P5 Reggie Miller 1.00 2.50
P6 Alonzo Mourning 1.00 2.50
P7 Dikembe Mutombo .75 2.00
P8 Hakeem Olajuwon 1.00 2.50
P9 Robert Parish .75 2.00
P10 John Stockton 1.00 2.50

1995-96 SP Championship

The 1995-96 SP Championship set was issued in one series totaling 146 cards. The 6-card packs retailed for $2.99 each. The set, issued in early-May, 1996 to retail outlets only, features full color action shots against an all-foil background with player name, team and a head shot along the front borders. The set is sequenced in alphabetical order by team and includes many of the top stars in the 1996 playoffs along with a special subset: Race for the Playoffs (118-146). Rookie Cards of note include Michael Finley, Kevin Garnett, Antonio McDyess, Jerry Stackhouse and Damon Stoudamire.
COMPLETE SET (146) 15.00 40.00
1 Stacey Augmon .20 .50
2 Mookie Blaylock .15 .40
3 Alan Henderson RC .25 .60
4 Steve Smith .20 .50
5 Dana Barros .15 .40
6 Dee Brown .15 .40
7 Eric Montross .15 .40
8 Dino Radja .15 .40
9 Eric Williams RC .25 .60
10 Kenny Anderson .20 .50
11 Larry Johnson .25 .60
12 Glen Rice .25 .60
13 George Zidek RC .20 .50
14 Toni Kukoc .25 .60
15 Scottie Pippen .40 1.00
16 Dennis Rodman .50 1.25
17 Michael Jordan 2.00 5.00
18 Terrell Brandon .15 .40
19 Danny Ferry .15 .40
20 Chris Mills .15 .40
21 Bobby Phills .15 .40
22 Jim Jackson .15 .40
23 Popeye Jones .15 .40
24 Jason Kidd .40 1.00
25 Jamal Mashburn .25 .60
26 Mahmoud Abdul-Rauf .15 .40
27 Dale Ellis .15 .40
28 Antonio McDyess RC .30 .75
29 Dikembe Mutombo .25 .60
30 Joe Dumars .25 .60
31 Grant Hill .40 1.00
32 Allan Houston .20 .50
33 Otis Thorpe .15 .40
34 Tim Hardaway .25 .60
35 Chris Mullin .25 .60
36 Latrell Sprewell .25 .60
37 Joe Smith RC .30 .75
38 Sam Cassell .25 .60
39 Clyde Drexler .30 .75
40 Robert Horry .20 .50
41 Hakeem Olajuwon .30 .75
42 Dale Davis .15 .40
43 Derrick McKey .15 .40
44 Reggie Miller .30 .75
45 Rik Smits .20 .50
46 Brent Barry RC .40 1.00
47 Lamond Murray .15 .40
48 Loy Vaught .15 .40
49 Brian Williams .15 .40
50 Cedric Ceballos .15 .40
51 Magic Johnson .60 1.50
52 Eddie Jones .25 .60
53 Nick Van Exel .25 .60
54 Sasha Danilovic RC .25 .60
55 Alonzo Mourning .30 .75
56 Billy Owens .15 .40
57 Kevin Willis .15 .40
58 Vin Baker .20 .50
59 Sherman Douglas .15 .40
60 Lee Mayberry .15 .40
61 Glenn Robinson .20 .50
62 Kevin Garnett RC 2.50 6.00
63 Tom Gugliotta .15 .40
64 Christian Laettner .20 .50
65 Isaiah Rider .25 .60
66 Chris Childs .15 .40
67 Kendall Gill .15 .40
68 Armon Gilliam .15 .40
69 Ed O'Bannon RC .20 .50
70 Patrick Ewing .30 .75
71 Derek Harper .20 .50
72 Charles Oakley .20 .50
73 John Starks .20 .50
74 Horace Grant .20 .50
75 Anfernee Hardaway .40 1.00
76 Shaquille O'Neal .60 1.50
77 Dennis Scott .15 .40
78 Derrick Coleman .20 .50
79 Trevor Ruffin .15 .40
80 Jerry Stackhouse RC .75 2.00
81 Clarence Weatherspoon .15 .40
82 Charles Barkley .40 1.00
83 Michael Finley RC .75 2.00
84 Kevin Johnson .25 .60
85 Danny Manning .20 .50
86 Randolph Childress RC .20 .50
87 Clifford Robinson .15 .40
88 Arvydas Sabonis RC .50 1.25
89 Rod Strickland .15 .40
90 Tyus Edney RC .25 .60
91 Brian Grant .20 .50
92 Mitch Richmond .25 .60
93 Walt Williams .15 .40
94 Sean Elliott .25 .60
95 Avery Johnson .20 .50
96 Chuck Person .20 .50
97 David Robinson .40 1.00
98 Shawn Kemp .25 .60
99 Gary Payton .25 .60
100 Sam Perkins .15 .40
101 Detlef Schrempf .25 .60
102 Ed Pinckney .15 .40
103 Tracy Murray .15 .40
104 Alvin Robertson .15 .40
105 Damon Stoudamire RC .60 1.50
106 Jeff Hornacek .20 .50
107 Karl Malone .30 .75
108 Chris Morris .15 .40
109 John Stockton .30 .75
110 Greg Anthony .15 .40
111 Blue Edwards .15 .40
112 Bryant Reeves RC .20 .50
113 Byron Scott .20 .50
114 Juwan Howard .25 .60
115 Gheorghe Muresan .15 .40
116 Rasheed Wallace RC .75 2.00
117 Chris Webber .30 .75
118 Mookie Blaylock RP .15 .40
119 Dana Barros RP .15 .40
120 Larry Johnson RP .25 .60
121 Michael Jordan RP 2.00 5.00
122 Terrell Brandon RP .15 .40
123 Jason Kidd RP .40 1.00
124 Mahmoud Abdul-Rauf RP .15 .40
125 Grant Hill RP .40 1.00
126 Latrell Sprewell RP .25 .60
127 Hakeem Olajuwon RP .30 .75
128 Reggie Miller RP .30 .75
129 Loy Vaught RP .15 .40
130 Magic Johnson RP .60 1.50
131 Alonzo Mourning RP .30 .75
132 Vin Baker RP .20 .50
133 Tom Gugliotta RP .15 .40
134 Ed O'Bannon RP .20 .50
135 Patrick Ewing RP .30 .75
136 Anfernee Hardaway RP .40 1.00
137 Jerry Stackhouse RP .50 1.25
138 Charles Barkley RP .40 1.00
139 Clifford Robinson RP .15 .40
140 Mitch Richmond RP .25 .60
141 David Robinson RP .40 1.00
142 Shawn Kemp RP .25 .60
143 Damon Stoudamire RP .40 1.00
144 John Stockton RP .30 .75
145 Bryant Reeves RP .12 .30
146 Juwan Howard RP .25 .60

1995-96 SP Championship Champions of the Court

Randomly inserted in packs at a rate of one in 6, cards from this 30-card set feature one top star from each NBA team and an additional card of Michael Jordan. In this special horizontal design, there is one action color photo on the left side and the same action photo in black and white on the right side. The main feature of the card is a cel photo featuring a headshot with a protective film covering the cell photo on the front of the card. When you turn the card over you see the same photo of the player. Each card is printed on special transparent chromium material. Unpeeled cards are priced below. Peeled cards are valued at about ten to twenty-five percent less.
COMPLETE SET (30) 30.00 80.00
STATED ODDS 1:6
*DIE CUTS: 2.5X TO 6X HI COLUMN
DIE CUTS: STATED ODDS 1:75
C1 Steve Smith .75 2.00
C2 Dino Radja .60 1.50
C3 Glen Rice 1.00 2.50
C4 Scottie Pippen 1.50 4.00
C5 Terrell Brandon .60 1.50
C6 Jason Kidd 1.50 4.00
C7 Dikembe Mutombo 1.00 2.50
C8 Grant Hill 1.50 4.00
C9 Joe Smith .60 1.50
C10 Hakeem Olajuwon 1.25 3.00
C11 Reggie Miller 1.25 3.00
C12 Loy Vaught .60 1.50
C13 Magic Johnson 2.50 6.00
C14 Alonzo Mourning 1.25 3.00
C15 Vin Baker .75 2.00
C16 Kevin Garnett 4.00 10.00
C17 Ed O'Bannon .40 1.00
C18 Patrick Ewing 1.25 3.00
C19 Shaquille O'Neal 2.50 6.00
C20 Jerry Stackhouse 1.50 4.00
C21 Charles Barkley 1.50 4.00
C22 Clifford Robinson .60 1.50
C23 Mitch Richmond 1.00 2.50
C24 David Robinson 1.50 4.00
C25 Shawn Kemp 1.00 2.50
C26 Damon Stoudamire 1.25 3.00
C27 John Stockton 1.25 3.00
C28 Bryant Reeves .40 1.00
C29 Juwan Howard 1.00 2.50
C30 Michael Jordan 8.00 20.00

1995-96 SP Championship Championship Shots

Inserted at a rate of one per magazine and Wal-Mart pack, as well as randomly in one in every three regular retail packs, this 20-card set features intense, closeup shots of many of the top NBA stars. Despite their status as inserts, these cards are actually easier to pull from packs than regular-issue cards. The design is highlighted by a horizontal, silver-foil, saw-tooth die cut element on the side border.
COMPLETE SET (20) 10.00 20.00
STATED ODDS 1:3
ONE PER SPECIAL RETAIL PACK
*GOLD: 3X TO 8X HI COLUMN
GOLD: STATED ODDS 1:62
S1 Antonio McDyess .30 .75
S2 Nick Van Exel .50 1.25
S3 Michael Finley .75 2.00
S4 Anfernee Hardaway .75 2.00
S5 Latrell Sprewell .50 1.25
S6 Brian Grant .40 1.00
S7 Juwan Howard .50 1.25
S8 Ed O'Bannon .20 .50
S9 Kevin Garnett 2.00 5.00
S10 Charles Barkley .75 2.00
S11 Joe Smith .30 .75
S12 Patrick Ewing .60 1.50
S13 Brent Barry .40 1.00
S14 Dennis Rodman 1.00 2.50
S15 Jerry Stackhouse .75 2.00
S16 Michael Jordan 4.00 10.00
S17 Jalen Rose .60 1.50
S18 Jamal Mashburn .50 1.25
S19 Theo Ratliff .40 1.00
S20 Shaquille O'Neal 1.25 3.00

1995-96 SP Championship Jordan Collection

Randomly inserted in packs at a rate of one in 29, this 4-card set completes the run of Jordan cards across Upper Deck's 1995-96 brands.
COMPLETE SET (4) 12.00 30.00
COMMON CARD (JC21-JC24) 4.00 10.00
RANDOM INSERTS IN PACKS

2000-01 SP Game Floor

The 2000-01 SP Game Floor product was released in May, 2001 and featured a 100-card base set that was broken into tiers as follows: Base Veterans (1-60), and Rookies (61-100) that were serial numbered to 300. Each pack contained three cards, and carried a suggested retail price of $19.99 per pack.
61-100 PRINT RUN 300 SERIAL #'d SETS
1 Jason Terry 1.00 2.50
2 Toni Kukoc 1.00 2.50
3 Antoine Walker .75 2.00
4 Paul Pierce 1.00 2.50
5 Jamal Mashburn .75 2.00
6 Baron Davis 1.00 2.50
7 Elton Brand 1.00 2.50
8 Ron Mercer .60 1.50
9 Andre Miller .75 2.00
10 Lamond Murray .60 1.50
11 Michael Finley 1.00 2.50
12 Dirk Nowitzki 1.50 4.00
13 Antonio McDyess .75 2.00
14 Nick Van Exel .75 2.00
15 Jerry Stackhouse .75 2.00
16 Joe Smith .75 2.00
17 Antawn Jamison 1.00 2.50
18 Larry Hughes .75 2.00
19 Steve Francis .75 2.00
20 Maurice Taylor .60 1.50
21 Jalen Rose .75 2.00
22 Reggie Miller 1.00 2.50
23 Lamar Odom .75 2.00
24 Corey Maggette .75 2.00
25 Kobe Bryant 6.00 15.00
26 Shaquille O'Neal 2.50 6.00
27 Horace Grant .75 2.00
28 Eddie Jones 1.00 2.50
29 Tim Hardaway 1.00 2.50
30 Glenn Robinson .75 2.00
31 Ray Allen 1.00 2.50
32 Kevin Garnett 1.50 4.00
33 Terrell Brandon .60 1.50
34 Wally Szczerbiak .75 2.00
35 Stephon Marbury .75 2.00
36 Keith Van Horn .75 2.00
37 Latrell Sprewell .75 2.00
38 Allan Houston .75 2.00
39 Tracy McGrady 1.50 4.00
40 Darrell Armstrong .60 1.50
41 Allen Iverson 2.00 5.00
42 Dikembe Mutombo 1.00 2.50
43 Jason Kidd 1.50 4.00
44 Shawn Marion .75 2.00
45 Rasheed Wallace 1.00 2.50
46 Damon Stoudamire .75 2.00
47 Chris Webber 1.00 2.50
48 Jason Williams 1.00 2.50
49 Tim Duncan 2.00 5.00
50 David Robinson 1.50 4.00
51 Gary Payton 1.00 2.50
52 Rashard Lewis 1.00 2.50
53 Vince Carter 2.00 5.00
54 Charles Oakley .75 2.00
55 Karl Malone 1.25 3.00
56 John Stockton 1.25 3.00
57 Shareef Abdur-Rahim .75 2.00
58 Mike Bibby 1.00 2.50
59 Richard Hamilton .75 2.00
60 Mitch Richmond .75 2.00
61 Kenyon Martin RC 6.00 15.00
62 Marc Jackson RC 2.00 5.00
63 Darius Miles RC 2.50 6.00
64 Morris Peterson RC 2.50 6.00
65 Mike Miller RC 4.00 10.00
66 Quentin Richardson RC 2.50 6.00
67 DerMarr Johnson RC 2.00 5.00
68 Chris Mihm RC 2.00 5.00
69 Jamal Crawford RC 6.00 15.00
70 Joel Przybilla RC 2.00 5.00
71 Keyon Dooling RC 2.50 6.00
72 Jerome Moiso RC 1.50 4.00
73 Mike Penberthy RC 2.50 6.00
74 Courtney Alexander RC 2.00 5.00
75 Mateen Cleaves RC 2.00 5.00
76 Wang Zhizhi RC 6.00 15.00
77 Hedo Turkoglu RC 4.00 10.00
78 Desmond Mason RC 3.00 8.00
79 Marcus Fizer RC 2.50 6.00
80 Jamaal Magloire RC 2.50 6.00
81 Stromile Swift RC 2.50 6.00
82 DeShawn Stevenson RC 2.50 6.00
83 Stephen Jackson RC 4.00 10.00
84 Erick Barkley RC 1.50 4.00
85 Mark Madsen RC 2.50 6.00
86 Dan Langhi RC 1.50 4.00
87 Hanno Mottola RC 1.50 4.00
88 Paul McPherson RC 1.50 4.00
89 Eddie House RC 2.00 5.00
90 Chris Porter RC 1.50 4.00
91 Jason Collier RC 2.50 6.00
92 Speedy Claxton RC 2.50 6.00
93 Ruben Wolkowyski RC 1.50 4.00
94 A.J. Guyton RC 1.50 4.00
95 Donnell Harvey RC 2.00 5.00
96 Ira Newble RC 2.00 5.00
97 Lee Nailon 2.50 6.00
98 Pepe Sanchez RC 2.50 6.00
99 Eduardo Najera RC 2.50 6.00
100 David Vanterpool RC 2.50 6.00

2000-01 SP Game Floor Authentic Fabric/Floor Combos

Randomly inserted into packs at one in 10, this 14-card insert features a swatch of both game-used jersey and floor. Card backs carry the player's initials followed by the letter "C". A gold version sequentially numbered to 25 was also issued.

STATED ODDS 1:10
*GOLD: 2.5X TO 6X HI
GOLD PRINT RUN 25 SER.#'d SETS
AIC Allen Iverson 6.00 15.00
DMC Darius Miles 3.00 8.00
JKC Jason Kidd 5.00 12.00
JMC Jamal Mashburn 2.50 6.00
KAC Karl Malone 4.00 10.00
KBC Kobe Bryant 12.00 30.00
KGC Kevin Garnett 5.00 12.00
MAC Marc Jackson 2.50 6.00
MDC Antonio McDyess 2.50 6.00
PPC Paul Pierce 3.00 8.00
RLC Rashard Lewis 3.00 8.00
SMC Stephon Marbury 2.50 6.00
SOC Shaquille O'Neal 8.00 20.00
TMC Tracy McGrady 5.00 12.00

2000-01 SP Game Floor Authentic Floor

Randomly inserted into packs at one per pack, this 60-card insert features a swatch of actual game-used floor. Card backs carry the player's initials as numbering.

STATED ODDS 1:1
AH Allan Houston AS 2.00 5.00
AH2 Allan Houston 2.00 5.00
AI Allen Iverson 5.00 12.00
AM Andre Miller 2.00 5.00
BD Baron Davis 2.50 6.00
CA Courtney Alexander 2.00 5.00
CP Chris Porter 1.50 4.00
CW Chris Webber 2.50 6.00
DE Desmond Mason 3.00 8.00
DJ DerMarr Johnson 2.00 5.00
DM Darius Miles 2.50 6.00
DS DeShawn Stevenson 2.50 6.00
DV David Robinson 4.00 10.00
EJ Eddie Jones 2.50 6.00
FI Marcus Fizer 2.50 6.00
GP Gary Payton 2.50 6.00
GR Glenn Robinson 2.00 5.00
JK Jason Kidd 4.00 10.00
JM Jamaal Magloire 2.50 6.00
JP Joel Przybilla 2.00 5.00
JS Jerry Stackhouse 2.00 5.00
JT Jason Terry 2.50 6.00
JW Jason Williams 2.50 6.00
KA Karl Malone 3.00 8.00
KB Kobe Bryant AS 10.00 25.00
KB2 Kobe Bryant 10.00 25.00
KE Khalid El-Amin 1.50 4.00
KG Kevin Garnett AS 4.00 10.00
KG2 Kevin Garnett 4.00 10.00
KM Kenyon Martin 6.00 15.00
LS Latrell Sprewell AS 2.00 5.00
LS2 Latrell Sprewell 2.00 5.00
MA Marc Jackson 2.00 5.00
MC Mateen Cleaves 2.00 5.00
MD Antonio McDyess AS 2.00 5.00
MD2 Antonio McDyess 2.00 5.00
MF Michael Finley 2.50 6.00
MJ Michael Jordan 20.00 50.00
MM Mike Miller 4.00 10.00
MP Morris Peterson 2.50 6.00
MT Dikembe Mutombo 2.50 6.00
PP Paul Pierce 2.50 6.00
PS Peja Stojakovic 2.50 6.00
QR Quentin Richardson 2.50 6.00
RA Ray Allen 2.50 6.00
RA2 Ray Allen AS 2.50 6.00
RL Rashard Lewis 2.50 6.00
RW Rasheed Wallace AS 2.50 6.00
RW2 Rasheed Wallace 2.50 6.00
SA Shareef Abdur-Rahim 2.00 5.00
SF Steve Francis 2.00 5.00
SH Shawn Marion 2.00 5.00
SJ Stephen Jackson 4.00 10.00
SM Stephon Marbury AS 2.00 5.00
SM2 Stephon Marbury 2.00 5.00
SO Shaquille O'Neal 6.00 15.00
SP Scottie Pippen 4.00 10.00
SS Stromile Swift 2.50 6.00
TM Tracy McGrady 4.00 10.00
WS Wally Szczerbiak 2.00 5.00

2000-01 SP Game Floor Authentic Floor Autographs

Randomly inserted into packs, this 17-card insert features a swatch of actual game-used floor plus an authentic autograph from the depicted player. Card backs carry the player's initials followed by the letter "A" as numbering. Please note that there were only 200 of each of these cards produced (with exception to Bryant, Jordan, and Garnett).

STATED PRINT RUN 200 SERIAL #'d SETS
CAA Courtney Alexander/200 4.00 10.00
DJA DerMarr Johnson/200 4.00 10.00
DMA Darius Miles/200 5.00 12.00
DSA DeShawn Stevenson/200 5.00 12.00
FIA Marcus Fizer/200 5.00 12.00
JPA Joel Przybilla/200 4.00 10.00
JSA Jerry Stackhouse/200 8.00 20.00
KGA Kevin Garnett/21 150.00 300.00
KMA Kenyon Martin/200 8.00 20.00
MAA Marc Jackson/200 4.00 10.00
MJA Michael Jordan/23 400.00 800.00
MMA Mike Miller/200 8.00 20.00
MPA Morris Peterson/200 5.00 12.00
SFA Steve Francis/200 12.00 30.00
SJA Stephen Jackson/200 8.00 20.00
SSA Stromile Swift/200 5.00 12.00

2000-01 SP Game Floor Authentic Floor Combos

Randomly inserted into packs at one in ten, this 30-card insert features two swatches of game-used floor. Card backs carry a "C" prefix. A gold version sequentially numbered to 100 was also issued.

STATED ODDS 1:10
*GOLD: .75X TO 2X BASE COMBO HI
GOLD PRINT RUN 100 SER.#'d SETS
C1 A.Iverson/S.O'Neal 10.00 25.00
C2 M.Jackson/S.Jackson 4.00 10.00
C3 S.Marbury/S.Francis 5.00 12.00
C4 C.Webber/J.Williams 5.00 12.00
C5 D.Miles/M.Jackson 4.00 10.00
C6 M.Jordan/L.Bird 60.00 120.00
C7 K.Martin/C.Webber 5.00 12.00
C8 K.Martin/D.Johnson 4.00 10.00
C9 K.Martin/M.Jackson 4.00 10.00
C10 K.Martin/S.Jackson 4.00 10.00
C11 K.Garnett/C.Webber 6.00 15.00
C12 K.Garnett/T.McGrady 6.00 15.00
C13 K.Bryant/A.Iverson 10.00 25.00
C14 K.Bryant/C.Webber 10.00 25.00
C15 K.Bryant/D.Miles 6.00 15.00
C16 K.Bryant/J.Kidd 10.00 25.00
C17 M.Jordan/K.Malone 50.00 120.00
C18 K.Malone/J.Stockton 15.00 40.00
C19 K.Bryant/K.Martin 8.00 20.00
C20 K.Bryant/K.Garnett 10.00 25.00
C21 K.Bryant/K.Garnett 10.00 25.00
C22 K.Bryant/L.Bird 50.00 100.00
C23 J.Williams/P.Stojakovic 5.00 12.00
C24 K.Bryant/M.Jordan 40.00 100.00
C25 K.Bryant/S.O'Neal 12.00 30.00
C26 K.Bryant/S.Francis 8.00 20.00
C27 K.Bryant/T.McGrady 8.00 20.00
C28 J.Kidd/S.Marion 8.00 20.00
C29 M.Cleaves/M.Peterson 4.00 10.00
C30 K.Garnett/R.Wallace 5.00 12.00

2002-03 SP Game Used

Released in September 2002, SP Game Used boasts a 144-card set with several different components. Card numbers 1-102 feature veteran players and place full color action photos agains a white and blue or gray background on the side of the card where the player picture is. Several jersey cards are mixed in with these 102 cards. Jersey cards are denoted by "JSY" in the price guide. Overall odds point to at least one Jersey and or Autographed card per pack. Rookie cards share most design aspects except the blue or gray background is centered with two blocks of color on either side set to match the featured player's team colors. All rookie cards are sequentially numbered to 900. SP Game Used was packaged in six pack boxes where packs contained three cards and carried a suggested retail price of $29.99.

OVERALL ODDS JSY/AU's 1:1
103-144 PRINT RUN 900 SER.#'d SETS
1 Shareef Abdur-Rahim JSY 2.50 6.00
2 DerMarr Johnson JSY 2.00 5.00
3 Jason Terry JSY 2.50 6.00
4 Antoine Walker JSY 2.50 6.00
5 Paul Pierce SP JSY 12.50 30.00
6 Kedrick Brown JSY 2.00 5.00
7 Tony Battie 1.25 3.00
8 Jamal Mashburn JSY 2.50 6.00
9 Baron Davis 1.50 4.00
10 David Wesley 1.25 3.00
11 Jalen Rose 1.50 4.00
12 Eddy Curry JSY 2.00 5.00
13 Tyson Chandler JSY 3.00 8.00
14 Marcus Fizer JSY 2.00 5.00
15 Lamond Murray 1.25 3.00
16 Andre Miller JSY 2.50 6.00
17 Chris Mihm JSY 2.00 5.00
18 Ricky Davis 1.50 4.00
19 Dirk Nowitzki 3.00 8.00
20 Michael Finley 2.00 5.00
21 Steve Nash 2.50 6.00
22 Nick Van Exel 1.50 4.00
23 Antonio McDyess JSY 2.50 6.00
24 Juwan Howard 1.50 4.00
25 James Posey 1.25 3.00
26 Jerry Stackhouse 1.50 4.00
27 Clifford Robinson 1.25 3.00
28 Ben Wallace 1.50 4.00
29 Antawn Jamison 2.00 5.00
30 Jason Richardson SP JSY 3.00 8.00
31 Gilbert Arenas 2.00 5.00
32 Steve Francis 1.50 4.00
33 Cuttino Mobley 1.25 3.00
34 Eddie Griffin JSY 2.00 5.00
35 Reggie Miller JSY 3.00 8.00
36 Jermaine O'Neal 1.50 4.00
37 Jamaal Tinsley JSY 2.00 5.00
38 Elton Brand 2.00 5.00
39 Darius Miles JSY 2.00 5.00
40 Lamar Odom JSY 2.50 6.00
41 Corey Maggette JSY 2.50 6.00
42 Kobe Bryant SP JSY 10.00 25.00
43 Shaquille O'Neal 5.00 12.00
44 Derek Fisher 1.50 4.00
45 Devean George 1.25 3.00
46 Pau Gasol 2.50 6.00
47 Jason Williams 1.50 4.00
48 Shane Battier 2.00 5.00
49 Stromile Swift 1.25 3.00
50 Alonzo Mourning 2.50 6.00
51 Eddie Jones 1.50 4.00
52 Brian Grant 1.25 3.00
53 Ray Allen 2.00 5.00
54 Glenn Robinson 1.50 4.00
55 Sam Cassell 1.50 4.00
56 Kevin Garnett SP JSY 12.50 30.00
57 Wally Szczerbiak JSY 2.50 6.00
58 Terrell Brandon JSY 2.00 5.00
59 Chauncey Billups JSY 3.00 8.00
60 Jason Kidd SP JSY 12.50 30.00
61 Richard Jefferson 2.00 5.00
62 Kenyon Martin JSY 2.50 6.00
63 Brandon Armstrong JSY 2.00 5.00
64 Keith Van Horn 1.50 4.00
65 Allan Houston 1.50 4.00
66 Latrell Sprewell 1.50 4.00
67 Kurt Thomas 1.25 3.00
68 Tracy McGrady 3.00 8.00
69 Mike Miller JSY 2.50 6.00
70 Darrell Armstrong JSY 2.00 5.00
71 Allen Iverson JSY 5.00 12.00
72 Dikembe Mutombo JSY 3.00 8.00
73 Aaron McKie 1.25 3.00
74 Stephon Marbury 1.50 4.00
75 Shawn Marion 1.50 4.00
76 Joe Johnson JSY 2.50 6.00
77 Anfernee Hardaway 3.00 8.00
78 Rasheed Wallace 2.00 5.00
79 Damon Stoudamire 1.50 4.00
80 Scottie Pippen 3.00 8.00
81 Chris Webber 2.00 5.00
82 Peja Stojakovic 2.00 5.00
83 Mike Bibby JSY 3.00 8.00
84 Gerald Wallace JSY 2.50 6.00
85 Tim Duncan 4.00 10.00
86 David Robinson 3.00 8.00
87 Tony Parker JSY 4.00 10.00
88 Gary Payton 2.00 5.00
89 Rashard Lewis 2.00 5.00
90 Desmond Mason 1.50 4.00
91 V.Radmanovic JSY 2.00 5.00
92 Morris Peterson 1.25 3.00
93 Antonio Davis 1.25 3.00
94 Vince Carter 3.00 8.00
95 Karl Malone 2.50 6.00
96 John Stockton JSY 4.00 10.00
97 Donyell Marshall 1.25 3.00
98 Andrei Kirilenko 2.00 5.00
99 Richard Hamilton 1.50 4.00
100 Michael Jordan SP JSY 40.00 100.00
101 Courtney Alexander JSY 2.00 5.00
102 Kwame Brown JSY 2.00 5.00
103 Jay Williams RC 4.00 10.00
104 Yao Ming RC 8.00 20.00
105 Drew Gooden RC 4.00 10.00
106 DaJuan Wagner RC 3.00 8.00
107 Curtis Borchardt RC 2.50 6.00
108 Amare Stoudemire RC 5.00 12.00
109 Caron Butler RC 4.00 10.00
110 Jared Jeffries RC 3.00 8.00
111 Chris Wilcox RC 3.00 8.00
112 Qyntel Woods RC 3.00 8.00
113 Casey Jacobsen RC 3.00 8.00
114 Melvin Ely RC 3.00 8.00
115 Kareem Rush RC 3.00 8.00
116 Mike Dunleavy RC 4.00 10.00
117 Dan Dickau RC 3.00 8.00
118 Juan Dixon RC 4.00 10.00
119 Sam Clancy RC 3.00 8.00
120 Tayshaun Prince RC 5.00 12.00
121 Dan Gadzuric RC 3.00 8.00
122 Chris Jefferies RC 2.50 6.00
123 Steve Logan RC 4.00 10.00
124 Vincent Yarbrough RC 2.50 6.00
125 Fred Jones RC 3.00 8.00
126 Efthimios Rentzias RC 2.50 6.00
127 Nene Hilario RC 4.00 10.00
128 Rod Grizzard RC 2.50 6.00
129 Matt Barnes RC 5.00 12.00
130 Nikoloz Tskitishvili RC 2.50 6.00
131 Bostjan Nachbar RC 3.00 8.00
132 Marcus Haislip RC 3.00 8.00
133 Jamal Sampson RC 4.00 10.00
134 Frank Williams RC 2.50 6.00
135 Tito Maddox RC 2.50 6.00
136 Carlos Boozer RC 4.00 10.00
137 Jiri Welsch RC 3.00 8.00
138 John Salmons RC 4.00 10.00
139 Predrag Savovic RC 3.00 8.00
140 Marko Jaric 4.00 10.00
141 Robert Archibald RC 2.50 6.00
142 Manu Ginobili RC 10.00 25.00
143 Chris Owens RC 2.50 6.00
144 Ryan Humphrey RC 3.00 8.00

2002-03 SP Game Used Autographed Jerseys

Randomly inserted in packs, this 24-card set parallels the base SP Game Used set design enhanced with a square swatch of game jersey somewhere on the bottom quarter of the card and authentic player autographs. Each card is sequentially numbered to 100.

PRINT RUN 100 SERIAL #'D SETS
1 Shareef Abdur-Rahim 8.00 20.00
2 DerMarr Johnson 5.00 12.00
4 Antoine Walker 10.00 25.00
6 Kedrick Brown 5.00 12.00
12 Eddy Curry 5.00 12.00
13 Tyson Chandler 10.00 25.00
14 Marcus Fizer 8.00 20.00
16 Andre Miller 10.00 25.00
34 Eddie Griffin 8.00 20.00
39 Darius Miles 5.00 12.00
40 Lamar Odom 6.00 15.00
41 Corey Maggette 8.00 20.00
57 Wally Szczerbiak 10.00 25.00
58 Terrell Brandon 5.00 12.00
61 Richard Jefferson 8.00 20.00
62 Kenyon Martin 15.00 40.00
63 Brandon Armstrong 5.00 12.00
69 Mike Miller 12.00 30.00
84 Gerald Wallace 12.00 30.00
87 Tony Parker 15.00 40.00
91 Vladimir Radmanovic 8.00 20.00
101 Courtney Alexander 5.00 12.00
102 Kwame Brown 5.00 12.00

2002-03 SP Game Used Autographed SP Jerseys

PRINT RUN 25 SERIAL #'D SETS
42 Kobe Bryant 200.00 400.00
56 Kevin Garnett 50.00 120.00
60 Jason Kidd 40.00 100.00
100 Michael Jordan 500.00 800.00

2002-03 SP Game Used Rookies Gold

Randomly inserted in packs, this 42-card set parallels the base SP Game Used set enhanced with gold backgrounds and gold SP Game Used logos. Each card is sequentially numbered to 50.

*GOLD: 1.25X TO 3X BASE CARD HI
PRINT RUN 50 SER.#'d SETS

2002-03 SP Game Used All-Star Apparel

Randomly inserted in packs at the combined odds of one in one for all jersey and autograph sets, this 24-card set places a small portrait style photograph in the upper right hand corner tinted in a color to match the player's team below which is a square swatch of game worn jersey on a silver/blue background.

STATED OVERALL JSY ODDS 1:1
*GOLD: .75X TO 2X HI
GOLD: STATED PRINT RUN 100 SETS
AKAS Andrei Kirilenko 2.50 6.00
AMAS Alonzo Mourning 3.00 8.00
BHAS Brendan Haywood 1.50 4.00
CMAS Chris Mihm 1.50 4.00
DMAS Desmond Mason 2.00 5.00
DNAS Dirk Nowitzki 4.00 10.00
GIAS Gilbert Arenas 2.50 6.00
GPAS Gary Payton 2.50 6.00
GWAS Gerald Wallace 2.00 5.00
KBAS Kobe Bryant 10.00 25.00
KDAS Jason Kidd 4.00 10.00
KMAS Kenyon Martin 2.00 5.00
LNAS Lee Nailon 1.50 4.00
MFAS Marcus Fizer 1.50 4.00
MGAS Magic Johnson 6.00 15.00
MJAS Michael Jordan 30.00 60.00
MMAS Mike Miller 2.00 5.00
PGAS Pau Gasol 3.00 8.00
QRAS Quentin Richardson 2.00 5.00
SFAS Steve Francis 2.00 5.00
SNAS Steve Nash 3.00 8.00
SSAS Steve Smith 2.00 5.00
WSAS Wally Szczerbiak 2.00 5.00
ZRAS Zelijko Rebraca 1.50 4.00

2002-03 SP Game Used Authentic Fabrics Dual

Randomly inserted in packs, this 28-card set showcases two players with small full color photos centered at the top and two small swatchs of game used memorabilia along the bottom. Each card is sequentially numbered to 100.

PRINT RUN 100 SERIAL #'d SETS
UNPRICED QUAD PRINT RUN 10 SETS
UNPRICED DUAL AU PRINT RUN 10 SETS
AMCMJ A.Miller/C.Mihm 6.00 15.00
BDJMJ B.Davis/J.Mashburn 6.00 15.00
CMLOJ C.Maggette/L.Odom 6.00 15.00
CWPSJ C.Webber/P.Stojakovic 10.00 25.00
DNMFJ D.Nowitzki/M.Finley 15.00 40.00
DNSNJ D.Nowitzki/S.Nash 15.00 40.00
DRTPJ D.Robinson/T.Parker 10.00 25.00
EBKMJ E.Brand/K.Malone 12.50 30.00
ECTCJ E.Curry/T.Chandler 6.00 15.00
JPJHJ J.Posey/J.Howard 6.00 15.00
JTTPJ J.Tinsley/T.Parker 10.00 25.00
KBAIJ K.Bryant/A.Iverson 30.00 80.00
KBKGJ K.Bryant/K.Garnett 20.00 50.00
KGTBJ K.Garnett/T.Brandon 8.00 20.00
KGWSJ K.Garnett/W.Szczerbiak 8.00 20.00
KMJSJ K.Malone/J.Stockton 8.00 20.00
KMKVJ K.Martin/K.Van Horn 6.00 15.00
KWCAJ K.Brown/C.Alexander 6.00 15.00
MFTHJ M.Fizer/T.Hassell 6.00 15.00
MJKBJ M.Jordan/K.Bryant 60.00 150.00
MJMGJ M.Jordan/M.Johnson 50.00 120.00
PPAWJ P.Pierce/A.Walker 6.00 15.00
RAGRJ R.Allen/G.Robinson 12.50 30.00
RMJOJ R.Miller/J.O'Neal 15.00 40.00
RWDSJ R.Wallace/D.Stoudamire 12.50 30.00
SADJJ S.Abdur-Rahim/D.Johnson 6.00 15.00
SMSMJ S.Marbury/S.Marion 10.00 25.00
TMMMJ T.McGrady/M.Miller 12.50 30.00

2002-03 SP Game Used Authentic Fabrics Triple

Randomly seeded in packs, this eight card set features three players with three pictures centered along the top of the card and three swatches of game used memorabilia along the bottom. Note: The cards are not numbered numerically on the card backs. They're listed this way to fit in our publications-ie: #1 is actually AW/PP/KA-J and so on. Each card is sequentially numbered to 25.

PRINT RUN 25 SERIAL #'d SETS
1 Walker/Pierce/Anderson 30.00 80.00
2 Webber/Stojakovic/Bibby 30.00 80.00
3 Terry/Abdur-Rahim/Johnson 20.00 50.00
4 Bryant/Fox/Horry 100.00 200.00
5 Malone/Stockton/Kirilenko 25.00 60.00
6 McDyess/Howard/Posey 20.00 50.00
7 Jordan/Bryant/Garnett 100.00 200.00
8 Marbury/Marion/Hardaway 50.00 120.00

2002-03 SP Game Used Authentic Patches

Inserted in packs, this 18-card set places a blue-tone portrait photo of the featured player on the left side of the card and a multi-color patch swatch in the upper right hand corner. A stripe of color runs from the patch down to the bottom of the card in the showcased team's colors. Each card is sequentially numbered to 100.

PRINT RUN 100 SERIAL #'d SETS
UNPRICED TRIPLE PRINT RUN 10 SETS
AWP Antoine Walker 10.00 25.00
BDP Baron Davis 10.00 25.00
CMP Corey Maggette 10.00 25.00
DJP DerMarr Johnson 8.00 20.00
DMP Darius Miles 8.00 20.00
GWP Gerald Wallace 10.00 25.00
JRP Jason Richardson 12.00 30.00
KBP Kobe Bryant 75.00 200.00
KGP Kevin Garnett 30.00 80.00
KWP Kwame Brown 8.00 20.00
LSP Latrell Sprewell 15.00 40.00
MJP Michael Jordan 100.00 200.00
PPP Paul Pierce 12.00 30.00
QRP Quentin Richardson 10.00 25.00
SAP Shareef Abdur-Rahim 10.00 25.00
TBP Terrell Brandon 8.00 20.00
TPP Tony Parker 15.00 40.00
WSP Wally Szczerbiak 10.00 25.00

2002-03 SP Game Used Autographed Authentic Patches

Randomly inserted in packs, this 15-card set parallels the design of the base Authentic Patches insert enhanced with authentic player autographs and sequential numbering to 50.

PRINT RUN 50 SERIAL #'d SETS
UNPRICED DUAL PRINT RUN 5 SETS
AWAP Antoine Walker 30.00 80.00
CMAP Corey Maggette 15.00 40.00
DJAP DerMarr Johnson 15.00 40.00
DMAP Darius Miles 15.00 40.00
GWAP Gerald Wallace 30.00 80.00
KBAP Kobe Bryant 400.00 800.00
KGAP Kevin Garnett 125.00 250.00
KWAP Kwame Brown 15.00 40.00
MJAP Michael Jordan 600.00 1200.00
PPAP Paul Pierce 40.00 100.00
QRAP Quentin Richardson 15.00 40.00
TBAP Terrell Brandon 15.00 40.00
TPAP Tony Parker 40.00 100.00
WSAP Wally Szczerbiak 15.00 40.00

2002-03 SP Game Used Dual Authentic Patches

Randomly seeded in packs, this six card set features a horizontal card design with a patch swatch in the upper left hand corner and lower right hand corner next to which is a streached black and gray-scale portrait of each player. Cards are sequentially numbered to 25.

PRINT RUN 25 SERIAL #'d SETS
KBJKP K.Bryant/J.Kidd 100.00 250.00
KBJRP K.Bryant/J.Richardson 100.00 250.00
KBKGP K.Bryant/K.Garnett 125.00 300.00
KBMGP K.Bryant/M.Johnson 100.00 200.00
MJKBP M.Jordan/K.Bryant 250.00 500.00
MJMGP M.Jordan/M.Johnson 300.00 500.00

2002-03 SP Game Used Extra SIGnificance

Randomly inserted in packs, this 10-card set is divided in half with a color photo and autograph of each of the featured players, one on the top and one on the bottom. Each card is sequentially numbered to 25. A Gold version sequentially numbered to 5 was also released.

PRINT RUN 25 SERIAL #'D SETS
DMLO D.Miles/L.Odom 25.00 60.00
JKKM J.Kidd/K.Martin 40.00 100.00
JRJT J.Richardson/J.Tinsley 25.00 60.00
KBJK K.Bryant/J.Kidd 150.00 300.00
KBJR K.Bryant/J.Richardson 100.00 250.00
KBKG K.Bryant/K.Garnett 200.00 400.00
KBMA K.Bryant/M.Johnson 300.00 600.00
KGTC K.Garnett/T.Chandler 40.00 100.00
MJKB M.Jordan/K.Bryant 800.00 1200.00
MJMA M.Jordan/M.Johnson 400.00 800.00

2002-03 SP Game Used SIGnificance

Randomly seeded in packs, this 29-card set looks very similar to the base SP Game Used cards with the word, SIGnificance in the upper right hand corner and an authentic player autograph in the lower right hand corner. A Gold version sequentially numbered to 50 was also issued.

STATED PRINT RUN 100 SERIAL #'d SETS
*GOLD: .75X TO 2X SIGNIFICANCE HI
GOLD PRINT RUN 50 SER.#'d SETS
AW Antoine Walker 6.00 15.00
CM Corey Maggette 4.00 10.00
DJ DerMarr Johnson 4.00 10.00
DS DeShawn Stevenson 4.00 10.00
EG Eddie Griffin 4.00 10.00
HM Hanno Mottola 4.00 10.00
JA Jamaal Magloire 4.00 10.00
JS Jerry Stackhouse 6.00 15.00
JT Jamaal Tinsley 4.00 10.00
KE Kedrick Brown 4.00 10.00
KM Kenyon Martin 6.00 15.00
KW Kwame Brown 4.00 10.00
LH Larry Hughes 4.00 10.00
LM Lamond Murray 4.00 10.00
LW Loren Woods 4.00 10.00
MB Michael Bradley 4.00 10.00
MF Marcus Fizer 4.00 10.00
MK Mark Madsen 4.00 10.00
MM Mike Miller 6.00 15.00
MO Terence Morris 4.00 10.00
MP Morris Peterson 4.00 10.00
QR Quentin Richardson 4.00 10.00
RJ Richard Jefferson 5.00 12.00
RM Ron Mercer 4.00 10.00
RW Rodney White 4.00 10.00
SD Samuel Dalembert 4.00 10.00
TC Tyson Chandler 8.00 20.00
TM Troy Murphy 4.00 10.00
WS Wally Szczerbiak 4.00 10.00

2002-03 SP Game Used Special SIGnificance

Seeded in packs, this 10-card set looks similar to the SIGnificance set with the words, "Special SIGnificance" in a black box in the upper right hand corner with an authentic player autograph in the lower right hand corner. Each card is sequentially numbered to 50. A Gold version sequentially numbered to 10 was also inserted in packs.

STATED PRINT RUN 50 SERIAL #'d SETS
AM Andre Miller 10.00 25.00
DM Darius Miles 10.00 25.00
JK Jason Kidd 30.00 80.00
JR Jason Richardson 15.00 40.00
KB Kobe Bryant 150.00 300.00
KG Kevin Garnett 75.00 150.00
LO Lamar Odom 15.00 40.00
MJ Michael Jordan 400.00 800.00
PP Paul Pierce 25.00 60.00
SA Shareef Abdur-Rahim 10.00 25.00
TM Troy Murphy 10.00 25.00

2002-03 SP Game Used UD Rookie Exclusive Autographs

Randomly inserted in packs, this 23-card set places full color player action photography on the left side of the card and a cut authentic player autograph on the right side of the card. Each card is sequentially numbered to 100.

PRINT RUN 100 SERIAL #'d SETS
RKAS Amare Stoudemire 50.00 120.00
RKCA Caron Butler 6.00 15.00
RKCH Chris Jefferies 4.00 10.00
RKCJ Casey Jacobsen 5.00 12.00
RKCW Chris Wilcox 5.00 12.00
RKDD Dan Dickau 5.00 12.00
RKDG Drew Gooden 6.00 15.00
RKDW DaJuan Wagner 5.00 12.00
RKEL Melvin Ely 5.00 12.00
RKFJ Fred Jones 5.00 12.00
RKFW Frank Williams 4.00 10.00
RKJD Juan Dixon 6.00 15.00
RKJJ Jared Jeffries 5.00 12.00
RKJS John Salmons 6.00 15.00
RKJW Jay Williams 6.00 15.00
RKKR Kareem Rush 5.00 12.00
RKMH Marcus Haislip 5.00 12.00
RKNH Nene Hilario 6.00 15.00
RKNT Nikoloz Tskitishvili 4.00 10.00
RKQW Qyntel Woods 5.00 12.00
RKRH Ryan Humphrey 5.00 12.00
RKTP Tayshaun Prince 8.00 20.00
RKYM Yao Ming 50.00 120.00

2003-04 SP Game Used

Issued in August 2003, this 148-card set is divided up into 94 veteran player cards which are a mix of base and jersey cards (inserted overall at 1:1 along with the Legendary Fabrics, All-Star Apparel and Authentic Fabrics), 12 Michael Jordan Tribute cards sequentially numbered to 999 (card numbers 95-106) and 41 rookie cards (card numbers 107-148) sequentially numbered to 999. Base cards have white borders with accent colors to match team jerseys, the MJ Tribute cards have red and blue borders around the photos and white borders on the outside of the card and rookie cards have colored backgrounds to match jersey color and black and white designs towards the bottom of the card. SP Game Used was packaged in six-pack boxes where packs contained three cards and carried a suggested retail price of $29.99.

OVERALL JSY STATED ODDS ONE PER PACK
95-106 MJ PRINT RUN 999 SER.#'d SETS
107-148 PRINT RUN 999 SER.#'d SETS
1 Shareef Abdur-Rahim 1.25 3.00
2 Glenn Robinson 1.25 3.00
3 Jason Terry JSY 2.50 6.00
4 Paul Pierce 1.50 4.00
5 Antoine Walker 1.50 4.00
6 Eddy Curry 1.00 2.50
7 Tyson Chandler JSY 2.50 6.00
8 Jalen Rose JSY 2.50 6.00
9 Jay Williams JSY 2.00 5.00
10 DaJuan Wagner JSY 2.00 5.00
11 Darius Miles JSY 2.00 5.00
12 Carlos Boozer JSY 2.50 6.00
13 Steve Nash 2.00 5.00
14 Michael Finley 1.50 4.00
15 Nick Van Exel 1.25 3.00
16 Dirk Nowitzki JSY 5.00 12.00
17 Rodney White 1.00 2.50
18 Marcus Camby 1.25 3.00
19 Nikoloz Tskitishvili 1.00 2.50
20 Nene Hilario JSY 2.50 6.00
21 Richard Hamilton 1.25 3.00
22 Chauncey Billups 1.50 4.00
23 Ben Wallace 1.25 3.00
24 Gilbert Arenas 1.25 3.00
25 Troy Murphy 1.00 2.50
26 Jason Richardson JSY 3.00 8.00
27 Antawn Jamison JSY 2.50 6.00
28 Cuttino Mobley 1.00 2.50
29 Steve Francis 1.25 3.00
30 Eddie Griffin 1.00 2.50
31 Jermaine O'Neal 1.25 3.00
32 Reggie Miller 1.50 4.00
33 Jamaal Tinsley JSY 2.00 5.00
34 Lamar Odom 1.25 3.00
35 Chris Wilcox 1.00 2.50
36 Marko Jaric 1.00 2.50
37 Elton Brand JSY 3.00 8.00
38 Andre Miller JSY 2.50 6.00
39 Kobe Bryant 6.00 15.00
40 Shaquille O'Neal 4.00 10.00
41 Gary Payton 1.50 4.00
42 Kareem Rush JSY 2.00 5.00
43 Mike Miller 1.25 3.00
44 Shane Battier JSY 2.50 6.00
45 Pau Gasol JSY 3.00 8.00
46 Eddie Jones 1.25 3.00
47 Brian Grant 1.00 2.50
48 Caron Butler JSY 2.50 6.00
49 Joe Smith 1.25 3.00
50 Desmond Mason 1.25 3.00
51 Toni Kukoc 1.50 4.00
52 Wally Szczerbiak 1.25 3.00
53 Kevin Garnett JSY 5.00 12.00
54 Alonzo Mourning 2.00 5.00
55 Kenyon Martin 1.25 3.00
56 Jason Kidd JSY 5.00 12.00
57 Richard Jefferson JSY 2.50 6.00
58 Baron Davis 1.25 3.00
59 Jamal Mashburn JSY 2.50 6.00
60 Latrell Sprewell 1.25 3.00
61 Allan Houston 1.25 3.00
62 Antonio McDyess 1.25 3.00
63 Juwan Howard 1.25 3.00
64 Drew Gooden JSY 2.50 6.00
65 Tracy McGrady JSY 4.00 10.00
66 Keith Van Horn 1.25 3.00
67 Aaron McKie 1.00 2.50
68 Allen Iverson JSY 5.00 12.00
69 Stephon Marbury 1.25 3.00
70 Shawn Marion 1.25 3.00
71 Anfernee Hardaway 2.50 6.00
72 Joe Johnson 1.25 3.00
73 Amare Stoudemire JSY 4.00 10.00
74 Rasheed Wallace 1.50 4.00
75 Scottie Pippen 2.50 6.00
76 Mike Bibby 1.50 4.00
77 Peja Stojakovic 1.50 4.00
78 Gerald Wallace 1.25 3.00
79 Chris Webber JSY 3.00 8.00
80 Tim Duncan 2.50 6.00
81 Manu Ginobili 2.00 5.00
82 Tony Parker JSY 3.00 8.00
83 Ray Allen 1.50 4.00
84 Rashard Lewis JSY 3.00 8.00
85 Morris Peterson 1.00 2.50
86 Antonio Davis 1.00 2.50
87 Vince Carter 2.50 6.00
88 John Stockton JSY 4.00 10.00
89 Karl Malone JSY 4.00 10.00
90 Jerry Stackhouse 1.25 3.00
91 Michael Jordan 10.00 25.00
92 Michael Jordan JSY 30.00 80.00
93 Kobe Bryant JSY 12.00 30.00
94 Yao Ming JSY 6.00 15.00
95 Michael Jordan Tribute 6.00 15.00
96 Michael Jordan Tribute 6.00 15.00
97 Michael Jordan Tribute 6.00 15.00
98 Michael Jordan Tribute 6.00 15.00
99 Michael Jordan Tribute 6.00 15.00
100 Michael Jordan Tribute 6.00 15.00
101 Michael Jordan Tribute 6.00 15.00
102 Michael Jordan Tribute 6.00 15.00
103 Michael Jordan Tribute 6.00 15.00
104 Michael Jordan Tribute 6.00 15.00
105 Michael Jordan Tribute 6.00 15.00
106 Michael Jordan Tribute 6.00 15.00
107 LeBron James RC 75.00 200.00
108 Darko Milicic RC 2.50 6.00
109 Carmelo Anthony RC 10.00 25.00
110 Chris Bosh RC 5.00 12.00
111 Dwyane Wade RC 8.00 20.00
112 Chris Kaman RC 3.00 8.00
113 Kirk Hinrich RC 3.00 8.00
114 T.J. Ford RC 2.50 6.00
115 Mike Sweetney RC 2.00 5.00
116 Jarvis Hayes RC 2.00 5.00
117 Mickael Pietrus RC 2.50 6.00
118 Nick Collison RC 2.50 6.00
119 Marcus Banks RC 2.00 5.00
120 Luke Ridnour RC 2.50 6.00
121 Reece Gaines RC 2.00 5.00
122 Troy Bell RC 2.00 5.00
123 Zarko Cabarkapa RC 2.00 5.00
124 David West RC 3.00 8.00
125 Aleksandar Pavlovic RC 2.50 6.00
126 Dahntay Jones RC 2.50 6.00
127 Boris Diaw RC 3.00 8.00
128 Zoran Planinic RC 2.00 5.00
129 Travis Outlaw RC 2.50 6.00
130 Brian Cook RC 2.00 5.00
131 Carlos Delfino RC 2.50 6.00
132 Ndudi Ebi RC 2.00 5.00
133 Kendrick Perkins RC 2.50 6.00
134 Leandro Barbosa RC 3.00 8.00
135 Josh Howard RC 3.00 8.00
136 Maciej Lampe RC 2.00 5.00
137 Jason Kapono RC 2.00 5.00
138 Luke Walton RC 3.00 8.00
139 Jerome Beasley RC 2.00 5.00
140 Sofoklis Schortsanitis RC 2.00 5.00
141 Mario Austin RC 3.00 8.00
142 Travis Hansen RC 2.00 5.00
143 Steve Blake RC 2.50 6.00
144 Slavko Vranes RC 2.00 5.00
145 Zaur Pachulia RC 3.00 8.00
146 Keith Bogans RC 2.00 5.00
147 Matt Bonner RC 3.00 8.00
148 Maurice Williams RC 3.00 8.00

2003-04 SP Game Used Gold

*1-94 SINGLES: .5X TO 1.25X BASE HI
*1-94 JSY SINGLES: .6X TO 1.5X BASE HI
1-94 PRINT RUN 100 SER.#'d SETS
1-94 JSY PRINT RUN 50 SER.#'d SETS
COMMON MJ TRIB (95-106) 20.00 50.00
95-106 MJ PRINT RUN 50 SER.#'d SETS
*107-148 RC SINGLES: 1X TO 2.5X BASE HI
107-148 RC PRINT RUN 50 SER.#'d SETS
107 Lebron James 200.00 400.00
111 Dwyane Wade 50.00 120.00

2003-04 SP Game Used All Star Apparel

Randomly inserted at one in one along with the other memorabilia cards mentioned in the main set blurb, this 18-card set features a black background with full color player action photography along with a swatch of All-Star worn memorabilia. A gold version was also issued and is sequentially numbered to 100.

OVERALL JERSEY ODDS ONE PER PACK
*GOLD SINGLES: .75X TO 2X BASE CARD HI
GOLD PRINT RUN 100 SER.#'d SETS
AKAS Andrei Kirilenko 2.50 6.00
BWAS Ben Wallace 2.00 5.00
DGAS Drew Gooden 2.00 5.00
DMAS Desmond Mason 2.00 5.00
GAAS Gilbert Arenas 2.00 5.00
GGAS Gordan Giricek 1.50 4.00
JAAS Marko Jaric 1.50 4.00
JRAS Jason Richardson 2.50 6.00
JTAS Jamaal Tinsley 1.50 4.00
KBAS Kobe Bryant 10.00 25.00
NHAS Nene Hilario 2.00 5.00
RJAS Richard Jefferson 2.00 5.00
SMAS Shawn Marion 2.00 5.00
TDAS Tim Duncan 4.00 10.00
TMAS Troy Murphy 1.50 4.00
TPAS Tony Parker 2.50 6.00
YMAS Yao Ming 5.00 12.00
ZIAS Zydrunas Ilgauskas 2.00 5.00

2003-04 SP Game Used Authentic Fabrics

Randomly inserted at one in one along with the other sets mentioned in the main set blurb, this 77-card set places full-color player action photos on the right of the card and a square swatch of memorabilia in the upper left. The far upper left-hand corner prominently displays the SP Game Used Logo. A Gold version of this set was also inserted and cards are sequentially numbered to 100.

OVERALL JERSEY ODDS ONE PER PACK
ADJ Antonio Davis 2.00 5.00
AHJ Allan Houston 2.00 5.00
AHJ Anfernee Hardaway 4.00 10.00
AMJ Alonzo Mourning 3.00 8.00
AMJ Aaron McKie 2.00 5.00
AWJ Antoine Walker 2.50 6.00
BDJ Baron Davis 2.00 5.00
BNJ Bostjan Nachbar 2.00 5.00
BWJ Ben Wallace 2.00 5.00
CBJ Chauncey Billups 2.50 6.00
CJD Chris Jefferies 2.00 5.00
CWJ Chris Wilcox 2.00 5.00
DDJ Dan Dickau 2.00 5.00
DGJ Devean George 2.00 5.00
DMJ Dikembe Mutombo 2.50 6.00
DMJ Desmond Mason 2.00 5.00
DRJ David Robinson 4.00 10.00
DWJ David Wesley 2.00 5.00
ECJ Eddy Curry 1.50 4.00
EGJ Eddie Griffin 2.00 5.00
EGJ Manu Ginobili 3.00 8.00
EJJ Eddie Jones 2.00 5.00
ESJ Eric Snow 2.00 5.00
FIJ Marcus Fizer 2.00 5.00
FJJ Fred Jones 2.00 5.00
FWJ Frank Williams 2.00 5.00
GGJ Gordan Giricek 2.00 5.00
GHJ Grant Hill 3.00 8.00
GPJ Gary Payton 2.50 6.00
GRJ Glenn Robinson 2.00 5.00
GWJ Gerald Wallace 2.00 5.00
JAJ Marko Jaric 2.00 5.00
JDJ Juan Dixon 2.00 5.00
JEJ Jared Jeffries 2.00 5.00
JJJ Joe Johnson 2.00 5.00
JOJ Jermaine O'Neal 2.00 5.00
JSJ John Salmons 2.00 5.00
JWJ Jiri Welsch 2.00 5.00
KBJ Kobe Bryant 10.00 25.00
KBJ Kwame Brown 2.00 5.00
KEJ Kedrick Brown 2.00 5.00
KMJ Kenyon Martin 2.00 5.00
KTJ Kurt Thomas 2.00 5.00
KVJ Keith Van Horn 2.00 5.00
LJJ LeBron James 40.00 100.00
LOJ Lamar Odom 2.00 5.00
LSJ Latrell Sprewell 2.00 5.00
MAJ Shawn Marion 2.00 5.00
MBJ Mike Bibby 2.50 6.00
MCJ Marcus Camby 2.00 5.00
MEJ Melvin Ely 2.00 5.00
MFJ Michael Finley 2.50 6.00
MHJ Marcus Haislip 2.00 5.00
MJJ Michael Jordan 30.00 60.00
MMJ Mike Miller 2.00 5.00
MPJ Morris Peterson 1.50 4.00
NTJ Nikoloz Tskitishvilli 2.00 5.00
PPJ Paul Pierce 2.50 6.00
PSJ Peja Stojakovic 2.50 6.00
QRJ Quentin Richardson 2.00 5.00
QWJ Qyntel Woods 2.00 5.00
RAJ Ray Allen 2.50 6.00
RBJ Rasual Butler 2.00 5.00
RHJ Richard Hamilton 2.00 5.00
RMJ Reggie Miller 5.00 12.00
RWJ Rasheed Wallace 2.50 6.00
SAJ Shareef Abdur Rahim 2.00 5.00
SFJ Steve Francis 2.00 5.00
SMJ Stephon Marbury 2.00 5.00
SNJ Steve Nash 3.00 8.00
SPJ Scottie Pippen 5.00 12.00
STJ Jerry Stackhouse 2.00 5.00
TDJ Tim Duncan 4.00 10.00
TKJ Toni Kukoc 2.50 6.00
VBJ Vin Baker 2.00 5.00
WAJ Charlie Ward 2.00 5.00
WSJ Wally Szczerbiak 2.00 5.00

2003-04 SP Game Used Authentic Fabrics Autographs

Randomly seeded in packs, this 29-card set parallels the look of the Authentic Fabrics insert set enhanced with a fade to white bottom and authentic player autographs. Each card is sequentially numbered to 100.

PRINT RUN 100 SER.#'d SETS
AJAJ Antawn Jamison 5.00 12.00
ASAJ Amare Stoudemire 8.00 20.00
CMAJ Corey Maggette 5.00 12.00
DRAJ David Robinson 30.00 80.00
DWAJ DaJuan Wagner 4.00 10.00
EGAJ Manu Ginobili 15.00 40.00
ETAJ Etan Thomas 4.00 10.00
FJAJ Fred Jones 5.00 12.00
GAAJ Gilbert Arenas 5.00 12.00
GWAJ Gerald Wallace 5.00 12.00
JKAJ Jason Kidd 25.00 60.00
JMAJ Jerome Moiso 4.00 10.00
JOAJ Jermaine O'Neal 5.00 12.00
JRAJ Jason Richardson 10.00 25.00
JSAJ Jerry Stackhouse 5.00 12.00
JTAJ Jamaal Tinsley 4.00 10.00
JWAJ Jay Williams 4.00 10.00
KBAJ Kobe Bryant 125.00 250.00
LOAJ Lamar Odom 5.00 12.00
MBAJ Mike Bibby 6.00 15.00
PPAJ Paul Pierce 15.00 40.00
PSAJ Peja Stojakovic 10.00 25.00
RJAJ Richard Jefferson 5.00 12.00
ROAJ Jalen Rose 5.00 12.00
SFAJ Steve Francis 5.00 12.00
SMAJ Shawn Marion 10.00 25.00
TMAJ Tracy McGrady 20.00 50.00
TPAJ Tony Parker 12.00 30.00
YMAJ Yao Ming 30.00 80.00

2003-04 SP Game Used Authentic Fabrics Gold

*GOLD SINGLES: .6X TO 1.5X BASE HI
PRINT RUN 100 SER.#'d SETS
AHJ Anfernee Hardaway 10.00 25.00
SPJ Scottie Pippen 10.00 25.00

2003-04 SP Game Used Authentic Fabrics Dual

Randomly inserted in packs, this 38-card set features a horizontal design with player photos on both the left and right of the card and two swatches of game used memorabilia. Each card is sequentially numbered to 100.

PRINT RUN 100 SER.#'d SETS
UNPRICED QUAD PRINT RUN 10 SETS
AIKVJ Iverson/V.Horn 10.00 25.00
AMQRJ A.Miller/Q-Rich 5.00 12.00

ASCJJ Amare/C.Jacobsen	6.00	15.00
AWVBJ Walker/V.Baker	5.00	12.00
BDJMJ B.Davis/J-Mash	5.00	12.00
BWCBJ B.Wallace/Billups	8.00	20.00
CBDMJ Boozer/Miles	5.00	12.00
CBRBJ C.Butler/R.Butler	5.00	12.00
DMKMJ K-Mart/Mutombo	6.00	15.00
DNSNJ Nowitzki/Nash	10.00	25.00
EBMEJ Brand/M.Ely	5.00	12.00
EJAMJ E.Jones/Mourning	6.00	15.00
GAAJJ Arenas/Jamison	5.00	12.00
GHDGJ G.Hill/Gooden	6.00	15.00
GPTKJ Payton/Kukoc	6.00	15.00
JHMCJ Howard/Camby	5.00	12.00
JRECJ Rose/E.Curry	5.00	12.00
JSWZJ J.Smith/Szczerb	5.00	12.00
JTDDJ Terry/Dickau	5.00	12.00
JTJOJ Tinsley/J.O'Neal	5.00	12.00
KBDFJ Bryant/Fisher	20.00	50.00
KGTHJ Garnett/Hudson	10.00	25.00
KMJSJ Stockton/Malone	15.00	30.00
LSAHJ Spree/Houston	5.00	12.00
MFRLJ Finley/LaFrentz	5.00	12.00
MJKBJ Jordan/Bryant	60.00	150.00
MJMAJ Jordan/Magic	75.00	150.00
NHNTJ Nene/Tskitishvili	5.00	12.00
PGMMJ Gasol/M.Miller	5.00	12.00
PPKBJ Pierce/Ke.Brown	5.00	12.00
RJJKJ R.Jefferson/Kidd	6.00	15.00
RMFJJ R.Miller/F.Jones	5.00	12.00
RWSPJ R.Wallace/Pippen	15.00	30.00
SAGRJ A-Rahim/G.Robinsn	5.00	12.00
SMAHJ Marbury/A.Hard	12.00	30.00
TMGGJ T-Mac/Giricek	8.00	20.00
TPRHJ Prince/R.Hamilton	6.00	15.00
WZCWJ Zhi Zhi/Wilcox	5.00	12.00

2003-04 SP Game Used Authentic Fabrics Dual Autographs

Randomly seeded, this 48-card set parallels the design of the Authentic Fabrics Dual set enhanced with a fade to white bottom and two authentic player autographs. Each card is sequentially numbered to 50. Also included were several cards numbered to 15. Those cards are denoted in our checklist.
PRINT RUN 15 TO 50 SER.#'d SETS
SOME NOT PRICED DUE TO SCARCITY

1 A.Miller/J.Kidd	30.00	60.00
2 A.Miller/L.Odom	20.00	40.00
3 A.Miller/M.Jaric	10.00	25.00
4 C.Billups/T.Prince	12.00	30.00
5 C.Maggette/A.Miller	10.00	25.00
6 G.Giricek/D.Gooden	10.00	25.00
7 D.Gooden/P.Pierce	20.00	50.00
8 D.Wagner/C.Boozer	15.00	30.00
9 M.Ginobili/M.Jaric	12.00	30.00
10 E.Griffin/S.Francis	10.00	25.00
11 G.Arenas/J-Rich	10.00	25.00
12 G.Giricek/T.Parker	20.00	40.00
13 Stojakovic/Wallace	10.00	25.00
14 J.Kidd/J.Tinsley	20.00	50.00
16 J.Kidd/R.Jefferson	20.00	50.00
17 J.O'Neal/K.Garnett	40.00	100.00
18 J.Rose/M.Fizer	10.00	25.00
19 J-Rich/R.Jefferson	10.00	25.00
20 J-Rich/T.Parker	20.00	40.00
22 Stack/J.Dixon	10.00	25.00
23 J.Tinsley/T.Parker	15.00	30.00
24 J-Will/C.Boozer	20.00	40.00
25 J-Will/M.Fizer	15.00	30.00
26 K.Bryant/M.Bibby	100.00	200.00
28 L.Odom/C.Wilcox	10.00	25.00
29 Bibby/P.Stojakovic	10.00	25.00
31 M.Ely/L.Odom	10.00	25.00
32 M.Pete/J.Richardson	10.00	25.00
33 R.Hamilton/C.Billups	12.00	30.00
34 R.Jefferson/M.Bibby	15.00	30.00
35 S.Francis/K.Bryant/15	150.00	300.00
36 S.Francis/Y.Ming	40.00	80.00
37 Marion/A.Stoudemire	12.00	30.00
39 T.McGrady/Garnett/15	100.00	200.00
41 T.Parker/M.Ginobili	40.00	80.00
42 T.Parker/M.Jaric	10.00	25.00

2003-04 SP Game Used Authentic Fabrics Triple

Randomly inserted, this six-card set places three players and three swatches of authentic memorabilia on the card. Each card is sequentially numbered to 25, and note the prominent display of the SP Game Used logo.
PRINT RUN 25 SER.#'d SETS

2 Wagner/Miles/Bzer	12.50	30.00
3 Rose/Chandler/Williams	12.50	30.00
4 Stockton/Malone/AK47	30.00	80.00
6 Jefferies/Peterson/Davis	12.50	30.00
8 Gasol/Battier/Miller	20.00	50.00
9 Allen/Lewis/Forte	12.50	30.00

2003-04 SP Game Used Authentic Patches

Randomly seeded, this 59-card set places full-color player photos at the top of the card and a centered square swatch of game-used patch on the bottom. Each card is sequentially numbered to 100.
PRINT RUN 100 SER.#'d SETS

AHP Allan Houston	8.00	20.00
AIP Allen Iverson	20.00	50.00
AJP Antawn Jamison	8.00	20.00
AMP Alonzo Mourning	20.00	50.00
ASP Amare Stoudemire	12.00	30.00
AWP Antoine Walker	10.00	25.00
BDP Baron Davis	8.00	20.00
CBP Caron Butler	8.00	20.00
CWP Chris Webber	20.00	50.00
DNP Dirk Nowitzki	15.00	40.00
DRR David Robinson	12.00	30.00
DWP DaJuan Wagner	6.00	15.00
EBP Elton Brand	10.00	25.00
EJP Eddie Jones	15.00	40.00
GAP Gilbert Arenas	8.00	20.00
GHP Grant Hill	12.00	30.00
GPP Gary Payton	10.00	25.00
HAP Anfernee Hardaway	20.00	50.00
HTP Hedo Turkoglu	8.00	20.00
JJP Jared Jeffries	6.00	15.00
JKP Jason Kidd	15.00	40.00
JMP Jamal Mashburn	8.00	20.00
JOP Jermaine O'Neal	8.00	20.00
JRP Jason Richardson	10.00	25.00
JSP John Stockton	12.00	30.00
JTP Jamaal Tinsley	6.00	15.00
JWP Jay Williams	6.00	15.00
KAP Karl Malone	12.00	30.00
KBP Kobe Bryant	40.00	100.00
KGP Kevin Garnett	15.00	40.00
KJP Kareem Abdul-Jabbar	15.00	40.00
KMP Kenyon Martin	8.00	20.00
KRP Kareem Rush	6.00	15.00
KVP Keith Van Horn	8.00	20.00
LOP Lamar Odom	8.00	20.00
LSP Latrell Sprewell	10.00	25.00
MAP Magic Johnson	20.00	50.00
MBP Mike Bibby	10.00	25.00
MCP Antonio McDyess	8.00	20.00
MIP Andre Miller	8.00	20.00
MJP Michael Jordan	60.00	150.00
NHP Nene Hilario	10.00	25.00
PGP Pau Gasol	10.00	25.00
PPP Paul Pierce	10.00	25.00
RAP Ray Allen	10.00	25.00
RHP Richard Hamilton	8.00	20.00
RJP Richard Jefferson	8.00	20.00
RLP Rashard Lewis	10.00	25.00
RMP Reggie Miller	10.00	25.00
RWP Rasheed Wallace	10.00	25.00
SBP Shane Battier	8.00	20.00
SFP Steve Francis	8.00	20.00
SHP Shawn Marion	8.00	20.00
SMP Stephon Marbury	8.00	20.00
SPP Scottie Pippen	30.00	80.00
TMP Tracy McGrady	12.00	30.00
WSP Wally Szczerbiak	8.00	20.00
WZP Wang Zhi Zhi	10.00	25.00
YMP Yao Ming	20.00	50.00

2003-04 SP Game Used Authentic Patches Autographs

Randomly inserted in packs, this 35-card set parallels the design of the Authentic Patches insert set enhanced with authentic player autographs. Each card is sequentially numbered to 50.
PRINT RUN 50 SER.#'d SETS

AJAP Antawn Jamison	15.00	40.00
ASAP Amare Stoudemire	20.00	50.00
BIAP Chauncey Billups	15.00	40.00
BOAP Carlos Boozer	15.00	40.00
CBAP Caron Butler	30.00	60.00
DDAP Dan Dickau	15.00	40.00
DGAP Drew Gooden	15.00	40.00
DJAP DerMarr Johnson	15.00	40.00
DWAP DaJuan Wagner	15.00	40.00
EGAP Manu Ginobili	30.00	80.00
ETAP Etan Thomas	15.00	40.00
GAAP Gilbert Arenas	25.00	50.00
GWAP Gerald Wallace	15.00	40.00
JDAP Juan Dixon	15.00	40.00
JKAP Jason Kidd	50.00	120.00
JMAP Jerome Moiso	15.00	40.00
JOAP Jermaine O'Neal	15.00	40.00
JRAP Jason Richardson	20.00	50.00
JSAP Jerry Stackhouse	25.00	60.00
JWAP Jay Williams	25.00	50.00
KBAP Kobe Bryant	400.00	800.00
LOAP Lamar Odom	15.00	40.00
MBAP Mike Bibby	15.00	40.00
MJAP Michael Jordan	1000.00	1500.00
NHAP Nene Hilario	15.00	40.00
PPAP Paul Pierce	40.00	80.00
PSAP Peja Stojakovic	20.00	50.00
RHAP Richard Hamilton	20.00	50.00
RJAP Richard Jefferson	15.00	40.00
ROAP Jalen Rose	15.00	40.00
SFAP Steve Francis	15.00	40.00
SMAP Shawn Marion	25.00	60.00
TMAP Tracy McGrady	75.00	200.00
TPAP Tony Parker	50.00	120.00
YMAP Yao Ming	75.00	200.00

2003-04 SP Game Used Authentic Patches Dual

Randomly inserted, this eight-card set utilizes the design of the Authentic Patches set but places two players and two patch swatches on each card. Cards are sequentially numbered to 25. An autographed version was also issued and these cards are sequentially numbered to five.
PRINT RUN 25 SER.#'d SETS
UNPRICED AUTO PRINT RUN 5 SETS
UNPRICED TRIPLE PRINT RUN 10 SETS

2 J.Richardson/A.Jamison	25.00	60.00
3 K.Bryant/K.Rush	30.00	80.00
4 M.Jordan/K.Bryant	100.00	250.00
5 M.Jordan/L.Bird	125.00	300.00
6 P.Stojakovic/G.Giricek	25.00	60.00
7 S.Nash/R.Fox	40.00	100.00
8 T.McGrady/D.Miles	25.00	60.00

2003-04 SP Game Used Extra SIGnificance

Randomly inserted in packs, this 10-card set features a horizontal design with one player photo appearing on the right and the other on the left with both autographs in the middle. Each card is sequentially numbered to 25. A Gold parallel version of this set was also produced and those cards are sequentially numbered to five.
PRINT RUN 25 SER.#'d SETS

ASTM Amare/T.McGrady	50.00	120.00
KAMJ Abdul-Jabbar/Magic	150.00	300.00
MJLB M.Jordan/L.Bird	350.00	650.00
PSMB Stojakovic/M.Bibby	25.00	60.00
YMKA Y.Ming/Abdul-Jabbar	75.00	200.00

2003-04 SP Game Used Legendary Fabrics

Randomly inserted at the rate of one in one along with the rest of the sets mentioned in the main set blurb, this 11-card set focuses on retired NBA Greats. Each card places a black and white image of the player on the left side of the card and a swatch of memorabilia on the right. An autographed version including most of the players from this set was issued.
OVERALL JERSEY ODDS ONE PER PACK

BRLO Bill Russell	20.00	50.00
DWL Dominique Wilkins	6.00	15.00
EJL Magic Johnson	12.00	30.00
JEL Julius Erving	8.00	20.00
KML Kevin McHale	6.00	15.00
LBL Larry Bird	12.00	30.00
MJL Michael Jordan	40.00	100.00
ORL Oscar Robertson	6.00	15.00
WCL Wilt Chamberlain	10.00	25.00

2003-04 SP Game Used Legendary Fabrics Autographs

This set is an autographed parallel to the Legendary Fabrics set, limited to just 100 serial numbered sets.
PRINT RUN 100 SER.#'d SETS

2 Bill Russell	100.00	250.00
3 Larry Bird	80.00	200.00
4 Julius Erving	60.00	150.00
5 Magic Johnson	60.00	150.00
6 Kareem Abdul-Jabbar	40.00	100.00
7 Dominique Wilkins	40.00	100.00

2003-04 SP Game Used Rookie Exclusive Autographs

This 42-card set is sequentially numbered to 100 and was randomly inserted in packs. Player photos appear on the right side of the card while an embedded cut signature appears centered below the photo.
PRINT RUN 100 SER.#'d SETS

RE1 Lebron James	1200.00	2000.00
RE2 Darko Milicic	5.00	12.00
RE3 Carmelo Anthony	60.00	150.00
RE4 Chris Bosh	25.00	60.00
RE5 Chris Kaman	6.00	15.00
RE6 Reece Gaines	4.00	10.00
RE7 Mickael Pietrus	5.00	12.00
RE8 Marcus Banks	4.00	10.00
RE9 Troy Bell	4.00	10.00
RE10 Zarko Cabarkapa	4.00	10.00
RE11 David West	6.00	15.00
RE12 Aleksandar Pavlovic	5.00	12.00
RE13 Dahntay Jones	5.00	12.00
RE14 Boris Diaw	6.00	15.00
RE15 Zoran Planinic	4.00	10.00
RE16 Travis Outlaw	5.00	12.00
RE17 Brian Cook	4.00	10.00
RE18 Leandro Barbosa	4.00	10.00
RE19 Josh Howard	4.00	10.00
RE20 Maciej Lampe	4.00	10.00
RE21 Jason Kapono	4.00	10.00
RE22 Luke Walton	6.00	15.00
RE23 Jerome Beasley	4.00	10.00
RE24 Sofoklis Schortsanitis	4.00	10.00
RE25 Mario Austin	6.00	15.00
RE26 Travis Hansen	4.00	10.00
RE27 Steve Blake	5.00	12.00
RE28 Slavko Vranes	4.00	10.00
RE29 Zaur Pachulia	6.00	15.00
RE30 Keith Bogans	4.00	10.00
RE31 Matt Bonner	6.00	15.00
RE32 Maurice Williams	6.00	15.00
RE33 Kyle Korver	8.00	20.00
RE34 Rick Rickert	4.00	10.00
RE35 Brandon Hunter	4.00	10.00
RE36 Jarvis Hayes	4.00	10.00
RE37 Ndudi Ebi	4.00	10.00
RE38 Kendrick Perkins	5.00	12.00
RE39 Dwyane Wade	100.00	250.00
RE40 Luke Ridnour	5.00	12.00
RE41 James Lang	4.00	10.00
RE42 Carlos Delfino	5.00	12.00

2003-04 SP Game Used SIGnificance

Inserted in packs, this 58-card set places full-color player photos along the top and leaves a low-detailed area on the bottom for player autographs. Each card is sequentially numbered to 100. Two other versions of this set were inserted: a Gold version sequentially numbered to 10, and a Marks version sequentially numbered to 75.
PRINT RUN 23 TO 100 SER.#'d SETS

AJ Antawn Jamison	6.00	15.00
AM Andre Miller	4.00	10.00
AM Antonio McDyess	5.00	12.00
AS Amare Stoudemire	12.00	30.00
BI Chauncey Billups	8.00	20.00
BO Carlos Boozer	6.00	15.00
BW Bill Walton	8.00	20.00
CB Caron Butler	8.00	20.00
CJ Chris Jefferies	4.00	10.00
CM Corey Maggette	4.00	10.00
DA Dan Gadzuric	4.00	10.00
DD Dan Dickau	4.00	10.00
DG Drew Gooden	4.00	10.00
DJ DerMarr Johnson	4.00	10.00
DR David Robinson	30.00	80.00
DWO DaJuan Wagner	6.00	15.00
EGO Manu Ginobili	25.00	60.00
ET Etan Thomas	4.00	10.00
FJ Fred Jones	4.00	10.00
GA Gilbert Arenas	8.00	20.00
GG Gordon Giricek	4.00	10.00
GR Eddie Griffin	4.00	10.00
GW Gerald Wallace	6.00	15.00
HU Ryan Humphrey	4.00	10.00
IM George Gervin	10.00	25.00
JD Juan Dixon	4.00	10.00
JK Jason Kidd	20.00	50.00
JM Jerome Moiso	6.00	15.00
JO Jermaine O'Neal	8.00	20.00
JR Jason Richardson	6.00	15.00
JS Jerry Stackhouse	8.00	20.00
JT Jamaal Tinsley	6.00	15.00
JW Jay Williams	8.00	20.00
KA Kareem Abdul-Jabbar	30.00	80.00
KB Kobe Bryant	100.00	200.00
KG Kevin Garnett	30.00	80.00
LO Lamar Odom	8.00	20.00
MB Mike Bibby	8.00	20.00
MJ Michael Jordan/23	300.00	600.00
MP Morris Peterson	4.00	10.00
NH Nene Hilario	5.00	12.00
NW Dominique Wilkins	15.00	40.00
PP Paul Pierce	12.00	30.00
PS Peja Stojakovic	6.00	15.00
QW Qyntel Woods	4.00	10.00
RE Reggie Evans	4.00	10.00
RH Richard Hamilton	8.00	20.00
RJ Richard Jefferson	4.00	10.00
RO Jalen Rose	6.00	15.00
SF Steve Francis	8.00	20.00
SM Shawn Marion	8.00	20.00
TM Tracy McGrady	10.00	25.00
TP Tony Parker	15.00	40.00
WI Chris Wilcox	4.00	10.00
WZ Wang Zhi Zhi	8.00	20.00
YM Yao Ming	20.00	50.00

2003-04 SP Game Used SIGnificant Marks

PRINT RUN 75 SER.#'d SETS

AJSM Antawn Jamison	10.00	25.00
AMSM Andre Miller	8.00	20.00
ANSM Antonio McDyess	10.00	25.00
ASSM Amare Stoudemire	25.00	60.00
BOSM Carlos Boozer	10.00	25.00
BWSM Bill Walton	12.00	30.00
CBSM Caron Butler	15.00	40.00
CMSM Corey Maggette	8.00	20.00
CWSM Chris Wilcox	8.00	20.00
DGSM Drew Gooden	8.00	20.00
DJSM DerMarr Johnson	8.00	20.00
DRSM David Robinson	25.00	60.00
DWSM DaJuan Wagner	8.00	20.00
EGSM Manu Ginobili	20.00	50.00
ETSM Etan Thomas	8.00	20.00
GASM Gilbert Arenas	10.00	25.00
GESM George Gervin	10.00	25.00
GGSM Gordon Giricek	8.00	20.00
GRSM Eddie Griffin	8.00	20.00
GWSM Gerald Wallace	10.00	25.00
JDSM Juan Dixon	8.00	20.00
JKSM Jason Kidd	25.00	60.00
JMSM Jerome Moiso	8.00	20.00
JOSM Jermaine O'Neal	10.00	25.00
JRSM Jason Richardson	10.00	25.00
JSSM Jerry Stackhouse	10.00	25.00
JWSM Jay Williams	10.00	25.00
LOSM Lamar Odom	15.00	30.00
MBSM Mike Bibby	15.00	30.00
MPSM Morris Peterson	8.00	20.00
PPSM Paul Pierce	10.00	25.00
PSSM Peja Stojakovic	12.50	30.00
RHSM Richard Hamilton	10.00	25.00
RJSM Richard Jefferson	10.00	25.00
ROSM Jalen Rose	10.00	25.00
SFSM Steve Francis	10.00	25.00
SMSM Shawn Marion	12.50	30.00
TMSM Tracy McGrady	20.00	50.00
TPSM Tony Parker	20.00	50.00
YMSM Yao Ming	30.00	80.00

2003-04 SP Game Used SIGnificant Numbers

This set is a parallel insert to the SIGnificance set and each player signed copies totaling his jersey number.
PRINT RUNS LISTED IN CHECKLIST
MOST NOT PRICED DUE TO SCARCITY

AS32 Amare Stoudemire/32	40.00	100.00
JR23 Jason Richardson/23	25.00	60.00
KG21 Kevin Garnett/21	100.00	200.00
MJ23 Michael Jordan/23	500.00	800.00
PP34 Paul Pierce/34	40.00	100.00

2004-05 SP Game Used

Issued in September 2004, SP Game Used consists of 162 card where cards 1-60 are base veterans, cards 61-90 are veteran jersey cards inserted at the combined rate for all memorabilia at one per pack, cards 91-132 feature rookies and are sequentially numbered to 999 and cards 133-162 are part of a LeBron James season in review subset and are sequentially numbered to 999. SP Game used was packaged in six pack boxes where packs contained three cards each and carried a SRP of $29.99..
ALL JSY's LISTED AT STATED ODDS 1:1
91-132 RC PRINT RUN 999 SER.#'d SETS
133-162 SIR PRINT RUN 999 SER.#'d SETS
UNPRICED LIMITED PARALLEL PRINT RUN ONE SET

1 Tony Delk	.60	1.50
2 Boris Diaw	.75	2.00
3 Ricky Davis	.75	2.00
4 Gary Payton	1.00	2.50
5 Gerald Wallace	.75	2.00
6 Jason Kapono	.60	1.50
7 Tyson Chandler	.75	2.00
8 Kirk Hinrich	.75	2.00
9 Dajuan Wagner	.60	1.50
10 Zydrunas Ilgauskas	.75	2.00
11 Jerry Stackhouse	.75	2.00
12 Michael Finley	1.00	2.50
13 Andre Miller	.75	2.00
14 Nene	.75	2.00
15 Richard Hamilton	.75	2.00
16 Rasheed Wallace	1.00	2.50
17 Derek Fisher	.75	2.00
18 Mike Dunleavy	.75	2.00
19 Tracy McGrady	1.25	3.00
20 Jim Jackson	.60	1.50
21 Reggie Miller	1.00	2.50
22 Jermaine O'Neal	.75	2.00
23 Elton Brand	1.00	2.50
24 Corey Maggette	.75	2.00
25 Lamar Odom	.75	2.00
26 Caron Butler	.75	2.00
27 Pau Gasol	1.00	2.50
28 Bonzi Wells	.60	1.50
29 Dwyane Wade	1.50	4.00
30 Shaquille O'Neal	2.50	6.00
31 Michael Redd	.75	2.00
32 T.J. Ford	.60	1.50
33 Latrell Sprewell	.75	2.00
34 Sam Cassell	.75	2.00
35 Jason Kidd	1.50	4.00
36 Richard Jefferson	.75	2.00
37 Baron Davis	.75	2.00
38 Jamaal Magloire	.60	1.50
39 Allan Houston	.75	2.00
40 Stephon Marbury	.75	2.00
41 Steve Francis	.75	2.00
42 Cuttino Mobley	.60	1.50
43 Glenn Robinson	.75	2.00
44 Kenny Thomas	.60	1.50
45 Shawn Marion	.75	2.00
46 Amare Stoudemire	.75	2.00
47 Zach Randolph	.75	2.00
48 Damon Stoudamire	.75	2.00
49 Chris Webber	1.00	2.50
50 Peja Stojakovic	1.00	2.50
51 Manu Ginobili	1.25	3.00
52 Tim Duncan	1.50	4.00
53 Rashard Lewis	1.00	2.50
54 Ray Allen	1.00	2.50
55 Jalen Rose	.75	2.00
56 Vince Carter	1.50	4.00
57 Carlos Boozer	.75	2.00
58 Andrei Kirilenko	.75	2.00
59 Larry Hughes	.75	2.00
60 Gilbert Arenas	.75	2.00
61 Paul Pierce JSY	2.50	6.00
62 Eddy Curry JSY	1.50	4.00
63 LeBron James JSY	12.50	30.00
64 Antawn Jamison JSY	2.00	5.00
65 Dirk Nowitzki JSY	4.00	10.00
66 Antoine Walker JSY	2.50	6.00
67 Carmelo Anthony JSY	5.00	12.00
68 Ben Wallace JSY	2.00	5.00
69 Jason Richardson JSY	2.50	6.00
70 Yao Ming JSY	5.00	12.00
71 Michael Jordan JSY	40.00	100.00
72 Kobe Bryant JSY	10.00	25.00
73 Quentin Richardson JSY	2.00	5.00
74 Jason Williams JSY	2.00	5.00
75 Eddie Jones JSY	2.00	5.00
76 Keith Van Horn JSY	2.00	5.00
77 Kevin Garnett JSY	4.00	10.00
78 Kenyon Martin JSY	2.00	5.00
79 Jamal Mashburn JSY	2.00	5.00
80 Kurt Thomas JSY	2.00	5.00
81 Juwan Howard JSY	2.00	5.00
82 Allen Iverson JSY	4.00	10.00
83 Joe Johnson JSY	2.00	5.00
84 Shareef Abdur-Rahim JSY	2.00	5.00
85 Mike Bibby JSY	2.50	6.00
86 Tony Parker JSY	2.50	6.00
87 Luke Ridnour JSY	2.00	5.00
88 Jalen Rose JSY	2.00	5.00
89 Gordan Giricek JSY	2.00	5.00
90 Juan Dixon JSY	2.00	5.00
91 Emeka Okafor RC	2.50	6.00
92 Dwight Howard RC	6.00	15.00
93 Shaun Livingston RC	3.00	8.00
94 Luol Deng RC	3.00	8.00
95 Ben Gordon RC	3.00	8.00
96 Devin Harris RC	2.50	6.00
97 Andre Iguodala RC	4.00	10.00
98 Andris Biedrins RC	2.00	5.00
99 Josh Childress RC	2.50	6.00
100 Josh Smith RC	3.00	8.00
101 Jameer Nelson RC	3.00	8.00
102 J.R. Smith RC	3.00	8.00
103 Sergei Monia RC	2.00	5.00
104 Sebastian Telfair RC	2.50	6.00
105 Pavel Podkolzin RC	2.00	5.00
106 Luke Jackson RC	2.00	5.00
107 Dorell Wright RC	3.00	8.00
108 Robert Swift RC	2.00	5.00
109 Anderson Varejao RC	2.50	6.00
110 Sasha Vujacic RC	3.00	8.00
111 Rafael Araujo RC	2.00	5.00
112 Al Jefferson RC	4.00	10.00
113 Kris Humphries RC	3.00	8.00
114 Kirk Snyder RC	2.00	5.00
115 Peter John Ramos RC	2.00	5.00
116 Beno Udrih RC	2.50	6.00
117 Viktor Khryapa RC	2.00	5.00
118 David Harrison RC	2.00	5.00
119 Trevor Ariza RC	3.00	8.00
120 Ha Seung-Jin RC	3.00	8.00
121 Kevin Martin RC	4.00	10.00
122 Delonte West RC	3.00	8.00
123 Blake Stepp RC	3.00	8.00
124 Chris Duhon RC	3.00	8.00
125 Tony Allen RC	3.00	8.00
126 Donta Smith RC	2.00	5.00
127 Andre Emmett RC	2.00	5.00
128 Royal Ivey RC	2.50	6.00
129 Nenad Krstic RC	3.00	8.00
130 Romain Sato RC	2.00	5.00
131 Antonio Burks RC	2.50	6.00
132 Lionel Chalmers RC	3.00	8.00
133 LeBron James SIR	4.00	10.00
134 LeBron James SIR	4.00	10.00
135 LeBron James SIR	4.00	10.00
136 LeBron James SIR	4.00	10.00
137 LeBron James SIR	4.00	10.00
138 LeBron James SIR	4.00	10.00
139 LeBron James SIR	4.00	10.00
140 LeBron James SIR	4.00	10.00
141 LeBron James SIR	4.00	10.00
142 LeBron James SIR	4.00	10.00
143 LeBron James SIR	4.00	10.00
144 LeBron James SIR	4.00	10.00
145 LeBron James SIR	4.00	10.00
146 LeBron James SIR	4.00	10.00
147 LeBron James SIR	4.00	10.00
148 LeBron James SIR	4.00	10.00
149 LeBron James SIR	4.00	10.00
150 LeBron James SIR	4.00	10.00
151 LeBron James SIR	4.00	10.00
152 LeBron James SIR	4.00	10.00
153 LeBron James SIR	4.00	10.00
154 LeBron James SIR	4.00	10.00
155 LeBron James SIR	4.00	10.00
156 LeBron James SIR	4.00	10.00
157 LeBron James SIR	4.00	10.00
158 LeBron James SIR	4.00	10.00
159 LeBron James SIR	4.00	10.00
160 LeBron James SIR	4.00	10.00
161 LeBron James SIR	4.00	10.00
162 LeBron James SIR	4.00	10.00

2004-05 SP Game Used Parallel

*1-60: .75X TO 2X BASE HI
*61-90: .6X TO 1.5X BASE HI
1-90 PRINT RUN 100 SER.#'d SETS
*91-132: 1X TO 2.5X BASE HI
*133-162: 1X TO 2.5X BASE HI
91-162 PRINT RUN 50 SER.#'d SETS

2004-05 SP Game Used All-Star Apparel

Randomly seeded with all memorabilia cards at the rate of one in one, this six-card set features jerseys of players from the Got Milk Rookie Challenge game and the logo from the 2004 NBA All-Star Game in Los Angeles. A Gold Parallel version was also inserted and these cards are numbered to 100.
ALL JSY's LISTED AT STATED ODDS 1:1
*GOLD SINGLES: .6X TO 1.5X BASE JSY HI
GOLD PRINT RUN 100 SER.#'d SETS

BO Carlos Boozer	2.00	5.00
CM Cuttino Mobley	1.50	4.00
MD Mike Dunleavy	2.00	5.00
NH Nene	2.00	5.00
RM Ronald Murray	2.00	5.00
UH Udonis Haslem	1.50	4.00

2004-05 SP Game Used All-Star Sigs

Limited to 25 copies, this 30-card set features a small head shot of some of the games greatest all-stars along with a sticker autograph. A Gold parallel version of this set was also produced and these cards are numbered to the featured player's total number of All-Star appearances.
PRINT RUN 25 SER.#'d SETS
UNPRICED GOLD PRINT RUN ONE TO 14 SETS

AK Andrei Kirilenko	12.00	30.00
BD Baron Davis	12.00	30.00
BM Brad Miller	10.00	25.00
BR Bill Russell	100.00	200.00
CD Clyde Drexler	30.00	80.00
DE Dennis Rodman	75.00	150.00
DR David Robinson	90.00	175.00
GP Gary Payton	20.00	50.00
JE Julius Erving	40.00	100.00
JK Jason Kidd	25.00	60.00
JS John Stockton	60.00	150.00
KB Kobe Bryant	125.00	250.00
KG Kevin Garnett	50.00	120.00
LB Larry Bird	75.00	150.00
MJ Michael Jordan	400.00	700.00
MR Michael Redd	10.00	25.00
PP Paul Pierce	25.00	60.00
RM Reggie Miller	40.00	100.00
RP Robert Parish	15.00	40.00
SA Shareef Abdur-Rahim	10.00	25.00
SM Stephon Marbury	10.00	25.00
WF Walt Frazier	15.00	40.00
YM Yao Ming	30.00	80.00
ZO Alonzo Mourning	60.00	150.00

2004-05 SP Game Used Authentic Fabrics

Inserted at the combined odds of one per pack for all memorabilia cards, this 83-card set features colored backgrounds and a square swatch of memorabilia centered towards the bottom of the card. A Gold version sequentially numbered to 100 and a Patch version in a one of one format were also inserted.
ALL JSY's LISTED AT STATED ODDS 1:1
SP INFO.PROVIDED BY UPPER DECK
*GOLD SINGLES: .6X TO 1.5X BASE JSY HI
GOLD PRINT RUN 100 SER.#'d SETS

AH Anfernee Hardaway	6.00	15.00
AJ Antawn Jamison	2.00	5.00
AK Andrei Kirilenko	2.00	5.00
AM Aaron McKie	2.00	5.00
AN Andre Miller	2.00	5.00
AS Amare Stoudemire	2.00	5.00
BD Baron Davis	2.00	5.00
BO Boris Diaw	2.00	5.00
CA Carlos Boozer	2.00	5.00
CB Caron Butler	2.00	5.00
CH Chauncey Billups	2.50	6.00
CJ Casey Jacobsen SP	2.00	5.00
CM Corey Maggette	2.00	5.00
CW Chris Wilcox	2.00	5.00
DA Derek Anderson	1.50	4.00
DB Shane Battier	2.00	5.00
DF Derek Fisher	2.00	5.00
DG Drew Gooden	1.50	4.00
DI Dikembe Mutombo	2.50	6.00
DM Darius Miles	2.00	5.00
DW David Wesley	2.00	5.00
EB Elton Brand	2.50	6.00
EC Eddy Curry	1.50	4.00
EG Manu Ginobili	3.00	8.00
EJ Eddie Jones SP	2.00	5.00
FJ Fred Jones	2.00	5.00
GA Gilbert Arenas	2.00	5.00
GG Gordan Giricek SP	2.00	5.00
GR Glenn Robinson	2.00	5.00
JA Marko Jaric SP	2.00	5.00
JD Juan Dixon SP	2.00	5.00
JH Jarvis Hayes	2.00	5.00
JI Jiri Welsch	2.00	5.00
JJ Joe Johnson	2.00	5.00
JK Jason Kidd SP	4.00	10.00
JM Jamaal Magloire	2.00	5.00
JO Jermaine O'Neal	2.00	5.00
JR Jalen Rose	2.00	5.00
JS Jerry Stackhouse	2.00	5.00
JT Jason Terry	2.00	5.00
JW Jason Williams	2.00	5.00
KB Kobe Bryant SP	10.00	25.00
KK Kerry Kittles	1.50	4.00
KR Kareem Rush SP	2.00	5.00
KT Kurt Thomas SP	2.00	5.00
KV Keith Van Horn SP	2.00	5.00
LE Rashard Lewis	2.50	6.00
LH Larry Hughes SP	2.00	5.00
LJ LeBron James	12.00	30.00
LO Lamar Odom	2.00	5.00
LR Luke Ridnour	2.00	5.00
LS Latrell Sprewell	2.00	5.00
MA Jamal Mashburn	2.00	5.00
MB Mike Bibby	2.50	6.00
MD Antonio McDyess	2.00	5.00
MI Mike Dunleavy	2.00	5.00
MJ Michael Jordan SP	50.00	100.00
MM Mike Miller	2.00	5.00
MO Morris Peterson	1.50	4.00
MP Mickael Pietrus	2.00	5.00
MR Michael Redd	2.00	5.00
NH Nene	2.00	5.00
NV Nick Van Exel	2.00	5.00
OL Michael Olowokandi	2.00	5.00
PG Pau Gasol	2.50	6.00
PR Tayshaun Prince	2.00	5.00
PS Peja Stojakovic	2.50	6.00
QR Quentin Richardson	2.00	5.00
RA Ray Allen	2.50	6.00
RH Richard Hamilton	2.00	5.00
RL Raef LaFrentz	2.00	5.00
RM Reggie Miller	3.00	8.00
SB Shane Battier	2.00	5.00
SJ Stephen Jackson	2.00	5.00
SM Shawn Marion SP	2.00	5.00
SS Stromile Swift SP	2.00	5.00
ST Stephon Marbury	2.00	5.00
TC Tyson Chandler	2.00	5.00
TD Tim Duncan	4.00	10.00
TK Toni Kukoc	2.50	6.00
TP Tony Parker	2.50	6.00
TR Theo Ratliff	2.00	5.00
WS Wally Szczerbiak	2.00	5.00
ZI Zydrunas Ilgauskas SP	2.00	5.00

2004-05 SP Game Used Authentic Fabrics Autographs

Randomly inserted in packs, this 31-card set parallels the design aspects of the base Authentic Fabrics set enhanced with a player autograph and sequential numbering to 100.
PRINT RUN 100 SER.#'d SETS

AJ Antawn Jamison	6.00	15.00
AK Andrei Kirilenko	6.00	15.00
AM Andre Miller	6.00	15.00
AN Antonio McDyess	6.00	15.00
AS Amare Stoudemire	8.00	20.00
BD Baron Davis	10.00	25.00
CA Carmelo Anthony	25.00	60.00
CM Corey Maggette	6.00	15.00
DW Dwyane Wade	60.00	150.00
GA Gilbert Arenas	6.00	15.00
GP Gary Payton	20.00	50.00
JC Jamal Crawford	6.00	15.00
JK Jason Kidd	25.00	60.00
JR Jason Richardson	10.00	25.00
KB Kobe Bryant	100.00	200.00
KG Kevin Garnett	50.00	100.00
LJ LeBron James	200.00	500.00
LO Lamar Odom	10.00	25.00
MB Mike Bibby	6.00	15.00
MJ Michael Jordan	300.00	600.00
PG Pau Gasol	20.00	50.00
PP Paul Pierce	15.00	40.00
RJ Richard Jefferson	6.00	15.00
RM Reggie Miller	100.00	200.00
SA Shareef Abdur-Rahim	6.00	15.00
SC Sam Cassell	6.00	15.00
SH Shawn Marion	6.00	15.00
SM Stephon Marbury	20.00	50.00
TM Tracy McGrady	20.00	50.00
YM Yao Ming	25.00	60.00
ZR Zach Randolph	10.00	25.00

2004-05 SP Game Used Authentic Fabrics Dual

Randomly inserted, this 38-card set utilizes some design aspects of the single player Authentic Fabrics cards but is horizontally designed with two players and two swatches of memorabilia. Each card is sequentially numbered to 100.
PRINT RUN 100 SER.#'d SETS
UNPRICED DUAL PATCH PRINT RUN 10 SETS
UNPRICED LOGO PRINT RUN ONE SET
UNPRICED QUAD PRINT RUN 10 SETS

AL R.Allen/R.Lewis	4.00	10.00
BJ K.Bryant/L.James	25.00	60.00
BM E.Brand/C.Maggette	4.00	10.00
BR C.Bosh/J.Rose	4.00	10.00
CB W.Chamberlain/Kobe	40.00	100.00
CC J.Crawford/T.Chandler	4.00	10.00
DM B.Davis/J.Mashburn	3.00	8.00
FM S.Francis/Y.Ming	8.00	20.00
GF D.George/D.Fisher	3.00	8.00
GP M.Ginobili/T.Parker	5.00	12.00
GW P.Gasol/J.Williams	4.00	10.00
HG J.Howard/R.Gaines	3.00	8.00
HH L.Hughes/J.Hayes	3.00	8.00
IS A.Iverson/E.Snow	6.00	15.00
JB M.Jordan/K.Bryant	60.00	150.00
JJ L.James/M.Jordan	75.00	200.00
JT M.Jordan/I.Thomas	40.00	100.00
KM J.Kidd/K.Martin	6.00	15.00
MA D.Miles/S.Abdur-Rahim	3.00	8.00
MB M.Miller/S.Battier	3.00	8.00
MI T.McGrady/A.Iverson	6.00	15.00
NN D.Nowitzki/S.Nash	6.00	15.00
OM S.O'Neal/K.Malone	10.00	25.00
PB P.Pierce/L.Bird	10.00	25.00
PS J.Posey/S.Swift	2.50	6.00
RA Z.Randolph/S.Abdur-Rahim	3.00	8.00
RD D.Robinson/T.Duncan	6.00	15.00
RJ J.Richardson/R.Jefferson	4.00	10.00
RK G.Robinson/K.Korver	3.00	8.00
RV M.Redd/K.Van Horn	3.00	8.00
RW K.Rush/L.Walton	2.50	6.00
SC L.Sprewell/S.Cassell	3.00	8.00
SK J.Stockton/A.Kirilenko	6.00	15.00
SM A.Stoudemire/S.Marion	3.00	8.00
SW P.Stojakovic/C.Webber	4.00	10.00
TS K.Thomas/M.Sweetney	2.50	6.00
WH B.Wallace/R.Hamilton	3.00	8.00
WO D.Wade/L.Odom	6.00	15.00

2004-05 SP Game Used Authentic Fabrics Dual Autographs

Randomly inserted, this 42-card set utilizes some design aspects of the single player Authentic Fabrics cards but is horizontally designed with two players, two swatches of memorabilia and two autographs. Each card is sequentially numbered to 50.
PRINT RUN 15 TO 50 SER.#'d SETS

AJ C.Anthony/L.James/15	250.00	500.00
AM C.Anthony/A.Miller	40.00	80.00
AR S.Abdur-R/Z.Randolph	20.00	50.00
AS G.Arenas/J.Stackhouse	12.00	30.00
BA M.Bibby/G.Arenas	12.00	30.00
BG C.Billups/K.Garnett	60.00	120.00
BH C.Billups/R.Hamilton	15.00	40.00
BJ M.Bibby/R.Jefferson	12.00	30.00
BM S.Battier/C.Maggette	12.00	30.00
BP K.Bryant/G.Payton	100.00	200.00
BS C.Bosh/S.Marbury	15.00	40.00
DM B.Davis/R.Miller	40.00	80.00
GB P.Gasol/S.Battier	12.00	30.00
GC K.Garnett/S.Cassell	50.00	100.00
GM K.Garnett/McGrady/15	100.00	200.00
JB L.James/C.Boozer	150.00	300.00
JJ M.Jordan/L.James/15	1000.00	1500.00
JM L.James/Y.Ming	200.00	400.00
KG A.Kirilenko/P.Gasol	20.00	50.00
KJ J.Kidd/R.Jefferson	30.00	80.00
MA D.Miles/S.Abdur-Rahim	12.00	30.00
MG T.McGrady/D.Gooden	30.00	60.00
MH A.Miller/Nene	12.00	30.00
MJ R.Miller/F.Jones	40.00	100.00
MK S.Marbury/J.Kidd	30.00	80.00
MM S.Marion/A.McDyess	12.00	30.00
MP T.McGrady/P.Pierce	40.00	80.00
MR A.Mourning/R.Jefferson	60.00	120.00
MW C.Maggette/C.Wilcox	12.00	30.00
PB P.Pierce/L.Bird/15	125.00	250.00
PF G.Payton/D.Fisher	25.00	60.00
PM P.Pierce.M.Banks	12.00	30.00
RJ J-Rich/F.Jones	12.00	30.00
RP J-Rich/M.Pietrus	12.00	30.00
RR Z.Randolph/J-Rich	12.00	30.00
SA S.Marion/Amare	40.00	80.00
SM A.Stoudemire/A.McDyess	30.00	60.00
WD C.Wilcox/J.Dixon	12.00	30.00
WH D.Wade/U.Haslem	60.00	120.00
WO D.Wade/L.Odom	20.00	50.00

2004-05 SP Game Used Authentic Fabrics Triple

Limted to 25 and randomly seeded, this nine card set features three players and three swatches of game worn memorabilia.
PRINT RUN 25 SER.#'d SETS

JBJ Jordan/Kobe/LeBron	125.00	250.00
JBW LeBron/Boozer/Wagner	20.00	50.00
MKJ Martin/Kittles/Jefferson	10.00	25.00
PDW Pierce/Davis/Welsch	12.00	30.00
RSA Randolph/Stoud/Anderson	10.00	25.00
RVD JRich/Van Exel/Dunleavy	10.00	25.00

2004-05 SP Game Used Authentic Patches

Randomly seeded and limited to 100 serial numbered copies, this 57-card set has a gray border along the bottom and a premium patch swatch in the lower left hand corner. Dual player versions serially numbered to 25 and Triple player versions serially numbered to 10 were also produced and inserted.
PRINT RUN 100 SER.#'d SETS
UNPRICED TRIPLE PRINT RUN 10 SETS

AK Andrei Kirilenko	5.00	12.00
AL Ray Allen	10.00	25.00
AM Andre Miller	5.00	12.00
AS Amare Stoudemire	5.00	12.00
AW Antoine Walker	6.00	15.00
BW Ben Wallace	5.00	12.00
CA Carmelo Anthony	12.00	30.00
CB Chris Bosh	6.00	15.00
CH Chauncey Billups	6.00	15.00
CM Cuttino Mobley	4.00	10.00
CO Corey Maggette	5.00	12.00
CW Chris Webber	8.00	20.00
DG Drew Gooden	4.00	10.00
DM Darius Miles	4.00	10.00
DN Dirk Nowitzki	10.00	25.00
DW Dwyane Wade	12.00	30.00
EC Eddy Curry	4.00	10.00
EG Manu Ginobili	8.00	20.00
GA Gilbert Arenas	5.00	12.00
GP Gary Payton	8.00	20.00
JC Jamal Crawford	6.00	15.00
JH Jarvis Hayes	4.00	10.00
JR Jalen Rose	5.00	12.00
JS Jerry Stackhouse	5.00	12.00
JT Jason Terry	5.00	12.00
JW Jason Williams	10.00	25.00
KB Kobe Bryant	50.00	125.00
KE Kenyon Martin	5.00	12.00
KG Kevin Garnett	10.00	25.00
KM Karl Malone	8.00	20.00
LH Larry Hughes	5.00	12.00
LJ LeBron James	30.00	80.00
LO Lamar Odom	5.00	12.00
LS Latrell Sprewell	6.00	15.00
MB Mike Bibby	6.00	15.00
MF Michael Finley	6.00	15.00
MJ Michael Jordan	100.00	200.00
MP Morris Peterson	4.00	10.00
MR Michael Redd	5.00	12.00
NH Nene	5.00	12.00
NV Nick Van Exel	5.00	12.00
PG Pau Gasol	6.00	15.00
PP Paul Pierce	6.00	15.00
PS Peja Stojakovic	6.00	15.00
QR Quentin Richardson	5.00	12.00
RH Richard Hamilton	5.00	12.00
RJ Richard Jefferson	5.00	12.00
RL Rashard Lewis	6.00	15.00
RM Reggie Miller	12.50	30.00
SA Shareef Abdur-Rahim	5.00	12.00
SF Steve Francis	5.00	12.00
SH Shawn Marion	5.00	12.00
SM Stephon Marbury	5.00	12.00
SN Steve Nash	8.00	20.00
TM Tracy McGrady	8.00	20.00
TP Tony Parker	6.00	15.00
ZR Zach Randolph	5.00	12.00

2004-05 SP Game Used Authentic Patches Autographs

Randomly seeded in packs, this 30-card set parallels the design of the Authentic Patches set enhanced with a player autograph and sequential numbering to 50. Dual Autographed versions serially numbered to five were also inserted.
PRINT RUN 50 SER.#'d SETS
AJ Antawn Jamison 15.00 40.00
AK Andrei Kirilenko 15.00 40.00
AM Andre Miller 15.00 40.00
AN Antonio McDyess 15.00 40.00
AS Amare Stoudemire 20.00 50.00
BD Baron Davis 15.00 40.00
CA Carmelo Anthony 40.00 100.00
CM Corey Maggette 15.00 40.00
DW Dwyane Wade 125.00 250.00
GA Gilbert Arenas 15.00 40.00
GP Gary Payton 25.00 60.00
JC Jamal Crawford 15.00 40.00
JK Jason Kidd 60.00 120.00
JR Jason Richardson 15.00 40.00
KB Kobe Bryant 150.00 300.00
KG Kevin Garnett 100.00 200.00
LJ LeBron James 200.00 400.00
LO Lamar Odom 20.00 50.00
MB Mike Bibby 15.00 40.00
PG Pau Gasol 20.00 50.00
PP Paul Pierce 40.00 80.00
RJ Richard Jefferson 15.00 40.00
RM Reggie Miller 75.00 200.00
SA Shareef Abdur-Rahim 15.00 40.00
SC Sam Cassell 15.00 40.00
SH Shawn Marion 15.00 40.00
SM Stephon Marbury 25.00 60.00
TM Tracy McGrady 40.00 100.00
YM Yao Ming 60.00 150.00
ZR Zach Randolph 15.00 40.00

2004-05 SP Game Used Authentic Patches Dual

Inserted randomly in packs, this eight card set utilizes some of the design aspects of the Authentic Patches set but is horizontally designed with two players and two memorabilia patches. Each card is limited to 25 serially numbered copies.
PRINT RUN 25 SER.#'d SETS
AG A.Jamison/G.Arenas 20.00 50.00
CR W.Chamberlain/B.Russell 175.00 300.00
JA L.James/C.Anthony 50.00 120.00
JB M.Jordan/K.Bryant 175.00 300.00
JR M.Jordan/D.Rodman 100.00 200.00
PM G.Payton/K.Malone 25.00 60.00

2004-05 SP Game Used Endorsed Numbers

Inserted randomly, this 88-card set is limited to each specific player's jersey number and has a sticker signature across the middle.
PRINT RUNS LISTED IN CHECKLIST
SOME NOT PRICED DUE TO SCARCITY
AJ Antawn Jamison/33 12.00 30.00
AK Andrei Kirilenko/47 20.00 50.00
AN Antonio McDyess/24 20.00 50.00
BB Brent Barry/31 15.00 40.00
BH Brandon Hunter/56 5.00 12.00
BM Brad Miller/52 12.50 30.00
CD Clyde Drexler/22 100.00 200.00
CK Chris Kaman/35 5.00 12.00
CM Cedric Maxwell/31 10.00 25.00
CW Chris Wilcox/54 5.00 12.00
DA David Robinson/50 50.00 125.00
DJ Dahntay Jones/30 5.00 12.00
DM Darko Milicic/31 15.00 40.00
DR Dennis Rodman/91 50.00 120.00
FE Francisco Elson/56 6.00 15.00
GP Gary Payton/20 20.00 50.00
GR Glenn Robinson/31 12.00 30.00
JA Jason Kapono/24 5.00 12.00
JJ James Jones/33 6.00 15.00
KG Kevin Garnett/21 30.00 80.00
KK Kyle Korver/26 15.00 40.00
LB Larry Bird/33 100.00 200.00
LJ LeBron James/23 200.00 400.00
MA Magic Johnson/32 75.00 150.00
MJ Michael Jordan/23 300.00 600.00
ML Maciej Lampe/30 8.00 20.00
MR Michael Redd/22 12.00 30.00
MS Mike Sweetney/50 5.00 12.00
MW Maurice Williams/25 5.00 12.00
NH Nene/31 8.00 20.00
PG Pau Gasol/16 30.00 80.00
PP Paul Pierce/34 20.00 50.00
RH Richard Hamilton/32 12.00 30.00
RJ Richard Jefferson/24 10.00 25.00
RM Reggie Miller/31 40.00 100.00
SA Shareef Abdur-Rahim/33 10.00 25.00
SC Sam Cassell/19 15.00 40.00
SH Shawn Marion/31 15.00 40.00
TO Travis Outlaw/25 6.00 15.00
WG Willie Green/33 5.00 12.00
WZ Wang Zhizhi/15 15.00 40.00
ZO Alonzo Mourning/33 75.00 150.00
ZP Zaza Pachulia/27 5.00 12.00
ZR Zach Randolph/50 10.00 25.00

2004-05 SP Game Used Legendary Fabrics

Inserted at the combined rate for memorabilia cards at one per pack, this 11-card set places a player photo above an "L" shaped swatch of game used memorabilia.
ALL JSY'S LISTED AT STATED ODDS 1:1
BR Bill Russell 8.00 20.00
CD Clyde Drexler 6.00 15.00
DR Dennis Rodman 10.00 25.00
GG George Gervin 5.00 12.00
IT Isiah Thomas 5.00 12.00
JE Julius Erving 8.00 20.00
JS John Stockton 8.00 20.00
LB Larry Bird 12.00 30.00
MA Magic Johnson 12.00 30.00
MJ Michael Jordan 40.00 100.00
WF Walt Frazier 5.00 12.00

2004-05 SP Game Used Legendary Fabrics Autographs

Seeded in packs randomly, this 11-card set parallels the Legendary Fabrics set enhanced with player autographs and sequential numbering to 100.
PRINT RUN 100 SER.#'d SETS
BR Bill Russell 100.00 200.00
CD Clyde Drexler 25.00 60.00
DR Dennis Rodman 100.00 250.00
GG George Gervin 15.00 40.00
IT Isiah Thomas 25.00 60.00
JE Julius Erving 50.00 100.00
JS John Stockton 75.00 150.00
LB Larry Bird 100.00 200.00
MA Magic Johnson 75.00 150.00
MJ Michael Jordan 300.00 550.00
WF Walt Frazier 15.00 40.00

2004-05 SP Game Used Rookie Exclusive Autographs

Randomly inserted in packs, this 51-card set is horizontally designed with a player photo and either a cut signature or a sticker signature centered along the bottom. Each card is limited to 100 serially numbered copies.
PRINT RUN 100 SER.#'d SETS
RE1 Andre Emmett 4.00 10.00
RE2 Andre Iguodala 20.00 50.00
RE3 Al Jefferson 10.00 25.00
RE4 Anderson Varejao 12.00 30.00
RE5 Ben Gordon 15.00 40.00
RE6 Andris Biedrins 4.00 10.00
RE7 Blake Stepp 6.00 15.00
RE8 Antonio Burks 5.00 12.00
RE9 Beno Udrih 5.00 12.00
RE10 Chris Duhon 6.00 15.00
RE11 David Harrison 4.00 10.00
RE12 Delonte West 10.00 25.00
RE13 Dwight Howard 20.00 50.00
RE14 Dorell Wright 6.00 15.00
RE15 Donta Smith 4.00 10.00
RE16 Devin Harris 12.00 30.00
RE17 Ha Seung-Jin 10.00 25.00
RE18 Josh Childress 5.00 12.00
RE19 Jameer Nelson 10.00 25.00
RE20 J.R. Smith 6.00 15.00
RE21 Pape Sow 5.00 12.00
RE22 Jackson Vroman 4.00 10.00
RE23 Kris Humphries 6.00 15.00
RE24 Kevin Martin 25.00 60.00
RE25 Kirk Snyder 4.00 10.00
RE26 Lionel Chalmers 6.00 15.00
RE27 Luol Deng 12.00 30.00
RE28 Luke Jackson 4.00 10.00
RE29 Matt Freije 5.00 12.00
RE30 Pavel Podkolzin 4.00 10.00
RE31 Peter John Ramos 4.00 10.00
RE32 Rafael Araujo 4.00 10.00
RE33 Robert Swift 4.00 10.00
RE34 Romain Sato 4.00 10.00
RE35 Shaun Livingston 10.00 25.00
RE36 Sergei Monia 4.00 10.00
RE37 Sebastian Telfair 5.00 12.00
RE38 Sasha Vujacic 6.00 15.00
RE39 Tony Allen 6.00 15.00
RE40 Tim Pickett 6.00 15.00
RE41 Trevor Ariza 6.00 15.00
RE42 Viktor Khryapa 4.00 10.00
RE43 David Young 6.00 15.00
RE44 Royal Ivey 5.00 12.00
RE45 Christian Drejer 6.00 15.00
RE46 Bernard Robinson 5.00 12.00
RE48 Justin Reed 4.00 10.00
RE49 Darius Rice 6.00 15.00
RE50 Ricky Minard 5.00 12.00
RE51 Nenad Krstic 6.00 15.00
NNO Josh Smith 20.00 50.00

2004-05 SP Game Used SIGnificance

Limited to 100 copies, this 111-card set features player photos and an unshaded basketball along the bottom in which autographs appear. Gold versions limited to 10 were produced along with dual signatures, numbered to 25, and dual gold signatures, numbered to five.
PRINT RUN 100 SER.#'d SETS
AJ Antawn Jamison 5.00 12.00
AK Andrei Kirilenko 6.00 15.00
AL Al Harrington 5.00 12.00
AM Andre Miller 5.00 12.00
AS Amare Stoudemire 12.00 30.00
BB Brent Barry 5.00 12.00
BC Bob Cousy 25.00 60.00
BD Baron Davis 5.00 12.00
BE Jerome Beasley 5.00 12.00
BH Brandon Hunter 5.00 12.00
BL Steve Blake 5.00 12.00
BM Brad Miller 6.00 15.00
BO Carlos Boozer 5.00 12.00
BR Bill Russell 50.00 125.00
BW Bill Walton 10.00 25.00
CA Carmelo Anthony 25.00 60.00
CD Clyde Drexler 12.00 30.00
CE Cedric Maxwell 5.00 12.00
CH Chauncey Billups 8.00 20.00
CK Chris Kaman 5.00 12.00
CM Corey Maggette 5.00 12.00
DA Chuck Daly 20.00 40.00
DD Darryl Dawkins 10.00 25.00
DF Derek Fisher 6.00 15.00
DG Drew Gooden 5.00 12.00
DI Dan Dickau 5.00 12.00
DM Darko Milicic 5.00 12.00
DR David Robinson 40.00 80.00
DT David Thompson 5.00 12.00
DW Dwyane Wade 25.00 60.00
DY Dahntay Jones 5.00 12.00
EC Eddy Curry 5.00 12.00
FE Francisco Elson 5.00 12.00
FJ Fred Jones 5.00 12.00
GA Gilbert Arenas 6.00 15.00
GG George Gervin 8.00 20.00
GO Gordan Giricek 5.00 12.00
GP Gary Payton 10.00 25.00
GR Glenn Robinson 5.00 12.00
GW Gerald Wallace 5.00 12.00
IT Isiah Thomas 20.00 50.00
JA Jamaal Wilkes 8.00 20.00
JB Jon Barry 5.00 12.00
JD Juan Dixon 5.00 12.00
JE Julius Erving 30.00 80.00
JH Josh Howard 5.00 12.00
JJ James Jones 5.00 12.00
JK Jason Kidd 12.00 30.00
JM Jerome Moiso 5.00 12.00
JO John Salley 8.00 20.00
JR Jalen Rose 6.00 15.00
JS John Stockton 40.00 100.00
JT Jamaal Tinsley 5.00 12.00
JW James Worthy 30.00 60.00
KA Jason Kapono 5.00 12.00
KB Kobe Bryant 100.00 200.00
KC K.C. Jones 8.00 20.00
KE Keith Bogans 5.00 12.00
KG Kevin Garnett 30.00 80.00
KK Kyle Korver 8.00 20.00
KR Kareem Rush 5.00 12.00
KU Kurt Rambis 5.00 12.00
LA Larry Bird 50.00 120.00
LB Leandro Barbosa 5.00 12.00
LJ LeBron James 150.00 300.00
LO Lamar Odom 6.00 15.00
LR Luke Ridnour 5.00 12.00
MA Magic Johnson 50.00 120.00
MB Mike Bibby 6.00 15.00
MI Mickael Pietrus 5.00 12.00
MJ Michael Jordan 400.00 800.00
MP Morris Peterson 5.00 12.00
MR Michael Redd 5.00 12.00
MS Mike Sweetney 5.00 12.00
MW Maurice Williams 5.00 12.00
NH Nene 5.00 12.00
PB Primoz Brezec 5.00 12.00
PG Pau Gasol 10.00 25.00
PL Zoran Planinic 5.00 12.00
PP Paul Pierce 10.00 25.00
PR Pat Riley 15.00 40.00
RG Reece Gaines 5.00 12.00
RH Richard Hamilton 6.00 15.00
RI Jason Richardson 5.00 12.00
RJ Richard Jefferson 5.00 12.00
RM Reggie Miller 60.00 150.00
RO Dennis Rodman 50.00 120.00
RP Robert Parish 8.00 20.00
SA Shareef Abdur-Rahim 5.00 12.00
SB Shane Battier 6.00 15.00
SC Sam Cassell 5.00 12.00
SH Shawn Marion 8.00 20.00
SM Stephon Marbury 12.00 30.00
ST Jerry Stackhouse 6.00 15.00
SW Spud Webb 8.00 20.00
TB Troy Bell 5.00 12.00
TM Tracy McGrady 20.00 50.00
TO Travis Outlaw 5.00 12.00
TP Tony Parker 6.00 15.00
TS Theron Smith 5.00 12.00
WF Walt Frazier 8.00 20.00
WG Willie Green 5.00 12.00
WR Willis Reed 10.00 25.00
WU Wes Unseld 8.00 20.00
WZ Wang Zhizhi 8.00 20.00
YM Yao Ming 20.00 50.00
ZC Zarko Cabarkapa 5.00 12.00
ZO Alonzo Mourning 20.00 50.00
ZP Zaza Pachulia 5.00 12.00
ZR Zach Randolph 6.00 15.00

2004-05 SP Game Used SIGnificance Duals

Randomly inserted and limited to 25 copies, this 30-card set places two players and two autographs on each card.
PRINT RUN 25 SER.#'d SETS
UNPRICED GOLD PRINT RUN 5 SETS
AJ C.Anthony/M.Jordan 300.00 600.00
BB B.Barry/J.Barry 15.00 40.00
BJ K.Bryant/M.Johnson 150.00 300.00
BK C.Boozer/A.Kirilenko 20.00 50.00
CC E.Curry/J.Crawford 20.00 50.00
DE D.Dawkins/J.Erving 60.00 150.00
DT B.Davis/I.Thomas 20.00 50.00
GC K.Garnett/S.Cassell 75.00 150.00
GR K.Garnett/B.Russell 150.00 300.00
JC K.C.Jones/B.Cousy 30.00 80.00
JJ L.James/M.Jordan 800.00 1500.00
KS J.Kidd/J.Stockton 100.00 200.00
LK L.Bird/K.C.Jones 100.00 200.00
MD T.McGrady/C.Drexler 75.00 150.00
MJ C.Maxwell/K.C.Jones 15.00 40.00
MP C.Maxwell/R.Parish 40.00 100.00
MS S.Marbury/M.Sweetney 20.00 50.00
PB P.Pierce/L.Bird 75.00 150.00
RJ K.Rambis/M.Johnson 40.00 100.00
RP M.Redd/Z.Pachulia 15.00 40.00
RW K.Rush/L.Walton 15.00 40.00
SE A.Stoudemire/J.Erving 75.00 150.00
WE D.Wade/J.Erving 125.00 250.00

2004-05 SP Game Used SIGnificant Numbers

Randomly seeded in packs, this 12-card set is horizontally designed with both an autograph and a swatch of memorabilia. Each card is limited to the featured player's jersey number.
STATED PRINT RUN ONE TO 50 SETS
SOME NOT PRICED DUE TO SCARCITY
AK Andrei Kirilenko/47 25.00 60.00
AS Amare Stoudemire/32 12.00 30.00
CA Carmelo Anthony/15 30.00 80.00
DR David Robinson/50 40.00 100.00
LJ LeBron James/23 400.00 800.00
MA Magic Johnson/32 100.00 250.00
MJ Michael Jordan/23 400.00 800.00

2004-05 SP Game Used Wood Impressions

Limited to 75 copies and randomly seeded in packs, this 42-card set places a player photo above a swatch of wood that is autographed.
STATED PRINT RUN 75 SER.#'d SETS
AK Andrei Kirilenko 15.00 40.00
AM Andre Miller 10.00 25.00
AS Amare Stoudemire 15.00 40.00
BC Bob Cousy 50.00 100.00
BD Baron Davis 12.00 30.00
CA Carmelo Anthony 30.00 80.00
CD Clyde Drexler 30.00 80.00
CH Chauncey Billups 15.00 40.00
CM Corey Maggette 10.00 25.00
DR Dennis Rodman 100.00 200.00
DT David Thompson 15.00 40.00
DW Dwyane Wade 60.00 150.00
FE Francisco Elson 10.00 25.00
GG George Gervin 12.00 30.00
GP Gary Payton 12.00 30.00
IT Isiah Thomas 15.00 40.00
JC Jamal Crawford 12.00 30.00
JE Julius Erving 40.00 80.00
JH Josh Howard 10.00 25.00
JK Jason Kidd 30.00 80.00
JR Jason Richardson 10.00 25.00
JS John Stockton 75.00 150.00
JW James Worthy 25.00 60.00
KB Kobe Bryant 150.00 400.00
KG Kevin Garnett 75.00 200.00
KK Kyle Korver 12.00 30.00
LJ LeBron James 500.00 1000.00
LO Lamar Odom 10.00 25.00
MA Magic Johnson 75.00 150.00
MD Marquis Daniels 10.00 25.00
MJ Michael Jordan 600.00 1200.00
PG Pau Gasol 20.00 50.00
PP Paul Pierce 15.00 40.00
RJ Richard Jefferson 10.00 25.00
RM Reggie Miller 75.00 200.00
SA Shareef Abdur-Rahim 10.00 25.00
SM Shawn Marion 12.00 30.00
SW Spud Webb 12.00 30.00
TM Tracy McGrady 40.00 100.00
WR Willis Reed 15.00 40.00
YM Yao Ming 60.00 150.00
ZR Zach Randolph 10.00 25.00

2005-06 SP Game Used

Released in November 2004, SP Game Used boasts a 150-card set where cards 1-100 feature veterans and cards 101-150 feature rookie players serially numbered to 999. Base cards have white and gray backgrounds with highlights set to match team colors. SP Game Used was packaged in six pack boxes of three cards each and carried a suggested retail price of $29.99. Each pack contains either an autograph or memorabilia cards.
UNPRICED PARALLEL PRINT RUN ONE SET
UNPRICED PARALLEL PRINT RUN 10 SETS
1 Al Harrington .75 2.00
2 Josh Smith .75 2.00
3 Josh Childress .75 2.00
4 Joe Johnson .75 2.00
5 Paul Pierce 1.00 2.50
6 Antoine Walker .75 2.00
7 Gary Payton 1.00 2.50
8 Al Jefferson .75 2.00
9 Emeka Okafor .75 2.00
10 Primoz Brezec .60 1.50
11 Gerald Wallace .75 2.00
12 Michael Jordan 8.00 20.00
13 Ben Gordon .75 2.00
14 Luol Deng .75 2.00
15 Eddy Curry .60 1.50
16 LeBron James 4.00 10.00
17 Dajuan Wagner .60 1.50
18 Drew Gooden .75 2.00
19 Larry Hughes .75 2.00
20 Dirk Nowitzki 1.50 4.00
21 Marquis Daniels .60 1.50
22 Michael Finley 1.00 2.50
23 Jerry Stackhouse .75 2.00
24 Andre Miller .75 2.00
25 Carmelo Anthony 2.00 5.00
26 Kenyon Martin .75 2.00
27 Nene .75 2.00
28 Rasheed Wallace 1.00 2.50
29 Ben Wallace .75 2.00
30 Richard Hamilton .75 2.00
31 Chauncey Billups 1.00 2.50
32 Baron Davis .75 2.00
33 Derek Fisher .75 2.00
34 Jason Richardson 1.00 2.50
35 Tracy McGrady 1.25 3.00
36 Yao Ming 1.25 3.00
37 Juwan Howard .75 2.00
38 Jermaine O'Neal .75 2.00
39 Ron Artest 1.00 2.50
40 Jamaal Tinsley .60 1.50
41 Corey Maggette .75 2.00
42 Elton Brand 1.00 2.50
43 Shaun Livingston .60 1.50
44 Kobe Bryant 4.00 10.00
45 Brian Cook .60 1.50
46 Lamar Odom .75 2.00
47 Bonzi Wells .60 1.50
48 Pau Gasol 1.00 2.50
49 Shane Battier .75 2.00
50 Shaquille O'Neal 2.00 5.00
51 Dwyane Wade 1.50 4.00
52 Dorell Wright .60 1.50
53 Eddie Jones .75 2.00
54 Joe Smith .75 2.00
55 Michael Redd .75 2.00
56 Desmond Mason .60 1.50
57 Kevin Garnett 1.50 4.00
58 Wally Szczerbiak .75 2.00
59 Sam Cassell .75 2.00
60 Vince Carter 1.50 4.00
61 Jason Kidd 1.50 4.00
62 Richard Jefferson .75 2.00
63 Jamaal Magloire .60 1.50
64 J.R. Smith .75 2.00
65 Bostjan Nachbar .60 1.50
66 Allan Houston .75 2.00
67 Stephon Marbury .75 2.00
68 Jamal Crawford 1.00 2.50
69 Dwight Howard .75 2.00
70 Grant Hill 1.25 3.00
71 Jameer Nelson .60 1.50
72 Steve Francis .75 2.00
73 Allen Iverson 1.50 4.00
74 Andre Iguodala .75 2.00
75 Chris Webber 1.00 2.50
76 Samuel Dalembert .60 1.50
77 Amare Stoudemire .75 2.00
78 Steve Nash 1.25 3.00
79 Quentin Richardson .75 2.00
80 Shawn Marion .75 2.00
81 Darius Miles .60 1.50
82 Zach Randolph .75 2.00
83 Shareef Abdur-Rahim .75 2.00
84 Peja Stojakovic 1.00 2.50
85 Mike Bibby 1.00 2.50
86 Manu Ginobili 1.00 2.50
87 Tim Duncan 1.50 4.00
88 Tony Parker 1.00 2.50
89 Ray Allen 1.00 2.50
90 Rashard Lewis 1.00 2.50
91 Robert Swift .60 1.50
92 Ronald Murray .60 1.50
93 Chris Bosh 1.00 2.50
94 Morris Peterson .60 1.50
95 Rafael Araujo .60 1.50
96 Andrei Kirilenko .75 2.00
97 Raul Lopez .60 1.50
98 Carlos Boozer .75 2.00
99 Antawn Jamison .75 2.00
100 Gilbert Arenas .75 2.00
101 Andrew Bynum RC 2.50 6.00
102 Julius Hodge RC 2.00 5.00
103 David Lee RC 3.00 8.00
104 Sarunas Jasikevicius RC 3.00 8.00
105 Ike Diogu RC 2.00 5.00
106 Luther Head RC 2.50 6.00
107 Jason Maxiell RC 2.50 6.00
108 Linas Kleiza RC 2.00 5.00
109 Amir Johnson RC 3.00 8.00
110 Andray Blatche RC 3.00 8.00
111 Sean May RC 2.00 5.00
112 Alex Acker RC 2.00 5.00
113 Nate Robinson RC 3.00 8.00
114 Brandon Bass RC 2.50 6.00
115 Ricky Sanchez RC 3.00 8.00
116 Daniel Ewing RC 2.50 6.00
117 Salim Stoudamire RC 2.50 6.00
118 Dijon Thompson RC 2.00 5.00
119 Danny Granger RC 4.00 10.00
120 Raymond Felton RC 3.00 8.00
121 Louis Williams RC 3.00 8.00
122 Channing Frye RC 3.00 8.00
123 Francisco Garcia RC 2.50 6.00
124 Ryan Gomes RC 2.50 6.00
125 Ersan Ilyasova RC 3.00 8.00
126 Jarrett Jack RC 3.00 8.00
127 Lawrence Roberts RC 2.00 5.00
128 Bracey Wright RC 2.00 5.00
129 C.J. Miles RC 3.00 8.00
130 Will Bynum RC 2.50 6.00
131 Travis Diener RC 2.00 5.00
132 Monta Ellis RC 4.00 10.00
133 Martell Webster RC 2.50 6.00
134 Johan Petro RC 2.00 5.00
135 Uros Slokar RC 3.00 8.00
136 Von Wafer RC 2.00 5.00
137 Martynas Andriuskevicius RC 2.00 5.00
138 Charlie Villanueva RC 3.00 8.00
139 Antoine Wright RC 2.50 6.00
140 Joey Graham RC 2.50 6.00
141 Wayne Simien RC 2.00 5.00
142 Hakim Warrick RC 2.50 6.00
143 Gerald Green RC 3.00 8.00
144 Marvin Williams RC 3.00 8.00
145 Deron Williams RC 4.00 10.00
146 Rashad McCants RC 2.50 6.00
147 Robert Whaley RC 2.00 5.00
148 Chris Taft RC 2.50 6.00
149 Chris Paul RC 12.00 30.00
150 Andrew Bogut RC 4.00 10.00

2005-06 SP Game Used 100

*1-100 VETERANS: .75X TO 2X BASE HI
*101-150 RC's: .5X TO 1.25X BASE HI
PRINT RUN 100 SER.#'d SETS

2005-06 SP Game Used 50

*1-100 VETERANS: 1.25X TO 3X BASE HI
*101-150 RCs: .6X TO 1.5X BASE HI
PRINT RUN 50 SER.#'d SETS
12 Michael Jordan 40.00 100.00

2005-06 SP Game Used 25

*1-100 VETERANS: 2X TO 5X BASE HI
*101-150 RCs: .75X TO 2X BASE HI
PRINT RUN 25 SER.#'d SETS
12 Michael Jordan 50.00 125.00

2005-06 SP Game Used Jerseys

PRINT RUN 100 SER.#'d SETS
1J Al Harrington 2.50 6.00
2J Josh Smith 2.50 6.00
3J Josh Childress 2.50 6.00
4J Joe Johnson 2.50 6.00
5J Paul Pierce 3.00 8.00
6J Antoine Walker 2.50 6.00
7J Gary Payton 3.00 8.00
8J Al Jefferson 2.50 6.00
10J Primoz Brezec 2.00 5.00
11J Gerald Wallace 2.50 6.00
12J Michael Jordan 40.00 100.00
13J Ben Gordon 2.50 6.00
14J Luol Deng 2.50 6.00
15J Eddy Curry 2.00 5.00
16J LeBron James 15.00 40.00
17J Dajuan Wagner 2.00 5.00
18J Drew Gooden 2.50 6.00
19J Larry Hughes 2.50 6.00
20J Dirk Nowitzki 5.00 12.00
21J Marquis Daniels 2.00 5.00
22J Michael Finley 3.00 8.00
23J Jerry Stackhouse 2.50 6.00
24J Andre Miller 2.50 6.00
25J Carmelo Anthony 6.00 15.00
26J Kenyon Martin 2.50 6.00
27J Nene 2.50 6.00
28J Rasheed Wallace 3.00 8.00
29J Ben Wallace 2.50 6.00
30J Richard Hamilton 2.50 6.00
31J Chauncey Billups 3.00 8.00
32J Baron Davis 2.50 6.00
33J Derek Fisher 2.50 6.00
34J Jason Richardson 3.00 8.00
35J Tracy McGrady 4.00 10.00
36J Yao Ming 4.00 10.00
37J Juwan Howard 2.50 6.00
38J Jermaine O'Neal 2.50 6.00
39J Ron Artest 3.00 8.00
40J Jamaal Tinsley 2.00 5.00
41J Corey Maggette 2.50 6.00
42J Elton Brand 3.00 8.00
43J Shaun Livingston 2.00 5.00
44J Kobe Bryant 12.00 30.00
45J Brian Cook 2.00 5.00
46J Lamar Odom 2.50 6.00
47J Bonzi Wells 2.00 5.00
48J Pau Gasol 3.00 8.00
49J Shane Battier 2.50 6.00
50J Shaquille O'Neal 6.00 15.00
51J Dwyane Wade 5.00 12.00
52J Dorell Wright 2.00 5.00
53J Eddie Jones 2.50 6.00
54J Joe Smith 2.50 6.00
55J Michael Redd 2.50 6.00
56J Desmond Mason 2.00 5.00
57J Kevin Garnett 5.00 12.00
58J Wally Szczerbiak 2.50 6.00
59J Sam Cassell 2.50 6.00
61J Jason Kidd 5.00 12.00
62J Richard Jefferson 2.50 6.00
63J Jamaal Magloire 2.00 5.00
64J J.R. Smith 2.50 6.00
65J Bostjan Nachbar 2.00 5.00
66J Allan Houston 2.50 6.00
67J Stephon Marbury 2.50 6.00
68J Jamal Crawford 3.00 8.00
69J Dwight Howard 2.50 6.00
70J Grant Hill 4.00 10.00
71J Jameer Nelson 2.00 5.00
72J Steve Francis 2.50 6.00
74J Andre Iguodala 2.50 6.00
75J Chris Webber 3.00 8.00
76J Samuel Dalembert 2.00 5.00
77J Amare Stoudemire 2.50 6.00
78J Steve Nash 4.00 10.00
79J Quentin Richardson 2.50 6.00
80J Shawn Marion 2.50 6.00
81J Darius Miles 2.00 5.00
82J Zach Randolph 2.50 6.00
83J Shareef Abdur-Rahim 2.50 6.00
84J Peja Stojakovic 3.00 8.00
85J Mike Bibby 3.00 8.00
86J Manu Ginobili 3.00 8.00
87J Tim Duncan 5.00 12.00
88J Tony Parker 3.00 8.00
89J Ray Allen 3.00 8.00
90J Rashard Lewis 3.00 8.00
91J Robert Swift 2.00 5.00
92J Ronald Murray 2.00 5.00
93J Chris Bosh 3.00 8.00
94J Morris Peterson 2.00 5.00
95J Rafael Araujo 2.00 5.00
96J Andrei Kirilenko 2.50 6.00
97J Raul Lopez 2.00 5.00
98J Carlos Boozer 2.50 6.00
99J Antawn Jamison 2.50 6.00
100J Gilbert Arenas 2.50 6.00

2005-06 SP Game Used Authentic Fabrics

Inserted at the rate of one per pack, this 100-card set features both veteran and rookie players with a centered image at the top of the card and a centered swatch of jersey at the bottom.
STATED ODDS ONE PER PACK
*GOLD: .5X TO 1.25X BASE FAB HI
GOLD PRINT RUN 100 SER.#'d SETS
UNPRICED LOGO PRINT RUN ONE SET
AB Andris Biedrins 1.50 4.00
AE Andre Emmett 2.00 5.00
AH Anfernee Hardaway 6.00 15.00
AI Andre Iguodala 2.00 5.00
AJ Al Jefferson 2.00 5.00
AK Andrei Kirilenko 2.00 5.00
AM Antonio McDyess 2.00 5.00
AN Antawn Jamison 2.00 5.00
AR Ron Artest 2.50 6.00
AS Amare Stoudemire 2.00 5.00
BC Brian Cook 2.00 5.00
BD Baron Davis 2.00 5.00
BE Ben Wallace 2.00 5.00
BG Ben Gordon 2.00 5.00
BJ Bobby Jackson 2.00 5.00
BR Bernard Robinson 2.00 5.00
BW Bonzi Wells 2.00 5.00
CA Carmelo Anthony 5.00 12.00
CB Carlos Boozer 2.00 5.00
CD Carlos Delfino 2.00 5.00
CM Corey Maggette 2.00 5.00
CU Cuttino Mobley 1.50 4.00
CW Corliss Williamson 2.00 5.00
DE Devean George 2.00 5.00
DG Drew Gooden 2.00 5.00
DH Dwight Howard 2.00 5.00
DJ Damon Jones 2.00 5.00
DM Darius Miles 2.00 5.00
DN Dirk Nowitzki 4.00 10.00
DS Darius Songaila 2.00 5.00
EB Elton Brand 2.50 6.00
EC Eddy Curry 1.50 4.00
EJ Eddie Jones 2.00 5.00
GP Gary Payton 2.50 6.00
GR Glenn Robinson 2.00 5.00
GW Gerald Wallace 2.00 5.00
JA Jason Kapono 2.00 5.00
JD Juan Dixon 2.00 5.00
JH Jarvis Hayes 2.00 5.00
JJ Jim Jackson 2.00 5.00
JK Jason Kidd 4.00 10.00
JM Jamaal Magloire 2.00 5.00
JN Jameer Nelson 1.50 4.00
JO Jermaine O'Neal 2.00 5.00
JR Jason Richardson 2.50 6.00
JS Joe Smith 2.00 5.00
KB Kobe Bryant 10.00 25.00
KE Kevin Martin 2.00 5.00
KG Kevin Garnett 4.00 10.00
KH Kris Humphries 2.00 5.00
KM Kenyon Martin 2.00 5.00
KS Kirk Snyder 2.00 5.00
KW Kwame Brown 2.00 5.00
LA Larry Hughes 2.00 5.00
LD Luol Deng 2.00 5.00
LH Lucious Harris 2.00 5.00
LJ LeBron James 15.00 40.00
LO Raul Lopez 2.00 5.00
LU Luke Jackson 2.00 5.00
MA Malik Rose 2.00 5.00
MB Mike Bibby 2.50 6.00
MD Marquis Daniels 2.00 5.00
MG Manu Ginobili 2.50 6.00
MI Mike Dunleavy 2.00 5.00
MJ Michael Jordan 30.00 80.00
MP Morris Peterson SP 1.50 4.00
MR Michael Redd SP 2.00 5.00
MT Maurice Taylor 2.00 5.00
NK Nenad Krstic 2.00 5.00
NT Nikoloz Tskitishvili 2.00 5.00
PP Paul Pierce 2.50 6.00
PS Peja Stojakovic 2.50 6.00
QR Quentin Richardson 2.00 5.00
RA Ray Allen 2.50 6.00
RF Rafael Araujo 2.00 5.00
RG Reece Gaines 2.00 5.00
RH Richard Hamilton 2.00 5.00
RJ Richard Jefferson 2.00 5.00
RL Rashard Lewis 2.50 6.00
RM Ronald Murray 2.00 5.00
RR Rodney Rogers 2.00 5.00
SD Samuel Dalembert 2.00 5.00
SF Steve Francis 2.00 5.00
SM Stephon Marbury 2.00 5.00
SN Steve Nash 3.00 8.00
SO Shaquille O'Neal 5.00 12.00
ST Sebastian Telfair 2.00 5.00
SV Sasha Vujacic 2.00 5.00
TA Tony Allen SP 2.00 5.00
TC Tyson Chandler 2.00 5.00
TD Tim Duncan 4.00 10.00
TH Troy Hudson 2.00 5.00
TM Tracy McGrady 3.00 8.00
TP Tony Parker 2.50 6.00
UH Udonis Haslem 1.50 4.00
VR Vladimir Radmanovic 2.00 5.00
WG Willie Green 2.00 5.00
WI Kevin Willis 2.00 5.00
WS Wally Szczerbiak 2.00 5.00
YM Yao Ming 3.00 8.00

2005-06 SP Game Used Authentic Fabrics Patches

*PATCHES: 2X TO 5X BASE HI
PRINT RUN 75 SER.#'d SETS
KB Kobe Bryant 75.00 200.00
MJ Michael Jordan 200.00 500.00

2005-06 SP Game Used Authentic Fabrics Autographs

Randomly seeded in packs, this 29-card set places player photos at the top of the card, a swatch of memorabilia in the center and a player autograph along the bottom. Each card is serially numbered to 100.
PRINT RUN 23 TO 100 SER.#'d SETS
AB Andris Biedrins/100 5.00 12.00
AH Al Harrington/100 5.00 12.00
AJ Antawn Jamison/100 5.00 12.00
AK Andrei Kirilenko/100 8.00 20.00
AR Carlos Arroyo/100 15.00 40.00
BD Baron Davis/100 5.00 12.00
BG Ben Gordon/100 12.50 30.00
BM Brad Miller/100 5.00 12.00
CM Corey Maggette/100 5.00 12.00
DG Drew Gooden/100 5.00 12.00
DH Dwight Howard/100 20.00 50.00
DM Desmond Mason/100 5.00 12.00
DS Damon Stoudamire/100 5.00 12.00
DW Dorell Wright/100 5.00 12.00
GA Gilbert Arenas/100 8.00 20.00
JM Jamaal Magloire/100 5.00 12.00
JW Jason Williams/100 15.00 40.00
KH Kirk Hinrich/100 12.50 30.00
LJ LeBron James/100 175.00 350.00
MB Mike Bibby/100 5.00 12.00
MJ Michael Jordan/23 500.00 900.00
MR Michael Redd/100 5.00 12.00
PP Paul Pierce/100 12.00 30.00
QR Quentin Richardson/100 5.00 12.00
RJ Richard Jefferson/100 5.00 12.00
SM Shawn Marion/100 6.00 15.00
SN Steve Nash/100 50.00 120.00
TM Tracy McGrady/100 20.00 50.00

2005-06 SP Game Used Authentic Fabrics Autographs Patches

Randomly seeded in packs, this 30-card set parallels the design of the Authentic Fabrics Autographs set enhanced with a patch swatch gold highlights and sequential numbering to 25.
PRINT RUN 10 TO 25 SER.#'d SETS
AB Andris Biedrins/25 15.00 40.00
AH Al Harrington/25 15.00 40.00
AJ Antawn Jamison/25 15.00 40.00
AK Andrei Kirilenko/25 25.00 60.00
AR Carlos Arroyo/25 40.00 80.00
BD Baron Davis/25 15.00 40.00
BM Brad Miller/25 15.00 40.00
CM Corey Maggette/25 15.00 40.00
DG Drew Gooden/25 15.00 40.00
DH Dwight Howard/25 40.00 100.00
DM Desmond Mason/25 15.00 40.00
DW Dorell Wright/25 15.00 40.00
GA Gilbert Arenas/25 15.00 40.00
JM Jamaal Magloire/25 15.00 40.00
JW Jason Williams/25 60.00 150.00
KH Kirk Hinrich/25 25.00 60.00
LJ LeBron James/25 800.00 1200.00
MB Mike Bibby/25 15.00 40.00
MR Michael Redd/25 15.00 40.00
PP Paul Pierce/25 25.00 60.00
QR Quentin Richardson/25 15.00 40.00
RJ Richard Jefferson/25 15.00 40.00
SM Shawn Marion/25 20.00 50.00
SN Steve Nash/25 80.00 160.00
TM Tracy McGrady/25 60.00 120.00

2005-06 SP Game Used Authentic Fabrics Dual

Randomly seeded in packs, this 41-card set features two players side by side, two swatches of memorabilia and sequential numbering to 100. A Gold version sequentially numbered to 50, a Patches version sequentially numbered to 15 and a Patches Gold version sequentially numbered to 10 were also produced.
PRINT RUN 100 SER.#'d SETS
*GOLD: .5X TO 1.25X BASE FAB HI
GOLD PRINT RUN 50 SER.#'d SETS
UNPRICED PATCH PRINT RUN 15 SETS
UNPRICED PATCH GOLD PRINT RUN 10 SETS
AL R.Allen/R.Lewis 8.00 20.00
AT A.Jefferson/T.Allen 5.00 12.00
BC B.Miller/C.Mobley 5.00 12.00
BJ K.Bryant/L.James 40.00 80.00
BL C.Boozer/R.Lopez 5.00 12.00
BO K.Bryant/L.Odom 15.00 40.00
BP C.Bosh/M.Peterson 5.00 12.00
CS S.Cassell/W.Szczerbiak 5.00 12.00
DH J.Dixon/J.Hayes 5.00 12.00
DS M.Daniels/J.Stackhouse 5.00 12.00
GJ D.Gooden/L.Jackson 5.00 12.00
GP M.Ginobili/T.Parker 8.00 20.00
GW P.Gasol/B.Wells 5.00 12.00
HB R.Hamilton/C.Billups 6.00 15.00
HC K.Hinrich/E.Curry 5.00 12.00
HN D.Howard/J.Nelson 5.00 12.00
HS K.Humphries/K.Snyder 5.00 12.00
JA A.Jamison/G.Arenas 5.00 12.00
JH D.Jones/U.Haslem 5.00 12.00
JJ L.James/M.Jordan 60.00 120.00
JS J.Johnson/S.Marion 5.00 12.00
KJ J.Kidd/R.Jefferson 8.00 20.00
MB C.Maggette/E.Brand 5.00 12.00
MC S.Marbury/J.Crawford 5.00 12.00
MM A.Miller/K.Martin 5.00 12.00
MR R.Murray/V.Radmanovic 5.00 12.00
MS J.Magloire/J.R.Smith 5.00 12.00
MT D.Miles/S.Telfair 5.00 12.00
NF D.Nowitzki/M.Finley 5.00 12.00
OA J.O'Neal/R.Artest 5.00 12.00
OJ S.O'Neal/E.Jones 10.00 25.00
RA Z.Randolph/S.Abdur-Rahim 5.00 12.00
RF J.Richardson/D.Fisher 5.00 12.00
RK B.Robinson/J.Kapono 5.00 12.00
RM M.Redd/D.Mason 5.00 12.00
RP D.Rodman/S.Pippen 25.00 60.00
SC Jsh.Smith/J.Childress 5.00 12.00
TS I.Thomas/J.Stockton 8.00 20.00
WI C.Webber/A.Iguodala 5.00 12.00
WP A.Walker/G.Payton 5.00 12.00
WW R.Wallace/B.Wallace 5.00 12.00

2005-06 SP Game Used Authentic Fabrics Dual Autographs

Randomly seeded in packs, this 30-card set parallels the design of the Authentic Fabrics Dual set enhanced with player autographs and sequential numbering to 50.
PRINT RUN 50 SER.#'d SETS
UNPRICED PATCH PRINT RUN 5 SETS
AJ K.Abdul-Jabbar/M.Johnson 150.00 300.00
AM C.Anthony/A.Miller 20.00 50.00
AT A.Jefferson/T.Allen 12.00 30.00
BH C.Billups/R.Hamilton 15.00 40.00
BS M.Bibby/P.Stojakovic 20.00 40.00
CH Childress/Harrington 12.50 30.00
DD B.Davis/M.Dunleavy 20.00 40.00
GH B.Gordon/K.Hinrich 20.00 50.00
GW P.Gasol/J.Williams 25.00 60.00
HN D.Howard/J.Nelson 20.00 50.00
IK A.Iguodala/K.Korver 25.00 50.00
JA A.Jamison/G.Arenas 15.00 40.00
JJ L.James/M.Jordan 800.00 1200.00
KB A.Kirilenko/C.Boozer 12.50 30.00
KJ J.Kidd/R.Jefferson 20.00 50.00
ML C.Maggette/S.Livingston 12.50 30.00
MW C.Maggette/C.Wilcox 12.50 30.00
MY T.McGrady/Y.Ming 40.00 100.00
PP P.Pierce/G.Payton 40.00 100.00
PR S.Pippen/D.Rodman 225.00 400.00
RM M.Redd/D.Mason 12.50 30.00
RP J.Rose/M.Peterson 12.50 30.00
SD J.Stackhouse/M.Daniels 12.50 30.00
SM J.R.Smith/J.Magloire 12.50 30.00
ST D.Stoudamire/Telfair 12.50 30.00
VO S.Vujacic/L.Odom 12.50 30.00
WB G.Wallace/P.Brezec 12.50 30.00

2005-06 SP Game Used Authentic Fabrics Triple

Randomly seeded in packs, this 10-card set features three player photos along the top of the card and three swatches of memorabilia along the bottom. Each card is serially numbered to 25.
PRINT RUN 25 SER.#'d SETS
UNPRICED TRIPLE GOLD PRINT RUN 15 SETS
UNPRICED TRIPLE PATCH PRINT RUN 10 SETS
UNPRICED TRIPLE PATCH GOLD PRINT RUN 3 SETS
BML Brand/Maggette/Livingston 12.50 30.00
DIW Dalembert/Iggy/Webber 15.00 40.00
DPG Duncan/Parker/Ginobili 20.00 50.00
DRD B.Davis/J-Rich/Dunleavy 12.50 30.00
JAH Jamison/Arenas/Hayes 12.50 30.00
JJB LeBron/MJ/Kobe 175.00 350.00
NFD Nowitzki/Finley/Daniels 20.00 50.00
OAT J.O'Neal/Artest/Tinsley 12.50 30.00
PJA Pierce/Big Al/T.Allen 15.00 40.00

2005-06 SP Game Used Authentic Tags

Randomly inserted in packs, this 21-card set features a player image along the top and three swatches of memorabilia from jersey logos and tags along the bottom. Cards are serially numbered to just three copies.
NOT PRICED DUE TO SCARCITY
UNPRICED AUTO PRINT RUN ONE SET

2005-06 SP Game Used By the Letter

Seeded in packs randomly, this 10-card set features a player image on the left of the card and a full letter from the player's nameplate on the back of his uniform. The total number of cards for each player is limited to the number of letters in the player's last name.
NOT PRICED DUE TO SCARCITY

2005-06 SP Game Used Legendary Fabrics

Randomly seeded in packs, this 12-card set features NBA legends along with a swatch of memorabilia.
RANDOM INSERTS IN PACKS
BK Bernard King 6.00 15.00
BR Bill Russell 12.50 30.00
CD Clyde Drexler 6.00 15.00
DR Dennis Rodman 10.00 25.00
GG George Gervin 6.00 15.00
HO Hakeem Olajuwon 6.00 15.00
JS John Stockton 10.00 25.00
KA Kareem Abdul-Jabbar 8.00 20.00
LB Larry Bird 15.00 40.00
MJ Michael Jordan 50.00 120.00
MJ2 Magic Johnson 12.50 30.00
SP Scottie Pippen 15.00 40.00

2005-06 SP Game Used Legendary Fabrics Autographs

Found in packs randomly, this set features NBA legends, a swatch of memorabilia and an authentic autograph. Each card is serially numbered to 23 or 50 copies.
PRINT RUN 23 TO 50 SER.#'d SETS
BK Bernard King/50 12.00 30.00
BR Bill Russell/50 125.00 300.00
DR Dennis Rodman/50 75.00 150.00
GG George Gervin/50 12.50 30.00
HO Hakeem Olajuwon/50 30.00 80.00
JS John Stockton/50 60.00 150.00
KA Kareem Abdul-Jabbar/50 50.00 120.00
LB Larry Bird/50 75.00 150.00
MA Magic Johnson/50 50.00 125.00
MJ Michael Jordan/23 700.00 1000.00
SP Scottie Pippen/50 100.00 200.00

2005-06 SP Game Used Materials

Limited to 10 serially numbered copies, this seven card set features both current players and NBA legends along with a swatch of memorabilia.
NOT PRICED DUE TO SCARCITY
UNPRICED LIMITED PRINT RUN 5 SETS
UNPRICED EXTRA PRINT RUN ONE SET

2005-06 SP Game Used Rookie Exclusive Autographs

Found in packs randomly, this 52-card set is horizontally designed with a player photo along the top and a cut signature embedded in the middle. Cards are serially numbered to 100.
PRINT RUN 100 SER.#'d SETS
AA Alex Acker 5.00 12.00
AB Andray Blatche 8.00 20.00
AJ Amir Johnson 8.00 20.00
AN Andrew Bogut 10.00 25.00
AW Antoine Wright 6.00 15.00
BB Brandon Bass 6.00 15.00
BW Bracey Wright 5.00 12.00
BY Andrew Bynum 6.00 15.00
CF Channing Frye 8.00 20.00
CJ C.J. Miles 8.00 20.00
CP Chris Paul 50.00 100.00
CT Chris Taft 6.00 15.00
CV Charlie Villanueva 5.00 12.00
DE Daniel Ewing 6.00 15.00
DG Danny Granger 10.00 25.00
DL David Lee 8.00 20.00
DT Dijon Thompson 5.00 12.00
DW Deron Williams 40.00 100.00
EI Ersan Ilyasova 8.00 20.00
FG Francisco Garcia 6.00 15.00
GG Gerald Green 8.00 20.00
HW Hakim Warrick 6.00 15.00
ID Ike Diogu 5.00 12.00
JG Joey Graham 6.00 15.00
JH Julius Hodge 5.00 12.00
JJ Jarrett Jack 8.00 20.00
JM Jason Maxiell 6.00 15.00
JP Johan Petro 5.00 12.00
LH Luther Head 6.00 15.00
LK Linas Kleiza 5.00 12.00
LR Lawrence Roberts 5.00 12.00
LW Louis Williams 8.00 20.00
MA Martell Webster 6.00 15.00
ME Monta Ellis 20.00 50.00
MG Mickael Gelabale 8.00 20.00
MW Marvin Williams 8.00 20.00
MY Martynas Andriuskevicius 5.00 12.00
NR Nate Robinson 15.00 40.00
RA Rashad McCants 6.00 15.00
RF Raymond Felton 8.00 20.00
RG Ryan Gomes 6.00 15.00
RS Ricky Sanchez 8.00 20.00
RT Ronny Turiaf 8.00 20.00
RW Robert Whaley 5.00 12.00
SJ Sarunas Jasikevicius 8.00 20.00
SM Sean May 5.00 12.00
SS Salim Stoudamire 6.00 15.00
TD Travis Diener 5.00 12.00
US Uros Slokar 8.00 20.00
VW Von Wafer 5.00 12.00
WB Will Bynum 6.00 15.00
WS Wayne Simien 5.00 12.00

2005-06 SP Game Used Signature Numbers

Found randomly inserted in packs, this 40-card set features a player photo set against a background that displays his jersey number along with a player autograph. Cards are serially numbered to each specific player's jersey number.
CARDS #'d TO PLAYER JSY NUMBER
SOME NOT PRICED DUE TO SCARCITY
AKO Andrei Kirilenko/47 ERR 12.00 30.00
CA Carmelo Anthony/15 25.00 60.00
DR Dennis Rodman/91 50.00 100.00
HO Hakeem Olajuwon/34 20.00 50.00
JN Jameer Nelson/14 12.00 30.00
JR J.R. Smith/23 15.00 40.00
KK Kyle Korver/26 12.00 30.00
LB Larry Bird/33 100.00 250.00
LJ LeBron James/23 1000.00 1500.00
MA Magic Johnson/32 60.00 120.00
MJ Michael Jordan/23 1000.00 1500.00
MR Michael Redd/22 12.00 30.00
PG Pau Gasol/16 20.00 50.00
PP Paul Pierce/34 15.00 40.00
ST Sebastian Telfair/31 12.00 30.00
UH Udonis Haslem/40 12.00 30.00

2005-06 SP Game Used SIGnificance

Seeded in packs randomly, this 120-card set is horizontally designed and utilizes some of the design elements of the base set along with player autographs and sequential numbering to 100.
PRINT RUN 100 SER.#'d SETS
*SIG 25: .75X TO 2X BASE HI
SIG 25 PRINT RUN 25 SER.#'d SETS
UNPRICED SIG 10 PRINT RUN 10 SETS
AB Andray Blatche 5.00 12.00
AH Al Harrington 4.00 10.00
AI Andre Iguodala 5.00 12.00
AJ Antawn Jamison 4.00 10.00
AKO Andrei Kirilenko ERR 8.00 20.00
AL Al Jefferson 4.00 10.00
AM Antonio McDyess 6.00 15.00
AN Martynas Andriuskevicius 4.00 10.00
AR Carlos Arroyo 10.00 25.00
AW Antoine Wright 4.00 10.00
BB Brandon Bass 5.00 12.00
BD Baron Davis 5.00 12.00
BE Bernard King 8.00 20.00
BG Ben Gordon 8.00 20.00
BK Bob Knight 25.00 50.00
BL Bill Laimbeer 6.00 15.00
BM Brad Miller 4.00 10.00
BO Andrew Bogut 8.00 20.00
BU Beno Udrih 4.00 10.00
BW Bracey Wright 4.00 10.00
BY Andrew Bynum 4.00 10.00
CB Carlos Boozer 4.00 10.00
CD Clyde Drexler 15.00 40.00
CF Channing Frye 6.00 15.00
CH Chauncey Billups 6.00 15.00
CJ C.J. Miles 5.00 12.00
CM Corey Maggette 4.00 10.00
CN Curly Neal 20.00 40.00
CO Michael Cooper 6.00 15.00
CP Chris Paul 30.00 80.00
CS Chris Bosh 8.00 20.00
CT Chris Taft 4.00 10.00
CV Charlie Villanueva 5.00 12.00
DA Daniel Ewing 4.00 10.00
DD Dan Dickau 4.00 10.00
DE Desmond Mason 4.00 10.00
DF Derek Fisher 6.00 15.00
DG Danny Granger 15.00 30.00
DH Dwight Howard 15.00 30.00
DL David Lee 6.00 15.00
DM Darko Milicic 4.00 10.00
DP Dan Patrick 15.00 30.00
DR Dennis Rodman 25.00 60.00
DS Damon Stoudamire 4.00 10.00
DT Dijon Thompson 4.00 10.00
DW Deron Williams 20.00 50.00
ED Erik Daniels 4.00 10.00
EH Elvin Hayes 6.00 15.00
EI Ersan Ilyasova 5.00 12.00
FG Francisco Garcia 5.00 12.00
GA Gilbert Arenas 6.00 15.00
GG George Gervin 10.00 25.00
GW Gerald Wallace 5.00 12.00
HO Hakeem Olajuwon 12.00 30.00
HW Hakim Warrick 10.00 25.00
ID Ike Diogu 4.00 10.00
IT Isiah Thomas 20.00 50.00
JA Jamal Crawford 4.00 10.00
JC Josh Childress 4.00 10.00
JD Juan Dixon 4.00 10.00
JG Joey Graham 4.00 10.00
JH Julius Hodge 4.00 10.00
JJ Jarrett Jack 4.00 10.00
JK Jason Kidd 12.00 30.00
JM Jamaal Magloire 4.00 10.00
JO John Edwards 4.00 10.00
JP Johan Petro 4.00 10.00
JR J.R. Smith 5.00 12.00
JV Jackson Vroman 4.00 10.00
JW John Wooden 50.00 120.00
KA Jason Kapono 4.00 10.00
KE Kevin Martin 5.00 12.00
KH Kris Humphries 4.00 10.00
KI Kirk Hinrich 6.00 15.00
KK Kyle Korver 5.00 12.00
KM Kenny Mayne 6.00 15.00
LA Larry Brown 5.00 12.00
LC Linda Cohn 10.00 25.00
LD Luol Deng 6.00 15.00
LF Luis Flores 4.00 10.00
LH Luther Head 4.00 10.00
LJ LeBron James 200.00 500.00
LO Lamar Odom 5.00 12.00
LR Lawrence Roberts 4.00 10.00
LU Louis Williams 6.00 15.00
LW Lenny Wilkens 10.00 25.00
MA Marvin Williams 5.00 12.00
MB Mike Bibby 5.00 12.00
MC Mark Cuban 15.00 40.00
MD Marquis Daniels 4.00 10.00
ME Monta Ellis 12.00 30.00
MI Andre Miller 4.00 10.00
MJ Michael Jordan 300.00 600.00
ML Meadowlark Lemon 12.50 30.00
MP Morris Peterson 4.00 10.00
MR Michael Redd 4.00 10.00
MW Maurice Williams 4.00 10.00
NR Nate Robinson 6.00 15.00
PG Pau Gasol 8.00 20.00
PS Pape Sow 4.00 10.00
QR Quentin Richardson 4.00 10.00
RF Raymond Felton 8.00 20.00
RJ Richard Jefferson 4.00 10.00
RM Ronald Murray 4.00 10.00
RT Ronny Turiaf 6.00 15.00
SB Steve Blake 4.00 10.00
SH Shane Battier 4.00 10.00
SV Sasha Vujacic 4.00 10.00
TA Tony Allen 4.00 10.00
TD Travis Diener 4.00 10.00
TR Trevor Ariza 4.00 10.00
UH Udonis Haslem 4.00 10.00
VK Viktor Khryapa 4.00 10.00
VW Von Wafer 4.00 10.00
WE Martell Webster 4.00 10.00
WF Walt Frazier 10.00 25.00
WI Jason Williams 20.00 50.00
WR Willis Reed 8.00 20.00
WS Wayne Simien 4.00 10.00

2005-06 SP Game Used SIGnificance Dual

Randomly inserted in packs, this 30 cards set utilizes some of the design elements of the SIGnificance set but places two players and two autographs on each card along with sequential numbering to 25.
PRINT RUN 25 SER.#'d SETS
UNPRICED DUAL GOLD PRINT RUN 5 SETS
BW L.Brown/L.Wilkens 30.00 80.00
DO C.Drexler/H.Olajuwon 75.00 150.00
EI J.Erving/A.Iguodala 50.00 120.00
FR W.Frazier/W.Reed 35.00 75.00
FS C.Frye/S.Stoudamire 15.00 40.00
GH G.Green/H.Warrick 15.00 40.00
GW P.Gasol/J.Williams 30.00 80.00
HG K.Hinrich/B.Gordon 15.00 40.00
HH D.Harris/J.Howard 15.00 40.00
HN D.Howard/J.Nelson 20.00 50.00
IS A.Iguodala/J.R.Smith 50.00 100.00
JJ M.Jordan/L.James 500.00 1000.00
KB A.Kirilenko/C.Boozer 15.00 40.00
KJ J.Kidd/R.Jefferson 30.00 80.00
KW B.Knight/J.Wooden 125.00 250.00
MA S.Marbury/T.Ariza 15.00 40.00
MM M.Johnson/M.Jordan 450.00 750.00
MP M.Bibby/P.Stojakovic 40.00 60.00
NL C.Neal/M.Lemon 75.00 150.00
NR S.Nash/Q.Richardson 60.00 150.00
PF C.Paul/R.Felton 60.00 150.00
PR S.Pippen/D.Rodman 250.00 500.00
RB B.Russell/L.Bird 200.00 350.00
TJ I.Thomas/M.Johnson 80.00 160.00
TL S.Telfair/S.Livingston 15.00 40.00
WH D.Williams/L.Head 60.00 120.00
WM M.Williams/S.May 15.00 40.00
YM Y.Ming/T.McGrady 150.00 300.00

2005-06 SP Game Used SIGnificant Numbers Autographs

Found randomly in packs, this 12-card set features the same design as the SIGnificance set enhanced with a swatch of memorabilia and sequential numbering to the featured players jersey number.
CARDS #'d TO PLAYER JSY NUMBER
SOME NOT PRICED DUE TO SCARCITY
UNPRICED PATCH PRINT RUN FIVE SETS
DR Dennis Rodman/91 50.00 120.00
KA Kareem Abdul-Jabbar/33 50.00 125.00
LB Larry Bird/33 80.00 200.00
LJ LeBron James/23 1000.00 1500.00
MA Magic Johnson/32 60.00 150.00
MJ Michael Jordan/23 1000.00 1500.00

2005-06 SP Game Used Superstar Exclusive Autographs

Randomly seeded in packs, this 35-card set parallels the design of the Rookie Exclusive Autographs with player photos, cut signatures and sequential numbering to either 25 or 100.
PRINT RUN 25 TO 100 SER.#'d SETS
AJ Antawn Jamison/25 10.00 25.00
BD Baron Davis/25 10.00 25.00
BG Ben Gordon/25 15.00 40.00
BK Bernard King/100 10.00 25.00
CB Chris Bosh/25 12.50 30.00
DE Devin Harris/25 10.00 25.00
DH Dwight Howard/25 35.00 70.00
JC Josh Childress/25 10.00 25.00
JK Jason Kidd/25 20.00 50.00
JN Jameer Nelson/25 10.00 25.00
JS John Salley/100 10.00 25.00
KH Kirk Hinrich/25 10.00 25.00
LD Luol Deng/25 12.50 30.00
LJ LeBron James/25 150.00 300.00
MB Mike Bibby/25 10.00 25.00
MJ Michael Jordan/25 300.00 600.00
MR Michael Redd/25 10.00 25.00
PG Pau Gasol/25 15.00 40.00
PS Peja Stojakovic/25 15.00 40.00
RH Richard Hamilton/25 12.00 30.00
RJ Richard Jefferson/25 10.00 25.00
SL Shaun Livingston/25 10.00 25.00
SM Stephon Marbury/25 15.00 40.00
SN Steve Nash/25 60.00 120.00
TM Tracy McGrady/25 30.00 80.00
WR Willis Reed/100 10.00 25.00
YM Yao Ming/25 25.00 60.00

2006-07 SP Game Used

Issued in late October 2006, SP Game Used boasts a 249-card base set where card numbers 1-100 picture veteran players, cards 101-200 picture veteran players along with a swatch jersey and card numbers 201-249 picture rookies sequentially numbered to 999. SP Game Used is packaged in single packs of five cards each and carried an initial suggested retail price of $29.99.
COMP.SET w/o SP's (100) 25.00 60.00
JSY ODDS APPROXIMATELY ONE PER PACK
RC PRINT RUN 999 SER.#'d SETS
UNPRICED RAINBOW PRINT RUN 10 SETS
1 Al Harrington .60 1.50
2 Joe Johnson .60 1.50
3 Salim Stoudamire .50 1.25
4 Tony Allen .50 1.25
5 Dan Dickau .50 1.25
6 Gerald Green .60 1.50
7 Michael Olowokandi .50 1.25
8 Brevin Knight .50 1.25
9 Peja Stojakovic .75 2.00
10 Gerald Wallace .60 1.50
11 Luol Deng .60 1.50
12 Chris Duhon .50 1.25
13 Mike Sweetney .50 1.25
14 Drew Gooden .60 1.50
15 Luke Jackson .50 1.25
16 Damon Jones .50 1.25
17 Eric Snow .50 1.25
18 Erick Dampier .50 1.25
19 Marquis Daniels .50 1.25
20 Jerry Stackhouse .60 1.50
21 Jason Terry .60 1.50
22 Earl Boykins .50 1.25
23 Marcus Camby .60 1.50
24 Kenyon Martin .60 1.50
25 Andre Miller .60 1.50
26 Kelvin Cato .50 1.25
27 Lindsey Hunter .50 1.25
28 Antonio McDyess .60 1.50
29 Mike Dunleavy .60 1.50
30 Derek Fisher .60 1.50
31 Troy Murphy .50 1.25
32 Rafer Alston .50 1.25
33 Juwan Howard .60 1.50
34 Stromile Swift .50 1.25
35 Austin Croshere .50 1.25
36 Stephen Jackson .60 1.50
37 Jamaal Tinsley .50 1.25
38 Sam Cassell .60 1.50
39 Chris Kaman .60 1.50
40 Yaroslav Korolev .50 1.25
41 Cuttino Mobley .50 1.25
42 Devean George .50 1.25
43 Smush Parker .50 1.25
44 Ronny Turiaf .60 1.50
45 Shane Battier .60 1.50
46 Bobby Jackson .50 1.25
47 Mike Miller .60 1.50
48 Damon Stoudamire .60 1.50
49 Alonzo Mourning 1.00 2.50
50 Gary Payton .75 2.00
51 Dwyane Wade 1.25 3.00
52 Jason Williams .60 1.50
53 T.J. Ford .50 1.25
54 Jamaal Magloire .50 1.25
55 Maurice Williams .60 1.50
56 Marcus Banks .50 1.25
57 Eddie Griffin .50 1.25
58 Troy Hudson .50 1.25
59 Jason Collins .50 1.25
60 Nenad Krstic .50 1.25
61 Antoine Wright .50 1.25
62 P.J. Brown .50 1.25
63 Speedy Claxton .50 1.25
64 Marc Jackson .50 1.25
65 Jamal Crawford .75 2.00
66 Eddy Curry .60 1.50
67 Quentin Richardson .60 1.50
68 Carlos Arroyo .50 1.25
69 Keyon Dooling .50 1.25
70 Darko Milicic .50 1.25
71 Steven Hunter .50 1.25
72 Allen Iverson 1.00 2.50
73 Kyle Korver .60 1.50
74 Raja Bell .60 1.50
75 Boris Diaw .60 1.50
76 Kurt Thomas .50 1.25
77 Steve Blake .50 1.25
78 Darius Miles .50 1.25
79 Joel Przybilla .50 1.25
80 Ha Seung-Jin .50 1.25
81 Shareef Abdur-Rahim .60 1.50
82 Brad Miller .60 1.50
83 Kenny Thomas .50 1.25
84 Bonzi Wells .50 1.25
85 Brent Barry .50 1.25
86 Bruce Bowen .50 1.25
87 Michael Finley .75 2.00
88 Robert Horry .60 1.50
89 Luke Ridnour .60 1.50
90 Robert Swift .50 1.25
91 Chris Wilcox .50 1.25
92 Rafael Araujo .50 1.25
93 Jose Calderon .50 1.25
94 Mike James .50 1.25
95 Matt Harpring .50 1.25
96 Kris Humphries .50 1.25
97 Jason Richardson .75 2.00
98 Gilbert Arenas .60 1.50
99 Antonio Daniels .50 1.25
100 Brendan Haywood .50 1.25
101 Josh Childress JSY 2.00 5.00
102 Josh Smith JSY 2.00 5.00
103 Marvin Williams JSY 2.00 5.00
104 Al Jefferson JSY 2.00 5.00
105 Paul Pierce JSY 2.50 6.00
106 Wally Szczerbiak JSY 2.00 5.00
107 Raymond Felton JSY 2.00 5.00
108 Sean May JSY 1.50 4.00
109 Emeka Okafor JSY 2.00 5.00
110 Tyson Chandler JSY 2.00 5.00
111 Ben Gordon JSY 2.00 5.00
112 Kirk Hinrich JSY 2.00 5.00
113 Michael Jordan SP JSY 30.00 80.00
114 Larry Hughes JSY 2.00 5.00
115 Zydrunas Ilgauskas JSY 2.00 5.00
116 LeBron James JSY 10.00 25.00
117 Devin Harris JSY 1.50 4.00
118 Josh Howard JSY 2.00 5.00
119 Dirk Nowitzki JSY 4.00 10.00
120 Carmelo Anthony JSY 3.00 8.00
121 Julius Hodge JSY 2.00 5.00
122 Linas Kleiza JSY 2.00 5.00
123 Chauncey Billups JSY 2.50 6.00
124 Tayshaun Prince JSY 2.00 5.00
125 Ben Wallace JSY 2.00 5.00
126 Rasheed Wallace JSY 2.50 6.00
127 Baron Davis JSY 2.00 5.00
128 Ike Diogu JSY 2.00 5.00
129 Jason Richardson JSY 2.50 6.00
130 Chris Taft JSY 2.00 5.00
131 Luther Head JSY 2.00 5.00
132 Tracy McGrady JSY 3.00 8.00
133 Yao Ming JSY 3.00 8.00
134 Danny Granger JSY 2.00 5.00
135 Sarunas Jasikevicius JSY 2.00 5.00
136 Jermaine O'Neal JSY 2.00 5.00
137 Peja Stojakovic SP JSY 2.50 6.00
138 Elton Brand JSY 2.50 6.00
139 Shaun Livingston JSY 2.00 5.00
140 Corey Maggette JSY 2.00 5.00
141 Kwame Brown JSY 2.00 5.00
142 Kobe Bryant JSY 10.00 25.00
143 Andrew Bynum JSY 1.50 4.00
144 Lamar Odom JSY 2.00 5.00
145 Pau Gasol JSY 2.50 6.00
146 Eddie Jones JSY 2.00 5.00
147 Hakim Warrick JSY 2.00 5.00
148 Shaquille O'Neal JSY 5.00 12.00
149 Wayne Simien JSY 2.00 5.00
150 Antoine Walker JSY 2.00 5.00
151 Andrew Bogut JSY 2.00 5.00
152 Ersan Ilyasova JSY 2.00 5.00
153 Michael Redd JSY 2.00 5.00
154 Ricky Davis JSY 2.00 5.00
155 Kevin Garnett JSY 4.00 10.00
156 Rashad McCants JSY 2.00 5.00
157 Bracey Wright JSY 2.00 5.00
158 Vince Carter JSY 3.00 8.00
159 Richard Jefferson JSY 2.00 5.00
160 Jason Kidd JSY 4.00 10.00
161 Jeff McInnis JSY 2.00 5.00
163 Chris Paul JSY 3.00 8.00
164 J.R. Smith JSY 2.00 5.00
165 David West JSY 2.00 5.00
166 Steve Francis JSY 2.00 5.00
167 Channing Frye JSY 2.00 5.00
168 Stephon Marbury JSY 2.00 5.00
169 Nate Robinson JSY 1.50 4.00
170 Grant Hill JSY 3.00 8.00
171 Dwight Howard JSY 2.00 5.00
172 Jameer Nelson JSY 1.50 4.00
173 Samuel Dalembert JSY 2.00 5.00
174 Andre Iguodala JSY 2.00 5.00
175 Chris Webber JSY 2.50 6.00
176 Shawn Marion JSY 2.00 5.00
177 Steve Nash JSY 3.00 8.00
178 Amare Stoudemire JSY 2.00 5.00
179 Zach Randolph JSY 2.00 5.00
180 Sebastian Telfair JSY 1.50 4.00
181 Martell Webster JSY 2.00 5.00
182 Ron Artest JSY 2.50 6.00
183 Mike Bibby JSY 2.50 6.00
184 Francisco Garcia JSY 1.50 4.00
185 Tim Duncan JSY 4.00 10.00
186 Manu Ginobili JSY 2.50 6.00
187 Tony Parker JSY 2.50 6.00
188 Ray Allen JSY 2.50 6.00
189 Rashard Lewis JSY 2.50 6.00
190 Johan Petro JSY 2.00 5.00
191 Chris Bosh JSY 2.50 6.00
192 Joey Graham JSY 2.00 5.00
193 Charlie Villanueva JSY 1.50 4.00
194 Carlos Boozer JSY 2.00 5.00
195 Andrei Kirilenko JSY 2.00 5.00
196 C.J. Miles JSY 2.00 5.00
197 Deron Williams JSY 2.00 5.00
198 Andray Blatche JSY 2.00 5.00
199 Caron Butler JSY 2.00 5.00
200 Antawn Jamison JSY 2.00 5.00
201 Andrea Bargnani RC 2.50 6.00
202 LaMarcus Aldridge RC 6.00 15.00
203 Adam Morrison RC 2.50 6.00
204 Tyrus Thomas RC 2.00 5.00
205 Shelden Williams RC 2.00 5.00
206 Brandon Roy RC 2.50 6.00
207 Randy Foye RC 2.50 6.00
208 Rudy Gay RC 3.00 8.00
209 Patrick O'Bryant RC 1.50 4.00
210 Saer Sene RC 1.50 4.00
211 J.J. Redick RC 3.00 8.00
212 Hilton Armstrong RC 1.50 4.00
213 Thabo Sefolosha RC 2.50 6.00
214 Ronnie Brewer RC 2.50 6.00
215 Cedric Simmons RC 1.50 4.00
216 Rodney Carney RC 1.50 4.00
217 Shawne Williams RC 1.50 4.00
218 Hassan Adams RC 1.50 4.00
219 Quincy Douby RC 1.50 4.00
220 Renaldo Balkman RC 2.00 5.00
221 Rajon Rondo RC 4.00 10.00
222 Marcus Williams RC 1.50 4.00
223 Josh Boone RC 1.50 4.00
224 Kyle Lowry RC 3.00 8.00
225 Shannon Brown RC 1.50 4.00
226 Jordan Farmar RC 2.50 6.00
227 Maurice Ager RC 1.50 4.00
228 Mardy Collins RC 1.50 4.00
229 Will Blalock RC 1.50 4.00
230 James White RC 1.50 4.00
231 Steve Novak RC 2.00 5.00
232 Solomon Jones RC 1.50 4.00
233 Paul Davis RC 1.50 4.00
234 P.J. Tucker RC 2.00 5.00
235 Craig Smith RC 2.00 5.00
236 Bobby Jones RC 1.50 4.00
237 David Noel RC 1.50 4.00
238 Denham Brown RC 1.50 4.00
239 James Augustine RC 1.50 4.00
240 Daniel Gibson RC 2.00 5.00
241 Ryan Hollins RC 2.00 5.00
242 Alexander Johnson RC 1.50 4.00
243 Dee Brown RC 1.50 4.00
244 Paul Millsap RC 3.00 8.00
245 Leon Powe RC 2.00 5.00
246 Mike Gansey RC 1.50 4.00
247 Tarence Kinsey RC 1.50 4.00
248 Damir Markota RC 1.50 4.00
249 J.R. Pinnock RC 1.50 4.00
250 Kevin Pittsnogle RC 2.00 5.00

2006-07 SP Game Used Gold

*1-100 GOLD: .75X TO 2X BASE HI
*101-200 JSY GOLD: .5X TO 1.25X BASE HI
*201-249 RCs GOLD: .6X TO 1.5X BASE HI
PRINT RUN 100 SER.#'d SETS

2006-07 SP Game Used Patches

*PATCH: 1.25X TO 3X BASE HI
STATED PRINT RUN 25 SER.#'d SETS
170 Grant Hill 12.00 30.00
175 Chris Webber 15.00 40.00

2006-07 SP Game Used All-Star Memorabilia

PRINT RUN 100 SER.#'d SETS
*PATCHES: .75X TO 2X BASE HI
PATCH PRINT RUN 25 SER.#'d SETS
AB Andrew Bogut 3.00 8.00
AI Andre Iguodala 3.00 8.00
AN Andres Nocioni 2.50 6.00
BG Ben Gordon 3.00 8.00
BO Chris Bosh 4.00 10.00
BW Ben Wallace 3.00 8.00
CB Chauncey Billups 4.00 10.00
CF Channing Frye 3.00 8.00
CP Chris Paul 5.00 12.00
CV Charlie Villanueva 2.50 6.00
DG Danny Granger 3.00 8.00
DH Devin Harris 2.50 6.00
DJ Dahntay Jones 2.50 6.00
DN Dirk Nowitzki 6.00 15.00
DW Delonte West 2.50 6.00
EB Elton Brand 4.00 10.00
EO Emeka Okafor 3.00 8.00
GA Gilbert Arenas 3.00 8.00
HW Hakim Warrick 3.00 8.00
JS Josh Smith 3.00 8.00
JT Jason Terry 3.00 8.00
KB Kobe Bryant 12.00 30.00
LD Luol Deng 3.00 8.00
LH Luther Head 3.00 8.00
LJ LeBron James 15.00 40.00
NK Nenad Krstic 2.50 6.00
NR Nate Robinson 2.50 6.00
PG Pau Gasol 4.00 10.00
PP Paul Pierce 4.00 10.00
QR Quentin Richardson 3.00 8.00
RA Ray Allen 5.00 12.00
RH Richard Hamilton 3.00 8.00
RI Royal Ivey 2.50 6.00
RW Rasheed Wallace 4.00 10.00
SJ Sarunas Jasikevicius 3.00 8.00
SM Shawn Marion 3.00 8.00
SO Shaquille O'Neal 8.00 20.00
TD Tim Duncan 6.00 15.00
TF T.J. Ford 2.50 6.00
TP Tony Parker 4.00 10.00
VC Vince Carter 5.00 12.00
WI Deron Williams 3.00 8.00

2006-07 SP Game Used Authentic Fabrics Dual

PRINT RUN 100 SER.#'d SETS
AD R.Artest/Q.Douby 3.00 8.00
AI A.Iverson/A.Iguodala 6.00 15.00
AJ A.Jefferson/T.Allen 3.00 8.00
AR R.Jefferson/A.Wright 3.00 8.00
AW R.Allen/C.Wilcox 3.00 8.00
BF C.Bosh/T.J.Ford 3.00 8.00
BG C.Butler/B.Gordon 3.00 8.00
BM C.J.Miles/R.Brewer 3.00 8.00
CA T.Chandler/H.Armstrong 3.00 8.00
CJ J.Childress/S.Jones 3.00 8.00
CL L.James/C.Anthony 12.00 30.00
CM C.Maggette/S.Cassell 3.00 8.00
DI S.Dalembert/A.Iguodala 3.00 8.00
DM R.Davis/R.McCants 3.00 8.00
DR B.Davis/J.Richardson 3.00 8.00
DS D.Gooden/S.Brown 3.00 8.00
DT M.Dunleavy/C.Taft 3.00 8.00
FC E.Curry/C.Frye 3.00 8.00
FM S.Francis/S.Marbury 3.00 8.00
FR S.Francis/N.Robinson 3.00 8.00
FW R.Felton/Mv.Williams 4.00 10.00
GB M.Bibby/F.Garcia 3.00 8.00
GC J.Graham/J.Calderon 3.00 8.00
GW H.Warrick/R.Gay 3.00 8.00
HB R.Hamilton/C.Billups 4.00 10.00
HH J.Howard/D.Harris 3.00 8.00
HJ L.James/L.Hughes 8.00 20.00
HM A.Miller/J.Hodge 3.00 8.00
HS K.Hinrich/M.Sweetney 3.00 8.00
HT K.Hinrich/T.Thomas 4.00 10.00
IC A.Iverson/R.Carney 4.00 10.00
IJ Z.Ilgauskas/L.James 10.00 25.00
JA A.Jamison/G.Arenas 3.00 8.00
JB M.Johnson/L.Bird 20.00 50.00
JJ M.Jordan/L.James 40.00 80.00
JM J.Jack/M.Webster 3.00 8.00
JS J.Johnson/J.Smith 3.00 8.00
JW J.Johnson/Mv.Williams 3.00 8.00
KF B.King/W.Frazier 3.00 8.00
KW A.Kirilenko/D.Williams 3.00 8.00
LC S.Livingston/J.Childress 3.00 8.00
LP R.Lewis/J.Petro 3.00 8.00
MA J.Magloire/L.Aldridge 3.00 8.00
MF R.Felton/S.May 3.00 8.00
MH J.Howard/T.McGrady 4.00 10.00
ML C.Mobley/S.Livingston 3.00 8.00
MM C.Maggette/C.Mobley 3.00 8.00
NG D.Nowitzki/P.Gasol 5.00 12.00
NH G.Hill/J.Nelson 3.00 8.00
OD H.Olajuwon/C.Drexler 8.00 20.00
OF L.Odom/J.Farmar 4.00 10.00
OM E.Okafor/S.May 3.00 8.00
RA Z.Randolph/M.Ager 3.00 8.00
RJ L.Ridnour/L.Jackson 4.00 10.00
RP P.Pierce/R.Rondo 4.00 10.00
RR R.McCants/R.Foye 4.00 10.00
RV M.Redd/C.Villanueva 3.00 8.00
SA W.Szczerbiak/T.Allen 3.00 8.00
ST W.Szczerbiak/S.Telfair 3.00 8.00
SW J.Williams/W.Simien 3.00 8.00
TC M.Taylor/E.Curry 3.00 8.00
TD C.Taft/I.Diogu 3.00 8.00
TH J.Terry/J.Howard 3.00 8.00
TS K.Thomas/A.Stoudemire 4.00 10.00
TW J.Tinsley/S.Williams 3.00 8.00
WB D.Williams/D.Brown 6.00 15.00
WD J.Dixon/M.Webster 3.00 8.00
WK C.Webber/K.Korver 5.00 12.00
WS D.West/C.Simmons 3.00 8.00
WW Mv.Williams/S.Williams 3.00 8.00

2006-07 SP Game Used Authentic Fabrics Dual Autographs

STATED PRINT RUN 15 TO 50 SER.#'d SETS
AL R.Artest/B.Laimbeer 12.00 30.00
AP C.Paul/H.Armstrong 12.00 30.00
AS R.Artest/P.Stojakovic 10.00 25.00
BA M.Bibby/R.Artest 12.00 30.00
BC T.Chandler/A.Bogut 12.00 30.00
BG E.Brand/K.Garnett 25.00 60.00
BI A.Bogut/E.Ilyasova 10.00 25.00
BM M.Bibby/B.Miller 8.00 20.00
BP C.Billups/T.Prince 15.00 40.00
BR N.Robinson/R.Balkman 12.00 30.00
BW C.Boozer/D.Williams 20.00 50.00
CB T.Chandler/Kw.Brown 8.00 20.00
CJ V.Carter/R.Jefferson 15.00 40.00
DL M.Daniels/S.Livingston 8.00 20.00
DT B.Davis/C.Taft 8.00 20.00
FT T.J.Ford/P.J.Tucker 8.00 20.00
GB M.Bibby/F.Garcia 8.00 20.00
GH K.Garnett/D.Howard 50.00 120.00
GM K.Garnett/R.McCants 20.00 50.00
HG H.Warrick/R.Gay 12.00 30.00
HM L.Hughes/D.Marshall 8.00 20.00
IK K.Korver/A.Iguodala 12.00 30.00
IR A.Iguodala/N.Robinson 8.00 20.00
JA L.James/C.Anthony/15 150.00 300.00
JJ M.Jordan/L.James/15 800.00 1200.00
JW J.Johnson/Mv.Williams 10.00 25.00
KC J.Kidd/V.Carter 25.00 60.00
KD J.Kidd/B.Davis 20.00 50.00
KF B.King/W.Frazier 20.00 50.00
KJ J.Kidd/R.Jefferson 12.00 30.00
KS K.Korver/P.Stojakovic 8.00 20.00
LS S.Livingston/J.R.Smith 8.00 20.00
MA Y.Ming/Abdul-Jabbar/15 50.00 120.00
MB D.Marshall/C.Boozer 8.00 20.00
MF R.McCants/R.Felton 10.00 25.00
MJ T.McGrady/L.James/15 150.00 300.00
ML C.Mobley/S.Livingston 8.00 20.00
MM C.Maggette/C.Mobley 8.00 20.00
NB S.Nash/C.Billups/15 50.00 120.00
OB L.Odom/Kw.Brown 8.00 20.00
OD Olajuwon/Drexler/15 75.00 150.00
OG L.Odom/J.Graham 8.00 20.00
OJ L.Odom/A.Jefferson 8.00 20.00
PJ P.Pierce/A.Jefferson 20.00 50.00
PT S.Telfair/K.Pittsnogle 8.00 20.00
RC Q.Richardson/E.Curry 8.00 20.00
RH L.Ridnour/K.Hinrich 8.00 20.00
RJ Q.Richardson/J.Johnson 8.00 20.00
SC T.Chandler/C.Simmons 8.00 20.00
TG C.Taft/F.Garcia 8.00 20.00
TR S.Telfair/N.Robinson 8.00 20.00
WB A.Bogut/Mv.Williams 12.00 30.00
WJ A.Jamison/Mv.Williams 8.00 20.00
WP C.Paul/D.Williams 40.00 100.00

2006-07 SP Game Used Authentic Fabrics Dual Patches

*PATCHES: 1X TO 2.5X BASE HI
PRINT RUN 25 SER.#'d SETS
CL L.James/C.Anthony 30.00 80.00

2006-07 SP Game Used Authentic Fabrics Dual Patches Autographs

STATED PRINT RUN 5 TO 25 SER.#'d SETS
SOME UNPRICED DUE TO SCARCITY
AL R.Artest/B.Laimbeer/25 15.00 40.00
AP C.Paul/H.Armstrong/25 40.00 100.00
BC T.Chandler/A.Bogut/25 20.00 50.00
BM M.Bibby/B.Miller/25 20.00 50.00
BW C.Boozer/D.Williams/25 10.00 25.00
CB T.Chandler/Kw.Brown/25 10.00 25.00
CJ V.Carter/R.Jefferson/25 20.00 50.00
DL M.Daniels/S.Livingston/25 10.00 25.00
DT B.Davis/C.Taft/25 10.00 25.00
GM K.Garnett/R.McCants/25 25.00 60.00
HG H.Warrick/R.Gay/25 10.00 25.00
IK K.Korver/A.Iguodala/25 15.00 40.00
IR A.Iguodala/N.Robinson/25 10.00 25.00
KC J.Kidd/V.Carter/25 30.00 80.00
KD J.Kidd/B.Davis/25 15.00 40.00
KF B.King/W.Frazier/25 25.00 60.00
KJ J.Kidd/R.Jefferson/25 25.00 60.00
KS K.Korver/P.Stojakovic/25 10.00 25.00
MB D.Marshall/C.Boozer/25 10.00 25.00
MF R.McCants/R.Felton/25 12.00 30.00
MM C.Maggette/C.Mobley/25 10.00 25.00
OJ L.Odom/A.Jefferson/25 10.00 25.00
PT S.Telfair/K.Pittsnogle/25 10.00 25.00
RH L.Ridnour/K.Hinrich/25 10.00 25.00
TG C.Taft/F.Garcia/25 10.00 25.00
TR S.Telfair/N.Robinson/25 10.00 25.00
WP C.Paul/D.Williams/25 30.00 80.00

2006-07 SP Game Used Authentic Fabrics Triple

INT RUN 25 SER.#'d SETS
UNPRICED PATCH PRINT RUN 10 SETS
ASJ Szcz/A.Jefferson/T.Allen 12.00 30.00
BAJ Kobe/LeBron/Melo 30.00 80.00
BBB Brand/Battier/Boozer 12.00 30.00
BGF Bosh/T.J.Ford/Graham 12.00 30.00
BOV Odom/Kw.Brown/Vujacic 12.00 30.00
DMO Duncan/Olajuwon/Yao 20.00 50.00
DPG Duncan/Parker/Manu 25.00 60.00
DRD J-Rich/Dunleavy/Diogu 12.00 30.00
GHO KG/D.Howard/J.O'Neal 20.00 50.00
HBP Hamilton/Billups/Prince 15.00 40.00
HDG Hinrich/Deng/Gordon 15.00 40.00
IKB Ilgauskas/Krstic/Bogut 12.00 30.00
JMM Jamison/McInnis/May 12.00 30.00
KCJ Kidd/Vince/R.Jefferson 15.00 40.00
MRR Marbury/Q-Rich/N.Robinson 12.00 30.00
MWP Mason/West/Paul 15.00 40.00
NKS Nowitzki/Kirilenko/Peja 15.00 40.00
NMS Nash/Marion/Amare 20.00 50.00
WIK Webber/Iverson/Korver 15.00 40.00

2006-07 SP Game Used Legendary Fabrics

PRINT RUN 100 SER.#'d SETS
BK Bernard King 5.00 12.00
BL Bill Laimbeer 6.00 15.00
BR Bill Russell 15.00 40.00
CD Clyde Drexler 8.00 20.00
DR Dennis Rodman 8.00 20.00
GG George Gervin 5.00 12.00
HO Hakeem Olajuwon 8.00 20.00
JE Julius Erving 10.00 25.00
JH Jeff Hornacek 6.00 15.00
JS John Starks 5.00 12.00
KA Kareem Abdul-Jabbar 8.00 20.00
LB Larry Bird 10.00 25.00
MA Magic Johnson 10.00 25.00
MJ Michael Jordan 30.00 75.00
NA Nate Archibald 5.00 12.00
RP Robert Parish 5.00 12.00
SE Sean Elliott 5.00 12.00
SK Steve Kerr 5.00 12.00
ST John Stockton 8.00 20.00
WF Walt Frazier 5.00 12.00

2006-07 SP Game Used Legendary Fabrics Autographs

PRINT RUN 10 TO 50 SER.#'d SETS
BK Bernard King/50 10.00 25.00
BL Bill Laimbeer/50 10.00 25.00
CD Clyde Drexler/50 30.00 80.00
GG George Gervin/50 10.00 25.00
HO Hakeem Olajuwon/50 25.00 60.00
JE Julius Erving/10 75.00 150.00
JH Jeff Hornacek/50 20.00 50.00
JS John Starks/50 30.00 60.00
KA Kareem Abdul-Jabbar/10 60.00 120.00
LB Larry Bird/10 125.00 225.00
MA Magic Johnson/50 75.00 150.00
MJ Michael Jordan/50 500.00 1000.00
NA Nate Archibald/50 12.00 30.00
RP Robert Parish/50 12.00 30.00
SK Steve Kerr/50 12.00 30.00
WF Walt Frazier/50 12.00 30.00

2006-07 SP Game Used Rookie Exclusive Autographs

PRINT RUN 100 SER.#'d SETS
AB Andrea Bargnani 6.00 15.00
AD Hassan Adams 4.00 10.00
AR Allan Ray 4.00 10.00
BA Renaldo Balkman 5.00 12.00
BJ Bobby Jones 4.00 10.00
BR Brandon Roy 6.00 15.00
CS Cedric Simmons 4.00 10.00
DB Denham Brown 4.00 10.00
DE Dee Brown 4.00 10.00
DG Daniel Gibson 5.00 12.00
DN David Noel 4.00 10.00
HA Hilton Armstrong 4.00 10.00
JA James Augustine 4.00 10.00
JB Josh Boone 4.00 10.00
JF Jordan Farmar 6.00 15.00
JW James White 4.00 10.00
KL Kyle Lowry 8.00 20.00
KP Kevin Pittsnogle 5.00 12.00
LA LaMarcus Aldridge 25.00 60.00
MA Maurice Ager 4.00 10.00
MC Mardy Collins 4.00 10.00
MG Mike Gansey 4.00 10.00
MW Marcus Williams 4.00 10.00
PD Paul Davis 4.00 10.00
PO Patrick O'Bryant 4.00 10.00
PT P.J. Tucker 5.00 12.00
QD Quincy Douby 4.00 10.00
RB Ronnie Brewer 6.00 15.00
RC Rodney Carney 4.00 10.00
RF Randy Foye 6.00 15.00
RG Rudy Gay 8.00 20.00
RH Ryan Hollins 5.00 12.00
RR Rajon Rondo 30.00 80.00
SB Shannon Brown 4.00 10.00
SJ Solomon Jones 4.00 10.00
SM Craig Smith 5.00 12.00
SN Steve Novak 5.00 12.00
SS Saer Sene 4.00 10.00
SW Shelden Williams 5.00 12.00
TT Tyrus Thomas 5.00 12.00
WI Shawne Williams 4.00 10.00

2006-07 SP Game Used SIGnificance

PRINT RUN 23 TO 100 SER.#'d SETS
AB Andrew Bogut/100 5.00 12.00
AH Hilton Armstrong/100 2.50 6.00
AI Andre Iguodala/100 4.00 10.00
AJ Al Jefferson/100 4.00 10.00
AU James Augustine/25 2.50 6.00
BA Andrea Bargnani/100 8.00 20.00
BB Brent Barry/100 4.00 10.00
BI Chauncey Billups/100 6.00 15.00
BJ Bobby Jackson/100 4.00 10.00
BK Bernard King/100 6.00 15.00
BM Brad Miller/100 4.00 10.00
BN Denham Brown/100 2.50 6.00
BR Brandon Roy/100 12.00 30.00
BW Bill Walton/100 8.00 20.00
CA Carmelo Anthony/50 20.00 50.00
CB Carlos Boozer/100 4.00 10.00
CD Clyde Drexler/100 12.50 30.00
CE Cedric Simmons/25 2.50 6.00
CM Cuttino Mobley/100 4.00 10.00
CS Craig Smith/100 3.00 8.00
CT Chris Taft/100 4.00 10.00
DB Dee Brown/100 2.50 6.00
DE Daniel Ewing/100 4.00 10.00
DG Daniel Gibson/100 3.00 8.00
DH Dwight Howard/100 12.50 30.00
DJ Dwayne Jones/100 4.00 10.00
DM Donyell Marshall/100 4.00 10.00
DN David Noel/100 2.50 6.00
DS DeShawn Stevenson/100 4.00 10.00
DW Deron Williams/100 3.00 8.00
EC Eddy Curry/100 4.00 10.00
EI Ersan Ilyasova/100 4.00 10.00
FG Francisco Garcia/100 4.00 10.00
FR Randy Foye/100 6.00 15.00
HA Hassan Adams/100 2.50 6.00
HW Hakim Warrick/100 4.00 10.00
JB Bobby Jones/100 2.50 6.00
JG Joey Graham/100 4.00 10.00
JK Jason Kapono/100 4.00 10.00

JO Amir Johnson/100 4.00 10.00
JW James White/100 2.50 6.00
KB Kwame Brown/100 4.00 10.00
KG Kevin Garnett/100 25.00 60.00
KH Kirk Hinrich/100 6.00 15.00
KK Kyle Korver/100 4.00 10.00
KL Kyle Lowry/100 5.00 12.00
LA LaMarcus Aldridge/100 15.00 40.00
LB Larry Bird/25 75.00 150.00
LH Larry Hughes/100 4.00 10.00
LJ LeBron James/23 300.00 600.00
LO Lamar Odom/100 5.00 12.00
LR Luke Ridnour/100 4.00 10.00
MA Maurice Ager/100 2.50 6.00
MB Mike Bibby/100 4.00 10.00
MD Marquis Daniels/100 4.00 10.00
MI Michael Jordan/23 300.00 550.00
NR Nate Robinson/100 4.00 10.00
NS Steve Novak/100 3.00 8.00
PO Patrick O'Bryant/100 2.50 6.00
PP Paul Pierce/100 10.00 25.00
PS Peja Stojakovic/100 5.00 12.00
QD Quincy Douby/100 2.50 6.00
RB Renaldo Balkman/100 3.00 8.00
RC Rodney Carney/100 2.50 6.00
RG Rudy Gay/100 5.00 12.00
RH Ryan Hollins/100 3.00 8.00
RJ Richard Jefferson/100 4.00 10.00
RM Rashad McCants/100 4.00 10.00
RT Ronny Turiaf/100 8.00 20.00
SB Shannon Brown/100 2.50 6.00
SC Speedy Claxton/100 4.00 10.00
SW Shelden Williams/100 3.00 8.00
TP Tayshaun Prince/100 6.00 15.00
TT Tyrus Thomas/100 3.00 8.00
VC Vince Carter/100 12.50 30.00
VW Von Wafer/100 4.00 10.00
WI Marvin Williams/100 3.00 8.00
WM Marcus Williams/100 2.50 6.00
YK Yaroslav Korolev/100 4.00 10.00
YM Yao Ming/100 15.00 40.00

2006-07 SP Game Used SIGnificance Dual

PRINT RUN 10 TO 50 SER.#'d SETS
SOME UNPRICED DUE TO SCARCITY
AL R.Artest/B.Laimbeer 20.00 50.00
AP C.Paul/H.Armstrong 15.00 40.00
AR L.Aldridge/B.Roy 40.00 100.00
AS R.Artest/P.Stojakovic 12.00 30.00
AT L.Aldridge/P.J.Tucker 20.00 50.00
BE C.Boozer/D.Ewing 8.00 20.00
BJ A.Johnson/W.Blalock 8.00 20.00
BP C.Billups/T.Prince 8.00 20.00
BR B.Barry/N.Robinson 8.00 20.00
BT Kw.Brown/R.Turiaf 8.00 20.00
BW A.Bogut/Mv.Williams 8.00 20.00
CB T.Chandler/A.Bogut 8.00 20.00
CJ V.Carter/R.Jefferson 10.00 25.00
DL M.Daniels/S.Livingston 8.00 20.00
EK D.Ewing/Y.Korolev 8.00 20.00
FO F.Garcia/O.Greene 8.00 20.00
FS R.Foye/C.Smith 8.00 20.00
FT T.J.Ford/P.J.Tucker 8.00 20.00
GG J.Graham/S.Graham 8.00 20.00
GH K.Garnett/D.Howard 40.00 100.00
GM K.Garnett/R.McCants 20.00 50.00
HR R.Jefferson/H.Adams 8.00 20.00
IR A.Iguodala/N.Robinson 8.00 20.00
JR A.Jefferson/R.Rondo 15.00 40.00
JS J.Johnson/S.Stoudamire 8.00 20.00
JW A.Jamison/Mv.Williams 8.00 20.00
KF B.King/W.Frazier 25.00 60.00
KS K.Korver/P.Stojakovic 8.00 20.00
LD S.Livingston/P.Davis 8.00 20.00
ME C.Mobley/D.Ewing 8.00 20.00
MF R.McCants/R.Felton 8.00 20.00
MK C.Mobley/C.Kaman 8.00 20.00
OJ L.Odom/A.Jefferson 8.00 20.00
OW L.Odom/V.Wafer 8.00 20.00
PJ P.Pierce/A.Jefferson 12.00 30.00
PR R.Rondo/K.Pittsnogle 8.00 20.00
RC Q.Richardson/E.Curry 8.00 20.00
RJ Q.Richardson/J.Johnson 8.00 20.00
RK Q.Richardson/B.King 10.00 25.00
SI B.Simmons/E.Ilyasova 8.00 20.00
TE C.Taft/M.Ellis 8.00 20.00
TH K.Hinrich/T.Thomas 8.00 20.00
TR S.Telfair/N.Robinson 8.00 20.00
WB Mar.Williams/J.Boone 8.00 20.00
WE D.Williams/D.Ewing 8.00 20.00
WJ B.Jackson/H.Warrick 8.00 20.00
WS S.Williams/S.Jones 8.00 20.00

2006-07 SP Game Used Significant Numbers

CARDS #'d TO PLAYER'S JSY NUMBER
SOME UNPRICED DUE TO SCARCITY
BK Bernard King/30 15.00 40.00
BL Bill Laimbeer/40 30.00 80.00
BM Brad Miller/52 6.00 15.00
BO Bobby Jones/11 15.00 40.00
CA Carmelo Anthony/15 20.00 50.00
CD Clyde Drexler/22 50.00 100.00
CO Corey Maggette/50 8.00 20.00
CT Chris Taft/21 10.00 25.00
DM Donyell Marshall/24 6.00 15.00
DR Dennis Rodman/91 30.00 80.00
EC Eddy Curry/34 6.00 15.00
EI Ersan Ilyasova/23 6.00 15.00
FG Francisco Garcia/32 6.00 15.00
GG George Gervin/44 10.00 25.00
HA Hilton Armstrong/12 15.00 40.00
HO Hakeem Olajuwon/34 40.00 80.00
HW Hakim Warrick/21 10.00 25.00
JM Jamaal Magloire/20 8.00 20.00
JO Michael Jordan/23 1000.00 2000.00
JW James White/100 6.00 15.00
KA Kareem Abdul-Jabbar/33 75.00 150.00
KG Kevin Garnett/21 40.00 80.00
KK Kyle Korver/26 12.00 30.00
KW Kwame Brown/54 10.00 25.00
LA LaMarcus Aldridge/12 30.00 60.00
LB Larry Bird/33 125.00 250.00
LH Larry Hughes/32 15.00 40.00
LJ LeBron James/23 300.00 600.00
NS Steve Novak/20 10.00 25.00
PO Patrick O'Bryant/26 10.00 25.00
PP Paul Pierce/34 20.00 50.00
PS Peja Stojakovic/16 15.00 40.00
RC Rodney Carney/25 12.00 30.00
RE Renaldo Balkman/32 10.00 25.00
RF Raymond Felton/20 20.00 50.00
RG Rudy Gay/22 12.00 30.00
RJ Richard Jefferson/24 6.00 15.00
RP Robert Parish/100 8.00 20.00
SE Sean Elliott/32 15.00 40.00
SJ Solomon Jones/44 6.00 15.00
SK Steve Kerr/25 40.00 75.00
SL Shaun Livingston/14 20.00 50.00
SM J.R. Smith/23 12.00 30.00
SN Steve Nash/13 60.00 120.00
TE Sebastian Telfair/31 12.00 30.00
TP Tayshaun Prince/22 20.00 50.00
TT Tyrus Thomas/24 20.00 50.00
VC Vince Carter/15 30.00 80.00
WF Walt Frazier/10 25.00 60.00
WI Marvin Williams/24 12.00 30.00
YM Yao Ming/11 60.00 120.00

2007-08 SP Game Used

This 190-card set was released in September, 2007. The set was issued in five-card packs which came six packs to a box and 10 boxes to a case where packs carried an initial SRP of $50. Cards numbered 1-100 feature veterans in team alphabetical order while cards 101-140 feature veterans with game-used jersey swatches attached and the set concludes with cards 141-190 featuring 2007-08 rookies. The jersey cards were issued at a stated rate of approximately one per pack and the rookies were issued to a stated print run of 999 serial numbered sets.

COMP.SET w/o SP's (100) 35.00 70.00
JSY APPROXIMATE ODDS ONE PER PACK
RC PRINT RUN 999 SER.#'d SETS
1 Joe Johnson .75 2.00
2 Marvin Williams .75 2.00
3 Josh Smith .75 2.00
4 Al Jefferson .75 2.00
5 Paul Pierce 1.00 2.50
6 Delonte West .60 1.50
7 Raymond Felton 1.00 2.50
8 Gerald Wallace .75 2.00
9 Emeka Okafor .75 2.00
10 Michael Jordan 8.00 20.00
11 Ben Gordon .75 2.00
12 Luol Deng .75 2.00
13 Kirk Hinrich .75 2.00
14 LeBron James 4.00 10.00
15 Larry Hughes .75 2.00
16 Zydrunas Ilgauskas .75 2.00
17 Dirk Nowitzki 1.25 3.00
18 Josh Howard .75 2.00
19 Jason Terry .75 2.00
20 Allen Iverson 1.25 3.00
21 Carmelo Anthony 1.25 3.00
22 Marcus Camby .60 1.50
23 J.R. Smith .75 2.00
24 Chauncey Billups 1.00 2.50
25 Rasheed Wallace 1.00 2.50
26 Richard Hamilton .75 2.00
27 Tayshaun Prince .75 2.00
28 Jason Richardson 1.00 2.50
29 Baron Davis .75 2.00
30 Monta Ellis .75 2.00
31 Tracy McGrady 1.00 2.50
32 Yao Ming 1.25 3.00
33 Rafer Alston .60 1.50
34 Jermaine O'Neal .75 2.00
35 Danny Granger .75 2.00
36 Jamaal Tinsley .60 1.50
37 Elton Brand 1.00 2.50
38 Corey Maggette .75 2.00
39 Cuttino Mobley .75 2.00
40 Kobe Bryant 4.00 10.00
41 Lamar Odom .75 2.00
42 Luke Walton .60 1.50
43 Kwame Brown .60 1.50
44 Pau Gasol 1.00 2.50
45 Mike Miller .75 2.00
46 Hakim Warrick .75 2.00
47 Dwyane Wade 1.50 4.00
48 Shaquille O'Neal 2.00 5.00
49 Jason Williams .75 2.00
50 Michael Redd .75 2.00
51 Mo Williams .75 2.00
52 Andrew Bogut .75 2.00
53 Kevin Garnett 1.50 4.00
54 Ricky Davis .75 2.00
55 Mike James .60 1.50
56 Vince Carter 1.25 3.00
57 Jason Kidd 1.00 2.50
58 Nenad Krstic .60 1.50
59 Richard Jefferson .75 2.00
60 Stephon Marbury .75 2.00
61 Eddy Curry .60 1.50
62 Jamal Crawford 1.00 2.50
63 David Lee .60 1.50
64 Chris Paul 1.25 3.00
65 Tyson Chandler .75 2.00
66 David West .75 2.00
67 Peja Stojakovic 1.00 2.50
68 Dwight Howard .75 2.00
69 Grant Hill 1.25 3.00
70 Jameer Nelson .60 1.50
71 Andre Miller .75 2.00
72 Andre Iguodala .75 2.00
73 Kyle Korver .75 2.00
74 Steve Nash 1.25 3.00
75 Amare Stoudemire .75 2.00
76 Shawn Marion .75 2.00
77 Leandro Barbosa .75 2.00
78 Brandon Roy 1.00 2.50
79 Zach Randolph .75 2.00
80 LaMarcus Aldridge 1.25 3.00
81 Mike Bibby 1.00 2.50
82 Kevin Martin .75 2.00
83 Ron Artest 1.00 2.50
84 Tony Parker 1.00 2.50
85 Manu Ginobili 1.00 2.50
86 Tim Duncan 1.50 4.00
87 Rashard Lewis .75 2.00
88 Ray Allen 1.00 2.50
89 Chris Wilcox .60 1.50
90 T.J. Ford .60 1.50
91 Chris Bosh 1.00 2.50
92 Juan Dixon .60 1.50
93 Andrea Bargnani 1.00 2.50
94 Carlos Boozer .75 2.00
95 Mehmet Okur .60 1.50
96 Deron Williams .75 2.00
97 Gilbert Arenas .75 2.00
98 Antawn Jamison .75 2.00
99 Caron Butler .75 2.00
100 DeShawn Stevenson .60 1.50
101 Al Jefferson JSY 2.50 6.00
102 Allen Iverson JSY 4.00 10.00
103 Amare Stoudemire JSY 2.50 6.00
104 Andre Iguodala JSY 2.50 6.00
105 Andre Miller JSY 2.50 6.00
106 Ben Gordon JSY 2.50 6.00
107 Bruce Bowen JSY 2.00 5.00
108 Carmelo Anthony JSY 4.00 10.00
109 Charlie Villanueva JSY 2.00 5.00
110 Corey Maggette JSY 2.50 6.00
111 Danny Granger JSY 2.50 6.00
112 Darko Milicic JSY 2.00 5.00
113 Devin Harris JSY 2.00 5.00
114 Dirk Nowitzki JSY 4.00 10.00
115 Donyell Marshall JSY 2.00 5.00
116 Drew Gooden JSY 2.50 6.00
117 Dwight Howard JSY 2.50 6.00
118 Elton Brand JSY 3.00 8.00
119 Gilbert Arenas JSY 2.50 6.00
120 Grant Hill JSY 4.00 10.00
121 Jason Kidd JSY 3.00 8.00
122 Jason Richardson JSY 3.00 8.00
123 Jermaine O'Neal JSY 2.50 6.00
124 Kevin Garnett JSY 5.00 12.00
125 Kobe Bryant JSY 8.00 20.00
126 LeBron James JSY 10.00 25.00
127 Luol Deng JSY 2.50 6.00
128 Manu Ginobili JSY 3.00 8.00
129 Mike Bibby JSY 3.00 8.00
130 Nenad Krstic JSY 2.00 5.00
131 Pau Gasol JSY 3.00 8.00
132 Paul Pierce JSY 3.00 8.00
133 Rashard Lewis JSY 2.50 6.00
134 Ray Allen JSY 3.00 8.00
135 Richard Jefferson JSY 2.50 6.00
136 Shaquille O'Neal JSY 6.00 15.00
137 Shaun Livingston JSY 2.00 5.00
138 Shawn Marion JSY 2.50 6.00
139 Tayshaun Prince JSY 2.50 6.00
140 Tim Duncan JSY 5.00 12.00
141 Greg Oden RC 2.00 5.00
142 Kevin Durant RC 20.00 50.00
143 Al Horford RC 2.50 6.00
144 Mike Conley Jr. RC 2.50 6.00
145 Jeff Green RC 2.00 5.00
146 Dominic McGuire RC 1.25 3.00
147 Corey Brewer RC 2.00 5.00
148 Brandan Wright RC 2.00 5.00
149 Joakim Noah RC 2.00 5.00
150 Spencer Hawes RC 1.50 4.00
151 Acie Law RC 1.25 3.00
152 Thaddeus Young RC 2.00 5.00
153 Julian Wright RC 1.25 3.00
154 Al Thornton RC 1.50 4.00
155 Rodney Stuckey RC 1.50 4.00
156 Nick Young RC 2.50 6.00
157 Sean Williams RC 1.25 3.00
158 Marco Belinelli RC 2.00 5.00
159 Javaris Crittenton RC 1.25 3.00
160 Jason Smith RC 1.50 4.00
161 Daequan Cook RC 1.50 4.00
162 Jared Dudley RC 1.50 4.00
163 Wilson Chandler RC 1.50 4.00
164 Morris Almond RC 1.25 3.00
165 Aaron Brooks RC 1.50 4.00
166 Arron Afflalo RC 2.00 5.00
167 Alando Tucker RC 1.25 3.00
168 Petteri Koponen RC 2.00 5.00
169 Carl Landry RC 1.25 3.00
170 Gabe Pruitt RC 1.25 3.00
171 Marcus Williams RC 1.25 3.00
172 Nick Fazekas RC 1.25 3.00
173 Glen Davis RC 1.50 4.00
174 Jermareo Davidson RC 1.25 3.00
175 Josh McRoberts RC 1.50 4.00
176 Chris Richard RC 1.25 3.00
177 Derrick Byars RC 1.25 3.00
178 Adam Haluska RC 1.25 3.00
179 Reyshawn Terry RC 1.25 3.00
180 Jared Jordan RC 1.25 3.00
181 Aaron Gray RC 1.25 3.00
182 JamesOn Curry RC 1.25 3.00
183 Taurean Green RC 1.25 3.00
184 Demetris Nichols RC 1.25 3.00
185 Herbert Hill RC 1.25 3.00
186 Brad Newley RC 2.00 5.00
187 Ramon Sessions RC 2.00 5.00
188 Sammy Mejia RC 1.25 3.00
189 D.J. Strawberry RC 1.25 3.00
190 Stephane Lasme RC 1.25 3.00

2007-08 SP Game Used Gold

*1-100 GOLD: 1.5X TO 4X BASE HI
*101-140 GOLD JSY: 1X TO 2.5X BASE HI
*141-190 GOLD RC: 1.5X TO 4X BASE HI
PRINT RUN 25 SER.#'d SETS
142 Kevin Durant 200.00 500.00

2007-08 SP Game Used All-Star Jersey

PRINT RUN 199 SER.#'d SETS
*PATCHES: 1.25X TO 3X BASE HI
PATCH PRINT RUN 50 SER.#'d SETS
ASAB Andrew Bogut 2.50 6.00
ASBG Ben Gordon 2.50 6.00
ASBO Carlos Boozer 2.50 6.00
ASBR Brandon Roy 3.00 8.00
ASBY Andrew Bynum 2.00 5.00
ASCB Chauncey Billups 3.00 8.00
ASCP Chris Paul 4.00 10.00
ASDH Dwight Howard 2.50 6.00
ASDJ Damon Jones 2.00 5.00
ASDL David Lee 2.00 5.00
ASDN Dirk Nowitzki 4.00 10.00
ASFE Raymond Felton 3.00 8.00
ASGA Gilbert Arenas 2.50 6.00
ASGG Gerald Green 2.50 6.00
ASJF Jordan Farmar 2.00 5.00
ASJG Jorge Garbajosa 2.50 6.00
ASJH Josh Howard 2.50 6.00
ASJJ Joe Johnson 2.50 6.00
ASJK Jason Kidd 3.00 8.00
ASJO Jermaine O'Neal 2.50 6.00
ASKB Kobe Bryant 10.00 25.00
ASLH Luther Head 2.50 6.00
ASLJ LeBron James 8.00 20.00
ASMM Mike Miller 2.50 6.00
ASMO Mehmet Okur 2.00 5.00
ASMW Marcus Williams 2.00 5.00
ASPM Paul Millsap 2.50 6.00
ASPP Paul Pierce 3.00 8.00
ASRA Ray Allen 3.00 8.00
ASRF Randy Foye 3.00 8.00
ASSN Steve Nash 4.00 10.00
ASSP Smush Parker 2.00 5.00
ASTP Tony Parker 4.00 10.00
ASTT Tyrus Thomas 2.00 5.00
ASYM Yao Ming 4.00 10.00

2007-08 SP Game Used Authentic Fabrics

APPROXIMATE ODDS ONE PER BOX
*PATCHES: 1X TO 2.5X BASE HI
PATCH PRINT RUN 75 SER.#'d SETS
AFAB Andrew Bynum 2.00 5.00
AFAI Allen Iverson 4.00 10.00
AFAJ Antawn Jamison 2.50 6.00
AFAM Alonzo Mourning 5.00 12.00
AFBR Brandon Roy 3.00 8.00
AFCB Chauncey Billups 3.00 8.00
AFCP Chris Paul 4.00 10.00
AFCW Chris Webber 3.00 8.00
AFDW Deron Williams 2.50 6.00
AFEB Elton Brand 3.00 8.00
AFGW Gerald Wallace 2.50 6.00
AFJO Jermaine O'Neal 2.50 6.00
AFJR Jason Richardson 3.00 8.00
AFLJ LeBron James 8.00 20.00
AFMG Manu Ginobili 3.00 8.00
AFMJ Michael Jordan 25.00 60.00
AFPG Pau Gasol 3.00 8.00
AFQD Quincy Douby 2.00 5.00
AFRW Rasheed Wallace 3.00 8.00
AFYM Yao Ming 4.00 10.00

2007-08 SP Game Used Authentic Fabrics Dual

PRINT RUN 99 SER.#'d SETS
*PATCH: .75X TO 2X BASE HI
PATCH PRINT RUN 50 SER.#'d SETS
AB G.Arenas/C.Butler 4.00 10.00
AI A.Iverson/C.Anthony 8.00 20.00
AW R.Artest/A.Walker 4.00 10.00
BJ M.Bibby/M.James 4.00 10.00
BS B.Bowen/J.Smith 4.00 10.00
BV A.Bogut/C.Villanueva 4.00 10.00
CJ V.Carter/R.Jefferson 5.00 12.00
CO M.Camby/M.Okur 4.00 10.00
DB A.Daniels/A.Blatche 4.00 10.00
DM R.Davis/K.Martin 4.00 10.00
DW L.Deng/M.Williams 4.00 10.00
FL R.Felton/S.Livingston 4.00 10.00
GD M.Ginobili/T.Duncan 6.00 15.00
GJ K.Garnett/M.James 5.00 12.00
HB B.Haywood/K.Brown 4.00 10.00
HD L.Hughes/M.Daniels 4.00 10.00
HJ A.Harrington/A.Jamison 4.00 10.00
HP R.Hamilton/T.Prince 4.00 10.00
HT D.Harris/J.Tinsley 4.00 10.00
HW R.Wallace/R.Hamilton 4.00 10.00
JJ L.James/M.Jordan 60.00 150.00
JK J.Williams/K.Hinrich 4.00 10.00
JP R.Jefferson/T.Prince 4.00 10.00
JS J.Smith/J.Childress 4.00 10.00
KN N.Krstic/Nene 4.00 10.00
KR K.Korver/M.Redd 4.00 10.00
LB D.Lee/C.Boozer 4.00 10.00
LP R.Lewis/M.Peterson 4.00 10.00
MD A.Miller/B.Davis 4.00 10.00
MG C.Maggette/D.Granger 4.00 10.00
MH S.May/U.Haslem 4.00 10.00
MI Y.Ming/Z.Ilgauskas 5.00 12.00
MK A.Mourning/A.Kirilenko 5.00 12.00
MN D.Milicic/J.Nelson 4.00 10.00
MT S.Marbury/J.Terry 4.00 10.00
OW L.Odom/L.Walton 4.00 10.00
PD M.Pietrus/M.Dunleavy 4.00 10.00
PS P.Pierce/P.Stojakovic 4.00 10.00
RB Z.Randolph/A.Bynum 4.00 10.00
RH J.Rose/G.Hill 8.00 20.00
RR N.Robinson/Q.Richardson 4.00 10.00
RW L.Ridnour/C.Wilcox 4.00 10.00
SK S.Swift/T.Kinsey 4.00 10.00
SR W.Szczerbiak/A.Ray 4.00 10.00
WA C.Webber/L.Aldridge 5.00 12.00
WB D.West/E.Boykins 4.00 10.00
WC D.Gooden/T.Chandler 4.00 10.00
WH G.Wallace/J.Howard 4.00 10.00
WM B.Wallace/B.Miller 4.00 10.00
WS D.West/J.Smith 4.00 10.00

2007-08 SP Game Used Authentic Fabrics Triple

PRINT RUN 50 SER.#'d SETS
*PATCHES: .75X TO 2X BASE HI
PATCH PRINT RUN 25 SER.#'d SETS
AMB Artest/Douby/Bibby 5.00 12.00
ASO Armstrong/Sene/O'Bryant 5.00 12.00
BBA Blatche/Bynum/Aldridge 5.00 12.00
BGM Bryant/Garnett/McGrady 30.00 75.00
BMK Udrih/Ginobili/Kerr 5.00 12.00
CBW Cook/Brown/Walton 5.00 12.00
FMW Felton/May/Wallace 5.00 12.00
HJB Harrington/Jamison/Boozer 5.00 12.00
HLN Harris/Livingston/Noel 5.00 12.00
ICA Iverson/Camby/Anthony 8.00 20.00
IKD Iguodala/Korver/Dalembert 5.00 12.00
JGC Jones/Green/Carter 6.00 15.00
JJJ James/Jordan/Johnson 75.00 200.00
KNM Krstic/Nene/Milicic 5.00 12.00
LAR Lewis/Allen/Ridnour 5.00 12.00
LRR Lee/Robinson/Richardson 5.00 12.00
MCI Mourning/Chandler/Ilgauskas 10.00 25.00
MHG Marshall/Hughes/Gooden 5.00 12.00
MHR Miller/Haslem/Randolph 5.00 12.00
MNS Marion/Nash/Stoudemire 10.00 25.00
MTW Miller/Tinsley/Williams 5.00 12.00
NBW Nelson/Boykins/West 5.00 12.00
PGD Parker/Ginobili/Duncan 12.00 30.00
PWH Prince/Webber/Hamilton 8.00 20.00
RSD Redick/Smith/Dunleavy 8.00 20.00
SKW Stockton/Kirilenko/Williams 6.00 15.00
SRC Smith/Richardson/Childress 5.00 12.00
WBB Wallace/Bowen/Battier 5.00 12.00
WGP Webster/Granger/Petro 5.00 12.00
WRR Webster/Roy/Randolph 6.00 15.00

2007-08 SP Game Used Authentic Fabrics Quad

PRINT RUN 25 SER.#'d SETS
UNPRICED PATCH PRINT RUN 10 SETS
ABPB Artest/Bowen/Pietrus/Butler 20.00 40.00
BHWR Brand/Hill/Wallace/Randolph 15.00 30.00
ESDO Eaton/Stock/Drexler/Olajuwn 30.00 60.00
GCMM KG/Carter/T-Mac/Marion 25.00 60.00
JDSH Jefferson/Davis/Smith/Hughes 15.00 30.00
JOHK James/O'Neal/Howard/Kidd 40.00 80.00
KDNF Kirilenko/Davis/Nene/Frye 15.00 30.00
MOVG May/Odom/Villanueva/Gooden 15.00 30.00
NDAS Dirk/Duncan/Anthony/Amare 20.00 40.00
RFSH Redd/Finley/Stojak/Rip 30.00 60.00
RMLC Ray/Steph/Lvngstn/Cssll 15.00 30.00
WMMB BigBen/Miller/Darko/Brown 15.00 30.00

2007-08 SP Game Used Cut from the Cloth

APPROXIMATELY ONE PER BOX
*PATCHES: 1.25X TO 3X BASE HI
PATCH PRINT RUN 25 SER.#'d SETS
CCAB Andrew Bogut 2.00 5.00
CCAH Al Harrington 2.00 5.00
CCAK Andrei Kirilenko 2.00 5.00
CCAM Alonzo Mourning 6.00 15.00
CCBC Brian Cook 2.00 5.00
CCBH Brendan Haywood 2.00 5.00
CCBR Brandon Roy 2.50 6.00
CCCB Caron Butler 2.00 5.00
CCCH Chauncey Billups 2.50 6.00
CCCP Chris Paul 3.00 8.00
CCCR Charlie Villanueva 1.50 4.00
CCDW Deron Williams 2.00 5.00
CCEB Elton Brand 2.50 6.00
CCJH Josh Howard 2.00 5.00
CCJJ J.J. Redick 2.50 6.00
CCJR Jason Richardson 2.50 6.00
CCJS Josh Smith 2.00 5.00
CCKH Kirk Hinrich 2.00 5.00
CCLH Larry Hughes 2.00 5.00
CCLO Lamar Odom 2.00 5.00
CCMR Michael Redd 2.00 5.00
CCMW Martell Webster 2.00 5.00
CCNR Nate Robinson 1.50 4.00
CCPS Peja Stojakovic 2.50 6.00
CCRW Rasheed Wallace 2.50 6.00
CCSM Stephon Marbury 2.00 5.00
CCSN Steve Nash 3.00 8.00
CCTM Tracy McGrady 2.50 6.00
CCTP Tony Parker 2.50 6.00
CCVC Vince Carter 3.00 8.00

2007-08 SP Game Used Hardcourt Classics

PRINT RUN 199 SER.#'d SETS
*PATCH: 1X TO 2.5X BASE HI
PATCH PRINT RUN 25 SER.#'d SETS
HCAD Antonio Daniels 2.00 5.00
HCAS Amare Stoudemire 2.50 6.00
HCBC Brian Cardinal 2.00 5.00
HCBH Brendan Haywood 2.00 5.00
HCBL Andray Blatche 2.00 5.00
HCBW Ben Wallace 2.50 6.00
HCCD Chris Duhon 2.00 5.00
HCCF Channing Frye 2.50 6.00
HCCM Corey Maggette 2.50 6.00
HCDH Dwight Howard 2.50 6.00
HCDS Damon Stoudamire 2.50 6.00
HCDT Donell Taylor 2.00 5.00
HCDW Dorell Wright 2.00 5.00
HCEH Eddie House 2.00 5.00
HCEP Eric Piatkowski 2.00 5.00
HCGO Ben Gordon 2.50 6.00
HCHW Hakim Warrick 2.50 6.00
HCJC Jason Collins 2.00 5.00
HCJH Juwan Howard 2.50 6.00
HCJJ Jerome James 2.00 5.00
HCJK Jason Kapono 2.00 5.00
HCJM Jeff McInnis 2.00 5.00
HCJN Jameer Nelson 2.00 5.00
HCJP James Posey 2.00 5.00
HCJR Jalen Rose 2.50 6.00
HCJS James Singleton 2.00 5.00
HCJT Jake Tsakalidis 2.00 5.00
HCJW Jason Williams 2.50 6.00
HCKB Keith Bogans 2.00 5.00
HCKG Kevin Garnett 5.00 12.00
HCKH Kirk Hinrich 2.50 6.00
HCLA LeBron James 8.00 20.00
HCLD Luol Deng 2.50 6.00
HCLH Luther Head 2.50 6.00
HCLJ Linton Johnson 2.00 5.00
HCLW Lorenzen Wright 2.00 5.00
HCMJ Marc Jackson 2.00 5.00
HCMM Mikki Moore 2.00 5.00
HCMR Michael Redd 2.50 6.00
HCMS Mike Sweetney 2.00 5.00
HCMW Mike Wilks 2.00 5.00
HCNR Nate Robinson 2.00 5.00
HCOH Othella Harrington 2.00 5.00
HCPA Jannero Pargo 2.00 5.00
HCPB Pat Burke 2.00 5.00
HCPG Pau Gasol 3.00 8.00
HCQD Quincy Douby 2.00 5.00
HCQR Quentin Richardson 2.50 6.00
HCSB Shannon Brown 2.00 5.00
HCSM Shawn Marion 2.50 6.00
HCSO Shaquille O'Neal 6.00 15.00
HCST DeShawn Stevenson 2.00 5.00
HCTA Trevor Ariza 2.00 5.00
HCUH Udonis Haslem 2.00 5.00
HCWS Wally Szczerbiak 2.50 6.00

2007-08 SP Game Used Rookie Exclusives Autographs

PRINT RUN 100 SER.#'d SETS
REAA Arron Afflalo 6.00 15.00
REAB Aaron Brooks 5.00 12.00
REAG Aaron Gray 4.00 10.00
REAH Adam Haluska 4.00 10.00
REAL Acie Law 4.00 10.00
REAT Al Thornton 5.00 12.00
RECB Corey Brewer 6.00 15.00
RECL Carl Landry 4.00 10.00
RECU JamesOn Curry 4.00 10.00
REDA Jermareo Davidson 4.00 10.00
REDB Derrick Byars 4.00 10.00
REDC Daequan Cook 5.00 12.00
REDS D.J. Strawberry 4.00 10.00
REGD Glen Davis 5.00 12.00
REGP Gabe Pruitt 4.00 10.00
REHH Herbert Hill 4.00 10.00
REHO Al Horford 15.00 40.00
REJC Javaris Crittenton 4.00 10.00
REJD Jared Dudley 5.00 12.00
REJG Jeff Green 12.00 30.00
REJJ Jared Jordan 4.00 10.00
REJM Josh McRoberts 5.00 12.00
REJN Joakim Noah 12.00 30.00
REJS Jason Smith 5.00 12.00
REJW Julian Wright 4.00 10.00
REKD Kevin Durant 150.00 300.00
REMC Mike Conley Jr. 8.00 20.00
REMW Marcus Williams 4.00 10.00
RENF Nick Fazekas 4.00 10.00
REPK Petteri Koponen 6.00 15.00
RERS Rodney Stuckey 5.00 12.00
RERT Reyshawn Terry 4.00 10.00
RESH Spencer Hawes 5.00 12.00
RESL Stephane Lasme 4.00 10.00
RETG Taurean Green 4.00 10.00
RETU Alando Tucker 4.00 10.00
REWC Wilson Chandler 5.00 12.00

2007-08 SP Game Used Signature Swatch

PRINT RUN 30 SER.#'d SETS
SSAI Andre Iguodala 6.00 15.00
SSAJ Antawn Jamison 10.00 25.00
SSAM Alonzo Mourning 30.00 80.00
SSAR Allan Ray 6.00 15.00
SSBB Bruce Bowen 8.00 20.00
SSBD Baron Davis 12.50 30.00
SSBG Ben Gordon 12.50 30.00
SSBJ Bobby Jones 6.00 15.00
SSBM Brad Miller 6.00 15.00
SSBR Brandon Roy 15.00 30.00
SSCA Carmelo Anthony 20.00 50.00
SSCB Chris Bosh 15.00 40.00
SSCF Channing Frye 6.00 15.00
SSCM Corey Maggette 6.00 15.00
SSCP Chris Paul 20.00 50.00
SSCS Cedric Simmons 6.00 15.00
SSDN David Noel 6.00 15.00
SSDS DeShawn Stevenson 6.00 15.00
SSDW Deron Williams 20.00 40.00
SSEO Emeka Okafor 6.00 15.00
SSFO Randy Foye 8.00 20.00
SSGW Gerald Wallace 8.00 20.00
SSHA Hilton Armstrong 6.00 15.00
SSJK Jason Kidd 20.00 40.00
SSJM Jamaal Magloire 6.00 15.00
SSJO Jermaine O'Neal 10.00 25.00
SSJS J.R. Smith 6.00 15.00
SSKB Kobe Bryant 100.00 200.00
SSLA LaMarcus Aldridge 20.00 40.00
SSLH Larry Hughes 6.00 15.00
SSLJ LeBron James 100.00 200.00
SSMA Maurice Ager 6.00 15.00
SSMB Mike Bibby 8.00 20.00
SSMC Mardy Collins 6.00 15.00
SSMI Andre Miller 6.00 15.00
SSMJ Michael Jordan 300.00 550.00
SSNO Steve Novak 6.00 15.00
SSPA Tony Parker 10.00 25.00
SSPD Paul Davis 6.00 15.00
SSPP Paul Pierce 20.00 50.00
SSPS Peja Stojakovic 8.00 20.00
SSQD Quincy Douby 6.00 15.00
SSQR Quentin Richardson 6.00 15.00
SSRF Raymond Felton 6.00 15.00
SSRH Richard Hamilton 8.00 20.00
SSRJ Richard Jefferson 6.00 15.00
SSSA Sean May 6.00 15.00
SSSB Shannon Brown 6.00 15.00
SSSM Craig Smith 6.00 15.00
SSSN Steve Nash 25.00 60.00
SSSS Saer Sene 6.00 15.00
SSTM Tracy McGrady 20.00 50.00
SSTP Tayshaun Prince 6.00 15.00
SSVC Vince Carter 20.00 50.00
SSWB Will Blalock 6.00 15.00
SSYM Yao Ming 25.00 60.00

2007-08 SP Game Used Signature Swatch Patch

*PATCH: .75X TO 2X HI COLUMN
PATCH PRINT RUN 15 SER.#'d SETS
SSAM Alonzo Mourning 100.00 200.00
SSCP Chris Paul 75.00 150.00

2007-08 SP Game Used SIGnificance

APPROXIMATE ODDS ONE PER BOX
SIAI Andre Iguodala 4.00 10.00
SIAJ Antawn Jamison 4.00 10.00
SIAM Andre Miller 4.00 10.00
SIBA Leandro Barbosa 4.00 10.00
SIBD Baron Davis 5.00 12.00
SIBG Ben Gordon 8.00 20.00
SIBM Brad Miller 4.00 10.00
SIBR Brandon Roy 8.00 20.00
SICA Carmelo Anthony 20.00 50.00
SICB Chris Bosh 10.00 25.00
SICD Chris Duhon 4.00 10.00
SICM Corey Maggette 4.00 10.00
SICP Chris Paul 15.00 40.00
SICS Craig Smith 4.00 10.00
SIDB Dee Brown 4.00 10.00
SIDR Clyde Drexler 20.00 40.00
SIDW Deron Williams 8.00 20.00
SIHA Hassan Adams 4.00 10.00
SIHO Hakeem Olajuwon 20.00 50.00
SIHW Hakim Warrick 4.00 10.00
SIIU Ime Udoka 4.00 10.00
SIJA James Augustine 4.00 10.00
SIJE Julius Erving 40.00 80.00
SIJG Joey Graham 4.00 10.00
SIJJ Jarrett Jack 4.00 10.00
SIJK Jason Kidd 12.50 30.00
SIJS J.R. Smith 4.00 10.00
SIKB Kobe Bryant 75.00 150.00
SILA LaMarcus Aldridge 8.00 20.00
SILB Larry Bird 40.00 100.00
SILJ LeBron James 80.00 160.00
SIMC Mardy Collins 4.00 10.00
SINO Steve Novak 4.00 10.00
SIPM Paul Millsap 4.00 10.00
SIPP Paul Pierce 10.00 25.00
SIRB Raja Bell 4.00 10.00
SIRG Rudy Gay 6.00 15.00
SISN Steve Nash 20.00 50.00
SIST John Stockton 50.00 100.00
SISW Shelden Williams 4.00 10.00
SITM Tracy McGrady 15.00 30.00
SITS Thabo Sefolosha 4.00 10.00
SIVC Vince Carter 15.00 40.00
SIVS Vassilis Spanoulis 4.00 10.00
SIWB Will Blalock 4.00 10.00

2007-08 SP Game Used SIGnificance Dual

PRINT RUN 50 SER.#'d SETS
SP PRINT RUN 25 SER.#'d SETS
UNLESS LISTED IN CHECKLIST
SDAR L.Aldridge/B.Roy 15.00 40.00
SDBA N.Archibald/M.Bogues 12.00 30.00
SDBB R.Bell/L.Barbosa 15.00 30.00
SDBJ K.Bryant/L.James SP 200.00 325.00
SDBM M.Bibby/B.Miller 10.00 25.00
SDBO J.O'Neal/K.Bryant SP 75.00 150.00
SDCL T.Chandler/D.Lee 10.00 25.00
SDCM V.Carter/McGrady SP 40.00 80.00
SDCO E.Curry/E.Okafor 10.00 25.00
SDCS T.Chandler/P.Stojakovic 10.00 25.00
SDDH A.Harrington/B.Davis 10.00 25.00
SDDS C.Duhon/T.Sefolosha 10.00 25.00
SDER J.Erving/W.Frazier SP 125.00 225.00
SDFC W.Frazier/M.Collins 10.00 25.00
SDFG J.Garbajosa/T.Ford 10.00 25.00
SDFR C.Russell/Frazier SP 35.00 75.00
SDFS C.Smith/R.Foye 10.00 25.00
SDGR R.Gay/B.Roy SP 30.00 60.00
SDHD C.Duhon/K.Hinrich/15 30.00 60.00
SDJI R.Jefferson/M.Ilic 10.00 25.00
SDJS A.Jamison/D.Stevenson 10.00 25.00
SDKC J.Kidd/V.Carter SP 30.00 60.00
SDKK S.Kerr/J.Kapono 6.00 15.00
SDKR D.Rodman/S.Kerr SP 60.00 120.00
SDLF C.Frye/D.Lee 10.00 25.00
SDLM Mahorn/Laimbeer SP 40.00 80.00
SDMI A.Miller/A.Iguodala 10.00 25.00
SDMM McGrady/Y.Ming SP 60.00 150.00
SDMW S.May/M.Williams 10.00 25.00
SDNB S.Novak/W.Blalock 10.00 25.00
SDOF R.Felton/E.Okafor 10.00 25.00
SDOM Murphy/Olajuwon/20 40.00 80.00
SDPB M.Bogues/R.Parish 15.00 40.00
SDPC V.Carter/P.Pierce SP 30.00 80.00
SDSP P.Stojakovic/C.Paul 20.00 40.00
SDSS Stockton/Nash SP 125.00 225.00
SDST T.Thomas/J.Smith 10.00 25.00
SDTB T.Prince/W.Blalock 10.00 25.00

2007-08 SP Game Used Significant Numbers Autographs

PRINT RUNS LISTED IN CHECKLIST
SOME UNPRICED DUE TO SCARCITY
AM Alonzo Mourning/33 60.00 150.00
AR Allan Ray/20 8.00 20.00
BL Bill Laimbeer/40 15.00 40.00
BM Brad Miller/52 8.00 20.00
CA Carmelo Anthony/15 40.00 100.00
CD Clyde Drexler/22 60.00 120.00
CF Channing Frye/44 15.00 30.00
CM Corey Maggette/50 8.00 20.00
CS Cedric Simmons/15 8.00 20.00
DD Darryl Dawkins/53 10.00 25.00
DL David Lee/42 20.00 40.00
DM Donyell Marshall/24 8.00 20.00
DN David Noel/34 8.00 20.00
HW Hakim Warrick/21 8.00 20.00
KB Kobe Bryant/24 175.00 350.00
KK Kyle Korver/26 8.00 20.00
LA LaMarcus Aldridge/12 40.00 80.00
LB Larry Bird/33 100.00 200.00
LJ1 LeBron James/23 175.00 350.00
LJ2 LeBron James/23 175.00 350.00
MC Mardy Collins/25 8.00 20.00
ME Mark Eaton/53 8.00 20.00
MJ Michael Jordan/23 500.00 800.00
MP Morris Peterson/24 8.00 20.00
MS Saer Sene/18 8.00 20.00
NO Steve Novak/20 8.00 20.00
PD Paul Davis/40 8.00 20.00
PP Paul Pierce/34 50.00 120.00
QR Quentin Richardson/23 8.00 20.00
RC Rodney Carney/25 8.00 20.00
RG Rudy Gay/22 20.00 40.00
RH Richard Hamilton/32 15.00 40.00
SK Steve Kerr/25 15.00 40.00
SM Sean May/42 8.00 20.00
SN Steve Nash/13 50.00 120.00
ST John Stockton/12 100.00 200.00
TP Tayshaun Prince/22 20.00 40.00
TT Tyrus Thomas/24 20.00 50.00
YM Yao Ming/11 75.00 150.00

2007-08 SP Game Used Significant Numbers Non-Auto Patch

PRINT RUNS LISTED IN CHECKLIST
SOME UNPRICED DUE TO SCARCITY
AG Maurice Ager/13 6.00 15.00
AM Alonzo Mourning/33 40.00 80.00
AR Allan Ray/20 6.00 15.00
BJ Bobby Jackson/35 6.00 15.00
BL Bill Laimbeer/40 10.00 25.00
BM Brad Miller/52 6.00 15.00
CA Carmelo Anthony/15 25.00 50.00
CF Channing Frye/44 6.00 15.00
CM Corey Maggette/50 6.00 15.00
CS Cedric Simmons/15 6.00 15.00
DD Darryl Dawkins/53 6.00 15.00
DH Dwight Howard/12 25.00 50.00
DM Donyell Marshall/24 6.00 15.00
DN David Noel/34 6.00 15.00
DR David Robinson/55 12.00 30.00
EB Elton Brand/42 6.00 15.00
HW Hakim Warrick/21 6.00 15.00
JN Jameer Nelson/14 6.00 15.00
JR Jason Richardson/23 20.00 40.00
KB Kobe Bryant/24 50.00 120.00
KH Kirk Hinrich/12 20.00 40.00
KK Kyle Korver/26 15.00 30.00
LA LaMarcus Aldridge/35 15.00 30.00
LB Larry Bird/33 25.00 50.00
LH Larry Hughes/32 6.00 15.00
LJ1 LeBron James/35 60.00 120.00
LJ2 LeBron James/23 60.00 120.00
MA Magic Johnson/32 30.00 60.00
MB Mike Bibby/10 15.00 30.00
MC Mardy Collins/25 6.00 15.00
ME Mark Eaton/53 15.00 30.00
MG Manu Ginobili/20 10.00 25.00
MJ Michael Jordan/23 125.00 225.00
MP Morris Peterson/35 6.00 15.00
MS Saer Sene/18 6.00 15.00
MW Marvin Williams/24 6.00 15.00
NO Steve Novak/20 6.00 15.00
PD Paul Davis/40 6.00 15.00
PP Paul Pierce/34 15.00 30.00
PS Peja Stojakovic/16 10.00 25.00
QR Quentin Richardson/23 6.00 15.00
RC Rodney Carney/25 6.00 15.00
RG Rudy Gay/22 10.00 25.00
RH Richard Hamilton/32 10.00 25.00
RJ Richard Jefferson/24 6.00 15.00
RO Dennis Rodman/91 20.00 50.00
SE Sean Elliott/32 10.00 25.00
SK Steve Kerr/25 8.00 20.00
SM Sean May/42 6.00 15.00
SN Steve Nash/13 25.00 50.00
ST John Stockton/12 12.00 30.00
TT Tyrus Thomas/24 6.00 15.00
VC Vince Carter/15 20.00 50.00
WF Walt Frazier/10 20.00 40.00
YM Yao Ming/11 20.00 40.00

2007-08 SP Game Used Swatch of Class

APPROXIMATE ODDS ONE PER BOX
*PATCHES: 1.5X TO 4X BASE HI
PATCH PRINT RUN 25 SER.#'d SETS
SCCD Clyde Drexler 5.00 12.00
SCDD Darryl Dawkins 4.00 10.00
SCDE Dennis Rodman 6.00 15.00
SCDR David Robinson 5.00 12.00
SCJE Julius Erving 6.00 15.00
SCJS John Stockton 4.00 10.00
SCLB Larry Bird 6.00 15.00
SCMA Magic Johnson 6.00 15.00
SCMJ Michael Jordan 20.00 50.00
SCRP Robert Parish 4.00 10.00

2009-10 SP Game Used

COMP. SET w/o SPs (100) 30.00 60.00
ROOKIE PRINT RUN 399 SER.#'d SETS
1 Al Harrington .75 2.00
2 Al Horford 1.00 2.50
3 Al Jefferson .75 2.00
4 Al Thornton .75 2.00
5 Allen Iverson 1.25 3.00
6 Andre Iguodala .75 2.00
7 Andre Miller .75 2.00
8 Andrea Bargnani .75 2.00
9 Antawn Jamison .75 2.00
10 Baron Davis .75 2.00
11 Ben Gordon .75 2.00
12 Ben Wallace .75 2.00
13 Beno Udrih .60 1.50
14 Brad Miller .75 2.00
15 Brandon Roy 1.00 2.50
16 Carlos Boozer .75 2.00
17 Carmelo Anthony 1.25 3.00
18 Chauncey Billups 1.00 2.50
19 Chris Bosh 1.00 2.50
20 Chris Duhon .60 1.50
21 Chris Paul 1.25 3.00
22 Courtney Lee .75 2.00
23 D.J. Augustin .60 1.50
24 Danny Granger .75 2.00
25 David Lee .60 1.50
26 David West .75 2.00
27 Derek Fisher .75 2.00
28 Deron Williams .75 2.00
29 Derrick Rose 1.50 4.00
30 DeShawn Stevenson .60 1.50
31 Devin Harris .60 1.50

32 Dirk Nowitzki 1.25 3.00
33 Dwight Howard .75 2.00
34 Dwyane Wade 1.50 4.00
35 Elton Brand 1.00 2.50
36 Eric Gordon .75 2.00
37 Gilbert Arenas .75 2.00
38 Hedo Turkoglu .75 2.00
39 Jamal Crawford 1.00 2.50
40 Jason Kidd 1.00 2.50
41 Jason Richardson 1.00 2.50
42 Jeff Green .75 2.00
43 Jermaine O'Neal .75 2.00
44 Jerryd Bayless .75 2.00
45 Joe Johnson .75 2.00
46 Jose Calderon .60 1.50
47 Josh Howard .75 2.00
48 Josh Smith .75 2.00
49 Kenyon Martin .75 2.00
50 Kevin Durant 2.50 6.00
51 Kevin Garnett 1.50 4.00
52 Kevin Love 1.00 2.50
53 Kevin Martin .75 2.00
54 Kobe Bryant 4.00 10.00
55 Lamar Odom .75 2.00
56 LaMarcus Aldridge 1.00 2.50
57 LeBron James 4.00 10.00
58 Luis Scola .75 2.00
59 Luke Ridnour .75 2.00
60 Luol Deng .75 2.00
61 Manu Ginobili 1.00 2.50
62 Marc Gasol 1.00 2.50
63 Mario Chalmers .75 2.00
64 Michael Beasley .60 1.50
65 Michael Redd .75 2.00
66 Mike Bibby .75 2.00
67 Mike Dunleavy .60 1.50
68 Mo Williams .75 2.00
69 Monta Ellis .75 2.00
70 O.J. Mayo .60 1.50
71 Pau Gasol 1.00 2.50
72 Paul Pierce 1.00 2.50
73 Peja Stojakovic 1.00 2.50
74 Quentin Richardson .75 2.00
75 Raja Bell .75 2.00
76 Ray Allen 1.00 2.50
77 Raymond Felton .75 2.00
78 Richard Hamilton .75 2.00
79 Richard Jefferson .75 2.00
80 Rodney Stuckey .60 1.50
81 Ron Artest 1.00 2.50
82 Ronnie Brewer .75 2.00
83 Rudy Fernandez .60 1.50
84 Rudy Gay 1.00 2.50
85 Russell Westbrook 2.50 6.00
86 Sebastian Telfair .60 1.50
87 Shaquille O'Neal 2.00 5.00
88 Shawn Marion .75 2.00
89 Stephen Jackson .75 2.00
90 Steve Nash 1.00 2.50
91 T.J. Ford .60 1.50
92 Tayshaun Prince .75 2.00
93 Thaddeus Young .60 1.50
94 Tim Duncan 1.50 4.00
95 Tony Parker 1.00 2.50
96 Tracy McGrady 1.00 2.50
97 Tyson Chandler .75 2.00
98 Vince Carter 1.25 3.00
99 Yao Ming 1.25 3.00
100 Yi Jianlian .75 2.00
101 A.J. Price RC 1.50 4.00
102 B.J. Mullens RC 1.50 4.00
103 Blake Griffin RC 10.00 25.00
104 Brandon Jennings RC 2.50 6.00
105 Chase Budinger RC 2.00 5.00
106 DaJuan Summers RC 1.50 4.00
107 Rodrigue Beaubois RC 1.50 4.00
108 Danny Green RC 3.00 8.00
109 Dante Cunningham RC 1.50 4.00
110 Darren Collison RC 2.50 6.00
111 DeJuan Blair RC 2.00 5.00
112 DeMar DeRozan RC 6.00 15.00
113 Derrick Brown RC 1.50 4.00
114 Earl Clark RC 2.00 5.00
115 Eric Maynor RC 1.50 4.00
116 Gerald Henderson RC 2.00 5.00
117 Hasheem Thabeet RC 1.50 4.00
118 James Harden RC 12.00 30.00
119 James Johnson RC 2.00 5.00
120 Jeff Pendergraph RC 1.50 4.00
121 Jeff Teague RC 2.50 6.00
122 Jonny Flynn RC 1.50 4.00
123 Jordan Hill RC 2.00 5.00
124 Austin Daye RC 1.50 4.00
125 Jrue Holiday RC 3.00 8.00
126 Marcus Thornton RC 2.00 5.00
127 Nick Calathes RC 1.50 4.00
128 Omri Casspi RC 2.00 5.00
129 Patrick Mills RC 5.00 12.00
130 Ricky Rubio RC 4.00 10.00
131 Sam Young RC 1.50 4.00
132 Sergio Llull RC 1.50 4.00
133 Stephen Curry RC 100.00 250.00
134 Taj Gibson RC 2.50 6.00
135 Terrence Williams RC 1.50 4.00
136 Toney Douglas RC 1.50 4.00
137 Ty Lawson RC 2.50 6.00
138 Tyler Hansbrough RC 2.00 5.00
139 Jermaine Taylor RC 1.50 4.00
140 Tyreke Evans RC 2.00 5.00
141 DeMarre Carroll RC 2.00 5.00
142 Wayne Ellington RC 2.50 6.00

2009-10 SP Game Used 3 Star Swatches

PRINT RUN 299 SER.#'d SETS
*SWATCH 125: .5X TO 1.25X BASE HI
*SWATCH 50: .6X TO 1.5X BASE HI
*SWATCH 35: .75X TO 2X BASE HI
3SAGA Arenas/Allen/Garnett 5.00 12.00
3SAHW Allen/Gordon/Hamilton 4.00 10.00
3SARB Roy/Aldridge/Bayless 4.00 10.00
3SASY O'Neal/Bynum/Ming 5.00 12.00
3SAWI Walton/Iguodala/Arenas 4.00 10.00
3SBAH Bryant/Artest/Howard 12.00 30.00
3SBFR Foye/Bogans/Rush 4.00 10.00
3SBGJ James/Bryant/Garnett 20.00 50.00
3SBHM Howard/Butler/Millsap 4.00 10.00
3SBIM Malone/Iguodala/Brand 4.00 10.00
3SBJD Bryant/James/Durant 25.00 60.00
3SBMH Bryant/Howard/McGrady 8.00 20.00
3SBMJ Bryant/James/Robertson 20.00 50.00
3SBOB Bargnani/Bosh/O'Neal 4.00 10.00
3SBOF Bryant/Grant/O'Neal 8.00 20.00
3SBWC Wright/Brown/Chandler 4.00 10.00
3SBWM Millsap/Williams/Boozer 4.00 10.00
3SCFM Carter/Felton/May 5.00 12.00
3SCGM Carter/McGrady/Gervin 5.00 12.00
3SCMA Anthony/Marion/Carter 5.00 12.00
3SCMP Carter/McGrady/Pippen 6.00 15.00
3SDFA Farmar/Davis/Afflalo 4.00 10.00
3SDGP Gervin/Duncan/Parker 5.00 12.00
3SDGR Duncan/Gervin/Robinson 5.00 12.00
3SDHP Duncan/Howard/Paul 5.00 12.00
3SDMF Davis/Farmar/Webb 4.00 10.00
3SDMO Duncan/Ming/O'Neal 6.00 15.00
3SDPR Duncan/Parker/Robinson 8.00 20.00
3SDWC Chalmers/D-Roberts/White 4.00 10.00
3SEFC Ellis/Crittenton/Farmar 4.00 10.00
3SEGH Ewing/Hibbert/Green 4.00 10.00
3SEHO O'Neal/Ewing/Howard 6.00 15.00
3SELR Ewing/Robinson/Lee 4.00 10.00
3SGAS Greene/Sharpe/Alexander 4.00 10.00
3SGCH Carter/Hill/Garnett 5.00 12.00
3SGCO Garnett/O'Neal/Carter 5.00 12.00
3SGMN Garnett/Nowitzki/Marion 5.00 12.00
3SGMO Ming/Gasol/O'Neal 5.00 12.00
3SGNA Garnett/Nowitzki/Anthony 6.00 15.00
3SGNB Nowitzki/Garnett/Bosh 5.00 12.00
3SGPA Garnett/Anthony/Prince 5.00 12.00
3SGYL Lopez/Gray/Young 4.00 10.00
3SHAR Allen/Redick/Hornacek 4.00 10.00
3SHBA Hamilton/Arenas/Billups 4.00 10.00
3SHDP Pippen/Rose/Deng 12.00 30.00
3SHFT Fernandez/Hamilton/Tucker 4.00 10.00
3SHHL Head/Landry/Howard 4.00 10.00
3SHIP Hamilton/Iverson/Prince 4.00 10.00
3SHIW Iverson/Hamilton/Wallace 4.00 10.00
3SHJK Jordan/Hibbert/Koufos 4.00 10.00
3SHMS Hornacek/Stockton/Malone 5.00 12.00
3SHWD Walton/Douby/Harrington 4.00 10.00
3SIBJ Johnson/Billups/Iverson 6.00 15.00
3SJBJ James/Jordan/Bryant 50.00 125.00
3SJGP Grant/Jordan/Pippen 25.00 60.00
3SJMJ Jordan/Johnson/Malone 25.00 60.00
3SJWS Stockton/Williams/Johnson 6.00 15.00
3SKPS Kidd/Stockton/Paul 5.00 12.00
3SLGH Grant/Lewis/Howard 5.00 12.00
3SLHD Lee/Haslem/Davis 4.00 10.00
3SMBD Maggette/Boozer/Deng 4.00 10.00
3SMBO Ming/Bynum/O'Neal 5.00 12.00
3SMBR Mayo/Rose/Beasley 10.00 25.00
3SMCD Cooper/Drexler/Malone 5.00 12.00
3SMCK Malone/Boozer/Okur 4.00 10.00
3SMDO Maggette/Davis/Odom 4.00 10.00
3SMER Maggette/Ellis/Randolph 4.00 10.00
3SMGP Malone/Pippen/Gervin 6.00 15.00
3SMHH Howard/Hughes/Maggette 4.00 10.00
3SMHL Landry/Scola/McGrady 4.00 10.00
3SMME Maggette/Ellis/Mullin 4.00 10.00
3SMMO Marion/O'Neal/Martin 4.00 10.00
3SMPT Pippen/Thomas/Maggette 5.00 12.00
3SMSM Stoudemire/Malone/Ming 6.00 15.00
3SMTO Harrington/O'Neal/Tinsley 4.00 10.00
3SMUW Williams/Udrih/Miller 4.00 10.00
3SMWH O'Neal/Haslem/Wade 5.00 12.00
3SNAK Anderson/Koufos/Novak 4.00 10.00
3SNAR Roy/Arenas/Nash 5.00 12.00
3SNGM Nash/Ming/Garnett 6.00 15.00
3SNHB Noah/Horford/Brewer 4.00 10.00
3SNIM Nash/Iverson/Marbury 6.00 15.00
3SNKP Parker/Kidd/Nash 6.00 15.00
3SOJC Odom/Cooper/Johnson 6.00 15.00
3SPAG Garnett/Allen/Pierce 8.00 20.00
3SPMG Robinson/Grant/Malone 5.00 12.00
3SRBG Rush/Giddens/Beasley 5.00 12.00
3SSJC Kidd/Nash/Paul 6.00 15.00
3SSMR Szczerbiak/Ridnour/Miller 4.00 10.00
3SSOT Swift/O'Neal/Thomas 5.00 12.00
3STBS Thomas/Brewer/Simmons 4.00 10.00
3STFP Tinsley/Ford/Paul 5.00 12.00
3STGW Gordon/Thomas/White 4.00 10.00
3STRC Crittenton/Tinsley/Robinson 4.00 10.00
3STSN Thomas/Noah/Deng 4.00 10.00
3STUW Tinsley/Udrih/Williams 4.00 10.00
3STWB Tinsley/West/Felton 4.00 10.00
3SWDG Durant/Green/Westbrook 10.00 25.00
3SWTR Thornton/Randolph/Thompson 4.00 10.00
3SWWH Wallace/Wallace/Howard 5.00 12.00

2009-10 SP Game Used 4 on 4 Fabrics

STATED PRINT RUN 99 SER.#'d SETS
*SWATCH 65: .4X TO 1X BASE HI
FFGUARD Guard Legends 40.00 100.00
FFSTARS NBA All-Stars 12.00 30.00
FF01CFINL 2001 NBA Playoffs 12.00 30.00
FF02CFINL 2002 NBA Playoffs 12.00 30.00
FF03FINL 2003 NBA Finals 12.00 30.00
FF04FINL 2004 NBA Finals 12.50 30.00
FF05FINL 2005 NBA Finals 10.00 25.00
FF06FINL 2006 NBA Finals 12.00 30.00
FF07FINL 2007 NBA Finals 15.00 40.00
FF2009AS 2009 NBA All-Stars 25.00 60.00
FF80STAR 1980s Stars 20.00 50.00
FF90EAST 1990s E.Conf.Stars 40.00 100.00
FF90STAR 1990s Stars 40.00 100.00
FF90WEST 1990s W.Conf.Stars 15.00 40.00
FF91FINL 1991 NBA Finals 40.00 100.00
FFATLCHA Hawks/Bobcats 8.00 20.00
FFATLDAL Hawks/Mavericks 8.00 20.00
FFATLMIA Hawks/Heat 8.00 20.00
FFATLORL Hawks/Magic 8.00 20.00
FFATLWAS Hawks/Wizards 8.00 20.00
FFBOSLAL Celtics/Lakers 12.00 30.00
FFBOSNET Celtics/Nets 10.00 25.00
FFBOSNYK Celtics/Knicks 10.00 25.00
FFBOSPHI Celtics/76ers 10.00 25.00
FFBOSTOR Celtics/Raptors 10.00 25.00
FFCENTER Center Legends 20.00 50.00
FFCHAMIA Bobcats/Heat 8.00 20.00
FFCHAORL Bobcats/Magic 8.00 20.00
FFCHAWAS Bobcats/Wizards 8.00 20.00
FFCHICLE Bulls/Cavaliers 12.00 30.00
FFCHIDET Bulls/Pistons 12.00 30.00
FFCHIIND Bulls/Pacers 10.00 25.00
FFCHIMIL Bulls/Bucks 10.00 25.00
FFCLEDET Cavaliers/Pistons 12.00 30.00
FFCLEIND Cavaliers/Pacers 12.00 30.00
FFCLEMIL Cavaliers/Bucks 12.00 30.00
FFCLEPHO Cavaliers/Suns 12.00 30.00
FFDALHOU Mavericks/Rockets 8.00 20.00
FFDALMEM Mavericks/Grizzlies 8.00 20.00
FFDALNEW Mavericks/Hornets 8.00 20.00
FFDALSAN Mavericks/Spurs 8.00 20.00
FFDENMIN Nuggets/Timberwolves 8.00 20.00
FFDENOKL Nuggets/Thunder 8.00 20.00
FFDENPOR Nuggets/Trail Blazers 8.00 20.00
FFDENUTA Nuggets/Jazz 10.00 25.00
FFDETIND Pistons/Pacers 8.00 20.00
FFDETMIL Pistons/Bucks 8.00 20.00
FFDETNEW Pistons/Hornets 8.00 20.00
FFEAST6M E.Conference 6th Men 8.00 20.00
FFEASTAS E.Conference All-Stars 20.00 50.00
FFEASTCE E.Conference Centers 8.00 20.00
FFEASTPF E.Conference PF 10.00 25.00
FFEASTPG E.Conference PG 10.00 25.00
FFEASTSF E.Conference SF 15.00 40.00
FFEASTSG E.Conference SG 10.00 25.00
FFEASVWES East vs West 20.00 50.00
FFFORWRD Forward Legends 15.00 40.00
FFGOLLAC Warriors/Clippers 8.00 20.00
FFGOLLAL Warriors/Lakers 12.00 30.00
FFGOLPHO Warriors/Suns 8.00 20.00
FFGOLSAC Warriors/Kings 8.00 20.00
FFHOUMEM Rockets/Grizzlies 10.00 25.00
FFHOUNEW Rockets/Hornets 8.00 20.00
FFHOUSAN Rockets/Spurs 8.00 20.00
FFINDMIL Pacers/Bucks 8.00 20.00
FFLACLAL Clippers/Lakers 12.00 30.00
FFLACPHO Clippers/Suns 8.00 20.00
FFLACSAC Clippers/Kings 8.00 20.00
FFLALPHO Lakers/Suns 12.00 30.00
FFLALSAC Lakers/Kings 12.00 30.00
FFMEMNEW Grizzlies/Hornets 8.00 20.00
FFMEMSAN Grizzlies/Spurs 8.00 20.00
FFMIAORL Heat/Magic 10.00 25.00
FFMIAUTA Heat/Jazz 8.00 20.00
FFMIAWAS Heat/Wizards 8.00 20.00
FFMINOKL Timberwolves/Thunder 8.00 20.00
FFMINPOR Timberwolves/Blazers 8.00 20.00
FFMINUTA Timberwolves/Jazz 8.00 20.00
FFNETNYK Nets/Knicks 8.00 20.00
FFNETPHI Nets/76ers 10.00 25.00
FFNETTOR Nets/Raptors 10.00 25.00
FFNEWMEM Hornets/Grizzlies 8.00 20.00
FFNEWSAN Hornets/Spurs 8.00 20.00
FFNYKPHI Knicks/76ers 8.00 20.00
FFNYKTOR Knicks/Raptors 8.00 20.00
FFOKLPOR Thunder/Trail Blazers 10.00 25.00
FFOKLUTA Thunder/Jazz 8.00 20.00
FFORLPOR Magic/Trail Blazers 10.00 25.00
FFORLWAS Magic/Wizards 8.00 20.00
FFPHITOR 76ers/Raptors 8.00 20.00
FFPHOSAC Suns/Kings 10.00 25.00
FFPORUTA Trail Blazers/Jazz 8.00 20.00
FFSACLAC Kings/Clippers 8.00 20.00
FFWEST6M W.Conference 6th Men 8.00 20.00
FFWESTAS W.Conference All-Stars 20.00 50.00
FFWESTCE W.Conference Centers 10.00 25.00
FFWESTPF W.Conference PF 10.00 25.00
FFWESTPG W.Conference PG 10.00 25.00
FFWESTSF W.Conference SF 10.00 25.00
FFWESTSG W.Conference SG 12.50 30.00

2009-10 SP Game Used Combo Materials

STATED PRINT RUN 499 SER.#'d SETS
*MATERIAL 155: .5X TO 1.25X BASE HI
*MATERIAL 50: .6X TO 1.5X BASE HI
*MATERIAL 35: .6X TO 1.5X BASE HI
CM23 L.James/M.Jordan 30.00 80.00
CMAA C.Anthony/G.Arenas 4.00 10.00
CMAB G.Arenas/C.Butler 3.00 8.00
CMAG K.Garnett/R.Allen 5.00 12.00
CMAN R.Allen/D.Nowitzki 4.00 10.00
CMAP T.Parker/G.Arenas 4.00 10.00
CMAT C.Anthony/T.Thomas 4.00 10.00
CMBA C.Billups/G.Arenas 3.00 8.00
CMBH U.Haslem/E.Brand 3.00 8.00
CMBJ K.Bryant/L.James 15.00 40.00
CMBL C.Boozer/D.Lee 3.00 8.00
CMBM A.Bargnani/Y.Ming 4.00 10.00
CMBO K.Bryant/L.Odom 8.00 20.00
CMBP C.Billups/T.Parker 3.00 8.00
CMBS K.Bryant/S.O'Neal 10.00 25.00
CMCA V.Carter/C.Anthony 6.00 15.00
CMCB C.Bosh/V.Carter 4.00 10.00
CMCG R.Gay/M.Cooper 3.00 8.00
CMCH V.Carter/G.Hill 4.00 10.00
CMCJ C.Maggette/J.Howard 3.00 8.00
CMCN D.Nowitzki/V.Carter 5.00 12.00
CMCR C.Maggette/R.Gay 3.00 8.00
CMCS C.Bosh/S.Marion 3.00 8.00
CMCT T.Thomas/V.Carter 4.00 10.00
CMDB B.Davis/C.Billups 3.00 8.00
CMDD B.Davis/C.Kaman 3.00 8.00
CMDG H.Grant/V.Divac 3.00 8.00
CMDH D.Howard/T.Duncan 5.00 12.00
CMDJ M.Johnson/B.Davis 5.00 12.00
CMDO J.O'Neal/L.Deng 3.00 8.00
CMDR D.Howard/R.Wallace 4.00 10.00
CMDT T.McGrady/D.Wade 5.00 12.00
CMDW B.Davis/D.Williams 4.00 10.00
CMFB J.Farmar/K.Bryant 8.00 20.00
CMFF T.Ford/R.Felton 3.00 8.00
CMGA G.Arenas/K.Garnett 5.00 12.00
CMGB K.Garnett/C.Bosh 5.00 12.00
CMGN K.Garnett/D.Nowitzki 6.00 15.00
CMGO K.Garnett/S.O'Neal 5.00 12.00
CMGP H.Grant/S.Pippen 8.00 20.00
CMGS S.Pippen/G.Gervin 8.00 20.00
CMHB C.Billups/R.Hamilton 3.00 8.00
CMHD L.Deng/L.Hughes 3.00 8.00
CMHG R.Hamilton/R.Gay 3.00 8.00
CMHI L.Hughes/A.Iguodala 3.00 8.00
CMHJ J.Johnson/G.Hill 3.00 8.00
CMHM J.Hornacek/K.Malone 4.00 10.00
CMHO G.Hill/S.O'Neal 5.00 12.00
CMHS J.Hornacek/J.Stockton 6.00 15.00
CMHT J.Tinsley/L.Hughes 3.00 8.00
CMIB C.Billups/A.Iverson 4.00 10.00
CMIM Z.Ilgauskas/Y.Ming 4.00 10.00
CMIP A.Iverson/C.Paul 4.00 10.00
CMIT A.Thornton/A.Iguodala 3.00 8.00
CMIW A.Iverson/D.Williams 4.00 10.00
CMJA M.Jordan/R.Allen 15.00 40.00
CMJB K.Bryant/M.Jordan 30.00 80.00
CMJD M.Johnson/C.Drexler 5.00 12.00
CMJJ M.Johnson/M.Jordan 25.00 60.00
CMJK J.Johnson/K.Bryant 8.00 20.00
CMJL L.Odom/J.O'Neal 3.00 8.00
CMJM J.Howard/S.Marion 3.00 8.00
CMJP M.Jordan/S.Pippen 30.00 80.00
CMKK K.Garnett/K.Malone 5.00 12.00
CMKM J.Kidd/T.McGrady 5.00 12.00
CMKP K.Garnett/P.Pierce 5.00 12.00
CMKT J.Kidd/J.Tinsley 4.00 10.00
CMLG R.Lewis/J.Green 3.00 8.00
CMLM M.Johnson/L.James 12.00 30.00
CMLO M.Okur/R.Lewis 3.00 8.00
CMLS S.Pippen/L.James 12.00 30.00
CMMB Y.Ming/A.Bargnani 4.00 10.00
CMMC M.Cooper/K.Malone 4.00 10.00
CMMD M.Miller/D.Gooden 3.00 8.00
CMMG M.Miller/R.Gay 3.00 8.00
CMMH J.Howard/S.Marion 3.00 8.00
CMMJ L.James/K.Malone 10.00 25.00
CMMN D.Majerle/S.Nash 4.00 10.00
CMMO S.O'Neal/Y.Ming 5.00 12.00
CMMP S.Pippen/K.Malone 6.00 15.00
CMMS K.Malone/J.Stockton 6.00 15.00
CMMT A.Thornton/D.Mason 3.00 8.00
CMMW K.Martin/L.Walton 3.00 8.00
CMNS J.Stockton/S.Nash 5.00 12.00
CMOC V.Carter/L.Odom 4.00 10.00
CMOG L.Odom/P.Gasol 3.00 8.00
CMOO M.Okur/S.O'Neal 4.00 10.00
CMPG C.Anthony/P.Pierce 4.00 10.00
CMPI P.Pierce/A.Iguodala 3.00 8.00
CMPR C.Paul/B.Roy 4.00 10.00
CMRE L.Ridnour/M.Ellis 3.00 8.00
CMRJ J.Farmar/R.Felton 3.00 8.00
CMSA S.Marbury/A.Iverson 4.00 10.00
CMSM W.Szczerbiak/C.Mullin 3.00 8.00
CMSO S.O'Neal/A.Stoudemire 5.00 12.00
CMSS S.Swift/W.Szczerbiak 3.00 8.00
CMUS J.Stockton/B.Udrih 4.00 10.00
CMWG B.Wallace/P.Gasol 3.00 8.00
CMWH L.Head/D.Williams 4.00 10.00
CMWM S.Williams/J.McGee 3.00 8.00

2009-10 SP Game Used Combo Patches

STATED PRINT RUN 99 SER.#'d SETS
CPR Nene/Z.Randolph 5.00 12.00
CPAA J.Alexander/R.Anderson 5.00 12.00
CPAB B.Wallace/A.McDyess 8.00 20.00
CPAG T.Ariza/J.Green 5.00 12.00
CPAM M.Camby/A.McDyess 6.00 15.00
CPAT A.Afflalo/A.Tucker 5.00 12.00
CPAW R.Anderson/S.Williams 5.00 12.00
CPBB B.Cardinal/B.Wallace 5.00 12.00
CPBC R.Carney/S.Battier 5.00 12.00
CPBF M.Bibby/R.Felton 6.00 15.00
CPBJ J.Collins/B.Wright 5.00 12.00
CPBW B.Wright/B.Wallace 8.00 20.00
CPBY T.Young/S.Brown 6.00 15.00
CPCC M.Conley/J.Crittenton 6.00 15.00
CPCE T.Chandler/M.Camby 6.00 15.00
CPCH B.Haywood/B.Cardinal 5.00 12.00
CPCI J.Crawford/A.Iverson 10.00 25.00
CPCM J.Crittenton/D.McGuire 5.00 12.00
CPCS R.Stuckey/S.Claxton 6.00 15.00
CPCW W.Chandler/S.Williams 5.00 12.00
CPDA R.Anderson/S.Dalembert 5.00 12.00
CPDG K.Durant/J.Green 10.00 25.00
CPDH V.Divac/S.Hawes 6.00 15.00
CPDW J.Wright/K.Durant 15.00 40.00
CPEM K.Malone/P.Ewing 12.00 30.00
CPER R.Lewis/E.Gordon 5.00 12.00
CPFD M.Finley/K.Durant 12.00 30.00
CPFG M.Finley/M.Ginobili 6.00 15.00
CPGA C.Anthony/K.Garnett 12.00 30.00
CPGB M.Ginobili/J.Bayless 5.00 12.00
CPGC A.Gray/W.Chandler 5.00 12.00
CPGF M.Ginobili/R.Fernandez 6.00 15.00
CPGG K.Garnett/P.Gasol 10.00 25.00
CPGH M.Ginobili/G.Hill 6.00 15.00
CPGK M.Ginobili/J.Kapono 5.00 12.00
CPGL D.Lee/D.Gooden 6.00 15.00
CPGM M.Ginobili/A.Morrison 8.00 20.00
CPGO P.Gasol/J.O'Neal 5.00 12.00
CPGS G.Green/W.Szczerbiak 5.00 12.00
CPHG K.Hinrich/M.Ginobili 6.00 15.00
CPHW B.Haywood/B.Wright 5.00 12.00
CPID A.Iverson/K.Durant 12.00 30.00
CPIS A.Iverson/R.Stuckey 15.00 40.00
CPIW A.Iverson/R.Wallace 8.00 20.00
CPJB K.Bogans/R.Jefferson 5.00 12.00
CPJC J.Collins/J.Smith 5.00 12.00
CPJG M.Ginobili/R.Jefferson 5.00 12.00
CPJL R.Lopez/D.Jordan 5.00 12.00
CPJR J.Tinsley/B.Udrih 5.00 12.00
CPJT R.Jefferson/A.Tucker 5.00 12.00
CPKG M.Ginobili/S.Kerr 6.00 15.00
CPKK K.Malone/K.McHale 12.00 30.00
CPMC D.Milicic/M.Conley 5.00 12.00
CPMD M.Almond/M.Dunleavy 5.00 12.00
CPMG J.McRoberts/J.Green 5.00 12.00
CPMI Z.Ilgauskas/M.Moore 8.00 20.00
CPMK K.Koufos/K.Malone 8.00 20.00
CPMN J.McRoberts/J.Noah 5.00 12.00
CPMP S.Pippen/K.Malone 20.00 50.00
CPMT J.Thompson/J.McGee 6.00 15.00
CPMW J.Wright/J.McRoberts 5.00 12.00
CPNB M.Bibby/N.Young 5.00 12.00
CPND J.Noah/K.Durant 15.00 40.00
CPNG J.Green/J.Noah 8.00 20.00
CPNH G.Hill/S.Nash 10.00 25.00
CPNI S.Nash/A.Iverson 8.00 20.00
CPNL R.Lopez/J.Noah 5.00 12.00
CPNW J.Noah/J.Wright 6.00 15.00
CPOB J.Bayless/T.Outlaw 5.00 12.00
CPOD C.Kaman/P.O'Bryant 5.00 12.00
CPPC J.Crittenton/O.Pecherov 6.00 15.00
CPPK K.Malone/P.Gasol 8.00 20.00
CPPM G.Pruitt/D.McGuire 5.00 12.00
CPRH G.Hill/D.Robinson 6.00 15.00
CPRP D.Robinson/R.Parish 8.00 20.00
CPRR Z.Randolph/J.Richardson 6.00 15.00
CPRS A.Randolph/W.Sharpe 5.00 12.00
CPSB J.Bayless/J.Smith 5.00 12.00
CPSR J.Richardson/W.Szczerbiak 6.00 15.00
CPST T.Chandler/S.Williams 5.00 12.00
CPSW B.Wright/J.Smith 5.00 12.00
CPTC J.Tinsley/M.Conley 5.00 12.00
CPTL R.Lopez/J.Thompson 5.00 12.00
CPTS J.Thompson/M.Speights 5.00 12.00
CPTY N.Young/R.Theus 5.00 12.00
CPWA S.Williams/R.Anderson 5.00 12.00
CPWB L.Wright/K.Brown 5.00 12.00
CPWH S.Hawes/B.Wright 5.00 12.00
CPWM M.Speights/W.Chandler 5.00 12.00
CPWW B.Wright/H.Warrick 6.00 15.00

2009-10 SP Game Used Fabric Foursomes

PRINT RUN 199 SER.#'d SETS
*MATERIAL 125: SAME VALUE
*MATERIAL 50: .75X TO 2X HI
*MATERIAL 35: .75X TO 2X HI
F4AATB Brks/Affl/Almnd/Tckr 4.00 10.00
F4AHLB Brks/Lndry/Artest/Ming 4.00 10.00
F4ALAH Lee/Hill/Anderson/Arthur 4.00 10.00
F4ALTB Bylss/Agstn/Lpz/Thmpsn 4.00 10.00
F4AWDA D-Rbrts/Andrsn/Wllms/Agr 4.00 10.00
F4BDGP Duncn/Pippen/KG/Kobe 12.50 30.00
F4BGBR Kobe/Ice/Rbinsn/Bird 10.00 25.00
F4BIJO Kobe/Shaq/AI/LeBron 12.00 30.00
F4BJWL Law/Wllms/Jhnsn/Bbby 4.00 10.00
F4BMCS Smith/Kobe/Crtr/Mson 10.00 25.00
F4BMDI Iggy/Miller/Dlmbrt/Brnd 5.00 12.00
F4BMGS Brnd/Pau/Amare/Miller 5.00 12.00
F4BMMJ James/Yao/Brnd/Martin 10.00 25.00
F4BNGN Kobe/KG/Dirk/Nash 10.00 25.00
F4BOGB Byum/Odom/Kobe/Pau 15.00 30.00
F4BOWB Bozer/Okur/Wllms/Brwr 4.00 10.00
F4CGAW Artest/KG/Wllce/Cmby 6.00 15.00
F4CHBL Crtr/Boone/Lpez/Hrris 4.00 10.00
F4DBCM Dxn/McGee/Crttntn/Btler 4.00 10.00
F4DBPH Hill/Dncn/Bwn/Prkr 8.00 20.00
F4DDFG Grngr/Ford/Dniels/Dnlvy 5.00 12.00
F4DFPG Prkr/Ginbili/Dncn/Fnly 6.00 15.00
F4DGNR Grdn/Deng/Noah/Rose 10.00 25.00
F4DHGC Hrfrd/Conly/Drnt/Green 8.00 20.00
F4DIOR AI/Shaq/Dncn/Rbnsn 10.00 25.00
F4DKIC Dncn/Kidd/Crtr/AI 6.00 15.00
F4DMBA Agstn/May/Diaw/Wllce 5.00 12.00
F4DMIO AI/Malone/Shaq/Dncn 8.00 20.00
F4DTGJ Davis/Jrdn/Grdn/Thrntn 6.00 15.00
F4EMHO Shaq/Yao/Hwrd/Ewng 8.00 20.00
F4FCDC Chndlr/Cook/Ddly/Frnndz 4.00 10.00
F4GCGM Gsol/Mayo/Cnly/Gay 5.00 12.00
F4GCKS Chmbrs/Stcktn/King/KG 8.00 20.00
F4GFRW Wllms/Foye/Roy/Gay 4.00 10.00
F4GGLA Grdn/Alxndr/Love/Lopz 6.00 15.00
F4GHTG Gray/Thms/Deng/Hnrch 4.00 10.00
F4HAPD Pruitt/Dvis/Alln/House 4.00 10.00
F4HBAS Rip/Affllo/Shrp/Brwn 4.00 10.00
F4HBYM Hywd/Bltch/Yung/McGuir 4.00 10.00
F4HCRG Curry/Rbnsn/Hrringtn/Richrdsn 4.00 10.00
F4HEOR Ewing/Rbnsn/Shaq/Hill 10.00 25.00
F4HMHA Hib/JVle/J.J./Ajinca 4.00 10.00
F4HNSS Smmns/Nconi/Hghs/Thabo 4.00 10.00
F4HOBA Hwrd/Wllce/Okfr/Agstin 4.00 10.00
F4HSGR Rbnsn/Hwrd/Green/Smith 4.00 10.00
F4IDPD Parish/Drxlr/AI/Dntley 10.00 25.00
F4IWJW LBJ/Wllce/Ilgask/West 8.00 20.00
F4IWPS Prince/AI/Wllce/Stcky 6.00 15.00
F4JASB Btlr/Arnas/Jmison/Stvnsn 4.00 10.00
F4JBVA Alxndr/Bogut/Vllnva/RJeff 4.00 10.00
F4JDWC Jrdn/Drsy/Chlmrs/Wevr 4.00 10.00
F4JMCA Jrdn/Wilt/Kareem/Mail 75.00 150.00
F4JOMR Mail/Olaj/Jordan/Rbnsn 30.00 80.00
F4JORD LBJ/Roy/Okfr/Durant 10.00 25.00
F4JPST Paul/Isiah/Stock/Jhnsn 10.00 25.00
F4JRRB RJeff/Bgut/Ridnur/Redd 5.00 12.00
F4JSWH Smith/Wllms/Hrfrd/Jhnsn 4.00 10.00
F4KBCB Brgnni/Cldrn/Kpno/Bosh 8.00 20.00
F4KKMM Miles/Millsp/AK47/Krvr 4.00 10.00
F4KNHW Wrght/Kidd/Hwrd/Dirk 6.00 15.00
F4LHBR Lewis/Nlsn/Rdck/Hwrd 5.00 12.00
F4LHNL Hwrd/Lee/Nlsn/Lewis 6.00 15.00
F4MBAN Mrtn/Melo/Billups/Nene 5.00 12.00
F4MBMS TMac/Battier/Yao/Scola 6.00 15.00
F4MBRW Beasly/Rose/Mayo/Wstbrk 6.00 15.00
F4MDGW Wstbrk/Masn/Green/Durnt 6.00 15.00
F4MEWR Rndlph/Wrght/Mggtt/Ellis 4.00 10.00
F4MMBL Love/Brwr/Miller/Jffrsn 4.00 10.00
F4MMMD Drsey/Yao/TMac/Mtmbo 5.00 12.00
F4MNDG Millsp/Gay/Nvk/Gbsn 4.00 10.00
F4MUDT Ncioni/Hws/Udrih/Thmpsn 4.00 10.00
F4MWCB Bsley/Cook/Wrght/Mglore 5.00 12.00
F4MWHC Wade/Hslm/Shaq/Chlmrs 5.00 12.00
F4MYSS Smth/Spights/Mrshll/Yng 4.00 10.00
F4NHSO Hill/Shaq/Amare/Nash 6.00 15.00
F4NKMW Nash/Wllms/Miller/Kidd 5.00 12.00
F4NWBL Law/Noah/Wright/Brwr 4.00 10.00
F4ODRB Outlw/Rdrgz/Roy/Bylss 4.00 10.00
F4ORMW Mlne/Rbrtsn/Wlkns/Olaj 6.00 15.00
F4PAGR KG/Allen/Rnd/Pierce 12.50 30.00
F4PCSP Chndlr/Paul/Ptrsn/Stojak 5.00 12.00
F4POMR Shaq/Rbnsn/Zo/Olaj 8.00 20.00
F4SJMG Miller/Jmisn/Grdn/Strks 4.00 10.00
F4SKBW Blkmn/Weems/Klz/Smth 4.00 10.00
F4SWGH Gbsn/Wrght/Hcksn/Szcz 4.00 10.00
F4TAMB Aldrdg/Tyrs/Brgn/Mrrsn 4.00 10.00
F4TGSW Grg/Sngletn/Wllms/Jet 4.00 10.00
F4TJFS BigAl/Tlfr/Foye/Smth 4.00 10.00
F4TMRH Rush/Hbbrt/McRob/Tinsl 4.00 10.00
F4TYSW Wright/Thrntn/Stcky/Yng 4.00 10.00
F4WARF Wbstr/Frndz/Aldrdg/Roy 5.00 12.00
F4WBOF Okfr/Wllce/Bell/Felfn 4.00 10.00
F4WGGS Whte/Shrp/Green/Gddns 4.00 10.00
F4WKWW Whte/Weav/Wstbrk/Krstc 4.00 10.00
F4WMEO West/Ewing/Mail/Shaq 10.00 25.00
F4YCSW Wllms/Yng/Crttntn/Smth 4.00 10.00

2009-10 SP Game Used Logo Men

STATED PRINT RUN ONE TO 18 SER.#'d SETS
MOST UNPRICED DUE TO SCARCITY
LOGOBI Chauncey Billups/16 50.00 120.00
LOGODN Dirk Nowitzki/14 250.00 500.00
LOGOJO Jermaine O'Neal/15 50.00 120.00
LOGOKG Kevin Garnett/18 250.00 400.00
LOGOPP Paul Pierce/14 150.00 300.00

2009-10 SP Game Used Multi Marks Dual

RANDOM INSERTS IN PACKS
MDAA A.Biedrins/A.Blatche 8.00 20.00
MDAB C.Brewer/R.Artest 8.00 20.00
MDAD A.Horford/D.Arthur 8.00 20.00
MDAG D.Augustin/E.Gordon 8.00 20.00
MDAH L.Aldridge/A.Horford 10.00 25.00
MDAN J.Noah/L.Aldridge 10.00 25.00
MDAT T.Chandler/A.Bynum 15.00 30.00
MDAW S.Webb/K.Anderson 10.00 25.00
MDBA J.Boone/R.Anderson 8.00 20.00
MDBB C.Brewer/B.Brown 8.00 20.00
MDBC M.Conley/A.Bynum 10.00 25.00
MDBJ B.Brown/J.Barea 10.00 25.00
MDBL B.Bass/R.Lopez 8.00 20.00
MDBM T.McGrady/M.Beasley 20.00 40.00
MDBN J.Noah/A.Blatche 10.00 25.00
MDBR B.Rush/C.Bosh 8.00 20.00
MDBS M.Speights/A.Blatche 8.00 20.00
MDBT A.Thornton/A.Bynum 10.00 25.00
MDBW B.Brown/K.Weaver 8.00 20.00
MDCA T.Chandler/H.Armstrong 8.00 20.00
MDCB V.Carter/M.Beasley 15.00 40.00
MDCG A.Gilmore/T.Chambers 8.00 20.00
MDCH T.Chandler/D.Howard 15.00 40.00
MDCM O.Mayo/M.Conley 12.00 30.00
MDCT M.Conley/M.Taylor 8.00 20.00
MDDA A.Afflalo/K.Dooling 8.00 20.00
MDDG E.Gordon/B.Diaw 10.00 25.00
MDDW M.Williams/K.Durant 40.00 100.00
MDDX W.Bynum/M.Almond 8.00 20.00
MDEB L.Bird/J.Erving 60.00 120.00
MDEW J.Erving/D.Wilkins 50.00 100.00
MDFB R.Fernandez/N.Batum 8.00 20.00
MDGB A.Bogut/K.Garnett 30.00 60.00
MDGD G.Goodrich/K.Durant 40.00 100.00
MDGL C.Landry/A.Gray 8.00 20.00
MDGN J.Nelson/P.Gasol 15.00 30.00
MDGP K.Garnett/T.Parker 30.00 80.00
MDGR D.Granger/B.Rush 15.00 40.00
MDGT J.Thompson/E.Gordon 8.00 20.00
MDGW E.Gordon/R.Westbrook 40.00 100.00
MDHG S.Haywood/J.Green 8.00 20.00
MDHM Y.Ming/D.Howard 20.00 50.00
MDHR M.Redd/J.Hornacek 12.50 30.00
MDJB A.Jamison/C.Bosh 10.00 25.00
MDJD C.Duhon/B.Jackson 8.00 20.00
MDJK K.Love/J.Wright 10.00 25.00
MDJM J.Wright/M.Beasley 8.00 20.00
MDJS D.Jordan/W.Sharpe 8.00 20.00
MDJW M.Williams/L.James 100.00 200.00
MDKD A.Dantley/B.King 8.00 20.00
MDKT J.Kidd/I.Thomas 25.00 60.00
MDLB K.Love/C.Brewer 12.50 30.00
MDLM L.James/M.Williams 100.00 200.00
MDLP T.Prince/B.Lanier 12.50 30.00
MDLS R.Sessions/A.Law 8.00 20.00
MDLW B.Lopez/S.Williams 8.00 20.00
MDMB O.Mayo/M.Beasley 15.00 40.00
MDMD C.Drexler/Y.Ming 30.00 80.00
MDMH J.McRoberts/S.Hawes 8.00 20.00
MDML K.Love/O.Mayo 10.00 25.00
MDMR Y.Ming/D.Robinson 50.00 100.00
MDNM Y.Ming/S.Nash 40.00 80.00
MDNS D.Wilkins/M.Jordan 250.00 500.00
MDNT D.West/A.Jamison 8.00 20.00
MDPB C.Brewer/T.Parker 12.00 30.00
MDPH A.Horford/B.Pettit 12.50 30.00
MDPS T.Prince/R.Stuckey 10.00 25.00
MDRA D.Augustin/M.Richardson 8.00 20.00
MDRB J.Bayless/B.Roy 10.00 25.00
MDRM D.Rose/O.Mayo 60.00 120.00
MDRN J.Noah/D.Rodman 40.00 80.00
MDRS B.Roy/R.Stuckey 15.00 30.00
MDSC D.Stoudamire/S.Cassell 8.00 20.00
MDSN B.Bowen/J.Bayless 8.00 20.00
MDSR R.Stuckey/D.Rose 20.00 50.00
MDSW C.Walker/J.Stockton 30.00 60.00
MDTG A.Thornton/D.Gallinari 8.00 20.00
MDTR D.Rose/T.Thomas 20.00 50.00
MDVB M.Beasley/Vandeweghe 15.00 30.00
MDVF J.Farmar/S.Vujacic 8.00 20.00
MDVP K.Vandeweghe/R.Parish 15.00 30.00
MDWA A.Ajinca/S.Williams 8.00 20.00
MDWB J.Wright/J.Bayless 8.00 20.00
MDWC M.Conley/M.Williams 8.00 20.00
MDWD J.Dorsey/C.Wilcox 8.00 20.00
MDWJ D.Jackson/J.Wright 8.00 20.00
MDWL B.Lopez/S.Williams 8.00 20.00
MDWR M.Williams/R.Rondo 10.00 25.00

2009-10 SP Game Used Multi Marks Triple

STATED PRINT RUN 4 TO 100 SER.#'d SETS
SOME UNPRICED DUE TO SCARCITY
MTARB Brewer/Roy/Armstrong/50 10.00 25.00
MTARC Armstrong/Roy/Conley/75 10.00 25.00
MTBAT Aldridge/Thrntn/Bosh/60 20.00 50.00
MTBBC Conley/Brewer/Brown/100 10.00 25.00
MTBBS Boone/Batum/Speights/75 10.00 25.00
MTBCT Conley/Taylor/Brewer/100 10.00 25.00
MTBMG McRob/Bosh/Glinri/50 12.50 30.00
MTBNT Thornton/Boone/Noah/100 10.00 25.00
MTBWJ Jordan/Wright/Balkman/75 10.00 25.00
MTDLW Deng/Lee/Westbrook/75 40.00 100.00
MTFBA Barea/Afflalo/Foye/75 15.00 40.00
MTFBG Brown/Gordon/Fernandez/100 10.00 25.00
MTFHS Fernandez/Singletary/Hickson/75 10.00 25.00
MTFNC Conley/Fernandez/Noah/100 10.00 25.00
MTGNW Noah/Gay/Wright/50 15.00 40.00
MTGWA Wright/Alexander/Garcia/75 10.00 25.00
MTHAB Hrnck/Bylss/Allen/14 30.00 60.00
MTJGJ LJ/Garnett/Jordan/25 700.00 1000.00
MTJWJ LJ/Jackson/Williams/75 100.00 200.00
MTMBH Marshall/Horford/Biedrins/50 10.00 25.00
MTMHT Thomas/Howard/Yao/18 50.00 100.00
MTMLW Mayo/Love/Westbrk/100 60.00 150.00
MTMNW McRob/Wright/Noah/25 15.00 30.00
MTMRG Rose/Gallinari/Rush/75 40.00 100.00
MTMWH Ming/Walton/Horford/40 25.00 50.00
MTMWS West/McRoberts/Sharpe/50 10.00 25.00
MTNBC Conley/Brewer/Noah/100 10.00 25.00
MTNSB Smith/Noah/Brown/75 10.00 25.00
MTNTB Batum/Thornton/Noah/75 10.00 25.00
MTOBG Odom/Gordon/Brown/75 10.00 25.00
MTOMM Ming/McGrady/Olaj/25 75.00 150.00
MTPBG Bynum/Peterson/Green/75 10.00 25.00
MTRWK Riley/Karl/Westphal/14 30.00 80.00
MTSCC Chalmers/Stuckey/Conley/75 10.00 25.00
MTWGB Byls/Gordon/Webb/75 10.00 25.00
MTWGK Williams/Gay/Koufos/100 10.00 25.00
MTWMG McRoberts/West/Green/50 10.00 25.00
MTWTC Conley/Williams/Tucker/75 10.00 25.00

2009-10 SP Game Used Multi Marks Quad

STATED PRINT RUN 5 TO 99 SER.#'d SETS
SOME UNPRICED DUE TO SCARCITY
MQBBMG Brwn/Brwr/Myo/Gnari/25 10.00 25.00
MQBBRW Brwn/Bsly/Rose/Wstbrk/25 75.00 200.00
MQBCMG Brwn/Myo/Cnly/Grdn/25 20.00 50.00
MQBHHS Sharp/Jcksn/Hbbrt/Brwn/99 10.00 25.00
MQBLGA Gnari/Brwn/Lpz/Ajnc/99 10.00 25.00
MQBRBG Bwn/Roy/Grdn/Brwn/50 10.00 25.00
MQBRRB Andrs/Rndp/Roy/Bylss/50 10.00 25.00
MQCBWL VC/Wllms/Brwr/Lve/50 30.00 80.00
MQCMRB Bls/Cnly/Myo/Rose/50 50.00 125.00
MQGBNG Noah/Gal/Bosh/KG/50 40.00 100.00
MQGJNB Gasol/Nelson/Bsly/LJ/25 125.00 250.00
MQGMHB Bsly/Hrfrd/KG/Yao/50 50.00 100.00
MQGTGW Gib/EG/Thrtn/Wstb/50 30.00 80.00
MQHGWD Wright/Douglas-Roberts/Harrington/Gordon/50 10.00 25.00
MQHJWH Hinrich/Hill/Jack/Weaver/99 10.00 25.00
MQHNCL Lopez/Noah Harrington/Chandler/50 10.00 25.00
MQHNHL DH/Noah/Hrfrd/Lve/50 40.00 100.00
MQJBRW LJ/Rose/Bsly/Wstbrk/25 200.00 400.00
MQJMBR Noah/Blch/Jmsn/Rndph/50 15.00 40.00
MQJWWW Williams Williams/Jamison/Wright/32 10.00 25.00
MQKBPW Kidd/Bllps/Prkr/Wllms/50 40.00 80.00
MQMBRW Bea/Ros/May/Wst/50 75.00 200.00
MQMDMH Divac/Hws/Yao/McG/50 40.00 100.00
MQMDSF Frazier/Zo/Stock/Dghty/15 75.00 150.00
MQMMBO Zo/Shaq/Yao/Bynm/25 75.00 200.00
MQMPBR Balkman/Marshall Prince/Randolph/99 10.00 25.00
MQMSCM McCants/Mbah a Moute/Stuckey/Conley/50 10.00 25.00
MQNBRL Brwr/Lve/Rose/Noah/50 75.00 150.00
MQOCHL DH/Odom/Love/VC/50 40.00 100.00
MQPBMG Gallinari/Pruitt Mayo/Brewer/50 10.00 25.00
MQRCMR Mayo/Cnly/Roy/Rose/50 50.00 120.00
MQTCMG Cnly/Myo/Thrtn/Grdn/50 15.00 40.00
MQTHLA Ajinca/Lopez/Hawes/Thomas/50 10.00 25.00
MQWPBB Prin/West/Brew/Bosh/50 15.00 40.00

2009-10 SP Game Used Retro Rookie Exclusives

STATED PRINT RUN 5 TO 300 SER.#'d SETS
SOME UNPRICED DUE TO SCARCITY
RRAE Alex English/180 6.00 15.00
RRAM Alonzo Mourning/25 60.00 120.00
RRAR B.J. Armstrong/278 6.00 15.00
RRAS Amare Stoudemire/15 25.00 50.00
RRBC Bill Cartwright/150 6.00 15.00
RRBD Brad Daugherty/300 6.00 15.00
RRBK Bernard King/250 6.00 15.00
RRBM Bob McAdoo/300 6.00 15.00
RRBP Bob Pettit/70 15.00 40.00
RRBR Brandon Roy/50 10.00 25.00
RRBS Bill Sharman/100 6.00 15.00
RRBW Bill Walton/100 10.00 25.00
RRCB Chauncey Billups/100 6.00 15.00
RRCD Clyde Drexler/25 25.00 60.00
RRCR Cazzie Russell/75 6.00 15.00
RRDH Dwight Howard/25 12.00 30.00
RRDN Don Nelson/100 12.00 30.00
RRDR Dennis Rodman/35 25.00 60.00
RRDW Dominique Wilkins/50 20.00 40.00
RREB Elgin Baylor/50 6.00 15.00
RRGG George Gervin/75 6.00 15.00
RRGO Gail Goodrich/100 6.00 15.00
RRGR Glen Rice/55 12.50 30.00
RRHA Connie Hawkins/20 10.00 25.00
RRHG Horace Grant/50 6.00 15.00
RRHL Hal Greer/50 6.00 15.00
RRJA LeBron James/23 150.00 300.00
RRJK Jason Kidd/25 20.00 40.00
RRJO Jermaine O'Neal/60 10.00 25.00
RRJW James Worthy/25 20.00 50.00
RRKA Kareem Abdul-Jabbar/25 40.00 100.00
RRKD Kevin Durant/25 75.00 150.00
RRKG Kevin Garnett/25 25.00 60.00
RRKV Kiki Vandeweghe/170 6.00 15.00
RRLA LaMarcus Aldridge/50 10.00 25.00
RRLD Luol Deng/100 6.00 15.00
RRLJ Larry Johnson/25 30.00 60.00
RRLO Lamar Odom/100 6.00 15.00
RRMJ Michael Jordan/23 300.00 500.00
RRMP Mark Price/300 10.00 25.00
RROR Oscar Robertson/25 30.00 80.00
RRPA Tony Parker/25 15.00 30.00
RRPR Pat Riley/25 15.00 30.00
RRQR Quentin Richardson/250 6.00 15.00
RRRB Rick Barry/75 15.00 30.00
RRRG Rudy Gay/100 6.00 15.00
RRRM Rick Mahorn/80 6.00 15.00
RRRO Rolondo Blackman/165 6.00 15.00
RRSC Bill Laimbeer/260 6.00 15.00
RRTC Tom Chambers/100 6.00 15.00
RRTM Tracy McGrady/25 20.00 40.00
RRVC Vince Carter/25 20.00 40.00
RRYM Yao Ming/25 20.00 40.00

2009-10 SP Game Used Rookie Exclusive Signatures

STATED PRINT RUN 100 SER.#'d SETS
READ Austin Daye 4.00 10.00
REAP A.J. Price 4.00 10.00
REBM B.J. Mullens 4.00 10.00
REBR Derrick Brown 4.00 10.00
REBU Chase Budinger 5.00 12.00
RECA DeMarre Carroll 5.00 12.00
RECU Dante Cunningham 4.00 10.00
REDC Darren Collison 6.00 15.00
REDG Danny Green 8.00 20.00
REDS DaJuan Summers 4.00 10.00
REEC Earl Clark 5.00 12.00
REEM Eric Maynor 4.00 10.00
REGH Gerald Henderson 5.00 12.00
REGR Taylor Griffin 4.00 10.00
REGS Goran Suton 4.00 10.00
REHA James Harden 50.00 120.00
REJB Jon Brockman 4.00 10.00
REJE Jonas Jerebko 8.00 20.00
REJF Jonny Flynn 4.00 10.00
REJH Jrue Holiday 8.00 20.00
REJJ James Johnson 5.00 12.00
REJM Jack McClinton 4.00 10.00
REJP Jeff Pendergraph 4.00 10.00
REJT Jeff Teague 6.00 15.00
RELH Lester Hudson 4.00 10.00
REMT Marcus Thornton 5.00 12.00
RENC Nick Calathes 4.00 10.00
REOC Omri Casspi 5.00 12.00
REPB Patrick Beverley 6.00 15.00
RERB Rodrigue Beaubois 4.00 10.00
RERR Ricky Rubio 40.00 100.00
RERV Robert Vaden 5.00 12.00
RESC Stephen Curry 600.00 800.00
RESL Sergio Llull 4.00 10.00
RESY Sam Young 4.00 10.00
RETA Jermaine Taylor 4.00 10.00
RETD Toney Douglas 4.00 10.00
RETG Taj Gibson 6.00 15.00
RETL Ty Lawson 12.00 30.00
REWE Wayne Ellington 6.00 15.00

2009-10 SP Game Used Signature Fabrics

RANDOM INSERTS IN PACKS
SFAA Arron Afflalo 4.00 10.00
SFAB Andrew Bogut 5.00 12.00
SFAJ Al Jefferson 4.00 10.00
SFAL Morris Almond 4.00 10.00
SFAM Alonzo Mourning 25.00 60.00
SFAR Anthony Randolph 5.00 12.00
SFAT Al Thornton 4.00 10.00
SFBD Boris Diaw 4.00 10.00
SFBL Brook Lopez 6.00 15.00
SFBO Bruce Bowen 5.00 12.00
SFBR Brandon Roy 4.00 10.00
SFBY Andrew Bynum 6.00 15.00
SFCB Chauncey Billups 6.00 15.00
SFCD Clyde Drexler 30.00 80.00
SFCH Chris Bosh 10.00 25.00
SFCJ C.J. Miles 4.00 10.00
SFCL Carl Landry 4.00 10.00
SFCO Corey Brewer 4.00 10.00
SFCR Javaris Crittenton 4.00 10.00
SFDC Daequan Cook 4.00 10.00
SFDE Derrick Rose 75.00 150.00
SFDG Chris Douglas-Roberts 4.00 10.00
SFDH Dwight Howard 20.00 40.00
SFDM Desmond Mason 4.00 10.00
SFDO Donyell Marshall 4.00 10.00
SFDR David Robinson 40.00 80.00
SFDS DeShawn Stevenson 5.00 12.00
SFDW Dominique Wilkins 15.00 30.00
SFEG Eric Gordon 5.00 12.00
SFGR Jeff Green 6.00 15.00
SFHA Spencer Hawes 4.00 10.00
SFJA Antawn Jamison 5.00 12.00
SFJC Javaris Crittenton 4.00 10.00
SFJD Joey Dorsey 4.00 10.00
SFJF Jordan Farmar 5.00 12.00
SFJG Jeff Green 5.00 12.00
SFJH J.J. Hickson 4.00 10.00
SFJK Jason Kidd 12.50 30.00
SFJM Javale McGee 5.00 12.00
SFJN Joakim Noah 6.00 15.00
SFJO DeAndre Jordan 6.00 15.00
SFJR J.R. Giddens 4.00 10.00
SFJS Jason Smith 4.00 10.00
SFJW Julian Wright 4.00 10.00
SFJY Jared Dudley 4.00 10.00
SFKD Kevin Durant 50.00 125.00
SFKG Kevin Garnett 30.00 80.00
SFKK Kosta Koufos 4.00 10.00
SFKL Kevin Love 10.00 25.00
SFKW Kyle Weaver 4.00 10.00
SFLB Larry Bird 50.00 125.00
SFLD Luol Deng 5.00 12.00
SFLE Courtney Lee 5.00 12.00
SFLJ LeBron James 175.00 350.00
SFLK Linas Kleiza 4.00 10.00
SFLO Lamar Odom 6.00 15.00
SFLS Luis Scola 5.00 12.00
SFMA Mario Chalmers 5.00 12.00
SFMB Michael Beasley 5.00 12.00
SFMC Mike Conley Jr. 5.00 12.00
SFMI Mike Conley Jr. 5.00 12.00
SFMJ Michael Jordan 350.00 650.00
SFMO Jamario Moon 5.00 12.00
SFMP Morris Peterson 4.00 10.00
SFMS Josh McRoberts 5.00 12.00
SFMW Marvin Williams 5.00 12.00
SFNE Donte Greene 4.00 10.00
SFNO Joakim Noah 5.00 12.00
SFPA Tony Parker 10.00 25.00
SFPG Pau Gasol 20.00 50.00
SFQR Quentin Richardson 4.00 10.00
SFRA Ron Artest 10.00 25.00
SFRB Renaldo Balkman 4.00 10.00
SFRF Rudy Fernandez 6.00 15.00
SFRG Rudy Gay 6.00 15.00
SFRJ Richard Jefferson 6.00 15.00
SFRO Dennis Rodman 25.00 60.00
SFRS Ramon Sessions 6.00 15.00
SFRU Brandon Rush 4.00 10.00
SFRW Russell Westbrook 40.00 100.00
SFSM Josh Smith 5.00 12.00
SFSW Sean Williams 4.00 10.00
SFTA Trevor Ariza 5.00 12.00
SFTM Tracy McGrady 12.00 30.00
SFTP Tayshaun Prince 5.00 12.00
SFTT Tyrus Thomas 6.00 15.00
SFTU Alando Tucker 4.00 10.00
SFVC Vince Carter 50.00 100.00
SFWI Mo Williams 5.00 12.00
SFWR Julian Wright 5.00 12.00
SFWS Walter Sharpe 4.00 10.00

2009-10 SP Game Used SIGnificance

RANDOM INSERTS IN PACKS

UNPRICED GOLD PRINT RUN 10 SETS
SAA Alexis Ajinca 3.00 8.00
SAB Andrew Bogut 4.00 10.00
SAG Aaron Gray 3.00 8.00
SAJ Al Jefferson 4.00 10.00
SAL Acie Law 3.00 8.00
SAN Ryan Anderson 4.00 10.00
SAR Darrell Arthur 4.00 10.00
SAT Al Thornton 4.00 10.00
SAV Anderson Varejao 3.00 8.00
SBB Bobby Brown 3.00 8.00
SBC Corey Brewer 3.00 8.00
SBD Boris Diaw 4.00 10.00
SBJ Josh Boone 3.00 8.00
SBL Brook Lopez 4.00 10.00
SBP Bob Pettit 6.00 15.00
SBR Bobby Brown 3.00 8.00
SBU Beno Udrih 3.00 8.00
SBW Bill Walker 3.00 8.00
SBY Andrew Bynum 3.00 8.00
SCA M.L. Carr 6.00 15.00
SCB Chauncey Billups 6.00 15.00
SCD Chris Duhon 3.00 8.00
SCH Chris Bosh 6.00 15.00
SCL Carl Landry 3.00 8.00
SCM Chris Mihm 3.00 8.00
SCO Corey Brewer 3.00 8.00
SCR Caron Butler 4.00 10.00
SDA D.J. Augustin 3.00 8.00
SDC Daequan Cook 3.00 8.00
SDE DeAndre Jordan 5.00 12.00
SDG Danilo Gallinari 4.00 10.00
SDJ Darnell Jackson 3.00 8.00
SDO Joey Dorsey 4.00 10.00
SDR Derrick Rose 25.00 60.00
SDW Dominique Wilkins 6.00 15.00
SEG Eric Gordon 6.00 15.00
SGA Danilo Gallinari 4.00 10.00
SGI Artis Gilmore 6.00 15.00
SGP Gabe Pruitt 3.00 8.00
SJA Antawn Jamison 4.00 10.00
SJB Jerryd Bayless 4.00 10.00
SJC Javaris Crittenton 3.00 8.00
SJD Jared Dudley 3.00 8.00
SJF Jordan Farmar 3.00 8.00
SJG Jeff Green 4.00 10.00
SJH J.J. Hickson 3.00 8.00
SJJ Jarrett Jack 4.00 10.00
SJM Javale McGee 4.00 10.00
SJN Joakim Noah 4.00 10.00
SJO Joe Alexander 3.00 8.00
SJS Jason Smith 3.00 8.00
SJT Jason Thompson 3.00 8.00
SKD Kevin Durant 100.00 200.00
SKG Kevin Garnett 40.00 100.00
SKK Kosta Koufos 3.00 8.00
SKL Kevin Love 15.00 40.00
SKW Kyle Weaver 3.00 8.00
SLA Louis Amundson 3.00 8.00
SLD Luol Deng 4.00 10.00
SLE Courtney Lee 4.00 10.00
SLM Luc Mbah A Moute 3.00 8.00
SLO Kyle Lowry 4.00 10.00
SMA Morris Almond 3.00 8.00
SMJ Josh McRoberts 3.00 8.00
SMK Maurice Cheeks 5.00 12.00
SMS Marreese Speights 4.00 10.00
SMT Mike Taylor 3.00 8.00
SMW Mo Williams 4.00 10.00
SNO Joakim Noah 4.00 10.00
SOD Lamar Odom 4.00 10.00
SOM O.J. Mayo 3.00 8.00
SOR Oscar Robertson 75.00 150.00
SPA Tony Parker 6.00 15.00
SPM Paul Millsap 4.00 10.00
SQR Quentin Richardson 4.00 10.00
SRA Ron Artest 6.00 15.00
SRJ Richard Jefferson 4.00 10.00
SRL Robin Lopez 3.00 8.00
SRM Rashad McCants 3.00 8.00
SRS Ramon Sessions 4.00 10.00
SRU Brandon Rush 3.00 8.00
SRW Russell Westbrook 60.00 150.00
SSH Spencer Hawes 3.00 8.00
SSJ Josh Smith 4.00 10.00
SSM Jason Smith 3.00 8.00
SSS Sean Singletary 3.00 8.00
SST Rodney Stuckey 3.00 8.00
SSV Sasha Vujacic 3.00 8.00
SSW Spud Webb 5.00 12.00
STC Tom Chambers 5.00 12.00
STY Tyson Chandler 5.00 12.00
SWA Walter Sharpe 3.00 8.00
SWI Deron Williams 4.00 10.00
SWS Shelden Williams 3.00 8.00
SYM Yao Ming 10.00 25.00

2009-10 SP Game Used Six Star Swatches 65

STATED PRINT RUN 65 SER.#'d SETS
*BASE SIX STAR: .4X TO 1X BASE HI
BASE SIX STAR PRINT RUN 99 SETS
6SAGWMHM OM/DW/AH/CA/BG/AM 12.00 30.00
6SAIDENO KB/MJ/KG/DH/MJ/SO 40.00 100.00
6SAJBWHO GA/LJ/DW/JO/DH/CB 20.00 50.00
6SALLBWS CL/MS/JB/DA/BL/KW 8.00 20.00
6SAMNDSG MA/PM/CS/DG/SN/SB 8.00 20.00
6SAWGGDS JD/JG/WS/DA/DG/DW 8.00 20.00
6SBAGCPR VC/TP/RA/DR/KG/KB 20.00 50.00
6SBAMMDL CL/SM/RA/MB/CM/MD 10.00 25.00
6SBAMPSA AS/RA/TP/CA/SM/KB 15.00 30.00
6SBDGIJO KB/KG/TD/SO/LJ/AI 25.00 50.00
6SBDKGWW LJ/RW/TD/KG/KB/JK 20.00 50.00
6SBDNGIN DN/KB/KG/TD/AI/SN 20.00 50.00
6SBISHOP SO/GG/LB/MJ/MJ/DH 40.00 100.00
6SBJKAHD BK/CD/DH/KB/CA/RJ 15.00 30.00
6SBLHAKH KK/RA/JH/MC/GH/CL 8.00 20.00
6SBMDMFV AB/CF/ID/RM/CV/SM 8.00 20.00
6SBNAIMI SN/ZI/AI/KB/SM/RA 20.00 50.00
6SBNAMIJ RA/KB/MJ/AI/CP/SN 25.00 50.00
6SBPCJHN VC/AJ/DN/LH/PP/MB 15.00 30.00
6SBPFWWW MW/CP/MW/DW/AB/RF 8.00 20.00
6SBROCKR MJ/SK/SP/MJ/VD/JW 30.00 80.00
6SBSWDSB QD/RB/SW/CS/RB/TS 8.00 20.00
6SCBCRBG JR/KB/TC/SB/EC/PG 8.00 20.00
6SCBKFCS JK/TM/MB/TC/MC/SS 10.00 25.00
6SCBRKSO AK/ZR/TC/PS/JO/SB 8.00 20.00
6SCJMGGP BG/MG/AJ/KM/VC/MM 10.00 25.00
6SCMGMAW MC/BW/AM/DM/RA/KG 8.00 20.00
6SCMSOSB AB/DM/JS/PS/EO/TC 8.00 20.00
6SDACKSC DA/SW/CB/AH/CD/KD 8.00 20.00
6SDBICMG PG/TD/EB/MM/VC/AI 20.00 40.00
6SDBJBPS TP/CB/JD/CB/CB/LS 8.00 20.00
6SDGMKGS PG/KG/KM/TD/AK/AS 12.50 30.00
6SDGMNOH MO/TD/KG/JH/DN/TM 10.00 25.00
6SDHCBRW AH/MB/DR/MC/KD/RW 15.00 30.00
6SDICBMC MC/AI/BD/SN/AM/CB 10.00 25.00
6SDIHSHJ TD/DH/AS/AJ/ZI/BH 10.00 25.00
6SDIMJHR AI/LJ/DH/YM/TD/DR 12.00 30.00
6SDKMNPM TD/TP/YM/TM/DN/JK 15.00 30.00
6SDNSAPR DN/TD/CA/BR/CP/AS 15.00 30.00
6SDSHBOM RH/WS/BD/AM/EB/LO 8.00 20.00
6SDWHBGC AH/MC/CB/BW/KD/JG 8.00 20.00
6SEGMBJB CB/LJ/LB/GG/JE/SM 20.00 40.00
6SFACDCB WC/AB/DC/RF/MA/JD 8.00 20.00
6SFRLBRB JB/SR/RR/KL/JF/SB 8.00 20.00
6SGAALBT EG/JA/JB/DA/BL/JT 8.00 20.00
6SGFOARS RF/HA/RG/MS/JR/PO 8.00 20.00
6SGGMBPO CB/YM/KG/PG/JO/CP 10.00 25.00
6SGWGWGR HW/DG/GG/AW/JG/NR 8.00 20.00
6SHCBJBO JJ/CB/SO/VC/CB/RH 10.00 25.00
6SHCNAGH RH/GA/VC/BG/DH/DN 10.00 25.00
6SHKSAPT LH/GP/JT/KK/MA/RS 8.00 20.00
6SJAHPGG DG/RG/CP/LJ/CA/DH 10.00 25.00
6SJMAKBW CB/CA/DW/LJ/CK/DM 15.00 30.00
6SKAJBWH LJ/DW/RA/CB/DH/JK 20.00 40.00
6SKASCDY KB/YM/AI/DW/SN/CB 12.00 30.00
6SKJEMCA MO/EO/JM/CF/KG/AH 10.00 25.00
6SLADKAY YM/DH/AB/KB/LJ/AB 12.00 30.00
6SLILYRO JS/KM/IT/MJ/MJ/SP 30.00 80.00
6SLKJGHM LH/LK/DL/ME/FG/JJ 8.00 20.00
6SLOGANO MJ/KB/KG/DR/MJ/RW 25.00 60.00
6SMASONC MJ/DR/MJ/HO/SO/KM 40.00 100.00
6SMBRGLW KL/EG/OM/DR/MB/RW 15.00 40.00
6SMGSADR CA/DR/CD/KG/AS/KM 12.50 30.00
6SMGSWDN AS/MD/YM/CW/DW/NH 10.00 25.00
6SMJSSRN NH/JS/KM/JS/RJ/BR 8.00 20.00
6SMMMGEK KM/GG/AM/BK/PE/HO 15.00 40.00
6SMMMMCS KM/JC/SS/MM/DM/DM 8.00 20.00
6SMOWADB KD/DM/EO/LA/MB/MW 10.00 25.00
6SMTMAGK RA/SM/JT/DG/CM/AK 8.00 20.00
6SNBKDBP SN/CP/BD/JK/MB/CB 15.00 30.00
6SNOAHLU MJ/JE/KG/KB/LJ/KD 50.00 125.00
6SNTHMWG RH/DG/SN/DW/JT/AM 10.00 25.00
6SNTYHWL JN/AL/TY/SH/AT/JW 8.00 20.00
6SNWVUMD KM/BU/DW/JN/SV/CD 8.00 20.00
6SOBPTCW CB/LO/TT/CP/MC/RW 8.00 20.00
6SOHDGHI EO/BG/LD/AI/DH/DH 10.00 25.00
6SOMNJHP HO/TM/DW/DN/RP/LJ 12.00 30.00
6SPBMFGO VD/KM/SO/HG/DR/KB 20.00 40.00
6SPEJBMB PP/LB/JE/MB/LJ/OM 25.00 60.00
6SPHJWBJ AJ/RH/RW/CB/PP/JJ 10.00 25.00
6SPNCJRM PP/ND/LJ/OM/RJ/MR 12.00 30.00
6SPWSDFA AS/MP/JA/BW/LD/RF 8.00 20.00
6SRAGDRL AC/GH/DS/RJ/LR/RM 8.00 20.00
6SRHMRLS AR/RL/BR/RH/JM/MS 8.00 20.00
6SRHOWHF KH/LW/JH/TO/LR/TF 8.00 20.00
6SRHSPWD MR/DW/CP/DH/JS/KD 10.00 25.00
6SRWJJCH GW/JJ/BH/ZR/RJ/JC 8.00 20.00
6SSJOPRD AS/LJ/BR/CP/EO/KD 20.00 40.00
6SSKWRGC WS/DG/AK/MW/RR/WC 8.00 20.00
6SSLRADS RA/RL/JS/JR/MD/WS 8.00 20.00
6SSOHSBO EO/SS/JS/JO/AB/DH 8.00 20.00
6SSSTSJH JS/JS/RR/AJ/SB/RS 8.00 20.00
6STADCPO JT/MO/JC/GA/SD/TP 8.00 20.00
6STAMBRW TT/AB/AM/BR/LA/SW 8.00 20.00
6STEAKKS SO/AI/KB/EB/KM/TD 10.00 25.00
6STORGER MJ/KA/WC/HO/MM/KM 50.00 100.00
6SWAPDTL AT/AA/CL/WC/GP/GD 8.00 20.00
6SWDJWWC SW/MC/DJ/BL/CD/KW 8.00 20.00
6SWHFWGL JG/RF/SW/KL/DW/DH 10.00 25.00
6SYCSSBW JS/SW/MB/RS/JC/NY 8.00 20.00

2009-10 SP Game Used Triple Patch

STATED PRINT RUN 60 SER.#'d SETS
TPADD Douby/Allen/Dunleavy 10.00 25.00
TPAMS Stojakovic/Allen/Ginobili 10.00 25.00
TPASG Allen/KG/Szczerbiak 12.00 30.00
TPASR Stojakovic/Randolph/Artest 8.00 20.00
TPAWA Anderson/Arthur/Weaver 8.00 20.00
TPAYS Young/Stuckey/Archibald 8.00 20.00
TPBDL Bryant/Love/Durant 25.00 60.00
TPBFC Conley/Bibby/Hinrich 8.00 20.00
TPBGW Gray/Blatche/Wright 8.00 20.00
TPBHG Haywood/Brand/Gooden 8.00 20.00
TPBLM McGuire/Brewer/Landry 8.00 20.00
TPBMN Noah/McRob/Brown 12.00 30.00
TPBRJ Brown/James/Rose 8.00 20.00
TPBSW Battier/Swift/Williams 8.00 20.00
TPCCD Collins/Collins/Davis 8.00 20.00
TPCMB Davis/Marion/Bayless 8.00 20.00
TPCOY Chambers/Outlaw/Young 8.00 20.00
TPDAD Davis/Armstrong/Diogu 8.00 20.00
TPDBM Duncan/Brand/Zo 15.00 40.00
TPDCC Daniels/Crittenton/Collins 8.00 20.00
TPDCO O'Neal/Collins/Dalembert 12.00 30.00
TPDCS Davis/Chandler/Sefolosha 8.00 20.00
TPDMD Douglas-Roberts/Deng/Morrison 8.00 20.00
TPDSB Brown/Stojakovic/Davis 8.00 20.00
TPDSG Peja/Dunleavy/Ginobili 8.00 20.00
TPDWA Wright/Daniels/Afflalo 8.00 20.00
TPDYC Dixon/Crittenton/Young 8.00 20.00
TPFRT Rodriguez/Tucker/Foye 8.00 20.00
TPFRY Rndlph/Thornton/Young 8.00 20.00
TPGCN Nene/Garnett/Chandler 15.00 30.00
TPGHT Gray/Horford/Thompson 8.00 20.00
TPGKS Sene/Krstic/Gasol 12.50 30.00
TPGPD Davis/Pruitt/Garnett 10.00 25.00
TPGRA KG/Robinson/Arthur 12.50 30.00
TPGRB Randolph/Biedrins/KG 10.00 25.00
TPHAW Wright/Afflalo/Haywood 8.00 20.00
TPHCY Chandler/Hrrngtn/Yng 10.00 25.00
TPHGC Ginobili/Hughes/Collins 8.00 20.00
TPHGF Fernandez/Garcia/Howard 8.00 20.00
TPIAG Iverson/Gordon/Agstn 10.00 25.00
TPICG Iverson/Gibson/Rondo 25.00 60.00
TPIMR Rose/Iverson/Mayo 25.00 60.00
TPITF Iverson/Telfair/Felton 10.00 25.00
TPJLB Brooks/Law/Jackson 8.00 20.00
TPJRB Barry/Dirk/Dunleavy 8.00 20.00
TPJSC Dunleavy/Simmons/Cook 8.00 20.00
TPKKM Beasley/KG/Malone 25.00 50.00
TPKSN Sene/Krstic/Nene 8.00 20.00
TPLAR Rondo/Artest/Lewis 8.00 20.00
TPLGB Lowry/Giddens/Bayless 8.00 20.00
TPLGR Gay/Rondo/Lewis 10.00 25.00
TPLJA Lewis/Almond/Jefferson 8.00 20.00
TPMCT Tlfr/Chndlr/Marion 8.00 20.00
TPMCY Marion/Young/Chandler 8.00 20.00
TPMGB Brewer/George/Mason 8.00 20.00
TPMGF Garnett/Reed/Malone 20.00 50.00
TPMGK Malone/King/Garnett 20.00 40.00
TPMJG James/Gay/Garnett 25.00 60.00
TPMMM Malone/Ewing/Mutombo 20.00 50.00
TPMMS Smith/Jefferson/Mason 8.00 20.00
TPMNG Green/McRob/Noah 8.00 20.00
TPMRH Rose/Hill/Mayo 20.00 50.00
TPMRW Maggette/Wade/Rich 10.00 25.00
TPMWW Miller/Wright/Williams 8.00 20.00
TPNFT Hinrich/Telfair/Nash 8.00 20.00
TPNGD Nash/Garnett/Durant 15.00 40.00
TPOWD Davis/Williams/Okur 8.00 20.00
TPPFF Farmar/Brown/Ariza 8.00 20.00
TPPSW Wright/Smith/Petro 8.00 20.00
TPRAW Richardson/Wright/Aldridge 8.00 20.00
TPRDS Dixon/Richardson/Smith 8.00 20.00
TPRGB Giddens/Randolph/Bayless 8.00 20.00
TPSAY Young/Stojakovic/Almons 8.00 20.00
TPSDG Davis/Smith/Green 8.00 20.00
TPSIA Aldridge/Szczerbiak/Ilgauskas 8.00 20.00
TPSRD Redd/Dunleavy/Szczerbiak 8.00 20.00
TPSSW Szczerbiak/Stojakovic/Williams 8.00 20.00
TPSWB Brewer/Stevenson/West 8.00 20.00
TPSYC Szczerbiak/Young/Chandler 8.00 20.00
TPSYW Young/Swift/Williams 8.00 20.00
TPTFD Dudley/Tinsley/Farmar 8.00 20.00
TPTNS Nelson/Tinsley/Singleton 8.00 20.00
TPVSG Villanueva/Simmons/Giddens 8.00 20.00
TPWAJ Dorsey/Randolph/Szczerbiak 8.00 20.00
TPWAT Afflalo/Conley/Tucker 8.00 20.00
TPWMD Wallace/Thornton/May 8.00 20.00
TPWRW Walton/Malone/Rodman 20.00 50.00
TPYHS Horford/Young/Sharpe 8.00 20.00

2012 SP Game Used

COMP.SET w/o SP's (30) 20.00 40.00
SP1 STATED ODDS 1:72
23 Michael Jordan 4.00 10.00

2012 SP Game Used Inked Drivers Black

STATED PRINT RUN 3-25

2012 SP Game Used Inked Drivers Light Orange

*LT.ORANGE/15-35: .5X TO 1.2X SILVER
STATED PRINT RUN 5-35

2012 SP Game Used Scorecard Signatures

STATED ODDS 1:15
GROUP A STATED ODDS 1:1,790
GROUP B STATED ODDS 1:203
GROUP C STATED ODDS 1:63
GROUP D STATED ODDS 1:23
SSMJ Michael Jordan A 300.00 500.00

2012 SP Game Used Spectrum Autographs

STATED PRINT RUN 5-100
23 Michael Jordan/5

2014 SP Game Used

COMP.SET w/o SP's (30) 25.00 50.00
OVERALL RC SHIRT AU ODDS 1:3 PACKS
23 Michael Jordan 4.00 10.00

2014 SP Game Used Inked Drivers

*BLONDE/35: .5X TO 1.2X BASIC DRIVER
IDMJ Michael Jordan A

2014 SP Game Used Inked Drivers Black

*BLACK/25: .5X TO 1.2X BASIC DRIVER
STATED PRINT RUN 3-25

2014 SP Game Used Leader Board Letter Marks

SERIAL NUMBERS B/WN 2-35 COPIES PER
ALL VERSIONS OF PLAYERS EQUALLY PRICED

2014 SP Game Used Spectrum Autographs

STATED PRINT RUN 10-100

2009 SP Legendary Cuts Mystery Cuts

Each card in this set is number "LC-MC". For cataloging purposes, we have assigned card numbers based on the subject's initials.
STATED ODDS ONE PER CASE
HL Harry Litwack/49 10.00 25.00
RA Red Auerbach/35 50.00 100.00

2007-08 SP Rookie Edition

Released in March 2008, SP Rookie Edition boasts a 210-card set where cards 1-60 feature veteran players on a horizontal design with black borders and gold foil highlights, cards 61-104 feature rookie players on a similar design, cards 105-120 feature rookie players on a cards which employ the design of the 1996-97 SP set, cards 121-150 feature rookie players on cards which employ the design of the 1997-98 SP Authentic set, cards 151-180 feature rookie players on cards which employ the design of the 1994-95 SP rookie foil set, and cards 181-210 feature a mix of retired legends, veteran players and rookies on cards which frame a color portrait style photo against a white background. SP Rookie Edition is packaged in 14-pack boxes of eight cards each and carried an intial SRP of $4.99 per pack.

61-104 RC ODDS THREE PER PACK
105-120 ODDS ONE PER PACK
121-150 STATED ODDS 1:12
151-180 STATED ODDS 1:12
181-210 STATED ODDS 1:12
1 Andre Iguodala .40 1.00
2 Andre Miller .40 1.00
3 Gerald Wallace .40 1.00
4 Jason Richardson .50 1.25
5 Andrew Bogut .40 1.00
6 Michael Redd .40 1.00
7 Ben Gordon .40 1.00
8 Ben Wallace .40 1.00
9 LeBron James 2.00 5.00
10 Larry Hughes .40 1.00
11 Paul Pierce .50 1.25
12 Ray Allen .50 1.25
13 Elton Brand .50 1.25
14 Pau Gasol .50 1.25
15 Kyle Lowry .50 1.25
16 Joe Johnson .40 1.00
17 Josh Smith .40 1.00
18 Dwyane Wade .75 2.00
19 Shaquille O'Neal 1.00 2.50
20 Chris Paul .60 1.50
21 Morris Peterson .30 .75
22 Carlos Boozer .40 1.00
23 Michael Jordan 4.00 10.00
24 Deron Williams .40 1.00
25 Mehmet Okur .30 .75
26 Ron Artest .50 1.25
27 Mike Bibby .50 1.25
28 Eddy Curry .30 .75
29 Zach Randolph .40 1.00
30 Kobe Bryant 2.00 5.00
31 Lamar Odom .40 1.00
32 Dwight Howard .40 1.00
33 Rashard Lewis .40 1.00
34 Dirk Nowitzki .60 1.50
35 Josh Howard .40 1.00
36 Jason Kidd .50 1.25
37 Vince Carter .60 1.50
38 Allen Iverson .60 1.50
39 Carmelo Anthony .60 1.50
40 Jermaine O'Neal .40 1.00
41 Tayshaun Prince .40 1.00
42 Chauncey Billups .50 1.25
43 Richard Hamilton .40 1.00
44 T.J. Ford .30 .75
45 Chris Bosh .50 1.25
46 Tracy McGrady .50 1.25
47 Yao Ming .60 1.50
48 Tim Duncan .75 2.00
49 Tony Parker .50 1.25
50 Amare Stoudemire .40 1.00
51 Shawn Marion .40 1.00
52 Steve Nash .60 1.50
53 Chris Wilcox .30 .75
54 Kevin Garnett .75 2.00
55 Brandon Roy .50 1.25
56 LaMarcus Aldridge .60 1.50
57 Baron Davis .40 1.00
58 Caron Butler .40 1.00
59 Gilbert Arenas .40 1.00
60 Antawn Jamison .40 1.00
61 Kevin Durant RC 6.00 15.00
62 Al Horford RC .75 2.00
63 Mike Conley Jr. RC .75 2.00
64 Jeff Green RC .60 1.50
65 Corey Brewer RC .60 1.50
66 Joakim Noah RC .60 1.50
67 Spencer Hawes RC .50 1.25
68 Acie Law RC .40 1.00
69 Julian Wright RC .40 1.00
70 Al Thornton RC .50 1.25
71 Rodney Stuckey RC .50 1.25
72 Sean Williams RC .40 1.00
73 Marco Belinelli RC .60 1.50
74 Javaris Crittenton RC .40 1.00
75 Jason Smith RC .50 1.25
76 Daequan Cook RC .50 1.25
77 Jared Dudley RC .50 1.25
78 Wilson Chandler RC .50 1.25
79 Morris Almond RC .40 1.00
80 Aaron Brooks RC .50 1.25
81 Arron Afflalo RC .60 1.50
82 Alando Tucker RC .40 1.00
83 Carl Landry RC .40 1.00
84 Gabe Pruitt RC .40 1.00
85 Juan Carlos Navarro RC .50 1.25
86 Yi Jianlian RC .75 2.00
87 Glen Davis RC .50 1.25
88 Jermareo Davidson RC .40 1.00
89 Thaddeus Young RC .60 1.50
90 Brandan Wright RC .60 1.50
91 Luis Scola RC .75 2.00
92 Chris Richard RC .40 1.00
93 Adam Haluska RC .40 1.00
94 D.J. Strawberry RC .40 1.00
95 Darryl Watkins RC .40 1.00
96 Cheikh Samb RC .40 1.00
97 Greg Oden RC .60 1.50
98 Aaron Gray RC .40 1.00
99 JamesOn Curry RC .40 1.00
100 Taurean Green RC .40 1.00
101 Demetris Nichols RC .40 1.00
102 Nick Young RC .75 2.00
103 Ramon Sessions RC .60 1.50
104 Coby Karl RC .40 1.00
105 Jason Smith 96-97 .60 1.50
106 Kevin Durant 96-97 8.00 20.00
107 Al Horford 96-97 1.00 2.50
108 Mike Conley Jr. 96-97 1.00 2.50
109 Jeff Green 96-97 .75 2.00
110 Corey Brewer 96-97 .75 2.00
111 Joakim Noah 96-97 .75 2.00
112 Spencer Hawes 96-97 .60 1.50
113 Acie Law 96-97 .50 1.25
114 Julian Wright 96-97 .50 1.25
115 Al Thornton 96-97 .60 1.50
116 Rodney Stuckey 96-97 .60 1.50
117 Sean Williams 96-97 .50 1.25
118 Marco Belinelli 96-97 .75 2.00
119 Javaris Crittenton 96-97 .50 1.25
120 Jason Smith 96-97 .60 1.50
121 Kevin Durant 97-98 12.00 30.00
122 Al Horford 97-98 2.00 5.00
123 Mike Conley Jr. 97-98 2.00 5.00
124 Jeff Green 97-98 1.50 4.00
125 Corey Brewer 97-98 1.50 4.00
126 Joakim Noah 97-98 1.50 4.00
127 Spencer Hawes 97-98 1.25 3.00
128 Acie Law 97-98 1.00 2.50
129 Julian Wright 97-98 1.00 2.50
130 Al Thornton 97-98 1.25 3.00
131 Rodney Stuckey 97-98 1.25 3.00
132 Sean Williams 97-98 1.00 2.50
133 Marco Belinelli 97-98 1.50 4.00
134 Javaris Crittenton 97-98 1.00 2.50
135 Jason Smith 97-98 1.25 3.00
136 Daequan Cook 97-98 1.25 3.00
137 Jared Dudley 97-98 1.25 3.00
138 Wilson Chandler 97-98 1.25 3.00
139 Brandan Wright 97-98 1.50 4.00
140 Aaron Brooks 97-98 1.25 3.00
141 Alando Tucker 97-98 1.00 2.50
142 Carl Landry 97-98 1.00 2.50
143 Gabe Pruitt 97-98 1.00 2.50
144 D.J. Strawberry 97-98 1.00 2.50
145 Yi Jianlian 97-98 2.00 5.00
146 Glen Davis 97-98 1.25 3.00
147 Greg Oden 97-98 1.50 4.00
148 Aaron Gray 97-98 1.00 2.50
149 Taurean Green 97-98 1.00 2.50
150 D.J. Strawberry 97-98 1.00 2.50
151 Kevin Durant 94-95 15.00 40.00
152 Al Horford 94-95 2.00 5.00
153 Mike Conley Jr. 94-95 2.00 5.00
154 Jeff Green 94-95 1.50 4.00
155 Corey Brewer 94-95 1.50 4.00
156 Joakim Noah 94-95 1.50 4.00
157 Spencer Hawes 94-95 1.25 3.00
158 Acie Law 94-95 1.00 2.50
159 Julian Wright 94-95 1.00 2.50
160 Al Thornton 94-95 1.25 3.00
161 Rodney Stuckey 94-95 1.25 3.00
162 Sean Williams 94-95 1.00 2.50
163 Marco Belinelli 94-95 1.50 4.00
164 Javaris Crittenton 94-95 1.00 2.50
165 Jason Smith 94-95 1.25 3.00
166 Daequan Cook 94-95 1.25 3.00
167 Jared Dudley 94-95 1.25 3.00
168 Wilson Chandler 94-95 1.25 3.00
169 Morris Almond 94-95 1.00 2.50
170 Aaron Brooks 94-95 1.25 3.00
171 Arron Afflalo 94-95 1.50 4.00
172 Alando Tucker 94-95 1.00 2.50
173 Carl Landry 94-95 1.00 2.50
174 Gabe Pruitt 94-95 1.00 2.50
175 Ramon Sessions 94-95 1.50 4.00
176 Oleksiy Pecherov 94-95 1.50 4.00
177 Luis Scola 94-95 2.00 5.00
178 Greg Oden 94-95 1.50 4.00
179 Doninique Wilkins 94-95 2.00 5.00
180 Yi Jianlian 94-95 2.00 5.00
181 Carmelo Anthony 98-99 2.00 5.00
182 B.J. Armstrong 98-99 1.50 4.00
183 Larry Bird 98-99 4.00 10.00
184 Steve Novak 98-99 1.00 2.50
185 Kobe Bryant 98-99 6.00 15.00
186 Vince Carter 98-99 2.00 5.00
187 Tom Chambers 98-99 1.25 3.00
188 Baron Davis 98-99 1.25 3.00
189 Boris Diaw 98-99 1.25 3.00
190 Hilton Armstrong 98-99 1.00 2.50
191 Hal Greer 98-99 1.25 3.00
192 Keyon Dooling 98-99 1.00 2.50
193 LeBron James 98-99 6.00 15.00
194 Antawn Jamison 98-99 1.25 3.00
195 Magic Johnson 98-99 4.00 10.00
196 Michael Jordan 98-99 12.00 30.00
197 Danny Manning 98-99 1.25 3.00
198 Tracy McGrady 98-99 1.50 4.00
199 Chris Mihm 98-99 1.00 2.50
200 Yao Ming 98-99 2.00 5.00
201 Steve Nash 98-99 2.00 5.00
202 Hakeem Olajuwon 98-99 2.00 5.00
203 Tony Parker 98-99 1.50 4.00
204 Paul Pierce 98-99 1.50 4.00
205 Quentin Richardson 98-99 1.25 3.00
206 Dennis Rodman 98-99 3.00 8.00
207 DeShawn Stevenson 98-99 1.00 2.50
208 John Stockton 98-99 2.50 6.00
209 Shelden Williams 98-99 1.00 2.50
210 Dominique Wilkins 98-99 2.00 5.00

2007-08 SP Rookie Edition 1994-95 SP Rookie Autographs

OVERALL AUTO ODDS 1:7
151 Kevin Durant 100.00 200.00
152 Al Horford 6.00 15.00
153 Mike Conley Jr. 6.00 15.00
154 Jeff Green 5.00 12.00
155 Corey Brewer 5.00 12.00
156 Joakim Noah 5.00 12.00
157 Spencer Hawes 4.00 10.00
158 Acie Law 3.00 8.00
159 Julian Wright 3.00 8.00
160 Al Thornton 4.00 10.00
161 Rodney Stuckey 4.00 10.00
162 Sean Williams 3.00 8.00
163 Marco Belinelli 5.00 12.00
164 Javaris Crittenton 3.00 8.00
165 Jason Smith 4.00 10.00
166 Daequan Cook 4.00 10.00
167 Jared Dudley 4.00 10.00
168 Wilson Chandler 4.00 10.00
169 Morris Almond 3.00 8.00
170 Aaron Brooks 4.00 10.00
171 Arron Afflalo 5.00 12.00
172 Alando Tucker 3.00 8.00
173 Carl Landry 3.00 8.00
174 Gabe Pruitt 3.00 8.00
175 Ramon Sessions 5.00 12.00
176 Oleksiy Pecherov 5.00 12.00
179 Ramon Sessions 5.00 12.00

2007-08 SP Rookie Edition 1996-97 SP Rookie Autographs

OVERALL AUTO ODDS 1:7
106 Kevin Durant 90.00 150.00
107 Al Horford 6.00 15.00
108 Mike Conley Jr. 6.00 15.00
109 Jeff Green 5.00 12.00
110 Corey Brewer 5.00 12.00
111 Joakim Noah 5.00 12.00
112 Spencer Hawes 4.00 10.00
113 Acie Law 3.00 8.00
114 Julian Wright 3.00 8.00
115 Al Thornton 4.00 10.00
116 Rodney Stuckey 4.00 10.00
117 Sean Williams 3.00 8.00
118 Marco Belinelli 5.00 12.00
119 Javaris Crittenton 3.00 8.00
120 Jason Smith 4.00 10.00

2007-08 SP Rookie Edition 1997-98 SP Rookie Autographs

OVERALL AUTO ODDS 1:7
121 Kevin Durant 100.00 250.00
122 Al Horford 6.00 15.00
123 Mike Conley Jr. 6.00 15.00
124 Jeff Green 5.00 12.00
125 Corey Brewer 5.00 12.00
126 Joakim Noah 5.00 12.00
127 Spencer Hawes 4.00 10.00
128 Acie Law 3.00 8.00
129 Julian Wright 3.00 8.00
130 Al Thornton 4.00 10.00
131 Rodney Stuckey 4.00 10.00
132 Sean Williams 3.00 8.00
133 Marco Belinelli 5.00 12.00
134 Javaris Crittenton 3.00 8.00
135 Jason Smith 4.00 10.00
136 Daequan Cook 4.00 10.00
137 Jared Dudley 4.00 10.00
138 Wilson Chandler 4.00 10.00
140 Aaron Brooks 4.00 10.00
141 Alando Tucker 3.00 8.00
142 Carl Landry 3.00 8.00
143 Gabe Pruitt 3.00 8.00
146 Glen Davis 4.00 10.00
148 Aaron Gray 3.00 8.00
149 Taurean Green 3.00 8.00
144 D.J. Strawberry 3.00 8.00

2007-08 SP Rookie Edition 1998-99 SP Autographs

OVERALL AUTO ODDS 1:7
181 Carmelo Anthony 20.00 50.00
182 B.J. Armstrong 6.00 15.00
183 Larry Bird 40.00 80.00
184 Steve Novak 5.00 12.00
185 Kobe Bryant 80.00 160.00
186 Vince Carter 20.00 40.00
187 Tom Chambers 5.00 12.00
188 Baron Davis 6.00 15.00
189 Boris Diaw 5.00 12.00
190 Hilton Armstrong 5.00 12.00
191 Hal Greer 6.00 15.00
193 LeBron James 150.00 300.00
194 Antawn Jamison 6.00 15.00
195 Magic Johnson 40.00 80.00
196 Michael Jordan 700.00 1000.00
197 Danny Manning 8.00 20.00
198 Tracy McGrady 15.00 30.00
199 Chris Mihm 5.00 12.00
200 Yao Ming 15.00 40.00
201 Steve Nash 30.00 80.00
202 Hakeem Olajuwon 20.00 50.00
203 Tony Parker 12.00 30.00
204 Paul Pierce 12.00 30.00
205 Quentin Richardson 5.00 12.00
206 Dennis Rodman 25.00 60.00
207 DeShawn Stevenson 5.00 12.00
208 John Stockton 50.00 100.00
209 Shelden Williams 5.00 12.00

2007-08 SP Rookie Edition Rookie Autographs

OVERALL AUTO ODDS 1:7
61 Kevin Durant 100.00 250.00
62 Al Horford 6.00 15.00
63 Mike Conley Jr. 6.00 15.00
64 Jeff Green 5.00 12.00
65 Corey Brewer 5.00 12.00
66 Joakim Noah 5.00 12.00
67 Spencer Hawes 4.00 10.00
68 Acie Law 3.00 8.00
69 Julian Wright 3.00 8.00
70 Al Thornton 4.00 10.00
71 Rodney Stuckey 4.00 10.00
72 Sean Williams 3.00 8.00
73 Marco Belinelli 5.00 12.00
74 Javaris Crittenton 3.00 8.00
75 Jason Smith 4.00 10.00
76 Daequan Cook 4.00 10.00
77 Jared Dudley 4.00 10.00
78 Wilson Chandler 4.00 10.00
79 Morris Almond 3.00 8.00
80 Aaron Brooks 4.00 10.00
81 Arron Afflalo 5.00 12.00
82 Alando Tucker 3.00 8.00
83 Carl Landry 3.00 8.00
84 Gabe Pruitt 3.00 8.00
85 Juan Navarro 4.00 10.00
87 Glen Davis 4.00 10.00
88 Jermareo Davidson 3.00 8.00
92 Chris Richard 3.00 8.00
93 Adam Haluska 3.00 8.00
94 D.J. Strawberry 3.00 8.00
96 Cheikh Samb 3.00 8.00
98 Aaron Gray 3.00 8.00
99 JamesOn Curry 3.00 8.00
100 Taurean Green 3.00 8.00
101 Demetris Nichols 3.00 8.00
103 Ramon Sessions 5.00 12.00
104 Coby Karl 3.00 8.00
105 D.J. Strawberry 3.00 8.00

2007-08 SP Rookie Edition SP Limited Jerseys

RANDOM INSERTS IN PACKS
SPAB Andrea Bargnani 2.50 6.00
SPAH Al Horford 3.00 8.00
SPAJ Antawn Jamison 2.00 5.00
SPAL Acie Law 1.50 4.00
SPAS Amare Stoudemire 2.00 5.00
SPAT Al Thornton 2.00 5.00
SPBI Chauncey Billups 2.50 6.00
SPBO Chris Bosh 2.50 6.00
SPBW Brandan Wright 2.50 6.00
SPCA Carmelo Anthony 3.00 8.00
SPCB Corey Brewer 2.50 6.00
SPCP Chris Paul 3.00 8.00
SPDC Daequan Cook 2.00 5.00
SPDH Dwight Howard 2.00 5.00
SPDW Deron Williams 2.00 5.00
SPEO Emeka Okafor 2.00 5.00
SPGD Glen Davis 2.00 5.00
SPJC Javaris Crittenton 1.50 4.00
SPJD Jared Dudley 2.00 5.00
SPJG Jeff Green 2.50 6.00
SPJN Joakim Noah 2.50 6.00
SPJS Jason Smith 2.00 5.00
SPJW Julian Wright 1.50 4.00
SPKB Kobe Bryant 8.00 20.00
SPKD Kevin Durant 15.00 40.00
SPKG Kevin Garnett 4.00 10.00
SPLA LaMarcus Aldridge 3.00 8.00
SPLJ LeBron James 8.00 20.00
SPMC Mike Conley Jr. 3.00 8.00
SPNY Nick Young 3.00 8.00
SPRG Rudy Gay 2.50 6.00
SPRS Rodney Stuckey 2.00 5.00
SPSH Spencer Hawes 2.00 5.00
SPSO Shaquille O'Neal 5.00 12.00
SPSW Sean Williams 1.50 4.00
SPTD Tim Duncan 4.00 10.00
SPTM Tracy McGrady 2.50 6.00
SPTP Tayshaun Prince 2.00 5.00
SPTT Tyrus Thomas 1.50 4.00
SPTY Thaddeus Young 2.50 6.00
SPVC Vince Carter 3.00 8.00
SPYM Yao Ming 3.00 8.00

2007-08 SP Rookie Threads

Released in April 2008, SP Rookie Threads boasts an 83-card base set where cards 1-42 feature veterans, cards 43-48 feature rookies serially numbered to 199, cards 49-60 feature rookies with autographs sequentially numbered to 199 and cards 61-83 feature rookies with autographs sequentially numbered to 799. SP Rookie Threads is packaged in six-pack boxes where packs contain five cards and carried an initial SRP of $50 per pack.

COMP.SET w/o SP's (42) 12.00 30.00
43-48 RC PRINT RUN 199 SER.#'d SETS
49-60 AU RC PRINT RUN 199 SER.#'d SETS
61-83 AU RC PRINT RUN 799 SER.#'d SETS
1 Allen Iverson .60 1.50
2 Amare Stoudemire .40 1.00
3 Andre Iquodala .40 1.00
4 Andrea Bargnani .50 1.25
5 Baron Davis .40 1.00
6 Ben Gordon .40 1.00
7 Brandon Roy .50 1.25
8 Carmelo Anthony .60 1.50
9 Chauncey Billups .50 1.25
10 Chris Bosh .50 1.25
11 Chris Paul .60 1.50
12 David Lee .30 .75
13 Deron Williams .40 1.00
14 Dirk Nowitzki .60 1.50
15 Dwight Howard .40 1.00
16 Dwyane Wade .75 2.00
17 Elton Brand .50 1.25
18 Emeka Okafor .40 1.00
19 Gilbert Arenas .40 1.00
20 Jason Kidd .50 1.25
21 Jermaine O'Neal .40 1.00
22 Kevin Garnett .75 2.00
23 Kirk Hinrich .40 1.00
24 Kobe Bryant 2.00 5.00
25 LaMarcus Aldridge .60 1.50
26 LeBron James 2.00 5.00
27 Luke Ridnour .40 1.00
28 Marvin Williams .40 1.00
29 Michael Jordan 4.00 10.00
30 Michael Redd .40 1.00
31 Mike Bibby .50 1.25
32 Paul Pierce .50 1.25
33 Randy Foye .50 1.25
34 Rudy Gay .50 1.25
35 Shaquille O'Neal 1.00 2.50
36 Stephon Marbury .40 1.00
37 Steve Nash .60 1.50
38 Tim Duncan .75 2.00
39 Tony Parker .50 1.25
40 Tracy McGrady .50 1.25
41 Vince Carter .60 1.50
42 Yao Ming .60 1.50
43 Greg Oden RC 1.50 4.00
44 Yi Jianlian RC 2.00 5.00
45 Brandan Wright RC 1.50 4.00
46 Thaddeus Young RC 1.50 4.00
47 Nick Young RC 2.00 5.00
48 Juan Carlos Navarro RC 1.25 3.00
49 Kevin Durant JSY AU RC 250.00 450.00
50 Al Horford JSY AU RC 6.00 15.00
51 M.Conley Jr. JSY AU RC 6.00 15.00
52 Jeff Green JSY AU RC 5.00 12.00
53 Corey Brewer JSY AU RC 5.00 12.00
54 Joakim Noah JSY AU RC 5.00 12.00
55 Spencer Hawes JSY AU RC 4.00 10.00
56 Acie Law JSY AU RC 3.00 8.00
57 Julian Wright JSY AU RC 3.00 8.00
58 Al Thornton JSY AU RC 4.00 10.00
59 Rodney Stuckey JSY AU RC 4.00 10.00
60 Jason Smith JSY AU RC 4.00 10.00
61 Taurean Green JSY AU RC 1.50 4.00
62 Javaris Crittenton JSY AU RC 1.50 4.00
63 Sean Williams JSY AU RC 1.50 4.00
64 Daequan Cook JSY AU RC 2.00 5.00
65 Jared Dudley JSY AU RC 2.00 5.00
66 W.Chandler JSY AU RC 2.00 5.00
67 Morris Almond JSY AU RC 1.50 4.00
68 Aaron Brooks JSY AU RC 2.00 5.00
69 Arron Afflalo JSY AU RC 2.50 6.00
70 Alando Tucker JSY AU RC 1.50 4.00
71 Aaron Gray JSY AU RC 1.50 4.00
72 Carl Landry JSY AU RC 1.50 4.00
73 Gabe Pruitt JSY AU RC 1.50 4.00
74 Nick Fazekas JSY AU RC 1.50 4.00
75 Adam Haluska JSY AU RC 1.50 4.00
76 Glen Davis JSY AU RC 2.00 5.00
77 Josh McRoberts JSY AU RC 2.00 5.00
78 Herbert Hill JSY AU RC 1.50 4.00
79 Jermareo Davidson JSY AU RC 1.50 4.00
80 Chris Richard JSY AU RC 1.50 4.00
81 Dominic McGuire JSY AU RC 1.50 4.00
83 Demetris Nichols JSY AU RC 1.50 4.00
84 D.J. Strawberry JSY AU RC 1.50 4.00

2007-08 SP Rookie Threads Maximum Threads

PRINT RUN 25 SER.#'d SETS
MTBG Ben Gordon 5.00 12.00
MTCA Carmelo Anthony 8.00 20.00
MTCB Chris Bosh 6.00 15.00
MTDH Dwight Howard 5.00 12.00
MTDN Dirk Nowitzki 10.00 25.00
MTDR David Robinson 15.00 30.00
MTDW Deron Williams 5.00 12.00
MTHO Hakeem Olajuwon 8.00 20.00
MTJS John Stockton 10.00 25.00
MTKA Kareem Abdul-Jabbar 10.00 25.00
MTKB Kobe Bryant 25.00 60.00
MTKG Kevin Garnett 10.00 25.00
MTLA LaMarcus Aldridge 8.00 20.00
MTLB Larry Bird 15.00 40.00
MTLJ LeBron James 25.00 60.00
MTSO Shaquille O'Neal 12.00 30.00
MTTM Tracy McGrady 6.00 15.00
MTTT Tyrus Thomas 4.00 10.00
MTVC Vince Carter 8.00 20.00
MTYM Yao Ming 8.00 20.00

2007-08 SP Rookie Threads Portraits Autographs

STATED COMBINED AUTO ODDS 1:1.2
POAJ Al Jefferson 5.00 12.00
POBG Ben Gordon 5.00 12.00
POCA Carmelo Anthony 15.00 30.00
PODR David Robinson 25.00 60.00
POHO Hakeem Olajuwon 15.00 40.00
POJE Julius Erving 25.00 60.00
POJO Michael Jordan 1000.00 1500.00
POKB Kobe Bryant 75.00 150.00
POLB Larry Bird 40.00 80.00
POLJ LeBron James 200.00 500.00
POMB Mike Bibby 5.00 12.00
POMJ Magic Johnson 30.00 80.00
POSN Steve Nash 20.00 50.00
POTP Tayshaun Prince 6.00 15.00
POVC Vince Carter 10.00 25.00

2007-08 SP Rookie Threads Rookie Threads

ONE MEMORABILIA CARD PER PACK
*PARALLEL: .5X TO 1.25X BASE HI
PRINT RUN 199 SER.#'d SETS
RTAA Arron Afflalo 2.50 6.00
RTAB Aaron Brooks 2.00 5.00
RTAG Aaron Gray 1.50 4.00
RTAH Al Horford 3.00 8.00
RTAL Acie Law 1.50 4.00
RTAT Al Thornton 2.00 5.00
RTBW Brandan Wright 2.50 6.00
RTCB Corey Brewer 2.50 6.00
RTCL Carl Landry 1.50 4.00
RTCR Chris Richard 1.50 4.00
RTDA Jermareo Davidson 1.50 4.00
RTDC Daequan Cook 2.00 5.00
RTDM Dominic McGuire 1.50 4.00
RTDN Demetris Nichols 1.50 4.00
RTDS D.J. Strawberry 1.50 4.00
RTGD Glen Davis 2.00 5.00
RTGP Gabe Pruitt 1.50 4.00
RTHA Adam Haluska 1.50 4.00
RTHH Herbert Hill 1.50 4.00
RTJC Javaris Crittenton 1.50 4.00
RTJD Jared Dudley 2.00 5.00
RTJG Jeff Green 2.50 6.00
RTJM Josh McRoberts 2.00 5.00
RTJN Joakim Noah 2.50 6.00
RTJS Jason Smith 2.00 5.00
RTJW Julian Wright 1.50 4.00
RTKD Kevin Durant 20.00 50.00
RTMA Morris Almond 1.50 4.00
RTMC Mike Conley Jr. 3.00 8.00
RTNF Nick Fazekas 1.50 4.00
RTNY Nick Young 3.00 8.00
RTRS Rodney Stuckey 2.00 5.00
RTSH Spencer Hawes 2.00 5.00
RTSW Sean Williams 1.50 4.00
RTTG Taurean Green 1.50 4.00
RTTU Alando Tucker 1.50 4.00
RTTY Thaddeus Young 2.50 6.00
RTWC Wilson Chandler 2.00 5.00

2007-08 SP Rookie Threads Rookie Threads Patch

*PATCH: .6X TO 1.5X BASE HI
PATCH PRINT RUN 50 SER.#'d SETS
RTKD Kevin Durant 50.00 120.00

2007-08 SP Rookie Threads Rookie Threads Dual

ONE MEMORABILIA CARD PER PACK
*PARALLEL: .5X TO 1.25X BASE HI
PARALLEL PRINT RUN 99 SER.#'d SETS
AS M.Almond/R.Stuckey 3.00 8.00
BR C.Brewer/C.Richard 3.00 8.00
CC M.Conley/D.Cook 3.00 8.00
DG K.Durant/J.Green 6.00 15.00
DH K.Durant/A.Horford 6.00 15.00
HB A.Horford/C.Brewer 3.00 8.00
HL A.Horford/A.Law 3.00 8.00
LB A.Brooks/C.Landry 3.00 8.00
MD G.Davis/J.McRoberts 4.00 10.00
NB C.Brewer/J.Noah 4.00 10.00
NC W.Chandler/D.Nichols 3.00 8.00
SA A.Afflalo/R.Stuckey 4.00 10.00
SH S.Hawes/R.Stuckey 4.00 10.00
TS A.Tucker/D.Strawberry 4.00 10.00
TW J.Wright/A.Thornton 4.00 10.00
WW B.Wright/J.Wright 3.00 8.00
WY B.Wright/T.Young 3.00 8.00
YC T.Young/J.Crittenton 3.00 8.00
YP N.Young/G.Pruitt 3.00 8.00
YY N.Young/T.Young 3.00 8.00

2007-08 SP Rookie Threads Rookie Threads Patch Dual

PRINT RUN 25 SER.#'d SETS

AS M.Almond/R.Stuckey 6.00 15.00
DG K.Durant/J.Green 30.00 60.00
DH K.Durant/A.Horford 30.00 60.00
MD J.McRoberts/G.Davis 8.00 20.00
NB J.Noah/C.Brewer 8.00 20.00
YC T.Young/J.Crittenton 6.00 15.00
YY T.Young/N.Young 6.00 15.00

2007-08 SP Rookie Threads Rookie Threads Triple

MEMORABILIA ODDS ON PER PACK
*PARALLEL: .5X TO 1.25X BASE HI
PARALLEL PRINT RUN 50 SER.#'d SETS
ACB Afflalo/Brooks/Cook 5.00 12.00
DCW Williams/Chandler/Davis 4.00 10.00
DGW Durant/Green/Wright 10.00 25.00
DHC Horford/Conley/Durant 10.00 25.00
DYW Durant/Young/Wright 10.00 25.00
GSP Pruitt/Green/Strawberry 4.00 10.00
GYC Gray/Young/Crittenton 4.00 10.00
NDS Strawberry/Davis/Noah 5.00 12.00
NGR Richard/Green/Noah 5.00 12.00
NHB Noah/Brewer/Horford 5.00 12.00
PLC Pruitt/Conley/Law 4.00 10.00
SHW Smith/Williams/Hawes 4.00 10.00
TCB Thornton/Cook/Brewer 4.00 10.00
TLC Tucker/Landry/Conley 4.00 10.00
TYW Young/Wright/Thornton 4.00 10.00
YCS Young/Crittenton/Stuckey 4.00 10.00
YYW Young/Wright/Young 4.00 10.00

2007-08 SP Rookie Threads Rookie Threads Patch Triple

INT RUN 15 SER.#'d SETS
ACB Afflalo/Cook/Brooks 10.00 25.00
DCW Davis/Chandler/Williams 10.00 25.00
DGW Durant/Green/Wright 50.00 100.00
DHC Durant/Horford/Conley 50.00 100.00
GSP Pruitt/Green/Strawberry 8.00 20.00
NDS Noah/Davis/Strawberry 15.00 30.00
NHB Noah/Horford/Brewer 15.00 30.00
SHW Smith/Hawes/Williams 8.00 20.00
TYW Thornton/Young/Wright 15.00 30.00
YYW Young/Young/Wright 10.00 25.00

2007-08 SP Rookie Threads Rookie Threads Patch Autographs

PRINT RUN 25 SER.#'d SETS
RTAA Arron Afflalo 10.00 25.00
RTAB Aaron Brooks 8.00 20.00
RTAH Al Horford 12.00 30.00
RTAL Acie Law 6.00 15.00
RTAT Al Thornton 8.00 20.00
RTCL Carl Landry 6.00 15.00
RTDS D.J. Strawberry 6.00 15.00
RTGD Glen Davis 8.00 20.00
RTJD Jared Dudley 8.00 20.00
RTJG Jeff Green 10.00 25.00
RTJN Joakim Noah 20.00 50.00
RTJS Jason Smith 8.00 20.00
RTKD Kevin Durant 400.00 700.00
RTMC Mike Conley Jr. 12.00 30.00
RTRS Rodney Stuckey 8.00 20.00
RTSH Spencer Hawes 8.00 20.00
RTSW Sean Williams 6.00 15.00
RTTG Taurean Green 6.00 15.00
RTTU Alando Tucker 6.00 15.00
RTWC Wilson Chandler 8.00 20.00

2007-08 SP Rookie Threads Rookie Threads Patch Dual Autographs

PRINT RUN 15 SER.#'d SETS
UNPRICED TRIPLE PRINT RUN 10 SETS
BR C.Brewer/C.Richard 12.00 30.00
CC D.Cook/M.Conley 20.00 40.00
DH K.Durant/A.Horford 250.00 450.00
HB A.Horford/C.Brewer 40.00 75.00
HL A.Horford/A.Law 15.00 40.00
NB J.Noah/C.Brewer 25.00 60.00
SA A.Afflalo/R.Stuckey 25.00 50.00
SH R.Stuckey/S.Hawes 25.00 50.00
TW A.Thornton/J.Wright 15.00 40.00

2007-08 SP Rookie Threads Rookies Gold

*43-48 GOLD: .75X TO 2X BASE HI
*49-60 GOLD: SAME VALUE AS BASE
*61-84 GOLD: .75X TO 2X BASE HI
GOLD PRINT RUN 50 SER.#'d SETS
UNPRICED SILVER PRINT RUN ONE SET
49 Kevin Durant JSY AU 300.00 550.00

2007-08 SP Rookie Threads Scripted in Time

COMBINED AUTO ODDS 1:1.2
AJ Al Jefferson 4.00 10.00
BB Bruce Bowen 4.00 10.00
BD Baron Davis 6.00 15.00
CP Chris Paul 25.00 60.00
DG Daniel Gibson 5.00 12.00
DH Dwight Howard 20.00 40.00
DL David Lee 4.00 10.00
EO Emeka Okafor 4.00 10.00
GR Danny Granger 5.00 12.00
JO Jermaine O'Neal 4.00 10.00
KH Kirk Hinrich 4.00 10.00
KK Kyle Korver 4.00 10.00
KL Kyle Lowry 4.00 10.00
LA LaMarcus Aldridge 6.00 15.00
LB Leandro Barbosa 4.00 10.00
LH Larry Hughes 4.00 10.00
LP Leon Powe 5.00 12.00
PO Patrick O'Bryant 4.00 10.00
PP Paul Pierce 10.00 25.00
RC Rodney Carney 4.00 10.00
RR Rajon Rondo 8.00 20.00
SB Shannon Brown 4.00 10.00
TF T.J. Ford 4.00 10.00
TM Tracy McGrady 10.00 25.00
TT Tyrus Thomas 4.00 10.00
YM Yao Ming 15.00 30.00

2007-08 SP Rookie Threads Signing Day

COMBINED AUTO ODDS 1:1.2
SDAA Arron Afflalo 3.00 8.00
SDAB Aaron Brooks 2.50 6.00
SDAG Aaron Gray 2.00 5.00
SDAH Al Horford 6.00 15.00
SDAL Acie Law 2.00 5.00
SDAT Al Thornton 2.50 6.00
SDCB Corey Brewer 3.00 8.00
SDCK Coby Karl 2.00 5.00
SDCL Carl Landry 2.00 5.00
SDCR Chris Richard 2.00 5.00
SDDA Jermareo Davidson 2.00 5.00
SDDC Daequan Cook 2.50 6.00
SDDN Demetris Nichols 2.00 5.00
SDDS D.J. Strawberry 2.00 5.00
SDGD Glen Davis 2.50 6.00
SDGP Gabe Pruitt 2.00 5.00
SDHA Adam Haluska 2.00 5.00
SDHH Herbert Hill 2.00 5.00
SDJC Javaris Crittenton 2.00 5.00
SDJD Jared Dudley 2.50 6.00
SDJG Jeff Green 3.00 8.00
SDJM Josh McRoberts 2.50 6.00
SDJN Joakim Noah 3.00 8.00
SDJS Jason Smith 2.50 6.00
SDJW Julian Wright 2.00 5.00
SDKD Kevin Durant 150.00 300.00
SDLS Luis Scola 4.00 10.00
SDMA Morris Almond 2.00 5.00
SDMB Marco Belinelli 3.00 8.00
SDMC Mike Conley Jr. 4.00 10.00
SDNF Nick Fazekas 2.00 5.00
SDRS Ramon Sessions 3.00 8.00
SDRS Rodney Stuckey 2.50 6.00
SDSH Spencer Hawes 2.50 6.00
SDSW Sean Williams 2.00 5.00
SDTG Taurean Green 2.00 5.00
SDTU Alando Tucker 2.00 5.00
SDWC Wilson Chandler 2.50 6.00

2007-08 SP Rookie Threads SP Marks Dual

PRINT RUN 50 SER.#'d SETS
UNPRICED QUAD PRINT RUN 10 SER.#'d SETS
UNPRICED SIX PRINT RUN 5 SER.#'d SETS
MDAR L.Aldridge/B.Roy 20.00 40.00
MDAS A.Afflalo/R.Stuckey 10.00 25.00
MDCJ V.Carter/A.Jamison 20.00 40.00
MDCM V.Carter/T.McGrady 25.00 60.00
MDDA A.Mourning/D.Cook 20.00 40.00
MDDB B.Davis/M.Belinelli 15.00 40.00
MDDG K.Durant/J.Green 125.00 250.00
MDDH B.Davis/A.Harrington 10.00 25.00
MDGC R.Gay/M.Conley 8.00 20.00
MDHB S.Hawes/M.Bibby 8.00 20.00
MDHD H.Grant/D.Howard 10.00 25.00
MDHG K.Hinrich/B.Gordon 12.50 30.00
MDJP T.Prince/R.Jefferson 8.00 20.00
MDKA S.Kerr/B.Armstrong 20.00 40.00
MDKP J.Kidd/T.Parker 20.00 50.00
MDLG D.Lee/R.Gay 8.00 20.00
MDMW Y.Ming/B.Walton 20.00 40.00
MDOM Y.Ming/H.Olajuwon 30.00 60.00
MDPD P.Pierce/A.Dantley/26 20.00 40.00
MDPS R.Stuckey/T.Prince 12.00 30.00
MDPW C.Paul/D.Williams 30.00 80.00
MDRG T.Green/B.Roy 10.00 25.00
MDRR D.Robinson/D.Rodman 40.00 80.00
MDTM A.Thornton/D.Manning 20.00 40.00
MDTN T.Thomas/J.Noah 15.00 30.00
MDWH A.Horford/D.Wilkins 25.00 50.00

2007-08 SP Rookie Threads SP Marks Triple

PRINT RUN 25 SER.#'d SETS
ARM Aldridge/Roy/McRoberts 12.00 30.00
CAW Chandler/Armstrong/Wright 10.00 25.00
CBP Carney/Boone/Powe 10.00 25.00
CRA Collins/Rondo/Afflalo 10.00 25.00
FFR Foye/Rondo/Felton 20.00 40.00
GGP Garcia/Gibson/Pruitt 10.00 25.00
GIS Gordon/Iguodala/Stuckey 10.00 25.00
JBJ Bryant/James/Jordan 800.00 1200.00
JFB Foye/Brewer/Jefferson 15.00 30.00
JGH Gordon/Haluska/Jamison 20.00 40.00
JMN Jamison/May/Noel 10.00 25.00
MRC Mourning/Riley/Cook 50.00 100.00
OMM Mourning/Ming/Olajuwon 50.00 100.00
PAJ Anthony/Jefferson/Prince 20.00 50.00
PDB Peterson/Brown/Davis 10.00 25.00
PJH Jamison/Harrington/Pierce 12.00 30.00
PRM Rondo/Morris/Prince 12.00 30.00

2007-08 SP Rookie Threads SP Threads

SPAI Andre Iguodala 3.00 8.00
SPAK Andrei Kirilenko 3.00 8.00
SPAS Amare Stoudemire 3.00 8.00
SPBL Bill Laimbeer 3.00 8.00
SPCA Carmelo Anthony 5.00 12.00
SPCD Clyde Drexler 5.00 12.00
SPCF Channing Frye 3.00 8.00
SPCP Chris Paul 5.00 12.00
SPDG Drew Gooden 3.00 8.00
SPDH Dwight Howard 3.00 8.00
SPDN Dirk Nowitzki 5.00 12.00
SPDR David Robinson 6.00 15.00
SPDW Deron Williams 3.00 8.00
SPIV Allen Iverson 5.00 12.00
SPJA LeBron James 12.00 30.00
SPJK Jason Kidd 4.00 10.00
SPKB Kobe Bryant 12.50 30.00
SPKG Kevin Garnett 6.00 15.00
SPLA LaMarcus Aldridge 5.00 12.00
SPLJ LeBron James 12.00 30.00
SPMJ Michael Jordan 30.00 80.00
SPPR Tayshaun Prince 3.00 8.00
SPRH Richard Hamilton 3.00 8.00
SPRO Dennis Rodman 8.00 20.00
SPSL Shaun Livingston 3.00 8.00
SPSM Shawn Marion 3.00 8.00
SPSN Steve Nash 5.00 12.00
SPSO Shaquille O'Neal 8.00 20.00
SPST Stephon Marbury 3.00 8.00
SPTD Tim Duncan 6.00 15.00
SPTP Tony Parker 4.00 10.00
SPVC Vince Carter 5.00 12.00
SPYM Yao Ming 5.00 12.00

2007-08 SP Rookie Threads SP Threads Patch

*PATCH: .75X TO 2X BASE HI
ONE MEMORABILIA CARD PER PACK
SPKB Kobe Bryant 40.00 100.00

2008-09 SP Rookie Threads

This set was released on December 10, 2008. The base set consists of 100 cards. Cards 1-60 feature veterans, while cards 61-66 are rookies serial numbered of 99. Cards 67-94 feature autographed jersey rookies serial numbered of 599, and cards 95-100 are autographed jersey rookies serial numbered of 399.

COMP.SET w/o SPs (60) 20.00 50.00
61-66 RC PRINT RUN 99 SER.#'d SETS
67-94 JSY AU RC PRINT RUN 599 SETS
95-100 JSY AU RC PRINT RUN 399 SETS
1 Antawn Jamison .50 1.25
2 Gilbert Arenas .50 1.25
3 Carlos Boozer .50 1.25
4 Deron Williams .50 1.25
5 Jermaine O'Neal .50 1.25
6 Chris Bosh .60 1.50
7 Jeff Green .50 1.25
8 Kevin Durant 1.50 4.00
9 Tim Duncan 1.00 2.50
10 Tony Parker .60 1.50
11 Beno Udrih .40 1.00
12 Kevin Martin .50 1.25
13 Brandon Roy .60 1.50
14 Greg Oden .50 1.25
15 Amare Stoudemire .50 1.25
16 Steve Nash .60 1.50
17 Thaddeus Young .50 1.25
18 Andre Iguodala .50 1.25
19 Hedo Turkoglu .50 1.25
20 Dwight Howard .50 1.25
21 Jamal Crawford .60 1.50
22 Stephon Marbury .50 1.25
23 David West .50 1.25
24 Chris Paul .75 2.00
25 Yi Jianlian .60 1.50
26 Vince Carter .75 2.00
27 Al Jefferson .50 1.25
28 Corey Brewer .50 1.25
29 Richard Jefferson .50 1.25
30 Michael Redd .50 1.25
31 Dwyane Wade 1.00 2.50
32 Shawn Marion .50 1.25
33 Mike Conley Jr. .50 1.25
34 Rudy Gay .60 1.50
35 Pau Gasol .60 1.50
36 Kobe Bryant 2.50 6.00
37 Al Thornton .50 1.25
38 Baron Davis .50 1.25
39 Danny Granger .50 1.25
40 T.J. Ford .40 1.00
41 Tracy McGrady .60 1.50
42 Yao Ming .75 2.00
43 Stephen Jackson .50 1.25
44 Monta Ellis .50 1.25
45 Richard Hamilton .50 1.25
46 Chauncey Billups .60 1.50
47 Allen Iverson .75 2.00
48 Carmelo Anthony .75 2.00
49 Jason Kidd .60 1.50
50 Dirk Nowitzki .75 2.00
51 LeBron James 2.50 6.00
52 Ben Wallace .50 1.25
53 Ben Gordon .50 1.25
54 Joakim Noah .50 1.25
55 Gerald Wallace .50 1.25
56 Jason Richardson .60 1.50
57 Kevin Garnett 1.00 2.50
58 Paul Pierce .60 1.50
59 Al Horford .60 1.50
60 Joe Johnson .50 1.25
61 James Gist RC 1.25 3.00
62 Danilo Gallinari RC 3.00 8.00
63 Malik Hairston RC 1.25 3.00
64 Mike Taylor RC 1.25 3.00
65 Joe Crawford RC 1.25 3.00
66 Trent Plaisted RC 1.25 3.00
67 R. Westbrook JSY AU RC 100.00 250.00
68 Sonny Weems JSY AU RC 3.00 8.00
69 Joe Alexander JSY AU RC 3.00 8.00
70 D.J. Augustin JSY AU RC 4.00 10.00
71 Brook Lopez JSY AU RC 10.00 25.00
72 Jason Thompson JSY AU RC 3.00 8.00
73 Brandon Rush JSY AU RC 4.00 10.00
74 Anthony Randolph JSY AU RC 3.00 8.00
75 Robin Lopez JSY AU RC 5.00 12.00
76 Marreese Speights JSY AU RC 4.00 10.00
77 Roy Hibbert JSY AU RC 5.00 12.00
78 JaVale McGee JSY AU RC 6.00 15.00
79 J.J. Hickson JSY AU RC 4.00 10.00
80 Kyle Weaver JSY AU RC 3.00 8.00
81 Ryan Anderson JSY AU RC 4.00 10.00
82 Courtney Lee JSY AU RC 4.00 10.00
83 Kosta Koufos JSY AU RC 4.00 10.00
84 George Hill JSY AU RC 5.00 12.00
85 Darrell Arthur JSY AU RC 4.00 10.00
86 Donte Greene JSY AU RC 3.00 8.00
87 D.J. White JSY AU RC 4.00 10.00
88 J.R. Giddens JSY AU RC 3.00 8.00
89 Walter Sharpe JSY AU RC 3.00 8.00
90 Joey Dorsey JSY AU RC 3.00 8.00
91 Mario Chalmers JSY AU RC 5.00 12.00
92 DeAndre Jordan JSY AU RC 12.00 30.00
93 C.Douglas-Roberts JSY AU RC 3.00 8.00
94 Patrick Ewing Jr. JSY AU RC 3.00 8.00
95 Derrick Rose JSY AU RC 30.00 80.00
96 Michael Beasley JSY AU RC 6.00 15.00
97 O.J. Mayo JSY AU RC 6.00 15.00
98 Kevin Love JSY AU RC 20.00 50.00
99 Eric Gordon JSY AU RC 10.00 25.00
100 Jerryd Bayless JSY AU RC 5.00 12.00

2008-09 SP Rookie Threads Authorization

APPROXIMATE ODDS 1:12
AUAB Andrew Bynum 2.50 6.00
AUAH Al Horford 4.00 10.00
AUBR Bill Russell 60.00 120.00
AUBW Bill Walton 4.00 10.00
AUCB Chauncey Billups 4.00 10.00
AUCP Chris Paul 20.00 50.00
AUCW Chris Wilcox 2.50 6.00
AUDH Dwight Howard 15.00 40.00
AUJA LeBron James 200.00 400.00
AUJM Jamario Moon 2.50 6.00
AUJP John Paxson 3.00 8.00
AUKA Kareem Abdul-Jabbar 50.00 100.00
AUKB Kobe Bryant 100.00 200.00
AUKD Kevin Durant 75.00 200.00
AULJ Larry Johnson 25.00 60.00
AULS Luis Scola 3.00 8.00
AUMJ Michael Jordan 300.00 500.00
AUMW Maurice Williams 3.00 8.00
AURG Rudy Gay 4.00 10.00
AUTC Tom Chambers 3.00 8.00
AUWF Walt Frazier 4.00 10.00

2008-09 SP Rookie Threads Letters of Introduction

CARDS #'d TO LETTERS IN FULL NAME
SOME NOT PRICED DUE TO SCARCITY
LICD Chris Douglas-Roberts/19* 8.00 20.00
LIJB Jerryd Bayless/13* 10.00 25.00
LIMB Michael Beasley/14* 12.00 30.00
LIMS Marreese Speights/16* 10.00 25.00

2008-09 SP Rookie Threads Rookie Threads

APPROXIMATE ODDS 1:3
*PARALLEL 125: .4X TO 1X BASE HI
PARALLEL PRINT RUN 125 SER.#'d SETS
*PATCH: 1X TO 2.5X HI COLUMN
PATCH PRINT RUN 35 SER.#'d SETS
RTAR Anthony Randolph 1.25 3.00
RTBR Brandon Rush 1.50 4.00
RTCL Courtney Lee 1.50 4.00
RTDA D.J. Augustin 1.50 4.00
RTDR Derrick Rose 8.00 20.00
RTEG Eric Gordon 3.00 8.00
RTGH George Hill 2.00 5.00
RTGR Donte Greene 1.25 3.00
RTJA Joe Alexander 1.25 3.00
RTJB Jerryd Bayless 1.50 4.00
RTJD Joey Dorsey 1.25 3.00
RTJG J.R. Giddens 1.25 3.00
RTJH J.J. Hickson 1.50 4.00
RTJT Jason Thompson 1.25 3.00
RTKL Kevin Love 6.00 15.00
RTMB Michael Beasley 2.00 5.00
RTMC Mario Chalmers 2.00 5.00
RTMS Marreese Speights 1.50 4.00
RTOM O.J. Mayo 2.00 5.00
RTSW Sonny Weems 1.25 3.00

2008-09 SP Rookie Threads Rookie Threads Dual

APPROXIMATE ODDS 1:6
RTDAB D.Augustin/J.Bayless 2.50 6.00
RTDAL K.Love/J.Alexander 3.00 8.00
RTDBC M.Beasley/M.Chalmers 2.50 6.00
RTDBH J.Bayless/G.Hill 2.50 6.00
RTDBR D.Rose/M.Beasley 3.00 8.00
RTDDD J.Dorsey/C.Douglas-Roberts 2.50 6.00
RTDGA E.Gordon/J.Alexander 2.50 6.00
RTDGD D.Greene/J.Dorsey 2.50 6.00
RTDGW E.Gordon/D.White 2.50 6.00
RTDLL B.Lopez/R.Lopez 2.50 6.00
RTDLW R.Westbrook/K.Love 8.00 20.00
RTDMR O.Mayo/D.Rose 3.00 8.00
RTDRC B.Rush/M.Chalmers 2.50 6.00
RTDWH S.Weems/G.Hill 2.50 6.00

2008-09 SP Rookie Threads Rookie Threads Dual Parallel

*PARALLEL: .5X TO 1.25X BASE HI
PRINT RUN 50 SER.#'d SETS
RTDAM O.Mayo/D.Arthur 3.00 8.00
RTDAW D.Augustin/K.Weaver 3.00 8.00
RTDDA R.Anderson/Douglas-Roberts 3.00 8.00
RTDGJ E.Gordon/D.Jordan 5.00 12.00
RTDHM R.Hibbert/J.McGee 3.00 8.00
RTDRL B.Rush/C.Lee 3.00 8.00
RTDTE J.Thompson/Ewing Jr. 3.00 8.00
RTDTS J.Thompson/Speights 3.00 8.00
RTDWW R.Westbrook/D.White 5.00 12.00

2008-09 SP Rookie Threads Rookie Threads Dual Patch

*PATCH: 1X TO 2.5X BASE HI
PRINT RUN 25 SER.#'d SETS
RTDAM O.Mayo/D.Arthur 6.00 15.00
RTDAW D.Augustin/K.Weaver 6.00 15.00
RTDDA R.Anderson/Douglas-Roberts 6.00 15.00
RTDGJ E.Gordon/D.Jordan 10.00 25.00
RTDHM R.Hibbert/J.McGee 6.00 15.00
RTDRL B.Rush/C.Lee 6.00 15.00
RTDTE J.Thompson/Ewing Jr. 6.00 15.00
RTDTS J.Thompson/Speights 6.00 15.00
RTDWW R.Westbrook/D.White 10.00 25.00

2008-09 SP Rookie Threads Rookie Threads Triple

APPROXIMATE ODDS 1:6
*PARALLEL: .75X TO 2X BASE HI
PARALLEL PRINT RUN 15 SER.#'d SETS
*PATCH: 1.25X TO 3X BASE HI
PATCH PRINT RUN 15 SER.#'d SETS
RTTAGH Hill/Arthur/Greene 2.50 6.00
RTTAGW Westbrook/Gordon/Augustin 4.00 10.00
RTTALA Lopez/Alexander/Augustin 2.50 6.00
RTTARW Rose/Westbrook/Augustin 6.00 15.00
RTTBLA Beasley/Love/Alexander 3.00 8.00
RTTDWE Weems/Douglas Roberts/Ewing Jr. 2.50 6.00
RTTGWH Weems/Hill/Greene 2.50 6.00
RTTHGS Giddens/Sharpe/Hickson 2.50 6.00
RTTHMH Hickson/Hibbert/McGee 2.50 6.00
RTTJLK Jordan/Koufos/Lopez 3.00 8.00
RTTJWC Chalmers/Jordan/Weaver 3.00 8.00
RTTLAK Anderson/Lee/Koufos 2.50 6.00
RTTLDA Lopez/Anderson Douglas-Roberts 2.50 6.00
RTTMBR Rose/Beasley/Mayo 3.00 8.00
RTTMGB Mayo/Gordon/Bayless 2.50 6.00
RTTMRG Rose/Mayo/Gordon 3.00 8.00
RTTRAC Rush/Arthur/Chalmers 2.50 6.00
RTTRDD Rose/Dorsey/Douglas-Roberts 3.00 8.00
RTTRLS Speights/Randolph/Lopez 2.50 6.00
RTTRSC Chalmers/Speights/Rush 2.50 6.00
RTTRTB Rush/Bayless/Thompson 2.50 6.00
RTTWES Ewing Jr./Sharpe/White 2.50 6.00
RTTWGD White/Giddens/Dorsey 2.50 6.00

2008-09 SP Rookie Threads Rookies Parallel

PRINT RUNS LISTED IN CHECKLIST
SOME NOT PRICED DUE TO SCARCITY
61 James Gist/59 2.00 5.00
63 Malik Hairston/47 2.00 5.00
64 Mike Taylor/55 2.00 5.00
65 Joe Crawford/58 2.00 5.00
66 Trent Plaisted/37 2.00 5.00
68 Sonny Weems JSY AU/39 6.00 15.00
71 Brook Lopez JSY AU/10 50.00 120.00
73 Brandon Rush JSY AU/13 12.00 30.00
74 A. Randolph JSY AU/14 60.00 120.00
75 Robin Lopez JSY AU/15 15.00 40.00
76 M. Speights JSY AU/16 20.00 50.00
77 Roy Hibbert JSY AU/17 10.00 25.00
78 Javale McGee JSY AU/18 20.00 50.00
79 J.J. Hickson JSY AU/19 15.00 40.00
80 Kyle Weaver JSY AU/38 6.00 15.00
81 Ryan Anderson JSY AU/21 8.00 20.00
82 Courtney Lee JSY AU/22 8.00 20.00
83 Kosta Koufos JSY AU/23 8.00 20.00
84 George Hill JSY AU/26 10.00 25.00
85 Darrell Arthur JSY AU/27 8.00 20.00
86 Donte Greene JSY AU/28 6.00 15.00
87 D.J. White JSY AU/29 8.00 20.00
88 J.R. Giddens JSY AU/30 6.00 15.00
89 Walter Sharpe JSY AU/32 6.00 15.00
90 Joey Dorsey JSY AU/33 6.00 15.00
91 Mario Chalmers JSY AU/34 10.00 25.00
92 DeAndre Jordan JSY AU/35 25.00 60.00
93 Chris Douglas-Roberts JSY AU/40 6.00 15.00
94 Patrick Ewing Jr. JSY AU/43 6.00 15.00

2008-09 SP Rookie Threads Scripted in Time

RANDOM INSERTS IN PACKS
SITAB Andrew Bynum 4.00 10.00
SITAJ Al Jefferson 4.00 10.00
SITBB Bruce Bowen 4.00 10.00
SITBD Baron Davis 4.00 10.00
SITBG Ben Gordon 4.00 10.00
SITDH Dwight Howard 8.00 20.00
SITEO Emeka Okafor 4.00 10.00
SITGR Danny Granger 4.00 10.00
SITHA Hilton Armstrong 4.00 10.00
SITHE Luther Head 4.00 10.00
SITJG Jeff Green 4.00 10.00
SITJS Jason Smith 4.00 10.00
SITKA Kelenna Azubuike 6.00 15.00
SITKL Kyle Lowry 4.00 10.00
SITLA LaMarcus Aldridge 6.00 15.00
SITLH Larry Hughes 4.00 10.00
SITLP Leon Powe 4.00 10.00
SITPM Paul Millsap 8.00 20.00
SITPP Paul Pierce 12.00 30.00
SITRA Ray Allen 12.00 30.00
SITRC Rodney Carney 4.00 10.00
SITRJ Richard Jefferson 4.00 10.00
SITRS Rodney Stuckey 4.00 10.00
SITSB Shane Battier 4.00 10.00
SITSJ Solomon Jones 4.00 10.00
SITTF T.J. Ford 4.00 10.00
SITTM Tracy McGrady 12.00 30.00
SITTP Tayshaun Prince 5.00 12.00
SITTT Tyrus Thomas 4.00 10.00
SITYM Yao Ming 20.00 50.00

2008-09 SP Rookie Threads Signing Day

APPROXIMATE ODDS 1:6
SDAR Anthony Randolph 2.50 6.00
SDBL Brook Lopez 5.00 12.00
SDBR Brandon Rush 3.00 8.00
SDCD Chris Douglas-Roberts 2.50 6.00
SDDA D.J. Augustin 3.00 8.00
SDDG Danilo Gallinari 6.00 15.00
SDDR Derrick Rose 20.00 50.00
SDDW D.J. White 3.00 8.00
SDEG Eric Gordon 6.00 15.00
SDGH George Hill 4.00 10.00
SDGR Donte Greene 2.50 6.00
SDJA Joe Alexander 2.50 6.00
SDJB Jerryd Bayless 3.00 8.00
SDJC Joe Crawford 2.50 6.00
SDJD Joey Dorsey 2.50 6.00
SDJG J.R. Giddens 2.50 6.00
SDJH J.J. Hickson 3.00 8.00
SDJT Jason Thompson 2.50 6.00
SDKK Kosta Koufos 3.00 8.00
SDKL Kevin Love 20.00 50.00
SDMB Michael Beasley 4.00 10.00
SDMC Mario Chalmers 4.00 10.00
SDMH Malik Hairston 2.50 6.00
SDMS Marreese Speights 3.00 8.00
SDOM O.J. Mayo 4.00 10.00
SDPE Patrick Ewing Jr. 2.50 6.00
SDRH Roy Hibbert 4.00 10.00
SDRL Robin Lopez 4.00 10.00
SDRW Russell Westbrook 75.00 200.00
SDSW Sonny Weems 2.50 6.00

2008-09 SP Rookie Threads SP Threads

APPROXIMATE ODDS 1:4
TAB Andrea Bargnani 2.00 5.00
TAI Allen Iverson 5.00 12.00
TAK Andrei Kirilenko 2.00 5.00
TAS Amare Stoudemire 2.00 5.00
TBO Andrew Bogut 2.00 5.00
TCB Caron Butler 2.00 5.00
TCH Chris Bosh 2.50 6.00
TDG Daniel Gibson 2.00 5.00
TDH Devin Harris 1.50 4.00
TDN Dirk Nowitzki 3.00 8.00
TEB Elton Brand 2.50 6.00
TGH Grant Hill 4.00 10.00
THO Dwight Howard 2.00 5.00
TJG Jeff Green 2.00 5.00
TJH Josh Howard 2.00 5.00
TJJ Joe Johnson 2.00 5.00
TJK Jason Kidd 2.50 6.00
TJR Jason Richardson 2.50 6.00
TJS Josh Smith 2.00 5.00
TKD Kevin Durant 12.00 30.00
TKG Kevin Garnett 4.00 10.00
TKH Kirk Hinrich 2.00 5.00
TLD Luol Deng 2.00 5.00
TLJ LeBron James 12.00 30.00
TMG Manu Ginobili 2.50 6.00
TPG Pau Gasol 2.50 6.00
TRA Ray Allen 2.50 6.00
TRH Richard Hamilton 2.00 5.00
TSL Shaun Livingston 2.00 5.00
TSM Shawn Marion 2.00 5.00
TTD Tim Duncan 4.00 10.00

2008-09 SP Rookie Threads SP Threads Patch

*PATCH: 1X TO 2.5X BASE HI
RANDOM INSERTS IN PACKS
TGH Grant Hill 20.00 50.00

2008-09 SP Rookie Threads SP Threads Dual

APPROXIMATE ODDS 1:5
TDAP S.Pippen/C.Anthony 15.00 40.00
TDBJ K.Bryant/M.Jordan 40.00 80.00
TDDD C.Drexler/K.Durant 10.00 25.00
TDEA J.Erving/G.Arenas 5.00 12.00
TDEJ P.Ewing/A.Jefferson 6.00 15.00
TDGM K.McHale/K.Garnett 6.00 15.00
TDHK J.Hornacek/K.Korver 6.00 15.00
TDHO S.O'Neal/D.Howard 8.00 20.00
TDIR A.Iverson/B.Roy 6.00 15.00
TDJB L.Bird/L.James 12.00 30.00
TDKJ M.Johnson/J.Kidd 8.00 20.00
TDMB C.Boozer/K.Malone 5.00 12.00
TDMW A.Mourning/S.Williams 5.00 12.00
TDPT I.Thomas/C.Paul 5.00 12.00
TDRM D.Majerle/M.Redd 5.00 12.00
TDSP J.Starks/T.Parker 5.00 12.00
TDSR D.Robinson/A.Stoudemire 6.00 15.00
TDWL B.Laimbeer/R.Wallace 5.00 12.00
TDWS D.Williams/J.Stockton 5.00 12.00

2008-09 SP Rookie Threads SP Threads Dual Patch

RANDOM INSERTS IN PACKS
TDAP C.Anthony/S.Pippen 30.00 80.00
TDBJ M.Jordan/K.Bryant 40.00 100.00
TDDD C.Drexler/K.Durant 12.00 30.00
TDEA J.Erving/G.Arenas 15.00 40.00
TDEJ P.Ewing/A.Jefferson 10.00 25.00
TDGM K.Garnett/K.McHale 15.00 40.00
TDHK J.Hornacek/K.Korver 10.00 25.00
TDHO D.Howard/S.O'Neal 12.00 30.00
TDIR A.Iverson/B.Roy 12.00 30.00
TDJB L.James/L.Bird 20.00 50.00
TDKJ J.Kidd/M.Johnson 15.00 40.00
TDMW S.Williams/A.Mourning 12.50 30.00
TDPT I.Thomas/C.Paul 12.50 30.00
TDRM M.Redd/D.Majerle 10.00 25.00
TDSP J.Starks/T.Parker 15.00 30.00
TDWL R.Wallace/B.Laimbeer 10.00 25.00

2003-04 SP Signature Edition

Released in March 2004, SP Signature Edition boasts a 225-card set divided up as follows: Cards 1-100 are veteran base cards with player photos on the left and colored borders on the right to match the player's team; cards 101-142 are rookies sequentially numbered to 499 which are horizontally designed with player photos on the right and the player's team logo on the left; cards 143-222 are sequentially numbered to the player's jersey number and have a colored border along the bottom and gray background on the top; and cards 223-225 feature celebrities Spike Lee, Summer Sanders and Cheryl Miller. A Legendary Cut Chick Hearn one of one autograph was also inserted. SP Signature Edition was packaged in one-pack boxes of three cards each and carried a suggested retail price of $60. Each "Pack" came with a collectible metal tin-both black and white versions were available for each player.

COMP.SET w/o SP's (100) 30.00 80.00
143-222 SER.#'d TO PLAYER JERSEY #
223-225 PRINT RUN 250 SER.#'d SETS
1 Shareef Abdur-Rahim .50 1.25
2 Jason Terry .50 1.25
3 Theo Ratliff .40 1.00
4 Raef LaFrentz .40 1.00
5 Paul Pierce .60 1.50
6 Larry Bird 1.50 4.00
7 Jalen Rose .50 1.25
8 Scottie Pippen 1.00 2.50
9 Michael Jordan 5.00 12.00
10 Dennis Rodman 1.25 3.00
11 Dajuan Wagner .40 1.00
12 Darius Miles .40 1.00
13 Carlos Boozer .50 1.25
14 Zydrunas Ilgauskas .50 1.25
15 Dirk Nowitzki 1.00 2.50
16 Steve Nash .75 2.00
17 Antoine Walker .60 1.50
18 Antawn Jamison .50 1.25
19 Andre Miller .50 1.25
20 Nene .50 1.25
21 Nikoloz Tskitishvili .40 1.00
22 Ben Wallace .50 1.25
23 Richard Hamilton .50 1.25
24 Chauncey Billups .60 1.50
25 Nick Van Exel .50 1.25
26 Jason Richardson .60 1.50
27 Mike Dunleavy .50 1.25
28 Yao Ming 1.25 3.00
29 Steve Francis .50 1.25
30 Cuttino Mobley .40 1.00
31 Reggie Miller .60 1.50
32 Jermaine O'Neal .50 1.25
33 Jamaal Tinsley .40 1.00
34 Chris Wilcox .40 1.00
35 Elton Brand .60 1.50
36 Wang Zhizhi .50 1.25
37 Corey Maggette .50 1.25
38 Kobe Bryant 2.50 6.00
39 Shaquille O'Neal 1.50 4.00
40 Gary Payton .60 1.50
41 Karl Malone .75 2.00
42 Pau Gasol .60 1.50
43 Shane Battier .50 1.25
44 Mike Miller .50 1.25
45 Caron Butler .50 1.25
46 Eddie Jones .50 1.25
47 Lamar Odom .50 1.25
48 Brian Grant .40 1.00
49 Desmond Mason .50 1.25
50 Michael Redd .60 1.50
51 Tim Thomas .40 1.00
52 Wally Szczerbiak .50 1.25
53 Kevin Garnett 1.00 2.50
54 Latrell Sprewell .50 1.25
55 Sam Cassell .50 1.25
56 Richard Jefferson .50 1.25
57 Kenyon Martin .50 1.25
58 Jason Kidd 1.00 2.50
59 Alonzo Mourning .75 2.00
60 Jamal Mashburn .50 1.25
61 Baron Davis .50 1.25
62 David Wesley .40 1.00
63 Allan Houston .50 1.25
64 Keith Van Horn .50 1.25
65 Antonio McDyess .50 1.25
66 Gordan Giricek .40 1.00
67 Tracy McGrady .75 2.00
68 Drew Gooden .50 1.25
69 Grant Hill .75 2.00
70 Glenn Robinson .50 1.25
71 Allen Iverson 1.00 2.50
72 Julius Erving 1.00 2.50
73 Eric Snow .40 1.00
74 Shawn Marion .50 1.25
75 Amare Stoudemire .75 2.00
76 Stephon Marbury .50 1.25
77 Bonzi Wells .40 1.00
78 Rasheed Wallace .60 1.50
79 Derek Anderson .40 1.00
80 Zach Randolph .50 1.25
81 Mike Bibby .60 1.50
82 Chris Webber .60 1.50
83 Peja Stojakovic .60 1.50
84 Brad Miller .50 1.25
85 Tony Parker .60 1.50
86 Tim Duncan 1.00 2.50
87 Manu Ginobili .75 2.00
88 David Robinson 1.00 2.50
89 Rashard Lewis .60 1.50
90 Ray Allen .60 1.50
91 Vladimir Radmanovic .40 1.00
92 Morris Peterson .40 1.00
93 Vince Carter 1.00 2.50
94 Antonio Davis .40 1.00
95 Andrei Kirilenko .60 1.50
96 Matt Harpring .40 1.00
97 Jarron Collins .40 1.00
98 Gilbert Arenas .50 1.25
99 Jerry Stackhouse .50 1.25
100 Kwame Brown .40 1.00
101 LeBron James RC 75.00 200.00
102 Darko Milicic RC 3.00 8.00
103 Carmelo Anthony RC 12.00 30.00
104 Chris Bosh RC 6.00 15.00
105 Dwyane Wade RC 12.00 30.00
106 Chris Kaman RC 4.00 10.00
107 Kirk Hinrich RC 4.00 10.00
108 T.J. Ford RC 3.00 8.00
109 Mike Sweetney RC 2.50 6.00
110 Jarvis Hayes RC 2.50 6.00
111 Mickael Pietrus RC 3.00 8.00
112 Nick Collison RC 3.00 8.00
113 Marcus Banks RC 2.50 6.00
114 Luke Ridnour RC 3.00 8.00
115 Reece Gaines RC 2.50 6.00
116 Troy Bell RC 2.50 6.00
117 Zarko Cabarkapa RC 2.50 6.00
118 David West RC 4.00 10.00
119 Aleksandar Pavlovic RC 3.00 8.00
120 Dahntay Jones RC 3.00 8.00
121 Boris Diaw RC 4.00 10.00
122 Zoran Planinic RC 2.50 6.00
123 Travis Outlaw RC 3.00 8.00
124 Brian Cook RC 2.50 6.00
125 James Lang RC 2.50 6.00
126 Ndudi Ebi RC 2.50 6.00
127 Kendrick Perkins RC 3.00 8.00
128 Leandro Barbosa RC 4.00 10.00
129 Josh Howard RC 4.00 10.00
130 Maciej Lampe RC 2.50 6.00
131 Jason Kapono RC 2.50 6.00
132 Luke Walton RC 4.00 10.00
133 Jerome Beasley RC 2.50 6.00
134 Willie Green RC 2.50 6.00
135 James Jones RC 2.50 6.00
136 Travis Hansen RC 2.50 6.00
137 Steve Blake RC 3.00 8.00
138 Slavko Vranes RC 2.50 6.00
139 Zaur Pachulia RC 4.00 10.00
140 Keith Bogans RC 2.50 6.00
141 Kyle Korver RC 5.00 12.00
142 Brandon Hunter RC 2.50 6.00
144 LeBron James/23 600.00 800.00
145 Michael Jordan/23 75.00 150.00
146 Darius Miles/21 6.00 15.00
148 Gary Payton/20 12.50 30.00
152 Ray Allen/34 10.00 25.00
153 Paul Pierce/34 12.50 30.00
154 Carmelo Anthony/15 25.00 60.00
160 Andrei Kirilenko/47 6.00 15.00
162 Nene/31 6.00 15.00
163 Elton Brand/42 6.00 15.00
168 Jerry Stackhouse/42 8.00 20.00
171 Darko Milicic/31 15.00 40.00
174 Glenn Robinson/31 6.00 15.00
175 Tim Duncan/21 25.00 60.00
177 Scottie Pippen/33 50.00 120.00
178 Richard Hamilton/32 8.00 20.00
179 Corey Maggette/50 6.00 15.00
182 Amare Stoudemire/32 12.50 30.00
185 Dirk Nowitzki/41 12.50 30.00
187 Magic Johnson/32 25.00 60.00
188 Michael Redd/22 6.00 15.00
190 Rasheed Wallace/30 6.00 15.00
192 Jason Terry/31 6.00 15.00
196 Kevin Garnett/21 25.00 60.00
203 Mike Miller/33 6.00 15.00
207 Morris Peterson/24 6.00 15.00
209 Jason Richardson/23 6.00 15.00
210 Shaquille O'Neal/34 15.00 40.00
211 Desmond Mason/24 6.00 15.00
212 Jamal Mashburn/24 6.00 15.00
213 Shawn Marion/31 8.00 20.00
214 Manu Ginobili/20 10.00 25.00
215 Larry Bird/33 60.00 150.00
216 Antawn Jamison/33 6.00 15.00
217 Reggie Miller/31 15.00 40.00
218 Pau Gasol/16 10.00 25.00
222 Vince Carter/15 20.00 50.00
223 Spike Lee 1.50 4.00
224 Summer Sanders 1.25 3.00
225 Cheryl Miller .75 2.00

2003-04 SP Signature Edition Gold

*GOLD SINGLES: 1.5X TO 4X BASE HI
GOLD PRINT RUN 100 SER.#'d SETS
GOLD PARALLEL FOR 1-100 ONLY
38 Kobe Bryant 15.00 40.00

2003-04 SP Signature Edition Autographed Parallel

1-100 SER.#'d TO PLAYER JERSEY #
SOME NOT PRICED DUE TO SCARCITY
RC AU PRINT RUN 25 SER.#'d SETS
SKIP-NUMBERED PARALLEL SET
A5 Paul Pierce/34 30.00 80.00
A6 Larry Bird/33 125.00 250.00
A9 Michael Jordan/23 500.00 800.00
A10 Dennis Rodman/91 60.00 150.00
A12 Darius Miles/21 10.00 25.00
A18 Antawn Jamison/33 15.00 40.00
A20 Nene/31 15.00 40.00
A23 Richard Hamilton/32 15.00 40.00
A26 Jason Richardson/23 15.00 40.00
A31 Reggie Miller/31 80.00 160.00
A34 Chris Wilcox/54 10.00 25.00
A36 Wang Zhizhi/16 15.00 40.00
A37 Corey Maggette/50 10.00 25.00
A40 Gary Payton/20 30.00 80.00
A43 Shane Battier/31 15.00 40.00
A53 Kevin Garnett/21 100.00 200.00
A56 Richard Jefferson/24 15.00 40.00
A65 Antonio McDyess/34 20.00 40.00
A74 Shawn Marion/31 12.00 30.00
A83 Peja Stojakovic/16 50.00 120.00
A87 Manu Ginobili/20 40.00 100.00
A92 Morris Peterson/24 10.00 25.00
A99 Jerry Stackhouse/42 15.00 40.00
A101 LeBron James 1000.00 1500.00
A102 Darko Milicic 10.00 25.00
A103 Carmelo Anthony 150.00 300.00
A104 Chris Bosh 100.00 200.00
A105 Dwyane Wade 400.00 750.00
A106 Chris Kaman 12.00 30.00
A107 Kirk Hinrich 12.00 30.00
A108 T.J. Ford 10.00 25.00
A109 Mike Sweetney 8.00 20.00
A110 Jarvis Hayes 8.00 20.00
A111 Mickael Pietrus 10.00 25.00
A112 Nick Collison 10.00 25.00
A113 Marcus Banks 8.00 20.00
A114 Luke Ridnour 10.00 25.00
A115 Reece Gaines 8.00 20.00
A116 Troy Bell 8.00 20.00
A117 Zarko Cabarkapa 8.00 20.00
A118 David West 20.00 50.00
A119 Aleksandar Pavlovic 10.00 25.00
A120 Dahntay Jones 10.00 25.00
A121 Boris Diaw 12.00 30.00
A122 Zoran Planinic 8.00 20.00
A123 Travis Outlaw 10.00 25.00
A124 Brian Cook 8.00 20.00
A125 James Lang 8.00 20.00
A126 Ndudi Ebi 8.00 20.00
A127 Kendrick Perkins 10.00 25.00
A128 Leandro Barbosa 12.00 30.00
A129 Josh Howard 12.00 30.00
A130 Maciej Lampe 8.00 20.00
A131 Jason Kapono 8.00 20.00
A132 Luke Walton 12.00 30.00
A133 Jerome Beasley 8.00 20.00
A134 Willie Green 8.00 20.00
A135 James Jones 8.00 20.00
A136 Travis Hansen 8.00 20.00
A137 Steve Blake 10.00 25.00
A138 Slavko Vranes 8.00 20.00
A139 Zaur Pachulia 12.00 30.00
A140 Keith Bogans 8.00 20.00
A141 Kyle Korver 15.00 40.00
A142 Brandon Hunter 8.00 20.00

2003-04 SP Signature Edition Alumni Associates Signatures

Randomly inserted, this 11-card set pairs players from the same college, with one on the top and one on the bottom, where each player signed the card. Each card is sequentially numbered to 100.

PRINT RUN 100 SER.#'d SETS
AK S.A-Rahim/J.Kidd 15.00 40.00
AW G.Arenas/L.Walton 10.00 25.00
BJ M.Bibby/R.Jefferson 10.00 25.00
DB M.Dunleavy/S.Battier 15.00 40.00

FD S.Francis/J.Dixon	10.00	25.00
MJ C.Maggette/D.Jones	10.00	25.00
MW A.McDyess/G.Wallace	15.00	40.00
PG Pierce/Gooden	20.00	50.00
PR M.Peterson/J.Richardson	10.00	25.00
SJ J.Stack/A.Jamison	10.00	25.00
WM B.Walton/R.Miller	50.00	125.00

2003-04 SP Signature Edition Celebrity Signings

Randomly inserted in packs, this three-card set features celebrities and their autographs. No odds were given for Cheryl Miller and Summer Sanders, but Spike Lee's card is sequentially numbered to 32. A gold version where Cheryl and Summer are sequentially numbered to 50 and Spike is sequentially numbered to 15 was also inserted in packs.
RANDOM INSERTS IN PACKS
*GOLD: .6X TO 1.5X BASE AU HI
GOLD PRINT RUN 15 TO 50 SER.#'d SETS

CM Cheryl Miller	12.50	30.00
SL Spike Lee/32	100.00	200.00
SS Summer Sanders	20.00	50.00

2003-04 SP Signature Edition Famous Nicknames

Randomly seeded in packs, this 30-card set places player photos on the left side of the card and autographs on the right along with a caption stating the player's nickname. Several players have more than one version and others signed to specific amounts listed in our checklist whereas everone else signed to 25.
PRINT RUN 25 TO 100 SER.#'d SETS

AS Amare Stoudemire/25	75.00	150.00
BB Brent Barry/25	25.00	60.00
CA Carmelo Anthony/25	200.00	400.00
CB Chauncey Billups/25	25.00	60.00
CM Cuttino Mobley/25	25.00	60.00
DM Desmond Mason/25	25.00	60.00
DR Dennis Rodman/100	150.00	300.00
EG Manu Ginobili/25	125.00	225.00
GA Gilbert Arenas/25	50.00	120.00
GG George Gervin/25	40.00	100.00
GP Gary Payton/25	50.00	120.00
GR Glenn Robinson/25	25.00	60.00
JE Julius Erving/25	100.00	225.00
JR Jason Richardson/25	25.00	60.00
KG1 Kevin Garnett/25	125.00	250.00
KG2 Kevin Garnett/25	125.00	250.00
LJ1 L.James King/25	750.00	1500.00
LJ2 L.James Bron/25	750.00	1500.00
LJ3 L.James Chosen/25	750.00	1500.00
LO Lamar Odom/25	25.00	60.00
MB Mike Bibby/25	40.00	100.00
NH Nene/25	25.00	60.00
PP Paul Pierce/25	150.00	400.00
RH Richard Hamilton/25	25.00	60.00
RO David Robinson/100	100.00	200.00
SF Steve Francis/25	40.00	100.00
SL Spike Lee/25	150.00	300.00
SM Shawn Marion/25	40.00	100.00
TM Tracy McGrady/25	100.00	200.00
YM Yao Ming/25	100.00	200.00

2003-04 SP Signature Edition INKcredible INKscriptions

Randomly inserted, this 13-card set features a full-color player photo on the left and an authentic autograph with a special caption on the right. Several players have more than one version, and each card is sequentially numbered to 25.
PRINT RUN 25 SER.#'d SETS

BW Bill Walton	20.00	50.00
CA Carmelo Anthony	150.00	300.00
DM Darko Milicic	15.00	40.00
GG George Gervin	40.00	100.00
GP Gary Payton	30.00	80.00
JE Julius Erving	75.00	200.00
JK Jason Kidd	50.00	120.00
JR1 Jason Richardson	20.00	50.00
JR2 Jason Richardson	20.00	50.00
KG Kevin Garnett	75.00	200.00
LJ LeBron James	700.00	1200.00
PS Peja Stojakovic	40.00	100.00

2003-04 SP Signature Edition Marquee Marks

Inserted in packs, this nine card set pairs two players from a team, one in the upper left corner and the other in the lower right where they signed next to their picture. Each card is sequentially numbered to 100 unless specified in our checklist.
PRINT RUN 100 SER.#'d SETS

AN C.Anthony/Nene/75	25.00	60.00
BP K.Bryant/G.Payton/100	125.00	250.00
DD Dunleavy Sr./Dunleavy Jr./100	12.00	30.00
JM0 L.James/D.Miles/100	150.00	300.00
JS Magic/J.Stockton/75	150.00	300.00
LM Spike Lee/R.Miller/25	250.00	500.00
MM C.Miller/R.Miller/100	75.00	150.00
MS C.Miller/S.Sanders/100	15.00	40.00
WW B.Walton/L.Walton/100	12.00	30.00

2003-04 SP Signature Edition National Treasures

This six-card set pairs players who hail from the same country. Small head-shots appear of each player, one on the top and the other on the bottom and both autographs appear in the middle of the card. Each card is sequentially numbered to 100.
PRINT RUN 100 SER.#'d SETS

NT1 L.Barbosa/Nene	12.50	30.00
NT2 Z.Cabarkapa/P.Stojakovic	12.50	30.00
NT3 M.Pietrus/B.Diaw	12.50	30.00
NT4 Y.Ming/W.Zhi Zhi	100.00	200.00
NT5 T.Parker/M.Pietrus	20.00	50.00
NT6 Planinic/Milicic	12.50	30.00

2003-04 SP Signature Edition Rookie INKorporated

Randomly inserted in packs, this 28-card set showcases this year's rookies with a small photo in the lower left hand corner and an autograph on the right. Each card is sequentially numbered to 100.
PRINT RUN 100 SER.#'d SETS

AP Aleksandar Pavlovic	4.00	10.00
BC Brian Cook	3.00	8.00
BD Boris Diaw	5.00	12.00
CA Carmelo Anthony	50.00	120.00
CB Chris Bosh	25.00	60.00
CK Chris Kaman	5.00	12.00
DJ Dahntay Jones	4.00	10.00
DM Darko Milicic	4.00	10.00
DY Dwyane Wade	125.00	250.00
HO Josh Howard	5.00	12.00
JH Jarvis Hayes	3.00	8.00
JK Jason Kapono	3.00	8.00
KP Kendrick Perkins	4.00	10.00
LB Leandro Barbosa	5.00	12.00
LJ LeBron James	500.00	800.00
LR Luke Ridnour	4.00	10.00
LW Luke Walton	5.00	12.00
MB Marcus Banks	3.00	8.00
ML Maciej Lampe	3.00	8.00
MP Mickael Pietrus	4.00	10.00
MS Mike Sweetney	3.00	8.00
NE Ndudi Ebi	3.00	8.00
RG Reece Gaines	3.00	8.00
TB Troy Bell	3.00	8.00
TO Travis Outlaw	4.00	10.00
WE David West	5.00	12.00
ZC Zarko Cabarkapa	3.00	8.00
ZP Zoran Planinic	3.00	8.00

2003-04 SP Signature Edition Scripts for Success

Randomly inserted in packs, this 28-card set features a horizontal design where full-color player action photos appear on the right and an authentic player autograph appears on the left. Each card is sequentially numbered to 250.
PRINT RUN 250 SER.#'d SETS

AP Aleksandar Pavlovic	3.00	8.00
BC Brian Cook	2.50	6.00
BD Boris Diaw	4.00	10.00
CB Chris Bosh	15.00	40.00
CK Chris Kaman	4.00	10.00
DJ Dahntay Jones	3.00	8.00
DM Darko Milicic	3.00	8.00
DY Dwyane Wade	50.00	125.00
HO Josh Howard	4.00	10.00
JH Jarvis Hayes	2.50	6.00
JK Jason Kapono	2.50	6.00
KP Kendrick Perkins	3.00	8.00
LB Leandro Barbosa	4.00	10.00
LR Luke Ridnour	3.00	8.00
LW Luke Walton	4.00	10.00
MB Marcus Banks	2.50	6.00
ML Maciej Lampe	2.50	6.00
MP Mickael Pietrus	3.00	8.00
MS Mike Sweetney	2.50	6.00
MW Maurice Williams	4.00	10.00
NE Ndudi Ebi	2.50	6.00
RG Reece Gaines	2.50	6.00
TB Troy Bell	2.50	6.00
TO Travis Outlaw	3.00	8.00
WE David West	4.00	10.00
ZA Zaur Pachulia	4.00	10.00
ZC Zarko Cabarkapa	2.50	6.00
ZP Zoran Planinic	2.50	6.00

2003-04 SP Signature Edition Signatures

Randomly seeded in packs at the rate of one in one along with the sets mentioned in the main set blurb, this 77-card set places player busts (from the waist up) on the left side of the card and authentic autographs on the right. Each card is highlighted with silver foil.
STATED ODDS FOR ANY AUTOGRAPH 1:1

AJ Antawn Jamison	4.00	10.00
AM Antonio McDyess SP	5.00	12.00
AP Aleksandar Pavlovic	2.50	6.00
BA Marcus Banks	2.00	5.00
BD Boris Diaw	3.00	8.00
BO Carlos Boozer	3.00	8.00
CA Carmelo Anthony SP	40.00	80.00
CB Chauncey Billups	3.00	8.00
CH Chris Bosh	8.00	20.00
CK Chris Kaman	3.00	8.00
CM Corey Maggette	3.00	8.00
CW Chris Wilcox	3.00	8.00
DA Darius Miles SP	5.00	12.00
DG Drew Gooden	3.00	8.00
DJ Dahntay Jones	2.50	6.00
DM Darko Milicic	2.50	6.00
DR Dennis Rodman SP	40.00	80.00
DU Mike Dunleavy Sr.	5.00	12.00
DY Dwyane Wade	40.00	100.00
EG Manu Ginobili	15.00	40.00
GA Gilbert Arenas	2.50	6.00
GG George Gervin	8.00	20.00
GP Gary Payton SP	8.00	20.00
HW Josh Howard	3.00	8.00
JD Juan Dixon	3.00	8.00
JE Julius Erving SP	30.00	80.00
JH Jarvis Hayes	2.00	5.00
JK Jason Kidd	8.00	20.00
JL James Lang	2.00	5.00
JR Jason Richardson	6.00	15.00
JS Jerry Stackhouse	6.00	15.00
KB Kobe Bryant	100.00	200.00
KG Kevin Garnett	25.00	60.00
KO Jason Kapono	2.00	5.00
KP Kendrick Perkins	10.00	25.00
LB Larry Bird SP	75.00	150.00
LE Leandro Barbosa	3.00	8.00
LJ LeBron James	1500.00	2000.00
LO Lamar Odom SP	6.00	15.00
LR Luke Ridnour	2.50	6.00
LW Luke Walton	3.00	8.00
MA Magic Johnson SP	60.00	150.00
MB Mike Bibby	6.00	15.00
MD Mike Dunleavy	5.00	12.00
MI Andre Miller	3.00	8.00
MJ Michael Jordan	400.00	700.00
MK Mickael Pietrus	2.50	6.00
ML Maciej Lampe	2.00	5.00
MP Morris Peterson	3.00	8.00
MS Mike Sweetney SP	2.00	5.00
MW Maurice Williams	3.00	8.00
NE Ndudi Ebi	2.00	5.00
NH Nene	3.00	8.00
PE Patrick Ewing	125.00	225.00
PP Paul Pierce	15.00	30.00
PS Peja Stojakovic	6.00	15.00
RG Reece Gaines	2.00	5.00
RH Richard Hamilton	6.00	15.00
RJ Richard Jefferson	3.00	8.00
RL Rashard Lewis SP	6.00	15.00
RM Reggie Miller	50.00	125.00
RO Jalen Rose	6.00	15.00
SA Shareef Abdur-Rahim SP	6.00	15.00
SF Steve Francis	6.00	15.00
SM Shawn Marion SP	6.00	15.00
ST John Stockton SP	50.00	120.00
TB Troy Bell	2.00	5.00
TM Tracy McGrady	12.50	30.00
TO Travis Outlaw	2.50	6.00
TP Tony Parker	10.00	25.00
WA Bill Walton SP	12.50	30.00
WE David West	3.00	8.00
WG Dajuan Wagner SP	3.00	8.00
WZ Wang Zhizhi SP	6.00	15.00
YM Yao Ming	15.00	40.00
ZC Zarko Cabarkapa	2.00	5.00
ZP Zoran Planinic	2.00	5.00

2003-04 SP Signature Edition Signatures Gold

*GOLD SINGLES: .75X TO 2X BASE AU HI
GOLD PRINT RUN 50 SER.#'d SETS

CA Carmelo Anthony	100.00	200.00
CH Chris Bosh	40.00	100.00
DM Darko Milicic	5.00	12.00
DR Dennis Rodman	100.00	200.00
DY Dwyane Wade	150.00	300.00
GP Gary Payton	12.00	30.00
LB Larry Bird	80.00	200.00
MA Magic Johnson	100.00	200.00
MJ Michael Jordan	600.00	1000.00
PE Patrick Ewing	200.00	400.00
RM Reggie Miller	250.00	500.00
WA Bill Walton	15.00	40.00
YM Yao Ming	60.00	150.00

2003-04 SP Signature Edition Signatures Triple

Randomly seeded in packs, this 10-card set lines up three player photos and autographs, from top to bottom, and cards are sequentially numbered to 25.
PRINT RUN 25 SER.#'d SETS

BPG Kobe/Payton/KG	250.00	500.00
BSW Bibby/Peja/Wallace	100.00	200.00
JJM LeBron/MJ/McGrady	1000.00	2000.00
JMA LeBron/Darko/Carmelo	600.00	1000.00
KJP Kidd/Jefferson/Zoran	75.00	150.00
MGG McGrady/Gaines/Gooden	75.00	150.00
MGJ McGrady/KG/LeBron	400.00	800.00
MHB Darko/Hamilton/Billups	75.00	150.00
MJM A.Miller/Rose/R.Miller	200.00	500.00
RJP J-Rich/Jamison/Pietrus	30.00	80.00

2003-04 SP Signature Edition Tins

COMPLETE SET	6.00	15.00
*BLACK TINS: .6X TO 1.5X BASE HI		
NNO Tracy McGrady	.40	1.00
NNO Kobe Bryant	1.25	3.00
NNO Darko Milicic	.25	.60
NNO LeBron James	3.00	8.00
NNO Carmelo Anthony	1.00	2.50
NNO Michael Jordan	2.50	6.00

2004-05 SP Signature Edition

Released in June 2005, SP Signature Edition is made up of a 242-card set where cards 1-100 feature veteran players, 101-142 feature rookie jersey sequentially numbered to 499 and cards 143-242 are serially numbered to the featured player's jersey number. SP Signature was sold in three card tins and the SRP was $60.
101-142 PRINT RUN 499 SER.#'d SETS
143-242 #'d TO PLAYER JSY NUMBER

1 Antoine Walker	.60	1.50
2 Al Harrington	.50	1.25
3 Boris Diaw	.50	1.25
4 Paul Pierce	.60	1.50
5 Ricky Davis	.50	1.25
6 Gary Payton	.60	1.50
7 Gerald Wallace	.50	1.25
8 Emeka Okafor RC	1.50	4.00
9 Jahidi White	.40	1.00
10 Eddy Curry	.40	1.00
11 Kirk Hinrich	.50	1.25
12 Michael Jordan	5.00	12.00
13 LeBron James	4.00	10.00
14 Dajuan Wagner	.40	1.00
15 Jeff McInnis	.40	1.00
16 Drew Gooden	.40	1.00
17 Dirk Nowitzki	1.00	2.50
18 Michael Finley	.60	1.50
19 Jerry Stackhouse	.50	1.25
20 Jason Terry	.50	1.25
21 Kenyon Martin	.50	1.25
22 Andre Miller	.50	1.25
23 Carmelo Anthony	1.25	3.00
24 Nene	.50	1.25
25 Chauncey Billups	.60	1.50
26 Rasheed Wallace	.60	1.50
27 Ben Wallace	.50	1.25
28 Richard Hamilton	.50	1.25
29 Derek Fisher	.50	1.25
30 Jason Richardson	.60	1.50
31 Mike Dunleavy	.50	1.25
32 Yao Ming	1.25	3.00
33 Tracy McGrady	.75	2.00
34 Juwan Howard	.50	1.25
35 Jermaine O'Neal	.50	1.25
36 Reggie Miller	.60	1.50
37 Ron Artest	.60	1.50
38 Jamaal Tinsley	.40	1.00
39 Elton Brand	.60	1.50
40 Corey Maggette	.50	1.25
41 Marko Jaric	.40	1.00
42 Kerry Kittles	.40	1.00
43 Kobe Bryant	2.50	6.00
44 Chucky Atkins	.40	1.00
45 Lamar Odom	.50	1.25
46 Caron Butler	.50	1.25
47 Pau Gasol	.60	1.50
48 Jason Williams	.50	1.25
49 Bonzi Wells	.40	1.00
50 Shaquille O'Neal	1.50	4.00
51 Dwyane Wade	1.00	2.50
52 Eddie Jones	.50	1.25
53 Michael Redd	.50	1.25
54 Desmond Mason	.50	1.25
55 T.J. Ford	.40	1.00
56 Latrell Sprewell	.50	1.25
57 Kevin Garnett	1.00	2.50
58 Sam Cassell	.50	1.25
59 Troy Hudson	.40	1.00
60 Vince Carter	1.00	2.50
61 Richard Jefferson	.50	1.25
62 Jason Kidd	1.00	2.50
63 Lee Nailon	.40	1.00
64 Baron Davis	.50	1.25
65 Jamaal Magloire	.40	1.00
66 Allan Houston	.50	1.25
67 Jamal Crawford	.60	1.50
68 Stephon Marbury	.50	1.25
69 Grant Hill	.75	2.00
70 Cuttino Mobley	.40	1.00
71 Steve Francis	.50	1.25
72 Glenn Robinson	.50	1.25
73 Allen Iverson	1.00	2.50
74 Kyle Korver	.50	1.25
75 Amare Stoudemire	.50	1.25
76 Steve Nash	.75	2.00
77 Quentin Richardson	.50	1.25
78 Shawn Marion	.50	1.25
79 Shareef Abdur-Rahim	.50	1.25
80 Damon Stoudamire	.50	1.25
81 Zach Randolph	.50	1.25
82 Darius Miles	.40	1.00
83 Peja Stojakovic	.60	1.50
84 Chris Webber	.60	1.50
85 Mike Bibby	.60	1.50
86 Tony Parker	.60	1.50
87 Tim Duncan	1.00	2.50
88 Manu Ginobili	.75	2.00
89 Ronald Murray	.40	1.00
90 Ray Allen	.60	1.50
91 Rashard Lewis	.60	1.50
92 Chris Bosh	.60	1.50
93 Jalen Rose	.50	1.25
94 Rafer Alston	.40	1.00
95 Andrei Kirilenko	.50	1.25
96 Matt Harpring	.40	1.00
97 Carlos Boozer	.50	1.25
98 Gilbert Arenas	.50	1.25
99 Jarvis Hayes	.40	1.00
100 Antawn Jamison	.50	1.25
101 Dwight Howard JSY RC	6.00	15.00
102 Ben Gordon JSY RC	3.00	8.00
103 Shaun Livingston JSY RC	3.00	8.00
104 Devin Harris JSY RC	2.50	6.00
105 Josh Childress JSY RC	2.50	6.00
106 Luol Deng JSY RC	3.00	8.00
107 Rafael Araujo JSY RC	2.00	5.00
108 Andre Iguodala JSY RC	4.00	10.00
109 Luke Jackson JSY RC	2.00	5.00
110 Sebastian Telfair JSY RC	2.50	6.00
111 Kris Humphries JSY RC	3.00	8.00
112 Al Jefferson JSY RC	4.00	10.00
113 Kirk Snyder JSY RC	2.00	5.00
114 Josh Smith JSY RC	3.00	8.00
115 J.R. Smith JSY RC	3.00	8.00
116 Dorell Wright JSY RC	3.00	8.00
117 Jameer Nelson JSY RC	3.00	8.00
118 Delonte West JSY RC	3.00	8.00
119 Tony Allen JSY RC	3.00	8.00
120 Kevin Martin JSY RC	4.00	10.00
121 David Harrison JSY RC	2.00	5.00
122 Anderson Varejao JSY RC	2.50	6.00
123 Jackson Vroman JSY RC	2.00	5.00
124 Lionel Chalmers JSY RC	3.00	8.00
125 Andre Emmett JSY RC	2.00	5.00
126 Chris Duhon JSY RC	3.00	8.00
127 Bernard Robinson JSY RC	2.50	6.00
128 Tim Pickett RC	2.00	5.00
129 Nenad Krstic JSY RC	3.00	8.00
130 Andris Biedrins JSY RC	2.00	5.00
131 Robert Swift RC	1.25	3.00
132 Andres Nocioni RC	2.00	5.00
133 Justin Reed RC	1.25	3.00
134 Romain Sato RC	1.25	3.00
135 Sasha Vujacic JSY RC	3.00	8.00
136 Beno Udrih RC	1.50	4.00
137 Peter John Ramos JSY RC	2.00	5.00
138 Donta Smith JSY RC	2.00	5.00
139 Antonio Burks RC	1.50	4.00
140 Yuta Tabuse JSY RC	3.00	8.00
141 Trevor Ariza JSY RC	3.00	8.00
142 Matt Freije JSY RC	2.50	6.00
143 Drew Gooden/90	4.00	10.00
144 Elton Brand/42	4.00	10.00
145 Shawn Marion/31	6.00	15.00
148 Dirk Nowitzki/41	6.00	15.00
149 Pau Gasol/16	6.00	15.00
152 Devin Harris/34	6.00	15.00
165 Shaquille O'Neal/32	12.50	30.00
166 Shareef Abdur-Rahim/33	4.00	10.00
167 Jason Terry/31	4.00	10.00
171 Zach Randolph/50	5.00	12.00
172 Dave DeBusschere/22	10.00	25.00
176 Gary Payton/20	8.00	20.00
180 Michael Redd/22	4.00	10.00
181 Peja Stojakovic/16	8.00	20.00
183 Luke Jackson/33	4.00	10.00
184 Richard Hamilton/32	6.00	15.00
185 Kevin Garnett/21	12.00	30.00
188 Sebastian Telfair/31	4.00	10.00
191 David Robinson/50	10.00	25.00
192 Jerry Stackhouse/42	4.00	10.00
193 Kris Humphries/43	4.00	10.00
194 Dennis Rodman/91	6.00	15.00
199 Michael Jordan/23	75.00	150.00
200 Magic Johnson/32	15.00	40.00
207 George Gervin/44	6.00	15.00
212 Bernard King/30	4.00	10.00
214 Grant Hill/33	8.00	20.00
215 J.R. Smith/23	8.00	20.00
216 LeBron James/23	25.00	60.00
218 Amare Stoudemire/32	8.00	20.00
221 Larry Bird/33	15.00	40.00
222 Reggie Miller/31	12.00	30.00
224 Andrei Kirilenko/47	6.00	15.00
228 Corey Maggette/50	4.00	10.00
233 Hakeem Olajuwon/34	6.00	15.00
234 Richard Jefferson/24	4.00	10.00
235 Tim Duncan/21	12.00	30.00
236 Ray Allen/34	10.00	25.00
238 Paul Pierce/34	8.00	20.00
240 Willis Reed/19	5.00	12.00
242 Manu Ginobili/20	6.00	15.00

2004-05 SP Signature Edition 25

PRINT RUN 25 SER.#'d SETS
MOST RC PLAYERS ARE AUTOGRAPHED
SOME NOT PRICED DUE TO SCARCITY

12 Michael Jordan	75.00	150.00
69 Grant Hill	12.00	30.00
101 Dwight Howard JSY AU	175.00	350.00
102 Ben Gordon JSY AU	20.00	50.00
104 Devin Harris JSY AU	20.00	50.00
108 Andre Iguodala JSY AU	40.00	100.00
112 Al Jefferson JSY AU	40.00	100.00
114 Josh Smith JSY AU	20.00	50.00
117 Jameer Nelson JSY AU	10.00	25.00
118 Delonte West JSY AU	10.00	25.00
119 Tony Allen JSY AU	10.00	25.00
122 Anderson Varejao JSY AU	8.00	20.00
126 Chris Duhon JSY AU	10.00	25.00
129 Nenad Krstic JSY AU	10.00	25.00
130 Andris Biedrins JSY AU	6.00	15.00
141 Trevor Ariza JSY AU	10.00	25.00

2004-05 SP Signature Edition Autographed Parallel

CARDS #'d TO PLAYER JSY NUMBER
CARDS WITH ASTERISK ISSUED AS EXCH

A4 Paul Pierce/34*	20.00	50.00
A6 Gary Payton/20	25.00	60.00
A12 Michael Jordan/23*	300.00	600.00
A13 LeBron James/23	400.00	800.00
A19 Jerry Stackhouse/42	15.00	40.00
A22 Andre Miller/24	12.00	30.00
A23 Carmelo Anthony/15	50.00	120.00
A28 Richard Hamilton/32	15.00	40.00
A30 Jason Richardson/23	12.00	30.00
A36 Reggie Miller/31	50.00	120.00
A40 Corey Maggette/50	12.00	30.00
A47 Pau Gasol/16	25.00	60.00
A53 Michael Redd/22	12.00	30.00
A57 Kevin Garnett/21	75.00	200.00
A65 Jamaal Magloire/21	12.00	30.00
A75 Amare Stoudemire/32	25.00	60.00
A78 Shawn Marion/31	15.00	40.00
A79 Shareef Abdur-Rahim/33	15.00	40.00
A81 Zach Randolph/50	12.00	30.00
A95 Andrei Kirilenko/47	15.00	40.00

2004-05 SP Signature Edition AKA Autographs

Limited to either 50 or 100 copies, this 49-card set is horizontally designed and features both an autograph and a nickname inscription.
PRINT RUNS LISTED IN CHECKLIST

AL A.Jefferson Big Al/100	12.00	30.00
AM A.McDyess/100	10.00	25.00
AR R.Araujo Hoffa/100	6.00	15.00
AS A.Stoudemire Future/50	15.00	40.00
BC Bob Cousy Cooz/50	20.00	50.00
BG B.Gordon M.S.G./50	12.00	30.00
BW B.Wallace Big Ben/50	40.00	80.00
CA C.Arroyo New Maestro/100	25.00	60.00
CD C.Drexler The Glide/50	60.00	150.00
CH C.Duhon C-Doo/100	10.00	25.00
DF Derek Fisher Fish/100	15.00	40.00
DG Drew Gooden Truth/100	10.00	25.00
DH D.Howard DeBo/100	12.00	30.00
DR D.Rodman The Worm/50	60.00	120.00
DS D.Stoud ROY 96/100	12.00	30.00
DW Delonte West Redz/100	10.00	25.00
EC Eddy Curry ECity/100	10.00	25.00
GP Gary Payton	10.00	25.00
GW Gerald Wallace	10.00	25.00
HO H.Olajuwon The Dream/50	75.00	150.00
JA Jason Williams JW/100	50.00	120.00
JC J.Childress Real Deal/50	15.00	40.00
JM J.Magloire Big Cat/100	10.00	25.00
JS Josh Smith JSmoove/100	10.00	25.00
JV J.Vroman Jax/100	6.00	15.00
JW John Wooden	75.00	150.00
KA Kenny Anderson	10.00	25.00
KE Kv.Martin K-Mart/100	6.00	15.00
KG Kevin Garnett KG/100	50.00	125.00
KH K.Hinrich Capt. Kirk/50	25.00	60.00
LJ LeBron James Bron/100	150.00	300.00
LO Lamar Odom/50	15.00	40.00
MB Mike Bibby	25.00	60.00
MR Michael Redd Silky/50	15.00	40.00
PP Paul Pierce Truth/50	100.00	200.00
RH R.Hamilton RIP/50	25.00	60.00
RM R.Murray Flip/100	10.00	25.00
RT R.Traylor Tractor/100	10.00	25.00
RY Ray Allen	20.00	50.00
SA S.Abdur-Rahim Reef/50	15.00	40.00
SE S.Telfair Bassy/50	15.00	40.00
SM Shawn Marion Matrix/50	8.00	20.00
ST Stephon Marbury	20.00	50.00
TK1 Kukoc Croat. Sensation/100	25.00	60.00
TK2 Kukoc Pink Panther/100	20.00	50.00
TM Tracy McGrady T-Mac/50	40.00	80.00
AU S.Augmon Plastic Man/100	6.00	15.00

2004-05 SP Signature Edition Alumni Associates

Inserted in packs randomly, this 11-card set places two players who attended the same college along with their autographs. Each card is sequentially numbered to 100.
PRINT RUN 100 SER.#'d SETS

AB G.Arenas/M.Bibby	15.00	40.00
BD C.Boozer/C.Duhon	15.00	40.00
CS L.Chalmers/R.Sato	10.00	25.00
DA B.Davis/T.Ariza	10.00	25.00
HG R.Hamilton/B.Gordon	15.00	40.00
JI R.Jefferson/A.Iguodala	15.00	40.00
JJ F.Jones/L.Jackson	10.00	25.00
KD K.Hinrich/D.Gooden	10.00	25.00
MD C.Maggette/L.Deng	15.00	40.00
NW J.Nelson/Del.West	15.00	30.00

2004-05 SP Signature Edition Celebrity Signings

No odds were given on the packs for this set, but the three cards are of celebrities and place a photo on the top of the card and an autograph on the bottom.
OVERALL AUTOGRAPH ODDS 1:1

CS7 Nelly	25.00	60.00
CS8 Jamie Foxx	25.00	60.00
CS9 Mark Cuban	40.00	100.00

2004-05 SP Signature Edition INKredible INKscriptions

Randomly seeded and sequentially numbered to 25, this 45-card set is horizontally designed with a player photo on the left and an autograph and an inscription on the right.
PRINT RUN 25 SER.#'d SETS

AK Andrei Kirilenko	15.00	40.00
AS Amare Stoudemire	30.00	80.00
BD B.Davis Bdiddy	30.00	80.00
BG B.Gordon 04 NCAA Champ	40.00	100.00
BG2 B.Gordon Draft Pick #3	40.00	100.00
BK Bob Knight	25.00	60.00
CA1 C.Anthony Final 4 MVP	60.00	150.00
CA2 Anthony 03 NCAA Champ	50.00	120.00
CA3 Carmelo Anthony Melo	60.00	150.00
CD Drexler Phi Slamma Jamma	100.00	200.00
CH C.Billups 04 Finals MVP	25.00	60.00
DE Devin Harris Big 10 POY	20.00	50.00
DE2 Devin Harris Draft Pick #5	20.00	50.00
DH D.Howard 04 Naismith AW	75.00	150.00
DH2 D.Howard Draft Pick #1	75.00	150.00
DH3 Dwight Howard	75.00	150.00
DR D.Robinson The Admiral	75.00	150.00
HO Olajuwon Phi Slamma Jamma	100.00	200.00
JA Jalen Rose Fab Five	20.00	50.00
JC J.Childress 04 Pac 10 POY	15.00	40.00
JE Julius Erving Dr. J	125.00	250.00
JH Josh Howard	15.00	40.00
JN J.Nelson John Wooden AW	15.00	40.00
JR J.R.Smith McDonald's MVP	30.00	80.00
JR2 J.R. Smith	20.00	50.00
KG Kevin Garnett 2004 MVP	200.00	400.00
KS Kirk Snyder 04 WAC POY	15.00	40.00
LJ1 LeBron James King James	600.00	900.00
LJ2 L.James 04 Naismith AW	600.00	900.00
LJ3 LeBron James 04 ROY	600.00	900.00
MA Magic Johnson	150.00	300.00
PS P.Stojakovic 3 Time All-Star	30.00	80.00
RA1 Araujo 04 Mount.West POY	15.00	40.00
RH R.Hamilton 04 NBA Champs	25.00	60.00
SL1 S.Livingston Draft Pick #4	15.00	40.00
SL2 Shaun Livingston Geezy	15.00	40.00
ST1 Telfair 3 Time PSAL Champ	15.00	40.00
TA1 Tony Allen 2004 Big 12 POY	15.00	40.00
TA2 Tony Allen	15.00	40.00
TM T.McGrady 5 Time All-Star	40.00	100.00
WI J.Williams White Chocolate	75.00	150.00

2004-05 SP Signature Edition Marks of Distinction

Randomly inserted and sequentially numbered to 25, this 30-card set places player photos towards the top and autographs on the bottom.
PRINT RUN 25 SER.#'d SETS

AK Andrei Kirilenko	10.00	25.00
BD Baron Davis	10.00	25.00
BK Bernard King	12.00	30.00
BR Bill Russell	125.00	300.00
BW Ben Wallace	20.00	50.00
CA Carmelo Anthony	40.00	100.00
CD Clyde Drexler	40.00	100.00
DH Dwight Howard	75.00	150.00
DR David Robinson	75.00	150.00
HO Hakeem Olajuwon	30.00	80.00
IT Isiah Thomas	25.00	60.00
JE Julius Erving	50.00	120.00
JK Jason Kidd	40.00	100.00
JR Jason Richardson	12.00	30.00
JS John Stockton	75.00	200.00
KB Kobe Bryant	125.00	250.00
KG Kevin Garnett	50.00	120.00
KH Kirk Hinrich	20.00	50.00
LB Larry Bird	100.00	200.00
LJ LeBron James	150.00	300.00
MA Magic Johnson	75.00	150.00
MJ Michael Jordan	350.00	600.00
PG Pau Gasol	8.00	20.00
PP Paul Pierce	15.00	40.00
PS Peja Stojakovic	15.00	40.00
RA Ray Allen	20.00	50.00
SM Stephon Marbury	15.00	40.00
TM Tracy McGrady	40.00	100.00
YM Yao Ming	40.00	100.00

2004-05 SP Signature Edition Marquee Marks

This seven card set was randomly seeded in packs and is horizontally designed with two great players from the same franchise along with their autographs. Each card is limited to 100 copies.
PRINT RUN 100 SER.#'d SETS

JB M.Johnson/K.Bryant	150.00	300.00
KR B.King/W.Reed	12.00	30.00
MM Y.Ming/T.McGrady	30.00	80.00
MT S.Marbury/S.Telfair	12.00	30.00
NL C.Neal/M.Lemon	50.00	100.00
SB P.Stojakovic/M.Bibby	15.00	40.00
SH J.R.Smith/D.Howard	40.00	100.00

2004-05 SP Signature Edition Pride of a Nation

Randomly inserted in packs, this five-card set places two players from the same nation along with their autographs and country flag on the card front. Each card is sequentially numbered to 100.
PRINT RUN 100 SER.#'d SETS

BV P.Brezec/S.Vujacic	10.00	25.00
KG T.Kukoc/G.Giricek	15.00	40.00
KK V.Khryapa/A.Kirilenko	10.00	25.00
KP A.Kirilenko/P.Podkolzin	10.00	25.00
VU S.Vujacic/B.Udrih	10.00	25.00

2004-05 SP Signature Edition Quadruple Authentic Signatures

Randomly inserted, this nine-card set features four players and four signatures on gold foil on the card front. Each card is sequentially numbered to 15.
PRINT RUN 15 SER.#'d SETS
SOME NOT PRICED DUE TO SCARCITY

BJJB Kobe/Magic/LeBron/Bird	500.00	800.00
CBPP Cousy/Bird/Pierce/Payton*	125.00	250.00
KSJM Kidd/Stcktn/Magic/Mrbry*	200.00	400.00
SMGK Peja/Yao/Gasol/Kirilenko	100.00	200.00
WOMR Wallace/Hakeem/Yao/D.Rob	200.00	350.00

2004-05 SP Signature Edition Rookie Auto Drafts

Limited to each specific player's draft position, this 44-card set is horizontally designed with a player photo on the left and the draft board and an authentic autograph on the right.
CARDS #'D TO DRAFT POSITION
MOST NOT PRICED DUE TO SCARCITY

AE Andre Emmett/35	4.00	10.00
AN Antonio Burks/36	5.00	12.00
AV Anderson Varejao/30	10.00	25.00
BR Bernard Robinson/45	5.00	12.00
BU Beno Udrih/28	15.00	40.00
CD Chris Duhon/38	10.00	25.00
DA David Harrison/29	4.00	10.00
DW Dorell Wright/19	20.00	50.00
JN Jameer Nelson/20	10.00	25.00
JR J.R. Smith/18	25.00	60.00
JS Josh Smith/17	25.00	60.00
JU Justin Reed/40	4.00	10.00
KM Kevin Martin/26	8.00	20.00
KS Kirk Snyder/16	4.00	10.00
LC Lionel Chalmers/33	6.00	15.00
LF Luis Flores/55	5.00	12.00
MF Matt Freije/53	5.00	12.00
NK Nenad Krstic/24	6.00	15.00
PP Pavel Podkolzin/21	4.00	10.00
PR Peter John Ramos/32	4.00	10.00
PS Pape Sow/47	5.00	12.00
RI Royal Ivey/37	5.00	12.00
RO Romain Sato/52	4.00	10.00
SV Sasha Vujacic/27	6.00	15.00
TP Tim Pickett/44	6.00	15.00
TR Trevor Ariza/43	6.00	15.00
WE Delonte West/24	6.00	15.00

2004-05 SP Signature Edition Rookie GRAPHiti

Randomly seeded in packs, this 40-card set is horizontally designed with a player photo and an autograph in the foreground and a graphiti style background. Each card is serially numbered to 200.
PRINT RUN 200 SER.#'d SETS

AB Andris Biedrins	2.50	6.00
AE Andre Emmett	2.50	6.00
AI Andre Iguodala	5.00	12.00
AJ Al Jefferson	5.00	12.00
AN Andres Nocioni	4.00	10.00
AV Anderson Varejao	3.00	8.00
BG Ben Gordon	4.00	10.00
BR Bernard Robinson	3.00	8.00
BU Beno Udrih	3.00	8.00
CD Chris Duhon	4.00	10.00
DA David Harrison	2.50	6.00
DE Devin Harris	3.00	8.00
DH Dwight Howard	12.00	30.00
DW Dorell Wright	4.00	10.00
JC Josh Childress	3.00	8.00
JN Jameer Nelson	4.00	10.00
JR J.R. Smith	4.00	10.00
JS Josh Smith	4.00	10.00
JU Justin Reed	2.50	6.00
JV Jackson Vroman	2.50	6.00
KH Kris Humphries	4.00	10.00
KM Kevin Martin	5.00	12.00
KS Kirk Snyder	2.50	6.00
LC Lionel Chalmers	4.00	10.00
LD Luol Deng	4.00	10.00
LF Luis Flores	3.00	8.00
LJ Luke Jackson	2.50	6.00
MF Matt Freije	3.00	8.00
NK Nenad Krstic	4.00	10.00
PR Peter John Ramos	2.50	6.00
RA Rafael Araujo	2.50	6.00
RS Robert Swift	2.50	6.00
SL Shaun Livingston	4.00	10.00
ST Sebastian Telfair	3.00	8.00
SV Sasha Vujacic	4.00	10.00
TA Tony Allen	4.00	10.00
TP Tim Pickett	4.00	10.00
TR Trevor Ariza	4.00	10.00
WE Delonte West	4.00	10.00
YT Yuta Tabuse	4.00	10.00

2004-05 SP Signature Edition Rookies INKorporated

Limited to 100 serially numbered copies, this 40-card set places rookie photos on the left and has a white-out box on the right for autographs.
PRINT RUN 100 SER.#'d SET

AB Andris Biedrins	3.00	8.00
AE Andre Emmett	3.00	8.00
AI Andre Iguodala	6.00	15.00
AJ Al Jefferson	6.00	15.00
AN Andres Nocioni	5.00	12.00
AV Anderson Varejao	4.00	10.00
BG Ben Gordon	5.00	12.00
BR Bernard Robinson	4.00	10.00
BU Beno Udrih	4.00	10.00
CD Chris Duhon	5.00	12.00
DA David Harrison	3.00	8.00
DE Devin Harris	4.00	10.00
DH Dwight Howard	40.00	80.00
DW Dorell Wright	5.00	12.00
JC Josh Childress	4.00	10.00
JN Jameer Nelson	5.00	12.00
JR J.R. Smith	5.00	12.00
JS Josh Smith	5.00	12.00
JV Jackson Vroman	3.00	8.00
KH Kris Humphries	5.00	12.00
KM Kevin Martin	6.00	15.00
KS Kirk Snyder	3.00	8.00
LC Lionel Chalmers	5.00	12.00
LD Luol Deng	5.00	12.00
LF Luis Flores	4.00	10.00
LJ Luke Jackson	3.00	8.00
MF Matt Freije	4.00	10.00
NK Nenad Krstic	5.00	12.00
PR Peter John Ramos	3.00	8.00
RA Rafael Araujo	3.00	8.00
RS Robert Swift	3.00	8.00
SL Shaun Livingston	5.00	12.00
ST Sebastian Telfair	4.00	10.00
SV Sasha Vujacic	5.00	12.00
TA Tony Allen	5.00	12.00
TP Tim Pickett	5.00	12.00
TR Trevor Ariza	5.00	12.00
WE Delonte West	5.00	12.00
YT Yuta Tabuse	5.00	12.00

2004-05 SP Signature Edition Scripts for Success

Seeded in packs randomly and limited to 25 copies, this 40-card set is horizontally designed, has a colored border along the bottom and a player photo and autograph set to a white background on the top.
PRINT RUN 25 SER.#'d SETS

AB Andris Biedrins	5.00	12.00
AE Andre Emmett	5.00	12.00
AI Andre Iguodala	10.00	25.00
AJ Al Jefferson	10.00	25.00
BG Ben Gordon	8.00	20.00
BR Bernard Robinson	6.00	15.00
BU Beno Udrih	6.00	15.00
CD Chris Duhon	8.00	20.00
DA David Harrison	5.00	12.00
DE Devin Harris	6.00	15.00
DH Dwight Howard	40.00	100.00
DW Dorell Wright	8.00	20.00
JN Jameer Nelson	8.00	20.00
JR J.R. Smith	8.00	20.00
JS Josh Smith	8.00	20.00
JV Jackson Vroman	5.00	12.00
KH Kris Humphries	8.00	20.00
KM Kevin Martin	10.00	25.00
KS Kirk Snyder	5.00	12.00
LD Luol Deng	8.00	20.00
MF Matt Freije	6.00	15.00
NK Nenad Krstic	8.00	20.00
PR Peter John Ramos	5.00	12.00
RA Rafael Araujo	5.00	12.00
RS Robert Swift	5.00	12.00
SL Shaun Livingston	8.00	20.00
ST Sebastian Telfair	6.00	15.00
SV Sasha Vujacic	8.00	20.00
TA Tony Allen	8.00	20.00
TP Tim Pickett	8.00	20.00
TR Trevor Ariza	8.00	20.00
WE Delonte West	8.00	20.00
YT Yuta Tabuse	8.00	20.00

2004-05 SP Signature Edition Signatures

Inserted at the overall odds of one per pack along with all other autographs, this 99-card set is horizontally designed with a player photo on the left and autographed gold foil on the right. A gold parallel was also inserted and those cards are sequentially numbered to ten.
OVERALL AUTOGRAPH ODDS 1:1

AB Andris Biedrins	2.00	5.00
AE Andre Emmett	2.00	5.00
AH Al Harrington	2.50	6.00
AI Andre Iguodala	10.00	25.00
AJ Al Jefferson	4.00	10.00
AK Andrei Kirilenko	6.00	15.00
AL Ray Allen	10.00	25.00
AN Antawn Jamison	6.00	15.00
AR Carlos Arroyo	6.00	15.00
AS Amare Stoudemire	5.00	12.00
AV Anderson Varejao	2.50	6.00
BC Bob Cousy	20.00	50.00
BD Baron Davis	5.00	12.00
BE Beno Udrih	2.50	6.00
BG Ben Gordon	5.00	12.00
BK Bernard King	6.00	15.00
BM Brad Miller	3.00	8.00
BO Carlos Boozer	4.00	10.00
BR Bill Russell SP	75.00	150.00
BU Antonio Burks	2.50	6.00
BW Ben Wallace	10.00	25.00
CA Carmelo Anthony SP	20.00	50.00
CD Chris Duhon	3.00	8.00
CL Clyde Drexler	15.00	40.00
CM Corey Maggette	3.00	8.00
CR Jamal Crawford SP	8.00	20.00
DA David Harrison	2.00	5.00
DE Dennis Rodman	50.00	100.00
DF Derek Fisher	6.00	15.00
DH Dwight Howard	15.00	40.00
DM Desmond Mason	3.00	8.00
DR David Robinson SP	30.00	80.00
DS Donta Smith	2.00	5.00
GG George Gervin	8.00	20.00
HA Devin Harris	2.50	6.00
IT Isiah Thomas SP	12.00	30.00
IV Royal Ivey	2.50	6.00
JA Jason Richardson	5.00	12.00
JE Julius Erving SP	40.00	100.00
JH Josh Howard	4.00	10.00
JK Jason Kidd SP	12.00	30.00
JN Jameer Nelson	3.00	8.00
JR J.R. Smith	3.00	8.00
JV Jackson Vroman	2.00	5.00
KB Kobe Bryant SP	80.00	160.00
KG Kevin Garnett SP	25.00	60.00
KH Kris Humphries	3.00	8.00
KI Kirk Hinrich	2.50	6.00
KM Kevin Martin	4.00	10.00
KR Kareem Rush	3.00	8.00
KS Kirk Snyder	2.00	5.00
LB Larry Bird SP	50.00	120.00
LC Lionel Chalmers	3.00	8.00
LD Luol Deng	3.00	8.00
LF Luis Flores	2.50	6.00
LJ LeBron James	200.00	400.00
LO Lamar Odom SP	20.00	50.00

LU Luke Jackson 2.00 5.00
MB Mike Bibby SP 5.00 12.00
MD Marquis Daniels 3.00 8.00
MJ Michael Jordan SP 500.00 800.00
MR Michael Redd 5.00 12.00
NK Nenad Krstic 3.00 8.00
NO Andres Nocioni 3.00 8.00
PG Pau Gasol 8.00 20.00
PP Paul Pierce SP 25.00 60.00
PR Peter John Ramos 2.00 5.00
RA Rafael Araujo 2.00 5.00
RE Justin Reed 2.00 5.00
RH Richard Hamilton 5.00 12.00
RJ Richard Jefferson 2.50 6.00
RM Reggie Miller SP 50.00 120.00
RO Bernard Robinson 2.50 6.00
RS Robert Swift 2.00 5.00
SA Romain Sato 2.00 5.00
SC Sam Cassell 4.00 10.00
SF Shareef Abdur-Rahim 5.00 12.00
SH Shawn Marion 6.00 15.00
SL Shaun Livingston 3.00 8.00
SM Josh Smith 3.00 8.00
SV Sasha Vujacic 3.00 8.00
TA Tony Allen 3.00 8.00
TE Sebastian Telfair SP 2.50 6.00
TM Tracy McGrady SP 15.00 40.00
TP Tony Parker 12.00 30.00
TP2 T.Parker AU Both Sides 15.00 40.00
TR Trevor Ariza 3.00 8.00
WE Delonte West 3.00 8.00
WR Dorell Wright 3.00 8.00
YM Yao Ming SP 20.00 50.00
ZO Alonzo Mourning SP 30.00 80.00
ZR Zach Randolph 3.00 8.00

2004-05 SP Signature Edition Signatures Dual

Limited to 100 copies for most and 25 copies for the short printed cards, this 38-card set utilizes some of the design elements of the Signatures set but is horizontally designed and places two players on the card front.

PRINT RUN 100 SER.#'d SETS
SP PRINT RUN 25 SER.#'d SETS
AA A.Emmett/A.Burks 8.00 20.00
AM C.Anthony/T.McGrady SP 50.00 120.00
AT S.Abdur-Rahim/S.Telfair 8.00 20.00
BH C.Billups/R.Hamilton 10.00 25.00
BJ K.Bryant/M.Jordan SP 900.00 1400.00
BM M.Bibby/Kv.Martin 10.00 25.00
BS C.Boozer/K.Snyder 8.00 20.00
CS J.Childress/Josh Smith* 10.00 25.00
DH M.Daniels/D.Harris 10.00 25.00
DP B.Davis/T.Parker 12.50 30.00
DS B.Davis/J.R.Smith 10.00 25.00
DT Del.West/T.Allen 10.00 25.00
EJ J.Erving/M.Jordan SP* 400.00 700.00
GC K.Garnett/S.Cassell* 25.00 60.00
GD B.Gordon/L.Deng 10.00 25.00
GH K.Garnett/D.Howard SP 75.00 150.00
HN D.Howard/J.Nelson 12.00 30.00
JB L.James/K.Bryant SP 400.00 800.00
JH L.James/D.Howard SP 150.00 300.00
JJ M.Jordan/L.James SP 800.00 1200.00
JR A.Jamison/P.J.Ramos 8.00 20.00
JV L.Jackson/A.Varejao 8.00 20.00
KH Kirilenko/Humphries 8.00 20.00
KJ J.Kidd/R.Jefferson 15.00 40.00
KM B.King/S.Marbury SP 8.00 20.00
LC S.Livingston/L.Chalmers 8.00 20.00
LM L.Bird/M.Johnson SP* 250.00 400.00
MG T.McGrady/K.Garnett SP 40.00 100.00
MH R.Miller/D.Harrison 25.00 60.00
OR L.Odom/K.Rush 8.00 20.00
PA M.Peterson/R.Araujo* 8.00 20.00
PP P.Pierce/G.Payton* 20.00 50.00
RB B.Russell/L.Bird SP 175.00 350.00
RS Z.Randolph/D.Stoudamire 8.00 20.00
SM A.Stoudamire/S.Marion* 15.00 40.00
VM J.Vroman/S.Marion 8.00 20.00
WR B.Wallace/D.Rodman SP 25.00 60.00

2004-05 SP Signature Edition SP Signs

Serially numbered to either 100 or 50, this 90-card set places a player photo and an autograph on a design that is highlighted by the featured player's team colors.

PRINT RUN 50 TO 100 SER.#'d SETS
AE Andre Emmett/100 3.00 8.00
AH Al Harrington/100 5.00 12.00
AI Andre Iguodala/50 12.00 30.00
AJ Al Jefferson/100 6.00 15.00
AK Andrei Kirilenko/50 8.00 20.00
AL Ray Allen/100 10.00 25.00
AM Andre Miller/100 5.00 12.00
AN Antawn Jamison/100 5.00 12.00
AR Carlos Arroyo/100 8.00 20.00
AS Amare Stoudemire/100 15.00 40.00
AV Anderson Varejao/100 4.00 10.00
BC Bob Cousy/50 20.00 50.00
BD Baron Davis/50 8.00 20.00
BE Beno Udrih/100 4.00 10.00
BG Ben Gordon/50 6.00 15.00
BI Bill Walton/100 10.00 25.00
BK Bernard King/50 6.00 15.00
BM Brad Miller/100 5.00 12.00
BO Carlos Boozer/100 5.00 12.00
BR Bill Russell/50 75.00 150.00
BU Antonio Burks/100 4.00 10.00
BW Ben Wallace/50 15.00 40.00
CA Carmelo Anthony/50 15.00 40.00
CB Chauncey Billups/100 8.00 20.00
CD Chris Duhon/100 5.00 12.00
CL Clyde Drexler/50 25.00 60.00
CM Corey Maggette/100 5.00 12.00
DA David Harrison/100 3.00 8.00
DE Dennis Rodman/50 40.00 100.00
DG Drew Gooden/100 5.00 12.00
DH Dwight Howard/100 12.00 30.00
DW Dorell Wright/100 5.00 12.00
ED Erik Daniels/100 4.00 10.00
GG George Gervin/100 10.00 25.00
HA Devin Harris/50 5.00 12.00
HO Hakeem Olajuwon/50 25.00 60.00
HS Ha Seung-Jin/100 5.00 12.00
IT Isiah Thomas/100 15.00 40.00
JC Josh Childress/50 5.00 12.00
JE Julius Erving/50 40.00 100.00
JH Josh Howard/100 5.00 12.00
JK Jason Kidd/50 12.00 30.00
JM Jamaal Magloire/100 5.00 12.00
JN Jameer Nelson/100 5.00 12.00
JR J.R. Smith/100 5.00 12.00
JS John Stockton/50 60.00 150.00
JU Justin Reed/100 3.00 8.00
JV Jackson Vroman/100 3.00 8.00
JW Jason Williams/100 25.00 60.00
KB Kobe Bryant/50 100.00 200.00
KH Kris Humphries/100 5.00 12.00
KI Kirk Hinrich/50 8.00 20.00
KM Kevin Martin/100 6.00 15.00
KS Kirk Snyder/100 3.00 8.00
LB Larry Bird/50 75.00 120.00
LC Lionel Chalmers/100 5.00 12.00
LD Luol Deng/50 6.00 15.00
LF Luis Flores/100 4.00 10.00
LJ LeBron James/50 250.00 500.00
LO Lamar Odom/50 10.00 25.00
LU Luke Jackson/100 3.00 8.00
MA Magic Johnson/100 50.00 120.00
MB Mike Bibby/100 8.00 20.00
MC Michael Cooper/100 10.00 25.00
MJ Michael Jordan/100 300.00 600.00
MR Michael Redd/50 4.00 10.00
NO Andres Nocioni/100 5.00 12.00
PA Pape Sow/100 4.00 10.00
PG Pau Gasol/100 8.00 20.00
PP Paul Pierce/50 12.00 30.00
PR Pat Riley/50 15.00 40.00
PS Peja Stojakovic/50 12.00 30.00
RA Rafael Araujo/100 3.00 8.00
RH Richard Hamilton/50 6.00 15.00
RJ Richard Jefferson/100 5.00 12.00
SA Romain Sato/100 3.00 8.00
SC Sam Cassell/100 5.00 12.00
SF Shareef Abdur-Rahim/100 6.00 15.00
SL Shaun Livingston/50 6.00 15.00
SM Josh Smith/50 6.00 15.00
SP Scottie Pippen/100 125.00 250.00
ST Stephon Marbury/100 8.00 20.00
TA Tony Allen/100 5.00 12.00
TE Sebastian Telfair/100 4.00 10.00
TM Tracy McGrady/100 20.00 50.00
TP Tony Parker/100 12.00 30.00
TR Trevor Ariza/100 5.00 12.00
WE Delonte West/100 5.00 12.00
WF Walt Frazier/100 6.00 15.00
YM Yao Ming/50 20.00 50.00

2004-05 SP Signature Edition Triple Authentic Signatures

Randomly seeded and serially numbered to 25, this 15-card set parallels the design of the Sigantures but places three players and their autographs on the card front.

PRINT RUN 25 SER.#'d SETS
ARD Shareef/Randolph/Drexler* 30.00 80.00
BJA Kobe/Magic/Kareem* 250.00 450.00
BJE Bird/Magic/Erving* 250.00 500.00
BPJ Bird/Pierce/A.Jefferson* 75.00 150.00
DMS Baron/Magloire/J.R.Smith 20.00 50.00
GDH Gordon/Deng/Hinrich 25.00 60.00
GMH KG/McGrady/D.Howard 100.00 200.00
HBW Hamilton/Billups/Wallace 25.00 60.00
JAJ LeBron/Carmelo/Jordan* 600.00 1000.00
JBJ Jordan/Kobe/LeBron 1200.00 1600.00
JHA LeBron/Howard/Carmelo* 250.00 500.00
LTH Livingston/Telfair/D.Harris 12.00 30.00
OMM Olajuwon/Yao/McGrady 100.00 200.00
SCS Jo.Smith/Childress/D.Smith 12.00 30.00
SKH Stockton/Kirilenko/Humph 100.00 200.00

2005-06 SP Signature Edition

Issued in March 2006, SP Signature Edition features a 142-card set where cards 1-100 picture veterans and cards 101-142 picture rookies serially numbered to 499. Base cards have a white border with the player's name on the right and background colors to match player jersey colors. Signature Edition was packaged in three-card tins that carried an initial $60 SRP.

COMP.SET w/o SP's (100) 50.00 100.00
1 Josh Smith .50 1.25
2 Josh Childress .50 1.25
3 Joe Johnson .50 1.25
4 Paul Pierce .60 1.50
5 Ricky Davis .50 1.25
6 Al Jefferson .50 1.25
7 Emeka Okafor .50 1.25
8 Kareem Rush .40 1.00
9 Gerald Wallace .50 1.25
10 Michael Jordan 5.00 12.00
11 Ben Gordon .50 1.25
12 Luol Deng .50 1.25
13 Kirk Hinrich .50 1.25
14 LeBron James 2.50 6.00
15 Larry Hughes .50 1.25
16 Zydrunas Ilgauskas .50 1.25
17 Donyell Marshall .40 1.00
18 Dirk Nowitzki 1.00 2.50
19 Jason Terry .50 1.25
20 Josh Howard .60 1.50
21 Devin Harris .40 1.00
22 Carmelo Anthony 1.25 3.00
23 Marcus Camby .50 1.25
24 Andre Miller .50 1.25
25 Kenyon Martin .50 1.25
26 Chauncey Billups .60 1.50
27 Ben Wallace .50 1.25
28 Richard Hamilton .50 1.25
29 Jason Richardson .60 1.50
30 Troy Murphy .40 1.00
31 Baron Davis .50 1.25
32 Tracy McGrady .75 2.00
33 Yao Ming .75 2.00
34 Stromile Swift .40 1.00
35 Jermaine O'Neal .50 1.25
36 Ron Artest .60 1.50
37 Stephen Jackson .50 1.25
38 Corey Maggette .50 1.25
39 Shaun Livingston .40 1.00
40 Chris Wilcox .40 1.00
41 Elton Brand .60 1.50
42 Kobe Bryant 2.50 6.00
43 Kwame Brown .40 1.00
44 Lamar Odom .50 1.25
45 Pau Gasol .60 1.50
46 Damon Stoudamire .50 1.25
47 Lorenzen Wright .40 1.00
48 Shaquille O'Neal 1.25 3.00
49 Dwyane Wade 1.00 2.50
50 Antoine Walker .50 1.25
51 Jason Williams .50 1.25
52 Desmond Mason .40 1.00
53 Michael Redd .50 1.25
54 Maurice Williams .50 1.25
55 Kevin Garnett 1.00 2.50
56 Marko Jaric .40 1.00
57 Wally Szczerbiak .50 1.25
58 Jason Kidd 1.00 2.50
59 Richard Jefferson .50 1.25
60 Vince Carter 1.00 2.50
61 Jamaal Magloire .40 1.00
62 J.R. Smith .50 1.25
63 Speedy Claxton .40 1.00
64 Stephon Marbury .50 1.25
65 Quentin Richardson .50 1.25
66 Mike Sweetney .40 1.00
67 Grant Hill .75 2.00
68 Dwight Howard .50 1.25
69 Steve Francis .50 1.25
70 Allen Iverson 1.00 2.50
71 Samuel Dalembert .40 1.00
72 Kyle Korver .50 1.25
73 Chris Webber .60 1.50
74 Steve Nash .75 2.00
75 Amare Stoudemire .50 1.25
76 Shawn Marion .50 1.25
77 Sebastian Telfair .50 1.25
78 Zach Randolph .50 1.25
79 Juan Dixon .40 1.00
80 Mike Bibby .60 1.50
81 Peja Stojakovic .60 1.50
82 Brad Miller .50 1.25
83 Tim Duncan 1.00 2.50
84 Manu Ginobili .60 1.50
85 Robert Horry .50 1.25
86 Tony Parker .60 1.50
87 Ray Allen .60 1.50
88 Rashard Lewis .60 1.50
89 Vladimir Radmanovic .40 1.00
90 Chris Bosh .60 1.50
91 Rafer Alston .40 1.00
92 Jalen Rose .60 1.50
93 Andrei Kirilenko .50 1.25
94 Matt Harpring .40 1.00
95 Carlos Boozer .50 1.25
96 Mehmet Okur .40 1.00
97 Gilbert Arenas .50 1.25
98 Antawn Jamison .50 1.25
99 Caron Butler .50 1.25
100 Antonio Daniels .40 1.00
101 Andrew Bogut RC 3.00 8.00
102 Marvin Williams RC 2.50 6.00
103 Deron Williams RC 3.00 8.00
104 Chris Paul RC 10.00 25.00
105 Raymond Felton RC 2.50 6.00
106 Martell Webster RC 2.00 5.00
107 Charlie Villanueva RC 2.50 6.00
108 Channing Frye RC 2.50 6.00
109 Ike Diogu RC 1.50 4.00
110 Andrew Bynum RC 2.00 5.00
111 Sean May RC 1.50 4.00
112 Rashad McCants RC 2.00 5.00
113 Antoine Wright RC 2.00 5.00
114 Joey Graham RC 2.00 5.00
115 Danny Granger RC 3.00 8.00
116 Gerald Green RC 2.50 6.00
117 Hakim Warrick RC 2.00 5.00
118 Julius Hodge RC 1.50 4.00
119 Nate Robinson RC 2.50 6.00
120 Jarrett Jack RC 2.50 6.00
121 Francisco Garcia RC 2.00 5.00
122 Luther Head RC 2.00 5.00
123 Johan Petro RC 1.50 4.00
124 Jason Maxiell RC 2.00 5.00
125 Linas Kleiza RC 1.50 4.00
126 Wayne Simien RC 1.50 4.00
127 David Lee RC 2.50 6.00
128 Salim Stoudamire RC 2.00 5.00
129 Daniel Ewing RC 2.00 5.00
130 Brandon Bass RC 2.00 5.00
131 C.J. Miles RC 2.50 6.00
132 Ersan Ilyasova RC 2.50 6.00
133 Travis Diener RC 1.50 4.00
134 Monta Ellis RC 3.00 8.00
135 Chris Taft RC 2.00 5.00
136 Martynas Andriuskevicius RC 1.50 4.00
137 Louis Williams RC 2.50 6.00
138 Bracey Wright RC 1.50 4.00
139 Robert Whaley RC 1.50 4.00
140 Andray Blatche RC 2.50 6.00
141 Ryan Gomes RC 2.00 5.00
142 Sarunas Jasikevicius RC 2.50 6.00

2005-06 SP Signature Edition Gold

*1-100 GOLD: 3X TO 8X BASE HI
*101-142 GOLD: 1.25X TO 3X BASE HI
GOLD PRINT RUN 25 SER.#'d SETS
10 Michael Jordan 40.00 100.00

2005-06 SP Signature Edition INKredible INKscriptions

Found randomly in packs, these cards are serially numbered to either 50 or 100 and horizontally designed with player photos on the left and authentic autographs on the right. Some players signed inscriptions rather than their names.

PRINT RUNS 50 TO 100 SER.#'d SETS
AB Andrew Bogut/50 20.00 50.00
AJ Al Jefferson/100 6.00 15.00
AK Andrei Kirilenko/50 12.00 30.00
BB Brent Barry/100 10.00 25.00
BI Bill Walton/100 20.00 50.00
BJ Bobby Jackson/100 8.00 20.00
BK Bob Knight/50 40.00 80.00
BL Bill Laimbeer/100 30.00 80.00
BR Brandon Bass/100 10.00 25.00
CB Chris Bosh/50 8.00 20.00
CH Chauncey Billups/100 25.00 60.00
CP Chris Paul/50 50.00 120.00
DA David Robinson/50 60.00 150.00
DR Dennis Rodman/50 50.00 100.00
EB Elton Brand/50 8.00 20.00
EH Elvin Hayes/100 12.00 30.00
EO Emeka Okafor/100 12.00 30.00
GE George Gervin/100 15.00 40.00
GG Gerald Green/100 8.00 20.00
HO Hakeem Olajuwon/50 100.00 250.00
HW Hakim Warrick/100 6.00 15.00
IT Isiah Thomas/50 20.00 50.00
JE Julius Erving/50 150.00 300.00
JG Joey Graham/100 6.00 15.00
JH Julius Hodge/100 6.00 15.00
KA Kareem Abdul-Jabbar/50 100.00 200.00
KW Kwame Brown/100 6.00 15.00
LB LeBron James/50 300.00 600.00
LH Larry Hughes/100 8.00 20.00
LW Louis Williams/100 10.00 25.00
MJ Magic Johnson/50 150.00 300.00
MW Marvin Williams/50 10.00 25.00
NR Nate Robinson/100 20.00 50.00
PP Paul Pierce/50 100.00 200.00
QR Quentin Richardson/100 6.00 15.00
RA Ron Artest/50 15.00 40.00
RF Raymond Felton/100 6.00 15.00
RM Rashad McCants/100 6.00 15.00
RP Robert Parish/50 12.00 30.00
SE Sean May/100 6.00 15.00
SM Stephon Marbury/50 12.00 30.00
SN Steve Nash/50 125.00 250.00
SP Scottie Pippen/50 125.00 250.00
SS Salim Stoudamire/100 6.00 15.00
TM Tracy McGrady/50 20.00 50.00
WS Wayne Simien/100 6.00 15.00
YM Yao Ming/50 30.00 80.00

2005-06 SP Signature Edition Marks of Distinction

Limited to 40 serially numbered copies, this 41-card set places full color player photos along the top of the card and sticker autograph on the bottom over a white background.

PRINT RUN 40 SER.#'d SETS
AB Andrew Bogut 8.00 20.00
AJ Antawn Jamison 8.00 20.00
AN Andrew Bynum 8.00 20.00
AW Antoine Wright 8.00 20.00
CB Chris Bosh 12.00 30.00
CF Channing Frye 8.00 20.00
CH Chauncey Billups 10.00 25.00
CM Cuttino Mobley 8.00 20.00
CP Chris Paul 60.00 150.00
CV Charlie Villanueva 8.00 20.00
DG Danny Granger 8.00 20.00
DH Dwight Howard 15.00 40.00
DR Dennis Rodman 20.00 50.00
DW Deron Williams 8.00 20.00
FG Francisco Garcia 8.00 20.00
GG Gerald Green 8.00 20.00
HO Hakeem Olajuwon 20.00 50.00
HW Hakim Warrick 8.00 20.00
IT Isiah Thomas 20.00 50.00
JG Joey Graham 8.00 20.00
JH Julius Hodge 8.00 20.00
JJ Jarrett Jack 8.00 20.00
JK Jason Kidd 15.00 50.00
JS J.R. Smith 8.00 20.00
LB Larry Bird 50.00 120.00
LJ LeBron James 200.00 500.00
LO Lamar Odom 8.00 20.00
MA Magic Johnson 50.00 120.00
MJ Michael Jordan 400.00 700.00
MR Michael Redd 8.00 20.00
MV Marvin Williams 8.00 20.00
MW Martell Webster 8.00 20.00
NR Nate Robinson 8.00 20.00
PP Paul Pierce 12.00 30.00
RF Raymond Felton 8.00 20.00
RM Rashad McCants 8.00 20.00
SM Sean May 8.00 20.00
ST Stephon Marbury 12.50 30.00
TC Tyson Chandler 8.00 20.00
TM Tracy McGrady 20.00 50.00
YM Yao Ming 20.00 50.00

2005-06 SP Signature Edition Rookie GRAPHiti

Randomly inserted in packs, this horizontally designed cards places full color player photos on the left and autograph on the right of a yellow and orange background. Each card is serially numbered to 100.

PRINT RUN 100 SER.#'d SETS
AB Andray Blatche 5.00 12.00
AW Antoine Wright 4.00 10.00
BB Brandon Bass 4.00 10.00
BW Bracey Wright 3.00 8.00
CT Chris Taft 4.00 10.00
DE Daniel Ewing 4.00 10.00
DL David Lee 5.00 12.00
DT Dijon Thompson 3.00 8.00
EI Ersan Ilyasova 5.00 12.00
GG Gerald Green 5.00 12.00
HW Hakim Warrick 4.00 10.00
JG Joey Graham 4.00 10.00
JH Julius Hodge 3.00 8.00
JM Jason Maxiell 4.00 10.00
LK Linas Kleiza 3.00 8.00
LR Lawrence Roberts 3.00 8.00
LW Louis Williams 5.00 12.00
MA Martynas Andriuskevicius 3.00 8.00
ME Monta Ellis 15.00 40.00
NR Nate Robinson 10.00 25.00
RG Ryan Gomes 4.00 10.00
SJ Sarunas Jasikevicius 5.00 12.00
SM Sean May 3.00 8.00
SS Salim Stoudamire 4.00 10.00
TD Travis Diener 3.00 8.00

2005-06 SP Signature Edition Rookies INKorporated

Randomly seeded an serially numbered out of 50, this 25-card set has bronze highlights and borders to match team colors around a portrait-style photo of the featured player. Autographs are centered along the bottom of the card.

PRINT RUN 50 SER.#'d SETS
AB Andrew Bogut 12.50 30.00
AN Andrew Bynum 5.00 12.00
AW Antoine Wright 5.00 12.00
CF Channing Frye 6.00 15.00
CP Chris Paul 50.00 120.00
CV Charlie Villanueva 6.00 15.00
DG Danny Granger 8.00 20.00
DW Deron Williams 8.00 20.00
FG Francisco Garcia 5.00 12.00
GG Gerald Green 6.00 15.00
HW Hakim Warrick 5.00 12.00
ID Ike Diogu 4.00 10.00
JG Joey Graham 5.00 12.00
JH Julius Hodge 4.00 10.00
JJ Jarrett Jack 6.00 15.00
JM Jason Maxiell 5.00 12.00
JP Johan Petro 4.00 10.00
MA Marvin Williams 6.00 15.00
MW Martell Webster 5.00 12.00
NR Nate Robinson 12.50 30.00
RF Raymond Felton 12.50 30.00
RM Rashad McCants 5.00 12.00
SM Sean May 4.00 10.00
WS Wayne Simien 4.00 10.00

2005-06 SP Signature Edition Scripts for Success

Randomly inserted in packs, this 54-card set is horizontally designed with a player photo on the left and an autograph on the right. Each card features blue-silver highlights and is sequentially numbered to 200.

PRINT RUN 200 SER.#'d SETS
*SILVER: .6X TO 1.5X BASE HI
SILVER PRINT RUN 50 SER.#'d SETS
*GOLD: .75X TO 2X BASE HI
GOLD PRINT RUN 25 SER.#'d SETS
AB Andrew Bogut 5.00 12.00
AD Andray Blatche 4.00 10.00
AL Al Jefferson 4.00 10.00
AN Andrew Bynum 3.00 8.00
AW Antoine Wright 3.00 8.00
BB Brandon Bass 3.00 8.00
BR Bruce Bowen 5.00 12.00
BW Bracey Wright 2.50 6.00
CF Channing Frye 4.00 10.00
CP Chris Paul 25.00 60.00
CT Chris Taft 3.00 8.00
CV Charlie Villanueva 4.00 10.00
DD Dan Dickau 4.00 10.00
DE Daniel Ewing 3.00 8.00
DG Danny Granger 5.00 12.00
DH Dwight Howard 12.00 30.00
DL David Lee 4.00 10.00
DS Damon Stoudamire 4.00 10.00
DT Dijon Thompson 2.50 6.00
DW Deron Williams 5.00 12.00
EI Ersan Ilyasova 4.00 10.00
FG Francisco Garcia 3.00 8.00
GG Gerald Green 4.00 10.00
HW Hakim Warrick 3.00 8.00
ID Ike Diogu 2.50 6.00
IT Isiah Thomas 10.00 25.00
JA Jamaal Magloire 4.00 10.00
JG Joey Graham 3.00 8.00
JH Julius Hodge 2.50 6.00
JJ Jarrett Jack 4.00 10.00
JM Jason Maxiell 3.00 8.00
JP Johan Petro 2.50 6.00
JR J.R. Smith 4.00 10.00
KK Kyle Korver 4.00 10.00
LH Luther Head 3.00 8.00
LK Linas Kleiza 2.50 6.00
LO Lamar Odom 5.00 12.00
LR Lawrence Roberts 2.50 6.00
MA Martynas Andriuskevicius 2.50 6.00
MD Marquis Daniels 4.00 10.00
ME Monta Ellis 12.00 30.00
MV Marvin Williams 4.00 10.00
PP Paul Pierce 10.00 25.00
QR Quentin Richardson 4.00 10.00
RF Raymond Felton 4.00 10.00
RG Ryan Gomes 3.00 8.00
RM Rashad McCants 3.00 8.00
RP Robert Parish 8.00 20.00
SA Shareef Abdur-Rahim 4.00 10.00
SJ Sarunas Jasikevicius 4.00 10.00
SM Sean May 2.50 6.00
SS Salim Stoudamire 3.00 8.00
TD Travis Diener 2.50 6.00
WS Wayne Simien 2.50 6.00

2005-06 SP Signature Edition Signatures

Inserted at approximately one per pack, this 127-card set places a player photo at the top of the card, an autograph along the bottom, a strip between the two in team uniform colors and black and gray borders.

RANDOM INSERTS IN PACKS
*GOLD: .75X TO 2X BASE AU HI
GOLD PRINT RUN 25 SER.#'d SETS
UNPRICED TRIPLE PRINT RUN 10 SETS
AB Andrew Bogut 5.00 12.00
AD Andre Miller 4.00 10.00
AI Andre Iguodala 5.00 12.00
AJ Antawn Jamison 4.00 10.00
AK Andrei Kirilenko 4.00 10.00
AL Al Jefferson 4.00 10.00
AN Andrew Bynum 3.00 8.00
AN Andris Biedrins 4.00 10.00
AR Amir Johnson 4.00 10.00
AW Antoine Wright 3.00 8.00
AY Carlos Arroyo 10.00 25.00
BA Bracey Wright 2.50 6.00
BB Brent Barry 4.00 10.00
BD Baron Davis 4.00 10.00
BJ Bobby Jackson 4.00 10.00
BK Bernard King 5.00 12.00
BL Bill Laimbeer 12.00 30.00
BM Brad Miller 4.00 10.00
BO Bob Knight SP 25.00 60.00
BR Brandon Bass 3.00 8.00
BS Bobby Simmons 4.00 10.00
BT Andray Blatche 4.00 10.00
BW Bruce Bowen 5.00 12.00
CA Carmelo Anthony SP 20.00 40.00
CB Carlos Boozer SP 4.00 10.00
CD Chris Duhon 4.00 10.00
CF Channing Frye 4.00 10.00
CH Chauncey Billups 6.00 15.00
CJ C.J. Miles 4.00 10.00
CM Corey Maggette 4.00 10.00
CP Chris Paul 20.00 50.00
CR Chris Bosh 8.00 20.00
CT Chris Taft 3.00 8.00
CU Cuttino Mobley 4.00 10.00
CV Charlie Villanueva 4.00 10.00
CW Chris Wilcox 4.00 10.00
DA Darko Milicic 4.00 10.00
DD Dan Dickau 4.00 10.00
DE Daniel Ewing 3.00 8.00
DG Danny Granger 5.00 12.00
DH David Harrison 4.00 10.00
DL David Lee 4.00 10.00
DM Desmond Mason 4.00 10.00
DO Donyell Marshall 4.00 10.00
DR Dennis Rodman 20.00 50.00
DS Damon Stoudamire 4.00 10.00
DW Deron Williams 12.00 30.00
EB Elton Brand SP 4.00 10.00
EH Elvin Hayes 6.00 15.00
EO Emeka Okafor 4.00 10.00
ES Ersan Ilyasova 4.00 10.00
FG Francisco Garcia 3.00 8.00
GE George Gervin 8.00 20.00
GG Gerald Green 4.00 10.00
GO Gordan Giricek 4.00 10.00
GP Gary Payton 8.00 20.00
GW Gerald Wallace 5.00 12.00
HA Josh Howard 4.00 10.00
HD Dwight Howard 12.00 30.00
HO Hakeem Olajuwon SP 20.00 50.00
HW Hakim Warrick 3.00 8.00
ID Ike Diogu 2.50 6.00
IT Isiah Thomas 10.00 25.00
JA Jason Kidd 10.00 25.00
JC Josh Childress 4.00 10.00
JG Joey Graham 3.00 8.00
JH Julius Hodge 2.50 6.00
JJ Jarrett Jack 4.00 10.00
JK Jason Kapono 4.00 10.00
JM Jason Maxiell 3.00 8.00
JO Joe Johnson 5.00 12.00
JP Johan Petro 2.50 6.00
JR J.R. Smith 4.00 10.00
JS James Singleton 2.50 6.00
KA Kareem Abdul-Jabbar SP 50.00 100.00
KB Kwame Brown 4.00 10.00
KD Keyon Dooling 4.00 10.00
KH Kirk Hinrich 6.00 15.00
KK Kyle Korver 4.00 10.00
KR Kris Humphries 4.00 10.00
LE Luke Jackson 4.00 10.00
LH Larry Hughes 4.00 10.00
LJ LeBron James 125.00 250.00
LK Linas Kleiza 2.50 6.00
LO Lamar Odom 5.00 12.00
LR Lawrence Roberts 2.50 6.00
LU Luther Head 3.00 8.00
LW Louis Williams 4.00 10.00
MA Martynas Andriuskevicius 2.50 6.00
MC Antonio McDyess 4.00 10.00
MD Marquis Daniels 4.00 10.00
ME Monta Ellis 10.00 25.00
MJ Michael Jordan SP 250.00 500.00
ML Jamaal Magloire 4.00 10.00
MP Morris Peterson 4.00 10.00
MR Michael Redd 4.00 10.00
MW Marvin Williams 4.00 10.00
NR Nate Robinson 6.00 15.00
OG Orien Greene 3.00 8.00
PP Paul Pierce 15.00 40.00
RA Ron Artest 6.00 15.00
RF Raymond Felton 4.00 10.00
RG Ryan Gomes 3.00 8.00
RH Richard Hamilton 5.00 12.00
RI Luke Ridnour 4.00 10.00
RM Rashad McCants 3.00 8.00
RP Robert Parish 10.00 25.00
SA Shareef Abdur-Rahim 4.00 10.00
SE Sean May 2.50 6.00
SI Scottie Pippen 75.00 150.00
SJ Sarunas Jasikevicius 4.00 10.00
SK Steve Kerr 8.00 20.00
SM Stephon Marbury 6.00 15.00
SP Speedy Claxton 4.00 10.00
SS Salim Stoudamire 3.00 8.00
ST Stromile Swift 4.00 10.00
TA Tony Allen 4.00 10.00
TC Tyson Chandler 4.00 10.00
TD Travis Diener 2.50 6.00
TM Tracy McGrady 12.00 30.00
TP Tayshaun Prince 6.00 15.00
VC Vince Carter 15.00 40.00
VR Vladimir Radmanovic 4.00 10.00
VW Von Wafer 2.50 6.00
WA Bill Walton 8.00 20.00
WS Wayne Simien 2.50 6.00
YM Yao Ming 20.00 50.00

2005-06 SP Signature Edition Signatures Dual

Serially numbered to 25, this 29-card set places two player photos and two autographs surrounded by team colors on a horizontally designed card with black and bronze highlights.

PRINT RUN 25 SER.#'d SETS
AH C.Anthony/J.Hodge 30.00 80.00
BB A.Bogut/A.Bynum 25.00 60.00
BJ L.Bird/M.Johnson 200.00 300.00
BM E.Brand/C.Maggette 10.00 25.00
BP C.Billups/T.Prince 40.00 80.00
DD I.Diogu/B.Davis 10.00 25.00
FM R.Felton/S.May 10.00 25.00
FR C.Frye/N.Robinson 10.00 25.00
GS B.Gordon/J.R.Smith 10.00 25.00
GW P.Gasol/H.Warrick 10.00 25.00
JG A.Jefferson/G.Green 25.00 60.00
JH L.James/L.Hughes 200.00 300.00
MK S.Marbury/J.Kidd 30.00 80.00
MM Y.Ming/T.McGrady 40.00 100.00
MR S.Marbury/N.Robinson 10.00 25.00
MS T.McGrady/S.Swift 10.00 25.00
NB S.Nash/C.Billups 30.00 80.00
PG P.Pierce/G.Green 20.00 50.00
PS C.Paul/J.R.Smith 60.00 120.00
RP D.Rodman/S.Pippen 200.00 400.00
TS I.Thomas/J.Stockton 100.00 200.00
VG C.Villanueva/J.Graham 10.00 25.00
WD H.Warrick/I.Diogu 10.00 25.00
WJ M.Webster/J.Jack 10.00 25.00
WM D.Williams/C.J.Miles 25.00 60.00
WP Mv.Williams/C.Paul 50.00 100.00
WS Mv.Williams/S.Stoudamire 10.00 25.00

2006-07 SP Signature Edition

Released in late March 2007, SP Signature Edition showcases a 142-card set where veteran players serially numbered to 499 are pictured on card numbers 1-100 and rookie players serially numbered to 299 are pictured on card numbers 101-142. SP Signature Edition is packaged in single-pack tins of five cards each and carried an initial suggested retail price of $60.00.

1-100 PRINT RUN 499 SER.#'d SETS
1 Josh Childress .75 2.00
2 Joe Johnson .75 2.00
3 Marvin Williams .75 2.00
4 Al Jefferson .75 2.00
5 Paul Pierce 1.00 2.50
6 Sebastian Telfair .60 1.50
7 Raymond Felton .75 2.00
8 Emeka Okafor .75 2.00
9 Gerald Wallace .75 2.00
10 Ben Gordon .75 2.00
11 Kirk Hinrich .75 2.00
12 Ben Wallace .75 2.00
13 Drew Gooden .75 2.00
14 LeBron James 4.00 10.00
15 Donyell Marshall .60 1.50
16 Devin Harris .60 1.50
17 Josh Howard .75 2.00
18 Dirk Nowitzki 1.50 4.00
19 Jason Terry .75 2.00
20 Carmelo Anthony 1.25 3.00
21 Kenyon Martin .75 2.00
22 J.R. Smith .75 2.00
23 Chauncey Billups 1.00 2.50
24 Richard Hamilton .75 2.00
25 Rasheed Wallace 1.00 2.50
26 Baron Davis .75 2.00
27 Troy Murphy .60 1.50
28 Jason Richardson 1.00 2.50
29 Rafer Alston .60 1.50
30 Shane Battier .75 2.00
31 Tracy McGrady 1.25 3.00
32 Yao Ming 1.25 3.00
33 Marquis Daniels .60 1.50
34 Al Harrington .75 2.00
35 Jermaine O'Neal .75 2.00
36 Elton Brand 1.00 2.50
37 Sam Cassell .75 2.00
38 Chris Kaman .75 2.00
39 Corey Maggette .75 2.00
40 Kobe Bryant 4.00 10.00
41 Lamar Odom .75 2.00
42 Kwame Brown .60 1.50
43 Eddie Jones .75 2.00
44 Mike Miller .75 2.00
45 Hakim Warrick .75 2.00
46 Pau Gasol 1.00 2.50
47 Alonzo Mourning 1.25 3.00
48 Shaquille O'Neal 2.00 5.00
49 Dwyane Wade 1.50 4.00
50 Jason Williams .75 2.00
51 Andrew Bogut .75 2.00
52 Michael Redd .75 2.00
53 Charlie Villanueva .60 1.50
54 Kevin Garnett 1.50 4.00
55 Mike James .60 1.50
56 Rashad McCants .60 1.50
57 Vince Carter 1.25 3.00
58 Richard Jefferson .75 2.00
59 Jason Kidd 1.50 4.00
60 Tyson Chandler .75 2.00
61 Desmond Mason .60 1.50
62 Chris Paul 1.25 3.00
63 Peja Stojakovic 1.00 2.50
64 Steve Francis .75 2.00
65 Stephon Marbury .75 2.00
66 Quentin Richardson .75 2.00
67 Nate Robinson .60 1.50
68 Carlos Arroyo .60 1.50
69 Dwight Howard .75 2.00
70 Darko Milicic .60 1.50
71 Andre Iguodala .75 2.00
72 Allen Iverson 1.25 3.00
73 Kyle Korver .75 2.00
74 Chris Webber 1.00 2.50
75 Boris Diaw .75 2.00
76 Shawn Marion .75 2.00
77 Steve Nash 1.25 3.00
78 Amare Stoudemire .75 2.00
79 Jamaal Magloire .60 1.50
80 Zach Randolph .75 2.00
81 Martell Webster .75 2.00
82 Ron Artest 1.00 2.50
83 Brad Miller .75 2.00
84 Mike Bibby 1.00 2.50
85 Tim Duncan 1.50 4.00
86 Michael Finley 1.00 2.50
87 Manu Ginobili 1.00 2.50
88 Tony Parker 1.00 2.50
89 Ray Allen 1.00 2.50
90 Rashard Lewis 1.00 2.50
91 Luke Ridnour .75 2.00
92 Chris Bosh 1.00 2.50
93 T.J. Ford .60 1.50
94 Joey Graham .60 1.50
95 Carlos Boozer .75 2.00
96 Andrei Kirilenko .75 2.00
97 Deron Williams .75 2.00
98 Gilbert Arenas .75 2.00
99 Caron Butler .75 2.00
100 Antawn Jamison .75 2.00
101 Andrea Bargnani RC 2.50 6.00
102 LaMarcus Aldridge RC 6.00 15.00
103 Adam Morrison RC 2.50 6.00
104 Tyrus Thomas RC 2.00 5.00
105 Shelden Williams RC 2.00 5.00
106 Brandon Roy RC 2.50 6.00
107 Randy Foye RC 2.50 6.00
108 Rudy Gay RC 3.00 8.00
109 Patrick O'Bryant RC 1.50 4.00
110 Saer Sene RC 1.50 4.00
111 J.J. Redick RC 3.00 8.00
112 Hilton Armstrong RC 1.50 4.00
113 Thabo Sefolosha RC 2.50 6.00
114 Ronnie Brewer RC 2.50 6.00
115 Cedric Simmons RC 1.50 4.00
116 Rodney Carney RC 1.50 4.00
117 Shawne Williams RC 1.50 4.00
118 Quincy Douby RC 1.50 4.00
119 Renaldo Balkman RC 2.00 5.00
120 Rajon Rondo RC 4.00 10.00
121 Marcus Williams RC 1.50 4.00
122 Josh Boone RC 1.50 4.00
123 Kyle Lowry RC 3.00 8.00
124 Shannon Brown RC 1.50 4.00
125 Jordan Farmar RC 2.50 6.00
126 Sergio Rodriguez RC 2.50 6.00
127 Maurice Ager RC 1.50 4.00
128 Mardy Collins RC 1.50 4.00
129 James White RC 1.50 4.00
130 Steve Novak RC 2.00 5.00
131 Solomon Jones RC 1.50 4.00
132 Paul Davis RC 1.50 4.00
133 P.J. Tucker RC 2.00 5.00
134 Craig Smith RC 2.00 5.00
135 Bobby Jones RC 1.50 4.00
136 David Noel RC 1.50 4.00
137 James Augustine RC 1.50 4.00
138 Daniel Gibson RC 2.00 5.00
139 Marcus Vinicius RC 1.50 4.00
140 Dee Brown RC 1.50 4.00
141 Ryan Hollins RC 2.00 5.00
142 Hassan Adams RC 1.50 4.00

2006-07 SP Signature Edition Gold

*1-100 GOLD: 2.5X TO 6X BASE HI
*101-142 GOLD: 1.25X TO 3X BASE HI
PRINT RUN 25 SER.#'d SETS

2006-07 SP Signature Edition AKA Signings

INT RUN 25 TO 50 SER.#'d SETS
AB Andrea Bargnani/25 20.00 50.00
AD Adrian Dantley/50 8.00 20.00
BB Brent Barry/50 8.00 20.00
BG Ben Gordon/25 20.00 50.00
BL Bill Laimbeer/50 20.00 50.00
BR Bill Russell/25 100.00 225.00
BS Byron Scott/50 12.00 30.00
CA Carmelo Anthony/25 50.00 100.00
CB Chauncey Billups/50 20.00 50.00
CD Clyde Drexler/25 50.00 100.00
CS Cedric Simmons/50 3.00 8.00
DD Darryl Dawkins/50 20.00 50.00
DN David Noel/50 3.00 8.00
DR Dennis Rodman/25 60.00 120.00
EH Elvin Hayes/25 15.00 40.00
GG George Gervin/50 20.00 50.00
HA Hilton Armstrong/50 3.00 8.00
HO Hakeem Olajuwon/25 30.00 75.00
JB Josh Boone/50 3.00 8.00
JE Julius Erving/25 30.00 80.00
JF Jordan Farmar/50 5.00 12.00
JK Jason Kidd/25 20.00 50.00
JW James White/50 3.00 8.00
KH Kirk Hinrich/25 40.00 80.00
LA LaMarcus Aldridge/25 30.00 60.00
LJ LeBron James/25 250.00 400.00
MA Maurice Ager/25 3.00 8.00
MJ Magic Johnson/25 60.00 120.00
MP Morris Peterson/50 5.00 12.00
NA Nate Archibald/50 12.00 30.00
PD Paul Davis/50 3.00 8.00
PO Patrick O'Bryant/50 3.00 8.00
PP Paul Pierce/25 40.00 100.00
QD Quincy Douby/50 3.00 8.00
RB Renaldo Balkman/50 4.00 10.00
RF Randy Foye/50 5.00 12.00
RJ Richard Jefferson/25 8.00 20.00
RR Rajon Rondo/50 25.00 60.00
SM Craig Smith/50 4.00 10.00
SW Shelden Williams/50 4.00 10.00
TM Tracy McGrady/25 20.00 50.00
TT Tyrus Thomas/25 10.00 25.00
VC Vince Carter/25 30.00 60.00

2006-07 SP Signature Edition Alumni Associations

PRINT RUN 50 SER.#'d SETS
AB H.Armstrong/J.Boone 10.00 25.00
AF L.Aldridge/T.Ford 10.00 25.00
AJ H.Adams/R.Jefferson 10.00 25.00
BA M.Ager/S.Brown 10.00 25.00
BJ C.Bosh/J.Jack 12.00 30.00
BT B.Bass/T.Thomas 10.00 25.00
DF B.Davis/J.Farmar 10.00 25.00
DJ D.Brown/J.Augustine 10.00 25.00
GG B.Gordon/R.Gay 25.00 60.00
GT D.Gibson/P.Tucker 10.00 25.00
JB J.Johnson/R.Brewer 12.00 30.00
JR B.Jones/B.Roy 20.00 50.00
MF R.McCants/R.Felton 15.00 40.00
NM D.Noel/S.May 10.00 25.00
RF A.Ray/R.Foye 10.00 25.00
RP R.Rondo/T.Prince 20.00 50.00
WC M.Williams/V.Carter 15.00 40.00
WO M.Williams/E.Okafor 10.00 25.00

2006-07 SP Signature Edition Five Star Autographs

PRINT RUN 10 SER.#'d SETS

BATFR Barg/Aldrd/Tyrus/Foye/Roy 150.00 300.00
DWEHF BD/Walton/Eat/Hllins/Frmr 30.00 60.00
HGDTS Kirk/Grdn/Dhn/Tyrus/Thbo 150.00 300.00
WDWAR Wltn/Glide/Wbstr/Aldr/Roy 150.00 300.00

2006-07 SP Signature Edition Four Star Autographs

PRINT RUN 15 SER.#'d SETS
APMJ Melo/Pierce/T-Mac/James 300.00 450.00
BATW Bargn/Aldrdg/Tyrus/Wllms 75.00 150.00
DWAR Glide/Wltn/Aldrdg/Roy 60.00 120.00
GHST Gordon/Hinrich/Sefolosha/Thomas 20.00 50.00
JEBJ Jordan/Erving/Bird/Johnson 900.00 1500.00
KICJ Korver/Iggy/Crny/Jones 20.00 50.00
ODMM Olaj/Glide/Ming/TMac 125.00 250.00
OGGH Okfr/Gordon/Gay/Rip 40.00 100.00
PKNB Paul/Kidd/Nash/Billups 100.00 225.00

2006-07 SP Signature Edition Hoops Inc. Autographs

PRINT RUN 50 SER.#'d SETS
*GOLD: .5X TO 1.25X BASE HI
GOLD PRINT RUN 25 SER.#'d SETS
AD Adrian Dantley 8.00 20.00
CH Connie Hawkins 8.00 20.00
DJ Dennis Johnson 25.00 60.00
EH Elvin Hayes 6.00 15.00
FW Walt Frazier 8.00 20.00
GG George Gervin 12.00 30.00
HG Hal Greer 6.00 15.00
JS Jack Sikma 6.00 15.00
MB Muggsy Bogues 8.00 20.00
MC Michael Cooper 8.00 20.00
ME Mark Eaton 6.00 15.00
MR Micheal Ray Richardson 6.00 15.00
NA Nate Archibald 8.00 20.00
NT Nate Thurmond 6.00 15.00
PW Paul Westphal 8.00 20.00
RP Robert Parish 10.00 25.00
RS Ralph Sampson 8.00 20.00
RT Reggie Theus 6.00 15.00
SK Steve Kerr 8.00 20.00
SP Sam Perkins 8.00 20.00
SW Spud Webb 10.00 25.00
WT Wayman Tisdale 6.00 15.00

2006-07 SP Signature Edition INKredible INKscriptions

PRINT RUN 50 TO 100 SER.#'d SETS
AB Andrea Bargnani/50 25.00 60.00
AJ Antawn Jamison/100 8.00 20.00
AR Allan Ray/50 3.00 8.00
BG Ben Gordon/50 8.00 20.00
BJ Bobby Jones/100 3.00 8.00
BM Brad Miller/100 5.00 12.00
BR Brandon Roy/50 20.00 50.00
CE Cedric Simmons/50 3.00 8.00
CS Craig Smith/100 4.00 10.00
DG Daniel Gibson/50 4.00 10.00
DM Damir Markota/100 3.00 8.00
DN David Noel/100 3.00 8.00
DW Deron Williams/50 25.00 60.00
GW Gerald Wallace/50 8.00 20.00
HA Hassan Adams/100 3.00 8.00
HI Hilton Armstrong/100 3.00 8.00
JA James Augustine/100 3.00 8.00
JB Josh Boone/50 3.00 8.00
JF Jordan Farmar/100 5.00 12.00
JW James White/100 3.00 8.00
KK Kyle Korver/50 15.00 40.00
LA LaMarcus Aldridge/50 15.00 40.00
LB Leandro Barbosa/100 5.00 12.00
MJ Mike James/100 5.00 12.00
NO Steve Novak/100 5.00 12.00
NR Nate Robinson/100 10.00 25.00
PD Paul Davis/50 3.00 8.00
PM Pops Mensah-Bonsu/100 3.00 8.00
PT P.J. Tucker/100 4.00 10.00
QD Quincy Douby/100 3.00 8.00
RB Raja Bell/50 15.00 40.00
RE Renaldo Balkman/100 4.00 10.00
RF Raymond Felton/100 12.00 30.00
RG Rudy Gay/50 20.00 50.00
RJ Richard Jefferson/50 6.00 15.00
SB Shannon Brown/50 12.00 30.00
SJ Solomon Jones/100 3.00 8.00
SN Steve Nash/50 125.00 250.00
SR Sergio Rodriguez/50 6.00 15.00
SS Saer Sene/100 3.00 8.00
SW Shelden Williams/50 4.00 10.00
TF T.J. Ford/100 5.00 12.00
TP Tayshaun Prince 12.00 30.00
TS Thabo Sefolosha/50 12.00 30.00
TT Tyrus Thomas/50 4.00 10.00
WB Will Blalock/100 3.00 8.00
WI Shawne Williams/50 3.00 8.00

2006-07 SP Signature Edition Marks of Distinction

PRINT RUN 50 SER.#'d SETS
AB Andrea Bargnani 15.00 40.00
AH Al Harrington 5.00 12.00
AI Andre Iguodala 5.00 12.00
BA Renaldo Balkman 4.00 10.00
BD Baron Davis 5.00 12.00
BG Ben Gordon 15.00 40.00
BM Brad Miller 5.00 12.00
BR Brandon Roy 12.00 30.00
CB Chauncey Billups 8.00 20.00
CH Chris Bosh 10.00 25.00
CM Corey Maggette 5.00 12.00
CS Cedric Simmons 3.00 8.00
DB Dee Brown 3.00 8.00
EO Emeka Okafor 10.00 25.00
HA Hassan Adams 3.00 8.00
JA James Augustine 3.00 8.00
JB Josh Boone 3.00 8.00
JF Jordan Farmar 5.00 12.00
JJ Jarrett Jack 5.00 12.00
JO Joe Johnson 8.00 20.00
KL Kyle Lowry 6.00 15.00
LB Leandro Barbosa 5.00 12.00
MA Maurice Ager 3.00 8.00
MB Mike Bibby 5.00 12.00
MC Mardy Collins 3.00 8.00
MJ Michael Jordan 300.00 550.00
MW Marcus Williams 3.00 8.00
ON Jermaine O'Neal 6.00 15.00
PO Patrick O'Bryant 3.00 8.00
PP Paul Pierce 10.00 25.00
PS Peja Stojakovic 5.00 12.00
QD Quincy Douby 3.00 8.00
RC Rodney Carney 3.00 8.00
RF Randy Foye 5.00 12.00
RG Rudy Gay 10.00 25.00
RH Richard Hamilton 8.00 20.00
RJ Richard Jefferson 5.00 12.00
RO Ronnie Brewer 5.00 12.00
RR Rajon Rondo 25.00 60.00
SN Steve Novak 4.00 10.00
SR Sergio Rodriguez 5.00 12.00
SS Saer Sene 3.00 8.00
SW Shawne Williams 3.00 8.00
TP Tayshaun Prince 8.00 20.00
TS Thabo Sefolosha 5.00 12.00
WI Shelden Williams 4.00 10.00

2006-07 SP Signature Edition Rookie GRAPHiti

PRINT RUN 50 SER.#'d SETS
*GOLD: .5X TO 1.25X BASE HI
GOLD PRINT RUN 25 SER.#'d SETS
AB Andrea Bargnani 15.00 40.00
BR Brandon Roy 5.00 12.00
CS Cedric Simmons 3.00 8.00
HA Hilton Armstrong 3.00 8.00
JB Josh Boone 3.00 8.00
JF Jordan Farmar 5.00 12.00
KL Kyle Lowry 6.00 15.00
LA LaMarcus Aldridge 15.00 40.00
MA Maurice Ager 3.00 8.00
MW Marcus Williams 3.00 8.00
PO Patrick O'Bryant 3.00 8.00
QD Quincy Douby 3.00 8.00
RB Renaldo Balkman 4.00 10.00
RC Rodney Carney 3.00 8.00
RF Randy Foye 5.00 12.00
RG Rudy Gay 6.00 15.00
RO Ronnie Brewer 5.00 12.00
RR Rajon Rondo 25.00 60.00
SB Shannon Brown 3.00 8.00
SR Sergio Rodriguez 5.00 12.00
SS Saer Sene 3.00 8.00
SW Shelden Williams 4.00 10.00
TS Thabo Sefolosha 5.00 12.00
TT Tyrus Thomas 4.00 10.00
WI Shawne Williams 3.00 8.00

2006-07 SP Signature Edition Signature Style

PRINT RUN 25 SER.#'d SETS
AI Andre Iguodala 8.00 20.00
BB Bruce Bowen 8.00 20.00
BG Ben Gordon 15.00 40.00
BL Bill Laimbeer 30.00 75.00
BM Brad Miller 8.00 20.00
CB Chris Bosh 10.00 25.00
CD Clyde Drexler 50.00 120.00
CP Chris Paul 25.00 60.00
DR David Robinson 60.00 150.00
GG George Gervin 20.00 50.00
HO Hakeem Olajuwon 20.00 50.00
JE Julius Erving 50.00 100.00
JK Jason Kidd 20.00 50.00
JS John Stockton 60.00 150.00
KA Kareem Abdul-Jabbar 60.00 120.00
KK Kyle Korver 10.00 25.00
LB Larry Bird 60.00 120.00
LJ LeBron James 125.00 250.00
MA Magic Johnson 60.00 120.00
MB Mike Bibby 8.00 20.00
PS Peja Stojakovic 8.00 20.00
RO Dennis Rodman 30.00 80.00
RP Robert Parish 12.50 30.00
SK Steve Kerr 30.00 60.00
SN Steve Nash 75.00 150.00
TM Tracy McGrady 25.00 60.00
VC Vince Carter 25.00 60.00
YM Yao Ming 25.00 60.00

2006-07 SP Signature Edition Signatures

APPROXIMATE ODDS ONE PER PACK
UNPRICED GOLD PRINT RUN 10 SETS
AB Andrea Bargnani 6.00 15.00
AH Al Harrington 3.00 8.00
AJ Al Jefferson 3.00 8.00
AM Maurice Ager 2.00 5.00
AR Hilton Armstrong 2.00 5.00
BA Leandro Barbosa 3.00 8.00
BB Brent Barry 3.00 8.00
BD Baron Davis 4.00 10.00
BO Chris Bosh 10.00 25.00
BR Ronnie Brewer 3.00 8.00
CA Carmelo Anthony 20.00 40.00
CB Chauncey Billups 6.00 15.00
CD Clyde Drexler 12.00 30.00
CM Corey Maggette 3.00 8.00
CP Chris Paul 20.00 50.00
CS Cedric Simmons 2.00 5.00
DB Dee Brown 2.00 5.00
DG Daniel Gibson 2.50 6.00
DM Damir Markota 2.00 5.00
DN David Noel 2.00 5.00
DR David Robinson 30.00 75.00
DS DeShawn Stevenson 3.00 8.00
EO Emeka Okafor 4.00 10.00
FO Randy Foye 3.00 8.00
GG George Gervin 8.00 20.00
GR Danny Granger 3.00 8.00
HA Hassan Adams 2.00 5.00
HO Hakeem Olajuwon 12.00 30.00
IU Ime Udoka 3.00 8.00
JA James Augustine 2.00 5.00
JB Josh Boone 2.00 5.00
JC Josh Childress 3.00 8.00
JF Jordan Farmar 3.00 8.00
JG Jorge Garbajosa 2.50 6.00
JJ Jarrett Jack 3.00 8.00
JK Jason Kidd 12.00 30.00
JM Mike James 3.00 8.00
JN Antawn Jamison 4.00 10.00
JO Avery Johnson 5.00 12.00
JS J.R. Smith 3.00 8.00
JW James White 2.00 5.00
KA Kareem Abdul-Jabbar 40.00 80.00
KK Kyle Korver 6.00 15.00
KL Kyle Lowry 4.00 10.00
LA LaMarcus Aldridge 15.00 40.00
LB Larry Bird 50.00 100.00
LJ LeBron James 100.00 250.00
LR Luke Ridnour 3.00 8.00
MA Magic Johnson 60.00 120.00
MC Mardy Collins 2.00 5.00
ME Pops Mensah-Bonsu 2.00 5.00
MI Mile Ilic 2.00 5.00
MJ Michael Jordan 400.00 800.00
MO Cuttino Mobley 3.00 8.00
MP Morris Peterson 3.00 8.00
MW Marvin Williams 2.50 6.00
NO Steve Novak 2.50 6.00
NR Nate Robinson 2.00 5.00
OG Orien Greene 3.00 8.00
PD Paul Davis 2.00 5.00
PM Paul Millsap 4.00 10.00
PO Patrick O'Bryant 2.00 5.00
PT P.J. Tucker 2.50 6.00
QD Quincy Douby 2.00 5.00
RA Allan Ray 2.00 5.00
RC Rodney Carney 2.00 5.00
RE Renaldo Balkman 2.50 6.00
RG Rudy Gay 4.00 10.00
RH Ryan Hollins 2.50 6.00
RM Rashad McCants 3.00 8.00
RO Dennis Rodman 25.00 60.00
RR Rajon Rondo 15.00 40.00
RT Reggie Theus 3.00 8.00
RU Bill Russell 75.00 150.00
RY Brandon Roy 8.00 20.00
SB Shannon Brown 2.00 5.00
SJ Solomon Jones 2.00 5.00
SK Steve Kerr 8.00 20.00
SM Craig Smith 2.50 6.00
SR Sergio Rodriguez 3.00 8.00
SS Saer Sene 2.00 5.00
ST John Stockton 30.00 60.00
SW Shawne Williams 2.00 5.00
TF T.J. Ford 3.00 8.00
TS Thabo Sefolosha 3.00 8.00
TT Tyrus Thomas 2.50 6.00
VC Vince Carter 8.00 20.00
WB Will Blalock 2.00 5.00
WE Spud Webb 5.00 12.00
WI Shelden Williams 2.50 6.00
WT Wayman Tisdale 10.00 25.00
YK Yaroslav Korolev 3.00 8.00
YM Yao Ming 10.00 25.00

2006-07 SP Signature Edition Signs of Success

PRINT RUN 25 SER.#'d SETS
UNPRICED GOLD PRINT RUN 10 SETS
AB Andrea Bargnani 25.00 60.00
AI Andre Iguodala 8.00 20.00
AR Allan Ray 3.00 8.00
BJ Bobby Jones 3.00 8.00
BR Brandon Roy 15.00 40.00
CS Cedric Simmons 3.00 8.00
DB Dee Brown 3.00 8.00
DG Danny Granger 6.00 15.00
DM Damir Markota 3.00 8.00
DN David Noel 3.00 8.00
GG Gerald Green 5.00 12.00
HA Hassan Adams 3.00 8.00
HI Hilton Armstrong 3.00 8.00
JB Josh Boone 3.00 8.00
JC Josh Childress 5.00 12.00
JF Jordan Farmar 5.00 12.00
JS J.R. Smith 8.00 20.00
KL Kyle Lowry 6.00 15.00
LA LaMarcus Aldridge 15.00 40.00
LB Leandro Barbosa 5.00 12.00
LR Luke Ridnour 5.00 12.00
MA Maurice Ager 3.00 8.00
ME Pops Mensah-Bonsu 3.00 8.00
MJ Mike James 5.00 12.00
MW Marcus Williams 3.00 8.00
OG Orien Greene 5.00 12.00
PM Paul Millsap 6.00 15.00
PO Patrick O'Bryant 3.00 8.00
PT P.J. Tucker 4.00 10.00
QD Quincy Douby 3.00 8.00
RC Rodney Carney 3.00 8.00
RF Randy Foye 5.00 12.00
RG Rudy Gay 6.00 15.00
RH Ryan Hollins 4.00 10.00
RO Ronnie Brewer 5.00 12.00
RR Rajon Rondo 25.00 60.00
SB Shannon Brown 3.00 8.00
SJ Solomon Jones 3.00 8.00
SM Craig Smith 4.00 10.00
SN Steve Novak 4.00 10.00
SR Sergio Rodriguez 5.00 12.00
SS Saer Sene 3.00 8.00
TS Thabo Sefolosha 5.00 12.00
TT Tyrus Thomas 4.00 10.00
WB Will Blalock 3.00 8.00
WE Martell Webster 5.00 12.00
WI Shelden Williams 4.00 10.00

2006-07 SP Signature Edition Three Star Autographs

PRINT RUN 25 SER.#'d SETS
ATG Aldridge/Tucker/Gibson 15.00 40.00
BBF Bargnani/Bosh/Ford 80.00 160.00
BBM Brewer/Brown/Millsap 15.00 40.00
BCF Balkman/Collins/Frye 15.00 40.00
BDM Bibby/Douby/Miller 15.00 40.00
BPB Billups/Prince/Blalock 15.00 40.00
CKJ Carter/Kidd/Jefferson 30.00 80.00
CWJ Childress/Williams/Jones 15.00 40.00
DFH Davis/Farmar/Hollins 15.00 40.00
GGW Granger/Greene/Williams 15.00 40.00
GLW Gay/Lowry/Warrick 20.00 50.00
JKC Jones/Korver/Carney 15.00 40.00
JMS James/McCants/Smith 15.00 40.00
MMN Ming/McGrady/Novak 50.00 100.00
OBM Okafor/Boone/Marshall 20.00 50.00
PRR Pierce/Rondo/Ray 60.00 120.00
PWF Paul/Williams/Felton 60.00 120.00
RFW Roy/Foye/Williams 20.00 50.00
SAC Simmons/Armstrong/Chandler 15.00 40.00
SSR Sene/Sefolosha/Rodriguez 20.00 50.00
TSG Thomas/Sefolosha/Gordon 40.00 80.00
WBA Williams/Boone/Adams 15.00 40.00

2006-07 SP Signature Edition Two Star Autographs

PRINT RUN 25 SER.#'d SETS
AM M.Ager/P.Mensah-Bonsu 8.00 20.00
BC R.Balkman/M.Collins 8.00 20.00
BG A.Bargnani/J.Garbajosa 60.00 120.00
BM R.Brewer/P.Millsap 20.00 50.00
BW B.Bowen/J.White 10.00 25.00
CJ R.Carney/B.Jones 8.00 20.00
DA C.Duhon/B.Armstrong 10.00 25.00
FT T.Ford/P.Tucker 8.00 20.00
GB S.Brown/D.Gibson 8.00 20.00
GG D.Granger/O.Greene 8.00 20.00
GL R.Gay/K.Lowry 8.00 20.00
HF R.Hollins/J.Farmar 10.00 25.00
HW C.Hawkins/P.Westphal 10.00 25.00
IR A.Iguodala/N.Robinson 12.00 30.00
JC J.Johnson/J.Childress 8.00 20.00
JD A.Jamison/B.Daugherty 10.00 25.00
JG A.Jefferson/G.Green 12.00 30.00
JS A.Jamison/D.Stevenson 8.00 20.00
JW J.Jack/M.Webster 8.00 20.00
KN K.Korver/S.Novak 12.00 30.00
MA B.Miller/S.Abdur-Rahim 8.00 20.00
MD C.Maggette/P.Davis 8.00 20.00
OG E.Okafor/B.Gordon 8.00 20.00
PB T.Prince/W.Blalock 8.00 20.00
PG M.Peterson/J.Graham 8.00 20.00
RR R.Rondo/A.Ray 15.00 40.00
RS L.Ridnour/S.Sene 8.00 20.00
SA C.Simmons/H.Armstrong 8.00 20.00
SF B.Scott/J.Farmar 25.00 50.00
SJ C.Smith/M.James 8.00 20.00
TT T.Thomas/T.Sefolosha 12.00 30.00
WB D.Brown/D.Williams 12.00 30.00
WH A.Harrington/S.Williams 8.00 20.00
WJ H.Warrick/R.Jefferson 8.00 20.00

2009-10 SP Signature Edition

COMPLETE SET (100) 30.00 60.00
1 Al Harrington .75 2.00
2 Al Horford 1.00 2.50
3 Al Jefferson .75 2.00
4 Al Thornton .75 2.00
5 Allen Iverson 1.25 3.00
6 Andre Iguodala .75 2.00
7 Andre Miller .75 2.00
8 Andrea Bargnani .75 2.00
9 Antawn Jamison .75 2.00
10 Baron Davis .75 2.00
11 Ben Gordon .75 2.00
12 Ben Wallace .75 2.00
13 Beno Udrih .60 1.50
14 Brad Miller .75 2.00
15 Brandon Roy 1.00 2.50
16 Carlos Boozer .75 2.00
17 Carmelo Anthony 1.25 3.00
18 Chauncey Billups 1.00 2.50
19 Chris Bosh 1.00 2.50
20 Chris Duhon .60 1.50
21 Chris Paul 1.25 3.00
22 Courtney Lee .75 2.00
23 D.J. Augustin .60 1.50
24 Danny Granger .75 2.00
25 David Lee .60 1.50
26 David West .75 2.00
27 Derek Fisher .75 2.00
28 Deron Williams .75 2.00
29 Derrick Rose 1.50 4.00
30 DeShawn Stevenson .60 1.50
31 Devin Harris .60 1.50
32 Dirk Nowitzki 1.25 3.00
33 Dwight Howard .75 2.00
34 Dwyane Wade 1.50 4.00
35 Elton Brand 1.00 2.50
36 Eric Gordon .75 2.00
37 Gilbert Arenas .75 2.00
38 Hedo Turkoglu .75 2.00
39 Jamal Crawford 1.00 2.50
40 Jason Kidd 1.00 2.50
41 Jason Richardson 1.00 2.50
42 Jeff Green .75 2.00
43 Jermaine O'Neal .75 2.00
44 Jerryd Bayless .75 2.00
45 Joe Johnson .75 2.00
46 Jose Calderon .60 1.50
47 Josh Howard .75 2.00
48 Josh Smith .75 2.00
49 Kenyon Martin .75 2.00
50 Kevin Durant 2.50 6.00
51 Kevin Garnett 1.50 4.00
52 Kevin Love 1.00 2.50
53 Kevin Martin .75 2.00
54 Kobe Bryant 4.00 10.00
55 Lamar Odom .75 2.00
56 LaMarcus Aldridge 1.00 2.50
57 LeBron James 4.00 10.00
58 Luis Scola .75 2.00
59 Luke Ridnour .75 2.00
60 Luol Deng .75 2.00
61 Manu Ginobili 1.00 2.50
62 Marc Gasol 1.00 2.50
63 Mario Chalmers .75 2.00
64 Michael Beasley .60 1.50
65 Michael Redd .75 2.00
66 Mike Bibby .75 2.00
67 Mike Dunleavy .60 1.50
68 Mo Williams .75 2.00
69 Monta Ellis .75 2.00
70 O.J. Mayo .60 1.50
71 Pau Gasol 1.00 2.50
72 Paul Pierce 1.00 2.50
73 Peja Stojakovic 1.00 2.50
74 Quentin Richardson .75 2.00
75 Raja Bell .75 2.00
76 Ray Allen 1.00 2.50
77 Raymond Felton .75 2.00
78 Richard Hamilton .75 2.00
79 Richard Jefferson .75 2.00
80 Rodney Stuckey .60 1.50
81 Ron Artest 1.00 2.50
82 Ronnie Brewer .75 2.00
83 Rudy Fernandez .60 1.50
84 Rudy Gay 1.00 2.50
85 Russell Westbrook 2.50 6.00
86 Sebastian Telfair .60 1.50
87 Shaquille O'Neal 2.00 5.00
88 Shawn Marion .75 2.00
89 Stephen Jackson .75 2.00
90 Steve Nash 1.00 2.50
91 T.J. Ford .60 1.50
92 Tayshaun Prince .75 2.00
93 Thaddeus Young .60 1.50
94 Tim Duncan 1.50 4.00
95 Tony Parker 1.00 2.50
96 Tracy McGrady 1.00 2.50
97 Tyson Chandler .75 2.00
98 Vince Carter 1.25 3.00
99 Yao Ming 1.25 3.00
100 Yi Jianlian .75 2.00

2009-10 SP Signature Edition 2 Star Signatures

ATED PRINT RUN 23 TO 299 SER.#'d SETS
2SAB M.Almond/A.Brooks/99 6.00 15.00
2SAH G.Hill/K.Azubuike/199 6.00 15.00
2SBA N.Batum/A.Ajinca/199 6.00 15.00
2SBG F.Brown/H.Greer/80 6.00 15.00
2SBO K.Brown/P.O'Bryant/65 6.00 15.00
2SBS J.Barea/R.Sessions/99 6.00 15.00
2SBW F.Brown/L.Wilkens/60 6.00 15.00
2SCV E.Vandeweghe/A.Cervi/60 6.00 15.00
2SDD K.Dooling/C.Douglas-Roberts/99 6.00 15.00
2SDS B.Davis/R.Stuckey/99 6.00 15.00
2SFB R.Fernandez/N.Batum/199 6.00 15.00
2SFJ J.Jack/R.Felton/60 6.00 15.00
2SFR R.Fernandez/Rondo/199 8.00 20.00
2SGB C.Boozer/H.Grant/49 10.00 25.00
2SGD P.Gasol/Daugherty/60 8.00 20.00
2SGS P.Gasol/J.Smith/30 15.00 30.00
2SHC E.Curry/A.Harrington/99 6.00 15.00
2SJA A.Afflalo/J.Barea/99 8.00 20.00
2SJJ L.James/Jordan/23 500.00 800.00
2SJR J.Paxson/R.Harper/35 40.00 100.00
2SKD Donovan/Knight/60 30.00 60.00
2SLB Sharman/L.Wilkens/30 15.00 30.00
2SLD Daugherty/Laimbeer/60 10.00 25.00
2SLG C.Lee/J.Giddens/199 6.00 15.00
2SLH G.Hill/C.Lee/199 6.00 15.00
2SLS J.Sikma/B.Laimbeer/65 6.00 15.00
2SMB C.Maggette/S.Battier/30 6.00 15.00
2SMD M.Bibby/D.Augustin/99 6.00 15.00
2SMS T.Sanders/McAdoo/89 15.00 30.00
2SMW B.Miller/C.Wilcox/119 6.00 15.00
2SND B.Daugherty/L.Nance/60 6.00 15.00
2SNH L.Nance/S.Haywood/60 6.00 15.00
2SPH Heinsohn/Parish/79 25.00 60.00
2SPS J.Smith/M.Peterson/40 6.00 15.00
2SRA M.Ray Richardson/K.Anderson/60 6.00 15.00
2SRB Rondo/A.Brooks/199 12.00 30.00
2SSA J.Smith/R.Anderson/60 6.00 15.00
2SSB J.Sikma/F.Brown/69 6.00 15.00
2SSD C.Daly/J.Sloan/40 6.00 15.00
2SSG J.Sloan/Goodrich/60 10.00 25.00
2SSM R.Sessions/L.Moute/99 8.00 20.00
2SSR S.Haywood/Parish/99 8.00 20.00
2SSS J.Smith/Stoudemire/40 12.00 30.00
2SSW S.Swift/S.Williams/60 6.00 15.00
2STS D.Thomp/J.Smith/30 10.00 25.00
2STT J.Thompson/A.Thornton/99 6.00 15.00
2SWA S.Webb/K.Anderson/60 6.00 15.00
2SWF S.Webb/D.Fisher/99 10.00 25.00
2SWI Iguodala/G.Wallace/30 8.00 20.00
2SWS J.Sloan/C.Walker/60 20.00 50.00

2009-10 SP Signature Edition 3 Star Signatures

STATED PRINT RUN 10 TO 199 SER.#'d SETS
SOME UNPRICED DUE TO SCARCITY
3SABA Batum/Ajinca/Amundson/199 6.00 15.00
3SABM Armst/Btum/McGee/199 10.00 25.00
3SACG Giddens/Crittenton/Augustin/99 6.00 15.00
3SADW Arthur/Dudley/White/99 6.00 15.00
3SALH Lee/Azubuike/Hill/199 8.00 20.00
3SBBG Gddns/Brks/Barea/199 10.00 25.00
3SBBW Bowen/Williams/Brewer/99 6.00 15.00
3SBDA Boone/Douglas-Roberts/Anderson/199 6.00
15.00
3SBDS Bibby/Stuckey/Davis/49 10.00 25.00
3SBGA Gsol/Batum/Andrsn/199 10.00 25.00
3SBSC Brooks/Chalmers/Sessions/199 6.00 15.00
3SCHV Crry/Hywd/Vndwgh/35 10.00 25.00
3SDSG Glmre/Skma/Dghrty/35 10.00 25.00
3SDWL Wllms/Lee/Dling/35 8.00 20.00
3SDWP Wltn/Prtr/Drxlr/49 30.00 60.00
3SESL Smmr/Ellngtn/Lwsn/99 10.00 25.00
3SFAH Frndz/Hllns/Andrsn/35 10.00 25.00
3SFBS Frndz/Sessns/Barea/199 10.00 25.00
3SFCH Cook/Hill/Fernandez/49 6.00 15.00
3SFRB Brks/Rondo/Frndz/199 8.00 20.00
3SFRS Sessions/Ford/Rondo/39 12.00 30.00
3SFWP Webb/Fisher/Porter/49 8.00 20.00
3SFWR Wllms/Fshr/Rndo/99 15.00 40.00
3SGRD Grnt/Rbnsn/Dnvn/25 40.00 80.00
3SGSM Greer/Sndrs/Mrtn/40 15.00 40.00
3SHBG Brwn/Hvlck/Gdrch/10 25.00 60.00
3SHHR Rubio/Hndrsn/Hrdn/99 75.00 200.00
3SHKH Hywd/King/Hrrngtn/35 8.00 20.00
3SHWB Hrrngtn/Bosh/Wllc/35 10.00 25.00
3SJFB Barea/Jcksn/Felton/49 8.00 20.00
3SJRA Kareem/Russell/MJ/10 900.00 1200.00
3SLGM Landry/Greene/Mbah A Moute/99 6.00 15.00
3SMGP Gasol/Miller/Parish/25 12.00 30.00
3SMPA Amundson/Pecherov/Marshall/95 6.00 15.00
3SMSW West/Stevenson/Maggette/120 6.00 15.00
3SOAI Iggy/Anthony/Odom/25 25.00 50.00
3SODO Odom/O'Bryant/Deng/15 10.00 25.00
3SOMH Zo/Hwrd/Olaj/35 60.00 120.00
3SOTW Thms/Okfr/Wrght/50 6.00 15.00
3SPPS Parish/Sanders/Pierce/49 15.00 30.00
3SPRP Parker/Redd/Paul/20 25.00 60.00
3SPTR Rdmn/Pxn/Theus/25 40.00 100.00
3SRAH Hill/Rondo/Almond/99 10.00 25.00
3SRSB Stcky/Rndo/Brks/49 15.00 30.00
3SRSC Rndo/Chlmrs/Sessns/99 10.00 25.00
3SSHG Haywd/Sikma/Green/49 10.00 25.00
3SSSB Amare/Smith/Bass/30 8.00 20.00
3SSWS Sndrs/Wlkr/Sloan/55 6.00 15.00
3STMB Tmpsn/Buse/McAd/55 15.00 30.00
3SWAP Andrsn/Prtr/Webb/35 12.00 30.00
3SWHW West/Wlkns/Hagan/30 30.00 80.00
3SWMS Mbah/Shrp/Wlkr/199 8.00 20.00
3SWRP Riley/Wilkes/Price/35 20.00 40.00

2009-10 SP Signature Edition 4 Star Signatures

STATED PRINT RUN 10 TO 99 SER.#'d SETS
SOME UNPRICED DUE TO SCARCITY
4SBCHH CB/GH/EC/JH/99 30.00 80.00
4SBPGG PP/KB/PG/KG/25 200.00 400.00
4SBWKO PO/CW/KB/CK/39 10.00 25.00
4SCMBK CK/CB/EC/BM/75 10.00 25.00
4SGBLL MB/BL/KL/MG/75 20.00 50.00
4SGCRV HG/EV/AR/AC/39 25.00 50.00
4SGLDG PG/HG/BL/BD/39 25.00 50.00
4SHHME GH/WE/EM/JH/99 12.00 30.00
4SJDFR BJ/KD/RR/RF/99 20.00 40.00
4SKDAP JK/KA/BD/TP/39 30.00 60.00
4SKPAH RH/SK/BA/JP/99 40.00 80.00
4SMESC DS/WE/EC/BM/99 15.00 30.00
4SMRGW RW/EG/OM/DR/75 100.00 250.00
4SNDSG PG/BD/JS/LN/39 20.00 40.00
4SOWMI LO/AI/DM/GW/39 10.00 25.00
4SPKJA PP/CA/BK/LJ/25 150.00 300.00
4SPLHR TH/JL/RP/DR/39 25.00 50.00
4SRBBS RR/AB/JB/RS/99 20.00 50.00
4SSSNK JS/DN/BS/GK/39 15.00 40.00
4SSWSG JS/TS/CW/GG/39 30.00 80.00
4STDJW LJ/DD/DT/DW/39 150.00 300.00
4SWFMG RF/PM/GW/JG/39 15.00 30.00
4SWGBS GW/CB/JS/PG/39 12.00 30.00
4SWRAP SW/RR/KA/TP/39 25.00 60.00
4SWSCM SM/DC/BS/JW/39 50.00 100.00

2009-10 SP Signature Edition INKcredible

STATED PRINT RUN 15 TO 499 SER.#'d SETS
SOME UNPRICED DUE TO SCARCITY
IAA Alexis Ajinca/499 3.00 8.00
IAB Aaron Brooks/399 4.00 10.00
IAC Al Cervi/99 8.00 20.00
IAF Arron Afflalo/399 3.00 8.00
IAM Alonzo Mourning/49 20.00 50.00
IAR Anthony Randolph/169 6.00 15.00
IAU D.J. Augustin/199 4.00 10.00
IBA Jose Barea/199 10.00 25.00
IBB Bobby Brown/499 3.00 8.00
IBC Bill Cartwright/99 8.00 20.00
IBD Baron Davis/75 4.00 10.00
IBE Michael Beasley/99 12.50 30.00
IBI Mike Bibby/50 4.00 10.00
IBL Andray Blatche/99 4.00 10.00
IBR Brad Davis/99 4.00 10.00
IBW Bill Walker/499 4.00 10.00
ICA Carmelo Anthony/49 20.00 50.00
ICB Corey Brewer/99 3.00 8.00
ICD Chris Douglas-Roberts/499 3.00 8.00
ICL Clyde Lovellette/99 6.00 15.00
ICM Corey Maggette/75 4.00 10.00
ICO Mike Conley Jr./99 4.00 10.00
ICW Chet Walker/99 6.00 15.00
IDA Brad Daugherty/139 5.00 12.00
IDF Derek Fisher/149 4.00 10.00
IDG Daniel Gibson/50 4.00 10.00
IDJ Darnell Jackson/499 3.00 8.00
IDM Donyell Marshall/199 3.00 8.00
IDO Billy Donovan/49 20.00 40.00
IDR Derrick Rose/99 75.00 150.00
IDW D.J. White/399 3.00 8.00
IEG Eric Gordon/99 6.00 15.00
IGA Danilo Gallinari/199 4.00 10.00
IGD Glen Davis/499 4.00 10.00
IGG George Gervin/149 6.00 15.00
IGH George Hill/399 4.00 10.00
IGP Gabe Pruitt/499 3.00 8.00
IGR Donte Greene/399 4.00 10.00
IJB Jerryd Bayless/199 4.00 10.00
IJD Joey Dorsey/499 3.00 8.00
IJG Jeff Green/99 4.00 10.00
IJL Jim Loscutoff/99 5.00 12.00
IJN Joakim Noah/149 6.00 15.00
IJO DeAndre Jordan/499 6.00 15.00
IJP Jim Price/99 3.00 8.00
IJS Jack Sikma/399 4.00 10.00
IJW Jerry West/49 25.00 50.00
IKA Kenny Anderson/99 5.00 12.00
IKL Kevin Love/199 10.00 25.00
ILA Louis Amundson/199 5.00 12.00
ILB Larry Bird/25 50.00 100.00
ILE Courtney Lee/99 6.00 15.00
ILJ LeBron James/23 125.00 250.00
ILM Luc Mbah A Moute/499 3.00 8.00
ILN Larry Nance/99 5.00 12.00
ILO Brook Lopez/199 5.00 12.00
IMA Morris Almond/99 3.00 8.00
IMB Marco Belinelli/399 3.00 8.00
IMC Mario Chalmers/499 4.00 10.00
IMJ Michael Jordan/23 350.00 650.00
IML Meadowlark Lemon/65 25.00 50.00
IMR Micheal Ray Richardson/149 4.00 10.00
IMT Mike Taylor/499 3.00 8.00
IMW Marvin Williams/99 4.00 10.00
INB Nicolas Batum/499 10.00 25.00
IOM O.J. Mayo/99 6.00 15.00
IPG Pau Gasol/75 15.00 30.00
IRA Ray Allen/25 20.00 50.00
IRB Renaldo Balkman/50 3.00 8.00
IRH Roy Hibbert/149 5.00 12.00
IRJ Richard Jefferson/115 5.00 12.00
IRP Robert Parish/149 6.00 15.00
IRR Rajon Rondo/299 6.00 15.00
IRS Ramon Sessions/199 4.00 10.00
IRU Brandon Rush/99 4.00 10.00
IRW Russell Westbrook/149 50.00 120.00
ISH Spencer Haywood/299 4.00 10.00
ISI James Silas/99 6.00 15.00
ISJ Sam Jones/35 20.00 40.00
ISL Jerry Sloan/99 6.00 15.00
ISM Josh Smith/119 4.00 10.00
ISO Sonny Weems/499 3.00 8.00
ISS Sean Singletary/499 3.00 8.00
ISW Spud Webb/299 5.00 12.00
ITS Tom Sanders/149 8.00 20.00
IWA Darrell Walker/99 4.00 10.00
IWE David West/149 4.00 10.00
IWI Chris Wilcox/279 3.00 8.00
IYM Yao Ming/49 15.00 30.00

2009-10 SP Signature Edition Signature Rookies

STATED PRINT RUN 199 SER.#'d SETS
RAD Austin Daye 3.00 8.00
RAJ A.J. Price 3.00 8.00
RBM B.J. Mullens 3.00 8.00
RBR Derrick Brown 3.00 8.00
RBU Chase Budinger 4.00 10.00
RCU Dante Cunningham 3.00 8.00
RDC Darren Collison 5.00 12.00
RDG Danny Green 15.00 40.00
RDS DaJuan Summers 3.00 8.00
REC Earl Clark 4.00 10.00
REM Eric Maynor 3.00 8.00
RGH Gerald Henderson 4.00 10.00
RGI Taylor Griffin 3.00 8.00
RHA James Harden 50.00 120.00
RHO Jrue Holiday 6.00 15.00
RJE Jonas Jerebko 5.00 12.00
RJF Jonny Flynn 3.00 8.00
RJJ James Johnson 4.00 10.00
RJP Jeff Pendergraph 3.00 8.00
RJT Jeff Teague 5.00 12.00
RMT Marcus Thornton 4.00 10.00
ROC Omri Casspi 4.00 10.00
RPB Patrick Beverley 5.00 12.00
RRR Ricky Rubio 25.00 60.00
RSC Stephen Curry 300.00 600.00
RSY Sam Young 3.00 8.00
RTA Jermaine Taylor 3.00 8.00
RTD Toney Douglas 3.00 8.00
RTG Taj Gibson 5.00 12.00
RTL Ty Lawson 5.00 12.00
RWE Wayne Ellington 8.00 20.00

2009-10 SP Signature Edition SIGnificance

STATED PRINT RUN 25 TO 499 SER.#'d SETS
SAA Alexis Ajinca/399 3.00 8.00
SAG Aaron Gray/499 3.00 8.00
SAJ Al Jefferson/249 4.00 10.00
SAL Acie Law/99 3.00 8.00
SAN Ryan Anderson/399 3.00 8.00
SAT Al Thornton/299 4.00 10.00
SAV Anderson Varejao/99 4.00 10.00
SBB Bobby Brown/499 3.00 8.00
SBC Corey Brewer/49 5.00 12.00
SBD Boris Diaw/109 5.00 12.00
SBJ Josh Boone/399 3.00 8.00
SBL Brook Lopez/199 4.00 10.00
SBR Bobby Brown/499 3.00 8.00
SBU Beno Udrih/99 3.00 8.00
SBW Bill Walker/499 3.00 8.00
SBY Andrew Bynum/199 8.00 20.00
SCA M.L. Carr/99 5.00 12.00
SCB Chauncey Billups/89 5.00 12.00
SCD Chris Duhon/99 3.00 8.00
SCH Chris Bosh/45 12.00 30.00
SCL Carl Landry/249 4.00 10.00
SCO Corey Brewer/49 4.00 10.00
SCR Caron Butler/99 5.00 12.00
SDA D.J. Augustin/199 4.00 10.00
SDC Daequan Cook/149 3.00 8.00
SDE DeAndre Jordan/499 6.00 15.00
SDG Danilo Gallinari/149 4.00 10.00
SDH Dwight Howard/49 15.00 30.00
SDJ Darnell Jackson/499 4.00 10.00
SDO Joey Dorsey/499 3.00 8.00
SDR Derrick Rose/49 75.00 200.00
SEG Eric Gordon/99 6.00 15.00
SGA Danilo Gallinari/149 5.00 12.00
SGI Artis Gilmore/25 10.00 25.00
SGP Gabe Pruitt/499 3.00 8.00
SJA Antawn Jamison/149 4.00 10.00
SJC Javaris Crittenton/105 3.00 8.00
SJD Jared Dudley/99 3.00 8.00
SJF Jordan Farmar/99 4.00 10.00
SJG Jeff Green/99 5.00 12.00
SJH J.J. Hickson/249 3.00 8.00
SJJ Jarrett Jack/30 4.00 10.00
SJM Javale McGee/399 4.00 10.00
SJN Joakim Noah/125 12.00 30.00
SJO Joe Alexander/249 4.00 10.00
SJS Jason Smith/399 3.00 8.00
SJT Jason Thompson/249 3.00 8.00
SKK Kosta Koufos/399 3.00 8.00
SKL Kevin Love/149 15.00 40.00
SKW Kyle Weaver/499 3.00 8.00
SLA Louis Amundson/349 3.00 8.00
SLD Luol Deng/40 5.00 12.00
SLE Courtney Lee/399 4.00 10.00
SLM Luc Mbah A Moute/499 3.00 8.00
SLO Kyle Lowry/99 3.00 8.00
SMA Morris Almond/199 3.00 8.00
SMB Michael Beasley/49 8.00 20.00
SMC Mario Chalmers 4.00 10.00
SMI Mike Conley Jr./49 6.00 15.00
SMJ Josh McRoberts/99 4.00 10.00
SMK Maurice Cheeks/99 4.00 10.00
SMS Marreese Speights/249 5.00 12.00
SMT Mike Taylor/499 3.00 8.00
SMW Mo Williams/299 5.00 12.00
SJO Joakim Noah/125 8.00 20.00
SOD Lamar Odom/149 8.00 20.00
SOM O.J. Mayo/99 10.00 25.00
SOR Oscar Robertson/25 40.00 80.00
SPA Tony Parker/65 10.00 25.00
SQR Quentin Richardson/379 4.00 10.00
SRA Ron Artest/25 6.00 15.00
SRL Robin Lopez/249 4.00 10.00
SRM Rashad McCants/99 4.00 10.00
SRS Ramon Sessions/199 4.00 10.00
SRU Brandon Rush/299 4.00 10.00
SRW Russell Westbrook/199 50.00 120.00
SSH Spencer Hawes/199 4.00 10.00
SSJ Josh Smith/99 5.00 12.00
SSM Jason Smith/399 3.00 8.00
SSS Sean Singletary/499 3.00 8.00
SST Rodney Stuckey/125 4.00 10.00
SSV Sasha Vujacic/99 5.00 12.00
SSW Spud Webb/199 5.00 12.00
STC Tom Chambers/99 5.00 12.00
STY Tyson Chandler/139 3.00 8.00
SWI Deron Williams/50 10.00 25.00
SWS Shelden Williams/199 4.00 10.00
SYM Yao Ming/49 15.00 40.00

1972-73 Spalding

Each of these seven photos measures 8 1/2" by 11". The fronts feature black-and-white action or posed player photos with a brown outer border that looks like a picture frame and a white inner border. The player's name and the words "Spalding Advisory Staff" appear in a gold bar under the photo. The backs are blank. The cards are unnumbered and checklisted below in alphabetical order.

COMPLETE SET (7) 150.00 300.00
1 Rick Barry 25.00 60.00
2 Rick Barry 25.00 60.00
(Action Shot)
3 Wilt Chamberlain 50.00 120.00
(Philadelphia)
4 Wilt Chamberlain 50.00 120.00
(San Francisco)
5 Julius Erving 40.00 100.00
6 Gail Goodrich 20.00 50.00
7 Luke Jackson 10.00 25.00

2001 Sparks Fleer WNBA

Sponsored by Melissa's and issued in conjunction with Fleer, this 9-card sheet was handed out at the August 8, 2001 game to the first 5000 ticket-holders. Cards feature perforated edges, as they were released in the form of a sheet, white borders, and a colored frame around the card to match the team's colors.

COMPLETE SET (9) 5.00 12.00
1 Temecka Dixon .40 1.00
2 Lisa Leslie 2.50 6.00
3 Ukari Figgs .40 1.00
4 Delisha Milton .40 1.00
5 L.A. Sparks .40 1.00
Melissa's
6 Mwadi Mabika .40 1.00
7 Rhonda Mapp .40 1.00
8 Michael Cooper .40 1.00
9 Latasha Byears .40 1.00

1953 Sport Magazine Premiums

This 10-card set features 5 1/2" by 7" color portraits and was issued as a subscription premium by Sport Magazine. These photos were taken by noted sports photographer Ozzie Sweet. Each features a top player from a number of different sports. The photo backs are blank and unnumbered. We've checklisted the set below in alphabetical order.

COMPLETE SET (10) 30.00 60.00
2 Bob Cousy BK 7.50 15.00

1996 Sported/Match

This 15-card set was produced by the British company Howitt Printing and features cards that "pop-up" when pulled. The basic card front for the first ten cards features a photo of the player against a black background with the title "Sported! World Class Winners" running vertically along the right-side of the card. The final five-cards feature a blue background with the title "Match World Class Winners" running vertically along the right side of the card. When the cards are pulled open, they reveal some statistics and the player's greatest Sported!or Match moment.

COMPLETE SET (15) 10.00 25.00
2 Michael Jordan BK 8.00 20.00
7 Shaquille O'Neal BK 3.00 8.00

1933 Sport Kings

The cards in this 48-card set measure 2 3/8" by 2 7/8". The 1933 Sport Kings set, issued by the Goudey Gum Company, contains cards for the most famous athletic heroes of the times. No less than 18 different sports are represented in the set. The baseball cards of Cobb, Hubbell, and Ruth, and the football cards of Rockne, Grange and Thorpe command premium prices. The cards were issued in one-card penny packs which came 100 packs to a box along with a piece of gum. The catalog designation for this set is R338.

COMPLETE SET 10000.00 16000.00
3 Nat Holman BK 200.00 350.00
5 Ed Wachter BK 75.00 125.00
32 Joe Lapchick BK 250.00 400.00
33 Eddie Burke BK 125.00 250.00

2007 Sportkings

4 Larry Bird 6.00 15.00
16 Magic Johnson 6.00 15.00
30 Bill Russell 15.00 30.00
44 Dominique Wilkins 4.00 10.00
46 John Wooden 6.00 15.00

2007 Sportkings Mini

*MINIS: 1X TO 2X BASIC
ONE PER PACK
ANNOUNCED PRINT RUN 93 SETS

2007 Sportkings Autograph Gold

*GOLD: 1.2X TO 2X BASIC
RANDOM INSERTS IN PACKS
ANNOUNCED PRINT RUN 10 SETS
ABR Bill Russell 125.00 200.00
ALB Larry Bird 90.00 150.00

2007 Sportkings Autograph Silver

RANDOM INSERTS IN PACKS
ANNOUNCED PRINT RUN B/WN 95-99 PER
ABR Bill Russell 75.00 125.00
ADW Dominique Wilkins 15.00 30.00
AJW John Wooden 50.00 120.00
ALB Larry Bird 60.00 100.00
AMJ Magic Johnson 50.00 80.00

2007 Sportkings Autograph Memorabilia Gold

*GOLD/10: 1.2X TO 2X SILVER/40

ANNOUNCED PRINT RUN 10 SETS
AMLB Larry Bird Jsy 125.00 200.00

2007 Sportkings Autograph Memorabilia Silver
RANDOM INSERTS IN PACKS
ANNOUNCED PRINT RUN 40 SETS
AMDW Dominique Wilkins Jsy 20.00 40.00
AMJW John Wooden Jkt 75.00 150.00
AMLB Larry Bird Jsy 70.00 120.00
AMMJ Magic Johnson Jsy 60.00 100.00

2007 Sportkings Cityscapes Silver
ANNOUNCED PRINT RUN 20 SETS
*GOLD: .5X TO 1.2X BASIC
GOLD ANNOUNCED PRINT RUN 10 SETS
RANDOM INSERTS IN PACKS
CS04 C.Yastrzemski/L.Bird 20.00 40.00
CS06 T.Williams/L.Bird 40.00 80.00
CS08 M.Johnson/T.Sawchuk 20.00 40.00

2007 Sportkings Decades Silver
ANNOUNCED PRINT RUN 20 SETS
*GOLD: .5X TO 1.2X BASIC
GOLD ANNOUNCED PRINT RUN 10 SETS
RANDOM INSERTS IN PACKS
D05 Hogan/Mattingly/Magic 50.00 100.00

2007 Sportkings Double Memorabilia Gold
*GOLD: .6X TO 1.5X BASIC
RANDOM INSERTS IN PACKS
ANNOUNCED PRINT RUN 10 SETS
DM15, DM16 ANNOUNCED PRINT RUN 1 PER
NO DM15, DM16 PRICING DUE TO SCARCITY

2007 Sportkings Double Memorabilia Silver
RANDOM INSERTS IN PACKS
ANNOUNCED PRINT RUN 4-40 SETS
DM15, DM16 ANNOUNCED PRINT RUN 4 PER
NO DM15, DM16 PRICING DUE TO SCARCITY
DM2 Larry Bird 15.00 40.00
DM3 Magic Johnson 12.50 30.00

2007 Sportkings Patch Silver
ANNOUNCED PRINT RUN 20 SETS
P28-P30 ANNOUNCED PRINT RUN 4 PER
NO P28-P30 PRICING DUE TO SCARCITY
*GOLD: .6X TO 1.2X BASIC
GOLD ANNOUNCED PRINT RUN 10 SETS
GOLD P28-P30 ANCD. PRINT RUN 1 PER
GOLD P28-P30 NO PRICING AVAILABLE
RANDOM INSERTS IN PACKS
P2 Domingue Wilkins Jsy 10.00 25.00
P5 John Wooden Jkt 20.00 50.00
P6 Larry Bird Jsy 30.00 60.00
P7 Larry Bird Jkt 30.00 60.00
P9 Magic Johnson Jsy 20.00 50.00

2007 Sportkings Single Memorabilia Silver
RANDOM INSERTS IN PACKS
ANNOUNCED PRINT RUN 90 SETS
SM3, SM13 ANNOUNCED PRINT RUN 4 PER
NO SM3, SM13 PRICING DUE TO SCARCITY
SM34 Dominique Wilkins Jsy 4.00 15.00
SM35 John Wooden Jkt 10.00 25.00
SM36 Larry Bird Shorts 10.00 25.00
SM37 Larry Bird Jsy 10.00 25.00
SM38 Larry Bird Jkt 10.00 25.00
SM39 Magic Johnson Jsy 8.00 20.00
SM40 Magic Johnson Shorts 8.00 20.00

2007 Sportkings Triple Memorabilia Silver
ANNOUNCED PRINT RUN 10 SETS
TM7, TM8 ANNOUNCED PRINT RUN 4 PER
NO TM7, TM8 PRICING DUE TO SCARCITY
GOLD ANNOUNCED PRINT RUN 1 SET
NO GOLD PRICING DUE TO SCARCITY
RANDOM INSERTS IN PACKS
TM01 Larry Bird 50.00 100.00
TM09 Bird/Johnson/Wilkins 50.00 100.00

2008 Sportkings
FIVE CARDS PER BOX
55 Hakeem Olajuwon 4.00 8.00
56 Dolph Schayes 5.00 10.00
57 Robert Parish 4.00 8.00
67 Meadowlark Lemon 5.00 10.00
85 Walt Frazier 4.00 8.00
108 Oscar Robertson 5.00 10.00

2008 Sportkings Mini
*MINI: 1X TO 2X BASIC
ONE PER BOX

2008 Sportkings Autograph Silver
ANNOUNCED PRINT RUN B/WN 20-90 PER
RANDOM INSERTS IN PACKS
DS Dolph Schayes/90 * 20.00 40.00
HO Hakeem Olajuwon/80 * 15.00 30.00
RP Robert Parish/80 * 10.00 25.00
OR1 Oscar Robertson/50 * 50.00 100.00
OR2 Oscar Robertson/50 * 50.00 100.00
WF1 Walt Frazier/40 * 15.00 30.00
WF2 Walt Frazier/40 * 15.00 30.00
MLE1 Meadowlark Lemon/40 * 25.00 50.00
MLE2 Meadowlark Lemon/40 * 25.00 50.00

2008 Sportkings Autograph Memorabilia Silver
ANNOUNCED PRINT RUN B/WN 15-50 PER
NO GOLD PRICING DUE TO SCARCITY
RANDOM INSERTS IN PACKS
HO Hakeem Olajuwon/40 * 20.00 40.00
MLE1 Meadowlark Lemon/40 * 30.00 60.00
MLE2 Meadowlark Lemon/30 * 30.00 60.00
RP Robert Parish/40 * 15.00 30.00
WF1 Walt Frazier/40 * 20.00 40.00
WF2 Walt Frazier/40 * 20.00 40.00

2008 Sportkings Cityscapes Double Silver
RANDOM INSERTS IN PACKS
2 D.Sanders/D.Wilkins 15.00 40.00

2008 Sportkings Cityscapes Triple Silver
RANDOM INSERTS IN PACKS
1 Bird/Clemens/Parish 30.00 60.00

2008 Sportkings Decades Silver
RANDOM INSERTS IN PACKS
4 Marino/Messier/Parish 30.00 60.00
5 Hull/Irvin/Olajuwon 20.00 50.00

2008 Sportkings Double Memorabilia Silver
RANDOM INSERTS IN PACKS
7 R.Parish/L.Bird 15.00 40.00

2008 Sportkings Passing the Torch Silver
RANDOM INSERTS IN PACKS

2008 Sportkings Patch Silver
RANDOM INSERTS IN PACKS
9 Hakeem Olajuwon 10.00 25.00
23 Robert Parish 12.50 30.00
25 Walt Frazier 12.50 30.00

2008 Sportkings Single Memorabilia Silver
RANDOM INSERTS IN PACKS
16 Hakeem Olajuwon 6.00 15.00
29 Meadowlark Lemon 8.00 20.00
35 Robert Parish 6.00 15.00
41 Walt Frazier 6.00 15.00

2008 Sportkings Triple Memorabilia Silver
RANDOM INSERTS IN PACKS
14 Olajuwon/Magic/Bird 20.00 50.00

2009 Sportkings
COMPLETE SET (52) 250.00 450.00
COMMON CARD (109-160) 5.00 12.00
SEMISTARS 6.00 15.00
UNLISTED STARS 8.00 20.00
112 Rick Barry 5.00 12.00
113 Jerry West 6.00 15.00
120 George Mikan 6.00 15.00
124 Pete Maravich 15.00 40.00
157 Lisa Leslie 8.00 20.00

2009 Sportkings Mini
*MINI: .6X TO 1.5X BASIC CARDS
STATED ODDS ONE PER BOX
UNPRICED SILVER PRINT RUN 7 SETS
UNPRICED GOLD PRINT RUN 3 SETS

2009 Sportkings Autograph Silver
ANNOUNCED PRINT RUN B/WN 15-70 PER
UNPRICED GOLD PRINT RUN 10
JWE1 Jerry West/50* 30.00 60.00
JWE2 Jerry West/50* 30.00 60.00
LLE1 Lisa Leslie/40* 25.00 50.00
LLE2 Lisa Leslie/40* 25.00 50.00
RBA1 Rick Barry/70* 20.00 40.00
RBA2 Rick Barry/70* 20.00 40.00

2009 Sportkings Autograph Memorabilia Silver
ANNOUNCED PRINT RUN B/WN 15-40 PER
UNPRICED GOLD PRINT RUN 10
RANDOM INSERTS IN PACKS
LLE1 Lisa Leslie Jsy/40* 25.00 50.00
LLE2 Lisa Leslie Jsy/40* 25.00 50.00

2009 Sportkings Double Memorabilia Silver
ANNOUNCED PRINT RUN B/WN 1-19
UNPRICED GOLD PRINT RUN 1
RANDOM INSERTS IN PACKS
14 Leslie/Jynr-Kersee/19* 20.00 40.00

2009 Sportkings Patch Silver
ANNOUNCED PRINT RUN B/WN 4-19
UNPRICED GOLD PRINT RUN 1 SET
RANDOM INSERTS IN PACKS
10 Lisa Leslie/19* 15.00 30.00

2009 Sportkings Single Memorabilia Silver
ANNOUNCED PRINT RUN B/WN 4-29
UNPRICED GOLD PRINT RUN B/WN 1-4
RANDOM INSERTS IN PACKS
19 Lisa Leslie Jsy/29* 10.00 25.00

2010 Sportkings
COMPLETE SET (48) 150.00 300.00
COMP.SET w/o ALI SP (47) 100.00 200.00
168 Wilt Chamberlain 6.00 15.00
169 Bobby Knight 5.00 12.00
173 Sheryl Swoopes 4.00 10.00
174 Dennis Rodman 5.00 12.00
202 Curly Neal 5.00 12.00

2010 Sportkings Mini
COMPLETE SET (48) 175.00 350.00
*MINI: .5X TO 1.2X BASIC CARDS
STATED ODDS 1:2

2010 Sportkings Autograph Silver
ANNOUNCED PRINT RUN 10-50
UNPRICED GOLD PRINT RUN 5-10
ACN1 Curly Neal/40* 20.00 40.00
ACN2 Curly Neal/40* 20.00 40.00
ADR1 Dennis Rodman/40* 25.00 50.00
ADR2 Dennis Rodman/40* 25.00 50.00
ABKN1 Bobby Knight/25* 30.00 60.00
ABKN2 Bobby Knight/25* 30.00 60.00
ABKN3 Bobby Knight/25* 30.00 60.00
ASSW1 Sheryl Swoopes/40* 15.00 30.00
ASSW2 Sheryl Swoopes/40* 15.00 30.00

2010 Sportkings Autograph Memorabilia Silver
ANNOUNCED PRINT RUN 10-40
UNPRICED GOLD PRINT RUN 5-10
AMCN1 Curly Neal Shorts/40* 25.00 50.00
AMCN2 Curly Neal Shorts/40* 25.00 50.00
AMDR1 Dennis Rodman/40* 30.00 60.00
AMDR2 Dennis Rodman/40* 30.00 60.00
AMBKN1 Bobby Knight Shirt/20* 40.00 80.00
AMBKN2 Bobby Knight Shirt/20* 40.00 80.00
AMBKN3 Bobby Knight Shirt/20* 40.00 80.00
AMSSW1 Sheryl Swoopes Jsy/40* 20.00 40.00
AMSSW2 Sheryl Swoopes Jsy/40* 20.00 40.00

2010 Sportkings Double Memorabilia Silver
STATED PRINT RUN 20 UNLESS NOTED
DM7 W.Chamberlain/C.Neal 40.00 100.00
DM9 S.Swoopes/L.Leslie 10.00 25.00

2010 Sportkings Patch Silver
STATED PRINT RUN 20
UNPRICED GOLD PRINT RUN 10
P4 Sheryl Swoopes 10.00 25.00

2010 Sportkings Single Memorabilia Silver
STATED PRINT RUN 26 UNLESS NOTED
SM4 Bobby Knight 10.00 20.00
SM7 Curly Neal 6.00 12.00
SM8 Dennis Rodman 10.00 20.00
SM26 Sheryl Swoopes 6.00 12.00
SM30 Wilt Chamberlain 20.00 40.00

2010 Sportkings Triple Memorabilia Silver
SILVER PRINT RUN 4-20
UNPRICED GOLD PRINT RUN 1-10
TM3 Chamberlain/Neal/Rodman 20.00 40.00

2012 Sportkings
218 Jackie Stiles 4.00 10.00
219 David Robinson 4.00 10.00
220 Bill Walton 4.00 10.00
221 Isiah Thomas 4.00 10.00
222 Dick Vitale 4.00 10.00

2012 Sportkings Mini
*MINI: .5X TO 1.2X BASIC CARDS
RANDOM INSERT IN PACKS

2012 Sportkings Autograph Memorabilia Silver
ANNOUNCED PRINT RUN 15-50
AMBW1 Bill Walton 12.00 25.00
AMBW2 Bill Walton 12.00 25.00
AMDRO1 David Robinson 40.00 80.00
AMDRO2 David Robinson 40.00 80.00
AMITH1 Isiah Thomas 12.00 25.00
AMITH2 Isiah Thomas 12.00 25.00
AMJST1 Jackie Stiles 12.00 25.00
AMJST2 Jackie Stiles 12.00 25.00

2012 Sportkings Autographs Silver
ANNOUNCED PRINT RUN 15-130
ABW1 Bill Walton 10.00 20.00
ABW2 Bill Walton 10.00 20.00
ADRO1 David Robinson 30.00 60.00
ADRO2 David Robinson 30.00 60.00
ADV1 Dick Vitale 20.00 40.00
ADV2 Dick Vitale 20.00 40.00
AITH1 Isiah Thomas 12.00 25.00
AITH2 Isiah Thomas 12.00 25.00
AJST1 Jackie Stiles 10.00 20.00
AJST2 Jackie Stiles 10.00 20.00

2012 Sportkings Cityscapes Double Silver
ANNOUNCED PRINT RUN 30
CS8 I.Thomas/G.Howe 15.00 30.00
CS10 S.Pippen/F.Thomas 25.00 50.00

2012 Sportkings Double Memorabilia Silver
ANNOUNCED PRINT RUN 60
DM5 D.Robinson/B.Walton 10.00 20.00

2012 Sportkings Premium Back
*SINGLES: .5X TO 1.2X BASIC CARDS
STATED ODDS ONE PER PACK

2012 Sportkings Quad Memorabilia Silver
ANNOUNCED PRINT RUN 30
QM5 Rbnsn/Waltn/Thoms/Pipp 15.00 30.00

2012 Sportkings Single Memorabilia Silver
ANNOUNCED PRINT RUN 90
SM9 David Robinson 7.50 15.00
SM10 Jackie Stiles 7.50 15.00
SM11 Isiah Thomas 7.50 15.00
SM12 Bill Walton 7.50 15.00

2012 Sportkings Triple Memorabilia Silver
ANNOUNCED PRINT RUN 30
TM5 Robinson/Petty/Sayers 15.00 30.00

2013 Sportkings
COMPLETE SET (48) 60.00 120.00
268 Clyde Drexler 3.00 8.00
287 Shaquille O'Neal 4.00 10.00
291 Scottie Pippen 4.00 10.00

2013 Sportkings Autograph Memorabilia Silver
PRINT RUN 20-50
AMCD1 Clyde Drexler/50* 12.00 30.00
AMCD2 Clyde Drexler/50* 12.00 30.00
AMSO1 Shaquille O'Neal/20* 40.00 80.00
AMSO2 Shaquille O'Neal/30* 40.00 80.00
AMSO3 Shaquille O'Neal/30* 40.00 80.00
AMSP1 Scottie Pippen/40* 40.00 80.00
AMSP2 Scottie Pippen/40* 40.00 80.00
AMSP3 Scottie Pippen/40* 40.00 80.00

2013 Sportkings Autographs Silver
PRINT RUN 15-60
ACD1 Clyde Drexler/50* 12.00 30.00
ACD2 Clyde Drexler/50* 12.00 30.00
ASO1 Shaquille O'Neal/20* 50.00 100.00
ASO2 Shaquille O'Neal/20* 50.00 100.00
ASO3 Shaquille O'Neal/20* 50.00 100.00
ASP1 Scottie Pippen/40* 35.00 70.00
ASP2 Scottie Pippen/40* 35.00 70.00
ASP3 Scottie Pippen/40* 35.00 70.00

2013 Sportkings Cityscapes Double Silver
ANNOUNCED PRINT RUN 40
CSD1 S.Pippen/B.Hull 10.00 25.00
CSD4 F.Valenzuela/S.O'Neal 6.00 15.00
CSD5 G.Howe/C.Drexler 8.00 20.00

2013 Sportkings Cityscapes Triple Silver
ANNOUNCED PRINT RUN 30
CST2 Thomas/Pippen/Hull 10.00 25.00
CST3 O'Neal/Valenzuela/Sawchuk

2013 Sportkings Decades Silver
ANNOUNCED PRINT RUN 40
D1 Orti/Rive/Shaq/Ortiz 8.00 20.00
D2 Thom/Pipp/Strg/Yzer 10.00 25.00
D3 Vale/Drex/Bogg/Chav 12.00 30.00

2013 Sportkings Double Memorabilia Silver
ANNOUNCED PRINT RUN 60
DM4 D.Robinson/S.O'Neal 6.00 15.00
DM6 S.Pippen/S.O'Neal 6.00 15.00

2013 Sportkings Four Sport Silver
ANNOUNCED PRINT RUN 19
FSQM1 Thom/Shaq/Cohn/Will 8.00 20.00
FSQM2 Vale/Pipp/Hays/Ortiz 10.00 25.00
FSQM3 Rive/Drex/Howe/Strug 12.00 30.00
FSQM4 Ortiz/Robi/Chav/Yama 12.00 30.00

2013 Sportkings Mini
*MINI: .5X TO 1.2X BASIC CARDS
STATED ODDS 1:2

2013 Sportkings Premium Back
*PREM.BACK: .5X TO 1.2X BASIC CARDS
ONE PREMIUM BACK PER BOX

2013 Sportkings Quad Memorabilia Silver
ANNOUNCED PRINT RUN 40
QM2 Shaq/Drex/Pipp/Robin 12.00 30.00

2013 Sportkings Single Memorabilia Silver
ANNOUNCED PRINT RUN 90
SM4 Clyde Drexler 6.00 15.00
SM17 Scottie Pippen 6.00 15.00
SM18 Shaquille O'Neal 5.00 12.00
SM19 Shaquille O'Neal 5.00 12.00

2013 Sportkings Triple Memorabilia Silver
ANNOUNCED PRINT RUN 40
TM1 Shaq/Pippen/Robinson 8.00 20.00

2008 Sportkings National Convention VIP Promo
7 Larry Bird 4.00 10.00
Nat Holman
13 Bill Russell 3.00 8.00
Joe Lapchick

2009 Sportkings National Convention VIP Promo
COMPLETE SET (7)
1 Lendl/Esposito/Wallace 4.00 10.00
Shamrock/Barry/Tyson
4 West/Nelson/Perry/Martin/Fats/Rice 5.00 12.00

2010 Sportkings National Convention VIP Promo
6 Wilt Chamberlain 1.50 4.00
8 Dennis Rodman 1.25 3.00
21 Curly Neal 1.25 3.00

1994-95 Sports Action Basket
Released during the 1994-95 season, this 172-card set packed out in Sports Action Basket magazine. Each card is numbered on the back, the first two digits refer to the issue number, and the last two digits refer to the individual card. The set features many NBA players, coaches, and cheerleaders. Oddities include Jack Nicholson and Michael Jordan as a baseball player.

COMPLETE SET (172) 200.00 500.00
5301 Dan Majerle 2.00 5.00
5302 Ron Harper 2.00 5.00
5303 Muggsy Bogues 1.50 4.00
5304 Shaquille O'Neal 8.00 20.00
5305 Larry Johnson 1.50 4.00
5306 Jalen Rose 3.00 8.00
5307 Nate McMillan 1.25 3.00
5308 Clippers Cheerleaders .40 1.00
5309 Kenny Smith 1.25 3.00
5310 Gorilla Mascot .60 1.50
5311 Michael Young 1.25 3.00
5312 David Robinson 5.00 12.00
5313 Jason Kidd 6.00 15.00
5314 Richard Dacoury 1.25 3.00
5315 Damon Bailey 1.50 4.00
5316 Dennis Rodman 3.00 8.00
5317 Michael Jordan 20.00 50.00
5318 B.J. Armstrong 1.25 3.00
5501 Billy Owens 1.25 3.00
5502 Alonzo Mourning 3.00 8.00
5503 Yann Bonato 1.25 3.00
5504 Isiah Thomas 2.50 6.00
5505 Glenn Robinson 3.00 8.00
5506 Karl Malone 5.00 12.00
5507 Dikembe Mutombo 2.50 6.00
5508 Hakeem Olajuwon 3.00 8.00
5509 Rony Seikaly 1.25 3.00
5510 Vernon Maxwell 1.25 3.00
5511 Stephane Ostrowski 1.25 3.00
5512 Arvydas Sabonis 3.00 8.00
5513 Yinka Dare 1.25 3.00
5514 Jamal Mashburn 3.00 8.00
5515 Buck Williams 1.50 4.00
5516 Mookie Blaylock 1.25 3.00
5517 Charles Barkley 5.00 12.00
5518 Patrick Ewing 3.00 8.00
5601 Scott Skiles 1.50 4.00
5602 Terry Porter 1.25 3.00
5603 Dominique Wilkins 3.00 8.00
5604 Stuff Mascot .40 1.00
5605 Anthony Peeler 1.25 3.00
5606 Donyell Marshall 1.50 4.00
5607 Chris Webber 3.00 8.00
5608 Alexander Volkov 2.00 5.00
5609 Pooh Richardson 1.25 3.00
5610 Robert Parish 1.50 4.00
5611 Isaiah Rider 1.50 4.00
5612 Steve Smith 1.50 4.00
5613 Michael Adams 1.25 3.00
5614 John Lucas Foundation .75 2.00
5615 Michael Jordan 20.00 50.00
5616 Sarunas Marciulionis 2.00 5.00
5617 Gerald Wilkins 1.50 4.00
5618 Miami Cheerleader .75 2.00
5701 Charlotte Mascot .40 1.00
5702 Brad Daugherty 1.25 3.00
5703 Chris Mullin 3.00 8.00
5704 Don MacLean 1.25 3.00
5705 Vlade Divac 1.50 4.00
5706 Danny Ainge 2.00 5.00
5707 Mark Jackson 2.00 5.00
5708 Lakers Cheerleaders 1.25 3.00
5709 B.J. Armstrong 1.50 4.00
5710 Nikos Gallis 2.00 5.00
5711 Joe Dumars 2.50 6.00
5712 Antoine Rigaudeau 2.00 5.00
5713 Rik Smits 1.25 3.00
5714 Charles Oakley 1.25 3.00
5715 Shawn Kemp 2.00 5.00
5716 Chris Webber 3.00 8.00
5717 Bill Varner 1.25 3.00
5718 Christian Laettner 2.00 5.00
5801 John Stockton 6.00 15.00
5802 Mitch Richmond 2.50 6.00
5803 Charles Barkley 5.00 12.00
5804 Latrell Sprewell 2.50 6.00
5805 Danny Manning 1.50 4.00
5806 Miami Mascot .40 1.00
5807 Bulls Mascot .40 1.00
5808 Kevin Willis 1.25 3.00
5809 Micheal Williams 1.25 3.00
5810 Magic Johnson 6.00 15.00
5811 Kevin Johnson 1.50 4.00
5812 Dennis Rodman 3.00 8.00
5813 John Starks 1.50 4.00
5814 Gheorghe Muresan 1.25 3.00
5815 Orlando Cheerleader 1.25 3.00
5816 Jeff Hornacek 2.00 5.00
5817 Clyde Drexler 4.00 10.00
5818 Dell Curry 1.25 3.00
5901 Jimmy Jackson 1.50 4.00
5902 Byron Scott 2.00 5.00
5903A Sam Cassell 2.00 5.00
5903B Otis Thorpe UER 1.25 3.00
Should have been numbered 5904
5905 San Antonio Mascot .40 1.00
5906 James Worthy 2.50 6.00
5907 A.C. Green 2.00 5.00
5908 Cleveland Cheerleader 1.25 3.00
5909 John Paxson 1.50 4.00
5910 Doug Christie 1.25 3.00
5911 Derrick Coleman 1.25 3.00
5912 Sean Rooks 1.25 3.00
5913 Turbo Mascot .40 1.00
5914 Charles Smith 1.25 3.00
5915 Derrick McKey 1.25 3.00
5916 Cherokee Parks 1.25 3.00
5917 Felton Spencer 1.25 3.00
5918 Derrick Phelps 1.25 3.00
6001 Steve Smith 1.50 4.00
6002 Tim Hardaway 2.00 5.00
6003 Dee Brown 1.25 3.00
6004 Reggie Miller 4.00 10.00
6005 Mark Price 2.00 5.00
6006 Jack Nicholson 2.00 5.00
6007 Kenny Anderson 1.25 3.00
6008 Jimmy Jackson 1.50 4.00
6009 Dikembe Mutombo 2.50 6.00
6010 Charles Oakley 1.25 3.00
6011 Muggsy Bogues 1.50 4.00
6012 Dan Majerle 2.00 5.00
6013 Mahmoud Abdul-Rauf .75 2.00
6014 B.J. Armstrong 1.50 4.00
6015 Nick Van Exel 2.50 6.00
6016 Kevin Johnson 1.50 4.00
6017 John Stockton 6.00 15.00
6018 Detlef Schrempf 1.50 4.00
6101 Scottie Pippen 5.00 12.00
6102 LaPhonso Ellis 1.25 3.00
6103 Sherman Douglas 1.25 3.00
6104 Isaiah Rider 1.50 4.00
6105 Vinny Del Negro 1.25 3.00
6106 Gary Payton 3.00 8.00
6107 Mookie Blaylock 1.25 3.00
6108 Christian Laettner 2.00 5.00
6109 Kevin Willis 1.25 3.00
6110 Harold Miner 1.25 3.00
6111 Chris Webber 3.00 8.00
6112 Rod Strickland 1.25 3.00
6113 Derrick Coleman 1.25 3.00
6114 Larry Johnson 1.50 4.00
6115 Rony Seikaly 1.25 3.00
6116 Derrick Coleman 1.25 3.00
6117 Larry Johnson 1.50 4.00
6118 Karl Malone 5.00 12.00
6201 Dell Curry 1.25 3.00
6202 Joe Dumars 2.50 6.00
6203 Robert Horry 2.00 5.00
6204 Glen Rice 2.00 5.00
6205 Hakeem Olajuwon 3.00 8.00
6206 Danny Ainge 1.50 4.00
6207 Oklahoma Cheerleader .75 2.00
6208 J.R. Reid 1.25 3.00
6209 Derrick McKey 1.25 3.00
6210 Shaquille O'Neal 6.00 15.00
6211 Christian Laettner 2.00 5.00
6212 John Starks 1.50 4.00
6213 Vernon Maxwell 1.25 3.00
6214 Charles Barkley 5.00 12.00
6215 Clyde Drexler 4.00 10.00
6216 Doug Smith 1.25 3.00
6217 Gators Cheerleader 1.25 3.00
6218 David Robinson 4.00 10.00
5406 Detlef Schrempf 1.50 4.00
5407 Anfernee Hardaway 3.00 8.00
5409 Reggie Miller 4.00 10.00
5410 Spud Webb 1.50 4.00
5412 Eric Montross 1.25 3.00
5415 Hakeem Olajuwon 3.00 8.00
5417 Glen Rice 2.00 5.00
5418 Kenny Anderson 1.25 3.00
6302 Craig Ehlo 1.25 3.00
6306 Jamal Mashburn 3.00 8.00

1995 Sports Action Basket
This oversized 41-card set was released in France in 1995. The set features four subsets: Ecris a ta Star (Write to your star) (ES), Legend of the NBA (LN), Star of the NBA (SN), and Back Court (BC). Please note that these cards are not numbered and are listed below in Alphabetical order.

COMPLETE SET (41) 150.00 300.00
1 Charles Barkley SN 2.50 6.00
2 Larry Bird LN 4.00 10.00
3 Dee Brown SN 1.00 2.50
4 Sam Cassell SN 1.50 4.00
5 Vlade Divac ES 1.50 4.00
6 Patrick Ewing SN 2.00 5.00
7 Horace Grant SN 1.25 3.00
8 Anfernee Hardaway ES 2.50 6.00
9 Anfernee Hardaway SN 2.50 6.00
10 Grant Hill ES 2.50 6.00
11 Jeff Hornacek SN 1.25 3.00
12 Bobby Hurley SN 1.00 2.50
13 Jim Jackson SN 1.00 2.50
14 Magic Johnson LN 4.00 10.00
15 Vinnie Johnson SN 1.50 4.00
16 Michael Jordan SN 12.00 30.00
17 Michael Jordan HOME UER ES 12.00 30.00
18 Michael Jordan AWAY ES 12.00 30.00
19 Shawn Kemp SN 1.50 4.00
20 Shawn Kemp BC 1.50 4.00
21 Jason Kidd SN 2.50 6.00
22 Toni Kukoc SN 1.50 4.00
23 Christian Laettner ES 1.25 3.00
24 Karl Malone HOME ES 2.00 5.00
25 Karl Malone AWAY UER ES 2.00 5.00
26 Anthony Mason SN 1.00 2.50
27 Antonio McDyess SN 2.00 5.00
28 Nate McMillan SN 1.00 2.50
29 Reggie Miller SN 2.00 5.00
30 Chris Mullin SN 1.50 4.00
31 Alonzo Mourning ES 2.00 5.00
32 Shaquille O'Neal ES 4.00 10.00
33 Hakeem Olajuwon UER ES 2.00 5.00
34 Hakeem Olajuwon SN 2.00 5.00
35 Gary Payton SN 1.50 4.00
36 Mitch Richmond SN 1.50 4.00
37 Mitch Richmond ES 1.50 4.00
38 Isaiah Rider SN 1.50 4.00
39 Dennis Rodman SN 3.00 8.00
40 Arvydas Sabonis SN 3.00 8.00
41 Nick Van Exel SN 1.50 4.00

1995 Sports Action Basket Sticker Panels
This set was released in France in 1995 by Sports Action Basket. The set features eight 4 5/8" by 6 1/2" sticker panels that features top NBA players and team logos. Please note that these panels are not numbered.

COMPLETE SET (7) 25.00 60.00
1 Hakeem Olajuwon 8.00 20.00
Michael Jordan
Jalen Rose
Charles Barkley
Chris Webber
Magic Cheerleader
Reggie Miller
Georgia Tech
Shawn Kemp
2 Miami Hurricanes 3.00 8.00
The Intimidator
Rebels Logo
Grant Hill
Dennis Rodman
Anfernee Hardaway
Lakers Cheerleader
Muggsy Bogues
Shaquille O'Neal
Scottie Pippen
3 Clyde Drexler 3.00 8.00
Robert Horry
Mitch Richmond
Mortal Kombat
Jimmy Jackson
Derek Harper
Mookie Blaylock
Vinny Del Negro
Dee Brown
4 Gorilla Mascot 3.00 8.00
Space Player
Horace Grant
James Robinson
Danny Ferry
David Robinson
Doug Smith
Kendall Gill
Mahmoud Abdul-Rauf
Mitch Richmond
5 Mitch Richmond 4.00 10.00
Dennis Rodman
Shaquille O'Neal
Jason Kidd
Knicks Cheerleader
Penny Hardaway
Larry Johnson
Charles Barkley
Isaiah Rider
6 Dee Brown 3.00 8.00
Karl Malone
Rik Smits
Chris Mullin
Joe Dumars
Shaquille O'Neal
Sean Elliott
John Starks
Pedrag Danilovic
7 KO 4.00 10.00
Playground Attitude
Dennis Rodman
Pacers Mascot
Charles Barkley
John Stockton
Don MacLean
Billy Owens
Coach Attitude

1996 Sports Action Basket Punch Outs
This 10-card set was released in 1996, and features players from the Chicago Bulls and the Seattle Supersonics. These player action-figures were printed on a very thick stock, and measure roughly 4 3/4" x 6 1/4". All of Bulls' players are featured on a white bordered card, the Sonics' players were issued on a light yellow bordered card.

COMPLETE SET (10) 50.00 125.00
1 Michael Jordan 25.00 60.00
2 Steve Kerr 2.00 5.00
3 Toni Kukoc 3.00 8.00
4 Scottie Pippen 5.00 12.00
5 Dennis Rodman 5.00 12.00
6 Frank Brickowski 2.00 5.00
7 Hersey Hawkins 2.00 5.00
8 Shawn Kemp 4.00 10.00
9 Gary Payton 4.00 10.00
10 Detlef Schrempf 2.00 5.00

1987 Sports Cube Game
3 1/2" by 5 3/8" cards with nine black and white portrait shots on front and questions on the back
COMPLETE SET (3) 8.00 20.00
1 James Naismith 6.00 15.00
Babe Ruth
America's Cup
Knute

1978 Sports I.D. Patches
This patch set was issued in 1978, and featured many of the NBA's top players or teams. Each patch was done in full color, and measured 3" x 5". Each patch is unnumbered and is listed below in alphabetical order.

COMPLETE SET (6) 60.00 120.00
1 Darryl Dawkins 5.00 10.00
2 Julius Erving 20.00 40.00
3 Dan Issel 12.50 25.00
4 Bobby Jones 7.50 15.00
5 Nuggets Team Photo 7.50 15.00
6 Spurs Team Photo 7.50 15.00
7 David Thompson 7.50 15.00

1989 Sports Illustrated for Kids I
Since its debut issue in January 1989, SI for Kids has included a perforated sheet of nine standard-size cards bound into each magazine. The cards were consecutively numbered 1-324 through December 1991. The athletes featured represent an extremely wide spectrum of sports. Each card features color photos with variously colored borders. The borders are as follows: aqua (1-108), green (109-207), woodgrain (208-216), red (217-315), marble (316-324). The player's name is printed in a white bar at the top, while his or her sport appears at the bottom. The backs carry biographical information, career highlights, and a trivia question with answer. The cards' magazine issue date appears on the back in very small type. Although originally distributed in sheet form, the cards are frequently traded as singles. Thus, they are priced individually. The value of an intact sheet is equal to the sum of the nine cards plus a premium of up to 20%.

4 Larry Bird BK 4.00 10.00
6 Isiah Thomas BK .60 1.50
10 Mark Jackson BK .40 1.00
16 Michael Jordan BK 20.00 35.00
23 Dominique Wilkins BK .40 1.00
27 Magic Johnson BK 4.00 10.00
29 Charles Barkley BK 2.00 5.00
34 Alex English BK .40 1.00
42 Kareem Abdul-Jabbar BK 1.50 4.00
44 Hakeem Olajuwon BK 1.50 4.00
77 Patrick Ewing BK 1.25 3.00
89 Karl Malone BK 2.00 5.00
91 Joe Dumars BK .40 1.00
93 Chris Mullin BK .40 1.00
97 Bridgette Gordon BK .40 1.00
101 Nancy Lieberman-Cline BK .40 1.00
104 John Stockton BK 1.00 2.50
107 Michael Cooper BK .40 1.00

1990 Sports Illustrated for Kids I
113 James Worthy BK .50 1.25
117 Jack Sikma BK .15 .40
119 Sandra Hodge BK .75 2.00
123 Brad Daugherty BK .10 .30
124 Dale Ellis BK .15 .40
129 Bill Laimbeer BK .10 .30
131 David Robinson BK 2.00 5.00
137 Moses Malone BK .50 1.25
139 J.R. Reid BK .10 .30
145 Reggie Miller BK .75 2.00
150 Rex Chapman BK .15 .40
160 Scottie Pippen BK 2.00 5.00
164 Jennifer Azzi BK .50 1.25
192 Dennis Rodman BK 2.00 5.00
199 Lynette Woodard BK .30 .75
200 Terry Cummings BK .15 .40
204 Kevin Johnson BK .50 1.25
208 Wilt Chamberlain BK 1.50 4.00

1991 Sports Illustrated for Kids I
217 Tom Chambers BK .15 .40
221 Clyde Drexler BK 1.25 3.00
223 Teresa Edwards BK .50 1.25
226 Ricky Pierce BK .15 .40
230 Bernard King BK .30 .75
235 Kevin McHale BK .50 1.25
239 Charles Smith HK .10 .30
244 Rolando Blackman BK .10 .30
246 Vlade Divac BK .30 .75
255 Kevin Duckworth BK .10 .30
263 Alvin Robertson BK .10 .30
274 Daedra Charles BK .60 1.50
281 Sonja Henning BK .40 1.00
302 Tim Hardaway BK .40 1.00
307 Chuck Person BK .15 .40
309 Hersey Hawkins BK .15 .40
310 Venus Lacy BK .75 2.00
323 Bill Russell BK 1.25 3.00

1992 Sports Illustrated for Kids II
Since its debut issue in January 1989, SI for Kids has included a perforated sheet of nine standard-size cards bound into each magazine. In January 1992, the card numbers started over again at 1. This listing comprises the cards contained from that magazine through the last 2000 issue. The athletes featured represent an extremely wide spectrum of sports. Each card features color photos with borders of various designs and colors. The borders are as follows: navy (1-9, 19-99), clouds (10-18, 55-63, 226-234), marble (100-108, 208-216, 316-324), pink (109-207), purple (217-225), blue (235-315), gold/silver (325-486), clouds (487-495) and gold/silver (496-621). The athlete's name is printed at the top while his or her sport appears at the bottom. The backs carry biographical information, career highlights, and a trivia question with answer. The cards' magazine issue date appears on the back in very small type. Although originally distributed in sheet form, the cards are frequently traded as singles. Thus, they are priced individually. The value of an intact sheet is equal to the sum of the nine cards plus a premium of up to 20 percent. The cards labeled as "MC" were issued in SI for Kids as part of a milk promotion.

4 Michael Jordan BK 8.00 20.00
8 Dee Brown BK .10 .30
19 Dominique Wilkins BK .40 1.00
25 Derrick Coleman BK .20 .50
31 Mitch Richmond BK .30 .75
35 David Robinson BK 1.25 3.00
37 Robert Parish BK .40 1.00
41 Dikembe Mutombo BK .60 1.50
46 Shawn Kemp BK .75 2.00
67 Dawn Staley BK .30 .75
85 Larry Johnson BK .40 1.00
92 Michael Adams BK .10 .30
97 Detlef Schrempf BK .30 .75
104 Julius Erving BK 1.25 3.00

1993 Sports Illustrated for Kids II
109 Drazen Petrovic BK .10 .30
122 Karl Malone BK 1.25 3.00
124 Horace Grant BK .60 1.50
127 Chris Mullin BK .20 .50
131 Shaquille O'Neal BK 3.00 8.00
140 Charles Barkley BK 1.25 3.00
147 Spud Webb BK .20 .50
155 Cliff Robinson BK .10 .30
164 Val Whiting BK .10 .30
166 Patrick Ewing BK .75 2.00
184 Sheryl Swoopes BK 1.25 3.00
193 Christian Laettner BK .30 .75
213 Oscar Robertson BK .75 2.00

1994 Sports Illustrated for Kids II
238 Hakeem Olajuwon BK .75 2.00
242 Dennis Rodman BK 1.25 3.00
249 Alonzo Mourning BK .75 2.00
250 John Starks BK .30 .75
260 Chris Webber BK .60 1.50
264 Danny Manning BK .20 .50
269 Lisa Leslie BK 1.25 3.00
279 Anfernee Hardaway BK 1.50 4.00
286 Mark Price BK .15 .40
295 Latrell Sprewell BK .40 1.00
299 Dikembe Mutombo BK .40 1.00
308 B.J. Armstrong BK .20 .50
316 Ann Meyers BK .30 .75
322 Bill Bradley BK .60 1.50

1996 Sports Illustrated for Kids II
440 Glen Rice BK .30 .75
444 Katrina McClain BK .30 .75
449 Alonzo Mourning BK .40 1.00
452 Teresa Edwards BK .20 .50
kid photo
458 David Robinson BK .40 1.00
kid photo
461 Mahmoud Abdul-Rauf BK .10 .30
468 Rik Smits BK .40 1.00
469 Juwan Howard BK .40 1.00
473 Magic Johnson BK 1.25 3.00
482 Dennis Rodman BK .75 2.00
484 Clifford Robinson BK .10 .30
487 Oscar Robertson BK .75 2.00
494 Cheryl Miller BK .30 .75
504 Jennifer Rizzotti BK .50 1.25
514 Shawn Kemp BK .75 2.00
522 Gheorghe Muresan BK .15 .40
523 Arvydas Sabonis BK .20 .50
530 Trooper Johnson BK .08 .25
533 Jerry Stackhouse BK .30 .75
534 Lisa Leslie BK .60 1.50
537 Michael Finley BK .40 1.00

1997 Sports Illustrated for Kids II
541 Kevin Garnett BK 1.25 3.00
545 Shaquille O'Neal BK 1.00 2.50
549 Kara Wolters BK .30 .75
550 Damon Stoudamire BK .60 1.50
556 Shawn Bradley BK .15 .40
560 Charles Barkley BK .75 2.00
572 Anfernee Hardaway .50 1.25
Ken Griffey Jr.
April Fool
580 Kevin Johnson BK .30 .75
584 Anfernee Hardaway BK .75 2.00
587 Grant Hill BK .60 1.50
597 Tom Gugliotta BK .20 .50
599 Hakeem Olajuwon BK .60 1.50
603 Chamique Holdsclaw BK .40 1.00
605 Mark Jackson BK .15 .40
612 Michele Timms BK .15 .40
614 Tim Hardaway BK .30 .75
622 Patrick Ewing BK .30 .75
cartoon
626 Lisa Leslie BK .40 1.00
cartoon
631 Scottie Pippen BK .50 1.25
635 Cynthia Cooper BK 1.25 3.00
637 John Stockton BK .60 1.50
642 Ruthie Bolton-Holifield BK 1.50 4.00
643 Gary Payton BK .40 1.00

1998 Sports Illustrated for Kids II
651 Natalie Williams BK .30 .75
653 Glen Rice BK .15 .40
655 Chris Webber BK .30 .75
668 Shawn Kemp BK .50 1.25
670 Tim Duncan BK .75 2.00
689 Reggie Miller BK .40 1.00
691 Keith Van Horn BK .30 .75
696 Rod Strickland BK .15 .40
698 Vin Baker BK .20 .50
700 Yolanda Griffith BK .20 .50
707 Dikembe Mutombo BK .30 .75
716 Jason Kidd BK .40 1.00
726 Antoine Walker BK .60 1.50
730 Dennis Rodman BK .30 .75
731 Karl Malone BK .60 1.50
739 Kobe Bryant BK 2.00 5.00
741 Mookie Blaylock BK .15 .40
745 Tina Thompson BK .30 .75

748 Stephon Marbury BK .30 .75
756 Katie Smith BK .20 .50

1999 Sports Illustrated for Kids II

760 Steve Kerr BK .15 .40
762 Debbie Black BK .08 .25
769 Shareef Abdur-Rahim BK .40 1.00
775 Michael Jordan BK 2.00 5.00
776 Michael Jordan BK 2.00 5.00
777 Michael Jordan BK 2.00 5.00
778 Michael Jordan BK 2.00 5.00
779 Michael Jordan BK 2.00 5.00
780 Michael Jordan BK 2.00 5.00
781 Michael Jordan BK 2.00 5.00
782 Michael Jordan BK 2.00 5.00
783 Michael Jordan BK 2.00 5.00
785 David Robinson BK .75 2.00
787 Sheryl Swoopes BK .75 2.00
793 Alonzo Mourning BK .30 .75
803 Eddie Jones BK .30 .75
810 Mitch Richmond BK .30 .75
811 Allen Iverson BK .75 2.00
819 Jennifer Gillom BK .40 1.00
821 Vince Carter BK 1.25 3.00
823 Teresa Weatherspoon BK .60 1.50
827 Brian Grant BK .15 .40
830 Darrell Armstrong BK .10 .30
835 Suzie McConnell-Serio BK .40 1.00
838 Gary Payton BK .40 1.00
842 Kobe Bryant BK 2.00 5.00
845 Cynthia Cooper BK .75 2.00
847 Avery Johnson BK .15 .40
851 Shaquille O'Neal BK 1.00 2.50
853 Ticha Penicheiro BK .20 .50
857 Kendall Gill BK .15 .40
859 Nykesha Sales BK .40 1.00

2000 Sports Illustrated for Kids II

871 Michael Jordan BK 2.00 5.00
876 Alonzo Mourning BK .30 .75
878 Reggie Miller BK .40 1.00
883 Scottie Pippen BK .30 .75
890 Allan Houston BK .15 .40
903 John Stockton BK .30 .75
905 Grant Hill BK .30 .75
911 Rasheed Wallace BK .40 1.00
919 Jeff Hornacek BK .15 .40
923 Tim Duncan BK .60 1.50
928 Sean Elliott BK .15 .40
937 Elton Brand BK .15 .40
942 Natalie Williams BK .20 .50
948 Glenn Robinson BK .15 .40
950 Vince Carter BK .75 2.00
952 Sheryl Swoopes .75 2.00
Cythnia Cooper
Tina Thompson
Basketball
956 Jalen Rose BK .10 .30
960 Katie Smith BK .20 .50
961 Jason Kidd BK .40 1.00

2001 Sports Illustrated for Kids

Since its debut issue in January 1989, SI for Kids has included a perforated sheet of nine standard-size cards bound into each magazine. In December 2000, for the second time, the card numbers started over again at 1. The athletes featured represent an extremely wide spectrum of sports. The athlete's name is printed at the top while his or her sport appears at the bottom. The backs carry biographical information, career highlights, and a trivia question with answer. The cards' magazine issue date appears on the back in very small type. Although originally distributed in sheet form, the cards are frequently traded as singles. Thus, they are priced individually. The value of an intact sheet is equal to the sum of the nine cards plus a premium of up to 20 percent.

COMPLETE SET (108) 25.00 50.00
2 Kevin Garnett BK .75 2.00
4 Jason Williams BK .07 .20
12 Steve Francis BK .20 .50
16 Ray Allen BK .40 1.00
23 Latrell Sprewell BK .08 .25
27 Tim Hardaway BK .08 .25
28 Allen Iverson BK 1.00 2.50
33 Stephon Marbury BK .15 .40
38 Sheryl Swoopes BK .40 1.00
42 Jerry Stackhouse BK .08 .25
51 Antonio McDyess BK .15 .40
52 Dirk Nowitzki BK .40 1.00
55 Dawn Staley BK .15 .40
59 Kobe Bryant BK 1.25 3.00
63 Damon Stoudamire BK .20 .50
65 Tracy McGrady BK .40 1.00
69 Ruth Riley BK .40 1.00
70 Karl Malone BK .30 .75
77 Tim Duncan BK .30 .75
83 Jackie Stiles BK .40 1.00
89 Dikembe Mutombo BK .08 .25
93 Shaquille O'Neal BK 1.00 2.50
97 Mike Miller BK .15 .40
103 Aaron McKie BK .10 .30
107 Predrag Stojakoic BK .30 .75

2002 Sports Illustrated for Kids

113 Vince Carter BK .60 1.50
117 Lisa Leslie BK .30 .75
120 Chris Webber BK .40 1.00
125 Glenn Robinson BK .10 .30
128 Kevin Garnett BK .50 1.25
130 Baron Davis BK .40 1.00
138 Jason Kidd BK .40 1.00
142 Darius Miles BK .60 1.50
147 Jermaine O'Neal BK .20 .50
149 Michael Jordan BK 2.00 5.00
154 Penny Hardaway BK .10 .30
156 Andre Miller BK .20 .50
161 Lauren Jackson BK .75 2.00
167 Antoine Walker BK .20 .50
171 Chamique Holdsclaw BK .20 .50
173 Ben Wallace BK .20 .50
175 Sue Bird BK .20 .50
184 Gary Payton BK .10 .30
188 Pau Gasol BK .07 .20
190 Mike Bibby BK .07 .20
192 Corliss Williamson BK .07 .20
200 Robert Horry BK .07 .20
202 Tamika Catchings BK .10 .30
210 Jason Richardson BK .08 .25
212 Alonzo Mourning BK .20 .50
219 Antoine Walker BK .20 .50
224 Nikki Teasley BK .07 .20

2003 Sports Illustrated for Kids

Since its debut issue in January 1989, SI for Kids has included a perforated sheet of nine standard-size cards bound into each magazine. In January 2001, for the second time, the card numbers started over at 1. Listed below are the cards issued in magazines that carry 2003 cover dates. The athletes featured represent an extremely wide spectrum of sports. Although originally distributed in sheet form, the cards are frequently traded as singles. Thus, they are priced individually. The value of an intact sheet is equal to the sum of the nine cards plus a premium of up to 20 percent.

227 Tracy McGrady BK .40 1.00
231 Rasheed Wallace BK .30 .75
236 Luke Walton BK .20 .50
240 Shareef Abdur-Rahim BK .20 .50
244 Sheryl Swoopes BK .30 .75
249 Kenyon Martin BK .20 .50
254 Steve Nash BK .40 1.00
256 Jerry Stackhouse BK .20 .50
264 LeBron James BK 4.00 10.00
266 Tim Duncan BK .40 1.00
268 Diana Taurasi WNBA .40 1.00
273 Stephon Marbury BK .30 .75
275 Jamal Mashburn BK .20 .50
282 Chris Webber BK .20 .50
284 Carmelo Anthony BK .50 1.25
288 Tony Parker BK .30 .75
291 Paul Pierce BK .30 .75
293 Kobe Bryant BK 1.25 3.00
297 Tina Thompson WNBA .20 .50
299 Nick Van Exel BK .20 .50
303 Richard Jefferson BK .20 .50
305 Shannon Johnson WNBA .30 .75
309 Yao Ming BK .75 1.25
311 Richard Hamilton BK .20 .50
317 Drew Gooden BK .20 .50
323 Michael Finley BK .20 .50
326 Allen Iverson BK .40 1.00
328 Jermaine O'Neal BK .20 .50
332 Swin Cash Women's BK .40 1.00

2004 Sports Illustrated for Kids

ONE NINE-CARD SHEET PER MAGAZINE
334 Shaquille O'Neal BK .40 1.00
338 Michael Jordan BK 2.00 5.00
344 Steve Francis BK .20 .50
350 Raymond Felton BK .20 .50
354 Vince Carter BK .40 1.00
355 Lauren Jackson BK .40 1.00
362 Peja Stojakovic BK .20 .50
368 Nicole Powell Women's BK .30 .75
372 Jason Kidd BK .30 .75
378 Michael Redd BK .20 .50
380 Kevin Garnett BK .30 .75
382 Sue Bird WNBA .60 1.50
387 Andrei Kirilenko BK .20 .50
390 Mike Bibby BK .20 .50
392 LeBron James BK 1.25 3.00
397 Theo Ratliff BK .20 .50
401 Corey Maggette BK .20 .50
407 Dwayne Wade BK .60 1.50
412 Chamique Holdsclaw WNBA .40 1.00
419 Carmelo Anthony BK .40 1.00
425 Dirk Nowitzki BK .40 1.00
432 Diana Taurasi WNBA 1.00 2.50
433 Ron Artest BK .20 .50
437 Manu Ginobili BK .20 .50

2005 Sports Illustrated for Kids

445 Nykesha Sales WNBA .30 .75
449 Sam Cassell BK .20 .50
456 Carlos Boozer BK .20 .50
457 Chris Paul BK .75 2.00
464 Amare Stoudemire BK .30 .75
468 Rashad McCants BK .20 .50
473 Shaquille O'Neal BK .40 1.00
477 Emeka Okafor BK .20 .50
482 Allen Iverson BK .40 1.00
486 Seimone Augustus College BK .30 .75
489 Lisa Leslie WNBA .50 1.25
491 Ray Allen BK .30 .75
500 Shawn Marion BK .20 .50
502 Gilbert Arenas BK .30 .75
510 Ben Wallace BK .20 .50
511 Cuttino Mobley BK .20 .50
515 Chris Bosh BK .30 .75
517 Tina Thompson WNBA .40 1.00
525 Paul Pierce BK .30 .75
529 Vince Carter BK .40 1.00
533 Ben Gordon BK .30 .75
539 Troy Murphy BK .20 .50

2006 Sports Illustrated for Kids

6 Dee Brown BK .20 .50
8 Sheryl Swoopes BK .40 1.00
14 Jason Richardson BK .20 .50
16 Chris Webber BK .20 .50
19 Richard Hamilton BK .20 .50
23 Manu Ginobili BK .20 .50
29 Marcus Camby BK .20 .50
31 J.J. Redick BK .60 1.50
38 Dirk Nowitzki BK .40 1.00
43 Cheryl Ford WNBA .40 1.00
46 Adam Morrison BK .60 1.50
51 Steve Nash BK .40 1.00
56 Jason Terry BK .20 .50
58 Ivory Latta Women's BK .60 1.50
63 Pau Gasol BK .20 .50
64 Lindsay Whalen WNBA .30 .75
66 Dwight Howard BK .40 1.00
71 Courtney Paris BK .40 1.00
74 Chauncey Billups BK .20 .50
80 Tamika Catchings WNBA .40 1.00
84 Tracy McGrady BK .40 1.00
89 Alana Beard WNBA .30 .75
97 Boris Diaw BK .20 .50
99 Swin Cash WNBA .40 1.00
101 Kirk Hinrich BK .20 .50
105 Joakim Noah BK .20 .50
107 Cappie Pondexter WNBA .40 1.00

2007 Sports Illustrated for Kids

ONE NINE-CARD SHEET PER MAGAZINE
116 Chris Paul BK 1.25 3.00
118 Kevin Love HS BK 1.00 2.50
122 O.J. Mayo HS BK 1.25 3.00
126 Maya Moore HS BK .20 .50
129 Tim Duncan BK .40 1.00
130 Joe Johnson BK .20 .50
134 Lindsey Harding BK .20 .50
137 Zach Randolph BK .20 .50
141 Tyler Hansbrough BK .75 2.00
142 Candace Parker BK 2.00 5.00
147 Kevin Durant BK 4.00 10.00
148 Andre Iguodala BK .30 .75
152 Crystal Langhorne BK .20 .50
155 Josh Howard BK .30 .75
157 DeAnna Nolan WNBA .20 .50
161 Caron Butler BK .20 .50
163 Tina Charles BK .20 .50
167 Carlos Boozer BK .20 .50
174 Luol Deng BK .20 .50
175 Katie Douglas WBNA .30 .75
186 Brandon Roy BK .75 2.00
188 Michelle Snow WNBA .20 .50
194 Tony Parker BK .40 1.00
199 Candice Wiggins BK .20 .50
204 Kevin Martin BK .20 .50
208 Penny Taylor WNBA .30 .75
212 Kobe Bryant BK .75 2.00
214 D.J. Augustin BK .30 .75

2008 Sports Illustrated for Kids

226 Armintie Price BK .20 .50
230 Yao Ming BK .30 .75
234 Deron Williams BK .40 1.00
237 Kevin Garnett BK .75 2.00
238 Michael Beasley BK .40 1.00
245 Derrick Rose BK 3.00 8.00
249 Chris Kaman BK .20 .50
250 Rashard Lewis BK .20 .50
255 Ray Allen BK .30 .75
256 Epiphanny Prince BK .20 .50
260 Al Jefferson BK .20 .50
263 David West BK .20 .50
270 Lauren Jackson BK .40 1.00
276 Allen Iverson BK .40 1.00
281 Rudy Gay BK .25 .60
283 Sophia Young BK .20 .50
289 Chris Bosh BK .25 .60
302 Paul Pierce BK .30 .75
304 Stephen Curry BK 20.00 50.00
312 Kobe Bryant BK .75 2.00
317 Al Horford BK .20 .50
321 Luke Harangody BK .40 1.00

2009 Sports Illustrated for Kids

335 Manu Ginobili BK .30 .75
342 Alana Beard BK .20 .50
347 Kevin Garnett ART BK .40 1.00
351 Dwyane Wade ART BK .60 1.50
353 Nate Robinson BK .20 .50
357 Kevin Durant BK .60 1.50
364 Candace Parker BK .40 1.00
368 Mo Williams BK .20 .50
372 Derrick Rose BK .75 2.00
373 Maya Moore BK .75 2.00
381 LeBron James BK .75 2.00
383 Dwight Howard BK .40 1.00
388 Danny Granger BK .20 .50
395 Diana Taurasi BK .40 1.00
397 Pau Gasol BK .20 .50
401 Carmelo Anthony BK .30 .75
408 Rajon Rondo BK .30 .75
409 Swin Cash BK .40 1.00
417 Dirk Nowitzki BK .40 1.00
429 Devin Harris BK .20 .50
431 Jayne Appel BK .20 .50

2010 Sports Illustrated for Kids

433 Marc Gasol BK .25 .60
440 Joakim Noah BK .40 1.00
444 Amare Stoudemire BK .25 .60
448 Tyreke Evans BK .30 .75
453 Tim Duncan BK .40 1.00
458 Monta Ellis BK .20 .50
462 Deron Williams BK .30 .75
467 Sherron Collins BK .20 .50
471 Steve Nash BK .40 1.00
472 Russell Westbrook BK .40 1.00
478 Joe Johnson BK .20 .50
483 Carlos Boozer BK .20 .50
492 Derek Fisher BK .20 .50
494 Rebekkah Brunson BK .20 .50
498 Josh Smith BK .20 .50
505 Jason Kidd BK .30 .75
512 Zach Randolph BK .20 .50
517 Lauren Jackson BK .40 1.00
522 Andre Iguodala BK .20 .50
523 Diana Taurasi BK
528 Kobe Bryant BK .75 2.00
530 Andrew Bogut BK .25 .60

2011 Sports Illustrated for Kids

5 Chris Paul BK .40 1.00
9 John Wall BK .40 1.00
15 Blake Griffin BK .40 1.00
17 Kevin Love BK .40 1.00
23 LeBron James BK .75 2.00
25 Brittney Griner BK 1.25 3.00
30 Kevin Durant BK .75 2.00
35 Jimmer Fredette BK 1.50 4.00
37 Kemba Walker BK 1.25 3.00
41 Derrick Rose BK .75 2.00
48 Dirk Nowitzki BK .40 1.00
59 Jason Terry BK .20 .50
65 Tina Charles BK .20 .50
72 Dwyane Wade BK .60 1.50
78 Dwight Howard BK .40 1.00
85 Angel McCoughtry BK .20 .50
87 Harrison Barnes BK 1.25 3.00
93 Carmelo Anthony BK .30 .75
94 Skylar Diggins BK .20 .50

2012 Sports Illustrated for Kids

105 Terrence Jones BK .40 1.00
114 LaMarcus Aldridge BK .25 .60
116 Kyle Lowry BK .20 .50
122 Kevin Durant BK .75 2.00
124 Deron Williams BK .25 .60
129 Kobe Bryant BK .75 2.00
130 Joakim Noah BK .25 .60
138 Chris Paul BK .40 1.00
143 Seimone Augustus BK .20 .50
145 Rajon Rondo BK .40 1.00
149 LeBron James BK .75 2.00
154 Sylvia Fowles BK .20 .50
158 Tim Duncan BK .40 1.00
163 Kyrie Irving BK
168 James Harden BK
174 Danny Granger BK
178 Tony Parker BK
186 Marc Gasol BK
188 Kristi Toliver BK
191 Brandon Jennings BK
193 Kaleena Mosqueda-Lewis BK

2013 Sports Illustrated for Kids

200 Zach Randolph BK
204 Jrue Holiday BK
212 Blake Griffin BK
216 Damian Lillard BK
222 Tyson Chandler BK
224 Skylar Diggins BK
226 Brittney Griner BK
230 Dwight Howard BK
234 Greivis Vasquez BK
237 Brook Lopez BK
242 Jabari Parker BK
246 Tamika Catchings BK
249 Jeremy Lin BK
250 Russ Smith BK
255 Andrew Wiggins BK
259 Elena Delle Donne BK
261 Paul George BK
267 Russell Westbrook BK
269 Candace Parker BK
271 Kenneth Faried BK
273 Chris Davis BK
276 Marcus Smart BK
287 Stephen Curry BK
295 Blake Sniffin BK
Dog head caricature

1997 Sports Time USBL

Distributed in two 25-card series sets, this 50-card set was produced by Sports Time, Inc. and features some of the best players who have played in the United States Basketball League. Card fronts feature a somewhat fuzzy action photo with the player's name running vertically along the left border. Card backs feature same photo as front, with bio and statistics.

COMPLETE SET (50) 8.00 20.00
1 Norris Coleman .08 .25
2 Anthony Mason 1.25 3.00
3 Michael Anderson .08 .25
4 Dallas Comegys .20 .50
5 Anthony Pullard .08 .25
6 Darrell Armstrong .08 .25
7 Kermit Holmes .08 .25
8 Lloyd Daniels .30 .75
9 Roy Tarpley .40 1.00
10 Paul Graham .20 .50
11 Nantambu Willingham .08 .25
12 Michael Ray Richardson .40 1.00
World B. Free
13 Richard Dumas .20 .50
14 International All-Star Tour .08 .25
15 Keith Jennings .20 .50
16 Duane Washington .20 .50
17 Wes Matthews .20 .50
18 Michael Adams .40 1.00
19 First USBL Game .30 .75
John Hot Rod Williams
20 Chuck Nevitt .20 .50
21 The Awards .40 1.00
Muggsy Bogues
22 The First Game .08 .25
Michael Adams
23 The Beginning .08 .25
Daniel T. Meisenheimer
24 Charlie Ward .75 2.00
25 Oliver Lee .08 .25
26 Greg Sutton .08 .25
27 1991 USBL Championship .08 .25
Paul Graham
28 Miami Tropics .08 .25
29 New Haven Skyhawks .08 .25
30 Back to Back Champions .08 .25
Miami Tropics
31 Springfield Fame .08 .25
32 Nate Johnson .08 .25
33 Muggsy Bogues 1.25 3.00
34 Chris Collier .08 .25
35 Sandhi Ortiz-Delvalle .08 .25
36 Henri Abrams .08 .25
37 Dan Cyrulik .08 .25
38 Charles Smith .30 .75
39 Mark Boyd .08 .25
40 Tim Legler .40 1.00
41 Jerry Ice Reynolds .20 .50
42 Road to the NBA .08 .25
Richard Dumas
43 Anthony Mason CL .40 1.00
44 Richard Dumas CL .08 .25
45 Atlanta Trojans .08 .25
Atlantic City Seagulls
46 Connecticut Skyhawks .08 .25
Florida Sharks
47 Jacksonville Barracudas .08 .25
Long Island Surf
48 New Hampshire Thunder Loons .08 .25
Philadelphia Power
49 Portland Wave .08 .25
Raleigh Cougars
50 Tampa Bay Windjammers .08 .25
Westchester Kings

1997 Sports Weekly Michael Jordan Promo

13 Michael Jordan 2.00 5.00

1998 Sports Weekly Michael Jordan Promo

23 Michael Jordan 2.00 5.00

1977-79 Sportscaster Series 1

COMPLETE SET (24) 17.50 35.00
124 Pete Maravich 3.00 8.00

1977-79 Sportscaster Series 2

COMPLETE SET (24) 30.00 60.00
203 Kareem Abdul-Jabbar 2.00 4.00
209 USA-USSR 1.00 2.00

1977-79 Sportscaster Series 3

COMPLETE SET (24) 15.00 30.00
315 Julius Erving 3.00 6.00

1977-79 Sportscaster Series 4

COMPLETE SET (24) 15.00 30.00
412 Bill Russell 3.00 6.00
414 Dave Cowens 1.00 2.00
415 Rick Barry 1.00 2.00

1977-79 Sportscaster Series 5

COMPLETE SET (24) 12.50 25.00
510 Referee's Signals .75 1.50
519 The 1969-70 1.00 2.00

1977-79 Sportscaster Series 6

COMPLETE SET (24) 12.50 25.00
608 The UCLA Dynasty 1.50 3.00
621 George McGinnis .75 1.50

1977-79 Sportscaster Series 7

COMPLETE SET (24) 15.00 30.00
712 A Laboratory Sport 1.00 2.00
713 Walt Frazier 1.50 3.00
720 Wilt Chamberlain 5.00 10.00

1977-79 Sportscaster Series 8

COMPLETE SET (24) 12.50 25.00
810 Jerry West 2.50 5.00

1977-79 Sportscaster Series 9

COMPLETE SET (24) 15.00 30.00
912 Nate Archibald 1.00 2.00
916 A Game for Giants 1.25 2.50

1977-79 Sportscaster Series 10

COMPLETE SET (24) 17.50 35.00
1018 John Havlicek 1.50 4.00

1977-79 Sportscaster Series 11

COMPLETE SET (25) 20.00 40.00
1124A UCLA vs Houston ERR 10.00 20.00
Bill Walton
1124B UCLA vs. Houston 5.00 10.00

1977-79 Sportscaster Series 12

COMPLETE SET (24) 12.50 25.00
1213 Wes Unseld 1.00 2.50

1977-79 Sportscaster Series 13

COMPLETE SET (24) 12.50 25.00
1304 The European .50 1.00
1310 Lakers Win 33 In 2.00 4.00

1977-79 Sportscaster Series 14

COMPLETE SET (24) 17.50 35.00
1412 Emil Zatopek .50 1.00
1418 Oscar Robertson 2.00 4.00

1977-79 Sportscaster Series 16

COMPLETE SET (24) 15.00 30.00
1614 Elgin Baylor 1.25 2.50
1624 Dick Button 1.00 2.00

1977-79 Sportscaster Series 18

COMPLETE SET (24) 12.50 25.00
1820 Jackie Chazalon .50 1.00

1977-79 Sportscaster Series 19

COMPLETE SET (24) 25.00 50.00
1914 Bob Pettit 1.00 2.00

1977-79 Sportscaster Series 20

COMPLETE SET (24) 7.50 15.00
2021 24-Second Clock .75 1.50

1977-79 Sportscaster Series 21

COMPLETE SET (24) 15.00 30.00
2114 Clarence(Bevo) .50 1.00

1977-79 Sportscaster Series 22

COMPLETE SET (24) 15.00 30.00
2208 Milwaukee Bucks 1.50 3.00

1977-79 Sportscaster Series 23

COMPLETE SET (24) 20.00 40.00
2303 Lingo 1.50 3.00

1977-79 Sportscaster Series 26

COMPLETE SET (24) 15.00 30.00
2624 Villeurbanne .25 .50

1977-79 Sportscaster Series 30

COMPLETE SET (24) 12.50 25.00
3010 Fouls and Penalties .50 1.00
3012 Podoloff Cup 1.50 3.00
3013 NBA All-Star Game 1.00 2.00

1977-79 Sportscaster Series 33

COMPLETE SET (24) 10.00 20.00
3304 Pivot Play 2.50 5.00

1977-79 Sportscaster Series 34

COMPLETE SET (24) 15.00 30.00
3414 Defenses .50 1.00

1977-79 Sportscaster Series 35

COMPLETE SET (24) 15.00 30.00
3506 The Highest Scoring 3.00 6.00

1977-79 Sportscaster Series 36

COMPLETE SET (24) 15.00 30.00
3608A Artis Gilmore UER 1.50 3.00
3608B Artis Gilmore COR 1.50 3.00
Basketball
3612A The Four Corner UER 1.50 3.00
3612B Phil Ford COR 1.50 3.00
Basketball
3622 The NCAA Tournament 2.50 5.00

1977-79 Sportscaster Series 38

COMPLETE SET (24) 20.00 40.00
3811 Paul Westphal 1.00 2.00
3812 Biddy-Basket .50 1.00

1977-79 Sportscaster Series 39

COMPLETE SET (24) 7.50 15.00
3910 Maccabi of Tel Aviv .50 1.00
3915 Doug Collins 1.50 3.00

1977-79 Sportscaster Series 40

COMPLETE SET (24) 10.00 20.00
4007 Marques Johnson 2.00 4.00
4009 Walter Davis 2.00 4.00

1977-79 Sportscaster Series 42

COMPLETE SET (24) 15.00 30.00
4202 Bernard King 1.00 2.00

1977-79 Sportscaster Series 43

COMPLETE SET (24) 12.50 25.00
4301 The Washington 1.00 2.00
4318 Power Forward 1.25 2.50

1977-79 Sportscaster Series 44

COMPLETE SET (24) 12.50 25.00
4416 Butch Lee .75 1.50
4421 3-Guard Offense 1.00 2.00

1977-79 Sportscaster Series 52

COMPLETE SET (24) 10.00 20.00
5224 Hank Luisetti 1.25 2.50

1977-79 Sportscaster Series 53

COMPLETE SET (24) 15.00 30.00
5322 Jack Sikma 1.25 2.50
5323 John Walker .75 1.50

1977-79 Sportscaster Series 54

COMPLETE SET (24) 15.00 30.00
5415 George Mikan 5.00 10.00
5423 Manuel Raga .75 1.50

1977-79 Sportscaster Series 55

COMPLETE SET (24) 12.50 25.00
5518 Leonard Robinson .75 1.50

1977-79 Sportscaster Series 56

COMPLETE SET (24) 37.50 75.00
5611 Marvin Webster 2.00 4.00

1977-79 Sportscaster Series 59

COMPLETE SET (24) 50.00 100.00
5905 David Thompson 4.00 8.00

1977-79 Sportscaster Series 60

COMPLETE SET (24) 37.50 75.00
6008 Carol Blazejowski 3.00 6.00

1977-79 Sportscaster Series 61

COMPLETE SET (24) 50.00 100.00
6110 Bill Bradley 5.00 12.00

1977-79 Sportscaster Series 62

COMPLETE SET (24) 40.00 80.00
6209 Calvin Murphy 2.50 5.00

1977-79 Sportscaster Series 63

COMPLETE SET (24) 30.00 60.00
6305 First TV Game 1.00 2.00
6320 Austin Carr 2.00 4.00

1977-79 Sportscaster Series 64

COMPLETE SET (24) 25.00 50.00
6404 Chinese Tour 1.00 2.00
6405 Olympic Games 2.50 5.00
6424 Three Officials 1.00 2.00

1977-79 Sportscaster Series 65

COMPLETE SET (24) 40.00 80.00
6502 Wilt Chamberlain 6.00 12.00
6515 20000 Point Club 2.50 5.00

1977-79 Sportscaster Series 66

COMPLETE SET (24) 37.50 75.00
6611 Hall of Fame 2.00 4.00

1977-79 Sportscaster Series 67

COMPLETE SET (24) 40.00 80.00
6702 Nancy Lieberman 5.00 10.00
6711 Bob Morse 2.00 4.00

1977-79 Sportscaster Series 70

COMPLETE SET (24) 30.00 60.00
7021 Kurt Thomas 3.00 6.00

1977-79 Sportscaster Series 73

COMPLETE SET (24) 40.00 80.00
7303 Rudy Tomjanovich 5.00 10.00

1977-79 Sportscaster Series 74

COMPLETE SET (24) 200.00 400.00
7407 A Pro Oddity 2.00 4.00
7418 Larry Bird 125.00 250.00

1977-79 Sportscaster Series 76

COMPLETE SET (24) 30.00 60.00
7608 The Longest Shot 1.00 2.00
7614 Inge Nissen 2.00 4.00

1977-79 Sportscaster Series 77

COMPLETE SET (24) 150.00 300.00
7705 Kevin Porter 2.50 5.00
7721 Nat Holman 4.00 8.00

1977-79 Sportscaster Series 78

COMPLETE SET (24) 150.00 300.00
7802 Earvin Johnson 100.00 200.00
7824 Dave Bing 4.00 8.00

1977-79 Sportscaster Series 79

COMPLETE SET (24) 60.00 120.00
7910 Ouliana Semenova 4.00 8.00
7915 Phil Ford 2.50 5.00
7919 Women's Basketball 2.00 4.00

1977-79 Sportscaster Series 81

COMPLETE SET (24) 62.50 125.00
8102 Lenny Wilkens 7.50 15.00

1977-79 Sportscaster Series 82

COMPLETE SET (24) 50.00 100.00
8202 Moses Malone 7.50 15.00
8215 Academic Basketball 3.00 6.00

1977-79 Sportscaster Series 83

COMPLETE SET (24) 62.50 125.00
8307 Three-Point Field 3.00 6.00
8317 Dutch Dehnert 3.00 6.00

1977-79 Sportscaster Series 84

COMPLETE SET (24) 60.00 120.00
8409 United Basketball 3.00 6.00

1977-79 Sportscaster Series 85

COMPLETE SET (24) 62.50 125.00
8515 Women's Draft 2.00 4.00
8522 F.P. Naismith Award 3.00 6.00

1977-79 Sportscaster Series 86

COMPLETE SET (24) 50.00 100.00
8608 Danny Ainge 15.00 40.00

1977-79 Sportscaster Series 102

COMPLETE SET (24) 75.00 150.00
10202 Ray Meyer 7.50 15.00

1977-79 Sportscaster Series 103

COMPLETE SET (24) 87.50 175.00
10304 Ann Meyers 10.00 20.00

1972 Sportscope Arena Great Moments in Basketball

Issued in 1972 by Sportscope, Inc. these items have been described as arena card booklets. We are not sure if the checklist is complete and will continue to add as we find other players.

1 Lew Alcindor/Wilt Chamberlain 40.00 75.00
2 Lew Alcindor/Bob Lanier 40.00 75.00
3 Lew Alcindor/Willis Reed/Bill Bradley 40.00 75.00
4 Dave Bing/Oscar Robertson 25.00 50.00
5 Austin Carr 15.00 30.00
6 Wilt Chamberlain/Lew Alcindor 50.00 100.00
7 Wilt Chamberlain/Jerry Lucas 75.00 150.00
8 Dave Cowens 25.00 50.00
9 Billy Cunningham/Phil Jackson 25.00 50.00
10 Dave DeBusschere 25.00 50.00
11 Walt Frazier 25.00 50.00
12 Gail Goodrich 20.00 40.00
13 John Havlicek 25.00 50.00
14 Pete Maravich 75.00 150.00
15 Jack Marin 15.00 30.00
16 Jack Newman 15.00 30.00
17 Unidentified Chicago Bulls #18 15.00 30.00
18 Dick VanArsdale/Walt Frazier 20.00 40.00
19 Lenny Wilkens 25.00 50.00

1976 Sportstix

This blank-backed irregularly shaped sticker features a borderless color player action photo. The team markings were crudely obliterated from the photo. The one basketball sticker is part of a larger multi-sport release. The stickers came in packs of five.

1 Dave DeBusschere 7.50 15.00

1996 SPx

The premier edition of Upper Deck's super-premium SPx basketball set contains 50 cards featuring only the top stars and youngsters in the NBA. The set marked a number of technological "firsts" in the basketball card market including first stand-alone all-Holoview set and first complete, perimeter die cut set. To create the holoview imagery, each athlete was videotaped while rotating on a turntable. The individual frames of videotape were then synthesized to produce a 50-degree, three-dimensional picture. Each card features super premium 32 point thick stock. Each pack contained only one card and carried a suggested retail price of $2.99. Each box contained 36 packs. In addition, to the 50 regular cards, a special Record Breaker card commemorating Michael Jordan's eighth scoring title (1:75 packs) and Tribute card commemorating Anfernee Hardaway's accomplishments in the NBA (1:24 packs) were issued. Also, two separate trade cards were available for signed Jordan and Hardaway cards. The odds of receiving a Jordan trade card were 1:34,560 packs. The Hardaway trade card was more than 25 times easier to pull at a rate of 1,345 packs. The Jordan AU was issued with a card sized certificate of authenticity, and the Upper Deck Authenticated hologram sticker on these cards carries a "BAC" or "BAD" prefix to the serial number.

COMPLETE SET (50) 20.00 50.00
R1: STATED ODDS 1:75
T1: STATED ODDS 1:95
1 Stacey Augmon .60 1.50
2 Mookie Blaylock .50 1.25
3 Eric Montross .50 1.25
4 Eric Williams .50 1.25
5 Larry Johnson .75 2.00
6 George Zidek .50 1.25
7 Jason Caffey .50 1.25
8 Michael Jordan 8.00 20.00
9 Chris Mills .50 1.25
10 Bob Sura .50 1.25
11 Jason Kidd 1.25 3.00
12 Jamal Mashburn .60 1.50
13 Antonio McDyess .75 2.00
14 Jalen Rose .60 1.50
15 Grant Hill 1.25 3.00
16 Theo Ratliff .60 1.50
17 Joe Smith .60 1.50
18 Latrell Sprewell .75 2.00
19 Hakeem Olajuwon 1.00 2.50
20 Reggie Miller 1.00 2.50
21 Rik Smits .60 1.50
22 Brent Barry .60 1.50
23 Lamond Murray .50 1.25
24 Magic Johnson 2.00 5.00
25 Eddie Jones .75 2.00
26 Nick Van Exel .75 2.00
27 Alonzo Mourning 1.00 2.50
28 Kurt Thomas .50 1.25
29 Vin Baker .60 1.50
30 Glenn Robinson .60 1.50
31 Kevin Garnett 2.00 5.00
32 Ed O'Bannon .50 1.25
33 Patrick Ewing 1.00 2.50
34 Anfernee Hardaway 1.25 3.00
35 Shaquille O'Neal 2.00 5.00
36 Jerry Stackhouse 1.00 2.50
37 Charles Barkley 1.25 3.00
38 Michael Finley 1.00 2.50
39 Randolph Childress .75 2.00
40 Gary Trent .50 1.25
41 Brian Grant .60 1.50
42 Mitch Richmond .75 2.00
43 David Robinson 1.25 3.00
44 Shawn Kemp .75 2.00
45 Gary Payton .75 2.00
46 Damon Stoudamire .60 1.50
47 Karl Malone 1.00 2.50
48 John Stockton 1.00 2.50
49 Bryant Reeves .50 1.25
50 Rasheed Wallace 1.00 2.50
R1 Michael Jordan RB 8.00 20.00
T1 Anfernee Hardaway TRIB 1.50 4.00
NNO Anfernee Hardaway AU 40.00 100.00
NNO A.Hardaway Expired 15.00 30.00
NNO Michael Jordan AU 600.00 1200.00
NNO M.Jordan Expired 300.00 600.00

1996 SPx Gold

COMPLETE SET (50) 50.00 120.00
*GOLD: .75X TO 2X BASE CARD HI
STATED ODDS 1:7

1996 SPx Holoview Heroes

Cards in this set of ten were randomly issued at a rate of one in every 24 packs and feature ten NBA players with the potential to be named to the NBA Hall of Fame. These die-cut cards feature a combination of lithograph and holoview technology.

COMPLETE SET (10) 20.00 50.00
STATED ODDS 1:24
H1 Michael Jordan 12.00 30.00
H2 Jason Kidd 2.50 6.00
H3 Grant Hill 2.50 6.00
H4 Joe Smith 1.25 3.00
H5 Magic Johnson 4.00 10.00
H6 Antonio McDyess 1.50 4.00
H7 Anfernee Hardaway 2.50 6.00
H8 Jerry Stackhouse 2.00 5.00
H9 Damon Stoudamire 1.25 3.00
H10 Shaquille O'Neal 2.50 6.00

1997 SPx

The 1997 SPx set was issued in one series totaling 50 cards and was distributed in one-card packs at a suggested retail of $3.49. This perimeter die-cut set features combinations of holographic, lithographic and Holoview images printed on super premium 32 point card stock. The cards were released after the 1997 NBA Playoffs and carry information from the first half of the 1996-97 NBA season. The cards are numbered with an "SPx" prefix. A Michael Jordan "sample" card was released prior to the regular set. It is listed below at the end of the set.

COMPLETE SET (50) 50.00 100.00
1 Mookie Blaylock .60 1.50
2 Antoine Walker 1.00 2.50
3 Eric Williams .60 1.50
4 Tony Delk .60 1.50
5 Michael Jordan 8.00 20.00
6 Dennis Rodman 2.00 5.00
7 Vitaly Potapenko .60 1.50
8 Bob Sura .60 1.50
9 Jamal Mashburn .75 2.00
10 Samaki Walker .60 1.50
11 Antonio McDyess .75 2.00
12 Joe Dumars .75 2.00
13 Grant Hill 1.50 4.00
14 Joe Smith .75 2.00
15 Latrell Sprewell 1.00 2.50
16 Charles Barkley 1.50 4.00
17 Hakeem Olajuwon 1.25 3.00
18 Erick Dampier .60 1.50
19 Reggie Miller 1.25 3.00
20 Brent Barry .75 2.00
21 Lorenzen Wright .60 1.50
22 Kobe Bryant 10.00 25.00
23 Eddie Jones 1.00 2.50
24 Shaquille O'Neal 2.50 6.00
25 Alonzo Mourning 1.25 3.00
26 Kurt Thomas .60 1.50
27 Vin Baker .75 2.00
28 Glenn Robinson .75 2.00
29 Kevin Garnett 1.50 4.00
30 Stephon Marbury 1.25 3.00
31 Kerry Kittles .60 1.50
32 Patrick Ewing 1.25 3.00
33 Larry Johnson 1.00 2.50
34 Anfernee Hardaway 1.50 4.00
35 Allen Iverson 2.00 5.00
36 Jerry Stackhouse 1.00 2.50
37 Kevin Johnson 1.00 2.50
38 Steve Nash 2.00 5.00
39 Jermaine O'Neal 1.25 3.00
40 Mitch Richmond 1.00 2.50
41 David Robinson 1.50 4.00
42 Shawn Kemp 1.00 2.50
43 Gary Payton 1.00 2.50
44 Marcus Camby 1.00 2.50
45 Damon Stoudamire 1.00 2.50
46 Karl Malone 1.25 3.00
47 John Stockton 1.25 3.00
48 Shareef Abdur-Rahim 1.00 2.50
49 Bryant Reeves .60 1.50
50 Juwan Howard .75 2.00
SPX5 Michael Jordan PROMO 10.00 25.00

1997 SPx Gold

*STARS: .75X TO 2X BASE CARD HI
STATED ODDS 1:9
5 Michael Jordan 20.00 50.00
22 Kobe Bryant 25.00 60.00

1997 SPx Holoview Heroes

Randomly inserted in packs at a rate of one in 75, this 20-card set features color photos of some of the best performers in the NBA on a vertical die-cut card format. Card backs are numbered with a "H" prefix.

COMPLETE SET (20) 150.00 300.00
STATED ODDS 1:75
H1 Michael Jordan 50.00 125.00
H2 Grant Hill 10.00 25.00
H3 Reggie Miller 8.00 20.00

H4 Joe Smith 5.00 12.00
H5 Kevin Garnett 10.00 25.00
H6 Mitch Richmond 6.00 15.00
H7 Allen Iverson 12.00 30.00
H8 Patrick Ewing 8.00 20.00
H9 Hakeem Olajuwon 8.00 20.00
H10 David Robinson 10.00 25.00
H11 Anfernee Hardaway 12.00 30.00
H12 Juwan Howard 5.00 12.00
H13 Gary Payton 6.00 15.00
H14 Dennis Rodman 12.00 30.00
H15 Shaquille O'Neal 15.00 40.00
H16 Charles Barkley 10.00 25.00
H17 Damon Stoudamire 6.00 15.00
H18 Shawn Kemp 6.00 15.00
H19 Glenn Robinson 5.00 12.00
H20 John Stockton 8.00 20.00

1997 SPx ProMotion

Randomly inserted in packs at a rate of one in 430, this five-card set features back-to-back Holoview images. Card fronts actually picture three shots of the player.

COMPLETE SET (5) 200.00 400.00
STATED ODDS 1:430
1 Michael Jordan 125.00 300.00
2 Damon Stoudamire 12.00 30.00
3 Anfernee Hardaway 20.00 50.00
4 Shawn Kemp 15.00 40.00
5 Antonio McDyess 10.00 25.00

1997 SPx ProMotion Autographs

1 Michael Jordan 2000.00 3500.00
2 Damon Stoudamire 75.00 125.00
3 Anfernee Hardaway 250.00 500.00
4 Shawn Kemp 125.00 250.00
5 Antonio McDyess 75.00 125.00

1997-98 SPx

The 1998 SPx set was the final that used the "holoview" technology. The 50-card set was packaged in three-card packs with a suggested retail price of $5.99. The set also featured redemption cards for a "Piece of History" which was a framed, uncut, Hardcourt HoloView sheet. That card is priced at the bottom of the set.

COMPLETE SET (50) 20.00 50.00
1 Mookie Blaylock .40 1.00
2 Dikembe Mutombo .60 1.50
3 Chauncey Billups RC 2.50 6.00
4 Antoine Walker .60 1.50
5 Glen Rice .60 1.50
6 Michael Jordan 5.00 12.00
7 Scottie Pippen 1.00 2.50
8 Dennis Rodman 1.25 3.00
9 Shawn Kemp .60 1.50
10 Michael Finley .60 1.50
11 Tony Battie RC .75 2.00
12 LaPhonso Ellis .40 1.00
13 Grant Hill 1.00 2.50
14 Joe Dumars .60 1.50
15 Joe Smith .50 1.25
16 Clyde Drexler .75 2.00
17 Charles Barkley 1.00 2.50
18 Hakeem Olajuwon .75 2.00
19 Reggie Miller .75 2.00
20 Brent Barry .50 1.25
21 Kobe Bryant 3.00 8.00
22 Shaquille O'Neal 1.50 4.00
23 Alonzo Mourning .75 2.00
24 Glenn Robinson .50 1.25
25 Kevin Garnett 1.00 2.50
26 Stephon Marbury .75 2.00
27 Keith Van Horn RC 1.25 3.00
28 Patrick Ewing .75 2.00
29 Anfernee Hardaway 1.00 2.50
30 Allen Iverson 1.25 3.00
31 Kevin Johnson .60 1.50
32 Antonio McDyess .50 1.25
33 Jason Kidd 1.00 2.50
34 Kenny Anderson .50 1.25
35 Rasheed Wallace .60 1.50
36 Mitch Richmond .60 1.50
37 Tim Duncan RC 4.00 10.00
38 David Robinson 1.00 2.50
39 Vin Baker .50 1.25
40 Gary Payton .60 1.50
41 Marcus Camby .60 1.50
42 Tracy McGrady RC 3.00 8.00
43 Damon Stoudamire .50 1.25
44 Karl Malone .75 2.00
45 John Stockton .75 2.00
46 Shareef Abdur-Rahim .60 1.50
47 Antonio Daniels RC .75 2.00
48 Bryant Reeves .40 1.00
49 Juwan Howard .50 1.25
50 Chris Webber .60 1.50
T1 Piece of History Trade 4.00 10.00

1997-98 SPx Sky

MPLETE SET (50) 30.00 80.00
*STARS: .5X TO 1.25X BASE CARD HI
*RCs: .4X TO 1X BASE HI
ONE PER PACK

1997-98 SPx Bronze

COMPLETE SET (50) 25.00 60.00
*STARS: .75X TO 2X BASE CARD HI
*RCs: .6X TO 1.5X BASE HI
STATED ODDS 1:3

1997-98 SPx Silver

*STARS: 1X TO 2.5X BASE CARD HI
*RCs: .75X TO 2X BASE HI
STATED ODDS 1:6

1997-98 SPx Gold

*STARS: 4X TO 10X BASE CARD HI
*RCs: 2X TO 5X BASE HI
STATED ODDS 1:17
6 Michael Jordan 200.00 500.00
37 Tim Duncan 30.00 80.00

1997-98 SPx Grand Finale

*STARS: 40X TO 100X BASE CARD HI
*RCs: 15X TO 40X BASE HI
STATED PRINT RUN 50 SERIAL #'d SETS
6 Michael Jordan 3000.00 5000.00
7 Scottie Pippen 200.00 400.00
8 Dennis Rodman 300.00 600.00
9 Shawn Kemp 100.00 200.00
16 Clyde Drexler 125.00 225.00
17 Charles Barkley 150.00 300.00
18 Hakeem Olajuwon 125.00 250.00
19 Reggie Miller 125.00 250.00
21 Kobe Bryant 2000.00 3500.00
22 Shaquille O'Neal 500.00 1000.00
23 Alonzo Mourning 150.00 400.00
25 Kevin Garnett 400.00 800.00
38 David Robinson 150.00 300.00
44 Karl Malone 125.00 250.00
45 John Stockton 125.00 250.00
50 Chris Webber 100.00 200.00

1997-98 SPx Hardcourt Holoview

Randomly inserted into packs at a rate of one in 54, this 20-card set features key NBA players using several "holoview" poses.

COMPLETE SET (20) 350.00 700.00
STATED ODDS 1:54
HH1 Michael Jordan 200.00 400.00
HH2 Allen Iverson 15.00 40.00
HH3 Antoine Walker 6.00 15.00
HH4 Chris Webber 6.00 15.00
HH5 Glenn Robinson 5.00 12.00
HH6 Kevin Garnett 10.00 25.00
HH7 Shareef Abdur-Rahim 6.00 15.00
HH8 Keith Van Horn 4.00 10.00
HH9 Kobe Bryant 40.00 100.00
HH10 Glen Rice 6.00 15.00
HH11 Damon Stoudamire 5.00 12.00
HH12 Hakeem Olajuwon 8.00 20.00
HH13 Mookie Blaylock 4.00 10.00
HH14 Shaquille O'Neal 20.00 50.00
HH15 Stephon Marbury 8.00 20.00
HH16 Chauncey Billups 8.00 20.00
HH17 Anfernee Hardaway 10.00 25.00
HH18 Tim Duncan 20.00 50.00
HH19 Mitch Richmond 6.00 15.00
HH20 Grant Hill 10.00 25.00

1997-98 SPx ProMotion

Randomly inserted into packs at a rate of one in 252, this 10-card set features the player against several "holoview" poses.

COMPLETE SET (10) 500.00 1000.00
STATED ODDS 1:252
PM1 Michael Jordan 400.00 800.00
PM2 Shaquille O'Neal 30.00 80.00
PM3 Tim Duncan 75.00 200.00
PM4 Shareef Abdur-Rahim 12.00 30.00
PM5 Grant Hill 20.00 50.00
PM6 Karl Malone 15.00 40.00
PM7 Anfernee Hardaway 40.00 100.00
PM8 Keith Van Horn 20.00 50.00
PM9 Kevin Garnett 40.00 100.00
PM10 Damon Stoudamire 10.00 25.00

1999-00 SPx

The 1999-00 version of SPx was released by Upper Deck as a 120-card set. The set was divided into 90 veterans and 30 rookies, which had either signed or unsigned cards. The unsigned rookies were serially numbered to 3500. The signed rookies were serially numbered to either 2500 or 500, depending on the player. The cards are designed below. Each pack contained four cards and carried a suggested retail price of $5.99. Please note that card "P32" was given out to dealers and members of the hobby press as a promotional card.

COMPLETE SET w/o RC (90) 18.00 30.00
91-120 UNSIGNED #'d TO 3500
91-120 SIGNED #'d TO 2500 UNLESS NOTED
UNPRICED SPECTRUM SERIAL #'d TO 1
1 Dikembe Mutombo .50 1.25
2 Alan Henderson .30 .75
3 Antoine Walker .50 1.25
4 Paul Pierce .60 1.50
5 Kenny Anderson .40 1.00
6 Eddie Jones .50 1.25
7 David Wesley .30 .75
8 Elden Campbell .30 .75
9 Toni Kukoc .50 1.25
10 Dickey Simpkins .30 .75
11 Shawn Kemp .50 1.25
12 Brevin Knight .30 .75
13 Michael Finley .50 1.25
14 Cedric Ceballos .30 .75
15 Dirk Nowitzki 1.00 2.50
16 Antonio McDyess .40 1.00
17 Nick Van Exel .40 1.00
18 Chauncey Billups .50 1.25
19 Grant Hill .60 1.50
20 Jerry Stackhouse .50 1.25
21 Bison Dele .30 .75
22 Lindsey Hunter .30 .75
23 Antawn Jamison .50 1.25
24 Donyell Marshall .30 .75
25 John Starks .40 1.00
26 Chris Mills .30 .75
27 Hakeem Olajuwon .60 1.50
28 Scottie Pippen .75 2.00
29 Charles Barkley .75 2.00
30 Reggie Miller .50 1.25
31 Rik Smits .50 1.25
32 Jalen Rose .40 1.00
33 Chris Mullin .50 1.25
34 Maurice Taylor .30 .75
35 Michael Olowokandi .30 .75
36 Shaquille O'Neal 1.25 3.00
37 Kobe Bryant 2.00 5.00
38 Glen Rice .50 1.25
39 Tim Hardaway .50 1.25
40 Alonzo Mourning .60 1.50
41 Dan Majerle .50 1.25
42 P.J. Brown .30 .75
43 Glenn Robinson .40 1.00
44 Ray Allen .50 1.25
45 Sam Cassell .40 1.00
46 Tim Thomas .40 1.00
47 Kevin Garnett .75 2.00
48 Bobby Jackson .30 .75
49 Joe Smith .40 1.00
50 Stephon Marbury .40 1.00
51 Keith Van Horn .40 1.00
52 Jayson Williams .30 .75
53 Patrick Ewing .60 1.50
54 Latrell Sprewell .50 1.25
55 Allan Houston .40 1.00
56 Marcus Camby .40 1.00
57 Bo Outlaw .30 .75
58 Darrell Armstrong .30 .75
59 Allen Iverson 1.00 2.50
60 Theo Ratliff .40 1.00
61 Larry Hughes .40 1.00
62 Jason Kidd .75 2.00
63 Tom Gugliotta .30 .75
64 Clifford Robinson .30 .75
65 Brian Grant .30 .75
66 Jermaine O'Neal .40 1.00
67 Rasheed Wallace .50 1.25
68 Damon Stoudamire .40 1.00
69 Jason Williams .60 1.50
70 Chris Webber .50 1.25
71 Vlade Divac .50 1.25
72 Avery Johnson .40 1.00
73 Tim Duncan 1.00 2.50
74 David Robinson .75 2.00
75 Sean Elliott .50 1.25
76 Gary Payton .50 1.25
77 Vin Baker .40 1.00
78 Jelani McCoy .30 .75
79 Charles Oakley .40 1.00
80 Vince Carter 1.00 2.50
81 Tracy McGrady .75 2.00
82 Doug Christie .40 1.00
83 Karl Malone .60 1.50
84 John Stockton .60 1.50
85 Shareef Abdur-Rahim .40 1.00
86 Bryant Reeves .30 .75
87 Mike Bibby .50 1.25
88 Juwan Howard .40 1.00
89 Mitch Richmond .50 1.25
90 Rod Strickland .30 .75
91 Elton Brand RC 5.00 12.00
92 Steve Francis AU/500 RC 15.00 40.00
93 Baron Davis AU/500 RC 30.00 60.00
94 Lamar Odom/3500 RC 5.00 12.00
95 Jonathan Bender/3500 RC 2.00 5.00
96 W.Szczerbiak AU/500 RC 6.00 15.00
97 R.Hamilton AU/2500 RC 4.00 10.00
98 Andre Miller AU/500 RC 6.00 15.00
99 Shawn Marion AU/2500 RC 4.00 10.00
100 Jason Terry AU/2500 RC 3.00 8.00
101 T.Langdon AU/2500 RC 2.00 5.00
102 Venson Hamilton/3500 RC 2.00 5.00
103 Corey Maggette AU/500 RC 5.00 12.00
104 William Avery AU/2500 RC 1.50 4.00
105 Dion Glover/3500 RC 1.50 4.00
106 Ron Artest AU RC 4.00 10.00
107 Cal Bowdler/3500 RC 1.25 3.00
108 James Posey AU/2500 RC 2.00 5.00
109 Quincy Lewis AU/2500 RC 1.25 3.00
110 D.George AU/2500 RC 2.00 5.00
111 Tim James AU/2500 RC 1.25 3.00
112 V.Cummings/3500 RC 1.25 3.00
113 Jumaine Jones AU/2500 RC 1.50 4.00
114 Scott Padgett AU/2500 RC 1.50 4.00
115 Kenny Thomas/3500 RC 2.00 5.00
116 Jeff Foster/3500 RC 2.00 5.00
117 Ryan Robertson/3500 RC 1.25 3.00
118 Chris Herren AU/2500 RC 6.00 15.00
119 E.Eschmeyer AU/2500 RC 1.50 4.00
120 A.J. Bramlett AU/2500 RC 2.00 5.00
P32 Karl Malone PROMO .50 1.25

1999-00 SPx Radiance

*STARS: 8X TO 20X BASE CARD HI
STATED PRINT RUN 100 SERIAL #'d SETS
4 Paul Pierce 15.00 40.00
11 Shawn Kemp 20.00 50.00
19 Grant Hill 20.00 50.00
28 Scottie Pippen 25.00 60.00
29 Charles Barkley 20.00 50.00
37 Kobe Bryant 60.00 150.00
59 Allen Iverson 40.00 100.00
81 Tracy McGrady 30.00 80.00
91 Elton Brand 20.00 50.00
92 Steve Francis 20.00 50.00
93 Baron Davis 20.00 50.00
94 Lamar Odom 20.00 50.00
95 Jonathan Bender 8.00 20.00
96 Wally Szczerbiak 15.00 40.00
97 Richard Hamilton 15.00 40.00
98 Andre Miller 15.00 40.00
99 Shawn Marion 15.00 40.00
100 Jason Terry 12.00 30.00
101 Trajan Langdon 8.00 20.00
102 Venson Hamilton 8.00 20.00
103 Corey Maggette 12.00 30.00
104 William Avery 6.00 15.00
105 Dion Glover 6.00 15.00
106 Ron Artest 15.00 40.00
107 Cal Bowdler 5.00 12.00
108 James Posey 8.00 20.00
109 Quincy Lewis 5.00 12.00
110 Devean George 8.00 20.00
111 Tim James 5.00 12.00
112 Vonteego Cummings 5.00 12.00
113 Jumaine Jones 6.00 15.00
114 Scott Padgett 6.00 15.00
115 Kenny Thomas 8.00 20.00
116 Jeff Foster 8.00 20.00
117 Ryan Robertson 5.00 12.00
118 Chris Herren 6.00 15.00
119 Evan Eschmeyer 6.00 15.00
120 A.J. Bramlett 8.00 20.00

1999-00 SPx Decade of Jordan

Randomly inserted in packs at one in nine, this 10-card set features each card dedicated to each year of the decade of the 90's. Card backs carry a "J" prefix.

COMPLETE SET (10) 15.00 30.00
COMMON CARD (J1-J10) 2.00 5.00
STATED ODDS 1:9

1999-00 SPx Masters

Randomly inserted in packs at one in 17, this 15-card set features the most masterful offensive performers in the NBA. Card backs carry a "M" prefix.

COMPLETE SET (15) 15.00 40.00
STATED ODDS 1:17
M1 Michael Jordan 8.00 20.00
M2 Vince Carter 2.00 5.00
M3 Tim Duncan 2.00 5.00
M4 Allen Iverson 2.00 5.00
M5 Gary Payton 1.00 2.50
M6 Shareef Abdur-Rahim .75 2.00
M7 Keith Van Horn .75 2.00
M8 Grant Hill 1.25 3.00
M9 Kobe Bryant 4.00 10.00
M10 Kevin Garnett 1.50 4.00
M11 Karl Malone 1.25 3.00
M12 Allan Houston .75 2.00
M13 Jason Kidd 1.50 4.00
M14 Antoine Walker 1.00 2.50
M15 Jason Williams 1.25 3.00

1999-00 SPx Prolifics

Randomly inserted in packs at one in 17, this 15-card set highlights stars who command the attention of the finest defenders in the league. Card backs carry a "P" prefix.

COMPLETE SET (15) 12.50 25.00
STATED ODDS 1:17
P1 Michael Jordan 12.00 30.00
P2 Karl Malone 1.00 2.50
P3 Jason Kidd 1.25 3.00
P4 Reggie Miller .75 2.00
P5 Glen Rice .75 2.00
P6 Hakeem Olajuwon 1.00 2.50
P7 Mitch Richmond .75 2.00
P8 Shawn Kemp .75 2.00
P9 Patrick Ewing 1.00 2.50
P10 Dikembe Mutombo .75 2.00
P11 Scottie Pippen 1.25 3.00
P12 John Stockton 1.00 2.50
P13 David Robinson 1.25 3.00
P14 Tim Hardaway .75 2.00
P15 Charles Barkley 1.25 3.00

1999-00 SPx Spxcitement

Randomly inserted in packs at one in three, this 20-card set features the top players in the league who provide fans with the most electrifying moves. Card backs carry a "S" prefix.

COMPLETE SET (20) 15.00 40.00
STATED ODDS 1:3
S1 Antoine Walker .40 1.00
S2 Antonio McDyess .30 .75
S3 Antawn Jamison .40 1.00
S4 Vin Baker .30 .75
S5 Juwan Howard .30 .75
S6 Brian Grant .25 .60
S7 Brevin Knight .25 .60
S8 Glenn Robinson .30 .75
S9 Stephon Marbury .30 .75
S10 Reggie Miller .40 1.00
S11 Nick Van Exel .30 .75
S12 Alonzo Mourning .50 1.25
S13 David Robinson .60 1.50
S14 Hakeem Olajuwon .50 1.25
S15 Toni Kukoc .40 1.00
S16 Maurice Taylor .25 .60
S17 Darrell Armstrong .25 .60
S18 Latrell Sprewell .40 1.00
S19 Tom Gugliotta .25 .60
S20 Michael Jordan 12.00 30.00

1999-00 SPx Spxtreme

Randomly inserted in packs at one in six, this 20-card set focuses on the most collectible players that makes them the fan favorites that they are. Card backs carry a "X" prefix.

COMPLETE SET (20) 8.00 20.00
STATED ODDS 1:6
X1 Michael Jordan 5.00 12.00
X2 Tim Hardaway .60 1.50
X3 Marcus Camby .50 1.25
X4 Jason Williams .75 2.00
X5 Shareef Abdur-Rahim .50 1.25
X6 Keith Van Horn .50 1.25
X7 Glen Rice .60 1.50
X8 Gary Payton .60 1.50
X9 Grant Hill .75 2.00
X10 Allan Houston .50 1.25
X11 Ray Allen .60 1.50
X12 Michael Finley .60 1.50
X13 Shawn Kemp .60 1.50
X14 Shaquille O'Neal 1.50 4.00
X15 Paul Pierce .75 2.00
X16 Mike Bibby .60 1.50
X17 Michael Olowokandi .40 1.00
X18 Damon Stoudamire .50 1.25
X19 Mitch Richmond .60 1.50
X20 Eddie Jones .60 1.50

1999-00 SPx Starscape

Randomly inserted in packs at one in nine, this 10-card set features the players that are worth the price of admission, every time they take the court. Card backs carry a "ST" prefix.

COMPLETE SET (10) 12.00 30.00
STATED ODDS 1:9
ST1 Michael Jordan 8.00 20.00
ST2 John Stockton .60 1.50
ST3 Antonio McDyess .40 1.00
ST4 Alonzo Mourning .60 1.50
ST5 Shaquille O'Neal 1.25 3.00
ST6 Stephon Marbury .40 1.00
ST7 Chris Webber .50 1.25
ST8 Charles Barkley .75 2.00
ST9 Antawn Jamison .50 1.25
ST10 Scottie Pippen .75 2.00

1999-00 SPx Winning Materials

Randomly inserted in packs at one in 252, this eight-card set features an authentic jersey swatch and a piece of a game-worn shoe or uniform from some of the top players in the NBA. WM3 and WM7 do not exist. Two signed versions of Winning Material also exist, each numbered to the player's jersey number. The two were Michael Jordan to 23 and Karl Malone to 32. Card backs carry a "WM" prefix.

STATED ODDS 1:252
CARDS WM3 AND WM7 DO NOT EXIST
WM1 Michael Jordan 250.00 500.00
WM1A M.Jordan AU/23 2000.00 3500.00
WM2 Karl Malone 12.00 30.00
WM2A K.Malone AU/32 100.00 200.00
WM4 Kobe Bryant 40.00 100.00
WM5 Paul Pierce 12.00 30.00
WM6 Kevin Garnett 15.00 40.00
WM8 Shaquille O'Neal 20.00 50.00
WM9 David Robinson 12.00 30.00
WM10 Charles Barkley 20.00 50.00

2000-01 SPx

The 2000-01 SPx product was released in early December, 2001, and features a 138-card base set. The base set is broken into tiers as follows: 90 Veterans (1-90), and 48 Rookies. Rookies 91/93-98/138 are serial numbered to 4500, Rookies 99-104 are serial numbered to 2500, Rookies 105-110 are serial numbered to 500, Rookies 92/111-130/136-137 are serial numbered to 2500, and Rookies 131-15 are serial numbered to 900. Each pack contains four cards are carried a suggested retail price of $4.99.

COMPLETE SET w/o RC (90) 20.00 40.00
1 Dikembe Mutombo .50 1.25
2 Jim Jackson .30 .75
3 Jason Terry .50 1.25
4 Paul Pierce .50 1.25
5 Kenny Anderson .40 1.00
6 Antoine Walker .40 1.00
7 Derrick Coleman .40 1.00
8 Baron Davis .50 1.25
9 David Wesley .30 .75
10 Elton Brand .50 1.25
11 Ron Artest .50 1.25
12 Corey Benjamin .30 .75
13 Trajan Langdon .30 .75
14 Lamond Murray .30 .75
15 Andre Miller .40 1.00
16 Michael Finley .50 1.25
17 Gary Trent .30 .75
18 Dirk Nowitzki .75 2.00
19 Antonio McDyess .40 1.00
20 Nick Van Exel .40 1.00
21 Raef LaFrentz .30 .75
22 Jerry Stackhouse .40 1.00
23 Michael Curry .30 .75
24 Jerome Williams .30 .75
25 Larry Hughes .40 1.00
26 Antawn Jamison .50 1.25
27 Mookie Blaylock .30 .75
28 Hakeem Olajuwon .60 1.50
29 Steve Francis .40 1.00
30 Shandon Anderson .30 .75
31 Reggie Miller .50 1.25
32 Jalen Rose .40 1.00
33 Austin Croshere .30 .75
34 Lamar Odom .40 1.00
35 Michael Olowokandi .30 .75
36 Tyrone Nesby .50 1.25
37 Shaquille O'Neal 1.25 3.00
38 Kobe Bryant 2.00 5.00
39 Robert Horry .40 1.00
40 Ron Harper .40 1.00
41 Alonzo Mourning .60 1.50
42 Eddie Jones .50 1.25
43 Tim Hardaway .50 1.25
44 Glenn Robinson .40 1.00
45 Sam Cassell .40 1.00
46 Ray Allen .50 1.25
47 Tim Thomas .30 .75
48 Kevin Garnett .75 2.00
49 Terrell Brandon .30 .75
50 Wally Szczerbiak .40 1.00
51 Keith Van Horn .40 1.00
52 Stephon Marbury .40 1.00
53 Jamie Feick .30 .75
54 Latrell Sprewell .40 1.00
55 Marcus Camby .40 1.00
56 Allan Houston .40 1.00
57 Grant Hill .60 1.50
58 Tracy McGrady .75 2.00
59 Darrell Armstrong .30 .75
60 Allen Iverson 1.00 2.50
61 Toni Kukoc .50 1.25
62 Theo Ratliff .30 .75
63 Anfernee Hardaway .75 2.00
64 Jason Kidd .75 2.00
65 Shawn Marion .40 1.00
66 Steve Smith .40 1.00
67 Rasheed Wallace .50 1.25
68 Scottie Pippen .75 2.00
69 Bonzi Wells .30 .75
70 Jason Williams .50 1.25
71 Vlade Divac .40 1.00
72 Chris Webber .50 1.25
73 David Robinson .75 2.00
74 Sean Elliott .50 1.25
75 Tim Duncan 1.00 2.50
76 Gary Payton .50 1.25
77 Rashard Lewis .50 1.25
78 Vin Baker .40 1.00
79 Vince Carter 1.00 2.50
80 Muggsy Bogues .40 1.00
81 Antonio Davis .30 .75
82 Karl Malone .60 1.50
83 John Stockton .60 1.50
84 Bryon Russell .30 .75
85 Shareef Abdur-Rahim .40 1.00
86 Michael Dickerson .30 .75
87 Mike Bibby .50 1.25
88 Mitch Richmond .40 1.00
89 Richard Hamilton .40 1.00
90 Juwan Howard .40 1.00
91 Lavor Postell RC .60 1.50
92 Mark Madsen JSY AU RC 3.00 8.00
93 Soumaila Samake RC .60 1.50
94 Michael Redd RC 2.50 6.00
95 Paul McPherson RC .60 1.50
96 Ruben Wolkowyski RC .60 1.50
97 Daniel Santiago RC 1.00 2.50
98 Pepe Sanchez RC 1.00 2.50
99 Marc Jackson RC 1.25 3.00
100 Khalid El-Amin RC 1.00 2.50
101 Iakovos Tsakalidis RC 1.00 2.50
102 Jabari Smith RC 1.00 2.50
103 Jason Hart RC 1.50 4.00
104 Stephen Jackson RC 2.50 6.00
105 Eduardo Najera RC 2.50 6.00
106 Hanno Mottola RC 1.50 4.00
107 Eddie House RC 2.00 5.00
108 Dan Langhi RC 1.50 4.00
109 A.J. Guyton RC 1.50 4.00
110 Chris Porter RC 1.50 4.00
111 Mike Miller JSY AU RC 5.00 12.00
112 Keyon Dooling JSY AU RC 3.00 8.00
113 C.Alexander JSY AU RC 2.50 6.00
114 Desmond Mason JSY AU RC 4.00 10.00
115 Jamaal Magloire JSY AU RC 3.00 8.00
116 D.Stevenson JSY AU RC 3.00 8.00
117 Dermarr Johnson JSY AU RC 2.50 6.00
118 Mateen Cleaves JSY AU RC 2.50 6.00
119 Morris Peterson JSY AU RC 3.00 8.00
120 Jerome Moiso JSY AU RC 2.00 5.00
121 Donnell Harvey JSY AU RC 2.50 6.00
122 Q.Richardson JSY AU RC 3.00 8.00
123 Jamal Crawford JSY AU RC 8.00 20.00
124 Erick Barkley JSY AU RC 2.00 5.00
125 Hedo Turkoglu JSY AU RC 5.00 12.00
126 Etan Thomas JSY AU RC 3.00 8.00
127 Mamadou N'Diaye JSY AU RC 2.00 5.00
128 Joel Przybilla JSY AU RC 2.50 6.00
129 Jason Collier JSY AU RC 3.00 8.00
130 Speedy Claxton JSY AU RC 3.00 8.00
131 Kenyon Martin JSY AU RC 10.00 25.00
132 Stromile Swift JSY AU RC 4.00 10.00
133 Darius Miles JSY AU RC 4.00 10.00
134 Marcus Fizer JSY AU RC 4.00 10.00
135 Chris Mihm JSY AU RC 3.00 8.00
136 Jake Voskuhl JSY AU RC 2.00 5.00
137 Pete Mickeal JSY AU RC 3.00 8.00
138 Dalibor Bagaric RC .75 2.00

2000-01 SPx Spectrum

*STARS: 15X TO 40X BASE CARD HI
STATED PRINT RUN 25 SERIAL #'d SETS
57 Grant Hill 30.00 80.00
91 Lavor Postell 6.00 15.00
92 Mark Madsen JSY AU 20.00 50.00
93 Soumaila Samake 6.00 15.00
94 Michael Redd 25.00 60.00
95 Paul McPherson 6.00 15.00
96 Ruben Wolkowyski 6.00 15.00
97 Daniel Santiago 10.00 25.00
98 Pepe Sanchez 10.00 25.00
99 Marc Jackson 8.00 20.00
100 Khalid El-Amin 6.00 15.00
101 Iakovos Tsakalidis 6.00 15.00
102 Jabari Smith 6.00 15.00
103 Jason Hart 10.00 25.00
104 Stephen Jackson 15.00 40.00
105 Eduardo Najera 10.00 25.00
106 Hanno Mottola 6.00 15.00
107 Eddie House 8.00 20.00
108 Dan Langhi 6.00 15.00
109 A.J. Guyton 6.00 15.00
110 Chris Porter 6.00 15.00
111 Mike Miller JSY AU 30.00 80.00
112 Keyon Dooling JSY AU 20.00 50.00
113 Courtney Alexander JSY AU 15.00 40.00
114 Desmond Mason JSY AU 25.00 60.00
115 Jamaal Magloire JSY AU 20.00 50.00
116 DeShawn Stevenson JSY AU 20.00 50.00
117 Dermarr Johnson JSY AU 15.00 40.00
118 Mateen Cleaves JSY AU 15.00 40.00
119 Morris Peterson JSY AU 20.00 50.00
120 Jerome Moiso JSY AU 12.00 30.00
121 Donnell Harvey JSY AU 15.00 40.00
122 Quentin Richardson JSY AU 20.00 50.00
123 Jamal Crawford JSY AU 50.00 125.00
124 Erick Barkley JSY AU 12.00 30.00
125 Hedo Turkoglu JSY AU 30.00 80.00
126 Etan Thomas JSY AU 20.00 50.00
127 Mamadou N'Diaye JSY AU 12.00 30.00
128 Joel Przybilla JSY AU 15.00 40.00
129 Jason Collier JSY AU 20.00 50.00
130 Speedy Claxton JSY AU 20.00 50.00
131 Kenyon Martin JSY AU 50.00 125.00
132 Stromile Swift JSY AU 20.00 50.00
133 Darius Miles JSY AU 20.00 50.00
134 Marcus Fizer JSY AU 20.00 50.00
135 Chris Mihm JSY AU 15.00 40.00
136 Jake Voskuhl JSY AU 12.00 30.00
137 Pete Mickeal JSY AU 20.00 50.00
138 Dalibor Bagaric 8.00 20.00

2000-01 SPx Masters

Randomly inserted in packs at one in 8, this 11-card insert set features NBA players that have mastered the game of basketball. Card backs carry a "M" prefix.

COMPLETE SET (11) 6.00 15.00
STATED ODDS 1:8
M1 Michael Jordan 3.00 8.00
M2 Kobe Bryant 1.50 4.00
M3 Steve Francis .30 .75
M4 Elton Brand .40 1.00
M5 Tim Duncan .75 2.00
M6 Jason Kidd .60 1.50
M7 Kevin Garnett .60 1.50
M8 Karl Malone .50 1.25
M9 Shaquille O'Neal 1.00 2.50
M10 Gary Payton .40 1.00
M11 Vince Carter .75 2.00

2000-01 SPx Spxcitement

Randomly inserted into packs at one in 5, this 20-card insert set features players that always bring excitement to the game. Card backs carry a "S" prefix.

COMPLETE SET (20) 7.50 15.00
STATED ODDS 1:5
S1 Kobe Bryant 1.50 4.00
S2 Gary Payton .40 1.00
S3 Rasheed Wallace .40 1.00
S4 Jason Williams .40 1.00
S5 Ray Allen .40 1.00
S6 Tim Duncan .75 2.00
S7 Stephon Marbury .30 .75
S8 Allen Iverson .75 2.00
S9 Jerry Stackhouse .30 .75
S10 Kevin Garnett .60 1.50
S11 Antawn Jamison .40 1.00
S12 Paul Pierce .40 1.00
S13 Lamar Odom .30 .75
S14 Elton Brand .40 1.00
S15 Vince Carter .75 2.00
S16 Antonio McDyess .30 .75
S17 Michael Finley .40 1.00
S18 Jalen Rose .30 .75
S19 Richard Hamilton .30 .75
S20 Jason Kidd .60 1.50

2000-01 SPx Spxtreme

Randomly inserted into packs at one in 8, this 11-card insert set features players that play extremely hard every night . Card backs carry a "X" prefix.

COMPLETE SET (11) 5.00 12.00
STATED ODDS 1:8
X1 Kevin Garnett .60 1.50
X2 Steve Francis .30 .75
X3 Chris Webber .40 1.00
X4 Elton Brand .40 1.00
X5 Shareef Abdur-Rahim .30 .75
X6 Larry Hughes .30 .75
X7 Vince Carter .75 2.00
X8 Kobe Bryant 1.50 4.00
X9 Scottie Pippen .60 1.50
X10 Anfernee Hardaway .60 1.50
X11 Shaquille O'Neal 1.00 2.50

2000-01 SPx UD Authentics Rookie Exclusives

Randomly inserted into packs, this 5-card insert features authentic autographs of top rookies from the 2000-01 season. Card backs carry the player's initials as numbering. Please note that the Kenyon Martin card packed out as an exchange card and must be redeemed by 8/03/01.

RANDOM INSERTS IN PACKS
DM Darius Miles 8.00 20.00
KM Kenyon Martin 20.00 50.00
MF Marcus Fizer 8.00 20.00
MI Mike Miller 12.00 30.00
SS Stromile Swift 8.00 20.00

2000-01 SPx Winning Materials

Randomly inserted in packs at one in 72, this 27-card set features an authentic jersey swatch and another swatch of memorabilia including shorts, shoes, and warm-ups. Card backs carry the players initials as numbering. Also note that there are autographed versions of these cards that were seeded into packs at one in 252.

STATED ODDS 1:72
AU STATED ODDS 1:252
BR1 Bryon Russell 3.00 8.00
CM1 Chris Mihm 3.00 8.00
DM1 DerMarr Johnson 3.00 8.00
JS1 John Stockton 6.00 15.00
KB1 K.Bryant JSY/WM 10.00 25.00
KB2 K.Bryant JSY/Shoe 30.00 80.00
KB3 K.Bryant WM/Shoe 30.00 80.00
KG1 K.Garnett JSY/WM 6.00 15.00
KG2 K.Garnett JSY/SS 6.00 15.00
KG3 K.Garnett JSY/Shorts 6.00 15.00
KM1 Kenyon Martin 10.00 25.00
MF1 Marcus Fizer 4.00 10.00
MM1 K.Malone JSY/Shorts 6.00 15.00
MM3 K.Malone JSY/Shoe 6.00 15.00
TB1 Terrell Brandon JSY/WM 3.00 8.00
WS1 W.Szczerbiak JSY/WM 4.00 10.00
WS2 W.Szczerbiak JSY/SS 4.00 10.00
DMA1 DerMarr Johnson AU 5.00 12.00
KBA1 K.Bryant JSY/WM AU 100.00 250.00
KBA2 K.Bryant JSY/Shoe AU 100.00 250.00
KBA3 K.Bryant WM/Shoe AU 100.00 250.00
KGA1 K.Garnett JSY/WM AU 50.00 120.00
KGA2 K.Garnett JSY/SS AU 60.00 150.00
KMA1 Kenyon Martin AU 8.00 20.00
MFA1 Marcus Fizer AU 6.00 15.00
MJA1 M.Jordan JSY/WM AU 1500.00 1800.00
MJA2 M.Jordan WM/Sh AU 1000.00 1200.00

2001-02 SPx

Released in February 2002, SPx features a 173-card set consisting of 90 base cards and 50 rookie players with three versions of card numbers 91-111. Rookie versions are differentiated as follows: version "A" has a blue background, version "B" has a green background, and version "C" has a red background. These cards are horizontally designed with a player photo, a swatch of a jersey, and a "cut signature" placed inside the card. Card numbers 91-105 are sequentially numbered to 800, and card numbers 106-111 are sequentially numbered to 250. The set was released without card numbers 112-120, and card numbers 121-140 feature a purple letter "R" on the left side of the card and player photos on the right, and are squentially numbered to 1999. SPx was packaged in 18-pack boxes where packs contained four cards and carried a suggested retail price of $6.99.

COMP.SET w/o SP's (90) 15.00 40.00
91-105 THREE VERSIONS SER.#'d TO 800
106-111 THREE VERSIONS SER.#'d TO 250
121-140 PRINT RUN 1999 SER.#'d SETS
THREE VERSIONS OF EACH JSY AU RC EXIST
1 Jason Terry .50 1.25
2 Shareef Abdur-Rahim .40 1.00
3 DerMarr Johnson .30 .75
4 Paul Pierce .50 1.25
5 Antoine Walker .40 1.00
6 Kenny Anderson .40 1.00
7 Baron Davis .50 1.25
8 Jamal Mashburn .40 1.00
9 David Wesley .30 .75
10 Ron Mercer .30 .75
11 Ron Artest .50 1.25
12 Marcus Fizer .30 .75
13 Andre Miller .40 1.00
14 Lamond Murray .30 .75
15 Chris Mihm .30 .75
16 Michael Finley .50 1.25
17 Dirk Nowitzki .75 2.00
18 Steve Nash .75 2.00
19 Antonio McDyess .40 1.00
20 Nick Van Exel .40 1.00
21 Raef LaFrentz .30 .75
22 Jerry Stackhouse .40 1.00
23 Chucky Atkins .30 .75
24 Corliss Williamson .30 .75
25 Antawn Jamison .50 1.25
26 Larry Hughes .40 1.00
27 Chris Porter .30 .75
28 Steve Francis .40 1.00
29 Cuttino Mobley .30 .75
30 Maurice Taylor .30 .75
31 Reggie Miller .50 1.25
32 Jalen Rose .40 1.00
33 Jermaine O'Neal .40 1.00
34 Darius Miles .30 .75
35 Elton Brand .50 1.25
36 Lamar Odom .40 1.00
37 Quentin Richardson .40 1.00
38 Kobe Bryant 2.00 5.00
39 Shaquille O'Neal 1.25 3.00
40 Rick Fox .30 .75
41 Derek Fisher .40 1.00
42 Stromile Swift .30 .75
43 Jason Williams .40 1.00
44 Michael Dickerson .30 .75
45 Alonzo Mourning .60 1.50
46 Eddie Jones .40 1.00
47 Anthony Carter .30 .75
48 Glenn Robinson .40 1.00
49 Ray Allen .50 1.25
50 Sam Cassell .40 1.00
51 Kevin Garnett .75 2.00
52 Wally Szczerbiak .40 1.00
53 Terrell Brandon .30 .75
54 Chauncey Billups .50 1.25
55 Kenyon Martin .50 1.25
56 Keith Van Horn .40 1.00
57 Jason Kidd .75 2.00
58 Latrell Sprewell .40 1.00
59 Allan Houston .40 1.00
60 Marcus Camby .40 1.00
61 Tracy McGrady .75 2.00
62 Mike Miller .40 1.00
63 Grant Hill .60 1.50
64 Allen Iverson 1.00 2.50
65 Dikembe Mutombo .50 1.25
66 Aaron McKie .30 .75
67 Stephon Marbury .40 1.00
68 Shawn Marion .40 1.00
69 Tom Gugliotta .30 .75
70 Rasheed Wallace .50 1.25
71 Damon Stoudamire .40 1.00
72 Bonzi Wells .30 .75
73 Chris Webber .50 1.25
74 Peja Stojakovic .50 1.25
75 Mike Bibby .50 1.25
76 Tim Duncan 1.00 2.50
77 David Robinson .75 2.00
78 Antonio Daniels .30 .75
79 Gary Payton .50 1.25
80 Rashard Lewis .50 1.25
81 Desmond Mason .40 1.00
82 Vince Carter .75 2.00
83 Morris Peterson .30 .75
84 Antonio Davis .30 .75
85 Karl Malone .60 1.50
86 John Stockton .60 1.50
87 Donyell Marshall .30 .75
88 Richard Hamilton .40 1.00
89 Courtney Alexander .30 .75
90 Michael Jordan 8.00 20.00
91A Tony Parker JSY AU RC 25.00 60.00
91B Tony Parker JSY AU RC 25.00 60.00
91C Tony Parker JSY AU RC 25.00 60.00
92A Jamaal Tinsley JSY AU RC 3.00 8.00
92B Jamaal Tinsley JSY AU RC 3.00 8.00
92C Jamaal Tinsley JSY AU RC 3.00 8.00
93A S.Dalembert JSY AU RC 3.00 8.00
93B S.Dalembert JSY AU RC 3.00 8.00
93C S.Dalembert JSY AU RC 3.00 8.00
94A Gerald Wallace JSY AU RC 4.00 10.00
94B Gerald Wallace JSY AU RC 4.00 10.00
94C Gerald Wallace JSY AU RC 4.00 10.00
95A B.Armstrong JSY AU RC 2.00 5.00
95B B.Armstrong JSY AU RC 2.00 5.00
95C B.Armstrong JSY AU RC 2.00 5.00
96A Jeryl Sasser JSY AU RC 2.00 5.00
96B Jeryl Sasser JSY AU RC 2.00 5.00
96C Jeryl Sasser JSY AU RC 2.00 5.00
97A Jason Collins JSY AU RC 6.00 15.00
97B Jason Collins JSY AU RC 6.00 15.00
97C Jason Collins JSY AU RC 6.00 15.00
98A M.Bradley JSY AU RC 2.00 5.00
98B M.Bradley JSY AU RC 2.00 5.00
98C M.Bradley JSY AU RC 2.00 5.00
99A Steven Hunter JSY AU RC 2.50 6.00
99B Steven Hunter JSY AU RC 2.50 6.00
99C Steven Hunter JSY AU RC 2.50 6.00
100A Troy Murphy JSY AU RC 3.00 8.00
100B Troy Murphy JSY AU RC 3.00 8.00
100C Troy Murphy JSY AU RC 3.00 8.00
101A R.Jefferson JSY AU RC 5.00 12.00
101B R.Jefferson JSY AU RC 5.00 12.00
101C R.Jefferson JSY AU RC 5.00 12.00
102A V.Radmanov JSY AU RC 3.00 8.00
102B V.Radmanov JSY AU RC 3.00 8.00
102C V.Radmanov JSY AU RC 3.00 8.00
103A Kedrick Brown JSY AU RC 2.00 5.00
103B Kedrick Brown JSY AU RC 2.00 5.00
103C Kedrick Brown JSY AU RC 2.00 5.00
104A J.Johnson JSY AU ERR RC 4.00 10.00
104B J.Johnson JSY AU ERR RC 4.00 10.00
104C J.Johnson JSY AU ERR RC 4.00 10.00
104D J.Johnson JSY AU COR RC 4.00 10.00
104E J.Johnson JSY AU COR RC 4.00 10.00
104F J.Johnson JSY AU COR RC 4.00 10.00
105A Kirk Haston JSY AU RC 2.00 5.00
105B Kirk Haston JSY AU RC 2.00 5.00
105C Kirk Haston JSY AU RC 2.00 5.00
106A Rodney White JSY AU RC 3.00 8.00
106B Rodney White JSY AU RC 3.00 8.00
106C Rodney White JSY AU RC 3.00 8.00
107A Eddie Griffin JSY AU RC 4.00 10.00
107B Eddie Griffin JSY AU RC 4.00 10.00
107C Eddie Griffin JSY AU RC 4.00 10.00
108A J.Richardson JSY AU RC 6.00 15.00
108B J.Richardson JSY AU RC 6.00 15.00
108C J.Richardson JSY AU RC 6.00 15.00
109A Eddy Curry JSY AU RC 5.00 12.00
109B Eddy Curry JSY AU RC 5.00 12.00
109C Eddy Curry JSY AU RC 5.00 12.00
110A T.Chandler JSY AU RC 8.00 20.00
110B T.Chandler JSY AU RC 8.00 20.00
110C T.Chandler JSY AU RC 8.00 20.00

111A Kwame Brown JSY AU RC 5.00 12.00
111B Kwame Brown JSY AU RC 5.00 12.00
111C Kwame Brown JSY AU RC 5.00 12.00
121 Shane Battier RC 4.00 10.00
122 Brendan Haywood RC 2.00 5.00
123 Joseph Forte RC 1.25 3.00
124 Zach Randolph RC 6.00 15.00
125 DeSagana Diop RC 1.50 4.00
126 Damone Brown RC 1.25 3.00
127 Andrei Kirilenko RC 3.00 8.00
128 Trenton Hassell RC 1.50 4.00
129 Gilbert Arenas RC 3.00 8.00
130 Earl Watson RC 2.00 5.00
131 Kenny Satterfield RC 1.25 3.00
132 Will Solomon RC 2.00 5.00
133 Bobby Simmons RC 2.00 5.00
134 Brian Scalabrine RC 2.00 5.00
135 Charlie Bell RC 2.00 5.00
136 Zeljko Rebraca RC 2.00 5.00
137 Loren Woods RC 1.25 3.00
138 Terence Morris RC 2.00 5.00
139 Jamison Brewer RC 2.00 5.00
140 Pau Gasol RC 6.00 15.00
NNO Kobe Bryant PROMO 2.00 5.00

2001-02 SPx Spectrum

*1-90 STARS: 12X TO 30X BASE CARD HI
*91-105 RCs: 1.5X TO 4X HI
*106-111 RCs: 1X TO 2.5X HI
*121-140 RCs: 2X TO 5X HI
STATED PRINT RUN 25 SERIAL #'d SETS
91-111 HAS THREE VERSIONS ALL EQUAL
91A Tony Parker JSY AU 75.00 200.00
108A Jason Richardson JSY AU 40.00 100.00
110A Tyson Chandler JSY AU 30.00 80.00

2001-02 SPx Winning Materials

Randomly inserted in packs at the rate of one in 18, this 20-card set features a horizontal design with a player photo on the left and two swatches of game materials on the right. The breakdown of materials on each card appears after the player's name in the descriptions below.
STATED ODDS 1:18
AH Anfernee Hardaway Shorts/WU 6.00 15.00
AI Allen Iverson JSY/Shorts 8.00 20.00
CB Chauncey Billups JSY/WU 4.00 10.00
KB Kobe Bryant JSY/WU 12.00 30.00
KE Kenyon Martin Shorts/Shirt 4.00 10.00
KG Kevin Garnett JSY/WU 6.00 15.00
KG2 Kevin Garnett WU/Shirt 6.00 15.00
KM Karl Malone JSY/JSY 5.00 12.00
KM2 Karl Malone WU/Shorts 5.00 12.00
KV Keith Van Horn WU/JSY 3.00 8.00
LP Lavor Postell Shirt/Pr.JSY 2.50 6.00
MM Mike Miller WU/Shirt 3.00 8.00
MO Michael Olowokandi Shirt/WU 2.50 6.00
RH Richard Hamilton WU/Shirt 3.00 8.00
SM Shawn Marion WU/Shirt 3.00 8.00
SS Stromile Swift WU/Shirt 2.50 6.00
ST John Stockton JSY/Pr.JSY 5.00 12.00
ST2 John Stockton JSY/Shirt 5.00 12.00
TB Terrell Brandon WU/Shirt 2.50 6.00
WS Wally Szczerbiak WU/Shirt 3.00 8.00

2002-03 SPx

Released in December 2002, SPx conatins 162 cards and is broken down as follows: Cards 1-90 are veterans, cards 91-110 are Flashback Fabrics veteran jersey autographs, cards 111-132 are rookie jersey autographs (sequentially numbered to 999), cards 133-138 are rookies sequentially numbered to 1599, cards 139-147 are rookies sequentially numbered to 2599, and cards 148-162 are rookies sequentaılly numbered to 2999. Base cards showcase a horizontal design which places a full color player action photo next to a close-up portrait style photo. All Autograph cards have "cut signatures" embedded in them, and the Flashback Fabrics have an F shaped jersey swatch and the rookies have an R shaped jersey swatch. SPx was packaged in 18-pack boxes where packs contained four cards and carried a suggested retail price of $4.99.
COMP.SET w/o SP's (90) 12.00 30.00
111-132 PRINT RUN 999 SER.#'d SETS
133-138 PRINT RUN 1599 SER.#'d SETS
137-147 PRINT RUN 2599 SER.#'d SETS
148-162 PRINT RUN 2999 SER.#'d SETS
1 Shareef Abdur-Rahim .40 1.00
2 Jason Terry .40 1.00
3 Glenn Robinson .40 1.00
4 Paul Pierce .50 1.25
5 Antoine Walker .40 1.00
6 Kedrick Brown .30 .75
7 Vin Baker .40 1.00
8 Jalen Rose .40 1.00
9 Tyson Chandler .50 1.25
10 Eddy Curry .30 .75
11 Ricky Davis .40 1.00
12 Chris Mihm .30 .75
13 Darius Miles .30 .75
14 Dirk Nowitzki .75 2.00
15 Michael Finley .50 1.25
16 Steve Nash .60 1.50
17 Raef LaFrentz .30 .75
18 James Posey .30 .75
19 Juwan Howard .40 1.00
20 Richard Hamilton .40 1.00
21 Ben Wallace .40 1.00
22 Chauncey Billups .50 1.25
23 Antawn Jamison .50 1.25
24 Jason Richardson .50 1.25
25 Steve Francis .40 1.00
26 Eddie Griffin .30 .75
27 Cuttino Mobley .30 .75
28 Reggie Miller .50 1.25
29 Jamaal Tinsley .30 .75
30 Jermaine O'Neal .40 1.00
31 Elton Brand .50 1.25
32 Andre Miller .40 1.00
33 Lamar Odom .40 1.00
34 Kobe Bryant 2.00 5.00
35 Shaquille O'Neal 1.25 3.00
36 Robert Horry .40 1.00
37 Devean George .30 .75
38 Pau Gasol .60 1.50
39 Shane Battier .50 1.25
40 Jason Williams .40 1.00
41 Alonzo Mourning .60 1.50
42 Eddie Jones .40 1.00
43 Brian Grant .30 .75
44 Ray Allen .50 1.25
45 Tim Thomas .30 .75
46 Kevin Garnett .75 2.00
47 Terrell Brandon .30 .75
48 Wally Szczerbiak .40 1.00
49 Jason Kidd .75 2.00
50 Richard Jefferson .50 1.25
51 Kenyon Martin .40 1.00
52 Baron Davis .40 1.00
53 Jamal Mashburn .40 1.00
54 David Wesley .30 .75
55 P.J. Brown .30 .75
56 Allan Houston .40 1.00
57 Antonio McDyess .40 1.00
58 Latrell Sprewell .40 1.00
59 Tracy McGrady .75 2.00
60 Mike Miller .40 1.00
61 Darrell Armstrong .30 .75
62 Allen Iverson .75 2.00
63 Keith Van Horn .40 1.00
64 Stephon Marbury .40 1.00
65 Shawn Marion .40 1.00
66 Anfernee Hardaway .75 2.00
67 Rasheed Wallace .50 1.25
68 Damon Stoudamire .40 1.00
69 Scottie Pippen .75 2.00
70 Chris Webber .50 1.25
71 Mike Bibby .50 1.25
72 Peja Stojakovic .50 1.25
73 Hedo Turkoglu .40 1.00
74 Tim Duncan 1.00 2.50
75 David Robinson .75 2.00
76 Tony Parker .60 1.50
77 Steve Smith .40 1.00
78 Gary Payton .50 1.25
79 Rashard Lewis .50 1.25
80 Brent Barry .30 .75
81 Desmond Mason .40 1.00
82 Vince Carter .75 2.00
83 Morris Peterson .30 .75
84 Antonio Davis .30 .75
85 Karl Malone .60 1.50
86 John Stockton .60 1.50
87 Andrei Kirilenko .50 1.25
88 Jerry Stackhouse .40 1.00
89 Michael Jordan 4.00 10.00
90 Kwame Brown .30 .75
91 Jason Richardson JSY AU 6.00 15.00
92 Tyson Chandler JSY AU 6.00 15.00
93 Kenyon Martin JSY AU 15.00 30.00
94 Gerald Wallace JSY AU SP 6.00 15.00
95 K.Abdul-Jabbar JSY AU SP 60.00 120.00
96 Morris Peterson JSY AU SP 6.00 15.00
97 Andre Miller JSY AU 6.00 15.00
98 Quentin Richardson JSY AU 6.00 15.00
99 Mike Miller JSY AU 6.00 15.00
100 Jer. O'Neal JSY AU SP 10.00 25.00
101 Marcus Fizer JSY AU 6.00 15.00
102 Mike Bibby JSY AU 6.00 15.00
103 C. Billups JSY AU SP 6.00 15.00
104 Lamar Odom JSY AU SP 12.50 30.00
105 Antoine Walker JSY AU 10.00 25.00
106 Paul Pierce JSY AU 15.00 30.00
107 Jason Kidd JSY AU SP 20.00 40.00
108 Kevin Garnett JSY AU SP 75.00 150.00
109 Kobe Bryant JSY AU SP 150.00 300.00
110 M. Jordan JSY AU SP 500.00 750.00
111 Chris Jefferies JSY AU RC 2.50 6.00
112 John Salmons JSY AU RC 4.00 10.00
113 Tayshaun Prince JSY AU RC 5.00 12.00
114 Casey Jacobsen JSY AU RC 3.00 8.00
115 Qyntel Woods JSY AU RC 3.00 8.00
116 Kareem Rush JSY AU RC 3.00 8.00
117 Ryan Humphrey JSY AU RC 3.00 8.00
118 Carlos Boozer JSY AU RC 4.00 10.00
119 Sam Clancy JSY AU RC 3.00 8.00
120 Fred Jones JSY AU RC 3.00 8.00
121 Marcus Haislip JSY AU RC 3.00 8.00
122 Melvin Ely JSY AU RC 3.00 8.00
123 Jared Jeffries JSY AU RC 3.00 8.00
124 Dan Gadzuric JSY AU RC 3.00 8.00
125 A.Stoudemire JSY AU RC 6.00 15.00
126 Caron Butler JSY AU RC 4.00 10.00
127 Nene Hilario JSY AU RC 6.00 15.00
128 DaJuan Wagner JSY AU RC 3.00 8.00
129 N.Tskitishvili JSY AU RC 2.50 6.00
130 Drew Gooden JSY AU RC 4.00 10.00
131 Jay Williams JSY AU RC 4.00 10.00
132 Yao Ming JSY AU RC 30.00 80.00
133 Mike Dunleavy RC 1.50 4.00
134 Frank Williams RC 1.00 2.50
135 Jiri Welsch RC 1.25 3.00
136 Dan Dickau RC 1.25 3.00
137 Efthimios Rentzias RC 1.00 2.50
138 Chris Wilcox RC 1.25 3.00
139 Curtis Borchardt RC 1.00 2.50
140 Predrag Savovic RC 1.25 3.00
141 Tito Maddox RC 1.00 2.50
142 Roger Mason RC 1.25 3.00
143 Juan Dixon RC 1.50 4.00
144 Pat Burke RC 1.00 2.50
145 Marko Jaric 1.50 4.00
146 Gordan Giricek RC 1.50 4.00
147 Juaquin Hawkins RC 1.00 2.50
148 Vincent Yarbrough RC 1.00 2.50
149 Robert Archibald RC 1.00 2.50
150 Bostjan Nachbar RC 1.25 3.00
151 Jamal Sampson RC 1.50 4.00
152 Lonny Baxter RC 1.00 2.50
153 J.R. Bremer RC 1.00 2.50
154 Cezary Trybanski RC 1.50 4.00
155 Manu Ginobili RC 4.00 10.00
156 Raul Lopez RC 1.50 4.00
157 Rasual Butler RC 1.50 4.00
158 Tamar Slay RC 1.00 2.50
159 Ronald Murray RC 1.50 4.00
160 Igor Rakocevic RC 1.00 2.50
161 Reggie Evans RC 1.50 4.00
162 Jannero Pargo RC 1.00 2.50

2002-03 SPx Spectrum

*1-90 STARS: 10X TO 25X BASE CARD HI
*111-132 RCs: 1.5X TO 4X HI
*133-162 RCs: 3X TO 8X HI
STATED PRINT RUN 25 SER.#'d SETS
28 Reggie Miller 15.00 40.00
34 Kobe Bryant 100.00 200.00
89 Michael Jordan 150.00 300.00
125 Amare Stoudemire JSY AU 125.00 250.00
132 Yao Ming JSY AU 350.00 700.00

2002-03 SPx Winning Combos

Inserted in packs at the rate of one in 18, this 20-card set places player photos in the upper left hand corner and in the lower right hand corner. Next to the player photos, there is an X shaped swatch of game worn memorabilia. An Autograph parallel for six cards was also inserted and sequentially numbered to 10.
STATED ODDS 1:18
AIJK A.Iverson/J.Kidd SP 6.00 15.00
BDJM B.Davis/J.Mashburn 4.00 10.00
BHKW B.Haywood/K.Brown 4.00 10.00
CWPS C.Webber/P.Stojakovic 4.00 10.00
ECTC E.Curry/T.Chandler 4.00 10.00
JTJO J.Tinsley/J.O'Neal 4.00 10.00
KBAI Bryant/Iverson SP 12.50 30.00
KBJK K.Bryant/J.Kidd 10.00 25.00
KBTM K.Bryant/T.McGrady SP 12.50 30.00
KGWS K.Garnett/W.Szczerbiak 5.00 12.00
KMJS K.Malone/J.Stockton 6.00 15.00
KMRJ K.Martin/R.Jefferson 4.00 10.00
MJKB M.Jordan/K.Bryant SP 50.00 120.00
PPAW P.Pierce/A.Walker 5.00 12.00
QRLO Q.Richardson/L.Odom 4.00 10.00
SADJ S.Abdur-Rahim/D.Johnson 4.00 10.00
SMSM S.Marbury/S.Marion 4.00 10.00
TMMM T.McGrady/M.Miller SP 6.00 15.00
WCKB Chamberlain/Bryant SP 50.00 120.00
WCMJ Chamberlain/Jordan SP 100.00 250.00

2002-03 SPx Winning Materials

Inserted in packs at the rate of one in 18, this 19-card set features a horizontal design with a player photo in the lower right hand corner and two X shaped swatches of game used memorabilia.
STATED ODDS 1:18
AMW A.McDyess JSY/WU 3.00 8.00
BDW Baron Davis JSY/WU 3.00 8.00
CWW Chris Webber JSY/WU 4.00 10.00
DNW D.Nowitzki Shorts/WU 6.00 15.00
DRW D.Robinson JSY/WU 6.00 15.00
EBW Elton Brand Shorts/WU 4.00 10.00
JKW Jason Kidd Shirt/WU 6.00 15.00
KBW K.Bryant Shorts/WU 15.00 40.00
KGW K.Garnett Shorts/WU 6.00 15.00
KMW K.Martin Shirt/WU 3.00 8.00
MJW M.Jordan Shirt/JSY SP 30.00 80.00
MMW Mike Miller JSY/Shirt 3.00 8.00
PPW Paul Pierce Shirt/WU 4.00 10.00
PSW P.Stojakovic JSY/WU 4.00 10.00
RHW R.Hamilton Shirt/WU 3.00 8.00
RJW R.Jefferson Shirt/WU 4.00 10.00
SHW S.Marion Shirt/WU 3.00 8.00
SMW S.Marbury Shirt/WU 3.00 8.00
TMW T.McGrady Shirt/WU SP 8.00 20.00

2002-03 SPx Winning Materials Autographs

Randomly seeded in packs, this 12-card set uses the same design as the Winning Materials insert set enhanced with a gold background and an authentic player autograph. Each card is sequentially numbered to 23 or 100.
PRINT RUN 23 TO 100 SER.#'d SETS
AMA Andre Miller/100 6.00 15.00
JKA Jason Kidd/100 20.00 50.00
JWA Jay Williams/100 6.00 15.00
KBA Kobe Bryant/100 125.00 250.00
KGA Kevin Garnett/100 40.00 100.00
KMA Kenyon Martin/100 12.00 30.00
MBA Mike Bibby/100 6.00 15.00
MJA Michael Jordan/23 500.00 1000.00
MMA Mike Miller/100 6.00 15.00
PPA Paul Pierce/100 20.00 50.00
QRA Quentin Richardson/100 6.00 15.00
TCA Tyson Chandler/100 6.00 15.00

2003-04 SPx

Released in December 2003, this 206-card set is broken down as follows: Cards 1-90 feature veteran players on a horizontal design with full-color player action photos on the right and a gray-scale portrait photo on the left; cards 91-132 are Spxcellence cards sequentially numbered to 3999; cards 133-150 are rookie cards sequentially numbered to 2999; cards 151-156 feature rookie jersey autograph cards sequentially numbered to 750; cards 157-165 feature rookie jersey autograph cards sequentially numbered to 1250; cards 166-185 feature rookie jersey autograph cards sequentially numbered to 1999; and cards 186-206 feature veteran jersey autograph cards sequentially numbered to random amounts. SPx was packaged in 18-pack boxes where packs contained four cards plus one promo and carried a suggested retail price of $6.99
COMP.SET w/o SP's (90) 25.00 60.00
91-132 PRINT RUN 3999 SER.#'d SETS
151-156 RC PRINT RUN 750 SER.#'d SETS
157-165 PRINT RUN 1250 SER.#'d SETS
166-185 RC PRINT RUN 1999 SER.#'d SETS
186-206 PRINT RUNS LISTED BELOW
1 Shafreef Abdur-Rahim .40 1.00
2 Jason Terry .40 1.00
3 Theo Ratliff .30 .75
4 Paul Pierce .50 1.25
5 Raef LaFrentz .30 .75
6 Vin Baker .30 .75
7 Jalen Rose .40 1.00
8 Tyson Chandler .40 1.00
9 Michael Jordan 4.00 10.00
10 Dajuan Wagner .30 .75
11 Darius Miles .30 .75
12 Carlos Boozer .40 1.00
13 Dirk Nowitzki .75 2.00
14 Antoine Walker .50 1.25
15 Steve Nash .60 1.50
16 Nene .40 1.00
17 Marcus Camby .40 1.00
18 Andre Miller .40 1.00
19 Richard Hamilton .40 1.00
20 Ben Wallace .40 1.00
21 Chauncey Billups .50 1.25
22 Nick Van Exel .40 1.00
23 Jason Richardson .50 1.25
24 Speedy Claxton .30 .75
25 Steve Francis .40 1.00
26 Yao Ming 1.00 2.50
27 Cuttino Mobley .30 .75
28 Reggie Miller .50 1.25
29 Jamaal Tinsley .30 .75
30 Jermaine O'Neal .40 1.00
31 Elton Brand .50 1.25
32 Corey Maggette .40 1.00
33 Quentin Richardson .40 1.00
34 Kobe Bryant 2.00 5.00
35 Karl Malone .60 1.50
36 Shaquille O'Neal 1.25 3.00
37 Gary Payton .50 1.25
38 Pau Gasol .50 1.25
39 Shane Battier .40 1.00
40 Mike Miller .40 1.00
41 Eddie Jones .40 1.00
42 Lamar Odom .40 1.00
43 Caron Butler .40 1.00
44 Michael Redd .50 1.25
45 Joe Smith .40 1.00
46 Desmond Mason .40 1.00
47 Kevin Garnett .75 2.00
48 Latrell Sprewell .40 1.00
49 Michael Olowokandi .30 .75
50 Jason Kidd .75 2.00
51 Richard Jefferson .40 1.00
52 Kenyon Martin .40 1.00
53 Baron Davis .40 1.00
54 Jamal Mashburn .40 1.00
55 David Wesley .30 .75
56 Allan Houston .40 1.00
57 Antonio McDyess .40 1.00
58 Keith Van Horn .40 1.00
59 Tracy McGrady .60 1.50
60 Grant Hill .60 1.50
61 Drew Gooden .40 1.00
62 Juwan Howard .40 1.00
63 Allen Iverson .75 2.00
64 Glenn Robinson .40 1.00
65 Eric Snow .30 .75
66 Stephon Marbury .40 1.00
67 Shawn Marion .40 1.00
68 Amare Stoudemire .60 1.50
69 Rasheed Wallace .50 1.25
70 Bonzi Wells .30 .75
71 Damon Stoudamire .40 1.00
72 Chris Webber .50 1.25
73 Mike Bibby .50 1.25
74 Peja Stojakovic .50 1.25
75 Brad Miller .40 1.00
76 Tim Duncan .75 2.00
77 Tony Parker .50 1.25
78 Manu Ginobili .60 1.50
79 Ray Allen .50 1.25
80 Rashard Lewis .50 1.25
81 Vladimir Radmanovic .30 .75
82 Vince Carter .75 2.00
83 Morris Peterson .30 .75
84 Antonio Davis .30 .75
85 Raul Lopez .50 1.25
86 Matt Harpring .30 .75
87 Andrei Kirilenko .50 1.25
88 Jerry Stackhouse .40 1.00
89 Gilbert Arenas .40 1.00
90 Larry Hughes .40 1.00
91 Allen Iverson 1.50 4.00
92 Dirk Nowitzki 1.50 4.00
93 Kobe Bryant 4.00 10.00
94 Michael Jordan 8.00 20.00
95 Vince Carter 1.50 4.00
96 Shaquille O'Neal 2.50 6.00
97 Yao Ming 2.00 5.00
98 Amare Stoudemire 1.25 3.00
99 Paul Pierce 1.00 2.50
100 Jason Richardson 1.00 2.50
101 Steve Francis .75 2.00
102 Jermaine O'Neal .75 2.00
103 Karl Malone 1.25 3.00
104 Tracy McGrady 1.25 3.00
105 Stephon Marbury .75 2.00
106 Chris Webber 1.00 2.50
107 Tim Duncan 1.50 4.00
108 Ray Allen 1.00 2.50
109 Antoine Walker 1.00 2.50
110 Steve Nash 1.25 3.00
111 Elton Brand 1.00 2.50
112 Rashard Lewis 1.00 2.50
113 Jerry Stackhouse .75 2.00
114 Shawn Marion .75 2.00
115 Mike Bibby 1.00 2.50
116 Tony Parker 1.00 2.50
117 Michael Finley 1.00 2.50
118 Allan Houston .75 2.00
119 Richard Hamilton .75 2.00
120 Ben Wallace .75 2.00
121 Reggie Miller 1.00 2.50
122 Richard Jefferson .75 2.00
123 Glenn Robinson .75 2.00
124 Rasheed Wallace 1.00 2.50
125 Gilbert Arenas .75 2.00
126 Jason Kidd 1.50 4.00
127 Latrell Sprewell .75 2.00
128 Kevin Garnett 1.50 4.00
129 Caron Butler .75 2.00
130 Pau Gasol 1.00 2.50
131 Alonzo Mourning 1.25 3.00
132 Gary Payton 1.00 2.50
133 Kirk Hinrich RC 3.00 8.00
134 T.J. Ford RC 2.50 6.00
135 Nick Collison RC 2.50 6.00
136 Keith McLeod RC 2.00 5.00
137 Jon Stefansson RC 2.00 5.00
138 Britton Johnsen RC 2.00 5.00
139 Matt Carroll RC 2.00 5.00
140 Linton Johnson RC 2.00 5.00
141 Francisco Elson RC 2.00 5.00
142 Willie Green RC 2.00 5.00
143 Kyle Korver RC 4.00 10.00
144 Theron Smith RC 2.00 5.00
145 Brandon Hunter RC 2.00 5.00
146 Josh Moore RC 2.00 5.00
147 Marquis Daniels RC 2.50 6.00
148 James Lang RC 2.00 5.00
149 Udonis Haslem RC 2.50 6.00
150 Alex Garcia RC 2.00 5.00
151 LeBron James JSY AU RC 2000.00 2500.00
152 Darko Milicic JSY AU RC 5.00 12.00
153 Carmelo Anthony JSY AU RC 40.00 100.00
154 Chris Bosh JSY AU RC 12.00 30.00
155 Dwyane Wade JSY AU RC 50.00 120.00
156 Chris Kaman JSY AU RC 6.00 15.00
157 Jarvis Hayes JSY AU RC 3.00 8.00
158 Mickael Pietrus JSY AU RC 4.00 10.00
159 Dahntay Jones JSY AU RC 4.00 10.00
160 Marcus Banks JSY AU RC 3.00 8.00
161 Luke Ridnour JSY AU RC 4.00 10.00
162 Reece Gaines JSY AU RC 3.00 8.00
163 Troy Bell JSY AU RC 3.00 8.00
164 Mike Sweetney JSY AU RC 3.00 8.00
165 David West JSY AU RC 5.00 12.00
166 Aleksandar Pavlovic JSY AU RC 3.00 8.00
167 Mo Williams JSY AU RC 2.50 6.00
168 Boris Diaw JSY AU RC 4.00 10.00
169 Zoran Planinic JSY AU RC 2.50 6.00
170 Travis Outlaw JSY AU RC 3.00 8.00
171 Brian Cook JSY AU RC 2.50 6.00
172 Jerome Beasley JSY AU RC 2.50 6.00
173 Ndudi Ebi JSY AU RC 2.50 6.00
174 Kendrick Perkins JSY AU RC 3.00 8.00
175 Leandro Barbosa JSY AU RC 4.00 10.00
176 Josh Howard JSY AU RC 4.00 10.00
177 Maciej Lampe JSY AU RC 2.50 6.00
178 Jason Kapono JSY AU RC 2.50 6.00
179 Luke Walton JSY AU RC 4.00 10.00
180 Slavko Vranes JSY AU RC 2.50 6.00
181 Zarko Cabarkapa JSY AU RC 2.50 6.00
182 Travis Hansen JSY AU RC 2.50 6.00
183 Steve Blake JSY AU RC 3.00 8.00
184 Zaur Pachulia JSY AU RC 4.00 10.00
185 Keith Bogans JSY AU RC 2.50 6.00
186 Michael Jordan JSY AU/23 500.00 800.00
187 Kobe Bryant JSY AU/25 150.00 300.00
188 Kevin Garnett JSY AU/150 40.00 80.00
189 Richard Jefferson JSY AU/215 8.00 20.00
190 Gilbert Arenas JSY AU/215 8.00 20.00
191 Antawn Jamison JSY AU/215 8.00 20.00
192 Tracy McGrady JSY AU/50 15.00 40.00
193 Steve Francis JSY AU/100 15.00 40.00
194 Yao Ming JSY AU/100 30.00 60.00
195 A.Stoudemire JSY AU/215 10.00 25.00
196 S.Abdur-Rahim JSY AU/342 8.00 20.00
197 Shane Battier JSY AU/280 8.00 20.00
198 Tony Parker JSY AU/200 10.00 25.00
199 Andre Miller JSY AU/215 8.00 20.00
200 Shawn Marion JSY AU/265 8.00 20.00
201 Richard Hamilton JSY AU/215 8.00 20.00
202 Lamar Odom JSY AU/215 8.00 20.00
203 Jerry Stackhouse JSY AU/215 8.00 20.00
204 Antonio McDyess JSY AU/230 8.00 20.00
205 Manu Ginobili JSY AU/215 25.00 60.00
206 Drew Gooden JSY AU/215 8.00 20.00

2003-04 SPx Spectrum

*1-90 SINGLES: 8X TO 20X BASE HI
*91-132 SINGLES: 4X TO 10X BASE HI
*133-150 RCs: 1X TO 2.5X BASE HI
*151-156 RCs: .75X TO 2X BASE HI
*157-165 RCs: 1X TO 2.5X BASE HI
*166-185 RCs: 1.25X TO 3X BASE HI
1-185 PRINT RUN 25 SER.#'d SETS
9 Michael Jordan 125.00 250.00
34 Kobe Bryant 60.00 150.00
93 Kobe Bryant 60.00 150.00
94 Michael Jordan 125.00 250.00
151 LeBron James JSY AU 6000.00 8000.00
153 Carmelo Anthony JSY AU 300.00 600.00
154 Chris Bosh JSY AU 150.00 300.00
155 Dwyane Wade JSY AU 400.00 800.00

2003-04 SPx Winning Materials

Randomly seeded at the rate of one in 18, this 42-card set features a horizontal design where player photos appear on the left and swatches of game-worn memorabilia appear in the center.
STATED ODDS 1:18
WM1 Shaquille O'Neal SP 10.00 25.00
WM2 Paul Pierce 4.00 10.00
WM3 Anfernee Hardaway 6.00 15.00
WM4 Nene 3.00 8.00
WM5 Jay Williams 2.50 6.00
WM6 Tony Parker 4.00 10.00
WM7 Stephon Marbury 3.00 8.00
WM8 Gary Payton 4.00 10.00
WM9 Vlade Divac 3.00 8.00
WM10 Reggie Miller SP 8.00 20.00
WM11 Jermaine O'Neal 3.00 8.00
WM12 Baron Davis 3.00 8.00
WM13 Jamal Mashburn 3.00 8.00
WM14 Darius Miles 2.50 6.00
WM15 David Robinson 6.00 15.00
WM16 Kwame Brown 2.50 6.00
WM17 Karl Malone 5.00 12.00
WM18 Joe Smith 3.00 8.00
WM19 Steve Nash 5.00 12.00
WM20 Richard Jefferson 3.00 8.00
WM21 Antonio McDyess 3.00 8.00
WM22 Caron Butler 3.00 8.00
WM23 Andre Miller 3.00 8.00
WM24 Shane Battier 3.00 8.00
WM25 Steve Francis 3.00 8.00
WM26 Elton Brand 4.00 10.00
WM27 Lamar Odom 3.00 8.00
WM28 Jason Richardson 4.00 10.00
WM29 Antawn Jamison 3.00 8.00
WM30 Kurt Thomas 2.50 6.00
WM31 Pau Gasol 4.00 10.00
WM32 Allen Iverson 6.00 15.00
WM33 Jason Kidd 6.00 15.00
WM34 Dirk Nowitzki 6.00 15.00
WM35 Chris Webber 4.00 10.00
WM36 Amare Stoudemire 5.00 12.00
WM37 Tracy McGrady 5.00 12.00
WM38 Tim Duncan 6.00 15.00
WM39 Kevin Garnett 6.00 15.00
WM40 LeBron James SP 50.00 120.00
WM41 Kobe Bryant SP 12.00 30.00
WM42 Michael Jordan SP 30.00 80.00

2003-04 SPx Winning Materials Autographs

Randomly seeded in packs, this 15-card set parallels the design of the base Winning Materials insert set enhanced with a second swatch of memorabilia, authentic player autographs and sequentail numbering to 100.
PRINT RUN 100 SERIAL #'d SETS
AJ Antawn Jamison 6.00 15.00
AM Andre Miller 6.00 15.00
CB Caron Butler 6.00 15.00
DW Dajuan Wagner 5.00 12.00
JM Jerome Moiso 5.00 12.00
JT Jamaal Tinsley 5.00 12.00
KB Kobe Bryant 125.00 250.00
MA Marko Jaric 5.00 12.00
MB Mike Bibby 8.00 20.00
NH Nene 6.00 15.00
PS Peja Stojakovic 8.00 20.00
RH Richard Hamilton 6.00 15.00
RJ Richard Jefferson 6.00 15.00
SF Steve Francis 15.00 40.00
YM Yao Ming 30.00 80.00

2003-04 SPx Winning Materials Combos

Randomly inserted at the rate of one in 18, this 42-card set places one player on the left and another on the right with a swatch of game worn material from each. An autographed version of the set was also produced where cards are sequentially numbered to 10.
STATED ODDS 1:18
WC1 P.Gasol/S.Swift 5.00 12.00
WC2 M.Jaric/A.Miller 5.00 12.00
WC3 P.Stojakovic/M.Bibby 6.00 15.00
WC4 R.Jefferson/J.Kidd 6.00 15.00
WC5 G.Arenas/J.Richardson 4.00 10.00
WC6 T.Parker/R.Nesterovic 5.00 12.00
WC7 M.Fizer/T.Chandler 4.00 10.00
WC8 T.McGrady/A.Stoudemire 8.00 20.00
WC9 K.Garnett/W.Szczerbiak 8.00 20.00
WC10 B.Miller/R.Miller 5.00 12.00
WC11 C.Mobley/S.Francis 4.00 10.00
WC12 M.Finley/S.Nash 5.00 12.00
WC13 D.Nowitzki/E.Najera 5.00 12.00
WC14 D.Mason/G.Payton 4.00 10.00
WC15 J.Erving/M.Johnson 6.00 15.00
WC16 A.Kirilenko/K.Malone 5.00 12.00
WC17 J.Rose/E.Curry 4.00 10.00
WC18 J.Howard/Nene 4.00 10.00
WC19 K.Van Horn/A.McKie 4.00 10.00
WC20 C.Boozer/C.Mihm 4.00 10.00
WC21 C.Maggette/M.Olowokandi 4.00 10.00
WC22 D.Fisher/K.Bryant 5.00 12.00
WC23 L.Hughes/Kw.Brown 4.00 10.00
WC24 M.Miller/S.Battier 4.00 10.00
WC25 Q.Richardson/L.Odom 4.00 10.00
WC26 T.Ratliff/J.Terry 4.00 10.00
WC27 S.Abdur-Rahim/J.Terry 4.00 10.00
WC28 P.Stojakovic/B.Miller 5.00 12.00
WC29 D.Mutombo/B.Armstrong 4.00 10.00
WC30 D.Miles/C.Boozer 4.00 10.00
WC31 B.Davis/D.Wesley 4.00 10.00
WC32 E.Brand/C.Maggette 4.00 10.00
WC33 R.Allen/R.Lewis 4.00 10.00
WC34 K.Martin/D.Mutombo 4.00 10.00
WC35 A.Kirilenko/D.Stevenson 4.00 10.00
WC36 A.Hardaway/J.Johnson 5.00 12.00
WC37 C.Billups/R.Hamilton 4.00 10.00
WC38 C.Webber/H.Turkoglu 5.00 12.00
WC39 J.Magliore/J.Mashburn 4.00 10.00
WC40 D.Johnson/J.Terry 4.00 10.00
WC41 L.James/D.Milicic SP 25.00 60.00
WC42 K.Bryant/M.Jordan SP 40.00 100.00

2003-04 SPx Winning Materials Combos Autographs

This six-card set is a partial parallel of the Winning Materials Combos set enhanced with autographs and sequential numbering to 10.

2004-05 SPx

Released in November 2004, this 168 card set features veteran players on cards 1-90, rookies serially numbered to 1999 on cards 91-111, rookies serially numbered to 99 on cards 112-117, jersey/autographed rookies serially numbered to 1999 on cards 118-139, jersey/autographed rookies serially numbered to 750 on cards 140-147, and veteran flashback autograph on cards 148-168. Every card in the set is horizontally designed. SPx was packaged in 18 pack boxes where packs contained four cards and carried a SRP of $6.99.
COMP.SET w/o SP's (90) 15.00 40.00
91-111 PRINT RUN 1999 SER.#'d SETS
112-117 PRINT RUN 99 SER.#'d SETS
108, 118-139 PRINT RUN 1999 #'d SETS
140-147 PRINT RUN 750 SER.#'d SETS
148-168 STATED ODDS
1 Antoine Walker .50 1.25
2 Al Harrington .40 1.00
3 Boris Diaw .40 1.00
4 Paul Pierce .50 1.25
5 Ricky Davis .40 1.00
6 Gary Payton .50 1.25
7 Jahidi White .30 .75
8 Jason Kapono .30 .75
9 Gerald Wallace .40 1.00
10 Eddy Curry .30 .75
11 Kirk Hinrich .40 1.00
12 Tyson Chandler .40 1.00
13 LeBron James 3.00 8.00
14 Drew Gooden .30 .75
15 Dajuan Wagner .30 .75
16 Dirk Nowitzki .75 2.00
17 Michael Finley .50 1.25
18 Jerry Stackhouse .40 1.00
19 Carmelo Anthony 1.00 2.50
20 Kenyon Martin .40 1.00
21 Nene .40 1.00
22 Chauncey Billups .50 1.25
23 Richard Hamilton .40 1.00
24 Ben Wallace .40 1.00
25 Mike Dunleavy .40 1.00
26 Jason Richardson .50 1.25
27 Derek Fisher .40 1.00
28 Yao Ming 1.00 2.50
29 Jim Jackson .30 .75
30 Tracy McGrady .60 1.50
31 Jermaine O'Neal .40 1.00
32 Reggie Miller .50 1.25
33 Stephen Jackson .40 1.00
34 Elton Brand .50 1.25
35 Corey Maggette .40 1.00
36 Chris Kaman .40 1.00
37 Kobe Bryant 2.00 5.00
38 Chris Mihm .30 .75
39 Lamar Odom .40 1.00
40 Pau Gasol .50 1.25
41 Jason Williams .40 1.00
42 Bonzi Wells .30 .75
43 Shaquille O'Neal 1.25 3.00
44 Dwyane Wade .75 2.00
45 Eddie Jones .40 1.00
46 Michael Redd .40 1.00
47 Desmond Mason .40 1.00
48 T.J. Ford .30 .75
49 Latrell Sprewell .40 1.00
50 Kevin Garnett .75 2.00
51 Sam Cassell .40 1.00
52 Richard Jefferson .40 1.00
53 Alonzo Mourning .60 1.50
54 Jason Kidd .75 2.00
55 Jamal Mashburn .40 1.00
56 Baron Davis .40 1.00
57 Jamaal Magloire .30 .75
58 Allan Houston .40 1.00
59 Jamal Crawford .50 1.25
60 Stephon Marbury .40 1.00
61 Cuttino Mobley .30 .75
62 Hedo Turkoglu .40 1.00
63 Steve Francis .40 1.00
64 Glenn Robinson .40 1.00
65 Allen Iverson .75 2.00
66 Aaron McKie .30 .75
67 Amare Stoudemire .40 1.00
68 Steve Nash .60 1.50
69 Shawn Marion .40 1.00
70 Shareef Abdur-Rahim .40 1.00
71 Damon Stoudamire .40 1.00
72 Zach Randolph .40 1.00
73 Peja Stojakovic .50 1.25
74 Chris Webber .50 1.25
75 Mike Bibby .50 1.25
76 Tony Parker .50 1.25
77 Tim Duncan .75 2.00
78 Manu Ginobili .60 1.50
79 Ronald Murray .30 .75
80 Ray Allen .50 1.25
81 Rashard Lewis .50 1.25
82 Chris Bosh .50 1.25
83 Vince Carter .75 2.00
84 Jalen Rose .40 1.00
85 Andrei Kirilenko .40 1.00
86 Carlos Boozer .40 1.00
87 Carlos Arroyo .30 .75
88 Gilbert Arenas .40 1.00
89 Jarvis Hayes .30 .75
90 Antawn Jamison .40 1.00
91 Matt Freije RC 2.00 5.00
92 Horace Jenkins RC 2.50 6.00
93 Luis Flores RC 2.00 5.00
94 Jared Reiner RC 2.50 6.00
95 D.J. Mbenga RC 2.00 5.00
96 Pape Sow RC 2.00 5.00
97 Erik Daniels RC 2.00 5.00
98 Arthur Johnson RC 2.50 6.00
99 John Edwards RC 1.50 4.00
100 Andre Barrett RC 2.50 6.00
101 Romain Sato RC 1.50 4.00
102 Tim Pickett RC 2.50 6.00
103 Bernard Robinson RC 2.00 5.00
104 Justin Reed RC 1.50 4.00
105 Andres Nocioni RC 2.50 6.00
106 Awvee Storey RC 2.50 6.00
107 Damien Wilkins RC 2.00 5.00
108 Nenad Krstic JSY AU RC 4.00 10.00
109 Viktor Khryapa RC 1.50 4.00
110 Royal Ivey RC 2.00 5.00
111 Antonio Burks RC 2.00 5.00
112 Robert Swift RC 8.00 20.00
113 Trevor Ariza RC 12.00 30.00
114 Chris Duhon RC 12.00 30.00
115 Beno Udrih RC 10.00 25.00
116 Pavel Podkolzin RC 8.00 20.00
117 Emeka Okafor RC 10.00 25.00
118 Yuta Tabuse JSY AU RC 4.00 10.00
119 Andre Emmett JSY AU RC 2.50 6.00
120 Sasha Vujacic JSY AU RC 4.00 10.00
121 Lionel Chalmers JSY AU RC 4.00 10.00
122 J.R. Smith JSY AU RC 4.00 10.00
123 Dorell Wright JSY AU RC 4.00 10.00
124 Jameer Nelson JSY AU RC 4.00 10.00
125 Andris Biedrins JSY AU RC 2.50 6.00
126 Jackson Vroman JSY AU RC 2.50 6.00
127 A.Varejao JSY AU RC 2.50 6.00
128 Delonte West JSY AU RC 4.00 10.00
129 Tony Allen JSY AU RC 4.00 10.00
130 Kevin Martin JSY AU RC 2.50 6.00
131 Rafael Araujo JSY AU RC 2.50 6.00
132 David Harrison JSY AU RC 2.50 6.00
133 Kris Humphries JSY AU RC 4.00 10.00
134 Al Jefferson JSY AU RC 5.00 12.00
135 Kirk Snyder JSY AU RC 2.50 6.00
136 Peter J.Ramos JSY AU RC 2.50 6.00
137 Luke Jackson JSY AU RC 2.50 6.00
138 Donta Smith JSY AU RC 2.50 6.00
139 Josh Smith JSY AU RC 4.00 10.00
140 Sebastian Telfair JSY AU RC 5.00 12.00
141 Andre Iguodala JSY AU RC 12.00 30.00
142 Luol Deng JSY AU RC 6.00 15.00
143 Josh Childress JSY AU RC 5.00 12.00
144 Devin Harris JSY AU RC 5.00 12.00
145 S.Livingston JSY AU RC 6.00 15.00
146 Ben Gordon JSY AU RC 6.00 15.00
147 Dwight Howard JSY AU RC 20.00 50.00
149 Pau Gasol AU 12.50 30.00
150 Jason Kidd AU 20.00 50.00
151 Richard Hamilton AU 12.50 30.00
152 Amare Stoudemire AU 15.00 40.00
153 Chauncey Billups AU 12.50 30.00
154 Mike Bibby AU 12.50 30.00
155 Jason Richardson AU 12.50 30.00
156 LeBron James AU SP 200.00 500.00
157 Larry Bird AU SP 75.00 150.00
158 Reggie Miller AU 75.00 200.00
159 Kevin Garnett AU 40.00 100.00
160 Baron Davis AU 12.50 30.00
162 Magic Johnson AU SP 50.00 120.00
163 Tracy McGrady AU 40.00 80.00
164 Yao Ming AU 25.00 60.00
165 Michael Jordan AU SP 300.00 500.00
166 Andrei Kirilenko AU 12.50 30.00
167 Stephon Marbury AU 12.50 30.00
168 Shawn Marion AU 12.50 30.00

2004-05 SPx Spectrum

*1-90: 4X TO 10X BASE HI
*91-111: 1.25X TO 3X BASE HI
*112-117: .25X TO .6X BASE HI
*108, 118-139: 1.5X TO 4X BASE HI
*140-147: 1X TO 2.5X BASE HI
1-147 PRINT RUN 25 SER.#'d SETS
148-168 PRINT RUN ONE SET
139 Josh Smith JSY AU 40.00 100.00
144 Devin Harris JSY AU 50.00 120.00
146 Ben Gordon JSY AU 40.00 100.00

2004-05 SPx Throwback

*1-90 THROW: .75X TO 2X BASE HI
1-90 PRINT RUN 500 SER.#'d SETS
*118-139 JSY RCs: .75X TO 2X BASE HI
*140-147 JSY RCs: .5X TO 1.25X BASE HI

2004-05 SPx Winning Materials

Seeded in packs at the rate of one in 15, this 40-card set is horizontally designed with a player photo on the left and an "X" shaped swatch of memorabilia on the right.
STATED ODDS 1:15
AI Allen Iverson 5.00 12.00
AK Andrei Kirilenko 2.50 6.00
AS Amare Stoudemire 2.50 6.00
BD Baron Davis 2.50 6.00
BM Brad Miller 2.50 6.00
BW Ben Wallace 2.50 6.00
CA Carmelo Anthony 6.00 15.00
CB Carlos Boozer 2.50 6.00
DA David Wesley 2.00 5.00
DH Dwight Howard 8.00 20.00
DM Darius Miles 2.00 5.00
DN Dirk Nowitzki 5.00 12.00
DS DeShawn Stevenson 2.00 5.00
DW Dajuan Wagner 2.00 5.00
EB Elton Brand 3.00 8.00
EC Eddy Curry 2.00 5.00
JC Jamal Crawford 3.00 8.00
JK Jason Kidd 5.00 12.00
JM Jamaal Magloire 2.00 5.00
JO Jermaine O'Neal 2.50 6.00
KB Kobe Bryant 10.00 25.00
KG Kevin Garnett 5.00 12.00
LJ LeBron James SP 12.00 30.00
MB Mike Bibby 3.00 8.00
MJ Michael Jordan SP 30.00 80.00
PG Pau Gasol 3.00 8.00
PP Paul Pierce 3.00 8.00
PS Peja Stojakovic 3.00 8.00
RA Ray Allen 3.00 8.00
RJ Richard Jefferson 2.50 6.00
RM Reggie Miller 3.00 8.00
SA Shareef Abdur-Rahim 2.50 6.00
SM Shawn Marion 2.50 6.00
SN Steve Nash 4.00 10.00
SO Shaquille O'Neal 8.00 20.00
ST Stephon Marbury 2.50 6.00
TD Tim Duncan 5.00 12.00
TM Tracy McGrady 4.00 10.00
WS Wally Szczerbiak 2.50 6.00
YM Yao Ming 6.00 15.00

2004-05 SPx Winning Materials Autographs

Serially numbered to 100, this 34-card set parallels the design of the Winning Materials insert enhanced with an autograph.
PRINT RUN 100 SER.#'d SETS
AI Andre Iguodala 10.00 25.00
AK Andrei Kirilenko 10.00 25.00
AS Amare Stoudemire 12.00 30.00
BD Baron Davis 8.00 20.00
BG Ben Gordon 10.00 25.00
BM Brad Miller 10.00 25.00
CA Carmelo Anthony 15.00 40.00
CB Carlos Boozer 10.00 25.00
DE Devin Harris 8.00 20.00
DF Derek Fisher 8.00 20.00
DH Dwight Howard 15.00 40.00
JA Jason Richardson 10.00 25.00
JC Jamal Crawford 10.00 25.00
JK Jason Kidd 20.00 50.00
JR Jalen Rose 8.00 20.00
JS John Stockton 60.00 150.00
KB Kobe Bryant 100.00 200.00
KG Kevin Garnett 50.00 100.00
LB Larry Bird 75.00 150.00
LD Luol Deng 10.00 25.00
LJO LeBron James 400.00 800.00
LO Lamar Odom 8.00 20.00
MA Magic Johnson 75.00 150.00
MJ Michael Jordan 500.00 1000.00
PP Paul Pierce 15.00 40.00
RJ Richard Jefferson 10.00 25.00
RM Reggie Miller 75.00 200.00
SA Shareef Abdur-Rahim 10.00 25.00
SL Shaun Livingston 10.00 25.00
SM Shawn Marion 8.00 20.00
ST Stephon Marbury 8.00 20.00
TE Sebastian Telfair 8.00 20.00
TM Tracy McGrady 30.00 80.00
YM Yao Ming 30.00 80.00

2004-05 SPx Winning Materials Combos

Inserted at the rate of one in 15, this 42-card set uses some of the design elements from the Winning Materials set but places two players with swatches of memorabilia. An Autographed version sequentially numbered to 10 was also inserted.
STATED ODDS 1:15
UNPRICED AUTO PRINT RUN 10 SETS

AJ A.Walker/Josh Smith 4.00 10.00
AK A.Jamison/K.Brown 4.00 10.00
AM C.Anthony/A.Miller 5.00 12.00
BA C.Bosh/R.Araujo 4.00 10.00
BJ K.Bryant/L.James 20.00 50.00
BO K.Bryant/L.Odom 8.00 20.00
BP M.Banks/G.Payton 4.00 10.00
DG L.Deng/B.Gordon 4.00 10.00
DM B.Davis/J.Magloire 4.00 10.00
DP T.Duncan/T.Parker 8.00 20.00
ES A.Emmett/S.Swift 4.00 10.00
FM S.Francis/C.Mobley 4.00 10.00
GC K.Garnett/S.Cassell 8.00 20.00
GD M.Ginobili/T.Duncan 8.00 20.00
GM K.Garnett/T.McGrady 8.00 20.00
II A.Iverson/A.Iguodala 8.00 20.00
JB M.Jordan/K.Bryant 40.00 100.00
JC J.Stockton/C.Boozer 6.00 15.00
JJ L.James/M.Jordan SP 60.00 150.00
JS L.James/E.Snow 8.00 20.00
KA K.Martin/A.Miller 4.00 10.00
KB A.Kirilenko/C.Boozer SP 4.00 10.00
KC K.Malone/C.Butler 4.00 10.00
KJ J.Kidd/R.Jefferson 5.00 12.00
LA L.James/C.Anthony SP 10.00 25.00
MB C.Maggette/E.Brand 4.00 10.00
MC S.Marbury/J.Crawford 4.00 10.00
MH S.Marbury/A.Houston 4.00 10.00
MM Y.Ming/T.McGrady 8.00 20.00
MS S.Marion/A.Stoudemire 5.00 12.00
MT D.Miles/S.Telfair 4.00 10.00
NH D.Nowitzki/D.Harris 5.00 12.00
NW J.Nelson/Del.West 4.00 10.00
OH S.O'Neal/D.Howard 6.00 15.00
OM J.O'Neal/R.Miller 5.00 12.00
PJ P.Pierce/A.Jefferson 5.00 12.00
PM P.Gasol/M.Miller 4.00 10.00
RD J.Richardson/M.Dunleavy 4.00 10.00
SB P.Stojakovic/M.Bibby 4.00 10.00
SD S.Abdur-R/D.Miles 4.00 10.00
SN A.Stoudemire/S.Nash 6.00 15.00
TH J.Tinsley/D.Harrison 4.00 10.00

2005-06 SPx

Released in December 2005, SPx consists of a 154-card set where cards 1-90 picture veterans on all-foil cards with an "X" design behind full color player photos, cards 91-120 picture rookies on an all foil cards stock and are sequentially numbered to 1499, cards 121-146 are horizontally designed and picture rookie players with a swatch of memorabilia and an embedded cut signature serially numbered to 1499 (with a few exceptions--card 124 is serially numbered to 99, card 133 is serially numbered to 99, card 136 is serially numbered to 1458 and card 141 is serially numbered to 99), and cards 147-154 picture rookies, same design as cards 121-146, but are serially numbered to 750. SPx was packaged in 18-pack boxes where packs contain four cards and carried an initial SRP of $6.99.
COMP.SET w/o SP's (90) 20.00 50.00
91-120 RC PRINT RUN 1499 SER.#'d SETS
UNLESS LISTED IN CHECKLIST
147-154 RC PRINT RUN 750 SER.#'d SETS

1 Josh Childress .40 1.00
2 Josh Smith .40 1.00
3 Al Harrington .40 1.00
4 Antoine Walker .40 1.00
5 Gary Payton .50 1.25
6 Paul Pierce .50 1.25
7 Kareem Rush .30 .75
8 Emeka Okafor .40 1.00
9 Gerald Wallace .40 1.00
10 Michael Jordan 4.00 10.00
11 Kirk Hinrich .40 1.00
12 Ben Gordon .40 1.00
13 Drew Gooden .40 1.00
14 Larry Hughes .40 1.00
15 LeBron James 2.00 5.00
16 Zydrunas Ilgauskas .40 1.00
17 Dirk Nowitzki .75 2.00
18 Jason Terry .40 1.00
19 Michael Finley .50 1.25
20 Carmelo Anthony 1.00 2.50
21 Kenyon Martin .40 1.00
22 Andre Miller .40 1.00
23 Ben Wallace .40 1.00
24 Chauncey Billups .50 1.25
25 Richard Hamilton .40 1.00
26 Troy Murphy .30 .75
27 Jason Richardson .50 1.25
28 Baron Davis .40 1.00
29 Tracy McGrady .60 1.50
30 Yao Ming .60 1.50
31 David Wesley .30 .75
32 Jermaine O'Neal .40 1.00
33 Jamaal Tinsley .30 .75
34 Ron Artest .50 1.25
35 Corey Maggette .40 1.00
36 Elton Brand .50 1.25
37 Bobby Simmons .30 .75
38 Caron Butler .40 1.00
39 Kobe Bryant 2.00 5.00
40 Lamar Odom .40 1.00
41 Mike Miller .40 1.00
42 Jason Williams .40 1.00
43 Pau Gasol .50 1.25
44 Dwyane Wade .75 2.00
45 Eddie Jones .40 1.00
46 Shaquille O'Neal 1.00 2.50
47 Desmond Mason .30 .75
48 Keith Van Horn .40 1.00
49 Michael Redd .40 1.00
50 Kevin Garnett .75 2.00
51 Latrell Sprewell .40 1.00
52 Sam Cassell .40 1.00
53 Vince Carter .75 2.00
54 Jason Kidd .75 2.00
55 Richard Jefferson .40 1.00
56 Dan Dickau .30 .75
57 Jamaal Magloire .30 .75
58 J.R. Smith .40 1.00
59 Jamal Crawford .50 1.25
60 Stephon Marbury .40 1.00
61 Quentin Richardson .40 1.00
62 Dwight Howard .40 1.00
63 Grant Hill .60 1.50
64 Steve Francis .40 1.00
65 Allen Iverson .75 2.00
66 Andre Iguodala .40 1.00
67 Chris Webber .50 1.25
68 Amare Stoudemire .40 1.00
69 Shawn Marion .40 1.00
70 Steve Nash .60 1.50
71 Damon Stoudamire .40 1.00
72 Shareef Abdur-Rahim .40 1.00
73 Zach Randolph .40 1.00
74 Brad Miller .40 1.00
75 Mike Bibby .50 1.25
76 Peja Stojakovic .50 1.25
77 Manu Ginobili .50 1.25
78 Tim Duncan .75 2.00
79 Tony Parker .50 1.25
80 Rashard Lewis .50 1.25
81 Ray Allen .50 1.25
82 Luke Ridnour .40 1.00
83 Rafer Alston .30 .75
84 Jalen Rose .50 1.25
85 Chris Bosh .50 1.25
86 Andrei Kirilenko .40 1.00
87 Carlos Boozer .40 1.00
88 Matt Harpring .30 .75
89 Antawn Jamison .40 1.00
90 Gilbert Arenas .40 1.00
91 Bracey Wright RC 1.25 3.00
92 Chris Taft RC 1.50 4.00
93 Jose Calderon RC 2.00 5.00
94 Dijon Thompson RC 1.25 3.00
95 Esteban Batista RC 1.25 3.00
96 Linas Kleiza RC 1.25 3.00
97 Earl Barron RC 1.50 4.00
98 Ike Diogu RC 1.25 3.00
99 Alan Anderson RC 1.25 3.00
100 Shavlik Randolph RC 1.50 4.00
101 Eddie Basden RC 1.25 3.00
102 Johan Petro RC 1.25 3.00
103 Ersan Ilyasova RC 2.00 5.00
104 Dwayne Jones RC 1.25 3.00
105 Aaron Miles RC 1.50 4.00
106 James Singleton RC 1.50 4.00
107 Von Wafer RC 1.25 3.00
108 Josh Powell RC 1.50 4.00
109 Yaroslav Korolev RC 1.25 3.00
110 Ronnie Price RC 1.50 4.00
111 Andray Blatche RC 2.00 5.00
112 Robert Whaley RC 1.25 3.00
113 Donell Taylor RC 1.25 3.00
114 Orien Greene RC 1.50 4.00
115 Lawrence Roberts RC 1.25 3.00
116 Amir Johnson RC 2.00 5.00
117 Matt Walsh RC 2.00 5.00
118 Fabricio Oberto RC 1.50 4.00
119 Arvydas Macijauskas RC 1.25 3.00
120 Alex Acker RC 1.25 3.00
121 Salim Stoudamire JSY AU RC 3.00 8.00
122 Francisco Garcia JSY AU RC 3.00 8.00
123 Daniel Ewing JSY AU RC 3.00 8.00
124 N.Robinson JSY AU/199 RC 30.00 75.00
125 Luther Head JSY AU RC 3.00 8.00
126 Louis Williams JSY AU RC 4.00 10.00
127 Jarrett Jack JSY AU RC 4.00 10.00
128 J.Maxiell JSY AU/1453 RC 3.00 8.00
129 Wayne Simien JSY AU RC 2.50 6.00
130 Julius Hodge JSY AU RC 2.50 6.00
131 C.J. Miles JSY AU RC 4.00 10.00
132 Andrew Bynum JSY AU RC 3.00 8.00
133 Monta Ellis JSY AU/99 RC 15.00 40.00
134 Joey Graham JSY AU RC 3.00 8.00
135 Antoine Wright JSY AU RC 3.00 8.00
136 Sean May JSY AU/1458 RC 2.50 6.00
137 Channing Frye JSY AU RC 4.00 10.00
138 Gerald Green JSY AU RC 4.00 10.00
139 S.Jasikevicius JSY AU RC 4.00 10.00
140 Danny Granger JSY AU RC 5.00 12.00
141 H.Warrick JSY AU/99 RC 15.00 40.00
142 David Lee JSY AU RC 4.00 10.00
143 Brandon Bass JSY AU RC 3.00 8.00
144 Ryan Gomes JSY AU RC 3.00 8.00
145 M.Andriuskevicius JSY AU RC 2.50 6.00
146 Travis Diener JSY AU RC 2.50 6.00
147 Martell Webster JSY AU RC 5.00 12.00
148 Rashad McCants JSY AU RC 5.00 12.00
149 Deron Williams JSY AU RC 8.00 20.00
150 Charlie Villanueva JSY AU RC 6.00 15.00
151 Raymond Felton JSY AU RC 6.00 15.00
152 Andrew Bogut JSY AU RC 8.00 20.00
153 Chris Paul JSY AU RC 50.00 120.00
154 Marvin Williams JSY AU RC 6.00 15.00

2005-06 SPx Spectrum

*1-90 SPECTRUM: 4X TO 10X BASE HI
*91-120 RCs: 1.25X TO 3X BASE HI
*121-146 RCs: 1.5X TO 4X BASE HI
*147-154 RCs: 1X TO 2.5X BASE HI
*124, 133, 141 RC SP: .75X TO 2X BASE HI
PRINT RUN 25 SER.#'d SETS

10 Michael Jordan 50.00 120.00
133 Monta Ellis JSY AU 150.00 300.00
149 Deron Williams JSY AU 40.00 100.00
153 Chris Paul JSY AU 250.00 500.00

2005-06 SPx Flashback Fabrics

Randomly seeded in packs, this 40-card set features a horizontal design with player photos on the left, a jersey swatch on the right and an embedded signature towards the bottom of the card. Though print runs or odds were never released, it is believed 25 cards for each player are in circulation.
RANDOM INSERTS IN PACKS
UNPRICED SPECTRUM PRINT RUN ONE SET

AK Andrei Kirilenko 8.00 20.00
BD Baron Davis 8.00 20.00
BG Ben Gordon 10.00 25.00
BO Carlos Boozer 8.00 20.00
BW Ben Wallace 8.00 20.00
CA Carmelo Anthony 20.00 50.00
CB Chauncey Billups 10.00 25.00
CH Chris Bosh 12.00 30.00
DH Dwight Howard 15.00 40.00
DR David Robinson 25.00 60.00
GA Gilbert Arenas 10.00 25.00
HO Hakeem Olajuwon 20.00 50.00
IT Isiah Thomas 20.00 50.00
JC Josh Childress 8.00 20.00
JK Jason Kidd 12.00 30.00
JR J.R. Smith 8.00 20.00
JS John Stockton 30.00 80.00
KH Kirk Hinrich 10.00 25.00
LB Larry Bird 60.00 120.00
LD Luol Deng 8.00 20.00
LJ LeBron James SP 200.00 400.00
LO Lamar Odom 10.00 25.00
MA Magic Johnson 50.00 100.00
MB Mike Bibby 8.00 20.00
MJ Michael Jordan SP 300.00 600.00
PG Pau Gasol 8.00 20.00
PP Paul Pierce 12.00 30.00
PS Peja Stojakovic 8.00 20.00
QR Quentin Richardson 8.00 20.00
RH Richard Hamilton 8.00 20.00
RJ Richard Jefferson 8.00 20.00
SE Sean May 8.00 20.00
SL Shaun Livingston 8.00 20.00
SN Steve Nash 15.00 40.00
ST Stephon Marbury 8.00 20.00
TM Tracy McGrady 15.00 40.00
UH Udonis Haslem 8.00 20.00
VC Vince Carter 15.00 40.00
WF Walt Frazier 12.00 30.00
YM Yao Ming 30.00 80.00

2005-06 SPx SPxcitement Rookies

Serially numbered to 1999, this 20-card set features full color player action photos, and a border along the left that morphs into a SPxcitement logo along the bottom of the card.
PRINT RUN 1999 SER.#'d SETS
*SPECTRUM: 1.25X TO 3X BASE HI
SPECTRUM PRINT RUN 99 SER.#'d SETS
UNPRICED AUTO PRINT RUN 5 SETS

XCR1 Chris Paul 4.00 10.00
XCR2 Marvin Williams 1.00 2.50
XCR3 Andrew Bogut 1.25 3.00
XCR4 Hakim Warrick .75 2.00
XCR5 Rashad McCants .75 2.00
XCR6 Raymond Felton 1.00 2.50
XCR7 Sean May .60 1.50
XCR8 Charlie Villanueva 1.00 2.50
XCR9 Gerald Green 1.00 2.50
XCR10 Danny Granger 1.25 3.00
XCR11 Deron Williams 1.25 3.00
XCR12 Martell Webster .75 2.00
XCR13 Andrew Bynum .75 2.00
XCR14 Channing Frye 1.00 2.50
XCR15 Joey Graham .75 2.00
XCR16 Ike Diogu .60 1.50
XCR17 Antoine Wright .75 2.00
XCR18 Julius Hodge .60 1.50
XCR19 Nate Robinson 1.00 2.50
XCR20 Jarrett Jack 1.00 2.50

2005-06 SPx SPxcitement Veterans

Limited to 999 serially numbered copies, this 40-card set places full color player photos in the center of a design that features a colored square in the background set to match team colors with white borders along the top and bottom and black borders on the sides.
PRINT RUN 999 SER.#'d SETS
*SPECTRUM: 1X TO 2.5X BASE HI
SPECTRUM PRINT RUN 99 SER.#'d SETS
UNPRICED AUTO PRINT RUN 5 SETS

XCV1 Gary Payton 1.00 2.50
XCV2 Paul Pierce 1.00 2.50
XCV3 Michael Jordan 8.00 20.00
XCV4 Ben Gordon .75 2.00
XCV5 Kirk Hinrich .75 2.00
XCV6 LeBron James 4.00 10.00
XCV7 Carmelo Anthony 2.00 5.00
XCV8 Ben Wallace .75 2.00
XCV9 Chauncey Billups 1.00 2.50
XCV10 Richard Hamilton .75 2.00
XCV11 Baron Davis .75 2.00
XCV12 Tracy McGrady 1.25 3.00
XCV13 Yao Ming 1.25 3.00
XCV14 Kobe Bryant 4.00 10.00
XCV15 Lamar Odom .75 2.00
XCV16 Pau Gasol 1.00 2.50
XCV17 Jason Williams .75 2.00
XCV18 Michael Redd .75 2.00
XCV19 Jason Kidd 1.50 4.00
XCV20 Richard Jefferson .75 2.00
XCV21 J.R. Smith .75 2.00
XCV22 Stephon Marbury .75 2.00
XCV23 Dwight Howard .75 2.00
XCV24 Jameer Nelson .60 1.50
XCV25 Andre Iguodala .75 2.00
XCV26 Kyle Korver .75 2.00
XCV27 Quentin Richardson .75 2.00
XCV28 Steve Nash 1.25 3.00
XCV29 Damon Stoudamire .75 2.00
XCV30 Mike Bibby 1.00 2.50
XCV31 Peja Stojakovic 1.00 2.50
XCV32 Chris Bosh 1.00 2.50
XCV33 Andrei Kirilenko .75 2.00
XCV34 Antawn Jamison .75 2.00
XCV35 Carlos Boozer .75 2.00
XCV36 Hakeem Olajuwon 1.25 3.00
XCV37 Isiah Thomas 1.00 2.50
XCV38 Dennis Rodman 2.00 5.00
XCV39 Scottie Pippen 1.50 4.00
XCV40 John Stockton 2.00 5.00

2005-06 SPx Winning Materials

Inserted in packs at the rate of one in 18, this 41-card set is horizontally designed with a player photo in the middle and a two swatches of memorabilia, one on each side of the player.
STATED ODDS 1:18
*SPECTRUM: .75X TO 2X BASE HI
SPECTRUM PRINT RUN 25 SER.#'d SETS.

AB Andrew Bogut 4.00 10.00
AS Amare Stoudemire 2.50 6.00
BD Baron Davis 2.50 6.00
CA Carmelo Anthony 6.00 15.00
CB Chris Bosh 3.00 8.00
CP Chris Paul 8.00 20.00
CW Chris Webber 3.00 8.00
DE Deron Williams 6.00 15.00
DN Dirk Nowitzki 5.00 12.00
EB Elton Brand 3.00 8.00
GA Gilbert Arenas 2.50 6.00
GG Gerald Green 3.00 8.00
GH Grant Hill 4.00 10.00
JK Jason Kidd 5.00 12.00
JO Jermaine O'Neal 2.50 6.00
JR Jason Richardson 3.00 8.00
KB Kobe Bryant 10.00 25.00
KG Kevin Garnett 5.00 12.00
KM Kenyon Martin 2.50 6.00
LJ LeBron James 10.00 25.00
MF Michael Finley 3.00 8.00
MG Manu Ginobili 3.00 8.00
MJ Michael Jordan 30.00 80.00
MW Marvin Williams 3.00 8.00
PG Pau Gasol 3.00 8.00
PP Paul Pierce 3.00 8.00
PS Peja Stojakovic 3.00 8.00
QR Quentin Richardson 2.50 6.00
RA Ray Allen 3.00 8.00
RL Rashard Lewis 3.00 8.00
SF Steve Francis 2.50 6.00
SM Shawn Marion 2.50 6.00
SN Steve Nash 4.00 10.00
SO Shaquille O'Neal 6.00 15.00
ST Stephon Marbury 2.50 6.00
TD Tim Duncan 5.00 12.00
TM Tracy McGrady 4.00 10.00
TP Tony Parker 3.00 8.00
VC Vince Carter 5.00 12.00
YM Yao Ming 4.00 10.00
ZI Zydrunas Ilgauskas 2.50 6.00

2005-06 SPx Winning Materials Autographs

Serially numbered to either 50 or 25 copies, this 18-card set parallels the design of the Winning Materials set enhanced with player autographs. See checklist for serial number details.
PRINT RUN 25 TO 50 SER.#'d SETS

AB Andrew Bogut/50 12.00 30.00
BG Ben Gordon/50 6.00 15.00
CA Carmelo Anthony/25 30.00 80.00
CB Chauncey Billups/50 15.00 40.00
CH Chris Bosh/50 12.00 30.00
CP Chris Paul/50 60.00 150.00
DE Deron Williams/50 10.00 25.00
GG Gerald Green/50 6.00 15.00
KH Kirk Hinrich/50 12.00 30.00
LJ LeBron James/25 200.00 350.00
MB Mike Bibby/50 12.00 30.00
MJ Michael Jordan/25 400.00 700.00
MW Marvin Williams/50 12.00 30.00
PS Peja Stojakovic/50 12.00 30.00
QR Quentin Richardson/50 6.00 15.00
SN Steve Nash/25 60.00 120.00

2005-06 SPx Winning Materials Combos

Inserted at the rate of one in 18, this 42-card set features two players and two swatches of memorabilia.
STATED ODDS 1:18
*SPECTRUM: .75X TO 2X BASE HI
SPECTRUM PRINT RUN 25 SER.#'d SETS
UNPRICED AUTO PRINT RUN 10 SETS

AL R.Allen/R.Lewis 4.00 10.00
AN C.Anthony/Nene 5.00 12.00
BB K.Bryant/C.Butler 8.00 20.00
BH C.Billups/R.Hamilton 6.00 15.00
BP B.Miller/P.Stojakovic 4.00 10.00
BS R.Bowen/S.Swift 4.00 10.00
CL S.Cassell/S.Livingston 4.00 10.00
DC L.Deng/T.Chandler 4.00 10.00
DG T.Duncan/M.Ginobili 6.00 15.00
DW S.Dalembert/C.Webber 4.00 10.00
FN S.Francis/J.Nelson 4.00 10.00
GC D.George/B.Cook 4.00 10.00
GH B.Gordon/K.Hinrich 4.00 10.00
GS K.Garnett/W.Szczerbiak 6.00 15.00
HH D.Howard/G.Hill 6.00 15.00
HM A.Houston/S.Marbury 4.00 10.00
HW U.Haslem/D.Wright 4.00 10.00
JA A.Jamison/G.Arenas 4.00 10.00
JI L.James/Z.Ilgauskas 8.00 20.00
JJ M.Jordan/L.James SP 40.00 100.00
KB A.Kirilenko/C.Boozer 4.00 10.00
KJ J.Kidd/R.Jefferson 5.00 12.00
KM L.Kleiza/K.Martin 4.00 10.00
MB C.Maggette/E.Brand 4.00 10.00
MS S.Marion/A.Stoudemire 5.00 12.00
MY T.McGrady/Y.Ming 6.00 15.00
NR S.Nash/S.Marion 5.00 12.00
NT D.Nowitzki/J.Terry 4.00 10.00
OT J.O'Neal/J.Tinsley 4.00 10.00
PJ P.Pierce/A.Jefferson 4.00 10.00
PU T.Parker/B.Udrih 4.00 10.00
RA J.Rose/R.Araujo 4.00 10.00
RD J.Richardson/B.Davis 4.00 10.00
RM Z.Randolph/D.Miles 4.00 10.00
RR L.Ridnour/V.Radmanovic 4.00 10.00
RW K.Rush/G.Wallace 4.00 10.00
SM J.R.Smith/J.Magloire 4.00 10.00
TH J.Terry/D.Harris 4.00 10.00
WP A.Walker/G.Payton 4.00 10.00
WS D.Wagner/E.Snow 4.00 10.00
WW D.Wesley/C.Ward 4.00 10.00
YO Y.Ming/S.O'Neal 6.00 15.00

2006-07 SPx

Released in late February 2007, SPx features a 152-card set where cards 1-100 utilize a foil-board design with an "X" in the background and picture veterans, cards 101-121 utilize a similar design and picture rookies serially numbered to 1999, cards 122-127 utilize a horizontal design including both a cut signature and a jersey swatch and picture rookies serially numbered to 299, and cards 127-152 utilize the same horizontal design and picture rookies serially numbered to 1199. SPx is packaged in 18-pack boxes of four cards each and carried a suggested retail price of $6.99 per pack.
COMP.SET w/o RC's (100) 25.00 60.00
122-127 RC PRINT RUN 299 SER.#'d SETS
128-152 RC PRINT RUN 1199 SER.#'d SETS

1 Joe Johnson .40 1.00
2 Salim Stoudamire .30 .75
3 Marvin Williams .40 1.00
4 Tony Allen .30 .75
5 Al Jefferson .40 1.00
6 Paul Pierce .50 1.25
7 Raymond Felton .40 1.00
8 Emeka Okafor .40 1.00
9 Gerald Wallace .40 1.00
10 Tyson Chandler .40 1.00
11 Ben Gordon .40 1.00
12 Michael Jordan 4.00 10.00
13 Drew Gooden .40 1.00
14 Zydrunas Ilgauskas .40 1.00
15 LeBron James 2.00 5.00
16 Devin Harris .30 .75
17 Dirk Nowitzki .75 2.00
18 Jason Terry .40 1.00
19 Carmelo Anthony .60 1.50
20 Andre Miller .40 1.00
21 Eduardo Najera .30 .75
22 Chauncey Billups .50 1.25
23 Richard Hamilton .40 1.00
24 Ben Wallace .40 1.00
25 Rasheed Wallace .50 1.25
26 Baron Davis .40 1.00
27 Troy Murphy .30 .75
28 Jason Richardson .50 1.25
29 Rafer Alston .30 .75
30 Tracy McGrady .60 1.50
31 Yao Ming .60 1.50
32 Sarunas Jasikevicius .40 1.00
33 Jermaine O'Neal .40 1.00
34 Peja Stojakovic .50 1.25
35 Elton Brand .50 1.25
36 Sam Cassell .40 1.00
37 Chris Kaman .40 1.00
38 Shaun Livingston .30 .75
39 Kobe Bryant 2.00 5.00
40 Lamar Odom .40 1.00
41 Ronny Turiaf .40 1.00
42 Pau Gasol .50 1.25
43 Mike Miller .40 1.00
44 Damon Stoudamire .40 1.00
45 Shaquille O'Neal 1.00 2.50
46 Wayne Simien .30 .75
47 Dwyane Wade .75 2.00
48 Jason Williams .40 1.00
49 Andrew Bogut .40 1.00
50 T.J. Ford .30 .75
51 Jamaal Magloire .30 .75
52 Michael Redd .40 1.00
53 Ricky Davis .40 1.00
54 Kevin Garnett .75 2.00
55 Rashad McCants .30 .75
56 Vince Carter .60 1.50
57 Richard Jefferson .40 1.00
58 Jason Kidd .75 2.00
59 Speedy Claxton .30 .75
60 Desmond Mason .30 .75
61 Chris Paul .60 1.50
62 Steve Francis .40 1.00
63 Channing Frye .40 1.00
64 Stephon Marbury .40 1.00
65 Nate Robinson .30 .75
66 Carlos Arroyo .30 .75
67 Grant Hill .60 1.50
68 Dwight Howard .40 1.00
69 Jameer Nelson .30 .75
70 Andre Iguodala .40 1.00
71 Allen Iverson .60 1.50
72 Chris Webber .50 1.25
73 Boris Diaw .40 1.00
74 Shawn Marion .40 1.00
75 Steve Nash .60 1.50
76 Amare Stoudemire .40 1.00
77 Zach Randolph .40 1.00
78 Sebastian Telfair .30 .75
79 Martell Webster .40 1.00
80 Shareef Abdur-Rahim .40 1.00
81 Ron Artest .50 1.25
82 Mike Bibby .50 1.25
83 Brad Miller .40 1.00
84 Tim Duncan .75 2.00
85 Michael Finley .50 1.25
86 Manu Ginobili .50 1.25
87 Tony Parker .50 1.25
88 Ray Allen .50 1.25
89 Rashard Lewis .50 1.25
90 Chris Wilcox .30 .75
91 Chris Bosh .50 1.25
92 Joey Graham .30 .75
93 Charlie Villanueva .30 .75
94 Carlos Boozer .40 1.00
95 Andrei Kirilenko .40 1.00
96 C.J. Miles .40 1.00
97 Deron Williams .40 1.00
98 Gilbert Arenas .40 1.00
99 Caron Butler .40 1.00
100 Antawn Jamison .40 1.00
101 Adam Morrison RC 2.00 5.00
102 Alexander Johnson RC 1.25 3.00
103 Damir Markota RC 1.25 3.00
104 J.J. Redick RC 2.50 6.00
105 Will Blalock RC 1.25 3.00
106 Leon Powe RC 1.50 4.00
107 Thabo Sefolosha RC 2.00 5.00
108 Pops Mensah-Bonsu RC 1.25 3.00
109 Robert Hite RC 1.25 3.00
110 Tarence Kinsey RC 1.25 3.00
111 Vassilis Spanoulis RC 1.25 3.00
112 Yakhouba Diawara RC 1.25 3.00
113 Daniel Gibson RC 1.50 4.00
114 Hassan Adams RC 1.25 3.00
115 James Augustine RC 1.25 3.00
116 Chris Quinn RC 1.25 3.00
117 Mardy Collins RC 1.25 3.00
118 Paul Millsap RC 2.50 6.00
119 P.J. Tucker RC 1.50 4.00
120 Ryan Hollins RC 1.50 4.00
121 Saer Sene RC 1.25 3.00
122 Andrea Bargnani JSY AU RC 8.00 20.00
123 LaMarcus Aldridge JSY AU RC 30.00 80.00
124 Tyrus Thomas JSY AU RC 6.00 15.00
125 Shelden Williams JSY AU RC 6.00 15.00
126 Brandon Roy JSY AU RC 8.00 20.00
127 Randy Foye JSY AU RC 8.00 20.00
128 Paul Davis JSY AU RC 3.00 8.00
129 Solomon Jones JSY AU RC 3.00 8.00
130 David Noel JSY AU RC 3.00 8.00
131 Allan Ray JSY AU RC 3.00 8.00
132 Bobby Jones JSY AU RC 3.00 8.00
133 Cedric Simmons JSY AU RC 3.00 8.00
134 Dee Brown JSY AU RC 3.00 8.00
135 Shawne Williams JSY AU RC 3.00 8.00
136 Hilton Armstrong JSY AU RC 3.00 8.00
137 James White JSY AU RC 3.00 8.00
138 Jordan Farmar JSY AU RC 5.00 12.00
139 Josh Boone JSY AU RC 3.00 8.00
140 Kyle Lowry JSY AU RC 6.00 15.00
141 Marcus Williams JSY AU RC 3.00 8.00
142 Maurice Ager JSY AU RC 3.00 8.00
143 Patrick O'Bryant JSY AU RC 3.00 8.00
144 Quincy Douby JSY AU RC 3.00 8.00
145 Rajon Rondo JSY AU RC 8.00 20.00
146 Renaldo Balkman JSY AU RC 4.00 10.00
147 Rodney Carney JSY AU RC 3.00 8.00
148 Ronnie Brewer JSY AU RC 5.00 12.00
149 Rudy Gay JSY AU RC 6.00 15.00
150 Shannon Brown JSY AU RC 3.00 8.00
151 Steve Novak JSY AU RC 4.00 10.00
152 Craig Smith JSY AU RC 4.00 10.00

2006-07 SPx Spectrum

*1-100 SPECTRUM: 4X TO 10X BASE HI
*101-121 RCs: 1.25X TO 3X BASE HI
*122-127 RCs: 1.25X TO 3X BASE HI
*128-152 RCs: 1.25X TO 3X BASE HI
SPECTRUM PRINT RUN 25 SER.#'d SETS

12 Michael Jordan 60.00 150.00
39 Kobe Bryant 30.00 80.00
71 Allen Iverson 10.00 25.00
126 Brandon Roy JSY AU 100.00 250.00

2006-07 SPx Flashback Fabrics

APPROXIMATE ODDS 1:72
UNPRICED SPECTRUM PRINT RUN ONE SET

FFAB Andrew Bynum 2.00 5.00
FFAI Allen Iverson 4.00 10.00
FFAJ Antawn Jamison 2.50 6.00
FFAK Andrei Kirilenko 2.50 6.00
FFAW Antoine Walker 2.50 6.00
FFBB Bruce Bowen 2.00 5.00
FFBG Ben Gordon 2.50 6.00
FFBM Brad Miller 2.50 6.00
FFCB Carlos Boozer 2.50 6.00
FFCF Channing Frye 2.50 6.00
FFCW Chris Webber 3.00 8.00
FFDG Drew Gooden 2.50 6.00
FFDH Devin Harris 2.00 5.00
FFDM Desmond Mason 2.00 5.00
FFDR Dennis Rodman 10.00 25.00
FFGA Gilbert Arenas 2.50 6.00
FFGE Devean George 2.00 5.00
FFGG George Gervin 5.00 12.00
FFGH Grant Hill 4.00 10.00
FFID Ike Diogu 2.00 5.00
FFJC Jamal Crawford 3.00 8.00
FFJN Jameer Nelson 2.00 5.00
FFJR Jason Richardson 3.00 8.00
FFJS John Stockton 8.00 20.00
FFJT Jason Terry 2.50 6.00
FFLD Luol Deng 2.50 6.00
FFLH Luther Head 2.50 6.00
FFLO Lamar Odom 2.50 6.00
FFMG Manu Ginobili 3.00 8.00
FFMJ Magic Johnson 8.00 20.00
FFQR Quentin Richardson 2.50 6.00
FFRJ Richard Jefferson 2.50 6.00
FFRO David Robinson 6.00 15.00
FFRW Rasheed Wallace 3.00 8.00
FFSD Samuel Dalembert 2.00 5.00
FFSE Sean Elliott 3.00 8.00
FFSJ Sarunas Jasikevicius 2.50 6.00
FFSM Sean May 2.00 5.00
FFWF Walt Frazier 5.00 12.00
FFWR Antoine Wright 2.00 5.00
FFWS Wally Szczerbiak 2.50 6.00

2006-07 SPx Flashback Fabrics Autographs

APPROXIMATE ODDS 1:144
UNPRICED SPECTRUM PRINT RUN ONE SET

FFBD Baron Davis 6.00 15.00
AFFAB Andrew Bogut 8.00 20.00
AFFAI Andre Iguodala 8.00 20.00
AFFAJ Al Jefferson 6.00 15.00
AFFBK Bernard King 10.00 25.00
AFFBL Bill Laimbeer 10.00 25.00
AFFCA Carmelo Anthony 20.00 50.00
AFFCB Chris Bosh 15.00 40.00
AFFCD Clyde Drexler 25.00 60.00
AFFCM Corey Maggette 6.00 15.00
AFFDG Danny Granger 6.00 15.00
AFFDW Deron Williams 12.00 30.00
AFFFG Francisco Garcia 6.00 15.00
AFFHO Hakeem Olajuwon 20.00 50.00
AFFHW Hakim Warrick 6.00 15.00
AFFJG Joey Graham 6.00 15.00
AFFJS J.R. Smith 6.00 15.00
AFFKK Kyle Korver 8.00 20.00
AFFLB Larry Bird 75.00 150.00
AFFLH Larry Hughes 8.00 20.00
AFFLJ LeBron James 150.00 300.00
AFFMD Marquis Daniels 6.00 15.00
AFFMJ Michael Jordan 300.00 600.00
AFFMW Marvin Williams 6.00 15.00
AFFNR Nate Robinson 6.00 15.00
AFFPP Paul Pierce 10.00 25.00
AFFPS Peja Stojakovic 8.00 20.00
AFFRA Ron Artest 8.00 20.00
AFFRF Raymond Felton 6.00 15.00
AFFRP Robert Parish 6.00 15.00
AFFSK Steve Kerr 20.00 50.00
AFFSL Shaun Livingston 6.00 15.00
AFFSN Steve Nash 30.00 60.00
AFFST Sebastian Telfair 6.00 15.00
AFFTC Tyson Chandler 6.00 15.00
AFFTM Tracy McGrady 30.00 60.00
AFFVC Vince Carter 25.00 50.00
AFFWE Martell Webster 6.00 15.00
AFFYK Yaroslav Korolev 6.00 15.00
AFFYM Yao Ming 15.00 40.00

2006-07 SPx SPxcitement

MPLETE SET 20.00 50.00
APPROXIMATE ODDS ONE PER PACK
UNPRICED AUTO PRINT RUN 10 SETS

SPX1 Andrea Bargnani .50 1.25
SPX2 LaMarcus Aldridge 1.25 3.00
SPX3 Adam Morrison .50 1.25
SPX4 Tyrus Thomas .40 1.00
SPX5 Shelden Williams .40 1.00
SPX6 Brandon Roy .50 1.25
SPX7 Rudy Gay .60 1.50
SPX8 Saer Sene .30 .75
SPX9 Hilton Armstrong .30 .75
SPX10 Thabo Sefolosha .50 1.25
SPX11 Ronnie Brewer .50 1.25
SPX12 Cedric Simmons .30 .75
SPX13 Rodney Carney .30 .75
SPX14 Quincy Douby .30 .75
SPX15 Rajon Rondo .75 2.00
SPX16 Renaldo Balkman .40 1.00
SPX17 Steve Novak .40 1.00
SPX18 Maurice Ager .30 .75
SPX19 Mardy Collins .30 .75
SPX20 James White .30 .75
SPX21 Craig Smith .40 1.00
SPX22 Bobby Jones .30 .75
SPX23 Dee Brown .30 .75
SPX24 Will Blalock .30 .75
SPX25 Daniel Gibson .40 1.00
SPX26 Michael Jordan 4.00 10.00
SPX27 Larry Bird 1.25 3.00
SPX28 Bill Russell 1.00 2.50
SPX29 Julius Erving .75 2.00
SPX30 Moses Malone .50 1.25
SPX31 Robert Parish .50 1.25
SPX32 Magic Johnson 1.25 3.00
SPX33 Walt Frazier .50 1.25
SPX34 Dennis Rodman 1.00 2.50
SPX35 Kareem Abdul-Jabbar .75 2.00
SPX36 Hakeem Olajuwon .60 1.50
SPX37 Zach Randolph .40 1.00
SPX38 Clyde Drexler .60 1.50
SPX39 David Robinson .75 2.00
SPX40 John Stockton .75 2.00
SPX41 Marvin Williams .40 1.00
SPX42 Joe Johnson .40 1.00
SPX43 Paul Pierce .50 1.25
SPX44 Emeka Okafor .40 1.00
SPX45 Raymond Felton .40 1.00
SPX46 Ben Gordon .40 1.00
SPX47 Kirk Hinrich .40 1.00
SPX48 LeBron James 2.00 5.00
SPX49 Zydrunas Ilgauskas .40 1.00
SPX50 Dirk Nowitzki .75 2.00
SPX51 Jason Terry .40 1.00
SPX52 Carmelo Anthony .60 1.50
SPX53 Kenyon Martin .40 1.00
SPX54 Chauncey Billups .50 1.25
SPX55 Richard Hamilton .40 1.00
SPX56 Ben Wallace .40 1.00
SPX57 Baron Davis .40 1.00
SPX58 Jason Richardson .50 1.25
SPX59 Tracy McGrady .60 1.50
SPX60 Yao Ming .60 1.50
SPX61 Jermaine O'Neal .40 1.00
SPX62 Peja Stojakovic .50 1.25
SPX63 Elton Brand .50 1.25
SPX64 Sam Cassell .40 1.00
SPX65 Kobe Bryant 2.00 5.00
SPX66 Pau Gasol .50 1.25
SPX67 Shaquille O'Neal 1.00 2.50
SPX68 Dwyane Wade .75 2.00
SPX69 Gary Payton .50 1.25
SPX70 Kevin Garnett .75 2.00
SPX71 Vince Carter .60 1.50
SPX72 Jason Kidd .75 2.00
SPX73 Chris Paul .60 1.50
SPX74 Stephon Marbury .40 1.00
SPX75 Grant Hill .60 1.50
SPX76 Dwight Howard .40 1.00
SPX77 Allen Iverson .60 1.50
SPX78 Chris Webber .50 1.25
SPX79 Shawn Marion .40 1.00
SPX80 Amare Stoudemire .40 1.00
SPX81 Steve Nash .60 1.50
SPX82 Ron Artest .50 1.25
SPX83 Tim Duncan .75 2.00
SPX84 Manu Ginobili .50 1.25
SPX85 Tony Parker .50 1.25
SPX86 Ray Allen .50 1.25
SPX87 Chris Bosh .50 1.25
SPX88 Charlie Villanueva .30 .75
SPX89 Andrei Kirilenko .40 1.00
SPX90 Gilbert Arenas .40 1.00
SPX91 Antawn Jamison .40 1.00
SPX92 Carlos Boozer .40 1.00
SPX93 Deron Williams .40 1.00
SPX94 Rashard Lewis .50 1.25
SPX95 Michael Finley .50 1.25
SPX96 Josh Howard .40 1.00
SPX97 Boris Diaw .40 1.00
SPX98 Andre Iguodala .40 1.00
SPX99 Mike Bibby .50 1.25

2006-07 SPx Winning Combos

APPROXIMATE ODDS 1:20

WCAP R.Allen/J.Petro 5.00 12.00
WCBB K.Brown/A.Bynum 3.00 8.00
WCBG M.Bibby/F.Garcia 3.00 8.00
WCBM K.Bryant/T.McGrady 8.00 20.00
WCBV C.Bosh/C.Villanueva 3.00 8.00
WCCD T.Chandler/L.Deng 3.00 8.00
WCCF E.Curry/C.Frye 3.00 8.00
WCCR J.Crawford/N.Robinson 3.00 8.00
WCDG L.Deng/B.Gordon 3.00 8.00
WCDH M.Daniels/D.Harris 3.00 8.00
WCDI S.Dalembert/A.Iguodala 3.00 8.00
WCDP T.Duncan/T.Parker 5.00 12.00
WCDR B.Davis/J.Richardson 3.00 8.00
WCGH K.Garnett/D.Howard 8.00 20.00
WCGJ D.Granger/S.Jasikevicius 3.00 8.00
WCGW D.George/L.Walton 3.00 8.00
WCHB R.Hamilton/C.Billups 3.00 8.00
WCHG L.Hughes/D.Gooden 3.00 8.00
WCHN G.Hill/J.Nelson 3.00 8.00
WCHS K.Hinrich/W.Simien 3.00 8.00
WCIK Z.Ilgauskas/N.Krstic 3.00 8.00
WCJA A.Jefferson/T.Allen 3.00 8.00
WCJB A.Jamison/C.Butler 3.00 8.00
WCJG E.Jones/P.Gasol 3.00 8.00
WCJJ M.Jordan/L.James 40.00 100.00
WCJW R.Jefferson/A.Wright 3.00 8.00
WCKC J.Kidd/V.Carter 4.00 10.00
WCKW A.Kirilenko/D.Williams 3.00 8.00
WCMB C.Maggette/E.Brand 3.00 8.00
WCMI J.Magloire/E.Ilyasova 3.00 8.00
WCMO Y.Ming/S.O'Neal 6.00 15.00
WCMR S.Marbury/Q.Richardson 3.00 8.00
WCNS S.Nash/A.Stoudemire 5.00 12.00
WCOM E.Okafor/S.May 3.00 8.00
WCPD D.West/P.Stojakovic 3.00 8.00
WCPM P.Pierce/S.Marion 3.00 8.00
WCRB M.Redd/A.Bogut 3.00 8.00
WCRD Z.Randolph/J.Dixon 3.00 8.00
WCSA A.Stoudemire/C.Anthony 5.00 12.00
WCSH S.Swift/L.Head 3.00 8.00
WCSP J.Smith/C.Paul 4.00 10.00
WCSW W.Szczerbiak/D.West 3.00 8.00
WCTN J.Terry/D.Nowitzki 3.00 8.00
WCTO J.Tinsley/J.O'Neal 3.00 8.00
WCTW S.Telfair/M.Webster 3.00 8.00
WCWJ D.Jones/H.Warrick 3.00 8.00
WCWK C.Webber/K.Korver 3.00 8.00
WCWM R.McCants/B.Wright 3.00 8.00
WCWS A.Walker/W.Simien 3.00 8.00
WCWW R.Wallace/B.Wallace 3.00 8.00

2006-07 SPx Winning Materials

RANDOM INSERTS IN PACKS

WMAI Andre Iguodala 2.50 6.00
WMAJ Al Jefferson 2.50 6.00
WMBD Baron Davis 2.50 6.00
WMBO Chris Bosh 3.00 8.00
WMBW Ben Wallace 2.50 6.00
WMCA Carmelo Anthony 4.00 10.00
WMCB Chauncey Billups 3.00 8.00
WMCF Channing Frye 2.50 6.00
WMCM Corey Maggette 2.50 6.00
WMCP Chris Paul 4.00 10.00
WMCV Charlie Villanueva 2.00 5.00
WMDG Drew Gooden 2.50 6.00
WMDH Dwight Howard 2.50 6.00
WMDJ Dahntay Jones 2.00 5.00
WMDN Dirk Nowitzki 5.00 12.00
WMDW Delonte West 2.00 5.00
WMEB Elton Brand 3.00 8.00
WMEO Emeka Okafor 2.50 6.00
WMGA Gilbert Arenas 2.50 6.00
WMGR Danny Granger 2.50 6.00
WMID Ike Diogu 2.00 5.00
WMJH Josh Howard 2.50 6.00
WMJK Jason Kidd 5.00 12.00
WMJO Jermaine O'Neal 2.50 6.00
WMKB Kobe Bryant 10.00 25.00
WMKG Kevin Garnett 5.00 12.00
WMLD Luol Deng 2.50 6.00
WMLH Luther Head 2.50 6.00
WMLJ LeBron James 10.00 25.00
WMMA Shawn Marion 2.50 6.00
WMMJ Michael Jordan 30.00 75.00
WMMR Michael Redd 2.50 6.00
WMNK Nenad Krstic 2.00 5.00
WMPG Pau Gasol 3.00 8.00
WMPP Paul Pierce 3.00 8.00
WMRA Ray Allen 3.00 8.00
WMRH Richard Hamilton 2.50 6.00
WMRW Rasheed Wallace 3.00 8.00
WMSD Samuel Dalembert 2.00 5.00
WMSL Shaun Livingston 2.00 5.00
WMSM Stephon Marbury 2.50 6.00
WMSN Steve Nash 4.00 10.00
WMSO Shaquille O'Neal 6.00 15.00
WMTD Tim Duncan 5.00 12.00
WMTM Tracy McGrady 4.00 10.00
WMTP Tony Parker 3.00 8.00
WMVC Vince Carter 4.00 10.00
WMWS Wally Szczerbiak 2.50 6.00
WMYM Yao Ming 4.00 10.00
WMZI Zydrunas Ilgauskas 2.50 6.00

2007-08 SPx

This 140-card set was released in December, 2007. The set was issued into the hobby in three-card packs which came 10 packs to a box and 10 boxes to a case. Cards numbered 1-90 feature veterans while cards 91-140 feature 2007-08 NBA rookies. In that grouping, cards numbered 101-140 have both a signature and a player-worn jersey swatch. The serial numbering for the rookies was arranged this way: Cards numbered 91-110 were issued to a stated print run of 299 serial numbered sets while cards 111-140 were issued to a stated print run of 825 serial numbered sets. SPx is packaged in 10-pack boxes where packs contain three cards and carried an initial SRP of $20.
COMP.SET w/o SP's (90) 15.00 40.00
101-110 PRINT RUN 299 SER.#'d SETS
111-140 PRINT RUN 825 SER.#'d SETS
UNPRICED SPECTRUM PRINT RUN 10 SETS

1 Chauncey Billups .50 1.25
2 Tayshaun Prince .40 1.00
3 Richard Hamilton .40 1.00
4 Rasheed Wallace .50 1.25
5 Zydrunas Ilgauskas .40 1.00
6 Larry Hughes .40 1.00
7 LeBron James 2.00 5.00
8 T.J. Ford .30 .75
9 Andrea Bargnani .50 1.25

10 Chris Bosh .50 1.25
11 Shaquille O'Neal 1.00 2.50
12 Dwyane Wade .75 2.00
13 Udonis Haslem .30 .75
14 Ben Wallace .40 1.00
15 Ben Gordon .40 1.00
16 Luol Deng .40 1.00
17 Kirk Hinrich .40 1.00
18 Vince Carter .60 1.50
19 Richard Jefferson .40 1.00
20 Jason Kidd .50 1.25
21 Gilbert Arenas .40 1.00
22 Caron Butler .40 1.00
23 Antawn Jamison .40 1.00
24 Dwight Howard .40 1.00
25 Jameer Nelson .30 .75
26 Jermaine O'Neal .40 1.00
27 Danny Granger .40 1.00
28 Mike Dunleavy .40 1.00
29 Andre Iguodala .40 1.00
30 Kyle Korver .40 1.00
31 Gerald Wallace .40 1.00
32 Emeka Okafor .40 1.00
33 Jason Richardson .50 1.25
34 Eddy Curry .30 .75
35 Stephon Marbury .40 1.00
36 Quentin Richardson .40 1.00
37 David Lee .30 .75
38 Marvin Williams .40 1.00
39 Josh Smith .40 1.00
40 Joe Johnson .40 1.00
41 Michael Redd .40 1.00
42 Andrew Bogut .40 1.00
43 Paul Pierce .50 1.25
44 Al Jefferson .40 1.00
45 Ray Allen .50 1.25
46 Dirk Nowitzki .60 1.50
47 Jerry Stackhouse .40 1.00
48 Jason Terry .40 1.00
49 Josh Howard .40 1.00
50 Amare Stoudemire .40 1.00
51 Steve Nash .60 1.50
52 Leandro Barbosa .40 1.00
53 Shawn Marion .40 1.00
54 Tony Parker .50 1.25
55 Tim Duncan .75 2.00
56 Manu Ginobili .50 1.25
57 Michael Finley .50 1.25
58 Andrei Kirilenko .40 1.00
59 Carlos Boozer .40 1.00
60 Deron Williams .40 1.00
61 Mehmet Okur .30 .75
62 Tracy McGrady .50 1.25
63 Yao Ming .60 1.50
64 Carmelo Anthony .60 1.50
65 Allen Iverson .60 1.50
66 Marcus Camby .30 .75
67 Kobe Bryant 2.00 5.00
68 Lamar Odom .40 1.00
69 Baron Davis .40 1.00
70 Al Harrington .40 1.00
71 Stephen Jackson .40 1.00
72 Elton Brand .50 1.25
73 Corey Maggette .40 1.00
74 Shaun Livingston .30 .75
75 David West .40 1.00
76 Chris Paul .60 1.50
77 Tyson Chandler .40 1.00
78 Kevin Garnett .75 2.00
79 Ricky Davis .40 1.00
80 Randy Foye .50 1.25
81 Kevin Martin .40 1.00
82 Ron Artest .50 1.25
83 Mike Bibby .50 1.25
84 Steve Francis .40 1.00
85 Brandon Roy .50 1.25
86 Jarrett Jack .40 1.00
87 Delonte West .30 .75
88 Rashard Lewis .40 1.00
89 Pau Gasol .50 1.25
90 Mike Miller .40 1.00
91 Greg Oden RC 8.00 20.00
92 Thaddeus Young RC 3.00 8.00
93 Brandan Wright RC 3.00 8.00
94 Yi Jianlian RC 4.00 10.00
95 Nick Young RC 4.00 10.00
96 Chris Richard RC 2.00 5.00
97 Marco Belinelli RC 3.00 8.00
98 Juan Carlos Navarro RC 2.50 6.00
99 Sammy Mejia RC 2.00 5.00
100 Kyrylo Fesenko RC 2.00 5.00
101 Kevin Durant JSY AU RC 150.00 300.00
102 Al Horford JSY AU RC 8.00 20.00
103 Mike Conley Jr. JSY AU RC 12.00 30.00
104 Jeff Green JSY AU RC 6.00 15.00
105 Corey Brewer JSY AU RC 6.00 15.00
106 Joakim Noah JSY AU RC 6.00 15.00
107 Spencer Hawes JSY AU RC 5.00 12.00
108 Acie Law JSY AU RC 4.00 10.00
109 Julian Wright JSY AU RC 4.00 10.00
110 Al Thornton JSY AU RC 5.00 12.00
111 Javaris Crittenton JSY AU RC 3.00 8.00
112 Daequan Cook JSY AU RC 4.00 10.00
113 Jared Dudley JSY AU RC 4.00 10.00
114 Wilson Chandler JSY AU RC 4.00 10.00
115 Morris Almond JSY AU RC 3.00 8.00
116 Arron Afflalo JSY AU RC 5.00 12.00
117 Alando Tucker JSY AU RC 3.00 8.00
118 Carl Landry JSY AU RC 3.00 8.00
119 Gabe Pruitt JSY AU RC 3.00 8.00
120 Marcus Williams JSY AU RC 3.00 8.00
121 Nick Fazekas JSY AU RC 3.00 8.00
122 Jermareo Davidson JSY AU RC 3.00 8.00
123 Josh McRoberts JSY AU RC 4.00 10.00
124 Glen Davis JSY AU RC 4.00 10.00
125 Adam Haluska JSY AU RC 3.00 8.00
126 Reyshawn Terry JSY AU RC 3.00 8.00
127 Jared Jordan JSY AU RC 3.00 8.00
128 Stephane Lasme JSY AU RC 3.00 8.00
129 Aaron Gray JSY AU RC 3.00 8.00
130 Taurean Green JSY AU RC 3.00 8.00
131 Demetris Nichols JSY AU RC 3.00 8.00
132 Herbert Hill JSY AU RC 3.00 8.00
133 Aaron Brooks JSY AU RC 4.00 10.00
134 D.J. Strawberry JSY AU RC 3.00 8.00
135 Dominic McGuire JSY AU RC 3.00 8.00
136 Jason Smith JSY AU RC 4.00 10.00
137 Sean Williams JSY AU RC 3.00 8.00
138 Derrick Byars JSY AU RC 3.00 8.00
139 Ramon Sessions JSY AU RC 5.00 12.00
140 Rodney Stuckey JSY AU RC 4.00 10.00

2007-08 SPx Radiance

*1-90 RADIANCE: 3X TO 8X BASE HI
*91-10 RC RAD: 1X TO 2.5X BASE HI
*101-110 RC RAD: 1.25X TO 3X BASE HI
*111-140 RC RAD: 1.5X TO 4X BASE HI
RADIANCE PRINT RUN 25 SER.#'d SETS
101 Kevin Durant JSY AU 800.00 1200.00

2007-08 SPx Duel Scripts

PRINT RUN 10 TO 25 SER.#'d SETS
SOME UNPRICED DUE TO SCARCITY
BB B.Bowen/Barbosa/25 10.00 25.00
BJ L.James/K.Bryant/10 350.00 500.00
CJ C.Brewer/J.Noah/25 12.00 30.00
EB L.Bird/J.Erving/25 100.00 200.00
GD C.Drexler/G.Gervin/25 40.00 80.00
HG R.Hamilton/Gibson/25 10.00 25.00
HH R.Hamilton/Hughes/25 20.00 40.00
IJ A.Jefferson/Iguodala/25 20.00 40.00
JA L.James/C.Anthony/25 225.00 350.00
JE M.Jordan/J.Erving/25 400.00 650.00
LM L.Bird/M.Johnson/25 150.00 300.00
NA N.Nixon/Archibald/25 15.00 30.00
NP S.Nash/T.Parker/25 60.00 120.00
SJ M.Johnson/Stockton/25 100.00 200.00
WR B.Russell/J.West/25 125.00 250.00

2007-08 SPx Endorsements

NDOM INSERTS IN PACKS
AA Arron Afflalo 2.50 6.00
AH Al Horford 5.00 12.00
AI Andre Iguodala 3.00 8.00
AL Acie Law 2.50 6.00
BR Bill Russell 75.00 150.00
BW Bill Walton 8.00 20.00
CA Carmelo Anthony 15.00 30.00
CB Corey Brewer 4.00 10.00
CD Clyde Drexler 15.00 40.00
DH Dwight Howard 10.00 25.00
GG George Gervin 8.00 20.00
HO Hakeem Olajuwon 15.00 40.00
JG Jeff Green 4.00 10.00
JN Joakim Noah 4.00 10.00
JO Jermaine O'Neal 4.00 10.00
KB Kobe Bryant 100.00 200.00
KD Kevin Durant 100.00 200.00
LB Larry Bird 50.00 120.00
LJ LeBron James 250.00 500.00
MC Mike Conley Jr. 5.00 12.00
MI Michael Jordan 500.00 1000.00
RJ Richard Jefferson 3.00 8.00
SH Spencer Hawes 3.00 8.00
TM Tracy McGrady 10.00 25.00
TP Tony Parker 8.00 20.00
VC Vince Carter 15.00 40.00
WF Walt Frazier 10.00 25.00
YM Yao Ming 20.00 40.00

2007-08 SPx Flashback Fabrics

RANDOM INSERTS IN PACKS
*PARALLEL: 1X TO 2.5X BASE HI
PARALLEL PRINT RUN 25 SER.#'d SETS
AW Antoine Walker 2.00 5.00
BB Bruce Bowen 2.00 5.00
BD Boris Diaw 2.00 5.00
BU Caron Butler 2.00 5.00
CB Carlos Boozer 2.00 5.00
CV Charlie Villanueva 1.50 4.00
CW Chris Webber 2.50 6.00
DG Danny Granger 2.00 5.00
DN Dirk Nowitzki 3.00 8.00
DW Deron Williams 2.00 5.00
EO Emeka Okafor 2.00 5.00
GA Gilbert Arenas 2.00 5.00
JK Jason Kidd 2.50 6.00
JR Jason Richardson 2.50 6.00
JT Jason Terry 2.00 5.00
JW Jason Williams 2.00 5.00
KA Jason Kapono 2.00 5.00
KG Kevin Garnett 4.00 10.00
KM Kenyon Martin 2.00 5.00
LJ LeBron James 12.00 30.00
LO Lamar Odom 2.00 5.00
MA Stephon Marbury 2.00 5.00
MB Mike Bibby 2.50 6.00
MC Marcus Camby 2.00 5.00
MF Michael Finley 2.50 6.00
MO Alonzo Mourning 6.00 15.00
N Nene 2.00 5.00
PG Pau Gasol 2.50 6.00
PP Paul Pierce 2.50 6.00
PS Peja Stojakovic 2.50 6.00
RA Ray Allen 2.50 6.00
RL Rashard Lewis 2.00 5.00
RW Rasheed Wallace 2.50 6.00
SC Sam Cassell 2.00 5.00
SF Steve Francis 2.00 5.00
SM Shawn Marion 2.00 5.00
SO Shaquille O'Neal 5.00 12.00
TC Tyson Chandler 2.00 5.00
TD Tim Duncan 4.00 10.00
UH Udonis Haslem 1.50 4.00
ZR Zach Randolph 2.00 5.00

2007-08 SPx Flashback Fabrics Autographs

STATED PRINT RUN 10 TO 25 SER.#'d SETS
SOME UNPRICED DUE TO SCARCITY
UNPRICED PARALLEL PRINT RUN ONE TO 10 SETS
AD Adrian Dantley/25 8.00 20.00
AH Al Harrington/25 8.00 20.00
AI Andre Iguodala/25 8.00 20.00
AJ Al Jefferson/25 8.00 20.00
BD Baron Davis/25 12.00 30.00
BG Ben Gordon/25 12.00 30.00
BO Chris Bosh/25 15.00 40.00
BR Bill Russell/25 75.00 150.00
CD Clyde Drexler/25 25.00 50.00
CP Chris Paul/25 40.00 80.00
DH Dwight Howard/25 40.00 80.00
GG George Gervin/25 12.00 30.00
HO Hakeem Olajuwon/25 25.00 60.00
JA Antawn Jamison/25 8.00 20.00
JE Julius Erving/25 40.00 100.00
JO Jermaine O'Neal/25 8.00 20.00
JS John Stockton/25 50.00 100.00
LB Larry Bird/25 75.00 150.00
LJ LeBron James/25 125.00 250.00
MI Michael Jordan/25 350.00 650.00
MJ Magic Johnson/25 40.00 100.00
MR Michael Ray Richardson/25 8.00 20.00
NA Nate Archibald/25 15.00 30.00
PA Tony Parker/25 15.00 30.00
QR Quentin Richardson/25 8.00 20.00
RH Richard Hamilton/25 15.00 30.00
RJ Richard Jefferson/25 8.00 20.00
RO Brandon Roy/25 15.00 30.00
RT Reggie Theus/25 15.00 30.00
SK Steve Kerr/25 15.00 30.00
SN Steve Nash/25 40.00 100.00
TC Tyson Chandler/25 8.00 20.00
TM Tracy McGrady/25 20.00 50.00
TP Tayshaun Prince/25 8.00 20.00
VC Vince Carter/25 15.00 40.00
WF Walt Frazier/25 15.00 40.00
YM Yao Ming/25 25.00 60.00

2007-08 SPx Freshman Orientation

APPROXIMATE ODDS TWO PER BOX
*PATCHES: 1X TO 2.5X BASE HI
PATCH PRINT RUN 25 SER.#'d SETS
AA Arron Afflalo 2.50 6.00
AB Aaron Brooks 2.00 5.00
AH Al Horford 3.00 8.00
AL Acie Law 1.50 4.00
AT Al Thornton 2.00 5.00
BW Brandan Wright 2.50 6.00
CB Corey Brewer 2.50 6.00
CL Carl Landry 1.50 4.00
DC Daequan Cook 2.00 5.00
GD Glen Davis 2.00 5.00
GP Gabe Pruitt 1.50 4.00
JC Javaris Crittenton 1.50 4.00
JD Jared Dudley 2.00 5.00
JG Jeff Green 2.50 6.00
JM Josh McRoberts 2.00 5.00
JN Joakim Noah 2.50 6.00
JS Jason Smith 2.00 5.00
JW Julian Wright 1.50 4.00
KD Kevin Durant 10.00 25.00
MA Morris Almond 1.50 4.00
MC Mike Conley Jr. 3.00 8.00
MW Marcus Williams 1.50 4.00
NF Nick Fazekas 1.50 4.00
NY Nick Young 3.00 8.00
RS Rodney Stuckey 2.00 5.00
SH Spencer Hawes 2.00 5.00
SW Sean Williams 1.50 4.00
TU Alando Tucker 1.50 4.00
TY Thaddeus Young 2.50 6.00
WC Wilson Chandler 2.00 5.00

2007-08 SPx Freshman Orientation Autographs

PRINT RUN 25 TO 50 SER.#'d SETS
UNPRICED LOGO PRINT RUN ONE SET
AA Arron Afflalo/50 6.00 15.00
AB Aaron Brooks/25 5.00 12.00
AH Al Horford/25 8.00 20.00
AL Acie Law/25 4.00 10.00
AT Al Thornton/25 5.00 12.00
CB Corey Brewer/25 6.00 15.00
CL Carl Landry/50 4.00 10.00
GP Gabe Pruitt/50 4.00 10.00
JC Javaris Crittenton/25 4.00 10.00
JD Jared Dudley/25 5.00 12.00
JG Jeff Green/25 6.00 15.00
JM Josh McRoberts/50 5.00 12.00
JN Joakim Noah/25 25.00 60.00
KD Kevin Durant/25 200.00 400.00
MA Morris Almond/50 4.00 10.00
MC Mike Conley Jr./25 8.00 20.00
NF Nick Fazekas/50 4.00 10.00
NY Nick Young/25 8.00 20.00
RS Rodney Stuckey/25 5.00 12.00
SW Sean Williams/25 4.00 10.00
TU Alando Tucker/25 4.00 10.00
WC Wilson Chandler/50 5.00 12.00

2007-08 SPx Freshman Orientation Tandems

RANDOM INSERTS IN PACKS
*PATCHES: .75X TO 2X BASE HI
PATCH PRINT RUN 15 SER.#'d SETS
UNPRICED AUTO PRINT RUN 10 SER.#'d SETS
AA A.Brooks/A.Afflalo 4.00 10.00
AB M.Almond/A.Brooks 3.00 8.00
AS R.Stuckey/A.Afflalo 4.00 10.00
CW S.Williams/W.Chandler 3.00 8.00
DD J.Dudley/J.Davidson 3.00 8.00
DG K.Durant/J.Green 8.00 20.00
DH K.Durant/A.Horford 8.00 20.00
DW S.Williams/J.Dudley 3.00 8.00
HB A.Horford/C.Brewer 5.00 12.00
HS S.Hawes/J.Smith 3.00 8.00
LC M.Conley/A.Law 3.00 8.00
NB C.Brewer/J.Noah 5.00 12.00
PD G.Davis/G.Pruitt 4.00 10.00
TC A.Thornton/J.Crittenton 3.00 8.00
TL A.Tucker/C.Landry 3.00 8.00
WW J.Wright/B.Wright 3.00 8.00
YC T.Young/J.Crittenton 3.00 8.00
YP N.Young/G.Pruitt 3.00 8.00
YS T.Young/J.Smith 3.00 8.00

2007-08 SPx Freshman Orientation Triples

RANDOM INSERTS IN PACKS
UNPRICED PATCH PRINT RUN 5 SETS
UNPRICED AUTO PRINT RUN 5 SER.#'d SETS
ACC Cook/Crittenton/Almond 3.00 8.00
DGC Durant/Green/Conley 10.00 25.00
DLC Landry/Chandler/Davis 3.00 8.00
NHB Horford/Brewer/Noah 6.00 15.00
SLC Conley/Law/Stuckey 4.00 10.00
STW Williams/Smith/Tucker 3.00 8.00
TYD Young/Thornton/Dudley 3.00 8.00
WGW Green/Wright/Wright 4.00 10.00
YAB Young/Brooks/Afflalo 4.00 10.00

2007-08 SPx Super Scripts

APPROXIMATELY ONE PER BOX
AB Andrea Bargnani 4.00 10.00
AH Al Horford 5.00 12.00
AI Andre Iguodala 4.00 10.00
AJ Antawn Jamison 4.00 10.00
AL Acie Law 2.50 6.00
AT Al Thornton 3.00 8.00
BD Boris Diaw 4.00 10.00
BO Chris Bosh 10.00 25.00
BR Brandon Roy 6.00 15.00
CA Carmelo Anthony 15.00 40.00
CP Chris Paul 20.00 50.00
DA Baron Davis 6.00 15.00
DG Daniel Gibson 4.00 10.00
DH Dwight Howard 15.00 40.00
DJ D.J. Strawberry 2.50 6.00
EO Emeka Okafor 4.00 10.00
JE Al Jefferson 4.00 10.00
JG Jeff Green 4.00 10.00
JJ Jarrett Jack 4.00 10.00
JN Joakim Noah 10.00 25.00
KB Kobe Bryant 125.00 250.00
KD Kevin Durant 100.00 250.00
KK Kyle Korver 4.00 10.00
LB Leandro Barbosa 4.00 10.00
LH Larry Hughes 4.00 10.00
LJ LeBron James 150.00 300.00
MC Mike Conley Jr. 5.00 12.00
PR Tayshaun Prince 4.00 10.00
QR Quentin Richardson 4.00 10.00
RF Randy Foye 4.00 10.00
RH Richard Hamilton 4.00 10.00
RJ Richard Jefferson 4.00 10.00
RM Rashad McCants 4.00 10.00
SH Spencer Hawes 3.00 8.00
SM Sean May 4.00 10.00
TC Tyson Chandler 4.00 10.00
TF T.J. Ford 4.00 10.00
TP Tony Parker 8.00 20.00
VC Vince Carter 5.00 12.00

2007-08 SPx Winning Materials Jersey Numbers

APPROXIMATELY TWO PER BOX
UNPRICED PATCH PRINT RUN 15 SETS
*STAT JSY: SAME VALUE
APPROXIMATELY TWO PER BOX
UNPRICED STAT PATCH PRINT RUN 10 SETS
AB Andrea Bargnani 2.50 6.00
AH Al Harrington 2.00 5.00
AJ Al Jefferson 2.00 5.00
AK Andrei Kirilenko 2.00 5.00
AM Alonzo Mourning 5.00 12.00
AR Ron Artest 2.50 6.00
AS Amare Stoudemire 2.00 5.00
AW Antoine Walker 2.00 5.00
BB Bruce Bowen 2.00 5.00
BD Baron Davis 2.00 5.00
BG Ben Gordon 2.00 5.00
BI Chauncey Billups 2.50 6.00
BM Brad Miller 2.00 5.00
BO Andrew Bogut 2.00 5.00
BR Brandon Roy 2.50 6.00
BU Caron Butler 2.00 5.00
BY Andrew Bynum 1.50 4.00
CA Carmelo Anthony 3.00 8.00
CB Carlos Boozer 2.00 5.00
CH Chris Bosh 2.50 6.00
CM Corey Maggette 2.00 5.00
CP Chris Paul 3.00 8.00
CV Charlie Villanueva 1.50 4.00
CW Chris Webber 2.50 6.00
DE Deron Williams 2.00 5.00
DG Danny Granger 2.00 5.00
DH Dwight Howard 2.00 5.00
DI Boris Diaw 2.00 5.00
DW Delonte West 1.50 4.00
EC Eddy Curry 2.00 5.00
GG Gerald Green 2.00 5.00
GH Grant Hill 3.00 8.00
GO Drew Gooden 2.00 5.00
GP Gary Payton 2.50 6.00
HA Devin Harris 1.50 4.00
IG Andre Iguodala 2.00 5.00
JA Antawn Jamison 2.00 5.00
JH Josh Howard 2.00 5.00
JJ Joe Johnson 2.00 5.00
JK Jarrett Jack 2.00 5.00
JO Jermaine O'Neal 2.00 5.00
JR Jason Richardson 2.50 6.00
JS J.R. Smith 2.00 5.00
JT Jason Terry 2.00 5.00
JW Jason Williams 2.00 5.00
KB Kobe Bryant 8.00 20.00
KG Kevin Garnett 4.00 10.00
KH Kirk Hinrich 2.00 5.00
KM Kenyon Martin 2.00 5.00
LD Luol Deng 2.00 5.00
LH Larry Hughes 2.00 5.00
LJ LeBron James 10.00 25.00
LO Lamar Odom 2.00 5.00
MA Sean May 2.00 5.00
MB Mike Bibby 2.50 6.00
MC Antonio McDyess 2.00 5.00
MF Michael Finley 2.50 6.00
MG Manu Ginobili 2.50 6.00
MI Andre Miller 2.00 5.00
MR Michael Redd 2.00 5.00
MW Marvin Williams 2.00 5.00
NH Nene 2.00 5.00
PG Pau Gasol 2.50 6.00
PS Peja Stojakovic 2.50 6.00
QR Quentin Richardson 2.00 5.00
RA Ray Allen 2.50 6.00
RF Raymond Felton 2.50 6.00
RG Rudy Gay 2.50 6.00
RH Richard Hamilton 2.00 5.00
RJ Richard Jefferson 2.00 5.00
RL Rashard Lewis 2.00 5.00
RW Rasheed Wallace 2.50 6.00
SC Sam Cassell 2.00 5.00
SH Shawn Marion 2.00 5.00
SL Shaun Livingston 2.00 5.00
SM Josh Smith 2.00 5.00
SN Steve Nash 3.00 8.00
SO Shaquille O'Neal 5.00 12.00
ST Stephon Marbury 2.00 5.00
TD Tim Duncan 4.00 10.00
TJ T.J. Ford 1.50 4.00
TM Tracy McGrady 2.50 6.00
TP Tayshaun Prince 2.00 5.00
VC Vince Carter 3.00 8.00
WE David West 2.00 5.00
WI Chris Wilcox 2.00 5.00
WS Wally Szczerbiak 2.00 5.00
YM Yao Ming 3.00 8.00
ZI Zydrunas Ilgauskas 2.00 5.00
ZR Zach Randolph 2.00 5.00

2007-08 SPx Winning Materials Combos

RANDOM INSERTS IN PACKS
*PATCHES: 1X TO 2.5X BASE HI
PATCH PRINT RUN 50 SER.#'d SETS
AA A.Iverson/A.Mourning 6.00 15.00
BA R.Artest/M.Bibby 3.00 8.00
BF C.Bosh/T.Ford 4.00 10.00
BO C.Bosh/J.O'Neal 3.00 8.00
BP C.Billups/T.Prince 3.00 8.00
CL E.Curry/D.Lee 3.00 8.00
DH B.Davis/A.Harrington 3.00 8.00
DP T.Duncan/T.Parker 4.00 10.00
FM R.Felton/S.May 3.00 8.00
GF K.Garnett/R.Foye 4.00 10.00
GG P.Gasol/R.Gay 3.00 8.00
GH D.Gooden/K.Hinrich 3.00 8.00
GO J.O'Neal/D.Granger 3.00 8.00
HB R.Hamilton/C.Billups 4.00 10.00
HH D.Howard/G.Hill 5.00 12.00
HJ L.James/L.Hughes 6.00 15.00
JA G.Arenas/A.Jamison 3.00 8.00
JG A.Jefferson/G.Green 3.00 8.00
KB C.Boozer/A.Kirilenko 3.00 8.00
KC V.Carter/J.Kidd 4.00 10.00
KL K.Bryant/L.Odom 6.00 15.00
LW R.Lewis/C.Wilcox 3.00 8.00
MA C.Anthony/K.Martin 4.00 10.00
MB E.Brand/C.Maggette 3.00 8.00
MI A.Iguodala/A.Miller 3.00 8.00
MM Y.Ming/T.McGrady 5.00 12.00
MR S.Marbury/Z.Randolph 3.00 8.00
NH D.Nowitzki/J.Howard 4.00 10.00
NJ Nene/J.Smith 3.00 8.00
PA R.Allen/P.Pierce 5.00 12.00
RB A.Bogut/M.Redd 3.00 8.00
RO E.Okafor/J.Richardson 3.00 8.00
SD A.Stoudemire/B.Diaw 4.00 10.00
SW M.Williams/J.Smith 3.00 8.00
WG B.Gordon/B.Wallace 3.00 8.00
WM D.Williams/P.Millsap 4.00 10.00
WP J.Williams/G.Payton 4.00 10.00
WW C.Webber/R.Wallace 4.00 10.00

2007-08 SPx Winning Materials Combos Patches Autographs

PRINT RUN 8 TO 25 SER.#'d SETS
SOME UNPRICED DUE TO SCARCITY
BP C.Billups/T.Prince/15 25.00 60.00
GG P.Gasol/R.Gay/25 30.00 60.00
SD A.Stoudemire/B.Diaw/25 30.00 80.00
SW M.Williams/J.Smith/25 12.00 30.00
WM D.Williams/P.Millsap/25 30.00 60.00

2007-08 SPx Winning Materials Triples

RANDOM INSERTS IN PACKS
*PATCHES: .75X TO 2X BASE HI
PATCH PRINT RUN 25 SER.#'d SETS
UNPRICED AUTO PRINT RUN 5 SER.#'d SETS
AMN Anthony/Martin/Nene 6.00 15.00
BMJ Bryant/James/McGrady 12.00 30.00
CAW Camby/Wallace/Artest 4.00 10.00
HPM Hamilton/Prince/McDyess 5.00 12.00
JAB Arenas/Butler/Jamison 4.00 10.00
JSW Johnson/Williams/Smith 4.00 10.00
KCJ Carter/Kidd/Jefferson 5.00 12.00
MBL Brand/Maggette/Livingston 4.00 10.00
NIP Nash/Parker/Iverson 6.00 15.00
NMS Nash/Stoudemire/Marion 5.00 12.00
PAG Pierce/Jefferson/Green 4.00 10.00
PGB Parker/Ginobili/Bowen 5.00 12.00
PMO O'Neal/Mourning/Payton 8.00 20.00
RBV Bogut/Redd/Villanueva 4.00 10.00
RMF Okafor/May/Felton 4.00 10.00
TNH Nowitzki/Howard/Terry 5.00 12.00
WDG Wallace/Deng/Gordon 4.00 10.00
WHR Webber/Howard/Rose 4.00 10.00
ZGJ Ilgauskas/Hughes/Gooden 4.00 10.00

2008-09 SPx

This set was released on November 19, 2008. The base set consists of 178 cards. Cards 1-90 feature veterans, and cards 91-110 are rookies serial numbered of 99. Cards 111-130 are autographed jersey rookie cards serial numbered of 99, and cards 131-178 are autographed jersey rookie cards serial numbered of 699. Each of these has both home and away versions, which are valued the same.

COMP.SET w/o SP's (90) 30.00 60.00
131-178 RC PRINT RUN 599 SER.#'d SETS
UNPRICED SPECTRUM PRINT RUN ONE SET
1 Kevin Garnett 1.00 2.50
2 Ray Allen .60 1.50
3 Paul Pierce .60 1.50
4 Chauncey Billups .60 1.50
5 Rasheed Wallace .60 1.50
6 Richard Hamilton .50 1.25
7 Tayshaun Prince .50 1.25
8 Dwight Howard .50 1.25
9 Hedo Turkoglu .50 1.25
10 Rashard Lewis .50 1.25
11 Daniel Gibson .50 1.25
12 Ben Wallace .50 1.25
13 LeBron James 2.50 6.00
14 Antawn Jamison .50 1.25
15 Caron Butler .50 1.25
16 Gilbert Arenas .50 1.25
17 Chris Bosh .60 1.50
18 Jamario Moon .40 1.00
19 T.J. Ford .40 1.00
20 Andre Iguodala .50 1.25
21 Andre Miller .50 1.25
22 Thaddeus Young .50 1.25
23 Al Horford .60 1.50
24 Joe Johnson .50 1.25
25 Josh Smith .50 1.25
26 Danny Granger .50 1.25
27 Jermaine O'Neal .50 1.25
28 Devin Harris .40 1.00
29 Richard Jefferson .50 1.25
30 Vince Carter .75 2.00
31 Ben Gordon .50 1.25
32 Joakim Noah .50 1.25
33 Luol Deng .50 1.25
34 Emeka Okafor .50 1.25
35 Gerald Wallace .50 1.25
36 Jason Richardson .60 1.50
37 Andrew Bogut .50 1.25
38 Michael Redd .50 1.25
39 Yi Jianlian .60 1.50
40 Eddy Curry .40 1.00
41 Jamal Crawford .60 1.50
42 Stephon Marbury .50 1.25
43 Zach Randolph .50 1.25
44 Daequan Cook .40 1.00
45 Dwyane Wade 1.00 2.50
46 Shawn Marion .50 1.25
47 Jordan Farmar .40 1.00
48 Kobe Bryant 2.50 6.00
49 Pau Gasol .60 1.50
50 Lamar Odom .50 1.25
51 Chris Paul .75 2.00
52 David West .50 1.25
53 Peja Stojakovic .60 1.50
54 Manu Ginobili .60 1.50
55 Tim Duncan 1.00 2.50
56 Tony Parker .60 1.50
57 Carlos Boozer .50 1.25
58 Deron Williams .50 1.25
59 Mehmet Okur .40 1.00
60 Luis Scola .50 1.25
61 Tracy McGrady .60 1.50
62 Yao Ming .75 2.00
63 Amare Stoudemire .50 1.25
64 Shaquille O'Neal 1.25 3.00
65 Steve Nash .60 1.50
66 Jason Kidd .60 1.50
67 Dirk Nowitzki .75 2.00
68 Josh Howard .50 1.25
69 Allen Iverson .75 2.00
70 Carmelo Anthony .75 2.00
71 Kenyon Martin .50 1.25
72 Baron Davis .50 1.25
73 Monta Ellis .50 1.25
74 Stephen Jackson .50 1.25
75 Brandon Roy .60 1.50
76 Greg Oden .50 1.25
77 LaMarcus Aldridge .60 1.50
78 Francisco Garcia .40 1.00
79 Kevin Martin .50 1.25
80 Ron Artest .60 1.50
81 Al Thornton .50 1.25
82 Chris Kaman .50 1.25
83 Elton Brand .60 1.50
84 Al Jefferson .50 1.25
85 Corey Brewer .50 1.25
86 Mike Conley Jr. .50 1.25
87 Rudy Gay .60 1.50
88 Damien Wilkins .40 1.00
89 Jeff Green .50 1.25
90 Kevin Durant 1.50 4.00
91 Danilo Gallinari RC 5.00 12.00
92 Rudy Fernandez RC 2.50 6.00
93 Sean Singletary RC 2.00 5.00
94 Othello Hunter RC 3.00 8.00
95 Shan Foster RC 2.00 5.00
96 Mike Taylor RC 2.00 5.00
97 Joe Crawford RC 2.00 5.00
98 Thomas Gardner RC 3.00 8.00
99 Nicolas Batum RC 10.00 25.00
100 Malik Hairston RC 2.00 5.00
101 Danilo Gallinari RC 5.00 12.00
102 Rudy Fernandez RC 2.50 6.00
103 Sean Singletary RC 2.00 5.00
104 Othello Hunter RC 3.00 8.00
105 Shan Foster RC 2.00 5.00
106 Mike Taylor RC 2.00 5.00
107 Joe Crawford RC 2.00 5.00
108 Thomas Gardner RC 3.00 8.00
109 Nicolas Batum RC 10.00 25.00
110 Malik Hairston RC 2.00 5.00
111 Derrick Rose JSY AU RC 75.00 200.00
112 Michael Beasley JSY AU RC 10.00 25.00
113 O.J. Mayo JSY AU RC 25.00 60.00
114 R.Westbrook JSY AU RC 200.00 400.00
115 Kevin Love JSY AU RC 30.00 80.00
116 Eric Gordon JSY AU RC 12.00 30.00
117 D.J. Augustin JSY AU RC 6.00 15.00
118 Jerryd Bayless JSY AU RC 6.00 15.00
119 Brook Lopez JSY AU RC 10.00 25.00
120 Brandon Rush JSY AU RC 6.00 15.00
121 Derrick Rose JSY AU RC 75.00 200.00
122 Michael Beasley JSY AU RC 10.00 25.00
123 O.J. Mayo JSY AU RC 10.00 25.00
124 R. Westbrook JSY AU RC 200.00 400.00
125 Kevin Love JSY AU RC 30.00 80.00
126 Eric Gordon JSY AU RC 12.00 30.00
127 D.J. Augustin JSY AU RC 6.00 15.00
128 Jerryd Bayless JSY AU RC 6.00 15.00
129 Brook Lopez JSY AU RC 10.00 25.00
130 Brandon Rush JSY AU RC 6.00 15.00
131 Joe Alexander JSY AU RC 3.00 8.00
132 Jason Thompson JSY AU RC 3.00 8.00
133 Anthony Randolph JSY AU RC 3.00 8.00
134 Robin Lopez JSY AU RC 5.00 12.00
135 Marreese Speights JSY AU RC 4.00 10.00
136 Roy Hibbert JSY AU RC 5.00 12.00
137 Javale McGee JSY AU RC 6.00 15.00
138 J.J. Hickson JSY AU RC 4.00 10.00
139 Ryan Anderson JSY AU RC 4.00 10.00
140 Courtney Lee JSY AU RC 4.00 10.00
141 Kosta Koufos JSY AU RC 4.00 10.00
142 George Hill JSY AU RC 5.00 12.00
143 Darrell Arthur JSY AU RC 4.00 10.00
144 Donte Greene JSY AU RC 3.00 8.00
145 D.J. White JSY AU RC 4.00 10.00
146 J.R. Giddens JSY AU RC 3.00 8.00
147 Walter Sharpe JSY AU RC 3.00 8.00
148 Joey Dorsey JSY AU RC 3.00 8.00
149 Mario Chalmers JSY AU RC 5.00 12.00
150 DeAndre Jordan JSY AU RC 12.00 30.00
151 Kyle Weaver JSY AU RC 3.00 8.00
152 Sonny Weems JSY AU RC 3.00 8.00
153 C.Douglas-Roberts JSY AU RC 3.00 8.00
154 Patrick Ewing Jr. JSY AU RC 3.00 8.00
155 Joe Alexander JSY AU RC 3.00 8.00
156 Jason Thompson JSY AU RC 3.00 8.00
157 Anthony Randolph JSY AU RC 3.00 8.00
158 Robin Lopez JSY AU RC 5.00 12.00
159 Marreese Speights JSY AU RC 4.00 10.00
160 Roy Hibbert JSY AU RC 10.00 25.00
161 Javale McGee JSY AU RC 6.00 15.00
162 J.J. Hickson JSY AU RC 4.00 10.00
163 Ryan Anderson JSY AU RC 4.00 10.00
164 Courtney Lee JSY AU RC 4.00 10.00
165 Kosta Koufos JSY AU RC 4.00 10.00
166 George Hill JSY AU RC 5.00 12.00
167 Darrell Arthur JSY AU RC 4.00 10.00
168 Donte Greene JSY AU RC 3.00 8.00
169 D.J. White JSY AU RC 4.00 10.00
170 J.R. Giddens JSY AU RC 3.00 8.00
171 Walter Sharpe JSY AU RC 3.00 8.00
172 Joey Dorsey JSY AU RC 3.00 8.00
173 Mario Chalmers JSY AU RC 5.00 12.00
174 DeAndre Jordan JSY AU RC 12.00 30.00
175 Kyle Weaver JSY AU RC 3.00 8.00
176 Sonny Weems JSY AU RC 3.00 8.00
177 Chris Douglas-Roberts JSY AU RC 3.00 8.00
178 Patrick Ewing Jr. JSY AU RC 3.00 8.00

2008-09 SPx Radiance

*1-90 RADIANCE: 5X TO 12X BASE HI
*91-110 RAD: .6X TO 1.5X BASE HI
*111-178 RAD: .75X TO 2X BASE HI
PRINT RUN 25 SER.#'d SETS
137 Javale McGee JSY AU 20.00 50.00
139 Ryan Anderson JSY AU 8.00 20.00

2008-09 SPx Dual Scripts

STATED PRINT RUN 25 TO 50 SER.#'d SETS
DSAB Almond/A.Brooks/50 5.00 12.00
DSAG E.Gordon/Augustin/50 8.00 20.00
DSAT Tucker/Azubuike/50 5.00 12.00
DSBA A.Afflalo/M.Bibby/50 5.00 12.00
DSBG C.Brewer/J.Green/50 5.00 12.00
DSBM C.Billups/A.Miller/50 5.00 12.00
DSBR D.Rose/Beasley/50 100.00 250.00
DSBT Thornton/Bynum/50 10.00 25.00
DSCB Crittenton/Brooks/50 5.00 12.00
DSCP P.Pierce/V.Carter/50 30.00 80.00
DSEE Ewing/Ewing Jr./25 60.00 120.00
DSFL A.Law/R.Felton/50 6.00 15.00
DSFS Strawberry/Farmar/50 5.00 12.00
DSGL K.Love/Gallinari/50 30.00 80.00
DSGS Sessions/Gibson/50 5.00 12.00
DSGW J.Wright/R.Gay/50 5.00 12.00
DSIM Moon/Iguodala/50 5.00 12.00
DSKH Hawes/Kaman/50 6.00 15.00
DSLL B.Lopez/R.Lopez/50 10.00 25.00
DSMW Mayo/Westbrook/50 40.00 80.00
DSPC M.Conley/C.Paul/50 25.00 60.00
DSPN J.Noah/T.Prince/50 15.00 40.00
DSPS G.Pruitt/Sessions/50 6.00 15.00
DSPW S.Williams/Powe/50 5.00 12.00
DSRB Bayless/B.Rush/50 6.00 15.00
DSSS J.Smith/Stuckey/50 5.00 12.00
DSTA Alexander/Thompson/50 5.00 12.00
DSWL D.West/C.Landry/50 5.00 12.00

2008-09 SPx Endorsements

STATED PRINT RUN 12 TO 25 SER.#'d SETS
SPXBR Bill Russell/25 75.00 150.00
SPXCP Chris Paul/25 30.00 80.00
SPXDR David Robinson/25 30.00 80.00
SPXJE Julius Erving/25 30.00 80.00
SPXJS John Stockton/12 60.00 120.00
SPXKB Kobe Bryant/24 100.00 225.00
SPXKD Kevin Durant/25 60.00 120.00
SPXKG Kevin Garnett/25 50.00 100.00
SPXLB Larry Bird/25 50.00 100.00
SPXLJ LeBron James/23 200.00 500.00
SPXMJ Magic Johnson/25 30.00 80.00
SPXOR Oscar Robertson/25 50.00 100.00
SPXSN Steve Nash/25 30.00 80.00
SPXYM Yao Ming/25 30.00 80.00

2008-09 SPx Freshman Orientation

STATED ODDS 1:1.5
*PATCH: .75X TO 2X BASE HI
PATCH PRINT RUN 25 SER.#'d SETS
FOAD Darrell Arthur 2.00 5.00
FOAR Anthony Randolph 1.50 4.00
FOBL Brook Lopez 3.00 8.00
FOBR Brandon Rush 2.00 5.00
FOCD Chris Douglas-Roberts 1.50 4.00
FODA D.J. Augustin 2.00 5.00
FODG Donte Greene 1.50 4.00
FODR Derrick Rose 10.00 25.00
FODW D.J. White 2.00 5.00
FOEG Eric Gordon 4.00 10.00
FOGH George Hill 2.50 6.00
FOJA Joe Alexander 1.50 4.00
FOJB Jerryd Bayless 2.00 5.00
FOJG J.R. Giddens 1.50 4.00
FOJH J.J. Hickson 2.00 5.00
FOJM Javale McGee 3.00 8.00
FOJT Jason Thompson 1.50 4.00
FOKK Kosta Koufos 2.00 5.00
FOKL Kevin Love 8.00 20.00
FOMB Michael Beasley 2.50 6.00
FOMC Mario Chalmers 2.50 6.00
FOMS Marreese Speights 2.00 5.00
FOOM O.J. Mayo 2.50 6.00
FOPE Patrick Ewing Jr. 1.50 4.00
FORA Ryan Anderson 2.00 5.00
FORH Roy Hibbert 2.50 6.00
FORL Robin Lopez 2.50 6.00
FORW Russell Westbrook 8.00 20.00
FOSW Sonny Weems 1.50 4.00
FOWS Walter Sharpe 1.50 4.00

2008-09 SPx Signature Block

COMBINED AUTO/MEM ODDS 1:10
SBAJ Antawn Jamison 4.00 10.00
SBAM Alonzo Mourning 40.00 100.00
SBBA B.J. Armstrong 4.00 10.00
SBCM Chris Mullin 10.00 25.00
SBDF Derek Fisher 8.00 20.00
SBDH Dwight Howard 12.00 30.00
SBDM Danny Manning 5.00 12.00
SBDW Dominique Wilkins 15.00 30.00
SBFG Francisco Garcia 4.00 10.00
SBKG Kevin Garnett 30.00 80.00
SBLH Larry Hughes 4.00 10.00
SBLO Lamar Odom 8.00 20.00
SBLS Luis Scola 4.00 10.00
SBMC Maurice Cheeks 5.00 12.00
SBMJ Michael Jordan 400.00 800.00
SBMR Micheal Ray Richardson 4.00 10.00
SBPO Patrick O'Bryant 4.00 10.00
SBQR Quentin Richardson 4.00 10.00
SBSM Sidney Moncrief 4.00 10.00
SBSP Sam Perkins 4.00 10.00
SBTC Tom Chambers 4.00 10.00
SBVC Vince Carter 12.00 30.00

2008-09 SPx Super Scripts

COMBINED AUTO/MEM ODDS 1:10
SSAL Acie Law 3.00 8.00
SSBI Chauncey Billups 4.00 10.00
SSBO Chris Bosh 8.00 20.00
SSCM Chris Mihm 3.00 8.00
SSDH Dwight Howard 10.00 25.00
SSDS D.J. Strawberry 3.00 8.00
SSFG Francisco Garcia 3.00 8.00
SSJC Javaris Crittenton 3.00 8.00
SSJD Jared Dudley 3.00 8.00
SSJF Jordan Farmar 5.00 12.00
SSJN Joakim Noah 8.00 20.00
SSJS Jason Smith 3.00 8.00
SSJW Julian Wright 3.00 8.00
SSKB Kobe Bryant 100.00 250.00
SSKD Kevin Durant 40.00 100.00
SSKG Kevin Garnett 30.00 80.00
SSKK Kyle Korver 3.00 8.00
SSMA Morris Almond 3.00 8.00
SSMW Mario West 3.00 8.00
SSRS Ramon Sessions 4.00 10.00
SSSH Spencer Hawes 3.00 8.00
SSSW Sean Williams 3.00 8.00
SSWI Shelden Williams 3.00 8.00

2008-09 SPx Triple Scripts

PRINT RUN 25 SER.#'d SETS
TSBWA Bryant/Kareem/West 200.00 400.00
TSMMS McGrady/Ming/Scola 40.00 100.00
TSNKP Parker/Kidd/Nash 75.00 150.00
TSPAG Garnett/Pierce/Allen 300.00 600.00
TSPWR Paul/Williams/Roy 50.00 120.00
TSRBM Rose/Beasley/Mayo 150.00 300.00
TSSHB Howard/Stoudemire/Bynum 60.00 150.00
TSWJA James/Anthony/West 150.00 300.00

2008-09 SPx Winning Materials Initials

STATED ODDS 1:1.5
*JSY NUM: .4X TO 1X BASE HI
*PATCHES: 1X TO 2.5X BASE HI
PATCH PRINT RUN 25 SER.#'d SETS
UNPRICED JSY AUTO PRINT RUN 10 SETS
UNPRICED PATCH AUTO PRINT RUN 5 SETS
WMIAB Andrew Bynum 1.50 4.00
WMIAI Allen Iverson 3.00 8.00
WMIAJ Antawn Jamison 2.00 5.00
WMIAM Andre Miller 2.00 5.00
WMIAS Amare Stoudemire 2.00 5.00
WMIAT Al Thornton 2.00 5.00
WMIBG Ben Gordon 2.00 5.00
WMIBR Brandon Roy 2.50 6.00
WMICA Carmelo Anthony 3.00 8.00
WMICB Chris Bosh 2.50 6.00
WMICM Corey Maggette 2.00 5.00
WMICP Chris Paul 3.00 8.00
WMIDG Daniel Gibson 2.00 5.00
WMIDH Dwight Howard 2.00 5.00
WMIDN Dirk Nowitzki 3.00 8.00
WMIEB Elton Brand 2.50 6.00
WMIEO Emeka Okafor 2.00 5.00
WMIGD Glen Davis 1.50 4.00
WMIHA Hilton Armstrong 2.00 5.00
WMIIG Andre Iguodala 2.00 5.00
WMIJF Jordan Farmar 1.50 4.00
WMIJG Jeff Green 2.00 5.00
WMIJH Josh Howard 2.00 5.00
WMIJK Jason Kidd 2.50 6.00
WMIJO Jermaine O'Neal 2.00 5.00
WMIJS J.R. Smith 2.00 5.00
WMIKB Kobe Bryant 10.00 25.00
WMIKD Kevin Durant 6.00 15.00
WMIKG Kevin Garnett 4.00 10.00
WMIKH Kirk Hinrich 2.00 5.00
WMILA LaMarcus Aldridge 2.50 6.00
WMILH Larry Hughes 2.00 5.00
WMILJ LeBron James 10.00 25.00
WMILO Lamar Odom 2.00 5.00
WMIPP Paul Pierce 2.50 6.00
WMIRA Ray Allen 2.50 6.00
WMIRF Raymond Felton 2.00 5.00
WMIRG Rudy Gay 2.50 6.00

WMIRL Rashard Lewis 2.00 5.00
WMISO Shaquille O'Neal 5.00 12.00
WMISW Shelden Williams 2.00 5.00
WMITM Tracy McGrady 2.50 6.00
WMITP Tayshaun Prince 2.00 5.00
WMIVC Vince Carter 3.00 8.00
WMIYM Yao Ming 3.00 8.00

2008-09 SPx Winning Materials Combos

COMMON CARD 3.00 8.00
STATED ODDS 1:1.5
*PATCHES: 1.25X TO 3X HI COLUMN
PATCH PRINT RUN 25 SER.#'d SETS
UNPRICED AUTO PRINT RUN 5 SETS
WMCAD K.Durant/C.Anthony 8.00 20.00
WMCAG R.Allen/K.Garnett 6.00 15.00
WMCAR B.Roy/L.Aldridge 3.00 8.00
WMCBB A.Bargnani/C.Bosh 3.00 8.00
WMCBF J.Farmer/A.Bynum 4.00 10.00
WMCBG K.Bryant/P.Gasol 6.00 15.00
WMCBJ L.James/K.Bryant 15.00 40.00
WMCBL A.Law/M.Bibby 3.00 8.00
WMCBM R.Brewer/P.Millsap 3.00 8.00
WMCBO A.Bargnani/J.O'Neal 3.00 8.00
WMCBW D.Williams/C.Boozer 3.00 8.00
WMCCH D.Harris/V.Carter 3.00 8.00
WMCCL S.Livingston/M.Camby 3.00 8.00
WMCCN K.Martin/Nene 3.00 8.00
WMCCT A.Thornton/M.Camby 3.00 8.00
WMCDG J.Green/K.Durant 6.00 15.00
WMCDM M.Ginobili/T.Duncan 4.00 10.00
WMCEJ M.Johnson/J.Erving 6.00 15.00
WMCEW B.Wright/M.Ellis 3.00 8.00
WMCFD R.Felton/J.Davidson 3.00 8.00
WMCFW M.Webster/C.Frye 3.00 8.00
WMCGD B.Gordon/L.Deng 3.00 8.00
WMCGP P.Pierce/K.Garnett 6.00 15.00
WMCHB C.Billups/R.Hamilton 3.00 8.00
WMCHG D.Gooden/L.Hughes 3.00 8.00
WMCHN D.Nowitzki/J.Howard 3.00 8.00
WMCIA C.Anthony/A.Iverson 4.00 10.00
WMCIY A.Iguodala/T.Young 3.00 8.00
WMCJB A.Jamison/C.Butler 3.00 8.00
WMCJF R.Foye/A.Jefferson 3.00 8.00
WMCJH J.Johnson/A.Horford 3.00 8.00
WMCJP M.Jordan/S.Pippen 30.00 80.00
WMCJS J.Smith/J.Johnson 3.00 8.00
WMCKN D.Nowitzki/J.Kidd 4.00 10.00
WMCKO A.Kirilenko/M.Okur 3.00 8.00
WMCLH D.Howard/R.Lewis 3.00 8.00
WMCMB E.Brand/A.Miller 3.00 8.00
WMCMD K.Martin/Q.Douby 3.00 8.00
WMCMH S.Marion/U.Haslem 3.00 8.00
WMCMM T.McGrady/Y.Ming 4.00 10.00
WMCMR N.Robinson/S.Marbury 3.00 8.00
WMCMS J.Stockton/K.Malone 4.00 10.00
WMCNH S.Nash/G.Hill 6.00 15.00
WMCPG T.Parker/M.Ginobili 4.00 10.00
WMCPM D.Majerle/M.Price 3.00 8.00
WMCPW C.Paul/D.Williams 5.00 12.00
WMCPY N.Young/O.Pecherov 3.00 8.00
WMCRB A.Bogut/M.Redd 3.00 8.00
WMCRP G.Pruitt/R.Rondo 3.00 8.00
WMCRR Q.Richardson/Z.Randolph 3.00 8.00
WMCRT I.Thomas/D.Rodman 5.00 12.00
WMCRW J.Richardson/G.Wallace 3.00 8.00
WMCSE J.Starks/P.Ewing 6.00 15.00
WMCSH D.Howard/A.Stoudemire 4.00 10.00
WMCSO A.Stoudemire/S.O'Neal 4.00 10.00
WMCSP P.Stojackovic/C.Paul 4.00 10.00
WMCTN J.Noah/T.Thomas 3.00 8.00
WMCWJ B.Wallace/L.James 6.00 15.00
WMCWO E.Okafor/G.Wallace 3.00 8.00
WMCWP T.Prince/R.Wallace 4.00 10.00

2008-09 SPx Winning Materials Trios

COMBINED MEM STATED ODDS 1:1.5
*PATCH: 1.5X TO 4X BASE HI
PATCH PRINT RUN 15 SER.#'d SETS
UNPRICED AUTO PRINT RUN 3 SER.#'d SETS
WMTBBG Bargnani/Bosh/Graham 4.00 10.00
WMTBGB Bryant/Gasol/Bynum 10.00 25.00
WMTBJS Smith/Johnson/Bibby 4.00 10.00
WMTBLS Scola/Landry/Battier 4.00 10.00
WMTBWB Williams/Boozer/Brewer 5.00 12.00
WMTCBH Boone/Carter/Harris 4.00 10.00
WMTCKT Thornton/Camby/Kaman 4.00 10.00
WMTCSP Stojakovic/Paul/Chandler 5.00 12.00
WMTDMG Martin/Douby/Garcia 4.00 10.00
WMTDPG Parker/Duncan/Ginobili 8.00 20.00
WMTGFW Granger/Ford/Williams 4.00 10.00
WMTHDG Gordon/Deng/Hinrich 4.00 10.00
WMTHWS Stuckey/Hamilton/Wallace 4.00 10.00
WMTJBY Jamison/Butler/Young 4.00 10.00
WMTJMF Foye/Jefferson/McCants 4.00 10.00
WMTKIA Anthony/Iverson/Martin 6.00 15.00
WMTKNH Nowitzki/Howard/Kidd 5.00 12.00
WMTLAH Howard/Lewis/Arroyo 5.00 12.00
WMTMEW Wright/Ellis/Maggette 4.00 10.00
WMTMIY Iguodala/Miller/Young 4.00 10.00
WMTMMH Marion/Haslem/Mourning 4.00 10.00
WMTMRC Crawford/Marbury/Randolph 4.00 10.00
WMTNSO Stoudemire/O'Neal/Nash 6.00 15.00
WMTPAG Allen/Garnett/Pierce 10.00 25.00
WMTPDG Green/Durant/Petro 6.00 15.00
WMTRRB Bogut/Redd/Ridnour 4.00 10.00
WMTRWO Okafor/Wallace/Richardson 4.00 10.00
WMTTGF Gay/Thomas/Farmar 4.00 10.00
WMTWAR Roy/Aldridge/Webster 4.00 10.00
WMTWJG Wallace/James/Gibson 6.00 15.00

2014-15 SPx

JSY AU PRINT RUN B/WN 250-499 COPIES PER
1 Pervis Ellison .60 1.50
2 Alonzo Mourning 1.25 3.00
3 Anfernee Hardaway 2.50 6.00
4 Antonio McDyess .75 2.00
5 Bill Russell 1.50 4.00
6 Bill Walton 1.00 2.50
7 Shaquille O'Neal 2.00 5.00
8 A.C. Green 1.00 2.50
9 Christian Laettner .75 2.00
10 Alex English .75 2.00
11 Danny Manning .75 2.00
12 Bo Kimble SP .60 1.50
13 David Robinson 1.50 4.00
14 Doc Rivers 1.00 2.50
15 Dave Cowens .60 1.50
16 Grant Hill 1.25 3.00
17 David Thompson .75 2.00
18 Kenny Anderson .75 2.00
19 Vinny Del Negro .75 2.00
20 Allan Houston .75 2.00
21 James Harden 1.50 4.00
22 James Worthy 1.25 3.00
23 Jerry West 1.25 3.00
24 Jerry Lucas 1.00 2.50
25 Byron Scott .75 2.00
26 John Stockton 1.50 4.00
27 John Salley .60 1.50
28 Julius Erving 1.50 4.00
29 Elvin Hayes 1.00 2.50
30 Eric Piatkowski .60 1.50
31 Micheal Ray Richardson .75 2.00
32 Larry Bird 2.50 6.00
33 Joe Smith .75 2.00
34 LeBron James 4.00 10.00
35 Magic Johnson 2.50 6.00
36 Michael Jordan 8.00 20.00
37 Harold Miner .60 1.50
38 Bo Outlaw .60 1.50
39 Donyell Marshall .60 1.50
40 Jay Williams .60 1.50
41 Reggie Theus .75 2.00
42 Keith Smart 1.00 2.50
43 Stacey Augmon .60 1.50
44 Nick Van Exel 1.00 2.50
45 Sleepy Floyd .60 1.50
46 Stephen Curry 4.00 10.00
47 Bill Laimbeer .75 2.00
48 Brad Daugherty .75 2.00
49 Yao Ming 1.25 3.00
50 Jerry Stackhouse .75 2.00
51 Clint Capela 1.00 2.50
52 P.J. Hairston .75 2.00
53 Dario Saric 2.00 5.00
54 Kyle Anderson 1.25 3.00
55 Joe Harris .75 2.00
56 Elfrid Payton 1.25 3.00
57 Josh Huestis .75 2.00
58 Aaron Gordon 2.00 5.00
59 Jordan Adams .75 2.00
60 Jusuf Nurkic 1.25 3.00
61 C.J. Wilcox .75 2.00
62 Gary Harris 1.25 3.00
63 Doug McDermott 1.25 3.00
64 Zach LaVine 2.00 5.00
65 Mitch McGary .75 2.00
66 James Young .75 2.00
67 T.J. Warren 1.25 3.00
68 Nik Stauskas 1.00 2.50
69 Nikola Mirotic 1.50 4.00
70 Adreian Payne 1.00 2.50
71 Rodney Hood 1.25 3.00
72 Cleanthony Early .75 2.00
73 Shabazz Napier 1.00 2.50
74 Glenn Robinson III .75 2.00
75 Thanasis Antetokounmpo .75 2.00
76 Clint Capela JSY AU/499 4.00 10.00
77 P.J. Hairston JSY AU/499 3.00 8.00
79 C.J. Wilcox JSY AU/499 3.00 8.00
80 Josh Huestis JSY AU/499 3.00 8.00
81 T.J. Warren JSY AU/499 5.00 12.00
82 Jordan Adams JSY AU/499 3.00 8.00
83 Joe Harris JSY AU/499 3.00 8.00
84 Nikola Mirotic JSY AU/499 6.00 15.00
85 Gary Harris JSY AU/499 6.00 15.00
86 Doug McDermott JSY AU/499 8.00 20.00
87 Zach LaVine JSY AU/499 8.00 20.00
88 Mitch McGary JSY AU/499 3.00 8.00
89 James Young JSY AU/499 3.00 8.00
90 Elfrid Payton JSY AU/499 5.00 12.00
91 Nik Stauskas JSY AU/499 4.00 10.00
92 Jusuf Nurkic JSY AU/499 5.00 12.00
93 Adreian Payne JSY AU/499 4.00 10.00
94 Rodney Hood JSY AU/499 5.00 12.00
96 Shabazz Napier JSY AU/499 4.00 10.00
97 Glenn Robinson III JSY AU/499 3.00 8.00
98 Thanasis Antetokounmpo JSY AU/499 3.00 8.00
99 Kyle Anderson JSY AU/250 5.00 12.00
100 Aaron Gordon JSY AU/250 8.00 20.00

2014-15 SPx Rookie Patch Autographs

*RK PATCH AUTO: 1.5X TO 4X BASE HI
STATED PRINT RUN 30 SER.#'d SETS

2014-15 SPx '96 Inserts

STATED ODDS 1:7 PACKS
961 Yao Ming 3.00 8.00
962 Jerry Stackhouse 2.00 5.00
963 Alonzo Mourning 3.00 8.00
964 Anfernee Hardaway 3.00 8.00
965 Bill Russell 4.00 10.00
966 Doc Rivers 2.50 6.00
967 Christian Laettner 2.00 5.00
968 Stephen Curry 10.00 25.00
969 David Robinson 4.00 10.00
9610 Grant Hill 3.00 8.00
9611 Antonio McDyess 2.00 5.00
9612 Bill Walton 2.50 6.00
9613 Shaquille O'Neal 5.00 12.00
9614 James Harden 4.00 10.00
9615 James Worthy 3.00 8.00
9616 Jerry West 3.00 8.00
9617 John Stockton 4.00 10.00
9618 Julius Erving 4.00 10.00
9619 Kenny Anderson 2.00 5.00
9620 John Salley 1.50 4.00
9621 Joe Smith 2.00 5.00
9622 Larry Bird 6.00 15.00
9623 Dave Cowens 1.50 4.00
9624 LeBron James 10.00 25.00
9625 Magic Johnson 6.00 15.00
9626 Michael Jordan 20.00 50.00
9627 A.C. Green 2.50 6.00
9628 Jay Williams 1.50 4.00
9629 Aaron Gordon 4.00 10.00
9630 Elfrid Payton 2.50 6.00

2014-15 SPx '97 Inserts

STATED ODDS 1:7 PACKS
971 Alonzo Mourning 2.00 5.00
972 Anfernee Hardaway 4.00 10.00
973 Antonio McDyess 1.25 3.00
974 Bill Russell 2.50 6.00
975 Bill Walton 1.50 4.00
976 Doc Rivers 1.50 4.00
977 Byron Scott 1.25 3.00
978 Christian Laettner 1.25 3.00
979 Danny Manning 1.25 3.00
9710 David Robinson 2.50 6.00
9711 John Salley 1.50 4.00
9712 Grant Hill 3.00 8.00
9713 Jerry Stackhouse 3.00 8.00
9714 Donyell Marshall 1.00 2.50
9715 Shabazz Napier 1.25 3.00
9716 James Worthy 2.00 5.00
9717 Jerry West 2.00 5.00
9718 John Stockton 2.50 6.00
9719 Julius Erving 2.50 6.00
9720 Jerry Lucas 1.50 4.00
9721 Larry Bird 4.00 10.00
9722 Stephen Curry 6.00 15.00
9723 LeBron James 6.00 15.00
9724 Magic Johnson 8.00 20.00
9725 Michael Jordan 15.00 40.00
9726 Tracy McGrady 1.50 4.00
9727 Harold Miner 1.00 2.50
9728 Yao Ming 2.00 5.00
9729 Aaron Gordon 2.50 6.00
9730 T.J. Warren 1.50 4.00

2014-15 SPx Autographs

GROUP A ODDS 1:4,870 PACKS
GROUP B ODDS 1:1,723 PACKS
GROUP C ODDS 1:200 PACKS
GROUP D ODDS 1:85 PACKS
GROUP E ODDS 1:25 PACKS
GROUP F ODDS 1:20 PACKS
1 Pervis Ellison D 5.00 12.00
3 Anfernee Hardaway C 30.00 80.00
4 Antonio McDyess D 4.00 10.00
5 Bill Russell A 60.00 150.00
6 Bill Walton C 25.00 60.00
9 Christian Laettner C 4.00 10.00
10 Alex English B 8.00 20.00
12 Bo Kimble D 3.00 8.00
14 Doc Rivers D 5.00 12.00
15 Dave Cowens C 8.00 20.00
18 Kenny Anderson D 4.00 10.00
20 Allan Houston D 4.00 10.00
24 Jerry Lucas C 5.00 12.00
26 John Stockton D 20.00 50.00
29 Elvin Hayes B 5.00 12.00
30 Eric Piatkowski C 3.00 8.00
33 Joe Smith B 10.00 25.00
34 LeBron James C EXCH 200.00 300.00
36 Michael Jordan C 250.00 400.00
37 Harold Miner D 6.00 15.00
38 Bo Outlaw C 3.00 8.00
40 Jay Williams D 10.00 25.00
43 Stacey Augmon D 3.00 8.00
44 Nick Van Exel D 5.00 12.00
45 Sleepy Floyd D 3.00 8.00
47 Bill Laimbeer B 4.00 10.00
48 Brad Daugherty D 4.00 10.00
50 Jerry Stackhouse C 4.00 10.00
51 Clint Capela F 4.00 10.00
52 P.J. Hairston F 3.00 8.00
53 Dario Saric E 10.00 25.00
54 Kyle Anderson E 5.00 12.00
55 Joe Harris F 3.00 8.00
56 Elfrid Payton E 5.00 12.00
57 Josh Huestis E 3.00 8.00
58 Aaron Gordon E 8.00 20.00
59 Jordan Adams E 3.00 8.00
60 Jusuf Nurkic E 5.00 12.00
61 C.J. Wilcox E 3.00 8.00
62 Gary Harris E 5.00 12.00
63 Doug McDermott E 5.00 12.00
64 Zach LaVine E 8.00 20.00
65 Mitch McGary F EXCH 3.00 8.00
66 James Young E 3.00 8.00
67 T.J. Warren E 5.00 12.00
68 Nik Stauskas E 4.00 10.00
69 Nikola Mirotic E 8.00 20.00
70 Adreian Payne F 4.00 10.00
71 Rodney Hood F 5.00 12.00
73 Shabazz Napier F 4.00 10.00
74 Glenn Robinson III F 3.00 8.00
75 Thanasis Antetokounmpo F 3.00 8.00

2014-15 SPx Finite Legends

STATED PRINT RUN 799 SER.#'d SETS
FAH Allan Houston 1.50 4.00
FAM Alonzo Mourning 2.50 6.00
FBD Brad Daugherty 1.50 4.00
FBR Bill Russell 3.00 8.00
FBS Byron Scott 1.50 4.00
FBW Bill Walton 2.00 5.00
FDM Danny Manning 1.50 4.00
FDR David Robinson 3.00 8.00
FEH Elvin Hayes 2.00 5.00
FGH Grant Hill 4.00 10.00
FHA Anfernee Hardaway 5.00 12.00
FJA LeBron James 2.50 6.00
FJE Julius Erving 3.00 8.00
FJH James Harden 3.00 8.00
FJO Michael Jordan 8.00 20.00
FJS John Salley 1.25 3.00
FJW Jay Williams 1.25 3.00
FKA Kenny Anderson 1.50 4.00
FLB Larry Bird 3.00 8.00
FMJ Magic Johnson 5.00 12.00
FMR Micheal Ray Richardson 1.50 4.00
FNE Nick Van Exel 2.00 5.00
FRI Doc Rivers 2.00 5.00
FRT Reggie Theus 1.50 4.00
FSC Stephen Curry 8.00 20.00
FSM Joe Smith 1.50 4.00
FST John Stockton 2.00 5.00
FWE Jerry West 2.50 6.00
FWO James Worthy 2.50 6.00
FYM Yao Ming 2.50 6.00

2014-15 SPx Finite Legends Radiance

*RADIANCE: .5X TO 1.2X BASE HI
STATED PRINT RUN 99 SER.#'d SETS
FJA LeBron James 10.00 25.00
FJO Michael Jordan 20.00 50.00
FMJ Magic Johnson 10.00 25.00

2014-15 SPx Finite Rookies

*RADIANCE: .5X TO 1.2X BASE HI
STATED PRINT RUN 499 SER.#'d SETS
FIAG Aaron Gordon 3.00 8.00
FIAP Adreian Payne 3.00 8.00
FIDM Doug McDermott 4.00 10.00
FIEP Elfrid Payton 4.00 10.00
FIGH Gary Harris 4.00 10.00
FIJN Dario Saric 6.00 15.00
FIJY James Young 2.50 6.00
FIMM Mitch McGary 2.50 6.00
FINS Nik Stauskas 3.00 8.00
FISN Shabazz Napier 2.50 6.00
FITW T.J. Warren 4.00 10.00
FIZL Zach LaVine 8.00 20.00

2014-15 SPx Signatures

GROUP A ODDS 1:2,760 PACKS
GROUP B ODDS 1:1,258 PACKS
GROUP C ODDS 1:1,500 PACKS
GROUP D ODDS 1:250 PACKS
GROUP E ODDS 1:150 PACKS
SAD Jordan Adams D 4.00 10.00
SAG Aaron Gordon B 10.00 25.00
SBK Bo Kimble E 4.00 10.00
SCW Corliss Williamson E 4.00 10.00
SDR David Robinson A 15.00 40.00
SGH Grant Hill A 15.00 40.00
SJA LeBron James C 200.00 300.00
SJH James Harden A 8.00 20.00
SJS Jerry Stackhouse D 12.00 30.00
SJW James Worthy A 8.00 20.00
SLO Lute Olson B 6.00 15.00
SMC Doug McDermott B 6.00 15.00
SMJ Michael Jordan C 200.00 300.00
SMM Mitch McGary D 8.00 20.00
SPE Pervis Ellison E 4.00 10.00
SSA Stacey Augmon E 4.00 10.00
SSF Sleepy Floyd E 4.00 10.00
STW T.J. Warren B 10.00 25.00
SVD Vinny Del Negro D 5.00 12.00
SZL Zach LaVine C 20.00 50.00

2014-15 SPx Super Scripts Autographs

GROUP A ODDS 1:5,900 PACKS
GROUP B ODDS 1:2,800 PACKS
GROUP C ODDS 1:1,244 PACKS
GROUP D ODDS 1:300 PACKS
GROUP E ODDS 1:120 PACKS
SSAG A.C. Green E 4.00 10.00
SSBK Bo Kimble E 4.00 10.00
SSBR Bill Russell A 50.00 120.00
SSBW Bill Walton C 10.00 25.00
SSCE Cleanthony Early D 4.00 10.00
SSGH Grant Hill C 20.00 50.00
SSGO Aaron Gordon D 10.00 25.00
SSJO Michael Jordan D 200.00 300.00
SSJS Jerry Stackhouse C 8.00 20.00
SSMC Antonio McDyess E 5.00 12.00
SSPE Pervis Ellison E 8.00 20.00
SSRH Rodney Hood E 6.00 15.00
SSRI Doc Rivers C 6.00 15.00
SSSA Stacey Augmon E 4.00 10.00
SSSN Shabazz Napier D 5.00 12.00

2014-15 SPx UD Premier Jersey Autographs

STATED PRINT RUN B/WN 15-80 COPIES PER
NO PRICING ON QTY 15 OR LESS
1 T.J. Warren/80 8.00 20.00
2 Kyle Anderson/80 12.00 30.00
3 DeAndre Daniels/80 8.00 20.00
4 Thanasis Antetokounmpo/80 5.00 12.00
5 Dwight Powell/80 5.00 12.00
6 Clint Capela/80 6.00 15.00
7 P.J. Hairston/80 5.00 12.00
9 Josh Huestis/80 5.00 12.00
10 Jordan Clarkson/80 8.00 20.00
11 Jusuf Nurkic/80 10.00 25.00
12 Jordan Adams/80 8.00 20.00
13 Nikola Mirotic/80 40.00 100.00
14 Gary Harris/80 10.00 25.00
15 Doug McDermott/80 25.00 60.00
16 Zach LaVine/80 30.00 80.00
17 Mitch McGary/80 5.00 12.00
18 James Young/80 5.00 12.00
19 C.J. Wilcox/80 5.00 12.00
20 Joe Harris/80 5.00 12.00
21 Spencer Dinwiddie/80 6.00 15.00
22 Adreian Payne/80 6.00 15.00
23 Rodney Hood/80 8.00 20.00
25 Shabazz Napier/80 6.00 15.00
26 Glenn Robinson III/80 5.00 12.00
27 James Michael McAdoo/80 6.00 15.00
28 Elfrid Payton/30 8.00 20.00
30 Nik Stauskas/30 6.00 15.00

2014-15 SPx UD Premier Jersey Autographs Patch

*PATCH: .6X TO 1.5X BASE HI
STATED PRINT RUN B/WN 3-30 COPIES PER
NO PRICING ON QTY 10 OR LESS
LACK OF PRICING DUE TO MARKET INFO

2014-15 SPx Winning Big Materials

STATED ODDS 1:9 PACKS
WMAG A.C. Green 3.00 8.00
WMAH Allan Houston 3.00 8.00
WMAM Alonzo Mourning 4.00 10.00
WMAP Adreian Payne 3.00 8.00
WMBD Brad Daugherty 2.50 6.00
WMBW Bill Walton 3.00 8.00
WMCJ C.J. Wilcox 2.00 5.00
WMCL Christian Laettner 2.50 6.00
WMCW Corliss Williamson 2.00 5.00
WMDM Donyell Marshall 2.00 5.00
WMEP Elfrid Payton 2.50 6.00
WMGH Gary Harris 3.00 8.00
WMGO Aaron Gordon 5.00 12.00
WMHA Anfernee Hardaway 5.00 12.00
WMJA Jordan Adams 2.00 5.00
WMJH James Harden 5.00 12.00
WMJN Jusuf Nurkic 3.00 8.00
WMJS Joe Smith 2.50 6.00
WMJW Jay Williams 10.00 25.00
WMJY James Young 2.00 5.00
WMKS Keith Smart 3.00 8.00
WMLJ LeBron James 10.00 25.00
WMMA Danny Manning 2.50 6.00
WMMC Doug McDermott 3.00 8.00
WMMM Mitch McGary 2.00 5.00
WMMR Micheal Ray Richardson 2.50 6.00
WMNM Nikola Mirotic 4.00 10.00
WMNS Nik Stauskas 2.50 6.00
WMPH P.J. Hairston 2.00 5.00
WMRH Rodney Hood 3.00 8.00
WMSC Stephen Curry 12.00 30.00
WMSN Shabazz Napier 2.50 6.00
WMTW T.J. Warren 3.00 8.00
WMWE Jerry West 4.00 10.00
WMWI Buck Williams 3.00 8.00
WMZL Zach LaVine 5.00 12.00

2014-15 SPx Winning Big Materials Patch

*PATCH: 1X TO 2.5X BASE HI
STATED PRINT RUN B/WN 5-25 COPIES PER
NO PRICING ON QTY 5 OR LESS
WMJH James Harden/25 20.00 50.00
WMMA Danny Manning/25 12.00 30.00
WMPH P.J. Hairston/25 5.00 12.00
WMRH Rodney Hood/25 15.00 40.00
WMTW T.J. Warren/25 15.00 40.00

2014-15 SPx Winning Materials Combos

STATED ODDS 1:45 PACKS
WM2CJ C.Laettner/J.Williams 10.00 25.00
WM2GS A.Gordon/N.Stauskas 4.00 10.00
WM2HH A.Houston/A.Hardaway 6.00 15.00
WM2HP A.Payne/G.Harris 6.00 15.00
WM2JC L.James/S.Curry 25.00 60.00
WM2LS K.Smart/C.Laettner 5.00 12.00
WM2MF A.Mourning/S.Floyd 4.00 10.00
WM2MJ L.Johnson/A.Mourning 5.00 12.00
WM2ND D.Daniels/S.Napier 5.00 12.00
WM2SG L.Shelton/A.Green 6.00 15.00
WM2SM N.Stauskas/M.McGary 5.00 12.00
WM2SW B.Williams/J.Smith 10.00 25.00
WM2WL C.Laettner/B.Walton 4.00 10.00

2014-15 SPx Winning Materials Trios

STATED ODDS 1:160 PACKS
WMTGLW Warren/LaVine/Gordon 3.00 8.00
WMTGSP Gordon/Payton/Stauskas 3.00 8.00
WMTHSH Smith/Houston/Hardaway

1998-99 SPx Finite

This was the first year for SPx to move from a "Holoview" based set to a serially numbered set. The full set consists of 210 cards that carried an SRP of $5.99. The base set was divided up into five smaller sets all with different numbering. The base set contained 90 cards, serially numbered to 10,000. The Star Power subset contained 60 cards, serially numbered to 5,400. The SPx 2000 subset contained 30 cards, serially numbered to 4,050. The Top Flight subset contained 20 cards, serially numbered to 3,390. Finally, the Finite Excellence subset contained 10 cards, serially numbered to 1,770. In addition, rookie cards were inserted into boxes of Upper Deck 2 in two-card packs. The cards were serially numbered to 2,500. Cards 227 and 228 do not exist, since those particular rookies did not sign NBA contracts. The cards are considered rookie cards, but the set is not included in the complete set price.

BASE CARD PRINT RUN 10000 SERIAL #'d SETS
SP PRINT RUN 5400 SERIAL #'d SETS
SPx STATED PRINT RUN 4050 SERIAL #'d SETS
TF STATED PRINT RUN 3390 SERIAL #'d SETS
FE STATED PRINT RUN 1770 SERIAL #'d SETS
RC STATED PRINT RUN 2500 SERIAL #'d SETS
RCs DISTRIBUTED IN UD 2 BOXES
UNPRICED EXTREME SERIAL #'d TO 1
1 Michael Jordan 6.00 15.00
2 Hakeem Olajuwon 1.00 2.50
3 Keith Van Horn .75 2.00
4 Rasheed Wallace .75 2.00
5 Mookie Blaylock .50 1.25
6 Bobby Jackson .50 1.25
7 Detlef Schrempf .75 2.00
8 Antonio McDyess .60 1.50
9 Lamond Murray .50 1.25
10 Chris Mullin .75 2.00
11 Zydrunas Ilgauskas .75 2.00
12 Tracy Murray .50 1.25
13 Jerry Stackhouse .75 2.00
14 Avery Johnson .60 1.50
15 Larry Johnson .75 2.00
16 Alan Henderson .50 1.25
17 David Wesley .50 1.25
18 Kevin Willis .50 1.25
19 Eddie Jones .75 2.00
20 Horace Grant .60 1.50
21 Ray Allen 1.00 2.50
22 Derrick Coleman .60 1.50
23 Derek Anderson .50 1.25
24 Tim Hardaway .75 2.00
25 Danny Fortson .50 1.25
26 Tariq Abdul-Wahad .50 1.25
27 Charles Barkley 1.25 3.00
28 Sam Cassell .60 1.50
29 Kevin Garnett 1.25 3.00
30 Jeff Hornacek .60 1.50
31 Isaac Austin .50 1.25
32 Allan Houston .60 1.50
33 David Robinson 1.25 3.00
34 Tracy McGrady 1.25 3.00
35 LaPhonso Ellis .50 1.25
36 Shawn Kemp .75 2.00
37 Glenn Robinson .60 1.50
38 Shareef Abdur-Rahim .75 2.00
39 Vin Baker .60 1.50
40 Rik Smits .60 1.50
41 Jason Kidd 1.25 3.00
42 Erick Dampier .50 1.25
43 Shawn Bradley .50 1.25
44 Anfernee Hardaway 1.25 3.00
45 John Stockton 1.00 2.50
46 Calbert Cheaney .50 1.25
47 Terrell Brandon .50 1.25
48 Hubert Davis .50 1.25
49 Patrick Ewing 1.00 2.50
50 Kobe Bryant 3.00 8.00
51 Gary Payton .75 2.00
52 Marcus Camby .60 1.50
53 Bryant Reeves .50 1.25
54 Reggie Miller 1.00 2.50
55 Antoine Walker .75 2.00
56 Scottie Pippen 1.25 3.00
57 Hersey Hawkins .50 1.25
58 John Starks .60 1.50
59 Dikembe Mutombo .75 2.00
60 Damon Stoudamire .60 1.50
61 Rodney Rogers .50 1.25
62 Nick Anderson .50 1.25
63 Brian Williams .50 1.25
64 Ron Mercer .60 1.50
65 Donyell Marshall .50 1.25
66 Glen Rice .75 2.00
67 Michael Finley .75 2.00
68 Tim Duncan 1.50 4.00
69 Stephon Marbury 1.00 2.50
70 Antonio Daniels .50 1.25
71 Chauncey Billups 1.00 2.50
72 Kerry Kittles .50 1.25
73 Brian Grant .50 1.25
74 Anthony Mason .50 1.25
75 Allen Iverson 1.50 4.00
76 Juwan Howard .60 1.50
77 Grant Hill 1.25 3.00
78 Tony Delk .50 1.25
79 Olden Polynice .50 1.25
80 Alonzo Mourning 1.00 2.50
81 Karl Malone 1.00 2.50
82 Isaiah Rider .60 1.50
83 Shaquille O'Neal 2.00 5.00
84 Steve Smith .60 1.50
85 Kenny Anderson .60 1.50
86 Toni Kukoc .75 2.00
87 Anthony Peeler .50 1.25
88 Tim Thomas .75 2.00
89 Nick Van Exel .60 1.50
90 Jamal Mashburn .60 1.50
91 Reggie Miller SP 1.50 4.00
92 Juwan Howard SP 1.00 2.50
93 Glen Rice SP 1.25 3.00
94 Grant Hill SP 2.00 5.00
95 Maurice Taylor SP .75 2.00
96 Vin Baker SP 1.00 2.50
97 Tim Thomas SP 1.25 3.00
98 Bobby Jackson SP .75 2.00
99 Damon Stoudamire SP 1.00 2.50
100 Michael Jordan SP 10.00 25.00
101 Eddie Jones SP 1.25 3.00
102 Keith Van Horn SP 1.25 3.00
103 Dikembe Mutombo SP 1.25 3.00
104 Brevin Knight SP .75 2.00
105 Shawn Bradley SP .75 2.00
106 Lamond Murray SP .75 2.00
107 Tim Duncan SP 2.50 6.00
108 Bryant Reeves SP .75 2.00
109 Antoine Walker SP 1.25 3.00
110 John Stockton SP 1.50 4.00
111 Nick Anderson SP .75 2.00
112 Chris Mullin SP 1.25 3.00
113 Glenn Robinson SP 1.00 2.50
114 Kevin Garnett SP 2.00 5.00
115 Michael Stewart SP .75 2.00
116 Antonio McDyess SP 1.00 2.50
117 Jim Jackson SP .75 2.00
118 Chauncey Billups SP 1.50 4.00
119 Sam Cassell SP 1.00 2.50
120 Dennis Rodman SP 2.50 6.00
121 Rasheed Wallace SP 1.25 3.00
122 Brian Williams SP .75 2.00
123 Anfernee Hardaway SP 2.00 5.00
124 Scottie Pippen SP 2.00 5.00
125 Terrell Brandon SP .75 2.00
126 Michael Finley SP 1.25 3.00
127 Kerry Kittles SP .75 2.00
128 Toni Kukoc SP 1.25 3.00
129 Hakeem Olajuwon SP 1.50 4.00
130 Tim Hardaway SP 1.25 3.00
131 Shareef Abdur-Rahim SP 1.25 3.00
132 Donyell Marshall SP .75 2.00
133 David Robinson SP 2.00 5.00
134 LaPhonso Ellis SP .75 2.00
135 Ray Allen SP 1.50 4.00
136 Nick Van Exel SP 1.00 2.50
137 Patrick Ewing SP 1.50 4.00
138 Anthony Mason SP .75 2.00
139 Shaquille O'Neal SP 3.00 8.00
140 Shawn Kemp SP 1.25 3.00
141 Stephon Marbury SP 1.50 4.00
142 Karl Malone SP 1.50 4.00
143 Allen Iverson SP 2.50 6.00
144 Kenny Anderson SP 1.00 2.50
145 Marcus Camby SP 1.00 2.50
146 Steve Smith SP 1.00 2.50
147 Gary Payton SP 1.25 3.00
148 Jason Kidd SP 2.00 5.00
149 Alonzo Mourning SP 1.50 4.00
150 Charles Barkley SP 2.00 5.00
151 Kobe Bryant SPx 8.00 20.00
152 Ron Mercer SPx 1.50 4.00
153 Maurice Taylor SPx 1.25 3.00
154 Tim Duncan SPx 4.00 10.00
155 Shareef Abdur-Rahim SPx 2.00 5.00
156 Eddie Jones SPx 2.00 5.00
157 Chauncey Billups SPx 2.50 6.00
158 Derek Anderson SPx 1.25 3.00
159 Bobby Jackson SPx 1.25 3.00
160 Stephon Marbury SPx 2.50 6.00
161 Anfernee Hardaway SPx 3.00 8.00
162 Zydrunas Ilgauskas SPx 2.00 5.00
163 Allen Iverson SPx 4.00 10.00
164 Antoine Walker SPx 2.00 5.00
165 Tracy McGrady SPx 3.00 8.00
166 Rasheed Wallace SPx 2.00 5.00
167 Jason Kidd SPx 3.00 8.00
168 Kevin Garnett SPx 3.00 8.00
169 Damon Stoudamire SPx 1.50 4.00
170 Brevin Knight SPx 1.25 3.00
171 Tim Thomas SPx 2.00 5.00
172 Danny Fortson SPx 1.25 3.00
173 Jermaine O'Neal SPx 2.00 5.00
174 Keith Van Horn SPx 2.00 5.00
175 Ray Allen SPx 2.50 6.00
176 Kerry Kittles SPx 1.25 3.00
177 Vin Baker SPx 1.50 4.00
178 Allan Houston SPx 1.50 4.00
179 Alan Henderson SPx 1.25 3.00
180 Bryon Russell SPx 1.25 3.00
181 Michael Jordan TF 20.00 50.00
182 Maurice Taylor TF 1.50 4.00
183 Isaiah Rider TF 2.00 5.00
184 Antonio McDyess TF 2.00 5.00
185 Anfernee Hardaway TF 4.00 10.00
186 Glenn Robinson TF 2.00 5.00
187 Dikembe Mutombo TF 2.50 6.00
188 Shawn Kemp TF 2.50 6.00
189 Tracy McGrady TF 4.00 10.00
190 Reggie Miller TF 3.00 8.00
191 Derek Anderson TF 1.50 4.00
192 Allan Houston TF 2.00 5.00
193 Michael Finley TF 2.50 6.00
194 Nick Van Exel TF 2.00 5.00
195 Juwan Howard TF 2.00 5.00
196 LaPhonso Ellis TF 1.50 4.00
197 Ron Mercer TF 2.00 5.00
198 Glen Rice TF 2.50 6.00
199 Joe Smith TF 2.00 5.00
200 Kobe Bryant TF 10.00 25.00
201 Michael Jordan FE 20.00 50.00
202 Karl Malone FE 5.00 12.00
203 Hakeem Olajuwon FE 5.00 12.00
204 David Robinson FE 6.00 15.00
205 Shaquille O'Neal FE 10.00 25.00
206 John Stockton FE 5.00 12.00
207 Grant Hill FE 6.00 15.00
208 Tim Hardaway FE 4.00 10.00
209 Scottie Pippen FE 6.00 15.00
210 Gary Payton FE 4.00 10.00
211 Michael Olowokandi RC 3.00 8.00
212 Mike Bibby RC 4.00 10.00
213 Raef LaFrentz RC 3.00 8.00
214 Antawn Jamison RC 4.00 10.00
215 Vince Carter RC 12.00 30.00
216 Robert Traylor RC 2.50 6.00
217 Jason Williams RC 6.00 15.00
218 Larry Hughes RC 5.00 12.00
219 Dirk Nowitzki RC 20.00 50.00
220 Paul Pierce RC 10.00 25.00
221 Bonzi Wells RC 2.50 6.00
222 Michael Doleac RC 2.00 5.00
223 Keon Clark RC 2.50 6.00
224 Michael Dickerson RC 2.50 6.00
225 Matt Harpring RC 2.50 6.00
226 Bryce Drew RC 1.50 4.00
229 Pat Garrity RC 2.00 5.00
230 Roshown McLeod RC 1.50 4.00
231 Ricky Davis RC 4.00 10.00
232 Brian Skinner RC 2.50 6.00
233 Tyronn Lue RC 2.50 6.00
234 Felipe Lopez RC 1.50 4.00
235 Al Harrington RC 4.00 10.00
236 Ruben Patterson RC 2.50 6.00
237 Jelani McCoy RC 2.50 6.00
238 Corey Benjamin RC 1.50 4.00
239 Nazr Mohammed RC 2.50 6.00
240 Rashard Lewis RC 6.00 15.00
S1 Michael Jordan PROMO 5.00 12.00

1998-99 SPx Finite Radiance

*1-90 STARS: .6X TO 1.5X BASE HI
1-90 PRINT RUN 5000 SERIAL #'d SETS
*91-150 STARS: .6X TO 1.5X BASE HI
91-150 PRINT RUN 2700 SERIAL #'d SETS
*151-180 STARS: .6X TO 1.5X BASE HI
151-180 PRINT RUN 2025 SERIAL #'d SETS
*181-200 STARS: .75X TO 2X BASE HI
181-200 PRINT RUN 1130 SERIAL #'d SETS
*201-210 STARS: .75X TO 2X BASE HI
201-210 PRINT RUN 590 SERIAL #'d SETS
211-240 RCs: .4X TO 1X BASE HI
211-240 RC PRINT RUN 1500 SERIAL #'d SETS
215 Vince Carter 15.00 40.00
219 Dirk Nowitzki 25.00 60.00

1998-99 SPx Finite Spectrum

*1-90 STARS: 3X TO 8X BASE HI
1-90 PRINT RUN 350 SERIAL #'d SETS
*91-150 STARS: 2.5X TO 6X BASE HI
91-150 PRINT RUN 250 SERIAL #'d SETS
*151-180 STARS: 2.5X TO 6X BASE HI
151-180 PRINT RUN 75 SERIAL #'d SETS
*181-200 STARS: 3X TO 8X BASE HI
181-200 PRINT RUN 50 SERIAL #'d SETS
*201-210 STARS: 5X TO 12X BASE HI
201-210 PRINT RUN 25 SERIAL #'d SETS
*211-240 RCs: 8X TO 20X BASE HI
211-240 PRINT RUN 25 SERIAL #'d SETS
1 Michael Jordan 200.00 400.00
100 Michael Jordan SP 200.00 400.00
151 Kobe Bryant SPx 175.00 350.00
181 Michael Jordan TF 750.00 1500.00
185 Anfernee Hardaway TF 30.00 80.00
188 Shawn Kemp TF 40.00 100.00
200 Kobe Bryant TF 300.00 600.00
201 Michael Jordan FE 2200.00 3000.00
209 Scottie Pippen FE 100.00 250.00
215 Vince Carter 500.00 1000.00
219 Dirk Nowitzki 600.00 1200.00
240 Rashard Lewis 125.00 300.00

1979-80 Spurs Police

This set contains 15 cards measuring approximately 2 5/8" by 4 1/8" featuring the San Antonio Spurs. Backs contain safety tips, "Tips from the Spurs." The set was also sponsored by Handy Dan and were put out by Express News and Handy Dan in conjunction with the Police Department.

COMPLETE SET (15) 3.00 6.00
1 Bob Bass .25 .60
2 Mike Evans .25 .60
3 Mike Gale .25 .60
4 George Gervin 1.50 4.00
5 Paul Griffin .25 .60
6 George Karl ACO .40 1.00
7 Larry Kenon .30 .75
8 Irv Kiffin .25 .60
9 Bernie LaReau .25 .60
10 Doug Moe CO .40 1.00
11 Mark Olberding .25 .60
12 Billy Paultz .30 .75
13 Wiley Peck .25 .60
14 Kevin Restani .25 .60
15 James Silas .30 .75

1988-89 Spurs Police/Diamond Shamrock

This eight-card set of San Antonio Spurs is one of two that were sponsored by Diamond Shamrock, a regional oil retailer and convenience store chain headquartered in San Antonio. One set had a tear-off tab, and one card was given out each week at San Antonio Diamond Shamrock CornerStore locations with each 3.00 purchase or purchase of eight gallons of gas. It is reported that 100,000 sets were printed. This promotion included weekly drawings for pairs of tickets and a final drawing to determine the winners of the Grand Prize and other prizes. The expiration of the contest to "Win A Road Trip With The Spurs" was May 21, 1989. The other set was donated to the San Antonio Police Department and distributed to kids in the San Antonio area by patrolmen on the night shift; 50,000 sets were produced. The cards measure approximately 2 1/2" by 3 9/16" and except for the tear-off tab, the two sets are identical. The front features a color action player photo with a white border (only the Robinson card has a posed shot). The card front has a distinctive black background with a white pinstripe pattern. Three color bands (aqua, red, and orange) overlay the top of the picture, with the team logo in the middle. The player's name is given in the aqua band below the picture. The back has biographical information and a player safety tip in a gray box. The San Antonio Police and sponsor logos appear at the bottom. The cards are unnumbered and checklisted below in alphabetical order, with jersey number after the player's name. The set may have received additional multiple printings in order to capitalize on the popularity of the David Robinson card, which was printed a year earlier than his 1989-90 Hoops Rookie Card.

COMPLETE SET (8) 3.50 7.00
1 Greg Anderson 33 .20 .50
2 Willie Anderson 40 .25 .60
3 Frank Brickowski 43 .25 .60
4 Larry Brown CO .40 1.00
5 Dallas Comegys 22 .25 .60
6 Johnny Dawkins 24 .30 .75
7 Alvin Robertson 21 .20 .50
8 David Robinson 50 2.50 6.00

1976-77 Spurs Team Issue

This 8" x 10" set was produced for the San Antonio Spurs during the 1976-77 season. The set features eight black and white cards of the team's players.

COMPLETE SET (8) 12.50 25.00
1 Mike D'Antoni 2.00 5.00
2 Louie Dampier 2.00 5.00
3 Coby Dietrick 1.25 3.00
4 Mike Gale 1.25 3.00
5 Billy Paultz 1.50 4.00
6 James Silas 1.50 4.00
7 Ken Smith 1.25 3.00
8 Henry Ward 1.25 3.00

2007 Spurs Upper Deck

Distributed by Upper Deck, this set originally was available in three 9-card perforated sheets.

COMPLETE SET (27) 10.00 20.00
1 Tony Parker .75 2.00
2 Brent Barry .40 1.00
3 Tony Parker .75 2.00
4 Jackie Butler .40 1.00
5 2007 NBA Champions .40 1.00
6 Matt Bonner .40 1.00
7 Bruce Bowen .40 1.00
8 Gregg Popovich CO .60 1.50
9 Bruce Bowen/Michael Finley .60 1.50
10 Manu Ginobili .75 2.00
11 Francisco Elson .40 1.00
12 Manu Ginobili .75 2.00
13 James White .40 1.00
14 4 Time NBA Champions .40 1.00
15 Melvin Ely .40 1.00
16 Michael Finley .75 2.00
17 The Coyote .40 1.00
18 Fabricio Oberto/Brent Barry .40 1.00
19 Tim Duncan 1.00 2.50
20 Jacque Vaughn .40 1.00
21 Tim Duncan 1.00 2.50
22 Fabricio Oberto .40 1.00
23 2007 Conference Champs .40 1.00
24 Beno Udrih .40 1.00
25 Robert Horry .75 2.00
26 Tim Duncan/Tony Parker CL 1.00 2.50
27 Robert Horry .75 2.00

1971-72 Squires Virginia Team Issue

Each of these team-issued photos measure approximately 8" by 10" and feature black and white player portraits on two sheets. The player's name and vitals are listed below the photo. Each sheet contains either seven or eight player portraits. The backs are blank. The photos are unnumbered and listed below alphabetically. Julius Erving is featured in his rookie season.

COMPLETE SET (2) 25.00 50.00
1 Bill Bunting 20.00 40.00
Jim Eakins
Julius Erving
George Irvine
Neil Johnson
Mike Maloy
Doug Moe
Dana Pagett

2 Al Bianchi CO 7.50 15.00
Earl M. Foreman PRES
Charlie Scott
Ray Scott
Willie Sojourner
Adrian Smith
Roland Taylor

2000 St. Vincent Stamps

NNO1 Michael Jordan 2.00 5.00
NNO2 Michael Jordan Full Sheet 8.00 20.00

1992-93 Stadium Club

The complete 1992-93 Stadium Club basketball set (created by Topps) consists of 400 standard-size cards, having been issued in two 200-card series. Both first and second series packs contained 15 cards with a suggested retail price of $1.79 per pack. Topps also issued, late in the season, second series 23-card jumbo packs. A Stadium Club membership form was inserted in every 15-card pack. The basic card fronts feature full-bleed color action player photos. The team name and player's name appear in gold foil stripes that cut across the bottom of the card and intersect the Stadium Club logo. On a colorful background of a basketball in a net, the horizontal backs present biography, The Sporting News Skills Rating System, player evaluation, 1991-92 season and career statistics, and a miniature representation of the player's first Topps card, which is confusingly referenced as "Topps Rookie Card" by Topps. The first series closes and the second series begins with a Members Choice (191-210) subset. Rookie Cards of note include Tom Gugliotta, Robert Horry, Christian Laettner, Alonzo Mourning, Shaquille O'Neal, Latrell Sprewell and Clarence Weatherspoon.

COMPLETE SET (400) 12.50 30.00
COMPLETE SERIES 1 (200) 6.00 15.00
COMPLETE SERIES 2 (200) 6.00 15.00
1 Michael Jordan 3.00 8.00
2 Greg Anthony .02 .10
3 Otis Thorpe .10 .30
4 Jim Les .02 .10
5 Kevin Willis .02 .10
6 Derek Harper .10 .30
7 Elden Campbell .10 .30
8 A.J. English .02 .10
9 Kenny Gattison .02 .10
10 Drazen Petrovic .02 .10
11 Chris Mullin .25 .60
12 Mark Price .02 .10
13 Karl Malone .40 1.00
14 Gerald Glass .02 .10
15 Negele Knight .02 .10
16 Mark Macon .02 .10
17 Michael Cage .02 .10
18 Kevin Edwards .02 .10
19 Sherman Douglas .02 .10
20 Ron Harper .10 .30
21 Clifford Robinson .10 .30
22 Byron Scott .10 .30
23 Antoine Carr .02 .10
24 Greg Dreiling .02 .10
25 Bill Laimbeer .10 .30
26 Hersey Hawkins .10 .30
27 Will Perdue .02 .10
28 Todd Lichti .02 .10
29 Gary Grant .02 .10
30 Sam Perkins .10 .30
31 Jayson Williams .10 .30
32 Magic Johnson .75 2.00
33 Larry Bird 1.00 2.50
34 Chris Morris .02 .10
35 Nick Anderson .10 .30
36 Scott Hastings .02 .10
37 Ledell Eackles .02 .10
38 Robert Pack .02 .10
39 Dana Barros .02 .10
40 Anthony Bonner .02 .10
41 J.R. Reid .02 .10
42 Tyrone Hill .02 .10
43 Rik Smits .10 .30
44 Kevin Duckworth .02 .10
45 LaSalle Thompson .02 .10
46 Brian Williams .02 .10
47 Willie Anderson .02 .10
48 Ken Norman .02 .10
49 Mike Iuzzolino .02 .10
50 Isiah Thomas .25 .60
51 Alec Kessler .02 .10
52 Johnny Dawkins .02 .10
53 Avery Johnson .02 .10
54 Stacey Augmon .10 .30
55 Charles Oakley .10 .30
56 Rex Chapman .02 .10
57 Charles Shackleford .02 .10
58 Jeff Ruland .02 .10
59 Craig Ehlo .02 .10
60 Jon Koncak .02 .10
61 Danny Schayes .02 .10
62 David Benoit .02 .10
63 Robert Parish .10 .30
64 Mookie Blaylock .10 .30
65 Sean Elliott .10 .30
66 Mark Aguirre .02 .10
67 Scott Williams .02 .10
68 Doug West .02 .10
69 Kenny Anderson .25 .60
70 Randy Brown .02 .10
71 Muggsy Bogues .10 .30
72 Spud Webb .10 .30
73 Sedale Threatt .02 .10
74 Chris Gatling .02 .10
75 Derrick McKey .02 .10
76 Sleepy Floyd .02 .10
77 Chris Jackson .02 .10
78 Thurl Bailey .02 .10
79 Steve Smith .30 .75
80 Cedric Ceballos .02 .10
81 Anthony Bowie .02 .10
82 John Williams .02 .10
83 Paul Graham .02 .10
84 Willie Burton .02 .10
85 Vernon Maxwell .02 .10
86 Stacey King .02 .10
87 B.J. Armstrong .02 .10
88 Kevin Gamble .02 .10
89 Terry Catledge .02 .10
90 Jeff Malone .02 .10
91 Sam Bowie .02 .10
92 Orlando Woolridge .02 .10
93 Steve Kerr .10 .30
94 Eric Leckner .02 .10
95 Loy Vaught .02 .10
96 Jud Buechler .02 .10
97 Doug Smith .02 .10
98 Sidney Green .02 .10
99 Jerome Kersey .02 .10
100 Patrick Ewing .25 .60
101 Ed Nealy .02 .10
102 Shawn Kemp .50 1.25
103 Luc Longley .10 .30
104 George McCloud .02 .10
105 Ron Anderson .02 .10
106 Moses Malone UER .25 .60
107 Tony Smith .02 .10
108 Terry Porter .02 .10
109 Blair Rasmussen .02 .10
110 Bimbo Coles .02 .10
111 Grant Long .02 .10
112 John Battle .02 .10
113 Brian Oliver .02 .10
114 Tyrone Corbin .02 .10
115 Benoit Benjamin .02 .10
116 Rick Fox .10 .30
117 Rafael Addison .02 .10
118 Danny Young .02 .10
119 Fat Lever .02 .10
120 Terry Cummings .10 .30
121 Felton Spencer .02 .10
122 Joe Kleine .02 .10
123 Johnny Newman .02 .10
124 Gary Payton .50 1.25
125 Kurt Rambis .02 .10
126 Vlade Divac .10 .30
127 John Paxson .02 .10
128 Lionel Simmons .02 .10
129 Randy Wittman .02 .10
130 Winston Garland .02 .10
131 Jerry Reynolds .02 .10
132 Dell Curry .02 .10
133 Fred Roberts .02 .10
134 Michael Adams .02 .10
135 Charles Jones .02 .10
136 Frank Brickowski .02 .10
137 Alton Lister .02 .10
138 Horace Grant .10 .30
139 Greg Sutton .02 .10
140 John Starks .10 .30
141 Detlef Schrempf .10 .30
142 Rodney Monroe .02 .10
143 Pete Chilcutt .02 .10
144 Mike Brown .02 .10
145 Rony Seikaly .02 .10
146 Donald Hodge .02 .10
147 Kevin McHale .25 .60
148 Ricky Pierce .02 .10
149 Brian Shaw .02 .10
150 Reggie Williams .02 .10
151 Kendall Gill .10 .30
152 Tom Chambers .02 .10
153 Jack Haley .02 .10
154 Terrell Brandon .25 .60
155 Dennis Scott .10 .30
156 Mark Randall .02 .10
157 Kenny Payne .02 .10
158 Bernard King .02 .10
159 Tate George .02 .10
160 Scott Skiles .02 .10
161 Pervis Ellison .02 .10
162 Marcus Liberty .02 .10
163 Rumeal Robinson .02 .10
164 Anthony Mason .25 .60
165 Les Jepsen .02 .10
166 Kenny Smith .02 .10
167 Randy White .02 .10
168 Dee Brown .02 .10
169 Chris Dudley .02 .10
170 Armon Gilliam .02 .10
171 Eddie Johnson .02 .10
172 A.C. Green .10 .30
173 Darrell Walker .02 .10
174 Bill Cartwright .02 .10
175 Mike Gminski .02 .10
176 Tom Tolbert .02 .10
177 Buck Williams .10 .30
178 Mark Eaton .02 .10
179 Danny Manning .10 .30
180 Glen Rice .25 .60
181 Sarunas Marciulionis .02 .10
182 Danny Ferry .02 .10
183 Chris Corchiani .02 .10
184 Dan Majerle .10 .30
185 Alvin Robertson .02 .10
186 Vern Fleming .02 .10
187 Kevin Lynch .02 .10
188 John Williams .02 .10
189 Checklist 1-100 .02 .10
190 Checklist 101-200 .02 .10
191 David Robinson MC .25 .60
192 Larry Johnson MC .25 .60
193 Derrick Coleman MC .02 .10
194 Larry Bird MC .50 1.25
195 Billy Owens MC .02 .10
196 Dikembe Mutombo MC .25 .60
197 Charles Barkley MC .25 .60
198 Scottie Pippen MC .40 1.00
199 Clyde Drexler MC .10 .30
200 John Stockton MC .10 .30
201 Shaquille O'Neal MC 3.00 8.00
202 Chris Mullin MC .10 .30
203 Glen Rice MC .10 .30
204 Isiah Thomas MC .10 .30
205 Karl Malone MC .25 .60
206 Christian Laettner MC .25 .60
207 Patrick Ewing MC .10 .30
208 Dominique Wilkins MC .10 .30
209 Alonzo Mourning MC .50 1.25
210 Michael Jordan MC 1.50 4.00
211 Tim Hardaway .30 .75
212 Rodney McCray .02 .10
213 Larry Johnson .30 .75
214 Charles Smith .02 .10
215 Kevin Brooks .02 .10
216 Kevin Johnson .25 .60
217 Duane Cooper RC .02 .10
218 Christian Laettner UER RC .50 1.25
219 Tim Perry .02 .10
220 Hakeem Olajuwon .40 1.00
221 Lee Mayberry RC .02 .10
222 Mark Bryant .02 .10
223 Robert Horry RC .25 .60
224 Tracy Murray UER RC .10 .30
225 Greg Grant .02 .10
226 Rolando Blackman .02 .10
227 James Edwards UER .02 .10
228 Sean Green .02 .10
229 Buck Johnson .02 .10
230 Andrew Lang .02 .10
231 Tracy Moore RC .02 .10
232 Adam Keefe UER RC .02 .10
233 Tony Campbell .02 .10
234 Rod Strickland .25 .60
235 Terry Mills .02 .10
236 Billy Owens .10 .30
237 Bryant Stith UER RC .10 .30
238 Tony Bennett UER RC .02 .10
239 David Wood .02 .10
240 Jay Humphries .02 .10
241 Doc Rivers .10 .30
242 Wayman Tisdale .02 .10
243 Litterial Green RC .02 .10
244 Jon Barry .10 .30
245 Brad Daugherty .02 .10
246 Nate McMillan .02 .10
247 Shaquille O'Neal RC 4.00 10.00
248 Chris Smith RC .02 .10
249 Duane Ferrell .02 .10
250 Anthony Peeler RC .10 .30
251 Gundars Vetra RC .02 .10
252 Danny Ainge .10 .30
253 Mitch Richmond .25 .60
254 Malik Sealy RC .10 .30
255 Brent Price RC .10 .30
256 Xavier McDaniel .02 .10
257 Bobby Phills RC .25 .60
258 Donald Royal .02 .10
259 Olden Polynice .02 .10
260 Dominique Wilkins UER .25 .60
261 Larry Krystkowiak .02 .10
262 Duane Causwell .02 .10
263 Todd Day RC .10 .30
264 Sam Mack RC .10 .30
265 John Stockton .25 .60
266 Eddie Lee Wilkins .02 .10
267 Gerald Glass .02 .10
268 Robert Pack .02 .10
269 Gerald Wilkins .02 .10
270 Reggie Lewis .10 .30
271 Scott Brooks .02 .10
272 Randy Woods UER RC .02 .10
273 Dikembe Mutombo .30 .75
274 Kiki Vandeweghe .02 .10
275 Rich King .02 .10
276 Jeff Turner .02 .10
277 Vinny Del Negro .02 .10
278 Marlon Maxey RC .02 .10
279 Elmore Spencer UER RC .02 .10
280 Cedric Ceballos .10 .30
281 Alex Blackwell RC .02 .10
282 Terry Davis .02 .10
283 Morlon Wiley .02 .10
284 Trent Tucker .02 .10
285 Carl Herrera .02 .10
286 Eric Anderson RC .02 .10
287 Clyde Drexler .25 .60
288 Tom Gugliotta RC .75 2.00
289 Dale Ellis .02 .10
290 Lance Blanks .02 .10
291 Tom Hammonds .02 .10
292 Eric Murdock .02 .10
293 Walt Williams RC .25 .60
294 Gerald Paddio .02 .10
295 Brian Howard RC .02 .10
296 Ken Williams .02 .10
297 Alonzo Mourning RC 1.50 4.00
298 Larry Nance .02 .10
299 Jeff Grayer .02 .10
300 Dave Johnson RC .02 .10
301 Bob McCann RC .02 .10
302 Bart Kofoed .02 .10
303 Anthony Cook .02 .10
304 Radisav Curcic RC .02 .10
305 John Crotty RC .02 .10
306 Brad Sellers .02 .10
307 Marcus Webb RC .02 .10
308 Winston Garland .02 .10
309 Walter Palmer .02 .10
310 Rod Higgins .02 .10
311 Travis Mays .02 .10
312 Alex Stivrins RC .02 .10
313 Greg Kite .02 .10
314 Dennis Rodman .50 1.25
315 Mike Sanders .02 .10
316 Ed Pinckney .02 .10
317 Harold Miner RC .10 .30
318 Pooh Richardson .02 .10
319 Oliver Miller RC .10 .30
320 Latrell Sprewell RC 2.00 5.00
321 Anthony Pullard RC .02 .10
322 Mark Randall .02 .10
323 Jeff Hornacek .10 .30
324 Rick Mahorn UER .02 .10
325 Sean Rooks RC .02 .10
326 Paul Pressey .02 .10
327 James Worthy .25 .60
328 Matt Bullard .02 .10
329 Reggie Smith RC .02 .10
330 Don MacLean UER RC .02 .10
331 John Williams UER .02 .10
332 Frank Johnson .02 .10
333 Hubert Davis UER RC .10 .30
334 Lloyd Daniels RC .02 .10
335 Steve Bardo RC .02 .10
336 Jeff Sanders .02 .10
337 Tree Rollins .02 .10
338 Micheal Williams .02 .10
339 Lorenzo Williams RC .02 .10
340 Harvey Grant .02 .10
341 Avery Johnson .02 .10
342 Bo Kimble .02 .10
343 LaPhonso Ellis UER RC .25 .60
344 Mookie Blaylock .10 .30
345 Isaiah Morris UER RC .02 .10
346 Clarence Weatherspoon RC .25 .60
347 Manute Bol .02 .10
348 Victor Alexander .02 .10
349 Corey Williams RC .02 .10
350 Byron Houston RC .02 .10
351 Stanley Roberts .02 .10
352 Anthony Avent RC .02 .10
353 Vincent Askew .02 .10
354 Herb Williams .02 .10
355 J.R. Reid .02 .10
356 Brad Lohaus .02 .10
357 Reggie Miller .25 .60
358 Blue Edwards .02 .10
359 Tom Tolbert .02 .10
360 Charles Barkley .40 1.00
361 David Robinson .40 1.00
362 Dale Davis .02 .10
363 Robert Werdann UER RC .02 .10
364 Chuck Person .02 .10
365 Alaa Abdelnaby .02 .10
366 Dave Jamerson .02 .10
367 Scottie Pippen .75 2.00
368 Mark Jackson .10 .30
369 Keith Askins .02 .10
370 Marty Conlon .02 .10
371 Chucky Brown .02 .10
372 LaBradford Smith .02 .10
373 Tim Kempton .02 .10
374 Sam Mitchell .02 .10
375 John Salley .02 .10
376 Mario Elie .10 .30
377 Mark West .02 .10
378 David Wingate .02 .10
379 Jaren Jackson RC .10 .30
380 Rumeal Robinson .02 .10
381 Kennard Winchester .02 .10
382 Walter Bond RC .02 .10
383 Isaac Austin RC .10 .30
384 Derrick Coleman .10 .30
385 Larry Smith .02 .10
386 Joe Dumars .25 .60
387 Matt Geiger UER RC .10 .30
388 Stephen Howard RC .02 .10
389 William Bedford .02 .10
390 Jayson Williams .10 .30
391 Kurt Rambis .02 .10
392 Keith Jennings RC .02 .10
393 Steve Kerr UER .10 .30
394 Larry Stewart .02 .10
395 Danny Young .02 .10
396 Doug Overton .02 .10
397 Mark Acres .02 .10
398 John Bagley .02 .10
399 Checklist 201-300 .02 .10
400 Checklist 301-400 .02 .10

1992-93 Stadium Club Beam Team

Comprised of some of the NBA's biggest stars, "Beam Team" cards commemorate Topps' 1993 sponsorship of a six-minute NBA laser animation show called Beams Above the Rim. The show premiered at the 1993 NBA All-Star Game. Afterwards, the laser show embarked on a ten-city tour and was featured in either the pre-game or half-time events in ten NBA arenas. These cards were randomly inserted in second series 15-card packs at a rate of one in 36. The color action player photos on the fronts are bordered on two sides by an angled silver light beam border design with a light refracting pattern. The player's name appears on a white-outlined burnt orange bar superimposed over a basketball icon at the bottom. The backs present a color head shot and, on a basketball icon, career highlights.

COMPLETE SET (21) 60.00 120.00
SER.2 STATED ODDS 1:36
1 Michael Jordan 25.00 60.00
2 Dominique Wilkins 1.50 4.00
3 Shawn Kemp 2.50 6.00
4 Clyde Drexler 1.50 4.00
5 Scottie Pippen 5.00 12.00
6 Chris Mullin 1.50 4.00
7 Reggie Miller 1.50 4.00
8 Glen Rice 1.50 4.00
9 Jeff Hornacek .75 2.00
10 Jeff Malone .60 1.50
11 John Stockton 1.50 4.00
12 Kevin Johnson 1.50 4.00
13 Mark Price .60 1.50
14 Tim Hardaway 2.00 5.00
15 Charles Barkley 2.50 6.00
16 Hakeem Olajuwon 2.50 6.00
17 Karl Malone 2.50 6.00
18 Patrick Ewing 1.50 4.00
19 Dennis Rodman 3.00 8.00
20 David Robinson 2.50 6.00
21 Shaquille O'Neal 25.00 60.00

1993-94 Stadium Club

The 1993-94 Stadium Club set consists of 360 standard-size cards issued in two series of 180 cards. Cards were issued in 12 and 20-card packs. There were 24 twelve-card packs per box. The full-bleed fronts feature glossy color action photos. The player's name is superimposed on the lower portion of the picture in white and gold foil lettering. The borderless backs are divided in half vertically with a torn effect. The left side sports a vertical player photo and on the right side, over a purple background, is biography and player's name and team. A brief section named "The Buzz" provides career highlights. A multi-colored box lists the 1992-93 statistics, career statistics and a Topps Skills Rating System that provides a score including player intimidation, mobility, shooting range and defense. Subsets featured are Triple Double (1-11, 101-111) and High Court (61-69, 170-178) and interspersed NBA Draft Picks. Card number 345 was never issued. Due to an error in numbering, both Toni Kukoc and Chris Corchiani are numbered 336. Corchiani is actually listed on the checklist card as number 345, thus we've listed him below in that order. Also, card number 290 was never issued. Both Nick Van Exel and Terry Cummings are numbered 273. Cummings is listed on the checklist card as number 290, thus we've listed him below in that order. Rookie Cards of note in this set include Vin Baker, Anfernee Hardaway, Allan Houston, Toni Kukoc, Jamal Mashburn, Nick Van Exel and Chris Webber.

COMPLETE SET (360) 20.00 40.00
COMPLETE SERIES 1 (180) 10.00 20.00
COMPLETE SERIES 2 (180) 10.00 20.00
NUMBER 345 NEVER ISSUED
KUKOC AND CORCHIANI NUMBERED 336
1 Michael Jordan TD 1.25 3.00
2 Kenny Anderson TD .12 .30
3 Steve Smith TD .12 .30
4 Kevin Gamble TD .10 .25
5 Detlef Schrempf TD .15 .40
6 Larry Johnson TD .15 .40
7 Brad Daugherty TD .12 .30
8 Rumeal Robinson TD .10 .25
9 Micheal Williams TD .10 .25
10 David Robinson TD .25 .60
11 Sam Perkins TD .10 .25
12 Thurl Bailey .10 .25
13 Sherman Douglas .10 .25
14 Larry Stewart .10 .25
15 Kevin Johnson .15 .40
16 Bill Cartwright .12 .30
17 Larry Nance .12 .30
18 P.J. Brown RC .20 .50
19 Tony Bennett .10 .25
20 Robert Parish .15 .40
21 David Benoit .10 .25
22 Detlef Schrempf .15 .40
23 Hubert Davis .10 .25
24 Donald Hodge .10 .25
25 Hersey Hawkins .10 .25
26 Mark Jackson .12 .30
27 Reggie Williams .10 .25
28 Lionel Simmons .10 .25
29 Ron Harper .12 .30
30 Chris Mills RC .20 .50
31 Danny Schayes .10 .25
32 J.R. Reid .10 .25
33 Willie Burton .10 .25
34 Greg Anthony .10 .25
35 Elden Campbell .10 .25
36 Ervin Johnson RC .20 .50
37 Scott Brooks .10 .25
38 Johnny Newman .10 .25
39 Rex Chapman .10 .25
40 Chuck Person .12 .30
41 John Williams .10 .25
42 Anthony Bowie .10 .25
43 Negele Knight .10 .25
44 Tyrone Corbin .10 .25
45 Jud Buechler .10 .25
46 Adam Keefe .10 .25
47 Glen Rice .15 .40
48 Tracy Murray .10 .25
49 Rick Mahorn .10 .25
50 Vlade Divac .15 .40
51 Eric Murdock .10 .25
52 Isaiah Morris .10 .25
53 Bobby Hurley RC .20 .50
54 Mitch Richmond .15 .40
55 Danny Ainge .15 .40
56 Dikembe Mutombo .15 .40
57 Jeff Hornacek .12 .30
58 Tony Campbell .10 .25
59 Vinny Del Negro .10 .25
60 Xavier McDaniel HC .10 .25
61 Scottie Pippen HC .30 .75
62 Larry Nance HC .12 .30
63 Dikembe Mutombo HC .15 .40
64 Hakeem Olajuwon HC .20 .50
65 Dominique Wilkins HC .20 .50
66 Clarence Weatherspoon HC .10 .25
67 Chris Morris HC .10 .25
68 Patrick Ewing HC .20 .50
69 Kevin Willis HC .10 .25
70 Jon Barry .10 .25
71 Jerry Reynolds .10 .25
72 Sarunas Marciulionis .10 .25
73 Mark West .10 .25
74 B.J. Armstrong .10 .25
75 Greg Kite .10 .25
76 LaSalle Thompson .10 .25
77 Randy White .10 .25
78 Alaa Abdelnaby .10 .25
79 Kevin Brooks .10 .25
80 Vern Fleming .10 .25
81 Doc Rivers .12 .30
82 Shawn Bradley RC .20 .50
83 Wayman Tisdale .10 .25
84 Olden Polynice .10 .25
85 Michael Cage .10 .25
86 Harold Miner .10 .25
87 Doug Smith .10 .25
88 Tom Gugliotta .12 .30
89 Hakeem Olajuwon .20 .50
90 Loy Vaught .10 .25
91 James Worthy .20 .50
92 John Paxson .12 .30
93 Jon Koncak .10 .25
94 Lee Mayberry .10 .25
95 Clarence Weatherspoon .10 .25
96 Mark Eaton .10 .25
97 Rex Walters RC .20 .50
98 Alvin Robertson .10 .25
99 Dan Majerle .15 .40
100 Shaquille O'Neal .60 1.50
101 Derrick Coleman TD .12 .30
102 Hersey Hawkins TD .10 .25
103 Scottie Pippen TD .30 .75
104 Scott Skiles TD .10 .25
105 Rod Strickland TD .10 .25
106 Pooh Richardson TD .10 .25
107 Tom Gugliotta TD .12 .30
108 Mark Jackson TD .12 .30
109 Dikembe Mutombo TD .15 .40
110 Charles Barkley TD .25 .60
111 Otis Thorpe TD .10 .25
112 Malik Sealy .10 .25
113 Mark Macon .10 .25
114 Dee Brown .10 .25
115 Nate McMillan .10 .25
116 John Starks .12 .30
117 Clyde Drexler .20 .50
118 Antoine Carr .10 .25
119 Doug West .10 .25
120 Victor Alexander .10 .25
121 Kenny Gattison .10 .25
122 Spud Webb .12 .30
123 Rumeal Robinson .10 .25
124 Tim Kempton .10 .25
125 Karl Malone .20 .50
126 Randy Woods .10 .25
127 Calbert Cheaney RC .20 .50
128 Johnny Dawkins .10 .25
129 Dominique Wilkins .20 .50
130 Horace Grant .12 .30
131 Bill Laimbeer .12 .30
132 Kenny Smith .12 .30
133 Sedale Threatt .10 .25
134 Brian Shaw .10 .25
135 Dennis Scott .10 .25
136 Mark Bryant .10 .25
137 Xavier McDaniel .10 .25
138 David Wood .10 .25
139 Luther Wright RC .20 .50
140 Lloyd Daniels .10 .25
141 Marlon Maxey UER .10 .25
142 Pooh Richardson .10 .25
143 Jeff Grayer .10 .25
144 LaPhonso Ellis .10 .25
145 Gerald Wilkins .10 .25
146 Dell Curry .10 .25
147 Duane Causwell .10 .25
148 Tim Hardaway .15 .40
149 Isiah Thomas .15 .40
150 Doug Edwards RC .20 .50
151 Anthony Peeler .10 .25
152 Tate George .10 .25
153 Terry Davis .10 .25
154 Sam Perkins .10 .25
155 John Salley .10 .25
156 Vernon Maxwell .10 .25
157 Anthony Avent .10 .25
158 Clifford Robinson .10 .25
159 Corie Blount RC .20 .50
160 Gerald Paddio .10 .25
161 Blair Rasmussen .10 .25
162 Carl Herrera .10 .25
163 Chris Smith .10 .25
164 Pervis Ellison .10 .25
165 Rod Strickland .10 .25
166 Jeff Malone .10 .25
167 Danny Ferry .10 .25
168 Kevin Lynch .10 .25
169 Michael Jordan 1.25 3.00
170 Derrick Coleman HC .12 .30
171 Jerome Kersey HC .10 .25
172 David Robinson HC .25 .60
173 Shawn Kemp HC .20 .50
174 Karl Malone HC .20 .50
175 Shaquille O'Neal HC .60 1.50
176 Alonzo Mourning HC .25 .60
177 Charles Barkley HC .25 .60
178 Larry Johnson HC .15 .40
179 Checklist 1-90 .10 .25
180 Checklist 91-180 .10 .25
181 Michael Jordan FF 1.25 3.00
182 Dominique Wilkins FF .20 .50
183 Dennis Rodman FF .30 .75
184 Scottie Pippen FF .30 .75
185 Larry Johnson FF .15 .40
186 Karl Malone FF .20 .50
187 Clarence Weatherspoon FF .10 .25
188 Charles Barkley FF .25 .60
189 Patrick Ewing FF .20 .50
190 Derrick Coleman FF .12 .30
191 LaBradford Smith .10 .25
192 Derek Harper .12 .30
193 Ken Norman .10 .25
194 Rodney Rogers RC .20 .50
195 Chris Dudley .10 .25
196 Gary Payton .20 .50
197 Andrew Lang .10 .25
198 Billy Owens .10 .25
199 Bryon Russell RC .20 .50
200 Patrick Ewing .20 .50
201 Stacey King .10 .25
202 Grant Long .10 .25
203 Sean Elliott .15 .40
204 Muggsy Bogues .12 .30
205 Kevin Edwards .10 .25
206 Dale Davis .10 .25
207 Dale Ellis .10 .25
208 Terrell Brandon .12 .30
209 Kevin Gamble .10 .25
210 Robert Horry .15 .40
211 Moses Malone UER .15 .40
212 Gary Grant .10 .25
213 Bobby Hurley .15 .40
214 Larry Krystkowiak .10 .25
215 A.C. Green .12 .30
216 Christian Laettner .12 .30
217 Orlando Woolridge .10 .25
218 Craig Ehlo .10 .25
219 Terry Porter .10 .25
220 Jamal Mashburn RC .30 .75
221 Kevin Duckworth .10 .25
222 Shawn Kemp .20 .50
223 Frank Brickowski .10 .25
224 Chris Webber RC 1.00 2.50
225 Charles Oakley .12 .30
226 Jay Humphries .10 .25
227 Steve Kerr .12 .30
228 Tim Perry .10 .25
229 Sleepy Floyd .10 .25
230 Bimbo Coles .10 .25
231 Eddie Johnson .10 .25
232 Terry Mills .10 .25
233 Danny Manning .12 .30
234 Isaiah Rider RC .30 .75
235 Darnell Mee RC .20 .50
236 Haywoode Workman .10 .25
237 Scott Skiles .10 .25
238 Otis Thorpe .10 .25
239 Mike Peplowski RC .20 .50
240 Eric Leckner .10 .25
241 Johnny Newman .10 .25
242 Benoit Benjamin .10 .25
243 Doug Christie .10 .25
244 Acie Earl RC .20 .50
245 Luc Longley .12 .30
246 Tyrone Hill .10 .25
247 Allan Houston RC .40 1.00
248 Joe Kleine .10 .25
249 Mookie Blaylock .10 .25
250 Anthony Bonner .10 .25
251 Luther Wright .10 .25
252 Todd Day .10 .25
253 Kendall Gill .10 .25
254 Mario Elie .10 .25
255 Pete Myers UER .10 .25
256 Jim Les .10 .25
257 Stanley Roberts .10 .25
258 Michael Adams .10 .25
259 Hersey Hawkins .10 .25
260 Shawn Bradley .10 .25
261 Scott Haskin RC .20 .50
262 Corie Blount .10 .25
263 Charles Smith .10 .25
264 Armon Gilliam .10 .25
265 Jamal Mashburn NW .15 .40
266 Anfernee Hardaway NW .50 1.25
267 Shawn Bradley NW .10 .25
268 Chris Webber NW .50 1.25
269 Bobby Hurley NW .10 .25
270 Isaiah Rider NW .15 .40
271 Dino Radja NW .10 .25
272 Chris Mills NW .10 .25
273 Nick Van Exel NW .20 .50
274 Lindsey Hunter NW .10 .25
275 Toni Kukoc NW .25 .60
276 Popeye Jones NW .10 .25
277 Chris Mills .15 .40
278 Ricky Pierce .10 .25
279 Negele Knight .10 .25
280 Kenny Walker .10 .25
281 Nick Van Exel RC .40 1.00
282 Derrick Coleman UER .12 .30
283 Popeye Jones RC .20 .50
284 Derrick McKey .10 .25
285 Rick Fox .10 .25
286 Jerome Kersey .10 .25
287 Steve Smith .12 .30
288 Brian Williams .10 .25
289 Chris Mullin .15 .40
290 Terry Cummings .12 .30
291 Donald Royal .10 .25
292 Alonzo Mourning .25 .60
293 Mike Brown .10 .25
294 Latrell Sprewell .25 .60
295 Oliver Miller .10 .25
296 Terry Dehere RC .20 .50
297 Detlef Schrempf .15 .40
298 Sam Bowie UER .10 .25
299 Chris Morris .10 .25
300 Scottie Pippen .30 .75
301 Warren Kidd RC .20 .50
302 Don MacLean .10 .25
303 Sean Rooks .10 .25
304 Matt Geiger .10 .25
305 Dennis Rodman .30 .75
306 Reggie Miller .20 .50
307 Vin Baker RC .30 .75
308 Anfernee Hardaway RC 1.00 2.50
309 Lindsey Hunter RC .20 .50
310 Stacey Augmon .12 .30
311 Randy Brown .10 .25
312 Anthony Mason .10 .25
313 John Stockton .20 .50
314 Sam Cassell RC .40 1.00
315 Buck Williams .10 .25
316 Bryant Stith .10 .25
317 Brad Daugherty .12 .30
318 Dino Radja RC .20 .50
319 Rony Seikaly .10 .25
320 Charles Barkley .25 .60
321 Avery Johnson .12 .30
322 Mahmoud Abdul-Rauf .10 .25
323 Larry Johnson .15 .40
324 Micheal Williams .10 .25
325 Mark Aguirre .12 .30
326 Jim Jackson .12 .30
327 Antonio Harvey RC .20 .50
328 David Robinson .25 .60
329 Calbert Cheaney .10 .25
330 Kenny Anderson .12 .30
331 Walt Williams .10 .25
332 Kevin Willis .10 .25
333 Nick Anderson .10 .25
334 Rik Smits .12 .30
335 Joe Dumars .15 .40
336 Toni Kukoc RC .50 1.25
337 Harvey Grant .10 .25
338 Tom Chambers .12 .30
339 Blue Edwards .10 .25
340 Mark Price .15 .40
341 Ervin Johnson .10 .25
342 Rolando Blackman .12 .30
343 Scott Burrell RC .20 .50
344 Gheorghe Muresan RC .20 .50
345 Chris Corchiani UER 336 .10 .25
346 Richard Petruska RC .20 .50
347 Dana Barros .10 .25
348 Hakeem Olajuwon FF .20 .50
349 Dee Brown FF .10 .25
350 John Starks FF .12 .30
351 Ron Harper FF .12 .30
352 Chris Webber FF .50 1.25
353 Dan Majerle FF .15 .40
354 Clyde Drexler FF .20 .50
355 Shawn Kemp FF .20 .50
356 David Robinson FF .25 .60
357 Chris Morris FF .10 .25
358 Shaquille O'Neal FF .60 1.50
359 Checklist .10 .25
360 Checklist .10 .25

1993-94 Stadium Club First Day Issue

*FDI: 5X TO 12X BASE CARD HI
SER.1/2 STATED ODDS 1:24
1 Michael Jordan TD 20.00 50.00
100 Shaquille O'Neal 12.00 30.00
169 Michael Jordan 25.00 60.00
181 Michael Jordan FF 25.00 60.00
266 Anfernee Hardaway NW 10.00 25.00
268 Chris Webber NW 10.00 25.00
352 Chris Webber FF 10.00 25.00

1993-94 Stadium Club Beam Team

Randomly inserted in first and second series 12-card and 20-card foil packs at a rate of one in 24, cards from this standard-size 27-card set features a selection of top NBA stars and rookies. Cards were issued in two series of 13 and 14, respectively. The design consists of borderless fronts with color player action photos set against game-crowd backgrounds. Silver metallic beams appear near the bottom above the player's name. The horizontal back carries a color action photo on one side, with player profile on the other. The cards are numbered on the back as "X of 27."

COMPLETE SET (27) 25.00 60.00
COMPLETE SERIES 1 (13) 15.00 40.00
COMPLETE SERIES 2 (14) 8.00 20.00
SER.1/2 STATED ODDS 1:24
1 Shaquille O'Neal 3.00 8.00
2 Mark Price .40 1.00
3 Patrick Ewing .50 1.25
4 Michael Jordan 15.00 40.00
5 Charles Barkley .60 1.50
6 Reggie Miller .50 1.25
7 Derrick Coleman .30 .75
8 Dominique Wilkins .50 1.25
9 Karl Malone .50 1.25
10 Alonzo Mourning .60 1.50
11 Tim Hardaway .40 1.00
12 Hakeem Olajuwon .50 1.25
13 David Robinson .60 1.50
14 Dan Majerle .40 1.00
15 Larry Johnson .40 1.00
16 LaPhonso Ellis .25 .60
17 Nick Van Exel .75 2.00
18 Scottie Pippen .75 2.00
19 John Stockton .50 1.25
20 Bobby Hurley .40 1.00
21 Chris Webber 2.00 5.00
22 Jamal Mashburn .60 1.50
23 Anfernee Hardaway 2.00 5.00
24 Isaiah Rider .60 1.50
25 Ken Norman .25 .60
26 Danny Manning .30 .75
27 Calbert Cheaney .40 1.00

1993-94 Stadium Club Big Tips

Randomly inserted about one in every four packs, these 27 team logo cards measure the standard size. The horizontal black fronts are framed by a thin white line and carry the words "NBA Showdown '94," the NBA logo and the team name and logo within a team-colored stripe across the bottom. The back carries game hints for the Electronic Arts NBA Showdown '94 and a videogame offer. The logo cards are unnumbered and checklisted below in alphabetical team order.

COMPLETE SET (27) 2.50 5.00
COMMON CARD (1-27) .08 .25

1993-94 Stadium Club Frequent Flyer Points

Randomly inserted in second series packs were 100 different Frequent Flyer point cards with 20 of the best NBA jumpshot stars each having five different point cards. The insertion rate was one in every six packs. Upon collecting 50 points or more for one particular player the collector could send the cards to Topps and receive a limited edition Frequent Flyer Upgrade card for the same player. The blue-bordered fronts features a rainbow colored map of the United States with a diagram of when, where and how many points the player scored. The players name appears in yellow in the upper right. The purple-bordered back features the rules on a ghosted sky background.

COMPLETE SET (100) 10.00 25.00
1 Charles Barkley .15 .40
2 Dee Brown .05 .15
3 Derrick Coleman .07 .20
4 Clyde Drexler .12 .30
5 Patrick Ewing .12 .30
6 Ron Harper .07 .20
7 Larry Johnson .10 .25
8 Shawn Kemp .12 .30
9 Dan Majerle .10 .25
10 Karl Malone .12 .30
11 Chris Morris .05 .15
12 Hakeem Olajuwon .12 .30
13 Shaquille O'Neal .40 1.00
14 Scottie Pippen .20 .50
15 David Robinson .15 .40
16 Dennis Rodman .20 .50
17 John Starks .07 .20
18 Clarence Weatherspoon .05 .15
19 Chris Webber .50 1.25
20 Dominique Wilkins .12 .30

1993-94 Stadium Club Frequent Flyer Upgrades

Cards from this 20-card standard size set are based upon the Frequent Flyer subsets in the basic 1993-94 Stadium Club issue. Upgrades are identical to the basic cards with the exception of a chromium like metallic gloss and Upgrade logo on front. Upgrades were available only through a mail offer based on Frequent Flyer Point cards which were randomly inserted at a rate of 1 in every 6 second series packs. Each of the 21 players featured in the Frequent Flyer subsets (except for Michael Jordan) had five different point cards (based upon point totals derived from actual games during the season) making for a total of 100 different point cards. Since none of the point cards feature player photos, none trade for a premium and are priced below as expired point cards. To obtain a

Frequent Flyer Upgrade card, collectors had to accumulate 50 points or more of an individual player and redeem them by September 15, 1994.

COMPLETE SET (20) 25.00 60.00
POINT CARDS: SER.2 STATED ODDS 1:6
182 Dominique Wilkins 2.00 5.00
183 Dennis Rodman 3.00 8.00
184 Scottie Pippen 3.00 8.00
185 Larry Johnson 1.50 4.00
186 Karl Malone 2.00 5.00
187 Clarence Weatherspoon 1.00 2.50
188 Charles Barkley 2.50 6.00
189 Patrick Ewing 2.00 5.00
190 Derrick Coleman 1.25 3.00
348 Hakeem Olajuwon 2.00 5.00
349 Dee Brown 1.00 2.50
350 John Starks 1.25 3.00
351 Ron Harper 1.25 3.00
352 Chris Webber 5.00 12.00
353 Dan Majerle 1.50 4.00
354 Clyde Drexler 2.00 5.00
355 Shawn Kemp 2.00 5.00
356 David Robinson 2.50 6.00
357 Chris Morris 1.00 2.50
358 Shaquille O'Neal 4.00 10.00

1993-94 Stadium Club Rim Rockers

Randomly inserted in second series 12-card packs at a rate of one in 24, these six standard-size cards feature some of the NBA's top dunkers. Fronts contain color player action shots. The player's name appears near the bottom. His first name is printed in white lowercase lettering; his last is gold-foil stamped in uppercase lettering. The back carries another borderless color player action shot, but its right side is ghosted, blue-screened, and overprinted with career highlights in white lettering. The cards are numbered on the back as "X of 6."

COMPLETE SET (6) 2.00 5.00
SER.2 STATED ODDS 1:24
1 Shaquille O'Neal 1.50 4.00
2 Harold Miner .15 .40
3 Charles Barkley .40 1.00
4 Dominique Wilkins .30 .75
5 Shawn Kemp .30 .75
6 Robert Horry .25 .60

1993-94 Stadium Club Super Teams

Randomly inserted in first series 12 and 20-card foil packs at a rate of one in 24, cards from this standard-size 27-card set feature borderless fronts with color team action photos. The team name appears in gold-foil lettering at the bottom. The back features the NBA Super Team Card rules. If the team shown on the card won its division, conference or league championship, the collector could have redeemed it for special prizes until Nov. 1, 1994. Atlanta, Houston, New York and Seattle were all winners. Their cards are currently in shorter supply than non-winner Super Team cards. The four winning teams are designated below with a "W". In addition, Conference, Division and Finals winner cards have "C", "D" and "F" designations.

COMPLETE SET (27) 7.50 15.00
SER.1 STATED ODDS 1:24
1 Atlanta/D.Wilkins WD .30 .75
2 Boston Celtics .25 .60
(Xavier McDaniel
Robert Parish)
3 Charlotte/LJ/Mourning .40 1.00
4 Chicago Bulls .20 .50
(Horace Grant)
5 Cleveland Cavaliers .20 .50
(Brad Daugherty
John Williams)
6 Dallas Mavericks .15 .40
(Group photo)
7 Denver Nuggets .25 .60
(Dikembe Mutombo
Kevin Brooks)
8 Detroit Pistons .15 .40
(Group photo)
9 Golden State Warriors .15 .40
(Group photo)
10 Houston/Group WCDF 2.50 6.00
11 Indiana Pacers .15 .40
(Group photo)
12 Los Angeles Clippers .20 .50
(Danny Manning
Ron Harper)
13 Los Angeles Lakers .15 .40
(Group photo)
14 Miami Heat .15 .40
(John Salley
Willie Burton)
15 Milwaukee Bucks .15 .40
(Group photo)
16 Minnesota Timberwolves .20 .50
(Christian Laettner
Felton Spencer)
17 New Jersey Nets .20 .50
(Derrick Coleman)
18 New York/P.Ewing WCD 1.00 2.50
19 Orlando/S.O'Neal 2.50 6.00
20 Philadelphia 76ers .20 .50
(Clarence Weatherspoon
Jeff Hornacek)
21 Phoenix/C.Barkley .40 1.00
22 Portland Trail Blazers .15 .40
(Buck Williams)
23 Sacramento Kings .15 .40
(Lionel Simmons)
24 San Antonio/D.Robinson .40 1.00
25 Seattle/S.Kemp WD .75 2.00
26 Utah Jazz .15 .40
(Group photo)
27 Washington Bullets .15 .40
(Group photo)

1993-94 Stadium Club Super Teams Division Winners

Collectors who pulled either a Hawks, Knicks, Rockets or Sonics Super Team insert card (randomly inserted in 1993-94 Stadium Club series 1 packs) could exchange the card for an 11-card Division Winners team set. The offer expired November 1, 1994. The cards are identical to their regular issue counterparts, except for the gold-foil Division Winner logo on their fronts. In the listing below, the suffixes H, K, R, and S have been added to denote Hawks, Knicks, Rockets and Supersonics.

COMPLETE BAG HAWKS (11) 2.00 5.00
COMPLETE BAG KNICKS (11) 3.00 6.00
COMPLETE BAG ROCKETS (11) 5.00 10.00
COMPLETE BAG SONICS (11) 5.00 10.00
H46 Adam Keefe .25 .60
H93 Jon Koncak .25 .60
H129 Dominique Wilkins .50 1.25
H150 Doug Edwards .40 1.00
H197 Andrew Lang .25 .60
H218 Craig Ehlo .25 .60
H233 Danny Manning .30 .75
H249 Mookie Blaylock .25 .60
H310 Stacey Augmon .30 .75
H332 Kevin Willis .25 .60
K23 Hubert Davis .25 .60
K34 Greg Anthony .25 .60
K81 Doc Rivers .30 .75
K116 John Starks .30 .75
K192 Derek Harper .30 .75
K200 Patrick Ewing 1.00 2.50
K225 Charles Oakley .30 .75
K250 Anthony Bonner .25 .60
K263 Charles Smith .25 .60
K312 Anthony Mason .25 .60
R37 Scott Brooks .25 .60
R89 Hakeem Olajuwon 2.50 6.00
R132 Kenny Smith .30 .75
R156 Vernon Maxwell .25 .60
R162 Carl Herrera .25 .60
R210 Robert Horry 1.00 2.50
R238 Otis Thorpe .25 .60
R254 Mario Elie .25 .60
R314 Sam Cassell .75 2.00
R346 Richard Petruska .40 1.00
S85 Michael Cage .25 .60
S115 Nate McMillan .25 .60
S154 Sam Perkins .25 .60
S173 Shawn Kemp HC .50 1.25
S196 Gary Payton 2.50 6.00
S222 Shawn Kemp 2.50 6.00
S253 Kendall Gill .25 .60
S278 Ricky Pierce .25 .60
S297 Detlef Schrempf .40 1.00
S341 Ervin Johnson .40 1.00
HD1 Hawks DW Super Team .40 1.00
KD18 Knicks DW Super Team .40 1.00
RD10 Rocket DW Super Team .40 1.00
SD25 Sonics DW Super Team .40 1.00

1993-94 Stadium Club Super Teams Master Photos

Collectors who pulled either a Knicks or Rockets Super Team insert card (randomly inserted in 1993-94 Stadium Club series 1 packs) could exchange the card via mail for a 11-card Master Photo set. The expiration date for the offer was November 1, 1994. Measuring 5" by 7", the cards are numbered on the back "X of 10." In the listing below, the suffixes K and R have been added to denote Knicks and Rockets.

COMPLETE BAG KNICKS (11) 5.00 10.00
COMPLETE BAG ROCKETS (11) 7.50 15.00
K1 Greg Anthony .60 1.50
K2 Anthony Bonner .60 1.50
K3 Hubert Davis .60 1.50
K4 Patrick Ewing 1.50 4.00
K5 Derek Harper .75 2.00
K6 Anthony Mason .60 1.50
K7 Charles Oakley .75 2.00
K8 Doc Rivers .75 2.00
K9 Charles Smith .60 1.50
K10 John Starks .75 2.00
KMP Knicks MP Superteam .40 1.00
R1 Scott Brooks .60 1.50
R2 Sam Cassell 2.00 5.00
R3 Mario Elie .60 1.50
R4 Carl Herrera .60 1.50
R5 Robert Horry 1.00 2.50
R6 Vernon Maxwell .60 1.50
R7 Hakeem Olajuwon 4.00 10.00
R8 Richard Petruska 1.00 2.50
R9 Kenny Smith .75 2.00
R10 Otis Thorpe .60 1.50
RMP Rockets MP Superteam .40 1.00

1993-94 Stadium Club Super Teams NBA Finals

COMPLETE SET (361) 20.00 50.00
*STARS: .75X TO 2X HI COLUMN
*RCs: .6X TO 1.5X HI
169 Michael Jordan 5.00 12.00

1994-95 Stadium Club

The 362 standard size cards that comprise the 1994-95 Stadium Club set were issued in two separate series of 182 and 180 cards each. Cards were primarily distributed in 12-card packs, each with a suggested retail price of $2.00. Full-bleed fronts feature full-color action shots with player's name placed along the bottom in foil. Topical subsets featured are College Teammates (100-114), Draft Picks (172, 179-182), All-Import (201-205, 251-255), Back Court Tandem (226-230, 276-280, 326-330), and Faces of the Game (353-362). Other topical subsets, such as Thru the Glass as well as First and Second Round '94 Draft Picks, are scattered throughout the set. Autographed cards of Reggie Miller were randomly inserted one per box into special retail boxes. Rookie Cards of note include Grant Hill, Juwan Howard, Eddie Jones, Jason Kidd and Glenn Robinson.

COMPLETE SET (362) 15.00 40.00
COMPLETE SERIES 1 (182) 8.00 20.00
COMPLETE SERIES 2 (180) 8.00 20.00
1 Patrick Ewing .20 .50
2 Patrick Ewing TG .20 .50
3 Bimbo Coles .10 .25
4 Elden Campbell .10 .25
5 Brent Price .10 .25
6 Hubert Davis .10 .25
7 Donald Royal .10 .25
8 Tim Perry .10 .25
9 Chris Webber .25 .60
10 Chris Webber TG .25 .60
11 Brad Daugherty .12 .30
12 P.J. Brown .10 .25
13 Charles Barkley .25 .60
14 Mario Elie .10 .25
15 Tyrone Hill .10 .25
16 Anfernee Hardaway .25 .60
17 Anfernee Hardaway TG .25 .60
18 Toni Kukoc .20 .50
19 Chris Morris .10 .25
20 Gerald Wilkins .10 .25
21 David Benoit .10 .25
22 Kevin Duckworth .10 .25
23 Derrick Coleman .12 .30
24 Adam Keefe .10 .25
25 Marlon Maxey .10 .25
26 Vern Fleming .10 .25
27 Jeff Malone .10 .25
28 Rodney Rogers .10 .25
29 Terry Mills .10 .25
30 Doug West .10 .25
31 Doug West TTG .10 .25
32 Shaquille O'Neal .40 1.00
33 Scottie Pippen .30 .75
34 Lee Mayberry .10 .25
35 Dale Ellis .10 .25
36 Cedric Ceballos .10 .25
37 Lionel Simmons .10 .25
38 Kenny Gattison .10 .25
39 Popeye Jones .10 .25
40 Jerome Kersey .10 .25
41 Jerome Kersey TTG .10 .25
42 Larry Stewart .10 .25
43 Rod Strickland .10 .25
44 Chris Mills .10 .25
45 Latrell Sprewell .20 .50
46 Haywoode Workman .10 .25
47 Charles Smith .10 .25
48 Detlef Schrempf .15 .40
49 Gary Grant .10 .25
50 Gary Grant TTG .10 .25
51 Tom Chambers .12 .30
52 J.R. Reid .10 .25
53 Mookie Blaylock .10 .25
54 Mookie Blaylock TTG .10 .25
55 Rony Seikaly .10 .25
56 Isaiah Rider .15 .40
57 Isaiah Rider TTG .15 .40
58 Nick Anderson .10 .25
59 Victor Alexander .10 .25
60 Lucious Harris .10 .25
61 Mark Macon .10 .25
62 Otis Thorpe .10 .25
63 Randy Woods .10 .25
64 Clyde Drexler .20 .50
65 Dikembe Mutombo .15 .40
66 Todd Day .10 .25
67 Greg Anthony .10 .25
68 Sherman Douglas .10 .25
69 Chris Mullin .15 .40
70 Kevin Johnson .15 .40
71 Kendall Gill .10 .25
72 Dennis Rodman .30 .75
73 Dennis Rodman TG .30 .75
74 Jeff Turner .10 .25
75 John Stockton .20 .50
76 John Stockton TTG .20 .50
77 Doug Edwards .10 .25
78 Jim Jackson .10 .25
79 Hakeem Olajuwon .20 .50
80 Glen Rice .15 .40
81 Christian Laettner .12 .30
82 Terry Porter .10 .25
83 Joe Dumars .15 .40
84 David Wingate .10 .25
85 B.J. Armstrong .10 .25
86 Derrick McKey .10 .25
87 Elmore Spencer .10 .25
88 Walt Williams .10 .25
89 Shawn Bradley .10 .25
90 Acie Earl .10 .25
91 Acie Earl TTG .10 .25
92 Randy Brown .10 .25
93 Grant Long .10 .25
94 Terry Dehere .10 .25
95 Spud Webb .12 .30
96 Lindsey Hunter .10 .25
97 Blair Rasmussen .10 .25
98 Tim Hardaway .15 .40
99 Kevin Edwards .10 .25
100 P.Ewing/R.Williams CT .20 .50
101 C.Person/C.Barkley CT .25 .60
102 Abdul-Rauf/S.O'Neal CT .40 1.00
103 R.Seikaly/D.Coleman CT .12 .30
104 H.Olajuwon/C.Drexler CT .20 .50
105 C.Mullin/M.Jackson CT .15 .40
106 R.Horry/L.Sprewell CT .20 .50
107 P.Richardson/R.Miller CT .20 .50
108 D.Scott/K.Anderson CT .12 .30
109 K.Gill/K.Norman CT .10 .25
110 S.Skiles/K.Willis CT .10 .25
111 T.Mills/G.Rice CT .15 .40
112 C.Laettner/B.Hurley CT .12 .30
113 S.Augmon/L.Johnson CT .15 .40
114 S.Perkins/J.Worthy CT .20 .50
115 Carl Herrera .10 .25
116 Sam Bowie .10 .25
117 Gary Payton .15 .40
118 Danny Ainge .15 .40
119 Danny Ainge TTG .15 .40
120 Luc Longley .12 .30
121 Antonio Davis .10 .25
122 Terry Cummings .12 .30
123 Terry Cummings TTG .12 .30
124 Mark Price .15 .40
125 Jamal Mashburn .15 .40
126 Mahmoud Abdul-Rauf .10 .25
127 Charles Oakley .12 .30
128 Steve Smith .12 .30
129 Vin Baker .15 .40
130 Robert Horry .15 .40
131 Doug Christie .10 .25
132 Wayman Tisdale .10 .25
133 Wayman Tisdale TTG .10 .25
134 Muggsy Bogues .12 .30
135 Dino Radja .10 .25
136 Jeff Hornacek .12 .30
137 Gheorghe Muresan .10 .25
138 Loy Vaught .10 .25
139 Loy Vaught TTG .10 .25
140 Benoit Benjamin .10 .25
141 Johnny Dawkins .10 .25
142 Allan Houston .15 .40
143 Jon Barry .10 .25
144 Reggie Miller .20 .50
145 Kevin Willis .10 .25
146 James Worthy .20 .50
147 James Worthy TTG .20 .50
148 Scott Burrell .10 .25
149 Tom Gugliotta .10 .25
150 LaPhonso Ellis .10 .25
151 Doug Smith .10 .25
152 A.C. Green .12 .30
153 A.C. Green TTG .12 .30
154 George Lynch .10 .25
155 Sam Perkins .10 .25
156 Corie Blount .10 .25
157 Xavier McDaniel .10 .25
158 Xavier McDaniel TTG .10 .25
159 Eric Murdock .10 .25
160 David Robinson .25 .60
161 Karl Malone .20 .50
162 Karl Malone TTG .20 .50
163 Clarence Weatherspoon .10 .25
164 Calbert Cheaney .10 .25
165 Tom Hammonds .10 .25
166 Tom Hammonds TTG .10 .25
167 Alonzo Mourning .20 .50
168 Clifford Robinson .10 .25
169 Micheal Williams .10 .25
170 Ervin Johnson .10 .25
171 Mike Gminski .10 .25
172 Jason Kidd RC .75 2.00
173 Anthony Bonner .10 .25
174 Stacey King .10 .25
175 Rex Chapman .10 .25
176 Greg Graham .10 .25
177 Stanley Roberts .10 .25
178 Mitch Richmond .15 .40
179 Eric Montross RC .12 .30
180 Eddie Jones RC .50 1.25
181 Grant Hill RC .75 2.00
182 Donyell Marshall RC .15 .40
183 Glenn Robinson RC .30 .75
184 Dominique Wilkins .20 .50
185 Mark Price .15 .40
186 Anthony Mason .10 .25
187 Tyrone Corbin .10 .25
188 Dale Davis .10 .25
189 Nate McMillan .10 .25
190 Jason Kidd .50 1.25
191 John Salley .10 .25
192 Keith Jennings .10 .25
193 Mark Bryant .10 .25
194 Sleepy Floyd .10 .25
195 Grant Hill .50 1.25
196 Joe Kleine .10 .25
197 Anthony Peeler .10 .25
198 Malik Sealy .10 .25
199 Kenny Walker .10 .25
200 Donyell Marshall .15 .40
201 Vlade Divac AI .15 .40
202 Dino Radja AI .10 .25
203 Carl Herrera AI .10 .25
204 Olden Polynice AI .10 .25
205 Patrick Ewing AI .20 .50
206 Willie Anderson .10 .25
207 Mitch Richmond .15 .40
208 John Crotty .10 .25
209 Tracy Murray .10 .25
210 Juwan Howard RC .25 .60
211 Robert Parish .15 .40
212 Steve Kerr .12 .30
213 Anthony Bowie .10 .25
214 Tim Breaux .10 .25
215 Sharone Wright RC .12 .30
216 Brian Williams .10 .25
217 Rick Fox .10 .25
218 Harold Miner .10 .25
219 Duane Ferrell .10 .25
220 Lamond Murray RC .15 .40
221 Blue Edwards .10 .25
222 Bill Cartwright .12 .30
223 Sergei Bazarevich RC .15 .40
224 Herb Williams .10 .25
225 Brian Grant RC .25 .60
226 D.Harper/J.Starks BCT .12 .30
227 R.Strickland/C.Drexler BCT .20 .50
228 K.Johnson/D.Majerle BCT .15 .40
229 L.Hunter/J.Dumars BCT .15 .40
230 T.Hardaway/L.Sprewell BCT .20 .50
231 Bill Wennington .10 .25
232 Brian Shaw .10 .25
233 Jamie Watson RC .10 .25
234 Chris Whitney .10 .25
235 Eric Montross .07 .20
236 Kenny Smith .12 .30
237 Andrew Lang .10 .25
238 Lorenzo Williams .10 .25
239 Dana Barros .10 .25
240 Eddie Jones .30 .75
241 Harold Ellis .10 .25
242 James Edwards .10 .25
243 Don MacLean .10 .25
244 Ed Pinckney .10 .25
245 Carlos Rogers RC .12 .30
246 Michael Adams .10 .25
247 Rex Walters .10 .25
248 John Starks .12 .30
249 Terrell Brandon .10 .25
250 Khalid Reeves RC .12 .30
251 Dominique Wilkins AI .20 .50
252 Toni Kukoc AI .20 .50
253 Rick Fox AI .10 .25
254 Detlef Schrempf AI .15 .40
255 Rik Smits AI .12 .30
256 Johnny Dawkins .10 .25
257 Dan Majerle .15 .40
258 Mike Brown .10 .25
259 Byron Scott .12 .30
260 Jalen Rose RC .40 1.00
261 Byron Houston .10 .25
262 Frank Brickowski .10 .25
263 Vernon Maxwell .10 .25
264 Craig Ehlo .10 .25
265 Yinka Dare RC .10 .25
266 Dee Brown .10 .25
267 Felton Spencer .10 .25
268 Harvey Grant .10 .25
269 Nick Van Exel .15 .40
270 Bob Martin .10 .25
271 Hersey Hawkins .10 .25
272 Scott Williams .10 .25
273 Sarunas Marciulionis .10 .25
274 Kevin Gamble .10 .25
275 Clifford Rozier RC .10 .25
276 B.J. Armstrong/R.Harper BCT .12 .30
277 J.Stockton/J.Hornacek BCT .20 .50
278 B.Hurley/M.Richmond BCT .15 .40
279 A.Hardaway/D.Scott BCT .25 .60
280 J.Kidd/J.Jackson BCT .50 1.25
281 Ron Harper .12 .30
282 Chuck Person .12 .30
283 John Williams .10 .25
284 Robert Pack .10 .25
285 Aaron McKie RC .15 .40
286 Chris Smith .10 .25
287 Horace Grant .12 .30
288 Oliver Miller .10 .25
289 Derek Harper .12 .30
290 Eric Mobley RC .10 .25
291 Scott Skiles .10 .25
292 Olden Polynice .10 .25
293 Mark Jackson .12 .30
294 Wayman Tisdale .10 .25
295 Tony Dumas RC .15 .40
296 Bryon Russell .10 .25
297 Vlade Divac .15 .40
298 David Wesley .10 .25
299 Askia Jones RC .15 .40
300 B.J. Tyler RC .10 .25
301 Hakeem Olajuwon AI .20 .50
302 Luc Longley AI .12 .30
303 Rony Seikaly AI .10 .25
304 Sarunas Marciulionis AI .10 .25
305 Dikembe Mutombo AI .15 .40
306 Ken Norman .10 .25
307 Dell Curry .10 .25
308 Danny Ferry .10 .25
309 Shawn Kemp .15 .40
310 Dickey Simpkins RC .12 .30
311 Johnny Newman .10 .25
312 Dwayne Schintzius .10 .25
313 Sean Elliott .15 .40
314 Sean Rooks .10 .25
315 Bill Curley RC .10 .25
316 Bryant Stith .10 .25
317 Pooh Richardson .10 .25
318 Jim McIlvaine RC .12 .30
319 Dennis Scott .10 .25
320 Wesley Person RC .15 .40
321 Bobby Hurley .10 .25
322 Armon Gilliam .10 .25
323 Rik Smits .12 .30
324 Tony Smith .10 .25
325 Monty Williams RC .12 .30
326 G.Payton/K.Gill BCT .15 .40
327 M.Blaylock/S.Augmon BCT .12 .30
328 M.Jackson/R.Miller BCT .20 .50
329 S.Cassell/V.Maxwell BCT .15 .40
330 H.Miner/K.Reeves BCT .12 .30
331 Vinny Del Negro .10 .25
332 Billy Owens .10 .25
333 Mark West .10 .25
334 Matt Geiger .10 .25
335 Greg Minor RC .15 .40
336 Larry Johnson .15 .40
337 Donald Hodge .10 .25
338 Aaron Williams RC .15 .40
339 Jay Humphries .10 .25
340 Charlie Ward RC .15 .40
341 Scott Brooks .10 .25
342 Stacey Augmon .12 .30
343 Will Perdue .10 .25
344 Dale Ellis .10 .25
345 Brooks Thompson RC .12 .30
346 Manute Bol .10 .25
347 Kenny Anderson .12 .30
348 Willie Burton .10 .25
349 Michael Cage .10 .25
350 Danny Manning .12 .30
351 Ricky Pierce .10 .25
352 Sam Cassell .15 .40
353 Reggie Miller FG .20 .50
354 David Robinson FG .25 .60
355 Shaquille O'Neal FG .40 1.00
356 Scottie Pippen FG .30 .75
357 Alonzo Mourning FG .20 .50
358 Clarence Weatherspoon FG .10 .25
359 Derrick Coleman FG .12 .30
360 Charles Barkley FG .25 .60
361 Karl Malone FG .20 .50
362 Chris Webber FG .25 .60
NNO Reggie Miller AU 20.00 50.00

1994-95 Stadium Club First Day Issue

*STARS: 6X TO 15X BASE CARD HI
*RCs: 5X TO 12X BASE HI
SER.1/2 STATED ODDS 1:24

1994-95 Stadium Club Beam Team

Randomly inserted at a rate of 1 in every 24 second series packs, this 27-card standard-size set features a star player from each NBA team spotlit with lazer light foil. The borderless fronts feature a player photo with his name in the upper left corner and the words "Beam Team" in funky lettering on the bottom. The backs are split between a player photo and some notes. Vital statistics are in the lower left corner and the cards are numbered in the lower corner as "X" of 27. The set is sequenced in alphabetical order by team.

COMPLETE SET (27) 25.00 50.00
SER.2 STATED ODDS 1:24
1 Mookie Blaylock .50 1.25
2 Dominique Wilkins 1.00 2.50
3 Alonzo Mourning 1.00 2.50
4 Toni Kukoc 1.00 2.50
5 Mark Price .75 2.00
6 Jason Kidd 4.00 10.00
7 Jalen Rose 2.00 5.00
8 Grant Hill 4.00 10.00
9 Latrell Sprewell 1.00 2.50
10 Hakeem Olajuwon 1.00 2.50
11 Reggie Miller 1.00 2.50
12 Lamond Murray .75 2.00
13 George Lynch .50 1.25
14 Khalid Reeves .60 1.50
15 Glenn Robinson 1.50 4.00
16 Donyell Marshall .75 2.00
17 Derrick Coleman .60 1.50
18 Patrick Ewing 1.00 2.50
19 Shaquille O'Neal 4.00 10.00
20 Clarence Weatherspoon .50 1.25
21 Charles Barkley 1.25 3.00
22 Clifford Robinson .50 1.25
23 Bobby Hurley .50 1.25
24 David Robinson 1.25 3.00
25 Shawn Kemp .75 2.00
26 Karl Malone 1.00 2.50
27 Chris Webber 1.25 3.00

1994-95 Stadium Club Clear Cut

Randomly inserted in all first series packs at a rate of one in 12, cards from this 27-card acetate set spotlight one key player from each NBA team. The set has "see through" fronts with some statistical information on the back. The player is identified on the right side of the card and the words "Clear Cut" are located in the bottom right. The set is sequenced in alphabetical order by team.

COMPLETE SET (27) 10.00 25.00
SER.1 STATED ODDS 1:12
1 Stacey Augmon .50 1.25
2 Dino Radja .40 1.00
3 Alonzo Mourning .75 2.00
4 Scottie Pippen 2.50 6.00
5 Gerald Wilkins .40 1.00
6 Jamal Mashburn .60 1.50
7 Dikembe Mutombo .60 1.50
8 Lindsey Hunter .40 1.00
9 Chris Mullin .60 1.50
10 Hakeem Olajuwon .75 2.00
11 Reggie Miller .75 2.00
12 Gary Grant .40 1.00
13 Doug Christie .40 1.00
14 Steve Smith .50 1.25
15 Vin Baker .60 1.50
16 Christian Laettner .50 1.25
17 Derrick Coleman .50 1.25
18 Charles Oakley .50 1.25
19 Dennis Scott .40 1.00
20 Clarence Weatherspoon .40 1.00
21 Charles Barkley 1.50 4.00
22 Clifford Robinson .40 1.00
23 Mitch Richmond .60 1.50
24 David Robinson 1.00 2.50
25 Shawn Kemp .60 1.50
26 Karl Malone .75 2.00
27 Don MacLean .40 1.00

1994-95 Stadium Club Dynasty and Destiny

This 20-card standard-size set was randomly inserted in first series foil packs at a rate of one in six and were also inserted one per first series rack pack. This set features a mixture of youthful phenoms paired up with a matching veteran star. The borderless fronts feature player photos, the player's name in the upper left corner and either the word "Destiny" or "Dynasty" in the lower right. The back has a player photo in a lower corner with a brief note and stats on the other side.

COMPLETE SET (20) 4.00 10.00
SER.1 STATED ODDS 1:6
1A Mark Price .40 1.00
1B Kenny Anderson .30 .75
2A Karl Malone .50 1.25
2B Derrick Coleman .30 .75
3A John Stockton .50 1.25
3B Anfernee Hardaway .60 1.50
4A Mitch Richmond .40 1.00
4B Jim Jackson .25 .60
5A James Worthy .50 1.25
5B Jamal Mashburn .40 1.00
6A Patrick Ewing .50 1.25
6B Alonzo Mourning .50 1.25
7A Hakeem Olajuwon .50 1.25
7B Shaquille O'Neal 1.00 2.50
8A Clyde Drexler .50 1.25
8B Isaiah Rider .40 1.00
9A Scottie Pippen .75 2.00
9B Latrell Sprewell .50 1.25
10A Charles Barkley .60 1.50
10B Chris Webber .60 1.50

1994-95 Stadium Club Rising Stars

Randomly inserted in all first series packs at a rate of one in 24, cards from this 10-card standard-size set feature a selection of young NBA stars. Card fronts feature full-color player action shots cut out against etched-foil backgrounds, with a prismatic galaxy design.

COMPLETE SET (12) 15.00 40.00
SER.1 STATED ODDS 1:24
1 Kenny Anderson 1.00 2.50
2 Latrell Sprewell 1.50 4.00
3 Jamal Mashburn 1.25 3.00
4 Alonzo Mourning 1.50 4.00
5 Shaquille O'Neal 6.00 15.00
6 LaPhonso Ellis .75 2.00
7 Chris Webber 3.00 8.00
8 Isaiah Rider 1.25 3.00
9 Dikembe Mutombo 1.25 3.00
10 Anfernee Hardaway 3.00 8.00
11 Antonio Davis .75 2.00
12 Robert Horry 1.25 3.00

1994-95 Stadium Club Super Skills

Randomly inserted at a rate of 1 in every 24 second series 12-card packs and seeded one per second series retail rack pack, cards from this 25-card standard-size set feature Topps selection of the five top players at each position in the NBA. Card fronts feature a multi-hued rainbow foil background.

COMPLETE SET (25) 10.00 25.00
SER.2 STATED ODDS 1:24
1 Mark Price .50 1.25
2 Tim Hardaway .50 1.25
3 Kevin Johnson .50 1.25
4 John Stockton .60 1.50
5 Mookie Blaylock .30 .75
6 Reggie Miller .60 1.50
7 Jeff Hornacek .40 1.00
8 Latrell Sprewell .60 1.50
9 John Starks .40 1.00
10 Nate McMillan .30 .75
11 Chris Mullin .50 1.25
12 Toni Kukoc .60 1.50
13 Anthony Mason .30 .75
14 Robert Horry .50 1.25
15 Scottie Pippen 1.00 2.50
16 Charles Barkley .75 2.00
17 Dennis Rodman 1.00 2.50
18 Karl Malone .60 1.50
19 Chris Webber .75 2.00
20 Charles Oakley .40 1.00
21 Patrick Ewing .60 1.50
22 Shaquille O'Neal 1.25 3.00
23 Dikembe Mutombo .50 1.25
24 David Robinson .75 2.00
25 Hakeem Olajuwon .60 1.50

1994-95 Stadium Club Super Teams

Randomly inserted in all first series packs at a rate of one in 24, cards from this 27-card standard-size set feature an action shot or group photo from each team in the league. Teams that won either their Division, their Conference or the NBA Finals were redeemable for special team sets or other prizes. The expiration date for Super Team cards was December 31st, 1995. The five winning cards (Houston, Indiana, Orlando, Phoenix and San Antonio) carry "W" designations. In addition "C", "D" and "F" designations are used to denote conference, division and finals winners.

COMPLETE SET (27) 12.00 30.00
SER.1 STATED ODDS 1:24
SUP.TEAMS RANDOM INSERTS IN SER.1 PACKS
1 Atlanta Hawks .40 1.00
Kevin Willis
2 Boston/Group .40 1.00
3 Charlotte Hornets .40 1.00
Muggsy Bogues
4 Chicago Bulls .40 1.00
Group
5 Cleveland Cavaliers .40 1.00
Danny Ferry
6 Dallas/J.Jackson .40 1.00
7 Denver/R.Rogers .40 1.00
8 Detroit/J.Dumars .40 1.00
9 Golden State/C.Webber 2.00 5.00
10 Houston/Olajuwon WCF 4.00 10.00
11 Indiana/Group WD .40 1.00
12 LA Clippers .40 1.00
Group
13 L.A.Lakers/N.Van Exel .40 1.00
14 Miami/G.Rice .40 1.00
15 Milwaukee/V.Baker .40 1.00
16 Minnesota/Laettner .40 1.00
17 New Jersey/C.Morris .40 1.00
18 New York Knicks .40 1.00
Group
19 Orlando/S.O'Neal WCD 6.00 15.00
20 Philadelphia/D.Barros .40 1.00
21 Phoenix/C.Barkley WD 2.00 5.00
22 Portland Trail Blazers .40 1.00
Group
23 Sacramento Kings .40 1.00
Olden Polynice
24 San Antonio/Group WD .40 1.00
25 Seattle Supersonics .40 1.00
Group
26 Utah/J.Stockton 1.00 2.50
27 Washington/Group .40 1.00

1994-95 Stadium Club Super Teams Division Winners

Each of these four team sets was available exclusively by mailing in the corresponding winning Super Team card before the December 31st, 1995 deadline. Super Team cards were randomly seeded in all first series Stadium Club packs at a rate of one in 24. The card design parallels the regular issue Stadium Club cards except for the gold foil "Division Winner" logo on each card front. The cards are listed below alphabetically according to teams; the prefixes M, P, SP, and SU have been added to denote Magic, Pacers, Spurs and Suns respectively.

COMP.BAG MAGIC (11) 6.00 12.00
COMP.BAG PACERS (11) 1.50 3.00
COMP.BAG SPURS (11) 2.50 5.00
COMP.BAG SUNS (11) 3.00 6.00
M7 Donald Royal .20 .50
M16 Anfernee Hardaway 1.50 4.00
M32 Shaquille O'Neal 2.50 6.00
M58 Nick Anderson .20 .50
M74 Jeff Turner .20 .50
M213 Anthony Bowie .20 .50
M232 Brian Shaw .20 .50
M287 Horace Grant .25 .60
M319 Dennis Scott .20 .50
M345 Brooks Thompson .25 .60
MD19 Magic DW Super Team .40 1.00
P26 Vern Fleming .20 .50
P46 Haywoode Workman .20 .50
P86 Derrick McKey .20 .50
P121 Antonio Davis .20 .50
P144 Reggie Miller .40 1.00
P188 Dale Davis .20 .50
P219 Duane Ferrell .20 .50
P259 Byron Scott .25 .60
P293 Mark Jackson .25 .60
P323 Rik Smits .25 .60
PD11 Pacers DW Super Team .40 1.00
SP52 J.R. Reid .20 .50
SP72 Dennis Rodman 1.00 2.50
SP73 Dennis Rodman TG 1.00 2.50
SP122 Terry Cummings .25 .60
SP160 David Robinson .75 2.00
SP206 Willie Anderson .20 .50
SP282 Chuck Person .25 .60
SP313 Sean Elliott .30 .75
SP331 Vinny Del Negro .20 .50
SP354 David Robinson FG .75 2.00
SPD24 Spurs DW Super Team .40 1.00
SU13 Charles Barkley 1.00 2.50
SU70 Kevin Johnson .30 .75
SU118 Danny Ainge .30 .75
SU152 A.C. Green .25 .60
SU196 Joe Kleine .20 .50
SU257 Dan Majerle .30 .75
SU294 Wayman Tisdale .20 .50
SU320 Wesley Person .30 .75
SU350 Danny Manning .25 .60
SU360 Charles Barkley FG 1.00 2.50
SUD21 Suns DW Super Team .40 1.00

1994-95 Stadium Club Super Teams Master Photos

Each of these two over-sized (5" by 7") team sets were available exclusively by mailing in the corresponding winning Super Team card before the December 31st, 1995 deadline. Super Team cards were randomly seeded in all first series Stadium Club packs at a rate of one in 24. The card design loosely parallels the corresponding regular issue Stadium Club cards but the bold, wildly designed borders and separate numbering sequences create distinctive differences. The cards are listed below alphabetically according to teams; the prefixes M and R have been added to denote Magic and Rockets respectively.

COMP.BAG MAGIC (11) 7.50 15.00
COMP.BAG ROCKETS (11) 4.00 8.00
M1 Nick Anderson .30 .75
M2 Anthony Bowie .30 .75
M3 Jeff Turner .30 .75
M4 Dennis Scott .30 .75
M5 Horace Grant .40 1.00
M6 Shaquille O'Neal 4.00 10.00
M7 Brooks Thompson .40 1.00
M8 Anfernee Hardaway 2.00 5.00
M9 Donald Royal .30 .75
M10 Brian Shaw .30 .75
MM19 Magic MP Super Team .40 1.00
R1 Tim Breaux .30 .75
R2 Scott Brooks .30 .75
R3 Clyde Drexler 1.25 3.00
Hakeem Olajuwon CT
R4 Hakeem Olajuwon 1.50 4.00
R5 Sam Cassell .50 1.25
R6 Vernon Maxwell .30 .75
R7 Mario Elie .30 .75
R8 Carl Herrera .30 .75
R9 Kenny Smith .40 1.00
R10 Robert Horry .50 1.25
MR10 Rockets MP Super Team .40 1.00

1994-95 Stadium Club Super Teams NBA Finals

COMPLETE SET (363) 20.00 50.00
*FINALS: 1.25X TO 2.5X HI COLUMN

1994-95 Stadium Club Team of the Future

Randomly inserted at a rate of 1 in every 24 second series packs, this 10-card standard-size set is comprised of tomorrow's superstars. Card fronts feature color player action shots against brilliant gold, etched-foil backgrounds.

COMPLETE SET (10) 10.00 25.00
SER.2 STATED ODDS 1:24
1 Anfernee Hardaway 2.00 5.00
2 Latrell Sprewell 1.50 4.00
3 Grant Hill 3.00 8.00
4 Chris Webber 2.00 5.00
5 Shaquille O'Neal 3.00 8.00
6 Jason Kidd 3.00 8.00
7 Jim Jackson .75 2.00
8 Jamal Mashburn 1.25 3.00
9 Glenn Robinson 1.25 3.00
10 Alonzo Mourning 1.50 4.00

1995-96 Stadium Club

The 1995-96 Stadium Club basketball set was issued in two series of 180 and 181 standard-size cards, for a total of 361. Cards were distributed in 13-card regular packs at a suggested retail price of $2.50, and in 24-card jumbo packs. The packs were distributed in 24-piece boxes. Fronts are full-bleed full-color action player shots. The player's name appears in etched foil against an exploding star background and his team's name is printed in gold foil at the bottom. Backs feature a close-up head shot and a full-color action photo with a blue background. The player's name is printed at the top as is his biography, player profile and '94-95 statistics. A category statistic chart appears on the lower right side of the chart. Second series cards included these variations. The "Rookie Cards" as well as other subset cards were issued in basic hobby and retail packs with a silver prismatic foil. These cards were also issued one per special retail pack with a gold/orange-type foil background. Subsets include 10 cards of players from the two expansion teams (Vancouver Grizzlies and Toronto Raptors), 29 "Extreme Corps" and six "Trans-Action" cards. A parallel version of every subset card was inserted in rack and jumbo packs. The parallel versions of the subset cards feature silver and blue diffraction foil around the player's name and team name. These foil variations are priced at equal value.

COMPLETE SET (361) 15.00 40.00
COMPLETE SERIES 1 (180) 15.00 25.00
COMPLETE SERIES 2 (181) 10.00 25.00
1 Michael Jordan 2.00 5.00
2 Glenn Robinson .20 .50
3 Jason Kidd .40 1.00
4 Clyde Drexler .30 .75
5 Horace Grant .20 .50
6 Allan Houston .20 .50

7 Xavier McDaniel .15 .40
8 Jeff Hornacek .20 .50
9 Vlade Divac .25 .60
10 Juwan Howard .25 .60
11B Keith Jennings EXP Blue .15 .40
11R Keith Jennings EXP Red .15 .40
12 Grant Long .15 .40
13 Jalen Rose .30 .75
14 Malik Sealy .15 .40
15 Gary Payton .25 .60
16 Danny Ferry .15 .40
17 Glen Rice .25 .60
18 Randy Brown .15 .40
19 Greg Graham .15 .40
20 Kenny Anderson UER .20 .50
21 Aaron McKie .15 .40
22 John Salley EXP .15 .40
23 Darrin Hancock .15 .40
24 Carlos Rogers .15 .40
25 Vin Baker .20 .50
26 Bill Wennington .15 .40
27 Kenny Smith .20 .50
28 Sherman Douglas .15 .40
29 Terry Davis .15 .40
30 Grant Hill .40 1.00
31 Reggie Miller .30 .75
32 Anfernee Hardaway .40 1.00
33 Patrick Ewing .30 .75
34 Charles Barkley .40 1.00
35 Eddie Jones .25 .60
36 Kevin Duckworth .15 .40
37 Tom Hammonds .15 .40
38 Craig Ehlo .15 .40
39 Micheal Williams .15 .40
40 Alonzo Mourning .30 .75
41 John Williams .15 .40
42 Felton Spencer .15 .40
43 Lamond Murray .15 .40
44B Dontonio Wingfield EXP Blue .15 .40
44R Dontonio Wingfield EXP Red .15 .40
45 Rik Smits .20 .50
46 Donyell Marshall .15 .40
47 Clarence Weatherspoon .15 .40
48 Kevin Edwards .15 .40
49 Charlie Ward .15 .40
50 David Robinson .40 1.00
51 James Robinson .15 .40
52 Bill Cartwright .20 .50
53 Bobby Hurley .15 .40
54 Kevin Gamble .15 .40
55B B.J. Tyler EXP Blue .15 .40
55R B.J. Tyler EXP Red .15 .40
56 Chris Smith .15 .40
57 Wesley Person .15 .40
58 Tim Breaux .15 .40
59 Mitchell Butler .15 .40
60 Toni Kukoc .25 .60
61 Roy Tarpley .15 .40
62 Todd Day .15 .40
63 Anthony Peeler .15 .40
64 Brian Williams .15 .40
65 Muggsy Bogues .20 .50
66B Jerome Kersey EXP Blue .15 .40
66R Jerome Kersey EXP Red .15 .40
67 Eric Piatkowski .20 .50
68 Tim Perry .15 .40
69 Chris Gatling .15 .40
70 Mark Price .25 .60
71 Terry Mills .15 .40
72 Anthony Avent .15 .40
73 Matt Geiger .15 .40
74 Walt Williams .15 .40
75 Sean Elliott .25 .60
76 Ken Norman .15 .40
77B Kendall Gill TA Blue .15 .40
77R Kendall Gill TA Red .15 .40
78 Byron Houston .15 .40
79 Rick Fox .15 .40
80 Derek Harper .20 .50
81 Rod Strickland .15 .40
82 Bryon Russell .15 .40
83 Antonio Davis .15 .40
84 Isaiah Rider .25 .60
85 Kevin Johnson .25 .60
86 Derrick Coleman .20 .50
87 Doug Overton .15 .40
88B Hersey Hawkins TA Blue .15 .40
88R Hersey Hawkins TA Red .15 .40
89 Popeye Jones .15 .40
90 Dickey Simpkins .15 .40
91B Rodney Rogers TA Blue .15 .40
91R Rodney Rogers TA Red .15 .40
92B Rex Chapman TA Blue .15 .40
92R Rex Chapman TA Red .15 .40
93B Spud Webb TA Blue .20 .50
93R Spud Webb TA Red .20 .50
94 Lee Mayberry .15 .40
95 Cedric Ceballos .15 .40
96 Tyrone Hill .15 .40
97 Bill Curley .15 .40
98 Jeff Turner .15 .40
99B Tyrone Corbin TA Blue .15 .40
99R Tyrone Corbin TA Red .15 .40
100 John Stockton .30 .75
101B Mookie Blaylock EC Blue .15 .40
101R Mookie Blaylock EC Red .15 .40
102B Dino Radja EC Blue .15 .40
102R Dino Radja EC Red .15 .40
103B Alonzo Mourning EC Blue .30 .75
103R Alonzo Mourning EC Red .30 .75
104B Scottie Pippen EC Blue .40 1.00
104R Scottie Pippen EC Red .40 1.00
105B Terrell Brandon EC Blue .15 .40
105R Terrell Brandon EC Red .15 .40
106B Jim Jackson EC Blue .15 .40
106R Jim Jackson EC Red .15 .40
107B Mahmoud Abdul-Rauf EC Blue .15 .40
107R Mahmoud Abdul-Rauf EC Red .15 .40
108B Grant Hill EC Blue .40 1.00
108R Grant Hill EC Red .40 1.00
109B Tim Hardaway EC Blue .25 .60
109R Tim Hardaway EC Red .25 .60
110B Hakeem Olajuwon EC Blue .30 .75
110R Hakeem Olajuwon EC Red .30 .75
111B Rik Smits EC Blue .20 .50
111R Rik Smits EC Red .20 .50
112B Loy Vaught EC Blue .15 .40
112R Loy Vaught EC Red .15 .40
113B Vlade Divac EC Blue .25 .60
113R Vlade Divac EC Red .25 .60
114B Kevin Willis EC Blue .15 .40
114R Kevin Willis EC Red .15 .40
115B Glenn Robinson EC Blue .20 .50
115R Glenn Robinson EC Red .20 .50
116B Christian Laettner EC Blue .20 .50
116R Christian Laettner EC Red .20 .50
117B Derrick Coleman EC Blue .20 .50
117R Derrick Coleman EC Red .20 .50
118B Patrick Ewing EC Blue .30 .75
118R Patrick Ewing EC Red .30 .75
119B Shaquille O'Neal EC Blue .60 1.50
119R Shaquille O'Neal EC Red .60 1.50
120B Dana Barros EC Blue .15 .40
120R Dana Barros EC Red .15 .40
121B Charles Barkley EC Blue .40 1.00
121R Charles Barkley EC Red .40 1.00
122B Rod Strickland EC Blue .15 .40
122R Rod Strickland EC Red .15 .40
123B Brian Grant EC Blue .20 .50
123R Brian Grant EC Red .20 .50
124B David Robinson EC Blue .40 1.00
124R David Robinson EC Red .40 1.00
125B Shawn Kemp EC Blue .25 .60
125R Shawn Kemp EC Red .25 .60
126B Oliver Miller EC Blue .15 .40
126R Oliver Miller EC Red .15 .40
127B Karl Malone EC Blue .30 .75
127R Karl Malone EC Red .30 .75
128B Benoit Benjamin EC Blue .15 .40
128R Benoit Benjamin EC Red .15 .40
129B Chris Webber EC Blue .30 .75
129R Chris Webber EC Red .30 .75
130 Dan Majerle .25 .60
131 Calbert Cheaney .15 .40
132 Mark Jackson .20 .50
133B Greg Anthony EXP Blue .15 .40
133R Greg Anthony EXP Red .15 .40
134 Scott Burrell .15 .40
135 Detlef Schrempf .25 .60
136 Marty Conlon .15 .40
137 Rony Seikaly .15 .40
138 Olden Polynice .15 .40
139 Terry Cummings .20 .50
140 Stacey Augmon .20 .50
141 Bryant Stith .15 .40
142 Sean Higgins .15 .40
143 Antoine Carr .15 .40
144B Blue Edwards EXP Blue .15 .40
144R Blue Edwards EXP Red .15 .40
145 A.C. Green .20 .50
146 Bobby Phills .15 .40
147 Terry Dehere .15 .40
148 Sharone Wright .15 .40
149 Nick Anderson .15 .40
150 Jim Jackson .15 .40
151 Eric Montross .15 .40
152 Doug West .15 .40
153 Charles Smith .15 .40
154 Will Perdue .15 .40
155B Gerald Wilkins EXP Blue .15 .40
155R Gerald Wilkins EXP Red .15 .40
156 Robert Horry .20 .50
157 Robert Parish .25 .60
158 Lindsey Hunter .15 .40
159 Harvey Grant .15 .40
160 Tim Hardaway .25 .60
161 Sarunas Marciulionis .15 .40
162 Khalid Reeves .15 .40
163 Bo Outlaw .15 .40
164 Dale Davis .15 .40
165 Nick Van Exel .25 .60
166B Byron Scott EXP Blue .20 .50
166R Byron Scott EXP Red .20 .50
167 Steve Smith .20 .50
168 Brian Grant .20 .50
169 Avery Johnson .20 .50
170 Dikembe Mutombo .25 .60
171 Tom Gugliotta .15 .40
172 Armon Gilliam .15 .40
173 Shawn Bradley .15 .40
174 Herb Williams .15 .40
175 Dino Radja .15 .40
176 Billy Owens .15 .40
177B Kenny Gattison EXP Blue .15 .40
177R Kenny Gattison EXP Red .15 .40
178 J.R. Reid .15 .40
179 Otis Thorpe .15 .40
180 Sam Cassell .25 .60
181 Sam Cassell .25 .60
182 Pooh Richardson .15 .40
183 Johnny Newman .15 .40
184 Dennis Scott .15 .40
185 Will Perdue .15 .40
186 Andrew Lang .15 .40
187 Karl Malone .30 .75
188 Buck Williams .15 .40
189 P.J. Brown .15 .40
190 Khalid Reeves .15 .40
191 Kevin Willis .15 .40
192 Robert Pack .15 .40
193 Joe Dumars .25 .60
194 Sam Perkins .15 .40
195 Dan Majerle .25 .60
196 John Williams .15 .40
197 Reggie Williams .15 .40
198 Greg Anthony .15 .40
199 Steve Kerr .20 .50
200 Richard Dumas .15 .40
201 Dee Brown .15 .40
202 Zan Tabak .15 .40
203 David Wood .15 .40
204 Duane Causwell .15 .40
205 Sedale Threatt .15 .40
206 Hubert Davis .15 .40
207 Donald Hodge .15 .40
208 Duane Ferrell .15 .40
209 Sam Mitchell .15 .40
210 Adam Keefe .15 .40
211 Clifford Robinson .15 .40
212 Rodney Rogers .15 .40
213 Jayson Williams .15 .40
214 Brian Shaw .15 .40
215 Luc Longley .20 .50
216 Don MacLean .15 .40
217 Rex Chapman .15 .40
218 Wayman Tisdale .15 .40
219 Shawn Kemp .25 .60
220 Chris Webber .30 .75
221 Antonio Harvey .15 .40
222 Sarunas Marciulionis .15 .40
223 Jeff Malone .15 .40
224 Chucky Brown .15 .40
225 Greg Minor .15 .40
226 Clifford Rozier .15 .40
227 Derrick McKey .15 .40
228 Tony Dumas .15 .40
229 Oliver Miller .15 .40
230 Charles Oakley .20 .50
231 Fred Roberts .15 .40
232 Glen Rice .25 .60
233 Terry Porter .15 .40
234 Mark Macon .15 .40
235 Michael Cage .15 .40
236 Eric Murdock .15 .40
237 Vinny Del Negro .15 .40
238 Spud Webb .20 .50
239 Mario Elie .15 .40
240 Blue Edwards .15 .40
241 Dontonio Wingfield .15 .40
242 Brooks Thompson .15 .40
243 Alonzo Mourning .30 .75
244 Dennis Rodman .50 1.25
245 Lorenzo Williams .15 .40
246 Haywoode Workman .15 .40
247 Loy Vaught .15 .40
248 Vernon Maxwell .15 .40
249 Lionel Simmons .15 .40
250 Chris Childs .15 .40
251 Mahmoud Abdul-Rauf .15 .40
252 Vincent Askew .15 .40
253 Chris Morris .15 .40
254 Elliot Perry .15 .40
255 Dell Curry .15 .40
256 Dana Barros .15 .40
257 Terrell Brandon .15 .40
258 Monty Williams .15 .40
259 Corie Blount .15 .40
260 B.J. Armstrong .15 .40
261 Jim McIlvaine .15 .40
262 Otis Thorpe .15 .40
263 Sean Rooks .15 .40
264 Tony Massenburg .15 .40
265 Steve Smith .20 .50
266 Ron Harper .20 .50
267 Dale Ellis .15 .40
268 Clyde Drexler .30 .75
269 Jamie Watson .15 .40
270 Doc Rivers .20 .50
271 Derrick Alston .15 .40
272 Eric Mobley .15 .40
273 Ricky Pierce .15 .40
274 David Wesley .15 .40
275 John Starks .20 .50
276 Chris Mullin .25 .60
277 Ervin Johnson .15 .40
278 Jamal Mashburn .25 .60
279 Joe Kleine .15 .40
280 Mitch Richmond .25 .60
281 Chris Mills .15 .40
282 Bimbo Coles .15 .40
283 Larry Johnson .25 .60
284 Stanley Roberts .15 .40
285 Rex Walters .15 .40
286 Donald Royal .15 .40
287 Benoit Benjamin .15 .40
288 Chris Dudley .15 .40
289 Elden Campbell .15 .40
290 Mookie Blaylock .15 .40
291 Hersey Hawkins .15 .40
292 Anthony Mason .15 .40
293 Latrell Sprewell .25 .60
294 Harold Miner .15 .40
295 Scott Williams .15 .40
296 David Benoit .15 .40
297 Christian Laettner .20 .50
298 LaPhonso Ellis .15 .40
299 Gheorghe Muresan .15 .40
300 Kendall Gill .15 .40
301 Eddie Johnson .15 .40
302 Terry Cummings .20 .50
303 Chuck Person .20 .50
304 Michael Smith .15 .40
305 Mark West .15 .40
306 Willie Anderson .15 .40
307 Pervis Ellison .15 .40
308 Brian Williams .15 .40
309 Danny Manning .20 .50
310 Hakeem Olajuwon .30 .75
311 Scottie Pippen .40 1.00
312 Jon Koncak .15 .40
313 Sasha Danilovic RC .25 .60
314 Lucious Harris .15 .40
315 Yinka Dare .15 .40
316 Eric Williams RC .25 .60
317 Gary Trent RC .25 .60
318 Theo Ratliff RC .40 1.00
319 Lawrence Moten RC .25 .60
320 Jerome Allen RC .25 .60
321 Tyus Edney RC .25 .60
322 Loren Meyer RC .15 .40
323 Michael Finley RC .75 2.00
324 Alan Henderson RC .25 .60
325 Bob Sura RC .20 .50
326 Joe Smith RC .30 .75
327 Damon Stoudamire RC .60 1.50
328 Sherrell Ford RC .20 .50
329 Jerry Stackhouse RC .75 2.00
330 George Zidek RC .20 .50
331 Brent Barry RC .40 1.00
332 Shawn Respert RC .20 .50
333 Rasheed Wallace RC .75 2.00
334 Antonio McDyess RC .30 .75
335 David Vaughn RC .25 .60
336 Cory Alexander RC .25 .60
337 Jason Caffey RC .25 .60
338 Frankie King RC .25 .60
339 Travis Best RC .25 .60
340 Greg Ostertag RC .25 .60
341 Ed O'Bannon RC .20 .50
342 Kurt Thomas RC .25 .60
343 Kevin Garnett RC 2.00 5.00
344 Bryant Reeves RC .20 .50
345 Corliss Williamson RC .25 .60
346 Cherokee Parks RC .20 .50
347 Junior Burrough RC .25 .60
348 Randolph Childress RC .20 .50
349 Lou Roe RC .25 .60
350 Mario Bennett RC .20 .50
351 Dikembe Mutombo XP .25 .60
352 Larry Johnson XP .25 .60
353 Vlade Divac XP .25 .60
354 Karl Malone XP .30 .75
355 John Stockton XP .30 .75
356 Alonzo Mourning TA .30 .75
357 Glen Rice TA .25 .60
358 Dan Majerle TA .25 .60
359 John Williams TA .15 .40
360 Mark Price TA .25 .60
361 Magic Johnson .60 1.50

1995-96 Stadium Club Retail Orange

*ORANGE: 3X TO 8X BASE HI
RANDOM INSERTS IN SPECIAL RETAIL PACKS

1995-96 Stadium Club Beam Team

Randomly inserted in all first and second series packs, this 20-card standard-size set features Topps' annual selection of their Beam Team stars. First series cards were randomly seeded into one in every 18 hobby and retail packs. Second series cards were randomly seeded into one in every 36 hobby packs and one in every 72 retail packs. Card front design from first to second series is radically different. First series cards feature borderless fronts with full-color action player cutouts set against a dark background of laser beams. Second series cards feature very bright neon green, yellow and red die cut backgrounds set against a cut out action shot of the featured player.

COMPLETE SET (20) 60.00 150.00
COMPLETE SERIES 1 (10) 5.00 12.00
COMPLETE SERIES 2 (10) 50.00 120.00
SER.1 STATED ODDS 1:18 HOB/RET, 1:9 JUM
SER.2 STATED ODDS 1:36 HOB, 1:144 JUM
SER.2 STATED ODDS 1:72 RETAIL
BT1 David Robinson 1.50 4.00
BT2 Juwan Howard 1.00 2.50
BT3 Mitch Richmond 1.00 2.50
BT4 Reggie Miller 1.25 3.00
BT5 Glenn Robinson .75 2.00
BT6 Shaquille O'Neal 2.50 6.00
BT7 Shawn Kemp 1.00 2.50
BT8 Karl Malone 1.25 3.00
BT9 Jamal Mashburn 1.00 2.50
BT10 Alonzo Mourning 1.25 3.00
BT11 Charles Barkley 4.00 10.00
BT12 Hakeem Olajuwon 2.50 6.00
BT13 Kenny Anderson 1.50 4.00
BT14 Michael Jordan 40.00 100.00
BT15 Dikembe Mutombo 2.00 5.00
BT16 Rod Strickland 1.25 3.00
BT17 Patrick Ewing 2.50 6.00
BT18 Latrell Sprewell 2.00 5.00
BT19 Grant Hill 4.00 10.00
BT20 Cedric Ceballos 1.25 3.00

1995-96 Stadium Club Draft Picks

Randomly inserted in series one packs, this set of 15 skip-numbered standard-size cards is numbered in the order of the 1995 NBA draft. Some draft picks are missing in the series one collection but those cards were not included in the second series. Full-bleed fronts picture the player in full-color action shots with the TSC logo at the top. "NBA Draft Pick" and the player's name are printed in red type at the bottom of the card. Blue and white backs are numbered according to place in draft with the player's name is printed in lower case white type at the top. The white areas resemble torn, crumpled paper and contain the player's biography, college statistics and a player profile, which is printed vertically in black type on the lower right side of the back.

COMPLETE SET (15) 3.00 8.00
RANDOM INSERTS IN ALL SER.1 PACKS
SKIP-NUMBERED SET
2 Antonio McDyess .30 .75
3 Jerry Stackhouse .75 2.00
4 Rasheed Wallace .75 2.00
5 Kevin Garnett 2.00 5.00
6 Bryant Reeves .20 .50
8 Shawn Respert .20 .50
9 Ed O'Bannon .20 .50
11 Gary Trent .25 .60
12 Cherokee Parks .20 .50
15 Brent Barry .40 1.00
16 Alan Henderson .25 .60
17 Bob Sura .20 .50
18 Theo Ratliff .40 1.00
19 Randolph Childress .20 .50
22 George Zidek .20 .50

1995-96 Stadium Club Extreme

This 24-card set was randomly inserted in packs at a rate of 1:9; however, special cards like Power Zone and Warp Speed were inserted in packs at a rate of 1:18. The cards are borderless and standard sized. They carry color action shots that are up close and personal! The Topps logo can be found in either upper corner. The player's name is written in gold lettering at either bottom corner and is set in a firework-type display of colors. The player's team name is also written in gold and is also located in either bottom corner of the card. The backs have another action shot of the player along with a head shot. His career stats are listed as well as a short bio.

13 Jalen Rose .30 .75
26 Bill Wennington .15 .40
31 Reggie Miller .30 .75
34 Charles Barkley .40 1.00
41 John Williams .15 .40
49 Charlie Ward .15 .40
56 Chris Smith .15 .40
64 Brian Williams .15 .40
65 Muggsy Bogues .20 .50
72 Anthony Avent .15 .40
96 Tyrone Hill .15 .40
117 Derrick Coleman .20 .50
125 Shawn Kemp .25 .60
143 Antoine Carr .15 .40
147 Terry Dehere .15 .40
148 Sharone Wright .15 .40
149 Nick Anderson .15 .40
153 Charles Smith .15 .40
168 Brian Grant .20 .50
179 Otis Thorpe .15 .40

1995-96 Stadium Club Intercontinental

Featuring NBA stars born outside the U.S., this 10-card set was a special bonus found only in 1995-96 Stadium Club Australian packs. On the horizontal fronts, color action player cutouts are superposed over longitude and latitude markings (in silver foil) and continents (in gold foil). On a computer-generated background, the backs provide biographical information and career highlight.

COMPLETE SET (10) 4.00 10.00
IC1 Hakeem Olajuwon 3.00 8.00
IC2 Dikembe Mutombo 1.00 2.50
IC3 Bill Wennington .60 1.50
IC4 Rick Fox .60 1.50
IC5 Carl Herrera .60 1.50
IC6 Rony Seikaly .60 1.50
IC7 Rik Smits .75 2.00
IC8 Dino Radja .60 1.50
IC9 Sarunas Marciulionis .60 1.50
IC10 Luc Longley .75 2.00

1995-96 Stadium Club Nemeses

Randomly inserted in series one packs at a rate of one in 18, this 10-card standard-size set portrays arch rivals on each side of the card. Both sides are silver and blue etched foil with alternating full-color action cutouts of the players. Both sides carry a smaller full-color shot of each player's nemesis looking on. Each side carries a highlight of a game when one player got the better of the other. The "Nemeses" logo appears at the top of each side in gold etched foil.

COMPLETE SET (10) 10.00 25.00
SER.1 STATED ODDS 1:18 HOB/RET, 1:9 JUM
N1 H.Olajuwon/D.Robinson 1.25 3.00
N2 P.Ewing/R.Smits 1.00 2.50
N3 J.Stockton/K.Johnson 1.00 2.50
N4 S.O'Neal/A.Mourning 2.00 5.00
N5 C.Barkley/K.Malone 1.25 3.00
N6 S.Pippen/G.Hill 1.25 3.00
N7 A.Hardaway/K.Anderson 1.25 3.00
N8 R.Miller/J.Starks 1.00 2.50
N9 T.Kukoc/D.Radja .75 2.00
N10 M.Jordan/J.Dumars 6.00 15.00

1995-96 Stadium Club Power Zone

Randomly inserted in first and second series packs, this set of twelve standard-size cards feature the men who drive to the basket with authority. First series cards were randomly seeded into one in every 36 hobby and retail packs. Second series cards were randomly seeded into one in every 48 hobby and retail packs. First and second series card design differ radically. The first series cards feature borderless fronts with full-color action player cutouts set against a silver diffracted foil background. Second series cards contain a foil-etched background.

COMPLETE SET (12) 8.00 20.00
COMPLETE SERIES 1 (6) 4.00 10.00
COMPLETE SERIES 2 (6) 4.00 10.00
SER.1 STATED ODDS 1:36 H/R, 1:18 JUM
SER.2 STATED ODDS 1:48 HOB/JUM/RET
PZ1 Shaquille O'Neal 2.50 6.00
PZ2 Charles Barkley 1.50 4.00
PZ3 Patrick Ewing 1.25 3.00
PZ4 Karl Malone 1.25 3.00
PZ5 Larry Johnson 1.00 2.50
PZ6 Derrick Coleman .75 2.00
PZ7 Hakeem Olajuwon 1.25 3.00
PZ8 David Robinson 1.50 4.00
PZ9 Shawn Kemp 1.00 2.50
PZ10 Dennis Rodman 2.00 5.00
PZ11 Alonzo Mourning 1.25 3.00
PZ12 Vin Baker .75 2.00

1995-96 Stadium Club Reign Men

Randomly inserted in second-series hobby and retail packs at a rate of one in 48, this 10-card set features the NBA's slam dunk kings. Card fronts have a foil-etched background with the card name "Reign Men" running vertically along the right side. Card backs are horizontal with a head shot of the player, biographical information and a brief commentary. The cards are numbered with an "RM" prefix.

COMPLETE SET (10) 20.00 50.00
SER.2 STATED ODDS 1:48 HOB, 1:96 JUM
SER.2 STATED ODDS 1:24 RETAIL
RM1 Shawn Kemp 1.50 4.00
RM2 Michael Jordan 15.00 40.00
RM3 Larry Johnson 1.50 4.00
RM4 Grant Hill 2.50 6.00
RM5 Isaiah Rider 1.50 4.00
RM6 Sean Elliott 1.50 4.00
RM7 Scottie Pippen 2.50 6.00
RM8 Robert Horry 1.25 3.00
RM9 Kendall Gill 1.00 2.50
RM10 Jerry Stackhouse 5.00 12.00

1995-96 Stadium Club Spike Says

Filmmaker Spike Lee picks his 10 favorite NBA players and tells us all about them in his inimitable style. Cards in this 10-piece set were randomly inserted at a rate of one in every 12 retail packs and one in every 24 hobby packs. Card fronts are full bleed action shots with the player's name and the set name in silver refractive foil. Spike Lee is also pictured on each card front in a small circle in the lower right. Card backs are horizontal with Spike Lee's commentary on the player. The cards are numbered with a "SS" prefix.

COMPLETE SET (10) 8.00 20.00
SER.2 STATED ODDS 1:24 HOB, 1:12 RET
SS1 Michael Jordan 5.00 12.00
SS2 Alonzo Mourning .75 2.00
SS3 Reggie Miller .75 2.00
SS4 Patrick Ewing .75 2.00
SS5 Charles Barkley 1.00 2.50
SS6 Kenny Anderson .50 1.25
SS7 Scottie Pippen 1.00 2.50
SS8 Jerry Stackhouse 2.00 5.00
SS9 Shaquille O'Neal 1.50 4.00
SS10 John Starks .50 1.25

1995-96 Stadium Club Warp Speed

Randomly inserted in first and second series packs, this 12-card standard-size set features the players with the quickest first steps in the league. First series cards were randomly seeded in hobby and retail packs at a rate of one in 36. Second series cards were randonmly seeded in hobby and retail packs at a rate of one in 48. First and second series card designs differ radically. First series features full-bleed fronts, a full-color action player cutout with a trailing ghost image set against a silver foil "outer space" background with shiny silver flecks. The "Warp Speed" logo appears vertically on the left side and the player's name printed in red at the bottom. Second series cards feature cur out action shots of each player set against a silver foil, vortex background.

COMPLETE SET (12) 30.00 80.00
COMPLETE SERIES 1 (6) 25.00 60.00
COMPLETE SERIES 2 (6) 6.00 15.00
SER.1 STATED ODDS 1:36 H/R, 1:18 JUM
SER.2 STATED ODDS 1:48 H/R, 1:48 JUM
WS1 Michael Jordan 20.00 50.00
WS2 Kevin Johnson 1.25 3.00
WS3 Gary Payton 1.25 3.00
WS4 Anfernee Hardaway 2.00 5.00
WS5 Mookie Blaylock .75 2.00
WS6 Tim Hardaway 1.25 3.00
WS7 Scottie Pippen 2.00 5.00
WS8 Jason Kidd 2.00 5.00
WS9 Grant Hill 2.00 5.00
WS10 Nick Van Exel 1.25 3.00
WS11 Kenny Anderson 1.00 2.50
WS12 Latrell Sprewell 1.25 3.00

1995-96 Stadium Club Wizards

Randomly inserted exclusively in series one hobby packs at a rate of one in 24, this 10-card standard-size set features the best ball handlers in the game. Borderless etched foil fronts feature the player in a full-color action cutout with the Blue etched foil "Wizard" logo at the top. The player's name is stamped in gold foil at the bottom.

COMPLETE SET (10) 12.50 30.00
SER.1 STATED ODDS 1:24 HOB, 1:9 JUM
W1 Nick Van Exel 2.00 5.00
W2 Tim Hardaway 2.00 5.00
W3 Mookie Blaylock 1.25 3.00
W4 Gary Payton 2.00 5.00
W5 Jason Kidd 3.00 8.00
W6 Kenny Anderson 1.50 4.00
W7 John Stockton 2.50 6.00
W8 Kevin Johnson 2.00 5.00
W9 Muggsy Bogues 1.50 4.00
W10 Anfernee Hardaway 3.00 8.00

1995-96 Stadium Club X-2

Randomly inserted exclusively in second series hobby packs at a rate of one in 24 and second series retail packs at one in 48, this 10-card set showcases elite players who averaged double-doubles last season. Card fronts have an etched "X" in the background with an action shot. Card backs contain the same background with biographical and statistical information.

COMPLETE SET (10) 10.00 25.00
SER.2 STATED ODDS 1:24 HOB, 1:96 JUM
SER.2 STATED ODDS 1:48 RETAIL
X1 Hakeem Olajuwon 2.00 5.00
X2 Shaquille O'Neal 4.00 10.00
X3 David Robinson 2.50 6.00
X4 Patrick Ewing 2.00 5.00
X5 Charles Barkley 2.50 6.00
X6 Karl Malone 2.00 5.00
X7 Derrick Coleman 1.25 3.00
X8 Shawn Kemp 1.50 4.00
X9 Vin Baker 1.25 3.00
X10 Vlade Divac 1.50 4.00

1996-97 Stadium Club Promos

These promotional cards, issued before the product's release date, look identical to the 1996-97 Stadium Club cards bearing the same card numbers. The only differentiation can be found in the copyright information on the backs of the cards. The promos have only two lines of white type whereas the cards from the regular set have four lines. The front of the Damon Stoudamire promo has his name correctly written so it reads from the bottom to the top of the card unlike the regular issue that has the name reading from top to bottom.

COMPLETE SET (6) 1.50 4.00
1 Scottie Pippen .60 1.50
33 Arvydas Sabonis .30 .75
46 Damon Stoudamire .30 .75
47 Elden Campbell .25 .60
77 Nick Anderson .25 .60
78 David Robinson .60 1.50

1996-97 Stadium Club

The 180-card Stadium Club set features embossed, foil color action player photos printed on 20 pt. stock, making them noticeably sturdier than previous Stadium Club releases. The cards were released in two series, each containing 90 cards. Cards were distributed in eight-card packs with a suggested retail price of $2.50. The fronts feature full-color game action phoptography with the players name running vertically up the right side of the card in an embossed foil strip. No subsets or Rookie Cards were included in the first series set. Two Moments or Rookies insert cards were guaranteed to be in each first series pack.

COMPLETE SET (180) 10.00 25.00
COMPLETE SERIES 1 (90) 4.00 10.00
COMPLETE SERIES 2 (90) 6.00 15.00
1 Scottie Pippen .40 1.00
2 Dale Davis .15 .40
3 Horace Grant .20 .50
4 Gheorghe Muresan .15 .40
5 Elliot Perry .15 .40
6 Carlos Rogers .15 .40
7 Glenn Robinson .20 .50
8 Avery Johnson .20 .50
9 Dee Brown .15 .40
10 Grant Hill .40 1.00
11 Tyus Edney .15 .40
12 Patrick Ewing .30 .75
13 Jason Kidd .40 1.00
14 Clifford Robinson .15 .40
15 Robert Horry .20 .50
16 Dell Curry .15 .40
17 Terry Porter .15 .40
18 Shaquille O'Neal .60 1.50
19 Bryant Stith .15 .40
20 Shawn Kemp .25 .60
21 Kurt Thomas .15 .40
22 Pooh Richardson .15 .40
23 Bob Sura .15 .40
24 Olden Polynice .15 .40
25 Lawrence Moten .15 .40
26 Kendall Gill .15 .40
27 Cedric Ceballos .15 .40
28 Latrell Sprewell .25 .60
29 Christian Laettner .20 .50
30 Jamal Mashburn .20 .50
31 Jerry Stackhouse .30 .75
32 John Stockton .30 .75
33 Arvydas Sabonis .20 .50
34 Detlef Schrempf .25 .60
35 Toni Kukoc .25 .60
36 Sasha Danilovic .15 .40
37 Dana Barros .15 .40
38 Loy Vaught .15 .40
39 John Starks .20 .50
40 Marty Conlon .15 .40
41 Antonio McDyess .25 .60
42 Michael Finley .30 .75
43 Tom Gugliotta .15 .40
44 Terrell Brandon .15 .40
45 Derrick McKey .15 .40
46 Damon Stoudamire .20 .50
47 Elden Campbell .15 .40
48 Luc Longley .20 .50
49 B.J. Armstrong .15 .40
50 Lindsey Hunter .15 .40
51 Glen Rice .25 .60
52 Shawn Respert .15 .40
53 Cory Alexander .15 .40
54 Tim Legler .15 .40
55 Bryant Reeves .15 .40
56 Anfernee Hardaway .40 1.00
57 Charles Barkley .40 1.00
58 Mookie Blaylock .15 .40
59 Kevin Garnett .60 1.50
60 Hersey Hawkins .15 .40
61 Ed O'Bannon .15 .40
62 George Zidek .15 .40
63 Mitch Richmond .25 .60
64 Derrick Coleman .20 .50
65 Chris Webber .30 .75
66 Bobby Phills .15 .40
67 Rik Smits .20 .50
68 Jeff Hornacek .20 .50
69 Sam Cassell .20 .50
70 Gary Trent .15 .40
71 LaPhonso Ellis .15 .40
72 Oliver Miller .15 .40
73 Rex Chapman .15 .40
74 Jim Jackson .15 .40
75 Eric Williams .15 .40
76 Brent Barry .20 .50
77 Nick Anderson .15 .40
78 David Robinson .40 1.00
79 Calbert Cheaney .15 .40
80 Joe Smith .20 .50
81 Steve Kerr .20 .50
82 Wayman Tisdale .15 .40
83 Steve Smith .20 .50
84 Clyde Drexler .30 .75
85 Theo Ratliff .15 .40
86 Charlie Ward .15 .40
87 Karl Malone .30 .75
88 Clarence Weatherspoon .15 .40
89 Greg Anthony .15 .40
90 Shawn Bradley .15 .40
91 Otis Thorpe .15 .40
92 Larry Johnson .25 .60
93 Sharone Wright .15 .40
94 Charles Barkley .40 1.00
95 Wesley Person .15 .40
96 Dikembe Mutombo .25 .60
97 Eddie Jones .25 .60
98 Juwan Howard .20 .50
99 Grant Hill .40 1.00
100 Chris Carr RC .25 .60
101 Michael Jordan 2.00 5.00
102 Vincent Askew .15 .40
103 Gary Payton .25 .60
104 Chris Mills .15 .40
105 Reggie Miller .30 .75
106 Don MacLean .15 .40
107 John Stockton .30 .75
108 Mahmoud Abdul-Rauf .15 .40
109 P.J. Brown .15 .40
110 Kenny Anderson .20 .50
111 Mark Price .25 .60
112 Derek Harper .20 .50
113 Dino Radja .15 .40
114 Terry Dehere .15 .40
115 Mark Jackson .20 .50
116 Vin Baker .20 .50
117 Dennis Scott .15 .40
118 Sean Elliott .25 .60
119 Lee Mayberry .15 .40
120 Vlade Divac .25 .60
121 Joe Dumars .25 .60
122 Isaiah Rider .20 .50
123 Hakeem Olajuwon .30 .75
124 Robert Pack .15 .40
125 Jalen Rose .20 .50
126 Allan Houston .20 .50
127 Nate McMillan .15 .40
128 Rod Strickland .15 .40
129 Sean Rooks .15 .40
130 Dennis Rodman .50 1.25
131 Alonzo Mourning .30 .75
132 Danny Ferry .15 .40
133 Sam Cassell .20 .50
134 Brian Grant .20 .50
135 Karl Malone .30 .75
136 Chris Gatling .15 .40
137 Tom Gugliotta .15 .40
138 Hubert Davis .15 .40
139 Lucious Harris .15 .40
140 Rony Seikaly .15 .40
141 Alan Henderson .15 .40
142 Mario Elie .15 .40
143 Vinny Del Negro .15 .40
144 Harvey Grant .15 .40
145 Muggsy Bogues .20 .50
146 Rodney Rogers .15 .40
147 Kevin Johnson .25 .60
148 Anthony Peeler .15 .40
149 Jon Koncak .15 .40
150 Ricky Pierce .15 .40
151 Todd Day .15 .40
152 Tyrone Hill .15 .40
153 Nick Van Exel .25 .60
154 Rasheed Wallace .30 .75
155 Jayson Williams .15 .40
156 Sherman Douglas .15 .40
157 Bryon Russell .15 .40
158 Ron Harper .20 .50
159 Stacey Augmon .20 .50
160 Antonio Davis .15 .40
161 Tim Hardaway .25 .60
162 Charles Oakley .20 .50
163 Billy Owens .15 .40
164 Sam Perkins .15 .40
165 Chris Whitney .15 .40
166 Matt Geiger .15 .40
167 Andrew Lang .15 .40
168 Danny Manning .20 .50
169 Doug Christie .15 .40
170 George Lynch .15 .40
171 Malik Sealy .15 .40
172 Eric Montross .15 .40
173 Rick Fox .15 .40
174 Chris Mullin .25 .60
175 Ken Norman .15 .40
176 Sarunas Marciulionis .15 .40
177 Kevin Garnett .60 1.50
178 Brian Shaw .15 .40
179 Will Perdue .15 .40
180 Scott Williams .15 .40
NNO Checklist .15 .40

1996-97 Stadium Club Matrix

*STARS: 5X TO 12X BASE CARD HI
RANDOM INSERTS IN ALL SER.1 PACKS
SER.1 STATED ODDS 1:12 H, 1:10 R

1996-97 Stadium Club Class Acts

Randomly inserted in all series two packs at a rate of one in 24, this 20-card dual player set features players who were either college teammates or went to the same school. The cards incorporated the use of the Finest technology. Card backs were numbered with a "CA" prefix.

COMPLETE SET (10) 10.00 25.00
SER.2 STATED ODDS 1:24 HOBBY/RETAIL
*ATO.REF: 5X TO 12X HI
ATO.REF: SER.2 STATED ODDS 1:192 H/R
*REF: 1.5X TO 4X HI COLUMN
REF: SER.2 STATED ODDS 1:96 H/R
CA1 M.Jordan/J.Stackhouse 5.00 12.00
CA2 P.Ewing/A.Mourning .75 2.00
CA3 G.Payton/B.Barry .60 1.50
CA4 C.Webber/J.Howard .75 2.00
CA5 C.Laettner/G.Hill 1.00 2.50
CA6 S.Abdur-Rahim/J.Kidd 1.00 2.50
CA7 C.Drexler/H.Olajuwon .75 2.00
CA8 S.Marbury/K.Anderson 1.50 4.00
CA9 A.Hardaway/L.Wright 1.00 2.50
CA10 A.Iverson/D.Mutombo 3.00 8.00

1996-97 Stadium Club Finest Reprints

Randomly inserted in series one packs at the rate of one in 24 hobby and one in 20 retail, this 25-card set features reprints of 25 of the 50 greatest NBA players as they appeared on their first Topps, Star Co., or Bowman cards. Cards utilize the Finest technology. The remaining 25 cards were issued in 1996-97 Topps series two.

SER.1 STATED ODDS 1:24 HOB, 1:20 RET
2 Nate Archibald 1.00 2.50
4 Charles Barkley 3.00 8.00
5 Rick Barry 1.00 2.50
6 Elgin Baylor 1.25 3.00
7 Dave Bing 1.25 3.00
8 Bird/Erving/Johnson 6.00 15.00
10 Bob Cousy 3.00 8.00
12 Billy Cunningham 1.25 3.00
13 Dave DeBusschere 1.25 3.00
15 Julius Erving 2.00 5.00
17 Walt Frazier 1.25 3.00
18 George Gervin 1.25 3.00
19 Hal Greer 1.00 2.50
24 Michael Jordan 30.00 80.00
26 Karl Malone 3.00 8.00
28 Pete Maravich 3.00 8.00
29 Kevin McHale 1.50 4.00
34 Robert Parish 1.25 3.00
35 Bob Pettit 1.25 3.00
36 Scottie Pippen 3.00 8.00
41 Dolph Schayes 1.25 3.00
44 Isiah Thomas 1.25 3.00
48 Jerry West 3.00 8.00
49 Lenny Wilkens UER 1.25 3.00
50 James Worthy 1.50 4.00

1996-97 Stadium Club Finest Reprints Refractors

*STARS: 1.25X TO 3X VALUE
SER.1 STATED ODDS 1:96 HOB, 1:80 RET
SERIES 2 SET LISTED UNDER TOPPS
24 Michael Jordan 150.00 400.00

1996-97 Stadium Club Fusion

Randomly inserted in both series hobby packs at a rate of one in 24, this 32-card set features color player photos on fusion laser cut cards. Each card displays one player and fits together with another card creating a larger image. Only the cards displaying the correct teammates can be "fused" together. Card backs are numbered with a "F" prefix.

COMPLETE SET (32) 70.00 140.00
COMPLETE SERIES 1 (16) 50.00 100.00
COMPLETE SERIES 2 (16) 25.00 50.00
SER.1/2 STATED ODDS 1:24 HOBBY
F1 Michael Jordan 25.00 60.00
F2 Chris Webber 2.50 6.00
F3 Glenn Robinson 1.50 4.00
F4 Glen Rice 2.00 5.00
F5 Gary Payton 2.00 5.00
F6 Rik Smits 1.50 4.00
F7 Grant Hill 3.00 8.00
F8 Horace Grant 1.50 4.00
F9 Scottie Pippen 3.00 8.00
F10 Gheorghe Muresan 1.25 3.00
F11 Vin Baker 1.50 4.00
F12 Dell Curry 1.25 3.00
F13 Shawn Kemp 2.00 5.00
F14 Reggie Miller 2.50 6.00
F15 Joe Dumars 2.00 5.00
F16 Anfernee Hardaway 3.00 8.00
F17 Charles Barkley 3.00 8.00
F18 Juwan Howard 1.50 4.00
F19 Patrick Ewing 2.50 6.00
F20 John Stockton 2.50 6.00
F21 David Robinson 3.00 8.00
F22 Cedric Ceballos 1.25 3.00
F23 Alonzo Mourning 2.50 6.00
F24 Mookie Blaylock 1.25 3.00
F25 Clyde Drexler 2.50 6.00
F26 Rod Strickland 1.25 3.00
F27 Larry Johnson 2.00 5.00
F28 Karl Malone 2.50 6.00
F29 Sean Elliott 2.00 5.00
F30 Shaquille O'Neal 5.00 12.00
F31 Tim Hardaway 2.00 5.00
F32 Dikembe Mutombo 2.00 5.00

1996-97 Stadium Club Gallery Player's Private Issue

Randomly inserted at a rate of one in 96 series 2 hobby packs, this 18-card set completes the 1995-96 Topps Gallery Player's Private Issue set. Cards are identical to the 1995-96 release. For pricing, please refer to the 1995-96 Topps Gallery Player's Private Issue set.

COMPLETE SET (18) 200.00 400.00

1996-97 Stadium Club Golden Moments

Five Golden Moment cards (GM1-M5) highlighted memorable events in the NBA from 1995 and 1996. These cards feature record-breaking occasions. The cards feature sturdy 20 pt. stock, actual event photography and were seeded at an approximate rate of one per first series pack.

COMPLETE SET (5) 1.50 4.00
RANDOM INSERTS IN ALL SER.1 PACKS
GM1 Robert Parish .25 .60
GM2 John Stockton .30 .75
GM3 M.Jordan/D.Rodman 1.50 4.00
GM4 Dennis Scott .15 .40
GM5 Hakeem Olajuwon .30 .75

1996-97 Stadium Club High Risers

Randomly inserted in second series packs at a rate of one in 36, this 15-card set features a combination of Power Matrix and embossed technologies. The set features some of the NBA's best players above the rim. Card backs carry a "HR" prefix.

COMPLETE SET (15) 25.00 60.00
SER.2 STATED ODDS 1:36 HOBBY/RETAIL
HR1 Scottie Pippen 2.50 6.00
HR2 Anfernee Hardaway 2.50 6.00
HR3 Vin Baker 1.25 3.00
HR4 Brent Barry 1.25 3.00
HR5 Clyde Drexler 2.00 5.00
HR6 Kevin Garnett 4.00 10.00
HR7 Grant Hill 2.50 6.00
HR8 Michael Finley 2.00 5.00
HR9 Jerry Stackhouse 2.00 5.00
HR10 Isaiah Rider 1.25 3.00
HR11 Shaquille O'Neal 4.00 10.00
HR12 Antonio McDyess 1.50 4.00
HR13 Shawn Kemp 1.50 4.00
HR14 Michael Jordan 12.00 30.00
HR15 Juwan Howard 1.25 3.00

1996-97 Stadium Club Mega Heroes

Randomly inserted in second series retail packs only at a rate of one in 20, this 9-card set features NBA players who have famous nicknames. Card fronts feature different themes depending on the player's particular nickname. Card backs carry a "MH" prefix.

COMPLETE SET (9) 6.00 15.00
SER.2 STATED ODDS 1:20 RETAIL
MH1 Dennis Rodman 2.00 5.00
MH2 David Robinson 1.50 4.00
MH3 Karl Malone 1.25 3.00
MH4 Clyde Drexler 1.25 3.00
MH5 Anfernee Hardaway 1.50 4.00
MH6 Hakeem Olajuwon 1.25 3.00
MH7 Charles Oakley .75 2.00
MH8 Joe Smith .75 2.00
MH9 Glenn Robinson .75 2.00

1996-97 Stadium Club Rookie Showcase

Randomly inserted in all series two packs at a rate of one in 12, this 25-card set features Topps first shot at holography. The cards focus on rookies and feature a "two-shot" hologram. Card backs carry a "RS" prefix.

COMPLETE SET (25) 20.00 50.00
SER.2 STATED ODDS 1:12 HOBBY/RETAIL
RS1 Marcus Camby 1.50 4.00
RS2 Shareef Abdur-Rahim 1.50 4.00
RS3 Stephon Marbury 2.50 6.00
RS4 Ray Allen 4.00 10.00
RS5 Antoine Walker 1.50 4.00
RS6 Lorenzen Wright .75 2.00
RS7 Kerry Kittles 1.00 2.50
RS8 Samaki Walker .75 2.00
RS9 Erick Dampier 1.00 2.50
RS10 Todd Fuller .60 1.50
RS11 Kobe Bryant 12.00 30.00
RS12 Steve Nash 5.00 12.00
RS13 Tony Delk 1.00 2.50
RS14 Jermaine O'Neal 1.50 4.00
RS15 John Wallace 1.00 2.50
RS16 Walter McCarty 1.00 2.50
RS17 Dontae' Jones 1.00 2.50
RS18 Roy Rogers .75 2.00
RS19 Derek Fisher 1.25 3.00
RS20 Martin Muursepp .60 1.50
RS21 Jerome Williams .75 2.00
RS22 Brian Evans 1.00 2.50
RS23 Priest Lauderdale .60 1.50
RS24 Travis Knight 1.00 2.50
RS25 Allen Iverson 5.00 12.00

1996-97 Stadium Club Rookies 1

This set of 25 standard-sized cards feature most of the top rookies selected in the first round of the 1996 NBA Draft. These cards were seeded at an approximate rate of one per first series pack. Cards are printed on sturdy 20 pt. stock and were the first cards released to picture the rookies in their pro uniforms. Card fronts feature full color, borderless photographs with the word "Rookie" running down the side of the card. A number of the top foreign draft picks were excluded from the set.

COMPLETE SET (25) 7.50 15.00
RANDOM INSERTS IN ALL SER.1 PACKS
R1 Allen Iverson 1.25 3.00
R2 Marcus Camby .40 1.00
R3 Shareef Abdur-Rahim .40 1.00
R4 Stephon Marbury .60 1.50
R5 Ray Allen 1.00 2.50
R6 Antoine Walker .40 1.00
R7 Lorenzen Wright .20 .50
R8 Kerry Kittles .25 .60
R9 Samaki Walker .20 .50
R10 Erick Dampier .25 .60
R11 Todd Fuller .15 .40
R12 Kobe Bryant 4.00 10.00
R13 Steve Nash 1.25 3.00
R14 Tony Delk .25 .60
R15 Jermaine O'Neal .40 1.00
R16 John Wallace .25 .60
R17 Walter McCarty .25 .60
R18 Dontae Jones .25 .60
R19 Roy Rogers .20 .50
R20 Derek Fisher .30 .75
R21 Martin Muursepp .15 .40
R22 Jerome Williams .20 .50
R23 Brian Evans .25 .60
R24 Priest Lauderdale .15 .40
R25 Travis Knight .25 .60

1996-97 Stadium Club Rookies 2

This set of 20 standard-sized cards feature most of the top rookies selected in the first round of the 1996 NBA Draft. These cards were seeded at an approximate rate of one per second series pack. Cards are printed on 20 pt. stock.

COMPLETE SET (20) 7.50 15.00
RANDOM INSERTS IN ALL SER.2 PACKS
R1 Shareef Abdur-Rahim .40 1.00
R2 Tony Delk .25 .60
R3 Priest Lauderdale .15 .40
R4 Roy Rogers .20 .50
R5 Lorenzen Wright .20 .50
R6 Stephon Marbury .60 1.50
R7 Derek Fisher .30 .75
R8 John Wallace .25 .60
R9 Kobe Bryant 4.00 10.00
R10 Kerry Kittles .25 .60
R11 Antoine Walker .40 1.00
R12 Steve Nash 1.25 3.00
R13 Erick Dampier .25 .60
R14 Walter McCarty .25 .60
R15 Vitaly Potapenko .20 .50
R16 Allen Iverson 1.25 3.00
R17 Marcus Camby .40 1.00
R18 Todd Fuller .15 .40
R19 Ray Allen 1.00 2.50
R20 Jermaine O'Neal .40 1.00

1996-97 Stadium Club Shining Moments

The fifteen Shining Moments cards showcase the slamming and jamming plays that made the '95-96 season memorable. The cards feature sturdy 20 pt. stock, actual event photography and were seeded at an approximate rate of one per first series pack

COMPLETE SET (15) 3.00 8.00
RANDOM INSERTS IN ALL SER.1 PACKS
SM1 Charles Barkley .40 1.00
SM2 Michael Jordan 2.00 5.00
SM3 Karl Malone .30 .75
SM4 Hakeem Olajuwon .30 .75
SM5 John Stockton .30 .75
SM6 Patrick Ewing .30 .75
SM7 Reggie Miller .30 .75
SM8 David Robinson .40 1.00
SM9 Dennis Rodman .50 1.25
SM10 Damon Stoudamire .20 .50
SM11 Brent Barry .20 .50
SM12 Tim Legler .15 .40
SM13 Jason Kidd .40 1.00
SM14 Terrell Brandon .15 .40
SM15 Allen Iverson 1.25 3.00

1996-97 Stadium Club Special Forces

Randomly inserted in series one packs at a rate of one in 20, this 10-card retail only set features color action photos of super-charged stars printed with the Electra-Etch foil technology. There appears to be different levels of etching on the cards, with some etched very deep and heavy and some barely etched, if at all.

COMPLETE SET (10) 30.00 80.00
SER.1 STATED ODDS 1:20 RETAIL
SF1 Anfernee Hardaway 2.00 5.00
SF2 Grant Hill 2.00 5.00
SF3 Shawn Kemp 1.25 3.00
SF4 Michael Jordan 25.00 60.00
SF5 Shaquille O'Neal 3.00 8.00
SF6 Scottie Pippen 2.00 5.00
SF7 Damon Stoudamire 1.00 2.50
SF8 Jerry Stackhouse 1.50 4.00
SF9 Gary Payton 1.25 3.00
SF10 Dennis Rodman 2.50 6.00

1996-97 Stadium Club Top Crop

Randomly inserted in series one packs at a rate of one in 24, this 12-card set features color action player photos on double-sided Power Matrix cards with NBA All-Stars from both the East and the West Conferences pitted against each other. One side displays an all-star player from the Eastern Conference with the other side carrying the corresponding Western Conference all-star player.

COMPLETE SET (12) 15.00 40.00
SER.1 STATED ODDS 1:24 HOB, 1:20 RET
TC1 S.O'Neal/H.Olajuwon 4.00 10.00
TC2 A.Mourning/D.Mutombo 1.25 3.00
TC3 P.Ewing/D.Robinson 1.50 4.00
TC4 G.Hill/S.Elliott 1.50 4.00
TC5 S.Pippen/S.Kemp 1.50 4.00
TC6 V.Baker/K.Malone 1.25 3.00
TC7 J.Howard/C.Barkley 1.50 4.00
TC8 G.Rice/C.Drexler 1.25 3.00
TC9 M.Jordan/G.Payton 10.00 25.00
TC10 T.Brandon/J.Stockton 1.25 3.00
TC11 R.Miller/M.Richmond 1.50 4.00
TC12 A.Hardaway/J.Kidd 1.50 4.00

1996-97 Stadium Club Welcome Additions

The 25 Welcome Addition cards showcase the new additions that NBA teams made in the off-season. The cards feature sturdy 20 pt. stock and were seeded at an approximate rate of one per second series pack.

COMPLETE SET (25) 2.00 5.00
RANDOM INSERTS IN ALL SER.2 PACKS
WA1 Charles Barkley .40 1.00
WA2 Armon Gilliam .15 .40
WA3 Larry Johnson .25 .60
WA4 Felton Spencer .15 .40
WA5 Isaiah Rider .20 .50
WA6 Kevin Willis .15 .40
WA7 Mahmoud Abdul-Rauf .15 .40
WA8 Chris Childs .15 .40
WA9 Robert Horry .20 .50
WA10 Dan Majerle .25 .60
WA11 Robert Pack .15 .40
WA12 Rod Strickland .15 .40
WA13 Tyrone Corbin .15 .40
WA14 Anthony Mason .15 .40
WA15 Derek Harper .20 .50
WA16 Kenny Anderson .20 .50
WA17 Hubert Davis .15 .40
WA18 Allan Houston .20 .50
WA19 Shaquille O'Neal .60 1.50
WA20 Brent Price .15 .40
WA21 Ervin Johnson .15 .40
WA22 Craig Ehlo .15 .40
WA23 Jalen Rose .20 .50
WA24 Oliver Miller .15 .40
WA25 Mark West .15 .40

1997-98 Stadium Club Promos

These six standard-size promo cards issued to preview the 97-98 Stadium Club set. They are numbered the same as the regular cards in the 97-8 Stadium Club set. The cards have slick photo stock on the front with a shiny foil-embossed logo. The player's name is found at the bottom inside an effervescent blue strip. The backs are filled with commentary and player statistics. The last three years of the player's performance are highlighted and given rankings based on others who played the same position. Most likely, the only difference between these promos and the regular set will be the small white lines of trademark information on the back of the card. This is not definite, but if past trends are followed, it may very well be the case.

COMPLETE SET (6) 2.00 5.00
21 Glen Rice .50 1.25
41 Reggie Miller .60 1.50
87 Patrick Ewing .60 1.50
95 Antoine Walker .50 1.25
115 Karl Malone .60 1.50
169 Kenny Anderson .40 1.00

1997-98 Stadium Club

The 1997-98 Stadium Club first series was issued with a total of 120 cards and was distributed in 10-card packs for a suggested retail price of $3.00. The fronts feature full-bleed color action player photos embossed and printed on 20 pt. stock and containing a new holographic foil logo. The backs carry expanded career and previous season statistics, including the player's ranking among other players at the same position. The cards of series one are the odd numbered cards.

COMPLETE SET (240) 22.50 45.00
COMPLETE SERIES 1 (120) 12.50 25.00
COMPLETE SERIES 2 (120) 10.00 20.00
1 Scottie Pippen .40 1.00
2 Bryon Russell .15 .40
3 Muggsy Bogues .20 .50
4 Gary Payton .25 .60
5 Bulls - Team of the 90s 2.00 5.00
6 Corliss Williamson .15 .40
7 Samaki Walker .15 .40
8 Allan Houston .20 .50
9 Ray Allen .30 .75
10 Nick Van Exel .20 .50
11 Chris Mullin .25 .60
12 Popeye Jones .15 .40
13 Horace Grant .20 .50
14 Rik Smits .20 .50
15 Wayman Tisdale .15 .40
16 Donny Marshall .15 .40
17 Rod Strickland .15 .40
18 Rod Strickland .15 .40
19 Greg Anthony .15 .40
20 Lindsey Hunter .15 .40
21 Glen Rice .25 .60
22 Anthony Goldwire .15 .40
23 Mahmoud Abdul-Rauf .15 .40
24 Sean Elliott .25 .60
25 Cory Alexander .15 .40
26 Tyrone Corbin .15 .40
27 Sam Perkins .15 .40
28 Brian Shaw .15 .40
29 Doug Christie .15 .40
30 Mark Jackson .20 .50
31 Christian Laettner .20 .50
32 Damon Stoudamire .20 .50
33 Eric Williams .15 .40
34 Glenn Robinson .20 .50
35 Brooks Thompson .15 .40
36 Derrick Coleman .20 .50
37 Theo Ratliff .20 .50
38 Ron Harper .20 .50
39 Hakeem Olajuwon .30 .75
40 Mitch Richmond .25 .60
41 Reggie Miller .30 .75
42 Reggie Miller .30 .75
43 Shaquille O'Neal .60 1.50
44 Zydrunas Ilgauskas .25 .60
45 Jamal Mashburn .20 .50
46 Isaiah Rider .20 .50
47 Tom Gugliotta .15 .40
48 Rex Chapman .15 .40
49 Lorenzen Wright .15 .40
50 Pooh Richardson .15 .40
51 Armon Gilliam .15 .40
52 Kevin Johnson .25 .60
53 Kerry Kittles .15 .40
54 Kerry Kittles .15 .40
55 Charles Oakley .20 .50
56 Dennis Rodman .50 1.25
57 Greg Ostertag .15 .40
58 Todd Fuller .15 .40
59 Mark Davis .15 .40
60 Erick Strickland RC .20 .50
61 Clifford Robinson .15 .40
62 Nate McMillan .15 .40
63 Steve Kerr .20 .50
64 Bob Sura .15 .40
65 Danny Ferry .15 .40
66 Loy Vaught .15 .40
67 A.C. Green .20 .50
68 John Stockton .30 .75
69 Terry Mills .15 .40
70 Voshon Lenard .15 .40
71 Matt Maloney .15 .40
72 Charlie Ward .15 .40
73 Brent Barry .20 .50
74 Chris Webber .25 .60
75 Stephon Marbury .30 .75
76 Bryant Stith .15 .40
77 Shareef Abdur-Rahim .25 .60
78 Sean Rooks .15 .40
79 Rony Seikaly .15 .40
80 Brent Price .15 .40
81 Wesley Person .15 .40
82 Michael Smith .15 .40
83 Gary Trent .15 .40
84 Dan Majerle .25 .60
85 Rex Walters .15 .40
86 Clarence Weatherspoon .15 .40
87 Patrick Ewing .30 .75
88 B.J. Armstrong .15 .40
89 Travis Best .15 .40
90 Steve Smith .20 .50
91 Vitaly Potapenko .15 .40
92 Derek Strong .15 .40
93 Michael Finley .25 .60
94 Will Perdue .15 .40
95 Antoine Walker .25 .60
96 Chuck Person .20 .50
97 Mookie Blaylock .15 .40
98 Eric Snow .15 .40
99 Tony Delk .15 .40
100 Mario Elie .15 .40
101 Terrell Brandon .15 .40
102 Shawn Bradley .15 .40
103 Latrell Sprewell .25 .60
104 Latrell Sprewell .25 .60
105 Tim Hardaway .25 .60
106 Terry Porter .15 .40
107 Darrell Armstrong .15 .40
108 Rasheed Wallace .25 .60
109 Vinny Del Negro .15 .40
110 Tracy Murray .15 .40
111 Lawrence Moten .15 .40
112 Lamond Murray .15 .40
113 Juwan Howard .20 .50
114 Juwan Howard .20 .50
115 Karl Malone .30 .75
116 Aaron McKie .15 .40
117 Shawn Respert .15 .40
118 Michael Jordan 2.00 5.00
119 Shawn Kemp .25 .60
120 Arvydas Sabonis .20 .50
121 Tyus Edney .15 .40
122 Bryant Reeves .15 .40
123 Jason Kidd .40 1.00
124 Dikembe Mutombo .25 .60
125 Allen Iverson .50 1.25
126 Allen Iverson .50 1.25
127 Larry Johnson .25 .60
128 Jerry Stackhouse .25 .60
129 Kendall Gill .15 .40
130 Kendall Gill .15 .40
131 Vin Baker .20 .50
132 Joe Dumars .25 .60
133 Calbert Cheaney .15 .40
134 Alonzo Mourning .30 .75
135 Isaac Austin .15 .40
136 Joe Smith .20 .50
137 Elden Campbell .15 .40
138 Kevin Garnett .40 1.00
139 Malik Sealy .15 .40
140 John Starks .20 .50
141 Clyde Drexler .30 .75
142 Matt Geiger .15 .40
143 Mark Price .25 .60
144 Buck Williams .15 .40
145 Grant Hill .40 1.00
146 Kobe Bryant 1.25 3.00
147 Dale Ellis .15 .40
148 Jason Caffey .15 .40
149 Toni Kukoc .25 .60
150 Avery Johnson .20 .50
151 Alan Henderson .15 .40
152 Walt Williams .15 .40
153 Greg Minor .15 .40
154 Calbert Cheaney .15 .40
155 Vlade Divac .25 .60
156 Greg Foster .15 .40
157 LaPhonso Ellis .15 .40
158 Charles Barkley .40 1.00
159 Antonio Davis .15 .40
160 Roy Rogers .15 .40
161 Robert Horry .20 .50
162 Sam Cassell .20 .50
163 Chris Carr .15 .40
164 Robert Pack .15 .40
165 Sam Cassell .20 .50
166 Rodney Rogers .15 .40
167 Chris Childs .15 .40
168 Shandon Anderson .15 .40
169 Kenny Anderson .20 .50
170 Anthony Mason .15 .40
171 Olden Polynice .15 .40
172 David Wingate .15 .40
173 David Robinson .40 1.00
174 Billy Owens .15 .40
175 Detlef Schrempf .25 .60
176 Carlos Rogers .15 .40
177 Marcus Camby .25 .60
178 Dana Barros .15 .40
179 Shandon Anderson .15 .40
180 Jayson Williams .15 .40
181 Eldridge Recasner .15 .40
182 Doug West .15 .40
183 Kevin Willis .15 .40
184 Eddie Johnson .15 .40
185 Derek Fisher .25 .60
186 Eddie Jones .25 .60
187 Sherman Douglas .15 .40
188 Anthony Peeler .15 .40
189 Danny Manning .20 .50
190 Stacey Augmon .20 .50
191 Hersey Hawkins .15 .40
192 Micheal Williams .15 .40
193 Jeff Hornacek .20 .50
194 Anfernee Hardaway .40 1.00
195 Harvey Grant .15 .40
196 Nick Anderson .15 .40
197 Luc Longley .20 .50
198 Andrew Lang .15 .40
199 P.J. Brown .15 .40
200 Cedric Ceballos .15 .40
201 Tim Duncan RC 1.25 3.00
202 Ervin Johnson TRAN .15 .40
203 Keith Van Horn RC .40 1.00
204 David Wesley TRAN .15 .40
205 Chauncey Billups RC .75 2.00
206 Jim Jackson TRAN .15 .40
207 Antonio Daniels RC .25 .60
208 Travis Knight TRAN .15 .40
209 Tony Battie RC .25 .60
210 Bobby Phills TRAN .15 .40
211 Bobby Jackson RC .30 .75
212 Otis Thorpe TRAN .15 .40
213 Tim Thomas RC .30 .75
214 Chris Mullin TRAN .25 .60
215 Adonal Foyle RC .20 .50
216 Brian Williams TRAN .15 .40
217 Tracy McGrady RC 1.00 2.50
218 Tyus Edney TRAN .15 .40
219 Danny Fortson RC .25 .60
220 Clifford Robinson TRAN .15 .40
221 Olivier Saint-Jean RC .20 .50
222 Vin Baker TRAN .20 .50
223 Austin Croshere RC .20 .50
224 John Wallace TRAN .15 .40
225 Derek Anderson RC .25 .60
226 Kelvin Cato RC .20 .50
227 Maurice Taylor RC .25 .60
228 Scot Pollard RC .25 .60
229 John Thomas RC .15 .40
230 Dean Garrett TRAN .15 .40
231 Brevin Knight RC .25 .60
232 Ron Mercer RC .30 .75
233 Johnny Taylor RC .20 .50
234 Antonio McDyess TRAN .20 .50
235 Ed Gray RC .25 .60
236 Terrell Brandon TRAN .15 .40
237 Anthony Parker RC .25 .60
238 Shawn Kemp TRAN .25 .60
239 Paul Grant RC .15 .40
240 Dennis Scott TRAN .15 .40

1997-98 Stadium Club First Day Issue

*STARS: 10X TO 25X BASE CARD HI
*RCs: 5X TO 12X BASE HI
STATED PRINT RUN 200 SETS
5 Bulls - Team of the 90's 125.00 250.00
118 Michael Jordan 100.00 200.00

1997-98 Stadium Club One Of A Kind

*STARS: 25X TO 60X BASE CARD HI
*RCs: 12.5X TO 30X BASE HI
STATED PRINT RUN 150 SERIAL #'d SETS
5 Bulls - Team of the 90s 125.00 250.00
118 Michael Jordan 450.00 750.00
146 Kobe Bryant 100.00 250.00

1997-98 Stadium Club Bowman's Best Previews

Randomly inserted in packs at the rate of one in 24, this 10-card set is a sneak preview of the Bowman's Best series and features color action player photos with a section of a large gold basketball in the background. Card backs are numbered with a BBP prefix.

SER.1/2 STATED ODDS 1:24 HOB/RET
*ATO.REF: 2X TO 5X HI
ATO.REF: SER.1/2 STATED ODDS 1:192 H/R
*REF: 1.25X TO 3X HI COLUMN
REF: SER.1/2 STATED ODDS 1:96 H/R
BBP1 Allen Iverson 2.00 5.00
BBP2 Gary Payton 1.00 2.50
BBP3 Grant Hill 1.50 4.00
BBP4 Anfernee Hardaway 1.50 4.00
BBP5 Karl Malone 1.25 3.00
BBP6 Glen Rice 1.00 2.50
BBP7 Antoine Walker 1.00 2.50
BBP8 Alonzo Mourning 1.25 3.00
BBP9 Shareef Abdur-Rahim 1.00 2.50
BBP10 Shaquille O'Neal 2.50 6.00
BBP11 Maurice Taylor .50 1.25
BBP12 Chauncey Billups 1.50 4.00
BBP13 Paul Grant .30 .75
BBP14 Tony Battie .50 1.25
BBP15 Austin Croshere .40 1.00
BBP16 Brevin Knight .50 1.25
BBP17 Bobby Jackson .60 1.50
BBP18 Johnny Taylor .40 1.00
BBP19 Scot Pollard .50 1.25
BBP20 Tariq Abdul-Wahad .40 1.00

1997-98 Stadium Club Co-Signers

Randomly inserted in both series, with series one inserted at one in 387 hobby and series two at one in 309 hobby, this 12-card set features a color action photo of a different player on each side of the card along with an authentic authograph of each player. Each of these double-sided cards are stamped with the Topps Certified Autograph issue stamp to ensure authenticity. The cards were inserted within three groups at different levels. Group "A", or cards CO1-CO4 were inserted at one in 15,483. Group "B", or cards CO5-CO8 were inserted at one in 5,161. Group "C", or cards CO9-CO12 were inserted at one in 430 packs. Card backs carry a CO prefix.

SER.1 STATED ODDS 1:387 HOB
SER.2 STATED ODDS 1:309 HOB
CO1 K.Malone/K.Bryant 350.00 700.00
CO2 J.Howard/H.Olajuwon 75.00 150.00
CO3 J.Starks/J.Smith 25.00 60.00
CO4 C.Drexler/T.Hardaway 100.00 200.00
CO5 K.Bryant/J.Starks 150.00 300.00
CO6 H.Olajuwon/C.Drexler 100.00 200.00
CO7 T.Hardaway/J.Howard 12.00 30.00
CO8 J.Smith/K.Malone 50.00 125.00
CO9 J.Howard/C.Drexler 12.00 30.00
CO10 H.Olajuwon/T.Hardaway 15.00 40.00
CO11 J.Smith/K.Bryant 75.00 150.00
CO12 K.Malone/J.Starks 50.00 120.00
CO13 D.Mutombo/C.Billups 40.00 100.00
CO14 K.Van Horn/C.Webber 125.00 250.00
CO15 K.Malone/K.Kittles 75.00 150.00
CO16 R.Mercer/A.Walker 25.00 60.00
CO17 C.Webber/K.Malone 125.00 250.00
CO18 A.Walker/D.Mutombo 40.00 80.00
CO19 K.Kittles/K.Van Horn 12.00 30.00
CO20 C.Billups/R.Mercer 12.00 30.00
CO21 A.Walker/C.Billups 12.00 30.00
CO22 D.Mutombo/R.Mercer 12.00 30.00
CO23 K.Van Horn/K.Malone 30.00 80.00
CO24 C.Webber/K.Kittles 50.00 120.00

1997-98 Stadium Club Hardcourt Heroics

Randomly inserted in series one packs at the rate of one in 12, this 10-card set features color player images of some of the greatest NBA stars printed on a bright, colorful background with uniluster technology. Card backs are numbered with a H prefix.

COMPLETE SET (10) 8.00 20.00
SER.1 STATED ODDS 1:12 HOB/RET
H1 Michael Jordan 6.00 15.00
H2 Gary Payton .60 1.50
H3 Charles Barkley 1.00 2.50
H4 Mitch Richmond .60 1.50
H5 Shawn Kemp .60 1.50
H6 Anfernee Hardaway 1.00 2.50
H7 Vin Baker .50 1.25
H8 Shaquille O'Neal 1.50 4.00
H9 Scottie Pippen 1.00 2.50
H10 Grant Hill 1.00 2.50

1997-98 Stadium Club Hardwood Hopefuls

Randomly inserted in series one packs at the rate of one in 36, this 10-card set features color action photos of the top 1997 NBA Draft Picks printed on rainbow foil cards. Card backs are numbered with a HH prefix.

COMPLETE SET (10) 6.00 15.00
SER.1 STATED ODDS 1:36 HOB/RET
HH1 Brevin Knight .50 1.25
HH2 Adonal Foyle .40 1.00
HH3 Keith Van Horn .75 2.00
HH4 Tim Duncan 2.50 6.00
HH5 Danny Fortson .50 1.25
HH6 Tracy McGrady 2.00 5.00
HH7 Tony Battie .50 1.25
HH8 Chauncey Billups 1.50 4.00
HH9 Austin Croshere .40 1.00
HH10 Antonio Daniels .50 1.25

1997-98 Stadium Club Hoop Screams

Randomly inserted in series one packs at the rate of one in 12, this 10-card set features color action photos of players who display intensity around the rim by their game faces. Card backs are numbered with a HS prefix.

COMPLETE SET (10) 6.00 15.00
SER.1 STATED ODDS 1:12 HOB/RET
HS1 Shaquille O'Neal 1.25 3.00
HS2 Cedric Ceballos .30 .75
HS3 Kevin Garnett .75 2.00
HS4 Shawn Kemp .50 1.25
HS5 Jerry Stackhouse .50 1.25
HS6 Grant Hill .75 2.00
HS7 Patrick Ewing .60 1.50
HS8 Marcus Camby .50 1.25
HS9 Kobe Bryant 2.50 6.00
HS10 Michael Jordan 5.00 12.00

1997-98 Stadium Club Never Compromise

Randomly inserted ifito series two packs at a rate of one in 36, this 20-card set focuses on players who never compromise in their game play. Card backs carry a "NC" prefix.

COMPLETE SET (20) 30.00 80.00
SER.2 STATED ODDS 1:36 HOB/RET
NC1 Michael Jordan 15.00 40.00
NC2 Karl Malone 2.00 5.00
NC3 Hakeem Olajuwon 2.00 5.00
NC4 Kevin Garnett 2.50 6.00
NC5 Dikembe Mutombo 1.50 4.00
NC6 Gary Payton 1.50 4.00
NC7 Grant Hill 2.50 6.00
NC8 Charles Barkley 2.50 6.00
NC9 Shaquille O'Neal 4.00 10.00
NC10 Anfernee Hardaway 2.50 6.00
NC11 Tim Duncan 4.00 10.00
NC12 Keith Van Horn 1.25 3.00
NC13 Tracy McGrady 3.00 8.00
NC14 Tim Thomas 1.00 2.50
NC15 Austin Croshere .60 1.50
NC16 Maurice Taylor .75 2.00
NC17 Chauncey Billups 2.50 6.00
NC18 Adonal Foyle .60 1.50
NC19 Tony Battie .75 2.00
NC20 Bobby Jackson 1.00 2.50

1997-98 Stadium Club Royal Court

Randomly inserted into series two packs at a rate of one in 12, this 20-card set features the elite players in the NBA. The card fronts feature a Royal Court logo against a silver foil background. Card backs carry a "RC" prefix.

COMPLETE SET (20) 20.00 50.00
SER.2 STATED ODDS 1:12 HOB/RET
RC1 Scottie Pippen 1.50 4.00
RC2 Karl Malone 1.25 3.00
RC3 Gary Payton 1.00 2.50
RC4 Kobe Bryant 5.00 12.00
RC5 Antoine Walker 1.00 2.50
RC6 Michael Jordan 8.00 20.00
RC7 Shaquille O'Neal 2.50 6.00
RC8 Dikembe Mutombo 1.00 2.50
RC9 Hakeem Olajuwon 1.25 3.00
RC10 Grant Hill 1.50 4.00
RC11 Tim Duncan 3.00 8.00
RC12 Keith Van Horn .75 2.00
RC13 Chauncey Billups 1.50 4.00
RC14 Antonio Daniels .50 1.25
RC15 Tony Battie .50 1.25
RC16 Bobby Jackson .60 1.50
RC17 Tim Thomas .60 1.50
RC18 Adonal Foyle .40 1.00
RC19 Tracy McGrady 2.00 5.00
RC20 Danny Fortson .50 1.25

1997-98 Stadium Club Triumvirate

Randomly inserted in both series retail packs only at one in 48, these cards feature three NBA teammates that can be fused together. These laser cut cards use Luminous technology. Card backs are numbered with a "T" prefix.

SER.1/2 STATED ODDS 1:48 RETAIL
*LUM.CARDS: 1.25X TO 3X BASE TRIUMV.
LUM: SER.1/2 STATED ODDS 1:192 RET
*ILLUM.CARDS: 2X TO 5X BASE TRIUMV.
ILLUM: SER.1/2 STATED ODDS 1:384 RET
T1A Scottie Pippen 5.00 12.00
T1B Michael Jordan 125.00 250.00
T1C Dennis Rodman 10.00 25.00
T2A Ray Allen 4.00 10.00
T2B Vin Baker 2.50 6.00
T2C Glenn Robinson 2.50 6.00
T3A Juwan Howard 2.50 6.00
T3B Chris Webber 3.00 8.00
T3C Rod Strickland 2.00 5.00
T4A Christian Laettner 2.50 6.00
T4B Dikembe Mutombo 3.00 8.00
T4C Steve Smith 2.50 6.00
T5A Tom Gugliotta 2.00 5.00
T5B Kevin Garnett 8.00 20.00
T5C Stephon Marbury 4.00 10.00
T6A Charles Barkley 5.00 12.00
T6B Hakeem Olajuwon 4.00 10.00
T6C Clyde Drexler 4.00 10.00
T7A John Stockton 4.00 10.00
T7B Karl Malone 4.00 10.00
T7C Bryon Russell 2.00 5.00
T8A Larry Johnson 3.00 8.00
T8B Patrick Ewing 4.00 10.00
T8C Allan Houston 2.50 6.00
T9A Tim Hardaway 3.00 8.00
T9B Michael Jordan 125.00 250.00
T9C Anfernee Hardaway 5.00 12.00
T10A Glen Rice 3.00 8.00
T10B Scottie Pippen 5.00 12.00
T10C Grant Hill 5.00 12.00
T11A Dikembe Mutombo 3.00 8.00
T11B Patrick Ewing 4.00 10.00
T11C Alonzo Mourning 4.00 10.00
T12A Ron Mercer 2.00 5.00
T12B Keith Van Horn 2.50 6.00
T12C Tracy McGrady 6.00 15.00
T13A Gary Payton 3.00 8.00
T13B John Stockton 4.00 10.00
T13C Stephon Marbury 4.00 10.00
T14A Karl Malone 4.00 10.00
T14B Charles Barkley 5.00 12.00
T14C Kevin Garnett 5.00 12.00
T15A David Robinson 5.00 12.00
T15B Hakeem Olajuwon 4.00 10.00
T15C Shaquille O'Neal 8.00 20.00
T16A Antonio Daniels 1.50 4.00
T16B Tim Duncan 8.00 20.00
T16C Adonal Foyle 1.25 3.00

1998-99 Stadium Club Promos

This 6-card promotional set was issued to dealers and members of the press to promote the 1998-99 Stadium Club product. Please note that the card backs carry a "PP" prefix.

COMPLETE SET (6) 2.00 5.00
PP1 Shareef Abdur-Rahim .40 1.00
PP2 Shaquille O'Neal 1.00 2.50
PP3 Keith Van Horn .40 1.00
PP4 Kevin Garnett .60 1.50
PP5 Tracy McGrady .60 1.50
PP6 Tim Hardaway .40 1.00

1998-99 Stadium Club

The 1998-99 Stadium Club set was issued with a total of 240 standard size cards, with each series containing 120 cards. The 10-card packs retail for a suggested price of $3.00 each. The fronts feature color action photography on a borderless design and were printed on a 20-point stock card. The rookies were redemption cards, originally numbered DP1-DP20. The redemption cards came back as cards numbered 101-120, thus making them rookie cards.

COMPLETE SET (240) 25.00 60.00
COMPLETE SERIES 1 (120) 15.00 30.00
COMP.SERIES 1 w/o RC (100) 7.50 15.00
COMPLETE SERIES 2 (120) 15.00 30.00
SER.1 ROOKIE REDEMPTION ODDS 1:6
1 Eddie Jones .25 .60
2 Matt Geiger .15 .40
3 Ray Allen .30 .75
4 Billy Owens .15 .40
5 Larry Johnson .25 .60
6 Jerry Stackhouse .25 .60
7 Travis Best .15 .40
8 Sam Cassell .20 .50
9 Isaiah Rider .20 .50
10 Walter McCarty .15 .40
11 Hakeem Olajuwon .30 .75
12 Detlef Schrempf .25 .60
13 Chris Garner .15 .40
14 Voshon Lenard .15 .40
15 Kevin Garnett .40 1.00
16 Doug Christie .15 .40
17 Dikembe Mutombo .25 .60
18 Terrell Brandon .15 .40
19 Brevin Knight .15 .40
20 Dan Majerle .25 .60
21 Keith Van Horn .25 .60
22 Jim Jackson .15 .40
23 Theo Ratliff .20 .50
24 Anthony Peeler .15 .40
25 Tim Hardaway .25 .60
26 Bo Outlaw .15 .40
27 Blue Edwards .15 .40
28 Khalid Reeves .15 .40
29 David Wesley .15 .40
30 Toni Kukoc .25 .60
31 Jaren Jackson .15 .40
32 Mario Elie .15 .40
33 Nick Anderson .15 .40
34 Derek Anderson .15 .40
35 Rodney Rogers .15 .40
36 Jalen Rose .20 .50
37 Corliss Williamson .15 .40
38 Tyrone Corbin .15 .40
39 Antonio Davis .15 .40
40 Chris Mills .15 .40
41 Clarence Weatherspoon .15 .40
42 George Lynch .15 .40
43 Kelvin Cato .15 .40
44 Anthony Mason .15 .40
45 Tracy McGrady .40 1.00
46 Lamond Murray .15 .40
47 Mookie Blaylock .15 .40
48 Tracy Murray .15 .40
49 Ron Harper .20 .50
50 Tom Gugliotta .15 .40
51 Allan Houston .20 .50
52 Arvydas Sabonis .20 .50
53 Brian Williams .15 .40
54 Brian Shaw .15 .40
55 John Stockton .30 .75
56 Rick Fox .15 .40
57 Hersey Hawkins .15 .40
58 Danny Manning .20 .50
59 Chris Carr .15 .40
60 Lindsey Hunter .15 .40
61 Donyell Marshall .15 .40
62 Michael Jordan 2.00 5.00
63 Mark Strickland .15 .40
64 LaPhonso Ellis .15 .40
65 Rod Strickland .15 .40
66 David Robinson .40 1.00
67 Cedric Ceballos .15 .40
68 Christian Laettner .20 .50
69 Anthony Goldwire .15 .40
70 Armon Gilliam .15 .40
71 Shaquille O'Neal .60 1.50
72 Sherman Douglas .15 .40
73 Kendall Gill .15 .40
74 Charlie Ward .15 .40
75 Allen Iverson .50 1.25
76 Shawn Kemp .25 .60
77 Travis Knight .15 .40
78 Gary Payton .25 .60
79 Cedric Henderson .15 .40
80 Matt Bullard .15 .40
81 Steve Kerr .20 .50
82 Shawn Bradley .15 .40
83 Antonio McDyess .20 .50
84 Robert Horry .20 .50
85 Darrick Martin .15 .40
86 Derek Strong .15 .40
87 Shandon Anderson .15 .40
88 Lawrence Funderburke .15 .40
89 Brent Price .15 .40
90 Reggie Miller .30 .75
91 Shareef Abdur-Rahim .25 .60

92 Jeff Hornacek .20 .50
93 Antoine Carr .15 .40
94 Greg Anthony .15 .40
95 Rex Chapman .15 .40
96 Antoine Walker .25 .60
97 Bobby Jackson .15 .40
98 Calbert Cheaney .15 .40
99 Avery Johnson .20 .50
100 Jason Kidd .40 1.00
101 Michael Olowokandi RC 2.50 6.00
102 Mike Bibby RC 3.00 8.00
103 Raef LaFrentz RC 2.50 6.00
104 Antawn Jamison RC 3.00 8.00
105 Vince Carter RC 10.00 25.00
106 Robert Traylor RC 2.00 5.00
107 Jason Williams RC 5.00 12.00
108 Larry Hughes RC 4.00 10.00
109 Dirk Nowitzki RC 12.00 30.00
110 Paul Pierce RC 8.00 20.00
111 Bonzi Wells RC 2.00 5.00
112 Michael Doleac RC 1.50 4.00
113 Keon Clark RC 2.00 5.00
114 Michael Dickerson RC 2.00 5.00
115 Matt Harpring RC 2.00 5.00
116 Bryce Drew RC 1.25 3.00
117 Pat Garrity RC 1.50 4.00
118 Roshown McLeod RC 1.25 3.00
119 Ricky Davis RC 3.00 8.00
120 Brian Skinner RC 2.00 5.00
121 Dee Brown .15 .40
122 Hubert Davis .15 .40
123 Vitaly Potapenko .15 .40
124 Ervin Johnson .15 .40
125 Chris Gatling .15 .40
126 Darrell Armstrong .15 .40
127 Glen Rice .25 .60
128 Ben Wallace .20 .50
129 Sam Mitchell .15 .40
130 Joe Dumars .25 .60
131 Terry Davis .15 .40
132 A.C. Green .20 .50
133 Alan Henderson .15 .40
134 Ron Mercer .20 .50
135 Brian Grant .15 .40
136 Chris Childs .15 .40
137 Rony Seikaly .15 .40
138 Pete Chilcutt .15 .40
139 Anfernee Hardaway .40 1.00
140 Bryon Russell .15 .40
141 Tim Thomas .25 .60
142 Erick Dampier .15 .40
143 Charles Barkley .40 1.00
144 Mark Jackson .20 .50
145 Bryant Reeves .15 .40
146 Tyrone Hill .15 .40
147 Rasheed Wallace .25 .60
148 Tim Duncan .50 1.25
149 Steve Smith .20 .50
150 Alonzo Mourning .30 .75
151 Danny Fortson .15 .40
152 Aaron Williams .15 .40
153 Andrew DeClercq .15 .40
154 Elden Campbell .15 .40
155 Don Reid .15 .40
156 Rik Smits .20 .50
157 Adonal Foyle .15 .40
158 Muggsy Bogues .20 .50
159 Chris Mullin .25 .60
160 Randy Brown .15 .40
161 Kenny Anderson .20 .50
162 Tariq Abdul-Wahad .15 .40
163 P.J. Brown .15 .40
164 Jayson Williams .15 .40
165 Grant Hill .40 1.00
166 Clifford Robinson .15 .40
167 Damon Stoudamire .20 .50
168 Aaron McKie .15 .40
169 Erick Strickland .15 .40
170 Kobe Bryant 1.00 2.50
171 Karl Malone .30 .75
172 Eric Piatkowski .20 .50
173 Rodrick Rhodes .15 .40
174 Sean Elliott .25 .60
175 John Wallace .15 .40
176 Derek Fisher .25 .60
177 Maurice Taylor .15 .40
178 Wesley Person .15 .40
179 Jamal Mashburn .20 .50
180 Patrick Ewing .30 .75
181 Howard Eisley .15 .40
182 Michael Finley .25 .60
183 Juwan Howard .20 .50
184 Matt Maloney .15 .40
185 Glenn Robinson .20 .50
186 Zydrunas Ilgauskas .25 .60
187 Dana Barros .15 .40
188 Stacey Augmon .20 .50
189 Bobby Phills .15 .40
190 Kerry Kittles .15 .40
191 Vin Baker .20 .50
192 Stephon Marbury .30 .75
193 Peja Stojakovic RC .60 1.50
194 Michael Olowokandi .30 .75
195 Mike Bibby .40 1.00
196 Raef LaFrentz .30 .75
197 Antawn Jamison .40 1.00
198 Vince Carter 1.25 3.00
199 Robert Traylor .25 .60
200 Jason Williams .60 1.50
201 Larry Hughes .50 1.25
202 Dirk Nowitzki 1.50 4.00
203 Paul Pierce 1.00 2.50
204 Bonzi Wells .25 .60
205 Michael Doleac .20 .50
206 Keon Clark .25 .60
207 Michael Dickerson .25 .60
208 Matt Harpring .25 .60
209 Bryce Drew .15 .40
210 Pat Garrity .20 .50
211 Roshown McLeod .15 .40
212 Ricky Davis .40 1.00
213 Brian Skinner .25 .60
214 Tyronn Lue RC .25 .60
215 Felipe Lopez RC .15 .40
216 Al Harrington RC .40 1.00
217 Sam Jacobson RC .20 .50
218 Vladimir Stepania RC .25 .60
219 Corey Benjamin RC .15 .40
220 Nazr Mohammed RC .25 .60
221 Tom Gugliotta TRAN .15 .40
222 Derrick Coleman TRAN .20 .50
223 Mitch Richmond TRAN .25 .60
224 John Starks TRAN .20 .50
225 Antonio McDyess TRAN .20 .50
226 Joe Smith TRAN .20 .50
227 Bobby Jackson TRAN .15 .40
228 Luc Longley TRAN .20 .50
229 Isaac Austin TRAN .15 .40
230 Chris Webber TRAN .25 .60
231 Chauncey Billups TRAN .30 .75
232 Sam Perkins TRAN .15 .40
233 Loy Vaught TRAN .20 .50
234 Antonio Daniels TRAN .15 .40
235 Brent Barry TRAN .20 .50
236 Latrell Sprewell TRAN .25 .60
237 Vlade Divac TRAN .25 .60
238 Marcus Camby TRAN .20 .50
239 Charles Oakley TRAN .20 .50
240 Scottie Pippen TRAN .40 1.00

1998-99 Stadium Club First Day Issue

*STARS: 12.5X TO 30X BASE CARD HI
*SER.1 RCs: 1X TO 2.5X BASE HI
*SER.2 RCs: 6X TO 15X BASE HI
STATED PRINT RUN 200 SERIAL #'d SETS
62 Michael Jordan 250.00 500.00
105 Vince Carter 40.00 100.00
109 Dirk Nowitzki 50.00 120.00
198 Vince Carter 25.00 60.00
202 Dirk Nowitzki 30.00 80.00
203 Paul Pierce 25.00 60.00

1998-99 Stadium Club One Of A Kind

*STARS: 15X TO 40X BASE CARD HI
*SER.1 RCs: 1.25X TO 3X BASE HI
*SER.2 RCs: 8X TO 20X BASE HI
SER.1 STATED ODDS 1:56 HOBBY
SER.2 STATED ODDS 1:55 HOBBY
STATED PRINT RUN 150 SERIAL #'d SETS
62 Michael Jordan 250.00 500.00
105 Vince Carter 50.00 120.00
109 Dirk Nowitzki 75.00 200.00
202 Dirk Nowitzki 40.00 100.00

1998-99 Stadium Club Chrome

Randomly inserted into both series packs at a rate of one in 12, this 20-card set features NBA stars on a chromium background. The card backs are numbered with a SCC prefix.
COMPLETE SET (40) 20.00 50.00
COMPLETE SERIES 1 (20) 10.00 25.00
COMPLETE SERIES 2 (20) 10.00 25.00
SER.1/2 STATED ODDS 1:12 HOB/RET
*REF: 1X TO 2.5X HI COLUMN
REF: SER.1/2 STATED ODDS 1:48 H/R
SCC1 Alonzo Mourning 1.00 2.50
SCC2 Scottie Pippen 1.25 3.00
SCC3 Patrick Ewing 1.00 2.50
SCC4 Vin Baker .60 1.50
SCC5 Glenn Robinson .60 1.50
SCC6 Kobe Bryant 3.00 8.00
SCC7 Charles Barkley 1.25 3.00
SCC8 Chris Mullin .75 2.00
SCC9 Steve Smith .60 1.50
SCC10 Stephon Marbury 1.00 2.50
SCC11 Zydrunas Ilgauskas .75 2.00
SCC12 Jayson Williams .50 1.25
SCC13 Juwan Howard .60 1.50
SCC14 Grant Hill 1.25 3.00
SCC15 Damon Stoudamire .60 1.50
SCC16 Ron Mercer .60 1.50
SCC17 Tim Duncan 1.50 4.00
SCC18 Michael Finley .75 2.00
SCC19 Glen Rice .75 2.00
SCC20 Karl Malone 1.00 2.50
SCC21 Eddie Jones .75 2.00
SCC22 Dikembe Mutombo .75 2.00
SCC23 Keith Van Horn .75 2.00
SCC24 Jason Kidd 1.25 3.00
SCC25 Shaquille O'Neal 2.00 5.00
SCC26 Kevin Garnett 1.25 3.00
SCC27 Allen Iverson 1.50 4.00
SCC28 Shawn Kemp .75 2.00
SCC29 Gary Payton .75 2.00
SCC30 Shareef Abdur-Rahim .75 2.00
SCC31 Mike Bibby 1.00 2.50
SCC32 Raef LaFrentz .75 2.00
SCC33 Jason Williams 1.50 4.00
SCC34 Paul Pierce 2.50 6.00
SCC35 Michael Doleac .50 1.25
SCC36 Michael Dickerson .60 1.50
SCC37 Bryce Drew .40 1.00
SCC38 Roshown McLeod .40 1.00
SCC39 Felipe Lopez .40 1.00
SCC40 Al Harrington 1.00 2.50

1998-99 Stadium Club Co-Signers

Randomly inserted into both series hobby packs an overall rate of one in 209, this 24-card set features two autographs of NBA players on one side. The cards are stamped with the "Certified Autograph Issue" stamp to ensure authenticity. Specific odds on Group A (CO1-CO4) are one in 8,337, Group B (CO5-CO8) are one in 2,792, Group C (CO9-CO12) are one in 233, Group A (CO13-CO16) are one in 11,618, Group B (CO17-CO20) are one in 3,873 and Group C (CO21-CO24) are 1:323. The card backs are numbered with a CO prefix.
SER.1 STATED OVERALL ODDS 1:209 HOB
SER.2 STATED OVERALL ODDS 1:290 HOB
CO1 T.Duncan/K.Bryant 900.00 1500.00
CO2 L.Johnson/D.Stoudamire 100.00 200.00
CO3 A.Walker/J.Kidd 125.00 225.00
CO4 G.Payton/S.Abdur-Rahim 20.00 50.00
CO5 K.Bryant/L.Johnson 150.00 300.00
CO6 T.Duncan/D.Stoudamire 80.00 200.00
CO7 S.Abdur-Rahim/A.Walker 15.00 40.00
CO8 G.Payton/J.Kidd 80.00 200.00
CO9 D.Stoudamire/K.Bryant 60.00 150.00
CO10 L.Johnson/T.Duncan 100.00 250.00
CO11 J.Kidd/S.Abdur-Rahim 15.00 40.00
CO12 A.Walker/G.Payton 15.00 40.00
CO13 T.Duncan/E.Jones 300.00 500.00
CO14 J.Williams/V.Baker 30.00 80.00
CO15 E.Jones/J.Williams 15.00 40.00
CO16 V.Baker/T.Duncan 100.00 250.00
CO17 E.Jones/V.Baker 15.00 40.00
CO18 T.Duncan/J.Williams 60.00 150.00
CO19 A.Jamison/M.Olowo. 15.00 40.00
CO20 V.Carter/M.Bibby 25.00 60.00
CO21 M.Olowokandi/V.Carter 20.00 50.00
CO22 M.Bibby/A.Jamison 40.00 100.00
CO23 A.Jamison/V.Carter 60.00 150.00
CO24 M.Bibby/M.Olowo. 25.00 60.00

1998-99 Stadium Club Never Compromise

Randomly inserted in both series packs at a rate of one in 12, this 20-card set features ten of the most dependable players in the NBA. Card backs are numbered with a NC prefix.
COMPLETE SET (20) 12.00 30.00
COMPLETE SERIES 1 (10) 6.00 15.00
COMPLETE SERIES 2 (10) 6.00 15.00
SER.1/2 STATED ODDS 1:12 HOB/RET
NC1 Michael Jordan 5.00 12.00
NC2 Kobe Bryant 2.00 5.00
NC3 Vin Baker .40 1.00
NC4 Tim Duncan 1.00 2.50
NC5 Eddie Jones .50 1.25
NC6 Shawn Kemp .50 1.25
NC7 Grant Hill .75 2.00
NC8 Antoine Walker .50 1.25
NC9 Karl Malone .60 1.50
NC10 Scottie Pippen .75 2.00
NC11 Michael Olowokandi .50 1.25
NC12 Mike Bibby .60 1.50
NC13 Raef LaFrentz .50 1.25
NC14 Antawn Jamison .60 1.50
NC15 Vince Carter 2.00 5.00
NC16 Robert Traylor .40 1.00
NC17 Jason Williams 1.00 2.50
NC18 Bryce Drew .25 .60
NC19 Paul Pierce 1.50 4.00
NC20 Felipe Lopez .25 .60

1998-99 Stadium Club Never Compromise Oversized

1 Kobe Bryant 2.50 6.00
2 Vin Baker .50 1.25
3 Tim Duncan 1.25 3.00
4 Eddie Jones .60 1.50
5 Shawn Kemp .60 1.50
6 Antoine Walker .60 1.50
7 Karl Malone .75 2.00
8 Scottie Pippen 1.00 2.50

1998-99 Stadium Club Prime Rookies

Randomly inserted in packs at a rate of one in 16, this 10-card set features redemption cards for some of the top rookies from the 1998 class. The card backs are numbered with a P prefix.
COMPLETE SET (10) 30.00 60.00
SER.1 STATED ODDS 1:16 HOB/RET
P1 Michael Olowokandi 2.00 5.00
P2 Mike Bibby 2.50 6.00
P3 Raef LaFrentz 2.00 5.00
P4 Antawn Jamison 2.50 6.00
P5 Vince Carter 10.00 25.00
P6 Robert Traylor 1.50 4.00
P7 Jason Williams 4.00 10.00
P8 Larry Hughes 3.00 8.00
P9 Dirk Nowitzki 12.00 30.00
P10 Paul Pierce 6.00 15.00

1998-99 Stadium Club Royal Court

Randomly inserted in series two packs at one in 24, this 15-card set features the best veteran player's - and some top rookies in the NBA against a holographic card front. Card backs are numbered with a RC prefix.
COMPLETE SET (15) 15.00 40.00
SER.2 STATED ODDS 1:16 HOB/RET
RC1 Gary Payton .75 2.00
RC2 Kobe Bryant 3.00 8.00
RC3 Tim Duncan 1.50 4.00
RC4 Scottie Pippen 1.25 3.00
RC5 Allen Iverson 1.50 4.00
RC6 Shaquille O'Neal 2.00 5.00
RC7 Stephon Marbury 1.00 2.50
RC8 Antoine Walker .75 2.00
RC9 Michael Jordan 10.00 25.00
RC10 Keith Van Horn .75 2.00
RC11 Michael Olowokandi .75 2.00
RC12 Mike Bibby 1.00 2.50
RC13 Antawn Jamison 1.00 2.50
RC14 Robert Traylor .60 1.50
RC15 Roshown McLeod .40 1.00

1998-99 Stadium Club Statliners

Randomly inserted into series one packs at a rate of one in 8, this 20-card set features some of the NBA's premier veterans featuring a photo from their finest statistical performance of the previous season. Card backs are numbered with a S prefix.
COMPLETE SET (20) 15.00 40.00
SER.1 STATED ODDS 1:8 HOB/RET
S1 Karl Malone .75 2.00
S2 Michael Jordan 5.00 12.00
S3 Antoine Walker .60 1.50
S4 Tim Duncan 1.25 3.00
S5 Grant Hill 1.00 2.50
S6 Allen Iverson 1.25 3.00
S7 Kevin Garnett 1.00 2.50
S8 Gary Payton .60 1.50
S9 Shareef Abdur-Rahim .60 1.50
S10 Shawn Kemp .60 1.50
S11 Stephon Marbury .75 2.00
S12 Vin Baker .50 1.25
S13 Ray Allen .75 2.00
S14 Glen Rice .60 1.50
S15 Dikembe Mutombo .60 1.50
S16 Shaquille O'Neal 1.50 4.00
S17 Kobe Bryant 2.50 6.00
S18 Scottie Pippen 1.00 2.50
S19 Keith Van Horn .60 1.50
S20 David Robinson 1.00 2.50

1998-99 Stadium Club Triumvirate

Randomly inserted into both series hobby packs at a rate of one in 24, this 48-card set features three players from the same team or same theme that interlock to form one card. The non-clear background of the cards are "solid". Card backs are numbered with a T prefix.
SER.1/2 STATED ODDS 1:24 HOBBY
*LUMINESCENT: 1X TO 2.5X HI COLUMN
LUM: SER.1/2 STATED ODDS 1:96 HOB
*ILLUMINATOR: 2X TO 5X HI
ILLUM: SER.1/2 STATED ODDS 1:192 HOB
T1A Kenny Anderson 1.00 2.50
T1B Antoine Walker 1.25 3.00
T1C Ron Mercer 1.00 2.50
T2A Kobe Bryant 8.00 20.00
T2B Shaquille O'Neal 3.00 8.00
T2C Eddie Jones 1.25 3.00
T3A Stephon Marbury 1.50 4.00
T3B Kevin Garnett 2.00 5.00
T3C Tom Gugliotta .75 2.00
T4A Jayson Williams .75 2.00
T4B Keith Van Horn 1.25 3.00
T4C Kerry Kittles .75 2.00
T5A Kevin Johnson 1.25 3.00
T5B Antonio McDyess 1.00 2.50
T5C Jason Kidd 2.00 5.00
T6A Avery Johnson 1.00 2.50
T6B David Robinson 2.00 5.00
T6C Tim Duncan 2.50 6.00
T7A Vin Baker 1.00 2.50
T7B Gary Payton 1.25 3.00
T7C Detlef Schrempf 1.25 3.00
T8A John Stockton 1.50 4.00
T8B Karl Malone 1.50 4.00
T8C Jeff Hornacek 1.00 2.50
T9A Shaquille O'Neal 3.00 8.00
T9B David Robinson 2.00 5.00
T9C Hakeem Olajuwon 1.50 4.00
T10A Dikembe Mutombo 1.25 3.00
T10B Alonzo Mourning 1.50 4.00
T10C Patrick Ewing 1.50 4.00
T11A Tim Duncan 2.50 6.00
T11B Kevin Garnett 2.00 5.00
T11C Shareef Abdur-Rahim 1.25 3.00
T12A Shawn Kemp 1.25 3.00
T12B Grant Hill 2.00 5.00
T12C Antoine Walker 1.25 3.00
T13A Kobe Bryant 5.00 12.00
T13B Gary Payton 1.25 3.00
T13C Stephon Marbury 1.50 4.00
T14A Ray Allen 1.50 4.00
T14B Allen Iverson 2.50 6.00
T14C Anfernee Hardaway 2.00 5.00
T15A Antawn Jamison 2.00 5.00
T15B Michael Olowokandi 1.50 4.00
T15C Raef LaFrentz 1.50 4.00
T16A Robert Traylor 1.25 3.00
T16B Larry Hughes 2.50 6.00
T16C Vince Carter 6.00 15.00

1998-99 Stadium Club Wing Men

Randomly inserted in series two packs at one in 12, this 20-card set features superstar player moves on the hardcourt. Card backs carry a "W" prefix.
COMPLETE SET (20) 15.00 30.00
SER.2 STATED ODDS 1:8 HOB/RET
W1 Kobe Bryant 2.50 6.00
W2 Tim Duncan 1.25 3.00
W3 Michael Finley .60 1.50
W4 Kevin Garnett 1.00 2.50
W5 Shawn Kemp .60 1.50
W6 Grant Hill 1.00 2.50
W7 Eddie Jones .60 1.50
W8 Tim Thomas .60 1.50
W9 Vin Baker .50 1.25
W10 Antoine Walker .60 1.50
W11 Steve Smith .50 1.25
W12 Glen Rice .60 1.50
W13 Ron Mercer .50 1.25
W14 Allen Iverson 1.25 3.00
W15 Ray Allen .75 2.00
W16 Glenn Robinson .50 1.25
W17 Kerry Kittles .40 1.00
W18 Vince Carter 2.50 6.00
W19 Larry Hughes 1.00 2.50
W20 Paul Pierce 2.00 5.00

1999-00 Stadium Club

The 1999-00 version of Stadium Club was released in just one series, containing 201 cards. The cards were issued in six-card packs with a suggested retail price of $2. Within the base set, there were 150 veterans, 16 Transaction subset cards, 9 USA Women's Basketball Team subset cards and 26 Rookie cards, inserted one in three.
COMPLETE SET (201) 25.00 60.00
COMPLETE SET w/o RC (175) 12.50 30.00
RC SUBSET STATED ODDS 1:3
1 Allen Iverson .50 1.25
2 Chris Crawford .15 .40
3 Chris Webber .25 .60
4 Antawn Jamison .25 .60
5 Karl Malone .30 .75
6 Sam Cassell .20 .50
7 Kerry Kittles .15 .40
8 Tim Thomas .20 .50
9 Chauncey Billups .25 .60
10 Shawn Bradley .15 .40
11 Alan Henderson .15 .40
12 David Wesley .15 .40
13 Glenn Robinson .20 .50
14 Mitch Richmond .25 .60
15 Luc Longley .20 .50
16 Shareef Abdur-Rahim .20 .50
17 Christian Laettner .20 .50
18 Anthony Mason .15 .40
19 Randy Brown .15 .40
20 Charles Barkley .40 1.00
21 Bob Sura .15 .40
22 Bobby Jackson .15 .40
23 Arvydas Sabonis .20 .50
24 Tracy Murray .15 .40
25 Matt Harpring .15 .40
26 Shawn Kemp .25 .60
27 Travis Best .15 .40
28 Ruben Patterson .15 .40
29 Mike Bibby .25 .60
30 Vlade Divac .25 .60
31 Tyrone Hill .15 .40
32 David Robinson .40 1.00
33 Keith Van Horn .20 .50
34 Alvin Williams .15 .40
35 Juwan Howard .20 .50
36 Shaquille O'Neal .60 1.50
37 Dale Davis .15 .40
38 Alonzo Mourning .30 .75
39 Michael Olowokandi .15 .40
40 Jason Caffey .15 .40
41 Andrew DeClercq .15 .40
42 Jud Buechler .15 .40
43 Toni Kukoc .25 .60
44 Dikembe Mutombo .25 .60
45 Steve Nash .40 1.00
46 Eddie Jones .25 .60
47 Reggie Miller .25 .60
48 Rick Fox .15 .40
49 Larry Hughes .20 .50
50 Tim Duncan .50 1.25
51 Jerome Williams .15 .40
52 Rod Strickland .15 .40
53 Anthony Peeler .15 .40
54 Greg Ostertag .15 .40
55 Patrick Ewing .30 .75
56 Grant Hill .30 .75
57 Derrick Coleman .20 .50
58 Raef LaFrentz .20 .50
59 Mark Bryant .15 .40
60 Rik Smits .25 .60
61 Latrell Sprewell .25 .60
62 John Starks .20 .50
63 Brevin Knight .15 .40
64 Cuttino Mobley .15 .40
65 Clarence Weatherspoon .15 .40
66 Marcus Camby .20 .50
67 Stephon Marbury .20 .50
68 Tom Gugliotta .15 .40
69 Vince Carter .50 1.25
70 Vladimir Stepania .15 .40
71 Chris Mullin .25 .60
72 Tyrone Nesby RC .20 .50
73 Kornel David RC .20 .50
74 Elden Campbell .15 .40
75 Lindsey Hunter .15 .40
76 Chris Childs .15 .40
77 Ervin Johnson .15 .40
78 Rasheed Wallace .25 .60
79 Jeff Hornacek .20 .50
80 Matt Geiger .15 .40
81 Antoine Walker .25 .60
82 Jason Williams .30 .75
83 Robert Horry .20 .50
84 Jaren Jackson .15 .40
85 Kendall Gill .15 .40
86 Dan Majerle .25 .60
87 Bobby Phills .15 .40
88 Eric Piatkowski .20 .50
89 Robert Traylor .15 .40
90 Cory Carr .15 .40
91 P.J. Brown .15 .40
92 Terrell Brandon .15 .40
93 Corliss Williamson .15 .40
94 Bryant Reeves .15 .40
95 Larry Johnson .25 .60
96 Keith Closs .15 .40
97 Gary Trent .15 .40
98 Walter McCarty .15 .40
99 Wesley Person .15 .40
100 Chris Mills .15 .40
101 Glen Rice .25 .60
102 Peja Stojakovic .25 .60
103 Jason Kidd .40 1.00
104 Dirk Nowitzki .50 1.25
105 Bryon Russell .15 .40
106 Vin Baker .20 .50
107 Darrell Armstrong .15 .40
108 Eric Snow .20 .50
109 Hakeem Olajuwon .30 .75
110 Tracy McGrady .40 1.00
111 Kenny Anderson .20 .50
112 Jalen Rose .20 .50
113 Greg Anthony .15 .40
114 Tim Hardaway .25 .60
115 Doug Christie .20 .50
116 Allan Houston .20 .50
117 Kobe Bryant 1.00 2.50
118 Kevin Garnett .40 1.00
119 Vitaly Potapenko .15 .40
120 Steve Kerr .20 .50
121 Nick Van Exel .20 .50
122 Jerry Stackhouse .25 .60
123 Derek Fisher .25 .60
124 Donyell Marshall .15 .40
125 Mark Jackson .20 .50
126 Ray Allen .25 .60
127 Avery Johnson .20 .50
128 Michael Doleac .15 .40
129 Charles Oakley .20 .50
130 Gary Payton .25 .60
131 Theo Ratliff .20 .50
132 Cedric Ceballos .15 .40
133 Paul Pierce .30 .75
134 Michael Finley .25 .60
135 Malik Sealy .15 .40
136 Brian Grant .15 .40
137 John Stockton .30 .75
138 Chris Whitney .15 .40
139 Maurice Taylor .15 .40
140 Antonio McDyess .20 .50
141 Adrian Griffin RC .25 .60
142 Vernon Maxwell .15 .40
143 Jamal Mashburn .20 .50
144 Jayson Williams .15 .40
145 Joe Smith .20 .50
146 Clifford Robinson .15 .40
147 Mario Elie .15 .40
148 Damon Stoudamire .20 .50
149 Felipe Lopez .15 .40
150 Rex Chapman .15 .40
151 Antonio Davis TRAN .15 .40
152 Mookie Blaylock TRAN .15 .40
153 Ron Mercer TRAN .20 .50
154 Horace Grant TRAN .20 .50
155 Steve Smith TRAN .20 .50
156 Isaiah Rider TRAN .20 .50
157 Tariq Abdul-Wahad TRAN .15 .40
158 Michael Dickerson TRAN .15 .40
159 Nick Anderson TRAN .15 .40
160 Jim Jackson TRAN .15 .40
161 Hersey Hawkins TRAN .15 .40
162 Brent Barry TRAN .20 .50
163 Shandon Anderson TRAN .15 .40
164 Scottie Pippen TRAN .40 1.00
165 Isaac Austin TRAN .15 .40
166 Anfernee Hardaway TRAN .40 1.00
167 Natalie Williams USA .30 .75
168 Teresa Edwards USA .30 .75
169 Yolanda Griffith USA .40 1.00
170 Nikki McCray USA .30 .75
171 Katie Smith USA .50 1.25
172 Chamique Holdsclaw USA 1.50 4.00
173 Dawn Staley USA .40 1.00
174 R.Bolton-Holifield USA .30 .75
175 Lisa Leslie USA .75 2.00
176 Elton Brand RC 1.25 3.00
177 Steve Francis RC 1.25 3.00
178 Baron Davis RC 1.25 3.00
179 Lamar Odom RC 1.25 3.00
180 Jonathan Bender RC .50 1.25
181 Wally Szczerbiak RC 1.00 2.50
182 Richard Hamilton RC 1.00 2.50
183 Andre Miller RC 1.00 2.50
184 Shawn Marion RC 1.00 2.50
185 Jason Terry RC .75 2.00
186 Trajan Langdon RC .50 1.25
187 A.Radojevic RC .30 .75
188 Corey Maggette RC .75 2.00
189 William Avery RC .40 1.00
190 DeMarco Johnson RC .50 1.25
191 Ron Artest RC 1.00 2.50
192 Cal Bowdler RC .30 .75
193 James Posey RC .50 1.25
194 Quincy Lewis RC .30 .75
195 Scott Padgett RC .40 1.00
196 Jeff Foster RC .50 1.25
197 Kenny Thomas RC .50 1.25
198 Devean George RC .50 1.25
199 Tim James RC .30 .75
200 Vonteego Cummings RC .30 .75
201 Jumaine Jones RC .40 1.00

1999-00 Stadium Club First Day Issue

*STARS: 10X TO 25X BASE CARD HI
*RCs: 2X TO 5X BASE HI
STATED ODDS 1:26 RETAIL
STATED PRINT RUN 150 SERIAL #'d SETS

1999-00 Stadium Club One of a Kind

*STARS: 10X TO 25X BASE CARD HI
*RCs: 2X TO 5X BASE HI
STATED ODDS 1:22 HOBBY, 1:9 HTA
STATED PRINT RUN 150 SERIAL #'d SETS

1999-00 Stadium Club 3x3

Randomly inserted in packs at one in 27, this 30-card set features ten groups of three top-notch players arranged by position with laser cut designs.
COMPLETE SET (30) 50.00 120.00
STATED ODDS 1:27 H/R, 1:14 HTA
*LUMINESCENT: .75X TO 2X HI COLUMN
LUM: STATED ODDS 1:108 H/R, 1:54 HTA
ILLUMINATOR: 1.5X TO 4X HI COLUMN
ILLUM: STATED ODDS 1:216 H/R, 1:108 HTA
1A Vince Carter 3.00 8.00
1B Shareef Abdur-Rahim 1.25 3.00
1C Grant Hill 2.00 5.00
2A Allen Iverson 3.00 8.00
2B Stephon Marbury 1.25 3.00
2C Jason Williams 2.00 5.00
3A Kevin Garnett 2.50 6.00
3B Antoine Walker 1.50 4.00
3C Scottie Pippen 2.50 6.00
4A Kobe Bryant 6.00 15.00
4B Eddie Jones 1.50 4.00
4C Michael Finley 1.50 4.00
5A Tim Duncan 3.00 8.00
5B Keith Van Horn 1.25 3.00
5C Antonio McDyess 1.25 3.00
6A Shaquille O'Neal 4.00 10.00
6B Alonzo Mourning 2.00 5.00
6C Dikembe Mutombo 1.50 4.00
7A Karl Malone 2.00 5.00
7B Chris Webber 1.50 4.00
7C Shawn Kemp 1.50 4.00
8A John Stockton 2.00 5.00
8B Gary Payton 1.50 4.00
8C Jason Kidd 2.50 6.00
9A Elton Brand 2.50 6.00
9B Lamar Odom 2.50 6.00
9C Wally Szczerbiak 2.00 5.00
10A Steve Francis 2.50 6.00
10B Baron Davis 2.50 6.00
10C Jason Terry 1.50 4.00

1999-00 Stadium Club Chrome Previews

Randomly inserted in packs at one in 24, this 20-card set parallels some of the base cards using chromium technology. Card backs carry a "SCC" prefix.
COMPLETE SET (20) 15.00 40.00
STATED ODDS 1:24 H/R, 1:12 HTA
*REF: 1.25X TO 3X HI COLUMN
REF: STATED ODDS 1:120 H/R, 1:60 HTA
*JUMBO: .4X TO 1X HI
JUMBO: ONE PER HOB/HTA BOX
*JUMBO.REF: 1.5X TO 4X HI
JUMBO.REF: STATED ODDS 1:12 H, 1:8 HTA
SCC1 Kevin Garnett 1.25 3.00
SCC2 Grant Hill 1.00 2.50
SCC3 Vince Carter 1.50 4.00
SCC4 Allen Iverson 1.50 4.00
SCC5 Shareef Abdur-Rahim .60 1.50
SCC6 Stephon Marbury .60 1.50
SCC7 Kobe Bryant 3.00 8.00
SCC8 Keith Van Horn .60 1.50
SCC9 Tim Duncan 1.50 4.00
SCC10 Shaquille O'Neal 2.00 5.00
SCC11 Jason Williams 1.00 2.50
SCC12 Scottie Pippen 1.25 3.00
SCC13 Gary Payton .75 2.00
SCC14 Karl Malone 1.00 2.50
SCC15 Elton Brand 2.00 5.00
SCC16 Steve Francis 2.00 5.00
SCC17 Baron Davis 2.00 5.00
SCC18 Lamar Odom 2.00 5.00
SCC19 Ron Artest 1.50 4.00
SCC20 Corey Maggette 1.25 3.00

1999-00 Stadium Club Co-Signers

Randomly inserted in hobby packs only at an overall rate of one in 254, this 26-card set features double-autographed cards. The insert rate on each individual group is: "A" 1:3294, "B" 1:2202, "C" 1:733 and "D" 1:550. Group A features cards CS1-CS8, Group B cards CS9-CS14, Group C features cards CS15-CS20 and Group D cards CS21-CS26. Card backs carry a "CS" prefix.
OVERALL STATED ODDS 1:254 H, 1:102 HTA
CS1 T.Duncan/T.McGrady 150.00 300.00
CS2 T.Duncan/M.Camby 60.00 120.00
CS3 T.Duncan/E.Brand 100.00 200.00
CS4 T.Duncan/S.Francis 125.00 250.00
CS5 T.Duncan/S.Marion 75.00 150.00
CS6 T.Duncan/J.Bender 50.00 120.00
CS7 T.Duncan/W.Szcz 50.00 120.00
CS8 T.Duncan/C.Maggette 125.00 250.00
CS9 T.McGrady/S.Francis 50.00 100.00
CS10 C.Maggette/S.Marion 10.00 25.00
CS11 M.Camby/G.Payton 25.00 50.00
CS12 E.Brand/S.A-Rahim 20.00 40.00
CS13 P.Pierce/J.Bender 20.00 50.00
CS14 T.Gugliotta/W.Szcz 10.00 25.00
CS15 T.McGrady/C.Maggette 20.00 50.00
CS16 S.Francis/S.Marion 25.00 60.00
CS17 G.Payton/J.Bender 10.00 25.00
CS18 P.Pierce/M.Camby 15.00 40.00
CS19 E.Brand/T.Gugliotta 10.00 25.00
CS20 W.Szcz/S.A-Rahim 15.00 40.00
CS21 T.McGrady/S.Marion 15.00 40.00
CS22 S.Francis/C.Maggette 10.00 25.00
CS23 G.Payton/P.Pierce 25.00 60.00
CS24 J.Bender/M.Camby 10.00 25.00
CS25 E.Brand/W.Szcz 15.00 40.00
CS26 T.Gugliotta/S.A-Rahim 10.00 25.00

1999-00 Stadium Club Lone Star Signatures

Randomly inserted in packs, this 13-card set features autographs of top NBA stars and rookies. The cards were inserted at an overall rate of one in 389. The cards are broken up into the following groups: Group 1 (LS1) 1:28620, Group 2 (LS2-LS5) 1:4871, Group 3 (LS6-LS7) 1:7269, Group 4 (LS8-LS10) 1:1024, Group 5 (LS11-LS12) 1:1215 and Group 6 (LS13) 1:2544.
OVERALL STATED ODDS 1:389 H, 1:156 HTA
LS1 Tim Duncan 400.00 800.00
LS2 Shawn Marion 8.00 20.00
LS3 Jonathan Bender 6.00 15.00
LS4 Wally Szczerbiak 8.00 20.00
LS5 Corey Maggette 10.00 25.00
LS6 Gary Payton 15.00 40.00
LS7 Tom Gugliotta 20.00 40.00
LS8 Steve Francis 8.00 20.00
LS9 Elton Brand 8.00 20.00
LS10 Tracy McGrady 20.00 50.00
LS11 Paul Pierce 12.00 30.00
LS12 Shareef Abdur-Rahim 6.00 15.00
LS13 Marcus Camby 6.00 15.00

1999-00 Stadium Club Never Compromise

Randomly inserted in packs at one in 12, this 30-card set features players who leave it all on the hardwood divided into three groups of ten - Rookies, Stars and Legends. Card backs carry a "NC" prefix.
COMPLETE SET (30) 15.00 40.00
*GAME-VIEW STARS: 8X TO 20X HI COLUMN
*GAME-VIEW RCs: 5X TO 12X HI COLUMN
GAME-VIEW: STATED ODDS 1:220 H, 1:88 HTA
GAME-VIEW: PRINT RUN 100 SERIAL #'d SETS
NC1 Elton Brand 1.00 2.50
NC2 Steve Francis 1.00 2.50
NC3 Baron Davis 1.00 2.50
NC4 Lamar Odom 1.00 2.50
NC5 Jonathan Bender .40 1.00
NC6 Wally Szczerbiak .75 2.00
NC7 Richard Hamilton .75 2.00
NC8 Andre Miller .75 2.00
NC9 Corey Maggette .60 1.50
NC10 Jason Terry .60 1.50
NC11 Kevin Garnett 1.00 2.50
NC12 Grant Hill .75 2.00
NC13 Vince Carter 1.25 3.00
NC14 Allen Iverson 1.25 3.00
NC15 Shareef Abdur-Rahim .50 1.25
NC16 Stephon Marbury .50 1.25
NC17 Kobe Bryant 2.50 6.00
NC18 Keith Van Horn .50 1.25
NC19 Tim Duncan 1.25 3.00
NC20 Shaquille O'Neal 1.50 4.00
NC21 Karl Malone .75 2.00
NC22 Scottie Pippen 1.00 2.50
NC23 David Robinson 1.00 2.50
NC24 John Stockton .75 2.00
NC25 Charles Barkley 1.00 2.50
NC26 Gary Payton .60 1.50
NC27 Shawn Kemp .60 1.50
NC28 Alonzo Mourning .75 2.00
NC29 Reggie Miller .60 1.50
NC30 Mitch Richmond .60 1.50

1999-00 Stadium Club Onyx Extreme

Randomly inserted in packs at one in eight, this 10-card set features black styrene cards with silver foil stamping that highlights players whose moves defy the norm. Card backs carry an "OE" prefix.
COMPLETE SET (10) 3.00 8.00
STATED ODDS 1:8 H/R, 1:6 HTA
*DIE CUTS: 1.25X TO 3X HI COLUMN
DIE CUTS: STATED ODDS 1:40 H/R, 1:30 HTA
OE1 Antonio McDyess .40 1.00
OE2 Antoine Walker .50 1.25
OE3 Jason Williams .60 1.50
OE4 Chris Webber .50 1.25
OE5 David Robinson .75 2.00
OE6 Wally Szczerbiak 1.00 2.50
OE7 Jason Kidd .75 2.00
OE8 Shawn Kemp .50 1.25
OE9 Aleksandar Radojevic .30 .75
OE10 Tim Duncan 1.00 2.50

1999-00 Stadium Club Picture Ending

Randomly inserted in packs at one in 12, this 10-card set features memorable buzzer-beating plays from the 1999 NBA Playoffs. Card backs carry a "PE" prefix.
COMPLETE SET (10) 2.50 6.00
STATED ODDS 1:12 H/R, 1:6 HTA
PE1 Allan Houston .40 1.00
PE2 John Stockton .60 1.50
PE3 Sean Elliott .50 1.25
PE4 Latrell Sprewell .50 1.25
PE5 Darrell Armstrong .30 .75
PE6 Marcus Camby .40 1.00
PE7 Keith Van Horn .40 1.00
PE8 Antoine Walker .50 1.25
PE9 Larry Johnson .50 1.25
PE10 Avery Johnson .40 1.00

1999-00 Stadium Club Pieces of Patriotism

Randomly inserted in hobby packs at one in 147, this nine-card set features game-used jersey cards from player's who particiapted in the qualifiying Tournament of the Americas for the 2000 Summer Olympic Games. Card backs carry a "P" prefix.
STATED ODDS 1:147 HOB, 1:59 HTA
P1 Allan Houston 6.00 15.00
P2 Kevin Garnett 10.00 25.00
P3 Gary Payton 8.00 20.00
P4 Steve Smith 6.00 15.00
P5 Tim Hardaway 6.00 15.00
P6 Tim Duncan 12.00 30.00
P7 Jason Kidd 8.00 20.00
P8 Tom Gugliotta 6.00 15.00
P9 Vin Baker 6.00 15.00

2000-01 Stadium Club Promos

This 6-card promotional set was issued to dealers and members of the press to promote the 2000-01 Stadium Club product. Please note that the card backs carry a "PP" prefix.
COMPLETE SET (6) 2.00 5.00
PP1 Shaquille O'Neal 1.25 3.00
PP2 Latrell Sprewell .40 1.00
PP3 Ray Allen .50 1.25
PP4 Clifford Robinson .30 .75
PP5 Corey Maggette .40 1.00
PP6 John Stockton .60 1.50

2000-01 Stadium Club

The 2000-01 Stadium Club product was released in January, 2001 and featured a 175-card base set that was broken into tiers as follows: Base Veterans (1-150), and Rookies (151-175) that were inserted into packs at 1:4 hobby/retail and 1:1 HTA. Each pack contained seven cards, and carried a suggested retail price of $2.50.
COMPLETE SET (175) 30.00 60.00
COMPLETE SET w/o RC (150) 10.00 25.00
151-175 STATED ODDS 1:4 H, 1:1 HTA
1 Baron Davis .25 .60
2 Adrian Griffin .15 .40
3 Dikembe Mutombo .25 .60
4 Andre Miller .20 .50
5 Kenny Anderson .20 .50
6 Keon Clark .15 .40
7 Larry Hughes .20 .50
8 Ruben Patterson .15 .40
9 Shandon Anderson .15 .40
10 Reggie Miller .25 .60
11 Lamar Odom .20 .50
12 John Stockton .30 .75
13 Rod Strickland .15 .40
14 Michael Dickerson .15 .40
15 Quincy Lewis .15 .40
16 Vin Baker .20 .50
17 Vince Carter .50 1.25
18 Avery Johnson .20 .50
19 Michael Finley .25 .60
20 Eric Snow .15 .40
21 Kevin Garnett .40 1.00
22 Rodney Rogers .15 .40
23 Bonzi Wells .15 .40
24 Jason Kidd .40 1.00
25 Toni Kukoc .25 .60
26 Darrell Armstrong .15 .40
27 Larry Johnson .25 .60
28 Kendall Gill .15 .40
29 Wally Szczerbiak .20 .50
30 Tim Thomas .15 .40
31 Dan Majerle .25 .60
32 Karl Malone .30 .75
33 Juwan Howard .20 .50
34 Kobe Bryant 1.00 2.50
35 Bryant Reeves .15 .40
36 Cuttino Mobley .15 .40
37 Mookie Blaylock .15 .40
38 Jerome Williams .15 .40
39 James Posey .15 .40
40 Shawn Bradley .15 .40
41 Tim Hardaway .25 .60
42 Theo Ratliff .15 .40
43 Damon Stoudamire .20 .50
44 Derrick Coleman .20 .50
45 Ron Artest .25 .60
46 Antoine Walker .20 .50
47 Jason Terry .25 .60
48 Antonio McDyess .20 .50
49 Jonathan Bender .15 .40
50 Shaquille O'Neal .60 1.50
51 Anthony Carter .15 .40
52 Ray Allen .25 .60
53 Joe Smith .20 .50
54 Marcus Camby .20 .50
55 Keith Van Horn .20 .50
56 Charlie Ward .15 .40
57 John Amaechi .15 .40

58 Tom Gugliotta .15 .40
59 Allan Houston .20 .50
60 Anfernee Hardaway .40 1.00
61 Scottie Pippen .40 1.00
62 Jason Williams .25 .60
63 Steve Smith .20 .50
64 David Robinson .40 1.00
65 Gary Payton .25 .60
66 Robert Horry .20 .50
67 Greg Ostertag .15 .40
68 Mike Bibby .25 .60
69 Tim Duncan .50 1.25
70 Richard Hamilton .20 .50
71 Bryon Russell .15 .40
72 Charles Oakley .20 .50
73 Rashard Lewis .25 .60
74 Chris Webber .25 .60
75 Arvydas Sabonis .20 .50
76 Allen Iverson .50 1.25
77 Bo Outlaw .15 .40
78 Elden Campbell .15 .40
79 Dirk Nowitzki .40 1.00
80 Elton Brand .25 .60
81 Brevin Knight .15 .40
82 David Wesley .15 .40
83 Raef LaFrentz .15 .40
84 Antawn Jamison .25 .60
85 Hakeem Olajuwon .30 .75
86 Jamie Feick .15 .40
87 Jalen Rose .20 .50
88 Michael Olowokandi .15 .40
89 Rick Fox .15 .40
90 Austin Croshere .15 .40
91 Glenn Robinson .20 .50
92 Stephon Marbury .20 .50
93 Clifford Robinson .15 .40
94 Derek Fisher .25 .60
95 Vlade Divac .20 .50
96 Jim Jackson .15 .40
97 Paul Pierce .25 .60
98 Corey Benjamin .15 .40
99 Lamond Murray .15 .40
100 Steve Francis .20 .50
101 Mitch Richmond .20 .50
102 Othella Harrington .15 .40
103 Nick Anderson .15 .40
104 Antonio Davis .15 .40
105 Ervin Johnson .15 .40
106 Rasheed Wallace .25 .60
107 Shawn Marion .20 .50
108 Latrell Sprewell .20 .50
109 Terrell Brandon .15 .40
110 Sam Cassell .20 .50
111 Shareef Abdur-Rahim .20 .50
112 Travis Best .15 .40
113 Tyrone Nesby .25 .60
114 Alan Henderson .15 .40
115 Vonteego Cummings .15 .40
116 Kelvin Cato .15 .40
117 Jerry Stackhouse .20 .50
118 Nick Van Exel .20 .50
119 Corliss Williamson TRAN .15 .40
120 Doug Christie TRAN .15 .40
121 Horace Grant TRAN .20 .50
122 Glen Rice TRAN .20 .50
123 Patrick Ewing TRAN .30 .75
124 Dale Davis TRAN .15 .40
125 Brian Grant TRAN .15 .40
126 Shawn Kemp TRAN .25 .60
127 Cedric Ceballos TRAN .15 .40
128 Christian Laettner TRAN .20 .50
129 Lindsey Hunter TRAN .15 .40
130 Donyell Marshall TRAN .15 .40
131 Robert Pack TRAN .15 .40
132 Danny Fortson TRAN .15 .40
133 Howard Eisley TRAN .15 .40
134 Andrew DeClercq TRAN .15 .40
135 Mark Jackson TRAN .20 .50
136 Grant Hill TRAN .30 .75
137 Tracy McGrady TRAN .40 1.00
138 Maurice Taylor TRAN .15 .40
139 Derek Anderson TRAN .15 .40
140 Corey Maggette TRAN .20 .50
141 Jermaine O'Neal TRAN .20 .50
142 Ben Wallace TRAN .20 .50
143 Ron Mercer TRAN .15 .40
144 John Starks TRAN .20 .50
145 Erick Strickland TRAN .15 .40
146 Isaiah Rider TRAN .20 .50
147 Eddie Jones TRAN .25 .60
148 Anthony Mason TRAN .15 .40
149 P.J. Brown TRAN .15 .40
150 Jamal Mashburn TRAN .20 .50
151 Kenyon Martin RC 1.00 2.50
152 Stromile Swift RC .40 1.00
153 Darius Miles RC .40 1.00
154 Marcus Fizer RC .40 1.00
155 Mike Miller RC .60 1.50
156 DerMarr Johnson RC .30 .75
157 Chris Mihm RC .30 .75
158 Jamal Crawford RC 1.00 2.50
159 Joel Przybilla RC .30 .75
160 Keyon Dooling RC .40 1.00
161 Jerome Moiso RC .25 .60
162 Etan Thomas RC .40 1.00
163 Courtney Alexander RC .30 .75
164 Mateen Cleaves RC .30 .75
165 Jason Collier RC .40 1.00
166 Desmond Mason RC .50 1.25
167 Quentin Richardson RC .40 1.00
168 Jamaal Magloire RC .40 1.00
169 Speedy Claxton RC .40 1.00
170 Morris Peterson RC .40 1.00
171 Donnell Harvey RC .30 .75
172 DeShawn Stevenson RC .40 1.00
173 Mamadou N'Diaye RC .25 .60
174 Erick Barkley RC .25 .60
175 Mark Madsen RC .40 1.00

2000-01 Stadium Club 11 x 14 Autographs

Randomly inserted into packs at one in 1675 Hobby/Retail, and 1:656 HTA, this 12-card exchange set features 11x14 autographs of some of the most popular players in the NBA. Please note that each of these 11x14's originally packed out as exchange cards. Each player is listed below in alphabetical order.
NNO CARDS LISTED BELOW ALPHABETICALLY
IVERSON WAS NEVER REDEEMED
STATED ODDS 1:1675 H/R 1:656 HTA
1 Ron Artest 8.00 20.00
2 Elton Brand 8.00 20.00
3 Mateen Cleaves 8.00 20.00
4 Jamal Crawford 8.00 20.00
5 Tim Duncan 60.00 120.00
6 Steve Francis 8.00 20.00
7 Larry Hughes 8.00 20.00
9 Magic Johnson 60.00 120.00
10 Tracy McGrady 20.00 50.00
11 Shaquille O'Neal 60.00 120.00
12 Latrell Sprewell 30.00 80.00

2000-01 Stadium Club Beam Team

Randomly inserted in packs at one in 67 Hobby/Retail, and 1:26 HTA, this 30-card set features the NBA's key players. Card backs carry a "BT" prefix.
STATED PRINT RUN 500 SERIAL #'d SETS
STATED ODDS 1:67 H/R, 1:26 HTA
BT1 Tim Duncan 20.00 50.00
BT2 Shaquille O'Neal 25.00 60.00
BT3 Kevin Garnett 20.00 50.00
BT4 Vince Carter 20.00 50.00
BT5 Kobe Bryant 75.00 200.00
BT6 Allen Iverson 20.00 50.00
BT7 Steve Francis 4.00 10.00
BT8 Chris Webber 20.00 50.00
BT9 Elton Brand 5.00 12.00
BT10 Larry Hughes 4.00 10.00
BT11 Lamar Odom 4.00 10.00
BT12 Shareef Abdur-Rahim 4.00 10.00
BT13 Jason Kidd 8.00 20.00
BT14 Gary Payton 12.00 30.00
BT15 Antonio McDyess 4.00 10.00
BT16 Jason Williams 20.00 50.00
BT17 Karl Malone 10.00 25.00
BT18 Eddie Jones 5.00 12.00
BT19 Scottie Pippen 8.00 20.00
BT20 Latrell Sprewell 20.00 50.00
BT21 Paul Pierce 5.00 12.00
BT22 Michael Finley 5.00 12.00
BT23 Jerry Stackhouse 4.00 10.00
BT24 Jalen Rose 4.00 10.00
BT25 Antoine Walker 4.00 10.00
BT26 Anfernee Hardaway 12.00 30.00
BT27 Mike Bibby 5.00 12.00
BT28 Kenyon Martin 10.00 25.00
BT29 Stromile Swift 5.00 12.00
BT30 Darius Miles 5.00 12.00

2000-01 Stadium Club Capture the Action

Randomly inserted into packs at one in 8 hobby/retail, and 1:2 HTA, this 14-card insert features players that capture the attention of the fans better than anyone else on the court. Card backs carry a "CA" prefix.
COMPLETE SET (14) 8.00 20.00
STATED ODDS 1:8 H/R, 1:2 HTA
CA1 Shaquille O'Neal 1.25 3.00
CA2 Kobe Bryant 3.00 8.00
CA3 Vince Carter 1.00 2.50
CA4 Kevin Garnett .75 2.00
CA5 Allen Iverson -1.00 2.50
CA6 Steve Francis .40 1.00
CA7 Tracy McGrady .75 2.00
CA8 Tim Duncan 1.00 2.50
CA9 Elton Brand .50 1.25
CA10 Lamar Odom .40 1.00
CA11 Larry Hughes .40 1.00
CA12 Chris Webber .50 1.25
CA13 Antonio McDyess .40 1.00
CA14 Gary Payton .50 1.25

2000-01 Stadium Club Capture the Action Game View

*GAME VIEW: 5X TO 12X BASE HI
STATED PRINT RUN 100 SERIAL #'d SETS
STATED ODDS 1:278 H/R, 1:108 HTA
CA2 Kobe Bryant 100.00 200.00

2000-01 Stadium Club Co-Signers

Randomly inserted into packs at one in 649 hobby/retail and 1:252 HTA, this 12-card insert set features authentic dual-autgraphs from players like Magic Johnson and Shaquille O'Neal. Card backs carry a "CS" prefix.
OVERALL STATED ODDS 1:649 H, 1:252 HTA
CS1 M.Johnson/S.O'Neal 200.00 400.00
CS2 M.Johnson/M.Cleaves 60.00 150.00
CS3 S.O'Neal/T.Duncan 250.00 450.00
CS4 T.Duncan/E.Brand 100.00 250.00
CS5 E.Brand/R.Artest 15.00 40.00
CS6 A.Iverson/S.Francis 100.00 200.00
CS7 S.Francis/M.Cleaves 12.00 30.00
CS9 T.McGrady/L.Sprewell 30.00 80.00
CS10 A.Iverson/J.Crawford 75.00 150.00
CS11 T.McGrady/E.Jones 30.00 80.00
CS12 R.Artest/J.Crawford 12.00 30.00

2000-01 Stadium Club Game Jerseys

Randomly inserted into packs at one in 20 hobby/retail and 1:8 HTA, this 96-card insert set features authentic swatches of game-used jerseys from players like Paul Pierce and Grant Hill. Card backs carry a "SC" prefix followed by the city's initials.
OVERALL STATED ODDS 1:20 H/R 1:8 HTA
SCAH1 Dikembe Mutombo 3.00 8.00
SCAH2 Jason Terry 3.00 8.00
SCAH3 Jim Jackson 2.00 5.00
SCAH4 Alan Henderson 2.00 5.00
SCAH5 Cal Bowdler 2.00 5.00
SCAH6 DerMarr Johnson 1.50 4.00
SCAH7 Chris Crawford 2.00 5.00
SCAH8 Lorenzen Wright 2.00 5.00
SCAH9 Roshown McLeod 2.00 5.00
SCAH10 Dion Glover 2.00 5.00
SCAH11 Anthony Johnson 2.00 5.00
SCAH12 Hanno Mottola 1.25 3.00
SCBC1 Antoine Walker 2.50 6.00
SCBC2 Paul Pierce 3.00 8.00
SCBC3 Kenny Anderson 2.50 6.00
SCBC4 Adrian Griffin 2.00 5.00
SCBC5 Vitaly Potapenko 2.00 5.00
SCBC6 Walter McCarty 2.00 5.00
SCBC7 Tony Battie 2.00 5.00
SCLC1 Jeff McInnis 2.00 5.00
SCLC2 Michael Olowokandi 2.00 5.00
SCLC3 Tyrone Nesby 3.00 8.00
SCLC4 Derek Strong 2.00 5.00
SCLC5 Corey Maggette 2.50 6.00
SCLC6 Eric Piatkowski 2.00 5.00
SCLC7 Brian Skinner 2.00 5.00
SCLC8 Darius Miles 2.00 5.00
SCLC9 Keyon Dooling 3.00 8.00
SCLC10 Quentin Richardson 2.00 5.00
SCLC11 Sean Rooks 2.00 5.00
SCLL1 Shaquille O'Neal 8.00 20.00
SCLL2 Horace Grant 2.50 6.00
SCLL3 Robert Horry 2.50 6.00
SCLL4 Rick Fox 2.00 5.00
SCLL5 Brian Shaw 2.00 5.00
SCLL6 Ron Harper 2.50 6.00
SCLL7 Tyronn Lue 2.00 5.00
SCLL8 Isaiah Rider 2.50 6.00
SCLL9 Greg Foster 2.00 5.00
SCLL10 Mark Madsen 2.00 5.00
SCLL11 Devean George 2.00 5.00
SCNJ1 Stephon Marbury 2.50 6.00
SCNJ2 Keith Van Horn 2.50 6.00
SCNJ3 Kendall Gill 2.00 5.00
SCNJ4 Evan Eschmeyer 2.00 5.00
SCNJ5 Soumaila Samake 1.25 3.00
SCNJ6 Stephen Jackson 3.00 8.00
SCNJ7 Johnny Newman 2.00 5.00
SCNJ8 Jim McIlvaine 2.00 5.00
SCNJ9 Lucious Harris 2.00 5.00
SCNJ10 Sherman Douglas 2.00 5.00
SCNJ11 Kenyon Martin 5.00 12.00
SCNJ12 Aaron Williams 2.00 5.00
SCOM1 Grant Hill 4.00 10.00
SCOM2 Tracy McGrady 5.00 12.00
SCOM3 Darrell Armstrong 2.00 5.00
SCOM4 Michael Doleac 2.00 5.00
SCOM5 Pat Garrity 2.00 5.00
SCOM6 Dee Brown 2.00 5.00
SCOM7 Bo Outlaw 2.00 5.00
SCOM8 John Amaechi 2.00 5.00
SCOM9 Mike Miller 3.00 8.00
SCOM10 Monty Williams 2.00 5.00
SCOM11 Andrew DeClercq 2.00 5.00
SCOM12 Don Reid 2.00 5.00
SCPS1 Jason Kidd 5.00 12.00
SCPS2 Anfernee Hardaway 5.00 12.00
SCPS3 Tom Gugliotta 2.00 5.00
SCPS4 Shawn Marion 2.50 6.00
SCPS5 Clifford Robinson 2.00 5.00
SCPS6 Rodney Rogers 2.00 5.00
SCPS7 Chris Dudley 2.00 5.00
SCPS8 Rex Chapman 2.00 5.00
SCPS9 Iakovos Tsakalidis 1.25 3.00
SCPS10 Tony Delk 2.00 5.00
SCPS11 Mario Elie 2.00 5.00
SCPS12 Corie Blount 2.00 5.00
SCVG1 Shareef Abdur-Rahim 2.50 6.00
SCVG2 Mike Bibby 3.00 8.00
SCVG3 Michael Dickerson 2.00 5.00
SCVG4 Othella Harrington 2.00 5.00
SCVG5 Bryant Reeves 2.00 5.00
SCVG6 Damon Jones 3.00 8.00
SCVG7 Brent Price 2.00 5.00
SCVG8 Stromile Swift 2.00 5.00
SCVG9 Grant Long 2.00 5.00
SCVG10 Doug West 2.00 5.00
SCVG11 Tony Massenburg 2.00 5.00
SCVG12 Isaac Austin 2.00 5.00
SCWW1 Mitch Richmond 2.50 6.00
SCWW2 Juwan Howard 2.50 6.00
SCWW3 Rod Strickland 2.00 5.00
SCWW4 Richard Hamilton 2.50 6.00
SCWW5 Jahidi White 2.00 5.00
SCWW6 Michael Smith 2.00 5.00
SCWW7 Chris Whitney 2.00 5.00

2000-01 Stadium Club Head to Head Game Jerseys

Randomly inserted into packs at one in 96 HTA, this 10-card insert set features authentic swatches of game-used jerseys from players like Grant Hill and Jason Kidd. Card backs carry a "HH" prefix.
STATED ODDS 1:96 HTA
HH1 K.Martin/A.Walker 5.00 12.00
HH2 S.Swift/D.Miles 5.00 12.00
HH3 G.Hill/S.Abdur-Rahim 6.00 15.00
HH4 J.Howard/K.Van Horn 5.00 12.00
HH5 K.Dooling/J.Kidd 6.00 15.00
HH6 D.Johnson/P.Pierce 5.00 12.00
HH7 Q.Richardson/S.Marion 5.00 12.00
HH8 S.Marbury/K.Anderson 5.00 12.00
HH9 T.McGrady/A.Hardaway 15.00 40.00
HH10 J.Terry/M.Bibby 5.00 12.00

2000-01 Stadium Club Lone Star Signatures

Randomly inserted into packs at one in 237 hobby/retail and 1:92 HTA, this 12-card insert set features authentic autgraphs from players like Magic Johnson and Shaquille O'Neal. Card backs carry a "LS" prefix followed by the player's initials.
OVERALL STATED ODDS 1:237 H/R 1:92 HTA
LSAI Allen Iverson 150.00 400.00
LSEB Elton Brand 6.00 15.00
LSEJ Eddie Jones 8.00 20.00
LSJC Jamal Crawford 20.00 50.00
LSLS Latrell Sprewell 25.00 60.00
LSMC Mateen Cleaves 6.00 15.00
LSMJ Magic Johnson 40.00 100.00
LSRA Ron Artest 6.00 15.00
LSSF Steve Francis 8.00 20.00
LSSO Shaquille O'Neal 60.00 120.00
LSTD Tim Duncan 400.00 800.00
LSTM Tracy McGrady 20.00 50.00

2000-01 Stadium Club Starting Five Game Jerseys

Randomly inserted into packs at one in 2234 hobby and 1:858 HTA, this 7-card insert set features authentic swatches of game-used jerseys. Card backs carry a "SF" prefix followed by the team's initials.
STATED ODDS 1:2234 H, 1:858 HTA
SFAH Atlanta Hawks 15.00 40.00
SFBC Boston Celtics 50.00 120.00
SFNJN New Jersey Nets 40.00 80.00
SFOM Orlando Magic 40.00 80.00
SFPS Phoenix Suns 75.00 150.00
SFVG Vancouver Grizzles 30.00 80.00
SFWW Washington Wizards 30.00 80.00

2000-01 Stadium Club Striking Distance

Randomly inserted into packs at one in 8 hobby/retail and 1:3 HTA, this 20-card insert set features players that are capable of taking over the game at any time. Card backs carry a "SD" prefix.
COMPLETE SET (20) 15.00 30.00
STATED ODDS 1:8 H/R, 1:3 HTA
SD1 Reggie Miller .60 1.50
SD2 Tim Duncan 1.25 3.00
SD3 Allen Iverson 1.25 3.00
SD4 Kevin Garnett 1.00 2.50
SD5 Vince Carter 1.25 3.00
SD6 Kobe Bryant 2.50 6.00
SD7 Shaquille O'Neal 1.50 4.00
SD8 Chris Webber .60 1.50
SD9 Elton Brand .60 1.50
SD10 Steve Francis .50 1.25
SD11 Lamar Odom .50 1.25
SD12 Gary Payton .60 1.50
SD13 Karl Malone .75 2.00
SD14 Latrell Sprewell .50 1.25
SD15 Ray Allen .60 1.50
SD16 Stephon Marbury .50 1.25
SD17 Rasheed Wallace .60 1.50
SD18 Jason Williams .60 1.50
SD19 Scottie Pippen 1.00 2.50
SD20 Eddie Jones .60 1.50

2001-02 Stadium Club

Released in late October 2001, this 134-card set features full color action photography on a borderless card stock with a colored bar containing the player's name and the Stadium Club logo along the bottom. The set is divided up into 101 veteran cards and 33 rookies inserted at the rate of one in four and one per pack in Home Team Advantage. In addition to the rookie card, HTA packs also contain two parallel cards. Stadium Club was packed out in six card packs and sixteen card HTA packs. Regular boxes contained 24 packs and retailed for $3.00 per pack, while HTA boxes contained 10 packs and retailed for $6.00 per pack.
COMP.SET w/o SP's (101) 12.50 25.00
RC STATED ODDS 1:4, 1:1 HTA
1 Dikembe Mutombo .25 .60
2 Clifford Robinson .15 .40
3 Bonzi Wells .15 .40
4 Peja Stojakovic .25 .60
5 Gary Payton .25 .60
6 Morris Peterson .15 .40
7 Patrick Ewing .30 .75
8 Terrell Brandon .15 .40
9 Tim Thomas .15 .40
10 Kobe Bryant 1.00 2.50
11 Hakeem Olajuwon .30 .75
12 Marc Jackson .15 .40
13 Wang Zhizhi .20 .50
14 Andre Miller .20 .50
15 Elton Brand .25 .60
16 Eddie Robinson .15 .40
17 Jason Terry .25 .60
18 Allan Houston .20 .50
19 Grant Hill .30 .75
20 Tim Duncan .50 1.25
21 Kevin Garnett .40 1.00
22 Jahidi White .15 .40
23 Michael Dickerson .15 .40
24 Karl Malone .30 .75
25 Chris Webber .25 .60
26 Scottie Pippen .40 1.00
27 Latrell Sprewell .20 .50
28 Keith Van Horn .20 .50
29 Ray Allen .25 .60
30 Alonzo Mourning .30 .75
31 Lamar Odom .20 .50
32 Jalen Rose .20 .50
33 Ben Wallace .20 .50
34 Shaquille O'Neal .60 1.50
35 Antonio McDyess .20 .50
36 Dirk Nowitzki .40 1.00
37 Marcus Fizer .15 .40
38 Jamal Mashburn .20 .50
39 Paul Pierce .25 .60
40 DerMarr Johnson .15 .40
41 Steve Nash .40 1.00
42 Jerry Stackhouse .20 .50
43 Larry Hughes .20 .50
44 Cuttino Mobley .15 .40
45 Horace Grant .20 .50
46 Eddie Jones .20 .50
47 Wally Szczerbiak .20 .50
48 Marcus Camby .20 .50
49 Jamal Crawford .25 .60
50 Vince Carter .40 1.00
51 Donyell Marshall .15 .40
52 Shareef Abdur-Rahim .20 .50
53 Courtney Alexander .15 .40
54 Kenny Anderson .20 .50
55 Ron Mercer .15 .40
56 Lamond Murray .15 .40
57 Michael Finley .25 .60
58 Raef LaFrentz .15 .40
59 Reggie Miller .25 .60
60 Steve Francis .20 .50
61 Rick Fox .15 .40
62 Tim Hardaway .25 .60
63 Glenn Robinson .20 .50
64 LaPhonso Ellis .20 .50
65 Kenyon Martin .25 .60
66 Jason Williams .20 .50
67 Derek Anderson .15 .40
68 Eric Snow .15 .40
69 Darius Miles .15 .40
70 Antawn Jamison .25 .60
71 Mateen Cleaves .15 .40
72 Jason Kidd .40 1.00
73 Rasheed Wallace .25 .60
74 Chris Porter .15 .40
75 Tracy McGrady .40 1.00
76 Aaron McKie .15 .40
77 Baron Davis .25 .60
78 Toni Kukoc .25 .60
79 Antoine Walker .20 .50
80 Shawn Marion .20 .50
81 Mike Miller .20 .50
82 Stephon Marbury .20 .50
83 Glen Rice .20 .50
84 David Robinson .40 1.00
85 Rashard Lewis .25 .60
86 John Stockton .30 .75
87 Stromile Swift .15 .40
88 Richard Hamilton .20 .50
89 Desmond Mason .20 .50
90 Brian Grant .15 .40
91 Keyon Dooling .15 .40
92 Jermaine O'Neal .20 .50
93 Nick Van Exel .20 .50
94 Tom Gugliotta .15 .40
95 Darrell Armstrong .15 .40
96 Sam Cassell .20 .50
97 Mike Bibby .25 .60
98 DeShawn Stevenson .15 .40
99 Antonio Davis .15 .40
100 Allen Iverson .50 1.25
101 Kwame Brown RC .75 2.00
102 Tyson Chandler RC 1.25 3.00
103 Pau Gasol RC 2.50 6.00
104 Eddy Curry RC .75 2.00
105 Jason Richardson RC 1.00 2.50
106 Shane Battier RC 1.50 4.00
107 Eddie Griffin RC .60 1.50
108 DeSagana Diop RC .60 1.50
109 Rodney White RC .50 1.25
110 Joe Johnson RC 1.00 2.50
111 Kedrick Brown RC .50 1.25
112 Vladimir Radmanovic RC .75 2.00
113 Richard Jefferson RC 1.25 3.00
114 Troy Murphy RC .75 2.00
115 Steven Hunter RC .60 1.50
116 Kirk Haston RC .50 1.25
117 Michael Bradley RC .50 1.25
118 Jason Collins RC .60 1.50
119 Zach Randolph RC 1.25 3.00
120 Brendan Haywood RC .75 2.00
121 Joseph Forte RC .50 1.25
122 Jeryl Sasser RC .50 1.25
123 Brandon Armstrong RC .50 1.25
124 Gerald Wallace RC 1.00 2.50
125 Samuel Dalembert RC .75 2.00
126 Jamaal Tinsley RC .75 2.00
127 Tony Parker RC 3.00 8.00
128 Trenton Hassell RC .60 1.50
129 Gilbert Arenas RC 1.25 3.00
130 Omar Cook RC .75 2.00
131 Jeff Trepagnier RC .50 1.25
132 Loren Woods RC .50 1.25
133 Terence Morris RC .75 2.00
134 Michael Jordan 6.00 15.00

2001-02 Stadium Club Parallel

1-100 STATED ODDS 1:4
101-133 STATED ODDS 1:12
134 Michael Jordan 15.00 40.00

2001-02 Stadium Club Co-Signers

Randomly inserted in packs at a rate of 1:68, this 4-card hobby exclusive insert set features dual players and their autographs. The horizontally designed set is standard size and set on borderless cards. The fronts include color photos of each featured player along with his printed name, autograph, and team name.
DUAL STAT.ODDS 1:1647 HOBBY
TRIPLE STAT.ODDS 1:10168 HOBBY
CS2 S.O'Neal/Abdul-Jabbar 150.00 300.00
CS3 B.Davis/J.Terry 25.00 60.00
SCATRI Magic/Kareem/Shaq 300.00 500.00

2001-02 Stadium Club Dunkus Colossus

Randomly inserted in packs at a rate of 1:4, this 15-card insert set showcases NBA leapers flaunting their most powerful and acrobatic dunks.
COMPLETE SET (15) 5.00 12.00
STATED ODDS 1:4
DC1 Baron Davis .40 1.00
DC2 Vince Carter .60 1.50
DC3 Tracy McGrady .60 1.50
DC4 Shawn Marion .30 .75
DC5 Kevin Garnett .60 1.50
DC6 Darius Miles .25 .60
DC7 Steve Francis .30 .75
DC8 Chris Webber .40 1.00
DC9 Alonzo Mourning .50 1.25
DC10 Rasheed Wallace .40 1.00
DC11 Tim Duncan .75 2.00
DC12 Antonio McDyess .30 .75
DC13 Jerry Stackhouse .30 .75
DC14 Jermaine O'Neal .30 .75
DC15 Shaquille O'Neal 1.00 2.50

2001-02 Stadium Club Lone Star Signatures

Randomly inserted in packs at the rate of one in 18, this 18-card set features full color player action photography coupled with authentic player autographs. Each card is enhanced with the "Topps Certified Autograph" stamp of authenticity.
STATED ODDS 1:18
LSAH Al Harrington 5.00 12.00
LSAJ Antawn Jamison 5.00 12.00
LSCA Courtney Alexander 5.00 12.00
LSEB Elton Brand 5.00 12.00
LSEMJ Magic Johnson 40.00 100.00
LSGA Gilbert Arenas 6.00 15.00
LSHT Hedo Turkoglu 5.00 12.00
LSIT Iakovos Tsakalidis 5.00 12.00
LSJF Joseph Forte 5.00 12.00
LSJT Jason Terry 5.00 12.00
LSKAJ Kareem Abdul-Jabbar 40.00 80.00
LSKS Kenny Satterfield 5.00 12.00
LSMJ Marc Jackson 5.00 12.00
LSPS Peja Stojakovic 6.00 15.00
LSSB Shane Battier 5.00 12.00
LSSM Shawn Marion 5.00 12.00
LSSO Shaquille O'Neal 40.00 100.00
LSTM Troy Murphy 6.00 15.00

2001-02 Stadium Club Maximus Rejectus

This 10-card insert set is randomly inserted in packs at a rate of 1:8. The standard size set features the 10 top shot-swatters in the league set against a borderless background. Color action shots grace the front of the cards as the featured player "swats" for the ball.
STATED ODDS 1:8
MR1 Chris Webber .50 1.25
MR2 Shaquille O'Neal 1.25 3.00
MR3 Tim Duncan 1.00 2.50
MR4 Kevin Garnett .75 2.00
MR5 Darius Miles .30 .75
MR6 Theo Ratliff .30 .75
MR7 Dikembe Mutombo .50 1.25
MR8 Jermaine O'Neal .40 1.00
MR9 Alonzo Mourning .60 1.50
MR10 Marcus Camby .40 1.00

2001-02 Stadium Club NBA Call Signs

This 10-card insert set is randomly inserted in packs at a rate of 1:24. The set highlights 10 NBA stars and their nicknames. The standard size cards have a full color action shot set against a borderless backdrop. The featured player's nickname is boldly printed below the photo along with his actual name.
COMPLETE SET (10) 10.00 25.00
STATED ODDS 1:24
CS1 Steve Francis .75 2.00
CS2 Shaquille O'Neal 2.50 6.00
CS3 Allen Iverson 2.00 5.00
CS4 Tracy McGrady 1.50 4.00
CS5 Vince Carter 1.50 4.00
CS6 Lamar Odom .75 2.00
CS7 Gary Payton 1.00 2.50
CS8 Stephon Marbury .75 2.00
CS9 Karl Malone 1.25 3.00
CS10 Glenn Robinson .75 2.00

2001-02 Stadium Club Stroke of Genius

Randomly inserted along with Traction and Touch of Class cards at the rate of one per box, this 15-card set features a horizontal card design with full color player action photos on the right side of the card and a circular game worn memorabilia swatch on the left. Cards are enhanced with gold foil stamping.
STATED ODDS 1:40
SGAI Allen Iverson 5.00 12.00
SGBD Baron Davis 2.50 6.00
SGCW Chris Webber 2.50 6.00
SGDM Darius Miles 1.50 4.00
SGGP Gary Payton 2.50 6.00
SGGR Glenn Robinson 2.00 5.00
SGJK Jason Kidd 4.00 10.00
SGJS John Stockton 3.00 8.00
SGKM Karl Malone 3.00 8.00
SGKW Jason Williams 2.00 5.00
SGRM Reggie Miller 2.50 6.00
SGRW Rasheed Wallace 2.50 6.00
SGSM Shawn Marion 2.00 5.00
SGSO Shaquille O'Neal 6.00 15.00
SGSXM Stephon Marbury 2.00 5.00

2001-02 Stadium Club Stroke of Genius Autographs

PRINT RUNS LISTED BELOW
SGASM Shawn Marion/31 10.00 25.00
SGASO Shaquille O'Neal/34 125.00 250.00

2001-02 Stadium Club Touch of Class

Randomly inserted along with Traction and Stroke of Genius cards at the rate of one per box, this 15-card set features a horizontal card design with full color player action photos on the right side of the card and a circular game worn sneaker swatch on the left. Cards are enhanced with gold foil stamping.
STATED ODDS 1:40
TCAFM Antonio McDyess 3.00 8.00
TCAM Andre Miller 3.00 8.00
TCDN Dirk Nowitzki 6.00 15.00
TCEB Elton Brand 4.00 10.00
TCJS Jerry Stackhouse 3.00 8.00
TCJT Jason Terry 4.00 10.00
TCKM Kenyon Martin 4.00 10.00
TCMF Michael Finley 4.00 10.00
TCMJ Marc Jackson 2.50 6.00
TCMM Mike Miller 3.00 8.00
TCPP Paul Pierce 4.00 10.00
TCRA Ray Allen 4.00 10.00
TCSF Steve Francis 3.00 8.00
TCTD Tim Duncan 8.00 20.00
TCTM Tracy McGrady 6.00 15.00

2001-02 Stadium Club Touch of Class Autographs

INT RUNS LISTED BELOW
TCAEB Elton Brand/42 20.00 50.00
TCATD Tim Duncan/21 1000.00 1500.00

2001-02 Stadium Club Traction

Randomly inserted along with Touch of Class and Stroke of Genius cards at the rate of one per box, this nine card set features full color player action photos set with a circular swatch of a game used shoe. The right edge of the card is white and contains the Stadium Club Logo in the top corner.
STATED ODDS 1:844
TAJ Antawn Jamison 6.00 15.00
TBD Baron Davis 6.00 15.00
TEB Elton Brand 6.00 15.00
TJT Jason Terry 6.00 15.00
TPS Peja Stojakovic 6.00 15.00
TRH Richard Hamilton 5.00 12.00
TSM Shawn Marion 5.00 12.00
TSO Shaquille O'Neal 15.00 40.00
TTD Tim Duncan 12.00 30.00

2001-02 Stadium Club Traction Autographs

PRINT RUNS LISTED BELOW
SOME NOT PRICED DUE TO SCARCITY
TAJ Antawn Jamison/33 25.00 60.00
TEB Elton Brand/21 25.00 60.00
TJT Jason Terry/31 25.00 60.00
TPS Peja Stojakovic/16 40.00 100.00
TRH Richard Hamilton/16 40.00 100.00
TSM Shawn Marion/31 30.00 80.00
TSO Shaquille O'Neal/34 150.00 300.00

2002-03 Stadium Club

Released in late October 2002, this 133-card set is divided up into 100 veteran players and 33 rookie players. Base cards are extra glossy and borderless, and in the spirit of the Stadium Club line, the photography is incredible. Along the bottom of each card, note: both horizontal and vertical versions were available, is a gold stripe with the players name off to the left and above and the Stadium Club logo off to the right and below. Rookie card stated odds were one in three. Stadium Club was packaged in 24-pack boxes where packs contained six cards and carried a suggested retail price of $3.00.
COMPLETE SET (133) 50.00 100.00
COMP.SET w/o SP's (100) 10.00 25.00
101-133 STATED ODDS 1:3
1 Shaquille O'Neal .60 1.50
2 Pau Gasol .30 .75
3 Allen Iverson .40 1.00
4 Bonzi Wells .15 .40
5 Mike Bibby .25 .60
6 Rashard Lewis .25 .60
7 Aaron McKie .15 .40
8 Shane Battier .25 .60
9 Kenyon Martin .20 .50
10 Tim Duncan .50 1.25
11 Richard Jefferson .25 .60
12 Jalen Rose .20 .50
13 Antoine Walker .20 .50
14 Michael Finley .25 .60
15 Clifford Robinson .15 .40
16 Antawn Jamison .25 .60
17 Reggie Miller .25 .60
18 Elton Brand .25 .60
19 Robert Horry .20 .50
20 Kevin Garnett .40 1.00
21 Baron Davis .20 .50
22 Latrell Sprewell .20 .50
23 Glenn Robinson .20 .50
24 Wally Szczerbiak .20 .50
25 Tracy McGrady .40 1.00
26 Stephon Marbury .20 .50
27 Rasheed Wallace .25 .60
28 Doug Christie .15 .40
29 Desmond Mason .20 .50
30 Vince Carter .40 1.00
31 Andrei Kirilenko .25 .60
32 Richard Hamilton .20 .50
33 Jamaal Tinsley .15 .40
34 Steve Francis .20 .50
35 Ben Wallace .20 .50
36 Juwan Howard .20 .50
37 Dirk Nowitzki .40 1.00
38 Andre Miller .20 .50
39 Elden Campbell .15 .40
40 Paul Pierce .25 .60
41 Shareef Abdur-Rahim .20 .50
42 John Stockton .30 .75
43 Gary Payton .25 .60
44 David Robinson .40 1.00
45 Scottie Pippen .40 1.00
46 Morris Peterson .15 .40
47 Mike Miller .20 .50
48 Marcus Camby .20 .50
49 Joe Smith .20 .50
50 Kobe Bryant 1.00 2.50
51 Alonzo Mourning .30 .75
52 Ray Allen .25 .60
53 Keith Van Horn .20 .50
54 Grant Hill .30 .75
55 Dikembe Mutombo .25 .60
56 Shawn Marion .20 .50
57 Peja Stojakovic .25 .60
58 Tony Parker .30 .75
59 Keon Clark .15 .40
60 Brendan Haywood .15 .40
61 Derek Anderson .15 .40
62 Allan Houston .20 .50
63 Brian Grant .15 .40
64 Lamar Odom .20 .50
65 Jermaine O'Neal .20 .50
66 Kenny Anderson .20 .50
67 Dermarr Johnson .15 .40
68 Lamond Murray .15 .40
69 Jason Richardson .25 .60
70 Rodney Rogers .15 .40
71 Rick Fox .15 .40
72 Tim Thomas .15 .40
73 Darrell Armstrong .15 .40
74 Anfernee Hardaway .40 1.00
75 Chris Webber .25 .60
76 Derrick Coleman .20 .50
77 Karl Malone .30 .75
78 Antonio Davis .15 .40
79 Jason Terry .20 .50
80 Wang Zhizhi .15 .40
81 Steve Nash .30 .75
82 Eddy Curry UER .15 .40
83 Tim Hardaway .25 .60
84 Corliss Williamson .15 .40
85 Eddie Griffin .15 .40
86 Darius Miles .15 .40
87 Jason Williams .20 .50
88 Sam Cassell .20 .50
89 Kwame Brown .15 .40
90 Jason Kidd .40 1.00
91 Jamal Mashburn .20 .50
92 Jamaal Magloire .15 .40
93 Tyson Chandler .25 .60
94 Jumaine Jones .15 .40
95 Antonio McDyess .20 .50
96 Jerry Stackhouse .20 .50
97 Gilbert Arenas .25 .60
98 Cuttino Mobley .15 .40
99 Eddie Jones .20 .50
100 Michael Jordan 2.00 5.00
101 Yao Ming RC 1.50 4.00
102 Jay Williams RC .75 2.00
103 Mike Dunleavy RC .75 2.00
104 Drew Gooden RC .75 2.00
105 Nikoloz Tskitishvili RC .50 1.25
106 DaJuan Wagner RC .60 1.50
107 Nene Hilario RC .75 2.00
108 Chris Wilcox RC .60 1.50
109 Amare Stoudemire RC 1.00 2.50
110 Caron Butler RC .75 2.00
111 Jared Jeffries RC .60 1.50
112 Melvin Ely RC .60 1.50
113 Marcus Haislip RC .60 1.50
114 Fred Jones RC .60 1.50
115 Bostjan Nachbar RC .60 1.50
116 Dan Dickau RC .60 1.50
117 Juan Dixon RC .75 2.00
118 Dan Gadzuric RC .60 1.50
119 Ryan Humphrey RC .60 1.50
120 Kareem Rush RC .60 1.50
121 Qyntel Woods RC .60 1.50
122 Casey Jacobsen RC .60 1.50
123 Tayshaun Prince RC 1.00 2.50
124 Frank Williams RC .50 1.25
125 John Salmons RC .75 2.00
126 Chris Jefferies RC .50 1.25
127 Sam Clancy RC .60 1.50
128 Ronald Murray RC .75 2.00
129 Roger Mason RC .60 1.50
130 Robert Archibald RC .50 1.25
131 Vincent Yarbrough RC .50 1.25
132 Darius Songaila RC .75 2.00
133 Carlos Boozer RC .75 2.00

2002-03 Stadium Club 10th Anniversary Parallel

*STARS: .5X TO 1.25X BASE CARD HI
*RCs: .75X TO 2X BASE CARD HI
ONE 10th ANNAV. OR INSERT PER PACK
101-133 PRINT RUN 1000 SER.#'d SETS
100 Michael Jordan 4.00 10.00

2002-03 Stadium Club Photo Proof Parallel

*STARS: 3X TO 8X BASE CARD HI
*RCs: 3X TO 8X BASE CARD HI
1-100 PRINT RUN 500 SER.#'d SETS
101-133 PRINT RUN 100 SER.#'d SETS
100 Michael Jordan 20.00 50.00

2002-03 Stadium Club All-Star Coverage Relics

Inserted in packs, this 15-card set features a horizontal design with a red white and blue motif. A red stripe appears along the left side of the card, full color player photos appear next to this and are set against a gray background featuring the Ben Franklin Philadelphia All-Star Game logo in white. Next to this is a blue stripe in which a circular piece of game used memorabilia is placed and another gray stripe next to that with the player's name in white. Each card is sequentially numbered to 700.
PRINT RUN 700 SER.#'d SETS
ASAI Allen Iverson 5.00 12.00
ASBH Brendan Haywood 2.00 5.00
ASDLM Darius Miles 2.00 5.00
ASEB Elton Brand 3.00 8.00
ASJK Jason Kidd 5.00 12.00
ASJO Jermaine O'Neal 2.50 6.00
ASJR Jason Richardson 3.00 8.00
ASKM Kenyon Martin 2.50 6.00
ASPG Pau Gasol 4.00 10.00
ASPS Peja Stojakovic 3.00 8.00
ASSB Shane Battier 3.00 8.00
ASSF Steve Francis 2.50 6.00
ASTD Tim Duncan 6.00 15.00
ASTM Tracy McGrady 5.00 12.00
ASTP Tony Parker 4.00 10.00

2002-03 Stadium Club All-Star Coverage Relics Autographs

Randomly seeded in packs, this five card set parallels the look of the base All-Star Coverage Relics insert set enhanced with authentic player autographs. Each card is sequentially numbered to 25.
PRINT RUN 25 SER.#'d SETS
ASAEB Elton Brand 25.00 60.00
ASAJO Jermaine O'Neal 25.00 60.00
ASASB Shane Battier 25.00 60.00
ASATD Tim Duncan 125.00 250.00

2002-03 Stadium Club Beam Team

Inserted in packs, this 20-card set showcases the brightest stars of the NBA on an all foil-board card with full-color player action photos set against a silver background with a gold arch through it. Each card is sequentially numbered to 500.
PRINT RUN 500 SER.#'d SETS
BT1 Shaquille O'Neal 25.00 60.00
BT2 Michael Jordan 100.00 250.00
BT3 Antoine Walker 4.00 10.00
BT4 Vince Carter 8.00 20.00
BT5 Darius Miles 3.00 8.00
BT6 Jerry Stackhouse 4.00 10.00
BT7 Kevin Garnett 15.00 40.00
BT8 Tim Duncan 15.00 40.00
BT9 Kobe Bryant 20.00 50.00
BT10 Steve Francis 4.00 10.00
BT11 Tony Parker 6.00 15.00
BT12 Richard Jefferson 5.00 12.00
BT13 Dirk Nowitzki 8.00 20.00
BT14 Antawn Jamison 5.00 12.00
BT15 DaJuan Wagner 4.00 10.00
BT16 Caron Butler 5.00 12.00
BT17 Mike Dunleavy 5.00 12.00
BT18 Kareem Rush 4.00 10.00
BT19 Amare Stoudemire 6.00 15.00
BT20 Drew Gooden 5.00 12.00

2002-03 Stadium Club Co-Signers

Seeded in packs at the rate of 1:2224, this two card set pairs players on cards with two authentic player autographs and two full color player photos.

STATED ODDS 1:2224
CS1 S.O'Neal/T.Duncan 175.00 350.00
CS2 E.Brand/S.Marion 30.00 80.00

2002-03 Stadium Club Dual Relics

Randomly seeded, this 10-card set places two players, one on each side of the card in full-color action with a gray strip and two circular swatches of game used memorabilia through the middle. Each card is sequentially numbered to 100.

PRINT RUN 100 SER.#'d SETS
CC1 T.McGrady/S.Francis 15.00 40.00
CC2 S.O'Neal/T.Duncan 20.00 50.00
CC3 A.Iverson/S.O'Neal 20.00 50.00
CC4 T.Duncan JSY/WU 15.00 40.00
CC5 S.O'Neal JSY/WU 25.00 60.00
CC6 M.Finley/D.Nowitzki 15.00 40.00
CC7 J.Stockton/K.Malone 15.00 40.00
CC8 R.Allen/G.Robinson 15.00 40.00
CC9 C.Webber/P.Stojakovic 15.00 40.00
CC10 P.Pierce/B.Davis 15.00 40.00

2002-03 Stadium Club Frequent Flyers Relics

Inserted in packs, this 14-card set showcases players in mid air with a trapezoidal swatch of game used memorabilia. Backgrounds feature a cloudy sky along the top, a true-life stadium background in the middle and an all-white background along the bottom where the swatch of memorabilia resides. Each card is sequentially numbered-print runs are listed below.

PRINT RUNS LISTED BELOW
FFAH Anfernee Hardaway/700 5.00 12.00
FFDN Dirk Nowitzki/700 5.00 12.00
FFJT Jason Terry/200 4.00 10.00
FFPP Paul Pierce/700 3.00 8.00
FFQR Quentin Richardson/350 2.50 6.00
FFRA Ray Allen/700 3.00 8.00
FFRL Raef Lafrentz/700 2.00 5.00
FFRW Rasheed Wallace/350 3.00 8.00
FFSM Stephon Marbury/700 2.50 6.00
FFSO Shaquille O'Neal/700 8.00 20.00
FFSDM Shawn Marion/700 2.50 6.00
FFTD Tim Duncan/700 6.00 15.00
FFTM Tracy McGrady/700 5.00 12.00

2002-03 Stadium Club Frequent Flyers Relics Autographs

Randomly seeded in packs, this five card set utilizes the same design as the base Frequent Flyers Relics set enhanced with authentic player autographs. Each card is sequentially numbered to 25.

PRINT RUN 25 SER.#'d SETS
FFAJT Jason Terry 20.00 50.00
FFARL Raef LaFrentz 20.00 50.00
FFASO Shaquille O'Neal 150.00 300.00
FFATD Tim Duncan 125.00 250.00
FFASDM Shawn Marion 30.00 80.00

2002-03 Stadium Club Lone Star Signatures

Randomly inserted in packs, this 25-card set features a full color player action photo towards the top of the card, a border with a fingerprint pattern along the left side, and a red stripe through the middle (horizontally) to separate the white autograph space from the photo. Each card contains a gold foil Topps authentication stamp and is sequentially numbered. Print runs are listed below.

PRINT RUNS LISTED BELOW
LSAM Aaron McKie/250 5.00 12.00
LSDB Damone Brown/500 5.00 12.00
LSDG Drew Gooden/100 5.00 12.00
LSDW DaJuan Wagner/100 4.00 10.00
LSEB Elton Brand/100 8.00 20.00
LSFJ Fred Jones/100 4.00 10.00
LSFW Frank Williams/100 3.00 8.00
LSJF Joseph Forte/250 5.00 12.00
LSJT Jake Tsakalidis/500 5.00 12.00
LSKB Kwame Brown/250 5.00 12.00
LSKS Kenny Satterfield/250 5.00 12.00
LSLP Lavor Postell/1000 5.00 12.00
LSMB Mike Bibby/500 6.00 15.00
LSMD Mike Dunleavy/100 5.00 12.00
LSRH Richard Hamilton/500 6.00 15.00
LSSM Shawn Marion/200 8.00 20.00
LSSO Shaquille O'Neal/1000 40.00 80.00
LSTM Troy Murphy/250 5.00 12.00
LSYM Yao Ming/100 25.00 60.00

2002-03 Stadium Club Reprint Relics

Randomly inserted in packs, this 10-card set uses a horizontal design and places a photo of the featured player's Stadium Club rookie card on the left and a parallelogram-shaped swatch of game-used memorabilia on the right. Each card is sequentially numbered to 700.

PRINT RUN 700 SER.#'d SETS
SCCW Chris Webber 4.00 10.00
SCDM Darius Miles 2.50 6.00
SCDN Dirk Nowitzki 6.00 15.00
SCEB Elton Brand 4.00 10.00
SCJK Jason Kidd 6.00 15.00
SCMF Michael Finley 4.00 10.00
SCPG Pau Gasol 5.00 12.00
SCRA Ray Allen 4.00 10.00
SCSO Shaquille O'Neal 10.00 25.00
SCTD Tim Duncan 8.00 20.00

2002-03 Stadium Club The Hustlers

Randomly inserted in packs at the rate of one in four, this 20-card set is horizontally designed with gold and white borders along the left and right side of the card and full-color player action photos in the middle. The words, "The Hustlers" appear in the left border and the player's name appears in the right.

COMPLETE SET (20) 10.00 25.00
STATED ODDS 1:4
H1 Baron Davis .40 1.00
H2 Jamaal Tinsley .30 .75
H3 Karl Malone .60 1.50
H4 Kevin Garnett .75 2.00
H5 Tim Duncan 1.00 2.50
H6 Kenyon Martin .40 1.00
H7 Michael Jordan 4.00 10.00
H8 Vince Carter .75 2.00
H9 Kobe Bryant 2.00 5.00
H10 Alonzo Mourning .60 1.50
H11 Shaquille O'Neal 1.25 3.00
H12 Chris Webber .50 1.25
H13 Paul Pierce .50 1.25
H14 Tony Parker .60 1.50
H15 Jason Kidd .75 2.00
H16 Antonio McDyess .40 1.00
H17 Eddie Jones .40 1.00
H18 Michael Finley .50 1.25
H19 Tracy McGrady .75 2.00
H20 Gary Payton .50 1.25

2002-03 Stadium Club Urban Legends

Randomly seeded in packs at the rate of one in eight, this ten card set also uses a horizontal design with a background reminiscent of black top on the left side that contains a map quest map of the player's home town. Full color phots are set against an urban background with buildings and a chain link fence.

COMPLETE SET (10) 3.00 8.00
STATED ODDS 1:8
UL1 Allen Iverson .60 1.50
UL2 Kobe Bryant 1.50 4.00
UL3 Elton Brand .40 1.00
UL4 Jamaal Tinsley .25 .60
UL5 Vince Carter .60 1.50
UL6 Kevin Garnett .60 1.50
UL7 Gary Payton .40 1.00
UL8 Ron Artest .40 1.00
UL9 Kenny Anderson .30 .75
UL10 Stephon Marbury .30 .75

2002-03 Stadium Club Beckett.com Samples

*SINGLES: .75X TO 2X BASE STADIUM HI

2007-08 Stadium Club Promos

PP1 Dwyane Wade .60 1.50
PP2 Carmelo Anthony .50 1.25
PP3 Larry Bird/Magic Johnson 1.00 2.50

2007-08 Stadium Club

This 150-card set was released in December, 2007. The set was issued into the hobby in six card packs, with an $20 SRP, which came 12 packs to a box, six boxes to a carton and two cartons to a case. Cards numbered 1-80 feature veterans, with cards numbered 81-100 featuring retired greats and cards numbered 1-150 featuring 2007-08 NBA rookies. The Rookie Cards were issued to a stated print run of 1999 serial numbered sets. A card for a signed 8" by 10" Greg Oden photo was randomly inserted into packs as well.

COMP.SET w/o SP's (100) 20.00 50.00
RC PRINT RUN 1999 SER.#'d SETS
EXCH EXPIRE DATE 1/31/10
UNPRICED PP PLATINUM PRINT RUN ONE SET
UNPRICED RC SPRFRCTR PRINT RUN ONE SET
1 Amare Stoudemire .30 .75
2 Baron Davis .30 .75
3 Dwyane Wade .60 1.50
4 Chris Bosh .40 1.00
5 Josh Smith .30 .75
6 Tyson Chandler .30 .75
7 Al Jefferson .30 .75
8 Deron Williams .30 .75
9 Andre Iguodala .30 .75
10 Jermaine O'Neal .30 .75
11 Yao Ming .50 1.25
12 Kirk Hinrich .30 .75
13 Steve Nash .50 1.25
14 Jameer Nelson .25 .60
15 Carmelo Anthony .50 1.25
16 Pau Gasol .40 1.00
17 Andrew Bynum .25 .60
18 Gerald Wallace .30 .75
19 Carlos Boozer .30 .75
20 Rasheed Wallace .40 1.00
21 Tim Duncan .60 1.50
22 Michael Redd .30 .75
23 LeBron James 1.50 4.00
24 Kobe Bryant 1.50 4.00
25 Richard Jefferson .30 .75
26 Mike Bibby .40 1.00
27 Ben Gordon .30 .75
28 Caron Butler .30 .75
29 Corey Maggette .30 .75
30 Kevin Garnett .60 1.50
31 Shawn Marion .30 .75
32 Shaquille O'Neal .75 2.00
33 Allen Iverson .50 1.25
34 Eddy Curry .25 .60
35 Chris Wilcox .25 .60
36 T.J. Ford .25 .60
37 LaMarcus Aldridge .50 1.25
38 Drew Gooden .30 .75
39 Antawn Jamison .30 .75
40 Richard Hamilton .30 .75
41 Dirk Nowitzki .50 1.25
42 Elton Brand .40 1.00
43 Jason Richardson .40 1.00
44 Paul Pierce .40 1.00
45 Manu Ginobili .40 1.00
46 Danny Granger .30 .75
47 Andrei Kirilenko .30 .75
48 Jarrett Jack .30 .75
49 Andre Miller .30 .75
50 Gilbert Arenas .30 .75
51 Mehmet Okur .25 .60
52 Rudy Gay .40 1.00
53 Ben Wallace .30 .75
54 Tayshaun Prince .30 .75
55 Jason Kidd .40 1.00
56 Josh Howard .30 .75
57 Daniel Gibson .30 .75
58 Rafer Alston .25 .60
59 Monta Ellis .30 .75
60 Dwight Howard .30 .75
61 Chauncey Billups .40 1.00
62 Joe Johnson .30 .75
63 Kevin Martin .30 .75
64 Ray Allen .40 1.00
65 Luol Deng .30 .75
66 Raymond Felton .40 1.00
67 Lamar Odom .30 .75
68 Mo Williams .30 .75
69 Tony Parker .40 1.00
70 Brandon Roy .40 1.00
71 Tracy McGrady .40 1.00
72 Marcus Camby .25 .60
73 Stephon Marbury .30 .75
74 Jason Terry .30 .75
75 Randy Foye .40 1.00
76 Vince Carter .50 1.25
77 Andrea Bargnani .40 1.00
78 Chris Paul .50 1.25
79 Rashard Lewis .30 .75
80 Leandro Barbosa .30 .75
81 Larry Johnson 1.00 2.50
82 Patrick Ewing 1.25 3.00
83 Hakeem Olajuwon 1.25 3.00
84 Clyde Drexler 1.25 3.00
85 David Robinson 1.50 4.00
86 Bill Walton 1.00 2.50
87 Wilt Chamberlain 2.00 5.00
88 Bill Russell 1.50 4.00
89 Bob Lanier .75 2.00
90 Dennis Rodman 2.00 5.00
91 John Stockton 1.50 4.00
92 Isiah Thomas 1.00 2.50
93 Magic Johnson 2.50 6.00
94 Larry Bird 2.50 6.00
95 Elgin Baylor 1.00 2.50
96 Oscar Robertson 1.00 2.50
97 Joe Barry Carroll 1.00 2.50
98 James Worthy 1.25 3.00
99 Pete Maravich 1.50 4.00
100 Kenny Smith .75 2.00
101 Greg Oden RC 1.50 4.00
102 Kevin Durant RC 15.00 40.00
103 Al Horford RC 2.00 5.00
104 Mike Conley Jr. RC 2.00 5.00
105 Jeff Green RC 1.50 4.00
106 Yi Jianlian RC 2.00 5.00
107 Corey Brewer RC 1.50 4.00
108 Brandan Wright RC 1.50 4.00
109 Joakim Noah RC 1.50 4.00
110 Spencer Hawes RC 1.25 3.00
111 Acie Law RC 1.00 2.50
112 Thaddeus Young RC 1.50 4.00
113 Julian Wright RC 1.00 2.50
114 Al Thornton RC 1.25 3.00
115 Rodney Stuckey RC 1.25 3.00
116 Nick Young RC 2.00 5.00
117 Sean Williams RC 1.00 2.50
118 Marco Belinelli RC 1.50 4.00
119 Javaris Crittenton RC 1.00 2.50
120 Jason Smith RC 1.25 3.00
121 Daequan Cook RC 1.25 3.00
122 Jared Dudley RC 1.25 3.00
123 Wilson Chandler RC 1.25 3.00
124 D.J. Strawberry RC 1.00 2.50
125 Morris Almond RC 1.00 2.50
126 Aaron Brooks RC 1.25 3.00
127 Arron Afflalo RC 1.50 4.00
128 Luis Scola RC 2.00 5.00
129 Alando Tucker RC 1.00 2.50
130 Carl Landry RC 1.00 2.50
131 Gabe Pruitt RC 1.00 2.50
132 Marcus Williams RC 1.00 2.50
133 Nick Fazekas RC 1.00 2.50
134 Glen Davis RC 1.25 3.00
135 Jermareo Davidson RC 1.00 2.50
136 Josh McRoberts RC 1.25 3.00
137 Oleksiy Pecherov RC 1.50 4.00
138 Derrick Byars RC 1.00 2.50
139 Adam Haluska RC 1.00 2.50
140 Reyshawn Terry RC 1.00 2.50
141 Jared Jordan RC 1.00 2.50
142 Stephane Lasme RC 1.00 2.50
143 Dominic McGuire RC 1.00 2.50
144 Aaron Gray RC 1.00 2.50
145 JamesOn Curry RC 1.00 2.50
146 Taurean Green RC 1.00 2.50
147 Demetris Nichols RC 1.00 2.50
148 Herbert Hill RC 1.00 2.50
149 Ramon Sessions RC 1.50 4.00
150 Sammy Mejia RC 1.00 2.50
NNO G.Oden AU 8x10 100.00 200.00

2007-08 Stadium Club Chrome Rookie Refractors

*REFRACTORS: .5X TO 1.25X BASE HI
REF.PRINT RUN 999 SER.#'d SETS
102 Kevin Durant 25.00 60.00

2007-08 Stadium Club Chrome Rookie Refractors Gold

*REF.GOLD: 1.25X TO 3X BASE HI
PRINT RUN 99 SER.#'d SETS
102 Kevin Durant 100.00 250.00

2007-08 Stadium Club Chrome Rookie X-Fractors

*X-FRACTOR: 1.5X TO 4X BASE HI
PRINT RUN 50 SER.#'d SETS
102 Kevin Durant 175.00 400.00

2007-08 Stadium Club Chrome Rookie X-Fractors Autographs

OUP A ODDS 1:66, GROUP B 1:30
GROUP C ODDS 1:9
101 Greg Oden B 5.00 12.00
106 Yi Jianlian A 6.00 15.00
108 Brandan Wright A 5.00 12.00
110 Spencer Hawes B 4.00 10.00
111 Acie Law B 3.00 8.00
112 Thaddeus Young C 5.00 12.00
115 Rodney Stuckey C 4.00 10.00
116 Nick Young A 6.00 15.00
117 Sean Williams C 3.00 8.00
118 Marco Belinelli C 5.00 12.00
119 Javaris Crittenton C 3.00 8.00
120 Jason Smith B 4.00 10.00
121 Daequan Cook C 4.00 10.00
122 Jared Dudley B 4.00 10.00
123 Wilson Chandler C 4.00 10.00
125 Morris Almond C 3.00 8.00
126 Aaron Brooks C 4.00 10.00
127 Arron Afflalo C 5.00 12.00
132 Marcus Williams C 3.00 8.00
133 Nick Fazekas C 3.00 8.00

2007-08 Stadium Club First Day Issue

*1-80 VETS: .6X TO 1.5X BASE HI
*81-100 RETIRED: .5X TO 1.25X BASE HI
PRINT RUN 1999 SER.#'d SETS

2007-08 Stadium Club Photographer's Proof Silver

ILVER 1-80: .75X TO 2X BASE HI
*SILVER 81-100: .6X TO 1.5X BASE HI
SILVER PRINT RUN 199 SER.#'d SETS

2007-08 Stadium Club Beam Team Autographs

GROUP A ODDS 1:110, GROUP B 1:141
GROUP C ODDS 1:38, GROUP D 1:26
GROUP E ODDS 1:20, GROUP F 1:44
*AU GOLD: .5X TO 1.25X BASE HI
GOLD PRINT RUN 25 SER.#'d SETS
AB Andrea Bargnani A 5.00 12.00
ABY Andrew Bynum B 5.00 12.00
AI Andre Iguodala A 5.00 12.00
AM Adam Morrison A 5.00 12.00
BD Baron Davis C 5.00 12.00
BG Ben Gordon A 5.00 12.00
CA Carmelo Anthony A 20.00 50.00
CB Carlos Boozer A 5.00 12.00
CBI Chauncey Billups B 6.00 15.00
CBO Chris Bosh A 6.00 15.00
CD Chris Duhon D 5.00 12.00
CF Channing Frye D 5.00 12.00
CM Corey Maggette E 5.00 12.00
DG Danny Granger F 5.00 12.00
DL David Lee E 5.00 12.00
DW Dwyane Wade A 20.00 50.00
DWI Deron Williams C 5.00 12.00
EO Emeka Okafor A 5.00 12.00
GW Gerald Wallace C 5.00 12.00
HT Hedo Turkoglu E 5.00 12.00
JC Josh Childress C 5.00 12.00
JF Jordan Farmar A 6.00 15.00
JH Josh Howard B 5.00 12.00
JO Jermaine O'Neal A 5.00 12.00
KH Kirk Hinrich B 5.00 12.00
MJ Mike James E 5.00 12.00
MW Marcus Williams D 5.00 12.00
MWE Martell Webster D 5.00 12.00
RA Ray Allen A 15.00 30.00
RB Raja Bell E 5.00 12.00
RF Raymond Felton C 5.00 12.00
SC Speedy Claxton F 5.00 12.00
SD Samuel Dalembert E 5.00 12.00
SO Shaquille O'Neal A 80.00 160.00
TJF T.J. Ford C 5.00 12.00
TP Tony Parker A 12.00 30.00
UH Udonis Haslem D 5.00 12.00
VC Vince Carter A 15.00 40.00

2007-08 Stadium Club Beam Team Relics

GROUP A ODDS 1:30, GROUP B 1:40
GROUP C ODDS 1:6, GROUP D 1:6
*GOLD: .6X TO 1.5X BASE HI
GOLD PRINT RUN 99 SER.#'d SETS
AB Andrea Bargnani D 3.00 8.00
AI Allen Iverson A 4.00 10.00
AIG Andre Iguodala C 2.50 6.00
AS Amare Stoudemire A 2.50 6.00
BD Baron Davis B 2.50 6.00
BG Ben Gordon A 2.50 6.00
CA Carmelo Anthony A 4.00 10.00
CB Carlos Boozer A 2.50 6.00
CBI Chauncey Billups C 3.00 8.00
CBO Chris Bosh C 3.00 8.00
DH Dwight Howard C 2.50 6.00
DN Dirk Nowitzki D 4.00 10.00
DW Dwyane Wade D 3.00 8.00
DWI Deron Williams D 2.50 6.00
JK Jason Kidd A 3.00 8.00
JO Jermaine O'Neal D 2.50 6.00
KB Kobe Bryant C 8.00 20.00
LD Luol Deng D 2.50 6.00
SN Steve Nash C 2.00 5.00
SO Shaquille O'Neal D 4.00 10.00
TD Tim Duncan C 5.00 12.00
TM Tracy McGrady C 3.00 8.00
TP Tony Parker C 3.00 8.00
VC Vince Carter B 4.00 10.00
YM Yao Ming C 4.00 10.00

2007-08 Stadium Club Full Court Press Relics

PRINT RUN 499 SER.#'d SETS
*GOLD: .5X TO 1.25X BASE HI
GOLD PRINT RUN 50 SER.#'d SETS
*DUAL: SAME VALUE AS BASE
DUAL PRINT RUN 199 SER.#'d SETS
*DUAL GOLD: .6X TO 1.5X BASE HI
DUAL GOLD PRINT RUN 25 SER.#'d SETS
*TRIPLE: .5X TO 1.25X BASE HI
TRIPLE PRINT RUN 99 SET.#'d SETS
UNPRICED TRIPLE GOLD PRINT RUN 10 SETS
AA Arron Afflalo 2.50 6.00
AB Aaron Brooks 2.00 5.00
AH Al Horford 3.00 8.00
AJ Al Jefferson 2.00 5.00
AL Acie Law 1.50 4.00
AS Amare Stoudemire 2.00 5.00
AT Al Thornton 2.00 5.00
ATU Alando Tucker 1.50 4.00
BD Baron Davis 2.00 5.00
BW Brandan Wright 2.50 6.00
BWA Ben Wallace 2.00 5.00
CA Carmelo Anthony 3.00 8.00
CB Corey Brewer 2.50 6.00
CBO Chris Bosh 2.50 6.00
CP Chris Paul 3.00 8.00
DC Daequan Cook 2.00 5.00
DH Dwight Howard 2.00 5.00
DN Dirk Nowitzki 3.00 8.00
DR David Robinson 4.00 10.00
DW Dwyane Wade 4.00 10.00
DWI Dominique Wilkins 3.00 8.00
EB Elton Brand 2.50 6.00
GD Glen Davis 2.00 5.00
GO Greg Oden 2.50 6.00
IT Isiah Thomas 2.50 6.00
JC Javaris Crittenton 1.50 4.00
JD Jared Dudley 2.00 5.00
JG Jeff Green 2.50 6.00
JK Jason Kidd 2.50 6.00
JM Josh McRoberts 2.00 5.00
JN Joakim Noah 2.50 6.00
JS Jason Smith 2.00 5.00
JW Julian Wright 1.50 4.00
KB Kobe Bryant 8.00 20.00
LB Larry Bird 6.00 15.00
MC Mike Conley Jr. 3.00 8.00
MJ Magic Johnson 6.00 15.00
NY Nick Young 3.00 8.00
RJ Richard Jefferson 2.00 5.00
RS Rodney Stuckey 2.00 5.00
SH Spencer Hawes 2.00 5.00
SN Steve Nash 3.00 8.00
SO Shaquille O'Neal 5.00 12.00
SW Sean Williams 1.50 4.00
TD Tim Duncan 4.00 10.00
TM Tracy McGrady 2.50 6.00
TY Thaddeus Young 2.50 6.00
VC Vince Carter 3.00 8.00
WC Wilson Chandler 2.00 5.00
YM Yao Ming 3.00 8.00

2007-08 Stadium Club Future Foundation Autographs Relics Dual

GROUP A ODDS 1:2050, GROUP B 1:1175
GROUP C ODDS 1:176
AW C.Anthony/M.Williams B 15.00 40.00
BL C.Billups/A.Law C 15.00 40.00
BW C.Bosh/B.Wright B 20.00 50.00
DC B.Davis/J.Crittenton C 12.00 30.00
IY A.Iguodala/T.Young C 12.00 30.00
OH J.O'Neal/S.Hawes C 12.00 30.00
RO B.Russell/G.Oden A 75.00 150.00
RW D.Rodman/S.Williams C 15.00 40.00
WT D.Wilkins/A.Thornton C 15.00 40.00
WY D.Wade/N.Young A 30.00 80.00

2007-08 Stadium Club Super Teams

PRINT RUN 50 SER.#'d SETS
ATL Atlanta Hawks 5.00 12.00
BOS Boston Celtics 10.00 25.00
CHA Charlotte Bobcats 5.00 12.00
CHI Chicago Bulls 6.00 15.00
CLE Cleveland Cavaliers 10.00 25.00
DAL Dallas Mavericks 6.00 15.00
DEN Denver Nuggets 6.00 15.00
DET Detroit Pistons 5.00 12.00
GST Golden State Warriors 5.00 12.00
HOU Houston Rockets 5.00 12.00
IND Indiana Pacers 5.00 12.00
LAC Los Angeles Clippers 5.00 12.00
LAL Los Angeles Lakers 10.00 25.00
MEM Memphis Grizzlies 5.00 12.00
MIA Miami Heat 6.00 15.00
MIL Milwaukee Bucks 5.00 12.00
MIN Minnesota Timberwolves 5.00 12.00
NJE New Jersey Nets 5.00 12.00
NOR New Orleans Hornets 5.00 12.00
NYC New York Knicks 6.00 15.00
ORL Orlando Magic 6.00 15.00
PHI Philadelphia 76ers 5.00 12.00
PHO Phoenix Suns 6.00 15.00
POR Portland Trail Blazers 5.00 12.00
SAC Sacramento Kings 5.00 12.00
SAN San Antonio Spurs 6.00 15.00
SEA Seattle SuperSonics 6.00 15.00
TOR Toronto Raptors 5.00 12.00
UTA Utah Jazz 5.00 12.00
WAS Washington Wizards 5.00 12.00

2007-08 Stadium Club Super Teams Rookie Black Refractors

COMPLETE SET (50) 100.00 200.00
SET AVAILABLE VIA DIVISON ST WINNER
UNPRICED SUPERFR. VIA CHAMP.ST WINNER
UNPRICED X-FRACTOR VIA CONF.ST WINNER
101 Greg Oden 2.00 5.00
102 Kevin Durant 30.00 80.00
103 Al Horford 2.50 6.00
104 Mike Conley Jr. 2.50 6.00
105 Jeff Green 2.00 5.00
106 Yi Jianlian 2.50 6.00
107 Corey Brewer 2.00 5.00
108 Brandan Wright 2.00 5.00
109 Joakim Noah 2.00 5.00
110 Spencer Hawes 1.50 4.00
111 Acie Law 1.25 3.00
112 Thaddeus Young 2.00 5.00
113 Julian Wright 1.25 3.00
114 Al Thornton 1.50 4.00
115 Rodney Stuckey 1.50 4.00
116 Nick Young 2.50 6.00
117 Sean Williams 1.25 3.00
118 Marco Belinelli 2.00 5.00
119 Javaris Crittenton 1.25 3.00
120 Jason Smith 1.50 4.00
121 Daequan Cook 1.50 4.00
122 Jared Dudley 1.50 4.00
123 Wilson Chandler 1.50 4.00
124 D.J. Strawberry 1.25 3.00
125 Morris Almond 1.25 3.00
126 Aaron Brooks 1.50 4.00
127 Arron Afflalo 2.00 5.00
128 Luis Scola 2.50 6.00
129 Alando Tucker 1.25 3.00
130 Carl Landry 1.25 3.00
131 Gabe Pruitt 1.25 3.00
132 Marcus Williams 1.25 3.00
133 Nick Fazekas 1.25 3.00
134 Glen Davis 1.50 4.00
135 Jermareo Davidson 1.25 3.00
136 Josh McRoberts 1.50 4.00
137 Oleksiy Pecherov 2.00 5.00
138 Derrick Byars 1.25 3.00
139 Adam Haluska 1.25 3.00
140 Reyshawn Terry 1.25 3.00
141 Jared Jordan 1.25 3.00
142 Stephane Lasme 1.25 3.00
143 Dominic McGuire 1.25 3.00
144 Aaron Gray 1.25 3.00
145 JamesOn Curry 1.25 3.00
146 Taurean Green 1.25 3.00
147 Demetris Nichols 1.25 3.00
148 Herbert Hill 1.25 3.00
149 Ramon Sessions 2.00 5.00
150 Sammy Mejia 1.25 3.00

1999-00 Stadium Club Chrome

Debuting in 1999/00, the base set contained 150 cards printed on 23-point stock. Most of the cards were parallels of the Stadium Club set, with some updated photography on rookies and free agents. Each pack contained five cards with a suggested retail price of $4.00.

COMPLETE SET (150) 25.00 60.00
1 Allen Iverson .60 1.50
2 Chris Webber .30 .75
3 Antawn Jamison .30 .75
4 Karl Malone .40 1.00
5 Sam Cassell .25 .60
6 Kerry Kittles .20 .50
7 Tim Thomas .25 .60
8 Shawn Bradley .20 .50
9 David Wesley .20 .50
10 Glenn Robinson .25 .60
11 Mitch Richmond .30 .75
12 Shareef Abdur-Rahim .25 .60
13 Christian Laettner .25 .60
14 Anthony Mason .20 .50
15 Randy Brown .20 .50
16 Charles Barkley .50 1.25
17 Bobby Jackson .20 .50
18 Matt Harpring .20 .50
19 Shawn Kemp .30 .75
20 Ruben Patterson .20 .50
21 Mike Bibby .30 .75
22 Vlade Divac .30 .75
23 David Robinson .50 1.25
24 Keith Van Horn .25 .60
25 Juwan Howard .25 .60
26 Shaquille O'Neal .75 2.00
27 Alonzo Mourning .40 1.00
28 Michael Olowokandi .20 .50
29 Andrew DeClercq .20 .50
30 Toni Kukoc .30 .75
31 Dikembe Mutombo .30 .75
32 Steve Nash .50 1.25
33 Eddie Jones .30 .75
34 Reggie Miller .30 .75
35 Larry Hughes .25 .60
36 Tim Duncan .60 1.50
37 Jerome Williams .20 .50
38 Rod Strickland .20 .50
39 Patrick Ewing .40 1.00
40 Grant Hill .40 1.00
41 Derrick Coleman .25 .60
42 Raef LaFrentz .25 .60
43 Rik Smits .30 .75
44 Latrell Sprewell .30 .75
45 John Starks .25 .60
46 Cuttino Mobley .20 .50
47 Marcus Camby .25 .60
48 Stephon Marbury .25 .60
49 Tom Gugliotta .20 .50
50 Vince Carter .60 1.50
51 Chris Mullin .30 .75
52 Tyrone Nesby RC .40 1.00
53 Elden Campbell .20 .50
54 Lindsey Hunter .20 .50
55 Rasheed Wallace .30 .75
56 Jeff Hornacek .25 .60
57 Matt Geiger .20 .50
58 Antoine Walker .30 .75
59 Jason Williams .40 1.00
60 Robert Horry .25 .60
61 Kendall Gill .20 .50
62 Dan Majerle .30 .75
63 Robert Traylor .20 .50
64 P.J. Brown .20 .50
65 Terrell Brandon .20 .50
66 Corliss Williamson .20 .50
67 Bryant Reeves .20 .50
68 Larry Johnson .30 .75
69 Keith Closs .20 .50
70 Walter McCarty .20 .50
71 Wesley Person .20 .50
72 Chris Mills .20 .50
73 Glen Rice .30 .75
74 Jason Kidd .50 1.25
75 Dirk Nowitzki .60 1.50
76 Bryon Russell .20 .50
77 Vin Baker .25 .60
78 Darrell Armstrong .20 .50
79 Eric Snow .25 .60
80 Hakeem Olajuwon .40 1.00
81 Tracy McGrady .50 1.25
82 Kenny Anderson .25 .60
83 Jalen Rose .25 .60
84 Tim Hardaway .30 .75
85 Doug Christie .25 .60
86 Allan Houston .25 .60
87 Kobe Bryant 1.25 3.00
88 Kevin Garnett .50 1.25
89 Steve Kerr .25 .60
90 Nick Van Exel .25 .60
91 Jerry Stackhouse .30 .75
92 Derek Fisher .30 .75
93 Donyell Marshall .20 .50
94 Mark Jackson .25 .60
95 Ray Allen .30 .75
96 Avery Johnson .25 .60
97 Michael Doleac .20 .50
98 Charles Oakley .25 .60
99 Gary Payton .30 .75
100 Theo Ratliff .25 .60
101 Cedric Ceballos .20 .50
102 Paul Pierce .40 1.00
103 Michael Finley .30 .75
104 Brian Grant .20 .50
105 John Stockton .40 1.00
106 Maurice Taylor .20 .50
107 Antonio McDyess .25 .60
108 Adrian Griffin RC .50 1.25
109 Jamal Mashburn .25 .60
110 Jayson Williams .20 .50
111 Joe Smith .25 .60
112 Clifford Robinson .20 .50
113 Mario Elie .20 .50
114 Damon Stoudamire .25 .60
115 Felipe Lopez .20 .50
116 Antonio Davis TRAN .20 .50
117 Mookie Blaylock TRAN .20 .50
118 Ron Mercer TRAN .25 .60
119 Horace Grant TRAN .25 .60
120 Steve Smith TRAN .25 .60
121 Isaiah Rider TRAN .25 .60
122 Tariq Abdul-Wahad TRAN .20 .50
123 Michael Dickerson TRAN .20 .50
124 Nick Anderson TRAN .20 .50
125 Jim Jackson TRAN .20 .50
126 Hersey Hawkins TRAN .20 .50
127 Brent Barry TRAN .25 .60
128 Shandon Anderson TRAN .20 .50
129 Scottie Pippen TRAN .50 1.25
130 Isaac Austin TRAN .20 .50
131 Anfernee Hardaway TRAN .50 1.25
132 Elton Brand RC 1.25 3.00
133 Steve Francis RC 1.25 3.00
134 Baron Davis RC 1.25 3.00
135 Lamar Odom RC 1.25 3.00
136 Jonathan Bender RC .50 1.25
137 Wally Szczerbiak RC 1.00 2.50
138 Richard Hamilton RC 1.00 2.50
139 Andre Miller RC 1.00 2.50
140 Shawn Marion RC 1.00 2.50
141 Jason Terry RC .75 2.00
142 Trajan Langdon RC .50 1.25
143 A.Radojevic RC .30 .75
144 Corey Maggette RC .75 2.00
145 William Avery RC .40 1.00
146 Ron Artest RC 1.00 2.50
147 Cal Bowdler RC .30 .75
148 James Posey RC .50 1.25
149 Quincy Lewis RC .30 .75
150 Scott Padgett RC .40 1.00

1999-00 Stadium Club Chrome First Day Issue

*STARS: 10X TO 25X BASE CARD HI
*RCs: 3X TO 8X BASE HI
STATED PRINT RUN 100 SERIAL #'d SETS
STATED ODDS 1:47

1999-00 Stadium Club Chrome First Day Issue Refractors

*STARS: 30X TO 80X BASE CARD HI
*RCs: 8X TO 20X BASE HI
STATED PRINT RUN 25 SERIAL #'d SETS
STATED ODDS 1:186
87 Kobe Bryant 250.00 500.00

1999-00 Stadium Club Chrome Refractors

*STARS: 2X TO 5X BASE CARD HI
*RCs: 1.25X TO 3X BASE HI
STATED ODDS 1:12

1999-00 Stadium Club Chrome Clear Shots

Randomly inserted in packs at one in 16, this 10-card set features NBA rookies shot from both the front and the back at the same time. The cards are printed on ClearChrome technology. Card backs carry a "CS" prefix.

COMPLETE SET (10) 4.00 10.00
STATED ODDS 1:16
*REF: 1X TO 2.5X HI COLUMN
REF: STATED ODDS 1:80
CS1 Lamar Odom .75 2.00
CS2 Elton Brand .75 2.00
CS3 Steve Francis .75 2.00
CS4 Shawn Marion .60 1.50
CS5 Wally Szczerbiak .60 1.50
CS6 Richard Hamilton .60 1.50
CS7 Andre Miller .60 1.50
CS8 Jason Terry .50 1.25
CS9 Baron Davis .75 2.00
CS10 Jonathan Bender .30 .75

1999-00 Stadium Club Chrome Eyes of the Game

Randomly inserted in packs at one in 24, this 10-card set features players who possess the "eye" to hit the key shot or make the key pass. The cards are printed on ClearChrome techonology. Card backs carry an "EG" prefix.

COMPLETE SET (10) 20.00 50.00
STATED ODDS 1:24
*REF: 1.25X TO 3X HI COLUMN
REF: STATED ODDS 1:120
EG1 Jason Kidd 2.00 5.00
EG2 Jason Williams 1.50 4.00
EG3 Gary Payton 1.25 3.00
EG4 Kevin Garnett 2.00 5.00
EG5 Vince Carter 2.50 6.00
EG6 Kobe Bryant 5.00 12.00
EG7 Stephon Marbury 1.00 2.50
EG8 Allen Iverson 2.50 6.00
EG9 Alonzo Mourning 1.50 4.00
EG10 John Stockton 1.50 4.00

1999-00 Stadium Club Chrome True Colors

Randomly inserted in packs at one in eight, this 10-card set features players that show their "true colors" at crunch time. Card backs carry a "TC" prefix.

COMPLETE SET (10) 3.00 8.00
STATED ODDS 1:8
*REF: 1X TO 2.5X HI COLUMN
REF: STATED ODDS 1:40
TC1 Gary Payton .40 1.00
TC2 Stephon Marbury .30 .75
TC3 Karl Malone .50 1.25
TC4 Kevin Garnett .60 1.50
TC5 Allen Iverson .75 2.00
TC6 Vince Carter .75 2.00
TC7 Grant Hill .50 1.25
TC8 Shaquille O'Neal 1.00 2.50
TC9 Reggie Miller .40 1.00
TC10 Tim Duncan .75 2.00

1999-00 Stadium Club Chrome Visionaries

Randomly inserted in packs at one in 32, this 10-card set showcases young stars destined for NBA glory. Card backs carry a "V" prefix.

COMPLETE SET (10) 12.50 30.00
STATED ODDS 1:32
*REF: 1X TO 2.5X HI COLUMN
REF: STATED ODDS 1:160
V1 Vince Carter 2.50 6.00
V2 Tim Duncan 2.50 6.00
V3 Jason Williams 1.50 4.00
V4 Lamar Odom 3.00 8.00
V5 Steve Francis 3.00 8.00
V6 Paul Pierce 1.50 4.00
V7 Tracy McGrady 2.00 5.00
V8 Elton Brand 3.00 8.00
V9 Shawn Marion 2.50 6.00
V10 Antawn Jamison 1.25 3.00

1993 Stadium Club Members Only

This 59-card standard-size set was mailed out to Stadium Club Members in four separate mailings. Each box contained several sports. The fronts have full-bleed color action player photos with the words "Members Only" printed in gold foil at the bottom along with the player's name and the Stadium Club logo. On a multi-colored background, the horizontal backs carry player information and a computer generated drawing of a baseball player. The cards are unnumbered and checklisted below alphabetically according to sport as follows: baseball (1-28), basketball (29-44), football (45-53), and hockey (54-59).

COMPLETE SET (59) 10.00 20.00
29 Danny Ainge .08 .25
30 Mark Eaton .07 .20
31 Patrick Ewing .25 .60
32 Anfernee Hardaway .25 .60
33 Houston Rockets .08 .25
Carl Herrera
34 Michael Jordan 1.25 3.00
35 Hakeem Olajuwon .40 1.00
36 Shaquille O'Neal .75 2.00
37 Cliff Robinson .08 .25
38 David Robinson .40 1.00
39 Brian Shaw .07 .20
40 John Stockton .25 .60
41 Isiah Thomas .15 .40
42 Chris Webber .75 2.00
43 Dominique Wilkins .15 .40
44 Micheal Williams .07 .20

1994-95 Stadium Club Members Only 50

Topps produced a 50-card boxed set for each of the four major sports. With their club membership, members received one set of their choice and had the option of purchasing additional sets for $10.00 each. The 45 Stadium Club Cards in the basketball set represent 11 of the top NBA players in each division from 1994-95 with an extra player from the Central Division. The five Topps Rookie Picks cards (46-50) represent the top five players from the 1994 NBA Draft and are all given a special Finest style refractive foil coating. The color action photos on the fronts have brightly-colored backgrounds and carry the distinctive Topps Stadium Club Members Only gold foil seal. The backs present a second color photo and player profile.

COMP.FACT SET (50) 15.00 40.00
1 Shaquille O'Neal .75 2.00
2 Charles Oakley .25 .60
3 Chris Webber .50 1.25
4 Dominique Wilkins .40 1.00
5 Kenny Anderson .25 .60
6 Kevin Willis .20 .50
7 Anfernee Hardaway .50 1.25
8 Derrick Coleman .25 .60
9 Clarence Weatherspoon .20 .50
10 Glen Rice .30 .75
11 Patrick Ewing .40 1.00
12 Reggie Miller .40 1.00
13 Scottie Pippen .60 1.50
14 Steve Smith .25 .60
15 Alonzo Mourning .40 1.00
16 Vin Baker .30 .75
17 Tyrone Hill .20 .50
18 Joe Dumars .30 .75
19 Mookie Blaylock .20 .50
20 Michael Jordan 2.50 6.00
21 Larry Johnson .30 .75
22 Mark Price .30 .75
23 Rik Smits .25 .60
24 Hakeem Olajuwon .40 1.00
25 Karl Malone .40 1.00
26 Jamal Mashburn .30 .75
27 Sean Elliott .30 .75
28 Christian Laettner .25 .60
29 Dikembe Mutombo .30 .75
30 John Stockton .40 1.00
31 Clyde Drexler .40 1.00
32 Tom Gugliotta .20 .50
33 Mahmoud Abdul-Rauf .20 .50
34 David Robinson .50 1.25
35 Chris Mullin .30 .75
36 Shawn Kemp .30 .75
37 Mitch Richmond .30 .75
38 Clifford Robinson .20 .50
39 Cedric Ceballos .20 .50
40 Charles Barkley .50 1.25
41 Loy Vaught .20 .50
42 Gary Payton .30 .75
43 Walt Williams .20 .50
44 Nick Van Exel .30 .75
45 Kevin Johnson .30 .75
46 Glenn Robinson TRP 2.00 5.00
47 Jason Kidd TRP 5.00 12.00
48 Grant Hill TRP 5.00 12.00
49 Donyell Marshall TRP 1.00 2.50
50 Juwan Howard TRP 1.50 4.00

1995-96 Stadium Club Members Only 50

For the second straight season, Ttopps produced a 50-card boxed set for Basketball fans. Cards number 46 through 50 featured leading rookies and were printed using Finest technology.

COMP.FACT SET (50) 10.00 25.00
1 Magic Johnson .75 2.00
2 Steve Smith .25 .60
3 Scottie Pippen .50 1.25
4 David Robinson .50 1.25
5 Jason Kidd .50 1.25
6 Dikembe Mutombo .30 .75
7 Sean Elliott .30 .75
8 Rik Smits .25 .60
9 Brian Grant .25 .60
10 Hakeem Olajuwon .40 1.00
11 Greg Anthony .20 .50
12 Mitch Richmond .30 .75
13 Clyde Drexler .40 1.00
14 Mahmoud Abdul-Rauf .20 .50
15 Larry Johnson .30 .75
16 Mookie Blaylock .20 .50
17 Clarence Weatherspoon .20 .50
18 Grant Hill .50 1.25
19 Vin Baker .25 .60
20 Patrick Ewing .40 1.00
21 Charles Barkley .50 1.25
22 Glenn Robinson .25 .60
23 Dino Radja .20 .50
24 Charles Oakley .25 .60
25 Anfernee Hardaway .50 1.25
26 Jamal Mashburn .30 .75
27 John Stockton .40 1.00
28 Isaiah Rider .30 .75
29 Cedric Ceballos .20 .50
30 Shaquille O'Neal .75 2.00
31 Shawn Kemp .30 .75
32 Juwan Howard .30 .75
33 Alonzo Mourning .40 1.00
34 Tom Gugliotta .20 .50
35 Karl Malone .40 1.00
36 Clifford Robinson .20 .50
37 Chris Webber .40 1.00
38 Latrell Sprewell .30 .75
39 Loy Vaught .20 .50
40 Michael Jordan 2.50 6.00
41 Reggie Miller .40 1.00
42 Terrell Brandon .20 .50
43 Armon Gilliam .20 .50
44 Gary Payton .30 .75
45 Glen Rice .30 .75
46 Jerry Stackhouse FIN 2.00 5.00
47 Michael Finley FIN 2.00 5.00
48 Joe Smith FIN .75 2.00
49 Damon Stoudamire FIN 1.50 4.00
50 Brent Barry FIN 1.00 2.50

1996-97 Stadium Club Members Only 55

Topps produced a 55-card boxed set for each of the four major sports. With their club membership, members received one set of their choice and had the option of purchasing additional sets for $15.00 each. The 50 Stadium Club Cards in the basketball set represent the top NBA players in each division. The five Topps Rookie player cards (51-55) represent the top players from the 1996-97 NBA season and are all given a special Finest style foil coating. The color action photos on the fronts are full bleed with the player in a gold circle and carry the distinctive Topps Stadium Club Members Only gold foil seal. The backs present a second color photo and player profile.

COMP.FACT SET (55) 30.00 80.00
1 Scottie Pippen .50 1.25
2 Dikembe Mutombo .30 .75
3 Antonio McDyess .30 .75
4 Mark Jackson .25 .60
5 Vin Baker .25 .60
6 Kendall Gill .20 .50
7 Kenny Anderson .25 .60
8 Karl Malone .40 1.00
9 Chris Webber .40 1.00
10 David Robinson .50 1.25
11 Cedric Ceballos .20 .50
12 Patrick Ewing .40 1.00
13 Alonzo Mourning .40 1.00
14 Latrell Sprewell .30 .75
15 Terrell Brandon .20 .50
16 Anthony Mason .20 .50
17 Joe Dumars .30 .75
18 Hakeem Olajuwon .40 1.00
19 Brent Barry .25 .60
20 Shaquille O'Neal .75 2.00
21 Kevin Garnett .75 2.00
22 Anfernee Hardaway .50 1.25
23 Jerry Stackhouse .40 1.00
24 Mitch Richmond .30 .75
25 Gary Payton .30 .75
26 Damon Stoudamire .25 .60
27 Christian Laettner .25 .60
28 Dino Radja .20 .50
29 Shawn Bradley .20 .50
30 John Stockton .40 1.00
31 Sean Elliott .30 .75
32 Jason Kidd .50 1.25
33 Allan Houston .25 .60
34 Glenn Robinson .25 .60
35 Tim Hardaway .30 .75
36 Reggie Miller .40 1.00
37 Charles Barkley .50 1.25
38 Joe Smith .25 .60
39 Grant Hill .50 1.25
40 LaPhonso Ellis .20 .50
41 Michael Jordan 2.50 6.00
42 Glen Rice .30 .75
43 Rony Seikaly .20 .50
44 Shawn Kemp .30 .75
45 Juwan Howard .25 .60
46 Tyrone Hill .20 .50
47 Michael Finley .40 1.00
48 Loy Vaught .20 .50
49 Arvydas Sabonis .25 .60
50 Brian Grant .25 .60
51 Kerry Kittles Finest 3.00 8.00
52 Kobe Bryant Finest 30.00 80.00
53 Stephon Marbury Finest 8.00 20.00
54 Allen Iverson Finest 15.00 40.00
55 Shareef Abdur-Rahim Finest 5.00 12.00

1992-93 Stadium Club Members Only Parallel

Available exclusively through Topps members Only Club, this set was sold in complete factory set form for $199. A total of 10,000 factory sets were printed. The set includes parallel cards of the 400-card basic Stadium Club set from that year in addition to the 21-card Beam Team insert set. The numbering for Members Only cards is identical to the regular issue Stadium Club cards from that year. Members Only cards are readily distinguishable by the gold "Members Only" logo stamped onto the front of each card.

COMPLETE SET (421) 100.00 250.00
1 Michael Jordan 10.00 25.00
2 Greg Anthony .10 .30
3 Otis Thorpe .20 .50
4 Jim Les .10 .30
5 Kevin Willis .10 .30
6 Derek Harper .25 .60
7 Elden Campbell .20 .50
8 A.J. English .10 .30
9 Kenny Gattison .10 .30
10 Drazen Petrovic 1.50 4.00
11 Chris Mullin .75 2.00
12 Mark Price .60 1.50
13 Karl Malone 1.50 4.00
14 Gerald Glass .10 .30
15 Negele Knight .10 .30
16 Mark Macon .10 .30
17 Michael Cage .10 .30
18 Kevin Edwards .10 .30
19 Sherman Douglas .10 .30
20 Ron Harper .40 1.00
21 Clifford Robinson .20 .50
22 Byron Scott .40 1.00
23 Antoine Carr .10 .30
24 Greg Dreiling .10 .30
25 Bill Laimbeer .40 1.00
26 Hersey Hawkins .20 .50
27 Will Perdue .10 .30
28 Todd Lichti .10 .30
29 Gary Grant .10 .30
30 Sam Perkins .40 1.00
31 Jayson Williams .20 .50
32 Magic Johnson 2.50 6.00
33 Larry Bird 3.00 8.00
34 Chris Morris .10 .30
35 Nick Anderson .20 .50
36 Scott Hastings .10 .30
37 Ledell Eackles .10 .30
38 Robert Pack .10 .30
39 Dana Barros .10 .30
40 Anthony Bonner .10 .30
41 J.R. Reid .10 .30
42 Tyrone Hill .10 .30
43 Rik Smits .30 .75
44 Kevin Duckworth .10 .30
45 LaSalle Thompson .10 .30
46 Brian Williams .10 .30
47 Willie Anderson .10 .30
48 Ken Norman .10 .30
49 Mike Iuzzolino .10 .30
50 Isiah Thomas .75 2.00
51 Alec Kessler .10 .30
52 Johnny Dawkins .10 .30
53 Avery Johnson .40 1.00
54 Stacey Augmon .20 .50
55 Charles Oakley .20 .50
56 Rex Chapman .40 1.00
57 Charles Shackleford .10 .30
58 Jeff Ruland .10 .30
59 Craig Ehlo .10 .30
60 Jon Koncak .10 .30
61 Danny Schayes .10 .30
62 David Benoit .10 .30
63 Robert Parish .40 1.00
64 Mookie Blaylock .20 .50
65 Sean Elliott .40 1.00
66 Mark Aguirre .30 .75
67 Scott Williams .10 .30
68 Doug West .10 .30
69 Kenny Anderson .30 .75
70 Randy Brown .10 .30
71 Muggsy Bogues .40 1.00
72 Spud Webb .40 1.00
73 Sedale Threatt .10 .30
74 Chris Galling .10 .30
75 Derrick McKey .10 .30
76 Sleepy Floyd .10 .30
77 Chris Jackson .10 .30
78 Thurl Bailey .10 .30
79 Steve Smith .60 1.50
80 Cedric Ceballos .10 .30
81 Anthony Bowie .10 .30
82 John Williams .10 .30
83 Paul Graham .10 .30
84 Willie Burton .10 .30
85 Vernon Maxwell .10 .30
86 Stacey King .10 .30
87 B.J. Armstrong .20 .50
88 Kevin Gamble .10 .30
89 Terry Catledge .10 .30
90 Jeff Malone .20 .50
91 Sam Bowie .30 .75
92 Orlando Woolridge .10 .30
93 Steve Kerr .40 1.00
94 Eric Leckner .10 .30
95 Loy Vaught .10 .30
96 Jud Buechler .10 .30
97 Doug Smith .10 .30
98 Sidney Green .10 .30
99 Jerome Kersey .10 .30
100 Patrick Ewing 1.00 2.50
101 Ed Nealy .10 .30
102 Shawn Kemp 1.00 2.50
103 Luc Longley .30 .75
104 George McCloud .10 .30
105 Ron Anderson .10 .30
106 Moses Malone UER .40 1.00
(Rookie Card is 1975-76, not 1976-77)
107 Tony Smith .10 .30
108 Terry Porter .20 .50
109 Blair Rasmussen .10 .30
110 Bimbo Coles .10 .30
111 Grant Long .10 .30
112 John Battle .10 .30
113 Brian Oliver .10 .30
114 Tyrone Corbin .10 .30
115 Benoit Benjamin .10 .30
116 Rick Fox .30 .75
117 Rafael Addison .10 .30
118 Danny Young .10 .30
119 Fat Lever .10 .30
120 Terry Cummings .20 .50
121 Felton Spencer .10 .30
122 Joe Kleine .10 .30
123 Johnny Newman .10 .30
124 Gary Payton 1.50 4.00
125 Kurt Rambis .30 .75
126 Vlade Divac .30 .75
127 John Paxson .40 1.00
128 Lionel Simmons .10 .30
129 Randy Wittman .10 .30
130 Winston Garland .10 .30
131 Jerry Reynolds .10 .30
132 Dell Curry .10 .30
133 Fred Roberts .10 .30
134 Michael Adams .10 .30
135 Charles Jones .10 .30
136 Frank Brickowski .10 .30
137 Alton Lister .10 .30
138 Horace Grant .40 1.00
139 Greg Sutton .10 .30
140 John Starks .30 .75
141 Detlef Schrempf .30 .75
142 Rodney Monroe .10 .30
143 Pete Chilcutt .10 .30
144 Mike Brown .10 .30
145 Rony Seikaly .10 .30
146 Donald Hodge .10 .30
147 Kevin McHale .60 1.50
148 Ricky Pierce .10 .30
149 Brian Shaw .10 .30
150 Reggie Williams .10 .30
151 Kendall Gill .30 .75
152 Tom Chambers .30 .75
153 Jack Haley .10 .30
154 Terrell Brandon .30 .75
155 Dennis Scott .20 .50
156 Mark Randall .10 .30
157 Kenny Payne .10 .30
158 Bernard King .30 .75
159 Tate George .10 .30
160 Scott Skiles .40 1.00
161 Pervis Ellison .10 .30
162 Marcus Liberty .10 .30
163 Rumeal Robinson .10 .30
164 Anthony Mason .30 .75
165 Les Jepsen .10 .30
166 Kenny Smith .20 .50
167 Randy White .10 .30
168 Dee Brown .10 .30
169 Chris Dudley .10 .30
170 Armon Gilliam .10 .30
171 Eddie Johnson .10 .30
172 A.C. Green .40 1.00
173 Darrell Walker .10 .30
174 Bill Cartwright .20 .50
175 Mike Gminski .10 .30
176 Tom Tolbert .20 .50
177 Buck Williams .30 .75
178 Mark Eaton .10 .30
179 Danny Manning .30 .75
180 Glen Rice .40 1.00
181 Sarunas Marciulionis .30 .75
182 Danny Ferry .10 .30
183 Chris Corchiani .10 .30
184 Dan Majerle .50 1.25
185 Alvin Robertson .10 .30
186 Vern Fleming .10 .30
187 Kevin Lynch .10 .30
188 John Williams .10 .30
189 Checklist 1-100 .10 .30
190 Checklist 101-200 .10 .30
191 David Robinson MC .75 2.00
192 Larry Johnson MC .30 .75
193 Derrick Coleman MC .10 .30
194 Larry Bird MC 1.50 4.00
195 Billy Owens MC .10 .30
196 Dikembe Mutombo MC .40 1.00
197 Charles Barkley MC .75 2.00
198 Scottie Pippen MC 1.00 2.50
199 Clyde Drexler MC .75 2.00
200 John Stockton MC 1.00 2.50
201 Shaquille O'Neal MC 4.00 10.00
202 Chris Mullin MC .40 1.00
203 Glen Rice MC .30 .75
204 Isiah Thomas MC .50 1.25
205 Karl Malone MC .75 2.00
206 Christian Laettner MC 1.00 2.50
207 Patrick Ewing MC .50 1.25
208 Dominique Wilkins MC .60 1.50
209 Alonzo Mourning MC 2.00 5.00
210 Michael Jordan MC 5.00 12.00
211 Tim Hardaway MC .60 1.50
212 Rodney McCray .10 .30
213 Larry Johnson .30 .75
214 Charles Smith .10 .30
215 Kevin Brooks .10 .30
216 Kevin Johnson .30 .75
217 Duane Cooper .10 .30
218 Christian Laettner UER 2.00 5.00
(Missing '92 Draft Pick logo)
219 Tim Perry .10 .30
220 Hakeem Olajuwon 1.25 3.00
221 Lee Mayberry .10 .30
222 Mark Bryant .10 .30
223 Robert Horry 1.50 4.00
224 Tracy Murray UER .20 .50
(Missing '92 Draft Pick logo)
225 Greg Grant .10 .30
226 Rolando Blackman .30 .75
227 James Edwards UER .10 .30
(Rookie Card is 1978-79, not 1980-81)
228 Sean Green .10 .30
229 Buck Johnson .10 .30
230 Andrew Lang .10 .30
231 Tracy Moore .10 .30
232 Adam Keefe UER .20 .50
(Missing '92 Draft Pick logo)
233 Tony Campbell .10 .30
234 Rod Strickland .20 .50
235 Terry Mills .10 .30
236 Billy Owens .20 .50
237 Bryant Stith UER .20 .50
(Missing '92 Draft Pick logo)
238 Tony Bennett UER .10 .30
(Missing '92 Draft Pick logo)
239 David Wood .10 .30
240 Jay Humphries .10 .30
241 Doc Rivers .30 .75
242 Wayman Tisdale .10 .30
243 Litterial Green .10 .30
244 Jon Barry .30 .75
245 Brad Daugherty .10 .30
246 Nate McMillan .20 .50
247 Shaquille O'Neal 10.00 25.00
248 Chris Smith .10 .30
249 Duane Ferrell .10 .30
250 Anthony Peeler .30 .75
251 Gundars Vetra .10 .30
252 Danny Ainge .40 1.00
253 Mitch Richmond .60 1.50
254 Malik Sealy .40 1.00
255 Brent Price .20 .50
256 Xavier McDaniel .10 .30
257 Bobby Phills .30 .75
258 Donald Royal .10 .30
259 Olden Polynice .10 .30
260 Dominique Wilkins UER 1.00 2.50
(Scoring 10,000th point & should be 20,000th)
261 Larry Krystkowiak .10 .30
262 Duane Causwell .10 .30
263 Todd Day .20 .50
264 Sam Mack .20 .50
265 John Stockton 1.50 4.00
266 Eddie Lee Wilkins .10 .30
267 Gerald Glass .10 .30
268 Robert Pack .10 .30
269 Gerald Wilkins .10 .30
270 Reggie Lewis .20 .50
271 Scott Brooks .10 .30
272 Randy Woods UER .10 .30
(Missing '92 Draft Pick logo)
273 Dikembe Mutombo .60 1.50
274 Kiki Vandeweghe .40 1.00
275 Rich King .10 .30
276 Jeff Turner .20 .50
277 Vinny Del Negro .10 .30
278 Marlon Maxey .10 .30
279 Elmore Spencer UER .10 .30
(Missing '92 Draft Pick logo)
280 Cedric Ceballos .20 .50
281 Alex Blackwell .10 .30
282 Terry Davis .10 .30
283 Morlon Wiley .10 .30
284 Trent Tucker .10 .30
285 Carl Herrera .10 .30
286 Eric Anderson .10 .30
287 Clyde Drexler 1.25 3.00
288 Tom Gugliotta 2.50 6.00
289 Dale Ellis .10 .30
290 Lance Blanks .10 .30
291 Tom Hammonds .10 .30
292 Eric Murdock .10 .30
293 Walt Williams .30 .75
294 Gerald Paddio .10 .30
295 Brian Howard .10 .30
296 Ken Williams .10 .30
297 Alonzo Mourning 4.00 10.00
298 Larry Nance .30 .75
299 Jeff Grayer .10 .30
300 Dave Johnson .10 .30
301 Bob McCann .10 .30
302 Bart Kofoed .10 .30
303 Anthony Cook .10 .30
304 Radisav Curcic .10 .30
305 John Crotty .10 .30
306 Brad Sellers .10 .30
307 Marcus Webb .10 .30
308 Winston Garland .10 .30
309 Walter Palmer .10 .30
310 Rod Higgins .10 .30
311 Travis Mays .10 .30
312 Alex Stivrins .10 .30
313 Greg Kite .10 .30
314 Dennis Rodman 1.25 3.00
315 Mike Sanders .10 .30
316 Ed Pinckney .10 .30
317 Harold Miner .20 .50
318 Pooh Richardson .10 .30
319 Oliver Miller .20 .50
320 Latrell Sprewell 2.00 5.00
321 Anthony Pullard .10 .30
322 Mark Randall .10 .30
323 Jeff Hornacek .40 1.00
324 Rick Mahorn UER .10 .30
(Rookie Card is 1981-82, not 1992-93)
325 Sean Rooks .10 .30
326 Paul Pressey .10 .30
327 James Worthy .60 1.50
328 Matt Bullard .10 .30
329 Reggie Smith .10 .30
330 Don MacLean UER .20 .50
(Missing '92 Draft Pick logo)
331 John Williams UER .10 .30
(Rookie Card erroneously shows Hot Rod)
332 Frank Johnson .10 .30
333 Hubert Davis UER .20 .50
(Missing '92 Draft Pick logo)
334 Lloyd Daniels .10 .30
335 Steve Bardo .10 .30
336 Jeff Sanders .10 .30
337 Tree Rollins .10 .30
338 Micheal Williams .10 .30
339 Lorenzo Williams .10 .30
340 Harvey Grant .10 .30
341 Avery Johnson .40 1.00
342 Bo Kimble .10 .30
343 LaPhonso Ellis UER .30 .75
(Missing '92 Draft Pick logo)
344 Mookie Blaylock .20 .50
345 Isaiah Morris UER .10 .30
(Missing '92 Draft Pick logo)
346 Clarence Weatherspoon .30 .75
347 Manute Bol .10 .30
348 Victor Alexander .10 .30
349 Corey Williams .10 .30
350 Byron Houston .10 .30
351 Stanley Roberts .10 .30
352 Anthony Avent .10 .30
353 Vincent Askew .10 .30
354 Herb Williams .10 .30
355 J.R. Reid .10 .30
356 Brad Lohaus .10 .30
357 Reggie Miller 1.00 2.50
358 Blue Edwards .10 .30
359 Tom Tolbert .20 .50
360 Charles Barkley 1.25 3.00
361 David Robinson 1.25 3.00
362 Dale Davis .20 .50
363 Robert Werdann UER .10 .30
(Missing '92 Draft Pick logo)
364 Chuck Person .10 .30
365 Alaa Abdelnaby .10 .30
366 Dave Jamerson .10 .30
367 Scottie Pippen 2.00 5.00
368 Mark Jackson .50 1.25
369 Keith Askins .10 .30
370 Marty Conlon .10 .30
371 Chucky Brown .10 .30
372 LaBradford Smith .10 .30
373 Tim Kempton .10 .30
374 Sam Mitchell .10 .30
375 John Salley .20 .50
376 Mario Elie .20 .50
377 Mark West .10 .30
378 David Wingate .10 .30
379 Jaren Jackson .20 .50
380 Rumeal Robinson .10 .30
381 Kennard Winchester .10 .30
382 Walter Bond .10 .30
383 Isaac Austin .20 .50
384 Derrick Coleman .20 .50
385 Larry Smith .10 .30
386 Joe Dumars .60 1.50
387 Matt Geiger UER .10 .30
(Missing '92 Draft Pick logo)
388 Stephen Howard .10 .30
389 William Bedford .10 .30
390 Jayson Williams .20 .50
391 Kurt Rambis .30 .75
392 Keith Jennings .10 .30
393 Steve Kerr UER .30 .75
(The words key stat are repeated on back)
394 Larry Stewart .10 .30
395 Danny Young .10 .30
396 Doug Overton .10 .30
397 Mark Acres .10 .30
398 John Bagley .10 .30
399 Checklist 201-300 .10 .30
400 Checklist 301-400 .10 .30
BT1 Michael Jordan 30.00 80.00
BT2 Dominique Wilkins 2.50 6.00
BT3 Shawn Kemp 1.50 4.00
BT4 Clyde Drexler 2.50 6.00
BT5 Scottie Pippen 2.50 6.00
BT6 Chris Mullin 1.50 4.00
BT7 Reggie Miller 2.00 5.00
BT8 Glen Rice 1.25 3.00
BT9 Jeff Hornacek 1.25 3.00
BT10 Jeff Malone .75 2.00
BT11 John Stockton 3.00 8.00
BT12 Kevin Johnson 1.00 2.50
BT13 Mark Price 1.00 2.50
BT14 Tim Hardaway 1.50 4.00
BT15 Charles Barkley 2.50 6.00
BT16 Hakeem Olajuwon 2.00 5.00
BT17 Karl Malone 2.50 6.00
BT18 Patrick Ewing 1.50 4.00
BT19 Dennis Rodman 2.00 5.00
BT20 David Robinson 2.50 6.00
BT21 Shaquille O'Neal 30.00 80.00

1993-94 Stadium Club Members Only Parallel

For the second straight year, Topps offered a special parallel set of their complete Stadium Club product (regular-issue and insert cards included) through their Members Only club. The set was available to members only in factory set form and was offered for $229 plus shipping and handling.

COMPLETE SET (414) 40.00 100.00
1 Michael Jordan TD 5.00 12.00
2 Kenny Anderson TD .50 1.25
3 Steve Smith TD .50 1.25
4 Kevin Gamble TD .40 1.00
5 Detlef Schrempf TD .60 1.50
6 Larry Johnson TD .60 1.50
7 Brad Daugherty TD .50 1.25
8 Rumeal Robinson TD .40 1.00
9 Micheal Williams TD .40 1.00
10 David Robinson TD 1.00 2.50
11 Sam Perkins TD .40 1.00
12 Thurl Bailey .40 1.00
13 Sherman Douglas .40 1.00
14 Larry Stewart .40 1.00
15 Kevin Johnson .60 1.50
16 Bill Cartwright .50 1.25
17 Larry Nance .50 1.25
18 P.J. Brown .60 1.50
19 Tony Bennett .40 1.00
20 Robert Parish .60 1.50
21 David Benoit .40 1.00
22 Detlef Schrempf .60 1.50
23 Hubert Davis .40 1.00
24 Donald Hodge .40 1.00
25 Hersey Hawkins .40 1.00
26 Mark Jackson .50 1.25
27 Reggie Williams .40 1.00
28 Lionel Simmons .40 1.00
29 Ron Harper .50 1.25
30 Chris Mills .60 1.50
31 Danny Schayes .40 1.00
32 J.R. Reid .40 1.00
33 Willie Burton .40 1.00
34 Greg Anthony .40 1.00
35 Elden Campbell .40 1.00
36 Ervin Johnson .60 1.50
37 Scott Brooks .40 1.00
38 Johnny Newman .40 1.00
39 Rex Chapman .40 1.00
40 Chuck Person .50 1.25
41 John Williams .40 1.00
42 Anthony Bowie .40 1.00
43 Negele Knight .40 1.00
44 Tyrone Corbin .40 1.00
45 Jud Buechler .40 1.00
46 Adam Keefe .40 1.00
47 Glen Rice .60 1.50
48 Tracy Murray .40 1.00
49 Rick Mahorn .40 1.00
50 Vlade Divac .60 1.50
51 Eric Murdock .40 1.00
52 Isaiah Morris .40 1.00
53 Bobby Hurley .60 1.50
54 Mitch Richmond .60 1.50
55 Danny Ainge .60 1.50
56 Dikembe Mutombo .60 1.50
57 Jeff Hornacek .50 1.25
58 Tony Campbell .40 1.00
59 Vinny Del Negro .40 1.00
60 Xavier McDaniel HC .40 1.00
61 Scottie Pippen HC 1.25 3.00
62 Larry Nance HC .50 1.25
63 Dikembe Mutombo HC .60 1.50
64 Hakeem Olajuwon HC .75 2.00
65 Dominique Wilkins HC .75 2.00
66 Clarence Weatherspoon HC .40 1.00
67 Chris Morris HC .40 1.00
68 Patrick Ewing HC .75 2.00
69 Kevin Willis HC .40 1.00
70 Jon Barry .40 1.00
71 Jerry Reynolds .40 1.00
72 Sarunas Marciulionis .40 1.00
73 Mark West .40 1.00
74 B.J. Armstrong .40 1.00
75 Greg Kite .40 1.00
76 LaSalle Thompson .40 1.00
77 Randy White .40 1.00
78 Alaa Abdelnaby .40 1.00
79 Kevin Brooks .40 1.00
80 Vern Fleming .40 1.00
81 Doc Rivers .50 1.25
82 Shawn Bradley .60 1.50
83 Wayman Tisdale .40 1.00
84 Olden Polynice .40 1.00
85 Michael Cage .40 1.00
86 Harold Miner .40 1.00
87 Doug Smith .40 1.00
88 Tom Gugliotta .50 1.25
89 Hakeem Olajuwon .75 2.00
90 Loy Vaught .40 1.00
91 James Worthy .75 2.00
92 John Paxson .50 1.25
93 Jon Koncak .40 1.00
94 Lee Mayberry .40 1.00
95 Clarence Weatherspoon .40 1.00
96 Mark Eaton .40 1.00
97 Rex Walters .60 1.50
98 Alvin Robertson .40 1.00
99 Dan Majerle .60 1.50
100 Shaquille O'Neal 2.50 6.00
101 Derrick Coleman TD .50 1.25
102 Hersey Hawkins TD .40 1.00
103 Scottie Pippen TD 1.25 3.00
104 Scott Skiles TD .40 1.00
105 Rod Strickland TD .40 1.00
106 Pooh Richardson TD .40 1.00
107 Tom Gugliotta TD .50 1.25
108 Mark Jackson TD .50 1.25
109 Dikembe Mutombo TD .60 1.50
110 Charles Barkley TD 1.00 2.50
111 Otis Thorpe TD .40 1.00
112 Malik Sealy .40 1.00
113 Mark Macon .40 1.00
114 Dee Brown .40 1.00
115 Nate McMillan .40 1.00
116 John Starks .50 1.25
117 Clyde Drexler .75 2.00
118 Antoine Carr .40 1.00
119 Doug West .40 1.00
120 Victor Alexander .40 1.00
121 Kenny Gattison .40 1.00
122 Spud Webb .50 1.25
123 Rumeal Robinson .40 1.00
124 Tim Kempton .40 1.00
125 Karl Malone .75 2.00
126 Randy Woods .40 1.00
127 Calbert Cheaney .60 1.50
128 Johnny Dawkins .40 1.00
129 Dominique Wilkins .75 2.00
130 Horace Grant .50 1.25
131 Bill Laimbeer .50 1.25
132 Kenny Smith .50 1.25
133 Sedale Threatt .40 1.00
134 Brian Shaw .40 1.00
135 Dennis Scott .40 1.00
136 Mark Bryant .40 1.00
137 Xavier McDaniel .40 1.00
138 David Wood .40 1.00
139 Luther Wright .60 1.50
140 Lloyd Daniels .40 1.00
141 Marlon Maxey UER .40 1.00
142 Pooh Richardson .40 1.00
143 Jeff Grayer .40 1.00
144 LaPhonso Ellis .40 1.00
145 Gerald Wilkins .40 1.00
146 Dell Curry .40 1.00
147 Duane Causwell .40 1.00
148 Tim Hardaway .60 1.50
149 Isiah Thomas .60 1.50
150 Doug Edwards .60 1.50
151 Anthony Peeler .40 1.00
152 Tate George .40 1.00
153 Terry Davis .40 1.00
154 Sam Perkins .40 1.00
155 John Salley .40 1.00
156 Vernon Maxwell .40 1.00
157 Anthony Avent .40 1.00
158 Clifford Robinson .40 1.00
159 Corie Blount .60 1.50
160 Gerald Paddio .40 1.00
161 Blair Rasmussen .40 1.00
162 Carl Herrera .40 1.00
163 Chris Smith .40 1.00
164 Pervis Ellison .40 1.00
165 Rod Strickland .40 1.00
166 Jeff Malone .40 1.00
167 Danny Ferry .40 1.00
168 Kevin Lynch .40 1.00
169 Michael Jordan 5.00 12.00
170 Derrick Coleman HC .50 1.25
171 Jerome Kersey HC .40 1.00
172 David Robinson HC 1.00 2.50
173 Shawn Kemp HC .75 2.00
174 Karl Malone HC .75 2.00
175 Shaquille O'Neal HC 2.50 6.00
176 Alonzo Mourning HC 1.00 2.50
177 Charles Barkley HC 1.00 2.50
178 Larry Johnson HC .60 1.50
179 Checklist 1-90 .40 1.00
180 Checklist 91-180 .40 1.00
181 Michael Jordan FF 5.00 12.00
182 Dominique Wilkins FF .75 2.00
183 Dennis Rodman FF 1.25 3.00
184 Scottie Pippen FF 1.25 3.00
185 Larry Johnson FF .60 1.50
186 Karl Malone FF .75 2.00
187 Clarence Weatherspoon FF .40 1.00
188 Charles Barkley FF 1.00 2.50
189 Patrick Ewing FF .75 2.00
190 Derrick Coleman FF .50 1.25
191 LaBradford Smith .40 1.00
192 Derek Harper .50 1.25
193 Ken Norman .40 1.00
194 Rodney Rogers .60 1.50
195 Chris Dudley .40 1.00
196 Gary Payton .75 2.00
197 Andrew Lang .40 1.00
198 Billy Owens .40 1.00
199 Bryon Russell .60 1.50
200 Patrick Ewing .75 2.00
201 Stacey King .40 1.00
202 Grant Long .40 1.00
203 Sean Elliott .60 1.50
204 Muggsy Bogues .50 1.25
205 Kevin Edwards .40 1.00
206 Dale Davis .40 1.00
207 Dale Ellis .40 1.00
208 Terrell Brandon .50 1.25
209 Kevin Gamble .40 1.00
210 Robert Horry .60 1.50
211 Moses Malone UER .60 1.50
212 Gary Grant .40 1.00
213 Bobby Hurley .60 1.50
214 Larry Krystkowiak .40 1.00
215 A.C. Green .50 1.25
216 Christian Laettner .50 1.25
217 Orlando Woolridge .40 1.00
218 Craig Ehlo .40 1.00
219 Terry Porter .40 1.00
220 Jamal Mashburn 1.00 2.50
221 Kevin Duckworth .40 1.00
222 Shawn Kemp .75 2.00
223 Frank Brickowski .40 1.00
224 Chris Webber 3.00 8.00
225 Charles Oakley .50 1.25
226 Jay Humphries .40 1.00
227 Steve Kerr .50 1.25
228 Tim Perry .40 1.00
229 Sleepy Floyd .40 1.00
230 Bimbo Coles .40 1.00
231 Eddie Johnson .40 1.00
232 Terry Mills .40 1.00
233 Danny Manning .50 1.25
234 Isaiah Rider 1.00 2.50
235 Darnell Mee .60 1.50
236 Haywoode Workman .40 1.00
237 Scott Skiles .40 1.00
238 Otis Thorpe .40 1.00
239 Mike Peplowski .60 1.50
240 Eric Leckner .40 1.00
241 Johnny Newman .40 1.00
242 Benoit Benjamin .40 1.00
243 Doug Christie .40 1.00
244 Acie Earl .60 1.50
245 Luc Longley .50 1.25
246 Tyrone Hill .40 1.00
247 Allan Houston 1.25 3.00
248 Joe Kleine .40 1.00
249 Mookie Blaylock .40 1.00
250 Anthony Bonner .40 1.00
251 Luther Wright .60 1.50
252 Todd Day .40 1.00
253 Kendall Gill .40 1.00
254 Mario Elie .40 1.00
255 Pete Myers .40 1.00
256 Jim Les .40 1.00
257 Stanley Roberts .40 1.00
258 Michael Adams .40 1.00
259 Hersey Hawkins .40 1.00
260 Shawn Bradley .60 1.50
261 Scott Haskin .60 1.50
262 Corie Blount .60 1.50
263 Charles Smith .40 1.00
264 Armon Gilliam .40 1.00
265 Jamal Mashburn NW 1.00 2.50
266 Anfernee Hardaway NW 3.00 8.00
267 Shawn Bradley NW .60 1.50
268 Chris Webber NW 3.00 8.00
269 Bobby Hurley NW .60 1.50
270 Isaiah Rider NW 1.00 2.50
271 Dino Radja NW .60 1.50
272 Chris Mills NW .60 1.50
273 Nick Van Exel NW 1.25 3.00
274 Lindsey Hunter NW .60 1.50
275 Toni Kukoc NW 1.50 4.00
276 Popeye Jones NW .60 1.50
277 Chris Mills .60 1.50
278 Ricky Pierce .40 1.00
279 Negele Knight .40 1.00
280 Kenny Walker .40 1.00
281 Nick Van Exel 1.25 3.00
282 Derrick Coleman UER .50 1.25
283 Popeye Jones .60 1.50
284 Derrick McKey .40 1.00
285 Rick Fox .40 1.00
286 Jerome Kersey .40 1.00
287 Steve Smith .50 1.25
288 Brian Williams .40 1.00
289 Chris Mullin .60 1.50
290 Terry Cummings .50 1.25
291 Donald Royal .40 1.00
292 Alonzo Mourning 1.00 2.50
293 Mike Brown .40 1.00
294 Latrell Sprewell 1.00 2.50
295 Oliver Miller .40 1.00
296 Terry Dehere .60 1.50
297 Detlef Schrempf .60 1.50
298 Sam Bowie UER .40 1.00
299 Chris Morris .40 1.00
300 Scottie Pippen 1.25 3.00
301 Warren Kidd .60 1.50
302 Don MacLean .40 1.00
303 Sean Rooks .40 1.00
304 Matt Geiger .40 1.00
305 Dennis Rodman 1.25 3.00
306 Reggie Miller .75 2.00
307 Vin Baker 1.00 2.50
308 Anfernee Hardaway 3.00 8.00
309 Lindsey Hunter .60 1.50
310 Stacey Augmon .50 1.25
311 Randy Brown .40 1.00
312 Anthony Mason .40 1.00
313 John Stockton .75 2.00
314 Sam Cassell 1.25 3.00
315 Buck Williams .40 1.00
316 Bryant Stith .40 1.00
317 Brad Daugherty .50 1.25
318 Dino Radja .60 1.50
319 Rony Seikaly .40 1.00
320 Charles Barkley 1.00 2.50
321 Avery Johnson .50 1.25
322 Mahmoud Abdul-Rauf .40 1.00
323 Larry Johnson .60 1.50
324 Micheal Williams .40 1.00
325 Mark Aguirre .50 1.25
326 Jim Jackson .50 1.25
327 Antonio Harvey .60 1.50
328 David Robinson 1.00 2.50
329 Calbert Cheaney .60 1.50
330 Kenny Anderson .50 1.25
331 Walt Williams .40 1.00
332 Kevin Willis .40 1.00
333 Nick Anderson .40 1.00
334 Rik Smits .50 1.25
335 Joe Dumars .60 1.50
336 Toni Kukoc 1.50 4.00
337 Harvey Grant .40 1.00
338 Tom Chambers .50 1.25
339 Blue Edwards .40 1.00
340 Mark Price .60 1.50
341 Ervin Johnson .60 1.50
342 Rolando Blackman .50 1.25
343 Scott Burrell .60 1.50
344 Gheorghe Muresan .60 1.50
345 Chris Corchiani .40 1.00
346 Richard Petruska .60 1.50
347 Dana Barros .40 1.00
348 Hakeem Olajuwon FF .75 2.00
349 Dee Brown FF .40 1.00
350 John Starks FF .50 1.25
351 Ron Harper FF .50 1.25
352 Chris Webber FF 3.00 8.00
353 Dan Majerle FF .60 1.50
354 Clyde Drexler FF .75 2.00
355 Shawn Kemp FF .75 2.00
356 David Robinson FF 1.00 2.50
357 Chris Morris FF .40 1.00
358 Shaquille O'Neal FF 2.50 6.00
359 Checklist .40 1.00
360 Checklist .40 1.00
BT1 Shaquille O'Neal 5.00 12.00
BT2 Mark Price 1.25 3.00
BT3 Patrick Ewing 1.50 4.00
BT4 Michael Jordan 25.00 60.00
BT5 Charles Barkley 2.00 5.00
BT6 Reggie Miller 1.50 4.00
BT7 Derrick Coleman 1.00 2.50
BT8 Dominique Wilkins 1.50 4.00
BT9 Karl Malone 1.50 4.00
BT10 Alonzo Mourning 2.00 5.00
BT11 Tim Hardaway 1.25 3.00
BT12 Hakeem Olajuwon 1.50 4.00
BT13 David Robinson 2.00 5.00
BT14 Dan Majerle 1.25 3.00
BT15 Larry Johnson 1.25 3.00
BT16 LaPhonso Ellis .75 2.00
BT17 Nick Van Exel 2.50 6.00
BT18 Scottie Pippen 2.50 6.00
BT19 John Stockton 1.50 4.00
BT20 Bobby Hurley 1.25 3.00
BT21 Chris Webber 6.00 15.00
BT22 Jamal Mashburn 2.00 5.00
BT23 Anfernee Hardaway 6.00 15.00
BT24 Isaiah Rider 2.00 5.00
BT25 Ken Norman .75 2.00
BT26 Danny Manning 1.00 2.50
BT27 Calbert Cheaney 1.25 3.00
ST1 Atlanta .60 1.50
Dominique Wilkins
ST2 Boston .50 1.25
Robert Parish
ST3 Charlotte .75 2.00
Larry Johnson
Alonzo Mourning
ST4 Chicago .40 1.00
Horace Grant
ST5 Cleveland .40 1.00
Brad Daugherty
ST6 Dallas .40 1.00
Group
ST7 Denver .50 1.25
Dikembe Mutombo
ST8 Detroit .40 1.00
Group
ST9 Golden State .40 1.00
Group
ST10 Houston .40 1.00
Group
ST11 Indiana .40 1.00
Group
ST12 L.A.Clippers .40 1.00
Danny Manning
ST13 L.A.Lakers .40 1.00
Group
ST14 Miami .40 1.00
John Salley
ST15 Milwaukee .40 1.00
Group
ST16 Minnesota .40 1.00
Christian Laettner
ST17 New Jersey .40 1.00
Derrick Coleman

ST18 New York .60 1.50
Patrick Ewing
ST19 Orlando 2.00 5.00
Shaquille O'Neal
ST20 Philadelphia .40 1.00
Clarence Weatherspoon
ST21 Phoenix .75 2.00
Charles Barkley
ST22 Portland .40 1.00
Buck Williams
ST23 Sacramento .40 1.00
Lionel Simmons
ST24 San Antonio .75 2.00
David Robinson
ST25 Seattle .60 1.50
Shawn Kemp
ST26 Utah .40 1.00
Group
ST27 Washington .40 1.00
Group

1994-95 Stadium Club Members Only Parallel

This 509 card set parallels the complete mainstream 1994-95 Stadium Club run (including all basic issue and insert cards). Topps printed only as many sets as were ordered through their Members Only collector's club, until the maximum of 7,500 sets was reached. To reserve a set, members had to send in an order form or call a toll free number before February 28, 1995. The factory set cost 199.00 plus 10.00 for shipping and handling, and it included a Members Only Edition portfolio with display sheets. The fronts are identical to the regular issue, except for the Members Only emblem. Also the NBA Super Team cards have different backs than the retail product, making them ineligible for prizes. An embossed, autographed card featuring Reggie Miller was included in the set.

COMPLETE SET (509) 125.00 300.00
1 Patrick Ewing .75 2.00
2 Patrick Ewing TG .75 2.00
3 Bimbo Coles .40 1.00
4 Elden Campbell .40 1.00
5 Brent Price .40 1.00
6 Hubert Davis .40 1.00
7 Donald Royal .40 1.00
8 Tim Perry .40 1.00
9 Chris Webber 1.00 2.50
10 Chris Webber TG 1.00 2.50
11 Brad Daugherty .50 1.25
12 P.J. Brown .40 1.00
13 Charles Barkley 1.00 2.50
14 Mario Elie .40 1.00
15 Tyrone Hill .40 1.00
16 Anfernee Hardaway 1.00 2.50
17 Anfernee Hardaway TG 1.25 3.00
18 Toni Kukoc .75 2.00
19 Chris Morris .40 1.00
20 Gerald Wilkins .40 1.00
21 David Benoit .40 1.00
22 Kevin Duckworth .40 1.00
23 Derrick Coleman .50 1.25
24 Adam Keefe .40 1.00
25 Marlon Maxey .40 1.00
26 Vern Fleming .40 1.00
27 Jeff Malone .40 1.00
28 Rodney Rogers .40 1.00
29 Terry Mills .40 1.00
30 Doug West .40 1.00
31 Doug West TG .40 1.00
32 Shaquille O'Neal 2.50 6.00
33 Scottie Pippen 1.50 4.00
34 Lee Mayberry .40 1.00
35 Dale Ellis .40 1.00
36 Cedric Ceballos .40 1.00
37 Lionel Simmons .40 1.00
38 Kenny Gattison .40 1.00
39 Popeye Jones .40 1.00
40 Jerome Kersey .40 1.00
41 Jerome Kersey TG .40 1.00
42 Larry Stewart .40 1.00
43 Rod Strickland .40 1.00
44 Chris Mills .40 1.00
45 Latrell Sprewell .75 2.00
46 Haywoode Workman .40 1.00
47 Charles Smith .40 1.00
48 Detlef Schrempf .60 1.50
49 Gary Grant .40 1.00
50 Gary Grant TG .40 1.00
51 Tom Chambers .50 1.25
52 J.R. Reid .40 1.00
53 Mookie Blaylock .40 1.00
54 Mookie Blaylock TG .40 1.00
55 Rony Seikaly .40 1.00
56 Isaiah Rider .60 1.50
57 Isaiah Rider TG .60 1.50
58 Nick Anderson .40 1.00
59 Victor Alexander .40 1.00
60 Lucious Harris .40 1.00
61 Mark Macon .40 1.00
62 Otis Thorpe .40 1.00
63 Randy Woods .40 1.00
64 Clyde Drexler .75 2.00
65 Dikembe Mutombo .60 1.50
66 Todd Day .40 1.00
67 Greg Anthony .40 1.00
68 Sherman Douglas .40 1.00
69 Chris Mullin .60 1.50
70 Kevin Johnson .60 1.50
71 Kendall Gill .40 1.00
72 Dennis Rodman 1.25 3.00
73 Dennis Rodman TG 1.25 3.00
74 Jeff Turner .40 1.00
75 John Stockton .75 2.00
76 John Stockton TG .75 2.00
77 Doug Edwards .40 1.00
78 Jim Jackson .40 1.00
79 Hakeem Olajuwon .75 2.00
80 Glen Rice .60 1.50
81 Christian Laettner .50 1.25
82 Terry Porter .40 1.00
83 Joe Dumars .60 1.50
84 David Wingate .40 1.00
85 B.J. Armstrong .40 1.00
86 Derrick McKey .40 1.00
87 Elmore Spencer .40 1.00
88 Walt Williams .40 1.00
89 Shawn Bradley .40 1.00
90 Acie Earl .40 1.00
91 Acie Earl TTG .40 1.00
92 Randy Brown .40 1.00
93 Grant Long .40 1.00
94 Terry Dehere .40 1.00
95 Spud Webb .50 1.25
96 Lindsey Hunter .40 1.00
97 Blair Rasmussen .40 1.00
98 Tim Hardaway .60 1.50
99 Kevin Edwards .40 1.00
100 Patrick Ewing CT .75 2.00
Reggie Williams CT
101 Chuck Person CT 1.00 2.50
Charles Barkley CT
102 Mahmoud Abdul-Rauf CT 1.50 4.00
Shaquille O'Neal CT
103 Rony Seikaly CT .50 1.25
Derrick Coleman CT
104 Hakeem Olajuwon CT .75 2.00
Clyde Drexler CT
105 Chris Mullin CT .60 1.50
Mark Jackson CT
106 Robert Horry CT .75 2.00
Latrell Sprewell CT
107 Pooh Richardson CT .75 2.00
Reggie Miller CT
108 Dennis Scott CT .50 1.25
Kenny Anderson CT
109 Kendall Gill CT .40 1.00
Ken Norman CT
110 Scott Skiles CT .40 1.00
Kevin Willis CT
111 Terry Mills CT .60 1.50
Glen Rice CT
112 Christian Laettner CT .50 1.25
Bobby Hurley CT
113 Stacey Augmon CT .60 1.50
Larry Johnson CT
114 Sam Perkins CT .75 2.00
James Worthy CT
115 Carl Herrera .40 1.00
116 Sam Bowie .40 1.00
117 Gary Payton .60 1.50
118 Danny Ainge .60 1.50
119 Danny Ainge TG .60 1.50
120 Luc Longley .50 1.25
121 Antonio Davis .40 1.00
122 Terry Cummings .50 1.25
123 Terry Cummings TG .50 1.25
124 Mark Price .60 1.50
125 Jamal Mashburn .60 1.50
126 Mahmoud Abdul-Rauf .40 1.00
127 Charles Oakley .50 1.25
128 Steve Smith .50 1.25
129 Vin Baker .60 1.50
130 Robert Horry .60 1.50
131 Doug Christie .40 1.00
132 Wayman Tisdale .40 1.00
133 Wayman Tisdale TG .40 1.00
134 Muggsy Bogues .50 1.25
135 Dino Radja .40 1.00
136 Jeff Hornacek .50 1.25
137 Gheorghe Muresan .40 1.00
138 Loy Vaught .40 1.00
139 Loy Vaught TG .40 1.00
140 Benoit Benjamin .40 1.00
141 Johnny Dawkins .40 1.00
142 Allan Houston .60 1.50
143 Jon Barry .40 1.00
144 Reggie Miller .75 2.00
145 Kevin Willis .40 1.00
146 James Worthy .75 2.00
147 James Worthy TG .75 2.00
148 Scott Burrell .40 1.00
149 Tom Gugliotta .40 1.00
150 LaPhonso Ellis .40 1.00
151 Doug Smith .40 1.00
152 A.C. Green .50 1.25
153 A.C. Green TG .50 1.25
154 George Lynch .40 1.00
155 Sam Perkins .40 1.00
156 Corie Blount .40 1.00
157 Xavier McDaniel .40 1.00
158 Xavier McDaniel TG .40 1.00
159 Eric Murdock .40 1.00
160 David Robinson 1.00 2.50
161 Karl Malone .75 2.00
162 Karl Malone TG .75 2.00
163 Clarence Weatherspoon .40 1.00
164 Calbert Cheaney .40 1.00
165 Tom Hammonds .40 1.00
166 Tom Hammonds TG .40 1.00
167 Alonzo Mourning .75 2.00
168 Clifford Robinson .40 1.00
169 Micheal Williams .40 1.00
170 Ervin Johnson .40 1.00
171 Mike Gminski .40 1.00
172 Jason Kidd 4.00 10.00
173 Anthony Bonner .40 1.00
174 Stacey King .40 1.00
175 Rex Chapman .40 1.00
176 Greg Graham .40 1.00
177 Stanley Roberts .40 1.00
178 Mitch Richmond .60 1.50
179 Eric Montross .50 1.25
180 Eddie Jones 2.00 5.00
181 Grant Hill 4.00 10.00
182 Donyell Marshall .60 1.50
183 Glenn Robinson 1.25 3.00
184 Dominique Wilkins .75 2.00
185 Mark Price .60 1.50
186 Anthony Mason .40 1.00
187 Tyrone Corbin .40 1.00
188 Dale Davis .40 1.00
189 Nate McMillan .40 1.00
190 Jason Kidd 3.00 8.00
191 John Salley .40 1.00
192 Keith Jennings .40 1.00
193 Mark Bryant .40 1.00
194 Sleepy Floyd .40 1.00
195 Grant Hill 3.00 8.00
196 Joe Kleine .40 1.00
197 Anthony Peeler .40 1.00
198 Malik Sealy .40 1.00
199 Kenny Walker .40 1.00
200 Donyell Marshall .60 1.50
201 Vlade Divac AI .60 1.50
202 Dino Radja AI .40 1.00
203 Carl Herrera AI .40 1.00
204 Olden Polynice AI .40 1.00
205 Patrick Ewing AI .75 2.00
206 Willie Anderson .40 1.00
207 Mitch Richmond .60 1.50
208 John Crotty .40 1.00
209 Tracy Murray .40 1.00
210 Juwan Howard 1.00 2.50
211 Robert Parish .60 1.50
212 Steve Kerr .50 1.25
213 Anthony Bowie .40 1.00
214 Tim Breaux .40 1.00
215 Sharone Wright .50 1.25
216 Brian Williams .40 1.00
217 Rick Fox .40 1.00
218 Harold Miner .40 1.00
219 Duane Ferrell .40 1.00
220 Lamond Murray .60 1.50
221 Blue Edwards .40 1.00
222 Bill Cartwright .50 1.25
223 Sergei Bazarevich .60 1.50
224 Herb Williams .40 1.00
225 Brian Grant 1.00 2.50
226 Derek Harper BCT .50 1.25
John Starks
227 Rod Strickland BCT .75 2.00
Clyde Drexler
228 Kevin Johnson BCT .60 1.50
Dan Majerle
229 Lindsey Hunter BCT .60 1.50
Joe Dumars
230 Tim Hardaway BCT .75 2.00
Latrell Sprewell
231 Bill Wennington .40 1.00
232 Brian Shaw .40 1.00
233 Jamie Watson .40 1.00
234 Chris Whitney .40 1.00
235 Eric Montross .50 1.25
236 Kenny Smith .50 1.25
237 Andrew Lang .40 1.00
238 Lorenzo Williams .40 1.00
239 Dana Barros .40 1.00
240 Eddie Jones 2.00 5.00
241 Harold Ellis .40 1.00
242 James Edwards .40 1.00
243 Don MacLean .40 1.00
244 Ed Pinckney .40 1.00
245 Carlos Rogers .50 1.25
246 Michael Adams .40 1.00
247 Rex Walters .40 1.00
248 John Starks .50 1.25
249 Terrell Brandon .40 1.00
250 Khalid Reeves .50 1.25
251 Dominique Wilkins AI .75 2.00
252 Toni Kukoc AI .75 2.00
253 Rick Fox AI .40 1.00
254 Detlef Schrempf AI .60 1.50
255 Rik Smits AI .50 1.25
256 Johnny Dawkins .40 1.00
257 Dan Majerle .60 1.50
258 Mike Brown .40 1.00
259 Byron Scott .50 1.25
260 Jalen Rose 1.50 4.00
261 Byron Houston .40 1.00
262 Frank Brickowski .40 1.00
263 Vernon Maxwell .40 1.00
264 Craig Ehlo .40 1.00
265 Yinka Dare .40 1.00
266 Dee Brown .40 1.00
267 Felton Spencer .40 1.00
268 Harvey Grant .40 1.00
269 Nick Van Exel .60 1.50
270 Bob Martin .40 1.00
271 Hersey Hawkins .40 1.00
272 Scott Williams .40 1.00
273 Sarunas Marciulionis .40 1.00
274 Kevin Gamble .40 1.00
275 Clifford Rozier .40 1.00
276 B.J. Armstrong BCT .50 1.25
Ron Harper
277 John Stockton BCT .75 2.00
Jeff Hornacek
278 Bobby Hurley BCT .60 1.50
Mitch Richmond
279 Anfernee Hardaway BCT 1.00 2.50
Dennis Scott
280 Jason Kidd BCT 3.00 8.00
Jim Jackson
281 Ron Harper .50 1.25
282 Chuck Person .50 1.25
283 John Williams .40 1.00
284 Robert Pack .40 1.00
285 Aaron McKie .60 1.50
286 Chris Smith .40 1.00
287 Horace Grant .50 1.25
288 Oliver Miller .40 1.00
289 Derek Harper .50 1.25
290 Eric Mobley .40 1.00
291 Scott Skiles .40 1.00
292 Olden Polynice .40 1.00
293 Mark Jackson .50 1.25
294 Wayman Tisdale .40 1.00
295 Tony Dumas .60 1.50
296 Bryon Russell .40 1.00
297 Vlade Divac .60 1.50
298 David Wesley .40 1.00
299 Askia Jones .60 1.50
300 B.J. Tyler .40 1.00
301 Hakeem Olajuwon AI .75 2.00
302 Luc Longley AI .50 1.25
303 Rony Seikaly AI .40 1.00
304 Sarunas Marciulionis AI .40 1.00
305 Dikembe Mutombo AI .60 1.50
306 Ken Norman .40 1.00
307 Dell Curry .40 1.00
308 Danny Ferry .40 1.00
309 Shawn Kemp .60 1.50
310 Dickey Simpkins .50 1.25
311 Johnny Newman .40 1.00
312 Dwayne Schintzius .40 1.00
313 Sean Elliott .60 1.50
314 Sean Rooks .40 1.00
315 Bill Curley .40 1.00
316 Bryant Stith .40 1.00
317 Pooh Richardson .40 1.00
318 Jim McIlvaine .50 1.25
319 Dennis Scott .40 1.00
320 Wesley Person .60 1.50
321 Bobby Hurley .40 1.00
322 Armon Gilliam .40 1.00
323 Rik Smits .50 1.25
324 Tony Smith .40 1.00
325 Monty Williams .50 1.25
326 Gary Payton BCT .60 1.50
Kendall Gill
327 Mookie Blaylock BCT .50 1.25
Stacey Augmon
328 Mark Jackson BCT .75 2.00
Reggie Miller
329 Sam Cassell BCT .60 1.50
Vernon Maxwell
330 Harold Miner BCT .50 1.25
Khalid Reeves
331 Vinny Del Negro .40 1.00
332 Billy Owens .40 1.00
333 Mark West .40 1.00
334 Matt Geiger .40 1.00
335 Greg Minor .60 1.50
336 Larry Johnson .60 1.50
337 Donald Hodge .40 1.00
338 Aaron Williams .60 1.50
339 Jay Humphries .40 1.00
340 Charlie Ward .60 1.50
341 Scott Brooks .40 1.00
342 Stacey Augmon .50 1.25
343 Will Perdue .40 1.00
344 Dale Ellis .40 1.00
345 Brooks Thompson .50 1.25
346 Manute Bol .40 1.00
347 Kenny Anderson .50 1.25
348 Willie Burton .40 1.00
349 Michael Cage .40 1.00
350 Danny Manning .50 1.25
351 Ricky Pierce .40 1.00
352 Sam Cassell .60 1.50
353 Reggie Miller FG .75 2.00
354 David Robinson FG 1.00 2.50
355 Shaquille O'Neal FG 1.50 4.00
356 Scottie Pippen FG 1.25 3.00
357 Alonzo Mourning FG .75 2.00
358 Clarence Weatherspoon FG .40 1.00
359 Derrick Coleman FG .50 1.25
360 Charles Barkley FG 1.00 2.50
361 Karl Malone FG .75 2.00
362 Chris Webber FG 1.00 2.50
BT1 Mookie Blaylock .40 1.00
BT2 Dominique Wilkins .75 2.00
BT3 Alonzo Mourning .75 2.00
BT4 Toni Kukoc .75 2.00
BT5 Mark Price .60 1.50
BT6 Jason Kidd 3.00 8.00
BT7 Jalen Rose 1.50 4.00
BT8 Grant Hill 3.00 8.00
BT9 Latrell Sprewell .75 2.00
BT10 Hakeem Olajuwon .75 2.00
BT11 Reggie Miller .75 2.00
BT12 Lamond Murray .60 1.50
BT13 George Lynch .40 1.00
BT14 Khalid Reeves .50 1.25
BT15 Glenn Robinson 1.25 3.00
BT16 Donyell Marshall .60 1.50
BT17 Derrick Coleman .50 1.25
BT18 Patrick Ewing .75 2.00
BT19 Shaquille O'Neal 1.50 4.00
BT20 Clarence Weatherspoon .40 1.00
BT21 Charles Barkley 1.00 2.50
BT22 Clifford Robinson .40 1.00
BT23 Bobby Hurley .40 1.00
BT24 David Robinson 1.00 2.50
BT25 Shawn Kemp .60 1.50
BT26 Karl Malone .75 2.00
BT27 Chris Webber 1.00 2.50
CC1 Stacey Augmon .50 1.25
CC2 Dino Radja .40 1.00
CC3 Alonzo Mourning .75 2.00
CC4 Scottie Pippen 1.25 3.00
CC5 Gerald Wilkins .40 1.00
CC6 Jamal Mashburn .60 1.50
CC7 Dikembe Mutombo .60 1.50
CC8 Lindsey Hunter .40 1.00
CC9 Chris Mullin .60 1.50
CC10 Hakeem Olajuwon .75 2.00
CC11 Reggie Miller .75 2.00
CC12 Gary Grant .40 1.00
CC13 Doug Christie .40 1.00
CC14 Steve Smith .50 1.25
CC15 Vin Baker .60 1.50
CC16 Christian Laettner .50 1.25
CC17 Derrick Coleman .50 1.25
CC18 Charles Oakley .50 1.25
CC19 Dennis Scott .40 1.00
CC20 Clarence Weatherspoon .40 1.00
CC21 Charles Barkley 1.00 2.50
CC22 Clifford Robinson .40 1.00
CC23 Mitch Richmond .60 1.50
CC24 David Robinson 1.00 2.50
CC25 Shawn Kemp .60 1.50
CC26 Karl Malone .75 2.00
CC27 Don MacLean .40 1.00
DD1A Mark Price .60 1.50
DD1B Kenny Anderson .50 1.25
DD2A Karl Malone .75 2.00
DD2B Derrick Coleman .50 1.25
DD3A John Stockton .75 2.00
DD3B Anfernee Hardaway 1.00 2.50
DD4A Mitch Richmond .60 1.50
DD4B Jim Jackson .40 1.00
DD5A James Worthy .75 2.00
DD5B Jamal Mashburn .60 1.50
DD6A Patrick Ewing .75 2.00
DD6B Alonzo Mourning .75 2.00
DD7A Hakeem Olajuwon .75 2.00
DD7B Shaquille O'Neal 1.50 4.00
DD8A Clyde Drexler .75 2.00
DD8B Isaiah Rider .60 1.50
DD9A Scottie Pippen 1.25 3.00
DD9B Latrell Sprewell .75 2.00
DD10A Charles Barkley 1.00 2.50
DD10B Chris Webber 1.00 2.50
RS1 Kenny Anderson .50 1.25
RS2 Latrell Sprewell .75 2.00
RS3 Jamal Mashburn .60 1.50
RS4 Alonzo Mourning .75 2.00
RS5 Shaquille O'Neal 1.50 4.00
RS6 LaPhonso Ellis .40 1.00
RS7 Chris Webber 1.00 2.50
RS8 Isaiah Rider .60 1.50
RS9 Dikembe Mutombo .60 1.50
RS10 Anfernee Hardaway 1.00 2.50
RS11 Antonio Davis .40 1.00
RS12 Robert Horry .60 1.50
SS1 Mark Price .60 1.50
SS2 Tim Hardaway .60 1.50
SS3 Kevin Johnson .60 1.50
SS4 John Stockton .75 2.00
SS5 Mookie Blaylock .40 1.00
SS6 Reggie Miller .75 2.00
SS7 Jeff Hornacek .50 1.25
SS8 Latrell Sprewell .75 2.00
SS9 John Starks .50 1.25
SS10 Nate McMillan .40 1.00
SS11 Chris Mullin .60 1.50
SS12 Toni Kukoc .75 2.00
SS13 Anthony Mason .40 1.00
SS14 Robert Horry .60 1.50
SS15 Scottie Pippen 1.25 3.00
SS16 Charles Barkley 1.00 2.50
SS17 Dennis Rodman 1.25 3.00
SS18 Karl Malone .75 2.00
SS19 Chris Webber 1.00 2.50
SS20 Charles Oakley .50 1.25
SS21 Patrick Ewing .75 2.00
SS22 Shaquille O'Neal 1.50 4.00
SS23 Dikembe Mutombo .60 1.50
SS24 David Robinson 1.00 2.50
SS25 Hakeem Olajuwon .75 2.00
ST1 Atlanta Hawks .40 1.00
Craig Ehlo
ST2 Boston Celtics .40 1.00
Group
ST3 Charlotte Hornets .40 1.00
Group
ST4 Chicago Bulls .40 1.00
Group
ST5 Cleveland Cavaliers .40 1.00
Group
ST6 Dallas Mavericks .40 1.00
Jim Jackson
ST7 Denver Nuggets .40 1.00
Group
ST8 Detroit Pistons .40 1.00
Joe Dumars
ST9 Golden State Warriors 1.00 2.50
Chris Webber
ST10 Houston Rockets .75 2.00
Hakeem Olajuwon
ST11 Indiana Pacers .50 1.25
Rik Smits
ST12 Los Angeles Clippers .40 1.00
Group
ST13 Los Angeles Lakers .60 1.50
Nick Van Exel
ST14 Miami Heat .40 1.00
Group
ST15 Milwaukee Bucks .60 1.50
Vin Baker
ST16 Minnesota Timberwolves .40 1.00
Group
ST17 New Jersey Nets .40 1.00
Group
ST18 New York Knicks .40 1.00
Group
ST19 Orlando Magic 1.50 4.00
Shaquille O'Neal
ST20 Philadelphia 76ers .40 1.00
Group
ST21 Phoenix Suns .40 1.00
Group
ST22 Portland Trail Blazers .40 1.00
Group
ST23 Sacramento Kings .40 1.00
Olden Polynice
ST24 San Antonio Spurs .40 1.00
Group
ST25 Seattle Supersonics .40 1.00
Group
ST26 Utah Jazz .75 2.00
John Stockton
ST27 Washington Bullets .40 1.00
Group
TF1 Anfernee Hardaway 1.00 2.50
TF2 Latrell Sprewell .75 2.00
TF3 Grant Hill 3.00 8.00
TF4 Chris Webber 1.00 2.50
TF5 Shaquille O'Neal 1.50 4.00
TF6 Jason Kidd 3.00 8.00
TF7 Jim Jackson .40 1.00
TF8 Jamal Mashburn .60 1.50
TF9 Glenn Robinson 1.25 3.00
TF10 Alonzo Mourning .75 2.00
NNO Reggie Miller AU 15.00 40.00

1995-96 Stadium Club Members Only Parallel I

Unlike previous years, Topps decided to split up their Members Only parallel sets into separate series. Issued only in factory set form and offered for sale through their Members Only Collectors Club, this 292-card set parallels the cards offered from the mainstream 1995-96 Stadium Club first series product (including both regular issue and insert cards). The set consists of all 180 basic issue first series cards plus the following insert cards: Beam Team 1, Draft Picks (a skip-numbered set), Intercontinental (only offered elsewhere in Australian boxes), Nemeses, Power Zone 1, Warp Speed 1 and Wizards. In addition, Topps included both blue and red foil versions of all the subset cards within the 180-card basic issue (X-Pansion, Trans-Action and Extreme Corps).

COMPLETE SET (292) 120.00 300.00
1 Michael Jordan 8.00 20.00
2 Glenn Robinson .60 1.50
3 Jason Kidd 1.25 3.00
4 Clyde Drexler 1.00 2.50
5 Horace Grant .60 1.50
6 Allan Houston .60 1.50
7 Xavier McDaniel .50 1.25
8 Jeff Hornacek .60 1.50
9 Vlade Divac .75 2.00
10 Juwan Howard .75 2.00
11B Keith Jennings EXP Blue .50 1.25
11R Keith Jennings EXP Red .50 1.25
12 Grant Long .50 1.25
13 Jalen Rose 1.00 2.50
14 Malik Sealy .50 1.25
15 Gary Payton .75 2.00
16 Danny Ferry .50 1.25
17 Glen Rice .75 2.00
18 Randy Brown .50 1.25
19 Greg Graham .50 1.25
20 Kenny Anderson .60 1.50
21 Aaron McKie .50 1.25
22B John Salley EXP Blue .50 1.25
22R John Salley EXP Red .50 1.25
23 Darrin Hancock .50 1.25
24 Carlos Rogers .50 1.25
25 Vin Baker .60 1.50
26 Bill Wennington .50 1.25
27 Kenny Smith .60 1.50
28 Sherman Douglas .50 1.25
29 Terry Davis .50 1.25
30 Grant Hill 1.25 3.00
31 Reggie Miller 1.00 2.50
32 Anfernee Hardaway 1.25 3.00
33 Patrick Ewing 1.00 2.50
34 Charles Barkley 1.25 3.00
35 Eddie Jones .75 2.00
36 Kevin Duckworth .50 1.25
37 Tom Hammonds .50 1.25
38 Craig Ehlo .50 1.25
39 Micheal Williams .50 1.25
40 Alonzo Mourning 1.00 2.50
41 John Williams .50 1.25
42 Felton Spencer .50 1.25
43 Lamond Murray .50 1.25
44B Dontonio Wingfield EXP Blue .50 1.25
44R Dontonio Wingfield EXP Red .50 1.25
45 Rik Smits .60 1.50
46 Donyell Marshall .50 1.25
47 Clarence Weatherspoon .50 1.25
48 Kevin Edwards .50 1.25
49 Charlie Ward .50 1.25
50 David Robinson 1.25 3.00
51 James Robinson .50 1.25
52 Bill Cartwright .60 1.50
53 Bobby Hurley .50 1.25
54 Kevin Gamble .50 1.25
55B B.J. Tyler EXP Blue .50 1.25
55R B.J. Tyler EXP Red .50 1.25
56 Chris Smith .50 1.25
57 Wesley Person .50 1.25
58 Tim Breaux .50 1.25
59 Mitchell Butler .50 1.25
60 Toni Kukoc .75 2.00
61 Roy Tarpley .50 1.25
62 Todd Day .50 1.25
63 Anthony Peeler .50 1.25
64 Brian Williams .50 1.25
65 Muggsy Bogues .60 1.50
66B Jerome Kersey EXP Blue .50 1.25
66R Jerome Kersey EXP Red .50 1.25
67 Eric Piatkowski .60 1.50
68 Tim Perry .50 1.25
69 Chris Gatling .50 1.25
70 Mark Price .75 2.00
71 Terry Mills .50 1.25
72 Anthony Avent .50 1.25
73 Matt Geiger .50 1.25
74 Walt Williams .50 1.25
75 Sean Elliott .75 2.00
76 Ken Norman .50 1.25
77B Kendall Gill TA Blue .50 1.25
77R Kendall Gill TA Red .50 1.25
78 Byron Houston .50 1.25
79 Rick Fox .50 1.25
80 Derek Harper .60 1.50
81 Rod Strickland .50 1.25
82 Bryon Russell .50 1.25
83 Antonio Davis .50 1.25
84 Isaiah Rider .75 2.00
85 Kevin Johnson .75 2.00
86 Derrick Coleman .60 1.50
87 Doug Overton .50 1.25
88B Hersey Hawkins TA Blue .50 1.25
88R Hersey Hawkins TA Red .50 1.25
89 Popeye Jones .50 1.25
90 Dickey Simpkins .50 1.25
91B Rodney Rogers TA Blue .50 1.25
91R Rodney Rogers TA Red .50 1.25
92B Rex Chapman TA Blue .50 1.25
92R Rex Chapman TA Red .50 1.25
93B Spud Webb TA Blue .60 1.50
93R Spud Webb TA Red .60 1.50
94 Lee Mayberry .50 1.25
95 Cedric Ceballos .50 1.25
96 Tyrone Hill .50 1.25
97 Bill Curley .50 1.25
98 Jeff Turner .50 1.25
99B Tyrone Corbin TA Blue .50 1.25
99R Tyrone Corbin TA Red .50 1.25
100 John Stockton 1.00 2.50
101B Mookie Blaylock EC Blue .50 1.25
101R Mookie Blaylock EC Red .50 1.25
102B Dino Radja EC Blue .50 1.25
102R Dino Radja EC Red .50 1.25
103B Alonzo Mourning EC Blue 1.00 2.50
103R Alonzo Mourning EC Red 1.00 2.50
104B Scottie Pippen EC Blue 1.25 3.00
104R Scottie Pippen EC Red 1.25 3.00
105B Terrell Brandon EC Blue .50 1.25
105R Terrell Brandon EC Red .50 1.25
106B Jim Jackson EC Blue .50 1.25
106R Jim Jackson EC Red .50 1.25
107B Mahmoud Abdul-Rauf EC Blue .50 1.25
107R Mahmoud Abdul-Rauf EC Red .50 1.25
108B Grant Hill EC Blue 1.25 3.00
108R Grant Hill EC Red 1.25 3.00
109B Tim Hardaway EC Blue .75 2.00
109R Tim Hardaway EC Red .75 2.00
110B Hakeem Olajuwon EC Blue 1.00 2.50
110R Hakeem Olajuwon EC Red 1.00 2.50
111B Rik Smits EC Blue .60 1.50
111R Rik Smits EC Red .60 1.50
112B Loy Vaught EC Blue .50 1.25
112R Loy Vaught EC Red .50 1.25
113B Vlade Divac EC Blue .75 2.00
113R Vlade Divac EC Red .75 2.00
114B Kevin Willis EC Blue .50 1.25
114R Kevin Willis EC Red .50 1.25
115B Glenn Robinson EC Blue .60 1.50
115R Glenn Robinson EC Red .60 1.50
116B Christian Laettner EC Blue .60 1.50
116R Christian Laettner EC Red .60 1.50
117B Derrick Coleman EC Blue .60 1.50
117R Derrick Coleman EC Red .60 1.50
118B Patrick Ewing EC Blue 1.00 2.50
118R Patrick Ewing EC Red 1.00 2.50
119B Shaquille O'Neal EC Blue 2.00 5.00
119R Shaquille O'Neal EC Red 2.00 5.00
120B Dana Barros EC Blue .50 1.25
120R Dana Barros EC Red .50 1.25
121B Charles Barkley EC Blue 1.25 3.00
121R Charles Barkley EC Red 1.25 3.00
122B Rod Strickland EC Blue .50 1.25
122R Rod Strickland EC Red .50 1.25
123B Brian Grant EC Blue .60 1.50
123R Brian Grant EC Red .60 1.50
124B David Robinson EC Blue 1.25 3.00
124R David Robinson EC Red 1.25 3.00
125B Shawn Kemp EC Blue .75 2.00
125R Shawn Kemp EC Red .75 2.00
126B Oliver Miller EC Blue .50 1.25
126R Oliver Miller EC Red .50 1.25
127B Karl Malone EC Blue 1.00 2.50
127R Karl Malone EC Red 1.00 2.50
128B Benoit Benjamin EC Blue .50 1.25
128R Benoit Benjamin EC Red .50 1.25
129B Chris Webber EC Blue 1.00 2.50
129R Chris Webber EC Red 1.00 2.50
130 Dan Majerle .75 2.00
131 Calbert Cheaney .50 1.25
132 Mark Jackson .60 1.50
133B Greg Anthony EXP Blue .50 1.25
133R Greg Anthony EXP Red .50 1.25
134 Scott Burrell .50 1.25
135 Detlef Schrempf .75 2.00
136 Marty Conlon .50 1.25
137 Rony Seikaly .50 1.25
138 Olden Polynice .50 1.25
139 Terry Cummings .60 1.50
140 Stacey Augmon .60 1.50
141 Bryant Stith .50 1.25
142 Sean Higgins .50 1.25
143 Antoine Carr .50 1.25
144B Blue Edwards EXP Blue .50 1.25
144R Blue Edwards EXP Red .50 1.25
145 A.C. Green .60 1.50
146 Bobby Phills .50 1.25
147 Terry Dehere .50 1.25
148 Sharone Wright .50 1.25
149 Nick Anderson .50 1.25
150 Jim Jackson .50 1.25
151 Eric Montross .50 1.25
152 Doug West .50 1.25
153 Charles Smith .50 1.25
154 Will Perdue .50 1.25
155B Gerald Wilkins EXP Blue .50 1.25
155R Gerald Wilkins EXP Red .50 1.25
156 Robert Horry .60 1.50
157 Robert Parish .75 2.00
158 Lindsey Hunter .50 1.25
159 Harvey Grant .50 1.25
160 Tim Hardaway .75 2.00
161 Sarunas Marciulionis .50 1.25
162 Khalid Reeves .50 1.25
163 Bo Outlaw .50 1.25
164 Dale Davis .50 1.25
165 Nick Van Exel .75 2.00
166B Byron Scott EXP Blue .60 1.50
166R Byron Scott EXP Red .60 1.50
167 Steve Smith .60 1.50
168 Brian Grant .60 1.50
169 Avery Johnson .60 1.50
170 Dikembe Mutombo .75 2.00
171 Tom Gugliotta .50 1.25
172 Armon Gilliam .50 1.25
173 Shawn Bradley .50 1.25
174 Herb Williams .50 1.25
175 Dino Radja .50 1.25
176 Billy Owens .50 1.25
177B Kenny Gattison EXP Blue .50 1.25
177R Kenny Gattison EXP Red .50 1.25
178 J.R. Reid .50 1.25
179 Otis Thorpe .50 1.25
180 Sam Cassell .75 2.00
N1 Hakeem Olajuwon 2.50 6.00
David Robinson
N2 Patrick Ewing 2.00 5.00
Rik Smits
N3 John Stockton 2.00 5.00
Kevin Johnson
N4 Shaquille O'Neal 4.00 10.00
Alonzo Mourning
N5 Charles Barkley 2.50 6.00
Karl Malone
N6 Scottie Pippen 2.50 6.00
Grant Hill
N7 Anfernee Hardaway 2.50 6.00
Kenny Anderson
N8 Reggie Miller 2.00 5.00
John Starks
N9 Toni Kukoc 1.50 4.00
Dino Radja
N10 Michael Jordan 15.00 40.00
Joe Dumars
BT1 David Robinson 2.50 6.00
BT2 Juwan Howard 1.50 4.00
BT3 Mitch Richmond 1.50 4.00
BT4 Reggie Miller 2.00 5.00
BT5 Vin Baker 1.25 3.00
BT6 Shaquille O'Neal 4.00 10.00
BT7 Shawn Kemp 1.50 4.00
BT8 Karl Malone 2.00 5.00
BT9 Jamal Mashburn 1.50 4.00
BT10 Alonzo Mourning 2.00 5.00
DP2 Antonio McDyess 1.25 3.00
DP3 Jerry Stackhouse 3.00 8.00
DP4 Rasheed Wallace 3.00 8.00
DP5 Kevin Garnett 8.00 20.00
DP6 Bryant Reeves .75 2.00
DP8 Shawn Respert .75 2.00
DP9 Ed O'Bannon .75 2.00
DP11 Gary Trent 1.00 2.50
DP12 Cherokee Parks .75 2.00
DP15 Brent Barry 1.50 4.00
DP16 Alan Henderson 1.00 2.50
DP17 Bob Sura .75 2.00
DP18 Theo Ratliff 1.50 4.00
DP19 Randolph Childress .75 2.00
DP22 George Zidek .75 2.00
IC1 Hakeem Olajuwon 2.00 5.00
IC2 Dikembe Mutombo 1.50 4.00
IC3 Bill Wennington 1.00 2.50
IC4 Rick Fox 1.00 2.50
IC5 Carl Herrera 1.00 2.50
IC6 Rony Seikaly 1.00 2.50
IC7 Rik Smits 1.25 3.00
IC8 Dino Radja 1.00 2.50
IC9 Sarunas Marciulionis 1.00 2.50
IC10 Luc Longley 1.25 3.00
PZ1 Shaquille O'Neal 4.00 10.00
PZ2 Charles Barkley 2.50 6.00
PZ3 Patrick Ewing 2.00 5.00
PZ4 Karl Malone 2.00 5.00
PZ5 Larry Johnson 1.50 4.00
PZ6 Derrick Coleman 1.25 3.00
WS1 Michael Jordan 15.00 40.00
WS2 Kevin Johnson 1.50 4.00
WS3 Gary Payton 1.50 4.00
WS4 Anfernee Hardaway 2.50 6.00
WS5 Mookie Blaylock 1.00 2.50
WS6 Tim Hardaway 1.50 4.00
WZ1 Nick Van Exel 1.50 4.00
WZ2 Tim Hardaway 1.50 4.00
WZ3 Mookie Blaylock 1.00 2.50
WZ4 Gary Payton 1.50 4.00
WZ5 Jason Kidd 2.50 6.00
WZ6 Kenny Anderson 1.25 3.00
WZ7 John Stockton 2.00 5.00
WZ8 Kevin Johnson 1.50 4.00
WZ9 Muggsy Bogues 1.25 3.00
WZ10 Anfernee Hardaway 2.50 6.00

1995-96 Stadium Club Members Only Parallel II

This 233-card set parallels the cards offered from the mainstream 1995-96 Stadium Club second series product (including both regular issue and insert cards). The set consists of all 181 basic issue second series cards plus the following insert cards: Beam Team 2, Power Zone 2, Reign Men, Spike Says, Warp Speed 2 and X-2.

COMPLETE SET (233) 120.00 300.00
181 Sam Cassell .75 2.00
182 Pooh Richardson .50 1.25
183 Johnny Newman .50 1.25
184 Dennis Scott .50 1.25
185 Will Perdue .50 1.25
186 Andrew Lang .50 1.25
187 Karl Malone 1.00 2.50
188 Buck Williams .50 1.25
189 P.J. Brown .50 1.25
190 Khalid Reeves .50 1.25
191 Kevin Willis .50 1.25
192 Robert Pack .50 1.25
193 Joe Dumars .75 2.00
194 Sam Perkins .50 1.25
195 Dan Majerle .75 2.00
196 John Williams .50 1.25
197 Reggie Williams .50 1.25
198 Greg Anthony .50 1.25
199 Steve Kerr .60 1.50
200 Richard Dumas .50 1.25
201 Dee Brown .50 1.25
202 Zan Tabak .50 1.25
203 David Wood .50 1.25
204 Duane Causwell .50 1.25
205 Sedale Threatt .50 1.25
206 Hubert Davis .50 1.25
207 Donald Hodge .50 1.25
208 Duane Ferrell .50 1.25
209 Sam Mitchell .50 1.25
210 Adam Keefe .50 1.25
211 Clifford Robinson .50 1.25
212 Rodney Rogers .50 1.25
213 Jayson Williams .50 1.25
214 Brian Shaw .50 1.25
215 Luc Longley .60 1.50
216 Don MacLean .50 1.25
217 Rex Chapman .50 1.25
218 Wayman Tisdale .50 1.25
219 Shawn Kemp .75 2.00
220 Chris Webber 1.00 2.50
221 Antonio Harvey .50 1.25
222 Sarunas Marciulionis .50 1.25
223 Jeff Malone .50 1.25
224 Chucky Brown .50 1.25
225 Greg Minor .50 1.25
226 Clifford Rozier .50 1.25
227 Derrick McKey .50 1.25
228 Tony Dumas .50 1.25
229 Oliver Miller .50 1.25
230 Charles Oakley .60 1.50
231 Fred Roberts .50 1.25
232 Glen Rice .75 2.00
233 Terry Porter .50 1.25
234 Mark Macon .50 1.25
235 Michael Cage .50 1.25
236 Eric Murdock .50 1.25
237 Vinny Del Negro .50 1.25
238 Spud Webb .60 1.50
239 Mario Elie .50 1.25
240 Blue Edwards .50 1.25
241 Dontonio Wingfield .50 1.25
242 Brooks Thompson .50 1.25

243 Alonzo Mourning 1.00 2.50
244 Dennis Rodman 1.50 4.00
245 Lorenzo Williams .50 1.25
246 Haywoode Workman .50 1.25
247 Loy Vaught .50 1.25
248 Vernon Maxwell .50 1.25
249 Lionel Simmons .50 1.25
250 Chris Childs .50 1.25
251 Mahmoud Abdul-Rauf .50 1.25
252 Vincent Askew .50 1.25
253 Chris Morris .50 1.25
254 Elliot Perry .50 1.25
255 Dell Curry .50 1.25
256 Dana Barros .50 1.25
257 Terrell Brandon .50 1.25
258 Monty Williams .50 1.25
259 Corie Blount .50 1.25
260 B.J. Armstrong .50 1.25
261 Jim McIlvaine .50 1.25
262 Otis Thorpe .50 1.25
263 Sean Rooks .50 1.25
264 Tony Massenburg .50 1.25
265 Steve Smith .60 1.50
266 Ron Harper .60 1.50
267 Dale Ellis .50 1.25
268 Clyde Drexler 1.00 2.50
269 Jamie Watson .50 1.25
270 Doc Rivers .60 1.50
271 Derrick Alston .50 1.25
272 Eric Mobley .50 1.25
273 Ricky Pierce .50 1.25
274 David Wesley .50 1.25
275 John Starks .60 1.50
276 Chris Mullin .75 2.00
277 Ervin Johnson .50 1.25
278 Jamal Mashburn .75 2.00
279 Joe Kleine .50 1.25
280 Mitch Richmond .75 2.00
281 Chris Mills .50 1.25
282 Bimbo Coles .50 1.25
283 Larry Johnson .75 2.00
284 Stanley Roberts .50 1.25
285 Rex Walters .50 1.25
286 Donald Royal .50 1.25
287 Benoit Benjamin .50 1.25
288 Chris Dudley .50 1.25
289 Elden Campbell .50 1.25
290 Mookie Blaylock .50 1.25
291 Hersey Hawkins .50 1.25
292 Anthony Mason .50 1.25
293 Latrell Sprewell .75 2.00
294 Harold Miner .50 1.25
295 Scott Williams .50 1.25
296 David Benoit .50 1.25
297 Christian Laettner .60 1.50
298 LaPhonso Ellis .50 1.25
299 Gheorghe Muresan .50 1.25
300 Kendall Gill .50 1.25
301 Eddie Johnson .50 1.25
302 Terry Cummings .60 1.50
303 Chuck Person .60 1.50
304 Michael Smith .50 1.25
305 Mark West .50 1.25
306 Willie Anderson .50 1.25
307 Pervis Ellison .50 1.25
308 Brian Williams .50 1.25
309 Danny Manning .60 1.50
310 Hakeem Olajuwon 1.00 2.50
311 Scottie Pippen 1.25 3.00
312 Jon Koncak .50 1.25
313 Sasha Danilovic .75 2.00
314 Lucious Harris .50 1.25
315 Yinka Dare .50 1.25
316 Eric Williams .75 2.00
317 Gary Trent .75 2.00
318 Theo Ratliff 1.25 3.00
319 Lawrence Moten .75 2.00
320 Jerome Allen .75 2.00
321 Tyus Edney .75 2.00
322 Loren Meyer .50 1.25
323 Michael Finley 2.50 6.00
324 Alan Henderson .75 2.00
325 Bob Sura .60 1.50
326 Joe Smith 1.00 2.50
327 Damon Stoudamire 2.00 5.00
328 Sherrell Ford .60 1.50
329 Jerry Stackhouse 2.50 6.00
330 George Zidek .60 1.50
331 Brent Barry 1.25 3.00
332 Shawn Respert .60 1.50
333 Rasheed Wallace 2.50 6.00
334 Antonio McDyess 1.00 2.50
335 David Vaughn .75 2.00
336 Cory Alexander .75 2.00
337 Jason Caffey .75 2.00
338 Frankie King .75 2.00
339 Travis Best .75 2.00
340 Greg Ostertag .75 2.00
341 Ed O'Bannon .60 1.50
342 Kurt Thomas .75 2.00
343 Kevin Garnett 12.50 30.00
344 Bryant Reeves .60 1.50
345 Corliss Williamson .75 2.00
346 Cherokee Parks .60 1.50
347 Junior Burrough .75 2.00
348 Randolph Childress .60 1.50
349 Lou Roe .75 2.00
350 Mario Bennett .60 1.50
351 Dikembe Mutombo .75 2.00
352 Larry Johnson .75 2.00
353 Vlade Divac .75 2.00
354 Karl Malone 1.00 2.50
355 John Stockton 1.00 2.50
356 Alonzo Mourning 1.00 2.50
357 Glen Rice .75 2.00
358 Dan Majerle .75 2.00
359 John Williams .50 1.25
360 Mark Price .75 2.00
361 Magic Johnson 2.00 5.00
B11 Charles Barkley 2.50 6.00
B12 Hakeem Olajuwon 2.00 5.00
B13 Kenny Anderson 1.25 3.00
B14 Michael Jordan 15.00 40.00
B15 Dikembe Mutombo 1.50 4.00
B16 Rod Strickland 1.00 2.50
B17 Patrick Ewing 2.00 5.00
B18 Latrell Sprewell 1.50 4.00
B19 Grant Hill 2.50 6.00
B20 Cedric Ceballos 1.00 2.50
X1 Hakeem Olajuwon 2.00 5.00
X2 Shaquille O'Neal 4.00 10.00
X3 David Robinson 2.50 6.00
X4 Patrick Ewing 2.00 5.00
X5 Charles Barkley 2.50 6.00
X6 Karl Malone 2.00 5.00
X7 Derrick Coleman 1.25 3.00
X8 Shawn Kemp 1.50 4.00
X9 Vin Baker 1.25 3.00
X10 Vlade Divac 1.50 4.00
PZ7 Hakeem Olajuwon 2.00 5.00
PZ8 David Robinson 2.50 6.00
PZ9 Shawn Kemp 1.50 4.00
PZ10 Dennis Rodman 3.00 8.00
PZ11 Alonzo Mourning 2.00 5.00
PZ12 Vin Baker 1.25 3.00

RM1 Shawn Kemp 1.50 4.00
RM2 Michael Jordan 15.00 40.00
RM3 Larry Johnson 1.50 4.00
RM4 Grant Hill 2.50 6.00
RM5 Isaiah Rider 1.50 4.00
RM6 Sean Elliott 1.50 4.00
RM7 Scottie Pippen 2.50 6.00
RM8 Robert Horry 1.25 3.00
RM9 Kendall Gill 1.00 2.50
RM10 Jerry Stackhouse 5.00 12.00
SS1 Michael Jordan 15.00 40.00
SS2 Alonzo Mourning 2.00 5.00
SS3 Reggie Miller 2.00 5.00
SS4 Patrick Ewing 2.00 5.00
SS5 Charles Barkley 2.50 6.00
SS6 Kenny Anderson 1.25 3.00
SS7 Scottie Pippen 2.50 6.00
SS8 Jerry Stackhouse 5.00 12.00
SS9 Shaquille O'Neal 4.00 10.00
SS10 John Starks 1.25 3.00
WS7 Scottie Pippen 2.50 6.00
WS8 Jason Kidd 2.50 6.00
WS9 Grant Hill 2.50 6.00
WS10 Nick Van Exel 1.50 4.00
WS11 Kenny Anderson 1.25 3.00
WS12 Latrell Sprewell 1.50 4.00

1996-97 Stadium Club Members Only Parallel I

This 173-card set parallels the cards offered from the mainstream 1996-97 Stadium Club first series product (including both regular issue and insert cards). The set consists of all 90 basic issue first series cards plus the following insert cards: Fusion 1, Golden Moments, Rookies 1, Shining Moments, Special Forces and Top Crop. Cards feature the Members Only logo running diagonally in the background.

COMPLETE SET (173) 150.00 400.00
1 Scottie Pippen 1.50 4.00
2 Dale Davis .60 1.50
3 Horace Grant .75 2.00
4 Gheorghe Muresan .60 1.50
5 Elliot Perry .60 1.50
6 Carlos Rogers .60 1.50
7 Glenn Robinson .75 2.00
8 Avery Johnson .75 2.00
9 Dee Brown .60 1.50
10 Grant Hill 1.50 4.00
11 Tyus Edney .60 1.50
12 Patrick Ewing 1.25 3.00
13 Jason Kidd 1.50 4.00
14 Clifford Robinson .60 1.50
15 Robert Horry .75 2.00
16 Dell Curry .60 1.50
17 Terry Porter .60 1.50
18 Shaquille O'Neal 2.50 6.00
19 Bryant Stith .60 1.50
20 Shawn Kemp 1.00 2.50
21 Kurt Thomas .60 1.50
22 Pooh Richardson .60 1.50
23 Bob Sura .60 1.50
24 Olden Polynice .60 1.50
25 Lawrence Moten .60 1.50
26 Kendall Gill .60 1.50
27 Cedric Ceballos .60 1.50
28 Latrell Sprewell 1.00 2.50
29 Christian Laettner .75 2.00
30 Jamal Mashburn .75 2.00
31 Jerry Stackhouse 1.25 3.00
32 John Stockton 1.25 3.00
33 Arvydas Sabonis .75 2.00
34 Detlef Schrempf 1.00 2.50
35 Toni Kukoc 1.00 2.50
36 Sasha Danilovic .60 1.50
37 Dana Barros .60 1.50
38 Loy Vaught .60 1.50
39 John Starks .75 2.00
40 Marty Conlon .60 1.50
41 Antonio McDyess 1.00 2.50
42 Michael Finley 1.25 3.00
43 Tom Gugliotta .60 1.50
44 Terrell Brandon .60 1.50
45 Derrick McKey .60 1.50
46 Damon Stoudamire .75 2.00
47 Elden Campbell .60 1.50
48 Luc Longley .75 2.00
49 B.J. Armstrong .60 1.50
50 Lindsey Hunter .60 1.50
51 Glen Rice 1.00 2.50
52 Shawn Respert .60 1.50
53 Cory Alexander .60 1.50
54 Tim Legler .60 1.50
55 Bryant Reeves .60 1.50
56 Anfernee Hardaway 1.50 4.00
57 Charles Barkley 1.50 4.00
58 Mookie Blaylock .60 1.50
59 Kevin Garnett 2.50 6.00
60 Hersey Hawkins .60 1.50
61 Ed O'Bannon .60 1.50
62 George Zidek .60 1.50
63 Mitch Richmond 1.00 2.50
64 Derrick Coleman .75 2.00
65 Chris Webber 1.25 3.00
66 Bobby Phills .60 1.50
67 Rik Smits .75 2.00
68 Jeff Hornacek .75 2.00
69 Sam Cassell .75 2.00
70 Gary Trent .60 1.50
71 LaPhonso Ellis .60 1.50
72 Oliver Miller .60 1.50
73 Rex Chapman .60 1.50
74 Jim Jackson .60 1.50
75 Eric Williams .60 1.50
76 Brent Barry .75 2.00
77 Nick Anderson .60 1.50
78 David Robinson 1.50 4.00
79 Calbert Cheaney .60 1.50
80 Joe Smith .75 2.00
81 Steve Kerr .75 2.00
82 Wayman Tisdale .60 1.50
83 Steve Smith .75 2.00
84 Clyde Drexler 1.25 3.00
85 Theo Ratliff .60 1.50
86 Charlie Ward .60 1.50
87 Karl Malone 1.25 3.00
88 Clarence Weatherspoon .60 1.50
89 Greg Anthony .60 1.50
90 Shawn Bradley .60 1.50
F1 Michael Jordan 20.00 50.00
F2 Chris Webber 2.00 5.00
F3 Glenn Robinson 1.25 3.00
F4 Glen Rice 1.50 4.00
F5 Gary Payton 1.50 4.00
F6 Rik Smits 1.25 3.00
F7 Grant Hill 2.50 6.00
F8 Horace Grant 1.25 3.00
F9 Scottie Pippen 2.50 6.00
F10 Gheorghe Muresan 1.00 2.50
F11 Vin Baker 1.25 3.00
F12 Dell Curry 1.00 2.50
F13 Shawn Kemp 1.50 4.00
F14 Reggie Miller 2.00 5.00
F15 Joe Dumars 1.50 4.00
F16 Anfernee Hardaway 2.50 6.00
R1 Allen Iverson 20.00 50.00
R2 Marcus Camby 6.00 15.00
R3 Shareef Abdur-Rahim 6.00 15.00
R4 Stephon Marbury 10.00 25.00
R5 Ray Allen 15.00 40.00
R6 Antoine Walker 6.00 15.00
R7 Lorenzen Wright 3.00 8.00
R8 Kerry Kittles 4.00 10.00
R9 Samaki Walker 3.00 8.00
R10 Erick Dampier 4.00 10.00
R11 Todd Fuller 2.50 6.00
R12 Kobe Bryant 60.00 150.00
R13 Steve Nash 20.00 50.00
R14 Tony Delk 4.00 10.00
R15 Jermaine O'Neal 6.00 15.00
R16 John Wallace 4.00 10.00
R17 Walter McCarty 4.00 10.00
R18 Dontae' Jones 4.00 10.00
R19 Roy Rogers 3.00 8.00
R20 Derek Fisher 5.00 12.00
R21 Martin Muursepp 2.50 6.00
R22 Jerome Williams 3.00 8.00
R23 Brian Evans 4.00 10.00
R24 Priest Lauderdale 2.50 6.00
R25 Travis Knight 4.00 10.00
GM1 Robert Parish 1.00 2.50
GM2 John Stockton 1.25 3.00
GM3 Michael Jordan 20.00 50.00
Toni Kukoc
Dennis Rodman
GM4 Dennis Scott .60 1.50
GM5 Hakeem Olajuwon 1.25 3.00
SF1 Anfernee Hardaway 2.50 6.00
SF2 Grant Hill 2.50 6.00
SF3 Shawn Kemp 1.50 4.00
SF4 Michael Jordan 30.00 80.00
SF5 Shaquille O'Neal 4.00 10.00
SF6 Scottie Pippen 2.50 6.00
SF7 Damon Stoudamire 1.25 3.00
SF8 Jerry Stackhouse 2.00 5.00
SF9 Gary Payton 1.50 4.00
SF10 Dennis Rodman 3.00 8.00
SM1 Charles Barkley 1.50 4.00
SM2 Michael Jordan 8.00 20.00
SM3 Karl Malone 1.25 3.00
SM4 Hakeem Olajuwon 1.25 3.00
SM5 John Stockton 1.25 3.00
SM6 Patrick Ewing 1.25 3.00
SM7 Reggie Miller 1.25 3.00
SM8 David Robinson 1.50 4.00
SM9 Dennis Rodman 2.00 5.00
SM10 Damon Stoudamire .75 2.00
SM11 Brent Barry .75 2.00
SM12 Tim Legler .60 1.50
SM13 Jason Kidd 1.50 4.00
SM14 Terrell Brandon .60 1.50
SM15 Allen Iverson 5.00 12.00
TC1 Hakeem Olajuwon 4.00 10.00
Shaquille O'Neal
TC2 Dikembe Mutombo 2.00 5.00
Alonzo Mourning
TC3 David Robinson 2.50 6.00
Patrick Ewing
TC4 Sean Elliott 2.50 6.00
Grant Hill
TC5 Shawn Kemp 2.50 6.00
Scottie Pippen
TC6 Karl Malone 2.00 5.00
Vin Baker
TC7 Charles Barkley 2.50 6.00
Juwan Howard
TC8 Clyde Drexler 2.00 5.00
Glen Rice
TC9 Gary Payton 15.00 40.00
Michael Jordan
TC10 John Stockton 2.00 5.00
Terrell Brandon
TC11 Mitch Richmond 2.00 5.00
Reggie Miller
TC12 Jason Kidd 2.50 6.00
Anfernee Hardaway

1996-97 Stadium Club Members Only Parallel II

This 210-card set parallels the cards offered from the mainstream 1996-97 Stadium Club second series product (including both regular issue and insert cards). The set consists of all 90 basic issue second series cards plus the following insert cards: Class Acts, Fusion 2, High Risers, Mega Heroes, Rookie Showcase, Rookies 2 and Welcome Additions. Cards feature the Members Only logo running diagonally in the background.

COMPLETE SET (210) 200.00 500.00
91 Otis Thorpe .60 1.50
92 Larry Johnson 1.00 2.50
93 Sharone Wright .60 1.50
94 Charles Barkley 1.50 4.00
95 Wesley Person .60 1.50
96 Dikembe Mutombo 1.00 2.50
97 Eddie Jones 1.00 2.50
98 Juwan Howard .75 2.00
99 Grant Hill 1.50 4.00
100 Chris Carr 1.00 2.50
101 Michael Jordan 8.00 20.00
102 Vincent Askew .60 1.50
103 Gary Payton 1.00 2.50
104 Chris Mills .60 1.50
105 Reggie Miller 1.25 3.00
106 Don MacLean .60 1.50
107 John Stockton 1.25 3.00
108 Mahmoud Abdul-Rauf .60 1.50
109 P.J. Brown .60 1.50
110 Kenny Anderson .75 2.00
111 Mark Price 1.00 2.50
112 Derek Harper .75 2.00
113 Dino Radja .60 1.50
114 Terry Dehere .60 1.50
115 Mark Jackson .75 2.00
116 Vin Baker .75 2.00
117 Dennis Scott .60 1.50
118 Sean Elliott 1.00 2.50
119 Lee Mayberry .60 1.50
120 Vlade Divac 1.00 2.50
121 Joe Dumars 1.00 2.50
122 Isaiah Rider .75 2.00
123 Hakeem Olajuwon 1.25 3.00
124 Robert Pack .60 1.50
125 Jalen Rose .75 2.00
126 Allan Houston .75 2.00
127 Nate McMillan .60 1.50
128 Rod Strickland .60 1.50
129 Sean Rooks .60 1.50
130 Dennis Rodman 2.00 5.00
131 Alonzo Mourning 1.25 3.00
132 Danny Ferry .60 1.50
133 Sam Cassell .75 2.00
134 Brian Grant .75 2.00
135 Karl Malone 1.25 3.00
136 Chris Gatling .60 1.50
137 Tom Gugliotta .60 1.50
138 Hubert Davis .60 1.50
139 Lucious Harris .60 1.50
140 Rony Seikaly .60 1.50
141 Alan Henderson .60 1.50
142 Mario Elie .60 1.50
143 Vinny Del Negro .60 1.50
144 Harvey Grant .60 1.50
145 Muggsy Bogues .75 2.00
146 Rodney Rogers .60 1.50
147 Kevin Johnson 1.00 2.50
148 Anthony Peeler .60 1.50
149 Jon Koncak .60 1.50
150 Ricky Pierce .60 1.50
151 Todd Day .60 1.50
152 Tyrone Hill .60 1.50
153 Nick Van Exel 1.00 2.50
154 Rasheed Wallace 1.25 3.00
155 Jayson Williams .60 1.50
156 Sherman Douglas .60 1.50
157 Bryon Russell .60 1.50
158 Ron Harper .75 2.00
159 Stacey Augmon .75 2.00
160 Antonio Davis .60 1.50
161 Tim Hardaway 1.00 2.50
162 Charles Oakley .75 2.00
163 Billy Owens .60 1.50
164 Sam Perkins .60 1.50
165 Chris Whitney .60 1.50
166 Matt Geiger .60 1.50
167 Andrew Lang .60 1.50
168 Danny Manning .75 2.00
169 Doug Christie .60 1.50
170 George Lynch .60 1.50
171 Malik Sealy .60 1.50
172 Eric Montross .60 1.50
173 Rick Fox .60 1.50
174 Chris Mullin 1.00 2.50
175 Ken Norman .60 1.50
176 Sarunas Marciulionis .60 1.50
177 Kevin Garnett 2.50 6.00
178 Brian Shaw .60 1.50
179 Will Perdue .60 1.50
180 Scott Williams .60 1.50
F17 Charles Barkley 2.50 6.00
F18 Juwan Howard 1.25 3.00
F19 Patrick Ewing 2.00 5.00
F20 John Stockton 2.00 5.00
F21 David Robinson 2.50 6.00
F22 Cedric Ceballos 1.00 2.50
F23 Alonzo Mourning 2.00 5.00
F24 Mookie Blaylock 1.00 2.50
F25 Clyde Drexler 2.00 5.00
F26 Rod Strickland 1.00 2.50
F27 Larry Johnson 1.50 4.00
F28 Karl Malone 2.00 5.00
F29 Sean Elliott 1.50 4.00
F30 Shaquille O'Neal 4.00 10.00
F31 Tim Hardaway 1.50 4.00
F32 Dikembe Mutombo 1.50 4.00
R1 Shareef Abdur-Rahim 6.00 15.00
R2 Tony Delk 4.00 10.00
R3 Priest Lauderdale 2.50 6.00
R4 Roy Rogers 3.00 8.00
R5 Lorenzen Wright 3.00 8.00
R6 Stephon Marbury 10.00 25.00
R7 Derek Fisher 5.00 12.00
R8 John Wallace 4.00 10.00
R9 Kobe Bryant 60.00 150.00
R10 Kerry Kittles 4.00 10.00
R11 Antoine Walker 6.00 15.00
R12 Steve Nash 20.00 50.00
R13 Erick Dampier 4.00 10.00
R14 Walter McCarty 4.00 10.00
R15 Vitaly Potapenko 3.00 8.00
R16 Allen Iverson 20.00 50.00
R17 Marcus Camby 6.00 15.00
R18 Todd Fuller 2.50 6.00
R19 Ray Allen 15.00 40.00
R20 Jermaine O'Neal 6.00 15.00
CA1 Michael Jordan 15.00 40.00
Jerry Stackhouse
CA2 Patrick Ewing 2.00 5.00
Alonzo Mourning
CA3 Brent Barry 1.50 4.00
Gary Payton
CA4 Chris Webber 2.00 5.00
Juwan Howard
CA5 Christian Laettner 2.50 6.00
Grant Hill
CA6 Jason Kidd 2.50 6.00
Shareef Abdur-Rahim
CA7 Clyde Drexler 2.00 5.00
Hakeem Olajuwon
CA8 Kenny Anderson 4.00 10.00
Stephon Marbury
CA9 Anfernee Hardaway 2.50 6.00
Lorenzen Wright
CA10 Dikembe Mutombo 8.00 20.00
Allen Iverson
HR1 Scottie Pippen 2.50 6.00
HR2 Anfernee Hardaway 2.50 6.00
HR3 Vin Baker 1.25 3.00
HR4 Brent Barry 1.25 3.00
HR5 Clyde Drexler 2.00 5.00
HR6 Kevin Garnett 4.00 10.00
HR7 Grant Hill 2.50 6.00
HR8 Michael Finley 2.00 5.00
HR9 Jerry Stackhouse 2.00 5.00
HR10 Isaiah Rider 1.25 3.00
HR11 Shaquille O'Neal 4.00 10.00
HR12 Antonio McDyess 1.50 4.00
HR13 Shawn Kemp 1.50 4.00
HR14 Michael Jordan 20.00 50.00
HR15 Juwan Howard 1.25 3.00
MH1 Dennis Rodman 3.00 8.00
MH2 David Robinson 2.50 6.00
MH3 Karl Malone 2.00 5.00
MH4 Clyde Drexler 2.00 5.00
MH5 Anfernee Hardaway 2.50 6.00
MH6 Hakeem Olajuwon 2.00 5.00
MH7 Charles Oakley 1.25 3.00
MH8 Joe Smith 1.25 3.00
MH9 Glenn Robinson 1.25 3.00
RS1 Marcus Camby 2.50 6.00
RS2 Shareef Abdur-Rahim 2.50 6.00
RS3 Stephon Marbury 4.00 10.00
RS4 Ray Allen 6.00 15.00
RS5 Antoine Walker 2.50 6.00
RS6 Lorenzen Wright 1.25 3.00
RS7 Kerry Kittles 1.50 4.00
RS8 Samaki Walker 1.25 3.00
RS9 Erick Dampier 1.50 4.00
RS10 Todd Fuller 1.00 2.50
RS11 Kobe Bryant 60.00 150.00
RS12 Steve Nash 8.00 20.00
RS13 Tony Delk 1.50 4.00
RS14 Jermaine O'Neal 2.50 6.00
RS15 John Wallace 1.50 4.00
RS16 Walter McCarty 1.50 4.00
RS17 Dontae' Jones 1.50 4.00
RS18 Roy Rogers 1.25 3.00
RS19 Derek Fisher 2.00 5.00
RS20 Martin Muursepp 1.00 2.50
RS21 Jerome Williams 1.25 3.00
RS22 Brian Evans 1.50 4.00
RS23 Priest Lauderdale 1.00 2.50
RS24 Travis Knight 1.50 4.00
RS25 Allen Iverson 8.00 20.00
WA1 Charles Barkley 1.50 4.00
WA2 Armon Gilliam .60 1.50
WA3 Larry Johnson 1.00 2.50
WA4 Felton Spencer .60 1.50
WA5 Isaiah Rider .75 2.00
WA6 Kevin Willis .60 1.50
WA7 Mahmoud Abdul-Rauf .60 1.50
WA8 Chris Childs .60 1.50
WA9 Robert Horry .75 2.00
WA10 Dan Majerle 1.00 2.50
WA11 Robert Pack .60 1.50
WA12 Rod Strickland .60 1.50
WA13 Tyrone Corbin .60 1.50
WA14 Anthony Mason .60 1.50
WA15 Derek Harper .75 2.00
WA16 Kenny Anderson .75 2.00
WA17 Hubert Davis .60 1.50
WA18 Allan Houston .75 2.00
WA19 Shaquille O'Neal 2.50 6.00
WA20 Brent Price .60 1.50
WA21 Ervin Johnson .60 1.50
WA22 Craig Ehlo .60 1.50
WA23 Jalen Rose .75 2.00
WA24 Oliver Miller .60 1.50
WA25 Mark West .60 1.50

1997-98 Stadium Club Members Only Parallel I

The series one version of the Members Only set contained 201 cards which included a parallel of the basic set and the following inserts: Bowman's Best Previews, Hardcourt Heroics, Hardwood Hopefuls, Hoop Screams and Triumvirate. All cards feature "Members Only" strips running diagonally along the card back except for Bowman's Best Previews, which have no distinguishing logos and Triumvirate which has the "Members Only" strip running diagonally on the card front.

COMPLETE SET (184) 200.00 400.00
1 Scottie Pippen 2.00 5.00
3 Muggsy Bogues 1.00 2.50
5 Bulls - Team of the 90's 12.00 30.00
Ron Harper
Michael Jordan
Scottie Pippen
Dennis Rodman
7 Samaki Walker .75 2.00
9 Ray Allen 1.50 4.00
11 Chris Mullin 1.25 3.00
13 Horace Grant 1.00 2.50
15 Wayman Tisdale .75 2.00
17 Rod Strickland .75 2.00
19 Greg Anthony .75 2.00
21 Glen Rice 1.25 3.00
23 Mahmoud Abdul-Rauf .75 2.00
25 Cory Alexander .75 2.00
27 Sam Perkins .75 2.00
29 Doug Christie .75 2.00
31 Christian Laettner 1.00 2.50
33 Eric Williams .75 2.00
35 Brooks Thompson .75 2.00
37 Theo Ratliff 1.00 2.50
39 Hakeem Olajuwon 1.50 4.00
41 Reggie Miller 1.50 4.00
43 Shaquille O'Neal 3.00 8.00
45 Jamal Mashburn 1.00 2.50
47 Tom Gugliotta .75 2.00
49 Lorenzen Wright .75 2.00
51 Armon Gilliam .75 2.00
53 Kerry Kittles .75 2.00
55 Bo Outlaw .75 2.00
57 Greg Ostertag .75 2.00
59 Mark Davis .75 2.00
61 Clifford Robinson .75 2.00
63 Steve Kerr 1.00 2.50
65 Danny Ferry .75 2.00
67 A.C. Green 1.00 2.50
69 Terry Mills .75 2.00
71 Matt Maloney .75 2.00
73 Brent Barry 1.00 2.50
75 Stephon Marbury 1.50 4.00
77 Shareef Abdur-Rahim 1.25 3.00
79 Rony Seikaly .75 2.00
81 Wesley Person .75 2.00
83 Gary Trent .75 2.00
85 Rex Walters .75 2.00
87 Patrick Ewing 1.50 4.00
89 Travis Best .75 2.00
91 Vitaly Potapenko .75 2.00
93 Michael Finley 1.25 3.00
95 Antoine Walker 1.25 3.00
97 Mookie Blaylock .75 2.00
99 Tony Delk .75 2.00
101 Terrell Brandon .75 2.00
103 Latrell Sprewell 1.25 3.00
105 Tim Hardaway 1.25 3.00
107 Darrell Armstrong .75 2.00
109 Vinny Del Negro .75 2.00
111 Lawrence Moten .75 2.00
113 Juwan Howard 1.00 2.50
115 Karl Malone 1.50 4.00
117 Shawn Respert .75 2.00
119 Shawn Kemp 1.25 3.00
121 Tyus Edney .75 2.00
123 Jason Kidd 2.00 5.00
125 Allen Iverson 2.50 6.00
127 Larry Johnson 1.25 3.00
129 Kendall Gill .75 2.00
131 Vin Baker 1.00 2.50
133 Calbert Cheaney .75 2.00
135 Isaac Austin .75 2.00
137 Elden Campbell .75 2.00
139 Malik Sealy .75 2.00
141 Clyde Drexler 1.50 4.00
143 Mark Price 1.25 3.00
145 Grant Hill 2.00 5.00
147 Dale Ellis .75 2.00
149 Toni Kukoc 1.25 3.00
151 Alan Henderson .75 2.00
153 Greg Minor .75 2.00
155 Vlade Divac 1.25 3.00
157 LaPhonso Ellis .75 2.00
159 Antonio Davis .75 2.00
161 Robert Horry 1.00 2.50
163 Chris Carr .75 2.00
165 Sam Cassell 1.00 2.50
167 Chris Childs .75 2.00
169 Kenny Anderson 1.00 2.50
171 Olden Polynice .75 2.00
173 David Robinson 2.00 5.00
175 Detlef Schrempf 1.25 3.00
177 Marcus Camby 1.25 3.00
179 Shandon Anderson .75 2.00
181 Eldridge Recasner .75 2.00
183 Kevin Willis .75 2.00
185 Derek Fisher 1.25 3.00
187 Sherman Douglas .75 2.00
189 Danny Manning 1.00 2.50
191 Hersey Hawkins .75 2.00
193 Jeff Hornacek 1.00 2.50
195 Harvey Grant .75 2.00
197 Luc Longley 1.00 2.50
199 P.J. Brown .75 2.00
201 Tim Duncan 6.00 15.00
203 Keith Van Horn 2.00 5.00
205 Chauncey Billups 4.00 10.00
207 Antonio Daniels 1.25 3.00
209 Tony Battie 1.25 3.00
211 Bobby Jackson 1.50 4.00
213 Tim Thomas 1.50 4.00
215 Adonal Foyle 1.00 2.50
217 Tracy McGrady 5.00 12.00
219 Danny Fortson 1.25 3.00
221 Olivier Saint-Jean 1.00 2.50
223 Austin Croshere 1.00 2.50
225 Derek Anderson 1.25 3.00
227 Maurice Taylor 1.25 3.00
229 John Thomas .75 2.00
231 Brevin Knight 1.25 3.00
233 Johnny Taylor 1.00 2.50
235 Ed Gray 1.25 3.00
237 Anthony Parker 1.25 3.00
239 Paul Grant .75 2.00
H1 Michael Jordan 15.00 40.00
H2 Gary Payton 1.50 4.00
H3 Charles Barkley 2.50 6.00
H4 Mitch Richmond 1.50 4.00
H5 Shawn Kemp 1.50 4.00
H6 Anfernee Hardaway 2.50 6.00
H7 Vin Baker 1.25 3.00
H8 Shaquille O'Neal 4.00 10.00
H9 Scottie Pippen 2.50 6.00
H10 Grant Hill 2.50 6.00
T1A Scottie Pippen 2.50 6.00
T1B Michael Jordan 15.00 40.00
T1C Dennis Rodman 3.00 8.00
T2A Ray Allen 2.00 5.00
T2B Vin Baker 1.25 3.00
T2C Glenn Robinson 1.25 3.00
T3A Juwan Howard 1.25 3.00
T3B Chris Webber 1.50 4.00
T3C Rod Strickland 1.00 2.50
T4A Christian Laettner 1.25 3.00
T4B Dikembe Mutombo 1.50 4.00
T4C Steve Smith 1.25 3.00
T5A Tom Gugliotta 1.00 2.50
T5B Kevin Garnett 2.50 6.00
T5C Stephon Marbury 2.00 5.00
T6A Charles Barkley 2.50 6.00
T6B Hakeem Olajuwon 2.00 5.00
T6C Clyde Drexler 2.00 5.00
T7A John Stockton 2.00 5.00
T7B Karl Malone 2.00 5.00
T7C Bryon Russell 1.00 2.50
T8A Larry Johnson 1.50 4.00
T8B Patrick Ewing 2.00 5.00
T8C Allan Houston 1.25 3.00
HH1 Brevin Knight .75 2.00
HH2 Adonal Foyle .60 1.50
HH3 Keith Van Horn 1.25 3.00
HH4 Tim Duncan 4.00 10.00
HH5 Danny Fortson .75 2.00
HH6 Tracy McGrady 3.00 8.00
HH7 Tony Battie .75 2.00
HH8 Chauncey Billups 2.50 6.00
HH9 Austin Croshere .60 1.50
HH10 Antonio Daniels .75 2.00
HS1 Shaquille O'Neal 4.00 10.00
HS2 Cedric Ceballos 1.00 2.50
HS3 Kevin Garnett 2.50 6.00
HS4 Shawn Kemp 1.50 4.00
HS5 Jerry Stackhouse 1.50 4.00
HS6 Grant Hill 2.50 6.00
HS7 Patrick Ewing 2.00 5.00
HS8 Marcus Camby 1.50 4.00
HS9 Kobe Bryant 8.00 20.00
HS10 Michael Jordan 15.00 40.00
BBP1 Allen Iverson 3.00 8.00
BBP2 Gary Payton 1.50 4.00
BBP3 Grant Hill 2.50 6.00
BBP4 Anfernee Hardaway 2.50 6.00
BBP5 Karl Malone 2.00 5.00
BBP6 Glen Rice 1.50 4.00
BBP7 Antoine Walker 1.50 4.00
BBP8 Alonzo Mourning 2.00 5.00
BBP9 Shareef Abdur-Rahim 1.50 4.00
BBP10 Shaquille O'Neal 4.00 10.00

1997-98 Stadium Club Members Only Parallel II

The series two version of the Members Only set contained cards which included a parallel of the basic set and the following inserts: Bowman's Best Previews, Never Comprimise, Royal Court and Triumvirate. All cards feature "Members Only" strips running diagonally along the card back.

COMPLETE SET (194) 200.00 400.00
2 Bryon Russell .75 2.00
4 Gary Payton 1.25 3.00
6 Corliss Williamson .75 2.00
8 Allan Houston 1.00 2.50
10 Nick Van Exel 1.00 2.50
12 Popeye Jones .75 2.00
14 Rik Smits 1.00 2.50
16 Donny Marshall .75 2.00
18 Rod Strickland .75 2.00
20 Lindsey Hunter .75 2.00
22 Anthony Goldwire .75 2.00
24 Tyrone Corbin .75 2.00
26 Sean Elliott 1.25 3.00
28 Brian Shaw .75 2.00
30 Mark Jackson 1.00 2.50
32 Damon Stoudamire 1.00 2.50
34 Glenn Robinson 1.00 2.50
36 Derrick Coleman 1.00 2.50
38 Ron Harper 1.00 2.50
40 Mitch Richmond 1.25 3.00
42 Reggie Miller 1.50 4.00
44 Zydrunas Ilgauskas 1.25 3.00
46 Isaiah Rider 1.00 2.50
48 Rex Chapman .75 2.00
50 Pooh Richardson .75 2.00
52 Kevin Johnson 1.25 3.00
54 Kerry Kittles .75 2.00
56 Dennis Rodman 2.50 6.00
58 Todd Fuller .75 2.00
60 Erick Strickland 1.00 2.50
62 Nate McMillan .75 2.00
64 Bob Sura .75 2.00
66 Loy Vaught .75 2.00
68 John Stockton 1.50 4.00
70 Voshon Lenard .75 2.00
72 Charlie Ward .75 2.00
74 Chris Webber 1.25 3.00
76 Bryant Stith .75 2.00
78 Sean Rooks .75 2.00
80 Brent Price .75 2.00
82 Michael Smith .75 2.00
84 Dan Majerle 1.25 3.00
86 Clarence Weatherspoon .75 2.00
88 B.J. Armstrong .75 2.00
90 Steve Smith 1.00 2.50
92 Derek Strong .75 2.00
94 Will Perdue .75 2.00
96 Chuck Person 1.00 2.50
98 Eric Snow .75 2.00
100 Mario Elie .75 2.00
102 Shawn Bradley .75 2.00
104 Latrell Sprewell 1.25 3.00
106 Terry Porter .75 2.00
108 Rasheed Wallace 1.25 3.00
110 Tracy Murray .75 2.00
112 Lamond Murray .75 2.00
114 Juwan Howard 1.00 2.50
116 Aaron McKie .75 2.00
118 Michael Jordan 10.00 25.00
120 Arvydas Sabonis 1.00 2.50
122 Bryant Reeves .75 2.00
124 Dikembe Mutombo 1.25 3.00
126 Allen Iverson 2.50 6.00
128 Jerry Stackhouse 1.25 3.00
130 Kendall Gill .75 2.00
132 Joe Dumars 1.25 3.00
134 Alonzo Mourning 1.50 4.00
136 Joe Smith 1.00 2.50
138 Kevin Garnett 2.00 5.00
140 John Starks 1.00 2.50
142 Matt Geiger .75 2.00
144 Buck Williams .75 2.00
146 Kobe Bryant 6.00 15.00
148 Jason Caffey .75 2.00
150 Avery Johnson 1.00 2.50
152 Walt Williams .75 2.00
154 Calbert Cheaney .75 2.00
156 Greg Foster .75 2.00
158 Charles Barkley 2.00 5.00
160 Roy Rogers .75 2.00
162 Sam Cassell 1.00 2.50
164 Robert Pack .75 2.00
166 Rodney Rogers .75 2.00
168 Shandon Anderson .75 2.00
170 Anthony Mason .75 2.00
172 David Wingate .75 2.00
174 Billy Owens .75 2.00
176 Carlos Rogers .75 2.00
178 Dana Barros .75 2.00
180 Jayson Williams .75 2.00
182 Doug West .75 2.00
184 Eddie Johnson .75 2.00
186 Eddie Jones 1.25 3.00
188 Anthony Peeler .75 2.00
190 Stacey Augmon 1.00 2.50
192 Micheal Williams .75 2.00
194 Anfernee Hardaway 2.00 5.00
196 Nick Anderson .75 2.00
198 Andrew Lang .75 2.00
200 Cedric Ceballos .75 2.00
202 Ervin Johnson TRAN .75 2.00
204 David Wesley TRAN .75 2.00
206 Jim Jackson TRAN .75 2.00
208 Travis Knight TRAN .75 2.00
210 Bobby Phills TRAN .75 2.00
212 Otis Thorpe TRAN .75 2.00
214 Chris Mullin TRAN 1.25 3.00
216 Brian Williams TRAN .75 2.00
218 Tyus Edney TRAN .75 2.00
220 Clifford Robinson TRAN .75 2.00
222 Vin Baker TRAN 1.00 2.50
224 John Wallace TRAN .75 2.00
226 Kelvin Cato 1.00 2.50
228 Scot Pollard 1.25 3.00
230 Dean Garrett TRAN .75 2.00
232 Ron Mercer 1.50 4.00
234 Antonio McDyess TRAN 1.00 2.50
236 Terrell Brandon TRAN .75 2.00
238 Shawn Kemp TRAN 1.25 3.00
240 Dennis Scott TRAN .75 2.00
T9A Tim Hardaway 1.50 4.00
T9B Michael Jordan 15.00 40.00
T9C Anfernee Hardaway 2.50 6.00
T10A Glen Rice 1.50 4.00
T10B Scottie Pippen 2.50 6.00
T10C Grant Hill 2.50 6.00
T11A Dikembe Mutombo 1.50 4.00
T11B Patrick Ewing 2.00 5.00
T11C Alonzo Mourning 2.00 5.00
T12A Ron Mercer 1.00 2.50
T12B Keith Van Horn 1.25 3.00
T12C Tracy McGrady 3.00 8.00
T13A Gary Payton 1.50 4.00
T13B John Stockton 2.00 5.00
T13C Stephon Marbury 2.00 5.00
T14A Karl Malone 2.00 5.00
T14B Charles Barkley 2.50 6.00
T14C Kevin Garnett 2.50 6.00
T15A David Robinson 2.50 6.00
T15B Hakeem Olajuwon 2.00 5.00
T15C Shaquille O'Neal 4.00 10.00
T16A Antonio Daniels .75 2.00
T16B Tim Duncan 4.00 10.00
T16C Adonal Foyle .60 1.50
NC1 Michael Jordan 15.00 40.00
NC2 Karl Malone 2.00 5.00
NC3 Hakeem Olajuwon 2.00 5.00
NC4 Kevin Garnett 2.50 6.00
NC5 Dikembe Mutombo 1.50 4.00
NC6 Gary Payton 1.50 4.00
NC7 Grant Hill 2.50 6.00
NC8 Charles Barkley 2.50 6.00
NC9 Shaquille O'Neal 4.00 10.00
NC10 Anfernee Hardaway 2.50 6.00
NC11 Tim Duncan 4.00 10.00
NC12 Keith Van Horn 1.25 3.00
NC13 Tracy McGrady 3.00 8.00
NC14 Tim Thomas 1.00 2.50
NC15 Austin Croshere .60 1.50
NC16 Maurice Taylor .75 2.00
NC17 Chauncey Billups 2.50 6.00
NC18 Adonal Foyle .60 1.50
NC19 Tony Battie .75 2.00
NC20 Bobby Jackson 1.00 2.50
RC1 Scottie Pippen 2.50 6.00
RC2 Karl Malone 2.00 5.00
RC3 Gary Payton 1.50 4.00
RC4 Kobe Bryant 8.00 20.00
RC5 Antoine Walker 1.50 4.00
RC6 Michael Jordan 20.00 50.00
RC7 Shaquille O'Neal 4.00 10.00
RC8 Dikembe Mutombo 1.50 4.00
RC9 Hakeem Olajuwon 2.00 5.00
RC10 Grant Hill 2.50 6.00
RC11 Tim Duncan 5.00 12.00
RC12 Keith Van Horn 1.25 3.00
RC13 Chauncey Billups 2.50 6.00
RC14 Antonio Daniels .75 2.00
RC15 Tony Battie .75 2.00
RC16 Bobby Jackson 1.00 2.50
RC17 Tim Thomas 1.00 2.50
RC18 Adonal Foyle .60 1.50
RC19 Tracy McGrady 3.00 8.00
RC20 Danny Fortson .75 2.00
BBP11 Maurice Taylor .75 2.00
BBP12 Chauncey Billups 2.50 6.00
BBP13 Paul Grant .50 1.25
BBP14 Tony Battie .75 2.00
BBP15 Austin Croshere .60 1.50
BBP16 Brevin Knight .75 2.00
BBP17 Bobby Jackson 1.00 2.50
BBP18 Johnny Taylor .60 1.50
BBP19 Scot Pollard .75 2.00
BBP20 Tariq Abdul-Wahad .60 1.50

1983 Star All-Star Game

This was the first NBA set issued by Star Company. The 30-card standard-size set was issued in a clear, sealed plastic bag and distributed through hobby dealers. According to information provided on the order forms, Star Company printed 15,000 sets. The sets originally retailed for $2.50 to $5.00 each. Each card has a blue border on the front and blue print on the back. The set commemorates the 1983 NBA All-Star Game held in Los Angeles. Many of the cards feature players in their All-Star uniforms. There are two unnumbered cards in the set listed at the end of the checklist below. The cards are numbered on the back with the order of the numbering essentially alphabetical according to the player's name. The set features the first professional card of Isiah Thomas.

COMPLETE SET (32)	30.00	80.00
1 Julius Erving CL !	3.00	8.00
2 Larry Bird	6.00	15.00
3 Maurice Cheeks	1.00	2.50
4 Julius Erving	3.00	8.00
5 Marques Johnson	1.00	2.50
6 Bill Laimbeer	1.00	2.50
7 Moses Malone	2.00	5.00
8 Sidney Moncrief	1.00	2.50
9 Robert Parish	2.00	5.00
10 Reggie Theus	1.00	2.50
11 Isiah Thomas	6.00	15.00
12 Andrew Toney	1.00	2.50
13 Buck Williams	1.00	2.50
14 Kareem Abdul-Jabbar	3.00	8.00
15 Alex English	2.00	5.00
16 George Gervin	2.50	6.00
17 Artis Gilmore	1.00	2.50
18 Magic Johnson	6.00	15.00
19 Maurice Lucas	1.00	2.50
20 Jim Paxson	1.00	2.50
21 Jack Sikma	1.00	2.50
22 David Thompson	2.00	5.00
23 Kiki Vandeweghe	1.00	2.50
24 Jamaal Wilkes	1.00	2.50
25 Gus Williams	1.00	2.50
26 Julius Erving MVP	4.00	10.00
27 R.Theus/M.Malone	2.00	5.00
28 All-Star ATL	1.00	2.50
29 L.Bird/R.Parish	5.00	12.00
30 Sidney Moncrief IA	1.00	2.50
xx A.Gilmore/A.English	1.00	2.50
xx Kareem Abdul-Jabbar	3.00	8.00
BAG Complete sealed bag (32)	30.00	80.00

1983-84 Star

This set of 276 standard-size cards was issued in four series during the first six months of 1984. Several teams in the first series (1-100) are difficult to obtain due to extensive miscuts (all of which, according to the company, were destroyed) in the initial production process. The team sets were issued in clear sealed bags. Many of the team bags were distributed to hobby dealers through a small group of Star Co. master distributors. According to Star Company's original sales materials and order forms, reportedly 5,000 team bags were printed for each team although quality control problems with the early sets apparently reduced that number considerably. The retail price per bag was $2.50 to $5 for most of the teams. Color borders around the fronts and color printing on the backs correspond to team colors. Cards are numbered according to team order. Extended Rookie Cards include Mark Aguirre, Danny Ainge, Rolando Blackman, Tom Chambers, Clyde Drexler, Dale Ellis, Derek Harper, Larry Nance, Rickey Pierce, Isiah Thomas, Dominique Wilkins, Buck Williams and James Worthy. A promotional card of Sidney Moncrief was produced in limited quantities, but it was numbered 39 rather than 38 as it was in the regular set. There is typically a slight discount on sales of opened team bags.

COMPLETE SET (275)	1200.00	1800.00
1 Julius Erving SP !	15.00	40.00
2 Maurice Cheeks SP	2.50	6.00
3 Franklin Edwards SP	1.50	4.00
4 Marc Iavaroni SP	2.50	6.00
5 Clemon Johnson SP	1.50	4.00
6 Bobby Jones SP	4.00	10.00
7 Moses Malone SP	8.00	20.00
8 Leo Rautins SP	1.50	4.00
9 Clint Richardson SP	1.50	4.00
10 Sedale Threatt SP XRC	4.00	10.00
11 Andrew Toney SP XRC	6.00	15.00
12 Sam Williams SP	1.50	4.00
13 Magic Johnson SP !	20.00	50.00
14 Kareem Abdul-Jabbar SP	15.00	40.00
15 Michael Cooper SP	6.00	15.00
16 Calvin Garrett SP	1.50	4.00
17 Mitch Kupchak SP	2.50	6.00
18 Bob McAdoo SP	5.00	12.00
19 Mike McGee SP	1.50	4.00
20 Swen Nater SP	1.50	4.00
21 Kurt Rambis SP XRC	8.00	20.00
22 Byron Scott SP XRC	10.00	25.00
23 Larry Spriggs SP	1.50	4.00
24 Jamaal Wilkes SP	5.00	12.00
25 James Worthy SP XRC	20.00	50.00
26 Larry Bird SP !	100.00	250.00
27 Danny Ainge SP XRC	30.00	50.00
28 Quinn Buckner SP	4.00	10.00
29 M.L. Carr SP	4.00	10.00
30 Carlos Clark SP	4.00	10.00
31 Gerald Henderson SP	4.00	10.00
32 Dennis Johnson SP	8.00	20.00
33 Cedric Maxwell SP	4.00	10.00
34 Kevin McHale SP !	12.00	30.00
35 Robert Parish SP !	10.00	25.00
36 Scott Wedman SP	4.00	10.00
37 Greg Kite SP XRC	4.00	10.00
38 Sidney Moncrief SP	5.00	12.00
39A Sidney Moncrief SP	8.00	20.00
39B Nate Archibald SP	6.00	15.00
40 Randy Breuer SP XRC	1.50	4.00
41 Junior Bridgeman SP	1.50	4.00
42 Harvey Catchings SP	1.50	4.00
43 Kevin Grevey SP	1.50	4.00
44A Marques Johnson SP UER	4.00	10.00
Bob Lanier pictured		
44B Marques Johnson SP	4.00	10.00
45 Bob Lanier SP	6.00	15.00
46 Alton Lister SP XRC	1.50	4.00
47 Paul Mokeski SP XRC	1.50	4.00
48 Paul Pressey SP XRC	1.50	4.00
49 Mark Aguirre SP XRC	25.00	60.00
50 Rolando Blackman SP XRC	25.00	60.00
51 Pat Cummings SP	6.00	15.00
52 Brad Davis SP XRC	8.00	20.00
53 Dale Ellis SP XRC	25.00	60.00
54 Bill Garnett SP	6.00	15.00
55 Derek Harper SP XRC	30.00	60.00
56 Kurt Nimphius SP	6.00	15.00
57 Jim Spanarkel SP	6.00	15.00
58 Elston Turner SP	6.00	15.00
59 Jay Vincent SP XRC	20.00	40.00
60 Mark West SP XRC	10.00	20.00
61 Bernard King	4.00	10.00
62 Bill Cartwright	2.50	6.00
63 Len Elmore	1.25	3.00
64 Eric Fernsten	1.25	3.00
65 Ernie Grunfeld	1.25	3.00
66 Louis Orr	1.25	3.00
67 Leonard Robinson	1.25	3.00
68 Rory Sparrow XRC	1.50	4.00
69 Trent Tucker XRC	1.50	4.00
70 Darrell Walker XRC	1.50	4.00
71 Marvin Webster	1.25	3.00
72 Ray Williams	1.25	3.00
73 Ralph Sampson XRC	5.00	12.00
74 James Bailey	1.25	3.00
75 Phil Ford	1.25	3.00
76 Elvin Hayes	4.00	10.00
77 Caldwell Jones	1.25	3.00
78 Major Jones	1.25	3.00
79 Allen Leavell	1.25	3.00
80 Lewis Lloyd	1.25	3.00
81 Rodney McCray XRC	1.50	4.00
82 Robert Reid	1.50	4.00
83 Terry Teagle XRC	1.50	4.00
84 Wally Walker	1.25	3.00
85 Kelly Tripucka XRC	1.50	4.00
86 Kent Benson	1.25	3.00
87 Earl Cureton	1.25	3.00
88 Lionel Hollins	1.25	3.00
89 Vinnie Johnson	1.50	4.00
90 Bill Laimbeer	2.50	6.00
91 Cliff Levingston XRC	1.50	4.00
92 John Long	1.25	3.00
93 David Thirdkill	1.25	3.00
94 Isiah Thomas XRC	40.00	100.00
95 Ray Tolbert	1.25	3.00
96 Terry Tyler	1.25	3.00
97 Jim Paxson	2.50	6.00
98 Kenny Carr	1.25	3.00
99 Wayne Cooper	1.25	3.00
100 Clyde Drexler XRC	80.00	160.00
101 Jeff Lamp XRC	2.50	6.00
102 Lafayette Lever XRC	2.50	6.00
103 Calvin Natt	1.25	3.00
104 Audie Norris	1.25	3.00
105 Tom Piotrowski	1.25	3.00
106 Mychal Thompson	1.25	3.00
107 Darnell Valentine XRC	1.50	4.00
108 Pete Verhoeven	1.25	3.00
109 Walter Davis	2.50	6.00
110 Alvan Adams	1.50	4.00
111 James Edwards	1.50	4.00
112 Rod Foster XRC	1.50	4.00
113 Maurice Lucas	1.50	4.00
114 Kyle Macy	1.25	3.00
115 Larry Nance XRC	8.00	20.00
116 Charles Pittman	1.25	3.00
117 Rick Robey	1.25	3.00
118 Mike Sanders XRC	1.50	4.00
119 Alvin Scott	1.25	3.00
120 Paul Westphal	2.50	6.00
121 Bill Walton	6.00	15.00
122 Michael Brooks	1.25	3.00
123 Terry Cummings XRC	5.00	12.00
124 James Donaldson XRC	1.50	4.00
125 Craig Hodges XRC	1.50	4.00
126 Greg Kelser XRC	1.50	4.00
127 Hank McDowell	1.25	3.00
128 Billy McKinney	1.25	3.00
129 Norm Nixon	1.50	4.00
130 Ricky Pierce UER XRC	2.50	6.00
131 Derek Smith XRC	1.50	4.00
132 Jerome Whitehead	1.25	3.00
133 Adrian Dantley	4.00	10.00
134 Mitchell Anderson	1.25	3.00
135 Thurl Bailey XRC	2.50	6.00
136 Tom Boswell	1.25	3.00
137 John Drew	1.25	3.00
138 Mark Eaton XRC	4.00	10.00
139 Jerry Eaves	1.25	3.00
140 Rickey Green XRC	1.50	4.00
141 Darrell Griffith	1.25	3.00
142 Bobby Hansen XRC	1.50	4.00
143 Rich Kelley	1.25	3.00
144 Jeff Wilkins	1.25	3.00
145 Buck Williams XRC	7.50	15.00
146 Otis Birdsong	1.25	3.00
147 Darwin Cook	1.25	3.00
148 Darryl Dawkins	2.50	6.00
149 Mike Gminski	1.25	3.00
150 Reggie Johnson	1.25	3.00
151 Albert King XRC	1.50	4.00
152 Mike O'Koren	1.25	3.00
153 Kelvin Ransey	1.25	3.00
154 Micheal Ray Richardson	1.25	3.00
155 Clarence Walker	1.25	3.00
156 Bill Willoughby	1.25	3.00
157 Steve Stipanovich XRC	1.50	4.00
158 Butch Carter	1.25	3.00
159 Edwin Leroy Combs	1.25	3.00
160 George L. Johnson	1.25	3.00
161 Clark Kellogg XRC	2.50	6.00
162 Sidney Lowe XRC	1.50	4.00
163 Kevin McKenna	1.25	3.00
164 Jerry Sichting XRC	1.50	4.00
165 Brook Steppe	1.25	3.00
166 Jimmy Thomas	1.25	3.00
167 Granville Waiters	1.25	3.00
168 Herb Williams XRC	1.50	4.00
169 Dave Corzine	1.25	3.00
170 Wallace Bryant	1.25	3.00
171 Quintin Dailey XRC	1.50	4.00
172 Sidney Green XRC	1.50	4.00
173 David Greenwood	1.25	3.00
174 Rod Higgins XRC	1.50	4.00
175 Clarence Johnson	1.25	3.00
176 Ronnie Lester	2.50	6.00
177 Jawann Oldham	1.25	3.00
178 Ennis Whatley XRC	1.50	4.00
179 Mitchell Wiggins XRC	1.50	4.00
180 Orlando Woolridge XRC	2.50	6.00
181 Kiki Vandeweghe XRC	5.00	12.00
182 Richard Anderson	1.25	3.00
183 Howard Carter	1.25	3.00
184 T.R. Dunn	1.25	3.00
185 Keith Edmonson	1.25	3.00
186 Alex English	5.00	12.00
187 Mike Evans	1.25	3.00
188 Bill Hanzlik XRC	1.50	4.00
189 Dan Issel	4.00	10.00
190 Anthony Roberts	1.25	3.00
191 Danny Schayes XRC	1.50	4.00
192 Rob Williams	1.25	3.00
193 Jack Sikma	2.50	6.00
194 Fred Brown	1.25	3.00
195 Tom Chambers XRC	10.00	25.00
196 Steve Hawes	1.25	3.00
197 Steve Hayes	1.25	3.00
198 Reggie King	1.25	3.00
199 Scooter McCray	1.25	3.00
200 Jon Sundvold XRC	1.50	4.00
201 Danny Vranes	1.25	3.00
202 Gus Williams	1.50	4.00
203 Al Wood	1.25	3.00
204 Jeff Ruland XRC	1.50	4.00
205 Greg Ballard	1.25	3.00
206 Charles Davis	1.25	3.00
207 Darren Daye	1.25	3.00
208 Michael Gibson	1.25	3.00
209 Frank Johnson XRC	2.50	6.00
210 Joe Kopicki	1.25	3.00
211 Rick Mahorn	1.50	4.00
212 Jeff Malone XRC	2.50	6.00
213 Tom McMillen	1.25	3.00
214 Ricky Sobers	1.25	3.00
215 Bryan Warrick	1.25	3.00
216 Billy Knight	1.25	3.00
217 Don Buse	1.25	3.00
218 Larry Drew XRC	1.50	4.00
219 Eddie Johnson XRC	4.00	10.00
220 Joe Meriweather	1.25	3.00
221 Larry Micheaux	1.25	3.00
222 Ed Nealy XRC	1.50	4.00
223 Mark Olberding	1.25	3.00
224 Dave Robisch	1.25	3.00
225 Reggie Theus	2.50	6.00
226 LaSalle Thompson XRC	1.50	4.00
227 Mike Woodson	1.25	3.00
228 World B. Free	1.50	4.00
229 John Bagley XRC	1.50	4.00
230 Jeff Cook	1.25	3.00
231 Geoff Crompton	1.25	3.00
232 John Garris	1.25	3.00
233 Stewart Granger	1.25	3.00
234 Roy Hinson XRC	1.50	4.00
235 Phil Hubbard	1.25	3.00
236 Geoff Huston	1.25	3.00
237 Ben Poquette	1.25	3.00
238 Cliff Robinson	1.25	3.00
239 Lonnie Shelton	1.25	3.00
240 Paul Thompson	1.25	3.00
241 George Gervin	5.00	12.00
242 Gene Banks	1.25	3.00
243 Ron Brewer	1.25	3.00
244 Artis Gilmore	2.50	6.00
245 Edgar Jones	1.25	3.00
246 John Lucas	1.50	4.00
247A Mike Mitchell ERR	1.25	3.00
247B Mike Mitchell ERR	2.50	6.00
248A M.McNamara ERR XRC	1.50	4.00
248B M.McNamara ERR XRC	2.50	6.00
249 Johnny Moore	1.25	3.00
250 John Paxson XRC	6.00	15.00
251 Fred Roberts XRC	1.50	4.00
252 Joe Barry Carroll	1.25	3.00
253 Mike Bratz	1.25	3.00
254 Don Collins	1.25	3.00
255 Lester Conner	1.25	3.00
256 Chris Engler	1.25	3.00
257 Sleepy Floyd XRC	4.00	10.00
258 Wallace Johnson	1.25	3.00
259 Pace Mannion	1.25	3.00
260 Purvis Short	1.25	3.00
261 Larry Smith	1.25	3.00
262 Darren Tillis	1.25	3.00
263 Dominique Wilkins XRC	90.00	180.00
264 Rickey Brown	1.25	3.00
265 Johnny Davis	1.25	3.00
266 Mike Glenn XRC	1.50	4.00
267 Scott Hastings XRC	1.50	4.00
268 Eddie Johnson	1.25	3.00
269 Mark Landsberger	1.25	3.00
270 Billy Paultz	1.25	3.00
271 Doc Rivers XRC	12.00	30.00
272 Tree Rollins	1.50	4.00
273 Dan Roundfield	1.25	3.00
274 Sly Williams	1.25	3.00
275 Randy Wittman XRC	1.50	4.00
BAG1 76ers sealed bag (12)	50.00	100.00
BAG2 Blazers sealed bag (12)	100.00	200.00
BAG3 Bucks sealed bag (11)	25.00	50.00
BAG4 Bullets sealed bag (12)	12.50	30.00
BAG5 Bulls sealed bag (12)	20.00	50.00
BAG6 Cavs sealed bag (13)	12.50	30.00
BAG7 Celtics sealed bag (12)	150.00	350.00
BAG8 Clippers sealed bag (12)	20.00	50.00
BAG9 Hawks sealed bag (14)	125.00	225.00
BAG10 Jazz sealed bag (12)	12.50	30.00
BAG11 Kings sealed bag (12)	12.50	30.00
BAG12 Knicks sealed bag (12)	17.50	35.00
BAG13 Lakers sealed bag (13)	60.00	150.00
BAG14 Mavs sealed bag (12)	200.00	400.00
BAG15 Nets sealed bag (12)	12.50	30.00
BAG16 Nuggets sealed bag (12)	15.00	40.00
BAG17 Pacers sealed bag (12)	12.50	30.00
BAG18 Pistons sealed bag (12)	60.00	120.00
BAG19 Rockets sealed bag (12)	12.50	30.00
BAG20 Sonics sealed bag (11)	20.00	40.00
BAG21 Spurs sealed bag (11)	12.50	30.00
BAG22 Suns sealed bag (12)	20.00	50.00
BAG23 Warriors sealed bag (11)	12.50	30.00

1983-84 Star All-Rookies

This set features the ten members of the 1982-83 NBA All-Rookie Team. The standard-size cards have a yellow border around the fronts of the cards. The set was issued in a sealed plastic bag and distributed through hobby dealers. It originally retailed for about $2.50 to $5. The set was issued late summer of 1983 and features the Star '84 logo on the front of each card. The cards are numbered on the backs with the order of the numbering alphabetical according to the player's last name.

COMPLETE SET (10)	12.00	30.00
1 Terry Cummings	2.50	6.00
2 Quintin Dailey	.75	2.00
3 Rod Higgins	.75	2.00
4 Clark Kellogg	.75	2.00
5 Lafayette Lever	.75	2.00
6 Paul Pressey	.75	2.00
7 Trent Tucker	.75	2.00
8 Dominique Wilkins !	8.00	20.00
9 Rob Williams	.75	2.00
10 James Worthy	5.00	12.00
BAG Complete sealed bag (10)	12.50	30.00

1983-84 Star Sixers Champs

This set of 25 standard-size cards is devoted to Philadelphia's NBA Championship victory over the Los Angeles Lakers in 1983. Reportedly 10,000 sets were printed. Majority of the distribution was done at the Spectrum, the 76ers home arena. The cards have a red border around the fronts of the cards and red printing on the backs. The set was issued in late summer of 1983 and features the Star '84 logo on the front of each card.

COMPLETE SET (25)	20.00	50.00
1 Moses Malone CL	1.50	4.00
2 Billy Cunningham CO	.75	2.00
3 M.Malone/Abdul-Jabbar	2.50	6.00
4 Julius Erving IA	2.50	6.00
5 Clint Richardson IA	.75	2.00
6 Andrew Toney IA	.75	2.00
7 Phila. 113, LA 107	.75	2.00
Game 1 Boxscore		
8 Bobby Jones IA	.75	2.00
9 Maurice Cheeks IA	.75	2.00
10 Julius Erving IA	2.50	6.00
11 Andrew Toney IA	.75	2.00
12 Phila. 103, LA 93	.75	2.00
Game 2 Boxscore		
13 Serious Sixers	.75	2.00
14 Moses Malone IA	1.50	4.00
15 Clemon Johnson IA	.75	2.00
16 Maurice Cheeks IA	.75	2.00
17 Phila. 111, LA 94	.75	2.00
Game 3 Boxscore		
18 Julius Erving IA	2.50	6.00
19 Bobby Jones 6M	.75	2.00
20 Moses Malone IA	1.50	4.00
21 World Champs	.75	2.00
22 Julius Erving COMM	2.50	6.00
23 Moses Malone COMM	1.50	4.00
24 Julius Erving COMM	2.50	6.00
25 Moses Malone MVP	1.50	4.00
BAG Complete sealed bag (25)	20.00	50.00

1984 Star All-Star Game

This set of 25 standard-size cards features participants in the 34th Annual NBA All-Star Game held in Denver. The cards have a white border around the fronts of the cards and blue printing on the backs. Cards feature the Star '84 logo on the front. The cards are ordered with the East All-Stars on cards 2-13 and the West All-Stars on cards 14-25. The cards are on the backs and are in alphabetical order by division.

COMPLETE SET (25)	30.00	80.00
1 Isiah Thomas CL	4.00	10.00
2 Larry Bird	15.00	30.00
3 Otis Birdsong	.75	2.00
4 Julius Erving	6.00	15.00
5 Bernard King	1.25	3.00
6 Bill Laimbeer	2.50	6.00
7 Kevin McHale	3.00	8.00
8 Sidney Moncrief	1.25	3.00
9 Robert Parish	1.25	3.00
10 Jeff Ruland	.75	2.00
11 Isiah Thomas	5.00	12.00
12 Andrew Toney	.75	2.00
13 Kelly Tripucka	.75	2.00
14 Kareem Abdul-Jabbar	5.00	12.00
15 Mark Aguirre	.75	2.00
16 Adrian Dantley	1.25	3.00
17 Walter Davis	.75	2.00
18 Alex English	1.25	3.00
19 George Gervin	2.50	6.00
20 Rickey Green	.75	2.00
21 Magic Johnson	12.50	25.00
22 Jim Paxson	.75	2.00
23 Ralph Sampson	1.25	3.00
24 Jack Sikma	1.25	3.00
25 Kiki Vandeweghe	1.25	3.00
BAG Complete sealed bag (25)	40.00	100.00

1984 Star All-Star Game Denver Police

This 34-card standard-size set was distributed as individual cards by the Denver Police in the months following the NBA All-Star Game held in Denver. Reportedly 10,000 sets were produced. The set was composed of participants in the All-Star Game (1-25) and the Slam Dunk contest (26-34). The cards have a white border around the fronts and blue printing on the backs. Cards feature the Star '84 logo on the fronts and safety tips on the backs.

COMPLETE SET (34)	100.00	200.00
1 Isiah Thomas CL	3.00	8.00
2 Larry Bird	20.00	40.00
3 Otis Birdsong	1.25	3.00
4 Julius Erving	6.00	15.00
5 Bernard King	2.00	5.00
6 Bill Laimbeer	2.50	6.00
7 Kevin McHale	4.00	10.00
8 Sidney Moncrief	2.00	5.00
9 Robert Parish	3.00	8.00
10 Jeff Ruland	1.25	3.00
11 Isiah Thomas w/Magic	6.00	15.00
12 Andrew Toney	1.25	3.00
13 Kelly Tripucka	1.25	3.00
14 Kareem Abdul-Jabbar	6.00	15.00
15 Mark Aguirre	2.00	5.00
16 Adrian Dantley	2.00	5.00
17 Walter Davis	2.00	5.00
18 Alex English	2.50	6.00
19 George Gervin	2.50	6.00
20 Rickey Green	1.25	3.00
21 Magic Johnson	15.00	30.00
22 Jim Paxson	1.25	3.00
23 Ralph Sampson	2.00	5.00
24 Jack Sikma	2.00	5.00
25 Kiki Vandeweghe	2.00	5.00
26 Michael Cooper SD	2.00	5.00
27 Clyde Drexler SD	10.00	25.00
28 Julius Erving SD	6.00	15.00
29 Darrell Griffith SD	2.00	5.00
30 Edgar Jones SD	1.25	3.00
31 Larry Nance SD	2.50	6.00
32 Ralph Sampson SD	2.00	5.00
33 Dominique Wilkins SD	10.00	25.00
34 Orlando Woolridge SD	1.25	3.00

1984 Star Award Banquet

This 24-card standard-size set was produced for the NBA to be given away at the Awards Banquet which took place following the conclusion of the 1983-84 season. According to a 1984 Star Company press release, only 3,000 sets were produced. The cards highlighted award winners from the 1983-84 season. Cards have a blue border around the fronts of the cards and pink and blue printing on the backs. The set was issued in June of 1984 and features the Star '84 logo on the front of each card.

COMPLETE SET (24)	30.00	80.00
1 1984 Award Winners	.75	2.00
2 Frank Layden CO	.75	2.00
3 Ralph Sampson ROY	.75	2.00
4 Adrian Dantley POY	.75	2.00
5 Kevin McHale 6M	1.25	3.00
6 Magic Johnson POY	5.00	12.00
7 Sidney Moncrief DEF	.75	2.00
8 Larry Bird MVP	6.00	15.00
9 Larry Nance SD	1.25	3.00
10 Bird/Griff/Gilm/Dant LL	4.00	10.00
11 Magic/Green/Eat/Moses LL	3.00	8.00
12 Isiah Thomas AS MVP	2.50	6.00
13 Adrian Dantley LL	.75	2.00
14 Artis Gilmore LL	.75	2.00
15 Larry Bird LL	6.00	15.00
16 Darrell Griffith LL	.75	2.00
17 Magic Johnson LL	5.00	12.00
18 Rickey Green LL	.75	2.00
19 Mark Eaton LL	.75	3.00
20 Moses Malone LL	1.25	3.00
21 Abdul-Jabbar w/D.Stern	4.00	10.00
22 All-Defensive Team	1.25	3.00
23 All-Rookie Team	1.25	3.00
24 All-NBA Team	6.00	15.00
BAG Complete sealed bag (24)	30.00	80.00

1984 Star Larry Bird

This set contains 18 standard-size cards highlighting the career of basketball great Larry Bird. Cards have a green border around the fronts of the cards and green printing on the backs. Cards feature Star '84 logo on the front as they were released in May of 1984.

COMPLETE SET (18)	25.00	60.00
COMMON L.BIRD (1-18)	2.00	5.00
BAG Complete sealed bag (18)	25.00	60.00

1984 Star Celtics Champs

This set of 25 standard-size cards is devoted to Boston's NBA Championship victory over the Los Angeles Lakers in 1984. Cards have a green border around the fronts of the cards and green printing on the backs. The set was issued in summer of 1984 and features the Star '84 logo on the front of each card. The set includes two of the three Red Auerbach cards ever printed.

COMPLETE SET (25)	100.00	200.00
1 Auerbach/D.Stern CL	4.00	10.00
2 Abdul-Jabbar/Parish IA	4.00	10.00
3 Kevin McHale IA	2.50	6.00
4 Larry Bird IA	10.00	25.00
5 Magic Johnson IA	8.00	20.00
6 D.Ainge/K.C.Jones	2.50	6.00
7 Larry Bird IA	10.00	25.00
8 Abdul-Jabbar/McHale IA	3.00	8.00
9 James Worthy IA	2.50	6.00
10 Magic Johnson IA	8.00	20.00
11 Magic/Bird IA	25.00	50.00
12 Worthy/Ainge IA	3.00	8.00
13 Boston 129& LA 125	.75	2.00
14 Larry Bird IA	12.00	30.00
15 Pat Riley CO IA	3.00	8.00
16 Kareem Abdul-Jabbar	4.00	10.00
17 Robert Parish IA	1.25	3.00
18 Kareem Abdul-Jabbar IA	4.00	10.00
19 Dennis Johnson IA	1.25	3.00
20 Kareem Abdul-Jabbar IA	4.00	10.00
21 K.C. Jones CO	1.25	3.00
22 M.L. Carr IA	.75	2.00
23 Red Auerbach !	3.00	8.00
24 Larry Bird MVP !	15.00	40.00
25 Boston Garden !	4.00	10.00
BAG Complete sealed bag (25)	100.00	200.00

1984 Star Slam Dunk

An 11-card standard-size set highlighting the revival of the Slam Dunk contest (during the 1984 All-Star Weekend in Denver) was produced by the Star Company in 1984. The cards have a white border around the fronts and blue printing on the backs. The Star '84 logo are featured on the front.

COMPLETE SET (11)	30.00	60.00
1 Group Photo CL	6.00	15.00
2 Michael Cooper	1.25	3.00
3 Clyde Drexler	8.00	20.00
4 Julius Erving	6.00	15.00
5 Darrell Griffith	1.25	3.00
6 Edgar Jones	.75	2.00
7 Larry Nance	2.50	6.00
8 Ralph Sampson	1.25	3.00
9 Dominique Wilkins UER	8.00	20.00
10 Orlando Woolridge	1.25	3.00
11 Larry Nance Champion	2.50	6.00
BAG Complete sealed bag (11)	30.00	60.00

1984-85 Star

This set of 288 standard-size cards was issued in three series during the first five months of 1985 by Star Company. The set is comprised of team sets that were issued in clear sealed bags. Many of these team bags were distributed to hobby dealers through a small group of Star Company master distributors and retailed for $2.50-$5. According to Star Company's original sales materials and order forms, reportedly 3,000 team bags were printed for each team. The cards have a colored border around the fronts of the cards according to the team with corresponding color printing on the backs. Cards are organized numerically by team. The set also features a special subset (195-200) honoring Gold Medal-winning players from the 1984 Olympic basketball competition as well as a subset of NBA specials (281-288). Michael Jordan's Extended Rookie Card appears in this set. Other Extended Rookie's include Charles Barkley, Craig Ehlo, Hakeem Olajuwon, Alvin Robertson, Sam Perkins, John Stockton and Otis Thorpe. There is typically a slight discount on sales of opened team bags.

COMPLETE SET (288)	3500.00	4500.00
CONDITION SENSITIVE SET		
BEWARE JORDAN COUNTERFEITS		
1 Larry Bird	30.00	80.00
2 Danny Ainge	6.00	12.00
3 Quinn Buckner	1.25	3.00
4 Rick Carlisle	4.00	10.00
5 M.L. Carr	1.25	3.00
6 Dennis Johnson	2.50	6.00
7 Greg Kite	1.25	3.00
8 Cedric Maxwell	1.25	3.00
9 Kevin McHale	6.00	15.00
10 Robert Parish	5.00	12.00
11 Scott Wedman	1.25	3.00
12 Larry Bird MVP !	15.00	40.00
13 Marques Johnson	1.25	3.00
14 Junior Bridgeman	1.25	3.00
15 Michael Cage XRC	1.50	4.00
16 Harvey Catchings	1.25	3.00
17 James Donaldson	1.25	3.00
18 Lancaster Gordon	1.25	3.00
19 Jay Murphy	1.25	3.00
20 Norm Nixon	1.25	3.00
21 Derek Smith	1.25	3.00
22 Bill Walton	8.00	20.00
23 Bryan Warrick	1.25	3.00
24 Rory White	1.25	3.00
25 Bernard King	2.50	6.00
26 James Bailey	1.25	3.00
27 Ken Bannister	1.25	3.00
28 Butch Carter	1.25	3.00
29 Bill Cartwright	2.50	6.00
30 Pat Cummings	1.25	3.00
31 Ernie Grunfeld	1.25	3.00
32 Louis Orr	1.25	3.00
33 Leonard Robinson	1.25	3.00
34 Rory Sparrow	1.25	3.00
35 Trent Tucker	1.25	3.00
36 Darrell Walker	1.25	3.00
37 Eddie Lee Wilkins XRC	1.50	4.00
38 Alvan Adams	1.25	3.00
39 Walter Davis	1.50	4.00
40 James Edwards	1.25	3.00
41 Rod Foster	1.25	3.00
42 Michael Holton	1.25	3.00
43 Jay Humphries XRC	1.50	4.00
44 Charles Jones	1.25	3.00
45 Maurice Lucas	1.25	3.00
46 Kyle Macy	1.25	3.00
47 Larry Nance	4.00	10.00
48 Charles Pittman	1.25	3.00
49 Rick Robey	1.25	3.00
50 Mike Sanders	1.25	3.00
51 Alvin Scott	1.25	3.00
52 Clark Kellogg	1.25	3.00
53 Tony Brown	1.25	3.00
54 Devin Durrant	1.25	3.00
55 Vern Fleming XRC	1.50	4.00
56 Bill Garnett	1.25	3.00
57 Stuart Gray UER	1.25	3.00
58 Jerry Sichting	1.25	3.00
59 Terence Stansbury	1.25	3.00
60 Steve Stipanovich	1.25	3.00
61 Jimmy Thomas	1.25	3.00
62 Granville Waiters	1.25	3.00
63 Herb Williams	1.25	3.00
64 Artis Gilmore	1.50	4.00
65 Gene Banks	1.25	3.00
66 Ron Brewer	1.25	3.00
67 George Gervin	6.00	15.00
68 Edgar Jones	1.25	3.00
69 Ozell Jones	1.25	3.00
70 Mark McNamara	1.25	3.00
71 Mike Mitchell	1.25	3.00
72 Johnny Moore	1.25	3.00
73 John Paxson	1.50	4.00
74 Fred Roberts	1.25	3.00
75 Alvin Robertson XRC	1.50	4.00
76 Dominique Wilkins	15.00	40.00
77 Rickey Brown	1.25	3.00
78 Antoine Carr XRC	1.50	4.00
79 Mike Glenn	1.25	3.00
80 Scott Hastings	1.25	3.00
81 Eddie Johnson	1.25	3.00
82 Cliff Levingston	1.25	3.00
83 Leo Rautins	1.25	3.00
84 Doc Rivers	4.00	10.00
85 Tree Rollins	1.25	3.00
86 Randy Wittman	1.25	3.00
87 Sly Williams	1.25	3.00
88 Darryl Dawkins	1.50	4.00
89 Otis Birdsong	1.25	3.00
90 Darwin Cook	1.25	3.00
91 Mike Gminski	1.25	3.00
92 George L. Johnson	1.25	3.00
93 Albert King	1.25	3.00
94 Mike O'Koren	1.25	3.00
95 Kelvin Ransey	1.25	3.00
96 M.R. Richardson	1.25	3.00
97 Wayne Sappleton	1.25	3.00
98 Jeff Turner XRC	1.50	4.00
99 Buck Williams	1.50	4.00
100 Michael Wilson	1.25	3.00
101 Michael Jordan XRC	1200.00	2200.00
102 Dave Corzine	1.50	4.00
103 Quintin Dailey	1.50	4.00
104 Sidney Green	1.50	4.00
105 David Greenwood	1.50	4.00
106 Rod Higgins	1.50	4.00
107 Steve Johnson XRC	1.50	4.00
108 Caldwell Jones	1.50	4.00
109 Wes Matthews	1.50	4.00
110 Jawann Oldham	1.50	4.00
111 Ennis Whatley	1.50	4.00
112 Orlando Woolridge	1.50	4.00
113 Tom Chambers	2.50	6.00
114 Cory Blackwell	1.25	3.00
115 Frank Brickowski XRC	1.50	4.00
116 Gerald Henderson	1.25	3.00
117 Reggie King	1.25	3.00
118 Tim McCormick XRC	1.50	4.00
119 John Schweitz	1.25	3.00
120 Jack Sikma	1.50	4.00
121 Ricky Sobers	1.25	3.00
122 Jon Sundvold	1.25	3.00
123 Danny Vranes	1.25	3.00
124 Al Wood	1.25	3.00
125 Terry Cummings UER	2.50	6.00
126 Randy Breuer	1.25	3.00
127 Charles Davis	1.25	3.00
128 Mike Dunleavy	1.50	4.00
129 Kenny Fields	1.25	3.00
130 Kevin Grevey	1.25	3.00
131 Craig Hodges	1.25	3.00
132 Alton Lister	1.25	3.00
133 Larry Micheaux	1.25	3.00
134 Paul Mokeski	1.25	3.00
135 Sidney Moncrief	2.50	6.00
136 Paul Pressey	1.25	3.00
137 Alex English	2.50	6.00
138 Wayne Cooper	1.25	3.00
139 T.R. Dunn	1.25	3.00
140 Mike Evans	1.25	3.00
141 Bill Hanzlik	1.25	3.00
142 Dan Issel	5.00	12.00
143 Joe Kopicki	1.25	3.00
144 Lafayette Lever	1.50	4.00
145 Calvin Natt	1.25	3.00
146 Danny Schayes	1.25	3.00
147 Elston Turner	1.25	3.00
148 Willie White	1.25	3.00
149 Purvis Short	1.25	3.00
150 Chuck Aleksinas	1.25	3.00
151 Mike Bratz	1.25	3.00
152 Steve Burtt	1.25	3.00
153 Lester Conner	1.25	3.00
154 Sleepy Floyd	1.50	4.00
155 Mickey Johnson	1.25	3.00
156 Gary Plummer	1.25	3.00
157 Larry Smith	1.25	3.00
158 Peter Thibeaux	1.25	3.00
159 Jerome Whitehead	1.25	3.00
160 Othell Wilson	1.25	3.00
161 Kiki Vandeweghe	1.50	4.00
162 Sam Bowie XRC	4.00	10.00
163 Kenny Carr	1.25	3.00
164 Steve Colter	1.25	3.00
165 Clyde Drexler !	20.00	40.00
166 Audie Norris	1.25	3.00
167 Jim Paxson	1.25	3.00
168 Tom Scheffler	1.25	3.00
169 Bernard Thompson	1.25	3.00
170 Mychal Thompson	1.25	3.00
171 Darnell Valentine	1.25	3.00
172 Magic Johnson !	25.00	60.00
173 Kareem Abdul-Jabbar	15.00	40.00
174 Michael Cooper	4.00	10.00
175 Earl Jones	1.25	3.00
176 Mitch Kupchak	1.50	4.00
177 Ronnie Lester	1.25	3.00
178 Bob McAdoo	4.00	10.00
179 Mike McGee	1.25	3.00
180 Kurt Rambis	2.50	6.00
181 Byron Scott	4.00	10.00
182 Larry Spriggs	1.25	3.00
183 Jamaal Wilkes	2.50	6.00
184 James Worthy	6.00	15.00
185 Gus Williams	1.25	3.00
186 Greg Ballard	1.25	3.00
187 Dudley Bradley	1.25	3.00
188 Darren Daye	1.25	3.00
189 Frank Johnson	1.25	3.00
190 Charles Jones XRC	1.25	3.00
191 Rick Mahorn	1.25	3.00
192 Jeff Malone	1.25	3.00
193 Tom McMillen	1.25	3.00
194 Jeff Ruland	1.25	3.00
195 Michael Jordan OLY !	150.00	300.00
196 Vern Fleming OLY	1.50	4.00
197 Sam Perkins OLY	4.00	10.00
198 Alvin Robertson OLY	1.50	4.00
199 Jeff Turner OLY	1.50	4.00
200 Leon Wood OLY	1.50	4.00
201 Moses Malone	6.00	12.00
202 Charles Barkley XRC	100.00	200.00
203 Maurice Cheeks	1.50	4.00
204 Julius Erving	20.00	40.00
205 Clemon Johnson	1.25	3.00
206 George L. Johnson	1.25	3.00
207 Bobby Jones	2.50	6.00
208 Clint Richardson	1.25	3.00
209 Sedale Threatt	1.25	3.00
210 Andrew Toney	1.50	4.00
211 Sam Williams	1.25	3.00
212 Leon Wood XRC	1.50	4.00
213 Mel Turpin XRC	1.50	4.00
214 Ron Anderson XRC	1.50	4.00
215 John Bagley	1.25	3.00
216 Johnny Davis	1.25	3.00
217 World B. Free	1.25	3.00
218 Roy Hinson	1.25	3.00
219 Phil Hubbard	1.25	3.00
220 Edgar Jones	1.25	3.00
221 Ben Poquette	1.25	3.00
222 Lonnie Shelton	1.25	3.00
223 Mark West	1.25	3.00
224 Kevin Williams	1.25	3.00
225 Mark Eaton	1.50	4.00
226 Mitchell Anderson	1.25	3.00
227 Thurl Bailey	1.25	3.00
228 Adrian Dantley	2.50	6.00
229 Rickey Green	1.25	3.00
230 Darrell Griffith	1.25	3.00
231 Rich Kelley	1.25	3.00
232 Pace Mannion	1.25	3.00
233 Billy Paultz	1.25	3.00
234 Fred Roberts	1.25	3.00
235 John Stockton XRC	80.00	200.00
236 Jeff Wilkins	1.25	3.00
237 Hakeem Olajuwon XRC !	100.00	250.00
238 Craig Ehlo XRC	7.50	15.00
239 Lionel Hollins	1.25	3.00
240 Allen Leavell	1.25	3.00
241 Lewis Lloyd	1.25	3.00
242 John Lucas	1.25	3.00
243 Rodney McCray	1.25	3.00
244 Hank McDowell	1.25	3.00
245 Larry Micheaux	1.25	3.00
246 Jim Petersen XRC	1.50	4.00
247 Robert Reid	1.25	3.00
248 Ralph Sampson	1.50	4.00
249 Mitchell Wiggins	1.25	3.00
250 Mark Aguirre	1.50	4.00
251 Rolando Blackman	1.50	4.00
252 Wallace Bryant	1.25	3.00
253 Brad Davis	1.25	3.00
254 Dale Ellis	1.50	4.00
255 Derek Harper	1.50	4.00
256 Kurt Nimphius	1.25	3.00
257 Sam Perkins XRC	6.00	15.00
258 Charlie Sitton	1.25	3.00
259 Tom Sluby	1.25	3.00
260 Jay Vincent	1.25	3.00
261 Isiah Thomas	10.00	25.00
262 Kent Benson	1.25	3.00
263 Earl Cureton	1.25	3.00
264 Vinnie Johnson	1.25	3.00
265 Bill Laimbeer	1.50	4.00
266 John Long	1.25	3.00
267 Dan Roundfield	1.25	3.00
268 Kelly Tripucka	1.25	3.00
269 Terry Tyler	1.25	3.00
270 Reggie Theus	1.50	4.00
271 Don Buse	1.25	3.00
272 Larry Drew	1.25	3.00
273 Eddie Johnson	1.25	3.00
274 Billy Knight	1.25	3.00
275 Joe Meriweather	1.25	3.00
276 Mark Olberding	1.25	3.00
277 LaSalle Thompson	1.25	3.00
278 Otis Thorpe XRC	4.00	10.00
279 Pete Verhoeven	1.25	3.00
280 Mike Woodson	1.25	3.00
281 Julius Erving SPEC !	6.00	15.00
282 K.Abdul-Jabbar SPEC !	6.00	15.00
283 Dan Issel SPEC !	2.50	6.00
284 Bernard King SPEC !	1.50	4.00
285 Moses Malone SPEC !	4.00	10.00
286 Mark Eaton SPEC !	1.50	4.00
287 Isiah Thomas SPEC !	5.00	12.00
288 Michael Jordan SPEC !	125.00	300.00
BAG1 76ers sealed bag (12)	125.00	225.00
BAG2 Blazers sealed bag (11)	40.00	80.00
BAG3 Bucks sealed bag (12)	12.50	30.00
BAG4 Bullets sealed bag (10)	12.50	30.00
BAG5 Bulls sealed bag (12)	2000.00	2600.00
BAG6 Cavs sealed bag (12)	12.50	30.00
BAG7 Celtics sealed bag (12)	60.00	150.00
BAG8 Clippers sealed bag (12)	12.50	30.00
BAG9 Hawks sealed bag (12)	25.00	60.00
BAG10 Jazz sealed bag (12)	125.00	225.00
BAG11 Kings sealed bag (11)	10.00	25.00
BAG12 Knicks sealed bag (13)	12.00	30.00
BAG13 Lakers sealed bag (13)	60.00	150.00
BAG14 Mavs sealed bag (11)	15.00	40.00
BAG15 Nets sealed bag (13)	12.50	30.00
BAG16 Nuggets sealed bag (12)	12.50	30.00
BAG17 Pacers sealed bag (12)	12.50	30.00
BAG18 Pistons sealed bag (9)	20.00	50.00
BAG19 Rockets sealed bag (13)	125.00	225.00
BAG20 Sonics sealed bag (12)	12.50	30.00
BAG21 Spurs sealed bag (12)	15.00	40.00
BAG22 Suns sealed bag (14)	12.50	30.00
BAG23 Warriors sealed bag (12)	12.50	30.00
BAG24 Olympic sealed bag (14)	350.00	650.00

1984-85 Star Arena

These sets were produced to be sold in the arena of each of the five teams featured in this set. The teams are Boston, Dallas, Milwaukee, Los Angeles Lakers and Philadelphia. Each set is different from the team's regular issue set in that the photography and card backs are different. Shortly after distribution began, Bob Lanier announced his retirement and his cards were withdrawn from the Milwaukee set. Cards measure 2 1/2" by 3 1/2" and have a colored border around the fronts according to team. Corresponding color printing is on the backs. Celtics feature Star '85 logo on the front while the other four teams feature the Star '84 logo on the front. The cards are ordered alphabetically by team using prefixes A-E.

COMPLETE SET (48)	125.00	250.00
COMPLETE SET (49) w/Lanier	250.00	500.00
A1 Larry Bird	12.00	30.00
A2 Danny Ainge	1.50	4.00
A3 Rick Carlisle	1.50	4.00
A4 Dennis Johnson	2.50	6.00
A5 Cedric Maxwell	.75	2.00
A6 Kevin McHale	3.00	8.00
A7 Robert Parish	1.50	4.00
A8 Scott Wedman	.75	2.00
A9 Parr/Bird/McHa/Coaches	10.00	25.00
B1 Mark Aguirre UER	1.50	4.00
B2 Rolando Blackman	1.50	4.00
B3 Brad Davis	.75	2.00
B4 Dale Ellis	1.00	2.50
B5 Bill Garnett	.75	2.00
B6 Derek Harper UER	1.50	4.00
B7 Kurt Nimphius	.75	2.00
B8 Jim Spanarkel	.75	2.00
B9 Elston Turner	.75	2.00
B10 Jay Vincent	.75	2.00
B11 Mark West	.75	2.00
C1 Nate Archibald	1.50	4.00
C2 Junior Bridgeman	.75	2.00
C3 Mike Dunleavy	1.50	4.00
C4 Kevin Grevey	.75	2.00
C5 Marques Johnson	1.50	4.00
C6 Bob Lanier SP	125.00	250.00
C7 Alton Lister	.75	2.00
C8 Sidney Moncrief	1.50	4.00
C9 Paul Pressey	.75	2.00
D1 Kareem Abdul-Jabbar	8.00	20.00
D2 Michael Cooper	1.50	4.00

D3 Magic Johnson 12.50 30.00
D4 Mike McGee .75 2.00
D5 Swen Nater .75 2.00
D6 Kurt Rambis 3.00 8.00
D7 Byron Scott 3.00 8.00
D8 James Worthy 4.00 10.00
D9 Magic Johnson/Kareem 10.00 25.00
D10 Kareem Abdul-Jabbar LL 6.00 15.00
E1 Julius Erving 6.00 15.00
E2 Maurice Cheeks 1.00 2.50
E3 Franklin Edwards .75 2.00
E4 Marc Iavaroni 1.00 2.50
E5 Clemon Johnson .75 2.00
E6 Bobby Jones 1.50 4.00
E7 Moses Malone 3.00 8.00
E8 Clint Richardson .75 2.00
E9 Andrew Toney 1.00 2.50
E10 Sam Williams .75 2.00
BAG1 76ers sealed bag (10) 25.00 40.00
BAG2 Bucks sealed bag (8) 10.00 25.00
BAG3 Celtics sealed bag (9) 40.00 80.00
BAG4 Lakers sealed bag (10) 40.00 100.00
BAG5 Mavs sealed bag (11) 12.50 30.00

1984-85 Star Court Kings 5x7

This over-sized 50-card set was issued as two series of 25. Cards measure approximately 5" by 7" and have a yellow (first series 1-25) or blue (second series 26-50) colored border around the fronts of the cards and blue and yellow printing on the backs. These large cards feature the Star '85 logo on the front. The set features early professional cards of Charles Barkley, Michael Jordan and Hakeem Olajuwon.

COMPLETE SET (50) 200.00 400.00
1 Kareem Abdul-Jabbar 6.00 12.00
2 Jeff Ruland 1.25 3.00
3 Mark Aguirre 1.50 4.00
4 Julius Erving 5.00 12.00
5 Kelly Tripucka 1.25 3.00
6 Buck Williams 1.50 4.00
7 Sidney Moncrief 1.50 4.00
8 World B. Free 1.25 3.00
9 Bill Walton 2.50 6.00
10 Purvis Short 1.25 3.00
11 Rickey Green 1.25 3.00
12 Dominique Wilkins 5.00 12.00
13 Jim Paxson 1.25 3.00
14 Ralph Sampson 1.50 4.00
15 Magic Johnson 10.00 20.00
16 Reggie Theus 1.50 4.00
17 Moses Malone 2.50 6.00
18 Larry Bird 10.00 25.00
19 Larry Nance 1.50 4.00
20 Clark Kellogg 1.25 3.00
21 Jack Sikma 1.25 3.00
22 Alex English 1.50 4.00
23 Bernard King 1.25 3.00
24 Dave Corzine 1.25 3.00
25 George Gervin 2.50 6.00
26 Michael Jordan 100.00 200.00
27 Rolando Blackman 1.50 4.00
28 Dan Issel 2.50 6.00
29 Maurice Cheeks 1.25 3.00
30 Isiah Thomas 6.00 15.00
31 Robert Parish 2.50 6.00
32 Mark Eaton 1.25 3.00
33 Sam Perkins 2.50 6.00
34 Artis Gilmore 1.50 4.00
35 Andrew Toney 1.25 3.00
36 Adrian Dantley 1.25 3.00
37 Terry Cummings 1.25 3.00
38 Orlando Woolridge 1.25 3.00
39 Tom Chambers 1.50 4.00
40 Gus Williams 1.25 3.00
41 Charles Barkley 20.00 50.00
42 Kevin McHale 5.00 12.00
43 Otis Birdsong 1.25 3.00
44 Sam Bowie 1.50 4.00
45 Darrell Griffith 1.25 3.00
46 Kiki Vandeweghe 1.50 4.00
47 Hakeem Olajuwon 20.00 35.00
48 Marques Johnson 1.25 3.00
49 James Worthy 4.00 10.00
50 Mel Turpin 1.25 3.00
BAG1 Series 1 sealed bag (25) 60.00 120.00
BAG2 Series 2 sealed bag (25) 200.00 325.00

1984-85 Star Julius Erving

This set contains 18 standard-size cards highlighting the career of basketball great Julius Erving. The cards have a red border around the fronts of the cards and red printing on the backs. Cards feature Star '85 logo on the front although they were released in the summer of 1984.

COMPLETE SET (18) 40.00 80.00
COMMON J.ERVING (1-18) 2.00 5.00
1 Julius Erving CL 2.50 6.00
18 Julius Erving TF 2.50 6.00
BAG1 Complete sealed bag (19) 40.00 80.00

1985 Star Kareem Abdul-Jabbar

The 1985 Star Kareem Abdul-Jabbar set is an 18-card standard-size tribute set. Most of the photos on the fronts are from the early 1980s. Card backs provide various statistics and tidbits of information about Abdul-Jabbar. The set's basic design is identical to those of the Star Company's regular NBA sets. The cards show a Star '85 logo in the upper right corner. The front borders are Lakers' purple.

COMPLETE SET (18) 15.00 40.00
COMMON JABBAR (1-18) 1.50 4.00
1 Kareem Abdul-Jabbar CL 2.00 5.00
18 Kareem Abdul-Jabbar TF 2.00 5.00
BAG1 Complete sealed bag (18) 20.00 50.00

1985 Star Coaches

The 1984-85 Star NBA Coaches set is a ten-card standard-size set depicting some of the NBA's best known coaches. The set's basic design is identical to those of the Star Company's regular NBA sets. The front borders are royal blue, and the backs show each man's coaching records. Statistics for ex-players are NOT included. The cards show a Star '85 logo in the upper right corner. Coaching statistics on the card backs only go up through the 1983-84 NBA season.

COMPLETE SET (10) 8.00 20.00
1 John Bach 1.25 3.00
2 Hubie Brown 1.50 4.00
3 Cotton Fitzsimmons 1.25 3.00
4 Kevin Loughery 1.25 3.00
5 John MacLeod 1.25 3.00
6 Doug Moe 1.25 3.00
7 Don Nelson 1.25 3.00
8 Jack Ramsay 1.50 4.00
9 Pat Riley 2.50 6.00
10 Lenny Wilkens UER 2.00 5.00
BAG1 Complete sealed bag (10) 10.00 25.00

1985 Star Crunch'n'Munch All-Stars

The 1985 Star Crunch'n'Munch NBA All-Stars set is an 11-card standard-size set featuring the ten starting players in the 1985 NBA All-Star Game plus a checklist card. The set was produced for the Crunch 'n' Munch Food Company and was originally available to the hobby exclusively through Don Guilbert of Woonsocket, Rhode Island. The set's basic design is identical to those of the Star Company's regular NBA sets. The cards show a Star '85 logo in the upper right corner. The front borders are yellowish orange and the backs show each player's All-Star Game record.

COMPLETE SET (11) 250.00 400.00
1 All-Star CL 2.50 6.00
2 Larry Bird 40.00 80.00
3 Julius Erving 12.50 30.00
4 Michael Jordan ! 125.00 300.00
5 Moses Malone 4.00 10.00
6 Isiah Thomas 6.00 15.00
7 Kareem Abdul-Jabbar 8.00 20.00
8 Adrian Dantley 3.00 8.00
9 George Gervin 5.00 12.00
10 Magic Johnson 30.00 60.00
11 Ralph Sampson 3.00 8.00
BAG1 Complete sealed bag (11) 250.00 450.00

1985 Star Gatorade Slam Dunk

This nine-card set was given to the people who attended the 1985 All-Star Weekend Banquet at Indianapolis. Cards measure the standard size and have a green border around the fronts of the cards and green printing on the backs. Cards feature the Star '85 and Gatorade logos on the fronts. Since Terence Stansbury was a late substitute in the Slam Dunk contest for Charles Barkley, both cards were produced, but the Barkley card was not released at that time. However, the Barkley card has since surfaced in the marketplace. The Barkley card is unnumbered and shows him dunking.

COMPLETE SET (9) 150.00 275.00
1 Slam Dunk CL 1.50 4.00
2 Larry Nance 2.50 6.00
3 Terence Stansbury 1.25 3.00
4 Clyde Drexler 10.00 25.00
5 Julius Erving 10.00 25.00
6 Darrell Griffith 1.25 3.00
7 Michael Jordan 100.00 200.00
8 Dominique Wilkins 10.00 25.00
9 Orlando Woolridge 1.50 4.00
BAG1 Complete sealed bag (11) 150.00 275.00
NNO Charles Barkley SP 40.00 80.00

1985 Star Last 11 ROY's

The 1985 Star Rookies of the Year set is an 11-card standard-size set depicting each of the NBA's ROY award winners from the 1974-75 through 1984-85 seasons. Michael Jordan's card only shows his collegiate statistics while all others provide NBA statistics up through the 1983-84 season. Cards of Darrell Griffith and Jamaal Wilkes show the Star '86 logo in the upper right corner while all others in the set show Star '85. The set's basic design is identical to those of the Star Company's regular NBA sets and the front borders are off-white. The set is sequenced in reverse chronological order according to when each player won the ROY.

COMPLETE SET (11) 175.00 275.00
1 Michael Jordan 100.00 200.00
2 Ralph Sampson 1.50 4.00
3 Terry Cummings 1.50 4.00
4 Buck Williams 1.50 4.00
5 Darrell Griffith 1.50 4.00
6 Larry Bird 40.00 80.00
7 Phil Ford 1.50 4.00
8 Walter Davis 1.50 4.00
9 Adrian Dantley 2.00 5.00
10 Alvan Adams 1.50 4.00
11 Jamaal Wilkes 1.50 4.00
BAG1 Complete sealed bag (11) 150.00 300.00

1985 Star Lite All-Stars

This 13-card standard-size set was given to the people who attended the 1985 All-Star Weekend Banquet at Indianapolis. The set was issued in a clear, sealed plastic bag. Cards have a blue border around the fronts of the cards and blue printing on the backs. Cards feature the Star '85 and Lite Beer logos on the fronts. Players featured are the 1985 NBA All-Star starting line-ups and coaches. A cropping variation on card #4, Michael Jordan, has been noted in the checklist. The variation features Jordan's hair right up tight to the top white outline border.

COMPLETE SET (13) 125.00 250.00
1 1985 NBA All-Stars 2.00 5.00
2 Larry Bird 30.00 60.00
3 Julius Erving 8.00 20.00
4 Michael Jordan ! 100.00 200.00
4A Michael Jordan VAR
5 Moses Malone 2.50 6.00
6 Isiah Thomas 3.00 8.00
7 K.C. Jones CO 2.00 5.00
8 Kareem Abdul-Jabbar 7.50 15.00
9 Adrian Dantley 2.00 5.00
10 George Gervin 3.00 8.00
11 Magic Johnson 20.00 40.00
12 Ralph Sampson 2.00 5.00
13 Pat Riley CO 2.50 6.00
BAG1 Complete sealed bag (13) 150.00 300.00

1985 Star Schick Legends

This 24-card set was given to the people who attended the 1985 All-Star Weekend Banquet at Indianapolis. Cards measure 2 1/2" by 3 1/2" and have a yellow border around the fronts of the cards and yellow and black printing on the backs. Cards feature the Star '85 and Schick logos on the fronts. Players featured were participants in the Schick NBA Legends Classic. The cards are numbered on the back; the numbering corresponds to alphabetical order by player.

COMPLETE SET (25) 25.00 60.00
1 Schick NBA Legends CL 1.25 3.00
2 Rick Barry 2.50 6.00
3 Zelmo Beaty 1.25 3.00
4 Walt Bellamy 1.25 3.00
5 Dave Bing 1.50 4.00
6 Roger Brown 1.25 3.00
7 Bob Cousy 2.50 6.00
8 Mel Daniels 1.25 3.00
9 Bob Davies 1.25 3.00
10 Dave DeBusschere 2.00 5.00
11 Walt Frazier 2.50 6.00
12 John Havlicek 3.00 8.00
13 Connie Hawkins 2.50 6.00
14 Tom Heinsohn 2.00 5.00
15 Red Holzman CO 1.50 4.00
16 Johnny Kerr 1.25 3.00
17 Bobby Leonard 1.25 3.00
18 Pete Maravich 12.50 30.00
19 Earl Monroe 2.50 6.00
20 Bob Pettit 3.00 8.00
21 Oscar Robertson 4.00 10.00
22 Nate Thurmond 2.00 5.00
23 Dick Van Arsdale 1.25 3.00
24 Tom Van Arsdale 1.25 3.00
25 George Yardley 1.25 3.00
BAG1 Complete sealed bag (25) 30.00 80.00

1985 Star Slam Dunk Supers 5x7

This ten-card set uses actual photography from the 1985 Slam Dunk contest in Indianapolis held during the NBA All-Star Weekend. Cards measure approximately 5" by 7" and have a red border around the fronts of the cards and red printing on the backs. Cards feature Star '85 logo on the fronts. The set ordering for these numbered cards is alphabetical by subject's name.

COMPLETE SET (10) 125.00 250.00
1 Group Photo CL 20.00 40.00
2 Clyde Drexler 12.50 25.00
3 Julius Erving 10.00 25.00
4 Darrell Griffith 1.50 4.00
5 Michael Jordan 100.00 200.00
6 Larry Nance 3.00 8.00
7 Terence Stansbury 1.50 4.00
8 Dominique Wilkins 6.00 15.00
9 Orlando Woolridge 2.00 5.00
10 D.Wilkins Champion 6.00 15.00
BAG1 Complete sealed bag (10) 125.00 250.00

1985 Star Team Supers 5x7

This 40-card set is actually eight team sets of five each except for the Sixers having ten players included. Cards measure approximately 5" by 7" and have a colored border around the fronts of the cards according to the team with corresponding color printing on the backs. Cards feature Star '85 logo on the front. Cards are numbered below by assigning a team prefix based on the initials of the team, for example, BC for Boston Celtics.

COMPLETE SET (40) 250.00 450.00
BC1 Larry Bird 15.00 30.00
BC2 Robert Parish 2.50 6.00
BC3 Kevin McHale 3.00 8.00
BC4 Dennis Johnson 3.00 8.00
BC5 Danny Ainge 3.00 8.00
CB1 Michael Jordan 100.00 200.00
CB2 Orlando Woolridge 1.25 3.00
CB3 Quintin Dailey 1.25 3.00
CB4 Dave Corzine 1.25 3.00
CB5 Steve Johnson 1.25 3.00
DP1 Isiah Thomas 5.00 12.00
DP2 Kelly Tripucka 1.25 3.00
DP3 Vinnie Johnson 1.25 3.00
DP4 Bill Laimbeer 2.00 5.00
DP5 John Long 1.25 3.00
HR1 Ralph Sampson 2.00 5.00
HR2 Hakeem Olajuwon 20.00 40.00
HR3 Lewis Lloyd 1.25 3.00
HR4 Rodney McCray 1.25 3.00
HR5 Lionel Hollins 1.25 3.00
LA1 Kareem Abdul-Jabbar 8.00 20.00
LA2 Magic Johnson 15.00 40.00
LA3 James Worthy 4.00 10.00
LA4 Byron Scott 2.00 5.00
LA5 Bob McAdoo 3.00 8.00
MB1 Terry Cummings 2.00 5.00
MB2 Sidney Moncrief 2.00 5.00
MB3 Paul Pressey 1.25 3.00
MB4 Mike Dunleavy 2.00 5.00
MB5 Alton Lister 1.25 3.00
PS1 Julius Erving 8.00 20.00
PS2 Maurice Cheeks 2.00 5.00
PS3 Bobby Jones 2.00 5.00
PS4 Clemon Johnson 1.25 3.00
PS5 Leon Wood 2.00 5.00
PS6 Moses Malone 4.00 10.00
PS7 Andrew Toney 1.25 3.00
PS8 Charles Barkley 25.00 50.00
PS9 Clint Richardson 1.25 3.00
PS10 Sedale Threatt 1.25 3.00
BAG1a 76ers sealed blue bag (5) 30.00 60.00
BAG1b 76ers sealed white bag (5) 12.50 30.00
BAG2 Bucks sealed bag (5) 6.00 15.00
BAG3 Bulls sealed bag (5) 100.00 200.00
BAG4 Celtics sealed bag (5) 30.00 60.00
BAG5 Lakers sealed bag (5) 30.00 60.00
BAG6 Pistons sealed bag (5) 10.00 20.00
BAG7 Rockets sealed bag (5) 20.00 50.00

1985-86 Star

This 172-card standard-size set was produced by the Star Company and features players in the NBA. Cards were released in two groups, 1-94 and 95-172. The team sets were issued in clear sealed bags. Many of these team bags were distributed to hobby dealers through a small group of Star Company master distributors. The original wholesale price per bag was $2-$3 for most of the teams. According to Star Company's original sales materials and order forms, reportedly 2,000 team bags were printed for each team and an additional 2,200 team sets were printed for the more popular teams of that time. Cards are numbered in team order. Borders are colored according to team. Card backs are very similar to the other Star basketball sets except that the player statistics go up through the 1984-85 season. Extended Rookie Cards in this set include Patrick Ewing and Kevin Willis. There is typically a slight discount on sales of opened team bags. Cards of Celtics players (95-102) have either green or white borders. Many cards in this set (particularly 95-176) have been counterfeited and are prevalent on the market. Among those affected are the Ewing Extended Rookie Card (166) and Jordan (117).

COMPLETE SET (172) 500.00 1000.00
1 Maurice Cheeks ! 1.50 4.00
2 Charles Barkley ! 15.00 40.00
3 Julius Erving ! 8.00 20.00
4 Clemon Johnson .75 2.00
5 Bobby Jones ! 1.25 3.00
6 Moses Malone ! 3.00 8.00
7 Sedale Threatt ! .75 2.00
8 Andrew Toney 1.25 3.00
9 Leon Wood .75 2.00
10 Isiah Thomas UER 6.00 15.00
11 Kent Benson .75 2.00
12 Earl Cureton .75 2.00
13 Vinnie Johnson 1.25 3.00
14 Bill Laimbeer 1.50 4.00
15 John Long .75 2.00
16 Rick Mahorn .75 2.00
17 Kelly Tripucka .75 2.00
18 Hakeem Olajuwon ! 15.00 40.00
19 Allen Leavell .75 2.00
20 Lewis Lloyd .75 2.00
21 John Lucas .75 2.00
22 Rodney McCray .75 2.00
23 Robert Reid .75 2.00
24 Ralph Sampson 1.25 3.00
25 Mitchell Wiggins .75 2.00
26 Kareem Abdul-Jabbar 10.00 25.00
27 Michael Cooper 3.00 8.00
28 Magic Johnson 25.00 60.00
29 Mitch Kupchak 1.50 4.00
30 Maurice Lucas 1.50 4.00
31 Kurt Rambis 1.50 4.00
32 Byron Scott 3.00 8.00
33 James Worthy 6.00 15.00
34 Larry Nance 1.50 4.00
35 Alvan Adams 1.25 3.00
36 Walter Davis 1.25 3.00
37 James Edwards .75 2.00
38 Jay Humphries .75 2.00
39 Charles Pittman .75 2.00
40 Rick Robey .75 2.00
41 Mike Sanders .75 2.00
42 Dominique Wilkins 12.50 30.00
43 Scott Hastings .75 2.00
44 Eddie Johnson .75 2.00
45 Cliff Levingston .75 2.00
46 Tree Rollins .75 2.00
47 Doc Rivers UER 1.50 4.00
48 Kevin Willis XRC 5.00 12.00
49 Randy Wittman .75 2.00
50 Alex English 3.00 8.00
51 Wayne Cooper .75 2.00
52 T.R. Dunn .75 2.00
53 Mike Evans .75 2.00
54 Lafayette Lever 1.25 3.00
55 Calvin Natt .75 2.00
56 Danny Schayes 1.25 3.00
57 Elston Turner .75 2.00
58 Buck Williams 1.50 4.00
59 Otis Birdsong .75 2.00
60 Darwin Cook .75 2.00
61 Darryl Dawkins 1.25 3.00
62 Mike Gminski .75 2.00
63 Mickey Johnson .75 2.00
64 Mike O'Koren .75 2.00
65 Micheal Ray Richardson .75 2.00
66 Tom Chambers 1.50 4.00
67 Gerald Henderson .75 2.00
68 Tim McCormick .75 2.00
69 Jack Sikma 1.25 3.00
70 Ricky Sobers .75 2.00
71 Danny Vranes .75 2.00
72 Al Wood .75 2.00
73 Danny Young XRC 1.25 3.00
74 Reggie Theus 1.25 3.00
75 Larry Drew .75 2.00
76 Eddie Johnson 1.25 3.00
77 Mark Olberding .75 2.00
78 LaSalle Thompson .75 2.00
79 Otis Thorpe 1.25 3.00
80 Mike Woodson 1.25 3.00
81 Clark Kellogg 1.25 3.00
82 Quinn Buckner .75 2.00
83 Vern Fleming .75 2.00
84 Bill Garnett .75 2.00
85 Terence Stansbury .75 2.00
86 Steve Stipanovich .75 2.00
87 Herb Williams .75 2.00
88 Marques Johnson 1.25 3.00
89 Michael Cage 1.25 3.00
90 Franklin Edwards .75 2.00
91 Cedric Maxwell .75 2.00
92 Derek Smith .75 2.00
93 Rory White .75 2.00
94 Jamaal Wilkes 1.25 3.00
95G Larry Bird Green 20.00 40.00
95W Larry Bird White 25.00 60.00
96G Danny Ainge Green 4.00 10.00
96W Danny Ainge White 6.00 15.00
97G Dennis Johnson Green 3.00 8.00
98G Kevin McHale Green 4.00 10.00
98W Kevin McHale White 6.00 15.00
99G Robert Parish Green 3.00 8.00
99W Robert Parish White 5.00 12.00
100G Jerry Sichting Green .75 2.00
101G Bill Walton Green 6.00 12.00
102G Scott Wedman Green .75 2.00
103 Kiki Vandeweghe 1.25 3.00
104 Sam Bowie 1.25 3.00
105 Kenny Carr .75 2.00
106 Clyde Drexler ! 20.00 50.00
107 Jerome Kersey XRC 3.00 8.00
108 Jim Paxson 1.25 3.00
109 Mychal Thompson 1.25 3.00
110 Gus Williams 1.25 3.00
111 Darren Daye .75 2.00
112 Jeff Malone 1.25 3.00
113 Tom McMillen 1.25 3.00
114 Cliff Robinson .75 2.00
115 Dan Roundfield .75 2.00
116 Jeff Ruland 1.25 3.00
117 Michael Jordan ! 200.00 500.00
118 Gene Banks 1.25 3.00
119 Dave Corzine 1.25 3.00
120 Quintin Dailey 1.25 3.00
121 George Gervin 8.00 20.00
122 Jawann Oldham 1.25 3.00
123 Orlando Woolridge 1.25 3.00
124 Terry Cummings 1.50 4.00
125 Craig Hodges .75 2.00
126 Alton Lister .75 2.00
127 Paul Mokeski .75 2.00
128 Sidney Moncrief 1.50 4.00
129 Ricky Pierce 1.25 3.00
130 Paul Pressey .75 2.00
131 Purvis Short .75 2.00
132 Joe Barry Carroll .75 2.00
133 Lester Conner .75 2.00
134 Sleepy Floyd 1.25 3.00
135 Geoff Huston .75 2.00
136 Larry Smith .75 2.00
137 Jerome Whitehead .75 2.00
138 Adrian Dantley 1.50 4.00
139 Mitchell Anderson .75 2.00
140 Thurl Bailey 1.25 3.00
141 Mark Eaton 1.25 3.00
142 Rickey Green .75 2.00
143 Darrell Griffith 1.25 3.00
144 John Stockton 25.00 60.00
145 Artis Gilmore 1.50 4.00
146 Marc Iavaroni 1.25 3.00
147 Steve Johnson .75 2.00
148 Mike Mitchell .75 2.00
149 Johnny Moore .75 2.00
150 Alvin Robertson .75 2.00
151 Jon Sundvold .75 2.00
152 World B. Free 1.25 3.00
153 John Bagley .75 2.00
154 Johnny Davis .75 2.00
155 Roy Hinson .75 2.00
156 Phil Hubbard .75 2.00
157 Ben Poquette .75 2.00
158 Mel Turpin .75 2.00
159 Rolando Blackman 1.50 4.00
160 Mark Aguirre 1.50 4.00
161 Brad Davis 1.25 3.00
162 Dale Ellis 1.25 3.00
163 Derek Harper 1.50 4.00
164 Sam Perkins 1.50 4.00
165 Jay Vincent .75 2.00
166 Patrick Ewing XRC. 60.00 150.00
167 Bill Cartwright 1.25 3.00
168 Pat Cummings .75 2.00
169 Ernie Grunfeld 1.25 3.00
170 Rory Sparrow .75 2.00
171 Trent Tucker .75 2.00
172 Darrell Walker 1.25 3.00
97W Dennis Johnson White 4.00 10.00
100W Jerry Sichting White 1.25 3.00
101W Bill Walton White 6.00 15.00
102W Scott Wedman White 1.25 3.00
BAG1 76ers sealed bag (9) 30.00 70.00
BAG2 Blazers sealed bag (7) 30.00 70.00
BAG3 Bucks sealed bag (7) 8.00 20.00
BAG4 Bullets sealed bag (7) 8.00 20.00
BAG5 Bulls sealed bag (7) 400.00 600.00
BAG6 Cavs sealed bag (7) 8.00 20.00
BAG7 Celtics grn sealed bag (8) 30.00 80.00
BAG8 Celtics wht sealed bag (8) 50.00 120.00
BAG9 Clippers sealed bag (7) 8.00 20.00
BAG10 Hawks sealed bag (8) 20.00 40.00
BAG11 Jazz sealed bag (7) 30.00 80.00
BAG12 Kings sealed bag (7) 8.00 20.00
BAG13 Knicks sealed bag (7) 100.00 175.00
BAG14 Lakers SP sealed bag (8) 50.00 120.00
BAG15 Mavs sealed bag (7) 12.00 30.00
BAG16 Nets sealed bag (8) 8.00 20.00
BAG17 Nuggets sealed bag (8) 8.00 20.00
BAG18 Pacers sealed bag (7) 8.00 20.00
BAG19 Pistons sealed bag (8) 15.00 30.00
BAG20 Rockets sealed bag (8) 25.00 60.00
BAG21 Sonics sealed bag (8) 8.00 20.00
BAG22 Spurs sealed bag (7) 8.00 20.00
BAG23 Suns sealed bag (8) 8.00 20.00
BAG24 Warriors sealed bag (7) 8.00 20.00

1985-86 Star All-Rookie Team

The 1985-86 Star NBA All-Rookie Team is an 11-card standard-size set that features 11 top rookies from the previous (1984-85) season. The set's basic design is identical to those of the Star Company's regular NBA sets. The front borders are red and the backs include each player's collegiate statistics. Alvin Robertson's card shows the Star '86 logo in the upper right corner. All others in the set show Star '85.

COMPLETE SET (11) 250.00 350.00
1 Hakeem Olajuwon 15.00 40.00
2 Michael Jordan 100.00 250.00
3 Charles Barkley 20.00 50.00
4 Sam Bowie 2.50 6.00
5 Sam Perkins 2.50 6.00
6 Vern Fleming 2.00 5.00
7 Otis Thorpe 2.00 5.00
8 John Stockton 30.00 60.00
9 Kevin Willis 2.50 6.00
10 Tim McCormick 2.00 5.00
11 Alvin Robertson 2.00 5.00
BAG1 Complete sealed bag (11) 250.00 400.00

1985-86 Star Lakers Champs

The 1985-86 Star Lakers NBA Champs set is an 18-card standard-size set commemorating the Los Angeles Lakers' 1985 NBA Championship. Each card depicts action from the Championship series. The front borders are off-white. The backs feature game and series summaries plus other related information. The set's basic design is identical to those of the Star Company's regular NBA sets. The cards show a Star '86 logo in the upper right corner.

COMPLETE SET (18) 30.00 80.00
1 Kareem/J.Buss Champs 4.00 10.00
2 Larry Bird IA 6.00 15.00
3 Dennis Johnson IA 1.25 3.00
4 Danny Ainge IA 1.50 4.00
5 Byron Scott IA 1.25 3.00
6 Kevin McHale IA 2.50 6.00
7 Magic Johnson IA 6.00 15.00
8 Kareem/Parish IA 3.00 8.00
9 Larry Bird IA 6.00 15.00
10 K.Abdul-Jabbar IA 3.00 8.00
11 M.Cooper/Ainge IA 2.00 5.00
12 Pat Riley CO 2.00 5.00
13 K.C. Jones CO 1.25 3.00
14 Magic Johnson IA 6.00 15.00
15 Lakers/Celtics IA 2.50 6.00
16 Road To The Title 1.25 3.00
17 Prior World Champs I 1.25 3.00
18 Lakers Champs II/Reagan 15.00 30.00
BAG1 Complete sealed bag (18) 30.00 80.00

1986 Star Best of the Best

The Star Company reportedly produced only 1,400 sets and planned to release them in 1986. However, they were not issued until as late as 1990. This set and the Magic Johnson set were printed on the same uncut sheet. No factory-sealed bags exist for this set due to the fact that the sets were cut from the sheets years after the original printing. It is understood that the uncut sheets were sold to hobbyists who cut the sheets and packaged sets to be sold into the hobby. The cards measure the standard size. The fronts feature color action photos with white inner borders and a blue card face. The player's name, position, and team name appear at the bottom. The set title "Best of the Best" appears in a white circle at the lower left corner. The backs are white with blue borders and contain biography and statistics. The cards are numbered and arranged in alphabetical order.

COMPLETE SET (15) 50.00 120.00
1 Kareem Abdul-Jabbar 2.50 6.00
2 Charles Barkley 6.00 15.00
3 Larry Bird 5.00 12.00
4 Tom Chambers 1.00 2.50
5 Terry Cummings 1.00 2.50
6 Julius Erving 3.00 8.00
7 Patrick Ewing 4.00 10.00
8 Magic Johnson 5.00 12.00
9 Michael Jordan 40.00 80.00
10 Moses Malone 1.50 4.00
11 Hakeem Olajuwon 4.00 10.00
12 John Stockton 4.00 10.00
13 Isiah Thomas 2.50 6.00
14 Dominique Wilkins 3.00 8.00
15 James Worthy 2.50 6.00

1986 Star Best of the New/Old

The Star Company distributed these sets to dealers who purchased 1985-86 complete sets. Dealers received one set for every five regular sets purchased. The cards measure the standard size. The cards are unnumbered and checklisted below in alphabetical order. The Best of the New are numbered 1-4 and the Best of the Old are numbered 5-8. The numbering is alphabetical within each group. Counterfeiting has been a problem with the Best of the New series.

COMPLETE SET (8) 225.00 450.00
COMPLETE NEW SET (4) 75.00 150.00
COMPLETE OLD SET (4) 150.00 300.00
1 Patrick Ewing 10.00 25.00
2 Michael Jordan 60.00 150.00
3 Hakeem Olajuwon 10.00 25.00
4 Ralph Sampson 2.00 5.00
5 Kareem Abdul-Jabbar 50.00 100.00
6 Julius Erving 60.00 120.00
7 George Gervin 30.00 60.00
8 Bill Walton 30.00 60.00
BAG1 Complete old sealed bag (4) 150.00 350.00
BAG2 Complete new sealed bag (4) 125.00 250.00

1986 Star Court Kings

The 1986 Star Court Kings set contains 33 standard-size cards which feature many of the NBA's top players. The set's basic design is identical to those of the Star Company's regular NBA sets. The front borders are yellow, and the backs have career narrative summaries of each player but no statistics. The cards show a Star '86 logo in the upper right corner. The cards are numbered in the upper left corner of the reverse. The numbering is alphabetical by last name.

COMPLETE SET (33) 100.00 200.00
1 Mark Aguirre 1.25 3.00
2 Kareem Abdul-Jabbar 4.00 10.00
3 Charles Barkley ! 8.00 20.00
4 Larry Bird ! 8.00 20.00
5 Rolando Blackman 1.25 3.00
6 Tom Chambers 1.25 3.00
7 Maurice Cheeks 1.25 3.00
8 Terry Cummings 1.25 3.00
9 Adrian Dantley 1.25 3.00
10 Darryl Dawkins 1.25 3.00
11 Mark Eaton 1.25 3.00
12 Alex English 1.50 4.00
13 Julius Erving 4.00 10.00
14 Patrick Ewing ! 5.00 12.00
15 George Gervin 2.50 6.00
16 Darrell Griffith 1.25 3.00
17 Magic Johnson 6.00 15.00
18 Michael Jordan 75.00 150.00
19 Clark Kellogg 1.25 3.00
20 Bernard King 1.25 3.00
21 Moses Malone 1.50 4.00
22 Kevin McHale 2.50 6.00
23 Sidney Moncrief 1.50 4.00
24 Larry Nance 1.50 4.00
25 Hakeem Olajuwon 5.00 12.00
26 Robert Parish 2.00 5.00
27 Ralph Sampson 1.25 3.00
28 Isiah Thomas 2.50 6.00
29 Andrew Toney 1.25 3.00
30 Kelly Tripucka 1.25 3.00
31 Kiki Vandeweghe 1.25 3.00
32 Dominique Wilkins UER 4.00 10.00
33 James Worthy 3.00 8.00
BAG1 Complete sealed bag (33) 125.00 250.00

1986 Star Magic Johnson

This 10-card set highlights the career of Magic Johnson. The Star Company reportedly produced only 1,400 sets of these cards and planned to release them in 1986. However, they were not issued until perhaps as late as 1990. This set and the Best of the Best set were printed on the same uncut sheet. Star directly sold sheets to hobbyists who cut them and sold sets to the hobby. The cards measure the standard size. The cards are unnumbered and checklisted below in alphabetical order.

COMPLETE SET (10) 15.00 40.00
COMMON CARD (1-10) 2.50 6.00

1986 Star Michael Jordan

The 1986 Star Michael Jordan set contains ten cards highlighting his career. There were reportedly only 2,800 sets produced. They were originally available to the hobby exclusively through Dan Stickney of Michigan. Sets were originally issued in sealed plastic bags. The card backs contain various bits of information about Jordan. The set's basic design is identical to those of the Star Company's regular NBA sets. The front borders are red. The cards show a Star '86 logo in the upper right corner. The cards measure approximately 2 1/2" by 3 1/2". The cards are numbered in the upper left corner of the reverse. Collectors should beware of counterfeits.

COMPLETE SET (10) 250.00 450.00
COMMON CARD (1-10) 30.00 60.00
BAG1 Complete sealed bag (10) 300.00 500.00

1990 Star Charles Barkley

This 11-card set measures the standard size. The fronts feature color action shots, with red borders that wash out in the middle of the card face. The horizontally oriented backs are printed in red on white and have various kinds of player information. Reportedly there were 5000 regular sets produced; 250 limited edition glossy sets. Glossy cards are valued at five times the values of the regular cards.

COMPLETE SET (11) 1.25 3.00
COMMON CARD (1-11) .20 .50

1990 Star Dee Brown

This 11-card set measures the standard size. The fronts feature color action shots, with green borders that wash out in the middle of the card face. The horizontally oriented backs are printed in green on white and have various kinds of player information. Reportedly there were 5000 regular sets produced; 250 limited edition glossy sets. Glossy cards are valued at five times the values of the regular cards.

COMPLETE SET (11) .75 2.00
COMMON CARD (1-11) .10 .25

1990 Star Tom Chambers

This 11-card set measures the standard size. The fronts feature color action shots, with orange borders that wash out in the middle of the card face. The horizontally oriented backs are printed in orange on white and have various kinds of player information. Reportedly there were 5000 regular sets produced; 250 limited edition glossy sets. Glossy cards are valued at five times the values of the regular cards.

COMPLETE SET (11) .75 2.00
COMMON CARD (1-11) .12 .30

1990 Star Derrick Coleman I

This 11-card set measures the standard size. The fronts feature color action shots, with blue borders that wash out in the middle of the card face. The horizontally oriented backs are printed in blue on white and have various kinds of player information. Reportedly there were 5000 regular sets produced; 250 limited edition glossy sets. Glossy cards are valued at five times the values of the regular cards.

COMPLETE SET (11) .75 2.00
COMMON CARD (1-11) .12 .30

1990 Star Derrick Coleman II

This 11-card set measures the standard size. The fronts feature color action shots, with red borders that wash out in the middle of the card face. The horizontally oriented backs are printed in red on white and have various kinds of player information. Reportedly there were 5000 regular sets produced; 250 limited edition glossy sets. Glossy cards are valued at five times the values of the regular cards.

COMPLETE SET (11) .75 2.00
COMMON CARD (1-11) .12 .30

1990 Star Clyde Drexler

This 11-card set measures the standard size. The fronts feature color action shots, with red borders that wash out in the middle of the card face. The horizontally oriented backs are printed in red on white and have various kinds of player information. Reportedly there were 5000 regular sets produced; 250 limited edition glossy sets. Glossy cards are valued at five times the values of the regular cards.

COMPLETE SET (11) 1.25 3.00
COMMON CARD (1-11) .25 .60

1990 Star Patrick Ewing

This 11-card set measures the standard size. The fronts feature color action shots, with orange borders that wash out in the middle of the card face. The horizontally oriented backs are printed in blue on white and have various kinds of player information. Reportedly there were 5000 regular sets produced; 250 limited edition glossy sets. Glossy cards are valued at five times the values of the regular cards.

COMPLETE SET (11) 1.25 3.00
COMMON CARD (1-11) .15 .40

1990 Star Tim Hardaway

This 11-card set measures the standard size. The fronts feature color action shots, with yellow borders that wash out in the middle of the card face. The horizontally oriented backs are printed in blue on white and have various kinds of player information. Reportedly there were 5000 regular sets produced; 250 limited edition glossy sets. Glossy cards are valued at five times the values of the regular cards.

COMPLETE SET (11) .75 2.00
COMMON CARD (1-11) .15 .40

1990 Star Kevin Johnson

This 11-card set measures the standard size. The fronts feature color action shots, with orange borders that wash out in the middle of the card face. The horizontally oriented backs are printed in purple on white and have various kinds of player information. Reportedly there were 5000 regular sets produced; 250 limited edition glossy sets. Glossy cards are valued at five times the values of the regular cards.

COMPLETE SET (11) .75 2.00
COMMON CARD (1-11) .10 .30

1990 Star Karl Malone

This 11-card set measures the standard size. The fronts feature color action shots, with green borders that wash out in the middle of the card face. The horizontally oriented backs are printed in green on white and have various kinds of player information. Reportedly there were 5000 regular sets produced; 250 limited edition glossy sets. Glossy cards are valued at five times the values of the regular cards.

COMPLETE SET (11) 1.25 3.00
COMMON CARD (1-11) .20 .50

1990 Star Hakeem Olajuwon

This 11-card set measures the standard size. The fronts feature color action shots, with yellow borders that wash out in the middle of the card face. The horizontally oriented backs are printed in red on white and have various kinds of player information. Reportedly there were 5000 regular sets produced; 250 limited edition glossy sets. Glossy cards are valued at five times the values of the regular cards.

COMPLETE SET (11) 1.25 3.00
COMMON CARD (1-11) .20 .50

1990 Star David Robinson I

This 11-card set measures the standard size. The fronts feature color action shots, with blue borders that wash out in the middle of the card face. The horizontally oriented backs are printed in blue on white and have various kinds of player information. Reportedly there were 5000 regular sets produced; 250 limited edition glossy sets. Glossy cards are valued at five times the values of the regular cards.

COMPLETE SET (11) 2.00 5.00
COMMON CARD (1-11) .30 .75

1990 Star David Robinson II

This 11-card set measures the standard size. The fronts feature color action shots, with black borders that wash out in the middle of the card face. The horizontally oriented backs are printed in black on white and have various kinds of player information. Reportedly there were 5000 regular sets produced; 250 limited edition glossy sets. Glossy cards are valued at five times the values of the regular cards.

COMPLETE SET (11) 1.50 4.00
COMMON CARD (1-11) .25 .60

1990 Star David Robinson III

This 11-card set measures the standard size. The fronts feature color action shots, with purple borders that wash out in the middle of the card face. The horizontally oriented backs are printed in purple on white and have various kinds of player information. Reportedly there were 5000 regular sets produced; 250 limited edition glossy sets. Glossy cards are valued at five times the values of the regular cards.

COMPLETE SET (11) 1.50 4.00
COMMON CARD (1-11) .30 .75

1990 Star John Stockton

This 11-card set measures the standard size. The fronts feature color action shots, with purple borders that wash out in the middle of the card face. The horizontally oriented backs are printed in purple on white and have various kinds of player information. Reportedly there were 5000 regular sets produced; 250 limited edition glossy sets. Glossy cards are valued at five times the values of the regular cards.

COMPLETE SET (11) 1.50 4.00
COMMON CARD (1-11) .20 .50

1990 Star Isiah Thomas

This 11-card set measures the standard size. The fronts feature color action shots, with purple borders that wash out in the middle of the card face. The horizontally oriented backs are printed in purple on white and have various kinds of player information. Reportedly there were 5000 regular sets produced; 250 limited edition glossy sets. Glossy cards are valued at five times the values of the regular cards.

COMPLETE SET (11) 1.25 3.00
COMMON CARD (1-11) .20 .50

1990 Star Dominique Wilkins

This 11-card set measures the standard size. The fronts feature color action shots, with yellow borders that wash out in the middle of the card face. The horizontally oriented backs are printed in red on white and have various kinds of player information. Reportedly there were 5000 regular sets produced; 250 limited edition glossy sets. Glossy cards are valued at five times the values of the regular cards.

COMPLETE SET (11) 1.25 3.00
COMMON CARD (1-11) .20 .50

1990 Star James Worthy

This 11-card set measures the standard size. The fronts feature color action shots, with yellow borders that wash out in the middle of the card face. The horizontally oriented backs are printed in purple on white and have various kinds of player information. Reportedly there were 5000 regular sets produced; 250 limited edition glossy sets. Glossy cards are valued at five times the values of the regular cards.

COMPLETE SET (11) 1.25 3.00
COMMON CARD (1-11) .15 .40

1990-91 Star Promos

These 18 promo cards showcase outstanding NBA players. The standard-size cards feature color action player photos on the obverse. The pictures have different color borders, which wash out as one approaches the middle of the card face. In white lettering the player's name, team, and "Promo" appear below the picture. The reverses are blank. The cards are unnumbered and are checklisted below in alphabetical order. Reportedly there were 1400 promo sets and 50 glossy promo sets produced. The glossy promos are valued at four times the values of the regular cards.

COMPLETE SET (18) 16.00 40.00
1 Charles Barkley 2.50 6.00
2 Dee Brown .40 1.00
3 Tom Chambers .40 1.00
4 Derrick Coleman I .60 1.50
5 Derrick Coleman II .40 1.00
6 Clyde Drexler 1.25 3.00
7 Patrick Ewing 1.25 3.00
8 Tim Hardaway 1.50 4.00
9 Kevin Johnson .75 2.00
10 Karl Malone 3.00 8.00
11 Hakeem Olajuwon 2.00 5.00
12 David Robinson I 2.00 5.00
13 David Robinson II 2.00 5.00
14 David Robinson III 2.00 5.00
15 John Stockton 2.00 5.00
16 Isiah Thomas .75 2.00
17 Dominique Wilkins .75 2.00
18 James Worthy .75 2.00

1993-94 Star

The 1993-94 Star basketball set consists of 100 standard-size cards featuring past and current NBA players. The cards were packaged in nine-card foil packs, and randomly inserted special coupons enabled the collector to win special autograph cards, uncut sheets, and other memorabilia. The fronts feature color player action photos with team color-coded borders. The player's name appears above the photo at the upper right. The card's subtitle appears below the photo at the lower left. The back has a color player action shot on the left side with the player's name, bio and profile alongside to the right. All NBA team names and logos have been airbrushed from the players' uniforms.

COMPLETE SET (100) 6.00 15.00
1 Larry Bird .40 1.00
Career Stats 1979-1987
2 Chris Mullin .12 .30
Pro Season Stats
3 Harold Miner .07 .20
Collegiate Record
4 Tom Gugliotta UER .10 .25
Personal Data/(Misspelled Guggliotta on front and back)
5 Christian Laettner .10 .25
College and NBA Record
6 Tim Hardaway .12 .30
Collegiate Stats
7 Shawn Kemp .15 .40
NBA Regular Season Stats
8 Walt Frazier .12 .30
Collegiate Record
9 John Starks .10 .25
Career Highlights
10 Charles Barkley .20 .50
Collegiate Stats
11 Robert Parish .12 .30
Pro Stats 1
12 Chris Mullin .12 .30
Playoff Stats
13 Kevin McHale .15 .40
Collegiate Stats
14 Scott Burrell .12 .30
Career Stats
15 Harold Miner .07 .20
1992/93 Season 1
16 Richard Dumas .07 .20
Career Stats
17 Larry Bird .40 1.00
Career Stats 1988-1992
18 Xavier McDaniel .07 .20
Collegiate Stats
19 Christian Laettner .10 .25
1992-93 Season 1
20 Shawn Kemp .15 .40
NBA Playoff Stats
21 Tom Gugliotta UER .10 .25
Collegiate Record/(Misspelled Guggliotta on front and back)
22 Walt Frazier .12 .30
Career Stats 1
23 Tim Hardaway .12 .30
Regular Season Stats
24 John Starks .10 .25
Personal Info
25 Charles Barkley .20 .50
Pro Season Stats
26 Robert Parish .12 .30
Pro Stats 2
27 Bill Walton .12 .30
Collegiate Stats
28 Xavier McDaniel .07 .20
Regular Season Stats
29 Chris Mullin .12 .30
All-Star Stats
30 Scott Burrell .12 .30
1992/93 Season
31 Shawn Kemp .15 .40
1992/93 Season
32 Oliver Miller .07 .20
Career Stats
33 Larry Bird .40 1.00
All-Star Stats
34 Richard Dumas .07 .20
1992/93 Season
35 Kevin McHale .15 .40
Pro Stats
36 Oliver Miller .07 .20
Collegiate Info
37 Harold Miner .07 .20
1992/93 Season 2
38 Christian Laettner .10 .25
1992/93 Season 2
39 Charles Barkley .20 .50
Pro Season Stats
40 Tom Gugliotta UER .10 .25
Career Highs/(Misspelled Guggliotta on front and back)
41 John Starks .10 .25
1992/93 Season 1
42 Tim Hardaway .12 .30
Playoff
All-Star Stats
43 Robert Parish .12 .30
All-Star Stats
44 Scott Burrell .12 .30
Collegiate Info 1
45 Bill Walton .12 .30
Regular Season Stats
46 Xavier McDaniel .07 .20
Playoff Stats
47 Richard Dumas .07 .20
Career Highs
48 Walt Frazier .12 .30
Career Stats 2
49 Oliver Miller .07 .20
1992/93 Season 1
50 Charles Barkley .20 .50
All-Star Stats
51 Larry Bird .40 1.00
Playoff Stats
52 Chris Mullin .12 .30
Career Best
53 Shawn Kemp .15 .40
Pro Info
54 Christian Laettner .10 .25
College Info
55 Robert Parish .12 .30
Playoff Stats
56 John Starks .10 .25
1992/93 Season 2
57 Xavier McDaniel .07 .20
Pro Info
58 Bill Walton .12 .30
Playoff
All-Star Stats
59 Harold Miner .07 .20
Personal Info
60 Richard Dumas .07 .20
Collegiate Info
61 Oliver Miller .07 .20
1992/93 Season 2
62 Tom Gugliotta UER .10 .25
Colliegiate Info/(Misspelled Guggliotta on front and back)
63 Scott Burrell .12 .30
Collegiate Info 2
64 Tim Hardaway .12 .30
Pro Info 1
65 Walt Frazier .12 .30
NBA Playoff Record
66 Larry Bird .40 1.00
Career Highlights
67 Shawn Kemp .15 .40
Personal Info
68 Kevin McHale .15 .40
All-Star Stats
69 Xavier McDaniel .07 .20
Personal Data
70 John Starks .10 .25
NBA Regular Season and Playoff Record
71 Bill Walton .12 .30
Career Info 1
72 Christian Laettner .10 .25
Personal Datta and Collegiate Record
73 Chris Mullin .12 .30
1992/93 Season
74 Walt Frazier .12 .30
NBA All-Star Game Record
75 Charles Barkley .20 .50
Playoff Stats
76 Oliver Miller .07 .20
Personal Info
77 Kevin McHale .15 .40
Playoff Stats
78 Robert Parish .12 .30
Career Highs
79 Larry Bird .40 1.00
All-Time Standings
80 Harold Miner .07 .20
Collegiate Info
81 Kevin McHale .15 .40
Career Highs
82 Tim Hardaway .12 .30
Pro Info 2
83 Tom Gugliotta UER .10 .25
Personal Data and 1992/93 Stats (Misspelled Guggliotta on front and back)
84 Bill Walton .12 .30
Career Info 2
85 Shawn Kemp .15 .40
Personal Data
86 Scott Burrell .12 .30
Personal Data
87 Richard Dumas .07 .20
Personal Info
88 Charles Barkley .20 .50
Pro Info
89 Bill Walton .12 .30
Personal Info
90 Kevin McHale .15 .40
Personal Data
91 Christian Laettner .10 .25
Personal Info
92 Walt Frazier .12 .30
Personal Data
93 John Starks .10 .25
Collegiate and CBA Regular Season Record
94 Harold Miner .07 .20
Personal Data and NBA Regular Season Record
95 Robert Parish .12 .30
Personal Info
96 Tim Hardaway .12 .30
Personal Data
97 Tom Gugliotta UER .10 .25
1992/93 Season Misspelled Guggliotta on front and back)
98 Larry Bird .40 1.00
Personal Data
99 Chris Mullin .12 .30
Personal Info
100 Charles Barkley .20 .50
Personal Info

2009-10 Studio

COMPLETE SET (150) 30.00 60.00
COMMON ROOKIE (121-150) 1.00 2.50
UNPRICED PLATINUM PRINT RUN ONE SET
UNPRICED PRESS PLATES PRINT RUN ONE SET
1 Andrew Bynum .30 .75
2 Derek Fisher .40 1.00
3 Kobe Bryant 2.00 5.00
4 Lamar Odom .40 1.00
5 Carmelo Anthony .60 1.50
6 Chauncey Billups .50 1.25
7 Chris Andersen .40 1.00
8 Brandon Roy .50 1.25
9 LaMarcus Aldridge .50 1.25
10 Rudy Fernandez .30 .75
11 Manu Ginobili .50 1.25
12 Tim Duncan .75 2.00
13 Tony Parker .50 1.25
14 Luis Scola .40 1.00
15 Shane Battier .50 1.25
16 Tracy McGrady .50 1.25
17 Dirk Nowitzki .60 1.50
18 Jason Kidd .50 1.25
19 Jason Terry .40 1.00
20 Josh Howard .40 1.00
21 Chris Paul .60 1.50
22 David West .40 1.00
23 Peja Stojakovic .50 1.25
24 Rasual Butler .30 .75
25 Andrei Kirilenko .40 1.00
26 Carlos Boozer .40 1.00
27 Deron Williams .40 1.00
28 Amare Stoudemire .40 1.00
29 Grant Hill .60 1.50
30 Jason Richardson .50 1.25
31 Steve Nash .50 1.25
32 Anthony Randolph .30 .75
33 Corey Maggette .40 1.00
34 Monta Ellis .40 1.00
35 Raja Bell .40 1.00
36 Marc Gasol .50 1.25
37 Mike Conley Jr. .40 1.00
38 O.J. Mayo .30 .75
39 Rudy Gay .50 1.25
40 Al Jefferson .40 1.00
41 Kevin Love .50 1.25
42 Ryan Gomes .30 .75
43 Jeff Green .40 1.00
44 Kevin Durant 1.25 3.00
45 Russell Westbrook 1.25 3.00
46 Al Thornton .40 1.00
47 Chris Kaman .40 1.00
48 Eric Gordon .40 1.00
49 Andres Nocioni .30 .75
50 Francisco Garcia .30 .75
51 Kevin Martin .40 1.00
52 LeBron James 2.00 5.00
53 Mo Williams .40 1.00
54 Shaquille O'Neal 1.00 2.50
55 Kevin Garnett .75 2.00
56 Paul Pierce .50 1.25
57 Rajon Rondo .50 1.25
58 Ray Allen .50 1.25
59 Dwight Howard .40 1.00
60 Jameer Nelson .30 .75
61 Rashard Lewis .40 1.00
62 Al Horford .50 1.25
63 Joe Johnson .40 1.00
64 Josh Smith .40 1.00
65 Mike Bibby .40 1.00
66 Dwyane Wade .75 2.00
67 Jermaine O'Neal .40 1.00
68 Michael Beasley .30 .75
69 Derrick Rose .75 2.00
70 Joakim Noah .40 1.00
71 John Salmons .40 1.00
72 Andre Iguodala .40 1.00
73 Elton Brand .50 1.25
74 Thaddeus Young .30 .75
75 Ben Gordon .40 1.00
76 Richard Hamilton .40 1.00
77 Tayshaun Prince .40 1.00
78 Danny Granger .40 1.00
79 Mike Dunleavy .30 .75
80 T.J. Ford .30 .75
81 Troy Murphy .30 .75
82 Boris Diaw .40 1.00
83 Gerald Wallace .40 1.00
84 Stephen Jackson .40 1.00
85 Raymond Felton .40 1.00
86 Andrew Bogut .40 1.00
87 Luke Ridnour .40 1.00
88 Michael Redd .40 1.00
89 Brook Lopez .40 1.00
90 Devin Harris .30 .75
91 Yi Jianlian .40 1.00
92 Andrea Bargnani .40 1.00
93 Chris Bosh .50 1.25
94 Jose Calderon .30 .75
95 Al Harrington .40 1.00
96 David Lee .30 .75
97 Wilson Chandler .40 1.00
98 Antawn Jamison .40 1.00
99 Caron Butler .40 1.00
100 Mike Miller .40 1.00
101 Wes Unseld .50 1.25
102 Arnie Risen .50 1.25
103 Bailey Howell .50 1.25
104 Bill Cartwright .40 1.00
105 Byron Scott .40 1.00
106 Darryl Dawkins .30 .75
107 Jeff Hornacek .40 1.00
108 Jerry Lucas .50 1.25
109 Kelly Tripucka .30 .75
110 Manute Bol .50 1.25
111 Mark Eaton .30 .75
112 Michael Cage .30 .75
113 Mitch Richmond .50 1.25
114 Norm Nixon .30 .75
115 Paul Westphal .50 1.25
116 Rick Barry .40 1.00
117 Ron Harper .50 1.25
118 Spencer Haywood .30 .75
119 Dennis Rodman 1.00 2.50
120 Anfernee Hardaway 1.25 3.00
121 Ty Lawson RC 1.00 2.50
122 Jeff Pendergraph RC .60 1.50
123 DeJuan Blair RC .75 2.00
124 Jermaine Taylor RC .60 1.50
125 Rodrigue Beaubois RC .60 1.50
126 Darren Collison RC 1.00 2.50
127 Eric Maynor RC .60 1.50
128 Earl Clark RC .75 2.00
129 Stephen Curry RC 10.00 25.00
130 DeMarre Carroll RC .75 2.00
131 Hasheem Thabeet RC .60 1.50
132 Jonny Flynn RC .60 1.50
133 Wayne Ellington RC 1.00 2.50
134 B.J. Mullens RC .60 1.50
135 James Harden RC 5.00 12.00
136 Blake Griffin RC 4.00 10.00
137 Omri Casspi RC .75 2.00
138 Tyreke Evans RC .75 2.00
139 Jeff Teague RC 1.00 2.50
140 James Johnson RC .75 2.00
141 Taj Gibson RC 1.00 2.50
142 Jrue Holiday RC 1.25 3.00
143 Austin Daye RC .60 1.50
144 Tyler Hansbrough RC .75 2.00
145 Gerald Henderson RC .75 2.00
146 Brandon Jennings RC 1.00 2.50
147 Terrence Williams RC .60 1.50
148 DeMar DeRozan RC 2.50 6.00
149 Jordan Hill RC .75 2.00
150 Toney Douglas RC .60 1.50

2009-10 Studio Proofs Bronze

*BRONZE: .6X TO 1.5X BASE HI
STATED PRINT RUN 199 SER.#'d SETS

2009-10 Studio Proofs Gold

*GOLD: 1.5X TO 4X BASE HI
STATED PRINT RUN 49 SER.#'d SETS
44 Kevin Durant 8.00 20.00

2009-10 Studio Proofs Gold Signatures

STATED PRINT RUN 5 TO 25 SER.#'d SETS
SOME UNPRICED DUE TO SCARCITY
UNPRICED PLAT.SIG PRINT RUN ONE SET
3 Kobe Bryant/25 125.00 250.00
13 Tony Parker/25 10.00 25.00
41 Kevin Love/25 15.00 40.00
48 Eric Gordon/25 8.00 20.00
57 Rajon Rondo/25 20.00 40.00
80 T.J. Ford/25 8.00 15.00
101 Wes Unseld/25 10.00 25.00
105 Byron Scott/25 8.00 20.00
107 Jeff Hornacek/25 10.00 25.00
121 Ty Lawson/25 15.00 40.00
122 Jeff Pendergraph/25 5.00 12.00
123 DeJuan Blair/25 6.00 15.00
124 Jermaine Taylor/25 5.00 12.00
125 Rodrigue Beaubois/25 5.00 12.00
126 Darren Collison/25 8.00 20.00
127 Eric Maynor/25 5.00 12.00
128 Earl Clark/25 6.00 15.00
129 Stephen Curry/25 800.00 1200.00
130 DeMarre Carroll/25 6.00 15.00
131 Hasheem Thabeet/25 5.00 12.00
132 Jonny Flynn/25 5.00 12.00
133 Wayne Ellington/25 8.00 20.00
134 B.J. Mullens/25 5.00 12.00
135 James Harden/25 60.00 150.00
136 Blake Griffin/25 125.00 250.00
137 Omri Casspi/25 6.00 15.00
138 Tyreke Evans/25 12.00 30.00
139 Jeff Teague/25 8.00 20.00
140 James Johnson/25 6.00 15.00
141 Taj Gibson/25 8.00 20.00
142 Jrue Holiday/25 20.00 50.00
143 Austin Daye/25 5.00 12.00
144 Tyler Hansbrough/25 6.00 15.00
145 Gerald Henderson/25 6.00 15.00
146 Brandon Jennings/25 8.00 20.00
147 Terrence Williams/25 5.00 12.00
149 Jordan Hill/25 6.00 15.00
150 Toney Douglas/25 5.00 12.00

2009-10 Studio Proofs Silver

*SILVER: .75X TO 2X BASE HI
STATED PRINT RUN 99 SER.#'d SETS

2009-10 Studio Proofs Silver Signatures

STATED PRINT RUN ONE TO 49 SER.#'d SETS
SOME UNPRICED DUE TO SCARCITY
3 Kobe Bryant/49 125.00 225.00
13 Tony Parker/49 12.50 30.00
41 Kevin Love/49 10.00 25.00
42 Ryan Gomes/25 5.00 12.00
45 Russell Westbrook/25 60.00 150.00
47 Chris Kaman/25 6.00 15.00
48 Eric Gordon/49 5.00 12.00
57 Rajon Rondo/49 12.00 30.00
58 Ray Allen/25 20.00 40.00
67 Jermaine O'Neal/25 6.00 15.00
68 Michael Beasley/25 8.00 20.00
78 Danny Granger/25 10.00 25.00
80 T.J. Ford/49 5.00 10.00
90 Devin Harris/25 8.00 20.00
96 David Lee/25 8.00 20.00
101 Wes Unseld/49 8.00 20.00
103 Bailey Howell/25 10.00 25.00
105 Byron Scott/49 6.00 15.00
107 Jeff Hornacek/49 6.00 15.00
110 Manute Bol/25 25.00 60.00
119 Dennis Rodman/25 20.00 50.00
121 Ty Lawson/49 6.00 15.00
122 Jeff Pendergraph/49 4.00 10.00
123 DeJuan Blair/49 5.00 12.00
124 Jermaine Taylor/49 4.00 10.00
125 Rodrigue Beaubois/49 4.00 10.00
126 Darren Collison/49 6.00 15.00
127 Eric Maynor/49 4.00 10.00
128 Earl Clark/49 5.00 12.00
129 Stephen Curry/49 800.00 1200.00
130 DeMarre Carroll/49 5.00 12.00
131 Hasheem Thabeet/49 4.00 10.00
132 Jonny Flynn/49 4.00 10.00
133 Wayne Ellington/49 6.00 15.00
134 B.J. Mullens/49 4.00 10.00
135 James Harden/49 75.00 200.00
136 Blake Griffin/49 40.00 100.00
137 Omri Casspi/49 5.00 12.00
138 Tyreke Evans/49 5.00 12.00
139 Jeff Teague/49 6.00 15.00
140 James Johnson/49 5.00 12.00
141 Taj Gibson/49 6.00 15.00
142 Jrue Holiday/49 15.00 40.00
143 Austin Daye/49 4.00 10.00
144 Tyler Hansbrough/49 5.00 12.00
145 Gerald Henderson/49 5.00 12.00
146 Brandon Jennings/49 6.00 15.00
147 Terrence Williams/49 4.00 10.00
149 Jordan Hill/49 5.00 12.00
150 Toney Douglas/49 4.00 10.00

2009-10 Studio Essence

COMPLETE SET (15) 7.50 15.00
RANDOM INSERTS IN PACKS
*PROOF: .75X TO 2X BASE HI
PROOF PRINT RUN 199 SER.#'d SETS
1 Al Jefferson .60 1.50
2 Andre Iguodala .60 1.50
3 Andrew Bynum .50 1.25
4 Baron Davis .60 1.50
5 Charlie Villanueva .50 1.25
6 Chris Bosh .75 2.00
7 Chris Kaman .60 1.50
8 Devin Harris .50 1.25
9 Emeka Okafor .60 1.50
10 Josh Howard .60 1.50
11 Rajon Rondo .75 2.00
12 Randy Foye .50 1.25
13 Ronnie Brewer .60 1.50
14 Rudy Fernandez .50 1.25
15 Trevor Ariza .50 1.25

2009-10 Studio Essence Materials

STATED PRINT RUN 149 TO 249 SER.#'d SETS
1 Al Jefferson/249 2.50 6.00
2 Andre Iguodala/249 2.50 6.00
3 Andrew Bynum/149 2.00 5.00
4 Baron Davis/249 2.50 6.00
5 Charlie Villanueva/249 2.00 5.00
6 Chris Bosh/249 3.00 8.00
7 Chris Kaman/149 2.50 6.00
10 Josh Howard/249 2.50 6.00

2009-10 Studio Essence Signatures

STATED PRINT RUN 49 TO 99 SER.#'d SETS
ASTERISK CARDS FROM PANINI UPDATE
2 Andre Iguodala/99 6.00 15.00
3 Andrew Bynum/49* 8.00 20.00
4 Baron Davis/49* 5.00 12.00
7 Chris Kaman/99 4.00 10.00
8 Devin Harris/99 4.00 10.00
10 Josh Howard/49 4.00 10.00
11 Rajon Rondo/49* 15.00 40.00
12 Randy Foye/99 4.00 10.00
13 Ronnie Brewer/99 4.00 10.00

2009-10 Studio Heritage

COMPLETE SET (20) 20.00 40.00
RANDOM INSERTS IN PACKS
*PROOFS: .6X TO 1.5X BASE HI
PROOF PRINT RUN 199 SER.#'d SETS
1 Elvin Hayes 1.25 3.00
2 Jerry West 1.50 4.00
3 Spencer Haywood .75 2.00
4 Sidney Moncrief .75 2.00
5 Sam Perkins .75 2.00
6 Robert Parish 1.25 3.00
7 Rick Barry 1.00 2.50
8 Paul Westphal 1.25 3.00
9 Nate Archibald 1.00 2.50
10 Moses Malone 1.25 3.00
11 Magic Johnson 3.00 8.00
12 Lou Hudson 1.25 3.00
13 Lenny Wilkens 1.25 3.00
14 Isiah Thomas 1.25 3.00
15 George Gervin 1.25 3.00
16 Frank Ramsey 1.25 3.00
17 Dolph Schayes 1.25 3.00
18 David Thompson 1.00 2.50
19 Darryl Dawkins .75 2.00
20 Connie Hawkins 1.25 3.00

2009-10 Studio Heritage Materials

STATED PRINT RUN 99 TO 249 SER.#'d SETS
2 Jerry West/99 6.00 15.00
6 Robert Parish/249 4.00 10.00
10 Moses Malone/99 4.00 10.00
11 Magic Johnson/249 8.00 20.00
14 Isiah Thomas/249 4.00 10.00
15 George Gervin/99 4.00 10.00

2009-10 Studio Heritage Signatures

STATED PRINT RUN 49 TO 99 SER.#'d SETS
1 Elvin Hayes/99 8.00 20.00
2 Jerry West/49 30.00 80.00
3 Spencer Haywood/99 8.00 20.00
4 Sidney Moncrief/99 8.00 20.00
5 Sam Perkins/99 8.00 20.00
6 Robert Parish/99 8.00 20.00
7 Rick Barry/99 8.00 20.00
8 Paul Westphal/99 8.00 20.00
9 Nate Archibald/99 8.00 20.00
11 Magic Johnson/49 40.00 100.00
13 Lenny Wilkens/99 8.00 20.00
14 Isiah Thomas/93 10.00 25.00
15 George Gervin/99 8.00 20.00
16 Frank Ramsey/99 8.00 20.00
17 Dolph Schayes/99 8.00 20.00
18 David Thompson/99 8.00 20.00

2009-10 Studio Masterstrokes

COMPLETE SET (20) 20.00 40.00
RANDOM INSERTS IN PACKS
*PROOFS: .6X TO 1.5X BASE HI
PROOF PRINT RUN 199 SER.#'d SETS
1 Al Jefferson .75 2.00
2 Andre Iguodala .75 2.00
3 Carlos Boozer .75 2.00
4 Carmelo Anthony 1.25 3.00
5 Danilo Gallinari .75 2.00
6 Dwight Howard .75 2.00
7 Jason Kidd 1.00 2.50
8 Joe Johnson .75 2.00
9 Kevin Martin .75 2.00
10 Kobe Bryant 4.00 10.00
11 LeBron James 4.00 10.00
12 Manu Ginobili 1.00 2.50
13 O.J. Mayo .60 1.50
14 Paul Pierce 1.00 2.50
15 Kevin Durant 2.50 6.00
16 Tracy McGrady 1.00 2.50
17 Dwyane Wade 1.50 4.00
18 Chris Bosh 1.00 2.50
19 Stephen Jackson .75 2.00
20 Tayshaun Prince .75 2.00

2009-10 Studio Masterstrokes Materials

STATED PRINT RUN 50 TO 249 SER.#'d SETS
1 Al Jefferson/249 2.50 6.00
2 Andre Iguodala/249 2.50 6.00
3 Carlos Boozer/249 2.50 6.00
4 Carmelo Anthony/249 4.00 10.00
5 Danilo Gallinari/249 2.50 6.00
6 Dwight Howard/249 2.50 6.00
8 Joe Johnson/50 2.50 6.00
10 Kobe Bryant/249 8.00 20.00
11 LeBron James/249 8.00 20.00
12 Manu Ginobili/249 3.00 8.00
14 Paul Pierce/199 3.00 8.00
16 Tracy McGrady/199 3.00 8.00
17 Dwyane Wade/249 5.00 12.00
18 Chris Bosh/249 3.00 8.00
20 Tayshaun Prince/249 2.50 6.00

2009-10 Studio Masterstrokes Signatures

STATED PRINT RUN 49 TO 99 SER.#'d SETS
2 Andre Iguodala/81 8.00 20.00
3 Carlos Boozer/99 6.00 15.00
7 Jason Kidd/49 10.00 25.00
10 Kobe Bryant/99 100.00 200.00
16 Tracy McGrady/49 15.00 40.00
18 Chris Bosh/99 8.00 20.00

2009-10 Studio Materials

STATED PRINT RUN 10 TO 249 SER.#'d SETS
SOME UNPRICED DUE TO SCARCITY
1 Andrew Bynum/249 2.00 5.00
3 Kobe Bryant/249 8.00 20.00
5 Carmelo Anthony/249 4.00 10.00
6 Chauncey Billups/249 3.00 8.00
7 Chris Andersen/249 2.50 6.00
8 Brandon Roy/249 3.00 8.00
9 LaMarcus Aldridge/249 3.00 8.00
11 Manu Ginobili/249 3.00 8.00
12 Tim Duncan/249 5.00 12.00
13 Tony Parker/249 3.00 8.00
14 Luis Scola/249 2.50 6.00
15 Shane Battier/249 3.00 8.00
16 Tracy McGrady/249 3.00 8.00
17 Dirk Nowitzki/249 4.00 10.00
18 Jason Kidd/249 3.00 8.00
19 Jason Terry/249 2.50 6.00
20 Josh Howard/249 2.50 6.00
21 Chris Paul/249 4.00 10.00
22 David West/249 2.50 6.00
25 Andrei Kirilenko/149 2.50 6.00
26 Carlos Boozer/249 2.50 6.00
27 Deron Williams/249 2.50 6.00
28 Amare Stoudemire/249 2.50 6.00
34 Monta Ellis/249 2.50 6.00
37 Mike Conley Jr./249 2.50 6.00
40 Al Jefferson/249 2.50 6.00
41 Kevin Love/249 3.00 8.00
42 Ryan Gomes/249 2.00 5.00
46 Al Thornton/249 2.50 6.00
47 Chris Kaman/149 2.50 6.00
49 Andres Nocioni/249 2.00 5.00
52 LeBron James/249 8.00 20.00
53 Mo Williams/249 2.50 6.00
54 Shaquille O'Neal/249 6.00 15.00
55 Kevin Garnett/249 5.00 12.00
56 Paul Pierce/199 3.00 8.00
58 Ray Allen/249 3.00 8.00
59 Dwight Howard/249 2.50 6.00
60 Jameer Nelson/249 2.00 5.00
61 Rashard Lewis/249 2.50 6.00
62 Al Horford/249 3.00 8.00
63 Joe Johnson/50 2.50 6.00
64 Josh Smith/249 2.50 6.00
65 Mike Bibby/50 2.50 6.00
66 Dwyane Wade/249 5.00 12.00
67 Jermaine O'Neal/50 2.50 6.00
68 Michael Beasley/249 2.00 5.00
69 Derrick Rose/50 5.00 12.00
70 Joakim Noah/249 2.50 6.00
72 Andre Iguodala/249 2.50 6.00
73 Elton Brand/249 3.00 8.00
74 Thaddeus Young/249 2.00 5.00
75 Ben Gordon/199 2.50 6.00
76 Richard Hamilton/249 2.50 6.00
77 Tayshaun Prince/249 2.50 6.00
82 Boris Diaw/249 2.50 6.00
83 Gerald Wallace/249 2.50 6.00
85 Raymond Felton/249 2.50 6.00
92 Andrea Bargnani/100 2.50 6.00
93 Chris Bosh/249 3.00 8.00
94 Jose Calderon/249 2.00 5.00
95 Al Harrington/25 2.50 6.00
96 David Lee/249 2.00 5.00
98 Antawn Jamison/249 2.50 6.00
113 Mitch Richmond/249 6.00 15.00
116 Rick Barry/199 2.50 6.00
117 Ron Harper/249 8.00 20.00
120 Anfernee Hardaway/249 10.00 25.00
121 Ty Lawson/249 2.00 5.00
122 Jeff Pendergraph/249 1.25 3.00
123 DeJuan Blair/249 1.50 4.00
124 Jermaine Taylor/249 1.25 3.00
125 Rodrigue Beaubois/249 1.25 3.00
126 Darren Collison/249 2.00 5.00
127 Eric Maynor/249 1.25 3.00
128 Earl Clark/249 1.50 4.00
129 Stephen Curry/249 40.00 100.00
130 DeMarre Carroll/249 1.50 4.00
131 Hasheem Thabeet/249 1.25 3.00
132 Jonny Flynn/249 1.25 3.00
133 Wayne Ellington/249 2.00 5.00
134 B.J. Mullens/249 1.25 3.00
135 James Harden/249 10.00 25.00
136 Blake Griffin/249 8.00 20.00
137 Omri Casspi/249 1.50 4.00
138 Tyreke Evans/249 1.50 4.00
139 Jeff Teague/249 2.00 5.00
140 James Johnson/249 1.50 4.00
141 Taj Gibson/249 2.00 5.00
142 Jrue Holiday/249 2.50 6.00
143 Austin Daye/249 1.25 3.00
144 Tyler Hansbrough/249 1.50 4.00
145 Gerald Henderson/249 1.50 4.00
146 Brandon Jennings/249 2.00 5.00
147 Terrence Williams/249 1.25 3.00
148 DeMar DeRozan/249 5.00 12.00
149 Jordan Hill/249 1.50 4.00
150 Toney Douglas/249 1.25 3.00

2009-10 Studio Signatures

STATED PRINT RUN 5 TO 199 SER.#'d SETS
SOME UNPRICED DUE TO SCARCITY
3 Kobe Bryant/49 75.00 150.00
13 Tony Parker/25 10.00 25.00
15 Shane Battier/50 5.00 12.00
41 Kevin Love/25 15.00 40.00
45 Russell Westbrook/99 50.00 120.00
47 Chris Kaman/99 5.00 12.00
48 Eric Gordon/99 6.00 15.00
57 Rajon Rondo/50 15.00 40.00
58 Ray Allen/25 25.00 60.00
67 Jermaine O'Neal/25 6.00 15.00
68 Michael Beasley/50 6.00 15.00
78 Danny Granger/25 6.00 15.00
80 T.J. Ford/99 5.00 10.00
90 Devin Harris/49 5.00 12.00
93 Chris Bosh/25 20.00 40.00
96 David Lee/25 8.00 20.00
101 Wes Unseld/50 8.00 20.00
103 Bailey Howell/49 10.00 25.00
110 Manute Bol/50 20.00 40.00
116 Rick Barry/25 10.00 25.00
119 Dennis Rodman/25 20.00 50.00
121 Ty Lawson/199 5.00 12.00
122 Jeff Pendergraph/199 3.00 8.00
123 DeJuan Blair/199 4.00 10.00
124 Jermaine Taylor/199 3.00 8.00
125 Rodrigue Beaubois/199 3.00 8.00
126 Darren Collison/199 5.00 12.00
127 Eric Maynor/199 3.00 8.00
128 Earl Clark/199 4.00 10.00
129 Stephen Curry/199 600.00 800.00
130 DeMarre Carroll/199 4.00 10.00
131 Hasheem Thabeet/199 3.00 8.00
132 Jonny Flynn/199 3.00 8.00
133 Wayne Ellington/199 5.00 12.00
134 B.J. Mullens/199 3.00 8.00
135 James Harden/199 50.00 120.00
136 Blake Griffin/199 30.00 80.00
137 Omri Casspi/199 4.00 10.00
138 Tyreke Evans/199 4.00 10.00
139 Jeff Teague/199 5.00 12.00
140 James Johnson/199 4.00 10.00
141 Taj Gibson/199 5.00 12.00
142 Jrue Holiday/199 12.00 30.00
143 Austin Daye/199 3.00 8.00
144 Tyler Hansbrough/199 4.00 10.00
145 Gerald Henderson/199 4.00 10.00
146 Brandon Jennings/199 5.00 12.00
147 Terrence Williams/199 3.00 8.00
149 Jordan Hill/199 4.00 10.00
150 Toney Douglas/199 3.00 8.00

2009-10 Studio Skylines

COMPLETE SET (30) 25.00 50.00
RANDOM INSERTS IN PACKS
*PROOFS: .6X TO 1.5X BASE HI
PROOF PRINT RUN 199 SER.#'d SETS
1 Mike Bibby .75 2.00
2 Rajon Rondo 1.00 2.50
3 Gerald Henderson .75 2.00
4 Derrick Rose 1.50 4.00
5 LeBron James 4.00 10.00
6 Jason Terry .75 2.00
7 Chauncey Billups 1.00 2.50
8 Ben Gordon .75 2.00
9 Stephen Curry 12.00 30.00
10 Tracy McGrady 1.00 2.50
11 Danny Granger .75 2.00
12 Blake Griffin 4.00 10.00
13 Kobe Bryant 4.00 10.00
14 O.J. Mayo .60 1.50
15 Dwyane Wade 1.50 4.00
16 Andrew Bogut .75 2.00
17 Kevin Love 1.00 2.50
18 Devin Harris .60 1.50
19 Chris Paul 1.25 3.00
20 Nate Robinson .60 1.50
21 Russell Westbrook 2.50 6.00
22 Dwight Howard .75 2.00
23 Elton Brand 1.00 2.50
24 Steve Nash 1.00 2.50
25 Brandon Roy 1.00 2.50
26 Kevin Martin .75 2.00
27 Tim Duncan 1.50 4.00
28 Chris Bosh 1.00 2.50
29 Deron Williams .75 2.00
30 Gilbert Arenas .75 2.00

2009-10 Studio Skylines Materials

STATED PRINT RUN 50 TO 249 SER.#'d SETS
1 Mike Bibby/50 2.50 6.00
3 Gerald Henderson/249 2.00 5.00
4 Derrick Rose/50 5.00 12.00
5 LeBron James/249 8.00 20.00
6 Jason Terry/249 2.50 6.00
7 Chauncey Billups/249 3.00 8.00
8 Ben Gordon/199 2.50 6.00
9 Stephen Curry/249 40.00 100.00
10 Tracy McGrady/249 3.00 8.00
12 Blake Griffin/249 10.00 25.00
13 Kobe Bryant/249 8.00 20.00
15 Dwyane Wade/249 5.00 12.00
17 Kevin Love/249 3.00 8.00
19 Chris Paul/249 4.00 10.00
20 Nate Robinson/249 2.00 5.00
22 Dwight Howard/249 2.50 6.00
23 Elton Brand/249 3.00 8.00
25 Brandon Roy/249 3.00 8.00
27 Tim Duncan/249 5.00 12.00
28 Chris Bosh/249 3.00 8.00
29 Deron Williams/249 2.50 6.00
30 Gilbert Arenas/249 2.50 6.00

2009-10 Studio Skylines Signatures

STATED PRINT RUN 49 TO 99 SER.#'d SETS
ASTERISK CARDS FROM PANINI UPDATE
1 Mike Bibby/99 6.00 15.00
2 Rajon Rondo/99* 15.00 40.00
3 Gerald Henderson/99 6.00 15.00
7 Chauncey Billups/99 8.00 20.00
9 Stephen Curry/99 800.00 1200.00
10 Tracy McGrady/49 10.00 25.00
11 Danny Granger/99* 6.00 15.00
12 Blake Griffin/99 50.00 120.00
13 Kobe Bryant/99 100.00 200.00
17 Kevin Love/99 15.00 40.00
18 Devin Harris/99 6.00 15.00
21 Russell Westbrook/99 60.00 150.00
28 Chris Bosh/99 10.00 25.00
29 Deron Williams/92 10.00 25.00

2009-10 Studio Team Studio

COMPLETE SET (15) 10.00 25.00
RANDOM INSERTS IN PACKS
*PROOFS: .75X TO 2X BASE HI
PROOF PRINT RUN 199 SER.#'d SETS
1 K.Bryant/P.Gasol 3.00 8.00
2 D.Howard/R.Lewis .60 1.50
3 T.Duncan/T.Parker 1.25 3.00
4 K.Garnett/R.Allen 1.25 3.00
5 D.Nowitzki/J.Howard 1.00 2.50
6 L.James/S.O'Neal 3.00 8.00
7 D.Wade/D.Cook 1.25 3.00
8 C.Anthony/C.Billups 1.00 2.50
9 C.Boozer/A.Kirilenko .60 1.50
10 A.Harrington/D.Lee .60 1.50
11 C.Bosh/A.Bargnani .75 2.00
12 B.Laimbeer/J.Dumars .75 2.00
13 L.Bird/K.McHale 2.00 5.00
14 M.Johnson/K.Abdul-Jabbar 2.00 5.00
15 G.McGinnis/M.Malone .75 2.00

2009-10 Studio Team Studio Materials

STATED PRINT RUN 25 TO 249 SER.#'d SETS
1 K.Bryant/P.Gasol/249 10.00 25.00
2 D.Howard/R.Lewis/249 4.00 10.00
3 T.Duncan/T.Parker/249 6.00 15.00
4 K.Garnett/R.Allen/249 6.00 15.00
5 D.Nowitzki/J.Howard/249 6.00 15.00
6 L.James/S.O'Neal/249 12.50 30.00
7 D.Wade/D.Cook/249 4.00 10.00
8 C.Anthony/C.Billups/249 5.00 12.00
9 C.Boozer/A.Kirilenko/249 4.00 10.00
10 A.Harrington/D.Lee/25 6.00 15.00
11 C.Bosh/A.Bargnani/249 4.00 10.00
13 L.Bird/K.McHale/249 10.00 25.00
14 Magic/Abdul-Jabbar/249 10.00 25.00
15 G.McGinnis/M.Malone/249 4.00 10.00

2016-17 Studio

1 Stephen Curry 2.00 5.00
2 Blake Griffin .50 1.25
3 Kyrie Irving 1.00 2.50
4 John Wall .60 1.50
5 Kevin Durant 1.25 3.00
6 Anthony Davis 1.00 2.50
7 Russell Westbrook 1.25 3.00
8 James Harden .75 2.00
9 Dirk Nowitzki .60 1.50
10 Carmelo Anthony .60 1.50
11 Dwyane Wade .75 2.00
12 Giannis Antetokounmpo 1.00 2.50
13 Chris Paul .60 1.50
14 Mike Conley .40 1.00
15 Kawhi Leonard .75 2.00
16 Jordan Clarkson .40 1.00
17 Aaron Gordon .40 1.00
18 LeBron James 2.00 5.00
19 Jahlil Okafor .40 1.00
20 Devin Booker .75 2.00
21 Emmanuel Mudiay .40 1.00
22 LaMarcus Aldridge .50 1.25
23 Paul George .60 1.50
24 DeMar DeRozan .50 1.25
25 Kemba Walker .50 1.25
26 Kyle Lowry .40 1.00
27 Eric Gordon .40 1.00
28 Pau Gasol .50 1.25
29 Jimmy Butler .50 1.25
30 Karl-Anthony Towns 1.25 3.00
31 Gordon Hayward .50 1.25
32 Dwight Howard .40 1.00
33 DeMarcus Cousins .50 1.25
34 Justise Winslow .40 1.00
35 Harrison Barnes .40 1.00
36 Damian Lillard 1.00 2.50
37 Klay Thompson .60 1.50
38 Tyson Chandler .40 1.00
39 Isaiah Thomas .50 1.25
40 Jabari Parker .60 1.50
41 Joel Embiid .75 2.00
42 Andre Drummond .50 1.25
43 Elfrid Payton .40 1.00
44 Zach LaVine .50 1.25
45 Kenneth Faried .40 1.00
46 Steven Adams .40 1.00
47 Derrick Rose .60 1.50
48 DeAndre Jordan .50 1.25
49 Andrew Wiggins .75 2.00
50 Marc Gasol .50 1.25
51 Magic Johnson 1.25 3.00
52 Larry Bird 1.25 3.00

Card	Low	High
53 Julius Erving	.75	2.00
54 Kareem Abdul-Jabbar	.75	2.00
55 Pete Maravich	.75	2.00
56 Scottie Pippen	1.00	2.50
57 Clyde Drexler	.60	1.50
58 David Robinson	.75	2.00
59 John Stockton	.75	2.00
60 Wilt Chamberlain	1.00	2.50
61 Patrick Ewing	.60	1.50
62 George Gervin	.50	1.25
63 Drazen Petrovic	.50	1.25
64 Jerry West	.60	1.50
65 Jason Kidd	.50	1.25
66 Karl Malone	.60	1.50
67 Bill Russell	.75	2.00
68 Oscar Robertson	.60	1.50
69 Isiah Thomas	.50	1.25
70 Hakeem Olajuwon	.60	1.50
71 John Havlicek	.60	1.50
72 Tim Duncan	.75	2.00
73 Shaquille O'Neal	1.25	3.00
74 Allen Iverson	.60	1.50
75 Kobe Bryant	2.00	5.00
76 Brandon Ingram RC	3.00	8.00
77 Malcolm Brogdon RC	1.25	3.00
78 Domantas Sabonis RC	.75	2.00
79 Denzel Valentine RC	.60	1.50
80 Buddy Hield RC	1.25	3.00
81 Juan Hernangomez RC	.60	1.50
82 Wade Baldwin IV RC	.50	1.25
83 Malik Beasley RC	.50	1.25
84 Ben Simmons RC	5.00	12.00
85 Henry Ellenson RC	.60	1.50
86 Jamal Murray RC	1.50	4.00
87 T. Luwawu-Cabarrot RC	1.00	2.50
88 Jaylen Brown RC	2.00	5.00
89 Patrick McCaw RC	1.00	2.50
90 Taurean Prince RC	.75	2.00
91 Marquese Chriss RC	1.25	3.00
92 DeAndre' Bembry RC	.50	1.25
93 Malachi Richardson RC	.60	1.50
94 Dragan Bender RC	.60	1.50
95 Isaiah Whitehead RC	.50	1.25
96 Dejounte Murray RC	1.00	2.50
97 Jakob Poeltl RC	.60	1.50
98 Kris Dunn RC	1.50	4.00
99 Pascal Siakam RC	.50	1.25
100 Thon Maker RC	1.50	4.00
101 Stephen Curry SE	2.50	6.00
102 Giannis Antetokounmpo SE	1.25	3.00
103 James Harden SE	1.00	2.50
104 Mike Conley SE	.50	1.25
105 Russell Westbrook SE	1.50	4.00
106 Brook Lopez SE	.50	1.25
107 Damian Lillard SE	1.25	3.00
108 Jahlil Okafor SE	.50	1.25
109 Stanley Johnson SE	.40	1.00
110 Pau Gasol SE	.60	1.50
111 Goran Dragic SE	.50	1.25
112 Thaddeus Young SE	.40	1.00
113 Rudy Gay SE	.60	1.50
114 Dwight Howard SE	.50	1.25
115 Elfrid Payton SE	.50	1.25
116 Devin Booker SE	1.00	2.50
117 Michael Kidd-Gilchrist SE	.50	1.25
118 Nerlens Noel SE	.50	1.25
119 Chris Paul SE	.75	2.00
120 Tony Parker SE	.60	1.50
121 Dwyane Wade SE	1.00	2.50
122 Julius Randle SE	.60	1.50
123 Jonas Valanciunas SE	.50	1.25
124 Blake Griffin SE	.60	1.50
125 Avery Bradley SE	.50	1.25
126 Victor Oladipo SE	.50	1.25
127 Dirk Nowitzki SE	.75	2.00
128 Rodney Hood SE	.50	1.25
129 Carmelo Anthony SE	.75	2.00
130 Kenneth Faried SE	.50	1.25
131 Eric Gordon SE	.50	1.25
132 Zach Randolph SE	.50	1.25
133 Dennis Schroder SE	.50	1.25
134 Gordon Hayward SE	.60	1.50
135 Joel Embiid SE	1.00	2.50
136 LeBron James SE	2.50	6.00
137 Kyle Korver SE	.50	1.25
138 Harrison Barnes SE	.50	1.25
139 Derrick Rose SE	.75	2.00
140 Dion Waiters SE	.50	1.25
141 Jeremy Lin SE	.60	1.50
142 Willie Cauley-Stein SE	.50	1.25
143 Andre Drummond SE	.60	1.50
144 C.J. McCollum SE	.50	1.25
145 Danilo Gallinari SE	.50	1.25
146 Al Horford SE	.50	1.25
147 J.J. Redick SE	.60	1.50
148 Paul Millsap SE	.60	1.50
149 Cody Zeller SE	.40	1.00
150 Kevin Durant SE	1.50	4.00
151 George Hill SE	.50	1.25
152 Greg Monroe SE	.50	1.25
153 Wesley Matthews SE	.40	1.00
154 Paul George SE	.75	2.00
155 Draymond Green SE	.75	2.00
156 Kemba Walker SE	.60	1.50
157 DeMar DeRozan SE	.60	1.50
158 Anthony Davis SE	1.25	3.00
159 Patrick Beverley SE	.40	1.00
160 Kawhi Leonard SE	1.00	2.50
161 Jimmy Butler SE	.60	1.50
162 DeMarcus Cousins SE	.60	1.50
163 Steven Adams SE	.50	1.25
164 Kevin Love SE	.60	1.50
165 LaMarcus Aldridge SE	.60	1.50
166 Brandon Knight SE	.50	1.25
167 Isaiah Thomas SE	.60	1.50
168 Aaron Gordon SE	.50	1.25
169 Kristaps Porzingis SE	1.25	3.00
170 Kyrie Irving SE	1.25	3.00
171 E'Twaun Moore SE	.40	1.00
172 Myles Turner SE	.50	1.25
173 Marcus Smart SE	.50	1.25
174 Nick Young SE	.50	1.25
175 Andre Iguodala SE	.50	1.25
176 Brandon Ingram SE	4.00	10.00
177 Malcolm Brogdon SE	1.50	4.00
178 Domantas Sabonis SE	1.00	2.50
179 Denzel Valentine SE	.75	2.00
180 Buddy Hield SE	1.50	4.00
181 Juan Hernangomez SE	.75	2.00
182 Wade Baldwin IV SE	.60	1.50
183 Malik Beasley SE	.60	1.50
184 Ben Simmons SE	6.00	15.00
185 Henry Ellenson SE	.75	2.00
186 Jamal Murray SE	2.00	5.00
187 T. Luwawu-Cabarrot SE	1.25	3.00
188 Jaylen Brown SE	2.50	6.00
189 Patrick McCaw SE	1.25	3.00
190 Taurean Prince SE	1.00	2.50
191 Marquese Chriss SE	1.50	4.00
192 DeAndre' Bembry SE	.60	1.50
193 Malachi Richardson SE	.75	2.00
194 Dragan Bender SE	.75	2.00
195 Isaiah Whitehead SE	.60	1.50
196 Dejounte Murray SE	1.25	3.00
197 Jakob Poeltl SE	.75	2.00
198 Kris Dunn SE	2.00	5.00
199 Pascal Siakam SE	.60	1.50
200 Thon Maker SE	2.00	5.00
201 Stephen Curry SK	20.00	50.00
202 Blake Griffin SK	5.00	12.00
203 Kyrie Irving SK	10.00	25.00
204 John Wall SK	6.00	15.00
205 Kevin Durant SK	12.00	30.00
206 Anthony Davis SK	10.00	25.00
207 Russell Westbrook SK	12.00	30.00
208 James Harden SK	8.00	20.00
209 Dirk Nowitzki SK	6.00	15.00
210 Carmelo Anthony SK	6.00	15.00
211 Dwyane Wade SK	8.00	20.00
212 G. Antetokounmpo SK	10.00	25.00
213 Chris Paul SK	6.00	15.00
214 Mike Conley SK	4.00	10.00
215 Kawhi Leonard SK	8.00	20.00
216 Jordan Clarkson SK	4.00	10.00
217 Aaron Gordon SK	4.00	10.00
218 LeBron James SK	20.00	50.00
219 Jahlil Okafor SK	4.00	10.00
220 Devin Booker SK	8.00	20.00
221 Emmanuel Mudiay SK	4.00	10.00
222 LaMarcus Aldridge SK	5.00	12.00
223 Paul George SK	6.00	15.00
224 DeMar DeRozan SK	5.00	12.00
225 Kemba Walker SK	5.00	12.00
226 Kyle Lowry SK	4.00	10.00
227 Eric Gordon SK	4.00	10.00
228 Pau Gasol SK	5.00	12.00
229 Jimmy Butler SK	5.00	12.00
230 Karl-Anthony Towns SK	12.00	30.00
231 Gordon Hayward SK	5.00	12.00
232 Dwight Howard SK	4.00	10.00
233 DeMarcus Cousins SK	5.00	12.00
234 Justise Winslow SK	4.00	10.00
235 Harrison Barnes SK	4.00	10.00
236 Damian Lillard SK	10.00	25.00
237 Klay Thompson SK	6.00	15.00
238 Tyson Chandler SK	4.00	10.00
239 Isaiah Thomas SK	5.00	12.00
240 Jabari Parker SK	6.00	15.00
241 Joel Embiid SK	8.00	20.00
242 Andre Drummond SK	5.00	12.00
243 Elfrid Payton SK	4.00	10.00
244 Zach LaVine SK	5.00	12.00
245 Kenneth Faried SK	4.00	10.00
246 Steven Adams SK	4.00	10.00
247 Derrick Rose SK	6.00	15.00
248 DeAndre Jordan SK	5.00	12.00
249 Andrew Wiggins SK	8.00	20.00
250 Marc Gasol SK	5.00	12.00
251 Magic Johnson SK	12.00	30.00
252 Larry Bird SK	12.00	30.00
253 Julius Erving SK	8.00	20.00
254 Kareem Abdul-Jabbar SK	8.00	20.00
255 Pete Maravich SK	8.00	20.00
256 Scottie Pippen SK	10.00	25.00
257 Clyde Drexler SK	6.00	15.00
258 David Robinson SK	8.00	20.00
259 John Stockton SK	8.00	20.00
260 Wilt Chamberlain SK	10.00	25.00
261 Patrick Ewing SK	6.00	15.00
262 George Gervin SK	5.00	12.00
263 Drazen Petrovic SK	5.00	12.00
264 Jerry West SK	6.00	15.00
265 Jason Kidd SK	5.00	12.00
266 Karl Malone SK	6.00	15.00
267 Bill Russell SK	8.00	20.00
268 Oscar Robertson SK	6.00	15.00
269 Isiah Thomas SK	5.00	12.00
270 Hakeem Olajuwon SK	6.00	15.00
271 John Havlicek SK	6.00	15.00
272 Tim Duncan SK	8.00	20.00
273 Shaquille O'Neal SK	12.00	30.00
274 Allen Iverson SK	8.00	20.00
275 Kobe Bryant SK	20.00	50.00
276 Brandon Ingram SK	40.00	100.00
277 Malcolm Brogdon SK	8.00	20.00
278 Domantas Sabonis SK	5.00	12.00
279 Denzel Valentine SK	4.00	10.00
280 Buddy Hield SK	8.00	20.00
281 Juan Hernangomez SK	4.00	10.00
282 Wade Baldwin IV SK	3.00	8.00
283 Malik Beasley SK	3.00	8.00
284 Ben Simmons SK	125.00	300.00
285 Henry Ellenson SK	4.00	10.00
286 Jamal Murray SK	10.00	25.00
287 T. Luwawu-Cabarrot SK	6.00	15.00
288 Jaylen Brown SK	12.00	30.00
289 Patrick McCaw SK	6.00	15.00
290 Taurean Prince SK	5.00	12.00
291 Marquese Chriss SK	8.00	20.00
292 DeAndre' Bembry SK	3.00	8.00
293 Malachi Richardson SK	4.00	10.00
294 Dragan Bender SK	4.00	10.00
295 Isaiah Whitehead SK	3.00	8.00
296 Dejounte Murray SK	6.00	15.00
297 Jakob Poeltl SK	4.00	10.00
298 Kris Dunn SK	10.00	25.00
299 Pascal Siakam SK	3.00	8.00
300 Thon Maker SK	10.00	25.00

2016-17 Studio Glossy

*GLOSSY 101-175: .75X TO 2X BASIC
*GLOSSY 176-200: .75X TO 2X BASIC
RANDOM INSERTS IN PACKS

Card	Low	High
176 Brandon Ingram SE	12.00	30.00
184 Ben Simmons SE	20.00	50.00

2016-17 Studio Breakout Signatures

RANDOM INSERTS IN PACKS
PRINT RUNS B/WN 49-299 COPIES PER
*MAGENTA/30: .6X TO 1.5X BASIC

Card	Low	High
1 Buddy Hield/299	12.00	30.00
2 Denzel Valentine/299	4.00	10.00
3 Kyle Wiltjer/299	3.00	8.00
4 Marshall Plumlee/299	3.00	8.00
5 Juan Hernangomez/299	4.00	10.00
6 Jake Layman/299	4.00	10.00
7 Malcolm Brogdon/299	12.00	30.00
8 Willy Hernangomez/299	4.00	10.00
9 Domantas Sabonis/299	5.00	12.00
10 Jaylen Brown/299	12.00	30.00
11 Wade Baldwin IV/299		
12 Marquese Chriss/199	6.00	15.00
13 Kris Dunn/199	6.00	15.00
14 Kay Felder/199		
15 Pascal Siakam/299		
16 Dario Saric/299	10.00	25.00
17 Brandon Ingram/99	30.00	80.00
18 Malcolm Delaney/299		
21 James Ennis/299	3.00	8.00
22 Trey Lyles/299	4.00	10.00
23 C.J. McCollum/299	5.00	12.00
24 Larry Nance Jr./299	4.00	10.00
25 Sean Kilpatrick/299	3.00	8.00
26 Justin Anderson/299		
27 Rodney McGruder/299	4.00	10.00
28 Josh Richardson/299	3.00	8.00
29 Norman Powell/299	3.00	8.00
30 Mario Hezonja/299	3.00	8.00
31 Brandon Knight/199	4.00	10.00
32 Maurice Harkless/299	3.00	8.00
33 Karl-Anthony Towns/49	25.00	60.00
34 Stephen Curry/49	60.00	150.00
35 Clint Capela/249	3.00	8.00
36 Michael Carter-Williams/199	3.00	8.00
37 Zach LaVine/99	10.00	25.00
38 Kyrie Irving/99	25.00	60.00
39 Anthony Davis/49	15.00	40.00
40 Andrew Wiggins/99	15.00	40.00

2016-17 Studio Celebrated Signatures

RANDOM INSERTS IN PACKS
STATED PRINT RUN 49 SER.#'d SETS
*MAGENTA/30: .6X TO 1.5X BASIC

Card	Low	High
1 Magic Johnson	25.00	60.00
2 Kyrie Irving	25.00	60.00
3 Dennis Rodman		
5 Oscar Robertson		
6 Patrick Ewing	30.00	80.00
7 Kareem Abdul-Jabbar	15.00	40.00
8 Shaquille O'Neal		
9 Scottie Pippen	30.00	80.00
10 Kobe Bryant	50.00	120.00
11 Nate Thurmond	8.00	20.00
12 Larry Bird	25.00	60.00
13 Pat Riley	20.00	50.00
14 Anthony Davis		
15 Stephen Curry	75.00	200.00

2016-17 Studio Defying Gravity Die Cut

RANDOM INSERTS IN PACKS

Card	Low	High
1 Blake Griffin	2.50	6.00
2 Zach LaVine	2.50	6.00
3 LeBron James	10.00	25.00
4 Kevin Durant	6.00	15.00
5 Aaron Gordon	2.00	5.00
6 Giannis Antetokounmpo	5.00	12.00
7 Russell Westbrook	6.00	15.00
8 Andrew Wiggins	4.00	10.00
9 John Wall	3.00	8.00
10 Jaylen Brown	5.00	12.00
11 Tracy McGrady	2.50	6.00
12 Clyde Drexler	3.00	8.00
13 Julius Erving	4.00	10.00
14 Dominique Wilkins	3.00	8.00
15 Shawn Kemp	4.00	10.00
16 Kobe Bryant	8.00	20.00

2016-17 Studio Driven

RANDOM INSERTS IN PACKS

Card	Low	High
1 Russell Westbrook	2.00	5.00
2 Isaiah Thomas	.75	2.00
3 Paul George	1.00	2.50
4 Mike Conley	.60	1.50
5 Giannis Antetokounmpo	1.50	4.00
6 Kristaps Porzingis	1.50	4.00
7 Elfrid Payton	.60	1.50
8 Rudy Gay	.75	2.00
9 Kawhi Leonard	1.25	3.00
10 LeBron James	3.00	8.00
11 James Harden	1.25	3.00
12 Kemba Walker	.75	2.00
13 Stephen Curry	3.00	8.00
14 D'Angelo Russell		
15 Josh Richardson	.50	1.25
16 Karl-Anthony Towns	2.00	5.00
17 Devin Booker	1.25	3.00
18 C.J. McCollum	.60	1.50
19 Kyle Lowry	.60	1.50
20 John Wall	1.00	2.50
21 Dennis Schroder	.60	1.50
22 Dwyane Wade	1.25	3.00
23 Kevin Durant	2.00	5.00
24 Chris Paul	1.00	2.50
25 Jabari Parker	1.00	2.50
26 Andrew Wiggins	1.25	3.00
27 Dario Saric	1.50	4.00
28 Damian Lillard	1.50	4.00
29 Gordon Hayward	.75	2.00
30 Bradley Beal	.75	2.00

2016-17 Studio First Impact Memorabilia

RANDOM INSERTS IN PACKS
*MAGENTA/23-30: 1X TO 2.5X BASIC

Card	Low	High
1 Brandon Ingram	8.00	20.00
2 Jaylen Brown	5.00	12.00
3 Dragan Bender	1.50	4.00
4 Kris Dunn	4.00	10.00
5 Buddy Hield	3.00	8.00
6 Jamal Murray	4.00	10.00
7 Marquese Chriss	3.00	8.00
8 Jakob Poeltl	1.50	4.00
9 Thon Maker	4.00	10.00
10 Domantas Sabonis	2.00	5.00
11 Taurean Prince	2.00	5.00
12 Denzel Valentine	1.50	4.00
13 Juan Hernangomez	1.50	4.00
14 Georgios Papagiannis	1.25	3.00
15 Wade Baldwin IV	1.25	3.00
16 Henry Ellenson	1.50	4.00
17 Malik Beasley	1.25	3.00
18 Caris LeVert	1.50	4.00
19 Malachi Richardson	1.50	4.00
20 Malcolm Brogdon	3.00	8.00
21 Dejounte Murray	2.50	6.00
22 Kay Felder	1.25	3.00
23 Patrick McCaw	2.50	6.00
24 Timothe Luwawu-Cabarrot	2.50	6.00
25 Isaiah Whitehead	1.25	3.00

2016-17 Studio From Downtown

RANDOM INSERTS IN PACKS

Card	Low	High
1 Stephen Curry	250.00	500.00
2 James Harden	75.00	200.00
3 Karl-Anthony Towns	80.00	200.00
4 Yogi Ferrell	30.00	80.00
5 Russell Westbrook	80.00	200.00
6 Damian Lillard	60.00	150.00
7 LeBron James	200.00	400.00
8 Jimmy Butler	50.00	120.00
9 Kristaps Porzingis	60.00	150.00
10 Ben Simmons	250.00	500.00
11 Isaiah Thomas	50.00	120.00
12 Kyrie Irving	125.00	300.00
13 Kevin Durant	200.00	400.00
14 Devin Booker	125.00	300.00
15 Andrew Wiggins	60.00	150.00
16 Dirk Nowitzki	75.00	200.00
17 J.J. Redick	30.00	80.00
18 Kobe Bryant	200.00	400.00
19 Gary Payton	30.00	80.00
20 Allen Iverson	75.00	200.00

2016-17 Studio Gamers Memorabilia

RANDOM INSERTS IN PACKS
*MAGENTA/30: 1X TO 2.5X BASIC

Card	Low	High
1 Steven Adams	1.50	4.00
2 LaMarcus Aldridge	2.00	5.00
3 Justin Anderson	1.50	4.00
4 Harrison Barnes	1.50	4.00
5 Nicolas Batum	1.50	4.00
6 Bradley Beal	2.00	5.00
7 Patrick Beverley	1.25	3.00
8 Devin Booker	3.00	8.00
9 Jordan Clarkson	1.50	4.00
10 Goran Dragic	1.50	4.00
11 Andre Drummond	2.00	5.00
12 Joel Embiid	3.00	8.00
13 Kenneth Faried	1.50	4.00
14 Marc Gasol	2.00	5.00
15 Pau Gasol	2.00	5.00
16 Rudy Gay	2.00	5.00
17 Taj Gibson	1.50	4.00
18 Rudy Gobert	2.00	5.00
19 Aaron Gordon	1.50	4.00
20 Draymond Green	2.50	6.00
21 Gordon Hayward	2.00	5.00
22 Al Horford	1.50	4.00
23 Dwight Howard	1.50	4.00
24 Reggie Jackson	1.50	4.00
25 DeAndre Jordan	2.00	5.00
26 Enes Kanter	1.25	3.00
27 Zach LaVine	2.00	5.00
28 Brook Lopez	1.50	4.00
29 Kevin Love	2.00	5.00
30 Wesley Matthews	1.25	3.00
31 C.J. McCollum	1.50	4.00
32 Emmanuel Mudiay	1.50	4.00
33 Joakim Noah	1.50	4.00
34 Victor Oladipo	1.50	4.00
35 Jabari Parker	2.50	6.00
36 Kristaps Porzingis	4.00	10.00
37 Julius Randle	2.00	5.00
38 J.J. Redick	2.00	5.00
39 D'Angelo Russell	2.50	6.00
40 Dennis Schroder	1.50	4.00
41 Marcus Smart	1.50	4.00
42 Isaiah Thomas	2.00	5.00
43 Tristan Thompson	1.50	4.00
44 Myles Turner	1.50	4.00
45 Hassan Whiteside	1.50	4.00
46 Andrew Wiggins	3.00	8.00

2016-17 Studio Rising to the Occasion

RANDOM INSERTS IN PACKS

Card	Low	High
1 James Harden	1.25	3.00
2 Russell Westbrook	2.00	5.00
3 Kyrie Irving	1.50	4.00
4 Stephen Curry	3.00	8.00
5 DeMarcus Cousins	.75	2.00
6 Damian Lillard	1.50	4.00
7 Kenneth Faried	.60	1.50
8 Karl-Anthony Towns	2.00	5.00
9 Jimmy Butler	.75	2.00
10 Kentavious Caldwell-Pope	.60	1.50
11 Dirk Nowitzki	1.00	2.50
12 Kawhi Leonard	1.25	3.00
13 LeBron James	3.00	8.00
14 John Wall	1.00	2.50
15 Giannis Antetokounmpo	1.50	4.00
16 Aaron Gordon	.60	1.50
17 Dennis Schroder	.60	1.50
18 Jordan Clarkson	.60	1.50
19 Isaiah Thomas	.75	2.00
20 Carmelo Anthony	1.00	2.50
21 Blake Griffin	.75	2.00
22 Devin Booker	1.25	3.00
23 DeMar DeRozan	.75	2.00
24 Paul George	1.00	2.50
25 George Hill	.60	1.50
26 Clyde Drexler	1.00	2.50
27 Tim Duncan	1.25	3.00
28 Tracy McGrady	.75	2.00
29 Chauncey Billups	.75	2.00
30 Robert Horry	.60	1.50
31 Larry Bird	2.00	5.00
32 Shaquille O'Neal	2.00	5.00
33 John Havlicek	1.00	2.50
34 Steve Nash	.75	2.00
35 Kobe Bryant	3.00	8.00

2016-17 Studio Rock Solid Die Cut

RANDOM INSERTS IN PACKS

Card	Low	High
1 Ben Wallace	5.00	12.00
2 Jae Crowder	5.00	12.00
3 Jimmy Butler	8.00	20.00
4 James Harden	10.00	25.00
5 Russell Westbrook	12.00	30.00
6 LeBron James	30.00	80.00
7 Shaquille O'Neal	10.00	25.00
8 Kyle Lowry	5.00	12.00
9 Kobe Bryant	25.00	60.00
10 Draymond Green	10.00	25.00
11 Joel Embiid	8.00	20.00
12 Eric Bledsoe	5.00	12.00
13 Karl-Anthony Towns	12.00	30.00
14 DeAndre Jordan	6.00	15.00

2016-17 Studio Signatures

RANDOM INSERTS IN PACKS
PRINT RUNS B/WN 49-299 COPIES PER
*MAGENTA/30: .6X TO 1.5X BASIC

Card	Low	High
1 Trey Lyles/299	4.00	10.00
2 C.J. McCollum/299	5.00	12.00
3 Jason Terry/299	4.00	10.00
4 Justin Anderson/299		
5 Josh Richardson/299	3.00	8.00
6 Mario Hezonja/299	3.00	8.00
7 Brandon Knight/299	4.00	10.00
8 Maurice Harkless/299	3.00	8.00
9 Jrue Holiday/299		
10 Karl-Anthony Towns/60	25.00	60.00
11 Al Horford/249	8.00	20.00
12 Khris Middleton/199		
13 Kobe Bryant/49	40.00	100.00
14 Evan Turner/165	3.00	8.00
15 J.J. Barea/125	15.00	40.00
16 Luol Deng/125	4.00	10.00
17 Andre Drummond/249	5.00	12.00
18 Alec Burks/299	3.00	8.00
20 Marcin Gortat/299	4.00	10.00
21 Cody Zeller/299	3.00	8.00
22 Devin Harris/299	3.00	8.00
23 Taurean Prince/299	5.00	12.00
24 Buddy Hield/299	12.00	30.00
25 Denzel Valentine/299	4.00	10.00
26 Joel Bolomboy/299	3.00	8.00
27 Diamond Stone/299	3.00	8.00
28 Deyonta Davis/299	3.00	8.00
29 DeAndre' Bembry/299		
30 Demetrius Jackson/299		
32 Cheick Diallo/299	3.00	8.00
33 Damian Jones/299	3.00	8.00
34 Brice Johnson/299	3.00	8.00
35 Ivica Zubac/299	5.00	12.00
36 Jaylen Brown/99	12.00	30.00
37 Wade Baldwin IV/299		
38 Marquese Chriss/249	6.00	15.00
39 Kris Dunn/175	12.00	30.00
40 Kristaps Porzingis/199	15.00	40.00
41 Larry Nance Jr./299	4.00	10.00
42 Brandon Ingram/99	30.00	80.00
43 Domantas Sabonis/299	5.00	12.00
44 Jamal Murray/199	15.00	40.00
45 Thon Maker/125	15.00	40.00

2016-17 Studio The Influencers Memorabilia

RANDOM INSERTS IN PACKS
*MAGENTA/30: 1X TO 2.5X BASIC

Card	Low	High
1 Stephen Curry	8.00	20.00
2 LeBron James	8.00	20.00
3 Kevin Durant	5.00	12.00
4 James Harden	3.00	8.00
5 Russell Westbrook	5.00	12.00
6 Damian Lillard	4.00	10.00
7 DeMarcus Cousins	2.00	5.00
8 Dwyane Wade	3.00	8.00
9 Carmelo Anthony	2.50	6.00
10 Paul George	2.50	6.00
11 Anthony Davis	4.00	10.00
12 Dirk Nowitzki	2.50	6.00
13 Kyrie Irving	4.00	10.00
14 Karl-Anthony Towns	5.00	12.00
15 Chris Paul	2.50	6.00
16 Andre Drummond	2.00	5.00
17 Jimmy Butler	2.00	5.00
18 Isaiah Thomas	2.00	5.00
19 Kawhi Leonard	3.00	8.00
20 John Wall	2.50	6.00
21 C.J. McCollum	1.50	4.00
22 Giannis Antetokounmpo	4.00	10.00
23 DeMar DeRozan	2.00	5.00
24 Gordon Hayward	2.00	5.00
25 Klay Thompson	2.50	6.00
26 Dwight Howard	1.50	4.00
27 Hassan Whiteside	1.50	4.00
28 Kemba Walker	2.00	5.00
29 Julius Randle	2.00	5.00

2016-17 Studio Top Five

RANDOM INSERTS IN PACKS

Card	Low	High
TOP1 Dario Saric	12.00	30.00
TOP2 Malcolm Brogdon	25.00	60.00
TOP3 Brandon Ingram	40.00	100.00
TOP4 Jaylen Brown	30.00	80.00
TOP5 Jamal Murray	12.00	30.00

1992-93 Suns 25th

Celebrating the 25th anniversary of the Suns' franchise, this 26-card standard-size set was sponsored by The Arizona Republic and The Phoenix Gazette. Each card pictures the Suns' team leader for a particular year, beginning in 1968-69 and ending in 1992-93. The cards feature action player photos. The entire card face, including the picture, exhibits a yellowish beige tint. The player's name appears below the photo, the year above. A purple border design frames the photo, name, and year. The outer edge of the card is enhanced by faded purple shading giving the card an older look. The horizontal backs present biographical information and team statistics for that particular year. There are two back versions with and without sponsor's logo; without seems to be slightly more difficult.

Card	Low	High
COMPLETE SET (26)	6.00	15.00
1 Gail Goodrich	.75	2.00
2 Connie Hawkins	.75	2.00
3 Dick Van Arsdale	.40	1.00
4 Paul Silas	.40	1.00
5 Neil Walk	.20	.50
6 Charlie Scott	.25	.60
7 Curtis Perry	.20	.50
8 Curtis Perry	.20	.50
9 Alvan Adams	.25	.60
10 Garfield Heard	.20	.50
11 Walter Davis	.40	1.00
12 Paul Westphal	.40	1.00
13 Don Buse	.20	.50
14 Truck Robinson	.25	.60
15 Kyle Macy	.40	1.00
16 Dennis Johnson	.50	1.25
17 Maurice Lucas	.40	1.00
18 Larry Nance	.40	1.00
19 Walter Davis	.40	1.00
20 Jeff Hornacek	.40	1.00
21 Eddie Johnson	.30	.75
22 Tyrone Corbin	.20	.50
23 Tom Chambers	.30	.75
24 Kevin Johnson	.40	1.00
25 Dan Majerle	.40	1.00
26 Charles Barkley	1.25	3.00

1976-77 Suns 8 x 10

This 8x10 set was produced for the Phoenix Suns during the 1976-77 season. The set features nice black and white cards of the team's players and coaches.

Card	Low	High
COMPLETE SET (9)	25.00	50.00
1 Dennis Awtrey	1.25	3.00
2 Al Bianchi CO	1.50	4.00
3 Jerry Colangelo GM	1.25	3.00
4 Keith Erickson	1.25	3.00
5 Butch Feher	1.25	3.00
6 Garfield Heard	2.00	5.00
7 Ron Lee	1.25	3.00
8 John McLeod CO	1.25	3.00
9 Curtis Perry	1.25	3.00
10 Joe Proski TR	1.25	3.00
11 Ricky Sobers	1.25	3.00
12 Ira Terrell	1.25	3.00
13 Dick Van Arsdale	2.00	5.00
14 Tom Van Arsdale	1.50	4.00
15 Dick Van Arsdale Tom Van Arsdale	2.00	5.00
16 Paul Westphal	2.50	6.00

1970-71 Suns A1 Premium Beer

These scarce cards are black and white and come with unperforated tabs. The cards were actually the advertising-oriented price tabs for six-packs of A1 Premium Beer. The set features members of the Phoenix Suns. There are three variations primarily based on the price marked on the tab; they are 95 cents (most common), 98 cents (tougher to find), and no price listed. Those not specifically identified in the checklist below are the 95 cents varieties. In terms of size, they resemble bookmarks, each measuring approximately 2 1/4" by 8 3/4". The top of each ad has a circular A-1 Premium Beer emblem. Immediately below the price for the six-pack appears; this can be either 95 or 98 cents, or on some ads no price was given. The black-and-white photo itself measures approximately 2 1/4" by 3 3/8" and features a posed action shot of the player. The backs are blank. The cards are unnumbered and are checklisted below in alphabetical order.

Card	Low	High
COMPLETE SET (13)	900.00	1700.00
1A Mel Counts (95 cents)	50.00	100.00
1B Mel Counts (98 cents)	60.00	120.00
2 Lamar Green	40.00	85.00
3 Clem Haskins	75.00	150.00
4 Connie Hawkins (98 cents)	250.00	450.00
5 Greg Howard	40.00	85.00
6 Paul Silas	125.00	225.00
7 Fred Taylor CO	40.00	85.00
8A Dick Van Arsdale ERR	100.00	175.00
8B Dick Van Arsdale COR	75.00	150.00
9A Neal Walk (95 cents)	50.00	100.00
9B Neal Walk (No price)	60.00	120.00
10 John Wetzel (No price)	50.00	100.00

1968-69 Suns Carnation Milk

This 12-card set of Phoenix Suns was sponsored by Carnation Milk and was issued as panels on the sides of milk cartons. The fronts feature a player pose and brief biographical information near the photo. The bottom of the panels indicate "WIN, 440 Home Game tickets to be given away." The cards measure approximately 3 1/2" by 7 1/2" and are blank backed. The cards are unnumbered and are checklisted below in alphabetical order. Bob Warlick was only with the Phoenix Suns during the last half of the 1968-69 season. The set features the first professional card of Gail Goodrich.

Card	Low	High
COMPLETE SET (12)	800.00	1400.00
1 Jim Fox	60.00	125.00
2 Gail Goodrich	200.00	400.00
3 Gary Gregor	50.00	100.00
4 Neil Johnson	60.00	125.00
5 John Kerr CO	90.00	170.00
6 Dave Lattin	60.00	125.00
7 Stan McKenzie	40.00	80.00
8 McCoy McLemore	40.00	80.00
9 Dick Snyder	40.00	80.00
10 Dick Van Arsdale	75.00	150.00
11 Bob Warlick	60.00	125.00
12 George Wilson	40.00	80.00

1969-70 Suns Carnation Milk

This ten-card set features members of the Phoenix Suns and was produced by Carnation Milk. The cards show white backgrounds with blue and white drawings of the players. Playing tips (in red type) are found at the bottom of each card. Player statistics were on the opposite milk carton panel and hence were not saved in most cases. The cards measure approximately 3 1/2" by 7 1/2". The backs are blank. The cards are unnumbered and are checklisted below in alphabetical order. The set features the first professional card of Connie Hawkins.

Card	Low	High
COMPLETE SET (10)	700.00	1100.00
1 Jerry Chambers	35.00	70.00
2 Jim Fox	35.00	70.00
3 Gail Goodrich	100.00	200.00
4 Connie Hawkins	200.00	400.00
5 Stan McKenzie	35.00	70.00
6 Paul Silas	100.00	200.00
7 Dick Snyder	35.00	70.00
8 Dick Van Arsdale	50.00	100.00
9 Neal Walk	60.00	120.00
10 Gene Williams	35.00	70.00

1970-71 Suns Carnation Milk

This ten-card set features members of the Phoenix Suns and was produced by Carnation Milk. The cards have solid red backgrounds or orange backgrounds if the cards were from diet milk cartons. Apparently the entire set was issued in both color backgrounds. The cards measure approximately 3 1/2" by 7 1/2". The backs are blank. The cards are unnumbered and are checklisted below in alphabetical order.

Card	Low	High
COMPLETE SET (10)	400.00	800.00
1 Mel Counts	30.00	60.00
2 Lamar Green	25.00	50.00
3 Art Harris	25.00	50.00
4 Clem Haskins	40.00	80.00
5 Connie Hawkins	125.00	250.00
6 Gus Johnson	60.00	120.00
7 Otto Moore	25.00	50.00
8 Paul Silas	60.00	120.00
9 Dick Van Arsdale	40.00	80.00
10 Neal Walk	30.00	60.00

1971-72 Suns Carnation Milk

This five-card set features members of the Phoenix Suns and was produced by Carnation Milk and issued as panels on the sides of milk cartons. The cards measure approximately 3 1/2" by 7 1/2". The backs are blank. The cards are unnumbered and are checklisted below in alphabetical order.

Card	Low	High
COMPLETE SET (5)	200.00	400.00
1 Connie Hawkins	100.00	200.00
2 Otto Moore	25.00	50.00
3 Fred Taylor CO	25.00	50.00
4 Neal Walk	30.00	60.00
5 John Wetzel	30.00	60.00

1972-73 Suns Carnation Milk

This 12-card set features members of the Phoenix Suns and was produced by Carnation Milk and issued as panels on the sides of milk cartons. The picture and text are in the team's colors, purple and orange. The cards measure approximately 3 1/2" by 7 1/2". The backs are blank. The cards are unnumbered and are checklisted below in alphabetical order.

Card	Low	High
COMPLETE SET (12)	400.00	800.00
1 Mel Counts	30.00	60.00
2 Lamar Green	25.00	50.00
3 Clem Haskins	40.00	80.00
4 Connie Hawkins	100.00	200.00
5 Gus Johnson	50.00	100.00
6 Dennis Layton	30.00	60.00
7 Otto Moore	25.00	50.00
8 Fred Taylor CO	25.00	50.00
9 Dick Van Arsdale	40.00	80.00
10 Bill VanBredaKolff CO	25.00	50.00
11 Neal Walk	30.00	60.00
12 John Wetzel	30.00	60.00

1987-88 Suns Circle K

This 15-card set was sponsored by Circle K stores. The cards were issued in three strips of five player cards each, plus a coupon. After perforation, the cards measure the standard size. The front features a posed color player photo, with white and purple borders on white card stock. Player information is given below the picture, and team and sponsor logos in the lower corners round out the card face. In a horizontal format the back has biographical and statistical information. The cards are unnumbered and are checklist below in alphabetical order. The set features the first professional cards of Jeff Hornacek and Armon Gilliam.

Card	Low	High
COMPLETE SET (15)	15.00	40.00
1 Alvan Adams	1.25	3.00
2 Herb Brown ACO	.75	2.00
3 Jeff Cook	.75	2.00
4 Winston Crite	.60	1.50
5 Walter Davis	1.50	4.00
6 James Edwards	1.00	2.50
7 Armon Gilliam	2.50	6.00
8 Jeff Hornacek	4.00	10.00
9 Jay Humphries	1.00	2.50
10 Eddie Johnson	1.50	4.00
11 Larry Nance	2.00	5.00
12 Joe Proski TR	.60	1.50
13 Mike Sanders	.60	1.50
14 Bernard Thompson	.60	1.50
15 John Wetzel CO	.60	1.50

1975-76 Suns Fan Grabber

The 1975-76 Phoenix Suns set contains 16 cards, including 12 player cards. The fronts feature black and white pictures, and the backs are blank. The dimensions are approximately 3 1/2" by 4 3/8". The set commemorates the Suns' Western Conference Championship. The cards are unnumbered and are checklisted below in alphabetical order. The set features Alvan Adams' first professional card. These cards were available through at the Fan Grabber concession stands at all Suns playoff games.

Card	Low	High
COMPLETE SET (16)	10.00	25.00
1 Alvan Adams	2.00	5.00
2 Dennis Awtrey	.60	1.50
3 Al Bianchi GM	.60	1.50
4 Jerry Colangelo VP	1.00	2.50
5 Keith Erickson	1.25	3.00
6 Nate Hawthorne	.60	1.50
7 Garfield Heard	1.00	2.50
8 Phil Lumpkin	.60	1.50
9 John MacLeod CO	.75	2.00
10 Curtis Perry	.75	2.00
11 Joe Proski TR	.60	1.50
12 Pat Riley	7.50	15.00
13 Ricky Sobers	1.00	2.50
14 Dick Van Arsdale	1.25	3.00
15 Paul Westphal	3.00	8.00
16 John Wetzel	.40	1.00

1982-83 Suns Giant Service

The 1982-83 Giant Self Service Stations Phoenix Suns set contains three cards each measuring approximately 3 1/4" by 4 1/2". The fronts have color photos while the backs show detailed career highlights and statistics. Each card has a safety tip on back. Apparently during the course of the promotion, one card was given out each month until the end of the season, Walter Davis in January, Maurice Lucas in February, and Larry Nance in March. In addition to being available at gas stations, the cards were also distributed at the Phoenix Suns' Arena on "Giant Service Station Night".

Card	Low	High
COMPLETE SET (3)	8.00	20.00
1 Walter Davis January	3.00	7.00
2 Maurice Lucas February	2.00	5.00
3 Larry Nance March	4.00	9.00

1972-73 Suns Holsum

Sponsored by Holsum Bread in Phoenix, Arizona, these inserts were available in loaves of bread. Each one measures approximately 2 1/2" by 4", is printed on glossy paper, and is devoted to a different Sun player and basketball topic. While the front displays a player portrait, the back carries a Holsum bread advertisement. The trifold insert unfolds to reveal player biography, basketball tips, and records and facts. All print is in light blue lettering; the fronts and backs are accented with red-orange as well. The inserts are unnumbered and checklisted below in alphabetical order.

Card	Low	High
COMPLETE SET (9)	100.00	175.00
1 Corky Calhoun	8.00	20.00
2 Lamar Green	8.00	20.00
3 Clem Haskins	15.00	30.00
4 Connie Hawkins	60.00	120.00
5 Dennis Layton	8.00	20.00
6 Charlie Scott	25.00	50.00
7 Dick Van Arsdale	15.00	30.00
8 Neal Walk	10.00	20.00
9 Walt Wesley	8.00	20.00

1977-78 Suns Humpty Dumpty Discs

The 1977-78 Humpty Dumpty Phoenix Suns set contains 12 discs measuring approximately 3 1/4" in diameter. The blankbacked discs are printed on thick stock. The fronts feature small black and white facial photos surrounded by a purple border with orange trim. Players are numbered below in alphabetical order by subject. The set features Walter Davis' first professional card.

Card	Low	High
COMPLETE SET (12)	15.00	30.00
1 Alvan Adams	1.25	3.00
2 Dennis Awtrey	.75	2.00
3 Mike Bratz	1.00	2.50
4 Don Buse	1.00	2.50
5 Walter Davis	7.50	15.00
6 Bayard Forrest	.75	2.00
7 Garfield Heard	1.25	3.00
8 Ron Lee	.75	2.00
9 Curtis Perry	.75	2.00
10 Alvin Scott	.75	2.00
11 Ira Terrell	1.00	2.50
12 Paul Westphal	2.50	6.00

1980-81 Suns Pepsi

The 1980-81 Pepsi Phoenix Suns set contains 12 numbered cards attached to a bumper sticker-sized promotional flyer/entry blank. The cards were part of a promotion featuring the fans' selection of their Suns' dream team. The entire strip measures approximately 2 7/8" by 11" whereas the cards themselves are standard size, 2 1/2" by 3 1/2". The strips were perforated twice to allow for the card and two ads. The strips were found in six-packs and eight-packs of Pepsi-Cola in the Phoenix area. The fronts feature color photos, and the backs include statistics and biographical information.

Card	Low	High
COMPLETE SET (12)	5.00	10.00
1 Walter Davis	1.25	3.00
2 Alvin Scott	.30	.75
3 Johnny High	.30	.75
4 Dennis Johnson	1.25	3.00
5 Alvan Adams	.75	2.00
6 Rich Kelley	.30	.75
7 Truck Robinson	.60	1.50
8 Joel Kramer	.50	1.25
9 Jeff Cook	.30	.75
10 Mike Niles	.30	.75
11 Kyle Macy	.60	1.50
12 John MacLeod CO	.30	.75

1981-82 Suns Pepsi

The 1981-82 Pepsi Phoenix Suns set contains 12 numbered cards attached to a bumper sticker-sized promotional flyer/entry blank. The cards were part of a promotion featuring the fans' selection of their Suns' dream team. A coupon attached to the card could be redeemed for a ticket to the game. The entire strip measures approximately 2 7/8" by 11" whereas the cards themselves are approximately standard size, 2 1/2" by 3 1/2". The strips were perforated twice to allow for the card and two ads. The strips were found in six-packs and eight-packs of Pepsi-Cola in the Phoenix area. The fronts feature color photos, and the

backs include statistics and biographical information. The set features Larry Nance's first professional card.
COMPLETE SET (12) 20.00 50.00
1 Alvan Adams 2.00 5.00
2 Dudley Bradley 1.25 3.00
3 Jeff Cooke 1.25 3.00
4 Walter Davis 4.00 10.00
5 The Gorilla 2.00 5.00
6 Dennis Johnson 4.00 10.00
7 Joel Kramer 1.50 4.00
8 John MacLeod CO 1.50 4.00
9 Kyle Macy 2.00 5.00
10 Larry Nance 6.00 15.00
11 Truck Robinson 2.00 5.00
12 Alvin Scott 1.25 3.00

1984-85 Suns Police

This set contains 16 cards measuring 2 5/8" by 4 1/8" featuring the Phoenix Suns. This set was issued in the Summer of 1984. Backs contain safety tips ("Suns Tips") and are written in purple print with an orange accent color. The set was sponsored by Kiwanis, the Suns, the NBA, and the Phoenix Police. The cards are unnumbered except for uniform number.
COMPLETE SET (16) 20.00 40.00
4 Kyle Macy 1.50 4.00
6 Walter Davis 3.00 8.00
7 Mike Sanders .75 2.00
8 Rick Robey 1.50 4.00
10 Rod Foster .75 2.00
14 Alvin Scott .75 2.00
20 Maurice Lucas 1.50 4.00
22 Larry Nance 4.00 10.00
32 Charles Pittman .75 2.00
33 Alvan Adams 1.50 4.00
44 Paul Westphal 2.50 6.00
53 James Edwards 1.50 4.00
NNO Suns Mascot 1.50 4.00
NNO John MacLeod CO .75 2.00
NNO Al Bianchi ACO .75 2.00
NNO Joe Proski TR .75 2.00

1990-91 Suns Smokey

This five-card set of Phoenix Suns was sponsored by the USDA Forest Service in cooperation with several other federal agencies. The cards were given away at a specific Phoenix Suns home game. The cards are oversized and measure approximately 3" by 5". The front features a color action player photo, with the Smokey Bear logo superimposed on the top left edge of the picture and the team logo on the bottom right edge. The picture is bordered in purple and has a shadow format. The team name and player's name are given in purple lettering on a peach-colored background. The back presents brief biographical information and features a fire prevention cartoon starring Smokey the Bear. The cards are unnumbered and are checklisted below in alphabetical order. Eddie Johnson was apparently pulled from distribution after he was traded and hence his card is a little tougher to find than the other four players.
COMPLETE SET (5) 9.00 18.00
1 Tom Chambers 1.50 4.00
2 Jeff Hornacek 1.50 4.00
3 Eddie Johnson SP 2.50 6.00
4 Kevin Johnson 2.50 6.00
5 Dan Majerle 2.00 5.00

1972-73 Suns Team Issue

Each of these team-issued photos measure approximately 8" by 10" and feature two black and white player photos - one a portrait and the other a posed action shot. The player's name is listed below the portrait. The backs are blank. The photos are unnumbered and listed below alphabetically.
COMPLETE SET (10) 25.00 50.00
1 Corky Calhoun 1.25 3.00
2 Mel Counts 1.25 3.00
3 Lamar Green 1.25 3.00
4 Clem Haskins 2.50 6.00
5 Connie Hawkins 7.50 15.00
6 Gus Johnson 2.00 5.00
7 Dennis Mo Layton 1.25 3.00
8 Charlie Scott 3.00 8.00
9 Dick Van Arsdale 2.00 5.00
10 Neal Walk 1.50 4.00

1973-74 Suns Team Issue

Measuring approximately 8" by 10", these photos feature members of the 1973-74 Phoenix Suns.
COMPLETE SET 15.00 30.00
1 Dick Van Arsdale 1.50 4.00
2 Neal Walk 1.25 3.00
3 Dennis Scott 1.50 4.00
4 Lamar Green 1.25 3.00
5 Clem Haskins 1.25 3.00
6 Mike Bantom 1.25 3.00
7 Jim Owens 1.25 3.00
8 Bob Christian 1.25 3.00
9 Corky Calhoun 1.25 3.00
10 Gary Melchionni 1.25 3.00
11 Keith Erickson 1.25 3.00
12 Bill Chamberlain 1.25 3.00

1974-75 Suns Team Issue

This set of 11 oversized cards picture a face shot of the player to the left, a posed shot to the right and career statistics at the bottom left. The set is black and white. The cards are not numbered and checklisted below in alphabetical order.
COMPLETE SET (11) 17.50 35.00
1 Dennis Awtrey 1.25 3.00
2 Mike Bantom 1.25 3.00
3 Keith Erickson 1.50 4.00
4 Nate Hawthorne 1.25 3.00
5 Gary Melchionni 1.25 3.00
6 Jim Owens 1.25 3.00
7 Curtis Perry 1.25 3.00
8 Fred Saunders 1.25 3.00
9 Charlie Scott 2.50 6.00
10 Dick Van Arsdale 1.50 4.00
11 Earl Williams 1.25 3.00

1975-76 Suns Team Issue

Measuring 8" by 10", this 14-card set features members of the Phoenix Suns. The set features black and white photos with the backs being blank. The cards are not numbered and checklisted below in alphabetical order.
COMPLETE SET (14) 12.00 30.00
1 Alvan Adams 1.50 4.00
2 Dennis Awtrey .75 2.00
3 Keith Erickson 1.25 3.00
4 Nate Hawthorne .75 2.00
5 Phil Lumpkin .75 2.00
6 John MacLeod CO 1.25 3.00
7 Curtis Perry .75 2.00
8 Joe Proski TR .75 2.00
9 Pat Riley 5.00 10.00
10 Fred Saunders .75 2.00
11 John Shumate 1.25 3.00
12 Ricky Sobers .75 2.00
13 Paul Westphal 2.00 5.00
14 John Wetzel .75 2.00

1977-78 Suns Team Issue

This 12-card set was released during the 1977-78 season, and features all of the Phoenix Suns players from that year. Please note that these cards are slightly oversized at 3x5, and the card backs are blank.
COMPLETE SET (12) 20.00 40.00
1 Alvan Adams 2.00 5.00
2 Dennis Awtrey 1.25 3.00
3 Mike Bratz 1.25 3.00
4 Don Buse 1.25 3.00
5 Walter Davis 3.00 8.00
6 Bayard Forrest 1.25 3.00
7 Greg Griffin 1.25 3.00
8 Garfield Heard 1.50 4.00
9 Ron Lee 1.25 3.00
10 Curtis Perry 1.25 3.00
11 Alvin Scott 1.25 3.00
12 Paul Westphal 2.00 5.00

1988-89 Suns Team Issue

This seven-card set of Phoenix Suns measures approximately 5" by 8". The front has a black and white action player photo with white borders. In the white space below the picture appears the player's name, jersey number, position, and the team logo. The backs are blank. The cards are unnumbered and we have checklisted them below in alphabetical order. Tyrone Corbin, Kevin Johnson, and Mark West came to the Suns on February 25, 1988. Tyrone Corbin was selected in the expansion draft on June 15, 1989 and Kenny Gattison was waived by the Suns on September 21, 1989. The set includes Kevin Johnson's first professional card.
COMPLETE SET (7) 10.00 25.00
1 Tyrone Corbin 1.50 4.00
2 Kenny Gattison 1.00 2.50
3 Armon Gilliam 1.50 4.00
4 Jeff Hornacek 2.00 5.00
5 Eddie Johnson 1.25 3.00
6 Kevin Johnson 5.00 12.00
7 Mark West 1.00 2.50

2001-02 Suns Topps

Released by Topps in conjunction with Sprite, this set features a horizontal design with the Suns logo in the background. Our information on this set is incomplete. If you have information regarding this release, please contact us at basketballmag@beckett.com.
COMPLETE SET (9) 2.00 5.00
PS1 Jason Kidd .75 2.00
PS2 Anfernee Hardaway .75 2.00
PS3 Tom Gugliotta .30 .75
PS5 Clifford Robinson .30 .75
PS6 Rodney Rogers .30 .75
PS7 Chris Dudley .30 .75
PS8 Scott Skiles CO .30 .75
PS9 The Gorilla MASCOT .25 .60
NNO Phoenix Suns .25 .60

1992-93 Suns Topps/Circle K Stickers

Issued in four three-sticker vertical strips, this 12-sticker set features white-bordered color player action photos, with the peel-away backs doubling as sweepstakes entry forms to win one of 50 autographed Suns posters. Each sticker measures approximately 2 3/8" by 3 3/8". The photos are framed by orange and white stripes, and each player's name appears at the bottom within a purple bar. The strips are numbered as Series 1-4, and the players are listed below in alphabetical order; S1 signifies sticker strip one. The set was sponsored by Circle K for the benefit of Boys Club charity.
COMPLETE SET (12) 4.00 10.00
1 Danny Ainge S1 .60 1.50
2 Charles Barkley S3 1.50 4.00
3 Cedric Ceballos S3 .30 .75
4 Tom Chambers S4 .60 1.50
5 Frank Johnson S1 .20 .50
6 Kevin Johnson S1 .60 1.50
7 Tom Kempton S4 .08 .25
8 Negele Knight S2 .08 .25
9 Dan Majerle S2 .60 1.50
10 Oliver Miller S3 .20 .50
11 Jerrod Mustaf S4 .08 .25
12 Mark West S2 .08 .25

1976-77 Suns

The 1976-77 Phoenix Suns set contains 12 horizontal player cards measuring 3 1/2" by 4 3/8". The fronts have circular black and white photos framed by the Suns' orange and purple logo. The backs are blank.
COMPLETE SET (12) 6.00 15.00
1 Alvan Adams 1.25 3.00
2 Dennis Awtrey .60 1.50
3 Keith Erickson 1.25 3.00
4 Butch Feher .60 1.50
5 Garfield Heard 1.00 2.50
6 Ron Lee .60 1.50
7 Curtis Perry .60 1.50
8 Ricky Sobers 1.00 2.50
9 Ira Terrell .75 2.00
10 Dick Van Arsdale 1.25 3.00
11 Tom Van Arsdale 1.25 3.00
12 Paul Westphal 2.00 5.00

1987-88 Suns Wendy's

This four-card set of Phoenix Suns was sponsored by Wendy's and measures approximately 5" by 8". Wendy's logo appears only on the Larry Nance card, whereas the others say "Don't Foul Out, Say No To Drugs" in the upper left corner. The front has a black and white action player photo with white borders. In the white action below the picture appears the player's name, jersey number, position, the team logo, and the words, "A commitment to quality." The backs are blank. The cards are unnumbered and we have checklisted them below in alphabetical order. Jay Humphries, Larry Nance, and Mike Sanders were traded away from the Suns on February 25, 1988.
COMPLETE SET (4) 6.00 15.00
1 Jay Humphries 2.00 5.00
2 Larry Nance 4.00 10.00
3 Mike Sanders 1.25 3.00
4 Bernard Thompson 1.25 3.00

1988 Supercampioni

This 56-sticker multisport set was available at Fina gas stations in Italy. Each sticker measures 1 3/4" by 2 7/16". The fronts display a color action photo inside a red inner border and a blue outer border. The bottom wider border carries the team emblem and, in a yellow bar, the player's name. The backs have a Fina advertisement and the sticker number. The players portrayed on stickers 31-38 are from Tracer Milano.
COMPLETE SET (8) 15.00 35.00
31 Robert Brunamonti .75 2.00
32 Michael D'Antoni 4.00 10.00
33 Walter Magnifico 3.00 8.00
34 Pier Luigi Marzorati .75 2.00
35 Bob McAdoo 5.00 12.00
36 Dino Meneghin 2.00 5.00
37 Antonello Riva 2.50 6.00
38 Renato Villalta .75 2.00

1974-75 Supersonics KTW-1250 Milk Cartons

These cards measure approximately 3 1/4" by 2 5/8" and feature drawings of the featured person in navy blue on a yellow background. A brief profile of the person appears in navy below the drawing. The cards are unnumbered and checklisted below in alphabetical order.
COMPLETE SET (2) 60.00 120.00
1 Wayne Cody ANN 10.00 20.00
2 Bill Russell GM 50.00 100.00

1990-91 Supersonics Kayo

This 14-card standard-size set was produced by Kayo Cards as a give-away to fans attending the April 13, 1991 Seattle Supersonics home game. A total of 10,000 sets supposedly were produced. The cards are numbered on the back. The set features early professional cards of Shawn Kemp and Gary Payton.
COMPLETE SET (14) 3.00 8.00
1 Shawn Kemp 1.00 2.50
2 Scott Meents .15 .40
3 Derrick McKey .25 .60
4 Michael Cage .25 .60
5 Benoit Benjamin .08 .25
6 Dave Corzine .08 .25
7 K.C. Jones CO .30 .75
8 Quintin Dailey .08 .25
9 Ricky Pierce .25 .60
10 Eddie Johnson .25 .60
11 Nate McMillan .40 1.00
12 Gary Payton 1.50 4.00
13 Sedale Threatt .08 .25
14 Dana Barros .20 .50

1993-94 Supersonics Playoff Taco Time

This four-card playoff subset was released in May 1994. Measuring 3 1/2" by 5" and featuring cartoon-like caricatures, these four cards combine to form 2 two-card pictures on their fronts (see 1-2 and 3-4 below); on their backs, they combine to form a four-card composite of Squatch wearing a Sonic uniform. The cards are unnumbered.
COMPLETE SET (4) 2.00 5.00
COMMON CARD (1-4) .50 1.25

1978-79 Supersonics Police

This set contains 16 unnumbered cards measuring 2 5/8" by 4 1/8" featuring the Seattle Supersonics. The set was sponsored by the Washington State Crime Prevention Association, Kiwanis Club, and local law enforcement agencies. The year of issue is printed in the lower right corner of the reverse. Backs contain safety tips ("Tips from the Sonics") and are written in black ink with blue accent. The cards are listed below in alphabetical order. The set features early professional cards of Dennis Johnson and Jack Sikma.
COMPLETE SET (16) 10.00 20.00
1 Fred Brown .75 2.00
2 Joe Hassett .30 .75
3 Dennis Johnson 1.50 4.00
4 John Johnson .30 .75
5 Tom LaGarde .40 1.00
6 Lonnie Shelton .50 1.25
7 Jack Sikma 1.00 2.50
8 Paul Silas 1.00 2.50
9 Dick Snyder .30 .75
10 Wally Walker .30 .75
11 Gus Williams .75 2.00
12 Len Wilkens CO 1.50 4.00
13 Les Habegger ACO .30 .75
14 Frank Furtado TR .30 .75
15 T. Wheedle mascot .30 .75
16 Team Photo .75 2.00

1979-80 Supersonics Police

This set contains 16 numbered cards measuring 2 5/8" by 4 1/8" featuring the Seattle Supersonics. Backs contain safety tips ("Tips for the Sonics") and are written in blue ink with red accent. The cards are numbered and dated in the lower right corner of the obverse. The set was sponsored by the Washington State Crime Prevention Association, Kiwanis, Coca Cola, Rainier Bank, and local area law enforcement agencies. The set features the first professional card of Vinnie Johnson.
COMPLETE SET (16) 7.50 15.00
1 Gus Williams .60 1.50
2 James Bailey .30 .75
3 Jack Sikma .60 1.50
4 Tom LaGarde .30 .75
5 Paul Silas .75 2.00
6 Lonnie Shelton .40 1.00
7 T. Wheedle (Mascot) .20 .50
8 Vinnie Johnson 1.25 3.00
9 Dennis Johnson 1.00 2.50
10 Wally Walker .40 1.00
11 Les Habegger ACO .25 .60
12 Frank Furtado TR .25 .60
13 Fred Brown .60 1.50
14 John Johnson .30 .75
15 Team Photo 1.00 2.50
16 Len Wilkens CO 1.00 2.50

1983-84 Supersonics Police

This set contains 16 cards measuring 2 5/8" by 4 1/8" featuring the Seattle Supersonics. Backs contain safety tips ("Tips from the Sonics") and are written in blue ink with a red accent. Set was also sponsored by the Washington State Crime Prevention Association, Kiwanis, Coca Cola, Ernst Home Centers, and area law enforcement agencies. The year of issue is given at the bottom right corner of the obverse. The cards are numbered on the back. The set features an early professional card of Tom Chambers.
COMPLETE SET (16) 3.00 8.00
1 Reggie King .30 .75
2 Frank Furtado TR .25 .60
3 Tom Chambers 1.25 3.00
4 Dave Harshman ACO .25 .60
5 Gus Williams .40 1.00
6 T. Wheedle (Mascot) .25 .60
7 Scooter McCray .30 .75
8 Jack Sikma .40 1.00
9 Al Wood .25 .60
10 Bob Blackburn ANN .25 .60
11 Danny Vranes .30 .75
12 Charles Bradley .25 .60
13 Steve Hawes .30 .75
14 Jon Sundvold .30 .75
15 Fred Brown .40 1.00
16 Lenny Wilkens CO .75 2.00

1979-80 Supersonics Portfolio

These limited collector prints of Seattle Supersonics were produced by artist Bill Vanderdasson and measure 11" by 14". Each print depicts a player in game action. While ten of the prints are in black and white on a gray background, the Sikma print is in full color. Each print has a hand-drawn border with rounded corners. The backs are blank. Dennis Awtrey was acquired from Boston on January 17, 1979 and left the SuperSonics via free agency on August 14, 1980. Dennis Johnson was traded to the Phoenix Suns on June 4, 1980.
COMPLETE SET (11) 22.50 45.00
1 Dennis Awtrey 1.25 3.00
2 Fred Brown 3.00 8.00
3 Dennis Johnson 5.00 10.00
4 John Johnson 1.25 3.00
5 Tom LaGarde 1.25 3.00
6 Lonnie Shelton 1.50 4.00
7 Jack Sikma 3.00 8.00
8 Paul Silas 3.00 8.00
9 Dick Snyder 1.25 3.00
10 Wally Walker 1.50 4.00
11 Gus Williams 2.50 6.00

1971-72 Supersonics Reed

These 13 pencil drawings of the 1971-72 Supersonics were drawn by Ashby Reed during the 1971-72 season. Each photo measures approximately 8 1/2" x 10". Each photo is black and white with a blank back.
COMPLETE SET (13) 25.00 50.00
1 Fred Brown 2.50 6.00
2 Barry Clemens 1.25 3.00
3 Pete Cross 1.25 3.00
4 Jake Ford 1.25 3.00
5 Spencer Haywood 3.00 8.00
6 Garfield Heard 1.50 4.00
7 Don Kojis 1.25 3.00
8 Bob Rule 1.25 3.00
9 Don Smith 1.25 3.00
10 Dick Snyder 1.25 3.00
11 Rod Thorn ACO 1.50 4.00
12 Lenny Wilkens 5.00 10.00
13 Lee Winfield 1.25 3.00

1973-74 Supersonics Shur-Fresh

The 1973-74 Shur-Fresh Seattle Supersonics set contains 12 cards measuring approximately 2 3/4" square. There are ten player cards and two coach cards. The cards have plastic bread ties attached to them. The fronts have color photos and the backs have biographical information. Cards are unnumbered so they are listed below in alphabetical order. The set features one of the few cards of Hall of Famer Bill Russell. Bill Russell's card may be slightly more difficult as a consumer could earn tickets to a Sonics game for five different cards of which one needed to be Russell's.
COMPLETE SET (12) 50.00 100.00
1 John Brisker 5.00 10.00
2 Fred Brown 10.00 20.00
3 Emmette Bryant ACO 3.00 8.00
4 Jim Fox 5.00 10.00
5 Dick Gibbs 3.00 8.00
6 Spencer Haywood 6.00 15.00
7 Bill Russell CO 30.00 60.00
8 Jim McDaniels 6.00 12.00
9 Kennedy McIntosh 3.00 8.00
10 Dick Snyder 3.00 8.00
11 Bud Stallworth 3.00 8.00
12 Lee Winfield 3.00 8.00

1990-91 Supersonics Smokey

This 16-card set was sponsored by the USDA Forest Service in conjunction with other federal agencies. The cards were issued in a sheet of four rows of four cards each. After perforation, they measure the standard size. The front features a color action player photo, with the Smokey the Bear logo in the lower left corner. The front is done in the team's colors: border and lettering in yellow on a green background. The team name is inscribed above the picture, with the player's name below. The back presents biographical information and a fire prevention cartoon starring Smokey. The set features early professional cards of Shawn Kemp and Gary Payton.
COMPLETE SET (16) 6.00 15.00
1 Dana Barros .60 1.50
2 Michael Cage .60 1.50
3 Dave Corzine .40 1.00
4 Quintin Dailey .40 1.00
5 Dale Ellis .60 1.50
6 K.C. Jones CO .60 1.50
7 Shawn Kemp 1.50 4.00
8 Bob Kloppenburg CO .40 1.00
9 Xavier McDaniel .40 1.00
10 Derrick McKey .60 1.50
11 Nate McMillan .75 2.00
12 Scott Meents .40 1.00
13 Kip Motta CO .40 1.00
14 Gary Payton 3.00 8.00
15 Olden Polynice .40 1.00
16 Sedale Threatt .40 1.00

1969-70 Supersonics Sunbeam Bread

This 11-card set consists of cards measuring approximately 2 3/4" by 2 3/4". The cards were attached to plastic bread ties and issued on loaves of Sunbeam Bread. The cards of either Tom Meschery or Len Wilkens along with any four other player cards could be redeemed by a fan 16 years of age or younger for a free ticket to a 1969-70 Seattle Supersonics game. The card fronts feature a color posed photo of each player shot from the waist up. The team and player name are given in white lettering in the picture. The photo has a thin red border, with the words "Sunbeam Enriched Bread" across the top of the card face. The words "Sonic Stars" are written vertically along the right side of the picture. Cards show the team's schedule for the 1969-70 season. Cards are unnumbered so they are listed below in alphabetical order.
COMPLETE SET (11) 50.00 100.00
1 Lucius Allen 10.00 20.00
2 Bob Boozer 6.00 12.00
3 Barry Clemens 5.00 10.00
4 Art Harris 5.00 10.00
5 Tom Meschery SP 7.50 15.00
6 Erwin Mueller 5.00 10.00
7 Dorie Murrey 5.00 10.00
8 Bob Rule 6.00 12.00
9 John Tresvant 5.00 10.00
10 Len Wilkens P/CO SP 20.00 40.00
11 Seattle Coliseum DP 5.00 10.00

1970-71 Supersonics Sunbeam Bread

This 11-card set consists of cards measuring approximately 2 3/4" by 2 3/4". The cards were attached to plastic bread ties and issued on loafs of Sunbeam Bread. The front features a color posed photo of each player shot from the waist up. The team and player name are given in white lettering in the picture. The photo has a thin red border, with the words "Sunbeam Enriched Bread" across the top of the card face. The words "Sonic Stars" are written vertically along the right side of the picture. The back has a career summary of the player and an offer for fans 16 years of age or younger to complete and send in a set of five different Sonic players (including Tom Meschery or Len Wilkens) for a complimentary ticket to a 1970-71 Seattle Supersonics home game. Cards are unnumbered so they are listed below in alphabetical order.
COMPLETE SET (11) 50.00 100.00
1 Tom Black 5.00 10.00
2 Barry Clemens 5.00 10.00
3 Pete Cross 5.00 10.00
4 Jake Ford 5.00 10.00
5 Garfield Heard 6.00 15.00
6 Don Kojis 6.00 12.00
7 Tom Meschery SP 6.00 15.00
8 Dick Snyder 5.00 10.00
9 Len Wilkens P/CO SP 20.00 40.00
10 Lee Winfield 5.00 10.00
11 Seattle Coliseum 5.00 10.00

1971-72 Supersonics Sunbeam Bread

This 11-card set consists of cards measuring approximately 2 3/4" by 2 3/4". The cards were attached to plastic bread ties and issued on loafs of Sunbeam Bread. The front features a color posed photo of each player shot from the waist up. The team and player name are given in white lettering in the picture. The photo has a thin red border, with the words "Sunbeam Enriched Bread" across the top of the card face. The words "Sonic Stars" are written vertically along the right side of the picture. Cards are unnumbered so they are listed below in alphabetical order.
COMPLETE SET (11) 50.00 100.00
1 Pete Cross 5.00 10.00
2 Jake Ford 5.00 10.00
3 Spencer Haywood 10.00 20.00
4 Garfield Heard 7.50 15.00
5 Don Kojis 6.00 12.00
6 Bob Rule 6.00 12.00
7 Don Smith 5.00 10.00
8 Dick Snyder 5.00 10.00
9 Len Wilkens P/CO 15.00 30.00
10 Lee Winfield 5.00 10.00
11 Sonics Coliseum 5.00 10.00

1993-94 Supersonics Taco Time

Alrak Enterprises produced this set as a promotion for Taco Time Restaurants of Western Washington. Individual cards were available free with the purchase of a Taco Time "Happy Meal" or could be purchased at participating restaurants for 99 cents with any food purchase. The promotion featured a different Sonic player each week for 12 consecutive weeks. There are two number 5 cards because Detlef Schrempf was added to the promotion after his trade to the Seattle Supersonics. It was reported that during week five, some stores were sent McKey by mistake while others were sent Schrempf in short numbers. The postcard-size cards measure approximately 3 1/2" by 5" and feature artwork by sports and comic book illustrator Larry Weber. On a colored background, the fronts feature cartoon-like caricatures, with the player's first name printed in gold-foil letters at the top. The team's logo and the words "Not in our house" also in gold-foil letters round out the front. With Seattle's night skyline as a background, the horizontal backs show a color player portrait, the player's name, biographical information, and his favorite Taco Time menu item. The cards are numbered on the back.
COMPLETE SET (9) 9.00 18.00
1 Nate McMillan 1.25 3.00
2 Sam Perkins 1.25 3.00
3 Gary Payton 2.50 6.00
4 Ricky Pierce .75 2.00
5A Derrick McKey .75 2.00
5B Detlef Schrempf 1.25 3.00
6 Shawn Kemp 1.50 4.00
7 George Karl CO .75 2.00
8 Kendall Gill 1.00 2.50
9 Michael Cage .75 2.00

1967-68 Supersonics Team Issue

Each of these team issued photos measure approximately 4" by 5" and feature black and white close-up player portraits. The backs are blank. The photos are not numbered and listed below alphabetically.
COMPLETE SET (12) 100.00 200.00
1 Henry Akin 7.50 15.00
2 Walt Hazzard 15.00 30.00
3 Tommy Kron 7.50 15.00
4 Plummer Lott 7.50 15.00
5 Tom Meschery 10.00 20.00
6 Dorie Murrey 7.50 15.00
7 Bud Olsen 7.50 15.00
8 Bob Rule 10.00 20.00
9 Rod Thorn 10.00 20.00
10 Al Tucker 7.50 15.00
11 Bob Weiss 10.00 20.00
12 George Wilson 7.50 15.00

1968-69 Supersonics Team Issue

This 5x7 set was produced for the Seattle Supersonics during the 1968-69 season. The set features 12 black and white cards of the team's players.
COMPLETE SET (12) 60.00 120.00
1 Dorie Murrey 5.00 10.00
2 Tom Meschery 6.00 12.00
3 Len Wilkens 12.50 25.00
4 Al Hairston 5.00 10.00
5 Art Harris 5.00 10.00
6 Bob Kauffman 5.00 10.00
7 Rod Thorn 6.00 12.00
8 Al Tucker 5.00 10.00
9 Bob Rule 6.00 12.00
10 Plummer Lott 5.00 10.00
11 Tommy Kron 5.00 10.00
12 Joe Kennedy 5.00 10.00

1975-76 Supersonics Team Issue

This 8" x10" set was produced for the Seattle Supersonics during the 1975-76 season. The set features eight black and white cards of the team's players.
COMPLETE SET (8) 10.00 20.00
1 Mike Bantom 1.25 3.00
2 Rod Derline 1.25 3.00
3 Herm Gilliam 1.25 3.00
4 Leonard Gray 1.25 3.00
5 Willie Norwood 1.25 3.00
6 Frank Oleynick 1.25 3.00
7 Bruce Seals 1.25 3.00
8 Talvin Skinner 1.25 3.00

1976-77 Supersonics Team Issue

This 8" x10" set was produced for the Seattle Supersonics during the 1976-77 season. The set features nine black and white cards of the team's players and coaches.
COMPLETE SET (9) 12.50 25.00
1 Mike Bantom 1.25 3.00
2 Tommy Burleson 1.50 4.00
3 Leonard Gray 1.25 3.00
4 Mike Green 1.25 3.00
5 Willie Norwood 1.25 3.00
6 Frank Oleynick 1.25 3.00
7 Bruce Seals 1.25 3.00
8 Slick Watts 1.25 3.00
9 Bob Wilkerson 1.50 4.00

1978-79 Supersonics Team Issue

Each of these team-issued photos measure approximately 5 7/8" by 9" and feature color close-up player portraits with white borders. A facsimile autograph appears at the bottom. The backs are blank. The photos are unnumbered and listed below alphabetically.
COMPLETE SET (11) 17.50 35.00
1 Fred Brown 2.50 6.00
2 Al Fleming .75 2.00
3 Joe Hassett .75 2.00
4 Dennis Johnson 3.00 8.00
5 John Johnson .75 2.00
6 Jack Sikma 2.50 6.00
7 Paul Silas 2.50 6.00
8 Wally Walker 1.00 2.50
9 Marvin Webster 1.25 3.00
10 Gus Williams 2.00 5.00
11 Cover Photo (Smaller versions of all ten photos) 2.00 5.00

1978-79 Supersonics Team Issue 8 X 10

This seven photo set was released during the 1978-79 season. The set features many of the players on that years team. Please note that these cards measure 8" x 10" and are listed below in alphabetical order.
COMPLETE SET (7) 12.50 25.00
1 Fred Brown 2.00 5.00
2 Dennis Johnson 2.00 5.00
3 John Johnson 1.50 4.00
4 Lonnie Shelton 1.25 3.00
5 Jack Sikma 2.00 5.00
6 Wally Walker 1.50 4.00
7 Gus Williams 1.25 3.00

1983-84 Supersonics Team Issue

This 6" x 8" set was produced for the Seattle Supersonics during the 1983-84 season. The set features 12 black and white cards of the team's players.
COMPLETE SET (12) 12.00 30.00
1 Fred Brown 1.50 4.00
2 Al Wood .75 2.00
3 David Thompson 1.50 4.00
4 Scooter McCray .75 2.00
5 Jack Sikma 1.50 4.00
6 Gus Williams 1.25 3.00
7 Lenny Wilkens CO 1.50 4.00
8 Tom Chambers 1.50 4.00
9 Steve Hawes .75 2.00
10 Steve Hayes .75 2.00
11 Clay Johnson .75 2.00
12 Danny Vranes .75 2.00

1990-91 Supersonics Team Issue

Measuring 3 3/8" by 4 3/4", these cards feature on their fronts black-and-white action photos. On white card stock, the backs carry a headshot, biography, and a facsimile autograph. The cards are unnumbered and checklisted below in alphabetical order.
COMPLETE SET (6) 10.00 25.00
1 Benoit Benjamin 1.25 3.00
2 Eddie Johnson 1.50 4.00
3 K.C. Jones CO 1.50 4.00
4 Shawn Kemp 3.00 8.00
5 Derrick McKey 1.50 4.00
6 Gary Payton 5.00 12.00

1980 Superstar Matchbook

These collector issued matchbooks were issued in the New England area in 1980 and featured superstars from all sports but with an emphasis on players who made their fame in New England. Since these are unnumbered, we have sequenced them in alphabetical order.
COMPLETE SET 30.00 60.00
2 Larry Bird 5.00 10.00

1975 SuperStar Sock Wrappers

1 Kareem Abdul-Jabbar 200.00 400.00
2 Lucius Allen 100.00 200.00
3 Nate Archibald 125.00 250.00
4 Rick Barry 125.00 250.00
5 Doug Collins 125.00 250.00
6 Elvin Hayes 150.00 300.00
7 Spencer Haywood 100.00 200.00
8 Bob Lanier 150.00 300.00
9 Pete Maravich 500.00 1000.00

2001-02 Sweet Shot

Released in December 2001, Upper Deck Sweet Shot is a 120-card set divided up into 90 base cards and 30 rookie cards. Veteran cards have a white border and a bronze background with a basketball centered in the desing. Photos are full color action shots, and the the bottom of the card has bronze foil highlights. The rookie breakdown is as follows: card numbers 91-110 utilize the same card design with a shift from bronze to silver on both the background and the foil highlights, and are sequentially numbered to 1200. Card numbers 111-120 have full color backgrounds, gold foil highlights, and are sequentially numbered to 600. Sweet Shot was packaged in 18-pack boxes with four cards per pack and carried a suggested retail price of $9.99.
COMP.SET w/o SP's 20.00 40.00
91-110 PRINT RUN 1200 SER.#'d SETS
110-120 PRINT RUN 600 SER.#'d SETS
1 Jason Terry .30 .75
2 Shareef Abdur-Rahim .25 .60
3 Toni Kukoc .30 .75
4 Paul Pierce .30 .75
5 Antoine Walker .25 .60
6 Kenny Anderson .25 .60
7 Baron Davis .30 .75
8 Jamal Mashburn .25 .60
9 David Wesley .20 .50
10 Ron Mercer .20 .50
11 Ron Artest .30 .75
12 A.J. Guyton .20 .50
13 Andre Miller .25 .60
14 Lamond Murray .20 .50
15 Chris Mihm .20 .50
16 Michael Finley .30 .75
17 Dirk Nowitzki .50 1.25
18 Steve Nash .50 1.25
19 Antonio McDyess .25 .60
20 Nick Van Exel .25 .60
21 Raef LaFrentz .20 .50
22 Jerry Stackhouse .25 .60
23 Chucky Atkins .20 .50
24 Corliss Williamson .20 .50
25 Antawn Jamison .30 .75
26 Marc Jackson .20 .50
27 Larry Hughes .25 .60
28 Steve Francis .25 .60
29 Cuttino Mobley .20 .50
30 Maurice Taylor .20 .50
31 Reggie Miller .30 .75
32 Jalen Rose .25 .60
33 Jermaine O'Neal .25 .60
34 Darius Miles .20 .50
35 Elton Brand .30 .75
36 Corey Maggette .25 .60
37 Quentin Richardson .25 .60
38 Kobe Bryant 1.25 3.00
39 Shaquille O'Neal .75 2.00
40 Rick Fox .20 .50
41 Derek Fisher .25 .60
42 Stromile Swift .20 .50
43 Jason Williams .25 .60
44 Michael Dickerson .20 .50
45 Alonzo Mourning .40 1.00
46 Eddie Jones .25 .60
47 Anthony Carter .20 .50
48 Glenn Robinson .25 .60
49 Ray Allen .30 .75
50 Sam Cassell .25 .60
51 Kevin Garnett .50 1.25
52 Chauncey Billups .30 .75
53 Terrell Brandon .20 .50
54 Joe Smith .25 .60
55 Kenyon Martin .30 .75
56 Keith Van Horn .25 .60
57 Jason Kidd .50 1.25
58 Latrell Sprewell .25 .60
59 Allan Houston .25 .60
60 Marcus Camby .25 .60
61 Tracy McGrady .50 1.25
62 Mike Miller .25 .60
63 Grant Hill .40 1.00
64 Allen Iverson .60 1.50
65 Dikembe Mutombo .30 .75
66 Aaron McKie .20 .50
67 Stephon Marbury .25 .60
68 Shawn Marion .25 .60
69 Tom Gugliotta .20 .50
70 Rasheed Wallace .30 .75
71 Damon Stoudamire .25 .60
72 Bonzi Wells .20 .50
73 Chris Webber .30 .75
74 Peja Stojakovic .30 .75
75 Mike Bibby .30 .75
76 Tim Duncan .60 1.50
77 David Robinson .50 1.25
78 Antonio Daniels .20 .50
79 Gary Payton .30 .75
80 Rashard Lewis .30 .75
81 Desmond Mason .25 .60
82 Vince Carter .50 1.25
83 Morris Peterson .20 .50
84 Antonio Davis .20 .50
85 Karl Malone .40 1.00
86 John Stockton .40 1.00
87 Donyell Marshall .20 .50
88 Richard Hamilton .25 .60
89 Courtney Alexander .20 .50
90 Michael Jordan 6.00 15.00
91 Zach Randolph RC 2.50 6.00
92 Troy Murphy RC 1.50 4.00
93 Michael Bradley RC 1.00 2.50
94 Vladimir Radmanovic RC 1.50 4.00
95 Kirk Haston RC 1.00 2.50
96 Joseph Forte RC 1.00 2.50
97 Jamaal Tinsley RC 1.50 4.00
98 Jason Collins RC 1.25 3.00
99 Brendan Haywood RC 1.50 4.00
100 Richard Jefferson RC 2.50 6.00
101 Gerald Wallace RC 2.00 5.00
102 Jeryl Sasser RC 1.00 2.50
103 Samuel Dalembert RC 1.50 4.00
104 Tony Parker RC 6.00 15.00
105 Kedrick Brown RC 1.00 2.50
106 Brandon Armstrong RC 1.00 2.50
107 Steven Hunter RC 1.25 3.00
108 Andrei Kirilenko RC 2.50 6.00
109 Primoz Brezec RC 1.50 4.00
110 Terence Morris RC 1.50 4.00
111 Eddie Griffin RC 1.50 4.00
112 DeSagana Diop RC 1.50 4.00
113 Tyson Chandler RC 3.00 8.00
114 Joe Johnson RC 2.50 6.00
115 Rodney White RC 1.25 3.00
116 Eddy Curry RC 2.00 5.00
117 Shane Battier RC 4.00 10.00
118 Jason Richardson RC 2.50 6.00
119 Kwame Brown RC 2.00 5.00
120 Pau Gasol RC 6.00 15.00

2001-02 Sweet Shot Rookie Memorabilia

91-110 PRINT RUN 1200 SER.#'d SETS
110-120 PRINT RUN 600 SER.#'d SETS
91 Zach Randolph 4.00 10.00
92 Troy Murphy 2.50 6.00
93 Michael Bradley 1.50 4.00
94 Vladimir Radmanovic 2.50 6.00
95 Kirk Haston 1.50 4.00
96 Joseph Forte 1.50 4.00
97 Jamaal Tinsley 2.50 6.00
98 Jason Collins 2.00 5.00
99 Brendan Haywood 2.50 6.00
100 Richard Jefferson 4.00 10.00
101 Gerald Wallace 3.00 8.00
102 Jeryl Sasser 1.50 4.00
104 Tony Parker 10.00 25.00
106 Brandon Armstrong 1.50 4.00
107 Steven Hunter 2.00 5.00
108 Andrei Kirilenko 4.00 10.00
109 Primoz Brezec 2.50 6.00
110 Terence Morris 2.50 6.00
111 Eddie Griffin 3.00 8.00
112 DeSagana Diop 3.00 8.00
113 Tyson Chandler 6.00 15.00
114 Joe Johnson 5.00 12.00
115 Rodney White 2.50 6.00
116 Eddy Curry 4.00 10.00
117 Shane Battier 8.00 20.00
118 Jason Richardson 5.00 12.00
119 Kwame Brown 4.00 10.00
120 Pau Gasol 12.00 30.00

2001-02 Sweet Shot Game Jerseys

Inserted one in every 18 packs, this 25-card set showcases an oval swatch of a jersey in the upper right hand corner. The card background is green with full color player action photos, a gray-scale portrait photo on the left side and silver foil highlights.
STATED ODDS 1:18
AI Allen Iverson 6.00 15.00
AJ Antawn Jamison 3.00 8.00
AW Antoine Walker 2.50 6.00
BD Baron Davis 3.00 8.00
CM Corey Maggette 2.50 6.00
CW Chris Webber 5.00 12.00
DJ DerMarr Johnson 2.00 5.00

DM Darius Miles 2.00 5.00
JM Jamal Mashburn 2.50 6.00
JT Jason Terry 3.00 8.00
KB Kobe Bryant 12.00 30.00
KE Kenyon Martin 3.00 8.00
KG Kevin Garnett 5.00 12.00
KM Karl Malone 4.00 10.00
KV Keith Van Horn 2.50 6.00
LH Larry Hughes 2.50 6.00
MF Marcus Fizer 2.00 5.00
MM Mike Miller 2.50 6.00
RM Ron Mercer 2.00 5.00
SM Shawn Marion 2.50 6.00
ST John Stockton 4.00 10.00
TB Terrell Brandon 2.00 5.00
TK Toni Kukoc 3.00 8.00
TM Tracy McGrady 5.00 12.00
WS Wally Szczerbiak 2.50 6.00

2001-02 Sweet Shot Hot Spot Floor

Inserted one in every 18 packs, this 28-card set features large swatches of floor set next to a full color player photo. The background fades from orange around the swatch into a "wood floor" background on the bottom and the words "Hot Spot Floor" on the top, and cards contain red foil highlights.
STATED ODDS 1:18
AHF Allan Houston 2.50 6.00
AMF Andre Miller 2.50 6.00
BWF Bonzi Wells 2.00 5.00
DEF Desmond Mason 2.50 6.00
DVF David Robinson 5.00 12.00
EJF Eddie Jones 2.50 6.00
JKF Jason Kidd 5.00 12.00
JMF Jamal Mashburn 2.50 6.00
JOF Jermaine O'Neal 2.50 6.00
JSF Jerry Stackhouse 2.50 6.00
JTF Jason Terry 3.00 8.00
KBF Kobe Bryant 12.00 30.00
KGF Kevin Garnett 5.00 12.00
LSF Latrell Sprewell 2.50 6.00
MAF Marc Jackson 2.00 5.00
MJF Michael Jordan 75.00 200.00
QRF Quentin Richardson 2.50 6.00
RAF Ray Allen 3.00 8.00
RHF Richard Hamilton 2.50 6.00
RLF Rashard Lewis 3.00 8.00
RMF Reggie Miller 5.00 12.00
RWF Rasheed Wallace 3.00 8.00
SFF Steve Francis 2.50 6.00
SHF Shawn Marion 2.50 6.00
SMF Stephon Marbury 2.50 6.00
SPF Scottie Pippen 8.00 20.00
TMF Tracy McGrady 5.00 12.00
WSF Wally Szczerbiak 2.50 6.00

2001-02 Sweet Shot Network Executives

Inserted one in every 108 packs, this 8 card set features combination of pieces of game used basketballs and nets on each card, with the corresponding player. Player action photos appear along the left side of the card, and the bottom background is a rim and basketball net. The swatch of basketball appears on the top half of the card, and the swatch of net is set to mix in with the bottom background.
STATED ODDS 1:108
AGN A.J. Guyton 6.00 15.00
AJN Antawn Jamison 10.00 25.00
DJN DerMarr Johnson 6.00 15.00
DMN Darius Miles 6.00 15.00
JAN Jason Terry 10.00 25.00
QRN Quentin Richardson 8.00 20.00
RHN Richard Hamilton 8.00 20.00
RMN Ron Mercer 6.00 15.00

2001-02 Sweet Shot Signature Shots

Inserted one in 18 packs, this 24 cards set features an authentic autograph signed on a piece of basketball-like material with the corresponding player on front. The back of the card is numbered with the player's initials.
STATED ODDS 1:18
AWS Antoine Walker 5.00 12.00
DAS Darrell Armstrong 5.00 12.00
DES Desmond Mason 5.00 12.00
DJS DerMarr Johnson 5.00 12.00
ECS Eddy Curry 5.00 12.00
EGS Eddie Griffin 5.00 12.00
HUS Steven Hunter 5.00 12.00
JJS Joe Johnson 8.00 20.00
JMS Jamal Mashburn 5.00 12.00
JPS Joel Przybilla 5.00 12.00
JRS Jason Richardson 6.00 15.00
JSS Jerry Stackhouse 6.00 15.00
KBS Kobe Bryant 125.00 250.00
KES Kenyon Martin 6.00 15.00
KGS Kevin Garnett 40.00 100.00
KWS Kwame Brown 5.00 12.00
LHS Larry Hughes 5.00 12.00
MJS Michael Jordan 800.00 1200.00
PPS Paul Pierce 12.00 30.00
RJS Richard Jefferson 5.00 12.00
SSS Stromile Swift 5.00 12.00
TCS Tyson Chandler 6.00 15.00
TMS Troy Murphy 6.00 15.00
WSS Wally Szczerbiak 6.00 15.00

2001-02 Sweet Shot Three-point Shots

Numbered to each player's jersey, this 15 card insert features a piece of game used jersey, floor, and autograph of the corresponding player shown on the front of the card. The back of the card is numbered with the player's initials.
NUMBERED TO PLAYER JSY
DE Desmond Mason/24 30.00 80.00
DM Darius Miles/21 20.00 50.00
JM Jamal Mashburn/24 30.00 80.00
JS Jerry Stackhouse/42 60.00 150.00
KG Kevin Garnett/21 100.00 250.00
MJ Michael Jordan/23 1000.00 1500.00
MM Mike Miller/50 40.00 100.00
PP Paul Pierce/34 75.00 200.00

2002-03 Sweet Shot

This 132-card standard-size was issued in four card packs with an $9.99 SRP which came 12 packs to a box. Cards numbered 1-90 featured veterans while cards 91 through 123 featured rookies and were issued to a stated print run of 999 copies and cards 124 through 132 featured rookies and were issued to a stated print run of 499 cards.
COMP.SET w/o SP's (90) 15.00 40.00
91-123 PRINT RUN 999 SER.#'d SETS
124-132 PRINT RUN 499 SER.#'d SETS
1 Shareef Abdur-Rahim .25 .60
2 Jason Terry .25 .60
3 Glenn Robinson .25 .60
4 Paul Pierce .30 .75
5 Antoine Walker .25 .60
6 Kedrick Brown .20 .50
7 Vin Baker .25 .60
8 Jalen Rose .25 .60
9 Eddy Curry .20 .50
10 Tyson Chandler .30 .75
11 Zydrunas Ilgauskas .25 .60
12 Chris Mihm .20 .50
13 Darius Miles .20 .50
14 Dirk Nowitzki .50 1.25
15 Michael Finley .30 .75
16 Steve Nash .40 1.00
17 Raef LaFrentz .20 .50
18 James Posey .20 .50
19 Juwan Howard .25 .60
20 Richard Hamilton .25 .60
21 Ben Wallace .25 .60
22 Chauncey Billups .30 .75
23 Jason Richardson .30 .75
24 Antawn Jamison .30 .75
25 Steve Francis .25 .60
26 Eddie Griffin .20 .50
27 Cuttino Mobley .20 .50
28 Reggie Miller .30 .75
29 Jamaal Tinsley .20 .50
30 Jermaine O'Neal .25 .60
31 Elton Brand .30 .75
32 Lamar Odom .25 .60
33 Andre Miller .25 .60
34 Kobe Bryant 1.25 3.00
35 Shaquille O'Neal .75 2.00
36 Devean George .20 .50
37 Pau Gasol .40 1.00
38 Shane Battier .30 .75
39 Jason Williams .25 .60
40 Eddie House .20 .50
41 Eddie Jones .25 .60
42 Brian Grant .20 .50
43 Ray Allen .30 .75
44 Tim Thomas .20 .50
45 Kevin Garnett .50 1.25
46 Terrell Brandon .20 .50
47 Wally Szczerbiak .25 .60
48 Joe Smith .25 .60
49 Jason Kidd .50 1.25
50 Richard Jefferson .30 .75
51 Kenyon Martin .25 .60
52 Dikembe Mutombo .30 .75
53 Jamal Mashburn .25 .60
54 Baron Davis .25 .60
55 David Wesley .20 .50
56 Allan Houston .25 .60
57 Antonio McDyess .25 .60
58 Latrell Sprewell .25 .60
59 Tracy McGrady .50 1.25
60 Mike Miller .25 .60
61 Darrell Armstrong .20 .50
62 Allen Iverson .50 1.25
63 Keith Van Horn .25 .60
64 Stephon Marbury .25 .60
65 Shawn Marion .25 .60
66 Anfernee Hardaway .50 1.25
67 Rasheed Wallace .30 .75
68 Bonzi Wells .20 .50
69 Scottie Pippen .50 1.25
70 Chris Webber .30 .75
71 Mike Bibby .30 .75
72 Peja Stojakovic .30 .75
73 Hedo Turkoglu .25 .60
74 Tim Duncan .60 1.50
75 David Robinson .50 1.25
76 Tony Parker .40 1.00
77 Steve Smith .25 .60
78 Gary Payton .30 .75
79 Rashard Lewis .30 .75
80 Desmond Mason .25 .60
81 Brent Barry .20 .50
82 Vince Carter .50 1.25
83 Morris Peterson .20 .50
84 Antonio Davis .20 .50
85 Karl Malone .40 1.00
86 John Stockton .40 1.00
87 Andrei Kirilenko .30 .75
88 Jerry Stackhouse .25 .60
89 Michael Jordan 2.50 6.00
90 Kwame Brown .20 .50
91 Efthimios Rentzias RC 1.25 3.00
92 Marko Jaric 2.00 5.00
93 Rasual Butler RC 2.00 5.00
94 Predrag Savovic RC 1.50 4.00
95 Sam Clancy RC 1.50 4.00
96 Lonny Baxter RC 1.25 3.00
97 Raul Lopez RC 2.00 5.00
98 Rod Grizzard RC 1.25 3.00
99 Tito Maddox RC 1.25 3.00
100 Carlos Boozer RC 2.00 5.00
101 Dan Gadzuric RC 1.50 4.00
102 Vincent Yarbrough RC 1.25 3.00
103 Robert Archibald RC 1.25 3.00
104 Roger Mason RC 1.50 4.00
105 Ronald Murray RC 2.00 5.00
106 Dan Dickau RC 1.50 4.00
107 Chris Jefferies RC 1.25 3.00
108 John Salmons RC 2.00 5.00
109 Frank Williams RC 1.25 3.00
110 Tayshaun Prince RC 2.50 6.00
111 Casey Jacobsen RC 1.50 4.00
112 Qyntel Woods RC 1.50 4.00
113 Kareem Rush RC 1.50 4.00
114 Ryan Humphrey RC 1.50 4.00
115 Curtis Borchardt RC 1.25 3.00
116 Juan Dixon RC 2.00 5.00
117 Jiri Welsch RC 1.50 4.00
118 Bostjan Nachbar RC 1.50 4.00
119 Fred Jones RC 1.50 4.00
120 Marcus Haislip RC 1.50 4.00
121 Melvin Ely RC 1.50 4.00
122 Jared Jeffries RC 1.50 4.00
123 Caron Butler RC 2.00 5.00
124 Amare Stoudemire RC 4.00 10.00
125 Chris Wilcox RC 2.50 6.00
126 Nene Hilario RC 3.00 8.00
127 DaJuan Wagner RC 2.50 6.00
128 Nikoloz Tskitishvili RC 2.00 5.00
129 Drew Gooden RC 3.00 8.00
130 Mike Dunleavy RC 3.00 8.00
131 Jay Williams RC 3.00 8.00
132 Yao Ming RC 6.00 15.00

2002-03 Sweet Shot Jerseys

Issued at a stated rate of one in 12, these 19 cards feature game-used jersey swatches of NBA players. A Gold version sequentially numbered to 50 was also inserted in packs.
STATED ODDS 1:12
*GOLD: .75X TO 2X JERSEYS HI
GOLD PRINT RUN 50 SER.#'d SETS
AIJ Allen Iverson 5.00 12.00
AJJ Antawn Jamison 3.00 8.00
BDJ Baron Davis 2.50 6.00
DJJ DerMarr Johnson 2.00 5.00
HTJ Hedo Turkoglu 2.50 6.00
JMJ Jamal Mashburn 2.50 6.00
JOJ Jermaine O'Neal 2.50 6.00
JSJ Joe Smith 2.50 6.00
KBJ Kobe Bryant 10.00 25.00
KGJ Kevin Garnett 5.00 12.00
KVJ Keith Van Horn 2.50 6.00
MCJ Antonio McDyess 2.50 6.00
MJJ Michael Jordan 30.00 80.00
PPJ Paul Pierce 3.00 8.00
RHJ Richard Hamilton 2.50 6.00
SFJ Steve Francis 2.50 6.00
SMJ Stephon Marbury 2.50 6.00
SNJ Steve Nash 4.00 10.00
WSJ Wally Szczerbiak 2.50 6.00

2002-03 Sweet Shot Off the Glass

Inserted at a stated rate of one in 84, these cards were made with a plexiglass feel and feature 12 leading NBA players.
STATED ODDS 1:84
G1 Michael Jordan 30.00 80.00
G2 Kobe Bryant 12.00 30.00
G3 Kevin Garnett 6.00 15.00
G4 Allen Iverson 6.00 15.00
G5 Shaquille O'Neal 10.00 25.00
G6 Vince Carter 6.00 15.00
G7 Paul Pierce 4.00 10.00
G8 Jason Kidd 6.00 15.00
G9 Steve Francis 3.00 8.00
G10 Tim Duncan 8.00 20.00
G11 Jay Williams 4.00 10.00
G12 Yao Ming 8.00 20.00

2002-03 Sweet Shot Signature Shots

Inserted at a stated rate of one in 24, these 30 cards feature authentic autographs from mainly current NBA players. Retired superstars Larry Bird, Magic Johnson and Julius Erving also signed cards in this set. A few of these cards were issued in shorter supply and we have printed the stated print run when known.
STATED ODDS 1:24
AS Amare Stoudemire 10.00 25.00
AW Antoine Walker 8.00 20.00
CB Caron Butler 5.00 12.00
CW Chris Wilcox 4.00 10.00
DG Drew Gooden 5.00 12.00
DS DeShawn Stevenson 5.00 12.00
DW DaJuan Wagner 4.00 10.00
JE Julius Erving SP 75.00 150.00
JJ Jared Jeffries 4.00 10.00
JK Jason Kidd 15.00 40.00
JR Jason Richardson 8.00 20.00
JW Jay Williams 5.00 12.00
KB Kobe Bryant SP 125.00 250.00
KM Kenyon Martin 4.00 10.00
LB Larry Bird 50.00 100.00
LO Lamar Odom 6.00 15.00
ME Melvin Ely 4.00 10.00
MF Marcus Fizer 3.00 8.00
MG Magic Johnson 50.00 100.00
MJ Michael Jordan SP 400.00 700.00
MP Morris Peterson 3.00 8.00
NH Nene Hilario 5.00 12.00
NT Nikoloz Tskitishvili 3.00 8.00
PP Paul Pierce 15.00 40.00
QR Quentin Richardson 5.00 12.00
RJ Richard Jefferson 6.00 15.00
RM Ron Mercer/34 6.00 15.00
SA Shareef Abdur-Rahim 5.00 12.00
TC Tyson Chandler 5.00 12.00
YM Yao Ming 40.00 100.00

2002-03 Sweet Shot Sweet Swatches

Inserted at a stated rate of one in 12, these 20 cards feature game-worn swatches from NBA players. A Gold version was also inserted in packs where cards are sequentially numbered to 100.
STATED ODDS 1:12
*GOLD: .6X TO 1.5X SWATCH HI
GOLD PRINT RUN 100 SER #'d SETS
AMS Andre Miller 2.50 6.00
AWS Antoine Walker 2.50 6.00
BDS Baron Davis 2.50 6.00
CWS Chris Webber 3.00 8.00
DMS Darius Miles 2.00 5.00
DNS Dirk Nowitzki 5.00 12.00
ECS Eddy Curry 2.00 5.00
JMS Jamal Mashburn 2.50 6.00
KBS Kobe Bryant 12.00 30.00
KES Kenyon Martin 2.50 6.00
KGS Kevin Garnett 5.00 12.00
KMS Karl Malone 4.00 10.00
KWS Kwame Brown 2.00 5.00
LOS Lamar Odom 2.50 6.00
MMS Mike Miller 2.50 6.00
RHS Robert Horry 2.50 6.00
SMS Shawn Marion 2.50 6.00
TBS Terrell Brandon 2.00 5.00
TMS Tracy McGrady 5.00 12.00
WSS Wally Szczerbiak 2.50 6.00

2002-03 Sweet Shot Three-Point Shots

Randomly inserted into packs, these 17 cards feature not only a "shirt" piece but also an authentic autograph of the featured player. Each of these cards were issued to the player's jersey number.
CARDS NUMBERED TO PLAYER JERSEY
MFA Marcus Fizer/21 20.00 50.00
MGA Magic Johnson/32 150.00 300.00
MJA Michael Jordan/23 500.00 1000.00
MMA Mike Miller/50 20.00 50.00
MPA Morris Peterson/24 20.00 50.00
PPA Paul Pierce/34 75.00 150.00

2003-04 Sweet Shot

Released in November 2003, Sweet Shot boasts a 144-card set divided up as follows: cards 1-90 are base veterans with a full color player action photo, borders set to look like a basketball and a colored ribbon on the left side of the card that matches the player's team colors. Cards 91-96 feature rookies and have white borders and are sequentially numbered to 799. Cards 97-132 feature rookies and a white border on the left and a basketball texture on the right. The middle of each card, where the player's photo is, is printed on metal. Cards 133-144 feature Michael Jordan and are seugentially numbered to 799. Sweet Shot was packaged in 12-pack boxes where packs contained four cards and carried a suggested retail price of $9.99.
COMP.SET w/o SP's (90) 15.00 40.00
91-96 PRINT RUN 799 SERIAL #'d SETS
97-132 PRINT RUN 999 SERIAL #'d SETS
MJ STATED PRINT RUN 799 SERIAL #'d SETS
1 Shareef Abdur-Rahim .25 .60
2 Jason Terry .25 .60
3 Theo Ratliff .20 .50
4 Paul Pierce .30 .75
5 Antoine Walker .30 .75
6 Vin Baker .20 .50
7 Jalen Rose .25 .60
8 Tyson Chandler .25 .60
9 Jay Williams .20 .50
10 Dajuan Wagner .20 .50
11 Zydrunas Ilgauskas .25 .60
12 Darius Miles .20 .50
13 Dirk Nowitzki .50 1.25
14 Antawn Jamison .25 .60
15 Steve Nash .40 1.00
16 Nene Hilario .25 .60
17 Marcus Camby .25 .60
18 Andre Miller .25 .60
19 Richard Hamilton .25 .60
20 Ben Wallace .25 .60
21 Chauncey Billups .30 .75
22 Nick Van Exel .25 .60
23 Jason Richardson .30 .75
24 Erick Dampier .20 .50
25 Steve Francis .25 .60
26 Yao Ming .60 1.50
27 Cuttino Mobley .20 .50
28 Reggie Miller .30 .75
29 Jamaal Tinsley .20 .50
30 Jermaine O'Neal .25 .60
31 Elton Brand .30 .75
32 Corey Maggette .25 .60
33 Marko Jaric .20 .50
34 Kobe Bryant 1.25 3.00
35 Gary Payton .30 .75
36 Shaquille O'Neal .75 2.00
37 Karl Malone .40 1.00
38 Pau Gasol .30 .75
39 Shane Battier .25 .60
40 Mike Miller .25 .60
41 Eddie Jones .25 .60
42 Lamar Odom .25 .60
43 Caron Butler .25 .60
44 Michael Redd .30 .75
45 Joe Smith .25 .60
46 Desmond Mason .25 .60
47 Kevin Garnett .50 1.25
48 Wally Szczerbiak .25 .60
49 Latrell Sprewell .25 .60
50 Jason Kidd .50 1.25
51 Richard Jefferson .25 .60
52 Kenyon Martin .25 .60
53 Baron Davis .25 .60
54 Jamal Mashburn .25 .60
55 David Wesley .20 .50
56 Allan Houston .25 .60
57 Antonio McDyess .25 .60
58 Keith Van Horn .25 .60
59 Tracy McGrady .40 1.00
60 Grant Hill .40 1.00
61 Drew Gooden .25 .60
62 Allen Iverson .50 1.25
64 Eric Snow .20 .50
64A Glenn Robinson .25 .60
65 Stephon Marbury .25 .60
66 Shawn Marion .25 .60
67 Amare Stoudemire .40 1.00
68 Rasheed Wallace .30 .75
69 Bonzi Wells .20 .50
70 Damon Stoudamire .25 .60
71 Chris Webber .30 .75
72 Mike Bibby .30 .75
73 Peja Stojakovic .30 .75
74 Vlade Divac .25 .60
75 Tim Duncan .50 1.25
76 David Robinson .50 1.25
77 Tony Parker .30 .75
78 Manu Ginobili .40 1.00
79 Ray Allen .30 .75
80 Rashard Lewis .30 .75
81 Vladimir Radmanovic .20 .50
82 Vince Carter .50 1.25
83 Morris Peterson .20 .50
84 Antonio Davis .20 .50
85 Keon Clark .20 .50
86 John Stockton .40 1.00
87 Andrei Kirilenko .30 .75
88 Jerry Stackhouse .25 .60
89 Kwame Brown .20 .50
90 Larry Hughes .25 .60
91 LeBron James RC 75.00 200.00
92 Darko Milicic RC 3.00 8.00
93 Carmelo Anthony RC 10.00 25.00
94 Chris Bosh RC 6.00 15.00
95 Dwyane Wade RC 8.00 20.00
96 Chris Kaman RC 4.00 10.00
97 Kirk Hinrich RC 3.00 8.00
98 T.J. Ford RC 2.50 6.00
99 Mike Sweetney RC 2.00 5.00
100 Jarvis Hayes RC 2.00 5.00
101 Mickael Pietrus RC 2.50 6.00
102 Nick Collison RC 2.50 6.00
103 Marcus Banks RC 2.00 5.00
104 Luke Ridnour RC 2.50 6.00
105 Reece Gaines RC 2.00 5.00
106 Troy Bell RC 2.00 5.00
107 Zarko Cabarkapa RC 2.00 5.00
108 David West RC 3.00 8.00
109 Aleksandar Pavlovic RC 2.50 6.00
110 Dahntay Jones RC 2.50 6.00
111 Boris Diaw RC 3.00 8.00
112 Zoran Planinic RC 2.00 5.00
113 Travis Outlaw RC 2.50 6.00
114 Brian Cook RC 2.00 5.00
115 Carlos Delfino RC 2.50 6.00
116 Ndudi Ebi RC 2.00 5.00
117 Kendrick Perkins RC 2.50 6.00
118 Leandro Barbosa RC 3.00 8.00
119 Josh Howard RC 3.00 8.00
120 Jason Kapono RC 2.00 5.00
121 Luke Walton RC 3.00 8.00
122 Jerome Beasley RC 2.00 5.00
123 Kyle Korver RC 4.00 10.00
124 Maciej Lampe RC 2.00 5.00
125 Travis Hansen RC 2.00 5.00
126 Steve Blake RC 2.50 6.00
127 Willie Green RC 2.00 5.00
128 Slavko Vranes RC 2.00 5.00
129 Keith Bogans RC 2.00 5.00
130 Maurice Williams RC 3.00 8.00
131 Matt Bonner RC 3.00 8.00
132 Zaur Pachulia RC 3.00 8.00
133 Michael Jordan 10.00 25.00
134 Michael Jordan 10.00 25.00
135 Michael Jordan 10.00 25.00
136 Michael Jordan 10.00 25.00
137 Michael Jordan 10.00 25.00
138 Michael Jordan 10.00 25.00
139 Michael Jordan 10.00 25.00
140 Michael Jordan 10.00 25.00
141 Michael Jordan 10.00 25.00
142 Michael Jordan 10.00 25.00
143 Michael Jordan 10.00 25.00
144 Michael Jordan 10.00 25.00

2003-04 Sweet Shot Jerseys

Inserted at the rate of one in 12, this 30-card set places full-color player photos on the left of the card and a swatch of game-worn jersey on the right.
STATED ODDS 1:12
AHJ Allan Houston 2.00 5.00
AIJ Allen Iverson 4.00 10.00
ASJ Amare Stoudemire 3.00 8.00
AWJ Antoine Walker 2.50 6.00
BDJ Baron Davis 2.00 5.00
CWJ Chris Webber 2.50 6.00
DNJ Dirk Nowitzki 4.00 10.00
DRJ David Robinson 6.00 15.00
DWJ DaJuan Wagner 2.00 5.00
GAJ Gilbert Arenas 2.00 5.00
GHJ Grant Hill 3.00 8.00
JKJ Jason Kidd 4.00 10.00
JOJ Jermaine O'Neal 2.00 5.00
JSJ John Stockton 3.00 8.00
KBJ Kobe Bryant SP 10.00 25.00
KGJ Kevin Garnett 4.00 10.00
KMJ Kenyon Martin 2.00 5.00
LJJ LeBron James 50.00 120.00
LSJ Latrell Sprewell 2.00 5.00
MAJ Shawn Marion 2.00 5.00
MJJ Michael Jordan SP 25.00 60.00
PPJ Paul Pierce 2.50 6.00
RAJ Ray Allen 2.50 6.00
SFJ Steve Francis 2.00 5.00
SMJ Stephon Marbury 2.00 5.00
SNJ Steve Nash 3.00 8.00
SPJ Scottie Pippen 6.00 15.00
TDJ Tim Duncan 4.00 10.00
TMJ Tracy McGrady 3.00 8.00
YMJ Yao Ming 5.00 12.00

2003-04 Sweet Shot Signature Shots

Inserted at the rate of one in 24, this 42-card set is horizontally desiged with a full-color player photo and an autographed swatch of basketball embedded in the card.
STATED ODDS 1:24
AJ Antawn Jamison 5.00 12.00
AM Antonio McDyess 5.00 12.00
AS Amare Stoudemire 10.00 25.00
BA Marcus Banks 3.00 8.00
BI Chauncey Billups 8.00 20.00
BW Bill Walton 5.00 12.00
CA Carmelo Anthony 30.00 60.00
CB Caron Butler 5.00 12.00
CK Chris Kaman 5.00 12.00
DJ DerMarr Johnson 5.00 12.00
DM Darko Milicic 4.00 10.00
DR David Robinson SP 30.00 60.00
DW DaJuan Wagner 5.00 12.00
EG Manu Ginobili 20.00 50.00
GA Gilbert Arenas 6.00 15.00
JE Julius Erving SP 30.00 80.00
JK Jason Kidd SP 15.00 40.00
JR Jason Richardson 6.00 15.00
JS Jerry Stackhouse 8.00 20.00
KA Kareem Abdul-Jabbar SP 40.00 80.00
KB Kobe Bryant SP 100.00 200.00
LB Larry Bird SP 50.00 120.00
LJ LeBron James 500.00 800.00
LR Luke Ridnour 4.00 10.00
MA Magic Johnson SP 50.00 100.00
MB Mike Bibby SP 8.00 20.00
MI Andre Miller 5.00 12.00
MJ Michael Jordan SP 300.00 600.00
MP Mickael Pietrus 4.00 10.00
PP Paul Pierce 15.00 30.00
PS Peja Stojakovic 6.00 15.00
RG Reece Gaines 3.00 8.00
RH Richard Hamilton 8.00 20.00
RJ Richard Jefferson 6.00 15.00
RO Jalen Rose SP 6.00 15.00
SB Shane Battier 6.00 15.00
SF Steve Francis 6.00 15.00
SM Shawn Marion 6.00 15.00
TM Tracy McGrady SP 12.00 30.00
TO Travis Outlaw 4.00 10.00
TP Tony Parker 12.00 30.00
YM Yao Ming 25.00 60.00

2003-04 Sweet Shot Sweet Spot Signatures

Inserted at the rate of one in 168, this 41-card set is horizontally designed with an embedded autographed baseball sweet spot swatch.
STATED ODDS 1:168
AJA Antawn Jamison/49 6.00 15.00
AMA Antonio McDyess 6.00 15.00
ASA Amare Stoudemire 12.00 30.00
BAA Marcus Banks/49 6.00 15.00
BIA Chauncey Billups 6.00 15.00
BWA Bill Walton 6.00 15.00
CAA Carmelo Anthony/49 125.00 225.00
CBA Caron Butler 6.00 15.00
CKA Chris Kaman/49 6.00 15.00
DJA DerMarr Johnson 6.00 15.00
DMA Darko Milicic/49 6.00 15.00
DRA David Robinson/49 75.00 150.00
EGA Manu Ginobili 30.00 80.00
GAA Gilbert Arenas 6.00 15.00
JEA Julius Erving 100.00 200.00
JKA Jason Kidd/44 40.00 100.00
JRA Jason Richardson 6.00 15.00
JSA Jerry Stackhouse/49 6.00 15.00
KAA Kareem Abdul-Jabbar/49 75.00 150.00
KBA Kobe Bryant/50 100.00 200.00
LBA Larry Bird/50 100.00 200.00
LJA LeBron James/49 750.00 1200.00
LRA Luke Ridnour/49 6.00 15.00
MAA Magic Johnson/49 75.00 200.00
MBA Mike Bibby/39 25.00 60.00
MIA Andre Miller 6.00 15.00
MJA Michael Jordan/23 500.00 1000.00
MPA Mickael Pietrus/49 6.00 15.00
PPA Paul Pierce 25.00 60.00
PSA Peja Stojakovic 6.00 15.00
RGA Reece Gaines 6.00 15.00
RHA Richard Hamilton 6.00 15.00
RJA Richard Jefferson/49 6.00 15.00
ROA Jalen Rose/44 6.00 15.00
SBA Shane Battier 6.00 15.00
SFA Steve Francis/40 20.00 50.00
SMA Shawn Marion 6.00 15.00
TMA Tracy McGrady/49 40.00 100.00
TOA Travis Outlaw/49 6.00 15.00
TPA Tony Parker 20.00 50.00
YMA Yao Ming 60.00 120.00

2003-04 Sweet Shot Sweet Swatches

Inserted at the rate of one in 12, this 33-card set is horizontally designed with a player photo to the left and a swatch of game-worn jersey in the upper right hand corner.
STATED ODDS 1:12
AHSS Allan Houston 2.00 5.00
AISS Allen Iverson 4.00 10.00
ASSS Amare Stoudemire 3.00 8.00
BDSS Baron Davis 2.00 5.00
CWSS Chris Webber SP 5.00 12.00
DNSS Dirk Nowitzki 4.00 10.00
DSSS Damon Stoudamire SP 2.00 5.00
ECSS Eddy Curry 1.50 4.00
JKSS Jason Kidd 4.00 10.00
JOSS Jermaine O'Neal 2.00 5.00
JRSS Jalen Rose 2.00 5.00
JSSS Joe Smith 2.00 5.00
JTSS Jamaal Tinsley 2.00 5.00
JWSS Jay Williams 2.00 5.00
KBSS Kobe Bryant SP 10.00 25.00
KGSS Kevin Garnett 4.00 10.00
LOSS Lamar Odom 2.00 5.00
LSSS Latrell Sprewell 2.00 5.00
MCSS Marcus Camby 2.00 5.00
MJSS Michael Jordan SP 20.00 50.00
MMSS Mike Miller 2.00 5.00
PPSS Paul Pierce 2.50 6.00
RISS Jason Richardson 2.50 6.00
RMSS Reggie Miller 2.50 6.00
SBSS Shane Battier 2.00 5.00
SFSS Steve Francis 2.00 5.00
SHSS Shawn Marion 2.00 5.00
SMSS Stephon Marbury 2.00 5.00
TBSS Terrell Brandon 2.00 5.00
TCSS Tyson Chandler 2.00 5.00
TMSS Tracy McGrady 3.00 8.00
WSSS Wally Szczerbiak 2.00 5.00
YMSS Yao Ming SP 6.00 15.00

2003-04 Sweet Shot Three-Point Shots

Randomly inserted, this 41-card set has cards sequentially numbered to featured player's jersey number and places two swatches of game-worn memorabilia along with a cut signature in the center of the card.
MOST UNPRICED DUE TO SCARCITY
AJ3 Antawn Jamison/33 15.00 40.00
AM3 Antonio McDyess/34 15.00 40.00
AS3 Amare Stoudemire/32 100.00 200.00
CA3 Carmelo Anthony/15 150.00 300.00
DR3 David Robinson/50 50.00 120.00
EG3 Manu Ginobili/20 30.00 80.00
JA3 Marko Jaric/20 15.00 40.00
JS3 Jerry Stackhouse/42 40.00 80.00
KA3 K.Abdul-Jabbar/33 75.00 200.00
LB3 Larry Bird/33 75.00 200.00
LJ3 LeBron James/23 900.00 1500.00
MA3 Magic Johnson/32 60.00 120.00
MI3 Andre Miller/24 15.00 40.00
MJ3 Michael Jordan/23 600.00 1000.00
MP3 Morris Peterson/24 15.00 40.00
PP3 Paul Pierce/34 30.00 80.00
PS3 Peja Stojakovic/16 60.00 150.00
RH3 Richard Hamilton/32 15.00 40.00
RJ3 Richard Jefferson/24 15.00 40.00
SB3 Shane Battier/31 15.00 40.00
SM3 Shawn Marion/31 30.00 60.00

2004-05 Sweet Shot

Released in February 2005, Sweet Shot consists of a 136-card set where cards 1-90 feature veteran players, cards 91-130 feature rookies sequentially numbered to 1250 and cards 131-136 feature rookies sequentially numbered to 499. Sweet Shot was packaged in 12-pack boxes with four cards per pack and a pack SRP of $9.99.
COMP.SET w/o SP's (90) 15.00 40.00
91-130 PRINT RUN 1250 SER.#'d SETS
131-136 PRINT RUN 499 SER.#'d SETS
1 Antoine Walker .30 .75
2 Al Harrington .25 .60
3 Boris Diaw .25 .60
4 Paul Pierce .30 .75
5 Ricky Davis .25 .60
6 Gary Payton .30 .75
7 Gerald Wallace .25 .60
8 Jason Kapono .20 .50
9 Jahidi White .20 .50
10 Eddy Curry .20 .50
11 Kirk Hinrich .25 .60
12 Antonio Davis .20 .50
13 LeBron James 2.00 5.00
14 Dajuan Wagner .20 .50
15 Jeff McInnis .20 .50
16 Dirk Nowitzki .50 1.25
17 Michael Finley .30 .75
18 Jerry Stackhouse .25 .60
19 Kenyon Martin .25 .60
20 Andre Miller .25 .60
21 Carmelo Anthony .60 1.50
22 Chauncey Billups .30 .75
23 Rasheed Wallace .30 .75
24 Ben Wallace .25 .60
25 Derek Fisher .25 .60
26 Jason Richardson .30 .75
27 Mike Dunleavy .25 .60
28 Yao Ming .60 1.50
29 Tracy McGrady .40 1.00
30 Juwan Howard .25 .60
31 Jermaine O'Neal .25 .60
32 Reggie Miller .30 .75
33 Ron Artest .30 .75
34 Elton Brand .30 .75
35 Corey Maggette .25 .60
36 Marko Jaric .20 .50
37 Kobe Bryant 1.25 3.00
38 Karl Malone .40 1.00
39 Lamar Odom .25 .60
40 Pau Gasol .30 .75
41 Jason Williams .25 .60
42 Bonzi Wells .20 .50
43 Shaquille O'Neal .75 2.00
44 Dwyane Wade .50 1.25
45 Eddie Jones .25 .60
46 Michael Redd .25 .60
47 Desmond Mason .25 .60
48 T.J. Ford .20 .50
49 Latrell Sprewell .25 .60
50 Kevin Garnett .50 1.25
51 Sam Cassell .25 .60
52 Aaron Williams .20 .50
53 Richard Jefferson .25 .60
54 Jason Kidd .50 1.25
55 Jamal Mashburn .25 .60
56 Baron Davis .25 .60
57 Jamaal Magloire .20 .50
58 Allan Houston .25 .60
59 Jamal Crawford .30 .75
60 Stephon Marbury .25 .60
61 Keith Bogans .20 .50
62 Cuttino Mobley .20 .50
63 Steve Francis .25 .60
64 Glenn Robinson .25 .60
65 Allen Iverson .50 1.25
66 Kenny Thomas .20 .50
67 Amare Stoudemire .25 .60
68 Steve Nash .40 1.00
69 Quentin Richardson .25 .60
70 Shareef Abdur-Rahim .25 .60
71 Damon Stoudamire .25 .60
72 Zach Randolph .25 .60
73 Peja Stojakovic .30 .75
74 Chris Webber .30 .75
75 Mike Bibby .30 .75
76 Tony Parker .30 .75
77 Tim Duncan .50 1.25
78 Manu Ginobili .40 1.00
79 Ronald Murray .20 .50
80 Ray Allen .30 .75
81 Rashard Lewis .30 .75
82 Chris Bosh .30 .75
83 Vince Carter .50 1.25
84 Jalen Rose .25 .60
85 Andrei Kirilenko .25 .60
86 Matt Harpring .20 .50
87 Carlos Boozer .25 .60
88 Gilbert Arenas .25 .60
89 Jarvis Hayes .20 .50
90 Antawn Jamison .25 .60
91 Anderson Varejao RC 1.50 4.00
92 Jackson Vroman RC 1.25 3.00
93 Peter John Ramos RC 1.25 3.00
94 Lionel Chalmers RC 2.00 5.00
95 Donta Smith RC 1.25 3.00
96 Andre Emmett RC 1.25 3.00
97 Antonio Burks RC 1.50 4.00
98 Royal Ivey RC 1.50 4.00
99 Chris Duhon RC 2.00 5.00
100 Albert Miralles RC 2.00 5.00
101 Justin Reed RC 1.25 3.00
102 David Young RC 2.00 5.00
103 Trevor Ariza RC 2.00 5.00
104 Luol Deng RC 2.00 5.00
105 Rafael Araujo RC 1.25 3.00
106 Andre Iguodala RC 2.50 6.00
107 Luke Jackson RC 1.25 3.00
108 Andris Biedrins RC 1.25 3.00
109 Robert Swift RC 1.25 3.00
110 Sebastian Telfair RC 1.50 4.00
111 Kris Humphries RC 2.00 5.00
112 Al Jefferson RC 2.50 6.00
113 Kirk Snyder RC 1.25 3.00
114 Josh Smith RC 2.00 5.00
115 J.R. Smith RC 2.00 5.00
116 Dorell Wright RC 2.00 5.00
117 Jameer Nelson RC 2.00 5.00
118 Pavel Podkolzin RC 1.25 3.00
119 Viktor Khryapa RC 1.25 3.00
120 Sergei Monia RC 1.25 3.00
121 Nenad Krstic RC 2.00 5.00
122 Tim Pickett RC 2.00 5.00
123 Bernard Robinson RC 1.50 4.00
124 Yuta Tabuse RC 2.00 5.00
125 Delonte West RC 2.00 5.00
126 Tony Allen RC 2.00 5.00
127 Kevin Martin RC 2.50 6.00
128 Sasha Vujacic RC 2.00 5.00
129 Beno Udrih RC 1.50 4.00
130 David Harrison RC 1.25 3.00
131 Dwight Howard RC 6.00 15.00
132 Emeka Okafor RC 2.50 6.00
133 Ben Gordon RC 3.00 8.00
134 Shaun Livingston RC 3.00 8.00
135 Devin Harris RC 2.50 6.00
136 Josh Childress RC 2.50 6.00

2004-05 Sweet Shot Jerseys

Inserted randomly in packs at the rate of one in 12, this 42-card set features borders along the top and bottom of the card, full color pictures and square swatch of jersey.
STATED ODDS 1:12
AI Allen Iverson 4.00 10.00
AJ Antawn Jamison SP 2.00 5.00
AK Andrei Kirilenko 2.00 5.00
AN Andre Iguodala 3.00 8.00
BG Ben Gordon 2.50 6.00
CA Carmelo Anthony 5.00 12.00
CB Chris Bosh 2.50 6.00
CW Chris Webber 2.50 6.00
DE Devin Harris 2.00 5.00
DH Dwight Howard 5.00 12.00
EB Elton Brand 2.50 6.00
EG Manu Ginobili SP 3.00 8.00
IT Isiah Thomas 2.50 6.00
JC Josh Childress 2.00 5.00
JK Jason Kidd 4.00 10.00
JN Jameer Nelson 2.50 6.00
JO Jermaine O'Neal 2.00 5.00
JR J.R. Smith 2.50 6.00
JS Josh Smith 2.50 6.00
KB Kobe Bryant 10.00 25.00
KG Kevin Garnett 4.00 10.00
KM Kenyon Martin 2.00 5.00
LB Larry Bird 10.00 25.00
LD Luol Deng 2.50 6.00
LJ LeBron James 10.00 25.00
LS Latrell Sprewell 2.00 5.00
LU Luke Jackson 1.50 4.00
MJ Michael Jordan SP 40.00 100.00
MR Michael Redd 2.00 5.00
PP Paul Pierce 2.50 6.00
PS Peja Stojakovic 2.50 6.00
RA Rafael Araujo 1.50 4.00
RH Richard Hamilton 2.00 5.00
RJ Richard Jefferson 2.00 5.00
SF Steve Francis 2.00 5.00
SL Shaun Livingston 2.50 6.00
SN Dirk Nowitzki 4.00 10.00
SN Steve Nash 3.00 8.00
SO Shaquille O'Neal 6.00 15.00
ST Sebastian Telfair 2.00 5.00
TD Tim Duncan 4.00 10.00
TM Tracy McGrady 3.00 8.00

2004-05 Sweet Shot Signature Shots

Inserted at one in 12, this 42-card set is horizontally designed with a player photo appearing along the top and an autographed swatch of basketball along the bottom.
STATED ODDS 1:12
*COLOR PARALLEL: 1X TO 2.5X BASE HI
*SP COLOR PARALLEL: .6X TO 1.5X BASE HI
WHITE/BLUE/RED STATED ODDS 1:960
UNPRICED STARS/STRIPES PRINT RUN 10 SETS
S & S NOT PRICED DUE TO SCARCITY
AI Andre Iguodala 4.00 10.00
AK Andrei Kirilenko 5.00 12.00
AS Amare Stoudemire 10.00 25.00
BG Ben Gordon 4.00 10.00
BK Bernard King 8.00 20.00
BM Brad Miller 4.00 10.00
CA Carmelo Anthony 20.00 50.00
CB Carlos Boozer 4.00 10.00
CD Clyde Drexler 12.00 30.00
CH Josh Childress 3.00 8.00
DE Devin Harris 3.00 8.00
DH Dwight Howard 15.00 40.00
DR Dennis Rodman 20.00 50.00
DW Dwyane Wade SP 40.00 100.00
HO Hakeem Olajuwon 20.00 50.00
JC Jamal Crawford SP 8.00 20.00
JE Julius Erving SP 40.00 100.00
JH Josh Howard 4.00 10.00
JK Jason Kidd 12.00 30.00
JN Jameer Nelson 4.00 10.00
JO John Stockton SP 50.00 120.00
JR J.R. Smith 4.00 10.00
JS Josh Smith 4.00 10.00
JW Jamaal Wilkes 8.00 20.00
KB Kobe Bryant SP 125.00 250.00

KG Kevin Garnett 40.00 80.00
LB Larry Bird SP 60.00 150.00
LD Luol Deng 4.00 10.00
LJ LeBron James 250.00 500.00
LU Luke Jackson 2.50 6.00
MA Magic Johnson SP 40.00 100.00
MD Marquis Daniels 4.00 10.00
MJ Michael Jordan SP 500.00 1000.00
PR Pat Riley 8.00 20.00
RA Rafael Araujo 2.50 6.00
SE Sebastian Telfair 3.00 8.00
SL Shaun Livingston 4.00 10.00
SM Shawn Marion 4.00 10.00
ST Stephon Marbury 6.00 15.00
TM Tracy McGrady 12.00 30.00
WF Walt Frazier SP 12.00 30.00
YM Yao Ming SP 30.00 60.00

2004-05 Sweet Shot Swatches

Seeded randomly in packs at the rate of one in 12, this 42-card set is bordered on the top and the bottom and has an "S" shaped swatch of memorabilia.
STATED ODDS 1:12
AH Allan Houston 2.00 5.00
AI Allen Iverson 4.00 10.00
AK Andrei Kirilenko 2.00 5.00
AM Andre Miller 2.00 5.00
AS Amare Stoudemire 2.00 5.00
AW Antoine Walker 2.50 6.00
BD Baron Davis 2.00 5.00
CA Carmelo Anthony 5.00 12.00
CB Carlos Boozer 2.00 5.00
CM Corey Maggette 2.00 5.00
DN Dirk Nowitzki 4.00 10.00
DR David Robinson 4.00 10.00
EC Eddy Curry 1.50 4.00
EG Manu Ginobili 3.00 8.00
GA Gilbert Arenas 2.00 5.00
GP Gary Payton 2.50 6.00
JA Jalen Rose 2.00 5.00
JO Jermaine O'Neal 2.00 5.00
JR Jason Richardson 2.50 6.00
JT Jason Terry 2.00 5.00
KB Kobe Bryant 10.00 25.00
KG Kevin Garnett 4.00 10.00
KM Kenyon Martin 2.00 5.00
LJ LeBron James 12.00 30.00
LO Lamar Odom 2.00 5.00
MF Michael Finley 2.50 6.00
MJ Michael Jordan SP 60.00 120.00
NH Nene 2.00 5.00
PP Paul Pierce 2.50 6.00
PS Peja Stojakovic 2.50 6.00
QR Quentin Richardson 2.00 5.00
RJ Richard Jefferson 2.00 5.00
RM Reggie Miller 2.50 6.00
RW Rasheed Wallace 2.50 6.00
SC Sam Cassell 2.00 5.00
SH Shawn Marion 2.00 5.00
SM Stephon Marbury 2.00 5.00
SO Shaquille O'Neal 6.00 15.00
TD Tim Duncan 4.00 10.00
TM Tracy McGrady 3.00 8.00
TP Tony Parker 2.50 6.00
YM Yao Ming 5.00 12.00

2004-05 Sweet Shot Sweet Spot Signatures

Randomly inserted in packs at the rate of one in 180, this 41-card set features an embedded and autographed sweet spot from a baseball.
STATED ODDS 1:180
AI Andre Iguodala 6.00 15.00
AK Andrei Kirilenko 15.00 40.00
AS Amare Stoudemire 20.00 50.00
BG Ben Gordon 5.00 12.00
BK Bernard King 25.00 60.00
BM Brad Miller 8.00 20.00
CA Carmelo Anthony 20.00 50.00
CB Carlos Boozer 8.00 20.00
CD Clyde Drexler 12.00 30.00
CH Josh Childress 4.00 10.00
CK Chris Kaman 8.00 20.00
DE Devin Harris 4.00 10.00
DH Dwight Howard 15.00 40.00
DR Dennis Rodman 50.00 120.00
DW Dwyane Wade 30.00 80.00
JC Jamal Crawford 8.00 20.00
JE Julius Erving 60.00 120.00
JH Josh Howard 8.00 20.00
JK Jason Kidd 20.00 50.00
JN Jameer Nelson 5.00 12.00
JO John Stockton 100.00 200.00
JR J.R. Smith 5.00 12.00
JS Josh Smith 5.00 12.00
JW Jamaal Wilkes 10.00 25.00
KB Kobe Bryant 125.00 250.00
KG Kevin Garnett 50.00 120.00
LB Larry Bird 125.00 250.00
LD Luol Deng 5.00 12.00
LJ LeBron James 125.00 300.00
LU Luke Jackson 3.00 8.00
MA Magic Johnson 60.00 150.00
MD Marquis Daniels 8.00 20.00
MJ Michael Jordan 350.00 600.00
PR Pat Riley 15.00 40.00
RA Rafael Araujo 3.00 8.00
SE Sebastian Telfair 4.00 10.00
SL Shaun Livingston 5.00 12.00
SM Shawn Marion 8.00 20.00
ST Stephon Marbury 15.00 40.00
TM Tracy McGrady 12.00 30.00
WF Walt Frazier 12.00 30.00

2004-05 Sweet Shot Three Point Shots

Randomly seeded in packs, this 41-card set features a horizontal design with two swatches of jersey and a cut signature. Each card is serially numbered to the player's jersey number.
CARDS #'d TO PLAYER JERSEY
SOME NOT PRICED DUE TO SCARCITY
AK Andrei Kirilenko/47 15.00 40.00
AS Amare Stoudemire/32 75.00 150.00
BM Brad Miller/52 15.00 40.00
CA Carmelo Anthony/15 100.00 200.00
CD Clyde Drexler/22 75.00 150.00
DE Devin Harris/34 20.00 50.00
DR Dennis Rodman/91 50.00 120.00
JA Jason Richardson/23 15.00 40.00
JR J.R. Smith/23 25.00 60.00
KG Kevin Garnett/21 75.00 150.00
LB Larry Bird/33 150.00 300.00
LJ LeBron James/23 250.00 450.00
LU Luke Jackson/33 15.00 40.00
MA Magic Johnson/32 100.00 200.00
MR Michael Redd/22 15.00 40.00
RA Rafael Araujo/55 15.00 40.00
RH Richard Hamilton/32 40.00 100.00
RJ Richard Jefferson/24 15.00 40.00
SM Shawn Marion/31 40.00 100.00

2005-06 Sweet Shot

Released in December 2005, Sweet Shot boasts a 150-card set where cards 1-100 feature veteran players on cards where the backgraound is oval and framing the player in colors to match team colors, cards 101-142 feature rookies on a basketball style background serially numbered to 1599 and cards 143-150 are serially numbered to 499. Sweet Shot was packaged in 12-pack boxes where each pack contained four cards and carried a $9.99 SRP.
COMP.SET w/o SP's (100) 15.00 40.00
143-150 RC PRINT RUN 499 SER.#'d SETS
1 Al Harrington .30 .75
2 Josh Smith .30 .75
3 Josh Childress .30 .75
4 Tyronn Lue .25 .60
5 Paul Pierce .40 1.00
6 Antoine Walker .30 .75
7 Gary Payton .40 1.00
8 Al Jefferson .30 .75
9 Emeka Okafor .30 .75
10 Primoz Brezec .25 .60
11 Gerald Wallace .30 .75
12 Michael Jordan 3.00 8.00
13 Ben Gordon .30 .75
14 Luol Deng .30 .75
15 Kirk Hinrich .30 .75
16 LeBron James 1.50 4.00
17 Luke Jackson .25 .60
18 Drew Gooden .30 .75
19 Larry Hughes .30 .75
20 Dirk Nowitzki .60 1.50
21 Jason Terry .30 .75
22 Michael Finley .40 1.00
23 Jerry Stackhouse .30 .75
24 Andre Miller .30 .75
25 Carmelo Anthony .75 2.00
26 Kenyon Martin .30 .75
27 Earl Boykins .25 .60
28 Rasheed Wallace .40 1.00
29 Ben Wallace .30 .75
30 Richard Hamilton .30 .75
31 Chauncey Billups .40 1.00
32 Baron Davis .30 .75
33 Derek Fisher .30 .75
34 Jason Richardson .40 1.00
35 Tracy McGrady .50 1.25
36 Yao Ming .50 1.25
37 Juwan Howard .30 .75
38 Jermaine O'Neal .30 .75
39 Ron Artest .40 1.00
40 Jamaal Tinsley .25 .60
41 Corey Maggette .30 .75
42 Elton Brand .40 1.00
43 Shaun Livingston .25 .60
44 Kobe Bryant 1.50 4.00
45 Brian Cook .25 .60
46 Lamar Odom .30 .75
47 Mike Miller .30 .75
48 Pau Gasol .40 1.00
49 Shane Battier .30 .75
50 Shaquille O'Neal .75 2.00
51 Dwyane Wade .60 1.50
52 Udonis Haslem .25 .60
53 Joe Smith .30 .75
54 Michael Redd .30 .75
55 Desmond Mason .25 .60
56 Kevin Garnett .60 1.50
57 Wally Szczerbiak .30 .75
58 Sam Cassell .30 .75
59 Vince Carter .60 1.50
60 Jason Kidd .60 1.50
61 Richard Jefferson .30 .75
62 Jamaal Magloire .25 .60
63 J.R. Smith .30 .75
64 Speedy Claxton .25 .60
65 Allan Houston .30 .75
66 Stephon Marbury .30 .75
67 Jamal Crawford .40 1.00
68 Dwight Howard .30 .75
69 Grant Hill .50 1.25
70 Jameer Nelson .25 .60
71 Steve Francis .30 .75
72 Allen Iverson .60 1.50
73 Andre Iguodala .30 .75
74 Chris Webber .40 1.00
75 Kyle Korver .30 .75
76 Amare Stoudemire .30 .75
77 Steve Nash .50 1.25
78 Quentin Richardson .30 .75
79 Shawn Marion .30 .75
80 Damon Stoudamire .30 .75
81 Zach Randolph .30 .75
82 Sebastian Telfair .30 .75
83 Peja Stojakovic .40 1.00
84 Mike Bibby .40 1.00
85 Cuttino Mobley .25 .60
86 Manu Ginobili .40 1.00
87 Tim Duncan .60 1.50
88 Tony Parker .40 1.00
89 Ray Allen .40 1.00
90 Rashard Lewis .40 1.00
91 Luke Ridnour .30 .75
92 Ronald Murray .25 .60
93 Chris Bosh .40 1.00
94 Morris Peterson .25 .60
95 Jalen Rose .40 1.00
96 Andrei Kirilenko .30 .75
97 Raul Lopez .25 .60
98 Carlos Boozer .30 .75
99 Antawn Jamison .30 .75
100 Gilbert Arenas .30 .75
101 Ike Diogu RC 1.25 3.00
102 Julius Hodge RC 1.25 3.00
103 David Lee RC 2.00 5.00
104 Linas Kleiza RC 1.25 3.00
105 Jason Maxiell RC 1.50 4.00
106 Luther Head RC 1.50 4.00
107 Jose Calderon RC 2.00 5.00
108 Brandon Bass RC 1.50 4.00
109 Ricky Sanchez RC 2.00 5.00
110 Andray Blatche RC 2.00 5.00
111 Sean May RC 1.25 3.00
112 Travis Diener RC 1.25 3.00
113 Nate Robinson RC 2.00 5.00
114 Von Wafer RC 1.25 3.00
115 James Singleton RC 1.25 3.00
116 Daniel Ewing RC 1.50 4.00
117 Salim Stoudamire RC 1.50 4.00
118 Dijon Thompson RC 1.25 3.00
119 Danny Granger RC 2.50 6.00
120 Will Bynum RC 1.50 4.00
121 Louis Williams RC 2.00 5.00
122 Channing Frye RC 2.00 5.00
123 Francisco Garcia RC 1.50 4.00
124 Ryan Gomes RC 1.50 4.00
125 Ronnie Price RC 1.50 4.00
126 Jarrett Jack RC 2.00 5.00
127 Alan Anderson RC 1.25 3.00
128 Ersan Ilyasova RC 2.00 5.00
129 C.J. Miles RC 2.00 5.00
130 Arvydas Macijauskas RC 1.25 3.00
131 Bracey Wright RC 1.25 3.00
132 Monta Ellis RC 2.50 6.00
133 Chris Taft RC 1.50 4.00
134 Johan Petro RC 1.25 3.00
135 Yaroslav Korolev RC 1.25 3.00
136 Andrew Bynum RC 1.50 4.00
137 Martynas Andriuskevicius RC 1.25 3.00
138 Charlie Villanueva RC 2.00 5.00
139 Antoine Wright RC 1.50 4.00
140 Joey Graham RC 1.50 4.00
141 Wayne Simien RC 1.25 3.00
142 Hakim Warrick RC 1.50 4.00
143 Gerald Green RC 3.00 8.00
144 Marvin Williams RC 3.00 8.00
145 Deron Williams RC 4.00 10.00
146 Rashad McCants RC 2.50 6.00
147 Raymond Felton RC 3.00 8.00
148 Martell Webster RC 2.50 6.00
149 Chris Paul RC 12.00 30.00
150 Andrew Bogut RC 4.00 10.00

2005-06 Sweet Shot Gold

*GOLD STARS: 1.25X TO 3X BASE HI
1-100 PRINT RUN 199 SER.#'d SETS
*GOLD RCs 101-142: .75X TO 2X BASE HI
*GOLD RCs 143-150: .5X TO 1.25X BASE HI

2005-06 Sweet Shot Spectrum

*SPEC STARS: 2X TO 5X BASE HI
1-100 PRINT RUN 75 SER.#'d SETS
*SPEC RCs 101-142: 1X TO 2.5X BASE HI
*SPEC RCs 143-150: .6X TO 1.5X BASE HI
101-150 PRINT RUN 50 SER.#'d SETS
12 Michael Jordan 25.00 60.00
16 LeBron James 20.00 50.00

2005-06 Sweet Shot Jerseys

Randomly inserted in packs, this 100-card set is horizontally designed with a full color player photo on the left and an "S" shaped swatch of memorabilia on the right. Cards are serially numbered to either 125 or 250.
*GOLD: .6X TO 1.5X BASE HI
GOLD PRINT RUN 50 TO 99 SER.#'d SETS
AB Andrew Bogut/125 4.00 10.00
AK Andrei Kirilenko/125 2.50 6.00
AN Andris Biedrins/125 2.00 5.00
AR Rafael Araujo/250 2.00 5.00
AS Amare Stoudemire/125 2.50 6.00
AT Antoine Wright/250 2.50 6.00
AW Antoine Walker/250 2.50 6.00
BB Bruce Bowen/125 2.00 5.00
BD Baron Davis/125 2.50 6.00
BG Ben Gordon/125 2.50 6.00
CA Carmelo Anthony/125 6.00 15.00
CB Caron Butler/250 2.50 6.00
CM Corey Maggette/125 2.50 6.00
CP Chris Paul/125 8.00 20.00
CV Charlie Villanueva/125 3.00 8.00
CW Chris Webber/250 3.00 8.00
DA Dajuan Wagner/250 2.00 5.00
DE Devin Harris/100 2.00 5.00
DF Derek Fisher/125 2.50 6.00
DG Devean George/125 2.00 5.00
DH Dwight Howard/125 2.50 6.00
DI Dikembe Mutombo/125 3.00 8.00
DM Darius Miles/250 2.00 5.00
DN Dirk Nowitzki/125 5.00 12.00
DO Dorell Wright/125 2.00 5.00
DR Dennis Rodman/125 6.00 15.00
DS DeShawn Stevenson/125 2.00 5.00
DW Deron Williams/125 6.00 15.00
EB Elton Brand/125 3.00 8.00
EC Eddy Curry/250 2.00 5.00
GA Gilbert Arenas/125 2.50 6.00
GG Gerald Green/250 3.00 8.00
GH Grant Hill/125 4.00 10.00
GR Danny Granger/250 4.00 10.00
HW Hakim Warrick/125 2.50 6.00
JA Jamal Crawford/125 3.00 8.00
JC Jason Collins/125 2.00 5.00
JH Josh Howard/50 3.00 8.00
JJ Jarrett Jack/250 3.00 8.00
JK Jason Kidd/125 5.00 12.00
JO Jermaine O'Neal/250 2.50 6.00
JR Jalen Rose/250 3.00 8.00
JS J.R. Smith/125 2.50 6.00
JT Jason Terry/250 2.50 6.00
JU Julius Hodge/125 2.00 5.00
KB Kobe Bryant/125 8.00 20.00
KD Keyon Dooling/250 2.00 5.00
KG Kevin Garnett/125 5.00 12.00
KM Kenyon Martin/250 2.50 6.00
KR Kareem Rush/250 2.00 5.00
KT Kurt Thomas/125 2.00 5.00
KW Kwame Brown/250 2.00 5.00
LB Larry Bird/125 8.00 20.00
LD Luol Deng/125 2.50 6.00
LH Larry Hughes/125 2.50 6.00
LJ LeBron James/125 10.00 25.00
LU Luke Jackson/125 2.00 5.00
LW Luke Walton/125 2.00 5.00
MA Magic Johnson/125 8.00 20.00
MD Mike Dunleavy/250 2.50 6.00
MG Manu Ginobili/250 3.00 8.00
MI Michael Finley/250 3.00 8.00
MJ Michael Jordan/125 40.00 80.00
MK Marko Jaric/125 2.00 5.00
MS Mike Sweetney/125 2.00 5.00
MW Marvin Williams/125 3.00 8.00
NH Nene/125 2.50 6.00
NR Nate Robinson/125 3.00 8.00
PG Pau Gasol/125 3.00 8.00
PP Paul Pierce/125 3.00 8.00
PS Peja Stojakovic/125 3.00 8.00
QR Quentin Richardson/125 2.50 6.00
RA Ray Allen/125 3.00 8.00
RD Ricky Davis/250 2.50 6.00
RF Raymond Felton/125 3.00 8.00
RI Jason Richardson/125 3.00 8.00
RJ Richard Jefferson/125 2.50 6.00
RL Rashard Lewis/125 3.00 8.00
RM Rashad McCants/125 2.50 6.00
RS Robert Swift/125 2.00 5.00
RW Rasheed Wallace/250 3.00 8.00
SC Sam Cassell/250 2.50 6.00
SD Samuel Dalembert/250 2.00 5.00
SF Steve Francis/250 2.50 6.00
SH Shawn Marion/125 2.50 6.00
SJ Sarunas Jasikevicius/125 3.00 8.00
SM Sean May/125 2.00 5.00
SN Steve Nash/125 4.00 10.00
SO Shaquille O'Neal/125 6.00 15.00
ST Stephon Marbury/125 2.50 6.00
TC Tyson Chandler/250 2.50 6.00
TD Tim Duncan/125 5.00 12.00
TM Tracy McGrady/250 4.00 10.00
WA Charlie Ward/250 2.00 5.00
WE Martell Webster/125 2.50 6.00
WI Chris Wilcox/125 2.00 5.00
WS Wayne Simien/250 2.00 5.00
YM Yao Ming/125 4.00 10.00
ZI Zydrunas Ilgauskas/125 2.50 6.00
ZR Zach Randolph/250 2.50 6.00

2005-06 Sweet Shot Signature Shots

Inserted in packs at the rate of one in 12, this 63-card set is horizontally designed with a player photo on the left and a cut signature embedded in the card on a basketball textured swatch.
SP INFO PROVIDED BY UPPER DECK
AB Andrew Bogut 4.00 10.00
AI Andre Iguodala 5.00 12.00
AK Andrei Kirilenko 5.00 12.00
BG Ben Gordon 6.00 15.00
BK Bob Knight SP 25.00 60.00
BM Brad Miller 5.00 12.00
CD Clyde Drexler 12.50 30.00
CF Channing Frye 5.00 12.00
CP Chris Paul 30.00 80.00
CV Charlie Villanueva 5.00 12.00
DE Devin Harris 5.00 12.00
DH Dwight Howard 12.00 30.00
DW Deron Williams 8.00 20.00
HW Hakim Warrick 4.00 10.00
ID Ike Diogu 3.00 8.00
JA Jamaal Wilkes 6.00 15.00
JG Joey Graham 4.00 10.00
JN Jameer Nelson 5.00 12.00
JR J.R. Smith 5.00 12.00
JW John Wooden SP 50.00 120.00
KA Kareem Abdul-Jabbar SP 50.00 100.00
LA Larry Brown 10.00 25.00
LB Larry Bird SP 50.00 120.00
LD Luol Deng 6.00 15.00
LJ LeBron James 200.00 400.00
MA Magic Johnson SP 50.00 120.00
MJ Michael Jordan SP 800.00 1200.00
MW Marvin Williams 5.00 12.00
RM Rashad McCants 4.00 10.00
SH Shawn Marion 5.00 12.00
SL Shaun Livingston 5.00 12.00
SM Sean May 3.00 8.00
SN Steve Nash SP 15.00 40.00
ST Sebastian Telfair 5.00 12.00
WE Martell Webster 4.00 10.00

2005-06 Sweet Shot Signature Shots Acetate

Randomly seeded and limited to 75 or 25 serially numbered copies, this horizontally designed set places full color pictures on the top of the card and an acetate cut signature in the middle.
PRINT RUN 25 TO 75 SER.#'d SETS
AB Andrew Bogut/75 8.00 20.00
AN Andrew Bynum/75 8.00 20.00
CA Carmelo Anthony/25 25.00 60.00
CF Channing Frye/75 10.00 25.00
CP Chris Paul/75 75.00 150.00
DH Dwight Howard/75 12.00 30.00
DR Dennis Rodman/75 60.00 150.00
DW Deron Williams/75 12.00 30.00
GE Gerald Green/75 10.00 25.00
HW Hakim Warrick/75 8.00 20.00
ID Ike Diogu/75 6.00 15.00
IT Isiah Thomas/75 10.00 25.00
JG Joey Graham/75 8.00 20.00
JK Jason Kidd/75 20.00 50.00
JW John Wooden/75 50.00 120.00
LB Larry Bird/25 75.00 150.00
LJ LeBron James/25 250.00 500.00
MJ Michael Jordan/25 350.00 700.00
MW Marvin Williams/75 10.00 25.00
RF Raymond Felton/75 10.00 25.00
RJ Richard Jefferson/75 8.00 20.00
RM Rashad McCants/75 8.00 20.00
SM Sean May/75 6.00 15.00
SN Steve Nash/75 40.00 100.00
SP Scottie Pippen/75 100.00 200.00
TM Tracy McGrady/75 25.00 50.00
WE Martell Webster/75 8.00 20.00
YM Yao Ming/75 25.00 60.00

2005-06 Sweet Shot Signature Shots Wood

PRINT RUN 15 TO 30 SER.#'d SETS
SOME UNPRICED DUE TO SCARCITY
AB Andrew Bogut/35 10.00 25.00
AN Andrew Bynum/35 10.00 25.00
CF Channing Frye/35 12.00 30.00
CP Chris Paul/35 20.00 50.00
DH Dwight Howard/35 25.00 60.00
DR Dennis Rodman/35 60.00 150.00
DW Deron Williams/35 15.00 40.00
GE Gerald Green/35 12.00 30.00
HW Hakim Warrick/35 10.00 25.00
ID Ike Diogu/35 8.00 20.00
IT Isiah Thomas/35 20.00 50.00
JG Joey Graham/35 10.00 25.00
JK Jason Kidd/35 20.00 50.00
JW John Wooden/35 40.00 100.00
MW Marvin Williams/35 12.00 30.00
RF Raymond Felton/35 12.00 30.00
RJ Richard Jefferson/35 10.00 25.00
RM Rashad McCants/35 10.00 25.00
SM Sean May/35 8.00 20.00
SN Steve Nash/35 60.00 150.00
SP Scottie Pippen/35 100.00 250.00
TM Tracy McGrady/35 30.00 60.00
WE Martell Webster/35 10.00 25.00
YM Yao Ming/35 30.00 80.00

2005-06 Sweet Shot Sweet Swatches

Randomly seeded in packs, this 99-card set is horizontally designed with player photos on the left and an "S" shaped swatch of memorabilia on the right. Cards are serially numbered to either 250 to 125.
PRINT RUN 125 TO 250 SER.#'d SETS
*GOLD: .6X TO 1.5X BASE HI
GOLD PRINT RUN 50 TO 99 SETS
AB Andrew Bogut/125 4.00 10.00
AK Andrei Kirilenko/125 2.50 6.00
AN Andris Biedrins/125 2.00 5.00
AR Rafael Araujo/125 2.00 5.00
AS Amare Stoudemire/125 2.50 6.00
AT Antoine Wright/250 2.50 6.00
AW Antoine Walker/250 2.50 6.00
BB Bruce Bowen/125 2.00 5.00
BD Baron Davis/250 2.50 6.00
BG Ben Gordon/125 2.50 6.00
CA Carmelo Anthony/125 6.00 15.00
CB Caron Butler/250 2.50 6.00
CM Corey Maggette/125 2.50 6.00
CP Chris Paul/125 8.00 20.00
CV Charlie Villanueva/125 3.00 8.00
CW Chris Webber/250 3.00 8.00
DA Dajuan Wagner/250 2.00 5.00
DE Devin Harris/125 2.00 5.00
DF Derek Fisher/250 2.50 6.00
DG Devean George/125 2.00 5.00
DH Dwight Howard/125 2.50 6.00
DI Dikembe Mutombo/250 3.00 8.00
DM Darius Miles/250 2.00 5.00
DN Dirk Nowitzki/125 5.00 12.00
DO Dorell Wright/125 2.00 5.00
DS DeShawn Stevenson/250 2.00 5.00
DW Deron Williams/125 6.00 15.00
EB Elton Brand/125 3.00 8.00
EC Eddy Curry/250 2.00 5.00
GA Gilbert Arenas/125 2.50 6.00
GG Gerald Green/125 3.00 8.00
GH Grant Hill/125 4.00 10.00
GR Danny Granger/250 4.00 10.00
HW Hakim Warrick/125 2.50 6.00
JA Jamal Crawford/125 3.00 8.00
JC Jason Collins/125 2.00 5.00
JH Josh Howard/125 3.00 8.00
JK Jason Kidd/125 5.00 12.00
JL Jalen Rose/250 3.00 8.00
JO Jermaine O'Neal/125 2.50 6.00
JR J.R. Smith/125 2.50 6.00
JT Jason Terry/250 2.50 6.00
JU Julius Hodge/125 2.00 5.00
KB Kobe Bryant/125 8.00 20.00
KD Keyon Dooling/250 2.00 5.00
KG Kevin Garnett/125 5.00 12.00
KK Kyle Korver/125 2.50 6.00
KM Kenyon Martin/250 2.50 6.00
KR Kareem Rush/250 2.00 5.00
KT Kurt Thomas/250 2.00 5.00
KW Kwame Brown/250 2.00 5.00
LD Luol Deng/125 2.50 6.00
LH Larry Hughes/125 2.50 6.00
LJ LeBron James/125 12.50 30.00
LR Luke Ridnour/250 2.50 6.00
LU Luke Jackson/125 2.00 5.00
LW Luke Walton/125 2.00 5.00
MB Mike Bibby/125 3.00 8.00
MD Mike Dunleavy/125 2.50 6.00
MG Manu Ginobili/125 3.00 8.00
MI Michael Finley/250 3.00 8.00
MJ Michael Jordan/125 40.00 80.00
MK Marko Jaric/250 2.00 5.00
MS Mike Sweetney/125 2.00 5.00
MW Marvin Williams/125 3.00 8.00
NH Nene/125 2.50 6.00
NR Nate Robinson/125 3.00 8.00
PG Pau Gasol/250 3.00 8.00
PP Paul Pierce/125 3.00 8.00
PS Peja Stojakovic/125 3.00 8.00
QR Quentin Richardson/250 2.50 6.00
RA Ray Allen/125 3.00 8.00
RD Ricky Davis/250 2.50 6.00
RF Raymond Felton/250 3.00 8.00
RI Jason Richardson/125 3.00 8.00
RL Rashard Lewis/125 3.00 8.00
RM Rashad McCants/125 2.50 6.00
RN Ron Artest/125 3.00 8.00
RS Robert Swift/250 2.00 5.00
RW Rasheed Wallace/250 3.00 8.00
SC Sam Cassell/250 2.50 6.00
SD Samuel Dalembert/250 2.00 5.00
SH Shawn Marion/125 2.50 6.00
SJ Sarunas Jasikevicius/250 3.00 8.00
SM Sean May/125 2.00 5.00
SN Steve Nash/125 4.00 10.00
SO Shaquille O'Neal/125 6.00 15.00
ST Stephon Marbury/125 2.50 6.00
TC Tyson Chandler/250 2.50 6.00
TD Tim Duncan/125 5.00 12.00
TM Tracy McGrady/250 4.00 10.00
TP Tony Parker/125 3.00 8.00
WA Charlie Ward/250 2.00 5.00
WE Martell Webster/125 2.50 6.00
WI Chris Wilcox/250 2.00 5.00
WS Wayne Simien/125 2.00 5.00
YM Yao Ming/125 4.00 10.00
ZI Zydrunas Ilgauskas/125 2.50 6.00
ZR Zach Randolph/125 2.50 6.00

2005-06 Sweet Shot Three Point Shots

Seeded in packs randomly, this 32-card set is horizontally designed with a full color player photo in the center, two swatches of memorabilia on the sides and an authentic player autograph centered at the bottom of the card on vellum. Print runs provided by Upper Deck.
PRINT RUNS PROVIDED BY UPPER DECK
CARDS ARE NOT SERIAL #'d
SOME UNPRICED DUE TO SCARCITY
CM Corey Maggette/50 10.00 25.00
DR Dennis Rodman/91 50.00 120.00
LB Larry Bird/33 75.00 150.00
LJ LeBron James/23 300.00 600.00
MJ Michael Jordan/23 400.00 700.00
PG Pau Gasol/16 20.00 50.00
PS Peja Stojakovic/16 20.00 50.00
RF Raymond Felton/20 25.00 60.00
RH Richard Hamilton/32 15.00 40.00
RJ Richard Jefferson/24 10.00 25.00
SM Sean May/42 10.00 25.00
SP Scottie Pippen/33 200.00 350.00

2006-07 Sweet Shot

Released in mid December 2006, the 137-card Sweet Shot set pictures veterans on cards 1-90, autograph rookies sequentially numbered to 799 on cards 91-115, autograph rookies sequentially numbered to 250 on cards 121-132 and rookies sequentially numbered to 99 on cards 133-137. All rookie autographs are signed on a swatch shaped like the surface of a basketball. Sweet Shot is packaged in 12-pack boxes of four cards each and carried an initial suggested retail price of $9.99 per pack.
COMP.SET w/o SP's (90) 15.00 40.00
91-115 AU RC PRINT RUN 799 SER.#'d SETS
116-135 AU RC PRINT RUN 250 SER.#'d SETS
133-140 AU RC PRINT RUN 99 SER.#'d SETS
1 Josh Childress .30 .75
2 Joe Johnson .30 .75
3 Marvin Williams .30 .75
4 Al Jefferson .30 .75
5 Paul Pierce .40 1.00
6 Wally Szczerbiak .30 .75
7 Raymond Felton .30 .75
8 Emeka Okafor .30 .75
9 Gerald Wallace .30 .75
10 Ben Gordon .30 .75
11 Kirk Hinrich .30 .75
12 Michael Jordan 3.00 8.00
13 Larry Hughes .30 .75
14 Zydrunas Ilgauskas .30 .75
15 LeBron James 1.50 4.00
16 Marquis Daniels .25 .60
17 Dirk Nowitzki .60 1.50
18 Jason Terry .30 .75
19 Carmelo Anthony .50 1.25
20 Marcus Camby .30 .75
21 Kenyon Martin .30 .75
22 Chauncey Billups .40 1.00
23 Richard Hamilton .30 .75
24 Ben Wallace .30 .75
25 Baron Davis .30 .75
26 Mike Dunleavy .30 .75
27 Jason Richardson .40 1.00
28 Rafer Alston .25 .60
29 Tracy McGrady .50 1.25
30 Yao Ming .50 1.25
31 Austin Croshere .25 .60
32 Jermaine O'Neal .30 .75
33 Peja Stojakovic .40 1.00
34 Elton Brand .40 1.00
35 Sam Cassell .30 .75
36 Shaun Livingston .25 .60
37 Kwame Brown .25 .60
38 Kobe Bryant 1.50 4.00
39 Lamar Odom .30 .75
40 Pau Gasol .40 1.00
41 Bobby Jackson .25 .60
42 Hakim Warrick .30 .75
43 Shaquille O'Neal .75 2.00
44 Dwyane Wade .60 1.50
45 Jason Williams .30 .75
46 Andrew Bogut .30 .75
47 T.J. Ford .25 .60
48 Jamaal Magloire .25 .60
49 Ricky Davis .30 .75
50 Kevin Garnett .60 1.50
51 Rashad McCants .25 .60
52 Vince Carter .50 1.25
53 Richard Jefferson .30 .75
54 Jason Kidd .60 1.50
55 Desmond Mason .25 .60
56 Chris Paul .50 1.25
57 J.R. Smith .30 .75
58 Channing Frye .30 .75
59 Stephon Marbury .30 .75
60 Quentin Richardson .30 .75
61 Carlos Arroyo .25 .60
62 Dwight Howard .30 .75
63 Darko Milicic .25 .60
64 Andre Iguodala .30 .75
65 Allen Iverson .50 1.25
66 Chris Webber .40 1.00
67 Boris Diaw .30 .75
68 Shawn Marion .30 .75
69 Steve Nash .50 1.25
70 Juan Dixon .25 .60
71 Zach Randolph .30 .75
72 Sebastian Telfair .25 .60
73 Ron Artest .40 1.00
74 Mike Bibby .40 1.00
75 Brad Miller .30 .75
76 Tim Duncan .60 1.50
77 Manu Ginobili .40 1.00
78 Tony Parker .40 1.00
79 Ray Allen .40 1.00
80 Rashard Lewis .40 1.00
81 Luke Ridnour .30 .75
82 Chris Bosh .40 1.00
83 Joey Graham .25 .60
84 Charlie Villanueva .25 .60
85 Carlos Boozer .30 .75
86 Andrei Kirilenko .30 .75
87 Deron Williams .30 .75
88 Gilbert Arenas .30 .75
89 Caron Butler .30 .75
90 Antawn Jamison .30 .75
91 David Noel AU RC 3.00 8.00
92 James Augustine AU RC 3.00 8.00
93 Kyle Lowry AU RC 6.00 15.00
94 Bobby Jones AU RC 3.00 8.00
95 Solomon Jones AU RC 3.00 8.00
96 Craig Smith AU RC 4.00 10.00
97 Josh Boone AU RC 3.00 8.00
98 Jordan Farmar AU RC 5.00 12.00
99 Marcus Williams AU RC 3.00 8.00
100 Hassan Adams AU RC 3.00 8.00
101 Dee Brown AU RC 3.00 8.00
102 Denham Brown AU RC 3.00 8.00
103 Steve Novak AU RC 4.00 10.00
104 James White AU RC 3.00 8.00
105 Daniel Gibson AU RC 4.00 10.00
106 Renaldo Balkman AU RC 4.00 10.00
107 P.J. Tucker AU RC 4.00 10.00
108 Saer Sene AU RC 3.00 8.00
109 Thabo Sefolosha AU RC 5.00 12.00
110 Maurice Ager AU RC 3.00 8.00
111 Rajon Rondo AU RC 10.00 25.00
112 Shawne Williams AU RC 3.00 8.00
113 Mardy Collins AU RC 3.00 8.00
114 Paul Davis AU RC 3.00 8.00
115 Quincy Douby AU RC 3.00 8.00
121 Rodney Carney AU RC 4.00 10.00
122 Randy Foye AU RC 5.00 12.00
123 Ronnie Brewer AU RC 6.00 15.00
124 Cedric Simmons AU RC 4.00 10.00
125 Andrea Bargnani AU RC 6.00 15.00
126 LaMarcus Aldridge AU RC 15.00 40.00
127 Tyrus Thomas AU RC 5.00 12.00
128 Rudy Gay AU RC 6.00 12.00
129 Shelden Williams AU RC 5.00 12.00
130 Patrick O'Bryant AU RC 4.00 10.00
131 Hilton Armstrong AU RC 4.00 10.00
132 Brandon Roy AU RC 6.00 15.00
133 Adam Morrison RC 5.00 12.00
134 J.J. Redick RC 6.00 15.00
135 Alexander Johnson RC 3.00 8.00
136 Damir Markota RC 3.00 8.00
137 Leon Powe RC 4.00 10.00
138 Ryan Hollins RC 4.00 10.00
139 Tarence Kinsey RC 3.00 8.00
140 Jorge Garbajosa RC 4.00 10.00

2006-07 Sweet Shot Gold

*1-90 GOLD: 1.25X TO 3X BASE HI
1-90 GOLD PRINT RUN 199 SER.#'d SETS
*91-115 AU RC GOLD: 1X TO 2.5X BASE HI
*116-132 AU RC GOLD: .75X TO 2X BASE HI
*133-140 ROOKIE GOLD: .75X TO 2X BASE HI
91-140 GOLD PRINT RUN 25 SER.#'d SETS

2006-07 Sweet Shot Signature Shots Acetate

INT RUN 25 SER.#'d SETS
BB Brent Barry 25.00 60.00
BD Baron Davis 10.00 25.00
CF Channing Frye 10.00 25.00
CP Chris Paul 30.00 80.00
DG Danny Granger 10.00 25.00
EI Ersan Ilyasova 10.00 25.00
GW Gerald Wallace 10.00 25.00
HW Hakim Warrick 12.00 30.00
JC Josh Childress 10.00 25.00
JJ Joe Johnson 10.00 25.00
JS J.R. Smith 10.00 25.00
KK Kyle Korver 10.00 25.00
KV Kiki Vandeweghe 10.00 25.00
LJ LeBron James 200.00 350.00
LW Louis Williams 10.00 25.00
MJ Michael Jordan 300.00 600.00
MW Marvin Williams 10.00 25.00
PP Paul Pierce 15.00 40.00
PS Peja Stojakovic 12.00 30.00
RF Raymond Felton 12.00 30.00
RM Rashad McCants 10.00 25.00
RT Ronny Turiaf 10.00 25.00
ST John Starks 20.00 50.00
TC Tyson Chandler 10.00 25.00
TP Tayshaun Prince 15.00 40.00
VC Vince Carter 40.00 80.00
WF Walt Frazier 12.00 30.00

2006-07 Sweet Shot Signature Shots Leather

APPROXIMATELY ONE PER BOX
AI Andre Iguodala 5.00 12.00
AU James Augustine 5.00 12.00
BB Brent Barry 6.00 15.00
BC Carlos Boozer 5.00 12.00
BJ Bobby Jones 5.00 12.00
BR Bill Russell SP 100.00 200.00
CA Carmelo Anthony 15.00 40.00
CB Chris Bosh SP 12.50 30.00
CD Chris Duhon 5.00 12.00
CF Channing Frye 5.00 12.00
CK Chris Kaman 5.00 12.00
CM Cuttino Mobley 5.00 12.00
CP Chris Paul SP 30.00 80.00
CT Chris Taft 5.00 12.00
DC Clyde Drexler 12.50 30.00
DG Danny Granger 5.00 12.00
DH Dwight Howard 12.50 30.00
DN David Noel 5.00 12.00
DR David Robinson SP 20.00 50.00
EC Eddy Curry 5.00 12.00
EI Ersan Ilyasova 5.00 12.00
FR Randy Foye 8.00 20.00
GW Gerald Wallace 5.00 12.00
HO Hakeem Olajuwon 15.00 40.00
HW Hakim Warrick 5.00 12.00
ID Ike Diogu 5.00 12.00
JA Al Jefferson 5.00 12.00
JB Josh Boone 5.00 12.00
JC Josh Childress 5.00 12.00
JE Julius Erving SP 25.00 60.00
JF Jordan Farmar 5.00 12.00
JJ Joe Johnson 6.00 15.00
JR Jalen Rose 5.00 12.00
JS J.R. Smith 5.00 12.00
KB Kwame Brown 5.00 12.00
KD Keyon Dooling 5.00 12.00
KK Kyle Korver 5.00 12.00
KL Kyle Lowry 6.00 15.00
KV Kiki Vandeweghe 6.00 15.00
LH Larry Hughes 5.00 12.00
LJ LeBron James SP 100.00 200.00
LR Luke Ridnour 5.00 12.00
LW Louis Williams 5.00 12.00
MC Corey Maggette 5.00 12.00
ME Monta Ellis 5.00 12.00
MW Marvin Williams 5.00 12.00
NR Nate Robinson 6.00 15.00
PS Peja Stojakovic SP 8.00 20.00
QR Quentin Richardson 5.00 12.00
RA Ron Artest SP 10.00 25.00
RB Ronnie Brewer 8.00 20.00
RC Rodney Carney 5.00 12.00
RF Raymond Felton 5.00 12.00
RJ Richard Jefferson 5.00 12.00
RM Rashad McCants 5.00 12.00
RT Ronny Turiaf 12.50 30.00
SC Craig Smith 5.00 12.00
SE Sean Elliott 8.00 20.00
SK Steve Kerr 8.00 20.00
SL Shaun Livingston 5.00 12.00
SO Solomon Jones 5.00 12.00
ST John Starks 20.00 50.00
SV Sasha Vujacic 5.00 12.00
TC Tyson Chandler 5.00 12.00
TM Tracy McGrady 10.00 25.00
TP Tayshaun Prince 6.00 15.00
TS Sebastian Telfair 5.00 12.00
VC Vince Carter SP 25.00 50.00
VW Von Wafer 5.00 12.00
WF Walt Frazier 6.00 15.00
WM Martell Webster 5.00 12.00
YK Yaroslav Korolev 5.00 12.00
YM Yao Ming 15.00 40.00

2006-07 Sweet Shot Stitches

APPROXIMATE ODDS ONE PER BOX
*GOLD: .6X TO 1.5X BASE HI
GOLD PRINT RUN 50 SER.#'d SETS
AK Andrei Kirilenko 2.00 5.00
AM Andre Miller 2.00 5.00
AS Amare Stoudemire 2.00 5.00
BD Baron Davis 2.00 5.00
CA Carmelo Anthony 3.00 8.00
CM Corey Maggette 2.00 5.00
DG Drew Gooden 2.00 5.00
DN Dirk Nowitzki 4.00 10.00
GA Gilbert Arenas 2.00 5.00
GH Grant Hill 3.00 8.00
JH Josh Howard 2.00 5.00
JK Jason Kidd 4.00 10.00
JM Jamaal Magloire 2.00 5.00
JO Jermaine O'Neal 2.00 5.00
JT Jamaal Tinsley 2.00 5.00
KG Kevin Garnett 4.00 10.00
KK Kyle Korver 2.00 5.00
LD Luol Deng 2.00 5.00
LJ LeBron James SP 10.00 25.00
MA Shawn Marion 2.00 5.00
MB Mike Bibby 2.50 6.00
MC Jeff McInnis 2.00 5.00
MJ Michael Jordan SP 40.00 80.00
MP Mickael Pietrus 2.00 5.00
PP Paul Pierce 2.50 6.00
RL Rashard Lewis 2.50 6.00
SD Samuel Dalembert 2.00 5.00
SF Steve Francis 2.00 5.00
SM Stephon Marbury 2.00 5.00
SO Shaquille O'Neal 5.00 12.00
SS Stromile Swift 2.00 5.00
TA Tony Allen 2.00 5.00
TC Tyson Chandler 2.00 5.00
TD Tim Duncan 4.00 10.00
TM Tracy McGrady 3.00 8.00
TP Tony Parker 2.50 6.00
VC Vince Carter 3.00 8.00
WS Wally Szczerbiak 2.00 5.00
YM Yao Ming 3.00 8.00
ZI Zydrunas Ilgauskas 2.00 5.00

2006-07 Sweet Shot Swatches Dual

PRINT RUN 199 SER.#'d SETS
*DUAL GOLD: .6X TO 1.5X BASE HI
GOLD PRINT RUN 25 SER.#'d SETS
AH R.Alston/L.Head 4.00 10.00
AK R.Allen/K.Korver 4.00 10.00
AL R.Allen/R.Lewis 4.00 10.00
AN C.Anthony/Nene 5.00 12.00
AT A.Jefferson/T.Allen 4.00 10.00
BB Kw.Brown/A.Bynum 4.00 10.00
BD A.Biedrins/I.Diogu 4.00 10.00
BG C.Bosh/J.Graham 4.00 10.00
BL E.Brand/S.Livingston 4.00 10.00
BM M.Bibby/B.Miller 4.00 10.00
BV A.Bogut/C.Villanueva 4.00 10.00
CH B.Haywood/C.Butler 4.00 10.00
CJ V.Carter/R.Jefferson 6.00 15.00
CP T.Chandler/C.Paul 5.00 12.00
CW Dv.West/T.Chandler 4.00 10.00
DB B.Davis/C.Billups 4.00 10.00
DG T.Duncan/M.Ginobili 6.00 15.00
DI S.Dalembert/A.Iguodala 4.00 10.00

DP T.Duncan/T.Parker 6.00 15.00
DW J.Dixon/M.Webster 4.00 10.00
FM S.Francis/S.Marbury 4.00 10.00
GJ D.Gooden/L.James 8.00 20.00
GM K.Garnett/S.Marion 5.00 12.00
GS P.Stojakovic/M.Ginobili 4.00 10.00
GW P.Gasol/H.Warrick 4.00 10.00
HB R.Hamilton/C.Billups 4.00 10.00
HG K.Hinrich/B.Gordon 4.00 10.00
HI L.Hughes/Z.Ilgauskas 4.00 10.00
JA A.Jamison/G.Arenas 4.00 10.00
JG D.Granger/S.Jasikevicius 4.00 10.00
JJ M.Jordan/L.James 40.00 80.00
JW J.Johnson/Mv.Williams 4.00 10.00
KJ J.Kidd/L.James 15.00 40.00
KW A.Kirilenko/D.Williams 5.00 12.00
LP R.Lewis/J.Petro 4.00 10.00
MB K.Bryant/T.McGrady 10.00 25.00
MD J.Magloire/J.Dixon 4.00 10.00
MH D.Milicic/D.Howard 5.00 12.00
MK J.McInnis/N.Krstic 4.00 10.00
MM T.McGrady/Y.Ming 6.00 15.00
MO Y.Ming/S.O'Neal 10.00 25.00
MR C.Maggette/M.Redd 4.00 10.00
MS A.Mourning/W.Simien 4.00 10.00
NH D.Nowitzki/J.Howard 6.00 15.00
NM S.Nash/S.Marion 6.00 15.00
OF E.Okafor/R.Felton 4.00 10.00
PP T.Parker/C.Paul 5.00 12.00
PS P.Pierce/W.Szczerbiak 4.00 10.00
RD J.Richardson/M.Dunleavy 4.00 10.00
RF N.Robinson/C.Frye 4.00 10.00
SD A.Stoudemire/B.Diaw 5.00 12.00
TC M.Taylor/E.Curry 4.00 10.00
TO J.Tinsley/J.O'Neal 4.00 10.00
TS K.Thomas/A.Stoudemire 5.00 12.00
UG B.Udrih/M.Ginobili 4.00 10.00
WC J.Childress/Mv.Williams 4.00 10.00
WD B.Wallace/L.Deng 5.00 12.00
WH R.Hamilton/B.Wallace 6.00 15.00
WK C.Webber/K.Korver 4.00 10.00
WP R.Wallace/T.Prince 6.00 15.00

2006-07 Sweet Shot Sweet Spot Signatures

RANDOM INSERTS IN PACKS
AJ Antawn Jamison 10.00 25.00
BD Baron Davis 10.00 25.00
CA Carmelo Anthony 30.00 80.00
CD Clyde Drexler 40.00 80.00
CP Chris Paul 35.00 75.00
HO Hakeem Olajuwon 15.00 40.00
JC Josh Childress 10.00 25.00
JO Magic Johnson 30.00 80.00
KA Kareem Abdul-Jabbar 60.00 120.00
KK Kyle Korver 10.00 25.00
LB Larry Bird 50.00 125.00
LJ LeBron James SP 125.00 250.00
PP Paul Pierce 20.00 50.00
PS Peja Stojakovic 12.50 30.00
RA Ron Artest 15.00 40.00
RF Raymond Felton 15.00 40.00
RM Rashad McCants 10.00 25.00
TC Tyson Chandler 10.00 25.00
TP Tayshaun Prince 10.00 25.00
VC Vince Carter 20.00 50.00
YM Yao Ming 25.00 60.00

2007-08 Sweet Shot

This 132-card set was released in December, 2007. The set was issued into the hobby in five-card packs (boxes) which came 20 to a case and packs carried an initial SRP of $75. Cards numbered 1-90 feature NBA veterans in their 2006-07 alphabetical team order while cards 91-132 feature NBA rookies all of which have signatures. Every card in this set is serial numbered with cards 1-90 having a stated print run of 350 serial numbered sets, cards 91-102 having a stated print run of 299 serial numbered sets and cards 103-132 having a stated print run of 699 serial numbered sets.
1-90 PRINT RUN 350 SER.#'d SETS
103-132 AU RC PRINT RUN 699 SER.#'d SETS
1 Joe Johnson .75 2.00
2 Marvin Williams .75 2.00
3 Josh Smith .75 2.00
4 Al Jefferson .75 2.00
5 Paul Pierce 1.00 2.50
6 Ray Allen 1.00 2.50
7 Adam Morrison .60 1.50
8 Raymond Felton 1.00 2.50
9 Gerald Wallace .75 2.00
10 Jason Richardson 1.00 2.50
11 Ben Gordon .75 2.00
12 Luol Deng .75 2.00
13 Ben Wallace .75 2.00
14 Michael Jordan 8.00 20.00
15 Larry Hughes .75 2.00
16 LeBron James 4.00 10.00
17 Zydrunas Ilgauskas .75 2.00
18 Dirk Nowitzki 1.25 3.00
19 Josh Howard .75 2.00
20 Jason Terry .75 2.00
21 Allen Iverson 1.25 3.00
22 Nene .75 2.00
23 Carmelo Anthony 1.25 3.00
24 Chauncey Billups 1.00 2.50
25 Richard Hamilton .75 2.00
26 Tayshaun Prince .75 2.00
27 Baron Davis .75 2.00
28 Stephen Jackson .75 2.00
29 Brandan Wright RC 1.50 4.00
30 Tracy McGrady 1.00 2.50
31 Yao Ming 1.25 3.00
32 Shane Battier .75 2.00
33 Jermaine O'Neal .75 2.00
34 Danny Granger .75 2.00
35 Elton Brand 1.00 2.50
36 Corey Maggette .75 2.00
37 Kobe Bryant 4.00 10.00
38 Lamar Odom .75 2.00
39 Luke Walton .60 1.50
40 Rudy Gay 1.00 2.50
41 Pau Gasol 1.00 2.50
42 Dwyane Wade 1.50 4.00
43 Antoine Walker .75 2.00
44 Shaquille O'Neal 2.00 5.00
45 Michael Redd .75 2.00
46 Maurice Williams .75 2.00
47 Andrew Bogut .75 2.00
48 Yi Jianlian RC 2.00 5.00
49 Kevin Garnett 1.50 4.00
50 Ricky Davis .75 2.00
51 Randy Foye 1.00 2.50
52 Vince Carter 1.25 3.00
53 Jason Kidd 1.00 2.50
54 Richard Jefferson .75 2.00
55 Tyson Chandler .75 2.00
56 David West .75 2.00
57 Chris Paul 1.25 3.00
58 Eddy Curry .60 1.50
59 Jamal Crawford 1.00 2.50
60 Stephon Marbury .75 2.00
61 Zach Randolph .75 2.00
62 Dwight Howard .75 2.00
63 Grant Hill 1.25 3.00
64 Andre Miller .75 2.00
65 Thaddeus Young RC 1.50 4.00
66 Andre Iguodala .75 2.00
67 Steve Nash 1.25 3.00
68 Amare Stoudemire .75 2.00
69 Shawn Marion .75 2.00
70 Brandon Roy 1.00 2.50
71 Greg Oden RC 1.50 4.00
72 Ron Artest 1.00 2.50
73 Mike Bibby 1.00 2.50
74 Kevin Martin .75 2.00
75 Tim Duncan 1.50 4.00
76 Manu Ginobili 1.00 2.50
77 Tony Parker 1.00 2.50
78 Wally Szczerbiak .75 2.00
79 Delonte West .60 1.50
80 Rashard Lewis .75 2.00
81 T.J. Ford .60 1.50
82 Chris Bosh 1.00 2.50
83 Andrea Bargnani 1.00 2.50
84 Carlos Boozer .75 2.00
85 Mehmet Okur .60 1.50
86 Deron Williams .75 2.00
87 Gilbert Arenas .75 2.00
88 Antawn Jamison .75 2.00
89 Caron Butler .75 2.00
90 Nick Young RC 2.00 5.00
91 Al Horford AU RC 6.00 15.00
92 Acie Law AU RC 3.00 8.00
93 Joakim Noah AU RC 10.00 25.00
94 Marco Belinelli AU RC 5.00 12.00
95 Al Thornton AU RC 4.00 10.00
96 Javaris Crittenton AU RC 3.00 8.00
97 Mike Conley Jr. AU RC 6.00 15.00
98 Corey Brewer AU RC 5.00 12.00
99 Julian Wright AU RC 3.00 8.00
100 Spencer Hawes AU RC 4.00 10.00
101 Kevin Durant AU RC 125.00 225.00
102 Jeff Green AU RC 5.00 12.00
103 Daequan Cook AU RC 3.00 8.00
104 Jared Dudley AU RC 3.00 8.00
105 Wilson Chandler AU RC 3.00 8.00
106 Rodney Stuckey AU RC 3.00 8.00
107 Morris Almond AU RC 2.50 6.00
108 Arron Afflalo AU RC 4.00 10.00
109 Alando Tucker AU RC 2.50 6.00
110 Sean Williams AU RC 2.50 6.00
111 Carl Landry AU RC 2.50 6.00
112 Gabe Pruitt AU RC 2.50 6.00
113 Marcus Williams AU RC 2.50 6.00
114 Nick Fazekas AU RC 2.50 6.00
115 Jermareo Davidson AU RC 2.50 6.00
116 Josh McRoberts AU RC 3.00 8.00
117 Aaron Brooks AU RC 3.00 8.00
118 Derrick Byars AU RC 2.50 6.00
119 Adam Haluska AU RC 2.50 6.00
120 Reyshawn Terry AU RC 2.50 6.00
121 Jared Jordan AU RC 2.50 6.00
122 Stephane Lasme AU RC 2.50 6.00
123 Aaron Gray AU RC 2.50 6.00
124 Renaldas Seibutis AU RC 4.00 10.00
125 Taurean Green AU RC 2.50 6.00
126 Demetris Nichols AU RC 2.50 6.00
127 Herbert Hill AU RC 2.50 6.00
128 Sammy Mejia AU RC 2.50 6.00
129 D.J. Strawberry AU RC 2.50 6.00
130 Chris Richard AU RC 2.50 6.00
131 Glen Davis AU RC 3.00 8.00
132 Jason Smith AU RC 3.00 8.00

2007-08 Sweet Shot Rookie Stitches

PRINT RUN 99 SER.#'d SETS
*PATCHES: 1X TO 2.5X BASE HI
PATCH PRINT RUN 10 SER.#'d SETS
AH Al Horford 3.00 8.00
AL Acie Law 1.50 4.00
AT Al Thornton 2.00 5.00
BW Brandan Wright 2.50 6.00
CB Corey Brewer 2.50 6.00
DC Daequan Cook 2.00 5.00
JC Javaris Crittenton 1.50 4.00
JD Jared Dudley 2.00 5.00
JG Jeff Green 2.50 6.00
JN Joakim Noah 2.50 6.00
JS Jason Smith 2.00 5.00
JW Julian Wright 1.50 4.00
KD Kevin Durant 25.00 60.00
MC Mike Conley Jr. 3.00 8.00
NY Nick Young 3.00 8.00
RS Rodney Stuckey 2.00 5.00
SH Spencer Hawes 2.00 5.00
SW Sean Williams 1.50 4.00
TY Thaddeus Young 2.50 6.00
WC Wilson Chandler 2.00 5.00

2007-08 Sweet Shot Signature Kicks White Leather

PRINT RUN 24 TO 40 SER.#'d SETS
UNPRICED BLACK PRINT RUN 5 TO 10 SETS
AA Arron Afflalo/40 8.00 20.00
AG Aaron Gray/40 8.00 20.00
AH Al Harrington/40 8.00 20.00
AJ Antawn Jamison/40 10.00 25.00
AL Morris Almond/40 5.00 12.00
BG Ben Gordon/40 10.00 25.00
BR Brandon Roy/40 10.00 25.00
CS Craig Smith/40 8.00 20.00
DG Daniel Gibson/40 10.00 25.00
DL David Lee/40 10.00 25.00
DN David Noel/40 8.00 20.00
DR Dennis Rodman/40 25.00 50.00
DW Deron Williams/40 6.00 15.00
HO Al Horford/40 12.50 30.00
JA James Augustine/40 8.00 20.00
JB Josh Boone/40 8.00 20.00
JC Javaris Crittenton/40 5.00 12.00
JG Jorge Garbajosa/40 10.00 25.00
JW Julian Wright/40 5.00 12.00
KB Kobe Bryant/24 175.00 325.00
KD Kevin Durant/40 100.00 200.00
KL Kyle Lowry/40 8.00 20.00
LA LaMarcus Aldridge/40 15.00 30.00
LB Leandro Barbosa/40 10.00 25.00
LJ LeBron James/40 100.00 200.00
LP Leon Powe/40 8.00 20.00
MC Mardy Collins/40 8.00 20.00
PM Paul Millsap/40 8.00 20.00
RF Randy Foye/40 8.00 20.00
RS Rodney Stuckey/40 6.00 15.00
SJ Solomon Jones/40 8.00 20.00
TP Tayshaun Prince/40 15.00 30.00

2007-08 Sweet Shot Signature Shots

PRINT RUNS LISTED IN CHECKLIST
SOME NOT PRICED DUE TO SCARCITY
AB Andrea Bargnani/25 10.00 25.00
AD Adrian Dantley/98 10.00 25.00
AH Al Harrington/50 4.00 10.00
AI Andre Iguodala/50 6.00 15.00
AJ Antawn Jamison/50 5.00 12.00
AM Alonzo Mourning/25 60.00 120.00
BA B.J. Armstrong/98 8.00 20.00
BB Bruce Bowen/97 4.00 10.00
BD Baron Davis/50 8.00 20.00
BE Raja Bell/25 5.00 12.00
BG Ben Gordon/369 4.00 10.00
BI Larry Bird/50 40.00 80.00
BL Bill Laimbeer/197 6.00 15.00
BM Brad Miller/99 4.00 10.00
BS Bill Sharman/50 10.00 25.00
BW Bill Walton/25 20.00 40.00
CD Chris Duhon/297 4.00 10.00
CH Tyson Chandler/98 4.00 10.00
CR Cazzie Russell/25 10.00 25.00
CS Cedric Simmons/98 4.00 10.00
CW Shawne Williams/195 4.00 10.00
DB Dee Brown/195 4.00 10.00
DH Dwight Howard/50 6.00 15.00
DL David Lee/197 4.00 10.00
DN David Noel/150 4.00 10.00
DO Keyon Dooling/197 4.00 10.00
DR Dennis Rodman/25 25.00 60.00
DW Deron Williams/409 5.00 12.00
DX Clyde Drexler/25 40.00 80.00
EO Emeka Okafor/25 10.00 25.00
FG Francisco Garcia/97 4.00 10.00
GR Glen Rice/50 4.00 10.00
HA Hilton Armstrong/195 4.00 10.00
HG Horace Grant/50 15.00 40.00
HK Connie Hawkins/50 8.00 20.00
HO Hakeem Olajuwon/25 20.00 40.00
JA James Augustine/195 4.00 10.00
JB Josh Boone/195 4.00 10.00
JG Jorge Garbajosa/97 4.00 10.00
JK Jason Kidd/20 20.00 40.00
JN Magic Johnson/50 40.00 100.00
JO Avery Johnson/50 8.00 20.00
JR J.R. Smith/197 8.00 20.00
JW Jamaal Wilkes/98 6.00 15.00
KA Kareem Abdul-Jabbar/50 30.00 60.00
KD Kevin Durant/99 100.00 200.00
KL Kyle Lowry/189 4.00 10.00
LB Leandro Barbosa/197 4.00 10.00
LH Larry Hughes/50 4.00 10.00
LJ LeBron James/54 100.00 250.00
LP Leon Powe/197 4.00 10.00
MA Maurice Ager/225 4.00 10.00
MC Mardy Collins/195 4.00 10.00
MD Marquis Daniels/195 4.00 10.00
MI Mile Ilic/195 4.00 10.00
PD Paul Davis/195 4.00 10.00
PM Paul Millsap/97 4.00 10.00
PO Patrick O'Bryant/197 4.00 10.00
PP Paul Pierce/50 25.00 60.00
PR Pat Riley/25 25.00 60.00
QR Quentin Richardson/25 4.00 10.00
RB Ronnie Brewer/149 4.00 10.00
RC Rodney Carney/220 4.00 10.00
RF Raymond Felton/197 5.00 12.00
RH Ryan Hollins/219 4.00 10.00
RI Rick Mahorn/97 6.00 15.00
RR Rajon Rondo/97 12.00 30.00
RS Randolph Morris/195 4.00 10.00
RT Ronny Turiaf/195 4.00 10.00
SB Shannon Brown/195 4.00 10.00
SC Craig Smith/195 4.00 10.00
SF Stromile Swift/220 4.00 10.00
SJ Solomon Jones/195 4.00 10.00
SK Steve Kerr/50 15.00 40.00
SN Steve Nash/25 40.00 80.00
SP Sam Perkins/98 5.00 12.00
SR Sergio Rodriguez/195 4.00 10.00
SS Saer Sene/195 4.00 10.00
SW Shelden Williams/197 4.00 10.00
TC Tom Chambers/195 4.00 10.00
TF T.J. Ford/197 4.00 10.00
TM Tracy McGrady/50 10.00 25.00
TP Tayshaun Prince/25 8.00 20.00
TT Tyrus Thomas/25 15.00 30.00
VC Vince Carter/25 25.00 60.00
WD Walter Davis/32 5.00 12.00
WF Walt Frazier/25 12.00 30.00
WI Marvin Williams/399 5.00 12.00
WI2 Damien Wilkins/195 4.00 10.00
WO John Wooden/103 40.00 80.00
WT Wayman Tisdale/97 10.00 25.00
WU Wes Unseld/25 10.00 25.00
YD Yakhouba Diawara/195 4.00 10.00

2007-08 Sweet Shot Signature Shots Acetate

PRINT RUN 10 TO 25 SER.#'d SETS
UNPRICED DUAL PRINT RUN 15 SER.#'d SETS
BR Brandon Roy/25 30.00 60.00
DH Dwight Howard/25 25.00 60.00
JB Josh Boone/25 6.00 15.00
KD Kevin Durant/25 175.00 350.00
LA LaMarcus Aldridge/25 10.00 25.00
LJ LeBron James/25 150.00 300.00
LW Lenny Wilkens/25 12.50 30.00
MA Maurice Ager/25 6.00 15.00
PP Paul Pierce/25 30.00 60.00
RF Randy Foye/25 8.00 20.00
RG Rudy Gay/25 15.00 40.00
RM Randolph Morris/25 10.00 25.00
SI Cedric Simmons/25 6.00 15.00
SN Steve Nash/25 50.00 100.00
YM Yao Ming/25 20.00 50.00

2007-08 Sweet Shot Signature Shots Black Ink

PRINT RUNS LISTED IN CHECKLIST
SOME NOT PRICED DUE TO SCARCITY
AD Adrian Dantley/50 6.00 15.00
AJ Antawn Jamison/50 5.00 12.00
BA B.J. Armstrong/50 10.00 25.00
BB Bruce Bowen/97 4.00 10.00
BG Ben Gordon/92 6.00 15.00
BI Larry Bird/50 40.00 100.00
BL Bill Laimbeer/25 15.00 30.00
BS Bill Sharman/32 10.00 25.00
CH Tyson Chandler/25 6.00 15.00
CM Corey Maggette/50 6.00 15.00
CR Cazzie Russell/50 6.00 15.00
CS Cedric Simmons/98 4.00 10.00
CW Shawne Williams/195 4.00 10.00
DB Dee Brown/195 4.00 10.00
DG Daniel Gibson/97 6.00 15.00
DH Dwight Howard/45 15.00 40.00
DL David Lee/98 4.00 10.00
DN David Noel/69 4.00 10.00
DO Keyon Dooling/98 4.00 10.00
FG Francisco Garcia/97 4.00 10.00
FO Randy Foye/99 4.00 10.00
HA Hilton Armstrong/97 4.00 10.00
JA James Augustine/195 4.00 10.00
JB Josh Boone/195 4.00 10.00
JG Jorge Garbajosa/97 4.00 10.00
JO Avery Johnson/98 6.00 15.00
JR J.R. Smith/25 8.00 20.00
JW Jamaal Wilkes/25 15.00 30.00
KB Kobe Bryant/24 150.00 300.00
KD Kevin Durant/99 100.00 200.00
KL Kyle Lowry/189 4.00 10.00
LB Leandro Barbosa/197 4.00 10.00
LJ LeBron James/23 125.00 250.00
LP Leon Powe/100 4.00 10.00
LR Luke Ridnour/98 4.00 10.00
MA Maurice Ager/97 4.00 10.00
MC Mardy Collins/97 4.00 10.00
MD Marquis Daniels/97 4.00 10.00
MI Mile Ilic/97 4.00 10.00
PD Paul Davis/97 4.00 10.00
PM Paul Millsap/97 4.00 10.00
PO Patrick O'Bryant/98 4.00 10.00
RB Ronnie Brewer/97 4.00 10.00
RC Rodney Carney/98 4.00 10.00
RF Raymond Felton/98 5.00 12.00
RH Ryan Hollins/97 4.00 10.00
RI Rick Mahorn/97 6.00 15.00
RR Rajon Rondo/97 20.00 50.00
RS Randolph Morris/97 4.00 10.00
RT Ronny Turiaf/99 6.00 15.00
SB Shannon Brown/49 8.00 20.00
SC Craig Smith/195 4.00 10.00
SF Stromile Swift/98 4.00 10.00
SJ Solomon Jones/97 4.00 10.00
SP Sam Perkins/98 5.00 12.00
SR Sergio Rodriguez/97 4.00 10.00
SS Saer Sene/97 4.00 10.00
SW Shelden Williams/50 4.00 10.00
TC Tom Chambers/50 5.00 12.00
TF T.J. Ford/25 6.00 15.00
TM Tracy McGrady/41 12.50 30.00
WI Marvin Williams/25 8.00 20.00
WI2 Damien Wilkins/195 4.00 10.00
WT Wayman Tisdale/97 10.00 25.00
YD Yakhouba Diawara/99 4.00 10.00

2007-08 Sweet Shot Signature Shots White Ink

STATED PRINT RUN ONE TO 191 SER.#'d SETS
MOST NOT PRICED DUE TO SCARCITY
KK Kyle Korver/191 4.00 10.00

2007-08 Sweet Shot Sweet Spot Signatures

INT RUNS LISTED IN CHECKLIST
SOME NOT PRICED DUE TO SCARCITY
UNPRICED GOLD PRINT RUN 1 TO 5 SETS
BR Brandon Roy/50 20.00 40.00
CS Craig Smith/50 6.00 15.00
DG Daniel Gibson/50 10.00 25.00
HG Horace Grant/25 15.00 40.00
HW Hakim Warrick/70 6.00 15.00
JN Joakim Noah/50 25.00 60.00
KD Kevin Durant/35 75.00 200.00
LA LaMarcus Aldridge/50 20.00 40.00
LJ LeBron James/23 150.00 300.00
MJ Michael Jordan/23 800.00 1200.00
MO Randolph Morris/50 6.00 15.00
RG Rudy Gay/50 12.50 30.00
RM Rick Mahorn/50 12.50 30.00
SR Sergio Rodriguez/50 6.00 15.00
TG Taurean Green/50 6.00 15.00
TT Tyrus Thomas/25 30.00 60.00
WF Walt Frazier/50 15.00 40.00
YD Yakhouba Diawara/50 6.00 15.00

2007-08 Sweet Shot Sweet Spot Signatures Silver Stitch

PRINT RUNS LISTED IN CHECKLIST
SOME NOT PRICED DUE TO SCARCITY
CS Craig Smith/20 8.00 20.00
DG Daniel Gibson/20 8.00 20.00
JG Jorge Garbajosa/20 8.00 20.00
RM Rick Mahorn/20 20.00 40.00
SR Sergio Rodriguez/20 8.00 20.00

2007-08 Sweet Shot Sweet Stitches

RANDOM INSERTS IN PACKS
*PATCHES: 1X TO 2.5X BASE HI
PATCH PRINT RUN 35 SER.#'d SETS
AI Allen Iverson 3.00 8.00
AR Ron Artest 2.50 6.00
BR Elton Brand 2.50 6.00
CA Carmelo Anthony 3.00 8.00
CM Corey Maggette 2.00 5.00
CW Chris Wilcox 2.00 5.00
DE Desmond Mason 2.00 5.00
DG Devean George 2.00 5.00
DH Devin Harris 1.50 4.00
DM Darko Milicic 2.00 5.00
DU Mike Dunleavy 2.00 5.00
FJ Fred Jones 2.00 5.00
GH Grant Hill 3.00 8.00
JO Jermaine O'Neal 2.00 5.00
JR Jason Richardson 2.50 6.00
JS J.R. Smith 2.00 5.00
KB Kobe Bryant 8.00 20.00
KG Kevin Garnett 4.00 10.00
LH Larry Hughes 2.00 5.00
LJ LeBron James 8.00 20.00
MA Martynas Andriuskevicius 2.00 5.00
MD Marquis Daniels 2.00 5.00
MG Manu Ginobili 2.50 6.00
PA Tony Parker 2.50 6.00
PG Pau Gasol 2.50 6.00
RA Ray Allen 2.50 6.00
RJ Richard Jefferson 2.00 5.00
RL Rashard Lewis 2.00 5.00
RW Rasheed Wallace 2.50 6.00
SD Samuel Dalembert 2.00 5.00
SF Steve Francis 2.00 5.00
SI Wayne Simien 2.00 5.00
SL Shaun Livingston 2.00 5.00
SM Sean May 2.00 5.00
SO Shaquille O'Neal 5.00 12.00
TD Tim Duncan 4.00 10.00
TP Tayshaun Prince 2.00 5.00
WS Wally Szczerbiak 2.00 5.00
ZI Zydrunas Ilgauskas 2.00 5.00
ZR Zach Randolph 2.00 5.00

2007-08 Sweet Shot Sweet Swatches Dual

RANDOM INSERTS IN PACKS
*PATCHES: 1.25X TO 3X BASE HI
PATCH PRINT RUN 25 SER.#'d SETS
AG R.Allen/K.Garnett 6.00 15.00
AS M.Andriuskevicius/T.Sefolosha 3.00 8.00
BB K.Brown/A.Bynum 3.00 8.00
BD E.Brand/P.Davis 3.00 8.00
BF K.Bryant/J.Farmar 8.00 20.00
BG M.Ginobili/B.Bowen 4.00 10.00
CJ R.Jefferson/V.Carter 5.00 12.00
CS T.Chandler/C.Simmons 3.00 8.00
DD M.Dunleavy/M.Daniels 3.00 8.00
DG L.Deng/B.Gordon 4.00 10.00
DP T.Duncan/T.Parker 5.00 12.00
DT R.Davis/S.Telfair 3.00 8.00
FB S.Battier/S.Francis 3.00 8.00
GH D.George/D.Harris 3.00 8.00
HB G.Hill/R.Bell 6.00 15.00
HJ L.James/L.Hughes 6.00 15.00
HW R.Hamilton/R.Wallace 3.00 8.00
IA A.Iverson/C.Anthony 6.00 15.00
IM D.Milicic/Z.Ilgauskas 3.00 8.00
JG L.Jackson/J.Graham 3.00 8.00
JJ M.Jordan/L.James 40.00 100.00
KB A.Kirilenko/C.Butler 3.00 8.00
LH D.Howard/R.Lewis 3.00 8.00
MC S.Marbury/M.Collins 3.00 8.00
MG D.Marshall/D.Gooden 3.00 8.00
MH Y.Ming/L.Head 4.00 10.00
ML C.Maggette/S.Livingston 3.00 8.00
MR D.Mason/M.Redd 3.00 8.00
MS A.Stoudemire/S.Marion 6.00 15.00
NA T.Ariza/J.Nelson 3.00 8.00
NH D.Nowitzki/J.Howard 4.00 10.00
PG K.Garnett/P.Pierce 5.00 12.00
RD R.Brewer/D.Brown 3.00 8.00
RF J.Richardson/R.Felton 3.00 8.00
SG P.Gasol/S.Swift 3.00 8.00
SP P.Stojakovic/C.Paul 4.00 10.00
SW W.Szczerbiak/D.West 3.00 8.00
TD I.Diogu/J.Tinsley 3.00 8.00
WR J.Rose/C.Webber 5.00 12.00
WW C.Wilcox/D.Wilkins 3.00 8.00

2009 Sweet Spot Signatures Red Stitch Blue Ink

OVERALL AUTO ODDS 1:3 HOBBY
PRINT RUNS B/WN 2-199 COPIES PER
NO PRICING ON QTY 25 OR LESS
EXCHANGE DEADLINE 10/7/2011
SLJ LeBron James/15 150.00 300.00

2009 Sweet Spot Signatures Red Stitch Green Ink

OVERALL AUTO ODDS 1:3 HOBBY
ANNOUNCED PRINT RUNS LISTED
PRINT RUN INFO PROVIDED BY UD
EXCHANGE DEADLINE 10/7/2011
SLJ LeBron James/25 * 125.00 250.00

2006 Sweet Spot Update Spokesmen Signatures

ERALL AUTO ODDS 1:6
UNPRICED AU PRINT RUN 5-20
4 Michael Jordan/20 400.00 700.00

1951 Syracuse National Glasses

These glasses were given out to a select few fans at a Syracuse National game in 1951. The glasses have a silhouette of the player on them along with their name. Since they are unnumbered we have sequenced them in alphabetical order.
COMPLETE SET (9) 500.00 850.00
1 Al Cervi 50.00 100.00
2 Billy Gabor 25.00 50.00
3 Alex Hannum 60.00 120.00
4 Noble Jorgensen 25.00 50.00
5 George Ratkovicz 25.00 50.00
6 Dolph Schayes 250.00 400.00
7 Paul Seymour 60.00 120.00
8 Front Office Personnel 25.00 50.00
9 Onodoga Cty War Memorial 25.00 50.00

1958-59 Syracuse Nationals

This set consists of 8" by 10" glossy photos of the 1955-56 Syracuse Nationals. Originally the photos sold for 25 cents each, or the entire set for $2.00. The order blank also included an offer for a 32-page record book that could be purchased for 50 cents. The photos are unnumbered and checklisted below in alphabetical order. We have dated this set 1958-59 as it was Hal Greer's and Connie Dierking's rookie NBA season and Togo Palazzi's last full NBA season.
COMPLETE SET (11) 800.00 1600.00
1 Al Bianchi 75.00 150.00
2 Ed Conlin 65.00 125.00
3 Larry Costello 75.00 150.00
4 Connie Dierking 75.00 150.00
5 Hal Greer 100.00 200.00
6 Bob Hopkins 65.00 125.00
7 John Kerr 100.00 200.00
8 Togo Palazzi 65.00 125.00
9 Dolph Schayes 150.00 300.00
10 Paul Seymour 65.00 125.00
11 Team Photo 75.00 150.00

1962-63 Syracuse Nationals

These photos, which measure 8" by 10", feature members of the Syracuse Nationals. Since these photos are unnumbered, we have sequenced them in alphabetical order.
COMPLETE SET 400.00 800.00
1 Al Bianchi 30.00 60.00
2 Len Chappell 25.00 50.00
3 Larry Costello 40.00 80.00
4 Dave Gambee 25.00 50.00
5 Hal Greer 60.00 120.00
6 Alex Hannum 30.00 60.00
7 Swede Halbrook 25.00 50.00
8 John Kerr 50.00 100.00
9 Paul Neuman 25.00 50.00
10 Joe Roberts 25.00 50.00
11 Dolph Schayes 75.00 150.00
12 Lee Shaffer 25.00 50.00

1998 Taco Bell Shaquille O'Neal

Inserted into various Taco Bell Home Original dinners, this card is shorter than a standard sized card and features a 3-D shot of Shaquille O'Neal dunking. The card back is not numbered and features a black and white promotional ad stating "Pile On The Fun with Taco Bell".
1 Shaquille O'Neal 4.00 10.00

1984-85 Tampa Bay Thrillers

This oversized card was released during the 1984-85 season by Eckerd Drug Store, it features ten of the Tampa Bay Thriller's players and coaches. Please note that this 8x11 black and white card is not numbered and has a blank back.
1 Jeff Rosenberg PRES 4.00 10.00
Bill Musselman CO
Charles Jones
James Banks
Les Craft
Marc Glass
Steve Hayes
Perry Moss
Freeman Williams
Ron Valentine

1980-81 TCMA CBA

The 1980-81 Continental Basketball Association set, produced by TCMA, features 45 black and white photos of the players along with the team name in red along the side of the front of the card. The sets were originally available direct from the CBA for 5.50. The backs contain brief biographical data and statistics, the CBA logo, the team logo and the card number. A 1981 TCMA copyright date also appears on the back. The standard-size cards are printed on white cardboard backs.
COMPLETE SET (45) 40.00 80.00
1 Chubby Cox 1.25 3.00
2 Sylvester Cuyler 1.00 2.50
3 Harry Davis .75 2.00
4 Danny Salisbury .75 2.00
5 Cazzie Russell 4.00 10.00
6 Al Green 1.00 2.50
7 Rick Wilson .75 2.00
8 Jim Brogan .75 2.00
9 Andre McCarter 2.50 6.00
10 Jerry Baskerville 1.25 3.00
11 James Woods .75 2.00
12 Geoff Crompton 1.25 3.00
13 Korky Nelson .75 2.00
14 George Karl CO 7.50 15.00
15 Stan Pietkiewicz 1.25 3.00
16 Raymond Townsend 2.00 5.00
17 Lenny Horton .75 2.00
18 Carl Bailey .75 2.00
19 Ken Jones .75 2.00
20 Rory Sparrow 3.00 8.00
21 Mauro Panaggio CO 1.50 4.00
22 Glenn Hagan 1.25 3.00
23 Larry Fogle 1.25 3.00
24 Wayne Abrams .75 2.00
25 Jerry Christian .75 2.00
26 Edgar Jones 1.50 4.00
27 Jerry Radocha .75 2.00
28 Greg Jackson 1.00 2.50
29 Eddie Mast P/CO 1.25 3.00
30 Ron Davis 1.25 3.00
31 Tico Brown 1.00 2.50
32 Freeman Blade 1.00 2.50
33 Bill Klucas CO 1.00 2.50
34 Melvin Davis 1.00 2.50
35 James Hardy .75 2.00
36 Brad Davis 4.00 10.00
37 Andre Wakefield .75 2.00
38 Brett Vroman 1.25 3.00
39 Larry Knight .75 2.00
40 Mel Bennett .75 2.00
41 Stan Eckwood .75 2.00
42 Andrew Parker .75 2.00
43 Billy Ray (Dunk) Bates 1.50 4.00
44 Matt Teahan .75 2.00
45 Carlton Green .75 2.00

1981-82 TCMA CBA

This 90-card standard-size set features black and white photos surrounded by a red frame line in which the player's name and team are printed. The Continental Basketball Association (CBA) logo appears in black on the front of the card. The back of the card contains the card number, career statistics, brief biographical data, and the team and CBA logos. A TCMA copyright date appears on the back.
COMPLETE SET (90) 60.00 150.00
1 1981 CBA Champions 2.00 5.00
Rochester Zeniths/(Previous champions listed on back)
2 Wayne Abrams .75 2.00
3 Pete Taylor .75 2.00
4 George Torres .75 2.00
5 Henry Bibby 3.00 8.00
6 Rufus Harris .75 2.00
7 Donnie Koonce .75 2.00
8 Jeff Wilkins 1.50 4.00
9 Kurt Nimphius 1.25 3.00
10 Billy Ray(Dunk) Bates 1.50 4.00
11 James Lee 1.25 3.00
12 Marlon Redmond .75 2.00
13 Gary Mazza CO .75 2.00
14 Tony Fuller 1.25 3.00
15 Brad Davis 3.00 8.00
16 Joe Cooper 1.25 3.00
17 Andra Griffin .75 2.00
18 Rudy White 1.25 3.00
19 Ricky Williams .75 2.00
20 Glenn Hagan 1.25 3.00
21 Ernie Graham .75 2.00
22 Kevin Graham .75 2.00
23 Billy Reid .75 2.00
24 Mauro Panaggio CO 1.25 3.00
25 Bo Ellis 1.50 4.00
26 Ollie Matson 1.25 3.00
27 Tony Turner .75 2.00
28 Leo Papile CO .75 2.00
29 Larry Holmes .75 2.00
30 Steve Hayes 2.00 5.00
31 Carl Bailey .75 2.00
32 Tico Brown 1.25 3.00
33 Percy Davis .75 2.00
34 Al Leslie .75 2.00
35 Ken Dennard 1.50 4.00
36 Larry Spriggs 3.00 8.00
37 John Smith .75 2.00
38 Kenny Natt 1.25 3.00
39 Harry Heineken .75 2.00
40 Lowes Moore .75 2.00
41 Curtis Berry .75 2.00
42 Freeman Blade CO 1.25 3.00
43 Larry Lawrence .75 2.00
44 Purvis Miller .75 2.00
45 Ron Valentine .75 2.00
46 Charles Floyd .75 2.00
47 Greg Cornelius .75 2.00
48 Clay Johnson 2.00 5.00
49 Bill Klucas CO 1.25 3.00
50 Cazzie Russell P/CO 4.00 10.00
51 Craig Shelton 1.50 4.00
52 Dave Britton .75 2.00
53 Ken Green .75 2.00
54 Stan Pawlak CO 1.25 3.00
55 Rich Yonakor .75 2.00
56 Darryl Gladden .75 2.00
57 Norman Black .75 2.00
58 Pete Harris .75 2.00
59 Anthony Roberts .75 2.00
60 Jawann Oldham 1.50 4.00
61 Sam Clancy 2.00 5.00
62 Andre McCarter 2.00 5.00
63 Joe Merten .75 2.00
64 Eddie Moss .75 2.00
65 Brad Branson .75 2.00
66 Lenny Horton .75 2.00
67 Jerome Henderson .75 2.00
68 Terry Stotts 2.00 5.00
69 Tony Wells .75 2.00
70 Rickey Green 3.00 8.00
71 Don Newman .75 2.00
72 Randy Owens .75 2.00
73 Erv Giddings .75 2.00
74 Barry Young .75 2.00
75 Jim Brogan .75 2.00
76 Richard Johnson .75 2.00
77 George Karl CO 4.00 10.00
78 U.S. Reed 1.25 3.00
79 Fran Greenberg .75 2.00
(PR Director)
80 Ron Davis .75 2.00
81 Larry Fogle 1.00 2.50
82 Clarence Kea .75 2.00
83 Steve Craig 1.25 3.00
84 Harry Davis .75 2.00
85 Jacky Dorsey .75 2.00
86 Herb Gray .75 2.00
87 Randy Johnson .75 2.00
88 Jim Drucker COMM .75 2.00
89 Lynbert Johnson .75 2.00
90 Checklist 1-90 .75 2.00

1982-83 TCMA CBA

This third Continental Basketball Association set from TCMA features 90 black and white standard-size cards with red frame lines. The CBA logo, the player's name, physical data, team name, and team logo appear on the front, as does the card number. The back of the cards form a large puzzle. The cards were apparently issued in two series of 45 cards each.
COMPLETE SET (90) 50.00 125.00
1 Cazzie Russell CO 3.00 8.00
2 Boot Bond .75 2.00
3 Ron Charles 1.00 2.50
4 Charles Pittman 1.50 4.00
5 Calvin Garrett 2.00 5.00
6 Willie Jones .60 1.50
7 Riley Clarida .60 1.50
8 Jim Johnstone .60 1.50
9 Bobby Potts .60 1.50
10 Lowes Moore .75 2.00
11 Dwight Anderson 2.50 6.00
12 John Coughran .60 1.50
13 Mike Evans 1.50 4.00
14 Alan Hardy .60 1.50
15 Willie Smith .60 1.50
16 Oliver Mack 2.00 5.00
17 Checklist 1-45 .60 1.50
18 Picture 1 .60 1.50
(Action under basket)
19 James Lee 1.25 3.00
20 Kenny Natt 1.25 3.00
21 Cyrus Mann .60 1.50
22 Bobby Cattage .75 2.00
23 Garry Witts .60 1.50
24 Bill Klucas CO .75 2.00
25 Al Smith 1.00 2.50
26 B.B. Fontenet .60 1.50
27 Chris Giles .60 1.50
28 Barry Young .75 2.00
29 Horace Wyatt 1.00 2.50
30 Robert Smith .75 2.00
31 Ron Baxter 1.00 2.50
32 Charlie Jones .75 2.00
33 Tico Brown 1.00 2.50
34 John McCullough .60 1.50
35 Dan Callandrillo 1.00 2.50
36 John Leonard 1.00 2.50
37 Sam Worthen 1.00 2.50
38 Dale Wilkinson .75 2.00
39 Gary Johnson .60 1.50
40 Dean Meminger CO 1.25 3.00
41 Lloyd Terry .60 1.50
42 Mike Schultz .75 2.00
43 Darryl Gladden .60 1.50
44 Clarence Kea .75 2.00
45 Charlie Floyd .60 1.50
46 Skip Dillard 1.25 3.00
47 Craig Tucker .60 1.50
48 Gib Hinz .60 1.50
49 Tom Sienkiewicz .75 2.00
50 Larry Spriggs 2.00 5.00
51 Perry Moss .60 1.50
52 Gerald Sims .60 1.50
53 Alan Taylor .60 1.50
54 James Terry .60 1.50
55 John Nillen CO .60 1.50
56 Steve Burks .60 1.50
57 Anthony Martin .60 1.50
58 Purvis Miller .75 2.00
59 Kevin Smith .60 1.50
60 John Neumann CO 1.00 2.50
61 Mike Davis 1.25 3.00
62 Gary Carter 1.25 3.00
63 Checklist 46-90 .60 1.50
64 Picture 2 .60 1.50
(Action under basket)
65 Charles Thompson .60 1.50
66 John Douglas .60 1.50
67 John Schweitz 1.25 3.00
68 Kevin Figaro .60 1.50
69 John Smith .60 1.50
70 Joe Cooper 1.00 2.50
71 Tony Brown 1.25 3.00
72 Mike Wilson .60 1.50
73 Wayne Abrams .60 1.50
74 T.X. Martin .60 1.50
75 Joe Merten .60 1.50
76 Joe Kopicki 1.00 2.50
77 Carl Nicks 1.00 2.50
78 Wayne Kreklow .60 1.50
79 Tony Guy .75 2.00
80 Dave Harshman CO .60 1.50
81 Bob Davis .60 1.50
82 Gary Mazza CO .60 1.50
83 Randy Owens .60 1.50
84 David Burns .60 1.50
85 Erv Giddings .60 1.50
86 JoJo Hunter 1.00 2.50
87 Frankie Sanders .60 1.50
88 Dave Richardson .60 1.50
89 Lionel Garrett .60 1.50
90 Marvin Barnes 3.00 8.00

1982-83 TCMA Lancaster CBA

This set features 30 black and white standard-sized cards with blue border on front. The card backs contain statistics and are numbered on the back. Many of the poses are in action shots. The set is printed on dark cardboard. All cards feature players or personnel of the Lancaster Lightning (Continental Basketball Association) team which won the 1981-82 CBA Championship.
COMPLETE SET (30) 14.00 35.00
1 Lightning Wins 1982 1.25 3.00
CBA Championship
2 1982-83 Lancaster .60 1.50
Lightning Team Picture
3 Dr. Seymour Kilstein PRES .40 1.00
4 Cazzie Russell CO 2.00 5.00
5 Cazzie Russell CO IA 2.00 5.00
6 Ed Koback 1.00 2.50
Operations
7 Bob Danforth .40 1.00
Marketing
8 Henry Bibby IA 1.25 3.00
9 Joe Cooper .75 2.00
10 Joe Cooper IA .60 1.50
11 Curtis Berry .75 2.00
12 Curtis Berry IA .60 1.50
13 James Lee 1.00 2.50
14 James Lee IA .75 2.00
15 Ed Sherod IA .60 1.50
16 Charlie Floyd .40 1.00
17 Charlie Floyd IA .40 1.00
18 Darryl Gladden .40 1.00
19 Darryl Gladden IA .40 1.00
20 Tom Sienkiewicz .75 2.00
21 Tom Sienkiewicz IA .60 1.50
22 Stan Williams .40 1.00
23 Willie Redden .40 1.00
24 Reginald Gaines .40 1.00

25 Gary (Cat) Johnson .75 2.00
26 Gary (Cat) Johnson IA .60 1.50
27 Keith Hilliard .40 1.00
28 Keith Hilliard IA .40 1.00
29 Donald Seals .40 1.00
30 Rufus Harris .75 2.00

1981 TCMA NBA

This 44-card standard-sized set features some of the all-time great basketball players. The fronts feature a color posed photo of the player, while the back has name, career summary, and career highlights.

COMPLETE SET (44) 50.00 125.00
1 Alex Hannum .75 2.00
2 Larry Foust .40 1.00
3 George Mikan 5.00 12.00
4 Mel(Hutch) Hutchins .40 1.00
5 Bob Pettit 1.50 4.00
6 Willis Reed 1.25 3.00
7 Adolph Schayes 1.25 3.00
8 Vern Mikkelsen SP 5.00 12.00
9 Cazzie Russell .60 1.50
10 Dick Van Arsdale .60 1.50
11 Lenny Wilkens 1.25 3.00
12 Ray Felix .60 1.50
13 Ed Macauley 1.00 2.50
14 Clyde Lovellette .75 2.00
15 Slater(Dugie) Martin .75 2.00
16 Bill Russell 6.00 15.00
17 Oscar Robertson SP 6.00 15.00
18 Bill Bradley 2.00 5.00
19 Elgin Baylor 3.00 8.00
20 Bill Sharman 2.00 5.00
21 Tom(Satch) Sanders 1.00 2.50
22 Dave Bing .75 2.00
23 Carl Braun .75 2.00
24 Frank Selvy .75 2.00
25 George Yardley .60 1.50
26 Dick McGuire .60 1.50
27 Leroy Ellis .40 1.00
28 Jack Twyman .75 2.00
29 Nate Thurmond 1.25 3.00
30 Walt Frazier 1.50 4.00
31 John(Red) Kerr 1.25 3.00
32 Jerry West 4.00 10.00
33 John Egan SP 2.50 6.00
34 Jim Loscutoff 1.00 2.50
35 Bob Leonard .60 1.50
36 Rick Barry 1.25 3.00
37 Gene Shue .75 2.00
38 Jerry Lucas 1.25 3.00
39 Dave DeBusschere 1.25 3.00
40 Johnny Green 1.00 2.50
Charles Tyra
Carl Braun
Richie Guerin
John George
41 Bob Cousy 4.00 10.00
42 Walter Bellamy .60 1.50
43 Billy Cunningham 1.25 3.00
44 Wilt Chamberlain 6.00 15.00

1990 The National Michael Jordan Promo

This standard-sized card was issued to promote the upcoming "The National" sports-only newspaper. The card front features the newspaper name at the top with Jordan shooting over Ewing. The card back features information about the new newspaper. The card is not numbered.

NNO Michael Jordan 12.00 30.00

2008-09 Thunder Upper Deck

COMPLETE SET (14) 2.50 6.00
1 Kevin Durant .75 2.00
2 Earl Watson .20 .50
3 Nick Collison .25 .60
4 Jeff Green .25 .60
5 Chris Wilcox .20 .50
6 Damien Wilkins .20 .50
7 Johan Petro .20 .50
8 Robert Swift .20 .50
9 Mouhamed Sene .20 .50
10 Desmond Mason .20 .50
11 Russell Westbrook 2.50 6.00
12 D.J. White .25 .60
13 P.J. Carlesimo CO .20 .50
14 Kyle Weaver .20 .50
NNO Checklist

1989-90 Timberwolves Burger King

This seven-card set was sponsored by Burger King to commemorate the inaugural season of the Minnesota Timberwolves. The cards were issued with a (9" by 12") Player Cards Collector Set, which included on the inside a 1989-90 game schedule and slots to hold the cards. The standard size cards feature on the fronts color action player photos, with dark blue borders on white card stock. A banner reading "Inaugural Season" overlays the top of the picture. The team name and logo at the top and player identification below the picture round out the card face. The backs have biographical and statistical information, with the team logo and a blue stripe (with player's name in white) appearing at the top of the cards. The cards are unnumbered. Brad Lohaus is considered somewhat tougher to find since he was supposedly pulled from the set and replaced by Randy Breuer during the promotion. The set features the first professional card of Jerome "Pooh" Richardson.

COMPLETE SET (7) 1.50 4.00
19 Tony Campbell .30 .75
23 Tyrone Corbin .40 1.00
24 Pooh Richardson .60 1.50
35 Sidney Lowe .30 .75
42 Sam Mitchell .40 1.00
45 Randy Breuer .30 .75
54 Brad Lohaus .30 .75

2009-10 Timeless Treasures

COMP.SET w/o SPs (100) 50.00 100.00
1-100 PRINT RUN 399 SER.#'d SETS
101-150 PRINT RUN 299 SER.#'d SETS
UNPRICED GOLD PRINT RUN 5 TO 10 SETS
UNPRICED PLATINUM PRINT RUN ONE SET
1 Kobe Bryant 4.00 10.00
2 LeBron James 4.00 10.00
3 Chris Paul 1.25 3.00
4 Dwight Howard .75 2.00
5 Dwyane Wade 1.50 4.00
6 Dirk Nowitzki 1.25 3.00
7 Danny Granger .75 2.00
8 Kevin Durant 2.50 6.00
9 Pau Gasol 1.00 2.50
10 Amare Stoudemire .75 2.00
11 Chris Bosh 1.00 2.50
12 Brandon Roy 1.00 2.50
13 Kevin Garnett 1.50 4.00
14 Al Jefferson .75 2.00
15 Deron Williams .75 2.00
16 Chauncey Billups 1.00 2.50
17 Steve Nash 1.00 2.50
18 Tim Duncan 1.50 4.00
19 Andre Iguodala .75 2.00
20 Jason Kidd 1.00 2.50
21 Devin Harris .60 1.50
22 Joe Johnson .75 2.00
23 Gerald Wallace .75 2.00
24 Vince Carter 1.25 3.00
25 Paul Pierce 1.00 2.50
26 Brook Lopez .75 2.00
27 Kevin Martin .75 2.00
28 Antawn Jamison .75 2.00
29 David West .75 2.00
30 Carmelo Anthony 1.25 3.00
31 Troy Murphy .60 1.50
32 Rashard Lewis .75 2.00
33 Elton Brand 1.00 2.50
34 Josh Smith .75 2.00
35 Baron Davis .75 2.00
36 Ray Allen 1.00 2.50
37 Carlos Boozer .75 2.00
38 David Lee .60 1.50
39 Derrick Rose 1.50 4.00
40 Rajon Rondo 1.00 2.50
41 O.J. Mayo .60 1.50
42 Nene .75 2.00
43 Andrea Bargnani .75 2.00
44 Charlie Villanueva .60 1.50
45 Ben Gordon .75 2.00
46 Mike Bibby .75 2.00
47 Tony Parker 1.00 2.50
48 Andrew Bynum .60 1.50
49 Russell Westbrook 2.50 6.00
50 Anthony Randolph .60 1.50
51 Eric Gordon .75 2.00
52 Jeff Green .75 2.00
53 Shaquille O'Neal 2.00 5.00
54 Aaron Brooks .60 1.50
55 Chris Kaman .75 2.00
56 D.J. Augustin .60 1.50
57 Emeka Okafor .75 2.00
58 Derek Fisher .75 2.00
59 Jermaine O'Neal .75 2.00
60 Josh Howard .75 2.00
61 Kevin Love 1.00 2.50
62 Lamar Odom .75 2.00
63 Michael Beasley .60 1.50
64 Richard Hamilton .75 2.00
65 Ron Artest 1.00 2.50
66 Ronnie Brewer .75 2.00
67 Rudy Fernandez .60 1.50
68 Ryan Gomes .60 1.50
69 Shane Battier 1.00 2.50
70 T.J. Ford .60 1.50
71 Tracy McGrady 1.00 2.50
72 Trevor Ariza .60 1.50
73 Greg Oden .75 2.00
74 Nate Archibald .75 2.00
75 Al Cervi 1.00 2.50
76 Bob Cousy 1.50 4.00
77 Harry Gallatin 1.00 2.50
78 Gail Goodrich .75 2.00
79 Hal Greer .75 2.00
80 John Havlicek 1.00 2.50
81 Connie Hawkins 1.00 2.50
82 Elvin Hayes 1.00 2.50
83 Bob McAdoo .75 2.00
84 Pete Maravich 1.50 4.00
85 Bill Russell 1.50 4.00
86 Dolph Schayes 1.00 2.50
87 Bill Sharman 1.00 2.50
88 David Thompson .75 2.00
89 Nate Thurmond .75 2.00
90 Jack Twyman 1.00 2.50
91 Wes Unseld 1.00 2.50
92 Bill Walton 1.00 2.50
93 Bobby Wanzer .60 1.50
94 Frank Ramsey 1.00 2.50
95 Willis Reed 1.00 2.50
96 Pat Riley 1.00 2.50
97 Xavier McDaniel .60 1.50
98 Oscar Robertson 1.00 2.50
99 Lenny Wilkens 1.00 2.50
100 James Worthy 1.25 3.00
101 Blake Griffin AU RC 20.00 50.00
102 Hasheem Thabeet AU RC 3.00 8.00
103 James Harden AU RC 50.00 120.00
104 Tyreke Evans AU RC 4.00 10.00
105 Jonny Flynn AU RC 3.00 8.00
106 Stephen Curry AU RC 250.00 500.00
107 Jordan Hill AU RC 4.00 10.00
108 Ricky Rubio AU RC 20.00 50.00
109 Brandon Jennings AU RC 5.00 12.00
110 Terrence Williams AU RC 3.00 8.00
111 Gerald Henderson AU RC 4.00 10.00
112 Tyler Hansbrough AU RC 4.00 10.00
113 Earl Clark AU RC 4.00 10.00
114 Austin Daye AU RC 3.00 8.00
115 James Johnson AU RC 4.00 10.00
116 Jrue Holiday AU RC 6.00 15.00
117 Ty Lawson AU RC 5.00 12.00
118 Jeff Teague AU RC 5.00 12.00
119 Eric Maynor AU RC 3.00 8.00
120 Darren Collison AU RC 5.00 12.00
121 Omri Casspi AU RC 4.00 10.00
122 B.J. Mullens AU RC 3.00 8.00
123 Rodrigue Beaubois AU RC 3.00 8.00
124 Taj Gibson AU RC 5.00 12.00
125 DeMarre Carroll AU RC 4.00 10.00
126 Wayne Ellington AU RC 5.00 12.00
127 Toney Douglas AU RC 3.00 8.00
128 Jeff Pendergraph AU RC 3.00 8.00
129 Jermaine Taylor AU RC 3.00 8.00
130 DaJuan Summers AU RC 3.00 8.00
131 Sam Young AU RC 3.00 8.00
132 DeJuan Blair AU RC 4.00 10.00
133 Jodie Meeks AU RC 5.00 12.00
134 Chase Budinger AU RC 4.00 10.00
135 Taylor Griffin AU RC 3.00 8.00
136 Marcus Thornton AU RC 4.00 10.00
137 Danny Green AU RC 6.00 15.00
138 Derrick Brown AU RC 3.00 8.00
139 Jonas Jerebko AU RC 5.00 12.00
140 Serge Ibaka AU RC 5.00 12.00
141 Jon Brockman AU RC 3.00 8.00
142 Dante Cunningham AU RC 3.00 8.00
143 Wesley Matthews AU RC 5.00 12.00
144 A.J. Price AU RC 3.00 8.00
145 Lester Hudson AU RC 3.00 8.00
146 Marcus Landry AU RC 3.00 8.00
147 Sundiata Gaines AU RC 3.00 8.00
148 David Andersen AU RC 3.00 8.00
149 Patrick Mills AU RC 12.00 30.00
150 DeMar DeRozan AU RC 20.00 40.00

2009-10 Timeless Treasures Silver

*SILVER 1-100: 1.5X TO 4X BASE HI
SILVER 1-100 PRINT RUN 25 SER.#'d SETS
*SILVER RC/25: .6X TO 1.5X BASE HI
SILVER/10 UNPRICED DUE TO SCARCITY
106 Stephen Curry AU/25 800.00 1200.00
116 Jrue Holiday AU/25 20.00 50.00

2009-10 Timeless Treasures Championship Season Combos Materials

STATED PRINT RUN 25 SER.#'d SETS
UNPRICED PRIME PRINT RUN 5 SER.#'d SETS
1 K.Garnett/R.Allen 10.00 25.00
2 K.Garnett/R.Rondo 8.00 20.00
3 R.Rondo/R.Allen 10.00 25.00
4 K.Bryant/P.Gasol 15.00 40.00

2009-10 Timeless Treasures Championship Season Materials

STATED PRINT RUN 50 TO 100 SER.#'d SETS
UNPRICED PRIME PRINT RUN 5 TO 25 SETS
UNPRICED TAG PRINT RUN 3 TO 6 SETS
UNPRICED TAG LOGO PRINT RUN 1 TO 2 SETS
UNPRICED TAG NBA SIGS PRINT RUN 1 TO 2 SETS
UNPRICED TEAM LOGO PRINT RUN 1 TO 2 SETS
UNPRICED TEAM LOGO SIGS PRINT RUN 1-3 SETS
UNPRICED NBA LOGO PRINT RUN 1 TO 3 SETS
UNPRICED NBA LOGO SIGS PRINT RUN 1 TO 3 SETS
1 Kevin Garnett/100 5.00 12.00
2 Rajon Rondo/100 3.00 8.00
3 Ray Allen/100 3.00 8.00
4 Pau Gasol/50 5.00 12.00
5 Kobe Bryant/100 10.00 25.00
6 Dwyane Wade/100 5.00 12.00
7 Tim Duncan/100 5.00 12.00
8 Tony Parker/100 3.00 8.00
10 Tom Heinsohn/100 3.00 8.00
11 Kareem Abdul-Jabbar/100 5.00 12.00
12 Manu Ginobili/100 3.00 8.00

2009-10 Timeless Treasures Championship Season Materials Laundry Tags Signatures

STATED PRINT RUN ONE TO 12 SER.#'d SETS
MOST UNPRICED DUE TO SCARCITY
3 Ray Allen/12 50.00 100.00

2009-10 Timeless Treasures Championship Season Materials Signatures

STATED PRINT RUN 5 TO 25 SER.#'d SETS
SOME UNPRICED DUE TO SCARCITY
UNPRICED PRIME PRINT RUN 5 TO 10 SETS
2 Rajon Rondo/25 40.00 70.00
3 Ray Allen/25 30.00 80.00
11 Kareem Abdul-Jabbar/25 40.00 80.00

2009-10 Timeless Treasures Championship Season Quad Materials

STATED PRINT RUN 25 TO 50 SER.#'d SETS
UNPRICED PRIME PRINT RUN 5 SER.#'d SETS
1 Wade/KG/Kobe/Duncan/50 10.00 25.00
2 Kareem/Kobe/Arch/Hnshn/25 15.00 30.00

2009-10 Timeless Treasures Championship Season Triple Materials

STATED PRINT RUN 25 SER.#'d SETS
UNPRICED PRIME PRINT RUN 5 SER.#'d SETS
1 Garnett/Rondo/Allen/25 15.00 40.00

2009-10 Timeless Treasures HOF Combos Materials

STATED PRINT RUN 10 TO 50 SER.#'d SETS
UNPRICED PRIME PRINT RUN 5 SER.#'d SETS
1 Kareem/G.Mikan/50 20.00 50.00
2 L.Bird/K.McHale/50 10.00 25.00
3 J.Dumars/I.Thomas/50 6.00 15.00
4 A.English/D.Issel/50 5.00 12.00
5 T.Heinsohn/D.Cowens/50 6.00 15.00
6 D.Cowens/J.Havlicek/50 6.00 15.00
7 H.Olajuwon/C.Drexler/50 10.00 25.00

2009-10 Timeless Treasures HOF Materials Jerseys

STATED PRINT RUN 5 TO 50 SER.#'d SETS
UNPRICED PRIME PRINT RUN 5 SER.#'d SETS
1 George Mikan/50 15.00 40.00
2 Kareem Abdul-Jabbar/50 6.00 15.00
3 John Stockton/50 6.00 15.00
4 Tom Heinsohn/50 5.00 12.00
5 Adrian Dantley/50 3.00 8.00
6 Alex English/50 3.00 8.00
7 Earl Monroe/50 5.00 12.00
8 George Gervin/50 5.00 12.00
9 Dominique Wilkins/50 5.00 12.00
10 Dave Cowens/50 5.00 12.00
11 Joe Dumars/50 5.00 12.00
12 Jerry West/50 6.00 15.00
13 Isiah Thomas/50 4.00 10.00
14 Walt Frazier/50 4.00 10.00
15 Robert Parish/50 4.00 10.00
16 Rick Barry/50 3.00 8.00
17 Moses Malone/50 4.00 10.00
18 Magic Johnson/50 8.00 20.00
21 Kevin McHale/50 5.00 12.00
22 Dan Issel/50 3.00 8.00
23 Bob Lanier/50 3.00 8.00
24 Clyde Drexler/50 5.00 12.00
25 Clyde Drexler/50 5.00 12.00
29 Hakeem Olajuwon/50 5.00 12.00
30 Patrick Ewing/50 8.00 20.00

2009-10 Timeless Treasures HOF Materials Jerseys Signatures

STATED PRINT RUN 5 TO 25 SER.#'d SETS
UNPRICED PRIME PRINT RUN 10 SER.#'d SETS
2 Kareem Abdul-Jabbar/25 50.00 120.00
8 George Gervin/25 12.50 30.00
9 Dominique Wilkins/25 12.50 30.00
10 Dave Cowens/25 12.50 30.00
13 Isiah Thomas/25 12.50 30.00
14 Walt Frazier/25 12.50 30.00
15 Robert Parish/25 12.50 30.00
18 Magic Johnson/25 50.00 100.00
19 Larry Bird/25 50.00 100.00
22 Dan Issel/25 12.50 30.00
24 Clyde Drexler/25 25.00 50.00
25 Clyde Drexler/25 25.00 50.00
26 John Havlicek/25 20.00 40.00

2009-10 Timeless Treasures HOF Quad Materials

STATED PRINT RUN 10 TO 50 SER.#'d SETS
SOME NOT PRICED DUE TO SCARCITY
UNPRICED PRIME PRINT RUN 5 SER.#'d SETS
1 Mikan/KAJ/West/Magic/50 30.00 80.00
2 Dant/Dumars/Isiah/Lanier/50 15.00 30.00
3 Hein/Cowns/Hav/Bird/50 20.00 40.00

2009-10 Timeless Treasures HOF Signatures Silver

STATED PRINT RUN 35 SER.#'d SETS
UNPRICED GOLD PRINT RUN 10 SER.#'d SETS
UNPRICED PLATINUM PRINT RUN ONE SET
2 Kareem Abdul-Jabbar 40.00 80.00
8 George Gervin 10.00 25.00
10 Dave Cowens 8.00 20.00
13 Isiah Thomas 8.00 20.00
15 Robert Parish 8.00 20.00
18 Magic Johnson 40.00 80.00
19 Larry Bird 40.00 80.00
24 Clyde Drexler 25.00 50.00
25 Clyde Drexler 20.00 50.00
26 John Havlicek 20.00 40.00
31 Wes Unseld 12.50 30.00
32 Bob Cousy 20.00 50.00
33 Oscar Robertson 40.00 80.00
34 Bill Russell 50.00 120.00

2009-10 Timeless Treasures Home and Road Gamers

STATED PRINT RUN 25 TO 100 SER.#'d SETS
UNPRICED PRIME PRINT RUNS 1 TO 10 SETS
1 Kevin Garnett/50 6.00 15.00
2 Deron Williams/50 3.00 8.00
3 Tracy McGrady/50 4.00 10.00
4 Tim Duncan/50 6.00 15.00
5 Kevin McHale/50 6.00 15.00
6 Kobe Bryant/50 12.00 30.00
7 Kareem Abdul-Jabbar/25 8.00 20.00
8 LeBron James/100 12.00 30.00
9 Dwight Howard/100 3.00 8.00
10 Shaquille O'Neal/100 8.00 20.00
11 Vince Carter/100 5.00 12.00
12 Dirk Nowitzki/100 5.00 12.00
14 Jason Kidd/100 4.00 10.00
15 Dan Issel/50 3.00 8.00
16 Chris Paul/100 5.00 12.00
17 LaMarcus Aldridge/100 4.00 10.00
18 Karl Malone/50 5.00 12.00
19 Dwyane Wade/50 6.00 15.00
20 Dikembe Mutombo/100 4.00 10.00
21 Kevin Durant/100 10.00 25.00
22 Hakeem Olajuwon/100 5.00 12.00
23 Elton Brand/100 4.00 10.00
24 Isiah Thomas/50 4.00 10.00
26 Brandon Roy/100 4.00 10.00
27 David Lee/50 4.00 10.00
28 Al Jefferson/100 3.00 8.00
29 Brook Lopez/100 3.00 8.00

2009-10 Timeless Treasures Home and Road Gamers Signatures

STATED PRINT RUN ONE TO 25 SER.#'d SETS
SOME NOT PRICED DUE TO SCARCITY
UNPRICED PRIME PRINT RUN ONE TO 10 SETS
2 Deron Williams/25 20.00 50.00
3 Tracy McGrady/25 20.00 40.00
6 Kobe Bryant/25 150.00 300.00
15 Dan Issel/25 12.00 30.00
20 Dikembe Mutombo/25 30.00 60.00
24 Isiah Thomas/25 20.00 40.00
27 David Lee/20 12.00 30.00

2009-10 Timeless Treasures Materials Jerseys

STATED PRINT RUN 50 TO 100 SER.#'d SETS
UNPRICED PRIME PRINT RUN 1 TO 10 SETS
TAGS PRINT RUN ONE SER.#'d SET
TAGS INK PRINT RUN ONE SER.#'d SET
TAGS NBA LOGO PRINT RUN ONE SET
TAGS NBA LOGO INK PRINT RUN ONE SET
TAGS TEAM LOGO PRINT RUN ONE SET
TAGS TEAM LOGO INK PRINT RUN ONE SET
TAGS NOT PRICED DUE TO SCARCITY
1 Kobe Bryant/100 8.00 20.00
2 LeBron James/100 8.00 20.00
3 Chris Paul/100 4.00 10.00
4 Dwight Howard/100 2.50 6.00
5 Dwyane Wade/100 5.00 12.00
6 Dirk Nowitzki/100 4.00 10.00
7 Danny Granger/100 2.50 6.00
8 Kevin Durant/100 8.00 20.00
9 Pau Gasol/100 3.00 8.00
10 Amare Stoudemire/100 2.50 6.00
11 Chris Bosh/100 3.00 8.00
12 Brandon Roy/100 3.00 8.00
13 Kevin Garnett/100 5.00 12.00
14 Al Jefferson/100 2.50 6.00
15 Deron Williams/100 2.50 6.00
16 Chauncey Billups/100 3.00 8.00
18 Tim Duncan/100 5.00 12.00
19 Andre Iguodala/100 2.50 6.00
20 Jason Kidd/100 3.00 8.00
21 Devin Harris/100 2.00 5.00
22 Joe Johnson/100 2.50 6.00
23 Gerald Wallace/100 2.50 6.00
24 Vince Carter/100 4.00 10.00
25 Paul Pierce/100 3.00 8.00
26 Brook Lopez/100 2.50 6.00
28 Antawn Jamison/100 2.50 6.00
29 David West/100 2.50 6.00
30 Carmelo Anthony/100 4.00 10.00
31 Troy Murphy/100 2.00 5.00
32 Rashard Lewis/100 2.50 6.00
33 Elton Brand/100 3.00 8.00
34 Josh Smith/100 2.50 6.00
35 Baron Davis/100 2.50 6.00
36 Ray Allen/100 3.00 8.00
37 Carlos Boozer/100 2.50 6.00
38 David Lee/100 2.00 5.00
40 Rajon Rondo/100 3.00 8.00
41 O.J. Mayo/100 2.00 5.00
42 Nene/100 2.50 6.00
43 Andrea Bargnani/100 2.50 6.00
44 Charlie Villanueva/100 2.00 5.00
45 Ben Gordon/100 2.50 6.00
46 Mike Bibby/100 2.50 6.00
48 Andrew Bynum/100 2.00 5.00
49 Russell Westbrook/100 8.00 20.00
50 Anthony Randolph/100 2.00 5.00
51 Eric Gordon/100 2.50 6.00
52 Jeff Green/100 2.50 6.00
53 Shaquille O'Neal/100 6.00 15.00
54 Aaron Brooks/100 2.00 5.00
55 Chris Kaman/100 2.50 6.00
56 D.J. Augustin/100 2.00 5.00
57 Emeka Okafor/100 2.50 6.00
61 Kevin Love/100 3.00 8.00
63 Michael Beasley/100 2.00 5.00
64 Richard Hamilton/100 2.50 6.00
67 Rudy Fernandez/100 2.00 5.00
68 Ryan Gomes/100 2.00 5.00
69 Shane Battier/100 3.00 8.00
70 T.J. Ford/100 2.00 5.00
71 Tracy McGrady/100 3.00 8.00
73 Greg Oden/100 2.50 6.00
80 John Havlicek/50 6.00 15.00
91 Wes Unseld/50 4.00 10.00

2009-10 Timeless Treasures Materials Jerseys Ink

STATED PRINT RUN ONE TO 100 SER.#'d SETS
SOME UNPRICED DUE TO SCARCITY
1 Kobe Bryant/100 100.00 200.00
3 Danny Granger/50 8.00 20.00
5 Chris Bosh/50 10.00 25.00
7 Deron Williams/50 12.50 30.00
10 Jason Kidd/25 25.00 50.00
11 Devin Harris/50 8.00 20.00
15 Ray Allen/50 15.00 40.00
18 Rajon Rondo/50 25.00 50.00
20 Tony Parker/45 10.00 25.00
22 Russell Westbrook/50 40.00 100.00
23 Eric Gordon/50 12.50 30.00
25 Tracy McGrady/50 15.00 30.00
27 Tyreke Evans/50 12.00 30.00
28 Brandon Jennings/100 8.00 20.00
29 Blake Griffin/100 40.00 100.00
30 Omri Casspi/50 8.00 20.00

2009-10 Timeless Treasures Materials Jerseys Prime Ink

STATED PRINT RUN ONE TO 25 SER.#'d SETS
SOME UNPRICED DUE TO SCARCITY
1 Kobe Bryant/25 200.00 350.00
3 Danny Granger/25 10.00 25.00
5 Chris Bosh/25 15.00 40.00
7 Deron Williams/25 15.00 40.00
11 Devin Harris/25 10.00 25.00
15 Ray Allen/25 30.00 60.00
16 Carlos Boozer/25 15.00 30.00
17 David Lee/25 10.00 25.00
18 Rajon Rondo/25 30.00 80.00
20 Tony Parker/25 20.00 40.00
22 Russell Westbrook/25 75.00 200.00
23 Eric Gordon/25 15.00 40.00
27 Tyreke Evans/25 75.00 150.00
28 Brandon Jennings/25 25.00 60.00
29 Blake Griffin/25 60.00 150.00
30 Omri Casspi/25 15.00 30.00

2009-10 Timeless Treasures MVP Materials

STATED PRINT RUN 10 TO 100 SER.#'d SETS
SOME UNPRICED DUE TO SCARCITY
TAGS NBA LOGO PRINT RUN ONE TO TWO SETS
TAGS NBA LOGO SIGS PRINT RUN ONE SET
TAGS TEAM LOGO PRINT RUN 1 TO 2 SETS
TAGS SIGS PRINT RUN 1 TO 4 SETS
TAGS TEAM LOGO SIGS PRINT RUN ONE SET
TAGS NOT PRICED DUE TO SCARCITY
1 Dirk Nowitzki/100 5.00 12.00
2 LeBron James/90 10.00 25.00
3 Kobe Bryant/100 10.00 25.00
6 Larry Bird/100 10.00 25.00
7 Karl Malone/100 5.00 12.00

2009-10 Timeless Treasures MVP Materials Prime

PRINT RUNS 10 TO 25 SER.#'d SETS
SOME UNPRICED DUE TO SCARCITY
2 LeBron James/25 15.00 40.00
5 Tim Duncan/25 12.00 30.00
7 Karl Malone/25 10.00 25.00

2009-10 Timeless Treasures MVP Materials MVP

STATED PRINT RUN 5 TO 25 SER.#'d SETS
SOME UNPRICED DUE TO SCARCITY
1 Dirk Nowitzki/25 8.00 20.00
2 LeBron James/25 15.00 40.00
3 Kobe Bryant/25 15.00 40.00
6 Larry Bird/25 15.00 40.00
7 Karl Malone/25 10.00 25.00

2009-10 Timeless Treasures MVP Materials MVP Prime

STATED PRINT RUN 5 TO 25 SER.#'d SETS
SOME UNPRICED DUE TO SCARCITY
5 Tim Duncan/25 20.00 50.00
7 Karl Malone/25 15.00 40.00

2009-10 Timeless Treasures MVP Materials Quads

STATED PRINT RUN 25 SER.#'d SETS
UNPRICED PRIME PRINT RUN 10 SETS
1 Dirk/Kobe/LBJ/Nash/25 30.00 60.00

2009-10 Timeless Treasures MVP Materials Signatures

STATED PRINT RUN 25 SER.#'d SETS
UNPRICED PRIME PRINT RUN 10 SER.#'d SETS
1 Dirk Nowitzki/25 50.00 120.00
3 Kobe Bryant/25 100.00 200.00
6 Larry Bird/25 50.00 100.00

2009-10 Timeless Treasures NBA Apprentice Materials

STATED PRINT RUN 100 SER.#'d SETS
*PRIME: .75X TO 2X BASE HI
PRIME PRINT RUNS 1 TO 99 SER.#'d SETS
SOME PRIME UNPRICED DUE TO SCARCITY
TAGS PRINT RUN ONE SET
TAGS NBA LOGO PRINT RUN ONE SET
TAGS NBA LOGO SIGS PRINT RUN ONE SET
TAGS SIGS PRINT RUN ONE SET
TAGS TEAM LOGO PRINT RUN ONE SET
TAGS TEAM LOGO SIGS PRINT RUN ONE SET
TAGS NOT PRICED DUE TO SCARCITY
1 Blake Griffin 12.50 30.00
2 Hasheem Thabeet 1.50 4.00
3 James Harden 12.00 30.00
4 Tyreke Evans 2.00 5.00
5 Jonny Flynn 1.50 4.00
6 Stephen Curry 40.00 100.00
7 Jordan Hill 2.00 5.00
8 DeMar DeRozan 6.00 15.00
9 Brandon Jennings 2.50 6.00
10 Terrence Williams 1.50 4.00
11 Gerald Henderson 2.00 5.00
12 Tyler Hansbrough 2.00 5.00
13 Earl Clark 2.00 5.00
14 Austin Daye 1.50 4.00
15 James Johnson 2.00 5.00
16 Jrue Holiday 3.00 8.00
17 Ty Lawson 2.50 6.00
18 Jeff Teague 2.50 6.00
19 Eric Maynor 1.50 4.00
20 Darren Collison 2.50 6.00
21 Omri Casspi 2.00 5.00
22 B.J. Mullens 1.50 4.00
23 Rodrigue Beaubois 1.50 4.00
24 Taj Gibson 2.50 6.00
25 DeMarre Carroll 2.00 5.00
26 Wayne Ellington 2.50 6.00
27 Toney Douglas 1.50 4.00
28 Jeff Pendergraph 1.50 4.00
29 Jermaine Taylor 1.50 4.00
30 DaJuan Summers 1.50 4.00
31 Sam Young 1.50 4.00
32 DeJuan Blair 2.00 5.00
33 Jodie Meeks 2.50 6.00
34 Chase Budinger 2.00 5.00
35 Taylor Griffin 1.50 4.00

2009-10 Timeless Treasures NBA Apprentice Materials Signatures

STATED PRINT RUN 50 SER.#'d SETS
UNPRICED PRIME PRINT RUN 10 SER.#'d SETS
1 Blake Griffin 60.00 120.00
2 Hasheem Thabeet 3.00 8.00
3 James Harden 60.00 150.00
4 Tyreke Evans 4.00 10.00
5 Jonny Flynn 3.00 8.00
6 Stephen Curry 300.00 600.00
7 Jordan Hill 4.00 10.00
9 Brandon Jennings 5.00 12.00
10 Terrence Williams 3.00 8.00
11 Gerald Henderson 4.00 10.00
12 Tyler Hansbrough 4.00 10.00
13 Earl Clark 4.00 10.00
14 Austin Daye 3.00 8.00
16 Jrue Holiday 6.00 15.00
18 Jeff Teague 5.00 12.00
19 Eric Maynor 3.00 8.00
20 Darren Collison 5.00 12.00
21 Omri Casspi 4.00 10.00
22 B.J. Mullens 3.00 8.00
23 Rodrigue Beaubois 3.00 8.00
24 Taj Gibson 5.00 12.00
25 DeMarre Carroll 4.00 10.00
26 Wayne Ellington 5.00 12.00
27 Toney Douglas 3.00 8.00
28 Jeff Pendergraph 3.00 8.00
30 DaJuan Summers 3.00 8.00
31 Sam Young 3.00 8.00
32 DeJuan Blair 4.00 10.00
33 Jodie Meeks 5.00 12.00
34 Chase Budinger 4.00 10.00
35 Taylor Griffin 3.00 8.00

2009-10 Timeless Treasures NBA Apprentice Combo Materials

STATED PRINT RUN 100 SER.#'d SETS
UNPRICED PRIME PRINT RUN 10 SER.#'d SETS
1 B.Griffin/B.Jennings 8.00 20.00
2 B.Griffin/T.Evans 8.00 20.00
3 B.Jennings/T.Evans 2.00 5.00
4 J.Johnson/T.Gibson 1.50 4.00
5 H.Thabeet/S.Young 1.25 3.00
6 B.Jennings/J.Meeks 2.00 5.00
7 J.Flynn/W.Ellington 1.25 3.00
8 J.Hill/T.Douglas 1.25 3.00
9 J.Harden/B.Mullens 10.00 25.00
10 T.Evans/O.Casspi 1.50 4.00
11 T.Lawson/T.Evans 2.00 5.00
12 T.Lawson/B.Jennings 2.00 5.00
13 S.Curry/J.Flynn 25.00 60.00
14 J.Harden/S.Curry 50.00 120.00
15 O.Casspi/D.Blair 1.50 4.00

2009-10 Timeless Treasures NBA Apprentice Combo Signatures

STATED PRINT RUN 25 SER.#'d SETS
1 B.Griffin/T.Griffin 75.00 150.00
2 H.Thabeet/S.Young 8.00 20.00
3 J.Harden/B.Mullens 30.00 80.00
4 T.Evans/O.Casspi 30.00 80.00
5 J.Flynn/W.Ellington 8.00 20.00
6 J.Hill/T.Douglas 8.00 20.00
7 B.Jennings/J.Meeks 15.00 40.00
9 T.Hansbrough/A.Price 10.00 25.00
10 E.Clark/T.Griffin 8.00 20.00
12 J.Johnson/T.Gibson 10.00 25.00
13 D.Collison/M.Thornton 15.00 40.00
16 H.Thabeet/A.Price 8.00 20.00
19 D.Blair/S.Young 8.00 20.00
20 J.Hill/C.Budinger 8.00 20.00
21 E.Clark/T.Williams 10.00 25.00
22 J.Holiday/D.Collison 15.00 30.00
23 J.Harden/J.Pendergraph 20.00 50.00
24 B.Jennings/T.Evans 75.00 150.00
25 B.Griffin/T.Hansbrough 100.00 200.00

2009-10 Timeless Treasures NBA Apprentice Quad Materials

STATED PRINT RUN 100 SER.#'d SETS
UNPRICED PRIME PRINT RUN ONE TO 10 SETS
1 Griffin/Thabeet/Harden/Evans 12.00 30.00
2 Flynn/Curry/Hill/DeRozan 15.00 40.00
3 Jennings/Wllms/Hndrsn/Hnsbrgh 5.00 12.00
4 Griffin/Hill/Blair/Hansbrgh 12.00 30.00
5 Evans/Flynn/Jennings/Lawson 6.00 15.00
6 Jennings/Evans/Harden/Lawson 6.00 15.00
7 Collisn/Blair/Flynn/Casspi 5.00 12.00
8 Blair/Casspi/Hnsbrgh/Griffin 12.50 30.00
9 Maynor/Collison/Curry/Douglas 15.00 40.00
10 Griffin/Harden/Evans/Jennings 12.00 30.00
11 DeRozan/Hill/Holiday/Wllms 5.00 12.00
12 Taj/Jennings/Hnsbrgh/Jhnsn 5.00 12.00
13 Ty/Ellngtn/Harden/Flynn 5.00 12.00
14 Blair/Budngr/Thabeet/Collison 5.00 12.00
15 Griffin/Casspi/Curry/Evans 15.00 40.00

2009-10 Timeless Treasures NBA Apprentice Triple Materials

STATED PRINT RUN 100 SER.#'d SETS
UNPRICED PRIME PRINT RUN ONE TO 10 SETS
1 Hansbrough/Lawson/Ellington 5.00 12.00
2 Griffin/Thabeet/Harden 10.00 25.00
3 Evans/Flynn/Curry 15.00 40.00
4 Hill/DeRozan/Jennings 5.00 12.00
5 Williams/Henderson/Hansbrough 5.00 12.00
6 Griffin/Evans/Jennings 10.00 25.00
7 Evans/Flynn/Curry 5.00 12.00
8 Evans/Lawson/Jennings 5.00 12.00
9 Harden/Curry/Budinger 15.00 40.00
10 Griffin/Hansbrough/Blair 10.00 25.00
11 Casspi/Griffin/Blair 6.00 15.00
12 Lawson/Flynn/Curry 15.00 40.00
13 Evans/Jennings/Casspi 5.00 12.00
14 Evans/Lawson/Casspi 5.00 12.00
15 Griffin/Hansbrough/Casspi 10.00 25.00

2009-10 Timeless Treasures Private Signings

STATED PRINT RUN 20 TO 100 SER.#'d SETS
1 Kobe Bryant/100 75.00 150.00
2 Steve Nash/20 40.00 100.00
3 Tracy McGrady/25 12.00 30.00
4 Danny Granger/25 10.00 25.00
5 Carmelo Anthony/25 25.00 50.00
6 Bill Russell/25 50.00 120.00
7 Bill Walton/25 15.00 30.00
8 Bob Cousy/25 20.00 50.00
9 Chris Bosh/20 20.00 40.00
10 Dave Cowens/25 15.00 30.00
11 David Thompson/25 10.00 25.00
12 Dennis Rodman/25 12.00 30.00
13 Isiah Thomas/25 10.00 25.00
14 Jerry West/25 30.00 60.00
15 John Havlicek/25 20.00 40.00
16 Kareem Abdul-Jabbar/25 40.00 80.00
17 Kevin Love/25 20.00 50.00
18 Kevin McHale/25 25.00 60.00
19 Larry Bird/25 40.00 100.00
20 Magic Johnson/25 40.00 100.00
21 Dominique Wilkins/20 12.00 30.00
22 Nate Thurmond/25 10.00 25.00
23 Oscar Robertson/25 40.00 80.00
24 Pau Gasol/25 30.00 60.00
25 Rajon Rondo/25 25.00 50.00
26 Ray Allen/25 25.00 60.00
27 Rick Barry/25 10.00 25.00
28 Robert Parish/25 10.00 25.00
29 Scottie Pippen/25 75.00 150.00
30 Tony Parker/20 15.00 30.00

2009-10 Timeless Treasures Rookie Year Materials

STATED PRINT RUN 25 TO 100 SER.#'d SETS
*PRIME: 1X TO 2.5X BASE HI
PRIME PRINT RUN 25 SER.#'d SETS
TAGS PRINT RUN ONE TO 6 SETS
TAGS NBA LOGO PRINT RUN 1 TO 3 SETS
TAGS NBA LOGO SIG.PRINT RUN ONE TO 3 SETS
TAGS SIGS PRINT RUN ONE TO 9 SETS
TAGS TEAM LOGO PRINT RUN 1 TO 3 SETS
TAGS TEAM LOGO SIG.PRINT RUN 1 TO 3 SETS
NBA LOGO PRINT RUN ONE TO 4 SETS
NBA LOGO SIGS PRINT RUN ONE TO 4 SETS
TAGS AND LOGOS UNPRICED DUE TO SCARCITY
1 Dwight Howard/50 2.50 6.00
2 Chris Paul/50 4.00 10.00
3 LeBron James/100 10.00 25.00
4 Kobe Bryant/100 10.00 25.00
5 Brandon Roy/100 3.00 8.00
6 Derrick Rose/50 5.00 12.00
7 Carmelo Anthony/100 4.00 10.00
8 Andre Iguodala/100 2.50 6.00
9 Shaquille O'Neal/100 6.00 15.00
10 Deron Williams/100 2.50 6.00
11 Kevin Garnett/100 5.00 12.00
12 Kevin Durant/100 8.00 20.00
13 Brandon Jennings/25 10.00 25.00
14 Dikembe Mutombo/100 6.00 15.00
15 Tracy McGrady/100 3.00 8.00

2009-10 Timeless Treasures Rookie Year Materials Signatures

STATED PRINT RUN ONE TO 50 SER.#'d SETS
SOME UNPRICED DUE TO SCARCITY
4 Kobe Bryant/50 100.00 225.00
6 Derrick Rose/25 125.00 250.00
10 Deron Williams/25 10.00 25.00
13 Brandon Jennings/25 8.00 20.00
14 Dikembe Mutombo/25 30.00 60.00
15 Tracy McGrady/25 25.00 50.00

2009-10 Timeless Treasures Rookie Year Materials Prime Signatures

STATED PRINT RUN ONE TO 25 SER.#'d SETS
SOME UNPRICED DUE TO SCARCITY
4 Kobe Bryant/25 200.00 350.00
6 Derrick Rose/25 150.00 300.00

2009-10 Timeless Treasures Rookie Year Materials Quads

STATED PRINT RUN 25 SER.#'d SETS
UNPRICED PRIME PRINT RUN 5 SER.#'d SETS
1 LBJ/Kobe/CP3/Dwight 25.00 50.00
2 KG/Shaq/Kobe/LBJ 40.00 100.00
3 LBJ/Dwight/Iggy/Melo 15.00 30.00
4 KG/Shaq/TMac/Kobe 25.00 60.00
5 KG/Howard/Mutmbo/Shaq 20.00 50.00

2009-10 Timeless Treasures Rookie Year Materials ROY

STATED PRINT RUN 25 TO 100 SER.#'d SETS
2 Chris Paul/25 12.50 30.00
3 LeBron James/100 15.00 40.00
5 Brandon Roy/25 6.00 15.00
9 Shaquille O'Neal/100 12.00 30.00
12 Kevin Durant/100 12.50 30.00

2009-10 Timeless Treasures Rookie Year Materials ROY Prime

STATED PRINT RUN ONE TO 25 SER.#'d SETS
SOME UNPRICED DUE TO SCARCITY
2 Chris Paul/25 50.00 40.00
3 LeBron James/25 50.00 125.00
12 Kevin Durant/25 25.00 60.00

2009-10 Timeless Treasures Rookie Year Materials ROY Prime Signatures

STATED PRINT RUN 25 SER.#'d SETS
UNPRICED ROY SIG PRINT RUN 10 SETS
6 Derrick Rose/25 250.00 400.00

2009-10 Timeless Treasures Signatures Silver

STATED PRINT RUN 25 TO 100 SER.#'d SETS
UNPRICED GOLD PRINT RUN 10 SER.#'d SETS
UNPRICED PLATINUM PRINT RUN ONE SET
1 Kobe Bryant 100.00 200.00
7 Danny Granger 5.00 12.00
9 Pau Gasol 25.00 50.00
11 Chris Bosh 12.50 30.00
15 Deron Williams 10.00 25.00
21 Devin Harris 5.00 12.00
36 Ray Allen 20.00 50.00
39 Derrick Rose 75.00 150.00
40 Rajon Rondo 20.00 40.00
41 O.J. Mayo 15.00 30.00
44 Charlie Villanueva 5.00 12.00
47 Tony Parker 8.00 20.00
49 Russell Westbrook 30.00 80.00
51 Eric Gordon 6.00 15.00
54 Aaron Brooks 5.00 12.00
56 D.J. Augustin 5.00 12.00
57 Emeka Okafor 6.00 15.00
59 Jermaine O'Neal 6.00 15.00
60 Josh Howard 5.00 12.00
61 Kevin Love 15.00 40.00
63 Michael Beasley 8.00 20.00
66 Ronnie Brewer 5.00 12.00
68 Ryan Gomes 8.00 20.00
69 Shane Battier 5.00 12.00
70 T.J. Ford 5.00 12.00
71 Tracy McGrady 15.00 40.00
72 Trevor Ariza 6.00 15.00
74 Nate Archibald 8.00 20.00
75 Al Cervi 6.00 15.00
76 Bob Cousy 20.00 50.00
77 Harry Gallatin 5.00 12.00
78 Gail Goodrich 8.00 20.00
79 Hal Greer 8.00 20.00
80 John Havlicek 15.00 30.00
82 Elvin Hayes 5.00 12.00
83 Bob McAdoo 10.00 25.00
86 Dolph Schayes 8.00 20.00
87 Bill Sharman 8.00 20.00
88 David Thompson 8.00 20.00
89 Nate Thurmond 8.00 20.00
91 Wes Unseld 6.00 15.00
92 Bill Walton 8.00 20.00
93 Bobby Wanzer 6.00 15.00
94 Frank Ramsey 10.00 25.00
95 Willis Reed 8.00 20.00
96 Pat Riley 15.00 30.00
98 Oscar Robertson 30.00 60.00
99 Lenny Wilkens 6.00 15.00
100 James Worthy 20.00 50.00

2009-10 Timeless Treasures Souvenir Cuts

STATED PRINT RUN ONE TO 25 SER.#'d SETS
SOME UNPRICED DUE TO SCARCITY
1 George Mikan/25 100.00 200.00
8 Hank Luisetti/15 50.00 125.00
9 Andy Phillip/15 100.00 175.00
13 Paul Arizin/25 20.00 50.00

2009-10 Timeless Treasures Souvenir Cuts Materials
STATED PRINT RUN 25 SER.#'d SETS
1 George Mikan/25 125.00 250.00

2009-10 Timeless Treasures Statistical Champions Materials
STATED PRINT RUN 50 TO 100 SER.#'d SETS
UNPRICED PRIME PRINT RUN 10 SER.#'d SETS
1 George Gervin/50 5.00 12.00
2 John Stockton/50 6.00 15.00
3 Dwight Howard/100 5.00 12.00
4 Kobe Bryant/100 10.00 25.00
5 Chris Paul/100 5.00 12.00

2009-10 Timeless Treasures Statistical Champions Materials Signatures
STATED PRINT RUN 50 SER.#'d SETS
UNPRICED PRIME PRINT RUN 10 SER.#'d SETS
1 George Gervin/50 15.00 40.00
4 Kobe Bryant/50 100.00 200.00

2010-11 Timeless Treasures
COMP.SET w/o RCs (100) 50.00 100.00
1-100 STATED PRINT RUN 399 SER.#'d SETS
AU RC PRINT RUN 249 TO 299 SER.#'d SETS
UNPRICED GOLD PRINT RUN 10 SETS
UNPRICED PLATINUM PRINT RUN ONE SET
1 Kobe Bryant 4.00 10.00
2 Pau Gasol 1.00 2.50
3 Derek Fisher .75 2.00
4 Andrew Bynum .60 1.50
5 Caron Butler .75 2.00
6 Dirk Nowitzki 1.25 3.00
7 Jason Kidd 1.00 2.50
8 Jason Terry .75 2.00
9 Grant Hill 1.25 3.00
10 Jason Richardson 1.00 2.50
11 Robin Lopez .60 1.50
12 Steve Nash 1.00 2.50
13 Carmelo Anthony 1.25 3.00
14 Chauncey Billups 1.00 2.50
15 Chris Andersen .75 2.00
16 Nene .75 2.00
17 Al Jefferson .75 2.00
18 Deron Williams .75 2.00
19 Mehmet Okur .60 1.50
20 Paul Millsap .75 2.00
21 Brandon Roy 1.00 2.50
22 Greg Oden .75 2.00
23 LaMarcus Aldridge 1.00 2.50
24 Marcus Camby .60 1.50
25 George Hill .75 2.00
26 Manu Ginobili 1.00 2.50
27 Tim Duncan 1.50 4.00
28 Tony Parker 1.00 2.50
29 James Harden 1.50 4.00
30 Jeff Green .75 2.00
31 Kevin Durant 2.50 6.00
32 Russell Westbrook 2.50 6.00
33 Aaron Brooks .60 1.50
34 Kevin Martin .75 2.00
35 Luis Scola .75 2.00
36 Yao Ming 1.25 3.00
37 Marc Gasol 1.00 2.50
38 Rudy Gay 1.00 2.50
39 Zach Randolph .75 2.00
40 Chris Paul 1.25 3.00
41 Marcus Thornton .60 1.50
42 Trevor Ariza .60 1.50
43 Chris Kaman .75 2.00
44 Eric Gordon .75 2.00
45 Baron Davis .75 2.00
46 David Lee .60 1.50
47 Monta Ellis .75 2.00
48 Stephen Curry 4.00 10.00
49 Carl Landry .60 1.50
50 Samuel Dalembert .60 1.50
51 Tyreke Evans .60 1.50
52 Kevin Love 1.00 2.50
53 Michael Beasley .60 1.50
54 Sebastian Telfair .60 1.50
55 Anderson Varejao .60 1.50
56 Antawn Jamison .75 2.00
57 Mo Williams .75 2.00
58 Dwight Howard .75 2.00
59 J.J. Redick 1.00 2.50
60 Vince Carter 1.25 3.00
61 Al Horford .75 2.00
62 Joe Johnson .75 2.00
63 Josh Smith .75 2.00
64 Kendrick Perkins .60 1.50
65 Paul Pierce 1.00 2.50
66 Rajon Rondo 1.00 2.50
67 Shaquille O'Neal 2.00 5.00
68 Chris Bosh 1.00 2.50
69 Dwyane Wade 1.50 4.00
70 LeBron James 5.00 12.00
71 Andrew Bogut .75 2.00
72 Brandon Jennings .60 1.50
73 Michael Redd .75 2.00
74 D.J. Augustin .60 1.50
75 Gerald Wallace .75 2.00
76 Stephen Jackson .75 2.00
77 Carlos Boozer .75 2.00
78 Derrick Rose 1.25 3.00
79 Luol Deng .75 2.00
80 Andrea Bargnani .75 2.00
81 DeMar DeRozan 1.00 2.50
82 Leandro Barbosa .75 2.00
83 Danny Granger .75 2.00
84 Darren Collison .75 2.00
85 Troy Murphy .60 1.50
86 Amare Stoudemire .75 2.00
87 Anthony Randolph .60 1.50
88 Danilo Gallinari .75 2.00
89 Ben Wallace .75 2.00
90 Richard Hamilton .75 2.00
91 Tracy McGrady 1.00 2.50
92 Andre Iguodala .75 2.00
93 Louis Williams .75 2.00
94 Thaddeus Young .60 1.50
95 Al Thornton .60 1.50
96 JaVale McGee .75 2.00
97 Josh Howard .75 2.00
98 Anthony Morrow .60 1.50
99 Brook Lopez .75 2.00
100 Devin Harris .60 1.50
101 John Wall AU/299 RC 25.00 60.00
102 Evan Turner AU/299 RC 3.00 8.00
103 Derrick Favors AU/299 RC 5.00 12.00
104 Wesley Johnson AU/299 RC 2.50 6.00
105 D.Cousins AU/299 RC 12.00 30.00
106 Ekpe Udoh AU/299 RC 2.50 6.00
107 Greg Monroe AU/299 RC 5.00 12.00
108 Al-Farouq Aminu AU/299 RC 4.00 10.00
109 Gordon Hayward AU/299 RC 12.00 30.00
110 Paul George AU/299 RC 20.00 50.00
111 Cole Aldrich AU/299 RC 3.00 8.00
112 Xavier Henry AU/299 RC 2.50 6.00
113 Ed Davis AU/298 RC 2.50 6.00
114 P.Patterson AU/299 RC 3.00 8.00
115 Larry Sanders AU/299 RC 2.50 6.00
116 Luke Babbitt AU/299 RC 3.00 8.00
117 Kevin Seraphin AU/299 RC 2.50 6.00
118 Eric Bledsoe AU/299 RC 5.00 12.00
119 Avery Bradley AU/299 RC 5.00 12.00
120 James Anderson AU/299 RC 2.50 6.00
121 Craig Brackins AU/299 RC 2.50 6.00
122 Elliot Williams AU/299 RC 2.50 6.00
123 Trevor Booker AU/299 RC 3.00 8.00
124 Damion James AU/299 RC 2.50 6.00
125 Dominique Jones AU/299 RC 2.50 6.00
126 Quincy Pondexter AU/299 RC 2.50 6.00
127 J.Crawford AU/299 RC 3.00 8.00
128 Greivis Vasquez AU/299 RC 3.00 8.00
129 Daniel Orton AU/299 RC 2.50 6.00
130 Lazar Hayward AU/299 RC 2.50 6.00
131 Jeremy Lin AU/299 RC 30.00 80.00
132 Dexter Pittman AU/299 RC 2.50 6.00
133 Hassan Whiteside AU/286 RC 20.00 50.00
134 Armon Johnson AU/299 RC 2.50 6.00
135 Terrico White AU/299 RC 2.50 6.00
136 Darington Hobson AU/298 RC 2.50 6.00
137 Andy Rautins AU/297 RC 2.50 6.00
138 Landry Fields AU/299 RC 3.00 8.00
139 Lance Stephenson AU/299 RC 4.00 10.00
140 Jarvis Varnado AU/299 RC 2.50 6.00
141 Sherron Collins AU/299 RC 2.50 6.00
142 Devin Ebanks AU/299 RC 2.50 6.00
143 Gani Lawal AU/249 RC 2.50 6.00
144 Timofey Mozgov AU/299 RC 4.00 10.00
145 Solomon Alabi AU/299 RC 2.50 6.00
146 L.Harangody AU/299 RC 2.50 6.00
147 Willie Warren AU/298 RC 2.50 6.00
148 Jeremy Evans AU/299 RC 2.50 6.00
149 Derrick Caracter AU/299 RC 2.50 6.00
150 Stanley Robinson AU/299 RC 2.50 6.00

2010-11 Timeless Treasures Silver
*1-100 SILVER: 1.5X TO 4X BASE HI
*101-150 SILVER: .6X TO 1.5X BASE HI
STATED PRINT RUN 25 SER.#'d SETS
9 Grant Hill 8.00 20.00

2010-11 Timeless Treasures Championship Season Materials
STATED PRINT RUN 10 TO 99 SER.#'d SETS
SOME UNPRICED DUE TO SCARCITY
UNPRICED LOGOMAN PRINT RUN ONE SET
UNPRICED TAG PRINT RUN 1 TO 5 SETS
UNPRICED TAG TEAM LOGO ONE SET
1 Andrew Bynum/99 2.50 6.00
2 Derek Fisher/99 3.00 8.00
3 Derek Fisher/99 3.00 8.00
4 Glen Davis/99 2.50 6.00
5 Hakeem Olajuwon/99 5.00 12.00
6 Joe Dumars/99 4.00 10.00
7 Kevin Garnett/99 6.00 15.00
8 Kobe Bryant/99 10.00 25.00
9 Lamar Odom/99 3.00 8.00
10 Luke Walton/99 2.50 6.00
12 Manu Ginobili/99 4.00 10.00
13 Pau Gasol/99 4.00 10.00
14 Pau Gasol/99 4.00 10.00
16 Ron Artest/99 4.00 10.00
17 Scottie Pippen/99 8.00 20.00
18 Tim Duncan/49 6.00 15.00
19 Tim Duncan/99 6.00 15.00
20 Tony Parker/49 4.00 10.00

2010-11 Timeless Treasures Championship Season Materials Combos
STATED PRINT RUN 10 TO 25 SER.#'d SETS
SOME UNPRICED DUE TO SCARCITY
UNPRICED PRIME PRINT RUN 5 SETS
1 A.Bynum/P.Gasol/25 8.00 20.00
2 L.Odom/L.Walton/25 6.00 15.00
3 D.Fisher/P.Gasol/25 8.00 20.00
5 T.Duncan/T.Parker/25 8.00 20.00
7 H.Olajuwon/S.Pippen/25 15.00 40.00
8 D.Fisher/R.Artest/25 10.00 25.00

2010-11 Timeless Treasures Championship Season Materials Prime
*PRIME: .6X TO 1.5X BASE HI
STATED PRINT RUN 5 TO 25 SER.#'d SETS
SOME UNPRICED DUE TO SCARCITY
6 Joe Dumars/25 8.00 20.00
13 Pau Gasol/25 8.00 20.00
14 Pau Gasol/25 8.00 20.00
15 Ray Allen/25 6.00 15.00

2010-11 Timeless Treasures Championship Season Materials Quads
STATED PRINT RUN 10 TO 25 SER.#'d SETS
SOME UNPRICED DUE TO SCARCITY
UNPRICED PRIME PRINT RUN 5 SER.#'d SETS
1 Bynum/Fisher/Bryant/Odom/25 15.00 40.00
2 Walton/Gasol/Artest/Bryant/25 20.00 50.00

2010-11 Timeless Treasures Championship Season Materials Signatures
STATED PRINT RUN 10 TO 25 SER.#'d SETS
SOME UNPRICED DUE TO SCARCITY
UNPRICED LOGOMAN SIG PRINT RUN ONE SET
UNPRICED PRIME SIG.PRINT RUN 5 TO 10 SETS
UNPRICED TAG SIGS PRINT RUN 1 TO 5 SETS
UNPRICED TAG TEAM LOGO SIG ONE SET
2 Derek Fisher/25 15.00 40.00
3 Derek Fisher/25 15.00 40.00
8 Kobe Bryant/25 100.00 200.00
16 Ron Artest/25 10.00 25.00
17 Scottie Pippen/25 75.00 150.00
20 Tony Parker/25 10.00 25.00

2010-11 Timeless Treasures Championship Season Materials Triple
STATED PRINT RUN 10 TO 25 SER.#'d SETS
SOME UNPRICED DUE TO SCARCITY
UNPRICED PRIME PRINT RUN 5 SER.#'d SETS
1 Ginobili/Duncan/Parker/25 10.00 25.00
2 Davis/Garnett/Allen/25 10.00 25.00

2010-11 Timeless Treasures HOF Materials Combos
STATED PRINT RUN 25 TO 50 SER.#'d SETS
1 L.Bird/M.Johnson/50 15.00 40.00
2 J.Stockton/K.Malone/50 8.00 20.00
3 I.Thomas/J.Dumars/25 6.00 15.00
5 D.Cowens/R.Parish/50 6.00 15.00
6 S.Pippen/C.Drexler/50 8.00 20.00
7 M.Malone/K.Malone/25 6.00 15.00
9 D.Wilkins/S.Pippen/50 10.00 25.00
10 G.Mikan/Abdul-Jabbar/50 15.00 40.00

2010-11 Timeless Treasures HOF Materials Combos Prime
STATED PRINT RUN 10 TO 50 SER.#'d SETS
SOME UNPRICED DUE TO SCARCITY
1 L.Bird/M.Johnson/50 25.00 60.00
2 J.Stockton/K.Malone/50 20.00 50.00
3 I.Thomas/J.Dumars/50 8.00 20.00
5 D.Cowens/R.Parish/25 8.00 20.00
7 M.Malone/K.Malone/50 10.00 25.00
8 R.Barry/D.Issel/45 8.00 20.00

2010-11 Timeless Treasures HOF Materials Jerseys
STATED PRINT RUN 5 TO 50 SER.#'d SETS
SOME UNPRICED DUE TO SCARCITY
UNPRICED PRIME PRINT RUN 5 SER.#'d SETS
5 David Robinson/50 6.00 15.00
6 Dave Cowens/50 2.50 6.00
7 Magic Johnson/50 6.00 15.00
15 Dominique Wilkins/50 5.00 12.00
21 Wes Unseld/50 4.00 10.00
28 Bob Lanier/50 3.00 8.00
33 Karl Malone/50 5.00 12.00
34 Kevin McHale/50 4.00 10.00
35 Hakeem Olajuwon/50 5.00 12.00

2010-11 Timeless Treasures HOF Materials Jerseys Signatures
STATED PRINT RUN 5 TO 25 SER.#'d SETS
SOME UNPRICED DUE TO SCARCITY
UNPRICED PRIME SIG PRINT RUN 4 TO 10 SETS
6 Dave Cowens/25 8.00 20.00
15 Dominique Wilkins/25 20.00 50.00
21 Wes Unseld/25 8.00 20.00
28 Bob Lanier/25 10.00 25.00
34 Kevin McHale/25 20.00 50.00

2010-11 Timeless Treasures HOF Materials Quads
STATED PRINT RUN 10 TO 50 SER.#'d SETS
SOME UNPRICED DUE TO SCARCITY
1 Mikan/Lanier/Ewing/Olaj/50 20.00 50.00
2 Bird/DJ/Parish/Cowens/50 12.00 30.00
3 Wilkins/Eng/McH/Malone/50 8.00 20.00
5 Bird/Magic/Kareem/Parish/50 25.00 60.00

2010-11 Timeless Treasures HOF Materials Quads Prime
STATED PRINT RUN 5 TO 50 SER.#'d SETS
SOME UNPRICED DUE TO SCARCITY
2 Bird/DJ/Parish/Cowens/50 20.00 50.00
5 Bird/Magic/Kareem/Parish/50 40.00 100.00

2010-11 Timeless Treasures HOF Signatures Silver
STATED PRINT RUN 10 TO 49 SER.#'d SETS
SOME UNPRICED DUE TO SCARCITY
UNPRICED GOLD PRINT RUN 5 TO 10 SETS
UNPRICED PLATINUM PRINT RUN ONE SET
2 Bill Walton/25 10.00 25.00
3 Elgin Baylor/25 12.00 30.00
4 Calvin Murphy/25 6.00 15.00
6 Dave Cowens/25 8.00 20.00
9 James Worthy/25 25.00 60.00
10 Bobby Wanzer/25 6.00 15.00
11 David Thompson/25 6.00 15.00
12 Adrian Dantley/25 6.00 15.00
13 Clyde Drexler/25 25.00 60.00
17 Joe Dumars/25 12.00 30.00
18 Oscar Robertson/25 40.00 100.00
19 Rick Barry/25 6.00 15.00
20 Gail Goodrich/49 6.00 15.00
21 Wes Unseld/25 8.00 20.00
22 K.C. Jones/25 6.00 15.00
23 Bob McAdoo/25 15.00 40.00
24 Dolph Schayes/25 6.00 15.00
25 Lenny Wilkens/25 6.00 15.00
26 Jerry West/25 30.00 80.00
27 Elvin Hayes/25 10.00 25.00
28 Bob Lanier/25 6.00 15.00
29 Sam Jones/25 12.00 30.00
30 Connie Hawkins/25 12.00 30.00
31 Hal Greer/25 6.00 15.00
32 George Gervin/25 15.00 40.00
34 Kevin McHale/25 20.00 50.00

2010-11 Timeless Treasures Home and Road Gamers
STATED PRINT RUN 10 TO 99 SER.#'d SETS
SOME UNPRICED DUE TO SCARCITY
UNPRICED PRIME PRINT RUN 1 TO 10 SETS
1 Hakeem Olajuwon/99 5.00 12.00
3 Dominique Wilkins/99 5.00 12.00
4 Kevin McHale/99 4.00 10.00
5 Dikembe Mutombo/99 4.00 10.00
6 Sleepy Floyd/49 2.50 6.00
7 Gary Payton/99 4.00 10.00
8 Glen Rice/99 3.00 8.00
9 Patrick Ewing/99 8.00 20.00
11 Karl Malone/99 5.00 12.00
12 Joe Johnson/49 3.00 8.00
13 Mike Bibby/99 3.00 8.00
14 Paul Pierce/99 4.00 10.00
15 Boris Diaw/99 3.00 8.00
16 Joakim Noah/99 3.00 8.00
17 Dirk Nowitzki/99 5.00 12.00
18 Jason Terry/99 3.00 8.00
19 Chris Andersen/99 3.00 8.00
20 J.R. Smith/99 3.00 8.00
21 Jeff Foster/99 2.50 6.00
22 Eric Gordon/49 3.00 8.00
23 Pau Gasol/99 4.00 10.00
25 Michael Redd/99 3.00 8.00
26 David West/99 3.00 8.00
27 James Harden/99 6.00 15.00
28 Dwight Howard/99 3.00 8.00
29 Jameer Nelson/99 2.50 6.00
30 LaMarcus Aldridge/99 4.00 10.00

2010-11 Timeless Treasures Home and Road Gamers Signatures
STATED PRINT RUN 10 TO 25 SER.#'d SETS
SOME UNPRICED DUE TO SCARCITY
UNPRICED PRIME PRINT RUN 5 TO 10 SETS
3 Dominique Wilkins/25 20.00 50.00
4 Kevin McHale/25 25.00 60.00
5 Dikembe Mutombo/25 20.00 50.00
6 Sleepy Floyd/25 10.00 25.00
7 Gary Payton/25 20.00 50.00
12 Joe Johnson/25 12.00 30.00
16 Joakim Noah/25 20.00 50.00
19 Chris Andersen/25 20.00 50.00
20 J.R. Smith/25 8.00 20.00
27 James Harden/25 25.00 60.00
30 LaMarcus Aldridge/25 12.00 30.00

2010-11 Timeless Treasures Materials Jerseys
STATED PRINT RUN ONE TO 99 SER.#'d SETS
SOME UNPRICED DUE TO SCARCITY
UNPRICED PRIME PRINT RUN 2 TO 10 SETS
UNPRICED TAG PRINT RUN ONE TO 5 SETS
UNPRICED TAG TEAM LOGO 1 TO 5 SETS
1 Kobe Bryant/99 10.00 25.00
2 Pau Gasol/49 3.00 8.00
5 Caron Butler/99 2.50 6.00
6 Dirk Nowitzki/99 4.00 10.00
7 Jason Kidd/99 3.00 8.00
8 Jason Terry/99 2.50 6.00
9 Grant Hill/99 4.00 10.00
10 Jason Richardson/99 3.00 8.00
12 Steve Nash/99 3.00 8.00
13 Carmelo Anthony/99 4.00 10.00
14 Chauncey Billups/99 3.00 8.00
16 Nene/99 2.50 6.00
17 Al Jefferson/99 2.50 6.00
18 Deron Williams/49 2.50 6.00
19 Mehmet Okur/99 2.00 5.00
21 Brandon Roy/99 3.00 8.00
22 Greg Oden/99 2.50 6.00
23 LaMarcus Aldridge/99 3.00 8.00
26 Manu Ginobili/99 3.00 8.00
27 Tim Duncan/99 5.00 12.00
28 Tony Parker/99 3.00 8.00
29 James Harden/99 5.00 12.00
32 Russell Westbrook/49 8.00 20.00
35 Luis Scola/99 2.50 6.00
37 Marc Gasol/99 3.00 8.00
38 Rudy Gay/35 3.00 8.00
39 Zach Randolph/99 2.50 6.00
40 Chris Paul/99 4.00 10.00
43 Chris Kaman/99 2.50 6.00
44 Eric Gordon/49 2.50 6.00
45 Baron Davis/99 2.50 6.00
48 Stephen Curry/30 20.00 50.00
50 Samuel Dalembert/99 2.00 5.00
51 Tyreke Evans/99 2.00 5.00
52 Kevin Love/99 3.00 8.00
56 Antawn Jamison/99 2.50 6.00
58 Dwight Howard/99 2.50 6.00
59 J.J. Redick/99 3.00 8.00
60 Vince Carter/99 4.00 10.00
61 Al Horford/99 2.50 6.00
62 Joe Johnson/99 2.50 6.00
63 Josh Smith/49 2.50 6.00
65 Paul Pierce/30 3.00 8.00
68 Chris Bosh/99 3.00 8.00
69 Dwyane Wade/99 5.00 12.00
70 LeBron James/99 10.00 25.00
72 Brandon Jennings/99 2.00 5.00
73 Michael Redd/99 2.50 6.00
74 D.J. Augustin/99 2.00 5.00
75 Gerald Wallace/25 2.50 6.00
78 Derrick Rose/99 4.00 10.00
79 Luol Deng/99 2.50 6.00
80 Andrea Bargnani/99 2.50 6.00
81 DeMar DeRozan/99 3.00 8.00
82 Leandro Barbosa/99 2.50 6.00
84 Darren Collison/49 2.50 6.00
86 Amare Stoudemire/49 2.50 6.00
88 Danilo Gallinari/99 2.50 6.00
92 Andre Iguodala/99 2.50 6.00
94 Thaddeus Young/99 2.00 5.00
97 Josh Howard/99 2.50 6.00
99 Brook Lopez/25 2.50 6.00

2010-11 Timeless Treasures Materials Jerseys Ink
STATED PRINT RUN ONE TO 99 SER.#'d SETS
SOME UNPRICED DUE TO SCARCITY
1 Al Horford/49 6.00 15.00
3 Baron Davis/49 6.00 15.00
4 Brandon Jennings/99 6.00 15.00
5 Brook Lopez/25 6.00 15.00
7 Derrick Rose/25 30.00 80.00
8 J.J. Redick/49 12.00 30.00
9 Joakim Noah/49 12.00 30.00
10 Joe Johnson/25 10.00 25.00
11 J.R. Smith/49 8.00 20.00
12 Kevin Love/49 12.00 30.00
13 LaMarcus Aldridge/49 10.00 25.00
16 Ron Artest/25 15.00 40.00
17 Stephen Curry/35 100.00 250.00
18 Steve Nash/20 30.00 80.00
19 Tony Parker/99 20.00 40.00
20 Alex English/25 8.00 20.00
21 Alvan Adams/99 6.00 15.00
22 Chris Mullin/99 10.00 25.00
24 Danny Manning/99 6.00 15.00
26 Gary Payton/49 12.00 30.00
28 John Stockton/25 40.00 100.00
29 Mark Aguirre/99 8.00 20.00
30 Robert Parish/25 8.00 20.00

2010-11 Timeless Treasures Materials Jerseys Prime Ink
STATED PRINT RUN 2 TO 25 SER.#'d SETS
SOME UNPRICED DUE TO SCARCITY
UNPRICED TAG PRINT RUN ONE TO TWO SETS
UNPRICED TAG TEAM PRINT RUN ONE SET
16 Ron Artest/20 20.00 50.00
17 Stephen Curry/25 150.00 300.00
19 Tony Parker/25 20.00 50.00
20 Alex English/25 10.00 25.00
21 Alvan Adams/25 10.00 25.00
30 Robert Parish/15 12.00 30.00

2010-11 Timeless Treasures MVP Materials
STATED PRINT RUN 10 TO 99 SER.#'d SETS
SOME UNPRICED DUE TO SCARCITY
UNPRICED LOGOMAN PRINT RUN ONE SET
UNPRICED TAG PRINT RUN ONE TO 5 SETS
UNPRICED TAG TEAM PRINT RUN ONE TO 4 SETS
1 Allen Iverson/99 5.00 12.00
2 Karl Malone/99 5.00 12.00
3 Kobe Bryant/25 15.00 40.00
4 LeBron James/99 10.00 25.00
7 Tim Duncan/49 6.00 15.00

2010-11 Timeless Treasures MVP Materials MVP
STATED PRINT RUN 5 TO 25 SER.#'d SETS
SOME UNPRICED DUE TO SCARCITY
UNPRICED SIG PRINT RUN 5 TO 10 SETS
UNPRICED SIG PRIME PRINT RUN 5 TO 10 SETS
1 Allen Iverson/25 6.00 15.00
2 Karl Malone/25 6.00 15.00
4 LeBron James/25 15.00 40.00

2010-11 Timeless Treasures MVP Materials MVP Prime
STATED PRINT RUN 5 TO 25 SER.#'d SETS
SOME UNPRICED DUE TO SCARCITY
1 Allen Iverson/25 12.00 30.00
2 Karl Malone/25 15.00 40.00
4 LeBron James/25 30.00 80.00
5 LeBron James/25 30.00 80.00

2010-11 Timeless Treasures MVP Materials Prime
STATED PRINT RUN 5 TO 25 SER.#'d SETS
SOME UNPRICED DUE TO SCARCITY
1 Allen Iverson/25 12.50 30.00
2 Karl Malone/25 15.00 40.00
4 LeBron James/25 50.00 120.00
5 LeBron James/25 25.00 60.00
7 Tim Duncan/25 12.50 30.00

2010-11 Timeless Treasures MVP Materials Quads
STATED PRINT RUN 25 SER.#'d SETS
UNPRICED PRIME PRINT RUN 10 SER.#'d SETS
1 Iverson/Malone/Magic/LJ 20.00 50.00
2 Iverson/Malone/Magic/Dncn 15.00 40.00

2010-11 Timeless Treasures MVP Materials Signatures
STATED PRINT RUN 10 TO 25 SER.#'d SETS
SOME UNPRICED DUE TO SCARCITY
UNPRICED LOGOMAN SIG PRINT RUN ONE SET
UNPRICED PRIME SIG PRINT RUN 5 TO 10 SETS
UNPRICED TAG SIG PRINT RUN ONE SET
UNPRICED TAG TEAM SIG PRINT RUN ONE SET
1 Allen Iverson/25 100.00 200.00
3 Kobe Bryant/25 125.00 250.00

2010-11 Timeless Treasures NBA Apprentice Materials
STATED PRINT RUN 99 SER.#'d SETS
*PRIME: .75X TO 2X BASE HI
PRIME PRINT RUN ONE TO 25 SETS
SOME UNPRICED DUE TO SCARCITY
UNPRICED LOGOMAN PRINT RUN ONE TO 5 SETS
UNPRICED TAG PRINT RUN ONE TO 5 SETS
1 John Wall 10.00 25.00
2 Evan Turner 1.50 4.00
3 Derrick Favors 2.50 6.00
4 Wesley Johnson 1.25 3.00
5 DeMarcus Cousins 6.00 15.00
6 Ekpe Udoh 1.25 3.00
7 Greg Monroe 2.50 6.00
8 Al-Farouq Aminu 2.00 5.00
9 Gordon Hayward 3.00 8.00
10 299 8.00 20.00
11 Cole Aldrich 1.50 4.00
12 Xavier Henry 1.25 3.00
13 Ed Davis 1.25 3.00
14 Patrick Patterson 1.50 4.00
15 Larry Sanders 1.25 3.00
16 Luke Babbitt 1.50 4.00
17 Eric Bledsoe 2.50 6.00
18 Avery Bradley 2.50 6.00
19 James Anderson 1.25 3.00
20 Craig Brackins 1.25 3.00
21 Elliot Williams 1.25 3.00
22 Trevor Booker 1.50 4.00
23 Damion James 1.25 3.00
24 Dominique Jones 1.25 3.00
25 Quincy Pondexter 1.25 3.00
26 Jordan Crawford 1.50 4.00
27 Greivis Vasquez 1.50 4.00
28 Daniel Orton 1.25 3.00
29 Lazar Hayward 1.25 3.00
30 Dexter Pittman 1.25 3.00
31 Hassan Whiteside 4.00 10.00
32 Terrico White 1.25 3.00
33 Andy Rautins 1.25 3.00
34 Lance Stephenson 2.00 5.00
35 Timofey Mozgov 2.00 5.00
36 Devin Ebanks 1.25 3.00
37 Gani Lawal 1.25 3.00
38 Kevin Seraphin 1.25 3.00
39 Luke Harangody 1.25 3.00
40 Willie Warren 1.25 3.00

2010-11 Timeless Treasures NBA Apprentice Materials Combos
STATED PRINT RUN 99 SER.#'d SETS
UNPRICED PRIME PRINT RUN 10 SETS
1 J.Wall/E.Turner 8.00 20.00
2 J.Wall/D.Cousins 10.00 25.00
3 E.Turner/D.Favors 5.00 12.00
4 D.Favors/W.Johnson 4.00 10.00
5 W.Johnson/D.Cousins 5.00 12.00
6 G.Monroe/T.White 3.00 8.00
7 A.Aminu/E.Bledsoe 4.00 10.00
8 L.Harangody/A.Bradley 3.00 8.00
9 G.Vasquez/X.Henry 3.00 8.00
10 C.Aldrich/X.Henry 3.00 8.00
11 E.Udoh/G.Hayward 4.00 10.00
12 P.George/L.Stephenson 12.00 30.00
13 D.James/D.Pittman 3.00 8.00
14 E.Davis/P.Patterson 4.00 10.00
15 E.Bledsoe/D.Orton 4.00 10.00

2010-11 Timeless Treasures NBA Apprentice Materials Quads
STATED PRINT RUN 99 SER.#'d SETS
UNPRICED PRIME PRINT RUN 4 TO 10 SETS
1 Wall/Turner/Favors/Johnson 10.00 25.00
2 Wall/Cousins/Pttrsn/Bledsoe 20.00 50.00
3 Cousins/Udoh/Monroe/Aminu 6.00 15.00
4 Hayward/George/Ald/Henry 4.00 10.00
5 Pittman/Whtsd/Aldrich/Orton 4.00 10.00
6 Udoh/Monroe/Pttrsn/Sanders 5.00 12.00
7 Davis/Vasquez/Aminu/Favors 5.00 12.00
8 Turner/Hrngdy/Davis/James 6.00 15.00
9 Sanders/George/Srphn/Monroe 4.00 10.00
10 Mozgov/Booker/Crwfrd/Pttmn 4.00 10.00
11 Williams/Jhnsn/Hywrd/Babbitt 5.00 12.00
12 Warren/Lawal/Whtsd/Ebanks 4.00 10.00
13 Jones/Pttrsn/Pndxtr/Anderson 5.00 12.00
14 Warren/Bradley/James/Srphn 4.00 10.00
15 Ebanks/Mzgv/Rautins/Johnson 4.00 10.00

2010-11 Timeless Treasures NBA Apprentice Materials Signatures
STATED PRINT RUN 50 SER.#'d SETS
UNPRICED LOGO.SIG PRINT RUN ONE TO 5 SETS
UNPRICED PRIME SIG PRINT RUN ONE TO 10 SETS
UNPRICED TAG SIG PRINT RUN ONE TO 5 SETS
UNPRICED TAG TEAM SIG PRINT RUN ONE SET
1 John Wall 30.00 80.00
2 Evan Turner 15.00 40.00
3 Derrick Favors 6.00 15.00
4 Wesley Johnson 3.00 8.00
5 DeMarcus Cousins 20.00 50.00
6 Ekpe Udoh 3.00 8.00
7 Greg Monroe 6.00 15.00
8 Al-Farouq Aminu 5.00 12.00
9 Gordon Hayward 20.00 50.00
10 Paul George 15.00 40.00
11 Cole Aldrich 4.00 10.00
12 Xavier Henry 3.00 8.00
13 Ed Davis 3.00 8.00
14 Patrick Patterson 4.00 10.00
15 Larry Sanders 3.00 8.00
16 Luke Babbitt 4.00 10.00
17 Eric Bledsoe 6.00 15.00
18 Avery Bradley 6.00 15.00
19 James Anderson 3.00 8.00
20 Craig Brackins 3.00 8.00
21 Elliot Williams 3.00 8.00
22 Trevor Booker 4.00 10.00
23 Damion James 3.00 8.00
24 Dominique Jones 3.00 8.00
25 Quincy Pondexter 3.00 8.00
26 Jordan Crawford 4.00 10.00
27 Greivis Vasquez 4.00 10.00
28 Daniel Orton 3.00 8.00
29 Lazar Hayward 3.00 8.00
30 Dexter Pittman 3.00 8.00
31 Hassan Whiteside 10.00 25.00
32 Terrico White 3.00 8.00
33 Andy Rautins 3.00 8.00
34 Lance Stephenson 5.00 12.00
35 Timofey Mozgov 15.00 40.00
36 Devin Ebanks 3.00 8.00
37 Gani Lawal 3.00 8.00
38 Kevin Seraphin 8.00 20.00
39 Luke Harangody 3.00 8.00
40 Willie Warren 3.00 8.00

2010-11 Timeless Treasures NBA Apprentice Materials Triple
STATED PRINT RUN 99 SER.#'d SETS
UNPRICED PRIME PRINT RUN 3 TO 10 SETS
1 Wall/Turner/Favors 8.00 20.00
2 Johnson/Cousins/Udoh 5.00 12.00
3 Monroe/Aminu/Hayward 4.00 10.00
4 George/Aldrich/Henry 3.00 8.00
5 Davis/Patterson/Sanders 4.00 10.00
6 Babbitt/Bledsoe/Bradley 4.00 10.00
7 Anderson/Brackins/Williams 3.00 8.00
8 Booker/James/Jones 3.00 8.00
9 Pondexter/Crawford/Vasquez 3.00 8.00
10 Orton/Hayward/Pittman 3.00 8.00
11 Whiteside/White/Rautins 3.00 8.00
12 Stephenson/Mozgov/Ebanks 3.00 8.00
13 Lawal/Seraphin/Harangody 3.00 8.00
14 Wall/Cousins/Patterson 12.00 30.00
15 Patterson/Bledsoe/Orton 5.00 12.00

2010-11 Timeless Treasures NBA Apprentice Signatures Combos
STATED PRINT RUN 25 SER.#'d SETS
1 J.Wall/E.Turner 50.00 125.00
2 J.Wall/D.Cousins 50.00 125.00
3 E.Turner/D.Favors 15.00 40.00
4 D.Favors/W.Johnson 8.00 20.00
5 W.Johnson/D.Cousins 10.00 25.00
6 G.Monroe/T.White 12.00 30.00
7 A.Aminu/E.Bledsoe 12.00 30.00
8 L.Harangody/A.Bradley 8.00 20.00
9 G.Vasquez/X.Henry 10.00 25.00
10 C.Aldrich/X.Henry 8.00 20.00
11 E.Udoh/G.Hayward 10.00 25.00
12 P.George/L.Stephenson 10.00 25.00
13 D.James/D.Pittman 8.00 20.00
14 E.Davis/P.Patterson 8.00 20.00
15 E.Bledsoe/D.Orton 12.00 30.00

2010-11 Timeless Treasures NBA Draft Lottery Patches
STATED PRINT RUN 10 TO 140 SER.#'d SETS
SOME UNPRICED DUE TO SCARCITY
1 John Wall/10
2 Evan Turner/20 25.00 60.00
3 Derrick Favors/30 15.00 40.00
4 Wesley Johnson/40 10.00 25.00
5 DeMarcus Cousins/50 20.00 50.00
6 Ekpe Udoh/60 6.00 15.00
7 Greg Monroe/70 6.00 15.00
8 Al-Farouq Aminu/80 6.00 15.00
9 Gordon Hayward/90 10.00 25.00
10 Paul George/100 30.00 60.00
11 Cole Aldrich/110 6.00 15.00
12 Xavier Henry/120 6.00 15.00
13 Ed Davis/130 6.00 15.00
14 Patrick Patterson/140 8.00 20.00

2010-11 Timeless Treasures Rookie Year Materials
STATED PRINT RUN ONE TO 99 SER.#'d SETS
SOME UNPRICED DUE TO SCARCITY
UNPRICED LOGO.PRINT RUN ONE TO 4 SETS
UNPRICED TAG PRINT RUN ONE TO 5 SETS
UNPRICED TAG TEAM PRINT RUN 1 TO 2 SETS
1 Al Horford/99 2.50 6.00
2 Al Thornton/99 2.00 5.00
3 Andre Iguodala/99 2.50 6.00
4 Andrea Bargnani/49 2.50 6.00
5 Chris Paul/99 4.00 10.00
6 Daequan Cook/99 2.00 5.00
7 Deron Williams/99 2.50 6.00
8 Dikembe Mutombo/99 3.00 8.00
9 Dwight Howard/99 2.50 6.00
10 Jameer Nelson/99 2.00 5.00
11 Jeff Green/99 2.50 6.00
12 Joakim Noah/49 2.50 6.00
13 Kevin Durant/99 8.00 20.00
14 Kevin Garnett/99 5.00 12.00
15 LeBron James/99 12.00 30.00
16 Luis Scola/99 2.50 6.00
17 Mike Conley Jr./20 3.00 8.00
18 Nate Robinson/49 2.00 5.00
19 O.J. Mayo/99 2.00 5.00
20 Patrick Ewing/99 5.00 12.00
22 Paul Pierce/99 5.00 12.00
23 Rodney Stuckey/49 2.50 6.00
24 Shaquille O'Neal/99 10.00 25.00
25 Thaddeus Young/49 2.00 5.00
26 Zydrunas Ilgauskas/99 2.50 6.00
27 Andrew Bogut/99 2.50 6.00

2010-11 Timeless Treasures Rookie Year Materials Prime
PRIME: .75X TO 2X BASE HI
STATED PRINT RUN ONE TO 25 SER.#'d SETS
SOME UNPRICED DUE TO SCARCITY
8 Dikembe Mutombo/25 10.00 25.00
12 Joakim Noah/25 8.00 20.00
17 Mike Conley Jr./25 6.00 15.00
26 Zydrunas Ilgauskas/25 5.00 12.00

2010-11 Timeless Treasures Rookie Year Materials Prime Signatures
STATED PRINT RUN 5 TO 25 SER.#'d SETS
SOME UNPRICED DUE TO SCARCITY
2 Al Thornton/25 10.00 25.00
3 Andre Iguodala/15 12.00 30.00
7 Deron Williams/25 10.00 25.00
8 Dikembe Mutombo/25 20.00 50.00
12 Joakim Noah/25 20.00 50.00
27 Andrew Bogut/25 10.00 25.00

2010-11 Timeless Treasures Rookie Year Materials Quads
STATED PRINT RUN 25 SER.#'d SETS
UNPRICED PRIME PRINT RUN 5 SETS
1 Paul/Rob/Williams/Bogut 12.00 30.00
2 Mutombo/Ewing/Shaq/Garnett 20.00 50.00
3 Pierce/James/Durant/Howard 25.00 60.00
4 Iguodala/Bargnani/Scola/Noah 6.00 15.00
5 Horford/Thornton/Conley/Stuckey 6.00 15.00

2010-11 Timeless Treasures Rookie Year Materials ROY
STATED PRINT RUN 99 SER.#'d SETS
*PRIME: .75X TO 2X BASE HI
PRIME PRINT RUN ONE TO 25 SETS
SOME PRIME UNPRICED DUE TO SCARCITY
5 Chris Paul 5.00 12.00
13 Kevin Durant 10.00 25.00
15 LeBron James 12.00 30.00
20 Patrick Ewing 5.00 12.00
24 Shaquille O'Neal 10.00 25.00

2010-11 Timeless Treasures Rookie Year Materials ROY Signatures
STATED PRINT RUN 10 TO 25 SER.#'d SETS
SOME UNPRICED DUE TO SCARCITY
13 Kevin Durant/25 125.00 250.00

2010-11 Timeless Treasures Rookie Year Materials Signatures
STATED PRINT RUN 10 TO 50 SER.#'d SETS
SOME UNPRICED DUE TO SCARCITY
UNPRICED LOGOMAN SIG PRINT RUN ONE SET
UNPRICED TAG SIG PRINT RUN ONE TO 2 SETS
UNPRICED TAG TEAM SIG PRINT RUN ONE SET
1 Al Horford/50 5.00 12.00
2 Al Thornton/50 5.00 12.00
3 Andre Iguodala/50 6.00 15.00
4 Andrea Bargnani/25 5.00 12.00
7 Deron Williams/50 6.00 15.00
8 Dikembe Mutombo/50 10.00 25.00
13 Kevin Durant/25 125.00 250.00
27 Andrew Bogut/50 8.00 20.00

2010-11 Timeless Treasures Signatures Silver
STATED PRINT RUN 10 TO 99 SER.#'d SETS
SOME UNPRICED DUE TO SCARCITY
UNPRICED GOLD PRINT RUN 5 TO 10 SETS
UNPRICED PLATINUM PRINT RUN ONE SET
1 Kobe Bryant/99 100.00 200.00
7 Jason Kidd/25 12.00 30.00
11 Robin Lopez/25 5.00 12.00
17 Al Jefferson/49 5.00 12.00
23 LaMarcus Aldridge/25 12.00 30.00
28 Tony Parker/99 8.00 20.00
29 James Harden/25 20.00 50.00
32 Russell Westbrook/99 75.00 200.00
33 Aaron Brooks/99 5.00 12.00
37 Marc Gasol/49 8.00 20.00
41 Marcus Thornton/15 5.00 12.00
46 David Lee/49 6.00 15.00
48 Stephen Curry/20 60.00 150.00
49 Carl Landry/99 6.00 15.00
51 Tyreke Evans/99 10.00 25.00
52 Kevin Love/19 15.00 40.00
53 Michael Beasley/49 12.00 30.00
57 Mo Williams/49 5.00 12.00
64 Kendrick Perkins/25 6.00 15.00
66 Rajon Rondo/25 20.00 50.00
68 Chris Bosh/49 10.00 25.00
71 Andrew Bogut/49 5.00 12.00
74 D.J. Augustin/99 5.00 12.00
78 Derrick Rose/25 75.00 150.00
80 Andrea Bargnani/49 5.00 12.00
81 DeMar DeRozan/49 6.00 15.00
83 Danny Granger/99 5.00 12.00
84 Darren Collison/99 5.00 12.00
87 Anthony Randolph/99 5.00 12.00
88 Danilo Gallinari/49 5.00 12.00
90 Richard Hamilton/25 6.00 15.00
91 Tracy McGrady/40 12.00 30.00
92 Andre Iguodala/49 5.00 12.00
97 Josh Howard/25 5.00 12.00
99 Brook Lopez/25 6.00 15.00
100 Devin Harris/49 5.00 12.00

2010-11 Timeless Treasures Timeless Signatures Silver
STATED PRINT RUN 10 TO 25 SER.#'d SETS
SOME UNPRICED DUE TO SCARCITY
UNPRICED GOLD PRINT RUN 5 TO 10 SETS
UNPRICED PLATINUM PRINT RUN ONE SET
10 John Stockton/25 15.00 40.00

2012-13 Timeless Treasures
COMP.SET w/o RCs (150) 40.00 100.00
AU RC PRINT RUN 188 TO 499 SER.#'d SETS
UNPRICED GOLD PRINT RUN 10 SETS
UNPRICED PLATINUM PRINT RUN ONE SET
1 Rajon Rondo 1.00 2.50
2 Kevin Durant 2.50 6.00
3 Hakim Warrick .75 2.00
4 Tyreke Evans .60 1.50
5 Jrue Holiday 1.00 2.50
6 Kevin Garnett 1.50 4.00
7 Evan Turner .60 1.50
8 Paul Pierce 1.00 2.50
9 Serge Ibaka .75 2.00
10 LaMarcus Aldridge 1.00 2.50
11 Jason Terry .75 2.00
12 Russell Westbrook 2.50 6.00
13 Greivis Vasquez .75 2.00
14 Vince Carter 1.25 3.00
15 Grant Hill 1.25 3.00
16 Thabo Sefolosha .60 1.50
17 J.J. Hickson .60 1.50
18 Nick Young .75 2.00
19 Dorell Wright .60 1.50
20 Jeremy Lin 1.00 2.50
21 Kevin Martin .75 2.00
22 Stephen Curry 4.00 10.00
23 Nick Collison .75 2.00
24 Amare Stoudemire .75 2.00
25 Eric Gordon .75 2.00
26 Darren Collison .75 2.00
27 Raymond Felton .75 2.00
28 Ryan Anderson .75 2.00
29 Chris Kaman .75 2.00
30 Jason Thompson .60 1.50
31 Tyson Chandler .75 2.00
32 Al Horford .75 2.00
33 Ben Gordon .75 2.00
34 Carlos Boozer .75 2.00
35 Daniel Gibson .75 2.00
36 Emeka Okafor .75 2.00
37 George Hill .75 2.00
38 Brendan Haywood .60 1.50
39 Kevin Love 1.00 2.50
40 Kobe Bryant 4.00 10.00
41 Andrew Bynum .60 1.50
42 Chauncey Billups 1.00 2.50
43 Chris Paul 1.25 3.00
44 Dirk Nowitzki 1.25 3.00
45 Brandon Bass .60 1.50
46 Steve Nash 1.00 2.50
47 Wesley Matthews .60 1.50
48 James Harden 1.50 4.00
49 Patrick Patterson .60 1.50
50 Landry Fields .60 1.50
51 Manu Ginobili 1.00 2.50
52 Nate Robinson .60 1.50
53 Paul George 1.25 3.00
54 Ramon Sessions .75 2.00
55 Stephen Jackson .75 2.00
56 Wilson Chandler .75 2.00
57 Zach Randolph .75 2.00
58 Al Jefferson .75 2.00
59 Brandon Jennings .60 1.50
60 Jose Calderon .60 1.50
61 Danny Granger .75 2.00
62 Ersan Ilyasova .60 1.50
63 Gerald Henderson .60 1.50
64 Jameer Nelson .60 1.50
65 Kirk Hinrich .75 2.00
66 LeBron James 4.00 10.00
67 Marc Gasol 1.00 2.50
68 Nene .75 2.00
69 Paul Millsap 1.00 2.50
70 Rashard Lewis .75 2.00
71 Tayshaun Prince .75 2.00
72 O.J. Mayo .60 1.50
73 Shawn Marion .75 2.00
74 Jarrett Jack .75 2.00
75 Courtney Lee .75 2.00
76 J.R. Smith .75 2.00
77 Carl Landry .60 1.50
78 DeMarcus Cousins 1.00 2.50
79 Alonzo Gee .60 1.50
80 Brandon Roy 1.00 2.50
81 Chris Bosh 1.00 2.50
82 Danny Green .75 2.00
83 Gerald Wallace .75 2.00

84 Jason Richardson 1.00 2.50
85 Kris Humphries .60 1.50
86 Louis Williams .75 2.00
87 Marcin Gortat .75 2.00
88 Ray Allen 1.00 2.50
89 Tim Duncan 1.50 4.00
90 Jason Kidd 1.00 2.50
91 Antawn Jamison .75 2.00
92 Andrew Bogut .75 2.00
93 Marcus Thornton .60 1.50
94 Metta World Peace 1.00 2.50
95 Anderson Varejao .60 1.50
96 Brook Lopez .75 2.00
97 Glen Davis .60 1.50
98 JaVale McGee .75 2.00
99 Kyle Korver .75 2.00
100 Luc Mbah a Moute .60 1.50
101 Mario Chalmers .75 2.00
102 Ricky Rubio 1.00 2.50
103 Tony Allen .60 1.50
104 Blake Griffin 1.00 2.50
105 Andre Iguodala .75 2.00
106 Pau Gasol 1.00 2.50
107 Carmelo Anthony 1.25 3.00
108 Nicolas Batum .75 2.00
109 David Lee .60 1.50
110 DeAndre Jordan 1.00 2.50
111 Jamal Crawford 1.00 2.50
112 Andre Miller .75 2.00
113 Darrell Arthur .60 1.50
114 Goran Dragic .75 2.00
115 Jeff Teague .75 2.00
116 Kyle Lowry .75 2.00
117 Luis Scola .75 2.00
118 Michael Beasley .60 1.50
119 Rodney Stuckey .75 2.00
120 Tony Parker 1.00 2.50
121 Andrea Bargnani .75 2.00
122 David West .75 2.00
123 Dwyane Wade 1.50 4.00
124 Gordon Hayward 1.00 2.50
125 J.J. Barea .75 2.00
126 Luol Deng .75 2.00
127 Mike Conley .75 2.00
128 Roy Hibbert .75 2.00
129 DeJuan Blair .60 1.50
130 Dwight Howard .75 2.00
131 Derrick Rose 1.25 3.00
132 Greg Monroe .75 2.00
133 J.J. Redick 1.00 2.50
134 Josh Smith .75 2.00
135 Mike Miller .75 2.00
136 Rudy Gay 1.00 2.50
137 DeMar DeRozan 1.00 2.50
138 Joakim Noah .75 2.00
139 Mo Williams .75 2.00
140 Andrei Kirilenko .75 2.00
141 Deron Williams .75 2.00
142 Joe Johnson .75 2.00
143 Monta Ellis .75 2.00
144 Derrick Favors .75 2.00
145 Devin Harris .60 1.50
146 John Wall 1.25 3.00
147 Arron Afflalo .75 2.00
148 Drew Gooden .75 2.00
149 Trevor Ariza .60 1.50
150 Ty Lawson .60 1.50
151 Alec Burks AU/499 RC EXCH 4.00 10.00
152 A.Drummond AU/499 RC 6.00 15.00
153 A.Nicholson AU/499 RC 2.50 6.00
154 Anthony Davis AU/188 RC 75.00 200.00
155 Arnett Moultrie AU/476 RC 2.50 6.00
156 Austin Rivers AU/499 RC 4.00 10.00
157 Bernard James AU/499 RC 2.50 6.00
158 Bismack Biyombo AU/499 RC 2.50 6.00
159 Bradley Beal AU/499 RC 8.00 20.00
160 Brandon Knight AU/476 RC 4.00 10.00
161 Chandler Parsons AU/499 RC 4.00 10.00
162 Charles Jenkins AU/476 RC 2.50 6.00
163 Chris Singleton AU/499 RC 2.50 6.00
164 Cory Joseph AU/499 RC 2.50 6.00
165 DeQuan Jones AU/499 RC EXCH 2.50 6.00
166 D.Johnson-Odom AU/499 RC 2.50 6.00
167 Darius Miller AU/499 RC EXCH 2.50 6.00
168 Darius Morris AU/499 RC 2.50 6.00
169 Derrick Williams AU/499 RC 2.50 6.00
170 Dion Waiters AU/349 RC EXCH 4.00 10.00
171 Doron Lamb AU/499 RC 2.50 6.00
172 Dray Green AU/499 RC 15.00 40.00
173 Enes Kanter AU/499 RC 3.00 8.00
174 E'Twaun Moore AU/499 RC 2.50 6.00
175 Evan Fournier AU/499 RC 4.00 10.00
176 Fab Melo AU/499 RC 2.50 6.00
177 Festus Ezeli AU/499 RC 3.00 8.00
178 Greg Stiemsma AU/499 RC 2.50 6.00
179 Gustavo Ayon AU/499 RC EXCH 2.50 6.00
180 Harrison Barnes AU/499 RC 6.00 15.00
181 Iman Shumpert AU/499 RC 4.00 10.00
182 Isaiah Thomas AU/499 RC 15.00 40.00
183 Ivan Johnson AU/499 RC 2.50 6.00
184 Jae Crowder AU/499 RC 3.00 8.00
186 Jan Vesely AU/499 RC 2.50 6.00
187 J.Cunningham AU/499 RC 2.50 6.00
188 Jeff Taylor AU/499 RC 2.50 6.00
189 J.Sullinger AU/399 RC EXCH 3.00 8.00
190 J.Lamb AU/399 RC EXCH 4.00 10.00
191 Jeremy Tyler AU/499 RC EXCH 2.50 6.00
192 Jimmer Fredette AU/499 RC 2.50 6.00
193 Jimmy Butler AU/499 RC 20.00 50.00
194 John Henson AU/499 RC 4.00 10.00
195 John Jenkins AU/476 RC 2.50 6.00
196 Jon Leuer AU/499 RC 3.00 8.00
197 Jordan Hamilton AU/499 RC 2.50 6.00
198 Josh Harrellson AU/499 RC EXCH 2.50 6.00
199 Josh Selby AU/499 RC EXCH 2.50 6.00
200 N.Colo AU/499 RC EXCH 2.50 6.00
201 C.Copeland AU/499 RC EXCH 2.50 6.00
202 Kawhi Leonard AU/499 RC 75.00 200.00
203 K.Walker AU/349 RC EXCH 8.00 20.00
204 Kendall Marshall AU/499 RC 2.50 6.00
205 Kenneth Faried AU/499 RC 4.00 10.00
206 Kevin Murphy AU/499 RC 2.50 6.00
207 Khris Middleton AU/499 RC 4.00 10.00
208 Kim English AU/499 RC 2.50 6.00
209 Klay Thompson AU/499 RC 25.00 60.00
210 Kris Joseph AU/499 RC 2.50 6.00
211 Kyle O'Quinn AU/499 RC EXCH 2.50 6.00
212 Kyrie Irving AU/399 RC 40.00 100.00
213 Lance Thomas AU/499 RC 2.50 6.00
214 Lavoy Allen AU/499 RC 2.50 6.00
215 Malcolm Lee AU/499 RC 2.50 6.00
216 J.Valanciunas AU/499 RC 4.00 10.00
217 Marc.Morris AU/499 RC EXCH 3.00 8.00
218 Mark.Morris AU/499 RC EXCH 4.00 10.00
219 Marquis Teague AU/438 RC 2.50 6.00
220 MarShon Brooks AU/499 RC 3.00 8.00
221 Meyers Leonard AU/499 RC 3.00 8.00
222 M.Kidd-Gilchrist AU/316 RC 4.00 10.00
223 Mike Scott AU/499 RC 2.50 6.00
224 Miles Plumlee AU/499 RC EXCH 2.50 6.00
225 Maurice Harkless AU/499 RC 4.00 10.00
226 Nikola Vucevic AU/499 RC 4.00 10.00
227 Nolan Smith AU/499 RC 2.50 6.00
228 Norris Cole AU/499 RC 2.50 6.00
229 Orlando Johnson AU/499 RC 2.50 6.00
230 Perry Jones AU/499 RC 2.50 6.00
231 Quincy Acy AU/499 RC 2.50 6.00
232 Quincy Miller AU/475 RC 2.50 6.00
233 Reggie Jackson AU/499 RC 4.00 10.00
234 Kyle Singler AU/499 RC 2.50 6.00
235 Robert Sacre AU/499 RC 2.50 6.00
236 Royce White AU/476 RC 2.50 6.00
237 Shelvin Mack AU/499 RC 3.00 8.00
238 Terrence Jones AU/476 RC 3.00 8.00
239 Terrence Ross AU/499 RC 4.00 10.00
240 T.Robinson AU/349 RC 3.00 8.00
241 Tobias Harris AU/499 RC 4.00 10.00
242 Tony Wroten AU/499 RC EXCH 3.00 8.00
244 T.Shengelia AU/476 RC 2.50 6.00
245 Trey Thompkins AU/499 RC 2.50 6.00
246 T.Thompson AU/499 RC 4.00 10.00
247 Tyler Honeycutt AU/499 RC 2.50 6.00
248 Tyler Zeller AU/499 RC 3.00 8.00
249 Tyshawn Taylor AU/475 RC 2.50 6.00
250 Will Barton AU/499 RC 3.00 8.00

2012-13 Timeless Treasures Silver

*VETS: 1.5X TO 4X BASE HI
*ROOKIES: .75X TO 2X BASE HI
STATED PRINT RUN 25 SER.#'d SETS
154 Anthony Davis AU 100.00 250.00

2012-13 Timeless Treasures All-Star Materials

STATED PRINT RUN 149 SER.#'d SETS
1 Blake Griffin 3.00 8.00
2 Kobe Bryant 8.00 20.00
3 Dwight Howard 2.50 6.00
4 Carmelo Anthony 5.00 12.00
5 Chris Paul 4.00 10.00
6 Deron Williams 2.50 6.00
7 Derrick Rose 6.00 15.00
8 Dirk Nowitzki 4.00 10.00
9 Dwyane Wade 4.00 10.00
10 Joe Johnson 2.50 6.00
11 Kevin Durant 8.00 20.00
12 Kevin Garnett 5.00 12.00
13 Kevin Love 3.00 8.00
14 Pau Gasol 3.00 8.00
15 Manu Ginobili 3.00 8.00
16 Paul Pierce 3.00 8.00
17 Rajon Rondo 3.00 8.00
18 Ray Allen 3.00 8.00
19 Russell Westbrook 8.00 20.00
20 Tim Duncan 5.00 12.00

2012-13 Timeless Treasures All-Star Materials Prime

*PRIME: 1X TO 2.5X BASE HI
STATED PRINT RUN 25 TO 49 SER.#'d SETS
18 Ray Allen/49 10.00 25.00

2012-13 Timeless Treasures Perennial Materials

STATED PRINT RUN 149 SER.#'d SETS
UNPRICED PRIME PRINT RUN 10 SETS
1 Patrick Ewing 6.00 15.00
2 Karl Malone 4.00 10.00
3 Shaquille O'Neal 6.00 15.00
4 Hakeem Olajuwon 4.00 10.00
5 Ron Harper 3.00 8.00
6 Sean Elliott 3.00 8.00
7 Joe Dumars 3.00 8.00
8 Clyde Drexler 4.00 10.00
9 Kevin McHale 3.00 8.00
10 Jeff Hornacek 2.50 6.00
11 Kenny Anderson 2.50 6.00
12 Alex English 2.50 6.00
13 Kareem Abdul-Jabbar 5.00 12.00
14 Chris Mullin 3.00 8.00
15 Reggie Lewis 6.00 15.00
16 Steve Smith 2.50 6.00
17 Dikembe Mutombo 3.00 8.00
18 Robert Parish 3.00 8.00
19 Manute Bol 8.00 20.00
20 Jalen Rose 3.00 8.00
21 Mark Price 3.00 8.00
22 Glen Rice 8.00 20.00
23 Kelly Tripucka 2.00 5.00
24 Lou Hudson 3.00 8.00
25 Shawn Kemp 12.00 30.00

2012-13 Timeless Treasures Promising Pros Materials

STATED PRINT RUN 99 TO 149 SER.#'d SETS
UNPRICED PRIME PRINT RUN ONE TO 10 SETS
1 Kyrie Irving/149 10.00 25.00
2 Derrick Williams/149 1.25 3.00
3 Tristan Thompson/149 2.00 5.00
4 Klay Thompson/149 8.00 20.00
5 Kawhi Leonard/99 10.00 25.00
6 Derrick Favors/149 2.00 5.00
7 DeMarcus Cousins/149 2.50 6.00
8 Iman Shumpert/149 2.00 5.00
9 Brandon Knight/149 2.00 5.00
10 Markieff Morris/149 2.00 5.00
11 Evan Turner/149 1.50 4.00
12 Gordon Hayward/149 2.50 6.00
13 MarShon Brooks/149 1.50 4.00
14 Kemba Walker/149 4.00 10.00
15 Kenneth Faried/149 2.00 5.00
16 Norris Cole/149 1.25 3.00
17 Jimmer Fredette/149 1.25 3.00
18 John Wall/149 3.00 8.00
19 Tiago Splitter/149 2.00 5.00
20 Ivan Johnson/149 1.25 3.00

2012-13 Timeless Treasures Revolution Memorabilia

STATED PRINT RUN 75 SER.#'d SETS
1 K.Bryant/L.James 20.00 50.00
2 K.Faried/K.Love 2.50 6.00
3 B.Griffin/K.Love 2.50 6.00
4 D.Rose/C.Paul 3.00 8.00
5 R.Rondo/R.Westbrook 6.00 15.00
6 T.Chandler/K.Garnett 4.00 10.00
7 K.Irving/K.Walker 12.00 30.00
8 P.Pierce/C.Anthony 3.00 8.00
9 T.Parker/J.Kidd 2.50 6.00
10 Z.Randolph/C.Bosh 2.50 6.00
11 D.Nowitzki/T.Duncan 4.00 10.00
12 T.Evans/T.Lawson 1.50 4.00
13 J.Wall/T.Evans 3.00 8.00
14 P.Gasol/A.Stoudemire 2.50 6.00
15 M.Ginobili/C.Billups 2.50 6.00
16 M.Gasol/S.Ibaka 2.50 6.00
17 D.Granger/R.Gay 2.50 6.00
18 B.Jennings/S.Curry 10.00 25.00
19 A.Iguodala/L.Deng 2.00 5.00
20 K.Durant/L.James 12.00 30.00

2012-13 Timeless Treasures Rookie Matchups

STATED PRINT RUN 99 SER.#'d SETS
1 K.Irving/B.Knight 5.00 12.00
2 T.Robinson/A.Davis 5.00 12.00
3 T.Thompson/D.Williams 1.00 2.50
4 M.Kidd-Gilchrist/H.Barnes 1.50 4.00
5 A.Drummond/J.Lamb 1.50 4.00
6 Marc.Morris/Mark.Morris 1.00 2.50
7 J.Henson/T.Zeller 1.00 2.50
8 D.Waiters/J.Sullinger 1.00 2.50
9 D.Lillard/I.Shumpert 4.00 10.00
10 K.Thompson/I.Thomas 4.00 10.00

2012-13 Timeless Treasures Three-Piece Puzzles

STATED PRINT RUN 199 SER.#'d SETS
1A Derrick Rose 2.00 5.00
1B Joakim Noah 1.25 3.00
1C Luol Deng 1.25 3.00
2A Chris Bosh 1.50 4.00
2B Dwyane Wade 2.50 6.00
2C LeBron James 6.00 15.00
3A Manu Ginobili 1.50 4.00
3B Tim Duncan 2.50 6.00
3C Tony Parker 1.50 4.00
4A Russell Westbrook 4.00 10.00
4B Kevin Durant 4.00 10.00
4C Serge Ibaka 1.25 3.00
5A Kevin Garnett 2.50 6.00
5B Paul Pierce 1.50 4.00
5C Rajon Rondo 1.50 4.00
6A Goran Dragic 1.25 3.00
6B Marcin Gortat 1.25 3.00
6C Michael Beasley 1.00 2.50
7A Brook Lopez 1.25 3.00
7B Deron Williams 1.25 3.00
7C Joe Johnson 1.25 3.00
8A Kobe Bryant 6.00 15.00
8B Pau Gasol 1.50 4.00
8C Steve Nash 1.50 4.00
9A Amare Stoudemire 1.25 3.00
9B Carmelo Anthony 2.00 5.00
9C Tyson Chandler 1.25 3.00
10A Marc Gasol 1.50 4.00
10B Rudy Gay 1.50 4.00
10C Zach Randolph 1.25 3.00
11A Darren Collison 1.25 3.00
11B Dirk Nowitzki 2.00 5.00
11C O.J. Mayo 1.00 2.50
12A Dion Waiters 1.50 4.00
12B Kyrie Irving 8.00 20.00
12C Tristan Thompson 1.50 4.00
13A Anthony Davis 8.00 20.00
13B Austin Rivers 1.50 4.00
13C Darius Miller 1.00 2.50

2012-13 Timeless Treasures Time to Shine Autographs

STATED PRINT RUN 49 TO 199 SER.#'d SETS
1 MarShon Brooks/199 4.00 10.00
2 Brandon Knight/199 5.00 12.00
3 Norris Cole/199 3.00 8.00
4 Kyrie Irving/99 40.00 100.00
5 Klay Thompson/199 30.00 80.00
6 Iman Shumpert/199 5.00 12.00
7 Kenneth Faried/199 5.00 12.00
8 Kawhi Leonard/199 50.00 120.00
9 Chandler Parsons/199 5.00 12.00
10 Isaiah Thomas/199 20.00 50.00
11 Tristan Thompson/99 5.00 12.00
12 Anthony Davis/49 75.00 150.00
13 Thomas Robinson/49 4.00 10.00
14 Michael Kidd-Gilchrist/49 5.00 12.00
15 Bradley Beal/99 10.00 25.00
16 Austin Rivers/99 5.00 12.00
17 Dion Waiters/199 5.00 12.00
18 Andre Drummond/99 8.00 20.00
19 Jimmer Fredette/199 3.00 8.00
20 Harrison Barnes/99 12.00 30.00

2012-13 Timeless Treasures Timeless Signatures

STATED PRINT RUN 25 TO 199 SER.#'d SETS
1 Jeff Hornacek/199 EXCH 4.00 10.00
2 John Starks/199 8.00 20.00
3 Bob Love/199 5.00 12.00
4 Larry Johnson/199 5.00 12.00
5 Spud Webb/199 6.00 15.00
6 Steve Smith/199 6.00 15.00
7 Jalen Rose/199 EXCH 4.00 10.00
8 Elgin Baylor/49 5.00 12.00
9 Dan Majerle/199 5.00 12.00
10 Bob McAdoo/99 10.00 25.00
11 Larry Bird/25
12 Alvan Adams/98
13 World B. Free/49 5.00 12.00
14 Steve Kerr/49 12.00 30.00
15 Hal Greer/99 4.00 10.00
16 Alonzo Mourning/49 12.00 30.00
17 Willis Reed/49 10.00 25.00
18 Anfernee Hardaway/49 20.00 50.00
19 George Gervin/49 10.00 25.00
20 Kenny Smith/49 6.00 15.00
21 Bruce Bowen/199 4.00 10.00
22 Sleepy Floyd/199 4.00 10.00
23 Rex Chapman/199 6.00 15.00
24 Sean Elliott/199 EXCH 6.00 15.00
25 Paul Silas/199 6.00 15.00
26 Magic Johnson/25 30.00 80.00
27 Cazzie Russell/199 4.00 10.00
28 Vlade Divac/199 4.00 10.00
29 Dan Issel/199 5.00 12.00
30 James Worthy/49 12.00 30.00
31 John Paxson/199 4.00 10.00
32 Bill Russell/25 40.00 100.00
33 Jamal Mashburn/199 4.00 10.00
34 Dikembe Mutombo/99 6.00 15.00
35 Terry Porter/199 4.00 10.00
36 Antoine Walker/199 4.00 10.00
37 Ralph Sampson/199 6.00 15.00
38 Lenny Wilkens/99 4.00 10.00
39 Dennis Scott/199 6.00 15.00
40 Calvin Murphy/99 4.00 10.00
41 John Stockton/25 40.00 100.00
42 Walt Frazier/99 10.00 25.00
43 Bill Walton/99 10.00 25.00
44 Allan Houston/99 6.00 15.00
45 George McGinnis/199 4.00 10.00
46 John Havlicek/25 12.00 30.00
47 Adrian Dantley/99 4.00 10.00
48 Bob Dandridge/199 4.00 10.00
49 Alex English/49 5.00 12.00
50 Yao Ming/25 20.00 50.00

2012-13 Timeless Treasures Timeless Talents Signatures

STATED PRINT RUN 25 TO 199 SER.#'d SETS
1 Brandon Roy/25
2 Jason Richardson/99 4.00 10.00
3 Carlos Boozer/99 4.00 10.00
4 Chauncey Billups/99 EXCH 6.00 15.00
5 Kobe Bryant/99 75.00 150.00
6 Pau Gasol/25 20.00 50.00
7 Deron Williams/25 12.00 30.00
8 Kevin Love/25 12.00 30.00
9 Luis Scola/99 4.00 10.00
10 Ryan Anderson/199 4.00 10.00
11 Kevin Durant/49 75.00 150.00
12 Channing Frye/99 EXCH 4.00 10.00
13 Nick Young/199 4.00 10.00
14 Thabo Sefolosha/199 4.00 10.00
15 D.J. Augustin/99 4.00 10.00
16 Al Horford/49 4.00 10.00
17 David West/99 4.00 10.00
18 Monta Ellis/99 4.00 10.00
19 Mike Conley/99 6.00 15.00
20 Caron Butler/49 4.00 10.00
21 Roy Hibbert/199 8.00 20.00
22 Gerald Henderson/199 4.00 10.00
23 James Harden/99 EXCH 25.00 60.00
24 Blake Griffin/49 25.00 60.00
25 Jose Calderon/99 EXCH 5.00 12.00
26 LaMarcus Aldridge/49 8.00 20.00
27 Zach Randolph/49 5.00 12.00
28 Shane Battier/49 12.00 30.00
29 David Lee/49 EXCH 6.00 15.00
30 Chris Bosh/25
31 Juwan Howard/99 4.00 10.00
32 Gerald Wallace/49 4.00 10.00
33 Andre Iguodala/49 6.00 15.00
34 Ben Gordon/49
35 Josh Smith/99 4.00 10.00
36 Chris Kaman/99 4.00 10.00
37 Jameer Nelson/99 4.00 10.00
38 Kevin Martin/99 8.00 20.00
39 Kris Humphries/199 EXCH 4.00 10.00
40 Stephen Curry/99 100.00 250.00
41 Antawn Jamison/99 4.00 10.00
42 Brook Lopez/99 5.00 12.00
43 Danny Granger/49 4.00 10.00
44 Taj Gibson/99 4.00 10.00
45 Wesley Matthews/199 4.00 10.00
46 Goran Dragic/99 4.00 10.00
47 Mario Chalmers/99 8.00 20.00
48 Drew Gooden/199 EXCH 4.00 10.00
49 Marcus Camby/199 6.00 15.00
50 Tyson Chandler/49 6.00 15.00

2012-13 Timeless Treasures Treasured Ink

STATED PRINT RUN 10 TO 199 SER.#'d SETS
1 David Robinson/25 50.00 125.00
2 Dolph Schayes/99 6.00 15.00
3 Mark Eaton/199 4.00 10.00
4 Bernard King/199 4.00 10.00
5 Kevin Durant/25 75.00 150.00
6 Andre Iguodala/49 4.00 10.00
7 Tom Heinsohn/199 20.00 50.00
8 Bill Walton/99 4.00 10.00
9 Kobe Bryant/99 75.00 150.00
10 Michael Cooper/199 4.00 10.00
11 Larry Bird/25 40.00 100.00
12 Gail Goodrich/99 6.00 15.00
13 Chris Mullin/199 6.00 15.00
14 Chris Paul/25 EXCH
15 Kareem Abdul-Jabbar/25
16 Gary Payton/25 10.00 25.00
17 Blake Griffin/49 15.00 40.00
18 Bill Russell/25 50.00 120.00
19 Tony Parker/49 15.00 40.00
20 Bill Sharman/49 4.00 10.00
21 LaMarcus Aldridge/49 8.00 20.00
22 Magic Johnson/25
23 Kevin Love/25 10.00 25.00
25 Steve Nash/25
26 Jerry West/25
27 Bailey Howell/199 4.00 10.00
28 Jeff Hornacek/199 4.00 10.00
29 Julius Erving/25 40.00 100.00
30 Kevin Willis/199 4.00 10.00

2012-13 Timeless Treasures Treasured Threads

STATED PRINT RUN 25 TO 99 SER.#'d SETS
UNPRICED PRIME PRINT RUN ONE TO 10 SETS
1 Tim Duncan/99 5.00 12.00
2 Jeff Hornacek/99 2.50 6.00
3 Chauncey Billups/99 3.00 8.00
4 Ben Wallace/99 2.50 6.00
5 Andre Miller/99 2.50 6.00
6 Vince Carter/99 4.00 10.00
7 Hedo Turkoglu/99 2.50 6.00
8 Tyson Chandler/99 2.50 6.00
9 Patrick Ewing/99 10.00 25.00
10 LeBron James/99 12.00 30.00
11 Dirk Nowitzki/99 4.00 10.00
12 Carmelo Anthony/99 5.00 12.00
13 Paul Pierce/99 5.00 12.00
14 Tayshaun Prince/99 2.50 6.00
15 Dwyane Wade/99 5.00 12.00
16 Amare Stoudemire/99 2.50 6.00
17 Alonzo Mourning/99 12.00 30.00
18 Kevin Durant/99 8.00 20.00
19 Chris Paul/99 4.00 10.00
20 Scottie Pippen/99 10.00 25.00
21 David Robinson/99 5.00 12.00
22 Jerry West/25 8.00 20.00
23 Julius Erving/25
24 Dennis Rodman/99 6.00 15.00
25 Gary Payton/25 6.00 15.00
26 Andre Iguodala/99 2.50 6.00
27 Derrick Rose/99 4.00 10.00
28 Pau Gasol/99 3.00 8.00
29 Hakeem Olajuwon/99 4.00 10.00
30 Blake Griffin/99 3.00 8.00

2012-13 Timeless Treasures Validating Marks Autographs

STATED PRINT RUN 49 TO 199 SER.#'d SETS
1 Brandon Bass/99 4.00 10.00
2 James Harden/49 30.00 80.00
3 Gordon Hayward/199 5.00 12.00
4 Paul George/199 15.00 40.00
5 Gary Neal/99 EXCH 4.00 10.00
6 Derrick Favors/99 4.00 10.00
7 Greg Monroe/99 4.00 10.00
8 Danny Green/199 4.00 10.00
9 Ersan Ilyasova/199 4.00 10.00
10 Brandon Jennings/49 EXCH 4.00 10.00
11 JaVale McGee/99 EXCH 4.00 10.00
12 Omri Casspi/199 EXCH 4.00 10.00
13 Omer Asik/199 EXCH 4.00 10.00
14 Landry Fields/199 4.00 10.00
15 Tiago Splitter/199 4.00 10.00
16 Greivis Vasquez/199 4.00 10.00
17 Patrick Patterson/199 4.00 10.00
18 Avery Bradley/199 EXCH 6.00 15.00
19 Ed Davis/199 4.00 10.00
20 Tyreke Evans/49 4.00 10.00
21 Al-Farouq Aminu/199 4.00 10.00
22 Ekpe Udoh/199 4.00 10.00
23 Quincy Pondexter/199 4.00 10.00
24 Jonas Jerebko/199 4.00 10.00
25 Jordan Crawford/199 EXCH 4.00 10.00
26 Jrue Holiday/99 8.00 20.00
27 Serge Ibaka/199 EXCH 5.00 12.00
28 Eric Gordon/49 5.00 12.00
29 Marcus Thornton/199 4.00 10.00
30 DeAndre Jordan/99 4.00 10.00
31 Ty Lawson/99 4.00 10.00
32 Elliot Williams/199 4.00 10.00
33 Stephen Curry/99 150.00 300.00
34 Gary Forbes/199 4.00 10.00
36 Xavier Henry/199 4.00 10.00
37 James Anderson/199 4.00 10.00
38 Nikola Pekovic/199 4.00 10.00
39 Eric Bledsoe/199 4.00 10.00
40 Devin Ebanks/199 4.00 10.00
41 DeMarcus Cousins/49 EXCH 10.00 25.00
42 Kyle Lowry/199 4.00 10.00
43 Ryan Anderson/199 EXCH 4.00 10.00
44 Timofey Mozgov/199 EXCH 4.00 10.00
45 Luke Babbitt/199 4.00 10.00
46 Luke Harangody/199 EXCH 4.00 10.00
47 Tyler Hansbrough/99 4.00 10.00
48 Jeff Teague/199 4.00 10.00
49 Austin Daye/199 4.00 10.00
50 Brandon Rush/199 4.00 10.00

2013-14 Timeless Treasures

100 PRINT RUN 299 SER.#'d SETS
EXCHANGE DEADLINE 6/11/2015
1 Kyrie Irving 2.50 6.00
2 Kobe Bryant 5.00 12.00
3 Kevin Durant 3.00 8.00
4 Kevin Love 1.25 3.00
5 Derrick Rose 1.50 4.00
6 Damian Lillard 2.50 6.00
7 Dirk Nowitzki 1.50 4.00
8 Blake Griffin 1.25 3.00
9 Anthony Davis 2.50 6.00
10 Deron Williams 1.00 2.50
11 Kenneth Faried 1.00 2.50
12 Jimmer Fredette .75 2.00
13 Al Horford 1.00 2.50
14 Marc Gasol 1.25 3.00
15 James Harden 2.00 5.00
16 Andre Drummond 1.25 3.00
17 Russell Westbrook 3.00 8.00
18 Carmelo Anthony 1.50 4.00
19 Tony Parker 1.25 3.00
20 Bradley Beal 1.25 3.00
21 Klay Thompson 1.50 4.00
22 Paul George 1.50 4.00
23 Tyreke Evans .75 2.00
24 Paul Pierce 1.25 3.00
25 Dwight Howard 1.00 2.50
26 LeBron James 5.00 12.00
27 Michael Kidd-Gilchrist 1.25 3.00
28 Jrue Holiday 1.25 3.00
29 Enes Kanter .75 2.00
30 LaMarcus Aldridge 1.25 3.00
31 Vince Carter 1.50 4.00
32 Monta Ellis 1.00 2.50
33 Isaiah Thomas 1.25 3.00
34 Ricky Rubio 1.25 3.00
35 Rudy Gay 1.25 3.00
36 Ty Lawson .75 2.00
37 MarShon Brooks 1.00 2.50
38 Roy Hibbert 1.00 2.50
39 Tim Duncan 2.00 5.00
40 Tristan Thompson 1.00 2.50
41 John Wall 1.50 4.00
42 Devin Harris .75 2.00
43 Goran Dragic 1.00 2.50
44 Zach Randolph 1.00 2.50
45 Joakim Noah 1.00 2.50
46 Dwyane Wade 2.00 5.00
47 Kemba Walker 1.25 3.00
48 Ersan Ilyasova .75 2.00
49 Greivis Vasquez 1.00 2.50
50 Amar'e Stoudemire 1.00 2.50
51 Steve Nash 1.25 3.00
52 Chandler Parsons 1.00 2.50
53 Danny Green 1.00 2.50
54 Rajon Rondo 1.25 3.00
55 DeMarcus Cousins 1.25 3.00
56 Jameer Nelson .75 2.00
57 Draymond Green 1.50 4.00
58 Brandon Knight 1.00 2.50
59 Gordon Hayward 1.25 3.00
60 Nick Young 1.25 3.00
61 Nene 1.00 2.50
62 Josh Smith 1.00 2.50
63 Joe Johnson 1.00 2.50
64 JaVale McGee 1.00 2.50
65 Kendall Marshall 1.00 2.50
66 Chris Bosh 1.25 3.00
67 Carlos Boozer 1.00 2.50
68 Stephen Curry 5.00 12.00
69 Gary Neal 1.00 2.50
70 Shawn Marion 1.00 2.50
71 Kyle Lowry 1.00 2.50
72 Chris Paul 1.50 4.00
73 Wesley Matthews .75 2.00
74 Lance Stephenson 1.00 2.50
75 Al Jefferson 1.00 2.50
76 Ray Allen 1.25 3.00
77 Ben Gordon 1.00 2.50
78 Brandon Jennings .75 2.00
79 Derrick Williams .75 2.00
80 Jeff Teague 1.00 2.50
81 Tyson Chandler 1.00 2.50
82 Austin Rivers 1.00 2.50
83 Greg Monroe 1.00 2.50
84 David West 1.00 2.50
85 Thaddeus Young .75 2.00
86 Kawhi Leonard 2.00 5.00
87 Brook Lopez 1.00 2.50
88 Marcin Gortat 1.00 2.50
89 Jimmy Butler 1.25 3.00
90 Metta World Peace 1.25 3.00
91 Andrea Bargnani 1.00 2.50
92 Jae Crowder 1.00 2.50
93 Kevin Garnett 2.00 5.00
94 Tobias Harris 1.00 2.50
95 DeAndre Jordan 1.25 3.00
96 Anderson Varejao .75 2.00
97 Jeremy Lin 1.25 3.00
98 Iman Shumpert .75 2.00
99 Harrison Barnes 1.00 2.50
100 Chris Andersen 1.00 2.50
101 Anthony Bennett JSY AU RC 4.00 10.00
102 Allen Crabbe JSY AU RC 4.00 10.00
103 Glen Rice Jr. JSY AU RC 3.00 8.00
104 Victor Oladipo JSY AU RC 10.00 25.00
105 Archie Goodwin JSY AU RC 4.00 10.00
106 Tony Mitchell JSY AU RC 3.00 8.00
107 Otto Porter JSY AU RC 5.00 12.00
108 Andre Roberson JSY AU RC 3.00 8.00
109 Nate Wolters JSY AU RC 4.00 10.00
110 Cody Zeller JSY AU RC 4.00 10.00
111 Reggie Bullock JSY AU RC 4.00 10.00
112 Jeff Withey JSY AU RC 3.00 8.00
113 Alex Len JSY AU RC 4.00 10.00
114 Tim Hardaway Jr. JSY AU RC 5.00 12.00
115 Grant Jerrett JSY AU RC 3.00 8.00
116 Nerlens Noel JSY AU RC 6.00 15.00
117 Solomon Hill JSY AU RC 3.00 8.00
118 Jamaal Franklin JSY AU RC 3.00 8.00
119 Ben McLemore JSY AU RC 4.00 10.00
120 Mason Plumlee JSY AU RC 5.00 12.00
121 Ryan Kelly JSY AU RC 3.00 8.00
122 Kentavious Caldwell Pope JSY AU RC 5.00 12.00
123 Tony Snell JSY AU RC 4.00 10.00
124 Erik Murphy JSY AU RC 3.00 8.00
125 Trey Burke JSY AU RC 4.00 10.00
126 Shane Larkin JSY AU RC 3.00 8.00
127 Peyton Siva JSY AU RC 3.00 8.00
128 C.J. McCollum JSY AU RC 15.00 40.00
129 Antetokounmpo JSY AU RC 75.00 200.00
130 Ricky Ledo JSY AU RC 3.00 8.00
131 M.Carter-Williams JSY AU RC 5.00 12.00
132 Shabazz Muhammad JSY AU RC 4.00 10.00
133 Isaiah Canaan JSY AU RC 3.00 8.00
134 Steven Adams JSY AU RC 5.00 12.00
135 Kelly Olynyk JSY AU RC 4.00 10.00

2013-14 Timeless Treasures Every Player Every Game Jerseys

STATED PRINT RUN 49 SER.#'d SETS
MOST NOT PRICED DUE TO LACK OF INFO
1 Russell Westbrook
2 Damian Lillard
3 Rodney Stuckey 3.00 8.00
4 Luol Deng 3.00 8.00
5 Gordon Hayward
6 Jonas Valanciunas 3.00 8.00
7 Tracy McGrady 6.00 15.00
8 Carlos Boozer
9 Tyreke Evans
10 Louis Williams
11 Klay Thompson
12 Tyson Chandler
13 Jeremy Lin 4.00 10.00
14 Paul Pierce 4.00 10.00
15 Al Horford
16 Evan Turner
17 Rajon Rondo 4.00 10.00
18 Tim Duncan 6.00 15.00
19 Pau Gasol
20 Tony Parker
21 Omer Asik 3.00 8.00
22 Kent Bazemore 3.00 8.00
23 Will Barton
24 David Lee 2.50 6.00
25 DeMar DeRozan
26 John Wall
27 Stephen Curry
28 Thaddeus Young 2.50 6.00
29 Mike Conley
30 Manu Ginobili
31 Joakim Noah 6.00 15.00
32 Grant Hill
33 Spencer Hawes
34 Harrison Barnes 3.00 8.00
35 Jimmer Fredette 2.50 6.00
36 Kemba Walker 4.00 10.00
37 Monta Ellis
38 Blake Griffin
39 Kyrie Irving
40 Dirk Nowitzki 5.00 12.00
41 Tyler Zeller
42 Jeff Green 3.00 8.00
43 Kyle Singler
44 Kobe Bryant
45 Tristan Thompson 3.00 8.00
46 DeMarcus Cousins
47 Brandon Roy
48 Terrence Jones
49 Ricky Rubio
50 Brandon Knight
51 Kevin Love
52 Carmelo Anthony 5.00 12.00
53 Michael Kidd-Gilchrist
54 Greg Monroe 3.00 8.00
55 Anthony Davis
56 Kevin Durant
57 Rasheed Wallace
58 Marc Gasol 4.00 10.00
59 Wesley Matthews
60 Bradley Beal 4.00 10.00
61 Jason Richardson 4.00 10.00
62 Kyle Lowry
63 Dwight Howard 3.00 8.00
64 Brandon Jennings 2.50 6.00
65 Dwyane Wade 6.00 15.00
66 LaMarcus Aldridge
67 Jason Kidd 4.00 10.00
68 Serge Ibaka 3.00 8.00
69 Thomas Robinson 6.00 15.00
70 Roy Hibbert
71 Ray Allen
72 J.R. Smith
73 Chris Bosh
74 Nick Young
75 LeBron James 20.00 50.00
76 Jeff Teague 3.00 8.00
77 Chandler Parsons 3.00 8.00
78 Goran Dragic
79 Joe Johnson
80 James Harden 6.00 15.00
81 Avery Bradley 3.00 8.00
82 Deron Williams
83 Eric Gordon 3.00 8.00
84 Pablo Prigioni
85 Danny Green 3.00 8.00
86 Amar'e Stoudemire 3.00 8.00
87 Kawhi Leonard
88 Eric Bledsoe 3.00 8.00
89 Orlando Johnson 2.50 6.00
90 Thabo Sefolosha
91 Steve Nash 4.00 10.00
92 Raymond Felton
93 Chris Paul 5.00 12.00
94 Shane Battier 3.00 8.00
95 Derrick Favors
96 Zach Randolph
97 Brandan Wright 2.50 6.00
98 Danny Granger
99 Kenneth Faried 3.00 8.00
100 Kevin Garnett

2013-14 Timeless Treasures Lottery Winners

1 Anthony Bennett 1.50 4.00
2 Victor Oladipo 2.50 6.00
3 Otto Porter 2.00 5.00
4 Cody Zeller 1.50 4.00
5 Alex Len 1.50 4.00
6 Nerlens Noel 2.50 6.00
7 Ben McLemore 1.50 4.00
8 Kentavious Caldwell-Pope 2.00 5.00
9 Trey Burke 1.50 4.00
10 C.J. McCollum 6.00 15.00
11 Michael Carter-Williams 2.00 5.00
12 Steven Adams 2.00 5.00
13 Kelly Olynyk 1.50 4.00
14 Shabazz Muhammad 1.50 4.00

2013-14 Timeless Treasures Perennial Materials

1 Dwyane Wade 5.00 12.00
2 Tony Parker 3.00 8.00
3 Deron Williams 2.50 6.00
4 Kevin Garnett 5.00 12.00
5 John Wall 4.00 10.00
6 Robert Parish 3.00 8.00
7 Raymond Felton 2.50 6.00
8 Luol Deng 2.50 6.00
9 Larry Bird 10.00 25.00
10 Shaquille O'Neal 12.00 30.00
11 Anfernee Hardaway
12 Dirk Nowitzki 4.00 10.00
13 Rajon Rondo 3.00 8.00
14 Blake Griffin 5.00 12.00
15 Danny Green 2.50 6.00
16 Kevin Durant 6.00 15.00
17 Brent Barry 2.00 5.00
18 J.R. Smith 2.50 6.00
19 Kevin McHale
20 Ty Lawson 2.00 5.00

2013-14 Timeless Treasures Perennial Materials Prime

*PRIME: .75X TO 2X BASIC
PRINT RUNS B/WN 7-25 COPIES PER
NO PRICING ON QTY 10 OR LESS
11 Anfernee Hardaway/25 30.00 80.00

2013-14 Timeless Treasures Promising Pros Materials

1 Kenneth Faried 3.00 8.00
2 Kawhi Leonard 6.00 15.00
3 Chandler Parsons 3.00 8.00
4 Brandon Knight
5 Anthony Davis 8.00 20.00
6 Bradley Beal 4.00 10.00
7 Klay Thompson 5.00 12.00
8 John Henson 3.00 8.00
9 Markieff Morris 2.50 6.00
10 Andre Drummond 4.00 10.00
11 Kyrie Irving 8.00 20.00
12 Iman Shumpert 2.50 6.00
13 Draymond Green 5.00 12.00
14 Dion Waiters 3.00 8.00
15 Michael Kidd-Gilchrist 4.00 10.00
16 Kemba Walker 4.00 10.00
17 Maurice Harkless
18 Jimmer Fredette 2.50 6.00
19 Tristan Thompson 3.00 8.00
20 Isaiah Thomas 4.00 10.00
21 Nikola Vucevic 3.00 8.00
22 Jrue Holiday 4.00 10.00
23 Avery Bradley
24 Paul George 8.00 20.00
25 Jeff Teague 3.00 8.00

2013-14 Timeless Treasures Promising Pros Materials Prime

*PRIME p/r 15: .75X TO 2X BASIC
*PRIME p/r 25: .75X TO 2X BASIC
PRINT RUNS B/WN 7-25 COPIES PER
NO PRICING ON QTY 10 OR LESS

2013-14 Timeless Treasures Rookie Jersey Autographs Prime

*PRIME: .5X TO 1.2X BASIC
STATED PRINT RUN 49 SER.#'d SETS
EXCHANGE DEADLINE 6/11/2015
108 Andre Roberson 5.00 12.00
128 C.J. McCollum 20.00 50.00
129 Giannis Antetokounmpo 75.00 150.00
134 Steven Adams 15.00 40.00

2013-14 Timeless Treasures Rookie Jersey Autographs Prime Ruby

*RUBY: .6X TO 1.5X BASIC
STATED PRINT RUN 25 SER.#'d SETS
EXCHANGE DEADLINE 6/11/2015
104 Victor Oladipo 30.00 80.00
125 Trey Burke 6.00 15.00
127 Peyton Siva 5.00 12.00
128 C.J. McCollum 25.00 60.00
129 Giannis Antetokounmpo
131 Michael Carter-Williams 8.00 20.00
132 Shabazz Muhammad 6.00 15.00
133 Isaiah Canaan 5.00 12.00
134 Steven Adams 8.00 20.00

2013-14 Timeless Treasures Three-Piece Puzzles

1A Tim Hardaway 2.00 5.00
1B Mitch Richmond 2.00 5.00
1C Chris Mullin 2.00 5.00
2A Bill Russell 3.00 8.00
2B Bob Cousy 3.00 8.00
2C Tom Heinsohn 2.00 5.00
3A Detlef Schrempf 2.00 5.00
3B Gary Payton 2.00 5.00
3C Shawn Kemp 3.00 8.00
4A Jeff Hornacek 1.50 4.00
4B Karl Malone 2.50 6.00
4C John Stockton 3.00 8.00
5A Dwight Howard 1.50 4.00
5B James Harden 3.00 8.00
5C Chandler Parsons 1.50 4.00
6A Carmelo Anthony 2.50 6.00
6B J.R. Smith 1.50 4.00
6C Tyson Chandler 1.50 4.00
7A Kobe Bryant 8.00 20.00
7B Pau Gasol 2.00 5.00
7C Steve Nash 2.00 5.00
8A Kevin Durant 5.00 12.00
8B Russell Westbrook 5.00 12.00
8C Serge Ibaka 1.50 4.00
9A Dion Waiters 1.50 4.00
9B Kyrie Irving 4.00 10.00
9C Anthony Bennett 1.50 4.00
10A Blake Griffin 2.00 5.00
10B Chris Paul 2.50 6.00
10C DeAndre Jordan 2.00 5.00
11A LeBron James 8.00 20.00
11B Dwyane Wade 3.00 8.00
11C Chris Bosh 2.00 5.00
12A Tony Parker 2.00 5.00
12B Tim Duncan 3.00 8.00
12C Manu Ginobili 2.00 5.00

2013-14 Timeless Treasures Time To Shine

PRINT RUNS B/WN 25-249 COPIES PER
EXCHANGE DEADLINE 6/11/2015
1 Tyson Chandler
2 Ersan Ilyasova 4.00 10.00
3 Nicolas Batum 5.00 12.00
4 Joakim Noah EXCH 5.00 12.00
5 Maurice Harkless 4.00 10.00
6 Austin Rivers
7 Nikola Vucevic 5.00 12.00
8 J.R. Smith 5.00 12.00
9 Tiago Splitter
10 Jeff Teague
11 Goran Dragic 5.00 12.00
12 Mike Conley
13 Lance Stephenson 5.00 12.00
14 Alexey Shved 4.00 10.00
15 James Jones 4.00 10.00
16 Steve Blake 8.00 20.00
17 Jeff Green 8.00 20.00
18 Jonas Valanciunas 6.00 15.00
19 George Hill 6.00 15.00
20 Alec Burks
21 Evan Fournier 5.00 12.00
22 E'Twaun Moore 4.00 10.00
23 Tyler Zeller 5.00 12.00
24 Kendall Marshall 5.00 12.00
25 Jerryd Bayless EXCH 5.00 12.00

2013-14 Timeless Treasures Timeless Signatures

PRINT RUNS B/WN 15-299 COPIES PER
EXCHANGE DEADLINE 6/11/2015
1 Gail Goodrich/15
2 Norm Nixon/299 4.00 10.00

3 Nate Archibald/15 10.00 25.00
4 Elgin Baylor/25
5 Scottie Pippen/25 100.00 200.00
6 Ralph Sampson/15 12.00 30.00
7 Reggie Theus/299 5.00 12.00
8 Bill Laimbeer/299 5.00 12.00
9 Connie Hawkins/15
10 Spencer Haywood/299 4.00 10.00
11 Isiah Thomas/25 12.00 30.00
12 David Thompson/15
13 Paul Westphal/299 6.00 15.00
14 Bill Walton/15 8.00 20.00
15 Rod Strickland/299 4.00 10.00
16 Bob Dandridge/299 4.00 10.00
17 David Robinson/35 60.00 120.00
18 George Gervin/15 60.00 120.00
19 Kendall Gill/299 4.00 10.00
20 Scott Skiles/299 5.00 12.00
21 Bobby Jones/299 6.00 15.00
22 Rolando Blackman/299 5.00 12.00
23 Cedric Maxwell/299 4.00 10.00
24 Mark Aguirre/299 5.00 12.00
25 Maurice Cheeks/299 4.00 10.00
26 Gary Payton/25 12.00 30.00
27 Sidney Moncrief/299 4.00 10.00
28 Dominique Wilkins/25 10.00 25.00
29 Artis Gilmore/15 12.00 30.00
30 Dikembe Mutombo/25
31 Jo Jo White/299 5.00 12.00
32 Sam Jones/15 15.00 40.00
33 Robert Parish/15
34 Jason Kidd/25 40.00 80.00
35 Bailey Howell/15 6.00 15.00
36 Alonzo Mourning/25 30.00 60.00
37 Danny Manning/15 10.00 25.00
38 Elvin Hayes/15
39 Mark Jackson/15
40 Harry Gallatin/15
41 Kareem Abdul-Jabbar/25 50.00 100.00
42 Cazzie Russell/299 5.00 12.00
43 Jack Sikma/299 5.00 12.00
44 Karl Malone/25
45 Lenny Wilkens/15 12.00 30.00
46 Kiki Vandeweghe/299 5.00 12.00
47 Hal Greer/15 10.00 25.00
48 Chris Mullin/15
50 Hakeem Olajuwon/25 30.00 60.00

2013-14 Timeless Treasures Timeless Talents

PRINT RUNS B/WN 23-49 COPIES PER
SOME CARDS NOT SERIAL #'d
EXCAHNGE DEADLINE 6/11/2015
2 Kevin Willis/25
3 Herb Williams 4.00 10.00
4 Michael Finley/25 15.00 40.00
7 Elvin Hayes/25
8 Dwight Howard/25
9 Rick Barry/49 5.00 12.00
10 Tyson Chandler/49
11 Steve Francis/25 5.00 12.00
12 David West/25
13 Steve Kerr/25
14 Nick Van Exel/25 12.00 30.00
15 Maurice Cheeks 4.00 10.00
16 Luc Longley 5.00 12.00
17 Zydrunas Ilgauskas 5.00 12.00
18 Vin Baker 4.00 10.00
19 Tom Chambers/25 8.00 20.00
21 Jason Terry/25 5.00 12.00
23 B.J. Armstrong/25 10.00 25.00
24 Bruce Bowen 6.00 15.00
25 Grant Hill/49 8.00 20.00
26 Alonzo Mourning/25 8.00 20.00
27 Deron Williams/25 5.00 12.00
28 Dwyane Wade/23
30 Harrison Barnes/25 5.00 12.00
31 Bradley Beal/25 12.00 30.00
32 Kyrie Irving/49 EXCH 50.00 120.00
33 Dan Majerle/25
34 Dan Issel 5.00 12.00
35 Joe Dumars/25 6.00 15.00
36 Sam Perkins/25 4.00 10.00
37 Len Elmore 4.00 10.00
38 Michael Cooper 5.00 12.00
39 Muggsy Bogues 5.00 12.00
40 Juwan Howard/25

2013-14 Timeless Treasures Timeless Talents Ruby

*RUBY p/r 20-25: .5X TO 1.2X BASIC
*RUBY p/r 99: .5X TO 1.2X BASIC
PRINT RUNS B/WN 10-99 COPIES PER
NO PRICING ON QTY 10
3 Herb Williams/99
8 Dwight Howard/20 40.00 80.00
9 Rick Barry/25
28 Dwyane Wade/20
32 Kyrie Irving/25 EXCH
39 Muggsy Bogues/99

2013-14 Timeless Treasures Timeless Talents Sapphire

*SAPPHIRE 15: .5X TO 1.2X BASIC
*SAPPHIRE 75: .5X TO 1.2X BASIC
PRINT RUNS B/WN 3-75 COPIES PER
NO PRICING ON QTY 5 OR LESS
3 Herb Williams/75
24 Bruce Bowen/75
39 Muggsy Bogues/75

2013-14 Timeless Treasures Timeless Teams

1 Bill Laimbeer 1.50 4.00
2 Dennis Rodman 4.00 10.00
3 Isiah Thomas 2.00 5.00
4 Joe Dumars 2.00 5.00
5 Mark Aguirre 1.50 4.00
6 Danny Ainge 2.00 5.00
7 Dennis Johnson 1.50 4.00
8 Kevin McHale 2.00 5.00
9 Larry Bird 5.00 12.00
10 Robert Parish 2.00 5.00
11 A.C. Green 2.00 5.00
12 Byron Scott 1.50 4.00
13 James Worthy 2.50 6.00
14 Kareem Abdul-Jabbar 3.00 8.00
15 Magic Johnson 5.00 12.00
16 Bobby Jones 1.50 4.00
17 Julius Erving 3.00 8.00
18 Maurice Cheeks 1.25 3.00
19 Moses Malone 2.00 5.00
20 Clint Richardson 1.25 3.00
21 Ron Harper 2.00 5.00
22 Scottie Pippen 4.00 10.00
23 Steve Kerr 2.00 5.00
24 Toni Kukoc 2.00 5.00
25 Luc Longley 1.50 4.00
26 Dick Barnett 2.00 5.00
27 Walt Frazier 2.00 5.00
28 Willis Reed 2.00 5.00
29 Dave DeBusschere 2.00 5.00
30 Cazzie Russell 1.50 4.00
31 Bob Dandridge 1.25 3.00
32 Kareem Abdul-Jabbar 3.00 8.00
33 Lucius Allen 2.00 5.00
34 Oscar Robertson 2.50 6.00
35 Jon McGlocklin 1.50 4.00
36 Dwyane Wade 3.00 8.00
37 LeBron James 8.00 20.00
38 Mario Chalmers 1.50 4.00
39 Ray Allen 2.00 5.00
40 Chris Bosh 2.00 5.00
41 Bruce Bowen 1.25 3.00
42 Tim Duncan 3.00 8.00
43 Tony Parker 2.00 5.00
44 David Robinson 3.00 8.00
45 Manu Ginobili 2.00 5.00
46 Clyde Drexler 2.50 6.00
47 Hakeem Olajuwon 2.50 6.00
48 Robert Horry 1.50 4.00
49 Sam Cassell 1.50 4.00
50 Vernon Maxwell 1.25 3.00

2013-14 Timeless Treasures Treasured Ink

PRINT RUNS B/WN 15-299 COPIES PER
EXCHANGE DEADLINE 6/11/2015
1 Kobe Bryant/49 100.00 200.00
2 Kevin Durant/49 60.00 150.00
3 Kyrie Irving/49 30.00 80.00
4 Blake Griffin/49 12.00 30.00
5 Steve Smith/299 5.00 12.00
6 Stephen Curry/25 100.00 200.00
7 Michael Finley/15
8 Nate Archibald/15 10.00 25.00
9 Karl Malone/25 15.00 40.00
10 Kareem Abdul-Jabbar/25 50.00 100.00
11 Jim Jackson/299 4.00 10.00
12 Horace Grant/15
13 Bailey Howell/49 6.00 15.00
14 Rolando Blackman/49 5.00 12.00
15 Tom Heinsohn/49 20.00 50.00
16 Antoine Walker/299 5.00 12.00
17 Anthony Mason/299 6.00 15.00
18 Nick Van Exel/15 12.00 30.00
19 Chris Bosh/25 15.00 40.00
20 Tony Parker/15 6.00 15.00
21 Sam Jones/15 15.00 40.00
22 A.C. Green/49 6.00 15.00
23 Larry Bird/25 EXCH 40.00 100.00
24 Jerry West/25 30.00 80.00
25 Vince Carter/25

2013-14 Timeless Treasures Treasured Picks Jerseys

1 Shane Larkin 2.00 5.00
2 Peyton Siva 2.00 5.00
3 Shabazz Muhammad 2.50 6.00
4 Kelly Olynyk 2.50 6.00
5 Anthony Bennett 2.50 6.00
6 Ryan Kelly 2.00 5.00
7 Jamaal Franklin 2.00 5.00
8 Michael Carter-Williams 3.00 8.00
9 Victor Oladipo 10.00 25.00
10 Andre Roberson 2.00 5.00
11 Mason Plumlee 3.00 8.00
12 C.J. McCollum 10.00 25.00
13 Otto Porter 3.00 8.00
14 Nate Wolters 2.50 6.00
15 Tim Hardaway Jr. 3.00 8.00
16 Trey Burke 2.50 6.00
17 Cody Zeller 2.50 6.00
18 Tony Mitchell 2.00 5.00
19 Archie Goodwin 2.50 6.00
20 Kentavious Caldwell-Pope 3.00 8.00
21 Alex Len 2.50 6.00
22 Glen Rice Jr. 2.00 5.00
23 Allen Crabbe 2.50 6.00
24 Ben McLemore 2.50 6.00
25 Nerlens Noel 4.00 10.00

2013-14 Timeless Treasures Treasured Picks Jerseys Prime

*PRIME: .75X TO 2X BASIC
STATED PRINT RUN 25 SER.#'d SETS

2013-14 Timeless Treasures Treasured Threads

1 Shaquille O'Neal 6.00 15.00
2 Grant Hill 4.00 10.00
3 Kiki Vandeweghe 2.50 6.00
4 Jeff Malone 2.00 5.00
5 Dee Brown 2.00 5.00
6 Jamal Mashburn 3.00 8.00
7 Gus Williams 2.00 5.00
8 Robert Horry 2.50 6.00
9 Mitch Richmond 3.00 8.00
10 Manute Bol 3.00 8.00
11 Karl Malone 4.00 10.00
12 Patrick Ewing 4.00 10.00
13 Tim Duncan 5.00 12.00
14 LeBron James 10.00 25.00
15 Kobe Bryant 10.00 25.00
16 Bernard King 2.50 6.00
17 Jeremy Lin 3.00 8.00
18 Reggie Lewis 10.00 25.00
19 Paul Westphal 3.00 8.00
20 Danny Manning 2.50 6.00
21 Paul Pierce 3.00 8.00
22 Manu Ginobili 3.00 8.00
23 Carmelo Anthony 4.00 10.00
24 Ray Allen 3.00 8.00
25 Dwyane Wade 5.00 12.00

2013-14 Timeless Treasures Treasured Threads Prime

*PRIME p/r 25: 1X TO 2.5X BASE
PRINT RUNS B/WN 5-25 COPIES PER
NO PRICING ON QTY 10 OR LESS

2013-14 Timeless Treasures Trophies

1 Kyrie Irving
2 Kobe Bryant
3 Karl Malone 60.00 150.00
4 Kevin Durant
5 Kareem Abdul-Jabbar

2013-14 Timeless Treasures Validating Marks

KOBE PRINT RUN 75 SER.#'d SETS
EXCHANGE DEADLINE 6/11/2015
1 Kendall Marshall 5.00 12.00
2 Kenyon Martin 5.00 12.00
3 Allan Houston
4 Maurice Harkless 4.00 10.00
5 Carl Landry
7 Lou Amundson 4.00 10.00
10 Jarrett Jack
12 J.J. Redick 10.00 25.00
13 Goran Dragic 5.00 12.00
15 Danny Green 5.00 12.00
16 Nikola Pekovic 4.00 10.00
17 Boris Diaw 12.00 30.00
18 Antawn Jamison
19 Corey Brewer 4.00 10.00
21 Kendrick Perkins 4.00 10.00
22 Ekpe Udoh 4.00 10.00
23 Earl Clark 4.00 10.00
24 Ersan Ilyasova
25 Mateen Cleaves 4.00 10.00
26 Tobias Harris
27 Kyle Lowry 5.00 12.00
28 Jonas Valanciunas
29 Kevin Love 12.00 30.00
30 Nick Young
31 Sam Cassell
32 Andre Drummond
33 Enes Kanter
34 Nicolas Batum 8.00 20.00
35 Marcin Gortat 5.00 12.00
36 Jared Sullinger
37 MarShon Brooks 5.00 12.00
38 Patrick Beverley 4.00 10.00
39 Eddie Johnson 4.00 10.00
40 Kobe Bryant/75 50.00 120.00
41 Willie Reed 4.00 10.00
42 Campy Russell 4.00 10.00
43 Justin Hamilton 4.00 10.00
44 Gus Williams 4.00 10.00
45 Kyrie Irving 30.00 80.00
46 Otis Birdsong 5.00 12.00
47 Kenny Walker
48 Will Bynum 4.00 10.00
49 James Johnson 4.00 10.00
50 Kevin Durant EXCH 60.00 150.00

2013-14 Timeless Treasures Validating Marks Ruby

*RUBY p/r 35-49: .5X TO 1.2X BASIC
*RUBY p/r 99: .5X TO 1.2X BASIC
PRINT RUNS B/WN 10-99 COPIES PER
NO PRICING ON QTY 10 OR LESS
EXCHANGE DEADLINE 6/11/2015
15 Danny Green/99
16 Nikola Pekovic/99
38 Patrick Beverley/99
42 Campy Russell/99
46 Otis Birdsong/99
48 Will Bynum/99

2013-14 Timeless Treasures Validating Marks Sapphire

*SAPPHIRE p/r 15-25: .5X TO 1.2X BASIC
*SAPPHIRE p/r 49: .5X TO 1.2X BASIC
PRINT RUNS B/WN 3-49 COPIES PER
NO PRICING ON QTY 5 OR LESS
EXCHANGE DEADLINE 6/11/2015
4 Maurice Harkless/49
7 Lou Amundson/49
19 Corey Brewer/49
22 Ekpe Udoh/49
37 MarShon Brooks/49
40 Kobe Bryant/25
41 Willie Reed/49
45 Kyrie Irving/15
46 Otis Birdsong/49
48 Will Bynum/49

1957-58 Topps

The 1957-58 Topps basketball set of 80 cards was Topps first basketball issue. Topps did not produce another basketball set until it released a test issue in 1968. A major set followed in 1969. Cards were issued in 5-cent packs (six cards per pack, 24 per box) and measure the standard size. A number of cards in the set were double printed (indicated by DP in checklist below). The set contains 49 double prints, 30 single prints and one quadruple print (No. 24 Bob Pettit). Card backs give statistical information from the 1956-57 NBA season. Bill Russell's Rookie Card is part of the set. Other Rookie Cards include Paul Arizin, Nat "Sweetwater" Clifton, Bob Cousy, Cliff Hagan, Tom Heinsohn, Rod Hundley, Red Kerr, Clyde Lovellette, Pettit, Dolph Schayes, Bill Sharman and Jack Twyman. The set contains the only card of Maurice Stokes. Topps also produced a three-card advertising panel featuring the fronts of Walt Davis, Joe Graboski and Cousy with an advertisement for the upcoming Topps basketball set on the combined reverse.

COMPLETE SET (80) 3000.00 5500.00
CONDITION SENSITIVE SET
CARDS PRICED IN EX-MT CONDITION
1 Nat Clifton DP RC 60.00 150.00
2 George Yardley DP RC 30.00 60.00
3 Neil Johnston DP RC 20.00 50.00
4 Carl Braun DP 30.00 50.00
5 Bill Sharman DP RC 65.00 125.00
6 George King DP RC 15.00 40.00
7 Kenny Sears DP RC 15.00 40.00
8 Dick Ricketts DP RC 15.00 40.00
9 Jack Nichols DP 15.00 40.00
10 Paul Arizin DP RC 30.00 80.00
11 Chuck Noble DP 15.00 25.00
12 Slater Martin DP RC 30.00 60.00
13 Dolph Schayes DP RC 25.00 60.00
14 Dick Atha DP 15.00 25.00
15 Frank Ramsey DP RC 40.00 80.00
16 Dick McGuire DP RC 25.00 50.00
17 Bob Cousy DP RC 175.00 350.00
18 Larry Foust DP RC 15.00 40.00
19 Tom Heinsohn RC 125.00 225.00
20 Bill Thieben DP 15.00 25.00
21 Don Meineke DP RC 15.00 40.00
22 Tom Marshall 25.00 40.00
23 Dick Garmaker 25.00 40.00
24 Bob Pettit QP RC 60.00 120.00
25 Jim Krebs DP RC 15.00 40.00
26 Gene Shue DP RC 30.00 60.00
27 Ed Macauley DP RC 30.00 60.00
28 Vern Mikkelsen RC 40.00 100.00
29 Willie Naulls RC 30.00 60.00
30 Walter Dukes DP RC 30.00 45.00
31 Dave Piontek DP 15.00 25.00
32 Johnny Red Kerr RC 50.00 100.00
33 Larry Costello DP RC 30.00 50.00
34 Woody Sauldsberry DP RC 15.00 40.00
35 Ray Felix RC 30.00 45.00
36 Ernie Beck 25.00 40.00
37 Cliff Hagan RC 60.00 100.00
38 Guy Sparrow DP 15.00 25.00
39 Jim Loscutoff RC 40.00 60.00
40 Arnie Risen DP 30.00 45.00
41 Joe Graboski 25.00 40.00
42 M.Stokes DP UER RC 60.00 100.00
43 Rod Hundley DP RC 50.00 100.00
44 Tom Gola DP RC 50.00 80.00
45 Med Park RC 30.00 45.00
46 Mel Hutchins DP 15.00 25.00
47 Larry Friend DP 15.00 25.00
48 Lennie Rosenbluth DP RC 30.00 50.00
49 Walt Davis 25.00 40.00
50 Richie Regan RC 25.00 40.00
51 Frank Selvy DP RC 25.00 50.00
52 Art Spoelstra DP 15.00 25.00
53 Bob Hopkins RC 25.00 40.00
54 Earl Lloyd RC 30.00 50.00
55 Phil Jordan DP 15.00 25.00
56 Bob Houbregs DP RC 25.00 40.00
57 Lou Tsioropoulos DP 15.00 25.00
58 Ed Conlin RC 30.00 45.00
59 Al Bianchi RC 50.00 80.00
60 George Dempsey RC 25.00 40.00
61 Chuck Share 25.00 40.00
62 Harry Gallatin DP RC 30.00 50.00
63 Bob Harrison 25.00 40.00
64 Bob Burrow DP 15.00 25.00
65 Win Wilfong DP 15.00 25.00
66 Jack McMahon DP RC 15.00 40.00
67 Jack George 25.00 40.00
68 Charlie Tyra DP 15.00 25.00
69 Ron Sobie 25.00 40.00
70 Jack Coleman 25.00 40.00
71 Jack Twyman DP RC 65.00 110.00
72 Paul Seymour RC 25.00 40.00
73 Jim Paxson DP RC 30.00 55.00
74 Bob Leonard RC 25.00 50.00
75 Andy Phillip 30.00 60.00
76 Joe Holup 25.00 40.00
77 Bill Russell RC 700.00 1100.00
78 Clyde Lovellette DP RC 40.00 100.00
79 Ed Fleming DP 15.00 25.00
80 Dick Schnittker RC 40.00 100.00

1968-69 Topps Test

This set was apparently a limited test issue produced by Topps. The cards measure the standard size. The fronts feature a black and white "action" pose of the player, on white card stock. The player's name, team, and height are given below the picture. The horizontally oriented card backs form a composite of Wilt Chamberlain. The set is dated as 1968-69 since Earl Monroe's first season was 1967-68. The set features the first professional cards of Dave Bing, Bill Bradley, Dave DeBusschere, John Havlicek, Earl Monroe, and Willis Reed, among others.

COMPLETE SET (22) 18000.00 24000.00
1 Wilt Chamberlain 3000.00 4000.00
2 Hal Greer 400.00 800.00
3 Chet Walker 250.00 500.00
4 Bill Russell 3000.00 4000.00
5 John Havlicek UER 1600.00 2200.00
6 Cazzie Russell 300.00 600.00
7 Willis Reed 500.00 850.00
8 Bill Bradley 500.00 850.00
9 Odie Smith 200.00 450.00
10 Dave Bing 500.00 850.00
11 Dave DeBusschere 500.00 850.00
12 Earl Monroe 500.00 850.00
13 Nate Thurmond 400.00 800.00
14 Jim King 200.00 450.00
15 Len Wilkens 500.00 900.00
16 Bill Bridges 250.00 500.00
17 Zelmo Beaty 300.00 600.00
18 Elgin Baylor 1400.00 2000.00
19 Jerry West 2400.00 3000.00
20 Jerry Sloan 600.00 900.00
21 Jerry Lucas 500.00 850.00
22 Oscar Robertson 1500.00 2000.00

1969-70 Topps

The 1969-70 Topps set of 99 cards was Topps' first major basketball issue since 1957. Cards were issued in 10-cent packs (10 cards per pack, 24 packs per box) and measure 2 1/2" by 4 11/16". The set features the first card of Lew Alcindor (later Kareem Abdul-Jabbar). Other notable Rookie Cards in the set are Dave Bing, Bill Bradley, Billy Cunningham, Dave DeBusschere, Walt Frazier, John Havlicek, Connie Hawkins, Elvin Hayes, Jerry Lucas, Earl Monroe, Don Nelson, Willis Reed, Nate Thurmond and Wes Unseld. The set was printed on a sheet of 99 cards (nine rows of eleven across) with the checklist card occupying the lower right corner of the sheet. As a result, the checklist is prone to wear and very difficult to obtain in Near Mint or better condition.

COMPLETE SET (99) 1000.00 1800.00
CONDITION SENSITIVE SET
CARDS PRICED IN NM CONDITION
1 Wilt Chamberlain 25.00 60.00
2 Gail Goodrich RC 15.00 30.00
3 Cazzie Russell RC 8.00 15.00
4 Darrall Imhoff RC 2.50 6.00
5 Bailey Howell 3.00 8.00
6 Lucius Allen RC 5.00 10.00
7 Tom Boerwinkle RC 2.50 6.00
8 Jimmy Walker RC 3.00 8.00
9 John Block RC 2.50 6.00
10 Nate Thurmond RC 12.00 30.00
11 Gary Gregor 1.50 4.00
12 Gus Johnson RC 6.00 15.00
13 Luther Rackley 1.50 4.00
14 Jon McGlocklin RC 15.00 30.00
15 Connie Hawkins RC 15.00 40.00
16 Johnny Egan 1.50 4.00
17 Jim Washington 1.50 4.00
18 Dick Barnett RC 3.00 8.00
19 Tom Meschery 3.00 8.00
20 John Havlicek RC 25.00 60.00
21 Eddie Miles 1.50 4.00
22 Walt Wesley 2.50 6.00
23 Rick Adelman RC 5.00 12.00
24 Al Attles 3.00 8.00
25 Lew Alcindor RC 125.00 250.00
26 Jack Marin RC 3.00 8.00
27 Walt Hazzard RC 4.00 10.00
28 Connie Dierking 1.50 4.00
29 Keith Erickson RC 4.00 10.00
30 Bob Rule RC 5.00 10.00
31 Dick Van Arsdale RC 4.00 10.00
32 Archie Clark RC 4.00 10.00
33 Terry Dischinger RC 1.50 4.00
34 Henry Finkel RC 1.50 4.00
35 Elgin Baylor 10.00 25.00
36 Ron Williams 1.50 4.00
37 Loy Petersen 1.50 4.00
38 Guy Rodgers 3.00 8.00
39 Toby Kimball 1.50 4.00
40 Billy Cunningham RC 10.00 25.00
41 Joe Caldwell RC 3.00 8.00
42 Leroy Ellis RC 2.50 6.00
43 Bill Bradley RC 15.00 40.00
44 Len Wilkens UER 10.00 25.00
45 Jerry Lucas RC 10.00 25.00
46 Neal Walk RC 2.50 6.00
47 Emmette Bryant RC 2.50 6.00
48 Bob Kauffman RC 1.50 4.00
49 Mel Counts RC 2.50 6.00
50 Oscar Robertson 15.00 40.00
51 Jim Barnett RC 3.00 8.00
52 Don Smith 1.50 4.00
53 Jim Davis 1.50 4.00
54 Wally Jones RC 2.50 6.00
55 Dave Bing RC 10.00 25.00
56 Wes Unseld RC 12.00 30.00
57 Joe Ellis 1.50 4.00
58 John Tresvant 1.50 4.00
59 Larry Siegfried RC 2.50 6.00
60 Willis Reed RC 12.50 30.00
61 Paul Silas RC 6.00 15.00
62 Bob Weiss RC 3.00 8.00
63 Willie McCarter 1.50 4.00
64 Don Kojis RC 1.50 4.00
65 Lou Hudson RC 8.00 20.00
66 Jim King 1.50 4.00
67 Luke Jackson RC 2.50 6.00
68 Len Chappell RC 1.50 4.00
69 Ray Scott 1.50 4.00
70 Jeff Mullins RC 4.00 10.00
71 Howie Komives 1.50 4.00
72 Tom Sanders RC 5.00 10.00
73 Dick Snyder 1.50 4.00
74 Dave Stallworth RC 2.50 6.00
75 Elvin Hayes RC 12.50 30.00
76 Art Harris 1.50 4.00
77 Don Ohl 2.50 6.00
78 Bob Love RC 15.00 30.00
79 Tom Van Arsdale RC 5.00 12.00
80 Earl Monroe RC 12.50 30.00
81 Greg Smith 1.50 4.00
82 Don Nelson RC 12.50 30.00
83 Happy Hairston RC 3.00 8.00
84 Hal Greer 6.00 12.00
85 Dave DeBusschere RC 12.50 30.00
86 Bill Bridges RC 3.00 8.00
87 Herm Gilliam RC 2.50 6.00
88 Jim Fox 1.50 4.00
89 Bob Boozer 2.50 6.00
90 Jerry West 20.00 50.00
91 Chet Walker RC 6.00 15.00
92 Flynn Robinson RC 2.50 6.00
93 Clyde Lee 1.50 4.00
94 Kevin Loughery RC 5.00 12.00
95 Walt Bellamy 5.00 10.00
96 Art Williams 1.50 4.00
97 Adrian Smith RC 2.50 6.00
98 Walt Frazier RC 20.00 50.00
99 Checklist 1-99 50.00 120.00

1969-70 Topps Rulers

The 1969-70 Topps basketball cartoon poster inserts are clever color cartoon drawings of NBA players, with "ruler" markings on the left edge of the insert. These paper-thin posters measure approximately 2 1/2" by 9 7/8". The player's height is indicated in an arrow pointing towards the ruler, and the top of the player's head corresponds to this line on the ruler. The inserts are numbered and contain the player's name and team in an oval near the bottom of the insert. As might be expected, these inserts make the players look both taller and thinner than they actually are. Insert number 5 was never issued; it was intended to be Bill Russell. The inserts came with gum packs (one per pack) of Topps regular issue basketball cards of that year.

COMPLETE SET (23) 200.00 400.00
1 Walt Bellamy 3.00 8.00
2 Jerry West 20.00 40.00
3 Bailey Howell 3.00 8.00
4 Elvin Hayes 7.50 15.00
6 Bob Rule 3.00 8.00
7 Gail Goodrich 5.00 10.00
8 Jeff Mullins 3.00 8.00
9 John Havlicek 15.00 30.00
10 Lew Alcindor 40.00 100.00
11 Wilt Chamberlain 30.00 80.00
12 Nate Thurmond 5.00 12.00
13 Hal Greer 4.00 10.00
14 Lou Hudson 3.00 8.00
15 Jerry Lucas 6.00 12.00
16 Dave Bing 6.00 12.00
17 Walt Frazier 7.50 15.00
18 Gus Johnson 3.00 8.00
19 Willis Reed 7.50 15.00
20 Earl Monroe 7.50 15.00
21 Billy Cunningham 6.00 15.00
22 Wes Unseld 5.00 12.00
23 Bob Boozer 3.00 8.00
24 Oscar Robertson 17.50 35.00

1970-71 Topps

The 1970-71 Topps basketball card set of 175 color cards continued the larger-size (2 1/2" by 4 11/16") format established the previous year. Cards were issued in 10-cent wax packs with 10 cards per pack and 24 packs per box. Cards numbered 106 to 115 contain the previous season's NBA first and second team All-Star selections. The first six cards in the set (1-6) feature the statistical league leaders from the previous season. The last eight cards in the set (168-175) summarize the results of the previous season's NBA championship playoff series won by the Knicks over the Lakers. The key Rookie Cards in this set are Pete Maravich, Calvin Murphy and Pat Riley. There are 22 short-printed cards in the first series which are marked SP in the checklist below.

COMPLETE SET (175) 700.00 1200.00
1 Alcind/West/Hayes LL ! 12.00 30.00
2 West/Alcin/Hayes LL SP 15.00 40.00
3 Green/Imhoff/Hudson LL 2.00 5.00
4 Rob/Walker/Mull LL SP ! 5.00 10.00
5 Hayes/Uns/Alcindor LL 12.50 30.00
6 Wilkens/Fraz/Hask LL SP 6.00 12.00
7 Bill Bradley 12.00 30.00
8 Ron Williams 1.00 2.50
9 Otto Moore 1.00 2.50
10 John Havlicek SP ! 25.00 60.00
11 George Wilson RC 1.00 2.50
12 John Trapp 1.00 2.50
13 Pat Riley RC 12.50 30.00
14 Jim Washington 1.00 2.50
15 Bob Rule 1.50 4.00
16 Bob Weiss 1.50 4.00
17 Neil Johnson 1.00 2.50
18 Walt Bellamy 2.50 6.00
19 McCoy McLemore 1.00 2.50
20 Earl Monroe 7.50 15.00
21 Wally Anderzunas 1.00 2.50
22 Guy Rodgers 1.50 4.00
23 Rick Roberson 1.00 2.50
24 Checklist 1-110 15.00 40.00
25 Jimmy Walker 1.50 4.00
26 Mike Riordan RC 2.50 6.00
27 Henry Finkel 1.00 2.50
28 Joe Ellis 1.00 2.50
29 Mike Davis 1.00 2.50
30 Lou Hudson 2.50 6.00
31 Lucius Allen SP 4.00 10.00
32 Toby Kimball SP 4.00 10.00
33 Luke Jackson SP 4.00 10.00
34 Johnny Egan 3.00 8.00
35 Leroy Ellis SP 4.00 10.00
36 Jack Marin SP 4.00 10.00
37 Joe Caldwell SP 4.00 10.00
38 Keith Erickson 2.50 6.00
39 Don Smith 1.00 2.50
40 Flynn Robinson 1.50 4.00
41 Bob Boozer 1.00 2.50
42 Howie Komives 1.00 2.50
43 Dick Barnett 1.50 4.00
44 Stu Lantz RC 1.50 4.00
45 Dick Van Arsdale 2.50 6.00
46 Jerry Lucas 5.00 10.00
47 Don Chaney RC 5.00 12.00
48 Ray Scott 1.00 2.50
49 Dick Cunningham SP 4.00 10.00
50 Wilt Chamberlain 20.00 50.00
51 Kevin Loughery 1.50 4.00
52 Stan McKenzie 1.00 2.50
53 Fred Foster 1.00 2.50
54 Jim Davis 1.00 2.50
55 Walt Wesley 1.00 2.50
56 Bill Hewitt 1.00 2.50
57 Darrall Imhoff 1.00 2.50
58 John Block 1.00 2.50
59 Al Attles SP 5.00 12.00
60 Chet Walker 2.50 6.00
61 Luther Rackley 1.00 2.50
62 Jerry Chambers SP RC 4.00 10.00
63 Bob Dandridge RC 3.00 8.00
64 Dick Snyder 1.00 2.50
65 Elgin Baylor 12.00 30.00
66 Connie Dierking 1.00 2.50
67 Steve Kuberski RC 1.00 2.50
68 Tom Boerwinkle 1.00 2.50
69 Paul Silas 2.50 6.00
70 Elvin Hayes 12.00 30.00
71 Bill Bridges 1.50 4.00
72 Wes Unseld 7.50 15.00
73 Herm Gilliam 1.00 2.50
74 Bobby Smith SP RC 4.00 10.00
75 Lew Alcindor 20.00 50.00
76 Jeff Mullins 1.50 4.00
77 Happy Hairston 1.50 4.00
78 Dave Stallworth SP 3.00 8.00
79 Fred Hetzel 1.00 2.50
80 Len Wilkens SP 12.00 25.00
81 Johnny Green RC 2.50 6.00
82 Erwin Mueller 1.00 2.50
83 Wally Jones 1.50 4.00
84 Bob Love 3.00 8.00
85 Dick Garrett RC 1.00 2.50
86 Don Nelson SP 12.00 25.00
87 Neal Walk SP 3.00 8.00
88 Larry Siegfried 1.00 2.50
89 Gary Gregor 1.00 2.50
90 Nate Thurmond 3.00 8.00
91 John Warren 1.00 2.50
92 Gus Johnson 2.50 6.00
93 Gail Goodrich 7.50 15.00
94 Dorie Murrey 1.00 2.50
95 Cazzie Russell SP 5.00 12.00
96 Terry Dischinger 1.00 2.50
97 Norm Van Lier SP RC 8.00 20.00
98 Jim Fox 1.00 2.50
99 Tom Meschery 1.00 2.50
100 Oscar Robertson 12.00 30.00
101A Checklist 111-175 12.00 30.00
101B Checklist 111-175 12.00 30.00
102 Rich Johnson 1.00 2.50
103 Mel Counts 1.50 4.00
104 Bill Hosket SP RC 3.00 8.00
105 Archie Clark 1.50 4.00
106 Walt Frazier AS 5.00 10.00
107 Jerry West AS 10.00 25.00
108 Billy Cunningham AS SP 5.00 12.00
109 Connie Hawkins AS 3.00 8.00
110 Willis Reed AS 3.00 8.00
111 Nate Thurmond AS 2.00 5.00
112 John Havlicek AS 15.00 30.00
113 Elgin Baylor AS 8.00 20.00
114 Oscar Robertson AS 12.00 20.00
115 Lou Hudson AS 1.25 3.00
116 Emmette Bryant 1.25 3.00
117 Greg Howard 1.25 3.00
118 Rick Adelman 2.50 6.00
119 Barry Clemens 1.25 3.00
120 Walt Frazier 18.00 30.00
121 Jim Barnes RC 1.25 3.00
122 Bernie Williams 1.25 3.00
123 Pete Maravich RC 150.00 300.00
124 Matt Guokas RC 3.00 8.00
125 Dave Bing 6.00 12.00
126 John Tresvant 1.25 3.00
127 Shaler Halimon 1.25 3.00
128 Don Ohl 1.25 3.00
129 Fred Carter RC 2.50 6.00
130 Connie Hawkins 8.00 20.00
131 Jim King 1.25 3.00
132 Ed Manning RC 2.50 6.00
133 Adrian Smith 1.25 3.00
134 Walt Hazzard 2.50 6.00
135 Dave DeBusschere 7.50 15.00
136 Don Kojis 1.25 3.00
137 Calvin Murphy RC 15.00 40.00
138 Nate Bowman 1.25 3.00
139 Jon McGlocklin 2.00 5.00
140 Billy Cunningham 8.00 20.00
141 Willie McCarter 1.25 3.00
142 Jim Barnett 1.25 3.00
143 Jo Jo White RC 8.00 20.00
144 Clyde Lee 1.25 3.00
145 Tom Van Arsdale 2.50 6.00
146 Len Chappell 1.25 3.00
147 Lee Winfield 1.25 3.00
148 Jerry Sloan RC 10.00 25.00
149 Art Harris 1.25 3.00
150 Willis Reed 10.00 20.00
151 Art Williams 1.25 3.00
152 Don May 1.25 3.00
153 Loy Petersen 1.25 3.00
154 Dave Gambee 1.25 3.00
155 Hal Greer 2.50 6.00
156 Dave Newmark 1.25 3.00
157 Jimmy Collins 1.25 3.00
158 Bill Turner 1.25 3.00
159 Eddie Miles 1.25 3.00
160 Jerry West 20.00 50.00
161 Bob Quick 1.25 3.00
162 Fred Crawford 1.25 3.00
163 Tom Sanders 2.50 6.00
164 Dale Schlueter 1.25 3.00
165 Clem Haskins RC 4.00 10.00
166 Greg Smith 1.25 3.00
167 Rod Thorn RC 3.00 8.00
168 Willis Reed PO 5.00 10.00
169 Dick Garnett PO 2.00 5.00
170 Dave DeBusschere PO 5.00 10.00
171 Jerry West PO 8.00 20.00
172 Bill Bradley PO 8.00 20.00
173 Wilt Chamberlain PO 8.00 20.00
174 Walt Frazier PO 6.00 12.00
175 Knicks Celebrate 10.00 20.00

1970-71 Topps Poster

This set of 24 large (8" by 10") thin paper posters was issued as an insert in second series wax packs along with the 1970-71 Topps regular basketball cards. The posters are in full color and contain the player's name and his team near the upper left of the poster. The number appears in the border at the lower right, and a Topps copyright date and a 1968 National Basketball Player's Association copyright date appears in the border at the left.

COMPLETE SET (24) 100.00 200.00
1 Walt Frazier 5.00 12.00
2 Joe Caldwell 2.00 5.00
3 Willis Reed 5.00 10.00
4 Elvin Hayes 10.00 20.00
5 Jeff Mullins 2.50 6.00
6 Oscar Robertson 12.50 25.00
7 Dave Bing 4.00 10.00
8 Jerry Sloan 4.00 10.00
9 Leroy Ellis 2.00 5.00
10 Hal Greer 3.00 8.00
11 Emmette Bryant 2.00 5.00
12 Bob Rule 6.00 12.00
13 Lew Alcindor 20.00 45.00
14 Chet Walker 3.00 8.00
15 Jerry West 15.00 30.00
16 Billy Cunningham 3.00 8.00
17 Wilt Chamberlain 15.00 40.00
18 John Havlicek 12.50 25.00
19 Lou Hudson 2.00 5.00
20 Earl Monroe 3.00 8.00
21 Wes Unseld 3.00 8.00
22 Connie Hawkins 5.00 10.00
23 Tom Van Arsdale 2.00 5.00
24 Len Chappell 2.00 5.00

1971-72 Topps

The 1971-72 Topps basketball set of 233 witnessed a return to the standard-sized card, i.e., 2 1/2" by 3 1/2". Cards were issued in 10-card, 10 cent packs with 24 packs per box. National Basketball Association players are depicted on cards 1 to 144 and American Basketball Association players are depicted on cards 145 to 233. The set was produced on two sheets. The second production sheet contained the ABA players (145-233) as well as 31 double-printed cards (NBA players) from the first sheet. These DP's are indicated in the checklist below. Subsets include NBA Playoffs (133-137), NBA Statistical Leaders (138-143) and ABA Statistical Leaders (146-151). The key Rookie Cards in this set are Nate Archibald, Rick Barry, Larry Brown, Dave Cowens, Spencer Haywood, Dan Issel, Bob Lanier, Rudy Tomjanovich and Doug Moe.

COMPLETE SET (233) 500.00 750.00
CARDS PRICED IN NM CONDITION
1 Oscar Robertson ! 8.00 20.00
2 Bill Bradley 6.00 15.00
3 Jim Fox .60 1.50
4 John Johnson RC .75 2.00
5 Luke Jackson .75 2.00
6 Don May DP .60 1.50
7 Kevin Loughery .75 2.00
8 Terry Dischinger .60 1.50
9 Neal Walk .75 2.00
10 Elgin Baylor 7.50 15.00
11 Rick Adelman .75 2.00
12 Clyde Lee .60 1.50
13 Jerry Chambers .60 1.50
14 Fred Carter .75 2.00
15 Tom Boerwinkle DP .60 1.50
16 John Block .60 1.50
17 Dick Barnett .75 2.00
18 Henry Finkel .60 1.50
19 Norm Van Lier 1.50 4.00
20 Spencer Haywood RC 4.00 10.00
21 George Johnson .60 1.50
22 Bobby Lewis .60 1.50
23 Bill Hewitt .60 1.50
24 Walt Hazzard DP 1.50 4.00
25 Happy Hairston .75 2.00
26 George Wilson .60 1.50
27 Lucius Allen .75 2.00
28 Jim Washington .60 1.50
29 Nate Archibald RC 8.00 20.00
30 Willis Reed 3.00 8.00
31 Erwin Mueller .60 1.50
32 Art Harris .60 1.50
33 Pete Cross .75 2.00
34 Geoff Petrie RC 2.00 5.00
35 John Havlicek 6.00 15.00
36 Larry Siegfried .60 1.50
37 John Tresvant DP .60 1.50
38 Ron Williams .60 1.50
39 Lamar Green DP .60 1.50
40 Bob Rule DP .75 2.00
41 Jim McMillian RC .75 2.00
42 Wally Jones .75 2.00
43 Bob Boozer .60 1.50
44 Eddie Miles .60 1.50
45 Bob Love DP 2.00 5.00
46 Claude English .60 1.50
47 Dave Cowens RC 10.00 25.00
48 Emmette Bryant .60 1.50
49 Dave Stallworth .75 2.00
50 Jerry West 8.00 20.00
51 Joe Ellis .60 1.50
52 Walt Wesley DP .60 1.50
53 Howie Komives .60 1.50
54 Paul Silas 1.50 4.00
55 Pete Maravich DP 10.00 25.00
56 Gary Gregor .60 1.50
57 Sam Lacey RC 1.50 4.00
58 Calvin Murphy DP 2.50 6.00
59 Bob Dandridge .75 2.00
60 Hal Greer 1.50 4.00
61 Keith Erickson 1.50 4.00
62 Joe Cooke .60 1.50
63 Bob Lanier RC 12.50 30.00
64 Don Kojis .60 1.50
65 Walt Frazier 5.00 12.00
66 Chet Walker DP 1.50 4.00
67 Dick Garrett .60 1.50
68 John Trapp .75 2.00
69 Jo Jo White 3.00 8.00
70 Wilt Chamberlain 17.50 35.00
71 Dave Sorenson .60 1.50
72 Jim King .60 1.50
73 Cazzie Russell 1.50 4.00
74 Jon McGlocklin .75 2.00
75 Tom Van Arsdale .75 2.00
76 Dale Schlueter .60 1.50
77 Gus Johnson DP 1.50 4.00
78 Dave Bing 3.00 8.00
79 Billy Cunningham 3.00 8.00
80 Len Wilkens 3.00 8.00
81 Jerry Lucas DP 2.00 5.00
82 Don Chaney 1.50 4.00
83 McCoy McLemore .60 1.50
84 Bob Kauffman DP .60 1.50
85 Dick Van Arsdale 1.50 4.00
86 Johnny Green .75 2.00
87 Jerry Sloan 2.00 5.00
88 Luther Rackley DP .60 1.50
89 Shaler Halimon .60 1.50
90 Jimmy Walker .75 2.00
91 Rudy Tomjanovich RC 6.00 15.00
92 Levi Fontaine .60 1.50
93 Bobby Smith .75 2.00
94 Bob Arnzen .60 1.50
95 Wes Unseld DP 3.00 8.00
96 Clem Haskins DP 1.50 4.00
97 Jim Davis .60 1.50
98 Steve Kuberski .60 1.50
99 Mike Davis DP .60 1.50
100 Lew Alcindor 12.00 30.00
101 Willie McCarter .60 1.50
102 Charlie Paulk .60 1.50
103 Lee Winfield .60 1.50
104 Jim Barnett .60 1.50
105 Connie Hawkins DP 2.50 6.00
106 Archie Clark DP .75 2.00
107 Dave DeBusschere 2.50 6.00
108 Stu Lantz DP .75 2.00

109 Don Smith .60 1.50
110 Lou Hudson 1.50 4.00
111 Leroy Ellis .60 1.50
112 Jack Marin .75 2.00
113 Matt Guokas .75 2.00
114 Don Nelson 3.00 8.00
115 Jeff Mullins DP .75 2.00
116 Walt Bellamy 2.50 6.00
117 Bob Quick .60 1.50
118 John Warren .60 1.50
119 Barry Clemens .60 1.50
120 Elvin Hayes DP 3.00 8.00
121 Gail Goodrich 3.00 8.00
122 Ed Manning .75 2.00
123 Herm Gilliam DP .60 1.50
124 Dennis Awtrey RC .75 2.00
125 John Hummer DP .60 1.50
126 Mike Riordan .75 2.00
127 Mel Counts .60 1.50
128 Bob Weiss DP .60 1.50
129 Greg Smith DP .60 1.50
130 Earl Monroe 3.00 8.00
131 Nate Thurmond DP 1.50 4.00
132 Bill Bridges DP .75 2.00
133 Lew Alcindor PO 3.00 8.00
134 NBA Playoffs G2 1.50 4.00
135 Bob Dandridge PO 1.50 4.00
136 Oscar Robertson PO 2.50 6.00
137 Oscar Robertson PO 5.00 12.00
138 Alcind/Hayes/Havl LL 5.00 12.00
139 Alcind/Havl/Hayes LL 5.00 12.00
140 Green/Alcind/Wilt LL 4.00 10.00
141 Walker/Oscar/Williams LL 2.00 5.00
142 Wilt/Hayes/Alcind LL 8.00 20.00
143 Van Lier/Oscar/West LL 3.00 8.00
144A NBA Checklist 1-144 6.00 15.00
144B NBA Checklist 1-144 6.00 15.00
145 ABA Checklist 145-233 6.00 15.00
146 Issel/Brisker/Scott LL 2.50 6.00
147 Issel/Barry/Brisker LL 4.00 10.00
148 ABA 2pt FG Pct Leaders 1.50 4.00
149 Barry/Carrier/Keller LL 3.00 8.00
150 ABA Rebound Leaders 1.50 4.00
151 ABA Assist Leaders 1.50 4.00
152 Larry Brown RC 6.00 15.00
153 Bob Bedell .75 2.00
154 Merv Jackson .75 2.00
155 Joe Caldwell 1.00 2.50
156 Billy Paultz RC 2.00 5.00
157 Les Hunter 1.00 2.50
158 Charlie Williams .75 2.00
159 Stew Johnson .75 2.00
160 Mack Calvin RC 2.00 5.00
161 Don Sidle .75 2.00
162 Mike Barrett .75 2.00
163 Tom Workman .75 2.00
164 Joe Hamilton 1.00 2.50
165 Zelmo Beaty RC 2.50 6.00
166 Dan Hester .75 2.00
167 Bob Verga .75 2.00
168 Wilbert Jones .75 2.00
169 Skeeter Swift .75 2.00
170 Rick Barry RC 12.50 30.00
171 Billy Keller RC 1.50 4.00
172 Ron Franz .75 2.00
173 Roland Taylor RC 1.00 2.50
174 Julian Hammond .75 2.00
175 Steve Jones RC 2.50 6.00
176 Gerald Govan 1.00 2.50
177 Darrell Carrier RC 1.00 2.50
178 Ron Boone RC 2.50 6.00
179 George Peeples .75 2.00
180 John Brisker 1.00 2.50
181 Doug Moe RC 2.50 6.00
182 Ollie Taylor .75 2.00
183 Bob Netolicky RC 1.00 2.50
184 Sam Robinson .75 2.00
...nes Jones 1.00 2.50
...s Keye 1.00 2.50
...e Hightower .75 2.00
...n Armstrong RC 1.00 2.50
... Lewis .75 2.00
...arlie Scott RC 2.00 5.00
...m Ard .75 2.00
...2 George Lehmann .75 2.00
193 Ira Harge .75 2.00
194 Willie Wise RC 2.00 5.00
195 Mel Daniels RC 2.50 6.00
196 Larry Cannon .75 2.00
197 Jim Eakins 1.00 2.50
198 Rich Jones 1.00 2.50
199 Bill Melchionni RC 1.50 4.00
200 Dan Issel RC 8.00 20.00
201 George Stone .75 2.00
202 George Thompson .75 2.00
203 Craig Raymond .75 2.00
204 Freddie Lewis RC 1.00 2.50
205 George Carter 1.00 2.50
206 Lonnie Wright .75 2.00
207 Cincy Powell 1.00 2.50
208 Larry Miller 1.00 2.50
209 Sonny Dove .75 2.00
210 Byron Beck RC 1.00 2.50
211 John Beasley .75 2.00
212 Lee Davis .75 2.00
213 Rick Mount RC 2.50 6.00
214 Walt Simon .75 2.00
215 Glen Combs .75 2.00
216 Neil Johnson .75 2.00
217 Manny Leaks .75 2.00
218 Chuck Williams 1.00 2.50
219 Warren Davis .75 2.00
220 Donnie Freeman RC 1.00 2.50
221 Randy Mahaffey .75 2.00
222 John Barnhill .75 2.00
223 Al Cueto .75 2.00
224 Louie Dampier RC 4.00 10.00
225 Roger Brown RC 2.50 6.00
226 Joe DePre .75 2.00
227 Ray Scott .75 2.00
228 Arvesta Kelly .75 2.00
229 Vann Williford .75 2.00
230 Larry Jones 1.00 2.50
231 Gene Moore .75 2.00
232 Ralph Simpson RC 1.50 4.00
233 Red Robbins RC 2.00 5.00

1971-72 Topps Trios

The 1971-72 Topps Trios (insert sticker panels) set contains 26 standard card-sized panels each with three player stickers. There are also three logo sticker panels. Each player sticker has a black border surrounding a color photo with a yellow player's name, and white team name. The NBA players are numbered by the number indicated; stickers of ABA players have the suffix "A" added to their numbers in order to differentiate them. The stickers were printed on a sheet of 77 (7 rows and 11 columns). There are a number of oddities with respect to the distribution on the sheet and hence also to the availability of respective cards in the set. The most difficult cards in the set (34, 37, 40, 43, 1A, 4A, 7A, 10A, 13A, 16A, 19A, 23A, and 24A) appeared on the sheet only twice; they are designated as short prints (SP) in the checklist below. Cards 1, 4, 7, 10, 13, 16, 19, 22, 25, 28, and 31 were all printed three times on the sheet and are hence 50 percent more available than the SP's. The rest of the sheet is comprised of 4 copies of card 22A and 14 copies of card 46; they are referenced as DP and QP respectively. The logo stickers are hard to find in good shape.

COMPLETE SET (26) 200.00 400.00
1 Hudson/Rule/Murphy 4.00 10.00
1A Jones/Wise/Issel SP 10.00 20.00
4 Wesley/White/Dand 3.00 8.00
4A Calvin/Brown/Verga SP 4.00 10.00
7 Thurm/Monroe/Hay 5.00 10.00
7A Melch/Daniels/Freem SP 4.00 10.00
10 DeBuss/Lanier/Van Ars 6.00 12.00
10A Cald/Dampier/Lewis SP 4.00 10.00
13 Greer/Green/Hayes 5.00 10.00
13A Barry/Jones/Keye SP 12.50 25.00
16 Walker/May/Clark 1.50 4.00
16A Cannon/Beaty/Scott SP 3.00 8.00
19 Hairston/Ellis/Sloan 4.00 10.00
19A Jones/Carter/Brisk SP 4.00 10.00
22 Maravich/Kauf/Hav 30.00 80.00
22A ABA Team DP 1.50 4.00
23A ABA Team SP 20.00 40.00
24A ABA Team SP 20.00 40.00
25 Frazier/Van Arsd/Bing 7.50 15.00
28 Love/Williams/Cowens 7.50 15.00
31 West/Reed/Walker 25.00 50.00
34 Rober/Unsel/Smith SP 25.00 45.00
37 Hawk/Mullins/Alcin 30.00 80.00
40 Cunn/Bellamy/Petrie SP 6.00 15.00
43 Cham/Johns/Van L SP 25.00 50.00
46 NBA Team QP 1.25 3.00

1972-73 Topps

The 1972-73 Topps set of 264 standard size cards contains NBA players (1-176) and ABA players (177-264). Cards were issued in 10-card packs with 24 packs per box. All-Star selections are depicted for the NBA on cards 161-170 and for the ABA on cards 249-258. Subsets include NBA Playoffs (154-159), NBA Statistical Leaders (171-176), ABA Playoffs (241-247) and ABA Statistical Leaders (259-264). The key Rookie Card is Julius Erving. Other Rookie Cards include Artis Gilmore and Phil Jackson.

COMPLETE SET (264) 350.00 700.00
CARDS PRICED IN NM CONDITION
1 Wilt Chamberlain ! 25.00 60.00
2 Stan Love .40 1.00
3 Geoff Petrie .60 1.50
4 Curtis Perry RC .40 1.00
5 Pete Maravich 15.00 40.00
6 Gus Johnson 1.25 3.00
7 Dave Cowens 7.50 15.00
8 Randy Smith RC 1.50 4.00
9 Matt Guokas .60 1.50
10 Spencer Haywood 1.50 4.00
11 Jerry Sloan 1.25 3.00
12 Dave Sorenson .40 1.00
13 Howie Komives .40 1.00
14 Joe Ellis .40 1.00
15 Jerry Lucas 2.00 5.00
16 Stu Lantz .60 1.50
17 Bill Bridges .60 1.50
18 Leroy Ellis .40 1.00
19 Art Williams .40 1.00
20 Sidney Wicks RC 3.00 8.00
21 Wes Unseld 2.50 6.00
22 Jim Washington .40 1.00
23 Fred Hilton .40 1.00
24 Curtis Rowe RC .60 1.50
25 Oscar Robertson 10.00 20.00
26 Larry Steele RC .60 1.50
27 Charlie Davis .40 1.00
28 Nate Thurmond 2.00 5.00
29 Fred Carter .60 1.50
30 Connie Hawkins 3.00 8.00
31 Calvin Murphy 2.00 5.00
32 Phil Jackson RC 15.00 40.00
33 Lee Winfield .40 1.00
34 Jim Fox .40 1.00
35 Dave Bing 2.50 6.00
36 Gary Gregor .40 1.00
37 Mike Riordan .60 1.50
38 George Trapp .40 1.00
39 Mike Davis .40 1.00
40 Bob Rule .60 1.50
41 John Block .40 1.00
42 Bob Dandridge .60 1.50
43 John Johnson .60 1.50
44 Rick Barry 8.00 20.00
45 Jo Jo White 1.50 4.00
46 Cliff Meely .40 1.00
47 Charlie Scott 1.25 3.00
48 Johnny Green .60 1.50
49 Pete Cross .40 1.00
50 Gail Goodrich 2.50 6.00
51 Jim Davis .40 1.00
52 Dick Barnett .60 1.50
53 Bob Christian .40 1.00
54 Jon McGlocklin .60 1.50
55 Paul Silas 1.25 3.00
56 Hal Greer 1.50 4.00
57 Barry Clemens .40 1.00
58 Nick Jones .40 1.00
59 Cornell Warner .40 1.00
60 Walt Frazier 5.00 10.00
61 Dorie Murrey .40 1.00
62 Dick Cunningham .40 1.00
63 Sam Lacey .60 1.50
64 John Warren .40 1.00
65 Tom Boerwinkle .40 1.00
66 Fred Foster .40 1.00
67 Mel Counts .40 1.00
68 Toby Kimball .40 1.00
69 Dale Schlueter .40 1.00
70 Jack Marin .60 1.50
71 Jim Barnett .40 1.00
72 Clem Haskins 1.25 3.00
73 Earl Monroe 2.50 6.00
74 Tom Sanders .60 1.50
75 Jerry West 12.50 25.00
76 Elmore Smith RC .60 1.50
77 Don Adams .40 1.00
78 Wally Jones .60 1.50
79 Tom Van Arsdale .60 1.50
80 Bob Lanier 10.00 20.00
81 Len Wilkens 3.00 8.00
82 Neal Walk .60 1.50
83 Kevin Loughery .60 1.50
84 Stan McKenzie .60 1.50
85 Jeff Mullins .60 1.50
86 Otto Moore .40 1.00
87 John Tresvant .40 1.00
88 Dean Meminger RC .40 1.00
89 Jim McMillian .60 1.50
90 Austin Carr RC 3.00 8.00
91 Clifford Ray RC .60 1.50
92 Don Nelson 1.50 4.00
93 Mahdi Abdul-Rahman .60 1.50
94 Willie Norwood .40 1.00
95 Dick Van Arsdale .60 1.50
96 Don May .40 1.00
97 Walt Bellamy 1.50 4.00
98 Garfield Heard RC 1.50 4.00
99 Dave Wohl .40 1.00
100 Kareem Abdul-Jabbar 12.00 30.00
101 Ron Knight .40 1.00
102 Phil Chenier RC 1.50 4.00
103 Rudy Tomjanovich 3.00 8.00
104 Flynn Robinson .40 1.00
105 Dave DeBusschere 2.50 6.00
106 Dennis Layton .40 1.00
107 Bill Hewitt .40 1.00
108 Dick Garrett .40 1.00
109 Walt Wesley .40 1.00
110 John Havlicek 12.00 25.00
111 Norm Van Lier .60 1.50
112 Cazzie Russell 1.25 3.00
113 Herm Gilliam .40 1.00
114 Greg Smith .40 1.00
115 Nate Archibald 2.50 6.00
116 Don Kojis .40 1.00
117 Rick Adelman .60 1.50
118 Luke Jackson .60 1.50
119 Lamar Green .40 1.00
120 Archie Clark .60 1.50
121 Happy Hairston .60 1.50
122 Bill Bradley 10.00 20.00
123 Ron Williams .40 1.00
124 Jimmy Walker .60 1.50
125 Bob Kauffman .40 1.00
126 Rick Roberson .60 1.50
127 Howard Porter RC .60 1.50
128 Mike Newlin RC .60 1.50
129 Willis Reed 3.00 8.00
130 Lou Hudson 1.25 3.00
131 Don Chaney 1.25 3.00
132 Dave Stallworth .40 1.00
133 Charlie Yelverton .40 1.00
134 Ken Durrett .40 1.00
135 John Brisker .60 1.50
136 Dick Snyder .40 1.00
137 Jim McDaniels .40 1.00
138 Clyde Lee .40 1.00
139 Dennis Awtrey UER .60 1.50
140 Keith Erickson .60 1.50
141 Bob Weiss .60 1.50
142 Butch Beard RC 1.25 3.00
143 Terry Dischinger .40 1.00
144 Pat Riley 8.00 20.00
145 Lucius Allen .60 1.50
146 John Mengelt RC .40 1.00
147 John Hummer .40 1.00
148 Bob Love 2.00 5.00
149 Bobby Smith .60 1.50
150 Elvin Hayes 5.00 10.00
151 Nate Williams .40 1.00
152 Chet Walker 1.25 3.00
153 Steve Kuberski .40 1.00
154 Earl Monroe PO 1.25 3.00
155 NBA Playoffs G2 1.25 3.00
156 NBA Playoffs G3 1.25 3.00
157 NBA Playoffs G4 1.25 3.00
158 Jerry West PO 3.00 8.00
159 Wilt Chamberlain PO 5.00 10.00
160 NBA Checklist 1-176 6.00 15.00
161 John Havlicek AS 5.00 10.00
162 Spencer Haywood AS 1.25 3.00
163 Kareem Abdul-Jabbar AS 12.50 25.00
164 Jerry West AS 8.00 20.00
165 Walt Frazier AS 2.00 5.00
166 Bob Love AS 1.25 3.00
167 Billy Cunningham AS 1.50 4.00
168 Wilt Chamberlain AS 10.00 25.00
169 Nate Archibald AS 2.00 5.00
170 Archie Clark AS 1.25 3.00
171 Jabbar/Havl/Arch LL 6.00 15.00
172 Jabbar/Arch/Havl LL 6.00 15.00
173 Wilt/Jabbar/Bell LL 6.00 15.00
174 Marin/Murphy/Goodr LL 1.25 3.00
175 Wilt/Jabbar/Unseld LL 6.00 15.00
176 Wilkens/West/Arch LL 6.00 12.00
177 Roland Taylor .60 1.50
178 Art Becker .60 1.50
179 Mack Calvin .75 2.00
180 Artis Gilmore RC 10.00 20.00
181 Collis Jones .60 1.50
182 John Roche RC .75 2.00
183 George McGinnis RC 6.00 15.00
184 Johnny Neumann .75 2.00
185 Willie Wise .75 2.00
186 Bernie Williams .60 1.50
187 Byron Beck .75 2.00
188 Larry Miller .75 2.00
189 Cincy Powell .60 1.50
190 Donnie Freeman .75 2.00
191 John Baum .60 1.50
192 Billy Keller .75 2.00
193 Wilbert Jones .60 1.50
194 Glen Combs .60 1.50
195 Julius Erving RC 75.00 150.00
196 Al Smith .60 1.50
197 George Carter .60 1.50
198 Louie Dampier 1.25 3.00
199 Rich Jones .60 1.50
200 Mel Daniels 1.25 3.00
201 Gene Moore .60 1.50
202 Randy Denton .60 1.50
203 Larry Jones .60 1.50
204 Jim Ligon .60 1.50
205 Warren Jabali .75 2.00
206 Joe Caldwell .75 2.00
207 Darrell Carrier .75 2.00
208 Gene Kennedy .60 1.50
209 Ollie Taylor .60 1.50
210 Roger Brown .75 2.00
211 George Lehmann .60 1.50
212 Red Robbins .75 2.00
213 Jim Eakins .75 2.00
214 Willie Long .60 1.50
215 Billy Cunningham 3.00 8.00
216 Steve Jones .75 2.00
217 Les Hunter .60 1.50
218 Billy Paultz .75 2.00
219 Freddie Lewis .75 2.00
220 Zelmo Beaty .75 2.00
221 George Thompson .60 1.50
222 Neil Johnson .60 1.50
223 Dave Robisch RC .75 2.00
224 Walt Simon .60 1.50
225 Bill Melchionni .75 2.00
226 Wendell Ladner RC .75 2.00
227 Joe Hamilton .60 1.50
228 Bob Netolicky .75 2.00
229 James Jones .75 2.00
230 Dan Issel 5.00 10.00
231 Charlie Williams .60 1.50
232 Willie Sojourner .60 1.50
233 Merv Jackson .60 1.50
234 Mike Lewis .60 1.50
235 Ralph Simpson .75 2.00
236 Darnell Hillman .75 2.00
237 Rick Mount 1.25 3.00
238 Gerald Govan .60 1.50
239 Ron Boone .75 2.00
240 Tom Washington .60 1.50
241 ABA Playoffs G1 1.25 3.00
242 Rick Barry PO 2.00 5.00
243 George McGinnis PO 1.50 4.00
244 Rick Barry PO 2.00 5.00
245 Billy Keller PO 1.25 3.00
246 ABA Playoffs G6 1.25 3.00
Tight Defense
247 ABA Champs: Pacers 1.25 3.00
248 ABA Checklist 177-264 6.00 15.00
249 Dan Issel AS 2.50 6.00
250 Rick Barry AS 3.00 8.00
251 Artis Gilmore AS 2.50 6.00
252 Donnie Freeman AS 1.25 3.00
253 Bill Melchionni AS 1.25 3.00
254 Willie Wise AS 1.25 3.00
255 Julius Erving AS 15.00 40.00
256 Zelmo Beaty AS 1.25 3.00
257 Ralph Simpson AS 1.25 3.00
258 Charlie Scott AS 1.25 3.00
259 Scott/Barry/Issel LL 3.00 8.00
260 Gilmore/Wash/Jones LL 1.50 4.00
261 Combs/Damp/Jabali LL 1.25 3.00
262 Barry/Calvin/Jones LL 1.50 4.00
263 Gilmore/Erving/Dan LL 10.00 20.00
264 Melch/Brown/Damp LL! 2.50 6.00

1973-74 Topps

The 1973-74 Topps set of 264 standard-size cards contains NBA players on cards numbered 1 to 176 and ABA players on cards numbered 177 to 264. Cards were issued in 10-card packs with 24 packs per box. All-Star selections (first and second team) for both leagues are noted on the respective player's regular cards. Card backs are printed in red and green on gray card stock. The backs feature year-by-year ABA and NBA statistics. Subsets include NBA Playoffs (62-68), NBA League Leaders (153-158), ABA Playoffs (202-208) and ABA League Leaders (234-239). The only notable Rookie Cards in this set are Chris Ford, Bob McAdoo, and Paul Westphal.

COMPLETE SET (264) 200.00 325.00
CONDITION SENSITIVE SET
CARDS PRICED IN NM CONDITION
1 Nate Archibald ! 5.00 10.00
2 Steve Kuberski .20 .50
3 John Mengelt .20 .50
4 Jim McMillian .40 1.00
5 Nate Thurmond 1.50 4.00
6 Dave Wohl .20 .50
7 John Brisker .20 .50
8 Charlie Davis .20 .50
9 Lamar Green .20 .50
10 Walt Frazier AS2 2.50 6.00
11 Bob Christian .20 .50
12 Cornell Warner .20 .50
13 Calvin Murphy 1.50 4.00
14 Dave Sorenson .20 .50
15 Archie Clark .40 1.00
16 Clifford Ray .40 1.00
17 Terry Driscoll .20 .50
18 Matt Guokas .60 1.50
19 Elmore Smith .40 1.00
20 John Havlicek AS1 7.50 15.00
21 Pat Riley 3.00 8.00
22 George Trapp .20 .50
23 Ron Williams .20 .50
24 Jim Fox .20 .50
25 Dick Van Arsdale .40 1.00
26 John Tresvant .20 .50
27 Rick Adelman .40 1.00
28 Eddie Mast .20 .50
29 Jim Cleamons .40 1.00
30 Dave DeBusschere AS2 2.00 5.00
31 Norm Van Lier .40 1.00
32 Stan McKenzie .20 .50
33 Bob Dandridge .40 1.00
34 Leroy Ellis .40 1.00
35 Mike Riordan .40 1.00
36 Fred Hilton .20 .50
37 Toby Kimball .20 .50
38 Jim Price .20 .50
39 Willie Norwood .20 .50
40 Dave Cowens AS2 5.00 10.00
41 Cazzie Russell .40 1.00
42 Lee Winfield .20 .50
43 Connie Hawkins 2.00 5.00
44 Mike Newlin .40 1.00
45 Chet Walker .40 1.00
46 Walt Bellamy 1.50 4.00
47 John Johnson .40 1.00
48 Henry Bibby RC 2.50 6.00
49 Bobby Smith .40 1.00
50 Kareem Abdul-Jabbar AS1 10.00 25.00
51 Mike Price .20 .50
52 John Hummer .20 .50
53 Kevin Porter RC 2.00 5.00
54 Nate Williams .20 .50
55 Gail Goodrich 1.50 4.00
56 Fred Foster .20 .50
57 Don Chaney .40 1.00
58 Bud Stallworth .20 .50
59 Clem Haskins .60 1.50
60 Bob Love AS2 1.25 3.00
61 Jimmy Walker .40 1.00
62 NBA Eastern Semis .40 1.00
63 NBA Eastern Semis .40 1.00
64 Wilt Chamberlain PO 3.00 8.00
65 NBA Western Semis .40 1.00
66 Willis Reed/H.Finkel PO 1.25 3.00
67 NBA Western Finals .40 1.00
68 W.Frazier/Erickson Champ 1.50 4.00
69 Larry Steele .40 1.00
70 Oscar Robertson 7.50 15.00
71 Phil Jackson 7.50 15.00
72 John Wetzel .20 .50
73 Steve Patterson RC .40 1.00
74 Manny Leaks .20 .50
75 Jeff Mullins .40 1.00
76 Stan Love .20 .50
77 Dick Garrett .20 .50
78 Don Nelson 1.50 4.00
79 Chris Ford RC 1.25 3.00
80 Wilt Chamberlain 15.00 25.00
81 Dennis Layton .20 .50
82 Bill Bradley 7.50 15.00
83 Jerry Sloan .40 1.00
84 Cliff Meely .20 .50
85 Sam Lacey .20 .50
86 Dick Snyder .20 .50
87 Jim Washington .20 .50
88 Lucius Allen .40 1.00
89 LaRue Martin RC .20 .50
90 Rick Barry 3.00 8.00
91 Fred Boyd .20 .50
92 Barry Clemens .20 .50
93 Dean Meminger .20 .50
94 Henry Finkel .20 .50
95 Elvin Hayes 2.50 6.00
96 Stu Lantz .40 1.00
97 Bill Hewitt .20 .50
98 Neal Walk .20 .50
99 Garfield Heard .40 1.00
100 Jerry West AS1 8.00 20.00
101 Otto Moore .20 .50
102 Don Kojis .20 .50
103 Fred Brown RC 2.50 6.00
104 Dwight Davis .20 .50
105 Willis Reed 2.50 6.00
106 Herm Gilliam .20 .50
107 Mickey Davis .40 1.00
108 Jim Barnett .20 .50
109 Ollie Johnson .20 .50
110 Bob Lanier 2.50 6.00
111 Fred Carter .40 1.00
112 Paul Silas 1.25 3.00
113 Phil Chenier .40 1.00
114 Dennis Awtrey .20 .50
115 Austin Carr .40 1.00
116 Bob Kauffman .20 .50
117 Keith Erickson .40 1.00
118 Walt Wesley .20 .50
119 Steve Bracey .20 .50
120 Spencer Haywood AS1 1.25 3.00
121 NBA Checklist 1-176 6.00 12.00
122 Jack Marin .40 1.00
123 Jon McGlocklin .20 .50
124 Johnny Green .40 1.00
125 Jerry Lucas 1.25 3.00
126 Paul Westphal RC 10.00 20.00
127 Curtis Rowe .40 1.00
128 Mahdi Abdul-Rahman .40 1.00
129 Lloyd Neal RC .40 1.00
130 Pete Maravich AS1 12.00 30.00
131 Don May .20 .50
132 Bob Weiss .40 1.00
133 Dave Stallworth .20 .50
134 Dick Cunningham .20 .50
135 Bob McAdoo RC 8.00 20.00
136 Butch Beard .40 1.00
137 Happy Hairston .40 1.00
138 Bob Rule .60 1.50
139 Don Adams .20 .50
140 Charlie Scott .40 1.00
141 Ron Riley .20 .50
142 Earl Monroe 1.50 4.00
143 Clyde Lee .20 .50
144 Rick Roberson .20 .50
145 Rudy Tomjanovich 2.50 6.00
146 Tom Van Arsdale .40 1.00
147 Art Williams .20 .50
148 Curtis Perry .20 .50
149 Rich Rinaldi .20 .50
150 Lou Hudson .40 1.00
151 Mel Counts .20 .50
152 Jim McDaniels .20 .50
153 Arch/Jabbar/Hayw LL 3.00 8.00
154 Arch/Jabbar/Hayw LL 3.00 8.00
155 Wilt/Guokas/Jabbar LL 6.00 12.00
156 Barry/Murphy/Newlin LL 1.50 4.00
157 Wilt/Thurm/Cowens LL 3.00 8.00
158 Arch/Wilkens/Bing LL 1.50 4.00
159 Don Smith .20 .50
160 Sidney Wicks 1.25 3.00
161 Howie Komives .20 .50
162 John Gianelli .20 .50
163 Jeff Halliburton .20 .50
164 Kennedy McIntosh .20 .50
165 Len Wilkens 3.00 8.00
166 Corky Calhoun .20 .50
167 Howard Porter .40 1.00
168 Jo Jo White 1.25 3.00
169 John Block .20 .50
170 Dave Bing 1.50 4.00
171 Joe Ellis .20 .50
172 Chuck Terry .20 .50
173 Randy Smith .40 1.00
174 Bill Bridges .40 1.00
175 Geoff Petrie .40 1.00
176 Wes Unseld 1.50 4.00
177 Skeeter Swift .40 1.00
178 Jim Eakins .60 1.50
179 Steve Jones .60 1.50
180 George McGinnis AS1 1.25 3.00
181 Al Smith .40 1.00
182 Tom Washington .40 1.00
183 Louie Dampier .60 1.50
184 Simmie Hill .40 1.00
185 George Thompson .40 1.00
186 Cincy Powell .60 1.50
187 Larry Jones .40 1.00
188 Neil Johnson .40 1.00
189 Tom Owens .40 1.00
190 Ralph Simpson AS2 .60 1.50
191 George Carter .60 1.50
192 Rick Mount .60 1.50
193 Red Robbins .60 1.50
194 George Lehmann .40 1.00
195 Mel Daniels AS2 .60 1.50
196 Bob Warren .40 1.00
197 Gene Kennedy .40 1.00
198 Mike Barr .40 1.00
199 Dave Robisch .40 1.00
200 Billy Cunningham AS1 2.00 5.00
201 John Roche .60 1.50
202 ABA Western Semis 1.25 3.00
203 ABA Western Semis 1.25 3.00
204 Dan Issel PO 1.25 3.00
205 ABA Eastern Semis 1.25 3.00
206 ABA Western Finals 1.25 3.00
207 Artis Gilmore PO 1.25 3.00
208 George McGinnis PO 1.25 3.00
209 Glen Combs .40 1.00
210 Dan Issel AS2 2.50 6.00
211 Randy Denton .40 1.00
212 Freddie Lewis .60 1.50
213 Stew Johnson .40 1.00
214 Roland Taylor .40 1.00
215 Rich Jones .40 1.00
216 Billy Paultz .60 1.50
217 Ron Boone .60 1.50
218 Walt Simon .40 1.00
219 Mike Lewis .40 1.00
220 Warren Jabali AS1 .60 1.50
221 Wilbert Jones .40 1.00
222 Don Buse RC .60 1.50
223 Gene Moore .40 1.00
224 Joe Hamilton .60 1.50
225 Zelmo Beaty .60 1.50
226 Brian Taylor RC .60 1.50
227 Julius Keye .40 1.00
228 Mike Gale RC .60 1.50
229 Warren Davis .40 1.00
230 Mack Calvin AS2 .60 1.50
231 Roger Brown .60 1.50
232 Chuck Williams .60 1.50
233 Gerald Govan .60 1.50
234 Erving/McG/Issel LL 5.00 10.00
235 Gil/Kenn/Owens LL 1.25 3.00
236 Comb/Brwn/Damp LL 1.25 3.00
237 Kellr/Boone/War LL 1.25 3.00
238 Gilmore/Daniels/Paultz LL 1.25 3.00
239 Mel/Will/Jabali LL 1.25 3.00
240 Julius Erving AS2 15.00 30.00
241 Jimmy O'Brien .40 1.00
242 ABA Checklist 177-264 6.00 12.00
243 Johnny Neumann .40 1.00
244 Darnell Hillman .60 1.50
245 Willie Wise .60 1.50
246 Collis Jones .40 1.00
247 Ted McClain .40 1.00
248 George Irvine RC .40 1.00
249 Bill Melchionni .60 1.50
250 Artis Gilmore AS1 2.50 6.00
251 Willie Long .40 1.00
252 Larry Miller .40 1.00
253 Lee Davis .40 1.00
254 Donnie Freeman .60 1.50
255 Joe Caldwell .60 1.50
256 Bob Netolicky .60 1.50
257 Bernie Williams .40 1.00
258 Byron Beck .60 1.50
259 Jim Chones RC 1.25 3.00
260 James Jones AS1 .60 1.50
261 Wendell Ladner .40 1.00
262 Ollie Taylor .40 1.00
263 Les Hunter .40 1.00
264 Billy Keller ! 1.25 3.00

1973-74 Topps Team Stickers

Measuring 2 1/2" by 3 1/2", these ABA and NBA team stickers were inserted one per wax pack. Two teams are represented on each color sticker. The larger (2 1/2" by 2 1/2") top sticker carries the team logo, while the smaller (1" by 2 1/2") bottom sticker displays only the team name on a banner. Only one of each ABA sticker was produced, while some NBA stickers exhibit two team combinations. The stickers are unnumbered and checklisted below in alphabetical order according to the top sticker for the ABA (1-10) and the NBA (11-33). The team represented on the bottom sticker is listed immediately below each entry.

COMPLETE SET (33) 60.00 125.00
1 Carolina Cougars 2.00 5.00
Stars
2 Denver Rockets 2.00 5.00
Spurs
3 Indiana Pacers 2.50 6.00
Squires
4 Kentucky Colonels 2.50 6.00
Tams
5 Memphis Tams 2.50 6.00
Cougars
6 New York Nets 2.50 6.00
Conquistadors
7 San Antonio Spurs 2.00 5.00
Nets
8 San Diego Conquistadors 2.00 5.00
Pacers
9 Utah Stars 2.00 5.00
Colonels
10 Virginia Squires 2.00 5.00
Rockets
11 Atlanta Hawks 1.25 3.00
Celtics
12 Atlanta Hawks 1.25 3.00
Supersonics
13 Boston Celtics 1.50 4.00
Braves
14 Boston Celtics/76ers 1.50 4.00
15 Buffalo Braves 1.50 4.00
Lakers
16 Buffalo Braves 1.50 4.00
Trail Blazers
17 Capitol Bullets 1.25 3.00
Knicks
18 Chicago Bulls 1.25 3.00
Pistons
19 Cleveland Cavaliers 1.25 3.00
Hawks
20 Detroit Pistons 1.25 3.00
Warriors
21 Golden State Warriors 1.25 3.00
Bucks
22 Golden State Warriors 1.25 3.00
Kings
23 Houston Rockets 1.25 3.00
Braves
24 Kansas City Kings 1.25 3.00
Lakers/76ers
25 Los Angeles Lakers 1.50 4.00
Bullets
26 Los Angeles Lakers 1.50 4.00
Celtics
27 Milwaukee Bucks 1.25 3.00
Knicks
28 New York Knicks 1.25 3.00
Bulls
29 New York Knicks 1.25 3.00
Warriors
30 Philadelphia 76ers 1.25 3.00
Hawks
31 Phoenix Suns 1.25 3.00
Cavaliers
32 Portland Trail Blazers 1.25 3.00
Rockets
33 Seattle Supersonics 1.25 3.00
Suns

1974-75 Topps

The 1974-75 Topps set of 264 standard-size cards contains NBA players on cards numbered 1 to 176 and ABA players on cards numbered 177 to 264. For the first time Team Leader (TL) cards are provided for each team. The cards were issued in 10-card packs with 24 packs per box. All-Star selections (first and second team) for both leagues are noted on the respective player's regular cards. The card backs are printed in blue and red on gray card stock. Subsets include NBA Team Leaders (81-98), NBA Statistical Leaders (144-149), NBA Playoffs (161-164), ABA Statistical Leaders (207-212), ABA Team Leaders (221-230) and ABA Playoffs (246-249). The key Rookie Cards in this set are Doug Collins, George Gervin and Bill Walton.

COMPLETE SET (264) 200.00 325.00
CARDS PRICED IN NM CONDITION
1 Kareem Abdul-Jabbar ! 10.00 25.00
2 Don May .20 .50
3 Bernie Fryer RC .40 1.00
4 Don Adams .20 .50
5 Herm Gilliam .20 .50
6 Jim Chones .40 1.00
7 Rick Adelman .40 1.00
8 Randy Smith .40 1.00
9 Paul Silas 1.25 3.00
10 Pete Maravich 8.00 20.00
11 Ron Behagen .20 .50
12 Kevin Porter .40 1.00
13 Bill Bridges .40 1.00
14 Charles Johnson RC .20 .50
15 Bob Love .40 1.00
16 Henry Bibby .40 1.00
17 Neal Walk .20 .50
18 John Brisker .20 .50
19 Lucius Allen .20 .50
20 Tom Van Arsdale .40 1.00
21 Larry Steele .20 .50
22 Curtis Rowe .40 1.00
23 Dean Meminger .20 .50
24 Steve Patterson .20 .50
25 Earl Monroe 1.25 3.00
26 Jack Marin .20 .50
27 Jo Jo White 1.25 3.00
28 Rudy Tomjanovich 2.50 6.00
29 Otto Moore .20 .50
30 Elvin Hayes AS2 2.00 5.00
31 Pat Riley 3.00 8.00
32 Clyde Lee .20 .50
33 Bob Weiss .20 .50
34 Jim Fox .20 .50
35 Charlie Scott .40 1.00
36 Cliff Meely .20 .50
37 Jon McGlocklin .20 .50
38 Jim McMillian .40 1.00
39 Bill Walton RC 20.00 50.00
40 Dave Bing AS2 1.25 3.00
41 Jim Washington .20 .50
42 Jim Cleamons .40 1.00
43 Mel Davis .20 .50
44 Garfield Heard .40 1.00
45 Jimmy Walker .40 1.00
46 Don Nelson .40 1.00
47 Jim Barnett .20 .50
48 Manny Leaks .20 .50
49 Elmore Smith .40 1.00
50 Rick Barry AS1 2.50 6.00
51 Jerry Sloan 1.25 3.00
52 John Hummer .20 .50
53 Keith Erickson .40 1.00
54 George E. Johnson .20 .50
55 Oscar Robertson 6.00 12.00
56 Steve Mix RC .40 1.00
57 Rick Roberson .20 .50
58 John Mengelt .20 .50
59 Dwight Jones RC .40 1.00
60 Austin Carr .40 1.00
61 Nick Weatherspoon RC .40 1.00
62 Clem Haskins .40 1.00
63 Don Kojis .20 .50
64 Paul Westphal 1.25 3.00
65 Walt Bellamy 1.50 4.00
66 John Johnson .40 1.00
67 Butch Beard .40 1.00
68 Happy Hairston .40 1.00
69 Tom Boerwinkle .20 .50
70 Spencer Haywood AS2 1.25 3.00
71 Gary Melchionni .20 .50
72 Ed Ratleff RC .40 1.00
73 Mickey Davis .20 .50
74 Dennis Awtrey .20 .50
75 Fred Carter .40 1.00
76 George Trapp .20 .50
77 John Wetzel .20 .50
78 Bobby Smith .40 1.00
79 John Gianelli .20 .50
80 Bob McAdoo AS2 2.50 6.00
81 Hawks TL/Maravich/Bell 2.50 6.00
82 Celtics TL/John Havlicek 2.00 5.00
83 Buffalo Braves TL .40 1.00
84 Bulls TL/Love/Walker 1.25 3.00
85 Cleveland Cavs TL .40 1.00
86 Detroit Pistons TL .40 1.00
87 Warriors TL/Rick Barry 1.25 3.00
88 Houston Rockets TL .40 1.00
89 Kansas City Omaha TL .40 1.00
90 Lakers TL/Gail Goodrich .40 1.00
91 Bucks TL/Jabbar/Oscar 6.00 12.00
92 New Orleans Jazz .40 1.00
93 Knicks TL/Fraz/Brad/DeB 2.00 5.00
94 Philadelphia 76ers TL .40 1.00
95 Phoenix Suns TL .40 1.00
96 Trail Blazers TL .40 1.00
97 Seattle Supersonics TL .40 1.00
98 Capitol Bullets TL .40 1.00
99 Sam Lacey .20 .50
100 John Havlicek AS1 5.00 10.00
101 Stu Lantz .40 1.00
102 Mike Riordan .20 .50
103 Larry Jones .20 .50
104 Connie Hawkins 1.50 4.00
105 Nate Thurmond 1.25 3.00
106 Dick Gibbs .20 .50
107 Corky Calhoun .20 .50
108 Dave Wohl .20 .50
109 Cornell Warner .20 .50
110 Geoff Petrie UER .40 1.00
111 Leroy Ellis .40 1.00
112 Chris Ford .40 1.00
113 Bill Bradley 5.00 10.00
114 Clifford Ray .40 1.00
115 Dick Snyder .20 .50
116 Nate Williams .20 .50
117 Matt Guokas .40 1.00
118 Henry Finkel .20 .50
119 Curtis Perry .20 .50
120 Gail Goodrich AS1 1.25 3.00
121 Wes Unseld 1.25 3.00
122 Howard Porter .40 1.00
123 Jeff Mullins .20 .50
124 Mike Bantom RC .40 1.00
125 Fred Brown .40 1.00
126 Bob Dandridge .40 1.00
127 Mike Newlin .40 1.00
128 Greg Smith .20 .50
129 Doug Collins RC 6.00 15.00
130 Lou Hudson .40 1.00
131 Bob Lanier 2.00 5.00
132 Phil Jackson 4.00 10.00
133 Don Chaney .40 1.00
134 Jim Brewer RC .40 1.00
135 Ernie DiGregorio RC 1.25 3.00
136 Steve Kuberski .20 .50
137 Jim Price .20 .50
138 Mike D'Antoni .20 .50
139 John Brown .20 .50
140 Norm Van Lier AS2 .40 1.00
141 NBA Checklist 1-176 5.00 10.00
142 Slick Watts RC .40 1.00
143 Walt Wesley .20 .50
144 McAd/Jabbar/Marav LL 6.00 12.00
145 McAd/Marav/Jabbar LL 6.00 12.00
146 McAd/Jabbar/Tomjan LL 5.00 10.00
147 NBA F.T. Pct. Leaders .40 1.00
148 Hayes/Cowens/McAd LL 1.50 4.00
149 NBA Assist Leaders .40 1.00
150 Walt Frazier AS1 2.00 5.00
151 Cazzie Russell .40 1.00
152 Calvin Murphy 1.25 3.00
153 Bob Kauffman .20 .50
154 Fred Boyd .20 .50
155 Dave Cowens 2.50 6.00
156 Willie Norwood .20 .50
157 Lee Winfield .20 .50
158 Dwight Davis .20 .50
159 George T. Johnson .20 .50
160 Dick Van Arsdale .40 1.00
161 NBA Eastern Semis .40 1.00
162 NBA Western Semis .40 1.00
163 NBA Div. Finals .40 1.00
164 NBA Championship .60 1.50
165 Phil Chenier .40 1.00

166 Kermit Washington RC .40 1.00
167 Dale Schlueter .20 .50
168 John Block .20 .50
169 Don Smith .20 .50
170 Nate Archibald 1.50 4.00
171 Chet Walker .40 1.00
172 Archie Clark .40 1.00
173 Kennedy McIntosh .20 .50
174 George Thompson .20 .50
175 Sidney Wicks 1.25 3.00
176 Jerry West 10.00 20.00
177 Dwight Lamar .40 1.00
178 George Carter .60 1.50
179 Wil Robinson .40 1.00
180 Artis Gilmore AS1 1.50 4.00
181 Brian Taylor .60 1.50
182 Darnell Hillman .60 1.50
183 Dave Robisch .60 1.50
184 Gene Littles RC .60 1.50
185 Willie Wise AS2 .60 1.50
186 James Silas RC 1.25 3.00
187 Caldwell Jones RC 1.25 3.00
188 Roland Taylor .40 1.00
189 Randy Denton .40 1.00
190 Dan Issel AS2 2.00 5.00
191 Mike Gale .40 1.00
192 Mel Daniels .60 1.50
193 Steve Jones .60 1.50
194 Marv Roberts .40 1.00
195 Ron Boone AS2 .60 1.50
196 George Gervin RC 15.00 40.00
197 Flynn Robinson .40 1.00
198 Cincy Powell .60 1.50
199 Glen Combs .40 1.00
200 Julius Erving UER 15.00 40.00
201 Billy Keller .60 1.50
202 Willie Long .40 1.00
203 ABA Checklist 177-264 5.00 10.00
204 Joe Caldwell .60 1.50
205 Swen Nater RC .60 1.50
206 Rick Mount .60 1.50
207 Erving/McG/Issel LL 5.00 10.00
208 ABA Two-Point Field 1.25 3.00
209 ABA Three-Point Field 1.25 3.00
210 ABA Free Throw 1.25 3.00
211 Gil/McGinn/Jones LL 1.25 3.00
212 ABA Assist Leaders 1.25 3.00
213 Larry Miller .40 1.00
214 Stew Johnson .40 1.00
215 Larry Finch RC 1.25 3.00
216 Larry Kenon RC 1.25 3.00
217 Joe Hamilton .60 1.50
218 Gerald Govan .60 1.50
219 Ralph Simpson .60 1.50
220 George McGinnis AS1 1.25 3.00
221 Carolina Cougars TL 1.25 3.00
222 Denver Nuggets TL 1.25 3.00
223 Indiana Pacers TL 1.25 3.00
224 Colonels TL/Dan Issel 1.25 3.00
225 Memphis Sounds TL 1.25 3.00
226 Nets TL/Erving 5.00 10.00
227 Spurs TL/George Gervin 2.50 6.00
228 San Diego Conq. TL 1.25 3.00
229 Utah Stars TL 1.25 3.00
230 Virginia Squires TL 1.25 3.00
231 Bird Averitt .40 1.00
232 John Roche .40 1.00
233 George Irvine .40 1.00
234 John Williamson RC .60 1.50
235 Billy Cunningham 1.50 4.00
236 Jimmy O'Brien .40 1.00
237 Wilbert Jones .40 1.00
238 Johnny Neumann .40 1.00
239 Al Smith .40 1.00
240 Roger Brown .60 1.50
241 Chuck Williams .60 1.50
242 Rich Jones .40 1.00
243 Dave Twardzik RC .60 1.50
244 Wendell Ladner .60 1.50
245 Mack Calvin AS1 .60 1.50
246 ABA Eastern Semis 1.25 3.00
247 ABA Western Semis 1.25 3.00
248 ABA Div. Finals 1.25 3.00
249 Julius Erving PO 6.00 12.00
250 Wilt Chamberlain CO 12.00 30.00
251 Ron Robinson .40 1.00
252 Zelmo Beaty .60 1.50
253 Donnie Freeman .60 1.50
254 Mike Green .40 1.00
255 Louie Dampier AS2 .60 1.50
256 Tom Owens .40 1.00
257 George Karl RC 5.00 10.00
258 Jim Eakins .60 1.50
259 Travis Grant .60 1.50
260 James Jones AS1 .60 1.50
261 Mike Jackson .40 1.00
262 Billy Paultz .60 1.50
263 Freddie Lewis .60 1.50
264 Byron Beck ! 1.25 3.00

1975-76 Topps

The 1975-76 Topps basketball card set of 330 standard-size cards was the largest basketball set ever produced up to that time. Cards were issued in 10-card which cost 15 cents per pack and had 24 packs per box. NBA players are depicted on cards 1-220 and ABA players on cards 221-330. Team Leaders (TL) cards are 116-133 (NBA teams) and 278-287 (ABA). Other subsets include NBA Statistical Leaders (1-6), NBA Playoffs (188-189), NBA Team Checklists (203-220), ABA Statistical Leaders (221-226), ABA Playoffs (309-310) and ABA Team Checklists (321-330). All-Star selections (first and second team) for both leagues are noted on the respective player's regular cards. Card backs are printed in blue and green on gray card stock. The set is particularly hard to sort numerically, as the small card number on the back is printed in blue on a dark green background. The set was printed on three large sheets each containing 110 different cards. Investigation of the second (series) sheet reveals that 22 of the cards were double printed; they are marked DP in the checklist below. Rookie Cards in this set include Bobby Jones, Maurice Lucas, Moses Malone and Keith (Jamaal) Wilkes.

COMPLETE SET (330) 250.00 400.00
CARDS PRICED IN NM CONDITION
1 McAd/Barry/Jabbar LL ! 6.00 12.00
2 Nelson/Beard/Tomj LL 1.50 4.00
3 Barry/Murphy/Bradley LL 2.00 5.00
4 Unseld/Cowens/Lacey LL 1.25 3.00
5 Porter/Bing/Arch LL 1.25 3.00
6 Barry/Frazier/Steele LL 1.50 4.00
7 Tom Van Arsdale .50 1.25
8 Paul Silas .50 1.25
9 Jerry Sloan 1.25 3.00
10 Bob McAdoo AS1 2.50 6.00
11 Dwight Davis .30 .75
12 John Mengelt .50 1.25
13 George Johnson .30 .75
14 Ed Ratleff .30 .75
15 Nate Archibald AS1 1.50 4.00
16 Elmore Smith .30 .75
17 Bob Dandridge .50 1.25
18 Louie Nelson RC .30 .75
19 Neal Walk .30 .75
20 Billy Cunningham 1.50 4.00
21 Gary Melchionni .30 .75
22 Barry Clemens .30 .75
23 Jimmy Jones .30 .75
24 Tom Burleson RC .50 1.25
25 Lou Hudson .50 1.25
26 Henry Finkel .30 .75
27 Jim McMillian .50 1.25
28 Matt Guokas .50 1.25
29 Fred Foster DP .30 .75
30 Bob Lanier 2.00 5.00
31 Jimmy Walker .50 1.25
32 Cliff Meely .30 .75
33 Butch Beard .75 2.00
34 Cazzie Russell .50 1.25
35 Jon McGlocklin .30 .75
36 Bernie Fryer .30 .75
37 Bill Bradley 5.00 10.00
38 Fred Carter .50 1.25
39 Dennis Awtrey DP .30 .75
40 Sidney Wicks .50 1.25
41 Fred Brown .50 1.25
42 Rowland Garrett .30 .75
43 Herm Gilliam .30 .75
44 Don Nelson .50 1.25
45 Ernie DiGregorio .75 2.00
46 Jim Brewer .30 .75
47 Chris Ford .75 2.00
48 Nick Weatherspoon .50 1.25
49 Zaid Abdul-Aziz .30 .75
50 Keith Wilkes RC 5.00 10.00
51 Ollie Johnson DP .30 .75
52 Lucius Allen .50 1.25
53 Mickey Davis .30 .75
54 Otto Moore .30 .75
55 Walt Frazier AS1 2.00 5.00
56 Steve Mix .50 1.25
57 Nate Hawthorne .30 .75
58 Lloyd Neal .30 .75
59 Slick Watts .50 1.25
60 Elvin Hayes 2.00 5.00
61 Checklist 1-110 3.00 8.00
62 Mike Sojourner .30 .75
63 Randy Smith .50 1.25
64 John Block DP .30 .75
65 Charlie Scott .50 1.25
66 Jim Chones .50 1.25
67 Rick Adelman .50 1.25
68 Curtis Rowe .30 .75
69 Derrek Dickey RC .50 1.25
70 Rudy Tomjanovich 2.00 5.00
71 Pat Riley 2.50 6.00
72 Cornell Warner .30 .75
73 Earl Monroe 1.25 3.00
74 Allan Bristow RC 1.25 3.00
75 Pete Maravich DP 12.00 20.00
76 Curtis Perry .30 .75
77 Bill Walton 10.00 20.00
78 Leonard Gray .30 .75
79 Kevin Porter .50 1.25
80 John Havlicek AS2 5.00 10.00
81 Dwight Jones .30 .75
82 Jack Marin .30 .75
83 Dick Snyder .30 .75
84 George Trapp .30 .75
85 Nate Thurmond 1.25 3.00
86 Charles Johnson .30 .75
87 Ron Riley .30 .75
88 Stu Lantz .50 1.25
89 Scott Wedman RC .60 1.50
90 Kareem Abdul-Jabbar 8.00 20.00
91 Aaron James .30 .75
92 Jim Barnett .30 .75
93 Clyde Lee .30 .75
94 Larry Steele .50 1.25
95 Mike Riordan .30 .75
96 Archie Clark .50 1.25
97 Mike Bantom .30 .75
98 Bob Kauffman .30 .75
99 Kevin Stacom RC .30 .75
100 Rick Barry AS1 2.50 6.00
101 Ken Charles .30 .75
102 Tom Boerwinkle .30 .75
103 Mike Newlin .50 1.25
104 Leroy Ellis .50 1.25
105 Austin Carr .50 1.25
106 Ron Behagen .30 .75
107 Jim Price .30 .75
108 Bud Stallworth .30 .75
109 Earl Williams .30 .75
110 Gail Goodrich 1.25 3.00
111 Phil Jackson 2.50 6.00
112 Rod Derline .30 .75
113 Keith Erickson .30 .75
114 Phil Lumpkin .30 .75
115 Wes Unseld 1.25 3.00
116 Atlanta Hawks TL .60 1.50
117 Cowens/White TL 1.25 3.00
118 Buffalo Braves TL 1.25 3.00
119 Love/Walk/Thur TL 1.25 3.00
120 Cleveland Cavs TL .60 1.50
121 Lanier/Bing TL 1.25 3.00
122 Rick Barry TL 1.25 3.00
123 Houston Rockets TL .75 2.00
124 Kansas City Kings TL .75 2.00
125 Los Angeles Lakers TL .60 1.50
126 K.Abdul-Jabbar TL 3.00 8.00
127 Pete Maravich TL 5.00 10.00
128 Frazier/Bradley TL DP 1.25 3.00
129 Car/Coll/Cunn TL DP .75 2.00
130 Phoenix Suns TL DP .60 1.50
131 Portland Blazers TL DP .60 1.50
132 Seattle Sonics TL .75 2.00
133 Hayes/Unseld TL 1.25 3.00
134 John Drew RC .50 1.25
135 Jo Jo White AS2 .75 2.00
136 Garfield Heard .50 1.25
137 Jim Cleamons .30 .75
138 Howard Porter .50 1.25
139 Phil Smith RC .50 1.25
140 Bob Love .50 1.25
141 John Gianelli DP .30 .75
142 Larry McNeill RC .30 .75
143 Brian Winters RC 1.25 3.00
144 George Thompson .30 .75
145 Kevin Kunnert .30 .75
146 Henry Bibby .50 1.25
147 John Johnson .30 .75
148 Doug Collins 1.50 4.00
149 John Brisker .30 .75
150 Dick Van Arsdale .50 1.25
151 Leonard Robinson RC 1.25 3.00
152 Dean Meminger .30 .75
153 Phil Hankinson .30 .75
154 Dale Schlueter .30 .75
155 Norm Van Lier .50 1.25
156 Campy Russell RC 1.50 4.00
157 Jeff Mullins .50 1.25
158 Sam Lacey .30 .75
159 Happy Hairston .50 1.25
160 Dave Bing DP 1.25 3.00
161 Kevin Restani RC .30 .75
162 Dave Wohl .30 .75
163 E.C. Coleman .30 .75
164 Jim Fox .30 .75
165 Geoff Petrie .50 1.25
166 Hawthorne Wingo DP UER .30 .75
167 Fred Boyd .30 .75
168 Willie Norwood .30 .75
169 Bob Wilson .30 .75
170 Dave Cowens 2.50 6.00
171 Tom Henderson RC .30 .75
172 Jim Washington .30 .75
173 Clem Haskins .50 1.25
174 Jim Davis .30 .75
175 Bobby Smith DP .30 .75
176 Mike D'Antoni .30 .75
177 Zelmo Beaty .50 1.25
178 Gary Brokaw RC .30 .75
179 Mel Davis .30 .75
180 Calvin Murphy 1.25 3.00
181 Checklist 111-220 DP 3.00 8.00
182 Nate Williams .30 .75
183 LaRue Martin .30 .75
184 George McGinnis 1.25 3.00
185 Clifford Ray .30 .75
186 Paul Westphal 1.50 4.00
187 Talvin Skinner .30 .75
188 NBA Playoff Semis DP 1.25 3.00
189 Clifford Ray PO 1.25 3.00
190 Phil Chenier AS2 DP .50 1.25
191 John Brown .30 .75
192 Lee Winfield .30 .75
193 Steve Patterson .30 .75
194 Charles Dudley .30 .75
195 Connie Hawkins DP 1.25 3.00
196 Leon Benbow .30 .75
197 Don Kojis .30 .75
198 Ron Williams .30 .75
199 Mel Counts .30 .75
200 Spencer Haywood AS2 1.25 3.00
201 Greg Jackson .30 .75
202 Tom Kozelko DP .30 .75
203 Atlanta Hawks CL .60 1.50
204 Boston Celtics CL 1.25 3.00
205 Buffalo Braves CL .60 1.50
206 Chicago Bulls CL 1.25 3.00
207 Cleveland Cavs CL .60 1.50
208 Detroit Pistons CL .60 1.50
209 Golden State CL .60 1.50
210 Houston Rockets CL .60 1.50
211 Kansas City Kings CL DP .60 1.50
212 Los Angeles Lakers CL DP .60 1.50
213 Milwaukee Bucks CL .60 1.50
214 New Orleans Jazz CL .60 1.50
215 New York Knicks CL .60 1.50
216 Philadelphia 76ers CL .60 1.50
217 Phoenix Suns CL DP .60 1.50
218 Portland Blazers CL .60 1.50
219 Sonics/B.Russell DP 5.00 10.00
220 Washington Bullets CL .60 1.50
221 McGin/Erving/Boone LL 3.00 8.00
222 Jones/Gilmore/Malone LL 3.00 8.00
223 ABA 3 Pt. Field Goal .75 2.00
224 ABA Free Throw .75 2.00
225 ABA Rebounds Leaders .75 2.00
226 ABA Assists Leaders .75 2.00
227 Mack Calvin AS1 .75 2.00
228 Billy Knight RC 1.25 3.00
229 Bird Averitt .60 1.50
230 George Carter .60 1.50
231 Swen Nater AS2 .75 2.00
232 Steve Jones .75 2.00
233 George Gervin 10.00 20.00
234 Lee Davis .60 1.50
235 Ron Boone AS1 .75 2.00
236 Mike Jackson .60 1.50
237 Kevin Joyce RC .60 1.50
238 Marv Roberts .60 1.50
239 Tom Owens .60 1.50
240 Ralph Simpson .75 2.00
241 Gus Gerard .60 1.50
242 Brian Taylor AS2 .75 2.00
243 Rich Jones .60 1.50
244 John Roche .60 1.50
245 Travis Grant .75 2.00
246 Dave Twardzik .75 2.00
247 Mike Green .60 1.50
248 Billy Keller .75 2.00
249 Stew Johnson .60 1.50
250 Artis Gilmore AS1 2.00 5.00
251 John Williamson .75 2.00
252 Marvin Barnes RC 1.50 4.00
253 James Silas AS2 .75 2.00
254 Moses Malone RC 15.00 40.00
255 Willie Wise .75 2.00
256 Dwight Lamar .60 1.50
257 Checklist 221-330 3.00 8.00
258 Byron Beck .75 2.00
259 Len Elmore RC 1.25 3.00
260 Dan Issel 2.00 5.00
261 Rick Mount .60 1.50
262 Billy Paultz .75 2.00
263 Donnie Freeman .60 1.50
264 George Adams .60 1.50
265 Don Chaney .75 2.00
266 Randy Denton .60 1.50
267 Don Washington .60 1.50
268 Roland Taylor .60 1.50
269 Charlie Edge .60 1.50
270 Louie Dampier .75 2.00
271 Collis Jones .60 1.50
272 Al Skinner RC .60 1.50
273 Coby Dietrick .60 1.50
274 Tim Bassett .60 1.50
275 Freddie Lewis .75 2.00
276 Gerald Govan .60 1.50
277 Ron Thomas .60 1.50
278 Denver Nuggets TL .75 2.00
279 McGinnis/Keller TL 1.00 2.50
280 Gilmore/Dampier TL 1.00 2.50
281 Memphis Sounds TL .75 2.00
282 Julius Erving TL 6.00 15.00
283 Barnes/Lewis TL 1.00 2.50
284 George Gervin TL 2.00 5.00
285 San Diego Sails TL .75 2.00
286 Malone/Boone TL 3.00 8.00
287 Virginia Squires TL .75 2.00
288 Claude Terry .60 1.50
289 Wilbert Jones .60 1.50
290 Darnell Hillman .75 2.00
291 Bill Melchionni .75 2.00
292 Mel Daniels .75 2.00
293 Fly Williams RC .75 2.00
294 Larry Kenon .75 2.00
295 Red Robbins .75 2.00
296 Warren Jabali .75 2.00
297 Jim Eakins .75 2.00
298 Bobby Jones RC 6.00 12.00
299 Don Buse .75 2.00
300 Julius Erving AS1 12.00 30.00
301 Billy Shepherd .60 1.50
302 Maurice Lucas RC 2.50 6.00
303 George Karl 2.00 5.00
304 Jim Bradley .60 1.50
305 Caldwell Jones .75 2.00
306 Al Smith .60 1.50
307 Jan Van Breda Kolff RC .75 2.00
308 Darrell Elston .60 1.50
309 ABA Playoff Semifinals .75 2.00
310 Artis Gilmore PO 1.00 2.50
311 Ted McClain .60 1.50
312 Willie Sojourner .60 1.50
313 Bob Warren .60 1.50
314 Bob Netolicky .75 2.00
315 Chuck Williams .60 1.50
316 Gene Kennedy .60 1.50
317 Jimmy O'Brien .60 1.50
318 Dave Robisch .60 1.50
319 Wali Jones .60 1.50
320 George Irvine .60 1.50
321 Denver Nuggets CL .75 2.00
322 Indiana Pacers CL .75 2.00
323 Kentucky Colonels CL .75 2.00
324 Memphis Sounds CL .75 2.00
325 New York Nets CL .75 2.00
326 St. Louis Spirits CL .75 2.00
(Spirits of St. Louis on card back)
327 San Antonio Spurs CL .75 2.00
328 San Diego Sails CL .75 2.00
329 Utah Stars CL .75 2.00
330 Virginia Squires CL ! 1.50 4.00

1975-76 Topps Team Checklist

These team checklists were issued in three panels, with nine teams per panel. The panels were available as a complete set via a mail-in offer. Each panel measures approximately 7 1/2" by 10 1/2" and are joined together to form one continuous sheet. The checklists are printed in blue and green on white card stock and list all NBA and ABA teams. They are numbered on the front and listed alphabetically according to the city names. The backs are blank. Since there was only room for 27 teams on the three-part sheet, Topps apparently left off card 324 (Memphis Sounds), which is in the regular set.

COMPLETE SET (27) 75.00 150.00
203 Atlanta Hawks 2.50 6.00
204 Boston Celtics 5.00 10.00
205 Buffalo Braves 2.50 6.00
206 Chicago Bulls 2.50 6.00
207 Cleveland Cavaliers 2.50 6.00
208 Detroit Pistons 2.50 6.00
209 Golden State Warriors 2.50 6.00
210 Houston Rockets 2.50 6.00
211 Kansas City Kings 2.50 6.00
212 Los Angeles Lakers 5.00 10.00
213 Milwaukee Bucks 2.50 6.00
214 New Orleans Jazz 2.50 6.00
215 New York Knicks 3.00 8.00
216 Philadelphia 76ers 2.50 6.00
217 Phoenix Suns 2.50 6.00
218 Portland Trail Blazers 3.00 8.00
219 Seattle SuperSonics 2.50 6.00
220 Washington Bullets 2.50 6.00
321 Denver Nuggets 3.00 8.00
322 Indiana Pacers 3.00 8.00
323 Kentucky Colonels 3.00 8.00
325 New York Nets 3.00 8.00
326 Spirits of St. Louis 3.00 8.00
327 San Antonio Spurs 3.00 8.00
328 San Diego Sails 3.00 8.00
329 Utah Stars 3.00 8.00
330 Virginia Squires 2.50 6.00

1976-77 Topps

Perhaps the most popular set of the seventies, the 144-card 1976-77 Topps set witnessed a return to the larger-size at 3 1/8" by 5 1/4". The larger size and excellent photo quality are appealing to collectors. Also, because of the size, they are attractive to autograph collectors. Cards were issued in 10-card packs which cost 15 cents with 24 packs per box. The fronts have a large color photo with the team name vertical on the left border. The player's name and position are at the bottom. Backs have statistical and biographical data. Cards numbered 126-135 are the previous season's NBA All-Star selections. The cards were printed on two large sheets, each with eight rows and nine columns. The checklist card was located in the lower right corner of the second sheet. Card No. 1, Julius Erving, is rarely found centered. Rookie Cards include Alvan Adams, Lloyd Free, Gus Williams and David Thompson.

COMPLETE SET (144) 175.00 375.00
CONDITION SENSITIVE SET
CARDS PRICED IN NM CONDITION
1 Julius Erving ! 15.00 40.00
2 Dick Snyder .75 2.00
3 Paul Silas 1.00 2.50
4 Keith Erickson .75 2.00
5 Wes Unseld 2.00 5.00
6 Butch Beard 1.00 2.50
7 Lloyd Neal .75 2.00
8 Tom Henderson .75 2.00
9 Jim McMillian 1.00 2.50
10 Bob Lanier 2.50 6.00
11 Junior Bridgeman RC 1.00 2.50
12 Corky Calhoun .75 2.00
13 Billy Keller 1.00 2.50
14 Mickey Johnson RC .75 2.00
15 Fred Brown 1.00 2.50
16 Keith Wilkes 1.00 2.50
17 Louie Nelson .75 2.00
18 Ed Ratleff .75 2.00
19 Billy Paultz 1.00 2.50
20 Nate Archibald 2.00 5.00
21 Steve Mix 1.00 2.50
22 Ralph Simpson .75 2.00
23 Campy Russell 1.00 2.50
24 Charlie Scott 1.00 2.50
25 Artis Gilmore 2.00 5.00
26 Dick Van Arsdale 1.00 2.50
27 Phil Chenier 1.00 2.50
28 Spencer Haywood 2.00 5.00
29 Chris Ford 1.00 2.50
30 Dave Cowens 5.00 12.00
31 Sidney Wicks 1.00 2.50
32 Jim Price .75 2.00
33 Dwight Jones .75 2.00
34 Lucius Allen .75 2.00
35 Marvin Barnes 1.00 2.50
36 Henry Bibby 1.00 2.50
37 Joe Meriweather RC .75 2.00
38 Doug Collins 2.50 6.00
39 Garfield Heard 1.00 2.50
40 Randy Smith 1.00 2.50
41 Tom Burleson 1.00 2.50
42 Dave Twardzik 1.00 2.50
43 Bill Bradley 6.00 12.00
44 Calvin Murphy 2.00 5.00
45 Bob Love 1.00 2.50
46 Brian Winters 1.00 2.50
47 Glenn McDonald .75 2.00
48 Checklist 1-144 10.00 25.00
49 Bird Averitt .75 2.00
50 Rick Barry 5.00 12.00
51 Ticky Burden RC .75 2.00
52 Rich Jones .75 2.00
53 Austin Carr 1.00 2.50
54 Steve Kuberski .75 2.00
55 Paul Westphal 1.00 2.50
56 Mike Riordan .75 2.00
57 Bill Walton 10.00 25.00
58 Eric Money RC .75 2.00
59 John Drew 1.00 2.50
60 Pete Maravich 12.00 30.00
61 John Shumate RC 1.00 2.50
62 Mack Calvin 1.00 2.50
63 Bruce Seals .75 2.00
64 Walt Frazier 3.00 8.00
65 Elmore Smith .75 2.00
66 Rudy Tomjanovich 2.50 6.00
67 Sam Lacey .75 2.00
68 George Gervin 12.50 25.00
69 Gus Williams RC 2.00 5.00
70 George McGinnis 1.00 2.50
71 Len Elmore .75 2.00
72 Jack Marin .75 2.00
73 Brian Taylor .75 2.00
74 Jim Brewer .75 2.00
75 Alvan Adams RC 2.50 6.00
76 Dave Bing 2.00 5.00
77 Phil Jackson 5.00 10.00
78 Geoff Petrie 1.00 2.50
79 Mike Sojourner .75 2.00
80 James Silas 1.00 2.50
81 Bob Dandridge 1.00 2.50
82 Ernie DiGregorio 1.00 2.50
83 Cazzie Russell 1.00 2.50
84 Kevin Porter 1.00 2.50
85 Tom Boerwinkle .75 2.00
86 Darnell Hillman 1.00 2.50
87 Herm Gilliam .75 2.00
88 Nate Williams .75 2.00
89 Phil Smith 1.00 2.50
90 John Havlicek 7.50 15.00
91 Kevin Kunnert .75 2.00
92 Jimmy Walker 1.00 2.50
93 Billy Cunningham 2.00 5.00
94 Dan Issel 2.50 6.00
95 Ron Boone 1.00 2.50
96 Lou Hudson 1.00 2.50
97 Jim Chones 1.00 2.50
98 Earl Monroe 2.50 6.00
99 Tom Van Arsdale 1.00 2.50
100 Kareem Abdul-Jabbar 15.00 40.00
101 Moses Malone 10.00 25.00
102 Ricky Sobers RC .75 2.00
103 Swen Nater 1.00 2.50
104 Leonard Robinson 1.00 2.50
105 Slick Watts 1.00 2.50
106 Otto Moore .75 2.00
107 Maurice Lucas 1.00 2.50
108 Norm Van Lier 1.00 2.50
109 Clifford Ray .75 2.00
110 David Thompson RC 15.00 40.00
111 Fred Carter 1.00 2.50
112 Caldwell Jones 1.00 2.50
113 John Williamson 1.00 2.50
114 Bobby Smith 1.00 2.50
115 Jo Jo White 1.00 2.50
116 Curtis Perry .75 2.00
117 John Gianelli .75 2.00
118 Curtis Rowe .75 2.00
119 Lionel Hollins RC 1.00 2.50
120 Elvin Hayes 2.50 6.00
121 Ken Charles .75 2.00
122 Dave Meyers RC 1.00 2.50
123 Jerry Sloan 1.00 2.50
124 Billy Knight 1.00 2.50
125 Gail Goodrich 1.00 2.50
126 K. Abdul-Jabbar AS 12.00 20.00
127 Julius Erving AS 10.00 25.00
128 George McGinnis AS 1.00 2.50
129 Nate Archibald AS 1.00 2.50
130 Pete Maravich AS 12.50 25.00
131 Dave Cowens AS 2.00 5.00
132 Rick Barry AS 2.00 5.00
133 Elvin Hayes AS 2.00 5.00
134 James Silas AS .75 2.00
135 Randy Smith AS .75 2.00
136 Leonard Gray .75 2.00
137 Charles Johnson .75 2.00
138 Ron Behagen .75 2.00
139 Mike Newlin 1.00 2.50
140 Bob McAdoo 2.50 6.00
141 Mike Gale .75 2.00
142 Scott Wedman 1.00 2.50
143 Lloyd Free RC 2.50 6.00
144 Bobby Jones ! 3.00 8.00

1977-78 Topps

The 1977-78 Topps basketball card set consists of 132 standard-size cards. Cards were issued in 10-card packs with 24 packs per box. Fronts feature team and player name at the bottom with the player's position in a basketball at bottom left of the photo. Card backs are printed in green and black on either white or gray card stock. The white card stock is considered more desirable by most collectors and may even be a little tougher to find. However, there is no difference in value for either card stock. Rookie Cards include Adrian Dantley, Darryl Dawkins, John Lucas, Tom McMillen and Robert Parish.

COMPLETE SET (132) 50.00 100.00
1 Kareem Abdul-Jabbar ! 7.50 15.00
2 Henry Bibby .15 .40
3 Curtis Rowe .10 .30
4 Norm Van Lier .15 .40
5 Darnell Hillman .15 .40
6 Earl Monroe .60 1.50
7 Leonard Gray .10 .30
8 Bird Averitt .10 .30
9 Jim Brewer .10 .30
10 Paul Westphal .40 1.00
11 Bob Gross RC .15 .40
12 Phil Smith .10 .30
13 Dan Roundfield RC .25 .60
14 Brian Taylor .10 .30
15 Rudy Tomjanovich .75 2.00
16 Kevin Porter .15 .40
17 Scott Wedman .15 .40
18 Lloyd Free .25 .60
19 Tom Boswell RC .10 .30
20 Pete Maravich 7.50 15.00
21 Cliff Pondexter .10 .30
22 Bubbles Hawkins .15 .40
23 Kevin Grevey RC .50 1.25
24 Ken Charles .10 .30
25 Bob Dandridge .15 .40
26 Lonnie Shelton RC .15 .40
27 Don Chaney .15 .40
28 Larry Kenon .15 .40
29 Checklist 1-132 1.25 3.00
30 Fred Brown .15 .40
31 John Gianelli UER .10 .30
32 Austin Carr .15 .40
33 Keith Wilkes .25 .60
34 Caldwell Jones .15 .40
35 Jo Jo White .40 1.00
36 Scott May RC .60 1.50
37 Mike Newlin .10 .30
38 Mel Davis .10 .30
39 Lionel Hollins .25 .60
40 Elvin Hayes 1.00 2.50
41 Dan Issel .75 2.00
42 Ricky Sobers .10 .30
43 Don Ford .10 .30
44 John Williamson .10 .30
45 Bob McAdoo .75 2.00
46 Geoff Petrie .15 .40
47 M.L. Carr RC .75 2.00
48 Brian Winters .20 .60
49 Sam Lacey .10 .30
50 George McGinnis .25 .60
51 Slick Watts .15 .40
52 Sidney Wicks .25 .60
53 Wilbur Holland .10 .30
54 Tim Bassett .15 .40
55 Phil Chenier .15 .40
56 Adrian Dantley RC 3.00 8.00
57 Jim Chones .15 .40
58 John Lucas RC 1.00 2.50
59 Cazzie Russell .15 .40
60 David Thompson 2.00 5.00
61 Bob Lanier .75 2.00
62 Dave Twardzik .15 .40
63 Wilbert Jones .10 .30
64 Clifford Ray .10 .30
65 Doug Collins .60 1.50
66 Tom McMillen RC 1.00 2.50
67 Rich Kelley RC .10 .30
68 Mike Bantom .10 .30
69 Tom Boerwinkle .10 .30
70 John Havlicek 2.50 6.00
71 Marvin Webster RC .25 .60
72 Curtis Perry .10 .30
73 George Gervin 3.00 8.00
74 Leonard Robinson .25 .60
75 Wes Unseld .60 1.50
76 Dave Meyers .15 .40
77 Gail Goodrich .25 .60
78 Richard Washington RC .25 .60
79 Mike Gale .10 .30
80 Maurice Lucas .25 .60
81 Harvey Catchings RC .15 .40
82 Randy Smith .10 .30
83 Campy Russell .15 .40
84 Kevin Kunnert .10 .30
85 Lou Hudson .15 .40
86 Mickey Johnson .10 .30
87 Lucius Allen .10 .30
88 Spencer Haywood .40 1.00
89 Gus Williams .25 .60
90 Dave Cowens 1.25 3.00
91 Al Skinner .10 .30
92 Swen Nater .10 .30
93 Tom Henderson .10 .30
94 Don Buse .15 .40
95 Alvan Adams .25 .60
96 Mack Calvin .15 .40
97 Tom Burleson .10 .30
98 John Drew .15 .40
99 Mike Green .10 .30
100 Julius Erving 7.50 15.00
101 John Mengelt .10 .30
102 Howard Porter .15 .40
103 Billy Paultz .15 .40
104 John Shumate .15 .40
105 Calvin Murphy .60 1.50
106 Elmore Smith .10 .30
107 Jim McMillian .10 .30
108 Kevin Stacom .10 .30
109 Jan Van Breda Kolff .10 .30
110 Billy Knight .25 .60
111 Robert Parish 10.00 25.00
112 Larry Wright .10 .30
113 Bruce Seals .10 .30
114 Junior Bridgeman .15 .40
115 Artis Gilmore .60 1.50
116 Steve Mix .15 .40
117 Ron Lee .15 .40
118 Bobby Jones .40 1.00
119 Ron Boone .15 .40
120 Bill Walton 4.00 10.00
121 Chris Ford .15 .40
122 Earl Tatum .10 .30
123 E.C. Coleman .10 .30
124 Moses Malone 2.50 6.00
125 Charlie Scott .25 .60
126 Bobby Smith .10 .30
127 Nate Archibald .75 2.00
128 Mitch Kupchak RC .50 1.25
129 Walt Frazier 1.00 2.50
130 Rick Barry 1.25 3.00
131 Ernie DiGregorio .15 .40
132 Darryl Dawkins RC 5.00 12.00

1978-79 Topps

The 1978-79 Topps basketball card set contains 132 standard-size cards. Cards were issued in 10-card packs with 36 packs per box. Card fronts feature the player and team name down the left border and a small head shot inserted at bottom right. Card backs are printed in orange and brown on gray card stock. The key Rookie Cards in this set inlcude Quinn Buckner, Walter Davis, James "Buddha" Edwards, Dennis Johnson, Marques Johnson, Bernard King, Norm Nixon and Jack Sikma.

COMPLETE SET (132) 25.00 60.00
1 Bill Walton ! 4.00 10.00
2 Doug Collins .60 1.50
3 Jamaal Wilkes .30 .75
4 Wilbur Holland .10 .30
5 Bob McAdoo .50 1.25
6 Lucius Allen .10 .30
7 Wes Unseld .50 1.25
8 Dave Meyers .20 .50
9 Austin Carr .20 .50
10 Walter Davis RC 3.00 8.00
11 John Williamson .10 .30
12 E.C. Coleman .10 .30
13 Calvin Murphy .50 1.25
14 Bobby Jones .30 .75
15 Chris Ford .20 .50
16 Kermit Washington .20 .50
17 Butch Beard .20 .50
18 Steve Mix .30 .75
19 Marvin Webster .20 .50
20 George Gervin 2.50 6.00
21 Steve Hawes .10 .30
22 Johnny Davis RC .20 .50
23 Swen Nater .10 .30
24 Lou Hudson .20 .50
25 Elvin Hayes .60 1.50
26 Nate Archibald .60 1.50
27 James Edwards RC 1.25 3.00
28 Howard Porter .20 .50
29 Quinn Buckner RC .50 1.25
30 Leonard Robinson .20 .50
31 Jim Cleamons .10 .30
32 Campy Russell .20 .50
33 Phil Smith .10 .30
34 Darryl Dawkins .75 2.00
35 Don Buse .20 .50
36 Mickey Johnson .10 .30
37 Mike Gale .10 .30
38 Moses Malone 1.50 4.00
39 Gus Williams .30 .75
40 Dave Cowens .75 2.00
41 Bobby Wilkerson RC .20 .50
42 Wilbert Jones .10 .30
43 Charlie Scott .20 .50
44 John Drew .20 .50
45 Earl Monroe .50 1.25
46 John Shumate .20 .50
47 Earl Tatum .10 .30
48 Mitch Kupchak .20 .50
49 Ron Boone .20 .50
50 Maurice Lucas .40 1.00
51 Louie Dampier .20 .50
52 Aaron James .10 .30
53 John Mengelt .10 .30
54 Garfield Heard .20 .50
55 George Johnson .10 .30
56 Junior Bridgeman .10 .30
57 Elmore Smith .10 .30
58 Rudy Tomjanovich .60 1.50
59 Fred Brown .20 .50
60 Rick Barry UER .75 2.00
61 Dave Bing .50 1.25
62 Anthony Roberts .20 .50
63 Norm Nixon RC .75 2.00
64 Leon Douglas RC .20 .50
65 Henry Bibby .20 .50
66 Lonnie Shelton .20 .50
67 Checklist 1-132 .75 2.00
68 Tom Henderson .10 .30
69 Dan Roundfield .20 .50
70 Armond Hill RC .20 .50
71 Larry Kenon .20 .50
72 Billy Knight .20 .50
73 Artis Gilmore .60 1.50
74 Lionel Hollins .20 .50
75 Bernard King RC 3.00 8.00
76 Brian Winters .30 .75
77 Alvan Adams .30 .75
78 Dennis Johnson RC 3.00 8.00
79 Scott Wedman .10 .30
80 Pete Maravich 5.00 10.00
81 Dan Issel .60 1.50
82 M.L. Carr .30 .75
83 Walt Frazier .60 1.50
84 Dwight Jones .10 .30
85 Jo Jo White .30 .75
86 Robert Parish 2.00 5.00
87 Charlie Criss RC .20 .50
88 Jim McMillian .10 .30
89 Chuck Williams .10 .30
90 George McGinnis .30 .75
91 Billy Paultz .20 .50
92 Bob Dandridge .20 .50
93 Ricky Sobers .10 .30
94 Paul Silas .20 .50
95 Gail Goodrich .30 [illegible]
96 Tim Bassett .20 [illegible]
97 Ron Lee .10 [illegible]
98 Bob Gross .20 [illegible]
99 Sam Lacey .20 [illegible]
100 David Thompson 1.50 [illegible]
101 John Gianelli .10 .30
102 Norm Van Lier .20 .50
103 Caldwell Jones .20 .50
104 Eric Money .10 .30
105 Jim Chones .20 .50
106 John Lucas .40 1.00
107 Spencer Haywood .30 .75
108 Eddie Johnson RC .10 .30
109 Sidney Wicks .30 .75
110 Kareem Abdul-Jabbar 3.00 8.00
111 Sonny Parker RC .20 .50
112 Randy Smith .10 .30
113 Kevin Grevey .20 .50
114 Rich Kelley .10 .30
115 Scott May .20 .50
116 Lloyd Free .30 .75
117 Jack Sikma RC .75 2.00
118 Kevin Porter .20 .50
119 Darnell Hillman .20 .50
120 Paul Westphal .40 1.00
121 Richard Washington .10 .30
122 Dave Twardzik .20 .50
123 Mike Bantom .10 .30
124 Mike Newlin .10 .30
125 Bob Lanier .60 1.50
126 Marques Johnson RC 1.50 4.00
127 Foots Walker RC .20 .50
128 Cedric Maxwell RC .60 1.50
129 Ray Williams RC .20 .50
130 Julius Erving 5.00 12.00
131 Clifford Ray .10 .30
132 Adrian Dantley ! 1.25 3.00

1979-80 Topps

The 1979-80 Topps basketball set contains 132 standard-size cards. Cards were issued in 12-card packs along with a stick of bubble gum. The player's name, team and position are at the bottom. The team name is wrapped around a basketball. Card backs are printed in red and black on gray card stock. All-Star selections are designated as AS1 for first team selections and AS2 for second team selections and are denoted on the front of the player's regular card. Notable Rookie Cards in this set include Alex English, Reggie Theus, and Mychal Thompson.

COMPLETE SET (132) 40.00 80.00
1 George Gervin ! 2.50 6.00
2 Mitch Kupchak .15 .40
3 Henry Bibby .15 .40
4 Bob Gross .25 .60
5 Dave Cowens .75 2.00
6 Dennis Johnson .60 1.50
7 Scott Wedman .15 .40
8 Earl Monroe .50 1.25
9 Mike Bantom .10 .30
10 Kareem Abdul-Jabbar AS 3.00 8.00
11 Jo Jo White .30 .75
12 Spencer Haywood .25 .60
13 Kevin Porter .15 .40
14 Bernard King .60 1.50
15 Mike Newlin .10 .30
16 Sidney Wicks .25 .60

17 Dan Issel .50 1.25
18 Tom Henderson .10 .30
19 Jim Chones .15 .40
20 Julius Erving 5.00 12.00
21 Brian Winters .25 .60
22 Billy Paultz .15 .40
23 Cedric Maxwell .15 .40
24 Eddie Johnson .10 .30
25 Artis Gilmore .30 .75
26 Maurice Lucas .25 .60
27 Gus Williams .25 .60
28 Sam Lacey .15 .40
29 Toby Knight .10 .30
30 Paul Westphal AS1 .25 .60
31 Alex English RC 5.00 12.00
32 Gail Goodrich .25 .60
33 Caldwell Jones .15 .40
34 Kevin Grevey .15 .40
35 Jamaal Wilkes .25 .60
36 Sonny Parker .10 .30
37 John Gianelli .10 .30
38 John Long RC .15 .40
39 George Johnson .10 .30
40 Lloyd Free AS2 .25 .60
41 Rudy Tomjanovich .50 1.25
42 Foots Walker .15 .40
43 Dan Roundfield .15 .40
44 Reggie Theus RC 1.25 3.00
45 Bill Walton 1.25 3.00
46 Fred Brown .15 .40
47 Darnell Hillman .15 .40
48 Ray Williams .10 .30
49 Larry Kenon .15 .40
50 David Thompson .75 2.00
51 Billy Knight .25 .60
52 Alvan Adams .25 .60
53 Phil Smith .10 .30
54 Adrian Dantley .50 1.25
55 John Williamson .10 .30
56 Campy Russell .15 .40
57 Armond Hill .15 .40
58 Bob Lanier .50 1.25
59 Mickey Johnson .10 .30
60 Pete Maravich 5.00 10.00
61 Nick Weatherspoon .10 .30
62 Robert Reid RC .25 .60
63 Mychal Thompson RC .60 1.50
64 Doug Collins .40 1.00
65 Wes Unseld .50 1.25
66 Jack Sikma .25 .60
67 Bobby Wilkerson .10 .30
68 Bill Robinzine .10 .30
69 Joe Meriweather .10 .30
70 Marques Johnson AS1 .15 .40
71 Ricky Sobers .10 .30
72 Clifford Ray .10 .30
73 Tim Bassett .15 .40
74 James Silas .15 .40
75 Bob McAdoo .30 .75
76 Austin Carr .15 .40
77 Don Ford .10 .30
78 Steve Hawes .10 .30
79 Ron Brewer RC .10 .30
80 Walter Davis .40 1.00
81 Calvin Murphy .40 1.00
82 Tom Boswell .10 .30
83 Lonnie Shelton .10 .30
84 Terry Tyler RC .15 .40
85 Randy Smith .10 .30
86 Rich Kelley .10 .30
87 Otis Birdsong RC .25 .60
88 Marvin Webster .10 .30
89 Eric Money .10 .30
90 Elvin Hayes AS1 .60 1.50
91 Junior Bridgeman .10 .30
92 Johnny Davis .10 .30
93 Robert Parish 1.50 4.00
94 Eddie Jordan .15 .40
95 Leonard Robinson .15 .40
96 Rick Robey RC .15 .40
97 Norm Nixon .25 .60
98 Mark Olberding .10 .30
99 Wilbur Holland .10 .30
100 Moses Malone AS1 1.25 3.00
101 Checklist 1-132 .75 2.00
102 Tom Owens .10 .30
103 Phil Chenier .15 .40
104 John Johnson .10 .30
105 Darryl Dawkins .40 1.00
106 Charlie Scott .15 .40
107 M.L. Carr .25 .60
108 Phil Ford RC 1.00 2.50
109 Swen Nater .10 .30
110 Nate Archibald .60 1.50
111 Aaron James .10 .30
112 Jim Cleamons .10 .30
113 James Edwards .25 .60
114 Don Buse .15 .40
115 Steve Mix .15 .40
116 Charles Johnson .10 .30
117 Elmore Smith .10 .30
118 John Drew .10 .30
119 Lou Hudson .15 .40
120 Rick Barry .75 2.00
121 Kent Benson RC .25 .60
122 Mike Gale .10 .30
123 Jan Van Breda Kolff .10 .30
124 Chris Ford .15 .40
125 George McGinnis .25 .60
126 Leon Douglas .10 .30
127 John Lucas .25 .60
128 Kermit Washington .15 .40
129 Lionel Hollins .15 .40
130 Bob Dandridge AS2 .15 .40
131 James McElroy .10 .30
132 Bobby Jones ! .60 1.50

1980-81 Topps

The 1980-81 Topps basketball card set contains 264 different individual players (1 1/6" by 2 1/2") on 176 different panels of three (2 1/2" by 3 1/2"). This set was issued in packs of eight cards costing 25 cents per pack which came 36 packs per box. The cards come with three individual players per standard card. A perforation line segments each card into three players. In all, there are 176 different complete cards, however, the same player will be on more than one card. The variations stem from the fact that the cards in this set were printed on two separate sheets. In the checklist below, the first 88 cards comprise a complete set of all 264 players. The second 88 cards (89-176) provide a slight rearrangement of players within the card, but still contain the same 264 players. The cards are numbered within each series of 88 by any ordering of the left-hand player's number when the card is viewed from the back. In the checklist below, SD refers to a "Slam Dunk" star card. The letters AS in the checklist refer to an All-Star selection pictured on the front of the checklist card. There are a number of Team Leader (TL) cards which depict the team's leader in assists, scoring or rebounds. Prices given below are for complete panels, as that is the typical way these cards are collected. Cards which have been separated into the three parts are relatively valueless. The key card in this set features Larry Bird, Julius Erving and Magic Johnson. It is the Rookie Card for Bird and Magic. In addition to Bird and Magic, other noteworthy players making their first card appearance in this set include Bill Cartwright, Maurice Cheeks, Michael Cooper, Sidney Moncrief and Tree Rollins. Other lesser-known players making their first card appearance include James Bailey, Greg Ballard, Dudley Bradley, Mike Bratz, Joe Bryant, Kenny Carr, Wayne Cooper, David Greenwood, Phil Hubbard, Geoff Huston, Abdul Jeelani, Greg Kelser, Reggie King, Tom LaGarde, Mark Landsberger, Allen Leavell, Calvin

COMPLETE SET (176) 250.00 450.00
1 3/Erving/258 Brewer 2.00 5.00
2 7 Malone AS/185/Parish TL .60 1.50
3 12 Gus Williams AS .25 .60
4 24/32/248 Elvin Hayes .40 1.00
5 29 Dan Roundfield .40 1.00
6 34 Bird RC/Erving/Magic RC 125.00 250.00
7 36 Cowens/186/Wilkes .60 1.50
8 38 Maravich/264/194 DJ 2.50 6.00
9 40 Rick Robey .25 .60
10 47 Scott May .25 .60
11 55 Don Ford .10 .30
12 58 Campy Russell .10 .30
13 60 Foots Walker .10 .30
14 61/Jabbar AS/200 Natt 1.25 3.00
15 63 Jim Cleamons .25 .60
16 69 Tom LaGarde .10 .30
17 71 Jerome Whitehead .25 .60
18 74 John Roche TL .10 .30
19 75 English/2/68 .50 1.25
20 82 Terry Tyler TL .10 .30
21 84 Kent Benson .25 .60
22 86/Parish TL/126 .60 1.50
23 88/Erving AS/Sobers 1.25 3.00
24 90 Eric Money .10 .30
25 95 Wayne Cooper .10 .30
26 97 Parish/187/46 .75 2.00
27 98 Sonny Parker .10 .30
28 105 Barry/122/48 .40 1.00
29 106 Allen Leavell .10 .30
30 108/176 Cheeks TL/87 .25 .60
31 110 Robert Reid .25 .60
32 111 Rudy Tomjanovich .25 .60
33 112/28 Tree Rollins/15 .10 .30
34 115 Mike Bantom .25 .60
35 116 Dudley Bradley .10 .30
36 118 James Edwards .10 .30
37 119 Mickey Johnson .10 .30
38 120 Billy Knight .25 .60
39 121 George McGinnis .25 .60
40 124 Phil Ford TL .10 .30
41 127 Phil Ford .25 .60
42 131 Scott Wedman .25 .60
43 132 Jabbar TL/Mitch/81 1.25 3.00
44 135 Jabbar/79/216 2.00 5.00
45 137 Coop/Malone TL/148 .60 1.50
46 140/Lanier AS/Walton .60 1.50
47 141 Norm Nixon .25 .60
48 143/30 Bird TL/Sikma 10.00 25.00
49 146/31 Bird TL/Brewer 8.00 20.00
50 147/133 Jabbar TL/207 1.25 3.00
51 149/262 Erving SD/62 1.25 3.00
52 151 Moncrief/260/220 1.25 3.00
53 156 George Johnson .25 .60
54 158 Maurice Lucas .25 .60
55 159 Mike Newlin .10 .30
56 160 Roger Phegley .10 .30
57 161 Cliff Robinson .10 .30
58 162 Jan V.Breda Kolff .25 .60
59 165/214/Gilmore .10 .30
60 166 Cartwright/244/25 .60 1.50
61 168/14/Dantley .10 .30
62 169 Joe Meriweather .25 .60
63 170 Monroe/27/85 .25 .60
64 172 Marvin Webster .25 .60
65 173 Ray Williams .10 .30
66 178 Cheeks/Magic AS/237 6.00 15.00
67 183 Bobby Jones .40 1.00
68 189/163/Issel .40 1.00
69 190 Don Buse .25 .60
70 191 Davis/Gervin AS/136 .40 1.00
71 192/Malone TL/64 .40 1.00
72 201 Tom Owens .10 .30
73 208 Gervin/Issel TL/249 .60 1.50
74 217/263/107 Malone .60 1.50
75 219 Swen Nater .25 .60
76 221 Brian Taylor .10 .30
77 228 Fred Brown .10 .30
78 230/W.Davis AS/Archibald .40 1.00
79 231 Lonnie Shelton .25 .60
80 233 Gus Williams .10 .30
81 236 Allan Bristow TL .10 .30
82 238/109/Lanier .40 1.00
83 241 Ben Poquette .40 1.00
84 245 Greg Ballard .10 .30
85 246 Bob Dandridge .25 .60
86 250 Kevin Porter .10 .30
87 251 Unseld/195/78 .25 .60
88 257 Hayes SD/144/McAdoo .25 .60
89 3 Dan Roundfield .25 .60
90 7 Malone AS/247/52 .40 1.00
91 12 Gus Williams .10 .30
92 24 Steve Hawes .10 .30
93 29 Dan Roundfield .10 .30
94 34 Bird/Cartwright/23 15.00 40.00
95 36 Cowens/16/59 .40 1.00
96 38 Maravich/187/46 3.00 8.00
97 40 Rick Robey .25 .60
98 47/30 Bird TL/Sikma 8.00 20.00
99 55 Don Ford .40 1.00
100 58 Campy Russell .25 .60
101 60 Foots Walker .10 .30
102 61 Austin Carr .10 .30
103 63 Jim Cleamons .10 .30
104 69/109/Bob Lanier .40 1.00
105 71 Jerome Whitehead .25 .60
106 74/28 Tree Rollins/15 .10 .30
107 75 English/Malone TL/64 .60 1.50
108 82 Terry Tyler TL .10 .30
109 84 Kent Benson .25 .60
110 86 Phil Hubbard .10 .30
111 88/18 Magic AS/237 6.00 15.00
112 90 Eric Money .10 .30
113 95 Wayne Cooper .10 .30
114 97 Parish/Malone TL/148 .75 2.00
115 98 Sonny Parker .25 .60
116 105 Barry/123/54 .40 1.00
117 106 Allen Leavell .10 .30
118 108 Calvin Murphy .25 .60
119 110 Robert Reid .25 .60
120 111 Rudy Tomjanovich .40 1.00
121 112/264/D.Johnson .40 1.00
122 115 Mike Bantom .25 .60
123 116 Dudley Bradley .40 1.00
124 118/Archibald TL/Hayes .50 1.25
125 119 Mickey Johnson .40 1.00
126 120 Billy Knight .10 .30
127 121/Lanier AS/Walton .60 1.50
128 124 Phil Ford TL .25 .60
129 127 Phil Ford .25 .60
130 131 Scott Wedman .10 .30
131 132 Jabbar TL/Par.TL/126 1.50 4.00
132 135 Jabbar/253/167 2.00 5.00
133 137 M.Cooper/212/229 .50 1.25
134 140/214/Gilmore .25 .60
135 141 Norm Nixon .25 .60
136 143 Marq.Johnson TL .10 .30
137 146/Erving AS/Sobers 1.25 3.00
138 147 Quinn Buckner .25 .60
139 149 Marques Johnson .10 .30
140 151 Moncrief/Jabb.TL/207 1.50 4.00
141 156 George Johnson .10 .30
142 158/262 Erving SD/62 1.25 3.00
143 159 Mike Newlin .25 .60
144 160 Roger Phegley .10 .30
145 161 Cliff Robinson .10 .30
146 162/Erving SD/139 Magic 15.00 40.00
147 165/185/Parish TL .40 1.00
148 166 Cartwright/13/179 .40 1.00
149 168 Toby Knight .25 .60
150 169 Joe Meriweather .10 .30
151 170 Monroe/206/91 .10 .30
152 172 Marvin Webster .25 .60
153 173 Ray Williams .10 .30
154 178 Cheeks/Gervin AS/136 1.50 4.00
155 183 Bobby Jones .25 .60
156 189/14/Dantley .25 .60
157 190 Don Buse .25 .60
158 191 Walter Davis .25 .60
159 192/263/107 Malone .60 1.50
160 201 Tom Owens .25 .60
161 208 Gervin/53/223 .60 1.50
162 217/8 Jabbar AS/Natt 1.25 3.00
163 219 Swen Nater .10 .30
164 221 Brian Taylor .10 .30
165 228/31 Bird TL/Brewer 7.50 15.00
166 230/163/Issel .40 1.00
167 231 Lonnie Shelton .10 .30
168 233 Gus Williams .25 .60
169 236 Allan Bristow TL .10 .30
170 238 Tom Boswell .10 .30
171 241/Cheeks TL/87 .40 1.00
172 245/W.Davis AS/Archibald .40 1.00
173 246 Bob Dandridge .10 .30
174 250 Kevin Porter .10 .30
175 251 Unseld/67/5 .40 1.00
176 257 Hayes SD/Erving/258 2.00 5.00

1980-81 Topps Team Posters

This set of 16 numbered team mini-posters was issued as a folded insert (one per pack) in regular wax packs of 1980-81 Topps basketball cards. The small posters feature a full-color posed team picture, with the team name in the frame line. These posters are on thin, white paper stock and measure approximately 4 7/8" by 6 7/8" when unfolded. Since the copies were originally folded by Topps prior to insertion into the packs, they are still considered Mint with fold lines.

COMPLETE SET (16) 12.00 30.00
1 Atlanta Hawks .40 1.00
2 Boston Celtics 3.00 8.00
3 Chicago Bulls .40 1.00
4 Cleveland Cavaliers .40 1.00
5 Detroit Pistons .40 1.00
6 Houston Rockets .40 1.00
7 Indiana Pacers .40 1.00
8 Los Angeles Lakers 2.50 6.00
9 Milwaukee Bucks .40 1.00
10 New Jersey Nets .40 1.00
11 New York Knicks .40 1.00
12 Philadelphia 76ers .75 2.00
13 Phoenix Suns .40 1.00
14 Portland Blazers .40 1.00
15 Seattle Sonics .40 1.00
16 Washington Bullets .40 1.00

1981-82 Topps

The 1981-82 Topps basketball card set contains a total of 198 standard-size cards that were issued in 13-card, 30-cent wax packs with 36 packs per box. These cards are numbered depending upon the regional distribution used in the issue. A 66-card national set was issued to all parts of the country, however, subsets of 44 cards each were issued in the East, Midwest and West. The national set is easier to acquire than any of the regional issues. Card numbers over 66 are prefaced on the card by the region in which they were distributed, e.g., East 96. The cards feature the Topps logo in the frame line and a quarter-round sunburst in the lower left-hand corner which lists the name, position and team of the player depicted. Cards 44-66 are Team Leader (TL) cards picturing each team's statistical leaders. The back, printed in orange and brown on gray stock, features standard Topps biographical data and career statistics. There are a number of Super Action (SA) cards in the set. Rookie Cards include Joe Barry Carroll, Mike Dunleavy, Mike Gminski, Darrell Griffith, Ernie Grunfeld, Vinnie Johnson, Bill Laimbeer, Rick Mahorn, Kevin McHale, Jim Paxson and Larry Smith. The card numbering sequence is alphabetical within team within each series. This was Topps' last basketball card issue until 1992.

COMPLETE SET (198) 25.00 60.00
1 John Drew .07 .20
2 Dan Roundfield .07 .20
3 Nate Archibald .25 .60
4 Larry Bird ! 5.00 12.00
5 Cedric Maxwell .07 .20
6 Robert Parish .60 1.50
7 Artis Gilmore .25 .60
8 Ricky Sobers .02 .10
9 Mike Mitchell .07 .20
10 Tom LaGarde .02 .10
11 Dan Issel .30 .75
12 David Thompson .30 .75
13 Lloyd Free .08 .25
14 Moses Malone .60 1.50
15 Calvin Murphy .08 .25
16 Johnny Davis .02 .10
17 Otis Birdsong .08 .25
18 Phil Ford .07 .20
19 Scott Wedman .02 .10
20 Kareem Abdul-Jabbar 3.00 8.00
21 Magic Johnson ! 4.00 10.00
22 Norm Nixon .08 .25
23 Jamaal Wilkes .08 .25
24 Marques Johnson .08 .25
25 Bob Lanier .30 .75
26 Bill Cartwright .20 .50
27 Michael Ray Richardson .07 .20
28 Ray Williams .07 .20
29 Darryl Dawkins .08 .25
30 Julius Erving 2.00 5.00
31 Lionel Hollins .02 .10
32 Bobby Jones .08 .25
33 Walter Davis .20 .50
34 Dennis Johnson .20 .50
35 Leonard Robinson .08 .25
36 Mychal Thompson .08 .25
37 George Gervin .75 2.00
38 Swen Nater .02 .10
39 Jack Sikma .08 .25
40 Adrian Dantley .25 .60
41 Darrell Griffith RC .40 1.00
42 Elvin Hayes .30 .75
43 Fred Brown .08 .25
44 Atlanta Hawks TL .05 .15
45 Celtics TL/Bird/Arch .75 2.00
46 Chicago Bulls TL .08 .25
47 Cleveland Cavs TL .05 .15
48 Dallas Mavericks TL .05 .15
49 Denver Nuggets TL .08 .25
50 Detroit Pistons TL .05 .15
51 Golden State TL .08 .25
52 Rockets TL/Malone .15 .40
53 Indiana Pacers TL .08 .25
54 Kansas City Kings TL .05 .15
55 Lakers TL/Jabbar .50 1.25
56 Milwaukee Bucks TL .08 .25
57 New Jersey Nets TL .05 .15
58 New York Knicks TL .08 .25
59 76ers TL/Erving .50 1.25
60 Phoenix Suns TL .08 .25
61 Trail Blazers TL .05 .15
62 San Antonio Spurs TL .08 .25
63 San Diego Clippers TL .05 .15
64 Seattle Sonics TL .08 .25
65 Utah Jazz TL .08 .25
66 Washington Bullets TL .08 .25
E67 Charlie Criss .08 .25
E68 Eddie Johnson .05 .15
E69 Wes Matthews .05 .15
E70 Tom McMillen .15 .40
E71 Tree Rollins .15 .40
E72 M.L. Carr .08 .25
E73 Chris Ford .08 .25
E74 Gerald Henderson RC .15 .40
E75 Kevin McHale RC 8.00 20.00
E76 Rick Robey .08 .25
E77 Darwin Cook RC .05 .15
E78 Mike Gminski RC .30 .75
E79 Maurice Lucas .08 .25
E80 Mike Newlin .08 .25
E81 Mike O'Koren RC .08 .25
E82 Steve Hawes .05 .15
E83 Foots Walker .08 .25
E84 Campy Russell .08 .25
E85 DeWayne Scales .05 .15
E86 Randy Smith .08 .25
E87 Marvin Webster .08 .25
E88 Sly Williams .05 .15
E89 Mike Woodson RC .08 .25
E90 Maurice Cheeks .60 1.50
E91 Caldwell Jones .08 .25
E92 Steve Mix .08 .25
E93A Checklist 1-110 ERR .75 2.00
E93B Checklist 1-110 COR .50 1.00
E94 Greg Ballard .05 .15
E95 Don Collins .05 .15
E96 Kevin Grevey .08 .25
E97 Mitch Kupchak .08 .25
E98 Rick Mahorn RC .30 .75
E99 Kevin Porter .08 .25
E100 Nate Archibald SA .08 .25
E101 Larry Bird SA 5.00 12.00
E102 Bill Cartwright SA .05 .15
E103 Darryl Dawkins SA .08 .25
E104 Julius Erving SA .75 2.00
E105 Kevin Porter SA .08 .25
E106 Bobby Jones SA .08 .25
E107 Cedric Maxwell SA .08 .25
E108 Robert Parish SA .40 1.00
E109 M.R.Richardson SA .08 .25
E110 Dan Roundfield SA .08 .25
W67 T.R. Dunn RC .20 .50
W68 Alex English .60 1.50
W69 Billy McKinney RC .08 .25
W70 Dave Robisch .08 .25
W71 Joe Barry Carroll RC .15 .40
W72 Bernard King .40 1.00
W73 Sonny Parker .05 .15
W74 Purvis Short .08 .25
W75 Larry Smith RC .15 .40
W76 Jim Chones .08 .25
W77 Michael Cooper .30 .75
W78 Mark Landsberger .05 .15
W79 Alvan Adams .08 .25
W80 Jeff Cook .05 .15
W81 Rich Kelley .05 .15
W82 Kyle Macy RC .15 .40
W83 Billy Ray Bates RC .20 .50
W84 Bob Gross .08 .25
W85 Calvin Natt .08 .25
W86 Lonnie Shelton .08 .25
W87 Jim Paxson RC .50 1.25
W88 Kelvin Ransey .05 .15
W89 Kermit Washington .08 .25
W90 Henry Bibby .08 .25
W91 Michael Brooks RC .05 .15
W92 Joe Bryant .08 .25
W93 Phil Smith .05 .15
W94 Brian Taylor .05 .15
W95 Freeman Williams .08 .25
W96 James Bailey .05 .15
W97 Checklist 1-110 .50 1.00
W98 John Johnson .05 .15
W99 Vinnie Johnson RC .60 1.50
W100 Wally Walker RC .08 .25
W101 Paul Westphal .08 .25
W102 Allan Bristow .08 .25
W103 Wayne Cooper .05 .15
W104 Carl Nicks .05 .15
W105 Ben Poquette .05 .15
W106 K.Abdul-Jabbar SA .75 2.00
W107 Dan Issel SA .20 .50
W108 Dennis Johnson SA .08 .25
W109 Magic Johnson SA ! 3.00 8.00
W110 Jack Sikma SA .08 .25
MW67 David Greenwood .08 .25
MW68 Dwight Jones .05 .15
MW69 Reggie Theus .15 .40
MW70 Bobby Wilkerson .05 .15
MW71 Mike Bratz .05 .15
MW72 Kenny Carr .05 .15
MW73 Geoff Huston .05 .15
MW74 Bill Laimbeer RC 1.25 4.00
MW75 Roger Phegley .05 .15
MW76 Checklist 1-110 .50 1.00
MW77 Abdul Jeelani .05 .15
MW78 Bill Robinzine .05 .15
MW79 Jim Spanarkel .05 .15
MW80 Kent Benson .08 .25
MW81 Keith Herron .05 .15
MW82 Phil Hubbard .05 .15
MW83 John Long .05 .15
MW84 Terry Tyler .05 .15
MW85 Mike Dunleavy RC .30 .75
MW86 Tom Henderson .05 .15
MW87 Billy Paultz .08 .25
MW88 Robert Reid .05 .15
MW89 Mike Bantom .05 .15
MW90 James Edwards .08 .25
MW91 Billy Knight .08 .25
MW92 George McGinnis .08 .25
MW93 Louis Orr .05 .15
MW94 Ernie Grunfeld RC .15 .40
MW95 Reggie King .05 .15
MW96 Sam Lacey .05 .15
MW97 Junior Bridgeman .08 .25
MW98 Mickey Johnson .08 .25
MW99 Sidney Moncrief .30 .75
MW100 Brian Winters .08 .25
MW101 Dave Corzine RC .15 .40
MW102 Paul Griffin .05 .15
MW103 Johnny Moore RC .08 .25
MW104 Mark Olberding .05 .15
MW105 James Silas .08 .25
MW106 George Gervin SA .30 .75
MW107 Artis Gilmore SA .08 .25
MW108 Marques Johnson SA .08 .25
MW109 Bob Lanier SA .20 .50
MW110 Moses Malone SA .40 1.00

1992-93 Topps

The complete 1992-93 Topps basketball set consists of 396 standard-size cards, issued in two 198-card series. Cards were issued in 15-card plastic wrap packs (suggested retail 79 cents, 36 packs per box), 18-card mini-jumbo packs, 45-card retail packs and 41-card magazine jumbo packs. In addition, factory sets were also released. On a white card face, the fronts display color action player photos framed by two-color border stripes. The player's name and team name appear in two different colored bars across the bottom of the picture. In addition to a color close-up photo, the horizontal backs have biography on a light blue panel as well as statistics and brief player profile on a yellow panel. Most Rookie Cards have the a gold-foil "'92 Draft Pix" emblem on their card fronts. Topical subsets included are Highlight (2-4), All-Star (100-126), 50 Point Club (199-215), and 20 Assist Club (216-224). Rookie Cards of note include Tom Gugliotta, Robert Horry, Christian Laettner, Alonzo Mourning, Shaquille O'Neal, Latrell Sprewell and Clarence Weatherspoon.

COMPLETE SET (396) 6.00 15.00
COMPLETE FACT. SET (408) 10.00 25.00
COMPLETE SERIES 1 (198) 2.00 4.00
COMPLETE SERIES 2 (198) 5.00 12.00
1 Larry Bird .25 .60
2 Magic Johnson HL .08 .25
3 Michael Jordan HL .40 1.00
4 David Robinson HL .05 .15
5 Johnny Newman .02 .10
6 Mike Iuzzolino .02 .10
7 Ken Norman .02 .10
8 Chris Jackson .02 .10
9 Duane Ferrell .02 .10
10 Sean Elliott .02 .10
11 Bernard King .02 .10
12 Armon Gilliam .02 .10
13 Reggie Williams .02 .10
14 Steve Kerr .02 .10
15 Anthony Bowie .02 .10
16 Alton Lister .02 .10
17 Dee Brown .02 .10
18 Tom Chambers .02 .10
19 Otis Thorpe .02 .10
20 Karl Malone .08 .25
21 Kenny Gattison .02 .10
22 Lionel Simmons UER .02 .10
23 Vern Fleming .02 .10
24 John Paxson .02 .10
25 Mitch Richmond .05 .15
26 Danny Schayes .02 .10
27 Derrick McKey .02 .10
28 Mark Randall .02 .10
29 Bill Laimbeer .02 .10
30 Chris Morris .02 .10
31 Alec Kessler .02 .10
32 Vlade Divac .02 .10
33 Rick Fox .02 .10
34 Charles Shackleford .02 .10
35 Dominique Wilkins .05 .15
36 Sleepy Floyd .02 .10
37 Doug West .02 .10
38 Pete Chilcutt .02 .10
39 Orlando Woolridge .02 .10
40 Eric Leckner .02 .10
41 Joe Kleine .02 .10
42 Scott Skiles .02 .10
43 Jerrod Mustaf .02 .10
44 John Starks .02 .10
45 Sedale Threatt .02 .10
46 Doug Smith .02 .10
47 Byron Scott .02 .10
48 Willie Anderson .02 .10
49 David Benoit .02 .10
50 Scott Hastings .02 .10
51 Terry Porter .02 .10
52 Sidney Green .02 .10
53 Danny Young .02 .10
54 Magic Johnson .20 .50
55 Brian Williams .02 .10
56 Randy Wittman .02 .10
57 Kevin McHale .05 .15
58 Dana Barros .02 .10
59 Thurl Bailey .02 .10
60 Kevin Duckworth .02 .10
61 John Williams .02 .10
62 Willie Burton .02 .10
63 Spud Webb .02 .10
64 Detlef Schrempf .02 .10
65 Sherman Douglas .02 .10
66 Patrick Ewing .05 .15
67 Michael Adams .02 .10
68 Vernon Maxwell .02 .10
69 Terrell Brandon .05 .15
70 Terry Catledge .02 .10
71 Mark Eaton .02 .10
72 Tony Smith .02 .10
73 B.J. Armstrong .02 .10
74 Moses Malone .05 .15
75 Anthony Bonner .02 .10
76 George McCloud .02 .10
77 Glen Rice .05 .15
78 Jon Koncak .02 .10
79 Michael Cage .02 .10
80 Ron Harper .02 .10
81 Tom Tolbert .02 .10
82 Brad Sellers .02 .10
83 Winston Garland .02 .10
84 Negele Knight .02 .10
85 Ricky Pierce .02 .10
86 Mark Aguirre .02 .10
87 Ron Anderson .02 .10
88 Loy Vaught .02 .10
89 Luc Longley .02 .10
90 Jerry Reynolds .02 .10
91 Terry Cummings .02 .10
92 Rony Seikaly .02 .10
93 Derek Harper .02 .10
94 Clifford Robinson .02 .10
95 Kenny Anderson .05 .15
96 Chris Gatling .02 .10
97 Stacey Augmon .02 .10
98 Chris Corchiani .02 .10
99 Pervis Ellison .02 .10
100 Larry Bird AS .10 .30
101 John Stockton AS UER .02 .10
102 Clyde Drexler AS .02 .10
103 Scottie Pippen AS .08 .25
104 Reggie Lewis AS .02 .10
105 Hakeem Olajuwon AS .05 .15
106 David Robinson AS .05 .15
107 Charles Barkley AS .05 .15
108 James Worthy AS .02 .10
109 Kevin Willis AS .02 .10
110 Dikembe Mutombo AS .05 .15
111 Joe Dumars AS .02 .10
112 Jeff Hornacek AS UER .02 .10
(5 or 7 shots should be 5 of 7 shots)
113 Mark Price AS .02 .10
114 Michael Adams AS .02 .10
115 Michael Jordan AS .40 1.00
116 Brad Daugherty AS .02 .10
117 Dennis Rodman AS .05 .15
118 Isiah Thomas AS .02 .10
119 Tim Hardaway AS .05 .15
120 Chris Mullin AS .02 .10
121 Patrick Ewing AS .02 .10
122 Dan Majerle AS .02 .10
123 Karl Malone AS .05 .15
124 Otis Thorpe AS .02 .10
125 Dominique Wilkins AS .02 .10
126 Magic Johnson AS .08 .25
127 Charles Oakley .02 .10
128 Robert Pack .02 .10
129 Billy Owens .02 .10
130 Jeff Malone .02 .10
131 Danny Ferry .02 .10
132 Sam Bowie .02 .10
133 Avery Johnson .02 .10
134 Jayson Williams .02 .10
135 Fred Roberts .02 .10
136 Greg Sutton .02 .10
137 Dennis Rodman .10 .30
138 John Williams .02 .10
139 Greg Dreiling .02 .10
140 Rik Smits .02 .10
141 Michael Jordan .75 2.00
142 Nick Anderson .02 .10
143 Jerome Kersey .02 .10
144 Fat Lever .02 .10
145 Tyrone Corbin .02 .10
146 Robert Parish .02 .10
147 Steve Smith .07 .20
148 Chris Dudley .02 .10
149 Antoine Carr .02 .10
150 Elden Campbell .02 .10
151 Randy White .02 .10
152 Felton Spencer .02 .10
153 Cedric Ceballos .02 .10
154 Mark Macon .02 .10
155 Jack Haley .02 .10
156 Bimbo Coles .02 .10
157 A.J. English .02 .10
158 Kendall Gill .02 .10
159 A.C. Green .02 .10
160 Mark West .02 .10
161 Benoit Benjamin .02 .10
162 Tyrone Hill .02 .10
163 Larry Nance .02 .10
164 Gary Grant .02 .10
165 Bill Cartwright .02 .10
166 Greg Anthony .02 .10
167 Jim Les .02 .10
168 Johnny Dawkins .02 .10
169 Alvin Robertson .02 .10
170 Kenny Smith .02 .10
171 Gerald Glass .02 .10
172 Harvey Grant .02 .10
173 Paul Graham .02 .10
174 Sam Perkins .02 .10
175 Manute Bol .02 .10
176 Muggsy Bogues .02 .10
177 Mike Brown .02 .10
178 Donald Hodge .02 .10
179 Dave Jamerson .02 .10
180 Mookie Blaylock .02 .10
181 Randy Brown .02 .10
182 Todd Lichti .02 .10
183 Kevin Gamble .02 .10
184 Gary Payton .10 .30
185 Brian Shaw .02 .10
186 Grant Long .02 .10
187 Frank Brickowski .02 .10
188 Tim Hardaway .07 .20
189 Danny Manning .02 .10
190 Kevin Johnson .05 .15
191 Craig Ehlo .02 .10
192 Dennis Scott .02 .10
193 Reggie Miller .05 .15
194 Darrell Walker .02 .10
195 Anthony Mason .05 .15
196 Buck Williams .02 .10
197 Checklist 1-99 .02 .10
198 Checklist 100-198 .02 .10
199 Karl Malone 50P .05 .15
200 Dominique Wilkins 50P .02 .10
201 Tom Chambers 50P .02 .10
202 Bernard King 50P .02 .10
203 Kiki Vandeweghe 50P .02 .10
204 Dale Ellis 50P .02 .10
205 Michael Jordan 50P .40 1.00
206 Michael Adams 50P .02 .10
207 Charles Smith 50P .02 .10
208 Moses Malone 50P .02 .10
209 Terry Cummings 50P .02 .10
210 Vernon Maxwell 50P .02 .10
211 Patrick Ewing 50P .02 .10
212 Clyde Drexler 50P .02 .10
213 Kevin McHale 50P .02 .10
214 Hakeem Olajuwon 50P .05 .15
215 Reggie Miller 50P .02 .10
216 Gary Grant 20A .02 .10
217 Doc Rivers 20A .02 .10
218 Mark Price 20A .02 .10
219 Isiah Thomas 20A .02 .10
220 Nate McMillan 20A .02 .10
221 Fat Lever 20A .02 .10
222 Kevin Johnson 20A .02 .10
223 John Stockton 20A .02 .10
224 Scott Skiles 20A .02 .10
225 Kevin Brooks .02 .10
226 Bobby Phills RC .05 .15
227 Oliver Miller RC .02 .10
228 John Williams .02 .10
229 Brad Lohaus .02 .10
230 Derrick Coleman .02 .10
231 Ed Pinckney .02 .10
232 Trent Tucker .02 .10
233 Lance Blanks .02 .10
234 Drazen Petrovic .02 .10
235 Mark Bryant .02 .10
236 Lloyd Daniels RC .02 .10
237 Dale Davis .02 .10
238 Jayson Williams .02 .10
239 Mike Sanders .02 .10
240 Mike Gminski .02 .10
241 William Bedford .02 .10
242 Dell Curry .02 .10
243 Gerald Paddio .02 .10
244 Chris Smith RC .02 .10
245 Jud Buechler .02 .10
246 Walter Palmer .02 .10
247 Larry Krystkowiak .02 .10
248 Marcus Liberty .02 .10
249 Sam Mitchell .02 .10
250 Kiki Vandeweghe .02 .10
251 Vincent Askew .02 .10
252 Travis Mays .02 .10
253 Charles Smith .02 .10
254 John Bagley .02 .10
255 James Worthy .05 .15
256 Paul Pressey P/CO .02 .10
257 Rumeal Robinson .02 .10
258 Tom Gugliotta RC .20 .50
259 Eric Anderson RC .02 .10
260 Hersey Hawkins .02 .10
261 Terry Davis .02 .10
262 Rex Chapman .02 .10
263 Chucky Brown .02 .10
264 Danny Young .02 .10
265 Olden Polynice .02 .10
266 Kevin Willis .02 .10
267 Shawn Kemp .10 .30
268 Mookie Blaylock .02 .10
269 Malik Sealy RC .02 .10
270 Charles Barkley .08 .25
271 Corey Williams RC .02 .10
272 Stephen Howard RC .02 .10
273 Keith Askins .02 .10
274 Matt Bullard .02 .10
275 John Battle .02 .10
276 Andrew Lang .02 .10
277 David Robinson .08 .25
278 Harold Miner RC .02 .10
279 Tracy Murray RC .02 .10
280 Pooh Richardson .02 .10
281 Dikembe Mutombo .07 .20
282 Wayman Tisdale .02 .10
283 Larry Johnson .07 .20
284 Todd Day RC .02 .10
285 Stanley Roberts .02 .10
286 Randy Woods UER RC .02 .10
287 Avery Johnson .02 .10
288 Anthony Peeler RC .02 .10
289 Mario Elie .02 .10
290 Doc Rivers .02 .10
291 Blue Edwards .02 .10
292 Sean Rooks RC .02 .10
293 Xavier McDaniel .02 .10
294 C.Weatherspoon RC .05 .15
295 Morlon Wiley .02 .10
296 LaBradford Smith .02 .10
297 Reggie Lewis .02 .10
298 Chris Mullin .05 .15
299 Litterial Green RC .02 .10
300 Elmore Spencer RC .02 .10
301 John Stockton .05 .15
302 Walt Williams RC .05 .15
303 Anthony Pullard RC .02 .10
304 Gundars Vetra RC .02 .10
305 LaSalle Thompson .02 .10
306 Nate McMillan .02 .10
307 Steve Bardo RC .02 .10
308 Robert Horry RC .05 .15
309 Scott Williams .02 .10
310 Bo Kimble .02 .10
311 Tree Rollins .02 .10
312 Tim Perry .02 .10
313 Isaac Austin RC .02 .10
314 Tate George .02 .10
315 Kevin Lynch .02 .10
316 Victor Alexander .02 .10
317 Doug Overton .02 .10
318 Tom Hammonds .02 .10
319 LaPhonso Ellis RC .05 .15
320 Scott Brooks .02 .10
321 Anthony Avent UER RC .02 .10
322 Matt Geiger RC .02 .10
323 Duane Causwell .02 .10
324 Horace Grant .02 .10
325 Mark Jackson .02 .10
326 Dan Majerle .02 .10
327 Chuck Person .02 .10
328 Buck Johnson .02 .10
329 Duane Cooper RC .02 .10
330 Rod Strickland .05 .15
331 Isiah Thomas .05 .15
332 Greg Kite .02 .10
333 Don MacLean RC .02 .10
334 Christian Laettner RC .10 .30
335 John Crotty RC .02 .10
336 Tracy Moore RC .02 .10
337 Hakeem Olajuwon .08 .25
338 Byron Houston RC .02 .10
339 Walter Bond RC .02 .10
340 Brent Price RC .02 .10
341 Bryant Stith RC .02 .10
342 Will Perdue .02 .10
343 Jeff Hornacek .02 .10
344 Adam Keefe RC .02 .10
345 Rafael Addison .02 .10
346 Marlon Maxey RC .02 .10
347 Joe Dumars .05 .15
348 Jon Barry RC .02 .10
349 Marty Conlon .02 .10
350 Alaa Abdelnaby .02 .10
351 Micheal Williams .02 .10
352 Brad Daugherty .02 .10
353 Tony Bennett RC .02 .10
354 Clyde Drexler .05 .15
355 Rolando Blackman .02 .10
356 Tom Tolbert .02 .10
357 Sarunas Marciulionis .02 .10
358 Jaren Jackson RC .02 .10
359 Stacey King .02 .10
360 Danny Ainge .02 .10
361 Dale Ellis .02 .10
362 Shaquille O'Neal RC 3.00 8.00
363 Bob McCann RC .02 .10
364 Reggie Smith RC .02 .10
365 Vinny Del Negro .02 .10
366 Robert Pack .02 .10
367 David Wood .02 .10
368 Rodney McCray .02 .10
369 Terry Mills .02 .10
370 Eric Murdock UER .02 .10
371 Alex Blackwell RC .02 .10
372 Jay Humphries .02 .10
373 Eddie Lee Wilkins .02 .10
374 James Edwards .02 .10
375 Tim Kempton .02 .10
376 J.R. Reid .02 .10
377 Sam Mack RC .02 .10
378 Donald Royal .02 .10
379 Mark Price .02 .10
380 Mark Acres .02 .10
381 Hubert Davis RC .02 .10
382 Dave Johnson RC .02 .10
383 John Salley .02 .10
384 Eddie Johnson .02 .10
385 Brian Howard RC .02 .10
386 Isaiah Morris RC .02 .10
387 Frank Johnson UER .02 .10
388 Rick Mahorn .02 .10
389 Scottie Pippen .20 .50
390 Lee Mayberry RC .02 .10
391 Tony Campbell .02 .10
392 Latrell Sprewell RC .50 1.25
393 Alonzo Mourning RC .40 1.00
394 Robert Werdann RC .02 .10
395 Checklist 199-297 UER .02 .10
396 Checklist 298-396 .04 .10

1992-93 Topps Gold

COMPLETE SET (396) 20.00 50.00
COMPLETE FACT.SET (403) 20.00 50.00
COMPLETE SERIES 1 (198) 8.00 20.00

COMPLETE SERIES 2 (198)	15.00	40.00
*STARS: 2X TO 5X BASE CARD HI		
*RCs: 1.25X TO 3X BASE HI		
ONE PER PACK		
197 Jeff Sanders	.20	.50
198 Elliot Perry UER	.20	.50
395 David Wingate	.20	.50
396 Carl Herrera	.20	.50

1992-93 Topps Beam Team

Comprised of some of the NBA's biggest stars, the Topps Beam Team set contains seven standard size cards. Inserted in 15-card second series packs at a ratio of one in 18, these special "Topps Beam Team" bonus cards commemorate Topps' 1993 sponsorship of a six-minute NBA laser animation show. Called Beams Above the Rim, the show premiered at the NBA All-Star Game on Feb. 21. Afterwards, the laser show embarked on a ten-city tour and was featured in either the pre-game or half-time events in ten NBA arenas. Three players are featured on each Topps Beam Team card. The horizontal fronts display three color action player photos on a dark blue background with a grid of brightly colored light beams. The set title "Beam Team" appears in pastel green block lettering across the top. The backs carry three light blue panels, with a close-up color photo, biography, and player profile on each panel.

COMPLETE SET (7)	5.00	10.00
SER.2 STATED ODDS 1:18		
*GOLD: 1.5X TO 4X HI COLUMN		
ONE GOLD BT SET PER GOLD FACTORY SET		
1 R.Miller/Barkley/Drexler	.40	1.00
2 Ewing/T.Hard/Hornacek	.40	1.00
3 K.Johnson/Jordan/Rodman	2.00	5.00
4 Wilkins/Stockton/K.Malon	.40	1.00
5 Olajuwon/M.Price/Kemp	.50	1.25
6 Pippen/D.Robinson/J.Malone	.50	1.25
7 Mullin/O'Neal/Rice	2.00	5.00

1993-94 Topps

The complete 1993-94 Topps basketball set consists of 396 standard-size cards issued in two 198-card series. Cards were issued in 12, 15 and 29-card packs. Factory sets contain 410 cards including 10 Gold, three Black Gold and one Finest Redemption card. The Finest Redemption card enabled a collector to mail away for two random Finest cards. The redemption deadline was July 31, 1994. The white bordered fronts display color action player photos with a team color coded inner border. The player's name is printed in white script at the lower left corner with the team name appearing on a team color coded bar at the very bottom. The horizontal backs carry a close-up player photo on the right with complete NBA statistics, biography, and career highlights on the left on a beige panel. Subsets featured are Highlights (1-5), 50 Point Club (50, 57, 64), Topps All-Star 1st Team (100-104), Topps All-Star 2nd Team (115-119), Topps All-Star 3rd Team (130-134), Topps All-Rookie 1st Team (150-154), Topps All-Rookie 2nd Team (175-179), Future Playoff MVP's (199-209) and Future Scoring Leaders (384-394). Rookie Cards of note in this set include Vin Baker, Anfernee Hardaway, Allan Houston, Jamal Mashburn, Nick Van Exel and Chris Webber.

COMPLETE SET (396)	10.00	20.00
COMPLETE FACT.SET (410)	12.50	25.00
COMPLETE SERIES 1 (198)	5.00	10.00
COMPLETE SERIES 2 (198)	5.00	10.00
SUBSET CARDS SAME VALUE AS BASE CARDS		
1 Charles Barkley HL	.15	.40
2 Hakeem Olajuwon HL	.12	.30
3 Shaquille O'Neal HL	.40	1.00
4 Chris Jackson HL	.05	.15
5 Clifford Robinson HL	.05	.15
6 Donald Hodge	.05	.15
7 Victor Alexander	.05	.15
8 Chris Morris	.05	.15
9 Muggsy Bogues	.07	.20
10 Steve Smith UER	.07	.20
11 Dave Johnson	.05	.15
12 Tom Gugliotta	.07	.20
13 Doug Edwards RC	.15	.40
14 Vlade Divac	.10	.25
15 Corie Blount RC	.15	.40
16 Derek Harper	.07	.20
17 Matt Bullard	.05	.15
18 Terry Catledge	.05	.15
19 Mark Eaton	.05	.15
20 Mark Jackson	.07	.20
21 Terry Mills	.05	.15
22 Johnny Dawkins	.05	.15
23 Michael Jordan UER	.75	2.00
24 Rick Fox UER	.05	.15
25 Charles Oakley	.07	.20
26 Derrick McKey	.05	.15
27 Christian Laettner	.07	.20
28 Todd Day	.05	.15
29 Danny Ferry	.05	.15
30 Kevin Johnson	.10	.25
31 Vinny Del Negro	.05	.15
32 Kevin Brooks	.05	.15
33 Pete Chilcutt	.05	.15
34 Larry Stewart	.05	.15
35 Dave Jamerson	.05	.15
36 Sidney Green	.05	.15
37 J.R. Reid	.05	.15
38 Jim Jackson	.07	.20
39 Micheal Williams UER	.05	.15
40 Rex Walters RC	.15	.40
41 Shawn Bradley RC	.15	.40
42 Jon Koncak	.05	.15
43 Byron Houston	.05	.15
44 Brian Shaw	.05	.15
45 Bill Cartwright	.07	.20
46 Jerome Kersey	.05	.15
47 Danny Schayes	.05	.15
48 Olden Polynice	.05	.15
49 Anthony Peeler	.05	.15
50 Nick Anderson 50P	.05	.15
51 David Benoit	.05	.15
52 David Robinson 50P	.15	.40
53 Greg Kite	.05	.15
54 Gerald Paddio	.05	.15
55 Don MacLean	.05	.15
56 Randy Woods	.05	.15
57 Reggie Miller 50P	.12	.30
58 Kevin Gamble	.05	.15
59 Sean Green	.05	.15
60 Jeff Hornacek	.07	.20
61 John Starks	.07	.20
62 Gerald Wilkins	.05	.15
63 Jim Les	.05	.15
64 Michael Jordan 50P	.75	2.00
65 Alvin Robertson	.05	.15
66 Tim Kempton	.05	.15
67 Bryant Stith	.05	.15
68 Jeff Turner	.05	.15
69 Malik Sealy	.05	.15
70 Dell Curry	.05	.15
71 Brent Price	.05	.15
72 Kevin Lynch	.05	.15
73 Bimbo Coles	.05	.15
74 Larry Nance	.07	.20
75 Luther Wright RC	.15	.40
76 Willie Anderson	.05	.15
77 Dennis Rodman	.20	.50
78 Anthony Mason	.05	.15
79 Chris Gatling	.05	.15
80 Antoine Carr	.05	.15
81 Kevin Willis	.05	.15
82 Thurl Bailey	.05	.15
83 Reggie Williams	.05	.15
84 Rod Strickland	.05	.15
85 Rolando Blackman	.07	.20
86 Bobby Hurley RC	.15	.40
87 Jeff Malone	.05	.15
88 James Worthy	.12	.30
89 Alaa Abdelnaby	.05	.15
90 Duane Ferrell	.05	.15
91 Anthony Avent	.05	.15
92 Scottie Pippen	.20	.50
93 Ricky Pierce	.05	.15
94 P.J. Brown RC	.15	.40
95 Jeff Grayer	.05	.15
96 Jerrod Mustaf	.05	.15
97 Elmore Spencer	.05	.15
98 Walt Williams	.05	.15
99 Otis Thorpe	.05	.15
100 Patrick Ewing AS	.12	.30
101 Michael Jordan AS	.75	2.00
102 John Stockton AS	.12	.30
103 Dominique Wilkins AS	.12	.30
104 Charles Barkley AS	.15	.40
105 Lee Mayberry	.05	.15
106 James Edwards	.05	.15
107 Scott Brooks	.05	.15
108 John Battle	.05	.15
109 Kenny Gattison	.05	.15
110 Pooh Richardson	.05	.15
111 Rony Seikaly	.05	.15
112 Mahmoud Abdul-Rauf	.05	.15
113 Nick Anderson	.05	.15
114 Gundars Vetra	.05	.15
115 Joe Dumars AS	.10	.25
116 Hakeem Olajuwon AS	.12	.30
117 Scottie Pippen AS	.20	.50
118 Mark Price AS	.10	.25
119 Karl Malone AS	.12	.30
120 Michael Cage	.05	.15
121 Ed Pinckney	.05	.15
122 Jay Humphries	.05	.15
123 Dale Davis	.05	.15
124 Sean Rooks	.05	.15
125 Mookie Blaylock	.05	.15
126 Buck Williams	.05	.15
127 John Williams	.05	.15
128 Stacey King	.05	.15
129 Tim Perry	.05	.15
130 Tim Hardaway AS	.10	.25
131 Larry Johnson AS	.10	.25
132 Detlef Schrempf AS	.10	.25
133 Reggie Miller AS	.12	.30
134 Shaquille O'Neal AS	.40	1.00
135 Dale Ellis	.05	.15
136 Duane Causwell	.05	.15
137 Rumeal Robinson	.05	.15
138 Billy Owens	.05	.15
139 Malcolm Mackey RC	.15	.40
140 Vernon Maxwell	.05	.15
141 LaPhonso Ellis	.05	.15
142 Robert Parish	.10	.25
143 LaBradford Smith	.05	.15
144 Charles Smith	.05	.15
145 Terry Porter	.05	.15
146 Elden Campbell	.05	.15
147 Bill Laimbeer	.07	.20
148 Chris Mills RC	.15	.40
149 Brad Lohaus	.05	.15
150 Jim Jackson ART	.07	.20
151 Tom Gugliotta ART	.07	.20
152 Shaquille O'Neal ART	.40	1.00
153 Latrell Sprewell ART	.15	.40
154 Walt Williams ART	.05	.15
155 Gary Payton	.12	.30
156 Orlando Woolridge	.05	.15
157 Adam Keefe	.05	.15
158 Calbert Cheaney RC	.15	.40
159 Rick Mahorn	.05	.15
160 Robert Horry	.10	.25
161 John Salley	.05	.15
162 Sam Mitchell	.05	.15
163 Stanley Roberts	.05	.15
164 Clarence Weatherspoon	.05	.15
165 Anthony Bowie	.05	.15
166 Derrick Coleman	.07	.20
167 Negele Knight	.05	.15
168 Marlon Maxey	.05	.15
169 Spud Webb UER	.07	.20
170 Alonzo Mourning	.15	.40
171 Ervin Johnson RC	.15	.40
172 Sedale Threatt	.05	.15
173 Mark Macon	.05	.15
174 B.J. Armstrong	.05	.15
175 Harold Miner ART	.05	.15
176 Anthony Peeler ART	.05	.15
177 Alonzo Mourning ART	.15	.40
178 Christian Laettner ART	.07	.20
179 Clarence Weatherspoon ART	.05	.15
180 Dee Brown	.05	.15
181 Shaquille O'Neal	.40	1.00
182 Loy Vaught	.05	.15
183 Terrell Brandon	.07	.20
184 Lionel Simmons	.05	.15
185 Mark Aguirre	.07	.20
186 Danny Ainge	.10	.25
187 Reggie Miller	.12	.30
188 Terry Davis	.05	.15
189 Mark Bryant	.05	.15
190 Tyrone Corbin	.05	.15
191 Chris Mullin	.10	.25
192 Johnny Newman	.05	.15
193 Doug West	.05	.15
194 Keith Askins	.05	.15
195 Bo Kimble	.05	.15
196 Sean Elliott	.10	.25
197 Checklist 1-99 UER	.05	.15
198 Checklist 100-198	.05	.15
199 Michael Jordan FPM	.75	2.00
200 Patrick Ewing FPM	.12	.30
201 John Stockton FPM	.12	.30
202 Shawn Kemp FPM	.12	.30
203 Mark Price FPM	.10	.25
204 Charles Barkley FPM	.15	.40
205 Hakeem Olajuwon FPM	.12	.30
206 Clyde Drexler FPM	.12	.30
207 Kevin Johnson FPM	.10	.25
208 John Starks FPM	.07	.20
209 Chris Mullin FPM	.10	.25
210 Doc Rivers	.07	.20
211 Kenny Walker	.05	.15
212 Doug Christie	.05	.15
213 James Robinson RC	.15	.40
214 Larry Krystkowiak	.05	.15
215 Manute Bol	.05	.15
216 Carl Herrera	.05	.15
217 Paul Graham	.05	.15
218 Jud Buechler	.05	.15
219 Mike Brown	.05	.15
220 Tom Chambers	.07	.20
221 Kendall Gill	.05	.15
222 Kenny Anderson	.07	.20
223 Larry Johnson	.10	.25
224 Chris Webber RC	.75	2.00
225 Randy White	.05	.15
226 Rik Smits	.07	.20
227 A.C. Green	.07	.20
228 David Robinson	.15	.40
229 Sean Elliott	.10	.25
230 Gary Grant	.05	.15
231 Dana Barros	.05	.15
232 Bobby Hurley	.10	.25
233 Blue Edwards	.05	.15
234 Tom Hammonds	.05	.15
235 Pete Myers UER	.05	.15
236 Acie Earl RC	.15	.40
237 Tony Smith	.05	.15
238 Bill Wennington	.05	.15
239 Andrew Lang	.05	.15
240 Ervin Johnson	.10	.25
241 Byron Scott	.10	.25
242 Eddie Johnson	.05	.15
243 Anthony Bonner	.05	.15
244 Luther Wright	.10	.25
245 LaSalle Thompson	.05	.15
246 Harold Miner	.05	.15
247 Chris Smith	.05	.15
248 John Williams	.05	.15
249 Clyde Drexler	.12	.30
250 Calbert Cheaney	.10	.25
251 Avery Johnson	.07	.20
252 Steve Kerr	.07	.20
253 Warren Kidd RC	.15	.40
254 Wayman Tisdale	.05	.15
255 Bob Martin RC	.15	.40
256 Popeye Jones RC	.15	.40
257 Jimmy Oliver	.05	.15
258 Kevin Edwards	.05	.15
259 Dan Majerle	.10	.25
260 Jon Barry	.05	.15
261 Allan Houston RC	.30	.75
262 Dikembe Mutombo	.10	.25
263 Sleepy Floyd	.05	.15
264 George Lynch RC	.15	.40
265 Stacey Augmon UER	.07	.20
266 Hakeem Olajuwon	.12	.30
267 Scott Skiles	.05	.15
268 Detlef Schrempf	.10	.25
269 Brian Davis RC	.15	.40
270 Tracy Murray	.05	.15
271 Gheorghe Muresan RC	.15	.40
272 Terry Dehere RC	.15	.40
273 Terry Cummings	.07	.20
274 Keith Jennings	.05	.15
275 Tyrone Hill	.05	.15
276 Hersey Hawkins	.05	.15
277 Grant Long	.05	.15
278 Herb Williams	.05	.15
279 Karl Malone	.12	.30
280 Mitch Richmond	.10	.25
281 Derek Strong RC	.15	.40
282 Dino Radja RC	.15	.40
283 Jack Haley	.05	.15
284 Derek Harper	.07	.20
285 Dwayne Schintzius	.05	.15
286 Michael Curry RC	.15	.40
287 Rodney Rogers RC	.15	.40
288 Horace Grant	.07	.20
289 Oliver Miller	.05	.15
290 Luc Longley	.07	.20
291 Walter Bond	.05	.15
292 Dominique Wilkins	.12	.30
293 Vern Fleming	.05	.15
294 Mark Price	.10	.25
295 Mark Aguirre	.07	.20
296 Shawn Kemp	.12	.30
297 Pervis Ellison	.05	.15
298 Josh Grant RC	.15	.40
299 Scott Burrell RC	.15	.40
300 Patrick Ewing	.12	.30
301 Sam Cassell RC	.30	.75
302 Nick Van Exel RC	.30	.75
303 Clifford Robinson	.05	.15
304 Frank Johnson	.05	.15
305 Matt Geiger	.05	.15
306 Vin Baker RC	.25	.60
307 Benoit Benjamin	.05	.15
308 Shawn Bradley	.10	.25
309 Chris Whitney RC	.15	.40
310 Eric Riley RC	.15	.40
311 Isiah Thomas	.10	.25
312 Jamal Mashburn RC	.25	.60
313 Xavier McDaniel	.05	.15
314 Mike Peplowski RC	.15	.40
315 Darnell Mee RC	.15	.40
316 Toni Kukoc RC	.40	1.00
317 Felton Spencer	.05	.15
318 Sam Bowie	.05	.15
319 Mario Elie	.05	.15
320 Tim Hardaway	.10	.25
321 Ken Norman	.05	.15
322 Isaiah Rider RC	.25	.60
323 Rex Chapman	.05	.15
324 Dennis Rodman	.20	.50
325 Derrick McKey	.05	.15
326 Corie Blount	.10	.25
327 Fat Lever	.07	.20
328 Ron Harper	.07	.20
329 Eric Anderson	.05	.15
330 Armon Gilliam	.05	.15
331 Lindsey Hunter RC	.15	.40
332 Eric Leckner	.05	.15
333 Chris Corchiani	.05	.15
334 Anfernee Hardaway RC	.75	2.00
335 Randy Brown	.05	.15
336 Sam Perkins	.05	.15
337 Glen Rice	.10	.25
338 Orlando Woolridge	.05	.15
339 Mike Gminski	.05	.15
340 Latrell Sprewell	.15	.40
341 Harvey Grant	.05	.15
342 Doug Smith	.05	.15
343 Kevin Duckworth	.05	.15
344 Cedric Ceballos	.07	.20
345 Chuck Person	.07	.20
346 Scott Haskin RC	.15	.40
347 Frank Brickowski	.05	.15
348 Scott Williams	.05	.15
349 Brad Daugherty	.07	.20
350 Willie Burton	.05	.15
351 Joe Dumars	.10	.25
352 Craig Ehlo	.05	.15
353 Lucious Harris RC	.15	.40
354 Danny Manning	.07	.20
355 Litterial Green	.05	.15
356 John Stockton	.12	.30
357 Nate McMillan	.05	.15
358 Greg Graham RC	.15	.40
359 Rex Walters	.10	.25
360 Lloyd Daniels	.05	.15
361 Antonio Harvey RC	.15	.40
362 Brian Williams	.05	.15
363 LeRon Ellis	.05	.15
364 Chris Dudley	.05	.15
365 Hubert Davis	.05	.15
366 Evers Burns RC	.15	.40
367 Sherman Douglas	.05	.15
368 Sarunas Marciulionis	.05	.15
369 Tom Tolbert	.05	.15
370 Robert Pack	.05	.15
371 Michael Adams	.05	.15
372 Negele Knight	.05	.15
373 Charles Barkley	.15	.40
374 Bryon Russell RC	.15	.40
375 Greg Anthony	.05	.15
376 Ken Williams	.05	.15
377 John Paxson	.07	.20
378 Corey Gaines	.05	.15
379 Eric Murdock	.05	.15
380 Kevin Thompson RC	.15	.40
381 Moses Malone	.10	.25
382 Kenny Smith	.07	.20
383 Dennis Scott	.05	.15
384 Michael Jordan FSL	.75	2.00
385 Hakeem Olajuwon FSL	.12	.30
386 Shaquille O'Neal FSL	.40	1.00
387 David Robinson FSL	.15	.40
388 Derrick Coleman FSL	.07	.20
389 Karl Malone FSL	.12	.30
390 Patrick Ewing FSL	.12	.30
391 Scottie Pippen FSL	.20	.50
392 Dominique Wilkins FSL	.12	.30
393 Charles Barkley FSL	.15	.40
394 Larry Johnson FSL	.10	.25
395 Checklist	.05	.15
396 Checklist	.05	.15
NNO Expired Finest Redempt.	.40	1.00

1993-94 Topps Gold

COMPLETE SET (396)	30.00	70.00
COMPLETE SERIES 1 (198)	12.00	30.00
COMPLETE SERIES 2 (198)	15.00	40.00
*STARS: 1X TO 2.5X BASE CARD HI		
*RCs: .6X TO 1.5X BASE HI		
ONE PER PACK		
23 Michael Jordan UER	4.00	10.00
197 Frank Johnson	.15	.40
198 David Wingate	.15	.40
395 Will Perdue	.15	.40
396 Mark West	.15	.40

1993-94 Topps Black Gold

Randomly inserted in first and second series packs and three per factory set, this 25-card standard size set features the top five draft picks each year from 1989-1993. Thirteen cards were inserts in series one and 12 in series two. They were inserted at a rate of one in 72 for 12-card packs and one in 18 for 29-card packs. Winner A cards, redeemable for a series 1 set, were randomly inserted into 1 in every 144 series 1 packs. Winner B cards, redeemable for a series 2 set, were randomly inserted into 1 in every 144 series 2 packs. The A/B Winner card (randomly inserted into 1 in every 288 series 2 packs only) was redeemable for a complete set. Each white-bordered front displays a color action player shot with the background tinted in black. Gold prismatic wavy stripes appear above and below the photo with the player's name reversed out of the black bar near the bottom. The white-bordered horizontal backs carry a close-up color cutout on a black background with white concentric stripes. The player's name appears in gold-foil lettering on a wood textured bar with the team name directly to the right in black lettering. Player statistics appear below in an orange background.

COMPLETE SET (25)	8.00	20.00
COMPLETE SERIES 1 (13)	2.00	5.00
COMPLETE SERIES 2 (12)	6.00	15.00
SER.1/2 STATED ODDS 1:72 HOB/RET		
SER.1/2 STATED ODDS 1:18 JUM/RACK		
1 Sean Elliott	.30	.75
2 Dennis Scott	.20	.50
3 Kenny Anderson	.25	.60
4 Alonzo Mourning	.50	1.25
5 Glen Rice	.30	.75
6 Billy Owens	.20	.50
7 Jim Jackson	.25	.60
8 Derrick Coleman	.25	.60
9 Larry Johnson	.30	.75
10 Gary Payton	.40	1.00
11 Christian Laettner	.25	.60
12 Dikembe Mutombo	.30	.75
13 Mahmoud Abdul-Rauf	.20	.50
14 Isaiah Rider	.60	1.50
15 Steve Smith	.25	.60
16 LaPhonso Ellis	.20	.50
17 Danny Ferry	.20	.50
18 Shaquille O'Neal	1.25	3.00
19 Anfernee Hardaway	2.00	5.00
20 J.R. Reid	.20	.50
21 Shawn Bradley	.40	1.00
22 Pervis Ellison	.20	.50
23 Chris Webber	2.00	5.00
24 Jamal Mashburn	.60	1.50
25 Kendall Gill	.15	.40
A1 Winner A 1-13 EXCH	2.00	5.00
A2 Winner A 1-13 Prize	.20	.50
B1 Winner B 14-25 EXCH	2.00	5.00
B2 Winner B 14-25 Prize	.20	.50
AB1 Winner AB 1-25 EXCH	3.00	8.00
AB2 Winner AB 1-25 Prize	.40	1.00

1994-95 Topps

The 396 standard-size cards that comprise the 1994-95 Topps set were issued in two separate series of 198 cards each. Cards were distributed primarily in 12-card packs that carried a suggested retail price of $1.00 each. Fronts feature full-color action photos framed by a jagged white border. Player's name and team are placed in gold foil along the bottom. The following subsets are included in this set: Eastern All-Star (1-13), Paint Patrol (100-109), and Western All-Star (183-195). In addition, various "From the Roof" subsets cards are intermingled within the set. Rookie Cards of note in this set include Grant Hill, Juwan Howard, Eddie Jones, Jason Kidd and Glenn Robinson.

COMPLETE SET (396)	12.50	25.00
COMPLETE SERIES 1 (198)	5.00	10.00
COMPLETE SERIES 2 (198)	7.50	15.00
1 Patrick Ewing AS	.15	.40
2 Mookie Blaylock AS	.07	.20
3 Charles Oakley AS	.10	.25
4 Mark Price AS	.12	.30
5 John Starks AS	.10	.25
6 Dominique Wilkins AS	.15	.40
7 Horace Grant AS	.10	.25
8 Alonzo Mourning AS	.15	.40
9 B.J. Armstrong AS	.07	.20
10 Kenny Anderson AS	.10	.25
11 Scottie Pippen AS	.25	.60
12 Derrick Coleman AS	.10	.25
13 Shaquille O'Neal AS	.30	.75
14 Anfernee Hardaway AS	.20	.50
15 Isaiah Rider SPEC	.12	.30
16 John Williams	.07	.20
17 Todd Day	.07	.20
18 Dale Davis	.07	.20
19 Sean Rooks	.07	.20
20 George Lynch	.07	.20
21 Mitchell Butler	.07	.20
22 Stacey King	.07	.20
23 Sherman Douglas	.07	.20
24 Derrick McKey	.07	.20
25 Joe Dumars	.12	.30
26 Scott Brooks	.07	.20
27 Clarence Weatherspoon	.07	.20
28 Jayson Williams	.07	.20
29 Scottie Pippen	.25	.60
30 John Starks	.10	.25
31 Robert Pack	.07	.20
32 Donald Royal	.07	.20
33 Haywoode Workman	.07	.20
34 Greg Graham	.07	.20
35 Terry Cummings	.10	.25
36 Andrew Lang	.07	.20
37 Jason Kidd RC	.60	1.50
38 Terry Mills	.07	.20
39 Alonzo Mourning	.15	.40
40 Shawn Kemp	.12	.30
41 Kevin Willis FTR	.07	.20
42 Kevin Willis	.07	.20
43 Armon Gilliam	.07	.20
44 Bobby Hurley	.07	.20
45 Jerome Kersey	.07	.20
46 Xavier McDaniel	.07	.20
47 Chris Webber	.20	.50
48 Chris Webber FTR	.20	.50
49 Jeff Malone	.07	.20
50 Dikembe Mutombo SPEC	.12	.30
51 Dan Majerle SPEC	.12	.30
52 Dee Brown SPEC	.07	.20
53 John Stockton SPEC	.15	.40
54 Dennis Rodman SPEC	.25	.60
55 Eric Murdock SPEC	.07	.20
56 Glen Rice	.12	.30
57 Glen Rice FTR	.12	.30
58 Dino Radja	.07	.20
59 Billy Owens	.07	.20
60 Doc Rivers	.10	.25
61 Don MacLean	.07	.20
62 Lindsey Hunter	.07	.20
63 Sam Cassell	.12	.30
64 James Worthy	.15	.40
65 Christian Laettner	.10	.25
66 Wesley Person RC	.12	.30
67 Rich King	.07	.20
68 Jon Koncak	.07	.20
69 Muggsy Bogues	.10	.25
70 Jamal Mashburn	.12	.30
71 Gary Grant	.07	.20
72 Eric Murdock	.07	.20
73 Scott Burrell	.07	.20
74 Scott Burrell FTR	.07	.20
75 Anfernee Hardaway	.20	.50
76 Anfernee Hardaway FTR	.20	.50
77 Yinka Dare RC	.07	.20
78 Anthony Avent	.07	.20
79 Jon Barry	.07	.20
80 Rodney Rogers	.07	.20
81 Chris Mills	.07	.20
82 Antonio Davis	.07	.20
83 Steve Smith	.10	.25
84 Buck Williams	.07	.20
85 Spud Webb	.10	.25
86 Stacey Augmon	.10	.25
87 Allan Houston	.12	.30
88 Will Perdue	.07	.20
89 Chris Gatling	.07	.20
90 Danny Ainge	.12	.30
91 Rick Mahorn	.07	.20
92 Elmore Spencer	.07	.20
93 Vin Baker	.12	.30
94 Rex Chapman	.07	.20
95 Dale Ellis	.07	.20
96 Doug Smith	.07	.20
97 Tim Perry	.07	.20
98 Toni Kukoc	.15	.40
99 Terry Dehere	.07	.20
100 Shaquille O'Neal PP	.30	.75
101 Shawn Kemp PP	.12	.30
102 Hakeem Olajuwon PP	.15	.40
103 Derrick Coleman PP	.10	.25
104 Alonzo Mourning PP	.15	.40
105 Dikembe Mutombo PP	.12	.30
106 Chris Webber PP	.20	.50
107 Dennis Rodman PP	.25	.60
108 David Robinson PP	.20	.50
109 Charles Barkley PP	.20	.50
110 Brad Daugherty	.10	.25
111 Derek Harper	.10	.25
112 Detlef Schrempf	.12	.30
113 Harvey Grant	.07	.20
114 Vlade Divac	.12	.30
115 Isaiah Rider	.12	.30
116 Mitch Richmond	.12	.30
117 Tom Chambers	.10	.25
118 Kenny Gattison	.07	.20
119 Kenny Gattison FTR	.07	.20
120 Vernon Maxwell	.07	.20
121 Reggie Williams	.07	.20
122 Chris Mullin	.12	.30
123 Harold Miner	.07	.20
124 Harold Miner FTR	.07	.20
125 Calbert Cheaney	.07	.20
126 Randy Woods	.07	.20
127 Mike Gminski	.07	.20
128 Willie Anderson	.07	.20
129 Mark Macon	.07	.20
130 Avery Johnson	.10	.25
131 Bimbo Coles	.07	.20
132 Kenny Smith	.10	.25
133 Dennis Scott	.07	.20
134 Lionel Simmons	.07	.20
135 Nate McMillan	.07	.20
136 Eric Montross RC	.10	.25
137 Sedale Threatt	.07	.20
138 Kenny Anderson	.10	.25
139 Micheal Williams	.07	.20
140 Grant Long	.07	.20
141 Grant Long FTR	.07	.20
142 Tyrone Corbin	.07	.20
143 Craig Ehlo	.07	.20
144 Gerald Wilkins	.07	.20
145 LaPhonso Ellis	.07	.20
146 Reggie Miller	.15	.40
147 Tracy Murray	.07	.20
148 Victor Alexander	.07	.20
149 Victor Alexander FTR	.07	.20
150 Clifford Robinson	.07	.20
151 Anthony Mason FTR	.07	.20
152 Anthony Mason	.07	.20
153 Jim Jackson	.07	.20
154 Jeff Hornacek	.10	.25
155 Nick Anderson	.07	.20
156 Mike Brown	.07	.20
157 Kevin Johnson	.12	.30
158 John Paxson	.10	.25
159 Loy Vaught	.07	.20
160 Carl Herrera	.07	.20
161 Shawn Bradley	.07	.20
162 Hubert Davis	.07	.20
163 David Benoit	.07	.20
164 Dell Curry	.07	.20
165 Dee Brown	.07	.20
166 LaSalle Thompson	.07	.20
167 Eddie Jones RC	.40	1.00
168 Walt Williams	.07	.20
169 A.C. Green	.10	.25
170 Kendall Gill	.07	.20
171 Kendall Gill FTR	.07	.20
172 Danny Ferry	.07	.20
173 Bryant Stith	.07	.20
174 John Salley	.07	.20
175 Cedric Ceballos	.07	.20
176 Derrick Coleman	.10	.25
177 Tony Bennett	.07	.20
178 Kevin Duckworth	.07	.20
179 Jay Humphries	.07	.20
180 Sean Elliott	.12	.30
181 Sam Perkins	.07	.20
182 Luc Longley	.10	.25
183 Mitch Richmond AS	.12	.30
184 Clyde Drexler AS	.15	.40
185 Karl Malone AS	.15	.40
186 Shawn Kemp AS	.12	.30
187 Hakeem Olajuwon AS	.15	.40
188 Danny Manning AS	.10	.25
189 Kevin Johnson AS	.12	.30
190 John Stockton AS	.15	.40
191 Latrell Sprewell AS	.15	.40
192 Gary Payton AS	.12	.30
193 Clifford Robinson AS	.07	.20
194 David Robinson AS	.20	.50
195 Charles Barkley AS	.20	.50
196 Mark Price SPEC	.12	.30
197 Checklist 1-99	.07	.20
198 Checklist 100-198	.07	.20
199 Patrick Ewing	.15	.40
200 Patrick Ewing FTR	.15	.40
201 Tracy Murray PP	.07	.20
202 Craig Ehlo PP	.07	.20
203 Nick Anderson PP	.07	.20
204 John Starks PP	.10	.25
205 Rex Chapman PP	.07	.20
206 Hersey Hawkins PP	.07	.20
207 Glen Rice PP	.12	.30
208 Jeff Malone PP	.07	.20
209 Dan Majerle PP	.12	.30
210 Chris Mullin PP	.12	.30
211 Grant Hill RC	.60	1.50
212 Bobby Phills	.07	.20
213 Dennis Rodman	.25	.60
214 Doug West	.07	.20
215 Harold Ellis	.07	.20
216 Kevin Edwards	.07	.20
217 Lorenzo Williams	.07	.20
218 Rick Fox	.07	.20
219 Mookie Blaylock	.07	.20
220 Mookie Blaylock FTR	.07	.20
221 John Williams	.07	.20
222 Keith Jennings	.07	.20
223 Nick Van Exel	.12	.30
224 Gary Payton	.12	.30
225 John Stockton	.15	.40
226 Ron Harper	.10	.25
227 Monty Williams RC	.10	.25
228 Marty Conlon	.07	.20
229 Hersey Hawkins	.07	.20
230 Rik Smits	.10	.25
231 James Robinson	.07	.20
232 Malik Sealy	.07	.20
233 Sergei Bazarevich RC	.12	.30
234 Brad Lohaus	.07	.20
235 Olden Polynice	.07	.20
236 Brian Williams	.07	.20
237 Tyrone Hill	.07	.20
238 Jim McIlvaine RC	.10	.25
239 Latrell Sprewell	.15	.40
240 Latrell Sprewell FTR	.15	.40
241 Popeye Jones	.07	.20
242 Scott Williams	.07	.20
243 Eddie Jones	.20	.50
244 Moses Malone	.12	.30
245 B.J. Armstrong	.07	.20
246 Jim Les	.07	.20
247 Greg Grant	.07	.20
248 Lee Mayberry	.07	.20
249 Mark Jackson	.10	.25
250 Larry Johnson	.12	.30
251 Terrell Brandon	.07	.20
252 Ledell Eackles	.07	.20
253 Yinka Dare	.07	.20
254 Dontonio Wingfield RC	.12	.30
255 Clyde Drexler	.15	.40
256 Andres Guibert	.07	.20
257 Gheorghe Muresan	.07	.20
258 Tom Hammonds	.07	.20
259 Charles Barkley	.20	.50
260 Charles Barkley FTR	.20	.50
261 Acie Earl	.07	.20
262 Lamond Murray RC	.12	.30
263 Dana Barros	.07	.20
264 Greg Anthony	.07	.20
265 Dan Majerle	.12	.30
266 Zan Tabak	.07	.20
267 Ricky Pierce	.07	.20
268 Eric Leckner	.07	.20
269 Duane Ferrell	.07	.20
270 Mark Price	.12	.30
271 Anthony Peeler	.07	.20
272 Adam Keefe	.07	.20
273 Rex Walters	.07	.20
274 Scott Skiles	.07	.20
275 Glenn Robinson RC	.25	.60
276 Tony Dumas RC	.12	.30
277 Elliot Perry	.07	.20
278 Bo Outlaw RC	.12	.30
279 Karl Malone	.15	.40
280 Karl Malone FTR	.15	.40
281 Herb Williams	.07	.20
282 Vincent Askew	.07	.20
283 Askia Jones RC	.12	.30
284 Shawn Bradley	.07	.20
285 Tim Hardaway	.12	.30
286 Mark West	.07	.20
287 Chuck Person	.10	.25
288 James Edwards	.07	.20
289 Antonio Lang RC	.12	.30
290 Dominique Wilkins	.15	.40
291 Khalid Reeves RC	.10	.25
292 Jamie Watson RC	.07	.20
293 Darnell Mee	.07	.20
294 Brian Grant RC	.20	.50
295 Hakeem Olajuwon	.15	.40
296 Dickey Simpkins RC	.10	.25
297 Tyrone Corbin	.07	.20
298 David Wingate	.07	.20
299 Shaquille O'Neal	.30	.75
300 Shaquille O'Neal FR	.30	.75
301 B.J. Armstrong PP	.07	.20
302 Mitch Richmond PP	.12	.30
303 Jim Jackson PP	.07	.20
304 Jeff Hornacek PP	.10	.25
305 Mark Price PP	.12	.30
306 Kendall Gill PP	.07	.20
307 Dale Ellis PP	.07	.20
308 Vernon Maxwell PP	.07	.20
309 Joe Dumars PP	.12	.30
310 Reggie Miller PP	.15	.40
311 Geert Hammink	.07	.20
312 Charles Smith	.07	.20
313 Bill Cartwright	.10	.25
314 Aaron McKie RC	.12	.30
315 Tom Gugliotta	.07	.20
316 P.J. Brown	.07	.20
317 David Wesley	.07	.20
318 Felton Spencer	.07	.20
319 Robert Horry	.12	.30
320 Robert Horry FR	.12	.30
321 Larry Krystkowiak	.07	.20
322 Eric Piatkowski RC	.15	.40
323 Anthony Bonner	.07	.20
324 Keith Askins	.07	.20
325 Mahmoud Abdul-Rauf	.07	.20
326 Darrin Hancock RC	.10	.25
327 Vern Fleming	.07	.20
328 Wayman Tisdale	.07	.20
329 Sam Bowie	.07	.20
330 Billy Owens	.07	.20
331 Donald Hodge	.07	.20
332 Derrick Alston RC	.07	.20
333 Doug Edwards	.07	.20
334 Johnny Newman	.07	.20
335 Otis Thorpe	.07	.20
336 Bill Curley RC	.07	.20
337 Michael Cage	.07	.20
338 Chris Smith	.07	.20
339 Dikembe Mutombo	.12	.30
340 Dikembe Mutombo FTR	.12	.30
341 Duane Causwell	.07	.20
342 Sean Higgins	.07	.20
343 Steve Kerr	.10	.25
344 Eric Montross	.10	.25
345 Charles Oakley	.10	.25
346 Brooks Thompson RC	.10	.25
347 Rony Seikaly	.07	.20
348 Chris Dudley	.07	.20
349 Sharone Wright RC	.10	.25
350 Sarunas Marciulionis	.07	.20
351 Anthony Miller RC	.12	.30
352 Pooh Richardson	.07	.20
353 Byron Scott	.10	.25
354 Michael Adams	.07	.20
355 Ken Norman	.07	.20
356 Clifford Rozier RC	.07	.20
357 Tim Breaux	.07	.20
358 Derek Strong	.07	.20
359 David Robinson	.20	.50
360 David Robinson FR	.20	.50
361 Benoit Benjamin	.07	.20
362 Terry Porter	.07	.20
363 Ervin Johnson	.07	.20
364 Alaa Abdelnaby	.07	.20
365 Robert Parish	.12	.30
366 Mario Elie	.07	.20
367 Antonio Harvey	.07	.20
368 Charlie Ward RC	.12	.30
369 Kevin Gamble	.07	.20
370 Rod Strickland	.07	.20
371 Jason Kidd	.30	.75
372 Oliver Miller	.07	.20
373 Eric Mobley RC	.07	.20
374 Brian Shaw	.07	.20
375 Horace Grant	.10	.25
376 Corie Blount	.07	.20
377 Sam Mitchell	.07	.20
378 Jalen Rose RC	.30	.75
379 Elden Campbell	.07	.20
380 Elden Campbell FTR	.07	.20
381 Donyell Marshall RC	.12	.30
382 Frank Brickowski	.07	.20
383 B.J. Tyler RC	.07	.20
384 Bryon Russell	.07	.20
385 Danny Manning	.10	.25
386 Manute Bol	.07	.20
387 Brent Price	.07	.20
388 J.R. Reid	.07	.20
389 Byron Houston	.07	.20
390 Blue Edwards	.07	.20
391 Adrian Caldwell	.07	.20
392 Wesley Person	.12	.30
393 Juwan Howard RC	.20	.50
394 Chris Morris	.07	.20
395 Checklist 199-296	.07	.20
396 Checklist 297-396	.07	.20

1994-95 Topps Spectralight

COMPLETE SET (396)	125.00	250.00
COMPLETE SERIES 1 (198)	50.00	100.00
COMPLETE SERIES 2 (198)	75.00	150.00
*SPECT: 2X TO 5X BASE CARD HI		
SER.1/2 STATED ODDS 1:4		
37 Jason Kidd	6.00	15.00
197 Keith Jennings	.40	1.00
198 Mark Price	.60	1.50
211 Grant Hill	4.00	10.00
371 Jason Kidd	4.00	10.00
395 Chris Webber	15.00	40.00
396 Mitch Richmond	4.00	10.00

1994-95 Topps Franchise/Futures

Randomly inserted into all second series packs at a rate of one in 18, cards from this 20-card set feature a selection of promising youngsters coupled with established stars from the same team. Card fronts feature full-color action shots surrounded by a white border.

COMPLETE SET (20)	8.00	20.00
SER.2 STATED ODDS 1:18		
1 Mookie Blaylock	.30	.75
2 Stacey Augmon	.40	1.00
3 Dominique Wilkins	.60	1.50
4 Eric Montross	.40	1.00
5 Dikembe Mutombo	.50	1.25
6 Jalen Rose	1.25	3.00
7 Joe Dumars	.50	1.25
8 Grant Hill	2.50	6.00
9 Chris Mullin	.50	1.25
10 Latrell Sprewell	.60	1.50
11 Glen Rice	.50	1.25
12 Khalid Reeves	.40	1.00
13 Derrick Coleman	.40	1.00
14 Yinka Dare	.30	.75
15 Patrick Ewing	.60	1.50
16 Monty Williams	.40	1.00
17 Shaquille O'Neal	2.00	5.00
18 Anfernee Hardaway	.75	2.00
19 Charles Barkley	.75	2.00
20 Wesley Person	.50	1.25

1994-95 Topps Own the Game

Randomly inserted in all first series packs (12-card packs one in 18, jumbo packs one in 9), cards from this 50-card standard-size unnumbered set featured nine top players in five different statistical categories (Super Passers, Super Rebounders, Super Scorers, Super Stealers and Super Swatters) in addition to five Field Cards. If the player pictured on the card (Field Card represented all other players in the league) led the league in that respective category, it became redeemable for a special 10-card Own the Game redemption set for that category.

COMPLETE SET (50) 15.00 40.00
SER.1 STATED ODDS 1:18
1 Kenny Anderson PASS .40 1.00
2 Charles Barkley SCORE .75 2.00
3 Mookie Blaylock PASS .30 .75
4 Mookie Blaylock STEAL .30 .75
5 Muggsy Bogues PASS .40 1.00
6 Shawn Bradley SWAT .30 .75
7 Derrick Coleman REB .40 1.00
8 Sherman Douglas PASS .30 .75
9 Patrick Ewing REB .60 1.50
10 Patrick Ewing SCORE .60 1.50
11 Patrick Ewing SWAT .60 1.50
12 Tom Gugliotta STEAL .30 .75
13 Anfernee Hardaway STEAL .75 2.00
14 Mark Jackson PASS .40 1.00
15 Kevin Johnson PASS .50 1.25
16 Karl Malone REB .60 1.50
17 Karl Malone SCORE .60 1.50
18 Nate McMillan STEAL .30 .75
19 Oliver Miller SWAT .30 .75
20 Alonzo Mourning SWAT .60 1.50
21 Eric Murdock STEAL .30 .75
22 Dikembe Mutombo REB .50 1.25
23 Dikembe Mutombo SWAT .50 1.25
24 Charles Oakley REB .40 1.00
25 Hakeem Olajuwon REB .60 1.50
26 Hakeem Olajuwon SCORE .60 1.50
27 Hakeem Olajuwon SWAT .60 1.50
28 Shaquille O'Neal REB 1.25 3.00
29 Shaquille O'Neal SCORE W 1.25 3.00
30 Shaquille O'Neal SWAT 1.25 3.00
31 Gary Payton STEAL .50 1.25
32 Scottie Pippen SCORE 1.00 2.50
33 Scottie Pippen STEAL W 1.00 2.50
34 Mark Price PASS .50 1.25
35 Mitch Richmond SCORE .50 1.25
36 David Robinson SCORE .75 2.00
37 David Robinson SWAT .75 2.00
38 Dennis Rodman REB W 1.00 2.50
39 Latrell Sprewell STEAL .60 1.50
40 John Stockton PASS W .60 1.50
41 John Stockton STEAL .60 1.50
42 Rod Strickland PASS .30 .75
43 Chris Webber SWAT .75 2.00
44 Kevin Willis REB .30 .75
45 Dominique Wilkins SCORE .60 1.50
46 Passers Field Card .30 .75
47 Rebounders Field Card .30 .75
48 Scorers Field Card .30 .75
49 Stealers Field Card .30 .75
50 Swatters Field Card .30 .75

1994-95 Topps Own the Game Redemption

MPLETE SET (10) 2.50 6.00
1 Shaquille O'Neal 1.25 3.00
2 Hakeem Olajuwon .60 1.50
3 Dennis Rodman 1.00 2.50
4 Patrick Ewing .60 1.50
5 John Stockton .60 1.50
6 Kenny Anderson .40 1.00
7 Scottie Pippen 1.00 2.50
8 Mookie Blaylock .30 .75
9 Dikembe Mutombo .50 1.25
10 Shawn Bradley .30 .75

1994-95 Topps Super Sophomores

Randomly inserted into all second series packs at a rate of one in 36, cards from this 10-card standard-size set spotlight a selection of young phenoms in their second NBA season. Fronts feature full-color player action shots cut out against silver-foil backgrounds.

COMPLETE SET (10) 6.00 15.00
SER.2 STATED ODDS 1:36
1 Chris Webber 1.50 4.00
2 Anfernee Hardaway 1.50 4.00
3 Vin Baker 1.00 2.50
4 Sam Cassell 1.00 2.50
5 Jamal Mashburn 1.00 2.50
6 Isaiah Rider 1.00 2.50
7 Chris Mills .60 1.50
8 Antonio Davis .60 1.50
9 Nick Van Exel 1.00 2.50
10 Lindsey Hunter .60 1.50

1995-96 Topps

The 1995-96 Topps Basketball set was issued in two separate series of 181 and 110 standard-size cards for a total of 291. Both first and second series cards were issued in 12-card hobby and retail packs (SRP $1.29). The white bordered fronts have a full-color action photo with the player's name in gold set against a black shadow. Horizontal backs have color head-shots with statistics and information. Subsets include Active Leaders (1-5), Scoring Leaders (6-10), Rebound Leaders (11-15), Assist Leaders (16-20), Steal Leaders (21-25) and Block Leaders (26-30). Rookie Cards of note in this set include Michael Finley, Kevin Garnett, Antonio McDyess, Joe Smith, Jerry Stackhouse and Damon Stoudamire.

COMPLETE SET (291) 15.00 40.00
COMPLETE SERIES 1 (181) 8.00 20.00
COMPLETE SERIES 2 (110) 8.00 20.00
1 Michael Jordan AL 1.00 2.50
2 Dennis Rodman AL .25 .60
3 John Stockton AL .15 .40
4 Michael Jordan AL 1.00 2.50
5 David Robinson AL .20 .50
6 Shaquille O'Neal LL .30 .75
7 Hakeem Olajuwon LL .15 .40
8 David Robinson LL .20 .50
9 Karl Malone LL .15 .40
10 Jamal Mashburn LL .12 .30
11 Dennis Rodman LL .25 .60
12 Dikembe Mutombo LL .12 .30
13 Shaquille O'Neal LL .30 .75
14 Patrick Ewing LL .15 .40
15 Tyrone Hill LL .07 .20
16 John Stockton LL .15 .40
17 Kenny Anderson LL .10 .25
18 Tim Hardaway LL .12 .30
19 Rod Strickland LL .07 .20
20 Muggsy Bogues LL .10 .25
21 Scottie Pippen LL .20 .50
22 Mookie Blaylock LL .07 .20
23 Gary Payton LL .12 .30
24 John Stockton LL .15 .40
25 Nate McMillan LL .07 .20
26 Dikembe Mutombo LL .12 .30
27 Hakeem Olajuwon LL .15 .40
28 Shawn Bradley LL .07 .20
29 David Robinson LL .20 .50
30 Alonzo Mourning LL .15 .40
31 Reggie Miller .15 .40
32 Karl Malone .15 .40
33 Grant Hill .20 .50
34 Charles Barkley .20 .50
35 Cedric Ceballos .07 .20
36 Gheorghe Muresan .07 .20
37 Doug West .07 .20
38 Tony Dumas .07 .20
39 Kenny Gattison .07 .20
40 Chris Mullin .12 .30
41 Pervis Ellison .07 .20
42 Vinny Del Negro .07 .20
43 Mario Elie .07 .20
44 Todd Day .07 .20
45 Scottie Pippen .20 .50
46 Buck Williams .07 .20
47 P.J. Brown .07 .20
48 Bimbo Coles .07 .20
49 Terrell Brandon .07 .20
50 Charles Oakley .10 .25
51 Sam Perkins .07 .20
52 Dale Ellis .07 .20
53 Andrew Lang .07 .20
54 Harold Ellis .07 .20
55 Clarence Weatherspoon .07 .20
56 Bill Curley .07 .20
57 Robert Parish .12 .30
58 David Benoit .07 .20
59 Anthony Avent .07 .20
60 Jamal Mashburn .12 .30
61 Duane Ferrell .07 .20
62 Elden Campbell .07 .20
63 Rex Chapman .07 .20
64 Wesley Person .07 .20
65 Mitch Richmond .12 .30
66 Micheal Williams .07 .20
67 Clifford Rozier .07 .20
68 Eric Montross .07 .20
69 Dennis Rodman .25 .60
70 Vin Baker .10 .25
71 Tyrone Hill .07 .20
72 Tyrone Corbin .07 .20
73 Chris Dudley .07 .20
74 Nate McMillan .07 .20
75 Kenny Anderson .10 .25
76 Monty Williams .07 .20
77 Kenny Smith .10 .25
78 Rodney Rogers .07 .20
79 Corie Blount .07 .20
80 Glen Rice .12 .30
81 Walt Williams .07 .20
82 Scott Williams .07 .20
83 Michael Adams .07 .20
84 Terry Mills .07 .20
85 Horace Grant .10 .25
86 Chuck Person .10 .25
87 Adam Keefe .07 .20
88 Scott Brooks .07 .20
89 George Lynch .07 .20
90 Kevin Johnson .12 .30
91 Armon Gilliam .07 .20
92 Greg Minor .07 .20
93 Derrick McKey .07 .20
94 Victor Alexander .07 .20
95 B.J. Armstrong .07 .20
96 Terry Dehere .07 .20
97 Christian Laettner .10 .25
98 Hubert Davis .07 .20
99 Aaron McKie .07 .20
100 Hakeem Olajuwon .15 .40
101 Michael Cage .07 .20
102 Grant Long .07 .20
103 Calbert Cheaney .07 .20
104 Olden Polynice .07 .20
105 Sharone Wright .07 .20
106 Lee Mayberry .07 .20
107 Robert Pack .07 .20
108 Loy Vaught .07 .20
109 Khalid Reeves .07 .20
110 Shawn Kemp .12 .30
111 Lindsey Hunter .07 .20
112 Dell Curry .07 .20
113 Dan Majerle .12 .30
114 Bryon Russell .07 .20
115 John Starks .10 .25
116 Roy Tarpley .07 .20
117 Dale Davis .07 .20
118 Nick Anderson .07 .20
119 Rex Walters .07 .20
120 Dominique Wilkins .15 .40
121 Sam Cassell .12 .30
122 Sean Elliott .12 .30
123 B.J. Tyler .07 .20
124 Eric Mobley .07 .20
125 Toni Kukoc .12 .30
126 Pooh Richardson .07 .20
127 Isaiah Rider .12 .30
128 Steve Smith .10 .25
129 Chris Mills .07 .20
130 Detlef Schrempf .12 .30
131 Donyell Marshall .07 .20
132 Eddie Jones .12 .30
133 Otis Thorpe .07 .20
134 Lionel Simmons .07 .20
135 Jeff Hornacek .10 .25
136 Jalen Rose .15 .40
137 Kevin Willis .07 .20
138 Don MacLean .07 .20
139 Dee Brown .07 .20
140 Glenn Robinson .10 .25
141 Joe Kleine .07 .20
142 Ron Harper .10 .25
143 Antonio Davis .07 .20
144 Jeff Malone .07 .20
145 Joe Dumars .12 .30
146 Jason Kidd .20 .50
147 J.R. Reid .07 .20
148 Lamond Murray .07 .20
149 Derrick Coleman .10 .25
150 Alonzo Mourning .15 .40
151 Clifford Robinson .07 .20
152 Kendall Gill .07 .20
153 Doug Christie .07 .20
154 Stacey Augmon .10 .25
155 Anfernee Hardaway .20 .50
156 Mahmoud Abdul-Rauf .07 .20
157 Latrell Sprewell .12 .30
158 Mark Price .12 .30
159 Brian Grant .10 .25
160 Clyde Drexler .15 .40
161 Juwan Howard .12 .30
162 Tom Gugliotta .07 .20
163 Nick Van Exel .12 .30
164 Billy Owens .07 .20
165 Brooks Thompson .07 .20
166 Acie Earl .07 .20
167 Ed Pinckney .07 .20
168 Oliver Miller .07 .20
169 John Salley .07 .20
170 Jerome Kersey .07 .20
171 Willie Anderson .07 .20
172 Keith Jennings .07 .20
173 Doug Smith .07 .20
174 Gerald Wilkins .07 .20
175 Byron Scott .10 .25
176 Benoit Benjamin .07 .20
177 Blue Edwards .07 .20
178 Greg Anthony .07 .20
179 Trevor Ruffin .07 .20
180 Kenny Gattison .07 .20
181 Checklist 1-181 .07 .20
182 Cherokee Parks RC .10 .25
183 Kurt Thomas RC .12 .30
184 Ervin Johnson .07 .20
185 Chucky Brown .07 .20
186 Luc Longley .10 .25
187 Anthony Miller .07 .20
188 Ed O'Bannon RC .10 .25
189 Bobby Hurley .07 .20
190 Dikembe Mutombo .12 .30
191 Robert Horry .10 .25
192 George Zidek RC .10 .25
193 Rasheed Wallace RC .40 1.00
194 Marty Conlon .07 .20
195 A.C. Green .10 .25
196 Mike Brown .07 .20
197 Oliver Miller .07 .20
198 Charles Smith .07 .20
199 Eric Williams RC .12 .30
200 Rik Smits .10 .25
201 Donald Royal .07 .20
202 Bryant Reeves RC .10 .25
203 Danny Ferry .07 .20
204 Brian Williams .07 .20
205 Joe Smith RC .15 .40
206 Gary Trent RC .12 .30
207 Greg Ostertag RC .12 .30
208 Ken Norman .07 .20
209 Avery Johnson .10 .25
210 Theo Ratliff UER RC .20 .50
211 Corie Blount .07 .20
212 Hersey Hawkins .07 .20
213 Loren Meyer RC .07 .20
214 Mario Bennett RC .10 .25
215 Randolph Childress RC .10 .25
216 Spud Webb .10 .25
217 Popeye Jones .07 .20
218 Shawn Respert RC .10 .25
219 Malik Sealy .07 .20
220 Dino Radja .07 .20
221 James Robinson .07 .20
222 David Vaughn .12 .30
223 Michael Smith .07 .20
224 Jamie Watson .07 .20
225 LaPhonso Ellis .07 .20
226 Kevin Gamble .07 .20
227 Dennis Rodman .25 .60
228 B.J. Armstrong .07 .20
229 Jerry Stackhouse RC .40 1.00
230 Muggsy Bogues .10 .25
231 Lawrence Moten RC .12 .30
232 Cory Alexander RC .12 .30
233 Carlos Rogers .07 .20
234 Tyus Edney RC .12 .30
235 Doc Rivers .10 .25
236 Antonio Harvey .07 .20
237 Kevin Garnett RC 1.00 2.50
238 Derek Harper .10 .25
239 Kevin Edwards .07 .20
240 Chris Smith .07 .20
241 Haywoode Workman .07 .20
242 Bobby Phills .07 .20
243 Sherrell Ford RC .10 .25
244 Corliss Williamson RC .12 .30
245 Shawn Bradley .07 .20
246 Jason Caffey RC .12 .30
247 Bryant Stith .07 .20
248 Mark West .07 .20
249 Dennis Scott .07 .20
250 Jim Jackson .07 .20
251 Travis Best RC .12 .30
252 Sean Rooks .07 .20
253 Yinka Dare .07 .20
254 Felton Spencer .07 .20
255 Vlade Divac .12 .30
256 Michael Finley RC .40 1.00
257 Damon Stoudamire RC .30 .75
258 Mark Bryant .07 .20
259 Brent Barry RC .20 .50
260 Rony Seikaly .07 .20
261 Alan Henderson RC .12 .30
262 Kendall Gill .07 .20
263 Rex Chapman .07 .20
264 Eric Murdock .07 .20
265 Rodney Rogers .07 .20
266 Greg Graham .07 .20
267 Jayson Williams .07 .20
268 Antonio McDyess RC .15 .40
269 Sedale Threatt .07 .20
270 Danny Manning .10 .25
271 Pete Chilcutt .07 .20
272 Bob Sura RC .10 .25
273 Dana Barros .07 .20
274 Allan Houston .10 .25
275 Tracy Murray .07 .20
276 Anthony Mason .07 .20
277 Michael Jordan 1.00 2.50
278 Patrick Ewing .15 .40
279 Shaquille O'Neal .30 .75
280 Larry Johnson .12 .30
281 Mark Jackson .10 .25
282 Chris Webber .15 .40
283 David Robinson .20 .50
284 John Stockton .15 .40
285 Mookie Blaylock .07 .20
286 Mark Price .12 .30
287 Tim Hardaway .12 .30
288 Rod Strickland .07 .20
289 Sherman Douglas .07 .20
290 Gary Payton .12 .30
291 Checklist (182-291) .07 .20

1995-96 Topps Draft Redemption

These 29 draft pick cards (covering the entire first round of the 1995 NBA draft) were available exclusively by redeeming one of the Topps Draft Redemption insert cards (randomly inserted in series one packs at a rate of one in 18). These cards feature all foil silver bordered fronts with a full-color action shot of the featured rookie. The first series exchange cards each featured a large number on the card front representing the player that was chosen at that slot in the 1995 NBA draft. Collectors had to then mail the card in to Topps to receive their player card. The redemption deadline for these cards was April 1, 1996.

COMPLETE SET (29) 100.00 200.00
EXCH.CARDS: SER.1 STATED ODDS 1:18
1 Joe Smith 3.00 8.00
2 Antonio McDyess 3.00 8.00
3 Jerry Stackhouse 8.00 20.00
4 Rasheed Wallace 8.00 20.00
5 Kevin Garnett 20.00 50.00
6 Bryant Reeves 2.00 5.00
7 Damon Stoudamire 6.00 15.00
8 Shawn Respert 2.00 5.00
9 Ed O'Bannon 2.00 5.00
10 Kurt Thomas 2.50 6.00
11 Gary Trent 2.50 6.00
12 Cherokee Parks 2.00 5.00
13 Corliss Williamson 2.50 6.00
14 Eric Williams 2.50 6.00
15 Brent Barry 4.00 10.00
16 Alan Henderson 2.50 6.00
17 Bob Sura 2.00 5.00
18 Theo Ratliff 4.00 10.00
19 Randolph Childress 2.00 5.00
20 Jason Caffey 2.50 6.00
21 Michael Finley 8.00 20.00
22 George Zidek 2.00 5.00
23 Travis Best 2.50 6.00
24 Loren Meyer 1.50 4.00
25 David Vaughn 2.50 6.00
26 Sherrell Ford 2.00 5.00
27 Mario Bennett 2.00 5.00
28 Greg Ostertag 2.50 6.00
29 Cory Alexander 2.50 6.00
NNO Expired Exchange Cards .40 1.00

1995-96 Topps Foreign Legion

Featuring foreign players who play in the NBA, this 10-card set was available in retail packs sold in Canada and Australia only. It was randomly inserted in 6-card packs at a rate of one in 36. On a white-bordered metallic background, the fronts feature color player cutouts. The player's name is gold foil stamped across the bottom. The backs carry a color closeup and a player profile, all on a blue background featuring a picture of the earth.

COMPLETE SET (10) 6.00 15.00
FL1 Luc Longley 1.00 2.50
FL2 Rick Fox .75 2.00
FL3 Dikembe Mutombo 1.25 3.00
FL4 Gheorghe Muresan .75 2.00
FL5 Sarunas Marciulionis .75 2.00
FL6 Dino Radja .75 2.00
FL7 Detlef Schrempf 1.25 3.00
FL8 Rony Seikaly .75 2.00
FL9 Bill Wennington .75 2.00
FL10 Rik Smits 1.00 2.50

1995-96 Topps Mystery Finest

Randomly inserted into all second series packs at a rate of one in 36, cards from this 22-card standard-size insert set spotlight a selection of top forwards and guards in the league. Each Mystery Finest card was inserted into packs with a black plastic coating on front. Hence, the "mystery" was to peel off the coating to see whether one had a basic card or a parallel refractor. Card fronts featur a silver foil border and a player action photo cut out against a galaxy design background. These cards are often found poorly centered.

COMPLETE SET (22) 30.00 80.00
SER.2 STATED ODDS 1:36 HOBBY/RETAIL
M1 Michael Jordan 12.00 30.00
M2 Anfernee Hardaway 2.50 6.00
M3 Clyde Drexler 2.00 5.00
M4 Mark Price 1.50 4.00
M5 Steve Smith 1.25 3.00
M6 Jim Jackson 1.00 2.50
M7 Nick Anderson 1.00 2.50
M8 Kenny Anderson 1.25 3.00
M9 Mookie Blaylock 1.00 2.50
M10 Jason Kidd 2.50 6.00
M11 Tim Hardaway 1.50 4.00
M12 Kevin Johnson 1.50 4.00
M13 Gary Payton 1.50 4.00
M14 John Stockton 2.00 5.00
M15 Rod Strickland 1.00 2.50
M16 Jamal Mashburn 1.50 4.00
M17 Danny Manning 1.25 3.00
M18 Billy Owens 1.00 2.50
M19 Grant Hill 2.50 6.00
M20 Scottie Pippen 2.50 6.00
M21 Isaiah Rider 1.50 4.00
M22 Latrell Sprewell 1.50 4.00

1995-96 Topps Mystery Finest Refractors

*REF: 2X TO 5X BASE HI
SER.2 STATED ODDS 1:36 HOB, 1:216 RET
CONDITION SENSITIVE SET
M1 Michael Jordan 100.00 250.00

1995-96 Topps Pan For Gold

Randomly inserted in first series retail packs only at a rate of one in eight, this 15-card standard-size set chronicles the play of NBA stars who came from small colleges and were drafted late. White-bordered fronts feature a full-color player cutout set against a mine shaft background. The player's team name is printed in silver across the top and his name is stamped in gold foil across the bottom. Horizontal backs have a full-color player head shot on the left third of the card with his name, biography and details of his draft and school information on the right. Pieces of gold serve as a background for the back. These cards are numbered with a "PFG" prefix.

COMPLETE SET (15) 20.00 50.00
SER.1 STATED ODDS 1:4 JUM, 1:8 RET
PFG1 Vin Baker 2.00 5.00
PFG2 John Stockton 3.00 8.00
PFG3 Dan Majerle 2.50 6.00
PFG4 Joe Dumars 2.50 6.00
PFG5 Rik Smits 2.00 5.00
PFG6 Tim Hardaway 2.50 6.00
PFG7 Charles Oakley 2.00 5.00
PFG8 Cedric Ceballos 1.50 4.00
PFG9 Karl Malone 3.00 8.00
PFG10 Scottie Pippen 4.00 10.00
PFG11 David Robinson 4.00 10.00
PFG12 Gary Payton 2.50 6.00
PFG13 Mitch Richmond 2.50 6.00
PFG14 Antonio Davis 1.50 4.00
PFG15 Dennis Rodman 5.00 12.00

1995-96 Topps Power Boosters

This 45-card insert standard-size set is printed on 28-point stock and features the leaders in points, rebounds, assists, steals and blocks paralleling the regular issue subset cards. The first 30 cards in the set (1-30) were seeded into first series packs at a rate of 1 in 36. The last 15 cards in the set (276-290) were seeded into second series packs also at a rate of one in 36. A Power Boosters card replaced two regular cards in every they came in. Full-bleed fronts carry a full-color action player cutout set against diffraction foil background with the player's name stamped in gold foil across the top. The Power Boosters logo appears at the bottom of the card with the individual's category listed above the logo. Borderless backs are one-color background with a full-color player head shot boxed on the right. Player name, team name, profile and biography appear on the back.

COMPLETE SET (45) 140.00 250.00
COMPLETE SERIES 1 (30) 100.00 175.00
COMPLETE SERIES 2 (15) 40.00 75.00
SER.1/2 STATED ODDS 1:36 HOBBY/RETAIL
1 Michael Jordan 25.00 60.00
2 Dennis Rodman 4.00 10.00
3 John Stockton 2.50 6.00
4 Michael Jordan 15.00 40.00
5 David Robinson 3.00 8.00
6 Shaquille O'Neal 5.00 12.00
7 Hakeem Olajuwon 2.50 6.00
8 David Robinson 3.00 8.00
9 Karl Malone 2.50 6.00
10 Jamal Mashburn 2.00 5.00
11 Dennis Rodman 4.00 10.00
12 Dikembe Mutombo 2.00 5.00
13 Shaquille O'Neal 5.00 12.00
14 Patrick Ewing 2.50 6.00
15 Tyrone Hill 1.25 3.00
16 John Stockton 2.50 6.00
17 Kenny Anderson 1.50 4.00
18 Tim Hardaway 2.00 5.00
19 Rod Strickland 1.25 3.00
20 Muggsy Bogues 1.50 4.00
21 Scottie Pippen 3.00 8.00
22 Mookie Blaylock 1.25 3.00
23 Gary Payton 2.00 5.00
24 John Stockton 2.50 6.00
25 Nate McMillan 1.25 3.00
26 Dikembe Mutombo 2.00 5.00
27 Hakeem Olajuwon 2.50 6.00
28 Shawn Bradley 1.25 3.00
29 David Robinson 3.00 8.00
30 Alonzo Mourning 2.50 6.00
276 Anthony Mason 1.25 3.00
277 Michael Jordan 20.00 50.00
278 Patrick Ewing 2.50 6.00
279 Shaquille O'Neal 5.00 12.00
280 Larry Johnson 2.00 5.00
281 Mark Jackson 1.50 4.00
282 Chris Webber 2.50 6.00
283 David Robinson 3.00 8.00
284 John Stockton 2.50 6.00
285 Mookie Blaylock 1.25 3.00
286 Mark Price 2.00 5.00
287 Tim Hardaway 2.00 5.00
288 Rod Strickland 1.25 3.00
289 Sherman Douglas 1.25 3.00
290 Gary Payton 2.00 5.00

1995-96 Topps Rattle and Roll

Randomly inserted in second series retail packs only at a rate of one in 12, this 10-card set takes aim at the power mongers of the NBA. Fronts are bordered in silver foil with a blue and red silver swirl pattern for a background. A full-color player cutout appears on the front with his name printed in a copper foil at the bottom. White-bordered backs contain a player head shot and his name printed underneath in red type. The blue and red swirl pattern continues and the player's biography and profile are printed in white type.

COMPLETE SET (10) 5.00 12.00
SER.2 STATED ODDS 1:12 RETAIL
R1 Juwan Howard 1.00 2.50
R2 Glenn Robinson .75 2.00
R3 Grant Hill 1.50 4.00
R4 Sharone Wright .60 1.50
R5 Brian Grant .75 2.00
R6 Antonio McDyess .60 1.50
R7 Bryant Reeves .40 1.00
R8 Gary Trent .50 1.25
R9 Jerry Stackhouse 1.50 4.00
R10 Joe Smith .60 1.50

1995-96 Topps Show Stoppers

Cards in this set of ten were randomly issued in first series hobby packs only at a rate of one in 24 and feature the top players of the NBA. Fronts are white bordered with silver foil and a full-color player action cutout. The player's name is printed in gold foil at the bottom. Backs have a player head shot with a spotlight description, a game high feature and a show stopper highlight.

COMPLETE SET (10) 20.00 50.00
SER.1 STATED ODDS 1:24 HOBBY
SS1 Michael Jordan 12.00 30.00
SS2 Grant Hill 2.50 6.00
SS3 Glenn Robinson 1.25 3.00
SS4 Anfernee Hardaway 2.50 6.00
SS5 Charles Barkley 2.50 6.00
SS6 Patrick Ewing 2.00 5.00
SS7 Shaquille O'Neal 4.00 10.00
SS8 Jason Kidd 2.50 6.00
SS9 Glen Rice 1.50 4.00
SS10 Karl Malone 2.00 5.00

1995-96 Topps Spark Plugs

Randomly inserted in all second series retail packs at a rate of one in 8, cards from this 10-card chase set highlight NBA scorers on full-foil fronts. Silver foil serves as a border and a blue and silver foil are background for a full-color action player cutout. A spark plug with sparks flying out and the player's name are printed in silver foil. Horizontal backs are white bordered with a full-color action shot on one side and a player biography and '94-95 season highlights on the other.

COMPLETE SET (10) 8.00 20.00
SER.2 STATED ODDS 1:8 HOBBY/RETAIL
SP1 Shaquille O'Neal 1.50 4.00
SP2 Michael Jordan 5.00 12.00
SP3 Reggie Miller .75 2.00
SP4 Anfernee Hardaway 1.00 2.50
SP5 John Stockton .75 2.00
SP6 David Robinson 1.00 2.50
SP7 Hakeem Olajuwon .75 2.00
SP8 Tim Hardaway .60 1.50
SP9 Grant Hill 1.00 2.50
SP10 Scottie Pippen 1.00 2.50

1995-96 Topps Sudden Impact

Sudden Impact is a hobby-exclusive insert set of ten rookies that were expected to make a significant impact on their teams. The horizontally designed "all foil" cards were randomly inserted at a rate of 1 in 72 second series hobby packs. The cards are numbered on the back with an "S" prefix.

COMPLETE SET (10) 20.00 50.00
SER.2 STATED ODDS 1:72 HOBBY
S1 Damon Stoudamire 5.00 12.00
S2 Cherokee Parks 1.50 4.00
S3 Kurt Thomas 2.00 5.00
S4 Gary Trent 2.00 5.00
S5 Bryant Reeves 1.50 4.00
S6 Ed O'Bannon 1.50 4.00
S7 Shawn Respert 1.50 4.00
S8 Antonio McDyess 2.50 6.00
S9 Joe Smith 2.50 6.00
S10 Jerry Stackhouse 6.00 15.00

1995-96 Topps Top Flight

Cards in this 20-piece set feature the high flyers of the NBA and were inserted one per retail pack. The white bordered fronts have a full-color player action cutout set against a background with two fighter jets. The player's name is printed in gold foil near the bottom above a gold foil swooshing jet whose vapor spells out "Top Flight." Backs have a ful-color head shot inset within a sky background of a jet in flight. A biography and special abilities box appear on the back.

COMPLETE SET (20) 15.00 40.00
ONE PER SPECIAL SER.1 RETAIL PACK
TF1 Michael Jordan 8.00 20.00
TF2 Isaiah Rider 1.25 3.00
TF3 Harold Miner .75 2.00
TF4 Dominique Wilkins 1.50 4.00
TF5 Clyde Drexler 1.50 4.00
TF6 Scottie Pippen 2.00 5.00
TF7 Shawn Kemp 1.25 3.00
TF8 Chris Webber 1.50 4.00
TF9 Anfernee Hardaway 2.00 5.00
TF10 Grant Hill 2.00 5.00
TF11 Kevin Johnson 1.25 3.00
TF12 John Starks 1.00 2.50
TF13 Dan Majerle 1.25 3.00
TF14 Latrell Sprewell 1.25 3.00
TF15 Dee Brown .75 2.00
TF16 Stacey Augmon 1.00 2.50
TF17 David Benoit .75 2.00
TF18 Sean Elliott 1.25 3.00
TF19 Cedric Ceballos .75 2.00
TF20 Robert Horry 1.00 2.50

1995-96 Topps Whiz Kids

Randomly inserted in all first series packs at a rate of one in 24, this set of 12 standard-size cards highlights the young power of the NBA. Etched silver foil fronts have a basketball court background and a full-color player action cutout. "Whiz Kids" is spelled out in children's letter blocks on the top. The players name is printed in red at the bottom. Borderless backs are numbered with the prefix "WK" and continue with a basketball court background. A full-color player head shot appears inside the key of the court and his name appears underneath the photo in red print on a blue banner. Career stats, biography and a trivia question appear on the lower half and the answer to the question on the preceding card appears at the bottom.

COMPLETE SET (12) 12.00 30.00
SER.1 STATED ODDS 1:24 HOBBY/RETAIL
WK1 Grant Hill 2.50 6.00
WK2 Nick Van Exel 1.50 4.00
WK3 Juwan Howard 1.50 4.00
WK4 Chris Webber 2.00 5.00
WK5 Brian Grant 1.25 3.00
WK6 Glenn Robinson 1.25 3.00
WK7 Donyell Marshall 1.00 2.50
WK8 Jason Kidd 2.50 6.00
WK9 Anfernee Hardaway 2.50 6.00
WK10 Jamal Mashburn 1.50 4.00
WK11 Vin Baker 1.25 3.00
WK12 Eddie Jones 1.50 4.00

1995-96 Topps World Class

This 10-card standard-size set was randomly inserted approximately one in every 18 second series International packs. These packs were intended for Australia and New Zealand only, but have found their way back to the United States. Card fronts are bordered with a photo of the player and the logo "World Class" clearly written on the front. Card backs are numbered with a "WC" prefix.

COMPLETE SET (10) 15.00 40.00
WC1 Michael Jordan 12.00 30.00
WC2 Karl Malone 1.50 4.00
WC3 Shaquille O'Neal 3.00 8.00
WC4 Reggie Miller 1.50 4.00
WC5 Hakeem Olajuwon 1.50 4.00
WC6 Grant Hill 2.00 5.00
WC7 Anfernee Hardaway 2.00 5.00
WC8 Scottie Pippen 2.00 5.00
WC9 David Robinson 2.00 5.00
WC10 Clyde Drexler 1.50 4.00

1996-97 Topps

The 1996-97 Topps basketball set was issued in two series totaling 222 standard-size cards, although the checklist card from series one (#111) is not considered part of the basic set. Both series cards were issued in 11-card hobby and retail packs carrying a suggested retail price of $1.29. The white-bordered fronts have a full-color action photo with the player's name in gold set against the trail of a moving basketball. Horizontal backs have color head shots with career statistics and information. The checklist card (#111) actually looks more like a premium Finest brand card than a Topps issue. Because it was so much tougher than a normal checklist, it is not considered part of the series one set. Rookie cards include Kobe Bryant, Marcus Camby, Allen Iverson, Stephon Marbury, Shareef Abdur-Rahim and Antoine Walker, among others. Several cards including Shawn Kemp and Damon Stoudamire were used for promotional purposes. The card numbers are identical to the regular issue, but on the front of the card, the Topps logo and the team logo are switched. In addition, Topps released factory sets for both the hobby and retail markets. Each set contained the full 221-card set, 2 of the Season's Best inserts, 1 card from the NBA at 50 parallel and 2 of the Pro File inserts. The hobby factory set also contained one of the 10 autographed cards originally released in the 1996 Topps NBA Stars Reprint Autograph set.

COMPLETE SET (221) 15.00 30.00
COMP.FACT.HOB.SET (227) 15.00 35.00
COMPLETE SERIES 1 (110) 6.00 12.00
COMPLETE SERIES 2 (111) 10.00 20.00
1 Patrick Ewing .20 .50
2 Christian Laettner .12 .30
3 Mahmoud Abdul-Rauf .10 .25
4 Chris Webber .20 .50
5 Jason Kidd .25 .60
6 Clifford Rozier .10 .25
7 Elden Campbell .10 .25
8 Chuck Person .12 .30
9 Jeff Hornacek .12 .30
10 Rik Smits .12 .30
11 Kurt Thomas .10 .25
12 Rod Strickland .10 .25
13 Kendall Gill .10 .25
14 Brian Williams .10 .25
15 Tom Gugliotta .10 .25
16 Ron Harper .12 .30
17 Eric Williams .10 .25
18 A.C. Green .12 .30
19 Scott Williams .10 .25
20 Damon Stoudamire .12 .30
21 Bryant Reeves .10 .25
22 Bob Sura .10 .25
23 Mitch Richmond .15 .40
24 Larry Johnson .15 .40
25 Vin Baker .12 .30
26 Mark Bryant .10 .25
27 Horace Grant .12 .30
28 Allan Houston .12 .30
29 Sam Perkins .10 .25
30 Antonio McDyess .15 .40
31 Rasheed Wallace .20 .50
32 Malik Sealy .10 .25
33 Scottie Pippen .25 .60
34 Charles Barkley .25 .60
35 Hakeem Olajuwon .20 .50
36 John Starks .12 .30
37 Byron Scott .12 .30
38 Arvydas Sabonis .12 .30
39 Vlade Divac .15 .40
40 Joe Dumars .15 .40
41 Danny Ferry .10 .25
42 Jerry Stackhouse .20 .50
43 B.J. Armstrong .10 .25
44 Shawn Bradley .10 .25
45 Kevin Garnett .40 1.00
46 Dee Brown .10 .25
47 Michael Smith .10 .25
48 Doug Christie .10 .25
49 Mark Jackson .12 .30
50 Shawn Kemp .15 .40
51 Sasha Danilovic .10 .25
52 Nick Anderson .10 .25
53 Matt Geiger .10 .25
54 Charles Smith .10 .25
55 Mookie Blaylock .10 .25
56 Johnny Newman .10 .25
57 George McCloud .10 .25
58 Greg Ostertag .10 .25
59 Reggie Williams .10 .25
60 Brent Barry .12 .30
61 Doug West .10 .25
62 Donald Royal .10 .25
63 Randy Brown .10 .25
64 Vincent Askew .10 .25
65 John Stockton .20 .50
66 Joe Kleine .10 .25
67 Keith Askins .10 .25
68 Bobby Phills .10 .25
69 Chris Mullin .15 .40
70 Nick Van Exel .15 .40
71 Rick Fox .10 .25
72 Chicago Bulls - 72 Wins .60 1.50
73 Shawn Respert .10 .25
74 Hubert Davis .10 .25
75 Jim Jackson .10 .25
76 Olden Polynice .10 .25
77 Gheorghe Muresan .10 .25
78 Theo Ratliff .10 .25
79 Khalid Reeves .10 .25
80 David Robinson .25 .60
81 Lawrence Moten .10 .25
82 Sam Cassell .12 .30
83 George Zidek .10 .25
84 Sharone Wright .10 .25
85 Clarence Weatherspoon .10 .25
86 Alan Henderson .10 .25
87 Chris Dudley .10 .25
88 Ed O'Bannon .10 .25
89 Calbert Cheaney .10 .25
90 Cedric Ceballos .10 .25
91 Michael Cage .10 .25
92 Ervin Johnson .10 .25
93 Gary Trent .10 .25
94 Sherman Douglas .10 .25
95 Joe Smith .12 .30
96 Dale Davis .10 .25
97 Tony Dumas .10 .25
98 Muggsy Bogues .12 .30
99 Toni Kukoc .15 .40
100 Grant Hill .25 .60
101 Michael Finley .20 .50
102 Isaiah Rider .12 .30
103 Bryant Stith .10 .25
104 Pooh Richardson .10 .25
105 Karl Malone .20 .50
106 Brian Grant .12 .30
107 Sean Elliott .15 .40
108 Charles Oakley .12 .30
109 Pervis Ellison .10 .25
110 Anfernee Hardaway .25 .60
111 Checklist SP .40 1.00
112 Dikembe Mutombo .15 .40
113 Alonzo Mourning .20 .50
114 Hubert Davis .10 .25
115 Rony Seikaly .10 .25
116 Danny Manning .12 .30
117 Donyell Marshall .10 .25
118 Gerald Wilkins .10 .25
119 Ervin Johnson .10 .25
120 Jalen Rose .12 .30
121 Dino Radja .10 .25
122 Glenn Robinson .12 .30
123 John Stockton .20 .50
124 Matt Maloney RC .12 .30
125 Clifford Robinson .10 .25
126 Steve Kerr .12 .30
127 Nate McMillan .10 .25
128 Shareef Abdur-Rahim RC .25 .60
129 Loy Vaught .10 .25
130 Anthony Mason .10 .25
131 Kevin Garnett .40 1.00
132 Roy Rogers RC .12 .30
133 Erick Dampier RC .15 .40
134 Tyus Edney .10 .25
135 Chris Mills .10 .25
136 Cory Alexander .10 .25
137 Juwan Howard .12 .30
138 Kobe Bryant RC 6.00 15.00
139 Michael Jordan 1.25 3.00
140 Jayson Williams .10 .25
141 Rod Strickland .10 .25
142 Lorenzen Wright RC .12 .30
143 Will Perdue .10 .25
144 Derek Harper .12 .30
145 Billy Owens .10 .25
146 Antoine Walker RC .25 .60
147 P.J. Brown .10 .25
148 Terrell Brandon .10 .25
149 Larry Johnson .15 .40
150 Steve Smith .12 .30
151 Eddie Jones .15 .40
152 Detlef Schrempf .15 .40
153 Dale Ellis .10 .25
154 Isaiah Rider .12 .30
155 Tony Delk RC .15 .40
156 Adrian Caldwell .10 .25
157 Jamal Mashburn .12 .30
158 Dennis Scott .10 .25
159 Dana Barros .10 .25
160 Martin Muursepp RC .10 .25
161 Marcus Camby RC .25 .60
162 Jerome Williams RC .12 .30
163 Wesley Person .10 .25
164 Luc Longley .12 .30
165 Charlie Ward .10 .25
166 Mark Jackson .12 .30
167 Derrick Coleman .12 .30
168 Dell Curry .10 .25
169 Armon Gilliam .10 .25
170 Vlade Divac .15 .40
171 Allen Iverson RC .75 2.00
172 Vitaly Potapenko RC .12 .30
173 Jon Koncak .10 .25
174 Lindsey Hunter .10 .25
175 Kevin Johnson .15 .40
176 Dennis Rodman .30 .75
177 Stephon Marbury RC .40 1.00
178 Karl Malone .20 .50
179 Charles Barkley .25 .60
180 Popeye Jones .10 .25
181 Samaki Walker RC .12 .30
182 Steve Nash RC 1.25 3.00
183 Latrell Sprewell .15 .40
184 Kenny Anderson .12 .30
185 Tyrone Hill .10 .25

186 Robert Pack .10 .25
187 Greg Anthony .10 .25
188 Derrick McKey .10 .25
189 John Wallace RC .15 .40
190 Bryon Russell .10 .25
191 Jermaine O'Neal RC .25 .60
192 Clyde Drexler .20 .50
193 Mahmoud Abdul-Rauf .10 .25
194 Eric Montross .10 .25
195 Allan Houston .12 .30
196 Harvey Grant .10 .25
197 Rodney Rogers .10 .25
198 Kerry Kittles RC .15 .40
199 Grant Hill .25 .60
200 Lionel Simmons .10 .25
201 Reggie Miller .20 .50
202 Avery Johnson .12 .30
203 LaPhonso Ellis .10 .25
204 Brian Shaw .10 .25
205 Priest Lauderdale RC .10 .25
206 Derek Fisher RC .20 .50
207 Terry Porter .10 .25
208 Todd Fuller RC .10 .25
209 Hersey Hawkins .10 .25
210 Tim Legler .10 .25
211 Terry Dehere .10 .25
212 Gary Payton .15 .40
213 Joe Dumars .15 .40
214 Don MacLean .10 .25
215 Greg Minor .10 .25
216 Tim Hardaway .15 .40
217 Ray Allen RC .60 1.50
218 Mario Elie .10 .25
219 Brooks Thompson .10 .25
220 Shaquille O'Neal .40 1.00

1996-97 Topps NBA at 50

*STARS: 2.5X TO 6X BASE CARD HI
*RCs: 2X TO 5X BASE HI
SER.1/2 STATED ODDS 1:3 HOB/RET
138 Kobe Bryant 20.00 50.00

1996-97 Topps Draft Redemption

These trade cards were randomly inserted in first series packs at a rate of one in 18. Each trade card has a number printed on front that corresponds to each draft position of the first round of the 1996 NBA draft. Collectors that exchanged their trade card would then receive an exchange card picturing the player selected at that spot in the draft. The Draft Redemption trade deadline was April 1, 1997. Cards number 14 and 23 were not issued as they did not sign NBA contracts during this promotion. Both Stojakovic and Retzias were foreign players who continued playing overseas.

EXCH.CARDS: SER.1 STATED ODDS 1:18 H/R
1 Allen Iverson 12.00 30.00
2 Marcus Camby 4.00 10.00
3 Shareef Abdur-Rahim 4.00 10.00
4 Stephon Marbury 6.00 15.00
5 Ray Allen 10.00 25.00
6 Antoine Walker 4.00 10.00
7 Lorenzen Wright 2.00 5.00
8 Kerry Kittles 2.50 6.00
9 Samaki Walker 2.00 5.00
10 Erick Dampier 2.50 6.00
11 Todd Fuller 1.50 4.00
12 Vitaly Potapenko 2.00 5.00
13 Kobe Bryant 50.00 120.00
15 Steve Nash 12.00 30.00
16 Tony Delk 2.50 6.00
17 Jermaine O'Neal 4.00 10.00
18 John Wallace 2.50 6.00
19 Walter McCarty 2.50 6.00
20 Zydrunas Ilgauskas 4.00 10.00
21 Dontae' Jones 2.50 6.00
22 Roy Rogers 2.00 5.00
26 Jerome Williams 2.00 5.00
27 Brian Evans 2.50 6.00
28 Priest Lauderdale 1.50 4.00
29 Travis Knight 2.50 6.00
24 Derek Fisher 3.00 8.00
25 Martin Muursepp 1.50 4.00
NNO Expired Trade Cards .20 .50

1996-97 Topps Finest Reprints

Randomly inserted in series two packs at the rate of one in 36, this 25-card set features reprints of 25 of the 50 greatest NBA players as they appeared on their first Topps, Star Co., or Bowman cards. Cards utilize the Finest technology. The first 25 cards were issued in 1996-97 Stadium Club series one. Card values below refer to unpeeled cards. Peeled cards generally trade for ten to twenty-five percent less.

COMPLETE SERIES 2 (25) 60.00 120.00
SER.2 STATED ODDS 1:36 HOBBY/RETAIL
*REF: 1.25X TO 3X HI COLUMN
REF: SER.2 STATED ODDS 1:144 HOB/RET
1 Lew Alcindor 4.00 10.00
3 Paul Arizin 1.25 3.00
9 Wilt Chamberlain 5.00 12.00
11 Dave Cowens .75 2.00
14 Clyde Drexler 2.50 6.00
16 Patrick Ewing 3.00 8.00
20 John Havlicek 3.00 8.00
21 Elvin Hayes 1.25 3.00
22 Bird/Erving/Johnson 10.00 25.00
23 Sam Jones 1.50 4.00
25 Jerry Lucas 1.25 3.00
27 Moses Malone 1.25 3.00
30 George Mikan 4.00 10.00
31 Earl Monroe 1.25 3.00
32 Shaquille O'Neal 4.00 10.00
33 Hakeem Olajuwon 3.00 8.00
37 Willis Reed 1.25 3.00
38 Oscar Robertson 3.00 8.00
39 David Robinson 2.50 6.00
40 Bill Russell 4.00 10.00
42 Bill Sharman 1.25 3.00
43 John Stockton 4.00 10.00
45 Nate Thurmond 1.00 2.50
46 Wes Unseld 1.25 3.00
47 Bill Walton 2.00 5.00

1996-97 Topps Hobby Masters

Randomly inserted exclusively into both series hobby packs at a rate of one in every 36, these inserts feature a selection of twenty top NBA stars as determined by Topps hobby dealer network. In addition to player selection, the dealers also determined the rate of insertion. Each card features 28 point full diffraction foil stock. Due to the thickness, a Hobby Masters insert replaced two regular issue cards within the packs they were seeded into. The card backs are numbered with an "HM" prefix. The cards are numbered 11-30 due to the fact that they are part of a cross-sport (football, baseball and basketball) insert program by Topps.

COMPLETE SET (20) 50.00 120.00
COMPLETE SERIES 1 (10) 25.00 60.00
COMPLETE SERIES 2 (10) 25.00 60.00
SER.1/2 STATED ODDS 1:36 HOBBY
HM11 Shaquille O'Neal 8.00 20.00
HM12 Jerry Stackhouse 4.00 10.00
HM13 Dennis Rodman 6.00 15.00
HM14 Joe Smith 2.50 6.00
HM15 Damon Stoudamire 2.50 6.00
HM16 Gary Payton 3.00 8.00
HM17 Mitch Richmond 3.00 8.00
HM18 Reggie Miller 4.00 10.00
HM19 Chris Webber 4.00 10.00
HM20 Vin Baker 2.50 6.00
HM21 Grant Hill 5.00 12.00
HM22 Scottie Pippen 5.00 12.00
HM23 Karl Malone 4.00 10.00
HM24 Patrick Ewing 4.00 10.00
HM25 Shawn Kemp 3.00 8.00
HM26 Anfernee Hardaway 5.00 12.00
HM27 Charles Barkley 5.00 12.00
HM28 Jason Kidd 5.00 12.00
HM29 Hakeem Olajuwon 4.00 10.00
HM30 Larry Johnson 3.00 8.00

1996-97 Topps Holding Court

Cards in this set of fifteen were randomly inserted in series one hobby and retail packs at a rate of one in 36 and feature the undeniable members of the NBA royalty, crowned "kings of the court" due to their impact on the game. Each card is printed utilizing Topps' exclusive Finest technology. Card backs are numbered with an "HC" prefix. Prices below refer to unpeeled cards. Peeled cards generally trade for ten to twenty-five percent less.

COMPLETE SET (15) 15.00 40.00
SER.1 ODDS 1:36 H/R, 1:24 JUMBO
*REF: 1.25X TO 3X HI COLUMN
REF: SER.1 ODDS 1:108 H/R, 1:72 JUMBO
HC1 Larry Johnson 1.00 2.50
HC2 Michael Jordan 10.00 25.00
HC3 Cedric Ceballos .60 1.50
HC4 Grant Hill 1.50 4.00
HC5 Anfernee Hardaway 1.50 4.00
HC6 Reggie Miller 1.25 3.00
HC7 Glenn Robinson .75 2.00
HC8 Patrick Ewing 1.25 3.00
HC9 Chris Webber 1.25 3.00
HC10 Shaquille O'Neal 2.50 6.00
HC11 John Stockton 1.25 3.00
HC12 Mitch Richmond 1.00 2.50
HC13 David Robinson 1.50 4.00
HC14 Gary Payton 1.00 2.50
HC15 Karl Malone 1.25 3.00

1996-97 Topps Mystery Finest

Randomly inserted in all second series packs at a rate of one 36, this 22-card set featues some of the top players from each division. Cards were issued with an opaque protector to keep the player a mystery until peeled. Card backs carry a "M" prefix.

COMPLETE SET (22) 30.00 80.00
SER.2 STATED ODDS 1:36 HOBBY/RETAIL
*BORDERLESS: .6X TO 1.5X HI COLUMN
BDLS: SER.2 STATED ODDS 1:72 HOB/RET
M1 Scottie Pippen 2.50 6.00
M2 Jason Kidd 2.50 6.00
M3 Anfernee Hardaway 2.50 6.00
M4 Gary Payton 1.50 4.00
M5 Juwan Howard 1.25 3.00
M6 Sean Elliott 1.50 4.00
M7 Dennis Rodman 3.00 8.00
M8 Shawn Kemp 1.50 4.00
M9 David Robinson 2.50 6.00
M10 Alonzo Mourning 2.00 5.00
M11 Dikembe Mutombo 1.50 4.00
M12 Shaquille O'Neal 4.00 10.00
M13 Clyde Drexler 2.00 5.00
M14 Michael Jordan 12.00 30.00
M15 Damon Stoudamire 1.25 3.00
M16 Mitch Richmond 1.50 4.00
M17 Patrick Ewing 2.00 5.00
M18 Vin Baker 1.25 3.00
M19 Hakeem Olajuwon 2.00 5.00
M20 Joe Smith 1.25 3.00
M21 Charles Barkley 2.50 6.00
M22 Reggie Miller 2.00 5.00

1996-97 Topps Mystery Finest Bordered Refractors

COMPLETE SET (22) 125.00 300.00
*BORDERED REF: 1.25X TO 3X BASE HI
SER.2 STATED ODDS 1:66 HOBBY JUMBO

1996-97 Topps Mystery Finest Borderless Refractors

*STARS: 1.5X TO 4X HI COLUMN
SER.2 STATED ODDS 1:216 HOBBY/RETAIL

1996-97 Topps Pro Files

Cards in this set of twenty were randomly issued in both series hobby and retail packs at a rate of one in 12. Topps' basketball spokesperson David Robinson was handed the assignment of writing all of the card backs for this insert set. "The Admiral" came through with flying colors as he gets up close and peronal with ten of the NBA's top stars. Card fronts contain a prismatic foil background with an action shot of the player and a head shot of David Robinson in the bottom left corner. Card backs are numbered with a "PF" prefix. In addition, two of these cards were inserted into Factory sets.

COMPLETE SET (20) 12.00 30.00
COMPLETE SERIES 1 (10) 10.00 25.00
COMPLETE SERIES 2 (10) 3.00 8.00
SER.1/2 STATED ODDS 1:12 H/R, 1:6 JUM
TWO PER FACTORY SET
PF1 Grant Hill .60 1.50
PF2 Shawn Kemp .40 1.00
PF3 Michael Jordan 6.00 15.00
PF4 Vin Baker .30 .75
PF5 Chris Webber .50 1.25
PF6 Joe Smith .30 .75
PF7 Shaquille O'Neal 1.00 2.50
PF8 Patrick Ewing .50 1.25
PF9 Scottie Pippen .60 1.50
PF10 Damon Stoudamire .30 .75
PF11 Anfernee Hardaway .60 1.50
PF12 Juwan Howard .30 .75
PF13 Dikembe Mutombo .40 1.00
PF14 Dennis Rodman .75 2.00
PF15 Kevin Garnett 1.00 2.50
PF16 Jerry Stackhouse .50 1.25
PF17 Alonzo Mourning .50 1.25
PF18 Karl Malone .50 1.25
PF19 Hakeem Olajuwon .50 1.25
PF20 Gary Payton .40 1.00

1996-97 Topps Season's Best

Cards in this set of 25 were randomly issued in first series hobby and retail packs at a rate of one in eight and feature five players who have excelled in the five key statistical categories of the game: Points - En Fuego; Rebounds - Board Members; Steals - Sticky Fingers; Assists - Dish Men and Blocks - Swat Team. Card fronts feature a prismatic background with the statistical theme title located around the action shot. Card backs are numbered with a "Season's Best" prefix. In addition, two of these cards were inserted in the Factory sets.

COMPLETE SET (25) 20.00 50.00
SER.1 STATED ODDS 1:8 HOB/RET, 1:4 JUM
TWO PER FACTORY SET
SB1 Michael Jordan 10.00 25.00
SB2 Hakeem Olajuwon 1.00 2.50
SB3 Shaquille O'Neal 2.00 5.00
SB4 Karl Malone 1.00 2.50
SB5 David Robinson 1.25 3.00
SB6 Dennis Rodman 1.50 4.00
SB7 David Robinson 1.25 3.00
SB8 Dikembe Mutombo .75 2.00
SB9 Charles Barkley 1.25 3.00
SB10 Shawn Kemp .75 2.00
SB11 John Stockton 1.00 2.50
SB12 Jason Kidd 1.25 3.00
SB13 Avery Johnson .60 1.50
SB14 Rod Strickland .50 1.25
SB15 Damon Stoudamire .60 1.50
SB16 Gary Payton .75 2.00
SB17 Mookie Blaylock .50 1.25
SB18 Michael Jordan 10.00 25.00
SB19 Jason Kidd 1.25 3.00
SB20 Alvin Robertson .50 1.25
SB21 Dikembe Mutombo .75 2.00
SB22 Shawn Bradley .50 1.25
SB23 David Robinson 1.25 3.00
SB24 Hakeem Olajuwon 1.00 2.50
SB25 Alonzo Mourning 1.00 2.50

1996-97 Topps Super Teams

After a one-year hiatus, Topps decided to transfer this insert set concept from their Stadium Club brand which had featured interactive Super Team inserts in 1993-94 and 1994-95. Cards from this set of 29 were randomly issued in first series hobby and retail packs at a rate of one in 36 and featured an action shot or group photo from each team in the league. Cards that feature teams that won either their division, their conference or the NBA finals or was the team selected to have the first draft pick in the 1997 NBA Draft are redeemable for various special Mystery Finest cards. The expiration date for Super Team cards is December 31, 1997.

COMPLETE SET (29) 30.00 60.00
SER.1 STATED ODDS 1:36 HOBBY/RETAIL
ST1 Atlanta Hawks 1.00 2.50
ST2 Boston Celtics 1.00 2.50
ST3 Charlotte Hornets 1.00 2.50
ST4 Chicago Bulls WCDF 10.00 25.00
ST5 Cleveland Cavaliers 1.00 2.50
ST6 Dallas Mavericks 1.00 2.50
ST7 Denver Nuggets 1.00 2.50
ST8 Detroit Pistons 1.00 2.50
ST9 Golden State Warriors 1.00 2.50
ST10 Houston Rockets 1.00 2.50
ST11 Indiana Pacers 1.00 2.50
ST12 Los Angeles Clippers 1.00 2.50
ST13 Los Angeles Lakers 1.50 4.00
ST14 Miami Heat WD 1.50 4.00
ST15 Milwaukee Bucks 1.00 2.50
ST16 Minnesota T'wolves 1.00 2.50
ST17 New Jersey Nets 1.00 2.50
ST18 New York Knicks 1.00 2.50
ST19 Orlando Magic 1.00 2.50
ST20 Philadelphia 76ers 1.00 2.50
ST21 Phoenix Suns 1.00 2.50
ST22 Portland Trail Blazers 1.00 2.50
ST23 Sacramento Kings 1.00 2.50
ST24 San Antonio Spurs W 5.00 12.00
ST25 Seattle Supersonics WD 1.00 2.50
ST26 Toronto Raptors 1.00 2.50
ST27 Utah Jazz WCD 5.00 12.00
ST28 Vancouver Grizzlies 1.00 2.50
ST29 Washington Bullets 1.00 2.50

1996-97 Topps Super Team Conference Winners

The following teams were eligible for the Conference Winner Super Team cards: Chicago and Utah. If you had one of those cards, you could redeem them for Mystery Finest Borderless Cards from the winners conference. The cards are similar in design to the regular Borderless cards issued in 1996-97 Topps series two. The cards differ by having a "Super Team Champion" logo on the card front. Each card was redeemable for 11 cards from each conference. The Eastern set is comprised of Reggie Miller, Vin Baker, Dennis Rodman, Damon Stoudamire, Michael Jordan, Scottie Pippen, Patrick Ewing, Alonzo Mourning, Juwan Howard, Anfernee Hardaway and Shaquille O'Neal. The Western set is comprised of Joe Smith, Mitch Richmond, Shawn Kemp, Gary Payton, Charles Barkley, Dikembe Mutombo, Hakeem Olajuwon, Clyde Drexler, David Robinson, Sean Elliott and Jason Kidd.

COMPLETE SET (22) 10.00 25.00
M1 Scottie Pippen 1.00 2.50
M2 Jason Kidd 1.00 2.50
M3 Anfernee Hardaway 1.00 2.50
M4 Gary Payton .60 1.50
M5 Juwan Howard .50 1.25
M6 Sean Elliott .60 1.50
M7 Dennis Rodman 1.25 3.00
M8 Shawn Kemp .60 1.50
M9 David Robinson 1.00 2.50
M10 Alonzo Mourning .75 2.00
M11 Dikembe Mutombo .60 1.50
M12 Shaquille O'Neal 1.50 4.00
M13 Clyde Drexler .75 2.00
M14 Michael Jordan 6.00 15.00
M15 Damon Stoudamire .50 1.25
M16 Mitch Richmond .60 1.50
M17 Patrick Ewing .75 2.00
M18 Vin Baker .50 1.25
M19 Hakeem Olajuwon .75 2.00
M20 Joe Smith .50 1.25
M21 Charles Barkley 1.00 2.50
M22 Reggie Miller .75 2.00

1996-97 Topps Super Team Division Winners

The following teams were eligible for the Division Winner Super Team cards: Chicago, Miami, Seattle and Utah. If you had one of those cards, you could redeem them for Mystery Finest Bordered Cards from the winners division. The cards are similar in design to the regular Bordered cards issued in 1996-97 Topps series two. The cards differ by having a "Super Team Champion" logo on the card front. The Bulls Central card returned six (Vin Baker, Michael Jordan, Reggie Miller, Scottie Pippen, Dennis Rodman and Damon Stoudamire), the Heat Atlantic five (Patrick Ewing, Anfernee Hardaway, Juwan Howard, Alonzo Mourning and Shaquille O'Neal), the Sonics Pacific five (Charles Barkley, Shawn Kemp, Gary Payton, Mitch Richmond and Joe Smith) and the Jazz Midwest six (Clyde Drexler, Sean Elliott, Jason Kidd, Dikembe Mutombo, Hakeem Olajuwon and David Robinson.)

COMPLETE SET (22) 8.00 20.00
M1 Scottie Pippen .75 2.00
M2 Jason Kidd .75 2.00
M3 Anfernee Hardaway .75 2.00
M4 Gary Payton .50 1.25
M5 Juwan Howard .40 1.00
M6 Sean Elliott .50 1.25
M7 Dennis Rodman 1.00 2.50
M8 Shawn Kemp .50 1.25
M9 David Robinson .75 2.00
M10 Alonzo Mourning .60 1.50
M11 Dikembe Mutombo .50 1.25
M12 Shaquille O'Neal 1.25 3.00
M13 Clyde Drexler .60 1.50
M14 Michael Jordan 4.00 10.00
M15 Damon Stoudamire .40 1.00
M16 Mitch Richmond .50 1.25
M17 Patrick Ewing .60 1.50
M18 Vin Baker .40 1.00
M19 Hakeem Olajuwon .60 1.50
M20 Joe Smith .40 1.00
M21 Charles Barkley .75 2.00
M22 Reggie Miller .60 1.50

1996-97 Topps Super Team NBA Finals

The following teams were eligible for the NBA Finals Super Team cards: Chicago and San Antonio. If you had one of those cards, you could redeem them for a set of Mystery Finest Bordered Refractor Cards - similar in design to the regular Bordered Refractors issued in 1996-97 Topps series two. The cards differ by having a "Super Team Champion" logo on the card front.

COMPLETE SET (22) 40.00 100.00
M1 Scottie Pippen 4.00 10.00
M2 Jason Kidd 4.00 10.00
M3 Anfernee Hardaway 4.00 10.00
M4 Gary Payton 2.50 6.00
M5 Juwan Howard 2.00 5.00
M6 Sean Elliott 2.50 6.00
M7 Dennis Rodman 5.00 12.00
M8 Shawn Kemp 2.50 6.00
M9 David Robinson 4.00 10.00
M10 Alonzo Mourning 3.00 8.00
M11 Dikembe Mutombo 2.50 6.00
M12 Shaquille O'Neal 6.00 15.00
M13 Clyde Drexler 3.00 8.00
M14 Michael Jordan 40.00 100.00
M15 Damon Stoudamire 2.00 5.00
M16 Mitch Richmond 2.50 6.00
M17 Patrick Ewing 3.00 8.00
M18 Vin Baker 2.00 5.00
M19 Hakeem Olajuwon 3.00 8.00
M20 Joe Smith 2.00 5.00
M21 Charles Barkley 4.00 10.00
M22 Reggie Miller 3.00 8.00

1996-97 Topps Youthquake

Randomly inserted into second series retail packs only at a rate of one in 36, this 15-card set features some of the NBA's top young stars. Cards are printed on wood. Card backs carry a "YQ" prefix.

COMPLETE SET (15) 25.00 60.00
SER.2 STATED ODDS 1:36 RETAIL
YQ1 Allen Iverson 5.00 12.00
YQ2 Samaki Walker .75 2.00
YQ3 Stephon Marbury 2.50 6.00
YQ4 Damon Stoudamire .75 2.00
YQ5 John Wallace 1.00 2.50
YQ6 Michael Finley 1.25 3.00
YQ7 Marcus Camby 1.50 4.00
YQ8 Kerry Kittles 1.00 2.50
YQ9 Ray Allen 4.00 10.00
YQ10 Jerry Stackhouse 1.25 3.00
YQ11 Shareef Abdur-Rahim 1.50 4.00
YQ12 Antonio McDyess 1.00 2.50
YQ13 Joe Smith .75 2.00
YQ14 Brent Barry .75 2.00
YQ15 Kobe Bryant 10.00 25.00

1997-98 Topps

The 1997-98 release from Topps contained 220 basic cards, with each series containing 110. The cards were distributed in 11-card packs with a suggested retail price of $1.29. The set features color player photos printed on 16 pt. card stock with foil stamping and spot UV-Coating.

COMPLETE SET (220) 15.00 30.00
COMPLETE SERIES 1 (110) 5.00 10.00
COMPLETE SERIES 2 (110) 10.00 20.00
1 Scottie Pippen .25 .60
2 Nate McMillan .10 .25
3 Byron Scott .12 .30
4 Mark Davis .10 .25
5 Rod Strickland .10 .25
6 Brian Grant .10 .25
7 Damon Stoudamire .12 .30
8 John Stockton .20 .50
9 Grant Long .10 .25
10 Darrell Armstrong .10 .25
11 Anthony Mason .10 .25
12 Travis Best .10 .25
13 Stephon Marbury .20 .50
14 Jamal Mashburn .12 .30
15 Detlef Schrempf .15 .40
16 Terrell Brandon .10 .25
17 Charles Barkley .25 .60
18 Vin Baker .12 .30
19 Gary Trent .10 .25
20 Vinny Del Negro .10 .25
21 Todd Day .10 .25
22 Malik Sealy .10 .25
23 Wesley Person .10 .25
24 Reggie Miller .20 .50
25 Dan Majerle .15 .40
26 Todd Fuller .10 .25
27 Juwan Howard .12 .30
28 Clarence Weatherspoon .10 .25
29 Grant Hill .25 .60
30 John Williams .10 .25
31 Ken Norman .10 .25
32 Patrick Ewing .20 .50
33 Bryon Russell .10 .25
34 Tony Smith .10 .25
35 Andrew Lang .10 .25
36 Rony Seikaly .10 .25
37 Billy Owens .10 .25
38 Dino Radja .10 .25
39 Chris Gatling .10 .25
40 Dale Davis .10 .25
41 Arvydas Sabonis .12 .30
42 Chris Mills .10 .25
43 A.C. Green .12 .30
44 Tyrone Hill .10 .25
45 Tracy Murray .10 .25
46 David Robinson .25 .60
47 Lee Mayberry .10 .25
48 Jayson Williams .10 .25
49 Jason Kidd .25 .60
50 Bryant Stith .10 .25
51 Latrell Sprewell .15 .40
52 Brent Barry .12 .30
53 Henry James .10 .25
54 Allen Iverson .30 .75
55 Shandon Anderson .10 .25
56 Mitch Richmond .15 .40
57 Allan Houston .12 .30
58 Ron Harper .12 .30
59 Gheorghe Muresan .10 .25
60 Vincent Askew .10 .25
61 Ray Allen .20 .50
62 Kenny Anderson .12 .30
63 Dikembe Mutombo .15 .40
64 Sam Perkins .10 .25
65 Walt Williams .10 .25
66 Chris Carr .10 .25
67 Vlade Divac .15 .40
68 LaPhonso Ellis .10 .25
69 B.J. Armstrong .10 .25
70 Jim Jackson .10 .25
71 Clyde Drexler .20 .50
72 Lindsey Hunter .10 .25
73 Sasha Danilovic .10 .25
74 Elden Campbell .10 .25
75 Robert Pack .10 .25
76 Dennis Scott .10 .25
77 Will Perdue .10 .25
78 Anthony Peeler .10 .25
79 Steve Smith .12 .30
80 Steve Kerr .12 .30
81 Buck Williams .10 .25
82 Terry Mills .10 .25
83 Michael Smith .10 .25
84 Adam Keefe .10 .25
85 Kevin Willis .10 .25
86 David Wesley .10 .25
87 Muggsy Bogues .12 .30
88 Bimbo Coles .10 .25
89 Tom Gugliotta .10 .25
90 Jermaine O'Neal .12 .30
91 Cedric Ceballos .10 .25
92 Shawn Kemp .15 .40
93 Horace Grant .12 .30
94 Shareef Abdur-Rahim .15 .40
95 Robert Horry .12 .30
96 Vitaly Potapenko .10 .25
97 Pooh Richardson .10 .25
98 Doug Christie .10 .25
99 Voshon Lenard .10 .25
100 Dominique Wilkins .20 .50
101 Alonzo Mourning .20 .50
102 Sam Cassell .12 .30
103 Sherman Douglas .10 .25
104 Shawn Bradley .10 .25
105 Mark Jackson .12 .30
106 Dennis Rodman .30 .75
107 Charles Oakley .12 .30
108 Matt Maloney .10 .25
109 Shaquille O'Neal .40 1.00
110 Checklist .10 .25
111 Antonio McDyess .12 .30
112 Bob Sura .10 .25
113 Terrell Brandon .10 .25
114 Tim Thomas RC .20 .50
115 Tim Duncan RC .75 2.00
116 Antonio Daniels RC .15 .40
117 Bryant Reeves .10 .25
118 Keith Van Horn RC .25 .60
119 Loy Vaught .10 .25
120 Rasheed Wallace .15 .40
121 Bobby Jackson RC .20 .50
122 Kevin Johnson .15 .40
123 Michael Jordan 1.25 3.00
124 Ron Mercer RC .20 .50
125 Tracy McGrady RC .60 1.50
126 Antoine Walker .15 .40
127 Carlos Rogers .10 .25
128 Isaac Austin .10 .25
129 Mookie Blaylock .10 .25
130 Rodrick Rhodes RC .12 .30
131 Dennis Scott .10 .25
132 Chris Mullin .15 .40
133 P.J. Brown .10 .25
134 Rex Chapman .10 .25
135 Sean Elliott .15 .40
136 Alan Henderson .10 .25
137 Austin Croshere RC .12 .30
138 Nick Van Exel .12 .30
139 Derek Strong .10 .25
140 Glenn Robinson .12 .30
141 Avery Johnson .12 .30
142 Calbert Cheaney .10 .25
143 Mahmoud Abdul-Rauf .10 .25
144 Stojko Vrankovic .10 .25
145 Chris Childs .10 .25
146 Danny Manning .12 .30
147 Jeff Hornacek .12 .30
148 Kevin Garnett .25 .60
149 Joe Dumars .15 .40
150 Johnny Taylor RC .12 .30
151 Mark Price .15 .40
152 Toni Kukoc .15 .40
153 Erick Dampier .10 .25
154 Lorenzen Wright .10 .25
155 Matt Geiger .10 .25
156 Tim Hardaway .15 .40
157 Charles Smith RC .12 .30
158 Hersey Hawkins .10 .25
159 Michael Finley .15 .40
160 Tyus Edney .10 .25
161 Christian Laettner .12 .30
162 Doug West .10 .25
163 Jim Jackson .10 .25
164 Larry Johnson .15 .40
165 Vin Baker .12 .30
166 Karl Malone .20 .50
167 Kelvin Cato RC .12 .30
168 Luc Longley .12 .30
169 Dale Davis .10 .25
170 Joe Smith .12 .30
171 Kobe Bryant .75 2.00
172 Scot Pollard RC .15 .40
173 Derek Anderson RC .15 .40
174 Erick Strickland RC .12 .30
175 Olden Polynice .10 .25
176 Chris Whitney .10 .25
177 Anthony Parker RC .15 .40
178 Armon Gilliam .10 .25
179 Gary Payton .15 .40
180 Glen Rice .15 .40
181 Chauncey Billups RC .50 1.25
182 Derek Fisher .15 .40
183 John Starks .12 .30
184 Mario Elie .10 .25
185 Chris Webber .15 .40
186 Shawn Kemp .15 .40
187 Greg Ostertag .10 .25
188 Olivier Saint-Jean RC .12 .30
189 Eric Snow .10 .25
190 Isaiah Rider .12 .30
191 Paul Grant RC .10 .25
192 Samaki Walker .10 .25
193 Cory Alexander .10 .25
194 Eddie Jones .15 .40
195 John Thomas RC .10 .25
196 Otis Thorpe .10 .25
197 Rod Strickland .10 .25
198 David Wesley .10 .25
199 Jacque Vaughn RC .12 .30
200 Rik Smits .12 .30
201 Brevin Knight RC .15 .40
202 Clifford Robinson .10 .25
203 Hakeem Olajuwon .20 .50
204 Jerry Stackhouse .15 .40
205 Tyrone Hill .10 .25
206 Kendall Gill .10 .25
207 Marcus Camby .15 .40
208 Tony Battie RC .15 .40
209 Brent Price .10 .25
210 Danny Fortson RC .15 .40
211 Jerome Williams .10 .25
212 Maurice Taylor RC .15 .40
213 Brian Williams .10 .25
214 Keith Booth RC .12 .30
215 Nick Anderson .10 .25
216 Travis Knight .10 .25
217 Adonal Foyle RC .12 .30
218 Anfernee Hardaway .25 .60
219 Kerry Kittles .10 .25
220 Checklist .10 .25

1997-98 Topps Minted in Springfield

*STARS: 2X TO 5X BASE CARD HI
*RCs: 1.25X TO 3X BASE HI
SER.1 STATED ODDS 1:6 HOBBY/RETAIL
SER.2 STATED ODDS 1:9 HOBBY/RETAIL

1997-98 Topps Autographs

Randomly inserted in first series hobby packs at a rate of one in 212, this eight-card set features autographs from some of the NBA's top players. The Hakeem Olajuwon card was available as both a redemption and an actual autograph from packs.

SER.1 STATED ODDS 1:212 HOBBY
1 John Starks 8.00 20.00
2 Juwan Howard 6.00 15.00
3 Mitch Richmond 8.00 20.00
4 Hakeem Olajuwon 15.00 40.00
5 Glenn Robinson 6.00 15.00
6 Steve Smith 5.00 12.00
7 Antoine Walker 6.00 15.00
8 Clyde Drexler 10.00 25.00

1997-98 Topps Bound for Glory

Randomly inserted in series one hobby packs only at a rate of one in 36, this 15-card set is printed on rainbow foilboard stock and features some of the NBA's top players. Card backs carry a "BG" prefix.

COMPLETE SET (15) 40.00 100.00
SER.1 STATED ODDS 1:36 HOBBY
BG1 Robert Parish 1.25 3.00
BG2 Grant Hill 2.00 5.00
BG3 Chris Mullin 1.25 3.00
BG4 Hakeem Olajuwon 1.50 4.00
BG5 Dennis Rodman 2.50 6.00
BG6 Patrick Ewing 1.50 4.00
BG7 Karl Malone 1.50 4.00
BG8 Charles Barkley 2.00 5.00
BG9 David Robinson 2.00 5.00
BG10 Michael Jordan 20.00 50.00
BG11 Dominique Wilkins 1.50 4.00
BG12 Shaquille O'Neal 3.00 8.00
BG13 Clyde Drexler 1.50 4.00
BG14 John Stockton 1.50 4.00
BG15 Scottie Pippen 2.00 5.00

1997-98 Topps Clutch Time

Randomly inserted into series two hobby packs only at a rate of one in 36, this 20-card set focuses on players who can get it done in the clutch. Card fronts feature a foil background with "Clutch Time" written across the top of the card as if it was a scoreboard. Card backs contain a "CT" prefix.

COMPLETE SET (20) 20.00 50.00
SER.2 STATED ODDS 1:36 HOBBY
CT1 Michael Jordan 12.00 30.00
CT2 Christian Laettner 1.00 2.50
CT3 Patrick Ewing 1.50 4.00
CT4 Glen Rice 1.25 3.00
CT5 Stephon Marbury 1.50 4.00
CT6 Tim Hardaway 1.25 3.00
CT7 Reggie Miller 1.50 4.00
CT8 Gary Payton 1.25 3.00
CT9 Charles Barkley 2.00 5.00
CT10 Grant Hill 2.00 5.00
CT11 Karl Malone 1.50 4.00
CT12 Dikembe Mutombo 1.25 3.00
CT13 Hakeem Olajuwon 1.50 4.00
CT14 Shawn Kemp 1.25 3.00
CT15 John Stockton 1.50 4.00
CT16 Anfernee Hardaway 2.00 5.00
CT17 Glenn Robinson 1.00 2.50
CT18 Chris Webber 1.25 3.00
CT19 Allen Iverson 2.50 6.00
CT20 Scottie Pippen 2.00 5.00

1997-98 Topps Destiny

Randomly inserted into retail packs only at a rate of one in 18, this 15-card set focuses on players who are destined to become NBA legends. Card fronts feature a full shot of the player surrounded by an embossed circle with the card theme "Destiny" also embossed across the top. Card backs carry a "D" prefix.

COMPLETE SET (15) 20.00 50.00
SER.2 STATED ODDS 1:18 RETAIL
D1 Grant Hill 2.00 5.00
D2 Kevin Garnett 2.00 5.00
D3 Vin Baker 1.00 2.50
D4 Antoine Walker 1.25 3.00
D5 Kobe Bryant 6.00 15.00
D6 Tracy McGrady 2.50 6.00
D7 Keith Van Horn 1.00 2.50
D8 Tim Duncan 3.00 8.00
D9 Eddie Jones 1.25 3.00
D10 Stephon Marbury 1.50 4.00
D11 Marcus Camby 1.25 3.00
D12 Antonio McDyess 1.00 2.50
D13 Shareef Abdur-Rahim 1.25 3.00
D14 Allen Iverson 2.50 6.00
D15 Shaquille O'Neal 3.00 8.00

1997-98 Topps Draft Redemption

Randomly inserted into series one hobby packs at a rate of 1:12 and retail packs at a rate of 1:18, this 29-card set features trade cards for the first 29 picks of the 1997 NBA Draft. Each redemption card had a number corresponding to each draft position of the first round, and could be exchanged for a special card of the player taken in that draft position once they signed their NBA Contract. The expiration date for the cards was April 1, 1998

SER.1 STATED ODDS 1:12 HOB, 1:18 RET
DP1 Tim Duncan 25.00 60.00
DP2 Keith Van Horn 3.00 8.00
DP3 Chauncey Billups 6.00 15.00
DP4 Antonio Daniels 2.00 5.00
DP5 Tony Battie 2.00 5.00
DP6 Ron Mercer 2.50 6.00
DP7 Tim Thomas 2.50 6.00
DP8 Adonal Foyle 1.50 4.00
DP9 Tracy McGrady 8.00 20.00
DP10 Danny Fortson 2.00 5.00
DP11 Olivier Saint-Jean 1.50 4.00
DP12 Austin Croshere 1.50 4.00
DP13 Derek Anderson 2.00 5.00
DP14 Maurice Taylor 2.00 5.00
DP15 Kelvin Cato 1.50 4.00
DP16 Brevin Knight 2.00 5.00
DP17 Johnny Taylor 1.50 4.00
DP18 Chris Anstey 1.25 3.00
DP19 Scot Pollard 2.00 5.00
DP20 Paul Grant 1.25 3.00
DP21 Anthony Parker 2.00 5.00
DP22 Ed Gray 2.00 5.00
DP23 Bobby Jackson 2.50 6.00
DP24 Rodrick Rhodes 1.50 4.00
DP25 John Thomas 1.25 3.00
DP26 Charles Smith 1.50 4.00
DP27 Jacque Vaughn 1.50 4.00
DP28 Keith Booth 1.50 4.00
DP29 Serge Zwikker 2.00 5.00

1997-98 Topps Fantastic 15

Randomly inserted in series one retail packs at a rate of one in 36, this 15-card set showcases up-and-comoing greats on holographic cards. Card backs carry a "F" prefix.

COMPLETE SET (15) 20.00 50.00
SER.1 STATED ODDS 1:36 RETAIL
F1 Antoine Walker 1.50 4.00
F2 Damon Stoudamire 1.25 3.00
F3 Brent Barry 1.25 3.00
F4 Michael Finley 1.50 4.00
F5 Ray Allen 2.00 5.00
F6 Allen Iverson 3.00 8.00
F7 Stephon Marbury 2.00 5.00
F8 Kerry Kittles 1.00 2.50
F9 John Wallace 1.00 2.50
F10 Kevin Garnett 2.50 6.00
F11 Jerry Stackhouse 1.50 4.00
F12 Kobe Bryant 8.00 20.00
F13 Marcus Camby 1.50 4.00
F14 Joe Smith 1.25 3.00
F15 Shareef Abdur-Rahim 1.50 4.00

1997-98 Topps Generations

Randomly inserted into series two packs at a rate of one in 36, this 30-card set features the best rookies from each draft class. The cards are die cut and finished in the Finest technology. Card backs are numbered with a "G" prefix.

COMPLETE SET (30) 75.00 150.00
SER.2 STATED ODDS 1:36 HOBBY/RETAIL
G1 Clyde Drexler 2.50 6.00
G2 Michael Jordan 25.00 60.00
G3 Charles Barkley 3.00 8.00
G4 Hakeem Olajuwon 2.50 6.00
G5 John Stockton 2.50 6.00
G6 Patrick Ewing 2.50 6.00
G7 Karl Malone 2.50 6.00
G8 Dennis Rodman 4.00 10.00
G9 Scottie Pippen 3.00 8.00
G10 David Robinson 3.00 8.00
G11 Mitch Richmond 2.00 5.00
G12 Glen Rice 2.00 5.00
G13 Shawn Kemp 2.00 5.00
G14 Gary Payton 2.00 5.00
G15 Dikembe Mutombo 2.00 5.00
G16 Steve Smith 1.50 4.00
G17 Christian Laettner 1.50 4.00
G18 Shaquille O'Neal 6.00 15.00
G19 Alonzo Mourning 2.50 6.00
G20 Tom Gugliotta 1.25 3.00
G21 Anfernee Hardaway 3.00 8.00
G22 Grant Hill 3.00 8.00
G23 Kevin Garnett 3.00 8.00
G24 Kobe Bryant 10.00 25.00
G25 Stephon Marbury 2.50 6.00
G26 Antoine Walker 2.00 5.00
G27 Shareef Abdur-Rahim 2.00 5.00
G28 Tim Duncan 5.00 12.00
G29 Keith Van Horn 1.50 4.00
G30 Tracy McGrady 4.00 10.00

1997-98 Topps Generations Refractors

*REF: 1X TO 2.5X HI COLUMN
SER.2 STATED ODDS 1:144 HOBBY/RETAIL
G2 Michael Jordan 125.00 300.00
G8 Dennis Rodman 15.00 40.00
G18 Shaquille O'Neal 12.00 30.00
G28 Tim Duncan 20.00 50.00

1997-98 Topps Inside Stuff

Randomly inserted into series two packs at a rate of one in 36, this 10-card set features some of the best plays from the 1997 NBA Playoffs. Card fronts have a foil background and card backs carry an "IS" prefix.

COMPLETE SET (10) 15.00 40.00
SER.2 STATED ODDS 1:36 HOBBY/RETAIL
IS1 Michael Jordan 10.00 25.00
IS2 Eddie Johnson .75 2.00
IS3 John Stockton 1.50 4.00
IS4 Patrick Ewing 1.50 4.00
IS5 Shaquille O'Neal 3.00 8.00
IS6 Rex Chapman .75 2.00
IS7 Shawn Kemp 1.25 3.00
IS8 Scottie Pippen 2.00 5.00
IS9 Kobe Bryant 6.00 15.00
IS10 Anfernee Hardaway 2.00 5.00

1997-98 Topps New School

Randomly inserted in series two hobby packs at a rate of one in 36 and series two retail packs at one in 18, this 15-card set focuses on the key rookies from the 1997 class. Card fronts feature the theme "New School" in a banner and the front is sprinkled in glitter. Card backs contain a "NS" prefix.

COMPLETE SET (15) 15.00 40.00
SER.2 STATED ODDS 1:36 HOBBY/RETAIL
NS1 Austin Croshere .60 1.50
NS2 Antonio Daniels .75 2.00
NS3 Tim Thomas 1.00 2.50
NS4 Keith Van Horn 1.25 3.00
NS5 Bobby Jackson 1.00 2.50
NS6 Derek Anderson .75 2.00
NS7 Adonal Foyle .60 1.50
NS8 Johnny Taylor .60 1.50
NS9 Jacque Vaughn .60 1.50
NS10 Chauncey Billups 2.50 6.00
NS11 Brevin Knight .75 2.00
NS12 Tracy McGrady 3.00 8.00
NS13 Tony Battie .75 2.00
NS14 Scot Pollard .75 2.00
NS15 Tim Duncan 4.00 10.00

1997-98 Topps Rock Stars

Randomly inserted in series one packs at a rate of one in 36, this 20-card set features a die-cut borderless Finest design. Card backs carry a "RS" prefix.

COMPLETE SET (20) 50.00 120.00
SER.1 STATED ODDS 1:36 HOBBY/RETAIL
*REF: 1.25X TO 3X BASE ROCK STARS
REF: SER.1 STATED ODDS 1:144 H/R
RS1 Michael Jordan 30.00 80.00
RS2 Jerry Stackhouse 2.00 5.00
RS3 Chris Webber 2.00 5.00
RS4 Charles Barkley 3.00 8.00
RS5 Dennis Rodman 4.00 10.00
RS6 Anfernee Hardaway 3.00 8.00
RS7 Juwan Howard 1.50 4.00
RS8 Tim Hardaway 2.00 5.00
RS9 Gary Payton 2.00 5.00
RS10 Dikembe Mutombo 2.00 5.00
RS11 Tom Gugliotta 1.25 3.00
RS12 Kevin Garnett 3.00 8.00
RS13 Shaquille O'Neal 5.00 12.00

RS14 Hakeem Olajuwon 2.50 6.00
RS15 Grant Hill 3.00 8.00
RS16 Karl Malone 2.50 6.00
RS17 Damon Stoudamire 1.50 4.00
RS18 Shawn Kemp 2.00 5.00
RS19 Alonzo Mourning 2.50 6.00
RS20 Scottie Pippen 3.00 8.00

1997-98 Topps Season's Best

Randomly inserted in series one packs at a rate of one in 16, this 30-card set showcases 25 superstars who have dominated the game in different statistical categories, and five rookies from the 1996 class featured on borderless prismatic illusion foilboard. The groupings used were Key Masters, Power Core, Shooting Stars, Frontcourt Finesse, Pressure Points and Hot Shots. Card backs carry a "SB" prefix.

COMPLETE SET (30) 20.00 50.00
SER.1 STATED ODDS 1:16 HOBBY/RETAIL
SB1 Gary Payton .75 2.00
SB2 Kevin Johnson .75 2.00
SB3 Tim Hardaway .75 2.00
SB4 John Stockton 1.00 2.50
SB5 Damon Stoudamire .60 1.50
SB6 Michael Jordan 15.00 40.00
SB7 Mitch Richmond .75 2.00
SB8 Latrell Sprewell .75 2.00
SB9 Reggie Miller 1.00 2.50
SB10 Clyde Drexler 1.00 2.50
SB11 Grant Hill 1.25 3.00
SB12 Scottie Pippen 1.25 3.00
SB13 Kendall Gill .50 1.25
SB14 Glen Rice .75 2.00
SB15 LaPhonso Ellis .50 1.25
SB16 Karl Malone 1.00 2.50
SB17 Charles Barkley 1.25 3.00
SB18 Vin Baker .60 1.50
SB19 Chris Webber .75 2.00
SB20 Tom Gugliotta .50 1.25
SB21 Shaquille O'Neal 2.00 5.00
SB22 Patrick Ewing 1.00 2.50
SB23 Hakeem Olajuwon 1.00 2.50
SB24 Alonzo Mourning 1.00 2.50
SB25 Dikembe Mutombo .75 2.00
SB26 Allen Iverson 1.50 4.00
SB27 Antoine Walker .75 2.00
SB28 Shareef Abdur-Rahim .75 2.00
SB29 Stephon Marbury 1.00 2.50
SB30 Kerry Kittles .50 1.25

1997-98 Topps Topps 40

Randomly inserted in both series packs at a rate of one in 12, this set of 40 cards was divided up among both series one and two packs and features 40 of the top players in the NBA as voted on by NBA players, coaches and writers. The cards are printed on foil-stamped mirrorboard cards. Card backs carry a "T40" prefix.

COMPLETE SET (40) 40.00 80.00
COMPLETE SERIES 1 (20) 15.00 40.00
COMPLETE SERIES 2 (20) 15.00 40.00
BOTH SERIES STATED ODDS 1:12 H/R
T1 Glen Rice 1.00 2.50
T2 Patrick Ewing 1.25 3.00
T3 Terrell Brandon .60 1.50
T4 Jerry Stackhouse 1.00 2.50
T5 Michael Jordan 8.00 20.00
T6 Christian Laettner .75 2.00
T7 Latrell Sprewell 1.00 2.50
T8 Reggie Miller 1.25 3.00
T9 Gary Payton 1.00 2.50
T10 Detlef Schrempf 1.00 2.50
T11 Kevin Garnett 1.50 4.00
T12 Eddie Jones 1.00 2.50
T13 Clyde Drexler 1.25 3.00
T14 Anfernee Hardaway 1.50 4.00
T15 Chris Webber 1.00 2.50
T16 Jayson Williams .60 1.50
T17 Joe Smith .75 2.00
T18 Karl Malone 1.25 3.00
T19 Tim Hardaway 1.00 2.50
T20 Vin Baker .75 2.00
T21 Tom Gugliotta .60 1.50
T22 Allen Iverson 2.00 5.00
T23 David Robinson 1.50 4.00
T24 Dikembe Mutombo 1.00 2.50
T25 John Stockton 1.25 3.00
T26 Charles Barkley 1.50 4.00
T27 Mitch Richmond 1.00 2.50
T28 Damon Stoudamire .75 2.00
T29 Anthony Mason .60 1.50
T30 Shaquille O'Neal 2.50 6.00
T31 Glenn Robinson .75 2.00
T32 Juwan Howard .75 2.00
T33 Shawn Kemp 1.00 2.50
T34 Dennis Rodman 2.00 5.00
T35 Grant Hill 1.50 4.00
T36 Kevin Johnson 1.00 2.50
T37 Alonzo Mourning 1.25 3.00
T38 Hakeem Olajuwon 1.25 3.00
T39 Joe Dumars 1.00 2.50
T40 Scottie Pippen 1.50 4.00

1998-99 Topps Promos

PP7 Kobe Bryant 2.50 6.00

1998-99 Topps

Both series of Topps was issued in 110-card sets (totalling 220 cards) in 11-card packs with a suggested retail price of $1.29. Each card was produced on a super gloss coated 16-point stock with foil-stamping.

COMPLETE SET (220) 15.00 40.00
COMPLETE SERIES 1 (110) 5.00 12.00
COMPLETE SERIES 2 (110) 10.00 25.00
1 Scottie Pippen .25 .60
2 Shareef Abdur-Rahim .15 .40
3 Rod Strickland .10 .25
4 Keith Van Horn .15 .40
5 Ray Allen .20 .50
6 Chris Mullin .15 .40
7 Anthony Parker .10 .25
8 Lindsey Hunter .10 .25
9 Mario Elie .10 .25
10 Jerry Stackhouse .15 .40
11 Eldridge Recasner .10 .25
12 Jeff Hornacek .12 .30
13 Chris Webber .15 .40
14 Lee Mayberry .10 .25
15 Erick Strickland .10 .25
16 Arvydas Sabonis .12 .30
17 Tim Thomas .15 .40
18 Luc Longley .12 .30
19 Detlef Schrempf .15 .40
20 Alonzo Mourning .20 .50
21 Adonal Foyle .10 .25
22 Tony Battie .12 .30
23 Robert Horry .12 .30
24 Derek Harper .12 .30
25 Jamal Mashburn .12 .30
26 Elliot Perry .10 .25
27 Jalen Rose .12 .30
28 Joe Smith .12 .30
29 Henry James .10 .25
30 Travis Knight .10 .25
31 Tom Gugliotta .10 .25
32 Chris Anstey .10 .25
33 Antonio Daniels .10 .25
34 Elden Campbell .10 .25
35 Charlie Ward .10 .25
36 Eddie Johnson .10 .25
37 John Wallace .10 .25
38 Antonio Davis .10 .25
39 Antoine Walker .15 .40
40 Patrick Ewing .20 .50
41 Doug Christie .10 .25
42 Andrew Lang .10 .25
43 Joe Dumars .15 .40
44 Jaren Jackson .10 .25
45 Loy Vaught .10 .25
46 Allan Houston .12 .30
47 Mark Jackson .12 .30
48 Tracy Murray .10 .25
49 Tim Duncan .30 .75
50 Micheal Williams .10 .25
51 Steve Nash .25 .60
52 Matt Maloney .10 .25
53 Sam Cassell .12 .30
54 Voshon Lenard .10 .25
55 Dikembe Mutombo .15 .40
56 Malik Sealy .10 .25
57 Dell Curry .10 .25
58 Stephon Marbury .20 .50
59 Tariq Abdul-Wahad .10 .25
60 Isaiah Rider .12 .30
61 Kelvin Cato .10 .25
62 LaPhonso Ellis .10 .25
63 Jim Jackson .10 .25
64 Greg Ostertag .10 .25
65 Glenn Robinson .12 .30
66 Chris Carr .10 .25
67 Marcus Camby .12 .30
68 Kobe Bryant .60 1.50
69 Bobby Jackson .10 .25
70 B.J. Armstrong .10 .25
71 Alan Henderson .10 .25
72 Terry Davis .10 .25
73 John Stockton .20 .50
74 Lamond Murray .10 .25
75 Mark Price .15 .40
76 Rex Chapman .10 .25
77 Michael Jordan 1.25 3.00
78 Terry Cummings .12 .30
79 Dan Majerle .15 .40
80 Bo Outlaw .10 .25
81 Michael Finley .15 .40
82 Vin Baker .12 .30
83 Clifford Robinson .10 .25
84 Greg Anthony .10 .25
85 Brevin Knight .10 .25
86 Jacque Vaughn .10 .25
87 Bobby Phills .10 .25
88 Sherman Douglas .10 .25
89 Kevin Johnson .15 .40
90 Mahmoud Abdul-Rauf .10 .25
91 Lorenzen Wright .10 .25
92 Eric Williams .10 .25
93 Will Perdue .10 .25
94 Charles Barkley .25 .60
95 Kendall Gill .10 .25
96 Wesley Person .10 .25
97 Buck Williams .10 .25
98 Erick Dampier .10 .25
99 Nate McMillan .10 .25
100 Sean Elliott .15 .40
101 Rasheed Wallace .15 .40
102 Zydrunas Ilgauskas .15 .40
103 Eddie Jones .15 .40
104 Ron Mercer .12 .30
105 Horace Grant .12 .30
106 Corliss Williamson .10 .25
107 Anthony Mason .10 .25
108 Mookie Blaylock .10 .25
109 Dennis Rodman .30 .75
110 Checklist .10 .25
111 Steve Smith .12 .30
112 Cedric Henderson .10 .25
113 Raef LaFrentz RC .40 1.00
114 Calbert Cheaney .10 .25
115 Rik Smits .12 .30
116 Rony Seikaly .10 .25
117 Lawrence Funderburke .10 .25
118 Ricky Davis RC .50 1.25
119 Howard Eisley .10 .25
120 Kenny Anderson .12 .30
121 Corey Benjamin RC .20 .50
122 Maurice Taylor .10 .25
123 Eric Murdock .10 .25
124 Derek Fisher .15 .40
125 Kevin Garnett .25 .60
126 Walt Williams .10 .25
127 Bryce Drew RC .20 .50
128 A.C. Green .12 .30
129 Ervin Johnson .10 .25
130 Christian Laettner .12 .30
131 Chauncey Billups .20 .50
132 Hakeem Olajuwon .20 .50
133 Al Harrington RC .50 1.25
134 Danny Manning .12 .30
135 Paul Pierce RC 1.25 3.00
136 Terrell Brandon .10 .25
137 Bob Sura .10 .25
138 Chris Gatling .10 .25
139 Donyell Marshall .10 .25
140 Marcus Camby .12 .30
141 Brian Skinner RC .30 .75
142 Charles Oakley .12 .30
143 Antawn Jamison RC .50 1.25
144 Nazr Mohammed RC .30 .75
145 Karl Malone .20 .50
146 Chris Mills .10 .25
147 Bison Dele .10 .25
148 Gary Payton .15 .40
149 Terry Porter .10 .25
150 Tim Hardaway .15 .40
151 Larry Hughes RC .60 1.50
152 Derek Anderson .10 .25
153 Jason Williams RC .75 2.00
154 Dirk Nowitzki RC 2.00 5.00
155 Juwan Howard .12 .30
156 Avery Johnson .12 .30
157 Matt Harpring RC .30 .75
158 Reggie Miller .20 .50
159 Walter McCarty .10 .25
160 Allen Iverson .30 .75
161 Felipe Lopez RC .20 .50
162 Tracy McGrady .25 .60
163 Damon Stoudamire .12 .30
164 Antonio McDyess .12 .30
165 Grant Hill .25 .60
166 Tyronn Lue RC .30 .75
167 P.J. Brown .10 .25
168 Antonio Daniels .10 .25
169 Mitch Richmond .15 .40
170 David Robinson .25 .60
171 Shawn Bradley .10 .25
172 Shandon Anderson .10 .25
173 Chris Childs .10 .25
174 Shawn Kemp .15 .40
175 Shaquille O'Neal .40 1.00
176 John Starks .12 .30
177 Tyrone Hill .10 .25
178 Jayson Williams .10 .25
179 Anfernee Hardaway .25 .60
180 Chris Webber .15 .40
181 Don Reid .10 .25
182 Stacey Augmon .12 .30
183 Hersey Hawkins .10 .25
184 Sam Mitchell .10 .25
185 Jason Kidd .25 .60
186 Nick Van Exel .12 .30
187 Larry Johnson .15 .40
188 Bryant Reeves .10 .25
189 Glen Rice .15 .40
190 Kerry Kittles .10 .25
191 Toni Kukoc .15 .40
192 Ron Harper .12 .30
193 Bryon Russell .10 .25
194 Vladimir Stepania RC .30 .75
195 Michael Olowokandi RC .40 1.00
196 Mike Bibby RC .50 1.25
197 Dale Ellis .10 .25
198 Muggsy Bogues .12 .30
199 Vince Carter RC 1.50 4.00
200 Robert Traylor RC .30 .75
201 Peja Stojakovic RC .75 2.00
202 Aaron McKie .10 .25
203 Hubert Davis .10 .25
204 Dana Barros .10 .25
205 Bonzi Wells RC .30 .75
206 Michael Doleac RC .25 .60
207 Keon Clark RC .30 .75
208 Michael Dickerson RC .30 .75
209 Nick Anderson .10 .25
210 Brent Price .10 .25
211 Cherokee Parks .10 .25
212 Sam Jacobson RC .25 .60
213 Pat Garrity RC .25 .60
214 Tyrone Corbin .10 .25
215 David Wesley .10 .25
216 Rodney Rogers .10 .25
217 Dean Garrett .10 .25
218 Roshown McLeod RC .20 .50
219 Dale Davis .10 .25
220 Checklist .10 .25

1998-99 Topps Apparitions

Randomly inserted in series one retail packs only at a rate of one in 36, this 15-card set features players whose moves defy the mind's eye. The cards feature micro-dyna etch technology. Card backs are numbered with an "A" prefix.

COMPLETE SET (15) 50.00 120.00
SER.1 STATED ODDS 1:36 RETAIL
A1 Kobe Bryant 5.00 12.00
A2 Stephon Marbury 1.50 4.00
A3 Brent Barry 1.00 2.50
A4 Karl Malone 1.50 4.00
A5 Shaquille O'Neal 3.00 8.00
A6 Chris Webber 1.25 3.00
A7 Shawn Kemp 1.25 3.00
A8 Hakeem Olajuwon 1.50 4.00
A9 Anfernee Hardaway 2.00 5.00
A10 Michael Finley 1.25 3.00
A11 Keith Van Horn 1.25 3.00
A12 Kevin Garnett 2.00 5.00
A13 Vin Baker 1.00 2.50
A14 Tim Duncan 2.50 6.00
A15 Michael Jordan 30.00 80.00

1998-99 Topps Autographs

Randomly inserted in series one hobby packs at a rate of one in 329 and one in 378 series two hobby packs, this 18-card set features certified autographs of some of the top players in the NBA. AG1-AG8 were included in the first series, while AG9-AG18 were in the second. Each card features a "Topps Certified Autograph Issue" stamp on the front. Card backs feature an "AG" prefix.

STATED ODDS 1:329 SER.1; 1:378 SER.2
AG1 Joe Smith 6.00 15.00
AG2 Kobe Bryant 100.00 175.00
AG3 Stephon Marbury 8.00 20.00
AG4 Dikembe Mutombo 6.00 15.00
AG5 Shareef Abdur-Rahim 6.00 15.00
AG6 Eddie Jones 8.00 20.00
AG7 Keith Van Horn 5.00 12.00
AG8 Glen Rice 6.00 15.00
AG9 Kobe Bryant 50.00 120.00
AG10 Ron Mercer 5.00 12.00
AG11 Glen Rice 6.00 15.00
AG12 Stephon Marbury 8.00 20.00
AG13 Kerry Kittles 5.00 12.00
AG14 Michael Olowokandi 5.00 12.00
AG15 Antawn Jamison 8.00 20.00
AG16 Mike Bibby 8.00 20.00
AG17 Robert Traylor 5.00 12.00
AG18 Paul Pierce 30.00 80.00

1998-99 Topps Chrome Preview

Randomly inserted in series two packs at one in 36, this 10-card set previews the 1998-99 Topps Chrome set. The set is skip-numbered.

COMPLETE SET (10) 30.00 60.00
SER.2 STATED ODDS 1:36 HOB/RET
6 Chris Mullin 3.00 8.00
10 Jerry Stackhouse 3.00 8.00
19 Detlef Schrempf 3.00 8.00
40 Patrick Ewing 4.00 10.00
43 Joe Dumars 3.00 8.00
60 Isaiah Rider 2.50 6.00
73 John Stockton 4.00 10.00
77 Michael Jordan 10.00 25.00
81 Michael Finley 3.00 8.00
100 Sean Elliott 3.00 8.00

1998-99 Topps Chrome Preview Refractors

REF: 2.5X TO 6X VALUE
SER.2 STATED ODDS 1:40 HCP
SKIP-NUMBERED SET
77 Michael Jordan 400.00 800.00

1998-99 Topps Classic Collection

Randomly inserted in series two packs at one in 12, this 10-card set focuses on some of the retired greats of the NBA. The card front features the player in the foreground with a special framed background photo. Card backs are numbered with a "CL" prefix.

COMPLETE SET (10) 5.00 10.00
SER.2 STATED ODDS 1:12 HOB/RET
CL1 Larry Bird 1.00 2.50
CL2 Magic Johnson 1.00 2.50
CL3 Kareem Abdul-Jabbar .60 1.50
CL4 Julius Erving .60 1.50
CL5 Bill Russell .60 1.50
CL6 Wilt Chamberlain .75 2.00
CL7 Oscar Robertson .50 1.25
CL8 Jerry West .50 1.25
CL9 Elgin Baylor .40 1.00
CL10 Bob Cousy .60 1.50

1998-99 Topps Coast to Coast

Randomly inserted in series two retail packs only at a-rate of one in 36, this 15-card set feature player's that have the ability to take it from one end of the court to the other. Card backs carry a "CC" prefix.

COMPLETE SET (15) 30.00 60.00
SER.2 STATED ODDS 1:36 RETAIL
CC1 Kobe Bryant 10.00 25.00
CC2 Scottie Pippen 3.00 8.00
CC3 Eddie Jones 2.00 5.00
CC4 Grant Hill 3.00 8.00
CC5 Jason Kidd 3.00 8.00
CC6 Antoine Walker 2.00 5.00
CC7 Michael Finley 2.00 5.00
CC8 Kevin Garnett 3.00 8.00
CC9 Allen Iverson 4.00 10.00
CC10 Shawn Kemp 2.00 5.00
CC11 Glenn Robinson 1.50 4.00
CC12 Anfernee Hardaway 3.00 8.00
CC13 Tim Hardaway 2.00 5.00
CC14 Ron Mercer 1.50 4.00
CC15 Kerry Kittles 1.25 3.00

1998-99 Topps Cornerstones

Randomly inserted in series one hobby packs only at a rate of one in 36, this 15-card set features players that teams would love to build entire teams around. The cards feature uniluster technology. Card backs feature a "C" prefix.

COMPLETE SET (15) 15.00 40.00
SER.1 STATED ODDS 1:36 HOBBY
C1 Keith Van Horn 1.25 3.00
C2 Kevin Garnett 2.00 5.00
C3 Shareef Abdur-Rahim 1.25 3.00
C4 Antoine Walker 1.25 3.00
C5 Allen Iverson 2.50 6.00
C6 Grant Hill 2.00 5.00
C7 Marcus Camby 1.00 2.50
C8 Stephon Marbury 1.50 4.00
C9 Kobe Bryant 5.00 12.00
C10 Bobby Jackson .75 2.00
C11 Kerry Kittles .75 2.00
C12 Ron Mercer 1.00 2.50
C13 Eddie Jones 1.25 3.00
C14 Tim Thomas 1.25 3.00
C15 Tim Duncan 2.50 6.00

1998-99 Topps Draft Redemption

Randomly inserted in series one packs at a rate of one in 18, this 29-card set features a redemption for the players drafted in the first round of the 1998 NBA Draft. Each card number contained a number corresponding to each draft position, and could be redeemed for a special card of that particular player selected. Cards had to be redemmed before April 1, 1999. Cards 17 and 18 do not exist, in redeemed form.

SER.1 STATED ODDS 1:18 HOB/RET
RED.CARDS NOT AVAILABLE FOR 17/18
1 Michael Olowokandi 3.00 8.00
2 Mike Bibby 4.00 10.00
3 Raef LaFrentz 3.00 8.00
4 Antawn Jamison 4.00 10.00
5 Vince Carter 12.00 30.00
6 Robert Traylor 2.50 6.00
7 Jason Williams 6.00 15.00
8 Larry Hughes 5.00 12.00
9 Dirk Nowitzki 15.00 40.00
10 Paul Pierce 10.00 25.00
11 Bonzi Wells 2.50 6.00
12 Michael Doleac 2.00 5.00
13 Keon Clark 2.50 6.00
14 Michael Dickerson 2.50 6.00
15 Matt Harpring 2.50 6.00
16 Bryce Drew 1.50 4.00
19 Pat Garrity 2.00 5.00
20 Roshown McLeod 1.50 4.00
21 Ricky Davis 4.00 10.00
22 Brian Skinner 2.50 6.00
23 Tyronn Lue 2.50 6.00
24 Felipe Lopez 1.50 4.00
25 Al Harrington 4.00 10.00
26 Sam Jacobson 2.00 5.00
27 Vladimir Stepania 2.50 6.00
28 Corey Benjamin 1.50 4.00
29 Nazr Mohammed 2.50 6.00

1998-99 Topps East/West

Randomly inserted in series two packs at one in 36, this 20-card double-sided set combines one superstar from the Eastern Conference with one from the Western Conference. The cards feature Finest technology. Card backs are numbered with an "EW" prefix.

COMPLETE SET (20) 40.00 80.00
SER.2 STATED ODDS 1:36 HOB/RET
*REF: 1.25X TO 3X HI COLUMN
REF: SER.2 STATED ODDS 1:144 H/R
EW1 A.Walker/S.Abdur-Rahim 1.25 3.00
EW2 A.Mourning/S.O'Neal 4.00 10.00
EW3 T.Hardaway/J.Stockton 1.50 4.00
EW4 S.Pippen/K.Garnett 3.00 8.00
EW5 M.Jordan/K.Bryant 12.00 30.00
EW6 G.Hill/M.Finley 1.50 4.00
EW7 D.Mutombo/H.Olajuwon 1.50 4.00
EW8 K.Van Horn/T.Duncan 1.50 4.00
EW9 A.Iverson/G.Payton 2.00 5.00
EW10 P.Ewing/D.Robinson 1.50 4.00
EW11 J.Howard/C.Webber 1.25 3.00
EW12 B.Knight/S.Marbury 1.25 3.00
EW13 S.Kemp/V.Baker 1.25 3.00
EW14 A.Mason/T.Gugliotta 1.00 2.50
EW15 A.Hardaway/D.Stoudamire 1.50 4.00
EW16 R.Mercer/E.Jones 1.25 3.00
EW17 R.Strickland/J.Kidd 2.00 5.00
EW18 T.Thomas/A.McDyess 1.00 2.50
EW19 J.Williams/K.Malone 1.50 4.00
EW20 R.Miller/J.Jackson 1.25 3.00

1998-99 Topps Emissaries

Randomly inserted in series one packs at a rate of one in 24, this 20-card set features players who have represented their country in tough international competition. The cards are produced with mirrorboard technology. Card backs are labeled with an "E" prefix.

COMPLETE SET (20) 25.00 50.00
SER.1 STATED ODDS 1:24 HOB/RET
E1 Scottie Pippen 2.50 6.00
E2 Karl Malone 2.00 5.00
E3 Chris Webber 1.50 4.00
E4 Anfernee Hardaway 2.50 6.00
E5 Detlef Schrempf 1.50 4.00
E6 Mitch Richmond 1.50 4.00
E7 Vlade Divac 1.50 4.00
E8 Shaquille O'Neal 4.00 10.00
E9 Luc Longley 1.25 3.00
E10 Grant Hill 2.50 6.00
E11 Christian Laettner 1.25 3.00
E12 Gary Payton 1.50 4.00
E13 Patrick Ewing 2.00 5.00
E14 Shawn Kemp 1.50 4.00
E15 Toni Kukoc 1.50 4.00
E16 David Robinson 2.50 6.00
E17 Hakeem Olajuwon 2.00 5.00
E18 Charles Barkley 2.50 6.00
E19 John Stockton 2.00 5.00
E20 Arvydas Sabonis 1.25 3.00

1998-99 Topps Gold Label

Randomly inserted in series two packs at one in 12, this 10-card set features players on a Gold Label card. This is not a preview set, since a Gold Label set was not released in 1998-99. Card backs carry a "GL" prefix.

COMPLETE SET (10) 12.00 30.00
SER.2 STATED ODDS 1:12 HOB/RET
*BLACK LABEL: .75X TO 2X HI COLUMN
BLACK: SER.2 STATED ODDS 1:96 H/R
*RED: 10X TO 25X HI
STATED PRINT RUN 100 SERIAL #'d SETS
GL1 Michael Jordan 6.00 15.00
GL2 Shaquille O'Neal 2.00 5.00
GL3 Kobe Bryant 3.00 8.00
GL4 Antoine Walker .75 2.00
GL5 Charles Barkley 1.25 3.00
GL6 Keith Van Horn .75 2.00
GL7 Tim Duncan 1.50 4.00
GL8 Stephon Marbury 1.00 2.50
GL9 Shareef Abdur-Rahim .75 2.00
GL10 Gary Payton .75 2.00

1998-99 Topps Kick Start

Randomly inserted in series two packs at a rate of one in 12, this 15-card set focuses on young players in the NBA who are expected to have a breakout year. The cards feature dot-matrix technology. Card backs carry a "KS" prefix.

COMPLETE SET (15) 10.00 25.00
SER.2 STATED ODDS 1:12 HOB/RET
KS1 Tim Duncan .75 2.00
KS2 Kobe Bryant 1.50 4.00
KS3 Antoine Walker .40 1.00
KS4 Stephon Marbury .50 1.25
KS5 Allen Iverson .75 2.00
KS6 Shareef Abdur-Rahim .40 1.00
KS7 Keith Van Horn .40 1.00
KS8 Ray Allen .50 1.25
KS9 Vince Carter 2.00 5.00
KS10 Kevin Garnett .60 1.50
KS11 Kerry Kittles .25 .60
KS12 Tim Thomas .40 1.00
KS13 Ron Mercer .30 .75
KS14 Antawn Jamison .60 1.50
KS15 Mike Bibby .60 1.50

1998-99 Topps Legacies

Randomly inserted in series two hobby packs only at one in 36, this 15-card set features the big superstars that bring excitement to the court every night. Card backs carry a "L" prefix.

COMPLETE SET (15) 30.00 60.00
SER.2 STATED ODDS 1:36 HOBBY
L1 Scottie Pippen 2.00 5.00
L2 Grant Hill 2.00 5.00
L3 Hakeem Olajuwon 1.50 4.00
L4 Alonzo Mourning 1.50 4.00
L5 Shaquille O'Neal 3.00 8.00
L6 Shawn Kemp 1.25 3.00
L7 Gary Payton 1.25 3.00
L8 Karl Malone 1.50 4.00
L9 Patrick Ewing 1.50 4.00
L10 Tim Hardaway 1.25 3.00
L11 Reggie Miller 1.50 4.00
L12 Glen Rice 1.25 3.00
L13 Dikembe Mutombo 1.25 3.00
L14 John Stockton 1.50 4.00
L15 Michael Jordan 30.00 80.00

1998-99 Topps Roundball Royalty

Randomly inserted in series one packs at a rate of one in 36, this 20-card set features the best in the NBA on Finest technology. Card backs are numbered with a "R" prefix.

COMPLETE SET (20) 40.00 100.00
SER.1 STATED ODDS 1:36 HOB/RET
R1 Michael Jordan 15.00 40.00
R2 Kevin Garnett 2.50 6.00
R3 David Robinson 2.50 6.00
R4 Allen Iverson 3.00 8.00
R5 Hakeem Olajuwon 2.00 5.00
R6 Anfernee Hardaway 2.50 6.00
R7 Gary Payton 1.50 4.00
R8 Scottie Pippen 2.50 6.00
R9 Shaquille O'Neal 4.00 10.00
R10 Mitch Richmond 1.50 4.00
R11 John Stockton 2.00 5.00
R12 Grant Hill 2.50 6.00
R13 Charles Barkley 2.50 6.00
R14 Dikembe Mutombo 1.50 4.00
R15 Karl Malone 2.00 5.00
R16 Shawn Kemp 1.50 4.00
R17 Patrick Ewing 2.00 5.00
R18 Kobe Bryant 6.00 15.00
R19 Terrell Brandon 1.00 2.50
R20 Vin Baker 1.25 3.00

1998-99 Topps Roundball Royalty Refractors

*REF: 1X TO 2.5X VALUE
SER.1 STATED ODDS 1:144 HOB/RET
R1 Michael Jordan 125.00 300.00

1998-99 Topps Season's Best

Randomly inserted in series one packs at a rate of one in 12, this 30-card set features 25 of the top players by position and five of the top rookies from 1997-98. This set is also broken into six themes: Postmen, Rockmen, Bombardiers, Navigators, Soarers and Newcomers. Card backs are numbered with a "SB" prefix.

COMPLETE SET (30) 25.00 60.00
SER.1 STATED ODDS 1:12 HOB/RET
SB1 Rod Strickland .60 1.50
SB2 Gary Payton 1.00 2.50
SB3 Tim Hardaway 1.00 2.50
SB4 Stephon Marbury 1.25 3.00
SB5 Sam Cassell .75 2.00
SB6 Michael Jordan 20.00 50.00
SB7 Mitch Richmond 1.00 2.50
SB8 Steve Smith .75 2.00
SB9 Ray Allen 1.25 3.00
SB10 Isaiah Rider .75 2.00
SB11 Grant Hill 1.50 4.00
SB12 Kevin Garnett 1.50 4.00
SB13 Shareef Abdur-Rahim 1.00 2.50
SB14 Glenn Robinson .75 2.00
SB15 Michael Finley 1.00 2.50
SB16 Karl Malone 1.25 3.00
SB17 Tim Duncan 2.00 5.00
SB18 Antoine Walker 1.00 2.50
SB19 Chris Webber 1.00 2.50
SB20 Vin Baker .75 2.00
SB21 Shaquille O'Neal 2.50 6.00
SB22 David Robinson 1.50 4.00
SB23 Alonzo Mourning 1.25 3.00
SB24 Dikembe Mutombo 1.00 2.50
SB25 Hakeem Olajuwon 1.25 3.00
SB26 Tim Duncan 2.00 5.00
SB27 Keith Van Horn 1.00 2.50
SB28 Zydrunas Ilgauskas 1.00 2.50
SB29 Brevin Knight .60 1.50
SB30 Bobby Jackson .60 1.50

1999-00 Topps

The first series of Topps was released as a 120-card set, while the second series contained 137 cards for a total of 257. The cards were released in 11-card packs that carried a suggested retail price of $1.29. Card fronts featured orange borders with the player's name in gold foil. The set also featured rookie subsets (cards 111-120 and cards 231-248) that were inserted at one in five packs. Series two packs also contained a nine-card Olympic subset that was also inserted at one in five.

COMPLETE SET (257) 30.00 60.00
COMPLETE SERIES 1 (120) 12.50 25.00
COMPLETE SERIES 2 (137) 17.50 35.00
COMP.SERIES 1 w/o SP (110) 6.00 12.00
COMP.SERIES 2 w/o SP (110) 5.00 10.00
SER.1/2 RC STATED ODDS 1:5 HOB/RET
USA STATED ODDS 1:5 HOB/RET
1 Steve Smith .15 .40
2 Ron Harper .12 .30
3 Michael Dickerson .12 .30
4 LaPhonso Ellis .12 .30
5 Chris Webber .20 .50
6 Jason Caffey .12 .30
7 Bryon Russell .12 .30
8 Bison Dele .12 .30
9 Isaiah Rider .15 .40
10 Dean Garrett .12 .30
11 Eric Murdock .12 .30
12 Juwan Howard .15 .40
13 Latrell Sprewell .20 .50
14 Jalen Rose .15 .40
15 Larry Johnson .20 .50
16 Eric Williams .12 .30
17 Bryant Reeves .12 .30
18 Tony Battie .15 .40
19 Luc Longley .15 .40
20 Gary Payton .20 .50
21 Tariq Abdul-Wahad .12 .30
22 Armen Gilliam UER .12 .30
23 Shaquille O'Neal .50 1.25
24 Gary Trent .12 .30
25 John Stockton .25 .60
26 Mark Jackson .15 .40
27 Cherokee Parks .12 .30
28 Michael Olowokandi .12 .30
29 Raef LaFrentz .15 .40
30 Dell Curry .12 .30
31 Travis Best .12 .30
32 Shawn Kemp .20 .50
33 Voshon Lenard .12 .30
34 Brian Grant .12 .30
35 Alvin Williams .12 .30
36 Derek Fisher .20 .50
37 Allan Houston .15 .40
38 Arvydas Sabonis .15 .40
39 Terry Cummings .15 .40
40 Dale Ellis .12 .30
41 Maurice Taylor .12 .30
42 Grant Hill .25 .60
43 Anthony Mason .12 .30
44 John Wallace .12 .30
45 David Wesley .12 .30
46 Nick Van Exel .15 .40
47 Cuttino Mobley .12 .30
48 Anfernee Hardaway .30 .75
49 Terry Porter .12 .30
50 Brent Barry .15 .40
51 Derek Harper .15 .40
52 Antoine Walker .20 .50
53 Karl Malone .25 .60
54 Ben Wallace .15 .40
55 Vlade Divac .20 .50
56 Sam Mitchell .12 .30
57 Joe Smith .15 .40
58 Shawn Bradley .12 .30
59 Darrell Armstrong .12 .30
60 Kenny Anderson .15 .40
61 Jason Williams .25 .60
62 Alonzo Mourning .25 .60
63 Matt Harpring .12 .30
64 Antonio Davis .12 .30
65 Lindsey Hunter .12 .30
66 Allen Iverson .40 1.00
67 Mookie Blaylock .12 .30
68 Wesley Person .12 .30
69 Bobby Phills .12 .30
70 Theo Ratliff .15 .40
71 Antonio Daniels .12 .30
72 P.J. Brown .12 .30
73 David Robinson .30 .75
74 Sean Elliott .20 .50
75 Zydrunas Ilgauskas .15 .40
76 Kerry Kittles .12 .30
77 Otis Thorpe .12 .30
78 John Starks .15 .40
79 Jaren Jackson .12 .30
80 Hersey Hawkins .12 .30
81 Glenn Robinson .15 .40
82 Paul Pierce .25 .60
83 Glen Rice .20 .50
84 Charlie Ward .12 .30
85 Dee Brown .12 .30
86 Danny Fortson .12 .30
87 Billy Owens .12 .30
88 Jason Kidd .30 .75
89 Brent Price .12 .30
90 Don Reid .12 .30
91 Mark Bryant .12 .30
92 Vinny Del Negro .12 .30
93 Stephon Marbury .15 .40
94 Donyell Marshall .12 .30
95 Jim Jackson .12 .30
96 Horace Grant .15 .40
97 Calbert Cheaney .12 .30
98 Vince Carter .40 1.00
99 Bobby Jackson .12 .30
100 Alan Henderson .12 .30
101 Mike Bibby .20 .50
102 Cedric Henderson .12 .30
103 Lamond Murray .12 .30
104 A.C. Green .15 .40
105 Hakeem Olajuwon .25 .60
106 George Lynch .12 .30
107 Kendall Gill .12 .30
108 Rex Chapman .12 .30
109 Eddie Jones .20 .50
110 Kornel David RC .25 .60
111 Jason Terry RC .50 1.25
112 Corey Maggette RC .50 1.25
113 Ron Artest RC .60 1.50
114 Richard Hamilton RC .60 1.50
115 Elton Brand RC .75 2.00
116 Baron Davis RC .75 2.00
117 Wally Szczerbiak RC .60 1.50
118 Steve Francis RC .75 2.00
119 James Posey RC .30 .75
120 Shawn Marion RC .60 1.50
121 Tim Duncan .40 1.00
122 Danny Manning .15 .40
123 Chris Mullin .20 .50
124 Antawn Jamison .20 .50
125 Kobe Bryant .75 2.00
126 Matt Geiger .12 .30
127 Rod Strickland .12 .30
128 Howard Eisley .12 .30
129 Steve Nash .30 .75
130 Felipe Lopez .12 .30
131 Ron Mercer .15 .40
132 Ruben Patterson .12 .30
133 Dana Barros .12 .30
134 Dale Davis .12 .30
135 Bo Outlaw .12 .30
136 Shandon Anderson .12 .30
137 Mitch Richmond .20 .50
138 Doug Christie .15 .40
139 Rasheed Wallace .20 .50
140 Chris Childs .12 .30
141 Jamal Mashburn .15 .40
142 Terrell Brandon .12 .30
143 Jamie Feick RC .15 .40
144 Robert Traylor .12 .30
145 Rick Fox .12 .30
146 Charles Barkley .30 .75
147 Tyrone Nesby RC .15 .40
148 Jerry Stackhouse .20 .50
149 Cedric Ceballos .12 .30
150 Dikembe Mutombo .20 .50
151 Anthony Peeler .12 .30
152 Larry Hughes .15 .40
153 Clifford Robinson .12 .30
154 Corliss Williamson .12 .30
155 Olden Polynice .12 .30
156 Avery Johnson .15 .40
157 Tracy Murray .12 .30
158 Tom Gugliotta .12 .30
159 Tim Thomas .15 .40
160 Reggie Miller .20 .50
161 Tim Hardaway .20 .50
162 Dan Majerle .20 .50
163 Will Perdue .12 .30
164 Brevin Knight .12 .30
165 Elden Campbell .12 .30
166 Chris Gatling .12 .30
167 Walter McCarty .12 .30
168 Chauncey Billups .20 .50
169 Chris Mills .12 .30
170 Christian Laettner .15 .40
171 Robert Pack .12 .30
172 Rik Smits .20 .50
173 Tyrone Hill .12 .30
174 Damon Stoudamire .15 .40
175 Nick Anderson .12 .30
176 Peja Stojakovic .20 .50
177 Vladimir Stepania .12 .30
178 Tracy McGrady .30 .75
179 Adam Keefe .12 .30
180 Shareef Abdur-Rahim .15 .40
181 Isaac Austin .12 .30
182 Mario Elie .12 .30
183 Rashard Lewis .20 .50
184 Scott Burrell .12 .30
185 Othella Harrington .12 .30
186 Eric Piatkowski .15 .40
187 Bryant Stith .12 .30
188 Michael Finley .20 .50
189 Chris Crawford .12 .30
190 Toni Kukoc .20 .50
191 Danny Ferry .12 .30
192 Erick Dampier .12 .30
193 Clarence Weatherspoon .12 .30
194 Bob Sura .12 .30
195 Jayson Williams .12 .30
196 Kurt Thomas .12 .30
197 Greg Anthony .12 .30
198 Rodney Rogers .12 .30
199 Detlef Schrempf .15 .40
200 Keith Van Horn .15 .40
201 Robert Horry .15 .40
202 Sam Cassell .15 .40
203 Malik Sealy .12 .30
204 Kelvin Cato .12 .30
205 Antonio McDyess .15 .40
206 Andrew DeClercq .12 .30
207 Ricky Davis .20 .50
208 Vitaly Potapenko .12 .30
209 Loy Vaught .12 .30
210 Kevin Garnett .30 .75
211 Eric Snow .15 .40
212 Anfernee Hardaway .30 .75
213 Vin Baker .15 .40
214 Lawrence Funderburke .12 .30
215 Jeff Hornacek .15 .40
216 Doug West .12 .30
217 Michael Doleac .12 .30
218 Ray Allen .20 .50
219 Derek Anderson .12 .30
220 Jerome Williams .12 .30
221 Derrick Coleman .15 .40
222 Randy Brown .12 .30
223 Patrick Ewing .25 .60
224 Walt Williams .12 .30
225 Charles Oakley .15 .40
226 Steve Kerr .15 .40
227 Muggsy Bogues .15 .40
228 Kevin Willis .12 .30
229 Marcus Camby .15 .40
230 Scottie Pippen .30 .75
231 Lamar Odom RC .75 2.00
232 Jonathan Bender RC .30 .75
233 Andre Miller RC .60 1.50
234 Trajan Langdon RC .30 .75
235 A.Radojevic RC .20 .50
236 William Avery RC .25 .60
237 Cal Bowdler RC .20 .50
238 Quincy Lewis RC .20 .50
239 Dion Glover RC .25 .60
240 Jeff Foster RC .30 .75
241 Kenny Thomas RC .30 .75
242 Devean George RC .30 .75
243 Tim James RC .20 .50
244 Vonteego Cummings RC .20 .50
245 Jumaine Jones RC .25 .60
246 Scott Padgett RC .25 .60
247 Adrian Griffin RC .30 .75

248 Chris Herren RC .25 .60
249 Allan Houston USA .20 .50
250 Kevin Garnett USA .40 1.00
251 Gary Payton USA .25 .60
252 Steve Smith USA .20 .50
253 Tim Hardaway USA .25 .60
254 Tim Duncan USA .50 1.25
255 Jason Kidd USA .40 1.00
256 Tom Gugliotta USA .15 .40
257 Vin Baker USA .20 .50

1999-00 Topps MVP Promotion

*MVP STARS: 10X TO 25X BASE CARD HI
*MVP RCs: 6X TO 15X BASE HI
SER.1 STATED ODDS 1:336
SER.2 STATED ODDS 1:172
STATED PRINT RUN 100 SETS

1999-00 Topps MVP Promotion Exchange

COMPLETE SET (22) 25.00 60.00
ONE SET VIA MAIL PER MVP WINNER
MVP1 Allen Iverson 2.50 6.00
MVP2 Alonzo Mourning 1.50 4.00
MVP3 Anthony Mason .75 2.00
MVP4 Chris Webber 1.25 3.00
MVP5 Eddie Jones 1.25 3.00
MVP6 Grant Hill 1.50 4.00
MVP7 Jason Kidd 2.00 5.00
MVP8 Karl Malone 1.50 4.00
MVP9 Kevin Garnett 2.00 5.00
MVP10 Kobe Bryant 5.00 12.00
MVP11 Michael Finley 1.25 3.00
MVP12 Sam Cassell 1.00 2.50
MVP13 Shaquille O'Neal 3.00 8.00
MVP14 Stephon Marbury 1.00 2.50
MVP15 Terrell Brandon .75 2.00
MVP16 Tim Duncan 2.50 6.00
MVP17 Vince Carter 2.50 6.00
MVP18 Steve Francis 3.00 8.00
MVP19 E.Brand/S.Francis 3.00 8.00
MVP20 Shaquille O'Neal 3.00 8.00
MVP21 Reggie Miller 1.25 3.00
MVP22 Shaquille O'Neal 3.00 8.00

1999-00 Topps 21st Century Topps

Randomly inserted in series two packs at one in 27, this 16-card set focuses on the 1999 NBA Draft Class. The cards are printed with holographic technology. Card backs carry a "C" prefix.

COMPLETE SET (16) 6.00 15.00
SER.2 STATED ODDS 1:27 HOB/RET
C1 Jason Terry .50 1.25
C2 Baron Davis .75 2.00
C3 Lamar Odom .75 2.00
C4 Jonathan Bender .30 .75
C5 Ron Artest .60 1.50
C6 Richard Hamilton .60 1.50
C7 Andre Miller .60 1.50
C8 Shawn Marion .60 1.50
C9 Steve Francis .75 2.00
C10 Elton Brand .75 2.00
C11 Wally Szczerbiak .60 1.50
C12 Corey Maggette .50 1.25
C13 James Posey .30 .75
C14 Trajan Langdon .30 .75
C15 Tim James .20 .50
C16 Cal Bowdler .20 .50

1999-00 Topps All-Matrix

Randomly inserted in series two packs at one in 15, this 30-card set showcases the top players in the league. The insert set was divided into three categories - Feature Force for the veterans, Instinctive Force for the younger stars and Future Force for the league's top rookies. Card backs carry a "AM" prefix.

COMPLETE SET (30) 30.00 80.00
SER.2 STATED ODDS 1:15 HOB/RET
AM1 Karl Malone 1.50 4.00
AM2 Scottie Pippen 2.00 5.00
AM3 Grant Hill 1.50 4.00
AM4 Shawn Kemp 1.25 3.00
AM5 Shaquille O'Neal 3.00 8.00
AM6 Anfernee Hardaway 2.00 5.00
AM7 Chris Webber 1.25 3.00
AM8 Gary Payton 1.25 3.00
AM9 Jason Kidd 2.00 5.00
AM10 John Stockton 1.50 4.00
AM11 Kevin Garnett 2.00 5.00
AM12 Vince Carter 2.50 6.00
AM13 Shareef Abdur-Rahim 1.00 2.50
AM14 Antoine Walker 1.25 3.00
AM15 Kobe Bryant 5.00 12.00
AM16 Tim Duncan 2.50 6.00
AM17 Keith Van Horn 1.00 2.50
AM18 Allen Iverson 2.50 6.00
AM19 Jason Williams 1.50 4.00
AM20 Stephon Marbury 1.00 2.50
AM21 Elton Brand 2.00 5.00
AM22 Jason Terry 1.25 3.00
AM23 Steve Francis 2.00 5.00
AM24 Corey Maggette 1.25 3.00
AM25 Lamar Odom 2.00 5.00
AM26 Ron Artest 1.50 4.00
AM27 Baron Davis 2.00 5.00
AM28 Andre Miller 1.50 4.00
AM29 Shawn Marion 1.50 4.00
AM30 Wally Szczerbiak 1.50 4.00

1999-00 Topps Autographs

Randomly inserted in series one hobby packs only at one in 877 for group A and one in 351 for group B and inserted at one in 196 for series two hobby packs, this 21-card set features autographs of top NBA stars. Card backs are labeled by the player's initials.

SER.1 STATED ODDS 1:877 (A) HOB
SER.1 STATED ODDS 1:351 (B) HOB
SER.2 STATED ODDS 1:196 (A/B) HOB
SER.2 OVERALL STATED ODDS 1:98 H
AM Antonio McDyess A 6.00 15.00
AM2 Antonio McDyess B 6.00 15.00
AW Antoine Walker A 6.00 15.00
BD Baron Davis A 8.00 20.00
CM Corey Maggette A 8.00 20.00
DS Damon Stoudamire A 6.00 15.00
EB Elton Brand B 6.00 15.00
GP Gary Payton B 15.00 40.00
GP2 Gary Payton A 12.00 30.00
JJ Jumaine Jones A 5.00 12.00
JK Jason Kidd A 20.00 50.00
MR Mitch Richmond A 6.00 15.00
PP Paul Pierce B 12.00 30.00
SF Steve Francis B 6.00 15.00
SP Scottie Pippen B 40.00 100.00
SS Steve Smith B 5.00 12.00
TD Tim Duncan A 300.00 600.00
TG Tom Gugliotta B 5.00 12.00
WA William Avery A 2.50 6.00
WS Wally Szczerbiak A 5.00 12.00
SAR Shareef Abdur-Rahim B 8.00 20.00

1999-00 Topps Highlight Reels

Randomly inserted in series one retail packs only at one in 14, this 15-card set focuses on players with the most heart-pounding, jaw-dropping moves in the NBA. Card backs carry a "HR" prefix.

COMPLETE SET (15) 8.00 20.00
SER.1 STATED ODDS 1:14 RETAIL
HR1 Stephon Marbury .60 1.50
HR2 Vince Carter 1.50 4.00
HR3 Kevin Garnett 1.25 3.00
HR4 Kobe Bryant 3.00 8.00
HR5 Chris Webber .75 2.00
HR6 Allen Iverson 1.50 4.00
HR7 Grant Hill 1.00 2.50
HR8 Antoine Walker .75 2.00
HR9 Jason Williams 1.00 2.50
HR10 Tim Duncan 1.50 4.00
HR11 Shareef Abdur-Rahim .60 1.50
HR12 Keith Van Horn .60 1.50
HR13 Antonio McDyess .60 1.50
HR14 Jason Kidd 1.25 3.00
HR15 Ron Mercer .60 1.50

1999-00 Topps Impact

Randomly inserted in series two packs at one in 24, this 20-card set was divided into three categories. Initial Impact features members of the 1999 NBA Draft Class, Present Impact highlights young stars and Lasting Impact showcases talented veterans. The cards are printed on Chromium technology. Card backs carry an "I" prefix.

COMPLETE SET (20) 25.00 60.00
SER.2 STATED ODDS 1:24 HOB/RET
*REF: 1X TO 2.5X HI COLUMN
REF: SER.2 STATED ODDS 1:120 H/R
I1 Elton Brand 2.00 5.00
I2 Lamar Odom 2.00 5.00
I3 Wally Szczerbiak 1.50 4.00
I4 Jason Terry 1.25 3.00
I5 Baron Davis 2.00 5.00
I6 Ron Artest 1.50 4.00
I7 Steve Francis 2.00 5.00
I8 Andre Miller 1.50 4.00
I9 Allen Iverson 2.50 6.00
I10 Jason Williams 1.50 4.00
I11 Keith Van Horn 1.00 2.50
I12 Vince Carter 2.50 6.00
I13 Kobe Bryant 5.00 12.00
I14 Tim Duncan 2.50 6.00
I15 Scottie Pippen 2.00 5.00
I16 Kevin Garnett 2.00 5.00
I17 Shaquille O'Neal 3.00 8.00
I18 Gary Payton 1.25 3.00
I19 Karl Malone 1.50 4.00
I20 Grant Hill 1.50 4.00

1999-00 Topps Jumbos

Inserted one per series one hobby box, this eight-card set features a jumbo-sized card of several NBA stars.

COMPLETE SET (8) 2.00 5.00
ONE PER SER.1 HOBBY BOX
1 Gary Payton .30 .75
2 Shaquille O'Neal .75 2.00
3 Antoine Walker .30 .75
4 Jason Williams .40 1.00
5 Alonzo Mourning .40 1.00
6 Allen Iverson .60 1.50
7 Stephon Marbury .25 .60
8 Vince Carter .60 1.50

1999-00 Topps Own the Game

Randomly inserted in series two packs at one in 44, this 10-card set highlights the statistical leaders from the 1998-99 season. Card backs carry an "OTG" prefix.

COMPLETE SET (10) 12.50 30.00
SER.2 STATED ODDS 1:44 HOB/RET
OTG1 Allen Iverson 2.50 6.00
OTG2 Shaquille O'Neal 3.00 8.00
OTG3 Jason Kidd 2.00 5.00
OTG4 Stephon Marbury 1.00 2.50
OTG5 Dikembe Mutombo 1.25 3.00
OTG6 Tim Duncan 2.50 6.00
OTG7 Wally Szczerbiak 2.50 6.00
OTG8 Quincy Lewis .75 2.00
OTG9 Elton Brand 3.00 8.00
OTG10 Aleksandar Radojevic .75 2.00

1999-00 Topps Patriarchs

Randomly inserted in series one packs at one in 22, this 15-card set. Card backs carry a "P" prefix.

COMPLETE SET (15) 10.00 25.00
SER.1 STATED ODDS 1:22 HOB/RET
P1 Patrick Ewing 1.25 3.00
P2 Reggie Miller 1.00 2.50
P3 Hakeem Olajuwon 1.25 3.00
P4 Scottie Pippen 1.50 4.00
P5 Grant Hill 1.25 3.00
P6 Shaquille O'Neal 2.50 6.00
P7 Mitch Richmond 1.00 2.50
P8 Glen Rice 1.00 2.50
P9 Charles Barkley 1.50 4.00
P10 Karl Malone 1.25 3.00
P11 John Stockton 1.25 3.00
P12 Gary Payton 1.00 2.50
P13 David Robinson 1.50 4.00
P14 Tim Hardaway 1.00 2.50
P15 Joe Dumars 1.00 2.50

1999-00 Topps Picture Perfect

Randomly inserted in series one packs at one in eight, this 10-card set features NBA stars against cards that are not quite correct. Card backs carry a "PIC" prefix.

COMPLETE SET (10) 2.00 5.00
SER.1 STATED ODDS 1:8 HOB/RET
PIC1 Shaquille O'Neal .75 2.00
PIC2 Alonzo Mourning .40 1.00
PIC3 Shareef Abdur-Rahim .25 .60
PIC4 Juwan Howard .25 .60
PIC5 Keith Van Horn .25 .60
PIC6 Ron Mercer .25 .60
PIC7 Tim Hardaway .30 .75
PIC8 Kevin Garnett .50 1.25
PIC9 David Robinson .50 1.25
PIC10 Kerry Kittles .20 .50

1999-00 Topps Prodigy

Randomly inserted in series one packs at one in 36, this 20-card set features the future stars of the NBA. The cards feature a chrome background and a "PR" prefix on the back.

COMPLETE SET (20) 30.00 80.00
SER.1 STATED ODDS 1:36 HOB/RET
PR1 Stephon Marbury 1.50 4.00
PR2 Jason Kidd 3.00 8.00
PR3 Kevin Garnett 3.00 8.00
PR4 Kobe Bryant 8.00 20.00
PR5 Antoine Walker 2.00 5.00
PR6 Ron Mercer 1.50 4.00
PR7 Shareef Abdur-Rahim 1.50 4.00
PR8 Tim Duncan 4.00 10.00
PR9 Keith Van Horn 1.50 4.00
PR10 Ray Allen 2.00 5.00
PR11 Michael Doleac 1.25 3.00
PR12 Jason Williams 2.50 6.00
PR13 Michael Dickerson 1.25 3.00
PR14 Mike Bibby 2.00 5.00
PR15 Paul Pierce 2.50 6.00
PR16 Michael Olowokandi 1.25 3.00
PR17 Vince Carter 4.00 10.00
PR18 Antawn Jamison 2.00 5.00
PR19 Felipe Lopez 1.25 3.00
PR20 Matt Harpring 1.25 3.00

1999-00 Topps Prodigy Refractors

*REF: .6X TO 1.5X HI COLUMN
SER.1 STATED ODDS 1:144 H/R
PR4 Kobe Bryant 20.00 50.00

1999-00 Topps Record Numbers

Randomly inserted in series one packs at one in 12, this 10-card set. Card backs carry a "RN" prefix.

COMPLETE SET (10) 2.00 5.00
SER.1 STATED ODDS 1:12 HOB/RET
RN1 Karl Malone .40 1.00
RN2 Kerry Kittles .20 .50
RN3 Reggie Miller .30 .75
RN4 Hakeem Olajuwon .40 1.00
RN5 John Stockton .40 1.00
RN6 Dikembe Mutombo .30 .75
RN7 Kobe Bryant 1.25 3.00
RN8 Tim Duncan .60 1.50
RN9 Allen Iverson .60 1.50
RN10 Patrick Ewing .40 1.00

1999-00 Topps Season's Best

Randomly inserted in packs at one in 12, this 30-card set features some of the top players in different categories from the previous year. Card backs carry a "SB" prefix.

COMPLETE SET (30) 15.00 40.00
SER.1 STATED ODDS 1:12 HOB/RET
SB1 David Robinson 1.25 3.00
SB2 Shaquille O'Neal 2.00 5.00
SB3 Patrick Ewing 1.00 2.50
SB4 Hakeem Olajuwon 1.00 2.50
SB5 Alonzo Mourning 1.00 2.50
SB6 Antonio McDyess .60 1.50
SB7 Tim Duncan 1.50 4.00
SB8 Keith Van Horn .60 1.50
SB9 Karl Malone 1.00 2.50
SB10 Chris Webber .75 2.00
SB11 Kevin Garnett 1.25 3.00
SB12 Juwan Howard .60 1.50
SB13 Shareef Abdur-Rahim .60 1.50
SB14 Glenn Robinson .60 1.50
SB15 Grant Hill 1.00 2.50
SB16 Michael Finley .75 2.00
SB17 Steve Smith .60 1.50
SB18 Mitch Richmond .75 2.00
SB19 Kobe Bryant 3.00 8.00
SB20 Ray Allen .75 2.00
SB21 Allen Iverson 1.50 4.00
SB22 Gary Payton .75 2.00
SB23 Stephon Marbury .60 1.50
SB24 Jason Kidd 1.25 3.00
SB25 Tim Hardaway .75 2.00
SB26 Jason Williams 1.00 2.50
SB27 Vince Carter 1.50 4.00
SB28 Paul Pierce 1.00 2.50
SB29 Mike Bibby .75 2.00
SB30 Michael Dickerson .50 1.25

1999-00 Topps Team Topps

Randomly inserted in series two packs at one in 18, this 24-card set features NBA All-Stars, past and present from both conferences. Card backs carry a "TT" prefix.

COMPLETE SET (24) 25.00 60.00
SER.2 STATED ODDS 1:18 HOB/RET
TT1 Gary Payton 1.25 3.00
TT2 Jason Kidd 2.00 5.00
TT3 Kobe Bryant 5.00 12.00
TT4 Anfernee Hardaway 2.00 5.00
TT5 Kevin Garnett 2.00 5.00
TT6 Patrick Ewing 1.50 4.00
TT7 Tim Duncan 2.50 6.00
TT8 Karl Malone 1.50 4.00
TT9 Shaquille O'Neal 3.00 8.00
TT10 Charles Barkley 2.00 5.00
TT11 John Stockton 1.50 4.00
TT12 Tim Hardaway 1.25 3.00
TT13 Hakeem Olajuwon 1.50 4.00
TT14 Jayson Williams .75 2.00
TT15 Reggie Miller 1.25 3.00
TT16 David Robinson 2.00 5.00
TT17 Grant Hill 1.50 4.00
TT18 Scottie Pippen 2.00 5.00
TT19 Chris Webber 1.25 3.00
TT20 Shawn Kemp 1.25 3.00
TT21 Alonzo Mourning 1.50 4.00
TT22 Mitch Richmond 1.25 3.00
TT23 Antoine Walker 1.25 3.00
TT24 Tom Gugliotta .75 2.00

2000-01 Topps Promos

These two cards were given to hobby dealers and members of the media to promote the 2000-01 Topps product. The set was shipped in a cello wrapper, and featured cards of Elton Brand and Tim Duncan. Card backs carry a "PP" prefix.

COMPLETE SET (2) 1.00 2.50
PP1 Elton Brand .40 1.00
PP2 Tim Duncan .75 2.00

2000-01 Topps

The 2000-01 Topps product was released in early September 2000 for series one and late November 2000 for series two. The sets featured a 295-card base set that is broken into tiers as follows:Base Veterans, Rookies, Season Leaders subset, Second Coming subset and one Team Championship card. Each pack contained 10 cards and carried a suggested retail price of $1.29.

COMPLETE SET (295) 40.00 80.00
COMPLETE SERIES 1 (155) 30.00 60.00
COMP.SERIES 1 w/o RC (130) 7.50 15.00
COMPLETE SERIES 2 (140) 12.50 25.00
COMP.SERIES 2 w/o RC (120) 7.50 15.00
RC SUBSET: STATED ODDS 1:5 H/R, 1:1 HTA
SOME RCs AVAILABLE VIA REDEMPTION
1 Elton Brand .20 .50
2 Marcus Camby .15 .40
3 Jalen Rose .15 .40
4 Jamie Feick .12 .30
5 Toni Kukoc .20 .50
6 Todd MacCulloch .12 .30
7 Mario Elie .12 .30
8 Doug Christie .12 .30
9 Sam Cassell .15 .40
10 Shaquille O'Neal .50 1.25
11 Larry Hughes .15 .40
12 Jerry Stackhouse .15 .40
13 Rick Fox .12 .30
14 Clifford Robinson .12 .30
15 Felipe Lopez .12 .30
16 Dirk Nowitzki .30 .75
17 Cuttino Mobley .12 .30
18 Latrell Sprewell .15 .40
19 Nick Anderson .12 .30
20 Kevin Garnett .30 .75
21 Rik Smits .12 .30
22 Jerome Williams .12 .30
23 Chris Webber .20 .50
24 Jason Terry .20 .50
25 Elden Campbell .12 .30
26 Kelvin Cato .12 .30
27 Tyrone Nesby .20 .50
28 Jonathan Bender .12 .30
29 Otis Thorpe .15 .40
30 Scottie Pippen .30 .75
31 Radoslav Nesterovic .12 .30
32 P.J. Brown .12 .30
33 Reggie Miller .20 .50
34 Andre Miller .15 .40
35 Tariq Abdul-Wahad .12 .30
36 Michael Doleac .12 .30
37 Rashard Lewis .20 .50
38 Jacque Vaughn .12 .30
39 Larry Johnson .20 .50
40 Steve Francis .15 .40
41 Arvydas Sabonis .15 .40
42 Jaren Jackson .12 .30
43 Howard Eisley .12 .30
44 Rod Strickland .12 .30
45 Tim Thomas .12 .30
46 Robert Horry .15 .40
47 Kenny Thomas .12 .30
48 Anthony Peeler .12 .30
49 Darrell Armstrong .12 .30
50 Vince Carter .40 1.00
51 Othella Harrington .12 .30
52 Derek Anderson .12 .30
53 Anthony Carter .12 .30
54 Scott Burrell .12 .30
55 Ray Allen .20 .50
56 Jason Kidd .30 .75
57 Sean Elliott .20 .50
58 Muggsy Bogues .15 .40
59 LaPhonso Ellis .15 .40
60 Tim Duncan .40 1.00
61 Adrian Griffin .12 .30
62 Wally Szczerbiak .15 .40
63 Austin Croshere .12 .30
64 Wesley Person .12 .30
65 James Posey .12 .30
66 Alan Henderson .12 .30
67 Ruben Patterson .12 .30
68 Jahidi White .12 .30
69 Shawn Marion .15 .40
70 Lamar Odom .15 .40
71 Lindsey Hunter .12 .30
72 Keon Clark .12 .30
73 Gary Trent .12 .30
74 Lamond Murray .12 .30
75 Paul Pierce .20 .50
76 Charlie Ward .12 .30
77 Matt Geiger .12 .30
78 Greg Anthony .12 .30
79 Horace Grant .15 .40
80 John Stockton .25 .60
81 Peja Stojakovic .20 .50
82 William Avery .12 .30
83 Dan Majerle .20 .50
84 Christian Laettner .15 .40
85 Dana Barros .12 .30
86 Corey Benjamin .12 .30
87 Keith Van Horn .15 .40
88 Patrick Ewing .25 .60
89 Steve Smith .15 .40
90 Antonio Davis .12 .30
91 Samaki Walker .12 .30
92 Mitch Richmond .15 .40
93 Michael Olowokandi .12 .30
94 Baron Davis .20 .50
95 Dikembe Mutombo .20 .50
96 Andrew DeClercq .12 .30
97 Raef LaFrentz .12 .30
98 Trajan Langdon .12 .30
99 Ervin Johnson .12 .30
100 Alonzo Mourning .25 .60
101 Kendall Gill .12 .30
102 George Lynch .12 .30
103 Detlef Schrempf .15 .40
104 Donyell Marshall .12 .30
105 Bo Outlaw .12 .30
106 Kenny Anderson .15 .40
107 Eddie Robinson .12 .30
108 Jermaine O'Neal .15 .40
109 John Amaechi .12 .30
110 Glen Rice .15 .40
111 Vlade Divac .15 .40
112 Vin Baker .15 .40
113 Mike Bibby .20 .50
114 Richard Hamilton .15 .40
115 Mookie Blaylock .12 .30
116 Vitaly Potapenko .12 .30
117 Anthony Mason .12 .30
118 Robert Pack .12 .30
119 Vonteego Cummings .12 .30
120 Michael Finley .20 .50
121 Ron Artest .20 .50
122 Tyrone Hill .12 .30
123 Rodney Rogers .12 .30
124 Quincy Lewis .12 .30
125 Kenyon Martin RC 1.00 2.50
126 Stromile Swift RC .40 1.00
127 Darius Miles RC .40 1.00
128 Marcus Fizer RC .40 1.00
129 Mike Miller RC .60 1.50
130 DerMarr Johnson RC .30 .75
131 Chris Mihm RC .30 .75
132 Jamal Crawford RC 1.00 2.50
133 Joel Przybilla RC .30 .75
134 Keyon Dooling RC .40 1.00
135 Jerome Moiso RC .25 .60
136 Etan Thomas RC .40 1.00
137 Courtney Alexander RC .30 .75
138 Mateen Cleaves RC .30 .75
139 Jason Collier RC .40 1.00
140 Desmond Mason RC .50 1.25
141 Quentin Richardson RC .40 1.00
142 Jamaal Magloire RC .40 1.00
143 Speedy Claxton RC .40 1.00
144 Morris Peterson RC .40 1.00
145 Donnell Harvey RC .30 .75
146 DeShawn Stevenson RC .40 1.00
147 Mamadou N'Diaye RC .25 .60
148 Erick Barkley RC .25 .60
149 Mark Madsen RC .40 1.00
150 Shaq/Iverson/G.Hill SL .15 .40
151 Kidd/Cassell/Van Exel SL .20 .50
152 Mutombo/Shaq/Duncan SL .25 .60
153 E.Jones/Pierce/Armstrong SL .10 .30
154 Mourning/Mutombo/Shaq SL .20 .50
155 Team Championship SL .30 .75
156 Jason Williams .12 .30
157 David Robinson .20 .50
158 Shammond Williams .12 .30
159 Charles Oakley .12 .30
160 Greg Ostertag .12 .30
161 Juwan Howard .15 .40
162 Antoine Walker .15 .40
163 Alan Henderson .12 .30
164 Eddie Jones .20 .50
165 Allen Iverson .40 1.00
166 Grant Hill .25 .60
167 Terrell Brandon .12 .30
168 Stephon Marbury .15 .40
169 Jason Caffey .12 .30
170 Sam Mitchell .12 .30
171 Jamal Mashburn .15 .40
172 Ron Harper .15 .40
173 Eric Piatkowski .12 .30
174 Sam Perkins .12 .30
175 Walt Williams .12 .30
176 Bob Sura .12 .30
177 Michael Curry .12 .30
178 Nick Van Exel .15 .40
179 Danny Ferry .12 .30
180 Randy Brown .12 .30
181 Danny Fortson .12 .30
182 Jim Jackson .12 .30
183 Brad Miller .15 .40
184 Shawn Bradley .12 .30
185 Voshon Lenard .12 .30
186 Erick Dampier .12 .30
187 Mark Jackson .15 .40
188 Maurice Taylor .12 .30
189 Kobe Bryant .75 2.00
190 Clarence Weatherspoon .12 .30
191 Bobby Jackson .12 .30
192 Eric Snow .12 .30
193 Allan Houston .15 .40
194 Kurt Thomas .12 .30
195 Chauncey Billups .20 .50
196 Tom Gugliotta .12 .30
197 Theo Ratliff .12 .30
198 Rasheed Wallace .20 .50
199 Jon Barry .12 .30
200 Malik Rose .12 .30
201 Vernon Maxwell .12 .30
202 Dee Brown .12 .30
203 Bryon Russell .12 .30
204 Brent Barry .12 .30
205 Tracy McGrady .30 .75
206 Bryant Reeves .12 .30
207 Isaac Austin .12 .30
208 Damon Stoudamire .15 .40
209 Anfernee Hardaway .30 .75
210 Aaron McKie .12 .30
211 Johnny Newman .12 .30
212 Scott Williams .12 .30
213 Brian Shaw .12 .30
214 Corey Maggette .15 .40
215 Travis Best .12 .30
216 Hakeem Olajuwon .25 .60
217 Antawn Jamison .20 .50
218 John Starks .15 .40
219 Antonio McDyess .15 .40
220 Cedric Ceballos .12 .30
221 Chris Carr .12 .30
222 Roshown McLeod .12 .30
223 Calbert Cheaney .12 .30
224 Gary Payton .20 .50
225 Karl Malone .25 .60
226 Michael Dickerson .12 .30
227 Tracy Murray .12 .30
228 Chris Childs .12 .30
229 Pat Garrity .12 .30
230 Rex Chapman .12 .30
231 Jumaine Jones .12 .30
232 Fred Hoiberg .12 .30
233 Bimbo Coles .12 .30
234 Shawn Kemp .20 .50
235 David Wesley .12 .30
236 Tony Battie .12 .30
237 Ron Mercer .12 .30
238 John Wallace .12 .30
239 Robert Traylor .12 .30
240 Derrick Coleman .15 .40
241 Steve Nash .30 .75
242 Ben Wallace .15 .40
243 Brian Skinner .12 .30
244 Chris Gatling .12 .30
245 Dale Davis .12 .30
246 Joe Smith .15 .40
247 Glenn Robinson .15 .40
248 Kerry Kittles .12 .30
249 Erick Strickland .12 .30
250 Sam Cassell .15 .40
251 Chucky Atkins .12 .30
252 Brian Grant .12 .30
253 Bonzi Wells .12 .30
254 Corliss Williamson .12 .30
255 Shareef Abdur-Rahim .15 .40
256 Kevin Willis .12 .30
257 Scott Padgett .12 .30
258 Terry Porter .12 .30
259 Tony Delk .12 .30
260 Avery Johnson .15 .40
261 Tim Hardaway .20 .50
262 Derek Fisher .20 .50
263 Isaiah Rider .15 .40
264 Shandon Anderson .12 .30
265 Adonal Foyle .12 .30
266 Hedo Turkoglu RC .60 1.50
267 Brian Cardinal RC .30 .75
268 Iakovos Tsakalidis RC .25 .60
269 Dalibor Bagaric RC .30 .75
270 Marko Jaric RC .40 1.00
271 Dan Langhi RC .25 .60
272 A.J. Guyton RC .25 .60
273 Jake Voskuhl RC .25 .60
274 Khalid El-Amin RC .25 .60
275 Mike Smith RC .25 .60
276 Soumaila Samake RC .25 .60
277 Eddie House RC .30 .75
278 Eduardo Najera RC .40 1.00
279 Lavor Postell RC .25 .60
280 Hanno Mottola RC .25 .60
281 Chris Carrawell RC .40 1.00
282 Olumide Oyedeji RC .25 .60
283 Michael Redd RC 1.00 2.50
284 Chris Porter RC .25 .60
285 Mark Karcher RC .25 .60
286 S.Francis/G.Payton SC .20 .50
287 D.Miles/K.Garnett SC .20 .50
288 L.Odom/Abdur-Rahim SC .15 .40
289 T.Duncan/A.Mourning SC .25 .60
290 E.Brand/K.Malone SC .20 .50
291 L.Hughes/A.Iverson SC .20 .50
292 K.Bryant/R.Miller SC .50 1.25
293 V.Carter/G.Hill SC .25 .60
294 T.McGrady/S.Pippen SC .40 1.00
295 K.Martin/M.Camby SC .60 1.50

2000-01 Topps MVP Promotion

*STARS: 20X TO 50X BASE CARD HI
*RCs: 2X TO 5X BASE CARD HI
SER.1 STATED ODDS 1:253 H/R, 1:51 HTA
SER.2 STATED ODDS 1:179 H/R, 1:41 HTA

2000-01 Topps Autographs

Randomly inserted into both series packs, this insert features autographed cards of some of the hottest names in basketball. The Tim Duncan autograph was inserted at one in 5,941 packs. Group A autographs were inserted into packs at 1:1009, Group B autographs were inserted at 1:137, Group C autographs were inserted into packs at 1:2511. Overall odds for series one autographs was one in 580, with series two at one in 465. Series Two autographs were inserted at the following rates: Group A 1:664, Group B 1:3113, Group C 1:7783, Group D 1:9398, and the overall odds were 1:465. The Co-Rookie autograph was inserted into packs at 1:11584.

SER.1 STATED ODDS 1:580 H/R, 1:115 HTA
SER.2 STATED ODDS 1:465 H/R, 1:89 HTA
DUNCAN AU: STATED ODDS 1:1239 HTA
ROY AU: STATED ODDS 1:11584
TAAI Allen Iverson A 75.00 150.00
TAAJ Antawn Jamison A 5.00 12.00
TAAM Antonio McDyess B 4.00 10.00
TAAJG A.J. Guyton A 2.50 6.00
TACA Courtney Alexander C 3.00 8.00
TAEB Elton Brand C 5.00 12.00
TAEB Elton Brand B 5.00 12.00
TAEMJ Magic Johnson A 40.00 80.00
TAJC Jamal Crawford A 10.00 25.00
TAJR Jalen Rose D 5.00 12.00
TAKD Keyon Dooling A 4.00 10.00
TALH Larry Hughes A 4.00 10.00
TALS Latrell Sprewell A 25.00 60.00
TAMC Mateen Cleaves B 3.00 8.00
TAMDC Marcus Camby B 5.00 12.00
TARA Ron Artest B 5.00 12.00
TAROY E.Brand/S.Francis 15.00 40.00
TASC Sam Cassell B 4.00 10.00
TASE Sean Elliott B 4.00 10.00
TASF Steve Francis B 5.00 12.00
TASO Shaquille O'Neal B 50.00 100.00
TASP Scoonie Penn B 4.00 10.00
TATB Terrell Brandon B 4.00 10.00
TATD Tim Duncan HTA 300.00 600.00
TATM Tracy McGrady B 15.00 40.00

2000-01 Topps Cards That Never Were

Randomly inserted in series two packs at one in 18 (one in six HTA), this 10-card set features new cards of Magic Johnson created with Topps classic designs from the years when Topps did not produced basketball cards. Card backs carry a "MJ" prefix.

COMPLETE SET (10) 15.00 30.00
COMMON CARD (MJ1-MJ10) 1.50 4.00
SER.2 STATED ODDS 1:18 H/R, 1:6 HTA

2000-01 Topps Chrome Previews

Randomly insert into series one packs at one in 18, this 20-card set gives collectors a taste of what the 2000-01 Topps Chrome set will look like. Card backs carry a "TCP" prefix.

COMPLETE SET (20) 15.00 40.00
SER.1 STATED ODDS 1:18 H/R, 1:5 HTA
TCP1 Shaquille O'Neal 2.00 5.00
TCP2 Kevin Garnett 1.25 3.00
TCP3 Vince Carter 1.50 4.00
TCP4 Tim Duncan 1.50 4.00
TCP5 Elton Brand .75 2.00
TCP6 Jason Kidd 1.25 3.00
TCP7 Lamar Odom .60 1.50
TCP8 Marcus Camby .60 1.50
TCP9 Paul Pierce .75 2.00
TCP10 Steve Francis .60 1.50
TCP11 Chris Webber .75 2.00
TCP12 Jalen Rose .60 1.50
TCP13 John Stockton 1.00 2.50
TCP14 Larry Hughes .60 1.50
TCP15 Ray Allen .75 2.00
TCP16 Alonzo Mourning 1.00 2.50
TCP17 Keith Van Horn .60 1.50
TCP18 Scottie Pippen 1.25 3.00
TCP19 Jerry Stackhouse .60 1.50
TCP20 Andre Miller .60 1.50

2000-01 Topps Combos 1

Randomly inserted into series one packs at one in 12, this 10-card insert pairs superstar caliber players together on the same card. Card backs carry a "TC" prefix.

COMPLETE SET (10) 6.00 15.00
SER.1 STATED ODDS 1:12 H/R, 1:4 HTA
TC1 S.O'Neal/K.Bryant 2.00 5.00
TC2 S.Marbury/A.Iverson .60 1.50
TC3 C.Webber/J.Williams .60 1.50
TC4 Ewing/Mutombo/Mourning .60 1.50
TC5 T.McGrady/V.Carter 2.00 5.00
TC6 T.Duncan/G.Hill 1.00 2.50
TC7 E.Brand/L.Odom/S.Francis .60 1.50
TC8 G.Payton/J.Kidd .75 2.00
TC9 Stoud/Pip/Smith/Wallace .75 2.00
TC10 T.Duncan/K.Garnett 1.25 3.00

2000-01 Topps Combos 2

Randomly inserted in series two packs at one in 12 (one in four HTA), this 10-card set features illustrated cards from NBA superstars and rookies as featured on the cover of Sports Collector's Digest. Card backs carry a "TC" prefix.

COMPLETE SET (10) 4.00 10.00
SER.2 STATED ODDS 1:12 H/R, 1:4 HTA
TC1 Hakeem Olajuwon .40 1.00
TC2 Patrick Ewing .40 1.00
TC3 Karl Malone .40 1.00
TC4 Scottie Pippen .60 1.50
TC5 Reggie Miller .40 1.00
TC6 S.O'Neal/M.Johnson 1.50 4.00
TC7 Fizer/Swift/K.Martin .40 1.00
TC8 Claxton/Dooling/Crawford .40 1.00
TC9 M.Miller/D.John/Miles .40 1.00
TC10 M.Johnson/M.Cleaves .60 1.50

2000-01 Topps East Meets West Game Jerseys

Randomly inserted in series two HTA packs only at one in 598, this two-card set features jersey swatches of two players who battled in the 2000 NBA Finals. Each card features the Topps "Genuine Issue" sticker. Card backs carry an "EMW" prefix.

SER.2 STATED ODDS 1:598 HTA
EMW1 S.O'Neal/R.Miller 50.00 100.00
EMW2 G.Rice/J.Rose 12.50 30.00

2000-01 Topps Final Piece Game Jerseys

Randomly inserted in series two packs at one in 517 (one in 52 HTA), this 23-card set features swatches of game-worn jerseys from the 2000 NBA Finals. Each card features the Topps "Genuine Issue" sticker. Card backs carry a "FP" prefix.

GROUP A ODDS 1:528
GROUP B ODDS 1:23719
SER.2 STATED ODDS 1:517 H/R, 1:52 HTA
FP1 Shaquille O'Neal A 25.00 60.00
FP2 Glen Rice A 6.00 15.00
FP3 Robert Horry A 8.00 20.00
FP4 Rick Fox A 8.00 20.00
FP5 Brian Shaw A 5.00 12.00
FP6 Ron Harper A 6.00 15.00
FP7 Derek Fisher A 8.00 20.00
FP8 A.C. Green B 6.00 15.00
FP9 John Salley A 5.00 12.00
FP10 Travis Knight A 5.00 12.00
FP11 Devean George A 5.00 12.00
FP12 Reggie Miller A 20.00 50.00
FP13 Jalen Rose A 6.00 15.00
FP14 Dale Davis A 5.00 12.00
FP15 Rik Smits A 6.00 15.00
FP16 Mark Jackson A 8.00 20.00
FP17 Travis Best A 5.00 12.00
FP18 Austin Croshere A 5.00 12.00
FP19 Derrick McKey A 5.00 12.00
FP20 Sam Perkins A 5.00 12.00
FP21 Chris Mullin A 15.00 40.00
FP22 Jonathan Bender A 5.00 12.00
FP23 Zan Tabak A 5.00 12.00

2000-01 Topps Flight Club

Randomly inserted in series two packs at one in 18 (one in six HTA), this 20-card set features players who spend their time above the rim. Card backs carry a "FC" prefix.

COMPLETE SET (20) 15.00 30.00
SER.2 STATED ODDS 1:18 H/R, 1:6 HTA
FC1 Vince Carter 1.50 4.00
FC2 Larry Hughes .60 1.50
FC3 Steve Francis .60 1.50
FC4 Tracy McGrady 1.25 3.00
FC5 Jerry Stackhouse .60 1.50
FC6 Kobe Bryant 3.00 8.00
FC7 Kevin Garnett 1.25 3.00
FC8 Michael Finley .75 2.00
FC9 Latrell Sprewell .60 1.50
FC10 Antonio McDyess .60 1.50
FC11 Lamar Odom .60 1.50
FC12 Shareef Abdur-Rahim .60 1.50
FC13 Chris Webber .75 2.00
FC14 Eddie Jones .75 2.00
FC15 Scottie Pippen 1.25 3.00
FC16 Grant Hill 1.00 2.50
FC17 Paul Pierce .75 2.00
FC18 Shawn Marion .60 1.50
FC19 Rasheed Wallace .75 2.00
FC20 Tim Duncan 1.50 4.00

2000-01 Topps Game Jerseys

Randomly inserted into series one packs at one in 502, this 20-card insert features game-used jersey cards of some of the best players in the NBA. Card backs carry a "TR" prefix. Please note that Group A were inserted into packs at 1:971 H/R and 1:151 HTA, and Group B were inserted at 1:1946 H/R and 1:302 HTA

GROUP A ODDS 1:971 H/R, 1:151 HTA
GROUP B ODDS 1:1946 H/R, 1:302 HTA
OVERALL ODDS 1:502 H/R, 1:101 HTA
TR1 Richard Hamilton A 2.50 6.00
TR2 Tracy Murray A 2.00 5.00
TR3 Chris Whitney B 2.00 5.00
TR4 Jahidi White A 2.00 5.00
TR5 Rod Strickland A 2.00 5.00
TR6 Mitch Richmond B 2.50 6.00
TR7 Juwan Howard B 2.50 6.00
TR8 Isaac Austin B 2.00 5.00
TR9 Michael Smith A 2.00 5.00
TR10 Lorenzo Williams B 2.00 5.00
TR11 Tony Battie B 2.00 5.00
TR12 Antoine Walker A 2.50 6.00
TR13 Adrian Griffin A 2.00 5.00
TR14 Vitaly Potapenko A 2.00 5.00
TR15 Pervis Ellison A 2.00 5.00
TR16 Paul Pierce B 3.00 8.00
TR17 Eric Williams B 2.00 5.00
TR18 Dana Barros B 2.00 5.00
TR19 Walter McCarty A 2.00 5.00
TR20 Danny Fortson B 2.00 5.00

2000-01 Topps Hidden Gems

Randomly inserted into series one packs at one in 11, this 10-card insert features players that quietly put up big numbers every year. Card backs carry a "HG" prefix.

COMPLETE SET (10) 2.50 6.00
SER.1 STATED ODDS 1:11 H/R, 1:3 HTA
HG1 Karl Malone .50 1.25
HG2 Latrell Sprewell .30 .75
HG3 Kobe Bryant 1.50 4.00
HG4 Michael Finley .40 1.00
HG5 Jalen Rose .30 .75
HG6 Reggie Miller .40 1.00
HG7 John Stockton .50 1.25
HG8 Terrell Brandon .25 .60
HG9 Nick Van Exel .30 .75
HG10 Allan Houston .30 .75

2000-01 Topps Hobby Masters

Randomly inserted into series one HTA packs only at one in 5, this 10-card insert features players that are in high demand in the hobby market. Card backs carry a "HM" prefix.

COMPLETE SET (10) 8.00 20.00
SER.1 STATED ODDS 1:5 HTA
HM1 Kevin Garnett 1.00 2.50
HM2 Jason Williams .60 1.50
HM3 Tim Duncan 1.25 3.00
HM4 Tracy McGrady 1.00 2.50
HM5 Kobe Bryant 2.50 6.00
HM6 Allen Iverson 1.25 3.00
HM7 Elton Brand .60 1.50
HM8 Steve Francis .50 1.25
HM9 Vince Carter 1.25 3.00
HM10 Chris Webber .60 1.50

2000-01 Topps Magic Johnson Reprints

Randomly inserted into series one packs, this 14-card set features 7 reprinted Magic Johnson cards (1:508), and 7 autographed Magic Johnson reprint cards (1:7088). According to Topps, less than 75 of each autographs exist.

COMPLETE SET (7) 40.00 70.00
COMMON CARD (1-7) 5.00 12.00
COMMON AU (1-7) 60.00 120.00
SER.1 STATED ODDS 1:508 H/R, 1:108 HTA
AU: SER.1 ST.ODDS 1:7088 H/R, 1:1506 HTA

2000-01 Topps Jumbos

Inserted as a series one box-topper in hobby boxes, this 10-card jumbo sized set pairs superstar caliber players together on the same card and parallels the Topps Combos insert. Card backs carry a "JC" prefix.

ONE PER SER.1 HOBBY BOX

2000-01 Topps No Limit

Randomly inserted in series two packs at one in six (one in two HTA), this 20-card set features NBA superstars that have propelled themselves past the competition. Card backs carry a "NL" prefix.

Card	Low	High
COMPLETE SET (20)	10.00	20.00
SER.2 STATED ODDS 1:6 H/R, 1:2 HTA		
NL1 Kobe Bryant	1.50	4.00
NL2 Kevin Garnett	.60	1.50
NL3 Vince Carter	.75	2.00
NL4 Tracy McGrady	.60	1.50
NL5 Tim Duncan	.75	2.00
NL6 Elton Brand	.40	1.00
NL7 Lamar Odom	.30	.75
NL8 Larry Hughes	.30	.75
NL9 Chris Webber	.40	1.00
NL10 Shareef Abdur-Rahim	.30	.75
NL11 Jason Kidd	.60	1.50
NL12 Gary Payton	.40	1.00
NL13 Paul Pierce	.40	1.00
NL14 Stromile Swift	.40	1.00
NL15 Darius Miles	.40	1.00
NL16 Mike Miller	.60	1.50
NL17 Jason Williams	.40	1.00
NL18 Jamal Crawford	1.00	2.50
NL19 Marcus Fizer	.40	1.00
NL20 DerMarr Johnson	.30	.75

2000-01 Topps Quantum Leaps

Randomly inserted into series one packs at one in 22, this 10-card insert features players that continue to show improvement everytime they step onto the court. Card backs carry a "QL" prefix.

Card	Low	High
COMPLETE SET (10)	6.00	15.00
SER.1 STATED ODDS 1:22 H/R, 1:6 HTA		
QL1 Chris Webber	.60	1.50
QL2 Antonio McDyess	.50	1.25
QL3 Stephon Marbury	.50	1.25
QL4 Shareef Abdur-Rahim	.50	1.25
QL5 Kobe Bryant	2.50	6.00
QL6 Jason Kidd	1.00	2.50
QL7 Elton Brand	.60	1.50
QL8 Lamar Odom	.50	1.25
QL9 Kevin Garnett	1.00	2.50
QL10 Jerry Stackhouse	.50	1.25

2000-01 Topps Rise to Stardom

Randomly inserted in series two packs at one in 36 (one in 12 HTA), this 10-card set depicts Rookie of the Year award winners from the past eight seasons. Card backs carry a "RS" prefix.

Card	Low	High
COMPLETE SET (10)	8.00	20.00
SER.2 STATED ODDS 1:36 H/R, 1:12 HTA		
RS1 Elton Brand	.75	2.00
RS2 Steve Francis	.60	1.50
RS3 Vince Carter	1.50	4.00
RS4 Tim Duncan	1.50	4.00
RS5 Allen Iverson	1.50	4.00
RS6 Damon Stoudamire	.60	1.50
RS7 Grant Hill	1.00	2.50
RS8 Jason Kidd	1.25	3.00
RS9 Chris Webber	.75	2.00
RS10 Shaquille O'Neal	2.00	5.00

2001-02 Topps Promos

This two-card cello pack was sent out to dealers and distributors with press material to debut the new Topps set design.

Card	Low	High
COMPLETE SET (2)	2.00	5.00
PP1 Shaquille O'Neal	1.50	4.00
PP2 Tim Duncan	1.25	3.00

2001-02 Topps

Released in August 2001, this 258-card base set contains 220 veterans and 35 rookies. The set also contains 1 NBA 2001 Championship Team photo card. The cards are standard size and have solid borders on the two vertical sides of the card. The borders on the horizontal sides of the card look as though they are crumbling apart. The cards feature color action shots with the Topps logo in the upper right-hand corner and the player's name in the lower right-hand corner. A special Preseason EXCH card was included in the product, and there was speculation that this would be a limited Michael Jordan card. In the end it was redeemed for a special Pau Gasol card. Topps was packaged in 36-pack boxes with ten cards per pack and packs carrying a suggested retail price of $1.49. HTA packs were packaged in 12-pack boxes with packs containing 38 cards, including one draft pick, and carried a suggested retail price of $5.00.

Card	Low	High
COMPLETE SET (257)	40.00	80.00
COMP.SET w/o RC (220)	15.00	30.00
221-256 STATED ODDS 1:4		
1 Shaquille O'Neal	.50	1.25
2 Travis Best	.12	.30
3 Allen Iverson	.40	1.00
4 Shawn Marion	.15	.40
5 Rasheed Wallace	.20	.50
6 Antonio Daniels	.12	.30
7 Rashard Lewis	.20	.50
8 John Starks	.12	.30
9 Stromile Swift	.12	.30
10 Vince Carter	.30	.75
11 George Lynch	.12	.30
12 Kendall Gill	.12	.30
13 Glen Rice	.15	.40
14 Glenn Robinson	.15	.40
15 Wally Szczerbiak	.15	.40
16 Rick Fox	.12	.30
17 Darius Miles	.12	.30
18 Jermaine O'Neal	.15	.40
19 Erick Dampier	.12	.30
20 Tracy McGrady	.30	.75
21 Kevin Garnett	.30	.75
22 Tim Thomas	.12	.30
23 Larry Hughes	.15	.40
24 Jerry Stackhouse	.15	.40
25 Voshon Lenard	.12	.30
26 Howard Eisley	.12	.30
27 Clarence Weatherspoon	.12	.30
28 Marcus Fizer	.12	.30
29 Elden Campbell	.12	.30
30 Tim Duncan	.40	1.00
31 Doug Christie	.12	.30
32 Keon Clark	.12	.30
33 Patrick Ewing	.25	.60
34 Hakeem Olajuwon	.25	.60
35 Stephen Jackson	.15	.40
36 Larry Johnson	.20	.50
37 Eric Snow	.12	.30
38 Tom Gugliotta	.12	.30
39 Scottie Pippen	.30	.75
40 Chris Webber	.20	.50
41 David Robinson	.30	.75
42 Elton Brand	.20	.50
43 Theo Ratliff	.12	.30
44 Paul Pierce	.20	.50
45 Jamal Mashburn	.15	.40
46 Eric Williams	.12	.30
47 DerMarr Johnson	.12	.30
48 Andre Miller	.15	.40
49 Dirk Nowitzki	.30	.75
50 Kobe Bryant	.75	2.00
51 Keyon Dooling	.12	.30
52 Brian Grant	.12	.30
53 Ervin Johnson	.12	.30
54 Anthony Peeler	.12	.30
55 Dikembe Mutombo	.20	.50
56 Steve Smith	.15	.40
57 Hedo Turkoglu	.15	.40
58 Terry Porter	.12	.30
59 Lorenzen Wright	.12	.30
60 Jason Terry	.20	.50
61 Vitaly Potapenko	.12	.30
62 Derrick Coleman	.15	.40
63 Ron Artest	.20	.50
64 Chris Gatling	.12	.30
65 Chris Mihm	.12	.30
66 Reggie Miller	.20	.50
67 Lamar Odom	.15	.40
68 Ron Harper	.15	.40
69 Baron Davis	.20	.50
70 Brad Miller	.20	.50
71 Shawn Bradley	.12	.30
72 James Posey	.12	.30
73 Ben Wallace	.15	.40
74 Marc Jackson	.12	.30
75 Maurice Taylor	.12	.30
76 Aaron McKie	.12	.30
77 Grant Hill	.25	.60
78 Arvydas Sabonis	.15	.40
79 Peja Stojakovic	.20	.50
80 Jason Kidd	.30	.75
81 Vin Baker	.15	.40
82 Morris Peterson	.12	.30
83 Bryon Russell	.12	.30
84 Michael Dickerson	.12	.30
85 Christian Laettner	.15	.40
86 Jerome Williams	.12	.30
87 Desmond Mason	.15	.40
88 Sean Elliott	.20	.50
89 Marcus Camby	.15	.40
90 Stephon Marbury	.15	.40
91 Joel Przybilla	.12	.30
92 Alonzo Mourning	.25	.60
93 Brian Shaw	.12	.30
94 Austin Croshere	.12	.30
95 Mookie Blaylock	.12	.30
96 Mateen Cleaves	.12	.30
97 Nick Van Exel	.15	.40
98 Michael Finley	.20	.50
99 Jamal Crawford	.20	.50
100 Steve Francis	.15	.40
101 Tim Hardaway	.20	.50
102 Sam Cassell	.15	.40
103 Shammond Williams	.12	.30
104 DeShawn Stevenson	.12	.30
105 Bryant Reeves	.12	.30
106 Richard Hamilton	.15	.40
107 Antonio Davis	.12	.30
108 Brent Barry	.12	.30
109 Derek Anderson	.12	.30
110 Kenny Anderson	.15	.40
111 Brevin Knight	.12	.30
112 Tyrone Nesby	.12	.30
113 Erick Strickland	.12	.30
114 Jacque Vaughn	.12	.30
115 John Stockton	.25	.60
116 Alvin Williams	.12	.30
117 Speedy Claxton	.12	.30
118 Bo Outlaw	.12	.30
119 Jahidi White	.12	.30
120 Karl Malone	.25	.60
121 Charles Oakley	.15	.40
122 Malik Rose	.12	.30
123 Avery Johnson	.15	.40
124 Toni Kukoc	.20	.50
125 Bryant Stith	.12	.30
126 P.J. Brown	.12	.30
127 Ron Mercer	.12	.30
128 Lamond Murray	.12	.30
129 Steve Nash	.30	.75
130 Raef LaFrentz	.12	.30
131 Corliss Williamson	.12	.30
132 Danny Fortson	.12	.30
133 Chris Porter	.12	.30
134 Shandon Anderson	.12	.30
135 Jalen Rose	.15	.40
136 Corey Maggette	.15	.40
137 Horace Grant	.15	.40
138 Eddie Jones	.15	.40
139 Chauncey Billups	.20	.50
140 Ray Allen	.20	.50
141 Terrell Brandon	.12	.30
142 Keith Van Horn	.15	.40
143 Allan Houston	.15	.40
144 Mark Jackson	.15	.40
145 Pat Garrity	.12	.30
146 Anfernee Hardaway	.30	.75
147 Iakovos Tsakalidis	.12	.30
148 Damon Stoudamire	.15	.40
149 Bobby Jackson	.12	.30
150 Antawn Jamison	.20	.50
151 Kenny Thomas	.12	.30
152 Jonathan Bender	.12	.30
153 Jeff McInnis	.12	.30
154 Robert Horry	.15	.40
155 Anthony Mason	.12	.30
156 Lindsey Hunter	.12	.30
157 LaPhonso Ellis	.15	.40
158 Jamie Feick	.12	.30
159 Kurt Thomas	.12	.30
160 Gary Payton	.20	.50
161 Rod Strickland	.12	.30
162 Bonzi Wells	.12	.30
163 Scot Pollard	.12	.30
164 Raja Bell RC	.75	2.00
165 Rodney Rogers	.12	.30
166 John Amaechi	.12	.30
167 Darrell Armstrong	.12	.30
168 Aaron Williams	.12	.30
169 Latrell Sprewell	.15	.40
170 Radoslav Nesterovic	.12	.30
171 Anthony Carter	.12	.30
172 Quentin Richardson	.15	.40
173 Primoz Brezec RC	.60	1.50
174 Michael Olowokandi	.12	.30
175 Jason Williams	.15	.40
176 Ruben Patterson	.12	.30
177 Chris Childs	.12	.30
178 Greg Ostertag	.12	.30
179 Mike Bibby	.20	.50
180 Mitch Richmond	.15	.40
181 Donyell Marshall	.12	.30
182 Dale Davis	.12	.30
183 Tony Delk	.12	.30
184 Mike Miller	.15	.40
185 Charlie Ward	.12	.30
186 Kenyon Martin	.20	.50
187 Walt Williams	.12	.30
188 Al Harrington	.15	.40
189 Chucky Atkins	.12	.30
190 Kevin Willis	.12	.30
191 Juwan Howard	.15	.40
192 Jim Jackson	.12	.30
193 Antonio McDyess	.15	.40
194 Jamaal Magloire	.12	.30
195 Mark Blount	.12	.30
196 Fred Hoiberg	.12	.30
197 Nazr Mohammed	.12	.30
198 Antoine Walker	.15	.40
199 Wang Zhizhi	.15	.40
200 Shareef Abdur-Rahim	.15	.40
201 Chris Whitney	.12	.30
202 David Wesley	.12	.30
203 Matt Harpring	.12	.30
204 George McCloud	.12	.30
205 Joe Smith	.15	.40
206 Cuttino Mobley	.12	.30
207 Tyrone Hill	.12	.30
208 Clifford Robinson	.12	.30
209 Vlade Divac	.15	.40
210 Eddie Robinson	.12	.30
211 Michael Curry	.12	.30
212 Courtney Alexander	.12	.30
213 Grant Long	.12	.30
214 Dan Majerle	.20	.50
215 Points Leaders	.20	.50
216 Rebounds Leaders	.20	.50
217 Assists Leaders	.20	.50
218 Steals Leaders	.20	.50
219 Blocks Leaders	.20	.50
220 Team Championship	.40	1.00
221 Kwame Brown RC	.60	1.50
222 Tyson Chandler RC	1.00	2.50
223 Pau Gasol RC	2.00	5.00
224 Eddy Curry RC	.60	1.50
225 Jason Richardson RC	.75	2.00
226 Shane Battier RC	1.25	3.00
227 Eddie Griffin RC	.50	1.25
228 DeSagana Diop RC	.50	1.25
229 Rodney White RC	.40	1.00
230 Joe Johnson RC	.75	2.00
231 Kedrick Brown RC	.40	1.00
232 Vladimir Radmanovic RC	.60	1.50
233 Richard Jefferson RC	1.00	2.50
234 Troy Murphy RC	.60	1.50
235 Steven Hunter RC	.50	1.25
236 Kirk Haston RC	.40	1.00
237 Michael Bradley RC	.40	1.00
238 Jason Collins RC	.50	1.25
239 Zach Randolph RC	1.00	2.50
240 Brendan Haywood RC	.60	1.50
241 Joseph Forte RC	.40	1.00
242 Jeryl Sasser RC	.40	1.00
243 Brandon Armstrong RC	.40	1.00
244 Gerald Wallace RC	.75	2.00
245 Samuel Dalembert RC	.60	1.50
246 Jamaal Tinsley RC	.60	1.50
247 Tony Parker RC	2.50	6.00
248 Trenton Hassell RC	.50	1.25
249 Gilbert Arenas RC	1.00	2.50
250 Jeff Trepagnier RC	.40	1.00
251 Damone Brown RC	.40	1.00
252 Loren Woods RC	.40	1.00
253 Ousmane Cisse RC	.60	1.50
254 Ken Johnson RC	.40	1.00
255 Kenny Satterfield RC	.40	1.00
256 Alvin Jones RC	.50	1.25
257 Pau Gasol Preseason	5.00	12.00
TRSC Shaq/Abdul-Jabbar JSY	100.00	200.00
NNO Gilbert Arenas SPEC AU	6.00	15.00

2001-02 Topps MVP Promotion

*MVP STARS: 12X TO 30X BASE CARD HI
*MVP RCs: 2X TO 5X BASE CARD HI
STATED ODDS 1:104 H, 1:80 R, 1:27 HTA
ANNOUNCED PRINT RUN 100 SETS
EXCHANGE DEADLINE 08/02/02

2001-02 Topps All-Star Remnants

This 21-card insert set is randomly inserted in hobby packs at a rate of 1:160; retail pack at a rate of 1:123; and 1:42 HTA. The set contains swatches of game-worn warm-ups. The cards are standard size, borderless, and printed with a horizontal design. The color action shot of the featured player is set on a background that resembles that of broken glass. The Topps logo is found in the upper right-hand corner with the featured player's team logo in the lower left-hand corner.

Card	Low	High
STATED ODDS 1:160 H, 1:123 R, 1:42 HTA		
TRAH Allan Houston	3.00	8.00
TRAM Andre Miller	3.00	8.00
TRBD Baron Davis	4.00	10.00
TRCW Chris Webber	4.00	10.00
TRDM Darius Miles	2.50	6.00
TRDN Dirk Nowitzki	6.00	15.00
TREB Elton Brand	4.00	10.00
TRJS Jerry Stackhouse	3.00	8.00
TRJT Jason Terry	4.00	10.00
TRJW Jason Williams	3.00	8.00
TRLO Lamar Odom	3.00	8.00
TRMB Mike Bibby	4.00	10.00
TRQR Quentin Richardson	3.00	8.00
TRRA Ray Allen	4.00	10.00
TRRH Richard Hamilton	3.00	8.00
TRRL Raef LaFrentz	2.50	6.00
TRRW Rasheed Wallace	4.00	10.00
TRSF Steve Francis	3.00	8.00
TRSM Shawn Marion	3.00	8.00
TRSO Shaquille O'Neal	10.00	25.00
TRTD Tim Duncan	8.00	20.00

2001-02 Topps All-Star Remnants Autographs

This 10-card insert set is randomly inserted in hobby packs in Groups A thru D. Group A: 1:5848; 1:1514 HTA, Group B: 1:8506; 1:2297 HTA, Group C: 1:17328; 1:4442 HTA, and Group D: 1:77976; 1:22208 HTA. The set contains both swatches of game-worn warm-ups and player autographs. The cards are standard size, borderless, and printed with a horizontal design. The color action shot of the featured player is set on a background that resembles that of broken glass. The Topps Certified Autograph logo is found in the lower right-hand corner.

Card	Low	High
GROUP A ODDS 1:5848 H, 1:1514 HTA		
GROUP B ODDS 1:8506 H, 1:2297 HTA		
GROUP C ODDS 1:17328 H, 1:4442 HTA		
GROUP D ODDS 1:77976 H, 1:22208 HTA		
TREB Elton Brand/42 B	20.00	50.00
TRJT Jason Terry/31 A	20.00	50.00
TRRH Richard Hamilton/32 A	20.00	50.00
TRRL Raef LaFrentz/45 B	10.00	25.00
TRSM Shawn Marion/32 A	50.00	100.00
TRSO Shaquille O'Neal/34 A	150.00	300.00
TRTD Tim Duncan/21 C	200.00	400.00

2001-02 Topps Autographs

This 12-card insert set is randomly inserted in Groups A thru C. Group A: 1:2515 H, 1:1958 R, 1:660 HTA; Group B: 1:1006 H, 1:766 R, 1:264 HTA; Group C: 1:838 H, 1:647 R, 1:221 HTA. The set is standard size and set on borderless cards. The set features players who have signed their Topps cards, including a group of Team Topps stars who exclusively sign with Topps. The cards of Team Topps members feature the "Team Topps" logo.

Card	Low	High
GROUP A 1:2515 H, 1:1958 R, 1:660 HTA		
GROUP B 1:1006 H, 1:766 R, 1:264 HTA		
GROUP C 1:838 H, 1:647 R, 1:221 HTA		
TAJB Jonathan Bender B	5.00	12.00
TAAJ Antawn Jamison C	5.00	12.00
TABD Baron Davis C	5.00	12.00
TADM Desmond Mason B	5.00	12.00
TAEB Elton Brand B	5.00	12.00
TAJT Jason Terry B	5.00	12.00
TAKAJ Kareem Abdul-Jabbar A	40.00	100.00
TALJ Larry Johnson A	30.00	80.00
TAMJ Magic Johnson A	50.00	100.00
TARH Richard Hamilton C	8.00	20.00
TASM Shawn Marion B	5.00	12.00
TASO Shaquille O'Neal A	50.00	120.00

2001-02 Topps Kareem Abdul-Jabbar Reprints

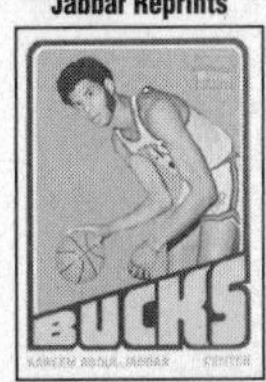

This 13-card insert set is randomly inserted in hobby packs at a rate of 1:14, retail packs at a rate of 1:11, and 1:4 HTA. These cards are reprints of some of Kareem Abdul-Jabbar's original Topps cards.

Card	Low	High
COMPLETE SET (13)	10.00	25.00
COMMON CARD (1-13)	1.25	3.00
STATED ODDS 1:14 H, 1:11 R, 1:4 HTA		

2001-02 Topps Kareem Abdul-Jabbar Reprints Autographs

This 13-card insert set is randomly inserted in packs at a rate of 1:9747 and 1:22208 HTA and parallels the base Kareem Abdul-Jabbar Reprints set enhanced with autographs.

Card	Low	High
COMMON CARD (1-13)	50.00	120.00
STATED ODDS 1:9747		
AU PROOF STATED ODDS 1:22208 HTA		
1 Lew Alcindor	100.00	200.00

2001-02 Topps Lottery Legends

Randomly inserted in hobby packs at the rate of one in six, retail packs at the rate of one in five, and HTA packs at the rate of one in two, this 13-card set features top draft picks from the past few years on an all foil card with two color player photos and the words "Lottery Legends" and player's draft number centered along the bottom of the card.

Card	Low	High
COMPLETE SET (13)	5.00	12.00
STATED ODDS 1:6 H, 1:5 R, 1:2 HTA		
LL1 Shaquille O'Neal	1.00	2.50
LL2 Steve Francis	.30	.75
LL3 Darius Miles	.25	.60
LL4 Stephon Marbury	.30	.75
LL5 Vince Carter	.60	1.50
LL6 Antoine Walker	.30	.75
LL7 Jason Williams	.30	.75
LL8 Larry Hughes	.30	.75
LL9 Tracy McGrady	.60	1.50
LL10 Paul Pierce	.40	1.00
LL11 Allan Houston	.30	.75
LL12 Austin Croshere	.25	.60
LL13 Kobe Bryant	1.50	4.00

2001-02 Topps Mad Game

Randomly inserted in hobby packs at the rate of one in 38, retail packs at the rate of one in 29, and HTA packs at the rate of one in 10, this 10-card set features a full color player action photo on an all foil backdrop where a "shadow" of his photo appears. The top of the card contains the words "Mad Game" which appears to be outlined in gold and filled with diamonds in a true bling-bling display.

Card	Low	High
COMPLETE SET (10)	10.00	25.00
STATED ODDS 1:38 H, 1:29 R, 1:10 HTA		
MG1 Allen Iverson	1.50	4.00
MG2 Shaquille O'Neal	2.00	5.00
MG3 Tim Duncan	1.50	4.00
MG4 Vince Carter	1.25	3.00
MG5 Kevin Garnett	1.25	3.00
MG6 Kobe Bryant	3.00	8.00
MG7 Tracy McGrady	1.25	3.00
MG8 Steve Francis	.60	1.50
MG9 Chris Webber	.75	2.00
MG10 Darius Miles	.50	1.25

2001-02 Topps NBA All-Star Jam Session

Produced by Topps, this set was given away at the All-Star Jam Session show from February 8th-10th exclusively at the Topps booth. These cards utilized the same card stock as the 2001-02 Topps set-blue borders and gold print, but are enhanced with the All-Star game logo in the lower left hand corner on an all holo-foil card stock.

Card	Low	High
COMPLETE SET (9)	6.00	15.00
1 Shaquille O'Neal	2.00	5.00
2 Tim Duncan	1.50	4.00
3 Allen Iverson	1.50	4.00
4 Tracy McGrady	1.25	3.00
5 Steve Francis	.60	1.50
6 Elton Brand	.75	2.00
7 Jamaal Tinsley	.75	2.00
8 Jamaal Tinsley	.75	2.00
9 Chris Webber	.75	2.00

2001-02 Topps Team Topps

Randomly inserted in hobby packs at the rate of one in eight, retail packs at the rate of one in seven, and HTA packs at the rate of one in two, this 10-card set features player's selected by Topps to represent the company as "Team Topps." Each card features an all-foil card stock with full color player action photos and player names printed vertically along the left edge of the card in white.

Card	Low	High
COMPLETE SET (9)	4.00	10.00
STATED ODDS 1:8 H, 1:7 R, 1:2 HTA		
TT1 Shaquille O'Neal	1.25	3.00
TT2 Tim Duncan	1.00	2.50
TT3 Antawn Jamison	.50	1.25
TT4 Jason Terry	.50	1.25
TT5 Baron Davis	.50	1.25
TT6 Elton Brand	.50	1.25
TT7 Peja Stojakovic	.50	1.25
TT8 Richard Hamilton	.40	1.00
TT9 Shawn Marion	.40	1.00
TT10 Team Shot	.75	2.00

2002-03 Topps Promos

This six-card cello pack was distributed with press material to dealers and distributors to debut the new design of 2002-03 Topps.

Card	Low	High
COMPLETE SET (6)	3.00	8.00
PP1 Tim Duncan	1.25	3.00
PP2 Steve Francis	.75	2.00
PP3 Ray Allen	.75	2.00
PP4 Steve Nash	1.00	2.50
PP5 Kenyon Martin	.75	2.00
PP6 Andre Miller	.75	2.00

2002-03 Topps

Released in late August 2002, Topps boasts a 220-card set divided up into 184 veteran player cards and 35 rookie cards. Card numbers 179-183 showcase six league leaders, Western Conference players on the front and Eastern Conference players on the back, and card number 184 features the NBA Championship winning Lakers from the 2001-02 season. Base cards have blue borders, full color player action photos, and silver foil highlights along the bottom for the player's name, team name, and the Topps logo. Topps was packaged in three different ways: Hobby, Retail, and Home Team Advantage packs. Hobby cases contained eight boxes, where boxes contained 36 packs, and packs contained 10 cards and carried a suggested retail price of $1.49. Retail boxes contained 24 packs where packs contained 13 cards and carried a suggested retail price of $1.99, and HTA cases had 12 boxes, where boxes contained six packs, and packs contained 34 cards and carried a suggested retail price of $5.00. Also included in packs were the Around the World scratch-off cards. These cards had five foil scratch-off circles around a three point arc where three or more "Hits" were winners. The The 10 Grand Prize winners received autographed jersey, one uncut sheet of Topps Basketball and one copy of the Around the World set. The 1000 First Prize winners received an uncut sheet of Topps basketball and one set of Around the World, and 5000 third prize winners received the Around the World set.

Card	Low	High
COMPLETE SET (220)	25.00	60.00
1 Shaquille O'Neal	.50	1.25
2 Pau Gasol	.25	.60
3 Allen Iverson	.30	.75
4 Tom Gugliotta	.12	.30
5 Rasheed Wallace	.20	.50
6 Peja Stojakovic	.20	.50
7 Jason Richardson	.20	.50
8 Rashard Lewis	.20	.50
9 Morris Peterson	.12	.30
10 Michael Jordan	1.50	4.00
11 Matt Harpring	.12	.30
12 Shareef Abdur-Rahim	.15	.40
13 Antoine Walker	.15	.40
14 Stephon Marbury	.15	.40
15 Jamal Mashburn	.15	.40
16 Eddy Curry	.12	.30
17 Jumaine Jones	.12	.30
18 Wang Zhizhi	.12	.30
19 James Posey	.12	.30
20 Jason Kidd	.30	.75
21 Jerry Stackhouse	.15	.40
22 Kenny Thomas	.12	.30
23 Ron Mercer	.12	.30
24 Jeff Mcinnis	.12	.30
25 Kobe Bryant	.75	2.00
26 Jason Williams	.15	.40
27 Eddie Jones	.15	.40
28 Anthony Mason	.12	.30
29 Kenyon Martin	.15	.40
30 Kevin Garnett	.30	.75
31 Kurt Thomas	.12	.30
32 Karl Malone	.25	.60
33 Patrick Ewing	.25	.60
34 Antonio McDyess	.15	.40
35 Dirk Nowitzki	.30	.75
36 Wesley Person	.12	.30
37 Theo Ratliff	.12	.30
38 Jarron Collins	.12	.30
39 Horace Grant	.15	.40
40 Vince Carter	.30	.75
41 Desmond Mason	.15	.40
42 Todd MacCulloch	.12	.30
43 Bobby Jackson	.12	.30
44 Vlade Divac	.15	.40
45 Keith Van Horn	.15	.40
46 Bo Outlaw	.12	.30
47 Eric Snow	.12	.30
48 Grant Hill	.25	.60
49 Terrell Brandon	.12	.30
50 Tracy Mcgrady	.30	.75
51 Tim Thomas	.12	.30
52 Loren Woods	.12	.30
53 Michael Redd	.15	.40
54 Stromile Swift	.12	.30
55 Dikembe Mutombo	.20	.50
56 Richard Jefferson	.20	.50
57 Glenn Robinson	.15	.40
58 Samaki Walker	.12	.30
59 Quentin Richardson	.15	.40
60 Elton Brand	.20	.50
61 Reggie Miller	.20	.50
62 Eddie Griffin	.12	.30
63 Gilbert Arenas	.20	.50
64 Zeljko Rebraca	.12	.30
65 Donnell Harvey	.12	.30
66 Juwan Howard	.15	.40
67 Nick Van Exel	.15	.40
68 Donyell Marshall	.12	.30
69 Tyson Chandler	.20	.50
70 Baron Davis	.15	.40
71 Nazr Mohammed	.12	.30
72 Marcus Camby	.15	.40
73 Jamaal Magloire	.12	.30
74 Marcus Fizer	.12	.30
75 Steve Francis	.15	.40
76 Aaron Mckie	.12	.30
77 Anfernee Hardaway	.30	.75
78 Scottie Pippen	.30	.75
79 Mike Bibby	.20	.50
80 Paul Pierce	.20	.50
81 Tony Delk	.12	.30
82 Kwame Brown	.12	.30
83 Andrei Kirilenko	.20	.50
84 Keon Clark	.12	.30
85 Alvin Williams	.12	.30
86 Brent Barry	.12	.30
87 David Robinson	.30	.75
88 Doug Christie	.12	.30
89 Derek Anderson	.12	.30
90 Chris Webber	.20	.50
91 Speedy Claxton	.12	.30
92 Robert Horry	.15	.40
93 Allan Houston	.15	.40
94 Kerry Kittles	.12	.30
95 Wally Szczerbiak	.15	.40
96 Jonathan Bender	.12	.30
97 Sam Cassell	.15	.40
98 Rod Strickland	.12	.30
99 Shane Battier	.20	.50
100 Tim Duncan	.40	1.00
101 Jermaine O'Neal	.15	.40
102 Cuttino Mobley	.12	.30
103 Danny Fortson	.12	.30
104 Clifford Robinson	.12	.30
105 Tim Hardaway	.20	.50
106 Steve Nash	.25	.60
107 Zydrunas Ilgauskas	.15	.40
108 Travis Best	.12	.30
109 Eddie Robinson	.12	.30
110 David Wesley	.12	.30
111 Kenny Anderson	.15	.40
112 DerMarr Johnson	.12	.30
113 Courtney Alexander	.12	.30
114 Brian Grant	.12	.30
115 Lorenzen Wright	.12	.30
116 Corliss Williamson	.12	.30
117 Malik Rose	.12	.30
118 Tony Parker	.25	.60
119 Vladimir Radmanovic	.12	.30
120 Hedo Turkoglu	.15	.40
121 Damon Stoudamire	.15	.40
122 Brendan Haywood	.12	.30
123 Jalen Rose	.15	.40
124 Mike Miller	.15	.40
125 Derrick Coleman	.15	.40
126 Mark Jackson	.15	.40
127 Raef Lafrentz	.12	.30
128 Ben Wallace	.15	.40
129 Larry Hughes	.15	.40
130 Ray Allen	.20	.50
131 Gary Payton	.20	.50
132 P.J. Brown	.12	.30
133 Derek Fisher	.15	.40
134 Michael Olowokandi	.12	.30
135 Jamaal Tinsley	.12	.30
136 Moochie Norris	.12	.30
137 Chris Mihm	.12	.30
138 Antawn Jamison	.20	.50
139 Chucky Atkins	.12	.30
140 Mengke Bateer	.12	.30
141 Brad Miller	.15	.40
142 Michael Finley	.20	.50
143 Andre Miller	.15	.40
144 Michael Dickerson	.12	.30
145 Elden Campbell	.12	.30
146 Kedrick Brown	.12	.30
147 Jason Terry	.15	.40
148 Chris Whitney	.12	.30
149 Bryon Russell	.12	.30
150 Darius Miles	.12	.30
151 Latrell Sprewell	.15	.40
152 Darrell Armstrong	.12	.30
153 Joe Johnson	.15	.40
154 Bonzi Wells	.12	.30
155 Jim Jackson	.12	.30
156 Steve Smith	.15	.40
157 Vin Baker	.15	.40
158 Antonio Davis	.12	.30
159 John Stockton	.25	.60
160 Shawn Marion	.15	.40
161 Devean George	.12	.30
162 Clarence Weatherspoon	.12	.30
163 Rick Fox	.12	.30
164 Chauncey Billups	.20	.50
165 Joe Smith	.15	.40
166 Laphonso Ellis	.15	.40
167 Maurice Taylor	.12	.30
168 Lamond Murray	.12	.30
169 Lamar Odom	.15	.40
170 Toni Kukoc	.20	.50
171 Alonzo Mourning	.25	.60
172 Antonio Daniels	.12	.30
173 Troy Murphy	.15	.40
174 Hakeem Olajuwon	.25	.60
175 Richard Hamilton	.15	.40
176 Rodney Rogers	.12	.30
177 Ruben Patterson	.12	.30
178 Dale Davis	.12	.30
179 League Leaders	.50	1.25
180 League Leaders	.20	.50
181 League Leaders	.20	.50
182 League Leaders	.20	.50
183 League Leaders	.20	.50
184 Team Championship Card	.60	1.50
185 Yao Ming RC	1.50	4.00
186 Jay Williams RC	.75	2.00
187 Mike Dunleavy RC	.75	2.00
188 Drew Gooden RC	.75	2.00
189 Nikoloz Tskitishvili RC	.50	1.25
190 DaJuan Wagner RC	.60	1.50
191 Nene Hilario RC	.75	2.00
192 Chris Wilcox RC	.60	1.50
193 Amare Stoudemire RC	1.00	2.50
194 Caron Butler RC	.75	2.00
195 Jared Jeffries RC	.60	1.50
196 Melvin Ely RC	.60	1.50
197 Marcus Haislip RC	.60	1.50
198 Fred Jones RC	.60	1.50
199 Bostjan Nachbar RC	.60	1.50
200 Jiri Welsch RC	.60	1.50
201 Juan Dixon RC	.75	2.00
202 Curtis Borchardt RC	.50	1.25
203 Ryan Humphrey RC	.60	1.50
204 Kareem Rush RC	.60	1.50
205 Qyntel Woods RC	.60	1.50
206 Casey Jacobsen RC	.60	1.50
207 Tayshaun Prince RC	1.00	2.50
208 Frank Williams RC	.50	1.25
209 John Salmons RC	.75	2.00
210 Chris Jefferies ERR RC	.50	1.25
211 Sam Clancy RC	.60	1.50
212 Dan Gadzuric RC	.60	1.50
213 Matt Barnes RC	1.00	2.50
214 Robert Archibald RC	.50	1.25
215 Vincent Yarbrough RC	.50	1.25
216 Dan Dickau RC	.60	1.50
217 Carlos Boozer RC	.75	2.00
218 Tito Maddox RC	.50	1.25
219 Chris Owens RC	.50	1.25
220 Ronald Murray RC	.75	2.00

2002-03 Topps Black

*BLACK STARS: 5X TO 12X BASE CARD HI
*BLACK RCs: 1.5X TO 4X BASE CARD HI
BLACK PRINT RUN 500 SER.#'d SETS

2002-03 Topps All-Star Relic Remnants

Randomly inserted in Hobby packs at the rate of one in 149, Retail packs at the rate of one in 540 and HTA packs at the rate of one in 40, this 15-card set places full color player action photos over a "wood court" backdrop featuring the NBA All-Star 2002 logo. The bottom right hand corner showcases an oval swatch of a pice of game worn memorabilia from the 2002 All-Star Game.

Card	Low	High
STAT.ODDS 1:149 H 1:540 R, 1:40 HTA		
TRAI Allen Iverson	6.00	15.00
TRAW Antoine Walker	3.00	8.00
TRCW Chris Webber	4.00	10.00
TREB Elton Brand	4.00	10.00
TRJK Jason Kidd	6.00	15.00
TRJO Jermaine O'Neal	3.00	8.00
TRPS Peja Stojakovic	4.00	10.00
TRRA Ray Allen	4.00	10.00
TRSF Steve Francis	3.00	8.00
TRSN Steve Nash	5.00	12.00
TRTD Tim Duncan	8.00	20.00
TRAEB Elton Brand AU	25.00	60.00
TRATD Tim Duncan AU/25	300.00	600.00

2002-03 Topps Around The World

Here's the information we have on that set in our database of cards, it's cataloged under the name 2002-03 Topps Around the World: This redemption set was available out of regular 2002-03 Topps packs as part of Around the World game pieces. These cards had five foil scratch-off circles around a three point arc where if three or more of they circles were "Hits" the card could be redeemed for a prize. The 10 Grand Prize winners received an autographed jersey, one uncut sheet of Topps basketball and one copy of the Around the World set. The 1000 First Prize winners received an uncut sheet of Topps basketball and one set of Around the World, and 5000 third prize winners received the Around the World set. The set contains 24 cards.

Card	Low	High
COMPLETE SET (24)	12.00	30.00
GAME CARDS IN TOPPS PACKS		
AW1 Tim Duncan	1.25	3.00
AW2 Dirk Nowitzki	1.00	2.50
AW3 Pau Gasol	.75	2.00
AW4 Steve Nash	.75	2.00
AW5 Peja Stojakovic	.60	1.50
AW6 Tony Parker	.75	2.00
AW7 Hedo Turkoglu	.50	1.25
AW8 Andrei Kirilenko	.60	1.50
AW9 Dikembe Mutombo	.60	1.50
AW10 Wang ZhiZhi	.40	1.00
AW11 Michael Olowokandi	.40	1.00
AW12 Vladimir Radmanovic	.40	1.00
AW13 Nikoloz Tskitishvili	.40	1.00
AW14 Shaquille O'Neal	1.50	4.00
AW15 Tracy McGrady	1.00	2.50
AW16 Nene Hilario	.60	1.50
AW17 Kevin Garnett	1.00	2.50
AW18 Yao Ming	1.25	3.00
AW19 DaJuan Wagner	.50	1.25
AW20 Mike Dunleavy	.60	1.50
AW21 Caron Butler	.60	1.50
AW22 Qyntel Woods	.50	1.25
AW23 Drew Gooden	.60	1.50
AW24 Chris Wilcox	.50	1.25

2002-03 Topps Autographs

Randomly seeded in Hobby packs at the rate of one in 303 and HTA packs at the rate of one in 80, this 11-card set places full color player photography against a basketball backdrop. The bottom of the card fades to white where authentic player autographs appear. These cards are garnished with gold foil highlights and the Topps stamp of authenticity.

Card	Low	High
STATED ODDS 1:303 H, 1:80 HTA		
TAAH Al Harrington	4.00	10.00
TACA Courtney Alexander	4.00	10.00
TACB Chauncey Billups	6.00	15.00
TACM Corey Maggette	4.00	10.00
TADH Donnell Harvey	4.00	10.00
TAEB Erick Barkley	4.00	10.00
TAKA Kareem Abdul-Jabbar	40.00	100.00
TAMD Michael Doleac	4.00	10.00
TAMJ Marc Jackson	4.00	10.00
TARM Roshown McLeod	4.00	10.00
TASO Shaquille O'Neal	30.00	80.00

2002-03 Topps Coast to Coast

Randomly inserted in Hobby packs at the rate of one in 13, retail packs at the rate of one in 10 and HTA packs at the rate of one in two, this 20-card set places top NBA stars on an all holofoil card stock with a street sign background theme.

Card	Low	High
COMPLETE SET (20)	12.00	30.00
STAT.ODDS 1:13 H, 1:10 R, 1:2 HTA		
CC1 Tracy McGrady	1.00	2.50
CC2 Jason Kidd	1.00	2.50
CC3 Mike Bibby	.60	1.50
CC4 Baron Davis	.50	1.25
CC5 Steve Francis	.50	1.25
CC6 Vince Carter	1.00	2.50
CC7 Kobe Bryant	2.50	6.00
CC8 Michael Jordan	5.00	12.00
CC9 Paul Pierce	.60	1.50
CC10 Stephon Marbury	.50	1.25
CC11 Ray Allen	.60	1.50
CC12 Gary Payton	.60	1.50
CC13 Shawn Marion	.50	1.25
CC14 Steve Nash	.75	2.00
CC15 Andre Miller	.50	1.25
CC16 Jerry Stackhouse	.50	1.25
CC17 Latrell Sprewell	.50	1.25
CC18 Jason Richardson	.60	1.50
CC19 Jamaal Tinsley	.40	1.00
CC20 Tony Parker	.75	2.00

2002-03 Topps Rookie Autographs

Randomly inserted in packs, this 15-card set features top draft picks at the NBA Rookie Photo Shoot in Jersey City, New Jersey in July 2002. The photos used on these cards were taken on Saturday, they were processed and printed, and the player's autographed the next day, Sunday. There are 50 of each card.

Card	Low	High
ANNOUNCED PRINT RUN 50 SETS		
1 Drew Gooden	25.00	60.00
2 Nikoloz Tskitishvili	6.00	15.00
3 Marcus Haislip	8.00	20.00
4 Melvin Ely	8.00	20.00
5 Tayshaun Prince	25.00	60.00
6 Sam Clancy	8.00	20.00
7 Dan Gadzuric	8.00	20.00
8 Ryan Humphrey	8.00	20.00
9 Jared Jeffries	8.00	20.00
10 Fred Jones	20.00	50.00
11 Kareem Rush	20.00	50.00
12 John Salmons	25.00	60.00
13 Amare Stoudemire	125.00	250.00
14 Vincent Yarbrough	6.00	15.00
15 Ronald Murray	10.00	25.00

2002-03 Topps Shaq Attack Relics

Randomly inserted in Hobby packs at the rate of one in 319, Retail packs at the rate of one in 451, and HTA packs at the rate of one in 90, this five card set features Shaquille O'Neal. The cards are horizontally designed with a picture of Shaq on the left and a white break towards the right side. The white side contains a "Shaq Attack" logo in silver foil and a highlight/signifigant place in Shaq's career. The jersey swatch is in the shape of the featured state.

Card	Low	High
COMPLETE SET (5)	50.00	100.00
COMMON CARD (SA1-SA5)	12.00	30.00
STAT.ODDS 1:319 H, 1:451 R, 1:90 HTA		

2002-03 Topps Shaq Attack Relics Autographs

Randomly inserted in HTA packs, this five card set features Shaquille O'Neal. The cards are horizontally designed with a picture of Shaq on the left and a white break towards the right side. The white side contains a "Shaq Attack" logo in silver foil and a highlight/signifigant place in Shaq's career. The jersey swatch is in the shape of the featured state. On the photo, an authentic Shaquille O'Neal autograph appears, and each card is sequentially numbered.

Card	Low	High
RANDOM INSERTS IN HTA PACKS		
SAA1 Shaquille O'Neal/72	75.00	200.00
SAA2 Shaquille O'Neal/33	150.00	300.00
SAA3 Shaquille O'Neal/92	75.00	200.00
SAA4 Shaquille O'Neal/32	150.00	300.00
SAA5 Shaquille O'Neal/34	150.00	300.00

2002-03 Topps Slam Duncan Relics

Randomly inserted in Hobby packs at the rate of one in 319, Retail packs at the rate of one in 451, and HTA packs at the rate of one in 90, this five card set pays tribute to Tim Duncan. Each card has an action photo of Duncan on the left coupled with a square swatch of a jersey, and a quick blurb about a signifigant event/place in Duncan's career.

Card	Low	High
COMPLETE SET (5)	30.00	60.00

COMMON CARD (SD1-SD5) 8.00 20.00
STAT.ODDS 1:319 H, 1:451 R, 1:90 HTA

2002-03 Topps Slam Duncan Relics Autographs

Randomly inserted in HTA packs, this five card set pays tribute to Tim Duncan. Each card has an action photo of Duncan on the left coupled with a square swatch of a jersey, and a quick blurb about a significant event/place in Duncan's career. Autographs are signed along the left edge of the card, and each card is sequentially numbered.

RANDOM INSERTS IN HTA PACKS
SDA1 Tim Duncan/76 150.00 300.00
SDA2 Tim Duncan/97 100.00 200.00
SDA3 Tim Duncan/21 200.00 400.00
SDA4 Tim Duncan/21 200.00 400.00
SDA5 Tim Duncan/21 200.00 400.00

2002-03 Topps Top Tandems

Randomly inserted in Hobby packs at the rate of one in five, Retail packs at the rate of one in ten and HTA packs at the rate of one in two, this 10-card set places two players from the same team on the card front. Two photos appear on this all holofoil card with the Topps Tandems logo in the upper left hand corner and the player's names along the right edge in red.

COMPLETE SET (10) 6.00 15.00
STAT.ODDS 1:5 H, 1:10 R, 1:2 HTA
TT1 A.Walker/P.Pierce .60 1.50
TT2 S.O'Neal/K.Bryant 2.50 6.00
TT3 D.Coleman/A.Iverson 1.00 2.50
TT4 S.Marion/S.Marbury .50 1.25
TT5 D.Nowitzki/M.Finley 1.00 2.50
TT6 M.Jordan/R.Hamilton 5.00 12.00
TT7 C.Webber/P.Stojakovic .60 1.50
TT8 V.Carter/M.Peterson 1.00 2.50
TT9 R.Allen/G.Robinson .60 1.50
TT10 S.Francis/C.Mobley .50 1.25

2002-03 Topps Verticality

Randomly seeded in Hobby packs at the rate of one in 10, Retail packs at the rate of one in eight, and HTA packs at the rate of one in three, this 15-card set places full color player action photos on a silver holofoil card stock with gold letter boxes running down both the left and right sides of the card. The left bar contains the player's name, and the right side contains the word, "Verticality" and the Topps logo.

COMPLETE SET (15) 10.00 25.00
STAT.ODDS 1:10 H, 1:8 R, 1:3 HTA
V1 Shawn Marion .50 1.25
V2 Darius Miles .40 1.00
V3 Vince Carter 1.00 2.50
V4 Tracy McGrady 1.00 2.50
V5 Kobe Bryant 2.50 6.00
V6 Jason Richardson .60 1.50
V7 Steve Francis .50 1.25
V8 Michael Jordan 8.00 20.00
V9 Jerry Stackhouse .50 1.25
V10 Baron Davis .50 1.25
V11 Pau Gasol .75 2.00
V12 Kevin Garnett 1.00 2.50
V13 Kenyon Martin .50 1.25
V14 Shaquille O'Neal 1.50 4.00
V15 Jermaine O'Neal .50 1.25

2003-04 Topps Promos

Sent out by Topps, this six-card cello pack accompanied press materials to dealers and distributors to debut the new design of 2003-04 Topps.

COMPLETE SET (6) 5.00 12.00
PP1 Shaquille O'Neal 1.50 4.00
PP2 Tracy McGrady .75 2.00
PP3 Chris Webber .60 1.50
PP4 Kevin Garnett 1.00 2.50
PP5 Tim Duncan 1.00 2.50
PP6 Steve Nash .75 2.00

2003-04 Topps

Released in September 2003, Topps boasts a 249-card base set divided up into 220 veterans and 29 rookie cards. Each card places full-color player action photography on a design with silver foil highlights and white borders. Several different packaging was available for the product. Hobby/Retail boxes contain 36 packs of ten cards each with a suggested retail price of $1.59. HTA Jumbo boxes contain 12 packs of 35 cards each and a suggested retail price of $5. HTA First Edition packs were also available to hobby shop account owners, and these were packaged in 20 pack boxes of 10 cards each with a suggested retail price of $1.59.

COMPLETE SET (249) 25.00 60.00
1 Tracy McGrady .25 .60
2 DaJuan Wagner .12 .30
3 Allen Iverson .30 .75
4 Chris Webber .20 .50
5 Jason Kidd .30 .75
6 Stephon Marbury .15 .40
7 Jermaine O'Neal .15 .40
8 Antoine Walker .20 .50
9 Tony Parker .20 .50
10 Mike Bibby .20 .50
11 Yao Ming .40 1.00
12 Walter McCarty .12 .30
13 Steve Nash .25 .60
14 Paul Pierce .20 .50
15 Vince Carter .30 .75
16 Peja Stojakovic .20 .50
17 Kenny Anderson .15 .40
18 Kenyon Martin .15 .40
19 Pau Gasol .20 .50
20 Gary Payton .20 .50
21 Tim Duncan .30 .75
22 Jay Williams .12 .30
23 Jason Richardson .20 .50
24 Andre Miller .15 .40
25 Latrell Sprewell .15 .40
26 Darius Miles .12 .30
27 Richard Jefferson .15 .40
28 Shawn Marion .15 .40
29 Baron Davis .15 .40
30 Ben Wallace .15 .40
31 Reggie Miller .20 .50
32 Karl Malone .25 .60
33 Grant Hill .25 .60
34 Shaquille O'Neal .50 1.25
35 Steve Francis .15 .40
36 Kobe Bryant .75 2.00
37 Mike Dunleavy .15 .40
38 Glenn Robinson .15 .40
39 Allan Houston .15 .40
40 Kevin Ollie .12 .30
41 Dirk Nowitzki .30 .75
42 Elton Brand .20 .50
43 Juan Dixon .12 .30
44 Brian Grant .12 .30
45 Jason Terry .15 .40
46 Richard Hamilton .15 .40
47 Morris Peterson .12 .30
48 Ray Allen .20 .50
49 Scottie Pippen .30 .75
50 David Robinson .30 .75
51 Cuttino Mobley .12 .30
52 Jerry Stackhouse .15 .40
53 Marcus Camby .15 .40
54 Jalen Rose .15 .40
55 Dikembe Mutombo .20 .50
56 P.J. Brown .12 .30
57 Jumaine Jones .12 .30
58 Shawn Bradley .12 .30
59 Juwan Howard .15 .40
60 Clifford Robinson .12 .30
61 Antawn Jamison .15 .40
62 Raef LaFrentz .12 .30
63 Kareem Rush .12 .30
64 LaPhonso Ellis .12 .30
65 Toni Kukoc .20 .50
66 Mike Miller .15 .40
67 Aaron McKie .12 .30
68 Tom Gugliotta .12 .30
69 Dale Davis .12 .30
70 Jared Jeffries .12 .30
71 Alvin Williams .12 .30
72 DeShawn Stevenson .12 .30
73 Doug Christie .12 .30
74 Troy Hudson .12 .30
75 Jason Collins .12 .30
76 Eddie Griffin .12 .30
77 Vladimir Radmanovic .12 .30
78 Michael Olowokandi .12 .30
79 Michael Redd .20 .50
80 Tim Thomas .12 .30
81 Ron Mercer .12 .30
82 Shareef Abdur-Rahim .15 .40
83 Eduardo Najera .12 .30
84 Jon Barry .12 .30
85 Erick Dampier .12 .30
86 Derek Fisher .15 .40
87 Drew Gooden .15 .40
88 Dan Gadzuric .12 .30
89 Antonio McDyess .15 .40
90 Derrick Coleman .15 .40
91 Carlos Boozer .15 .40
92 Rasheed Wallace .20 .50
93 Antonio Davis .12 .30
94 Kwame Brown .12 .30
95 Manu Ginobili .25 .60
96 Eric Williams .12 .30
97 Trenton Hassell .12 .30
98 Chris Whitney .12 .30
99 Chauncey Billups .20 .50
100 Kevin Garnett .30 .75
101 Marko Jaric .12 .30
102 Rasual Butler .12 .30
103 Gilbert Arenas .15 .40
104 Keith Van Horn .15 .40
105 Iakovos Tsakalidis .12 .30
106 Ruben Patterson .12 .30
107 Jarron Collins .12 .30
108 Rodney White .12 .30
109 Rashard Lewis .20 .50
110 Malik Rose .12 .30
111 Bobby Jackson .12 .30
112 Brendan Haywood .12 .30
113 Charlie Ward .12 .30
114 Courtney Alexander .12 .30
115 Kerry Kittles .12 .30
116 Wally Szczerbiak .15 .40
117 Darrell Armstrong .12 .30
118 Anfernee Hardaway .30 .75
119 Qyntel Woods .12 .30
120 Quentin Richardson .15 .40
121 Jonathan Bender .12 .30
122 Robert Horry .15 .40
123 Lorenzen Wright .12 .30
124 Malik Allen .12 .30
125 Sam Cassell .15 .40
126 Joe Smith .15 .40
127 Dion Glover .12 .30
128 Jamal Crawford .20 .50
129 Ricky Davis .15 .40
130 Nikoloz Tskitishvili .12 .30
131 Tyronn Lue .12 .30
132 Scott Padgett .12 .30
133 Jerome James .12 .30
134 Hedo Turkoglu .15 .40
135 Jamal Mashburn .15 .40
136 Pat Burke .12 .30
137 Joe Johnson .15 .40
138 Anthony Peeler .12 .30
139 Ron Artest .20 .50
140 Theo Ratliff .12 .30
141 Caron Butler .15 .40
142 Anthony Mason .12 .30
143 Vin Baker .12 .30
144 Donyell Marshall .12 .30
145 Nene .15 .40
146 Chucky Atkins .12 .30
147 Tyson Chandler .15 .40
148 Jason Williams .15 .40
149 Larry Hughes .15 .40
150 Stephen Jackson .15 .40
151 Kurt Thomas .12 .30
152 Mehmet Okur .15 .40
153 Amare Stoudemire .25 .60
154 Elden Campbell .12 .30
155 Jamaal Tinsley .12 .30
156 Chris Wilcox .12 .30
157 Rick Fox .12 .30
158 Gordan Giricek .12 .30
159 Voshon Lenard .12 .30
160 Brent Barry .12 .30
161 Dan Dickau .12 .30
162 Junior Harrington .12 .30
163 Jiri Welsch .12 .30
164 Vladimir Stepania .12 .30
165 Brad Miller .15 .40
166 Moochie Norris .12 .30
167 Wesley Person .12 .30
168 Greg Buckner .12 .30
169 Bonzi Wells .12 .30
170 Predrag Drobnjak .12 .30
171 Andrei Kirilenko .20 .50
172 Vlade Divac .15 .40
173 Rodney Rogers .12 .30
174 Kendall Gill .12 .30
175 Kenny Thomas .12 .30
176 Derek Anderson .12 .30
177 Steve Smith .15 .40
178 Christian Laettner .15 .40
179 Tony Delk .12 .30
180 Zydrunas Ilgauskas .15 .40
181 James Posey .12 .30
182 Tayshaun Prince .15 .40
183 Devean George .12 .30
184 Eddie Jones .15 .40
185 Corey Maggette .15 .40
186 Ira Newble .12 .30
187 Shane Battier .15 .40
188 Clarence Weatherspoon .12 .30
189 Eric Snow .12 .30
190 Damon Stoudamire .15 .40
191 Keon Clark .12 .30
192 Desmond Mason .15 .40
193 Matt Harpring .12 .30
194 Radoslav Nesterovic .12 .30
195 Jamaal Magloire .12 .30
196 Pat Garrity .12 .30
197 Fred Jones .15 .40
198 Tony Battie .12 .30
199 Tyrone Hill .12 .30
200 Adrian Griffin .12 .30
201 Nick Van Exel .15 .40
202 Shammond Williams .12 .30
203 Corliss Williamson .12 .30
204 Lamar Odom .15 .40
205 Travis Best .12 .30
206 Howard Eisley .12 .30
207 Jerome Williams .12 .30
208 David Wesley .12 .30
209 Bostjan Nachbar .12 .30
210 Marcus Fizer .12 .30
211 Michael Finley .20 .50
212 Troy Murphy .12 .30
213 Adonal Foyle .12 .30
214 Samaki Walker .12 .30
215 Lucious Harris .12 .30
216 Lindsey Hunter .12 .30
217 Stromile Swift .12 .30
218 Eddy Curry .12 .30
219 Kelvin Cato .12 .30
220 Chris Anderson .25 .60
221 LeBron James RC 50.00 120.00
222 Darko Milicic RC .75 2.00
223 Carmelo Anthony RC 3.00 8.00
224 Chris Bosh RC 1.50 4.00
225 Dwyane Wade RC 3.00 8.00
226 Chris Kaman RC 1.00 2.50
227 Kirk Hinrich RC 1.00 2.50
228 T.J. Ford RC .75 2.00
229 Mike Sweetney RC .60 1.50
230 Jarvis Hayes RC .60 1.50
231 Mickael Pietrus RC .75 2.00
232 Nick Collison RC .75 2.00
233 Marcus Banks RC .60 1.50
234 Luke Ridnour RC .75 2.00
235 Reece Gaines RC .60 1.50
236 Troy Bell RC .60 1.50
237 Zarko Cabarkapa RC .60 1.50
238 David West RC 1.00 2.50
239 Aleksandar Pavlovic RC .75 2.00
240 Dahntay Jones RC .75 2.00
241 Boris Diaw RC 1.00 2.50
242 Zoran Planinic RC .60 1.50
243 Travis Outlaw RC .75 2.00
244 Brian Cook RC .60 1.50
245 Carlos Delfino RC .75 2.00
246 Ndudi Ebi RC .60 1.50
247 Kendrick Perkins RC .75 2.00
248 Leandro Barbosa RC 1.00 2.50
249 Josh Howard RC 1.00 2.50

2003-04 Topps Black

1-220 SINGLES: 4X TO 10X BASE CARD HI
221-249 RCs: 1.25X TO 3X BASE CARD HI
STATED PRINT RUN 500 SER.#'d SETS
STATED ODDS 1:29 H, 1:26 R, 1:9 HTA
221 LeBron James 300.00 600.00

2003-04 Topps First Edition

1ST ED.SINGLES: 1.5X TO 4X BASE HI
1ST ED.RCs: 1X TO 2.5X BASE CARD HI
BOXES DISTRIBUTED TO HTA DEALERS
221 LeBron James 75.00 200.00

2003-04 Topps Gold

*1-220 SINGLES: 8X TO 20X BASE CARD HI
*221-249 RCs: 1.25X TO 3X BASE CARD HI
STATED PRINT RUN 99 SER.#'d SETS
STATED ODDS 1:91 H, 1:25 HTA
221 LeBron James 500.00 800.00

2003-04 Topps Highlight Zone

Inserted in Hobby packs at the rate of one in 16, Retail packs at the rate of one in 18 and HTA packs at the rate of one in six, this 20-card set features an all-foil card stock with full-color player photos set against an irridescent background designed to look like a TV.

COMPLETE SET (20) 12.50 30.00
STATED ODDS 1:16 H, 1:18R, 1:6 HTA
HZ1 Paul Pierce .75 2.00
HZ2 Shaquille O'Neal 2.00 5.00
HZ3 Chris Webber .75 2.00
HZ4 Steve Francis .60 1.50
HZ5 Shawn Marion .60 1.50
HZ6 Elton Brand .75 2.00
HZ7 Peja Stojakovic .75 2.00
HZ8 Vince Carter 1.25 3.00
HZ9 Stephon Marbury .60 1.50
HZ10 Jerry Stackhouse .60 1.50
HZ11 Ray Allen .75 2.00
HZ12 Baron Davis .60 1.50
HZ13 Antoine Walker .75 2.00
HZ14 Jason Kidd 1.25 3.00
HZ15 Antawn Jamison .60 1.50
HZ16 Steve Nash 1.00 2.50
HZ17 Jason Richardson .75 2.00
HZ18 Ricky Davis .60 1.50
HZ19 Latrell Sprewell .60 1.50
HZ20 Kobe Bryant 3.00 8.00

2003-04 Topps Justice of the Court

Inserted in Hobby packs at the rate of one in eight, Retail packs at the rate of one in nine and HTA packs at the rate of one in three, this 20-card set is horzontally designed with a full-color player action photo on a white bordered backdrop.

COMPLETE SET (20) 8.00 20.00
STATED ODDS 1:8 H, 1:9 R, 1:3 HTA
JC1 Ben Wallace .40 1.00
JC2 Gary Payton .50 1.25
JC3 Shaquille O'Neal 1.25 3.00
JC4 Tim Duncan .75 2.00
JC5 Chris Webber .50 1.25
JC6 Dirk Nowitzki .75 2.00
JC7 Kevin Garnett .75 2.00
JC8 Shawn Marion .40 1.00
JC9 Karl Malone .60 1.50
JC10 Nene .40 1.00
JC11 Yao Ming 1.00 2.50
JC12 Kobe Bryant 2.00 5.00
JC13 Vince Carter .75 2.00
JC14 Elton Brand .50 1.25
JC15 Kenyon Martin .40 1.00
JC16 Amare Stoudemire .60 1.50
JC17 Pau Gasol .50 1.25
JC18 Derrick Coleman .40 1.00
JC19 Ron Artest .50 1.25
JC20 Rasheed Wallace .50 1.25

2003-04 Topps Love it Live

Inserted in Hobby packs at the rate of one in eight, Retail packs at the rate of one in nine and HTA at the rate of one in three, this 20-card set is horizontally designed with a player action photo on the left and a portrait-style photo on the right.

COMPLETE SET (20) 10.00 25.00
STATED ODDS 1:8 H, 1:9 R, 1:3 HTA
LLAI Allen Iverson .75 2.00
LLAS Amare Stoudemire .60 1.50
LLBD Baron Davis .40 1.00
LLCB Caron Butler .40 1.00
LLCW Chris Webber .50 1.25
LLDG Drew Gooden .40 1.00
LLDN Dirk Nowitzki .75 2.00
LLDW DaJuan Wagner .30 .75
LLGP Gary Payton .50 1.25
LLJO Jermaine O'Neal .40 1.00
LLJS Jerry Stackhouse .40 1.00
LLKB Kobe Bryant 2.00 5.00
LLKG Kevin Garnett .75 2.00
LLPP Paul Pierce .50 1.25
LLSF Steve Francis .40 1.00
LLSO Shaquille O'Neal 1.25 3.00
LLTD Tim Duncan .75 2.00
LLTM Tracy McGrady .60 1.50
LLVC Vince Carter .75 2.00
LLYM Yao Ming 1.00 2.50

2003-04 Topps Love it Live Relics

Insert odds: Group A one in 48614 Hobby, one in 51840 Retail and one in 14090 HTA. Group B one in 2431 Hobby, one in 2142 Retail and one in 733 HTA. Group C one in 10568 Hobby, one in 9425 Retail and one in 3212 HTA. Group D one in 812 Hobby, one in 711 Retail and one in 244 HTA. Group E one in 5675 Hobby, one in 5040 Retail and one in 1712 HTA. This set parallels the design of the Love it Live set enhanced with a square swatch of memorabilia.

GROUP A 1:48614 H, 1:51840 R, 1:14090 HTA
GROUP B 1:2431 H, 1:2142 R, 1:733 HTA
GROUP C 1:10568 H, 1:9425 R, 1:3212 HTA
GROUP D 1:812 H, 1:711 R, 1:244 HTA
GROUP E 1:5675 H, 1:5040 R, 1:1712 HTS
AI Allen Iverson B 6.00 15.00
AS Amare Stoudemire D 5.00 12.00
CB Caron Butler B 3.00 8.00
DG Drew Gooden B 3.00 8.00
DN Dirk Nowitzki E 6.00 15.00
DW DaJuan Wagner B 2.50 6.00
GP Gary Payton D 4.00 10.00
JO Jermaine O'Neal D 3.00 8.00
PP Paul Pierce D 4.00 10.00
SF Steve Francis C 3.00 8.00
SO Shaquille O'Neal B 10.00 25.00
TD Tim Duncan D 6.00 15.00
YM Yao Ming D 8.00 20.00

2003-04 Topps Mark of Excellence Autographs

Insert odds: Group A one in 12256 Hobby, one in 10961 Retail, one in 3663 HTA. Group B one in 4051 Hobby, one in 3583 Retail and one in 1221 HTA. Group C one in 1306 Hobby, one in 1144 Retail and one in 391 HTA. Group D one in 1217 Hobby, one in 1069 Retail and one in 366 HTA. Group E one in 522 Hobby, one in 457 Retail and one in 157 HTA. Each card places a full-color player action photo along the top of the card that fades into an area of white on the bottom for player autographs.

GROUP A 1:12256 H, 1:10961 R, 1:3663 HTA
GROUP B 1:4051 H, 1:3583 R, 1:221 HTA
GROUP C 1:1306 H, 1:1144 R, 1:391 HTA
GROUP D 1:1217 H, 1:1069 R, 1:366 HTA
GROUP E 1:522 H, 1:457 R, 1:157 HTA
BB Brent Barry E 2.50 6.00
CA Carmelo Anthony B 30.00 80.00
EB Elton Brand D 4.00 10.00
FW Frank Williams E 2.50 6.00
JH Jarvis Hayes C 2.50 6.00
JO Jermaine O'Neal 3.00 8.00
JW Jerome Williams B 2.50 6.00
KH Kirk Hinrich D 4.00 10.00
KJ Ken Johnson E 2.50 6.00
LR Luke Ridnour C 3.00 8.00
MB Marcus Banks C 2.50 6.00
MP Morris Peterson E 2.50 6.00
MR Michael Redd B 4.00 10.00
MS Mike Sweetney C 2.50 6.00
NC Nick Collison D 3.00 8.00
RG Reece Gaines A 2.50 6.00
RR Rick Rickert C 2.50 6.00
SO Shaquille O'Neal E 30.00 80.00
TF T.J. Ford D 3.00 8.00
CBO Chris Bosh A 10.00 25.00
DGE Devean George E 2.50 6.00
DWE David West C 4.00 10.00
DWY Dwyane Wade C 25.00 60.00

2003-04 Topps Piece of a Dream Relics

Insert odds: Group A one in 37396 Hobby, one in 34560 Retail and one in 10775 HTA. Group B one in 27518 Hobby, one in 25920 Retail and one in 8326 HTA. Group C one in 4882 Hobby, one in 12960 Retail and one in 4361 HTA. Group De one in 1140 Hobby, one in 1002 Retail and one in 343 HTA. Group E one in 1620 Hobby, one in 1422 Retail and one in 487 HTA. Each card places a full-color player action photo on the top side of the card and a square swatch of memorabilia centered along the bottom.

GROUP A 1:37396 H, 1:34560 R, 1:10775 HTA
GROUP B 1:27518 H, 1:25920 R, 1:8326 HTA
GROUP C 1:14882 H, 1:12960 R, 1:4361 HTA
GROUP D 1:1140 H, 1:1002 R, 1:343 HTA
GROUP E 1:1620 H, 1:1422 R, 1:487 HTA
PDBD Baron Davis C 3.00 8.00
PDCW Chris Webber D 4.00 10.00
PDEB Elton Brand A 4.00 10.00
PDGH Grant Hill C 5.00 12.00
PDJK Jason Kidd A 6.00 15.00
PDJR Jason Richardson C 4.00 10.00
PDLS Latrell Sprewell B 3.00 8.00
PDMD Mike Dunleavy C 3.00 8.00
PDMP Morris Peterson C 2.50 6.00
PDMR Michael Redd C 4.00 10.00
PDNT Nikoloz Tskitishvili C 2.50 6.00
PDSB Shawn Bradley D 2.50 6.00
PDSM Stephon Marbury D 3.00 8.00
PDSN Steve Nash C 5.00 12.00

2003-04 Topps Rookie Photo Shoot Autographs

Inserted in packs at the rate of one in 458 Hobby and one in 438 HTA, this 27-card set was produced and autographed at the NBA's Rookie Photo Shoot. 56 of each card were inserted into the production run of Topps, however, several more were printed and given to the players themselves.

STATED PRINT RUN 56 SETS
TABC Brian Cook 10.00 25.00
TACA Carmelo Anthony 175.00 350.00
TACB Chris Bosh 150.00 300.00
TADJ Dahntay Jones 12.00 30.00
TADW1 David West 15.00 40.00
TADW2 Dwyane Wade 400.00 600.00
TAJH1 Jarvis Hayes 10.00 25.00
TAJH2 Josh Howard 15.00 40.00
TAJK Jason Kapono 10.00 25.00
TAKB Keith Bogans 10.00 25.00
TAKH Kirk Hinrich 15.00 40.00
TAKP Kendrick Perkins 12.00 30.00
TALB Leandro Barbosa 15.00 40.00
TALW Luke Walton 15.00 40.00
TAMB1 Marcus Banks 10.00 25.00
TAMB2 Matt Bonner 15.00 40.00
TAMP Mickael Pietrus 12.00 30.00
TAMS Mike Sweetney 10.00 25.00
TAMW Maurice Williams 15.00 40.00
TANE Ndudi Ebi 10.00 25.00
TARG Reece Gaines 10.00 25.00
TASB Steve Blake 12.00 30.00
TASV Slavko Vranes 10.00 25.00
TATB Troy Bell 10.00 25.00
TATF T.J. Ford 12.00 30.00
TATO Travis Outlaw 12.00 30.00
THAT Travis Hansen 10.00 25.00

2003-04 Topps Welcome to Atlanta Dual Relics

Welcome to Atlanta Dual Relics is divided up into two groups, Group A, cards WA1 to WA10, and Group B, WA11 to WA20. Group A was inserted at one in 1460 Hobby, one in 1283 Retail and one in 439 HTA, and Group B was inserted a one in 1042 Hobby, one in 1283 Retail and one in 190 HTA. The set is horizontally designed and places two players and two swatches of memorabilia from the 2003 All-Star Game in Atlanta.

WA1-WA10 GROUP A
WA11-WA20 GROUP B
GROUP A 1:1460 H, 1:1283 R, 1:439 HTA
GROUP B 1:1042 H, 1:1283 R, 1:190 HTA
WA1 A.Iverson/D.Wagner 10.00 25.00
WA2 S.O'Neal/A.Stoudemire 25.00 50.00
WA3 J.Kidd/T.Parker 10.00 25.00
WA4 T.McGrady/J-Rich 10.00 25.00
WA5 J.O'Neal/D.Gooden 8.00 20.00
WA6 S.Marion/R.Jefferson 8.00 20.00
WA7 P.Pierce/C.Butler 10.00 25.00
WA8 S.Marbury/G.Arenas 8.00 20.00
WA9 B.Wallace/C.Boozer 8.00 20.00
WA10 T.Duncan/Nene 10.00 25.00
WA11 A.Walker/D.Nowitzki 8.00 20.00
WA12 Nene/A.Kirilenko 8.00 20.00
WA13 P.Gasol/D.Gooden 8.00 20.00
WA14 J.Tinsley/D.Wagner 8.00 20.00
WA15 S.Marion/J.Mashburn 8.00 20.00
WA16 J.Kidd/G.Payton 10.00 25.00
WA17 Y.Ming/S.O'Neal 30.00 60.00
WA18 J.O'Neal/K.Garnett 8.00 20.00
WA19 T.McGrady/A.Iverson 10.00 25.00
WA20 S.Nash/S.Francis 10.00 25.00

2004-05 Topps

This 249-card set was released in July/August, 2004. The set was issued in 10-card packs. Cards number 1-220 feature veterans while cards 221-249 feature Rookie Cards.

COMPLETE SET (249) 15.00 40.00
1 Allen Iverson .30 .75
2 Eddy Curry .12 .30
3 Stephon Marbury .15 .40
4 Chris Bosh .20 .50
5 Jason Kidd .30 .75
6 Bonzi Wells .12 .30
7 Fred Jones .12 .30
8 Kobe Bryant .75 2.00
9 Ben Wallace .15 .40
10 Darrell Armstrong .12 .30
11 Yao Ming .40 1.00
12 Udonis Haslem .12 .30
13 Nene .15 .40
14 Michael Redd .15 .40
15 Carmelo Anthony .40 1.00
16 Gary Trent .12 .30
17 Larry Hughes .15 .40
18 Kareem Rush .12 .30
19 Antonio McDyess .15 .40
20 Drew Gooden .12 .30
21 Kevin Garnett .30 .75
22 DeShawn Stevenson .12 .30
23 LeBron James 1.25 3.00
24 Robert Horry .15 .40
25 Shareef Abdur-Rahim .15 .40
26 Antonio Daniels .12 .30
27 Scottie Pippen .30 .75
28 Mike Dunleavy .15 .40
29 Joe Smith .15 .40
30 Vince Carter .30 .75
31 Reggie Miller .20 .50
32 Chris Wilcox .12 .30
33 Rasheed Wallace .20 .50
34 Paul Pierce .20 .50
35 Tayshaun Prince .15 .40
36 Raja Bell .15 .40
37 Stephen Jackson .15 .40
38 Eric Snow .12 .30
39 Zydrunas Ilgauskas .15 .40
40 Andre Miller .15 .40
41 Dirk Nowitzki .30 .75
42 Steve Francis .15 .40
43 Ray Allen .20 .50
44 Donyell Marshall .12 .30
45 Pau Gasol .20 .50
46 T.J. Ford .12 .30
47 Andrei Kirilenko .15 .40
48 Jamaal Tinsley .12 .30
49 Earl Boykins .12 .30
50 Tim Duncan .30 .75
51 Erick Dampier .12 .30
52 Nazr Mohammed .12 .30
53 Tim Thomas .12 .30
54 Keyon Dooling .12 .30
55 Jason Kapono .12 .30
56 Kirk Hinrich .15 .40
57 Aaron McKie .12 .30
58 Brad Miller .15 .40
59 Al Harrington .15 .40
60 Gary Payton .20 .50
61 Nick Van Exel .15 .40
62 Cuttino Mobley .12 .30
63 Marcus Camby .15 .40
64 Desmond Mason .15 .40
65 Boris Diaw .15 .40
66 Kenyon Martin .15 .40
67 Mike Miller .15 .40
68 Dwyane Wade .30 .75
69 Allan Houston .15 .40
70 Jermaine O'Neal .15 .40
71 Travis Hansen .12 .30
72 Qyntel Woods .12 .30
73 Jamal Crawford .20 .50
74 Bobby Jackson .12 .30
75 Derrick Coleman .15 .40
76 Brian Skinner .12 .30
77 Elton Brand .20 .50
78 Rodney Rogers .12 .30
79 Zarko Cabarkapa .12 .30
80 Mike Bibby .20 .50
81 Jim Jackson .12 .30
82 Kurt Thomas .12 .30
83 Vin Baker .12 .30
84 Rodney White .12 .30
85 Gordan Giricek .12 .30
86 Jamal Mashburn .15 .40
87 Kenny Thomas .12 .30
88 Antoine Walker .20 .50
89 Rasho Nesterovic .12 .30
90 Shawn Marion .15 .40
91 Shane Battier .15 .40
92 Marquis Daniels .12 .30
93 Ruben Patterson .12 .30
94 Michael Olowokandi .12 .30
95 Bruce Bowen .12 .30
96 Caron Butler .15 .40
97 Corliss Williamson .12 .30
98 Jeff Foster .12 .30
99 Carlos Boozer .15 .40
100 Tracy McGrady .25 .60
101 Stromile Swift .12 .30
102 Keith Van Horn .15 .40
103 Derek Fisher .15 .40
104 Juwan Howard .15 .40
105 Tony Parker .20 .50
106 Jason Terry .15 .40
107 Vlade Divac .15 .40
108 Marcus Banks .12 .30
109 Derek Anderson .12 .30
110 Karl Malone .25 .60
111 Baron Davis .15 .40
112 Chris Crawford .12 .30
113 Kwame Brown .12 .30
114 Jiri Welsch .12 .30
115 Maciej Lampe .12 .30
116 Josh Howard .20 .50
117 Luke Walton .12 .30
118 John Salmons .15 .40
119 David West .15 .40
120 Amare Stoudemire .15 .40
121 Antawn Jamison .15 .40
122 Clarence Weatherspoon .12 .30
123 Aleksandar Pavlovic .12 .30
124 Kerry Kittles .12 .30
125 Rafer Alston .12 .30
126 Jarvis Hayes .12 .30
127 Toni Kukoc .20 .50
128 Latrell Sprewell .15 .40
129 Keith Bogans .12 .30
130 Jason Richardson .20 .50
131 Brent Barry .12 .30
132 Darko Milicic .12 .30
133 Peja Stojakovic .20 .50
134 Jerome Williams .12 .30
135 Malik Rose .12 .30
136 Quentin Richardson .15 .40
137 Wally Szczerbiak .15 .40
138 Theo Ratliff .12 .30
139 Gilbert Arenas .15 .40
140 Richard Hamilton .15 .40
141 Rashard Lewis .20 .50
142 Joe Johnson .15 .40
143 P.J. Brown .12 .30
144 Jason Collins .12 .30
145 Chauncey Billups .20 .50
146 Raef LaFrentz .12 .30
147 Mickael Pietrus .15 .40
148 Lamar Odom .15 .40
149 Vladimir Radmanovic .12 .30
150 Chris Webber .20 .50
151 Tony Delk .12 .30
152 Troy Hudson .12 .30
153 David Wesley .12 .30
154 Juan Dixon .12 .30
155 Darius Miles .12 .30
156 Gerald Wallace .15 .40
157 Jalen Rose .15 .40
158 Charlie Ward .12 .30
159 Michael Finley .20 .50
160 Jonathan Bender .12 .30
161 Lorenzen Wright .12 .30
162 George Lynch .12 .30
163 Leandro Barbosa .20 .50
164 Dajuan Wagner .12 .30
165 Francisco Elson .12 .30
166 Jerry Stackhouse .15 .40
167 Manu Ginobili .25 .60
168 Chris Kaman .15 .40
169 James Posey .12 .30
170 Doug Christie .12 .30
171 Zoran Planinic .12 .30
172 Maurice Taylor .12 .30
173 Carlos Arroyo .12 .30
174 Damon Stoudamire .15 .40
175 Brian Cardinal .12 .30
176 Devean George .12 .30
177 Hedo Turkoglu .15 .40
178 Anfernee Hardaway .50 1.25
179 Tony Battie .12 .30
180 Steve Nash .25 .60
181 Glenn Robinson .15 .40
182 Morris Peterson .12 .30
183 Luke Ridnour .15 .40
184 Mehmet Okur .15 .40
185 Eddie Jones .15 .40
186 Tyronn Lue .12 .30
187 Raul Lopez .12 .30
188 Lucious Harris .12 .30
189 Alvin Williams .12 .30
190 Zach Randolph .15 .40
191 Steve Blake .12 .30
192 Marko Jaric .12 .30
193 Anthony Peeler .12 .30
194 Troy Murphy .12 .30
195 Jamaal Magloire .12 .30
196 Brandon Hunter .12 .30
197 Jason Williams .15 .40
198 Corey Maggette .15 .40
199 Ron Artest .20 .50
200 Shaquille O'Neal .50 1.25
201 Richard Jefferson .15 .40
202 Kelvin Cato .12 .30
203 Mark Blount .12 .30
204 Eric Williams .12 .30
205 Sam Cassell .15 .40
206 Voshon Lenard .12 .30
207 Bob Sura .12 .30
208 Speedy Claxton .12 .30
209 Samuel Dalembert .12 .30
210 Tyson Chandler .15 .40
211 Brian Grant .12 .30
212 Stanislav Medvedenko .12 .30
213 Danny Fortson .12 .30
214 Chucky Atkins .12 .30
215 Matt Harpring .12 .30
216 Trenton Hassell .12 .30
217 Ronald Murray .12 .30
218 Jeff McInnis .12 .30
219 Primoz Brezec .12 .30
220 Ricky Davis .15 .40
221 Dwight Howard RC 1.50 4.00
222 Emeka Okafor RC .60 1.50
223 Ben Gordon RC .75 2.00
224 Shaun Livingston RC .75 2.00
225 Devin Harris RC .60 1.50
226 Josh Childress RC .60 1.50
227 Luol Deng RC .75 2.00
228 Rafael Araujo RC .50 1.25
229 Andre Iguodala RC 1.00 2.50
230 Luke Jackson RC .50 1.25
231 Andris Biedrins RC .50 1.25
232 Robert Swift RC .50 1.25
233 Sebastian Telfair RC .60 1.50
234 Kris Humphries RC .75 2.00
235 Al Jefferson RC 1.00 2.50
236 Kirk Snyder RC .50 1.25
237 Josh Smith RC .75 2.00
238 J.R. Smith RC .75 2.00
239 Dorell Wright RC .75 2.00
240 Jameer Nelson RC .75 2.00
241 Pavel Podkolzin RC .50 1.25
242 Viktor Khryapa RC .50 1.25
243 Sergei Monia RC .50 1.25
244 Delonte West RC .75 2.00
245 Tony Allen RC .75 2.00
246 Kevin Martin RC 1.00 2.50
247 Sasha Vujacic RC .75 2.00
248 Beno Udrih RC .60 1.50
249 David Harrison RC .50 1.25

2004-05 Topps Black

*BLACK STARS: 4X TO 10X BASE HI
*BLACK RCs: 1.5X TO 4X BASE HI
BLACK PRINT RUN 500 SER.#'d SETS
23 LeBron James 15.00 40.00

2004-05 Topps First Edition

*FIRST ED. STARS: 1.5X TO 4X BASE HI
*FIRST ED. RCs: .75X TO 2X BASE HI
BOXES DISTRIBUTED TO HTA DEALERS
23 LeBron James 10.00 25.00

2004-05 Topps Gold

*GOLD STARS: 5X TO 12X BASE HI
*GOLD RCs: 3X TO 8X BASE HI
PRINT RUN 99 SER.#'d SETS
8 Kobe Bryant 12.00 30.00
23 LeBron James 25.00 60.00

2004-05 Topps All-Star Support

These cards, of players who were teammates on either All-Star or Rookie Challenge teams, were issued at a stated rate of one in 18.

COMPLETE SET (20) 15.00 40.00
STATED ODDS 1:18
ASAW R.Artest/B.Wallace 1.00 2.50
ASBD C.Boozer/M.Dunleavy 1.00 2.50
ASBF K.Bryant/S.Francis 2.00 5.00
ASBW C.Bosh/D.Wade 2.00 5.00
ASCA S.Cassell/R.Allen 1.00 2.50
ASCP V.Carter/P.Pierce 1.50 4.00
ASDR B.Davis/M.Redd 1.00 2.50
ASGD K.Garnett/T.Duncan 1.50 4.00
ASGP M.Ginobili/T.Prince 1.00 2.50
ASHH K.Hinrich/J.Hayes 1.00 2.50
ASIK A.Iverson/J.Kidd 1.50 4.00
ASJA L.James/C.Anthony 3.00 8.00
ASKH C.Kaman/J.Howard 1.00 2.50
ASMJ R.Murray/M.Jaric 1.00 2.50
ASMK B.Miller/A.Kirilenko 1.00 2.50
ASMM J.Magloire/K.Martin 1.00 2.50
ASMO T.McGrady/J.O'Neal 1.25 3.00
ASNS Nene/A.Stoudemire 1.00 2.50
ASOM S.O'Neal/Y.Ming 1.50 4.00
ASSN P.Stojakovic/D.Nowitzki 1.25 3.00

2004-05 Topps All-Star Support Relics

These cards, featuring game-used relic pieces of players, were issued at a stated rate of one in 200 and issued to a stated print run of 250 serial numbered sets.

STATED ODDS 1:200
PRINT RUN 250 SER.#'d SETS
ASAW R.Artest/B.Wallace 5.00 12.00
ASBD C.Boozer/M.Dunleavy 8.00 20.00
ASBF Kobe NO JSY/S.Francis 6.00 15.00
ASBW C.Bosh/D.Wade 8.00 20.00
ASCA Cassell/R.Allen NO JSY 5.00 12.00
ASCP V.Carter NO JSY/P.Pierce 5.00 12.00
ASDR B.Davis/M.Redd 5.00 12.00
ASGD K.Garnett/T.Duncan 10.00 25.00
ASGP M.Ginobili/T.Prince 5.00 12.00
ASHH K.Hinrich/J.Hayes 5.00 12.00
ASJA LeBron NO JSY/Carmelo 8.00 20.00
ASKH C.Kaman/J.Howard 5.00 12.00
ASMJ R.Murray/M.Jaric 5.00 12.00
ASMK B.Miller/A.Kirilenko 5.00 12.00
ASMM J.Magloire/K.Martin 5.00 12.00
ASMO T.McGrady/J.O'Neal 6.00 15.00
ASNS Nene/A.Stoudemire 5.00 12.00
ASOM S.O'Neal/Y.Ming 10.00 25.00
ASSN P.Stojakovic/D.Nowitzki 5.00 12.00

2004-05 Topps Drive N Thrive Relics

STATED ODDS 1:318
N Nene 2.50 6.00
AI Allen Iverson 5.00 12.00
AK Andrei Kirilenko 2.50 6.00
BD Baron Davis 2.50 6.00
CM Corey Maggette 2.50 6.00
DM Desmond Mason 2.50 6.00
DW Dwyane Wade 8.00 20.00
EG Manu Ginobili 4.00 10.00
GP Gary Payton 3.00 8.00
JC Jamal Crawford 3.00 8.00
JH Jarvis Hayes 2.00 5.00
JR Jason Richardson 3.00 8.00
JS Jerry Stackhouse 2.50 6.00
JT Jason Terry 2.50 6.00
KH Kirk Hinrich 2.50 6.00
KR Kareem Rush 2.00 5.00
MT Maurice Taylor 2.00 5.00
QR Quentin Richardson 2.50 6.00
QW Qyntel Woods 2.00 5.00
RH Richard Hamilton 2.50 6.00
RJ Richard Jefferson 2.50 6.00
RL Rashard Lewis 3.00 8.00
SF Steve Francis 2.50 6.00
SM Shawn Marion 2.50 6.00
SN Steve Nash 4.00 10.00
TM Tracy McGrady 4.00 10.00
CBO Carlos Boozer 2.50 6.00
CBO2 Chris Bosh 3.00 8.00
CBU Caron Butler 2.50 6.00
SMA Stephon Marbury 2.50 6.00

2004-05 Topps Great Expectations

Inserted at a stated rate of one in nine, these 20 cards feature some of the leading young NBA players.

COMPLETE SET (20) 8.00 20.00
STATED ODDS 1:9
AS Amare Stoudemire .40 1.00
BD Boris Diaw .40 1.00
CA Carmelo Anthony 1.00 2.50
CB Chris Bosh .50 1.25
CK Chris Kaman .40 1.00
DW Dwyane Wade .75 2.00
JH Jarvis Hayes .30 .75
KH Kirk Hinrich .40 1.00
LJ LeBron James 3.00 8.00
MD Mike Dunleavy .40 1.00
MG Manu Ginobili .60 1.50

MS Mike Sweetney .30 .75
RM Ronald Murray .30 .75
TP Tayshaun Prince .40 1.00
YM Yao Ming 1.00 2.50
ZR Zach Randolph .40 1.00
CAR Carlos Arroyo .30 .75
CBZ Carlos Boozer .40 1.00
JHO Josh Howard .50 1.25
TJF T.J. Ford .30 .75

2004-05 Topps Marks of Excellence

Randomly Inserted into packs at different rates, these 30 cards all feature authentic autographs. Since there were six different groupings of autographs, we have notated the group next to the player's name in our checklist.
STATED ODDS: GROUP A 1:54432, GROUP B 1:2838, GROUP C 1:1531, GROUP D 1:548, GROUP E 1:2395
BD Baron Davis B 12.00 30.00
BG Ben Gordon D 5.00 12.00
CA Carmelo Anthony D 15.00 40.00
CD Chris Duhon C 5.00 12.00
DH Devin Harris D 4.00 10.00
EO Emeka Okafor E 8.00 20.00
FJ Fred Jones D 5.00 12.00
JC Josh Childress D 4.00 10.00
JK Jason Kidd C 15.00 40.00
JO Jermaine O'Neal B 5.00 12.00
KS Kirk Snyder C 3.00 8.00
LD Luol Deng D 5.00 12.00
LJ Luke Jackson D 3.00 8.00
LO Lamar Odom C 6.00 15.00
PS Peja Stojakovic C 6.00 15.00
RH Richard Hamilton B 10.00 25.00
SL Shaun Livingston D 5.00 12.00
SM Stephon Marbury C 10.00 25.00
SO Shaquille O'Neal B 30.00 80.00
ST Sebastian Telfair D 4.00 10.00
TA Tony Allen C 5.00 12.00
TD Tim Duncan B 200.00 400.00
TM Tracy McGrady B 30.00 80.00
RAL Rafer Alston B 25.00 50.00

2004-05 Topps Peak Performers Relics

Inserted into packs at a stated rate of one in 399, these 24 cards feature game-used relics of the featured player.
STATED ODDS 1:399
AS Amare Stoudemire 2.50 6.00
AW Antoine Walker 3.00 8.00
BW Ben Wallace 2.50 6.00
CA Carmelo Anthony 6.00 15.00
EB Elton Brand 3.00 8.00
GR Glenn Robinson 2.50 6.00
JM Jamal Mashburn 2.50 6.00
KB Kwame Brown 2.00 5.00
KG Kevin Garnett 5.00 12.00
MB Mike Bibby 3.00 8.00
MR Michael Redd 2.50 6.00
PG Pau Gasol 3.00 8.00
PP Paul Pierce 3.00 8.00
PS Peja Stojakovic 3.00 8.00
SO Shaquille O'Neal 8.00 20.00
TD Tim Duncan 5.00 12.00
TP Tony Parker 3.00 8.00
TT Tim Thomas 2.00 5.00
YM Yao Ming 6.00 15.00
ZI Zydrunas Ilgauskas 2.50 6.00
KMA Kenyon Martin 2.50 6.00
RAL Ray Allen 3.00 8.00

2004-05 Topps Rock Rhythm

Inserted at a stated rate of one in 12, these cards feature players who can do great things on the basketball court.
COMPLETE SET (15) 12.50 30.00
STATED ODDS 1:12
AI Allen Iverson 1.00 2.50
BD Baron Davis .50 1.25
BW Ben Wallace .50 1.25
CA Carmelo Anthony 1.25 3.00
JK Jason Kidd 1.00 2.50
JR Jason Richardson .60 1.50
KB Kobe Bryant 2.50 6.00
KG Kevin Garnett 1.00 2.50
LJ LeBron James 4.00 10.00
SM Stephon Marbury .50 1.25
SO Shaquille O'Neal 1.50 4.00
TD Tim Duncan 1.00 2.50
TM Tracy McGrady .75 2.00
VC Vince Carter 1.00 2.50
YM Yao Ming 1.25 3.00

2004-05 Topps Rookie Photo Shoot Autographs

Inserted at a stated rate of one in 721, these 39 cards feature autographs of players who participated in the Rookie Photo Shoot. Each of these cards were issued to a stated print run of 55 serial numbered sets.
STATED ODDS 1:721
STATED PRINT RUN 55 SETS
AE Andre Emmett 10.00 25.00
AJ Al Jefferson 50.00 125.00
AV Anderson Varejao 12.00 30.00
BG Ben Gordon 50.00 125.00
BR Bernard Robinson 12.00 30.00
CD Chris Duhon 15.00 40.00
DH Dwight Howard 200.00 400.00
DH2 David Harrison 10.00 25.00
DW Dorell Wright 15.00 40.00
DW Delonte West 15.00 40.00
EO Emeka Okafor 30.00 80.00
JC Josh Childress 12.00 30.00
JN Jameer Nelson 15.00 40.00
JS Josh Smith 30.00 80.00
JV Jackson Vroman 10.00 25.00
KH Kris Humphries 15.00 40.00
KM Kevin Martin 30.00 80.00
KS Kirk Snyder 10.00 25.00
LC Lionel Chalmers 15.00 40.00
LD Luol Deng 40.00 100.00
LJ Luke Jackson 10.00 25.00
RA Rafael Araujo 10.00 25.00
RP Rickey Paulding 10.00 25.00
SL Shaun Livingston 15.00 40.00
ST Sebastian Telfair 12.00 30.00
TA Tony Allen 15.00 40.00
TA2 Trevor Ariza 15.00 40.00
DHA Devin Harris 30.00 80.00
HSJ Ha Seung-Jin 15.00 40.00
JRS J.R. Smith 50.00 125.00

2005-06 Topps

Released in Late August, 2005-06 Topps features a 255-card base set divided up into 220 veteran players, 30 rookie players and five celebrities. Each card is full color with a white border in usual Topps fashion. Topps was packaged in 36-pack boxes with packs containing 10 cards and an SRP of $1.59, and Jumbo HTA boxes of 12 packs containing 35 cards and an SRP of $5.00.
COMPLETE SET (255) 20.00 50.00
UNPRICED OVERTIME PRINT RUN ONE SET .50 1.25
1 Grant Hill .25 .60
2 Keith Van Horn .15 .40
3 Quentin Richardson .15 .40
4 Damon Jones .12 .30
5 Lamar Odom .15 .40
6 Jamal Crawford .20 .50
7 Ben Gordon .15 .40
8 Zach Randolph .15 .40
9 Rafer Alston .12 .30
10 Gilbert Arenas .15 .40
11 Yao Ming .25 .60
12 Cuttino Mobley .12 .30
13 Josh Smith .15 .40
14 Ray Allen .20 .50
15 Vince Carter .30 .75
16 Kenyon Martin .15 .40
17 Mark Blount .12 .30
18 Carlos Arroyo .12 .30
19 Lee Nailon .12 .30
20 Bobby Simmons .12 .30
21 Tim Duncan .30 .75
22 Michael Redd .15 .40
23 Antawn Jamison .15 .40
24 Matt Bonner .12 .30
25 Shane Battier .15 .40
26 Nick Van Exel .20 .50
27 Jason Hart .12 .30
28 Nene .15 .40
29 Fred Jones .12 .30
30 Baron Davis .15 .40
31 Danny Fortson .12 .30
32 Caron Butler .15 .40
33 Allen Iverson .30 .75
34 Eddie Griffin .12 .30
35 Jameer Nelson .12 .30
36 Brent Barry .12 .30
37 Zydrunas Ilgauskas .15 .40
38 Jason Terry .15 .40
39 Mike Dunleavy .15 .40
40 Paul Pierce .20 .50
41 Reggie Miller .20 .50
42 Lorenzen Wright .12 .30
43 Peja Stojakovic .20 .50
44 Zaza Pachulia .12 .30
45 Dan Dickau .12 .30
46 Andre Iguodala .15 .40
47 Andrei Kirilenko .15 .40
48 Nenad Krstic .12 .30
49 Damon Stoudamire .15 .40
50 Emeka Okafor .15 .40
51 Jalen Rose .20 .50
52 Beno Udrih .12 .30
53 Jared Jeffries .12 .30
54 Ricky Davis .15 .40
55 Jason Kidd .30 .75
56 Eddy Curry .12 .30
57 Chauncey Billups .20 .50
58 Eric Snow .12 .30
59 Derek Fisher .15 .40
60 Amare Stoudemire .15 .40
61 Josh Childress .15 .40
62 Juwan Howard .15 .40
63 Mehmet Okur .12 .30
64 Jerome Williams .12 .30
65 Shaun Livingston .12 .30
66 Stephen Jackson .15 .40
67 Alonzo Mourning .25 .60
68 J.R. Smith .15 .40
69 Kobe Bryant .75 2.00
70 Dwight Howard .15 .40
71 Manu Ginobili .20 .50
72 Kyle Korver .15 .40
73 Reggie Evans .12 .30
74 Shareef Abdur-Rahim .15 .40
75 Rafael Araujo .12 .30
76 Kirk Snyder .12 .30
77 Jermaine O'Neal .15 .40
78 Melvin Ely .12 .30
79 Chris Kaman .15 .40
80 Stephon Marbury .15 .40
81 Joe Smith .15 .40
82 Samuel Dalembert .12 .30
83 Luke Ridnour .15 .40
84 Sebastian Telfair .15 .40
85 Larry Hughes .15 .40
86 Tyson Chandler .15 .40
87 Michael Finley .20 .50
88 Drew Gooden .15 .40
89 Marcus Camby .15 .40
90 Dwyane Wade .30 .75
91 Troy Murphy .12 .30
92 David Wesley .12 .30
93 Stromile Swift .12 .30
94 Clifford Robinson .12 .30
95 Sam Cassell .15 .40
96 Joe Johnson .15 .40
97 Bobby Jackson .12 .30
98 Derek Anderson .12 .30
99 Rashard Lewis .20 .50
100 Shaquille O'Neal .40 1.00
101 Keith McLeod .12 .30
102 Keith Bogans .12 .30
103 Al Harrington .15 .40
104 Anderson Varejao .12 .30
105 Al Jefferson .15 .40
106 Jerry Stackhouse .15 .40
107 Chris Duhon .12 .30
108 Earl Boykins .12 .30
109 Tayshaun Prince .15 .40
110 Carlos Boozer .15 .40
111 Rasual Butler .12 .30
112 Bonzi Wells .12 .30
113 Chris Wilcox .12 .30
114 Latrell Sprewell .15 .40
115 Richard Jefferson .15 .40
116 Toni Kukoc .20 .50
117 Doug Christie .12 .30
118 Brad Miller .15 .40
119 Antonio Daniels .12 .30
120 Richard Hamilton .15 .40
121 Kevin Garnett .30 .75
122 Tony Parker .20 .50
123 Mike Sweetney .12 .30
124 Speedy Claxton .12 .30
125 Udonis Haslem .12 .30
126 Chucky Atkins .12 .30
127 David Harrison .12 .30
128 Jason Collier .12 .30
129 Pau Gasol .20 .50
130 Chris Webber .20 .50
131 Kelvin Cato .12 .30
132 Michael Olowokandi .12 .30
133 Ben Wallace .15 .40
134 Antoine Walker .15 .40
135 Marquis Daniels .12 .30
136 Ira Newble .12 .30
137 Austin Croshere .12 .30
138 Mike James .12 .30
139 Michael Doleac .12 .30
140 Carmelo Anthony .40 1.00
141 Sasha Vujacic .15 .40
142 Brian Cardinal .12 .30
143 Ron Mercer .12 .30
144 Tim Thomas .12 .30
145 Juan Dixon .12 .30
146 Rodney Rogers .12 .30
147 Hedo Turkoglu .15 .40
148 Nazr Mohammed .12 .30
149 Gerald Wallace .15 .40
150 Dirk Nowitzki .30 .75
151 Tony Allen .12 .30
152 Adonal Foyle .12 .30
153 Corey Maggette .15 .40
154 Rasheed Wallace .20 .50
155 Andre Miller .15 .40
156 Luol Deng .15 .40
157 Mike Miller .15 .40
158 Wally Szczerbiak .15 .40
159 Maurice Williams .15 .40
160 Chris Bosh .20 .50
161 Jamaal Magloire .12 .30
162 Leandro Barbosa .15 .40
163 Kevin Martin .15 .40
164 Jeff Foster .12 .30
165 Nick Collison .15 .40
166 Matt Harpring .12 .30
167 Kirk Hinrich .15 .40
168 Antonio McDyess .15 .40
169 Josh Howard .20 .50
170 Elton Brand .20 .50
171 Kurt Thomas .12 .30
172 Tyronn Lue .12 .30
173 Bob Sura .12 .30
174 Chris Mihm .12 .30
175 Jason Williams .15 .40
176 Jim Jackson .12 .30
177 Brevin Knight .12 .30
178 Eduardo Najera .12 .30
179 Jeff McInnis .12 .30
180 Jason Richardson .20 .50
181 Vladimir Radmanovic .12 .30
182 Jamaal Tinsley .12 .30
183 Eddie Jones .15 .40
184 P.J. Brown .12 .30
185 Troy Hudson .12 .30
186 Steve Francis .15 .40
187 Marc Jackson .12 .30
188 Kenny Thomas .12 .30
189 Joel Przybilla .12 .30
190 Steve Nash .25 .60
191 Devin Brown .12 .30
192 Donyell Marshall .12 .30
193 Raja Bell .15 .40
194 Brendan Haywood .12 .30
195 Primoz Brezec .12 .30
196 Gary Payton .20 .50
197 Devin Harris .12 .30
198 Predrag Drobnjak .12 .30
199 Dikembe Mutombo .20 .50
200 LeBron James .75 2.00
201 Marko Jaric .12 .30
202 Mike Bibby .20 .50
203 Desmond Mason .12 .30
204 Morris Peterson .12 .30
205 Jarvis Hayes .12 .30
206 Bruce Bowen .12 .30
207 Trevor Ariza .12 .30
208 Raef LaFrentz .12 .30
209 Brian Grant .12 .30
210 Shawn Marion .15 .40
211 Dan Gadzuric .12 .30
212 Andres Nocioni .12 .30
213 Tony Delk .12 .30
214 Darius Miles .12 .30
215 Gordan Giricek .12 .30
216 Rasho Nesterovic .12 .30
217 Jason Collins .12 .30
218 Mickael Pietrus .15 .40
219 Erick Dampier .12 .30
220 Tracy McGrady .25 .60
221 Andrew Bogut RC 1.00 2.50
222 Marvin Williams RC .75 2.00
223 Deron Williams RC 1.00 2.50
224 Chris Paul RC 3.00 8.00
225 Raymond Felton RC .75 2.00
226 Martell Webster RC .60 1.50
227 Charlie Villanueva RC .75 2.00
228 Channing Frye RC .75 2.00
229 Ike Diogu RC .50 1.25
230 Andrew Bynum RC .60 1.50
231 Fran Vazquez RC .50 1.25
232 Daniel Ewing RC .60 1.50
233 Sean May RC .50 1.25
234 Rashad McCants RC .60 1.50
235 Antoine Wright RC .60 1.50
236 Joey Graham RC .60 1.50
237 Danny Granger RC 1.00 2.50
238 Gerald Green RC .75 2.00
239 Hakim Warrick RC .60 1.50
240 Julius Hodge RC .50 1.25
241 Nate Robinson RC .75 2.00
242 Jarrett Jack RC .75 2.00
243 Francisco Garcia RC .60 1.50
244 Luther Head RC .60 1.50
245 Johan Petro RC .50 1.25
246 Jason Maxiell RC .60 1.50
247 Linas Kleiza RC .50 1.25
248 Ryan Gomes RC .60 1.50
249 Wayne Simien RC .50 1.25
250 David Lee RC .75 2.00
251 Shannon Elizabeth 1.50 4.00
252 Carmen Electra 1.50 4.00
253 Jenny McCarthy 1.50 4.00
254 Christie Brinkley 1.50 4.00
255 Jay-Z 1.50 4.00

2005-06 Topps Black

*1-220 BLACK: 3X TO 8X BASE HI
*221-250 RC BLACK: 1X TO 2.5X BASE HI
*251-255 BLACK: 1X TO 2.5X BASE HI
PRINT RUN 500 SER.#'d SETS

2005-06 Topps First Edition

*1-220 1ST ED.: 1.5X TO 4X BASE HI
*221-255 1ST ED.: .75X TO 2X BASE HI
BOXES DISTRIBUTED TO HTA DEALERS

2005-06 Topps Gold

*1-220 GOLD: 5X TO 12X BASE HI
*221-250 RC GOLD: 2X TO 5X BASE HI
*251-255 GOLD: 1.5X TO 4X BASE HI
69 Kobe Bryant 15.00 40.00

2005-06 Topps All-Star Altitude

Inserted in packs at the rate of one in 10, this 25-card set features players in their All-Star jerseys from the 2005 NBA All-Star Game in Denver. Full color photos are placed agains a sky background.
COMPLETE SET (25) 15.00 30.00
STATED ODDS 1:10
ASAI Allen Iverson 1.00 2.50
ASAJ Antawn Jamison .50 1.25
ASAS Amare Stoudemire .50 1.25
ASBW Ben Wallace .50 1.25
ASDN Dirk Nowitzki 1.00 2.50
ASDW Dwyane Wade 1.00 2.50
ASGA Gilbert Arenas .50 1.25
ASGH Grant Hill .75 2.00
ASJO Jermaine O'Neal .50 1.25
ASKB Kobe Bryant 2.50 6.00
ASKG Kevin Garnett 1.00 2.50
ASLJ LeBron James 2.50 6.00
ASMG Manu Ginobili .60 1.50
ASPP Paul Pierce .60 1.50
ASRA Ray Allen .60 1.50
ASRL Rashard Lewis .60 1.50
ASSM Shawn Marion .50 1.25
ASSN Steve Nash .75 2.00
ASSO Shaquille O'Neal 1.25 3.00
ASTD Tim Duncan 1.00 2.50
ASTM Tracy McGrady .75 2.00
ASVC Vince Carter 1.00 2.50
ASYM Yao Ming .75 2.00
ASZI Zydrunas Ilgauskas .50 1.25

2005-06 Topps All-Star Altitude Relics

Randomly seeded at the rate of one in 488, this set parallels the base All-Star Altitude set enhanced with a star-shaped swatch of All-Star weekend worn memorabilia. The cards are serially numbered out of 250.
PRINT RUN 250 SER.#'d SETS
BW Ben Wallace 2.00 5.00
DN Dirk Nowitzki 4.00 10.00
GA Gilbert Arenas 2.00 5.00
GH Grant Hill 3.00 8.00
JO Jermaine O'Neal 2.00 5.00
MG Manu Ginobili 2.50 6.00
RA Ray Allen 2.50 6.00
SM Shawn Marion 2.00 5.00
SN Steve Nash 3.00 8.00
SO Shaquille O'Neal 5.00 12.00
TD Tim Duncan 4.00 10.00
TM Tracy McGrady 3.00 8.00
YM Yao Ming 3.00 8.00
ZI Zydrunas Ilgauskas 2.00 5.00
JRS J.R. Smith 2.00 5.00

2005-06 Topps Celebrity Threads

Inserted in packs at the rate of one in 2198, this five card set features various celebritys with their photo on the right and a swatch of worn material on the left set on a yellow and white background.
STATED ODDS 1:2198
CB Christie Brinkley 15.00 40.00
JZ Jay-Z 15.00 40.00
SE Shannon Elizabeth 15.00 40.00
CAE Carmen Electra 25.00 60.00
JMC Jenny McCarthy 25.00 60.00

2005-06 Topps Critical Component

Inserted in packs as the rate of one in 17, each card places a full-color photo of the player on the card front, set agains a blue background with the words, "Critical Component" in white along the top.
COMPLETE SET (15) 12.50 25.00
STATED ODDS 1:17
CC1 Ray Allen .75 2.00
CC2 Vince Carter 1.25 3.00
CC3 Tim Duncan 1.25 3.00
CC4 Steve Nash 1.00 2.50
CC5 Gilbert Arenas .60 1.50
CC6 Carmelo Anthony 1.50 4.00
CC7 Chris Bosh .75 2.00
CC8 Richard Hamilton .60 1.50
CC9 Tracy McGrady 1.00 2.50
CC10 Paul Pierce .75 2.00
CC11 Dirk Nowitzki 1.25 3.00
CC12 Amare Stoudemire .60 1.50
CC13 Kobe Bryant 3.00 8.00
CC14 Shaquille O'Neal 1.50 4.00
CC15 Mike Bibby .75 2.00

2005-06 Topps Finishing Touch Relics

Randomly inserted in packs at the rate of one in 246, this horizintally designed set features a star-shaped jersey swatch on the left and a full color player photo on the right set against a white background.
STATED ODDS 1:246
BG Ben Gordon 2.00 5.00
CA Carmelo Anthony 5.00 12.00
CB Chris Bosh 2.50 6.00
JK Jason Kidd 4.00 10.00
MC Marcus Camby 2.00 5.00
PG Pau Gasol 2.50 6.00
PP Paul Pierce 2.50 6.00
RM Reggie Miller 3.00 8.00
RW Rasheed Wallace 2.50 6.00
SF Steve Francis 2.00 5.00
SM Stephon Marbury 2.00 5.00
SO Shaquille O'Neal 5.00 12.00
TD Tim Duncan 4.00 10.00
WS Wally Szczerbiak 2.00 5.00
YM Yao Ming 3.00 8.00

2005-06 Topps Marks of Excellence

Inserted at the rate of one in 835 for group A, one in 419 for group B and one in 2016 for group C, this set utilizes oragne and red borders around a full color player photo along with a silver foil autographed sticker.
GROUP A ODDS 1:835, GRP B ODDS 1:419
GROUP C ODDS 1:2016
AI Allen Iverson 40.00 100.00
AS Amare Stoudemire A 8.00 20.00
BD Baron Davis A 8.00 20.00
BU Beno Udrih A 3.00 8.00
CA Carmelo Anthony C 12.00 30.00
DE Daniel Ewing B 4.00 10.00
DG Danny Granger B 6.00 15.00
DW Dorell Wright A 5.00 12.00
EO Emeka Okafor C 4.00 10.00
FV Fran Vazquez B 3.00 8.00
GG Gerald Green B 5.00 12.00
HW Hakim Warrick B 4.00 10.00
JG Joey Graham B 4.00 10.00
JH Julius Hodge B 3.00 8.00
JK Jason Kidd A 8.00 20.00
JM Jason Maxiell B 4.00 10.00
JN Jameer Nelson A 5.00 12.00
JS Josh Smith A 4.00 10.00
LD Luol Deng A 4.00 10.00
LH Luther Head B 4.00 10.00
LO Lamar Odom A 4.00 10.00
PP Pavel Podkolzin A 5.00 12.00
PS Pape Sow A 5.00 12.00
QR Quentin Richardson A 4.00 10.00
RA Rafer Alston A 12.50 30.00
RF Raymond Felton B 5.00 12.00
RH Richard Hamilton A 6.00 15.00
RM Rashad McCants B 4.00 10.00
SL Shaun Livingston A 5.00 12.00
SM Shawn Marion A 10.00 25.00
SO Shaquille O'Neal A 30.00 80.00
TD Tim Duncan A 700.00 1000.00
TM Tracy McGrady A 12.00 30.00
WS Wayne Simien B 3.00 8.00
ABO Andrew Bogut B 6.00 15.00
CTA Chris Taft B 4.00 10.00
DWI Deron Williams B 6.00 15.00
HSJ Ha Seung-Jin A 5.00 12.00
PST Peja Stojakovic A 6.00 15.00
SMA Stephon Marbury A 8.00 20.00
SMY Sean May B 3.00 8.00

2005-06 Topps Rise to the Occasion Relics

Randomly seeded at the rate of one in 257, this 16-card set features a player action photo on the left, an oval swatch of game-worn memorabilia on the right and is set against a swirling red, purple and green background.
STATED ODDS 1:257
AH Al Harrington 2.00 5.00
AI Andre Iguodala 2.00 5.00
AS Amare Stoudemire 2.00 5.00
CW Chris Webber 2.50 6.00
DF Derek Fisher 2.00 5.00
DG Drew Gooden 2.00 5.00
EB Elton Brand 2.50 6.00
EO Emeka Okafor 2.00 5.00
JC Josh Childress 2.00 5.00
JS Josh Smith 2.00 5.00
KM Kenyon Martin 2.00 5.00
LO Lamar Odom 2.00 5.00
LW Luke Walton 2.00 5.00
RJ Richard Jefferson 2.00 5.00
TM Tracy McGrady 3.00 8.00
JRS J.R. Smith 2.00 5.00

2005-06 Topps Rookie Photo Shoot Autographs

Inserted at the rate of one in 619, this 32-card set features cards made "same day" at the NBA Rookie photo shoot in August. Player photos appear at the top of the card while a white-out design is left on the bottom for the authentic player autographs. Fewer than sixty versions of each card are reported in existance.
STATED ODDS 1:619
UNPRICED TRIPLE STATED ODDS 1:28698
BB Brandon Bass 12.00 30.00
CV Charlie Villanueva 15.00 40.00
DE Daniel Ewing 12.00 30.00
DG Danny Granger 20.00 50.00
DL David Lee 15.00 40.00
DW Deron Williams 75.00 150.00
EI Ersan Ilyasova 15.00 40.00
FG Francisco Garcia 12.00 30.00
GG Gerald Green 15.00 40.00
HW Hakim Warrick 12.00 30.00
JG Joey Graham 12.00 30.00
JH Julius Hodge 10.00 25.00
JJ Jarrett Jack 15.00 40.00
JM Jason Maxiell 12.00 30.00
LH Luther Head 12.00 30.00
LW Louis Williams 15.00 40.00
ME Monta Ellis 40.00 100.00
NR Nate Robinson 15.00 40.00
RF Raymond Felton 15.00 40.00
RG Ryan Gomes 12.00 30.00
RM Rashad McCants 12.00 30.00
SJ Sarunas Jasikevicius 15.00 40.00
SM Sean May 10.00 25.00
WS Wayne Simien 10.00 25.00
ABL Andray Blatche 15.00 40.00
MWE Martell Webster 12.00 30.00

2005-06 Topps Rookie Photo Shoot Autographs Dual

Inserted in packs at the rate of one in 7998, this set parallels the design of the Rookie Photo Shoot Autographs, but is horizontally designed with two NBA rookies.
STATED ODDS 1:7998
FM R.Felton/S.May 30.00 80.00
GV Graham/Villanueva 20.00 50.00
GW G.Green/Webster 30.00 80.00
HJ J.Hodge/J.Jack 20.00 50.00
HW L.Head/D.Williams 30.00 80.00
MM S.May/R.McCants 30.00 80.00
WF D.Williams/R.Felton 30.00 80.00
FMC R.Felton/McCants 30.00 80.00
GWI F.Garcia/D.Williams 30.00 80.00

2005-06 Topps Signs of Stardom

Inserted in packs at the rate of one in 7391, this eight-card set is horizontally designed and features the members of Topps' celebrity lineup. Photos appear on the left of each card while a silver autographed sticker appears on the right.
STATED ODDS 1:7391
CB Christie Brinkley 40.00 100.00
JZ Jay-Z 40.00 100.00
SE Shannon Elizabeth 40.00 100.00
CAE Carmen Electra 20.00 50.00
JMC Jenny McCarthy 40.00 100.00

2005-06 Topps Target Hardwood Classics Jerseys

RANDOM INSERTS IN TARGET PACKS
AF Adonal Foyle 1.50 4.00
AI Allen Iverson 4.00 10.00
AJ Antawn Jamison 2.00 5.00
AM Andre Miller 2.00 5.00
AV Anderson Varejao 1.50 4.00
BS Bob Sura 1.50 4.00
CM Chris Mihm 1.50 4.00
DH Devin Harris 1.50 4.00
DM Darko Milicic 1.50 4.00
EB Earl Boykins 1.50 4.00
LW Luke Walton 1.50 4.00
RW Rasheed Wallace 2.50 6.00
SD Samuel Dalembert 1.50 4.00
ST Sebastian Telfair 2.00 5.00
TO Travis Outlaw 2.00 5.00
WG Willie Green 1.50 4.00
DHA David Harrison 1.50 4.00
HSJ Ha Seung-Jin 1.50 4.00

2005-06 Topps Versatile Velocity

Inserted in packs at the rate of one in 25, this 10-card set is horizontally designed and places player photos on the left of an orange background that features a graphic of an automobile speedometer.
COMPLETE SET (10) 10.00 25.00
STATED ODDS 1:25
VV1 Stephon Marbury .75 2.00
VV2 Kevin Garnett 1.50 4.00
VV3 Dwyane Wade 1.50 4.00
VV4 Shawn Marion .75 2.00
VV5 Ben Gordon .75 2.00
VV6 Corey Maggette .75 2.00
VV7 LeBron James 4.00 10.00
VV8 Gilbert Arenas .75 2.00
VV9 Manu Ginobili 1.00 2.50
VV10 Steve Francis .75 2.00

2006-07 Topps

Released in mid September 2006, Topps features a classic design placing full-color player photos on a white-bordered design with silver foil highlights. Veteran players are pictured on cards 1-215 and rookies are pictured on cards 216-275. For several of the first-round draft picks, two versions of each card were issued--one of the player in his college uniform and another of the player in his suit on NBA Draft night. Topps is packaged in 36-pack boxes of 12 cards each and carried an initial suggested retail price of $1.99. There were 33 variations for the #33 Larry Bird card (besides the base version) and all were numbered as #33 with no other identifiable features to label them.
COMPLETE SET (275) 25.00 60.00
COMP.SET w/o SP's (215) 12.50 30.00
UNPRICED PLATINUM PRINT RUN ONE SET
1 Elton Brand .20 .50
2 Tim Duncan .30 .75
3 Chris Paul .25 .60
4 Joe Johnson .15 .40
5 Chauncey Billups .20 .50
6 Al Harrington .15 .40
7 Andres Nocioni .12 .30
8 Kobe Bryant .75 2.00
9 Al Jefferson .15 .40
10 Gerald Wallace .15 .40
11 Jason Terry .15 .40
12 Dwight Howard .15 .40
13 Larry Hughes .15 .40
14 Sebastian Telfair .12 .30
15 Vince Carter .25 .60
16 Mike Bibby .20 .50
17 Ben Gordon .15 .40
18 Desmond Mason .12 .30
19 Eddie Jones .15 .40
20 Raymond Felton .15 .40
21 Paul Pierce .20 .50
22 Eddy Curry .15 .40
23 Jason Richardson .20 .50
24 Rasheed Wallace .20 .50
25 Andrew Bogut .15 .40
26 Stromile Swift .12 .30
27 Peja Stojakovic .20 .50
28 Deron Williams .15 .40
29 Kwame Brown .12 .30
30 Michael Redd .15 .40
31 Shawn Marion .15 .40
32 Shaquille O'Neal .40 1.00
33 Larry Bird 3.00 8.00
34 Ray Allen .20 .50
35 Marko Jaric .12 .30
36 Luther Head .15 .40
37 Robert Horry .15 .40
38 Jason Collins .12 .30
39 Cuttino Mobley .12 .30
40 Donyell Marshall .12 .30
41 Dirk Nowitzki .30 .75
42 Jermaine O'Neal .15 .40
43 Kurt Thomas .12 .30
44 Gerald Green .15 .40
45 Marvin Williams .15 .40
46 Bonzi Wells .12 .30
47 Andrei Kirilenko .15 .40
48 J.R. Smith .15 .40
49 Baron Davis .15 .40
50 Tracy McGrady .25 .60
51 Chris Kaman .15 .40
52 Luol Deng .15 .40
53 Emeka Okafor .15 .40
54 Grant Hill .25 .60
55 Amare Stoudemire .15 .40
56 Lamar Odom .15 .40
57 Eric Snow .12 .30
58 Ike Diogu .12 .30
59 Alonzo Mourning .25 .60
60 Maurice Evans .12 .30
61 Marcus Camby .15 .40
62 Bobby Simmons .12 .30
63 Vladimir Radmanovic .12 .30
64 Ryan Gomes .12 .30
65 Fred Jones .12 .30
66 Kirk Snyder .12 .30
67 Flip Murray .12 .30
68 T.J. Ford .12 .30
69 DeSagana Diop .12 .30
70 Josh Smith .15 .40
71 Lorenzen Wright .12 .30
72 Nate Robinson .12 .30
73 Brendan Haywood .12 .30
74 Darius Miles .12 .30
75 Keith Van Horn .15 .40
76 Johan Petro .12 .30
77 Yao Ming .25 .60
78 Darko Milicic .12 .30
79 Smush Parker .12 .30
80 Sarunas Jasikevicius .15 .40
81 Mike Dunleavy .15 .40
82 Joey Graham .12 .30
83 Jason Williams .15 .40
84 Melvin Ely .12 .30
85 Ricky Davis .15 .40
86 Michael Finley .20 .50
87 Steve Blake .12 .30
88 Nenad Krstic .12 .30
89 Earl Boykins .12 .30
90 Richard Hamilton .15 .40
91 Chris Duhon .12 .30
92 Hakim Warrick .15 .40
93 Wally Szczerbiak .15 .40
94 Corey Maggette .15 .40
95 Leandro Barbosa .15 .40
96 Jamaal Tinsley .12 .30
97 Kenyon Martin .15 .40
98 Kyle Korver .15 .40
99 Jason Kidd .30 .75
100 Dwyane Wade .30 .75
101 Ben Wallace .15 .40
102 Mike James .12 .30
103 Josh Howard .15 .40
104 Joe Smith .15 .40
105 Josh Childress .15 .40
106 Eddie Griffin .12 .30
107 Richard Jefferson .15 .40
108 Jalen Rose .15 .40
109 Mickael Pietrus .15 .40
110 Steve Nash .25 .60
111 Juwan Howard .15 .40
112 Drew Gooden .15 .40
113 Eduardo Najera .12 .30
114 Chris Mihm .12 .30
115 Jose Calderon .12 .30
116 Kevin Garnett .30 .75
117 Rafer Alston .12 .30
118 Delonte West .12 .30
119 Jamaal Magloire .12 .30
120 Channing Frye .15 .40
121 Andre Iguodala .15 .40
122 Pau Gasol .20 .50
123 LeBron James .75 2.00
124 Antonio Daniels .12 .30
125 James Posey .12 .30
126 Devean George .12 .30
127 Linas Kleiza .12 .30
128 Brian Cook .12 .30
129 Sean May .12 .30
130 Sam Cassell .15 .40
131 Mehmet Okur .12 .30
132 Bruce Bowen .12 .30
133 Kirk Hinrich .15 .40
134 Chris Wilcox .12 .30
135 Brad Miller .15 .40
136 Erick Dampier .12 .30
137 Primoz Brezec .12 .30
138 Derek Fisher .15 .40
139 Antonio McDyess .15 .40
140 Chris Bosh .20 .50
141 Jamal Crawford .20 .50
142 Mike Miller .15 .40
143 Danny Granger .15 .40
144 Quinton Ross .12 .30
145 Manu Ginobili .20 .50
146 Udonis Haslem .12 .30
147 Marquis Daniels .12 .30
148 Maurice Williams .15 .40
149 Viktor Khryapa .12 .30
150 Gilbert Arenas .15 .40
151 Tony Parker .20 .50
152 Carlos Boozer .15 .40
153 Quentin Richardson .15 .40
154 Clifford Robinson .12 .30
155 Speedy Claxton .12 .30
156 Charlie Villanueva .12 .30
157 Rashard Lewis .20 .50
158 DeShawn Stevenson .12 .30
159 Boris Diaw .15 .40
160 Francisco Garcia .12 .30
161 Zaza Pachulia .12 .30
162 Raja Bell .15 .40
163 Juan Dixon .12 .30
164 Shaun Livingston .12 .30
165 Shareef Abdur-Rahim .15 .40
166 Devin Harris .12 .30
167 Brevin Knight .12 .30
168 Troy Murphy .12 .30
169 Antawn Jamison .15 .40
170 Tyson Chandler .15 .40
171 Stephen Jackson .15 .40
172 Shane Battier .15 .40
173 Chris Webber .20 .50
174 Trenton Hassell .12 .30
175 Devin Brown .12 .30
176 Luke Ridnour .15 .40
177 Joel Przybilla .12 .30
178 David West .15 .40
179 John Salmons .15 .40
180 Nazr Mohammed .12 .30
181 Caron Butler .15 .40
182 Troy Hudson .12 .30
183 Zydrunas Ilgauskas .15 .40
184 David Wesley .12 .30
185 Andre Miller .15 .40
186 Nick Collison .15 .40
187 Ron Artest .20 .50
188 Samuel Dalembert .12 .30
189 Tayshaun Prince .15 .40
190 Jameer Nelson .12 .30
191 Zach Randolph .15 .40
192 Stephon Marbury .15 .40
193 Steve Francis .15 .40
194 Matt Harpring .12 .30
195 Kevin Martin .15 .40
196 Rashad McCants .12 .30
197 Carmelo Anthony .25 .60
198 Morris Peterson .12 .30
199 Etan Thomas .12 .30
200 Allen Iverson .25 .60
201 Antoine Walker .15 .40
202 Eddie House .12 .30
203 Adrian Griffin .12 .30
204 Salim Stoudamire .12 .30
205 Raef LaFrentz .12 .30
206 Jared Jeffries .12 .30
207 Rasual Butler .12 .30
208 Damon Jones .12 .30
209 Chuck Hayes .12 .30
210 James Singleton .12 .30
211 Marcus Banks .12 .30
212 P.J. Brown .12 .30
213 Hedo Turkoglu .20 .50
214 Jarrett Jack .15 .40
215 Kendrick Perkins .12 .30
216A Adam Morrison RC .75 2.00
216B Adam Morrison Draft RC .75 2.00
217 Leon Powe RC .60 1.50
218A Shelden Williams RC .60 1.50
218B Shelden Williams Draft RC .60 1.50
219 Alexander Johnson RC .50 1.25
220 Will Blalock RC .50 1.25
221 Steve Novak RC .60 1.50
222 Shawne Williams RC .50 1.25
223 Guillermo Diaz RC .50 1.25
224 Mardy Collins RC .50 1.25
225 Ryan Hollins RC .60 1.50
226 Kyle Lowry RC 1.00 2.50
227 Craig Smith RC .60 1.50
228 Denham Brown RC .50 1.25
229 Dee Brown RC .50 1.25
230 Daniel Gibson RC .60 1.50
231A Tyrus Thomas RC .60 1.50
231B Tyrus Thomas Draft RC .60 1.50
232A Patrick O'Bryant RC .50 1.25
232B Patrick O'Bryant Draft RC .50 1.25
233 Cedric Simmons RC .50 1.25
234 P.J. Tucker RC .60 1.50
235 Hassan Adams RC .50 1.25
236 Hilton Armstrong RC .50 1.25
237 James Augustine RC .50 1.25
238 Josh Boone RC .50 1.25
239 James White RC .50 1.25
240A J.J. Redick RC 1.00 2.50
240B J.J. Redick Draft RC 1.00 2.50
241A LaMarcus Aldridge RC 2.00 5.00
241B LaMarcus Aldridge Draft RC 2.00 5.00
242 Maurice Ager RC .50 1.25
243A Marcus Williams RC .50 1.25
243B Marcus Williams Draft RC .50 1.25
244 Paul Davis RC .50 1.25
245 Jordan Farmar RC .75 2.00
246A Brandon Roy RC .75 2.00
246B Brandon Roy Draft RC .75 2.00
247 Quincy Douby RC .50 1.25
248 Ronnie Brewer RC .75 2.00
249 Rodney Carney RC .50 1.25
250A Randy Foye RC .75 2.00
250B Randy Foye Draft RC .75 2.00
251 Rajon Rondo RC 1.25 3.00
252 Rudy Gay RC 1.00 2.50
253 Paul Millsap RC 1.00 2.50
254 Saer Sene RC .50 1.25
255A Andrea Bargnani RC .75 2.00
255B Andrea Bargnani Draft RC .75 2.00
256 Allan Ray RC .50 1.25
257 Thabo Sefolosha RC .75 2.00
258 Darius Washington RC .50 1.25
259 Renaldo Balkman RC .60 1.50
260 Mike Gansey RC .50 1.25
261 Solomon Jones RC .50 1.25
262 Bobby Jones RC .50 1.25

263 David Noel RC .50 1.25
264 Kevin Pittsnogle RC .60 1.50
265 Shannon Brown RC .50 1.25

2006-07 Topps Black

*1-215 BLACK: 4X TO 10X BASE HI
*216-275 BLACK: 1.25X TO 3X BASE HI
PRINT RUN 99 SER.#'d SETS
33 Larry Bird 10.00 25.00
251 Rajon Rondo 12.00 30.00

2006-07 Topps Gold

*1-215 GOLD: 1.5X TO 4X BASE HI
*216-275 GOLD: .75X TO 2X BASE HI
PRINT RUN 500 SER.#'d SETS
33 Larry Bird 2.00 5.00

2006-07 Topps 2K7 Promotion

COMPLETE SET (12) 8.00 20.00
APPROXIMATE ODDS 1:12
1 Allen Iverson .75 2.00
2 Dwyane Wade 1.00 2.50
3 Dwight Howard .50 1.25
4 LeBron James 2.50 6.00
5 Yao Ming .75 2.00
6 Tim Duncan 1.00 2.50
7 Kobe Bryant 2.50 6.00
8 Steven Nash .75 2.00
9 Kevin Garnett 1.00 2.50
10 Ben Wallace .50 1.25
11 Shaquille O'Neal 1.25 3.00
12 Dirk Nowitzki 1.00 2.50

2006-07 Topps Clutch City Prospects

COMPLETE SET (18) 6.00 15.00
STATED ODDS 1:9
1 Andrew Bogut .60 1.50
2 Luther Head .60 1.50
3 Channing Frye .60 1.50
4 Danny Granger .60 1.50
5 Chris Paul 1.00 2.50
6 Sarunas Jasikevicius .60 1.50
7 Nate Robinson .50 1.25
8 Charlie Villanueva .50 1.25
9 Deron Williams .60 1.50
10 Luol Deng .60 1.50
11 T.J. Ford .50 1.25
12 Ben Gordon .60 1.50
13 Devin Harris .50 1.25
14 Dwight Howard .60 1.50
15 Andre Iguodala .60 1.50
16 Nenad Krstic .50 1.25
17 Andres Nocioni .50 1.25
18 Delonte West .50 1.25

2006-07 Topps Clutch City Prospects Relics

GROUP A ODDS 1:1500, GROUP B 1:707
*BLACK: .5X TO 1.25X BASE HI
BLACK PRINT RUN 99 SER.#'d SETS
*GOLD: .6X TO 1.5X BASE HI
GOLD PRINT RUN 25 SER.#'d SETS
UNPRICED AUTO PRINT RUN 5 SETS
AB Andrew Bogut B 2.50 6.00
AN Andres Nocioni B 2.00 5.00
BG Ben Gordon B 2.50 6.00
CF Channing Frye B 2.50 6.00
CP Chris Paul B 4.00 10.00
CV Charlie Villanueva B 2.00 5.00
DH Dwight Howard B 2.50 6.00
DW Deron Williams B 2.50 6.00
HW Hakim Warrick B 2.50 6.00
LD Luol Deng B 2.50 6.00
NK Nenad Krstic B 2.00 5.00
NR Nate Robinson B 2.00 5.00
SJ Sarunas Jasikevicius A 2.50 6.00
DWE Delonte West B 2.00 5.00
TJF T.J. Ford B 2.00 5.00

2006-07 Topps Clutch City Stars

COMPLETE SET (24) 12.50 30.00
STATED ODDS 1:7
1 Allen Iverson .75 2.00
2 Dwyane Wade 1.00 2.50
3 LeBron James 2.50 6.00
4 Vince Carter .75 2.00
5 Shaquille O'Neal 1.25 3.00
6 Ben Wallace .50 1.25
7 Chris Bosh .60 1.50
8 Rasheed Wallace .60 1.50
9 Paul Pierce .60 1.50
10 Richard Hamilton .50 1.25
11 Gilbert Arenas .50 1.25
12 Chauncey Billups .60 1.50
13 Kobe Bryant 2.50 6.00
14 Steve Nash .75 2.00
15 Tim Duncan 1.00 2.50
16 Tracy McGrady .75 2.00
17 Yao Ming .75 2.00
18 Tony Parker .60 1.50
19 Kevin Garnett 1.00 2.50
20 Ray Allen .60 1.50
21 Dirk Nowitzki 1.00 2.50
22 Shawn Marion .50 1.25
23 Elton Brand .60 1.50
24 Pau Gasol .60 1.50

2006-07 Topps Clutch City Stars Relics

GROUP A ODDS: 1:115000, GROUP B 1:8200
GROUP C ODDS 1:1400
*BLACK: .5X TO 1.25X BASE HI
BLACK PRINT RUN 99 SER.#'d SETS
*GOLD: .6X TO 1.5X BASE HI
GOLD PRINT RUN 25 SER.#'d SETS
UNPRICED AUTO PRINT RUN 5 SETS
AI Allen Iverson C 4.00 10.00
BW Ben Wallace C 2.50 6.00
DN Dirk Nowitzki C 5.00 12.00
DW Dwyane Wade C 6.00 15.00
GA Gilbert Arenas C 2.50 6.00
KB Kobe Bryant C 8.00 20.00
KG Kevin Garnett A 5.00 12.00
PP Paul Pierce B 3.00 8.00
RH Richard Hamilton B 2.50 6.00
SN Steve Nash C 4.00 10.00
SO Shaquille O'Neal B 6.00 15.00
TD Tim Duncan C 5.00 12.00
TP Tony Parker C 3.00 8.00
VC Vince Carter C 4.00 10.00
YM Yao Ming A 4.00 10.00
CBI Chauncey Billups B 3.00 8.00

2006-07 Topps Hobby Masters

COMPLETE SET (20) 12.50 30.00
STATED ODDS 1:8
1 Kobe Bryant 2.50 6.00
2 Shaquille O'Neal 1.25 3.00
3 LeBron James 2.50 6.00
4 Allen Iverson .75 2.00
5 Tracy McGrady .75 2.00
6 Dwyane Wade 1.00 2.50
7 Vince Carter .75 2.00
8 Tim Duncan 1.00 2.50
9 Kevin Garnett 1.00 2.50
10 Yao Ming .75 2.00
11 Steve Nash .75 2.00
12 Carmelo Anthony .75 2.00
13 Jason Kidd 1.00 2.50
14 Jerry West .75 2.00
15 George Gervin .60 1.50
16 Larry Bird 1.50 4.00
17 Pete Maravich 1.00 2.50
18 Wilt Chamberlain 1.25 3.00
19 Oscar Robertson .60 1.50
20 Earl Monroe .60 1.50

2006-07 Topps Larry Bird The Missing Years

COMPLETE SET (10) 20.00 50.00
COMMON CARD (LB82-LB91) 3.00 8.00
STATED ODDS 1:18

2006-07 Topps Marks of Excellence

GROUP A ODDS 1:30000, GROUP B 1:1800
GROUP C ODDS 1:1800, GROUP D 1:1144
AI Allen Iverson D 50.00 120.00
AM Adam Morrison D 8.00 20.00
BH Ben Howland C 6.00 15.00
DR DaRoc D 5.00 12.00
DW Dwyane Wade B 15.00 40.00
EO Emeka Okafor D 6.00 15.00
FM Streetballer D 5.00 12.00
FT Future D 5.00 12.00
HS Hops D 5.00 12.00
HW Hakim Warrick B 5.00 12.00
JB Jim Boeheim D 10.00 25.00
JC Jim Calhoun C 10.00 25.00
LB Larry Bird B 40.00 80.00
LR Luke Ridnour D 5.00 12.00
LS Lil Scrappy D 5.00 12.00
RC Rodney Carney B 5.00 12.00
SO Shaquille O'Neal B 30.00 80.00
SW Shelden Williams B 5.00 12.00
TE Too EZ D 5.00 12.00
TW The Wizard D 5.00 12.00
WC White Chocolate D 5.00 12.00
BMA Bird Man D 5.00 12.00
DWE Delonte West D 5.00 12.00
JFK JFK D 5.00 12.00
JJR J.J. Redick D 5.00 12.00
JWO John Wooden C 40.00 100.00
RWI Roy Williams C 20.00 50.00

2006-07 Topps Own the Game

COMPLETE SET (28) 15.00 40.00
STATED ODDS 1:6
1 Kobe Bryant 2.50 6.00
2 Allen Iverson .75 2.00
3 LeBron James 2.50 6.00
4 Gilbert Arenas .50 1.25
5 Dwyane Wade 1.00 2.50
6 Kevin Garnett 1.00 2.50
7 Dwight Howard .50 1.25
8 Shawn Marion .50 1.25
9 Ben Wallace .50 1.25
10 Tim Duncan 1.00 2.50
11 Steve Nash .75 2.00
12 Baron Davis .50 1.25
13 Brevin Knight .40 1.00
14 Chauncey Billups .60 1.50
15 Jason Kidd 1.00 2.50
16 Marcus Camby .50 1.25
17 Andrei Kirilenko .50 1.25
18 Alonzo Mourning .75 2.00
19 Josh Smith .50 1.25
20 Elton Brand .60 1.50
21 Gerald Wallace .50 1.25
22 Brevin Knight .40 1.00
23 Chris Paul .75 2.00
24 Gilbert Arenas .50 1.25
25 Shawn Marion .50 1.25
26 Chris Paul .75 2.00
27 Larry Bird 1.50 4.00
28 Steve Nash .75 2.00

2006-07 Topps Own the Game Relics

GROUP A ODDS 1:35000, GROUP B 1:8200
GROUP C ODDS 1:1202, GROUP D 1:658
*BLACK: .5X TO 1.25X BASE HI
BLACK PRINT RUN 99 SER.#'d SETS
*GOLD: .6X TO 1.5X BASE HI
GOLD PRINT RUN 25 SER.#'d SETS
UNPRICED AUTO PRINT RUN 5 SETS
AI Allen Iverson D 4.00 10.00
CP Chris Paul D 4.00 10.00
DH Dwight Howard C 2.50 6.00
DN Dirk Nowitzki C 5.00 12.00
DW Dwyane Wade D 6.00 15.00
EB Elton Brand A 3.00 8.00
JS Josh Smith B 2.50 6.00
KB Kobe Bryant D 8.00 20.00
KG Kevin Garnett D 5.00 12.00
SN Steve Nash D 4.00 10.00
SO Shaquille O'Neal D 6.00 15.00
TD Tim Duncan D 5.00 12.00
TP Tony Parker D 3.00 8.00

2006-07 Topps Pride of the Program

COMPLETE SET (10) 12.50 30.00
STATED ODDS 1:16
PP1 Sheed/Chauncey/Rip 2.00 5.00
PP2 LeBron/Ilgauskas/Hughes 3.00 8.00
PP3 Vince/Kidd/Jefferson 2.00 5.00
PP4 Carmelo/Boykins/Camby 2.00 5.00
PP5 Wade/Walker/Shaq 3.00 8.00
PP6 Iverson/Dalembert/Iggy 2.00 5.00
PP7 Dirk/Terry/Howard 2.00 5.00
PP8 T-Mac/Yao/Head 2.50 6.00
PP9 Kobe/Odom/Bynum 2.50 6.00
PP10 Parker/Ginobili/Duncan 2.50 6.00

2006-07 Topps Pride of the Program Relics

STATED PRINT RUN 99 SER.#'d SETS
BBW Bynum/Kobe/Worthy 15.00 40.00
JPC Big Al/Pierce/Cowens 12.00 30.00
KBM AK-47/Boozer/Malone 8.00 20.00
MMD Yao/T-Mac/Drexler 12.00 30.00
PDG Parker/Duncan/Gervin 15.00 40.00
RFM Robinson/Frye/The Pearl 12.00 30.00

2006-07 Topps Rookie Photo Shoot Autographs

STATED ODDS 1:358
UNPRICED DUAL STATED ODDS 1:9050
UNPRICED TRIPLE STATED ODDS 1:22700
AM Adam Morrison 12.00 30.00
AR Allan Ray 8.00 20.00
CS Craig Smith 10.00 25.00
DN David Noel 8.00 20.00
JB Josh Boone 8.00 20.00
JF Jordan Farmar 12.00 30.00
KL Kyle Lowry 15.00 40.00
MA Maurice Ager 8.00 20.00
MC Mardy Collins 8.00 20.00
MW Marcus Williams 8.00 20.00
PD Paul Davis 8.00 20.00
QD Quincy Douby 8.00 20.00
RB Ronnie Brewer 12.00 30.00
RC Rodney Carney 8.00 20.00
RF Randy Foye 12.00 30.00
RR Rajon Rondo 30.00 80.00
SB Shannon Brown 8.00 20.00
SJ Solomon Jones 8.00 20.00
SN Steve Novak 10.00 25.00
SW Shelden Williams 10.00 25.00
CSI Cedric Simmons 8.00 20.00
DBR Denham Brown 8.00 20.00
DEE Dee Brown 8.00 20.00
HAR Hilton Armstrong 8.00 20.00
JJR J.J. Redick 40.00 100.00
KPI Kevin Pittsnogle 10.00 25.00
RBA Renaldo Balkman 10.00 25.00
SWI Shawne Williams 8.00 20.00

2007-08 Topps

This 135-card set was released in September, 2007. The set was issued into the hobby in nine-card packs with an $1.99 SRP which came 36 packs to a box. Cards numbered 1-110 feature veterans while cards numbered 111-135 feature 2007-08 NBA rookies.

COMPLETE SET (135) 12.00 30.00
UNPRICED SILVER PRINT RUN ONE SET
1 Amare Stoudemire .15 .40
2 Joe Johnson .15 .40
3 Dwyane Wade .30 .75
4 Chris Bosh .20 .50
5 Jason Kidd .20 .50
6 Bill Russell .30 .75
7 Jermaine O'Neal .15 .40
8 Mike Miller .15 .40
9 Ray Allen .20 .50
10 Elton Brand .20 .50
11 Yao Ming .25 .60
12 Al Harrington .15 .40
13 Steve Nash .25 .60
14 Dwight Howard .15 .40
15 Carmelo Anthony .25 .60
16 Pau Gasol .20 .50
17 Chauncey Billups .20 .50
18 Antawn Jamison .15 .40
19 Shane Battier .15 .40
20 Kevin Garnett .30 .75
21 Tim Duncan .30 .75
22 Michael Redd .15 .40
23 LeBron James .75 2.00
24 Kobe Bryant .75 2.00
25 Eddy Curry .12 .30
26 Peja Stojakovic .20 .50
27 Andrew Bogut .15 .40
28 Vince Carter .25 .60
29 Corey Maggette .15 .40
30 Rasheed Wallace .20 .50
31 Shawn Marion .15 .40
32 Shaquille O'Neal .40 1.00
33 Allen Iverson .25 .60
34 Paul Pierce .20 .50
35 Adam Morrison .12 .30
36 Tony Parker .20 .50
37 Mike Bibby .20 .50
38 Andrea Bargnani .20 .50
39 Luol Deng .15 .40
40 Chris Paul .25 .60
41 Dirk Nowitzki .25 .60
42 David Lee .12 .30
43 Paul Millsap .15 .40
44 Danny Granger .15 .40
45 Al Jefferson .15 .40
46 Rafer Alston .12 .30
47 Andrei Kirilenko .15 .40
48 Shaun Livingston .12 .30
49 Chris Wilcox .12 .30
50 Emeka Okafor .15 .40
51 Zach Randolph .15 .40
52 Devin Harris .12 .30
53 Mo Williams .15 .40
54 Leandro Barbosa .15 .40
55 Smush Parker .12 .30
56 Andre Miller .15 .40
57 Manu Ginobili .20 .50
58 Jason Richardson .20 .50
59 Jason Terry .15 .40
60 Gerald Wallace .15 .40
61 Richard Hamilton .15 .40
62 Ricky Davis .15 .40
63 Boris Diaw .15 .40
64 Carlos Boozer .15 .40
65 Rashard Lewis .15 .40
66 Josh Childress .15 .40
67 Lamar Odom .15 .40
68 Kyle Korver .15 .40
69 Stephon Marbury .15 .40
70 Luke Walton .12 .30
71 Baron Davis .15 .40
72 Larry Hughes .15 .40
73 Jameer Nelson .12 .30
74 Caron Butler .15 .40
75 Udonis Haslem .12 .30
76 Mike Dunleavy .15 .40
77 Ben Gordon .15 .40
78 Andrew Bynum .12 .30
79 Hakim Warrick .15 .40
80 Josh Smith .15 .40
81 Mehmet Okur .12 .30
82 J.R. Smith .15 .40
83 Raymond Felton .20 .50
84 Chris Webber .20 .50
85 Jamal Crawford .20 .50
86 Jarrett Jack .15 .40
87 Anderson Varejao .12 .30
88 Ryan Gomes .12 .30
89 Charlie Villanueva .12 .30
90 Marcus Camby .12 .30
91 Kirk Hinrich .15 .40
92 Tayshaun Prince .15 .40
93 Ron Artest .20 .50
94 T.J. Ford .12 .30
95 Richard Jefferson .15 .40
96 Zydrunas Ilgauskas .15 .40
97 Josh Howard .15 .40
98 Monta Ellis .15 .40
99 Deron Williams .15 .40
100 Gilbert Arenas .15 .40
101 Tracy McGrady .20 .50
102 Steve Blake .12 .30
103 Ben Wallace .15 .40
104 Kevin Martin .15 .40
105 Marcus Williams .12 .30
106 J.J. Redick .20 .50
107 Brandon Roy .20 .50
108 Desmond Mason .12 .30
109 Randy Foye .20 .50
110 Andre Iguodala .15 .40
111 Greg Oden RC .75 2.00
112 Kevin Durant RC 6.00 15.00
113 Al Horford RC 1.00 2.50
114 Mike Conley Jr. RC 1.00 2.50
115 Jeff Green RC .75 2.00
116 Yi Jianlian RC 1.00 2.50
117 Corey Brewer RC .75 2.00
118 Brandan Wright RC .75 2.00
119 Joakim Noah RC .75 2.00
120 Spencer Hawes RC .60 1.50
121 Acie Law RC .50 1.25
122 Thaddeus Young RC .75 2.00
123 Julian Wright RC .50 1.25
124 Al Thornton RC .60 1.50
125 Rodney Stuckey RC .60 1.50
126 Nick Young RC 1.00 2.50
127 Sean Williams RC .50 1.25
128 Marco Belinelli RC .75 2.00
129 Javaris Crittenton RC .50 1.25
130 Jason Smith RC .60 1.50
131 Daequan Cook RC .60 1.50
132 Jared Dudley RC .60 1.50
133 Wilson Chandler RC .60 1.50
134 Morris Almond RC .50 1.25
135 Aaron Brooks RC .60 1.50

2007-08 Topps Copper

*1-110 COPPER: 5X TO 12X BASE HI
*111-135 COPPER RC: 2.5X TO 6X BASE HI
COPPER PRINT RUN 50 SER.#'d SETS
112 Kevin Durant 200.00 500.00

2007-08 Topps First Edition

*1-110 1st EDITION: 3X TO 8X BASE HI
*111-135 1st ED.RC: 1.5X TO 4X BASE HI
1st EDITION PRINT RUN 119 SER.#'d SETS
112 Kevin Durant 100.00 250.00

2007-08 Topps Gold

*GOLD STARS: 1.25X TO 3X BASE HI
*GOLD RCs: .75X TO 2X BASE HI
PRINT RUN 2007 SER.#'d SETS
112 Kevin Durant 60.00 150.00

2007-08 Topps 1957-58 Variations

MPLETE SET (50) 15.00 40.00
ONE VARIATION CARD PER PACK
*1-110 COPPER: 1.25X TO 3X BASE HI
*COPPER RC: 2X TO 5X BASE HI
COPPER PRINT RUN 50 SER.#'d SETS
*1-110 1st ED: .6X TO 1.5X BASE HI
*1st ED.RC: 1.5X TO 4X BASE HI
1st EDITION PRINT RUN 119 SER.#'d SETS
*1-110 GOLD: SAME AS BASE
*GOLD RC: .75X TO 2X BASE HI
GOLD PRINT RUN 2007 SER.#'d SETS
UNPRICED SILVER PRINT RUN ONE SET
1 Amare Stoudemire .50 1.25
3 Dwyane Wade 1.00 2.50
4 Chris Bosh .60 1.50
5 Jason Kidd .60 1.50
7 Jermaine O'Neal .50 1.25
11 Yao Ming .75 2.00
13 Steve Nash .75 2.00
14 Dwight Howard .50 1.25
15 Carmelo Anthony .75 2.00
17 Chauncey Billups .60 1.50
20 Kevin Garnett 1.00 2.50
21 Tim Duncan 1.00 2.50
23 LeBron James 2.50 6.00
24 Kobe Bryant 2.50 6.00
25 Eddy Curry .40 1.00
28 Vince Carter .75 2.00
31 Shawn Marion .50 1.25
32 Shaquille O'Neal 1.25 3.00
33 Allen Iverson .75 2.00
41 Dirk Nowitzki .75 2.00
100 Gilbert Arenas .50 1.25
101 Tracy McGrady .60 1.50
104 Kevin Martin .50 1.25
107 Brandon Roy .60 1.50
110 Andre Iguodala .50 1.25
111 Greg Oden .75 2.00
112 Kevin Durant 8.00 20.00
113 Al Horford 1.00 2.50
114 Mike Conley Jr. 1.00 2.50
115 Jeff Green .75 2.00
116 Yi Jianlian 1.00 2.50
117 Corey Brewer .75 2.00
118 Brandan Wright .75 2.00
119 Joakim Noah .75 2.00
120 Spencer Hawes .60 1.50
121 Acie Law .50 1.25
122 Thaddeus Young .75 2.00
123 Julian Wright .50 1.25
124 Al Thornton .60 1.50
125 Rodney Stuckey .60 1.50
126 Nick Young 1.00 2.50
127 Sean Williams .50 1.25
128 Marco Belinelli .75 2.00
129 Javaris Crittenton .50 1.25
130 Jason Smith .60 1.50
131 Daequan Cook .60 1.50
132 Jared Dudley .60 1.50
133 Wilson Chandler .60 1.50
134 Morris Almond .50 1.25
135 Aaron Brooks .60 1.50

2007-08 Topps 1957-58 Variations Autographs

GROUP A ODDS 1:1700; B ODDS 1:325
GROUP C ODDS 1:299; D ODDS 1:285
3 Dwyane Wade A 25.00 60.00
4 Chris Bosh A 10.00 25.00
9 Ray Allen A 10.00 25.00
12 Al Harrington B 4.00 10.00
17 Chauncey Billups B 8.00 20.00
27 Andrew Bogut C 4.00 10.00
28 Vince Carter A 15.00 40.00
29 Corey Maggette D 4.00 10.00
35 Adam Morrison B 4.00 10.00
42 David Lee D 4.00 10.00
43 Paul Millsap A 4.00 10.00
47 Andrei Kirilenko C 4.00 10.00
54 Leandro Barbosa B 4.00 10.00
55 Smush Parker C 4.00 10.00
63 Boris Diaw D 4.00 10.00
64 Carlos Boozer C 4.00 10.00
70 Luke Walton D 4.00 10.00
73 Jameer Nelson B 4.00 10.00
79 Hakim Warrick D 4.00 10.00
86 Jarrett Jack C 4.00 10.00
89 Charlie Villanueva C 4.00 10.00
91 Kirk Hinrich B 4.00 10.00
97 Josh Howard B 4.00 10.00
106 J.J. Redick C 6.00 15.00
110 Andre Iguodala B 5.00 12.00

2007-08 Topps 1957-58 Variations Relics

STATED ODDS 1:71
1 Amare Stoudemire 2.50 6.00
2 Joe Johnson 2.50 6.00
3 Dwyane Wade 6.00 15.00
4 Chris Bosh 3.00 8.00
5 Jason Kidd 3.00 8.00
7 Jermaine O'Neal 2.50 6.00
11 Yao Ming 4.00 10.00
13 Steve Nash 4.00 10.00
14 Dwight Howard 2.50 6.00
17 Chauncey Billups 3.00 8.00
20 Kevin Garnett 5.00 12.00
21 Tim Duncan 5.00 12.00
24 Kobe Bryant 10.00 25.00
28 Vince Carter 4.00 10.00
31 Shawn Marion 2.50 6.00
32 Shaquille O'Neal 6.00 15.00
33 Allen Iverson 4.00 10.00
35 Adam Morrison 2.00 5.00
41 Dirk Nowitzki 4.00 10.00
61 Richard Hamilton 3.00 8.00
74 Caron Butler 2.50 6.00
91 Kirk Hinrich 2.50 6.00
101 Tracy McGrady 3.00 8.00
104 Kevin Martin 2.50 6.00
107 Brandon Roy 3.00 8.00

2007-08 Topps Bill Russell The Missing Years

COMPLETE SET (11) 10.00 25.00
COMMON CARD (BR58-BR69) 2.00 5.00
STATED ODDS 1:9
AUTOGRAPH ODDS 1:90000
AUTOS NOT PRICED DUE TO SCARCITY

2007-08 Topps Generation Now

COMPLETE SET (30) 6.00 15.00
STATED ODDS 1:3
GN1 LeBron James 1.25 3.00
GN2 Carmelo Anthony .40 1.00
GN3 Dwyane Wade .50 1.25
GN4 Chris Bosh .30 .75
GN5 Josh Howard .25 .60
GN6 Dwight Howard .25 .60
GN7 Emeka Okafor .25 .60
GN8 Ben Gordon .25 .60
GN9 Andre Iguodala .25 .60
GN10 Josh Smith .25 .60
GN11 Kevin Martin .25 .60
GN12 Chris Paul .40 1.00
GN13 Deron Williams .25 .60
GN14 Raymond Felton .30 .75
GN15 Marvin Williams .25 .60
GN16 David Lee .20 .50
GN17 Andrew Bynum .20 .50
GN18 Monta Ellis .25 .60
GN19 Jarrett Jack .25 .60
GN20 Hakim Warrick .25 .60
GN21 Ryan Gomes .20 .50
GN22 Sean May .20 .50
GN23 Charlie Villanueva .20 .50
GN24 Luke Walton .20 .50
GN25 Boris Diaw .25 .60
GN26 Brandon Roy .30 .75
GN27 Andrea Bargnani .30 .75
GN28 Randy Foye .30 .75
GN29 Marcus Williams .20 .50
GN30 Adam Morrison .20 .50

2007-08 Topps Generation Now Relics

STATED ODDS 1:71
GNRAB Andrew Bynum 2.00 5.00
GNRAI Andre Iguodala 2.50 6.00
GNRAM Adam Morrison 2.00 5.00
GNRBD Boris Diaw 2.50 6.00
GNRBG Ben Gordon 2.50 6.00
GNRBR Brandon Roy 3.00 8.00
GNRCA Carmelo Anthony 4.00 10.00
GNRCB Chris Bosh 3.00 8.00
GNRCP Chris Paul 4.00 10.00
GNRCV Charlie Villanueva 2.00 5.00
GNRDH Dwight Howard 2.50 6.00
GNRDW Dwyane Wade 6.00 15.00
GNREO Emeka Okafor 2.50 6.00
GNRHW Hakim Warrick 2.50 6.00
GNRJH Josh Howard 2.50 6.00
GNRJJ Jarrett Jack 2.50 6.00
GNRJS Josh Smith 2.50 6.00
GNRLW Luke Walton 2.00 5.00
GNRME Monta Ellis 2.50 6.00
GNRMW Marcus Williams 2.00 5.00
GNRRF Raymond Felton 3.00 8.00
GNRSM Sean May 2.00 5.00
GNRABA Andrea Bargnani 3.00 8.00
GNRDWI Deron Williams 2.50 6.00
GNRRFO Randy Foye 3.00 8.00

2007-08 Topps Mini Exclusives

ONE PER RIP CARD
MEAI Allen Iverson 4.00 10.00
MEBR Bill Russell 5.00 12.00
MEBW Bill Walton 3.00 8.00
MECA Carmelo Anthony 4.00 10.00
MECD Clyde Drexler 4.00 10.00
MECM Chris Mullin 3.00 8.00
MEDH Dwight Howard 2.50 6.00
MEDN Dirk Nowitzki 4.00 10.00
MEDR Dennis Rodman 6.00 15.00
MEEB Elgin Baylor 3.00 8.00
MEEM Earl Monroe 3.00 8.00
MEGA Gilbert Arenas 2.50 6.00
MEGG George Gervin 3.00 8.00
MEIT Isiah Thomas 3.00 8.00
MEJE Julius Erving 5.00 12.00
MEJH Josh Howard 3.00 8.00
MEJK Jason Kidd 3.00 8.00
MEJS John Stockton 5.00 12.00
MEJW James Worthy 4.00 10.00
MEKB Kobe Bryant 12.00 30.00
MEKG Kevin Garnett 5.00 12.00
MEKM Karl Malone 4.00 10.00
MELB Larry Bird 8.00 20.00
MELB Leandro Barbosa 3.00 8.00
MEOR Oscar Robertson 3.00 8.00
MERB Rick Barry 2.50 6.00
MESN Steve Nash 4.00 10.00
METD Tim Duncan 5.00 12.00
MEVC Vince Carter 4.00 10.00
MEWC Wilt Chamberlain 6.00 15.00
MEAIG Andre Iguodala 2.50 6.00
MEDWI Dominique Wilkins 4.00 10.00

2007-08 Topps Mini Exclusives Autographs

MOST UNPRICED DUE TO SCARCITY
MEDR Dennis Rodman 75.00 150.00
MEEB Elgin Baylor 10.00 25.00
MEJH Josh Howard 8.00 20.00
MEAIG Andre Iguodala 10.00 25.00
MEDWI Dominique Wilkins 15.00 40.00

2007-08 Topps Own the Game

COMPLETE SET (9) 6.00 15.00
STATED ODDS 1:11
OTG1 Mikki Moore .60 1.50
OTG2 Kyle Korver .75 2.00
OTG3 Jason Kapono .60 1.50
OTG4 Kevin Garnett 1.50 4.00
OTG5 Steve Nash 1.25 3.00
OTG6 Baron Davis .75 2.00
OTG7 Marcus Camby .60 1.50
OTG8 Kobe Bryant 4.00 10.00
OTG9 Jason Kidd 1.00 2.50

2007-08 Topps Rip Card Combinations

*RIPPED CARDS: HALF VALUE
PRINT RUN 99 SER.#'d SETS
VALUES FOR UNRIPPED CARDS
RIP1 James/Anthony/Wade 20.00 50.00
RIP2 Arenas/Iverson/Bryant 20.00 40.00
RIP3 Nash/Maravich/Kidd 20.00 50.00
RIP4 Howard/Duncan/Garnett 20.00 40.00
RIP5 Nowitzki/Garnett/Brand 20.00 40.00
RIP6 Bird/Erving/Johnson 30.00 60.00
RIP8 Russell/O'Neal/Chamberlain 30.00 80.00
RIP9 Rodman/Artest/Wallace 20.00 40.00
RIP10 Walton/Ming/Robinson 20.00 40.00
RIP11 Wilkins/Carter/Drexler 20.00 40.00
RIP12 Johnson/Thomas/Stockton 25.00 50.00
RIP13 Allen/Mullin/Nowitzki 12.00 30.00
RIP14 Robinson/Stoudemire/Malone 12.00 30.00
RIP15 Bryant/McGrady/James 30.00 60.00
RIP16 Monroe/Iverson/Robertson 12.00 30.00
RIP17 Smith/Gervin/Marion 12.00 30.00
RIP18 O'Neal/Worthy/Garnett 20.00 40.00
RIP19 O'Neal/Rodman/Malone 25.00 50.00
RIP20 Erving/Wade/Johnson 20.00 40.00
RIP21 Hill/Williams/Jamison 12.00 30.00
RIP22 Paul/Gordon/Iverson 25.00 60.00
RIP23 Bird/Johnson/Wade 25.00 60.00
RIP24 Erving/Bryant/Robertson 25.00 60.00
RIP25 Kidd/Stockton/Nash 25.00 50.00
RIP26 Arenas/Anthony/Pierce 20.00 40.00
RIP27 Mullin/Barry/Bird 20.00 40.00
RIP28 Ellis/Felton/Johnson 12.00 30.00
RIP30 Camby/Okafor/O'Neal 12.00 30.00
RIP31 Williams/Maravich/Stockton 25.00 50.00
RIP32 Erving/James/Wilkins 30.00 60.00
RIP34 Redd/Allen/Pierce 20.00 40.00
RIP35 Smith/Richardson/Mason 12.00 30.00
RIP36 Stoudemire/Gasol/Brand 12.00 30.00
RIP37 Marbury/Wade/Kidd 20.00 40.00
RIP38 James/O'Neal/Bryant 30.00 80.00

2007-08 Topps Rookie Photo Shoot Autographs

STATED ODDS 1:381
AA Arron Afflalo 8.00 20.00
AB Aaron Brooks 6.00 15.00
AG Aaron Gray 5.00 12.00
AT Al Thornton 6.00 15.00
BW Brandan Wright 8.00 20.00
CL Carl Landry 5.00 12.00
DB Derrick Byars 5.00 12.00
DC Daequan Cook 6.00 15.00
DM Dominic McGuire 5.00 12.00
GD Glen Davis 6.00 15.00
GO Greg Oden 12.00 30.00
GP Gabe Pruitt 5.00 12.00
HH Herbert Hill 5.00 12.00
JC Javaris Crittenton 5.00 12.00
JD Jared Dudley 6.00 15.00
JJ Jared Jordan 5.00 12.00
JM Josh McRoberts 6.00 15.00
JS Jason Smith 6.00 15.00
MA Morris Almond 5.00 12.00
MW Marcus Williams 5.00 12.00
NF Nick Fazekas 5.00 12.00
NY Nick Young 10.00 25.00
RS Rodney Stuckey 6.00 15.00
RT Reyshawn Terry 5.00 12.00
SH Spencer Hawes 6.00 15.00
SL Stephane Lasme 5.00 12.00
SW Sean Williams 5.00 12.00
TG Taurean Green 5.00 12.00
TY Thaddeus Young 8.00 20.00
WC Wilson Chandler 6.00 15.00
AL4 Acie Law 5.00 12.00
ATU Alando Tucker 5.00 12.00
JDA Jermareo Davidson 5.00 12.00

2007-08 Topps Rookie Photo Shoot Autographs Dual

STATED ODDS 1:2500
BL A.Brooks/A.Law 15.00 40.00
DB G.Davis/D.Byars 15.00 40.00
MH J.McRoberts/S.Hawes 15.00 40.00
OW G.Oden/B.Wright 30.00 80.00
SA R.Stuckey/A.Afflalo 15.00 40.00
SF J.Smith/N.Fazekas 15.00 40.00
TC A.Thornton/W.Chandler 15.00 40.00
WD S.Williams/J.Dudley 15.00 40.00
YP N.Young/G.Pruitt 15.00 40.00

2007-08 Topps Rookie Photo Shoot Autographs Triple

STATED ODDS 1:26000
BCA Brooks/Crittenton/Afflalo 20.00 50.00
CLY Cook/Law/Young 20.00 50.00
HFS Hawes/Fazekas/Smith 20.00 50.00
OYW Oden/Young/Wright 40.00 100.00
WTD Williams/Thornton/Dudley 20.00 50.00

2007-08 Topps Rookie Set

Issued as a set, this version of the 2007-08 Topps rookie set features white borders and was available in retail outlets for between $9.99 and $14.99.

COMPLETE SET (1-14) 6.00 15.00
1 Greg Oden .50 1.25
2 Kevin Durant 5.00 12.00
3 Al Horford .60 1.50
4 Mike Conley Jr. .60 1.50
5 Jeff Green .50 1.25
6 Yi Jianlian .60 1.50
7 Corey Brewer .50 1.25
8 Brandan Wright .50 1.25
9 Joakim Noah .50 1.25
10 Spencer Hawes .40 1.00
11 Acie Law .30 .75
12 Thaddeus Young .50 1.25
13 Julian Wright .30 .75
14 Al Thornton .40 1.00

2007-08 Topps Rookie Set Orange

Issued as a set, this version of the 2007-08 Topps rookie set features orange borders and was available at retail outlets.

COMPLETE SET (14) 6.00 15.00
*SAME VALUE AS REGULAR

2008-09 Topps

This set was released on September 11, 2008. The base set consists of 220 cards. Cards 1-195 feature veterans, and cards 196-220 are rookies.

COMPLETE SET (220) 20.00 50.00
ROOKIE STATED ODDS 1:3
UNPRICED PLATINUM PRINT RUN ONE SET
1 Chris Paul .25 .60
2 Joe Johnson .15 .40
3 Allen Iverson .25 .60
4 Luis Scola .15 .40
5 Kevin Garnett .30 .75
6 Andrew Bogut .15 .40
7 Ben Gordon .15 .40
8 Carlos Boozer .15 .40
9 Tony Parker .20 .50
10 Gilbert Arenas .15 .40
11 Yao Ming .25 .60
12 Dwight Howard .15 .40
13 Steve Nash .20 .50
14 Daequan Cook .12 .30
15 Carmelo Anthony .25 .60
16 Pau Gasol .20 .50
17 Mike Dunleavy .15 .40
18 Jason Maxiell .12 .30
19 Al Thornton .15 .40
20 Ray Allen .20 .50
21 Tim Duncan .30 .75
22 Michael Redd .15 .40
23 LeBron James .75 2.00
24 Kobe Bryant .75 2.00
25 Al Jefferson .15 .40
26 Raymond Felton .15 .40
27 LaMarcus Aldridge .20 .50
28 Jose Calderon .12 .30
29 Andris Biedrins .12 .30
30 Rasheed Wallace .20 .50
31 Shawn Marion .15 .40
32 Shaquille O'Neal .40 1.00
33 Mike Miller .15 .40
34 Paul Pierce .20 .50
35 Brad Miller .15 .40
36 Richard Jefferson .15 .40
37 DeShawn Stevenson .12 .30
38 Zach Randolph .15 .40
39 Daniel Gibson .15 .40
40 Nazr Mohammed .12 .30
41 Dirk Nowitzki .25 .60
42 Elton Brand .20 .50
43 Linas Kleiza .12 .30
44 Andrea Bargnani .15 .40
45 Josh Smith .15 .40
46 Luol Deng .15 .40
47 Andrei Kirilenko .15 .40
48 Danny Granger .15 .40
49 Rashad McCants .12 .30
50 Emeka Okafor .15 .40
51 Kyle Korver .15 .40
52 Jamario Moon .12 .30
53 Nick Young .15 .40
54 Rashard Lewis .15 .40
55 Jason Kidd .20 .50
56 Josh Howard .15 .40
57 Desmond Mason .12 .30
58 Andre Miller .15 .40
59 Rafer Alston .12 .30
60 Baron Davis .15 .40
61 Zydrunas Ilgauskas .15 .40
62 Marvin Williams .15 .40
63 Manu Ginobili .20 .50
64 David West .15 .40
65 Rajon Rondo .20 .50
66 Kenyon Martin .15 .40
67 Josh Boone .12 .30
68 Travis Outlaw .15 .40
69 Andre Iguodala .15 .40
70 Yi Jianlian .20 .50
71 Jordan Farmar .12 .30
72 Udonis Haslem .12 .30
73 Caron Butler .15 .40
74 Craig Smith .12 .30
75 Tayshaun Prince .15 .40
76 Rudy Gay .20 .50
77 Jermaine O'Neal .15 .40
78 Devin Harris .12 .30
79 Fabricio Oberto .12 .30
80 Hedo Turkoglu .15 .40
81 Jannero Pargo .12 .30
82 Corey Maggette .15 .40
83 Ricky Davis .15 .40
84 Grant Hill .25 .60
85 Josh Childress .15 .40
86 Jeff Green .15 .40
87 Lamar Odom .15 .40
88 Brandan Wright .15 .40
89 Sean Williams .15 .40
90 Drew Gooden .15 .40
91 Amare Stoudemire .15 .40
92 Charlie Villanueva .12 .30
93 Ron Artest .20 .50
94 Derek Fisher .15 .40
95 Willie Green .12 .30
96 Kirk Hinrich .15 .40
97 Jameer Nelson .12 .30
98 Al Harrington .15 .40
99 Ronnie Brewer .15 .40
100 Dwyane Wade .30 .75
101 Jamal Crawford .20 .50
102 Ryan Gomes .12 .30
103 Marcus Camby .12 .30
104 Antawn Jamison .15 .40
105 Cuttino Mobley .12 .30
106 Tyson Chandler .15 .40
107 Al Horford .20 .50
108 Chris Wilcox .12 .30
109 Gerald Wallace .15 .40
110 Andrew Bynum .12 .30
111 Tracy McGrady .20 .50
112 Mo Williams .15 .40
113 Nate Robinson .12 .30
114 Wally Szczerbiak .15 .40
115 Vince Carter .25 .60
116 T.J. Ford .12 .30
117 Kevin Martin .15 .40
118 Steve Blake .12 .30
119 Anderson Varejao .12 .30
120 Mike Conley Jr. .15 .40
121 Chris Kaman .15 .40
122 Louis Williams .15 .40
123 Jason Richardson .20 .50
124 John Salmons .15 .40
125 Martell Webster .15 .40
126 Juan Carlos Navarro .15 .40
127 Raja Bell .15 .40
128 Jason Terry .15 .40
129 Corey Brewer .15 .40
130 Bruce Bowen .12 .30
131 Glen Davis .12 .30
132 Richard Hamilton .15 .40
133 Ben Wallace .15 .40
134 Chris Bosh .20 .50
135 Beno Udrih .12 .30
136 Jarrett Jack .15 .40
137 Stephen Jackson .15 .40
138 Damien Wilkins .12 .30
139 Jamaal Tinsley .12 .30
140 Deron Williams .15 .40
141 Andres Nocioni .12 .30
142 David Lee .12 .30
143 Rodney Stuckey .15 .40
144 Luke Walton .12 .30
145 Jerry Stackhouse .15 .40
146 Samuel Dalembert .12 .30
147 Brandon Roy .20 .50
148 Chauncey Billups .20 .50
149 Michael Finley .20 .50
150 Leandro Barbosa .15 .40
151 Keith Bogans .12 .30
152 Mike Bibby .15 .40
153 Troy Murphy .12 .30
154 Eddy Curry .12 .30

155 Anthony Parker .12 .30
156 Kevin Durant .50 1.25
157 Larry Hughes .15 .40
158 Peja Stojakovic .20 .50
159 Shane Battier .15 .40
160 Kendrick Perkins .12 .30
161 Mehmet Okur .12 .30
162 Brendan Haywood .12 .30
163 Monta Ellis .15 .40
164 J.R. Smith .15 .40
165 Greg Oden .15 .40
166 John Stockton .30 .75
167 Tim Hardaway .20 .50
168 Dennis Rodman .40 1.00
169 Dominique Wilkins .25 .60
170 David Thompson .15 .40
171 Spencer Haywood .12 .30
172 Larry Bird .50 1.25
173 Isiah Thomas .20 .50
174 Magic Johnson .50 1.25
175 Bill Russell .30 .75
176 Moses Malone .20 .50
177 Sidney Moncrief .12 .30
178 George Gervin .25 .60
179 David Robinson .30 .75
180 Jerry West .25 .60
181 Rick Barry .15 .40
182 Sam Perkins .12 .30
183 Lenny Wilkens .20 .50
184 Jo Jo White .15 .40
185 Elgin Baylor .20 .50
186 Micheal Ray Richardson .15 .40
187 Otis Birdsong .15 .40
188 Derrick Coleman .20 .50
189 Mark Eaton .12 .30
190 Pete Maravich .30 .75
191 Wilt Chamberlain .40 1.00
192 Alex English .15 .40
193 Patrick Ewing .25 .60
194 Julius Erving .30 .75
195 Hakeem Olajuwon .25 .60
196 Derrick Rose RC 2.50 6.00
197 Michael Beasley RC .60 1.50
198 O.J. Mayo RC .60 1.50
199 Russell Westbrook RC 12.00 30.00
200 Kevin Love RC 2.00 5.00
201 Danilo Gallinari RC 1.00 2.50
202 Eric Gordon RC 1.00 2.50
203 Joe Alexander RC .40 1.00
204 D.J. Augustin RC .50 1.25
205 Brook Lopez RC .75 2.00
206 Jerryd Bayless RC .50 1.25
207 Jason Thompson RC .40 1.00
208 Brandon Rush RC .50 1.25
209 Anthony Randolph RC .50 1.25
210 Robin Lopez RC .60 1.50
211 Marreese Speights RC .50 1.25
212 Roy Hibbert RC .60 1.50
213 George Hill RC .60 1.50
214 J.J. Hickson RC .50 1.25
215 Alexis Ajinca RC .40 1.00
216 Ryan Anderson RC .50 1.25
217 Courtney Lee RC .50 1.25
218 Kosta Koufos RC .50 1.25
219 Darrell Arthur RC .50 1.25
220 Donte Greene RC .40 1.00
BO Barack Obama 20.00 50.00
JM John McCain 6.00 15.00

2008-09 Topps Black
*1-195 BLACK: 6X TO 15X BASE HI
*196-220 RC BLACK: 3X TO 8X BASE HI
PRINT RUN 51 SER.#'d SETS
199 Russell Westbrook 150.00 400.00

2008-09 Topps Gold Border
*GOLD BORDER: 1.25X TO 3X BASE HI
1-195 GOLD STATED ODDS 1:7
196-220 GOLD STATED ODDS 1:44

2008-09 Topps Gold Foil
*STARS: .75X TO 2X BASE HI
*RCs: .6X TO 1.5X BASE HI
1-195 GOLD FOIL ODDS 1:2
196-220 GOLD FOIL ODDS 1:11

2008-09 Topps Orange
*ORANGE: 1.25X TO 3X BASE HI
ORANGE PRINT RUN 1199 SETS

2008-09 Topps 1958-59 Variations
STATED ODDS 1:2
*GOLD: 1.25X TO 3X BASE HI
GOLD PRINT RUN 50 SER.#'d SETS
1 Chris Paul 1.00 2.50
5 Kevin Garnett 1.25 3.00
8 Carlos Boozer .60 1.50
10 Gilbert Arenas .60 1.50
12 Dwight Howard .60 1.50
15 Carmelo Anthony 1.00 2.50
23 LeBron James 3.00 8.00
24 Kobe Bryant 3.00 8.00
60 Baron Davis .60 1.50
100 Dwyane Wade 1.25 3.00
147 Brandon Roy .75 2.00
166 John Stockton 1.25 3.00
170 David Thompson .60 1.50
172 Larry Bird 2.00 5.00
173 Isiah Thomas .75 2.00
174 Magic Johnson 2.00 5.00
175 Bill Russell 1.25 3.00
179 David Robinson 1.25 3.00
180 Jerry West 1.00 2.50
183 Lenny Wilkens .75 2.00
196 Derrick Rose 3.00 8.00
197 Michael Beasley .75 2.00
198 O.J. Mayo .75 2.00
199 Russell Westbrook 8.00 20.00
200 Kevin Love 2.50 6.00
201 Danilo Gallinari 1.25 3.00
202 Eric Gordon 1.25 3.00
203 Joe Alexander .50 1.25
204 D.J. Augustin .60 1.50
205 Brook Lopez 1.00 2.50

2008-09 Topps 1958-59 Variations Autographs
GROUP A ODDS 1:3422; B ODDS 1:1665
GROUP C ODDS 1:846; D ODDS 1:1118
GROUP E ODDS 1:850; F ODDS 1:398
*GOLD: .5X TO 1.25X BASE HI
GOLD PRINT RUN 25 SER.#'d SETS
1 Chris Paul A 15.00 40.00
8 Carlos Boozer C 5.00 12.00
10 Gilbert Arenas C 8.00 20.00
12 Dwight Howard B 8.00 20.00
39 Daniel Gibson D 5.00 12.00
60 Baron Davis C 6.00 15.00
65 Rajon Rondo E 15.00 40.00
100 Dwyane Wade A 25.00 60.00
102 Ryan Gomes E 5.00 12.00
112 Mo Williams D 5.00 12.00
165 Greg Oden A 15.00 40.00
167 Tim Hardaway F 6.00 15.00
170 David Thompson F 5.00 12.00
171 Spencer Haywood B 6.00 15.00
172 Larry Bird A 40.00 100.00
174 Magic Johnson A 30.00 80.00
177 Sidney Moncrief F 5.00 12.00
182 Sam Perkins B 5.00 12.00
183 Lenny Wilkens B 8.00 20.00
184 Jo Jo White B 8.00 20.00
185 Elgin Baylor C 10.00 25.00
186 Micheal Ray Richardson B 5.00 12.00
187 Otis Birdsong B 5.00 12.00
188 Derrick Coleman F 5.00 12.00
189 Mark Eaton B 5.00 12.00

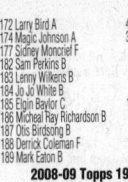

2008-09 Topps 1958-59 Variations Relics

GROUP A ODDS 1:5197; B ODDS 1:437
GROUP C ODDS 1:60
*GOLD: .6X TO 1.5X BASE HI
GOLD PRINT RUN 50 SER.#'d SETS
1 Chris Paul C 3.00 8.00
5 Kevin Garnett C 4.00 10.00
8 Carlos Boozer C 2.00 5.00
10 Gilbert Arenas B 2.00 5.00
12 Dwight Howard C 2.00 5.00
15 Carmelo Anthony C 3.00 8.00
24 Kobe Bryant C 6.00 15.00
39 Daniel Gibson C 2.00 5.00
60 Baron Davis C 2.00 5.00
65 Rajon Rondo C 2.50 6.00
100 Dwyane Wade C 4.00 10.00
102 Ryan Gomes C 2.00 5.00
112 Mo Williams C 2.00 5.00
147 Brandon Roy C 2.50 6.00
165 Greg Oden C 2.00 5.00
166 John Stockton C 4.00 10.00
170 David Thompson B 2.00 5.00
172 Larry Bird B 6.00 15.00
173 Isiah Thomas B 3.00 8.00
174 Magic Johnson C 6.00 15.00
175 Bill Russell A 8.00 20.00
178 George Gervin C 3.00 8.00
179 David Robinson C 4.00 10.00
180 Jerry West A 8.00 20.00
184 Jo Jo White B

2008-09 Topps In the Genes
STATED ODDS 1:9
*GOLD: .75X TO 2X BASE HI
GOLD PRINT RUN 50 SER.#'d SETS
IG1 K.Bryant/J.Bryant 2.50 6.00
IG2 C.Karl/G.Karl 1.50 4.00
IG3 K.Love/S.Love 2.00 5.00
IG4 M.Dunleavy Jr./M.Dunleavy Sr. 1.50 4.00
IG5 S.May/S.May 1.50 4.00
IG6 B.Barry/R.Barry 1.50 4.00
IG7 M.Bibby/H.Bibby 1.50 4.00
IG8 D.Wilkins/D.Wilkins 1.50 4.00
IG9 L.Walton/B.Walton 2.00 5.00
IG10 T.Green/S.Green 1.50 4.00

2008-09 Topps McDonald's All American Autographs
STATED ODDS 1:5908
B13 Darrell Arthur 10.00 25.00
B14 D.J. Augustin 10.00 25.00
B22 Brook Lopez 15.00 40.00
B23 Robin Lopez 12.00 30.00
DG Donte Greene 8.00 20.00
DR Derrick Rose 350.00 700.00
EG Eric Gordon 50.00 125.00
JB Jerryd Bayless 10.00 25.00
JJH J.J. Hickson 10.00 25.00
KK Kosta Koufos 10.00 25.00
KL Kevin Love 125.00 250.00
MB Michael Beasley 40.00 100.00
OJM O.J. Mayo 40.00 100.00

2008-09 Topps Mini Exclusives
MINIS INSERTED IN RIP CARDS
MEAI Allen Iverson 1.25 3.00
MEAJ Al Jefferson .75 2.00
MEBG Ben Gordon .75 2.00
MEBR Brandon Roy 1.00 2.50
MECA Carmelo Anthony 1.25 3.00
MECB Carlos Boozer .75 2.00
MECBI Chauncey Billups 1.00 2.50
MECM Corey Maggette .75 2.00
MECP Chris Paul 1.25 3.00
MEDH Dwight Howard .75 2.00
MEDL David Lee .60 1.50
MEDN Dirk Nowitzki 1.25 3.00
MEDR Dennis Rodman 2.00 5.00
MEDW Dwyane Wade 1.50 4.00
MEGA Gilbert Arenas .75 2.00
MEGO Greg Oden .75 2.00
MEJR Jason Richardson .60 1.50
MEJW Jerry West 1.25 3.00
MEKB Kobe Bryant 4.00 10.00
MELB Larry Bird 2.50 6.00
MELJ LeBron James 4.00 10.00
MEMJ Magic Johnson 2.50 6.00
MEMR Michael Redd .75 2.00
MENY Nick Young .75 2.00
MERA Ray Allen 1.00 2.50
MESN Steve Nash 1.00 2.50
MESO Shaquille O'Neal 2.00 5.00
METP Tony Parker 1.00 2.50
MEYJ Yi Jianlian 1.00 2.50
MEYM Yao Ming 1.25 3.00

2008-09 Topps Mini Exclusives Autographs
RANDOM INSERTS IN PACKS
MEACP Chris Paul 25.00 50.00

2008-09 Topps Own the Game
COMPLETE SET (20) 8.00 20.00
STATED ODDS 1:5
*GOLD: .75X TO 2X BASE HI
GOLD PRINT RUN 50 SER.#'d SETS
OTG1 Andris Biedrins .50 1.25
OTG2 Tyson Chandler .60 1.50
OTG3 Peja Stojakovic .75 2.00
OTG4 Chauncey Billups .75 2.00
OTG5 Jason Kapono .50 1.25
OTG6 Steve Nash .75 2.00
OTG7 Dwight Howard .60 1.50
OTG8 Marcus Camby .50 1.25
OTG9 Chris Paul 1.00 2.50
OTG10 Steve Nash 1.00 2.50
OTG11 Chris Paul 1.00 2.50
OTG12 Baron Davis .60 1.50
OTG13 Marcus Camby .50 1.25
OTG14 Josh Smith .60 1.50
OTG15 LeBron James 3.00 8.00
OTG16 Kobe Bryant 3.00 8.00
OTG17 Dwight Howard .60 1.50
OTG18 Chris Paul 1.00 2.50
OTG19 Allen Iverson 1.00 2.50
OTG20 Joe Johnson .60 1.50

2008-09 Topps Own the Game Relics
ATED ODDS 1:134
*GOLD: .5X TO 1.25X BASE HI
GOLD PRINT RUN 50 SER.#'d SETS
OTGR1 Andris Biedrins 2.00 5.00
OTGR2 Peja Stojakovic 2.50 6.00
OTGR3 Jason Kapono 2.00 5.00
OTGR4 Dwight Howard 2.00 5.00
OTGR5 Chris Paul 3.00 8.00
OTGR6 Baron Davis 2.00 5.00
OTGR7 Marcus Camby 2.00 5.00
OTGR8 Kobe Bryant 6.00 15.00
OTGR9 Dwight Howard 2.00 5.00
OTGR10 Allen Iverson 3.00 8.00

2008-09 Topps Retail Relics
RANDOM INSERTS IN RETAIL PACKS
TBKR1 Daequan Cook 2.00 5.00
TBKR2 Andrea Bargnani 2.00 5.00
TBKR3 LaMarcus Aldridge 2.50 6.00
TBKR4 Andrew Bynum 1.50 4.00
TBKR5 Caron Butler 2.00 5.00
TBKR6 Chris Bosh 2.50 6.00
TBKR7 Corey Brewer 2.00 5.00
TBKR8 Corey Maggette 2.00 5.00
TBKR9 Rashad McCants 2.00 5.00
TBKR10 Zach Randolph 2.00 5.00
TBKR11 Martell Webster 2.00 5.00
TBKR12 Dwight Howard 2.00 5.00
TBKR13 Eddy Curry 2.00 5.00
TBKR14 Gilbert Arenas 2.00 5.00
TBKR15 Greg Oden 2.00 5.00
TBKR16 Jamal Crawford 2.50 6.00
TBKR17 Ronnie Brewer 2.00 5.00
TBKR18 Juan Carlos Navarro 2.00 5.00
TBKR19 Joe Johnson 2.00 5.00
TBKR20 Brandan Wright 2.00 5.00
TBKR21 Kirk Hinrich 2.00 5.00
TBKR22 Lamar Odom 2.00 5.00
TBKR23 Mehmet Okur 2.00 5.00
TBKR24 Glen Davis 1.50 4.00
TBKR25 Monta Ellis 2.00 5.00
TBKR26 Paul Pierce 2.50 6.00
TBKR27 Peja Stojakovic 2.50 6.00
TBKR28 Yao Ming 3.00 8.00
TBKR29 Richard Hamilton 2.00 5.00
TBKR30 Ron Artest 2.50 6.00
TBKR31 Shawn Marion 2.00 5.00
TBKR32 Jarrett Jack 2.00 5.00
TBKR33 Tim Duncan 4.00 10.00
TBKR34 Vince Carter 3.00 8.00
TBKR35 Yi Jianlian 2.50 6.00

2008-09 Topps Rip Cards 99
PRINT RUN 99 SER.#'d SETS
*RIP 25: .5X TO 1.25X BASE HI
RIP 10 UNPRICED DUE TO SCARCITY
1 Chris Paul 6.00 15.00
2 Allen Iverson 6.00 15.00
3 Tony Parker 6.00 15.00
4 LeBron James 15.00 40.00
5 Kobe Bryant 10.00 25.00
6 Shaquille O'Neal 10.00 25.00
7 Larry Bird 15.00 40.00
8 Magic Johnson 10.00 25.00
9 Carlos Boozer 4.00 10.00
10 Jason Kidd 10.00 25.00
11 Chauncey Billups 5.00 12.00
12 Jason Richardson 5.00 12.00
13 Corey Maggette 4.00 10.00
14 David Lee 5.00 12.00
15 Dwyane Wade 8.00 20.00
16 Greg Oden 4.00 10.00
17 Yi Jianlian 5.00 12.00
18 Nick Young 5.00 12.00
19 Dennis Rodman 6.00 15.00
20 Ray Allen 6.00 15.00
21 Steve Nash 6.00 15.00
23 Michael Redd 5.00 12.00
24 Jerry West 6.00 15.00
25 Gilbert Arenas 6.00 15.00
26 Dwight Howard 6.00 15.00
27 Yao Ming 6.00 15.00
28 Carmelo Anthony 6.00 15.00
29 Ben Gordon 4.00 10.00
30 Dirk Nowitzki 6.00 15.00

2008-09 Topps Rookie Medallions
PRINT RUN 15 SER.#'d SETS
14KAR Anthony Randolph 12.00 30.00
14KBL Brook Lopez 25.00 60.00
14KBR Brandon Rush 15.00 40.00
14KDA Darrell Arthur 15.00 40.00
14KDG Danilo Gallinari 30.00 80.00
14KDJA D.J. Augustin 15.00 40.00
14KDR Derrick Rose 80.00 200.00
14KEG Eric Gordon 30.00 80.00
14KJA Joe Alexander 12.00 30.00
14KJB Jerryd Bayless 15.00 40.00
14KKL Kevin Love 60.00 150.00
14KMB Michael Beasley 20.00 50.00
14KOJM O.J. Mayo 20.00 50.00
14KRL Robin Lopez 20.00 50.00
14KRW Russell Westbrook 150.00 400.00

2008-09 Topps Rookie Photo Shoot Autographs
STATED ODDS 1:240 PACKS
*RED INK: .5X TO 1.25X BASE HI
RED INK STATED ODDS 1:243 PACKS
RPAR Anthony Randolph 4.00 10.00
RPBL Brook Lopez 6.00 15.00
RPBR Brandon Rush 5.00 12.00
RPCDR Chris Douglas-Roberts 4.00 10.00
RPCL Courtney Lee 5.00 12.00
RPDA Darrell Arthur 5.00 12.00
RPDG Donte Greene 4.00 10.00
RPDJ DeAndre Jordan 12.00 30.00
RPDJA D.J. Augustin 5.00 12.00
RPDJW D.J. White 5.00 12.00
RPDR Derrick Rose 125.00 250.00
RPEG Eric Gordon 15.00 40.00
RPGH George Hill 6.00 15.00
RPJA Joe Alexander 4.00 10.00
RPJB Jerryd Bayless 5.00 12.00
RPJD Joey Dorsey 4.00 10.00
RPJJH J.J. Hickson 5.00 12.00
RPJM JaVale McGee 6.00 15.00
RPJRG J.R. Giddens 4.00 10.00
RPJT Jason Thompson 4.00 10.00
RPKK Kosta Koufos 5.00 12.00
RPKL Kevin Love 40.00 100.00
RPKW Kyle Weaver 4.00 10.00
RPMB Michael Beasley 12.00 30.00
RPMC Mario Chalmers 6.00 15.00
RPMS Marreese Speights 6.00 15.00
RPOJM O.J. Mayo 15.00 40.00
RPPE Patrick Ewing Jr. 4.00 10.00
RPRA Ryan Anderson 5.00 12.00
RPRH Roy Hibbert 12.00 30.00
RPRL Robin Lopez 6.00 15.00
RPRW Russell Westbrook 50.00 125.00
RPSW Sonny Weems 4.00 10.00
RPWS Walter Sharpe 4.00 10.00

2008-09 Topps Rookie Photo Shoot Autographs Dual
STATED ODDS 1:1461
RPDAA R.Anderson/J.Alexander 12.00 30.00
RPDBL M.Beasley/K.Love 30.00 80.00
RPDGA E.Gordon/D.Augustin 12.00 30.00
RPDGB E.Gordon/J.Bayless 12.00 30.00
RPDGW E.Gordon/D.White 12.00 30.00
RPDHK J.Hickson/K.Koufos 12.00 30.00
RPDLL B.Lopez/R.Lopez 12.00 30.00
RPDMB O.Mayo/M.Beasley 15.00 40.00
RPDML O.Mayo/K.Love 30.00 80.00
RPDRB D.Rose/M.Beasley 60.00 150.00
RPDRC B.Rush/M.Chalmers 15.00 40.00
RPDRL D.Rose/K.Love 200.00 350.00
RPDRM D.Rose/O.Mayo 60.00 150.00
RPDTR J.Thompson/A.Randolph 12.00 30.00
RPDWB R.Westbrook/J.Bayless 50.00 125.00

2008-09 Topps Rookie Photo Shoot Autographs Dual Red
*RED: .5X TO 1.25X HI COLUMN
OVERALL STATED ODDS 1:243
SOME UNPRICED DUE TO SCARCITY
RPDRL D.Rose/K.Love 200.00 350.00

2008-09 Topps Rookie Photo Shoot Autographs Triple
STATED ODDS 1:5908
RPTABS Alexander/Love/Speights 25.00 60.00
RPTBLR Beasley/Love/Rose 100.00 200.00
RPTDRD Dorsey/Rose/D-Roberts 60.00 150.00
RPTGBW Grdn/Bayls/Wstbrk 30.00 80.00
RPTLKL Lopez/Koufos/Lopez 10.00 25.00
RPTMBA Mayo/Bayless/Augustin 10.00 25.00
RPTRAC Rush/Arthur/Chalmers 10.00 25.00
RPTRBM Rose/Beasley/Mayo 125.00 250.00

2008-09 Topps Rookie Photo Shoot Autographs Triple Red
*RED: .4X TO 1X HI COLUMN
OVERALL STATED ODDS 1:5908
SOME UNPRICED DUE TO SCARCITY

2009-10 Topps
MPLETE SET (330) 250.00 400.00
COMP SET w/o RCs (315) 12.00 30.00
UNPRICED TAGS PRINT RUN ONE SET
UNPRICED LOGOMEN PRINT RUN ONE SET
UNPRICED PRESS PLATE PRINT RUN ONE SET
1 Joe Johnson .15 .40
2 Josh Smith .15 .40
3 Mike Bibby .15 .40
4 Marvin Williams .15 .40
5 Al Horford .20 .50
6 Ronald Murray .12 .30
7 Zaza Pachulia .12 .30
8 Acie Law .12 .30
9 Solomon Jones .12 .30
10 Maurice Evans .12 .30
11 Mario West .12 .30
12 Paul Pierce .20 .50
13 Ray Allen .20 .50
14 Kevin Garnett .30 .75
15 Rajon Rondo .20 .50
16 Eddie House .12 .30
17 Kendrick Perkins .12 .30
18 Tony Allen .12 .30
19 Leon Powe .12 .30
20 Glen Davis .12 .30
21 Brian Scalabrine .12 .30
22 Stephon Marbury .15 .40
23 Gerald Wallace .15 .40
24 Boris Diaw .12 .30
25 Emeka Okafor .15 .40
26 Raymond Felton .15 .40
27 Raja Bell .12 .30
28 D.J. Augustin .15 .40
29 Vladimir Radmanovic .12 .30
30 Sean Singletary .12 .30
31 DeSagana Diop .12 .30
32 Ben Gordon .15 .40
33 Derrick Rose .30 .75
34 Luol Deng .15 .40
35 John Salmons .15 .40
36 Tim Thomas .12 .30
37 Brad Miller .15 .40
38 Kirk Hinrich .15 .40
39 Tyrus Thomas .12 .30
40 Joakim Noah .15 .40
41 Aaron Gray .12 .30
42 LeBron James .75 2.00
43 Mo Williams .15 .40
44 Zydrunas Ilgauskas .15 .40
45 Delonte West .12 .30
46 Anderson Varejao .12 .30
47 Daniel Gibson .12 .30
48 Ben Wallace .15 .40
49 J.J. Hickson .15 .40
50 Wally Szczerbiak .12 .30
51 Aleksandar Pavlovic .12 .30
52 Dirk Nowitzki .25 .60
53 Jason Terry .15 .40
54 Josh Howard .15 .40
55 Jason Kidd .20 .50
56 Brandon Bass .12 .30
57 Jose Barea .25 .60
58 Antoine Wright .12 .30
59 Gerald Green .12 .30
60 Erick Dampier .12 .30
61 Devean George .12 .30
62 Carmelo Anthony .25 .60
63 Chauncey Billups .20 .50
64 Nene .12 .30
65 J.R. Smith .15 .40
66 Kenyon Martin .15 .40
67 Linas Kleiza .12 .30
68 Dahntay Jones .12 .30
69 Chris Andersen .12 .30
70 Renaldo Balkman .12 .30
71 Anthony Carter .12 .30
72 Allen Iverson .25 .60
73 Richard Hamilton .15 .40
74 Tayshaun Prince .15 .40
75 Rodney Stuckey .12 .30
76 Rasheed Wallace .15 .40
77 Antonio McDyess .15 .40
78 Jason Maxiell .12 .30
79 Arron Afflalo .12 .30
80 Amir Johnson .12 .30
81 Walter Herrmann .12 .30
82 Stephen Jackson .12 .30
83 Corey Maggette .15 .40
84 Jamal Crawford .20 .50
85 Kelenna Azubuike .12 .30
86 Monta Ellis .15 .40
87 Andris Biedrins .15 .40
88 Marco Belinelli .12 .30
89 C.J. Watson .12 .30
90 Anthony Morrow .12 .30
91 Brandan Wright .12 .30
92 Anthony Randolph .15 .40
93 Yao Ming .25 .60
94 Ron Artest .20 .50
95 Tracy McGrady .20 .50
96 Luis Scola .15 .40
97 Von Wafer .12 .30
98 Aaron Brooks .12 .30
99 Carl Landry .12 .30
100 Shane Battier .15 .40
101 Kyle Lowry .12 .30
102 Chuck Hayes .12 .30
103 Danny Granger .15 .40
104 Mike Dunleavy .12 .30
105 T.J. Ford .12 .30
106 Marquis Daniels .12 .30
107 Troy Murphy .12 .30
108 Jarrett Jack .12 .30
109 Rasho Nesterovic .12 .30
110 Brandon Rush .12 .30
111 Roy Hibbert .15 .40
112 Jeff Foster .12 .30
113 Zach Randolph .15 .40
114 Al Thornton .15 .40
115 Baron Davis .15 .40
116 Eric Gordon .15 .40
117 Chris Kaman .12 .30
118 Marcus Camby .12 .30
119 Mardy Collins .12 .30
120 Ricky Davis .15 .40
121 DeAndre Jordan .20 .50
122 Steve Novak .12 .30
123 Kobe Bryant .75 2.00
124 Pau Gasol .20 .50
125 Andrew Bynum .15 .40
126 Derek Fisher .15 .40
127 Lamar Odom .15 .40
128 Trevor Ariza .12 .30
129 Jordan Farmar .12 .30
130 Adam Morrison .12 .30
131 Sasha Vujacic .12 .30
132 Luke Walton .12 .30
133 D.J. Mbenga .12 .30
134 O.J. Mayo .15 .40
135 Rudy Gay .20 .50
136 Hakim Warrick .12 .30
137 Marc Gasol .15 .40
138 Mike Conley Jr. .15 .40
139 Darko Milicic .12 .30
140 Darrell Arthur .12 .30
141 Hamed Haddadi .12 .30
142 Quinton Ross .12 .30
143 Dwyane Wade .30 .75
144 Michael Beasley .12 .30
145 Jermaine O'Neal .15 .40
146 Udonis Haslem .12 .30
147 Daequan Cook .12 .30
148 Mario Chalmers .12 .30
149 Chris Quinn .12 .30
150 Jamario Moon .12 .30
151 Joel Anthony RC .20 .50
152 Luther Head .12 .30
153 Michael Redd .15 .40
154 Richard Jefferson .15 .40
155 Charlie Villanueva .12 .30
156 Andrew Bogut .15 .40
157 Luke Ridnour .12 .30
158 Ramon Sessions .12 .30
159 Luc Mbah a Moute .12 .30
160 Joe Alexander .12 .30
161 Charlie Bell .12 .30
162 Keith Bogans .12 .30
163 Shelden Williams .12 .30
164 Al Jefferson .15 .40
165 Randy Foye .15 .40
166 Ryan Gomes .12 .30
167 Kevin Love .20 .50
168 Craig Smith .12 .30
169 Mike Miller .15 .40
170 Sebastian Telfair .12 .30
171 Corey Brewer .12 .30
172 Brian Cardinal .12 .30
173 Rodney Carney .12 .30
174 Devin Harris .15 .40
175 Vince Carter .25 .60
176 Brook Lopez .15 .40
177 Yi Jianlian .15 .40
178 Keyon Dooling .12 .30
179 Jarvis Hayes .12 .30
180 Bobby Simmons .12 .30
181 Ryan Anderson .12 .30
182 Josh Boone .12 .30
183 Chris Douglas-Roberts .12 .30
184 Sean Williams .12 .30
185 Chris Paul .25 .60
186 David West .15 .40
187 Peja Stojakovic .20 .50
188 Rasual Butler .12 .30
189 James Posey .12 .30
190 Tyson Chandler .12 .30
191 Devin Brown .12 .30
192 Morris Peterson .12 .30
193 Hilton Armstrong .12 .30
194 Julian Wright .12 .30
195 Antonio Daniels .12 .30
196 Chris Wilcox .12 .30
197 Al Harrington .15 .40
198 David Lee .15 .40
199 Nate Robinson .15 .40
200 Wilson Chandler .12 .30
201 Chris Duhon .12 .30
202 Quentin Richardson .15 .40
203 Larry Hughes .12 .30
204 Danilo Gallinari .15 .40
205 Jared Jeffries .12 .30
206 Russell Westbrook .50 1.25
207 Earl Watson .12 .30
208 Robert Swift .12 .30
209 Joe Smith .12 .30
210 Desmond Mason .12 .30
211 Kevin Durant .50 1.25
212 Jeff Green .15 .40
213 Nick Collison .12 .30
214 Thabo Sefolosha .12 .30
215 Damien Wilkins .12 .30
216 Rafer Alston .12 .30
217 Dwight Howard .25 .60
218 Rashard Lewis .15 .40
219 Hedo Turkoglu .15 .40
220 Jameer Nelson .15 .40
221 Mickael Pietrus .12 .30
222 Courtney Lee .15 .40
223 J.J. Redick .12 .30
224 Tyronn Lue .12 .30
225 Anthony Johnson .12 .30
226 Tony Battie .12 .30
227 Andre Iguodala .15 .40
228 Andre Miller .15 .40
229 Elton Brand .20 .50
230 Thaddeus Young .15 .40
231 Louis Williams .15 .40
232 Willie Green .12 .30
233 Marreese Speights .15 .40
234 Samuel Dalembert .12 .30
235 Reggie Evans .12 .30
236 Donyell Marshall .12 .30
237 Amare Stoudemire .15 .40
238 Shaquille O'Neal .40 1.00
239 Jason Richardson .20 .50
240 Steve Nash .20 .50
241 Leandro Barbosa .15 .40
242 Grant Hill .25 .60
243 Matt Barnes .12 .30
244 Alando Tucker .12 .30
245 Louis Amundson .12 .30
246 Robin Lopez .12 .30
247 Goran Dragic RC .40 1.00
248 Jared Dudley .12 .30
249 Brandon Roy .20 .50
250 LaMarcus Aldridge .20 .50
251 Travis Outlaw .15 .40
252 Steve Blake .12 .30
253 Rudy Fernandez .12 .30
254 Greg Oden .15 .40
255 Jerryd Bayless .15 .40
256 Joel Przybilla .12 .30
257 Nicolas Batum .15 .40
258 Sergio Rodriguez .12 .30
259 Martell Webster .12 .30
260 Channing Frye .15 .40
261 Kevin Martin .15 .40
262 Andres Nocioni .12 .30
263 Francisco Garcia .12 .30
264 Beno Udrih .12 .30
265 Jason Thompson .12 .30
266 Spencer Hawes .12 .30
267 Bobby Jackson .12 .30
268 Rashad McCants .12 .30
269 Donte Greene .12 .30
270 Quincy Douby .12 .30
271 Tony Parker .20 .50
272 Tim Duncan .30 .75
273 Manu Ginobili .20 .50
274 Roger Mason .12 .30
275 Michael Finley .20 .50
276 Matt Bonner .12 .30
277 George Hill .20 .50
278 Kurt Thomas .12 .30
279 Bruce Bowen .12 .30
280 Ime Udoka .12 .30
281 Drew Gooden .15 .40
282 Chris Bosh .20 .50
283 Andrea Bargnani .15 .40
284 Shawn Marion .15 .40
285 Jose Calderon .12 .30
286 Anthony Parker .12 .30
287 Jason Kapono .12 .30
288 Marcus Banks .12 .30
289 Joey Graham .12 .30
290 Roko Ukic .12 .30
291 Pops Mensah-Bonsu .12 .30
292 Kris Humphries .12 .30
293 Carlos Boozer .15 .40
294 Deron Williams .20 .50
295 Mehmet Okur .12 .30
296 Paul Millsap .15 .40
297 Ronnie Brewer .15 .40
298 Andrei Kirilenko .15 .40
299 C.J. Miles .12 .30
300 Ronnie Price .15 .40
301 Kyle Korver .15 .40
302 Kosta Koufos .15 .40
303 Matt Harpring .12 .30
304 Brevin Knight .12 .30
305 Antawn Jamison .15 .40
306 Caron Butler .15 .40
307 Nick Young .12 .30
308 Andray Blatche .12 .30
309 DeShawn Stevenson .12 .30
310 JaVale McGee .15 .40
311 Mike James .12 .30
312 Gilbert Arenas .15 .40
313 Juan Dixon .12 .30
314 Dominic McGuire .12 .30
315 Darius Songaila .12 .30
316 Blake Griffin RC 3.00 8.00
317 Ricky Rubio RC 1.25 3.00
318 Hasheem Thabeet RC .50 1.25
319 James Harden RC 12.00 30.00
320 DeMar DeRozan RC 5.00 12.00
321 Stephen Curry RC 60.00 150.00
322 Brandon Jennings RC .60 1.50
323 Jordan Hill RC .60 1.50
324 Earl Clark RC .60 1.50
325 Gerald Henderson RC .60 1.50
326 Jonny Flynn RC .60 1.50
327 Tyreke Evans RC .60 1.50
328 Tyler Hansbrough RC .60 1.50
329 Terrence Williams RC .60 1.50
330 Jrue Holiday RC 1.00 2.50

2009-10 Topps Black
*BLACK: 8X TO 20X BASE HI
*BLACK RC: 5X TO 12X BASE HI
PRINT RUN 50 SER.#'d SETS
42 LeBron James 150.00 250.00
206 Russell Westbrook 15.00 40.00
211 Kevin Durant 30.00 80.00
317 Ricky Rubio 20.00 50.00
319 James Harden 300.00 600.00
321 Stephen Curry 1000.00 2000.00

2009-10 Topps Gold
*1-309 GOLD: 2X TO 5X BASE HI
*310-330 GOLD: .75X TO 2X BASE HI
GOLD PRINT RUN 2009 SER.#'d SETS
321 Stephen Curry 125.00 300.00

2009-10 Topps All-Star Relics Dual
STATED PRINT RUN 199 SER.#'d SETS
*QUAD: .6X TO 1.5X BASE HI
QUAD PRINT RUN 100 SER.#'d SETS
ASDAI Allen Iverson 4.00 10.00
ASDAS Amare Stoudemire 2.50 6.00
ASDCB Chris Bosh 3.00 8.00
ASDDW Dwyane Wade 8.00 20.00
ASDGA Gilbert Arenas 2.50 6.00
ASDKB Kobe Bryant 10.00 25.00
ASDKG Kevin Garnett 5.00 12.00
ASDPG Pau Gasol 3.00 8.00
ASDPP Paul Pierce 3.00 8.00
ASDRH Richard Hamilton 2.00 5.00
ASDSM Shawn Marion 2.50 6.00
ASDSN Steve Nash 2.50 6.00
ASDSO Shaquille O'Neal 6.00 15.00
ASDTD Tim Duncan 5.00 12.00
ASDTM Tracy McGrady 3.00 8.00
ASDTP Tony Parker 3.00 8.00
ASDVC Vince Carter 4.00 10.00
ASDYM Yao Ming 4.00 10.00
ASDCBI Chauncey Billups 3.00 8.00

2009-10 Topps Autograph Relics
STATED PRINT RUN 299 SER.#'d SETS
TARAB Andrea Bargnani 6.00 15.00
TARBG Ben Gordon 6.00 15.00
TARBR Brandon Roy 6.00 15.00
TARCB Carlos Boozer 6.00 15.00
TARDG Danny Granger 6.00 15.00
TARGO Greg Oden 6.00 15.00
TARJB Jerryd Bayless 6.00 15.00
TARLW Luke Walton 6.00 15.00
TARNY Nick Young 6.00 15.00
TARRM Rashad McCants 6.00 15.00

2009-10 Topps Championship Materials
GROUP A ODDS 1:94, GROUP B ODDS 1:320
GROUP C ODDS 1:425, GROUP D ODDS 1:235
*PATCHES: .75X TO 2X BASE HI
PATCH PRINT RUN 50 SER.#'d SETS
CMAB Andrew Bynum A 2.00 5.00
CMBB Brent Barry A 2.50 6.00
CMBR Bill Russell D 8.00 20.00
CMBW Ben Wallace A 2.50 6.00
CMCD Clyde Drexler B 5.00 12.00
CMDR David Robinson A 6.00 15.00
CMDW Dwyane Wade C 5.00 12.00
CMEB Elgin Baylor C 4.00 10.00
CMIT Isiah Thomas D 4.00 10.00
CMJE Julius Erving B 6.00 15.00
CMJH John Havlicek C 5.00 12.00
CMKB Kobe Bryant D 8.00 20.00
CMKG Kevin Garnett D 5.00 12.00
CMMG Manu Ginobili D 3.00 8.00
CMMJ Magic Johnson D 6.00 15.00
CMMM Moses Malone B 4.00 10.00
CMPG Pau Gasol D 3.00 8.00
CMPP Paul Pierce A 3.00 8.00
CMRA Ray Allen D 3.00 8.00
CMRH Richard Hamilton C 2.50 6.00
CMRW Rasheed Wallace D 3.00 8.00
CMSC Sam Cassell A 2.50 6.00
CMSO Shaquille O'Neal A 6.00 15.00
CMSP Scottie Pippen D 8.00 20.00
CMTD Tim Duncan A 5.00 12.00
CMTP Tayshaun Prince A 2.50 6.00
CMBWA Bill Walton D 4.00 10.00
CMCBI Chauncey Billups 3.00 8.00
CMDRO Dennis Rodman C 8.00 20.00
CMTPA Tony Parker D 3.00 8.00

2009-10 Topps Draft Snapshot
COMPLETE SET (50) 15.00 40.00
STATED ODDS 1:6
DSN Nene .50 1.25
DSAH Allan Houston .50 1.25
DSAI Allen Iverson .75 2.00
DSAS Amare Stoudemire .50 1.25
DSBD Baron Davis .50 1.25
DSBG Ben Gordon .50 1.25
DSCA Carmelo Anthony .75 2.00
DSCB Caron Butler .50 1.25
DSCJ V.Carter/A.Jamison .75 2.00
DSCP Chris Paul .75 2.00
DSCW Chris Webber .60 1.50
DSDH Dwight Howard .50 1.25
DSDM Dikembe Mutombo .60 1.50
DSDR Derrick Rose 1.00 2.50
DSDW Dwyane Wade 1.00 2.50
DSEB Elton Brand .60 1.50
DSEO Emeka Okafor .50 1.25
DSGH Grant Hill .75 2.00
DSHO Hakeem Olajuwon .75 2.00
DSJJ Joe Johnson .50 1.25
DSJK Jason Kidd .60 1.50
DSJR Jason Richardson .60 1.50
DSJS Joe Smith .50 1.25
DSKA Kenny Anderson .50 1.25
DSKB Kobe Bryant 2.50 6.00
DSKD Kevin Durant 1.50 4.00
DSKG Kevin Garnett 1.00 2.50
DSLJ LeBron James 2.50 6.00
DSMC Marcus Camby .40 1.00
DSMF Michael Finley .60 1.50
DSMM Mike Miller .60 1.50
DSPE Patrick Ewing .75 2.00
DSPG Pau Gasol .60 1.50
DSPH Penny Hardaway 1.50 4.00
DSPP Paul Pierce .60 1.50
DSRA Ray Allen .60 1.50
DSRS Ralph Sampson .50 1.25
DSSN Steve Nash .60 1.50
DSSO Shaquille O'Neal 1.25 3.00
DSSP Scottie Pippen 1.25 3.00
DSTD Tim Duncan 1.00 2.50
DSTM Tracy McGrady .60 1.50
DSYM Yao Ming .75 2.00
DSCBO Chris Bosh .60 1.50
DSDHA Devin Harris .40 1.00
DSDMI Darko Milicic .40 1.00
DSDWI Deron Williams .50 1.25
DSJST Jerry Stackhouse .50 1.25
DSLJO Larry Johnson .60 1.50
DSTJF T.J. Ford .40 1.00

2009-10 Topps Franchise Fabrics Autographs
PRINT RUNS LISTED IN CHECKLIST
SOME UNPRICED DUE TO SCARCITY
FFBG Ben Gordon Number/149 8.00 20.00
FFCB Carlos Boozer Logo/41 8.00 20.00

2009-10 Topps McDonalds All-American Game Day Autographs
STATED ODDS 1:670
BG Blake Griffin 100.00 200.00
BJ Brandon Jennings 12.00 30.00
BM B.J. Mullens 8.00 20.00
CB Chase Budinger 10.00 25.00
DR DeMar DeRozan 25.00 60.00
EC Earl Clark 10.00 25.00
GH Gerald Henderson 10.00 25.00
JF Jonny Flynn 8.00 20.00
JH Jrue Holiday 15.00 40.00
JH James Harden 100.00 250.00
MC Mike Conley Jr. 20.00 50.00
TE Tyreke Evans 10.00 25.00
TL Ty Lawson 12.00 30.00
WE Wayne Ellington 12.00 30.00

2009-10 Topps Rookie Rewind Jumbo Jersey Autographs
STATED PRINT RUN 99 SER.#'d SETS
JJABL Brook Lopez 10.00 25.00
JJADG Donte Greene 8.00 20.00
JJAEG Eric Gordon 12.00 30.00
JJAGH George Hill 8.00 20.00
JJAKL Kevin Love 20.00 50.00
JJAMS Marreese Speights 10.00 25.00
JJARA Ryan Anderson 8.00 20.00
JJASW Sonny Weems 8.00 20.00

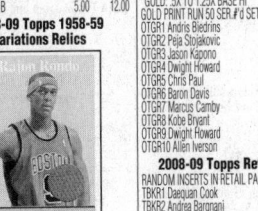

JJACDR Chris Douglas-Roberts 8.00 20.00
JJAJJH J.J. Hickson 8.00 20.00
JJAOJM O.J. Mayo 8.00 20.00

2009-10 Topps Roundball Remnants

GROUP A ODDS 1:65, GROUP B ODDS 1:33
GROUP C ODDS 1:166, GROUP D ODDS 1:955
*PATCHES: .75X TO 2X BASE HI
PATCH PRINT RUN 50 SER.#'d SETS
RRAA Arron Afflalo A 2.00 5.00
RRAB Aaron Brooks A 2.00 5.00
RRAG Aaron Gray B 2.00 5.00
RRAH Al Harrington B 2.50 6.00
RRAI Allen Iverson D 4.00 10.00
RRAJ Al Jefferson B 2.50 6.00
RRAK Andrei Kirilenko C 2.50 6.00
RRAL Acie Law A 2.00 5.00
RRAM Adam Morrison B 2.00 5.00
RRAS Amare Stoudemire D 2.50 6.00
RRAT Al Thornton B 2.50 6.00
RRAV Anderson Varejao D 2.00 5.00
RRBD Baron Davis C 2.50 6.00
RRBG Ben Gordon D 2.50 6.00
RRBM Brad Miller B 2.50 6.00
RRBR Brandon Roy D 3.00 8.00
RRBU Beno Udrih B 2.00 5.00
RRBW Brandan Wright A 2.00 5.00
RRCF Channing Frye B 2.50 6.00
RRCK Chris Kaman B 2.50 6.00
RRCL Carl Landry A 2.00 5.00
RRCM Corey Maggette D 2.50 6.00
RRCV Charlie Villanueva B 2.00 5.00
RRDC Daequan Cook B 2.00 5.00
RRDG Danny Granger B 2.50 6.00
RRDL David Lee B 2.00 5.00
RRDM Darko Milicic B 2.00 5.00
RRDW David West B 2.50 6.00
RRFG Francisco Garcia B 2.00 5.00
RRGD Glen Davis C 2.00 5.00
RRJC Jamal Crawford B 3.00 8.00
RRJH Josh Howard D 2.50 6.00
RRKM Kevin Martin B 2.50 6.00
RRLA LaMarcus Aldridge D 3.00 8.00
RRLB Leandro Barbosa B 2.50 6.00
RRLD Luol Deng B 2.50 6.00
RRMC Marcus Camby D 2.00 5.00
RRME Monta Ellis B 2.50 6.00
RRPG Pau Gasol D 3.00 8.00
RRRA Rafer Alston C 2.00 5.00
RRRB Ronnie Brewer B 2.50 6.00
RRRG Rudy Gay A 3.00 8.00
RRSB Shane Battier A 3.00 8.00
RRSD Samuel Dalembert C 2.00 5.00
RRSH Spencer Hawes C 2.00 5.00
RRTA Trevor Ariza B 2.00 5.00
RRTC Tyson Chandler B 2.50 6.00
RRTM Tracy McGrady C 3.00 8.00
RRUH Udonis Haslem A 2.00 5.00
RRVC Vince Carter C 4.00 10.00
RRWC Wilson Chandler B 2.50 6.00
RRYJ Yi Jianlian B 2.50 6.00
RRZI Zydrunas Ilgauskas B 2.50 6.00
RRABA Andrea Bargnani C 2.50 6.00
RRABI Andris Biedrins B 2.00 5.00
RRABO Andrew Bogut B 2.50 6.00
RRABY Andrew Bynum B 2.00 5.00
RRAIG Andre Iguodala C 2.50 6.00
RRAJA Antawn Jamison B 2.50 6.00
RRAMC Antonio McDyess B 2.50 6.00
RRAMI Andre Miller B 2.50 6.00
RRATU Alando Tucker A 2.00 5.00
RRBDI Boris Diaw B 2.50 6.00
RRCBH Chris Bosh C 3.00 8.00
RRCBO Carlos Boozer B 2.50 6.00
RRCBR Corey Brewer C 2.00 5.00
RRCBU Caron Butler B 2.50 6.00
RRMCO Mike Conley Jr. D 2.50 6.00
RRRAR Ron Artest C 3.00 8.00
RRTJF T.J. Ford D 2.00 5.00

2008 Topps All-Star Booklet Cards

CA Carmelo Anthony 4.00 10.00
CP Chris Paul 4.00 10.00
DW Dwyane Wade 6.00 15.00
GA Gilbert Arenas 3.00 8.00
YJ Yi Jianlian 3.00 8.00

2006 Topps Allen and Ginter

This 350-card set was release in August, 2006. The set was issued in seven-card hobby packs with an $4 SRP. Those packs came 24 to a box and there were 12 boxes in a case. In addition, there were also six-card retail packs issued and those packs came 24 packs to a box and 20 boxes to a case. There were some subsets included in this set including Rookies (251-265); Retired Greats (266-290); Managers (291-300); Modern Personalities (301-314); Reprinted Allen and Ginters (316-319); Famous People of the Past (326-349).`
COMPLETE SET (350) 60.00 120.00
COMP.SET w/o SP's (300) 15.00 40.00
SP STATED ODDS 1:2 HOBBY, 1:2 RETAIL
SP CL: 5/15/25/35/45/50-59/65/85/105/115
SP CL: 125/135/145/150-159/165/175/185
SP CL: 205/215/235/245/251/255-256/265
SP CL: 285/295/305/315/325/335/345
FRAMED ORIGINALS ODDS 1:3227 H, 1:3227 R
309 John Wooden .25 .60

2006 Topps Allen and Ginter Mini

*MINI 1-350: 1X TO 2.5X BASIC
*MINI 1-350: 1X TO 2.5X BASIC RC's
APPX.15 MINIS PER 24-CT SEALED BOX
*MINI SP 1-350: .6X TO 1.5X BASIC SP
*MINI SP 1-350: .6X TO 1.5X BASIC SP RC's
MINI SP ODDS 1:13 H, 1:13 R
COMMON CARD (351-375) 20.00 50.00
SEMISTARS 351-375 30.00 60.00
UNLISTED STARS 351-375 30.00 60.00
351-375 RANDOM WITHIN RIP CARDS
OVERALL PLATE ODDS 1:865 H, 1:865 R
PLATE PRINT RUN 1 SET PER COLOR
BLACK-CYAN-MAGENTA-YELLOW ISSUED
NO PLATE PRICING DUE TO SCARCITY

2006 Topps Allen and Ginter Mini A and G Back

*A & G BACK: 2X TO 5X BASIC
*A & G BACK: 1.5X TO 4X BASIC RC's
STATED ODDS 1:5 H, 1:5 R
*A & G BACK SP: 1X TO 2.5X BASIC SP
*A & G BACK SP: 1X TO 2.5X BASIC SP RC's
SP STATED ODDS 1:65 H, 1:65 R

2006 Topps Allen and Ginter Mini Black

*BLACK: 4X TO 10X BASIC
*BLACK: 2.5X TO 6X BASIC RC's
STATED ODDS 1:10 H, 1:10 R
*BLACK SP: 1.5X TO 4X BASIC SP
*BLACK SP: 1.5X TO 4X BASIC SP RC's
SP STATED ODDS 1:130 H, 1:130 R

2006 Topps Allen and Ginter Mini No Card Number

*NO NBR: 6X TO 15X BASIC
*NO NBR: 4X TO 10X BASIC RC's
*NO NBR: 2X TO 5X BASIC SP
*NO NBR: 2X TO 5X BASIC SP RC's
STATED ODDS 1:60 H, 1:168 R
STATED PRINT RUN 50 SETS
CARDS ARE NOT SERIAL-NUMBERED
PRINT RUN INFO PROVIDED BY TOPPS

2006 Topps Allen and Ginter Autographs

GROUP A ODDS 1:2467 H, 1:3850 R
GROUP B ODDS 1:14,500 H, 1:32,000 R
GROUP C ODDS 1:2200 H, 1:4300 R
GROUP D ODDS 1:548 H, 1:1090 R
GROUP E ODDS 1:473 H, 1:1000 R
GROUP F ODDS 1:250 H, 1:520 R
GROUP G ODDS 1:158 H, 1:299 R
GROUP A PRINT RUN 50 CARDS PER
GROUP A BONDS PRINT RUN 25 CARDS
GROUP B PRINT RUN 75 CARDS PER
GROUP C PRINT RUN 100 CARDS PER
GROUP D PRINT RUN 200 CARDS PER
GROUP A-D ARE NOT SERIAL-NUMBERED
A-D PRINT RUNS PROVIDED BY TOPPS
NO BONDS PRICING DUE TO SCARCITY
JW John Wooden D/200 * 125.00 250.00

2007 Topps Allen and Ginter

This 350-card set was released in August, 2007. The set was issued in both hobby and retail versions. The hobby packs, which had an $4 SRP, consisted of eight-cards which came 24 packs to a box and 12 boxes to a case. Similar to the 2006 set, many non-baseball players were interspersed throughout this set. There were also a group of short-printed cards, which were inserted at a stated rate of one in two hobby or retail packs. In addition, some original 19th century Allen and Ginter cards were repurchased for this product and those original cards (featuring both sports and non-sport subjects) were inserted at a stated rate of one in 17, 072 hobby and one in 34, 654 retail packs.
COMPLETE SET (350) 60.00 120.00
COMP.SET w/o SP's (300) 20.00 50.00
SP STATED ODDS 1:2 HOBBY, 1:2 RETAIL
SP CL: 5/43/48/58/63/107/110/119/130/137
SP CL: 152/159/178/193/194/203/219/222
SP CL: 224/243/263/301/302/303/306/307
SP CL: 308/309/310/316/317/318/319/320
SP CL: 321/322/325/326/327/330/331/334
SP CL: 335/336/339/340/345/348/349/350
FRAMED ORIGINALS ODDS 1:17,072 HOBBY
FRAMED ORIGINALS ODDS 1:34,654 RETAIL
331 Dennis Rodman SP 1.25 3.00
339 Jason McElwain SP 1.25 3.00

2007 Topps Allen and Ginter Mini

*MINI 1-350: 1X TO 2.5X BASIC
*MINI 1-350: .6X TO 1.5X BASIC RC's
APPX. ONE MINI PER PACK
*MINI SP 1-350: .6X TO 1.5X BASIC SP
*MINI SP 1-350: .6X TO 1.5X BASIC SP RC's
MINI SP ODDS 1:13 H, 1:13 R
COMMON CARD (351-390) 15.00 40.00
351-390 RANDOM WITHIN RIP CARDS
OVERALL PLATE ODDS 1:788 HOBBY
PLATE PRINT RUN 1 SET PER COLOR
BLACK-CYAN-MAGENTA-YELLOW ISSUED
NO PLATE PRICING DUE TO SCARCITY

2007 Topps Allen and Ginter Mini A and G Back

*A & G BACK: 1.25X TO 3X BASIC
*A & G BACK: .75X TO 2X BASIC RC's
STATED ODDS 1:5 H, 1:5 R
*A & G BACK SP: .75X TO 2X BASIC SP
*A & G BACK SP: .75X TO 2X BASIC SP RC's
SP STATED ODDS 1:65 H, 1:65 R

2007 Topps Allen and Ginter Mini Black

*BLACK: 2X TO 5X BASIC
*BLACK: 1.5X TO 4X BASIC RC's
STATED ODDS 1:10 H, 1:10 R
*BLACK SP: 1.5X TO 4X BASIC SP
*BLACK SP: 1.5X TO 4X BASIC SP RC's
SP STATED ODDS 1:130 H, 1:130 R

2007 Topps Allen and Ginter Mini Black No Number

*BLK NO NBR: 2.5X TO 6X BASIC
*BLK NO NBR: 2X TO 5X BASIC RC's
*BLK NO NBR: 1.5X TO 4X BASIC SP
*BLK NO NBR: 1.5X TO 4X BASIC SP RC's
RANDOM INSERTS IN PACKS

2007 Topps Allen and Ginter Mini No Card Number

*NO NBR: 10X TO 25X BASIC
*NO NBR: 6X TO 15X BASIC RC's
*NO NBR: 2.5X TO 6X BASIC SP
*NO NBR: 2.5X TO 6X BASIC SP RC's
STATED ODDS 1:106 H, 1:108 R
STATED PRINT RUN 50 SETS
CARDS ARE NOT SERIAL-NUMBERED
PRINT RUN INFO PROVIDED BY TOPPS

2007 Topps Allen and Ginter Autographs

GROUP A ODDS 1:64,496 H, 1:122200 R
GROUP B ODDS 1:3261 H, 1:6522 R
GROUP C ODDS 1:13,987 H, 1:27,642 R
GROUP D ODDS 1:288 H, 1:578 R
GROUP E ODDS 1:6789 H, 1:13,578 R
GROUP F ODDS 1:162 H, 1:324 R
GROUP G ODDS 1:680 H, 1:1362 R
GROUP A PRINT RUN 25 CARDS PER
GROUP B PRINT RUN 100 CARDS PER
GROUP C PRINT RUN 120 CARDS PER
GROUP D PRINT RUN 200 CARDS PER
GROUP A-D ARE NOT SERIAL-NUMBERED
A-D PRINT RUNS PROVIDED BY TOPPS
NO PUJOLS PRICING DUE TO SCARCITY
EXCH DEADLINE 7/31/2009
DR Dennis Rodman D/200 * 30.00 60.00
JMC Jason McElwain D/200 * 12.00 30.00

2007 Topps Allen and Ginter National Mini Promos

NCC7 Greg Oden 1.50 4.00

2007 Topps Allen and Ginter National Promos

NCC7 Greg Oden 1.50 4.00

2008 Topps Allen and Ginter

COMP.SET w/o FUKU.(350) 30.00 60.00
COMP.SET w/o SPs (300) 15.00 40.00
COMMON CARD (1-300) .15 .40
COMMON RC (1-300) .40 1.00
COMMON SP (301-350) 1.25 3.00
SP STATED ODDS 1:2 HOBBY
FRAMED ORIG.ODDS 1:26,500 HOBBY
247 Lisa Leslie .40 1.00

2008 Topps Allen and Ginter Mini

*MINI 1-300: .75X TO 2X BASIC
*MINI 1-300 RC: .5X TO 1.2X BASIC RC's
APPX. ONE MINI PER PACK
*MINI SP 300-350: .75X TO 2X BASIC SP
MINI SP ODDS 1:13 HOBBY
351-390 RANDOM WITHIN RIP CARDS
OVERALL PLATE ODDS 1:961 HOBBY
PLATE PRINT RUN 1 SET PER COLOR
BLACK-CYAN-MAGENTA-YELLOW ISSUED
NO PLATE PRICING DUE TO SCARCITY

2008 Topps Allen and Ginter Mini A and G Back

*A & G BACK: 1X TO 2.5X BASIC
*A & G BACK RCs: .6X TO 1.5X BASIC RCs
STATED ODDS 1:5 HOBBY
*A & G BACK SP: 1X TO 2.5X BASIC SP
SP STATED ODDS 1:65 HOBBY

2008 Topps Allen and Ginter Mini Black

*BLACK: 1.5X TO 4X BASIC
*BLACK RCs: .75X TO 2X BASIC RCs
STATED ODDS 1:10 HOBBY
*BLACK SP: 1.2X TO 3X BASIC SP
SP STATED ODDS 1:130 HOBBY

2008 Topps Allen and Ginter Mini No Card Number

*NO NBR: 10X TO 25X BASIC
*NO NBR RCs: 4X TO 10X BASIC RCs
*NO NBR: 1.5X TO 4X BASIC SP
STATED ODDS 1:151 HOBBY
STATED PRINT RUN 50 SETS
CARDS ARE NOT SERIAL-NUMBERED
PRINT RUN INFO PROVIDED BY TOPPS

2008 Topps Allen and Ginter Autographs

GROUP A ODDS 1:277 HOBBY
GROUP B ODDS 1:256 HOBBY
GROUP C ODDS 1:135 HOBBY
GRP A PRINT RUNS B/W 90-240 COPIES PER
CARDS ARE NOT SERIAL-NUMBERED
PRINT RUNS PROVIDED BY TOPPS
EXCHANGE DEADLINE 7/31/2010
LL Lisa Leslie A/190 * 12.50 30.00

2008 Topps Allen and Ginter Relics

GROUP A ODDS 1:280 HOBBY
GROUP B ODDS 1:71 HOBBY
GROUP C ODDS 1:20 HOBBY
RELIC AU ODDS 1:26,431 HOBBY
GROUP A B/W 100-250 COPIES PER
CARDS ARE NOT SERIAL NUMBERED
PRINT RUN INFO PROVIDED BY TOPPS
LL Lisa Leslie A/250 * 12.50 30.00

2009 Topps Allen and Ginter

COMPLETE SET (350) 30.00 60.00
COMP.SET w/o SP's (300) 12.50 30.00
COMMON CARD (1-300) .15 .40
COMMON RC (1-300) .40 1.00
COMMON SP (301-350) 1.25 3.00
SP STATED ODDS 1:2 HOBBY
346 Dominique Wilkins SP 1.25 3.00

2009 Topps Allen and Ginter Mini

COMP.SET w/o EXT (350) 125.00 250.00
*MINI 1-300: .75X TO 2X BASIC
*MINI 1-300 RC: .5X TO 1.2X BASIC RC's
APPX. ONE MINI PER PACK
*MINI SP 301-350: .5X TO 1.2X BASIC SP
MINI SP ODDS 1:13 HOBBY
351-390 RANDOM WITHIN RIP CARDS
OVERALL PLATE ODDS 1:608 HOBBY
PLATE PRINT RUN 1 SET PER COLOR
BLACK-CYAN-MAGENTA-YELLOW ISSUED
NO PLATE PRICING DUE TO SCARCITY

2009 Topps Allen and Ginter Mini A and G Back

*A & G BACK: 1X TO 2.5X BASIC
*A & G BACK RCs: .6X TO 1.5X BASIC RCs
STATED ODDS 1:5 HOBBY
*A & G BACK SP: .6X TO 1.5X BASIC SP
SP STATED ODDS 1:65 HOBBY

2009 Topps Allen and Ginter Mini Black

*BLACK: 2X TO 5X BASIC
*BLACK RCs: .75X TO 2X BASIC RCs
STATED ODDS 1:10 HOBBY
*BLACK SP: .75X TO 2X BASIC SP
SP STATED ODDS 1:130 HOBBY

2009 Topps Allen and Ginter Mini No Card Number

*NO NBR: 8X TO 20X BASIC
*NO NBR RCs: 3X TO 8X BASIC RCs
*NO NBR SP: 1.2X TO 3X BASIC SP
STATED ODDS 1:95 HOBBY
STATED PRINT RUN 50 SETS

2009 Topps Allen and Ginter Autographs

GROUP A ODDS 1:2730 HOBBY
GROUP B ODDS 1:51 HOBBY
CARDS ARE NOT SERIAL-NUMBERED
PRINT RUNS PROVIDED BY TOPPS
NO PHELPS PRICING DUE TO SCARCITY
EXCHANGE DEADLINE 6/30/2012
DOW D.Wilkins/239 * B 15.00 40.00

2009 Topps Allen and Ginter Relics

GROUP A ODDS 1:100 HOBBY
GROUP B ODDS 1:215 HOBBY
GROUP D ODDS 1:17 HOBBY
GROUP C ODDS 1:39 HOBBY
CARDS ARE NOT SERIAL-NUMBERED
PRINT RUNS PROVIDED BY TOPPS
DOW D.Wilkins/250 * A 10.00 25.00

2010 Topps Allen and Ginter

COMPLETE SET (350) 60.00 120.00
COMP.SET w/o SPs (300) 15.00 40.00
COMMON CARD (1-300) .15 .40
COMMON RC (1-300) .40 1.00
COMMON SP (301-350) 1.25 3.00
SP STATED ODDS 1:2 HOBBY
148 Anne Donovan .15 .40

2010 Topps Allen and Ginter Mini

*MINI 1-300: .75X TO 2X BASIC
*MINI 1-300 RC: .5X TO 1.2X BASIC RC's
APPX. ONE MINI PER PACK
*MINI SP 301-350: .5X TO 1.2X BASIC SP
MINI SP ODDS 1:13 HOBBY
COMMON CARD (351-400) 6.00 15.00
351-400 RANDOM WITHIN RIP CARDS
STRASBURG 401 ISSUED IN PACKS
OVERALL PLATE ODDS 1:799 HOBBY

2010 Topps Allen and Ginter Mini A and G Back

*A & G BACK: 1X TO 2.5X BASIC
*A & G BACK RCs: .6X TO 1.5X BASIC RCs
STATED ODDS 1:5 HOBBY
*A & G BACK SP: .6X TO 1.5X BASIC SP
SP STATED ODDS 1:65 HOBBY

2010 Topps Allen and Ginter Mini Black

*BLACK: 2X TO 5X BASIC
*BLACK RCs: .75X TO 2X BASIC RCs
STATED ODDS 1:10 HOBBY
*BLACK SP: .75X TO 2X BASIC SP
SP STATED ODDS 1:130 HOBBY

2010 Topps Allen and Ginter Mini No Card Number

*NO NBR: 8X TO 20X BASIC
*NO NBR RCs: 3X TO 8X BASIC RCs
*NO NBR SP: 1.2X TO 3X BASIC SP
STATED ODDS 1:140 HOBBY

2010 Topps Allen and Ginter Autographs

STATED ODDS 1:HOBBY
ASTERISK EQUALS PARTIAL EXCHANGE
AD Anne Donovan 6.00 15.00

2010 Topps Allen and Ginter Relics

STATED ODDS 1:11 HOBBY
AD Anne Donovan 5.00 12.00

2011 Topps Allen and Ginter

COMPLETE SET (350) 50.00 100.00
COMP.SET w/o SP's (300) 12.50 30.00
COMMON CARD (1-300) .15 .40
COMMON RC (1-300) .40 1.00
COMMON SP (301-350) 1.25 3.00
SP ODDS 1:2 HOBBY
15 Diana Taurasi .15 .40
133 Geno Auriemma .25 .60
136 Dick Vitale .15 .40
190 Sue Bird .15 .40

2011 Topps Allen and Ginter Glossy

ISSUED VIA TOPPS ONLINE STORE
STATED PRINT RUN 999 SER.#'d SETS
15 Diana Taurasi .75 2.00
133 Geno Auriemma 1.25 3.00
136 Dick Vitale .75 2.00
190 Sue Bird .75 2.00

2011 Topps Allen and Ginter Autographs

STATED ODDS 1:68 HOBBY
DUAL AUTO ODDS 1:56,000 HOBBY
EXCHANGE DEADLINE 6/30/2014
DTU Diana Taurasi 12.50 30.00
DVI Dick Vitale 10.00 25.00
GAU Geno Auriemma 12.50 30.00
SBI Sue Bird 20.00 50.00

2011 Topps Allen and Ginter Code Cards

*MINI 1-300: 1.5X TO 4X BASIC
*MINI 1-300 RC: .75X TO 2X BASIC RC's
OVERALL CODE ODDS 1:8 HOBBY

2011 Topps Allen and Ginter Mini

*MINI 1-300: .75X TO 2X BASIC
*MINI 1-300 RC: .5X TO 1.2X BASIC RC's
*MINI SP 301-350: .5X TO 1.2X BASIC SP
MINI SP ODDS 1:13 HOBBY
COMMON CARD (351-400) 10.00 25.00
351-400 RANDOM WITHIN RIP CARDS
STATED PLATE ODDS 1:751 HOBBY
PLATE PRINT RUN 1 SET PER COLOR
BLACK-CYAN-MAGENTA-YELLOW ISSUED
NO PLATE PRICING DUE TO SCARCITY

2011 Topps Allen and Ginter Mini A and G Back

*A & G BACK: 1X TO 2.5X BASIC
*A & G BACK RCs: .6X TO 1.5X BASIC RCs
A & G BACK ODDS 1:5 HOBBY
*A & G BACK SP: .6X TO 1.5X BASIC SP
A & G BACK SP ODDS 1:65 HOBBY

2011 Topps Allen and Ginter Mini Black

*BLACK: 2X TO 5X BASIC
*BLACK RCs: .75X TO 2X BASIC RCs
BLACK ODDS 1:10 HOBBY
BLACK SP ODDS 1:130 HOBBY
*BLACK SP: .75X TO 2X BASIC SP

2011 Topps Allen and Ginter Mini No Card Number

*NO NBR: 8X TO 20X BASIC
*NO NBR RCs: 3X TO 8X BASIC RCs
*NO NBR SP: 1.2X TO 3X BASIC SP
STATED ODDS 1:142 HOBBY

2011 Topps Allen and Ginter Relics

STATED ODDS 1:10 HOBBY
EXCHANGE DEADLINE 6/30/2014
DTU Diana Taurasi 6.00 15.00
DVA Dick Vitale 6.00 15.00
GAU Geno Auriemma 8.00 20.00
SBI Sue Bird 6.00 15.00

2012 Topps Allen and Ginter

COMPLETE SET (350) 30.00 60.00
COMP.SET w/o SP's (300) 15.00 40.00
SP ODDS 1:2 HOBBY
19 Bob Knight .50 1.25
85 Curly Neal .40 1.00
113 Meadowlark Lemon .40 1.00
154 Bob Hurley Sr. .15 .40
339 Swin Cash SP 3.00 8.00

2012 Topps Allen and Ginter Autographs

STATED ODDS 1:51 HOBBY
EXCHANGE DEADELINE 06/30/2015
BHS Bob Hurley Sr. 8.00 20.00
BKN Bob Knight 40.00 80.00
CNE Curly Neal 20.00 50.00
MLE Meadowlark Lemon 20.00 50.00
SCA Swin Cash 8.00 20.00

2012 Topps Allen and Ginter Mini

*MINI 1-300: .75X TO 2X BASIC
*MINI 1-300 RC: .5X TO 1.2X BASIC RC's
*MINI SP 301-350: .5X TO 1.2X BASIC SP
MINI SP ODDS 1:13 HOBBY
351-400 RANDOM WITHIN RIP CARDS
STATED PLATE ODDS 1:564 HOBBY
PLATE PRINT RUN 1 SET PER COLOR
NO PLATE PRICING DUE TO SCARCITY

2012 Topps Allen and Ginter Mini A and G Back

*A & G BACK: 1X TO 2.5X BASIC
*A & G BACK RCs: .6X TO 1.5X BASIC RCs
A & G BACK ODDS 1:5 HOBBY
*A & G BACK SP: .6X TO 1.5X BASIC SP
A & G BACK SP ODDS 1:65 HOBBY

2012 Topps Allen and Ginter Mini Black

*BLACK: 1.5X TO 4X BASIC
*BLACK RCs: .6X TO 1.5X BASIC RCs
BLACK ODDS 1:10 HOBBY
*BLACK SP: 1X TO 2.5X BASIC SP
BLACK SP ODDS 1:130 HOBBY

2012 Topps Allen and Ginter Mini Gold Border

*GOLD: .5X TO 1.2X BASIC
*GOLD RCs: .5X TO 1.2X BASIC RCs
COMMON SP (301-350) .40 1.00
SP SEMIS .60 1.50
SP UNLISTED 1.00 2.50
339 Swin Cash 1.00 2.50

2012 Topps Allen and Ginter Mini No Card Number

*NO NBR: 5X TO 12X BASIC
*NO NBR RCs: 2X TO 5X BASIC RCs
*NO NBR SP: 1.2X TO 3X BASIC SP
STATED ODDS 1:111 HOBBY
ANNC'D PRINT RUN OF 50 SETS

2012 Topps Allen and Ginter Relics

STATED ODDS 1:10 HOBBY
EXCHANGE DEADELINE 06/30/2015
BH Bob Hurley Sr. 3.00 8.00
BK Bob Knight 5.00 12.00
CN Curly Neal EXCH 6.00 15.00
MLE Meadowlark Lemon 6.00 15.00
SCA Swin Cash 3.00 8.00

2013 Topps Allen and Ginter

COMPLETE SET (350) 20.00 50.00
COMP.SET w/o SP's (300) 12.00 30.00
SP ODDS 1:2 HOBBY
100 Bill Walton .40 1.00
250 John Calipari .40 1.00
350 Bill Walton SP 1.25 3.00

2013 Topps Allen and Ginter Mini

*MINI 1-300: .75X TO 2X BASIC
*MINI 1-300 RC: .5X TO 1.2X BASIC RC's
*MINI SP 301-350: .5X TO 1.2X BASIC SP
MINI SP ODDS 1:13 HOBBY
351-400 RANDOM WITHIN RIP CARDS
STATED PLATE ODDS 1:594 HOBBY
PLATE PRINT RUN 1 SET PER COLOR
BLACK-CYAN-MAGENTA-YELLOW ISSUED
NO PLATE PRICING DUE TO SCARCITY

2013 Topps Allen and Ginter Mini A and G Back

*A & G BACK: 1X TO 2.5X BASIC
*A & G BACK RCs: .6X TO 1.5X BASIC RCs
A & G BACK ODDS 1:5 HOBBY
*A & G BACK SP: .6X TO 1.5X BASIC SP
A & G BACK SP ODDS 1:65 HOBBY

2013 Topps Allen and Ginter Mini Black

*BLACK: 1.5X TO 4X BASIC
*BLACK RCs: 1X TO 2.5X BASIC RCs
BLACK ODDS 1:10 HOBBY
*BLACK SP: 1X TO 2.5X BASIC SP
BLACK SP ODDS 1:130 HOBBY

2013 Topps Allen and Ginter Mini No Card Number

*NO NBR: 4X TO 10X BASIC
*NO NBR RCs: 2.5X TO 6X BASIC RCs
*NO NBR SP: 1.2X TO 3X BASIC SP
STATED ODDS 1:102 HOBBY
ANNC'D PRINT RUN OF 50 SETS

2013 Topps Allen and Ginter Autographs

STATED ODDS 1:49 HOBBY
EXCHANGE DEADLINE 07/31/2016
BW Bill Walton 12.00 30.00
JC John Calipari 20.00 50.00
MC Mark Cuban 30.00 80.00

2013 Topps Allen and Ginter Autographs Red Ink

STATED ODDS 1:931 HOBBY
PRINT RUNS B/WN 10-409 SER.#'d SETS
NO PRICING ON MOST DUE TO SCARCITY
EXCHANGE DEADLINE 07/31/2013

2013 Topps Allen and Ginter Framed Mini Relics

VERSION A ODDS 1:29 HOBBY
VERSION B ODDS 1:27 HOBBY
BW Bill Walton 3.00 8.00
JCA John Calipari 4.00 10.00
MCU Mark Cuban 4.00 10.00

2014 Topps Allen and Ginter

COMPLETE SET (350) 25.00 60.00
COMP.SET w/o SP's (300) 12.00 30.00
SP ODDS 1:2 HOBBY
259 Jim Calhoun .15 .40

2014 Topps Allen and Ginter Autographs

RANDOM INSERTS IN PACKS
AGFADM Doug McDermott 15.00 40.00

2014 Topps Allen and Ginter Framed Mini Autographs

STATED ODDS 1:52 HOBBY
EXCHANGE DEADLINE 6/30/2017
AGAJCL Jim Calhoun 8.00 20.00
AGASN Shabazz Napier 10.00 25.00

2014 Topps Allen and Ginter Mini

*MINI 1-300: 1X TO 2.5X BASIC
*MINI 1-300 RC: .6X TO 1.5X BASIC RCs
*MINI SP 301-350: .6X TO 1.5X BASIC SP
MINI SP ODDS 1:13 HOBBY
351-400 RANDOM WITHIN RIP CARDS
STATED PLATE ODDS 1:412 HOBBY
PLATE PRINT RUN 1 SET PER COLOR
BLACK-CYAN-MAGENTA-YELLOW ISSUED
NO PLATE PRICING DUE TO SCARCITY

2014 Topps Allen and Ginter Mini A and G Back

*A & G BACK: 1.2X TO 3X BASIC
*A & G BACK RCs: .75X TO 2X BASIC RCs
A & G BACK ODDS 1:5 HOBBY
*A & G BACK SP: .75X TO 2X BASIC SP
A & G BACK SP ODDS 1:65 HOBBY

2014 Topps Allen and Ginter Mini Black

*BLACK: 2X TO 5X BASIC
*BLACK RCs: 1.2X TO 3X BASIC RCs
BLACK ODDS 1:10 HOBBY
*BLACK SP: 1.2X TO 3X BASIC SP
BLACK SP ODDS 1:130 HOBBY

2014 Topps Allen and Ginter Mini Gold

*GOLD: 1.5X TO 4X BASIC
*GOLD RCs: 1X TO 2.5X BASIC RCs
*GOLD SP: 1X TO 2.5X BASIC SP
RANDOM INSERTS IN BACKS

2014 Topps Allen and Ginter Mini No Card Number

*NO NBR: 5X TO 12X BASIC
*NO NBR RCs: 3X TO 8X BASIC RCs
*NO NBR SP: 1.2X TO 3X BASIC SP
STATED ODDS 1:64 HOBBY
ANNC'D PRINT RUN OF 50 SETS

2014 Topps Allen and Ginter Mini Red

*RED: 12X TO 30X BASIC
*RED RCs: 8X TO 20X BASIC RCs
*RED SP: 5X TO 12X BASIC SP
STATED PRINT RUN 33 SER.#'d SETS

2015 Topps Allen and Ginter

COMPLETE SET (350) 30.00 80.00
ORIGINAL BUYBACK ODDS 1:7958 HOBBY
ORIG.BUYBACK PRINT RUN 1 SER.#'d SET
163 Zach Lowe .15 .40
319 Brian Windhorst .15 .40

2015 Topps Allen and Ginter Framed Mini Autographs

STATED ODDS 1:54 HOBBY
EXCHANGE DEADLINE 6/30/2018
AGABW Brian Windhorst 4.00 10.00
AGAKOU Kelly Oubre 10.00 25.00
AGASD Sam Dekker 12.00 30.00
AGAZL Zach Lowe 6.00 15.00

2015 Topps Allen and Ginter Mini

*MINI 1-300: 1X TO 2.5X BASIC
*MINI 1-300 RC: .5X TO 1.2X BASIC RCs
*MINI SP 301-350: .6X TO 1.5X BASIC
MINI SP ODDS 1:13 HOBBY
351-400 RANDOM WITHIN RIP CARDS
STATED PLATE ODDS 1:495 HOBBY
PLATE PRINT RUN 1 SET PER COLOR
BLACK-CYAN-MAGENTA-YELLOW ISSUED
NO PLATE PRICING DUE TO SCARCITY

2015 Topps Allen and Ginter Mini A and G Back

*MINI AG 1-300: 1.2X TO 3X BASIC
*MINI AG 1-300 RC: .6X TO 1.5X BASIC RCs
*MINI AG SP 301-350: .75X TO 2X BASIC
MINI AG ODDS 1:5 HOBBY
MINI AG SP ODDS 1:65 HOBBY

2015 Topps Allen and Ginter Mini Black

*MINI BLK 1-300: 2X TO 5X BASIC
*MINI BLK 1-300 RC: 1X TO 2.5X BASIC RCs
*MINI BLK SP 301-350: 1.2X TO 3X BASIC
MINI BLK ODDS 1:10 HOBBY
MINI BLK SP ODDS 1:130 HOBBY

2015 Topps Allen and Ginter Mini Flag Back

*MINI FLAG: 5X TO 12X BASIC
*MINI FLAG RC: 2.5X TO 6X BASIC RCs
MINI FLAG ODDS 1:157 HOBBY
STATED PRINT RUN 25 SER.#'d SETS

2015 Topps Allen and Ginter Mini No Card Number

*MINI NNO: 6X TO 15X BASIC
*MINI NNO RC: 3X TO 8X BASIC RCs
MINI NNO ODDS 1:79 HOBBY
ANNCD PRINT RUN OF 50 COPIES EACH

2015 Topps Allen and Ginter Mini Red

*MINI RED: 5X TO 12X BASIC
*MINI RED RC: 2.5X TO 6X BASIC RCs
MINI RED ODDS 1:12 HOBBY BOXES
STATED PRINT RUN 40 SER.#'d SETS

2015 Topps Allen and Ginter Relics

GROUP A ODDS 1:24 HOBBY
GROUP B ODDS 1:24 HOBBY
FSRABW Brian Windhorst A 2.50 6.00
FSRBZL Zach Lowe B 2.50 6.00

2002 Topps All-Star Game

Produced by Topps for distribution at the 2002 NBA All-Star Game Show via wrapper redemption, this nine card set utilizes the base 2001-02 Topps set design enhanced with a holofoil finish on the front and the All-Star Game 2002 Philadelphia logo.
COMPLETE SET (9) 8.00 20.00
1 Shaquille O'Neal 2.00 5.00
2 Tim Duncan 1.50 4.00
3 Allen Iverson 1.25 3.00
4 Tracy McGrady 1.00 2.50
5 Steve Francis .75 2.00
6 Elton Brand .75 2.00
7 Jason Richardson 1.25 3.00
8 Jamaal Tinsley .75 2.00
9 Chris Webber .75 2.00

2003 Topps All-Star Game

Distributed by Topps at the All-Star Jam Session show in Atlanta, this set was available via wrapper redemption at the Topps show booth. Collectors were required to turn in three packs of 2002-03 Topps products in exchange for this eight card set. The set uses the base card design of 2002-03 topps and is enhanced with a gold foil 2003 NBA All-Star Game logo in the lower left hand corner of the card front.
COMPLETE SET (8) 6.00 15.00
1 Shaquille O'Neal 1.50 4.00
2 Mike Dunleavy .75 2.00
3 Glenn Robinson .75 2.00
4 Tracy McGrady 1.50 4.00
5 Stephon Marbury .75 2.00
6 Allen Iverson 1.25 3.00
7 Dirk Nowitzki 1.00 2.50
8 Jason Kidd 1.00 2.50

2009 Topps American Heritage Heroes Heroes of Sport

COMPLETE SET (25) 12.50 25.00
STATED ODDS 1:4
*GOLD/199: 3X TO 8X BASIC INSERTS
*PLATINUM/25: 5X TO 12X BASIC INSERTS
HS5 Larry Bird .60 1.50
HS15 Bill Russell .60 1.50
HS24 Magic Johnson .40 1.00

2009 Topps American Heritage Heroes Heroes of Sport Relics

STATED ODDS 1:234
HSR5 Magic Johnson Jsy 10.00 25.00
HSR8 Larry Bird Jsy 10.00 25.00
HSR14 Bill Russell Jsy 15.00 40.00

1992-93 Topps Archives

Featuring the missing years of Topps basketball from 1981 through 1991, this 150-card set consists of 139 current NBA players and an 11-card subset of the Number One draft picks from 1981 to 1991. Production was limited to 10,000 24-box cases (24 packs per box). Each pack contained 14 cards and one Stadium Club membership card. Since Topps did not produce basketball cards when the photos were taken, the front designs are patterned after the Topps baseball cards issued during the same year. The horizontal backs display a small, square, current action player photo that overlaps a red, yellow, and white box containing biographical information, and statistics from college and the NBA. The set name, player's name, and team are printed in the upper left portion. The background is in varying shades of blue with a light beam design. After opening with a No. 1 Draft Pick (1-11) subset, the player cards are arranged by year in ascending chronological order and alphabetically within each season. The set closes with checklist (149-150) cards.
COMPLETE SET (150) 6.00 15.00
1 Mark Aguirre FDP .08 .15
2 James Worthy FDP .08 .15
3 Ralph Sampson FDP .08 .15
4 Hakeem Olajuwon FDP .10 .30
5 Patrick Ewing FDP .08 .25
6 Brad Daugherty FDP .08 .15
7 David Robinson FDP .10 .30
8 Danny Manning FDP .08 .15
9 Pervis Ellison FDP UER .08 .15
10 Derrick Coleman FDP .08 .15
11 Larry Johnson FDP .08 .15
12 Mark Aguirre .08 .15
13 Danny Ainge .08 .15
14 Rolando Blackman .08 .15
15 Tom Chambers .08 .15
16 Eddie Johnson .08 .15
17 Alton Lister .08 .15
18 Larry Nance .08 .15
19 Kurt Rambis .08 .15
20 Isiah Thomas .10 .30
21 Buck Williams .08 .15
22 Orlando Woolridge .08 .15
23 John Bagley .08 .15
24 Terry Cummings .08 .15
25 Mark Eaton .08 .15
26 Sleepy Floyd .08 .25
27 Fat Lever .08 .15
28 Ricky Pierce .08 .25
29 Trent Tucker .08 .15
30 Dominique Wilkins .10 .30
31 James Worthy .08 .25
32 Thurl Bailey .08 .15
33 Clyde Drexler .10 .30
34 Dale Ellis .08 .15
35 Sidney Green .08 .15
36 Derek Harper .08 .15
37 Jeff Malone .08 .15
38 Rodney McCray .08 .15
39 John Paxson .08 .15
40 Doc Rivers .08 .15
41 Byron Scott .08 .15
42 Sedale Threatt .08 .15
43 Ron Anderson .08 .15
44 Charles Barkley .25 .60
45 Sam Bowie .08 .15
46 Michael Cage .08 .15
47 Tony Campbell .08 .15
48 Antoine Carr .08 .25
49 Craig Ehlo .08 .15
50 Vern Fleming .08 .15
51 Jay Humphries .08 .15
52 Michael Jordan 2.50 6.00
53 Jerome Kersey .08 .15
54 Hakeem Olajuwon .25 .60
55 Sam Perkins .08 .15
56 Alvin Robertson .08 .15
57 John Stockton .15 .40
58 Otis Thorpe .08 .15
59 Kevin Willis .08 .15
60 Michael Adams .08 .15
61 Benoit Benjamin .08 .15
62 Terry Catledge .08 .15
63 Joe Dumars .08 .25
64 Patrick Ewing .15 .40
65 A.C. Green .08 .15
66 Karl Malone .25 .60
67 Reggie Miller .15 .40
68 Chris Mullin .08 .25
69 Xavier McDaniel .08 .15
70 Charles Oakley .08 .15
71 Terry Porter .08 .15
72 Jerry Reynolds .08 .15
73 Detlef Schrempf .08 .15
74 Wayman Tisdale .08 .15
75 Spud Webb .08 .15
76 Gerald Wilkins .08 .15
77 Dell Curry .08 .15
78 Brad Daugherty .08 .15
79 Johnny Dawkins .08 .15
80 Kevin Duckworth .08 .15
81 Ron Harper .08 .15
82 Jeff Hornacek .08 .15
83 Johnny Newman .08 .15
84 Chuck Person .08 .15
85 Mark Price .08 .15
86 Dennis Rodman .25 .60
87 John Salley .08 .15
88 Scott Skiles .08 .15
89 Muggsy Bogues .08 .15
90 Armon Gilliam .08 .15
91 Horace Grant .08 .15
92 Mark Jackson .08 .15
93 Kevin Johnson .08 .15
94 Reggie Lewis .08 .15
95 Derrick McKey .08 .15
96 Ken Norman .08 .15
97 Scottie Pippen .50 1.25
98 Olden Polynice .08 .15
99 Kenny Smith .08 .15
100 John Williams .08 .15
101 Willie Anderson .08 .15
102 Rex Chapman .08 .15
103 Harvey Grant .08 .25
104 Hersey Hawkins .08 .15
105 Dan Majerle .08 .15
106 Danny Manning .08 .15
107 Vernon Maxwell .08 .15
108 Chris Morris .08 .15
109 Mitch Richmond UER .08 .25
110 Rony Seikaly .08 .15
111 Brian Shaw .08 .15
112 Charles Smith .08 .15
113 Rod Strickland .08 .25
114 Micheal Williams .08 .15
115 Nick Anderson .08 .15
116 B.J. Armstrong .08 .15

117 Mookie Blaylock .08 .15
118 Vlade Divac .08 .15
119 Sherman Douglas .08 .15
120 Blue Edwards .08 .15
121 Sean Elliott .08 .15
122 Pervis Ellison .08 .15
123 Tim Hardaway .10 .30
124 Sarunas Marciulionis .08 .15
125 Drazen Petrovic .08 .15
126 J.R. Reid .08 .15
127 Glen Rice .08 .25
128 Pooh Richardson .08 .15
129 Clifford Robinson .08 .15
130 David Robinson .25 .60
131 Dee Brown .08 .15
132 Cedric Ceballos .08 .15
133 Derrick Coleman .08 .15
134 Kendall Gill .08 .15
135 Chris Jackson .08 .15
136 Shawn Kemp .30 .75
137 Gary Payton .30 .75
138 Dennis Scott .08 .15
139 Lionel Simmons .08 .15
140 Kenny Anderson .08 .25
141 Greg Anthony .08 .15
142 Stacey Augmon .08 .15
143 Rick Fox .08 .15
144 Larry Johnson .08 .25
145 Luc Longley .08 .15
146 Dikembe Mutombo .08 .25
147 Billy Owens .08 .15
148 Steve Smith .08 .25
149 Checklist 1-75 .08 .15
150 Checklist 76-150 .08 .15

1992-93 Topps Archives Gold

COMPLETE FACT.SET (150) 20.00 50.00
*STARS: 1.25X TO 3X BASE CARD HI
149G Rumeal Robinson .30 .40
150G Shaquille O'Neal 20.00 50.00

1992-93 Topps Archives Master Photos

In one out of 24 '92-93 Archives packs, the Stadium Club membership card was replaced by a mini-Master Photo Trade card (2 1/2" by 3 1/2") good for three of these full-size (5" by 7") Master Photos. The expiration date was January 31, 1994. Showcasing the 11 No. 1 NBA draft picks from the missing years of Topps basketball from 1981 through 1991, these 12 oversized cards feature white-bordered color player action shots framed by prismatic silver-foil lines. The player's name, team name and year of his being the No. 1 pick appear in diagonal red, yellow, and blue stripes near the bottom. The words "#1 Draft Pick" followed by a curving comet like prismatic silver-foil tail appear in one of the photo's upper corners. Aside from the Topps and NBA trademarks, the backs are blank. The cards are numbered on the front by year. The mini Master Photo cards are presently valued the same as the large.

COMPLETE SET (12) 4.00 10.00
1981 Mark Aguirre .40 1.00
1982 James Worthy .60 1.50
1983 Ralph Sampson .40 1.00
1984 Hakeem Olajuwon 1.00 2.50
1985 Patrick Ewing .75 2.00
1986 Brad Daugherty .40 1.00
1987 David Robinson 1.00 2.50
1988 Danny Manning .40 1.00
1989 Pervis Ellison .40 1.00
1990 Derrick Coleman .40 1.00
1991 Larry Johnson .60 1.50
NNO First Picks 1981-91 .40 1.00

2005-06 Topps Big Game

Released in October 2005, Big Game features an all-foil all serially numbered set consisting of 146 cards broken down as follows: 1-110 feature veterans and are serially numbered to 179, 111-141 feature rookies and are serially numbered to 529 and 142-146 feature celebrities serially numbered to 529. Base cards have white borders and a stat grid along the bottom with the player's name, position, team and some stats from career-best games. Big Game was packaged in tins containing five cards, a veteran, a rookie, a low-serially numbered parallel, a relic card and an autographed relic card and carried an initial SRP of $75.

1-110 PRINT RUN 179 SER.#'d SETS
142-146 PRINT RUN 529 SER.#'d SETS
UNPRICED BIG GAME 1 PRINT RUN ONE SET
1 Vince Carter 1.50 4.00
2 Mehmet Okur .60 1.50
3 Andre Iguodala .75 2.00
4 Baron Davis .75 2.00
5 Drew Gooden .75 2.00
6 Yao Ming 1.25 3.00
7 Gary Payton 1.00 2.50
8 Shaun Livingston .60 1.50
9 Marcus Camby .75 2.00
10 Ben Wallace .75 2.00
11 Mike Miller .75 2.00
12 Steve Francis .75 2.00
13 Sam Cassell .75 2.00
14 Gilbert Arenas .75 2.00
15 Chris Bosh 1.00 2.50
16 Jamaal Magloire .60 1.50
17 Zach Randolph .75 2.00
18 Josh Childress .75 2.00
19 Kirk Hinrich .75 2.00
20 Dirk Nowitzki 1.50 4.00
21 Trevor Ariza .60 1.50
22 Primoz Brezec .60 1.50
23 LeBron James 4.00 10.00
24 Vladimir Radmanovic .60 1.50
25 Tim Duncan 1.50 4.00
26 Damon Jones .60 1.50
27 Rasheed Wallace 1.00 2.50
28 Corey Maggette .75 2.00
29 Stephen Jackson .75 2.00
30 Amare Stoudemire .75 2.00
31 Jason Richardson 1.00 2.50
32 Brad Miller .75 2.00
33 Kenyon Martin .75 2.00
34 Paul Pierce 1.00 2.50
35 Lamar Odom .75 2.00
36 Marquis Daniels .60 1.50
37 Shane Battier .75 2.00
38 Eddy Curry .60 1.50
39 Michael Redd .75 2.00
40 Ray Allen 1.00 2.50
41 Latrell Sprewell .75 2.00
42 Rafer Alston .60 1.50
43 Brendan Haywood .60 1.50
44 Al Harrington .75 2.00
45 Udonis Haslem .60 1.50
46 Chauncey Billups 1.00 2.50
47 Andrei Kirilenko .75 2.00
48 Chris Webber 1.00 2.50
49 Stephon Marbury .75 2.00
50 Emeka Okafor .75 2.00
51 Cuttino Mobley .60 1.50
52 Shawn Marion .75 2.00
53 Jamaal Tinsley .60 1.50
54 Nenad Krstic .60 1.50
55 Bob Sura .60 1.50
56 Manu Ginobili 1.00 2.50
57 Dan Dickau .60 1.50
58 Wally Szczerbiak .75 2.00
59 Mike Dunleavy .75 2.00
60 Carmelo Anthony 2.00 5.00
61 Zydrunas Ilgauskas .75 2.00
62 Elton Brand 1.00 2.50
63 Jamal Crawford 1.00 2.50
64 Grant Hill 1.25 3.00
65 Ben Gordon .75 2.00
66 Rashard Lewis 1.00 2.50
67 Josh Howard 1.00 2.50
68 Jalen Rose 1.00 2.50
69 Pau Gasol 1.00 2.50
70 Steve Nash 1.25 3.00
71 Larry Hughes .75 2.00
72 J.R. Smith .75 2.00
73 Jason Kidd 1.50 4.00
74 Mike Bibby 1.00 2.50
75 Josh Smith .75 2.00
76 Richard Hamilton .75 2.00
77 Caron Butler .75 2.00
78 Richard Jefferson .75 2.00
79 Mike Sweetney .60 1.50
80 Shaquille O'Neal 2.00 5.00
81 Dwight Howard .75 2.00
82 Allen Iverson 1.50 4.00
83 Luol Deng .75 2.00
84 Luke Ridnour .75 2.00
85 Desmond Mason .60 1.50
86 Gerald Wallace .75 2.00
87 Carlos Boozer .75 2.00
88 Antoine Walker .75 2.00
89 Tony Parker 1.00 2.50
90 Tracy McGrady 1.25 3.00
91 Jermaine O'Neal .75 2.00
92 Andre Miller .75 2.00
93 Quentin Richardson .75 2.00
94 Dwyane Wade 1.50 4.00
95 Kevin Garnett 1.50 4.00
96 Peja Stojakovic 1.00 2.50
97 Antawn Jamison .75 2.00
98 Devin Harris .60 1.50
99 Kobe Bryant 4.00 10.00
100 Sebastian Telfair .75 2.00
101 Samuel Dalembert .60 1.50
102 Darius Miles .60 1.50
103 Al Jefferson .75 2.00
104 Brevin Knight .60 1.50
105 Anderson Varejao .60 1.50
106 Troy Murphy .60 1.50
107 Mike James .60 1.50
108 Maurice Williams .75 2.00
109 Robert Horry .75 2.00
110 Bobby Simmons .60 1.50
111 Andrew Bogut RC 2.50 6.00
112 Gerald Green RC 2.00 5.00
113 Raymond Felton RC 2.00 5.00
114 Francisco Garcia RC 1.50 4.00
115 Hakim Warrick RC 1.50 4.00
116 Jarrett Jack RC 2.00 5.00
117 Wayne Simien RC 1.25 3.00
118 Nate Robinson RC 2.00 5.00
119 Julius Hodge RC 1.25 3.00
120 Chris Paul RC 3.00 8.00
121 Rashad McCants RC 1.50 4.00
122 Ike Diogu RC 1.25 3.00
123 Antoine Wright RC 1.50 4.00
124 Luther Head RC 1.50 4.00
125 Ryan Gomes RC 1.50 4.00
126 David Lee RC 2.00 5.00
127 Andrew Bynum RC 1.50 4.00
128 Salim Stoudamire RC 1.50 4.00
129 Sean May RC 1.25 3.00
130 Deron Williams RC 2.50 6.00
131 Joey Graham RC 1.50 4.00
132 Fran Vazquez RC 1.25 3.00
133 Brandon Bass RC 1.50 4.00
134 Jason Maxiell RC 1.50 4.00
135 Charlie Villanueva RC 2.00 5.00
136 Daniel Ewing RC 1.50 4.00
137 Channing Frye RC 2.00 5.00
138 Chris Taft RC 1.50 4.00
139 Marvin Williams RC 2.00 5.00
140 Danny Granger RC 2.50 6.00
141 Travis Diener RC 1.25 3.00
142 Shannon Elizabeth 2.50 6.00
143 Jenny McCarthy 2.50 6.00
144 Christie Brinkley 2.50 6.00
145 Jay-Z 2.50 6.00
146 Carmen Electra 2.50 6.00

2005-06 Topps Big Game 99

*1-110 GAME 99: .6X TO 1.5X BASE HI
*111-141 GAME 99: .75X TO 2X BASE HI
*142-146 GAME 99: .75X TO 2X BASE HI
STATED PRINT RUN 99 SER.#'d SETS

2005-06 Topps Big Game 33

*1-110 GAME 33: 2X TO 5X BASE HI
*111-141 GAME 33: 1.25X TO 3X BASE HI
*142-146 GAME 33: 1.25X TO 3X BASE HI
64 Grant Hill 8.00 20.00
99 Kobe Bryant 30.00 80.00

2005-06 Topps Big Game All-Star Rally Relics

Randomly seeded in packs, this 20-card set features NBA All-Stars on a horizontally designed card with player images on the left and swatches of memorabilia on the right. Each card is sequentially numbered to 79.

PRINT RUN 79 SER.#'d SETS
AI Allen Iverson Shirt 10.00 25.00
AJ Al Jefferson RC Chall Shorts 2.50 6.00
AS Amare Stoudemire Warm 2.50 6.00
BW Ben Wallace Warm 2.50 6.00
CA C.Anthony RC Chall JSY 6.00 15.00
CB Chris Bosh Shorts 3.00 8.00
DH Dwight Howard Warm 2.50 6.00
EB Earl Boykins Warm 2.00 5.00
EO Emeka Okafor RC Chall JSY 2.50 6.00
GA Gilbert Arenas Shirt 2.50 6.00
GH Grant Hill Warm 4.00 10.00
MG Manu Ginobili Warm 3.00 8.00
RA Ray Allen JSY 3.00 8.00
RD Ronald Dupree JSY 2.00 5.00
SM Shawn Marion Warm 2.50 6.00
SN Steve Nash Warm 4.00 10.00
SO Shaquille O'Neal Warm 6.00 15.00
TM Tracy McGrady Shirt 4.00 10.00
UH U.Haslem RC Chall Shirt 2.00 5.00
YM Yao Ming Warm 4.00 10.00

2005-06 Topps Big Game All-Star Rally Relics Autographs

Randomly seeded in packs, this 11-card set parallels the design of the All-Star Rally Relics but is enahnced with sequential numbering and a silver autograph sticker. Cards are numbered to varying amounts. See checklist for details.

PRINT RUNS LISTED IN CHECKLIST
AS A.Stoudemire Shirt/67 12.50 30.00
BW Ben Wallace Pants/20 15.00 40.00
CA C.Anthony RC Chall JSY/199 20.00 50.00
DW Dwyane Wade Pants/199 30.00 80.00
EO E.Okafor RC Chall JSY/199 10.00 25.00
QR Q.Richardson Event Shirt/31 10.00 25.00
SN Steve Nash Pants/199 20.00 50.00
SO Shaquille O'Neal Shirt/199 20.00 50.00
TD Tim Duncan Shirt/111 100.00 250.00
TM Tracy McGrady Shirt/76 20.00 50.00
JRS J.R. Smith Event JSY/32 8.00 20.00

2005-06 Topps Big Game Draft Day Moments Relics

Inserted in packs, this set features 38 rookie players and places a photo of the player on the left and a swatch of memorabilia on the right. Most players have two versions, a draft day ball and a draft day hat, but Andrew Bogut has a jacket version. Cards are serially numbered to varying amounts, see checklist for details.

BALL PRINT RUN 75 SER.#'d SETS
HAT PRINT RUNS LISTED IN CHECKLIST
AB Andrew Bogut Hat/27 8.00 20.00
AB2 Andrew Bogut Ball/75 5.00 12.00
AW Antoine Wright Hat/27 5.00 12.00
AW2 Antoine Wright Ball/75 3.00 8.00
CF Channing Frye Hat/146 6.00 15.00
CF2 Channing Frye Ball/75 4.00 10.00
CP Chris Paul Hat/125 10.00 25.00
CP2 Chris Paul Ball/75 15.00 40.00
CV Charlie Villanueva Hat/33 6.00 15.00
CV2 Charlie Villanueva Ball/75 4.00 10.00
DG Danny Granger Hat/25 8.00 20.00
DG2 Danny Granger Ball/75 5.00 12.00
DW Deron Williams Hat/30 8.00 20.00
DW2 Deron Williams Ball/75 5.00 12.00
FV Fran Vazquez Hat/99 4.00 10.00
GG Gerald Green Hat/21 6.00 15.00
GG2 Gerald Green Ball/75 4.00 10.00
HW Hakim Warrick Hat/26 5.00 12.00
HW2 Hakim Warrick Ball/75 3.00 8.00
IM Ian Mahinmi Hat/124 6.00 15.00
IM2 Ian Mahinmi Ball/75 4.00 10.00
JH2 Julius Hodge Ball/75 2.50 6.00
JP Johan Petro Hat/34 8.00 20.00
JP2 Johan Petro Ball/75 2.50 6.00
RF Raymond Felton Hat/33 6.00 15.00
RF2 Raymond Felton Ball/75 4.00 10.00
RM2 Rashad McCants Ball/75 3.00 8.00
SM Sean May Hat/36 4.00 10.00
YK Yaroslav Korolev Hat/143 4.00 10.00
YK2 Yaroslav Korolev Ball/75 2.50 6.00
ABY Andrew Bynum Hat/30 5.00 12.00
ABY2 Andrew Bynum Ball/75 3.00 8.00
MWE2 Martell Webster Ball/75 3.00 8.00

2005-06 Topps Big Game Draft Day Moments Relics Autographs

Randomly seeded in packs, this set parallels somewhat the design of the Draft Day Moments Relics set and is enhanced with a silver autograph sticker. Players have multiple memorabilia versions, draft day balls which are sequentially numbered to 99 and draft day hats sequentially numbered to 129.

AU BALL PRINT RUN 99 SER.#'d SETS
AU HAT PRINT RUN 129 SER.#'d SETS
AB Andrew Bogut Hat 6.00 15.00
AB2 Andrew Bogut Ball 8.00 20.00
AW Antoine Wright Hat 5.00 12.00
AW2 Antoine Wright Ball 5.00 12.00
CV Charlie Villanueva Hat 6.00 15.00
CV2 Charlie Villanueva Ball 6.00 15.00
DG Danny Granger Hat 8.00 20.00
DG2 Danny Granger Ball 8.00 20.00
DW Deron Williams Hat 8.00 20.00
DW2 Deron Williams Ball 8.00 20.00
FV Fran Vazquez Hat 4.00 10.00
FV2 Fran Vazquez Ball 4.00 10.00
GG Gerald Green Hat 6.00 15.00
GG2 Gerald Green Ball 6.00 15.00
HW Hakim Warrick Hat 5.00 12.00
HW2 Hakim Warrick Ball 5.00 12.00
JH Julius Hodge Hat 4.00 10.00
JH2 Julius Hodge Ball 4.00 10.00
JP Johan Petro Hat 4.00 10.00
JP2 Johan Petro Ball 4.00 10.00
RF Raymond Felton Hat 6.00 15.00
RF2 Raymond Felton Ball 6.00 15.00
RM Rashad McCants Hat 5.00 12.00
RM2 Rashad McCants Ball 5.00 12.00
SM Sean May Hat 4.00 10.00
SM2 Sean May Ball 4.00 10.00
ABY Andrew Bynum Hat 5.00 12.00
ABY2 Andrew Bynum Ball 5.00 12.00
MWE Martell Webster Hat 5.00 12.00
MWE2 Martell Webster Ball 5.00 12.00

2005-06 Topps Big Game Final Score Relics

Randomly seeded in packs, this 24-card set features a horizontal design with player photos on the left and a circle swatch of memorabilia in the center. Cards are sequentially numbered to 133.

PRINT RUN 133 SER.#'d SETS
AM Antonio McDyess 2.50 6.00
BB Brent Barry 2.00 5.00
BU Beno Udrih 2.00 5.00
BW Ben Wallace 2.50 6.00
CA Carlos Arroyo 5.00 12.00
CB Chauncey Billups 3.00 8.00
DB Devin Brown 2.00 5.00
DH Darvin Ham 2.00 5.00
DM Darko Milicic 2.00 5.00
EC Elden Campbell 2.00 5.00
GR Glenn Robinson 2.50 6.00
LH Lindsey Hunter 2.00 5.00
MG Manu Ginobili 3.00 8.00
NM Nazr Mohammed 2.00 5.00
RD Ronald Dupree 2.00 5.00
RH Robert Horry 4.00 10.00
RN Rasho Nesterovic 2.00 5.00
RW Rasheed Wallace 3.00 8.00
TD Tim Duncan 5.00 12.00
TM Tony Massenburg 2.00 5.00
TP Tony Parker 3.00 8.00
BBO Bruce Bowen 2.00 5.00
RHA Richard Hamilton 2.50 6.00
TPR Tayshaun Prince 2.50 6.00

2005-06 Topps Big Game Final Score Relics Autographs

Seeded in packs, this four-card set parallels the design of the Final Score Relics set enhanced with a silver autograph sticker and sequential numbering to the featured player's jersey number.

PRINT RUNS LISTED IN CHECKLIST
BU Beno Udrih/50 6.00 15.00
BW Ben Wallace/30 20.00 50.00
RH Richard Hamilton/56 8.00 20.00
TD Tim Duncan/50 100.00 250.00

2005-06 Topps Big Game Picture Perfect Relics

Inserted randomly in packs, this 68-card set features a player photo on the right and a centered circular swatch of memorabilia. Each card is serially numbered to 129, and most players have multiple memorabilia versions. See checklist for details.

PRINT RUN 129 SER.#'d SETS
BOTH VERSIONS SAME VALUE
AB Andray Blatche JSY 2.50 6.00
AB2 Andray Blatche Shorts 2.50 6.00
AW Antoine Wright JSY 2.00 5.00
AW2 Antoine Wright Shorts 2.00 5.00
BB Brandon Bass JSY 2.00 5.00
BB2 Brandon Bass Shorts 2.00 5.00
CF Channing Frye JSY 2.50 6.00
CF2 Channing Frye Shorts 2.50 6.00
CP Chris Paul JSY 10.00 25.00
CP2 Chris Paul Shorts 10.00 25.00
CV Charlie Villanueva JSY 2.50 6.00
CV2 Charlie Villanueva Shorts 2.50 6.00
DE Daniel Ewing JSY 2.00 5.00
DE2 Daniel Ewing Shorts 2.00 5.00
DG Danny Granger JSY 3.00 8.00
DG2 Danny Granger Shorts 3.00 8.00
DL David Lee JSY 2.50 6.00
DL2 David Lee Shorts 2.50 6.00
DW Deron Williams JSY 3.00 8.00
DW2 Deron Williams Shorts 3.00 8.00
EI Ersan Ilyasova JSY 2.50 6.00
EI2 Ersan Ilyasova Shorts 2.50 6.00
FG Francisco Garcia JSY 2.00 5.00
FG2 Francisco Garcia Shorts 2.00 5.00
GG Gerald Green JSY 2.50 6.00
GG2 Gerald Green Shorts 2.50 6.00
HW Hakim Warrick JSY 2.00 5.00
HW2 Hakim Warrick Shorts 2.00 5.00
JG Joey Graham JSY 2.00 5.00
JG2 Joey Graham Shorts 2.00 5.00
JH Julius Hodge JSY 1.50 4.00
JH2 Julius Hodge Shorts 1.50 4.00
JJ Jarrett Jack JSY 2.50 6.00
JJ2 Jarrett Jack Shorts 2.50 6.00
JM Jason Maxiell JSY 2.00 5.00
JM2 Jason Maxiell Shorts 2.00 5.00
LH Luther Head JSY 2.00 5.00
LH2 Luther Head Shorts 2.00 5.00
LW Louis Williams JSY 2.50 6.00
LW2 Louis Williams Shorts 2.50 6.00
MA Martynas Andriuskevicius JSY 1.50 4.00
MA2 Martynas Andriuskevicius Shorts 1.50 4.00
ME Monta Ellis JSY 3.00 8.00
ME2 Monta Ellis Shorts 3.00 8.00
MW Martell Webster JSY 2.00 5.00
MW2 Martell Webster Shorts 2.00 5.00
NR Nate Robinson JSY 2.50 6.00
NR2 Nate Robinson Shorts 2.50 6.00
RF Raymond Felton JSY 2.50 6.00
RF2 Raymond Felton Shorts 2.50 6.00
RG Ryan Gomes JSY 2.00 5.00
RG2 Ryan Gomes Shorts 2.00 5.00
RM Rashad McCants JSY 2.00 5.00
RM2 Rashad McCants Shorts 2.00 5.00
SJ Sarunas Jasikevicius JSY 2.50 6.00
SJ2 Sarunas Jasikevicius Shorts 2.50 6.00
SM Sean May JSY 1.50 4.00
SM2 Sean May Shorts 1.50 4.00
SS Salim Stoudamire JSY 2.00 5.00
SS2 Salim Stoudamire Shorts 2.00 5.00
TD Travis Diener JSY 1.50 4.00
TD2 Travis Diener Shorts 1.50 4.00
WS Wayne Simien JSY 1.50 4.00
WS2 Wayne Simien Shorts 1.50 4.00
ABO Andrew Bogut JSY 3.00 8.00
ABO2 Andrew Bogut Jacket 3.00 8.00
CJM C.J. Miles JSY 2.50 6.00
CJM2 C.J. Miles Shorts 2.50 6.00

2005-06 Topps Big Game Picture Perfect Relics Autographs

Seeded randomly in packs, this 52-card set parallels the design of the Picture Perfect Relics set enahnced with a silver autograph sticker. Most cards are serially numbered to 199, but there are a few exceptions. See checklist for details.

PRINT RUN 199 SER.#'d SETS
UNLESS NOTED IN CHECKLIST
BOTH VERSIONS SAME VALUE
AB Andray Blatche JSY/129 5.00 12.00
AB2 Andray Blatche Shorts/179 5.00 12.00
AW Antoine Wright JSY 4.00 10.00
AW2 Antoine Wright Shorts 4.00 10.00
BB Brandon Bass JSY 4.00 10.00
BB2 Brandon Bass Shorts 4.00 10.00
CV Charlie Villanueva JSY 5.00 12.00
CV2 Charlie Villanueva Shorts 5.00 12.00
DE Daniel Ewing JSY 4.00 10.00
DE2 Daniel Ewing Shorts 4.00 10.00
DG Danny Granger JSY 6.00 15.00
DG2 Danny Granger Shorts 6.00 15.00
DL David Lee JSY 5.00 12.00
DL2 David Lee Shorts 5.00 12.00
DW Deron Williams JSY 6.00 15.00
DW2 Deron Williams Shorts 6.00 15.00
FG Francisco Garcia JSY 4.00 10.00
FG2 Francisco Garcia Shorts 4.00 10.00
GG Gerald Green JSY 5.00 12.00
GG2 Gerald Green Shorts 5.00 12.00
HW Hakim Warrick JSY 4.00 10.00
HW2 Hakim Warrick Shorts 4.00 10.00
JG Joey Graham JSY 4.00 10.00
JG2 Joey Graham Shorts 4.00 10.00
JH Julius Hodge JSY 3.00 8.00
JH2 Julius Hodge Shorts 3.00 8.00
JJ Jarrett Jack JSY 5.00 12.00
JJ2 Jarrett Jack Shorts 5.00 12.00
JM Jason Maxiell JSY 4.00 10.00
JM2 Jason Maxiell Shorts 4.00 10.00
LH Luther Head JSY 4.00 10.00
LH2 Luther Head Shorts 4.00 10.00
ME Monta Ellis JSY 6.00 15.00
ME2 Monta Ellis Shorts 10.00 25.00
MW Martell Webster JSY 4.00 10.00
MW2 Martell Webster Shorts 4.00 10.00
RF Raymond Felton JSY 5.00 12.00
RF2 Raymond Felton Shorts 5.00 12.00
RG Ryan Gomes JSY 4.00 10.00
RG2 Ryan Gomes Shorts 4.00 10.00
RM Rashad McCants JSY 4.00 10.00
RM2 Rashad McCants Shorts 4.00 10.00
SJ Sarunas Jasikevicius JSY 5.00 12.00
SJ2 Sarunas Jasikevicius Shorts 5.00 12.00
SM Sean May JSY 3.00 8.00
SM2 Sean May Shorts 3.00 8.00
TD Travis Diener JSY 3.00 8.00
TD2 Travis Diener Shorts 3.00 8.00
WS Wayne Simien JSY 3.00 8.00
WS2 Wayne Simien Shorts 3.00 8.00
ABO Andrew Bogut JSY 6.00 15.00
ABO2 Andrew Bogut Jacket 6.00 15.00

2005-06 Topps Big Game Relics

Randomly seeded in packs, this 36-card set showcases both NBA players and celebrities. Photos appear on the left side of the card and a circular swatch of memorabilia appears on the right in a design that resembles a bulls-eye. Each card is serially numbered to 99.

PRINT RUN 99 SER.#'d SETS
AI Allen Iverson JSY 5.00 12.00
AJ Al Jefferson JSY 2.50 6.00
AN Andres Nocioni JSY 2.00 5.00
AS Amare Stoudemire Shirt 2.50 6.00
BG Ben Gordon JSY 2.50 6.00
BW Ben Wallace Warm 2.50 6.00
CA Carmelo Anthony JSY 6.00 15.00
CB Christie Brinkley Jeans 12.50 30.00
CE Carmen Electra Jeans 12.50 30.00
DH Devin Harris JSY 2.00 5.00
DN Dirk Nowitzki JSY 5.00 12.00
EB Earl Boykins Warm 2.00 5.00
EO Emeka Okafor JSY 2.50 6.00
JM Jenny McCarthy Jeans 10.00 25.00
JO Jermaine O'Neal Warm 2.50 6.00
JS Josh Smith JSY 2.50 6.00
JZ Jay-Z Jeans 20.00 50.00
KB Kobe Bryant JSY 10.00 25.00
KG Kevin Garnett JSY 5.00 12.00
KH Kirk Hinrich JSY 2.50 6.00
KM Kenyon Martin JSY 2.50 6.00
LR Luke Ridnour JSY 2.50 6.00
MG Manu Ginobili Warm 3.00 8.00
NK Nenad Krstic JSY 2.00 5.00
RA Ray Allen JSY 3.00 8.00
RM Reggie Miller Warm 3.00 8.00
RW Rasheed Wallace JSY 3.00 8.00
SE Shannon Elizabeth Jeans 10.00 25.00
SN Steve Nash JSY 4.00 10.00
SO Shaquille O'Neal JSY 6.00 15.00
TD Tim Duncan JSY 5.00 12.00
TM Tracy McGrady JSY 4.00 10.00
YM Yao Ming JSY 4.00 10.00
AJA Antawn Jamison JSY 2.50 6.00
DHO Dwight Howard JSY 2.50 6.00
JRS J.R. Smith JSY 2.50 6.00

2005-06 Topps Big Game Relics Autographs

Inserted in packs randomly, this 42-card set parallels the design of the Relics set enhanced with a silver autograph sticker and sequential numbering. Serial numbers vary, see checklist for details.

PRINT RUNS LISTED IN CHECKLIST
SOME UNPRICED DUE TO SCARCITY
AI Allen Iverson/129 60.00 150.00
AS Amare Stoudemire Shirt/99 20.00 50.00
BD Baron Davis/128 5.00 12.00
BG Ben Gordon/101 10.00 25.00
BR Bernard Robinson/21 5.00 12.00
BU Beno Udrih Shirt/78 5.00 12.00
BW Ben Wallace Warm/20 20.00 50.00
CA Carmelo Anthony/199 20.00 40.00
CB Christie Brinkley Jeans/50 150.00 275.00
CE Carmen Electra Jeans/50 100.00 250.00
DH Devin Harris/32 8.00 20.00
DW Dwyane Wade/199 20.00 50.00
EO Emeka Okafor/199 10.00 25.00
FJ Fred Jones/199 5.00 12.00
JC Josh Childress/27 8.00 20.00
JK Jason Kidd/199 12.50 30.00
JM Jenny McCarthy Jeans/50 100.00 200.00
JN Jameer Nelson/199 5.00 12.00
JS Josh Smith/86 6.00 15.00
JZ Jay-Z/50 125.00 250.00
KH Kris Humphries/57 5.00 12.00
KM Kevin Martin Event JSY/199 5.00 12.00
KS Kirk Snyder/115 5.00 12.00
LD Luol Deng/147 6.00 15.00
RA Rafael Araujo Event JSY/79 5.00 12.00
RH Richard Hamilton Event Warm/199 5.00 12.00
SE Shannon Elizabeth Jeans/50 100.00 200.00
SL Shaun Livingston/199 5.00 12.00
SM Stephon Marbury/199 6.00 15.00
SN Steve Nash/199 20.00 50.00
SO Shaquille O'Neal/199 40.00 80.00
ST Sebastian Telfair/55 5.00 12.00
TA Trevor Ariza/99 5.00 12.00
TM Tracy McGrady/99 12.00 30.00
DWE Delonte West/23 15.00 40.00
DWR Dorell Wright/199 5.00 12.00

2006-07 Topps Big Game

Issued in December 2006, Topps Big Game employs a basic design with color player images on a white background with silver foil highlights. Card numbers 1-75 picture veteran players and are serially numbered to 269 and card numbers 76-110 picture rookie players are are serially numbered to 579. Big Game is packaged in single packs of five cards each and carried an original suggested retail price of $75.00.

1-75 PRINT RUN 269 SER.#'d SETS
RC PRINT RUN 579 SER.#'d SETS
UNPRICED GOLD PRINT RUN ONE SET
1 Dirk Nowitzki 1.25 3.00
2 Tracy McGrady 1.00 2.50
3 Elton Brand .75 2.00
4 Ricky Davis .60 1.50
5 Marcus Camby .60 1.50
6 Gilbert Arenas .60 1.50
7 Channing Frye .60 1.50
8 Chauncey Billups .75 2.00
9 Shaquille O'Neal 1.50 4.00
10 Lamar Odom .60 1.50
11 Pau Gasol .75 2.00
12 Charlie Villanueva .50 1.25
13 Larry Hughes .60 1.50
14 Peja Stojakovic .75 2.00
15 Andre Iguodala .60 1.50
16 Vince Carter 1.00 2.50
17 Jason Terry .60 1.50
18 Ron Artest .75 2.00
19 Luke Ridnour .60 1.50
20 Paul Pierce .75 2.00
21 Michael Redd .60 1.50
22 Rasheed Wallace .75 2.00
23 Baron Davis .60 1.50
24 Amare Stoudemire .60 1.50
25 Zach Randolph .60 1.50
26 Yao Ming 1.00 2.50
27 Raymond Felton .60 1.50
28 Stephon Marbury .60 1.50
29 Kirk Hinrich .60 1.50
30 Andre Miller .60 1.50
31 Jason Kidd 1.25 3.00
32 Tayshaun Prince .60 1.50
33 Antoine Walker .60 1.50
34 LeBron James 3.00 8.00
35 Brad Miller .60 1.50
36 Tim Duncan 1.25 3.00
37 Jermaine O'Neal .60 1.50
38 Josh Smith .60 1.50
39 Gerald Wallace .60 1.50
40 Delonte West .50 1.25
41 Darius Miles .50 1.25
42 Chris Paul 1.00 2.50
43 Mike Bibby .75 2.00
44 Sam Cassell .60 1.50
45 Josh Howard .60 1.50
46 Allen Iverson 1.00 2.50
47 Jameer Nelson .50 1.25
48 Mehmet Okur .50 1.25
49 Shawn Marion .60 1.50
50 Ray Allen .75 2.00
51 Joe Johnson .60 1.50
52 Richard Hamilton .60 1.50
53 Richard Jefferson .60 1.50
54 Kobe Bryant 3.00 8.00
55 Manu Ginobili .75 2.00
56 Carmelo Anthony 1.00 2.50
57 Ben Gordon .60 1.50
58 Andrew Bogut .60 1.50
59 Antawn Jamison .60 1.50
60 Chris Bosh .75 2.00
61 David West .60 1.50
62 Steve Nash 1.00 2.50
63 Ben Wallace .60 1.50
64 Chris Webber .75 2.00
65 Caron Butler .60 1.50
66 Danny Granger .60 1.50
67 Andrei Kirilenko .60 1.50
68 Kevin Garnett 1.25 3.00
69 Dwyane Wade 1.25 3.00
70 Tony Parker .75 2.00
71 Dwight Howard .60 1.50
72 Rashard Lewis .75 2.00
73 Mike Miller .60 1.50
74 Jason Richardson .75 2.00
75 T.J. Ford .50 1.25
76 J.J. Redick RC 2.00 5.00
77 Marcus Williams RC 1.00 2.50
78 Shelden Williams RC 1.25 3.00
79 Tyrus Thomas RC 1.25 3.00
80 LaMarcus Aldridge RC 4.00 10.00
81 Cedric Simmons RC 1.00 2.50
82 Saer Sene RC 1.00 2.50
83 Randy Foye RC 1.50 4.00
84 Patrick O'Bryant RC 1.00 2.50
85 Adam Morrison RC 1.50 4.00
86 Rudy Gay RC 2.00 5.00
87 Ronnie Brewer RC 1.50 4.00
88 Josh Boone RC 1.00 2.50
89 Maurice Ager RC 1.00 2.50
90 Shannon Brown RC 1.00 2.50
91 Renaldo Balkman RC 1.25 3.00
92 Thabo Sefolosha RC 1.50 4.00
93 Shawne Williams RC 1.00 2.50
94 Hilton Armstrong RC 1.00 2.50
95 Brandon Roy RC 1.50 4.00
96 Kyle Lowry RC 2.00 5.00
97 Steve Novak RC 1.25 3.00
98 Paul Davis RC 1.00 2.50
99 Solomon Jones RC 1.00 2.50
100 P.J. Tucker RC 1.25 3.00
101 Rajon Rondo RC 2.50 6.00
102 Dee Brown RC 1.00 2.50
103 Craig Smith RC 1.25 3.00
104 Bobby Jones RC 1.00 2.50
105 James White RC 1.00 2.50
106 Jordan Farmar RC 1.50 4.00
107 Mardy Collins RC 1.00 2.50
108 Quincy Douby RC 1.00 2.50
109 Rodney Carney RC 1.00 2.50
110 Andrea Bargnani RC 1.50 4.00

2006-07 Topps Big Game Blue

*BLUE: 1.25X TO 3X BASE HI
STATED PRINT RUN 59 SER.#'d SETS

2006-07 Topps Big Game Red

*1-75 RED: 1X TO 2.5X BASE HI
*76-110 RED: .5X TO 1.25X BASE HI
STATED PRINT RUN 129 SER.#'d SETS

2006-07 Topps Big Game All-Star Rally Relics Jerseys

PRINT RUN 99 SER.#'d SETS
UNPRICED DUAL PRINT RUN 15 SETS
UNPRICED PATCH PRINT RUN 10 SETS
UNPRICED PATCH AU PRINT RUN 10 SETS
AI Allen Iverson 4.00 10.00
AN Andres Nocioni 2.00 5.00
BW Ben Wallace 2.50 6.00
CB Chauncey Billups 3.00 8.00
CF Channing Frye 2.50 6.00
DN Dirk Nowitzki 5.00 12.00
DW Dwyane Wade 6.00 15.00
KB Kobe Bryant 10.00 25.00
KG Kevin Garnett 5.00 12.00
LH Luther Head 2.50 6.00
NK Nenad Krstic 2.00 5.00
PG Pau Gasol 3.00 8.00
RH Richard Hamilton 2.50 6.00
SM Shawn Marion 2.50 6.00
SN Steve Nash 4.00 10.00
SO Shaquille O'Neal 6.00 15.00
TD Tim Duncan 5.00 12.00
TM Tracy McGrady 4.00 10.00
TP Tony Parker 3.00 8.00
VC Vince Carter 4.00 10.00
AIG Andre Iguodala 2.50 6.00
CBO Chris Bosh 3.00 8.00

2006-07 Topps Big Game All-Star Rally Relics Jerseys Autographs

INT RUN 199 SER.#'d SETS
AI Allen Iverson 40.00 100.00
DW Dwyane Wade 20.00 50.00
SO Shaquille O'Neal 30.00 80.00
TP Tony Parker 12.00 30.00
VC Vince Carter 15.00 40.00
CBO Chris Bosh 10.00 25.00

2006-07 Topps Big Game All-Star Rally Relics Dual Autographs

PRINT RUN 25 SER.#'d SETS
AI Allen Iverson 50.00 120.00
DW Dwyane Wade 60.00 120.00
SO Shaquille O'Neal 50.00 100.00
TP Tony Parker 20.00 50.00
VC Vince Carter 30.00 60.00
CBO Chris Bosh 20.00 50.00

2006-07 Topps Big Game Draft Day Moments Jerseys

PRINT RUN 99 SER.#'d SETS
*JUMBO: .6X TO 1.5X BASE HI
JUMBO PRINT RUN 99 SER.#'d SETS
*BALL: 1X TO 2.5X BASE HI
BALL PRINT RUN 25 SER.#'d SETS
UNPRICED BALL AU PRINT RUN 10 SETS
*BALL/HAT: 1X TO 2.5X BASE HI
BALL/HAT PRINT RUN 25 SER.#'d SETS
UNPRICED BALL/HAT AU PRINT RUN 10 SETS
*BALL/JSY: .6X TO 1.5X BASE HI
BALL/JSY PRINT RUN 50 SER.#'d SETS
UNPRICED BALL/JSY AU PRINT RUN 10 SETS
*HAT: .75X TO 2X BASE HI
HAT PRINT RUN 50 SER.#'d SETS
*HAT/JSY: 1X TO 2.5X BASE HI
HAT/JSY PRINT RUN 25 SER.#'d SETS
UNPRICED HAT/JSY AU PRINT RUN 10 SETS
UNPRICED LOGO PRINT RUN ONE SET
*PATCHES: 1X TO 2.5X BASE HI
PATCH PRINT RUN 25 SER.#'d SETS
UNPRICED PATCH JUMBO PRINT RUN 5 SETS
UNPRICED TAG PRINT RUN ONE SET
AB Andrea Bargnani 2.50 6.00
AM Adam Morrison 2.50 6.00
BR Brandon Roy 2.50 6.00
CS Cedric Simmons 1.50 4.00
HA Hilton Armstrong 1.50 4.00
LA LaMarcus Aldridge 6.00 15.00
MA Maurice Ager 1.50 4.00
MW Marcus Williams 1.50 4.00
RB Ronnie Brewer 2.50 6.00
RC Rodney Carney 1.50 4.00
RF Randy Foye 2.50 6.00
RG Rudy Gay 3.00 8.00
SS Saer Sene 1.50 4.00
SW Shelden Williams 2.00 5.00
TS Thabo Sefolosha 2.50 6.00
JJR J.J. Redick 3.00 8.00
POB Patrick O'Bryant 1.50 4.00

2006-07 Topps Big Game Draft Day Moments Jerseys Autographs

PRINT RUN 199 SER.#'d SETS
AB Andrea Bargnani 12.50 30.00
AM Adam Morrison 4.00 10.00
CS Cedric Simmons 2.50 6.00
HA Hilton Armstrong 2.50 6.00
MA Maurice Ager 2.50 6.00
MW Marcus Williams 2.50 6.00
RB Ronnie Brewer 4.00 10.00
RC Rodney Carney 2.50 6.00
RF Randy Foye 4.00 10.00
SS Saer Sene 2.50 6.00
SW Shelden Williams 3.00 8.00
TS Thabo Sefolosha 4.00 10.00
JJR J.J. Redick 5.00 12.00
POB Patrick O'Bryant 2.50 6.00

2006-07 Topps Big Game Draft Day Moments Hat Autographs

INT RUN 25 SER.#'d SETS
AB Andrea Bargnani 25.00 60.00
AM Adam Morrison 8.00 20.00
CS Cedric Simmons 5.00 12.00
HA Hilton Armstrong 5.00 12.00
MA Maurice Ager 5.00 12.00
MW Marcus Williams 5.00 12.00
RB Ronnie Brewer 8.00 20.00
RC Rodney Carney 5.00 12.00
RF Randy Foye 8.00 20.00
SS Saer Sene 5.00 12.00
SW Shelden Williams 6.00 15.00
TS Thabo Sefolosha 8.00 20.00
JJR J.J. Redick 10.00 25.00
POB Patrick O'Bryant 5.00 12.00

2006-07 Topps Big Game Draft Day Moments Patches Autographs

INT RUN 25 SER.#'d SETS
AB Andrea Bargnani 25.00 60.00
AM Adam Morrison 8.00 20.00
CS Cedric Simmons 5.00 12.00
HA Hilton Armstrong 5.00 12.00
MA Maurice Ager 5.00 12.00
MW Marcus Williams 5.00 12.00
RB Ronnie Brewer 8.00 20.00
RC Rodney Carney 5.00 12.00
RF Randy Foye 8.00 20.00
SS Saer Sene 5.00 12.00
SW Shelden Williams 6.00 15.00
TS Thabo Sefolosha 8.00 20.00
JJR J.J. Redick 10.00 25.00
POB Patrick O'Bryant 5.00 12.00

2006-07 Topps Big Game Final Score Relics

PRINT RUN 99 SER.#'d SETS
*PATCHES: .75X TO 2X BASE HI
PATCH PRINT RUN 50 SER.#'d SETS
AM Alonzo Mourning 8.00 20.00
AW Antoine Walker 2.50 6.00
DW Dwyane Wade 6.00 15.00
GP Gary Payton 3.00 8.00
JK Jason Kapono 2.00 5.00
JP James Posey 2.00 5.00
JW Jason Williams 2.50 6.00
MD Michael Doleac 2.00 5.00
SA Shandon Anderson 2.00 5.00
SO Shaquille O'Neal 6.00 15.00
UH Udonis Haslem 2.00 5.00

2006-07 Topps Big Game Final Score Relics Autographs

PRINT RUN 199 SER.#'d SETS
DW Dwyane Wade 40.00 100.00
SO Shaquille O'Neal 25.00 60.00

2006-07 Topps Big Game Final Score Patches Autographs

PRINT RUN 50 SER.#'d SETS
DW Dwyane Wade 40.00 100.00
SO Shaquille O'Neal 40.00 100.00

2006-07 Topps Big Game Picture Perfect Jerseys

PRINT RUN 99 SER.#'d SETS
*JSY/SHORTS: .5X TO 1.25X BASE HI
JSY/SHRT PRINT RUN 99 SER.#'d SETS
*PATCHES: .75X TO 2X BASE HI
PATCH PRINT RUN 50 SER.#'d SETS
AM Adam Morrison 2.50 6.00
AR Allan Ray 1.50 4.00
BJ Bobby Jones 1.50 4.00
CS Cedric Simmons 1.50 4.00
DB Dee Brown 1.50 4.00
HA Hilton Armstrong 1.50 4.00
JB Josh Boone 1.50 4.00
JF Jordan Farmar 2.50 6.00
JW James White 1.50 4.00
KL Kyle Lowry 3.00 8.00
KP Kevin Pittsnogle 2.00 5.00
LA LaMarcus Aldridge 6.00 15.00
MA Maurice Ager 1.50 4.00
MC Mardy Collins 1.50 4.00
MW Marcus Williams 1.50 4.00
PD Paul Davis 1.50 4.00
PO Patrick O'Bryant 1.50 4.00
QD Quincy Douby 1.50 4.00
RB Renaldo Balkman 2.00 5.00
RC Rodney Carney 1.50 4.00
RF Randy Foye 2.50 6.00
RG Rudy Gay 3.00 8.00
RR Rajon Rondo 4.00 10.00
SB Shannon Brown 1.50 4.00
SN Steve Novak 2.00 5.00
SW Shelden Williams 2.00 5.00
CSM Craig Smith 2.00 5.00
JJR J.J. Redick 3.00 8.00
RBR Ronnie Brewer 2.50 6.00
SWI Shawne Williams 1.50 4.00

2006-07 Topps Big Game Picture Perfect Jerseys Autographs

PRINT RUN 199 SER.#'d SETS
*JSY/SHORTS: .4X TO 1X BASE HI
JSY/SHRT PRINT RUN 199 SER.#'d SETS
*PATCH AU: .6X TO 1.5X BASE HI
PATCH AU PRINT RUN 99 SETS
AM Adam Morrison 4.00 10.00
AR Allan Ray 2.50 6.00
BJ Bobby Jones 2.50 6.00
CS Cedric Simmons 2.50 6.00
DB Dee Brown 2.50 6.00
HA Hilton Armstrong 2.50 6.00
JB Josh Boone 2.50 6.00
JF Jordan Farmar 4.00 10.00
JW James White 2.50 6.00
KL Kyle Lowry 5.00 12.00
MA Maurice Ager 2.50 6.00
MC Mardy Collins 2.50 6.00
MW Marcus Williams 2.50 6.00
PO Patrick O'Bryant 2.50 6.00
QD Quincy Douby 2.50 6.00
RB Renaldo Balkman 3.00 8.00
RC Rodney Carney 2.50 6.00
RF Randy Foye 4.00 10.00
RR Rajon Rondo 12.00 30.00
SB Shannon Brown 2.50 6.00
SW Shelden Williams 3.00 8.00
CSM Craig Smith 3.00 8.00
JJR J.J. Redick 5.00 12.00
RBR Ronnie Brewer 4.00 10.00
SWI Shawne Williams 2.50 6.00

2006-07 Topps Big Game Relics

PRINT RUN 99 SER.#'d SETS
*PATCHES: .75X TO 2X BASE HI
PATCH PRINT RUN 25 SER.#'d SETS
AB Andrew Bogut 2.50 6.00
AI Allen Iverson 4.00 10.00
AM Adam Morrison 3.00 8.00
CA Carmelo Anthony 4.00 10.00
CB Chris Bosh 3.00 8.00
DE Daniel Ewing 2.00 5.00
DW Dwyane Wade 6.00 15.00
EO Emeka Okafor 2.50 6.00
HW Hakim Warrick 2.50 6.00
JC Josh Childress 2.50 6.00
KB Kobe Bryant 10.00 25.00
LD Luol Deng 2.50 6.00
PP Paul Pierce 3.00 8.00
RF Raymond Felton 2.50 6.00
SN Steve Nash 4.00 10.00
SO Shaquille O'Neal 6.00 15.00
TP Tony Parker 3.00 8.00
JJR J.J. Redick 4.00 10.00
TJF T.J. Ford 2.00 5.00

2006-07 Topps Big Game Relics Autographs

PRINT RUN 75 SER.#'d SETS
*PATCH AU: .6X TO 1.5X BASE HI
PATCH AU PRINT RUN 25 SER.#'d SETS
AB Andrew Bogut 8.00 20.00
AI Allen Iverson 40.00 100.00
AM Adam Morrison 8.00 20.00
CB Chris Bosh 10.00 25.00
DE Daniel Ewing 5.00 12.00
DW Dwyane Wade 30.00 80.00
EO Emeka Okafor 5.00 12.00
HW Hakim Warrick 5.00 12.00
JC Josh Childress 5.00 12.00
LD Luol Deng 5.00 12.00
RF Raymond Felton 5.00 12.00
SO Shaquille O'Neal 40.00 80.00
TP Tony Parker 10.00 25.00
JJR J.J. Redick 5.00 12.00
TJF T.J. Ford 5.00 12.00

2006-07 Topps Big Game Patches

*PATCHES: .75X TO 2X BASE HI
PRINT RUN 25 SER.#'d SETS
KB Kobe Bryant 25.00 60.00

1996-97 Topps Chrome

The debut 1996-97 Topps Chrome basketball set was issued in one series totaling 220 standard-size cards. The card design is very similar to the 1996-97 Topps issue, but utilizes a Chrome background and silver borders. This product was produced for retail outlets exclusively, but was carried in many hobby stores. The cards were issued in 4-card packs carrying a suggested retail price of $2.99. Rookie cards include Shareef Abdur-Rahim, Kobe Bryant, Marcus Camby, Allen Iverson, Stephon Marbury and Antoine Walker, among others. The set is condition sensitive.

COMPLETE SET (220) 200.00 450.00
CONDITION SENSITIVE SET
BEWARE KOBE COUNTERFEITS
1 Patrick Ewing .60 1.50
2 Christian Laettner .40 1.00
3 Mahmoud Abdul-Rauf .30 .75
4 Chris Webber .60 1.50
5 Jason Kidd .75 2.00
6 Clifford Rozier .30 .75
7 Elden Campbell .30 .75
8 Chuck Person .40 1.00
9 Jeff Hornacek .40 1.00
10 Rik Smits .40 1.00
11 Kurt Thomas .30 .75
12 Rod Strickland .30 .75
13 Kendall Gill .30 .75
14 Brian Williams .30 .75
15 Tom Gugliotta .30 .75
16 Ron Harper .40 1.00
17 Eric Williams .30 .75
18 A.C. Green .40 1.00
19 Scott Williams .30 .75
20 Damon Stoudamire .40 1.00
21 Bryant Reeves .30 .75
22 Bob Sura .30 .75
23 Mitch Richmond .50 1.25
24 Larry Johnson .50 1.25
25 Vin Baker .40 1.00
26 Mark Bryant .30 .75
27 Horace Grant .40 1.00
28 Allan Houston .40 1.00
29 Sam Perkins .30 .75
30 Antonio McDyess .50 1.25
31 Rasheed Wallace .60 1.50
32 Malik Sealy .30 .75
33 Scottie Pippen .75 2.00
34 Charles Barkley .75 2.00
35 Hakeem Olajuwon .60 1.50
36 John Starks .40 1.00
37 Byron Scott .40 1.00
38 Arvydas Sabonis .40 1.00
39 Vlade Divac .50 1.25
40 Joe Dumars .50 1.25
41 Danny Ferry .30 .75
42 Jerry Stackhouse .60 1.50
43 B.J. Armstrong .30 .75
44 Shawn Bradley .30 .75
45 Kevin Garnett 1.25 3.00
46 Dee Brown .30 .75
47 Michael Smith .30 .75
48 Doug Christie .30 .75
49 Mark Jackson .40 1.00
50 Shawn Kemp .50 1.25
51 Sasha Danilovic .30 .75
52 Nick Anderson .30 .75
53 Matt Geiger .30 .75
54 Charles Smith .30 .75
55 Mookie Blaylock .30 .75
56 Johnny Newman .30 .75
57 George McCloud .30 .75
58 Greg Ostertag .30 .75
59 Reggie Williams .30 .75
60 Brent Barry .40 1.00
61 Doug West .30 .75
62 Donald Royal .30 .75
63 Randy Brown .30 .75
64 Vincent Askew .30 .75
65 John Stockton .60 1.50
66 Joe Kleine .30 .75
67 Keith Askins .30 .75
68 Bobby Phills .30 .75
69 Chris Mullin .50 1.25
70 Nick Van Exel .50 1.25
71 Rick Fox .30 .75
72 Chicago Bulls - 72 Wins 1.50 4.00
73 Shawn Respert .30 .75
74 Hubert Davis .30 .75
75 Jim Jackson .30 .75
76 Olden Polynice .30 .75
77 Gheorghe Muresan .30 .75
78 Theo Ratliff .30 .75
79 Khalid Reeves .30 .75
80 David Robinson .75 2.00
81 Lawrence Moten .30 .75
82 Sam Cassell .40 1.00
83 George Zidek .30 .75
84 Sharone Wright .30 .75
85 Clarence Weatherspoon .30 .75
86 Alan Henderson .30 .75
87 Chris Dudley .30 .75
88 Ed O'Bannon .30 .75
89 Calbert Cheaney .30 .75
90 Cedric Ceballos .30 .75
91 Michael Cage .30 .75
92 Ervin Johnson .30 .75
93 Gary Trent .30 .75
94 Sherman Douglas .30 .75
95 Joe Smith .40 1.00
96 Dale Davis .30 .75
97 Tony Dumas .30 .75
98 Muggsy Bogues .40 1.00
99 Toni Kukoc .50 1.25
100 Grant Hill .75 2.00
101 Michael Finley .60 1.50
102 Isaiah Rider .40 1.00
103 Bryant Stith .30 .75
104 Pooh Richardson .30 .75
105 Karl Malone .60 1.50
106 Brian Grant .40 1.00
107 Sean Elliott .50 1.25
108 Charles Oakley .40 1.00
109 Pervis Ellison .30 .75
110 Anfernee Hardaway .75 2.00
111 Checklist (1-220) .30 .75
112 Dikembe Mutombo .50 1.25
113 Alonzo Mourning .60 1.50
114 Hubert Davis .30 .75
115 Rony Seikaly .30 .75
116 Danny Manning .40 1.00
117 Donyell Marshall .30 .75
118 Gerald Wilkins .30 .75
119 Ervin Johnson .30 .75
120 Jalen Rose .40 1.00
121 Dino Radja .30 .75
122 Glenn Robinson .40 1.00
123 John Stockton .60 1.50
124 Matt Maloney RC 1.25 3.00
125 Clifford Robinson .30 .75
126 Steve Kerr .40 1.00
127 Nate McMillan .30 .75
128 Shareef Abdur-Rahim RC 6.00 15.00
129 Loy Vaught .30 .75
130 Anthony Mason .30 .75
131 Kevin Garnett 1.25 3.00
132 Roy Rogers RC 1.25 3.00
133 Erick Dampier RC 1.50 4.00
134 Tyus Edney .30 .75
135 Chris Mills .30 .75
136 Cory Alexander .30 .75
137 Juwan Howard .40 1.00
138 Kobe Bryant RC 150.00 300.00
139 Michael Jordan 6.00 15.00
140 Jayson Williams .30 .75
141 Rod Strickland .30 .75
142 Lorenzen Wright RC 1.25 3.00
143 Will Perdue .30 .75
144 Derek Harper .40 1.00
145 Billy Owens .30 .75
146 Antoine Walker RC 3.00 8.00
147 P.J. Brown .30 .75
148 Terrell Brandon .30 .75
149 Larry Johnson .50 1.25
150 Steve Smith .40 1.00
151 Eddie Jones .50 1.25
152 Detlef Schrempf .50 1.25
153 Dale Ellis .30 .75
154 Isaiah Rider .40 1.00
155 Tony Delk RC 1.50 4.00
156 Adrian Caldwell .30 .75
157 Jamal Mashburn .40 1.00
158 Dennis Scott .30 .75
159 Dana Barros .30 .75
160 Martin Muursepp RC 1.00 2.50
161 Marcus Camby RC 2.50 6.00
162 Jerome Williams RC 1.25 3.00
163 Wesley Person .30 .75
164 Luc Longley .40 1.00
165 Charlie Ward .30 .75
166 Mark Jackson .40 1.00
167 Derrick Coleman .40 1.00
168 Dell Curry .30 .75
169 Armon Gilliam .30 .75
170 Vlade Divac .50 1.25
171 Allen Iverson RC 25.00 60.00
172 Vitaly Potapenko RC 1.25 3.00
173 Jon Koncak .30 .75
174 Lindsey Hunter .30 .75
175 Kevin Johnson .50 1.25
176 Dennis Rodman 1.00 2.50
177 Stephon Marbury RC 6.00 15.00
178 Karl Malone .60 1.50
179 Charles Barkley .75 2.00
180 Popeye Jones .30 .75
181 Samaki Walker RC 1.25 3.00
182 Steve Nash RC 10.00 25.00
183 Latrell Sprewell .50 1.25
184 Kenny Anderson .40 1.00
185 Tyrone Hill .30 .75
186 Robert Pack .30 .75
187 Greg Anthony .30 .75
188 Derrick McKey .30 .75
189 John Wallace RC 1.50 4.00
190 Bryon Russell .30 .75
191 Jermaine O'Neal RC 2.50 6.00
192 Clyde Drexler .60 1.50
193 Mahmoud Abdul-Rauf .30 .75
194 Eric Montross .30 .75
195 Allan Houston .40 1.00
196 Harvey Grant .30 .75
197 Rodney Rogers .30 .75
198 Kerry Kittles RC 1.50 4.00
199 Grant Hill .75 2.00
200 Lionel Simmons .30 .75
201 Reggie Miller .60 1.50
202 Avery Johnson .40 1.00
203 LaPhonso Ellis .30 .75
204 Brian Shaw .30 .75
205 Priest Lauderdale RC 1.00 2.50
206 Derek Fisher RC 2.00 5.00
207 Terry Porter .30 .75
208 Todd Fuller RC 1.00 2.50
209 Hersey Hawkins .30 .75
210 Tim Legler .30 .75
211 Terry Dehere .30 .75
212 Gary Payton .50 1.25
213 Joe Dumars .50 1.25
214 Don MacLean .30 .75
215 Greg Minor .30 .75
216 Tim Hardaway .50 1.25
217 Ray Allen RC 10.00 25.00
218 Mario Elie .30 .75
219 Brooks Thompson .30 .75
220 Shaquille O'Neal 1.25 3.00

1996-97 Topps Chrome Refractors

*STARS: 8X TO 20X HI COLUMN
*RCs: 1.5X TO 4X HI
STATED ODDS 1:12
CONDITION SENSITIVE SET
72 Chicago Bulls - 72 Wins 150.00 400.00
110 Anfernee Hardaway 20.00 50.00
128 Shareef Abdur-Rahim 40.00 100.00
138 Kobe Bryant 3000.00 4000.00
139 Michael Jordan 700.00 1200.00
151 Eddie Jones 12.00 30.00
155 Tony Delk 15.00 40.00
162 Jerome Williams 10.00 25.00
171 Allen Iverson 500.00 800.00
182 Steve Nash 200.00 500.00

1996-97 Topps Chrome Pro Files

Randomly inserted into packs at a rate of one in 8, this 20-card set parallels the Pro Files insert set from the regular 1996-97 Topps issue, but with a Chrome background. Card backs carry a "PF" prefix.

COMPLETE SET (20) 15.00 40.00
STATED ODDS 1:8
PF1 Grant Hill 1.50 4.00
PF2 Shawn Kemp 1.00 2.50
PF3 Michael Jordan 10.00 25.00
PF4 Vin Baker .75 2.00
PF5 Chris Webber 1.25 3.00
PF6 Joe Smith .75 2.00
PF7 Shaquille O'Neal 2.50 6.00
PF8 Patrick Ewing 1.25 3.00
PF9 Scottie Pippen 1.50 4.00
PF10 Damon Stoudamire .75 2.00
PF11 Anfernee Hardaway 1.50 4.00
PF12 Juwan Howard .75 2.00
PF13 Dikembe Mutombo 1.00 2.50
PF14 Dennis Rodman 2.00 5.00
PF15 Kevin Garnett 2.50 6.00
PF16 Jerry Stackhouse 1.25 3.00
PF17 Alonzo Mourning 1.25 3.00
PF18 Karl Malone 1.25 3.00
PF19 Hakeem Olajuwon 1.25 3.00
PF20 Gary Payton 1.00 2.50

1996-97 Topps Chrome Season's Best

Randomly inserted into packs at a rate of one in 6, this 25-card set parallels the Season's Best insert set from the regular 1996-97 Topps issue, but with a Chrome background. Card backs carry a "SB" prefix.

COMPLETE SET (25) 20.00 50.00
STATED ODDS 1:6
SB1 Michael Jordan 10.00 25.00
SB2 Hakeem Olajuwon 1.25 3.00
SB3 Shaquille O'Neal 2.50 6.00
SB4 Karl Malone 1.25 3.00
SB5 David Robinson 1.50 4.00
SB6 Dennis Rodman 2.00 5.00
SB7 David Robinson 1.50 4.00
SB8 Dikembe Mutombo 1.00 2.50
SB9 Charles Barkley 1.50 4.00
SB10 Shawn Kemp 1.00 2.50
SB11 John Stockton 1.25 3.00
SB12 Jason Kidd 1.50 4.00
SB13 Avery Johnson .75 2.00
SB14 Rod Strickland .60 1.50
SB15 Damon Stoudamire .75 2.00
SB16 Gary Payton 1.00 2.50
SB17 Mookie Blaylock .60 1.50
SB18 Michael Jordan 10.00 25.00
SB19 Jason Kidd 1.50 4.00
SB20 Alvin Robertson .60 1.50
SB21 Dikembe Mutombo 1.00 2.50
SB22 Shawn Bradley .60 1.50
SB23 David Robinson 1.50 4.00
SB24 Hakeem Olajuwon 1.25 3.00
SB25 Alonzo Mourning 1.25 3.00

1996-97 Topps Chrome Youthquake

Randomly inserted into packs at a rate of one in 12, this 15-card set parallels the Youthquake insert set from the regular 1996-97 Topps issue, but with a Chrome background. Card backs carry a "YQ" prefix.

COMPLETE SET (15) 40.00 100.00
STATED ODDS 1:12
YQ1 Allen Iverson 6.00 15.00
YQ2 Samaki Walker .75 2.00
YQ3 Stephon Marbury 2.50 6.00
YQ4 Damon Stoudamire 1.25 3.00
YQ5 John Wallace 1.00 2.50
YQ6 Michael Finley 2.00 5.00
YQ7 Marcus Camby 1.50 4.00
YQ8 Kerry Kittles 1.00 2.50
YQ9 Ray Allen 4.00 10.00
YQ10 Jerry Stackhouse 2.00 5.00
YQ11 Shareef Abdur-Rahim 1.50 4.00
YQ12 Antonio McDyess 1.00 2.50
YQ13 Joe Smith .75 2.00
YQ14 Brent Barry .75 2.00
YQ15 Kobe Bryant 50.00 120.00

1997-98 Topps Chrome

The 1997-98 Topps Chrome set was issued in one series totalling 220 cards. The cards are a semi-parallel of the regular Topps set - utilizing the same photography, but released in separate packaging at a suggested retail price of $3 per pack.

COMPLETE SET (220) 25.00 60.00
1 Scottie Pippen 1.00 2.50
2 Nate McMillan .40 1.00
3 Byron Scott .50 1.25
4 Mark Davis .40 1.00
5 Rod Strickland .40 1.00
6 Brian Grant .40 1.00
7 Damon Stoudamire .50 1.25
8 John Stockton .75 2.00
9 Grant Long .40 1.00
10 Darrell Armstrong .40 1.00
11 Anthony Mason .40 1.00
12 Travis Best .40 1.00
13 Stephon Marbury .75 2.00
14 Jamal Mashburn .50 1.25
15 Detlef Schrempf .60 1.50
16 Terrell Brandon .40 1.00
17 Charles Barkley 1.00 2.50
18 Vin Baker .50 1.25
19 Gary Trent .40 1.00
20 Vinny Del Negro .40 1.00
21 Todd Day .40 1.00
22 Malik Sealy .40 1.00
23 Wesley Person .40 1.00
24 Reggie Miller .75 2.00
25 Dan Majerle .60 1.50
26 Todd Fuller .40 1.00
27 Juwan Howard .50 1.25
28 Clarence Weatherspoon .40 1.00
29 Grant Hill 1.00 2.50
30 John Williams .40 1.00
31 Ken Norman .40 1.00
32 Patrick Ewing .75 2.00
33 Bryon Russell .40 1.00
34 Tony Smith .40 1.00
35 Andrew Lang .40 1.00
36 Rony Seikaly .40 1.00
37 Billy Owens .40 1.00
38 Dino Radja .40 1.00
39 Chris Gatling .40 1.00
40 Dale Davis .40 1.00
41 Arvydas Sabonis .50 1.25
42 Chris Mills .40 1.00
43 A.C. Green .50 1.25
44 Tyrone Hill .40 1.00
45 Tracy Murray .40 1.00
46 David Robinson 1.00 2.50
47 Lee Mayberry .40 1.00
48 Jayson Williams .40 1.00
49 Jason Kidd 1.00 2.50
50 Bryant Stith .40 1.00
51 CL/Bulls - Team of the 90s 1.50 4.00
52 Brent Barry .50 1.25
53 Henry James .40 1.00
54 Allen Iverson 1.25 3.00
55 Shandon Anderson .40 1.00
56 Mitch Richmond .60 1.50
57 Allan Houston .50 1.25
58 Ron Harper .50 1.25
59 Gheorghe Muresan .40 1.00
60 Vincent Askew .40 1.00
61 Ray Allen .75 2.00
62 Kenny Anderson .50 1.25
63 Dikembe Mutombo .60 1.50
64 Sam Perkins .40 1.00
65 Walt Williams .40 1.00
66 Chris Carr .40 1.00
67 Vlade Divac .60 1.50
68 LaPhonso Ellis .40 1.00
69 B.J. Armstrong .40 1.00
70 Jim Jackson .40 1.00
71 Clyde Drexler .75 2.00
72 Lindsey Hunter .40 1.00
73 Sasha Danilovic .40 1.00
74 Elden Campbell .40 1.00
75 Robert Pack .40 1.00
76 Dennis Scott .40 1.00
77 Will Perdue .40 1.00
78 Anthony Peeler .40 1.00
79 Steve Smith .50 1.25
80 Steve Kerr .50 1.25
81 Buck Williams .40 1.00
82 Terry Mills .40 1.00
83 Michael Smith .40 1.00
84 Adam Keefe .40 1.00
85 Kevin Willis .40 1.00
86 David Wesley .40 1.00
87 Muggsy Bogues .50 1.25
88 Bimbo Coles .40 1.00
89 Tom Gugliotta .40 1.00
90 Jermaine O'Neal .50 1.25
91 Cedric Ceballos .40 1.00
92 Shawn Kemp .60 1.50
93 Horace Grant .50 1.25
94 Shareef Abdur-Rahim .60 1.50
95 Robert Horry .50 1.25
96 Vitaly Potapenko .40 1.00
97 Pooh Richardson .40 1.00
98 Doug Christie .40 1.00
99 Voshon Lenard .40 1.00
100 Dominique Wilkins .75 2.00
101 Alonzo Mourning .75 2.00
102 Sam Cassell .50 1.25
103 Sherman Douglas .40 1.00
104 Shawn Bradley .40 1.00
105 Mark Jackson .50 1.25
106 Dennis Rodman 1.25 3.00
107 Charles Oakley .50 1.25
108 Matt Maloney .40 1.00
109 Shaquille O'Neal 1.50 4.00
110 K.Malone MVP CL .75 2.00
111 Antonio McDyess .50 1.25
112 Bob Sura .40 1.00
113 Terrell Brandon .40 1.00
114 Tim Thomas RC 1.25 3.00
115 Tim Duncan RC 30.00 80.00
116 Antonio Daniels RC 1.00 2.50
117 Bryant Reeves .40 1.00
118 Keith Van Horn RC 1.50 4.00
119 Loy Vaught .40 1.00
120 Rasheed Wallace .60 1.50
121 Bobby Jackson RC 1.25 3.00
122 Kevin Johnson .60 1.50
123 Michael Jordan 5.00 12.00
124 Ron Mercer RC 1.25 3.00
125 Tracy McGrady RC 4.00 10.00
126 Antoine Walker .60 1.50
127 Carlos Rogers .40 1.00
128 Isaac Austin .40 1.00
129 Mookie Blaylock .40 1.00
130 Rodrick Rhodes RC .75 2.00
131 Dennis Scott .40 1.00
132 Chris Mullin .60 1.50
133 P.J. Brown .40 1.00
134 Rex Chapman .40 1.00
135 Sean Elliott .60 1.50
136 Alan Henderson .40 1.00
137 Austin Croshere RC .75 2.00
138 Nick Van Exel .50 1.25
139 Derek Strong .40 1.00
140 Glenn Robinson .50 1.25
141 Avery Johnson .50 1.25
142 Calbert Cheaney .40 1.00
143 Mahmoud Abdul-Rauf .40 1.00
144 Stojko Vrankovic .40 1.00
145 Chris Childs .40 1.00
146 Danny Manning .50 1.25
147 Jeff Hornacek .50 1.25
148 Kevin Garnett 1.00 2.50
149 Joe Dumars .60 1.50
150 Johnny Taylor RC .75 2.00
151 Mark Price .60 1.50
152 Toni Kukoc .60 1.50
153 Erick Dampier .40 1.00
154 Lorenzen Wright .40 1.00
155 Matt Geiger .40 1.00
156 Tim Hardaway .60 1.50
157 Charles Smith RC .75 2.00
158 Hersey Hawkins .40 1.00
159 Michael Finley .60 1.50
160 Tyus Edney .40 1.00
161 Christian Laettner .50 1.25
162 Doug West .40 1.00
163 Jim Jackson .40 1.00
164 Larry Johnson .60 1.50
165 Vin Baker .50 1.25
166 Karl Malone .75 2.00
167 Kelvin Cato RC .75 2.00
168 Luc Longley .50 1.25
169 Dale Davis .40 1.00
170 Joe Smith .50 1.25
171 Kobe Bryant 3.00 8.00
172 Scot Pollard RC 1.00 2.50
173 Derek Anderson RC 1.00 2.50
174 Erick Strickland RC .75 2.00
175 Olden Polynice .40 1.00
176 Chris Whitney .40 1.00
177 Anthony Parker RC 1.00 2.50
178 Armon Gilliam .40 1.00
179 Gary Payton .60 1.50
180 Glen Rice .60 1.50
181 Chauncey Billups RC 3.00 8.00
182 Derek Fisher .60 1.50
183 John Starks .50 1.25
184 Mario Elie .40 1.00
185 Chris Webber .60 1.50
186 Shawn Kemp .60 1.50
187 Greg Ostertag .40 1.00
188 Olivier Saint-Jean RC .75 2.00
189 Eric Snow .40 1.00
190 Isaiah Rider .50 1.25
191 Paul Grant RC .60 1.50
192 Samaki Walker .40 1.00
193 Cory Alexander .40 1.00
194 Eddie Jones .60 1.50
195 John Thomas RC .60 1.50
196 Otis Thorpe .40 1.00
197 Rod Strickland .40 1.00
198 David Wesley .40 1.00
199 Jacque Vaughn RC .75 2.00
200 Rik Smits .50 1.25
201 Brevin Knight RC 1.00 2.50
202 Clifford Robinson .40 1.00
203 Hakeem Olajuwon .75 2.00
204 Jerry Stackhouse .60 1.50
205 Tyrone Hill .40 1.00
206 Kendall Gill .40 1.00
207 Marcus Camby .60 1.50
208 Tony Battie RC 1.00 2.50
209 Brent Price .40 1.00
210 Danny Fortson RC 1.00 2.50
211 Jerome Williams .40 1.00
212 Maurice Taylor RC 1.00 2.50
213 Brian Williams .40 1.00
214 Keith Booth RC .75 2.00
215 Nick Anderson .40 1.00
216 Travis Knight .40 1.00
217 Adonal Foyle RC .75 2.00
218 Anfernee Hardaway 1.00 2.50
219 Kerry Kittles .40 1.00
220 D.Mutombo POY CL .60 1.50

1997-98 Topps Chrome Refractors

*STARS: 3X TO 8X BASE CARD HI
*RCs: 2X TO 5X BASE HI
STATED ODDS 1:12
51 CL/Bulls - Team of the 90s 125.00 300.00
54 Allen Iverson 15.00 40.00
115 Tim Duncan 500.00 900.00
123 Michael Jordan 150.00 400.00
125 Tracy McGrady 100.00 250.00
171 Kobe Bryant 75.00 200.00
181 Chauncey Billups 15.00 40.00

1997-98 Topps Chrome Destiny

Randomly inserted into packs at a rate of one in 12, this 15-card set is a parallel of the regular Topps Destiny utilizing the Chrome technology. Card backs are numbered with a "D" prefix.

COMPLETE SET (15) 12.00 30.00
STATED ODDS 1:12
*REF: 1X TO 2.5X BASE DESTINY
REF: STATED ODDS 1:48
D1 Grant Hill 1.25 3.00
D2 Kevin Garnett 1.25 3.00
D3 Vin Baker .60 1.50
D4 Antoine Walker .75 2.00
D5 Kobe Bryant 4.00 10.00
D6 Tracy McGrady 1.50 4.00
D7 Keith Van Horn .60 1.50
D8 Tim Duncan 2.00 5.00
D9 Eddie Jones .75 2.00
D10 Stephon Marbury 1.00 2.50
D11 Marcus Camby .75 2.00
D12 Antonio McDyess .60 1.50
D13 Shareef Abdur-Rahim .75 2.00
D14 Allen Iverson 1.50 4.00
D15 Shaquille O'Neal 2.00 5.00

1997-98 Topps Chrome Season's Best

Randomly inserted into packs at a rate of one in eight, this 29-card set is a parallel of the regular Topps Season's Best set utilizing the Chrome technology. The only card not available is SB8, which was not produced. Card backs are numbered with a "SB" prefix.

COMPLETE SET (29) 20.00 50.00
STATED ODDS 1:8
*REF: 1.25X TO 3X BASE SEAS.BEST
REF: STATED ODDS 1:24
SB1 Gary Payton .75 2.00
SB2 Kevin Johnson .75 2.00
SB3 Tim Hardaway .75 2.00
SB4 John Stockton 1.00 2.50
SB5 Damon Stoudamire .60 1.50
SB6 Michael Jordan 12.00 30.00
SB7 Mitch Richmond .75 2.00
SB9 Reggie Miller 1.00 2.50
SB10 Clyde Drexler 1.00 2.50
SB11 Grant Hill 1.25 3.00
SB12 Scottie Pippen 1.25 3.00
SB13 Kendall Gill .50 1.25
SB14 Glen Rice .75 2.00
SB15 LaPhonso Ellis .50 1.25
SB16 Karl Malone 1.00 2.50
SB17 Charles Barkley 1.25 3.00
SB18 Vin Baker .60 1.50
SB19 Chris Webber .75 2.00
SB20 Tom Gugliotta .50 1.25
SB21 Shaquille O'Neal 2.00 5.00
SB22 Patrick Ewing 1.00 2.50
SB23 Hakeem Olajuwon 1.00 2.50
SB24 Alonzo Mourning 1.00 2.50
SB25 Dikembe Mutombo .75 2.00
SB26 Allen Iverson 1.50 4.00
SB27 Antoine Walker .75 2.00
SB28 Shareef Abdur-Rahim .75 2.00
SB29 Stephon Marbury 1.00 2.50
SB30 Kerry Kittles .50 1.25

1997-98 Topps Chrome Topps 40

Randomly inserted into packs at a rate of one in 6, this 39-card set is a parallel of the regular Topps 40 set utilizing the Chrome technology. Card T-40 7 was not produced. Card backs are numbered with a "T40" prefix.

COMPLETE SET (39) 30.00 60.00
STATED ODDS 1:6
*REF: 1.25X TO 3X BASE TOP 40
REF: STATED ODDS 1:18
CARD T-40 7 DOES NOT EXIST
T1 Glen Rice .60 1.50
T2 Patrick Ewing .75 2.00
T3 Terrell Brandon .40 1.00
T4 Jerry Stackhouse .60 1.50
T5 Michael Jordan 8.00 20.00
T6 Christian Laettner .50 1.25
T8 Reggie Miller .75 2.00
T9 Gary Payton .60 1.50
T10 Detlef Schrempf .60 1.50
T11 Kevin Garnett 1.00 2.50
T12 Eddie Jones .60 1.50
T13 Clyde Drexler .75 2.00
T14 Anfernee Hardaway 1.00 2.50
T15 Chris Webber .60 1.50
T16 Jayson Williams .40 1.00
T17 Joe Smith .50 1.25
T18 Karl Malone .75 2.00
T19 Tim Hardaway .60 1.50
T20 Vin Baker .50 1.25
T21 Tom Gugliotta .40 1.00
T22 Allen Iverson 1.25 3.00
T23 David Robinson 1.00 2.50
T24 Dikembe Mutombo .60 1.50
T25 John Stockton .75 2.00
T26 Charles Barkley 1.00 2.50
T27 Mitch Richmond .60 1.50
T28 Damon Stoudamire .50 1.25
T29 Anthony Mason .50 1.25
T30 Shaquille O'Neal 1.50 4.00
T31 Glenn Robinson .60 1.50
T32 Juwan Howard .60 1.50
T33 Shawn Kemp .75 2.00
T34 Dennis Rodman 1.50 4.00
T35 Grant Hill 1.00 2.50
T36 Kevin Johnson .75 2.00
T37 Alonzo Mourning 1.00 2.50
T38 Hakeem Olajuwon 1.00 2.50
T39 Joe Dumars .60 1.50
T40 Scottie Pippen 1.25 3.00

1998-99 Topps Chrome

Released in four-card packs, this 220-card set is a semi-parallel of the base 1998-99 Topps set. Cards #6, 10, 19, 40, 43, 60, 73, 75, 77, 81, 89, 90, 97, 99, and 100 either do not exist, due to player's not signing contracts or players no longer playing in the NBA, or were included in the Topps 2 preview set.

COMPLETE SET (220) 20.00 50.00
COMP.SET W/PREV (230) 60.00 150.00
THE FOLLOWING CARDS ARE IN PREVIEW:
6/10/19/40/43/60/73/77/81/100
PREV.SET: INSERTED IN TOPPS 2 PACKS
1 Scottie Pippen .60 1.50
2 Shareef Abdur-Rahim .40 1.00
3 Rod Strickland .25 .60
4 Keith Van Horn .40 1.00
5 Ray Allen .50 1.25
7 Anthony Parker .25 .60
8 Lindsey Hunter .25 .60
9 Mario Elie .25 .60
11 Eldridge Recasner .25 .60
12 Jeff Hornacek .30 .75
13 Chris Webber .40 1.00
14 Lee Mayberry .25 .60
15 Erick Strickland .25 .60
16 Arvydas Sabonis .30 .75
17 Tim Thomas .40 1.00
18 Luc Longley .30 .75
20 Alonzo Mourning .50 1.25
21 Adonal Foyle .25 .60
22 Tony Battie .30 .75
23 Robert Horry .30 .75
24 Derek Harper .30 .75
25 Jamal Mashburn .30 .75
26 Elliott Perry .25 .60
27 Jalen Rose .30 .75
28 Joe Smith .30 .75
29 Henry James .25 .60
30 Travis Knight .25 .60
31 Tom Gugliotta .25 .60
32 Chris Anstey .25 .60
33 Antonio Daniels .25 .60
34 Elden Campbell .25 .60
35 Charlie Ward .25 .60
36 Eddie Johnson .25 .60
37 John Wallace .25 .60
38 Antonio Davis .25 .60
39 Antoine Walker .40 1.00
41 Doug Christie .25 .60
42 Andrew Lang .25 .60
44 Jaren Jackson .25 .60
45 Loy Vaught .25 .60
46 Allan Houston .30 .75
47 Mark Jackson .30 .75
48 Tracy Murray .25 .60
49 Tim Duncan .75 2.00
50 Micheal Williams .25 .60
51 Steve Nash .60 1.50
52 Matt Maloney .25 .60
53 Sam Cassell .30 .75
54 Voshon Lenard .25 .60
55 Dikembe Mutombo .40 1.00
56 Malik Sealy .25 .60
57 Dell Curry .25 .60
58 Stephon Marbury .50 1.25
59 Tariq Abdul-Wahad .25 .60
61 Kelvin Cato .25 .60
62 LaPhonso Ellis .25 .60
63 Jim Jackson .25 .60
64 Greg Ostertag .25 .60
65 Glenn Robinson .30 .75
66 Chris Carr .25 .60
67 Marcus Camby .30 .75
68 Kobe Bryant 1.50 4.00
69 Bobby Jackson .25 .60
70 B.J. Armstrong .25 .60
71 Alan Henderson .25 .60
72 Terry Davis .25 .60
74 Lamond Murray .25 .60
76 Rex Chapman .25 .60
78 Terry Cummings .30 .75
79 Dan Majerle .40 1.00
80 Bo Outlaw .25 .60
82 Vin Baker .30 .75
83 Clifford Robinson .25 .60
84 Greg Anthony .25 .60
85 Brevin Knight .25 .60
86 Jacque Vaughn .25 .60
87 Bobby Phills .25 .60
88 Sherman Douglas .25 .60
91 Lorenzen Wright .25 .60
92 Eric Williams .25 .60
93 Will Perdue .25 .60
94 Charles Barkley .60 1.50
95 Kendall Gill .25 .60
96 Wesley Person .25 .60
98 Erick Dampier .25 .60
101 Rasheed Wallace .40 1.00
102 Zydrunas Ilgauskas .40 1.00
103 Eddie Jones .40 1.00
104 Ron Mercer .30 .75
105 Horace Grant .30 .75
106 Corliss Williamson .25 .60
107 Anthony Mason .25 .60
108 Mookie Blaylock .25 .60
109 Dennis Rodman .75 2.00
110 Checklist .25 .60
111 Steve Smith .30 .75
112 Cedric Henderson .25 .60
113 Raef LaFrentz RC 1.25 3.00
114 Calbert Cheaney .25 .60
115 Rik Smits .30 .75
116 Rony Seikaly .25 .60
117 Lawrence Funderburke .25 .60
118 Ricky Davis RC 1.50 4.00
119 Howard Eisley .25 .60
120 Kenny Anderson .30 .75
121 Corey Benjamin RC .60 1.50
122 Maurice Taylor .25 .60
123 Eric Murdock .25 .60
124 Derek Fisher .40 1.00
125 Kevin Garnett .60 1.50
126 Walt Williams .25 .60
127 Bryce Drew RC .60 1.50
128 A.C. Green .30 .75
129 Ervin Johnson .25 .60
130 Christian Laettner .30 .75
131 Chauncey Billups .50 1.25
132 Hakeem Olajuwon .50 1.25
133 Al Harrington RC 1.50 4.00
134 Danny Manning .30 .75
135 Paul Pierce RC 4.00 10.00
136 Terrell Brandon .25 .60
137 Bob Sura .25 .60
138 Chris Gatling .25 .60
139 Donyell Marshall .25 .60
140 Marcus Camby .30 .75
141 Brian Skinner RC 1.00 2.50
142 Charles Oakley .30 .75
143 Antawn Jamison RC 1.50 4.00
144 Nazr Mohammed RC 1.00 2.50
145 Karl Malone .50 1.25
146 Chris Mills .25 .60
147 Bison Dele .25 .60
148 Gary Payton .40 1.00
149 Terry Porter .25 .60
150 Tim Hardaway .40 1.00
151 Larry Hughes RC 2.00 5.00
152 Derek Anderson .25 .60
153 Jason Williams RC 2.50 6.00
154 Dirk Nowitzki RC 12.00 30.00
155 Juwan Howard .30 .75
156 Avery Johnson .30 .75
157 Matt Harpring RC 1.00 2.50
158 Reggie Miller .50 1.25
159 Walter McCarty .25 .60
160 Allen Iverson .75 2.00
161 Felipe Lopez RC .60 1.50
162 Tracy McGrady .60 1.50
163 Damon Stoudamire .30 .75
164 Antonio McDyess .30 .75
165 Grant Hill .60 1.50
166 Tyronn Lue RC 1.00 2.50
167 P.J. Brown .25 .60
168 Antonio Daniels .25 .60
169 Mitch Richmond .40 1.00
170 David Robinson .60 1.50
171 Shawn Bradley .25 .60
172 Shandon Anderson .25 .60
173 Chris Childs .25 .60
174 Shawn Kemp .40 1.00
175 Shaquille O'Neal 1.00 2.50
176 John Starks .30 .75
177 Tyrone Hill .25 .60
178 Jayson Williams .25 .60
179 Anfernee Hardaway .60 1.50
180 Chris Webber .40 1.00
181 Don Reid .25 .60
182 Stacey Augmon .30 .75
183 Hersey Hawkins .25 .60
184 Sam Mitchell .25 .60
185 Jason Kidd .60 1.50
186 Nick Van Exel .30 .75
187 Larry Johnson .40 1.00
188 Bryant Reeves .25 .60
189 Glen Rice .40 1.00
190 Kerry Kittles .25 .60
191 Toni Kukoc .40 1.00
192 Ron Harper .30 .75
193 Bryon Russell .25 .60
194 Vladimir Stepania RC 1.00 2.50
195 Michael Olowokandi RC 1.25 3.00
196 Mike Bibby RC 1.50 4.00
197 Dale Ellis .25 .60
198 Muggsy Bogues .30 .75
199 Vince Carter RC 5.00 12.00
200 Robert Traylor RC 1.00 2.50
201 Peja Stojakovic RC 2.50 6.00
202 Aaron McKie .25 .60
203 Hubert Davis .25 .60
204 Dana Barros .25 .60
205 Bonzi Wells RC 1.00 2.50
206 Michael Doleac RC .75 2.00
207 Keon Clark RC 1.00 2.50
208 Michael Dickerson RC 1.00 2.50
209 Nick Anderson .25 .60
210 Brent Price .25 .60
211 Cherokee Parks .25 .60
212 Sam Jacobson RC .75 2.00
213 Pat Garrity RC .75 2.00
214 Tyrone Corbin .25 .60
215 David Wesley .25 .60
216 Rodney Rogers .25 .60
217 Dean Garrett .25 .60
218 Roshown McLeod RC .60 1.50
219 Dale Davis .25 .60
220 Checklist .25 .60
221 Scottie Pippen MO .60 1.50
222 Antonio McDyess MO .30 .75
223 Stephon Marbury MO .50 1.25
224 Tom Gugliotta MO .25 .60
225 Chris Webber MO .40 1.00
226 Latrell Sprewell MO .40 1.00
227 Mitch Richmond MO .40 1.00
228 Joe Smith MO .30 .75
229 John Starks MO .30 .75
230 Charles Oakley MO .30 .75

231 Dennis Rodman MO .75 2.00
232 Eddie Jones MO .40 1.00
233 Nick Van Exel MO .30 .75
234 Bobby Jackson MO .25 .60
235 Glen Rice MO .40 1.00

1998-99 Topps Chrome Refractors

*STARS: 4X TO 10X HI COLUMN
*RCs: 1.5X TO 4X HI
STATED ODDS 1:12
THE FOLLOWING CARDS DO NOT EXIST:
75/89/90/97/99
THE FOLLOWING CARDS ARE IN PREVIEW:
6/10/19/40/43/60/73/77/81/100
PREV.SET: INSERTED IN TOPPS 2 HCP
68 Kobe Bryant 30.00 80.00
135 Paul Pierce 100.00 250.00
153 Jason Williams 60.00 150.00
154 Dirk Nowitzki 400.00 700.00
199 Vince Carter 100.00 250.00
201 Peja Stojakovic 12.00 30.00

1998-99 Topps Chrome Apparitions

Randomly inserted in packs at 1:24, this 14-card set features players that are known for their spectacular moves. Card backs carry an "A" prefix.
COMPLETE SET (14) 12.00 30.00
STATED ODDS 1:24
*REF: 6X TO 15X HI COLUMN
REF: STATED ODDS 1:1,015
REF: PRINT RUN 100 SERIAL #'d SETS
A1 Kobe Bryant 4.00 10.00
A2 Stephon Marbury 1.25 3.00
A3 Brent Barry .75 2.00
A4 Karl Malone 1.25 3.00
A5 Shaquille O'Neal 2.50 6.00
A6 Chris Webber 1.00 2.50
A7 Shawn Kemp 1.00 2.50
A8 Hakeem Olajuwon 1.25 3.00
A9 Anfernee Hardaway 1.50 4.00
A10 Michael Finley 1.00 2.50
A11 Keith Van Horn 1.00 2.50
A12 Kevin Garnett 1.50 4.00
A13 Vin Baker .75 2.00
A14 Tim Duncan 2.00 5.00

1998-99 Topps Chrome Back 2 Back

Randomly inserted in packs at one in 12, this 7-card set features player's who continually produce, resulting in either an individual or team title. Card backs carry a "B" prefix.
COMPLETE SET (7) 7.50 15.00
STATED ODDS 1:12
B1 Michael Jordan 5.00 12.00
B2 Scottie Pippen 1.00 2.50
B3 Dennis Rodman 1.25 3.00
B4 Hakeem Olajuwon .75 2.00
B5 John Stockton .75 2.00
B6 Dikembe Mutombo .60 1.50
B7 Grant Hill 1.00 2.50

1998-99 Topps Chrome Champion Spirit

Randomly inserted at one in 12, this 7-card set features players whose teams, either on the collegiate or professional level, have won team championships. Card backs feature a "CS" prefix.
COMPLETE SET (7) 7.50 15.00
STATED ODDS 1:12
CS1 Michael Jordan 6.00 15.00
CS2 Grant Hill 1.00 2.50
CS3 Ron Mercer .50 1.25
CS4 Mike Bibby 1.00 2.50
CS5 Michael Dickerson .60 1.50
CS6 Patrick Ewing .75 2.00
CS7 Scottie Pippen 1.00 2.50

1998-99 Topps Chrome Coast to Coast

Randomly inserted in packs at one in 24, this 15-card set focuses on player's who can take it "coast to coast" on the floor. Card backs carry a "CC" prefix.
COMPLETE SET (15) 12.00 30.00
STATED ODDS 1:24
*REF: 1.25X TO 3X HI COLUMN
REF: STATED ODDS 1:96
CC1 Kobe Bryant 4.00 10.00
CC2 Scottie Pippen 1.50 4.00
CC3 Eddie Jones 1.00 2.50
CC4 Grant Hill 1.50 4.00
CC5 Jason Kidd 1.50 4.00
CC6 Antoine Walker 1.00 2.50
CC7 Michael Finley 1.00 2.50
CC8 Kevin Garnett 1.50 4.00
CC9 Allen Iverson 2.00 5.00
CC10 Shawn Kemp 1.00 2.50
CC11 Glenn Robinson .75 2.00
CC12 Anfernee Hardaway 1.50 4.00
CC13 Tim Hardaway 1.00 2.50
CC14 Ron Mercer .75 2.00
CC15 Kerry Kittles .60 1.50

1998-99 Topps Chrome Instant Impact

Randomly inserted in packs at one in 36, this 10-card set features player's who make an immediate impact on the court. Card backs carry an "I" prefix.
COMPLETE SET (10) 12.00 30.00
STATED ODDS 1:36
*REF: 1.25X TO 3X HI COLUMN
REF: STATED ODDS 1:144
I1 Tim Duncan 2.50 6.00
I2 Keith Van Horn 1.25 3.00
I3 Stephon Marbury 1.50 4.00
I4 Hakeem Olajuwon 1.50 4.00
I5 Shaquille O'Neal 3.00 8.00
I6 Michael Olowokandi 1.00 2.50
I7 Raef LaFrentz 1.00 2.50
I8 Vince Carter 4.00 10.00
I9 Jason Williams 2.00 5.00
I10 Paul Pierce 3.00 8.00

1998-99 Topps Chrome Season's Best

Randomly inserted in packs at one in six, this 29-card set features player's who perform different "themes" very well. Card backs are numbered with a "SB" prefix. There is no card SB6.
COMPLETE SET (29) 8.00 20.00
STATED ODDS 1:6
*REF: 1.25X TO 3X HI COLUMN
REF: STATED ODDS 1:24
SB1 Rod Strickland .30 .75
SB2 Gary Payton .50 1.25
SB3 Tim Hardaway .50 1.25
SB4 Stephon Marbury .60 1.50
SB5 Sam Cassell .40 1.00
SB7 Mitch Richmond .50 1.25
SB8 Steve Smith .40 1.00
SB9 Ray Allen .60 1.50
SB10 Isaiah Rider .40 1.00
SB11 Grant Hill .75 2.00
SB12 Kevin Garnett .75 2.00
SB13 Shareef Abdur-Rahim .50 1.25
SB14 Glenn Robinson .40 1.00
SB15 Michael Finley .50 1.25
SB16 Karl Malone .60 1.50
SB17 Tim Duncan 1.00 2.50
SB18 Antoine Walker .50 1.25
SB19 Chris Webber .50 1.25
SB20 Vin Baker .40 1.00
SB21 Shaquille O'Neal 1.25 3.00
SB22 David Robinson .75 2.00
SB23 Alonzo Mourning .60 1.50
SB24 Dikembe Mutombo .50 1.25
SB25 Hakeem Olajuwon .60 1.50
SB26 Tim Duncan 1.00 2.50
SB27 Keith Van Horn .50 1.25
SB28 Zydrunas Ilgauskas .50 1.25
SB29 Brevin Knight .30 .75
SB30 Bobby Jackson .30 .75

1999-00 Topps Chrome

The 1999-00 Topps Chrome set was released in April 2000. The set contained 257 cards, with 220 veterans, 28 rookies and nine Team USA cards.
COMPLETE SET (257) 60.00 120.00
1 Steve Smith .30 .75
2 Ron Harper .25 .60
3 Michael Dickerson .25 .60
4 LaPhonso Ellis .25 .60
5 Chris Webber .40 1.00
6 Jason Caffey .25 .60
7 Bryon Russell .25 .60
8 Bison Dele .25 .60
9 Isaiah Rider .30 .75
10 Dean Garrett .25 .60
11 Eric Murdock .25 .60
12 Juwan Howard .30 .75
13 Latrell Sprewell .40 1.00
14 Jalen Rose .30 .75
15 Larry Johnson .40 1.00
16 Eric Williams .25 .60
17 Bryant Reeves .25 .60
18 Tony Battie .30 .75
19 Luc Longley .30 .75
20 Gary Payton .40 1.00
21 Tariq Abdul-Wahad .25 .60
22 Armon Gilliam UER .25 .60
23 Shaquille O'Neal 1.00 2.50
24 Gary Trent .25 .60
25 John Stockton .50 1.25
26 Mark Jackson .30 .75
27 Cherokee Parks .25 .60
28 Michael Olowokandi .25 .60
29 Raef LaFrentz .30 .75
30 Dell Curry .25 .60
31 Travis Best .25 .60
32 Shawn Kemp .40 1.00
33 Voshon Lenard .25 .60
34 Brian Grant .25 .60
35 Alvin Williams .25 .60
36 Derek Fisher .40 1.00
37 Allan Houston .30 .75
38 Arvydas Sabonis .30 .75
39 Terry Cummings .30 .75
40 Dale Ellis .25 .60
41 Maurice Taylor .25 .60
42 Grant Hill .50 1.25
43 Anthony Mason .25 .60
44 John Wallace .25 .60
45 David Wesley .25 .60
46 Nick Van Exel .30 .75
47 Cuttino Mobley .25 .60
48 Anfernee Hardaway .60 1.50
49 Terry Porter .25 .60
50 Brent Barry .30 .75
51 Derek Harper .30 .75
52 Antoine Walker .40 1.00
53 Karl Malone .50 1.25
54 Ben Wallace .30 .75
55 Vlade Divac .40 1.00
56 Sam Mitchell .25 .60
57 Joe Smith .30 .75
58 Shawn Bradley .25 .60
59 Darrell Armstrong .25 .60
60 Kenny Anderson .30 .75
61 Jason Williams .50 1.25
62 Alonzo Mourning .50 1.25
63 Matt Harpring .25 .60
64 Antonio Davis .25 .60
65 Lindsey Hunter .25 .60
66 Allen Iverson .75 2.00
67 Mookie Blaylock .25 .60
68 Wesley Person .25 .60
69 Bobby Phills .25 .60
70 Theo Ratliff .30 .75
71 Antonio Daniels .25 .60
72 P.J. Brown .25 .60
73 David Robinson .60 1.50
74 Sean Elliott .40 1.00
75 Zydrunas Ilgauskas .30 .75
76 Kerry Kittles .25 .60
77 Otis Thorpe .25 .60
78 John Starks .30 .75
79 Jaren Jackson .25 .60
80 Hersey Hawkins .25 .60
81 Glenn Robinson .30 .75
82 Paul Pierce .50 1.25
83 Glen Rice .40 1.00
84 Charlie Ward .25 .60
85 Dee Brown .25 .60
86 Danny Fortson .25 .60
87 Billy Owens .25 .60
88 Jason Kidd .60 1.50
89 Brent Price .25 .60
90 Don Reid .25 .60
91 Mark Bryant .25 .60
92 Vinny Del Negro .25 .60
93 Stephon Marbury .30 .75
94 Donyell Marshall .25 .60
95 Jim Jackson .25 .60
96 Horace Grant .30 .75
97 Calbert Cheaney .25 .60
98 Vince Carter .75 2.00
99 Bobby Jackson .25 .60
100 Alan Henderson .25 .60
101 Mike Bibby .40 1.00
102 Cedric Henderson .25 .60
103 Lamond Murray .25 .60
104 A.C. Green .30 .75
105 Hakeem Olajuwon .50 1.25
106 George Lynch .25 .60
107 Kendall Gill .25 .60
108 Rex Chapman .25 .60
109 Eddie Jones .40 1.00
110 Kornel David RC .60 1.50
111 Jason Terry RC 1.25 3.00
112 Corey Maggette RC 1.25 3.00
113 Ron Artest RC 1.50 4.00
114 Richard Hamilton RC 1.50 4.00
115 Elton Brand RC 2.00 5.00
116 Baron Davis RC 2.00 5.00
117 Wally Szczerbiak RC 1.50 4.00
118 Steve Francis RC 2.00 5.00
119 James Posey RC .75 2.00
120 Shawn Marion RC 1.50 4.00
121 Tim Duncan .75 2.00
122 Danny Manning .30 .75
123 Chris Mullin .40 1.00
124 Antawn Jamison .40 1.00
125 Kobe Bryant 1.50 4.00
126 Matt Geiger .25 .60
127 Rod Strickland .25 .60
128 Howard Eisley .25 .60
129 Steve Nash .60 1.50
130 Felipe Lopez .25 .60
131 Ron Mercer .30 .75
132 Ruben Patterson .25 .60
133 Dana Barros .25 .60
134 Dale Davis .25 .60
135 Bo Outlaw .25 .60
136 Shandon Anderson .25 .60
137 Mitch Richmond .40 1.00
138 Doug Christie .30 .75
139 Rasheed Wallace .40 1.00
140 Chris Childs .25 .60
141 Jamal Mashburn .30 .75
142 Terrell Brandon .25 .60
143 Jamie Feick RC .60 1.50
144 Robert Traylor .25 .60
145 Rick Fox .25 .60
146 Charles Barkley .60 1.50
147 Tyrone Nesby RC .60 1.50
148 Jerry Stackhouse .40 1.00
149 Cedric Ceballos .25 .60
150 Dikembe Mutombo .40 1.00
151 Anthony Peeler .25 .60
152 Larry Hughes .30 .75
153 Clifford Robinson .25 .60
154 Corliss Williamson .25 .60
155 Olden Polynice .25 .60
156 Avery Johnson .30 .75
157 Tracy Murray .25 .60
158 Tom Gugliotta .25 .60
159 Tim Thomas .30 .75
160 Reggie Miller .40 1.00
161 Tim Hardaway .40 1.00
162 Dan Majerle .40 1.00
163 Will Perdue .25 .60
164 Brevin Knight .25 .60
165 Elden Campbell .25 .60
166 Chris Gatling .25 .60
167 Walter McCarty .25 .60
168 Chauncey Billups .40 1.00
169 Chris Mills .25 .60
170 Christian Laettner .30 .75
171 Robert Pack .25 .60
172 Rik Smits .40 1.00
173 Tyrone Hill .25 .60
174 Damon Stoudamire .30 .75
175 Nick Anderson .25 .60
176 Peja Stojakovic .40 1.00
177 Vladimir Stepania .25 .60
178 Tracy McGrady .60 1.50
179 Adam Keefe .25 .60
180 Shareef Abdur-Rahim .30 .75
181 Isaac Austin .25 .60
182 Mario Elie .25 .60
183 Rashard Lewis .40 1.00
184 Scott Burrell .25 .60
185 Othella Harrington .25 .60
186 Eric Piatkowski .30 .75
187 Bryant Stith .25 .60
188 Michael Finley .40 1.00
189 Chris Crawford .25 .60
190 Toni Kukoc .40 1.00
191 Danny Ferry .25 .60
192 Erick Dampier .25 .60
193 Clarence Weatherspoon .25 .60
194 Bob Sura .25 .60
195 Jayson Williams .25 .60
196 Kurt Thomas .25 .60
197 Greg Anthony .25 .60
198 Rodney Rogers .25 .60
199 Detlef Schrempf .30 .75
200 Keith Van Horn .30 .75
201 Robert Horry .30 .75
202 Sam Cassell .30 .75
203 Malik Sealy .25 .60
204 Kelvin Cato .25 .60
205 Antonio McDyess .30 .75
206 Andrew DeClercq .25 .60
207 Ricky Davis .40 1.00
208 Vitaly Potapenko .25 .60
209 Loy Vaught .25 .60
210 Kevin Garnett .60 1.50
211 Eric Snow .30 .75
212 Anfernee Hardaway .60 1.50
213 Vin Baker .30 .75
214 Lawrence Funderburke .25 .60
215 Jeff Hornacek .30 .75
216 Doug West .25 .60
217 Michael Doleac .25 .60
218 Ray Allen .40 1.00
219 Derek Anderson .25 .60
220 Jerome Williams .25 .60
221 Derrick Coleman .30 .75
222 Randy Brown .25 .60
223 Patrick Ewing .50 1.25
224 Walt Williams .25 .60
225 Charles Oakley .30 .75
226 Steve Kerr .30 .75
227 Muggsy Bogues .30 .75
228 Kevin Willis .25 .60
229 Marcus Camby .30 .75
230 Scottie Pippen .60 1.50
231 Lamar Odom RC 2.00 5.00
232 Jonathan Bender RC .75 2.00
233 Andre Miller RC 1.50 4.00
234 Trajan Langdon RC .75 2.00
235 A.Radojevic RC .50 1.25
236 William Avery RC .60 1.50
237 Cal Bowdler RC .50 1.25
238 Quincy Lewis RC .50 1.25
239 Dion Glover RC .60 1.50
240 Jeff Foster RC .75 2.00
241 Kenny Thomas RC .75 2.00
242 Devean George RC .75 2.00
243 Tim James RC .50 1.25
244 Vonteego Cummings RC .50 1.25
245 Jumaine Jones RC .60 1.50
246 Scott Padgett RC .60 1.50
247 Adrian Griffin RC .75 2.00
248 Chris Herren RC .60 1.50
249 Allan Houston USA .60 1.50
250 Kevin Garnett USA 1.25 3.00
251 Gary Payton USA .75 2.00
252 Steve Smith USA .60 1.50
253 Tim Hardaway USA .75 2.00
254 Tim Duncan USA 1.50 4.00
255 Jason Kidd USA 1.25 3.00
256 Tom Gugliotta USA .50 1.25
257 Vin Baker USA .60 1.50

1999-00 Topps Chrome Refractors

*STARS: 3X TO 8X BASE CARD HI
*RCs: 2X TO 5X BASE HI
STATED ODDS 1:12
125 Kobe Bryant 50.00 120.00

1999-00 Topps Chrome All-Etch

Randomly inserted into packs at one in 100, this 30-card insert set features 10 veteran cards, 10 young stars, and 10 draft picks. Card backs carry an "AE" prefix.
COMPLETE SET (30) 25.00 60.00
STATED ODDS 1:10
*REF.STARS: 1.5X TO 4X HI COLUMN
REF: STATED ODDS 1:100
AE1 Karl Malone 1.25 3.00
AE2 Scottie Pippen 1.50 4.00
AE3 Grant Hill 1.25 3.00
AE4 Shawn Kemp 1.00 2.50
AE5 Shaquille O'Neal 2.50 6.00
AE6 Anfernee Hardaway 1.50 4.00
AE7 Chris Webber 1.00 2.50
AE8 Gary Payton 1.00 2.50
AE9 Jason Kidd 1.50 4.00
AE10 John Stockton 1.25 3.00
AE11 Kevin Garnett 1.50 4.00
AE12 Vince Carter 2.00 5.00
AE13 Shareef Abdur-Rahim .75 2.00
AE14 Antoine Walker 1.00 2.50
AE15 Kobe Bryant 4.00 10.00
AE16 Tim Duncan 2.00 5.00
AE17 Keith Van Horn .75 2.00
AE18 Allen Iverson 2.00 5.00
AE19 Jason Williams 1.25 3.00
AE20 Stephon Marbury .75 2.00
AE21 Elton Brand 2.00 5.00
AE22 Jason Terry 1.25 3.00
AE23 Steve Francis 2.00 5.00
AE24 Corey Maggette 1.25 3.00
AE25 Lamar Odom 2.00 5.00
AE26 Ron Artest 1.50 4.00
AE27 Baron Davis 2.00 5.00
AE28 Andre Miller 1.50 4.00
AE29 Shawn Marion 1.50 4.00
AE30 Wally Szczerbiak 1.50 4.00

1999-00 Topps Chrome All-Stars

Randomly inserted in packs at one in 30, this 10-card set focuses on veteran All-Stars in the NBA. Card backs carry an "AS" prefix.
COMPLETE SET (10) 8.00 20.00
STATED ODDS 1:30
*REF: 1.5X TO 4X HI COLUMN
REF: STATED ODDS 1:300
AS1 Patrick Ewing 1.25 3.00
AS2 Karl Malone 1.25 3.00
AS3 Hakeem Olajuwon 1.25 3.00
AS4 Scottie Pippen 1.50 4.00
AS5 Gary Payton 1.00 2.50
AS6 John Stockton 1.25 3.00
AS7 Shaquille O'Neal 2.50 6.00
AS8 Charles Barkley 1.50 4.00
AS9 David Robinson 1.50 4.00
AS10 Grant Hill 1.25 3.00

1999-00 Topps Chrome Highlight Reels

Randomly inserted in packs at one in ten, this 15-card set features some of the most exciting players in the NBA. Card backs carry a "HR" prefix.
COMPLETE SET (15) 8.00 20.00
STATED ODDS 1:10
*REF: 1.5X TO 4X HI COLUMN
REF: STATED ODDS 1:100
HR1 Stephon Marbury .50 1.25
HR2 Vince Carter 1.25 3.00
HR3 Kevin Garnett 1.00 2.50
HR4 Kobe Bryant 2.50 6.00
HR5 Chris Webber .60 1.50
HR6 Allen Iverson 1.25 3.00
HR7 Grant Hill .75 2.00
HR8 Antoine Walker .60 1.50
HR9 Jason Williams .75 2.00
HR10 Tim Duncan 1.25 3.00
HR11 Shareef Abdur-Rahim .50 1.25
HR12 Keith Van Horn .50 1.25
HR13 Antonio McDyess .50 1.25
HR14 Jason Kidd 1.00 2.50
HR15 Ron Mercer .50 1.25

1999-00 Topps Chrome Instant Impact

Randomly inserted in packs at one in 15, this 10-card set focuses on players traded during the 1999/2000 season. Card backs carry an "II" prefix.
COMPLETE SET (10) 2.50 6.00
STATED ODDS 1:15
*REF: 1.5X TO 4X HI COLUMN
REF: STATED ODDS 1:150
II1 Scottie Pippen 1.00 2.50
II2 Nick Anderson .40 1.00
II3 Isaiah Rider .50 1.25
II4 Antonio Davis .40 1.00
II5 Ron Mercer .50 1.25
II6 Anfernee Hardaway 1.00 2.50
II7 Isaac Austin .40 1.00
II8 Steve Smith .50 1.25
II9 Michael Dickerson .40 1.00
II10 Horace Grant .50 1.25

1999-00 Topps Chrome Keepers

Randomly inserted in packs at one in 30, this 10-card set features the top draft picks in the NBA. Card backs carry a "K" prefix.
COMPLETE SET (10) 5.00 12.00
STATED ODDS 1:30
*REF: 2X TO 5X HI COLUMN
REF: STATED ODDS 1:300
K1 Elton Brand .75 2.00
K2 Lamar Odom .75 2.00
K3 Steve Francis .75 2.00
K4 Shawn Marion .60 1.50
K5 Wally Szczerbiak .60 1.50
K6 Baron Davis .75 2.00
K7 Andre Miller .60 1.50
K8 Corey Maggette .50 1.25
K9 Jason Terry .50 1.25
K10 Richard Hamilton .60 1.50

2000-01 Topps Chrome

The 2000-01 Topps Chrome product was released in early April, 2001. The product featured a 200-card base set that was broken into tiers as follows:Base Veterans (1-150), and Rookies (151-200) that were inserted at 1:6 and serial numbered to 1999. Each pack contained four cards and carried a suggested retail price of $3.00.

COMPLETE SET (200) 150.00 300.00
COMPLETE SET w/o SP's (150) 15.00 40.00
151-200 PRINT RUN 1999 SERIAL #'d SETS
1 Elton Brand .40 1.00
2 Marcus Camby .30 .75
3 Jalen Rose .30 .75
4 Jamie Feick .25 .60
5 Toni Kukoc .40 1.00
6 Doug Christie .25 .60
7 Sam Cassell .30 .75
8 Shaquille O'Neal 1.00 2.50
9 Larry Hughes .30 .75
10 Jerry Stackhouse .30 .75
11 Rick Fox .25 .60
12 Clifford Robinson .25 .60
13 Dirk Nowitzki .60 1.50
14 Cuttino Mobley .25 .60
15 Latrell Sprewell .30 .75
16 Kevin Garnett .60 1.50
17 Jerome Williams .25 .60
18 Chris Webber .40 1.00
19 Jason Terry .40 1.00
20 Elden Campbell .25 .60
21 Jonathan Bender .25 .60
22 Scottie Pippen .60 1.50
23 Radoslav Nesterovic .25 .60
24 Reggie Miller .40 1.00
25 Andre Miller .30 .75
26 Rashard Lewis .40 1.00
27 Larry Johnson .40 1.00
28 Steve Francis .30 .75
29 Rod Strickland .25 .60
30 Tim Thomas .25 .60
31 Robert Horry .30 .75
32 Darrell Armstrong .25 .60
33 Vince Carter .75 2.00
34 Othella Harrington .25 .60
35 Derek Anderson .25 .60
36 Anthony Carter .25 .60
37 Ray Allen .40 1.00
38 Jason Kidd .60 1.50
39 Sean Elliott .40 1.00
40 Tim Duncan .75 2.00
41 Adrian Griffin .25 .60
42 Wally Szczerbiak .30 .75
43 Austin Croshere .25 .60
44 James Posey .25 .60
45 Alan Henderson .25 .60
46 Jahidi White .25 .60
47 Shawn Marion .30 .75
48 Lamar Odom .30 .75
49 Keon Clark .25 .60
50 Lamond Murray .25 .60
51 Paul Pierce .40 1.00
52 Charlie Ward .25 .60
53 Horace Grant .30 .75
54 John Stockton .50 1.25
55 Peja Stojakovic .40 1.00
56 Christian Laettner .30 .75
57 Keith Van Horn .30 .75
58 Patrick Ewing .50 1.25
59 Steve Smith .30 .75
60 Antonio Davis .25 .60
61 Mitch Richmond .30 .75
62 Michael Olowokandi .25 .60
63 Baron Davis .40 1.00
64 Dikembe Mutombo .40 1.00
65 Raef LaFrentz .25 .60
66 Ervin Johnson .25 .60
67 Alonzo Mourning .50 1.25
68 Kendall Gill .25 .60
69 George Lynch .25 .60
70 Donyell Marshall .25 .60
71 Bo Outlaw .25 .60
72 Kenny Anderson .30 .75
73 John Amaechi .25 .60
74 Vlade Divac .30 .75
75 Vin Baker .30 .75
76 Mike Bibby .40 1.00
77 Richard Hamilton .30 .75
78 Mookie Blaylock .25 .60
79 Vitaly Potapenko .25 .60
80 Anthony Mason .25 .60
81 Vonteego Cummings .25 .60
82 Michael Finley .40 1.00
83 Ron Artest .40 1.00
84 Rodney Rogers .25 .60
85 Team Championship .75 2.00
86 Jason Williams .40 1.00
87 David Robinson .60 1.50
88 Charles Oakley .30 .75
89 Juwan Howard .30 .75
90 Antoine Walker .30 .75
91 Roshown McLeod .25 .60
92 Eddie Jones .40 1.00
93 Allen Iverson .75 2.00
94 Grant Hill .50 1.25
95 Terrell Brandon .25 .60
96 Stephon Marbury .30 .75
97 Jamal Mashburn .30 .75
98 Ron Harper .30 .75
99 Jermaine O'Neal .30 .75
100 Nick Van Exel .30 .75
101 Danny Fortson .25 .60
102 Jim Jackson .25 .60
103 Brad Miller .30 .75
104 Shawn Bradley .25 .60
105 Mark Jackson .30 .75
106 Maurice Taylor .25 .60
107 Kobe Bryant 1.50 4.00
108 Clarence Weatherspoon .25 .60
109 Eric Snow .25 .60
110 Allan Houston .30 .75
111 Chauncey Billups .40 1.00
112 Tom Gugliotta .25 .60
113 Theo Ratliff .25 .60
114 Rasheed Wallace .40 1.00
115 Glen Rice .30 .75
116 Bryon Russell .25 .60
117 Tracy McGrady .60 1.50
118 Bryant Reeves .25 .60
119 Damon Stoudamire .30 .75
120 Anfernee Hardaway .60 1.50
121 Johnny Newman .25 .60
122 Corey Maggette .30 .75
123 Travis Best .25 .60
124 Hakeem Olajuwon .50 1.25
125 Antawn Jamison .40 1.00
126 John Starks .30 .75
127 Antonio McDyess .30 .75
128 Gary Payton .40 1.00
129 Karl Malone .50 1.25
130 Michael Dickerson .25 .60
131 Shawn Kemp .40 1.00
132 David Wesley .25 .60
133 P.J. Brown .25 .60
134 Ron Mercer .25 .60
135 Robert Traylor .25 .60
136 Derrick Coleman .30 .75
137 Steve Nash .60 1.50
138 Ben Wallace .30 .75
139 Brian Skinner .25 .60
140 Chris Gatling .25 .60
141 Dale Davis .25 .60
142 Glenn Robinson .30 .75
143 Chucky Atkins .25 .60
144 Brian Grant .25 .60
145 Corliss Williamson .25 .60
146 Shareef Abdur-Rahim .30 .75
147 Avery Johnson .30 .75
148 Tim Hardaway .40 1.00
149 Isaiah Rider .30 .75
150 Shandon Anderson .25 .60
151 Kenyon Martin RC 4.00 10.00
152 Stromile Swift RC 1.50 4.00
153 Darius Miles RC 1.50 4.00
154 Marcus Fizer RC 1.50 4.00
155 Mike Miller RC 2.50 6.00
156 DerMarr Johnson RC 1.25 3.00
157 Chris Mihm RC 1.25 3.00
158 Jamal Crawford RC 4.00 10.00
159 Joel Przybilla RC 1.25 3.00
160 Keyon Dooling RC 1.50 4.00
161 Jerome Moiso RC 1.00 2.50
162 Etan Thomas RC 1.50 4.00
163 Courtney Alexander RC 1.25 3.00
164 Mateen Cleaves RC 1.25 3.00
165 Jason Collier RC 1.50 4.00
166 Desmond Mason RC 2.00 5.00
167 Quentin Richardson RC 1.50 4.00
168 Jamaal Magloire RC 1.50 4.00
169 Speedy Claxton RC 1.50 4.00
170 Morris Peterson RC 1.50 4.00
171 Donnell Harvey RC 1.25 3.00
172 DeShawn Stevenson RC 1.50 4.00
173 Mamadou N'Diaye RC 1.00 2.50
174 Erick Barkley RC 1.00 2.50
175 Mark Madsen RC 1.50 4.00
176 Hedo Turkoglu RC 2.50 6.00
177 Brian Cardinal RC 1.25 3.00
178 Iakovos Tsakalidis RC 1.00 2.50
179 Dalibor Bagaric RC 1.25 3.00
180 Dragan Tarlac RC 1.00 2.50
181 Dan Langhi RC 1.00 2.50
182 A.J. Guyton RC 1.00 2.50
183 Jake Voskuhl RC 1.00 2.50
184 Khalid El-Amin RC 1.00 2.50
185 Mike Smith RC 1.00 2.50
186 Soumaila Samake RC 1.00 2.50
187 Eddie House RC 1.25 3.00
188 Eduardo Najera RC 1.50 4.00
189 Lavor Postell RC 1.00 2.50
190 Hanno Mottola RC 1.00 2.50
191 Olumide Oyedeji RC 1.00 2.50
192 Michael Redd RC 4.00 10.00
193 Chris Porter RC 1.00 2.50
194 Jabari Smith RC 1.00 2.50
195 Marc Jackson RC 1.25 3.00
196 Stephen Jackson RC 2.50 6.00
197 Pepe Sanchez RC 1.50 4.00
198 Daniel Santiago RC 1.50 4.00
199 Paul McPherson RC 1.00 2.50
200 Mike Penberthy RC 1.50 4.00

2000-01 Topps Chrome Refractors

*STARS: 3X TO 8X BASE CARD HI
1-150 STATED ODDS 1:12
*ROOKIES 151-200: 2X TO 5X BASE CARD HI
151-200 STATED ODDS 1:118
151-200 PRINT RUN 199 SERIAL #'d SETS

2000-01 Topps Chrome Aptitude for Altitude

Randomly inserted into packs at one in 20, this 10-card set features players that are very capable of dunking over their opponents. Card backs carry a "AA" prefix.
COMPLETE SET (10) 5.00 12.00
STATED ODDS 1:20
*REF: 1.25X TO 3X APTITUDE ALTITUDE HI
REF.STATED ODDS 1:200 PACKS
AA1 Larry Hughes .60 1.50
AA2 Steve Francis .60 1.50
AA3 Shawn Marion .60 1.50
AA4 Michael Finley .75 2.00
AA5 Allen Iverson 1.50 4.00
AA6 Jerry Stackhouse .60 1.50
AA7 Rashard Lewis .75 2.00
AA8 Tim Thomas .50 1.25
AA9 Baron Davis .75 2.00
AA10 Darius Miles .75 2.00

2000-01 Topps Chrome Cards That Never Were

Randomly inserted into packs, this 10-card insert set features cards of Magic Johnson that were never produced. Card backs carry a "MJ" prefix.
COMPLETE SET (10) 15.00 40.00
COMMON CARD (MJ1-MJ10) 2.00 5.00
RANDOM INSERTS IN PACKS
REF: 1.5X TO 4X HI COLUMN
RANDOM INSERTS IN PACKS

2000-01 Topps Chrome Combos

Randomly inserted into packs at one in 30, this 20-card insert set features different player combinations. Card backs carry a "TC" prefix.
COMPLETE SET (20) 25.00 60.00
STATED ODDS 1:30
*REF: 1.25X TO 3X COMBOS HI
REF.STATED ODDS 1:300
TC1 S.O'Neal/K.Bryant 5.00 12.00
TC2 S.Marbury/A.Iverson 2.00 5.00
TC3 C.Webber/J.Williams 1.25 3.00
TC4 Ewing/Mutombo/Mourning 1.25 3.00
TC5 T.McGrady/V.Carter 2.50 6.00
TC6 T.Duncan/G.Hill 2.00 5.00
TC7 E.Brand/L.Odom/S.Francis 1.25 3.00
TC8 G.Payton/J.Kidd 2.00 5.00
TC9 Stoud/Pip/Smith/Wallace 2.00 5.00
TC10 T.Duncan/K.Garnett 2.50 6.00
TC11 Hakeem Olajuwon 1.25 3.00
TC12 Patrick Ewing 1.25 3.00
TC13 Karl Malone 1.25 3.00
TC14 Scottie Pippen 2.00 5.00
TC15 Reggie Miller 1.25 3.00
TC16 S.O'Neal/M.Johnson 3.00 8.00
TC17 Fizer/Swift/K.Martin 1.25 3.00
TC18 Claxton/Dooling/Crawford 1.25 3.00
TC19 M.Miller/D.John/Miles 1.25 3.00
TC20 M.Johnson/M.Cleaves 2.00 5.00

2000-01 Topps Chrome Final Piece Game Jerseys

Randomly inserted into packs at one in 2025, this 23-card insert set features swatches of game-used jerseys from the NBA Finals . Card backs carry a "FP" prefix. A refractor version of this set was issued as well. Each of these cards is sequentially numbered to 10.
STATED ODDS 1:2025
PRINT RUN 25 SERIAL #'d SETS
FP1 Shaquille O'Neal 100.00 250.00
FP2 Glen Rice 30.00 80.00
FP3 Robert Horry 30.00 80.00
FP4 Rick Fox 25.00 60.00
FP5 Brian Shaw 25.00 60.00
FP6 Ron Harper 30.00 80.00
FP7 Derek Fisher 40.00 100.00
FP8 A.C. Green 30.00 80.00
FP9 John Salley 25.00 60.00
FP10 Travis Knight 25.00 60.00
FP11 Devean George 25.00 60.00
FP12 Reggie Miller 75.00 200.00
FP13 Jalen Rose 30.00 80.00
FP14 Dale Davis 25.00 60.00
FP15 Rik Smits 25.00 60.00
FP16 Mark Jackson 30.00 80.00
FP17 Travis Best 25.00 60.00
FP18 Austin Croshere 25.00 60.00
FP19 Derrick McKey 25.00 60.00
FP20 Sam Perkins 25.00 60.00
FP21 Chris Mullin 40.00 100.00
FP22 Jonathan Bender 25.00 60.00
FP23 Zan Tabak 25.00 60.00

2000-01 Topps Chrome Hobby Masters

Randomly inserted into packs at one in 30 hobby, this 10-card insert set features players that are the most popular in the Basketball trading card field. Card backs carry a "HM" prefix.
COMPLETE SET (10) 15.00 40.00
STATED ODDS 1:30 HOBBY
*REF: 2.5X TO 6X HOBBY MASTERS HI
REF.STATED ODDS 1:602 HOBBY
HM1 Kevin Garnett 2.00 5.00
HM2 Jason Williams 1.25 3.00
HM3 Tim Duncan 2.50 6.00
HM4 Tracy McGrady 2.00 5.00
HM5 Kobe Bryant 5.00 12.00
HM6 Allen Iverson 2.50 6.00
HM7 Elton Brand 1.25 3.00
HM8 Steve Francis 1.00 2.50
HM9 Vince Carter 2.50 6.00
HM10 Chris Webber 1.25 3.00

2000-01 Topps Chrome In The Paint

Randomly inserted into packs at one in 60, this 10-card insert set features players that can be found "in the paint" scoring points and grabbing rebounds . Card backs carry an "IP" prefix.
COMPLETE SET (10) 15.00 40.00
STATED ODDS 1:60
*REF: 1.25X TO 3X IN THE PAINT HI
REF.STATED ODDS 1:600
IP1 Elton Brand 2.00 5.00
IP2 Tim Duncan 4.00 10.00
IP3 Antonio McDyess 1.50 4.00
IP4 Karl Malone 2.50 6.00
IP5 Rasheed Wallace 2.00 5.00
IP6 Antoine Walker 1.50 4.00
IP7 Shareef Abdur-Rahim 1.50 4.00
IP8 Lamar Odom 1.50 4.00
IP9 Kenyon Martin 5.00 12.00
IP10 Stromile Swift 2.00 5.00

2000-01 Topps Chrome Magic Johnson Reprints

Randomly inserted into packs at one in 10, this 7-card insert set features reprinted Magic Johnson cards.
COMPLETE SET (7) 12.50 30.00
COMMON CARD (1-7) 2.00 5.00
STATED ODDS 1:10
REF.STATED ODDS 1:100

2000-01 Topps Chrome No Limit

Randomly inserted into packs at one in 15, this 20-card insert set features players whose game has no limits. Card backs carry a "NL" prefix.
COMPLETE SET (20) 20.00 50.00
STATED ODDS 1:15
*REF: 1.25X TO 3X NO LIMIT HI
REF.STATED ODDS 1:150
NL1 Kobe Bryant 4.00 10.00
NL2 Kevin Garnett 1.50 4.00
NL3 Vince Carter 2.00 5.00
NL4 Tracy McGrady 1.50 4.00
NL5 Tim Duncan 2.00 5.00
NL6 Elton Brand 1.00 2.50
NL7 Lamar Odom .75 2.00
NL8 Larry Hughes .75 2.00
NL9 Chris Webber 1.00 2.50
NL10 Shareef Abdur-Rahim .75 2.00
NL11 Jason Kidd 1.50 4.00
NL12 Gary Payton 1.00 2.50
NL13 Paul Pierce 1.00 2.50
NL14 Stromile Swift 1.00 2.50
NL15 Darius Miles 1.00 2.50
NL16 Mike Miller 1.50 4.00
NL17 Jason Williams 1.00 2.50
NL18 Jamal Crawford 2.50 6.00
NL19 Marcus Fizer 1.00 2.50
NL20 DerMarr Johnson .75 2.00

2001-02 Topps Chrome

This 165 card standard-size set was issued in March, 2002. These cards were issued in four card packs which came 24 packs to a box and 10 boxes to case. Each pack had an SRP of $3.00. Card numbers 1-129 feature veteran players and card numbers 130-165 feature rookies with the respective player's draft pick number. Each card boasts full color player action photos with blue borders on an all chromium card stock.
COMP.SET w/o RC's (129) 12.00 30.00
1 Shaquille O'Neal 1.00 2.50
2 Steve Nash .60 1.50
3 Allen Iverson .75 2.00
4 Shawn Marion .30 .75
5 Rasheed Wallace .40 1.00
6 Antonio Daniels .25 .60
7 Rashard Lewis .40 1.00
8 Raef LaFrentz .25 .60
9 Stromile Swift .25 .60
10 Vince Carter .60 1.50
11 Danny Fortson .25 .60
12 Jalen Rose .30 .75
13 Glen Rice .30 .75
14 Glenn Robinson .30 .75
15 Wally Szczerbiak .30 .75
16 Rick Fox .25 .60
17 Darius Miles .25 .60
18 Jermaine O'Neal .30 .75
19 Eddie Jones .30 .75
20 Tracy McGrady .60 1.50
21 Kevin Garnett .60 1.50
22 Tim Thomas .25 .60
23 Larry Hughes .30 .75
24 Jerry Stackhouse .30 .75
25 Ray Allen .40 1.00
26 Terrell Brandon .25 .60
27 Keith Van Horn .30 .75
28 Marcus Fizer .25 .60
29 Elden Campbell .25 .60
30 Tim Duncan .75 2.00
31 Doug Christie .25 .60
32 Allan Houston .30 .75
33 Patrick Ewing .50 1.25
34 Hakeem Olajuwon .50 1.25
35 Anfernee Hardaway .60 1.50
36 Clarence Weatherspoon .25 .60
37 Eric Snow .25 .60
38 Tom Gugliotta .25 .60
39 Scottie Pippen .60 1.50
40 Chris Webber .40 1.00
41 David Robinson .60 1.50
42 Elton Brand .40 1.00
43 Theo Ratliff .25 .60
44 Paul Pierce .40 1.00
45 Jamal Mashburn .30 .75
46 Damon Stoudamire .30 .75
47 DerMarr Johnson .25 .60
48 Andre Miller .30 .75
49 Dirk Nowitzki .60 1.50
50 Kobe Bryant 1.50 4.00

51 Keyon Dooling .25 .60
52 Brian Grant .25 .60
53 Antawn Jamison .40 1.00
54 Jonathan Bender .25 .60
55 Dikembe Mutombo .40 1.00
56 Steve Smith .30 .75
57 Hedo Turkoglu .30 .75
58 Robert Horry .30 .75
59 Kurt Thomas .25 .60
60 Jason Terry .40 1.00
61 Vitaly Potapenko .25 .60
62 Gary Payton .40 1.00
63 Bonzi Wells .25 .60
64 Raja Bell RC 1.25 3.00
65 Chris Mihm .25 .60
66 Reggie Miller .40 1.00
67 Lamar Odom .30 .75
68 Darrell Armstrong .25 .60
69 Baron Davis .40 1.00
70 Aaron Williams .25 .60
71 Latrell Sprewell .30 .75
72 James Posey .25 .60
73 Ben Wallace .30 .75
74 Marc Jackson .25 .60
75 Maurice Taylor .25 .60
76 Aaron McKie .25 .60
77 Grant Hill .50 1.25
78 Anthony Carter .25 .60
79 Peja Stojakovic .40 1.00
80 Jason Kidd .60 1.50
81 Vin Baker .30 .75
82 Morris Peterson .25 .60
83 Bryon Russell .25 .60
84 Michael Dickerson .25 .60
85 Quentin Richardson .30 .75
86 Primoz Brezec RC 1.00 2.50
87 Desmond Mason .30 .75
88 Jason Williams .30 .75
89 Marcus Camby .30 .75
90 Stephon Marbury .30 .75
91 Mike Bibby .40 1.00
92 Alonzo Mourning .50 1.25
93 Mitch Richmond .30 .75
94 Donyell Marshall .25 .60
95 Michael Jordan 4.00 10.00
96 Mike Miller .30 .75
97 Nick Van Exel .30 .75
98 Michael Finley .40 1.00
99 Jamal Crawford .40 1.00
100 Steve Francis .30 .75
101 Kenyon Martin .40 1.00
102 Sam Cassell .30 .75
103 Chucky Atkins .25 .60
104 Juwan Howard .30 .75
105 Bryant Reeves .25 .60
106 Richard Hamilton .30 .75
107 Antonio Davis .25 .60
108 Antonio McDyess .30 .75
109 Derek Anderson .25 .60
110 Kenny Anderson .30 .75
111 Antoine Walker .30 .75
112 Wang ZhiZhi .30 .75
113 Shareef Abdur-Rahim .30 .75
114 Chris Whitney .25 .60
115 John Stockton .50 1.25
116 Alvin Williams .25 .60
117 David Wesley .25 .60
118 Joe Smith .30 .75
119 Jahidi White .25 .60
120 Karl Malone .50 1.25
121 Cuttino Mobley .25 .60
122 Tyrone Hill .25 .60
123 Clifford Robinson .25 .60
124 Toni Kukoc .40 1.00
125 Eddie Robinson .25 .60
126 Courtney Alexander .25 .60
127 Ron Mercer .25 .60
128 Lamond Murray .25 .60
129 Rodney Rogers .25 .60
130 Tyson Chandler RC 1.50 4.00
131 Pau Gasol RC 3.00 8.00
132 Eddy Curry RC 1.00 2.50
133 Jason Richardson RC 1.25 3.00
134 Shane Battier RC 2.00 5.00
135 Eddie Griffin RC .75 2.00
136 DeSagana Diop RC .75 2.00
137 Rodney White RC .60 1.50
138 Joe Johnson RC 1.25 3.00
139 Kedrick Brown RC .60 1.50
140 Vladimir Radmanovic RC 1.00 2.50
141 Richard Jefferson RC 1.50 4.00
142 Troy Murphy RC 1.00 2.50
143 Steven Hunter RC .75 2.00
144 Kirk Haston RC .60 1.50
145 Michael Bradley RC .60 1.50
146 Jason Collins RC .75 2.00
147 Zach Randolph RC 1.50 4.00
148 Brendan Haywood RC 1.00 2.50
149 Joseph Forte RC .60 1.50
150 Jeryl Sasser RC .60 1.50
151 Brandon Armstrong RC .60 1.50
152 Gerald Wallace RC 1.25 3.00
153 Samuel Dalembert RC 1.00 2.50
154 Jamaal Tinsley RC 1.00 2.50
155 Tony Parker RC 4.00 10.00
156 Trenton Hassell RC .75 2.00
157 Gilbert Arenas RC 1.50 4.00
158 Jeff Trepagnier RC .60 1.50
159 Damone Brown RC .60 1.50
160 Loren Woods RC .60 1.50
161 Andrei Kirilenko RC 1.50 4.00
162 Zeljko Rebraca RC 1.00 2.50
163 Kenny Satterfield RC .60 1.50
164 Alvin Jones RC .75 2.00
165 Kwame Brown RC 1.00 2.50

2001-02 Topps Chrome Refractors

*REF.STARS: 2.5X TO 6X BASE CARD HI
*REF.RCs: 1.25X TO 3X BASE CARD HI
REF.STATED ODDS 1:4
35 Anfernee Hardaway 5.00 12.00
130 Tyson Chandler 8.00 20.00
131 Pau Gasol 20.00 50.00
155 Tony Parker 30.00 80.00

2001-02 Topps Chrome Refractors Black Border

*REF.BLK.STRS:12.5X TO 30X BASE CARD HI
*REF.BLK.RCs: 5X TO 12X BASE CARD HI
REF.BLACK PRINT RUN 50 SER.#'d SETS
3 Allen Iverson 50.00 120.00
30 Tim Duncan 100.00 250.00
35 Anfernee Hardaway 25.00 60.00
50 Kobe Bryant 150.00 400.00
95 Michael Jordan 200.00 500.00
155 Tony Parker 75.00 200.00

2001-02 Topps Chrome Autographs

Randomly inserted in packs at the rate of one in 257, this 10-card set features players signed to Team Topps. Full color player phtos are set against an orange and yellow background which fades to white at the bottom for authentic player autographs. The player names followed with the letter "H" were only available in hobby packs.

STATED ODDS 1:257
CARDS WITH "H" HOBBY PACKS ONLY
CAAD Antonio Daniels H 5.00 12.00
CAAJ Antawn Jamison 5.00 12.00
CABD Baron Davis H 10.00 25.00
CAEB Elton Brand H 5.00 12.00
CAJF Joseph Forte H 5.00 12.00
CAJJ Joe Johnson H 8.00 20.00
CAPS Peja Stojakovic 6.00 15.00
CASB Shane Battier 5.00 12.00
CASM Shawn Marion 5.00 12.00
CAZR Zach Randolph 8.00 20.00

2001-02 Topps Chrome Fast and Furious

Randomly seeded in packs at the rate of one in six, this 14-card set is printed on an all foil card stock with full color player action photos, colorful backgrounds and the words "Fast and Furious." A refractor version was also produced and was inserted at the rate of one in 30.

COMPLETE SET (14) 15.00 40.00
STATED ODDS 1:6
*REF: 1X TO 2.5X BASE HI
REF STATED ODDS 1:30
FF1 Steve Francis .50 1.25
FF2 Allen Iverson 1.25 3.00
FF3 Tracy McGrady 1.00 2.50
FF4 Vince Carter 1.00 2.50
FF5 Michael Jordan 5.00 12.00
FF6 Kobe Bryant 2.50 6.00
FF7 Kevin Garnett 1.00 2.50
FF8 Shaquille O'Neal 1.50 4.00
FF9 Ray Allen .60 1.50
FF10 Paul Pierce .60 1.50
FF11 Jerry Stackhouse .50 1.25
FF12 Antoine Walker .50 1.25
FF13 Chris Webber .60 1.50
FF14 Jason Richardson .75 2.00

2001-02 Topps Chrome Kareem Abdul-Jabbar Reprints

Randomly inserted in packs at the rate of one in 20, this 13-card reprints some of Kareem Abdul-Jabbars original Topps cards. A refractor version of this set was also inserted at the rate of one in 100.

COMPLETE SET (13) 20.00 40.00
COMMON CARD (1-13) 2.50 6.00
STATED ODDS 1:20
REFRACTOR STATED ODDS 1:100

2001-02 Topps Chrome Lacing Up

Randomly inserted in packs, this 14-card set is printed on an all-holofoil card stock with full color player action photos centered above a swatch of a shoe lace. The words "Lacing Up" appear along the right side, and each card is sequentially numbered to 50.

PRINT RUN 50 SER.#'d SETS
LUAJ Antawn Jamison 10.00 25.00
LUBD Baron Davis 10.00 25.00
LUEB Elton Brand 10.00 25.00
LUEC Eddy Curry 10.00 25.00
LUJF Joseph Forte 6.00 15.00
LUJT Jason Terry 10.00 25.00
LUKB Kwame Brown 10.00 25.00
LUPS Peja Stojakovic 10.00 25.00
LURH Richard Hamilton 8.00 20.00
LUSB Shane Battier 20.00 50.00
LUSM Shawn Marion 8.00 20.00
LUSO Shaquille O'Neal 25.00 60.00
LUTD Tim Duncan 20.00 50.00
LUVR Vladimir Radmanovic 10.00 25.00

2001-02 Topps Chrome Mad Game

Randomly inserted in packs at the rate of one in 13, this 10-card set features a full color player action photo on an all foil backdrop where a "shadow" of his photo appears. The top of the card contains the words "Mad Game" which appears to be outlined in gold and filled with diamonds. A refractor version was also inserted at the rate of one in 65.

COMPLETE SET (10) 12.50 30.00
STATED ODDS 1:13
*REF: 1.25X TO 3X MAD GAME HI
REF.STATED ODDS 1:65
MG1 Allen Iverson 2.00 5.00
MG2 Shaquille O'Neal 2.50 6.00
MG3 Tim Duncan 2.00 5.00
MG4 Vince Carter 1.50 4.00
MG5 Kevin Garnett 1.50 4.00
MG6 Kobe Bryant 4.00 10.00
MG7 Tracy McGrady 1.50 4.00
MG8 Steve Francis .75 2.00
MG9 Chris Webber 1.00 2.50
MG10 Darius Miles .60 1.50

2001-02 Topps Chrome Shorts Illustrated

Randomly inserted in packs at the rate of one in 180, this 10-card set boasts full color player action photos set against "shadows" of the featured player in the background. The right side contains a black strip from top to bottom with the set name and player's name in gold, and a circular swatch of game used shorts in the bottom corner. A refractor version was also inserted and is sequentially numbered to 50.

STATED ODDS 1:180
*REF: 1.25X TO 3X SHORT ILLUSTRATED HI
REF.PRINT RUN 50 SER.#'d SETS
SIAH Allan Houston 3.00 8.00
SICM Cuttino Mobley 2.50 6.00
SIDF Derek Fisher 3.00 8.00
SIDN Dirk Nowitzki 6.00 15.00
SIDW David Wesley 2.50 6.00
SIGP Gary Payton 4.00 10.00
SIMF Michael Finley 4.00 10.00
SIRH Richard Hamilton 3.00 8.00
SITD Tim Duncan 8.00 20.00
SIWS Wally Szczerbiak 3.00 8.00

2001-02 Topps Chrome Team Topps

Seeded in packs at the rate of one in 55, this 12-card set showcases the members of Team Topps on an all foil card. A refractor version was also inserted at the rate of one in 55.

COMPLETE SET (12) 12.50 30.00
STATED ODDS 1:30
*REF: 1X TO 2.5X TEAM TOPPS HI
REF.STATED ODDS 1:55
TT1 Shaquille O'Neal 3.00 8.00
TT2 Tim Duncan 2.50 6.00
TT3 Antawn Jamison 1.25 3.00
TT4 Jason Terry 1.25 3.00
TT5 Baron Davis 1.25 3.00
TT6 Elton Brand 1.25 3.00
TT7 Peja Stojakovic 1.25 3.00
TT8 Richard Hamilton 1.00 2.50
TT9 Shawn Marion 1.00 2.50
TT10 Team Photo 1.00 2.50
TT11 Shane Battier 2.50 6.00
TT12 Joseph Forte .75 2.00

2001-02 Topps Chrome Team Topps Jerseys

Randomly seeded in packs at the rate of one in 109, this 11-card set features the members of Team Topps on an all foil card with a rainbow colored background. Player portrait photos appear on the left side of the card, and a square jersey swatch appears on the right. A refractor version was also inserted at the rate of one in 682, and each card is sequentially numbered to 50.

STATED ODDS 1:109
*REF: 1.25X TO 3X HI
REF.PRINT RUN 50 SER.#'d SETS
TTAJ Antawn Jamison 2.00 5.00
TTBD Baron Davis 2.00 5.00
TTEB Elton Brand 2.00 5.00
TTJF Joseph Forte 1.25 3.00
TTJT Jason Terry 2.00 5.00
TTPS Peja Stojakovic 2.00 5.00
TTRH Richard Hamilton 1.50 4.00
TTSB Shane Battier 4.00 10.00
TTSM Shawn Marion 1.50 4.00
TTSO Shaquille O'Neal 5.00 12.00
TTTD Tim Duncan 4.00 10.00

2002-03 Topps Chrome

Released in late February 2003, Topps Chrome consists of 175 total cards but is only numbered consecutively through 165. Ten foreign born rookies have card "B" versions which feature the same photo as their regular card, but all the text is in the player's home language. Ex: Yao Ming has an English and Chinese version. Base cards are printed on an all chrome card stock with blue borders and silver highlights. Topps Chrome was packaged in 24-pack boxes where each pack contained four cards and carried a suggested retail price of $3.00.

COMPLETE SET (175) 40.00 100.00
RC CARD B VER. NOT IN ENGLISH
1 Shaquille O'Neal 1.00 2.50
2 Pau Gasol .50 1.25
3 Allen Iverson .60 1.50
4 Tom Gugliotta .25 .60
5 Rasheed Wallace .40 1.00
6 Peja Stojakovic .40 1.00
7 Jason Richardson .40 1.00
8 Rashard Lewis .40 1.00
9 Morris Peterson .25 .60
10 Michael Jordan 3.00 8.00
11 Matt Harpring .25 .60
12 Shareef Abdur-Rahim .30 .75
13 Antoine Walker .30 .75
14 Stephon Marbury .30 .75
15 Jamal Mashburn .30 .75
16 Eddy Curry .25 .60
17 Jumaine Jones .25 .60
18 Jason Kidd .60 1.50
19 Jerry Stackhouse .30 .75
20 Kenny Thomas .25 .60
21 Kobe Bryant 1.50 4.00
22 Jason Williams .30 .75
23 Eddie Jones .30 .75
24 Kenyon Martin .30 .75
25 Kevin Garnett .60 1.50
26 Kurt Thomas .25 .60
27 Karl Malone .50 1.25
28 Reggie Evans RC 1.50 4.00
29 Dirk Nowitzki .60 1.50
30 Vince Carter .60 1.50
31 Desmond Mason .30 .75
32 Todd MacCulloch .25 .60
33 Grant Hill .50 1.25
34 Terrell Brandon .25 .60
35 Tracy McGrady .60 1.50
36 Tim Thomas .25 .60
37 Loren Woods .25 .60
38 Michael Redd .30 .75
39 Stromile Swift .25 .60
40 Dikembe Mutombo .40 1.00
41 Richard Jefferson .40 1.00
42 Glenn Robinson .30 .75
43 Quentin Richardson .30 .75
44 Elton Brand .40 1.00
45 Reggie Miller .40 1.00
46 Eddie Griffin .25 .60
47 Gilbert Arenas .40 1.00
48 Zeljko Rebraca .25 .60
49 Mark Jackson .30 .75
50 Juwan Howard .30 .75
51 Nick Van Exel .30 .75
52 Donyell Marshall .25 .60
53 Tyson Chandler .40 1.00
54 Baron Davis .30 .75
55 Nate Huffman RC .25 .60
56 Jamaal Magloire .25 .60
57 Marcus Fizer .25 .60
58 Steve Francis .30 .75
59 Aaron McKie .25 .60
60 Scottie Pippen .60 1.50
61 Mike Bibby .40 1.00
62 Paul Pierce .40 1.00
63 Kwame Brown .25 .60
64 Andrei Kirilenko .40 1.00
65 Keon Clark .25 .60
66 Alvin Williams .25 .60
67 Brent Barry .25 .60
68 Doug Christie .25 .60
69 Chris Webber .40 1.00
70 Robert Horry .30 .75
71 Allan Houston .30 .75
72 Kerry Kittles .25 .60
73 Wally Szczerbiak .30 .75
74 Jonathan Bender .25 .60
75 Sam Cassell .30 .75
76 Rod Strickland .25 .60
77 Shane Battier .40 1.00
78 Tim Duncan .75 2.00
79 Jermaine O'Neal .30 .75
80 Cuttino Mobley .25 .60
81 Clifford Robinson .25 .60
82 Steve Nash .50 1.25
83 Dermarr Johnson .25 .60
84 Courtney Alexander .25 .60
85 Corliss Williamson .25 .60
86 Tony Parker .50 1.25
87 Damon Stoudamire .30 .75
88 Jalen Rose .30 .75
89 Mike Miller .30 .75
90 Raef Lafrentz .25 .60
91 Ben Wallace .30 .75
92 Ray Allen .40 1.00
93 Gary Payton .40 1.00
94 Derek Fisher .30 .75
95 Michael Olowokandi .25 .60
96 Jamaal Tinsley .25 .60
97 Chris Mihm .25 .60
98 Antawn Jamison .40 1.00
99 Mengke Bateer .25 .60
100 Michael Finley .40 1.00
101 Andre Miller .30 .75
102 Elden Campbell .25 .60
103 Kedrick Brown .25 .60
104 Jason Terry .30 .75
105 Kenny Anderson .30 .75
106 Darius Miles .25 .60
107 Latrell Sprewell .30 .75
108 Darrell Armstrong .25 .60
109 Joe Johnson .30 .75
110 Bonzi Wells .25 .60
111 LaPhonso Ellis .30 .75
112 Steve Smith .30 .75
113 Vin Baker .30 .75
114 Antonio Davis .25 .60
115 John Stockton .50 1.25
116 Shawn Marion .30 .75
117 Devean George .25 .60
118 Joe Smith .30 .75
119 Sean Lampley .25 .60
120 Lamar Odom .30 .75
121 Alonzo Mourning .50 1.25
122 Antonio Daniels .25 .60
123 Troy Murphy .30 .75
124A Manu Ginobili RC 4.00 10.00
124B Manu Ginobili RC 4.00 10.00
125 Richard Hamilton .30 .75
126 Amare Stoudemire RC 2.00 5.00
127 Carlos Boozer RC 1.50 4.00
128 Casey Jacobsen RC 1.25 3.00
129 Juaquin Hawkins RC 1.00 2.50
130 Pat Burke RC 1.00 2.50
131 Dan Dickau RC 1.25 3.00
132 Drew Gooden RC 1.50 4.00
133 Fred Jones RC 1.25 3.00
134 Jared Jeffries RC 1.25 3.00
135A Jiri Welsch RC 1.25 3.00
135B Jiri Welsch RC 1.25 3.00
136 Juan Dixon RC 1.50 4.00
137 Marcus Haislip RC 1.25 3.00
138 Melvin Ely RC 1.25 3.00
139A Nene Hilario RC 1.50 4.00
139B Nene Hilario RC 1.50 4.00
140 Qyntel Woods RC 1.25 3.00
141 Lonny Baxter RC 1.00 2.50
142 Ryan Humphrey RC 1.25 3.00
143 Smush Parker RC 1.50 4.00
144 Tayshaun Prince RC 2.00 5.00
145 Vincent Yarbrough RC 1.00 2.50
146A Yao Ming RC 3.00 8.00
146B Yao Ming RC 3.00 8.00
147 Pete Mickeal .25 .60
148 Tamar Slay RC 1.00 2.50
149A Efthimios Rentzias RC 1.00 2.50
149B Efthimios Rentzias RC 1.00 2.50
150A Igor Rakocevic RC 1.00 2.50
150B Igor Rakocevic RC 1.00 2.50
151A Gordan Giricek RC 1.50 4.00
151B Gordan Giricek RC 1.50 4.00
152A Nikoloz Tskitishvili RC 1.00 2.50
152B Nikoloz Tskitishvili RC 1.00 2.50
153 Mike Dunleavy RC 1.50 4.00
154A Marko Jaric 1.50 4.00
154B Marko Jaric 1.50 4.00
155 Kareem Rush RC 1.25 3.00
156 John Salmons RC 1.50 4.00
157 Jay Williams RC 1.50 4.00
158 J.R. Bremer RC 1.00 2.50
159 Frank Williams RC 1.00 2.50
160 Adam Harrington RC 1.00 2.50
161 DaJuan Wagner RC 1.25 3.00
162 Chris Wilcox RC 1.25 3.00
163 Chris Jefferies RC 1.00 2.50
164 Caron Butler RC 1.50 4.00
165A Bostjan Nachbar RC 1.25 3.00
165B Bostjan Nachbar RC 1.25 3.00

2002-03 Topps Chrome Refractors

*STARS: 2.5X TO 6X BASE CARD HI
*RCs: 1X TO 2.5X BASE CARD HI
STATED ODDS 1:4
10 Michael Jordan 30.00 80.00

2002-03 Topps Chrome Refractors Black Border

*STARS: 8X TO 20X BASE CARD HI
*RCs: 3X TO 8X BASE CARD HI
STATED ODDS 1:29
STATED PRINT RUN 99 SER #'d SETS
10 Michael Jordan 100.00 250.00
21 Kobe Bryant 50.00 125.00

2002-03 Topps Chrome Refractors White Border

*STARS: 5X TO 12X BASE CARD HI
*RCs: 1.5X TO 4X BASE CARD HI
PRINT RUN 249 SER.#'d SETS
10 Michael Jordan 75.00 200.00

2002-03 Topps Chrome Autographs

Topps Chrome Autographs were inserted in packs for Group A at 1:3796, Yao Ming-also sequentially numbered to 250, Group B at 1:949, Mike Dunleavy and Troy Murphy-also each sequentially numbered to 500, Group C at 1:1130, Shaquille O'Neal-also sequentially numbered to 850, and Group D at 1:862, Tito Maddox-also sequentially numbered to 1100. Each card features an all chrome card stock with a full color player image set agains a basketball background with a fade to white area along the bottom of the card for player autographs. Each card is also stamped in the upper left hand corner with a Topps Chrome Certified Autograph stamp.

GROUP A ODDS 1:3796; B ODDS 1:949
GROUP C ODDS 1:1130; D ODDS 1:862
TCAMD Mike Dunleavy/500 4.00 10.00
TCASO Shaquille O'Neal/850 40.00 100.00
TCATM Troy Murphy/500 4.00 10.00
TCATM Tito Maddox/1100 4.00 10.00
TCAYM Yao Ming/250 40.00 80.00

2002-03 Topps Chrome Coast to Coast

Randomy inserted in packs at the rate of one in eight, this 20-card set places full-color player action photos on a background littered with street signs. Along the top a green sign contains the words, "Coast to Coast," and the player's name appears in a yellow box along the bottom of the card. Refractor versions were inserted at the rate of one in 40 and utilize the rainbow holofoil refractor effect.

COMPLETE SET (20) 15.00 40.00
STATED ODDS 1:8
*REF: .75X TO 2X COAST TO COAST HI
REF. STATED ODDS 1:40
CC1 Tracy McGrady 1.25 3.00
CC2 Jason Kidd 1.25 3.00
CC3 Mike Bibby .75 2.00
CC4 Baron Davis .60 1.50
CC5 Steve Francis .60 1.50
CC6 Vince Carter 1.25 3.00
CC7 Kobe Bryant 3.00 8.00
CC8 Michael Jordan 6.00 15.00
CC9 Paul Pierce .75 2.00
CC10 Stephon Marbury .60 1.50
CC11 Ray Allen .75 2.00
CC12 Gary Payton .75 2.00
CC13 Shawn Marion .60 1.50
CC14 Steve Nash 1.00 2.50
CC15 Andre Miller .60 1.50
CC16 Jerry Stackhouse .60 1.50
CC17 Latrell Sprewell .60 1.50
CC18 Jason Richardson .75 2.00
CC19 Jamaal Tinsley .50 1.25
CC20 Tony Parker 1.00 2.50

2002-03 Topps Chrome Destination Relics

Randomly inserted in packs for Group A at one in 9310, Group B at one in 2373, Group C at one in 1898, Group D at one in 422, and Group E at one in 111. The cards are horizontally designed on an all-foil card stock with a player photo on the left and a circular swatch on the right. Under the swatch, the card tells what piece of clothing the material is from. Refractor versions were also randomly inserted and are sequentially numbered to 25.

GROUP A ODDS 1:9310; B: 1:2373
GROUP C ODDS 1:1898; D: 1:422; E: 1:111
*REF: 1.25X TO 3X HI
REF.PRINT RUN 25 SER.#'d SETS
FDBH Brendan Haywood 2.00 5.00
FDDR David Robinson 6.00 15.00
FDJJ Joe Johnson 2.50 6.00
FDLO Lamar Odom 2.50 6.00
FDMO Michael Olowokandi 2.00 5.00
FDNV Nick Van Exel 2.50 6.00
FDPS Peja Stojakovic 3.00 8.00
FDRW Rasheed Wallace 3.00 8.00
FDSF Steve Francis 2.50 6.00
FDSN Steve Nash 4.00 10.00
FDSS Steve Smith 2.50 6.00
FDWS Wally Szczerbiak 2.50 6.00

2002-03 Topps Chrome Franchise Fabric Relics

Inserted in packs at the rate of one in 11167 for Group A, one in 9099 for Group B, one in 316 for Group C, and one in 135 for Group D, this 13-card set places a full color player action photo on the top with gold borders on an all white background. Below the picture a star-shaped swatch of memorabilia appears. A refractor version of this set was issued and cards are sequentially numbered to 25.

GROUP A ODDS 1:11167; B ODDS 1:9099
GROUP C ODDS 1:316; D ODDS 1:135
*REF: 1.5X TO 4X HI
REF.PRINT RUN 25 SER.#'d SETS
FFCW Chris Webber 4.00 10.00
FFDW DaJuan Wagner 2.50 6.00
FFEB Elton Brand 3.00 8.00
FFJO Jermaine O'Neal 2.50 6.00
FFJR Jason Richardson 3.00 8.00
FFKG Kevin Garnett 5.00 12.00
FFKM Kenyon Martin 2.50 6.00
FFMD Mike Dunleavy 3.00 8.00
FFMO Michael Olowokandi 2.00 5.00
FFNH Nene Hilario 3.00 8.00
FFSO Shaquille O'Neal 8.00 20.00
FFTD Tim Duncan 6.00 15.00
FFYM Yao Ming 6.00 15.00

2002-03 Topps Chrome Shaq Attack Relics

Inserted in packs at the rate of one in 474, this five card set highlights Shaquille O'Neal's career from high school to the pros. Cards utilize a horizontal design with a picture of Shaq on the left and a timeline on the right with a white border. The memorabilia featured on the card is centered and in the shape of the state that the highlighted event occurred. A refractor version was also inserted and each card is sequentially numbered to 34.

COMMON CARD (1-5) 12.00 30.00
STATED ODDS 1:474
*REF: 1X TO 2.5X BASE HI
REF PRINT RUN 34 SER.#'d SETS

2002-03 Topps Chrome The Move

Randomly seeded in packs at the rate of one in 28, this 20-card set places full color player photos on a green background with the words "The Move" along the top of the card. A refractor version of this set was also inserted at the rate of one in 140.

COMPLETE SET (20) 30.00 80.00
STATED ODDS 1:28
*REF: 1X TO 2.5X THE MOVE HI
REF.STATED ODDS 1:140
TM1 Shaquille O'Neal 3.00 8.00
TM2 Reggie Miller 1.25 3.00
TM3 Allen Iverson 2.00 5.00
TM4 Kobe Bryant 5.00 12.00
TM5 Jason Kidd 2.00 5.00
TM6 Michael Jordan 10.00 25.00
TM7 Vince Carter 2.00 5.00
TM8 Ray Allen 1.25 3.00
TM9 Gary Payton 1.25 3.00
TM10 Jason Richardson 1.25 3.00
TM11 Tim Duncan 2.50 6.00
TM12 Scottie Pippen 2.00 5.00
TM13 Paul Pierce 1.25 3.00
TM14 Dikembe Mutombo 1.25 3.00
TM15 Tracy McGrady 2.00 5.00
TM16 Chris Wilcox 1.00 2.50
TM17 Yao Ming 2.50 6.00
TM18 Jay Williams 1.25 3.00
TM19 Mike Dunleavy 1.25 3.00
TM20 DaJuan Wagner 1.00 2.50

2002-03 Topps Chrome Zone Busters

Randomly inserted in packs at the rate of one in 12, this 15-card set places full color player action photos on a blue and yellow background. A white strip runs down the right side of the card containing the words, Zone Busters and the player's name. A refractor version was also inserted at one in 60.

COMPLETE SET (15) 12.50 30.00
STATED ODDS 1:12
*REF: .75X TO 2X ZONE BUSTER HI
REF.STATED ODDS 1:60
ZB1 Shaquille O'Neal 2.00 5.00
ZB2 Kevin Garnett 1.25 3.00
ZB3 Peja Stojakovic .75 2.00
ZB4 Kenyon Martin .60 1.50
ZB5 Latrell Sprewell .60 1.50
ZB6 Michael Finley .75 2.00
ZB7 Shawn Marion .60 1.50
ZB8 Kobe Bryant 3.00 8.00
ZB9 Mike Bibby .75 2.00
ZB10 Tracy McGrady 1.25 3.00
ZB11 Tony Parker 1.00 2.50
ZB12 Vince Carter 1.25 3.00
ZB13 Michael Jordan 6.00 15.00
ZB14 Elton Brand .75 2.00
ZB15 Jamaal Tinsley .50 1.25

2003-04 Topps Chrome

Issued in February 2004, Topps Chrome features a 174-card set divided up into 110 veteran player cards and 67 rookie cards (numbers 111-165) where several players have card variations in their native languages. The card design is set to match that of base topps, but is enhanced with an all-foil card stock. Chrome was packaged in 24-pack boxes where packs contained four cards and carried a suggested retail price of $3. Also included in each box was a sealed uncirculated X-Fractor card.

COMPLETE SET (165) 150.00 250.00
COMP.SET w/o RC's (110) 15.00 40.00
B VERSION FOR CARDS 112, 121, 127
129, 131, 132, 138, 140, 146, 147, 149, 154
CARD B VERSION FOREIGN, SAME VALUE
1 Tracy McGrady .50 1.25
2 Dajuan Wagner .25 .60
3 Allen Iverson .60 1.50
4 Chris Webber .40 1.00
5 Jason Kidd .60 1.50
6 Stephon Marbury .30 .75
7 Jermaine O'Neal .30 .75
8 Antoine Walker .40 1.00
9 Tony Parker .40 1.00
10 Mike Bibby .40 1.00
11 Yao Ming .75 2.00
12 Bobby Jackson .25 .60
13 Steve Nash .50 1.25
14 Paul Pierce .40 1.00
15 Vince Carter .60 1.50
16 Peja Stojakovic .40 1.00
17 Wally Szczerbiak .30 .75
18 Kenyon Martin .30 .75
19 Pau Gasol .40 1.00
20 Gary Payton .40 1.00
21 Tim Duncan .60 1.50
22 Anfernee Hardaway .60 1.50
23 Jason Richardson .40 1.00
24 Andre Miller .30 .75
25 Latrell Sprewell .30 .75
26 Darius Miles .25 .60
27 Richard Jefferson .30 .75
28 Shawn Marion .30 .75
29 Baron Davis .30 .75
30 Ben Wallace .30 .75
31 Reggie Miller .40 1.00
32 Karl Malone .50 1.25
33 Jonathan Bender .25 .60
34 Shaquille O'Neal 1.00 2.50
35 Steve Francis .30 .75
36 Kobe Bryant 1.50 4.00
37 Mike Dunleavy .30 .75
38 Glenn Robinson .30 .75
39 Allan Houston .30 .75
40 Sam Cassell .30 .75
41 Dirk Nowitzki .60 1.50
42 Elton Brand .40 1.00
43 Joe Smith .30 .75
44 Brian Grant .25 .60
45 Jason Terry .30 .75
46 Richard Hamilton .30 .75
47 Morris Peterson .25 .60
48 Ray Allen .40 1.00
49 Scottie Pippen .60 1.50
50 Jamal Crawford .40 1.00
51 Cuttino Mobley .25 .60
52 Jerry Stackhouse .30 .75
53 Marcus Camby .30 .75
54 Jalen Rose .30 .75
55 Ricky Davis .30 .75
56 Jamal Mashburn .30 .75
57 Ron Artest .40 1.00
58 Theo Ratliff .25 .60
59 Juwan Howard .30 .75
60 Caron Butler .30 .75
61 Antawn Jamison .30 .75
62 Nene .30 .75
63 Tyson Chandler .30 .75
64 Jason Williams .30 .75
65 Kurt Thomas .25 .60
66 Mike Miller .30 .75
67 Amare Stoudemire .50 1.25
68 Jamaal Tinsley .25 .60
69 Brent Barry .25 .60
70 Brad Miller .30 .75
71 Bonzi Wells .25 .60
72 Andrei Kirilenko .40 1.00
73 Kenny Thomas .25 .60
74 Derek Anderson .25 .60
75 Zydrunas Ilgauskas .30 .75
76 Eddie Griffin .25 .60
77 Tayshaun Prince .30 .75
78 Michael Olowokandi .25 .60
79 Michael Redd .40 1.00
80 Tim Thomas .25 .60
81 Eddie Jones .30 .75
82 Shareef Abdur-Rahim .30 .75
83 Corey Maggette .30 .75
84 Eric Snow .25 .60
85 Keon Clark .25 .60
86 Desmond Mason .30 .75
87 Drew Gooden .30 .75
88 Matt Harpring .25 .60
89 Antonio McDyess .30 .75
90 Radoslav Nesterovic .25 .60
91 Jamaal Magloire .25 .60
92 Rasheed Wallace .40 1.00
93 Antonio Davis .25 .60
94 Kwame Brown .25 .60
95 Manu Ginobili .50 1.25
96 Eric Williams .25 .60
97 Nick Van Exel .30 .75
98 Lamar Odom .30 .75
99 Chauncey Billups .40 1.00
100 Kevin Garnett .60 1.50
101 Marko Jaric .25 .60
102 David Wesley .25 .60
103 Gilbert Arenas .30 .75
104 Keith Van Horn .30 .75
105 Bostjan Nachbar .25 .60
106 Michael Finley .40 1.00
107 Troy Murphy .25 .60
108 Eddy Curry .25 .60
109 Rashard Lewis .40 1.00
110 Tony Battie .25 .60
111 LeBron James RC 250.00 500.00
112A Darko Milicic RC 1.50 4.00
112B Darko Milicic 1.50 4.00
113 Carmelo Anthony RC 5.00 12.00
114 Chris Bosh RC 3.00 8.00
115 Dwyane Wade RC 8.00 20.00
116 Chris Kaman RC 2.00 5.00
117 Kirk Hinrich RC 2.00 5.00
118 T.J. Ford RC 1.50 4.00
119 Mike Sweetney RC 1.25 3.00
120 Jarvis Hayes RC 1.25 3.00
121A Mickael Pietrus RC 1.50 4.00
121B Mickael Pietrus 1.50 4.00
122 Nick Collison RC 1.50 4.00
123 Marcus Banks RC 1.25 3.00
124 Luke Ridnour RC 1.50 4.00
125 Reece Gaines RC 1.25 3.00
126 Troy Bell RC 1.25 3.00
127A Zarko Cabarkapa RC 1.25 3.00
127B Zarko Cabarkapa 1.25 3.00
128 David West RC 2.00 5.00
129A Aleksandar Pavlovic RC 1.50 4.00
129B Aleksandar Pavlovic 1.50 4.00
130 Dahntay Jones RC 1.50 4.00
131A Boris Diaw RC 2.00 5.00
131B Boris Diaw RC 2.00 5.00
132A Zoran Planinic RC 1.25 3.00
132B Zoran Planinic 1.25 3.00
133 Travis Outlaw RC 1.50 4.00
134 Brian Cook RC 1.25 3.00
135 Matt Carroll RC 1.25 3.00
136 Ndudi Ebi RC 1.25 3.00
137 Kendrick Perkins RC 1.50 4.00
138A Leandro Barbosa RC 2.00 5.00
138B Leandro Barbosa 2.00 5.00
139 Josh Howard RC 2.00 5.00
140A Maciej Lampe RC 1.25 3.00
140B Maciej Lampe 1.25 3.00
141 Jason Kapono RC 1.25 3.00
142 Luke Walton RC 2.00 5.00
143 Jerome Beasley RC 1.25 3.00
144 Travis Hansen RC 1.25 3.00
145 Steve Blake RC 1.50 4.00
146A Slavko Vranes RC 1.25 3.00
146B Slavko Vranes 1.25 3.00
147A Francisco Elson RC 1.25 3.00
147B Francisco Elson 1.25 3.00
148 Willie Green RC 1.25 3.00
149A Zaur Pachulia RC 2.00 5.00
149B Zaur Pachulia 2.00 5.00
150 Keith Bogans RC 1.25 3.00
151 Maurice Williams RC 2.00 5.00
152 James Jones RC 1.25 3.00
153 Kyle Korver RC 2.50 6.00
154A Jon Stefansson RC 1.25 3.00
154B Jon Stefansson 1.25 3.00
155 Brandon Hunter RC 1.25 3.00
156 Josh Moore RC 1.25 3.00
157 Torraye Braggs RC 1.25 3.00
158 Devin Brown RC 1.25 3.00
159 James Lang RC 1.25 3.00
160 Theron Smith RC 1.25 3.00
161 Linton Johnson RC 1.25 3.00
162 Marquis Daniels RC 1.50 4.00
163 Keith McLeod RC 1.25 3.00
164 Udonis Haslem RC 1.50 4.00
165 Ben Handlogten RC 1.25 3.00

2003-04 Topps Chrome Refractors

*1-110 SINGLES: 2X TO 5X BASE HI
*111-165 RC SINGLES: 1X TO 2.5X BASE HI
1-110 STATED ODDS 1:6
111-165 STATED ODDS 1:12
36 Kobe Bryant 15.00 40.00
111 LeBron James 1800.00 2200.00
113 Carmelo Anthony 20.00 50.00
115 Dwyane Wade 50.00 120.00

2003-04 Topps Chrome Refractors Black

*1-110 SINGLES: 3X TO 8X BASE HI
*111-165 RC SINGLES: 2X TO 5X BASE HI
36 Kobe Bryant 30.00 80.00
111 LeBron James 2200.00 2500.00
113 Carmelo Anthony 40.00 100.00
115 Dwyane Wade 100.00 250.00

2003-04 Topps Chrome Refractors Gold

*1-110 SINGLES: 5X TO 12X BASE HI
*111-165 RC SINGLES: 3X TO 8X BASE HI
1-110 PRINT RUN 99 SER.#'d SETS
111-165 PRINT RUN 50 SER.#'d SETS
36 Kobe Bryant 200.00 500.00
111 LeBron James 5000.00 8000.00
113 Carmelo Anthony 150.00 400.00
114 Chris Bosh 75.00 150.00
115 Dwyane Wade 400.00 800.00

2003-04 Topps Chrome X-Fractors

*X-FRAC.SINGLES: 4X TO 10X BASE HI
*X-FRAC RC SINGLES: 2.5X TO 6X BASE HI
ONE PER BOX TOPPER
PRINT RUN 220 SER.#'d SETS
36 Kobe Bryant 100.00 250.00
111 LeBron James 3000.00 4000.00
113 Carmelo Anthony 75.00 200.00
115 Dwyane Wade 125.00 300.00

2003-04 Topps Chrome Autographs

Inserted at the following rates: Group A one in 300, Group B one in 622, Group C one in 2329 and Group D one in 595, this 11-card set features full-color player photos on the top of the card and a white space with an autograph at the bottom. The word, Chromograps, separates the two. A Refractor Parallel was also inserted in packs and those cards are sequentially numbered to 25.

STATED ODDS GROUP A 1:300; GROUP B 1:622
STATED ODDS GROUP C 1:2329; GROUP D 1:595
*REFRACTORS: 1.25X TO 3X BASE HI
REFRACTORS PRINT RUN 25 SETS
CACA Carmelo Anthony A 40.00 80.00
CADW Dwyane Wade A 50.00 125.00
CAKB Kwame Brown A 4.00 10.00
CAKH Kirk Hinrich B 8.00 20.00
CALR Luke Ridnour A 3.00 8.00
CAMR Michael Redd 5.00 12.00
CANC Nick Collison B 3.00 8.00
CARA Ray Allen D 12.00 30.00
CASO Shaquille O'Neal C 40.00 100.00
CASV Slavko Vranes B 2.50 6.00
CATF T.J. Ford D 3.00 8.00

2003-04 Topps Chrome Bonus Coverage Relics

Inserted at the following rates, Group A one in 1214, Group B one in 484, Group C one in 242 and Group D one in 102, this 23-card set is horizontally desiged with a player photo on the right and a swatch of memorabilia on the left. A Refractor parallel set was inserted in packs as well, and the print runs are as follows: Group A is sequentially numbered to five, Group B is sequentially numbered to 15, Group C is sequentially numbered to 20 and Group D is sequentially numbered to 25.

STATED ODDS GROUP A 1:1214; B 1:484
STATED ODDS GROUP C 1:242; D 1:102
*REFRACTORS: 1.25X TO 3X BASE HI
REFRACTORS PRINT RUN 5 TO 25 SETS
SOME REF.NOT PRICED DUE TO SCARCITY
AI Allen Iverson A 5.00 12.00
AW Antoine Walker D 3.00 8.00
BD Baron Davis A 2.50 6.00

CB Caron Butler B 2.50 6.00
CW Chris Webber D 3.00 8.00
DM Darius Miles B 2.00 5.00
DW Dajuan Wagner C 2.00 5.00
JM Jamal Mashburn C 2.50 6.00
JR Jason Richardson A 3.00 8.00
KB Kevin Garnett A 5.00 12.00
MD Mike Dunleavy A 2.50 6.00
MF Michael Finley A 3.00 8.00
PG Pau Gasol D 3.00 8.00
RJ Richard Jefferson C 2.50 6.00
SA Shareef Abdur-Rahim A 2.50 6.00
SF Steve Francis A 2.50 6.00
SM Shawn Marion C 2.50 6.00
SO Shaquille O'Neal D 8.00 20.00
TM Tracy McGrady D 4.00 10.00
SMA Stephon Marbury B 2.50 6.00

2003-04 Topps Chrome Cuts Relics

Inserted in packs at the following rates, Group A one in 1214, Group B one in 484, Group C one in 242 and Group D one in 102, this 23-card set places player photos on the right and memorabilia swatches in the shape of the letter "C" on the left. A Refractor parallel set was inserted in packs as well, and the print runs are as follows: Group A is sequentially numbered to five, Group B is sequentially numbered to 15, Group C is sequentially numbered to 20 and Group D is sequentially numbered to 25.

STATED ODDS GROUP A 1:1214; B 1:484
STATED ODDS GROUP C 1:242; D 1:102
*REFRACTORS: 1.25X TO 3X BASE HI
REFRACTORS PRINT RUN 5 TO 25 SETS
SOME REF.NOT PRICED DUE TO SCARCITY
BH Brendan Haywood B 2.00 5.00
BM Brad Miller C 2.50 6.00
BW Ben Wallace D 2.50 6.00
DF Derek Fisher A 2.50 6.00
EC Elden Campbell B 2.00 5.00
EG Manu Ginobili A 4.00 10.00
HT Hedo Turkoglu C 2.50 6.00
JS Jerry Stackhouse B 2.50 6.00
KM Kenyon Martin A 2.50 6.00
MB Mike Bibby B 3.00 8.00
MR Michael Redd B 3.00 8.00
NH Nene C 2.50 6.00
NT Nikoloz Tskitishvili B 2.00 5.00
RW Rasheed Wallace D 3.00 8.00
TC Tyson Chandler D 2.50 6.00
TD Tim Duncan 5.00 12.00
VR Vladimir Radmanovic A 2.00 5.00
ZI Zydrunas Ilgauskas D 2.50 6.00
AHA Anfernee Hardaway A 5.00 12.00

2003-04 Topps Chrome Gametime Gear Relics

Inserted in packs at the following rates, Group A one in 1214, Group B one in 484, Group C one in 242 and Group D one in 102, this 23-card set places player photos on the right and circular memorabilia swatches on the left. A Refractor parallel set was inserted in packs as well, and the print runs are as follows: Group A is sequentially numbered to five, Group B is sequentially numbered to 15, Group C is sequentially numbered to 20 and Group D is sequentially numbered to 25.

STATED ODDS GROUP A 1:1214; B 1:484
STATED ODDS GROUP C 1:242; D 1:102
*REFRACTORS: 1.25X TO 3X BASE HI
REFRACTORS PRINT RUN 5 TO 25 SETS
SOME REF.NOT PRICED DUE TO SCARCITY
AK Andrei Kirilenko A 3.00 8.00
AS Amare Stoudemire C 4.00 10.00
CB Carlos Boozer D 2.50 6.00
CM Cuttino Mobley D 2.00 5.00
DG Devean George A 2.00 5.00
DN Dirk Nowitzki D 5.00 12.00
DW David Wesley D 2.00 5.00
JD Juan Dixon B 2.00 5.00
JK Jason Kidd B 5.00 12.00
JW Jerome Williams D 2.00 5.00
LO Lamar Odom C 2.50 6.00
MP Morris Peterson B 2.00 5.00
PP Paul Pierce C 3.00 8.00
PS Peja Stojakovic D 3.00 8.00
QW Qyntel Woods C 2.00 5.00
RA Ray Allen D 3.00 8.00
TM Troy Murphy A 2.00 5.00
TP Tayshaun Prince A 2.50 6.00
WS Wally Szczerbiak C 2.50 6.00
YM Yao Ming D 6.00 15.00
TPA Tony Parker D 3.00 8.00

2004-05 Topps Chrome

This 220-card was released in February, 2005. The cards were issued in four-card packs with an $3 SRP which came 24 packs to a box and eight boxes to a case. Cards numbered 1-165 feature active veterans while cards 166-220 feature Rookie Cards.

COMPLETE SET (220) 75.00 200.00
COMP.SET w/o RC's (165) 15.00 40.00
UNPRICED SUPERFR.PRINT RUN ONE SET
1 Allen Iverson .60 1.50
2 Eddy Curry .25 .60
3 Stephon Marbury .30 .75
4 Chris Bosh .40 1.00
5 Jason Kidd .60 1.50
6 Baron Davis .30 .75
7 Kwame Brown .25 .60
8 Kobe Bryant 1.50 4.00
9 Ben Wallace .30 .75
10 Josh Howard .40 1.00
11 Yao Ming .75 2.00
12 Luke Walton .25 .60
13 Nene .30 .75
14 Michael Redd .30 .75
15 Carmelo Anthony .75 2.00
16 Amare Stoudemire .30 .75
17 Jarvis Hayes .25 .60
18 Toni Kukoc .40 1.00
19 Latrell Sprewell .30 .75
20 Jason Richardson .40 1.00
21 Kevin Garnett .60 1.50
22 Darko Milicic .25 .60
23 LeBron James 20.00 50.00
24 Peja Stojakovic .40 1.00
25 Wally Szczerbiak .30 .75
26 Theo Ratliff .25 .60
27 Gilbert Arenas .30 .75
28 Mike Dunleavy .30 .75
29 Joe Smith .30 .75
30 Vince Carter .60 1.50
31 Reggie Miller .40 1.00
32 Chris Wilcox .25 .60
33 Rasheed Wallace .40 1.00
34 Paul Pierce .40 1.00
35 Tayshaun Prince .30 .75
36 Richard Hamilton .30 .75
37 Rashard Lewis .40 1.00
38 Joe Johnson .30 .75
39 Zydrunas Ilgauskas .30 .75
40 Andre Miller .30 .75
41 Dirk Nowitzki .60 1.50
42 Chauncey Billups .40 1.00
43 Ray Allen .40 1.00
44 Raef LaFrentz .25 .60
45 Mickael Pietrus .30 .75
46 T.J. Ford .25 .60
47 Chris Webber .40 1.00
48 Jamaal Tinsley .25 .60
49 Earl Boykins .25 .60
50 Tim Duncan .60 1.50
51 Troy Hudson .25 .60
52 Juan Dixon .25 .60
53 Tim Thomas .25 .60
54 Darius Miles .25 .60
55 Jalen Rose .30 .75
56 Kirk Hinrich .30 .75
57 Michael Finley .40 1.00
58 Brad Miller .30 .75
59 Jonathan Bender .25 .60
60 Manu Ginobili .50 1.25
61 Chris Kaman .30 .75
62 Doug Christie .25 .60
63 Marcus Camby .30 .75
64 Desmond Mason .30 .75
65 Boris Diaw .30 .75
66 Maurice Taylor .25 .60
67 Damon Stoudamire .30 .75
68 Dwyane Wade .60 1.50
69 Allan Houston .30 .75
70 Jermaine O'Neal .30 .75
71 Glenn Robinson .30 .75
72 Morris Peterson .25 .60
73 Luke Ridnour .30 .75
74 Bobby Jackson .25 .60
75 Eddie Jones .30 .75
76 Alvin Williams .25 .60
77 Elton Brand .40 1.00
78 Zach Randolph .30 .75
79 Marko Jaric .25 .60
80 Mike Bibby .40 1.00
81 Jim Jackson .25 .60
82 Kurt Thomas .25 .60
83 Troy Murphy .25 .60
84 Rodney White .25 .60
85 Jamaal Magloire .25 .60
86 Jamal Mashburn .30 .75
87 Kenny Thomas .25 .60
88 Corey Maggette .30 .75
89 Rasho Nesterovic .25 .60
90 Shawn Marion .30 .75
91 Antonio Daniels .25 .60
92 Marquis Daniels .25 .60
93 Richard Jefferson .30 .75
94 Michael Olowokandi .25 .60
95 Bruce Bowen .25 .60
96 Mark Blount .25 .60
97 Sam Cassell .30 .75
98 Voshon Lenard .25 .60
99 Speedy Claxton .25 .60
100 Samuel Dalembert .25 .60
101 Tyson Chandler .30 .75
102 Keith Van Horn .30 .75
103 Udonis Haslem .25 .60
104 Trenton Hassell .25 .60
105 Tony Parker .40 1.00
106 Ronald Murray .25 .60
107 Jeff McInnis .25 .60
108 Marcus Banks .25 .60
109 Ricky Davis .30 .75
110 Karl Malone .50 1.25
111 Bonzi Wells .25 .60
112 Antonio McDyess .30 .75
113 Drew Gooden .25 .60
114 Stephen Jackson .30 .75
115 Eric Snow .25 .60
116 Steve Francis .30 .75
117 Pau Gasol .40 1.00
118 Andrei Kirilenko .30 .75
119 Erick Dampier .25 .60
120 Jason Kapono .25 .60
121 Al Harrington .30 .75
122 Gary Payton .40 1.00
123 Nick Van Exel .30 .75
124 Cuttino Mobley .25 .60
125 Kenyon Martin .30 .75
126 Mike Miller .30 .75
127 Jamal Crawford .40 1.00
128 Kerry Kittles .25 .60
129 Derrick Coleman .30 .75
130 Gordan Giricek .25 .60
131 Antoine Walker .40 1.00
132 Shane Battier .30 .75
133 Caron Butler .30 .75
134 Corliss Williamson .25 .60
135 Carlos Boozer .30 .75
136 Tracy McGrady .50 1.25
137 Stromile Swift .25 .60
138 Derek Fisher .30 .75
139 Juwan Howard .30 .75
140 Jason Terry .30 .75
141 Vlade Divac .30 .75
142 Antawn Jamison .30 .75
143 Aleksandar Pavlovic .25 .60
144 Rafer Alston .25 .60
145 Brent Barry .25 .60
146 Quentin Richardson .30 .75
147 Lamar Odom .30 .75
148 Gerald Wallace .30 .75
149 Charlie Ward .25 .60
150 Jerry Stackhouse .30 .75
151 Carlos Arroyo .25 .60
152 Hedo Turkoglu .30 .75
153 Steve Nash .50 1.25
154 Mehmet Okur .30 .75
155 Tyronn Lue .25 .60
156 Bob Sura .25 .60
157 Jason Williams .30 .75
158 Shaquille O'Neal 1.00 2.50
159 Kelvin Cato .25 .60
160 Eric Williams .25 .60
161 Brian Grant .25 .60
162 Danny Fortson .25 .60
163 Chucky Atkins .25 .60
164 Matt Harpring .25 .60
165 Primoz Brezec .25 .60
166 Dwight Howard RC 3.00 8.00
167 Emeka Okafor RC 1.25 3.00
168 Ben Gordon RC 1.50 4.00
169 Shaun Livingston RC 1.50 4.00
170 Devin Harris RC 1.25 3.00
171 Josh Childress RC 1.25 3.00
172 Luol Deng RC 1.50 4.00
173 Rafael Araujo RC 1.00 2.50
174 Andre Iguodala RC 2.00 5.00
175 Luke Jackson RC 1.00 2.50
176 Andris Biedrins RC 1.00 2.50
177 Robert Swift RC 1.00 2.50
178 Sebastian Telfair RC 1.25 3.00
179 Kris Humphries RC 1.50 4.00
180 Al Jefferson RC 2.00 5.00
181 Kirk Snyder RC 1.00 2.50
182 Josh Smith RC 1.50 4.00
183 J.R. Smith RC 1.50 4.00
184 Dorell Wright RC 1.50 4.00
185 Jameer Nelson RC 1.50 4.00
186 Pavel Podkolzin RC 1.00 2.50
187 Horace Jenkins RC 1.50 4.00
188 Luis Flores RC 1.25 3.00
189 Delonte West RC 1.50 4.00
190 Tony Allen RC 1.50 4.00
191 Kevin Martin RC 2.00 5.00
192 Sasha Vujacic RC 1.50 4.00
193 Beno Udrih RC 1.25 3.00
194 David Harrison RC 1.00 2.50
195 Yuta Tabuse RC 1.50 4.00
196 Peter John Ramos RC 1.00 2.50
197 Chris Duhon RC 1.50 4.00
198 Trevor Ariza RC 1.50 4.00
199 Bernard Robinson RC 1.25 3.00
200 Andre Emmett RC 1.00 2.50
201 Mario Kasun RC 1.25 3.00
202 Matt Freije RC 1.25 3.00
203 Maurice Evans RC 1.50 4.00
204 Erik Daniels RC 1.25 3.00
205 Lionel Chalmers RC 1.50 4.00
206 Jared Reiner RC 1.50 4.00
207 D.J. Mbenga RC 1.25 3.00
208 Antonio Burks RC 1.25 3.00
209 Justin Reed RC 1.00 2.50
210 Pape Sow RC 1.25 3.00
211 Jackson Vroman RC 1.00 2.50
212 Romain Sato RC 1.00 2.50
213 Nenad Kristic RC 1.50 4.00
214 Damien Wilkins RC 1.25 3.00
215 Arthur Johnson RC 1.50 4.00
216 Ibrahim Kutluay RC 1.50 4.00
217 Andres Nocioni RC 1.50 4.00
218 Josh Davis RC 1.50 4.00
219 Donta Smith RC 1.00 2.50
220 Anderson Varejao RC 1.25 3.00

2004-05 Topps Chrome Refractors

*1-165 REFRACTORS: 2X TO 5X BASE HI
*166-220 REF.RCs: .75X TO 2X BASE HI
STATED ODDS 1:4
8 Kobe Bryant 20.00 50.00
23 LeBron James 100.00 250.00

2004-05 Topps Chrome Refractors Black

*1-165 SINGLES: 3X TO 8X BASE HI
*166-220 RC SINGLES: 1.5X TO 4X BASE HI
PRINT RUN 500 SER.#'d SETS
8 Kobe Bryant 25.00 60.00
23 LeBron James 200.00 500.00

2004-05 Topps Chrome Refractors Gold

*1-165 SINGLES: 8X TO 20X BASE HI
*166-220 RC SINGLES: 2.5X TO 6X BASE HI
PRINT RUN 99 SER.#'d SETS
8 Kobe Bryant 60.00 150.00
23 LeBron James 500.00 1000.00

2004-05 Topps Chrome X-Fractors

*1-165 SINGLES: 4X TO 10X BASE HI
*166-220 RC SINGLES: 2.5X TO 6X BASE HI
PRINT RUN 110 SER.#'d SETS
ONE PER BOX AS A TOPPER
8 Kobe Bryant 25.00 60.00
23 LeBron James 500.00 1000.00

2004-05 Topps Chrome Autographs

Randomly inserted into packs, these 22 cards featuring autographs of leading NBA players. Since the players in group A, group B and group C are inserted at different odds, we have notated next to the player's name what group they are a part of. There is also a refractor parallel to this set. Those cards were issued to a stated print run of seven serial numbered sets.

GROUP A STATED ODDS 1:1264
GROUP B STATED ODDS 1:1073
GROUP C STATED ODDS 1:205
UNPRICED REFRACTOR PRINT RUN 7 SETS
AB Andris Biedrins C 3.00 8.00
AS Amare Stoudemire A 4.00 10.00
AV Anderson Varejao B 4.00 10.00
BG Ben Gordon C 5.00 12.00
CA Carmelo Anthony A 20.00 40.00
DH Devin Harris C 4.00 10.00
EO Emeka Okafor A 4.00 10.00
JC Josh Childress C 4.00 10.00
JK Jason Kidd A 15.00 40.00
JN Jameer Nelson C 3.00 8.00
JO Jermaine O'Neal A 10.00 25.00
JS Josh Smith C 5.00 12.00
LD Luol Deng A 8.00 20.00
LJ Luke Jackson B 3.00 8.00
RH Richard Hamilton A 6.00 15.00
RS Robert Swift B 3.00 8.00
SL Shaun Livingston C 5.00 12.00
SO Shaquille O'Neal A 30.00 80.00
ST Sebastian Telfair C 4.00 10.00
TM Tracy McGrady A 20.00 50.00
JRS J.R. Smith C 5.00 12.00
SMA Shawn Marion A 6.00 15.00

2004-05 Topps Chrome Chrome-Town Heroes

Randomly inserted into packs, these 29 cards featuring game-used swatches of leading veterans. For those players not in Group C, we have listed the stated print runs next to their name. Please note that Corey Maggette and Shaquille O'Neal were issued as exchange cards. There is also a refractor parallel of these cards, which were issued to a stated print run of 25 serial numbered sets.

PRINT RUNS LISTED IN CHECKLIST
*REFRACTOR: 1.25X TO 3X BASE HI
REFRACTOR PRINT RUN 25 SETS
AK Andrei Kirilenko/272 2.00 5.00
AS Amare Stoudemire/885 2.00 5.00
BW Ben Wallace/206 2.00 5.00
CA Carmelo Anthony/1000 5.00 12.00
CB Chris Bosh/859 2.50 6.00
CM Corey Maggette 2.00 5.00
CW Chris Webber/500 2.50 6.00
DM Desmond Mason/500 2.00 5.00
DN Dirk Nowitzki/500 4.00 10.00
GA Gilbert Arenas/287 2.00 5.00
GW Gerald Wallace/287 2.00 5.00
JO Jermaine O'Neal/336 2.00 5.00
JT Jason Terry/500 2.00 5.00
KG Kevin Garnett/500 4.00 10.00
KH Kirk Hinrich/1000 2.00 5.00
MD Mike Dunleavy/985 2.00 5.00
PG Pau Gasol/500 2.50 6.00
RJ Richard Jefferson/1000 2.00 5.00
RL Rashard Lewis/500 2.50 6.00
SO Shaquille O'Neal B 6.00 15.00
TP Tony Parker/385 2.50 6.00
YM Yao Ming/467 5.00 12.00
ZR Zach Randolph/364 2.00 5.00
CHB Chauncey Billups/211 2.50 6.00

2004-05 Topps Chrome Refined Remnants

Randomly inserted into packs, these 12 cards featuring game-used swatches of leading veterans. For those players not in Group C, we have listed the stated print runs next to their name. Please note that Gary Payton was issued as exchange cards. There is also a refractor parallel of these cards, which were issued to a stated print run of 25 serial numbered sets.

PRINT RUNS LISTED IN CHECKLIST
*REFRACTORS: 1.25X TO 3X BASE HI
REFRACTOR PRINT RUN 25 SETS
BD Baron Davis/780 2.00 5.00
EB Elton Brand/412 2.50 6.00
GP Gary Payton B 2.50 6.00
JK Jason Kidd/782 4.00 10.00
PP Paul Pierce/500 2.50 6.00
PS Peja Stojakovic/1000 2.50 6.00
RA Ray Allen/500 2.50 6.00
RM Reggie Miller/1000 2.50 6.00
SC Sam Cassell/385 2.00 5.00
SM Shawn Marion/332 2.00 5.00
TD Tim Duncan/939 4.00 10.00
TM Tracy McGrady/385 3.00 8.00

2004-05 Topps Chrome Slice of Success

Randomly inserted into packs, these 25 cards featuring game-used swatches of leading veterans. For those players not in Group C, we have listed the stated print runs next to their name. There is also a refractor parallel of these cards, which were issued to a stated print run of 25 serial numbered sets.

PRINT RUNS LISTED IN CHECKLIST
*REFRACTORS: 1.25X TO 3X BASE HI
REFRACTOR PRINT RUN 25 SETS
AJ Al Jefferson/976 3.00 8.00
AW Antoine Walker/900 2.50 6.00
BG Ben Gordon/500 2.50 6.00
DH Devin Harris/1000 2.00 5.00
EO Emeka Okafor/1000 2.00 5.00
JC Josh Childress/500 2.00 5.00
JH Jarvis Hayes/200 2.00 5.00
JM Jamaal Magloire/900 2.00 5.00
JT Jamaal Tinsley/500 2.00 5.00
KR Kareem Rush/500 2.00 5.00
KS Kirk Snyder/500 1.50 4.00
LD Luol Deng/307 2.50 6.00
LR Luke Ridnour/249 2.00 5.00
MB Mike Bibby/500 2.50 6.00
MJ Marko Jaric/1000 2.00 5.00
RN Rasho Nesterovic/754 2.00 5.00
SB Shane Battier/332 2.00 5.00
SF Steve Francis/500 2.00 5.00
SL Shaun Livingston/500 2.50 6.00
TA Tony Allen/500 2.50 6.00
TC Tyson Chandler/500 2.00 5.00
TP Tayshaun Prince/500 2.00 5.00
JHO Josh Howard/500 2.50 6.00
SAR Shareef Abdur-Rahim/1000 2.00 5.00

2004-05 Topps Chrome Total Recall

Randomly inserted into packs, these nine cards featuring game-used swatches of a leading rookie paired up with a leading veteran. Each of these cards were issued to a stated print run of 100 serial numbered sets. There is also a refractor parallel of these cards, which were issued to a stated print run of 25 serial numbered sets.

PRINT RUN 100 SER.#'d SETS
*REFRACTORS: 1X TO 2.5X BASE HI
REFRACTOR PRINT RUN 25 SETS
DD M.Dunleavy/L.Deng 5.00 12.00
DG B.Davis/B.Gordon 5.00 12.00
JI R.Jefferson/A.Iguodala 8.00 20.00
KH J.Kidd/D.Harris 8.00 20.00
MA B.Miller/R.Araujo 5.00 12.00
MC R.Miller/J.Childress 8.00 20.00
MT S.Marbury/S.Telfair 5.00 12.00
PJ T.Prince/L.Jackson 5.00 12.00
WO B.Wallace/E.Okafor 5.00 12.00

2005-06 Topps Chrome

Released in February 2006, this 274-card set pictures veteran players on cards 1-165, rookie players on cards 166-215, celebrities on cards 216-220 and NBA D-League players on cards 221-274. Base cards are printed on an all-foil card stock with white borders. Chrome was packaged in 24 pack boxes where packs contain four cards and carried an initial SRP of $3.00.

COMPLETE SET (274) 30.00 60.00
UNPRICED SUPERFR.PRINT RUN ONE SET
1 Grant Hill .50 1.25
2 Lamar Odom .30 .75
3 Jamal Crawford .40 1.00
4 Ben Gordon .30 .75
5 Zach Randolph .30 .75
6 Chris Duhon .25 .60
7 Gilbert Arenas .30 .75
8 Yao Ming .50 1.25
9 Josh Smith .30 .75
10 Ray Allen .40 1.00
11 Vince Carter .60 1.50
12 Kenyon Martin .30 .75
13 Tim Duncan .60 1.50
14 Michael Redd .30 .75
15 Antawn Jamison .30 .75
16 Shane Battier .30 .75
17 Baron Davis .30 .75
18 Allen Iverson .60 1.50
19 Jameer Nelson .25 .60
20 Brent Barry .25 .60
21 Zydrunas Ilgauskas .30 .75
22 Jason Terry .30 .75
23 Mike Dunleavy .30 .75
24 Paul Pierce .40 1.00
25 Peja Stojakovic .40 1.00
26 Andre Iguodala .30 .75
27 Andrei Kirilenko .30 .75
28 Nenad Krstic .25 .60
29 Emeka Okafor .30 .75
30 Jalen Rose .40 1.00
31 Ricky Davis .30 .75
32 Jason Kidd .60 1.50
33 Chauncey Billups .40 1.00
34 Amare Stoudemire .30 .75
35 Josh Childress .30 .75
36 Mehmet Okur .25 .60
37 Shaun Livingston .25 .60
38 Bruce Bowen .25 .60
39 J.R. Smith .30 .75
40 Kobe Bryant 1.50 4.00
41 Dwight Howard .30 .75
42 Manu Ginobili .40 1.00
43 Keith Van Horn .30 .75
44 Stephon Marbury .30 .75
45 Samuel Dalembert .25 .60
46 Luke Ridnour .30 .75
47 Sebastian Telfair .30 .75
48 Tyson Chandler .30 .75
49 Drew Gooden .30 .75
50 Marcus Camby .30 .75
51 Dwyane Wade .60 1.50
52 Troy Murphy .25 .60
53 Rashard Lewis .40 1.00
54 Shaquille O'Neal .75 2.00
55 Al Harrington .30 .75
56 Al Jefferson .30 .75
57 Earl Boykins .25 .60
58 Tayshaun Prince .30 .75
59 Carlos Boozer .30 .75
60 Richard Jefferson .30 .75
61 Toni Kukoc .40 1.00
62 Brad Miller .30 .75
63 Richard Hamilton .30 .75
64 Kevin Garnett .60 1.50
65 Tony Parker .40 1.00
66 Udonis Haslem .25 .60
67 Dikembe Mutombo .40 1.00
68 Pau Gasol .40 1.00
69 Chris Webber .40 1.00
70 Ben Wallace .30 .75
71 Carmelo Anthony .75 2.00
72 Dirk Nowitzki .60 1.50
73 Tony Allen .25 .60
74 Corey Maggette .30 .75
75 Rasheed Wallace .40 1.00
76 Andre Miller .30 .75
77 Luol Deng .30 .75
78 Mike Miller .30 .75
79 Wally Szczerbiak .30 .75
80 Chris Bosh .40 1.00
81 Marquis Daniels .25 .60
82 Nick Collison .30 .75
83 Matt Harpring .25 .60
84 Kirk Hinrich .30 .75
85 Josh Howard .40 1.00
86 Elton Brand .40 1.00
87 Tyronn Lue .25 .60
88 Bob Sura .25 .60
89 Chris Mihm .25 .60
90 Brevin Knight .25 .60
91 Jason Richardson .40 1.00
92 Vladimir Radmanovic .25 .60
93 Eddie Griffin .25 .60
94 P.J. Brown .25 .60
95 Troy Hudson .25 .60
96 Steve Francis .30 .75
97 Joel Przybilla .25 .60
98 Steve Nash .50 1.25
99 Brendan Haywood .25 .60
100 Primoz Brezec .25 .60
101 Devin Harris .25 .60
102 Lebron James 8.00 20.00
103 Mike Bibby .40 1.00
104 Jared Jeffries .25 .60
105 Morris Peterson .25 .60
106 Trevor Ariza .25 .60
107 Shawn Marion .30 .75
108 Andres Nocioni .25 .60
109 Darius Miles .25 .60
110 Tracy Mcgrady .50 1.25
111 Stephen Jackson .30 .75
112 Joe Johnson .30 .75
113 Bonzi Wells .25 .60
114 Damon Jones .25 .60
115 Rafer Alston .25 .60
116 Cuttino Mobley .25 .60
117 Nick Van Exel .40 1.00
118 Jason Hart .25 .60
119 Fred Jones .25 .60
120 Dan Dickau .25 .60
121 Damon Stoudamire .30 .75
122 Kirk Snyder .25 .60
123 Larry Hughes .30 .75
124 Michael Finley .40 1.00
125 Sam Cassell .30 .75
126 Bobby Jackson .25 .60
127 Austin Croshere .25 .60
128 Kwame Brown .25 .60
129 James Posey .25 .60
130 Antonio Daniels .25 .60
131 Eddy Curry .25 .60
132 Mike James .25 .60
133 Juan Dixon .25 .60
134 Jason Williams .30 .75
135 Jeff McInnis .25 .60
136 Jamaal Tinsley .25 .60
137 Derek Anderson .25 .60
138 Devin Brown .25 .60
139 Raja Bell .30 .75
140 Gary Payton .40 1.00
141 Marko Jaric .25 .60
142 Ron Artest .40 1.00
143 Zaza Pachulia .25 .60
144 Jermaine O'Neal .30 .75
145 Quentin Richardson .30 .75
146 Lee Nailon .25 .60
147 Bobby Simmons .25 .60
148 Caron Butler .30 .75
149 Shareef Abdur-Rahim .30 .75
150 Stromile Swift .25 .60
151 Rasual Butler .25 .60
152 Mike Sweetney .25 .60
153 Antoine Walker .30 .75
154 Eddie Jones .30 .75
155 David Harrison .25 .60
156 Kurt Thomas .25 .60
157 Donyell Marshall .25 .60
158 Brian Grant .25 .60
159 Desmond Mason .25 .60
160 Tim Thomas .25 .60
161 Marc Jackson .25 .60
162 Chucky Atkins .25 .60
163 Jeff Foster .25 .60
164 Jamaal Magloire .25 .60
165 Desagana Diop .25 .60
166 Danny Granger RC 2.00 5.00
167 Hakim Warrick RC 1.25 3.00
168 Chris Paul RC 8.00 20.00
169 Marvin Williams RC 1.50 4.00
170 Ike Diogu RC 1.00 2.50
171 Wayne Simien RC 1.00 2.50
172 James Singleton RC 1.00 2.50
173 Robert Whaley RC 1.00 2.50
174 Arvydas Macijauskas RC 1.00 2.50
175 Linas Kleiza RC 1.00 2.50
176 Raymond Felton RC 1.50 4.00
177 Ersan Ilyasova RC 1.50 4.00
178 Jarrett Jack RC 1.50 4.00
179 Antoine Wright RC 1.25 3.00
180 David Lee RC 1.50 4.00
181 Esteban Batista RC 1.00 2.50
182 Sarunas Jasikevicius RC 1.50 4.00
183 Francisco Garcia RC 1.25 3.00
184 C.J. Miles RC 1.50 4.00
185 Ryan Gomes RC 1.25 3.00
186 Andrew Bynum RC 1.25 3.00
187 Sean May RC 1.00 2.50
188 Jose Calderon RC 1.50 4.00
189 Rashad McCants RC 1.25 3.00
190 Johan Petro RC 1.00 2.50
191 Jason Maxiell RC 1.25 3.00
192 Martell Webster RC 1.25 3.00
193 Nate Robinson RC 1.50 4.00
194 Daniel Ewing RC 1.25 3.00
195 Fabricio Oberto RC 1.25 3.00
196 Travis Diener RC 1.00 2.50
197 Salim Stoudamire RC 1.25 3.00
198 Charlie Villanueva RC 1.50 4.00
199 Orien Greene RC 1.25 3.00
200 Deron Williams RC 2.00 5.00
201 Bracey Wright RC 1.00 2.50
202 Lawrence Roberts RC 1.00 2.50
203 Eddie Basden RC 1.00 2.50
204 Brandon Bass RC 1.25 3.00
205 Martynas Andriuskevicius RC 1.00 2.50
206 Channing Frye RC 1.50 4.00
207 Julius Hodge RC 1.00 2.50
208 Luther Head RC 1.25 3.00
209 Chris Taft RC 1.25 3.00
210 Andrew Bogut RC 2.00 5.00
211 Gerald Green RC 1.50 4.00
212 Joey Graham RC 1.25 3.00
213 Louis Williams RC 1.50 4.00
214 Yaroslav Korolev RC 1.00 2.50
215 Monta Ellis RC 2.00 5.00
216 Christie Brinkley 1.50 4.00
217 Jay-Z 1.50 4.00
218 Shannon Elizabeth 1.50 4.00
219 Carmen Electra 1.50 4.00
220 Jenny McCarthy Cut Out 30.00 80.00
221 Joe Shipp DL RC 1.00 2.50
222 Dwayne Jones DL RC .60 1.50
223 Will Conroy DL RC 1.00 2.50
224 Darnell Miller DL RC 1.00 2.50
225 Will Bynum DL RC .75 2.00
226 Jamar Smith DL RC 1.00 2.50
227 Daryl Dorsey DL RC 1.00 2.50
228 Tony Bland DL RC .60 1.50
229 Hiram Fuller DL RC 1.00 2.50
230 Tyrone Sally DL RC 1.00 2.50
231 Clay Tucker DL RC 1.00 2.50
232 George Leach DL RC 1.00 2.50
233 Marcus Douthit DL RC .60 1.50
234 Carlos Hurt DL RC 1.00 2.50
235 Seamus Boxley DL RC 1.00 2.50
236 Ramel Curry DL RC .60 1.50
237 Andreas Glyniadakis DL RC 1.00 2.50
238 Kareem Reid DL RC 1.00 2.50
239 Austin Nichols DL RC .60 1.50
240 Chris Shumate DL RC 1.00 2.50
241 Brandon Robinson DL RC 1.00 2.50
242 Harvey Thomas DL RC 1.00 2.50
243 Desmon Farmer DL RC 1.00 2.50
244 Marcus Hill DL RC 1.00 2.50
245 Robb Dryden DL RC 1.00 2.50
246 Nate Daniels DL RC 1.00 2.50
247 James Lang DL RC 1.00 2.50
248 Anthony Terrell DL RC 1.00 2.50
249 Jeff Hagen DL RC 1.00 2.50
250 Kevin Owens DL RC .60 1.50
251 Myron Allen DL RC 1.00 2.50
252 Ayudeji Akindele DL RC 1.00 2.50
253 T.J. Cummings DL RC 1.00 2.50
254 Mike King DL RC .60 1.50
255 Otis George DL RC 1.00 2.50
256 Ezra Williams DL RC 1.00 2.50
257 Anthony Wilkins DL RC 1.00 2.50
258 Scott Merritt DL RC 1.00 2.50
259 Seth Doliboa DL RC 1.00 2.50
260 Anthony Fuqua DL RC 1.00 2.50
261 Malik Moore DL RC .60 1.50
262 Randall Orr DL RC .60 1.50
263 Ricky Shields DL RC .60 1.50
264 John Lucas III DL RC .75 2.00
265 Butter Johnson DL RC 1.00 2.50
266 Isiah Victor DL RC 1.00 2.50
267 Roderick Riley DL RC 1.00 2.50
268 Bernard King DL RC 1.00 2.50
269 E.J. Rowland DL RC .60 1.50
270 Anthony Grundy DL RC 1.00 2.50
271 Brian Jackson DL RC .60 1.50
272 Keith Langford DL RC .75 2.00
273 Chuck Hayes DL RC 1.00 2.50
274 Jonathan Moore DL RC .60 1.50

2005-06 Topps Chrome Refractors

*1-165 REF: 1.5X TO 4X BASE HI
*166-274 REF: 1X TO 2.5X BASE HI
REFRACTOR PRINT RUN 999 SER.#'d SETS
40 Kobe Bryant 20.00 50.00
102 LeBron James 75.00 200.00
168 Chris Paul 60.00 150.00

2005-06 Topps Chrome Refractors Black

*1-165 REF.BLACK: 2X TO 5X BASE HI
*166-274 REF.BLACK: 1.25X TO 3X BASE HI
PRINT RUN 399 SER.#'d SETS
40 Kobe Bryant 25.00 60.00
102 LeBron James 125.00 300.00
168 Chris Paul 75.00 200.00

2005-06 Topps Chrome Refractors Gold

*REF.GOLD: 6X TO 15X BASE HI
*166-274 REF.GOLD: 3X TO 8X BASE HI
PRINT RUN 99 SER.#'d SETS
40 Kobe Bryant 60.00 150.00
64 Kevin Garnett 30.00 80.00
102 LeBron James 300.00 600.00
168 Chris Paul 125.00 300.00

2005-06 Topps Chrome X-Fractors

*1-165 X-FRACTORS: 4X TO 10X BASE HI
*166-274 X-FRAC: 3X TO 8X BASE HI
PRINT RUN 90 SER.#'d SETS
INSERTED ONE PER BOX AS TOPPER
40 Kobe Bryant 75.00 200.00
102 Lebron James 300.00 600.00
168 Chris Paul 125.00 300.00

2005-06 Topps Chrome Autographs

Inserted in packs randomly, this 23-card set actually contains cards from two differently designed sets, Topps Chrome Autographs and Topps Chrome Signs of Stardom. The Autographs cards have orange borders around the player photos with silver autograph stickers and the Signs of Stardom cards are horizontally desinged with a player photo on the left and a silver autograph sticker on the right. Each card is serially numbered, see checklist for details.

PRINT RUNS LISTED IN CHECKLIST
*REFRACTORS: .75X TO 2X BASE AU HI
REFRACTOR PRINT RUN 15 TO 25 SETS
UNPRICED REF.GOLD PRINT RUN 3 SETS
UNPRICED REF.SUPER PRINT RUN ONE SET
AI Allen Iverson/162 40.00 100.00
CA Carmelo Anthony/82 20.00 40.00
CB Christie Brinkley/30 40.00 100.00
DE Daniel Ewing/208 6.00 15.00
DG Danny Granger/112 12.50 30.00
EO Emeka Okafor/162 6.00 15.00
GG Gerald Green/208 8.00 20.00
HW Hakim Warrick/162 8.00 20.00
JG Joey Graham/84 6.00 15.00
JH Julius Hodge/84 6.00 15.00
JZ Jay-Z/208 50.00 125.00
LH Luther Head/208 6.00 15.00
OG Orien Greene/162 6.00 15.00
RF Raymond Felton/58 10.00 25.00
RM Rashad McCants/208 6.00 15.00
SE Shannon Elizabeth/30 60.00 120.00
SL Shaun Livingston/179 6.00 15.00
SM Sean May/208 6.00 15.00
SO Shaquille O'Neal/89 40.00 100.00
ABO Andrew Bogut/162 10.00 25.00
CAE Carmen Electra/30 60.00 120.00
DWA Dwyane Wade/162 40.00 100.00
DWI Deron Williams/162 10.00 25.00
JMC Jenny McCarthy/30 50.00 120.00

2005-06 Topps Chrome Chosen One Relics

Seeded in packs randomly, this 24-card set placed player photos on the right side of the card and a circular swatch of memorabilia in the lower left-hand corner. Every card is on a foil board card stock and serially numbered to 400.

PRINT RUN 400 SER.#'d SETS
*REFRACTORS: .6X TO 1.5X BASE HI
REF.PRINT RUN 99 SER.#'d SETS
*X-FRACTORS: 1.5X TO 4X BASE HI
X-FRAC.PRINT RUN 25 SER.#'d SETS
UNPRICED REF.GOLD PRINT RUN 9 SETS
UNPRICED SUPERFR.PRINT RUN ONE SET
AB Andrew Bogut 3.00 8.00
AI Allen Iverson 4.00 10.00
CA Carmelo Anthony 5.00 12.00
CB Chauncey Billups 2.50 6.00
CF Channing Frye 2.50 6.00
CP Chris Paul 10.00 25.00
DH Dwight Howard 2.00 5.00
DL David Lee 2.50 6.00
DN Dirk Nowitzki 4.00 10.00
DW Deron Williams 3.00 8.00
EB Elton Brand 2.50 6.00
EO Emeka Okafor 2.00 5.00
GG Gerald Green 2.50 6.00
HW Hakim Warrick 2.00 5.00
JM Jenny McCarthy 6.00 15.00
JO Jermaine O'Neal 2.00 5.00
JZ Jay-Z 6.00 15.00
PG Pau Gasol 2.50 6.00
RF Raymond Felton 2.50 6.00
SO Shaquille O'Neal 5.00 12.00
TD Tim Duncan 4.00 10.00
YM Yao Ming 3.00 8.00
CBR Christie Brinkley 6.00 15.00
DWA Dwyane Wade 4.00 10.00

2005-06 Topps Chrome Hardwood Heroics

Inserted randomly in packs, this 19-card set features a gray and tan background, player photos and a circular swatch of memorabilia. Each card is serially numbered to 400.

PRINT RUN 400 SER.#'d SETS
*REFRACTORS: .75X TO 2X BASE HI
REF.PRINT RUN 99 SER.#'d SETS
*X-FRACTORS: 1.5X TO 4X BASE HI
X-FRAC.PRINT RUN 25 SER.#'d SETS
UNPRICED REF.GOLD PRINT RUN 9 SETS
UNPRICED REF.SUPER PRINT RUN ONE SET
AS Amare Stoudemire 2.00 5.00
BG Ben Gordon 2.00 5.00
BW Ben Wallace 2.00 5.00
CB Chauncey Billups 2.50 6.00
DW Dwyane Wade 4.00 10.00
EO Emeka Okafor 2.00 5.00
GH Grant Hill 3.00 8.00
JK Jason Kidd 4.00 10.00
JO Jermaine O'Neal 2.00 5.00
KB Kobe Bryant 10.00 25.00
LH Larry Hughes 2.00 5.00
MB Mike Bibby 2.50 6.00
RA Ray Allen 2.50 6.00
RH Robert Horry 4.00 10.00
RL Rashard Lewis 2.50 6.00
SN Steve Nash 3.00 8.00
TD Tim Duncan 4.00 10.00
TM Tracy McGrady 3.00 8.00
VC Vince Carter 4.00 10.00

2005-06 Topps Chrome Premium Performers

Randomly seeded in packs, this 20-card set is horizontally designed with a player photo on the left and an oval swatch of memorabilia in the lower right hand corner. The background design contains color elements of white, brown, blue and yellow and cards are serially numbered to 400.

PRINT RUN 400 SER.#'d SETS
*REFRACTORS: .6X TO 1.5X BASE HI
REFRACTOR PRINT RUN 99 SER.#'d SETS
*X-FRACTORS: 1.5X TO 4X BASE HI
X-FRAC.PRINT RUN 25 SER.#'d SETS
UNPRICED REF.GOLD PRINT RUN 9 SETS
UNPRICED REF.SUPER PRINT RUN ONE SET
AB Andrew Bogut 3.00 8.00
CB Chris Bosh 2.50 6.00
CW Chris Webber 2.50 6.00
DN Dirk Nowitzki 4.00 10.00
EB Elton Brand 2.50 6.00
GG Gerald Green 2.50 6.00
JK Jason Kidd 4.00 10.00
JZ Jay-Z 10.00 25.00
KG Kevin Garnett 4.00 10.00
MB Mike Bibby 2.50 6.00
PG Pau Gasol 2.50 6.00
PP Paul Pierce 2.50 6.00
RM Rashad McCants 2.00 5.00
SM Shawn Marion 2.00 5.00
SN Steve Nash 3.00 8.00
SO Shaquille O'Neal 5.00 12.00
ST Sebastian Telfair 2.00 5.00
TD Tim Duncan 4.00 10.00
TM Tracy McGrady 3.00 8.00
TP Tony Parker 2.50 6.00

2005-06 Topps Chrome Second Unit

Randomly inserted in packs, this 25-card set places a player photo on the left, a swatch of memorabilia in the center and a tan-scale portrait photo of the player on the right of a horizontal design. Each card is serially numbered to 400.

PRINT RUN 400 SER.#'d SETS
*REFRACTORS: .5X TO 1.25X BASE HI
REFRACTOR PRINT RUN 99 SER.#'d SETS
*X-FRACTORS: 1.25X TO 3X BASE HI
X-FRAC.PRINT RUN 25 SER.#'d SETS
UNPRICED REF.GOLD PRINT RUN 9 SETS
UNPRICED REF.SUPER PRINT RUN ONE SET
AJ Al Jefferson 2.50 6.00
AV Anderson Varejao 2.00 5.00
BG Ben Gordon 2.50 6.00
BU Beno Udrih 2.00 5.00
CD Carlos Delfino 2.00 5.00
DF Derek Fisher 2.50 6.00
DH Devin Harris 2.00 5.00
DW Dorell Wright 2.00 5.00
FG Francisco Garcia 2.50 6.00
FJ Fred Jones 2.00 5.00
JH Jarvis Hayes 2.00 5.00

Card	Low	High
JJ Jim Jackson	2.00	5.00
JK Jason Kapono	2.00	5.00
KK Kyle Korver	2.50	6.00
LW Luke Walton	2.00	5.00
MD Marquis Daniels	2.00	5.00
MJ Marko Jaric	2.00	5.00
MO Mehmet Okur	2.00	5.00
NC Nick Collison	2.50	6.00
RA Rafer Alston	2.00	5.00
SM Sean May	2.00	5.00
WS Wayne Simien	2.00	5.00
JHO Josh Howard	3.00	8.00
JOJ Joe Johnson	2.50	6.00
RAR Rafael Araujo	2.00	5.00

2006-07 Topps Chrome

Released in early February 2007, Topps Chrome parallels the design of the base Topps set enhanced with holo-foil card stock. Card numbers 1-160 feature veteran players and retired NBA legends and card numbers 161-210 feature rookie players inserted at the rate of one in two packs. Please note that an alternate version of the rookies employing the 1996-97 Topps Chrome card design was also produced for insertion and these cards are not considered the player's actual rookie cards. Topps Chrome is packaged in 24-pack boxes of four cards each and carried an initial suggested retail price of $3.00.

Card	Low	High
COMPLETE SET (210)	60.00	120.00
COMP.SET w/o SP's (160)	20.00	50.00
UNPRICED SUPERFR.PRINT RUN ONE SET		
1 Elton Brand	.40	1.00
2 Tim Duncan	.60	1.50
3 Chris Paul	.50	1.25
4 Joe Johnson	.30	.75
5 Chauncey Billups	.40	1.00
6 Andres Nocioni	.25	.60
7 Al Jefferson	.30	.75
8 Gerald Wallace	.30	.75
9 Jason Terry	.30	.75
10 Dwight Howard	.30	.75
11 Larry Hughes	.30	.75
12 Vince Carter	.50	1.25
13 Mike Bibby	.40	1.00
14 Ben Gordon	.30	.75
15 Desmond Mason	.25	.60
16 Raymond Felton	.30	.75
17 Paul Pierce	.40	1.00
18 Jason Richardson	.40	1.00
19 Rasheed Wallace	.40	1.00
20 Leandro Barbosa	.30	.75
21 Deron Williams	.30	.75
22 Kwame Brown	.25	.60
23 Josh Childress	.30	.75
24 Shawn Marion	.30	.75
25 Shaquille O'Neal	.75	2.00
26 Ray Allen	.40	1.00
27 Cuttino Mobley	.25	.60
28 Dirk Nowitzki	.60	1.50
29 Jermaine O'Neal	.30	.75
30 Marvin Williams	.30	.75
31 Eddy Curry	.30	.75
32 Andrei Kirilenko	.30	.75
33 Baron Davis	.30	.75
34 Tracy McGrady	.50	1.25
35 Chris Kaman	.30	.75
36 Luol Deng	.30	.75
37 Emeka Okafor	.30	.75
38 Lamar Odom	.30	.75
39 Alonzo Mourning	.50	1.25
40 Marcus Camby	.30	.75
41 Ike Diogu	.25	.60
42 Josh Smith	.30	.75
43 Nate Robinson	.25	.60
44 Yao Ming	.50	1.25
45 Darko Milicic	.25	.60
46 Smush Parker	.25	.60
47 Mike Dunleavy	.30	.75
48 Ricky Davis	.30	.75
49 Michael Finley	.40	1.00
50 Nenad Krstic	.25	.60
51 Earl Boykins	.25	.60
52 Richard Hamilton	.30	.75
53 Hakim Warrick	.30	.75
54 Corey Maggette	.30	.75
55 Kenyon Martin	.30	.75
56 Jason Kidd	.60	1.50
57 Dwyane Wade	.60	1.50
58 Josh Howard	.30	.75
59 Richard Jefferson	.30	.75
60 Steve Nash	.50	1.25
61 Drew Gooden	.30	.75
62 Kevin Garnett	.60	1.50
63 Delonte West	.25	.60
64 Channing Frye	.30	.75
65 Andre Iguodala	.30	.75
66 Pau Gasol	.40	1.00
67 LeBron James	8.00	20.00
68 Sam Cassell	.30	.75
69 Mehmet Okur	.25	.60
70 Bruce Bowen	.25	.60
71 Kirk Hinrich	.30	.75
72 Chris Wilcox	.25	.60
73 Brad Miller	.30	.75
74 Chris Bosh	.40	1.00
75 Jamal Crawford	.40	1.00
76 Mike Miller	.30	.75
77 Danny Granger	.30	.75
78 Manu Ginobili	.40	1.00
79 Udonis Haslem	.25	.60
80 Gilbert Arenas	.30	.75
81 Tony Parker	.40	1.00
82 Carlos Boozer	.30	.75
83 Rashard Lewis	.40	1.00
84 Boris Diaw	.30	.75
85 Shaun Livingston	.25	.60
86 Shareef Abdur-Rahim	.30	.75
87 Devin Harris	.25	.60
88 Brevin Knight	.25	.60
89 Troy Murphy	.25	.60
90 Antawn Jamison	.30	.75
91 Stephen Jackson	.30	.75
92 Chris Webber	.40	1.00
93 Luke Ridnour	.30	.75
94 Joel Przybilla	.25	.60
95 David West	.30	.75
96 Caron Butler	.30	.75
97 Andre Miller	.30	.75
98 Ron Artest	.40	1.00
99 Samuel Dalembert	.25	.60
100 Tayshaun Prince	.30	.75
101 Jameer Nelson	.25	.60
102 Zach Randolph	.30	.75
103 Stephon Marbury	.30	.75
104 Steve Francis	.30	.75
105 Kevin Martin	.30	.75
106 Carmelo Anthony	.50	1.25
107 Morris Peterson	.25	.60
108 Allen Iverson	.50	1.25
109 Antoine Walker	.30	.75
110 Jarrett Jack	.30	.75
111 Ben Wallace	.30	.75
112 Vladimir Radmanovic	.25	.60
113 Andrew Bogut	.30	.75
114 Nazr Mohammed	.25	.60
115 Kirk Snyder	.25	.60
116 Marquis Daniels	.25	.60
117 T.J. Ford	.25	.60
118 Stromile Swift	.25	.60
119 Lorenzen Wright	.25	.60
120 Mike James	.25	.60
121 Amare Stoudemire	.30	.75
122 Raef LaFrentz	.25	.60
123 Adrian Griffin	.25	.60
124 Maurice Evans	.25	.60
125 David Wesley	.25	.60
126 J.R. Smith	.30	.75
127 Ronald Murray	.25	.60
128 Shane Battier	.30	.75
129 Kobe Bryant	1.50	4.00
130 Jamaal Magloire	.25	.60
131 Charlie Villanueva	.25	.60
132 Tyson Chandler	.30	.75
133 Eddie House	.25	.60
134 Marcus Banks	.25	.60
135 Derek Fisher	.30	.75
136 Bobby Simmons	.25	.60
137 Al Harrington	.30	.75
138 Speedy Claxton	.25	.60
139 Viktor Khryapa	.25	.60
140 Sean May	.25	.60
141 Devean George	.25	.60
142 Joe Smith	.30	.75
143 Peja Stojakovic	.40	1.00
144 DeShawn Stevenson	.25	.60
145 Fred Jones	.25	.60
146 P.J. Brown	.25	.60
147 Sebastian Telfair	.25	.60
148 Bonzi Wells	.25	.60
149 Michael Redd	.30	.75
150 Jared Jeffries	.25	.60
151 Larry Bird	1.00	2.50
152 Dominique Wilkins	.50	1.25
153 Isiah Thomas	.40	1.00
154 Wilt Chamberlain	.75	2.00
155 Bill Walton	.40	1.00
156 Oscar Robertson	.40	1.00
157 Walt Frazier	.40	1.00
158 Elgin Baylor	.40	1.00
159 George Gervin	.40	1.00
160 Moses Malone	.40	1.00
161 Solomon Jones RC	.75	2.00
162 Kyle Lowry RC	1.50	4.00
163 Maurice Ager RC	.75	2.00
164 Patrick O'Bryant RC	.75	2.00
165 Marcus Vinicius RC	.75	2.00
166 Jorge Garbajosa RC	1.00	2.50
167 Josh Boone RC	.75	2.00
168 Mardy Collins RC	.75	2.00
169 Rodney Carney RC	.75	2.00
170 P.J. Tucker RC	1.00	2.50
171 Shelden Williams RC	1.00	2.50
172 Ryan Hollins RC	1.00	2.50
173 Pops Mensah-Bonsu RC	.75	2.00
174 Steve Novak RC	1.00	2.50
175 Paul Davis RC	.75	2.00
176 David Noel RC	.75	2.00
177 Marcus Williams RC	.75	2.00
178 Renaldo Balkman RC	1.00	2.50
179 Quincy Douby RC	.75	2.00
180 Andrea Bargnani RC	1.25	3.00
181 Chris Quinn RC	.75	2.00
182 Thabo Sefolosha RC	1.25	3.00
183 LaMarcus Aldridge RC	3.00	8.00
184 Rudy Gay RC	1.50	4.00
185 Jordan Farmar RC	1.25	3.00
186 Damir Markota RC	.75	2.00
187 Mile Ilic RC	.75	2.00
188 James Augustine RC	.75	2.00
189 Tyrus Thomas RC	1.00	2.50
190 Brandon Roy RC	1.25	3.00
191 Allan Ray RC	.75	2.00
192 Shannon Brown RC	.75	2.00
193 Will Blalock RC	.75	2.00
194 James White RC	.75	2.00
195 Adam Morrison RC	1.25	3.00
196 Craig Smith RC	1.00	2.50
197 Cedric Simmons RC	.75	2.00
198 J.J. Redick RC	1.50	4.00
199 Sergio Rodriguez RC	1.25	3.00
200 Ronnie Brewer RC	1.25	3.00
201 Rajon Rondo RC	2.00	5.00
202 Daniel Gibson RC	1.00	2.50
203 Hassan Adams RC	.75	2.00
204 Shawne Williams RC	.75	2.00
205 Alexander Johnson RC	.75	2.00
206 Randy Foye RC	1.25	3.00
207 Hilton Armstrong RC	.75	2.00
208 Bobby Jones RC	.75	2.00
209 Saer Sene RC	.75	2.00
210 Dee Brown RC	.75	2.00

2006-07 Topps Chrome Refractors

*REF 1-160: 1.25X TO 3X BASE HI
1-160 STATED ODDS 1:4
*REF 161-210: 1.5X TO 4X BASE HI
161-210 REF PRINT RUN 199 SETS

Card	Low	High
67 LeBron James	75.00	200.00
129 Kobe Bryant	12.00	30.00

2006-07 Topps Chrome Refractors Black

*1-160 REF.BLACK: 5X TO 12X BASE HI
*161-210 REF.BLACK: 2X TO 5X BASE HI
REF.BLACK PRINT RUN 99 SER.#'d SETS

Card	Low	High
67 LeBron James	300.00	600.00
129 Kobe Bryant	40.00	100.00

2006-07 Topps Chrome Refractors Gold

*1-160 REF.GOLD: 12X TO 30X BASE HI
*161-210 REF.GOLD: 5X TO 12X BASE HI
REF.GOLD PRINT RUN 25 SER.#'d SETS

Card	Low	High
39 Alonzo Mourning	20.00	50.00
67 LeBron James	400.00	800.00
183 LaMarcus Aldridge	50.00	120.00
190 Brandon Roy	50.00	120.00

2006-07 Topps Chrome 1996-97 Variations

Card	Low	High
COMPLETE SET (10)	10.00	25.00

STATED ODDS 1:4
*REFRACTORS: 1.25X TO 3X BASE HI
REF.PRINT RUN 199 SER.#'d SETS
*REF.BLACK: 2.5X TO 6X BASE HI
REF.BLACK PRINT RUN 99 SER.#'d SETS
*REF.GOLD: 4X TO 10X BASE HI
REF.GOLD PRINT RUN 25 SER.#'d SETS
UNPRICED SUPERFR.PRINT RUN ONE SET
UNPRICED X-FRAC PRINT RUN 10 SETS

Card	Low	High
171 Shelden Williams	.75	2.00
177 Marcus Williams	.60	1.50
180 Andrea Bargnani	1.00	2.50
183 LaMarcus Aldridge	2.50	6.00
184 Rudy Gay	1.25	3.00
189 Tyrus Thomas	.75	2.00
190 Brandon Roy	1.00	2.50
195 Adam Morrison	1.00	2.50
198 J.J. Redick	1.25	3.00
200 Ronnie Brewer	1.00	2.50

2006-07 Topps Chrome Autographs Refractors Black

GROUP A ODDS 1:2575, GROUP B 1:590
GROUP C ODDS 1:1191
RC GROUP A ODDS 1:1295, GROUP B 1:1030
RC GROUP C ODDS 1:1192, GROUP D 1:161
RC GROUP E ODDS 1:113, GROUP F 1:73
*REF.GOLD: .75X TO 2X BASE HI
REF.GOLD PRINT RUN 25 SER.#'d SETS
UNPRICED SUPERFR.PRINT RUN ONE SET
UNPRICED X-FRAC PRINT RUN 10 SETS

Card	Low	High
12 Vince Carter B	20.00	50.00
14 Ben Gordon B	8.00	20.00
25 Shaquille O'Neal A	40.00	100.00
37 Emeka Okafor A	10.00	25.00
46 Smush Parker C	3.00	8.00
57 Dwyane Wade A	50.00	100.00
74 Chris Bosh B	5.00	12.00
108 Allen Iverson A	30.00	80.00
151 Larry Bird A	75.00	150.00
153 Isiah Thomas B	12.00	30.00
161 Solomon Jones D	3.00	8.00
162 Kyle Lowry C	6.00	15.00
163 Maurice Ager D	3.00	8.00
164 Patrick O'Bryant B	3.00	8.00
165 Marcus Vinicius F	3.00	8.00
166 Jorge Garbajosa C	4.00	10.00
167 Josh Boone C	3.00	8.00
168 Mardy Collins C	3.00	8.00
169 Rodney Carney C	3.00	8.00
170 P.J. Tucker D	4.00	10.00
171 Shelden Williams A	4.00	10.00
172 Ryan Hollins E	4.00	10.00
173 Pops Mensah-Bonsu F	3.00	8.00
174 Steve Novak E	4.00	10.00
175 Paul Davis D	3.00	8.00
176 David Noel E	3.00	8.00
177 Marcus Williams A	3.00	8.00
178 Renaldo Balkman B	4.00	10.00
179 Quincy Douby D	3.00	8.00
180 Andrea Bargnani A	12.00	30.00
181 Chris Quinn F	3.00	8.00
182 Thabo Sefolosha E	5.00	12.00
185 Jordan Farmar C	5.00	12.00
186 Damir Markota F	3.00	8.00
187 Mile Ilic F	3.00	8.00
188 James Augustine E	3.00	8.00
191 Allan Ray F	3.00	8.00
192 Shannon Brown C	3.00	8.00
193 Will Blalock F	3.00	8.00
194 James White F	3.00	8.00
195 Adam Morrison A	5.00	12.00
196 Craig Smith E	4.00	10.00
197 Cedric Simmons C	3.00	8.00
198 J.J. Redick A	15.00	40.00
199 Sergio Rodriguez C	5.00	12.00
200 Ronnie Brewer B	5.00	12.00
201 Rajon Rondo C	12.00	30.00
202 Daniel Gibson F	4.00	10.00
203 Hassan Adams F	3.00	8.00
204 Shawne Williams E	3.00	8.00
205 Alexander Johnson F	3.00	8.00
206 Randy Foye B	5.00	12.00
207 Hilton Armstrong B	3.00	8.00
208 Bobby Jones E	3.00	8.00
209 Saer Sene D	3.00	8.00
210 Dee Brown D	3.00	8.00

2007-08 Topps Chrome

This 160-card set was released in January, 2008. The set was issued into the hobby in four-card packs, with a $3 SRP, which came 24 packs to a box and 12 boxes to a case. Cards numbered 1-110 feature a mix of active players and retired greats and cards numbered 101-160 feature 2007-08 NBA rookies.

Card	Low	High
COMPLETE SET (160)	40.00	80.00
UNPRICED SUPFRACTOR PRINT RUN ONE SET		
1 Amare Stoudemire	.40	1.00
2 Joe Johnson	.40	1.00
3 Dwyane Wade	.75	2.00
4 Chris Bosh	.50	1.25
5 Jason Kidd	.50	1.25
6 Bill Russell	.75	2.00
7 Jermaine O'Neal	.40	1.00
8 Mike Miller	.40	1.00
9 Ray Allen	.50	1.25
10 Elton Brand	.50	1.25
11 Yao Ming	.60	1.50
12 Al Harrington	.40	1.00
13 Steve Nash	.60	1.50
14 Dwight Howard	.40	1.00
15 Carmelo Anthony	.60	1.50
16 Pau Gasol	.50	1.25
17 Chauncey Billups	.50	1.25
18 Bob Pettit	.60	1.50
19 Jason Kapono	.30	.75
20 Kevin Garnett	.75	2.00
21 Tim Duncan	.75	2.00
22 Michael Redd	.40	1.00
23 LeBron James	8.00	20.00
24 Kobe Bryant	2.00	5.00
25 Eddy Curry	.30	.75
26 Gerald Green	.40	1.00
27 Andrew Bogut	.40	1.00
28 Vince Carter	.60	1.50
29 Corey Maggette	.40	1.00
30 Morris Peterson	.30	.75
31 Shawn Marion	.40	1.00
32 Shaquille O'Neal	1.00	2.50
33 Allen Iverson	.60	1.50
34 Paul Pierce	.50	1.25
35 Bill Sharman	.50	1.25
36 Tony Parker	.50	1.25
37 Mike Bibby	.50	1.25
38 Andrea Bargnani	.50	1.25
39 Luol Deng	.40	1.00
40 Chris Paul	.60	1.50
41 Dirk Nowitzki	.60	1.50
42 David Lee	.30	.75
43 Vern Mikkelsen	.50	1.25
44 Darko Milicic	.30	.75
45 Al Jefferson	.40	1.00
46 Bob Cousy	.75	2.00
47 Andrei Kirilenko	.40	1.00
48 Anfernee Hardaway	1.25	3.00
49 Chris Wilcox	.30	.75
50 Dolph Schayes	.50	1.25
51 Zach Randolph	.40	1.00
52 Grant Hill	.60	1.50
53 Jim Loscutoff	.50	1.25
54 Leandro Barbosa	.40	1.00
55 Smush Parker	.30	.75
56 Sam Jones	.60	1.50
57 Manu Ginobili	.50	1.25
58 Jason Richardson	.50	1.25
59 Jason Terry	.40	1.00
60 Gerald Wallace	.40	1.00
61 Richard Hamilton	.40	1.00
62 Cliff Hagan	.40	1.00
63 Tom Heinsohn	.50	1.25
64 Carlos Boozer	.40	1.00
65 Rashard Lewis	.40	1.00
66 Josh Childress	.40	1.00
67 Channing Frye	.40	1.00
68 Mike James	.30	.75
69 Kurt Thomas	.30	.75
70 Mikki Moore	.30	.75
71 Baron Davis	.40	1.00
72 Reggie Theus	.40	1.00
73 Jameer Nelson	.30	.75
74 Caron Butler	.40	1.00
75 Jamaal Magloire	.30	.75
76 Darryl Dawkins	.30	.75
77 Ben Gordon	.40	1.00
78 Andrew Bynum	.30	.75
79 Oscar Robertson	.50	1.25
80 Josh Smith	.40	1.00
81 Spud Webb	.40	1.00
82 Chris Mullin	.50	1.25
83 Raymond Felton	.50	1.25
84 Sebastian Telfair	.30	.75
85 Clyde Drexler	.60	1.50
86 Jarrett Jack	.40	1.00
87 Anderson Varejao	.30	.75
88 Ryan Gomes	.30	.75
89 Bill Walton	.50	1.25
90 Marcus Camby	.30	.75
91 Kirk Hinrich	.40	1.00
92 David Robinson	.75	2.00
93 Dennis Rodman	1.00	2.50
94 Dominique Wilkins	.60	1.50
95 Richard Jefferson	.40	1.00
96 Isiah Thomas	.50	1.25
97 Josh Howard	.40	1.00
98 John Stockton	.75	2.00
99 Deron Williams	.40	1.00
100 Gilbert Arenas	.40	1.00
101 Tracy McGrady	.50	1.25
102 Steve Blake	.30	.75
103 Ben Wallace	.40	1.00
104 Kevin Martin	.40	1.00
105 Larry Bird	1.25	3.00
106 Magic Johnson	1.25	3.00
107 Brandon Roy	.50	1.25
108 Desmond Mason	.30	.75
109 Rick Barry	.40	1.00
110 Andre Iguodala	.40	1.00
111 Mike Conley Jr. RC	1.50	4.00
112 Glen Davis RC	1.00	2.50
113 Julian Wright RC	.75	2.00
114 Rodney Stuckey RC	1.00	2.50
115 Chris Richard RC	.75	2.00
116 Coby Karl RC	.75	2.00
117 Thaddeus Young RC	1.25	3.00
118 Spencer Hawes RC	1.00	2.50
119 Jermareo Davidson RC	.75	2.00
120 Daequan Cook RC	1.00	2.50
121 Josh McRoberts RC	1.00	2.50
122 Aaron Gray RC	.75	2.00
123 Wilson Chandler RC	1.00	2.50
124 Herbert Hill RC	.75	2.00
125 Stephane Lasme RC	.75	2.00
126 Cheikh Samb RC	.75	2.00
127 Adam Haluska RC	.75	2.00
128 Al Thornton RC	1.00	2.50
129 Corey Brewer RC	1.25	3.00
130 Ramon Sessions RC	1.25	3.00
131 Kevin Durant RC	75.00	200.00
132 Alando Tucker RC	.75	2.00
133 Marco Belinelli RC	1.25	3.00
134 Nick Fazekas RC	.75	2.00
135 Yi Jianlian RC	1.50	4.00
136 Luis Scola RC	1.50	4.00
137 Jared Dudley RC	1.00	2.50
138 Taurean Green RC	.75	2.00
139 Kosta Perovic RC	.75	2.00
140 Kyrylo Fesenko RC	.75	2.00
141 JamesOn Curry RC	.75	2.00
142 D.J. Strawberry RC	.75	2.00
143 Javaris Crittenton RC	.75	2.00
144 Acie Law RC	.75	2.00
145 Nick Young RC	1.50	4.00
146 Joakim Noah RC	1.25	3.00
147 Dominic McGuire RC	.75	2.00
148 Arron Afflalo RC	1.25	3.00
149 Gabe Pruitt RC	.75	2.00
150 Carl Landry RC	.75	2.00
151 Jeff Green RC	1.25	3.00
152 Greg Oden RC	1.25	3.00
153 Jason Smith RC	1.00	2.50
154 Morris Almond RC	.75	2.00
155 Juan Carlos Navarro RC	1.00	2.50
156 Brandon Wallace RC	.75	2.00
157 Aaron Brooks RC	1.00	2.50
158 Brandan Wright RC	1.25	3.00
159 Sean Williams RC	.75	2.00
160 Al Horford RC	1.50	4.00

2007-08 Topps Chrome Refractors

1-110 REF.PRINT RUN 999 SER.#'d SETS
111-160 REF.PRINT RUN 1499 SER.#'d SETS

Card	Low	High
23 LeBron James	75.00	200.00
24 Kobe Bryant	10.00	25.00
131 Kevin Durant	600.00	1200.00

2007-08 Topps Chrome Refractors Orange

*1-110 REF.ORANGE: 1.5X TO 4X BASE HI
*111-160 RC REF.ORNG: 1.5X TO 4X BASE HI
PRINT RUN 199 SER.#'d SETS

Card	Low	High
23 LeBron James	125.00	300.00
24 Kobe Bryant	15.00	40.00
131 Kevin Durant	1200.00	1600.00

2007-08 Topps Chrome Refractors White

*1-110 REF.WHITE: 2X TO 5X BASE HI
*111-160 RC.REF.WHT: 2X TO 5X BASE HI
REF.WHITE PRINT RUN 99 SER.#'d SETS

Card	Low	High
3 Dwyane Wade	8.00	20.00
23 LeBron James	300.00	600.00
24 Kobe Bryant	25.00	60.00
48 Anfernee Hardaway	12.00	30.00
52 Grant Hill	4.00	10.00
131 Kevin Durant	2000.00	2500.00

2007-08 Topps Chrome X-Fractors

*1-110 X-FRAC: 6X TO 15X BASE HI
*111-160 RC X-FRAC: 3X TO 8X BASE HI
X-FRAC PRINT RUN 50 SER.#'d SETS

Card	Low	High
23 LeBron James	400.00	800.00
24 Kobe Bryant	75.00	200.00
131 Kevin Durant	2200.00	3000.00

2007-08 Topps Chrome 1957-58 Variations

Card	Low	High
COMPLETE SET (50)	40.00	75.00

APPROXIMATE ODDS ONE PER PACK
*X-FRACTORS: 4X TO 10X BASE HI
X-FRAC.PRINT RUN 50 SER.#'d SETS
UNPRICED SUPERFR.PRINT RUN ONE SET

Card	Low	High
3 Dwyane Wade	1.00	2.50
6 Bill Russell	1.00	2.50
9 Ray Allen	.60	1.50
11 Yao Ming	.75	2.00
13 Steve Nash	.75	2.00
15 Carmelo Anthony	.75	2.00
18 Bob Pettit	.75	2.00
20 Kevin Garnett	1.00	2.50
21 Tim Duncan	1.00	2.50
23 LeBron James	2.50	6.00
24 Kobe Bryant	2.50	6.00
28 Vince Carter	.75	2.00
32 Shaquille O'Neal	1.25	3.00
33 Allen Iverson	.75	2.00
35 Bill Sharman	.60	1.50
36 Tony Parker	.60	1.50
40 Chris Paul	.75	2.00
41 Dirk Nowitzki	.75	2.00
42 David Lee	.40	1.00
43 Vern Mikkelsen	.60	1.50
46 Bob Cousy	1.00	2.50
50 Dolph Schayes	.60	1.50
53 Jim Loscutoff	.60	1.50
54 Leandro Barbosa	.50	1.25
56 Sam Jones	.75	2.00
58 Jason Richardson	.60	1.50
60 Gerald Wallace	.50	1.25
62 Cliff Hagan	.50	1.25
63 Tom Heinsohn	.60	1.50
64 Carlos Boozer	.50	1.25
71 Baron Davis	.50	1.25
72 Reggie Theus	.50	1.25
76 Darryl Dawkins	.40	1.00
79 Oscar Robertson	.60	1.50
81 Spud Webb	.50	1.25
82 Chris Mullin	.60	1.50
85 Clyde Drexler	.75	2.00
89 Bill Walton	.60	1.50
90 Marcus Camby	.40	1.00
92 David Robinson	1.00	2.50
93 Dennis Rodman	1.25	3.00
94 Dominique Wilkins	.75	2.00
96 Isiah Thomas	.60	1.50
98 John Stockton	1.00	2.50
99 Deron Williams	.50	1.25
100 Gilbert Arenas	.50	1.25
103 Ben Wallace	.50	1.25
105 Larry Bird	1.50	4.00
106 Magic Johnson	1.50	4.00
109 Rick Barry	.50	1.25

2007-08 Topps Chrome 1957-58 Variations Refractors

*REFRACTORS: .75X TO 2X BASE HI
PRINT RUN 999 SER.#'d SETS

Card	Low	High
23 LeBron James	25.00	60.00
24 Kobe Bryant	8.00	20.00

2007-08 Topps Chrome 1957-58 Variations Refractors Orange

*REF.ORANGE: 1.25X TO 3X BASE HI
PRINT RUN 199 SER.#'d SETS

Card	Low	High
23 LeBron James	60.00	150.00
24 Kobe Bryant	12.00	30.00

2007-08 Topps Chrome 1957-58 Variations Refractors White

*REF.WHITE: 1.5X TO 4X BASE HI
PRINT RUN 99 SER.#'d SETS

Card	Low	High
23 LeBron James	75.00	200.00
24 Kobe Bryant	20.00	50.00

2007-08 Topps Chrome 1957-58 Variations Autographs

PRINT RUN 29 TO 99 SER.#'d SETS
*REF.ORANGE: .5X TO 1.25X BASE HI
*REF.ORANGE SP's: SAME VALUE
PRINT RUN 25 SER.#'d SETS
UNPRICED REF.WHITE PRINT RUN 10 SETS
UNPRICED X-FRAC.PRINT RUN 5 SETS
UNPRICED SUPERFR.PRINT RUN ONE SET
EXCH.EXPIRATION DATE 1/31/10

Card	Low	High
3 Dwyane Wade/29	40.00	100.00
6 Bill Russell/29	100.00	200.00
9 Ray Allen/99	15.00	30.00
28 Vince Carter/99	15.00	40.00
32 Shaquille O'Neal/29	50.00	100.00
42 David Lee/99	6.00	15.00
54 Leandro Barbosa/99	6.00	15.00
60 Gerald Wallace/99	6.00	15.00
64 Carlos Boozer/99	6.00	15.00
71 Baron Davis/99	6.00	15.00
81 Spud Webb/99	8.00	20.00
89 Bill Walton/29	25.00	50.00
92 David Robinson/29	50.00	100.00
93 Dennis Rodman/29	25.00	50.00
94 Dominique Wilkins/99	15.00	30.00
96 Isiah Thomas/29	20.00	40.00
98 John Stockton/29	30.00	60.00
99 Deron Williams/99	20.00	40.00
105 Larry Bird/29	40.00	100.00
109 Rick Barry/99	12.50	30.00

2007-08 Topps Chrome Rookie Autographs

PRINT RUN 149 TO 999 SER.#'d SETS
*REF.ORANGE: .75X TO 2X BASE HI
REF.ORANGE PRINT RUN 25 SER.#'d SETS
UNPRICED REF.WHITE PRINT RUN 10 SETS
UNPRICED X-FRAC PRINT RUN 5 SETS
UNPRICED SUPERFR.PRINT RUN ONE SET
EXCH.EXPIRATION DATE 1/31/10

Card	Low	High
112 Glen Davis/999	4.00	10.00
114 Rodney Stuckey/999	4.00	10.00
117 Thaddeus Young/149	5.00	12.00
118 Spencer Hawes/149	4.00	10.00
119 Jermareo Davidson/999	3.00	8.00
120 Daequan Cook/539	4.00	10.00
121 Josh McRoberts/999	4.00	10.00
122 Aaron Gray/539	3.00	8.00
123 Wilson Chandler/539	4.00	10.00
124 Herbert Hill/999	3.00	8.00
125 Stephane Lasme/999	3.00	8.00
127 Adam Haluska/999	3.00	8.00
128 Al Thornton/149	4.00	10.00
132 Alando Tucker/539	3.00	8.00
133 Marco Belinelli/539	5.00	12.00
134 Nick Fazekas/999	3.00	8.00
135 Yi Jianlian/149	12.00	30.00
137 Jared Dudley/539	4.00	10.00
138 Taurean Green/999	3.00	8.00
141 JamesOn Curry/999	3.00	8.00
142 D.J. Strawberry/999	3.00	8.00
143 Javaris Crittenton/999	3.00	8.00
144 Acie Law/149	3.00	8.00
145 Nick Young/149	6.00	15.00
147 Dominic McGuire/999	3.00	8.00
148 Arron Afflalo/539	5.00	12.00
149 Gabe Pruitt/999	3.00	8.00
150 Carl Landry/999	3.00	8.00
152 Greg Oden/149	5.00	12.00
153 Jason Smith/149	4.00	10.00
154 Morris Almond/539	3.00	8.00
155 Juan Carlos Navarro/539	4.00	10.00
157 Aaron Brooks/539	4.00	10.00
158 Brandan Wright/999	5.00	12.00
159 Sean Williams/539	3.00	8.00

2008-09 Topps Chrome

This set was released on December 17, 2008. The base set consists of 255 cards. Cards 1-180 feature veterans. and cards 181-220 are rookies.

Card	Low	High
COMPLETE SET (255)	40.00	80.00
UNPRICED PRESS PLATE PRINT RUN ONE SET		
UNPRICED SUPERFR.PRINT RUN ONE SET		
1 Chris Paul	.60	1.50
2 Joe Johnson	.40	1.00
3 Allen Iverson	.60	1.50
4 Luis Scola	.40	1.00
5 Kevin Garnett	.75	2.00
6 Andrew Bogut	.40	1.00
7 Ben Gordon	.40	1.00
8 Carlos Boozer	.40	1.00
9 Tony Parker	.50	1.25
10 Gilbert Arenas	.40	1.00
11 Yao Ming	.60	1.50
12 Dwight Howard	.40	1.00
13 Steve Nash	.50	1.25
14 Daequan Cook	.30	.75
15 Carmelo Anthony	.60	1.50
16 Pau Gasol	.50	1.25
17 Mike Dunleavy	.40	1.00
18 Jason Maxiell	.30	.75
19 Al Thornton	.40	1.00
20 Ray Allen	.50	1.25
21 Tim Duncan	.75	2.00
22 Michael Redd	.40	1.00
23 LeBron James	8.00	20.00
24 Kobe Bryant	2.00	5.00
25 Al Jefferson	.40	1.00
26 Raymond Felton	.40	1.00
27 LaMarcus Aldridge	.50	1.25
28 Jose Calderon	.30	.75
29 Andris Biedrins	.30	.75
30 Rasheed Wallace	.50	1.25
31 Shawn Marion	.40	1.00
32 Shaquille O'Neal	1.00	2.50
33 Mike Miller	.40	1.00
34 Paul Pierce	.50	1.25
35 Brad Miller	.40	1.00
36 Richard Jefferson	.40	1.00
37 DeShawn Stevenson	.30	.75
38 Zach Randolph	.40	1.00
39 Daniel Gibson	.40	1.00
40 Nazr Mohammed	.30	.75
41 Dirk Nowitzki	.60	1.50
42 Elton Brand	.50	1.25
43 Linas Kleiza	.30	.75
44 Andrea Bargnani	.40	1.00
45 Josh Smith	.40	1.00
46 Luol Deng	.40	1.00
47 Andrei Kirilenko	.40	1.00
48 Danny Granger	.40	1.00
49 Rashad McCants	.30	.75
50 Emeka Okafor	.40	1.00
51 Kyle Korver	.40	1.00
52 Jamario Moon	.30	.75
53 Nick Young	.40	1.00
54 Rashard Lewis	.40	1.00
55 Jason Kidd	.50	1.25
56 Josh Howard	.40	1.00
57 Desmond Mason	.30	.75
58 Andre Miller	.40	1.00
59 Rafer Alston	.30	.75
60 Baron Davis	.40	1.00
61 Zydrunas Ilgauskas	.40	1.00
62 Marvin Williams	.40	1.00
63 Manu Ginobili	.50	1.25
64 David West	.40	1.00
65 Rajon Rondo	.50	1.25
66 Kenyon Martin	.40	1.00
67 Josh Boone	.30	.75
68 Travis Outlaw	.40	1.00
69 Andre Iguodala	.40	1.00
70 Yi Jianlian	.50	1.25
71 Jordan Farmar	.30	.75
72 Udonis Haslem	.30	.75
73 Caron Butler	.40	1.00
74 Craig Smith	.30	.75
75 Tayshaun Prince	.40	1.00
76 Rudy Gay	.50	1.25
77 Jermaine O'Neal	.40	1.00
78 Devin Harris	.30	.75
79 Fabricio Oberto	.30	.75
80 Hedo Turkoglu	.40	1.00
81 James Posey	.30	.75
82 Corey Maggette	.40	1.00
83 Ricky Davis	.40	1.00
84 Grant Hill	.60	1.50
85 Eddie House	.30	.75
86 Jeff Green	.40	1.00
87 Lamar Odom	.40	1.00
88 Brandan Wright	.40	1.00
89 Sean Williams	.40	1.00
90 Drew Gooden	.40	1.00
91 Amare Stoudemire	.40	1.00
92 Charlie Villanueva	.30	.75
93 Ron Artest	.50	1.25
94 Derek Fisher	.40	1.00
95 Willie Green	.30	.75
96 Kirk Hinrich	.40	1.00
97 Jameer Nelson	.30	.75
98 Al Harrington	.40	1.00
99 Ronnie Brewer	.40	1.00
100 Dwyane Wade	.75	2.00
101 Jamal Crawford	.50	1.25
102 Ryan Gomes	.30	.75
103 Marcus Camby	.30	.75
104 Antawn Jamison	.40	1.00
105 Cuttino Mobley	.30	.75
106 Tyson Chandler	.40	1.00
107 Al Horford	.50	1.25
108 Chris Wilcox	.30	.75
109 Gerald Wallace	.40	1.00
110 Andrew Bynum	.30	.75
111 Tracy McGrady	.50	1.25
112 Mo Williams	.40	1.00
113 Nate Robinson	.30	.75
114 Wally Szczerbiak	.40	1.00
115 Vince Carter	.60	1.50
116 T.J. Ford	.30	.75
117 Kevin Martin	.40	1.00
118 Steve Blake	.30	.75
119 Anderson Varejao	.30	.75
120 Mike Conley Jr.	.40	1.00
121 Chris Kaman	.40	1.00
122 Louis Williams	.40	1.00
123 Jason Richardson	.50	1.25
124 John Salmons	.40	1.00
125 Martell Webster	.40	1.00
126 Kurt Thomas	.30	.75
127 Raja Bell	.40	1.00
128 Jason Terry	.40	1.00
129 Corey Brewer	.40	1.00
130 Bruce Bowen	.30	.75
131 Glen Davis	.30	.75
132 Richard Hamilton	.40	1.00
133 Ben Wallace	.40	1.00
134 Chris Bosh	.50	1.25
135 Beno Udrih	.30	.75
136 Jarrett Jack	.40	1.00
137 Stephen Jackson	.40	1.00
138 Damien Wilkins	.30	.75
139 Jamaal Tinsley	.30	.75
140 Deron Williams	.40	1.00
141 Andres Nocioni	.30	.75
142 David Lee	.30	.75
143 Rodney Stuckey	.40	1.00
144 Luke Walton	.30	.75
145 Jerry Stackhouse	.40	1.00
146 Samuel Dalembert	.30	.75
147 Brandon Roy	.50	1.25
148 Chauncey Billups	.50	1.25
149 Michael Finley	.50	1.25
150 Leandro Barbosa	.40	1.00
151 Keith Bogans	.30	.75
152 Mike Bibby	.40	1.00
153 Troy Murphy	.30	.75
154 Eddy Curry	.30	.75
155 Anthony Parker	.30	.75
156 Kevin Durant	4.00	10.00
157 Larry Hughes	.40	1.00
158 Peja Stojakovic	.50	1.25
159 Shane Battier	.40	1.00
160 Kendrick Perkins	.30	.75
161 Mehmet Okur	.30	.75
162 Brendan Haywood	.30	.75
163 Monta Ellis	.40	1.00
164 J.R. Smith	.40	1.00
165 Greg Oden	.40	1.00
166 John Stockton	.75	2.00
167 Dennis Rodman	1.00	2.50
168 Dominique Wilkins	.60	1.50
169 Larry Bird	1.25	3.00
170 Isiah Thomas	.50	1.25
171 Magic Johnson	1.25	3.00
172 Bill Russell	.75	2.00
173 David Robinson	.75	2.00
174 Jerry West	.60	1.50
175 Micheal Ray Richardson	.40	1.00
176 Jo Jo White	.40	1.00
177 Pete Maravich	.75	2.00
178 Wilt Chamberlain	1.00	2.50
179 Patrick Ewing	.60	1.50
180 Julius Erving	.75	2.00
181 Derrick Rose RC	6.00	15.00
182 Michael Beasley RC	1.25	3.00
183 O.J. Mayo RC	1.25	3.00
184 Russell Westbrook RC	50.00	120.00
185 Kevin Love RC	6.00	15.00
186 Danilo Gallinari RC	2.00	5.00
187 Eric Gordon RC	2.00	5.00
188 Joe Alexander RC	.75	2.00
189 D.J. Augustin RC	1.00	2.50
190 Brook Lopez RC	1.50	4.00
191 Jerryd Bayless RC	1.00	2.50
192 Jason Thompson RC	.75	2.00
193 Anthony Randolph RC	.75	2.00
194 Robin Lopez RC	1.25	3.00
195 Marreese Speights RC	1.00	2.50
196 Roy Hibbert RC	1.25	3.00
197 JaVale McGee RC	1.50	4.00
198 J.J. Hickson RC	1.00	2.50
199 Alexis Ajinca RC	.75	2.00
200 Ryan Anderson RC	1.00	2.50
201 Courtney Lee RC	1.00	2.50
202 Kosta Koufos RC	1.00	2.50
203 Donte Greene RC	.75	2.00
204 George Hill RC	1.25	3.00
205 D.J. White RC	1.00	2.50
206 J.R. Giddens RC	.75	2.00
207 Joey Dorsey RC	.75	2.00
208 Mario Chalmers RC	1.25	3.00
209 DeAndre Jordan RC	1.50	4.00
210 Chris Douglas-Roberts RC	.75	2.00
211 Malik Hairston RC	.75	2.00
212 Marc Gasol RC	2.50	6.00
213 Kyle Weaver RC	.75	2.00
214 Patrick Ewing Jr. RC	.75	2.00
215 Walter Sharpe RC	.75	2.00
216 Sonny Weems RC	.75	2.00
217 Trent Plaisted RC	.75	2.00
218 Nicolas Batum RC	1.50	4.00
219 Brandon Rush RC	1.00	2.50
220 Darrell Arthur RC	1.00	2.50

2008-09 Topps Chrome Refractors

*STARS: .75X TO 2X BASE HI
*RCs: 1.25X TO 3X BASE HI
REF.STATED ODDS 1:4
AUTO GRP.A PRINT RUN 145 SETS
AUTO GRP.B PRINT RUN 245 SETS
AUTO GRP.C PRINT RUN 476 SETS
AUTO GRP.D PRINT RUN 795 SETS

Card	Low	High
23 LeBron James	75.00	200.00
24 Kobe Bryant	15.00	40.00
156 Kevin Durant	25.00	60.00
184 Russell Westbrook	150.00	400.00
221 Derrick Rose AU A	200.00	400.00
222 Michael Beasley AU A	10.00	25.00
223 O.J. Mayo AU A	12.00	30.00
224 Russell Westbrook AU A	700.00	1000.00
225 Kevin Love AU A	75.00	150.00
226 Danilo Gallinari AU A	15.00	40.00
227 Eric Gordon AU A	20.00	50.00
228 Joe Alexander AU B	4.00	10.00
229 D.J. Augustin AU B	5.00	12.00
230 Brook Lopez AU B	12.00	30.00
231 Jerryd Bayless AU B	5.00	12.00
232 Jason Thompson AU B	4.00	10.00
233 Anthony Randolph AU A	10.00	25.00
234 Robin Lopez AU A	6.00	15.00
235 Marreese Speights AU C	5.00	12.00
236 Roy Hibbert AU B	12.00	30.00
237 JaVale McGee AU C	8.00	20.00
238 J.J. Hickson AU C	5.00	12.00
239 Sonny Weems AU C	4.00	10.00
240 Ryan Anderson AU C	5.00	12.00
241 Courtney Lee AU B	5.00	12.00
242 Kosta Koufos AU C	5.00	12.00
243 Donte Greene AU B	4.00	10.00
244 George Hill AU B	6.00	15.00
245 D.J. White AU C	5.00	12.00
246 J.R. Giddens AU B	4.00	10.00
247 Joey Dorsey AU B	4.00	10.00
248 Mario Chalmers AU B	6.00	15.00
249 DeAndre Jordan AU C	12.00	30.00
250 Chris Douglas-Roberts AU D	4.00	10.00
251 Kyle Weaver AU D	4.00	10.00
252 Patrick Ewing Jr. AU D	4.00	10.00
253 Walter Sharpe AU D	4.00	10.00
254 Brandon Rush AU B	5.00	12.00
255 Darrell Arthur AU B	5.00	12.00

2008-09 Topps Chrome Refractors Gold

*1-180 REF.GOLD: 8X TO 20X BASE HI
*181-220 REF.GOLD: 4X TO 10X BASE HI
181-220 PRINT RUN 50 SER.#'d SETS
UNPRICED AUTO PRINT RUN 5 SETS

Card	Low	High
3 Allen Iverson	15.00	40.00
23 LeBron James	400.00	800.00

24 Kobe Bryant 75.00 200.00
32 Shaquille O'Neal 25.00 60.00
156 Kevin Durant 300.00 600.00
181 Derrick Rose 175.00 350.00
184 Russell Westbrook 1000.00 1500.00
186 Danilo Gallinari 40.00 70.00
187 Eric Gordon 50.00 120.00

2008-09 Topps Chrome Refractors Orange

*ORANGE STARS: 2X TO 5X BASE HI
*ORANGE RCs: 2X TO 5X BASE HI
PRINT RUN 499 SER.#'d SETS
23 LeBron James 100.00 250.00
156 Kevin Durant 40.00 100.00
184 Russell Westbrook 400.00 800.00

2008-09 Topps Chrome X-Fractors

*X-FRACTOR STARS: 1.5X TO 4X BASE HI
*X-FRACTOR RCs: 2X TO 5X BASE HI
PRINT RUN 288 SER.#'d SETS
UNPRICED AUTO PRINT RUN 15 SETS
23 LeBron James 150.00 400.00
24 Kobe Bryant 20.00 50.00
100 Dwyane Wade 6.00 15.00
156 Kevin Durant 60.00 150.00
184 Russell Westbrook 600.00 900.00

2008-09 Topps Chrome 1958-59 Variations Autographs Refractors

GROUP A PRINT RUN 20 SETS
GROUP B PRINT RUN 45 SETS
GROUP C PRINT RUN 60 SETS
GROUP D PRINT RUN 360 SETS
UNPRICED GOLD PRINT RUN FIVE SETS
UNPRICED RED PRINT RUN THREE SETS
UNPRICED SUPERFR.PRINT RUN ONE SET
*X-FRAC: .6X TO 1.5X BASE HI
X-FRAC.PRINT RUN 15 SER.#'d SETS
1 Chris Paul A 20.00 50.00
7 Ben Gordon B 8.00 20.00
8 Carlos Boozer B 8.00 20.00
12 Dwight Howard B 12.00 30.00
15 Carmelo Anthony A 25.00 60.00
34 Paul Pierce B 15.00 40.00
46 Luol Deng C 5.00 12.00
48 Danny Granger C 8.00 20.00
60 Baron Davis B 10.00 25.00
76 Rudy Gay D 5.00 12.00
111 Tracy McGrady A 10.00 25.00
147 Brandon Roy B 15.00 30.00
165 Greg Oden A 12.00 30.00
172 Larry Bird A 50.00 120.00

2008-09 Topps Chrome Youthquake Autographs Refractors

STATED PRINT RUN 30 TO 165 SETS
*X-FRACTORS: .75X TO 2X BASE HI
X-FRACTORS PRINT RUN 15 SETS
UNPRICED REF.GOLD PRINT RUN 5 SETS
UNPRICED REF.RED PRINT RUN 3 SETS
UNPRICED SUPERFR.PRINT RUN ONE SET
YQA1 Michael Beasley/30 30.00 80.00
YQA2 Jerryd Bayless/30 15.00 40.00
YQA3 Danilo Gallinari/30 15.00 40.00
YQA4 Eric Gordon/30 40.00 100.00
YQA5 Robin Lopez/165 6.00 15.00
YQA6 Kevin Love/30 100.00 250.00
YQA7 Derrick Rose/30 125.00 300.00
YQA8 Anthony Randolph/165 10.00 25.00
YQA9 O.J. Mayo/30 30.00 80.00
YQA10 Russell Westbrook/30 700.00 1000.00
YQA11 D.J. Augustin/45 10.00 25.00
YQA12 Brook Lopez/45 12.50 30.00
YQA13 Rudy Gay/165 6.00 15.00
YQA14 Al Thornton/45 8.00 20.00
YQA15 Thaddeus Young/30 8.00 20.00

2009-10 Topps Chrome

PRINT RUN 999 SER.#'d SETS
1 Joe Johnson .50 1.25
2 Josh Smith .50 1.25
3 Mike Bibby .50 1.25
4 Marvin Williams .50 1.25
5 Al Horford .60 1.50
6 Paul Pierce .60 1.50
7 Ray Allen .60 1.50
8 Kevin Garnett 1.00 2.50
9 Rajon Rondo .60 1.50
10 Glen Davis .40 1.00
11 Gerald Wallace .50 1.25
12 Raymond Felton .50 1.25
13 Ben Gordon .50 1.25
14 Derrick Rose 1.00 2.50
15 Luol Deng .50 1.25
16 LeBron James 60.00 150.00
17 Mo Williams .50 1.25
18 Anderson Varejao .40 1.00
19 Daniel Gibson .50 1.25
20 Ben Wallace .50 1.25
21 Dirk Nowitzki .75 2.00
22 Jason Terry .50 1.25
23 Josh Howard .50 1.25
24 Jason Kidd .60 1.50
25 Carmelo Anthony .75 2.00
26 Chauncey Billups .60 1.50
27 J.R. Smith .50 1.25
28 Allen Iverson .75 2.00
29 Richard Hamilton .50 1.25
30 Tayshaun Prince .50 1.25
31 Corey Maggette .50 1.25
32 Monta Ellis .50 1.25
33 Anthony Randolph .40 1.00
34 Yao Ming .75 2.00
35 Ron Artest .60 1.50
36 Tracy McGrady .60 1.50
37 Shane Battier .60 1.50
38 Danny Granger .50 1.25
39 T.J. Ford .40 1.00
40 Troy Murphy .40 1.00
41 Al Thornton .50 1.25
42 Baron Davis .50 1.25
43 Eric Gordon .50 1.25
44 Kobe Bryant 12.00 30.00
45 Pau Gasol .60 1.50
46 Andrew Bynum .40 1.00
47 Lamar Odom .50 1.25
48 O.J. Mayo .40 1.00
49 Rudy Gay .60 1.50
50 Marc Gasol .60 1.50
51 Dwyane Wade 1.00 2.50
52 Michael Beasley .40 1.00
53 Michael Redd .50 1.25
54 Richard Jefferson .50 1.25
55 Andrew Bogut .50 1.25
56 Al Jefferson .50 1.25
57 Kevin Love .60 1.50
58 Mike Miller .50 1.25
59 Devin Harris .40 1.00
60 Vince Carter .75 2.00
61 Brook Lopez .50 1.25
62 Yi Jianlian .50 1.25
63 Chris Paul .75 2.00
64 David West .50 1.25
65 David Lee .40 1.00
66 Nate Robinson .40 1.00
67 Russell Westbrook 12.00 30.00
68 Kevin Durant 10.00 25.00
69 Dwight Howard .50 1.25
70 Rashard Lewis .50 1.25
71 Hedo Turkoglu .50 1.25
72 Jameer Nelson .40 1.00
73 Andre Iguodala .50 1.25
74 Elton Brand .60 1.50
75 Thaddeus Young .40 1.00
76 Amare Stoudemire .50 1.25
77 Shaquille O'Neal 1.25 3.00
78 Jason Richardson .60 1.50
79 Steve Nash .60 1.50
80 Brandon Roy .60 1.50
81 LaMarcus Aldridge .60 1.50
82 Rudy Fernandez .40 1.00
83 Greg Oden .50 1.25
84 Kevin Martin .50 1.25
85 Tony Parker .60 1.50
86 Tim Duncan 1.00 2.50
87 Manu Ginobili .60 1.50
88 Chris Bosh .60 1.50
89 Andrea Bargnani .50 1.25
90 Shawn Marion .50 1.25
91 Jose Calderon .40 1.00
92 Carlos Boozer .50 1.25
93 Deron Williams .50 1.25
94 Antawn Jamison .50 1.25
95 Gilbert Arenas .50 1.25
96 Blake Griffin RC 30.00 80.00
97 Ricky Rubio RC 10.00 25.00
98 Hasheem Thabeet RC 4.00 10.00
99 James Harden RC 125.00 300.00
100 DeMar DeRozan RC 40.00 100.00
101 Stephen Curry RC 500.00 1000.00
102 Brandon Jennings RC 6.00 15.00
103 Jordan Hill RC 5.00 12.00
104 Earl Clark RC 5.00 12.00
105 Gerald Henderson RC 5.00 12.00
106 Jonny Flynn RC 4.00 10.00
107 Tyreke Evans RC 5.00 12.00
108 Tyler Hansbrough RC 5.00 12.00
109 Terrence Williams RC 4.00 10.00
110 Jrue Holiday RC 8.00 20.00

2009-10 Topps Chrome Refractors

*REF 1-95 : 2.5X TO 6X BASE HI
*REF RC: .6X TO 1.5X BASE HI
REF PRINT RUN 500 SER.#d SETS
16 LeBron James 100.00 250.00
44 Kobe Bryant 25.00 60.00
67 Russell Westbrook 25.00 60.00
68 Kevin Durant 50.00 120.00
97 Ricky Rubio 30.00 80.00
99 James Harden 300.00 600.00
101 Stephen Curry 2000.00 2500.00

2009-10 Topps Chrome Refractors Gold

*REF.GOLD 1-95: 6X TO 15X BASE HI
*REF.GOLD RC 96-110: 1.5X TO 4X BASE HI
PRINT RUN 50 SER.#'d SETS
16 LeBron James 400.00 800.00
44 Kobe Bryant 75.00 200.00
67 Russell Westbrook 75.00 200.00
68 Kevin Durant 150.00 400.00
96 Blake Griffin 200.00 400.00
97 Ricky Rubio 200.00 400.00
99 James Harden 800.00 1200.00
101 Stephen Curry 4000.00 6000.00

2003-04 Topps Collection

Released in time for Christmas, Topps Collection parallels the setup and design of the regular Topps set enhanced with gold foil highlights and new photography for some of the veterans and rookies. Initially Topps announced that a special Black Border LeBron James cards would be included in each box set, but this card was never issued. The suggested retail price was $40.

COMP.FACT.SET (265) 40.00 80.00
*SINGLES: .6X TO 1.5X BASE TOPPS HI
*RCs: .5X TO 1.25X BASE TOPPS HI
SOME PLAYERS HAVE PHOTO VARIATIONS
CARDS HAVE GOLD FOIL HIGHLIGHTS

2003-04 Topps Contemporary Collection

Released in April 2004, Topps Contemporary Collection is a 140-card set comprised of 20 rookie cards (numbers 1-20), 10 autographed rookie cards sequentially numbered to 499 (numbers 21-30), 100 veteran cards (numbers 31-130) and 10 autographed veteran cards sequentially numbered to 499 (numbers 131-140). Base cards are bordered and printed on irridescent foil board. Contemporary Collection was packaged in six-pack boxes with four cards per pack and carried a suggested retail price of $50.

1-20 RC RANDOM INSERTS IN PACKS
21-30 AU RC PRINT RUN 499 SER.#'d SETS
131-140 AU PRINT RUN 499 SER.#'d SETS
1 LeBron James RC 75.00 200.00
2 Darko Milicic RC 2.00 5.00
3 Chris Bosh RC 4.00 10.00
4 Dwyane Wade RC 8.00 20.00
5 Chris Kaman RC 2.50 6.00
6 Kirk Hinrich RC 2.50 6.00
7 Jarvis Hayes RC 1.50 4.00
8 Mickael Pietrus RC 2.00 5.00
9 Luke Ridnour RC 2.00 5.00
10 David West RC 2.50 6.00
11 Aleksandar Pavlovic RC 2.00 5.00
12 Boris Diaw RC 2.50 6.00
13 Zoran Planinic RC 1.50 4.00
14 Francisco Elson RC 1.50 4.00
15 Leandro Barbosa RC 2.50 6.00
16 Josh Howard RC 2.50 6.00
17 Luke Walton RC 2.50 6.00
18 Willie Green RC 1.50 4.00
19 Maurice Williams RC 2.50 6.00
20 Udonis Haslem RC 2.00 5.00
21 Reece Gaines AU RC 3.00 8.00
22 Carmelo Anthony AU RC 25.00 60.00
23 Zarko Cabarkapa AU RC 3.00 8.00
24 Troy Bell AU RC 3.00 8.00
25 Travis Outlaw AU RC 4.00 10.00
26 Marcus Banks AU RC 3.00 8.00
27 Kendrick Perkins AU RC 4.00 10.00
28 Dahntay Jones AU RC 4.00 10.00
29 T.J. Ford AU RC 4.00 10.00
30 Mike Sweetney AU RC 3.00 8.00
31 Jason Terry .75 2.00
32 Theo Ratliff .60 1.50
33 Raef LaFrentz .60 1.50
34 Eddy Curry .60 1.50
35 Ricky Davis .75 2.00
36 Zydrunas Ilgauskas .75 2.00
37 Darius Miles .60 1.50
38 Dirk Nowitzki 1.50 4.00
39 Steve Nash 1.25 3.00
40 Antawn Jamison .75 2.00
41 Antoine Walker 1.00 2.50
42 Andre Miller .75 2.00
43 Nene .75 2.00
44 Richard Hamilton .75 2.00
45 Ben Wallace .75 2.00
46 Jason Richardson 1.00 2.50
47 Nick Van Exel .75 2.00
48 Troy Murphy .60 1.50
49 Yao Ming 2.00 5.00
50 Steve Francis .75 2.00
51 Ron Artest 1.00 2.50
52 Jermaine O'Neal .75 2.00
53 Al Harrington .75 2.00
54 Marko Jaric .60 1.50
55 Corey Maggette .75 2.00
56 Kobe Bryant 4.00 10.00
57 Shaquille O'Neal 2.50 6.00
58 Devean George .60 1.50
59 Gary Payton 1.00 2.50
60 Pau Gasol 1.00 2.50
61 Stromile Swift .60 1.50
62 Mike Miller .75 2.00
63 Lamar Odom .75 2.00
64 Caron Butler .75 2.00
65 Eddie Jones .75 2.00
66 Brian Grant .60 1.50
67 Desmond Mason .75 2.00
68 Tim Thomas .60 1.50
69 Michael Redd 1.00 2.50
70 Sam Cassell .75 2.00
71 Kevin Garnett 1.50 4.00
72 Latrell Sprewell .75 2.00
73 Michael Olowokandi .60 1.50
74 Wally Szczerbiak .75 2.00
75 Richard Jefferson .75 2.00
76 Kenyon Martin .75 2.00
77 Alonzo Mourning 1.25 3.00
78 Baron Davis .75 2.00
79 Jamal Mashburn .75 2.00
80 Allan Houston .75 2.00
81 Keith Van Horn .75 2.00
82 Kurt Thomas .60 1.50
83 Tracy McGrady 1.25 3.00
84 Juwan Howard .75 2.00
85 Drew Gooden .75 2.00
86 Allen Iverson 1.50 4.00
87 Glenn Robinson .75 2.00
88 Derrick Coleman .75 2.00
89 Stephon Marbury .75 2.00
90 Shawn Marion .75 2.00
91 Amare Stoudemire 1.25 3.00
92 Zach Randolph .75 2.00
93 Rasheed Wallace 1.00 2.50
94 Bonzi Wells .60 1.50
95 Mike Bibby 1.00 2.50
96 Chris Webber 1.00 2.50
97 Brad Miller .75 2.00
98 Tim Duncan 1.50 4.00
99 Rasho Nesterovic .60 1.50
100 Tony Parker 1.00 2.50
101 Manu Ginobili 1.25 3.00
102 Brent Barry .60 1.50
103 Rashard Lewis 1.00 2.50
104 Ray Allen 1.00 2.50
105 Vince Carter 1.50 4.00
106 Jerome Williams .60 1.50
107 Carlos Arroyo .75 2.00
108 Matt Harpring .60 1.50
109 Andrei Kirilenko 1.00 2.50
110 Gilbert Arenas .75 2.00
111 Kwame Brown .60 1.50
112 Jerry Stackhouse .75 2.00
113 Darrell Armstrong .60 1.50
114 Alvin Williams .60 1.50
115 Kelvin Cato .60 1.50
116 Stephen Jackson .75 2.00
117 Shareef Abdur-Rahim .75 2.00
118 Eric Williams .60 1.50
119 Tony Battie .60 1.50
120 Tyson Chandler .75 2.00
121 Scottie Pippen 1.50 4.00
122 Nikoloz Tskitishvili .60 1.50
123 Chauncey Billups 1.00 2.50
124 Quentin Richardson .75 2.00
125 Dikembe Mutombo 1.00 2.50
126 Joe Smith .75 2.00
127 Qyntel Woods .60 1.50
128 Dajuan Wagner .60 1.50
129 Robert Horry .75 2.00
130 Cuttino Mobley .60 1.50
131 Bobby Jackson AU 5.00 12.00
132 Elton Brand AU 6.00 15.00
133 Peja Stojakovic AU 6.00 15.00
134 Jamal Crawford AU 6.00 15.00
135 Jalen Rose AU 8.00 20.00
136 Paul Pierce AU 10.00 25.00
137 Jason Kidd AU 8.00 20.00
138 Tayshaun Prince AU 6.00 12.00
139 Morris Peterson AU 5.00 12.00
140 Speedy Claxton AU 5.00 12.00

2003-04 Topps Contemporary Collection Gold

*1-20 RCs GOLD: 1.25X TO 3X BASE HI
*31-130 STARS GOLD: 3X TO 8X BASE HI
GOLD PRINT RUN 25 SER.#'d SETS
1 LeBron James 700.00 1200.00
56 Kobe Bryant 60.00 150.00

2003-04 Topps Contemporary Collection Red

*RED: .75X TO 2X BASE HI
1-20 PRINT RUN 225 SER.#'d SETS
21-30 AU PRINT RUN 50 SER.#'d SETS
31-130 PRINT RUN 225 SER.#'d SETS
131-140 AU PRINT RUN 50 SER.#'d SETS
1 LeBron James 200.00 500.00
56 Kobe Bryant 12.00 30.00

2003-04 Topps Contemporary Collection Caption Autographs

Randomly seeded in packs, this 40-card set features player's autographs along with a caption that has something to do with themselves. Most players have two different caption versions.

BJ1 B.Jackson Court Kings 8.00 20.00
BJ2 B.Jackson 6th Man 8.00 20.00
CA1 C.Anthony NCAA MVP 40.00 100.00
CA2 C.Anthony Mile High 40.00 80.00
DJ1 D.Jones Cameron 6.00 15.00
DJ2 D.Jones Grizzly Den 6.00 15.00
EB1 E.Brand ROY 99 10.00 25.00
EB2 E.Brand Hollywood 6.00 15.00
JC1 J.Crawford Go Blue 10.00 25.00
JC2 J.Crawford Windy City 15.00 40.00
JK1 J.Kidd ROY 94 20.00 50.00
JK2 J.Kidd Jersey Kidd 30.00 80.00
JR1 J.Rose FAB 5 15.00 30.00
JR2 J.Rose Hollywood North 10.00 25.00
KP1 K.Perkins Ozen Orig. 8.00 20.00
KP2 K.Perkins Celtic Pride 8.00 20.00
MB1 M.Banks Runnin Reb 8.00 20.00
MB2 M.Banks Celtic Pride 8.00 20.00
MP1 Mo Pete Rebel 6.00 15.00
MP2 Mo Pete Hollywood North 6.00 15.00
MS1 M.Sweetney HOYA 34 6.00 15.00
MS2 M.Sweetney Big Apple 6.00 15.00
PP1 P.Pierce The Truth 30.00 80.00
PP2 P.Pierce Celtic Pride 25.00 60.00
PS1 P.Stojakovic Court Kings 10.00 25.00
PS2 P.Stojakovic 3 Point King 8.00 20.00
RG1 R.Gaines Cardinals #1 6.00 15.00
RG2 R.Gaines Magic Tricks 6.00 15.00
SC1 S.Claxton Hofstra Pride 6.00 15.00
SC2 S.Claxton Oaktown 6.00 15.00
TB1 T.Bell BC Beast 6.00 15.00
TB2 T.Bell Grizzly Den 6.00 15.00
TO1 T.Outlaw Starkville's Son 6.00 15.00
TO2 T.Outlaw City of Roses 6.00 15.00
TP1 T.Prince UK Prince 15.00 40.00
TP2 T.Prince Motown Prince 15.00 40.00
ZC1 Cabarkapa Count of Mont. 6.00 15.00
ZC2 Cabarkapa Valley of Sun 6.00 15.00
TJF1 T.Ford Longhorn Legend 8.00 20.00
TJF2 T.Ford NCAA POY 03 12.50 30.00

2003-04 Topps Contemporary Collection Caption Autographs Dual

Randomly seeded, this 20-card set pairs players who have autographed and added a caption to each card.

SOME UNPRICED DUE TO SCARCITY
AF C.Anthony/T.Ford 100.00 200.00
BJ T.Bell/D.Jones 8.00 20.00
BP1 M.Banks/K.Perkins 10.00 25.00
BP2 M.Banks/MoPete 8.00 20.00
BS E.Brand/M.Sweetney 10.00 25.00
CR J.Crawford/J.Rose 30.00 80.00
GC R.Gaines/S.Claxton 8.00 20.00
OC T.Outlaw/Zarko 10.00 25.00
PC T.Prince/S.Claxton 10.00 25.00
PK P.Pierce/J.Kidd 100.00 200.00
PP P.Pierce/M.Peterson 40.00 100.00
SC Peja/Z.Cabarkapa 12.50 30.00
SJ P.Stojakovic/B.Jackson 12.50 30.00
SP M.Sweetney/T.Prince 12.50 30.00

2003-04 Topps Contemporary Collection Draft 03 Tribute

Randomly seeded in packs, this 23-card set showcases the top rookies from the 2003 NBA draft along with a swatch of memorabilia. Two other parallel version were inserted, a red one sequentially numbered to 50 and a gold one where cards are numbered one of one.

PRINT RUN 250 SER.#'d SETS
*RED SINGLES: .75X TO 2X BASE DRAFT HI
RED PRINT RUN 50 SER.#'d SETS
AP Aleksandar Pavlovic 2.00 5.00
BC Brian Cook 1.50 4.00
BD Boris Diaw 2.50 6.00
CA Carmelo Anthony 8.00 20.00
CB Chris Bosh 4.00 10.00
CK Chris Kaman 2.50 6.00
DJ Dahntay Jones 2.00 5.00
DW Dwyane Wade 8.00 20.00
JH Josh Howard 2.50 6.00
JK Jason Kapono 1.50 4.00
KH Kirk Hinrich 2.50 6.00
LB Leandro Barbosa 2.50 6.00
LR Luke Ridnour 2.00 5.00
LW Luke Walton 2.50 6.00
MB Marcus Banks 1.50 4.00
MP Mickael Pietrus 2.00 5.00
MW Maurice Williams 2.50 6.00
SB Steve Blake 2.00 5.00
TB Troy Bell 1.50 4.00
ZP Zoran Planinic 1.50 4.00
DWE David West 2.50 6.00
JHA Jarvis Hayes 1.50 4.00
TJF T.J. Ford 2.00 5.00

2003-04 Topps Contemporary Collection Lucky Draw

Randomly inserted in packs, this 25-card set is horizontally designed with a player photo on the left and the player's conference logo, Eastern or Western, on the right. Cards are sequentially numbered to 175. Two parallel versions were also issued, one sequentially numbered to 50 and one sequentially numbered to 25.

PRINT RUN 175 SER.#'d SETS
*50 SINGLES: .6X TO 1.5X BASE HI
*25 SINGLES: 1X TO 2.5X BASE HI
LD1 Carmelo Anthony 12.00 30.00
LD2 Marcus Banks 2.50 6.00
LD3 Chris Bosh 6.00 15.00
LD4 Dwyane Wade 12.00 30.00
LD5 Chris Kaman 4.00 10.00
LD6 Kirk Hinrich 4.00 10.00
LD7 Jarvis Hayes 2.50 6.00
LD8 Mickael Pietrus 3.00 8.00
LD9 Luke Ridnour 3.00 8.00
LD10 David West 4.00 10.00
LD11 Aleksandar Pavlovic 3.00 8.00
LD12 Boris Diaw 4.00 10.00
LD13 Zoran Planinic 2.50 6.00
LD14 Ndudi Ebi 2.50 6.00
LD15 Leandro Barbosa 4.00 10.00
LD16 Josh Howard 4.00 10.00
LD17 Luke Walton 4.00 10.00
LD18 Willie Green 2.50 6.00
LD19 Maurice Williams 4.00 10.00
LD20 Zarko Cabarkapa 2.50 6.00
LD21 Travis Outlaw 3.00 8.00
LD22 Dahntay Jones 3.00 8.00
LD23 Troy Bell 2.50 6.00
LD24 Reece Gaines 2.50 6.00
LD25 Mike Sweetney 2.50 6.00

2003-04 Topps Contemporary Collection Matching Marks Relics

Randomly inserted, this nine-card set pairs players who match in a specific statistical category on a horizontally designed card with two color photos and jersey swatches inside numbers and letters that spell out the stat category. Each card is sequentially numbered to 250. Two parallel versions of this set were issued, a red version sequentially numbered to 50 and a gold version numbered one of one.

PRINT RUN 250 SER.#'d SETS
*RED SINGLES: .5X TO 1.25X MATCH HI
RED PRINT RUN 50 SER.#'d SETS
AH R.Allen/A.Houston 6.00 15.00
GD K.Garnett/T.Duncan 10.00 25.00
IM A.Iverson/T.McGrady 8.00 20.00
KM J.Kidd/A.Miller 6.00 15.00
MM K.Malone/A.Mourning 8.00 20.00
OS Shaq/A.Stoudemire 10.00 25.00
WB C.Webber/E.Brand 6.00 15.00
WM B.Wallace/D.Mutombo 6.00 15.00
WR A.Walker/G.Robinson 6.00 15.00

2003-04 Topps Contemporary Collection Memorable Materials

Randomly inserted, this seven-card set places a player photo on the right side of the card and a square shaped swatch of memorabilia on the left. Each card is sequentially numbered to 250. Two parallel versions of this set were issued, a red version sequentially numbered to 50 and a gold version numbered one of one.

PRINT RUN 250 SER.#'d SETS
*RED SINGLES: .75X TO 2X MEM.MAT.HI
RED PRINT RUN 50 SER.#'d SETS
AI Allen Iverson 5.00 12.00
JR Jason Richardson 3.00 8.00
KG Kevin Garnett 5.00 12.00
RH Robert Horry 2.50 6.00
RM Reggie Miller 3.00 8.00
SM Stephon Marbury 2.50 6.00
TD Tim Duncan 5.00 12.00

2003-04 Topps Contemporary Collection Milestone Materials

Randomly inserted, this 13-card set places a player photo on the left and a swatch of memorabilia on the right. Each card is sequentially numbered to 250. Two parallel versions of this set were issued, a red version sequentially numbered to 50 and a gold version numbered one of one.

PRINT RUN 250 SER.#'d SETS
*RED SINGLES: .75X TO 2X MILE HI
RED PRINT RUN 50 SER.#'d SETS
DM Dikembe Mutombo 3.00 8.00
DN Dirk Nowitzki 5.00 12.00
GP Gary Payton 3.00 8.00
JS Jerry Stackhouse 2.50 6.00
KM Karl Malone 4.00 10.00
MB Mike Bibby 3.00 8.00
RA Ray Allen 3.00 8.00
SC Sam Cassell 2.50 6.00
SF Steve Francis 2.50 6.00
SO Shaquille O'Neal 8.00 20.00
TD Tim Duncan 5.00 12.00
NVE Nick Van Exel 2.50 6.00
RHA Richard Hamilton 2.50 6.00

2003-04 Topps Contemporary Collection Perennial All-Star Relics

Randomly inserted, this 16-card set showcases NBA All-Stars with a centered swatch of memorabilia. Each card is sequentially numbered to 250 unless noted. Two parallel versions of this set were issued, a red version sequentially numbered to 50 and a gold version numbered one of one.

PRINT RUN 175 TO 250 SER.#'d SETS
*RED SINGLES: .75X TO 2X ALL-STAR HI
RED PRINT RUN 50 SER.#'d SETS
AI Allen Iverson 5.00 12.00
AM Alonzo Mourning 5.00 12.00
CW Chris Webber/175 3.00 8.00
DN Dirk Nowitzki 5.00 12.00
GP Gary Payton 3.00 8.00
JK Jason Kidd 5.00 12.00
KG Kevin Garnett 5.00 12.00
KM Karl Malone 4.00 10.00
PP Paul Pierce 3.00 8.00
RA Ray Allen 3.00 8.00
RM Reggie Miller 3.00 8.00
SF Steve Francis 2.50 6.00
SN Steve Nash 4.00 10.00
SO Shaquille O'Neal 8.00 20.00
TD Tim Duncan 5.00 12.00
TM Tracy McGrady 4.00 10.00

2003-04 Topps Contemporary Collection Performance Tribute Doubles

Randomly seeded in packs, this nine-card set places two players and two swatches of memorabilia on each card. The cards are sequentially numbered to 250. Two parallel versions of this set were issued, a red version sequentially numbered to 50 and a gold version numbered one of one.

PRINT RUN 250 SER.#'d SETS
*RED SINGLES: .6X TO 1.5X PERF. HI
RED PRINT RUN 50 SER.#'d SETS
AM R.Artest/K.Martin 5.00 12.00
BW E.Brand/C.Webber 5.00 12.00
ML T.Murphy/R.Lafrentz 5.00 12.00
MW D.Mutombo/B.Wallace 5.00 12.00
NK S.Nash/J.Kidd 6.00 15.00
NS Nene/A.Stoudemire 5.00 12.00
PB S.Pippen/S.Battier 8.00 20.00
RW G.Robinson/R.Wallace 5.00 12.00
WB Jer.Williams/Boozer 5.00 12.00

2003-04 Topps Contemporary Collection Performance Tribute Triples

Randomly inserted, this nine-card set places three players and three swatches of memorabilia on each card. Cards are sequentially numbered to 250 unless noted below. Two parallel versions of this set were issued, a red version sequentially numbered to 50 and a gold version numbered one of one.

PRINT RUN 200 TO 250 SER.#'d SETS
*RED SINGLES: .75X TO 2X PERF.TRIP HI
RED PRINT RUN 50 SER.#'d SETS
FDR Francis/B.Davis/J-Rich 6.00 15.00
HJP Rip/R.Jeff/MoPete/200 6.00 15.00
JAB Jaric/Arenas/Butler 6.00 15.00
MGM Yao/Garnett/Mourning 8.00 20.00
MIS T-Mac/Iverson/Shaq 12.00 30.00
OMR Odom/Miles/Rose/200 6.00 15.00
PWM Pierce/Walker/Marion 6.00 15.00
RWO Ratliff/Big Ben/J.O'Neal 6.00 15.00
TMW Terry/Marbury/Wagner/200 6.00 15.00

2003-04 Topps Contemporary Collection Team Tribute Doubles

Randomly inserted, this 13-card set places two players from the same team along with two swatches of memorabilia on the card. Cards are sequentially numbered to 250. Two parallel versions of this set were issued, a red version sequentially numbered to 50 and a gold version numbered one of one.

PRINT RUN 250 SER.#'d SETS
*RED SINGLES: .6X TO 1.5X DOUBLE HI
RED PRINT RUN 50 SER.#'d SETS
AO R.Artest/J.O'Neal 5.00 12.00
GE K.Garnett/N.Ebi 6.00 15.00
HT R.Horry/H.Turkoglu 5.00 12.00
HV A.Houston/K.Van Horn 5.00 12.00
IR A.Iverson/G.Robinson 5.00 12.00
KP J.Kidd/Z.Planinic 5.00 12.00
MH R.Miller/A.Harrington 5.00 12.00
PB P.Pierce/M.Banks 5.00 12.00
PH T.Prince/R.Hamilton 6.00 15.00
SH J.Stack/J.Hayes 5.00 12.00
TS K.Thomas/M.Sweetney 5.00 12.00
WM C.Webber/B.Miller 5.00 12.00
PBO M.Peterson/C.Bosh 5.00 12.00

2003-04 Topps Contemporary Collection Team Tribute Triples

Randomly inserted, this 16-card set places three players from the same team along with three swatches of memorabilia on the card. Cards are sequentially numbered to 250. Two parallel versions of this set were issued, a red version sequentially numbered to 50 and a gold version numbered one of one.

PRINT RUN 200 TO 250 SER.#'d SETS
*RED SINGLES: .6X TO 1.5X TRIB.TRIP.HI
RED PRINT RUN 50 SER.#'d SETS
BMR Brand/Maggette/Q-Rich 6.00 15.00
BOW Butler/Odom/Wade 8.00 20.00
BSJ Bibby/Peja/B.Jcksn/200 8.00 20.00
BSM Barbosa/Amare/Marion 6.00 15.00
DMW B.Davis/Mash/West 6.00 15.00
DNP Duncan/Rasho/Parker 8.00 20.00
FMR Ford/Mason/Redd 6.00 15.00
MAN A.Miller/Melo/Nene 8.00 20.00
MFM Yao/Francis/Mobley 8.00 20.00
MGG T-Mac/Gaines/Gooden 6.00 15.00
NNF Nash/Dirk/Finley 10.00 25.00
PCK Planinic/Clark/AK-47 6.00 15.00
PMO Payton/Malone/Shaq 12.50 30.00
SOC Spree/Olowok/Cassell 6.00 15.00
WMB Wagner/Miles/Boozer 6.00 15.00
WOW R.Wallace/Outlaw/Woods 6.00 15.00

2003-04 Topps Contemporary Collection Tribute to the Stars Relics

Randomly inserted in packs, this 22-card set features a centered photo of each player and two star-shaped swatches of memorabilia. Each card is sequentially numbered to 50 unless noted.

PRINT RUN 21 TO 50 SER.#'d SETS
UNPRICED GOLD ONE OF ONE'S EXIST
N Nene/50 5.00 12.00
AK Andrei Kirilenko/50 6.00 15.00
AS Amare Stoudemire/50 8.00 20.00
BW Ben Wallace/50 5.00 12.00
CW Chris Webber/50 6.00 15.00
DM Desmond Mason/50 5.00 12.00
EB Elton Brand/50 6.00 15.00
EC Eddy Curry/50 4.00 10.00
JK Jason Kidd/50 10.00 25.00
JO Jermaine O'Neal/50 5.00 12.00
JR Jason Richardson/50 6.00 15.00
JT Jason Terry/50 5.00 12.00
KV Keith Van Horn/50 5.00 12.00
LO Lamar Odom/21 10.00 25.00
PG Pau Gasol/50 6.00 15.00
PP Paul Pierce/50 6.00 15.00
RW Rasheed Wallace/50 6.00 15.00
SM Stephon Marbury/50 5.00 12.00
TM Tracy McGrady/50 8.00 20.00
TP Tony Parker/50 6.00 15.00
YM Yao Ming/50 12.00 30.00

2007-08 Topps Co-Signers

This 100-card set was released in January, 2008. The set was issued into the hobby in six-card packs with an $10 SRP which came 12 packs per box and 24 boxes to a case. Cards numbered 1-30 featured NBA active stars, cards numbered 31-50 featured retired greats and cards numbered 51-100 featured 2007-08 NBA rookies. The Rookie Cards were all issued to a stated print run of 499 serial numbered sets.

COMP.SET w/o SP's (50) 20.00 40.00
ROOKIE PRINT RUN 499 SER.#'d SETS
1 Dwyane Wade .60 1.50
2 Chauncey Billups .40 1.00
3 Allen Iverson .50 1.25
4 Amare Stoudemire .30 .75
5 Jason Kidd .40 1.00
6 Dirk Nowitzki .50 1.25
7 Jermaine O'Neal .30 .75
8 Elton Brand .40 1.00
9 Carlos Boozer .30 .75
10 Ray Allen .40 1.00
11 Yao Ming .50 1.25
12 Dwight Howard .30 .75
13 Steve Nash .50 1.25
14 Chris Paul .50 1.25
15 Carmelo Anthony .50 1.25
16 Pau Gasol .40 1.00
17 Ben Gordon .30 .75
18 Andre Iguodala .30 .75
19 Paul Pierce .40 1.00
20 Tracy McGrady .40 1.00
21 Tim Duncan .60 1.50
22 Josh Smith .30 .75
23 LeBron James 1.50 4.00
24 Kobe Bryant 1.50 4.00
25 Vince Carter .50 1.25
26 Shaquille O'Neal .75 2.00
27 Kevin Garnett .60 1.50
28 Chris Bosh .40 1.00
29 Baron Davis .30 .75
30 Gilbert Arenas .30 .75
31 John Stockton 1.00 2.50
32 Magic Johnson 1.50 4.00
33 Larry Bird 1.50 4.00
34 Rick Barry .50 1.25
35 Isiah Thomas .60 1.50
36 Dominique Wilkins .75 2.00
37 Dennis Rodman 1.25 3.00
38 Wilt Chamberlain 1.25 3.00
39 Pete Maravich 1.00 2.50
40 Bill Russell 1.00 2.50
41 Byron Scott .50 1.25
42 Karl Malone .75 2.00
43 Chris Mullin .60 1.50
44 Kevin McHale .75 2.00
45 Clyde Drexler .75 2.00
46 James Worthy .75 2.00
47 Bill Walton .60 1.50
48 Earl Monroe .60 1.50
49 Elgin Baylor .60 1.50
50 David Robinson 1.00 2.50
51 Nick Young RC 2.50 6.00
52 Greg Oden RC 2.00 5.00
53 Morris Almond RC 1.25 3.00
54 Alando Tucker RC 1.25 3.00
55 Arron Afflalo RC 2.00 5.00
56 Derrick Byars RC 1.25 3.00
57 Adam Haluska RC 1.25 3.00
58 Corey Brewer RC 2.00 5.00
59 Ramon Sessions RC 2.00 5.00
60 Daequan Cook RC 1.50 4.00
61 Mike Conley Jr. RC 2.50 6.00
62 Javaris Crittenton RC 1.25 3.00
63 Jared Jordan RC 1.25 3.00
64 Aaron Brooks RC 1.50 4.00
65 Marco Belinelli RC 2.00 5.00
66 Sammy Mejia RC 1.25 3.00
67 Jared Dudley RC 1.50 4.00
68 Rodney Stuckey RC 1.50 4.00
69 JamesOn Curry RC 1.25 3.00
70 Gabe Pruitt RC 1.25 3.00
71 Acie Law RC 1.25 3.00
72 Dominic McGuire RC 1.25 3.00
73 Herbert Hill RC 1.25 3.00
74 Jeff Green RC 2.00 5.00
75 Wilson Chandler RC 1.50 4.00
76 Marcus Williams RC 1.25 3.00
77 Josh McRoberts RC 1.50 4.00
78 Thaddeus Young RC 2.00 5.00
79 Jared Newson RC 2.00 5.00
80 Stephane Lasme RC 1.25 3.00
81 Demetris Nichols RC 1.25 3.00
82 Julian Wright RC 1.25 3.00
83 Sean Williams RC 1.25 3.00
84 Chris Richard RC 1.25 3.00
85 Yi Jianlian RC 2.50 6.00
86 Al Thornton RC 1.50 4.00
87 Carl Landry RC 1.25 3.00
88 Kevin Durant RC 20.00 50.00
89 Brandan Wright RC 2.00 5.00
90 Nick Fazekas RC 1.25 3.00
91 Joakim Noah RC 2.00 5.00
92 Jermareo Davidson RC 1.25 3.00
93 D.J. Strawberry RC 1.25 3.00
94 Glen Davis RC 1.50 4.00
95 Al Horford RC 2.50 6.00
96 Spencer Hawes RC 1.50 4.00
97 Taurean Green RC 1.25 3.00
98 Jason Smith RC 1.50 4.00
99 Luis Scola RC 2.50 6.00
100 Aaron Gray RC 1.25 3.00

2007-08 Topps Co-Signers Gold Red

PRINT RUN 109 SER.#'d SETS
UNPRICED GOLD RED FOIL PRINT RUN 9 SETS
*GOLD BLUE: .5X TO 1.25X GOLD RED
GOLD BLUE PRINT RUN 89 SETS
UNPRICED GOLD BLUE FOIL PRINT RUN 5 SETS
*GOLD GREEN: .5X TO 1.25X GOLD RED
GOLD GREEN PRINT RUN 59 SETS
*G.GREEN FOIL: 1.5X TO 4X GOLD RED
GOLD GREEN FOIL PRINT RUN 19 SETS
*SILVER BLUE FOIL: 1.25X TO 3X GOLD RED
SILVER BLUE FOIL PRINT RUN 29 SETS
*SILVER GREEN FOIL: 1.5X TO 4X RED GOLD
SILVER GREEN FOIL PRINT RUN 19 SETS
*SILVER RED FOIL: 1.25X TO 3X BASE HI
SILVER RED FOIL PRINT RUN 39 SETS
1 D.Wade/S.O'Neal 1.50 4.00
1A D.Wade/A.Walker 1.25 3.00
2 C.Billups/R.Hamilton 1.25 3.00
2A C.Billups/T.Prince 1.25 3.00
3 A.Iverson/C.Anthony 1.25 3.00
3A A.Iverson/M.Camby 1.25 3.00
4 A.Stoudemire/S.Nash 1.25 3.00
4A A.Stoudemire/S.Marion 1.25 3.00
5 J.Kidd/V.Carter 1.25 3.00
5A J.Kidd/M.Williams 1.25 3.00
6 D.Nowitzki/J.Terry 1.25 3.00
6A D.Nowitzki/J.Howard 1.25 3.00
7 J.O'Neal/D.Granger 1.25 3.00
7A J.O'Neal/T.Murphy 1.25 3.00
8 E.Brand/C.Maggette 1.25 3.00
8A E.Brand/S.Livingston 1.25 3.00
9 C.Boozer/D.Williams 1.25 3.00
9A C.Boozer/A.Kirilenko 1.25 3.00
10 R.Allen/P.Pierce 1.25 3.00
10A R.Allen/K.Garnett 1.25 3.00
11 Y.Ming/T.McGrady 1.25 3.00
11A Y.Ming/S.Battier 1.25 3.00
12 D.Howard/R.Lewis 1.25 3.00
12A D.Howard/J.Nelson 1.25 3.00
13 S.Nash/S.Marion 1.25 3.00
13A S.Nash/A.Stoudemire 1.25 3.00
14 C.Paul/T.Chandler 1.25 3.00
14A C.Paul/D.West 1.25 3.00
15 C.Anthony/A.Iverson 1.25 3.00
15A C.Anthony/M.Camby 1.25 3.00
16 P.Gasol/M.Miller 1.25 3.00
16A P.Gasol/R.Gay 1.25 3.00
17 B.Gordon/L.Deng 1.25 3.00
17A B.Gordon/B.Wallace 1.25 3.00
18 A.Iguodala/K.Korver 1.25 3.00
18A A.Iguodala/A.Miller 1.25 3.00
19 P.Pierce/R.Allen 1.25 3.00
19A P.Pierce/K.Garnett 1.25 3.00
20 T.McGrady/Y.Ming 1.25 3.00
20A T.McGrady/S.Battier 1.25 3.00
21 T.Duncan/T.Parker 1.25 3.00
21A T.Duncan/M.Ginobili 1.25 3.00
22 J.Smith/M.Williams 1.25 3.00
22A J.Smith/J.Johnson 1.25 3.00
23 L.James/A.Varejao 2.50 6.00
23A L.James/D.Gibson 2.50 6.00
24 K.Bryant/A.Bynum 2.00 5.00
24A K.Bryant/L.Walton 1.50 4.00
25 V.Carter/J.Kidd 1.25 3.00
25A V.Carter/M.Williams 1.25 3.00
26 S.O'Neal/D.Wade 1.50 4.00
26A S.O'Neal/A.Walker 1.25 3.00
27 K.Garnett/P.Pierce 1.25 3.00
27A K.Garnett/R.Allen 1.25 3.00
28 C.Bosh/A.Bargnani 1.25 3.00
28A C.Bosh/T.Ford 1.25 3.00
29 B.Davis/A.Harrington 1.25 3.00
29A B.Davis/M.Ellis 1.25 3.00
30 G.Arenas/C.Butler 1.25 3.00
30A G.Arenas/A.Jamison 1.25 3.00
31 J.Stockton/D.Williams 1.25 3.00
31A J.Stockton/C.Boozer 1.25 3.00
32 M.Johnson/B.Scott 1.50 4.00
32A M.Johnson/K.Bryant 2.50 6.00
33 L.Bird/B.Russell 3.00 8.00
33A L.Bird/P.Pierce 2.50 6.00
34 R.Barry/B.Davis 1.25 3.00
34A R.Barry/C.Mullin 1.25 3.00
35 I.Thomas/C.Billups 1.25 3.00
35A I.Thomas/D.Rodman 1.50 4.00
36 D.Wilkins/J.Smith 1.25 3.00
36A D.Wilkins/J.Johnson 1.25 3.00
37 D.Rodman/B.Wallace 1.25 3.00
37A D.Rodman/L.Deng 1.25 3.00
38 W.Chamberlain/M.Malone 2.00 5.00
38A W.Chamberlain/M.Cheeks 2.00 5.00
39 P.Maravich/J.Stockton 4.00 10.00
39A P.Maravich/D.Williams 3.00 8.00
40 B.Russell/L.Bird 3.00 8.00
40A B.Russell/K.Garnett 3.00 8.00
41 B.Scott/M.Johnson 1.50 4.00
41A B.Scott/K.Bryant 2.00 5.00
42 K.Malone/J.Stockton 2.00 5.00
42A K.Malone/C.Boozer 1.25 3.00
43 C.Mullin/B.Davis 1.25 3.00
43A C.Mullin/R.Barry 1.25 3.00
44 K.McHale/L.Bird 1.50 4.00
44A K.McHale/J.Havlicek 1.50 4.00
45 C.Drexler/T.McGrady 1.25 3.00
45A C.Drexler/Y.Ming 1.25 3.00
46 J.Worthy/K.Bryant 1.25 3.00

46A J.Worthy/M.Johnson 2.00 5.00
47 B.Walton/G.Oden 1.25 3.00
47A B.Walton/B.Roy 1.25 3.00
48 E.Monroe/S.Marbury 1.25 3.00
48A E.Monroe/J.Crawford 1.25 3.00
49 E.Baylor/J.West 1.50 4.00
49A E.Baylor/K.Bryant 2.00 5.00
50 D.Robinson/T.Duncan 2.00 5.00
50A D.Robinson/T.Parker 1.50 4.00
51 N.Young/G.Arenas 1.25 3.00
51A N.Young/A.Jamison 1.25 3.00
52 G.Oden/B.Walton 2.50 6.00
52A G.Oden/B.Roy 2.50 6.00
53 M.Almond/C.Boozer 1.25 3.00
53A M.Almond/D.Williams 1.25 3.00
54 A.Tucker/S.Nash 1.25 3.00
54A A.Tucker/A.Stoudemire 1.25 3.00
55 A.Afflalo/C.Billups 1.25 3.00
55A A.Afflalo/R.Stuckey 1.50 4.00
56 D.Byars/A.Iguodala 1.25 3.00
56A D.Byars/J.Smith 1.25 3.00
57 A.Haluska/C.Paul 1.25 3.00
57A A.Haluska/T.Chandler 1.25 3.00
58 C.Brewer/A.Jefferson 1.50 4.00
58A C.Brewer/R.Foye 1.25 3.00
59 R.Sessions/M.Redd 1.25 3.00
59A R.Sessions/M.Williams 1.25 3.00
60 D.Cook/D.Wade 2.00 5.00
60A D.Cook/S.O'Neal 2.00 5.00
61 M.Conley/P.Gasol 1.25 3.00
61A M.Conley/R.Gay 1.25 3.00
62 J.Crittenton/K.Bryant 2.50 6.00
62A J.Crittenton/A.Bynum 1.25 3.00
63 J.Jordan/S.Marbury 1.25 3.00
63A J.Jordan/J.Crawford 1.25 3.00
64 A.Brooks/T.McGrady 1.50 4.00
64A A.Brooks/Y.Ming 2.00 5.00
65 M.Belinelli/B.Davis 1.25 3.00
65A M.Belinelli/A.Harrington 1.25 3.00
66 S.Mejia/A.Afflalo 1.25 3.00
66A S.Mejia/R.Stuckey 1.25 3.00
67 J.Dudley/E.Okafor 1.25 3.00
67A J.Dudley/R.Felton 1.25 3.00
68 R.Stuckey/A.Afflalo 1.25 3.00
68A R.Stuckey/C.Billups 1.25 3.00
69 J.Curry/B.Gordon 1.25 3.00
69A J.Curry/A.Gray 1.25 3.00
70 G.Pruitt/G.Davis 1.25 3.00
70A G.Pruitt/P.Pierce 1.25 3.00
71 A.Law/J.Smith 1.25 3.00
71A A.Law/J.Johnson 1.25 3.00
72 D.McGuire/G.Arenas 1.25 3.00
72A D.McGuire/N.Young 1.25 3.00
73 H.Hill/D.Byars 1.25 3.00
73A H.Hill/J.Smith 1.25 3.00
74 J.Green/K.Durant 6.00 15.00
74A J.Green/C.Wilcox 1.50 4.00
75 W.Chandler/S.Marbury 1.25 3.00
75A W.Chandler/J.Crawford 1.25 3.00
76 M.Williams/T.Duncan 1.50 4.00
76A M.Williams/T.Parker 1.25 3.00
77 J.McRoberts/G.Oden 2.00 5.00
77A J.McRoberts/T.Green 1.25 3.00
78 T.Young/A.Iguodala 1.25 3.00
78A T.Young/J.Smith 1.25 3.00
79 J.Newson/D.Nowitzki 1.25 3.00
79A J.Newson/J.Terry 1.25 3.00
80 S.Lasme/B.Wright 1.25 3.00
80A S.Lasme/B.Davis 1.25 3.00
81 D.Nichols/W.Chandler 1.25 3.00
81A D.Nichols/S.Marbury 1.25 3.00
82 J.Wright/C.Paul 1.50 4.00
82A J.Wright/D.West 1.25 3.00
83 S.Williams/J.Kidd 1.25 3.00
83A S.Williams/V.Carter 1.50 4.00
84 C.Richard/C.Brewer 1.25 3.00
84A C.Richard/A.Jefferson 1.25 3.00
85 Y.Jianlian/R.Sessions 2.00 5.00
85A Y.Jianlian/M.Redd 2.00 5.00
86 A.Thornton/E.Brand 1.25 3.00
86A A.Thornton/C.Maggette 1.25 3.00
87 C.Landry/Y.Ming 1.50 4.00
87A C.Landry/A.Brooks 1.50 4.00
88 K.Durant/J.Green 6.00 15.00
88A K.Durant/C.Wilcox 5.00 12.00
89 B.Wright/B.Davis 1.25 3.00
89A B.Wright/C.Mullin 1.25 3.00
90 N.Fazekas/D.Nowitzki 1.25 3.00
90A N.Fazekas/J.Newson 1.25 3.00
91 J.Noah/L.Deng 2.50 6.00
91A J.Noah/B.Wallace 1.50 4.00
92 J.Davidson/J.Dudley 1.25 3.00
92A J.Davidson/E.Okafor 1.25 3.00
93 D.Strawberry/S.Nash 1.25 3.00
93A D.Strawberry/A.Tucker 1.25 3.00
94 G.Davis/P.Pierce 1.50 4.00
94A G.Davis/G.Pruitt 1.25 3.00
95 A.Horford/J.Smith 2.00 5.00
95A A.Horford/A.Law 1.50 4.00
96 S.Hawes/M.Bibby 1.25 3.00
96A S.Hawes/B.Miller 1.25 3.00
97 T.Green/G.Oden 2.50 6.00
97A T.Green/J.McRoberts 1.25 3.00
98 J.Smith/D.Byars 1.25 3.00
98A J.Smith/H.Hill 1.25 3.00
99 L.Scola/T.McGrady 1.50 4.00
99A L.Scola/A.Brooks 1.50 4.00
100 A.Gray/B.Wallace 1.25 3.00
100A A.Gray/J.Noah 1.50 4.00

2007-08 Topps Co-Signers Dual Autographs

OUP A ODDS 1:494, GROUP B 1:191
GROUP C ODDS 1:79, GROUP D 1:327
GROUP E ODDS 1:33, GROUP F 1:122
GROUP G ODDS 1:94
UNPRICED GOLD PRINT RUN 9 SETS
UNPRICED GOLD FOIL PRINT RUN 5 SETS
SILVER FOIL PRINT RUN FIVE SETS
UNPRICED PLATE PRINT RUN ONE SET
EXCH EXPRE DATE 12/31/09
CS1 D.Wade/C.Anthony A 50.00 125.00
CS2 G.Oden/B.Walton A 40.00 100.00
CS3 D.Rodman/I.Thomas A 40.00 80.00
CS4 B.Russell/J.Havlicek A 100.00 225.00
CS5 R.Allen/P.Pierce B 35.00 75.00
CS7 S.O'Neal/D.Robinson A 50.00 100.00
CS8 E.Baylor/J.Havlicek B 20.00 50.00
CS9 R.Barry/B.Davis B 10.00 25.00
CS10 J.Stockton/D.Williams A 50.00 100.00
CS11 C.Bosh/A.Bargnani B 20.00 40.00
CS12 L.Walton/M.Williams E 6.00 15.00
CS13 D.Lee/T.Green E 6.00 15.00
CS14 D.McGuire/N.Fazekas E 6.00 15.00
CS15 D.Lee/W.Chandler E 8.00 20.00
CS16 H.Hill/D.Byars E 6.00 15.00
CS17 C.Hawkins/A.Tucker C 15.00 30.00
CS18 E.Okafor/J.Dudley D 6.00 15.00
CS19 M.Cheeks/M.Malone B 20.00 40.00
CS20 B.Love/K.Hinrich F 10.00 25.00
CS21 H.Turkoglu/J.Redick F 8.00 20.00
CS22 A.Bynum/J.Crittenton C 10.00 25.00
CS23 R.Tomjanovich/C.Landry G 8.00 20.00
CS24 M.Bol/J.Smith D 40.00 80.00
CS25 W.Chandler/S.Mejia E 6.00 15.00
CS26 S.Rodriguez/J.Jack E 6.00 15.00
CS27 R.Balkman/W.Chandler C 6.00 15.00
CS28 P.O'Bryant/S.Lasme F 6.00 15.00
CS29 D.Gibson/A.Law E 6.00 15.00
CS30 A.Iguodala/T.Young B 8.00 20.00
CS31 M.Williams/S.Williams C 6.00 15.00
CS32 D.Granger/I.Diogu G 6.00 15.00
CS33 G.Pruitt/G.Davis E 6.00 15.00
CS34 C.Maggette/A.Thornton C 6.00 15.00
CS35 A.Brooks/C.Landry E 8.00 20.00
CS37 B.Gordon/C.Duhon C 10.00 25.00
CS38 S.Dalembert/J.Smith C 6.00 15.00
CS39 R.Felton/J.Davidson C 6.00 15.00
CS40 L.Elmore/D.Strawberry G 6.00 15.00
CS41 R.Stuckey/A.Afflalo E 6.00 15.00
CS42 C.Boozer/M.Almond B 6.00 15.00
CS43 M.Belinelli/S.Lasme E 6.00 15.00
CS44 J.Smith/D.Cook C 6.00 15.00
CS45 T.Green/J.Jack E 6.00 15.00
CS46 S.Williams/J.Dudley C 6.00 15.00
CS47 G.Oden/J.Havlicek A 40.00 100.00
CS48 Y.Jianlian/M.Belinelli B 30.00 60.00
CS49 N.Young/G.Pruitt C 6.00 15.00
CS50 T.Young/J.Crittenton B 8.00 20.00

2007-08 Topps Co-Signers Rookie Autographs

GROUP A ODDS 1:112, GROUP B 1:1:16
*GOLD: .5X TO 1.25X BASE HI
GOLD PRINT RUN 25 SER.#'d SETS
UNPRICED GOLD FOIL PRINT RUN 10 SETS
UNPRICED SILVER FOIL PRINT RUN ONE SET
UNPRICED PLATE PRINT RUN ONE SET
51 Nick Young A 6.00 15.00
52 Greg Oden A 4.00 10.00
53 Morris Almond B 2.50 6.00
54 Alando Tucker A 2.50 6.00
55 Arron Afflalo B 4.00 10.00
56 Derrick Byars B 2.50 6.00
57 Adam Haluska B 2.50 6.00
62 Javaris Crittenton B 2.50 6.00
63 Jared Jordan B 2.50 6.00
64 Aaron Brooks B 3.00 8.00
68 Rodney Stuckey B 3.00 8.00
69 JamesOn Curry B 2.50 6.00
71 Acie Law A 2.50 6.00
72 Dominic McGuire B 2.50 6.00
73 Herbert Hill B 2.50 6.00
78 Thaddeus Young A 4.00 10.00
85 Yi Jianlian A 10.00 25.00
86 Al Thornton A 3.00 8.00
89 Brandan Wright A 4.00 10.00
90 Nick Fazekas B 2.50 6.00
92 Jermareo Davidson B 2.50 6.00
94 Glen Davis B 3.00 8.00
96 Spencer Hawes A 3.00 8.00
98 Jason Smith A 3.00 8.00
100 Aaron Gray B 2.50 6.00

2007-08 Topps Co-Signers Triple Autographs

ATED PRINT RUN 9 TO 19 SETS
UNLESS LISTED IN CHECKLIST
PRINT RUNS ANNOUNCED BY TOPPS
UNPRICED GOLD PRINT RUN 5 SER.#'d SETS
UNPRICED GOLD FOIL PRINT RUN 3 SETS
UNPRICED SILVER FOIL PRINT RUN ONE SET
TS3 Wilkins/Smith/Law 30.00 60.00
TS4 Wallace/Okafor/Felton 30.00 60.00
TS7 Anthony/Bosh/Wade 100.00 200.00
TS8 Parker/Wade/Billups 60.00 120.00
TS9 Williams/Birdsong/Rich 25.00 50.00
TS10 Thomas/Johnson/Stktn 100.00 200.00

2008-09 Topps Co-Signers

This set was released on November 28, 2008. The base set consists of 140 cards. Cards 1-100 feature veterans, and cards 101-140 are rookies serial numbered of 2008.

ROOKIE PRINT RUN 2008 SER.#'d SETS
UNPRICED HYP.PLAT.PRINT RUN ONE SET
UNPRICED PRESS PLATE PRINT RUN ONE SET
1 Tracy McGrady .50 1.25
2 Jason Kidd .50 1.25
3 Allen Iverson .60 1.50
4 Chris Bosh .50 1.25
5 Baron Davis .40 1.00
6 Chauncey Billups .50 1.25
7 Ben Gordon .40 1.00
8 Jermaine O'Neal .40 1.00
9 Jason Richardson .50 1.25
10 Gilbert Arenas .40 1.00
11 Jamal Crawford .50 1.25
12 Dwight Howard .40 1.00
13 Steve Nash .50 1.25
14 Vince Carter .60 1.50
15 Carmelo Anthony .60 1.50
16 Pau Gasol .50 1.25
17 Josh Smith .40 1.00
18 Yi Jianlian .50 1.25
19 Andre Iguodala .40 1.00
20 Ray Allen .50 1.25
21 Tim Duncan .75 2.00
22 Tayshaun Prince .40 1.00
23 LeBron James 2.00 5.00
24 Kobe Bryant 2.00 5.00
25 Rudy Gay .50 1.25
26 Caron Butler .40 1.00
27 Al Jefferson .40 1.00
28 Deron Williams .40 1.00
29 Luol Deng .40 1.00
30 Chris Paul .60 1.50
31 Brad Miller .40 1.00
32 Shaquille O'Neal 1.00 2.50
33 Dwyane Wade .75 2.00
34 Paul Pierce .50 1.25
35 Kevin Durant 1.25 3.00
36 Anderson Varejao .30 .75
37 Rashard Lewis .40 1.00
38 Jamario Moon .30 .75
39 Manu Ginobili .50 1.25
40 Mo Williams .40 1.00
41 Dirk Nowitzki .60 1.50
42 David Lee .30 .75
43 Stephen Jackson .40 1.00
44 Antawn Jamison .40 1.00
45 Mike Dunleavy .40 1.00
46 Devin Harris .30 .75
47 Andrei Kirilenko .40 1.00
48 Gerald Wallace .40 1.00
49 Mike Miller .40 1.00
50 Corey Maggette .40 1.00
51 Yao Ming .60 1.50
52 Greg Oden .40 1.00
53 Kevin Martin .40 1.00
54 Joe Johnson .40 1.00
55 Kevin Garnett .75 2.00
56 Ricky Davis .40 1.00
57 Chris Wilcox .30 .75
58 Rashad McCants .30 .75
59 T.J. Ford .30 .75
60 David West .40 1.00
61 Amare Stoudemire .40 1.00
62 Al Thornton .40 1.00
63 Kirk Hinrich .40 1.00
64 Samuel Dalembert .30 .75
65 Tony Parker .50 1.25
66 Ben Wallace .40 1.00
67 Shawn Marion .40 1.00
68 LaMarcus Aldridge .50 1.25
69 Eddy Curry .30 .75
70 Richard Hamilton .40 1.00
71 Danny Granger .40 1.00
72 Elton Brand .50 1.25
73 Raymond Felton .40 1.00
74 Richard Jefferson .40 1.00
75 Hedo Turkoglu .40 1.00
76 Peja Stojakovic .50 1.25
77 Brandon Roy .50 1.25
78 Ryan Gomes .30 .75
79 Jeff Green .40 1.00
80 Michael Redd .40 1.00
81 Andre Miller .40 1.00
82 Carlos Boozer .40 1.00
83 Marcus Camby .30 .75
84 Hakim Warrick .40 1.00
85 Mike Bibby .40 1.00
86 Josh Howard .40 1.00
87 Andrew Bynum .30 .75
88 Monta Ellis .40 1.00
89 Shane Battier .40 1.00
90 Ron Artest .50 1.25
91 Dennis Rodman 1.00 2.50
92 Dominique Wilkins .60 1.50
93 Larry Bird 1.25 3.00
94 John Stockton .75 2.00
95 Moses Malone .50 1.25
96 David Robinson .75 2.00
97 Jerry West .60 1.50
98 Bill Russell .75 2.00
99 George Gervin .60 1.50
100 Magic Johnson 1.25 3.00
101 Derrick Rose RC 4.00 10.00
102 Michael Beasley RC 1.00 2.50
103 O.J. Mayo RC 1.00 2.50
104 Russell Westbrook RC 8.00 20.00
105 Kevin Love RC 3.00 8.00
106 Danilo Gallinari RC 1.50 4.00
107 Eric Gordon RC 1.50 4.00
108 Joe Alexander RC .60 1.50
109 D.J. Augustin RC .75 2.00
110 Brook Lopez RC 1.25 3.00
111 Jerryd Bayless RC .75 2.00
112 Jason Thompson RC .60 1.50
113 Anthony Randolph RC .60 1.50
114 Robin Lopez RC 1.00 2.50
115 Marreese Speights RC .75 2.00
116 Roy Hibbert RC 1.00 2.50
117 JaVale McGee RC 1.25 3.00
118 J.J. Hickson RC .75 2.00
119 Alexis Ajinca RC .60 1.50
120 Ryan Anderson RC .75 2.00
121 Courtney Lee RC .75 2.00
122 Kosta Koufos RC .75 2.00
123 Donte Greene RC .60 1.50
124 George Hill RC 1.00 2.50
125 D.J. White RC .75 2.00
126 J.R. Giddens RC .60 1.50
127 Joey Dorsey RC .60 1.50
128 Mario Chalmers RC 1.00 2.50
129 DeAndre Jordan RC 1.25 3.00
130 Chris Douglas-Roberts RC .60 1.50
131 Malik Hairston RC .60 1.50
132 Sonny Weems RC .60 1.50
133 Kyle Weaver RC .60 1.50
134 Patrick Ewing Jr. RC .60 1.50
135 Mike Taylor RC .60 1.50
136 Walter Sharpe RC .60 1.50
137 Rudy Fernandez RC .75 2.00
138 Nicolas Batum RC 1.25 3.00
139 Brandon Rush RC .75 2.00
140 Darrell Arthur RC .75 2.00

2008-09 Topps Co-Signers Bronze

*1-100 BRONZE: .5X TO 1.25 BASE HI
*101-140 BRONZE: SAME AS BASE
BRONZE PRINT RUN 299 SER.#'d SETS
101 Derrick Rose 10.00 25.00

2008-09 Topps Co-Signers Gold

*1-100 GOLD: 1X TO 2.5X BASE HI
*101-140 GOLD: .75X TO 2X BASE HI
STATED PRINT RUN 99 SER.#'d SETS
101 Derrick Rose 20.00 50.00

2008-09 Topps Co-Signers Hyper Bronze

*1-100 HYP.BRNZ: 1.5X TO 4X BASE
*101-140 HYP.BRNZ: 1.25X TO 3X BASE
STATED PRINT RUN 50 SER.#'d SETS
23 LeBron James 15.00 40.00
24 Kobe Bryant 15.00 40.00

2008-09 Topps Co-Signers Hyper Silver

*1-100 HYP.SILV: 2X TO 5X BASE
*101-140 HYP.SILV: 1.5X TO 4X BASE
STATED PRINT RUN 25 SER.#'d SETS

2008-09 Topps Co-Signers Silver

*SILVER 1-100: .6X TO 1.5X BASE HI
*SILVER 101-140: .5X TO 1.25X BASE HI
STATED PRINT RUN 199 SER.#'d SETS
101 Derrick Rose 12.50 30.00

2008-09 Topps Co-Signers Changing Faces

STATED PRINT RUN 899 SER.#'d SETS
*BRONZE: .5X TO 1.25X BASE HI
BRONZE PRINT RUN 399 SER.#'d SETS
*GOLD: .6X TO 1.5X BASE HI
GOLD PRINT RUN 199 SER.#'d SETS
*SILVER: .75X TO 2X BASE HI
SILVER PRINT RUN 99 SER.#'d SETS
CF1 Tracy McGrady .60 1.50
CF2 Chris Bosh .60 1.50
CF3 Chauncey Billups .60 1.50
CF4 Gilbert Arenas .50 1.25
CF5 Dwight Howard .50 1.25
CF6 LeBron James 2.50 6.00
CF7 Kobe Bryant 2.50 6.00
CF8 Chris Paul .75 2.00
CF9 Paul Pierce .60 1.50
CF10 Kevin Durant 1.50 4.00
CF11 Dirk Nowitzki .75 2.00
CF12 Greg Oden .50 1.25
CF13 Tony Parker .60 1.50
CF14 Elton Brand .60 1.50
CF15 Brandon Roy .60 1.50
CF16 Carlos Boozer .50 1.25
CF17 Allen Iverson .75 2.00
CF18 Steve Nash .60 1.50
CF19 Vince Carter .75 2.00
CF20 Carmelo Anthony .75 2.00
CF21 Andre Iguodala .50 1.25
CF22 Ray Allen .60 1.50
CF23 Tim Duncan 1.00 2.50
CF24 Shaquille O'Neal 1.25 3.00
CF25 Dwyane Wade 1.00 2.50
CF26 Manu Ginobili .60 1.50
CF27 Yao Ming .75 2.00
CF28 Kevin Garnett 1.00 2.50
CF29 Amare Stoudemire .50 1.25
CF30 Michael Redd .50 1.25
CF31 Jason Kidd .60 1.50
CF32 Deron Williams .50 1.25
CF33 Kevin Martin .50 1.25
CF34 Joe Johnson .50 1.25
CF35 Richard Hamilton .50 1.25
CF36 Magic Johnson 1.50 4.00
CF37 Dominique Wilkins .75 2.00
CF38 Larry Bird 1.50 4.00
CF39 Jerry West .75 2.00
CF40 Bill Russell 1.00 2.50
CF41 Derrick Rose 2.50 6.00
CF42 Michael Beasley .60 1.50
CF43 O.J. Mayo .60 1.50
CF44 Russell Westbrook 5.00 12.00
CF45 Kevin Love 2.00 5.00
CF46 Brook Lopez .75 2.00
CF47 Eric Gordon 1.00 2.50
CF48 Joe Alexander .40 1.00
CF49 D.J. Augustin .50 1.25
CF50 Jerryd Bayless .50 1.25

2008-09 Topps Co-Signers Dual Autographs

GROUP A PRINT RUN 7 SER.#'d SETS
GROUP B PRINT RUN 43 SER.#'d SETS
GROUP C PRINT RUN 240 SER.#'d SETS
SOME UNPRICED DUE TO SCARCITY
UNPRICED GOLD PRINT RUN FIVE SETS
UNPRICED HYP.GOLD PRINT RUN 3 SETS
UNPRICED HYP.PLAT.PRINT RUN ONE SET
UNPRICED PRESS PLATE PRINT RUN ONE SET
CSAC D.Arthur/M.Chalmers C 8.00 20.00
CSBG A.Bargnani/D.Gallinari B 12.00 30.00
CSBJ C.Butler/A.Jamison C 8.00 20.00
CSBS E.Baylor/D.Schayes C 10.00 25.00
CSBT C.Billups/I.Thomas B 15.00 30.00
CSCB M.Chalmers/C.Boozer C 8.00 20.00
CSDG B.Davis/E.Gordon B 15.00 40.00
CSDM B.Davis/C.Maggette B 8.00 20.00
CSDRD C.Douglas-Roberts/J.Dorsey C 6.00 15.00
CSDT B.Davis/A.Thornton B 10.00 25.00
CSFA T.Ford/D.Augustin C 6.00 15.00
CSFG T.Ford/D.Granger B 8.00 20.00
CSFJ T.Ford/J.Jack C 6.00 15.00
CSGA B.Gordon/R.Allen B 12.50 30.00
CSGM R.Gay/J.Moon C 6.00 15.00
CSHB E.Hayes/R.Barry C 12.50 30.00
CSHE R.Hibbert/P.Ewing Jr. C 8.00 20.00
CSHT S.Hawes/J.Thompson C 8.00 20.00
CSHW J.Havlicek/J.White B 30.00 60.00
CSHWI D.Harris/S.Williams B 8.00 20.00
CSHWS J.Hickson/J.Williams C 8.00 20.00
CSIY A.Iguodala/T.Young B 6.00 15.00
CSJC Y.Jianlian/V.Carter B 25.00 50.00
CSLC D.Lee/W.Chandler C 6.00 15.00
CSLD C.Landry/J.Dorsey C 6.00 15.00
CSLJ A.Law/D.Jordan C 10.00 25.00
CSLL B.Lopez/R.Lopez C 8.00 20.00
CSLLO S.Love/K.Love B 10.00 25.00
CSLS D.Lee/M.Speights C 6.00 15.00
CSLW K.Love/R.Westbrook B 25.00 60.00
CSMG O.Mayo/R.Gay B 15.00 40.00
CSML M.Miller/K.Love B 15.00 40.00
CSMM P.McGee/J.McGee C 6.00 15.00
CSMS M.Miller/M.Speights C 6.00 15.00
CSMY O.Mayo/N.Young B 20.00 40.00
CSPE R.Parish/M.Eaton C 8.00 20.00
CSPW M.Pietrus/G.Wallace C 6.00 15.00
CSRB D.Rose/M.Beasley B 100.00 200.00
CSRD D.Rose/L.Deng B 75.00 150.00
CSRH B.Rush/R.Hibbert C 8.00 20.00
CSSS D.Schayes/D.Schayes C 6.00 15.00
CSSY R.Stuckey/N.Young B 8.00 20.00
CSTG A.Thornton/E.Gordon B 6.00 15.00
CSTH J.Thompson/G.Hill C 8.00 20.00
CSWC D.Wilkins/V.Carter B 25.00 50.00
CSWL S.Webb/F.Lever C 8.00 20.00

2008-09 Topps Co-Signers Rookie Autographs

GROUP A PRINT RUN 50 SER.#'d SETS
GROUP B PRINT RUN 100 SER.#'d SETS
GROUP C PRINT RUN 350 SER.#'d SETS
*GOLD: .75X TO 2X BASE HI
GOLD PRINT RUN 5 TO 25 SETS
UNPRICED HYP.PLAT PRINT RUN ONE SET
UNPRICED HYP.SIL.PRINT RUN 10 SETS
UNPRICED PRESS PLATE PRINT RUN ONE SET
101 Derrick Rose A 125.00 250.00
102 Michael Beasley A 4.00 10.00
103 O.J. Mayo A 4.00 10.00
104 Russell Westbrook B 75.00 200.00
105 Kevin Love A 25.00 60.00
106 Danilo Gallinari B 6.00 15.00
107 Eric Gordon A 12.00 30.00
108 Joe Alexander B 2.50 6.00
109 D.J. Augustin C 3.00 8.00
110 Brook Lopez B 5.00 12.00
111 Jerryd Bayless B 3.00 8.00
112 Jason Thompson C 2.50 6.00
113 Anthony Randolph C 2.50 6.00
114 Robin Lopez C 4.00 10.00
115 Marreese Speights C 3.00 8.00
116 Roy Hibbert C 4.00 10.00
117 JaVale McGee C 5.00 12.00
118 J.J. Hickson C 3.00 8.00
120 Ryan Anderson C 3.00 8.00
121 Courtney Lee C 3.00 8.00
122 Kosta Koufos C 3.00 8.00
123 Donte Greene C 2.50 6.00
124 George Hill C 4.00 10.00
125 D.J. White C 3.00 8.00
126 J.R. Giddens C 2.50 6.00
127 Joey Dorsey C 2.50 6.00
128 Mario Chalmers C 4.00 10.00
130 Chris Douglas-Roberts C 2.50 6.00
139 Brandon Rush B 3.00 8.00
140 Darrell Arthur C 3.00 8.00

2008-09 Topps Co-Signers Rookie Photo Shoot Quad Autographs

ANNOUNCED PRINT RUN 25 SETS
UNPRICED RED INK EXISTS
RPQABRM Agstn/Byls/Rse/Myo 50.00 120.00
RPQBLGA Bsly/Lve/Lpz/Alxndr 30.00 80.00
RPQBLRM Bsly/Lve/Rose/Myo 100.00 250.00
RPQRARD Rsh/Arthr/Rse/Dgls-Rbt 50.00 120.00
RPQRMWG Rse/Myo/Wstbk/Grdn 200.00 400.00

2008-09 Topps Co-Signers Triple Autographs

STATED PRINT RUN 36 SER.#'d SETS
UNPRICED HYP.PLAT.PRINT RUN ONE SET
UNPRICED PRESS PLATE PRINT RUN ONE SET
TSBLG Bsly/Love/Gallinari 50.00 100.00
TSGAB Gordon/Agstn/Bylss 20.00 50.00
TSGAR Gallinari/Alxndr/Rndlph 20.00 50.00
TSGGA Gallinari/Grdn/Alxndr 20.00 50.00
TSLTR Lpz/Thmpsn/Rndlph 20.00 50.00
TSMLB Mayo/Love/Bayless 40.00 100.00
TSRBM Rose/Beasley/Mayo 40.00 100.00
TSRGA Rose/Gordon/Agstn 100.00 250.00
TSRMB Rose/Mayo/Bayless 75.00 150.00
TSWLL Wstbrk/Love/Lopez 50.00 120.00

2008 Topps Draft Day Autographs

DDBL Brook Lopez/50 40.00 100.00
DDDR Derrick Rose/100 250.00 500.00
DDEG Eric Gordon/50 50.00 125.00
DDJB Jerryd Bayless/50 30.00 80.00
DDKL Kevin Love/50 75.00 200.00
DDMB Michael Beasley/100 40.00 100.00
DDOM O.J. Mayo/100 40.00 100.00

2007-08 Topps Echelon

This 85-card set was released in December, 2007. The set was issued into the hobby in four-card packs (mini-boxes) with an $125 SRP which came four to a full box. There were three full boxes to a carton and two cartons to a case. Cards numbered 1-40 feature veterans, while cards numbered 41-50 feature retired greats and cards numbered 51-85 feature NBA rookies. Every card in this set was serial numbered and the serial numbering was done thusly: Cards numbered 1-50 had a stated print run of 999 serial numbered sets, cards 51-54 were issued to a stated print run of 199 serial numbered sets, cards 55-62 had a stated print run of 399 serial numbered sets, cards 63-72 had a stated print run of 499 serial numbered sets and the set concludes with cards 73-85 which had a stated print run of 999 serial numbered sets.

55-62 RC PRINT RUN 399 SER.#'d SETS
63-72 RC PRINT RUN 499 SER.#'d SETS
73-85 RC PRINT RUN 999 SER.#'d SETS
1 Tracy McGrady 1.25 3.00
2 Chris Paul 1.50 4.00
3 Dwyane Wade 2.00 5.00
4 Elton Brand 1.25 3.00
5 Josh Smith 1.00 2.50
6 Brandon Roy 1.25 3.00
7 Andrea Bargnani 1.25 3.00
8 Deron Williams 1.00 2.50
9 Andre Iguodala 1.00 2.50
10 Mike Bibby 1.25 3.00
11 Yao Ming 1.50 4.00
12 Dwight Howard 1.00 2.50
13 Steve Nash 1.50 4.00
14 Randy Foye 1.25 3.00
15 Carmelo Anthony 1.50 4.00
16 Pau Gasol 1.25 3.00
17 Jermaine O'Neal 1.00 2.50
18 Ben Gordon 1.00 2.50
19 Vince Carter 1.50 4.00
20 Tim Duncan 2.00 5.00
21 Kevin Garnett 2.00 5.00
22 Michael Redd 1.00 2.50
23 LeBron James 5.00 12.00
24 Kobe Bryant 5.00 12.00
25 Chris Webber 1.25 3.00
26 Allen Iverson 1.50 4.00
27 Chauncey Billups 1.25 3.00
28 Paul Pierce 1.25 3.00
29 Amare Stoudemire 1.00 2.50
30 Emeka Okafor 1.00 2.50
31 Jason Kidd 1.25 3.00
32 Shaquille O'Neal 2.50 6.00
33 Grant Hill 1.50 4.00
34 Ray Allen 1.25 3.00
35 Adam Morrison .75 2.00
36 Gilbert Arenas 1.00 2.50
37 Baron Davis 1.00 2.50
38 Mike Miller 1.00 2.50
39 Chris Bosh 1.25 3.00
40 Dirk Nowitzki 1.50 4.00
41 Bob Pettit 2.00 5.00
42 Bill Russell 2.50 6.00
43 Rick Barry 1.25 3.00
44 Oscar Robertson 1.50 4.00
45 Jerry Lucas 1.50 4.00
46 Magic Johnson 4.00 10.00
47 Larry Bird 4.00 10.00
48 Wes Unseld 1.50 4.00
49 James Worthy 2.00 5.00
50 Bob McAdoo 1.25 3.00
51 Greg Oden RC 5.00 12.00
52 Yi Jianlian RC 6.00 15.00
53 Brandan Wright RC 5.00 12.00
54 Nick Young RC 6.00 15.00
55 Spencer Hawes RC 3.00 8.00
56 Acie Law RC 2.50 6.00
57 Rodney Stuckey RC 3.00 8.00
58 Al Thornton RC 3.00 8.00
59 Arron Afflalo RC 4.00 10.00
60 Marco Belinelli RC 4.00 10.00
61 Gabe Pruitt RC 2.50 6.00
62 Wilson Chandler RC 3.00 8.00
63 Jared Dudley RC 3.00 8.00
64 Marcus Williams RC 2.50 6.00
65 Aaron Brooks RC 3.00 8.00
66 Daequan Cook RC 3.00 8.00
67 Thaddeus Young RC 4.00 10.00
68 Josh McRoberts RC 3.00 8.00
69 Nick Fazekas RC 2.50 6.00
70 Javaris Crittenton RC 2.50 6.00
71 Alando Tucker RC 2.50 6.00
72 Carl Landry RC 2.50 6.00
73 Al Horford RC 4.00 10.00
74 Kevin Durant RC 20.00 50.00
75 Corey Brewer RC 3.00 8.00
76 Jeff Green RC 3.00 8.00
77 Mike Conley Jr. RC 4.00 10.00
78 Joakim Noah RC 3.00 8.00
79 Sean Williams RC 2.00 5.00
80 Julian Wright RC 2.00 5.00
81 Reyshawn Terry RC 2.00 5.00
82 Aaron Gray RC 2.00 5.00
83 Glen Davis RC 2.50 6.00
84 Jermareo Davidson RC 2.00 5.00
85 Taurean Green RC 2.00 5.00

2007-08 Topps Echelon Blue

*1-50 BLUE: 1.25X TO 3X BASE HI
1-50 BLUE PRINT RUN 25 SER.#'d SETS
51-85 BLUE PRINT RUN 10 SER.#'d SETS
51-85 BLUE UNPRICED DUE TO SCARCITY

2007-08 Topps Echelon Red

*1-40 RED: .75X TO 2X BASE HI
*41-50 RED: .6X TO 1.5X BASE HI
1-50 PRINT RUN 50 SER.#'d SETS
*51-85 RC RED: .75X TO 2X BASE HI
51-85 PRINT RUN 25 SER.#'d SETS
74 Kevin Durant 100.00 200.00

2007-08 Topps Echelon Autographs

PRINT RUN 99 SER.#'d SETS
*RELICS: .5X TO 1.25X BASE HI
RELIC PRINT RUN 99 TO 199 SETS
*RELICS GOLD: .6X TO 1.5X BASE HI
RELICS GOLD PRINT RUN 25 TO 50 SETS
UNPRICED GOLD PRINT RUN 10 SER.#'d SETS
UNPRICED LOGO PRINT RUN ONE SET
UNPRICED PATCH PRINT RUN 10 SER.#'d SETS
AI Andre Iguodala/99 4.00 10.00
AM Adam Morrison/99 3.00 8.00
BD Baron Davis/99 8.00 20.00
BG Ben Gordon/99 4.00 10.00
BL Bob Love/99 10.00 25.00
BR Bill Russell/50 50.00 120.00
BW Bill Walton/99 10.00 25.00
CA Carmelo Anthony/99 12.00 30.00
CB Chris Bosh/50 10.00 25.00
CBI Chauncey Billups/50 5.00 12.00
CBO Carlos Boozer/99 4.00 10.00
CM Corey Maggette/99 4.00 10.00
DEW Deron Williams/99 4.00 10.00
DR Dennis Rodman/99 20.00 50.00
DRO David Robinson/99 15.00 40.00
DW Dwyane Wade/99 15.00 40.00
DWI Dominique Wilkins/99 12.00 30.00
EM Earl Monroe/50 12.00 30.00
EO Emeka Okafor/99 4.00 10.00
GW Gerald Wallace/99 4.00 10.00
IT Isiah Thomas/99 8.00 20.00
JF Jordan Farmar/99 3.00 8.00
JH Josh Howard/99 4.00 10.00
JJR J.J. Redick/99 6.00 15.00
JO Jermaine O'Neal/99 6.00 15.00
JS Josh Smith/99 4.00 10.00
JST John Stockton/99 25.00 60.00
KH Kirk Hinrich/99 4.00 10.00
LB Larry Bird/50 50.00 120.00
LE Len Elmore/99 10.00 25.00
MB Manute Bol/99 20.00 40.00
MJ Magic Johnson/50 40.00 80.00
RA Ray Allen/99 12.00 30.00
RB Rick Barry/99 10.00 25.00
RF Randy Foye/99 5.00 12.00
RT Rudy Tomjanovich/99 10.00 25.00
SO Shaquille O'Neal/50 30.00 80.00
TJF T.J. Ford/99 5.00 12.00
TP Tony Parker/99 10.00 25.00
VC Vince Carter/50 10.00 25.00

2007-08 Topps Echelon McDonald's All-American Autographs

PRINT RUN 100 SER.#'d SETS
BW Brandan Wright 10.00 25.00
DC Daequan Cook 10.00 25.00
GO Greg Oden 15.00 40.00
JC Javaris Crittenton 10.00 25.00
TY Thaddeus Young 10.00 25.00

2007-08 Topps Echelon McDonald's All-American Autographs Five-Piece Relics

PRINT RUN 75 SER.#'d SETS
GAME/NAME LETTER CARDS #'d ONE OF ONE
GAME/NAME UNPRICED DUE TO SCARCITY
BW Brandan Wright 12.00 30.00
DC Daequan Cook 12.00 30.00
GO Greg Oden 12.00 30.00
JC Javaris Crittenton 12.00 30.00
SH Spencer Hawes 12.00 30.00
TY Thaddeus Young 12.00 30.00

2007-08 Topps Echelon McDonald's All-American Autographs Super Size Patches

PRINT RUN 25 SER.#'d SETS
BW Brandan Wright 30.00 80.00
DC Daequan Cook 30.00 80.00
JC Javaris Crittenton 30.00 80.00
SH Spencer Hawes 30.00 80.00
TY Thaddeus Young 30.00 80.00

2007-08 Topps Echelon Rookie Autographs

PRINT RUN 499 SER.#'d SETS
*GOLD: .5X TO 1.25X BASE HI
GOLD PRINT RUN 50 SER.#'d SETS
63 Jared Dudley 5.00 12.00
64 Marcus Williams 4.00 10.00
65 Aaron Brooks 5.00 12.00
66 Daequan Cook 5.00 12.00
67 Thaddeus Young 6.00 15.00
68 Josh McRoberts 5.00 12.00
69 Nick Fazekas 4.00 10.00
70 Javaris Crittenton 4.00 10.00
71 Alando Tucker 4.00 10.00
72 Carl Landry 4.00 10.00

2007-08 Topps Echelon Rookie Autographs Dual Relics

PRINT RUN 399 SER.#'d SETS
*GOLD: .6X TO 1.5X BASE HI
GOLD PRINT RUN 50 SER.#'d SETS
PATCHES: .75X TO 2X BASE HI
PATCH PRINT RUN 50 SER.#'d SETS
UNPRICED PATCH GOLD PRINT RUN 5 SETS
55 Spencer Hawes 5.00 12.00
56 Acie Law 4.00 10.00
57 Rodney Stuckey 5.00 12.00
58 Al Thornton 5.00 12.00
59 Arron Afflalo 6.00 15.00
60 Marco Belinelli 6.00 15.00
61 Gabe Pruitt 4.00 10.00
62 Wilson Chandler 5.00 12.00

2007-08 Topps Echelon Rookie Autographs Quad Relics

PRINT RUN 199 SER.#'d SETS
*GOLD: .5X TO 1.25X BASE HI
GOLD PRINT RUN 50 SER.#'d SETS
51 Greg Oden 12.00 30.00
52 Yi Jianlian 15.00 40.00
53 Brandan Wright 12.00 30.00
54 Nick Young 8.00 20.00

2007-08 Topps Echelon Rookie Autographs Quad Patches

PRINT RUN 25 SER.#'d SETS
UNPRICED GOLD PRINT RUN FIVE SETS
51 Greg Oden 125.00 250.00
52 Yi Jianlian 50.00 120.00
53 Brandan Wright 40.00 100.00
54 Nick Young 50.00 125.00

2005-06 Topps First Row

This 150-card set was released in January, 2006. The set was issued in 16-pack boxes which cames six boxes to a case. Each pack had three base cards plus one card which was either a serial numbered autograph, relic, autograph relic, parallel or insert card. Cards numbered 101 through 150 were issued to a stated print run of 549 serial numbered sets. Initial pack SRP was $6.99.

RC PRINT RUN 549 SER.#'d SETS
CELEB.PRINT RUN 549 SER.#'d SETS
1 Shaquille O'Neal 1.00 2.50
2 Marcus Camby .40 1.00
3 Caron Butler .40 1.00
4 Carlos Boozer .40 1.00
5 Peja Stojakovic .50 1.25
6 Chris Webber .50 1.25
7 Vince Carter .75 2.00
8 Bobby Simmons .30 .75
9 Pau Gasol .50 1.25
10 Stromile Swift .30 .75
11 Carmelo Anthony 1.00 2.50
12 Drew Gooden .40 1.00
13 Al Harrington .40 1.00
14 Emeka Okafor .40 1.00
15 Gilbert Arenas .40 1.00
16 Tony Parker .50 1.25
17 Steve Nash .60 1.50
18 Jamal Crawford .50 1.25
19 Troy Hudson .30 .75
20 Kobe Bryant 2.00 5.00
21 Tracy McGrady .60 1.50
22 Chauncey Billups .50 1.25
23 Devin Harris .30 .75
24 Brevin Knight .30 .75
25 Joe Johnson .40 1.00
26 Nenad Krstic .30 .75
27 Primoz Brezec .30 .75
28 Mehmet Okur .30 .75
29 Shareef Abdur-Rahim .40 1.00
30 Amare Stoudemire .40 1.00
31 Quentin Richardson .40 1.00
32 Kevin Garnett .75 2.00
33 Shane Battier .40 1.00
34 Elton Brand .50 1.25
35 Kenyon Martin .40 1.00
36 LeBron James 2.00 5.00
37 Al Jefferson .40 1.00
38 Jermaine O'Neal .40 1.00
39 Ron Artest .50 1.25
40 Luke Ridnour .40 1.00
41 Sebastian Telfair .40 1.00
42 Steve Francis .40 1.00
43 Jason Kidd .75 2.00
44 Ben Wallace .40 1.00
45 Mike Miller .40 1.00
46 Jamaal Tinsley .30 .75
47 Richard Hamilton .40 1.00
48 Jerry Stackhouse .40 1.00
49 Kirk Hinrich .40 1.00
50 Josh Childress .40 1.00
51 Jamaal Magloire .30 .75
52 Yao Ming .60 1.50
53 Tyson Chandler .40 1.00
54 Andrei Kirilenko .40 1.00
55 Rashard Lewis .50 1.25
56 Shawn Marion .40 1.00
57 Grant Hill .60 1.50
58 Wally Szczerbiak .40 1.00
59 Antoine Walker .40 1.00
60 Corey Maggette .40 1.00
61 Rasheed Wallace .50 1.25
62 Dirk Nowitzki .75 2.00
63 Paul Pierce .50 1.25
64 Tim Duncan .75 2.00
65 Desmond Mason .30 .75
66 Ray Allen .50 1.25
67 Mike Bibby .50 1.25
68 Andre Iguodala .40 1.00
69 J.R. Smith .40 1.00
70 Dwyane Wade .75 2.00
71 Shaun Livingston .30 .75
72 Jason Richardson .50 1.25
73 Earl Boykins .30 .75
74 Ben Gordon .40 1.00
75 Stephen Jackson .40 1.00
76 Samuel Dalembert .30 .75
77 Kwame Brown .30 .75
78 Zydrunas Ilgauskas .40 1.00
79 Antawn Jamison .40 1.00
80 Chris Bosh .50 1.25
81 Zach Randolph .40 1.00
82 Dwight Howard .40 1.00
83 Richard Jefferson .40 1.00
84 Udonis Haslem .30 .75
85 Lamar Odom .40 1.00
86 Mike Dunleavy .40 1.00
87 Josh Howard .50 1.25
88 Luol Deng .40 1.00
89 Josh Smith .40 1.00
90 Jalen Rose .50 1.25
91 Rafer Alston .30 .75
92 Manu Ginobili .50 1.25
93 Allen Iverson .75 2.00
94 Stephon Marbury .40 1.00
95 Michael Redd .40 1.00
96 Sam Cassell .40 1.00
97 Baron Davis .40 1.00
98 Andre Miller .40 1.00
99 Larry Hughes .40 1.00
100 Ricky Davis .40 1.00
101 Nate Robinson RC 2.00 5.00
102 Danny Granger RC 2.50 6.00
103 Marvin Williams RC 2.00 5.00
104 Rashad McCants RC 2.00 5.00
105 Jarrett Jack RC 2.00 5.00
106 Andrew Bogut RC 2.50 6.00
107 Ike Diogu RC 1.25 3.00
108 Chris Paul RC 8.00 20.00
109 Julius Hodge RC 1.25 3.00
110 C.J. Miles RC 2.00 5.00
111 Francisco Garcia RC 1.50 4.00
112 Channing Frye RC 2.00 5.00
113 Deron Williams RC 2.50 6.00
114 Hakim Warrick RC 1.50 4.00
115 Salim Stoudamire RC 1.50 4.00
116 Raymond Felton RC 2.00 5.00
117 Joey Graham RC 1.50 4.00
118 Wayne Simien RC 1.25 3.00
119 David Lee RC 2.00 5.00
120 Luther Head RC 1.50 4.00
121 Andrew Bynum RC 1.50 4.00
122 Monta Ellis RC 2.50 6.00
123 Brandon Bass RC 1.50 4.00
124 Antoine Wright RC 1.50 4.00
125 Gerald Green RC 2.00 5.00
126 Charlie Villanueva RC 2.00 5.00
127 Chris Taft RC 1.50 4.00
128 Sarunas Jasikevicius RC 2.00 5.00
129 Sean May RC 1.25 3.00
130 Martell Webster RC 1.50 4.00
131 Yaroslav Korolev RC 1.25 3.00
132 Eddie Basden RC 1.25 3.00
133 Ersan Ilyasova RC 2.00 5.00
134 Martynas Andriuskevicius RC 1.25 3.00
135 Orien Greene RC 1.50 4.00
136 Johan Petro RC 1.25 3.00
137 Linas Kleiza RC 1.25 3.00
138 Daniel Ewing RC 1.50 4.00
139 Fabricio Oberto RC 1.50 4.00
140 Travis Diener RC 1.25 3.00
141 Ryan Gomes RC 1.50 4.00
142 Andray Blatche RC 2.00 5.00
143 Louis Williams RC 2.00 5.00
144 Jose Calderon RC 2.00 5.00

145 Robert Whaley RC 1.25 3.00
146 Jay-Z 4.00 10.00
147 Carmen Electra 4.00 10.00
148 Christie Brinkley 4.00 10.00
149 Shannon Elizabeth 4.00 10.00
150 Jenny McCarthy 4.00 10.00

2005-06 Topps First Row 325

*1-100: .6X TO 1.5X BASE HI
*101-150: .5X TO 1.25X BASE HI
PRINT RUN 325 SER.#'d SETS

2005-06 Topps First Row 100

*ROW 100 VETS: 1.5X TO 4X BASE HI
*ROW 100 RCs: .75X TO 2X BASE HI
*ROW 100 CELEBS: .6X TO 1.5X BASE HI
ROW 100 PRINT RUN 100 SER.#'d SETS
20 Kobe Bryant 15.00 40.00

2005-06 Topps First Row Black and White

*BLACK/WHITE: .6X TO 1.5X BASE HI
STATED PRINT RUN 225 SER.#'d SETS

2005-06 Topps First Row Sepia

*SEPIA VETS: 5X TO 12X BASE HI
*SEPIA RCs: 1.5X TO 4X BASE HI
*SEPIA CELEB: 1.25X TO 3X BASE HI
STATED PRINT RUN 25 SER.'d SETS

2005-06 Topps First Row Alley Oop Dual Relics

These six card, each of which feature two jersey pieces, were issued to a stated print run of 200 serial numbered sets.
PRINT RUN 200 SER.#'d SETS
AB C.Anthony/E.Boykins 6.00 15.00
AJ G.Arenas/A.Jamison 5.00 12.00
FO R.Felton/E.Okafor 5.00 12.00
HC K.Hinrich/T.Chandler 5.00 12.00
NS S.Nash/A.Stoudemire 6.00 15.00
PS C.Paul/J.R. Smith 6.00 15.00

2005-06 Topps First Row Baseline

This set, issued as an insert, was issued to a stated print run of 149 serial numbered sets.
PRINT RUN 149 SER.#'d SETS
*BASELINE 99: .5X TO 1.25X BASE HI
*BASE.99 PRINT RUN 99 SER.#'d SETS
BASE.10 NOT PRICED DUE TO SCARCITY
1 Baron Davis 1.00 2.50
2 Dwyane Wade 2.00 5.00
3 Allen Iverson 2.00 5.00
4 Ben Gordon 1.00 2.50
5 Andre Miller 1.00 2.50
6 Mike Bibby 1.25 3.00
7 Jason Kidd 2.00 5.00
8 Shaun Livingston .75 2.00
9 Steve Francis 1.00 2.50
10 Steve Nash 1.50 4.00
11 Luke Ridnour 1.00 2.50
12 T.J. Ford .75 2.00
13 Stephon Marbury 1.00 2.50
14 Brevin Knight .75 2.00
15 Jamaal Tinsley .75 2.00
16 Rafer Alston .75 2.00
17 Damon Jones .75 2.00
18 Chauncey Billups 1.25 3.00
19 Kirk Hinrich 1.00 2.50
20 Devin Harris .75 2.00
21 Tony Parker 1.25 3.00
22 Jason Williams 1.00 2.50
23 Troy Hudson .75 2.00
24 Deron Williams 1.50 4.00
25 Chris Paul 5.00 12.00
26 Tracy McGrady 1.50 4.00
27 Earl Boykins .75 2.00
28 Marcus Banks .75 2.00
29 Gilbert Arenas 1.00 2.50
30 Jamal Crawford 1.25 3.00
31 Larry Hughes 1.00 2.50
32 Jarrett Jack 1.25 3.00
33 Kobe Bryant 5.00 12.00
34 Damon Stoudamire 1.00 2.50
35 Jameer Nelson .75 2.00
36 Raymond Felton 1.25 3.00
37 Tyronn Lue .75 2.00
38 Manu Ginobili 1.25 3.00
39 Rashad McCants 1.00 2.50
40 Andre Iguodala 1.00 2.50
41 Carlos Arroyo .75 2.00
42 Jason Terry 1.00 2.50
43 Nate Robinson 1.25 3.00
44 Luther Head 1.00 2.50
45 Joe Johnson 1.00 2.50
46 Vince Carter 2.00 5.00
47 Monta Ellis 1.50 4.00
48 Sebastian Telfair 1.00 2.50
49 Cuttino Mobley .75 2.00
50 J.R. Smith 1.00 2.50

2005-06 Topps First Row Center Court

Randomly inserted into packs, this is an insert to the First Row set and was issued to a stated print run of 149 serial numbered sets.
PRINT RUN 149 SER.#'d SETS
*CENTER 99: .5X TO 1.25X BASE HI
CENT.99 PRINT RUN 99 SER.#'d SETS
CENT.10 NOT PRICED DUE TO SCARCITY
1 Jason Kidd 2.00 5.00
2 Richard Hamilton 1.00 2.50
3 Manu Ginobili 1.25 3.00
4 Elton Brand 1.25 3.00
5 Jason Richardson 1.25 3.00
6 Emeka Okafor 1.00 2.50
7 Shawn Marion 1.00 2.50
8 Ben Gordon 1.00 2.50
9 Gilbert Arenas 1.00 2.50
10 Jermaine O'Neal 1.00 2.50
11 Ben Wallace 1.00 2.50
12 LeBron James 5.00 12.00
13 Allen Iverson 2.00 5.00
14 Dirk Nowitzki 2.00 5.00
15 Tracy McGrady 1.50 4.00
16 Steve Nash 1.50 4.00
17 Vince Carter 2.00 5.00
18 Carmelo Anthony 2.50 6.00
19 Kobe Bryant 5.00 12.00
20 Kevin Garnett 2.00 5.00
21 Tim Duncan 2.00 5.00
22 Stephon Marbury 1.00 2.50
23 Kirk Hinrich 1.00 2.50
24 Amare Stoudemire 1.00 2.50
25 Steve Francis 1.00 2.50
26 Yao Ming 1.50 4.00
27 Jamal Crawford 1.25 3.00
28 Ray Allen 1.25 3.00
29 Paul Pierce 1.25 3.00
30 Dwyane Wade 2.00 5.00
31 Corey Maggette 1.00 2.50
32 Rashard Lewis 1.25 3.00
33 Chris Bosh 1.25 3.00
34 Mike Bibby 1.25 3.00
35 Antoine Walker 1.00 2.50
36 Tony Parker 1.25 3.00
37 Kenyon Martin 1.00 2.50
38 Michael Redd 1.00 2.50
39 Baron Davis 1.00 2.50
40 Al Harrington 1.00 2.50
41 Jalen Rose 1.25 3.00
42 Antawn Jamison 1.00 2.50
43 Andre Miller 1.00 2.50
44 Rafer Alston .75 2.00
45 Jason Terry 1.00 2.50
46 Pau Gasol 1.25 3.00
47 Andrei Kirilenko 1.00 2.50
48 Rasheed Wallace 1.25 3.00
49 Richard Jefferson 1.00 2.50
50 Shaquille O'Neal 2.50 6.00

2005-06 Topps First Row Charity Stripe

Randomly inserted into packs, this is an insert in the First Row product. Each of these cards were issued to a stated print run of 149 serial numbered sets.
PRINT RUN 149 SER.#'d SETS
*STRIPE 99: .5X TO 1.25X BASE HI
STRIP.99 PRINT RUN 99 SER.#'d SETS
STRIP.10 UNPRICED DUE TO SCARCITY
1 Earl Boykins .75 2.00
2 Peja Stojakovic 1.25 3.00
3 Damon Stoudamire 1.00 2.50
4 Chauncey Billups 1.25 3.00
5 Steve Nash 1.50 4.00
6 Ray Allen 1.25 3.00
7 Austin Croshere .75 2.00
8 Dirk Nowitzki 2.00 5.00
9 Sam Cassell 1.00 2.50
10 Ben Gordon 1.00 2.50
11 Caron Butler 1.00 2.50
12 Derek Fisher 1.00 2.50
13 David Wesley .75 2.00
14 Wally Szczerbiak 1.00 2.50
15 Michael Redd 1.00 2.50
16 Jalen Rose 1.25 3.00
17 Fred Jones .75 2.00
18 Brian Cardinal .75 2.00
19 Danny Fortson .75 2.00
20 Shareef Abdur-Rahim 1.00 2.50
21 Corey Maggette 1.00 2.50
22 Mehmet Okur .75 2.00
23 Josh Childress 1.00 2.50
24 Shawn Marion 1.00 2.50
25 Hedo Turkoglu 1.00 2.50
26 Jerry Stackhouse 1.00 2.50
27 Bobby Simmons .75 2.00
28 Jamal Crawford 1.25 3.00
29 Marvin Williams 1.25 3.00
30 Richard Hamilton 1.00 2.50
31 Luke Ridnour 1.00 2.50
32 Julius Hodge .75 2.00
33 Danny Granger 1.50 4.00
34 Gerald Green 1.25 3.00
35 Francisco Garcia 1.00 2.50
36 Daniel Ewing 1.00 2.50
37 Antoine Wright 1.00 2.50
38 Martell Webster 1.00 2.50
39 Morris Peterson .75 2.00
40 Andrew Bogut 1.50 4.00
41 Salim Stoudamire 1.00 2.50
42 Paul Pierce 1.25 3.00
43 Sean May .75 2.00
44 Kobe Bryant 5.00 12.00
45 Grant Hill 1.50 4.00
46 P.J. Brown .75 2.00
47 Dan Dickau .75 2.00
48 Richard Jefferson 1.00 2.50
49 Stephen Jackson 1.00 2.50
50 Wayne Simien .75 2.00

2005-06 Topps First Row Direct Effect Relics

This is an insert in the First Row product. Each of these cards were issued to a stated print run of 200 serial numbered sets.
PRINT RUN 200 SER.#'d SETS
UNPRICED AUTO PRINT RUN 10 SETS
AI Allen Iverson 4.00 10.00
CP Chris Paul 10.00 25.00
DH Devin Harris 1.50 4.00
DW Dwyane Wade 4.00 10.00
EB Earl Boykins 2.00 5.00
ES Eric Snow 2.00 5.00
GA Gilbert Arenas 2.00 5.00
KH Kirk Hinrich 2.00 5.00
LR Luke Ridnour 2.00 5.00
MB Mike Bibby 2.50 6.00
RA Rafer Alston 2.00 5.00
RF Raymond Felton 2.50 6.00
SF Steve Francis 2.00 5.00
SL Shaun Livingston 2.00 5.00
SN Steve Nash 3.00 8.00
TM Tracy McGrady 3.00 8.00
DWI Deron Williams 3.00 8.00
TJF T.J. Ford 1.50 4.00

2005-06 Topps First Row In The Post

This is an insert to the First Row set. Each of these cards were issued to a stated print run of 149 serial numbered sets.
PRINT RUN 149 SER.#'d SETS
*POST 99: .5X TO 1.25X BASE HI
POST 99 PRINT RUN 99 SER.#'d SETS
POST 10 NOT PRICED DUE TO SCARCITY
1 Elton Brand 1.25 3.00
2 Emeka Okafor 1.00 2.50
3 Jermaine O'Neal 1.00 2.50
4 Ben Wallace 1.00 2.50
5 Dirk Nowitzki 2.00 5.00
6 Kevin Garnett 2.00 5.00
7 Tim Duncan 2.00 5.00
8 Amare Stoudemire 1.00 2.50
9 Yao Ming 1.50 4.00
10 Chris Bosh 1.25 3.00
11 Andrew Bogut 1.50 4.00
12 Zydrunas Ilgauskas 1.00 2.50
13 Pau Gasol 1.25 3.00
14 Shaquille O'Neal 2.50 6.00
15 Marcus Camby 1.00 2.50
16 Antawn Jamison 1.00 2.50
17 Charlie Villanueva 1.25 3.00
18 Carlos Boozer 1.00 2.50
19 Lamar Odom 1.00 2.50
20 Channing Frye 1.25 3.00
21 Zach Randolph 1.00 2.50
22 Carmelo Anthony 2.50 6.00
23 Ike Diogu .75 2.00
24 Chris Webber 1.25 3.00
25 Andrew Bynum 1.00 2.50
26 Sean May .75 2.00
27 Wayne Simien .75 2.00
28 Drew Gooden 1.00 2.50
29 Rasheed Wallace 1.25 3.00
30 Troy Murphy .75 2.00
31 Marvin Williams 1.25 3.00
32 Jason Kidd 2.00 5.00
33 Steve Francis 1.00 2.50
34 Tracy McGrady 1.50 4.00
35 Dwyane Wade 2.00 5.00
36 Quentin Richardson 1.00 2.50
37 Corey Maggette 1.00 2.50
38 Kobe Bryant 5.00 12.00
39 Paul Pierce 1.25 3.00
40 Jalen Rose 1.25 3.00
41 Danny Granger 1.50 4.00
42 Michael Finley 1.25 3.00
43 Tayshaun Prince 1.00 2.50
44 Kenyon Martin 1.00 2.50
45 Brad Miller 1.00 2.50
46 Joey Graham 1.00 2.50
47 Jason Maxiell 1.00 2.50
48 Primoz Brezec .75 2.00
49 Nenad Krstic .75 2.00
50 Ron Artest 1.25 3.00

2005-06 Topps First Row Pick n Roll Relics

Randomly inserted into packs, these six cards feature game-used jersey swatches from teammates. Each of these cards were issued to a stated print run of 200 serial numbered sets.
PRINT RUN 200 SER.#'d SETS
AL R.Allen/R.Lewis 5.00 12.00
BL E.Brand/S.Livingston 5.00 12.00
BW C.Boozer/D.Williams 6.00 15.00
GD M.Ginobili/T.Duncan 6.00 15.00
MM T.McGrady/Y.Ming 6.00 15.00
OW S.O'Neal/D.Wade 12.50 30.00

2005-06 Topps First Row PTP Dual Autographs

Randomly inserted into packs, these five cards feature authentic autographs from the featured players. Each of these cards were issued to a stated print run of 10 serial numbered sets and no pricing is available due to market scarcity.

2005-06 Topps First Row PTP Dual Relics

Randomly inserted into packs, these 32 cards feature two game-used relics from the featured players. Each of these cards were issued to a stated print run of 140 serial numbered sets.
PRINT RUN 140 SER.#'d SETS
UNPRICED AU PRINT RUNS 10 SETS
AW C.Anthony/H.Warrick 6.00 15.00
BO K.Bryant/S.O'Neal 10.00 25.00
DB T.Duncan/A.Bogut 6.00 15.00
IB A.Iverson/K.Bryant 12.50 30.00
IW A.Iverson/D.Wade 8.00 20.00
MG T.McGrady/G.Green 5.00 12.00
NW S.Nash/D.Williams 6.00 15.00
OI S.O'Neal/A.Iverson 10.00 25.00
OW S.O'Neal/D.Wade 15.00 40.00
PI C.Paul/A.Iverson 12.50 30.00
PM P.Pierce/R.McCants 6.00 15.00
WB D.Wade/K.Bryant 12.00 30.00
AB2 Andrew Bogut 4.00 10.00
AI2 Allen Iverson 5.00 12.00
BG2 Ben Gordon 2.50 6.00
CA2 Carmelo Anthony 6.00 15.00
CP2 Chris Paul 12.00 30.00
DN2 Dirk Nowitzki 5.00 12.00
DW1 Dwyane Wade 8.00 20.00
DW2 Deron Williams 4.00 10.00
EO2 Emeka Okafor 2.50 6.00
GA2 Gilbert Arenas 2.50 6.00
JT2 Jason Terry 2.50 6.00
KB2 Kobe Bryant 10.00 25.00
KM2 Kenyon Martin 2.50 6.00
RF2 Raymond Felton 3.00 8.00
SN2 Steve Nash 4.00 10.00
SO2 Shaquille O'Neal 6.00 15.00
TD2 Tim Duncan 5.00 12.00
TM2 Tracy McGrady 4.00 10.00
YM2 Yao Ming 4.00 10.00

2005-06 Topps First Row PTP Dual Relics Autographs

Randomly inserted into packs, these four cards feature both game-used material and authentic signatures from the featured players. These cards were issued to a stated print run of 10 serial numbered sets and no pricing is available due to market scarcity.

2005-06 Topps First Row Range Relics

Randomly inserted into packs, these 15-cards feature players who can shoot the ball from a long distance. Each of these cards were issued to a stated print run of 200 serial numbered sets.
PRINT RUN 200 SER.#'d SETS
AW Antoine Wright 2.00 5.00
BG Ben Gordon 2.00 5.00
DN Dirk Nowitzki 4.00 10.00
DW Dwyane Wade 6.00 15.00
JC Jamal Crawford 2.50 6.00
JH Julius Hodge 1.50 4.00
KB Kobe Bryant 8.00 20.00
KK Kyle Korver 2.00 5.00
MG Manu Ginobili 2.50 6.00
MP Morris Peterson 1.50 4.00
PP Paul Pierce 2.50 6.00
PS Peja Stojakovic 2.50 6.00
RA Ray Allen 2.50 6.00
SJ Sarunas Jasikevicius 2.50 6.00
TP Tayshaun Prince 2.00 5.00

2005-06 Topps First Row Signature Dish

Randomly inserted into packs, these 36 cards feature sticker-signed autographs of the featured players. Most of the players are active but Dave Bing, Earl Monroe and Jo Jo White are vintage players. Since the print run is different for many players, we have put the stated print run next to the player's name in our checklist.
PRINT RUNS LISTED IN CHECKLIST
AB Andrew Bogut/190 5.00 12.00
AI Allen Iverson/150 50.00 120.00
AJ Amir Johnson/190 4.00 10.00
AW Antoine Wright/190 3.00 8.00
BW Bracey Wright/190 2.50 6.00
CA Carmelo Anthony/65 20.00 50.00
CV Charlie Villanueva/190 4.00 10.00
DB Dave Bing/67 75.00 150.00
DG Danny Granger/190 5.00 12.00
DL David Lee/190 4.00 10.00
DW Dwyane Wade/190 30.00 80.00
EM Earl Monroe/83 15.00 40.00
FG Francisco Garcia/190 3.00 8.00
GG Gerald Green/190 4.00 10.00
JH Julius Hodge/190 2.50 6.00
JJ Jarrett Jack/190 4.00 10.00
JK Jason Kidd/120 12.50 30.00
JN Jameer Nelson/157 4.00 10.00
JP Johan Petro/190 2.50 6.00
LH Luther Head/190 3.00 8.00
LO Lamar Odom/100 3.00 8.00
LW Louis Williams/190 4.00 10.00
ME Monta Ellis/190 12.50 30.00
MW Martell Webster/190 3.00 8.00
RF Raymond Felton/190 4.00 10.00
RG Ryan Gomes/190 3.00 8.00
RM Rashad McCants/190 3.00 8.00
RS Robert Swift/124 4.00 10.00
RW Robert Whaley/190 2.50 6.00
SJ Sarunas Jasikevicius/190 4.00 10.00
SL Shaun Livingston/190 4.00 10.00
SM Sean May/190 2.50 6.00
TD Travis Diener/110 2.50 6.00
DWI Deron Williams/190 5.00 12.00
JJW Jo Jo White/79 8.00 20.00
PJR Peter John Ramos/190 4.00 10.00

2005-06 Topps First Row Signature Dunk

Randomly inserted into packs, these 37 cards feature sticker-signed autographs of the featured players. Most of the players are active but Dave Cowens, Elgin Baylor and Moses Malone are vintage players. Since the print run is different for many players, we have put the stated print run next to the player's name in our checklist.
PRINT RUNS LISTED IN CHECKLIST
AB Andrew Bogut/190 5.00 12.00
AI Allen Iverson/150 40.00 100.00
AW Antoine Wright/190 3.00 8.00
BB Brandon Bass/110 3.00 8.00
BW Bracey Wright/190 2.50 6.00
CA Carmelo Anthony/50 25.00 60.00
CT Chris Taft/190 3.00 8.00
CV Charlie Villanueva/190 4.00 10.00
DC Dave Cowens/83 6.00 15.00
DG Danny Granger/190 5.00 12.00
DL David Lee/190 4.00 10.00
DS Donta Smith/184 4.00 10.00
DW Dwyane Wade/190 30.00 80.00
EB Elgin Baylor/107 10.00 25.00
EO Emeka Okafor/190 3.00 8.00
FG Francisco Garcia/190 3.00 8.00
GG Gerald Green/190 4.00 10.00
ID Ike Diogu/190 2.50 6.00
JH Julius Hodge/190 2.50 6.00
JM Jason Maxiell/190 3.00 8.00
JP Johan Petro/190 2.50 6.00
LH Luther Head/190 3.00 8.00
LW Louis Williams/190 4.00 10.00
ME Mark Eaton/67 12.00 30.00
MM Moses Malone/78 10.00 25.00
MW Martell Webster/190 3.00 8.00
PP Pavel Podkolzin/190 4.00 10.00
RG Ryan Gomes/190 3.00 8.00
RM Rashad McCants/190 3.00 8.00
RW Robert Whaley/190 2.50 6.00
SJ Sarunas Jasikevicius/190 4.00 10.00
SM Sean May/190 2.50 6.00
SO Shaquille O'Neal/115 30.00 60.00
WS Wayne Simien/190 2.50 6.00
ABY Andrew Bynum/190 3.00 8.00
DWI Deron Williams/190 5.00 12.00
PJR Peter John Ramos/190 4.00 10.00

2005-06 Topps First Row Signature Swish

Randomly inserted into packs, these 41 cards feature sticker-signed autographs of the featured players. Most of the players are active but Bill Walton, Rick Barry are vintage players. In addition, celebrities such as Carmen Electra, Shannon Elizabeth, Jay-Z and Christine Brinkley also signed for this product. Since the print run is different for many players, we have put the stated print run next to the player's name in our checklist.
PRINT RUNS LISTED IN CHECKLIST
AI Allen Iverson/150 50.00 120.00
AJ Amir Johnson/190 4.00 10.00
AW Antoine Wright/190 3.00 8.00
BW Bill Walton/55 15.00 40.00
CA Carmelo Anthony/75 20.00 50.00
CB Christie Brinkley/50 50.00 120.00
CE Carmen Electra/50 60.00 120.00
CT Chris Taft/37 3.00 8.00
CV Charlie Villanueva/190 4.00 10.00
DE Daniel Ewing/85 3.00 8.00
DG Danny Granger/190 5.00 12.00
DL David Lee/190 4.00 10.00
DS Detlef Schrempf/91 12.50 30.00
DW Dwyane Wade/190 30.00 80.00
EO Emeka Okafor/190 3.00 8.00
FG Francisco Garcia/190 3.00 8.00
JG Joey Graham/190 3.00 8.00
JH Julius Hodge/190 2.50 6.00
JJ Jarrett Jack/190 4.00 10.00
JM Jenny McCarthy/50 60.00 120.00
JP Johan Petro/190 2.50 6.00
KM Kevin Martin/190 4.00 10.00
LH Luther Head/190 3.00 8.00
LO Lamar Odom/75 3.00 8.00
LW Louis Williams/190 4.00 10.00
MW Martell Webster/190 3.00 8.00
OG Orien Greene/190 3.00 8.00
RB Rick Barry/83 15.00 40.00
RG Ryan Gomes/190 3.00 8.00
RM Rashad McCants/190 3.00 8.00
RS Robert Swift/150 4.00 10.00
RW Robert Whaley/190 2.50 6.00
SE Shannon Elizabeth/50 50.00 120.00
SJ Sarunas Jasikevicius/190 4.00 10.00
SM Sean May/190 2.50 6.00
VW Von Wafer/190 2.50 6.00
BWR Bracey Wright/190 2.50 6.00
DWI Deron Williams/190 5.00 12.00
DWR Dorell Wright/190 4.00 10.00
PJR Peter John Ramos/190 4.00 10.00

2005-06 Topps First Row Spokesmen

Randomly inserted into packs, these nine cards feature signed cards of people whom Topps uses as spokesmen. Since each card was issued to a different print run, we have put this information next to the player's name in our checklist.
PRINT RUNS LISTED IN CHECKLIST
AUTOS UNPRICED DUE TO SCARCITY
SSRAI Allen Iverson JSY/200 5.00 12.00
SSRDW Dwyane Wade JSY/200 6.00 15.00
SSRJZ Jay-Z JSY/200 8.00 20.00

2005-06 Topps First Row Thunder Relics

Randomly inserted into packs, these 22-cards feature game-used relics of players known for their dunking ability. Each of these cards were issued to a stated print run of 200 serial numbered sets.
PRINT RUN 200 SER.#'d SETS
UNPRICED AUTO PRINT RUN 10 SETS
AI Andre Iguodala 2.00 5.00
AJ Antawn Jamison 2.00 5.00
AS Amare Stoudemire 2.00 5.00
BW Ben Wallace 2.00 5.00
CA Carmelo Anthony 5.00 12.00
CB Chris Bosh 2.50 6.00
DG Drew Gooden 2.00 5.00
DW Dwyane Wade 8.00 20.00
GG Gerald Green 2.50 6.00
HW Hakim Warrick 2.00 5.00
JO Jermaine O'Neal 2.00 5.00
JS Josh Smith 2.00 5.00
KB Kobe Bryant 8.00 20.00
LD Luol Deng 2.00 5.00
PG Pau Gasol 2.50 6.00
RJ Richard Jefferson 2.00 5.00
RL Rashard Lewis 2.50 6.00
SO Shaquille O'Neal 5.00 12.00
TD Tim Duncan 4.00 10.00
VC Vince Carter 4.00 10.00
YM Yao Ming 3.00 8.00
JRS J.R. Smith 2.00 5.00

2006-07 Topps Full Court

Released in mid March 2007, Topps Full Court features full-bleed photo veteran and retired legends cards for card numbers 1-100 and chromium card stock picturing rookies on card numbers 101-150. Full Court is packaged in 18-pack boxes of six cards each and carried an initial suggested retail price of $6.00 per pack.
COMP.SET w/o RC's (100) 12.50 30.00
101-150 RC PRINT RUN 999 SER.#'d SETS
UNPRICED PLATINUM PRINT RUN ONE SET
UNPRICED PLATES PRINT RUN ONE SET
1 Vince Carter .40 1.00
2 Josh Smith .25 .60
3 Dwyane Wade .50 1.25
4 Lamar Odom .25 .60
5 Jermaine O'Neal .25 .60
6 Andrei Kirilenko .25 .60
7 Rasheed Wallace .30 .75
8 Manu Ginobili .30 .75
9 Richard Hamilton .25 .60
10 Tim Duncan .50 1.25
11 Ricky Davis .25 .60
12 Antoine Walker .25 .60
13 Troy Murphy .20 .50
14 Ray Allen .30 .75
15 Ben Wallace .25 .60
16 Dwight Howard .25 .60
17 Joe Johnson .25 .60
18 Jason Kidd .50 1.25
19 Michael Redd .25 .60
20 Kobe Bryant 1.25 3.00
21 Al Harrington .25 .60
22 Mehmet Okur .20 .50
23 Danny Granger .25 .60
24 Caron Butler .25 .60
25 Elton Brand .30 .75
26 Gilbert Arenas .25 .60
27 Sam Cassell .25 .60
28 Antawn Jamison .25 .60
29 Carmelo Anthony .40 1.00
30 Zach Randolph .25 .60
31 Ben Gordon .25 .60
32 Andre Iguodala .25 .60
33 Paul Pierce .30 .75
34 Peja Stojakovic .30 .75
35 Andrew Bogut .25 .60
36 Mike Miller .25 .60
37 Mike James .20 .50
38 Shaquille O'Neal .60 1.50
39 Baron Davis .25 .60
40 Jason Richardson .30 .75
41 Rashard Lewis .30 .75
42 Marcus Camby .25 .60
43 Ron Artest .30 .75
44 Larry Hughes .25 .60
45 Allen Iverson .40 1.00
46 Al Jefferson .25 .60
47 Chris Paul .40 1.00
48 Tony Parker .30 .75
49 Pau Gasol .30 .75
50 Kevin Garnett .50 1.25
51 Richard Jefferson .25 .60
52 Corey Maggette .25 .60
53 Yao Ming .40 1.00
54 T.J. Ford .20 .50
55 Andre Miller .25 .60
56 Mike Bibby .30 .75
57 LeBron James 1.25 3.00
58 Chris Webber .30 .75
59 Emeka Okafor .25 .60
60 Tyson Chandler .25 .60
61 Raymond Felton .25 .60
62 Channing Frye .25 .60
63 Gerald Wallace .25 .60
64 Stephon Marbury .25 .60
65 Kirk Hinrich .25 .60
66 Jameer Nelson .20 .50
67 Charlie Villanueva .20 .50
68 Smush Parker .20 .50
69 Tracy McGrady .40 1.00
70 Chris Bosh .30 .75
71 Chauncey Billups .30 .75
72 Brad Miller .25 .60
73 Drew Gooden .25 .60
74 Amare Stoudemire .25 .60
75 Dirk Nowitzki .50 1.25
76 Shawn Marion .25 .60
77 Jason Terry .25 .60
78 Steve Nash .40 1.00
79 Josh Howard .25 .60
80 Darius Miles .20 .50
81 John Stockton 1.50 4.00
82 Wilt Chamberlain 2.00 5.00
83 Dennis Rodman 2.00 5.00
84 Karl Malone 1.25 3.00
85 Dominique Wilkins 1.25 3.00
86 Isiah Thomas 1.00 2.50
87 Earl Monroe 1.00 2.50
88 Hakeem Olajuwon 1.25 3.00
89 Clyde Drexler 1.25 3.00
90 George Gervin 1.00 2.50
91 Oscar Robertson 1.00 2.50
92 Rick Barry .75 2.00
93 Walt Frazier 1.00 2.50
94 Drazen Petrovic 1.25 3.00
95 Dan Majerle .75 2.00
96 Jerry West 1.25 3.00
97 Larry Bird 2.50 6.00
98 Moses Malone 1.00 2.50
99 Kareem Abdul-Jabbar 1.50 4.00
100 Bill Russell 2.00 5.00
101 Shelden Williams RC 1.25 3.00
102 Adam Morrison RC 1.50 4.00
103 Daniel Gibson RC 1.25 3.00
104 Mile Ilic RC 1.00 2.50
105 Jorge Garbajosa RC 1.25 3.00
106 David Noel RC 1.00 2.50
107 Hassan Adams RC 1.00 2.50
108 J.J. Redick RC 2.00 5.00
109 Brandon Roy RC 1.50 4.00
110 Damir Markota RC 1.00 2.50
111 Solomon Jones RC 1.00 2.50
112 Yakhouba Diawara RC 1.00 2.50
113 Maurice Ager RC 1.00 2.50
114 Steve Novak RC 1.25 3.00
115 Jordan Farmar RC 1.50 4.00
116 Randy Foye RC 1.50 4.00
117 Cedric Simmons RC 1.00 2.50
118 James Augustine RC 1.00 2.50
119 Sergio Rodriguez RC 1.50 4.00
120 P.J. Tucker RC 1.25 3.00
121 Rajon Rondo RC 2.50 6.00
122 Tyrus Thomas RC 1.25 3.00
123 Will Blalock RC 1.00 2.50
124 Shawne Williams RC 1.00 2.50
125 Rudy Gay RC 2.00 5.00
126 Craig Smith RC 1.25 3.00
127 Hilton Armstrong RC 1.00 2.50
128 Bobby Jones RC 1.00 2.50
129 Quincy Douby RC 1.00 2.50
130 Andrea Bargnani RC 1.50 4.00
131 Vassilis Spanoulis RC 1.00 2.50
132 Thabo Sefolosha RC 1.50 4.00
133 Pops Mensah-Bonsu RC 1.00 2.50
134 Paul Milsap RC 2.00 5.00
135 Kyle Lowry RC 2.00 5.00
136 Marcus Williams RC 1.00 2.50
137 Renaldo Balkman RC 1.25 3.00
138 Rodney Carney RC 1.00 2.50
139 Marcus Vinicius RC 1.00 2.50
140 Ronnie Brewer RC 1.50 4.00
141 Leon Powe RC 1.25 3.00
142 Shannon Brown RC 1.00 2.50
143 Patrick O'Bryant RC 1.00 2.50
144 Paul Davis RC 1.00 2.50
145 Alexander Johnson RC 1.00 2.50
146 Josh Boone RC 1.00 2.50
147 Mardy Collins RC 1.00 2.50
148 LaMarcus Aldridge RC 4.00 10.00
149 Saer Sene RC 1.00 2.50
150 Dee Brown RC 1.00 2.50

2006-07 Topps Full Court First Day Issue

*1-80 FIRST DAY: .75X TO 2X BASE HI
*81-100 FIRST DAY: .6X TO 1.5X BASE HI
PRINT RUN 429 SER.#'d SETS

2006-07 Topps Full Court Photographer's Proof

*1-80 PROOF: .6X TO 1.5X BASE HI
*81-100 PROOF: .5X TO 1.25X BASE HI
STATED PRINT RUN 1999 SER.#'d SETS

2006-07 Topps Full Court Photographer's Proof Gold

*1-80 PROOF GOLD: 1.25X TO 3X BASE HI
*81-100 PROOF GOLD: .75X TO 2X BASE HI
STATED PRINT RUN 199 SER.#'d SETS

2006-07 Topps Full Court Chrome Rookie Refractors

*REFRACTORS: .6X TO 1.5X BASE HI
PRINT RUN 199 SER.#'d SETS

2006-07 Topps Full Court Chrome Rookie Refractors Gold

*REF.GOLD: 1X TO 2.5X BASE HI
STATED PRINT RUN 50 SER.#'d SETS

2006-07 Topps Full Court Co-Signers

GROUP A ODDS 1:270, GROUP B 1:755
GROUP C ODDS 1:1100, GROUP D 1:375
GROUP E ODDS 1:470, GROUP F 1:218
GROUP G ODDS 1:82, GROUP H 1:36
CS1 A.Iverson/M.Cheeks 30.00 80.00
CS2 A.Morrison/L.Bird 50.00 120.00
CS3 D.Wade/S.O'Neal 150.00 300.00
CS4 B.Walton/J.Wooden 60.00 150.00
CS5 R.Felton/R.Williams 25.00 60.00
CS6 A.Morrison/J.Redick 15.00 40.00
CS7 V.Carter/D.Wilkins 40.00 80.00
CS8 B.Gordon/J.Calhoun 20.00 40.00
CS9 T.Parker/B.Diaw 10.00 25.00
CS10 C.Villanueva/E.Okafor 8.00 20.00
CS11 C.Anthony/J.Boeheim 40.00 100.00
CS12 J.O'Neal/L.Elmore 8.00 20.00
CS13 C.Bosh/C.Hawkins 15.00 40.00
CS14 T.Ford/S.Claxton 8.00 20.00
CS15 B.Lanier/S.O'Neal 40.00 80.00
CS16 A.Bargnani/A.Bogut 20.00 40.00
CS17 L.Deng/J.Redick 8.00 20.00
CS18 D.Ewing/C.Duhon 8.00 20.00
CS19 J.Farmer/B.Howland 8.00 20.00
CS20 B.Simmons/H.Turkoglu 8.00 20.00
CS21 J.Nelson/D.West 8.00 20.00
CS22 D.Brown/D.Williams 8.00 20.00
CS23 R.Bell/L.Barbosa 8.00 20.00
CS24 M.James/S.Parker 8.00 20.00
CS25 M.Bol/R.Barry 20.00 50.00
CS26 A.Ray/R.Foye 8.00 20.00
CS27 S.Brown/M.Ager 8.00 20.00
CS28 H.Armstrong/J.Boone 8.00 20.00
CS29 M.Williams/V.Carter 20.00 40.00
CS30 J.Farmar/R.Hollins 8.00 20.00
CS31 S.Williams/R.Carney 8.00 20.00
CS32 P.Tucker/D.Gibson 8.00 20.00
CS33 E.Monroe/I.Thomas 25.00 60.00
CS34 J.Redick/S.Williams 10.00 25.00
CS35 J.Howard/D.Harris 8.00 20.00
CS36 J.Howard/J.Smith 10.00 25.00
CS37 R.Rondo/Q.Douby 10.00 25.00
CS38 R.Balkman/M.Collins 8.00 20.00
CS39 P.O'Bryant/S.Sene 8.00 20.00
CS40 R.Allen/A.Iverson 75.00 150.00
CS41 R.Brewer/D.Brown 8.00 20.00
CS42 C.Smith/D.Noel 8.00 20.00
CS43 D.Wade/A.Morrison 25.00 60.00
CS44 B.Jones/S.Jones 8.00 20.00
CS45 A.Ray/K.Lowry 8.00 20.00
CS46 R.Carney/T.Sefolosha 8.00 20.00
CS47 R.Felton/B.Gordon 8.00 20.00
CS48 B.Walton/L.Walton 30.00 60.00
CS49 A.Iguodala/G.Wallace 8.00 20.00
CS50 M.Johnson/L.Bird 150.00 300.00

2006-07 Topps Full Court Court Records

COMPLETE SET (20) 10.00 25.00
PRINT RUN 1499 SER.#'d SETS
CR1 Larry Bird 1.50 4.00
CR2 Dwyane Wade 1.00 2.50
CR3 Adam Morrison .60 1.50
CR4 Allen Iverson .75 2.00
CR5 Shaquille O'Neal 1.25 3.00
CR6 Vince Carter .75 2.00
CR7 Chris Bosh .60 1.50
CR8 Ben Gordon .50 1.25
CR9 J.J. Redick .75 2.00
CR10 Dominique Wilkins .75 2.00
CR11 Isiah Thomas .60 1.50
CR12 Andre Iguodala .50 1.25
CR13 Earl Monroe .60 1.50
CR14 Shelden Williams .50 1.25
CR15 Dee Brown .40 1.00
CR16 Rodney Carney .40 1.00
CR17 Charlie Villanueva .40 1.00
CR18 Quincy Douby .40 1.00
CR19 Raymond Felton .50 1.25
CR20 Randy Foye .60 1.50

2006-07 Topps Full Court Court Records Relics

PRINT RUN 499 SER.#'d SETS
CR1 Larry Bird 6.00 15.00
CR2 Dwyane Wade 5.00 12.00
CR3 Adam Morrison 2.50 6.00
CR4 Allen Iverson 3.00 8.00
CR5 Shaquille O'Neal 5.00 12.00
CR6 Vince Carter 3.00 8.00
CR7 Chris Bosh 2.50 6.00
CR8 Ben Gordon 2.00 5.00
CR9 J.J. Redick 3.00 8.00
CR10 Dominique Wilkins 3.00 8.00
CR11 Isiah Thomas 2.50 6.00
CR12 Andre Iguodala 2.00 5.00
CR13 Earl Monroe 2.50 6.00
CR14 Shelden Williams 2.00 5.00
CR15 Dee Brown 1.50 4.00
CR16 Rodney Carney 1.50 4.00
CR17 Charlie Villanueva 1.50 4.00
CR18 Quincy Douby 1.50 4.00
CR19 Raymond Felton 2.00 5.00
CR20 Randy Foye 2.50 6.00

2006-07 Topps Full Court Court Records Relics Autographs

PRINT RUN 15 TO 50 SER.#'d SETS
CR1 Larry Bird/33 60.00 150.00
CR2 Dwyane Wade/50 30.00 80.00
CR3 Adam Morrison/50 10.00 25.00
CR4 Allen Iverson/50 40.00 100.00
CR5 Shaquille O'Neal/32 60.00 120.00
CR6 Vince Carter/50 20.00 50.00
CR7 Chris Bosh/50 15.00 40.00
CR8 Ben Gordon/50 12.50 30.00
CR9 J.J. Redick/50 12.50 30.00
CR10 Dominique Wilkins/21 25.00 60.00
CR11 Isiah Thomas/50 20.00 40.00
CR12 Andre Iguodala/50 10.00 25.00
CR13 Earl Monroe/15 30.00 60.00
CR14 Shelden Williams/50 10.00 25.00
CR15 Dee Brown/50 10.00 25.00
CR16 Rodney Carney/50 10.00 25.00
CR17 Charlie Villanueva/50 10.00 25.00
CR18 Quincy Douby/50 10.00 25.00

2006-07 Topps Full Court Full Court Press

COMPLETE SET (25) 12.50 30.00
PRINT RUN 1499 SER.#'d SETS
FCP1 Dwyane Wade 1.25 3.00
FCP2 Adam Morrison .75 2.00
FCP3 Joe Johnson .60 1.50
FCP4 Ben Gordon .60 1.50
FCP5 Jason Terry .60 1.50
FCP6 Baron Davis .60 1.50
FCP7 Jordan Farmar .75 2.00
FCP8 Randy Foye .75 2.00
FCP9 J.J. Redick 1.00 2.50
FCP10 Jason Kidd 1.25 3.00
FCP11 Allen Iverson 1.00 2.50
FCP12 Manu Ginobili .75 2.00
FCP13 Stephon Marbury .60 1.50
FCP14 Caron Butler .60 1.50
FCP15 T.J. Ford .50 1.25
FCP16 Ronnie Brewer .75 2.00
FCP17 Mike Bibby .75 2.00
FCP18 Rodney Carney .50 1.25
FCP19 Chauncey Billups .75 2.00
FCP20 Steve Nash 1.00 2.50
FCP21 Rudy Gay 1.00 2.50
FCP22 Rajon Rondo 1.25 3.00
FCP23 Raymond Felton .60 1.50
FCP24 Ron Artest .75 2.00
FCP25 Tony Parker .75 2.00

2006-07 Topps Full Court Full Court Press Relics

PRINT RUN 499 SER.#'d SETS
*DUAL: .5X TO 1.25X BASE HI
PRINT RUN 199 SER.#'d SETS
*TRIPLE: .6X TO 1.5X BASE HI
TRIPLE PRINT RUN 50 SER.#'d SETS
FCP1 Dwyane Wade 5.00 12.00
FCP3 Joe Johnson 2.00 5.00
FCP4 Ben Gordon 2.00 5.00
FCP5 Jason Terry 2.00 5.00
FCP6 Baron Davis 2.00 5.00
FCP7 Jordan Farmar 2.50 6.00
FCP8 Randy Foye 2.50 6.00
FCP9 J.J. Redick 3.00 8.00
FCP10 Jason Kidd 4.00 10.00
FCP11 Allen Iverson 3.00 8.00
FCP12 Manu Ginobili 2.50 6.00
FCP13 Stephon Marbury 2.00 5.00
FCP14 Caron Butler 2.00 5.00
FCP15 T.J. Ford 1.50 4.00
FCP16 Ronnie Brewer 2.50 6.00
FCP17 Mike Bibby 2.50 6.00
FCP18 Rodney Carney 1.50 4.00
FCP19 Chauncey Billups 2.50 6.00
FCP20 Steve Nash 3.00 8.00
FCP21 Rudy Gay 3.00 8.00
FCP22 Rajon Rondo 8.00 20.00
FCP23 Raymond Felton 2.00 5.00
FCP24 Ron Artest 2.50 6.00
FCP25 Tony Parker 2.50 6.00

2006-07 Topps Full Court Half Court Press

COMPLETE SET (25) 12.50 30.00
PRINT RUN 999 SER.#'d SETS
HCP1 Shaquille O'Neal 1.25 3.00
HCP2 Dirk Nowitzki 1.00 2.50
HCP3 Ben Wallace .50 1.25
HCP4 Carmelo Anthony .75 2.00
HCP5 Jermaine O'Neal .50 1.25
HCP6 Elton Brand .60 1.50
HCP7 J.J. Redick .75 2.00
HCP8 Andrew Bogut .50 1.25
HCP9 Chris Paul .75 2.00
HCP10 Dwyane Wade 1.00 2.50
HCP11 Kobe Bryant 2.50 6.00
HCP12 Dwight Howard .50 1.25
HCP13 Pau Gasol .60 1.50
HCP14 Tim Duncan 1.00 2.50
HCP15 LaMarcus Aldridge 1.50 4.00
HCP16 Ray Allen .60 1.50
HCP17 Yao Ming .75 2.00
HCP18 Allen Iverson .75 2.00
HCP19 Chris Bosh .60 1.50
HCP20 Adam Morrison .60 1.50
HCP21 Kevin Garnett 1.00 2.50
HCP22 Tracy McGrady .75 2.00
HCP23 Vince Carter .75 2.00
HCP24 Andrea Bargnani .60 1.50
HCP25 Gilbert Arenas .50 1.25

2006-07 Topps Full Court Half Court Press Relics

PRINT RUN 249 SER.#'d SETS
*DUAL: .5X TO 1.25X BASE HI
DUAL PRINT RUN 199 SER.#'d SETS
*TRIPLE: .75X TO 2X BASE HI
TRIPLE PRINT RUN 25 SER.#'d SETS
HCP1 Shaquille O'Neal 5.00 12.00

HCP2 Dirk Nowitzki 4.00 10.00
HCP3 Ben Wallace 2.00 5.00
HCP4 Carmelo Anthony 3.00 8.00
HCP5 Jermaine O'Neal 2.00 5.00
HCP6 Elton Brand 2.50 6.00
HCP7 J.J. Redick 3.00 8.00
HCP8 Andrew Bogut 2.00 5.00
HCP9 Chris Paul 3.00 8.00
HCP10 Dwyane Wade 5.00 12.00
HCP11 Kobe Bryant 6.00 15.00
HCP12 Dwight Howard 2.00 5.00
HCP13 Pau Gasol 2.50 6.00
HCP14 Tim Duncan 4.00 10.00
HCP15 LaMarcus Aldridge 6.00 15.00
HCP16 Ray Allen 2.50 6.00
HCP17 Yao Ming 3.00 8.00
HCP18 Allen Iverson 3.00 8.00
HCP19 Chris Bosh 2.50 6.00
HCP20 Adam Morrison 2.50 6.00
HCP21 Kevin Garnett 4.00 10.00
HCP22 Tracy McGrady 3.00 8.00
HCP23 Vince Carter 3.00 8.00
HCP24 Andrea Bargnani 2.50 6.00
HCP25 Gilbert Arenas 2.00 5.00

1995-96 Topps Gallery

The 1995-96 Topps Gallery set was issued in one series of 144 cards. The 8-card packs, offered exclusively to hobby outlets, retailed for $3.00 each. The set features the topical subsets: The Masters (1-18), The Modernists (19-36), New Editions (37-84) and The Classics (85-144). Each card is printed on 24-point stock, covered with an exclusive high-gloss film and etch stamped with one or more foils. Rookie Cards of note in this set include Michael Finley, Kevin Garnett, Antonio McDyess, Jerry Stackhouse and Damon Stoudamire.

COMPLETE SET (144) 15.00 30.00
1 Shaquille O'Neal .60 1.50
2 Shawn Kemp .25 .60
3 Reggie Miller .30 .75
4 Mitch Richmond .25 .60
5 Grant Hill .40 1.00
6 Magic Johnson .60 1.50
7 Vin Baker .20 .50
8 Charles Barkley .40 1.00
9 Hakeem Olajuwon .30 .75
10 Michael Jordan 2.00 5.00
11 Patrick Ewing .30 .75
12 David Robinson .40 1.00
13 Alonzo Mourning .30 .75
14 Karl Malone .30 .75
15 Chris Webber .30 .75
16 Dikembe Mutombo .25 .60
17 Larry Johnson .25 .60
18 Jamal Mashburn .25 .60
19 Anfernee Hardaway .40 1.00
20 Bryant Stith .15 .40
21 Juwan Howard .25 .60
22 Jason Kidd .40 1.00
23 Sharone Wright .15 .40
24 Tom Gugliotta .15 .40
25 Eric Montross .15 .40
26 Allan Houston .20 .50
27 Antonio Davis .15 .40
28 Brian Grant .20 .50
29 Terrell Brandon .15 .40
30 Eddie Jones .25 .60
31 James Robinson .15 .40
32 Wesley Person .15 .40
33 Glenn Robinson .20 .50
34 Donyell Marshall .15 .40
35 Sam Cassell .25 .60
36 Lamond Murray .15 .40
37 Damon Stoudamire RC .60 1.50
38 Tyus Edney RC .25 .60
39 Jerry Stackhouse RC .75 2.00
40 Arvydas Sabonis RC .50 1.25
41 Kevin Garnett RC 2.00 5.00
42 Brent Barry RC .40 1.00
43 Alan Henderson RC .25 .60
44 Bryant Reeves RC .20 .50
45 Shawn Respert RC .20 .50
46 Michael Finley RC .75 2.00
47 Gary Trent RC .25 .60
48 Antonio McDyess RC .30 .75
49 George Zidek RC .20 .50
50 Joe Smith RC .30 .75
51 Ed O'Bannon RC .20 .50
52 Rasheed Wallace RC .75 2.00
53 Eric Williams RC .25 .60
54 Kurt Thomas RC .25 .60
55 Mookie Blaylock .15 .40
56 Robert Pack .15 .40
57 Dana Barros .15 .40
58 Eric Murdock .15 .40
59 Glen Rice .25 .60
60 John Stockton .30 .75
61 Scottie Pippen .40 1.00
62 Oliver Miller .15 .40
63 Tyrone Hill .15 .40
64 Gary Payton .25 .60
65 Jim Jackson .15 .40
66 Avery Johnson .20 .50
67 Mahmoud Abdul-Rauf .15 .40
68 Olden Polynice .15 .40
69 Joe Dumars .25 .60
70 Rod Strickland .15 .40
71 Chris Mullin .25 .60
72 Kevin Johnson .25 .60
73 Derrick Coleman .20 .50
74 Clyde Drexler .30 .75
75 Dale Davis .15 .40
76 Horace Grant .20 .50
77 Loy Vaught .15 .40
78 Armon Gilliam .15 .40
79 Nick Van Exel .25 .60
80 Charles Oakley .20 .50
81 Kevin Willis .15 .40
82 Sherman Douglas .15 .40
83 Isaiah Rider .25 .60
84 Steve Smith .20 .50
85 Dee Brown .15 .40
86 Dell Curry .15 .40
87 Calbert Cheaney .15 .40
88 Greg Anthony .15 .40
89 Jeff Hornacek .20 .50
90 Dennis Rodman .50 1.25
91 Willie Anderson .15 .40
92 Chris Mills .15 .40
93 Hersey Hawkins .15 .40
94 Popeye Jones .15 .40
95 Chuck Person .20 .50
96 Reggie Williams .15 .40
97 A.C. Green .20 .50
98 Otis Thorpe .15 .40
99 Walt Williams .15 .40
100 Latrell Sprewell .25 .60
101 Buck Williams .15 .40
102 Robert Horry .20 .50
103 Clarence Weatherspoon .15 .40
104 Dennis Scott .15 .40
105 Rik Smits .20 .50
106 Jayson Williams .15 .40
107 Pooh Richardson .15 .40
108 Anthony Mason .15 .40
109 Cedric Ceballos .15 .40
110 Billy Owens .15 .40
111 Johnny Newman .15 .40
112 Christian Laettner .20 .50
113 Stacey Augmon .20 .50
114 Chris Morris .15 .40
115 Detlef Schrempf .25 .60
116 Dino Radja .15 .40
117 Sean Elliott .25 .60
118 Muggsy Bogues .20 .50
119 Toni Kukoc .25 .60
120 Clifford Robinson .15 .40
121 Bobby Hurley .15 .40
122 Lorenzo Williams .15 .40
123 Wayman Tisdale .15 .40
124 Bobby Phills .15 .40
125 Nick Anderson .15 .40
126 LaPhonso Ellis .15 .40
127 Scott Williams .15 .40
128 Mark West .15 .40
129 P.J. Brown .15 .40
130 Tim Hardaway .25 .60
131 Derek Harper .20 .50
132 Mario Elie .15 .40
133 Benoit Benjamin .15 .40
134 Terry Porter .15 .40
135 Derrick McKey .15 .40
136 Bimbo Coles .15 .40
137 John Salley .15 .40
138 Malik Sealy .15 .40
139 Byron Scott .20 .50
140 Vlade Divac .25 .60
141 Mark Price .25 .60
142 Rony Seikaly .15 .40
143 Mark Jackson .20 .50
144 John Starks .20 .50

1995-96 Topps Gallery Player's Private Issue

*STARS: 10X TO 25X BASE CARD HI
*RCs: 5X TO 12X BASE HI
STATED ODDS 1:12
1-18 INSERTED IN 96-97 STADIUM CLUB II
10 Michael Jordan 125.00 300.00
61 Scottie Pippen 12.00 30.00
100 Latrell Sprewell 8.00 20.00

1995-96 Topps Gallery Expressionists

Randomly inserted into 1 in every 24 packs, these inserts feature a collection of fifteen NBA team leaders. Each card attempts to capture the intensity and spirit of the featured player incorporating an embossed, textured, brush stroke effect.

COMPLETE SET (15) 30.00 80.00
STATED ODDS 1:24
EX1 Shawn Kemp 1.25 3.00
EX2 Michael Jordan 10.00 25.00
EX3 Reggie Miller 1.50 4.00
EX4 Kevin Willis .75 2.00
EX5 Jason Kidd 2.00 5.00
EX6 Larry Johnson 1.25 3.00
EX7 Patrick Ewing 1.50 4.00
EX8 Rasheed Wallace 4.00 10.00
EX9 Karl Malone 1.50 4.00
EX10 Shaquille O'Neal 3.00 8.00
EX11 Joe Smith 1.50 4.00
EX12 Jerry Stackhouse 4.00 10.00
EX13 Glen Rice 1.25 3.00
EX14 Clyde Drexler 1.50 4.00
EX15 Grant Hill 2.00 5.00

1995-96 Topps Gallery Photo Gallery

Randomly inserted into 1 in every 30 packs, this seventeen card set features a selection of premium quality photographs, chronicling classic moments from some of the NBA's biggest stars. Each card is custom-designed to compliment the photography. Multiple foils were also used on each card.

COMPLETE SET (17) 50.00 100.00
STATED ODDS 1:30
PG1 Vin Baker 2.50 6.00
PG2 Brian Grant 2.50 6.00
PG3 George Zidek 1.25 3.00
PG4 Hakeem Olajuwon 4.00 10.00
PG5 Stacey Augmon 2.50 6.00
PG6 Oliver Miller 2.00 5.00
PG7 Kenny Gattison 2.00 5.00
PG8 Dikembe Mutombo 3.00 8.00
PG9 Rony Seikaly 2.00 5.00
PG10 Tom Gugliotta 2.00 5.00
PG11 Scottie Pippen 5.00 12.00
PG12 David Robinson 5.00 12.00
PG13 Anfernee Hardaway 5.00 12.00
PG14 Dennis Rodman 6.00 15.00
PG15 Kevin Garnett 12.00 30.00
PG16 Damon Stoudamire 4.00 10.00
PG17 Charles Barkley 5.00 12.00

1999-00 Topps Gallery Promos

This six-card standard-size set was sent to dealers as a promotional set for the 1999-00 Topps Gallery issue. The cards carry a "PP" prefix.

COMPLETE SET (6) 1.25 3.00
PP1 Jason Williams .25 .60
PP2 Eddie Jones .20 .50
PP3 Allan Houston .15 .40
PP4 Alonzo Mourning .25 .60
PP5 Shareef Abdur-Rahim .15 .40
PP6 Wally Szczerbiak .40 1.00

1999-00 Topps Gallery

Released in May 2000, this set contained 150 base cards which were issued in five-card packs that carried a $3.00 suggested retail price. The base set was composed of 100 veteran cards and three subsets: 12 Masters, focusing on the top veteran players; 12 Artisans, focusing on younger players and 26 Apprentices featuring the top rookies.

COMPLETE SET (150) 20.00 50.00
PRIN.PLATES: STATED ODDS 1:1028
SUBSET CARDS SAME VALUE AS BASE
1 Gary Payton .30 .75
2 Derek Anderson .20 .50
3 Jalen Rose .25 .60
4 Tim Hardaway .30 .75
5 Jerry Stackhouse .30 .75
6 Antonio McDyess .25 .60
7 Paul Pierce .40 1.00
8 Reggie Miller .30 .75
9 Maurice Taylor .20 .50
10 Stephon Marbury .25 .60
11 Terrell Brandon .20 .50
12 Marcus Camby .25 .60
13 Michael Doleac .20 .50
14 Doug Christie .25 .60
15 Brent Barry .25 .60
16 John Stockton .40 1.00
17 Rod Strickland .20 .50
18 Shareef Abdur-Rahim .25 .60
19 Vin Baker .25 .60
20 Jason Kidd .50 1.25
21 Nick Anderson .20 .50
22 Brian Grant .20 .50
23 Chris Webber .30 .75
24 Tariq Abdul-Wahad .20 .50
25 Jason Williams .40 1.00
26 Joe Smith .25 .60
27 Ray Allen .30 .75
28 Glenn Robinson .25 .60
29 Alonzo Mourning .40 1.00
30 Scottie Pippen .50 1.25
31 Mookie Blaylock .20 .50
32 Christian Laettner .25 .60
33 Mark Jackson .25 .60
34 Shawn Kemp .30 .75
35 Anfernee Hardaway .50 1.25
36 Chris Mullin .30 .75
37 Dennis Rodman .60 1.50
38 Lamond Murray .20 .50
39 Jim Jackson .20 .50
40 Shaquille O'Neal .75 2.00
41 Randy Brown .20 .50
42 Nick Van Exel .25 .60
43 Robert Traylor .20 .50
44 Vlade Divac .30 .75
45 Karl Malone .40 1.00
46 Avery Johnson .25 .60
47 Jayson Williams .20 .50
48 Darrell Armstrong .20 .50
49 Michael Olowokandi .20 .50
50 Kevin Garnett .50 1.25
51 Dirk Nowitzki .60 1.50
52 Antawn Jamison .30 .75
53 Latrell Sprewell .30 .75
54 Ruben Patterson .20 .50
55 Vince Carter .60 1.50
56 Michael Dickerson .20 .50
57 Raef LaFrentz .25 .60
58 Keith Van Horn .25 .60
59 Tom Gugliotta .20 .50
60 Allen Iverson .60 1.50
61 Eric Snow .25 .60
62 Kerry Kittles .20 .50
63 Sam Cassell .25 .60
64 Rik Smits .30 .75
65 Isaiah Rider .25 .60
66 Anthony Mason .20 .50
67 Hersey Hawkins .20 .50
68 Cuttino Mobley .20 .50
69 Allan Houston .25 .60
70 Kobe Bryant 1.25 3.00
71 Damon Stoudamire .25 .60
72 Charles Oakley .25 .60
73 Mike Bibby .30 .75
74 David Robinson .50 1.25
75 Eddie Jones .30 .75
76 Juwan Howard .25 .60
77 Antoine Walker .30 .75
78 Michael Finley .30 .75
79 Larry Hughes .25 .60
80 Charles Barkley .50 1.25
81 Tracy McGrady .50 1.25
82 Dikembe Mutombo .30 .75
83 Rasheed Wallace .30 .75
84 Jeff Hornacek .25 .60
85 Patrick Ewing .40 1.00
86 P.J. Brown .20 .50
87 Brevin Knight .20 .50
88 Elden Campbell .20 .50
89 Kenny Anderson .25 .60
90 Grant Hill .40 1.00
91 Mitch Richmond .30 .75
92 Steve Smith .25 .60
93 Jamal Mashburn .25 .60
94 Toni Kukoc .30 .75
95 Hakeem Olajuwon .40 1.00
96 Ron Mercer .25 .60
97 John Starks .25 .60
98 Glen Rice .30 .75
99 Cedric Ceballos .20 .50
100 Tim Duncan .60 1.50
101 Karl Malone MAS .40 1.00
102 Alonzo Mourning MAS .40 1.00
103 Gary Payton MAS .30 .75
104 Scottie Pippen MAS .50 1.25
105 Shaquille O'Neal MAS .75 2.00
106 Charles Barkley MAS .50 1.25
107 Grant Hill MAS .40 1.00
108 John Stockton MAS .40 1.00
109 Jason Kidd MAS .50 1.25
110 Reggie Miller MAS .30 .75
111 Shawn Kemp MAS .30 .75
112 Patrick Ewing MAS .40 1.00
113 Kevin Garnett ART .50 1.25
114 Vince Carter ART .60 1.50
115 Kobe Bryant ART 1.25 3.00
116 Chris Webber ART .30 .75
117 Tracy McGrady ART .50 1.25
118 Shareef Abdur-Rahim ART .25 .60
119 Paul Pierce ART .40 1.00
120 Jason Williams ART .40 1.00
121 Tim Duncan ART .60 1.50
122 Eddie Jones ART .30 .75
123 Allen Iverson ART .60 1.50
124 Stephon Marbury ART .25 .60
125 Elton Brand RC 1.00 2.50
126 Lamar Odom RC 1.00 2.50
127 Steve Francis RC 1.00 2.50
128 Adrian Griffin RC .40 1.00
129 Wally Szczerbiak RC .75 2.00
130 Baron Davis RC 1.00 2.50
131 Richard Hamilton RC .75 2.00
132 Jonathan Bender RC .40 1.00
133 Andre Miller RC .75 2.00
134 Shawn Marion RC .75 2.00
135 Jason Terry RC .60 1.50
136 Trajan Langdon RC .40 1.00
137 Corey Maggette RC .60 1.50
138 William Avery RC .30 .75
139 Ron Artest RC .75 2.00
140 Cal Bowdler RC .25 .60
141 James Posey RC .40 1.00
142 Quincy Lewis RC .25 .60
143 Kenny Thomas RC .40 1.00
144 Vonteego Cummings RC .25 .60
145 Todd MacCulloch RC .40 1.00
146 Anthony Carter RC .30 .75
147 A.Radojevic RC .25 .60
148 Devean George RC .40 1.00
149 Scott Padgett RC .30 .75
150 Jumaine Jones RC .30 .75

1999-00 Topps Gallery Player's Private Issue

*STARS: 6X TO 15X BASE CARD HI
*RCs: 3X TO 8X BASE HI
STATED PRINT RUN 250 SERIAL #'d SETS
STATED ODDS 1:17

1999-00 Topps Gallery Autographs

Randomly inserted in packs at an overall rate of one in 375, this four-card set features authentic autographs from top NBA players. Group "A" cards were inserted at one in 437, while Group "B" cards were inserted at one in 2,637. Each card is stamped with the Topps Certified Autograph Issue logo and the Topps Authentication sticker. Card backs are numbered by the player's initials.

OVERALL STATED ODDS 1:375
GROUP B: STATED ODDS 1:2637
CM Corey Maggette A 6.00 15.00
EB Elton Brand B 6.00 15.00
TD Tim Duncan B 400.00 800.00
WS Wally Szczerbiak A 5.00 12.00

1999-00 Topps Gallery Exhibits

Randomly inserted in packs at one in 24, this 30-card set traces the history of art and features NBA stars in 10 different themes. Card backs carry a "GE" prefix.

COMPLETE SET (30) 50.00 100.00
STATED ODDS 1:24
GE1 Shaquille O'Neal 4.00 10.00
GE2 Chris Webber 1.50 4.00
GE3 Karl Malone 2.00 5.00
GE4 Hakeem Olajuwon 2.00 5.00
GE5 Scottie Pippen 2.50 6.00
GE6 Patrick Ewing 2.00 5.00
GE7 John Stockton 2.00 5.00
GE8 Tim Duncan 3.00 8.00
GE9 Grant Hill 2.00 5.00
GE10 Dennis Rodman 3.00 8.00
GE11 Reggie Miller 1.50 4.00
GE12 Brian Grant 1.00 2.50
GE13 Antoine Walker 1.50 4.00
GE14 Damon Stoudamire 1.25 3.00
GE15 Tracy McGrady 2.50 6.00
GE16 Alonzo Mourning 2.00 5.00
GE17 Shawn Kemp 1.50 4.00
GE18 Isaiah Rider 1.25 3.00
GE19 Vince Carter 3.00 8.00
GE20 Antonio McDyess 1.25 3.00
GE21 Jason Kidd 2.50 6.00
GE22 Kobe Bryant 10.00 25.00
GE23 Kevin Garnett 2.50 6.00
GE24 Latrell Sprewell 1.50 4.00
GE25 Michael Finley 1.50 4.00
GE26 Nick Van Exel 1.25 3.00
GE27 Anfernee Hardaway 2.50 6.00
GE28 Elton Brand 2.50 6.00
GE29 Lamar Odom 2.50 6.00
GE30 Baron Davis 2.50 6.00

1999-00 Topps Gallery Gallery of Heroes

Randomly inserted in packs at one in 24, this 10-card set features players on card stock that simulates stained glass. Card backs carry a "GH" prefix.

COMPLETE SET (10) 12.00 30.00
STATED ODDS 1:24
GH1 Kevin Garnett 1.50 4.00
GH2 Stephon Marbury .75 2.00
GH3 Kobe Bryant 10.00 25.00
GH4 Vince Carter 2.00 5.00
GH5 Tim Duncan 2.00 5.00
GH6 Gary Payton 1.00 2.50
GH7 Antoine Walker 1.00 2.50
GH8 Chris Webber 1.00 2.50
GH9 Alonzo Mourning 1.25 3.00
GH10 Karl Malone 1.25 3.00

1999-00 Topps Gallery Heritage

Randomly inserted in packs at one in 12, this 10-card set features players on artwork in the style of the 1956-57 Topps Baseball cards. Card backs carry a "TGH" prefix.

COMPLETE SET (10) 8.00 20.00
STATED ODDS 1:12
*PROOF: .75X TO 2X HI COLUMN
PROOF: STATED ODDS 1:36
TGH1 Tim Duncan 1.50 4.00
TGH2 Elton Brand 2.00 5.00
TGH3 Shaquille O'Neal 2.00 5.00
TGH4 Stephon Marbury .60 1.50
TGH5 Allen Iverson 1.50 4.00
TGH6 Grant Hill 1.00 2.50
TGH7 Charles Barkley 1.25 3.00
TGH8 Jason Williams 1.00 2.50
TGH9 Scottie Pippen 1.25 3.00
TGH10 Allan Houston .60 1.50

1999-00 Topps Gallery Originals

Randomly inserted in packs at one in 87, this 10-card set features swatches of player-worn jerseys from the 1999 NBA Rookie Photo Shoot. Card backs carry a "GO" prefix.

STATED ODDS 1:87
GO1 Elton Brand 4.00 10.00
GO2 Shawn Marion 3.00 8.00
GO3 Corey Maggette 2.50 6.00
GO4 Steve Francis 4.00 10.00
GO5 Wally Szczerbiak 3.00 8.00
GO6 Baron Davis 4.00 10.00
GO7 Jonathan Bender 1.50 4.00
GO8 Jason Terry 2.50 6.00
GO9 Richard Hamilton 3.00 8.00
GO10 Andre Miller 3.00 8.00

1999-00 Topps Gallery Photo Gallery

Randomly inserted in packs at one in 12, this 10-card set features cards that were created in a cross-promotion with NBA.com, where fans chose their favorite photos. Card backs carry a "PG" prefix.

COMPLETE SET (10) 2.00 5.00
STATED ODDS 1:12
PG1 Tim Duncan .50 1.25
PG2 Allen Iverson .50 1.25
PG3 Gary Payton .25 .60
PG4 Elton Brand .60 1.50
PG5 Steve Francis .60 1.50
PG6 Latrell Sprewell .25 .60
PG7 Jason Kidd .40 1.00
PG8 Shawn Marion .50 1.25
PG9 Shareef Abdur-Rahim .20 .50
PG10 Jason Williams .30 .75

2000-01 Topps Gallery

The 2000-01 Topps Gallery product was released in April, 2001 and featured a 150-card base set that was broken into tiers as follows: Base Veterans (1-125) and Rookies (126-150) serial numbered to 999. Each pack contained six cards and carried a suggested retail price of $2.99.

COMP.SET w/o RC's (125) 15.00 40.00
126-150 STATED PRINT RUN 999 SER.#'d SETS
SUBSET CARDS SAME VALUE AS BASE
1 Allen Iverson .50 1.25
2 Terrell Brandon .15 .40
3 Tracy McGrady .40 1.00
4 Shawn Marion .20 .50
5 Steve Smith .20 .50
6 Avery Johnson .20 .50
7 Gary Payton .25 .60
8 Mark Jackson .20 .50
9 Mike Bibby .25 .60
10 Karl Malone .30 .75
11 Kevin Garnett .40 1.00
12 Tim Hardaway .25 .60
13 Isaiah Rider .20 .50
14 Corey Maggette .20 .50
15 Vince Carter .50 1.25
16 Vin Baker .20 .50
17 Paul Pierce .25 .60
18 Matt Harpring .15 .40
19 Ron Artest .25 .60
20 Kenny Anderson .20 .50
21 Larry Hughes .20 .50
22 Antonio McDyess .20 .50
23 Shandon Anderson .15 .40
24 Joe Smith .20 .50
25 Jermaine O'Neal .20 .50
26 Horace Grant .20 .50
27 Ray Allen .25 .60
28 Keith Van Horn .20 .50
29 Darrell Armstrong .15 .40
30 Shaquille O'Neal .60 1.50
31 Reggie Miller .25 .60
32 Allan Houston .20 .50
33 Grant Hill .30 .75
34 David Robinson .40 1.00
35 Clifford Robinson .15 .40
36 Theo Ratliff .15 .40
37 Rashard Lewis .25 .60
38 Peja Stojakovic .25 .60
39 Jason Kidd .40 1.00
40 Latrell Sprewell .20 .50
41 Stephon Marbury .20 .50
42 Sam Cassell .20 .50
43 Brian Grant .15 .40
44 Jalen Rose .20 .50
45 Antawn Jamison .25 .60
46 Raef LaFrentz .15 .40
47 Dirk Nowitzki .40 1.00
48 Lamond Murray .15 .40
49 Derrick Coleman .20 .50
50 Steve Francis .20 .50
51 Dikembe Mutombo .25 .60
52 Elton Brand .25 .60
53 Christian Laettner .20 .50
54 Ben Wallace .20 .50
55 Jim Jackson .15 .40
56 Cuttino Mobley .15 .40
57 Jonathan Bender .15 .40
58 Anthony Mason .15 .40
59 Tim Thomas .15 .40
60 Lamar Odom .20 .50
61 Glenn Robinson .20 .50
62 Kendall Gill .15 .40
63 Glen Rice .20 .50
64 Anfernee Hardaway .40 1.00
65 Jason Williams .25 .60
66 Shawn Kemp .25 .60
67 Derek Anderson .15 .40
68 Patrick Ewing .30 .75
69 Shareef Abdur-Rahim .20 .50
70 Tim Duncan .50 1.25
71 Rod Strickland .15 .40
72 Bryon Russell .15 .40
73 Antonio Davis .15 .40
74 Rasheed Wallace .25 .60
75 Wally Szczerbiak .20 .50
76 Eric Snow .15 .40
77 Toni Kukoc .25 .60
78 Michael Olowokandi .15 .40
79 Hakeem Olajuwon .30 .75
80 Kobe Bryant 1.00 2.50
81 Mookie Blaylock .15 .40
82 Michael Finley .25 .60
83 Jerry Stackhouse .20 .50
84 Baron Davis .25 .60
85 Jason Terry .25 .60
86 Andre Miller .20 .50
87 Antoine Walker .20 .50
88 Jamal Mashburn .20 .50
89 Nick Van Exel .20 .50
90 Eddie Jones .25 .60
91 Marcus Camby .20 .50
92 Scottie Pippen .40 1.00
93 John Stockton .30 .75
94 Richard Hamilton .20 .50
95 John Starks .20 .50
96 Juwan Howard .20 .50
97 Michael Dickerson .15 .40
98 Ron Mercer .15 .40
99 Chris Webber .25 .60
100 Magic Johnson .60 1.50
101 Shaquille O'Neal MAS .60 1.50
102 Tim Duncan MAS .50 1.25
103 Chris Webber MAS .25 .60
104 Grant Hill MAS .30 .75
105 Kevin Garnett MAS .40 1.00
106 Vince Carter MAS .50 1.25
107 Gary Payton MAS .25 .60
108 Jason Kidd MAS .40 1.00
109 Kobe Bryant MAS 1.00 2.50
110 Karl Malone MAS .30 .75
111 Scottie Pippen MAS .40 1.00
112 Reggie Miller MAS .25 .60
113 John Stockton MAS .30 .75
114 Elton Brand ART .25 .60
115 Tracy McGrady ART .40 1.00
116 Steve Francis ART .20 .50
117 Lamar Odom ART .20 .50
118 Baron Davis ART .25 .60
119 Andre Miller ART .20 .50
120 Jonathan Bender ART .15 .40
121 Paul Pierce ART .25 .60
122 Jason Williams ART .25 .60
123 Rashard Lewis ART .25 .60
124 Larry Hughes ART .20 .50
125 Shawn Marion ART .20 .50
126 Kenyon Martin RC 3.00 8.00
127 Stromile Swift RC 1.25 3.00
128 Darius Miles RC 1.25 3.00
129 Marcus Fizer RC 1.25 3.00
130 Mike Miller RC 2.00 5.00
131 DerMarr Johnson RC 1.00 2.50
132 Chris Mihm RC 1.00 2.50
133 Jamal Crawford RC 3.00 8.00
134 Joel Przybilla RC 1.00 2.50
135 Keyon Dooling RC 1.25 3.00
136 Jerome Moiso RC .75 2.00
137 Etan Thomas RC 1.25 3.00
138 Courtney Alexander RC 1.00 2.50
139 Mateen Cleaves RC 1.00 2.50
140 Jason Collier RC 1.25 3.00
141 Hedo Turkoglu RC 2.00 5.00
142 Desmond Mason RC 1.50 4.00
143 Quentin Richardson RC 1.25 3.00
144 Jamaal Magloire RC 1.25 3.00
145 Speedy Claxton RC 1.25 3.00
146 Morris Peterson RC 1.25 3.00
147 Donnell Harvey RC 1.00 2.50
148 DeShawn Stevenson RC 1.25 3.00
149 Stephen Jackson RC 2.00 5.00
150 Marc Jackson RC 1.00 2.50

2000-01 Topps Gallery Charity Gallery

Randomly inserted into packs at one in 12, this 10-card insert features players that make a difference in the community. Card backs carry a "CG" prefix.

COMPLETE SET (10) 6.00 15.00
STATED ODDS 1:12
CG1 Eddie Jones 1.00 2.50
CG2 Ray Allen 1.00 2.50
CG3 Elton Brand 1.00 2.50
CG4 Jason Kidd 1.50 4.00
CG5 Derek Anderson .60 1.50
CG6 Karl Malone 1.25 3.00
CG7 Brian Grant .60 1.50
CG8 Shareef Abdur-Rahim .75 2.00
CG9 Rasheed Wallace 1.00 2.50
CG10 Marcus Camby .75 2.00

2000-01 Topps Gallery Extremes

Randomly inserted into packs at one in 18, this 20-card insert features players that have taken their game to the next level. Card backs carry a "E" prefix.

COMPLETE SET (20) 20.00 50.00
STATED ODDS 1:18
E1 Shaquille O'Neal 3.00 8.00
E2 Vince Carter 2.50 6.00
E3 Allen Iverson 2.50 6.00
E4 Kevin Garnett 2.00 5.00
E5 Chris Webber 1.25 3.00
E6 Larry Hughes 1.00 2.50
E7 Jason Williams 1.25 3.00
E8 Steve Francis 1.00 2.50
E9 Antonio McDyess 1.00 2.50
E10 Tim Duncan 2.50 6.00
E11 Gary Payton 1.25 3.00
E12 Lamar Odom 1.00 2.50
E13 Elton Brand 1.25 3.00
E14 Michael Finley 1.25 3.00
E15 Latrell Sprewell 1.00 2.50
E16 Shareef Abdur-Rahim 1.00 2.50
E17 Jerry Stackhouse 1.00 2.50
E18 Rashard Lewis 1.25 3.00
E19 Shawn Marion 1.00 2.50
E20 Darius Miles 1.25 3.00

2000-01 Topps Gallery Gallery of Heroes

Randomly inserted into packs at one in 24, this 10-card insert features players that have a knack for heroics. Card backs carry a "GH" prefix.

COMPLETE SET (10) 20.00 40.00
STATED ODDS 1:24
GH1 Allen Iverson 3.00 8.00
GH2 Tim Duncan 3.00 8.00
GH3 Kobe Bryant 10.00 25.00
GH4 Elton Brand 1.50 4.00
GH5 Ray Allen 1.50 4.00
GH6 Stephon Marbury 1.25 3.00
GH7 Eddie Jones 1.50 4.00
GH8 Gary Payton 1.50 4.00
GH9 Antonio McDyess 1.25 3.00
GH10 Shareef Abdur-Rahim 1.25 3.00

2000-01 Topps Gallery Heritage

Randomly inserted into packs at one in 10, this 10-card insert features some of the hottest players in the league. Card backs carry a "H" prefix. Please note that there is a parallel to this set that was inserted at 1:186.

COMPLETE SET (10) 8.00 20.00
STATED ODDS 1:10
*PROOFS: 1.5X TO 4X BASE CARD HI
PROOFS STATED ODDS 1:186
PROOFS PRINT RUN 250 SERIAL #'d SETS
H1 Tim Duncan 2.00 5.00
H2 Tracy McGrady 1.50 4.00
H3 Steve Francis .75 2.00
H4 Elton Brand 1.00 2.50
H5 Rashard Lewis 1.00 2.50
H6 Larry Hughes .75 2.00
H7 Shawn Marion .75 2.00
H8 Baron Davis 1.00 2.50
H9 Antawn Jamison 1.00 2.50
H10 Keyon Dooling 1.00 2.50

2000-01 Topps Gallery Originals

Randomly inserted into packs, this 31-card insert features swatches of actual game-used jerseys. Card backs carry a "GO" prefix. Please note that the insert was broken into tiers as follows: Group A was inserted at 1:153, Group B was inserted at one in 1:71, Group C was inserted at 1:255, and Group D at 1:1148.

GROUP A ODDS 1:153; B ODDS 1:71
GROUP C ODDS 1:255; D ODDS 1:1148
ROOKIE STATED ODDS 1:48 OVERALL
VETERAN STATED ODDS 1:209 OVERALL
GO1 Kenyon Martin B 5.00 12.00
GO2 Stromile Swift B 2.00 5.00
GO3 Darius Miles B 2.00 5.00
GO4 Marcus Fizer B 2.00 5.00
GO5 Mike Miller B 3.00 8.00
GO6 DerMarr Johnson B 1.50 4.00
GO7 Chris Mihm B 1.50 4.00
GO8 Joel Przybilla B 1.50 4.00
GO9 Keyon Dooling B 2.00 5.00
GO10 Jerome Moiso B 1.25 3.00
GO11 Etan Thomas B 2.00 5.00
GO12 Courtney Alexander B 1.50 4.00
GO13 Mateen Cleaves B 1.50 4.00
GO14 Jason Collier A 2.00 5.00
GO15 Hedo Turkoglu A 3.00 8.00
GO16 Desmond Mason A 2.50 6.00
GO17 Quentin Richardson A 2.00 5.00
GO18 Jamaal Magloire A 2.00 5.00
GO19 Speedy Claxton A 2.00 5.00
GO20 Morris Peterson A 2.00 5.00
GO21 Donnell Harvey A 1.50 4.00
GO22 DeShawn Stevenson A 2.00 5.00
GO23 Mamadou N'Diaye A 1.25 3.00
GO24 Erick Barkley A 1.25 3.00
GO25 Mark Madsen A 2.00 5.00
GO26 Tracy McGrady C 3.00 8.00
GO27 Shaquille O'Neal D 5.00 12.00
GO28 Grant Hill C 2.50 6.00
GO29 Tim Duncan D 4.00 10.00
GO30 Antoine Walker C 1.50 4.00
GO31 Jason Kidd C 3.00 8.00

2000-01 Topps Gallery Photo Gallery

Randomly inserted into packs at one in 10, this 10-card insert features great photos of some of the great young players in the game. Card backs carry a "PG" prefix.

COMPLETE SET (10) 10.00 25.00
STATED ODDS 1:10
PG1 Kevin Garnett 1.25 3.00
PG2 Grant Hill 1.00 2.50
PG3 Kobe Bryant 3.00 8.00
PG4 Vince Carter 1.50 4.00
PG5 Lamar Odom .60 1.50
PG6 Stephon Marbury .60 1.50
PG7 Baron Davis .75 2.00
PG8 Chris Webber .75 2.00
PG9 Ray Allen .75 2.00
PG10 Kenyon Martin 2.00 5.00

2000-01 Topps Gallery Signatures

Randomly inserted into packs, this 7-card insert features autographs from some of the hottest young players in the league. Card backs carry a "GS" prefix followed by the players initials. Please note that the insert was broken into tiers as follows: Group A inserted at 1:1836, Group B at 1:765, Group C at 1:574, Group D at 1:918, and Group E at 1:612.

GROUP A ODDS 1:1836; B ODDS 1:765
GROUP C ODDS 1:574; D ODDS 1:918
GROUP E ODDS 1:612
STATED ODDS 1:158 OVERALL
GSEB Elton Brand C 6.00 15.00
GSEJ Eddie Jones A 10.00 25.00
GSGP Gary Payton E 12.50 30.00
GSJC Jamal Crawford B 6.00 15.00
GSMC Mateen Cleaves D 5.00 12.00
GSMJ Magic Johnson B 40.00 100.00

1999-00 Topps Gold Label Class 1

Released for the first time in basketball for the 1999-2000 season, the set contained 100 cards, including 85 veterans and 15 rookies. The cards were available in five-card packs which carried a suggested retail price of $5. The base set, or Class 1, pictured the background photo as dribbling.

COMPLETE SET (100) 25.00 60.00
ONE TO ONE STATED ODDS 1:629
1 Tim Duncan .75 2.00
2 Steve Smith .30 .75
3 Jeff Hornacek .30 .75
4 Kevin Garnett .60 1.50
5 Paul Pierce .50 1.25
6 Doug Christie .30 .75
7 Charles Barkley .60 1.50
8 Nick Van Exel .30 .75
9 Shareef Abdur-Rahim .30 .75
10 Rod Strickland .25 .60
11 Keith Van Horn .30 .75
12 Matt Harpring .25 .60
13 Randy Brown .25 .60
14 Vin Baker .30 .75
15 Mark Jackson .30 .75
16 Latrell Sprewell .40 1.00
17 Anthony Mason .25 .60
18 Brian Grant .25 .60
19 Brevin Knight .25 .60
20 Elden Campbell .25 .60
21 Allen Iverson .75 2.00
22 Kobe Bryant 1.50 4.00
23 Antawn Jamison .40 1.00
24 Lindsey Hunter .25 .60
25 Eddie Jones .40 1.00
26 Michael Finley .40 1.00
27 Juwan Howard .30 .75
28 Antonio McDyess .30 .75
29 David Robinson .60 1.50
30 Karl Malone .60 1.50
31 Jason Kidd .60 1.50
32 Zydrunas Ilgauskas .30 .75
33 Vince Carter .75 2.00
34 Maurice Taylor .25 .60
35 Alonzo Mourning .50 1.25
36 Tim Thomas .30 .75
37 Dikembe Mutombo .40 1.00
38 Grant Hill .50 1.25
39 Jason Williams .50 1.25
40 Scottie Pippen .60 1.50
41 Stephon Marbury .30 .75
42 Reggie Miller .40 1.00
43 Tyrone Nesby RC .30 .75
44 Ron Mercer .30 .75
45 Terrell Brandon .25 .60
46 Darrell Armstrong .25 .60
47 Larry Hughes .30 .75
48 Alan Henderson .25 .60
49 Ray Allen .40 1.00
50 Rasheed Wallace .40 1.00
51 Toni Kukoc .40 1.00
52 Patrick Ewing .50 1.25
53 Tom Gugliotta .25 .60
54 Chris Mills .25 .60
55 Gary Payton .40 1.00
56 Michael Olowokandi .25 .60
57 Chris Mullin .40 1.00
58 Shawn Kemp .40 1.00
59 Joe Smith .30 .75
60 Steve Nash .60 1.50
61 Gary Trent .25 .60
62 Shaquille O'Neal 1.00 2.50
63 Kerry Kittles .25 .60
64 Tim Hardaway .40 1.00
65 Glenn Robinson .30 .75
66 Damon Stoudamire .30 .75
67 Anfernee Hardaway .60 1.50
68 Vlade Divac .40 1.00
69 John Starks .30 .75
70 Allan Houston .30 .75
71 Jerry Stackhouse .40 1.00
72 Avery Johnson .30 .75
73 Glen Rice .40 1.00
74 Felipe Lopez .25 .60
75 Clifford Robinson .25 .60
76 Jamal Mashburn .30 .75
77 Hakeem Olajuwon .50 1.25
78 Matt Geiger .25 .60
79 John Stockton .50 1.25
80 Chauncey Billups .40 1.00
81 Chris Webber .40 1.00
82 Antoine Walker .40 1.00
83 Mike Bibby .40 1.00
84 Tracy McGrady .60 1.50
85 Mitch Richmond .40 1.00
86 Elton Brand RC 1.00 2.50
87 Steve Francis RC 1.00 2.50
88 Baron Davis RC 1.00 2.50
89 Lamar Odom RC 1.00 2.50
90 Jonathan Bender RC .40 1.00
91 Wally Szczerbiak RC .75 2.00
92 Richard Hamilton RC .75 2.00
93 Andre Miller RC .75 2.00
94 Shawn Marion RC .75 2.00
95 Jason Terry RC .60 1.50
96 Trajan Langdon RC .40 1.00
97 A.Radojevic RC .25 .60
98 Corey Maggette RC .60 1.50
99 William Avery RC .30 .75
100 Cal Bowdler RC .25 .60

1999-00 Topps Gold Label Class 1 Black Label

*STARS: 1.5X TO 4X BASE HI
*RCs: 1.25X TO 3X BASE HI
STATED ODDS 1:8

1999-00 Topps Gold Label Class 1 Red Label

*STARS: 10X TO 25X BASE HI
*RCs: 6X TO 15X BASE HI
STATED PRINT RUN 100 SERIAL #'d SETS

1999-00 Topps Gold Label Class 2

COMPLETE SET (100) 40.00 100.00
*STARS: .75X TO 2X CLASS 1 BASE
*RCs: .6X TO 1.5X CLASS 1 BASE
STATED ODDS 1:2

1999-00 Topps Gold Label Class 2 Black Label

*STARS: 3X TO 8X CLASS 1 BASE
*RCs: 2.5X TO 6X CLASS 1 BASE
STATED ODDS 1:16

1999-00 Topps Gold Label Class 2 Red Label

*STARS: 15X TO 40X CLASS 1 BASE
*RCs: 8X TO 20X CLASS 1 BASE
STATED PRINT RUN 50 SERIAL #'d SETS

1999-00 Topps Gold Label Class 3

COMPLETE SET (100) 75.00 150.00
*STARS: 1.25X TO 3X CLASS 1 BASE
*RCs: 1X TO 2.5X CLASS 1 BASE
STATED ODDS 1:4

1999-00 Topps Gold Label Class 3 Black Label

*STARS: 5X TO 12X CLASS 1 BASE
*RCs: 4X TO 10X CLASS 1 BASE
STATED ODDS 1:32

1999-00 Topps Gold Label Class 3 Red Label

*STARS: 25X TO 60X CLASS 1 BASE
*RCs: 10X TO 25X CLASS 1 BASE
STATED PRINT RUN 25 SERIAL #'d SETS
30 Karl Malone 75.00 200.00
33 Vince Carter 100.00 250.00

1999-00 Topps Gold Label New Standard

Randomly inserted in packs at one in 12, this 15-card set features current and future stars with less than three years of NBA experience. The cards feature a "NS" prefix on the back.
COMPLETE SET (15) 15.00 40.00
STATED ODDS 1:12
*BLACK: 1X TO 2.5X HI COLUMN
BLACK: STATED ODDS 1:60
*RED STARS: 10X TO 25X HI
RED: STATED ODDS 1:1692
RED: PRINT RUN 25 SERIAL #'d SETS
NS1 Vince Carter 1.50 4.00
NS2 Kevin Garnett 1.25 3.00
NS3 Tim Duncan 1.50 4.00
NS4 Kobe Bryant 3.00 8.00
NS5 Allen Iverson 1.50 4.00
NS6 Jason Williams 1.00 2.50
NS7 Keith Van Horn .60 1.50
NS8 Elton Brand 1.50 4.00
NS9 Steve Francis 1.50 4.00
NS10 Baron Davis 1.50 4.00
NS11 Lamar Odom 1.50 4.00
NS12 Jonathan Bender .60 1.50
NS13 Wally Szczerbiak 1.25 3.00
NS14 Jason Terry 1.00 2.50
NS15 Corey Maggette 1.00 2.50

1999-00 Topps Gold Label Prime Gold

Randomly inserted in packs at one in 18, this 11-card set focuses on veteran players who have set the standard in the NBA. Card backs carry a "PG" prefix.
COMPLETE SET (11) 6.00 15.00
STATED ODDS 1:18
*BLACK: 1X TO 2.5X HI COLUMN
BLACK: STATED ODDS 1:90
*RED: 12X TO 30X HI
RED: STATED ODDS 1:2312
RED: PRINT RUN 25 SERIAL #'d SETS
PG1 John Stockton 1.00 2.50
PG2 Hakeem Olajuwon 1.00 2.50
PG3 Charles Barkley 1.25 3.00
PG4 Shaquille O'Neal 2.00 5.00
PG5 Alonzo Mourning 1.00 2.50
PG6 Scottie Pippen 1.25 3.00
PG7 Jason Kidd 1.25 3.00
PG8 David Robinson 1.25 3.00
PG9 Gary Payton .75 2.00
PG10 Karl Malone 1.00 2.50
PG11 Grant Hill 1.00 2.50

1999-00 Topps Gold Label Quest for the Gold

Randomly inserted in packs at one in nine, this nine-card set features players who will participate in the 2000 Summer Olympic Games for the USA Basketball team. Card backs carry a "Q" prefix.
STATED ODDS 1:9
*BLACK: 1X TO 2.5X HI COLUMN
BLACK: STATED ODDS 1:45
*RED: 15X TO 40X HI
RED: STATED ODDS 1:2813
RED: PRINT RUN 25 SERIAL #'d SETS
Q1 Allan Houston .50 1.25
Q2 Kevin Garnett 1.00 2.50
Q3 Gary Payton .60 1.50
Q4 Steve Smith .50 1.25
Q5 Tim Hardaway .60 1.50
Q6 Tim Duncan 1.25 3.00
Q7 Jason Kidd 1.00 2.50
Q8 Tom Gugliotta .40 1.00
Q9 Vin Baker .50 1.25

2000-01 Topps Gold Label Class 1

The 2000-01 Topps Gold Label product was released in December,2000. The product features a 100-card base set broken into tiers as follows: 80 Base Veterans (1-80), and 20 Rookies (81-100). Please note that there are four levels of the base set. Class one features the player dribbling, class two features the player shooting, class three features the player defending, and finally, there is a premium parallel that features the player dribbling, shooting, and defending on the same card. Each pack contained five cards and carried a suggested retail price of $5.00. Class 1 rookie cards were inserted at one in 29 and serially numbered to 1499.
COMPLETE SET w/o RC (80) 15.00 30.00
RCs: STATED ODDS 1:29
RCs: STATED PRINT RUN 1499 SERIAL #'d SETS
1 Steve Francis .30 .75
2 Jalen Rose .30 .75
3 Allen Iverson .75 2.00
4 Damon Stoudamire .30 .75
5 David Robinson .60 1.50
6 Bryon Russell .25 .60
7 Toni Kukoc .40 1.00
8 Tracy McGrady .60 1.50
9 John Stockton .50 1.25
10 Tim Duncan .75 2.00
11 Hakeem Olajuwon .50 1.25
12 Antoine Walker .30 .75
13 Dikembe Mutombo .40 1.00
14 Shawn Kemp .40 1.00
15 Ron Artest .40 1.00
16 Eddie Jones .40 1.00
17 Dirk Nowitzki .60 1.50
18 Nick Van Exel .30 .75
19 Grant Hill .50 1.25
20 Antawn Jamison .40 1.00
21 Cuttino Mobley .25 .60
22 Jonathan Bender .25 .60
23 Maurice Taylor .25 .60
24 Kobe Bryant 1.50 4.00
25 Tim Hardaway .40 1.00
26 Tim Thomas .25 .60
27 Terrell Brandon .25 .60
28 Marcus Camby .30 .75
29 Keith Van Horn .30 .75
30 Shawn Marion .30 .75
31 Rasheed Wallace .40 1.00
32 Corey Maggette .30 .75
33 Jason Kidd .60 1.50
34 Shaquille O'Neal 1.00 2.50
35 Rashard Lewis .40 1.00
36 Karl Malone .50 1.25
37 Michael Dickerson .25 .60
38 Richard Hamilton .30 .75
39 Darrell Armstrong .25 .60
40 Wally Szczerbiak .30 .75
41 Glen Rice .30 .75
42 Glenn Robinson .30 .75
43 Reggie Miller .40 1.00
44 Alonzo Mourning .50 1.25
45 Larry Hughes .30 .75
46 Antonio McDyess .30 .75
47 Derrick Coleman .30 .75
48 Brevin Knight .25 .60
49 Jason Terry .40 1.00
50 Elton Brand .40 1.00
51 Latrell Sprewell .30 .75
52 Theo Ratliff .25 .60
53 Scottie Pippen .60 1.50
54 Jason Williams .40 1.00
55 Gary Payton .40 1.00
56 Mitch Richmond .30 .75
57 Vin Baker .30 .75
58 Raef LaFrentz .25 .60
59 Anfernee Hardaway .60 1.50
60 Steve Smith .30 .75
61 Stephon Marbury .30 .75
62 Vlade Divac .30 .75
63 Jamal Mashburn .30 .75
64 Jerome Williams .25 .60
65 Patrick Ewing .50 1.25
66 Lamar Odom .30 .75
67 Jerry Stackhouse .30 .75
68 Michael Finley .40 1.00
69 Vince Carter .75 2.00
70 Andre Miller .30 .75
71 Paul Pierce .40 1.00
72 Baron Davis .40 1.00
73 Derek Anderson .25 .60
74 Chris Webber .40 1.00
75 Ray Allen .40 1.00
76 Kevin Garnett .60 1.50
77 Allan Houston .30 .75
78 Mike Bibby .40 1.00
79 Shareef Abdur-Rahim .30 .75
80 Juwan Howard .30 .75
81 Kenyon Martin RC 4.00 10.00
82 Stromile Swift RC 1.50 4.00
83 Darius Miles RC 1.50 4.00
84 Marcus Fizer RC 1.50 4.00
85 Mike Miller RC 2.50 6.00
86 DerMarr Johnson RC 1.25 3.00
87 Chris Mihm RC 1.25 3.00
88 Jamal Crawford RC 4.00 10.00
89 Joel Przybilla RC 1.25 3.00
90 Keyon Dooling RC 1.50 4.00
91 Jerome Moiso RC 1.00 2.50
92 Etan Thomas RC 1.50 4.00
93 Courtney Alexander RC 1.25 3.00
94 Mateen Cleaves RC 1.25 3.00
95 Jason Collier RC 1.50 4.00
96 Desmond Mason RC 2.00 5.00
97 Quentin Richardson RC 1.50 4.00
98 Jamaal Magloire RC 1.50 4.00
99 Speedy Claxton RC 1.50 4.00
100 Morris Peterson RC 1.50 4.00

2000-01 Topps Gold Label Class 2

*CLASS 2 VETS: .75X TO 2X CLASS 1 HI
*CLASS 2 RCs: .3X TO .8X CLASS 1 HI
CLASS 2 VETS: STATED ODDS 1:4
CLASS 2 RCs: PRINT RUN 999 SERIAL #'d SETS

2000-01 Topps Gold Label Class 3

*CLASS 3 VETS: 1.25X TO 3X CLASS 1 HI
*CLASS 3 RCs: .5X TO 1.25X CLASS 1 HI
CLASS 3 VETS: STATED ODDS 1:12
CLASS 3 RCs: PRINT RUN 499 SERIAL #'d SETS

2000-01 Topps Gold Label Premium

*STARS: 2.5X TO 6X BASE CARD HI
*RCs: .75X TO 2X BASE CARD HI
VETS: PRINT RUN 1000 SERIAL #'d SETS
RCs: PRINT RUN 100 SERIAL #'d SETS
RCs: STATED ODDS 1:430

2000-01 Topps Gold Label Autographs

Randomly inserted in packs at one in 1718, this two-card set features autographs of Shaquille O'Neal and Jalen Rose. Each card carries the Topps Genuine Issue seal.
STATED ODDS 1:1718
TTAJR Jalen Rose 10.00 25.00
TTASO Shaquille O'Neal 150.00 300.00

2000-01 Topps Gold Label Game Jerseys

Randomly inserted into packs at one in 40, this 34-card insert features swatches of game-used jersey. Please note that cards labeled "H" are from Laker home jerseys (yellow), and that cards labeled "A" are from the Lakers away jerseys (purple). Card backs carry a "TT" prefix. A leather version of this set was produced as well where the cards are actually printed on leather and inserted in packs at the rate of one in 1039
OVERALL STATED ODDS 1:40
LAKERS (H) JERSEYS ARE YELLOW
LAKERS (A) JERSEYS ARE PURPLE
*LEATHER: 2X TO 5X BASE JSY HI
LEATHER STATED ODDS 1:1039
TT1A Shaquille O'Neal 12.00 30.00
TT1H Shaquille O'Neal 12.00 30.00
TT2A Glen Rice 10.00 25.00
TT2H Glen Rice 10.00 25.00
TT3A Robert Horry 5.00 12.00
TT3H Robert Horry 5.00 12.00
TT4A Rick Fox 4.00 10.00
TT4H Rick Fox 4.00 10.00
TT5A Brian Shaw 4.00 10.00
TT5H Brian Shaw 4.00 10.00
TT6A Ron Harper 6.00 15.00
TT6H Ron Harper 6.00 15.00
TT7A Derek Fisher 10.00 25.00
TT7H Derek Fisher 10.00 25.00
TT8A A.C. Green 5.00 12.00
TT8H A.C. Green 5.00 12.00
TT9A John Salley 4.00 10.00
TT9H John Salley 4.00 10.00
TT10A Travis Knight 4.00 10.00
TT10H Travis Knight 4.00 10.00
TT11A Devean George 4.00 10.00
TT11H Devean George 4.00 10.00
TT12 Reggie Miller 25.00 60.00
TT13 Jalen Rose 8.00 20.00
TT14 Dale Davis 4.00 10.00
TT15 Rik Smits 5.00 12.00
TT16 Mark Jackson 5.00 12.00
TT17 Travis Best 4.00 10.00
TT18 Austin Croshere 6.00 15.00
TT19 Derrick McKey 4.00 10.00
TT20 Sam Perkins 4.00 10.00
TT21 Chris Mullin 12.00 30.00
TT22 Jonathan Bender 4.00 10.00
TT23 Zan Tabak 4.00 10.00

2000-01 Topps Gold Label Great Expectations

Randomly inserted in packs at one in 32, this 10-card set focuses on some of the younger players in the NBA. Card backs carry a "GE" prefix.
COMPLETE SET (10) 7.50 15.00
STATED ODDS 1:32
GE1 Elton Brand 1.00 2.50
GE2 Shawn Marion .75 2.00
GE3 Jason Williams 1.00 2.50
GE4 Baron Davis 1.00 2.50
GE5 Andre Miller .75 2.00
GE6 Paul Pierce 1.00 2.50
GE7 Lamar Odom .75 2.00
GE8 Dirk Nowitzki 1.50 4.00
GE9 Kenyon Martin 2.50 6.00
GE10 Marcus Fizer 1.00 2.50

2000-01 Topps Gold Label Home Court Advantage

Randomly inserted in packs at one in 40, this 15-card set focuses players that make it extemely tuff for opposing players to win on their courts. Card backs carry a "HCA" prefix.
COMPLETE SET (15) 15.00 40.00
STATED ODDS 1:40
HCA1 Tim Duncan 3.00 8.00
HCA2 Antoine Walker 1.25 3.00
HCA3 Chris Webber 1.50 4.00
HCA4 Alonzo Mourning 2.00 5.00
HCA5 Karl Malone 2.00 5.00
HCA6 Allen Iverson 3.00 8.00
HCA7 Jason Kidd 2.50 6.00
HCA8 Rasheed Wallace 1.50 4.00
HCA9 Gary Payton 1.50 4.00
HCA10 Shareef Abdur-Rahim 1.25 3.00
HCA11 Eddie Jones 1.50 4.00
HCA12 Stephon Marbury 1.25 3.00
HCA13 Scottie Pippen 2.50 6.00
HCA14 Raef LaFrentz 1.00 2.50
HCA15 Elton Brand 1.50 4.00

2000-01 Topps Gold Label Jam Artists

Randomly inserted in packs at one in 8, this 10-card set focuses players that have helped define the art of dunking in the NBA. Card backs carry a "JA" prefix.
COMPLETE SET (10) 4.00 10.00
STATED ODDS 1:8
JA1 Vince Carter .75 2.00
JA2 Tracy McGrady .60 1.50
JA3 Steve Francis .30 .75
JA4 Jerry Stackhouse .30 .75
JA5 Kevin Garnett .60 1.50
JA6 Michael Finley .40 1.00
JA7 Stromile Swift .40 1.00
JA8 Kobe Bryant 1.50 4.00
JA9 Darius Miles .40 1.00
JA10 Larry Hughes .30 .75

1998 Topps Golden Greats

The 1998 Topps Golden Greats set was issued in one series totalling 18 cards. The one card packs retailed for $9.99 each. The cards feature vintage footage on lenticular card technology utilizing Kodamotion technology.
COMPLETE SET (18) 25.00 60.00
1 Kareem Abdul-Jabbar 3.00 8.00
2 Elgin Baylor 2.00 5.00
3 Larry Bird 5.00 12.00
4 Wilt Chamberlain 4.00 10.00
5 Bob Cousy 3.00 8.00
6 Julius Erving 3.00 8.00
7 Walt Frazier 2.00 5.00
8 George Gervin 2.00 5.00
9 John Havlicek 2.50 6.00
10 Magic Johnson 5.00 12.00
11 Kevin McHale 2.50 6.00
12 Earl Monroe 2.00 5.00
13 Willis Reed 2.00 5.00
14 Oscar Robertson 2.50 6.00
15 Bill Russell 3.00 8.00
16 Bill Walton 2.00 5.00
17 Jerry West 2.50 6.00
18 Rick Barry 1.50 4.00

1998 Topps Golden Greats Laser Cuts

COMPLETE SET (18) 40.00 100.00
*LASER CUTS: .75X TO 2X BASE HI

2008-09 Topps Hardwood

This set was released on January 21, 2008. The base set consists of 125 cards. Cards 1-100 feature veterans, and cards 101-125 are rookies. Each rookie has two verisons, listed below, with both serially numbered to 2009.
COMP.SET w/o SPs (100) 20.00 40.00
RC PRINT RUN 2009 SER.#'d SETS
TWO VERSIONS EXIST FOR EACH RC
UNPRICED EBONY PRINT RUN ONE SET
UNPRICED PRESS PLATE PRINT RUN ONE SET
1 Paul Pierce .40 1.00
2 Andrew Bogut .30 .75
3 Greg Oden .30 .75
4 Monta Ellis .30 .75
5 Shaquille O'Neal .75 2.00
6 Al Horford .40 1.00
7 Al Thornton .30 .75
8 Anderson Varejao .25 .60
9 Andre Iguodala .30 .75
10 Carlos Boozer .30 .75
11 Chris Bosh .40 1.00
12 Corey Maggette .30 .75
13 Craig Smith .25 .60
14 Danny Granger .30 .75
15 David West .30 .75
16 Josh Howard .30 .75
17 Kevin Durant 1.00 2.50
18 Kevin Garnett .60 1.50
19 Luis Scola .30 .75
20 Luol Deng .30 .75
21 Yi Jianlian .40 1.00
22 Pau Gasol .40 1.00
23 Rasheed Wallace .40 1.00
24 Ben Gordon .30 .75
25 Dwyane Wade .60 1.50
26 Gilbert Arenas .30 .75
27 Jamal Crawford .40 1.00
28 Gerald Wallace .30 .75
29 Jason Richardson .40 1.00
30 Kevin Martin .30 .75
31 Mike Conley Jr. .30 .75
32 Richard Hamilton .30 .75
33 Tony Parker .40 1.00
34 Vince Carter .50 1.25
35 Brad Miller .30 .75
36 Al Jefferson .30 .75
37 Antawn Jamison .30 .75
38 Carmelo Anthony .50 1.25
39 David Lee .25 .60
40 Dirk Nowitzki .50 1.25
41 Elton Brand .40 1.00
42 Jose Calderon .25 .60
43 Josh Smith .30 .75
44 LaMarcus Aldridge .40 1.00
45 LeBron James 1.50 4.00
46 Peja Stojakovic .40 1.00
47 Rashard Lewis .30 .75
48 Richard Jefferson .30 .75
49 Devin Harris .25 .60
50 Joe Johnson .30 .75
51 Shawn Marion .30 .75
52 Stephen Jackson .30 .75
53 Tayshaun Prince .30 .75
54 Baron Davis .30 .75
55 Chris Paul .50 1.25
56 Mike Dunleavy .30 .75
57 Deron Williams .30 .75
58 Kobe Bryant 1.50 4.00
59 Jason Kidd .40 1.00
60 Ray Allen .40 1.00
61 Manu Ginobili .40 1.00
62 Michael Redd .30 .75
63 Rajon Rondo .40 1.00
64 Raymond Felton .30 .75
65 Steve Nash .40 1.00
66 T.J. Ford .25 .60
67 Tracy McGrady .40 1.00
68 Amare Stoudemire .30 .75
69 Andrew Bynum .25 .60
70 Ben Wallace .30 .75
71 Eddy Curry .25 .60
72 Marcus Camby .25 .60
73 Tyson Chandler .30 .75
74 Yao Ming .50 1.25
75 Andrei Kirilenko .30 .75
76 Andres Nocioni .25 .60
77 Caron Butler .30 .75
78 Hedo Turkoglu .30 .75
79 Jeff Green .30 .75
80 Mike Miller .30 .75
81 Ron Artest .40 1.00
82 Rudy Gay .40 1.00
83 Tim Duncan .60 1.50
84 Udonis Haslem .25 .60
85 Dwight Howard .30 .75
86 Jermaine O'Neal .30 .75
87 Allen Iverson .50 1.25
88 Andre Miller .30 .75
89 Brandon Roy .40 1.00
90 Chauncey Billups .40 1.00
91 Dominique Wilkins .50 1.25
92 Isiah Thomas .40 1.00
93 John Stockton .60 1.50
94 Magic Johnson 1.00 2.50
95 George Gervin .50 1.25
96 Bill Russell .60 1.50
97 David Robinson .60 1.50
98 Larry Bird 1.00 2.50
99 Jerry West .50 1.25
100 Dennis Rodman .75 2.00
101 Derrick Rose 1 Ball RC 4.00 10.00
101B Derrick Rose 2 Balls RC 4.00 10.00
102 M.Beasley Shooting RC 1.00 2.50
102B M.Beasley Pointing RC 1.00 2.50
103 O.J. Mayo Shooting RC 1.00 2.50
103B O.J. Mayo Standing RC 1.00 2.50
104 R.Westbrook Shooting RC 8.00 20.00
104B R.Westbrook Standing RC 8.00 20.00
105 Kevin Love Shooting RC 3.00 8.00
105B Kevin Love Posing RC 3.00 8.00
106 D.Gallinari Dribbling RC 1.50 4.00
106B D.Gallinari Standing RC 1.50 4.00
107 Eric Gordon Shooting RC 1.50 4.00
107B Eric Gordon Standing RC 1.50 4.00
108 Joe Alexander Shooting RC .60 1.50
108B Joe Alexander Passing RC .60 1.50
109 D.J. Augustin Shooting RC .75 2.00
109B D.J. Augustin Posing RC .75 2.00
110 Brook Lopez Shooting RC 1.25 3.00
110B Brook Lopez Posing RC 1.25 3.00
111 Jerryd Bayless Passing RC .75 2.00
111B Jerryd Bayless Posing RC .75 2.00
112 J.Thompson Shooting RC .60 1.50
112B Jason Thompson Posing RC .60 1.50
113 Brandon Rush Action RC .75 2.00
113B Brandon Rush Posing RC .75 2.00
114 A.Randolph Finger RC .60 1.50
114B A.Randolph Posing RC .60 1.50
115 Robin Lopez Shooting RC 1.00 2.50
115B Robin Lopez Posing RC 1.00 2.50
116 M.Speights Action RC .75 2.00
116B M.Speights Posing RC .75 2.00
117 Roy Hibbert Shooting RC 1.00 2.50
117B Roy Hibbert Posing RC 1.00 2.50
118 J.J.Hickson Ball in Front RC .75 2.00
118B J.J. Hickson Ball on Side RC .75 2.00
119 Ryan Anderson Ball RC .75 2.00
119B Ryan Anderson Posing RC .75 2.00
120 Courtney Lee Face Right RC .75 2.00
120B Courtney Lee Face Left RC .75 2.00
121 Kosta Koufos Shooting RC .75 2.00
121B Kosta Koufos Posing RC .75 2.00
122 Darrell Arthur Forward RC .75 2.00
122B Darrell Arthur Face Left RC .75 2.00
123 Donte Greene Ball Up RC .60 1.50
123B Donte Greene Ball Down RC .60 1.50
124 Mario Chalmers 2 Balls RC 1.00 2.50
124B Mario Chalmers 1 Ball RC 1.00 2.50
125 Rudy Fernandez 2 Balls RC .75 2.00
125B Rudy Fernandez 1 Ball RC .75 2.00

2008-09 Topps Hardwood Hardwood

*WOOD: .6X TO 1.5X BASE HI
WOOD PRINT RUN 299 SER.#'d SETS
101 Derrick Rose 1 Ball 6.00 15.00
101B Derrick Rose 2 Balls 6.00 15.00

2008-09 Topps Hardwood Mahogany

*1-100 MAHOGANY: 1.25X TO 3X HI
*101-125 MAHOG: 1X TO 2.5X HI
STATED PRINT RUN 75 SER.#'d SETS
101 Derrick Rose 1 Ball 10.00 25.00
101B Derrick Rose 2 Balls 10.00 25.00

2008-09 Topps Hardwood Maple

*1-100 MAPLE: 1X TO 2.5X BASE HI
*101-125 MAPLE: .75X TO 2X HI
STATED PRINT RUN 175 SER.#'d SETS

2008-09 Topps Hardwood Redwood

*1-100 RED: 6X TO 15X BASE HI
*101-125 RED: 2.5X TO 6X BASE HI
STATED PRINT RUN 15 SER.#'d SETS
101 Derrick Rose 1 Ball 25.00 60.00
101B Derrick Rose 2 Balls 25.00 60.00

2008-09 Topps Hardwood Fabric Signature Patches

ATED PRINT RUN 50 SER.#'d SETS
*MAPLE: .5X TO 1.25X BASE HI
MAPLE PRINT RUN 25 SER.#'d SETS
UNPRICED RED PRINT RUN 5 SER.#'d SETS
UNPRICED ONE OF ONES EXIST
HFSPBL Brook Lopez 12.00 30.00
HFSPBR Brandon Rush 8.00 20.00
HFSPCDR Chris Douglas-Roberts 6.00 15.00
HFSPDGR Donte Greene 6.00 15.00
HFSPEG Eric Gordon 15.00 40.00
HFSPGH George Hill 10.00 25.00
HFSPJJH J.J. Hickson 8.00 20.00
HFSPKL Kevin Love 15.00 40.00
HFSPMS Marreese Speights 8.00 20.00
HFSPOJM O.J. Mayo 10.00 25.00
HFSPRA Ryan Anderson 8.00 20.00
HFSPRH Roy Hibbert 10.00 25.00

2008-09 Topps Hardwood Relics

STATED PRINT RUN 175 SER.#'d SETS
*MAHOGANY: .5X TO 1.25X BASE HI
MAHOG.PRINT RUN 75 SER.#'d SETS
*MAPLE: .6X TO 1.5X BASE HI
MAPLE PRINT RUN 50 SER.#'d SETS
*RED: 1.25X TO 3X BASE HI
RED PRINT RUN 25 SER.#'d SETS
UNPRICED ONE OF ONES EXIST
HRAIG Andre Iguodala 2.00 5.00
HRAS Amare Stoudemire 2.00 5.00
HRBD Baron Davis 2.00 5.00
HRCA Carmelo Anthony 3.00 8.00
HRCB Chauncey Billups 2.50 6.00
HRCBH Chris Bosh 2.50 6.00
HRCBO Carlos Boozer 2.00 5.00
HRCM Corey Maggette 2.00 5.00
HRCP Chris Paul 3.00 8.00
HRDH Dwight Howard 2.00 5.00
HRDN Dirk Nowitzki 3.00 8.00
HRDR Derrick Rose 12.00 30.00
HRDW Dwyane Wade 4.00 10.00
HRDWI Deron Williams 2.00 5.00
HREB Elton Brand 2.50 6.00
HREG Eric Gordon 4.00 10.00
HRGA Gilbert Arenas 2.00 5.00
HRGO Greg Oden 2.00 5.00
HRJJ Joe Johnson 2.00 5.00
HRJO Jermaine O'Neal 2.00 5.00
HRJS Josh Smith 2.00 5.00
HRKB Kobe Bryant 8.00 20.00
HRKG Kevin Garnett 4.00 10.00
HRKL Kevin Love 8.00 20.00
HRKM Kevin Martin 2.00 5.00
HRMB Michael Beasley 2.50 6.00
HROJM O.J. Mayo 2.50 6.00
HRPP Paul Pierce 2.50 6.00
HRSN Steve Nash 2.50 6.00
HRSO Shaquille O'Neal 5.00 12.00
HRTD Tim Duncan 4.00 10.00
HRTM Tracy McGrady 2.50 6.00
HRTP Tony Parker 2.50 6.00
HRVC Vince Carter 3.00 8.00
HRYM Yao Ming 3.00 8.00

2008-09 Topps Hardwood Rookie Autographs

STATED PRINT RUN 69 SER.#'d SETS
MAHOGANY: .5X TO 1.25X BASE HI
MAHOGANY PRINT RUN 19 SER.#'d SETS
UNPRICED MAPLE PRINT RUN 9 SETS
UNPRICED RED PRINT RUN 5 SETS
UNPRICED PRESS PLATES PRINT RUN ONE SET
UNPRICED ONE OF ONES EXIST
101 Derrick Rose 25.00 60.00
102 Michael Beasley 6.00 15.00
103 O.J. Mayo 6.00 15.00
104 Russell Westbrook 100.00 250.00
105 Kevin Love 25.00 60.00
106 Danilo Gallinari 10.00 25.00
107 Eric Gordon 10.00 25.00
108 Joe Alexander 4.00 10.00
109 D.J. Augustin 5.00 12.00
110 Brook Lopez 8.00 20.00
111 Jerryd Bayless 5.00 12.00
112 Jason Thompson 4.00 10.00
113 Brandon Rush 5.00 12.00
114 Anthony Randolph 4.00 10.00
115 Robin Lopez 6.00 15.00
116 Marreese Speights 5.00 12.00
117 Roy Hibbert 6.00 15.00
118 J.J. Hickson 5.00 12.00
119 Ryan Anderson 5.00 12.00
120 Courtney Lee 5.00 12.00
121 Kosta Koufos 5.00 12.00
122 Darrell Arthur 5.00 12.00
123 Donte Greene 4.00 10.00
124 Mario Chalmers 6.00 15.00
125 Rudy Fernandez 5.00 12.00

2008-09 Topps Hardwood Signatures

STATED PRINT RUN 39 SER.#'d SETS
*MAHOGANY: .5X TO 1.25X BASE HI
MAHOGANY PRINT RUN 19 SER.#'d SETS
UNPRICED MAPLE PRINT RUN 9 SER.#'d SETS
UNPRICED RED PRINT RUN 5 SER.#'d SETS
UNPRICED PRESS PLATE PRINT RUN ONE SET
UNPRICED ONE OF ONES EXIST
HSAB Andrea Bargnani 4.00 10.00
HSABY Andrew Bynum 4.00 10.00
HSAJ Antawn Jamison 4.00 10.00
HSBG Ben Gordon 4.00 10.00
HSBR Brandon Roy 4.00 10.00
HSCA Carmelo Anthony 15.00 40.00
HSCB Chauncey Billups 4.00 10.00
HSCP Chris Paul 25.00 60.00
HSDG Danny Granger 4.00 10.00
HSDH Dwight Howard 12.00 30.00
HSDR David Robinson 25.00 60.00
HSDS Dolph Schayes 8.00 20.00
HSDW Dominique Wilkins 15.00 30.00
HSEH Elvin Hayes 5.00 12.00
HSGA Gilbert Arenas 4.00 10.00
HSGG George Gervin 12.00 30.00
HSGO Greg Oden 4.00 10.00
HSIT Isiah Thomas 12.00 30.00
HSJH John Havlicek 15.00 30.00
HSJJW Jo Jo White 6.00 15.00
HSJS John Stockton 20.00 50.00
HSLB Larry Bird 40.00 80.00
HSLW Lenny Wilkens 6.00 15.00
HSMJ Magic Johnson 40.00 80.00
HSPP Paul Pierce 15.00 30.00
HSRB Rick Barry 8.00 20.00
HSRG Rudy Gay 4.00 10.00
HSRP Robert Parish 8.00 20.00
HSRT Reggie Theus 6.00 15.00
HSSO Shaquille O'Neal 40.00 100.00
HSSP Sam Perkins 5.00 12.00
HSTJF T.J. Ford 4.00 10.00
HSTM Tracy McGrady 10.00 25.00
HSTY Thaddeus Young 6.00 15.00

2000-01 Topps Heritage

The 2000-01 Topps Heritage product released in Febuary, 2001. The base set featured 233 cards broken into tiers as follows: Base Veterans (1-24/61-233) and Rookies (25-60) that were inserted at 1:9 and serial numbered to 1972. Each pack contained eight cards, and carried a suggested retail price of $2.99.
COMPLETE SET w/o RC (197) 20.00 50.00
RCs: STATED ODDS 1:9
RCs: STATED PRINT RUN 1972 SERIAL #'d SETS
1 Jason Kidd .60 1.50
2 Allen Iverson .75 2.00
3 Tracy McGrady .60 1.50
4 Tim Duncan .75 2.00
5 Michael Finley .40 1.00
6 Jason Williams .40 1.00
7 Kobe Bryant 1.50 4.00
8 Gary Payton .40 1.00
9 Latrell Sprewell .30 .75
10 Antonio McDyess .30 .75
11 Antoine Walker .30 .75
12 Steve Francis .30 .75
13 Elton Brand .40 1.00
14 Larry Hughes .30 .75
15 Shaquille O'Neal 1.00 2.50
16 Lamar Odom .30 .75
17 Kevin Garnett .60 1.50
18 Vince Carter .75 2.00
19 Ray Allen .40 1.00
20 Grant Hill .50 1.25
21 Chris Webber .40 1.00
22 Paul Pierce .40 1.00
23 Shareef Abdur-Rahim .30 .75
24 Eddie Jones .40 1.00
25 Kenyon Martin RC 4.00 10.00
26 Stromile Swift RC 1.50 4.00
27 Darius Miles RC 1.50 4.00
28 Marcus Fizer RC 1.50 4.00
29 Mike Miller RC 2.50 6.00
30 DerMarr Johnson RC 1.25 3.00
31 Chris Mihm RC 1.25 3.00
32 Jamal Crawford RC 4.00 10.00
33 Joel Przybilla RC 1.25 3.00
34 Keyon Dooling RC 1.50 4.00
35 Jerome Moiso RC 1.00 2.50
36 Etan Thomas RC 1.50 4.00
37 Courtney Alexander RC 1.25 3.00
38 Mateen Cleaves RC 1.25 3.00
39 Jason Collier RC 1.50 4.00
40 Hedo Turkoglu RC 2.50 6.00
41 Desmond Mason RC 2.00 5.00
42 Quentin Richardson RC 1.50 4.00
43 Jamaal Magloire RC 1.50 4.00
44 Speedy Claxton RC 1.50 4.00
45 Morris Peterson RC 1.50 4.00
46 Donnell Harvey RC 1.25 3.00
47 DeShawn Stevenson RC 1.50 4.00
48 Dalibor Bagaric RC 1.25 3.00
49 Iakovos Tsakalidis RC 1.00 2.50
50 Mamadou N'Diaye RC 1.00 2.50
51 Erick Barkley RC 1.00 2.50
52 Mark Madsen RC 1.50 4.00
53 Dan Langhi RC 1.00 2.50
54 A.J. Guyton RC 1.00 2.50
55 Jake Voskuhl RC 1.00 2.50
56 Khalid El-Amin RC 1.00 2.50
57 Lavor Postell RC 1.00 2.50
58 Eduardo Najera RC 1.50 4.00
59 Michael Redd RC 4.00 10.00
60 Stephen Jackson RC 2.50 6.00
61 Andrew DeClercq .25 .60
62 Darrell Armstrong .25 .60
63 Al Harrington .30 .75
64 Johnny Newman .25 .60
65 Baron Davis .40 1.00
66 Adrian Griffin .25 .60
67 Anthony Mason .25 .60
68 Ron Harper .30 .75
69 Michael Olowokandi .25 .60
70 Maurice Taylor .25 .60
71 Travis Best .25 .60
72 Chucky Atkins .25 .60
73 Bob Sura .25 .60
74 Jason Terry .40 1.00
75 Ervin Johnson .25 .60
76 Eric Snow .25 .60
77 Shawn Bradley .25 .60
78 Christian Laettner .30 .75
79 Keith Van Horn .30 .75
80 Damon Stoudamire .30 .75
81 Peja Stojakovic .40 1.00
82 Clifford Robinson .25 .60
83 Elden Campbell .25 .60
84 Kenny Anderson .30 .75
85 Patrick Ewing .50 1.25
86 Mookie Blaylock .25 .60
87 Brian Skinner .25 .60
88 Rick Fox .25 .60
89 Tim Hardaway .40 1.00
90 Brian Grant .25 .60
91 Joe Smith .30 .75
92 Kerry Kittles .25 .60
93 Scottie Pippen .60 1.50
94 Steve Smith .30 .75
95 Sean Elliott .40 1.00
96 Rashard Lewis .40 1.00
97 Michael Dickerson .25 .60
98 Rod Strickland .25 .60
99 Sam Cassell .30 .75
100 Lew Alcindor .60 1.50
101 John Amaechi .25 .60
102 Kendall Gill .25 .60
103 Terrell Brandon .25 .60
104 Dan Majerle .40 1.00
105 Mark Jackson .30 .75
106 Hakeem Olajuwon .50 1.25
107 Antawn Jamison .40 1.00
108 Cedric Ceballos .25 .60
109 Shandon Anderson .25 .60
110 Gary Trent .25 .60
111 Wesley Person .25 .60
112 James Posey .25 .60
113 David Wesley .25 .60
114 Vitaly Potapenko .25 .60
115 P.J. Brown .25 .60
116 Alan Henderson .25 .60
117 Terry Porter .25 .60
118 Lindsey Hunter .25 .60
119 Chauncey Billups .40 1.00
120 Doug Christie .25 .60
121 Glen Rice .30 .75
122 Jamie Feick .25 .60
123 Tom Gugliotta .25 .60
124 Arvydas Sabonis .30 .75
125 Toni Kukoc .40 1.00
126 Shawn Marion .30 .75
127 Dale Davis .25 .60
128 Corliss Williamson .25 .60
129 Brent Barry .25 .60
130 Shammond Williams .25 .60
131 Nick Anderson .25 .60
132 Charles Oakley .30 .75
133 Shaquille O'Neal CHAMP .50 1.25
134 Ron Harper CHAMP .30 .75
135 Kobe Bryant CHAMP .75 2.00
136 Shaquille O'Neal CHAMP .50 1.25
137 L.A. Lakers CHAMP .40 1.00
138 V.Carter/Iverson/J.Stack .50 1.25
139 Iverson/G.Hill/V.Carter .40 1.00
140 Mutombo/Mourning/D.Davis .40 1.00
141 R.Miller/D.Arm/R.Allen .40 1.00
142 Mutombo/Brand/Je.Williams .40 1.00
143 S.Cassell/M.Jackson/E.Snow .40 1.00
144 Checklist .10 .30
145 Checklist .10 .30
146 Shaq/K.Malone/Payton .75 2.00
147 Shaq/K.Malone/Webber .60 1.50
148 Shaq/Patterson/R.Wallace .60 1.50
149 Hornacek/Brandon/Stojakovic .25 .60
150 Shaq/Garnett/Duncan .60 1.50
151 Payton/Van Exel/Stockton .40 1.00
152 Chris Whitney .25 .60
153 Isaac Austin .25 .60
154 Kevin Willis .25 .60
155 Vin Baker .30 .75
156 Avery Johnson .30 .75
157 Rodney Rogers .25 .60
158 Allan Houston .30 .75
159 Austin Croshere .25 .60
160 George Lynch .25 .60
161 Howard Eisley .25 .60
162 Jerome Williams .25 .60
163 LaPhonso Ellis .30 .75
164 Ron Mercer .25 .60
165 Andre Miller .30 .75
166 Tariq Abdul-Wahad .25 .60
167 Donyell Marshall .25 .60
168 Quincy Lewis .25 .60
169 Mitch Richmond .30 .75
170 Richard Hamilton .30 .75
171 Bryant Reeves .25 .60
172 Jim Jackson .25 .60
173 David Robinson .60 1.50
174 Derrick Coleman .30 .75
175 Anthony Peeler .25 .60
176 Theo Ratliff .25 .60
177 Roshown McLeod .25 .60
178 Ron Artest .40 1.00
179 Bryon Russell .25 .60
180 Othella Harrington .25 .60
181 Juwan Howard .30 .75
182 Antonio Davis .25 .60
183 Ruben Patterson .25 .60
184 Shawn Kemp .40 1.00
185 Larry Johnson .40 1.00
186 Marcus Camby .30 .75
187 Eric Piatkowski .25 .60
188 Reggie Miller .40 1.00
189 Anfernee Hardaway .60 1.50
190 Kelvin Cato .25 .60
191 Erick Dampier .25 .60
192 Keon Clark .25 .60
193 Dirk Nowitzki .60 1.50
194 Robert Traylor .25 .60
195 Lamond Murray .25 .60
196 John Wallace .25 .60
197 Robert Horry .30 .75
198 Robert Pack .25 .60
199 Jamal Mashburn .30 .75
200 Corey Benjamin .25 .60
201 Matt Harpring .25 .60
202 Nick Van Exel .30 .75
203 Vonteego Cummings .25 .60
204 Ben Wallace .30 .75
205 Karl Malone .50 1.25
206 Jonathan Bender .25 .60
207 Cuttino Mobley .25 .60
208 Isaiah Rider .30 .75
209 Tyrone Nesby .40 1.00
210 Jermaine O'Neal .30 .75
211 Corey Maggette .30 .75
212 Anthony Carter .25 .60
213 Horace Grant .30 .75
214 Tim Thomas .25 .60
215 Wally Szczerbiak .30 .75
216 Stephon Marbury .30 .75
217 Charlie Ward .25 .60
218 Bo Outlaw .25 .60
219 Matt Geiger .25 .60
220 Vlade Divac .30 .75
221 Rasheed Wallace .40 1.00
222 Derek Anderson .25 .60
223 John Stockton .50 1.25
224 Dikembe Mutombo .40 1.00
225 John Starks .30 .75
226 Mike Bibby .40 1.00
227 Jahidi White .25 .60
228 Jalen Rose .30 .75
229 Glenn Robinson .30 .75
230 Brevin Knight .25 .60
231 Jerry Stackhouse .30 .75
232 Raef LaFrentz .25 .60
233 Brad Miller .30 .75

2000-01 Topps Heritage Proofs

The original artwork for the Topps Heritage set was auctioned off by Topps. 175 Canvas Proof sets were produced and issued to the first 175 runners up in the bidding. Each card is sequentially numbered to 175 and features the autograph of the original artist, Bill Purdom.
*PROOF VETS: 4X TO 10X BASE HI
*PROOF RCs: .6X TO 1.5X

2000-01 Topps Heritage Retrofractors

*STARS: 4X TO 10X BASE CARD HI
*RCs: 1.25X TO 3X BASE CARD HI
STARS: PRINT RUN 272 SERIAL #'d SETS
STARS: STATED ODDS 1:95
RCs: PRINT RUN 72 SERIAL #'d SETS
RCs: STATED ODDS 1:613
15 Shaquille O'Neal 12.00 30.00

2000-01 Topps Heritage Authentic Arena

Randomly inserted into packs at one in 87, this 7-card insert set features swatches of actual arena seats. Card backs carry an "AAR" prefix.
STATED ODDS 1:87
AAR1 Shaquille O'Neal 10.00 25.00
AAR2 Gary Payton 4.00 10.00
AAR3 Anfernee Hardaway 6.00 15.00
AAR4 Hakeem Olajuwon 5.00 12.00
AAR5 Toni Kukoc 4.00 10.00
AAR6 Scottie Pippen 6.00 15.00
AAR7 Juwan Howard 3.00 8.00

2000-01 Topps Heritage Autographs

Randomly inserted into packs at one in 90, this 11-card insert set features different player combinations . Card backs carry a "HA" prefix followed by the player's initials. Please note that the Kareem Abdul-Jabbar proof was inserted at 1:25728.

STATED ODDS 1:90
A-J PROOF: STATED ODDS 1:25,728
IVERSON WAS NEVER REDEEMED
HACA Courtney Alexander 4.00 10.00
HADM Desmond Mason 4.00 10.00
HAKD Keyon Dooling 4.00 10.00
HALH Larry Hughes 4.00 10.00
HASF Steve Francis 5.00 12.00
HASM Shawn Marion 6.00 15.00
HASO Shaquille O'Neal 40.00 100.00
HATM Tracy McGrady 12.00 30.00
NNO K.Abdul-Jabbar PROOF 200.00 400.00

2000-01 Topps Heritage Back to the Future Game Jerseys

Randomly inserted into packs at one in 113, this 6-card insert set features actual game-used jersey swatches from players like Mark Madsen and Jonathan Bender. Card backs carry a "BF" prefix.

STATED ODDS 1:113
BF1 Joel Przybilla 2.00 5.00
BF2 Jerome Moiso 1.50 4.00
BF3 Mateen Cleaves 2.00 5.00
BF4 Speedy Claxton 2.50 6.00
BF5 Mark Madsen 2.50 6.00
BF6 Jonathan Bender 2.50 6.00

2000-01 Topps Heritage Blast from the Past

Randomly inserted into packs at one in 8, this 15-card insert set features present day players on a retro designed card. Card backs carry a "BP" prefix.

COMPLETE SET (15) 6.00 15.00
STATED ODDS 1:8
BP1 Chris Webber .50 1.25
BP2 Kevin Garnett .75 2.00
BP3 Allen Iverson 1.00 2.50
BP4 Rasheed Wallace .50 1.25
BP5 Elton Brand .50 1.25
BP6 Grant Hill .60 1.50
BP7 Ray Allen .50 1.25
BP8 Allan Houston .40 1.00
BP9 Tim Duncan 1.00 2.50
BP10 Eddie Jones .50 1.25
BP11 Tracy McGrady .75 2.00
BP12 Lamar Odom .40 1.00
BP13 Steve Francis .40 1.00
BP14 Jason Williams .50 1.25
BP15 Vince Carter 1.00 2.50

2000-01 Topps Heritage Deja Vu

Randomly inserted into packs at one in 5, this 10-card insert set features players that are so consistent on the court, you might believe that they suffer from Deja Vu . Card backs carry a "DV" prefix.

COMPLETE SET (10) 2.50 6.00
STATED ODDS 1:5
DV1 Larry Hughes .25 .60
DV2 Elton Brand .30 .75
DV3 Steve Francis .25 .60
DV4 Paul Pierce .30 .75
DV5 Allen Iverson .60 1.50
DV6 Gary Payton .30 .75
DV7 Rasheed Wallace .30 .75
DV8 Jason Kidd .50 1.25
DV9 Kobe Bryant 1.25 3.00
DV10 Ray Allen .30 .75

2000-01 Topps Heritage Dynamite Duds Game Jerseys

Randomly inserted into packs at one in 97, this 17-card insert set features actual game-used jersey swatches from players like Stephon Marbury and Darius Miles . Card backs carry a "DD" prefix.

STATED ODDS 1:97
DD1 Dikembe Mutombo 2.50 6.00
DD2 Hanno Mottola 1.50 4.00
DD3 Stephon Marbury 2.00 5.00
DD4 Keith Van Horn 2.00 5.00
DD5 Anfernee Hardaway 4.00 10.00
DD6 Shawn Marion 2.00 5.00
DD7 Shareef Abdur-Rahim 2.00 5.00
DD8 Paul Pierce 2.50 6.00
DD9 Juwan Howard 2.00 5.00
DD10 DerMarr Johnson 2.00 5.00
DD11 Kenyon Martin 6.00 15.00
DD12 Mike Miller 4.00 10.00
DD13 Darius Miles 2.50 6.00
DD14 Keyon Dooling 2.50 6.00
DD15 Quentin Richardson 2.50 6.00
DD16 Iakovos Tsakalidis 1.50 4.00
DD17 Stromile Swift 2.50 6.00

2000-01 Topps Heritage Off the Hook

Randomly inserted into packs at one in 8, this 15-card insert set features players that keep their teams off the hook with their specatular play on the court. Card backs carry a "OH" prefix.

COMPLETE SET (15) 8.00 20.00
STATED ODDS 1:8
OH1 Kevin Garnett .75 2.00
OH2 Vince Carter 1.00 2.50
OH3 Tim Duncan 1.00 2.50
OH4 Allen Iverson 1.00 2.50
OH5 Elton Brand .50 1.25
OH6 Jason Kidd .75 2.00
OH7 Lamar Odom .40 1.00
OH8 Kobe Bryant 2.00 5.00
OH9 Tracy McGrady .75 2.00
OH10 Steve Francis .40 1.00
OH11 Chris Webber .50 1.25
OH12 Larry Hughes .40 1.00
OH13 Jason Williams .50 1.25
OH14 Shareef Abdur-Rahim .40 1.00
OH15 Darius Miles .50 1.25

2001-02 Topps Heritage

Issued in early February 2002, this 264-card set contains veteran players, rookie players, league leader cards, playoff cards, team leader cards, and utilizes the set design for 1974-75 topps. Full color player photos are set against colored backgrounds, white borders, and have the player's team name appearing on the right border of the card. Heritage was packaged in 24-pack boxes where each pack contained eight cards and carried a suggested retail price of $3.00.

COMPLETE SET (264) 60.00 150.00
1 Shaquille O'Neal 1.00 2.50
2 Jalen Rose .30 .75
3 Kwame Brown RC .75 2.00
4 Bryon Russell .25 .60
5 Hakeem Olajuwon .50 1.25
6 Shammond Williams .25 .60
7 Aaron Mckie .25 .60
8 Anfernee Hardaway .60 1.50
9 Dale Davis .25 .60
10 Tracy McGrady .60 1.50
11 Speedy Claxton .25 .60
12 Kurt Thomas .25 .60
13 Keith Van Horn .30 .75
14 Tyson Chandler RC 1.25 3.00
15 Andre Miller .30 .75
16 Dirk Nowitzki .60 1.50
17 Raef Lafrentz .25 .60
18 Mateen Cleaves .25 .60
19 Danny Fortson .25 .60
20 Steve Francis .30 .75
21 Al Harrington .30 .75
22 Keyon Dooling .25 .60
23 Rick Fox .25 .60
24 Michael Dickerson .25 .60
25 Alonzo Mourning .50 1.25
26 Glenn Robinson .30 .75
27 Wally Szczerbiak .30 .75
28 Todd MacCulloch .25 .60
29 Shandon Anderson .25 .60
30 Kobe Bryant 1.50 4.00
31 Tyrone Hill .25 .60
32 Grant Hill .50 1.25
33 Shawn Marion .30 .75
34 Derek Anderson .25 .60
35 Hedo Turkoglu .30 .75
36 David Robinson .60 1.50
37 Gary Payton .40 1.00
38 Alvin Williams .25 .60
39 Pau Gasol RC 2.50 6.00
40 Tim Duncan .75 2.00
41 Rashard Lewis .40 1.00
42 Antonio Davis .25 .60
43 Donyell Marshall .25 .60
44 Jahidi White .25 .60
45 Shareef Abdur-Rahim .30 .75
46 Antoine Walker .30 .75
47 P.J. Brown .25 .60
48 Eddie Robinson .25 .60
49 Chris Mihm .25 .60
50 Kevin Garnett .60 1.50
51 Marcus Camby .30 .75
52 Mike Miller .30 .75
53 Tony Delk .25 .60
54 Mike Bibby .40 1.00
55 Dikembe Mutombo .40 1.00
56 Eddy Curry RC .75 2.00
57 Shawn Bradley .25 .60
58 James Posey .25 .60
59 Jason Richardson RC 1.00 2.50
60 Jason Kidd .60 1.50
61 Eddie Griffin RC .60 1.50
62 Larry Hughes .30 .75
63 Ben Wallace .30 .75
64 Antonio McDyess .30 .75
65 Tim Hardaway .40 1.00
66 Shawn Kemp .40 1.00
67 Bobby Jackson .25 .60
68 Tom Gugliotta .25 .60
69 Antawn Jamison .40 1.00
70 Lamar Odom .30 .75
71 Jamaal Tinsley RC .75 2.00
72 Moochie Norris .25 .60
73 Marc Jackson .25 .60
74 Andrei Kirilenko RC 1.25 3.00
75 Wang Zhizhi .30 .75
76 Eric Snow .25 .60
77 Rasheed Wallace .40 1.00
78 Antonio Daniels .25 .60
79 Vladimir Radmanovic RC .75 2.00
80 Morris Peterson .25 .60
81 Terry/Terry/Mutombo/Terry .40 1.00
82 Pierce/Pllcio/Walkr/Walkr .25 .60
83 Mash/Hawkins/Brwn/Davis .25 .60
84 Brand/Hoiberg/Brand/Hoiberg .40 1.00
85 Millr/Lngdn/Wthrspoon/Millr .25 .60
86 Nowitz/Nash/Nowitz/Nash .40 1.00
87 McDys/McCld/McDys/VnEx .25 .60
88 Stack/Barros/Wllce/Stack .40 1.00
89 Jmisn/Jcksn/Jmisn/Blaylck .40 1.00
90 Frncis/Mobly/Frncis/Frncis .10 .30
91 Rose/Miller/O'Neal/Best .40 1.00
92 Odm/Piatkow/Odm/Mclnns .40 1.00
93 Shaq/Penbrthy/Shaq/Kobe .60 1.50
94 Rahim/Rahim/Rahim/Bibby .40 1.00
95 Jones/Jones/Masn/Hrdawy .25 .60
96 Robnsn/Allen/Jhnsn/Cassll .40 1.00
97 Grntt/Brandn/Grntt/Brandn .50 1.25
98 Mrbry/Newmn/Wllams/Mrbry .25 .60
99 Deshawn Stevenson .25 .60
100 Allen Iverson .75 2.00
101 Jeryl Sasser RC .50 1.25
102 Jason Terry .40 1.00
103 Vitaly Potapenko .25 .60
104 Elden Campbell .25 .60
105 Jamal Crawford .40 1.00
106 Michael Finley .40 1.00
107 Earl Watson RC .75 2.00
108 Clifford Robinson .25 .60
109 Chucky Atkins .25 .60
110 Glen Rice .30 .75
111 Jermaine O'Neal .30 .75
112 Jonathan Bender .25 .60
113 Michael Olowokandi .25 .60
114 Derek Fisher .30 .75
115 Stromile Swift .25 .60
116 Toni Kukoc .40 1.00
117 Samuel Dalembert RC .75 2.00
118 Paul Pierce .40 1.00
119 Jamal Mashburn .30 .75
120 Ron Mercer .25 .60
121 Lamond Murray .25 .60
122 Steve Nash .60 1.50
123 Nick Van Exel .30 .75
124 Desagana Diop RC .60 1.50
125 Ron Artest .40 1.00
126 Marcus Fizer .25 .60
127 Jumaine Jones .25 .60
128 Corliss Williamson .25 .60
129 Rodney White RC .50 1.25
130 Cuttino Mobley .25 .60
131 Reggie Miller .40 1.00
132 Austin Croshere .25 .60
133 Jeff Mcinnis .25 .60
134 Joe Johnson RC 1.00 2.50
135 Kedrick Brown RC .50 1.25
136 Theo Ratliff .25 .60
137 Laphonso Ellis .30 .75
138 Ervin Johnson .25 .60
139 Terrell Brandon .25 .60
140 Chauncey Billups .40 1.00
141 Kenyon Martin .40 1.00
142 Richard Jefferson RC 1.25 3.00
143 Howard Eisley .25 .60
144 Stackhouse/Iverson/Shaq .50 1.25
145 Iverson/Stackhouse/Shaq .60 1.50
146 Shaq/Wells/Camby .40 1.00
147 Miller/Houston/Christie .25 .60
148 Mutombo/Wallace/Shaq .40 1.00
149 Kidd/Stockton/Van Exel .40 1.00
150 Vince Carter .60 1.50
151 Calvin Booth .25 .60
152 Chris Whitney .25 .60
153 John Amaechi .25 .60
154 Keon Clark .25 .60
155 Terry Porter .25 .60
156 Doug Christie .25 .60
157 Gerald Wallace RC 1.00 2.50
158 Zach Randolph RC 1.25 3.00
159 Iakovos Tsakalidis .25 .60
160 Damone Brown RC .50 1.25
161 Ivrsn/Miller/Grntt/Duncan .50 1.25
162 Allen/T-Mac/Shaq/Smith 1.00 2.50
163 Mornig/Dvis/Wbber/Hrdway .40 1.00
164 Houstn/Crtr/Nowitz/Malone .60 1.50
165 Christian Laettner .30 .75
166 John Starks .25 .60
167 Jerome Williams .25 .60
168 Brent Barry .25 .60
169 Malik Rose .25 .60
170 Vlade Divac .30 .75
171 Damon Stoudamire .30 .75
172 Rodney Rogers .25 .60
173 Alvin Jones RC .60 1.50
174 Darrell Armstrong .25 .60
175 Mark Jackson .30 .75
176 Kerry Kittles ERR .25 .60
177 Radoslav Nesterovic .25 .60
178 Brandon Armstrong RC .50 1.25
179 Joe Smith .30 .75
180 Ray Allen .40 1.00
181 Anthony Mason .25 .60
182 Bryant Reeves .25 .60
183 Jason Williams .30 .75
184 Terence Morris RC .75 2.00
185 Travis Best .25 .60
186 Troy Murphy RC .75 2.00
187 Gilbert Arenas RC 1.25 3.00
188 Avery Johnson .30 .75
189 Juwan Howard .30 .75
190 Checklist .10 .30
191 Courtney Alexander .25 .60
192 John Stockton .50 1.25
193 Vin Baker .30 .75
194 Desmond Mason .30 .75
195 Steve Smith .30 .75
196 Steven Hunter RC .60 1.50
197 Stephon Marbury .30 .75
198 Patrick Ewing .50 1.25
199 Allan Houston .30 .75
200 Karl Malone .50 1.25
201 Peja Stojakovic .40 1.00
202 Bonzi Wells .25 .60
203 Latrell Sprewell .30 .75
204 Rafer Alston .25 .60
205 Tony Parker RC 3.00 8.00
206 Michael Bradley RC .50 1.25
207 Richard Hamilton .30 .75
208 Zeljko Rebraca RC .75 2.00
209 Joel Przybilla .25 .60
210 Tim Thomas .25 .60
211 Eddie House .25 .60
212 Brian Grant .25 .60
213 Lindsey Hunter .25 .60
214 Corey Maggette .30 .75
215 Shane Battier RC 1.50 4.00
216 Will Solomon .40 1.00
217 Mitch Richmond .30 .75
218 Eddie Jones .30 .75
219 Elton Brand .40 1.00
220 Quentin Richardson .30 .75
221 Hustn/Houstn/Cmby/Ward .25 .60
222 T-Mc/Armstrong/Outlw/Arm .40 1.00
223 Ivrsn/Ivrsn/Hill/McKie .60 1.50
224 Mrion/Kidd/Mrion/Kidd .40 1.00
225 Wllce/Smth/Davis/Stoudmr .25 .60
226 Wbbr/Christi/Wbbr/Wllams .40 1.00
227 Duncn/Andrsn/Duncn/Dnils .40 1.00
228 Pytn/Williams/Ewing/Pytn .25 .60
229 Cartr/Curry/Davis/Jackson .40 1.00
230 Malon/Stock/Malon/Stock .40 1.00
231 Hwrd/Whtny/White/Whtny .25 .60
232 Brendan Haywood RC .75 2.00
233 Scottie Pippen .60 1.50
234 Loren Woods RC .50 1.25
235 Sam Cassell .30 .75
236 Anthony Carter .25 .60
237 Raja Bell RC 1.00 2.50
238 Robert Horry .30 .75
239 Maurice Taylor .25 .60
240 Zydrunas Ilgauskas .30 .75
241 Derrick Coleman .30 .75
242 Kenny Anderson .30 .75
243 Joseph Forte RC .50 1.25
244 Baron Davis .40 1.00
245 Nazr Mohammed .25 .60
246 Ivrsn/Cartr/Duncn/Bradly .50 1.25
247 Allen/Davis/Kobe/Divac .75 2.00
248 Mtmb/Robnsn/Robnsn/Lue .40 1.00
249 Bryant/Iverson .50 1.25
250 Darius Miles .25 .60
251 Samaki Walker .25 .60
252 Dermarr Johnson .25 .60
253 David Wesley .25 .60
254 Trenton Hassell RC .60 1.50
255 Jeff Trepagnier RC .50 1.25
256 Jacque Vaughn .25 .60
257 Kirk Haston RC .50 1.25
258 Jamaal Magloire .25 .60
259 Jason Collins RC .60 1.50
260 Chris Webber .40 1.00
261 Kenny Satterfield RC .50 1.25
262 Horace Grant .30 .75
263 Jerry Stackhouse .30 .75
264 Michael Jordan 6.00 15.00

2001-02 Topps Heritage Air Alert

Randomly inserted in packs at the rate of one in eight, this 12-card set features high flyers of the NBA in action on white bordered cards and set against colorful backgrounds.

COMPLETE SET (10) 12.50 30.00
STATED ODDS 1:8
1 Shawn Marion .50 1.25
2 Vince Carter 1.00 2.50
3 Tracy McGrady 1.00 2.50
4 Steve Francis .50 1.25
5 Kobe Bryant 2.50 6.00
6 Darius Miles .40 1.00
7 Jerry Stackhouse .50 1.25
8 Baron Davis .60 1.50
9 Kevin Garnett 1.00 2.50
10 Michael Jordan 8.00 20.00
11 Kwame Brown .60 1.50
12 Jason Richardson .75 2.00

2001-02 Topps Heritage Articles of the Arena Relics

Inserted in packs at the rate of one in 46, this 20-card set features a horizontal card design with white borders that places full color player action photos on the right side and swatches of memorabilia from The Boston Garden's parquet floor which is die cut in the shape of the letter A.

STATED ODDS 1:46
1 Shaquille O'Neal 10.00 25.00
2 Chris Webber 4.00 10.00
3 Jason Kidd 6.00 15.00
4 Latrell Sprewell 3.00 8.00
5 Jalen Rose 3.00 8.00
6 Grant Hill 5.00 12.00
7 Alonzo Mourning 5.00 12.00
8 Gary Payton 4.00 10.00
9 Anfernee Hardaway 6.00 15.00
10 Scottie Pippen 6.00 15.00
11 Tim Hardaway 4.00 10.00
12 Reggie Miller 4.00 10.00
13 Hakeem Olajuwon 5.00 12.00
14 Patrick Ewing 5.00 12.00
15 Karl Malone 5.00 12.00
16 John Stockton 5.00 12.00
17 Charles Oakley 3.00 8.00
18 Glenn Robinson 3.00 8.00
19 Dikembe Mutombo 4.00 10.00
20 Eddie Jones 3.00 8.00

2001-02 Topps Heritage Autographs

Randomly inserted in packs at the rate of one in 83, this 13-card set places full color player action photos on a white bordered card above a blank white spot set aside for authentic player autographs.

STATED ODDS 1:83
1 Antonio Daniels 4.00 10.00
2 Alvin Jones 4.00 10.00
3 Baron Davis 6.00 15.00
4 Damone Brown 4.00 10.00
5 Erick Barkley 4.00 10.00
6 Elton Brand 6.00 15.00
7 Joseph Forte 4.00 10.00
8 Mike Bibby 6.00 15.00
9 Peja Stojakovic 8.00 20.00
10 Richard Jefferson 4.00 10.00
11 Shane Battier 6.00 15.00
12 Shawn Marion 6.00 15.00
13 Vladimir Radmanovic 4.00 10.00

2001-02 Topps Heritage Ball Basics Relics

Inserted in packs at the rate of one in 627, this 11-card set features photos from the 2001 NBA Rookie Photo Shoot. Each card has a colored background, white borders, and a swatch of a basketball used in that shoot in the lower right hand corner.

STATED ODDS 1:627
1 Courtney Alexander 3.00 8.00
2 Speedy Claxton 3.00 8.00
3 DerMarr Johnson 3.00 8.00
4 Darius Miles 3.00 8.00
5 Desmond Mason 4.00 10.00
6 Hedo Turkoglu 4.00 10.00
7 Kenyon Martin 5.00 12.00
8 Marcus Fizer 3.00 8.00
9 Mike Miller 4.00 10.00
10 Morris Peterson 3.00 8.00
11 Stromile Swift 3.00 8.00

2001-02 Topps Heritage Competitive Threads

Inserted in packs at the rate of one in 61, this 15-card set boasts a horizontal card design with full color player action photos on the left and a swatch of a jersey on the right. The words "COMPETITIVE threads" appear along the right side border of the card.

STATED ODDS 1:61
1 Allan Houston 2.50 6.00
2 Allen Iverson 6.00 15.00
3 Andre Miller 2.50 6.00
4 Baron Davis 3.00 8.00
5 Chris Webber 3.00 8.00
6 Elton Brand 3.00 8.00
7 Jerry Stackhouse 2.50 6.00
8 Karl Malone 4.00 10.00
9 Latrell Sprewell 2.50 6.00
10 Michael Finley 3.00 8.00
11 Ray Allen 3.00 8.00
12 Rasheed Wallace 3.00 8.00
13 Tim Duncan 6.00 15.00
14 Tracy McGrady 5.00 12.00
15 Wally Szczerbiak 2.50 6.00

2001-02 Topps Heritage Competitive Threads Autographs

Randomly inserted in packs at the rate of one in 1862, this five card set parallels the base Competitive Threads set design enhanced with authentic player autographs in a white box below the player photo.

STATED ODDS 1:1862
1 Andre Miller 30.00 80.00
3 Elton Brand 30.00 80.00
4 Tim Duncan 150.00 300.00

2001-02 Topps Heritage Crossover

Randomly inserted in packs at the rate of one in 14, this 12-card set features some of the NBA's best ball-handlers in full color set against colored backgrounds with white borders.

COMPLETE SET (12) 20.00 40.00
STATED ODDS 1:14
1 Jamaal Tinsley 1.00 2.50
2 Steve Francis .75 2.00
3 Vince Carter 1.50 4.00
4 Baron Davis 1.00 2.50
5 Tracy McGrady 1.50 4.00
6 Kobe Bryant 4.00 10.00
7 Jason Terry 1.00 2.50
8 Stephon Marbury .75 2.00
9 Jason Williams .75 2.00
10 Tim Hardaway 1.00 2.50
11 Jason Richardson 1.25 3.00
12 Michael Jordan 10.00 25.00

2001-02 Topps Heritage Out of Bounds

Randomly seeded in packs at the rate of one in 10, this 10-card set showcases some of the NBA's foreign talent in full color with colorful backgrounds and white bordered cards.

COMPELTE SET (10) 8.00 20.00
STATED ODDS 1:10
1 Dirk Nowitzki 1.25 3.00
2 Peja Stojakovic .75 2.00
3 Wang ZhiZhi .60 1.50
4 Dikembe Mutombo .75 2.00
5 Steve Nash 1.25 3.00
6 Hedo Turkoglu .60 1.50
7 Hakeem Olajuwon 1.00 2.50
8 Tony Parker 3.00 8.00
9 Vladimir Radmanovic .75 2.00
10 Pau Gasol 2.50 6.00

2001-02 Topps Heritage Unity

Seeded in packs at the rate of one in 485, this eight card set places full color player action photos of the Charlotte Hornets roster with a swatch of a playoff used headband.

STATED ODDS 1:485
1 Baron Davis 10.00 25.00
2 Derrick Coleman 8.00 20.00
3 David Wesley 6.00 15.00
4 Elden Campbell 6.00 15.00
5 Eddie Robinson 6.00 15.00
6 Jamaal Magloire 6.00 15.00
7 Jamal Mashburn 8.00 20.00
8 P.J. Brown 6.00 15.00

2001-02 Topps High Topps

Released in mid-December 2001, Topps High Topps features a 164-card set divided up as follows: card numbers 1-81 are base veteran cards, card numbers 82-86 are 1st Team All-NBA players, card numbers 87-91 are 2nd Team All-NBA players, card numbers 92-101 are Stat Leaders showcasing top stats grabbers, card numbers 102-105 are Road to the Championship showcasing LA Lakers players, card numbers 106-113 are Super Veteran Autographed cards sequentially numberd to 850, card numbers 114-129 are Super Veteran Relics sequentially numbered to 425, card numbers 130-140 are Rookie Signatures sequentially numbered to 850, card numbers 141-153 are Rookie Relics sequentially numbered to 425, and card numbers 154-164 are rookies sequentially numbered to 1500. All cards feature a jumbo tall-boy design measuring 2 1/2" by 4 11/16" with full color player action photos, white borders and gold foil highlights. High Topps was packaged in six box cases with 24-pack boxes where packs contained eight cards and carried a suggested retail price of $7.00.

COMPLETE SET (164) 250.00 500.00
COMP.SET w/o SP's (105) 15.00 40.00
106-113 PRINT RUN 850 SER.#'d SETS
114-129 PRINT RUN 425 SER.#'d SETS
130-140 PRINT RUN 850 SER.#'d SETS
141-153 PRINT RUN 425 SER.#'d SETS
154-164 PRINT RUN 1500 SER.#'d SETS
1 Shaquille O'Neal 1.00 2.50
2 Reggie Miller .40 1.00
3 Steve Francis .30 .75
4 Jerry Stackhouse .30 .75
5 Nick Van Exel .30 .75
6 Dirk Nowitzki .60 1.50
7 Dikembe Mutombo .40 1.00
8 Terrell Brandon .25 .60
9 Allan Houston .30 .75
10 Kevin Garnett .60 1.50
11 Eric Snow .25 .60
12 Stephon Marbury .30 .75
13 Jalen Rose .30 .75
14 Rick Fox .25 .60
15 Alonzo Mourning .50 1.25
16 Tim Thomas .25 .60
17 Keith Van Horn .30 .75
18 Glen Rice .30 .75
19 Mike Miller .30 .75
20 Chris Webber .40 1.00
21 Larry Hughes .30 .75
22 Joe Smith .30 .75
23 Ron Mercer .25 .60
24 Jamal Mashburn .30 .75
25 Shareef Abdur-Rahim .30 .75
26 P.J. Brown .25 .60
27 Ben Wallace .30 .75
28 Wang Zhizhi .30 .75
29 Jermaine O'Neal .30 .75
30 Lamar Odom .30 .75
31 Stromile Swift .25 .60
32 Theo Ratliff .25 .60
33 Patrick Ewing .50 1.25
34 Antonio Davis .25 .60
35 John Stockton .50 1.25
36 Courtney Alexander .25 .60
37 Alvin Williams .25 .60
38 Rashard Lewis .40 1.00
39 Mike Bibby .40 1.00
40 Scottie Pippen .60 1.50
41 Anfernee Hardaway .60 1.50
42 Marcus Camby .30 .75
43 Glenn Robinson .30 .75
44 Jason Williams .30 .75
45 Horace Grant .30 .75
46 Chris Mihm .25 .60
47 Paul Pierce .40 1.00
48 DerMarr Johnson .25 .60
49 Steve Nash .60 1.50
50 Vince Carter .60 1.50
51 Michael Jordan 4.00 10.00
52 Donyell Marshall .25 .60
53 Desmond Mason .30 .75
54 Tom Gugliotta .25 .60
55 Hedo Turkoglu .30 .75
56 Grant Hill .50 1.25
57 Kenyon Martin .40 1.00
58 Wally Szczerbiak .30 .75
59 Eddie Jones .30 .75
60 Kobe Bryant 1.50 4.00
61 Cuttino Mobley .25 .60
62 Michael Dickerson .25 .60
63 Clifford Robinson .25 .60
64 Raef LaFrentz .25 .60
65 Lamond Murray .25 .60
66 Kenny Anderson .30 .75
67 Antonio Daniels .25 .60
68 Hakeem Olajuwon .50 1.25
69 Eddie Robinson .25 .60
70 Karl Malone .50 1.25
71 Richard Hamilton .30 .75
72 Derek Anderson .25 .60
73 Bonzi Wells .25 .60
74 Darrell Armstrong .25 .60
75 Gary Payton .40 1.00
76 Bryon Russell .25 .60
77 Steve Smith .30 .75
78 Sam Cassell .30 .75
79 Brian Grant .25 .60
80 Antoine Walker .30 .75
81 Marcus Fizer .25 .60
82 Tim Duncan AN .75 2.00
83 Chris Webber AN .40 1.00
84 Shaquille O'Neal AN 1.00 2.50
85 Allen Iverson AN .75 2.00
86 Jason Kidd AN .60 1.50
87 Kevin Garnett AN .60 1.50
88 Vince Carter AN .60 1.50
89 Dikembe Mutombo AN .40 1.00
90 Kobe Bryant AN 1.50 4.00
91 Tracy McGrady AN .60 1.50
92 Allen Iverson SL .50 1.25
93 Dikembe Mutombo SL .25 .60
94 Jason Kidd SL .40 1.00
95 Allen Iverson SL .50 1.25
96 Theo Ratliff SL .15 .40
97 Shaquille O'Neal SL .60 1.50
98 Reggie Miller SL .25 .60
99 Antoine Walker SL .20 .50
100 Michael Finley SL .25 .60
101 Jason Kidd SL .40 1.00
102 Shaquille O'Neal RTC .60 1.50
103 Kobe Bryant RTC 1.00 2.50
104 Derek Fisher RTC .20 .50
105 Shaquille O'Neal RTC .60 1.50
106 Shawn Marion AU 6.00 15.00
107 Antawn Jamison AU 8.00 20.00
108 Peja Stojakovic AU 15.00 40.00
109 Jason Terry AU 5.00 12.00
110 Aaron McKie AU 5.00 12.00
111 Keyon Dooling AU 5.00 12.00
112 Al Harrington AU 5.00 12.00
113 Chauncey Billups AU 6.00 15.00
114 Tim Duncan JSY 10.00 25.00
115 Tracy McGrady JSY 8.00 20.00
116 Jason Kidd JSY 8.00 20.00
117 Latrell Sprewell JSY 4.00 10.00
118 David Robinson JSY 8.00 20.00
119 Baron Davis JSY 5.00 12.00
120 Allen Iverson JSY 10.00 25.00
121 Ray Allen JSY 5.00 12.00
122 Rasheed Wallace JSY 5.00 12.00
123 Morris Peterson JSY 3.00 8.00
124 Darius Miles JSY 3.00 8.00
125 Marc Jackson JSY 3.00 8.00
126 Michael Finley JSY 5.00 12.00
127 Elton Brand JSY 5.00 12.00
128 Antonio McDyess JSY 4.00 10.00
129 Andre Miller JSY 4.00 10.00
130 Kwame Brown AU RC 5.00 12.00
131 Eddy Curry AU RC 5.00 12.00
132 Loren Woods AU RC 3.00 8.00
133 Joe Johnson AU RC 10.00 25.00
134 Richard Jefferson AU RC 8.00 20.00
135 Zach Randolph AU RC 15.00 40.00
136 Brendan Haywood AU RC 5.00 12.00
137 Gilbert Arenas AU RC 12.00 30.00
138 Damone Brown AU RC 3.00 8.00
139 Kenny Satterfield AU RC 3.00 8.00
140 Vladimir Radmanovic AU RC 5.00 12.00
141 Eddie Griffin JSY RC 2.50 6.00
142 Shane Battier JSY RC 6.00 15.00
143 Michael Bradley JSY RC 2.00 5.00
144 Gerald Wallace JSY RC 4.00 10.00
145 Samuel Dalembert JSY RC 3.00 8.00
146 Tyson Chandler JSY RC 5.00 12.00
147 Pau Gasol JSY RC 10.00 25.00
148 Steven Hunter JSY RC 2.50 6.00
149 Rodney White JSY RC 2.00 5.00
150 Jeryl Sasser JSY RC 2.00 5.00
151 Brandon Armstrong JSY RC 2.00 5.00
152 Jamaal Tinsley JSY RC 3.00 8.00
153 DeSagana Diop JSY RC 2.50 6.00
154 Jason Richardson RC 1.50 4.00
155 Kirk Haston RC .75 2.00
156 Joseph Forte RC .75 2.00
157 Jason Collins RC 1.00 2.50
158 Kedrick Brown RC .75 2.00
159 Troy Murphy RC 1.25 3.00
160 Tony Parker RC 5.00 12.00
161 Raja Bell RC 1.50 4.00
162 Jeff Trepagnier RC .75 2.00
163 Terence Morris RC 1.25 3.00
164 Zeljko Rebraca RC 1.25 3.00

2001-02 Topps High Topps Above and Beyond

Inserted in packs at the rate of one in 10, this seven card 2 1/2" by 4 11/16" design places some of the NBA's shortest stars in action with full color player action photos, white borders, and gold foil highlights.

COMPLETE SET (7) 10.00 25.00
STATED ODDS 1:10
AB1 John Stockton 1.25 3.00
AB2 Shawn Marion .75 2.00
AB3 Jason Terry 1.00 2.50
AB4 Alonzo Mourning 1.25 3.00
AB5 Theo Ratliff .60 1.50
AB6 Michael Jordan 8.00 20.00
AB7 Marcus Camby .75 2.00

2001-02 Topps High Topps Dominant Figures

Seeded in packs at the rate of one in nine, this 2 1/2" by 4 11/16" card design features eight perennial NBA All-Stars in action with full color player photos, white borders and gold foil highlights.

COMPLETE SET (8) 20.00 40.00
STATED ODDS 1:9
DF1 Alonzo Mourning 1.50 4.00
DF2 Shaquille O'Neal 3.00 8.00
DF3 Chris Webber 1.25 3.00
DF4 Michael Jordan 10.00 25.00
DF5 Kevin Garnett 2.00 5.00
DF6 Tracy McGrady 2.00 5.00
DF7 Vince Carter 2.00 5.00
DF8 Kobe Bryant 5.00 12.00

2001-02 Topps High Topps Giant Remains

Randomly seeded in packs at the rate of one in 16, this 20-card set measures 2 1/2" by 4 11/16". Full color player photos are separated from the white borders by black along the top and the bottom which are enhanced with gold foil highlights. A swatch of a jersey appears towards the bottom of the card and is die-cut in the shape of the Topps logo.

STATED ODDS 1:16
GRAD Antonio Davis 2.50 6.00
GRAH Allan Houston 3.00 8.00
GRAKM Antonio McDyess 3.00 8.00
GRAM Anthony Mason 2.50 6.00
GRCM Cuttino Mobley 2.50 6.00
GRCW Chris Webber 4.00 10.00
GRGR Glenn Robinson 3.00 8.00
GRJS Jerry Stackhouse 3.00 8.00
GRJT Jason Terry 4.00 10.00
GRKLM Kenyon Martin 4.00 10.00
GRKM Karl Malone 5.00 12.00
GRMM Mike Miller 3.00 8.00
GRRH Richard Hamilton 3.00 8.00
GRSDM Shawn Marion 3.00 8.00
GRSF Steve Francis 3.00 8.00
GRSM Stephon Marbury 3.00 8.00
GRSO Shaquille O'Neal 10.00 25.00
GRTD Tim Duncan 8.00 20.00
GRVD Vlade Divac 3.00 8.00
GRWS Wally Szczerbiak 3.00 8.00

2001-02 Topps High Topps Lofty Lettering

Randomly inserted in packs at the rate of one in 38, this 10-card set measures 2 1/2" by 4 11/16" and places full color player action photos on a white bordered card with gold foil highlights. The bottom of the card fades to white were authentic player autographs appear. These cards also contain a gold foil Topps stamp of authenticity.

STATED ODDS 1:38
LLBD Baron Davis 6.00 15.00
LLBJ Bobby Jackson 5.00 12.00
LLGW Gerald Wallace 12.50 30.00
LLHT Hedo Turkoglu 6.00 15.00
LLJF Joseph Forte 5.00 12.00
LLLP Lavor Postell 5.00 12.00
LLMB Mike Bibby 6.00 15.00
LLSB Shane Battier 6.00 15.00
LLTM Troy Murphy 6.00 15.00
LLTT Tim Thomas 5.00 12.00

2001-02 Topps High Topps Sky's The Limit

Seeded in packs at the rate of one in eight, this 13-card set measures 2 1/2" by 4 11/16". Thirteen players are showcased in full color with black separating the picture from the white borders at the bottom where the player's name appears in gold foil, while the set name appears at the top of the photo in gold foil.

COMPLETE SET (13) 20.00 40.00
STATED ODDS 1:8
SL1 Darius Miles .75 2.00
SL2 Vince Carter 2.00 5.00
SL3 Tracy McGrady 2.00 5.00
SL4 Steve Francis 1.00 2.50
SL5 Baron Davis 1.25 3.00
SL6 Tim Duncan 2.50 6.00
SL7 Shawn Marion 1.00 2.50
SL8 Paul Pierce 1.25 3.00
SL9 Rashard Lewis 1.25 3.00
SL10 Lamar Odom 1.00 2.50
SL11 Antawn Jamison 1.25 3.00
SL12 Dirk Nowitzki 2.00 5.00
SL13 Michael Jordan 10.00 25.00

1983 Topps History's Greatest Olympians

This 99-card boxed set was manufactured under license from the Los Angeles Olympic Organizing Committee. (Sporting a slightly different card design, the 1984 M and M's Olympic Heroes is a subset of this set.) Though widely known to have been produced by Topps, this company name appears nowhere on the cards. On a white card face, the fronts feature either color or black-and-white photos framed by a white inner border and a yellow outer border. The player's name appears in red print across the bottom of the front. On a red panel, the backs carry a headline and news brief. The cards are numbered on the upper left corner.

COMPLETE SET (99) 8.00 20.00
9 Bill Bradley .50 1.25
17 Don Bragg .12 .30
63 Oscar Robertson .60 1.50
91 Jerry West .75 2.00

2002-03 Topps Jersey Edition

Released in April 2003, Topps Jersey Edition consists of 166 cards. Most players have two card versions, a Home Cookin' and a Road Jersey version. Cards that have the "UER" connotation (Uncorrected Error) feature either the Road Jersey or Home Cookin' card stock, however, the opposite swatch was inserted due to the unavailibility of those specific jerseys. Also, a few cards appear with an asterisk, these cards are percieved to be much scarcer than the rest of the cards in the set. Multiple versions were available for the rookie players, so the more abundant version has been tagged as the RC card. Several NNO exchange cards were inserted at the end of the set and these are redeemable for two cards, one of each of the names that appear on the exchange. Note: on the Payton/Dixon EXCH card, Gary Payton was replaced by Jerry Stackhouse.

HOME JSY ON CARDS WITH H
ROAD JSY ON CARDS WITH R
ERR CARDS HAVE WRONG JSY SWATCH
STACKHOUSE REPLACE PAYTON ON EXCH
ASTERISKS PERCEIVED AS SP VERSION
JEAD Antonio Davis R UER 2.50 6.00
JEAI Allen Iverson R * 6.00 15.00
JEAJ Antawn Jamison R 4.00 10.00
JEAK Andrei Kirilenko R 4.00 10.00
JEAS Amare Stoudemire R RC 5.00 12.00
JEBD Baron Davis R 3.00 8.00
JEBG Brian Grant R 2.50 6.00
JEBW Ben Wallace R 3.00 8.00
JECA Courtney Alexander R UER 2.50 6.00
JECB Carlos Boozer R RC 4.00 10.00
JECJ Chris Jefferies H RC 2.50 6.00
JECM Cuttino Mobley R 2.50 6.00
JECW Chris Wilcox R UER RC 3.00 8.00
JEDD Dan Dickau R RC 3.00 8.00
JEDF Derek Fisher R 3.00 8.00
JEDN Dirk Nowitzki R 6.00 15.00
JEDW DaJuan Wagner R RC 3.00 8.00
JEEB Elton Brand R 4.00 10.00
JEEC Eddy Curry R 2.50 6.00
JEEG Eddie Griffin R UER 2.50 6.00
JEEJ Eddie Jones R 3.00 8.00
JEFJ Fred Jones R RC 3.00 8.00
JEGA Gilbert Arenas R UER 4.00 10.00
JEGG Gordan Giricek R RC 4.00 10.00
JEJH Juwan Howard R 3.00 8.00
JEJM Jamal Mashburn R 3.00 8.00
JEJO Jermaine O'Neal R 3.00 8.00
JEJR Jalen Rose R 3.00 8.00
JEJS Joe Smith R 3.00 8.00
JEJT Jamaal Tinsley R 2.50 6.00
JEKG Kevin Garnett R 6.00 15.00
JEKR Kareem Rush R RC 3.00 8.00
JEKS Kenny Satterfield R 2.50 6.00
JEKV Keith Van Horn R 3.00 8.00
JEMD Mike Dunleavy H RC 4.00 10.00
JEMF Michael Finley R 4.00 10.00
JEMO Mehmet Okur R RC 4.00 10.00
JEMP Morris Peterson R UER 2.50 6.00
JENT Nikoloz Tskitishvili R RC 2.50 6.00
JEPG Pau Gasol R 5.00 12.00
JEPP Paul Pierce R 4.00 10.00
JEQR Quentin Richardson R 3.00 8.00
JEQW Qyntel Woods R RC 3.00 8.00
JERA Ray Allen 4.00 10.00
JERB Rasual Butler R RC 4.00 10.00
JERM Reggie Miller R 4.00 10.00
JESA Shareef Abdur-Rahim R 3.00 8.00
JESM Stephon Marbury R 3.00 8.00
JESN Steve Nash R 5.00 12.00
JESO Shaquille O'Neal R 10.00 25.00
JETC Tyson Chandler R 4.00 10.00
JETH Troy Hudson R 2.50 6.00
JEWS Wally Szczerbiak R 3.00 8.00
JEYM Yao Ming R RC 8.00 20.00
JEAFM Aaron McKie R UER 2.50 6.00
JEAHO Allan Houston H 3.00 8.00
JEAIV Allen Iverson H 6.00 15.00
JEALM Andre Miller R 3.00 8.00
JEAMG Drew Gooden R RC 4.00 10.00
JEAMI Andre Miller H 3.00 8.00
JEAST Amare Stoudemire H RC 5.00 12.00
JEAWA Antoine Walker 3.00 8.00
JEBDA Baron Davis H 3.00 8.00
JEBWA Ben Wallace H 3.00 8.00
JECBU Caron Butler H RC 4.00 10.00
JEDAS Damon Stoudamire H 3.00 8.00
JEDDI Dan Dickau H UER RC 3.00 8.00
JEDGO Drew Gooden H RC 4.00 10.00
JEDJG Devean George R 2.50 6.00
JEDLM Darius Miles R 2.50 6.00
JEDMA Donyell Marshall R UER 2.50 6.00
JEDNO Dirk Nowitzki H 6.00 15.00
JEDWA DaJuan Wagner H RC 3.00 8.00
JEEBR Elton Brand H 4.00 10.00
JEECU Eddy Curry H 2.50 6.00

JEECW Elden Campbell R UER 2.50 6.00
JEECW Chris Webber 4.00 10.00
JEEGI Manu Ginobili H RC 10.00 25.00
JEGDW Bonzi Wells R 2.50 6.00
JEGRO Glenn Robinson H 3.00 8.00
JEJAR Jason Richardson R 4.00 10.00
JEJAT Jason Terry R 3.00 8.00
JEJCB Caron Butler R RC 4.00 10.00
JEJDM Jamaal Magloire R UER 2.50 6.00
JEJHS John Stockton R 5.00 12.00
JEJKI Jason Kidd H 6.00 15.00
JEJMJ Joe Johnson R 3.00 8.00
JEJON Jermaine O'Neal H 3.00 8.00
JEJOS John Stockton H 5.00 12.00
JEJRI Jason Richardson H 4.00 10.00
JEJRO Jalen Rose H 3.00 8.00
JEJRS John Salmons R RC 4.00 10.00
JEJWL Jerome Williams H 2.50 6.00
JEKAM Karl Malone R 5.00 12.00
JEKGA Kevin Garnett H 6.00 15.00
JEKMA Karl Malone H 5.00 12.00
JEKRU Kareem Rush H RC 3.00 8.00
JEKVH Keith Van Horn H 3.00 8.00
JELSP Latrell Sprewell H 3.00 8.00
JEMAF Marcus Fizer R 2.50 6.00
JEMOK Mehmet Okur H RC 4.00 10.00
JENTS Nikoloz Tskitishvili H RC 2.50 6.00
JEPGA Pau Gasol H 5.00 12.00
JEQRI Quentin Richardson H 3.00 8.00
JEQWO Qyntel Woods H RC 3.00 8.00
JERAO Ron Artest R 4.00 10.00
JERAW Rasheed Wallace R 4.00 10.00
JERBU Rasual Butler H RC 4.00 10.00
JERCH Richard Hamilton R 3.00 8.00
JERHO Robert Horry R 3.00 8.00
JERIH Richard Hamilton H 3.00 8.00
JERWA Rasheed Wallace H 4.00 10.00
JESCB Shane Battier R 4.00 10.00
JESDM Shawn Marion R 3.00 8.00
JESFR Steve Francis H 3.00 8.00
JESMA Shawn Marion H 3.00 8.00
JESNA Steve Nash H * 5.00 12.00
JESON Shaquille O'Neal H 10.00 25.00
JETCH Tyson Chandler H 4.00 10.00
JETDU Tim Duncan H 8.00 20.00
JETDU Tim Duncan R 8.00 20.00
JETLM Tracy McGrady R 6.00 15.00
JETPA Tony Parker H 5.00 12.00
JETPR Tayshaun Prince R RC 5.00 12.00
JEWSZ Wally Szczerbiak H 3.00 8.00

2002-03 Topps Jersey Edition Black

*BLACK: .6X TO 1.5X BASE CARD HI
STATED PRINT RUN 99 SER.#'d SETS
JEYM Yao Ming R 30.00 80.00

2002-03 Topps Jersey Edition Copper

*COPPER: .5X TO 1.25X BASE CARD HI
STATED PRINT RUN 299 SER.#'d SETS

2003-04 Topps Jersey Edition

Released in February 2004, Topps Jersey edition boasts 140-cards, all of which have some sort of memorabilia element to them. Several of the rookie cards have jerseys, Standout Selection patches (with the 2003 NBA Draft NY logo on them and inserted at the rate of one in nine) and autographs. Jersey Edition was packaged in 10-pack boxes with packs containing two cards and carried a suggested retail price of $20.

SS RC HAVE NBA DRAFT PATCH
SS RC STATED ODDS 1:9
UNPRICED LOGOMAN PRINT RUN ONE SET
AD Antonio Davis 2.00 5.00
AH Allan Houston 2.00 5.00
AI Allen Iverson 4.00 10.00
AJ Antawn Jamison 2.00 5.00
AK Andrei Kirilenko 2.50 6.00
AM Andre Miller 2.00 5.00
AP Aleksandar Pavlovic RC 2.50 6.00
AS Amare Stoudemire 3.00 8.00
BB Brent Barry 2.00 5.00
BC Brian Cook RC 2.00 5.00
BD Baron Davis 2.00 5.00
BH Brandon Hunter RC 2.00 5.00
BJ Bobby Jackson 2.00 5.00
BM Brad Miller 2.00 5.00
BW Ben Wallace 2.00 5.00
CA Carmelo Anthony SS RC 10.00 25.00
CB Caron Butler 2.00 5.00
CK Chris Kaman RC 3.00 8.00
CM Corey Maggette 2.00 5.00
CW Chris Webber 2.50 6.00
DC Derrick Coleman 2.00 5.00
DG Drew Gooden 2.00 5.00
DJ Dahntay Jones RC 2.50 6.00
DM Desmond Mason 2.00 5.00
DN Dirk Nowitzki 4.00 10.00
DW Dwyane Wade SS RC 15.00 40.00
EB Elton Brand AU 8.00 20.00
EC Eddy Curry 1.50 4.00
EG Manu Ginobili 3.00 8.00
GA Gilbert Arenas 2.00 5.00
GP Gary Payton 2.50 6.00
GR Glenn Robinson 2.00 5.00
HT Hedo Turkoglu 2.00 5.00
JB Jerome Beasley RC 2.00 5.00
JC Jamal Crawford 2.50 6.00
JH Juwan Howard 2.00 5.00
JJ James Jones RC 2.00 5.00
JK Jason Kidd 4.00 10.00
JM Jamal Mashburn 2.00 5.00
JO Jermaine O'Neal 2.00 5.00
JR Jalen Rose 2.00 5.00
JS Jerry Stackhouse 2.00 5.00
JT Jason Terry 2.00 5.00
JW Jason Williams 2.00 5.00
KB Kwame Brown 2.00 5.00
KC Keon Clark 2.00 5.00
KG Kevin Garnett 4.00 10.00
KH Kirk Hinrich AU RC 8.00 20.00
KM Karl Malone 3.00 8.00
KP Kendrick Perkins RC 2.50 6.00
KR Kareem Rush 2.00 5.00
KT Kurt Thomas 2.00 5.00
LB Leandro Barbosa SS RC 3.00 8.00
LJ LeBron James SS RC 125.00 300.00
LO Lamar Odom 2.00 5.00
LR Luke Ridnour AU RC 6.00 15.00
LS Latrell Sprewell 2.00 5.00
LW Luke Walton SS RC 3.00 8.00
MB Mike Bibby 2.50 6.00
MC Marcus Camby 2.00 5.00
MD Mike Dunleavy 2.00 5.00
MJ Marko Jaric 2.00 5.00
MM Mike Miller 2.00 5.00
MO Michael Olowokandi 2.00 5.00
MP Morris Peterson 1.50 4.00
MR Michael Redd 2.50 6.00
MS Mike Sweetney SS RC 2.00 5.00
MT Maurice Taylor 2.00 5.00
MW Maurice Williams RC 3.00 8.00
NE Ndudi Ebi RC 2.00 5.00
NH Nene 2.00 5.00
PG Pau Gasol 2.50 6.00
PP Paul Pierce 2.50 6.00
PS Peja Stojakovic 2.50 6.00
QR Quentin Richardson 2.00 5.00
QW Qyntel Woods 2.00 5.00
RA Ray Allen 2.50 6.00
RD Ricky Davis 2.00 5.00
RG Reece Gaines SS RC 2.00 5.00
RH Richard Hamilton 2.00 5.00
RJ Richard Jefferson 2.00 5.00
RL Raef LaFrentz 2.00 5.00
RL Rashard Lewis 2.50 6.00
RM Ron Mercer 2.00 5.00
RN Radoslav Nesterovic 2.00 5.00
RW Rasheed Wallace 2.50 6.00
SB Steve Blake RC 2.50 6.00
SC Sam Cassell 2.00 5.00
SF Steve Francis 2.00 5.00
SM Shawn Marion 2.00 5.00
SN Steve Nash 3.00 8.00
SO Shaquille O'Neal AU 30.00 80.00
SP Scottie Pippen 4.00 10.00
TB Troy Bell RC 3.00 8.00
TC Tyson Chandler 2.00 5.00
TD Tim Duncan 4.00 10.00
TM Tracy McGrady 3.00 8.00
TO Travis Outlaw RC 2.50 6.00
TP Tony Parker 2.50 6.00
TR Theo Ratliff 2.00 5.00
TS Theron Smith RC 2.00 5.00
TT Tim Thomas 2.00 5.00
WG Willie Green RC 2.00 5.00
YM Yao Ming 5.00 12.00
ZC Zarko Cabarkapa RC 2.00 5.00
ZI Zydrunas Ilgauskas 2.00 5.00
ZP Zoran Planinic RC 2.00 5.00
ZR Zach Randolph 2.00 5.00
AHA Al Harrington 2.00 5.00
BDR Boris Diaw RC 3.00 8.00
CBI Chauncey Billups 2.50 6.00
CBO Chris Bosh RC 5.00 12.00
CBO Carlos Boozer 2.00 5.00
CMO Cuttino Mobley 1.50 4.00
CWI Corliss Williamson 2.00 5.00
DAM Darko Milicic SS RC 2.50 6.00
DCH Doug Christie 2.00 5.00
DGE Devean George 2.00 5.00
DMI Darius Miles 2.00 5.00
DWA DaJuan Wagner 2.00 5.00
DWE David West SS RC 3.00 8.00
JHA Jarvis Hayes RC 2.00 5.00
JHO Josh Howard RC 3.00 8.00
JKA Jason Kapono SS RC 2.00 5.00
JMA Jamaal Magloire 2.00 5.00
JRI Jason Richardson 2.50 6.00
JSM Joe Smith 2.00 5.00
JWI Jerome Williams 2.00 5.00
KMA Kenyon Martin 2.00 5.00
KVH Keith Van Horn 2.00 5.00
MBA Marcus Banks RC 2.00 5.00
MJA Marc Jackson 2.00 5.00
MPI Mickael Pietrus RC 2.50 6.00
NVE Nick Van Exel 2.00 5.00
RAR Ron Artest 2.50 6.00
RHO Robert Horry 2.00 5.00
RLO Raul Lopez 2.50 6.00
RMI Reggie Miller 2.50 6.00
SAR Shareef Abdur-Rahim 2.00 5.00
SBA Shane Battier 2.00 5.00
SCL Speedy Claxton 2.00 5.00
SMA Stephon Marbury 2.00 5.00
TMU Troy Murphy 1.50 4.00
TPR Tayshaun Prince 2.00 5.00
ZPA Zaur Pachulia RC 3.00 8.00

2003-04 Topps Jersey Edition Black

*BLACK SINGLES: 1.25X TO 3X BASE HI
*BLACK AU: 1X TO 2.5X BASE HI
*BLACK RCs: 1X TO 2.5X BASE HI
*BLACK SS RCs: 1.5X TO 4X BASE HI
BLACK PRINT RUN 25 SER.#'d SETS
LJ Lebron James SS 600.00 1000.00
SP Scottie Pippen 25.00 60.00
RMI Reggie Miller 15.00 40.00

2003-04 Topps Jersey Edition Copper

*COPPER SINGLES: .6X TO 1.5X BASE HI
*COPPER AU: .5X TO 1.25X BASE HI
*COPPER RCs: .5X TO 1.25X BASE HI
*COPPER SS RCs: .75X TO 2X BASE HI
COPPER PRINT RUN 99 SER.#'d SETS
LJ Lebron James SS 300.00 600.00

2003-04 Topps Jersey Edition Double Team

Inserted in packs at the rate of one in 108, this 15-card set features two players, one on top and one on the bottom and two circular swatches of memorabilia.

STATED ODDS 1:108
1 T.McGrady/R.Gaines 6.00 15.00
2 P.Pierce/M.Banks 6.00 15.00
3 S.Nash/D.Nowitzki 8.00 20.00
4 B.Wallace/R.Hamilton 6.00 15.00
5 J.Richardson/M.Pietrus 6.00 15.00
6 Y.Ming/S.Francis 10.00 25.00
8 J.Kidd/K.Martin 8.00 20.00
9 A.Stoudemire/S.Marbury 6.00 15.00
10 C.Webber/P.Stojakovic 6.00 15.00
11 T.Duncan/T.Parker 15.00 30.00
12 C.Anthony/Nene 10.00 25.00
14 A.Iverson/G.Robinson 6.00 15.00
15 K.Hinrich/T.Chandler 8.00 20.00

2003-04 Topps Jersey Edition Draft Day Hits

Randomly seeded, this 24-card set features the newest rookies in their warmups on the right of the card and a swatch of memorabilia on the left. Each card is sequentially numbered to 75.

PRINT RUN 75 SER.#'d SETS
BC Brian Cook 2.00 5.00
CA Carmelo Anthony 10.00 25.00
CB Chris Bosh 5.00 12.00
CK Chris Kaman 3.00 8.00
DJ Dahntay Jones 2.50 6.00
DW Dwyane Wade 10.00 25.00
JH Jarvis Hayes 2.00 5.00
JK Jason Kapono 2.00 5.00
KH Kirk Hinrich 3.00 8.00
KP Kendrick Perkins 2.50 6.00
LB Leandro Barbosa 3.00 8.00
LR Luke Ridnour 2.50 6.00
LW Luke Walton 3.00 8.00
MB Marcus Banks 2.00 5.00
MP Mickael Pietrus 2.50 6.00
MS Mike Sweetney 2.00 5.00
NC Nick Collison 2.50 6.00
NE Ndudi Ebi 2.00 5.00
RG Reece Gaines 2.00 5.00
TB Troy Bell 2.00 5.00
TO Travis Outlaw 2.50 6.00
DWE David West 3.00 8.00
JHO Josh Howard 3.00 8.00
TJF T.J. Ford 2.50 6.00

2003-04 Topps Jersey Edition Patch Place

Randomly seeded, this 33-card set features full-color player photos on the left and a circular swatch or memorabilia on the right. Each card is sequentially numbered to 25.

PRINT RUN 25 SER.#'d SETS
1 Paul Pierce 10.00 25.00
2 Baron Davis 8.00 20.00
3 Steve Nash 12.00 30.00
4 Dirk Nowitzki 15.00 40.00
5 Steve Francis 8.00 20.00
6 Yao Ming 20.00 50.00
7 Jason Richardson 10.00 25.00
8 Pau Gasol 10.00 25.00
9 Tracy McGrady 12.00 30.00
10 Ben Wallace 8.00 20.00
11 Zoran Planinic 6.00 15.00
12 Dajuan Wagner 6.00 15.00
13 Darius Miles 6.00 15.00
14 Jermaine O'Neal 8.00 20.00
15 Elton Brand 10.00 25.00
16 Shaquille O'Neal 30.00 80.00
17 Lamar Odom 8.00 20.00
18 Michael Redd 10.00 25.00
19 Kevin Garnett 15.00 40.00
20 Jason Kidd 15.00 40.00
21 Kenyon Martin 8.00 20.00
22 Allen Iverson 15.00 40.00
23 Amare Stoudemire 12.00 30.00
24 Tim Duncan 15.00 40.00
25 Ray Allen 10.00 25.00
26 Carmelo Anthony 30.00 80.00
27 Kirk Hinrich 10.00 25.00
28 T.J. Ford 8.00 20.00
29 Reece Gaines 6.00 15.00
30 Chris Bosh 15.00 40.00
31 Mickael Pietrus 8.00 20.00
32 Mike Sweetney 6.00 15.00
33 Jarvis Hayes 6.00 15.00

2003-04 Topps Jersey Edition Prime Pieces

Randomly inserted, this 34-card set places player photos on the left and a premium swatch of memorabilia on the right. Each card is sequentially numbered to the featured player's jersey number.

STATED PRINT RUN ONE TO 43 SETS
11 Richard Hamilton/32 8.00 20.00
12 Allan Houston/20 8.00 20.00
15 Eddie Griffin/33 6.00 15.00
21 David West/30 10.00 25.00
24 Kendrick Perkins/43 8.00 20.00
31 Elton Brand/42 10.00 25.00
32 Shawn Marion/31 8.00 20.00

2003-04 Topps Jersey Edition Triple Threat

Inserted at the rate of one in 217, this 15-card set places three players on each card with a swatch of memorabilia. Players are lined up top to bottom and the swatches starting at the top and going down are shaped like 1, 2 and 3. Each card is sequentially numbered to 25.

PRINT RUN 25 SER.#'d SETS
2 Pierce/McG/J-Rich 10.00 25.00
4 Carmelo/Wade/Gaines 30.00 80.00
10 Heinrich/Ford/Pietrus 10.00 25.00

1996 Topps Kellogg's Raptors

This five card set was inserted at the rate of one card per specially marked box of Rice Krispies sold in the Toronto area. The cards are similar to the regular Topps design for this year except all of the printing on the front is in silver foil instead of gold. On the front of each card, there is a small silver foil emblem of the Raptor's logo and the words "Inaugural Season" and "1995-96". The backs have a Kellogg's Logo in red at the top just right of the player's photo.

COMPLETE SET (5) 2.50 6.00
1 Willie Anderson .40 1.00
2 Damon Stoudamire 2.00 5.00
3 Alvin Robertson .40 1.00
4 Tony Massenburg .40 1.00
5 Tracy Murray .40 1.00

2007-08 Topps Letterman

This set was released on September 4, 2008. The base set consists of 75 cards. Cards 1-50 feature veterans, and cards 51-75 are rookies. All cards are serially numbered to 599.

PRINT RUN 599 SER.#'d SETS
UNPRICED SUPERFR.PRINT RUN ONE SET
1 Dwyane Wade 1.50 4.00
2 Kobe Bryant 4.00 10.00
3 Allen Iverson 1.25 3.00
4 Jason Kidd 1.00 2.50
5 Kevin Garnett 1.50 4.00
6 Tony Parker 1.00 2.50
7 Gilbert Arenas .75 2.00
8 Dwight Howard .75 2.00
9 Steve Nash 1.25 3.00
10 Carmelo Anthony 1.25 3.00
11 Tim Duncan 1.50 4.00
12 Chris Bosh 1.00 2.50
13 LeBron James 4.00 10.00
14 Tracy McGrady 1.00 2.50
15 Vince Carter 1.25 3.00
16 Amare Stoudemire .75 2.00
17 Shaquille O'Neal 2.00 5.00
18 Paul Pierce 1.00 2.50
19 Yao Ming 1.25 3.00
20 Dirk Nowitzki 1.25 3.00
21 Pau Gasol 1.00 2.50
22 Michael Redd .75 2.00
23 Carlos Boozer .75 2.00
24 Baron Davis .75 2.00
25 Caron Butler .75 2.00
26 Joe Johnson .75 2.00
27 Gerald Wallace .75 2.00
28 Al Jefferson .75 2.00
29 Chris Paul 1.25 3.00
30 Rudy Gay 1.00 2.50
31 Manu Ginobili 1.00 2.50
32 Corey Maggette .75 2.00
33 Ray Allen 1.00 2.50
34 Ben Gordon .75 2.00
35 Jamal Crawford 1.00 2.50
36 David West .75 2.00
37 Andre Iguodala .75 2.00
38 Deron Williams .75 2.00
39 Brandon Roy 1.00 2.50
40 Richard Hamilton .75 2.00
41 Larry Bird 3.00 8.00
42 John Stockton 2.00 5.00
43 Bill Russell 2.00 5.00
44 David Robinson 2.00 5.00
45 Isiah Thomas 1.25 3.00
46 Dennis Rodman 2.50 6.00
47 Jerry West 1.50 4.00
48 Moses Malone 1.25 3.00
49 Dominique Wilkins 1.50 4.00
50 Magic Johnson 3.00 8.00
51 Jamario Moon RC 1.50 4.00
52 Juan Carlos Navarro RC 1.50 4.00
53 Spencer Hawes RC 1.50 4.00
54 Glen Davis RC 1.50 4.00
55 Rodney Stuckey RC 1.50 4.00
56 Kevin Durant RC 15.00 40.00
57 Corey Brewer RC 2.00 5.00
58 Joakim Noah RC 2.00 5.00
59 Mike Conley Jr. RC 2.50 6.00
60 Al Horford RC 2.50 6.00
61 Julian Wright RC 1.25 3.00
62 Jeff Green RC 2.00 5.00
63 Luis Scola RC 2.50 6.00
64 Yi Jianlian RC 2.50 6.00
65 Sean Williams RC 1.25 3.00
66 Arron Afflalo RC 2.00 5.00
67 Al Thornton RC 1.50 4.00
68 Marco Belinelli RC 2.00 5.00
69 Javaris Crittenton RC 1.25 3.00
70 Thaddeus Young RC 2.00 5.00
71 Daequan Cook RC 1.50 4.00
72 Brandan Wright RC 2.00 5.00
73 Acie Law RC 1.25 3.00
74 Nick Young RC 2.50 6.00
75 Greg Oden RC 2.00 5.00
NNO Lottery Exchange 20.00 40.00

2007-08 Topps Letterman Refractors

*REFRACTORS: .75X TO 2X BASE HI
REFRACTOR PRINT RUN 99 SETS
2 Kobe Bryant 12.00 30.00
13 LeBron James 12.00 30.00
56 Kevin Durant 50.00 100.00

2007-08 Topps Letterman Xfractors

*1-50 XFRACTORS: 2X TO 5X BASE HI
*51-75 XFRACTORS: 1.5X TO 4X HI
XFRACTORS PRINT RUN 25 SETS
2 Kobe Bryant 40.00 100.00
13 LeBron James 40.00 100.00
56 Kevin Durant 400.00 800.00

2007-08 Topps Letterman Authentic Relics Quad Autographs

GROUP A PRINT RUN 9 SETS
GROUP B PRINT RUN 75 SETS
UNPRICED GRP A REF.PRINT RUN 5 SETS
GRP B REF: .5X TO 1.25X BASE HI
GRP B REF.PRINT RUN 19 SETS
UNPRICED SUPERFR.PRINT RUN ONE SET
UNPRICED XFRACTOR PRINT RUN ONE SET
ABY Andrew Bynum B 10.00 25.00
AT Al Thornton B 6.00 15.00
ATU Alando Tucker B 6.00 15.00
CB Caron Butler B 8.00 20.00
DH Dwight Howard B 12.00 30.00
DM Darko Milicic B 6.00 15.00
DT David Thompson B 10.00 25.00
IT Isiah Thomas B 15.00 30.00
JJW Jo Jo White B 8.00 20.00
LD Luol Deng B 8.00 20.00
MW Maurice Williams B 6.00 15.00
RG Rudy Gay B 6.00 15.00
RR Rajon Rondo B 20.00 40.00
SM Shawn Marion B 10.00 25.00
YJ Yi Jianlian B 15.00 30.00
ZR Zach Randolph B 6.00 15.00

2007-08 Topps Letterman Booklet Autographs

PRINT RUN 19 SER.#'d SETS
UNPRICED REF.PRINT RUN 5 SETS
UNPRICED XF.PRINT RUN 3 SETS
UNPRICED SUPER PRINT RUN ONE SET
AJ Antawn Jamison 20.00 50.00
AL4 Acie Law 20.00 50.00
BR Bill Russell 150.00 300.00
BWR Brandan Wright 20.00 50.00
CA Carmelo Anthony 40.00 100.00
CB Carlos Boozer 30.00 80.00
CBI Chauncey Billups 30.00 60.00
CBO Chris Bosh 50.00 120.00
CP Chris Paul 50.00 100.00
DR Dennis Rodman 75.00 150.00
DW Dwyane Wade 125.00 225.00
DWI Dominique Wilkins 50.00 120.00
GA Gilbert Arenas 40.00 80.00
GO Greg Oden 20.00 50.00
JW Jerry West 75.00 150.00
LB Larry Bird 125.00 250.00
MJ Magic Johnson 75.00 150.00
MM Mike Miller 20.00 50.00
NY Nick Young 25.00 60.00
PP Paul Pierce 100.00 200.00
RA Ray Allen 50.00 100.00
RB Rick Barry 30.00 60.00
RS Rodney Stuckey 40.00 100.00
TY Thaddeus Young 30.00 80.00
VC Vince Carter 20.00 50.00
YJ Yi Jianlian 30.00 80.00

2007-08 Topps Letterman Patches

STATED PRINT RUN NINE SETS
TOTAL PRINT RUNS 36-99
*REFRACTORS: .5X TO 1.25X BASE HI
REFRACTOR PRINT RUN FIVE SETS
FIVE CARDS FOR EACH LETTER
UNPRICED XF.PRINT RUN ONE SET
UNPRICED SUPER PRINT RUN ONE SET
LPAA Arron Afflalo/63* 8.00 20.00
LPAH Al Horford/63* 6.00 15.00
LPAI Allen Iverson/63* 20.00 40.00
LPAL4 Acie Law/45* 6.00 15.00
LPAS Amare Stoudemire/90* 15.00 30.00
LPBD Baron Davis/45* 10.00 25.00
LPBG Ben Gordon/54* 6.00 15.00
LPBR Bill Russell/63* 15.00 40.00
LPBWR Brandan Wright/54* 6.00 15.00
LPCA Carmelo Anthony/63* 20.00 50.00
LPCB Corey Brewer/54* 6.00 15.00
LPCBO Carlos Boozer/54* 6.00 15.00
LPCP Chris Paul/36* 20.00 40.00
LPDN Dirk Nowitzki/72* 20.00 40.00
LPDR Dennis Rodman/54* 15.00 30.00
LPDW Dominique Wilkins/63* 8.00 20.00
LPDWA Dwyane Wade/36* 20.00 50.00
LPGA Gilbert Arenas/54* 15.00 30.00
LPGO Greg Oden/36* 20.00 40.00
LPJC Javaris Crittenton/90* 6.00 15.00
LPJG Jeff Green/45* 8.00 20.00
LPJW Julian Wright/54* 6.00 15.00
LPJWE Jerry West/36* 20.00 40.00
LPKB Kobe Bryant/54* 25.00 60.00
LPKD Kevin Durant/54* 25.00 60.00
LPKG Kevin Garnett/63* 15.00 40.00
LPLB Larry Bird/45* 20.00 50.00
LPLJ LeBron James/45* 30.00 80.00
LPMA Morris Almond/54* 6.00 15.00
LPMJ Magic Johnson/63* 20.00 40.00
LPMM Mike Miller/54* 6.00 15.00
LPNY Nick Young/45* 6.00 15.00
LPRS Rodney Stuckey/63* 6.00 15.00
LPSN Steve Nash/45* 15.00 30.00
LPSW Sean Williams/72* 6.00 15.00
LPTD Tim Duncan/54* 25.00 50.00
LPWC Wilt Chamberlain/99* 20.00 40.00
LPWCH Wilson Chandler/72* 8.00 20.00
LPYJ Yi Jianlian/72* 8.00 20.00
LPYM Yao Ming/27* 20.00 40.00

2007-08 Topps Letterman Patches Autographs

UNPRICED GROUP A PRINT RUN 5 SETS
UNPRICED GROUP B PRINT RUN 9 SETS
GROUP C PRINT RUN 33 SETS
UNPRICED GRP.A REF.PRINT RUN 3 SETS
UNPRICED GRP.B REF.PRINT RUN 5 SETS
GRP.C REF: .6X TO 1.5X BASE HI
GRP.C REF.PRINT RUN 15 SETS
UNPRICED X-F.PRINT RUN ONE SET
UNPRICED SUPER PRINT RUN ONE SET
AA Arron Afflalo C/231* 8.00 20.00
AL4 Acie Law C/165* 8.00 20.00
BD Baron Davis C/165* 10.00 25.00
BG Ben Gordon C/198* 8.00 20.00
DW Dominique Wilkins C/231* 15.00 40.00
JC Javaris Crittenton C/333* 8.00 20.00
MA Morris Almond C/198* 8.00 20.00
MM Mike Miller C/198* 10.00 25.00
NY Nick Young C/165* 10.00 25.00
RS Rodney Stuckey C/231* 12.00 30.00
SW Sean Williams C/264* 8.00 20.00
TY Thaddeus Young C/165* 8.00 20.00
WC Wilson Chandler C/264* 12.00 30.00

2007-08 Topps Letterman Patches Jersey Number Autographs

GROUP A PRINT RUN NINE SETS
GROUP B PRINT RUN 75 SETS
*REFRACTORS: .5X TO 1.25X BASE HI
GRP.A REF.PRINT RUN 19 SETS
UNPRICED GRP.B REF.PRINT RUN 5 SETS
UNPRICED SUPER PRINT RUN ONE SET
AA Arron Afflalo B 6.00 15.00
AI Andre Iguodala B 8.00 20.00
AJ Antawn Jamison B 6.00 15.00
AL Acie Law B 6.00 15.00
CB Carlos Boozer B 6.00 15.00
CBI Chauncey Billups B 8.00 20.00
CBO Chris Bosh B 15.00 30.00
DC Daequan Cook B 8.00 20.00
DR Dennis Rodman B 25.00 60.00
MA Morris Almond B 6.00 15.00
NY Nick Young B 10.00 25.00
RB Rick Barry B 10.00 25.00
RF Raymond Felton B 6.00 15.00
RS Rodney Stuckey B 12.50 30.00
SW Sean Williams B 6.00 15.00
YJ Yi Jianlian B 15.00 30.00

2007-08 Topps Letterman Patches Team Logo Autographs

GROUP A PRINT RUN NINE SETS
GROUP B PRINT RUN 75 SETS
*REFRACTORS: .5X TO 1.25X BASE HI
GRP.A REF.PRINT RUN 19 SETS
UNPRICED GRP.B REF.PRINT RUN 5 SETS
UNPRICED SUPER PRINT RUN ONE SET
AI Andre Iguodala B 6.00 15.00
AJ Antawn Jamison B 6.00 15.00
AL Acie Law B 6.00 15.00
BD Baron Davis B 10.00 25.00
CB Carlos Boozer B 6.00 15.00
DC Daequan Cook B 8.00 20.00
DW Dominique Wilkins B 15.00 30.00
MA Morris Almond B 6.00 15.00
NY Nick Young B 10.00 25.00
PP Paul Pierce B 20.00 50.00
RA Ray Allen B 20.00 40.00
RB Rick Barry B 10.00 25.00
RS Rodney Stuckey B 10.00 25.00
SH Spencer Hawes B 6.00 15.00
WC Wilson Chandler B 10.00 25.00

2007-08 Topps Letterman Redemptions

CARDS AVAILABLE VIA REDEMPTION
STATED PRINT RUN 25 SER.#'d SETS
BL Brook Lopez/125* 6.00 15.00
BR Brandon Rush/100* 3.00 8.00
DR Derrick Rose/100* 15.00 40.00
EG Eric Gordon/150* 8.00 20.00
JB Jerryd Bayless/175* 3.00 8.00
KL Kevin Love/100* 10.00 25.00
MB Michael Beasley/175* 4.00 10.00
RW Russell Westbrook/225* 30.00 80.00
DJA D.J. Augustin/200* 3.00 8.00
OJM O.J. Mayo/100* 4.00 10.00

2004-05 Topps Luxury Box

Released in March 2005, Luxury Box consists of a 150-card set divided up into 100 veteran players, 30 rookies and 20 retired legends. Cards are horizontally designed with a full-color player action photo and a foil likeness. Each pack of Luxury Box was packaged twice to hide the the inner packaged. Here's how the inner package breaks down: Tier Reserved packs have seven base cards and one season ticket parallel card. Every third Tier Reserved pack contains a sequentially numbered parallel card and each box contains five Tier Reserved packs. Loge Level packs have seven base cards and one sequentially numbered single or dual player relic card. Every third Loge Level pack contains a sequentially numbered single or dual player relic parallel and there are two Loge Level packs in each box. Main Reserved packs have seven base cards and one Sequentially numbered triple or quad-player relic card. Luxury Box packs have six base cards, one Season Ticket parallel and one sequentially numbered autograph card. Every third Luxury Box pack contains a sequentially numbered autograph parallel and each box contains one Luxury Box pack. Full boxes contain 10 mystery packs that carried a suggested retail price of $10.

UNPRICED ONE OF ONE PARALLEL EXISTS
1 Andrei Kirilenko .30 .75
2 Peja Stojakovic .40 1.00
3 Grant Hill .50 1.25
4 Baron Davis .30 .75
5 Wally Szczerbiak .30 .75
6 Ray Allen .40 1.00
7 Shawn Marion .30 .75
8 Gilbert Arenas .30 .75
9 Keith Van Horn .30 .75
10 Eddie Jones .30 .75
11 Lamar Odom .30 .75
12 Stephen Jackson .30 .75
13 Rasheed Wallace .40 1.00
14 Steve Smith .30 .75
15 Gary Payton .40 1.00
16 Jason Terry .30 .75
17 Eddy Curry .25 .60
18 Yao Ming .75 2.00
19 Kenyon Martin .30 .75
20 Jason Richardson .40 1.00
21 Bonzi Wells .25 .60
22 Richard Jefferson .30 .75
23 LeBron James 2.50 6.00
24 Marko Jaric .25 .60
25 Chauncey Billups .40 1.00
26 Jamal Crawford .40 1.00
27 Willie Green .25 .60
28 Zach Randolph .30 .75
29 Latrell Sprewell .30 .75
30 Tim Duncan .60 1.50
31 Cuttino Mobley .25 .60
32 Shaquille O'Neal 1.00 2.50
33 Carlos Arroyo .25 .60
34 Jamaal Tinsley .25 .60
35 Luke Ridnour .30 .75
36 Kenny Anderson .30 .75
37 Brad Miller .30 .75
38 Caron Butler .30 .75
39 Troy Murphy .25 .60
40 Vince Carter .60 1.50
41 Shane Battier .30 .75
42 Joe Johnson .30 .75
43 Jason Kapono .25 .60
44 Juwan Howard .30 .75
45 Zydrunas Ilgauskas .30 .75
46 Jerry Stackhouse .30 .75
47 Jamaal Magloire .25 .60
48 Steve Francis .30 .75
49 Kwame Brown .25 .60
50 Kevin Garnett .60 1.50
51 Shareef Abdur-Rahim .30 .75
52 Tony Parker .40 1.00
53 Marcus Camby .30 .75
54 Morris Peterson .25 .60
55 Antoine Walker .40 1.00
56 Elton Brand .40 1.00
57 Paul Pierce .40 1.00
58 Jason Kidd .60 1.50
59 Gerald Wallace .30 .75
60 Jason Williams .30 .75
61 Dwyane Wade .60 1.50
62 Amare Stoudemire .30 .75
63 T.J. Ford .25 .60
64 Tyson Chandler .30 .75
65 Alonzo Mourning .50 1.25
66 Dirk Nowitzki .60 1.50
67 Allan Houston .30 .75
68 Andre Miller .30 .75
69 Glenn Robinson .30 .75
70 Richard Hamilton .30 .75
71 Darius Miles .25 .60
72 Mike Dunleavy .30 .75
73 Mike Bibby .40 1.00
74 Tracy McGrady .50 1.25
75 Manu Ginobili .50 1.25
76 Jermaine O'Neal .30 .75
77 Rashard Lewis .40 1.00
78 Corey Maggette .30 .75
79 Chris Bosh .40 1.00
80 Pau Gasol .40 1.00
81 Carlos Boozer .30 .75
82 Desmond Mason .30 .75
83 Antawn Jamison .30 .75
84 Sam Cassell .30 .75
85 Al Harrington .30 .75
86 Steve Nash .50 1.25
87 Ricky Davis .30 .75
88 Chris Andersen .40 1.00
89 Kirk Hinrich .30 .75
90 Carmelo Anthony .75 2.00
91 Ron Mercer .25 .60
92 Ben Wallace .30 .75
93 Josh Howard .40 1.00
94 Reggie Miller .40 1.00
95 Chris Webber .40 1.00
96 Drew Gooden .25 .60
97 Michael Redd .30 .75
98 Allen Iverson .60 1.50
99 Kobe Bryant 1.50 4.00
100 Stephon Marbury .30 .75
101 Dwight Howard RC 2.00 5.00
102 Emeka Okafor RC .75 2.00
103 Ben Gordon RC 1.00 2.50
104 Shaun Livingston RC 1.00 2.50
105 Devin Harris RC .75 2.00
106 Josh Childress RC .75 2.00
107 Luol Deng RC 1.00 2.50
108 Rafael Araujo RC .60 1.50
109 Andre Iguodala RC 1.25 3.00
110 Luke Jackson RC .60 1.50
111 Andris Biedrins RC .60 1.50
112 Robert Swift RC .60 1.50
113 Sebastian Telfair RC .75 2.00
114 Kris Humphries RC 1.00 2.50
115 Al Jefferson RC 1.25 3.00
116 Kirk Snyder RC .60 1.50
117 Josh Smith RC 1.00 2.50
118 J.R. Smith RC 1.00 2.50
119 Dorell Wright RC 1.00 2.50
120 Jameer Nelson RC 1.00 2.50
121 Andres Nocioni RC 1.00 2.50
122 Kevin Martin RC 1.25 3.00
123 Tony Allen RC 1.00 2.50
124 Anderson Varejao RC .75 2.00
125 Nenad Krstic RC 1.00 2.50
126 Sasha Vujacic RC 1.00 2.50
127 David Harrison RC .60 1.50
128 Pavel Podkolzin RC .60 1.50
129 Trevor Ariza RC 1.00 2.50
130 Delonte West RC 1.00 2.50
131 Rick Barry .75 2.00
132 Elgin Baylor 1.00 2.50
133 Larry Bird 2.50 6.00
134 Bob Cousy 1.50 4.00
135 Bill Russell 1.50 4.00
136 Walt Frazier 1.00 2.50
137 George Gervin 1.00 2.50
138 John Havlicek 1.00 2.50
139 James Worthy 1.25 3.00
140 Wilt Chamberlain 2.00 5.00
141 Dave Cowens .60 1.50
142 Moses Malone 1.00 2.50
143 Kevin McHale 1.25 3.00
144 Earl Monroe 1.00 2.50
145 Pete Maravich 1.50 4.00
146 Willis Reed 1.00 2.50
147 Oscar Robertson 1.00 2.50
148 Isiah Thomas 1.00 2.50
149 Bill Walton 1.00 2.50
150 Kareem Abdul-Jabbar 1.50 4.00

2004-05 Topps Luxury Box Season Tickets

*SEASON TIX: .6X TO 1.5X BASE HI
*SEASON TIX RC's: .2X TO .5X BASE HI
ONE PER PACK w/o INSERT

2004-05 Topps Luxury Box 300

*BOX 300: .75X TO 2X BASE HI
*BOX 300 RC's: .5X TO 1.25X BASE HI
PRINT RUN 300 SER.#'d SETS

2004-05 Topps Luxury Box 100

*BOX 100: 2X TO 5X BASE HI
*BOX 100 RC's: 1X TO 2X BASE HI
*BOX 100 RET: 1.5X TO 4X BASE HI
PRINT RUN 100 SER.#'d SETS

2004-05 Topps Luxury Box 25

*BOX 25: 5X TO 12X BASE HI
*BOX 25 RCs: 2.5X TO 6X BASE HI
*BOX 25 RET: 2.5X TO 6X BASE HI
PRINT RUN 25 SER.#'d SETS

2004-05 Topps Luxury Box and 1

Randomly inserted into packs, these five cards feature four game-used relics on each card. Each of these cards were issued to a stated print run of 450 serial numbered sets. Parallel version of these cards were issued to stated print runs of 200, 75, 30 and 1.

PRINT RUN 450 SER.#'d SETS
*AND 1 200: .5X TO 1.25X BASE JSY HI
*AND 1 75: .6X TO 1.5X BASE JSY HI
*AND 1 30: .75X TO 2X BASE JSY HI
AMDB Melo/Yao/Baron/Brand 8.00 20.00
MIFK Marbury/AI/Francis/Kidd 8.00 20.00
OHIG Okafor/Howard/Iggy/Gordon 8.00 20.00
OWOO Shaq/BigBen/O'Neal/Okafor 8.00 20.00
PJPH Pierce/R-Jeff/Prince/Harring 8.00 20.00

2004-05 Topps Luxury Box Assist Dual Relics

Randomly inserted into packs, these 12 cards feature two game-used relics on each card. Each of these cards were issued to a stated print run of 350 serial numbered sets. Parallel relics were issued to stated print runs of 200, 75 and 30.

PRINT RUN 350 SER.#'d SETS
*ASSIST 200: .5X TO 1.25X BASE JSY HI
*ASSIST 75: .6X TO 1.5X BASE JSY HI
*ASSIST 30: .75X TO 2X BASE JSY HI
UNPRICED AUTO RANDOM INSERTS IN PACKS
ASAP R.Alston/M.Peterson 3.00 8.00
ASDS B.Davis/J.R.Smith 3.00 8.00
ASGD B.Gordon/L.Deng 8.00 20.00
ASID A.Iverson/S.Dalembert 4.00 10.00
ASJA A.Jamison/G.Arenas 3.00 8.00
ASKJ J.Kidd/R.Jefferson 4.00 10.00
ASLB S.Livingston/E.Brand 3.00 8.00
ASOJ J.O'Neal/F.Jones 3.00 8.00
ASPP G.Payton/P.Pierce 4.00 10.00
ASSN A.Stoudemire/S.Nash 6.00 15.00
ASTN J.Terry/D.Nowitzki 4.00 10.00
ASWW R.Wallace/B.Wallace 3.00 8.00

2004-05 Topps Luxury Box Champagne Toast Autographs

Randomly inserted into packs, these five cards feature autographs of the featured players. Each of these cards were issued to a stated print run of 100 serial numbered sets. Parallel versions of this set was issued to stated print runs of 75, 30 and 10.

PRINT RUN 100 SER.#'d SETS
*AUTO 75: .5X TO 1.25X BASE AU HI
*AUTO 30: .6X TO 1.5X BASE AU HI
BW Ben Wallace 12.50 30.00
EO Emeka Okafor 15.00 40.00
RH Richard Hamilton 12.50 30.00
SO Shaquille O'Neal 30.00 80.00
TD Tim Duncan 60.00 120.00

2004-05 Topps Luxury Box Lay-Up Relics

Randomly inserted into packs, these 30 cards feature game-used relics on each card. Each of these cards were issued to a stated print run of 500 serial numbered sets. Parallel relics were issued to stated print runs of 200, 75 and 30 and 1.

PRINT RUN 500 SER.#'d SETS
*LAY UP 200: .4X TO 1X BASE JSY HI
*LAY UP 75: .5X TO 1.25X BASE JSY HI
*LAY UP 30: .6X TO 1.5X BASE JSY HI
AI Andre Iguodala 3.00 8.00
AJ Antawn Jamison 2.00 5.00
AK Andrei Kirilenko 2.00 5.00
AS Amare Stoudemire 2.00 5.00
AW Antoine Walker 2.50 6.00
BD Baron Davis 2.00 5.00
CA Carmelo Anthony 5.00 12.00
DH Dwight Howard 5.00 12.00
EB Elton Brand 2.50 6.00
EO Emeka Okafor 2.00 5.00
GP Gary Payton 2.50 6.00
JO Jermaine O'Neal 2.00 5.00
JS Jerry Stackhouse 2.00 5.00
KG Kevin Garnett 4.00 10.00
KM Kenyon Martin 2.00 5.00
NK Nenad Krstic 2.50 6.00
PG Pau Gasol 2.50 6.00
PP Paul Pierce 2.50 6.00
PS Peja Stojakovic 2.50 6.00
RH Richard Hamilton 2.00 5.00
SF Steve Francis 2.00 5.00
SL Shaun Livingston 2.50 6.00
SM Stephon Marbury 2.00 5.00
SO Shaquille O'Neal 6.00 15.00
ST Sebastian Telfair 2.00 5.00
TD Tim Duncan 4.00 10.00
TM Tracy McGrady 3.00 8.00
YM Yao Ming 5.00 12.00
AIV Allen Iverson 4.00 10.00
JRS J.R. Smith 2.50 6.00

2004-05 Topps Luxury Box Lay-Up Relics Autographs

Randomly inserted in packs, this 7-card set parallels the Lay-Up Relics insert set design enhanced with player autographs and sequential numbering to 15.

PRINT RUN 15 SER.#'d SETS
SO Shaquille O'Neal 75.00 150.00
TD Tim Duncan 100.00 200.00
TM Tracy McGrady 40.00 100.00

2004-05 Topps Luxury Box Pre-Production

COMPLETE SET (6) 2.00 5.00
PP1 Emeka Okafor .40 1.00
PP2 Sebastian Telfair .40 1.00
PP3 Shaun Livingston .50 1.25
PP4 Shaquille O'Neal 1.25 3.00
PP5 Tracy McGrady .60 1.50
PP6 Carmelo Anthony 1.00 2.50

2004-05 Topps Luxury Box Red Carpet Autographs

Randomly inserted into packs, these 26 cards feature an autograph on each card. Each of these cards were issued to a stated print run of 135 serial numbered sets. Parallel relics were issued to stated print runs of 75 and 30 and 10.

PRINT RUN 135 SER.#'d SETS
*AUTO 75: .5X TO 1.2X BASE AU HI
*AUTO 30: .6X TO 1.5X BASE AU HI
AB Andris Biedrins 2.50 6.00
AV Anderson Varejao 3.00 8.00
BG Ben Gordon 4.00 10.00
BU Beno Udrih 3.00 8.00
CD Chris Duhon 4.00 10.00
EO Emeka Okafor 3.00 8.00
JC Josh Childress 3.00 8.00
JN Jameer Nelson 4.00 10.00
JR Justin Reed 2.50 6.00
JS Josh Smith 4.00 10.00
JV Jackson Vroman 2.50 6.00
KH Kris Humphries 4.00 10.00
KM Kevin Martin 5.00 12.00
LC Lionel Chalmers 4.00 10.00
LD Luol Deng 4.00 10.00

PP Pavel Podkolzin 2.50 6.00
RA Rafael Araujo 2.50 6.00
RS Romain Sato 2.50 6.00
SL Shaun Livingston 4.00 10.00
ST Sebastian Telfair 3.00 8.00
TA Tony Allen 4.00 10.00
DEH Devin Harris 3.00 8.00
DHA David Harrison 2.50 6.00
DWE Delonte West 4.00 10.00
DWR Dorell Wright 4.00 10.00
JRS J.R. Smith 4.00 10.00

2004-05 Topps Luxury Box Red Carpet Legends Autographs

Randomly inserted into packs, these 17 cards feature an autograph of a retired NBA great on each card. Please note that George Karl did not return his cards in time for pack out and was issued as an exchange card. Each of these cards were issued to a stated print run of 30 serial numbered sets. Parallel versions of these cards were issued to stated print runs of 10 and 1 serial numbered copies.

PRINT RUN 30 SER.#'d SETS
BL Bob Lanier 15.00 40.00
BW Bill Walton 15.00 40.00
CD Clyde Drexler 40.00 80.00
DB Dave Bing 50.00 100.00
DS Detlef Schrempf 15.00 40.00
EB Elgin Baylor 20.00 50.00
GG George Gervin 15.00 40.00
GK George Karl 15.00 40.00
ME Mark Eaton 20.00 50.00
MM Moses Malone 20.00 50.00
RB Rick Barry 20.00 50.00
RP Robert Parish 30.00 80.00

2004-05 Topps Luxury Box Signs of Luxury

Randomly inserted into packs, these 11 cards feature an autograph on each card. Each of these cards were issued to a stated print run of 100 serial numbered sets. Parallel relics were issued to stated print runs of 75 and 30 and 10.

PRINT RUN 100 SER.#'d SETS
*SIGS 75: .6X TO 1.5X BASE AU HI
*SIGS 30: .75X TO 2X BASE AU HI
AS Amare Stoudemire 12.50 30.00
BD Baron Davis 6.00 15.00
CA Carmelo Anthony 15.00 40.00
FJ Fred Jones 6.00 15.00
JK Jason Kidd 12.50 30.00
JO Jermaine O'Neal 6.00 15.00
LO Lamar Odom 6.00 15.00
PS Peja Stojakovic 6.00 15.00
RA Rafer Alston 15.00 40.00
TM Tracy McGrady 15.00 40.00
STM Stephon Marbury 6.00 15.00

2004-05 Topps Luxury Box Three-Point Play Relics

Randomly inserted into packs, these 13 cards feature three game-used relics on each card. Each of these cards were issued to a stated print run of 450 serial numbered sets. Parallel versions of these cards were issued to stated print runs of 200, 75 and 30 serial numbered sets.

PRINT RUN 450 SER.#'d SETS
*RELICS 200: .5X TO 1.25X BASE HI
*RELICS 75: .6X TO 1.5X BASE HI
*RELICS 30: .75X TO 2X BASE HI
AMM Carmelo/K-Mart/A.Miller 8.00 20.00
AWJ T.Allen/D.West/Big Al 4.00 10.00
DSM B.Davis/J.R.Smith/Magloire 4.00 10.00
GCS Garnett/Cassell/Spree 6.00 15.00
HFM D.Howard/Francis/Mobley 5.00 12.00
IID Iguodala/Iverson/Dalembert 5.00 12.00
KBA Kirilenko/Boozer/Arroyo 4.00 10.00
KMJ Kidd/Mourning/Jefferson 6.00 15.00
OBV Odom/Butler/Vujacic 4.00 10.00
OJW Shaq/E.Jones/D.Wright 8.00 20.00
RAT Randolph/Shareef/Telfair 4.00 10.00
WSC Walker/JoshSmith/Childress 6.00 15.00
WWH B.Wallace/R.Wallace/Rip 6.00 15.00

2004-05 Topps Luxury Box Triple Threat Relics

Randomly inserted into packs, these 12 cards feature three game-used relics on each card. Each of these cards were issued to a stated print run of 450 serial numbered sets. Parallel versions of these cards were issued to stated print runs of 200, 75 and 30 serial numbered sets.

PRINT RUN 450 SER.#'d SETS
*RELICS 200: .5X TO 1.25X BASE HI
*RELICS 75: .6X TO 1.5X BASE HI
*RELICS 30: .75X TO 2X BASE HI
ALK Shareef/R.Lewis/Kirilenko 4.00 10.00
CJM Childress/E.Jones/Mobley 4.00 10.00
DJD Deng/L.Jackson/Delfino 4.00 10.00
HBF Hinrich/Billups/Ford 4.00 10.00
HES Harris/Emmett/J.R.Smith 4.00 10.00
JBS Big Al/Bosh/Sweetney 4.00 10.00
JIA Big Al/Igoudala/Araujo 5.00 12.00
KAG Kirilenko/Carmelo/Garnett 8.00 20.00
MCA A.Miller/Cassell/Arroyo 4.00 10.00
MND Yao/Dirk/Duncan 6.00 15.00
RMM J-Rich/Marion/Maggette 4.00 10.00
WJH Walker/Jamison/Hill 4.00 10.00

2005-06 Topps Luxury Box

This 150-card set was released in March, 2006. The set was issued in six card packs with an $12.50 SRP which came eight packs to a box and 10 boxes to a case. The Rookie Cards numbered 101 through 145 were issued to a stated print run of 999 serial numbered sets.

COMP.SET w/o SP's (100) 20.00 50.00
101-145 RC PRINT RUN 999 SER.#'d SETS
UNPRICED LUX.BOX 1 PRINT RUN ONE SET
1 Dwyane Wade .60 1.50
2 Joe Johnson .30 .75
3 Larry Hughes .30 .75
4 Michael Finley .40 1.00
5 Josh Howard .40 1.00
6 Kenyon Martin .30 .75
7 Jermaine O'Neal .30 .75
8 Luke Ridnour .30 .75
9 Andre Iguodala .30 .75
10 Wally Szczerbiak .30 .75
11 Yao Ming .50 1.25
12 Dwight Howard .30 .75
13 Ricky Davis .30 .75
14 Baron Davis .30 .75
15 Carmelo Anthony .75 2.00
16 Pau Gasol .40 1.00
17 Robert Horry .30 .75
18 Andres Nocioni .25 .60
19 Sam Cassell .30 .75
20 Shareef Abdur-Rahim .30 .75
21 Gerald Wallace .30 .75
22 Vince Carter .60 1.50
23 LeBron James 1.50 4.00
24 Richard Hamilton .30 .75
25 Shawn Marion .30 .75
26 Stephon Marbury .30 .75
27 Chris Bosh .40 1.00
28 Darius Miles .25 .60
29 Jamaal Magloire .25 .60
30 Kevin Garnett .60 1.50
31 Lamar Odom .30 .75
32 Shaquille O'Neal .75 2.00
33 Allen Iverson .60 1.50
34 Paul Pierce .40 1.00
35 Keith Van Horn .30 .75
36 Damon Stoudamire .30 .75
37 Jason Richardson .40 1.00
38 Ben Gordon .30 .75
39 J.R. Smith .30 .75
40 Brad Miller .30 .75
41 Dirk Nowitzki .60 1.50
42 Bonzi Wells .25 .60
43 Corey Maggette .30 .75
44 Tracy McGrady .50 1.25
45 T.J. Ford .25 .60
46 Steve Francis .30 .75
47 Bobby Simmons .25 .60
48 Eddy Curry .25 .60
49 Antawn Jamison .30 .75
50 Emeka Okafor .30 .75
51 Tim Duncan .60 1.50
52 Chauncey Billups .40 1.00
53 Kwame Brown .25 .60
54 Ray Allen .40 1.00
55 Jason Kidd .60 1.50
56 Marcus Camby .30 .75
57 Stephen Jackson .30 .75
58 Rasheed Wallace .40 1.00
59 Rashard Lewis .40 1.00
60 Sebastian Telfair .30 .75
61 Manu Ginobili .40 1.00
62 Kurt Thomas .25 .60
63 Jamal Crawford .40 1.00
64 Jamaal Tinsley .25 .60
65 Donyell Marshall .25 .60
66 Chris Webber .40 1.00
67 Peja Stojakovic .40 1.00
68 P.J. Brown .25 .60
69 Nenad Krstic .25 .60
70 Ben Wallace .30 .75
71 Grant Hill .50 1.25
72 Elton Brand .40 1.00
73 Zach Randolph .30 .75
74 Josh Smith .30 .75
75 Samuel Dalembert .25 .60
76 Andre Miller .30 .75
77 Al Jefferson .30 .75
78 Caron Butler .30 .75
79 Shaun Livingston .25 .60
80 Richard Jefferson .30 .75
81 Rafer Alston .25 .60
82 Antoine Walker .30 .75
83 Zydrunas Ilgauskas .30 .75
84 Morris Peterson .25 .60
85 Marko Jaric .25 .60
86 Steve Nash .50 1.25
87 Kirk Hinrich .30 .75
88 Kobe Bryant 1.50 4.00
89 Eddie Jones .30 .75
90 Luol Deng .30 .75
91 Ron Artest .40 1.00
92 Desmond Mason .25 .60
93 Jason Terry .30 .75
94 Andrei Kirilenko .30 .75
95 Michael Redd .30 .75
96 Mehmet Okur .25 .60
97 Mike Dunleavy .30 .75
98 Mike Bibby .40 1.00
99 Amare Stoudemire .30 .75
100 Gilbert Arenas .30 .75
101 Daniel Ewing RC 1.00 2.50
102 Andray Blatche RC 1.25 3.00
103 Jose Calderon RC 1.25 3.00
104 Shavlik Randolph RC 1.00 2.50
105 Travis Diener RC .75 2.00
106 Brandon Bass RC 1.00 2.50
107 Fabricio Oberto RC 1.00 2.50
108 Ryan Gomes RC 1.00 2.50
109 Gerald Fitch RC .75 2.00
110 James Singleton RC .75 2.00
111 Deron Williams RC 1.50 4.00
112 Gerald Green RC 1.25 3.00
113 C.J. Miles RC 1.25 3.00
114 Chris Paul RC 5.00 12.00
115 Julius Hodge RC .75 2.00
116 Salim Stoudamire RC 1.00 2.50
117 Raymond Felton RC 1.25 3.00
118 Nate Robinson RC 1.25 3.00
119 Sarunas Jasikevicius RC 1.25 3.00
120 Monta Ellis RC 1.50 4.00
121 Jarrett Jack RC 1.25 3.00
122 Orien Greene RC 1.00 2.50
123 Rashad McCants RC 1.00 2.50
124 Francisco Garcia RC 1.00 2.50
125 Antoine Wright RC 1.00 2.50
126 Luther Head RC 1.00 2.50
127 Martell Webster RC 1.00 2.50
128 Eddie Basden RC .75 2.00
129 Marvin Williams RC 1.25 3.00
130 Danny Granger RC 1.50 4.00
131 Charlie Villanueva RC 1.25 3.00
132 Hakim Warrick RC 1.00 2.50
133 Ike Diogu RC .75 2.00
134 Wayne Simien RC .75 2.00
135 Yaroslav Korolev RC .75 2.00
136 David Lee RC 1.25 3.00
137 Sean May RC .75 2.00
138 Linas Kleiza RC .75 2.00
139 Joey Graham RC 1.00 2.50
140 Jason Maxiell RC 1.00 2.50
141 Andrew Bogut RC 1.50 4.00
142 Channing Frye RC 1.25 3.00
143 Andrew Bynum RC 1.00 2.50
144 Martynas Andriuskevicius RC .75 2.00
145 Johan Petro RC .75 2.00
146 Christie Brinkley 1.50 4.00
147 Jenny McCarthy 1.50 4.00
148 Shannon Elizabeth 1.50 4.00
149 Carmen Electra 1.50 4.00
150 Jay-Z 1.50 4.00

2005-06 Topps Luxury Box Season Ticket

*SEASON TICKET: .5X TO 1.25X BASE HI
STATED ODDS ONE PER PACK

2005-06 Topps Luxury Box 430

*BOX 430: .5X TO 1.25X BASE HI

2005-06 Topps Luxury Box 350

*BOX 350: .6X TO 1.5X BASE HI
PRINT RUN 350 SER.#'d SETS

2005-06 Topps Luxury Box 200

*BOX 200: .75X TO 2X BASE HI
PRINT RUN 200 SER.#'d SETS

2005-06 Topps Luxury Box 100

*BOX 100 VETS: 1.5X TO 4X BASE HI
*BOX 100 RCs: .75X TO 2X BASE HI
PRINT RUN 100 SER.#'d SETS

2005-06 Topps Luxury Box 25

*1-100 BOX 25: 3X TO 8X BASE HI
*101-145 BOX 25: 2X TO 5X BASE HI
*146-150 BOX 25: 4X TO 10X BASE HI
PRINT RUN 25 SER.#'d SETS

2005-06 Topps Luxury Box 4 on 2 Break 8 Relics

Randomly inserted into packs, these 10-cards feature eight players with game-used relics. Each of these cards were issued to a stated print run of 90 serial numbered sets.

PRINT RUN 90 SER.#'d SETS
*RELIC 25: .6X TO 1.5X BASE REL.HI
RELICS 1 NOT PRICED DUE TO SCARCITY
1 Jay-Z/NBA Stars 20.00 50.00
2 Jay-Z/NBA Guards 20.00 50.00
3 Jay-Z/NBA Stars 20.00 50.00
4 NBA Stars 25.00 60.00
5 Al/Wade/05 Draft Class 15.00 40.00
6 Al/Wade/J-Z/05 Draft Class 15.00 40.00
7 Jay-Z/NBA Guards 15.00 40.00
8 Jay-Z/NBA Guards 15.00 40.00
9 NBA Power Forwards 20.00 50.00
10 NBA Forwards 15.00 40.00

2005-06 Topps Luxury Box Box Out Quad Relics

Randomly inserted into packs, these cards feature relics from four people with something in common. Each of these cards were issued to a stated print run of 193 serial numbered sets.

PRINT RUN 193 SER.#'d SETS
*RELIC 25: .5X TO 1.25X BASE HI
RELICS 1 NOT PRICED DUE TO SCARCITY
1 Atlanta Hawks 5.00 12.00
2 Boston Celtics 8.00 20.00
3 Chicago Bulls 12.50 30.00
4 Cleveland Cavaliers 6.00 15.00
5 Dallas Mavericks 12.50 30.00
6 Denver Nuggets 6.00 15.00
7 Detroit Pistons 15.00 40.00
8 Golden State Warriors 5.00 12.00
9 Houston Rockets 8.00 20.00
10 Indiana Pacers 6.00 15.00
11 Los Angeles Clippers 6.00 15.00
12 Los Angeles Lakers 15.00 40.00
13 Memphis Grizzlies 6.00 15.00
14 Miami Heat 20.00 50.00
15 Milwaukee Bucks 5.00 12.00
16 Minnesota Timberwolves 8.00 20.00
17 New Jersey Nets 20.00 50.00
18 New York Knicks 6.00 15.00
19 New Orleans Hornets 6.00 15.00
20 Philadelphia 76ers 12.50 30.00
21 Phoenix Suns 10.00 25.00
22 Portland Trailblazers 5.00 12.00
23 Sacramento Kings 5.00 12.00
24 San Antonio Spurs 12.50 30.00
25 Seattle Supersonics 8.00 20.00
26 Toronto Raptors 6.00 15.00
27 Utah Jazz 5.00 12.00
28 Washington Wizards 6.00 15.00
29 Charlotte Bobcats 5.00 12.00
30 Orlando Magic 6.00 15.00
31 Celebrities 20.00 50.00
32 Jay-Z/Shaq/Ben/Yao 12.50 30.00
33 KG/Marion/Okafor/Ben 6.00 15.00
34 Bogut/Villan/Frye/Ike 5.00 12.00
35 Bynum/May/Warrk/Green 5.00 12.00
36 Jay-Z/Al/Wade/Melo 12.50 30.00
37 Duncan/Shaq/Al/Nash 12.50 30.00
38 Brand/Deng/Magg/Hill 6.00 15.00
39 Iggy/Frye/Arenas/R-Jeff 5.00 12.00
40 Okafor/Rip/Allen/Gordon 6.00 15.00

2005-06 Topps Luxury Box Box Seats Autographs

Randomly inserted into packs, these cards feature sticker-signed autographs of the featured player. For those players whom Topps released print run information on we have published the stated print run next to the player's name in our checklist.

PRINT RUNS LISTED IN CHECKLIST
*PARALLEL 25: .6X TO 1.5X BASE HI
PARALLEL PRINT RUN 25 SETS
AB Andrew Bogut/124 10.00 25.00
AI Allen Iverson/224 40.00 100.00
CB Christie Brinkley/74 30.00 80.00
CE Carmen Electra/74 8.00 20.00
DE Daniel Ewing/624 5.00 12.00
DW Dwyane Wade/224 20.00 50.00
EO Emeka Okafor/224 6.00 15.00
JJ Jarrett Jack/44 5.00 12.00
OG Orien Greene/624 5.00 12.00
RF Raymond Felton/424 8.00 20.00
SE Shannon Elizabeth/74 30.00 80.00
SL Shaun Livingston/124 5.00 12.00
SO Shaquille O'Neal/74 30.00 80.00
VC Vince Carter/224 15.00 40.00

2005-06 Topps Luxury Box Divisions 6 Relics

Randomly inserted into packs, these cards feature six players, with something in common, and game-used relics from those players. Each of these cards were issued to a stated print run of 192 serial numbered sets.

PRINT RUN 192 SER.#'d SETS
*RELIC 25: .5X TO 1.25X BASE REL.HI
RELICS 1 NOT PRICED DUE TO SCARCITY
1 2005 NBA Draft Class 8.00 20.00
2 NBA Guards 12.00 30.00
3 NBA Centers 12.50 30.00
4 NBA Forwards 12.50 30.00
5 High School Draftees 12.50 30.00
6 NBA Guards 8.00 20.00
7 NBA Forwards 12.50 30.00
8 NBA Point Guards 12.50 30.00
9 NBA Power Forwards 10.00 25.00
10 Top NBA Shooters 8.00 20.00
11 NBA Point Guards 10.00 25.00
12 Foreign NBA Forwards 10.00 25.00
13 NBA Forward/Centers 6.00 15.00
14 ACC Players 10.00 25.00
15 NBA Forward/Centers 8.00 20.00
16 2005 NBA Draft Class 8.00 20.00
17 NBA Swing Men 8.00 20.00
18 NBA Point Guards 8.00 20.00
19 NBA Guards 15.00 40.00
20 NBA Power Forwards 10.00 25.00

2005-06 Topps Luxury Box Industry Anchors

Randomly inserted into packs, this set features a few cards of each of these people, who are Topps spokesmen. The print run of each player is the same but each player has a different print run so we have that information in the headers of our checklist.

COMMON IVERSON (1-9) 1.50 4.00
COMMON WADE (1-9) 2.50 6.00
COMMON JAY-Z (1-8) 2.50 6.00
AI/WADE PRINT RUN 599 SER.#'d SETS
JAY-Z PRINT RUN 100 SER.#'d SETS
UNPRICED AUTO PRINT RUN 10 SETS
*RELICS: 1X TO 2.5X BASE HI
RELIC PRINT RUN 279 SER.#'d SETS

2005-06 Topps Luxury Box Industry Anchors Relics Dual

Randomly inserted into packs, these three cards feature two game-used relics from the featured players. Each of these cards were issued to a stated print run of 99 serial numbered sets.

PRINT RUN 99 SER.#'d SETS
IW A.Iverson/D.Wade 10.00 25.00
IZ A.Iverson/Jay-Z 10.00 25.00
WZ D.Wade/Jay-Z 10.00 25.00

2005-06 Topps Luxury Box Industry Anchors Relics Triple

Randomly inserted into packs, this card feature three game-used relics from the featured players. Each of these cards were issued to a stated print run of 25 serial numbered sets.

IWZ A.Iverson/D.Wade/Jay-Z 20.00 50.00

2005-06 Topps Luxury Box One-on-One Autographs Dual

Randomly inserted into packs, these five cards feature dual-signed cards. Each of these cards were issued to a stated print run of 25 serial numbered sets.

PRINT RUN 25 SER.#'d SETS
AUTO 1 NOT PRICE DUE TO SCARCITY
UNPRICED AU RELIC PRINT RUN 5 SETS
BO A.Bogut/S.O'Neal 75.00 150.00
WI D.Wade/A.Iverson 125.00 250.00
WW D.Williams/D.Wade 75.00 150.00

2005-06 Topps Luxury Box One Man Show Autographs

Randomly inserted into packs, these 21 cards feature sticker autographs from the players. For those players Topps released print runs for we have placed that information next to their name in our checklist.

PRINT RUNS LISTED IN CHECKLIST
*PARALLEL 25: .6X TO 1.5X BASE HI
PARALLEL PRINT RUN 25 SETS
UNPRICED AUTO RELIC PRINT RUN 10 SETS
AI Allen Iverson/124 40.00 100.00
AJ Amir Johnson/449 4.00 10.00
AW Antoine Wright/426 4.00 10.00
BB Brandon Bass/724 5.00 12.00
DL David Lee/559 6.00 15.00
DW Dwyane Wade/124 20.00 50.00
FG Francisco Garcia/1121 4.00 10.00
FO Fabricio Oberto/724 4.00 10.00
ID Ike Diogu/67 5.00 12.00
JG Joey Graham/724 4.00 10.00
MW Martell Webster/124 4.00 10.00
RW Robert Whaley/167 4.00 10.00
SO Shaquille O'Neal/74 30.00 75.00
VC Vince Carter/124 15.00 40.00
DWI Deron Williams/124 10.00 25.00

2005-06 Topps Luxury Box One Man Show Relics

Randomly inserted into packs, this is an insert to the Luxury Box product. Each of these cards were issued to a stated print run of 225 serial numbered sets.

PRINT RUN 225 SER.#'d SETS
*RELIC 25: .75X TO 2X BASE HI
*RELIC 25 PRINT RUN 25 SETS
RELIC 1 NOT PRICED DUE TO SCARICTY
AI Allen Iverson 4.00 10.00
AK Andrei Kirilenko 2.00 5.00
AS Amare Stoudemire 2.00 5.00
AW Antoine Walker 2.00 5.00
BG Ben Gordon 2.00 5.00
CA Carmelo Anthony 5.00 12.00
CM Corey Maggette 2.00 5.00
CP Chris Paul 8.00 20.00
DM Desmond Mason 2.00 5.00
DN Dirk Nowitzki 4.00 10.00
DW Dwyane Wade 4.00 10.00
GA Gilbert Arenas 2.00 5.00
GG Gerald Green 2.50 6.00
HW Hakim Warrick 2.00 5.00
ID Ike Diogu 1.50 4.00
JC Josh Childress 2.00 5.00
JJ Joe Johnson 2.00 5.00
JS Jerry Stackhouse 2.00 5.00
JT Jamaal Tinsley 2.00 5.00
JZ Jay-Z 4.00 10.00
KB Kobe Bryant 8.00 20.00
KG Kevin Garnett 4.00 10.00
LJ Luke Jackson 2.00 5.00
LR Luke Ridnour 2.00 5.00
MG Manu Ginobili 2.50 6.00
MP Morris Peterson 1.50 4.00
MR Michael Redd 2.00 5.00
MW Martell Webster 2.00 5.00
PP Paul Pierce 2.50 6.00
PS Peja Stojakovic 2.50 6.00
RA Ray Allen 2.50 6.00
RF Raymond Felton 2.50 6.00
RH Robert Horry 3.00 8.00
RJ Richard Jefferson 2.00 5.00
RW Rasheed Wallace 2.50 6.00
SF Steve Francis 2.00 5.00
SL Shaun Livingston 2.00 5.00
SM Stephon Marbury 2.00 5.00
ST Sebastian Telfair 2.00 5.00
TM Tracy McGrady 3.00 8.00
TP Tony Parker 2.50 6.00
VC Vince Carter 4.00 10.00
AIG Andre Iguodala 2.00 5.00
DWI Deron Williams 3.00 8.00
JSM Josh Smith 2.00 5.00
JTE Jason Terry 2.00 5.00
SAR Shareef Abdur-Rahim 2.00 5.00
SMA Shawn Marion 2.00 5.00
J.R. Jason Richardson 2.50 6.00
J.R.S J.R. Smith 2.00 5.00

2005-06 Topps Luxury Box One on One Dual Relics

Randomly inserted into packs, these 30-cards feature two game-used relics of the featured players. Each of these cards were issued to a stated print run of 225 serial numbered sets.

PRINT RUN 225 SER.#'d SET
*RELIC 25: .5X TO 1.25X BASE HI
RELIC 1 NOT PRICED DUE TO SCARCITY
AP C.Anthony/P.Pierce 5.00 12.00
AW R.Allen/B.Wells 4.00 10.00
BB K.Bryant/B.Bowen 8.00 20.00
BC E.Boykins/S.Cassell 4.00 10.00
BS K.Brown/S.Swift 4.00 10.00
CG M.Camby/P.Gasol 4.00 10.00
DG L.Deng/F.Garcia 4.00 10.00
DM T.Duncan/Y.Ming 5.00 12.00
FK C.Frye/N.Krstic 4.00 10.00
GB B.Gordon/C.Billups 5.00 12.00
HF J.Hodge/R.Felton 4.00 10.00
HM R.Hamilton/R.McCants 4.00 10.00
IF A.Iverson/S.Francis 6.00 15.00
JB A.Jamison/E.Brand 4.00 10.00
JP R.Jefferson/T.Prince 4.00 10.00
LW R.Lewis/R.Wallace 4.00 10.00
MG T.McGrady/M.Ginobili 5.00 12.00
MV J.Magloire/A.Varejao 4.00 10.00
NW A.Nocioni/A.Wright 4.00 10.00
OH E.Okafor/D.Howard 4.00 10.00
PC P.Pierce/V.Carter 5.00 12.00
PW C.Paul/D.Williams 6.00 15.00
RB Q.Richardson/C.Butler 4.00 10.00
SG A.Stoudemire/K.Garnett 6.00 15.00
TD J.Terry/B.Davis 4.00 10.00
TW K.Thomas/H.Warrick 4.00 10.00
WI D.Wade/A.Iguodala 5.00 12.00
WO B.Wallace/S.O'Neal 6.00 15.00
WT J.Williams/J.Tinsley 4.00 10.00
WW A.Walker/C.Webber 4.00 10.00

2005-06 Topps Luxury Box Stat Sheet 7 Relics

Randomly inserted into packs, these 20-cards feature seven game-used relics of the featured players. Each of these cards were issued to a stated print run of 140 serial numbered sets.

PRINT RUN 140 SER.#'d SETS
*RELIC 25: .5X TO 1.25X BASE REL.HI
RELIC 1 NOT PRICED DUE TO SCARCITY
1 Al/KG/Nash/Kirk+3 12.50 30.00
2 Kobe/Al/T-Mac/Wade+3 20.00 50.00
3 Dirk/Duncan/Al/Amare+3 12.50 30.00
4 Amare/Kobe/Al+4 15.00 40.00
5 T-Mac/Al/Steph+4 12.50 30.00
6 Shaq/T-Mac/Pierce+4 12.50 30.00
7 Vince/Shaq/Kobe+4 20.00 50.00
8 Wade/Brand/Pierce+4 12.50 30.00
9 Dirk/Wade/Yao/Manu+3 15.00 40.00
10 Hinrich/Wade/Dirk+4 15.00 40.00
11 Shaq/Brand/Melo+4 12.50 30.00
12 Al/Kobe/T-Mac/Vince+3 20.00 50.00
13 KG/Marion/Shaq+4 15.00 40.00
14 Nash/Kidd/Steph/Al+3 15.00 40.00
15 AK47/Duncan/Shaq+4 15.00 40.00
16 Al/Marion/T-Mac+4 12.50 30.00
17 Al/T-Mac/Kobe/Steph+3 15.00 40.00
18 Al/Wade/Pierce/Kobe+3 20.00 50.00
19 2005 NBA Draft Class 20.00 50.00
20 2005 NBA Draft Class 20.00 50.00

2005-06 Topps Luxury Box The Machine Autographs

Randomly inserted into packs, these cards feature sticker autographs of the featured players. Since the print run is different for each player, we have put that information next to the player's name in our checklist. Carmelo Anthony did not sign his stickers in time for release and those cards were issued as exchanges.

PRINT RUNS LISTED IN CHECKLIST
PARALLEL 25: .6X TO 1.5X BASE HI
PARALLEL PRINT RUN 25 SETS
AB Andrew Bogut/224 8.00 20.00
AI Allen Iverson/224 50.00 120.00
AN Andres Nocioni/349 5.00 12.00
BW Bracey Wright/167 5.00 12.00
CA Carmelo Anthony/74 15.00 40.00
CV Charlie Villanueva/441 6.00 15.00
DW Dwyane Wade/224 30.00 60.00
EO Emeka Okafor/224 6.00 15.00
HW Hakim Warrick/1192 5.00 12.00
JH Julius Hodge/474 5.00 12.00
JM Jason Maxiell/474 5.00 12.00
JP Johan Petro/124 5.00 12.00
NK Nenad Krstic/388 5.00 12.00
SJ Sarunas Jasikevicius/224 5.00 12.00
SM Sean May/474 5.00 12.00
SO Shaquille O'Neal/74 35.00 75.00
VC Vince Carter/124 15.00 40.00
ABY Andrew Bynum/116 20.00 50.00

2005-06 Topps Luxury Box The Machine Relics

Randomly inserted into packs, these 50-cards feature game-used relics of the players. Each of these cards were issued to a stated print run of 225 serial numbered sets.

PRINT RUN 225 SER.#'d SETS
*RELIC 25: .75X TO 2X BASE REL.HI
RELIC 25 PRINT RUN 25 SETS
RELIC 1 NOT PRICED DUE TO SCARCITY
AB Andrew Bogut 3.00 8.00
AH Al Harrington 2.00 5.00
AJ Al Jefferson 2.00 5.00
AN Andres Nocioni 2.00 5.00
AV Anderson Varejao 1.50 4.00
AW Antoine Wright 2.00 5.00
BB Brandon Bass 2.00 5.00
BD Baron Davis 2.00 5.00
BW Ben Wallace 2.00 5.00
CB Carlos Boozer 2.00 5.00
CF Channing Frye 2.50 6.00
CV Charlie Villanueva 2.50 6.00
CW Chris Webber 2.50 6.00
DG Drew Gooden 2.00 5.00
DH Dwight Howard 2.00 5.00
EB Elton Brand 2.50 6.00
EO Emeka Okafor 2.00 5.00
JF Jeff Foster 2.00 5.00
JH Josh Howard 2.50 6.00
JJ Jarrett Jack 2.50 6.00
JK Jason Kidd 4.00 10.00
JM Jamaal Magloire 2.00 5.00
JO Jermaine O'Neal 2.00 5.00
KH Kirk Hinrich 2.00 5.00
KM Kenyon Martin 2.00 5.00
KT Kurt Thomas 2.00 5.00
LO Lamar Odom 2.00 5.00
MB Mike Bibby 2.50 6.00
MC Marcus Camby 2.00 5.00
NR Nate Robinson 2.50 6.00
PG Pau Gasol 2.50 6.00
RH Richard Hamilton 2.00 5.00
RL Rashard Lewis 2.50 6.00
RM Rashad McCants 2.00 5.00
SD Samuel Dalembert 2.00 5.00
SM Sean May 1.50 4.00
SN Steve Nash 3.00 8.00
SO Shaquille O'Neal 5.00 12.00
TD Tim Duncan 4.00 10.00
TR Theo Ratliff 2.00 5.00
YM Yao Ming 3.00 8.00
ABY Andrew Bynum 2.00 5.00
AJA Antawn Jamison 2.00 5.00
BBA Brent Barry 2.00 5.00
BBO Bruce Bowen 2.00 5.00
CBI Chauncey Billups 2.50 6.00
CBO Chris Bosh 2.50 6.00
CBU Caron Butler 2.00 5.00
CDU Chris Duhon 2.00 5.00
KVH Keith Van Horn 2.00 5.00

2005-06 Topps Luxury Box Trinity Triple Relics

Randomly inserted into packs, these 50-cards feature three players and a relic piece from each player. This set was issued to a stated print run of 250 serial numbered sets.

PRINT RUN 250 SER.#'d SETS
*RELIC 25: .5X TO 1.25X BASE HI
RELIC 25 PRINT RUN 25 SETS
RELIC 1 NOT PRICED DUE TO SCARCITY
ABS Abdur-Rahim/Bibby/Stojakovic 5.00 12.00
BAM Boykins/Anthony/Martin 6.00 15.00
BBO Bynum/Bryant/Odom 10.00 30.00
BMI Bryant/McGrady/Iverson 10.00 25.00
BML Brand/Maggette/Livingston 5.00 12.00
BMR Bogut/Mason/Redd 5.00 12.00
CKJ Carter/Kidd/Jefferson 8.00 20.00
DDD Wade/Wade/Wade 15.00 40.00
DKI Dalembert/Korver/Iverson 6.00 15.00
DOI Duncan/O'Neal/Iverson 10.00 25.00
DRT Davis/Richardson/Taft 6.00 15.00
FMM Felton/May/McCants 5.00 12.00
FMR Frye/Marbury/Richardson 5.00 12.00
GJM Garnett/Jaric/McCants 5.00 12.00
GJP Green/Jefferson/Pierce 5.00 12.00
HBB Horry/Bowen/Barry 5.00 12.00
HFH Hill/Francis/Howard 6.00 15.00
HGN Hinrich/Gordon/Nocioni 8.00 20.00
HIG Hughes/Ilgauskas/Gooden 5.00 12.00
JBA Jamison/Butler/Arenas 5.00 12.00
KPI Kidd/Pierce/Iverson 8.00 20.00
MAI Marbury/Arenas/Iverson 6.00 15.00
MFO May/Felton/Okafor 5.00 12.00
MMS McGrady/Ming/Swift 6.00 15.00
NSM Nash/Stoudemire/Marion 8.00 20.00
OBM O'Neal/Bogut/Ming 6.00 15.00
OGA O'Neal/Granger/Artest 5.00 12.00
PBS Paul/Bass/Smith 6.00 15.00
PGD Parker/Ginobili/Duncan 10.00 25.00
RAL Ridnour/Allen/Lewis 5.00 12.00
RWT Ratliff/Webster/Telfair 5.00 12.00
SCJ Smith/Childress/Johnson 5.00 12.00
TND Terry/Nowitzki/Daniels 8.00 20.00
VGB Villanueva/Graham/Bosh 6.00 15.00
WAB Wade/Anthony/Bosh 10.00 25.00
WGA Wade/Gordon/Allen 6.00 15.00
WGJ Warrick/Gasol/Jones 5.00 12.00
WHD Wade/Hamilton/Davis 8.00 20.00
WHO Wade/O'Neal/Haslem 12.50 30.00
WHT Wade/Hinrich/Terry 8.00 20.00
WII Webber/Iguodala/Iverson 6.00 15.00
WKO Williams/Kirilenko/Okur 5.00 12.00
WMB Wade/McGrady/Bryant 12.50 30.00
WMK Wade/Marbury/Kidd 10.00 25.00
WPF Williams/Paul/Felton 8.00 20.00
WWF Wade/Wade/Felton 8.00 20.00
WWH Wallace/Wallace/Hamilton 10.00 25.00
WWP Williams/Walker/Posey 8.00 20.00
WWW Wade/Walker/Williams 12.50 30.00
WZI Wade/Jay-Z/Felton 10.00 25.00

2005-06 Topps Luxury Box Triple Double 5 Relics

Randomly inserted into packs, these 30-cards feature five game-used pieces from members of the same team. Each of these cards were issued to a stated print run of 193 serial numbered sets.

PRINT RUN 193 SER.#'d SETS
*RELIC 25: .5X TO 1.25X BASE HI
RELIC 25 PRINT RUN 25 SETS
RELIC 1 NOT PRICED DUE TO SCARCITY
1 Toronto Raptors 6.00 15.00
2 Utah Jazz 6.00 15.00
3 Phoenix Suns 12.00 30.00
4 Atlanta Hawks 6.00 15.00
5 Chicago Bulls 10.00 25.00
6 Cleveland Cavaliers 6.00 15.00
7 Dallas Mavericks 10.00 25.00
8 Denver Nuggets 6.00 15.00
9 Detroit Pistons 15.00 40.00
10 Golden State Warriors 6.00 15.00
11 Indiana Pacers 6.00 15.00
12 Los Angeles Clippers 6.00 15.00
13 Miami Heat 15.00 40.00
14 Milwaukee Bucks 6.00 15.00
15 New Jersey Nets 10.00 25.00
16 New York Knicks 6.00 15.00
17 Portland Trailblazers 6.00 15.00
18 Sacramento Kings 6.00 15.00
19 San Antonio Spurs 10.00 25.00
20 Seattle Supersonics 6.00 15.00
21 Washington Wizards 6.00 15.00
22 Boston Celtics 8.00 20.00
23 Charlotte Bobcats 6.00 15.00
24 Houston Rockets 10.00 25.00
25 Los Angeles Lakers 20.00 50.00
26 Memphis Grizzlies 6.00 15.00
27 Minnesota Timberwolves 8.00 20.00
28 New Orleans Hornets 10.00 25.00
29 Orlando Magic 8.00 20.00
30 Philadelphia 76ers 10.00 25.00

2005-06 Topps Luxury Box Two's Company Dual Relics

Randomly inserted into packs, these cards featuring two players and relics from each one were issued to a stated print run of 193 serial numbered sets.

PRINT RUN 193 SER.#'d SETS
*RELIC 25: .5X TO 1.25X BASE HI
RELIC 25 PRINT RUN 25 SETS
RELIC 1 NOT PRICED DUE TO SCARCITY
KW A.Kirilenko/D.Williams 5.00 12.00
AJ G.Arenas/A.Jamison 5.00 12.00
AW A.Iverson/C.Webber 10.00 25.00
BB K.Bryant/A.Bynum 8.00 25.00
BR A.Bogut/M.Redd 6.00 15.00
BV C.Bosh/C.Villanueva 5.00 12.00
CM S.Cassell/C.Mobley 5.00 12.00
DG T.Duncan/M.Ginobili 6.00 15.00
DR B.Davis/J.Richardson 5.00 12.00
HG K.Hinrich/B.Gordon 5.00 12.00
FM R.Felton/S.May 6.00 15.00
AM C.Anthony/K.Martin 5.00 12.00
GH D.Gooden/L.Hughes 5.00 12.00
GJ D.Granger/S.Jasikevicius 5.00 12.00
GM K.Garnett/R.McCants 6.00 15.00
GW P.Gasol/H.Warrick 5.00 12.00
HF D.Howard/S.Francis 6.00 15.00
JJ J.Smith/J.Johnson 5.00 12.00
KC J.Kidd/V.Carter 6.00 15.00
LP R.Lewis/J.Petro 5.00 12.00
MF S.Marbury/C.Frye 5.00 12.00
MM T.McGrady/Y.Ming 8.00 20.00
ND D.Nowitzki/M.Daniels 6.00 15.00
NS S.Nash/A.Stoudemire 6.00 15.00
PG P.Pierce/G.Green 5.00 12.00
PS C.Paul/J.R.Smith 6.00 15.00
SA P.Stojakovic/S.Abdur-Rahim 5.00 12.00
TW S.Telfair/M.Webster 5.00 12.00
WO D.Wade/S.O'Neal 12.50 30.00
WW B.Wallace/R.Wallace 8.00 20.00

2006-07 Topps Luxury Box

Released in mid May 2007, Topps Luxury Box boasts a 100-card set where veteran players are pictured on card numbers 1-40, retired NBA legends are pictured on card numbers 41-50 and rookies sequentially numbered to 999 are pictured on card numbers 51-100. The base card design places full color player photos on a design-heavy white and blue background showcasing a water-mark portrait of the featured player. Luxury Box is packaged in eight pack boxes of six cards each and originally carried a suggested retail price of $15.00 per pack.

COMP.SET w/o SP's (50) 20.00 50.00
51-100 RC PRINT RUN 999 SER.#'d SETS
UNPRICED GOLD PRINT RUN ONE SET
UNPRICED SILVER PRINT RUN 9 SETS
1 Chris Bosh .50 1.25
2 Dirk Nowitzki .75 2.00
3 Ben Wallace .40 1.00
4 Mike Bibby .50 1.25
5 Josh Howard .40 1.00
6 Vince Carter .60 1.50
7 Andrei Kirilenko .40 1.00
8 Richard Hamilton .40 1.00
9 Tony Parker .50 1.25
10 Dwyane Wade .75 2.00
11 Amare Stoudemire .40 1.00
12 Tim Duncan .75 2.00
13 Steve Nash .60 1.50
14 Dwight Howard .40 1.00
15 Carmelo Anthony .60 1.50
16 Pau Gasol .50 1.25
17 Zach Randolph .40 1.00
18 Kirk Hinrich .40 1.00
19 Stephon Marbury .40 1.00
20 Tracy McGrady .60 1.50
21 Kevin Garnett .75 2.00
22 Michael Redd .40 1.00
23 LeBron James 2.00 5.00
24 Kobe Bryant 2.00 5.00
25 Jason Kidd .75 2.00
26 Baron Davis .40 1.00
27 Jermaine O'Neal .40 1.00
28 Ray Allen .50 1.25
29 Joe Johnson .40 1.00
30 Elton Brand .50 1.25
31 Chris Paul .60 1.50
32 Shaquille O'Neal 1.00 2.50
33 Allen Iverson .60 1.50
34 Paul Pierce .50 1.25
35 Chauncey Billups .50 1.25
36 Gerald Wallace .40 1.00
37 Jason Richardson .50 1.25
38 Yao Ming .60 1.50
39 Andre Iguodala .40 1.00
40 Gilbert Arenas .40 1.00
41 Larry Bird 2.00 5.00
42 Isiah Thomas .75 2.00
43 Dominique Wilkins 1.00 2.50
44 Moses Malone .75 2.00
45 George Gervin .75 2.00
46 Chris Mullin .75 2.00
47 Karl Malone 1.00 2.50
48 Bob McAdoo .60 1.50
49 James Worthy .75 2.00
50 Walt Frazier .75 2.00
51 J.J. Redick RC 1.50 4.00
52 Tyrus Thomas RC 1.00 2.50
53 Rodney Carney RC .75 2.00
54 Jorge Garbajosa RC 1.00 2.50
55 Shawne Williams RC .75 2.00
56 Renaldo Balkman RC 1.00 2.50
57 Chris Quinn RC .75 2.00
58 Solomon Jones RC .75 2.00
59 Maurice Ager RC .75 2.00
60 Rudy Gay RC 1.50 4.00
61 Hassan Adams RC .75 2.00
62 Sergio Rodriguez RC 1.25 3.00
63 Dee Brown RC .75 2.00
64 Saer Sene RC .75 2.00
65 Allan Ray RC .75 2.00
66 Damir Markota RC .75 2.00
67 Bobby Jones RC .75 2.00
68 Kyle Lowry RC 1.50 4.00
69 Cedric Simmons RC .75 2.00
70 LaMarcus Aldridge RC 3.00 8.00
71 Mardy Collins RC .75 2.00
72 Daniel Gibson RC 1.00 2.50
73 Patrick O'Bryant RC .75 2.00
74 Josh Boone RC .75 2.00
75 Paul Davis RC .75 2.00
76 Craig Smith RC 1.00 2.50
77 Andrea Bargnani RC 1.25 3.00
78 Alexander Johnson RC .75 2.00
79 James Augustine RC .75 2.00
80 Jordan Farmar RC 1.25 3.00
81 Marcus Vinicius RC .75 2.00
82 Ryan Hollins RC 1.00 2.50
83 Marcus Williams RC .75 2.00
84 Will Blalock RC .75 2.00
85 Shannon Brown RC .75 2.00
86 Pops Mensah-Bonsu RC .75 2.00
87 P.J. Tucker RC 1.00 2.50
88 Steve Novak RC 1.00 2.50
89 Quincy Douby RC .75 2.00
90 Rajon Rondo RC 2.00 5.00
91 David Noel RC .75 2.00
92 Mile Ilic RC .75 2.00
93 Ronnie Brewer RC 1.25 3.00
94 James White RC .75 2.00
95 Hilton Armstrong RC .75 2.00
96 Randy Foye RC 1.25 3.00
97 Shelden Williams RC 1.00 2.50
98 Thabo Sefolosha RC 1.25 3.00
99 Brandon Roy RC 1.25 3.00
100 Adam Morrison RC 1.25 3.00

2006-07 Topps Luxury Box Blue

*BLUE: 2X TO 5X BASE HI
PRINT RUN 49 SER.#'d SETS

2006-07 Topps Luxury Box Green

*GREEN: .75X TO 2X BASE HI
PRINT RUN 329 SER.#'d SETS

2006-07 Topps Luxury Box Red

*RED: .6X TO 1.5X BASE HI
STATED PRINT RUN 499 SER.#'d SETS

2006-07 Topps Luxury Box Courtside Relics Dual

PRINT RUN 299 SER.#'d SETS
*BLUE: .5X TO 1.25X BASE HI
BLUE PRINT RUN 49 SER.#'d SETS
*BRONZE: .75X TO 2X BASE HI
BRONZE PRINT RUN 19 SER.#'d SETS
UNPRICED SILVER PRINT RUN 9 SETS
UNPRICED GOLD PRINT RUN ONE SET
AM A.Miller/R.Carney 3.00 8.00
BB A.Bargnani/C.Bosh 5.00 12.00
BJ C.Butler/A.Jamison 3.00 8.00
BO K.Bryant/L.Odom 5.00 12.00
BO A.Biedrins/P.O'Bryant 4.00 10.00
BP C.Billups/T.Prince 4.00 10.00
DP T.Duncan/T.Parker 5.00 12.00
DS L.Deng/T.Sefolosha 5.00 12.00
GB D.Gooden/S.Brown 3.00 8.00
GJ K.Garnett/M.James 3.00 8.00
GM P.Gasol/M.Miller 3.00 8.00

HH D.Harris/J.Howard 3.00 8.00
HM D.Howard/D.Milicic 3.00 8.00
IA A.Iverson/C.Anthony 5.00 12.00
II A.Iguodala/A.Iverson 4.00 10.00
JK R.Jefferson/N.Krstic 3.00 8.00
KC J.Kidd/V.Carter 5.00 12.00
LA R.Lewis/R.Allen 3.00 8.00
LB S.Livingston/E.Brand 3.00 8.00
MAR B.Miller/R.Artest 3.00 8.00
MC C.Maggette/S.Cassell 4.00 10.00
MF S.Marbury/S.Francis 3.00 8.00
MO D.Miles/T.Outlaw 3.00 8.00
MY T.McGrady/Y.Ming 5.00 12.00
NT D.Nowitzki/J.Terry 4.00 10.00
OF E.Okafor/R.Felton 3.00 8.00
OG J.O'Neal/D.Granger 3.00 8.00
PF M.Peterson/T.Ford 3.00 8.00
PS C.Paul/P.Stojakovic 4.00 10.00
PT P.Pierce/S.Telfair 3.00 8.00
RD J.Richardson/B.Davis 3.00 8.00
SJ J.Smith/J.Johnson 3.00 8.00
SM A.Stoudemire/S.Marion 4.00 10.00
VR C.Villanueva/M.Redd 3.00 8.00
WB L.Walton/A.Bynum 4.00 10.00
WG B.Wallace/B.Gordon 3.00 8.00
WH R.Wallace/R.Hamilton 4.00 10.00
WK D.Williams/A.Kirilenko 3.00 8.00
WM G.Wallace/A.Morrison 5.00 12.00
WO D.Wade/S.O'Neal 6.00 15.00

2006-07 Topps Luxury Box Courtside Relics Triple

PRINT RUN 249 SER.#'d SETS
*BLUE: .5X TO 1.25X BASE HI
BLUE PRINT RUN 49 SER.#'d SETS
*BRONZE: 1.25X TO 3X BASE HI
BRONZE PRINT RUN 19 SER.#'d SETS
UNPRICED SILVER PRINT RUN 9 SETS
UNPRICED GOLD PRINT RUN ONE SET
ABJ Arenas/Butler/Jamison 5.00 12.00
ACS Allen/Collison/Sene 4.00 10.00
AMB Artest/Martin/Bibby 5.00 12.00
ANI Anthony/Nene/Iverson 8.00 20.00
BDW Billups/Duncan/Wade 6.00 15.00
BGB Bosh/Garbajosa/Bargnani 6.00 15.00
BMM Brand/Maggette/Mobley 4.00 10.00
BOF Bryant/Odom/Farmar 8.00 20.00
BRV Bogut/Redd/Villanueva 4.00 10.00
CKJ Carter/Kidd/Jefferson 8.00 20.00
CWS Childress/Williams/Smith 5.00 12.00
DGN Duncan/Garnett/Nash 8.00 20.00
FOM Felton/Okafor/Morrison 6.00 15.00
GDP Ginobili/Duncan/Parker 8.00 20.00
GDW Gordon/Duhon/Wallace 4.00 10.00
GJF Garnett/Jaric/Foye 4.00 10.00
HHR Hill/Howard/Redick 8.00 20.00
IDM Iguodala/Dalembert/Miller 4.00 10.00
IVH Ilgauskas/Varejao/Hughes 5.00 12.00
JGM Jamison/Gordon/Miller 4.00 10.00
KOB Kirilenko/Okur/Brewer 4.00 10.00
MAW Mutombo/Artest/Wallace 5.00 12.00
MBH McDyess/Billups/Hamilton 6.00 15.00
MFR Marbury/Frye/Robinson 4.00 10.00
MIB McGrady/Iverson/Bryant 10.00 25.00
MJA Miles/Jack/Aldridge 4.00 10.00
MOW Mourning/O'Neal/Wade 10.00 25.00
MSD Marion/Stoudemire/Diaw 5.00 12.00
NHS Nowitzki/Howard/Stackhouse 5.00 12.00
OJT O'Neal/Granger/Tinsley 4.00 10.00
ORB O'Bryant/Richardson/Biedrins 5.00 12.00
PMA Paul/Mason/Armstrong 4.00 10.00
WGS Warrick/Gasol/Stoudamire 4.00 10.00
WJP West/Jefferson/Pierce 4.00 10.00
YMH Ming/McGrady/Head 6.00 15.00

2006-07 Topps Luxury Box Courtside Relics Autographs Dual

PRINT RUN 79 SER.#'d SETS
UNPRICED SILVER PRINT RUN 9 SETS
UNPRICED GOLD PRINT RUN ONE SET
AG C.Anthony/B.Gordon 25.00 50.00
AR R.Allen/J.Redick 15.00 30.00
BC C.Bosh/V.Carter 30.00 60.00
BG A.Bargnani/J.Garbajosa 30.00 60.00
BJ L.Bird/M.Johnson 200.00 300.00
DW B.Diaw/H.Warrick 10.00 25.00
FB T.Ford/C.Billups 10.00 25.00
FD J.Farmar/Q.Douby 10.00 25.00
HB D.Harris/L.Barbosa 10.00 25.00
JL M.James/K.Lowry 10.00 25.00
KW A.Kirilenko/G.Wallace 10.00 25.00
MR A.Morrison/J.Redick 10.00 25.00
OI J.O'Neal/A.Iguodala 10.00 25.00
OM E.Okafor/A.Morrison 10.00 25.00
SD T.Sefolosha/C.Duhon 10.00 25.00
SW D.Wilkins/J.Smith 15.00 40.00
VB C.Villanueva/A.Bogut 10.00 25.00
WB D.Wade/C.Billups 40.00 80.00
WF L.Walton/C.Frye 12.50 30.00
WW D.Williams/M.Williams 15.00 40.00

2006-07 Topps Luxury Box Courtside Relics Autographs Triple

PRINT RUN 29 SER.#'d SETS
UNPRICED SILVER PRINT RUN 9 SETS
UNPRICED GOLD PRINT RUN ONE SET
ABW Anthony/Bosh/Wade 100.00 225.00
BJW Billups/Johnson/Wade 50.00 120.00
IFW Iguodala/Frye/Walton 30.00 60.00
WOC Wade/O'Neal/Carter 75.00 150.00

2006-07 Topps Luxury Box Mezzanine Relics

PRINT RUN 349 SER.#'d SETS
*BLUE: .6X TO 1.5X BASE HI
BLUE PRINT RUN 49 SER.#'d SETS
*BRONZE: .75X TO 2X BASE HI
BRONZE PRINT RUN 19 SER.#'d SETS
UNPRICED SILVER PRINT RUN 9 SETS
UNPRICED GOLD PRINT RUN ONE SET
AB Andrew Bogut 2.00 5.00
ABY Andrew Bynum 1.50 4.00
AJ Antawn Jamison 2.00 5.00
AK Andrei Kirilenko 2.00 5.00
AS Amare Stoudemire 2.00 5.00
BR Brandon Roy 2.50 6.00
BW Ben Wallace 2.00 5.00
CD Chris Duhon 2.00 5.00
CF Channing Frye 2.00 5.00
CP Chris Paul 3.00 8.00
CV Charlie Villanueva 1.50 4.00
CW Chris Webber 2.50 6.00
DH Devin Harris 1.50 4.00
DHO Dwight Howard 2.00 5.00
DM Darko Milicic 2.00 5.00
DN Dirk Nowitzki 4.00 10.00
DW Deron Williams 2.00 5.00
EB Elton Brand 2.50 6.00
EO Emeka Okafor 2.00 5.00
GA Gilbert Arenas 2.00 5.00
GH Grant Hill 4.00 10.00
JF Jordan Farmar 2.50 6.00
JG Jorge Garbajosa 2.00 5.00
JK Jason Kidd 4.00 10.00
JO Jermaine O'Neal 2.00 5.00
JR Jason Richardson 2.50 6.00
JS Josh Smith 2.00 5.00
JT Jason Terry 2.00 5.00
KB Kobe Bryant 8.00 20.00
KG Kevin Garnett 4.00 10.00
KL Kyle Lowry 3.00 8.00
LA LaMarcus Aldridge 6.00 15.00
LH Larry Hughes 2.00 5.00
LO Lamar Odom 2.00 5.00
LW Luke Walton 1.50 4.00
MA Maurice Ager 1.50 4.00
MB Mike Bibby 2.50 6.00
MG Manu Ginobili 2.50 6.00
MJ Mike James 2.00 5.00
MP Morris Peterson 1.50 4.00
MR Michael Redd 2.00 5.00
MW Marcus Williams 1.50 4.00
MWE Martell Webster 2.00 5.00
MWI Marvin Williams 2.00 5.00
PG Pau Gasol 2.50 6.00
PP Paul Pierce 2.50 6.00
PS Peja Stojakovic 2.50 6.00
RA Ron Artest 2.50 6.00
RC Rodney Carney 1.50 4.00
RG Rudy Gay 3.00 8.00
RH Richard Hamilton 2.00 5.00
RJ Richard Jefferson 2.00 5.00
RL Rashard Lewis 2.50 6.00
SM Shawn Marion 2.00 5.00
SMA Stephon Marbury 2.00 5.00
TD Tim Duncan 4.00 10.00
TJF T.J. Ford 1.50 4.00
TM Tracy McGrady 3.00 8.00
TS Thabo Sefolosha 2.50 6.00
YM Yao Ming 3.00 8.00

2006-07 Topps Luxury Box Mezzanine Relics Autographs

STATED PRINT RUN 139 SER.#'d SETS
UNPRICED SILVER PRINT RUN 9 SETS
UNPRICED GOLD PRINT RUN ONE SET
AB Andrew Bogut 6.00 15.00
ABA Andrea Bargnani 10.00 25.00
ABY Andrew Bynum 6.00 15.00
AH Al Harrington 4.00 10.00
AIG Andre Iguodala 6.00 15.00
AK Andrei Kirilenko 4.00 10.00
AM Adam Morrison 4.00 10.00
BD Boris Diaw 4.00 10.00
BG Ben Gordon 6.00 15.00
CA Carmelo Anthony 15.00 40.00
CB Chauncey Billups 6.00 15.00
CD Chris Duhon 4.00 10.00
CF Channing Frye 4.00 10.00
CV Charlie Villanueva 4.00 10.00
DW Dwyane Wade 20.00 50.00
DWI Deron Williams 6.00 15.00
EO Emeka Okafor 4.00 10.00
GW Gerald Wallace 4.00 10.00
HT Hedo Turkoglu 5.00 12.00
HW Hakim Warrick 5.00 12.00
JF Jordan Farmar 4.00 10.00
JG Jorge Garbajosa 3.00 8.00
JH Josh Howard 4.00 10.00
JJ Jarrett Jack 4.00 10.00
JJR J.J. Redick 8.00 20.00
JS Josh Smith 8.00 20.00
KL Kyle Lowry 5.00 12.00
LB Leandro Barbosa 4.00 10.00
LW Luke Walton 4.00 10.00
MA Maurice Ager 2.50 6.00
MW Marcus Williams 2.50 6.00
MWE Martell Webster 4.00 10.00
RA Ray Allen 12.50 30.00
RC Rodney Carney 2.50 6.00
UH Udonis Haslem 5.00 12.00
VC Vince Carter 12.00 30.00

2006-07 Topps Luxury Box Relics Quad

PRINT RUN 199 SER.#'d SETS
*BLUE: .5X TO 1.25X BASE HI
BLUE PRINT RUN 49 SER.#'d SETS
*BRONZE: .6X TO 1.5X BASE HI
BRONZE PRINT RUN 19 SER.#'d SETS
UNPRICED SILVER PRINT RUN 9 SETS
UNPRICED GOLD PRINT RUN ONE SET
1 Marion/Terry/Mourning/Billups 10.00 25.00
2 Amare/Brand/Duncan/Dirk 10.00 25.00
3 Wade/Carter/Hughes/Hamilton 10.00 25.00
4 Ginobili/Bibby/Nash/Bryant 15.00 30.00
5 Anthony/Maggette/Harris/Gasol 8.00 20.00
6 Wallace/Redd/O'Neal/Gordon 15.00 30.00
7 Kidd/O'Neal/Gooden/Jamison 8.00 20.00
8 O'Neal/Wade/Nowitzki/Terry 30.00 70.00
9 Bosh/Marbury/Okafor/Webster 8.00 20.00
10 Smith/Garnett/Pierce/Ming 8.00 20.00
11 Richardson/Allen/Hill/Paul 8.00 20.00
12 Stoudemire/Harris/Williams/Wallace 8.00 20.00
13 Marion/Livingston/Bowen/Howard 8.00 20.00
14 Walker/Jefferson/Varejao/McDyess 8.00 20.00
15 Parker/Artest/Nash/Odom 10.00 25.00
16 Miller/Cassell/Stackhouse/Miller 8.00 20.00
17 Billups/Bogut/O'Neal/Deng 15.00 30.00
18 Krstic/Granger/Gooden/Arenas 8.00 20.00
19 Bargnani/Francis/Felton/Miles 6.00 15.00
20 Williams/James/Kirilenko/Iverson 8.00 20.00

2006-07 Topps Luxury Box Relics Five

PRINT RUN 179 SER.#'d SETS
*BLUE: .5X TO 1.25X BASE HI
BLUE PRINT RUN 49 SER.#'d SETS
*BRONZE: .6X TO 1.5X BASE HI
BRONZE PRINT RUN 19 SER.#'d SETS
UNPRICED SILVER PRINT RUN 9 SETS
UNPRICED GOLD PRINT RUN ONE SET
1 Telfair/Kidd/Iverson/Marbury/Ford 8.00 20.00
2 Billups/Hughes/Tinsley/Duhon/Redd 8.00 20.00
3 Redick/Arenas/Payton/Johnson/Felton 8.00 20.00
4 Parker/Harris/McGrady 8.00 20.00
Paul/Stoudamire
5 Williams/Boykins/James/Ridnour/Jack 8.00 20.00
6 Bryant/Nash/Cassell/Davis/Bibby 12.00 30.00
7 Jefferson/Jefferson 8.00 20.00
Webber/Frye/Peterson
8 Prince/Gooden/Granger 8.00 20.00
Deng/Villanueva
9 Hwrd/Jmisn/Wlkr/Willi/Mrrsn 10.00 25.00
10 Duncan/Dirk/Battier/Peja/Gay 8.00 20.00
11 Kirilenko/Nene/Garnett/Lewis/Miles 8.00 20.00
12 Odom/Marion/Brand/Dunleavy/Artest 8.00 20.00
13 Krstic/Dalembert 8.00 20.00
Ilgauskas/O'Neal/Wallace
14 Bogut/O'Neal/Okafor/Dampier/Ming 8.00 20.00
15 Okur/Sene/Aldridge/Bynum/Miller 8.00 20.00

2006-07 Topps Luxury Box Relics Six

PRINT RUN 149 SER.#'d SETS
*BLUE: .5X TO 1.25X BASE HI
BLUE PRINT RUN 49 SER.#'d SETS
*BRONZE: .6X TO 1.5X BASE HI
BRONZE PRINT RUN 19 SER.#'d SETS
UNPRICED SILVER PRINT RUN 9 SETS
UNPRICED GOLD PRINT RUN ONE SET
1 Felton/Wallace/Jamison 8.00 20.00
May/Noel/Stackhouse
2 Batt/Brnd/Deng/Hill/Magg/Rdck 10.00 25.00
3 Grdn/Rip/Allen/Villan/Okfr/Gay 8.00 20.00
4 Walton/Terry/Stoudamire 8.00 20.00
Bibby/Iguodala/Arenas
5 Stojakovic/Okur/Rodriguez 8.00 20.00
Diaw/Garbajosa/Ilgauskas
6 Dirk/Krst/Barg/Pau/AK47/Prkr 8.00 20.00
7 Baron/Roy/GP/Frmr/Nate/Walton 8.00 20.00
8 Wade/Wllms/Al/Dlmb/Melo/Doby 10.00 25.00
9 TD/Steph/Cssll/Cedric/Noel/J.J 10.00 25.00
10 Pierce/Aldridge/Battie 8.00 20.00
Billups/Tinsley/Wright
11 Rndo/Wlkr/Shq/McD/Udn/Balk 10.00 25.00
12 Deron/Wbb/Mgic/Redd/Hrrs/Rse 10.00 25.00
13 Telfair/McGrady/Smith 8.00 20.00
Brown/Livingston/Garnett
14 Kobe/Shaq/Amare/Mses/Hwrd/BigAl 12.50 30.00
15 Redick/Bogut/Nelson 8.00 20.00
Ford/Battier/Brand

2006-07 Topps Luxury Box Relics Seven

PRINT RUN 99 SER.#'d SETS
*BLUE: .5X TO 1.25X BASE HI
BLUE PRINT RUN 49 SER.#'d SETS
*BRONZE: .6X TO 1.5X BASE HI
BRONZE PRINT RUN 19 SER.#'d SETS
UNPRICED SILVER PRINT RUN 9 SETS
UNPRICED GOLD PRINT RUN ONE SET
1 CP/Vill/Bog/Will/Frye/Grngr/Felt 12.50 30.00
2 Kobe/Nash/Dirk/SO/Bllps/Wade/TD 12.00 30.00
3 Bnd/Wllce/Ivsn/Arns/Mrn/Athny/Yao 12.50 30.00
4 Bowen/Wallace/Kirilenko 10.00 25.00
Artest/Bryant/Kidd/Duncan
5 Nash/CP/Daw/Bylr/Wllce/Mllr/Wade 20.00 40.00
6 Kobe/Al/Arns/Wade/Prce/Dirk/CA 20.00 40.00
7 KG/Hwrd/Mrn/Wllce/Dncn/Mrp/Bnd 12.50 30.00
8 Nash/Dvs/Blps/Kid 12.50 30.00
Mill/CP/Ivsn
9 Hamilton/Barbosa/James 10.00 25.00
Nash/Gordon/Billups/Bowen
10 Cam/Kir/Mou/Smi/Bra/Dal/Prz 12.50 30.00

2006-07 Topps Luxury Box Relics Eight

PRINT RUN 79 SER.#'d SETS
*BLUE: .5X TO 1.25X BASE HI
BLUE PRINT RUN 49 SER.#'d SETS
*BRONZE: .6X TO 1.5X BASE HI
BRONZE PRINT RUN 19 SER.#'d SETS
UNPRICED SILVER PRINT RUN 9 SETS
UNPRICED GOLD PRINT RUN ONE SET
1 Bargnani/Aldridge 15.00 30.00
Morrison/Williams/Foye/Roy/Gay/Redick
2 Wade/Dirk/Wlkr/Jet 15.00 30.00
Shaq/JHo/JWill/Stack
3 Bargnani/Bogut/Howard 15.00 30.00
Ming/Brand/Duncan/Iverson/O'Neal
4 Kobe/KG/TMac/Hwrd/Amare/Shaq 20.00 50.00
5 Bird/Thms/Mgic/Nque/Stck/Glde 25.00 60.00

2006-07 Topps Luxury Box Rookie Relics Autographs

STATED PRINT RUN 249 SER.#'d SETS
UNPRICED SILVER PRINT RUN 9 SETS
UNPRICED GOLD PRINT RUN ONE SET
AB Andrea Bargnani 10.00 25.00
AM Adam Morrison 4.00 10.00
AR Allan Ray 2.50 6.00
CS Cedric Simmons 2.50 6.00
CSM Craig Smith 3.00 8.00
DB Dee Brown 2.50 6.00
DM Damir Markota 2.50 6.00
DN David Noel 2.50 6.00
HA Hilton Armstrong 2.50 6.00
JB Josh Boone 2.50 6.00
JF Jordan Farmar 4.00 10.00
JG Jorge Garbajosa 3.00 8.00
JJR J.J. Redick 8.00 20.00
JW James White 2.50 6.00
KL Kyle Lowry 5.00 12.00
MA Maurice Ager 2.50 6.00
MC Mardy Collins 2.50 6.00
MW Marcus Williams 2.50 6.00
PD Paul Davis 2.50 6.00
PJT P.J. Tucker 3.00 8.00
PO Patrick O'Bryant 2.50 6.00
QD Quincy Douby 2.50 6.00
RB Renaldo Balkman 3.00 8.00
RBR Ronnie Brewer 4.00 10.00
RC Rodney Carney 2.50 6.00
RF Randy Foye 4.00 10.00
RR Rajon Rondo 6.00 15.00
SB Shannon Brown 2.50 6.00
SEW Shawne Williams 2.50 6.00
SJ Solomon Jones 2.50 6.00
SN Steve Novak 3.00 8.00
SNW Shelden Williams 3.00 8.00
SR Sergio Rodriguez 4.00 10.00
SS Saer Sene 2.50 6.00
TS Thabo Sefolosha 4.00 10.00

2007-08 Topps Luxury Box

Released in April 2008, Topps Luxury Box features a 100-card base set where veterans appear on cards 1-50 and rookies appear on cards 21-100 and are serially numbered to 669. Luxury Box hit the market in 10-pack boxes of four cards each and carried an initial suggested retail price of $16.

COMP.SET w/o SPs (50) 15.00 40.00
51-100 RC PRINT RUN 699 SER.#'d SETS
UNPRICED GOLD PRINT RUN ONE SET
UNPRICED PLATINUM PRINT RUN ONE SET
1 Kevin Garnett .75 2.00
2 Kobe Bryant 2.00 5.00
3 Dwyane Wade .75 2.00
4 LeBron James 2.00 5.00
5 Baron Davis .40 1.00
6 Dirk Nowitzki .60 1.50
7 Jermaine O'Neal .40 1.00
8 Jason Richardson .50 1.25
9 Tony Parker .50 1.25
10 Chris Bosh .50 1.25
11 Yao Ming .60 1.50
12 Dwight Howard .40 1.00
13 Steve Nash .60 1.50
14 Luol Deng .40 1.00
15 Carmelo Anthony .60 1.50
16 Pau Gasol .50 1.25
17 Carlos Boozer .40 1.00
18 Vince Carter .60 1.50
19 Chauncey Billups .50 1.25
20 Ray Allen .50 1.25
21 Tim Duncan .75 2.00
22 Amare Stoudemire .40 1.00
23 Kevin Martin .40 1.00
24 Michael Redd .40 1.00
25 Corey Maggette .40 1.00
26 Al Jefferson .40 1.00
27 Brandon Roy .50 1.25
28 Chris Paul .60 1.50
29 Andre Iguodala .40 1.00
30 Gilbert Arenas .40 1.00
31 Tracy McGrady .50 1.25
32 Shaquille O'Neal 1.00 2.50
33 Allen Iverson .60 1.50
34 Paul Pierce .50 1.25
35 Jason Kidd .50 1.25
36 John Stockton 1.25 3.00
37 Tim Hardaway .75 2.00
38 Dennis Rodman 1.50 4.00
39 Dominique Wilkins 1.00 2.50
40 David Thompson .60 1.50
41 Spencer Haywood .50 1.25
42 Larry Bird 2.00 5.00
43 Isiah Thomas .75 2.00
44 Magic Johnson 2.00 5.00
45 Bill Russell 1.25 3.00
46 Moses Malone .75 2.00
47 Sidney Moncrief .50 1.25
48 Bill Walton .75 2.00
49 David Robinson 1.25 3.00
50 Jerry West 1.00 2.50
51 Thaddeus Young RC 1.25 3.00
52 Javaris Crittenton RC .75 2.00
53 Sean Williams RC .75 2.00
54 Jared Dudley RC 1.00 2.50
55 Wilson Chandler RC 1.00 2.50
56 Mario West RC 1.25 3.00
57 Chris Richard RC .75 2.00
58 Al Horford RC 1.50 4.00
59 Taurean Green RC .75 2.00
60 Corey Brewer RC 1.25 3.00
61 Joakim Noah RC 1.25 3.00
62 Al Thornton RC 1.00 2.50
63 Nick Young RC 1.50 4.00
64 Arron Afflalo RC 1.25 3.00
65 Juan Carlos Navarro RC 1.00 2.50
66 Marco Belinelli RC 1.25 3.00
67 Yi Jianlian RC 1.50 4.00
68 Luis Scola RC 1.50 4.00
69 Jeff Green RC 1.25 3.00
70 Herbert Hill RC .75 2.00
71 Aaron Gray RC .75 2.00
72 Kosta Perovic RC .75 2.00
73 Spencer Hawes RC 1.00 2.50
74 Aaron Brooks RC 1.00 2.50
75 Kevin Durant RC 12.00 30.00
76 Alando Tucker RC .75 2.00
77 Julian Wright RC .75 2.00
78 Carl Landry RC .75 2.00
79 Acie Law RC .75 2.00
80 Morris Almond RC .75 2.00
81 Nick Fazekas RC .75 2.00
82 Glen Davis RC 1.00 2.50
83 Jermareo Davidson RC .75 2.00
84 Jamario Moon RC 1.00 2.50
85 Jason Smith RC 1.00 2.50
86 Cheikh Samb RC .75 2.00
87 Coby Karl RC .75 2.00
88 Dominic McGuire RC .75 2.00
89 Ramon Sessions RC 1.25 3.00
90 Rodney Stuckey RC 1.00 2.50
91 JamesOn Curry RC .75 2.00
92 Gabe Pruitt RC .75 2.00
93 Adam Haluska RC .75 2.00
94 Kyrylo Fesenko RC .75 2.00
95 Josh McRoberts RC 1.00 2.50
96 D.J. Strawberry RC .75 2.00
97 Brandan Wright RC 1.25 3.00
98 Mike Conley Jr. RC 1.50 4.00
99 Daequan Cook RC 1.00 2.50
100 Greg Oden RC 1.25 3.00

2007-08 Topps Luxury Box Bronze

*BRONZE 1-50: .75X TO 2X BASE HI
*BRONZE 51-100: .5X TO 1.25X BASE
BRONZE PRINT RUN 249 SER.#'d SETS

2007-08 Topps Luxury Box Silver

*SILVER 1-50: 1X TO 2.5X BASE HI
*SILVER 51-100: .6X TO 1.5X BASE HI
PRINT RUN 75 SER.#'d SETS
75 Kevin Durant 50.00 100.00

2007-08 Topps Luxury Box Courtside Dual Relics

PRINT RUN 179 SER.#'d SETS
*GOLD: .5X TO 1.25X BASE HI
GOLD PRINT RUN 75 SER.#'d SETS
UNPRICED PLATINUM PRINT RUN ONE SET
UNPRICED AUTO PRINT RUN 10 SETS
UNPRICED AUTO GOLD PRINT RUN ONE SET
UNPRICED AUTO PLAT.PRINT RUN ONE SET
AH R.Allen/R.Hamilton 4.00 10.00
AM C.Anthony/T.McGrady 4.00 10.00
AW G.Arenas/D.Wade 5.00 12.00
CR V.Carter/J.Richardson 5.00 12.00
DB L.Deng/C.Boozer 4.00 10.00
DM T.Duncan/Y.Ming 5.00 12.00
GJ K.Garnett/A.Jefferson 5.00 12.00
HB D.Howard/C.Bosh 5.00 12.00
HP K.Hinrich/P.Pierce 4.00 10.00
IM A.Iverson/S.Marbury 4.00 10.00
MD K.Martin/B.Davis 4.00 10.00
NG D.Nowitzki/P.Gasol 4.00 10.00
NP S.Nash/T.Parker 5.00 12.00
OB S.O'Neal/K.Bryant 10.00 25.00
OH J.O'Neal/A.Harrington 4.00 10.00
RM M.Redd/M.Miller 4.00 10.00
RP B.Roy/C.Paul 5.00 12.00
RS J.Richardson/J.Smith 4.00 10.00
SK A.Stoudemire/J.Kidd 4.00 10.00
WC B.Wallace/M.Camby 4.00 10.00

2007-08 Topps Luxury Box Courtside Triple Relics

PRINT RUN 149 SER.#'d SETS
*GOLD: .5X TO 1.25X BASE HI
GOLD PRINT RUN 49 SER.#'d SETS
UNPRICED PLATINUM PRINT RUN ONE SET
UNPRICED AUTO PRINT RUN 10 SETS
UNPRICED AUTO GOLD PRINT RUN ONE SET
UNPRICED AUTO PLAT.PRINT RUN ONE SET
AAW Anthony/Arenas/Wade 6.00 15.00
AWM Artest/Wallace/Marion 5.00 12.00
BGN Bryant/Garnett/Nash 10.00 25.00
BIW Butler/Iguodala/Wallace 5.00 12.00
FGT Foye/Gay/Thomas 5.00 12.00
HBC Howard/Boozer/Camby 5.00 12.00
HCG Horford/Cook/Green 5.00 12.00
IMJ Iguodala/McGrady/Johnson 5.00 12.00
MOR Ming/O'Neal/Robinson 8.00 20.00
NOB Noah/Oden/Brewer 8.00 20.00
OGT Okur/Ginobili/Turkoglu 5.00 12.00
OOS Okafor/O'Neal/Smith 5.00 12.00
RAI Redd/Allen/Iverson 5.00 12.00
RMB Roy/Morrison/Bargnani 5.00 12.00
SDB Stoudemire/Duncan/Bosh 5.00 12.00
TLD Ford/Aldridge/Gibson 5.00 12.00
VFG Villanueva/Frye/Gomes 5.00 12.00
WKP Williams/Kidd/Paul 6.00 15.00
YWC Young/Wright/Crittenton 5.00 12.00

2007-08 Topps Luxury Box Quad Relics

PRINT RUN 99 SER.#'d SET
*GOLD: .5X TO 1.25X BASE HI
GOLD PRINT RUN 25 SER.#'d SETS
UNPRICED PLATINUM PRINT RUN ONE SET
QR2 Horfrd/Green/Brwer/Noah 8.00 20.00
QR3 Duncn/Parker/Manu/DRob 12.50 30.00
QR4 Arenas/Butler/Jamisn/Young 6.00 15.00
QR5 Steph/Lee/ZBo/Chandler 6.00 15.00
QR7 Bird/Magic/DRob/Malone 20.00 40.00
QR8 BigAl/Green/Foye/Gomes 6.00 15.00
QR9 Billups/Rip/Afflalo/Stuckey 6.00 15.00
QR10 Davis/Harring/Ellis/Marco 6.00 15.00
QR11 Nash/Amare/Barbo/O'Neal 8.00 20.00
QR12 Harris/Dirk/Terry/Howard 8.00 20.00
QR13 Kidd/RJeff/Vince/Williams 6.00 15.00
QR14 KG/Pierce/Allen/Rondo 10.00 25.00
QR15 TMac/Yao/Brooks/Landry 8.00 20.00

2007-08 Topps Luxury Box Five Piece Relics

PRINT RUN 75 SER.#'d SETS
*GOLD: .5X TO 1.25X BASE HI
GOLD PRINT RUN 25 SER.#'d SETS
UNPRICED PLATINUM PRINT RUN ONE SET
R1 Oden/Yi/Wright/Young 10.00 25.00
R2 Noah/Brewer/Horford+2 15.00 30.00
R3 Dirk/Duncn/Amare/Kobe+1 10.00 25.00
R4 Bosh/Yao/TMac/KG+1 8.00 20.00
R5 Melo/Howard/Wade+2 8.00 20.00
R6 Camby/Kidd/Wallace+2 8.00 20.00
R7 Battier/Marion/Artest/Zo+1 8.00 20.00
R8 Dirk/Nash/KG/Duncan/Al 8.00 20.00
R9 Shaq/Howard/DRob+2 10.00 25.00
R10 Roy/Amare/Paul/Pau+1 8.00 20.00
R11 Vince/Al/Kidd/Brand+1 10.00 25.00
R13 Deke/Bird/Nique/Webb+2 20.00 50.00
R14 Kobe/Al/Shaq/KG/Duncan 20.00 40.00
R15 Oden/Bargs/Bogut/Yao+1 20.00 40.00

2007-08 Topps Luxury Box Six Piece Relics

PRINT RUN 75 SER.#'d SET
*GOLD: .5X TO 1.25X BASE HI
GOLD PRINT RUN 25 SER.#'d SETS
UNPRICED PLATINUM PRINT RUN ONE SET
R1 Spurs and Suns 10.00 25.00
R2 Mavericks and Warriors 8.00 20.00
R3 Bulls and Heat 8.00 20.00
R4 Knicks and Nets 8.00 20.00
R5 Celtics and 76ers 10.00 25.00
R6 Trailblazers and Supersonics 8.00 20.00
R7 Magic and Hawks 8.00 20.00
R8 Nuggets and Jazz 8.00 20.00
R9 Rockets and Grizzlies 10.00 25.00
R10 Pistons and Wizards 8.00 20.00

2007-08 Topps Luxury Box Seven Piece Relics

PRINT RUN 50 SER.#'d SETS
UNPRICED GOLD PRINT RUN 10 SETS
UNPRICED PLATINUM PRINT RUN ONE SET
R1 NBA Point Guards 6.00 15.00
R2 Vince/Bosh/Wade/KG+3 8.00 20.00
R3 NBA Centers 8.00 20.00
R5 RJeff/Bargs/Prince/ZBo+3 6.00 15.00
R7 Kobe/Melo/Dirk/Amare+3 15.00 30.00
R8 NBA Centers/Forwards 8.00 20.00
R9 Marion/Magg/How/Okur+3 6.00 15.00
R10 2007-08 Rookies 8.00 20.00

2007-08 Topps Luxury Box Eight Piece Relics

PRINT RUN 25 SER.#'d SETS
UNPRICED GOLD PRINT RUN 10 SETS
UNPRICED PLATINUM PRINT RUN ONE SET
R1 Kidd/Wade/KG/Shaq+4 15.00 30.00
R2 Bilups/Arenas/Howard+5 10.00 25.00
R4 Pierce/JRich/Allen/+5 15.00 30.00
R5 Kobe/Al/Dirk/Duncn+4 20.00 50.00
R6 Yao/Melo/Amare/CP3+4 20.00 50.00
R7 Manu/KMart/Marion+5 15.00 30.00
R10 2007-08 Rookies 20.00 50.00

2007-08 Topps Luxury Box Mezzanine Relics

PRINT RUN 199 SER.#'d SETS
*GOLD: .5X TO 1.25X BASE HI
GOLD PRINT RUN 99 SER.#'d SETS
UNPRICED PLATINUM PRINT RUN ONE SET
AB Andrea Bargnani 2.50 6.00
AI Allen Iverson 3.00 8.00
AJ Al Jefferson 2.00 5.00
AJA Antawn Jamison 2.00 5.00
AS Amare Stoudemire 2.00 5.00
BG Ben Gordon 2.00 5.00
BR Brandon Roy 2.50 6.00
BW Buck Williams 1.50 4.00
CA Carmelo Anthony 3.00 8.00
CB Caron Butler 2.00 5.00
CBI Chauncey Billups 2.50 6.00
CBO Chris Bosh 2.50 6.00
CP Chris Paul 3.00 8.00
DL David Lee 1.50 4.00
DN Dirk Nowitzki 3.00 8.00
DW Dwyane Wade 4.00 10.00
EO Emeka Okafor 2.00 5.00
GA Gilbert Arenas 2.00 5.00
GG Gerald Green 2.00 5.00
JJ Joe Johnson 2.00 5.00
JJW Jo Jo White 2.00 5.00
JK Jason Kidd 2.50 6.00
JO Jermaine O'Neal 2.00 5.00
JR Jason Richardson 2.50 6.00
KB Kobe Bryant 8.00 20.00
KG Kevin Garnett 4.00 10.00
KM Kevin Martin 2.00 5.00
LA LaMarcus Aldridge 3.00 8.00
LB Leandro Barbosa 2.00 5.00
LD Luol Deng 2.00 5.00
LO Lamar Odom 2.00 5.00
MC Marcus Camby 2.00 5.00
MM Mike Miller 2.00 5.00
MO Mehmet Okur 2.00 5.00
MP Mickael Pietrus 2.00 5.00
MR Michael Redd 2.00 5.00
PG Pau Gasol 2.50 6.00
PP Paul Pierce 2.50 6.00
RA Ray Allen 2.50 6.00
RAR Ron Artest 2.50 6.00
RF Raymond Felton 2.50 6.00
RG Rudy Gay 2.50 6.00
RGO Ryan Gomes 2.00 5.00
RH Richard Hamilton 2.00 5.00
RJ Richard Jefferson 2.00 5.00
RL Rashard Lewis 2.00 5.00
RW Rasheed Wallace 2.50 6.00
SM Shawn Marion 2.00 5.00
SMA Stephon Marbury 2.00 5.00
SO Shaquille O'Neal 5.00 12.00
SW Spud Webb 2.00 5.00
TD Tim Duncan 4.00 10.00
TJF T.J. Ford 1.50 4.00
TM Tracy McGrady 2.50 6.00
TP Tony Parker 2.50 6.00
VC Vince Carter 3.00 8.00
YM Yao Ming 3.00 8.00
ZR Zach Randolph 2.00 5.00

2007-08 Topps Luxury Box Mezzanine Relics Autographs

PRINT RUN 39 SER.#'d SETS
*AUTO GOLD: .6X TO 1.5X BASE HI
GOLD PRINT RUN 25 SER.#'d SETS
UNPRICED LOGO PRINT RUN ONE SET
UNPRICED PLATINUM PRINT RUN ONE SET
AB Andrea Bargnani 5.00 12.00
AJ Al Jefferson 5.00 12.00
AJA Antawn Jamison 5.00 12.00
BG Ben Gordon 6.00 15.00
BW Buck Williams 6.00 15.00
CB Caron Butler 5.00 12.00
CBI Chauncey Billups 6.00 15.00
CBO Chris Bosh 12.00 30.00
DL David Lee 5.00 12.00
DW Dwyane Wade 25.00 60.00
GA Gilbert Arenas 8.00 20.00
JJW Jo Jo White 6.00 15.00
LB Leandro Barbosa 5.00 12.00
MP Mickael Pietrus 5.00 12.00
PP Paul Pierce 8.00 20.00
RA Ray Allen 15.00 40.00
RF Raymond Felton 5.00 12.00
RGO Ryan Gomes 5.00 12.00
SO Shaquille O'Neal 30.00 80.00
SW Spud Webb 15.00 30.00
TJF T.J. Ford 5.00 12.00
VC Vince Carter 20.00 40.00

2007-08 Topps Luxury Box Rookie Relics

PRINT RUN 499 SER.#'d SETS
*GOLD: .5X TO 1.25X BASE HI
GOLD PRINT RUN 149 SER.#'d SETS
UNPRICED LOGO PRINT RUN ONE SET
UNPRICED PLATINUM PRINT RUN ONE SET
AA Arron Afflalo 2.50 6.00
AB Aaron Brooks 2.00 5.00
AG Aaron Gray 1.50 4.00
AH Al Horford 3.00 8.00
AHA Adam Haluska 1.50 4.00
AL Acie Law 1.50 4.00
AT Al Thornton 2.00 5.00
ATU Alando Tucker 1.50 4.00
BW Brandan Wright 2.50 6.00
CB Corey Brewer 2.50 6.00
CL Carl Landry 1.50 4.00
CR Chris Richard 1.50 4.00
DC Daequan Cook 2.00 5.00
DJS D.J. Strawberry 1.50 4.00
DM Dominic McGuire 1.50 4.00
DN Demetris Nichols 1.50 4.00
GD Glen Davis 2.00 5.00
GO Greg Oden 2.50 6.00
GP Gabe Pruitt 1.50 4.00
HH Herbert Hill 1.50 4.00
JC Javaris Crittenton 1.50 4.00
JD Jared Dudley 2.00 5.00
JDA Jermareo Davidson 1.50 4.00
JG Jeff Green 2.50 6.00
JM Josh McRoberts 2.00 5.00
JN Joakim Noah 2.50 6.00
JS Jason Smith 2.00 5.00
JW Julian Wright 1.50 4.00
MA Morris Almond 1.50 4.00
MB Marco Belinelli 2.50 6.00
MC Mike Conley Jr. 3.00 8.00
NF Nick Fazekas 1.50 4.00
NY Nick Young 3.00 8.00
RS Rodney Stuckey 2.00 5.00
SH Spencer Hawes 2.00 5.00
SW Sean Williams 1.50 4.00
TG Taurean Green 1.50 4.00
TY Thaddeus Young 2.50 6.00
WC Wilson Chandler 2.00 5.00
YJ Yi Jianlian 3.00 8.00

2007-08 Topps Luxury Box Rookie Relics Autographs

PRINT RUN 99 TO 199 SER.#'d SETS
*GOLD: .5X TO 1.25X BASE HI
GOLD PRINT RUN 19 TO 39 SETS
UNPRICED LOGO PRINT RUN ONE SET
UNPRICED PLATINUM PRINT RUN ONE SET
AA Arron Afflalo 4.00 10.00
AB Aaron Brooks 3.00 8.00
AG Aaron Gray 2.50 6.00
AH Adam Haluska 2.50 6.00
AL Acie Law 2.50 6.00
AT Al Thornton 3.00 8.00
ATU Alando Tucker 2.50 6.00
BW Brandan Wright 4.00 10.00
CL Carl Landry 2.50 6.00
DC Daequan Cook 3.00 8.00
DJS D.J. Strawberry 2.50 6.00
DM Dominic McGuire 2.50 6.00
DN Demetris Nichols 2.50 6.00
GD Glen Davis 3.00 8.00
GO Greg Oden 25.00 60.00
GP Gabe Pruitt 2.50 6.00
HH Herbert Hill 2.50 6.00
JC Javaris Crittenton 2.50 6.00
JD Jared Dudley 3.00 8.00
JDA Jermareo Davidson 2.50 6.00
JM Josh McRoberts 3.00 8.00
JS Jason Smith 3.00 8.00
MA Morris Almond 2.50 6.00
MB Marco Belinelli 4.00 10.00
NF Nick Fazekas 2.50 6.00
NY Nick Young 5.00 12.00
RS Rodney Stuckey 3.00 8.00
SH Spencer Hawes 3.00 8.00
SW Sean Williams 2.50 6.00
TG Taurean Green 2.50 6.00
TY Thaddeus Young 4.00 10.00
WC Wilson Chandler 3.00 8.00
YJ Yi Jianlian 5.00 12.00

1983-84 Topps M&M's Olympic Heroes

This 44-card boxed standard-sized set is an abridgment of the 99-card 1983 Topps History's Greatest Olympians set. Though widely known to have been produced by Topps, this company name is found nowhere on the cards. On a white card face, the fronts display either color or black-and-white photos framed by a white inner border and a red outer border. The top of the red outer border carries the olympiad number, year, and city, while the player's name is printed across the bottom of the front. Inside a light blue border, the back carry a headline and news brief in brown ink. The M&M's logo adorns both sides of the cards. The cards are numbered on the back; note that numbering differs completely from that of the larger set.

COMPLETE SET (44) 8.00 20.00
3 Bill Bradley .50 1.25
33 Oscar Robertson .60 1.50
42 Jerry West .75 2.00

1948 Topps Magic Photos

The 1948 Topps Magic Photos set contains 252 small (approximately 7/8" by 1 7/16") individual cards featuring sport and non-sport subjects. They were issued in 19 lettered series with cards numbered within each series. The fronts were developed, much like a photograph, from a "blank" appearance by using moisture and sunlight. Due to varying degrees of photographic sensitivity, the clarity of these cards ranges from fully developed to poorly developed. This set contains Topps' first baseball cards. A premium album holding 126-cards was also issued. The set is sometimes confused with Topps' 1956 Hocus-Focus set, although the cards in this set are slightly smaller than those in the Hocus-Focus set. The checklist below is presented by series. Poorly developed cards are considered in lesser condition and hence have lesser value. The catalog designation for this set is R714-27. Each type of card subject has a letter prefix as follows: Boxing Champions (A), All-American Basketball (B), All-American Football (C), Wrestling Champions (D), Track and Field Champions (E), Stars of Stage and Screen (F), American Dogs (G), General Sports (H), Movie Stars (J), Baseball Hall of Fame (K), Aviation Pioneers (L), Famous Landmarks (M), American Inventors (N), American Military Leaders (O), American Explorers (P), Basketball Thrills (Q), Football Thrills (R), Figures of the Wild West (S), and General Sports (T).

COMPLETE SET (252) 3000.00 5000.00
B1 Ralph Beard 25.00 50.00
B2 Murray Weir 15.00 30.00
B3 Ed Macauley 40.00 80.00
B4 Kevin O'Shea 12.50 25.00
B5 Jim McIntyre 15.00 30.00
B6 Manhattan Beats 12.50 25.00

2012 Topps Magic Historical Coins

HISTORY COIN/25 ODDS 1:722 HOB
HCHG Harlem Globetrotters 15.00 40.00

2006 Topps McDonald's All-American

COMPLETE SET (48) 12.00 30.00
B1 Earl Clark 1.00 2.50
B2 Mike Conley Jr. 1.50 4.00
B3 Jarvaris Crittenton .75 2.00
B4 Wayne Ellington .75 2.00
B5 Gerald Henderson 1.50 4.00
B6 Ty Lawson 1.50 4.00
B7 Vernon Macklin .75 2.00
B8 Greg Oden 2.00 5.00
B9 Scottie Reynolds .75 2.00
B10 Lance Thomas .75 2.00
B11 Brandan Wright .75 2.00
B12 Thaddeus Young 1.25 3.00
B13 Darrell Arthur .75 2.00
B14 D.J. Augustin 1.00 2.50
B15 Chase Budinger 1.00 2.50
B16 Demond Carter .75 2.00
B17 Sherron Collins .75 2.00
B18 Daequan Cook 1.00 2.50
B19 Kevin Durant 6.00 15.00
B20 James Keefe .75 2.00
B21 Spencer Hawes 1.00 2.50
B22 Brook Lopez 2.00 5.00
B23 Robin Lopez 1.25 3.00
B24 Jon Scheyer .75 2.00
G1 Jessica Breland .75 2.00
G2 Tina Charles 1.00 2.50
G3 Joy Cheek .40 1.00
G4 Amber Harris .75 2.00
G5 Ashley Houts .40 1.00
G6 Kaili McLaren .40 1.00
G7 Bridgette Mitchell .40 1.00
G8 Porsha Phillips .40 1.00
G9 Epiphanny Prince .40 1.00
G10 Amber White .75 2.00
G11 Danielle Wilson .40 1.00
G12 Monica Wright .75 2.00
G13 Jayne Appel .40 1.00
G14 Jacki Gemelos .40 1.00
G15 Michelle Harrison .40 1.00
G16 Allison Hightower .40 1.00
G17 Dela Quese Jernigan .40 1.00
G18 Adrian McGowan .40 1.00
G19 Morghan Medlock .40 1.00
G20 Jordan Murphee .40 1.00
G21 Abi Olajuwon .75 2.00
G22 Brittainey Raven .40 1.00
G23 Dymond Simon .40 1.00
G24 Amanda Thompson .75 2.00

2007 Topps McDonald's All-American

This 48-card set was distributed in box set form and features action photos of both the men's and women's All-American team.

COMPLETE SET (48) 20.00 50.00
AB Angie Bjorklund W .40 1.00
AC Ashley Cimino W .40 1.00
AF Austin Freeman .75 2.00
AJ Alison Jackson W .40 1.00
AJ2 Amy Jaeschke W .40 1.00
BG Blake Griffin 6.00 15.00
CA Cole Aldrich 1.25 3.00
CD Cetera DeGraffenrein W .40 1.00
CS Corey Stokes .75 2.00
CW Chris Wright .75 2.00
DG Donte Greene 1.25 3.00
DM Drey Mingo W .40 1.00
DP Devereaux Peters W .40 1.00
DR Derrick Rose 8.00 20.00
EG Eric Gordon 2.50 6.00
EM Erica Morrow W .40 1.00
GL Gani Lawal .75 2.00
IL Italee Lucas W .40 1.00
JA James Anderson 1.50 4.00
JB Jerryd Bayless 1.25 3.00
JF Jonny Flynn 2.00 5.00
JH James Harden 2.50 6.00
JJH J.J. Hickson 1.00 2.50
JL Jai Lucas .75 2.00
JL2 Jantel Lavender W .40 1.00
JP Jeanette Pohlen W .40 1.00
JT Jasmine Thomas W .40 1.00
KC Kelley Cain W .40 1.00
KK Kosta Koufos .75 2.00
KL Kevin Love 3.00 8.00
KP Kayla Pedersen W .50 1.25
KR Khadijah Rushdan W .40 1.00
KS Kyle Singler 1.00 2.50
KT Krystal Thomas W .40 1.00
LD Lorin Dixon W .40 1.00
LS Lenita Sanford W .40 1.00
MB Michael Beasley 4.00 10.00
MM Maya Moore W 2.00 5.00
MS Marah Strickland W .40 1.00
NC Nick Calathes .75 2.00
NS Nolan Smith 2.00 5.00
OM O.J. Mayo 3.00 8.00
PP Patrick Patterson 1.50 4.00
SG Stefanie Galbreath W .40 1.00
TK Taylor King .75 2.00
TP Ta'Shia Phillips W .40 1.00
TW Tyra White W .40 1.00
VB Victoria Baugh W .40 1.00

2008 Topps McDonald's All-American

This 48-card set was distributed in box set form and features action photos of both the men's and women's All-American team.

COMPLETE SET (48) 25.00 60.00
AB Alyssia Brewer W .40 1.00

AC Ashley Corral W .40 1.00
AD Ayana Dunning W .40 1.00
AFA Al-Farouq Aminu 1.25 3.00
AG Amber Gray W .40 1.00
AG Ashley Gayle W .40 1.00
AM Alicia Manning W .40 1.00
AS April Sykes W .40 1.00
BG Briana Gilbreath W .40 1.00
BJ Brandon Jennings 4.00 10.00
BJM B.J. Mullens .75 2.00
BP Brooklyn Pope W .40 1.00
CL Chelsea Lee W .40 1.00
CS Chay Shegog W .40 1.00
CS Chris Singleton 2.00 5.00
DD DeMar DeRozan 2.00 5.00
DH Destiny Hughes W .40 1.00
ED Ed Davis 3.00 8.00
EDD Elena Delle Donna W .40 1.00
EW Elliot Williams 1.25 3.00
GJ Glory Johnson W .40 1.00
GM Greg Monroe 3.00 8.00
IS Iman Shumpert 2.50 6.00
JD Jasmine Dixon W .40 1.00
JG JaMychal Green 1.00 2.50
JH Jrue Holiday 3.00 8.00
KW Kemba Walker 6.00 15.00
LB Luke Babbitt 1.25 3.00
LD Larry Drew II 1.00 2.50
LK Lynetta Kizer W .40 1.00
LSB LaSondra Barrett W .40 1.00
MD Michael Dunigan .75 2.00
ML Malcolm Lee .75 2.00
MR Michael Rosario .75 2.00
NO Nnemkadi Ogwumike W .40 1.00
NS Nikki Speed W .40 1.00
SH Scotty Hopson 1.25 3.00
SJ Shenise Johnson W .40 1.00
SL Sylven Landesberg 1.25 3.00
SP Samantha Prahalis W .40 1.00
SS Shekinna Stricklen W .40 1.00
SS Samardo Samuels 1.25 3.00
SW She'la White W .40 1.00
TE Tyreke Evans 6.00 15.00
TH Tiffany Hayes W .40 1.00
TZ Tyler Zeller .75 2.00
WB William Buford .75 2.00
WW Willie Warren .75 2.00

2005-06 Topps NBA Collector Chips

COMPLETE SET (111) 80.00 160.00
1 Al Harrington .60 1.50
2 Al Jefferson .60 1.50
3 Allen Iverson 1.25 3.00
4 Amare Stoudemire .60 1.50
5 Anderson Varejao .50 1.25
6 Andre Iguodala .60 1.50
7 Andre Miller .60 1.50
8 Andrei Kirilenko .60 1.50
9 Andrew Bogut 1.00 2.50
10 Antawn Jamison .60 1.50
11 Antoine Walker .60 1.50
12 Antoine Wright .60 1.50
13 Baron Davis .60 1.50
14 Ben Gordon .60 1.50
15 Ben Wallace .60 1.50
16 Bob Sura .50 1.25
17 Brad Miller .60 1.50
18 Brevin Knight .50 1.25
19 Carlos Boozer .60 1.50
20 Carmelo Anthony 1.50 4.00
21 Caron Butler .60 1.50
22 Channing Frye .75 2.00
23 Charlie Villanueva .75 2.00
24 Chris Bosh .75 2.00
25 Chris Paul 3.00 8.00
26 Chris Taft .60 1.50
27 Chris Webber .75 2.00
28 Corey Maggette .60 1.50
29 Dan Dickau .50 1.25
30 Danny Granger 1.00 2.50
31 Darius Miles .50 1.25
32 Deron Williams 1.00 2.50
33 Desmond Mason .50 1.25
34 Dirk Nowitzki 1.25 3.00
35 Drew Gooden .60 1.50
36 Dwight Howard .60 1.50
37 Dwyane Wade 1.25 3.00
38 Elton Brand .75 2.00
39 Emeka Okafor .60 1.50
40 Gerald Green .75 2.00
41 Gilbert Arenas .60 1.50
42 Grant Hill 1.00 2.50
43 Hakim Warrick .60 1.50
44 Ike Diogu .50 1.25
45 J.R. Smith .60 1.50
46 Jalen Rose .75 2.00
47 Jamaal Magloire .50 1.25
48 Jamal Crawford .75 2.00
49 Jason Kidd 1.25 3.00
50 Jason Richardson .75 2.00
51 Jermaine O'Neal .60 1.50
52 Jerry West
53 Joey Graham .60 1.50
54 Josh Childress .60 1.50
55 Josh Howard .75 2.00
56 Josh Smith .60 1.50
57 Julius Hodge .50 1.25
58 Kenyon Martin .60 1.50
59 Kevin Garnett 1.25 3.00
60 Kirk Hinrich .60 1.50
61 Kobe Bryant 3.00 8.00
62 Lamar Odom .60 1.50
63 Larry Hughes .60 1.50
64 Latrell Sprewell .60 1.50
65 LeBron James 3.00 8.00
66 Luke Ridnour .60 1.50
67 Luol Deng .60 1.50
68 Manu Ginobili .75 2.00
69 Martell Webster .60 1.50
70 Marvin Williams .75 2.00
71 Maurice Williams .60 1.50
72 Mehmet Okur .50 1.25
73 Michael Finley .75 2.00
74 Michael Redd .60 1.50
75 Mike Bibby .75 2.00
76 Mike Miller .60 1.50
77 Monta Ellis 1.00 2.50
78 Morris Peterson .50 1.25
79 Pau Gasol .75 2.00
80 Paul Pierce .75 2.00
81 Peja Stojakovic .75 2.00
82 Primoz Brezec .50 1.25
83 Rashad McCants .60 1.50
84 Rashard Lewis .75 2.00
85 Rasheed Wallace .75 2.00
86 Ray Allen .75 2.00
87 Raymond Felton .75 2.00
88 Richard Hamilton .60 1.50
89 Richard Jefferson .60 1.50
90 Ron Artest .75 2.00
91 Sean May .50 1.25
92 Sebastian Telfair .60 1.50
93 Shane Battier .60 1.50
94 Shaquille O'Neal 1.50 4.00
95 Shaun Livingston .50 1.25
96 Shawn Marion .60 1.50
97 Stephen Jackson .60 1.50
98 Stephon Marbury .60 1.50
99 Steve Francis .60 1.50
100 Steve Nash 1.00 2.50
101 Tim Duncan 1.25 3.00
102 Tony Parker .75 2.00
103 Tracy McGrady 1.00 2.50
104 Trevor Ariza .50 1.25
105 Troy Murphy .50 1.25
106 Udonis Haslem .50 1.25
107 Vince Carter 1.25 3.00
108 Wally Szczerbiak .60 1.50
109 Wayne Simien .50 1.25
110 Yao Ming 1.00 2.50
111 Zach Randolph .60 1.50

2005-06 Topps NBA Collector Chips 599

*1-110 BLUE FOIL: .6X TO 1.5X CHIP 599 HI
*1-10 GREEN FOIL: .75X TO 2X CHIP 599 HI
*1-50 RED FOIL: .5X TO 1.25X CHIP 599 HI
1 Al Jefferson .75 2.00
2 Allen Iverson 1.50 4.00
3 Amare Stoudemire .75 2.00
4 Andre Iguodala .75 2.00
5 Andrei Kirilenko .75 2.00
6 Andrew Bogut 1.25 3.00
7 Antawn Jamison .75 2.00
8 Antoine Walker .75 2.00
9 Antoine Wright .75 2.00
10 Baron Davis .75 2.00
11 Ben Wallace .75 2.00
12 Bill Walton 1.00 2.50
13 Bob Cousy 1.50 4.00
14 Bob Sura .60 1.50
15 Brad Miller .75 2.00
16 Carlos Boozer .75 2.00
17 Carmelo Anthony 2.00 5.00
18 Caron Butler .75 2.00
19 Channing Frye 1.00 2.50
20 Charlie Villanueva 1.00 2.50
21 Chris Bosh 1.00 2.50
22 Chris Paul 4.00 10.00
23 Chris Taft .75 2.00
24 Chris Webber 1.00 2.50
25 Dan Dickau .60 1.50
26 Danny Granger 1.25 3.00
27 Darius Miles .60 1.50
28 Dave Cowens .60 1.50
29 Deron Williams 1.25 3.00
30 Dirk Nowitzki 1.50 4.00
31 Drazen Petrovic 1.00 2.50
32 Drew Gooden .75 2.00
33 Dwight Howard .75 2.00
34 Dwyane Wade 1.50 4.00
35 Earl Monroe 1.00 2.50
36 Emeka Okafor .75 2.00
37 George Gervin 1.00 2.50
38 Gerald Green 1.00 2.50
39 Gilbert Arenas .75 2.00
40 Grant Hill 1.25 3.00
41 Hakim Warrick .75 2.00
42 Ike Diogu .60 1.50
43 Isiah Thomas 1.00 2.50
44 Jamaal Magloire .60 1.50
45 Jamal Crawford 1.00 2.50
46 Jason Richardson 1.00 2.50
47 Jermaine O'Neal .75 2.00
48 Jerry West 1.25 3.00
49 Joey Graham .75 2.00
50 John Havlicek 1.00 2.50
51 Josh Howard 1.00 2.50
52 Julius Erving 1.50 4.00
53 Julius Hodge .60 1.50
54 Kareem Abdul-Jabbar 1.50 4.00
55 Kevin Garnett 1.50 4.00
56 Kirk Hinrich .75 2.00
57 Kobe Bryant 4.00 10.00
58 Lamar Odom .75 2.00
59 Larry Bird 2.50 6.00
60 Larry Hughes .75 2.00
61 Latrell Sprewell .75 2.00
62 LeBron James 4.00 10.00
63 Luke Ridnour .75 2.00
64 Luol Deng .75 2.00
65 Manu Ginobili 1.00 2.50
66 Martell Webster .75 2.00
67 Marvin Williams 1.00 2.50
68 Maurice Williams .75 2.00
69 Michael Finley 1.00 2.50
70 Michael Redd 1.00 2.50
71 Monta Ellis 1.25 3.00
72 Morris Peterson .60 1.50
73 Moses Malone 1.00 2.50
74 Oscar Robertson 1.00 2.50
75 Pau Gasol 1.00 2.50
76 Paul Pierce 1.00 2.50
77 Peja Stojakovic 1.00 2.50
78 Pete Maravich 1.50 4.00
79 Primoz Brezec .60 1.50
80 Quentin Richardson .75 2.00
81 Rashad McCants .75 2.00
82 Rashard Lewis 1.00 2.50
83 Rasheed Wallace 1.00 2.50
84 Ray Allen 1.00 2.50
85 Raymond Felton 1.00 2.50
86 Richard Jefferson .75 2.00
87 Richard Hamilton .75 2.00
88 Rick Barry .75 2.00
89 Ron Artest 1.00 2.50
90 Sean May .60 1.50
91 Sebastian Telfair .75 2.00
92 Shane Battier .75 2.00
93 Shaquille O'Neal 2.00 5.00
94 Shaun Livingston .60 1.50
95 Shawn Marion .75 2.00
96 Steve Francis .75 2.00
97 Steve Nash 1.25 3.00
98 Tim Duncan 1.50 4.00
99 Tracy McGrady 1.25 3.00
100 Trevor Ariza .60 1.50
101 Troy Murphy .60 1.50
102 Quentin Richardson .75 2.00
103 Vince Carter 1.50 4.00
104 Walt Frazier 1.00 2.50
105 Wayne Simien .60 1.50
106 Willis Reed 1.00 2.50
107 Wilt Chamberlain 2.00 5.00
108 Yao Ming 1.25 3.00
109 Zach Randolph .75 2.00
110 Zydrunas Ilgauskas .75 2.00

2005-06 Topps NBA Collector Chips Autographs

PRINT RUN 100 SER.#'d SETS
1 Allen Iverson 60.00 120.00
2 Carmelo Anthony 30.00 60.00
3 Charlie Villanueva 10.00 25.00
4 Chris Taft 8.00 20.00
5 Emeka Okafor 15.00 40.00
6 Gerald Green 8.00 20.00
7 Hakim Warrick 10.00 25.00
8 Joey Graham 8.00 20.00
9 Rashad McCants 10.00 25.00
10 Raymond Felton 15.00 30.00
11 Wayne Simien 8.00 20.00

2005-06 Topps NBA Collector Chips Blue

1 LeBron James 4.00 10.00
2 Dirk Nowitzki 1.50 4.00
3 Carmelo Anthony 2.00 5.00
4 Ben Wallace .75 2.00
5 Tracy McGrady 1.25 3.00
6 Yao Ming 1.25 3.00
7 Jermaine O'Neal .75 2.00
8 Kobe Bryant 4.00 10.00
9 Dwyane Wade 1.50 4.00
10 Shaquille O'Neal 2.00 5.00
11 Kevin Garnett 1.50 4.00
12 Vince Carter 1.50 4.00
13 Jason Kidd 1.50 4.00
14 Stephon Marbury .75 2.00
15 Steve Francis .75 2.00
16 Allen Iverson 1.50 4.00
17 Amare Stoudemire .75 2.00
18 Steve Nash 1.25 3.00
19 Ben Gordon .75 2.00
20 Tim Duncan 1.50 4.00
21 Manu Ginobili 1.00 2.50
22 Ray Allen 1.00 2.50
23 Emeka Okafor .75 2.00
24 Paul Pierce 1.00 2.50
25 Andrew Bogut 1.25 3.00
26 Marvin Williams 1.00 2.50
27 Chris Paul 4.00 10.00
28 Deron Williams 1.25 3.00
29 Gerald Green 1.00 2.50
30 Raymond Felton 1.00 2.50

2005-06 Topps NBA Collector Chips Green

1 LeBron James 5.00 12.00
2 Tracy McGrady 1.50 4.00
3 Steve Nash 1.50 4.00
4 Shaquille O'Neal 2.50 6.00
5 Tim Duncan 2.00 5.00
6 Dwyane Wade 2.00 5.00
7 Allen Iverson 2.00 5.00
8 Andrew Bogut 1.50 4.00
9 Marvin Williams 1.25 3.00
10 Chris Paul 5.00 12.00

2005-06 Topps NBA Collector Chips Red

1 Bill Russell 2.00 5.00
2 Wilt Chamberlain 2.00 5.00
3 Bob Cousy 1.50 4.00
4 Dave Cowens .60 1.50
5 Walt Frazier 1.00 2.50
6 John Havlicek 1.00 2.50
7 Earl Monroe 1.00 2.50
8 Oscar Robertson 1.00 2.50
9 Jerry West 1.25 3.00
10 Kareem Abdul-Jabbar 1.50 4.00
11 Moses Malone 1.00 2.50
12 George Gervin 1.00 2.50
13 Julius Erving 1.50 4.00
14 Drazen Petrovic 1.00 2.50
15 Pete Maravich 1.50 4.00
16 Larry Bird 2.50 6.00
17 Isiah Thomas 1.00 2.50
18 Rick Barry .75 2.00
19 Willis Reed 1.00 2.50
20 Bill Walton 1.00 2.50
21 Gilbert Arenas .75 2.00
22 Grant Hill 1.25 3.00
23 Zydrunas Ilgauskas .75 2.00
24 Allen Iverson 1.50 4.00
25 Antawn Jamison .75 2.00
26 Jermaine O'Neal .75 2.00
27 Shaquille O'Neal 2.00 5.00
28 Paul Pierce 1.00 2.50
29 Dwyane Wade 1.50 4.00
30 Ben Wallace .75 2.00
31 Ray Allen 1.00 2.50
32 Tim Duncan 1.50 4.00
33 Kevin Garnett 1.50 4.00
34 Manu Ginobili 1.00 2.50
35 Rashard Lewis 1.00 2.50
36 Shawn Marion .75 2.00
37 Tracy McGrady 1.25 3.00
38 Yao Ming 1.25 3.00
39 Steve Nash 1.25 3.00
40 Dirk Nowitzki 1.50 4.00
41 Amare Stoudemire .75 2.00
42 LeBron James 4.00 10.00
43 Vince Carter 1.50 4.00
44 Kobe Bryant 4.00 10.00
45 Allen Iverson 1.50 4.00
46 Carmelo Anthony 2.00 5.00
47 Quentin Richardson .75 2.00
48 Steve Nash 1.25 3.00
49 Josh Smith .75 2.00
50 Shawn Marion .75 2.00

1997-98 Topps O-Pee-Chee

Randomly inserted at a rate of one in three in Candian packs only, this 220-card set parallels the basic Topps set. The front and the back of the card looks identical, except an O-Pee-Chee logo replaces the normal Topps logo.

COMPLETE SET (219) 125.00 250.00
COMPLETE SERIES 1 (110) 50.00 100.00
COMPLETE SERIES 2 (110) 75.00 150.00
*OPC: 4X TO 10X BASE TOPPS HI
115 Tim Duncan 30.00 80.00
123 Michael Jordan 30.00 80.00
125 Tracy McGrady 8.00 20.00

1998-99 Topps O-Pee-Chee

COMPLETE SET (220) 50.00 120.00
*OPC STARS: 2X TO 5X BASE TOPPS HI
*OPC RCs: 1X TO 2.5X BASE TOPPS HI
77 Michael Jordan 30.00 80.00

2001-02 Topps Pristine

Released in Mid April 2002, this 110-card set features 50 Veteran players and 20 different Rookies. Three versions of each rookie player were produced, a base version, an uncommon version, and a rare version. Base cards are standard size with full color player photos set against colored and patterned backgrounds with player name bars along the bottom of the card and the "TP" Topps Pristine circular logo in the upper left-hand corner. Player photos are embossed and printed on an all chromium card stock. SRP for packs was $25, and packs were released in a 3 in 1 format. The outer pack contains one Topps Pristine Refractor card in a sealed protective case. The middle pack conatins one Relic card and the third outer pack. The outer pack conatins four veteran cards plus two base rookie cards. One Jumbo pack is inserted as a box-topper which features playoff-used memorabilia, and the sealed versions were inserted at the rate of one per case.

COMPLETE SET (110) 150.00 300.00
COMP.SET w/o SP's (50) 30.00 80.00
1 Allen Iverson 2.00 5.00
2 Shawn Marion .75 2.00
3 Baron Davis 1.00 2.50
4 Peja Stojakovic 1.00 2.50
5 Dirk Nowitzki 1.50 4.00
6 Michael Jordan 8.00 20.00
7 Dikembe Mutombo 1.00 2.50
8 Antoine Walker .75 2.00
9 David Robinson 1.50 4.00
10 Tracy McGrady 1.50 4.00
11 Rasheed Wallace 1.00 2.50
12 Kenyon Martin 1.00 2.50
13 Glenn Robinson .75 2.00
14 Shareef Abdur-Rahim .75 2.00
15 Lamar Odom .75 2.00
16 Alonzo Mourning 1.25 3.00
17 Latrell Sprewell .75 2.00
18 Stephon Marbury .75 2.00
19 Chris Webber 1.00 2.50
20 Darius Miles .60 1.50
21 Tim Duncan 2.00 5.00
22 Antawn Jamison 1.00 2.50
23 Jason Kidd 1.50 4.00
24 John Stockton 1.25 3.00
25 Michael Finley 1.00 2.50
26 Eddie Jones .75 2.00
27 Jamal Mashburn .75 2.00
28 Paul Pierce 1.00 2.50
29 Jason Terry 1.00 2.50
30 Kobe Bryant 4.00 10.00
31 Reggie Miller 1.00 2.50
32 Elton Brand 1.00 2.50
33 Antonio McDyess .75 2.00
34 Ray Allen 1.00 2.50
35 Kevin Garnett 1.50 4.00
36 Allan Houston .75 2.00
37 Grant Hill 1.25 3.00
38 Jalen Rose .75 2.00
39 Gary Payton .75 2.00
40 Vince Carter 1.50 4.00
41 Jerry Stackhouse .75 2.00
42 Karl Malone 1.25 3.00
43 Wang Zhizhi .75 2.00
44 Marcus Fizer .60 1.50
45 Marcus Camby .75 2.00
46 Andre Miller .75 2.00
47 Jason Williams .75 2.00
48 Hakeem Olajuwon 1.25 3.00
49 Shaquille O'Neal 2.50 6.00
50 Steve Francis .75 2.00
51 Eddie Griffin C RC .60 1.50
52 Eddie Griffin U .75 2.00
53 Eddie Griffin R 1.25 3.00
54 Kwame Brown C RC .75 2.00
55 Kwame Brown U 1.00 2.50
56 Kwame Brown R 1.50 4.00
57 Shane Battier C RC 1.50 4.00
58 Shane Battier U 2.00 5.00
59 Shane Battier R 3.00 8.00
60 Eddy Curry C RC .75 2.00
61 Eddy Curry U .75 2.00
62 Eddy Curry R 1.50 4.00
63 Tyson Chandler C RC 1.25 3.00
64 Tyson Chandler U 1.50 4.00
65 Tyson Chandler R 2.50 6.00
66 Rodney White C RC .50 1.25
67 Rodney White U .60 1.50
68 Rodney White R 1.00 2.50
69 Jason Richardson C RC 1.00 2.50
70 Jason Richardson U 1.25 3.00
71 Jason Richardson R 2.00 5.00
72 Joe Johnson C RC 1.00 2.50
73 Joe Johnson U 1.25 3.00
74 Joe Johnson R 2.00 5.00
75 Pau Gasol C RC 2.50 6.00
76 Pau Gasol U 3.00 8.00
77 Pau Gasol R 5.00 12.00
78 Desagana Diop C RC .60 1.50
79 Desagana Diop U .75 2.00
80 Desagana Diop R 1.25 3.00
81 Vladimir Radmanovic C RC .75 2.00
82 Vladimir Radmanovic U 1.00 2.50
83 Vladimir Radmanovic R 1.50 4.00
84 Troy Murphy C RC .75 2.00
85 Troy Murphy U 1.00 2.50
86 Troy Murphy R 1.50 4.00
87 Zach Randolph C RC 1.25 3.00
88 Zach Randolph U 1.50 4.00
89 Zach Randolph R 2.50 6.00
90 Jamaal Tinsley C RC .75 2.00
91 Jamaal Tinsley U 1.00 2.50
92 Jamaal Tinsley R 1.50 4.00
93 Richard Jefferson C RC 1.25 3.00
94 Richard Jefferson U 1.50 4.00
95 Richard Jefferson R 2.50 6.00
96 Loren Woods C RC .50 1.25
97 Loren Woods U .60 1.50
98 Loren Woods R 1.00 2.50
99 Joseph Forte C RC .50 1.25
100 Joseph Forte U .60 1.50
101 Joseph Forte R 1.00 2.50
102 Gerald Wallace C RC 1.25 3.00
103 Gerald Wallace U 1.25 3.00
104 Gerald Wallace R 2.00 5.00
105 Andrei Kirilenko C RC 1.25 3.00
106 Andrei Kirilenko U 1.50 4.00
107 Andrei Kirilenko R 2.50 6.00
108 Tony Parker C RC 3.00 8.00
109 Tony Parker U 4.00 10.00
110 Tony Parker R 6.00 15.00

2001-02 Topps Pristine Refractors

*STARS: 6X TO 15X BASE CARD HI
1-50 PRINT RUN 50 SERIAL #'d SETS
*RCs: 1X TO 2.5X BASE CARD HI
*RC/750: 1.25X TO 3X BASE RC C VERSION
*RCs/250: 2X TO 5X BASE RC C VERSION

2001-02 Topps Pristine Autographs

Randomly inserted in packs at the rate of one in four, this 32-card set features player photos on the top half of the card and a white space in the bottom right hand corner for player autographs. These cards also feature the rainbow holofoil refractor effect.

STATED ODDS 1:4
AAD Antonio Daniels 2.50 6.00
AAFM Aaron McKie 2.50 6.00
AAJ Antawn Jamison 4.00 10.00
AAM Andre Miller 3.00 8.00
ABD Baron Davis 4.00 10.00
ABH Brendan Haywood 4.00 10.00
ABJ Bobby Jackson 2.50 6.00
ACB Chauncey Billups 4.00 10.00
ADB Damone Brown 2.50 6.00
ADH Donnell Harvey 2.50 6.00
ADM Desmond Mason 3.00 8.00
AEB Elton Brand 4.00 10.00
AEC Eddy Curry 4.00 10.00
AGA Gilbert Arenas 6.00 15.00
AHT Hedo Turkoglu 6.00 15.00
AIT Iakovos Tsakalidis 2.50 6.00
AJB Jonathan Bender 2.50 6.00
AJF Joseph Forte 2.50 6.00
AJJ Joe Johnson 5.00 12.00
AJO Jermaine O'Neal 3.00 8.00
AJT Jason Terry 4.00 10.00
AJTR Jeff Trepagnier 2.50 6.00
AKAJ Kareem Abdul-Jabbar 50.00 120.00
AKB Kwame Brown 4.00 10.00
AKBR Kedrick Brown 2.50 6.00
AKS Kenny Satterfield 2.50 6.00
ALW Loren Woods 2.50 6.00
AMB Mike Bibby 4.00 10.00
AMJ Marc Jackson 2.50 6.00
APS Peja Stojakovic 4.00 10.00
ARH Richard Hamilton 8.00 20.00
ARJ Richard Jefferson 6.00 15.00
ARL Raef LaFrentz 2.50 6.00
ASB Shane Battier 6.00 15.00
ASM Shawn Marion 6.00 15.00
ASO Shaquille O'Neal 60.00 150.00
ATD Tim Duncan 300.00 600.00
ATMU Troy Murphy 4.00 10.00
AZR Zach Randolph 8.00 20.00

2001-02 Topps Pristine Oversized Relics

Randomly inserted at the rate of one per box, these jumbo cards feature player action photos set against a silver foil background. The cards also contain the NBA logo where "Jerry West" has been replaced with a jersey swatch.

STATED ODDS 1 PER BOX
BLAH Allan Houston 4.00 10.00
BLAI Allen Iverson 10.00 25.00
BLAM Alonzo Mourning 6.00 15.00
BLCM Cuttino Mobley 3.00 8.00
BLDM Dikembe Mutombo 5.00 12.00
BLDN Dirk Nowitzki 8.00 20.00
BLDR David Robinson 8.00 20.00
BLDW David Wesley 3.00 8.00
BLGR Glenn Robinson 4.00 10.00
BLJK Jason Kidd 8.00 20.00
BLJS Jerry Stackhouse 4.00 10.00
BLJHS John Stockton 6.00 15.00
BLKM Karl Malone 6.00 15.00
BLLO Lamar Odom 4.00 10.00
BLLS Latrell Sprewell 4.00 10.00
BLRH Richard Hamilton 4.00 10.00
BLRW Rasheed Wallace 5.00 12.00
BLTD Tim Duncan 10.00 25.00

2001-02 Topps Pristine Partners

Randomly seeded in packs at the rate of one in 11, this nine card set features full color player photos on the right side, colorful backgrounds, the word "Partners" along the top, and a circular swatch of a warm-up used by the featured player in the NBA All-Star 2-Ball competition.

STATED ODDS 1:11
PAAH Allan Houston 2.50 6.00
PACM Cuttino Mobley 2.00 5.00
PADF Derek Fisher 2.50 6.00
PAGH Grant Hill 4.00 10.00
PAJW Jason Williams 2.50 6.00
PARH Richard Hamilton 2.50 6.00
PASF Steve Francis 2.50 6.00
PATL Trajan Langdon 2.00 5.00
PATM Tracy McGrady 5.00 12.00

2001-02 Topps Pristine Portions

Randomly inserted in packs at the rate of one in three, this 18-card set features a horizontal design where a parobolic line that runs diagonally from the top right hand corner to the bottom left hand corner divides the card between black background on the left and gray background on the right. Full color player photos appear on the left, the word "Portions" appears along the top in white, and a swach of game worn relic in the upper left hand corner.

STATED ODDS 1:3
PPAM Alonzo Mourning 3.00 8.00
PPDM Dikembe Mutombo 2.50 6.00
PPDN Dirk Nowitzki 4.00 10.00
PPEJ Eddie Jones 2.00 5.00
PPGP Gary Payton 2.50 6.00
PPJK Jason Kidd 4.00 10.00
PPJP James Posey 1.50 4.00
PPMB Mike Bibby 2.50 6.00
PPMC Mateen Cleaves 1.50 4.00
PPMD Michael Dickerson 1.50 4.00
PPMO Michael Olowokandi 1.50 4.00
PPRD Ricky Davis 2.00 5.00
PPRH Richard Hamilton 2.00 5.00
PPSJ Stephen Jackson 2.00 5.00
PPSO Shaquille O'Neal 6.00 15.00
PPTD Tim Duncan 5.00 12.00
PPTM Todd MacCulloch 1.50 4.00
PPTP Terry Porter 1.50 4.00

2001-02 Topps Pristine Premier

Seeded in packs at the rate of one in six, this 14-card set features dark backgrounds with player photos on the left, the words Pristine Premier along the bottom, and a star-shaped swatch of a jersey worn in these player's first All-Star game appearances.

STATED ODDS 1:6
PRAD Antonio Davis 2.50 6.00
PRAH Allan Houston 3.00 8.00
PRAI Allen Iverson 8.00 20.00
PRAM Anthony Mason 2.50 6.00
PRAKM Antonio McDyess 3.00 8.00
PRDD Dale Davis 2.50 6.00
PRGR Glenn Robinson 3.00 8.00
PRJS Jerry Stackhouse 3.00 8.00
PRMF Michael Finley 4.00 10.00
PRRA Ray Allen 4.00 10.00
PRRW Rasheed Wallace 4.00 10.00
PRSM Stephon Marbury 3.00 8.00
PRTM Tracy McGrady 6.00 15.00
PRVD Vlade Divac 3.00 8.00

2001-02 Topps Pristine Slice of a Star

Randomly inserted in packs at the rate of one in three, this 18-card set features full color player photos on the left, the words "Slice of a Star" along the top in blue, and a diamond shaped swatch of a game worn relic on the right.

STATED ODDS 1:3
SAI Allen Iverson 6.00 15.00
SAM Alonzo Mourning 4.00 10.00
SBS Bob Sura 2.00 5.00
SCW Chris Webber 3.00 8.00
SDR David Robinson 5.00 12.00
SEJ Eddie Jones 2.50 6.00
SGH Grant Hill 4.00 10.00
SGP Gary Payton 3.00 8.00
SJDS Jerry Stackhouse 2.50 6.00
SJS John Stockton 4.00 10.00
SLH Larry Hughes 2.50 6.00
SLO Lamar Odom 2.50 6.00
SMF Michael Finley 3.00 8.00
SRA Ray Allen 3.00 8.00
SRM Reggie Miller 4.00 10.00
SSO Shaquille O'Neal 8.00 20.00
STD Tim Duncan 6.00 15.00
STP Terry Porter 2.00 5.00

2001-02 Topps Pristine Sweat and Tears

Randomly inserted in packs at the rate of one in eight, this 50-card set features full color player action photos on the right side, colorful backgrounds, and a swatch of a playoff game-used towel which is cut in the shape of the letter S.

STATED ODDS 1:8
CHBD Baron Davis 6.00 15.00
CHDC Derrick Coleman 5.00 12.00
CHDW David Wesley 4.00 10.00
CHEC Elden Campbell 4.00 10.00
CHER Eddie Robinson 4.00 10.00
CHJM Jamal Mashburn 5.00 12.00
CHJDM Jamaal Magloire 4.00 10.00
CHPB P.J. Brown 4.00 10.00
DMCB Calvin Booth 4.00 10.00
DMDN Dirk Nowitzki 10.00 25.00
DMHE Howard Eisley 4.00 10.00
DMJH Juwan Howard 5.00 12.00
DMMF Michael Finley 6.00 15.00
DMSB Shawn Bradley 4.00 10.00
DMSN Steve Nash 10.00 25.00
DMWZ Wang Zhizhi 12.00 30.00
IPAC Austin Croshere 4.00 10.00
IPAH Al Harrington 5.00 12.00
IPJB Jonathan Bender 4.00 10.00
IPJO Jermaine O'Neal 5.00 12.00
IPJR Jalen Rose 5.00 12.00
IPRM Reggie Miller 6.00 15.00
IPTB Travis Best 4.00 10.00
MBEJ Ervin Johnson 4.00 10.00
MBGR Glenn Robinson 5.00 12.00
MBJP Joel Przybilla 4.00 10.00
MBRA Ray Allen 15.00 40.00
MBSC Sam Cassell 5.00 12.00
MBTT Tim Thomas 4.00 10.00
OMAD Andrew DeClercq 4.00 10.00
OMBO Bo Outlaw 4.00 10.00
OMDA Darrell Armstrong 4.00 10.00
OMMM Mike Miller 5.00 12.00
OMPG Pat Garrity 4.00 10.00
OMTM Tracy McGrady 10.00 25.00
PSCR Clifford Robinson 4.00 10.00
PSDS Daniel Santiago 4.00 10.00
PSIT Iakovos Tsakalidis 4.00 10.00
PSJK Jason Kidd 10.00 25.00
PSRR Rodney Rogers 4.00 10.00
PSSM Shawn Marion 5.00 12.00
PSTD Tony Delk 4.00 10.00
PSTG Tom Gugliotta 4.00 10.00
SSAD Antonio Daniels 4.00 10.00
SSAJ Avery Johnson 5.00 12.00
SSDA Derek Anderson 4.00 10.00
SSDR David Robinson 20.00 50.00
SSSE Sean Elliott 6.00 15.00
SSTD Tim Duncan 20.00 50.00
SSTP Terry Porter 4.00 10.00

2001-02 Topps Pristine Team Topps Captain Oversized

Inserted one card per case this is a four by six inch card with a game-used piece of memorabilia.

STATED ODDS: ONE PER CASE
CLSO Shaquille O'Neal 12.00 30.00
CLTD Tim Duncan 10.00 25.00

2002-03 Topps Pristine

Released in January 2003, Topps Pristine followed in the footsteps of last year's set by once again utilizing the pack-in-a-pack-in-a-pack set up. Each pack conatined the following: Pack #1-one uncirculated refractor or relic refractor encased in plastic with a hologram seal on the end to prevent tampering. Pack #2-one game-used relic card. Pack #3-four veterans, two rookies and randomly inserted autograph cards. Veteran cards comprise the first 50 cards in the set. Rookie players appear on cards 51-125. Three versions of each rookie player were issued, the Common version, which is the actual RC card, an Uncommon version sequentially numbered to 1499 and a Rare version sequentially numbered to 499. Pristine was packaged where each box contained five tri-packs and the packs carried a suggested retail price of $30. Note that an Amare Stoudemire error card was discovered. This card appears to be the same as his base Common RC card but on the back contains the words, "Gold Refractor." It is unknown how many error versions were released, but initial reports place it as a low number.

COMP.SET w/o SP's (50) 20.00 50.00
UNCOMMON RC PRINT RUN 1499 SER.#'d SETS
RARE RC PRINT RUN 499 SER.#'d SETS
1 Shaquille O'Neal 1.50 4.00
2 Steve Nash .75 2.00
3 Vince Carter 1.00 2.50
4 Michael Jordan 5.00 12.00
5 Chris Webber .60 1.50
6 Tim Duncan 1.25 3.00
7 Vladimir Radmanovic .40 1.00
8 Kobe Bryant 2.50 6.00
9 Allan Houston .50 1.25
10 Tracy McGrady 1.00 2.50
11 Allen Iverson 1.00 2.50
12 Scottie Pippen 1.00 2.50
13 Steve Francis .50 1.25
14 Reggie Miller .60 1.50
15 Antoine Walker .50 1.25
16 Shawn Marion .50 1.25
17 Wally Szczerbiak .50 1.25
18 Elton Brand .60 1.50
19 Jerry Stackhouse .50 1.25
20 Andre Miller .50 1.25
21 Gary Payton .60 1.50
22 Richard Hamilton .50 1.25
23 Pau Gasol .75 2.00
24 Juwan Howard .50 1.25
25 Jalen Rose .50 1.25
26 Eddie Jones .50 1.25
27 Baron Davis .50 1.25
28 Darrell Armstrong .40 1.00
29 John Stockton .75 2.00
30 Mike Bibby .60 1.50
31 Eddy Curry .40 1.00
32 Kevin Garnett 1.00 2.50
33 Dikembe Mutombo .60 1.50
34 Jason Kidd 1.00 2.50
35 Clifford Robinson .40 1.00
36 Ray Allen .60 1.50
37 Paul Pierce .60 1.50
38 Shane Battier .60 1.50
39 Kenyon Martin .50 1.25
40 Rasheed Wallace .60 1.50
41 Latrell Sprewell .60 1.50
42 Cuttino Mobley .40 1.00
43 Karl Malone .75 2.00
44 Dirk Nowitzki 1.00 2.50
45 Antawn Jamison .60 1.50
46 Elden Campbell .40 1.00
47 Lamar Odom .50 1.25
48 Jason Richardson .50 1.25
49 Jermaine O'Neal .50 1.25
50 Shareef Abdur-Rahim .50 1.25
51 Yao Ming C RC 3.00 8.00
52 Yao Ming U 4.00 10.00
53 Yao Ming R 8.00 20.00
54 Jay Williams C RC 1.50 4.00
55 Jay Williams U 2.00 5.00
56 Jay Williams R 4.00 10.00
57 Mike Dunleavy C RC 1.50 4.00
58 Mike Dunleavy U 2.00 5.00
59 Mike Dunleavy R 4.00 10.00
60 Drew Gooden C RC 1.50 4.00
61 Drew Gooden U 2.00 5.00
62 Drew Gooden R 4.00 10.00
63 Nikoloz Tskitishvili C RC 1.00 2.50
64 Nikoloz Tskitishvili U 1.25 3.00
65 Nikoloz Tskitishvili R 2.50 6.00
66 DaJuan Wagner C RC 1.25 3.00
67 DaJuan Wagner U 1.50 4.00
68 DaJuan Wagner R 3.00 8.00
69 Nene Hilario C RC 1.50 4.00
70 Nene Hilario U 2.00 5.00
71 Nene Hilario R 4.00 10.00
72 Chris Wilcox C RC 1.25 3.00
73 Chris Wilcox U 1.50 4.00
74 Chris Wilcox R 3.00 8.00
75 Amare Stoudemire C RC 2.00 5.00
75A A.Stoudemire G.Ref ERR
76 Amare Stoudemire U 2.50 6.00
77 Amare Stoudemire R 5.00 12.00
78 Caron Butler C RC 1.50 4.00
79 Caron Butler U 2.00 5.00
80 Caron Butler R 4.00 10.00
81 Jared Jeffries C RC 1.25 3.00
82 Jared Jeffries U 1.50 4.00
83 Jared Jeffries R 3.00 8.00
84 Melvin Ely C RC 1.25 3.00
85 Melvin Ely U 1.50 4.00
86 Melvin Ely R 3.00 8.00
87 Marcus Haislip C RC 1.25 3.00
88 Marcus Haislip U 1.50 4.00
89 Marcus Haislip R 3.00 8.00
90 Fred Jones C RC 1.25 3.00
91 Fred Jones U 1.50 4.00
92 Fred Jones R 3.00 8.00
93 Casey Jacobsen C RC 1.25 3.00
94 Casey Jacobsen U 1.50 4.00
95 Casey Jacobsen R 3.00 8.00
96 John Salmons C RC 1.50 4.00
97 John Salmons U 2.00 5.00
98 John Salmons R 4.00 10.00
99 Juan Dixon C RC 1.50 4.00
100 Juan Dixon U 2.00 5.00
101 Juan Dixon R 4.00 10.00
102 Chris Jefferies C RC 1.00 2.50
103 Chris Jefferies U 1.25 3.00
104 Chris Jefferies R 2.50 6.00
105 Ryan Humphrey C RC 1.25 3.00
106 Ryan Humphrey U 1.50 4.00
107 Ryan Humphrey R 3.00 8.00
108 Kareem Rush C RC 1.25 3.00
109 Kareem Rush U 1.50 4.00
110 Kareem Rush R 3.00 8.00
111 Qyntel Woods C RC 1.25 3.00
112 Qyntel Woods U 1.50 4.00
113 Qyntel Woods R 3.00 8.00
114 Frank Williams C RC 1.00 2.50
115 Frank Williams U 1.25 3.00
116 Frank Williams R 2.50 6.00
117 Tayshaun Prince C RC 2.00 5.00
118 Tayshaun Prince U 2.50 6.00
119 Tayshaun Prince R 5.00 12.00
120 Carlos Boozer C RC 1.50 4.00
121 Carlos Boozer U 2.00 5.00
122 Carlos Boozer R 4.00 10.00
123 Dan Dickau C RC 1.25 3.00
124 Dan Dickau U 1.50 4.00
125 Dan Dickau R 3.00 8.00

2002-03 Topps Pristine Refractors

*STARS: 10X TO 25X BASE CARD HI
1-50 PRINT RUN 50 SERIAL #'d SETS
*RC's/1899: 1X TO 2X BASE RC C VER. HI
*RC's/499: 1.25X TO 3X BASE RC C VER. HI
*RC's/99: 2.5X TO 6X BASE RC C VER. HI
4 Michael Jordan 200.00 400.00
8 Kobe Bryant 150.00 300.00

2002-03 Topps Pristine Refractors Gold

*STARS: 5X TO 12X BASE CARD HI
*C RCs: 2.5X TO 6X BASE CARD HI
*U RCs: 2X TO 5X BASE CARD HI
*R RCs: 1X TO 2.5X BASE CARD HI
PRINT RUN 99 SERIAL #'d SETS
GOLD REFRACTORS ARE DIE-CUTS
AVAIL. AS HOBBY EXCLUSIVE BOX LOADER
1 Shaquille O'Neal 25.00 60.00
3 Vince Carter 15.00 40.00
4 Michael Jordan 125.00 300.00
8 Kobe Bryant 75.00 200.00

2002-03 Topps Pristine Personal Endorsements

Randomly inserted into pack #3, this 235-card set showcases a horizontal design with player photos on the left, a gray-scale portrait photo in the upper right-hand corner and a white-out background in the lower right-hand corner for player autographs. Each card is stamped with the "Topps Certified Autograph Issue" foil.

STATED ODDS ONE PER BOX
INSERTED INTO #3 PACKS
PEBJ Bobby Jackson 4.00 10.00
PEBN Bostjan Nachbar 3.00 8.00
PECJ Chris Jefferies 2.50 6.00
PECM Corey Maggette 4.00 10.00
PECW Chris Wilcox 3.00 8.00
PEDD Dan Dickau 3.00 8.00
PEDG Drew Gooden 4.00 10.00
PEDW DaJuan Wagner 3.00 8.00
PEFJ Fred Jones 3.00 8.00
PEFW Frank Williams 2.50 6.00
PEGA Gilbert Arenas 10.00 25.00
PEGW Gerald Wallace 6.00 15.00
PEJF Joseph Forte 4.00 10.00
PEJJ Joe Johnson 5.00 12.00
PEKB Kwame Brown 5.00 12.00
PEKD Keyon Dooling 4.00 10.00
PEKR Kareem Rush 3.00 8.00
PELP Lavor Postell 4.00 10.00
PELW Loren Woods 4.00 10.00
PEMD Mike Dunleavy 4.00 10.00
PEME Melvin Ely 3.00 8.00
PERJ Richard Jefferson 6.00 15.00
PESO Shaquille O'Neal 40.00 100.00
PETP Tayshaun Prince 5.00 12.00
PEYM Yao Ming 30.00 60.00

2002-03 Topps Pristine Popular Demand

Randomly inserted in pack #2, this 18-card set is designed horizontally and on a blue and green foil background. Full color player photos are set on the right and a swatch of game worn memorabilia appears on the left. A Refractor version encased in the Topps Uncirculated slab was inserted into #1 packs and cards are sequentially numbered to 25.

RANDOMLY INSERTED INTO #2 PACKS
*REF: 1.5X TO 4X HI
REFRACTOR PRINT RUN 25 SER.#'d SETS
PDAI Allen Iverson 5.00 12.00
PDBD Baron Davis 2.50 6.00
PDCW Chris Webber 3.00 8.00

PDDM Darius Miles 2.00 5.00
PDDN Dirk Nowitzki 5.00 12.00
PDDR David Robinson 5.00 12.00
PDJK Jason Kidd 5.00 12.00
PDJO Jermaine O'Neal 2.50 6.00
PDKA Kareem Abdul Jabbar 10.00 25.00
PDKG Kevin Garnett 5.00 12.00
PDKM Karl Malone 4.00 10.00
PDMB Mike Bibby 3.00 8.00
PDRA Ray Allen 3.00 8.00
PDSF Steve Francis 2.50 6.00
PDSM Shawn Marion 2.50 6.00
PDSO Shaquille O'Neal 8.00 20.00
PDTD Tim Duncan 6.00 15.00
PDTM Tracy McGrady 5.00 12.00

2002-03 Topps Pristine Patches

Randomly inserted in pack #2, this 19-card set places full-color player action photos on the left side with the background set to look like a quilt on the right side. A hexagonal swatch of a uniform patch appears on the right.

RANDOMLY INSERTED INTO #2 PACKS
PPAAI Allen Iverson 20.00 50.00
PPADM Darius Miles 8.00 20.00
PPAJO Jermaine O'Neal 10.00 25.00
PPAJR Jason Richardson 12.00 30.00
PPAKM Kenyon Martin 10.00 25.00
PPAMD Mike Dunleavy 12.00 30.00
PPAMM Mike Miller 10.00 25.00
PPAPG Pau Gasol 12.00 30.00
PPAPS Peja Stojakovic 20.00 50.00
PPAPS Predrag Savovic 10.00 25.00
PPAQR Quentin Richardson 10.00 25.00
PPARA Ray Allen 12.00 30.00
PPASB Shane Battier 12.00 30.00
PPASN Steve Nash 15.00 40.00
PPASO Shaquille O'Neal 30.00 80.00
PPASS Steve Smith 10.00 25.00
PPATD Tim Duncan 25.00 60.00

2002-03 Topps Pristine Performance

Randomly seeded in #2 packs, this 14-card set places player action photos to the right of a swatch of game-worn memorabilia. The memorabilia is set and centered on a printed basketball. A Refractor version encased in the Topps Uncirculated slab was inserted into #1 packs and cards are sequentially numbered to 25.

RANDOMLY INSERTED INTO #2 PACKS
*REF: 1.5X TO 4X HI
REFRACTOR PRINT RUN 25 SER.#'d SETS
PPEAW Antoine Walker 2.50 6.00
PPEBD Baron Davis 2.50 6.00
PPEBH Brendan Haywood 2.00 5.00
PPECM Cuttino Mobley 2.00 5.00
PPEEN Eduardo Najera 2.00 5.00
PPEGA Gilbert Arenas 3.00 8.00
PPEJM Jamal Mashburn 2.50 6.00
PPEKM Kenyon Martin 2.50 6.00
PPELN Lee Nailon 2.00 5.00
PPENV Nick Van Exel 2.50 6.00
PPEQR Quentin Richardson 2.50 6.00
PPESM Stephon Marbury 2.50 6.00
PPESO Shaquille O'Neal 8.00 20.00
PPETD Tim Duncan 6.00 15.00

2002-03 Topps Pristine Portions

Inserted randomly in #2 packs, this 21-card set utilizes a horizontal design with a centered swatch of game-used memorabilia. The words Pristine and Portions run from the upper left corner down to the lower right and connect in the center around the memorabilia swatch. The backgrounds on these cards are silver, blue and green, and a full-color player action shot is set on the right. A Refractor version encased in the Topps Uncirculated slab was inserted into #1 packs and cards are sequentially numbered to 25.

RANDOMLY INSERTED INTO #2 PACKS
*REF: 1.5X TO 4X HI
REFRACTOR PRINT RUN 25 SER.#'d SETS
PPOAH Allan Houston 2.50 6.00
PPOCM Cuttino Mobley 2.00 5.00
PPOCW Chris Webber 3.00 8.00
PPODG Devean George 2.00 5.00
PPODJ DerMarr Johnson 2.00 5.00
PPOGR Glenn Robinson 2.50 6.00
PPOJO Jermaine O'Neal 2.50 6.00
PPOJT Jason Terry 2.50 6.00
PPOKM Kenyon Martin 2.50 6.00
PPOLO Lamar Odom 2.50 6.00
PPOMM Mike Miller 2.50 6.00
PPOMO Michael Olowokandi 2.00 5.00
PPOPS Peja Stojakovic 3.00 8.00
PPORL Raef LaFrentz 2.00 5.00
PPOSB Shawn Bradley 2.00 5.00
PPOSM Shawn Marion 2.50 6.00
PPOSS Steve Smith 2.50 6.00
PPOTD Tim Duncan 6.00 15.00
PPOTG Tom Gugliotta 2.00 5.00
PPOVD Vlade Divac 2.50 6.00
PPOAHA Anfernee Hardaway 5.00 12.00

2002-03 Topps Pristine Rookie Club

Randomly seeded in #2 packs, this 11-card set features a horizontal design with the new rookie player set to a background that features his team's logo and a swatch of memorabilia. A Refractor version encased in the Topps Uncirculated slab was inserted into #1 packs and cards are sequentially numbered to 25.

RANDOMLY INSERTED INTO #2 PACKS
*REF: 1.25X TO 3X HI
REFRACTOR PRINT RUN 25 SER.#'d SETS
RCAS Amare Stoudemire 3.00 8.00
RCCB Caron Butler 2.50 6.00
RCCW Chris Wilcox 2.00 5.00
RCDG Drew Gooden 2.50 6.00
RCDW DaJuan Wagner 2.00 5.00
RCFJ Fred Jones 2.00 5.00
RCKR Kareem Rush 2.00 5.00
RCMD Mike Dunleavy 2.50 6.00
RCME Melvin Ely 2.00 5.00
RCPS Predrag Savovic 2.00 5.00
RCYM Yao Ming 5.00 12.00

2003-04 Topps Pristine

Released in December 2003, Pristine boasts a 199-card set divided up into 100 veteran player cards and 99 rookie player cards. The cards alternate where each player has three cards in a row and the first card is the common, also the rookie card, the second is uncommon sequentially numbered to 999 and the third is rare and sequentially numbered to 499. Pristine was packaged five packs per box where each pack contained three individual packs and cards were inserted as follows: Pack one (the outermost pack) contains one uncirculated Refractor, Relic Refractor or Gold Autograph sealed in a holder. Pack two contains one relic card plus pack three. Pack three contains four Topps Pristine veteran cards plus two Rookie cards. In the event that an autographed card is present in the third pack, it replaces one of the veteran cards. Also, a box-topper pack was inserted and those contain one mini card. Pristine packs (the large one containing the three small packs) carried a suggested retail price of $30.

COMP.SET w/o RC's (100) 25.00 60.00
RARE RC PRINT RUN 499 SER.#'d SETS
FOUR (1-100) CARDS IN PACK #3
TWO (101-199) CARDS IN PACK #3
1 Tracy McGrady .60 1.50
2 DaJuan Wagner .30 .75
3 Allen Iverson .75 2.00
4 Chris Webber .50 1.25
5 Jason Kidd .75 2.00
6 Eddie Jones .40 1.00
7 Jermaine O'Neal .40 1.00
8 Kobe Bryant 2.00 5.00
9 Tony Parker .50 1.25
10 Wally Szczerbiak .40 1.00
11 Yao Ming 1.00 2.50
12 Amare Stoudemire .60 1.50
13 Steve Nash .60 1.50
14 Baron Davis .40 1.00
15 Vince Carter .75 2.00
16 Peja Stojakovic .50 1.25
17 Desmond Mason .40 1.00
18 Antoine Walker .50 1.25
19 Steve Francis .40 1.00
20 Gary Payton .50 1.25
21 Tim Duncan .75 2.00
22 Jalen Rose .40 1.00
23 Jason Richardson .50 1.25
24 Andre Miller .40 1.00
25 Allan Houston .40 1.00
26 Ron Artest .50 1.25
27 Andrei Kirilenko .50 1.25
28 Kenyon Martin .40 1.00
29 Kevin Garnett .75 2.00
30 Rasheed Wallace .50 1.25
31 Shawn Marion .40 1.00
32 Karl Malone .60 1.50
33 Antawn Jamison .40 1.00
34 Shaquille O'Neal 1.25 3.00
35 Paul Pierce .50 1.25
36 Nene .40 1.00
37 Ray Allen .50 1.25
38 Bonzi Wells .30 .75
39 Ben Wallace .40 1.00
40 Jerry Stackhouse .40 1.00
41 Dirk Nowitzki .75 2.00
42 Elton Brand .50 1.25
43 Pau Gasol .50 1.25
44 Richard Hamilton .40 1.00
45 Shareef Abdur-Rahim .40 1.00
46 Jason Terry .40 1.00
47 Jamal Mashburn .40 1.00
48 Latrell Sprewell .40 1.00
49 Keith Van Horn .40 1.00
50 Mike Miller .40 1.00
51 Theo Ratliff .30 .75
52 Scottie Pippen .75 2.00
53 Nick Van Exel .40 1.00
54 Chauncey Billups .50 1.25
55 Al Harrington .40 1.00
56 Corey Maggette .40 1.00
57 Shane Battier .40 1.00
58 Tim Thomas .30 .75
59 Darius Miles .30 .75
60 Alonzo Mourning .60 1.50
61 Jamaal Magloire .30 .75
62 Antonio McDyess .40 1.00
63 Juwan Howard .40 1.00
64 Eric Snow .30 .75
65 Anfernee Hardaway .75 2.00
66 Tayshaun Prince .40 1.00
67 Derek Anderson .30 .75
68 Mike Bibby .50 1.25
69 Deshawn Stevenson .30 .75
70 Kwame Brown .30 .75
71 Jerome Williams .30 .75
72 Radoslav Nesterovic .30 .75
73 Stephon Marbury .40 1.00
74 P.J. Brown .30 .75
75 Sam Cassell .40 1.00
76 Kenny Thomas .30 .75
77 Jason Williams .40 1.00
78 Jamaal Tinsley .30 .75
79 Nikoloz Tskitishvili .30 .75
80 Michael Finley .50 1.25
81 Jamal Crawford .50 1.25
82 Brent Barry .30 .75
83 Gilbert Arenas .40 1.00
84 Morris Peterson .30 .75
85 Manu Ginobili .60 1.50
86 Dale Davis .30 .75
87 Aaron McKie .30 .75
88 Richard Jefferson .40 1.00
89 Michael Redd .50 1.25
90 Reggie Miller .50 1.25
91 Cuttino Mobley .30 .75
92 Marcus Camby .40 1.00
93 Tony Delk .30 .75
94 Tyson Chandler .40 1.00
95 Caron Butler .40 1.00
96 Kurt Thomas .30 .75
97 Glenn Robinson .40 1.00
98 Brad Miller .40 1.00
99 Matt Harpring .30 .75
100 Alvin Williams .30 .75
101 LeBron James C RC 40.00 100.00
102 LeBron James U 50.00 120.00
103 LeBron James R 60.00 150.00
104 Darko Milicic C RC 1.50 4.00
105 Darko Milicic U 2.00 5.00
106 Darko Milicic R 2.50 6.00
107 Carmelo Anthony C RC 6.00 15.00
108 Carmelo Anthony U 8.00 20.00
109 Carmelo Anthony R 10.00 25.00
110 Chris Bosh C RC 3.00 8.00
111 Chris Bosh U 4.00 10.00
112 Chris Bosh R 5.00 12.00
113 Dwyane Wade C RC 6.00 15.00
114 Dwyane Wade U 8.00 20.00
115 Dwyane Wade R 10.00 25.00
116 Chris Kaman C RC 2.00 5.00
117 Chris Kaman U 2.50 6.00
118 Chris Kaman R 3.00 8.00
119 Kirk Hinrich C RC 2.00 5.00
120 Kirk Hinrich U 2.50 6.00
121 Kirk Hinrich R 3.00 8.00
122 T.J. Ford C RC 1.50 4.00
123 T.J. Ford U 2.00 5.00
124 T.J. Ford R 2.50 6.00
125 Mike Sweetney C RC 1.25 3.00
126 Mike Sweetney U 1.50 4.00
127 Mike Sweetney R 2.00 5.00
128 Jarvis Hayes C RC 1.25 3.00
129 Jarvis Hayes U 1.50 4.00
130 Jarvis Hayes R 2.00 5.00
131 Mickael Pietrus C RC 1.50 4.00
132 Mickael Pietrus U 2.00 5.00
133 Mickael Pietrus R 2.50 6.00
134 Nick Collison C RC 1.50 4.00
135 Nick Collison U 2.00 5.00
136 Nick Collison R 2.50 6.00
137 Marcus Banks C RC 1.25 3.00
138 Marcus Banks U 1.50 4.00
139 Marcus Banks R 2.00 5.00
140 Luke Ridnour C RC 1.50 4.00
141 Luke Ridnour U 2.00 5.00
142 Luke Ridnour R 2.50 6.00
143 Reece Gaines C RC 1.25 3.00
144 Reece Gaines U 1.50 4.00
145 Reece Gaines R 2.00 5.00
146 Troy Bell C RC 1.25 3.00
147 Troy Bell U 1.50 4.00
148 Troy Bell R 2.00 5.00
149 Zarko Cabarkapa C RC 1.25 3.00
150 Zarko Cabarkapa U 1.50 4.00
151 Zarko Cabarkapa R 2.00 5.00
152 David West C RC 2.00 5.00
153 David West U 2.50 6.00
154 David West R 3.00 8.00
155 Aleksandar Pavlovic C RC 1.50 4.00
156 Aleksandar Pavlovic U 2.00 5.00
157 Aleksandar Pavlovic R 2.50 6.00
158 Dahntay Jones C RC 1.50 4.00
159 Dahntay Jones U 2.00 5.00
160 Dahntay Jones R 2.50 6.00
161 Boris Diaw C RC 2.00 5.00
162 Boris Diaw U 2.50 6.00
163 Boris Diaw R 3.00 8.00
164 Zoran Planinic C RC 1.25 3.00
165 Zoran Planinic U 1.50 4.00
166 Zoran Planinic R 2.00 5.00
167 Travis Outlaw C RC 1.50 4.00
168 Travis Outlaw U 2.00 5.00
169 Travis Outlaw R 2.50 6.00
170 Brian Cook C RC 1.25 3.00
171 Brian Cook U 1.50 4.00
172 Brian Cook R 2.00 5.00
173 Travis Hansen C RC 1.25 3.00
174 Travis Hansen U 1.50 4.00
175 Travis Hansen R 2.00 5.00
176 Ndudi Ebi C RC 1.25 3.00
177 Ndudi Ebi U 1.50 4.00
178 Ndudi Ebi R 2.00 5.00
179 Kendrick Perkins C RC 1.50 4.00
180 Kendrick Perkins U 2.00 5.00
181 Kendrick Perkins R 2.50 6.00
182 Leandro Barbosa C RC 2.00 5.00
183 Leandro Barbosa U 2.50 6.00
184 Leandro Barbosa R 3.00 8.00
185 Josh Howard C RC 2.00 5.00
186 Josh Howard U 2.50 6.00
187 Josh Howard R 3.00 8.00
188 Maciej Lampe C RC 1.25 3.00
189 Maciej Lampe U 1.50 4.00
190 Maciej Lampe R 2.00 5.00
191 Jason Kapono C RC 1.25 3.00
192 Jason Kapono U 1.50 4.00
193 Jason Kapono R 2.00 5.00
194 Luke Walton C RC 2.00 5.00
195 Luke Walton U 2.50 6.00
196 Luke Walton R 3.00 8.00
197 Jerome Beasley C RC 1.25 3.00
198 Jerome Beasley U 1.50 4.00
199 Jerome Beasley R 2.00 5.00

2003-04 Topps Pristine Refractors

*1-100 STARS: 3X TO 8X BASE HI
1-100 PRINT RUN 149 SER.#'d SETS
*RC's/1999: .75X TO 2X BASE RC C VER.HI
*RC's/499: 1X TO 2.5X BASE RC U VER.HI
*RC's/149: 1X TO 2.5X BASE RC R VER.HI
ALL CARDS ARE ENCASED
RANDOMLY INSERTED IN #1 PACKS
8 Kobe Bryant 40.00 100.00

2003-04 Topps Pristine Refractors Gold

*1-100 STARS: 4X TO 10X BASE HI
*RC C VER: 2X TO 5X RC C VER.BASE
*RC U VER: 1.5X TO 4X RC U VER.BASE
*RC R VER:1.25X TO 3X RC R VER.BASE
GOLD PRINT RUN 99 SER.#'d SETS
RANDOM INSERTS IN PACK #1
8 Kobe Bryant 50.00 120.00
101 LeBron James C 250.00 500.00
102 LeBron James U 400.00 800.00
103 LeBron James R 300.00 600.00
113 Dwyane Wade C 50.00 120.00
114 Dwyane Wade U 50.00 120.00
115 Dwyane Wade R 50.00 120.00

2003-04 Topps Pristine Borders Relics

Randomly seeded in packs at the following rates in pack #2: Group A one in 4433, Group B one in 41 and no odds given for group E. The cards are horizontally designed and focus on foreign players. Each card has a swatch of memorabilia and the player's home country flag. A sealed refractor parallel was also produced and these cards are sequentially numbered to 25 and were randomly inserted in #1 packs.

STATED ODDS: GROUP A 1:4433
GROUP B 1:41, NO ODDS FOR GROUP E
RANDOM INSERTS IN PACK #2
*REFRACTORS: 1.25X TO 3X BASE HI
REFRACTOR PRINT RUN 25 SER.#'d SETS
REFRACTORS INSERTED IN #1 PACKS
AK Andrei Kirilenko E 3.00 8.00
DN Dirk Nowitzki E 5.00 12.00
EG Manu Ginobili B 4.00 10.00
NH Nene E 2.50 6.00
PG Pau Gasol E 3.00 8.00
PS Peja Stojakovic 3.00 8.00
TD Tim Duncan E 5.00 12.00
TP Tony Parker E 3.00 8.00
YM Yao Ming B 6.00 15.00
ZI Zydrunas Ilgauskas E 2.50 6.00

2003-04 Topps Pristine Challenge Relics

Inserted in packs #2 for Group C at one in 51 and no odds given for Group E, this 14-card set places a circular swatch of memorabilia in the lower right-hand corner. A sealed refractor parallel was also produced and these cards are sequentially numbered to 25 and were randomly inserted in #1 packs.

STATED ODDS: GROUP C 1:51
NO ODDS GIVEN FOR GROUP E
RANDOM INSERTS IN PACK #2
*REFRACTORS: 1.25X TO 3X BASE HI
REFRACTOR PRINT RUN 25 SER.#'d SETS
REFRACTORS INSERTED IN #1 PACKS
AK Andrei Kirilenko E 3.00 8.00
AS Amare Stoudemire E 4.00 10.00
CB Carlos Boozer E 2.50 6.00
DG Drew Gooden E 2.50 6.00
DW Dajuan Wagner E 2.00 5.00
GA Gilbert Arenas E 2.50 6.00
JR Jason Richardson C 3.00 8.00
JT Jamaal Tinsley E 2.00 5.00
MJ Marko Jaric E 2.00 5.00
RJ Richard Jefferson E 2.50 6.00
TC Tyson Chandler E 2.50 6.00
TM Troy Murphy E 2.00 5.00
TP Tony Parker E 3.00 8.00
CBU Caron Butler E 2.50 6.00

2003-04 Topps Pristine Factor Relics

Randomly inserted in pack #2 at the rates of one in 156 for Group B, one in 48 for Group D and no odds given for Group E, this 22-card set places a circular swatch of memorabilia in the lower right-hand corner. A sealed refractor parallel was also produced and these cards are sequentially numbered to 25 and were randomly inserted in #1 packs.

STATED ODDS: GROUP B 1:156
GROUP D 1:48, NO ODDS FOR GROUP E
RANDOM INSERTS IN #2 PACKS
*REFRACTORS: 1.25X TO 3X BASE HI
REFRACTOR PRINT RUN 25 SER.#'d SETS
REFRACTORS INSERTED IN #1 PACKS
AI Allen Iverson B 5.00 12.00
BD Baron Davis D 2.50 6.00
DA Darrell Armstrong E 2.00 5.00
DM Darius Miles E 2.00 5.00
EG Eddie Griffin E 2.00 5.00
JK Jason Kidd D 5.00 12.00
JS Jerry Stackhouse E 2.50 6.00
KM Karl Malone E 4.00 10.00
LO Lamar Odom E 2.50 6.00
LS Latrell Sprewell E 2.50 6.00
MB Mike Bibby E 3.00 8.00
MP Morris Peterson E 2.00 5.00
PP Paul Pierce E 3.00 8.00
RL Rashard Lewis E 3.00 8.00
RW Rasheed Wallace B 3.00 8.00
SC Sam Cassell E 2.50 6.00
SF Steve Francis E 2.50 6.00
SM Stephon Marbury D 2.50 6.00
SO Shaquille O'Neal E 6.00 15.00
DMU Dikembe Mutombo E 3.00 8.00

2003-04 Topps Pristine Gems Relics

Randomly inserted in #2 packs at the rates of one in 41 for Group B, one in 51 for Group C, no odds given for Group E, one in nine for Group F and one in three for Group G, this 34-card set is horizontally designed and places a diamond-shaped swatch of memorabilia on the right side of the card. A sealed refractor parallel was also produced and these cards are sequentially numbered to 25 and were randomly inserted in #1 packs.

STATED ODDS GROUP B 1:41
GROUP C 1:51, NO ODDS FOR GROUP E
GROUP F 1:9, GROUP G 1:3
RANDOM INSTERS IN #2 PACKS
*REFRACTORS: 1.25X TO 3X BASE HI
REFRACTOR PRINT RUN 25 SER.#'d SETS
REFRACTORS INSERTED IN #1 PACKS
AH Allan Houston G 2.50 6.00
BW Ben Wallace G 2.50 6.00
CM Cuttino Mobley G 2.00 5.00
DD Dan Dickau G 2.00 5.00
DF Derek Fisher G 2.50 6.00
DG Drew Gooden F 2.50 6.00
DW David Wesley F 2.00 5.00
EG Eddie Griffin G 2.00 5.00
GH Grant Hill B 4.00 10.00
JJ Jared Jeffries G 2.00 5.00
JK Jason Kidd G 5.00 12.00
JO Jermaine O'Neal G 2.50 6.00
JR Jason Richardson F 3.00 8.00
MB Mike Bibby C 3.00 8.00
MD Mike Dunleavy C 2.50 6.00
MF Michael Finley E 3.00 8.00
MJ Marko Jaric G 2.00 5.00
PG Pat Garrity F 2.00 5.00
PS Peja Stojakovic E 3.00 8.00
RA Ray Allen F 3.00 8.00
RJ Richard Jefferson F 2.50 6.00
SC Sam Cassell G 2.50 6.00
SF Steve Francis F 2.50 6.00
SM Shawn Marion G 2.50 6.00
SN Steve Nash F 4.00 10.00
SO Shaquille O'Neal E 8.00 20.00
TC Tyson Chandler G 2.50 6.00
TD Tim Duncan F 5.00 12.00
TM Tracy McGrady G 4.00 10.00
TP Tayshaun Prince F 2.50 6.00
YM Yao Ming F 6.00 15.00
CBU Caron Butler G 2.50 6.00
PGA Pau Gasol F 3.00 8.00

2003-04 Topps Pristine Generals Relics

Randomly inserted in #2 packs at the rates of one in 41 for Group B, one in 28 for Group C, and no odds given for Group E, this 20-card set has white borders, color photos and a swatch of memorabilia. A sealed refractor parallel was also produced and these cards are sequentially numbered to 25 and were randomly inserted in #1 packs.

STATED ODDS GROUP B 1:41
GROUP C 1:28, NO ODDS FOR GROUP E
RANDOM INSERTS IN PACK #2
*REFRACTORS: 1.25X TO 3X BASE HI
REFRACTOR PRINT RUN 25 SER.#'d SETS
REFRACTORS INSERTED IN #1 PACKS
AH Anfernee Hardaway B 5.00 12.00
AI Allen Iverson B 5.00 12.00
AM Anthony Mason B 2.00 5.00
AW Antoine Walker E 3.00 8.00
BW Ben Wallace E 2.50 6.00
CM Cuttino Mobley E 2.00 5.00
CW Chris Webber 3.00 8.00
DD Dan Dickau E 2.00 5.00
EG Manu Ginobili B 4.00 10.00
GP Gary Payton E 3.00 8.00
JK Jason Kidd C 5.00 12.00
JM Jamal Mashburn E 2.50 6.00
KM Kenyon Martin E 2.50 6.00
MD Mike Dunleavy E 2.50 6.00
MF Michael Finley E 3.00 8.00
RA Ray Allen E 3.00 8.00
SO Shaquille O'Neal E 8.00 20.00
TD Tim Duncan E 5.00 12.00
VR Vladimir Radmanovic E 2.00 5.00
WS Wally Szczerbiak E 2.50 6.00

2003-04 Topps Pristine Minis

Inserted as a box-topper in a pack at one per box, these mini-cards have a black border along the right and photos are full-color portraits.

SHAQ AU INSERTED IN HOBBY ONLY
RANDOM INSERTS IN #3 PACKS
PM1 Paul Pierce 1.50 4.00
PM2 Dirk Nowitzki 2.50 6.00
PM3 Yao Ming 3.00 8.00
PM4 Steve Francis 1.25 3.00
PM5 Kobe Bryant 6.00 15.00
PM6 Shaquille O'Neal 4.00 10.00
PM7 Gary Payton 1.50 4.00
PM8 Kevin Garnett 2.50 6.00
PM9 Jason Kidd 2.50 6.00
PM10 Tracy Mcgrady 2.00 5.00
PM11 Allen Iverson 2.50 6.00
PM12 Chris Webber 1.50 4.00
PM13 Tim Duncan 2.50 6.00
PM14 Ray Allen 1.50 4.00
PM15 Vince Carter 2.50 6.00
PM16 Antoine Walker 1.50 4.00
PM17 Jermaine O'Neal 1.25 3.00
PM18 Elton Brand 1.50 4.00
PM19 Baron Davis 1.25 3.00
PM20 Shawn Marion 1.25 3.00
PM21 LeBron James 15.00 40.00
PM22 Darko Milicic 1.25 3.00
PM23 Carmelo Anthony 5.00 12.00
PM24 Chris Bosh 2.50 6.00
PM25 Dwyane Wade 5.00 12.00
PM26 Chris Kaman 1.50 4.00
PM27 Kirk Hinrich 1.50 4.00
PM28 T.J. Ford 1.25 3.00
PM29 Mike Sweetney 1.00 2.50
PM30 Jarvis Hayes 1.00 2.50
PM31 Mickael Pietrus 1.25 3.00
PM32 Nick Collison 1.25 3.00
PM33 Marcus Banks 1.00 2.50
PM34 Luke Ridnour 1.25 3.00
PM35 Reece Gaines 1.00 2.50
PM36 Troy Bell 1.00 2.50
PM37 Zarko Cabarkapa 1.00 2.50
PM38 David West 1.50 4.00
PM39 Aleksandar Pavlovic 1.25 3.00
PM40 Dahntay Jones 1.25 3.00
SO S.O'Neal AU/100 50.00 100.00

2003-04 Topps Pristine Personal Endorsements

Randomly seeded in #3 packs at the rates of one in 36 for Group A, one in 156 for Group B, one in 28 for Group C, one in 48 for Group D and one in nine for Group E, this 37-card set places player autographs below a black and white photo. A gold version sequentially numbered to 25 and sealed in a holder was also available in #1 packs.

STATED ODDS: GROUP A 1:36
GROUP B 1:156, GROUP C 1:28
GROUP D 1:48, GROUP E 1:9
RANDOM INSERTS IN #3 PACKS
*GOLD: 1.25X TO 3X BASE HI
GOLD PRINT RUN 25 SER.#'d SETS
ALL GOLD AU's ENCASED
GOLDS INSERTED IN #1 PACKS
BB Bruce Bowen C 5.00 12.00
BC Brian Cook B 2.50 6.00
BW Boris Diaw A 4.00 10.00
CA Carmelo Anthony D 25.00 60.00
CB Chris Bosh C 8.00 20.00
DG Drew Gooden D 4.00 10.00
DJ Dahntay Jones D 3.00 8.00
EB Elton Brand C 4.00 10.00
JK Jason Kapono D 2.50 6.00
KB Keith Bogans A 4.00 10.00
KH Kirk Hinrich D 4.00 10.00
KJ Ken Johnson D 4.00 10.00
KP Kendrick Perkins A 3.00 8.00
LBO Leandro Barbosa A 4.00 10.00
LR Luke Ridnour C 3.00 8.00
LW Luke Walton D 4.00 10.00
ML Maciej Lampe A 2.50 6.00
MP Mickael Pietrus C 3.00 8.00
MR Malik Rose A 4.00 10.00
MS Mike Sweetney D 2.50 6.00
NC Nick Collison E 6.00 15.00
NE Nduai Ebi A 2.50 6.00
RG Reece Gaines C 2.50 6.00
SB Steve Blake A 3.00 8.00
SO Shaquille O'Neal C 40.00 100.00
TB Troy Bell D 2.50 6.00
TF T.J. Ford B 3.00 8.00
TH Travis Hansen D 2.50 6.00
TO Travis Outlaw D 3.00 8.00
ZC Zarko Cabarkapa A 2.50 6.00
ZP Zaur Pachulia A 4.00 10.00
DWA Dwyane Wade C 20.00 50.00
DWE David West A 4.00 10.00
JHA Jarvis Hayes A 2.50 6.00
JHO Josh Howard E 4.00 10.00
MBA Marcus Banks E 2.50 6.00
ZPL Zoran Planinic D 2.50 6.00

2003-04 Topps Pristine Recruit Relics

Randomly inserted in number two packs at the rate of one in three, this 25-card set is horizontally designed with a red, black and white background and a square swatch of memorabilia. A sealed refractor parallel was also produced and these cards are sequentially numbered to 25 and were randomly inserted in #1 packs.

STATED ODDS 1:3
RANDOM INSERTS IN PACK #2
*REFRACTORS: 1X TO 2.5X BASE HI
REFRACTOR PRINT RUN 25 SER.#'d SETS
REFRACTORS INSERTED IN #1 PACKS
BC Brian Cook 1.50 4.00
CA Carmelo Anthony 8.00 20.00
CB Chris Bosh 4.00 10.00
CK Chris Kaman 2.50 6.00
DJ Dahntay Jones 2.00 5.00
DW David West 2.50 6.00
JH Jarvis Hayes 1.50 4.00
KH Kirk Hinrich 2.50 6.00
KP Kendrick Perkins 2.00 5.00
LB Leandro Barbosa 2.50 6.00
LR Luke Ridnour 2.00 5.00
LW Luke Walton 2.50 6.00
MB Marcus Banks 1.50 4.00
MP Mickael Pietrus 2.00 5.00
MS Mike Sweetney 1.50 4.00
NC Nick Collison 2.00 5.00
NE Ndudi Ebi 1.50 4.00
RG Reece Gaines 1.50 4.00
SB Steve Blake 2.00 5.00
SV Slavko Vranes 1.50 4.00
TB Troy Bell 1.50 4.00
TF T.J. Ford 2.00 5.00
TH Travis Hansen 1.50 4.00
TO Travis Outlaw 2.00 5.00
DWY Dwyane Wade 8.00 20.00

2004-05 Topps Pristine

Released in December 2004, Topps Pristine features a 199-card set divided up into 100 veteran players and 33 rookie players who appear on three cards each. The first card, numberwise, each rookie appears on is the common version and is tagged as the rookie card. The second card, Uncommon, is sequentially numbered to 739 and the third card, Rare, is sequentially numbered to 239. Pristine was packaged in its usual triple pack format where the first pack contains an uncirculated refractor card, the second pack contains relic cards and the third pack contains four base veterans and two rookies. One pack per box will contain a bonus fourth pack that holds a mini card. Each box contains five packs and upon release, SRP was $30 per pack.

COMP.SET w/o SP's (100) 25.00 60.00
RARE RC PRINT RUN 239 SER.#'d SETS
ONE UNCIRCULATED CARD PER PACK #1
ONE RELIC CARD PER PACK #2
FOUR VETS AND TWO RC'S PER PACK #3
ONE PACK #4 INSERTED PER BOX
1 Ben Wallace .40 1.00
2 Michael Redd .40 1.00
3 Dwyane Wade .75 2.00
4 Chris Webber .50 1.25
5 Cuttino Mobley .30 .75
6 Bonzi Wells .30 .75
7 Rashard Lewis .50 1.25
8 Kobe Bryant 2.00 5.00
9 Gilbert Arenas .40 1.00
10 Jeff Foster .30 .75
11 Yao Ming 1.00 2.50
12 Ricky Davis .40 1.00
13 Glenn Robinson .40 1.00
14 Chauncey Billups .50 1.25
15 Carmelo Anthony 1.00 2.50
16 Pau Gasol .50 1.25
17 Erick Dampier .30 .75
18 Jason Terry .40 1.00
19 Corey Maggette .40 1.00
20 Zach Randolph .40 1.00
21 Kevin Garnett .75 2.00
22 Steve Nash .60 1.50
23 LeBron James 3.00 8.00
24 Andre Miller .40 1.00
25 Manu Ginobili .60 1.50
26 Gordan Giricek .30 .75
27 Juwan Howard .40 1.00
28 Brad Miller .40 1.00
29 Al Harrington .40 1.00
30 Allen Iverson .75 2.00
31 Shawn Marion .40 1.00
32 Elton Brand .50 1.25
33 Steve Francis .40 1.00
34 Shaquille O'Neal 1.25 3.00
35 Marcus Camby .40 1.00
36 Tyson Chandler .40 1.00
37 Dirk Nowitzki .75 2.00
38 Damon Stoudamire .40 1.00
39 Richard Hamilton .40 1.00
40 Kurt Thomas .30 .75
41 Paul Pierce .50 1.25
42 Jarvis Hayes .30 .75
43 Ray Allen .50 1.25
44 Keith Van Horn .40 1.00
45 Kirk Hinrich .40 1.00
46 Caron Butler .40 1.00
47 Andrei Kirilenko .40 1.00
48 Jamaal Magloire .30 .75
49 Chris Kaman .40 1.00
50 Stephon Marbury .40 1.00
51 Mike Miller .40 1.00
52 Eddy Curry .30 .75
53 Sam Cassell .40 1.00
54 Vince Carter .75 2.00
55 Jason Kidd .75 2.00
56 Desmond Mason .40 1.00
57 Nene .40 1.00
58 Gerald Wallace .40 1.00
59 Baron Davis .40 1.00
60 Tim Duncan .75 2.00
61 Drew Gooden .30 .75
62 Jason Williams .40 1.00
63 Eddie Jones .40 1.00
64 Michael Finley .50 1.25
65 Gary Payton .50 1.25
66 Kenyon Martin .40 1.00
67 Mike Bibby .50 1.25
68 Jason Kapono .30 .75
69 Allan Houston .40 1.00
70 Ron Artest .50 1.25
71 Rasho Nesterovic .30 .75
72 Kwame Brown .30 .75
73 Wally Szczerbiak .40 1.00
74 Joe Johnson .40 1.00
75 Jamal Mashburn .40 1.00
76 Peja Stojakovic .50 1.25
77 Lamar Odom .40 1.00
78 Jalen Rose .40 1.00
79 Mike Dunleavy .40 1.00
80 Rasheed Wallace .50 1.25
81 Richard Jefferson .40 1.00
82 Luke Ridnour .40 1.00
83 Samuel Dalembert .30 .75
84 Zydrunas Ilgauskas .40 1.00
85 Carlos Arroyo .30 .75
86 Primoz Brezec .30 .75
87 Chris Bosh .50 1.25
88 Antoine Walker .50 1.25
89 Boris Diaw .40 1.00
90 Tracy McGrady .60 1.50
91 Amare Stoudemire .40 1.00
92 Karl Malone .60 1.50
93 Jamal Crawford .50 1.25
94 Shareef Abdur-Rahim .40 1.00
95 Jason Richardson .50 1.25
96 Marcus Banks .30 .75
97 Jermaine O'Neal .40 1.00
98 Latrell Sprewell .40 1.00
99 Tony Parker .50 1.25
100 Carlos Boozer .40 1.00
101 Dwight Howard C RC 3.00 8.00
102 Dwight Howard U 5.00 12.00
103 Dwight Howard R 6.00 15.00
104 Ben Gordon C RC 1.50 4.00
105 Ben Gordon U 2.50 6.00
106 Ben Gordon R 3.00 8.00
107 Devin Harris C RC 1.25 3.00
108 Devin Harris U 2.00 5.00
109 Devin Harris R 2.50 6.00
110 Rafael Araujo C RC 1.00 2.50
111 Rafael Araujo U 1.50 4.00
112 Rafael Araujo R 2.00 5.00
113 Luke Jackson C RC 1.00 2.50
114 Luke Jackson U 1.50 4.00
115 Luke Jackson R 2.00 5.00
116 Yuta Tabuse C RC 1.50 4.00
117 Yuta Tabuse U 2.50 6.00
118 Yuta Tabuse R 3.00 8.00
119 Kris Humphries C RC 1.50 4.00
120 Kris Humphries U 2.50 6.00
121 Kris Humphries R 3.00 8.00
122 Josh Smith C RC 1.50 4.00
123 Josh Smith U 2.50 6.00
124 Josh Smith R 3.00 8.00
125 Dorell Wright C RC 1.50 4.00
126 Dorell Wright U 2.50 6.00
127 Dorell Wright R 3.00 8.00
128 Jackson Vroman C RC 1.00 2.50
129 Jackson Vroman U 1.50 4.00
130 Jackson Vroman R 2.00 5.00
131 Sasha Vujacic C RC 1.50 4.00
132 Sasha Vujacic U 2.50 6.00
133 Sasha Vujacic R 3.00 8.00
134 David Harrison C RC 1.00 2.50
135 David Harrison U 1.50 4.00
136 David Harrison R 2.00 5.00
137 Blake Stepp C RC 1.50 4.00
138 Blake Stepp U 2.50 6.00
139 Blake Stepp R 3.00 8.00
140 Lionel Chalmers C RC 1.50 4.00
141 Lionel Chalmers U 2.50 6.00
142 Lionel Chalmers R 3.00 8.00
143 Delonte West C RC 1.50 4.00
144 Delonte West U 2.50 6.00
145 Delonte West R 3.00 8.00
146 Kevin Martin C RC 2.00 5.00
147 Kevin Martin U 3.00 8.00
148 Kevin Martin R 4.00 10.00
149 Robert Swift C RC 1.00 2.50
150 Robert Swift U 1.50 4.00
151 Robert Swift R 2.00 5.00
152 Trevor Ariza C RC 1.50 4.00
153 Trevor Ariza U 2.50 6.00
154 Trevor Ariza R 3.00 8.00
155 Peter John Ramos C RC 1.00 2.50
156 Peter John Ramos U 1.50 4.00
157 Peter John Ramos R 2.00 5.00
158 Anderson Varejao C RC 1.25 3.00
159 Anderson Varejao U 2.00 5.00
160 Anderson Varejao R 2.50 6.00
161 Andre Emmett C RC 1.00 2.50
162 Andre Emmett U 1.50 4.00
163 Andre Emmett R 2.00 5.00
164 Tony Allen C RC 1.50 4.00
165 Tony Allen U 2.50 6.00
166 Tony Allen R 3.00 8.00
167 Jameer Nelson C RC 1.50 4.00
168 Jameer Nelson U 2.50 6.00
169 Jameer Nelson R 3.00 8.00
170 J.R. Smith C RC 1.50 4.00
171 J.R. Smith U 2.50 6.00
172 J.R. Smith R 3.00 8.00
173 Kirk Snyder C RC 1.00 2.50
174 Kirk Snyder U 1.50 4.00
175 Kirk Snyder R 2.00 5.00
176 Al Jefferson C RC 2.00 5.00
177 Al Jefferson U 3.00 8.00
178 Al Jefferson R 4.00 10.00
179 Sebastian Telfair C RC 1.25 3.00
180 Sebastian Telfair U 2.00 5.00
181 Sebastian Telfair R 2.50 6.00
182 Andris Biedrins C RC 1.00 2.50
183 Andris Biedrins U 1.50 4.00
184 Andris Biedrins R 2.00 5.00
185 Andre Iguodala C RC 2.00 5.00
186 Andre Iguodala U 3.00 8.00
187 Andre Iguodala R 4.00 10.00
188 Luol Deng C RC 1.50 4.00
189 Luol Deng U 2.50 6.00
190 Luol Deng R 3.00 8.00
191 Josh Childress C RC 1.25 3.00
192 Josh Childress U 2.00 5.00
193 Josh Childress R 2.50 6.00
194 Shaun Livingston C RC 1.50 4.00
195 Shaun Livingston U 2.50 6.00
196 Shaun Livingston R 3.00 8.00
197 Emeka Okafor C RC 1.25 3.00
198 Emeka Okafor U 2.00 5.00
199 Emeka Okafor R 2.50 6.00

2004-05 Topps Pristine Refractors

*1-100: 6X TO 15X BASE HI
1-100 PRINT RUN 25 SER.#'d SETS
*COMMON RCs: .75X TO 2X BASE HI
COMMON RC PRINT RUN 599 SER.#'d SETS
*UNCOMMON RCs: .75X TO 2X BASE HI
UNCOMMON RC PRINT RUN 275 SER.#'d SETS
*RARE RCs: 1X TO 2.5X BASE HI
RARE RC PRINT RUN 49 SER.#'d SETS

2004-05 Topps Pristine Refractors Gold

*1-100: 8X TO 20X BASE HI
*COMMON RCs: 2.5X TO 6X BASE HI
*UNCOMMON RCs: 1.5X TO 4X BASE HI
*RARE RCs: 1.25X TO 3X BASE HI
PRINT RUN 27 SER.#'d SETS
3 Dwyane Wade 40.00 100.00
8 Kobe Bryant 75.00 200.00
101 Dwight Howard C 40.00 100.00
102 Dwight Howard U 40.00 100.00
103 Dwight Howard R 40.00 100.00

2004-05 Topps Pristine Court Clash

Inserted at stated odds of one in 47, these eight cards feature relics of each of the featured players. There is also a refractor parallel which was issued to a stated print run of 10 sets.

STATED ODDS 1:47
AG C.Anthony/K.Garnett 8.00 20.00
AP R.Artest/P.Pierce 5.00 12.00
DM T.Duncan/K.Malone 10.00 25.00
MK S.Marbury/J.Kidd 6.00 15.00
NW D.Nowitzki/C.Webber 8.00 20.00
OM S.O'Neal/Y.Ming 8.00 20.00
PP G.Payton/T.Parker 5.00 12.00
WO B.Wallace/J.O'Neal 6.00 15.00

2004-05 Topps Pristine Fantasy Favorites

Inserted at a stated rate of one in three, these 54 cards feature game-used relics of the featured player. There was also a refractor version of these cards issued. Those refractors were issued to a stated print run of 25 serial numbered sets.

STATED ODDS 1:3
*REFRACTORS: .75X TO 2X BASE HI
REFRACTOR PRINT RUN 25 SER.#'d SETS
N Nene 2.00 5.00
AK Andrei Kirilenko 2.00 5.00
AS Amare Stoudemire 2.00 5.00
AW Antoine Walker 2.50 6.00
BM Brad Miller 2.00 5.00
CB Chauncey Billups 2.50 6.00
CK Chris Kaman 2.00 5.00
CW Chris Wilcox 2.00 5.00
DD Dan Dickau 2.00 5.00
DF Derek Fisher 2.00 5.00
DM Darko Milicic 2.00 5.00
DW Dajuan Wagner 2.00 5.00
EB Elton Brand 2.50 6.00
FW Frank Williams 2.00 5.00
GA Gilbert Arenas 2.00 5.00
JH Jarvis Hayes 2.00 5.00
JJ Jim Jackson 2.00 5.00
JK Jason Kidd 4.00 10.00
JM Jamaal Magloire 2.00 5.00
JO Jermaine O'Neal 2.00 5.00
JT Jason Terry 2.00 5.00
KG Kevin Garnett 4.00 10.00
KH Kirk Hinrich 2.00 5.00
KR Kareem Rush 2.00 5.00
LB Leandro Barbosa 2.50 6.00
LR Luke Ridnour 2.00 5.00
MB Marcus Banks 2.00 5.00
MD Mike Dunleavy 2.00 5.00
MJ Marko Jaric 2.00 5.00
MO Michael Olowokandi 2.00 5.00
MP Morris Peterson 1.50 4.00
NM Nazr Mohammed 2.00 5.00
PP Paul Pierce 2.50 6.00

PS Peja Stojakovic 2.50 6.00
RA Ron Artest 2.50 6.00
RL Rashard Lewis 2.50 6.00
RM Reggie Miller 2.50 6.00
SF Steve Francis 2.00 5.00
SO Shaquille O'Neal 6.00 15.00
TO Travis Outlaw 2.00 5.00
TP Tayshaun Prince 2.00 5.00
UH Udonis Haslem 1.50 4.00
VR Vladimir Radmanovic 2.00 5.00
WS Wally Szczerbiak 2.00 5.00
YM Yao Ming 5.00 12.00
ZR Zach Randolph 2.00 5.00
CBH Chris Bosh 2.50 6.00
CBO Carlos Boozer 2.00 5.00
CBU Caron Butler 2.00 5.00
DWE David Wesley 2.00 5.00
JAM Jamal Mashburn 2.00 5.00
JHO Josh Howard 2.50 6.00
MPI Mickael Pietrus 2.00 5.00
SAR Shareef Abdur-Rahim 2.00 5.00

2004-05 Topps Pristine Mini

Inserted one per box in #4 packs, these "mini" cards feature some of the leading NBA players.
STATED ODDS ONE PER BOX IN #4 PACKS
AI Andre Iguodala 1.50 4.00
AJ Antawn Jamison 1.00 2.50
AK Andrei Kirilenko 1.00 2.50
BD Baron Davis 1.00 2.50
BG Ben Gordon 1.25 3.00
BW Ben Wallace 1.00 2.50
CA Carmelo Anthony 2.50 6.00
DH Dwight Howard 2.50 6.00
DN Dirk Nowitzki 2.00 5.00
DW Dwyane Wade 2.00 5.00
EO Emeka Okafor 1.00 2.50
JC Josh Childress 1.00 2.50
JK Jason Kidd 2.00 5.00
JN Jameer Nelson 1.25 3.00
JO Jermaine O'Neal 1.00 2.50
JR Jason Richardson 1.25 3.00
KB Kobe Bryant 5.00 12.00
KG Kevin Garnett 2.00 5.00
KH Kris Humphries 1.25 3.00
LD Luol Deng 1.25 3.00
LJ LeBron James 8.00 20.00
LJ Luke Jackson .75 2.00
PG Pau Gasol 1.25 3.00
PP Paul Pierce 1.25 3.00
PS Peja Stojakovic 1.25 3.00
RA Rafael Araujo .75 2.00
SF Steve Francis 1.00 2.50
SL Shaun Livingston 1.25 3.00
SM Stephon Marbury 1.00 2.50
SO Shaquille O'Neal 3.00 8.00
ST Sebastian Telfair 1.00 2.50
TD Tim Duncan 2.00 5.00
TM Tracy McGrady 1.50 4.00
VC Vince Carter 2.00 5.00
YM Yao Ming 2.50 6.00
ALJ Al Jefferson 1.50 4.00
DHA Devin Harris 1.00 2.50
JRS J.R. Smith 1.25 3.00
RAL Ray Allen 1.25 3.00
SMA Shawn Marion 1.00 2.50

2004-05 Topps Pristine Mini Relics

Inserted at a stated rate of one in 47, these eight cards feature game-used relics of the featured player.
STATED ODDS 1:47
AS Amare Stoudemire 2.00 5.00
BW Ben Wallace 2.00 5.00
CA Carmelo Anthony 5.00 12.00
KG Kevin Garnett 4.00 10.00
PS Peja Stojakovic 2.50 6.00
RA Ron Artest 2.50 6.00
SF Steve Francis 2.00 5.00
SM Stephon Marbury 2.00 5.00

2004-05 Topps Pristine Personal Endorsements

Inserted at different odds depending on what group the player belongs to, these cards feature authentic autographs of the featured player. We have notated which group the player belongs to next to his name in our checklist. In additon, parallel refractor gold cards of these players, issued to stated print runs of 10 or 25 sets were issued.
GROUP A STATED ODDS 1:47
GROUP B STATED ODDS 1:29
GROUP C STATED ODDS 1:7
AB Andris Biedrins C 3.00 8.00
AS Amare Stoudemire A 10.00 25.00
AV Anderson Varejao C 4.00 10.00
BD Baron Davis B 6.00 15.00
BG Ben Gordon C 5.00 12.00
BJ Bobby Jackson A 10.00 25.00
BW Ben Wallace A 12.00 30.00
CA Carmelo Anthony B 25.00 60.00
DH David Harrison C 3.00 8.00
DW Dorell Wright C 5.00 12.00
EB Elton Brand A 8.00 20.00
EO Emeka Okafor C 4.00 10.00
JK Jason Kidd B 12.00 30.00
JO Jermaine O'Neal B 6.00 15.00
JR Jalen Rose A 6.00 15.00
JS Josh Smith C 5.00 12.00
KH Kris Humphries C 5.00 12.00
KS Kirk Snyder C 3.00 8.00
LD Luol Deng C 5.00 12.00
LJ Luke Jackson C 3.00 8.00
PS Peja Stojakovic B 6.00 15.00
RA Rafael Araujo C 3.00 8.00
RH Richard Hamilton B 8.00 20.00
RS Robert Swift C 3.00 8.00
SC Speedy Claxton A 5.00. 12.00
SL Shaun Livingston C 5.00 12.00
SM Shawn Marion A 6.00 15.00
SO Shaquille O'Neal A 50.00 120.00
ST Sebastian Telfair C 4.00 10.00
SV Sasha Vujacic C 5.00 12.00
TA Tony Allen C 5.00 12.00
TD Tim Duncan A 200.00 400.00
TM Tracy McGrady A 12.00 30.00
TP Tayshaun Prince A 6.00 15.00
DEH Devin Harris C 4.00 10.00
JOC Josh Childress C 4.00 10.00
JRS J.R. Smith C 5.00 12.00
SMA Stephon Marbury C 8.00 20.00

2004-05 Topps Pristine Rookie Sign In

Inserted at a stated rate of one in eight, these 15 cards feature relics of NBA rookies. There is also a refractor version of each of these cards. Each of these cards were issued to a stated print run of 25 serial numbered sets.
STATED ODDS 1:8
*REFRACTORS: 1X TO 2.5X BASE HI
REFRACTOR PRINT RUN 25 SER.#'d SETS
AI Andre Iguodala 3.00 8.00
AJ Al Jefferson 3.00 8.00
BG Ben Gordon 2.50 6.00
DH Dwight Howard 5.00 12.00
DW Dorell Wright 2.50 6.00
JC Josh Childress 2.00 5.00
JN Jameer Nelson 2.50 6.00
JS Josh Smith 2.50 6.00
LD Luol Deng 2.50 6.00
LJ Luke Jackson 1.50 4.00
RA Rafael Araujo 1.50 4.00
SL Shaun Livingston 2.50 6.00
ST Sebastian Telfair 2.00 5.00
TA Tony Allen 2.50 6.00
DHA Devin Harris 2.00 5.00

2004-05 Topps Pristine Two of a Kind Autographs

Inserted into packs at a stated rate of one in 305, these 10 cards feature dual autographs of leading NBA players.
STATED ODDS 1:305
MOST NOT PRICED DUE TO SCARCITY
AO C.Anthony/E.Okafor 40.00 100.00
DO T.Duncan/E.Okafor 150.00 300.00

2004-05 Topps Pristine Verticality

Inserted into packs at differing rates, these 13-cards feature game-used relic pieces of the featured player. Each of these cards belong to either group A or group B and we have notated that information next to the player's name in our checklist. In addition, each card has a refractor parallel and those cards were issued to a stated print run of 25 serial numbered copies.
GROUP A STATED ODDS 1:252
GROUP B STATED ODDS 1:11
*REFRACTORS: .75X TO 2X BASE HI
REFRACTOR PRINT RUN 25 SER.#'d SETS
AK Andrei Kirilenko B 2.00 5.00
AS Amare Stoudemire B 2.00 5.00
CA Chris Anderson B 2.50 6.00
DG Devean George B 2.00 5.00
DM Desmond Mason A 2.00 5.00
DW David West B 2.00 5.00
JR Jason Richardson B 2.50 6.00
RG Reece Gaines B 2.00 5.00
RJ Richard Jefferson B 2.00 5.00
SM Shawn Marion B 2.00 5.00
TC Tyson Chandler B 2.00 5.00
TM Tracy McGrady B 3.00 8.00

2004-05 Topps Pristine Winning Wardrobe

Inserted into packs at differing rates, these 34 cards feature game-used relic pieces of the featured player. Each of these cards belong to either group A or group B and we have notated that information next to the player's name in our checklist. In addition, each card has a refractor parallel and those cards were issued to a stated print run of 25.
GROUP A STATED ODDS 1:252
GROUP B STATED ODDS 1:4
*REFRACTORS: 1X TO 2.5X BASE HI
REFRACTOR PRINT RUN 25 SER.#'d SETS
BD Baron Davis B 2.00 5.00
BW Ben Wallace B 2.00 5.00
CA Carmelo Anthony B 5.00 12.00
DF Derek Fisher B 2.00 5.00
DM Desmond Mason A 2.00 5.00
DN Dirk Nowitzki B 4.00 10.00
GP Gary Payton B 2.50 6.00
HT Hedo Turkoglu B 2.00 5.00
JK Jason Kidd B 4.00 10.00
JM Jamaal Magloire B 2.00 5.00
JO Jermaine O'Neal B 2.00 5.00
JT Jamaal Tinsley B 2.00 5.00
KH Kirk Hinrich B 2.00 5.00
KM Karl Malone B 3.00 8.00
MB Mike Bibby B 2.50 6.00
MJ Marko Jaric B 2.00 5.00
MR Michael Redd B 2.00 5.00
PG Pau Gasol B 2.50 6.00
PP Paul Pierce B 2.50 6.00
PS Peja Stojakovic B 2.50 6.00
RA Ray Allen B 2.50 6.00
RH Robert Horry B 2.00 5.00
RJ Richard Jefferson B 2.00 5.00
RM Reggie Miller B 2.50 6.00
RN Rasho Nesterovic B 2.00 5.00
SB Shane Battier B 2.00 5.00
SM Stephon Marbury B 2.00 5.00
SO Shaquille O'Neal B 6.00 15.00
TD Tim Duncan B 4.00 10.00
TM Tracy McGrady B 3.00 8.00
TP Tony Parker B 2.50 6.00
YM Yao Ming B 5.00 12.00
ZP Zoran Planinic B 2.00 5.00
TAP Tayshaun Prince B 2.00 5.00

2005-06 Topps Pristine

Released in December 2005, Pristine boasts a 210 card set where cards 1-100 feature veteran players where color photos are set against a plain white background, cards 101-130 feature rookies, cards 131-180 feature players with memorabilia swatches serially numbered to 500, cards 181-205 feature autographs where most players are serially numbered to 100 (see checklist for details) and cards 206-210 feature memorabilia autograph cards sequentially numbered to 50. Pristine was packaged in five pack boxes where packs contained eight cards, including a format where one of the cards is sealed in an uncirculated case and two more packs where at least one memorabilia cards will be present. SRP upon release was $30 per pack.
COMP.SET w/o SP's 25.00 60.00
RELIC PRINT RUN 500 SER.#'d SETS
AUTO PRINT RUN 60 TO 100 SETS
JSY AU PRINT RUN 50 SER.#'d SETS
1 Ray Allen .40 1.00
2 Cuttino Mobley .25 .60
3 Sebastian Telfair .30 .75
4 Dwight Howard .30 .75
5 Udonis Haslem .25 .60
6 Luol Deng .30 .75
7 Lamar Odom .30 .75
8 Paul Pierce .40 1.00
9 Stephen Jackson .30 .75
10 Mike Dunleavy .30 .75
11 Andre Miller .30 .75
12 Ben Gordon .30 .75
13 Caron Butler .30 .75
14 Al Jefferson .30 .75
15 Jamaal Tinsley .25 .60
16 Josh Childress .30 .75
17 Larry Hughes .30 .75
18 Andrei Kirilenko .30 .75
19 Brad Miller .30 .75
20 Steve Nash .50 1.25
21 Grant Hill .50 1.25
22 Samuel Dalembert .25 .60
23 Quentin Richardson .30 .75
24 Wally Szczerbiak .30 .75
25 Desmond Mason .25 .60
26 Dwyane Wade .60 1.50
27 Richard Hamilton .30 .75
28 Shane Battier .30 .75
29 Chauncey Billups .40 1.00
30 Shawn Marion .30 .75
31 Kenyon Martin .30 .75
32 Marquis Daniels .25 .60
33 Al Harrington .30 .75
34 Brendan Haywood .25 .60
35 Mehmet Okur .25 .60
36 Rafer Alston .25 .60
37 Luke Ridnour .30 .75
38 Tim Duncan .60 1.50
39 Mike Miller .30 .75
40 Allen Iverson .60 1.50
41 Jamal Crawford .40 1.00
42 J.R. Smith .30 .75
43 Kevin Garnett .60 1.50
44 Baron Davis .30 .75
45 Corey Maggette .30 .75
46 Jermaine O'Neal .30 .75
47 Yao Ming .50 1.25
48 Pau Gasol .40 1.00
49 Devin Harris .25 .60
50 Emeka Okafor .30 .75
51 Zydrunas Ilgauskas .30 .75
52 Vladimir Radmanovic .25 .60
53 Tracy McGrady .50 1.25
54 Steve Francis .30 .75
55 Stephon Marbury .30 .75
56 Shaun Livingston .25 .60
57 Sam Cassell .30 .75
58 Rasheed Wallace .40 1.00
59 Primoz Brezec .25 .60
60 Nenad Krstic .25 .60
61 Mike Bibby .40 1.00
62 Marcus Camby .30 .75
63 LeBron James 1.50 4.00
64 Kobe Bryant 3.00 8.00
65 Josh Smith .30 .75
66 Jason Richardson .40 1.00
67 Jamaal Magloire .25 .60
68 Gilbert Arenas .30 .75
69 Zach Randolph .30 .75
70 Vince Carter .60 1.50
71 Tony Parker .40 1.00
72 Shaquille O'Neal .75 2.00
73 Richard Jefferson .30 .75
74 Rashard Lewis .40 1.00
75 Peja Stojakovic .40 1.00
76 Mike Sweetney .25 .60
77 Elton Brand .40 1.00
78 Drew Gooden .30 .75
79 Chris Webber .40 1.00
80 Carmelo Anthony .75 2.00
81 Bobby Simmons .25 .60
82 Bob Sura .25 .60
83 Antoine Walker .30 .75
84 Andre Iguodala .30 .75
85 Michael Redd .30 .75
86 Manu Ginobili .40 1.00
87 Latrell Sprewell .30 .75
88 Kirk Hinrich .30 .75
89 Josh Howard .40 1.00
90 Jason Kidd .60 1.50
91 Jalen Rose .40 1.00
92 Gerald Wallace .30 .75
93 Eddy Curry .25 .60
94 Dirk Nowitzki .60 1.50
95 Joe Johnson .30 .75
96 Chris Bosh .40 1.00
97 Carlos Boozer .30 .75
98 Ben Wallace .30 .75
99 Antawn Jamison .30 .75
100 Amare Stoudemire .30 .75
101 Andrew Bogut RC 2.50 6.00
102 Marvin Williams RC 2.00 5.00
103 Deron Williams RC 2.50 6.00
104 Chris Paul RC 8.00 20.00
105 Raymond Felton RC 2.00 5.00
106 Martell Webster RC 1.50 4.00
107 Charlie Villanueva RC 2.00 5.00
108 Channing Frye RC 2.00 5.00
109 Ike Diogu RC 1.25 3.00
110 Andrew Bynum RC 1.50 4.00
111 Monta Ellis RC 2.50 6.00
112 Yaroslav Korolev RC 1.25 3.00
113 Sean May RC 1.25 3.00
114 Rashad McCants RC 1.50 4.00
115 Antoine Wright RC 1.50 4.00
116 Joey Graham RC 1.50 4.00
117 Danny Granger RC 2.50 6.00
118 Gerald Green RC 2.00 5.00
119 Hakim Warrick RC 1.50 4.00
120 Julius Hodge RC 1.25 3.00
121 Nate Robinson RC 2.00 5.00
122 Jarrett Jack RC 2.00 5.00
123 Francisco Garcia RC 1.50 4.00
124 Luther Head RC 1.50 4.00
125 C.J. Miles RC 2.00 5.00
126 Salim Stoudamire RC 1.50 4.00
127 Sarunas Jasikevicius RC 2.00 5.00
128 Wayne Simien RC 1.25 3.00
129 David Lee RC 2.00 5.00
130 Jay-Z 3.00 8.00
131 Tim Duncan JSY 5.00 12.00
132 Ray Allen JSY 3.00 8.00
133 Grant Hill Warm 4.00 10.00
134 Dwyane Wade Shorts 5.00 12.00
135 Shawn Marion JSY 2.50 6.00
136 Jermaine O'Neal JSY 2.50 6.00
137 Emeka Okafor JSY 2.50 6.00
138 Tracy McGrady JSY 4.00 10.00
139 Chris Bosh Shorts 3.00 8.00
140 Dwight Howard JSY 2.50 6.00
141 Elton Brand JSY 3.00 8.00
142 Manu Ginobili JSY 3.00 8.00
143 Dirk Nowitzki JSY 5.00 12.00
144 Ben Wallace Warm 2.50 6.00
145 Steve Nash Warm 4.00 10.00
146 Allen Iverson Shirt 5.00 12.00
147 Kevin Garnett JSY 5.00 12.00
148 Corey Maggette JSY 2.50 6.00
149 Yao Ming JSY 4.00 10.00
150 Kobe Bryant Shorts 8.00 20.00
151 Rasheed Wallace JSY 3.00 8.00
152 Ben Gordon JSY 2.50 6.00
153 Gilbert Arenas Shirt 2.50 6.00
154 Shaquille O'Neal Warm 6.00 15.00
155 Peja Stojakovic JSY 3.00 8.00
156 Carmelo Anthony JSY 6.00 15.00
157 Kirk Hinrich JSY 2.50 6.00
158 Paul Pierce Shirt 3.00 8.00
159 Antawn Jamison JSY 2.50 6.00
160 Amare Stoudemire Shirt 2.50 6.00
161 Sarunas Jasikevicius Shorts 3.00 8.00
162 Wayne Simien JSY 2.00 5.00
163 Channing Frye JSY 3.00 8.00
164 Antoine Wright JSY 2.50 6.00
165 Sean May JSY 2.00 5.00
166 Rashad McCants JSY 2.50 6.00
167 Julius Hodge JSY 2.00 5.00
168 Nate Robinson JSY 3.00 8.00
169 Jarrett Jack JSY 3.00 8.00
170 Francisco Garcia JSY 2.50 6.00
171 Charlie Villanueva JSY 3.00 8.00
172 Andrew Bogut JSY 4.00 10.00
173 David Lee JSY 3.00 8.00
174 Deron Williams JSY 6.00 15.00
175 Chris Paul JSY 8.00 20.00
176 Raymond Felton JSY 3.00 8.00
177 Martell Webster JSY 2.50 6.00
178 Danny Granger JSY 4.00 10.00
179 Gerald Green JSY 3.00 8.00
180 Hakim Warrick JSY 2.50 6.00
181 Shaun Livingston AU 6.00 15.00
182 Danny Granger AU 8.00 20.00
183 Ryan Gomes AU RC 5.00 12.00
184 Jermaine O'Neal AU/75 10.00 25.00
185 George Gervin AU/60 6.00 15.00
186 Allen Iverson AU 50.00 100.00
187 Sean May AU 4.00 10.00
188 Andrew Bogut AU 8.00 20.00
189 Deron Williams AU 8.00 20.00
190 Stephon Marbury AU 10.00 25.00
191 Jason Kidd AU 12.50 30.00
192 Raymond Felton AU 6.00 15.00
193 Rashad McCants AU 5.00 12.00
194 Gerald Green AU 6.00 15.00
195 Andrew Bynum AU 5.00 12.00
196 Charlie Villanueva AU 6.00 15.00
197 Antoine Wright AU 5.00 12.00
198 Martell Webster AU 5.00 12.00
199 Francisco Garcia AU 5.00 12.00
200 Emeka Okafor AU 8.00 20.00
201 Hakim Warrick AU 5.00 12.00
202 Joey Graham AU 5.00 12.00
203 Julius Hodge AU 4.00 10.00
204 Ike Diogu AU 4.00 10.00
205 Johan Petro AU RC 4.00 10.00
206 Shaquille O'Neal JSY AU 40.00 80.00
208 Andrew Bogut JSY AU 15.00 40.00
209 Deron Williams JSY AU 40.00 80.00
210 Jay-Z Jeans AU 75.00 150.00

2005-06 Topps Pristine Die Cut

*1-100 VET DIE CUT: 3X TO 8X BASE HI
*101-130 DIE CUT: 1X TO 2.5X BASE HI
PRINT RUN 50 SER.#'d SETS
UNPRICED JERSEY PRINT RUN 15 SETS
UNPRICED AU PRINT RUN 7 SETS
UNPRICED JSY AU PRINT RUN 2 SETS

2005-06 Topps Pristine Uncirculated

-100 UNCIR: 1.5X TO 4X BASE HI
1-100 PRINT RUN 325 SER.#'d SETS
*101-130 UNCIR: .6X TO 1.5X BASE HI
*131-180 UNCIR: .5X TO 1.25X BASE HI
131-180 JSY PRINT RUN 100 SER.#'d SETS
*181-205 UNCIR: .6X TO 1.5X BASE HI
181-205 AU PRINT RUN 20 SER.#'d SETS
UNPRICED JSY AU PRINT RUN ONE SET
150 Kobe Bryant Shorts 12.00 30.00
185 George Gervin AU/60 12.50 30.00
189 Deron Williams AU 40.00 100.00
195 Andrew Bynum AU 40.00 100.00

2005-06 Topps Pristine Personal Endorsements

Randomly seeded in packs, this 45-card set features a horizontal design with several different serially numbered tiers. Common cards are sequentially numbered to 215, Uncommons are sequentially numbered to 125 (unless noted in checklist), Rare cards are sequentially numbered to 50 and Scarce cards are sequentially numbered to 10.
COMMON PRINT RUN 215 SER.#'d SETS
RARE PRINT RUN 50 SER.#'d SETS
UNPRICED SCARCE PRINT RUN 10 SETS
UNCIR.COMMON PRINT RUN 7 SETS
UNCIR.UNCOMM.PRINT RUN 5 SETS
UNCIR.RARE PRINT RUN 3 SETS
UNCIR.SCARCE PRINT RUN ONE SET
UNCIR.NOT PRICED DUE TO SCARCITY
CAI Allen Iverson/215 30.00 80.00
CBB Brandon Bass/215 3.00 8.00
CBW Bracey Wright/215 2.50 6.00
CCA Carmelo Anthony/215 15.00 30.00
CCT Chris Taft/215 3.00 8.00
CDE Daniel Ewing/215 3.00 8.00
CDG Danny Granger/215 5.00 12.00
CDL David Lee/215 4.00 10.00
CDW Dorell Wright/215 4.00 10.00
CEO Emeka Okafor/215 10.00 25.00
CJJ Jarrett Jack/215 4.00 10.00
CJM Jason Maxiell/215 3.00 8.00
CJN Jameer Nelson/215 4.00 10.00
CLD Luol Deng/215 5.00 12.00
CLH Luther Head/215 3.00 8.00
CLW Louis Williams/215 4.00 10.00
CME Monta Ellis/215 5.00 12.00
CRS Robert Swift/215 4.00 10.00
CRW Robert Whaley/215 4.00 10.00
CSL Shaun Livingston/215 4.00 10.00
CTD Travis Diener/215 2.50 6.00
CVW Von Wafer/215 2.50 6.00
CWS Wayne Simien/215 2.50 6.00
RAI Allen Iverson/50 50.00 125.00
RCB Christie Brinkley/50 40.00 100.00
RCE Carmen Electra/50 25.00 60.00
RJM Jenny McCarthy/50 40.00 100.00
RSE Shannon Elizabeth/50 25.00 60.00
RSN Steve Nash/50 40.00 80.00
RSO Shaquille O'Neal/50 40.00 80.00
UBD Baron Davis/125 5.00 12.00
UBU Beno Udrih/125 5.00 12.00
UBW Bill Walton/125 10.00 25.00
UCD Clyde Drexler/105 12.50 30.00
UHW Hakim Warrick/125 6.00 15.00
UJS Josh Smith/125 5.00 12.00
UKS Kirk Snyder/125 5.00 12.00
ULD Luol Deng/125 6.00 15.00
URF Raymond Felton/125 8.00 20.00
URP Robert Parish/109 15.00 30.00
USM Stephon Marbury/125 6.00 15.00
CDWA Dwyane Wade/215 25.00 60.00
USMA Sean May/125 5.00 12.00

2005-06 Topps Pristine Personal Pieces

Randomly inserted in packs, this multi-level set is horizontally designed with square swatches of memorabilia in the lower left hand corner. Common cards are serially numbered to 350, Uncommon cards are serially numbered to 175, Rare cards are serially numbered to 75 and Scarce cards are serially numbered to 10.
COMMON PRINT RUN 350 SER.#'d SETS
RARE PRINT RUN 75 SER.#'d SETS
UNPRICED SCARCE PRINT RUN 10 SETS
UNCIR.COMMON PRINT RUN 7 SETS
UNCIR.UNCOMM.PRINT RUN 5 SETS
UNCIR.RARE PRINT RUN 3 SETS
UNCIR.SCARCE PRINT RUN ONE SET
UNCIR.NOT PRICED DUE TO SCARCITY
CAB Andrew Bogut Warm C 3.00 8.00
CAI Allen Iverson C 4.00 10.00
CAW Antoine Walker Shorts C 2.00 5.00
CBR Bernard Robinson C 2.00 5.00
CCA Carmelo Anthony C 5.00 12.00
CCB Chris Bosh C 2.50 6.00
CCE Carmen Electra Jeans C 8.00 20.00
CCF Channing Frye Warm C 2.50 6.00
CCK Chris Kaman C 2.00 5.00
CCP Chris Paul Warm C 8.00 20.00
CCV Charlie Villanueva Warm C 2.50 6.00
CDG Danny Granger Warm C 3.00 8.00
CDH David Harrison C 2.00 5.00
CDW Deron Williams Warm C 3.00 8.00
CEC Eddy Curry C 1.50 4.00
CEO Emeka Okafor C 2.00 5.00
CES Eric Snow C 2.00 5.00
CGA Gilbert Arenas C 2.00 5.00
CGG Gerald Green Warm C 2.50 6.00
CGP Gary Payton C 2.50 6.00
CHW Hakim Warrick Warm C 2.00 5.00
CJC Josh Childress C 2.00 5.00
CJH Julius Hodge Warm C 1.50 4.00
CJJ Jarrett Jack Warm C 2.50 6.00
CJM Jenny McCarthy Jeans C 8.00 20.00
CJS Josh Smith C 2.00 5.00
CJZ Jay-Z Jeans C 10.00 25.00
CKB Kobe Bryant Shorts C 8.00 20.00
CLR Luke Ridnour C 2.00 5.00
CMC Marcus Camby C 2.00 5.00
CMW Martell Webster Warm C 2.00 5.00
CPB Primoz Brezec C 2.00 5.00
CRF Raymond Felton Warm C 2.50 6.00
CRL Rashard Lewis C 2.50 6.00
CRW Rasheed Wallace C 2.50 6.00
CSD Samuel Dalembert C 2.00 5.00
CSE Shannon Elizabeth Jeans C 8.00 20.00
CSM Shawn Marion C 2.00 5.00
CSO S.O'Neal AS Shorts C 5.00 12.00
CSV Sasha Vujacic C 2.00 5.00
CTA Tony Allen C 2.00 5.00
CTD Tim Duncan AS Shorts C 4.00 10.00
CTM Troy Murphy C 1.50 4.00
CTP Tayshaun Prince C 2.00 5.00
CUH Udonis Haslem C 1.50 4.00
CWS Wally Szczerbiak C 2.00 5.00
CYM Yao Ming C 3.00 8.00
RAI Allen Iverson Shirt R 6.00 15.00
RCA Carmelo Anthony R 8.00 20.00
RDW Dwyane Wade Shorts R 6.00 15.00
REO Emeka Okafor R 3.00 8.00
RJZ Jay-Z Jeans R 15.00 40.00
RKB Kobe Bryant R 12.50 30.00
RMG Manu Ginobili Warm R 4.00 10.00
RSM Sean May R 2.50 6.00
RSO Shaquille O'Neal R 8.00 20.00
RYM Yao Ming R 5.00 12.00
SPP Paul Pierce S 4.00 10.00
UAB Andrew Bogut Shirt U 4.00 10.00
UAI Allen Iverson Shirt U 5.00 12.00
UBW Ben Wallace U 2.50 6.00
UCB Christie Brinkley Jeans U 10.00 25.00
UCE Carmen Electra Jeans U 10.00 25.00
UCP Chris Paul Shirt U 8.00 20.00
UDH Dwight Howard U 2.50 6.00
UDN Dirk Nowitzki U 5.00 12.00
UDW Deron Williams Shirt U 4.00 10.00
UGH Grant Hill U 4.00 10.00
UJM Jenny McCarthy Jeans U 10.00 25.00
UJZ Jay-Z Jeans U 12.50 30.00
UKB Kobe Bryant Warm U 10.00 25.00
UKG Kevin Garnett AS JSY U 5.00 12.00
UKH Kirk Hinrich U 2.50 6.00
UKM Kenyon Martin U 2.50 6.00
ULO Lamar Odom U 2.50 6.00
UMW Martell Webster Shirt U 2.50 6.00
URF Raymond Felton Shirt U 3.00 8.00
URM Rashad McCants Shirt U 2.50 6.00
USE Shannon Elizabeth Jeans U 10.00 25.00
USN Steve Nash Shorts U 4.00 10.00
UST Sebastian Telfair U 2.50 6.00
UTM Tracy McGrady U 4.00 10.00
CAIG Andre Iguodala C 2.00 5.00
CCBR Christie Brinkley Jeans C 8.00 20.00
CDWA Dwyane Wade C 4.00 10.00
UDWA Dwyane Wade Shorts U 5.00 12.00

2008 Topps Red Autographs

NNO Dwyane Wade 20.00 40.00
NNO Magic Johnson 40.00 80.00

2000-01 Topps Reserve

The 2000-01 Topps Reserve product was released in May, 2001 and featured a 134-card base set that was broken into tiers as follows: Base Veterans (1-100), and Rookies (101-134) that were serial numbered to either 499, 999, or 1499. Each pack contained five cards and carried a suggested retail price $115 a box. Please note that each box also contained an autographed 8x10 canvas.
COMPLETE SET (134) 125.00 250.00
COMP.SET w/o SP's (100) 40.00 80.00
1 Tim Duncan 1.00 2.50
2 Clifford Robinson .30 .75
3 Allen Iverson 1.00 2.50
4 Marcus Camby .40 1.00
5 Chauncey Billups .50 1.25
6 Anthony Mason .30 .75
7 Toni Kukoc .50 1.25
8 Tim Thomas .30 .75
9 Corey Maggette .40 1.00
10 Steve Francis .40 1.00
11 Larry Hughes .40 1.00
12 Jerome Williams .30 .75
13 Reggie Miller .50 1.25
14 Chris Gatling .30 .75
15 Ron Artest .50 1.25
16 Derrick Coleman .40 1.00
17 Paul Pierce .50 1.25
18 Dikembe Mutombo .50 1.25
19 Andre Miller .40 1.00
20 Gary Payton .50 1.25
21 Kevin Garnett .75 2.00
22 Allan Houston .40 1.00
23 Rasheed Wallace .50 1.25
24 Derek Anderson .30 .75
25 Vin Baker .40 1.00
26 John Stockton .60 1.50
27 Richard Hamilton .40 1.00
28 Mike Bibby .50 1.25
29 Dale Davis .30 .75
30 Vince Carter 1.00 2.50
31 Shawn Marion .40 1.00
32 Karl Malone .60 1.50
33 Patrick Ewing .60 1.50
34 Shaquille O'Neal 1.25 3.00
35 Jermaine O'Neal .40 1.00
36 Danny Fortson .30 .75
37 Steve Nash .75 2.00
38 Antoine Walker .40 1.00
39 Jason Terry .50 1.25
40 Vlade Divac .40 1.00
41 Avery Johnson .40 1.00
42 Elton Brand .50 1.25
43 Mitch Richmond .40 1.00
44 Antonio Davis .30 .75
45 Shawn Kemp .50 1.25
46 Anfernee Hardaway .75 2.00
47 Kendall Gill .30 .75
48 Glen Rice .40 1.00
49 Tim Hardaway .50 1.25
50 Tracy McGrady .75 2.00
51 Horace Grant .40 1.00
52 Hakeem Olajuwon .60 1.50
53 Antawn Jamison .50 1.25
54 Dirk Nowitzki .75 2.00
55 Antonio McDyess .40 1.00
56 Michael Dickerson .30 .75
57 Baron Davis .50 1.25
58 Nick Van Exel .40 1.00
59 Joe Smith .40 1.00
60 Kobe Bryant 2.00 5.00
61 Ray Allen .50 1.25
62 Keith Van Horn .40 1.00
63 Latrell Sprewell .40 1.00
64 Jason Kidd .75 2.00
65 Chris Webber .50 1.25
66 David Robinson .75 2.00
67 Mark Jackson .40 1.00
68 Bryon Russell .30 .75
69 Lamar Odom .40 1.00
70 Maurice Taylor .30 .75
71 Jonathan Bender .30 .75
72 Raef LaFrentz .30 .75
73 Sam Cassell .40 1.00
74 Wally Szczerbiak .40 1.00
75 Grant Hill .60 1.50
76 Theo Ratliff .30 .75
77 Rashard Lewis .50 1.25
78 Darrell Armstrong .30 .75
79 Glenn Robinson .40 1.00
80 Stephon Marbury .40 1.00
81 Michael Olowokandi .30 .75
82 Isaiah Rider .40 1.00
83 Jalen Rose .40 1.00
84 Cuttino Mobley .30 .75
85 Jerry Stackhouse .40 1.00
86 Jamal Mashburn .40 1.00
87 Kenny Anderson .40 1.00
88 Michael Finley .50 1.25
89 Lamond Murray .30 .75
90 Eddie Jones .50 1.25
91 Eric Snow .30 .75
92 Terrell Brandon .30 .75
93 Jason Williams .50 1.25
94 Scottie Pippen .75 2.00
95 Rod Strickland .30 .75
96 Jim Jackson .30 .75
97 Ron Mercer .30 .75
98 Juwan Howard .40 1.00
99 Brian Grant .30 .75
100 Shareef Abdur-Rahim .40 1.00
101 Kenyon Martin/499 RC 6.00 15.00
102 Stromile Swift/999 RC 2.00 5.00
103 Darius Miles/1499 RC 1.50 4.00
104 Marcus Fizer/499 RC 2.50 6.00
105 Mike Miller/999 RC 3.00 8.00
106 D.Johnson/1499 RC 1.25 3.00
107 Chris Mihm/499 RC 2.00 5.00
108 Jamal Crawford/999 RC 5.00 12.00
109 Joel Przybilla/1499 RC 1.25 3.00
110 Keyon Dooling/499 RC 2.50 6.00
111 Jerome Moiso/999 RC 1.25 3.00
112 Etan Thomas/1499 RC 1.50 4.00
113 C.Alexander/499 RC 2.00 5.00
114 Mateen Cleaves/999 RC 1.50 4.00
115 Jason Collier/1499 RC 1.50 4.00
116 Hedo Turkoglu/499 RC 4.00 10.00
117 Desmond Mason/999 RC 2.50 6.00
118 Q.Richardson/1499 RC 1.50 4.00
119 Jamaal Magloire/499 RC 2.50 6.00
120 Speedy Claxton/999 RC 2.00 5.00
121 Morris Peterson/1499 RC 1.50 4.00
122 Donnell Harvey/499 RC 2.00 5.00
123 D.Stevenson/999 RC 2.00 5.00
124 Dalibor Bagaric/1499 RC 1.25 3.00
125 I.Tsakalidis/499 RC 1.50 4.00
126 M.N'Diaye/999 RC 1.25 3.00
127 Erick Barkley/1499 RC 1.00 2.50
128 Mark Madsen/499 RC 2.50 6.00
129 A.J. Guyton/999 RC 1.25 3.00
130 Khalid El-Amin/1499 RC 1.00 2.50
131 Lavor Postell/499 RC 1.50 4.00
132 Marc Jackson/999 RC 1.50 4.00
133 S.Jackson/1499 RC 2.50 6.00
134 Wang Zhizhi/1499 RC 3.00 8.00

2000-01 Topps Reserve Canvas Autographs

Randomly inserted into boxes, this 13-canvas insert features autographs from some of the hottest players in the league. Card backs carry a "TR" prefix followed by the players initials. Please note that Shaquille O'Neal was inserted at 1:68 boxes, while Magic Johnson was inserted a 1:34 boxes.
OVERALL ODDS ONE PER HOBBY BOX
GROUP A STATED ODDS 1:68 BOXES
GROUP B STATED ODDS 1:34 BOXES
TRAJ Antawn Jamison E 6.00 15.00
TRAM Andre Miller F 6.00 15.00
TRBD Baron Davis E 6.00 15.00
TREB Elton Brand C 6.00 15.00
TRJO Jermaine O'Neal C 8.00 20.00
TRKD Keyon Dooling F 6.00 15.00
TRLH Larry Hughes D 6.00 15.00
TRMB Mike Bibby E 6.00 15.00
TRMJ Magic Johnson B 40.00 100.00
TRMT Maurice Taylor E 6.00 15.00
TRSM Shawn Marion E 8.00 20.00
TRSO Shaquille O'Neal A 50.00 120.00
TRWS Wally Szczerbiak E 6.00 15.00

2000-01 Topps Reserve Game Jerseys

Randomly inserted into packs, this 36-card insert features game-used jersey cards from some of the hottest players in the NBA. Card backs carry a "TAS" prefix.
OVERALL STATED ODDS ONE PER BOX
TAS1 Allen Iverson A 6.00 15.00
TAS2 Grant Hill A 4.00 10.00
TAS3 Alonzo Mourning A 4.00 10.00
TAS4 Eddie Jones A 3.00 8.00
TAS5 Allan Houston A 2.50 6.00
TAS6 Dale Davis A 2.00 5.00
TAS7 Reggie Miller A 3.00 8.00
TAS8 Dikembe Mutombo A 3.00 8.00
TAS9 Glenn Robinson A 2.50 6.00
TAS10 Ray Allen A 3.00 8.00
TAS11 Jerry Stackhouse A 2.50 6.00
TAS12 Tim Duncan A 6.00 15.00
TAS13 Shaquille O'Neal A 8.00 20.00
TAS14 Jason Kidd A 5.00 12.00
TAS15 Gary Payton A 3.00 8.00
TAS16 John Stockton A 4.00 10.00
TAS17 Karl Malone A 4.00 10.00
TAS18 David Robinson A 5.00 12.00
TAS19 Rasheed Wallace A 3.00 8.00
TAS20 Michael Finley A 3.00 8.00
TAS21 Chris Webber A 3.00 8.00
TAS22 Mike Bibby B 3.00 8.00
TAS23 Michael Dickerson B 2.00 5.00
TAS24 Cuttino Mobley B 2.00 5.00
TAS25 Raef LaFrentz B 2.00 5.00
TAS26 Dirk Nowitzki B 5.00 12.00
TAS27 Michael Olowokandi B 2.00 5.00
TAS28 Paul Pierce B 3.00 8.00
TAS29 Jason Williams B 3.00 8.00
TAS30 Elton Brand B 3.00 8.00
TAS31 Steve Francis B 2.50 6.00
TAS32 Adrian Griffin B 2.00 5.00
TAS33 Todd MacCulloch B 2.00 5.00
TAS34 Andre Miller B 2.50 6.00
TAS35 James Posey B 2.00 5.00
TAS36 Wally Szczerbiak B 2.50 6.00

2003-04 Topps Rookie Matrix Promos

COMPLETE SET (3) 10.00 25.00
PP1 Dwyane Wade 10.00 25.00
Carmelo Anthony
Chris Bosh
PP2 T.J. Ford 2.00 5.00
Kirk Hinrich
Marcus Banks
PP3 Elton Brand .40 1.00

2003-04 Topps Rookie Matrix

Released in April 2004, Topps Rookie Matrix boasts a 220-card set broken down into 110 veteran player cards and 110 triple player rookie cards. The rookie cards are not tagged RC's due to lack of space but are widely accepted as such by the Hobby. The cards are numbered by the first letter of each of the three rookies last names from left to right. Card backgrounds are that of streetball courts and the set was designed to appeal to video gamers. Rookie Matrix was packaged in 20-pack boxes where packs contained five veteran cards, two rookie cards, one mini parallel and one checklist and carried a suggested retail price of $4.
COMP.SET w/o RC's (110) 12.50 30.00
UNPRICED KEY POINTS PRINT RUN 5 SETS
1 Allen Iverson .50 1.25
2 Anfernee Hardaway .50 1.25
3 Bonzi Wells .20 .50
4 Bobby Jackson .20 .50
5 Manu Ginobili .40 1.00
6 Andrei Kirilenko .30 .75
7 Ray Allen .30 .75
8 Kwame Brown .20 .50
9 Jason Terry .25 .60
10 Paul Pierce .30 .75
11 Tyson Chandler .25 .60
12 Darius Miles .20 .50
13 Antoine Walker .30 .75
14 Antawn Jamison .25 .60
15 Steve Nash .40 1.00
16 Marcus Camby .25 .60
17 Chauncey Billups .30 .75
18 Jason Richardson .30 .75
19 Cuttino Mobley .20 .50
20 Yao Ming .60 1.50
21 Ron Artest .30 .75
22 Gary Payton .30 .75
23 Jason Williams .25 .60
24 Eddie Jones .25 .60
25 Kevin Garnett .50 1.25
26 Wally Szczerbiak .25 .60
27 Kenyon Martin .25 .60
28 Jamaal Magloire .20 .50
29 Keith Van Horn .25 .60
30 Tracy McGrady .40 1.00
31 Glenn Robinson .25 .60
32 Derek Anderson .20 .50
33 Chris Webber .30 .75
34 Tony Parker .30 .75
35 Morris Peterson .20 .50
36 Jerry Stackhouse .25 .60
37 Theo Ratliff .20 .50
38 Jalen Rose .20 .50
39 Dajuan Wagner .20 .50
40 Dirk Nowitzki .50 1.25
41 Nikoloz Tskitishvili .20 .50
42 Ben Wallace .25 .60
43 Tayshaun Prince .25 .60
44 Troy Murphy .25 .60
45 Jamaal Tinsley .25 .60
46 Corey Maggette .25 .60
47 Karl Malone .40 1.00
48 Mike Miller .25 .60
49 Lamar Odom .25 .60
50 Shaquille O'Neal .75 2.00
51 Michael Redd .30 .75
52 Sam Cassell .25 .60
53 Raef LaFrentz .20 .50
54 Baron Davis .25 .60
55 Allan Houston .25 .60
56 Drew Gooden .25 .60
57 Eric Snow .20 .50
58 Stephon Marbury .25 .60
59 Zach Randolph .25 .60
60 Peja Stojakovic .25 .60
61 Brent Barry .20 .50
62 Radoslav Nesterovic .20 .50
63 Antonio Davis .20 .50
64 Gilbert Arenas .25 .60
65 Shareef Abdur-Rahim .25 .60
66 Scottie Pippen .50 1.25
67 Ronald Murray .20 .50
68 Zydrunas Ilgauskas .25 .60
69 Nene .25 .60
70 Steve Francis .25 .60
71 Mike Dunleavy .25 .60
72 Jermaine O'Neal .25 .60
73 Elton Brand .30 .75
74 Caron Butler .25 .60
75 Kobe Bryant 1.25 3.00
76 Kenny Thomas .20 .50
77 Joe Smith .20 .50
78 Jason Kidd .50 1.25
79 Antonio McDyess .25 .60
80 Shawn Marion .25 .60
81 Rasheed Wallace .30 .75
82 Mike Bibby .30 .75
83 Tim Thomas .20 .50
84 Rashard Lewis .30 .75
85 Vince Carter .50 1.25
86 Matt Harpring .25 .60
87 Ricky Davis .20 .50
88 Michael Finley .30 .75
89 Andre Miller .25 .60
90 Pau Gasol .30 .75
91 Dion Glover .20 .50
92 Jamal Crawford .30 .75
93 Richard Hamilton .25 .60
94 Nick Van Exel .25 .60
95 Maurice Taylor .20 .50
96 Reggie Miller .25 .60
97 Marko Jaric .20 .50
98 Brian Grant .20 .50
99 Desmond Mason .20 .50
100 Tim Duncan .50 1.25
101 Latrell Sprewell .25 .60

102 Richard Jefferson .25 .60
103 David Wesley .20 .50
104 Kurt Thomas .20 .50
105 Juwan Howard .25 .60
106 Amare Stoudemire .40 1.00
107 Brad Miller .25 .60
108 Keon Clark .20 .50
109 Pat Garrity .20 .50
110 Jamal Mashburn .25 .60
AJF Carmelo/LeBron/Ford RC 4.00 10.00
AKM Carmelo/Kaman/Darko RC 2.00 5.00
AMB Carmelo/Darko/Bosh RC 3.00 8.00
AWB Carmelo/Wade/Bosh RC 5.00 12.00
BAH Bosh/Carmelo/Hinrich RC 2.50 6.00
BAJ Bosh/Carmelo/LeBron RC 8.00 20.00
BBG Barbosa/Bell/Gaines RC 1.25 3.00
BBR Banks/Bell/Ridnour RC 1.25 3.00
BCC Bell/Zarko/Collison RC 1.25 3.00
BCG Bell/Collison/Gaines RC 1.25 3.00
BCP Barbosa/Zarko/Pavlovic RC 1.25 3.00
BCP Banks/Collison/Pietrus RC 1.25 3.00
BHJ Bosh/Hinrich/LeBron RC 4.00 10.00
BJP Bell/Jones/Planinic RC 1.25 3.00
BKC Beasley/Kapono/Cook RC 1.25 3.00
BKS Banks/Kaman/Sweetney RC 1.25 3.00
BKW Bosh/Kaman/Wade RC 2.50 6.00
BPH Banks/Pietrus/Hayes RC 1.25 3.00
BPW Barbosa/Pavlovic/Williams RC 1.25 3.00
BRG Banks/Ridnour/Gaines RC 1.25 3.00
BWM Bosh/Wade/Darko RC 3.00 8.00
CEK Cook/Ebi/Kapono RC 1.25 3.00
CHB Collison/Hayes/Banks RC 1.25 3.00
CHC Cook/Howard/Zarko RC 1.25 3.00
CPD Zarko/Pietrus/Diaw RC 1.25 3.00
CPS Collison/Pietrus/Sweetney RC 1.25 3.00
CSH Collison/Sweetney/Hayes RC 1.25 3.00
CWC Cook/West/Collison RC 1.25 3.00
DPP Diaw/Pavlovic/Planinic RC 1.25 3.00
DPW Diaw/Pavlovic/West RC 1.25 3.00
EPW Ebi/Perkins/West RC 1.50 4.00
EWC Ebi/West/Cook RC 1.25 3.00
FAH Ford/Carmelo/Hinrich RC 2.00 5.00
FBH Ford/Banks/Hinrich RC 1.25 3.00
FBJ Ford/Bosh/LeBron RC 4.00 10.00
FBR Ford/Banks/Ridnour RC 1.25 3.00
FBW Ford/Bosh/Wade RC 2.50 6.00
FCH Ford/Collison/Hinrich RC 1.25 3.00
FGB Ford/Gaines/Banks RC 1.25 3.00
FKW Ford/Kaman/Wade RC 1.50 4.00
GBB Gaines/Banks/Bell RC 1.25 3.00
GBR Gaines/Bell/Ridnour RC 1.25 3.00
HAM Hinrich/Carmelo/Darko RC 2.50 6.00
HBM Hinrich/Bosh/Darko RC 1.50 4.00
HBS Hayes/Banks/Sweetney RC 1.25 3.00
HCJ Howard/Cook/Jones RC 1.25 3.00
HGP Hayes/Gaines/Pietrus RC 1.25 3.00
HJM Hinrich/LeBron/Darko RC 3.00 8.00
HKC Hayes/Kaman/Collison RC 1.25 3.00
HLC Howard/Lampe/Cook RC 1.25 3.00
HLK Howard/Lampe/Kapono RC 1.25 3.00
HPR Hayes/Peitrus/Ridnour RC 1.25 3.00
HSL Hayes/Sweetney/Lampe RC 1.25 3.00
HSP Hayes/Sweetney/Pietrus RC 1.25 3.00
HWS Hinrich/Wade/Sweetney RC 1.50 4.00
JAW LeBron/Carmelo/Wade RC 15.00 40.00
JBM LeBron/Bosh/Darko RC 4.00 10.00
JHA LeBron/Hinrich/Carmelo RC 6.00 15.00
JKA LeBron/Kaman/Carmelo RC 6.00 15.00
JMA LeBron/Darko/Carmelo RC 8.00 20.00
JMK LeBron/Darko/Kaman RC 4.00 10.00
JOB Jones/Outlaw/Barbosa RC 1.25 3.00
JWE Jones/Walton/Ebi RC 1.25 3.00
KCP Kaman/Zarko/Perkins RC 1.25 3.00
KEW Kapono/Ebi/Williams RC 1.25 3.00
KHW Kaman/Hinrich/Wade RC 1.50 4.00
KPH Kaman/Pietrus/Hayes RC 1.25 3.00
KSC Kaman/Sweetney/Collison RC 1.25 3.00
LBB Lampe/Barbosa/Beasley RC 1.25 3.00
LHC Lampe/Howard/Zarko RC 1.25 3.00
LSP Lampe/Sweetney/Planinic RC 1.25 3.00
MAF Darko/Carmelo/Ford RC 1.50 4.00
MBF Darko/Bosh/Ford RC 1.50 4.00
MFJ Darko/Ford/LeBron RC 3.00 8.00
MJW Darko/LeBron/Wade RC 5.00 12.00
OBD Outlaw/Barbosa/Diaw RC 1.25 3.00
OCB Outlaw/Cook/Beasley RC 1.25 3.00
OEJ Outlaw/Ebi/Jones RC 1.25 3.00
OPE Outlaw/Perkins/Ebi RC 1.25 3.00
PBE Perkins/Beasley/Ebi RC 1.25 3.00
PBG Perkins/Banks/Gaines RC 1.25 3.00
PBH Pietrus/Bell/Hayes RC 1.25 3.00
PCH Pietrus/Collison/Hayes RC 1.25 3.00
PCR Pietrus/Collison/Ridnour RC 1.25 3.00
PCW Perkins/Zarko/West RC 1.50 4.00
PDB Planinic/Diaw/Barbosa RC 1.25 3.00
PJD Pavlovic/Jones/Diaw RC 1.25 3.00
PLH Perkins/Lampe/Howard RC 1.25 3.00
POP Pavlovic/Outlaw/Planinic RC 1.25 3.00
PPC Pietrus/Pavlovic/Zarko RC 1.25 3.00
PSK Pietrus/Sweetney/Kaman RC 1.25 3.00
PWO Planinic/West/Outlaw RC 1.25 3.00
RFH Ridnour/Ford/Hinrich RC 1.25 3.00
RHC Ridnour/Hayes/Collison RC 1.25 3.00
SBC Sweetney/Banks/Collison RC 1.25 3.00
SHK Sweetney/Hayes/Kaman RC 1.25 3.00
SPB Sweetney/Pietrus/Banks RC 1.25 3.00
WBH Wade/Bosh/Hinrich RC 2.00 5.00
WBP Williams/Barbosa/Planinic RC 1.25 3.00
WDJ West/Diaw/Jones RC 1.25 3.00
WDP Williams/Diaw/Planinic RC 1.25 3.00
WFH Wade/Ford/Hinrich RC 2.00 5.00
WHL Walton/Howard/Lampe RC 1.25 3.00
WHO Walton/Outlaw/Howard RC 1.25 3.00
WJB Wade/LeBron/Bosh RC 20.00 50.00
WKP Walton/Kapono/Perkins RC 1.25 3.00
WKS Wade/Kaman/Sweetney RC 2.00 5.00
WMA Wade/Darko/Carmelo RC 5.00 12.00
WPJ West/Pavlovic/Jones RC 1.25 3.00
WWB Walton/Williams/Beasley RC 1.25 3.00

2003-04 Topps Rookie Matrix Minis

Randomly inserted in packs at the rate of one in one, this 143-card set parallels the base Rookie Matrix set on mini-cards. Several different card backs were issued for each mini: Topps backs are inserted at one in 5, Double Double backs are inserted at one in 13, Triple backs are inserted at one in 203, and Swish backs are inserted at one in 1693.

ONE PER PACK
*DOUBLE: .6X TO 1.5X MINI HI
DOUBLE STATED ODDS 1:13
*SWISH: 5X TO 12X MINI HI
SWISH STATED ODDS 1:1693
*TOPPS: .5X TO 1.25X MINI HI
TOPPS STATED ODDS 1:5
*TRIPLE: 1.25X TO 3X MINI HI
TRIPLE STATED ODDS 1:203
111 LeBron James 6.00 15.00
112 Darko Milicic .50 1.25
113 Carmelo Anthony 2.00 5.00
114 Chris Bosh 1.00 2.50
115 Dwyane Wade 2.00 5.00
116 Chris Kaman .60 1.50
117 Kirk Hinrich .60 1.50
118 T.J. Ford .50 1.25
119 Mike Sweetney .40 1.00
120 Jarvis Hayes .40 1.00
121 Mickael Pietrus .50 1.25
122 Nick Collison .50 1.25
123 Marcus Banks .40 1.00
124 Luke Ridnour .50 1.25
125 Reece Gaines .40 1.00
126 Troy Bell .40 1.00
127 Zarko Cabarkapa .40 1.00
128 David West .60 1.50
129 Aleksandar Pavlovic .50 1.25
130 Dahntay Jones .50 1.25
131 Boris Diaw .60 1.50
132 Zoran Planinic .40 1.00
133 Travis Outlaw .50 1.25
134 Brian Cook .40 1.00
135 Ndudi Ebi .40 1.00
136 Kendrick Perkins .50 1.25
137 Leandro Barbosa .60 1.50
138 Josh Howard .60 1.50
139 Maciej Lampe .40 1.00
140 Jason Kapono .40 1.00
141 Luke Walton .60 1.50
142 Jerome Beasley .40 1.00
143 Maurice Williams .60 1.50

2003-04 Topps Rookie Matrix Lottery Draw

Randomly inserted at the rate of one in 371, this 13-card set has a border and encased are small frame photos of each player. There are three different versions per card and features the "A" variation for dribbling, the "B" variation for passing and the "C" variation for shooting. All versions are valued equally.

THREE VERSIONS PER CARD VALUED SAME
STATED ODDS 1:371
LD1A LeBron James 30.00 80.00
LD2A Darko Milicic 2.50 6.00
LD3A Carmelo Anthony 10.00 25.00
LD4A Chris Bosh 5.00 12.00
LD5A Dwyane Wade 10.00 25.00
LD6A Chris Kaman 3.00 8.00
LD7A Kirk Hinrich 3.00 8.00
LD8A T.J. Ford 2.50 6.00
LD9A Mike Sweetney 2.00 5.00
LD10A Jarvis Hayes 2.00 5.00
LD11A Mickael Pietrus 2.50 6.00
LD12A Nick Collison 2.50 6.00
LD13A Marcus Banks 2.00 5.00

2003-04 Topps Rookie Matrix Mini Autographs

Randomly inserted in packs at the rates of one in 7164 for Group A, one in 3175 for Group B, one in 2039 for Group C, one in 412 for Group D, one in 913 for Group E, one in 148 for group F and one in 49 for Group G, this 25-card set is made up of mini-encased autographed cards.

GROUP A ODDS 1:7164, B 1:3175, C 1:2039
GROUP D ODDS 1:412, E 1:913, F 1:148
GROUP G ODDS 1:49
AK Andrei Kirilenko F 5.00 12.00
BM Brad Miller F 5.00 12.00
CA Carmelo Anthony/100 A 30.00 60.00
DW Dwyane Wade D 30.00 80.00
GA Gilbert Arenas D 4.00 10.00
JC Jason Collins G 3.00 8.00
JK Jason Kidd E 8.00 20.00
LW Luke Walton G 5.00 12.00
MC Michael Curry G 5.00 12.00
MR Malik Rose B 5.00 12.00
PP Paul Pierce C 12.00 30.00
RG Reece Gaines F 3.00 8.00
RH Richard Hamilton D 5.00 12.00
TB Troy Bell G 3.00 8.00
TH Travis Hansen G 3.00 8.00
TP Tayshaun Prince G 5.00 12.00
ZC Zarko Cabarkapa G 3.00 8.00
ZP Zoran Planinic G 3.00 8.00
TPA Tony Parker F 8.00 20.00

2003-04 Topps Rookie Matrix Mini Relics

Randomly inserted in packs at the rates of one in 1259 for Group A, one in 372 for Group B, one in 473 for Group C, one in 792 for Group D, one in 219 for Group E, one in 148 for Group F and one in 49 for Group G, this 87-card set is comprised of mini-encased memorabilia cards.

GROUP A ODDS 1:1259, B 1:372, C 1:473
GROUP D ODDS 1:792, E 1:219, F 1:148, G 1:49
AI Allen Iverson F 4.00 10.00
AJ Antawn Jamison/250 C 2.00 5.00
AM Andre Miller G 2.00 5.00
AS Amare Stoudemire G 3.00 8.00
BB Brent Barry/50 A 5.00 12.00
BW Ben Wallace G 2.00 5.00
CA Carmelo Anthony F 8.00 20.00
CB Caron Butler/250 C 2.00 5.00
CK Chris Kaman F 2.50 6.00
CM Corey Maggette A 2.00 5.00
CW Chris Webber/50 A 8.00 20.00
DG Drew Gooden E 2.00 5.00
DM Darius Miles G 2.00 5.00
DN Dirk Nowitzki G 4.00 10.00
DW Dajuan Wagner F 2.00 5.00
EB Elton Brand F 2.50 6.00
GR Glenn Robinson E 2.00 5.00
JH Jarvis Hayes F 1.50 4.00
JK Jason Kidd F 4.00 10.00
JO Jermaine O'Neal G 2.00 5.00
JR Jalen Rose F 2.00 5.00
JT Jason Terry/50 A 6.00 15.00
JW Jason Williams E 2.00 5.00
KB Kwame Brown/150 B 2.50 6.00
KG Kevin Garnett G 4.00 10.00
KH Kirk Hinrich F 2.50 6.00
KT Kurt Thomas/50 A 5.00 12.00
LO Lamar Odom F 2.00 5.00
LR Luke Ridnour F 2.00 5.00
LS Latrell Sprewell G 2.00 5.00
MB Marcus Banks F 1.50 4.00
MD Mike Dunleavy/50 A 5.00 12.00
MM Mike Miller F 2.00 5.00
MO Michael Olowokandi G 1.50 4.00
MP Mickael Pietrus/50 A 5.00 12.00
MS Mike Sweetney F 1.50 4.00
NH Nene G 2.00 5.00
PG Pau Gasol G 2.50 6.00
PP Paul Pierce G 2.50 6.00
QR Quentin Richardson/50 A 2.00 5.00
RA Ray Allen/150 B 5.00 12.00
RG Reece Gaines G 1.50 4.00
RH Richard Hamilton G 2.00 5.00
RJ Richard Jefferson D 2.00 5.00
RL Rashard Lewis/250 C 2.50 6.00
RM Reggie Miller D 2.50 6.00
RW Rasheed Wallace/50 A 6.00 15.00
SF Steve Francis F 2.00 5.00
SM Shawn Marion G 2.00 5.00
SN Steve Nash F 3.00 8.00
SO Shaquille O'Neal G 6.00 15.00
TB Troy Bell F 1.50 4.00
TD Tim Duncan F 4.00 10.00
TM Tracy McGrady G 3.00 8.00
TP Tayshaun Prince/150 B 2.00 5.00
YM Yao Ming F 5.00 12.00
ZC Zarko Cabarkapa/150 B 1.50 4.00
ZI Zydrunas Ilgauskas G 2.00 5.00
CBO Chris Bosh F 4.00 10.00
CMO Cuttino Mobley G 1.50 4.00
DWA Dwyane Wade F 8.00 20.00
JHO Juwan Howard E 2.00 5.00
JRI Jason Richardson/50 A 6.00 15.00
JWI Jerome Williams E 2.00 5.00
KMA Kenyon Martin/50 A 6.00 15.00
MBI Mike Bibby/150 B 2.50 6.00
MPE Morris Peterson F 1.50 4.00
RAR Ron Artest/150 B 2.50 6.00
SMA Stephon Marbury/150 B 2.00 5.00
TMU Troy Murphy E 1.50 4.00
TPA Tony Parker/250 C 2.50 6.00

2003-04 Topps Rookie Matrix Rookie Frames

Randomly inserted, this 33-card set parallels the rookie players with mini-cards encased in a frame. Several different card back versions were inserted: Double Doubles at one in 125, Topps at one in 51, Triple Doubles at one in 2235 and Swish at one in 10348.

STATED ODDS 1:13
*DOUBLE: .6X TO 1.5X BASE FRAME HI
DOUBLE STATED ODDS 1:125
*TOPPS: .5X TO 1.25X BASE FRAME
TOPPS STATED ODDS 1:51
*TRIPLE: 3X TO 8X BASE FRAME HI
TRIPLE STATED ODDS 1:2235
UNPRICED SWISH STATED ODDS 1:10348
111 LeBron James 12.00 30.00
112 Darko Milicic 1.00 2.50
113 Carmelo Anthony 4.00 10.00
114 Chris Bosh 2.00 5.00
115 Dwyane Wade 4.00 10.00
116 Chris Kaman 1.25 3.00
117 Kirk Hinrich 1.25 3.00
118 T.J. Ford 1.00 2.50
119 Mike Sweetney .75 2.00
120 Jarvis Hayes .75 2.00
121 Mickael Pietrus 1.00 2.50
122 Nick Collison 1.00 2.50
123 Marcus Banks .75 2.00
124 Luke Ridnour 1.00 2.50
125 Reece Gaines .75 2.00
126 Troy Bell .75 2.00
127 Zarko Cabarkapa .75 2.00
128 David West 1.25 3.00
129 Aleksandar Pavlovic 1.00 2.50
130 Dahntay Jones 1.00 2.50
131 Boris Diaw 1.25 3.00
132 Zoran Planinic .75 2.00
133 Travis Outlaw 1.00 2.50
134 Brian Cook .75 2.00
135 Ndudi Ebi .75 2.00
136 Kendrick Perkins 1.00 2.50
137 Leandro Barbosa 1.25 3.00
138 Josh Howard 1.25 3.00
139 Maciej Lampe .75 2.00
140 Jason Kapono .75 2.00
141 Luke Walton 1.25 3.00
142 Jerome Beasley .75 2.00
143 Maurice Williams 1.25 3.00

2001 Topps Sean Elliott National Kidney Foundation

Given away to the first 10,000 fans on March 14, 2001, this set was issued by Topps in association with the National Kidney Foundation. The two card set commemorates the one year anniversary of Sean Elliott's return to basketball.

COMPLETE SET (2) .75 2.00
SE Sean Elliott .75 2.00
NNO Nation Kidney Foundation .05 .15

2008-09 Topps Signature

COMPLETE SET (85) 75.00 150.00
PRINT RUN 2325 SER.#'d SETS
TSAA Arron Afflalo .60 1.50
TSAT Al Thornton .75 2.00
TSBD Baron Davis .75 2.00
TSBR Brandon Roy 1.00 2.50
TSBW Brandan Wright .75 2.00
TSCL Courtney Lee RC 1.00 2.50
TSCP Chris Paul 1.25 3.00
TSDC Daequan Cook .60 1.50
TSDE Dale Ellis .60 1.50
TSDH Dwight Howard .75 2.00
TSDJ DeAndre Jordan RC 1.50 4.00
TSDR Derrick Rose RC 5.00 12.00
TSDS Dolph Schayes 1.00 2.50
TSEB Elgin Baylor 1.00 2.50
TSEG Eric Gordon RC 2.00 5.00
TSEH Elvin Hayes 1.00 2.50
TSFL Fat Lever .75 2.00
TSGA Gilbert Arenas .75 2.00
TSGG George Gervin 1.25 3.00
TSGH George Hill RC 1.25 3.00
TSGP Gabe Pruitt .60 1.50
TSGW Gerald Wallace .75 2.00
TSIT Isiah Thomas 1.00 2.50
TSJA Joe Alexander RC .75 2.00
TSJD Joey Dorsey RC .75 2.00
TSJH Josh Howard .75 2.00
TSJM JaVale McGee RC 1.50 4.00
TSJS John Stockton 1.50 4.00
TSJW Jerry West 1.25 3.00
TSKW Kyle Weaver RC .75 2.00
TSLB Larry Bird 2.50 6.00
TSLW Lenny Wilkens 1.00 2.50
TSMA Morris Almond .60 1.50
TSME Mark Eaton .60 1.50
TSMJ Magic Johnson 2.50 6.00
TSML Maurice Lucas 1.00 2.50
TSMP Mickael Pietrus .60 1.50
TSMW Marcus Williams .60 1.50
TSNY Nick Young .75 2.00
TSOB Otis Birdsong .75 2.00
TSPP Paul Pierce 1.00 2.50
TSRA Ryan Anderson RC 1.00 2.50
TSRF Raymond Felton .75 2.00
TSRG Rudy Gay 1.00 2.50
TSRP Robert Parish 1.00 2.50
TSRR Rajon Rondo 1.00 2.50
TSRS Rodney Stuckey .75 2.00
TSRT Reggie Theus .75 2.00
TSRW Russell Westbrook RC 10.00 25.00
TSSC Speedy Claxton .60 1.50
TSSD Samuel Dalembert .60 1.50
TSSH Spencer Hawes .60 1.50
TSSO Shaquille O'Neal 2.00 5.00
TSSP Sam Perkins .60 1.50
TSSS Sean Singletary RC .75 2.00
TSSW Sonny Weems RC .75 2.00
TSTY Thaddeus Young .75 2.00
TSVC Vince Carter 1.25 3.00
TSWS Walter Sharpe RC .75 2.00
TSYJ Yi Jianlian 1.00 2.50
TSZR Zach Randolph .75 2.00
TSABR Aaron Brooks .60 1.50
TSATU Alando Tucker .60 1.50
TSBRU Bill Russell 1.50 4.00
TSBWA Bill Walker RC .75 2.00
TSBWI Buck Williams .60 1.50
TSCBU Caron Butler .75 2.00
TSDGA Danilo Gallinari RC 2.00 5.00
TSDGI Daniel Gibson .75 2.00
TSDGR Donte Greene RC .75 2.00
TSDRD Dennis Rodman 2.00 5.00
TSDRO David Robinson 1.50 4.00
TSDSC Danny Schayes 1.00 2.50
TSDWA Dwyane Wade 1.50 4.00
TSJHA John Havlicek 1.00 2.50
TSJJH J.J. Hickson RC 1.00 2.50
TSJJW Jo Jo White .75 2.00
TSJRG J.R. Giddens RC .75 2.00
TSMRR Micheal Ray Richardson .75 2.00
TSOJM O.J. Mayo RC 1.25 3.00
TSRAL Ray Allen 1.00 2.50
TSRPI Ricky Pierce .60 1.50
TSSHA Spencer Haywood .60 1.50
TSSWE Spud Webb .75 2.00
TSJHRW John "Hot Rod" Williams .60 1.50

2008-09 Topps Signature Facsimile Black

*BLACK: .6X TO 1.5X BASE HI
STATED PRINT RUN 289 SER.#'d SETS
TSRW Russell Westbrook 30.00 80.00

2008-09 Topps Signature Facsimile Red

*RED: .5X TO 1.25X BASE HI
STATED PRINT RUN 869 SER.#'d SETS
TSRW Russell Westbrook 25.00 60.00

2008-09 Topps Signature Autographs

PRINT RUNS LISTED IN CHECKLIST
TSAAA Arron Afflalo/917 4.00 10.00
TSAAT Al Thornton/1799 4.00 10.00
TSABD Baron Davis/1079 5.00 12.00
TSABR Brandon Roy/649 6.00 15.00
TSABW Brandan Wright/3645 4.00 10.00
TSACL Courtney Lee/149 4.00 10.00
TSACP Chris Paul/649 15.00 40.00
TSADC Daequan Cook/1199 4.00 10.00
TSADE Dale Ellis/999 4.00 10.00
TSADH Dwight Howard/2499 6.00 15.00
TSADJ DeAndre Jordan/149 12.00 30.00
TSADR Derrick Rose/649 25.00 60.00
TSADS Dolph Schayes/425 4.00 10.00
TSAEB Elgin Baylor/1299 8.00 20.00
TSAEG Eric Gordon/275 5.00 12.00
TSAEH Elvin Hayes/625 6.00 15.00
TSAFL Fat Lever/750 4.00 10.00
TSAGA Gilbert Arenas/1199 4.00 10.00
TSAGG George Gervin/875 8.00 20.00
TSAGH George Hill/550 4.00 10.00
TSAGP Gabe Pruitt/1199 4.00 10.00
TSAGW Gerald Wallace/1499 4.00 10.00
TSAIT Isiah Thomas/999 8.00 20.00
TSAJA Joe Alexander/147 4.00 10.00
TSAJD Joey Dorsey/299 4.00 10.00
TSAJH Josh Howard/625 4.00 10.00
TSAJM JaVale McGee/275 5.00 12.00
TSAJS John Stockton/676 15.00 40.00
TSAJW Jerry West/649 15.00 40.00
TSAKW Kyle Weaver/699 4.00 10.00
TSALB Larry Bird/499 30.00 80.00
TSALW Lenny Wilkens/650 6.00 15.00
TSAMA Morris Almond/599 4.00 10.00
TSAME Mark Eaton/1029 4.00 10.00
TSAMJ Magic Johnson/499 15.00 40.00
TSAML Maurice Lucas/999 4.00 10.00
TSAMP Mickael Pietrus/1399 4.00 10.00
TSAMW Marcus Williams/1199 4.00 10.00
TSANY Nick Young/6225 4.00 10.00
TSAOB Otis Birdsong/1199 4.00 10.00
TSAPP Paul Pierce/1999 8.00 20.00
TSARA Ryan Anderson/499 4.00 10.00
TSARF Raymond Felton/1799 4.00 10.00
TSARG Rudy Gay/3640 4.00 10.00
TSARP Robert Parish/650 8.00 20.00
TSARR Rajon Rondo/1299 5.00 12.00
TSARS Rodney Stuckey/450 4.00 10.00
TSART Reggie Theus/940 4.00 10.00
TSARW R. Westbrook/184 150.00 300.00
TSASC Speedy Claxton/599 4.00 10.00
TSASD Samuel Dalembert/750 4.00 10.00
TSASH Spencer Hawes/999 4.00 10.00
TSASO Shaquille O'Neal/825 30.00 80.00
TSASP Sam Perkins/1199 4.00 10.00
TSASS Sean Singletary/1999 4.00 10.00
TSASW Sonny Weems/799 4.00 10.00
TSATY Thaddeus Young/5775 4.00 10.00
TSAVC Vince Carter/599 10.00 25.00
TSAWS Walter Sharpe/350 4.00 10.00
TSAYJ Yi Jianlian/6225 5.00 12.00
TSAZR Zach Randolph/1799 4.00 10.00
TSAABR Aaron Brooks/492 4.00 10.00
TSAATU Alando Tucker/2999 4.00 10.00
TSABRU Bill Russell/499 40.00 100.00
TSABWA Bill Walker/1999 5.00 12.00
TSABWI Buck Williams/1299 5.00 12.00
TSACBU Caron Butler/1309 4.00 10.00
TSADGA Danilo Gallinari/439 8.00 20.00
TSADGI Daniel Gibson/1799 4.00 10.00
TSADGR Donte Greene/1199 4.00 10.00
TSADRD Dennis Rodman/1299 12.00 30.00
TSADRO David Robinson/899 15.00 40.00
TSADSC Danny Schayes/750 4.00 10.00
TSADWA Dwyane Wade/649 15.00 40.00
TSAJHA John Havlicek/799 10.00 25.00
TSAJJH J.J. Hickson/125 4.00 10.00
TSAJJW Jo Jo White/989 5.00 12.00
TSAJRG J.R. Giddens/625 4.00 10.00
TSAMRR Micheal Ray Richardson/1199 4.00 10.00
TSAOJM O.J. Mayo/599 4.00 10.00
TSARAL Ray Allen/799 15.00 40.00
TSARPI Ricky Pierce/999 4.00 10.00
TSASHA Spencer Haywood/1179 4.00 10.00
TSASWE Spud Webb/1899 5.00 12.00
TSAJHRW Hot Rod Williams/750 5.00 12.00

2008-09 Topps Signature Autographs Dual

STATED PRINT RUN 49 SER.#'d SETS
TSDBA C.Billups/C.Anthony 25.00 50.00
TSDGM R.Gay/O.Mayo 15.00 30.00
TSDHW D.Howard/D.Wade 25.00 60.00
TSDIG A.Iguodala/D.Granger 8.00 20.00
TSDOR G.Oden/B.Roy 30.00 60.00
TSDPR C.Paul/D.Rose 125.00 250.00
TSDRG D.Robinson/G.Gervin 40.00 100.00
TSDSJ J.Stockton/M.Johnson 60.00 120.00
TSDWC D.Wilkins/V.Carter 25.00 50.00
TSDWR J.West/B.Russell 75.00 150.00

2008-09 Topps Signature Autographs Triple

PRINT RUNS B/WN 9-36 COPI ES PER
TSTARM Arenas/Roy/Mayo 40.00 100.00
TSTHOR Howard/O'Neal/D.Rob 150.00 300.00
TSTJWB Magic/West/Baylor 125.00 250.00

2005 Topps Special Edition Authentic

AU ISSUED AS REPLACEMENT
E01 Emeka Okafor/499 5.00 12.00
E02 Emeka Okafor/99 8.00 20.00
E03 Emeka Okafor/25 12.00 30.00

1992 Topps Stadium of Stars

This 12-card standard-size set measures the standard size and features stars from different sports and entertainment. The cards have the same design as the regular 1992 Topps cards. The fronts feature color portraits with red and white inner borders and white outer borders. The star's name and the set name appear in two short color stripes respectively at the bottom. The backs carry a short biography and personal information. The cards are unnumbered and checklisted below in alphabetical order

COMPLETE SET (12) 5.00 12.00
9 Ann Meyers BK .40 1.00
12 John Wooden CO BK 1.00 2.50

1996 Topps Stars

This set was created to commemorate the NBA's announcement of their top 50 players of all time. The set contained 150-cards and was issued in 8-card packs that carried a suggested retail price of $3.00. Each player had three cards - a Golden Season card highlighting their best year and two versions of a Commemorative card, in which the card fronts were the same but one had an all-text back and the other featured all the career statistics showing why each player is among the NBA's top 50. Each player has three different cards, but only one card is priced below. All cards carry the same value. All the cards were full-bleed, double-foil stamped and printed on 20-point stock.

COMPLETE SET (150) 20.00 40.00
CL (NNO) .08 .25
1 Kareem Abdul-Jabbar .25 .60
2 Nate Archibald .12 .30
3 Paul Arizin .15 .40
4 Charles Barkley .25 .60
5 Rick Barry .12 .30
6 Elgin Baylor .15 .40
7 Dave Bing .15 .40
8 Larry Bird .40 1.00
9 Wilt Chamberlain .30 .75
10 Bob Cousy .25 .60
11 Dave Cowens .10 .25
12 Billy Cunningham .15 .40
13 Dave DeBusschere .15 .40
14 Clyde Drexler .20 .50
15 Julius Erving .25 .60
16 Patrick Ewing .20 .50
17 Walt Frazier .15 .40
18 George Gervin .15 .40
19 Hal Greer .12 .30
20 John Havlicek .20 .50
21 Elvin Hayes .15 .40
22 Magic Johnson .40 1.00
23 Sam Jones .20 .50
24 Michael Jordan 1.25 3.00
25 Jerry Lucas .15 .40
26 Karl Malone .20 .50
27 Moses Malone .15 .40
28 Pete Maravich .25 .60
29 Kevin McHale .20 .50
30 George Mikan .25 .60
31 Earl Monroe .15 .40
32 Shaquille O'Neal .40 1.00
33 Hakeem Olajuwon .20 .50
34 Robert Parish .15 .40
35 Bob Pettit .15 .40
36 Scottie Pippen .25 .60
37 Willis Reed .15 .40
38 Oscar Robertson .20 .50
39 David Robinson .25 .60
40 Bill Russell .25 .60
41 Dolph Schayes .15 .40
42 Bill Sharman .15 .40
43 John Stockton .20 .50
44 Isiah Thomas .15 .40
45 Nate Thurmond .12 .30
46 Wes Unseld .15 .40
47 Bill Walton .15 .40
48 Jerry West .20 .50
49 Lenny Wilkens .15 .40
50 James Worthy .20 .50
51 Kareem Abdul-Jabbar GS .25 .60
52 Nate Archibald GS .12 .30
53 Paul Arizin GS .15 .40
54 Charles Barkley GS .25 .60
55 Rick Barry GS .12 .30
56 Elgin Baylor GS .15 .40
57 Dave Bing GS .15 .40
58 Larry Bird GS .40 1.00
59 Wilt Chamberlain GS .30 .75
60 Bob Cousy GS .25 .60
61 Dave Cowens GS .10 .25
62 Billy Cunningham GS .15 .40
63 Dave DeBusschere GS .15 .40
64 Clyde Drexler GS .20 .50
65 Julius Erving GS .25 .60
66 Patrick Ewing GS .20 .50
67 Walt Frazier GS .15 .40
68 George Gervin GS .15 .40
69 Hal Greer GS .12 .30
70 John Havlicek GS .20 .50
71 Elvin Hayes GS .15 .40
72 Magic Johnson GS .40 1.00
73 Sam Jones GS .20 .50
74 Michael Jordan GS 1.25 3.00
75 Jerry Lucas GS .15 .40
76 Karl Malone GS .20 .50
77 Moses Malone GS .15 .40
78 Pete Maravich GS .25 .60
79 Kevin McHale GS .20 .50
80 George Mikan GS .25 .60
81 Earl Monroe GS .15 .40
82 Shaquille O'Neal GS .40 1.00
83 Hakeem Olajuwon GS .20 .50
84 Robert Parish GS .15 .40
85 Bob Pettit GS .15 .40
86 Scottie Pippen GS .25 .60
87 Willis Reed GS .15 .40
88 Oscar Robertson GS .20 .50
89 David Robinson GS .25 .60
90 Bill Russell GS .25 .60
91 Dolph Schayes GS .15 .40
92 Bill Sharman GS .15 .40
93 John Stockton GS .20 .50
94 Isiah Thomas GS .15 .40
95 Nate Thurmond GS .12 .30
96 Wes Unseld GS .15 .40
97 Bill Walton GS .15 .40
98 Jerry West GS .20 .50
99 Lenny Wilkens GS .15 .40
100 James Worthy GS .20 .50
101 Kareem Abdul-Jabbar .25 .60
102 Nate Archibald .12 .30
103 Paul Arizin .15 .40
104 Charles Barkley .25 .60
105 Rick Barry .12 .30
106 Elgin Baylor .15 .40
107 Dave Bing .15 .40
108 Larry Bird .40 1.00
109 Wilt Chamberlain .30 .75
110 Bob Cousy .25 .60
111 Dave Cowens .10 .25
112 Billy Cunningham .15 .40
113 Dave DeBusschere .15 .40
114 Clyde Drexler .20 .50
115 Julius Erving .25 .60
116 Patrick Ewing .20 .50
117 Walt Frazier .15 .40
118 George Gervin .15 .40
119 Hal Greer .12 .30
120 John Havlicek .20 .50
121 Elvin Hayes .15 .40
122 Magic Johnson .40 1.00
123 Sam Jones .20 .50
124 Michael Jordan 1.25 3.00
125 Jerry Lucas .15 .40
126 Karl Malone .20 .50
127 Moses Malone .15 .40
128 Pete Maravich .25 .60
129 Kevin McHale .20 .50
130 George Mikan .25 .60
131 Earl Monroe .15 .40
132 Shaquille O'Neal .40 1.00
133 Hakeem Olajuwon .20 .50
134 Robert Parish .15 .40
135 Bob Pettit .15 .40
136 Scottie Pippen .25 .60
137 Willis Reed .15 .40
138 Oscar Robertson .20 .50
139 David Robinson .25 .60
140 Bill Russell .25 .60
141 Dolph Schayes .15 .40
142 Bill Sharman .15 .40
143 John Stockton .20 .50
144 Isiah Thomas .15 .40
145 Nate Thurmond .12 .30
146 Wes Unseld .15 .40
147 Bill Walton .15 .40
148 Jerry West .20 .50
149 Lenny Wilkens .15 .40
150 James Worthy .20 .50

1996 Topps Stars Finest

COMPLETE SET (150) 150.00 300.00
*STARS: 2.5X TO 6X BASIC

1996 Topps Stars Finest Atomic Refractors

*ATOMIC: 25X TO 60X BASE HI

1996 Topps Stars Finest Refractors

*REFRACTORS: 8X TO 20X BASIC

1996 Topps Stars Imagine

Randomly inserted into all packs at a rate of one in 18, this 25-card dual player set uses computer imagery to pit two players from different eras against one another. Card backs carry an "I" prefix.

COMPLETE SET (25) 65.00 125.00
I1 Shaquille O'Neal 5.00 12.00
Wilt Chamberlain
I2 David Robinson 2.00 5.00
Dave Cowens
I3 Kareem Abdul-Jabbar 4.00 10.00
Bill Russell
I4 Scottie Pippen 4.00 10.00
Julius Erving
I5 Hakeem Olajuwon 2.00 5.00
Elvin Hayes
I6 Michael Jordan 8.00 20.00
Oscar Robertson
I7 Clyde Drexler 1.50 4.00
Earl Monroe
I8 Magic Johnson 4.00 10.00
Jerry West
I9 Larry Bird 3.00 8.00
Rick Barry
I10 Kevin McHale 1.50 4.00
Dave DeBusschere
I11 Moses Malone 1.25 3.00
Jerry Lucas
I12 Robert Parish 1.25 3.00
Nate Thurmond
I13 Pete Maravich 2.00 5.00
Sam Jones
I14 John Stockton 3.00 8.00
Bob Cousy
I15 Isiah Thomas 1.25 3.00
Bill Sharman
I16 Karl Malone 3.00 8.00
Bob Pettit
I17 Bill Walton 2.50 6.00
George Mikan
I18 Patrick Ewing 1.50 4.00
Willis Reed
I19 Billy Cunningham 1.25 3.00
James Worthy
I20 George Gervin 1.25 3.00
Hal Greer
I21 Wes Unseld 1.25 3.00
Dolph Schayes
I22 Nate Archibald 1.25 3.00
Lenny Wilkens
I23 Walt Frazier 1.25 3.00
Paul Arizin
I24 Charles Barkley 2.50 6.00
Elgin Baylor
I25 Dave Bing 2.50 6.00
John Havlicek

1996 Topps Stars Reprints

Randomly inserted into hobby packs at a rate of one in nine and retail at one in six, this 50-card set features reprints of each player's first Topps, Bowman or Star Company cards.

COMPLETE SET (50) 150.00 250.00
1 Lew Alcindor 5.00 12.00
2 Nate Archibald 1.25 3.00
3 Paul Arizin .75 2.00
4 Charles Barkley 5.00 12.00
5 Rick Barry 1.00 2.50
6 Elgin Baylor .75 2.00
7 Dave Bing .75 2.00
8 Larry Bird 12.00 30.00
Julius Erving
Magic Johnson
9 Wilt Chamberlain 5.00 12.00
10 Bob Cousy 3.00 8.00
11 Dave Cowens .75 2.00
12 Billy Cunningham .75 2.00
13 Dave DeBusschere .75 2.00
14 Clyde Drexler 1.50 4.00
15 Julius Erving 5.00 12.00
16 Patrick Ewing 1.50 4.00
17 Walt Frazier 1.25 3.00
18 George Gervin 1.25 3.00
19 Hal Greer .75 2.00
20 John Havlicek 3.00 8.00
21 Elvin Hayes 1.25 3.00
22 Larry Bird 10.00 25.00
Julius Erving
Magic Johnson
23 Sam Jones .75 2.00
24 Michael Jordan 20.00 50.00
25 Jerry Lucas .75 2.00
26 Karl Malone 3.00 8.00
27 Moses Malone 1.50 4.00
28 Pete Maravich 3.00 8.00
29 Kevin McHale 1.25 3.00
30 George Mikan 3.00 8.00
31 Earl Monroe 1.25 3.00
32 Shaquille O'Neal 3.00 8.00
33 Hakeem Olajuwon 4.00 10.00
34 Robert Parish 1.25 3.00
35 Bob Pettit 1.00 2.50
36 Scottie Pippen 4.00 10.00
37 Willis Reed .75 2.00
38 Oscar Robertson 3.00 8.00
39 David Robinson 2.50 6.00
40 Bill Russell 5.00 12.00
41 Dolph Schayes 1.50 4.00
42 Bill Sharman .75 2.00
43 John Stockton 1.50 4.00
44 Isiah Thomas 1.50 4.00
45 Nate Thurmond .75 2.00
46 Wes Unseld .75 2.00
47 Bill Walton 1.25 3.00
48 Jerry West 4.00 10.00
49 Len Wilkens UER .75 2.00
50 James Worthy 1.50 4.00

1996 Topps Stars Reprint Autographs

Inserted one per retail box, 10 of the 50 players from the Topps NBA Stars signed their reprint cards. Each card has a gold seal of authenticity and is signed on the front of the card in black ink. The set is skip-numbered. In addition, one of the ten cards were inserted into 1996-97 Topps Factory Hobby sets.

COMPLETE SET (10) 150.00 300.00
2 Nate Archibald 10.00 25.00
5 Rick Barry 10.00 25.00
17 Walt Frazier 10.00 25.00
18 George Gervin 12.00 30.00
21 Elvin Hayes 12.00 30.00
23 Sam Jones 10.00 25.00
30 George Mikan 80.00 200.00
31 Earl Monroe 10.00 25.00
37 Willis Reed 12.00 30.00
47 Bill Walton 8.00 20.00

1996 Topps Stars Members Only Parallel

COMPLETE SET (150) 300.00 500.00
*MO: 5X TO 12X BASE TOPPS STARS HI

1996 Topps Stars Imagine Members Only Parallel

COMPLETE SET (25) 60.00 150.00
*MO: .6X TO 1.5X BASE IMAGINE HI

1996 Topps Stars Reprints Members Only Parallel

COMPLETE SET (50) 150.00 300.00
*MO: .6X TO 1.5X BASE REPRINT HI

1996 Topps Stars Uncut Sheets

These two sheets were prizes awarded to collector's who received a Fan Favorite ballot card in Topps NBA Stars (around 1:6 packs), filled out their vote for the top five NBA players of all time, and correctly matched them with the overall tally taken from Topps' "blue ribbon media panel". Topps reported that only a small fraction (a total of 1,073 voters) correctly matched the top five players: Kareem Abdul-Jabar, Larry Bird, Wilt Chamberlain, Magic Johnson and Bill Russell. The 33 Basketball Hall of Famers that were in the top 50 NBA list had their Topps reprints on this two-sided, uncut sheet. There are two variations: a Gold bordered sheet awarded to correct entries from hobby packs (a reported 402) and a black bordered sheet awarded to correct entries from retail packs (a reported 671). The sheets were shipped in a round tube, so many of these thick stock sheets are curved as opposed to flat.

COMPLETE SET (2) 20.00 50.00
1 Black Bordered Sheet 10.00 25.00
2 Gold Bordered Sheet 10.00 25.00

2000-01 Topps Stars Promos

These six cards were given to hobby dealers and members of the media to promote the 2000-01 Topps Stars product. The set was shipped in a cello wrapper, and the card backs carry a "PP" prefix.

COMPLETE SET (6) 2.00 5.00
PP1 Allen Iverson 1.00 2.50
PP2 Jason Williams .50 1.25
PP3 Antonio McDyess .40 1.00
PP4 Alonzo Mourning .60 1.50
PP5 Ray Allen .50 1.25
PP6 Larry Hughes .40 1.00

2000-01 Topps Stars

Released in November 2000, the Topps Stars base set was comprised of 150 cards. Cards were available in six-card packs that carried a suggested retail price of $3.00. The base set was broken into the following themes: 100 veterans, 25 rookies, and 25 Spotlight subset cards.

COMPLETE SET (150) 20.00 50.00
SUBSET CARDS SAME VALUE AS BASE
1 Elton Brand .25 .60
2 Paul Pierce .25 .60
3 Baron Davis .25 .60
4 Corey Benjamin .15 .40
5 Jason Kidd .40 1.00
6 Stephon Marbury .20 .50
7 Eric Snow .15 .40
8 Joe Smith .20 .50
9 Larry Hughes .20 .50
10 Tim Duncan .50 1.25
11 Theo Ratliff .15 .40
12 Dikembe Mutombo .25 .60
13 Tim Hardaway .25 .60
14 Glenn Robinson .20 .50
15 Grant Hill .30 .75
16 Patrick Ewing .30 .75
17 Ron Mercer .15 .40
18 Ron Artest .25 .60
19 Tom Gugliotta .15 .40
20 Steve Smith .20 .50
21 Vlade Divac .20 .50
22 Rashard Lewis .25 .60
23 Tracy McGrady .40 1.00
24 Bryon Russell .15 .40
25 Michael Dickerson .15 .40
26 Juwan Howard .20 .50
27 Damon Stoudamire .20 .50
28 Hakeem Olajuwon .30 .75
29 Antonio McDyess .20 .50
30 Kobe Bryant 1.00 2.50
31 Lindsey Hunter .15 .40
32 Magic Johnson .60 1.50
33 Alonzo Mourning .30 .75
34 Kenny Anderson .20 .50
35 Allan Houston .20 .50
36 Keith Van Horn .20 .50
37 Shawn Marion .20 .50
38 David Robinson .40 1.00
39 Mitch Richmond .20 .50
40 Shaquille O'Neal .60 1.50
41 Gary Payton .25 .60
42 Sean Elliott .25 .60
43 Sam Cassell .20 .50
44 Dale Davis .15 .40
45 Derek Anderson .15 .40

46 Jonathan Bender .15 .40
47 Shandon Anderson .15 .40
48 Raef LaFrentz .15 .40
49 Michael Finley .25 .60
50 Toni Kukoc .25 .60
51 Anthony Mason .15 .40
52 Jim Jackson .15 .40
53 Glen Rice .20 .50
54 Jalen Rose .20 .50
55 Keon Clark .15 .40
56 Anfernee Hardaway .40 1.00
57 Vin Baker .20 .50
58 Shawn Kemp .25 .60
59 John Stockton .30 .75
60 Shareef Abdur-Rahim .20 .50
61 Doug Christie .15 .40
62 Lamond Murray .15 .40
63 Scottie Pippen .40 1.00
64 Darrell Armstrong .15 .40
65 Marcus Camby .20 .50
66 Wally Szczerbiak .20 .50
67 Jamal Mashburn .20 .50
68 Antonio Davis .15 .40
69 Kevin Garnett .40 1.00
70 Cuttino Mobley .15 .40
71 Jerry Stackhouse .20 .50
72 Cedric Ceballos .15 .40
73 Nick Van Exel .20 .50
74 Latrell Sprewell .20 .50
75 Antoine Walker .20 .50
76 Allen Iverson .50 1.25
77 Antawn Jamison .25 .60
78 Derrick Coleman .20 .50
79 Jason Terry .25 .60
80 Steve Francis .20 .50
81 Reggie Miller .25 .60
82 Rasheed Wallace .25 .60
83 Chris Webber .25 .60
84 Donyell Marshall .15 .40
85 Ruben Patterson .15 .40
86 Terrell Brandon .15 .40
87 Mike Bibby .25 .60
88 Richard Hamilton .20 .50
89 Jason Williams .25 .60
90 Corey Maggette .20 .50
91 Kerry Kittles .15 .40
92 Karl Malone .30 .75
93 Rod Strickland .15 .40
94 Eddie Jones .25 .60
95 Maurice Taylor .15 .40
96 Dirk Nowitzki .40 1.00
97 Andre Miller .20 .50
98 Lamar Odom .20 .50
99 Ray Allen .25 .60
100 Vince Carter .50 1.25
101 Chris Mihm RC .20 .50
102 Kenyon Martin RC .60 1.50
103 Stromile Swift RC .25 .60
104 Joel Przybilla RC .20 .50
105 Marcus Fizer RC .25 .60
106 Mike Miller RC .40 1.00
107 Darius Miles RC .25 .60
108 Mark Madsen RC .25 .60
109 Courtney Alexander RC .20 .50
110 DeShawn Stevenson RC .25 .60
111 DerMarr Johnson RC .20 .50
112 Mamadou N'Diaye RC .15 .40
113 Mateen Cleaves RC .20 .50
114 Morris Peterson RC .25 .60
115 Etan Thomas RC .25 .60
116 Erick Barkley RC .15 .40
117 Quentin Richardson RC .25 .60
118 Keyon Dooling RC .25 .60
119 Jerome Moiso RC .15 .40
120 Desmond Mason RC .30 .75
121 Speedy Claxton RC .25 .60
122 Jamaal Magloire RC .25 .60
123 Donnell Harvey RC .20 .50
124 Jamal Crawford RC .60 1.50
125 Jason Collier RC .25 .60
126 Tim Duncan SPOT .50 1.25
127 Shaquille O'Neal SPOT .60 1.50
128 Vince Carter SPOT .50 1.25
129 Allen Iverson SPOT .50 1.25
130 Jason Kidd SPOT .40 1.00
131 Kevin Garnett SPOT .40 1.00
132 Gary Payton SPOT .25 .60
133 Tracy McGrady SPOT .40 1.00
134 Jason Williams SPOT .25 .60
135 Kobe Bryant SPOT 1.00 2.50
136 Elton Brand SPOT .25 .60
137 Ray Allen SPOT .25 .60
138 Grant Hill SPOT .30 .75
139 Chris Webber SPOT .25 .60
140 Latrell Sprewell SPOT .20 .50
141 Alonzo Mourning SPOT .30 .75
142 Lamar Odom SPOT .20 .50
143 Shareef Abdur-Rahim SPOT .20 .50
144 Steve Francis SPOT .20 .50
145 Magic Johnson SPOT .60 1.50
146 Darius Miles SPOT .25 .60
147 Kenyon Martin SPOT .60 1.50
148 Marcus Fizer SPOT .25 .60
149 Mateen Cleaves SPOT .20 .50
150 Stromile Swift SPOT .25 .60

2000-01 Topps Stars Parallel

*BASE STARS: 5X TO 12X BASE CARD HI
*BASE RCs: 2.5X TO 6X BASE CARD HI
BASE: PRINT RUN 299 SERIAL #'d SETS
*SUB.STARS: 10X TO 25X SUBSET CARD HI
*SUB.RCs: 10X TO 25X SUBSET CARD HI
SUBSET: PRINT RUN 99 SERIAL #'d SETS
SUBSET: STATED ODDS 1:261
135 Kobe Bryant SPOT 40.00 100.00

2000-01 Topps Stars All-Star Authority

Randomly inserted in packs at one in 12, this 15-card set features All-Star players who continuously demonstrate their dominance of the NBA. Card backs carry an "ASA" prefix.
COMPLETE SET (15) 7.50 15.00
STATED ODDS 1:12 HOB/RET
ASA1 John Stockton .75 2.00
ASA2 Shaquille O'Neal 1.50 4.00
ASA3 Patrick Ewing .75 2.00
ASA4 Hakeem Olajuwon .75 2.00
ASA5 Karl Malone .75 2.00
ASA6 Grant Hill .75 2.00
ASA7 Alonzo Mourning .75 2.00
ASA8 Jason Kidd 1.00 2.50
ASA9 Gary Payton .60 1.50
ASA10 Scottie Pippen 1.00 2.50
ASA11 Tim Duncan 1.25 3.00
ASA12 Kevin Garnett 1.00 2.50
ASA13 Reggie Miller .60 1.50
ASA14 David Robinson 1.00 2.50
ASA15 Dikembe Mutombo .60 1.50

2000-01 Topps Stars Autographs

Randomly inserted in packs at an overall rate of one in 316, this 10-card set features autographs of top players in the NBA. Each card features the Topps "Certified Autograph Issue" stamp. The autographs were broken into two levels: Level "A" were inserted at one in 359 packs, while Level "B" were inserted at one in 2,599 packs.
GROUP A: STATED ODDS 1:359
GROUP B: STATED ODDS 1:2599
OVERALL STATED ODDS 1:316
TSAJ Antawn Jamison A 4.00 10.00
TSCA Courtney Alexander A 4.00 10.00
TSEB Elton Brand A 5.00 12.00
TSJC Jamal Crawford A 10.00 25.00
TSJR Jalen Rose A 5.00 12.00
TSMC Mateen Cleaves A 4.00 10.00
TSMJ Magic Johnson A 40.00 100.00
TSSF Steve Francis A 5.00 12.00
TSTD Tim Duncan B 200.00 400.00
TSTM Tracy McGrady A 20.00 50.00

2000-01 Topps Stars Game Jerseys

Randomly inserted in packs at an overall rate of one in 71, this 34-card set features swatches of game-worn jersey from players who participated in the 2000 NBA Finals.
LAKERS HOME GJ: STATED ODDS 1:646
LAKERS AWAY GJ: STATED ODDS 1:117
PACERS HOME GJ: STATED ODDS 1:359
OVERALL STATED ODDS 1:71
LAKERS (H) JERSEYS ARE YELLOW
LAKERS (A) JERSEYS ARE PURPLE
TSR1A Shaquille O'Neal 12.00 30.00
TSR1H Shaquille O'Neal 12.00 30.00
TSR2A Glen Rice 6.00 15.00
TSR2H Glen Rice 6.00 15.00
TSR3A Robert Horry 6.00 15.00
TSR3H Robert Horry 6.00 15.00
TSR4A Rick Fox 5.00 12.00
TSR4H Rick Fox 5.00 12.00
TSR5A Brian Shaw 5.00 12.00
TSR5H Brian Shaw 5.00 12.00
TSR6A Ron Harper 6.00 15.00
TSR6H Ron Harper 6.00 15.00
TSR7A Derek Fisher 8.00 20.00
TSR7H Derek Fisher 8.00 20.00
TSR8A A.C. Green 10.00 25.00
TSR8H A.C. Green 10.00 25.00
TSR9A John Salley 5.00 12.00
TSR9H John Salley 5.00 12.00
TSR10A Travis Knight 5.00 12.00
TSR10H Travis Knight 5.00 12.00
TSR11A Devean George 5.00 12.00
TSR11H Devean George 5.00 12.00
TSR12 Reggie Miller 15.00 40.00
TSR13 Jalen Rose 6.00 15.00
TSR14 Dale Davis 5.00 12.00
TSR15 Rik Smits 5.00 12.00
TSR16 Mark Jackson 6.00 15.00
TSR17 Travis Best 5.00 12.00
TSR18 Austin Croshere 5.00 12.00
TSR19 Derrick McKey 5.00 12.00
TSR20 Sam Perkins 5.00 12.00
TSR21 Chris Mullin 15.00 40.00
TSR22 Jonathan Bender 5.00 12.00
TSR23 Zan Tabak 5.00 12.00
TSRMJ Magic Johnson 12.00 30.00

2000-01 Topps Stars On the Horizon

Randomly inserted in packs at one in 36, this 10-card set takes a look at young stars ready to explode in the NBA. Card backs carry a "H" prefix.
COMPLETE SET (10) 6.00 15.00
STATED ODDS 1:36 HOB/RET
H1 Steve Francis .60 1.50
H2 Elton Brand .75 2.00
H3 Tracy McGrady 1.25 3.00
H4 Stephon Marbury .60 1.50
H5 Lamar Odom .60 1.50
H6 Kenyon Martin 2.00 5.00
H7 Shareef Abdur-Rahim .60 1.50
H8 Marcus Fizer .75 2.00
H9 Larry Hughes .60 1.50
H10 Darius Miles .75 2.00

2000-01 Topps Stars Progression

Randomly inserted in packs at one in 24, this five-card set showcases players from the past, present and future on one card. Card backs carry a "P" prefix.
COMPLETE SET (5) 5.00 12.00
STATED ODDS 1:24 HOB/RET
P1 Ewing/Zo/Mihm .75 2.00
P2 K.Malone/Brand/K.Martin 2.00 5.00
P3 Pippen/V.Carter/Miles 1.00 2.50
P4 Richmond/Kobe/C.Alex 1.50 4.00
P5 Magic/Stockton/Crawford 1.25 3.00

2000-01 Topps Stars Walk of Fame

Randomly inserted in packs at one in eight, this 15-card set features current superstars compared against all-time greats at their position. Card backs carry a "WF" prefix.
COMPLETE SET (15) 7.50 15.00
STATED ODDS 1:8 HOB/RET
WF1 Grant Hill .60 1.50
WF2 Vince Carter 1.00 2.50
WF3 Kevin Garnett .75 2.00
WF4 Jason Kidd .75 2.00
WF5 Gary Payton .50 1.25
WF6 Tim Duncan 1.00 2.50
WF7 Allen Iverson 1.00 2.50
WF8 Kobe Bryant 2.00 5.00
WF9 Ray Allen .50 1.25
WF10 Shareef Abdur-Rahim .40 1.00
WF11 Chris Webber .50 1.25
WF12 Karl Malone .60 1.50
WF13 Reggie Miller .50 1.25
WF14 Jason Williams .50 1.25
WF15 Elton Brand .50 1.25

1997 Topps Stickers

Released in some retail outlets, or through the Topps Stadium Club Members Only catalog, these stickers were issued on five different sheets. Each sheet contained 12 players and had a suggested retail price of $1.49. Boxes were available for $19.95.
COMPLETE SET (5) 3.00 8.00
1 Glen Rice .75 2.00
Dino Radja
Grant Hill
Clifford Robinson
Jerry Stackhouse
Horace Grant
Terrell Brandon
Lorenzen Wright
Sean Elliott
Stephon Marbury
Shaquille O'Neal
Ray Allen
2 Hakeem Olajuwon .75 2.00
Marcus Camby
Kobe Bryant
Chris Webber
Jayson Williams
Kenny Anderson
David Robinson
Joe Dumars
Michael Finley
Reggie Miller
Scottie Pippen
Latrell Sprewell
3 Alonzo Mourning .75 2.00
Bobby Phills
Christian Laettner
Dennis Rodman
Jason Kidd
Joe Smith
John Starks
Juwan Howard
Karl Malone
Kevin Garnett
Bryant Reeves
Mitch Richmond
4 Brent Barry .75 2.00
Anthony Mason
Antonio McDyess
Allen Iverson
Brian Grant
Charles Barkley
Dikembe Mutombo
John Stockton
Kerry Kittles
Rik Smits
Shawn Kemp
Tim Hardaway
5 Derek Harper .75 2.00
Patrick Ewing
Greg Anthony
Gary Payton
Kevin Johnson
Doug Christie
LaPhonso Ellis
Antoine Walker
Damon Stoudamire
Rony Seikaly
Vin Baker
Shareef Abdur-Rahim

2005-06 Topps Style

Released in May 2006, Style boasts a 165-card set where numbers 1-130 feature veteran players, numbers 131-160 feature rookie players and numbers 161-165 feature celebrites. Also printed was card number seven, a special Mickey Mantle basketball card. The set design is that of the 1952 Topps baseball set which utilizes white borders, colorful backgrounds, images that appear as though they were painted and a white-out name box along the bottom with the player's name and a fascimile signature. Style was packaged in 18-pack boxes where packs contain nine cards and carried an initial SRP of $6.00.
COMPLETE SET (165) 30.00 80.00
UNPRICED SUPERFR.PRINT RUN ONE SET
1 Ben Wallace .40 1.00
2 Joe Johnson .40 1.00
3 Luol Deng .40 1.00
4 Morris Peterson .30 .75
5 Jason Terry .40 1.00
6 Carmelo Anthony 1.00 2.50
7 Mickey Mantle 3.00 8.00
8 Ron Artest .50 1.25
9 Elton Brand .50 1.25
10 Chris Mihm .30 .75
11 Shane Battier .40 1.00
12 Speedy Claxton .30 .75
13 Baron Davis .40 1.00
14 Damon Stoudamire .40 1.00
15 Desmond Mason .30 .75
16 Marko Jaric .30 .75
17 Vince Carter .75 2.00
18 Sam Cassell .40 1.00
19 J.R. Smith .40 1.00
20 Trevor Ariza .30 .75
21 Quentin Richardson .40 1.00
22 Jamal Crawford .50 1.25
23 Dwight Howard .40 1.00
24 Kyle Korver .40 1.00
25 Steve Nash .60 1.50
26 Amare Stoudemire .40 1.00
27 Zach Randolph .40 1.00
28 Brad Miller .40 1.00
29 Tim Duncan .75 2.00
30 Michael Finley .50 1.25
31 Ray Allen .50 1.25
32 Luke Ridnour .40 1.00
33 Andrei Kirilenko .40 1.00
34 Tony Allen .30 .75
35 Paul Pierce .50 1.25
36 Al Jefferson .40 1.00
37 Emeka Okafor .40 1.00
38 Al Harrington .40 1.00
39 Ben Gordon .40 1.00
40 Andres Nocioni .30 .75
41 Zydrunas Ilgauskas .40 1.00
42 Anderson Varejao .30 .75
43 Keith Van Horn .40 1.00
44 Richard Hamilton .40 1.00
45 Stromile Swift .30 .75
46 Dirk Nowitzki .75 2.00
47 Stephen Jackson .40 1.00
48 Pau Gasol .50 1.25
49 Lamar Odom .40 1.00
50 Kobe Bryant 2.00 5.00
51 Shaquille O'Neal 1.00 2.50
52 Jason Williams .40 1.00
53 Dwyane Wade .75 2.00
54 Michael Redd .40 1.00
55 Joe Smith .40 1.00
56 Troy Hudson .30 .75
57 Jameer Nelson .30 .75
58 Chris Webber .50 1.25
59 Darius Miles .30 .75
60 Chris Wilcox .30 .75
61 Rafer Alston .30 .75
62 Kirk Hinrich .40 1.00
63 Jalen Rose .50 1.25
64 Matt Harpring .30 .75
65 Caron Butler .40 1.00
66 Shareef Abdur-Rahim .40 1.00
67 Josh Childress .40 1.00
68 Delonte West .30 .75
69 Brevin Knight .30 .75
70 Larry Hughes .40 1.00
71 Dikembe Mutombo .50 1.25
72 Kenyon Martin .40 1.00
73 Earl Boykins .30 .75
74 Tayshaun Prince .40 1.00
75 Chauncey Billups .50 1.25
76 Josh Smith .40 1.00
77 Troy Murphy .30 .75
78 Jermaine O'Neal .40 1.00
79 Corey Maggette .40 1.00
80 Wally Szczerbiak .40 1.00
81 Richard Jefferson .40 1.00
82 Nenad Krstic .30 .75
83 Jason Kidd .75 2.00
84 Jamaal Magloire .30 .75
85 Stephon Marbury .40 1.00
86 Samuel Dalembert .30 .75
87 Andre Iguodala .40 1.00
88 Yao Ming .60 1.50
89 Kurt Thomas .30 .75
90 Brendan Haywood .30 .75
91 Peja Stojakovic .50 1.25
92 Mike Bibby .50 1.25
93 Tony Parker .50 1.25
94 Manu Ginobili .50 1.25
95 Rashard Lewis .50 1.25
96 Mehmet Okur .30 .75
97 Gilbert Arenas .40 1.00
98 Antawn Jamison .40 1.00
99 Ricky Davis .40 1.00
100 Shawn Marion .40 1.00
101 Melvin Ely .30 .75
102 Tyson Chandler .40 1.00
103 Jason Richardson .50 1.25
104 Drew Gooden .40 1.00
105 Josh Howard .50 1.25
106 Marcus Camby .40 1.00
107 Jerry Stackhouse .40 1.00
108 Andre Miller .40 1.00
109 Rasheed Wallace .50 1.25
110 Mike Dunleavy .40 1.00
111 LeBron James 2.00 5.00
112 Allen Iverson .75 2.00
113 Tracy McGrady .60 1.50
114 Jamaal Tinsley .30 .75
115 Cuttino Mobley .30 .75
116 Kwame Brown .30 .75
117 Derek Anderson .30 .75
118 Eddie Jones .40 1.00
119 Antoine Walker .40 1.00
120 Alonzo Mourning .60 1.50
121 Bobby Simmons .30 .75
122 Kevin Garnett .75 2.00
123 P.J. Brown .30 .75
124 Steve Francis .40 1.00
125 Grant Hill .60 1.50
126 Primoz Brezec .30 .75
127 Mike Miller .40 1.00
128 Sebastian Telfair .40 1.00
129 Chris Bosh .50 1.25
130 Carlos Boozer .40 1.00
131 Andrew Bogut RC 1.50 4.00
132 Raymond Felton RC 1.25 3.00
133 Ike Diogu RC .75 2.00
134 Rashad McCants RC 1.00 2.50
135 Gerald Green RC 1.25 3.00
136 Jarrett Jack RC 1.25 3.00
137 Linas Kleiza RC .75 2.00
138 Brandon Bass RC 1.00 2.50
139 Marvin Williams RC 1.25 3.00
140 Martell Webster RC 1.00 2.50
141 Sarunas Jasikevicius RC 1.25 3.00
142 Antoine Wright RC 1.00 2.50
143 Hakim Warrick RC 1.00 2.50
144 Francisco Garcia RC 1.00 2.50
145 Wayne Simien RC .75 2.00
146 Monta Ellis RC 1.50 4.00
147 Deron Williams RC 1.50 4.00
148 Charlie Villanueva RC 1.25 3.00
149 Chris Taft RC 1.00 2.50
150 Joey Graham RC 1.00 2.50
151 Julius Hodge RC .75 2.00
152 Luther Head RC 1.00 2.50
153 David Lee RC 1.25 3.00
154 Chris Paul RC 5.00 12.00
155 Channing Frye RC 1.25 3.00
156 Sean May RC .75 2.00
157 Danny Granger RC 1.50 4.00
158 Nate Robinson RC 1.25 3.00
159 Jason Maxiell RC 1.00 2.50
160 Salim Stoudamire RC 1.00 2.50
161 Christie Brinkley 2.00 5.00
162 Carmen Electra 2.00 5.00
163 Shannon Elizabeth 2.00 5.00
164 Jenny McCarthy 2.00 5.00
165 Jay-Z 2.00 5.00

2005-06 Topps Style Chrome

*1-130 CHROME: .75X TO 2X BASE HI
*131-165 CHROME: .6X TO 1.5X BASE HI
CHROME PRINT RUN 499 SER.#'d SETS
111 LeBron James 20.00 50.00

2005-06 Topps Style Chrome Refractors

*1-130 REF: 1.5X TO 4X BASE HI
*131-165 REF: .75X TO 2X BASE HI
PRINT RUN 299 SER.#'d SETS
111 LeBron James 75.00 200.00

2005-06 Topps Style Chrome Refractors Blue

*1-130 REF.BLUE: 2.5X TO 6X BASE HI
*131-165 REF.BLUE: 1X TO 2.5X BASE HI
PRINT RUN 149 SER.#'d SETS
50 Kobe Bryant 20.00 50.00
111 LeBron James 100.00 250.00
154 Chris Paul 20.00 50.00

2005-06 Topps Style Chrome Refractors Gold

*1-130 GOLD: 10X TO 25X BASE HI
*131-160 GOLD: 4X TO 10X BASE HI
*161-165 GOLD: 3X TO 8X BASE HI
PRINT RUN 25 SER.#'d SETS
7 Mickey Mantle 50.00 120.00
50 Kobe Bryant 100.00 250.00
58 Chris Webber 40.00 100.00
111 LeBron James 300.00 600.00
154 Chris Paul 125.00 250.00

2005-06 Topps Style Dwyane Wade Comics

Inserted randomly in packs, this four-card set features comic images of Dwyane Wade on a white background serially numbered to 499.
COMPLETE SET (4) 4.00 10.00
COMMON CARD (1-4) 1.50 4.00
PRINT RUN 499 SER.#'d SETS
COMMON AUTO (1-4) 40.00 100.00
AUTO STATED ODDS 1:2991
COMMON ART.AU (1-4) 10.00 25.00
ART.AU PRINT RUN 75 SER.#'d SETS
AU DUAL STATED ODDS 1:7704
JSY AU STATED ODDS 1:14124
COMMON RELIC (1-4) 6.00 15.00
RELIC PRINT RUN 99 SER.#'d SETS

2005-06 Topps Style Fan Favorites Autographs

Inserted randomly in packs at the rate of one in 10, this 188-card set uses card designs from both previous year's baseball and basketball sets where each card contains an authentic player autograph. These cards are not serially numbered but print runs were provided by Topps as announced print runs.
STATED ODDS 1:10
ASTERISK: ANNOUNCED PRINT RUNS
UNPRICED CHROME PRINT RUN 8-10 SETS
AA Al Attles/176* 6.00 15.00
AB Andrew Bogut/417* 8.00 20.00
AC Archie Clark/212* 12.00 30.00
AD Adrian Dantley/320* 8.00 20.00
AG Artis Gilmore/188* 10.00 25.00
AG A.C. Green/406* 10.00 25.00
AJ Aaron James/192* 6.00 15.00
AK Albert King/216* 6.00 15.00
BB Bill Bradley/223* 100.00 175.00
BC Billy Cunningham/214* 40.00 100.00
BH Bailey Howell/219* 12.50 30.00
BJ Bobby Jones/220* 15.00 40.00
BK Bernard King/420* 8.00 20.00
BL Bob Lanier/217* 10.00 25.00
BP Billy Paultz/220* 8.00 20.00
BS Bud Stallworth/196* 8.00 20.00
BT Brian Taylor/220* 8.00 20.00
BW Bill Walton/220* 10.00 25.00
CD Chris Dudley/210* 6.00 15.00
CE Craig Ehlo/318* 6.00 15.00
CH Clem Haskins/220* 8.00 20.00
CM Chris Morris/228* 6.00 15.00
CM Calvin Murphy/219* 10.00 25.00
CR Campy Russell/200* 6.00 15.00
CS Charles Smith/199* 8.00 20.00
CW Chuck Williams/220* 6.00 15.00
DA Dan Anderson/194* 6.00 15.00
DB Dee Brown/405* 8.00 20.00
DC Darwin Cook/217* 8.00 20.00
DD Darryl Dawkins/219* 10.00 25.00
DE Dale Ellis/212* 8.00 20.00
DG Danny Granger/410* 8.00 20.00
DI Dan Issel/220* 15.00 40.00
DK Don Kojis/215* 15.00 40.00
DL Dennis Layton/220* 6.00 15.00
DM Dan Majerle/220* 12.00 30.00
DR Dennis Rodman/218* 50.00 120.00
DS Danny Schayes/220* 8.00 20.00
DT David Thompson/220* 8.00 20.00
DW Deron Williams/419* 6.00 15.00
EB Elgin Baylor/417* 12.00 30.00
EJ Eddie Johnson/405* 6.00 15.00
EK Eugene Kennedy/205* 10.00 25.00
EM Eric Money/203* 6.00 15.00
EM Earl Monroe/85* 25.00 60.00
FB Frank Brickowski/213* 10.00 25.00
FC Fred Carter/220* 6.00 15.00
FE Franklin Edwards/219* 6.00 15.00
FL Fat Lever/219* 6.00 15.00
FR Flynn Robinson/209* 8.00 20.00
GG George Gervin/220* 10.00 25.00
GH Gar Heard/420* 8.00 20.00
GM Glenn McDonald/220* 6.00 15.00
GT George Tinsley/218* 6.00 15.00
GW Gerald Wilkens/415* 6.00 15.00
HC Harvey Catchings/219* 6.00 15.00
HG Harry Gallatin/220* 6.00 15.00
HH Hersey Hawkins/320* 6.00 15.00
HP Howard Porter/211* 10.00 25.00
HW Herb Williams/318* 8.00 20.00
JB Junior Bridgeman/220* 6.00 15.00
JE Johnny Egan/214* 6.00 15.00
JG Johnny Green/218* 12.00 30.00
JH Jeff Hornacek/420* 8.00 20.00
JJ J.J. Johnson/413* 6.00 15.00
JL John Lambert/217* 6.00 15.00
JM Jeff Mullins/220* 6.00 15.00
JN Johnny Newman/320* 6.00 15.00
JR Joe Roberts/409* 10.00 25.00
JS Jack Sikma/404* 6.00 15.00
JW Jim Washington/210* 6.00 15.00
KB Kent Benson/217* 6.00 15.00
KC Kenny Charles/215* 6.00 15.00
KE Keith Edmonson/218* 8.00 20.00
KH Keith Herron/220* 6.00 15.00
KT Kelly Tripucka/220* 6.00 15.00
KV Kiki Vandeweghe/420* 6.00 15.00
LC Len Chappell/219* 6.00 15.00
LE Len Elmore/215* 6.00 15.00
LG Lamar Green/199* 6.00 15.00
LH Lou Hudson/401* 6.00 15.00
LM Larue Martin/215* 6.00 15.00
LN Larry Nance/420* 8.00 20.00
LW Lenny Wilkens/405* 10.00 25.00
MB Muggsy Bogues/219* 10.00 25.00
MC Maurice Cheeks/218* 6.00 15.00
MD Mel Davis/215* 6.00 15.00
ME Mark Eaton/209* 6.00 15.00
MG Mike Gale/220* 6.00 15.00
MJ Magic Johnson/220* 40.00 100.00
ML Maurice Lucas/217* 8.00 20.00
MM Moses Malone/212* 30.00 80.00
MW Mark West/221* 6.00 15.00
NA Nate Archibald/220* 8.00 20.00
NN Norm Nixon/219* 8.00 20.00
OB Otis Birdsong/200* 6.00 15.00
OG Orien Greene/420* 6.00 15.00
OR Oscar Robertson/215* 100.00 200.00
OT Ollie Taylor/220* 6.00 15.00
PA Paul Arizin/219* 30.00 80.00
PW Paul Westphal/409* 6.00 15.00
RB Rick Barry/220* 15.00 40.00
RD Rick Darnell/217* 6.00 15.00
RF Raymond Felton/419* 8.00 20.00
RG Richie Guerin/219* 10.00 25.00
RH Roy Hinson/217* 6.00 15.00
RK Rich Kelley/220* 6.00 15.00
RM Rodney McCray/220* 6.00 15.00
RP Ricky Pierce/219* 6.00 15.00
RR Rich Rinaldi/190* 8.00 20.00
RR Robert Reid/220* 6.00 15.00
RS Rik Smits/384* 8.00 20.00
RT Reggie Theus/420* 6.00 15.00
SG Sidney Green/339* 6.00 15.00
SH Spencer Haywood Red/207* 6.00 15.00
SL Sam Lacey/220* 6.00 15.00
SM Sean May/417* 6.00 15.00
ST Sedric Toney/213* 6.00 15.00
SW Samuel Williams/220* 6.00 15.00
TC Terry Cummings/320* 8.00 20.00
TG Tate George/219* 8.00 20.00
TH Tom Hoover/219* 6.00 15.00
TR Tree Rollins/405* 6.00 15.00
TS Tom Sanders/220* 6.00 15.00
TT Thomas Thacker/219* 6.00 15.00
TW Reggie Williams/214* 6.00 15.00
WD Walter Davis/418* 8.00 20.00
WF Walt Frazier/217* 15.00 40.00
WH Walt Hazzard/218* 8.00 20.00
WJ Wali Jones/203* 6.00 15.00
WN Willie Norwood/205* 6.00 15.00
WT Wayman Tisdale/218* 6.00 15.00
WW Walt Wesley/220* 6.00 15.00
XM Xavier McDaniel/208* 8.00 20.00
ZA Zaid Abdul-Aziz/218* 6.00 15.00
AC2 Austin Carr/203* 8.00 20.00
AJ2 Alfonso Buck Johnson/215* 6.00 15.00
BB2 Bob Boozer/220* 12.00 30.00
BH2 Bobby Hansen/406* 10.00 25.00
BL2 Bob Love/208* 10.00 25.00
BS2 Byron Scott/420* 6.00 15.00
BW2 Buck Williams/211* 8.00 20.00
CD2 Clyde Drexler/419* 15.00 40.00
CH2 Cliff Hagan/189* 8.00 20.00
CH3 Connie Hawkins/420* 10.00 25.00
CM2 Cliff Meely/187* 8.00 20.00
DA2 Dennis Awtrey/219* 6.00 15.00
DA3 Don Adams/210* 8.00 20.00
DC2 Dave Cowens/220* 15.00 40.00
DC3 Duane Causwell/220* 6.00 15.00
DD2 Dwight Davis/219* 6.00 15.00
DM2 Dick McGuire/220* 10.00 25.00
DS2 Detlef Schrempf/420* 6.00 15.00
DS3 Dick Schnittker/220* 12.00 30.00
DS4 Dick Snyder/219* 10.00 25.00
DS5 Dolph Schayes/219* 15.00 30.00
DW2 Dominique Wilkins/213* 15.00 40.00
EB2 Em Bryant/217* 6.00 15.00
FB2 Fred Brown/216* 6.00 15.00
FC2 Fred Crawford/201* 10.00 25.00
GH2 Geoff Huston/205* 8.00 20.00
GM2 Greg Minor/210* 6.00 15.00
GW2 Gus Williams/218* 10.00 25.00
JJ2 Jimmy Jones/222* 8.00 20.00
JL2 John Lucas/218* 6.00 15.00
JM2 Jerrod Mustaf/209* 6.00 15.00
JS2 James Silas/206* 15.00 40.00
JS3 John Starks/196* 10.00 25.00
JW2 Jo Jo White/200* 12.00 30.00
KE2 Keith Erickson/218* 6.00 15.00
LG2 Leonard Gray/201* 8.00 20.00
LN2 Louie Nelson/194* 6.00 15.00
MD2 Mike Davis/180* 6.00 15.00
MJ2 Major Jones/204* 6.00 15.00
RB2 Rolando Blackman/218* 8.00 20.00
RB3 Ron Behagen/213* 8.00 20.00
RB4 Ron Boone/213* 8.00 20.00
RP2 Robert Parish/420* 10.00 25.00
RS2 Rory Sparrow/219* 6.00 15.00
SH2 Spencer Haywood/194* 8.00 20.00
SW2 Slick Watts/218* 15.00 30.00
TC2 Tom Chambers/405* 6.00 15.00
TC4 Tyrone Corbin/219* 10.00 25.00
TC3 Tony Campbell/218* 6.00 15.00
TH2 Tommy Hawkins/220* 8.00 20.00
TT2 Trent Tucker/421* 6.00 15.00
WF2 World B. Free/216* 15.00 30.00

2005-06 Topps Style Hardwood Classics

Inserted in packs at the rate of one in six, this 75-card set is horizontally designed with a player image on the right and an "H" shaped swatch of memorabilia on the left. Though unconfirmed, it appears every swatch of memorabilia was taken from some form of throwback apparel.
N Nene 2.00 5.00
AH Alan Henderson 2.00 5.00
AI Andre Iguodala 2.00 5.00
AJ Anthony Johnson 2.00 5.00
AM Aaron McKie 2.00 5.00
BC Brian Cook 2.00 5.00
BG Brian Grant 2.00 5.00
BR Bryon Russell 2.00 5.00
BW Ben Wallace 2.00 5.00
CA Carmelo Anthony 5.00 12.00
CB Caron Butler 2.00 5.00
CR Cliff Robinson 2.00 5.00
CW Corliss Williamson 2.00 5.00
DA Darrell Armstrong 2.00 5.00
DC Doug Christie 2.00 5.00
DD Dale Davis 2.00 5.00
DG Drew Gooden 2.00 5.00
DJ DerMarr Johnson 2.00 5.00
DW David Wesley 2.00 5.00
ED Erick Dampier 2.00 5.00
EN Eduardo Najera 1.50 4.00
ES Eric Snow 2.00 5.00
ET Etan Thomas 2.00 5.00
GA Gilbert Arenas 2.00 5.00
GO Greg Ostertag 2.00 5.00
HT Hedo Turkoglu 2.00 5.00
IN Ira Newble 2.00 5.00
JF Jeff Foster 2.00 5.00
JH Juwan Howard 2.00 5.00
JJ Jared Jeffries 2.00 5.00
JP Joel Przybilla 2.00 5.00
JS Jerry Stackhouse 2.00 5.00
JT Jamaal Tinsley 2.00 5.00
KB Kobe Bryant 10.00 25.00
KM Kenyon Martin 2.00 5.00
KO Kevin Ollie 2.00 5.00
KT Kurt Thomas 2.00 5.00
LH Lindsey Hunter 2.00 5.00
MB Michael Bradley 2.00 5.00
MD Mike Dunleavy 2.00 5.00
ME Maurice Evans 2.00 5.00
MJ Marc Jackson 2.00 5.00
MN Moochie Norris 2.00 5.00
MT Maurice Taylor 2.00 5.00
PG Pat Garrity 2.00 5.00
RB Ryan Bowen 2.00 5.00
RP Ruben Patterson 2.00 5.00
SA Stacey Augmon 2.00 5.00
SB Steve Blake 2.00 5.00
SJ Stephen Jackson 2.00 5.00
SM Stephon Marbury 2.00 5.00
SP Scott Padgett 2.00 5.00
TA Trevor Ariza 1.50 4.00
TB Tony Battie 2.00 5.00
TM Troy Murphy 1.50 4.00
TR Theo Ratliff 2.00 5.00
TT Tim Thomas 2.00 5.00
CAT Chucky Atkins 2.00 5.00
DAN Derek Anderson 1.50 4.00
DST Damon Stoudamire 2.00 5.00
JBA Jon Barry 2.00 5.00
JJO Jumaine Jones 2.00 5.00
JJS James Jones 2.00 5.00
JWI Jerome Williams 2.00 5.00
KBR Kwame Brown 2.00 5.00
KVH Keith Van Horn 2.00 5.00
MDA Marquis Daniels 2.00 5.00
NVE Nick Van Exel 2.50 6.00
SAR Shareef Abdur-Rahim 2.00 5.00
SBR Shawn Bradley 2.00 5.00
SME Slava Medvedenko 2.00 5.00

2008-09 Topps T51 Murad

This set was released on February 26, 2009. The base set consists of 230 cards. Cards 1-170 feature veterans, and cards 171-200 are rookies. Cards 201-230 are short-printed veterans.
COMPLETE SET (230) 100.00 200.00
SP STATED ODDS 1:3
UNPRICED PRESS PLATE PRINT RUN ONE SET
1 Elton Brand .50 1.25
2 Ray Allen .50 1.25
3 Allen Iverson .60 1.50
4 Luis Scola .40 1.00
5 Jason Kidd .50 1.25
6 Lamar Odom .40 1.00
7 Yi Jianlian .50 1.25
8 Marcus Camby .30 .75
9 Jamal Crawford .50 1.25
10 Steve Nash .50 1.25
11 Al Harrington .40 1.00
12 Carmelo Anthony .60 1.50
13 Peja Stojakovic .50 1.25
14 Mike Dunleavy .40 1.00
15 Larry Hughes .40 1.00
16 Josh Smith .40 1.00
17 Emeka Okafor .40 1.00
18 Ron Artest .50 1.25
19 Vince Carter .60 1.50
20 Jamario Moon .30 .75
21 Mike Miller .40 1.00
22 Brendan Haywood .30 .75
23 Kirk Hinrich .40 1.00
24 Jason Terry .40 1.00
25 Brandan Wright .40 1.00
26 Derek Fisher .40 1.00
27 Desmond Mason .30 .75
28 Tyson Chandler .40 1.00
29 Mickael Pietrus .30 .75
30 Ronnie Brewer .40 1.00
31 Gerald Wallace .40 1.00
32 Daniel Gibson .40 1.00
33 J.R. Smith .40 1.00
34 Monta Ellis .40 1.00
35 Kobe Bryant 2.00 5.00
36 Ramon Sessions .40 1.00
37 Zach Randolph .40 1.00
38 Andre Miller .40 1.00
39 Tony Parker .50 1.25
40 Nick Young .40 1.00
41 Kevin Garnett .75 2.00
42 Luol Deng .40 1.00
43 Josh Howard .40 1.00
44 Corey Maggette .40 1.00
45 Cuttino Mobley .30 .75
46 James Posey .30 .75
47 Hedo Turkoglu .40 1.00
48 Brad Miller .40 1.00
49 Andrei Kirilenko .40 1.00
50 Raymond Felton .40 1.00
51 Zydrunas Ilgauskas .40 1.00
52 Jason Maxiell .30 .75
53 Yao Ming .60 1.50
54 Luke Walton .30 .75
55 Mo Williams .40 1.00
56 David Lee .30 .75
57 Thaddeus Young .40 1.00
58 Raja Bell .40 1.00
59 Ime Udoka .30 .75
60 Gilbert Arenas .40 1.00
61 Glen Davis .30 .75
62 Ben Wallace .40 1.00
63 Kenyon Martin .40 1.00
64 Stephen Jackson .40 1.00
65 Andrew Bynum .30 .75
66 Richard Jefferson .40 1.00
67 Chris Duhon .30 .75
68 John Salmons .40 1.00
69 DeShawn Stevenson .30 .75
70 Zaza Pachulia .30 .75
71 Jason Richardson .50 1.25
72 Anderson Varejao .30 .75
73 Rasheed Wallace .50 1.25
74 Rafer Alston .30 .75
75 Troy Murphy .30 .75
76 T.J. Ford .30 .75
77 Chris Kaman .40 1.00
78 Hakim Warrick .40 1.00
79 Daequan Cook .30 .75
80 Al Jefferson .40 1.00
81 Sean Williams .40 1.00
82 Eddy Curry .30 .75
83 Chris Wilcox .30 .75
84 Willie Green .30 .75
85 Martell Webster .40 1.00
86 Travis Outlaw .40 1.00
87 Bruce Bowen .30 .75
88 Jermaine O'Neal .40 1.00
89 Ben Gordon .40 1.00
90 Antawn Jamison .40 1.00
91 Al Horford .50 1.25
92 Andres Nocioni .30 .75
93 Rodney Stuckey .40 1.00
94 Shane Battier .40 1.00
95 Jarrett Jack .40 1.00
96 Al Thornton .40 1.00
97 Mike Conley Jr. .40 1.00
98 Udonis Haslem .30 .75
99 Rashad McCants .30 .75
100 Marcus Williams .30 .75
101 Jeff Green .40 1.00
102 Jameer Nelson .30 .75
103 Shaquille O'Neal 1.00 2.50
104 LaMarcus Aldridge .50 1.25
105 Brandon Roy .50 1.25
106 Manu Ginobili .50 1.25
107 Jose Calderon .30 .75
108 Jason Kapono .30 .75
109 Mike Bibby .40 1.00
110 Andrea Bargnani .40 1.00
111 Jerry Stackhouse .40 1.00
112 Richard Hamilton .40 1.00
113 Brent Barry .30 .75
114 Baron Davis .40 1.00
115 Darko Milicic .30 .75
116 Ricky Davis .40 1.00
117 Corey Brewer .40 1.00
118 Nick Collison .40 1.00
119 Rashard Lewis .40 1.00
120 Amare Stoudemire .40 1.00
121 Steve Blake .30 .75
122 Kevin Martin .40 1.00
123 Fabricio Oberto .30 .75
124 Mehmet Okur .30 .75
125 Wally Szczerbiak .40 1.00
126 Mark Aguirre .60 1.50
127 Danny Ainge .75 2.00
128 Rick Barry .60 1.50
129 Elgin Baylor .75 2.00
130 Dave Bing .75 2.00
131 Otis Birdsong .60 1.50
132 Gail Goodrich .60 1.50
133 Bill Bradley 1.00 2.50
134 Bill Cartwright .60 1.50
135 James Worthy .75 2.00
136 Tom Chambers .60 1.50
137 Maurice Cheeks .50 1.25
138 Archie Clark .75 2.00
139 Michael Cooper .60 1.50
140 Bob Cousy 1.25 3.00
141 Dave Cowens .50 1.25
142 Billy Cunningham .75 2.00
143 Adrian Dantley .60 1.50
144 Darryl Dawkins .50 1.25
145 Clyde Drexler 1.00 2.50
146 Joe Dumars .75 2.00
147 Mario Elie .50 1.25
148 Walt Frazier .75 2.00
149 George Gervin 1.00 2.50
150 Tim Hardaway .75 2.00
151 John Havlicek .75 2.00
152 Bill Russell 1.25 3.00
153 Bill Laimbeer .60 1.50
154 Karl Malone 1.00 2.50
155 Bob McAdoo .60 1.50

156 Larry Bird 2.00 5.00
157 Magic Johnson 2.00 5.00
158 Willis Reed .75 2.00
159 Wilt Chamberlain 1.50 4.00
160 Pete Maravich 1.25 3.00
161 George Mikan 1.50 4.00
162 Hakeem Olajuwon 1.00 2.50
163 Patrick Ewing 1.00 2.50
164 Oscar Robertson .75 2.00
165 Bill Sharman .75 2.00
166 Dennis Rodman 1.50 4.00
167 David Robinson 1.25 3.00
168 Dominique Wilkins 1.00 2.50
169 Isiah Thomas .75 2.00
170 Jerry West 1.00 2.50
171A Derrick Rose Dribbling RC 4.00 10.00
171B Derrick Rose Standing 5.00 12.00
172A Michael Beasley 1BK RC 1.00 2.50
172B Michael Beasley 2BK 1.25 3.00
173A O.J. Mayo Dribbling RC 1.00 2.50
173B O.J. Mayo Standing 1.25 3.00
174A Russell Westbrook Red RC 8.00 20.00
174B Russell Westbrook Blue 10.00 25.00
175A Kevin Love Shooting RC 3.00 8.00
175B Kevin Love Standing 4.00 10.00
176A Danilo Gallinari Standing RC 1.50 4.00
176B Danilo Gallinari Dribbling 2.00 5.00
177A Eric Gordon Dribbling RC 1.50 4.00
177B Eric Gordon Standing 2.00 5.00
178A Joe Alexander Dribbling RC .60 1.50
178B Joe Alexander Standing .75 2.00
179A D.J. Augustin Dribbling RC .75 2.00
179B D.J. Augustin Standing 1.00 2.50
180A Brook Lopez Blue RC 1.25 3.00
180B Brook Lopez Red 1.50 4.00
181A Jerryd Bayless Layup RC .75 2.00
181B Jerryd Bayless Standing 1.00 2.50
182 Jason Thompson RC .60 1.50
183A A.Randolph Crouching RC .60 1.50
183B A.Randolph Standing .75 2.00
184A Robin Lopez Standing RC 1.00 2.50
184B Robin Lopez Crouching 1.25 3.00
185 Marreese Speights RC .75 2.00
186 Roy Hibbert RC 1.00 2.50
187 JaVale McGee RC 1.25 3.00
188A J.J. Hickson Dribbling RC .75 2.00
188B J.J. Hickson Standing 1.00 2.50
189A Brandon Rush Dribbling RC .75 2.00
189B Brandon Rush Standing 1.00 2.50
190 Ryan Anderson RC .75 2.00
191A Courtney Lee Dribbling RC .75 2.00
191B Courtney Lee Standing 1.00 2.50
192A Kosta Koufos Dribbling RC .75 2.00
192B Kosta Koufos Standing 1.00 2.50
193 Rudy Fernandez RC .75 2.00
194 George Hill RC 1.00 2.50
195 D.J. White RC .75 2.00
196 J.R. Giddens RC .60 1.50
197A C.Douglas-Roberts Red RC .60 1.50
197B C.Douglas-Roberts Blue .75 2.00
198A Mario Chalmers Dribbling RC 1.00 2.50
198B Mario Chalmers Standing 1.25 3.00
199 DeAndre Jordan RC 1.25 3.00
200A Darrell Arthur Blue RC .75 2.00
200B Darrell Arthur Gold 1.00 2.50
201 Joe Johnson SP .75 2.00
202 Paul Pierce SP 1.00 2.50
203 LeBron James SP 4.00 10.00
204 Tayshaun Prince SP .75 2.00
205 Danny Granger SP .75 2.00
206 Pau Gasol SP 1.00 2.50
207 Shawn Marion SP .75 2.00
208 Michael Redd SP .75 2.00
209 Devin Harris SP .60 1.50
210 David West SP .75 2.00
211 Kevin Durant SP 2.50 6.00
212 Dwight Howard SP .75 2.00
213 Samuel Dalembert SP .75 2.00
214 Greg Oden SP .75 2.00
215 Tim Duncan SP 1.50 4.00
216 Carlos Boozer SP .75 2.00
217 Caron Butler SP .75 2.00
218 Chris Bosh SP 1.00 2.50
219 Leandro Barbosa SP .75 2.00
220 Tracy McGrady SP 1.00 2.50
221 Andrew Bogut SP .75 2.00
222 Rudy Gay SP 1.00 2.50
223 Andre Iguodala SP .75 2.00
224 Dirk Nowitzki SP 1.25 3.00
225 Deron Williams SP .75 2.00
226 Chauncey Billups SP 1.00 2.50
227 Rajon Rondo SP 1.00 2.50
228 Beno Udrih SP .75 2.00
229 Dwyane Wade SP 1.50 4.00
230 Chris Paul SP 1.25 3.00

2008-09 Topps T51 Murad Mini

*1-170 MINI: .75X TO 2X BASE HI
*171-200 RC MINI: .5X TO 1.25X BASE
*201-250 SP MINI: .6X TO 1.5X BASE
ONE MINI PER PACK
171-200 RC STATED ODDS 1:18
201-250 SP ODDS 1:12

2008-09 Topps T51 Murad Mini Black

*1-170 BLACK: 1X TO 2.5X BASE HI
*171-200 RC BLACK: .6X TO 1.5X BASE HI
*201-230 SP BLACK: .75X TO 2X BASE HI

2008-09 Topps T51 Murad Silk

*1-125 SILK: 10X TO 25X BASE HI
*126-170/201-230 SILK: 5X TO 12X BASE HI
*171-200 SILK: 4X TO 10X BASE HI
RC VARIATIONS: SAME VALUE
PRINT RUN 25 SER.#'d SETS
167 David Robinson 20.00 50.00

2008-09 Topps T51 Murad Autographs

*BLACK: .6X TO 1.5X BASE
BLACK PRINT RUN 25 SER.#'d SETS
UNPRICED SILVER PRINT RUN 10 SETS
UNPRICED LEATHER PRINT RUN ONE SET
T51AAB Andrea Bargnani 6.00 15.00
T51AABY Andrew Bynum 15.00 40.00
T51AAIG Andre Iguodala 5.00 12.00
T51AAJ Antawn Jamison 4.00 10.00
T51AAR Anthony Randolph 2.50 6.00
T51ABD Baron Davis 6.00 15.00
T51ABL Brook Lopez 5.00 12.00
T51ABR Brandon Roy 10.00 25.00
T51ABRA Brandon Rush 3.00 8.00
T51ABRL Bill Russell 50.00 100.00
T51ACBI Chauncey Billups 6.00 15.00
T51ACBO Carlos Boozer 4.00 10.00
T51ACM Corey Maggette 4.00 10.00
T51ACP Chris Paul 20.00 50.00
T51ADA Darrell Arthur 3.00 8.00
T51ADG Danny Granger 5.00 12.00
T51ADGA Danilo Gallinari 10.00 25.00
T51ADH Devin Harris 8.00 20.00
T51ADHO Dwight Howard 15.00 40.00
T51ADJA D.J. Augustin 3.00 8.00
T51ADJW D.J. White 3.00 8.00
T51ADL David Lee 5.00 12.00
T51ADR Derrick Rose 30.00 80.00
T51AEG Eric Gordon 6.00 15.00
T51AGO Greg Oden 12.00 30.00
T51AGW Gerald Wallace 4.00 10.00
T51AJA Joe Alexander 2.50 6.00
T51AJB Jerryd Bayless 3.00 8.00
T51AJJ Jarrett Jack 4.00 10.00
T51AJJH J.J. Hickson 3.00 8.00
T51AJRG J.R. Giddens 2.50 6.00
T51AKH Kirk Hinrich 8.00 20.00
T51AKK Kosta Koufos 3.00 8.00
T51AKL Kevin Love 30.00 80.00
T51ALB Larry Bird 50.00 100.00
T51AMB Michael Beasley 12.00 30.00
T51AMC Mario Chalmers 4.00 10.00
T51AMJ Magic Johnson 40.00 80.00
T51AMM Mike Miller 4.00 10.00
T51AMP Mickeal Pietrus 4.00 10.00
T51AOJM O.J. Mayo 12.00 30.00
T51APP Paul Pierce 10.00 25.00
T51ARG Rudy Gay 6.00 15.00
T51ARH Roy Hibbert 4.00 10.00
T51ARL Robin Lopez 4.00 10.00
T51ARM Rashad McCants 4.00 10.00
T51ARWE Russell Westbrook 100.00 250.00
T51ATJF T.J. Ford 4.00 10.00
T51ATM Tracy McGrady 10.00 25.00
T51AVC Vince Carter 20.00 40.00

2008-09 Topps T51 Murad Checklists

COMPLETE SET (30) 6.00 15.00
APPROXIMATE ODDS ONE PER PACK
CL1 Dwyane Wade .75 2.00
CL2 Travis Outlaw .40 1.00
CL3 Los Angeles Clippers .50 1.25
CL4 Michael Redd .40 1.00
CL5 E.Okafor/A.Jefferson .50 1.25
CL6 Tracy McGrady .50 1.25
CL7 Andre Iguodala .40 1.00
CL8 Brown/Brewer/Jefferson .50 1.25
CL9 Rudy Gay .50 1.25
CL10 J.Kidd/S.Nash 1.25 3.00
CL11 Shaquille O'Neal 1.00 2.50
CL12 Carmelo Anthony .60 1.50
CL13 Chris Bosh .50 1.25
CL14 Tony Parker .50 1.25
CL15 Gilbert Arenas .40 1.00
CL16 Sacramento Kings .54 1.25
CL17 Utah Jazz 1.00 2.50
CL18 A.Biedrins/M.Moore .75 1.25
CL19 Dwight Howard .40 1.00
CL20 Cleveland Cavaliers 1.25 3.00
CL21 Ray Allen .50 1.25
CL22 Detroit Pistons .50 1.25
CL23 Dallas Mavericks .75 2.00
CL24 Jamal Crawford .50 1.25
CL25 Danny Granger .40 1.00
CL26 Chauncey Billups .50 1.25
CL27 Atlanta Hawks .50 1.25
CL28 Kevin Garnett .75 2.00
CL29 Kobe Bryant 2.00 5.00
CL30 Larry Bird 1.25 3.00

2008-09 Topps T51 Murad Relics

APPROXIMATE ODDS 1:24 PACKS
*GOLD: .6X TO 1.5X BASE
GOLD PRINT RUN 51 SER.#'d SETS
UNPRICED LEATHER PRINT RUN ONE SET
UNPRICED SILVER PRINT RUN 10 SETS
T51RAI Allen Iverson 4.00 10.00
T51RAIG Andre Iguodala 2.50 6.00
T51RAS Amare Stoudemire 2.50 6.00
T51RBK Bernard King 2.50 6.00
T51RBL Bill Laimbeer 2.50 6.00
T51RBR Brandon Roy 3.00 8.00
T51RBW Bill Walton 4.00 10.00
T51RCA Carmelo Anthony 4.00 10.00
T51RCBI Chauncey Billups 3.00 8.00
T51RCBO Chris Bosh 3.00 8.00
T51RCBU Caron Butler 2.50 6.00
T51RCBZ Carlos Boozer 2.50 6.00
T51RCD Clyde Drexler 4.00 10.00
T51RCM Chris Mullin 3.00 8.00
T51RCP Chris Paul 4.00 10.00
T51RDH Dwight Howard 2.50 6.00
T51RDN Dirk Nowitzki 4.00 10.00
T51RDR Dennis Rodman 6.00 15.00
T51RDW Dwyane Wade 5.00 12.00
T51RDWI Deron Williams 2.50 6.00
T51REM Earl Monroe 3.00 8.00
T51RGA Gilbert Arenas 2.50 6.00
T51RGG George Gervin 4.00 10.00
T51RGO Greg Oden 2.50 6.00
T51RIT Isiah Thomas 3.00 8.00
T51RJJ Joe Johnson 2.50 6.00
T51RJK Jason Kidd 3.00 8.00
T51RJS Josh Smith 2.50 6.00
T51RKB Kobe Bryant 8.00 20.00
T51RKG Kevin Garnett 5.00 12.00
T51RKM Kevin Martin 2.50 6.00
T51RLB Larry Bird 8.00 20.00
T51RMC Michael Cooper 2.50 6.00
T51RMG Manu Ginobili 3.00 8.00
T51RMJ Magic Johnson 10.00 25.00
T51RMR Michael Redd 2.50 6.00
T51RMRI Mitch Richmond 3.00 8.00
T51RPG Pau Gasol 3.00 8.00
T51RPM Pete Maravich 30.00 80.00
T51RPP Paul Pierce 3.00 8.00
T51RRG Rudy Gay 3.00 8.00
T51RRR Rajon Rondo 3.00 8.00
T51RSN Steve Nash 3.00 8.00
T51RSO Shaquille O'Neal 6.00 15.00
T51RSP Scottie Pippen 10.00 25.00
T51RTD Tim Duncan 5.00 12.00
T51RTM Tracy McGrady 3.00 8.00
T51RTP Tony Parker 3.00 8.00
T51RVC Vince Carter 4.00 10.00
T51RYM Yao Ming 4.00 10.00

2008-09 Topps T51 Murad T6 Cabinets

ONE CABINET PER BOX
*BLACK: .75X TO 2X BASE HI
BLACK STATED PRINT RUN 51 SETS
UNPRICED SILVER PRINT RUN 10 SETS
T6BR Brandon Roy 1.00 2.50
T6CA Carmelo Anthony 1.25 3.00
T6CP Chris Paul 1.25 3.00
T6DH Dwight Howard .75 2.00
T6DR Derrick Rose 10.00 25.00
T6DW Dwyane Wade 1.50 4.00
T6GO Greg Oden .75 2.00
T6KB Kobe Bryant 4.00 10.00
T6KG Kevin Garnett 1.50 4.00
T6LB Larry Bird 2.50 6.00
T6LJ LeBron James 4.00 10.00
T6MB Michael Beasley 1.00 2.50
T6MJ Magic Johnson 2.50 6.00
T6OJM O.J. Mayo 1.00 2.50
T6PP Paul Pierce 1.00 2.50
T6YM Yao Ming 1.25 3.00

2001-02 Topps TCC

Released in late April 2002, Topps TCC boasts a 150-card set divided up as follows: card numbers 1-120 feature veterans and are further divided into Playoff Bound, Playoff Hopefuls, Making Strides, and Opportunity knocks; and card numbers 118-150 feature rookie players. Base cards place full color player action photos on a white background with orange trim along the right and bottom of the card, where rookies have this replaced with gold, and gold foil highlights. TCC was released in 10 box cases with 24 packs per box and six card packs which carried a suggested retail price of $2.00. Each pack contained one extra thick insert card which also served to deter collectors from searching packs.

COMPLETE SET (150) 20.00 50.00
1 Shaquille O'Neal .60 1.50
2 Jason Williams .20 .50
3 Eddie Jones .20 .50
4 Anthony Mason .15 .40
5 Joe Smith .20 .50
6 Kenyon Martin .25 .60
7 Tracy McGrady .40 1.00
8 Horace Grant .20 .50
9 Andre Miller .20 .50
10 Allen Iverson .50 1.25
11 Shawn Marion .20 .50
12 Derek Anderson .15 .40
13 Chris Webber .25 .60
14 Bruce Bowen .15 .40
15 Alvin Williams .15 .40
16 Brent Barry .15 .40
17 Donyell Marshall .15 .40
18 Richard Hamilton .20 .50
19 Vlade Divac .20 .50
20 Vince Carter .40 1.00
21 Kevin Garnett .40 1.00
22 Jason Terry .25 .60
23 Antoine Walker .20 .50
24 P.J. Brown .15 .40
25 Baron Davis .25 .60
26 Eddie Robinson .15 .40
27 Chris Mihm .15 .40
28 Michael Finley .25 .60
29 Nick Van Exel .20 .50
30 Steve Francis .20 .50
31 Chucky Atkins .15 .40
32 Raef LaFrentz .15 .40
33 Antawn Jamison .25 .60
34 Jalen Rose .20 .50
35 Lamar Odom .20 .50
36 Elton Brand .25 .60
37 Derek Fisher .20 .50
38 Alonzo Mourning .30 .75
39 Ervin Johnson .15 .40
40 Tim Duncan .50 1.25
41 Kurt Thomas .15 .40
42 Latrell Sprewell .20 .50
43 Darrell Armstrong .15 .40
44 Tom Gugliotta .15 .40
45 Derrick Coleman .20 .50
46 Dale Davis .15 .40
47 David Robinson .40 1.00
48 Scottie Pippen .40 1.00
49 Hakeem Olajuwon .30 .75
50 Darius Miles .15 .40
51 Greg Ostertag .15 .40
52 Karl Malone .30 .75
53 Morris Peterson .15 .40
54 Shareef Abdur-Rahim .20 .50
55 Dikembe Mutombo .25 .60
56 Elden Campbell .15 .40
57 Ron Mercer .15 .40
58 Jumaine Jones .15 .40
59 Wang ZhiZhi .20 .50
60 Ray Allen .25 .60
61 Marcus Camby .20 .50
62 Jermaine O'Neal .20 .50
63 Kenny Thomas .15 .40
64 Danny Fortson .15 .40
65 Ben Wallace .20 .50
66 DeShawn Stevenson .15 .40
67 Antonio Davis .15 .40
68 Doug Christie .15 .40
69 Rasheed Wallace .25 .60
70 Stephon Marbury .20 .50
71 Allan Houston .20 .50
72 Kerry Kittles .15 .40
73 Todd MacCulloch .15 .40
74 Sam Cassell .20 .50
75 Kobe Bryant 1.00 2.50
76 Aaron McKie .15 .40
77 Terrell Brandon .15 .40
78 Brian Grant .15 .40
79 Michael Dickerson .15 .40
80 Jerry Stackhouse .20 .50
81 Antonio McDyess .20 .50
82 Steve Nash .40 1.00
83 Paul Pierce .25 .60
84 Jamal Mashburn .20 .50
85 Toni Kukoc .25 .60
86 James Posey .15 .40
87 Larry Hughes .20 .50
88 Cuttino Mobley .15 .40
89 Jeff Foster .15 .40
90 Jason Kidd .40 1.00
91 Keith Van Horn .20 .50
92 Mike Miller .20 .50
93 Anfernee Hardaway .40 1.00
94 Bonzi Wells .15 .40
95 Mike Bibby .25 .60
96 Steve Smith .20 .50
97 Gary Payton .25 .60
98 John Stockton .30 .75
99 Peja Stojakovic .25 .60
100 Michael Jordan 5.00 12.00
101 Iakovos Tsakalidis .15 .40
102 Mark Jackson .20 .50
103 Wally Szczerbiak .20 .50
104 Rod Strickland .15 .40
105 Rick Fox .15 .40
106 Glenn Robinson .20 .50
107 Michael Olowokandi .15 .40
108 Reggie Miller .25 .60
109 Kelvin Cato .15 .40
110 Clifford Robinson .15 .40
111 Dirk Nowitzki .40 1.00
112 Brad Miller .25 .60
113 David Wesley .15 .40
114 Kenny Anderson .20 .50
115 Theo Ratliff .15 .40
116 Rashard Lewis .25 .60
117 Matt Harpring .15 .40
118 Eddie Griffin RC .30 .75
119 Brendan Haywood RC .40 1.00
120 Steven Hunter RC .30 .75
121 Jamaal Tinsley RC .40 1.00
122 Jason Richardson RC .50 1.25
123 Tony Parker RC 1.50 4.00
124 Pau Gasol RC 1.25 3.00
125 Shane Battier RC .75 2.00
126 Joe Johnson RC .50 1.25
127 Leon Smith RC .40 1.00
128 Mengke Bateer RC .40 1.00
129 Loren Woods RC .25 .60
130 Kwame Brown RC .40 1.00
131 Tyson Chandler RC .60 1.50
132 Eddy Curry RC .40 1.00
133 Kedrick Brown RC .25 .60
134 Joseph Forte RC .25 .60
135 Troy Murphy RC .40 1.00
136 Richard Jefferson RC .60 1.50
137 DeSagana Diop RC .30 .75
138 Vladimir Radmanovic RC .40 1.00
139 Zach Randolph RC .60 1.50
140 Gerald Wallace RC .50 1.25
141 Brandon Armstrong RC .25 .60
142 Jeryl Sasser RC .25 .60
143 Rodney White RC .25 .60
144 Samuel Dalembert RC .40 1.00
145 Jason Collins RC .30 .75
146 Michael Bradley RC .25 .60
147 Oscar Torres RC .40 1.00
148 Zeljko Rebraca RC .40 1.00
149 Andrei Kirilenko RC .60 1.50
150 Trenton Hassell RC .30 .75

2001-02 Topps TCC Red

*STARS: 1.25X TO 3X BASE CARD HI
*RC's: .75X TO 2X BASE CARD HI
STATED ODDS 1:2

2001-02 Topps TCC Autographs

Randomly seeded in packs at the rate of one in 48, this 27-card set features full color player action photos along the top, a gold line with the player's name in the middle, and an authentic autograph on the bottom. Each card is highlighted with gold foil and contains the Topps stamp of authenticity.

STATED ODDS 1:48
CCAAM Andre Miller 5.00 12.00
CCABJ Bobby Jackson 5.00 12.00
CCADB Damone Brown 2.50 6.00
CCADH Donnell Harvey 4.00 10.00
CCADM Desmond Mason 4.00 10.00
CCAGA Gilbert Arenas 6.00 15.00
CCAHT Hedo Turkoglu 5.00 12.00
CCAJF Joseph Forte 2.50 6.00
CCAJJ Joe Johnson 5.00 12.00
CCAJT Jason Terry 4.00 10.00
CCAKB Kedrick Brown 2.50 6.00
CCAKD Keyon Dooling 4.00 10.00
CCAKS Kenny Satterfield 2.50 6.00
CCALP Lavor Postell 4.00 10.00
CCALW Loren Woods 2.50 6.00
CCAMB Mike Bibby 6.00 15.00
CCAMD Michael Doleac 4.00 10.00
CCAPS Peja Stojakovic 8.00 20.00
CCARH Richard Hamilton 3.00 8.00
CCARL Raef LaFrentz 4.00 10.00
CCARM Roshown McLeod 4.00 10.00
CCASB Shane Battier 8.00 20.00
CCASM Shawn Marion 6.00 15.00
CCATM Troy Murphy 4.00 10.00
CCAAJO Alvin Jones 3.00 8.00
CCAJTR Jeff Trepagnier 2.50 6.00

2001-02 Topps TCC Challenging the Champ

Randomly inserted in packs at the rate of one in 32, this 16-card set showcases player's aiming for a shot on the right and a diamond shaped swatch of game memorabilia on the left. All TCC memorabilia swatches are encased with plastic borders to deter replacement or tampering with the swatch.

STATED ODDS 1:32
CCAH Anfernee Hardaway 5.00 12.00
CCBD Baron Davis 3.00 8.00
CCDN Dirk Nowitzki 5.00 12.00
CCEB Elton Brand 3.00 8.00
CCJM Jamal Mashburn 2.50 6.00
CCJT Jason Terry 3.00 8.00
CCMF Michael Finley 3.00 8.00
CCSA Shareef Abdur-Rahim 2.50 6.00
CCSM Stephon Marbury 2.50 6.00
CCSN Steve Nash 5.00 12.00
CCSDM Shawn Marion 2.50 6.00
CCTD Tim Duncan 6.00 15.00
CCTG Tom Gugliotta 2.00 5.00
CCTK Toni Kukoc 3.00 8.00
CCTR Theo Ratliff 2.00 5.00
CCWZ Wang Zhizhi 2.50 6.00

2001-02 Topps TCC Crowning Moment

Seeded in packs at the rate of one in five, this 10-card set features an all foil card stock with a colored background and a player photo as he recieves an award centered and circled with gold foil. All TCC inserts are thicker than standard size cards.

COMPLETE SET (10) 8.00 20.00
STATED ODDS 1:5
CM1 Karl Malone .60 1.50
CM2 Shaquille O'Neal 1.25 3.00
CM3 Tim Duncan 1.00 2.50
CM4 Michael Jordan 4.00 10.00
CM5 Kobe Bryant 2.00 5.00
CM6 Vince Carter .75 2.00
CM7 Dikembe Mutombo .50 1.25
CM8 Elton Brand .50 1.25
CM9 Jason Kidd .75 2.00
CM10 Steve Francis .40 1.00

2001-02 Topps TCC Finals Journey

Inserted in packs at the rate of one in 22, this 23-card set features full color player action phots on the left and a circular swatch of a game worn finals jersey on the right. All TCC memorabilia swatches are encased with plastic borders to deter replacement or tampering with the swatch.

STATED ODDS 1:22
FJAI Allen Iverson 6.00 15.00
FJAM Aaron McKie 2.00 5.00
FJBS Brian Shaw 2.00 5.00
FJDF Derek Fisher 2.50 6.00
FJDG Devean George 2.00 5.00
FJDM Dikembe Mutombo 3.00 8.00
FJES Eric Snow 2.00 5.00
FJGF Greg Foster 2.00 5.00
FJGL George Lynch 2.00 5.00
FJHG Horace Grant 2.50 6.00
FJJJ Jumaine Jones 2.00 5.00
FJKO Kevin Ollie 2.00 5.00
FJMG Matt Geiger 2.00 5.00
FJMM Mark Madsen 2.00 5.00
FJRB Raja Bell 4.00 10.00
FJRF Rick Fox 2.00 5.00
FJRH Robert Horry 2.50 6.00
FJRAB Rodney Buford 2.00 5.00
FJRKH Ron Harper 2.50 6.00
FJSO Shaquille O'Neal 6.00 15.00
FJTH Tyrone Hill 2.00 5.00
FJTL Tyronn Lue 2.00 5.00
FJTM Todd MacCulloch 2.00 5.00

2001-02 Topps TCC First Step Sneakers

Seeded in packs at the rate of one in 222, this 14-card set showcases young stars who have yet to win an NBA Championship. Player color photos appear on the left, and a circular swatch of a game worn sneaker appears in the upper right hand corner. All TCC memorabilia swatches are encased with plastic borders to deter replacement or tampering with the swatch.

STATED ODDS 1:222
FSAJ Antawn Jamison 5.00 12.00
FSBD Baron Davis 5.00 12.00
FSEB Elton Brand 5.00 12.00
FSEC Eddy Curry 5.00 12.00
FSJF Joseph Forte 3.00 8.00
FSJT Jason Terry 5.00 12.00
FSKB Kwame Brown 5.00 12.00
FSPS Peja Stojakovic 5.00 12.00
FSRH Richard Hamilton 4.00 10.00
FSSB Shane Battier 10.00 25.00
FSSM Shawn Marion 4.00 10.00
FSSO Shaquille O'Neal 12.00 30.00
FSTD Tim Duncan 10.00 25.00
FSVR Vladimir Radmanovic 5.00 12.00

2001-02 Topps TCC Heart of a Champion

Inserted in packs at the rate of one in 19, this 10-card set features an all foil card stock with full color player photos centered and surrounded by a border that is shaped like a heart.

COMPLETE SET (10) 25.00 60.00
STATED ODDS 1:19
HC1 Tim Duncan 2.00 5.00
HC2 Shaquille O'Neal 2.50 6.00
HC3 Michael Jordan 12.50 30.00
HC4 Karl Malone 1.25 3.00
HC5 Hakeem Olajuwon 1.25 3.00
HC6 David Robinson 1.50 4.00
HC7 Kobe Bryant 4.00 10.00
HC8 Scottie Pippen 1.50 4.00
HC9 Shane Battier 2.00 5.00
HC10 Jason Richardson 1.25 3.00

2001-02 Topps TCC Heroes Honor

Seeded in packs at the rate of one in five, this six card set features an all foil card stock with full color player photos centered between red white and blue ribbins falling from the words, "Heroes Honor."

COMPLETE SET (6) 3.00 8.00
STATED ODDS 1:5
HH1 Tim Duncan 1.25 3.00
HH2 Vince Carter 1.00 2.50
HH3 Tracy McGrady 1.00 2.50
HH4 Chris Webber .60 1.50
HH5 Baron Davis .60 1.50
HH6 Allan Houston .50 1.25

2001-02 Topps TCC Jump Ball

Randomly seeded in packs at the rate of one in 540, this nine card set showcases full color player action photos set agaist a white background. The right edge of the card has a gold stripe with the words, "Jump Ball" and on the inside of that stripe is a purple stripe with the featured player's name. A swatch of game used basketball appears in the lower right-hand corner.

STATED ODDS 1:540
JBAI Allen Iverson 8.00 20.00
JBBD Baron Davis 4.00 10.00
JBCW Chris Webber 6.00 15.00
JBGR Glenn Robinson 3.00 8.00
JBPS Peja Stojakovic 4.00 10.00
JBRA Ray Allen 4.00 10.00
JBSC Sam Cassell 3.00 8.00
JBSM Shawn Marion 3.00 8.00
JBTM Tracy McGrady 6.00 15.00

2001-02 Topps TCC Setting the Stage

Randomly inserted in packs at the rate of one in 19, this 10-card set showcases some of the NBA's best matchups. Both players are featured on the front of this all foil insert set. The words "Setting the Stage" appear along the bottom of the card which fades to black and places both player's names and team logos.

COMPLETE SET (10) 25.00 60.00
STATED ODDS 1:19
SS1 T.McGrady/R.Allen 3.00 8.00
SS2 K.Bryant/A.Iverson 4.00 10.00
SS3 S.O'Neal/D.Mutombo 2.50 6.00
SS4 S.O'Neal/T.Duncan 4.00 10.00
SS5 P.Ewing/A.Mourning 2.50 6.00
SS6 L.Sprewell/V.Carter 2.00 5.00
SS7 S.O'Neal/H.Olajuwon 3.00 8.00
SS8 M.Jordan/R.Miller 6.00 15.00
SS9 K.Malone/C.Webber 2.00 5.00
SS10 J.Stockton/G.Payton 2.00 5.00

2000 Topps Team USA

Released in June 2000, this 96-card set focuses on both the men's and women's Team USA players for the Olympics. The cards were released in seven-card packs that carried a suggested retail price of $1.99. Card number 16 does not exist (Nikki McCray). Instead, two number 40's were produced.

COMPLETE SET (96) 12.50 30.00
1 Tim Duncan ACH .40 1.00
2 Jason Kidd ACH .25 .60
3 Vin Baker ACH .15 .40
4 Steve Smith ACH .07 .20
5 Grant Hill ACH .25 .60
6 Gary Payton ACH .25 .60
7 Vince Carter ACH .50 1.25
8 Ray Allen ACH .25 .60
9 Kevin Garnett ACH .40 1.00
10 Tim Hardaway ACH .25 .60
11 Allan Houston ACH .25 .60
12 Alonzo Mourning ACH .25 .60
13 Lisa Leslie ACH .75 2.00
14 Dawn Staley ACH .40 1.00
15 Katie Smith ACH .40 1.00
16 Nikki McCray ACH UER .40 1.00
numbered as 40
17 Ruthie Bolton-Holifield ACH .40 1.00
18 Chamique Holdsclaw ACH 1.00 2.50
19 Yolanda Griffith ACH .50 1.25
20 Teresa Edwards ACH .30 .75
21 Natalie Williams ACH .50 1.25
22 Delisha Milton ACH .15 .40
23 Kara Wolters ACH .25 .60
24 Gary Payton ST .15 .40
25 Kevin Garnett ST .40 1.00
26 Tim Hardaway ST .15 .40
27 Steve Smith ST .07 .20
28 Ray Allen ST .15 .40
29 Alonzo Mourning ST .15 .40
30 Allan Houston ST .15 .40
31 Vince Carter ST .50 1.25
32 Grant Hill ST .15 .40
33 Tim Duncan ST .40 1.00
34 Jason Kidd ST .25 .60
35 Vin Baker ST .15 .40
36 Ruthie Bolton-Holifield ST .40 1.00
37 Natalie Williams ST .50 1.25
38 Lisa Leslie ST .75 2.00
39 Chamique Holdsclaw ST 1.00 2.50
40 Nikki McCray ST .40 1.00
41 Dawn Staley ST .40 1.00
42 Teresa Edwards ST .30 .75
43 Yolanda Griffith ST .50 1.25
44 Katie Smith ST .40 1.00
45 Delisha Milton ST .15 .40
46 Kara Wolters ST .25 .60
47 Vin Baker PAI .15 .40
48 Jason Kidd PAI .25 .60
49 Allan Houston PAI .15 .40
50 Ray Allen PAI .15 .40
51 Alonzo Mourning PAI .15 .40
52 Kevin Garnett PAI .40 1.00
53 Gary Payton PAI .15 .40
54 Steve Smith PAI .07 .20
55 Vince Carter PAI .50 1.25
56 Grant Hill PAI .15 .40
57 Tim Duncan PAI .40 1.00
58 Tim Hardaway PAI .15 .40
59 Chamique Holdsclaw PAI 1.00 2.50
60 Katie Smith PAI .40 1.00
61 Yolanda Griffith PAI .50 1.25
62 Nikki McCray PAI .40 1.00
63 Lisa Leslie PAI .75 2.00
64 Teresa Edwards PAI .30 .75
65 Dawn Staley PAI .40 1.00
66 Ruthie Bolton-Holifield PAI .40 1.00
67 Natalie Williams PAI .50 1.25
68 Delisha Milton PAI .15 .40
69 Kara Wolters PAI .25 .60
70 Allan Houston QU .15 .40
71 Kevin Garnett QU .40 1.00
72 Tim Duncan QU .40 1.00
73 Tim Hardaway QU .15 .40
74 Gary Payton QU .15 .40
75 Ray Allen QU .15 .40
76 Vince Carter QU .50 1.25
77 Grant Hill QU .15 .40
78 Vin Baker QU .15 .40
79 Alonzo Mourning QU .15 .40
80 Steve Smith QU .07 .20
81 Jason Kidd QU .25 .60
82 Chamique Holdsclaw QU 1.00 2.50
83 Lisa Leslie QU .75 2.00
84 Dawn Staley QU .40 1.00
85 Natalie Williams QU .50 1.25
86 Nikki McCray QU .40 1.00
87 Katie Smith QU .40 1.00
88 Teresa Edwards QU .30 .75
89 Yolanda Griffith QU .50 1.25
90 Ruthie Bolton-Holifield QU .40 1.00
91 Delisha Milton QU .15 .40
92 Kara Wolters QU .25 .60
93 Team USA Men's .40 1.00
94 Team USA Women's .40 1.00
95 Group Shot .60 1.50
96 Checklist .07 .20

2000 Topps Team USA Gold

*GOLD: 1.25X TO 3X BASE CARD HI

2000 Topps Team USA Autographs

Randomly inserted in packs at one in 291, this 10-card set features autographs from the women of Team USA. Card backs are numbered with the player's initials.

CH Chamique Holdsclaw 100.00 200.00
DM Delisha Milton 10.00 25.00
DS Dawn Staley 10.00 25.00
KS Katie Smith 40.00 80.00
LL Lisa Leslie 40.00 100.00
NM Nikki McCray 40.00 80.00
NW Natalie Williams 10.00 25.00
RH Ruthie Bolton-Holifield 10.00 25.00
TE Teresa Edwards 40.00 80.00
YG Yolanda Griffith 40.00 80.00

2000 Topps Team USA National Spirit

Randomly inserted in packs at one in eight, this 23-card set features every player on Team USA against foilboard technology. Card backs carry a "NS" prefix.

COMPLETE SET (23) 20.00 40.00
NS1 Steve Smith .20 .50
NS2 Ray Allen .60 1.50
NS3 Grant Hill .60 1.50
NS4 Vince Carter 1.50 4.00
NS5 Tim Hardaway .40 1.00
NS6 Jason Kidd 1.00 2.50
NS7 Vin Baker .40 1.00
NS8 Alonzo Mourning .40 1.00
NS9 Tim Duncan 1.25 3.00
NS10 Gary Payton .60 1.50
NS11 Allan Houston .40 1.00
NS12 Kevin Garnett 1.25 3.00
NS13 Nikki McCray 1.25 3.00
NS14 Dawn Staley 1.25 3.00
NS15 Lisa Leslie 2.50 6.00
NS16 Teresa Edwards .75 2.00
NS17 Yolanda Griffith 1.50 4.00
NS18 Chamique Holdsclaw 3.00 8.00
NS19 Katie Smith 1.25 3.00
NS20 Ruthie Bolton-Holifield 1.25 3.00
NS21 Natalie Williams 1.50 4.00
NS22 Delisha Milton .50 1.25
NS23 Kara Wolters .75 2.00

2000 Topps Team USA Side by Side

Randomly inserted in packs at one in 12, this 12-card set highlights a player from both the men's and women's team who share something in common. Prices below are for the Non-Refractor/Refractor technology.

COMPLETE SET (12) 12.00 30.00
RIGHT/LEFT VARIATIONS EQUAL VALUE
*DUAL REF: .75X TO 2X HI COLUMN
DUAL REF: STATED ODDS 1:36
SS1 Tim Duncan 2.50 6.00
Lisa Leslie
SS2 Allan Houston 1.50 4.00
Ruthie Bolton-Holifield
SS3 Kevin Garnett 2.50 6.00
Chamique Holdsclaw
SS4 Jason Kidd 1.50 4.00
Katie Smith
SS5 Vin Baker 1.25 3.00
Natalie Williams
SS6 Gary Payton 1.25 3.00
Dawn Staley
SS7 Vince Carter 1.25 3.00
Theresa Edwards
SS8 Tim Hardaway 1.00 2.50
Dawn Staley
SS9 Steve Smith 1.00 2.50
Kara Wolters
SS10 Alonzo Mourning 1.25 3.00
Yolanda Griffith
SS11 Ray Allen 1.00 2.50
Delisha Milton
SS12 Grant Hill 1.00 2.50
Nikki McCray

2000 Topps Team USA USArchival

Randomly inserted in packs at one in 323, this nine-card set features pieces of game-worn USA jerseys from the 1999 Olympic qualifying tournament in Puerto Rice. Card backs carry a "US" prefix. According to Topps, only 250 sets were produced.

USAR1 Tom Gugliotta 10.00 25.00
USAR2 Allan Houston 15.00 40.00
USAR3 Vin Baker 10.00 25.00
USAR4 Kevin Garnett 20.00 50.00
USAR5 Gary Payton 12.50 30.00
USAR6 Steve Smith 12.50 30.00
USAR7 Tim Duncan 30.00 80.00
USAR8 Jason Kidd 20.00 50.00
USAR9 Tim Hardaway 10.00 25.00

2002-03 Topps Ten

Topps Ten consisted of 150-cards broken down into 120 veteran players and 30 rookie players. Veteran were divided up into 12 different categories: Points Per Game, Points Per 48 Minutes, Rebounds Per Game, Assists Per Game, Blocks Per Game, Steals Per Game, Double-Doubles, Field Goal %, Three-Point FG %, Minutes Per Game, Free Throw %, and Rookie Points Per Game; and Rookies were divided up into: Top 10 Rookie Guards, Top 10 Rookie Small Forwards, and Top 10 Rookie Power Forwards/Centers. Each player is ranked between one and ten. Topps Ten was issue in 24-pack boxes where packs contained eight cards and carried a suggested retail price of $300.

COMPLETE SET (150) 20.00 50.00
1 Allen Iverson .40 1.00
2 Shaquille O'Neal .60 1.50
3 Paul Pierce .25 .60
4 Tracy McGrady .40 1.00
5 Tim Duncan .50 1.25
6 Kobe Bryant 1.00 2.50
7 Dirk Nowitzki .40 1.00
8 Karl Malone .30 .75
9 Antoine Walker .20 .50
10 Gary Payton .25 .60
11 Shaquille O'Neal .60 1.50
12 Allen Iverson .40 1.00
13 Tracy McGrady .40 1.00
14 Kobe Bryant 1.00 2.50
15 Michael Jordan 2.00 5.00
16 Paul Pierce .25 .60
17 Chris Webber .25 .60
18 Tim Duncan .50 1.25
19 Corliss Williamson .15 .40
20 Dirk Nowitzki .40 1.00
21 Ben Wallace .20 .50
22 Tim Duncan .50 1.25
23 Kevin Garnett .40 1.00
24 Danny Fortson .15 .40
25 Elton Brand .25 .60
26 Dikembe Mutombo .25 .60
27 Jermaine O'Neal .20 .50
28 Dirk Nowitzki .40 1.00
29 Shawn Marion .20 .50
30 P.J. Brown .15 .40
31 Andre Miller .20 .50
32 Jason Kidd .40 1.00
33 Gary Payton .25 .60
34 Baron Davis .20 .50
35 John Stockton .30 .75
36 Stephon Marbury .20 .50
37 Jamaal Tinsley .15 .40
38 Jason Williams .20 .50
39 Steve Nash .30 .75
40 Mark Jackson .20 .50
41 Ben Wallace .20 .50
42 Raef LaFrentz .15 .40
43 Alonzo Mourning .30 .75
44 Tim Duncan .50 1.25
45 Dikembe Mutombo .25 .60
46 Jermaine O'Neal .20 .50
47 Erick Dampier .15 .40
48 Adonal Foyle .15 .40
49 Pau Gasol .30 .75
50 Shaquille O'Neal .60 1.50
51 Allen Iverson .40 1.00
52 Ron Artest .25 .60
53 Jason Kidd .40 1.00
54 Baron Davis .20 .50
55 Doug Christie .15 .40
56 Darrell Armstrong .15 .40
57 Karl Malone .30 .75
58 Paul Pierce .25 .60
59 Kenny Anderson .20 .50
60 John Stockton .30 .75
61 Shaquille O'Neal .60 1.50
62 Elton Brand .25 .60
63 Donyell Marshall .15 .40
64 Pau Gasol .30 .75
65 John Stockton .30 .75
66 Alonzo Mourning .30 .75
67 Ruben Patterson .15 .40
68 Corliss Williamson .15 .40
69 Tim Duncan .50 1.25
70 Brent Barry .15 .40
71 Steve Smith .20 .50
72 Jon Barry .15 .40
73 Eric Piatkowski .15 .40
74 Wally Szczerbiak .20 .50
75 Steve Nash .30 .75
76 Hubert Davis .15 .40
77 Tyronn Lue .15 .40
78 Michael Redd .20 .50
79 Wesley Person .15 .40
80 Ray Allen .25 .60
81 Reggie Miller .25 .60
82 Richard Hamilton .20 .50
83 Darrell Armstrong .15 .40
84 Damon Stoudamire .20 .50
85 Steve Nash .30 .75
86 Chauncey Billups .25 .60
87 Chris Whitney .15 .40
88 Steve Smith .20 .50
89 Peja Stojakovic .25 .60
90 Troy Hudson .15 .40
91 Allen Iverson .40 1.00
92 Cuttino Mobley .15 .40
93 Antoine Walker .20 .50
94 Steve Francis .20 .50
95 Latrell Sprewell .20 .50
96 Tim Duncan .50 1.25
97 Baron Davis .20 .50
98 Paul Pierce .25 .60
99 Gary Payton .25 .60
100 Michael Finley .25 .60
101 Tim Duncan .50 1.25
102 Kevin Garnett .40 1.00
103 Elton Brand .25 .60
104 Jason Kidd .40 1.00
105 Shawn Marion .20 .50
106 Andre Miller .20 .50
107 Shaquille O'Neal .60 1.50
108 Jermaine O'Neal .20 .50
109 Dirk Nowitzki .40 1.00
110 Pau Gasol .30 .75
111 Pau Gasol .30 .75
112 Shane Battier .25 .60
113 Jason Richardson .25 .60
114 Gilbert Arenas .25 .60

115 Andrei Kirilenko .25 .60
116 Richard Jefferson .25 .60
117 Jamaal Tinsley .15 .40
118 Tony Parker .30 .75
119 Eddie Griffin .15 .40
120 Trenton Hassell .15 .40
121 Jay Williams RC .75 2.00
122 DaJuan Wagner RC .60 1.50
123 Fred Jones RC .60 1.50
124 Jiri Welsch RC .60 1.50
125 Juan Dixon RC .75 2.00
126 Kareem Rush RC .60 1.50
127 Casey Jacobsen RC .60 1.50
128 Frank Williams RC .50 1.25
129 John Salmons RC .75 2.00
130 Dan Dickau RC .60 1.50
131 Mike Dunleavy RC .75 2.00
132 Nikoloz Tskitishvili RC .50 1.25
133 Caron Butler RC .75 2.00
134 Jared Jeffries RC .60 1.50
135 Bostjan Nachbar RC .60 1.50
136 Ryan Humphrey RC .60 1.50
137 Qyntel Woods RC .60 1.50
138 Tayshaun Prince RC 1.00 2.50
139 Chris Jefferies RC .50 1.25
140 Vincent Yarbrough RC .50 1.25
141 Yao Ming RC 1.50 4.00
142 Drew Gooden RC .75 2.00
143 Nene Hilario RC .75 2.00
144 Chris Wilcox RC .60 1.50
145 Amare Stoudemire RC 1.00 2.50
146 Melvin Ely RC .60 1.50
147 Marcus Haislip RC .60 1.50
148 Curtis Borchardt RC .50 1.25
149 Robert Archibald RC .50 1.25
150 Dan Gadzuric RC .60 1.50

2002-03 Topps Ten Parallel

*STARS: 1X TO 2.5X BASE CARD HI
*RC's: .75X TO 2X BASE CARD HI
ONE PARALLEL OR RELIC PER PACK

2002-03 Topps Ten Relic Parallel

ONE PARALLEL OR RELIC PER PACK
4 Tracy McGrady/1500 5.00 12.00
7 Dirk Nowitzki/1500 5.00 12.00
8 Karl Malone/1500 4.00 10.00
10 Gary Payton/300 3.00 8.00
11 Shaquille O'Neal/1500 8.00 20.00
17 Chris Webber/1500 3.00 8.00
22 Tim Duncan/1500 6.00 15.00
23 Kevin Garnett/1500 5.00 12.00
31 Andre Miller/300 2.50 6.00
34 Baron Davis/1500 2.50 6.00
51 Allen Iverson/1500 5.00 12.00
62 Elton Brand/750 3.00 8.00
66 Alonzo Mourning/300 4.00 10.00
75 Steve Nash/300 4.00 10.00
80 Ray Allen/1500 3.00 8.00
89 Peja Stojakovic/300 3.00 8.00
92 Cuttino Mobley/1500 2.00 5.00
93 Antoine Walker/1500 2.50 6.00
94 Steve Francis/750 2.50 6.00
95 Latrell Sprewell/300 2.50 6.00
108 Jermaine O'Neal/1500 2.50 6.00
111 Pau Gasol/400 4.00 10.00
114 Gilbert Arenas/750 3.00 8.00
115 Andrei Kirilenko/750 3.00 8.00
118 Tony Parker/300 4.00 10.00

2002-03 Topps Ten Autographs

Topps Ten Autographs consists of 20 cards divided up into five different groups: A, B, C, D, and E; and the inserted odds are as follows: Group A 1:335, Group B 1:679, Group C 1:220, Group D 1:283 and Group E 1:184. Each card places full-color player photography on a white bordered card with a box across the bottom third of the card reserved for autographs.

STATED ODDS AS FOLLOWS:
GROUP A 1:335, GROUP B 1:679
GROUP C 1:220, GROUP D 1:283
GROUP E 1:184
TAAM Aaron McKie C 4.00 10.00
TABH Brendan Haywood B 5.00 12.00
TACB Chauncey Billups E 6.00 15.00
TAEC Eddy Curry B 4.00 10.00
TAGA Gilbert Arenas B 6.00 15.00
TAJJ Joe Johnson A 6.00 15.00
TAJO Jermaine O'Neal A 8.00 20.00
TAJT Jason Terry D 4.00 10.00
TAKS Kenny Satterfield E 4.00 10.00
TAMB Mike Bibby C 6.00 15.00
TAMD Mike Dunleavy A 6.00 15.00
TAPS Peja Stojakovic E 6.00 15.00
TARJ Richard Jefferson C 4.00 10.00
TARL Raef LaFrentz A 6.00 15.00
TASB Shane Battier D 5.00 12.00
TASM Shawn Marion A 6.00 15.00
TASO Shaquille O'Neal B 50.00 125.00
TATM Troy Murphy C 4.00 10.00
TAVR Vladimir Radmanovic C 4.00 10.00
TAYM Yao Ming 30.00 80.00

2002-03 Topps Ten Team Leader Relics

Randomly inserted in packs, this 28-card set features players who led their teams in a specific statistical category. Each card is sequentially numbered and contains a swatch of game-worn memorabilia.

ONE PARALLEL OR RELIC PER PACK
TLAD Antonio Davis/1000 2.00 5.00
TLAH Allan Houston/1000 2.50 6.00
TLAM Antonio McDyess/290 2.50 6.00
TLAMI Andre Miller/400 2.50 6.00
TLBH Brendan Haywood/400 2.00 5.00
TLCM Cuttino Mobley/1000 2.00 5.00
TLDM Dikembe Mutombo/400 3.00 8.00
TLDMI Darius Miles/1500 2.00 5.00
TLGR Glenn Robinson/1500 2.50 6.00
TLJM Jamal Mashburn/1500 2.50 6.00
TLJS John Stockton/400 4.00 10.00
TLJSH Jerry Stackhouse/1000 2.50 6.00
TLKM Kenyon Martin/1500 2.50 6.00
TLMF Michael Finley/1000 3.00 8.00
TLPG Pat Garrity/400 2.00 5.00
TLPS Peja Stojakovic/1500 3.00 8.00
TLRA Ray Allen/1290 3.00 8.00
TLRH Richard Hamilton/1000 2.50 6.00
TLRM Reggie Miller/400 8.00 20.00
TLRW Rasheed Wallace/125 3.00 8.00
TLSA Shareef Abdur-Rahim/400 2.50 6.00
TLSF Steve Francis/1000 2.50 6.00
TLSM Shawn Marion/400 2.50 6.00
TLSO Shaquille O'Neal/1500 8.00 20.00
TLSS Steve Smith/1000 2.50 6.00
TLTD Tim Duncan/1500 6.00 15.00
TLTM Tracy McGrady/1500 5.00 12.00
TLWS Wally Szczerbiak/1500 2.50 6.00

2005-06 Topps The Finals Promos

COMPLETE SET (4) 2.50 6.00
SCDW Dwyane Wade .75 2.00
SCMJ Magic Johnson 1.25 3.00
NBAF1 Allen Iverson .75 2.00
NBAF2 Dwyane Wade .75 2.00

1981 Topps Thirst Break

This is a 56-card set of individual wax paper gum wrappers, similar to a Bazooka Comic. These wrappers were issued in Thirst Break Orange Gum, which was reportedly distributed in Pennsylvania and Ohio. Each of these small gum wrappers has a comic-style image of a particular great moment in sports. As the checklist below shows, many different sports are represented in this set. The wrappers each measure approximately 2 9/16" by 1 5/8". The wrappers are numbered in small print at the top. The backs of the wrappers are blank. The "1981 Topps" copyright is at the bottom of each card. There was an orange and green outer wrapper that did not have player images.

COMPLETE SET (56) 60.00 150.00
16 Wilt Chamberlain 2.00 5.00
17 Wilt Chamberlain 2.00 5.00
18 Wilt Chamberlain 2.00 5.00
25 John Havlicek 1.60 4.00
26 Oscar Robertson 1.60 4.00
27 Calvin Murphy .80 2.00

1999-00 Topps Tip-Off

Intended as a retail-only release, this 132-card set is a semi-parallel of the regular Topps set. The cards feature silver foil.

COMPLETE SET (132) 12.50 30.00
1 Steve Smith .15 .40
2 Ron Harper .12 .30
3 Michael Dickerson .12 .30
4 LaPhonso Ellis .12 .30
5 Chris Webber .20 .50
6 Jason Caffey .12 .30
7 Bryon Russell .12 .30
8 Bison Dele .12 .30
9 Isaiah Rider .15 .40
10 Dean Garrett .12 .30
11 Eric Murdock .12 .30
12 Juwan Howard .15 .40
13 Latrell Sprewell .20 .50
14 Jalen Rose .15 .40
15 Larry Johnson .20 .50
16 Eric Williams .12 .30
17 Bryant Reeves .12 .30
18 Tony Battie .15 .40
19 Luc Longley .15 .40
20 Gary Payton .20 .50
21 Tariq Abdul-Wahad .12 .30
22 Armen Gilliam .12 .30
23 Shaquille O'Neal .50 1.25
24 Gary Trent .12 .30
25 John Stockton .25 .60
26 Mark Jackson .15 .40
27 Cherokee Parks .12 .30
28 Michael Olowokandi .12 .30
29 Raef LaFrentz .15 .40
30 Dell Curry .12 .30
31 Travis Best .12 .30
32 Shawn Kemp .20 .50
33 Voshon Lenard .12 .30
34 Brian Grant .12 .30
35 Alvin Williams .12 .30
36 Derek Fisher .20 .50
37 Allan Houston .15 .40
38 Arvydas Sabonis .15 .40
39 Terry Cummings .15 .40
40 Dale Ellis .12 .30
41 Maurice Taylor .12 .30
42 Grant Hill .25 .60
43 Anthony Mason .12 .30
44 John Wallace .12 .30
45 David Wesley .12 .30
46 Nick Van Exel .15 .40
47 Cuttino Mobley .12 .30
48 Anfernee Hardaway .30 .75
49 Terry Porter .12 .30
50 Brent Barry .15 .40
51 Derek Harper .15 .40
52 Antoine Walker .20 .50
53 Karl Malone .25 .60
54 Ben Wallace .15 .40
55 Vlade Divac .20 .50
56 Sam Mitchell .12 .30
57 Joe Smith .15 .40
58 Shawn Bradley .12 .30
59 Darrell Armstrong .12 .30
60 Kenny Anderson .15 .40
61 Jason Williams .25 .60
62 Alonzo Mourning .25 .60
63 Matt Harpring .12 .30
64 Antonio Davis .12 .30
65 Lindsey Hunter .12 .30
66 Allen Iverson .40 1.00
67 Mookie Blaylock .12 .30
68 Wesley Person .12 .30
69 Bobby Phills .12 .30
70 Theo Ratliff .15 .40
71 Antonio Daniels .12 .30
72 P.J. Brown .12 .30
73 David Robinson .30 .75
74 Sean Elliott .20 .50
75 Zydrunas Ilgauskas .15 .40
76 Kerry Kittles .12 .30
77 Otis Thorpe .12 .30
78 John Starks .15 .40
79 Jaren Jackson .12 .30
80 Hersey Hawkins .12 .30
81 Glenn Robinson .15 .40
82 Paul Pierce .25 .60
83 Glen Rice .20 .50
84 Charlie Ward .12 .30
85 Dee Brown .12 .30
86 Danny Fortson .12 .30
87 Billy Owens .12 .30
88 Jason Kidd .30 .75
89 Brent Price .12 .30
90 Don Reid .12 .30
91 Mark Bryant .12 .30
92 Vinny Del Negro .12 .30
93 Stephon Marbury .15 .40
94 Donyell Marshall .12 .30
95 Jim Jackson .12 .30
96 Horace Grant .15 .40
97 Calbert Cheaney .12 .30
98 Vince Carter .40 1.00
99 Bobby Jackson .12 .30
100 Alan Henderson .12 .30
101 Mike Bibby .20 .50
102 Cedric Henderson .12 .30
103 Lamond Murray .12 .30
104 A.C. Green .15 .40
105 Hakeem Olajuwon .25 .60
106 George Lynch .12 .30
107 Kendall Gill .12 .30
108 Rex Chapman .12 .30
109 Eddie Jones .20 .50
110 Kornel David RC .50 1.25
111 Jason Terry RC 1.00 2.50
112 Corey Maggette RC 1.00 2.50
113 Ron Artest RC 1.25 3.00
114 Richard Hamilton RC 1.25 3.00
115 Elton Brand RC 1.50 4.00
116 Baron Davis RC 1.50 4.00
117 Wally Szczerbiak RC 1.25 3.00
118 Steve Francis RC 1.50 4.00
119 James Posey RC .60 1.50
120 Shawn Marion RC 1.25 3.00
121 Tim Duncan .40 1.00
122 Danny Manning .15 .40
123 Chris Mullin .20 .50
124 Antawn Jamison .20 .50
125 Kobe Bryant .75 2.00
126 Matt Geiger .12 .30
127 Rod Strickland .12 .30
128 Howard Eisley .12 .30
129 Steve Nash .30 .75
130 Felipe Lopez .12 .30
131 Ron Mercer .15 .40
132 Checklist .05 .15

1999-00 Topps Tip-Off Autographs

Randomly inserted in packs, this three-card set features autographs of some top stars in the NBA. The cards were inserted at different ratios, with Duncan at one in 12,910, Carter at one in 4,303 and Iverson at one in 6,455. Vince Carter did not end up signing the card, thus only the redemption exists. Card backs feature an "AG" prefix.

AG1 STATED ODDS 1:12,910
AG2 STATED ODDS 1:4,303
AG3 STATED ODDS 1:6,455
CARTER DID NOT SIGN EXCH.CARDS
AG1 Tim Duncan 150.00 300.00

2000-01 Topps Tip-Off

The 2000-01 Topps Tip-Off product was released in late October 2000. The set includes 124 Veterans, 10 Rookies, 6 Season Highlights, 10 Topps Series 2 Previews, 9 Coming Soon cards, and 1 Checklist. Each pack contained six cards and carried a suggested retail price of $.99.

COMPLETE SET (160) 15.00 40.00
SUBSET CARDS SAME VALUE AS BASE
1 Elton Brand .20 .50
2 Marcus Camby .15 .40
3 Jalen Rose .15 .40
4 Jamie Feick .12 .30
5 Toni Kukoc .20 .50
6 Todd MacCulloch .12 .30
7 Mario Elie .12 .30
8 Doug Christie .12 .30
9 Sam Cassell .15 .40
10 Shaquille O'Neal .50 1.25
11 Larry Hughes .15 .40
12 Jerry Stackhouse .15 .40
13 Rick Fox .12 .30
14 Clifford Robinson .12 .30
15 Felipe Lopez .12 .30
16 Dirk Nowitzki .30 .75
17 Cuttino Mobley .12 .30
18 Latrell Sprewell .15 .40
19 Nick Anderson .12 .30
20 Kevin Garnett .30 .75
21 Rik Smits .12 .30
22 Jerome Williams .12 .30
23 Chris Webber .20 .50
24 Jason Terry .20 .50
25 Elden Campbell .12 .30
26 Kelvin Cato .12 .30
27 Tyrone Nesby .20 .50
28 Jonathan Bender .12 .30
29 Otis Thorpe .15 .40
30 Scottie Pippen .30 .75
31 Radoslav Nesterovic .12 .30
32 P.J. Brown .12 .30
33 Reggie Miller .20 .50
34 Andre Miller .15 .40
35 Tariq Abdul-Wahad .12 .30
36 Michael Doleac .12 .30
37 Rashard Lewis .20 .50
38 Jacque Vaughn .12 .30
39 Larry Johnson .20 .50
40 Steve Francis .15 .40
41 Arvydas Sabonis .15 .40
42 Jaren Jackson .12 .30
43 Howard Eisley .12 .30
44 Rod Strickland .12 .30
45 Tim Thomas .12 .30
46 Robert Horry .15 .40
47 Kenny Thomas .12 .30
48 Anthony Peeler .12 .30
49 Darrell Armstrong .12 .30
50 Vince Carter .40 1.00
51 Othella Harrington .12 .30
52 Derek Anderson .12 .30
53 Anthony Carter .12 .30
54 Scott Burrell .12 .30
55 Ray Allen .20 .50
56 Jason Kidd .30 .75
57 Sean Elliott .20 .50
58 Muggsy Bogues .15 .40
59 LaPhonso Ellis .15 .40
60 Tim Duncan .40 1.00
61 Adrian Griffin .12 .30
62 Wally Szczerbiak .15 .40
63 Austin Croshere .12 .30
64 Wesley Person .12 .30
65 James Posey .12 .30
66 Alan Henderson .12 .30
67 Ruben Patterson .12 .30
68 Jahidi White .12 .30
69 Shawn Marion .15 .40
70 Lamar Odom .15 .40
71 Lindsey Hunter .12 .30
72 Keon Clark .12 .30
73 Gary Trent .12 .30
74 Lamond Murray .12 .30
75 Paul Pierce .20 .50
76 Charlie Ward .12 .30
77 Matt Geiger .12 .30
78 Greg Anthony .12 .30
79 Horace Grant .15 .40
80 John Stockton .25 .60
81 Peja Stojakovic .20 .50
82 William Avery .12 .30
83 Dan Majerle .20 .50
84 Christian Laettner .15 .40
85 Dana Barros .12 .30
86 Corey Benjamin .12 .30
87 Keith Van Horn .15 .40
88 Patrick Ewing .25 .60
89 Steve Smith .15 .40
90 Antonio Davis .12 .30
91 Samaki Walker .12 .30
92 Mitch Richmond .15 .40
93 Michael Olowokandi .12 .30
94 Baron Davis .20 .50
95 Dikembe Mutombo .20 .50
96 Andrew DeClercq .12 .30
97 Raef LaFrentz .12 .30
98 Trajan Langdon .12 .30
99 Ervin Johnson .12 .30
100 Alonzo Mourning .25 .60
101 Kendall Gill .12 .30
102 George Lynch .12 .30
103 Detlef Schrempf .15 .40
104 Donyell Marshall .12 .30
105 Bo Outlaw .12 .30
106 Kenny Anderson .15 .40
107 Eddie Robinson .12 .30
108 Jermaine O'Neal .15 .40
109 John Amaechi .12 .30
110 Glen Rice .15 .40
111 Vlade Divac .15 .40
112 Vin Baker .15 .40
113 Mike Bibby .20 .50
114 Richard Hamilton .15 .40
115 Mookie Blaylock .12 .30
116 Vitaly Potapenko .12 .30
117 Anthony Mason .12 .30
118 Robert Pack .12 .30
119 Vonteego Cummings .12 .30
120 Michael Finley .20 .50
121 Ron Artest .20 .50
122 Tyrone Hill .12 .30
123 Rodney Rogers .12 .30
124 Quincy Lewis .12 .30
125 Kenyon Martin RC .75 2.00
126 Stromile Swift RC .30 .75
127 Darius Miles RC .30 .75
128 Marcus Fizer RC .30 .75
129 Mike Miller RC .50 1.25
130 DerMarr Johnson RC .25 .60
131 Chris Mihm RC .25 .60
132 Jamal Crawford RC .75 2.00
133 Joel Przybilla RC .25 .60
134 Keyon Dooling RC .30 .75
135 Shaq/Iverson/G.Hill SL .15 .40
136 Kidd/Van Exel/Cassell SL .20 .50
137 Mutombo/Shaq/Duncan SL .25 .60
138 E.Jones/Pierce/Armstrong SL .10 .30
139 Mourning/Mutombo/Shaq SL .20 .50
140 Team Championship SL .30 .75
141 Kobe Bryant .75 2.00
142 Stephon Marbury .15 .40
143 Antoine Walker .15 .40
144 Jason Williams .20 .50
145 Shareef Abdur-Rahim .15 .40
146 Gary Payton .20 .50
147 Grant Hill .25 .60
148 Allen Iverson .40 1.00
149 Khalid El-Amin RC .20 .50
150 Chris Carrawell RC .30 .75
151 Shaquille O'Neal CS .50 1.25
152 Allen Iverson CS .40 1.00
153 Kevin Garnett CS .30 .75
154 Vince Carter CS .40 1.00
155 Tim Duncan CS .40 1.00
156 Karl Malone CS .25 .60
157 Chris Webber CS .20 .50
158 Latrell Sprewell CS .15 .40
159 Alonzo Mourning CS .25 .60
160 Checklist .12 .30

2000-01 Topps Tip-Off Autographs

Randomly inserted in packs at overall odds of one in 1,404, this four-card set features autographs from NBA stars. The autographs were broken into two groups, A and B, and were inserted at one in 1,989 for group A and one in 4,773 for group B. The groupings are marked after the player's name.

GROUP A STATED ODDS 1:1,989
GROUP B STATED ODDS 1:4,773
OVERALL STATED ODDS 1:1,404
TOAEB Elton Brand B 10.00 25.00
TOAEJ Eddie Jones A 10.00 25.00
TOASF Steve Francis A 10.00 25.00
TOATM Tracy McGrady A 15.00 40.00

2008-09 Topps Tip-Off

This set was released on November 26, 2008. The base set consists of 143 cards. Cards 1-110 feature veterans, and cards 111-143 are rookies.

COMPLETE SET (143) 15.00 30.00
UNPRICED PRESS PLATE PRINT RUN ONE SET
1 Kobe Bryant .75 2.00
2 Kevin Garnett .30 .75
3 Chris Paul .25 .60
4 Chris Bosh .20 .50
5 Caron Butler .15 .40
6 Andrew Bogut .15 .40
7 Brandon Roy .20 .50
8 Richard Hamilton .15 .40
9 Tony Parker .20 .50
10 Yao Ming .25 .60
11 Jamal Crawford .20 .50
12 Dwight Howard .15 .40
13 Steve Nash .20 .50
14 Mike Miller .15 .40
15 Vince Carter .25 .60
16 Pau Gasol .20 .50
17 Mike Dunleavy .15 .40
18 Josh Smith .15 .40
19 Kevin Martin .15 .40
20 Ray Allen .20 .50
21 Tim Duncan .30 .75
22 Michael Redd .15 .40
23 LeBron James .75 2.00
24 Richard Jefferson .15 .40
25 Al Jefferson .15 .40
26 Corey Maggette .15 .40
27 Hedo Turkoglu .15 .40
28 Mo Williams .15 .40
29 Andre Iguodala .15 .40
30 David West .15 .40
31 Tracy McGrady .20 .50
32 Shaquille O'Neal .40 1.00
33 Dwyane Wade .30 .75
34 Paul Pierce .20 .50
35 Kevin Durant .50 1.25
36 Tayshaun Prince .15 .40
37 Shawn Marion .15 .40
38 Anderson Varejao .12 .30
39 Stephen Jackson .15 .40
40 Marcus Camby .12 .30
41 Brad Miller .15 .40
42 David Lee .12 .30
43 Allen Iverson .25 .60
44 Antawn Jamison .15 .40
45 Peja Stojakovic .20 .50
46 Rashad McCants .12 .30
47 Andrei Kirilenko .15 .40
48 Luol Deng .15 .40
49 Hakim Warrick .15 .40
50 Zach Randolph .15 .40
51 Danny Granger .15 .40
52 Greg Oden .15 .40
53 Jason Kidd .20 .50
54 Al Horford .20 .50
55 Carlos Boozer .15 .40
56 Jameer Nelson .12 .30
57 Andre Miller .15 .40
58 Ricky Davis .15 .40
59 Elton Brand .20 .50
60 Kirk Hinrich .15 .40
61 Amare Stoudemire .15 .40
62 Chris Wilcox .12 .30
63 Baron Davis .15 .40
64 Jason Richardson .20 .50
65 Jamario Moon .12 .30
66 LaMarcus Aldridge .20 .50
67 Jermaine O'Neal .15 .40
68 Joe Johnson .15 .40
69 Ben Wallace .15 .40
70 Carmelo Anthony .25 .60
71 T.J. Ford .12 .30
72 Dirk Nowitzki .25 .60
73 Ryan Gomes .12 .30
74 Ben Gordon .15 .40
75 Gerald Wallace .15 .40
76 Rudy Gay .20 .50
77 Lamar Odom .15 .40
78 Jeff Green .15 .40
79 Devin Harris .12 .30
80 Monta Ellis .15 .40
81 Samuel Dalembert .12 .30
82 Raymond Felton .15 .40
83 Ron Artest .20 .50
84 Chauncey Billups .20 .50
85 Josh Howard .15 .40
86 Rafer Alston .12 .30
87 Chris Kaman .15 .40
88 Deron Williams .15 .40
89 Manu Ginobili .20 .50
90 Gilbert Arenas .15 .40
91 Bill Russell .30 .75
92 David Robinson .30 .75
93 Bill Cartwright .15 .40
94 Dominique Wilkins .25 .60
95 Larry Bird .50 1.25
96 Dennis Rodman .40 1.00
97 Jerry West .25 .60
98 George Gervin .25 .60
99 Rick Barry .15 .40
100 Bernard King .15 .40
101 Karl Malone .25 .60
102 Gail Goodrich .15 .40
103 Bill Bradley .25 .60
104 Adrian Dantley .15 .40
105 Joe Dumars .20 .50
106 Sam Jones .25 .60
107 John Stockton .30 .75
108 Magic Johnson .50 1.25
109 Larry Nance .15 .40
110 Dave Bing .20 .50
111 Derrick Rose RC 5.00 12.00
112 Michael Beasley RC .40 1.00
113 O.J. Mayo RC .40 1.00
114 Russell Westbrook RC 3.00 8.00
115 Kevin Love RC 1.25 3.00
116 Danilo Gallinari RC .60 1.50
117 Eric Gordon RC .60 1.50
118 Joe Alexander RC .25 .60
119 D.J. Augustin RC .30 .75
120 Brook Lopez RC .50 1.25
121 Jerryd Bayless RC .30 .75
122 Jason Thompson RC .25 .60
123 Brandon Rush RC .30 .75
124 Anthony Randolph RC .25 .60
125 Robin Lopez RC .40 1.00
126 Marreese Speights RC .30 .75
127 Roy Hibbert RC .40 1.00
128 JaVale McGee RC .50 1.25
129 J.J. Hickson RC .30 .75
130 Alexis Ajinca RC .25 .60
131 Ryan Anderson RC .30 .75
132 Courtney Lee RC .30 .75
133 Kosta Koufos RC .30 .75
134 Darrell Arthur RC .30 .75
135 Donte Greene RC .25 .60
136 Nicolas Batum RC .50 1.25
137 George Hill RC .40 1.00
138 D.J. White RC .30 .75
139 J.R. Giddens RC .25 .60
140 Walter Sharpe RC .25 .60
141 Joey Dorsey RC .25 .60
142 Mario Chalmers RC .40 1.00
143 Chris Douglas-Roberts RC .25 .60

2008-09 Topps Tip-Off Gold

*1-110 GOLD: 2.5X TO 6X BASE HI
*111-143 GOLD RC: 2X TO 5X BASE
STATED PRINT RUN 99 SER.#'d SETS

2008-09 Topps Tip-Off Red

*1-110 RED: .75X TO 2X BASE HI
*111-143 RED RC: .6X TO 1.5X BASE
RED PRINT RUN 2008 SER.#'d SETS

2008-09 Topps Tip-Off Rookie Autographs

STATED PRINT RUN 20 SER.#'d SETS
111 Derrick Rose 150.00 300.00
112 Michael Beasley 25.00 50.00
113 O.J. Mayo 25.00 50.00
114 Russell Westbrook 60.00 150.00
116 Danilo Gallinari 15.00 40.00
117 Eric Gordon 15.00 40.00
118 Joe Alexander 6.00 15.00
120 Brook Lopez 12.00 30.00
123 Brandon Rush 8.00 20.00
124 Anthony Randolph 6.00 15.00
125 Robin Lopez 10.00 25.00
126 Marreese Speights 8.00 20.00
127 Roy Hibbert 10.00 25.00
131 Ryan Anderson 8.00 20.00
137 George Hill 10.00 25.00

2008-09 Topps Tip-Off Team Tattoos

COMPLETE SET (30) 6.00 15.00
1 Atlanta Hawks .40 1.00
2 Boston Celtics .75 2.00
3 Charlotte Bobcats .40 1.00
4 Chicago Bulls .75 2.00
5 Cleveland Cavaliers .40 1.00
6 Dallas Mavericks .40 1.00
7 Denver Nuggets .40 1.00
8 Detroit Pistons .40 1.00
9 Golden State Warriors .40 1.00
10 Houston Rockets .40 1.00
11 Indiana Pacers .40 1.00
12 Los Angeles Clippers .40 1.00
13 Los Angeles Lakers .75 2.00
14 Memphis Grizzlies .40 1.00
15 Miami Heat .40 1.00
16 Milwaukee Bucks .40 1.00
17 Minnesota Timberwolves .40 1.00
18 New Jersey Nets .40 1.00
19 New Orleans Hornets .40 1.00
20 New York Knicks .75 2.00
21 Oklahoma City Thunder .40 1.00
22 Orlando Magic .40 1.00
23 Philadelphia 76ers .40 1.00
24 Phoenix Suns .40 1.00
25 Portland Trail Blazers .40 1.00
26 Sacramento Kings .40 1.00
27 San Antonio Spurs .40 1.00
28 Toronto Raptors .40 1.00
29 Utah Jazz .40 1.00
30 Washington Wizards .40 1.00

2004-05 Topps Total

Released in April 2005, Topps Total boasts a large 440-card checklist including most players in the NBA during the 2004-05 season. All cards feature a silver and white bordered design with the Topps Total logo in red. The breaks down as follows: cards 1-311 feature veteran players, cards 312-360 feature rookies, cards 361-420 feature coaches and cards 421-440 feature team mascots. Total was packaged in 36-pack boxes where each pack contained 10 cards.

COMPLETE SET (440) 20.00 50.00
1 Antoine Walker .20 .50
2 Paul Pierce .20 .50
3 Tyson Chandler .15 .40
4 Lebron James 1.25 3.00
5 Dirk Nowitzki .30 .75
6 Carmelo Anthony .40 1.00
7 Chauncey Billups .20 .50
8 Juwan Howard .15 .40
9 Eddie Gill .12 .30
10 Elton Brand .20 .50
11 Chucky Atkins .12 .30
12 Shane Battier .15 .40
13 Shaquille O'Neal .50 1.25
14 T.J. Ford .12 .30
15 Sam Cassell .15 .40
16 Rodney Buford .12 .30
17 David West .15 .40
18 Stephon Marbury .15 .40
19 Steve Francis .15 .40
20 Samuel Dalembert .12 .30
21 Steve Nash .25 .60
22 Shareef Abdur-Rahim .15 .40
23 Mike Bibby .20 .50
24 Tim Duncan .30 .75
25 Ray Allen .20 .50
26 Vince Carter .30 .75
27 Carlos Arroyo .12 .30
28 Gilbert Arenas .15 .40
29 Mark Blount .12 .30
30 Primoz Brezec .12 .30
31 Eddy Curry .12 .30
32 Lucious Harris .12 .30
33 Shawn Bradley .12 .30
34 Earl Boykins .12 .30
35 Elden Campbell .12 .30
36 Calbert Cheaney .12 .30
37 Jim Jackson .12 .30
38 Jonathan Bender .12 .30
39 Kobe Bryant .75 2.00
40 Malik Allen .12 .30
41 Dan Gadzuric .12 .30
42 Eddie Griffin .12 .30
43 Jason Collins .12 .30
44 Chris Andersen .20 .50
45 Marc Jackson .12 .30
46 Leandro Barbosa .20 .50
47 Derek Anderson .12 .30
48 Doug Christie .12 .30
49 Brent Barry .12 .30
50 Nick Collison .15 .40
51 Carlos Boozer .15 .40
52 Steve Blake .12 .30
53 Al Harrington .15 .40
54 Melvin Ely .12 .30
55 Zydrunas Ilgauskas .15 .40
56 Erick Dampier .12 .30
57 Marcus Camby .15 .40
58 Derrick Coleman .15 .40
59 Speedy Claxton .12 .30
60 Tyronn Lue .12 .30
61 Austin Croshere .12 .30
62 Marko Jaric .12 .30
63 Caron Butler .15 .40
64 Pau Gasol .20 .50
65 Christian Laettner .15 .40
66 Daniel Santiago .12 .30
67 Kevin Garnett .30 .75
68 Richard Jefferson .15 .40
69 David Wesley .12 .30
70 Vin Baker .12 .30
71 Tony Battie .12 .30
72 Allen Iverson .30 .75
73 Darius Miles .12 .30
74 Bobby Jackson .12 .30
75 Bruce Bowen .12 .30
76 Antonio Daniels .12 .30
77 Chris Bosh .20 .50
78 Gordan Giricek .12 .30
79 Kwame Brown .12 .30
80 Raef Lafrentz .12 .30
81 Jason Hart .12 .30
82 Marquis Daniels .12 .30
83 Francisco Elson .12 .30
84 Carlos Delfino .12 .30
85 Dale Davis .12 .30
86 Tracy McGrady .25 .60
87 Jeff Foster .12 .30
88 Chris Kaman .15 .40
89 Brian Cook .12 .30
90 Mike Miller .15 .40
91 Rasual Butler .12 .30
92 Mike James .12 .30
93 Trenton Hassell .12 .30
94 Jason Kidd .30 .75
95 Lee Nailon .12 .30
96 Jerome Williams .12 .30
97 Stacey Augmon .12 .30
98 Willie Green .12 .30
99 Amare Stoudemire .15 .40
100 Ruben Patterson .12 .30
101 Chris Webber .20 .50
102 Manu Ginobili .25 .60
103 Danny Fortson .12 .30
104 Donyell Marshall .12 .30
105 Matt Harpring .12 .30
106 Juan Dixon .12 .30
107 Boris Diaw .15 .40
108 Ricky Davis .15 .40
109 Kareem Rush .12 .30
110 Kirk Hinrich .15 .40
111 Jeff Mcinnis .12 .30
112 Michael Finley .20 .50
113 Voshon Lenard .12 .30
114 Darvin Ham .12 .30
115 Mike Dunleavy .15 .40
116 Dikembe Mutombo .20 .50
117 Kerry Kittles .12 .30
118 Vlade Divac .15 .40
119 James Posey .12 .30
120 Michael Doleac .12 .30
121 Toni Kukoc .20 .50
122 Troy Hudson .12 .30
123 Jamal Crawford .20 .50
124 Grant Hill .25 .60
125 Corliss Williamson .12 .30
126 Quentin Richardson .15 .40
127 Zach Randolph .15 .40
128 Peja Stojakovic .20 .50
129 Robert Horry .15 .40
130 Jerome James .12 .30
131 Morris Peterson .12 .30
132 Jarvis Hayes .12 .30
133 Tony Delk .12 .30
134 Jason Kapono .12 .30
135 Adrian Griffin .12 .30
136 Aleksandar Pavlovic .12 .30
137 Kenyon Martin .15 .40
138 Richard Hamilton .15 .40
139 Derek Fisher .15 .40
140 Bob Sura .12 .30
141 Stephen Jackson .15 .40
142 Devean George .12 .30
143 Stromile Swift .12 .30
144 Keyon Dooling .12 .30
145 Desmond Mason .15 .40
146 Michael Olowokandi .12 .30
147 Ron Mercer .12 .30
148 P.J. Brown .12 .30
149 Tim Thomas .12 .30
150 Kelvin Cato .12 .30
151 Kenny Thomas .12 .30
152 Theo Ratliff .12 .30
153 Rasho Nesterovic .12 .30
154 Rashard Lewis .20 .50
155 Jalen Rose .15 .40
156 Brendan Haywood .12 .30
157 Kevin Willis .12 .30
158 Gary Payton .20 .50
159 Brevin Knight .12 .30
160 Othella Harrington .12 .30
161 Eric Snow .12 .30
162 Josh Howard .20 .50
163 Andre Miller .15 .40
164 Lindsey Hunter .12 .30
165 Adonal Foyle .12 .30
166 Maurice Taylor .12 .30
167 Fred Jones .12 .30
168 Corey Maggette .15 .40
169 Brian Grant .12 .30
170 Bonzi Wells .12 .30
171 Michael Redd .15 .40
172 Latrell Sprewell .15 .40
173 Steven Hunter .12 .30
174 Rodney Rogers .12 .30
175 Anfernee Hardaway .50 1.25
176 Pat Garrity .12 .30
177 Brian Skinner .12 .30
178 Zarko Cabarkapa .12 .30
179 Damon Stoudamire .15 .40
180 Tony Parker .20 .50
181 Ronald Murray .12 .30
182 Alvin Williams .12 .30
183 Raul Lopez .12 .30
184 Larry Hughes .15 .40
185 Predrag Drobnjak .12 .30
186 Jiri Welsch .12 .30
187 Robert Traylor .12 .30
188 Nene .15 .40
189 Antonio McDyess .15 .40
190 Troy Murphy .12 .30
191 Charlie Ward .12 .30
192 Reggie Miller .20 .50
193 Bobby Simmons .12 .30
194 Stanislav Medvedenko .12 .30
195 Jason Williams .15 .40
196 Dwyane Wade .30 .75
197 Joe Smith .15 .40
198 Wally Szczerbiak .15 .40
199 Zoran Planinic .12 .30
200 Baron Davis .15 .40
201 Kurt Thomas .12 .30
202 Deshawn Stevenson .12 .30
203 John Salmons .15 .40
204 Maciej Lampe .12 .30
205 Greg Ostertag .12 .30
206 Malik Rose .12 .30
207 Matt Bonner .12 .30
208 Keith McLeod .12 .30
209 Antawn Jamison .15 .40
210 Marcus Banks .12 .30
211 Keith Bogans .12 .30
212 Antonio Davis .12 .30
213 Jerry Stackhouse .15 .40
214 Nikoloz Tskitishvili .12 .30
215 Darko Milicic .12 .30
216 Eduardo Najera .12 .30
217 Yao Ming .40 1.00
218 Jermaine O'Neal .15 .40
219 Chris Wilcox .12 .30
220 Lamar Odom .15 .40
221 Lorenzen Wright .12 .30
222 Damon Jones .12 .30
223 Keith Van Horn .15 .40
224 Fred Hoiberg .12 .30
225 Brian Scalabrine .12 .30
226 Jamaal Magloire .12 .30
227 Mike Sweetney .12 .30
228 Hedo Turkoglu .15 .40
229 Glenn Robinson .15 .40
230 Casey Jacobsen .12 .30
231 Nick Van Exel .15 .40
232 Matt Barnes .12 .30
233 Luke Ridnour .15 .40
234 Loren Woods .12 .30
235 Raja Bell .15 .40
236 Walter McCarty .12 .30
237 Steve Smith .15 .40
238 Frank Williams .12 .30
239 Dajuan Wagner .12 .30
240 Jason Terry .15 .40
241 Rodney White .12 .30
242 Tayshaun Prince .15 .40
243 Mickael Pietrus .15 .40
244 Reece Gaines .12 .30
245 Jamaal Tinsley .12 .30
246 Zeljko Rebraca .12 .30
247 Chris Mihm .12 .30
248 Eddie Jones .15 .40
249 Zaza Pachulia .12 .30
250 Ervin Johnson .12 .30
251 Jabari Smith .12 .30
252 Nazr Mohammed .12 .30
253 Andrew Declercq .12 .30
254 Kyle Korver .15 .40
255 Jake Voskuhl .12 .30
256 Travis Outlaw .15 .40
257 Vladimir Radmanovic .12 .30
258 Lamond Murray .12 .30
259 Jarron Collins .12 .30
260 Jared Jeffries .12 .30
261 Jason Collier .12 .30
262 Tom Gugliotta .12 .30
263 Gerald Wallace .15 .40
264 Eric Piatkowski .12 .30
265 Desagana Diop .12 .30
266 Alan Henderson .12 .30
267 Greg Buckner .12 .30
268 Ben Wallace .15 .40
269 Jason Richardson .20 .50
270 Ryan Bowen .12 .30
271 Mikki Moore .12 .30
272 Brian Cardinal .12 .30
273 Maurice Williams .15 .40
274 Mark Madsen .12 .30
275 Jacque Vaughn .12 .30
276 George Lynch .12 .30
277 Allan Houston .15 .40
278 Aaron McKie .12 .30
279 Joe Johnson .15 .40
280 Qyntel Woods .12 .30
281 Darius Songaila .12 .30
282 Devin Brown .12 .30
283 Mehmet Okur .15 .40
284 Kenny Anderson .15 .40
285 Jahidi White .12 .30
286 Jon Barry .12 .30
287 Drew Gooden .12 .30
288 Wesley Person .12 .30
289 Rasheed Wallace .20 .50
290 Clifford Robinson .12 .30
291 Bostjan Nachbar .12 .30
292 Scot Pollard .12 .30
293 Quinton Ross .12 .30
294 Luke Walton .12 .30
295 Earl Watson .12 .30
296 Udonis Haslem .12 .30
297 Erick Strickland .12 .30
298 Eric Williams .12 .30
299 Junior Harrington .12 .30
300 Moochie Norris .12 .30
301 Cuttino Mobley .12 .30

Card	Low	High
302 Shawn Marion	.15	.40
303 Richie Frahm	.12	.30
304 Brad Miller	.15	.40
305 Michael Wilks	.12	.30
306 Rafer Alston	.12	.30
307 Andrei Kirilenko	.15	.40
308 Etan Thomas	.12	.30
309 Ndudi Ebi	.12	.30
310 Anthony Peeler	.12	.30
311 Pavel Podkolzin RC	.20	.50
312 Lionel Chalmers RC	.30	.75
313 Andre Emmett RC	.20	.50
314 Trevor Ariza RC	.30	.75
315 Dwight Howard RC	.60	1.50
316 Rafael Araujo RC	.20	.50
317 Tony Allen RC	.30	.75
318 Luol Deng RC	.30	.75
319 Jackson Vroman RC	.20	.50
320 Josh Smith RC	.30	.75
321 Ben Gordon RC	.30	.75
322 Luke Jackson RC	.20	.50
323 David Harrison RC	.20	.50
324 Nenad Krstic RC	.30	.75
325 J.R. Smith RC	.30	.75
326 Kris Humphries RC	.30	.75
327 Al Jefferson RC	.40	1.00
328 Devin Harris RC	.25	.60
329 Shaun Livingston RC	.30	.75
330 Kaniel Dickens RC	.30	.75
331 Kevin Martin RC	.40	1.00
332 Kirk Snyder RC	.20	.50
333 Josh Childress RC	.25	.60
334 Erik Daniels RC	.25	.60
335 Bernard Robinson RC	.25	.60
336 Andres Nocioni RC	.30	.75
337 D.J. Mbenga RC	.25	.60
338 Sebastian Telfair RC	.25	.60
339 Robert Swift RC	.20	.50
340 Royal Ivey RC	.25	.60
341 Anderson Varejao RC	.25	.60
342 Romain Sato RC	.20	.50
343 Peter John Ramos RC	.20	.50
344 Chris Duhon RC	.30	.75
345 Emeka Okafor RC	.25	.60
346 Matt Freije RC	.25	.60
347 Maurice Evans RC	.30	.75
348 Beno Udrih RC	.25	.60
349 John Edwards RC	.20	.50
350 Sasha Vujacic RC	.30	.75
351 Dorell Wright RC	.30	.75
352 Jameer Nelson RC	.30	.75
353 Damien Wilkins RC	.25	.60
354 Pape Sow RC	.25	.60
355 Andris Biedrins RC	.20	.50
356 Delonte West RC	.30	.75
357 Arthur Johnson RC	.30	.75
358 Antonio Burks RC	.25	.60
359 Andre Iguodala RC	.40	1.00
360 Ibrahim Kutluay RC	.30	.75
361 Mike Woodson CO	.20	.50
362 Larry Drew CO	.20	.50
363 Doc Rivers CO	.40	1.00
364 Tony Brown CO	.20	.50
365 Bernie Bickerstaff CO	.20	.50
366 Gary Brokaw CO	.20	.50
367 Scott Skiles CO	.40	1.00
368 Ron Adams CO	.20	.50
369 Paul Silas CO	.20	.50
370 Brendan Malone CO	.20	.50
371 Don Nelson CO	.40	1.00
372 Donnie Nelson CO RC	.20	.50
373 Jeff Bzdelik CO	.20	.50
374 Michael Cooper CO	.20	.50
375 Larry Brown CO	.50	1.25
376 Dave Hanners CO	.20	.50
377 Mike Montgomery CO	.40	1.00
378 Terry Stotts CO	.20	.50
379 Jeff Van Gundy CO	.40	1.00
380 Tom Thibodeau CO	.20	.50
381 Rick Carlisle CO	.20	.50
382 Mike Brown CO	.20	.50
383 Mike Dunleavy Sr. CO	.40	1.00
384 Jim Eyen CO	.20	.50
385 Rudy Tomjanovich CO	.40	1.00
386 Frank Hamblen CO	.20	.50
387 Mike Fratello CO	.40	1.00
388 Eric Musselman CO	.20	.50
389 Stan Van Gundy CO	.40	1.00
390 Bob Mcadoo CO	.40	1.00
391 Terry Porter CO	.20	.50
392 Mike Schuler CO	.20	.50
393 Flip Saunders CO	.40	1.00
394 Jerry Sichting CO	.20	.50
395 Lawrence Frank CO	.40	1.00
396 Brian Hill CO	.20	.50
397 Byron Scott CO	.20	.50
398 Darrell Walker CO	.20	.50
399 Lenny Wilkens CO	.50	1.25
400 Mark Aguirre CO	.20	.50
401 Johnny Davis CO	.20	.50
402 Paul Westhead CO	.20	.50
403 Jim O'Brien CO	.40	1.00
404 Lester Conner CO	.20	.50
405 Mike D'Antoni CO	.40	1.00
406 Marc Iavaroni CO	.20	.50
407 Maurice Cheeks CO	.40	1.00
408 Jim Lynam CO	.20	.50
409 Rick Adelman CO	.40	1.00
410 Elston Turner CO	.20	.50
411 Gregg Popovich CO	.50	1.25
412 P.J. Carlesimo CO	.40	1.00
413 Nate Mcmillan CO	.20	.50
414 Dwane Casey CO	.20	.50
415 Sam Mitchell CO	.20	.50
416 Alex English CO	.40	1.00
417 Jerry Sloan CO	.40	1.00
418 Phil Johnson CO	.20	.50
419 Eddie Jordan CO	.20	.50
420 Mike O'Koren CO	.20	.50
421 Harry The Hawk	.30	.75
422 Blaze	.30	.75
423 Benny Da Bull	.30	.75
424 Slamson	.30	.75
425 Champ	.30	.75
426 Rocky	.30	.75
427 Clutch	.30	.75
428 Squatch	.30	.75
429 Boomer	.30	.75
430 The Raptor	.30	.75
431 Super Grizz	.30	.75
432 G-Wiz	.30	.75
433 Crunch	.30	.75
434 Sly The Fox	.30	.75
435 Hip Hop	.30	.75
436 The Gorilla	.30	.75
437 Skyhawk	.30	.75
438 Turbo	.30	.75
439 Bowser	.30	.75
440 Da Bull	.30	.75

2004-05 Topps Total Silver

*PARALLEL: 1X TO 2.5X BASE HI
STATED ODDS ONE PER PACK

2004-05 Topps Total Domination

Inserted at one in nine packs, this 20-card set utilizes a borderless design with a blue bar through the bottom contianing the player's name.

Card	Low	High
COMPLETE SET (20)	4.00	10.00
STATED ODDS 1:9		
TD1 Shaquille O'Neal	.75	2.00
TD2 Allen Iverson	.50	1.25
TD3 Tim Duncan	.50	1.25
TD4 Tracy McGrady	.40	1.00
TD5 Emeka Okafor	.25	.60
TD6 Vince Carter	.50	1.25
TD7 Jermaine O'Neal	.25	.60
TD8 Jason Kidd	.50	1.25
TD9 Ben Wallace	.25	.60
TD10 Dirk Nowitzki	.50	1.25
TD11 Peja Stojakovic	.30	.75
TD12 Michael Redd	.25	.60
TD13 Amare Stoudemire	.25	.60
TD14 Yao Ming	.60	1.50
TD15 Lamar Odom	.25	.60
TD16 Steve Francis	.25	.60
TD17 Sebastian Telfair	.25	.60
TD18 Devin Harris	.25	.60
TD19 Luol Deng	.30	.75
TD20 Elton Brand	.30	.75

2004-05 Topps Total Package

Inserted at one in nine packs, this 20-card set is gold bordered and places players against colored backgrounds.

Card	Low	High
COMPLETE SET (20)	6.00	15.00
STATED ODDS 1:9		
TP1 Kevin Garnett	.50	1.25
TP2 Kobe Bryant	1.25	3.00
TP3 Lebron James	2.00	5.00
TP4 Dwyane Wade	.50	1.25
TP5 Richard Jefferson	.25	.60
TP6 Dwight Howard	.60	1.50
TP7 Ben Gordon	.30	.75
TP8 Shaun Livingston	.30	.75
TP9 Carmelo Anthony	.60	1.50
TP10 Paul Pierce	.30	.75
TP11 Baron Davis	.25	.60
TP12 Chris Webber	.30	.75
TP13 Shawn Marion	.25	.60
TP14 Andrei Kirilenko	.25	.60
TP15 Ray Allen	.30	.75
TP16 Pau Gasol	.30	.75
TP17 Richard Hamilton	.25	.60
TP18 Stephon Marbury	.25	.60
TP19 Jason Richardson	.30	.75
TP20 Andre Iguodala	.40	1.00

2004-05 Topps Total Signatures

ndomly seeded in packs for Group A at one in 15948, Group B at one in 1492 and Group C at one in 537, this 18-card set is bordered on the top and bottom in gold and has a sticker containing the player's autograph towards the bottom.

Card	Low	High
GROUP C ODDS 1:537		
CA Carmelo Anthony	20.00	50.00
DH Devin Harris	5.00	12.00
EO Emeka Okafor	5.00	12.00
JR Justin Reed	4.00	10.00
KH Kris Humphries	6.00	15.00
LC Lionel Chalmers	6.00	15.00
LD Luol Deng	6.00	15.00
RS Romain Sato	4.00	10.00
SO Shaquille O'Neal	50.00	100.00
YT Yuta Tabuse	6.00	15.00
RSW Robert Swift	4.00	10.00

2004-05 Topps Total Success

Seeded in packs at one in 18, this 10-card set is printed on foil and places full-color player action photos on a design with a white line through it towards the left.

Card	Low	High
COMPLETE SET (10)	2.50	6.00
STATED ODDS 1:18		
TS1 Carlos Boozer	.40	1.00
TS2 Zach Randolph	.40	1.00
TS3 Brad Miller	.40	1.00
TS4 Ben Wallace	.40	1.00
TS5 Cuttino Mobley	.30	.75
TS6 Rashard Lewis	.50	1.25
TS7 Rafer Alston	.30	.75
TS8 Carlos Arroyo	.30	.75
TS9 Manu Ginobili	.60	1.50
TS10 Sam Cassell	.40	1.00

2004-05 Topps Total Team Checklists

serted in packs at one in 4, this 30-card set showcases one of the team's top players on the front and a listing for all the players who appear on cards on the back.

Card	Low	High
COMPLETE SET (30)	10.00	25.00
STATED ODDS 1:4		
1 Antoine Walker	.40	1.00
2 Paul Pierce	.40	1.00
3 Emeka Okafor	.30	.75
4 Kirk Hinrich	.30	.75
5 Lebron James	2.50	6.00
6 Dirk Nowitzki	.60	1.50
7 Carmelo Anthony	.75	2.00
8 Ben Wallace	.30	.75
9 Mike Dunleavy	.30	.75
10 Yao Ming	.75	2.00
11 Jermaine O'Neal	.30	.75
12 Elton Brand	.40	1.00
13 Kobe Bryant	1.50	4.00
14 Pau Gasol	.40	1.00
15 Shaquille O'Neal	1.00	2.50
16 Michael Redd	.30	.75
17 Kevin Garnett	.60	1.50
18 Richard Jefferson	.30	.75
19 Baron Davis	.30	.75
20 Stephon Marbury	.30	.75
21 Dwight Howard	.75	2.00
22 Allen Iverson	.60	1.50
23 Amare Stoudemire	.30	.75
24 Zach Randolph	.30	.75
25 Mike Bibby	.40	1.00
26 Tim Duncan	.60	1.50
27 Rashard Lewis	.40	1.00
28 Vince Carter	.60	1.50
29 Andrei Kirilenko	.30	.75
30 Antawn Jamison	.30	.75

2005-06 Topps Total

leased in January 2006, This 440-card set is the largest base set issued during the 2005-06 season. Cards 1-360 feature a mix of veteran and rookie players, cards 361-420 feature team coaching staffs, cards 421-435 feature team mascots and cards 436-440 feature Topps celebrities. Base cards have white borders and photos outlined in team colors. Total was packaged in 36-pack boxes where each pack contains 10 cards and carried an initial SRP of $1.00.

Card	Low	High
COMPLETE SET (440)	20.00	50.00
UNPRICED GOLD PRINT RUN 10 SETS		
UNPRICED PRESS PLATES 1/1 EXISTS		
1 Josh Childress	.15	.40
2 Emeka Okafor	.15	.40
3 Luol Deng	.15	.40
4 Carmelo Anthony	.40	1.00
5 Carlos Arroyo	.12	.30
6 Shane Battier	.15	.40
7 Vince Carter	.30	.75
8 Samuel Dalembert	.12	.30
9 Leandro Barbosa	.15	.40
10 Mike Bibby	.20	.50
11 Brent Barry	.12	.30
12 Ray Allen	.20	.50
13 Rafer Alston	.12	.30
14 Gilbert Arenas	.15	.40
15 Al Harrington	.15	.40
16 Primoz Brezec	.12	.30
17 Antonio Davis	.12	.30
18 Earl Boykins	.12	.30
19 Chauncey Billups	.20	.50
20 Antonio Burks	.12	.30
21 Jason Collins	.12	.30
22 P.J. Brown	.12	.30
23 Andre Iguodala	.15	.40
24 Bruce Bowen	.12	.30
25 Nick Collison	.15	.40
26 Rafael Araujo	.12	.30
27 Josh Smith	.15	.40
28 Melvin Ely	.12	.30
29 Ben Gordon	.15	.40
30 Zydrunas Ilgauskas	.15	.40
31 Marcus Camby	.15	.40
32 Carlos Delfino	.12	.30
33 Mike James	.12	.30
34 Brian Cardinal	.12	.30
35 Udonis Haslem	.12	.30
36 Toni Kukoc	.20	.50
37 Kevin Garnett	.30	.75
38 Richard Jefferson	.15	.40
39 Jamal Crawford	.20	.50
40 Allen Iverson	.30	.75
41 Tim Duncan	.30	.75
42 Danny Fortson	.12	.30
43 Chris Bosh	.20	.50
44 Ricky Davis	.15	.40
45 LeBron James	.75	2.00
46 Devin Harris	.12	.30
47 Tracy McGrady	.25	.60
48 Chris Kaman	.15	.40
49 Pau Gasol	.20	.50
50 Jamaal Magloire	.12	.30
51 Trenton Hassell	.12	.30
52 Jason Kidd	.30	.75
53 Speedy Claxton	.12	.30
54 Kevin Martin	.15	.40
55 Manu Ginobili	.20	.50
56 Rashard Lewis	.20	.50
57 Matt Harpring	.12	.30
58 Kenyon Martin	.15	.40
59 Al Jefferson	.15	.40
60 Josh Howard	.20	.50
61 Bob Sura	.12	.30
62 David Harrison	.12	.30
63 Shaun Livingston	.12	.30
64 Alonzo Mourning	.25	.60
65 Michael Redd	.15	.40
66 Mark Madsen	.12	.30
67 Brad Miller	.15	.40
68 Robert Horry	.15	.40
69 Luke Ridnour	.15	.40
70 Paul Pierce	.20	.50
71 Anderson Varejao	.12	.30
72 Dirk Nowitzki	.30	.75
73 Stephen Jackson	.15	.40
74 Corey Maggette	.15	.40
75 Shaquille O'Neal	.40	1.00
76 Joe Smith	.15	.40
77 Troy Hudson	.12	.30
78 Steve Francis	.15	.40
79 Shawn Marion	.15	.40
80 Ruben Patterson	.12	.30
81 Morris Peterson	.12	.30
82 Jarvis Hayes	.12	.30
83 Derek Fisher	.15	.40
84 Fred Jones	.12	.30
85 Chris Mihm	.12	.30
86 Stephon Marbury	.15	.40
87 Grant Hill	.25	.60
88 Steve Nash	.25	.60
89 Joel Przybilla	.12	.30
90 Jalen Rose	.20	.50
91 Brendan Haywood	.12	.30
92 Jerry Stackhouse	.15	.40
93 Adonal Foyle	.12	.30
94 Lamar Odom	.15	.40
95 Dwight Howard	.15	.40
96 Amare Stoudemire	.15	.40
97 Zach Randolph	.15	.40
98 Peja Stojakovic	.20	.50
99 Mehmet Okur	.12	.30
100 Antawn Jamison	.15	.40
101 Jason Terry	.15	.40
102 Troy Murphy	.12	.30
103 Sasha Vujacic	.15	.40
104 Dwyane Wade	.30	.75
105 Jameer Nelson	.12	.30
106 Jared Jeffries	.12	.30
107 J.R. Smith	.15	.40
108 Mike Sweetney	.12	.30
109 DeShawn Stevenson	.12	.30
110 Sebastian Telfair	.15	.40
111 Eddie Griffin	.12	.30
112 Tyronn Lue	.12	.30
113 Jon Barry	.12	.30
114 Eric Williams	.12	.30
115 Rasho Nesterovic	.12	.30
116 Keith Van Horn	.15	.40
117 Kenny Thomas	.12	.30
118 Chris Wilcox	.12	.30
119 Chris Webber	.20	.50
120 Nene	.15	.40
121 John Salmons	.15	.40
122 Chris Andersen	.20	.50
123 Lindsey Hunter	.12	.30
124 Matt Bonner	.12	.30
125 Darius Miles	.12	.30
126 Orien Greene RC	.15	.40
127 Jarron Collins	.12	.30
128 Trevor Ariza	.12	.30
129 Dan Gadzuric	.12	.30
130 Loren Woods	.12	.30
131 Jason Richardson	.20	.50
132 Corliss Williamson	.12	.30
133 Zeljko Rebraca	.12	.30
134 Othella Harrington	.12	.30
135 Theo Ratliff	.12	.30
136 David Wesley	.12	.30
137 Bostjan Nachbar	.12	.30
138 Eric Snow	.12	.30
139 Desmond Mason	.12	.30
140 Dahntay Jones	.12	.30
141 Andre Miller	.15	.40
142 Travis Outlaw	.15	.40
143 Jim Jackson	.12	.30
144 Gordan Giricek	.12	.30
145 Kelvin Cato	.12	.30
146 Michael Doleac	.12	.30
147 Lorenzen Wright	.12	.30
148 Vladimir Radmanovic	.12	.30
149 Maurice Evans	.12	.30
150 Hedo Turkoglu	.15	.40
151 Ryan Bowen	.12	.30
152 Brevin Knight	.12	.30
153 Jacque Vaughn	.12	.30
154 Tayshaun Prince	.15	.40
155 Clifford Robinson	.12	.30
156 Delonte West	.12	.30
157 Zoran Planinic	.12	.30
158 Slava Medvedenko	.12	.30
159 Andres Nocioni	.12	.30
160 Kyle Korver	.15	.40
161 Brian Cook	.12	.30
162 Viktor Khryapa	.12	.30
163 Malik Rose	.12	.30
164 Elton Brand	.20	.50
165 Gerald Wallace	.15	.40
166 Michael Bradley	.12	.30
167 DerMarr Johnson	.12	.30
168 Reece Gaines	.12	.30
169 Mickael Pietrus	.15	.40
170 Donta Smith	.12	.30
171 Wally Szczerbiak	.15	.40
172 Aleksandar Pavlovic	.12	.30
173 Michael Olowokandi	.12	.30
174 Jose Calderon RC	.20	.50
175 Jiri Welsch	.12	.30
176 Antonio McDyess	.15	.40
177 Andrei Kirilenko	.15	.40
178 Nenad Krstic	.12	.30
179 Richard Hamilton	.15	.40
180 Stacey Augmon	.12	.30
181 Kobe Bryant	.75	2.00
182 Erick Dampier	.12	.30
183 Raef LaFrentz	.12	.30
184 Jackie Butler RC	.12	.30
185 Ira Newble	.12	.30
186 Luke Walton	.12	.30
187 Rasheed Wallace	.20	.50
188 Alvin Williams	.12	.30
189 Ben Wallace	.15	.40
190 Chris Duhon	.12	.30
191 Maurice Williams	.15	.40
192 Ronald Murray	.12	.30
193 Yao Ming	.25	.60
194 Eduardo Najera	.12	.30
195 Nazr Mohammed	.12	.30
196 Devean George	.12	.30
197 Kirk Hinrich	.15	.40
198 Baron Davis	.15	.40
199 Juwan Howard	.15	.40
200 Drew Gooden	.15	.40
201 Carlos Boozer	.15	.40
202 Tony Delk	.12	.30
203 David West	.15	.40
204 Keith Bogans	.12	.30
205 Quinton Ross	.12	.30
206 Darrell Armstrong	.12	.30
207 Damien Wilkins	.12	.30
208 Voshon Lenard	.12	.30
209 Vitaly Potapenko	.12	.30
210 Mike Miller	.15	.40
211 Beno Udrih	.12	.30
212 Darko Milicic	.12	.30
213 Tony Parker	.20	.50
214 Brian Skinner	.12	.30
215 Mike Dunleavy	.15	.40
216 Kris Humphries	.12	.30
217 Mark Blount	.12	.30
218 Marquis Daniels	.12	.30
219 Tony Allen	.12	.30
220 Tony Battie	.12	.30
221 Luther Head RC	.15	.40
222 Richie Frahm	.12	.30
223 Arvydas Macijauskas RC	.12	.30
224 Eddie Jones	.15	.40
225 Dan Dickau	.12	.30
226 Marko Jaric	.12	.30
227 Daniel Ewing RC	.15	.40
228 Keyon Dooling	.12	.30
229 James Posey	.12	.30
230 Earl Watson	.12	.30
231 Juan Dixon	.12	.30
232 Rasual Butler	.12	.30
233 Bernard Robinson	.12	.30
234 Joe Johnson	.15	.40
235 Antoine Walker	.15	.40
236 Andris Biedrins	.12	.30
237 Gary Payton	.20	.50
238 Monta Ellis RC	.25	.60
239 Quentin Richardson	.15	.40
240 Martynas Andriuskevicius RC	.12	.30
241 Kwame Brown	.12	.30
242 Travis Diener RC	.12	.30
243 Stromile Swift	.12	.30
244 Wayne Simien RC	.12	.30
245 Zaza Pachulia	.12	.30
246 Andrew Bogut RC	.25	.60
247 Marvin Williams RC	.20	.50
248 David Lee RC	.20	.50
249 Nate Robinson RC	.20	.50
250 Jason Williams	.15	.40
251 Larry Hughes	.15	.40
252 Ike Diogu RC	.12	.30
253 Marc Jackson	.12	.30
254 Luke Jackson	.12	.30
255 Lee Nailon	.12	.30
256 T.J. Ford	.12	.30
257 Shavlik Randolph RC	.15	.40
258 Eddie Basden RC	.12	.30
259 Yaroslav Korolev RC	.12	.30
260 James Jones	.12	.30
261 Raja Bell	.15	.40
262 Salim Stoudamire RC	.15	.40
263 Cuttino Mobley	.12	.30
264 Kurt Thomas	.12	.30
265 D.J. Mbenga	.12	.30
266 Zarko Cabarkapa	.12	.30
267 Bobby Jackson	.12	.30
268 Rashad McCants RC	.15	.40
269 Antoine Wright RC	.15	.40
270 Josh Powell RC	.15	.40
271 Francisco Garcia RC	.15	.40
272 Robert Swift	.12	.30
273 Gerald Green RC	.20	.50
274 Peter John Ramos	.12	.30
275 Nick Van Exel	.20	.50
276 Jarrett Jack RC	.20	.50
277 Ronnie Price RC	.15	.40
278 Jamaal Tinsley	.12	.30
279 Jake Voskuhl	.12	.30
280 Devin Brown	.12	.30
281 James Singleton RC	.12	.30
282 C.J. Miles RC	.20	.50
283 Charlie Villanueva RC	.20	.50
284 Jeff McInnis	.12	.30
285 Eddie House	.12	.30
286 Rawle Marshall RC	.12	.30
287 Royal Ivey	.12	.30
288 Dikembe Mutombo	.20	.50
289 Fabricio Oberto RC	.15	.40
290 Damon Jones	.12	.30
291 Jason Hart	.12	.30
292 Jumaine Jones	.12	.30
293 Greg Ostertag	.12	.30
294 Ryan Gomes RC	.15	.40
295 Derek Anderson	.12	.30
296 Raymond Felton RC	.20	.50
297 Johan Petro RC	.12	.30
298 Bonzi Wells	.12	.30
299 Tyson Chandler	.15	.40
300 Sarunas Jasikevicius RC	.20	.50
301 Joey Graham RC	.15	.40
302 Alan Anderson RC	.12	.30
303 Steve Blake	.12	.30
304 Nikoloz Tskitishvili	.12	.30
305 Shareef Abdur-Rahim	.15	.40
306 Sean May RC	.12	.30
307 Julius Hodge RC	.12	.30
308 Deron Williams RC	.25	.60
309 Michael Ruffin	.12	.30
310 Darius Songaila	.12	.30
311 Donyell Marshall	.12	.30
312 Jermaine O'Neal	.15	.40
313 Bracey Wright RC	.12	.30
314 Scot Pollard	.12	.30
315 Linas Kleiza RC	.12	.30
316 Jerome James	.12	.30
317 Brian Scalabrine	.12	.30
318 Tim Thomas	.12	.30
319 Reggie Evans	.12	.30
320 Jason Maxiell RC	.15	.40
321 Jannero Pargo	.12	.30
322 Michael Finley	.20	.50
323 Ersan Ilyasova RC	.20	.50
324 Robert Whaley RC	.12	.30
325 Chris Taft RC	.15	.40
326 Esteban Batista RC	.12	.30
327 Louis Williams RC	.20	.50
328 Austin Croshere	.12	.30
329 Martell Webster RC	.15	.40
330 Etan Thomas	.12	.30
331 Brandon Bass RC	.15	.40
332 Ron Artest	.20	.50
333 Gerald Fitch RC	.12	.30
334 Chucky Atkins	.12	.30
335 Jonathan Bender	.12	.30
336 Boris Diaw	.15	.40
337 Andray Blatche RC	.20	.50
338 Jeff Foster	.12	.30
339 Andrew Bynum RC	.15	.40
340 Caron Butler	.15	.40
341 Danny Granger RC	.25	.60
342 Channing Frye RC	.20	.50
343 Antonio Daniels	.12	.30
344 Brian Grant	.12	.30
345 Steven Hunter	.12	.30
346 Chris Paul RC	.75	2.00
347 Lawrence Roberts RC	.12	.30
348 Bobby Simmons	.12	.30
349 Dijon Thompson RC	.12	.30
350 Von Wafer RC	.12	.30
351 Damon Stoudamire	.15	.40
352 Kevin Ollie	.12	.30
353 Kirk Snyder	.12	.30
354 Hakim Warrick RC	.15	.40
355 Eddy Curry	.12	.30
356 Aaron McKie	.12	.30
357 Sam Cassell	.15	.40
358 Dorell Wright	.12	.30
359 Scott Padgett	.12	.30
360 Pat Garrity	.12	.30
361 Mike Woodson	.20	.50
362 Larry Drew	.20	.50
363 Doc Rivers	.20	.50
364 Tony Brown	.12	.30
365 Bernie Bickerstaff	.20	.50
366 Gary Brokaw	.20	.50
367 Scott Skiles	.15	.40
368 Ron Adams	.20	.50
369 Mike Brown	.20	.50
370 Kenny Natt	.20	.50
371 Avery Johnson	.15	.40
372 Del Harris	.20	.50
373 George Karl	.20	.50
374 Scott Brooks	.12	.30
375 Flip Saunders	.20	.50
376 Sid Lowe	.20	.50
377 Mike Montgomery	.20	.50
378 Mario Elie	.12	.30
379 Jeff Van Gundy	.20	.50
380 Tom Thibodeau	.20	.50
381 Rick Carlisle	.20	.50
382 Kevin O'Neill	.20	.50
383 Mike Dunleavy Sr.	.20	.50
384 Jim Eyen	.20	.50
385 Phil Jackson	.25	.60
386 Frank Hamblen	.20	.50
387 Mike Fratello	.25	.60
388 Eric Musselman	.20	.50
389 Pat Riley	.20	.50
390 Bob McAdoo	.15	.40
391 Terry Stotts	.20	.50
392 Lester Conner	.20	.50
393 Dwane Casey	.20	.50
394 Johnny Davis	.20	.50
395 Lawrence Frank	.20	.50
396 Bill Cartwright	.15	.40
397 Byron Scott	.15	.40
398 Darrell Walker	.20	.50
399 Larry Brown	.20	.50
400 Herb Williams	.12	.30
401 Brian Hill	.20	.50
402 Randy Ayers	.20	.50
403 Maurice Cheeks	.12	.30
404 John Kuester	.20	.50
405 Mike D'Antoni	.20	.50
406 Marc Iavaroni	.20	.50
407 Nate McMillan	.20	.50
408 Dean Demopoulos	.20	.50
409 Rick Adelman	.20	.50
410 Elston Turner	.20	.50
411 Gregg Popovich	.25	.60
412 P.J. Carlesimo	.20	.50
413 Bob Weiss	.20	.50
414 Jack Sikma	.15	.40
415 Sam Mitchell	.12	.30
416 Jim Todd	.20	.50
417 Jerry Sloan	.20	.50
418 Phil D. Johnson	.20	.50
419 Eddie Jordan	.20	.50
420 Mike O'Koren	.20	.50
421 The Gorilla	.30	.75
422 Rocky	.30	.75
423 Slamson	.30	.75
424 The Raptor	.30	.75
425 Squatch	.30	.75
426 Blaze	.30	.75
427 Crunch	.30	.75
428 Harry the Hawk	.30	.75
429 Champ	.30	.75
430 Hip Hop	.30	.75
431 Sly the Silver Fox	.30	.75
432 Benny the Bull	.30	.75
433 G-Wiz	.30	.75
434 Clutch	.30	.75
435 Boomer	.30	.75
436 Shannon Elizabeth	.40	1.00
437 Christie Brinkley	.40	1.00
438 Jenny McCarthy	.40	1.00
439 Carmen Electra	.40	1.00
440 Jay-Z	.60	1.50

2005-06 Topps Total Silver

*SILVER: .75X TO 2X BASE HI
STATED ODDS ONE PER PACK

2005-06 Topps Total Competition

Card	Low	High
COMPLETE SET (10)	3.00	8.00
STATED ODDS 1:18		
TC1 Jason Kidd	1.00	2.50
TC2 Richard Hamilton	.50	1.25
TC3 Manu Ginobili	.60	1.50
TC4 Elton Brand	.60	1.50
TC5 Jason Richardson	.60	1.50
TC6 Emeka Okafor	.50	1.25
TC7 Allen Iverson	1.00	2.50
TC8 Shawn Marion	.50	1.25
TC9 Ben Gordon	.50	1.25
TC10 Dwyane Wade	1.00	2.50

2005-06 Topps Total Performance

Card	Low	High
COMPLETE SET (20)	8.00	20.00
STATED ODDS 1:9		
TP1 Shaquille O'Neal	1.00	2.50
TP2 LeBron James	2.00	5.00
TP3 Allen Iverson	.75	2.00
TP4 Dirk Nowitzki	.75	2.00
TP5 Tracy McGrady	.60	1.50
TP6 Steve Nash	.60	1.50
TP7 Vince Carter	.75	2.00
TP8 Carmelo Anthony	1.00	2.50
TP9 Kobe Bryant	2.00	5.00
TP10 Kevin Garnett	.75	2.00
TP11 Tim Duncan	.75	2.00
TP12 Stephon Marbury	.40	1.00
TP13 Kirk Hinrich	.40	1.00
TP14 Amare Stoudemire	.40	1.00
TP15 Steve Francis	.40	1.00
TP16 Yao Ming	.60	1.50
TP17 Gilbert Arenas	.40	1.00
TP18 Ray Allen	.50	1.25
TP19 Paul Pierce	.50	1.25
TP20 Dwyane Wade	.75	2.00

2005-06 Topps Total Signatures

Inserted in packs at the rate of one in 1634, this set places player photos on backgrounds set to match team colors along with a silver autograph sticker on each card.

Card	Low	High
STATED ODDS 1:1634		
TSAB Andrew Bogut	25.00	60.00
TSABY Andrew Bynum	15.00	40.00
TSDWA Dwyane Wade	50.00	120.00
TSJM Jenny McCarthy	50.00	125.00
TSJZ Jay-Z	50.00	125.00
TSSL Shaun Livingston	8.00	20.00
TSSO Shaquille O'Neal	40.00	100.00

2005-06 Topps Total Surprise

Inserted in packs at the rate of one in 18, this 10-card set is printed on an all-foil card stock and places player photos on a colorful background with black borders along the bottom and the words, "Total Surprise" along the top.

Card	Low	High
COMPLETE SET (10)	2.50	6.00
STATED ODDS 1:18		
TS1 Chauncey Billups	.60	1.50
TS2 Gilbert Arenas	.50	1.25
TS3 Jermaine O'Neal	.50	1.25
TS4 Marquis Daniels	.40	1.00
TS5 Ben Wallace	.50	1.25
TS6 Michael Redd	.50	1.25
TS7 Earl Boykins	.40	1.00
TS8 Shawn Marion	.50	1.25
TS9 Rafer Alston	.40	1.00
TS10 Manu Ginobili	.60	1.50

2005-06 Topps Total Team Checklists

Card	Low	High
COMPLETE SET (30)	15.00	30.00
RANDOM INSERTS IN PACKS		
1 Josh Smith	.50	1.25
2 Paul Pierce	.60	1.50
3 Emeka Okafor	.50	1.25
4 Kirk Hinrich	.50	1.25
5 LeBron James	2.50	6.00
6 Dirk Nowitzki	1.00	2.50
7 Carmelo Anthony	1.25	3.00
8 Ben Wallace	.50	1.25
9 Baron davis	.50	1.25
10 Yao Ming	.75	2.00
11 Jermaine O'Neal	.50	1.25
12 Elton Brand	.60	1.50
13 Kobe Bryant	2.50	6.00
14 Pau Gasol	.60	1.50
15 Dwyane Wade	1.00	2.50
16 T.J. Ford	.40	1.00
17 Kevin Garnett	1.00	2.50
18 Jason Kidd	1.00	2.50
19 J.R. Smith	.50	1.25
20 Stephon Marbury	.50	1.25
21 Dwight Howard	.50	1.25
22 Allen Iverson	1.00	2.50
23 Steve Nash	.75	2.00
24 Sebastian Telfair	.50	1.25
25 Mike Bibby	.60	1.50
26 Tim Duncan	1.00	2.50
27 Ray Allen	.60	1.50
28 Chris Bosh	.60	1.50
29 Andrei Kirilenko	.50	1.25
30 Gilbert Arenas	.50	1.25

2005-06 Topps Total Transfer

Randomly seeded in packs at the rate of one in 18, this 10-card set is printed on an all-foil card stock where player photos are framed by a circular border with the setname and player name along with black borders on the top and bottom of the card.

Card	Low	High
COMPLETE SET (10)	2.50	6.00
STATED ODDS 1:18		
TT1 Michael Finley	.60	1.50
TT2 Joe Johnson	.50	1.25
TT3 Larry Hughes	.50	1.25
TT4 Caron Butler	.50	1.25
TT5 Quentin Richardson	.50	1.25
TT6 Antoine Walker	.50	1.25
TT7 Sam Cassell	.50	1.25
TT8 Damon Stoudamire	.50	1.25
TT9 Bobby Simmons	.40	1.00
TT10 Shareef Abdur-Rahim	.50	1.25

2006-07 Topps Trademark Moves

Released in early March 2007, Topps Trademark Moves features a 150-card base set with a white background design that places a full-color player photo inside an oval that runs from the top right to the bottom left of the card. Card numbers 1-80 picture veterans, card numbers 81-100 picture retired NBA legends, and card numbers 101-150 picture rookie autographs sequentially numbered to either 149 or 75 (see checklist for details) where rookie autographs are signed on stickers. Trademark Moves is packaged in 18-pack boxes of five cards each and carried an original suggested retail price of $10.00 per pack.

Card	Low	High
COMP.SET w/o SP's (100)	8.00	20.00
AU RC's SER.#'d TO 75 OR 149		
1 Dwyane Wade	.50	1.25
2 Richard Jefferson	.25	.60
3 Raymond Felton	.25	.60
4 Ray Allen	.30	.75
5 Peja Stojakovic	.30	.75
6 Mike Miller	.25	.60
7 Mike Bibby	.30	.75
8 Marcus Camby	.25	.60
9 LeBron James	1.25	3.00
10 Joe Johnson	.25	.60
11 Corey Maggette	.25	.60
12 Charlie Villanueva	.20	.50
13 Caron Butler	.25	.60
14 Amare Stoudemire	.25	.60
15 Vince Carter	.40	1.00
16 Tracy McGrady	.40	1.00
17 Shawn Marion	.25	.60
18 Ron Artest	.30	.75
19 Pau Gasol	.30	.75
20 Smush Parker	.20	.50
21 Josh Smith	.25	.60
22 Gilbert Arenas	.25	.60
23 Elton Brand	.30	.75
24 Dwight Howard	.25	.60
25 Dirk Nowitzki	.50	1.25
26 Chris Bosh	.30	.75
27 Chauncey Billups	.30	.75
28 Ben Gordon	.25	.60
29 Yao Ming	.40	1.00
30 Tyson Chandler	.25	.60
31 T.J. Ford	.20	.50
32 Steve Nash	.40	1.00
33 Sam Cassell	.25	.60
34 Speedy Claxton	.20	.50
35 Manu Ginobili	.30	.75
36 Kevin Garnett	.50	1.25
37 Jason Terry	.25	.60
38 Jameer Nelson	.20	.50
39 Ben Wallace	.25	.60
40 Antoine Walker	.25	.60
41 Al Jefferson	.25	.60
42 Tim Duncan	.50	1.25
43 Richard Hamilton	.25	.60
44 Paul Pierce	.30	.75
45 Mike James	.20	.50
46 Martell Webster	.25	.60
47 Kobe Bryant	1.25	3.00
48 Kirk Hinrich	.25	.60
49 Josh Howard	.25	.60
50 Bobby Simmons	.20	.50
51 Channing Frye	.25	.60
52 Andrei Kirilenko	.25	.60
53 Allen Iverson	.40	1.00
54 Al Harrington	.25	.60
55 Zach Randolph	.25	.60
56 Tony Parker	.30	.75
57 Stephon Marbury	.25	.60
58 Shaquille O'Neal	.60	1.50
59 Ricky Davis	.25	.60
60 Lamar Odom	.25	.60
61 Emeka Okafor	.25	.60
62 Raja Bell	.25	.60
63 Deron Williams	.25	.60
64 Danny Granger	.25	.60
65 Baron Davis	.25	.60
66 Andre Miller	.25	.60
67 Andre Iguodala	.25	.60
68 Michael Redd	.25	.60
69 Rashard Lewis	.30	.75
70 Larry Hughes	.25	.60
71 Jermaine O'Neal	.25	.60
72 Jason Richardson	.30	.75
73 Jason Kidd	.50	1.25
74 Gerald Wallace	.25	.60
75 Leandro Barbosa	.25	.60
76 Chris Paul	.40	1.00
77 Carmelo Anthony	.40	1.00
78 Brad Miller	.25	.60
79 Antawn Jamison	.25	.60
80 Andrew Bogut	.25	.60
81 Dominique Wilkins	.60	1.50
82 Larry Bird	1.25	3.00
83 Clyde Drexler	.60	1.50
84 Dennis Rodman	1.00	2.50
85 Isiah Thomas	.50	1.25
86 Rick Barry	.40	1.00
87 Hakeem Olajuwon	.60	1.50
88 George Gervin	.50	1.25
89 Spud Webb	.40	1.00
90 Kareem Abdul-Jabbar	.75	2.00
91 Oscar Robertson	.50	1.25
92 Earl Monroe	.50	1.25
93 Walt Frazier	.50	1.25
94 Moses Malone	.50	1.25
95 Wilt Chamberlain	1.00	2.50
96 Karl Malone	.60	1.50
97 Manute Bol	.50	1.25
98 Bill Walton	.50	1.25
99 Maurice Cheeks	.30	.75
100 Bob Lanier	.40	1.00
101 Solomon Jones AU/149 RC	2.00	5.00
102 Kyle Lowry AU/149 RC	4.00	10.00
103 Maurice Ager AU/149 RC	2.00	5.00
104 Patrick O'Bryant AU/75 RC	2.50	6.00
105 Pops Mensah-Bonsu AU/149 RC	2.00	5.00
106 Marcus Vinicius AU/149 RC	2.00	5.00
107 Josh Boone AU/149 RC	2.00	5.00
108 Mardy Collins AU/149 RC	2.00	5.00
109 Rodney Carney AU/75 RC	2.50	6.00
110 P.J. Tucker AU/149 RC	2.50	6.00
111 Shelden Williams AU/75 RC	3.00	8.00
112 Ryan Hollins AU/149 RC	2.50	6.00
113 Sergio Rodriguez AU/149 RC	3.00	8.00
114 Steve Novak AU/149 RC	2.50	6.00
115 Paul Davis AU/149 RC	2.00	5.00
116 David Noel AU/149 RC	2.00	5.00
117 Marcus Williams AU/75 RC	2.50	6.00
118 Renaldo Balkman AU/75 RC	3.00	8.00
119 Quincy Douby AU/149 RC	2.00	5.00
120 Andrea Bargnani AU/75 RC	4.00	10.00
121 Chris Quinn AU/149 RC	2.00	5.00
122 Thabo Sefolosha AU/75 RC	4.00	10.00
123 Hassan Adams AU/149 RC	2.00	5.00
124 James White AU/149 RC	2.00	5.00
125 Jordan Farmar AU/75 RC	4.00	10.00
126 Damir Markota AU/149 RC	2.00	5.00
127 Mile Ilic AU/149 RC	2.00	5.00
128 James Augustine AU/149 RC	2.00	5.00
129 Paul Millsap AU/149 RC	4.00	10.00
130 Jorge Garbajosa AU/149 RC	2.50	6.00
131 Allan Ray AU/75 RC	2.50	6.00
132 Shannon Brown AU/149 RC	2.00	5.00
133 Will Blalock AU/149 RC	2.00	5.00
134 Vassilis Spanoulis AU/149 RC	2.00	5.00
135 Adam Morrison AU/75 RC	4.00	10.00
136 Craig Smith AU/149 RC	2.50	6.00
137 Cedric Simmons AU/149 RC	2.00	5.00
138 J.J. Redick AU/75 RC	5.00	12.00
140 Ronnie Brewer AU/75 RC	4.00	10.00
141 Rajon Rondo AU/149 RC	15.00	40.00
142 Daniel Gibson AU/149 RC	2.50	6.00
143 Mickael Gelabale AU/75 RC	2.50	6.00
144 Shawne Williams AU/75 RC	2.50	6.00
145 Alexander Johnson AU/149 RC	2.00	5.00
146 Randy Foye AU/75 RC	4.00	10.00
148 Bobby Jones AU/149 RC	2.00	5.00
149 Saer Sene AU/149 RC	2.00	5.00
150 Dee Brown AU/75 RC	2.50	6.00

2006-07 Topps Trademark Moves Foil
*1-100 FOIL: .75X TO 2X BASE HI
1-100 PRINT RUN 299 SER.#'d SETS
*101-150 AU/75 FOIL: .4X TO 1X BASE HI
*101-150 AU/35 FOIL: .5X TO 1.25X BASE

2006-07 Topps Trademark Moves Rainbow
*1-100 RAINBOW: 1X TO 2.5X BASE
1-100 RAINBOW PRINT RUN 149 SER.#'d SETS
*101-150 AU/35 RAINBOW: .6X TO 1.5X BASE
*101-150 AU/19 RAINBOW: .75 TO 2X BASE
47 Kobe Bryant 10.00 25.00

2006-07 Topps Trademark Moves Wood
*1-100 WOOD: 1.5X TO 4X BASE
1-100 WOOD PRINT RUN 75 SETS
*101-150 AU/19 WOOD: .75X TO 3X BASE
101-150 AU/10 WOOD NOT PRICED

2006-07 Topps Trademark Moves Wood Red
*1-80 WOOD RED: 4X TO 10X BASE
*81-100 WOOD RED: 3X TO 8X BASE
1-100 WOOD RED PRINT RUN 35 SETS
101-150 AU PRINT RUN 10 OR 3 SETS
RED WOOD AU NOT PRICED

2006-07 Topps Trademark Moves Autographs
PRINT RUNS 75 TO 149 SER.#'d SETS
*FOIL AU/75: SAME VALUE AS BASE
*FOIL AU/35: .5X TO 1.25X BASE HI
*RAINBOW AU/35: .5X TO 1.25X BASE
*RAINBOW AU/19: .6X TO 1.5X BASE
*WOOD AU/19: .75X TO 2X BASE
WOOD AU/10 NOT PRICED
UNPRICED WOOD RED PRINT RUN 3 TO 10 SETS
1 Dwyane Wade/75 25.00 60.00
3 Raymond Felton/149 4.00 10.00
12 Charlie Villanueva/149 3.00 8.00
15 Vince Carter/75 8.00 20.00
20 Smush Parker/149 3.00 8.00
21 Josh Smith/149 4.00 10.00
26 Chris Bosh/149 10.00 25.00
28 Ben Gordon/149 6.00 15.00
31 T.J. Ford/149 3.00 8.00
34 Speedy Claxton/149 3.00 8.00
38 Jameer Nelson/149 3.00 8.00
45 Mike James/149 3.00 8.00
46 Martell Webster/149 3.00 8.00
50 Bobby Simmons/149 3.00 8.00
53 Allen Iverson/75 40.00 80.00
56 Tony Parker/149 6.00 15.00
58 Shaquille O'Neal/75 20.00 50.00
61 Emeka Okafor/149 3.00 8.00
62 Raja Bell/149 6.00 15.00
74 Gerald Wallace/149 3.00 8.00
75 Leandro Barbosa/149 3.00 8.00
80 Andrew Bogut/149 6.00 15.00
81 Dominique Wilkins/75 10.00 25.00
82 Larry Bird/75 40.00 80.00
85 Isiah Thomas/75 8.00 20.00
94 Moses Malone/149 8.00 20.00
98 Bill Walton/75 8.00 20.00
99 Maurice Cheeks/149 3.00 8.00
100 Bob Lanier/75 6.00 15.00

2006-07 Topps Trademark Moves Dish
COMPLETE SET (10) 4.00 10.00
*FOIL: .5X TO 1.25X BASE HI
FOIL PRINT RUN 299 SER.#'d SETS
*RAINBOW: .6X TO 1.5X BASE HI
RAINBOW PRINT RUN 149 SER.#'d SETS
*WOOD: 1X TO 2.5X BASE HI
WOOD PRINT RUN 75 SER.#'d SETS
*WOOD RED: 1.25X TO 3X BASE HI
WOOD RED PRINT RUN 35 SER.#'d SETS
TDI1 Allen Iverson 1.00 2.50
TDI2 Tony Parker .75 2.00
TDI3 Jarrett Jack .60 1.50
TDI4 Delonte West .50 1.25
TDI5 Chris Duhon .50 1.25
TDI6 Jameer Nelson .50 1.25
TDI7 Marcus Williams .50 1.25
TDI8 Dee Brown .50 1.25
TDI9 Luke Walton .50 1.25
TDI10 Jordan Farmar .75 2.00

2006-07 Topps Trademark Moves Dish Autographs
PRINT RUN 75 TO 149 SER.#'d SETS
*FOIL AU/75: .4X TO 1X BASE HI
*FOIL AU/35: .5X TO 1.25X BASE HI
*RAIN AU/35: .6X TO 1.5X BASE HI
*RAIN AU/19: .75X TO 2X BASE HI
*WOOD AU/19: 1.25X TO 3X BASE HI
WOOD AU/10 NOT PRICED
UNPRICED WOOD RED PRINT RUN 3 TO 10 SETS
SDI1 Allen Iverson/75 40.00 80.00
SDI2 Tony Parker/75 6.00 15.00
SDI3 Jarrett Jack/149 3.00 8.00
SDI4 Delonte West/75 4.00 10.00
SDI5 Chris Duhon/149 3.00 8.00
SDI6 Jameer Nelson/75 4.00 10.00
SDI7 Marcus Williams/75 3.00 8.00
SDI8 Dee Brown/149 3.00 8.00
SDI9 Luke Walton/149 3.00 8.00
SDI10 Jordan Farmar/149 4.00 10.00

2006-07 Topps Trademark Moves Dunk
COMPLETE SET (20) 10.00 25.00
*FOIL: .5X TO 1.25X BASE HI
FOIL PRINT RUN 299 SER.#'d SETS
*RAINBOW: .6X TO 1.5X BASE HI
RAIN PRINT RUN 149 SER.#'d SETS
*WOOD: 1X TO 2.5X BASE HI
WOOD PRINT RUN 75 SER.#'d SETS
*WOOD RED: 1.25X TO 3X BASE HI
WOOD RED PRINT RUN 35 SER.#'d SETS
TDU1 Shaquille O'Neal 2.00 5.00
TDU2 Chris Bosh 1.00 2.50
TDU3 Dwyane Wade 1.50 4.00
TDU4 Hakim Warrick .75 2.00
TDU5 Josh Smith .75 2.00
TDU6 Andrew Bogut .75 2.00
TDU7 Ike Diogu .60 1.50
TDU8 J.R. Smith .75 2.00
TDU9 Josh Childress .75 2.00
TDU10 Emeka Okafor .75 2.00
TDU11 Shawne Williams .60 1.50
TDU12 Renaldo Balkman .75 2.00
TDU13 Gerald Wallace .75 2.00
TDU14 Craig Smith .75 2.00
TDU15 Andre Iguodala .75 2.00
TDU16 Shelden Williams .75 2.00
TDU17 Hilton Armstrong .60 1.50
TDU18 Vince Carter 1.25 3.00
TDU19 Connie Hawkins 1.00 2.50
TDU20 Dominique Wilkins 1.25 3.00

2006-07 Topps Trademark Moves Dunk Autographs
PRINT RUN 75 TO 149 SER.#'d SETS
*FOIL AU/75: .4X TO 1X BASE HI
*FOIL AU/35: .5X TO 1.25X BASE HI
*RAIN AU/35: .6X TO 1.5X BASE HI
*RAIN AU/19: .75X TO 2X BASE HI
*WOOD AU/19: 1.25X TO 3X BASE HI
WOOD AU/10 NOT PRICED
UNPRICED WOOD RED PRINT RUN 3 TO 10 SETS
SDU1 Shaquille O'Neal/75 25.00 60.00
SDU2 Chris Bosh/75 10.00 25.00
SDU3 Dwyane Wade/75 25.00 60.00
SDU4 Hakim Warrick/149 3.00 8.00
SDU5 Josh Smith/75 5.00 12.00
SDU6 Andrew Bogut/75 5.00 12.00
SDU7 Ike Diogu/149 3.00 8.00
SDU8 J.R. Smith/149 3.00 8.00
SDU9 Josh Childress/75 4.00 10.00
SDU10 Emeka Okafor/75 4.00 10.00
SDU11 Shawne Williams/149 3.00 8.00
SDU12 Renaldo Balkman/149 3.00 8.00
SDU13 Gerald Wallace/149 3.00 8.00
SDU14 Craig Smith/149 3.00 8.00
SDU15 Andre Iguodala/149 3.00 8.00
SDU16 Shelden Williams/75 5.00 12.00
SDU17 Hilton Armstrong/149 3.00 8.00
SDU18 Vince Carter/75 12.50 30.00
SDU19 Connie Hawkins/149 8.00 20.00
SDU20 Dominique Wilkins/75 12.50 30.00

2006-07 Topps Trademark Moves Swish
COMPLETE SET (20) 10.00 25.00
*FOIL: .5X TO 1.25X BASE HI
FOIL PRINT RUN 299 SER.#'d SETS
*RAINBOW: .6X TO 1.5X BASE HI
RAIN PRINT RUN 149 SER.#'d SETS
*WOOD: 1X TO 2.5X BASE HI
WOOD PRINT RUN 75 SER.#'d SETS
*WOOD RED: 1.25X TO 3X BASE HI
WOOD RED PRINT RUN 35 SER.#'d SETS
TSW1 Adam Morrison 1.00 2.50
TSW2 Randy Foye 1.00 2.50
TSW3 Andrea Bargnani 1.00 2.50
TSW4 Thabo Sefolosha 1.00 2.50
TSW5 Maurice Ager .60 1.50
TSW6 Mike James .60 1.50
TSW7 J.J. Redick 1.25 3.00
TSW8 Quincy Douby .60 1.50
TSW9 Chauncey Billups 1.00 2.50
TSW10 Carmelo Anthony 1.25 3.00
TSW11 Ray Allen 1.00 2.50
TSW12 Rodney Carney .60 1.50
TSW13 Rick Barry .75 2.00
TSW14 Larry Bird 2.50 6.00
TSW15 Elgin Baylor 1.00 2.50
TSW16 Luol Deng .75 2.00
TSW17 Devin Harris .60 1.50
TSW18 Rashad McCants .60 1.50
TSW19 Martell Webster .75 2.00
TSW20 Ben Gordon .75 2.00

2006-07 Topps Trademark Moves Swish Autographs
PRINT RUN 75 TO 149 SER.#'d SETS
*FOIL AU/75: SAME VALUE AS BASE
*FOIL AU/35: .5X TO 1.25X BASE HI
*RAIN AU/35: .6X TO 1.5X BASE HI
*RAIN AU/19: .75X TO 2X BASE HI
*WOOD AU/19: 1.25X TO 3X BASE HI
WOOD AU/10 NOT PRICED
UNPRICED WOOD RED PRINT RUN 3 TO 10 SETS
SSW1 Adam Morrison/75 5.00 12.00
SSW2 Randy Foye/149 5.00 12.00
SSW3 Andrea Bargnani/75 15.00 30.00
SSW4 Thabo Sefolosha/149 5.00 12.00
SSW5 Maurice Ager/149 3.00 8.00
SSW6 Mike James/149 3.00 8.00
SSW7 J.J. Redick/149 6.00 15.00
SSW8 Quincy Douby/149 3.00 8.00
SSW9 Chauncey Billups/75 4.00 10.00
SSW10 Carmelo Anthony/75 12.50 30.00
SSW11 Ray Allen/75 8.00 20.00
SSW12 Rodney Carney/149 3.00 8.00
SSW13 Rick Barry/75 8.00 20.00
SSW14 Larry Bird/75 40.00 100.00
SSW15 Elgin Baylor/75 15.00 40.00
SSW16 Luol Deng/75 8.00 20.00
SSW17 Devin Harris/149 3.00 8.00
SSW18 Rashad McCants/149 3.00 8.00
SSW19 Martell Webster/149 3.00 8.00
SSW20 Ben Gordon/75 10.00 25.00

2007-08 Topps Trademark Moves
This 100-card set was released in December, 2007. The set was issued into the hobby in five-card packs, with an $30 SRP, which came 12 packs to a box, four boxes to a carton and two cartons per case. Cards numbered 1-40 feature veterans, cards numbered 41-50 feature retired greats and cards numbered 51-100 feature 2007-08 NBA rookies. The Rookie Cards were issued to a stated print run of 1999 serial numbered sets.
COMP.SET w/o SP's (50) 15.00 30.00
RC PRINT RUN 1999 SER.#'d SETS
1 Amare Stoudemire .40 1.00
2 Elton Brand .50 1.25
3 Dwyane Wade .75 2.00
4 Dirk Nowitzki .60 1.50
5 Baron Davis .40 1.00
6 Brandon Roy .50 1.25
7 Ben Gordon .40 1.00
8 Richard Hamilton .40 1.00
9 Andre Iguodala .40 1.00
10 Tim Duncan .75 2.00
11 Yao Ming .60 1.50
12 Jason Kidd .50 1.25
13 Steve Nash .60 1.50
14 Chris Paul .60 1.50
15 Carmelo Anthony .60 1.50
16 Pau Gasol .50 1.25
17 Dwight Howard .40 1.00
18 Ray Allen .50 1.25
19 Deron Williams .40 1.00
20 Vince Carter .60 1.50
21 Kevin Garnett .75 2.00
22 Michael Redd .40 1.00
23 LeBron James 2.00 5.00
24 Kobe Bryant 2.00 5.00
25 Josh Smith .40 1.00
26 Gilbert Arenas .40 1.00
27 Jermaine O'Neal .40 1.00
28 Kirk Hinrich .40 1.00
29 Eddy Curry .30 .75
30 Chauncey Billups .50 1.25
31 Shawn Marion .40 1.00
32 Shaquille O'Neal 1.00 2.50
33 Allen Iverson .60 1.50
34 Paul Pierce .50 1.25
35 Tony Parker .50 1.25
36 Gerald Wallace .40 1.00
37 Carlos Boozer .40 1.00
38 Chris Bosh .50 1.25
39 Mike Bibby .50 1.25
40 Tracy McGrady .50 1.25
41 Rick Barry .40 1.00
42 David Robinson .75 2.00
43 John Stockton .75 2.00
44 Bill Walton .50 1.25
45 Larry Bird 1.25 3.00
46 Isiah Thomas .50 1.25
47 Magic Johnson 1.25 3.00
48 Dennis Rodman 1.00 2.50
49 Dominique Wilkins .60 1.50
50 Bill Russell .75 2.00
51 Yi Jianlian RC 1.25 3.00
52 Greg Oden RC 1.00 2.50
53 Mike Conley Jr. RC 1.25 3.00
54 Jeff Green RC 1.00 2.50
55 Corey Brewer RC 1.00 2.50
56 Joakim Noah RC 1.00 2.50
57 Julian Wright RC .60 1.50
58 Ramon Sessions RC 1.00 2.50
59 Sammy Mejia RC .60 1.50
60 Dominic McGuire RC .60 1.50
61 Kevin Durant RC 12.00 30.00
62 Arron Afflalo RC 1.00 2.50
63 Acie Law RC .60 1.50
64 Alando Tucker RC .60 1.50
65 Gabe Pruitt RC .60 1.50
66 Marcus Williams RC .60 1.50
67 Spencer Hawes RC .75 2.00
68 Carl Landry RC .60 1.50
69 Thaddeus Young RC 1.00 2.50
70 Nick Fazekas RC .60 1.50
71 Al Thornton RC .75 2.00
72 Rodney Stuckey RC .75 2.00
73 Nick Young RC 1.25 3.00
74 Glen Davis RC .75 2.00
75 Jermareo Davidson RC .60 1.50
76 Luis Scola RC 1.25 3.00
77 Jason Smith RC .75 2.00
78 Daequan Cook RC .75 2.00
79 Jared Dudley RC .75 2.00
80 Derrick Byars RC .60 1.50
81 Josh McRoberts RC .75 2.00
82 Adam Haluska RC .60 1.50
83 Juan Carlos Navarro RC .75 2.00
84 Aaron Gray RC .60 1.50
85 Herbert Hill RC .60 1.50
86 Jared Jordan RC .60 1.50
87 Wilson Chandler RC .75 2.00
88 Morris Almond RC .60 1.50
89 Aaron Brooks RC .75 2.00
90 Chris Richard RC .60 1.50
91 JamesOn Curry RC .60 1.50
92 Al Horford RC 1.25 3.00
93 Stephane Lasme RC .60 1.50
94 D.J. Strawberry RC .60 1.50
95 Sean Williams RC .60 1.50
96 Marco Belinelli RC 1.00 2.50
97 Javaris Crittenton RC .60 1.50
98 Demetris Nichols RC .60 1.50
99 Taurean Green RC .60 1.50
100 Brandan Wright RC 1.00 2.50

2007-08 Topps Trademark Moves Blue
*BLUE 1-50: 3X TO 8X BASE HI
BLUE 1-50 PRINT RUN 25 SER.#'d SETS
UNPRICED BLUE RC PRINT RUN 10 SETS

2007-08 Topps Trademark Moves Orange
*1-50 ORANGE: .6X TO 1.5X BASE HI
1-50 ORANGE PRINT RUN 399 SETS
*RC ORANGE: 1.5X TO 4X BASE HI
RC ORANGE PRINT RUN 99 SETS

2007-08 Topps Trademark Moves Red
*1-50 RED: 1.25X TO 3X BASE HI
1-50 RED PRINT RUN 99 SER.#'d SETS
*RC RED: 2X TO 5X BASE HI
RC RED PRINT RUN 50 SER.#'d SETS
61 Kevin Durant 50.00 120.00

2007-08 Topps Trademark Moves Rookies Wood
*WOOD: .5X TO 1.25X BASE HI
PRINT RUN 199 SER.#'d SETS
61 Kevin Durant 12.00 30.00

2007-08 Topps Trademark Moves Ink
PRINT RUN 49 SER.#'d SETS
UNPRICED BLACK PRINT RUN ONE SET
UNPRICED BLUE PRINT RUN 5 SETS
*ORANGE: .5X TO 1.25X BASE HI
ORANGE PRINT RUN 25 SER.#'d SETS
UNPRICED RED PRINT RUN 10 SETS
AB Andrew Bynum 20.00 40.00
AG Aaron Gray 4.00 10.00
AM Adam Morrison 5.00 12.00
AT Al Thornton 4.00 10.00
ATU Alando Tucker 4.00 10.00
BD Baron Davis 6.00 15.00
BR Bill Russell 75.00 150.00
BW Brandan Wright 4.00 10.00
CA Carmelo Anthony 15.00 40.00
DG Danny Granger 4.00 10.00
DH Devin Harris 6.00 15.00
DJS D.J. Strawberry 4.00 10.00
DL David Lee 4.00 10.00
DM Dominic McGuire 4.00 10.00
DR David Robinson 40.00 80.00
DRO Dennis Rodman 25.00 60.00
DW Dominique Wilkins 15.00 30.00
DWA Dwyane Wade 30.00 60.00
DWI Deron Williams 15.00 30.00
EM Earl Monroe 10.00 25.00
GD Glen Davis 6.00 15.00
GO Greg Oden 8.00 20.00
GW Gerald Wallace 6.00 15.00
HA Hilton Armstrong 4.00 10.00
HT Hedo Turkoglu 4.00 10.00
ID Ike Diogu 4.00 10.00
IT Isiah Thomas 15.00 30.00
JH John Havlicek 12.00 30.00
JS John Stockton 30.00 80.00
KH Kirk Hinrich 8.00 20.00
LB Larry Bird 50.00 100.00
MB Marco Belinelli 4.00 10.00
MJ Magic Johnson 40.00 100.00
MJA Mike James 4.00 10.00
MW Marcus Williams 4.00 10.00
MWE Martell Webster 4.00 10.00
NY Nick Young 6.00 15.00
RB Rick Barry 10.00 25.00
RF Randy Foye 4.00 10.00
RFE Raymond Felton 4.00 10.00
SC Speedy Claxton 4.00 10.00
SD Samuel Dalembert 4.00 10.00
TG Taurean Green 4.00 10.00
TJF T.J. Ford 4.00 10.00
TP Tony Parker 10.00 25.00
TY Thaddeus Young 8.00 20.00
UH Udonis Haslem 4.00 10.00
VC Vince Carter 20.00 40.00
YJ Yi Jianlian 10.00 25.00

2007-08 Topps Trademark Moves Relics
PRINT RUN 299 SER.#'d SETS
UNPRICED BLACK PRINT RUN 10 SETS
*ORANGE: SAME VALUE AS BASE
ORANGE PRINT RUN 199 SER.#'d SETS
*RED: .5X TO 1.25X BASE HI
RED PRINT RUN 50 SER.#'d SETS
AH Al Horford 3.00 8.00
AS Amare Stoudemire 2.00 5.00
CA Carmelo Anthony 3.00 8.00
CB Caron Butler 2.00 5.00
CBI Chauncey Billups 2.50 6.00
CBO Chris Bosh 2.50 6.00
CBR Corey Brewer 2.50 6.00
CBZ Carlos Boozer 2.00 5.00
DH Dwight Howard 2.00 5.00
DN Dirk Nowitzki 3.00 8.00
DW Dwyane Wade 4.00 10.00
GA Gilbert Arenas 2.00 5.00
GO Greg Oden 2.50 6.00
JG Jeff Green 2.50 6.00
JH Josh Howard 2.00 5.00
JJ Joe Johnson 2.00 5.00
JK Jason Kidd 2.50 6.00
JN Joakim Noah 2.50 6.00
JO Jermaine O'Neal 2.00 5.00
JW Julian Wright 1.50 4.00
KB Kobe Bryant 8.00 20.00
KG Kevin Garnett 4.00 10.00
MC Mike Conley Jr. 3.00 8.00
MO Mehmet Okur 2.00 5.00
RA Ray Allen 2.50 6.00
RH Richard Hamilton 2.00 5.00
SM Shawn Marion 2.00 5.00
SN Steve Nash 3.00 8.00
SO Shaquille O'Neal 5.00 12.00
TD Tim Duncan 4.00 10.00
TM Tracy McGrady 2.50 6.00
TP Tony Parker 2.50 6.00
VC Vince Carter 3.00 8.00
YJ Yi Jianlian 3.00 8.00
YM Yao Ming 3.00 8.00

2007-08 Topps Trademark Moves Rookie Relic Ink
PRINT RUN 149 OR 79 SER.#'d SETS
UNPRICED BLACK PRINT RUN ONE SET
UNPRICED BLUE PRINT RUN 10 SETS
*ORANGE: .5X TO 1.25X BASE HI
ORANGE PRINT RUN 50 SER.#'d SETS
*RED: .6X TO 1.5X BASE HI
RED PRINT RUN 25 SER.#'d SETS
EXCH.EXPIRATION DATE 11/30/09
51 Yi Jianlian/79 12.00 30.00
52 Greg Oden/139 5.00 12.00
60 Dominic McGuire/139 3.00 8.00
62 Arron Afflalo/139 5.00 12.00
63 Acie Law/79 3.00 8.00
65 Gabe Pruitt/139 3.00 8.00
66 Marcus Williams/139 3.00 8.00
67 Spencer Hawes/79 4.00 10.00
68 Carl Landry/139 3.00 8.00
69 Thaddeus Young/79 5.00 12.00
70 Nick Fazekas/139 3.00 8.00
72 Rodney Stuckey/79 4.00 10.00
73 Nick Young/79 6.00 15.00
74 Glen Davis/139 4.00 10.00
75 Jermareo Davidson/139 3.00 8.00
77 Jason Smith/79 4.00 10.00
78 Daequan Cook/139 4.00 10.00
79 Jared Dudley/79 4.00 10.00
80 Derrick Byars/139 3.00 8.00
81 Josh McRoberts/139 4.00 10.00
82 Adam Haluska/139 3.00 8.00
84 Aaron Gray/139 3.00 8.00
87 Wilson Chandler/139 4.00 10.00
88 Morris Almond/79 3.00 8.00
89 Aaron Brooks/139 4.00 10.00
93 Stephane Lasme/139 3.00 8.00
97 Javaris Crittenton/79 3.00 8.00
99 Taurean Green/139 3.00 8.00
100 Brandan Wright/79 5.00 12.00

2007-08 Topps Trademark Moves Triple Ink
PRINT RUN 39 SER.#'d SETS
UNPRICED BLACK PRINT RUN ONE SET
UNPRICED BLUE PRINT RUN 3 SETS
UNPRICED ORANGE PRINT RUN 10 SETS
UNPRICED RED PRINT RUN 5 SETS
APD Allen/Pruitt/Davis 12.00 30.00
ASY Allen/Stuckey/Young 12.00 30.00
AYT Anthony/Young/Thornton 25.00 50.00
BBF Bosh/Bargnani/Ford 25.00 50.00
BLC Billups/Law/Crittenton 10.00 25.00
BSA Billups/Stuckey/Afflalo 25.00 50.00
BTS Barbosa/Tucker/Strawberry 20.00 40.00
BWA Boozer/Williams/Almond 25.00 60.00
BWB Barry/Wright/Belinelli 15.00 30.00
BYC Bosh/Young/Crittenton 10.00 25.00
CAA Cook/Almond/Afflalo 10.00 25.00
CAW Carter/Anthony/Wade 50.00 120.00
CWW Carter/Williams/Williams 15.00 40.00
CYA Carter/Young/Almond 12.00 30.00
DPL Davis/Parker/Law 15.00 40.00
FBP Ford/Brooks/Pruitt 15.00 30.00
GGC Gordon/Gray/Curry 10.00 25.00
HFM Hawes/Fazekas/McRoberts 10.00 25.00
HSG Hawes/Smith/Gray 10.00 25.00
JBL James/Brooks/Landry 10.00 25.00
JBT Johnson/Bird/Thomas 100.00 225.00
LCB Law/Crittenton/Brooks 10.00 25.00
LCN Lee/Chandler/Nichols 10.00 25.00
OMF Okafor/Morrison/Felton 15.00 30.00
OOY O'Neal/Okafor/Jianlian 12.50 30.00
OWD Okafor/Wallace/Dudley 10.00 25.00
OWY Oden/Wright/Young 12.00 30.00
PBF Parker/Billups/Ford 20.00 40.00
PBY Parker/Belinelli/Jianlian 30.00 60.00
RBH Russell/Baylor/Havlicek 75.00 150.00
ROO Robinson/O'Neal/Oden 100.00 225.00
RRO Russell/Robinson/O'Neal 100.00 225.00
RWD Rodman/Williams/Dudley 20.00 50.00
SBH Smith/Byars/Hill 10.00 25.00
SBW Stockton/Boozer/Williams 30.00 60.00
SYB Stuckey/Young/Belinelli 20.00 40.00
TCM Thornton/Crittenton/Maggette 15.00 30.00
TWS Tucker/Williams/Strawberry 15.00 30.00
WDA Walton/Davis/Afflalo 30.00 60.00
WGM Wallace/Granger/Maggette 10.00 25.00
WSR Wilkins/Stockton/Rodman 60.00 120.00
WTD Williams/Thornton/Dudley 10.00 25.00
WTY Wilkins/Thornton/Young 25.00 50.00
YBL Jianlian/Belinelli/Lasme 30.00 60.00
YSB Young/Smith/Byars 10.00 25.00
YTD Young/Thornton/Dudley 10.00 25.00

2007-08 Topps Trademark Moves Triple Relics
PRINT RUN 199 SER.#'d SETS
UNPRICED BLACK PRINT RUN 10 SETS
*BLUE: 1X TO 2.5X BASE HI
BLUE PRINT RUN 25 SER.#'d SETS
*ORANGE: .5X TO 1.25X BASE HI
ORANGE PRINT RUN 99 SER.#'d SETS
*RED: .6X TO 1.5X BASE HI
RED PRINT RUN 50 SER.#'d SETS
ABB Arenas/Butler/Bosh 4.00 10.00
AHM Anthony/Howard/McGrady 6.00 15.00
BEF Bogut/Ellis/Felton 4.00 10.00
BFF Bargnani/Farmar/Foye 4.00 10.00
BGH Bynum/Granger/Head 4.00 10.00
BGP Billups/Gordon/Parker 5.00 12.00
BSG Bryant/Stoudemire/Garnett 10.00 25.00
BSY Brewer/Stuckey/Young 4.00 10.00
CHW Carter/Howard/Wade 6.00 15.00
CLC Conley/Law/Crittenton 4.00 10.00
GDN Garnett/Duncan/Nowitzki 8.00 20.00
GGM Garbajosa/Gay/Millsap 4.00 10.00
GRH Green/Robinson/Howard 4.00 10.00
GYW Green/Young/Wright 4.00 10.00
HBB Hamilton/Billups/Bosh 4.00 10.00
HBN Horford/Brewer/Noah 6.00 15.00
HWW Horford/Wright/Williams 4.00 10.00
KAN Kapono/Arenas/Nowitzki 4.00 10.00
KNB Kidd/Nash/Boozer 6.00 15.00
LPW Lee/Paul/Williams 4.00 10.00
MJT Miller/Jones/Terry 4.00 10.00
MRW Morrison/Roy/Williams 4.00 10.00
NSM Nash/Stoudemire/Marion 5.00 12.00
OCC Oden/Conley/Cook 5.00 12.00
OGM Okur/Garnett/McGrady 4.00 10.00
OHA O'Neal/Howard/Arenas 5.00 12.00
OHS Oden/Hawes/Smith 4.00 10.00
PDA Parker/Duncan/Anthony 6.00 15.00
WBP Wade/Bryant/Paul 10.00 25.00
WOO Wade/O'Neal/O'Neal 6.00 15.00

2008-09 Topps Treasury
This set was released on October 1, 2008. The base set consists of 120 cards. Cards 1-100 feature veterans, and cards 101-120 are rookies.
COMPLETE SET (120) 30.00 60.00
UNPRICED X-FRCT PRINT RUN ONE SET
1 Kobe Bryant 2.00 5.00
2 Ray Allen .50 1.25
3 Chris Paul .60 1.50
4 Tim Duncan .75 2.00
5 Josh Smith .40 1.00
6 Luis Scola .40 1.00
7 Rashad McCants .30 .75
8 Vince Carter .60 1.50
9 LeBron James 2.00 5.00
10 Mike Dunleavy .40 1.00
11 Chauncey Billups .50 1.25
12 Dwight Howard .40 1.00
13 Steve Nash .50 1.25
14 Monta Ellis .40 1.00
15 Carmelo Anthony .60 1.50
16 Pau Gasol .50 1.25
17 Anderson Varejao .30 .75
18 Yi Jianlian .50 1.25
19 Deron Williams .40 1.00
20 Joe Johnson .40 1.00
21 Yao Ming .60 1.50
22 Rudy Gay .50 1.25
23 Jason Richardson .50 1.25
24 Andrew Bogut .40 1.00
25 Kevin Garnett .75 2.00
26 Chris Wilcox .30 .75
27 Zach Randolph .40 1.00
28 Kirk Hinrich .40 1.00
29 Tony Parker .50 1.25
30 Allen Iverson .60 1.50
31 David West .40 1.00
32 Shaquille O'Neal 1.00 2.50
33 Dwyane Wade .75 2.00
34 Paul Pierce .50 1.25
35 Mike Miller .40 1.00
36 Hedo Turkoglu .40 1.00
37 LaMarcus Aldridge .50 1.25
38 Kevin Martin .40 1.00
39 Jamal Crawford .50 1.25
40 Gilbert Arenas .40 1.00
41 Dirk Nowitzki .60 1.50
42 Amare Stoudemire .40 1.00
43 Danny Granger .40 1.00
44 Chris Bosh .50 1.25
45 Luol Deng .40 1.00
46 Al Thornton .40 1.00
47 Andrei Kirilenko .40 1.00
48 Tayshaun Prince .40 1.00
49 Gerald Wallace .40 1.00
50 Corey Maggette .40 1.00
51 Andre Iguodala .40 1.00
52 Greg Oden .40 1.00
53 Al Jefferson .40 1.00
54 Devin Harris .30 .75
55 Baron Davis .40 1.00
56 Marcus Camby .30 .75
57 Udonis Haslem .30 .75
58 Ron Artest .50 1.25
59 Jeff Green .40 1.00
60 Richard Hamilton .40 1.00
61 Samuel Dalembert .30 .75
62 Antawn Jamison .40 1.00
63 Mike Conley Jr. .40 1.00
64 Raymond Felton .40 1.00
65 Carlos Boozer .40 1.00
66 Ben Gordon .40 1.00
67 Jermaine O'Neal .40 1.00
68 Peja Stojakovic .50 1.25
69 Ryan Gomes .30 .75
70 Michael Redd .40 1.00
71 Manu Ginobili .50 1.25
72 Elton Brand .50 1.25
73 Josh Howard .40 1.00
74 Stephen Jackson .40 1.00
75 Richard Jefferson .40 1.00
76 Andrew Bynum .30 .75
77 Shawn Marion .40 1.00
78 David Lee .30 .75
79 Jamario Moon .30 .75
80 Caron Butler .40 1.00
81 Tracy McGrady .50 1.25
82 Al Horford .50 1.25
83 Brandon Roy .50 1.25
84 Ben Wallace .40 1.00
85 Andre Miller .40 1.00
86 Brad Miller .40 1.00
87 Jameer Nelson .30 .75
88 Andrea Bargnani .40 1.00
89 Kevin Durant 1.25 3.00
90 Jason Kidd .50 1.25
91 Dennis Rodman 1.00 2.50
92 Larry Bird 1.25 3.00
93 Moses Malone .50 1.25
94 Jerry West .60 1.50
95 Bill Russell .75 2.00
96 David Robinson .75 2.00
97 John Stockton .75 2.00
98 Magic Johnson 1.25 3.00
99 George Gervin .60 1.50
100 Dominique Wilkins .60 1.50
101 Derrick Rose RC 2.50 6.00
102 Michael Beasley RC .60 1.50
103 O.J. Mayo RC .60 1.50
104 Russell Westbrook RC 5.00 12.00
105 Kevin Love RC 2.00 5.00
106 Danilo Gallinari RC 1.00 2.50
107 Eric Gordon RC 1.00 2.50
108 Joe Alexander RC .40 1.00
109 D.J. Augustin RC .50 1.25
110 Brook Lopez RC .75 2.00
111 Jerryd Bayless RC .50 1.25
112 Brandon Rush RC .50 1.25
113 Anthony Randolph RC .40 1.00
114 Robin Lopez RC .60 1.50
115 Courtney Lee RC .50 1.25
116 Darrell Arthur RC .50 1.25
117 Joey Dorsey RC .40 1.00
118 Mario Chalmers RC .60 1.50
119 DeAndre Jordan RC .75 2.00
120 Kosta Koufos RC .50 1.25

2008-09 Topps Treasury Refractors Bronze
*BRONZE: .6X TO 1.5X BASE HI
*BRONZE 101-120: 1X TO 2.5X BASE HI
1-100 PRINT RUN 999 SER.#'d SETS
101-120 PRINT RUN 2008 SER.#'d SETS
1 Kobe Bryant 5.00 12.00
9 LeBron James 10.00 25.00
104 Russell Westbrook 20.00 50.00

2008-09 Topps Treasury Refractors Gold
*GOLD 1-100: 3X TO 8X BASE HI
*GOLD 101-120: 3X TO 8X BASE HI
STATED PRINT RUN 50 SER.#'d SETS
9 LeBron James 40.00 100.00
104 Russell Westbrook 125.00 300.00

2008-09 Topps Treasury Refractors Silver
*SILVER 1-100: 1X TO 2.5X BASE HI
*SILVER 101-120: 2X TO 5X BASE HI
STATED PRINT RUN 199 SER.#'d SETS
1 Kobe Bryant 8.00 20.00
9 LeBron James 20.00 50.00
104 Russell Westbrook 50.00 120.00

2008-09 Topps Treasury Bird's All Rookie Team Autographs Dual
ATED PRINT RUN 39 SER.#'d SETS
UNPRICED GREEN PRINT RUN ONE SET
UNPRICED RED PRINT RUN 5 SETS
BA L.Bird/J.Alexander 30.00 80.00
BAU L.Bird/D.Augustin 30.00 80.00
BB L.Bird/M.Beasley 30.00 80.00
BBA L.Bird/J.Bayless 30.00 80.00
BG L.Bird/B.Rush 30.00 80.00
BGO L.Bird/E.Gordon 40.00 100.00
BL L.Bird/K.Love 50.00 120.00
BM L.Bird/O.Mayo 30.00 80.00
BR L.Bird/D.Rose 50.00 120.00
BW L.Bird/R.Westbrook 125.00 300.00

2008-09 Topps Treasury Magic's All Rookie Team Autographs Dual
STATED PRINT RUN 39 SER.#'d SETS
UNPRICED GREEN PRINT RUN ONE SET
UNPRICED RED PRINT RUN FIVE SETS
JA M.Johnson/J.Alexander 30.00 80.00
JAU M.Johnson/D.Augustin 30.00 80.00
JB M.Johnson/M.Beasley 30.00 80.00
JBA M.Johnson/J.Bayless 30.00 80.00
JG M.Johnson/E.Gordon 30.00 80.00
JL M.Johnson/K.Love 50.00 120.00
JLO M.Johnson/B.Lopez 30.00 80.00
JM M.Johnson/O.Mayo 30.00 80.00
JR M.Johnson/D.Rose 50.00 120.00
JW M.Johnson/R.Westbrook 125.00 300.00

2008-09 Topps Treasury Mini Exclusives
COMPLETE SET (50) 30.00 60.00
STATED PRINT RUN 278 SER.#'d SETS
ONE MINI CARD PER RIP CARD
*BRONZE: .5X TO 1.25X BASE HI
BRONZE PRINT RUN 99 SER.#'d SETS
*SILVER: 1.5X TO 4X BASE HI
SILVER PRINT RUN 25 SER.#'d SETS
UNPRICED GOLD PRINT RUN ONE SET
UNPRICED LOGOMAN PRINT RUN ONE SET
MEAH Al Horford .75 2.00
MEAI Allen Iverson 1.00 2.50
MEAIG Andre Iguodala .60 1.50
MEAK Andrei Kirilenko .60 1.50
MEAS Amare Stoudemire .60 1.50
MEAT Al Thornton .60 1.50
MEBD Baron Davis .60 1.50
MEBG Ben Gordon .60 1.50
MEBR Bill Russell 1.25 3.00
MEBRO Brandon Roy .75 2.00
MECA Carmelo Anthony 1.00 2.50
MECB Chris Bosh .75 2.00
MECBO Carlos Boozer .60 1.50
MECBU Caron Butler .60 1.50
MECM Corey Maggette .60 1.50
MECP Chris Paul 1.00 2.50
MEDH Dwight Howard .60 1.50
MEDN Dirk Nowitzki 1.00 2.50
MEDR Dennis Rodman 1.50 4.00
MEDW Deron Williams .60 1.50
MEDWA Dwyane Wade 1.25 3.00
MEDWE David West .60 1.50
MEDWI Dominique Wilkins 1.00 2.50
MEGA Gilbert Arenas .60 1.50
MEGO Greg Oden .60 1.50
MEJJ Joe Johnson .60 1.50
MEJK Jason Kidd .75 2.00
MEJW Jerry West 1.00 2.50
MEKB Kobe Bryant 3.00 8.00
MEKD Kevin Durant 2.00 5.00
MEKG Kevin Garnett 1.25 3.00
MEKM Kevin Martin .60 1.50
MELA LaMarcus Aldridge .75 2.00
MELB Larry Bird 2.00 5.00
MELJ LeBron James 3.00 8.00
MEMG Manu Ginobili .75 2.00
MEMJ Magic Johnson 2.00 5.00
MEMM Mike Miller .60 1.50
MEMR Michael Redd .60 1.50
MEPG Pau Gasol .75 2.00
MEPP Paul Pierce .75 2.00
MERG Rudy Gay .75 2.00
MESN Steve Nash .75 2.00
MESO Shaquille O'Neal 1.50 4.00
METD Tim Duncan 1.25 3.00
METM Tracy McGrady .75 2.00
METP Tony Parker .75 2.00
MEVC Vince Carter 1.00 2.50
MEYJ Yi Jianlian .75 2.00
MEYM Yao Ming 1.00 2.50

2008-09 Topps Treasury Mini Exclusives Autographs
ONE MINI CARD PER RIP CARD
RANDOM INSERTS IN PACKS
BD Baron Davis 10.00 25.00
BL Brook Lopez 10.00 25.00
BR Brandon Roy 8.00 20.00
CA Carmelo Anthony 30.00 80.00
CB Chris Bosh 12.00 30.00
CBO Carlos Boozer 8.00 20.00
CP Chris Paul 25.00 60.00
DJA D.J. Augustin 6.00 15.00
DR Derrick Rose 30.00 80.00
DW Dwyane Wade 30.00 60.00
EG Eric Gordon 12.00 30.00
GO Greg Oden 6.00 15.00
JB Jerryd Bayless 6.00 15.00
JJH J.J. Hickson 6.00 15.00
KL Kevin Love 25.00 60.00
MB Michael Beasley 8.00 20.00
MM Mike Miller 8.00 20.00
OJM O.J. Mayo 8.00 20.00
RL Robin Lopez 8.00 20.00
YJ Yi Jianlian 8.00 20.00

2008-09 Topps Treasury Relics
RANDOM INSERTS IN RETAIL PACKS
AB Andrea Bargnani 2.00 5.00
AH Al Horford 2.50 6.00
AT Al Thornton 2.00 5.00
CB Corey Brewer 2.00 5.00
CF Channing Frye 2.00 5.00
DW Dwyane Wade 4.00 10.00
GO Greg Oden 2.00 5.00
JC Javaris Crittenton 2.00 5.00
JH Josh Howard 2.00 5.00
JJ Jarrett Jack 2.00 5.00
JT Jason Terry 2.00 5.00
KB Kobe Bryant 10.00 25.00
PG Pau Gasol 2.50 6.00
RJ Richard Jefferson 2.00 5.00
SC Sam Cassell 2.00 5.00
SO Shaquille O'Neal 5.00 12.00
TY Thaddeus Young 2.00 5.00
DWI Deron Williams 2.00 5.00
JTI Jamaal Tinsley 2.00 5.00

2008-09 Topps Treasury Rip Cards
PRINT RUN 299 SER.#'d SETS
*BRONZE: .5X TO 1.25X BASE HI
BRONZE PRINT RUN 99 SER.#'d SETS
*SILVER: .6X TO 1.5X BASE HI
SILVER PRINT RUN 25 SETS
UNPRICED GOLD PRINT RUN 10 SETS
UNPRICED PLATINUM PRINT RUN ONE SET
1 Kobe Bryant 20.00 50.00
2 Chris Paul 10.00 25.00
3 Tim Duncan 10.00 25.00
4 Vince Carter 8.00 20.00
5 LeBron James 20.00 50.00
6 Dwight Howard 10.00 25.00
7 Steve Nash 10.00 25.00
8 Carmelo Anthony 10.00 25.00
9 Pau Gasol 6.00 15.00
10 Yi Jianlian 8.00 20.00
11 Deron Williams 10.00 25.00
12 Joe Johnson 6.00 15.00
13 Yao Ming 10.00 25.00
14 Rudy Gay 6.00 15.00
15 Kevin Garnett 10.00 25.00
16 Tony Parker 8.00 20.00
17 Allen Iverson 8.00 20.00
18 David West 6.00 15.00
19 Shaquille O'Neal 12.00 30.00
20 Dwyane Wade 10.00 25.00
21 Paul Pierce 10.00 25.00
22 Mike Miller 6.00 15.00
23 Kevin Martin 10.00 25.00
24 Gilbert Arenas 10.00 25.00
25 Dirk Nowitzki 10.00 25.00
26 Amare Stoudemire 8.00 20.00
27 Chris Bosh 10.00 25.00
28 Corey Maggette 6.00 15.00
29 Andre Iguodala 6.00 15.00
30 Greg Oden 6.00 15.00
31 Baron Davis 8.00 20.00
32 Carlos Boozer 6.00 15.00
33 Ben Gordon 8.00 20.00
34 Michael Redd 8.00 20.00
35 Manu Ginobili 8.00 20.00
36 Caron Butler 6.00 15.00
37 Tracy McGrady 8.00 20.00
38 Al Horford 6.00 15.00
39 Brandon Roy 8.00 20.00
40 Kevin Durant 20.00 50.00
41 Jason Kidd 8.00 20.00
42 LaMarcus Aldridge 6.00 15.00
43 Al Thornton 6.00 15.00
44 Andrei Kirilenko 6.00 15.00
45 Jerry West 8.00 20.00
46 Bill Russell 8.00 20.00
47 Dennis Rodman 8.00 20.00
48 Dominique Wilkins 6.00 15.00
49 Larry Bird 15.00 40.00
50 Magic Johnson 12.00 30.00

2008-09 Topps Treasury Rookie Autographs
ATED ODDS 1:23 PACKS
*BRONZE: .5X TO 1.25X BASE HI
BRONZE PRINT RUN 50 SETS
*SILVER: .6X TO 1.5X BASE HI
SILVER PRINT RUN 25 SER.#'d SETS
UNPRICED GOLD PRINT RUN 10 SETS
UNPRICED X-FRAC PRINT RUN ONE SET
121 Derrick Rose 30.00 80.00
122 Michael Beasley 5.00 12.00
123 O.J. Mayo 5.00 12.00
124 Russell Westbrook 100.00 250.00
125 Kevin Love 25.00 60.00
126 Danilo Gallinari 10.00 25.00
127 Eric Gordon 6.00 15.00
128 Joe Alexander 3.00 8.00
129 D.J. Augustin 4.00 10.00
130 Brook Lopez 6.00 15.00

131 Jerryd Bayless 4.00 10.00
132 Brandon Rush 4.00 10.00
133 Anthony Randolph 3.00 8.00
134 Robin Lopez 5.00 12.00
135 Courtney Lee 4.00 10.00
136 Darrell Arthur 4.00 10.00
137 Joey Dorsey 3.00 8.00
138 Mario Chalmers 5.00 12.00
139 DeAndre Jordan 12.00 30.00
140 Kosta Koufos 4.00 10.00

2008-09 Topps Treasury Rookie Medallions

STATED PRINT RUN 19 SER.#'d SETS
UNPRICED GOLD PRINT RUN ONE SET
AR Anthony Randolph 12.00 30.00
BL Brook Lopez 25.00 60.00
BR Brandon Rush 15.00 40.00
DA Darrell Arthur 15.00 40.00
DG Danilo Gallinari 30.00 80.00
DJA D.J. Augustin 15.00 40.00
DR Derrick Rose 125.00 250.00
EG Eric Gordon 30.00 80.00
JA Joe Alexander 12.00 30.00
JB Jerryd Bayless 15.00 40.00
KL Kevin Love 60.00 150.00
MB Michael Beasley 20.00 50.00
OJM O.J. Mayo 20.00 50.00
RL Robin Lopez 20.00 50.00
RW Russell Westbrook 150.00 400.00

2008-09 Topps Treasury They're Money Rip Cards

STATED PRINT RUN 42 SER.#'d SETS
1 Kobe Bryant 75.00 200.00
2 LeBron James 75.00 200.00
3 Carmelo Anthony 60.00 120.00
4 Kevin Garnett 50.00 100.00
5 Allen Iverson 50.00 100.00
8 Dirk Nowitzki 40.00 80.00
10 Chris Paul 75.00 150.00

2006-07 Topps Triple Threads

Released in late April 2007, Triple Threads is Topps' premium 2006-07 basketball product. With a 130-card set, Triple Threads pictures veteran players on cards 1-86, rookie players on cards 87-90 and retired players on cards 91-100 which are serially numbered to 899. Cards 1-100 share the same design which utilizes a white background with a centered grey-ish/blue oval framing a full-color player action photo. Card numbers 101-130 showcase a horizontal design which places a framed autograph sticker between two premium swatches of jersey. 101-130 are rookie cards and are sequentially numbered to 99. Triple Threads is packaged in two-pack boxes of six cards each and carried an initial suggested retail price of $100.00 per pack. Each pack contains three base cards, two parallels and one triple memorabilia card. In each box, one of the two packs contains a triple memorabilia autographs card.

1-100 PRINT RUN 899 SER.#'d SETS
JSY AU RC PRINT RUN 99 SER.#'d SETS
UNPRICED PLATINUM PRINT RUN ONE SET
1 Amare Stoudemire .75 2.00
2 Dirk Nowitzki 1.50 4.00
3 Dwyane Wade 1.50 4.00
4 Allen Iverson 1.25 3.00
5 LeBron James 4.00 10.00
6 Tracy McGrady 1.25 3.00
7 Ben Wallace .75 2.00
8 Jason Richardson 1.00 2.50
9 Vince Carter 1.25 3.00
10 Joe Johnson .75 2.00
11 Paul Pierce 1.00 2.50
12 Gerald Wallace .75 2.00
13 Elton Brand 1.00 2.50
14 Gilbert Arenas .75 2.00
15 Marcus Camby .75 2.00
16 Andrew Bogut .75 2.00
17 Stephon Marbury .75 2.00
18 Kevin Garnett 1.50 4.00
19 Al Harrington .75 2.00
20 Tim Duncan 1.50 4.00
21 Pau Gasol 1.00 2.50
22 Kobe Bryant 4.00 10.00
23 Dwight Howard .75 2.00
24 Jarrett Jack .75 2.00
25 T.J. Ford .60 1.50
26 Ron Artest 1.00 2.50
27 Deron Williams .75 2.00
28 Rasheed Wallace 1.00 2.50
29 Shaquille O'Neal 2.00 5.00
30 Ray Allen 1.00 2.50
31 Peja Stojakovic 1.00 2.50
32 Jermaine O'Neal .75 2.00
33 Larry Hughes .75 2.00
34 Brad Miller .75 2.00
35 Caron Butler .75 2.00
36 Andre Miller .75 2.00
37 Kirk Hinrich .75 2.00
38 Andrei Kirilenko .75 2.00
39 Charlie Villanueva .60 1.50
40 Sebastian Telfair .60 1.50
41 Josh Howard .75 2.00
42 Emeka Okafor .75 2.00
43 Danny Granger .75 2.00
44 Tony Parker 1.00 2.50
45 Zach Randolph .75 2.00
46 Ricky Davis .75 2.00
47 Chris Webber 1.00 2.50
48 Mike Bibby 1.00 2.50
49 Troy Murphy .60 1.50
50 Josh Smith .75 2.00
51 Steve Nash 1.25 3.00
52 Chris Paul 1.25 3.00
53 Rashard Lewis 1.00 2.50
54 Ben Gordon .75 2.00
55 Mehmet Okur .60 1.50
56 Chris Bosh 1.00 2.50
57 Drew Gooden .75 2.00
58 Corey Maggette .75 2.00
59 Eddy Curry .75 2.00
60 Yao Ming 1.25 3.00
61 Al Jefferson .75 2.00
62 Smush Parker .60 1.50
63 Jason Kidd 1.50 4.00
64 Hakim Warrick .75 2.00
65 Richard Hamilton .75 2.00
66 Luke Ridnour .75 2.00
67 Raymond Felton .75 2.00
68 Andre Iguodala .75 2.00
69 Jason Terry .75 2.00
70 Richard Jefferson .75 2.00
71 Lamar Odom .75 2.00
72 Jameer Nelson .60 1.50
73 Mike James .60 1.50
74 Antawn Jamison .75 2.00
75 Shaun Livingston .60 1.50
76 Manu Ginobili 1.00 2.50
77 Antoine Walker .75 2.00
78 Desmond Mason .60 1.50
79 Channing Frye .75 2.00
80 Morris Peterson .60 1.50
81 Michael Redd .75 2.00
82 Shawn Marion .75 2.00
83 Bonzi Wells .60 1.50
84 Chauncey Billups 1.00 2.50
85 Baron Davis .75 2.00
86 Carmelo Anthony 1.25 3.00
87 Brandon Roy RC 1.50 4.00
88 Rudy Gay RC 2.00 5.00
89 Tyrus Thomas RC 1.25 3.00
90 LaMarcus Aldridge RC 4.00 10.00
91 Wilt Chamberlain 3.00 8.00
92 Larry Bird 4.00 10.00
93 Isiah Thomas 1.50 4.00
94 Bernard King 1.25 3.00
95 Elgin Baylor 1.50 4.00
96 Oscar Robertson 1.50 4.00
97 Walt Frazier 1.50 4.00
98 Chris Mullin 1.50 4.00
99 Bill Laimbeer 1.25 3.00
100 George Gervin 1.50 4.00
101 Dee Brown JSY AU RC 4.00 10.00
102 Renaldo Balkman JSY AU RC 5.00 12.00
103 Maurice Ager JSY AU RC 4.00 10.00
104 Shelden Williams JSY AU RC 5.00 12.00
105 Rodney Carney JSY AU RC 4.00 10.00
106 J.J. Redick JSY AU RC 8.00 20.00
107 Hilton Armstrong JSY AU RC 4.00 10.00
108 Craig Smith JSY AU RC 5.00 12.00
109 Kyle Lowry JSY AU RC 8.00 20.00
110 Josh Boone JSY AU RC 4.00 10.00
111 Saer Sene JSY AU RC 4.00 10.00
112 Jorge Garbajosa JSY AU RC 5.00 12.00
113 Paul Davis JSY AU RC 4.00 10.00
114 Thabo Sefolosha JSY AU RC 6.00 15.00
115 Shannon Brown JSY AU RC 4.00 10.00
116 Bobby Jones JSY AU RC 4.00 10.00
117 Jordan Farmar JSY AU RC 6.00 15.00
118 Allan Ray JSY AU RC 4.00 10.00
119 Randy Foye JSY AU RC 6.00 15.00
120 Marcus Williams JSY AU RC 4.00 10.00
121 Adam Morrison JSY AU RC 6.00 15.00
122 Cedric Simmons JSY AU RC 4.00 10.00
123 Rajon Rondo JSY AU RC 20.00 50.00
124 Patrick O'Bryant JSY AU RC 4.00 10.00
125 Shawne Williams JSY AU RC 4.00 10.00
126 Mardy Collins JSY AU RC 4.00 10.00
127 Steve Novak JSY AU RC 5.00 12.00
128 Ronnie Brewer JSY AU RC 6.00 15.00
129 Quincy Douby JSY AU RC 4.00 10.00
130 Andrea Bargnani JSY AU RC 6.00 15.00

2006-07 Topps Triple Threads Emerald

*EMERALD: .5X TO 1.25X BASE HI
1-100 EMERALD PRINT RUN 199 SER.#'d SETS
101-130 EMERALD PRINT RUN 50 SER.#'d SETS

2006-07 Topps Triple Threads Gold

*GOLD: .75X TO 2X BASE HI
1-100 PRINT RUN 99 SER.#'d SETS
101-130 PRINT RUN 25 SER.#'d SETS

2006-07 Topps Triple Threads Sapphire

*1-100 SAPPH: 1.25X TO 3X BASE HI
1-100 PRINT RUN 25 SER.#'d SETS
101-130 PRINT RUN 10 SER.#'d SETS
101-130 NOT PRICED DUE TO SCARCITY

2006-07 Topps Triple Threads Sepia

SEPIA: .4X TO 1X BASE HI
STATED PRINT RUN 299 SER.#'d SETS

2006-07 Topps Triple Threads Relics

PRINT RUN 36 SER.#'d SETS
EACH PLAYER HAS THREE VERSIONS
ALL VERSIONS SAME VALUE
*EMERALD: .6X TO 1.5X BASE HI
EMERALD PRINT RUN 18 SER.#'d SETS
UNPRICED GOLD PRINT RUN 9 SETS
UNPRICED PLATINUM PRINT RUN ONE SET
UNPRICED SAPPHIRE PRINT RUN 3 SETS
*SEPIA: .5X TO 1.25X BASE HI
SEPIA PRINT RUN 27 SER.#'d SETS
1 Adam Morrison NBA 5.00 12.00
4 Amare Stoudemire NBA 4.00 10.00
7 Andrea Bargnani NBA 5.00 12.00
10 Andrei Kirilenko AK47 4.00 10.00
13 Antawn Jamison NBA 4.00 10.00
16 Ben Wallace NBA 4.00 10.00
19 Brandon Roy NBA 5.00 12.00
22 Carmelo Anthony Nuggets 6.00 15.00
25 Charlie Villanueva NBA 3.00 8.00
28 Chauncey Billups NBA 5.00 12.00
31 Chris Paul NBA 6.00 15.00
34 Dirk Nowitzki Symbol 8.00 20.00
37 Dominique Wilkins HOF 6.00 15.00
40 Dwight Howard NBA 4.00 10.00
43 Dwyane Wade NBA 8.00 20.00
46 Isiah Thomas HOF 6.00 15.00
49 J.J. Redick NBA 6.00 15.00
52 Jason Kidd Symbol 8.00 20.00
55 Josh Smith NBA 4.00 10.00
58 Kevin Garnett KG 8.00 20.00
61 Kobe Bryant NBA 20.00 40.00
64 LaMarcus Aldridge Blazers 12.00 30.00
67 Larry Bird #33 20.00 50.00
70 Magic Johnson #32 12.00 30.00
73 Manu Ginobili Spurs 5.00 12.00
76 Pau Gasol #16 5.00 12.00
79 Paul Pierce #34 5.00 12.00
82 Rudy Gay NBA 6.00 15.00
85 Shaquille O'Neal MVP 10.00 25.00
88 Shawn Marion NBA 4.00 10.00
91 Steve Nash #13 6.00 15.00
94 Tim Duncan #21 8.00 20.00
97 Tracy McGrady NBA 6.00 15.00
100 Vince Carter NBA 6.00 15.00
103 Yao Ming Rockets 6.00 15.00

2006-07 Topps Triple Threads Relics Autographs

PRINT RUN 36 SER.#'d SETS
EACH PLAYER HAS THREE VERSIONS
ALL VERSIONS SAME VALUE
*EMERALD: .6X TO 1.5X BASE HI
EMERALD PRINT RUN 18 SER.#'d SETS
UNPRICED GOLD PRINT RUN 9 SETS
UNPRICED PLATINUM PRINT RUN ONE SET
UNPRICED PR.PLATE PRINT RUN ONE SET
UNPRICED SAPPHIRE PRINT RUN 3 SETS
1 Adam Morrison #35 6.00 15.00
4 Chauncey Billups NBA 6.00 15.00
7 Andre Iguodala NBA 6.00 15.00
10 Andrea Bargnani Raptors 8.00 20.00
13 Andrew Bogut NBA 6.00 15.00
16 Ben Gordon Bulls 12.50 30.00
19 Bill Walton NBA 8.00 20.00
22 Bob Lanier NBA 6.00 15.00
25 Channing Frye NBA 6.00 15.00
28 Charlie Villanueva NBA 6.00 15.00
31 Chris Bosh Raptors 15.00 40.00
34 Chris Duhon NBA 6.00 15.00
37 Devin Harris NBA 6.00 15.00
40 Dominique Wilkins HOF 12.00 30.00
43 Dwyane Wade NBA 15.00 40.00
46 Earl Monroe #15 15.00 40.00
49 Emeka Okafor #50 6.00 15.00
52 Gerald Wallace NBA 6.00 15.00
55 Hakim Warrick NBA 6.00 15.00
58 John Stockton #12 40.00 100.00
61 Isiah Thomas HOF 15.00 40.00
64 J.J. Redick Magic 12.50 30.00
67 Jameer Nelson NBA 6.00 15.00
70 Jarrett Jack NBA 6.00 15.00
73 Josh Smith Dunking 6.00 15.00
76 Larry Bird Legend 75.00 150.00
77 Larry Bird BOS 75.00 150.00
78 Larry Bird #33 75.00 150.00
79 Luol Deng NBA 6.00 15.00
82 Magic Johnson #32 60.00 120.00
85 Dennis Rodman #91 30.00 75.00
88 Martell Webster Blazers 6.00 15.00
91 Randy Foye NBA 6.00 15.00
94 Ray Allen NBA 25.00 50.00
97 Luke Walton NBA 6.00 15.00
100 Ronnie Brewer NBA 6.00 15.00
103 Andrei Kirilenko AK47 6.00 15.00
106 Jermaine O'Neal NBA 6.00 15.00
109 Carmelo Anthony Nuggets 20.00 50.00
112 Shelden Williams #33 6.00 15.00
115 T.J. Ford NBA 6.00 15.00
118 Vince Carter NBA 20.00 40.00

2006-07 Topps Triple Threads Relics Combos

PRINT RUN 36 SER.#'d SETS
*EMERALD: .5X TO 1.25X BASE HI
EMERALD PRINT RUN 18 SER.#'d SETS
UNPRICED GOLD PRINT RUN 9 SETS
UNPRICED SAPPHIRE PRINT RUN 3 SETS
*SEPIA: .4X TO 1X BASE HI
SEPIA PRINT RUN 27 SER.#'d SETS
1 Morrison/Wade/Redick 12.00 30.00
2 Amare/Nash/Marion 15.00 40.00
3 Marion/Nash/Barbosa 10.00 25.00
4 Yao/T-Mac/Novak 12.50 30.00
5 Bargnani/Bogut/D.Howard 10.00 25.00
6 Wade/Shaq/Mourning 40.00 100.00
7 Wade/Bosh/Carmelo 15.00 40.00
8 T-Mac/Vince/Kobe 25.00 60.00
9 Kobe/Odom/Magic 20.00 50.00
10 Allen/Lewis/Ridnour 10.00 25.00
11 Duncan/Ginobili/Parker 15.00 40.00
12 Simmons/Redick/Sd.Williams 10.00 25.00
13 Gay/Morrison/Carney 10.00 25.00
14 Foye/Ray/Lowry 10.00 25.00
15 Allen/Gordon/Okafor 10.00 25.00
16 Barry/Allen/Bird 15.00 40.00
17 Bird/Magic/Isiah 30.00 80.00
18 Isiah/Hamilton/Billups 10.00 25.00
19 Garnett/Duncan/Amare 12.50 30.00
20 Morrison/Bird/Redick 15.00 50.00
21 Dirk/Bargnani/Kirilenko 10.00 25.00
22 D.Howard/Okafor/Gordon 10.00 25.00
23 D.Wilkins/J.Smith/Childress 12.50 30.00
24 Iggy/D.Wilkins/Vince 12.50 30.00
26 D.Howard/Nelson/Hill 10.00 25.00
27 Vince/Rasheed/Jamison 10.00 25.00
28 Morrison/Bogut/Okafor 10.00 25.00
29 Nash/Magic/Kidd 20.00 50.00
30 C.Paul/Okafor/Amare 10.00 25.00
31 Gasol/Brand/Vince 10.00 25.00
32 Duncan/Iverson/Kidd 15.00 40.00
33 Hill/Richmond/Shaq 15.00 30.00
34 Gay/Aldridge/Foye 10.00 25.00
35 Worthy/Shaq/Duncan 15.00 40.00
36 Bird/Magic/Isiah 30.00 80.00
37 Barry/M.Malone/D.Wade 12.50 30.00
38 Parker/Arenas/Billups 10.00 25.00
39 Redd/Ginobili/Arenas 10.00 25.00
40 Iverson/Kobe/T-Mac 20.00 50.00
41 Isiah/Magic/Bird 20.00 50.00
42 Garnett/Amare/Kobe 20.00 50.00
43 Duncan/Shaq/Garnett 15.00 40.00
44 Kobe/Iverson/K.Malone 15.00 40.00
45 D.Wilkins/Drexler/Erving 25.00 60.00
46 Duncan/Gervin/Parker 12.50 30.00
47 M.Malone/Iggy/Erving 15.00 40.00
48 J.West/Magic/Baylor 25.00 50.00
49 Marbury/E.Monroe/Frye 10.00 25.00
50 Magic/Kobe/Baylor 25.00 50.00
51 Lanier/Isiah/Rodman 15.00 40.00
52 Yao/Duncan/Iverson 15.00 40.00
53 Bird/Cowens/Walton 25.00 60.00
54 Bosh/Redick/Felton 10.00 25.00
55 Webber/Rose/Howard 20.00 50.00

2006-07 Topps Triple Threads Relics Combos Autographs

PRINT RUN 36 SER.#'d SETS
*EMERALD: .5X TO 1.25X BASE HI
EMERALD PRINT RUN 18 SER.#'d SETS
UNPRICED GOLD PRINT RUN 9 SETS
UNPRICED PR.PLATE PRINT RUNS ONE SET
UNPRICED SAPPHIRE PRINT RUN 3 SETS
1 Wade/Morrison/Anthony 50.00 120.00
2 Bird/Magic/Barry 100.00 200.00
3 Nique/J.Smith/Vince 30.00 80.00
4 Elgin/Earl/Isiah 40.00 100.00
5 Bird/Morrison/Stockton 100.00 200.00
6 Walton/Magic/Bird 125.00 250.00
7 Lanier/Malone/Walton 40.00 100.00
8 Wade/Magic/Bird 150.00 300.00
9 Bird/Magic/Isiah 125.00 250.00
10 Bargnani/Morrison/Foye 25.00 60.00

2007-08 Topps Triple Threads

Released in February 2008, Topps Triple Threads boasts a 150-card set where cards 1-90 feature NBA veterans serially numbered to 33, cards 91-100 feature retired NBA legends serially numbered to 333 and cards 101-150 feature NBA rookies serially numbered to 99. Triple Threads released in two-pack boxes of three cards each and packs carried an initial suggested retail price of $150.

1-100 PRINT RUN 333 SER.#'d SETS
ROOKIE PRINT RUN 99 SER.#'d SETS
UNPRICED PLATINUM PRINT RUN ONE SET
UNPRICED SAPPHIRE PRINT RUN ONE SET
1 Yao Ming 1.00 2.50
2 Michael Redd .60 1.50
3 Dwyane Wade 1.25 3.00
4 Chris Bosh .75 2.00
5 Kevin Garnett 1.25 3.00
6 Sam Cassell .60 1.50
7 Ben Gordon .60 1.50
8 Deron Williams .60 1.50
9 Andre Iguodala .60 1.50
10 Mike Bibby .75 2.00
11 Chauncey Billups .75 2.00
12 Dwight Howard .60 1.50
13 Steve Nash 1.00 2.50
14 Raymond Felton .75 2.00
15 Carmelo Anthony 1.00 2.50
16 Pau Gasol .75 2.00
17 Brandon Roy .75 2.00
18 Chris Wilcox .50 1.25
19 Josh Howard .60 1.50
20 Ray Allen .75 2.00
21 Tim Duncan 1.25 3.00
22 Tayshaun Prince .60 1.50
23 LeBron James 3.00 8.00
24 Kobe Bryant 3.00 8.00
25 Al Jefferson .60 1.50
26 Stephon Marbury .60 1.50
27 Mike Miller .60 1.50
28 Jason Terry .60 1.50
29 Corey Maggette .60 1.50
30 Allen Iverson 1.00 2.50
31 Tracy McGrady .75 2.00
32 Shaquille O'Neal 1.50 4.00
33 Ben Wallace .60 1.50
34 Paul Pierce .75 2.00
35 Vince Carter 1.00 2.50
36 Chris Paul 1.00 2.50
37 Kyle Korver .60 1.50
38 LaMarcus Aldridge 1.00 2.50
39 Al Harrington .60 1.50
40 Gilbert Arenas .60 1.50
41 Dirk Nowitzki 1.00 2.50
42 David Lee .50 1.25
43 Gerald Wallace .60 1.50
44 Luke Walton .50 1.25
45 Manu Ginobili .75 2.00
46 Charlie Villanueva .50 1.25
47 Andrei Kirilenko .60 1.50
48 Richard Jefferson .60 1.50
49 Joe Johnson .60 1.50
50 Zach Randolph .60 1.50
51 Andrea Bargnani .75 2.00
52 Elton Brand .75 2.00
53 Anderson Varejao .50 1.25
54 Kirk Hinrich .60 1.50
55 Baron Davis .60 1.50
56 Shane Battier .60 1.50
57 Jameer Nelson .50 1.25
58 Antawn Jamison .60 1.50
59 Andrew Bynum .50 1.25
60 Kevin Martin .60 1.50
61 Amare Stoudemire .60 1.50
62 Randy Foye .75 2.00
63 Marcus Camby .50 1.25
64 Larry Hughes .60 1.50
65 Luol Deng .60 1.50
66 Danny Granger .60 1.50
67 Eddy Curry .50 1.25
68 David West .60 1.50
69 Tony Parker .75 2.00
70 Jason Kidd .75 2.00
71 Monta Ellis .60 1.50
72 Richard Hamilton .60 1.50
73 Udonis Haslem .50 1.25
74 Rudy Gay .75 2.00
75 Carlos Boozer .60 1.50
76 Luke Ridnour .60 1.50
77 Jermaine O'Neal .60 1.50
78 Ricky Davis .60 1.50
79 Desmond Mason .50 1.25
80 Lamar Odom .60 1.50
81 T.J. Ford .50 1.25
82 Jarrett Jack .60 1.50
83 Ron Artest .75 2.00
84 Sam Dalembert .50 1.25
85 Josh Smith .60 1.50
86 Tyson Chandler .60 1.50
87 Shawn Marion .60 1.50
88 Caron Butler .60 1.50
89 Jason Richardson .75 2.00
90 Rashard Lewis .60 1.50
91 Larry Bird 2.00 5.00
92 Isiah Thomas .75 2.00
93 Magic Johnson 2.00 5.00
94 John Stockton 1.25 3.00
95 Bill Russell 1.25 3.00
96 Dennis Rodman 1.50 4.00
97 Dominique Wilkins 1.00 2.50
98 David Robinson 1.25 3.00
99 Bill Walton .75 2.00
100 Jerry West 1.00 2.50
101 Greg Oden RC 2.50 6.00
102 Daequan Cook RC 2.00 5.00
103 Morris Almond RC 1.50 4.00
104 Sean Williams RC 1.50 4.00
105 Arron Afflalo RC 2.50 6.00
106 Coby Karl RC 1.50 4.00
107 Adam Haluska RC 1.50 4.00
108 Corey Brewer RC 2.50 6.00
109 Herbert Hill RC 1.50 4.00
110 Nick Young RC 3.00 8.00
111 Joakim Noah RC 2.50 6.00
112 Mike Conley Jr. RC 3.00 8.00
113 Kyrylo Fesenko RC 1.50 4.00
114 Aaron Brooks RC 2.00 5.00
115 Marco Belinelli RC 2.50 6.00
116 Juan Carlos Navarro RC 2.00 5.00
117 Jared Dudley RC 2.00 5.00
118 Rodney Stuckey RC 2.00 5.00
119 JamesOn Curry RC 1.50 4.00
120 Gabe Pruitt RC 1.50 4.00
121 Acie Law RC 1.50 4.00
122 Dominic McGuire RC 1.50 4.00
123 Ramon Sessions RC 2.50 6.00
124 Jeff Green RC 2.50 6.00
125 Wilson Chandler RC 2.00 5.00
126 Kosta Perovic RC 1.50 4.00
127 Josh McRoberts RC 2.00 5.00
128 Jason Smith RC 2.00 5.00
129 Cheik Samb RC 1.50 4.00
130 Stephane Lasme RC 1.50 4.00
131 Brandon Wallace RC 1.50 4.00
132 Alando Tucker RC 1.50 4.00
133 Javaris Crittenton RC 1.50 4.00
134 Chris Richard RC 1.50 4.00
135 Kevin Durant RC 40.00 80.00
136 Al Thornton RC 2.00 5.00
137 Carl Landry RC 1.50 4.00
138 Yi Jianlian RC 3.00 8.00
139 Brandan Wright RC 2.50 6.00
140 Nick Fazekas RC 1.50 4.00
141 Al Horford RC 3.00 8.00
142 Jermareo Davidson RC 1.50 4.00
143 D.J. Strawberry RC 1.50 4.00
144 Glen Davis RC 2.00 5.00
145 Julian Wright RC 1.50 4.00
146 Spencer Hawes RC 2.00 5.00
147 Taurean Green RC 1.50 4.00
148 Luis Scola RC 3.00 8.00
149 Aaron Gray RC 1.50 4.00
150 Thaddeus Young RC 2.50 6.00

2007-08 Topps Triple Threads Emerald

*1-100 EMERALD: 1X TO 2.5X BASE HI
*101-150 EMERALD RCs: 1X TO 2.5X BASE HI
1-100 EMERALD PRINT RUN 66 SER.#'d SETS
101-150 EMERALD RC PRINT RUN 33 SETS

2007-08 Topps Triple Threads Gold

*1-100 GOLD: 1.5X TO 4X BASE HI
1-100 PRINT RUN 33 SER.#'d SETS
101-150 PRINT RUN 3 SER.#'d SET
101-150 UNPRICED DUE TO SCARCITY

2007-08 Topps Triple Threads Sepia

*1-100 SEPIA: .75X TO 2X BASE HI
*101-150 SEPIA RCs: .6X TO 1.5X BASE HI
1-100 SEPIA PRINT RUN 99 SET.#'d SETS
101-150 SEPIA RC PRINT RUN 66 SETS

2007-08 Topps Triple Threads Relics

PRINT RUN 18 SER.#'d SETS
THREE VERSIONS OF EACH EXIST
ALL VERSIONS SAME VALUE
UNPRICED EMERALD PRINT RUN 5 SETS
UNPRICED GOLD PRINT RUN ONE SET
UNPRICED PLATINUM PRINT RUN ONE SET
UNPRICED SAPPHIRE PRINT RUN ONE SET
*SEPIA: .75X TO 2X BASE HI
SEPIA PRINT RUN NINE SETS
1 Kobe Bryant KB24 25.00 50.00
2 Kobe Bryant Ball 25.00 50.00
3 Kobe Bryant 81 Points 25.00 50.00
4 Allen Iverson Nuggets 15.00 30.00
5 Allen Iverson Answer 15.00 30.00
6 Allen Iverson MVP 15.00 30.00
7 Gilbert Arenas Ball 6.00 15.00
8 Gilbert Arenas Hibachi 6.00 15.00
9 Gilbert Arenas WAS 6.00 15.00
10 Kevin Garnett #5 20.00 40.00
11 Kevin Garnett Shamrock 20.00 40.00
12 Kevin Garnett Big Ticket 20.00 40.00
13 Dwight Howard 10.00 25.00
14 Dwight Howard Dunk 10.00 25.00
15 Dwight Howard Magic 10.00 25.00
16 Chris Paul ROY 20.00 40.00
17 Chris Paul Shoot 20.00 40.00
18 Chris Paul Hornets 20.00 40.00
19 Steve Nash APG 10.00 25.00
20 Steve Nash Floor General 10.00 25.00
21 Steve Nash Captain Canada 10.00 25.00
22 Tim Duncan Slam Duncan 10.00 25.00
23 Tim Duncan Spurs 10.00 25.00
24 Tim Duncan MVP 10.00 25.00
25 Jason Kidd JK5 10.00 25.00
26 Jason Kidd Trip.Double 10.00 25.00
27 Jason Kidd APG 10.00 25.00
28 Tracy McGrady Tmac 10.00 25.00
29 Tracy McGrady #1 10.00 25.00
30 Tracy McGrady Ball 10.00 25.00
31 Dirk Nowitzki MVP 15.00 30.00
32 Dirk Nowitzki All-Star 15.00 30.00
33 Dirk Nowitzki 3PT 15.00 30.00
34 Amare Stoudemire ROY 10.00 25.00
35 Amare Stoudemire Double 10.00 25.00
36 Amare Stoudemire Dunk 10.00 25.00
37 Joe Johnson NBA 6.00 15.00
38 Joe Johnson ATL 6.00 15.00
39 Joe Johnson Ball 6.00 15.00
40 Pau Gasol ROY 6.00 15.00
41 Pau Gasol Grizzlies 6.00 15.00
42 Pau Gasol Dunk 6.00 15.00
43 Baron Davis GSW 10.00 25.00
44 Baron Davis #5 10.00 25.00
45 Baron Davis Shoot 10.00 25.00
46 Richard Hamilton DET 6.00 15.00
47 Richard Hamilton RIP 6.00 15.00
48 Richard Hamilton Ball 6.00 15.00
49 Manu Ginobili Argentina 10.00 25.00
50 Manu Ginobili Ball 10.00 25.00
51 Manu Ginobili Manu 10.00 25.00
52 Lamar Odom LAL 6.00 15.00
53 Lamar Odom #7 6.00 15.00
54 Lamar Odom Shoot 6.00 15.00
55 Josh Smith #5 6.00 15.00
56 Josh Smith Jsmooth 6.00 15.00
57 Josh Smith Dunk 6.00 15.00
58 Yao Ming Chinese 10.00 25.00
59 Yao Ming #1 Pick 10.00 25.00
60 Yao Ming Ball 10.00 25.00
61 Jermaine O'Neal Pacers 6.00 15.00
62 Jermaine O'Neal #7 6.00 15.00
63 Jermaine O'Neal Double 6.00 15.00
64 Michael Redd PTS 6.00 15.00
65 Michael Redd 3PT 6.00 15.00
66 Michael Redd Ball 6.00 15.00
67 Shawn Marion Suns 6.00 15.00
68 Shawn Marion Dunk 6.00 15.00
69 Shawn Marion All-Star 6.00 15.00
70 Josh Howard DAL 6.00 15.00
71 Josh Howard #5 6.00 15.00
72 Josh Howard NBA 6.00 15.00
73 Ben Wallace Big Ben 6.00 15.00
74 Ben Wallace Bulls 6.00 15.00
75 Ben Wallace Defense 6.00 15.00
76 Kevin Martin #23 6.00 15.00
77 Kevin Martin SAC 6.00 15.00
78 Kevin Martin NBA 6.00 15.00
79 Carmelo Anthony Ball 10.00 25.00
80 Carmelo Anthony Melo 10.00 25.00
81 Carmelo Anthony PTS 10.00 25.00
82 Mike Conley Jr. MEM 6.00 15.00
83 Mike Conley Jr. #11 6.00 15.00
84 Mike Conley Jr. NBA 6.00 15.00
85 Al Horford ATL 10.00 25.00
86 Al Horford #15 10.00 25.00
87 Al Horford NBA 10.00 25.00
88 Corey Brewer MIN 8.00 20.00
89 Corey Brewer #22 8.00 20.00
90 Corey Brewer NBA 8.00 20.00
91 Joakim Noah CHI 8.00 20.00
92 Joakim Noah NBA 8.00 20.00
93 Joakim Noah #13 8.00 20.00
94 Greg Oden #52 12.50 30.00
95 Greg Oden #1 Pick 12.50 30.00
96 Greg Oden POR 12.50 30.00
97 Eddy Curry NYK 6.00 15.00
98 Eddy Curry #34 6.00 15.00
99 Eddy Curry NBA 6.00 15.00
100 Mike Miller #33 6.00 15.00
101 Mike Miller MEM 6.00 15.00
102 Mike Miller Ball 6.00 15.00
103 Dwyane Wade Heat 15.00 30.00
104 Dwyane Wade Flash 15.00 30.00
105 Dwyane Wade DW3 15.00 30.00

2007-08 Topps Triple Threads Relics Autographs

PRINT RUN NINE SETS
THREE VERSIONS OF EACH CARD EXIST
ALL VERSIONS SAME VALUE
UNPRICED EMERALD PRINT RUN ONE SET
UNPRICED GOLD PRINT RUN ONE SET
UNPRICED PLATINUM PRINT RUN ONE SET
UNPRICED SAPPHIRE PRINT RUN ONE SET
1 Dwyane Wade Heat 40.00 80.00
2 Dwyane Wade Flash 40.00 80.00
3 Dwyane Wade DW3 40.00 80.00
7 Nick Young NY1 30.00 60.00
8 Nick Young WAS 30.00 60.00
9 Nick Young Ball 30.00 60.00
10 Brandan Wright #32 20.00 50.00
11 Brandan Wright GSW 20.00 50.00
12 Brandan Wright Ball 20.00 50.00
13 Yi Jianlian YI 40.00 80.00
14 Yi Jianlian MIL 40.00 80.00
15 Yi Jianlian Chinese 40.00 80.00
19 Paul Pierce #34 40.00 80.00
20 Paul Pierce Ball 40.00 80.00
21 Paul Pierce Shamrock 40.00 80.00
22 Vince Carter Nets 25.00 60.00
23 Vince Carter Dunk 25.00 60.00
24 Vince Carter Vinsanity 25.00 60.00
25 Andre Iguodala 73ers 15.00 30.00
26 Andre Iguodala Dunk 15.00 30.00
27 Andre Iguodala AI9 15.00 30.00
28 Corey Maggette LAC 15.00 30.00
29 Corey Maggette #50 15.00 30.00
30 Corey Maggette NBA 15.00 30.00
31 Mickael Pietrus MP2 15.00 30.00
32 Mickael Pietrus GSW 15.00 30.00
33 Mickael Pietrus Shoot 15.00 30.00
34 Raymond Felton CHA 15.00 30.00
35 Raymond Felton Floor Gen. 15.00 30.00
36 Raymond Felton #20 15.00 30.00
37 Rajon Rondo Bean Town 30.00 80.00
38 Rajon Rondo BOS 30.00 80.00
39 Rajon Rondo Ball 30.00 80.00
46 Craig Smith MIN 15.00 30.00
47 Craig Smith Dunk 15.00 30.00
48 Craig Smith #5 15.00 30.00
49 Magic Johnson Ball 100.00 200.00
50 Magic Johnson MVP 100.00 200.00
51 Magic Johnson Champ 100.00 200.00
52 Larry Bird MVP 100.00 200.00
53 Larry Bird Ball 100.00 200.00
54 Larry Bird All-Star 100.00 200.00
55 Rick Barry GSW 30.00 60.00
56 Rick Barry Under Hand 30.00 60.00
57 Rick Barry FT% 30.00 60.00
58 Dominique Wilkins HHFilm 20.00 50.00
59 Dominique Wilkins Dunk 20.00 50.00
60 Dominique Wilkins 23 FTs 20.00 50.00
61 David Robinson Admiral 100.00 200.00
62 David Robinson #50 100.00 200.00
63 David Robinson MVP 100.00 200.00
67 John Stockton APG 60.00 120.00
68 John Stockton Double 60.00 120.00
69 John Stockton SPG 60.00 120.00
70 Dennis Rodman Worm 50.00 100.00
71 Dennis Rodman RPG 50.00 100.00
72 Dennis Rodman Defense 50.00 100.00
73 Isiah Thomas ZEKE 25.00 50.00
74 Isiah Thomas MVP 25.00 50.00
75 Isiah Thomas Shoot 25.00 50.00
76 Ray Allen #20 40.00 80.00
77 Ray Allen Bean Town 40.00 80.00
78 Ray Allen 3PT 40.00 80.00
82 David Lee #42 15.00 30.00
83 David Lee NYK 15.00 30.00
84 David Lee Lee 15.00 30.00
85 Bill Walton Bean Town 20.00 50.00
86 Bill Walton Shamrock 20.00 50.00
87 Bill Walton Red Head 20.00 50.00
88 Chauncey Billups Big Shot 25.00 50.00
89 Chauncey Billups Pistons 25.00 50.00
90 Chauncey Billups MVP 25.00 50.00
91 Al Jefferson MIN 20.00 40.00
92 Al Jefferson #25 20.00 40.00
93 Al Jefferson Dunk 20.00 40.00
94 Luke Walton Shoot 15.00 30.00
95 Luke Walton #4 15.00 30.00
96 Luke Walton Walton 15.00 30.00
97 Ben Gordon #7 15.00 30.00
98 Ben Gordon 3PT 15.00 30.00
99 Ben Gordon 6th Man 15.00 30.00
100 Shaquille O'Neal Double 75.00 200.00
101 Shaquille O'Neal Dunk 75.00 200.00
102 Shaquille O'Neal MVP 75.00 200.00
103 Carmelo Anthony Ball 30.00 60.00
104 Carmelo Anthony Melo 30.00 60.00
105 Carmelo Anthony PTS 30.00 60.00
106 Chris Paul ROY 50.00 100.00
107 Chris Paul Shoot 50.00 100.00
108 Chris Paul Hornets 50.00 100.00
109 Deron Williams Jazz 30.00 60.00
110 Deron Williams UTA 30.00 60.00
111 Deron Williams Ball 30.00 60.00
112 Antawn Jamison WAS 15.00 30.00
113 Antawn Jamison 6th Man 15.00 30.00
114 Antawn Jamison PTS 15.00 30.00
118 Ryan Gomes Wolves #8 15.00 30.00
119 Ryan Gomes Shoot 15.00 30.00
120 Ryan Gomes MIN 15.00 30.00
121 David Thompson #33 10.00 25.00
122 David Thompson All-Star 10.00 25.00
123 David Thompson DEN 10.00 25.00
124 Moses Malone HOF 20.00 40.00
125 Moses Malone PTS 20.00 40.00
126 Moses Malone MVP 20.00 40.00
127 Dwight Howard Magic 12 20.00 50.00
128 Dwight Howard Dunk 20.00 50.00
129 Dwight Howard REB 20.00 50.00
130 Thaddeus Young PHI 30.00 80.00
131 Thaddeus Young #21 30.00 80.00
132 Thaddeus Young Shoot 30.00 80.00
133 Adam Morrison Cats 35 15.00 30.00
134 Adam Morrison Ball 15.00 30.00
135 Adam Morrison 3PT 15.00 30.00

2007-08 Topps Triple Threads Relics Autographs Sepia

PRINT RUN FIVE SETS
THREE VERSIONS OF EACH CARD
UNLISTED VERSIONS SAME VALUE
1 Dwyane Wade Heat 50.00 100.00
2 Dwyane Wade Flash 50.00 100.00
3 Dwyane Wade DW3 50.00 100.00
4 Greg Oden #52 60.00 150.00
5 Greg Oden #1Pick 60.00 150.00
6 Greg Oden POR 60.00 150.00
13 Yi Jianlian YI 50.00 100.00
14 Yi Jianlian MIL 50.00 100.00
15 Yi Jianlian Chinese 50.00 100.00
16 Chris Bosh CB4 30.00 60.00
17 Chris Bosh TOR 30.00 60.00
18 Chris Bosh All-Star 30.00 60.00
19 Paul Pierce #34 60.00 120.00
20 Paul Pierce Ball 60.00 120.00
21 Paul Pierce Shamrock 60.00 120.00
22 Vince Carter Nets 30.00 80.00
23 Vince Carter Dunk 30.00 80.00
24 Vince Carter Vinsanity 30.00 80.00
25 Andre Iguodala 73ers 15.00 30.00
26 Andre Iguodala Dunk 15.00 30.00
27 Andre Iguodala AI9 15.00 30.00
28 Corey Maggette LAC 20.00 40.00
29 Corey Maggette #50 20.00 40.00
30 Corey Maggette NBA 20.00 40.00
31 Mickael Pietrus MP2 20.00 40.00
32 Mickael Pietrus GSW 20.00 40.00
33 Mickael Pietrus Shoot 20.00 40.00
34 Raymond Felton CHA 20.00 40.00
35 Raymond Felton Floor Gen. 20.00 40.00
36 Raymond Felton #20 20.00 40.00
37 Rajon Rondo Bean Town 40.00 100.00
38 Rajon Rondo BOS 40.00 100.00
39 Rajon Rondo Ball 40.00 100.00
40 Jarrett Jack POR 20.00 40.00
41 Jarrett Jack NBA 20.00 40.00
42 Jarrett Jack Ball 20.00 40.00
46 Craig Smith MIN 20.00 40.00
47 Craig Smith Dunk 20.00 40.00
48 Craig Smith #5 20.00 40.00
49 Magic Johnson Ball 100.00 200.00
50 Magic Johnson MVP 100.00 200.00
51 Magic Johnson Champ 100.00 200.00
52 Larry Bird MVP 100.00 200.00
53 Larry Bird Ball 100.00 200.00
54 Larry Bird All-Star 100.00 200.00
55 Rick Barry GSW 50.00 100.00
56 Rick Barry Under Hand 50.00 100.00
57 Rick Barry FT 50.00 100.00
58 Dominique Wilkins HHFilm 30.00 60.00
59 Dominique Wilkins Dunk 30.00 60.00
60 Dominique Wilkins 23 FTs 30.00 60.00
64 Mike Miller MEM 20.00 40.00
65 Mike Miller #33 20.00 40.00
66 Mike Miller Ball 20.00 40.00
67 John Stockton APG 80.00 160.00
68 John Stockton Double 80.00 160.00
69 John Stockton SPG 80.00 160.00
73 Isiah Thomas ZEKE 25.00 50.00
74 Isiah Thomas MVP 25.00 50.00
75 Isiah Thomas Shoot 25.00 50.00
76 Ray Allen #20 60.00 120.00
77 Ray Allen Bean Town 60.00 120.00
78 Ray Allen 3PT 60.00 120.00
79 Gilbert Arenas Ball 40.00 100.00
80 Gilbert Arenas Hibachi 40.00 100.00
81 Gilbert Arenas WAS 40.00 100.00
85 Bill Walton Bean Town 30.00 75.00
86 Bill Walton Shamrock 30.00 75.00
87 Bill Walton Red Head 30.00 75.00
88 Chauncey Billups Big Shot 30.00 75.00
89 Chauncey Billups Pistons 30.00 75.00
90 Chauncey Billups MVP 30.00 75.00
94 Luke Walton Shoot 20.00 40.00
95 Luke Walton #4 20.00 40.00
96 Luke Walton Walton 20.00 40.00
97 Ben Gordon #7 20.00 40.00
98 Ben Gordon 3PT 20.00 40.00
99 Ben Gordon 6th Man 20.00 40.00
100 Shaquille O'Neal Double 80.00 160.00
101 Shaquille O'Neal Dunk 80.00 160.00
102 Shaquille O'Neal MVP 80.00 160.00
103 Carmelo Anthony Ball 50.00 100.00
104 Carmelo Anthony Melo 50.00 100.00
105 Carmelo Anthony PTS 50.00 100.00
106 Chris Paul ROY 100.00 200.00
107 Chris Paul Shoot 100.00 200.00
108 Chris Paul Hornets 100.00 200.00
109 Deron Williams Jazz 40.00 80.00
110 Deron Williams UTA 40.00 80.00
111 Deron Williams Ball 40.00 80.00
112 Antawn Jamison WAS 25.00 50.00
113 Antawn Jamison 6th Man 25.00 50.00
114 Antawn Jamison PTS 25.00 50.00
115 Joe Johnson ATL 20.00 40.00
116 Joe Johnson Ball 20.00 40.00
117 Joe Johnson Hawks #2 20.00 40.00
118 Ryan Gomes Wolves #8 20.00 40.00
119 Ryan Gomes Shoot 20.00 40.00
120 Ryan Gomes MIN 20.00 40.00
121 David Thompson #33 25.00 50.00
122 David Thompson All-Star 25.00 50.00
123 David Thompson DEN 25.00 50.00
124 Moses Malone HOF 30.00 60.00
125 Moses Malone PTS 30.00 60.00
126 Moses Malone MVP 30.00 60.00
127 Dwight Howard Magic 12 30.00 80.00
128 Dwight Howard Dunk 30.00 80.00
129 Dwight Howard REB 30.00 80.00
130 Thaddeus Young PHI 40.00 80.00
131 Thaddeus Young #21 40.00 80.00
132 Thaddeus Young Shoot 40.00 80.00
133 Adam Morrison Cats 35 15.00 30.00
134 Adam Morrison Ball 15.00 30.00
135 Adam Morrison 3PT 15.00 30.00

2007-08 Topps Triple Threads Relics Combos

PRINT RUN 18 SER.#'d SETS
UNPRICED EMERALD PRINT RUN 3 SETS
UNPRICED GOLD PRINT RUN ONE SET
UNPRICED PLATINUM PRINT RUN ONE SET
UNPRICED SEPIA PRINT RUN 9 SETS
1 Pierce/Allen/Garnett 40.00 100.00
2 Iverson/Camby/Anthony 25.00 50.00
3 Oden/Roy/Aldridge 50.00 100.00
4 Wallace/Noah/Gordon 20.00 40.00
5 Conley/Gasol/Miller 10.00 25.00
6 Smith/Horford/Johnson 25.00 50.00
7 Jefferson/Brewer/Foye 10.00 25.00
8 Jianlian/Nowitzki/Ming 12.50 30.00
9 Nowitzki/Nash/Duncan 20.00 40.00
10 O'Neal/Malone/Robinson 30.00 60.00
11 Bird/Garnett/Walton 40.00 80.00
12 Wade/Thomas/Parker 20.00 40.00
13 Bryant/Arenas/Anthony 15.00 40.00
14 Redd/Allen/Iverson 25.00 50.00
15 Davis/Wright/Ellis 10.00 25.00
16 Jamison/Young/Butler 10.00 25.00
17 Young/Iguodala/Dalembert 10.00 25.00
18 Bird/Robinson/O'Neal 40.00 80.00
19 Roy/Paul/Carter 20.00 40.00
20 Stockton/Johnson/Thomas 25.00 50.00
21 Kidd/Marbury/Nash 20.00 40.00
22 Russell/Baylor/Rodman 25.00 50.00
23 O'Neal/Duncan/Wallace 12.00 30.00
24 Allen/Jones/Walker 10.00 25.00
25 Iverson/McGrady/Carter 20.00 40.00
26 Wilkins/Drexler/Johnson 25.00 50.00
27 Hardaway/Richmond/Mullin 25.00 50.00
29 McGrady/Battier/Ming 15.00 30.00
30 Marion/Iguodala/Artest 10.00 25.00
31 Young/Wade/Young 15.00 30.00
32 Camby/Prince/Wallace 10.00 25.00
33 Barbosa/Miller/Gordon 10.00 25.00
35 Arenas/O'Neal/McGrady 10.00 25.00
36 Ming/Stoudemire/Boozer 20.00 40.00
37 Hinrich/Ford/Howard 10.00 25.00
38 Richardson/Felton/Wallace 10.00 25.00
39 Afflalo/Billups/Stuckey 10.00 25.00
42 Bosh/McGrady/Anthony 15.00 30.00
43 Garnett/Howard/Wade 20.00 40.00
44 Ridnour/Green/West 10.00 25.00
46 Jefferson/Williams/Kidd 10.00 25.00
47 Horford/Brewer/Noah 20.00 40.00
48 Barry/Baylor/Bird 25.00 50.00
49 Johnson/O'Neal/Malone 40.00 80.00
50 Stockton/Walton/Thomas 20.00 40.00

2007-08 Topps Triple Threads Rookie Relics Autographs

SKIP-NUMBERED SET
PRINT RUN 50 SER.#'d SETS
UNPRICED EMERALD PRINT RUN ONE SET
UNPRICED GOLD PRINT RUN ONE SET
UNPRICED PLATINUM PRINT RUN ONE SET
UNPRICED SAPPHIRE PRINT RUN ONE SET
*SEPIA: .5X TO 1.25X BASE HI
SEPIA PRINT RUN 23 SER.#'d SETS
101 Greg Oden 8.00 20.00
102 Daequan Cook 6.00 15.00
103 Morris Almond 5.00 12.00
104 Sean Williams 5.00 12.00

105 Arron Afflalo 8.00 20.00
107 Adam Haluska 5.00 12.00
109 Herbert Hill 5.00 12.00
110 Nick Young 10.00 25.00
113 Jared Jordan 5.00 12.00
114 Aaron Brooks 6.00 15.00
115 Marco Belinelli 8.00 20.00
117 Jared Dudley 6.00 15.00
118 Rodney Stuckey 6.00 15.00
120 Gabe Pruitt 5.00 12.00
121 Acie Law 5.00 12.00
122 Dominic McGuire 5.00 12.00
125 Wilson Chandler 6.00 15.00
126 Marcus Williams 5.00 12.00
127 Josh McRoberts 6.00 15.00
128 Jason Smith 6.00 15.00
130 Stephane Lasme 5.00 12.00
132 Alando Tucker 5.00 12.00
133 Javaris Crittenton 5.00 12.00
136 Al Thornton 6.00 15.00
137 Carl Landry 5.00 12.00
138 Yi Jianlian 10.00 25.00
139 Brandan Wright 8.00 20.00
140 Nick Fazekas 5.00 12.00
142 Jermareo Davidson 5.00 12.00
143 D.J. Strawberry 5.00 12.00
144 Glen Davis 6.00 15.00
146 Spencer Hawes 6.00 15.00
147 Taurean Green 5.00 12.00
149 Aaron Gray 5.00 12.00
150 Thaddeus Young 8.00 20.00

2006-07 Topps Turkey Red

Released in early February 2007, Turkey Red employs an old-school design which resembles a framed portrait of each player painted on a textured card stock. The 275-card base set pictures veteran players on cards 1-175 where short prints are labeled as "SP" (inserted at the rate of one in four packs), rookies are pictured on cards 176-225, retired NBA legends are pictured on cards 226-250 and cards 251-260 are checklist cards. Also inserted were a series of advertisement-back variations. These are noted in the checklist with "Ad." Turkey Red is packaged in 24-pack boxes of eight cards each and carried an original suggested retail price of $4.00 per pack.

COMPLETE SET (275) 60.00 120.00
COMP.SET w/o RC's (175) 15.00 40.00
UNPRICED GOLD PRINT RUN 5 SETS
UNPRICED SUEDE PRINT RUN 3 SETS
UNPRICED WOOD PRINT RUN ONE SET
1 Dwyane Wade SP 1.00 2.50
2 LeBron James 1.50 4.00
3 Allen Iverson SP .75 2.00
4 Sebastian Telfair .25 .60
5 Bonzi Wells .25 .60
6 Antawn Jamison .30 .75
7 Joe Johnson .30 .75
8 DeSagana Diop .25 .60
9 Stromile Swift .25 .60
10 Shaun Livingston .25 .60
11 Baron Davis .30 .75
12 Richard Hamilton .30 .75
13 Andrei Kirilenko SP .50 1.25
14 Richard Jefferson .30 .75
15 T.J. Ford .25 .60
16 Luke Ridnour .30 .75
17 Carlos Boozer .30 .75
18 Al Jefferson .30 .75
19 Andrew Bogut SP .50 1.25
20 Kobe Bryant 1.50 4.00
21 Tim Duncan .60 1.50
22 Ben Gordon .30 .75
22B Ben Gordon Ad .50 1.25
23 Stephen Jackson .30 .75
24 Peja Stojakovic .40 1.00
25 Mike Miller .30 .75
26 Ricky Davis SP .50 1.25
27 Boris Diaw SP .50 1.25
28 Shareef Abdur-Rahim .30 .75
29 Caron Butler .30 .75
30 Al Harrington .30 .75
31 Ben Wallace SP .50 1.25
32 Jason Richardson .40 1.00
33 Channing Frye .30 .75
34 Paul Pierce .40 1.00
35 Andre Iguodala .30 .75
35B Andre Iguodala Ad .50 1.25
36 Joey Graham .25 .60
37 Corey Maggette .30 .75
38 Sarunas Jasikevicius .30 .75
39 Lamar Odom .30 .75
40 Shaquille O'Neal .75 2.00
40B Shaquille O'Neal Ad 1.25 3.00
41 Larry Hughes SP .50 1.25
42 Darko Milicic SP .40 1.00
43 Jerry Stackhouse .30 .75
44 Raymond Felton .30 .75
45 Nenad Krstic SP .40 1.00
46 Michael Redd .30 .75
47 Shane Battier .30 .75
48 Kevin Garnett .60 1.50
49 Deron Williams .30 .75
50 Chris Paul SP .75 2.00
51 Rashard Lewis .40 1.00
52 Kevin Martin SP .50 1.25
53 Zach Randolph .30 .75
54 Jared Jeffries .25 .60
55 Donyell Marshall .25 .60
56 Josh Howard SP .50 1.25
57 Stephon Marbury .30 .75
58 Raja Bell .30 .75
59 Tony Parker .40 1.00
60 Dwight Howard .30 .75
61 Kirk Hinrich .30 .75
62 Emeka Okafor .30 .75
63 Zaza Pachulia .25 .60
64 Troy Murphy .25 .60
65 Chris Duhon .25 .60
65B Chris Duhon Ad .40 1.00
66 Earl Boykins SP .40 1.00
67 Tracy McGrady .50 1.25
68 Hakim Warrick .30 .75
69 Charlie Villanueva SP .40 1.00
70 Jason Kidd .60 1.50
71 Joel Przybilla SP .40 1.00
72 Antonio Daniels .25 .60
73 Wally Szczerbiak .30 .75
74 Drew Gooden .30 .75
75 Antonio McDyess .30 .75
76 Ray Allen SP .60 1.50
77 Rashad McCants .25 .60
78 Eddy Curry .30 .75
79 Chris Webber .40 1.00
80 Yao Ming SP .75 2.00
81 Tyson Chandler .30 .75
82 Bobby Simmons .25 .60
83 Jarrett Jack .30 .75
84 Jameer Nelson SP .40 1.00
85 Luol Deng .30 .75
86 Kurt Thomas .25 .60
87 Mickael Pietrus .30 .75
88 Chris Bosh SP .60 1.50
89 Devin Harris .25 .60
90 Jermaine O'Neal .30 .75
91 Luther Head .30 .75
92 Elton Brand SP .60 1.50
93 Antoine Walker .30 .75
94 Smush Parker .25 .60
95 Nate Robinson SP .40 1.00
96 Marvin Williams SP .50 1.25
97 Primoz Brezec .25 .60
98 Desmond Mason .25 .60
99 Ron Artest SP .60 1.50
100 Jason Terry .30 .75
101 Mehmet Okur .25 .60
102 Kenyon Martin .30 .75
103 Ike Diogu SP .40 1.00
104 Eddie Griffin .25 .60
105 Amare Stoudemire .30 .75
106 Kwame Brown SP .40 1.00
107 Hedo Turkoglu .40 1.00
108 Chauncey Billups .40 1.00
108B Chauncey Billups Ad .60 1.50
109 Rafer Alston .25 .60
110 Dirk Nowitzki SP 1.00 2.50
111 Steve Francis .30 .75
112 Mike Bibby .40 1.00
113 Kirk Snyder .25 .60
114 Luke Walton .25 .60
114B Luke Walton Ad .40 1.00
115 Maurice Williams .30 .75
116 Nick Collison .30 .75
117 Brendan Haywood .25 .60
118 Delonte West SP .40 1.00
119 Mike Dunleavy .30 .75
120 Vince Carter .50 1.25
120B Vince Carter Ad .75 2.00
121 Juwan Howard .30 .75
122 J.R. Smith .30 .75
123 Gerald Wallace SP .50 1.25
124 Cuttino Mobley .25 .60
125 James Posey .25 .60
126 Tayshaun Prince SP .50 1.25
127 Anderson Varejao .25 .60
128 Trenton Hassell .25 .60
129 Matt Harpring .25 .60
130 Gilbert Arenas SP .50 1.25
131 Leandro Barbosa .30 .75
132 Bruce Bowen .25 .60
133 Morris Peterson .25 .60
134 David West SP .50 1.25
135 Joe Smith .30 .75
136 Rasheed Wallace .40 1.00
137 Nene .30 .75
138 Alonzo Mourning .50 1.25
139 Jamal Crawford .40 1.00
140 Carmelo Anthony SP .75 2.00
141 Brad Miller .30 .75
142 Tim Thomas .25 .60
143 Jose Calderon .25 .60
144 Sean May .25 .60
145 Andres Nocioni SP .40 1.00
146 Samuel Dalembert .25 .60
147 Chris Wilcox .25 .60
148 Jason Williams .30 .75
149 DeShawn Stevenson .25 .60
150 Josh Smith SP .50 1.25
151 Andre Miller .30 .75
152 Michael Finley .40 1.00
153 Marquis Daniels .25 .60
154 Martell Webster .30 .75
155 Brevin Knight .25 .60
156 Steve Nash SP .75 2.00
157 Vladimir Radmanovic .25 .60
158 Speedy Claxton .25 .60
158B Speedy Claxton Ad .40 1.00
159 Darius Miles .25 .60
160 Pau Gasol SP .60 1.50
161 Sam Cassell .30 .75
162 Nazr Mohammed .25 .60
163 Shawn Marion .30 .75
164 Francisco Garcia .25 .60
165 Kyle Korver .30 .75
166 Udonis Haslem .25 .60
167 Manu Ginobili SP .60 1.50
168 Zydrunas Ilgauskas .30 .75
169 Eddie Jones .30 .75
170 Danny Granger SP .50 1.25
171 Mike James .25 .60
172 Ryan Gomes .25 .60
173 Josh Childress .30 .75
174 Marcus Camby .30 .75
175 Chris Kaman SP .50 1.25
176 Brandon Roy RC 1.00 2.50
177 Kyle Lowry RC 1.25 3.00
178 Tyrus Thomas RC .75 2.00
179 Hilton Armstrong RC .60 1.50
180 LaMarcus Aldridge RC 2.50 6.00
181 Ronnie Brewer RC 1.00 2.50
182 Rajon Rondo RC 1.50 4.00
183 Marcus Vinicius RC .60 1.50
184 Solomon Jones RC .60 1.50
185 Leon Powe RC .75 2.00
186 Shawne Williams RC .60 1.50
187 Craig Smith RC .75 2.00
187B Craig Smith Ad RC .75 2.00
188 Patrick O'Bryant RC .60 1.50
189 James Augustine RC .60 1.50
190 Maurice Ager RC .60 1.50
191 Quincy Douby RC .60 1.50
192 Rudy Gay RC 1.25 3.00
193 Thabo Sefolosha RC 1.00 2.50
194 Bobby Jones RC .60 1.50
195 Shelden Williams RC .75 2.00
195B Shelden Williams Ad RC .75 2.00
196 Mile Ilic RC .60 1.50
197 Jorge Garbajosa RC .75 2.00
198 Cedric Simmons RC .60 1.50
199 Josh Boone RC .60 1.50
200 Adam Morrison RC 1.00 2.50
200B Adam Morrison Ad RC 1.00 2.50
201 Marcus Williams RC .60 1.50
201B Marcus Williams Ad RC .60 1.50
202 Steve Novak RC .75 2.00
203 Vassilis Spanoulis RC .60 1.50
204 Allan Ray RC .60 1.50
205 David Noel RC .60 1.50
206 Alexander Johnson RC .60 1.50
207 Mardy Collins RC .60 1.50
208 Dee Brown RC .60 1.50
209 P.J. Tucker RC .75 2.00
210 Paul Millsap RC 1.25 3.00
211 Paul Davis RC .60 1.50
212 Rodney Carney RC .60 1.50
212B Rodney Carney Ad RC .60 1.50
213 Saer Sene RC .60 1.50
214 Renaldo Balkman RC .75 2.00
215 Ryan Hollins RC .75 2.00
216 Will Blalock RC .60 1.50
217 Mickael Gelabale RC .60 1.50
218 Daniel Gibson RC .75 2.00
219 Hassan Adams RC .60 1.50
220 J.J. Redick RC 1.25 3.00
221 Jordan Farmar RC 1.00 2.50
221B Jordan Farmar Ad RC 1.00 2.50
222 Randy Foye RC 1.00 2.50
223 Shannon Brown RC .60 1.50
224 Sergio Rodriguez RC 1.00 2.50
225 Andrea Bargnani RC 1.00 2.50
225B Andrea Bargnani Ad RC 1.00 2.50
226 Larry Bird 2.50 6.00
227 George Gervin 1.00 2.50
228 Earl Monroe 1.00 2.50
229 Kareem Abdul-Jabbar 1.50 4.00
230 Wilt Chamberlain 2.00 5.00
231 Bill Walton 1.00 2.50
232 Isiah Thomas 1.00 2.50
233 Oscar Robertson 1.00 2.50
234 Pete Maravich 6.00 15.00
235 Bill Russell 2.00 5.00
236 James Worthy 1.00 2.50
237 Rick Barry .75 2.00
238 Walt Frazier 1.00 2.50
239 Elgin Baylor 1.00 2.50
240 Karl Malone 1.25 3.00
241 Connie Hawkins 1.00 2.50
242 Dennis Rodman 2.00 5.00
243 John Stockton 1.50 4.00
244 Jerry West 1.25 3.00
245 Bob Cousy 1.50 4.00
246 Hakeem Olajuwon 1.25 3.00
247 John Havlicek 1.00 2.50
248 Spencer Haywood .60 1.50
249 Moses Malone 1.00 2.50
250 Willis Reed 1.00 2.50
251 LeBron James CL 1.00 2.50
252 Shaquille O'Neal CL .50 1.25
253 Dwyane Wade CL .40 1.00
254 Y.Ming/T.McGrady CL .60 1.50
255 Carmelo Anthony CL .30 .75
256 K.Garnett/D.Howard CL .75 2.00
257 Nate Robinson CL .15 .40
258 Kobe Bryant/Team CL 1.00 2.50
259 Larry Bird CL 2.00 5.00
260 S.Nash/K.Thomas CL .60 1.50

2006-07 Topps Turkey Red Black

*1-175 BLACK: .75X TO 2X BASE HI
*176-225 BLACK RC: .4X TO 1X BASE HI
*226-260 BLACK: .75X TO 2X BASE HI
STATED ODDS 1:4

2006-07 Topps Turkey Red Red

*RED: .4X TO 1X BASE HI
STATED ODDS ONE PER PACK

2006-07 Topps Turkey Red White

*1-175 WHITE: .5X TO 1.25X BASE HI
*176-225 WHITE RC: .3X TO .75X BASE HI
*226-260 WHITE: .5X TO 1.25X BASE HI
STATED ODDS 1:4

2006-07 Topps Turkey Red Autographs

GROUP A ODDS 1:505, GROUP B ODDS 1:186
UNPRICED BLACK PRINT RUN 10 SETS
UNPRICED GOLD PRINT RUN 5 SETS
UNPRICED SUEDE PRINT RUN 3 SETS
AB Andrea Bargnani A 4.00 10.00
ABO Andrew Bogut A 6.00 15.00
AI Allen Iverson A 30.00 80.00
AM Adam Morrison A 4.00 10.00
BG Ben Gordon A 4.00 10.00
CB Chris Bosh A 6.00 15.00
CD Chris Duhon B 4.00 10.00
CS Cedric Simmons B 4.00 10.00
CV Charlie Villanueva A 4.00 10.00
DH Devin Harris A 4.00 10.00
DW Dwyane Wade A 25.00 60.00
EO Emeka Okafor A 4.00 10.00
HA Hilton Armstrong B 4.00 10.00
HW Hakim Warrick B 4.00 10.00
JB Josh Boone B 4.00 10.00
JF Jordan Farmar B 4.00 10.00
JJR J.J. Redick A 12.50 30.00
JO Jermaine O'Neal A 5.00 12.00
KL Kyle Lowry B 5.00 12.00
LB Larry Bird A 50.00 120.00
LD Luol Deng A 4.00 10.00
LR Luke Ridnour B 4.00 10.00
MA Maurice Ager B 4.00 10.00
MC Mardy Collins B 4.00 10.00
MW Marcus Williams A 4.00 10.00
POB Patrick O'Bryant B 4.00 10.00
QD Quincy Douby B 4.00 10.00
RB Ronnie Brewer B 4.00 10.00
RBA Renaldo Balkman B 4.00 10.00
RC Rodney Carney B 4.00 10.00
RF Randy Foye B 4.00 10.00
RFE Raymond Felton A 4.00 10.00
RR Rajon Rondo B 12.00 30.00
SO Shaquille O'Neal A 40.00 100.00
ST Sebastian Telfair A 4.00 10.00
SW Shelden Williams A 4.00 10.00
SWI Shawne Williams B 4.00 10.00
TJF T.J. Ford B 4.00 10.00
TP Vince Carter A 15.00 40.00
TPA Tony Parker A 8.00 20.00

2006-07 Topps Turkey Red Autographs Red

PRINT RUN 25 TO 99 SER.#'d SETS
*WHITE: .5X TO 1.25X BASE HI
WHITE PRINT RUN 15 TO 50 SER.#'d SETS
AB Andrea Bargnani/25 6.00 15.00
AI Allen Iverson/25 40.00 100.00
AM Adam Morrison/25 6.00 15.00
BG Ben Gordon/25 6.00 15.00
CB Chris Bosh/25 8.00 20.00
CD Chris Duhon/99 5.00 12.00
CS Cedric Simmons/99 5.00 12.00
CV Charlie Villanueva/25 5.00 12.00
DH Devin Harris/25 6.00 15.00
DW Dwyane Wade/25 30.00 80.00
EO Emeka Okafor/25 6.00 15.00
HA Hilton Armstrong/99 5.00 12.00
HW Hakim Warrick/99 5.00 12.00
JB Josh Boone/99 5.00 12.00
JF Jordan Farmar/99 5.00 12.00
JO Jermaine O'Neal/25 6.00 15.00
KL Kyle Lowry/99 6.00 15.00
LB Larry Bird/25 60.00 150.00
LD Luol Deng/25 6.00 15.00
LR Luke Ridnour/99 5.00 12.00
MA Maurice Ager/99 5.00 12.00
MC Mardy Collins/99 5.00 12.00
MW Marcus Williams/25 5.00 12.00
QD Quincy Douby/99 5.00 12.00
RB Ronnie Brewer/99 6.00 15.00
RC Rodney Carney/99 5.00 12.00
RF Randy Foye/99 5.00 12.00
RR Rajon Rondo/99 15.00 40.00
SO Shaquille O'Neal/25 50.00 120.00
ST Sebastian Telfair/25 5.00 12.00
SW Shelden Williams/25 6.00 15.00
TP Vince Carter/25 20.00 50.00
ABO Andrew Bogut/25 8.00 20.00
JJR J.J. Redick/25 15.00 40.00
POB Patrick O'Bryant/99 5.00 12.00
RBA Renaldo Balkman/99 5.00 12.00
RFE Raymond Felton/25 6.00 15.00
SWI Shawne Williams/99 5.00 12.00
TJF T.J. Ford/99 5.00 12.00
TPA Tony Parker/25 10.00 25.00

2006-07 Topps Turkey Red Cabinet Jumbos

*GOLD: .5X TO 1.25X BASE HI
GOLD PRINT RUN 50 SER.#'d SET
ONE PER BOX AS TOPPER
UNPRICED SUEDE PRINT RUN 3 SETS
UNPRICED AUTO PRINT RUN 10 SETS
UNPRICED AUTO GOLD PRINT RUN 5 SETS
UNPRICED AUTO SUEDE PRINT RUN ONE SET
UNPRICED AUTO DUAL PRINT RUN 10 SETS
UNPRICED AUTO DUAL GOLD PRINT RUN 5 SETS
UNPRICED AUTO DUAL SUEDE PRINT RUN ONE SET
1 Chris Paul 2.00 5.00
2 Gilbert Arenas 1.25 3.00
3 Dwyane Wade 2.50 6.00
4 Joe Johnson 1.25 3.00
5 Carmelo Anthony 2.00 5.00
6 Shane Battier 1.25 3.00
7 Bruce Bowen 1.00 2.50
8 LeBron James 6.00 15.00
9 Elton Brand 1.50 4.00
10 Antawn Jamison 1.25 3.00
11 Chris Bosh 1.50 4.00
12 Dwight Howard 1.25 3.00
13 Brad Miller 1.25 3.00
14 Kirk Hinrich 1.25 3.00
15 Amare Stoudemire 1.25 3.00
16 Andrea Bargnani 1.50 4.00
17 LaMarcus Aldridge 4.00 10.00
18 Adam Morrison 1.50 4.00
19 Tyrus Thomas 1.25 3.00
20 Shelden Williams 1.25 3.00
21 Brandon Roy 1.50 4.00
22 Randy Foye 1.50 4.00
23 Rudy Gay 2.00 5.00
24 Patrick O'Bryant 1.00 2.50
25 Saer Sene 1.00 2.50
26 J.J. Redick 2.00 5.00
27 Hilton Armstrong 1.00 2.50
28 Thabo Sefolosha 1.50 4.00
29 Ronnie Brewer 1.50 4.00
30 Cedric Simmons 1.00 2.50

2006-07 Topps Turkey Red Relics

GROUP A ODDS 1:88, GROUP B ODDS 1:23
UNPRICED BLACK PRINT RUN 10 SETS
UNPRICED GOLD PRINT RUN 5 SETS
*RED: .5X TO 1.25X BASE HI
RED PRINT RUN 99 SER.#'d SETS
*WHITE: .6X TO 1.5X BASE HI
WHITE PRINT RUN 50 SER.#'d SETS
AI Allen Iverson B 3.00 8.00
AM Adam Morrison A 2.50 6.00
BG Ben Gordon B 2.00 5.00
BR Brandon Roy A 2.50 6.00
CB Chris Bosh A 2.50 6.00
CP Chris Paul A 3.00 8.00
CS Cedric Simmons B 1.50 4.00
DH Dwight Howard B 2.00 5.00
DW Dwyane Wade B 4.00 10.00
GA Gilbert Arenas B 2.00 5.00
GW Gerald Wallace A 2.00 5.00
HA Hilton Armstrong B 1.50 4.00
JB Josh Boone B 1.50 4.00
JF Jordan Farmar B 2.50 6.00
JR Jason Richardson A 2.50 6.00
JT Jason Terry A 2.00 5.00
KB Kobe Bryant B 6.00 15.00
KG Kevin Garnett A 4.00 10.00
KL Kyle Lowry B 3.00 8.00
LA LaMarcus Aldridge B 6.00 15.00
MA Maurice Ager A 1.50 4.00
MW Marcus Williams A 1.50 4.00
PP Paul Pierce A 2.50 6.00
QD Quincy Douby B 1.50 4.00
RA Ray Allen B 2.50 6.00
RB Ronnie Brewer B 2.50 6.00
RC Rodney Carney B 1.50 4.00
RF Randy Foye B 2.50 6.00
RG Rudy Gay B 3.00 8.00
RR Rajon Rondo A 8.00 20.00
SM Shawn Marion B 2.00 5.00
SO Shaquille O'Neal B 5.00 12.00
SW Shelden Williams B 2.00 5.00
TD Tim Duncan B 4.00 10.00
TM Tracy McGrady A 3.00 8.00
VC Vince Carter A 3.00 8.00
AIG Andre Iguodala A 2.00 5.00
JJR J.J. Redick B 3.00 8.00
POB Patrick O'Bryant B 1.50 4.00
SWI Shawne Williams B 1.50 4.00

2012 Topps U.S. Olympic Team

COMPLETE SET (100) 10.00 25.00
20 Sue Bird .40 1.00
46 Candace Parker .25 .60
60 Maya Moore .50 1.25
91 Seimone Augustus .25 .60

2012 Topps U.S. Olympic Team Bronze

*BRONZE: .5X TO 1.2X BASIC CARDS
STATED ODDS 1:1

2012 Topps U.S. Olympic Team Gold

*GOLD: .8X TO 2X BASIC CARDS
STATED ODDS 1:3

2012 Topps U.S. Olympic Team Silver

*SILVER: .6X TO 1.5X BASIC CARDS
STATED ODDS 1:2

2012 Topps U.S. Olympic Team Autographs

STATED ODDS 1:23
20 Sue Bird 15.00 40.00
60 Maya Moore 25.00 50.00

2012 Topps U.S. Olympic Team Autographs Bronze

*BRONZE: SAME AS BASIC AUTO
STATED ODDS 1:202
STATED PRINT RUN 50 SER. #'d SETS

2012 Topps U.S. Olympic Team Autographs Gold

*GOLD: .6X TO 1.5X BASIC CARDS
STATED ODDS 1:577
STATED PRINT RUN 15 SER. #'d SETS

2012 Topps U.S. Olympic Team Autographs Silver

*SILVER: .5X TO 1.2X BASIC CARDS
STATED ODDS 1:286
STATED PRINT RUN 30 SER. #'d SETS

2012 Topps U.S. Olympic Team Event Pins

STATED ODDS 1:92
ELPCP Candace Parker 5.00 12.00
ELPMM Maya Moore 10.00 25.00
ELPSA Seimone Augustus 5.00 12.00
ELPSB Sue Bird 8.00 20.00

2012 Topps U.S. Olympic Team Games of the XXX Olympiad

COMPLETE SET (25) 12.00 30.00
STATED ODDS 1:4
OLY3 Maya Moore 2.00 5.00

2012 Topps U.S. Olympic Team Olympic Team Patch

STATED ODDS 1:131
ULPCP Candace Parker 5.00 12.00
ULPMM Maya Moore 10.00 25.00
ULPSA Seimone Augustus 5.00 12.00
ULPSB Sue Bird 8.00 20.00

2012 Topps U.S. Olympic Team Relics

STATED ODDS 1:31
ORMM Maya Moore 8.00 20.00
ORSB Sue Bird 8.00 20.00

2012 Topps U.S. Olympic Team Relics Bronze

*BRONZE: SAME PRICE AS BASIC CARDS
STATED ODDS 1:222
STATED PRINT RUN 75 SER. #'d SETS

2012 Topps U.S. Olympic Team Relics Gold

*GOLD: .6X TO 1.5X BASIC CARDS
STATED ODDS 1:666
STATED PRINT RUN 25 SER. #'d SETS

2012 Topps U.S. Olympic Team Relics Silver

*SILVER: .5X TO 1.2X BASIC CARDS
STATED ODDS 1:333
STATED PRINT RUN 50 SER. #'d SETS

2012 Topps U.S. Olympic Team U.S. Flag Patch

STATED ODDS 1:131
FLPCP Candace Parker 5.00 12.00
FLPMM Maya Moore 10.00 25.00
FLPSA Seimone Augustus 5.00 12.00
FLPSB Sue Bird 8.00 20.00

2012 Topps U.S. Olympic Team USOC Pins

STATED ODDS 1:92
PINCP Candace Parker 5.00 12.00
PINMM Maya Moore 10.00 25.00
PINSA Seimone Augustus 5.00 12.00
PINSB Sue Bird 8.00 20.00

1996 Topps USA Women's National Team

Topps, a corporate sponsor of the USA Women's National team, issued this 24-card set featuring the core of the team that represented the United States at the Olympic Games in Atlanta. The cards were available in 8-card packs. The set consists of two cards each (a regular card [1-11] and a "Profiles" card [13-23]) of the 11 players on the team, a coach card, and a team photo card listing a complete pre-Olympics tour schedule. The cards were sold in 10-card packs for a suggested retail price of $1.29. Against a background featuring an American flag, the fronts of the regular cards display a color action cutout of each athlete in her U.S.A. Basketball uniform. The backs provide complete biographical information and collegiate statistics. The horizontal fronts of the "Profiles" cards have a color closeup and a gold foil-stamped facsimile autograph. The backs list a variety of questions and answers that provide a glimpse into the players' personal lives.

COMPLETE SET (24) 10.00 25.00
1 Jennifer Azzi 1.25 3.00
2 Ruthie Bolton 1.00 2.50
3 Teresa Edwards .75 2.00
4 Lisa Leslie 1.50 4.00
5 Rebecca Lobo 1.25 3.00
6 Katrina McClain .20 .50
7 Nikki McCray 1.25 3.00
8 Carla McGhee .20 .50
9 Dawn Staley 1.25 3.00
10 Katy Steding .20 .50
11 Sheryl Swoopes 2.00 5.00
12 Team Photo 1.25 3.00
13 Jennifer Azzi PRO .60 1.50
14 Ruthie Bolton PRO .50 1.25
15 Teresa Edwards PRO .40 1.00
16 Lisa Leslie PRO .75 2.00
17 Rebecca Lobo PRO .60 1.50
18 Katrina McClain PRO .08 .25
19 Nikki McCray PRO .60 1.50
20 Carla McGhee PRO .08 .25
21 Dawn Staley PRO .60 1.50
22 Katy Steding PRO .08 .25
23 Sheryl Swoopes PRO 1.00 2.50
24 Tara VanDerveer CO .20 .50

2001 Topps Wilkins Oversized

This oversized card was given to each fan coming through the turnstile for the 2000-01 Hawks-Clippers game. This exclusive-issued Topps card, lists Wilkins' Atanta Hawks career stats on the back.

NNO Dominique Wilkins 2.00 5.00

2001-02 Topps Xpectations Promos

Released with the press material, this six card promo set debuts the future design of the Topps Xpectations set which was to be released in November 2001.

COMPLETE SET (6) .75 2.00
P1 Antawn Jamison .30 .75
P2 Paul Pierce .30 .75
P3 Larry Hughes .25 .60
P4 Derek Anderson .20 .50
P5 Bonzi Wells .20 .50
P6 Wally Szczerbiak .25 .60

2001-02 Topps Xpectations

Released in November of 2001, this 151-card base set includes 101 veterans and 50 rookies. The 100 veteran cards were selected by NBA Drafts (1997-2000) and NBA Drafts (before 1997). The 50 rookie cards feature reel game footage and carry the Xpectations "Rookie Card" logo. Cards of six of the rookies have been selected to be sequentially numbered to 250. The cards are standard size and are set on borderless cards. Xpectations was issued in 10 box cases with 20 packs per box and six cards per pack which carried a suggested retail price of $6.00.

COMP.SET w/o SP's (145) 50.00 120.00
ROOKIES/250 STATED ODDS 1:191
1 Baron Davis .30 .75
2 Jason Terry .30 .75
3 Paul Pierce .30 .75
4 Ron Mercer .20 .50
5 Dirk Nowitzki .50 1.25
6 Marc Jackson .20 .50
7 Cuttino Mobley .20 .50
8 Al Harrington .25 .60
9 Keyon Dooling .20 .50
10 Mark Madsen .20 .50
11 Jumaine Jones .20 .50
12 Shawn Marion .25 .60
13 Mike Bibby .30 .75
14 Antonio Daniels .20 .50
15 Vince Carter .50 1.25
16 Stromile Swift .20 .50
17 Courtney Alexander .20 .50
18 Desmond Mason .25 .60
19 Hedo Turkoglu .25 .60
20 Speedy Claxton .20 .50
21 Lavor Postell .20 .50
22 Chauncey Billups .30 .75
23 Eddie House .20 .50
24 Maurice Taylor .20 .50
25 Lamar Odom .25 .60
26 Antawn Jamison .30 .75
27 Raef LaFrentz .20 .50
28 Marcus Fizer .20 .50
29 Chris Mihm .20 .50
30 Eddie Robinson .20 .50
31 Mark Blount .20 .50
32 DerMarr Johnson .20 .50
33 Wang Zhizhi .25 .60
34 Danny Fortson .20 .50
35 Elton Brand .30 .75
36 Anthony Carter .20 .50
37 Wally Szczerbiak .25 .60
38 Mike Miller .25 .60
39 Bonzi Wells .20 .50
40 Tim Duncan .60 1.50
41 Ruben Patterson .20 .50
42 Keon Clark .20 .50
43 Jason Williams .25 .60
44 Richard Hamilton .25 .60
45 Scott Padgett .20 .50
46 Derek Anderson .20 .50
47 Keith Van Horn .25 .60
48 Tim Thomas .20 .50
49 Jonathan Bender .20 .50
50 Tracy McGrady .50 1.25
51 Tyronn Lue .20 .50
52 Austin Croshere .20 .50
53 James Posey .20 .50
54 Mateen Cleaves .20 .50
55 Matt Harpring .20 .50
56 Calvin Booth .20 .50
57 Quentin Richardson .25 .60
58 Joel Przybilla .20 .50
59 Kenyon Martin .30 .75
60 Iakovos Tsakalidis .20 .50
61 Peja Stojakovic .30 .75
62 Shammond Williams .20 .50
63 Alvin Williams .20 .50
64 Jahidi White .20 .50
65 Morris Peterson .20 .50
66 Larry Hughes .25 .60
67 Andre Miller .25 .60
68 Jamaal Magloire .20 .50
69 Steve Francis .25 .60
70 Todd MacCulloch .20 .50
71 Rashard Lewis .30 .75
72 Michael Dickerson .20 .50
73 Nazr Mohammed .20 .50
74 Jamal Crawford .30 .75
75 Darius Miles .20 .50
76 Allen Iverson .60 1.50
77 Shaquille O'Neal .75 2.00
78 Michael Finley .30 .75
79 Antonio McDyess .25 .60
80 Jerry Stackhouse .25 .60
81 Chris Webber .30 .75
82 Eddie Jones .25 .60
83 Reggie Miller .30 .75
84 Antoine Walker .25 .60
85 Latrell Sprewell .25 .60
86 Alonzo Mourning .40 1.00
87 Jalen Rose .25 .60
88 Ray Allen .30 .75
89 Gary Payton .30 .75
90 Jason Kidd .50 1.25
91 Stephon Marbury .25 .60
92 Kobe Bryant 1.25 3.00
93 Grant Hill .40 1.00
94 Karl Malone .40 1.00
95 John Stockton .40 1.00
96 Anfernee Hardaway .50 1.25
97 Rasheed Wallace .30 .75
98 Hakeem Olajuwon .40 1.00
99 Shareef Abdur-Rahim .25 .60
100 Kevin Garnett .50 1.25
101 Kwame Brown/250 RC 6.00 15.00
102 Tyson Chandler RC 1.25 3.00
103 Pau Gasol RC 2.50 6.00
104 Eddy Curry RC .75 2.00
105 J.Richardson/250 RC 8.00 20.00
106 Shane Battier/250 RC 12.00 30.00
107 Eddie Griffin RC .60 1.50
108 DeSagana Diop RC .60 1.50
109 Rodney White RC .50 1.25
110 Joe Johnson/250 RC 8.00 20.00
111 Kedrick Brown RC .50 1.25
112 Vladimir Radmanovic RC .75 2.00
113 Richard Jefferson RC 1.25 3.00
114 Troy Murphy/250 RC 6.00 15.00
115 Steven Hunter RC .60 1.50
116 Kirk Haston RC .50 1.25
117 Michael Bradley RC .50 1.25
118 Jason Collins RC .60 1.50
119 Zach Randolph/250 RC 10.00 25.00
120 Brendan Haywood RC .75 2.00
121 Joseph Forte RC .50 1.25
122 Jeryl Sasser RC .50 1.25
123 Brandon Armstrong RC .50 1.25
124 Gerald Wallace RC 1.00 2.50
125 Samuel Dalembert RC .75 2.00
126 Jamaal Tinsley RC .75 2.00
127 Tony Parker RC 3.00 8.00
128 Trenton Hassell RC .60 1.50
129 Gilbert Arenas RC 1.25 3.00
130 Raja Bell RC 1.00 2.50
131 Will Solomon RC .75 2.00
132 Terence Morris RC .75 2.00
133 Brian Scalabrine RC .75 2.00
134 Jeff Trepagnier RC .50 1.25
135 Damone Brown RC .50 1.25
136 Carlos Arroyo RC 4.00 10.00
137 Earl Watson RC .75 2.00
138 Jamison Brewer RC .75 2.00
139 Bobby Simmons RC .75 2.00
140 Andrei Kirilenko RC 1.25 3.00
141 Zeljko Rebraca RC .75 2.00
142 Sean Lampley RC .75 2.00
143 Loren Woods RC .50 1.25
144 Alton Ford RC .75 2.00
145 Antonis Fotsis RC .50 1.25
146 Charlie Bell RC .75 2.00
147 R.Boumtje-Boumtje RC .75 2.00
148 Jarron Collins RC .75 2.00
149 Kenny Satterfield RC .50 1.25
150 Alvin Jones RC .60 1.50
151 Michael Jordan 2.50 6.00

2001-02 Topps Xpectations Autographs

This 42-card insert set is randomly inserted in packs at a rate of 1:13. The set features signed cards of NBA athletes who are quickly on their way to becoming elite ranked all-stars. The cards are standard size and have solid black borders on two of its four sides. There is a color action shot in the center. The Certified Autograph Issue logo is in the lower right-hand corner and the featured player's name and team name is in the lower left-hand corner.

STATED ODDS 1:13
TXAAD Antonio Daniels 4.00 10.00
TXAAJ Antawn Jamison 5.00 12.00
TXAAM Andre Miller 4.00 10.00
TXABD Baron Davis 6.00 15.00
TXABH Brendan Haywood 4.00 10.00
TXABJ Bobby Jackson 4.00 10.00
TXACA Courtney Alexander 4.00 10.00
TXACB Chauncey Billups 6.00 15.00
TXADB Damone Brown 2.50 6.00
TXADH Donnell Harvey 4.00 10.00
TXAEB Erick Barkley 4.00 10.00
TXAEC Eddy Curry 4.00 10.00
TXAGA Gilbert Arenas 6.00 15.00
TXAGW Gerald Wallace 5.00 12.00
TXAHT Hedo Turkoglu 4.00 10.00
TXAIT Iakovos Tsakalidis 4.00 10.00
TXAJB Jonathan Bender 4.00 10.00
TXAJF Joseph Forte 2.50 6.00
TXAJO Jermaine O'Neal 6.00 15.00
TXAJT Jason Terry 5.00 12.00
TXAKB Kwame Brown 4.00 10.00
TXAKD Keyon Dooling 4.00 10.00
TXALP Lavor Postell 4.00 10.00
TXALW Loren Woods 2.50 6.00
TXAMB Mike Bibby 5.00 12.00
TXAMD Michael Doleac 4.00 10.00
TXAMJ Marc Jackson 4.00 10.00
TXAPS Peja Stojakovic 6.00 15.00
TXARH Richard Hamilton 5.00 12.00
TXARL Raef LaFrentz 4.00 10.00
TXARM Roshown McLeod 4.00 10.00
TXASB Shane Battier 8.00 20.00
TXASM Shawn Marion 5.00 12.00
TXATT Tim Thomas 4.00 10.00
TXAVR Vladimir Radmanovic 4.00 10.00
TXAZR Zach Randolph 4.00 10.00
TXAAJO Alvin Jones 3.00 8.00
TXADTM Desmond Mason 4.00 10.00
TXAETB Elton Brand 5.00 12.00
TXAJTR Jeff Trepagnier 2.50 6.00
TXAKBR Kedrick Brown 2.50 6.00

2001-02 Topps Xpectations Bowman's Best

With the cancellation of the Bowman's best brand in 2001-02, Topps inserted some of the better inserts that were slated for the Bowman's Best set. This nine card set features both jersey and autograph cards of Magic Johnson, Shaquille O'Neal, and Kareem Abdul-Jabbar.

RANDOM INSERTS IN PACKS
FF1 Magic Johnson JSY 12.00 30.00
FF2 Kareem Abdul-Jabbar JSY 15.00 40.00
FF3 Shaquille O'Neal JSY 15.00 40.00
FF4 Kareem/Magic JSY 40.00 100.00
FF5 Shaq/Kareem JSY 30.00 80.00
FF6 Shaq/Magic JSY 30.00 60.00
FF7 Kareem/Shaq/Magic JSY/50 60.00 120.00
FFA1 K.Abdul-Jabbar JSY AU/50 100.00 200.00
FFA1A Magic Johnson JSY AU/50 75.00 150.00
FFA3 S.O'Neal JSY AU/50 75.00 150.00
FFA4 Kareem/Magic JSY AU/25 125.00 250.00

2001-02 Topps Xpectations Changing of the Guard

Randomly inserted in packs at a rate of 1:10, this 10-card insert set features the top 10 guards in the NBA.

COMPLETE SET (10) 8.00 20.00
STATED ODDS 1:10
CG1 Allen Iverson 1.50 4.00
CG2 Kobe Bryant 3.00 8.00
CG3 Vince Carter 1.25 3.00
CG4 Tracy McGrady 1.25 3.00
CG5 Jason Kidd 1.25 3.00
CG6 Steve Francis .60 1.50
CG7 Stephon Marbury .60 1.50
CG8 Gary Payton .75 2.00
CG9 Michael Finley .75 2.00
CG10 Baron Davis .75 2.00

2001-02 Topps Xpectations Class Challenge

Randomly inserted in packs at a rate of 1:9, this 28-card insert set is horizontally designed and measures standard size. The cards feature swatches of game-worn warm-ups from the 2000/01 NBA Rookie Challenge All-Star Weekends. The card fronts carry an "X" design with the player's name running across one arm of the "X". The Topps logo is found in the upper left-hand corner. A color action shot of the player is also featured.

STATED ODDS 1:9
CCAG Adrian Griffin 2.00 5.00
CCAM Andre Miller 2.50 6.00
CCBD Baron Davis 3.00 8.00
CCCM Cuttino Mobley 2.00 5.00
CCDM Darius Miles 2.00 5.00
CCDN Dirk Nowitzki 5.00 12.00
CCEB Elton Brand 3.00 8.00
CCJP James Posey 2.00 5.00
CCJT Jason Terry 3.00 8.00
CCJW Jason Williams 2.50 6.00
CCKM Kenyon Martin 3.00 8.00
CCLO Lamar Odom 2.50 6.00
CCMB Mike Bibby 3.00 8.00
CCMC Mateen Cleaves 2.00 5.00
CCMD Michael Dickerson 2.00 5.00
CCMJ Marc Jackson 2.00 5.00
CCMM Mike Miller 2.50 6.00
CCMO Michael Olowokandi 2.00 5.00
CCMP Morris Peterson 2.00 5.00
CCPP Paul Pierce 3.00 8.00
CCQR Quentin Richardson 2.50 6.00
CCRH Richard Hamilton 2.50 6.00
CCRL Raef LaFrentz 2.00 5.00
CCSF Steve Francis 2.50 6.00
CCSJ Stephen Jackson 2.50 6.00
CCSM Shawn Marion 2.50 6.00
CCTM Todd MacCulloch 2.00 5.00
CCWS Wally Szczerbiak 2.50 6.00

2001-02 Topps Xpectations Class Challenge Autographs

PRINT RUNS LISTED BELOW
CCAEB Elton Brand/43 25.00 60.00

CCAJT Jason Terry/31 25.00 60.00
CCARH Richard Hamilton/32 25.00 60.00
CCARL Raef LaFrentz/45 8.00 20.00
CCASM Shawn Marion/31 30.00 80.00

2001-02 Topps Xpectations First Shot

Randomly inserted in packs at a rate of 1:17, this 25-card insert set features top draft picks from the 2001 NBA draft, a photo of each in their respective team's jersey, and a swatch of jersey.
STATED ODDS 1:17
FS1 Kwame Brown 2.00 5.00
FS2 Tyson Chandler 3.00 8.00
FS3 Pau Gasol 6.00 15.00
FS4 Eddy Curry 2.00 5.00
FS5 Jason Richardson 2.50 6.00
FS6 Shane Battier 4.00 10.00
FS7 Eddie Griffin 1.50 4.00
FS8 DeSagana Diop 1.50 4.00
FS9 Rodney White 1.25 3.00
FS10 Joe Johnson 2.50 6.00
FS11 Kedrick Brown 1.25 3.00
FS12 Vladimir Radmanovic 2.00 5.00
FS13 Richard Jefferson 3.00 8.00
FS14 Troy Murphy 2.00 5.00
FS15 Steven Hunter 1.50 4.00
FS16 Kirk Haston 1.25 3.00
FS17 Michael Bradley 1.25 3.00
FS18 Zach Randolph 3.00 8.00
FS19 Brendan Haywood 2.00 5.00
FS20 Joseph Forte 1.25 3.00
FS21 Jeryl Sasser 1.25 3.00
FS22 Brandon Armstrong 1.25 3.00
FS23 Primoz Brezec 2.00 5.00
FS24 Jamaal Tinsley 2.00 5.00
FS25 Tony Parker 8.00 20.00

2001-02 Topps Xpectations Forward Thinking

Randomly inserted in packs at a rate of 1:10, this 10-card insert set honors the integral position of the NBA Forward. The set is borderless and comes on standard size cards. The card design is a color action shot of the featured player with a multiple linear background. The set name, team logo, and player name are all found at the bottom of the card. The Topps logo is found in the upper left-hand corner.
COMPLETE SET (10) 8.00 20.00
STATED ODDS 1:10
FT1 Chris Webber 1.00 2.50
FT2 Kevin Garnett 1.50 4.00
FT3 Lamar Odom .75 2.00
FT4 Tim Duncan 2.00 5.00
FT5 Dirk Nowitzki 1.50 4.00
FT6 Karl Malone 1.25 3.00
FT7 Paul Pierce 1.00 2.50
FT8 Shawn Marion .75 2.00
FT9 Scottie Pippen 1.50 4.00
FT10 Darius Miles .60 1.50

2001-02 Topps Xpectations Future Features

Randomly inserted in packs at a rate of 1:31, this 10-card insert set is horizontally designed and measures standard size. The cards feature swatches of authentic NBA All-Star game-worn shooting shirts. The card fronts carry an "X" design. The Topps logo is found in the upper left-hand corner. A color action shot of the player is also featured along with his name and team logo.
STATED ODDS 1:31
FFAM Andre Miller 3.00 8.00
FFDM Darius Miles 2.50 6.00
FFDN Dirk Nowitzki 6.00 15.00
FFEB Elton Brand 4.00 10.00
FFJT Jason Terry 4.00 10.00
FFPP Paul Pierce 4.00 10.00
FFRH Richard Hamilton 3.00 8.00
FFRW Rasheed Wallace 4.00 10.00
FFSF Steve Francis 3.00 8.00
FFSM Shawn Marion 3.00 8.00

2001-02 Topps Xpectations Future Features Autographs

STATED ODDS 1:812
FFAEB Elton Brand/42 20.00 50.00
FFAJT Jason Terry/31 20.00 50.00
FFARH Richard Hamilton/32 20.00 50.00
FFASM Shawn Marion/31 30.00 80.00

2001-02 Topps Xpectations In The Center

This six-card insert set is randomly inserted in packs at a rate of 1:17. The standard size cards are borderless and pay tribute to legendary NBA centers. The cards feature a center court design with a color action shot of the featured player "In the Center". The player name and team name are found at the bottom and the Topps logo is found in the upper left-hand corner.
COMPLETE SET (6) 4.00 10.00
STATED ODDS 1:17
IC1 Shaquille O'Neal 2.50 6.00
IC2 Alonzo Mourning 1.25 3.00
IC3 Jermaine O'Neal .75 2.00
IC4 Hakeem Olajuwon 1.25 3.00
IC5 David Robinson 1.50 4.00
IC6 Dikembe Mutombo 1.00 2.50

2002-03 Topps Xpectations

Released in November 2002, Topps Xpectations was issued as a 178-card set divided up into 100 base cards, 53 Rookie cards, where card numbers 134-153 are sequentially numbered to 500, and 24 Xceeding Xpectations cards (154-178) which were inserted one in 14 packs and are sequentially numbered to 750. All base cards feature a colored background with an "X" behind the player photo and are highlighted with gold foil. The Xceeding Xpectations cards have a true life background inside the "X" and white around it. Xpectations was packaged in 20-pack boxes where each pack contained five cards and carried a suggested retail price of $6.00.
COMPLETE SET (178) 125.00 300.00
COMP.SET w/o SP's (100) 10.00 25.00
134-153 PRINT RUN 500 SER.#'d SETS
154-178 PRINT RUN 750 SER.#'d SETS
1 Darius Miles .15 .40
2 Jason Williams .20 .50
3 Speedy Claxton .15 .40
4 Eduardo Najera .15 .40
5 Chris Mihm .15 .40
6 Eddie Robinson .15 .40
7 Lee Nailon .15 .40
8 Joseph Forte .15 .40
9 Jason Terry .20 .50
10 Vince Carter .40 1.00
11 Matt Harpring .15 .40
12 Bonzi Wells .15 .40
13 Mike Bibby .25 .60
14 Jerome James .15 .40
15 Morris Peterson .15 .40
16 Jarron Collins .15 .40
17 Brendan Haywood .15 .40
18 Dermarr Johnson .15 .40
19 Kirk Haston .15 .40
20 Paul Pierce .25 .60
21 Eddy Curry .15 .40
22 Ricky Davis .20 .50
23 James Posey .15 .40
24 Zeljko Rebraca .15 .40
25 Jason Richardson .25 .60
26 Ron Artest .25 .60
27 Jonathan Bender .15 .40
28 Elton Brand .25 .60
29 Stromile Swift .15 .40
30 Steve Francis .20 .50
31 Devean George .15 .40
32 Eddie House .15 .40
33 Loren Woods .15 .40
34 Richard Jefferson .25 .60
35 Mike Miller .20 .50
36 Joe Johnson .20 .50
37 Zach Randolph .20 .50
38 Peja Stojakovic .25 .60
39 Predrag Drobnjak .15 .40
40 Kwame Brown .15 .40
41 DeShawn Stevenson .15 .40
42 Desmond Mason .20 .50
43 Stephen Jackson .20 .50
44 Ruben Patterson .15 .40
45 Samuel Dalembert .15 .40
46 Pat Garrity .15 .40
47 Jason Collins .15 .40
48 Marc Jackson .15 .40
49 Rafer Alston .15 .40
50 Shawn Marion .20 .50
51 Joel Przybilla .15 .40
52 Shane Battier .25 .60
53 Quentin Richardson .20 .50
54 Jamaal Tinsley .15 .40
55 Cuttino Mobley .15 .40
56 Antawn Jamison .25 .60
57 Chucky Atkins .15 .40
58 Raef Lafrentz .15 .40
59 Jumaine Jones .15 .40
60 Dirk Nowitzki .40 1.00
61 Marcus Fizer .15 .40
62 Kedrick Brown .15 .40
63 Nazr Mohammed .15 .40
64 Jamaal Magloire .15 .40
65 Tyson Chandler .25 .60
66 Andre Miller .20 .50
67 Wang Zhizhi .15 .40
68 Mengke Bateer .15 .40
69 Gilbert Arenas .25 .60
70 Baron Davis .20 .50
71 Lamar Odom .20 .50
72 Mark Madsen .15 .40
73 Pau Gasol .30 .75
74 Anthony Carter .15 .40
75 Wally Szczerbiak .20 .50
76 Todd MacCulloch .15 .40
77 Steven Hunter .15 .40
78 Iakovos Tsakalidis .15 .40
79 Ruben Boumtje-Boumtje .15 .40
80 Gerald Wallace .20 .50
81 Vladimir Radmanovic .15 .40
82 Keon Clark .15 .40
83 Andrei Kirilenko .25 .60
84 Richard Hamilton .20 .50
85 Trenton Hassell .15 .40
86 Donnell Harvey .15 .40
87 Rodney White .15 .40
88 Troy Murphy .20 .50
89 Terence Morris .15 .40
90 Al Harrington .20 .50
91 Michael Redd .20 .50
92 Kenyon Martin .20 .50
93 Lavor Postell .15 .40
94 Jeryl Sasser .15 .40
95 Hedo Turkoglu .20 .50
96 Tony Parker .30 .75
97 Rashard Lewis .25 .60
98 Michael Bradley .15 .40
99 Courtney Alexander .15 .40
100 Eddie Griffin .15 .40
101 Yao Ming RC 1.50 4.00
102 Dan Gadzuric RC .60 1.50
103 Mike Dunleavy RC .75 2.00
104 Drew Gooden RC .75 2.00
105 Nikoloz Tskitishvili RC .50 1.25
106 Roger Mason RC .60 1.50
107 Nene Hilario RC .75 2.00
108 Chris Wilcox RC .60 1.50
109 Rod Grizzard RC .50 1.25
110 Chris Owens RC .50 1.25
111 Jared Jeffries RC .60 1.50
112 Efthimios Rentzias RC .50 1.25
113 Marcus Haislip RC .60 1.50
114 Fred Jones RC .60 1.50
115 Bostjan Nachbar RC .60 1.50
116 Jiri Welsch RC .60 1.50
117 Jannero Pargo RC .50 1.25
118 Curtis Borchardt RC .50 1.25
119 Ryan Humphrey RC .60 1.50
120 Raul Lopez RC .75 2.00
121 Cezary Trybanski RC .75 2.00
122 Predrag Savovic RC .60 1.50
123 Tayshaun Prince RC 1.00 2.50
124 Frank Williams RC .50 1.25
125 John Salmons RC .75 2.00
126 Chris Jefferies RC .50 1.25
127 Luke Recker RC .75 2.00
128 Tamar Slay RC .50 1.25
129 Matt Barnes RC 1.00 2.50
130 Rasual Butler RC .75 2.00
131 Vincent Yarbrough RC .50 1.25
132 Junior Harrington RC .50 1.25
133 Carlos Boozer RC .75 2.00
134 DaJuan Wagner/500 RC 2.00 5.00
135 Jay Williams/500 RC 2.50 6.00
136 Amare Stoudemire/500 RC 3.00 8.00
137 Caron Butler/500 RC 2.50 6.00
138 Melvin Ely/500 RC 2.00 5.00
139 Juan Dixon/500 RC 2.50 6.00
140 Kareem Rush/500 RC 2.00 5.00
141 Qyntel Woods/500 RC 2.00 5.00
142 Casey Jacobsen/500 RC 2.00 5.00
143 Robert Archibald/500 RC 1.50 4.00
144 Tito Maddox/500 RC 1.50 4.00
145 Ronald Murray/500 RC 2.50 6.00
146 Sam Clancy/500 RC 2.00 5.00
147 Dan Dickau/500 RC 2.00 5.00
148 Mehmet Okur/500 RC 2.50 6.00
149 Marko Jaric/500 2.50 6.00
150 Gordan Giricek/500 RC 2.50 6.00
151 Manu Ginobili/500 RC 6.00 15.00
152 J.R. Bremer/500 RC 1.50 4.00
153 Corsley Edwards/500 RC 2.00 5.00
154 Michael Jordan XX 8.00 20.00
155 Allen Iverson XX 1.50 4.00
156 Shaquille O'Neal XX 2.50 6.00
157 Tim Duncan XX 2.00 5.00
158 Tracy McGrady XX 1.50 4.00
159 Kevin Garnett XX 1.50 4.00
160 Chris Webber XX 1.00 2.50
161 Alonzo Mourning XX 1.25 3.00
162 Antoine Walker XX .75 2.00
163 Latrell Sprewell XX .75 2.00
164 Eddie Jones XX .75 2.00
165 Kobe Bryant XX 4.00 10.00
166 Allan Houston XX .75 2.00
167 Ray Allen XX 1.00 2.50
168 Gary Payton XX 1.00 2.50
169 Antonio McDyess XX .75 2.00
170 Jason Kidd XX 1.50 4.00
171 Jerry Stackhouse XX .75 2.00
172 Stephon Marbury XX .75 2.00
173 Karl Malone XX 1.25 3.00
174 Reggie Miller XX 1.00 2.50
175 Shareef Abdur-Rahim XX .75 2.00
176 Rasheed Wallace XX 1.00 2.50
177 John Stockton XX 1.25 3.00
178 Grant Hill XX 1.25 3.00

2002-03 Topps Xpectations Parallel

*1-100 STARS: .6X TO 1.5X BASE CARD HI
*101-133 RCs: .6X TO 1.5X BASE CARD HI
*134-153 RCs: .2X TO .5X BASE CARD HI
*154-178 STARS: .15X TO .4X BASE CARD HI
STATED ODDS 1 PER PACK

2002-03 Topps Xpectations Parallel Xtra

*1-100 STARS: 6X TO 15X BASE CARD HI
*101-133 RCs: 2.5X TO 6X BASE CARD HI
*134-153 RCs: .75X TO 2X BASE CARD HI
*154-178 STARS: 1.5X TO 4X BASE CARD HI
PRINT RUN 99 SER.#'d SETS

2002-03 Topps Xpectations Autographs

Xpectations autographs were divided up into five different groups and were inserted at the following rates: Group A at one in 177 packs, Group B at one in 312 packs, Group C at one in 42 packs, Group D at one in 412 packs and Group E at one in 332 packs. Each card places a full color player action photo in the background with the lower half of the card faded in an X shape so the autograph stands out. All cards are enahanced with the Topps Certified Autograph Issue stamp and gold foil highlights.
GROUP A ODDS 1:117; B ODDS 1:312
GROUP C ODDS 1:42; D ODDS 1:412
GROUP E ODDS 1:332
XAAH Al Harrington C 4.00 10.00
XACM Corey Maggette E 3.00 8.00
XACBC Curtis Borchardt E 2.50 6.00
XACBO Carlos Boozer C 4.00 10.00
XADB Damone Brown A 4.00 10.00
XADG Drew Gooden A 4.00 10.00
XADH Donnell Harvey A 4.00 10.00
XADW DaJuan Wagner C 3.00 8.00
XAEC Eddy Curry C 4.00 10.00
XAFW Frank Williams B 2.50 6.00
XAHT Hedo Turkoglu E 3.00 8.00
XAJB Jonathan Bender B 4.00 10.00
XAJF Joseph Forte E 4.00 10.00
XAJJ Joe Johnson A 8.00 20.00
XAJT Iakovos Tsakalidis A 4.00 10.00
XAJJE Jared Jeffries C 3.00 8.00
XAJTR Jeff Trepagnier A 4.00 10.00
XAKBR Kedrick Brown C 2.50 6.00
XALW Loren Woods A 4.00 10.00
XAMD Mike Dunleavy C 4.00 10.00
XAMJ Marc Jackson A 4.00 10.00
XANT Nikoloz Tskitishvili C 2.50 6.00
XASB Shane Battier C 5.00 12.00
XASM Shawn Marion A 3.00 8.00
XATD Tim Duncan B 250.00 500.00
XATM Troy Murphy C 3.00 8.00
XATT Tim Thomas A 4.00 10.00
XAVY Vincent Yarbrough C 2.50 6.00
XAYM Yao Ming C 30.00 80.00
XAZR Zach Randolph D 6.00 15.00

2002-03 Topps Xpectations Class Challenge Relics

Xpectations Class Challenge Relics was divided up into four different groups and inserted as follows: Group A at one in 298 packs, Group B at one in 30 packs and group C and D combined at one per box. The set showcases young NBA talent and places a portrait style photograph on the left and a swatch of game-worn memorabilia on the right. Brandon Haywood and Shane Battier signed versions of these cards that were inserted at the rate of one in 3804.
GROUP A ODDS: 1:298; B ODDS 1:30
AUTO's NOT PRICED DUE TO SCARCITY
CCAK Andrei Kirilenko D 3.00 8.00
CCBH Brendan Haywood D 2.00 5.00
CCCM Chris Mihm D 2.00 5.00
CCDM Darius Miles D 2.00 5.00
CCJR Jason Richardson D 3.00 8.00
CCKM Kenyon Martin D 2.50 6.00
CCLN Lee Nailon D 2.00 5.00
CCMF Marcus Fizer D 2.00 5.00
CCMM Mike Miller D 2.50 6.00
CCPG Pau Gasol C 4.00 10.00
CCQR Quentin Richardson C 2.50 6.00
CCSB Shane Battier A 3.00 8.00
CCTP Tony Parker B 4.00 10.00
CCZR Zeljko Rebraca D 2.00 5.00

2002-03 Topps Xpectations First Shot Relics

ndomly inserted in packs at the rate of one in 10, this 25-card set places a full-color action photo of the player on the right and a swatch of jersey worn at the NBA Photo Shoot on the left. Background colors on the left side of the card are white and gold.
STATED ODDS 1:10
FSAS Amare Stoudemire 4.00 10.00
FSCB Caron Butler 3.00 8.00
FSCB Carlos Boozer 3.00 8.00
FSCW Chris Wilcox 2.50 6.00
FSCJA Casey Jacobsen 2.50 6.00
FSCJE Chris Jefferies 2.00 5.00
FSDW DaJuan Wagner 2.50 6.00
FSDGO Drew Gooden 3.00 8.00
FSFJ Fred Jones 2.50 6.00
FSJD Juan Dixon 3.00 8.00
FSJJ Jared Jeffries 2.50 6.00
FSJS John Salmons 3.00 8.00
FSKR Kareem Rush 2.50 6.00
FSMD Mike Dunleavy 3.00 8.00
FSME Melvin Ely 2.50 6.00
FSMH Marcus Haislip 2.50 6.00
FSNH Nene Hilario 3.00 8.00
FSNT Nikoloz Tskitishvili 2.00 5.00
FSPS Predrag Savovic 2.50 6.00
FSQW Qyntel Woods 2.50 6.00
FSRH Ryan Humphrey 2.50 6.00
FSSC Sam Clancy 2.50 6.00
FSSL Steve Logan 3.00 8.00
FSTP Tayshaun Prince 4.00 10.00
FSVY Vincent Yarbrough 2.00 5.00

2002-03 Topps Xpectations Future Features Relics

Inserted overall at the rate of one in 40, this 15-card set places a full-color player photo on the right of the card and a swatch of game-worn material on the left. The background is composed of different color circles coming from around the player photo.
STATED ODDS 1:40
FFAM Andre Miller C 1.50 4.00
FFBH Brendan Haywood C 1.25 3.00
FFDN Dirk Nowitzki A 3.00 8.00
FFGW Gerald Wallace C 1.50 4.00
FFJJ Joe Johnson A 1.50 4.00
FFMM Mike Miller C 1.50 4.00
FFPP Paul Pierce C 2.00 5.00
FFPS Peja Stojakovic C 2.00 5.00
FFQR Quentin Richardson B 1.50 4.00
FFRL Raef LaFrentz A 1.25 3.00
FFSF Steve Francis A 1.50 4.00
FFSM Stephon Marbury C 1.50 4.00
FFSN Steve Nash A 2.50 6.00
FFSDM Shawn Marion C 1.50 4.00
FFWS Wally Szczerbiak C 1.50 4.00

2002-03 Topps Xpectations Future Features Relics Autographs

Inserted in packs at the rate of one in 1259, this five card set parallels the design of the Xpectations Future Features Relics set enhanced with authentic player autographs.
STATED ODDS 1:1259
FFAGW Gerald Wallace 10.00 25.00
FFAJJ Joe Johnson 10.00 25.00
FFAPS Peja Stojakovic 30.00 60.00

2002-03 Topps Xpectations Xtra Threads Relics

Inserted in packs overall at the rate of one in 25, this 16-card set places full color player action photography on the right side of the card and an "X" shaped swatch of memorabilia on the left. Background colors are set to match the featured player's team colors.
STATED ODDS 1:25
XTAH Anfernee Hardaway C 4.00 10.00
XTAI Allen Iverson C 4.00 10.00
XTAHO Allan Houston A 2.00 5.00
XTCW Chris Webber C 2.50 6.00
XTGR Glenn Robinson C 2.00 5.00
XTJK Jason Kidd C 4.00 10.00
XTJO Jermaine O'Neal C 2.00 5.00
XTMJ Michael Finley C 2.50 6.00
XTMO Michael Olowokandi C 1.50 4.00
XTNV Nick Van Exel C 2.00 5.00
XTRA Ray Allen C 2.50 6.00
XTSN Steve Nash C 3.00 8.00
XTSO Shaquille O'Neal C 6.00 15.00
XTTD Tim Duncan C 5.00 12.00
XTTG Tom Gugliotta C 1.50 4.00
XTTM Tracy McGrady B 4.00 10.00

2010-11 Totally Certified

COMP.SET w/o RCs (150) 40.00 100.00
1-150 PRINT RUN 1849 SER.#'d SETS
JSY AU RC PRINT RUN 575 TO 599 SETS
UNPRICED BLACK PRINT RUN ONE SET
UNPRICED GREEN PRINT RUN 5 SETS
1 Andre Iguodala .60 1.50
2 Elton Brand .75 2.00
3 Jrue Holiday .75 2.00
4 Thaddeus Young .50 1.25
5 D.J. Augustin .50 1.25
6 Boris Diaw .60 1.50
7 Gerald Henderson .50 1.25
8 Stephen Jackson .60 1.50
9 Brandon Jennings .50 1.25
10 Andrew Bogut .60 1.50
11 John Salmons .60 1.50
12 Corey Maggette .60 1.50
13 Luc Mbah a Moute .50 1.25
14 Derrick Rose 1.00 2.50
15 Carlos Boozer .60 1.50
16 Luol Deng .60 1.50
17 Joakim Noah .60 1.50
18 Taj Gibson .60 1.50
19 Antawn Jamison .60 1.50
20 Daniel Gibson .60 1.50
21 Baron Davis .60 1.50
22 Anderson Varejao .50 1.25
23 Paul Pierce .75 2.00
24 Rajon Rondo .75 2.00
25 Kevin Garnett 1.25 3.00
26 Shaquille O'Neal 1.50 4.00
27 Ray Allen .75 2.00
28 Troy Murphy .50 1.25
29 Blake Griffin .75 2.00
30 DeAndre Jordan .75 2.00
31 Eric Gordon .60 1.50
32 Ryan Gomes .50 1.25
33 Chris Kaman .60 1.50
34 Shane Battier .60 1.50
35 Marc Gasol .75 2.00
36 Zach Randolph .60 1.50
37 Rudy Gay .75 2.00
38 O.J. Mayo .50 1.25
39 Joe Johnson .60 1.50
40 Josh Smith .60 1.50
41 Al Horford .60 1.50
42 Jamal Crawford .75 2.00
43 Kirk Hinrich .60 1.50
44 Dwyane Wade 1.25 3.00
45 LeBron James 4.00 10.00
46 Chris Bosh .75 2.00
47 Eddie House .50 1.25
48 Mike Bibby .60 1.50
49 Chris Paul 1.00 2.50
50 David West .60 1.50
51 Trevor Ariza .50 1.25
52 Emeka Okafor .60 1.50
53 Jarrett Jack .60 1.50
54 Al Jefferson .60 1.50
55 Devin Harris .50 1.25
56 Andrei Kirilenko .60 1.50
57 Paul Millsap .60 1.50
58 Mehmet Okur .50 1.25
59 Tyreke Evans .50 1.25
60 Omri Casspi .50 1.25
61 Samuel Dalembert .50 1.25
62 Marcus Thornton .50 1.25
63 Beno Udrih .50 1.25
64 Amare Stoudemire .60 1.50
65 Carmelo Anthony 1.00 2.50
66 Chauncey Billups .75 2.00
67 Toney Douglas .50 1.25
68 Ronny Turiaf .50 1.25
69 Kobe Bryant 3.00 8.00
70 Pau Gasol .75 2.00
71 Ron Artest .75 2.00
72 Lamar Odom .60 1.50
73 Derek Fisher .60 1.50
74 Matt Barnes .50 1.25
75 Dwight Howard .60 1.50
76 Jameer Nelson .50 1.25
77 Gilbert Arenas .60 1.50
78 J.J. Redick .75 2.00
79 Hedo Turkoglu .60 1.50
80 Dirk Nowitzki 1.00 2.50
81 Caron Butler .60 1.50
82 Shawn Marion .60 1.50
83 Jason Terry .60 1.50
84 Tyson Chandler .60 1.50
85 Jason Kidd .75 2.00
86 Deron Williams .60 1.50
87 Brook Lopez .60 1.50
88 Anthony Morrow .50 1.25
89 Sasha Vujacic .50 1.25
90 Travis Outlaw .60 1.50
91 Nene .60 1.50
92 Raymond Felton .60 1.50
93 Chris Andersen .60 1.50
94 Danilo Gallinari .60 1.50
95 Al Harrington .60 1.50
96 Danny Granger .60 1.50
97 Darren Collison .60 1.50
98 Mike Dunleavy .50 1.25
99 T.J. Ford .50 1.25
100 Jeff Foster .50 1.25
101 Ben Gordon .60 1.50
102 Richard Hamilton .60 1.50
103 Tracy McGrady .75 2.00
104 Tayshaun Prince .60 1.50
105 Rodney Stuckey .60 1.50
106 DeMar DeRozan .75 2.00
107 Jose Calderon .50 1.25
108 Andrea Bargnani .60 1.50
109 Leandro Barbosa .60 1.50
110 Linas Kleiza .50 1.25
111 Kevin Martin .60 1.50
112 Luis Scola .60 1.50
113 Goran Dragic .60 1.50
114 Chase Budinger .50 1.25
115 Kyle Lowry .60 1.50
116 Tim Duncan 1.25 3.00
117 Tony Parker .75 2.00
118 Manu Ginobili .75 2.00
119 Richard Jefferson .60 1.50
120 DeJuan Blair .50 1.25
121 Steve Nash .75 2.00
122 Grant Hill 1.00 2.50
123 Channing Frye .60 1.50
124 Aaron Brooks .50 1.25
125 Vince Carter 1.00 2.50
126 Kevin Durant 2.00 5.00
127 Russell Westbrook 2.00 5.00
128 Serge Ibaka .60 1.50
129 James Harden 1.25 3.00
130 Kendrick Perkins .50 1.25
131 Kevin Love .75 2.00
132 Michael Beasley .50 1.25
133 Jonny Flynn .50 1.25
134 Anthony Randolph .50 1.25
135 Darko Milicic .50 1.25
136 LaMarcus Aldridge .75 2.00
137 Brandon Roy .75 2.00
138 Andre Miller .60 1.50
139 Rudy Fernandez .50 1.25
140 Marcus Camby .50 1.25
141 Monta Ellis .60 1.50
142 Stephen Curry 3.00 8.00
143 David Lee .50 1.25
144 Al Thornton .50 1.25
145 Dorell Wright .50 1.25
146 Josh Howard .60 1.50
147 Nick Young .60 1.50
148 JaVale McGee .60 1.50
149 Rashard Lewis .60 1.50
150 Yi Jianlian .60 1.50
151 John Wall/599 JSY AU RC 30.00 80.00
152 D.Cousins/593 JSY AU RC 20.00 50.00
153 Quincy Pondexter/585 JSY AU RC 3.00 8.00
154 G.Hayward/579 JSY AU RC 20.00 50.00
155 Al-Farouq Aminu/596 JSY AU RC 5.00 12.00
156 Ed Davis/599 JSY AU RC 3.00 8.00
157 G.Vasquez/599 JSY AU RC 4.00 10.00
158 Ekpe Udoh/599 JSY AU RC 3.00 8.00
159 Damion James/599 JSY AU RC 3.00 8.00
160 Landry Fields/599 JSY AU RC 4.00 10.00
161 Greg Monroe/599 JSY AU RC 6.00 15.00
162 Cole Aldrich/599 JSY AU RC 4.00 10.00
163 Evan Turner/599 JSY AU RC 4.00 10.00
164 Luke Babbitt/597 JSY AU RC 4.00 10.00
165 Derrick Favors/599 JSY AU RC 6.00 15.00
166 Xavier Henry/599 JSY AU RC 3.00 8.00
167 J.Crawford/595 JSY AU RC 4.00 10.00
168 Larry Sanders/583 JSY AU RC 3.00 8.00
169 Wesley Johnson/599 JSY AU RC 3.00 8.00
170 Eric Bledsoe/599 JSY AU RC 6.00 15.00
171 Avery Bradley/575 JSY AU RC 6.00 15.00
172 Daniel Orton/599 JSY AU RC 3.00 8.00
173 Paul George/599 JSY AU RC 40.00 100.00
174 J.Anderson/599 JSY AU RC 3.00 8.00
175 Elliot Williams/599 JSY AU RC 3.00 8.00
176 Dominique Jones/599 JSY AU RC 3.00 8.00
177 Dexter Pittman/599 JSY AU RC 3.00 8.00
178 Lazar Hayward/599 JSY AU RC 3.00 8.00
179 Trevor Booker/599 JSY AU RC 4.00 10.00
180 Luke Harangody/599 JSY AU RC 3.00 8.00
181 P.Patterson/599 JSY AU RC 4.00 10.00
182 H. Whiteside/565 JSY AU RC 10.00 25.00
183 Willie Warren/599 JSY AU RC 3.00 8.00
184 Terrico White/599 JSY AU RC 3.00 8.00
185 Andy Rautins/599 JSY AU RC 3.00 8.00

2010-11 Totally Certified Blue

*BLUE: .75X TO 2X BASE HI
STATED PRINT RUN 299 SER.#'d SETS
122 Grant Hill 4.00 10.00

2010-11 Totally Certified Blue Autographs

*BLUE RC AUTOGRAPHS: .5X TO 1.25X BASE HI
STATED PRINT RUN 32 TO 49 SER.#'d SETS
151 John Wall JSY AU/49 50.00 120.00
152 D.Cousins JSY AU/49 30.00 80.00
161 Greg Monroe JSY AU/49 12.00 30.00
170 Eric Bledsoe JSY AU/49 15.00 40.00
173 Paul George JSY AU/49 100.00 200.00

2010-11 Totally Certified Blue Materials

*BLUE MATERIALS: 2X TO 5X BASE HI
STATED PRINT RUN 49 TO 99 SER.#'d SETS
45 LeBron James/99 12.00 30.00
69 Kobe Bryant/99 12.00 30.00
122 Grant Hill/99 10.00 25.00
126 Kevin Durant/99 10.00 25.00

2010-11 Totally Certified Gold

*GOLD: 6X TO 15X BASE HI
STATED PRINT RUN 25 SER.#'d SETS
14 Derrick Rose 50.00 125.00
26 Shaquille O'Neal 30.00 80.00
45 LeBron James 75.00 200.00
126 Kevin Durant 50.00 125.00

2010-11 Totally Certified Gold Autographs

*GOLD RC AUTOGRAPHS: 1.25X TO 3X BASE HI
STATED PRINT RUN 10 TO 25 SER.#'d SETS
SOME UNPRICED DUE TO SCARCITY
1 Andre Iguodala/25 8.00 20.00
3 Jrue Holiday/25 10.00 25.00
5 D.J. Augustin/25 6.00 15.00
6 Boris Diaw/25 6.00 15.00
7 Gerald Henderson/25 6.00 15.00
8 Stephen Jackson/25 6.00 15.00
9 Brandon Jennings/25 12.00 30.00
10 Andrew Bogut/25 15.00 40.00
15 Carlos Boozer/25 12.00 30.00
17 Joakim Noah/25 15.00 40.00
18 Taj Gibson/25 10.00 25.00
19 Antawn Jamison/25 6.00 15.00
20 Daniel Gibson/25 6.00 15.00
21 Baron Davis/25 6.00 15.00
23 Paul Pierce/25 40.00 100.00
24 Rajon Rondo/25 10.00 25.00
27 Ray Allen/25 50.00 120.00
29 Blake Griffin/25 100.00 200.00
31 Eric Gordon/25 10.00 25.00
32 Ryan Gomes/25 6.00 15.00
34 Shane Battier/25 8.00 20.00
35 Marc Gasol/25 12.00 30.00
36 Zach Randolph/25 12.00 30.00
39 Joe Johnson/25 10.00 25.00
40 Josh Smith/25 8.00 20.00
41 Al Horford/25 6.00 15.00
46 Chris Bosh/25 25.00 60.00
48 Mike Bibby/25 10.00 25.00
51 Trevor Ariza/25 6.00 15.00
52 Emeka Okafor/25 6.00 15.00
54 Al Jefferson/25 6.00 15.00
55 Devin Harris/25 6.00 15.00
56 Andrei Kirilenko/25 6.00 15.00
59 Tyreke Evans/25 15.00 40.00
60 Omri Casspi/25 6.00 15.00
61 Samuel Dalembert/25 6.00 15.00
62 Marcus Thornton/25 6.00 15.00
63 Beno Udrih/25 6.00 15.00
66 Chauncey Billups/25 10.00 25.00
67 Toney Douglas/25 6.00 15.00
69 Kobe Bryant/25 100.00 200.00
72 Lamar Odom/25 12.00 30.00
73 Derek Fisher/25 20.00 50.00
78 J.J. Redick/25 10.00 25.00
79 Hedo Turkoglu/25 6.00 15.00
81 Caron Butler/25 8.00 20.00
85 Jason Kidd/25 30.00 80.00
86 Deron Williams/25 8.00 20.00
87 Brook Lopez/25 10.00 25.00
93 Chris Andersen/25 30.00 80.00
94 Danilo Gallinari/25 6.00 15.00
96 Danny Granger/25 8.00 20.00
97 Darren Collison/25 6.00 15.00
98 Mike Dunleavy/25 6.00 15.00
99 T.J. Ford/25 6.00 15.00
101 Ben Gordon/25 10.00 25.00
102 Richard Hamilton/25 12.00 30.00
106 DeMar DeRozan/25 8.00 20.00
108 Andrea Bargnani/25 8.00 20.00
113 Goran Dragic/25 15.00 40.00
114 Chase Budinger/25 6.00 15.00
117 Tony Parker/25 15.00 40.00
120 DeJuan Blair/25 6.00 15.00
122 Grant Hill/25 100.00 250.00
123 Channing Frye/25 6.00 15.00
124 Aaron Brooks/25 6.00 15.00
125 Vince Carter/25 25.00 60.00
127 Russell Westbrook/25 50.00 120.00
128 Serge Ibaka/25 15.00 40.00
129 James Harden/25 40.00 100.00
130 Kendrick Perkins/25 8.00 20.00
131 Kevin Love/25 15.00 40.00
132 Michael Beasley/25 10.00 25.00
133 Jonny Flynn/25 6.00 15.00
135 Darko Milicic/25 6.00 15.00
136 LaMarcus Aldridge/25 12.00 30.00
137 Brandon Roy/25 10.00 25.00
138 Andre Miller/25 8.00 20.00
139 Rudy Fernandez/25 6.00 15.00
140 Marcus Camby/25 10.00 25.00
141 Monta Ellis/25 15.00 40.00
142 Stephen Curry/25 125.00 300.00
143 David Lee/25 8.00 20.00
144 Al Thornton/25 6.00 15.00
146 Josh Howard/25 6.00 15.00
148 JaVale McGee/25 6.00 15.00
151 John Wall JSY AU/25 150.00 300.00
152 D.Cousins JSY AU/25 125.00 300.00
173 Paul George JSY AU/25 150.00 300.00

2010-11 Totally Certified Gold Materials Prime

*GOLD MATERIALS: 6X TO 15X BASE HI
STATED PRINT RUN 3 TO 25 SER.#'d SETS
SOME UNPRICED DUE TO SCARCITY
46 Chris Bosh/25 20.00 50.00
49 Chris Paul/25 25.00 60.00
85 Jason Kidd/25 15.00 40.00
122 Grant Hill/25 50.00 125.00
126 Kevin Durant/25 40.00 100.00

2010-11 Totally Certified Red

*RED: .5X TO 1.25X BASE HI
STATED PRINT RUN 499 SER.#'d SETS

2010-11 Totally Certified Red Autographs

*RED RC AUTOGRAPHS: .4X TO 1X BASE HI
STATED PRINT RUN 3 TO 99 SER.#'d SETS
SOME UNPRICED DUE TO SCARCITY
1 Andre Iguodala/25 6.00 15.00
3 Jrue Holiday/49 12.00 30.00
5 D.J. Augustin/49 4.00 10.00
6 Boris Diaw/49 4.00 10.00
7 Gerald Henderson/99 4.00 10.00
8 Stephen Jackson/49 4.00 10.00
9 Brandon Jennings/25 15.00 40.00
10 Andrew Bogut/49 10.00 25.00
15 Carlos Boozer/49 8.00 20.00
17 Joakim Noah/49 10.00 25.00
18 Taj Gibson/99 6.00 15.00
19 Antawn Jamison/49 4.00 10.00
20 Daniel Gibson/49 4.00 10.00
21 Baron Davis/25 8.00 20.00
24 Rajon Rondo/25 20.00 50.00
31 Eric Gordon/99 6.00 15.00
32 Ryan Gomes/99 4.00 10.00
33 Chris Kaman/25 4.00 10.00
34 Shane Battier/25 6.00 15.00
35 Marc Gasol/25 12.00 30.00
36 Zach Randolph/25 10.00 25.00
38 O.J. Mayo/20 6.00 15.00
39 Joe Johnson/25 10.00 25.00
40 Josh Smith/25 8.00 20.00
41 Al Horford/25 6.00 15.00
48 Mike Bibby/25 10.00 25.00
51 Trevor Ariza/25 6.00 15.00
52 Emeka Okafor/25 6.00 15.00
54 Al Jefferson/25 6.00 15.00
55 Devin Harris/25 6.00 15.00
56 Andrei Kirilenko/25 6.00 15.00
59 Tyreke Evans/49 12.00 30.00
60 Omri Casspi/99 4.00 10.00
61 Samuel Dalembert/49 4.00 10.00
62 Marcus Thornton/99 4.00 10.00
63 Beno Udrih/99 4.00 10.00
66 Chauncey Billups/25 10.00 25.00
67 Toney Douglas/49 4.00 10.00
69 Kobe Bryant/49 125.00 250.00
70 Pau Gasol/15 25.00 60.00
73 Derek Fisher/49 10.00 25.00
78 J.J. Redick/49 6.00 15.00
79 Hedo Turkoglu/49 4.00 10.00
81 Caron Butler/49 5.00 12.00
87 Brook Lopez/25 10.00 25.00
93 Chris Andersen/25 20.00 50.00
94 Danilo Gallinari/49 10.00 25.00
97 Darren Collison/49 4.00 10.00
98 Mike Dunleavy/49 4.00 10.00
99 T.J. Ford/99 4.00 10.00
101 Ben Gordon/25 10.00 25.00
102 Richard Hamilton/25 10.00 25.00
106 DeMar DeRozan/25 8.00 20.00
108 Andrea Bargnani/25 6.00 15.00
113 Goran Dragic/99 8.00 20.00
114 Chase Budinger/99 4.00 10.00
117 Tony Parker/25 12.00 30.00
120 DeJuan Blair/99 4.00 10.00
123 Channing Frye/49 4.00 10.00
124 Aaron Brooks/49 4.00 10.00
127 Russell Westbrook/25 50.00 120.00
128 Serge Ibaka/99 10.00 25.00
129 James Harden/25 15.00 40.00
130 Kendrick Perkins/49 6.00 15.00
131 Kevin Love/25 15.00 40.00
133 Jonny Flynn/99 4.00 10.00
134 Anthony Randolph/25 5.00 12.00
135 Darko Milicic/99 4.00 10.00
136 LaMarcus Aldridge/49 10.00 25.00
137 Brandon Roy/25 12.00 30.00
138 Andre Miller/49 4.00 10.00
139 Rudy Fernandez/99 4.00 10.00
140 Marcus Camby/25 10.00 25.00
141 Monta Ellis/25 15.00 40.00
142 Stephen Curry/99 100.00 250.00
143 David Lee/25 8.00 20.00
144 Al Thornton/99 4.00 10.00
146 Josh Howard/25 6.00 15.00
148 JaVale McGee/49 4.00 10.00
151 John Wall JSY AU/99 40.00 100.00
152 D.Cousins JSY AU/99 30.00 80.00
153 Quincy Pondexter JSY AU/99 3.00 8.00
155 Al-Farouq Aminu JSY AU/98 5.00 12.00
156 Ed Davis JSY AU/99 3.00 8.00
157 Greivis Vasquez JSY AU/99 4.00 10.00
158 Ekpe Udoh JSY AU/99 3.00 8.00
159 Damion James JSY AU/99 3.00 8.00
160 Landry Fields JSY AU/98 4.00 10.00
161 Greg Monroe JSY AU/99 12.00 30.00
162 Cole Aldrich JSY AU/99 4.00 10.00
164 Luke Babbitt JSY AU/99 4.00 10.00
169 Wesley Johnson JSY AU/99 3.00 8.00
170 Eric Bledsoe JSY AU/99 6.00 15.00
171 Avery Bradley JSY AU/99 6.00 15.00
172 Daniel Orton JSY AU/99 3.00 8.00
173 Paul George JSY AU/99 125.00 250.00
174 James Anderson JSY AU/99 3.00 8.00
175 Elliot Williams JSY AU/99 3.00 8.00
176 Dominique Jones JSY AU/99 3.00 8.00
177 Dexter Pittman JSY AU/99 3.00 8.00
178 Lazar Hayward JSY AU/99 3.00 8.00
179 Trevor Booker JSY AU/99 4.00 10.00
180 Luke Harangody JSY AU/99 3.00 8.00
181 Patrick Patterson JSY AU/99 4.00 10.00
183 Willie Warren JSY AU/99 3.00 8.00
184 Terrico White JSY AU/99 3.00 8.00
185 Andy Rautins JSY AU/99 3.00 8.00

2010-11 Totally Certified Red Materials

*RED MATERIALS: 1.5X TO 4X BASE HI
STATED PRINT RUN 199 TO 249 SER.#'d SETS
45 LeBron James/249 10.00 25.00
69 Kobe Bryant/249 8.00 20.00
122 Grant Hill/249 8.00 20.00
126 Kevin Durant/249 6.00 15.00

2010-11 Totally Certified Fabric of the Game Jumbo Jersey Number

STATED PRINT RUN ONE TO 299 SETS
1 Patrick Ewing/99 8.00 20.00
2 Dirk Nowitzki/299 4.00 10.00
3 Chris Andersen/299 2.50 6.00
4 Dwyane Wade/299 5.00 12.00
5 Chris Paul/299 4.00 10.00
6 Dwight Howard/299 2.50 6.00
7 Elton Brand/299 3.00 8.00
8 Grant Hill/299 5.00 12.00
9 Rudy Fernandez/299 2.00 5.00
10 LeBron James/299 10.00 25.00
11 Manu Ginobili/99 3.00 8.00
12 Karl Malone/299 4.00 10.00
13 Al Horford/299 2.50 6.00
14 Kevin McHale/99 3.00 8.00
15 Andres Nocioni/299 2.00 5.00
16 Larry Johnson/99 8.00 20.00
17 Scottie Pippen/299 8.00 20.00
18 Jason Terry/299 2.50 6.00
19 Tim Duncan/299 5.00 12.00
20 Dikembe Mutombo/99 5.00 12.00
21 Omri Casspi/299 2.00 5.00
22 Luis Scola/299 2.50 6.00
23 Chris Kaman/299 2.50 6.00
24 Ron Artest/299 3.00 8.00
25 O.J. Mayo/299 2.00 5.00
26 Andrew Bogut/299 2.50 6.00
27 Brook Lopez/299 2.50 6.00
28 Shawn Marion/299 2.50 6.00
30 Jonny Flynn/299 2.00 5.00
31 James Harden/299 5.00 12.00
32 Toni Kukoc/299 3.00 8.00
33 Udonis Haslem/299 2.00 5.00
34 LaMarcus Aldridge/299 3.00 8.00
35 Shawn Kemp/99 20.00 50.00
36 John Stockton/299 5.00 12.00
37 Josh Smith/299 2.50 6.00
38 Paul Pierce/299 3.00 8.00
39 Luol Deng/299 2.50 6.00
40 Ty Lawson/299 2.00 5.00
41 Joe Dumars/99 3.00 8.00
42 Nick Van Exel/99 4.00 10.00
43 Charles Oakley/99 6.00 15.00
44 Maurice Cheeks/99 2.00 5.00
45 David West/299 2.50 6.00
46 Andre Iguodala/299 2.50 6.00
47 Rasheed Wallace/299 3.00 8.00
48 Boris Diaw/299 2.50 6.00
49 Arron Afflalo/299 2.00 5.00
50 Andre Miller/299 2.50 6.00

2010-11 Totally Certified Fabric of the Game Jumbo Jersey Number Prime

*PRIME: 1X TO 2.5X BASE HI
STATED PRINT RUN ONE TO 25 SER.#'d SETS
1 Patrick Ewing/25 25.00 60.00
2 Dirk Nowitzki/25 12.00 30.00
4 Dwyane Wade/20 20.00 50.00
8 Grant Hill/25 20.00 50.00
10 LeBron James/25 30.00 80.00
16 Larry Johnson/25 25.00 60.00
29 Hakeem Olajuwon/25 10.00 25.00
32 Toni Kukoc/25 10.00 25.00

42 Nick Van Exel/25 12.00 30.00
43 Charles Oakley/25 10.00 25.00

2010-11 Totally Certified Fabric of the Game Jumbo Team

STATED PRINT RUN 5 TO 299 SER.#'d SETS
1 Ray Allen/5
2 Brook Lopez/99 2.50 6.00
3 Amare Stoudemire/49 2.50 6.00
4 Elton Brand/299 3.00 8.00
5 DeMar DeRozan/299 3.00 8.00
6 Derrick Rose/299 6.00 15.00
7 Antawn Jamison/299 2.50 6.00
8 Ben Gordon/299 2.50 6.00
9 Danny Granger/299 2.50 6.00
10 Brandon Jennings/299 2.00 5.00
11 Joe Johnson/299 2.50 6.00
12 Stephen Jackson/299 2.50 6.00
13 LeBron James/299 10.00 25.00
14 Dwight Howard/299 2.50 6.00
15 Jason Kidd/299 3.00 8.00
16 Luis Scola/299 2.50 6.00
17 Marc Gasol/299 3.00 8.00
18 Chris Paul/299 4.00 10.00
19 Tony Parker/25 6.00 15.00
20 Nene/99 2.50 6.00
21 Michael Beasley/299 2.00 5.00
22 Brandon Roy/299 3.00 8.00
23 Kevin Durant/299 8.00 20.00
24 Al Jefferson/49 2.50 6.00
25 Monta Ellis/299 2.50 6.00
26 Blake Griffin/49 3.00 8.00
27 Kobe Bryant/299 10.00 25.00
28 Steve Nash/299 3.00 8.00
29 Tyreke Evans/299 2.00 5.00
30 JaVale McGee/299 2.50 6.00
31 Shaquille O'Neal/299 6.00 15.00
32 Andre Iguodala/190 2.50 6.00
33 Andrea Bargnani/299 2.50 6.00
34 Carlos Boozer/299 2.50 6.00
35 Andrew Bogut/299 2.50 6.00
36 Dwyane Wade/299 5.00 12.00
37 Caron Butler/299 2.50 6.00
38 LaMarcus Aldridge/299 3.00 8.00
39 Stephen Curry/99 12.00 30.00
40 Eric Gordon/299 2.50 6.00
41 Pau Gasol/299 3.00 8.00
42 Tim Duncan/299 5.00 12.00
43 Kevin Love/299 3.00 8.00
44 Russell Westbrook/299 8.00 20.00
45 Joakim Noah/199 2.50 6.00
46 Chris Bosh/99 3.00 8.00
47 Chris Kaman/299 2.50 6.00
48 Manu Ginobili/99 3.00 8.00
49 Andrei Kirilenko/99 2.50 6.00
50 Tyson Chandler/299 2.50 6.00

2010-11 Totally Certified Fabric of the Game Jumbo Team Prime

*PRIME: 1X TO 2.5X BASE HI
STATED PRINT RUN ONE TO 25 SER.#'d SETS
1 Ray Allen/25 12.00 30.00
13 LeBron James/25 20.00 50.00
19 Tony Parker/25 8.00 20.00
23 Kevin Durant/25 20.00 50.00
28 Steve Nash/25 12.00 30.00
31 Shaquille O'Neal/25 25.00 60.00

2010-11 Totally Certified HRX Video Cards

STATED PRINT RUN 40 SER.#'d SETS
UNPRICED AUTO PRINT RUN 10 SETS
UNPRICED AUTO GOLD PRINT RUN ONE SET
1 Kobe Bryant 175.00 350.00
2 Kevin Durant 125.00 250.00
3 Blake Griffin 60.00 150.00
4 John Wall 60.00 150.00

2010-11 Totally Certified Potential

STATED PRINT RUN 249 SER.#'d SETS
*BLUE: .75X TO 2X BASE HI
BLUE PRINT RUN 49 SER.#'d SETS
*GOLD: 2X TO 5X BASE HI
GOLD PRINT RUN 25 SER.#'d SETS
*RED: .6X TO 1.5X BASE HI
RED PRINT RUN 99 SER.#'d SETS
UNPRICED BLACK PRINT RUN ONE SET
UNPRICED GREEN PRINT RUN 5 SETS
1 Blake Griffin 1.25 3.00
2 Derrick Rose 1.50 4.00
3 Stephen Curry 5.00 12.00
4 Tyreke Evans .75 2.00
5 DeJuan Blair .75 2.00
6 Eric Gordon 1.00 2.50
7 Brandon Jennings .75 2.00
8 Kevin Love 1.25 3.00
9 Michael Beasley .75 2.00
10 Wesley Matthews .75 2.00
11 Zach Randolph 1.00 2.50
12 Russell Westbrook 3.00 8.00
13 Taj Gibson 1.00 2.50
14 James Harden 2.00 5.00
15 JaVale McGee 1.00 2.50

2010-11 Totally Certified Potential Autographs Gold

ATED PRINT RUN 25 SER.#'d SETS
UNPRICED BLACK PRINT RUN ONE SET
UNPRICED GREEN PRINT RUN 5 SETS
1 Blake Griffin 30.00 80.00
2 Derrick Rose 100.00 200.00
3 Stephen Curry 125.00 250.00
4 Tyreke Evans 15.00 40.00
5 DeJuan Blair 6.00 15.00
6 Eric Gordon 8.00 20.00
7 Brandon Jennings 15.00 40.00
8 Kevin Love 15.00 40.00
9 Michael Beasley 12.50 30.00
10 Wesley Matthews 15.00 40.00
11 Zach Randolph 10.00 25.00
12 Russell Westbrook 40.00 100.00
13 Taj Gibson 12.00 30.00
14 James Harden 15.00 40.00
15 JaVale McGee 6.00 15.00

2010-11 Totally Certified Potential Jerseys Prime Gold

*GOLD PRIME: 3X TO 8X BASE HI
STATED PRINT RUN 15 TO 25 SER.#'d SETS
UNPRICED BLACK PRINT RUN ONE SET
UNPRICED GREEN PRINT RUN 5 SETS

2012-13 Totally Certified

COMPLETE SET (300) 125.00 250.00
UNPRICED BLACK PRINT RUN ONE SET
UNPRICED GREEN PRINT RUN 5 SETS
1 Arron Afflalo .60 1.50
2 LaMarcus Aldridge .75 2.00
3 Drew Gooden .60 1.50
4 Tony Allen .50 1.25
5 Al-Farouq Aminu .60 1.50
6 Kenneth Faried RC 1.00 2.50
7 Carmelo Anthony 1.00 2.50
8 Trevor Ariza .50 1.25
9 Darrell Arthur .50 1.25
10 Thomas Robinson RC .75 2.00
11 Kawhi Leonard RC 5.00 12.00
12 Kyrie Irving RC 5.00 12.00
13 Brandon Bass .50 1.25
14 Matt Barnes .50 1.25
15 Shane Battier .60 1.50
16 Michael Kidd-Gilchrist RC 1.00 2.50
17 Jerryd Bayless .60 1.50
18 Iman Shumpert RC 1.00 2.50
19 Rodrigue Beaubois .50 1.25
20 Marco Belinelli .50 1.25
21 Andris Biedrins .50 1.25
22 Chauncey Billups .75 2.00
23 DeJuan Blair .50 1.25
24 Will Barton RC .75 2.00
25 Eric Bledsoe .60 1.50
26 Andrew Bogut .60 1.50
27 Matt Bonner .50 1.25
28 Trevor Booker .50 1.25
29 Anthony Davis RC 8.00 20.00
30 Chris Bosh .75 2.00
31 Avery Bradley .60 1.50
32 Elton Brand .75 2.00
33 Tobias Harris RC 1.00 2.50
34 Chase Budinger .50 1.25
35 Caron Butler .60 1.50
36 Andrew Bynum .50 1.25
37 Jose Calderon .50 1.25
38 Enes Kanter RC .75 2.00
39 Jordan Williams RC .75 2.00
40 Vince Carter 1.00 2.50
41 Omri Casspi .50 1.25
42 Mario Chalmers .60 1.50
43 Tyson Chandler .60 1.50
44 Darren Collison .60 1.50
45 Nick Collison .60 1.50
46 Nolan Smith RC .60 1.50
47 DeMarcus Cousins .75 2.00
48 Jamal Crawford .75 2.00
49 Stephen Curry 3.00 8.00
50 Malcolm Lee RC .60 1.50
51 JaJuan Johnson RC .60 1.50
52 Glen Davis .50 1.25
53 Carlos Delfino .50 1.25
54 Luol Deng .60 1.50
55 DeMar DeRozan .75 2.00
56 Goran Dragic .60 1.50
57 Josh Selby RC .60 1.50
58 Tim Duncan 1.25 3.00
59 Bradley Beal RC 1.50 4.00
60 Devin Ebanks .50 1.25
61 Monta Ellis .60 1.50
62 Tyreke Evans .50 1.25
63 Johan Petro .50 1.25
64 Raymond Felton .60 1.50
65 Wilson Chandler .60 1.50
66 Landry Fields .50 1.25
67 Dion Waiters RC 1.00 2.50
68 Jonny Flynn .50 1.25
69 Randy Foye .50 1.25
70 Damian Lillard RC 4.00 10.00
71 Danilo Gallinari .50 1.25
72 Kevin Garnett 1.25 3.00
73 Terrence Ross RC 1.00 2.50
74 Pau Gasol .75 2.00
75 Rudy Gay .75 2.00
76 Paul George 1.00 2.50
77 Harrison Barnes RC 1.50 4.00
78 Daniel Gibson .60 1.50
79 Taj Gibson .60 1.50
80 Manu Ginobili .75 2.00
81 Kobe Bryant 3.00 8.00
82 Kevin Durant 2.00 5.00
83 Amare Stoudemire .60 1.50
84 Marcin Gortat .60 1.50
85 Danny Granger .60 1.50
86 Andre Drummond RC 1.50 4.00
87 Blake Griffin .75 2.00
88 Richard Hamilton .60 1.50
89 Tyler Hansbrough .60 1.50
90 James Harden 1.25 3.00
91 Al Harrington .60 1.50
92 Devin Harris .50 1.25
93 Udonis Haslem .50 1.25
94 Austin Rivers RC 1.00 2.50
95 Gordon Hayward .75 2.00
96 Brendan Haywood .50 1.25
97 Gerald Henderson .50 1.25
98 Xavier Henry .50 1.25
99 Roy Hibbert .60 1.50
100 J.J. Hickson .50 1.25
101 George Hill .60 1.50
102 Jimmer Fredette RC .60 1.50
103 Kirk Hinrich .60 1.50
104 Jrue Holiday .75 2.00
105 Al Horford .60 1.50
106 Dwight Howard .60 1.50
107 Kris Humphries .50 1.25
108 Serge Ibaka .60 1.50
109 Andre Iguodala .60 1.50
110 Ersan Ilyasova .50 1.25
111 J.J. Barea .60 1.50
112 Stephen Jackson .60 1.50
113 LeBron James 3.00 8.00
114 Al Jefferson .60 1.50
115 Antawn Jamison .60 1.50
116 Brandon Jennings .50 1.25
117 James Johnson .50 1.25
118 Joe Johnson .60 1.50
119 Wesley Johnson .60 1.50
120 DeAndre Jordan .75 2.00
121 Chris Kaman .60 1.50
122 Jason Kidd .75 2.00
123 Linas Kleiza .50 1.25
124 Kyle Korver .60 1.50
125 Carl Landry .50 1.25
126 Norris Cole RC .60 1.50
127 Courtney Lee .60 1.50
128 David Lee .50 1.25
129 Jeremy Lin .75 2.00
130 Brook Lopez .60 1.50
131 Kevin Love .75 2.00
132 Kyle Lowry .60 1.50
133 John Lucas III .50 1.25
134 Corey Maggette .60 1.50
135 Ian Mahinmi .50 1.25
136 Shawn Marion .60 1.50
137 Cartier Martin RC 1.00 2.50
138 Kevin Martin .60 1.50
139 Wesley Matthews .50 1.25
140 Jordan Hamilton RC .60 1.50
141 Luc Mbah a Moute .50 1.25
142 JaVale McGee .60 1.50
143 DeShawn Stevenson .50 1.25
144 C.J. Miles .60 1.50
145 Andre Miller .60 1.50
146 Mike Miller .60 1.50
147 Paul Millsap .75 2.00
148 Greg Monroe .60 1.50
149 Timofey Mozgov .50 1.25
150 Marcus Morris RC .75 2.00
151 Steve Nash .75 2.00
152 Gary Neal .60 1.50
153 Jameer Nelson .50 1.25
154 Nene .60 1.50
155 Joakim Noah .60 1.50
156 Steve Novak .50 1.25
157 Dirk Nowitzki 1.00 2.50
158 Emeka Okafor .60 1.50
159 Daniel Orton .50 1.25
160 Tony Parker .75 2.00
161 Patrick Patterson .50 1.25
162 Chris Paul 1.00 2.50
163 Meyers Leonard RC .75 2.00
164 Paul Pierce .75 2.00
165 Tayshaun Prince .60 1.50
166 Anthony Randolph .60 1.50
167 Zach Randolph .60 1.50
168 J.J. Redick .75 2.00
169 Jason Richardson .75 2.00
170 Luke Ridnour .60 1.50
171 Nate Robinson .50 1.25
172 Derrick Rose 1.00 2.50
173 Rajon Rondo .75 2.00
174 Ricky Rubio .75 2.00
175 Brandon Rush .50 1.25
176 John Salmons .60 1.50
177 Alonzo Gee .50 1.25
178 Ramon Sessions .60 1.50
179 Jeremy Lamb RC 1.00 2.50
180 Josh Smith .60 1.50
181 Marreese Speights .50 1.25
182 Jerry Stackhouse .60 1.50
183 Eric Gordon .60 1.50
184 Rodney Stuckey .60 1.50
185 Jeff Teague .60 1.50
186 Jason Terry .60 1.50
187 Tyrus Thomas .50 1.25
188 Marcus Thornton .50 1.25
189 Hedo Turkoglu .60 1.50
190 Evan Turner .50 1.25
191 D.J. Augustin .50 1.25
192 Anderson Varejao .50 1.25
193 Greivis Vasquez .60 1.50
194 Dwyane Wade 1.25 3.00
195 John Wall 1.00 2.50
196 Hakim Warrick .60 1.50
197 Kendall Marshall RC .60 1.50
198 David West .60 1.50
199 Delonte West .50 1.25
200 Russell Westbrook 2.00 5.00
201 Deron Williams .60 1.50
202 Louis Williams .60 1.50
203 Mo Williams .60 1.50
204 Metta World Peace .75 2.00
205 Nick Young .60 1.50
206 Ryan Anderson .60 1.50
207 Jordan Crawford .50 1.25
208 Kendrick Perkins .50 1.25
209 Jason Smith .50 1.25
210 Marvin Williams .60 1.50
211 Jarrett Jack .60 1.50
212 Andrea Bargnani .60 1.50
213 Brandon Knight RC 1.00 2.50
214 MarShon Brooks RC .75 2.00
215 Klay Thompson RC 4.00 10.00
216 Kemba Walker RC 2.00 5.00
217 Isaiah Thomas RC 1.50 4.00
218 Michael Beasley .50 1.25
219 Chandler Parsons RC 1.00 2.50
220 Derrick Williams RC .60 1.50
221 Tristan Thompson RC 1.00 2.50
222 Grant Hill 1.00 2.50
223 Doron Lamb RC .60 1.50
224 Markieff Morris RC 1.00 2.50
225 Alec Burks RC 1.00 2.50
226 Ty Lawson .50 1.25
227 Ivan Johnson RC .60 1.50
228 Gustavo Ayon RC .60 1.50
229 Charles Jenkins RC .60 1.50
230 Nikola Vucevic RC 1.00 2.50
231 Donald Sloan RC .60 1.50
232 Bismack Biyombo RC .60 1.50
233 Ray Allen .75 2.00
234 Jeremy Tyler RC .60 1.50
235 Jon Leuer RC .75 2.00
236 Jan Vesely RC .60 1.50
237 Chris Singleton RC .60 1.50
238 Marcus Camby .60 1.50
239 DeMarre Carroll .50 1.25
240 O.J. Mayo .50 1.25
241 Kyle Singler RC .60 1.50
242 Andrew Goudelock RC .60 1.50
243 Lavoy Allen RC .60 1.50
244 Lance Thomas RC .60 1.50
245 Cory Higgins RC .60 1.50
246 Mike Conley .60 1.50
247 Elliot Williams .50 1.25
248 Terrel Harris RC .60 1.50
249 Shelvin Mack RC .75 2.00
250 Samuel Dalembert .50 1.25
251 Baron Davis .60 1.50
252 Reggie Jackson RC 1.00 2.50
253 Greg Stiemsma RC .60 1.50
254 Maalik Wayns RC 1.00 2.50
255 Cory Joseph RC .60 1.50
256 Jimmy Butler RC 3.00 8.00
257 Jared Dudley .50 1.25
258 Julyan Stone RC .60 1.50
259 Jeremy Pargo RC .60 1.50
260 Byron Mullens .50 1.25
261 John Henson RC 1.00 2.50
262 Moe Harkless RC 1.00 2.50
263 Nikola Pekovic .50 1.25
264 Royce White RC .60 1.50
265 Tyler Zeller RC .75 2.00
266 Terrence Jones RC .75 2.00
267 Derek Fisher .60 1.50
268 Andrew Nicholson RC .60 1.50
269 Evan Fournier RC 1.00 2.50
270 Channing Frye .60 1.50
271 Jared Sullinger RC .75 2.00
272 Fab Melo RC .60 1.50
273 Marc Gasol .75 2.00
274 John Jenkins RC .60 1.50
275 Jared Cunningham RC .60 1.50
276 Tony Wroten RC .75 2.00
277 Luis Scola .60 1.50
278 Miles Plumlee RC .60 1.50
279 J.R. Smith .60 1.50
280 Arnett Moultrie RC .60 1.50
281 Perry Jones RC .60 1.50
282 Ben Gordon .60 1.50
283 Thabo Sefolosha .50 1.25
284 Festus Ezeli RC .75 2.00
285 Marquis Teague RC .60 1.50
286 Danny Green .60 1.50
287 Jeff Taylor RC .60 1.50
288 Bernard James RC .60 1.50
289 Nicolas Batum .60 1.50
290 Jae Crowder RC .75 2.00
291 Carlos Boozer .60 1.50
292 Draymond Green RC 3.00 8.00
293 Orlando Johnson RC .60 1.50
294 Spencer Hawes .50 1.25
295 Quincy Acy RC .60 1.50
296 Quincy Miller RC .60 1.50
297 C.J. Watson .50 1.25
298 Khris Middleton RC 1.00 2.50
299 Tyshawn Taylor RC .60 1.50
300 Ekpe Udoh .50 1.25

2012-13 Totally Certified Blue

*BLUE: .75X TO 2X BASE HI
STATED PRINT RUN 299 SER.#'d SETS

2012-13 Totally Certified Gold

*VETS: 4X TO 10X BASE HI
*ROOKIES: 3X TO 8X BASE HI
STATED PRINT RUN 25 SER.#'d SETS
7 Carmelo Anthony 12.00 30.00
10 Thomas Robinson 25.00 60.00
82 Kevin Durant 30.00 80.00
86 Andre Drummond 12.00 30.00
106 Dwight Howard 20.00 50.00
122 Jason Kidd 10.00 25.00
222 Grant Hill 15.00 40.00
233 Ray Allen 15.00 40.00

2012-13 Totally Certified Red

*RED: .5X TO 1.25X BASE HI
STATED PRINT RUN 499 SER.#'d SETS
67 Dion Waiters 4.00 10.00
113 LeBron James 5.00 12.00
129 Jeremy Lin 3.00 8.00

2012-13 Totally Certified Autographs

STATED PRINT RUN 25 TO 49 SER.#'d SETS
UNPRICED BLACK PRINT RUN ONE SET
UNPRICED GREEN PRINT RUN 5 SETS
UNPRICED GOLD PRINT RUN 10 SETS
1 Brook Lopez/49 5.00 12.00
2 Danilo Gallinari/49 4.00 10.00
3 David Lee/49 6.00 15.00
4 Eric Gordon/49 6.00 15.00
5 Gordon Hayward/49 5.00 12.00
6 Kevin Durant/49 40.00 100.00
7 Chris Kaman/49 4.00 10.00
8 Jamal Crawford/44 10.00 25.00
9 Richard Hamilton/49 6.00 15.00
10 Ricky Rubio/49 30.00 60.00
11 Reggie Evans/49 4.00 10.00
12 Steve Nash/49 20.00 50.00
13 Ty Lawson/49 EXCH 10.00 25.00
14 Tyreke Evans/49 8.00 20.00
15 Wesley Matthews/49 4.00 10.00
16 Xavier Henry/49 4.00 10.00
17 Andrew Bogut/44
18 Avery Bradley/49 EXCH 4.00 10.00
19 Ben Gordon/49 4.00 10.00
20 Channing Frye/49 EXCH 4.00 10.00
21 DeJuan Blair/49 EXCH 5.00 12.00
22 DeMarcus Cousins/49 8.00 20.00
23 Derrick Favors/46 5.00 12.00
24 Jeff Teague/49 4.00 10.00
25 Jrue Holiday/49 6.00 15.00
26 Kobe Bryant/49 EXCH 100.00 175.00
27 Jared Dudley/49 4.00 10.00
28 Omri Casspi/49 4.00 10.00
29 Zach Randolph/49 8.00 20.00
30 Kevin Love/49 8.00 20.00
31 Serge Ibaka/49 12.00 30.00
32 Tony Parker/49 8.00 20.00
33 Chris Bosh/49 12.00 30.00
34 DeAndre Jordan/49 5.00 12.00
35 Deron Williams/49 5.00 12.00
36 Stephen Curry/49 60.00 150.00
37 Mike Bibby/49 4.00 10.00
38 James Harden/49 12.00 30.00
39 Luol Deng/49 6.00 15.00
40 Brandon Jennings/49 EXCH 10.00 25.00
41 Blake Griffin/49 12.00 30.00
42 Jose Calderon/49 6.00 15.00
43 Chris Paul/49 EXCH 20.00 50.00
44 Stephen Jackson/49 4.00 10.00
45 Andre Iguodala/49 8.00 20.00
46 David West/49 4.00 10.00
47 Andrew Bynum/49 6.00 15.00
48 Shane Battier/49
49 Mike Conley/49 5.00 12.00
50 Darren Collison/49 4.00 10.00
51 JaVale McGee/49 5.00 12.00
52 Gary Neal/49 EXCH 5.00 12.00
53 Grant Hill/49 12.00 30.00
54 Jason Kidd/25 12.00 30.00
55 Kris Humphries/49 5.00 12.00
56 Tyson Chandler/49 6.00 15.00
57 Wesley Johnson/49 4.00 10.00
58 Delonte West/49 4.00 10.00
59 Joakim Noah/49 8.00 20.00
60 Greg Monroe/49 8.00 20.00
61 Monta Ellis/49 6.00 15.00
62 Roy Hibbert/49 4.00 10.00
63 Vince Carter/49 12.00 30.00
64 Derek Fisher/49 8.00 20.00
65 Raymond Felton/49 4.00 10.00
66 LaMarcus Aldridge/49 8.00 20.00
67 Josh Smith/49 4.00 10.00
68 Steve Novak/49 4.00 10.00
69 Marcin Gortat/49 15.00 40.00
70 Kyle Lowry/49 4.00 10.00
71 Pau Gasol/49 EXCH 10.00 25.00
72 Ersan Ilyasova/49 4.00 10.00
73 Nick Young/49 4.00 10.00
74 Al Horford/49 4.00 10.00
76 Adrian Dantley/49 4.00 10.00
77 Artis Gilmore/49 6.00 15.00
78 Magic Johnson/49 30.00 80.00
79 Mark Eaton/49 4.00 10.00
80 Ron Harper/34 10.00 25.00
81 Tim Hardaway/49 8.00 20.00
82 Bill Laimbeer/49 4.00 10.00
83 Dolph Schayes/49 4.00 10.00
84 Calvin Murphy/49 4.00 10.00
85 Rick Barry/49 6.00 15.00
86 Bill Russell/49 50.00 100.00
87 Chris Mullin/49 8.00 20.00
88 David Robinson/49 25.00 60.00
89 Bernard King/49 4.00 10.00
90 Detlef Schrempf/49 10.00 25.00
91 Cedric Ceballos/49 4.00 10.00
92 John Starks/49 6.00 15.00
93 Gail Goodrich/49 5.00 12.00
94 John Havlicek/49 10.00 25.00
95 James Worthy/49 15.00 40.00
96 Toni Kukoc/49 8.00 20.00
97 Larry Bird/49 40.00 100.00
98 Mark Jackson/49 6.00 15.00
99 Vlade Divac/49 6.00 15.00
100 Robert Horry/49 6.00 15.00

2012-13 Totally Certified Blue Autographs

*BLUE: .6X TO 1.5X BASE HI
STATED PRINT RUN 15 SER.#'d SETS
42 Jose Calderon 12.00 30.00
44 Stephen Jackson 10.00 25.00
54 Jason Kidd 15.00 40.00
79 Mark Eaton 12.00 30.00
88 David Robinson 40.00 100.00
97 Larry Bird 50.00 125.00
98 Mark Jackson 8.00 20.00
100 Robert Horry 15.00 40.00

2012-13 Totally Certified Red Autographs

*RED: .5X TO 1.25X BASE HI
STATED PRINT RUN 25 SER.#'d SETS
32 Tony Parker 10.00 25.00
75 Dirk Nowitzki 40.00 100.00

2012-13 Totally Certified HRX Video Cards

STATED PRINT RUN 40 SER.#'d SETS
UNPRICED AUTO PRINT RUN 10 SETS
UNPRICED AUTO GOLD PRINT RUN ONE SET
1 Kobe Bryant 175.00 350.00
2 Kevin Durant 125.00 250.00
3 Kyrie Irving 75.00 200.00
4 Anthony Davis 75.00 200.00

2012-13 Totally Certified Red Materials

RANDOM INSERTS IN PACKS
UNPRICED BLACK PRINT RUN ONE SET
UNPRICED GREEN PRINT RUN 5 SETS
UNPRICED GOLD PRINT RUN 7 TO 10 SETS
1 Kobe Bryant 8.00 20.00
2 Kevin Durant 6.00 15.00
3 Chris Bosh 2.50 6.00
4 Brook Lopez 2.00 5.00
5 Al Jefferson 2.00 5.00
6 Amare Stoudemire 2.00 5.00
7 Andre Miller 2.00 5.00
8 Antawn Jamison 2.00 5.00
10 Carl Landry 1.50 4.00
11 Carmelo Anthony 3.00 8.00
13 Chris Paul 3.00 8.00
15 David West 2.00 5.00
17 Derrick Rose 3.00 8.00
19 Dwight Howard 2.00 5.00
21 Jalen Rose 2.50 6.00
22 Jason Richardson 2.50 6.00
23 Joakim Noah 2.00 5.00
24 Kirk Hinrich 2.00 5.00
25 Joe Johnson 2.00 5.00
26 John Salmons 2.00 5.00
27 John Stockton 4.00 10.00
28 Karl Malone 3.00 8.00
29 Kawhi Leonard 10.00 25.00
30 Kyrie Irving 10.00 25.00
32 Kevin Martin 2.00 5.00
34 LaMarcus Aldridge 2.50 6.00
35 Leandro Barbosa 2.00 5.00
36 LeBron James 10.00 25.00
37 Manu Ginobili 2.50 6.00
38 Landry Fields 1.50 4.00
39 MarShon Brooks 1.50 4.00
41 Patrick Ewing 3.00 8.00
42 Pau Gasol 2.50 6.00
43 Paul Pierce 2.50 6.00
44 Ray Allen 2.50 6.00
45 Raymond Felton 2.00 5.00
46 Shaquille O'Neal 5.00 12.00
47 Tayshaun Prince 2.00 5.00
48 Tim Duncan 4.00 10.00
50 Tony Parker 2.50 6.00
51 Tracy McGrady 2.50 6.00
52 Tristan Thompson 2.00 5.00
53 Tyrus Thomas 1.50 4.00
54 Vince Carter 3.00 8.00
55 Zach Randolph 2.00 5.00
56 Alonzo Mourning 3.00 8.00
57 Andre Iguodala 2.00 5.00
58 Blake Griffin 2.50 6.00
59 Carlos Boozer 2.00 5.00
60 Darren Collison 2.00 5.00
61 David Lee 1.50 4.00
62 Dennis Rodman 5.00 12.00
63 Derrick Favors 2.00 5.00
64 Dirk Nowitzki 3.00 8.00
65 Grant Hill 6.00 15.00
66 Hedo Turkoglu 2.00 5.00
67 J.J. Redick 2.50 6.00
68 Jameer Nelson 1.50 4.00
69 JaVale McGee 2.00 5.00
70 Josh Howard 2.00 5.00
72 Kemba Walker 4.00 10.00
73 Luol Deng 2.00 5.00
74 Markieff Morris 2.00 5.00
75 Michael Beasley 1.50 4.00
78 Metta World Peace 2.50 6.00
79 Ryan Gomes 1.50 4.00
80 Russell Westbrook 6.00 15.00
81 Steve Nash 2.50 6.00
82 Terrence Williams 1.50 4.00
83 Thaddeus Young 1.50 4.00
84 Ty Lawson 1.50 4.00
85 Alex English 2.00 5.00
86 Andrew Bynum 1.50 4.00
88 Derrick Williams 1.25 3.00
89 Wesley Matthews 1.50 4.00
90 Tyreke Evans 1.50 4.00
91 Jermaine O'Neal 2.00 5.00
92 Joe Dumars 2.50 6.00
93 Klay Thompson 8.00 20.00
94 Kenny Anderson 2.00 5.00
96 Josh Smith 2.00 5.00
97 Kevin Love 2.50 6.00
98 Marc Gasol 2.50 6.00
99 Mark Jackson 2.00 5.00
100 Raja Bell 2.00 5.00
101 Larry Bird 6.00 15.00
102 Taj Gibson 2.00 5.00
103 Steve Smith 2.00 5.00
104 Tyler Hansbrough 2.00 5.00
106 Jrue Holiday 2.50 6.00
107 Evan Turner 1.50 4.00
108 Emeka Okafor 2.00 5.00
109 Dikembe Mutombo 2.50 6.00
110 DeMar DeRozan 2.50 6.00
111 Marcus Morris 1.50 4.00
112 Chuck Person 2.00 5.00
113 Danny Granger 2.00 5.00
114 Chase Budinger 1.50 4.00
115 Channing Frye 2.00 5.00
116 Caron Butler 2.00 5.00
117 Bismack Biyombo 1.25 3.00
118 Ben Wallace 2.00 5.00
119 Al Horford 2.00 5.00
120 Dwyane Wade 4.00 10.00
121 Earl Monroe 2.50 6.00
122 Iman Shumpert 2.00 5.00
123 James Harden 4.00 10.00
124 Jimmer Fredette 1.25 3.00
126 Brandon Jennings 1.50 4.00
128 Mike Conley 2.00 5.00
129 Tiago Splitter 2.00 5.00
130 Andrea Bargnani 2.00 5.00
131 Wesley Johnson 2.00 5.00
132 Zydrunas Ilgauskas 2.00 5.00
133 Udonis Haslem 1.50 4.00
134 Spencer Hawes 1.50 4.00
136 Rudy Gay 2.50 6.00
137 Luke Ridnour 2.00 5.00
138 Jose Calderon 1.50 4.00
139 Carlos Delfino 1.50 4.00
141 Jason Williams 2.50 6.00
143 Joel Anthony 1.50 4.00
144 Larry Johnson 4.00 10.00
145 D.J. Augustin 1.50 4.00
146 Daniel Gibson 2.00 5.00
148 DeMarcus Cousins 2.50 6.00
149 Ed Davis 1.50 4.00
151 Enes Kanter 1.50 4.00
155 J.J. Barea 4.00 10.00
156 Jamaal Wilkes 2.50 6.00
157 Jamal Crawford 2.50 6.00
158 Jeff Foster 1.50 4.00
159 Jeff Teague 2.00 5.00
160 Jim Jackson 1.50 4.00
161 Kenneth Faried 2.00 5.00
162 Luis Scola 2.00 5.00
163 Mark Price 2.50 6.00
164 Marvin Williams 2.00 5.00
165 Maurice Cheeks 1.50 4.00
166 Nick Collison 2.00 5.00
168 Peja Stojakovic 2.50 6.00
169 Randy Foye 1.50 4.00
170 Bill Laimbeer 2.00 5.00
171 Richard Hamilton 2.00 5.00
172 Rodrigue Beaubois 1.50 4.00
174 Shawn Kemp 12.00 30.00
175 Stephen Curry 10.00 25.00
176 Trevor Booker 1.50 4.00
177 Vinnie Johnson 2.50 6.00
178 Allan Houston 2.00 5.00
179 Alvan Adams 1.50 4.00
180 Anderson Varejao 1.50 4.00
181 Toni Kukoc 2.50 6.00
182 Anthony Mason 2.00 5.00
183 Baron Davis 2.00 5.00
185 Bobby Jackson 1.50 4.00
186 Brendan Haywood 1.50 4.00
187 Charles Jenkins 1.25 3.00
188 Chauncey Billups 2.50 6.00
189 Eric Gordon 2.00 5.00
190 Goran Dragic 2.00 5.00
191 Gordon Hayward 2.50 6.00
192 Brandon Knight 2.00 5.00
193 Gary Neal 2.00 5.00
194 Chandler Parsons 2.00 5.00
195 Clyde Drexler 3.00 8.00
196 Tyson Chandler 2.00 5.00
197 David Robinson 4.00 10.00
198 Cedric Maxwell 1.50 4.00
199 Charles Oakley 2.50 6.00
200 Yao Ming 3.00 8.00

2012-13 Totally Certified Red Materials Prime

*RED PRIME: 1X TO 2.5X RED MAT HI
STATED PRINT RUN 49 SER.#'d SETS
2 Kevin Durant 20.00 50.00
27 John Stockton 12.00 30.00
36 LeBron James 25.00 60.00
41 Patrick Ewing 25.00 60.00
51 Tracy McGrady 12.00 30.00
56 Alonzo Mourning 12.00 30.00
81 Steve Nash 8.00 20.00
94 Kenny Anderson 8.00 20.00
109 Dikembe Mutombo 15.00 40.00
141 Jason Williams 10.00 25.00
144 Larry Johnson 25.00 60.00
153 Glen Rice 8.00 20.00
163 Mark Price 8.00 20.00
177 Vinnie Johnson 8.00 20.00
181 Toni Kukoc 8.00 20.00
195 Clyde Drexler 12.00 30.00
199 Charles Oakley 10.00 25.00

2012-13 Totally Certified Blue Materials

*BLUE: .5X TO 1.25X RED MAT HI
STATED PRINT RUN 5 TO 99 SER.#'d SETS
31 Kevin Garnett/35 8.00 20.00
36 LeBron James/99 10.00 25.00
41 Patrick Ewing/99 8.00 20.00
46 Shaquille O'Neal/99 12.00 30.00
56 Alonzo Mourning/99 6.00 15.00
65 Grant Hill/99 10.00 25.00
71 Julius Erving/99 5.00 12.00
76 Mo Williams/15 6.00 15.00
77 Rajon Rondo/99 5.00 12.00
81 Steve Nash/99 4.00 10.00
87 Dominique Wilkins/99 4.00 10.00
94 Kenny Anderson/99 6.00 15.00
109 Dikembe Mutombo/99 4.00 10.00
121 Earl Monroe/99 12.00 30.00
144 Larry Johnson/99 6.00 15.00
153 Glen Rice/99 5.00 12.00
173 Scottie Pippen/25 20.00 50.00
174 Shawn Kemp/99 20.00 50.00
181 Toni Kukoc/99 3.00 8.00

2012-13 Totally Certified Blue Materials Prime

*BLUE PRIME: 1.25X TO 3X RED MAT HI
STATED PRINT RUN 5 TO 25 SER.#'d SETS
2 Kevin Durant/25 30.00 80.00
36 LeBron James/25 30.00 60.00
41 Patrick Ewing/25 30.00 80.00
46 Shaquille O'Neal/25 30.00 80.00
56 Alonzo Mourning/25 15.00 40.00
58 Blake Griffin/25 25.00 60.00
62 Dennis Rodman/25 20.00 50.00
72 Kemba Walker/25 40.00 70.00
81 Steve Nash/25 12.00 30.00
109 Dikembe Mutombo/25 20.00 50.00
141 Jason Williams/25 10.00 25.00
144 Larry Johnson/25 25.00 60.00
152 Gary Payton/25 25.00 60.00
153 Glen Rice/25 15.00 40.00
155 J.J. Barea/25 20.00 50.00
163 Mark Price/25 15.00 40.00
195 Clyde Drexler/25 15.00 40.00

2012-13 Totally Certified Private Signings

RANDOM INSERTS IN PACKS
1 Alvan Adams 6.00 15.00
2 Adrian Dantley 6.00 15.00
3 Al Attles 6.00 15.00
4 Kelly Tripucka 6.00 15.00
5 Larry Johnson 12.00 30.00
6 Al Horford 8.00 20.00
7 Roy Hibbert 8.00 20.00
8 Hedo Turkoglu 3.00 8.00
9 Darryl Dawkins 8.00 20.00
10 Campy Russell 6.00 15.00
11 Paul Millsap 8.00 20.00
12 Emeka Okafor 6.00 15.00
13 Ty Lawson 8.00 20.00
14 Glen Rice 8.00 20.00
15 Luke Ridnour 6.00 15.00
16 Juwan Howard 6.00 15.00
17 Jeff Teague 3.00 8.00
18 Michael Cooper 8.00 20.00
19 Josh Smith 6.00 15.00
20 Bernard King 3.00 8.00

2012-13 Totally Certified Rookie Roll Call Autographs

RANDOM INSERTS IN PACKS
UNPRICED BLACK PRINT RUN ONE SET
UNPRICED GREEN PRINT RUN 5 SETS
1 Kawhi Leonard 50.00 120.00
2 Iman Shumpert 8.00 20.00
3 Anthony Davis 75.00 150.00
4 Michael Kidd-Gilchrist 15.00 40.00
5 Chandler Parsons 5.00 12.00
6 Kyrie Irving 50.00 120.00
7 Thomas Robinson 3.00 8.00
8 Andre Drummond 25.00 60.00
9 Kenneth Faried 4.00 10.00
10 Isaiah Thomas 12.00 30.00
11 Harrison Barnes 10.00 25.00
12 Jeremy Lamb 4.00 10.00
13 Brandon Knight 4.00 10.00
14 MarShon Brooks 3.00 8.00
15 Bradley Beal 10.00 25.00
17 Klay Thompson 40.00 100.00
18 Jimmer Fredette 2.50 6.00
19 Austin Rivers 4.00 10.00
20 Lance Thomas 2.50 6.00
21 Kemba Walker 8.00 20.00
22 Bismack Biyombo 2.50 6.00
23 Tyler Zeller 3.00 8.00
24 Meyers Leonard 8.00 20.00
25 Derrick Williams 2.50 6.00
26 Enes Kanter 3.00 8.00
28 Kendall Marshall 2.50 6.00
29 Alec Burks 4.00 10.00
30 Jan Vesely 2.50 6.00
31 Jared Sullinger 5.00 12.00
32 John Henson 4.00 10.00
33 Markieff Morris 4.00 10.00
34 Norris Cole 2.50 6.00
35 Moe Harkless 6.00 15.00
36 Dion Waiters 3.00 8.00
37 Lavoy Allen 2.50 6.00
38 Tristan Thompson 4.00 10.00
39 Terrence Ross 4.00 10.00
41 Gustavo Ayon 2.50 6.00
42 Charles Jenkins 2.50 6.00
43 Terrence Jones 3.00 8.00
44 Andrew Nicholson 2.50 6.00
46 Jeremy Tyler 2.50 6.00
47 Julyan Stone 2.50 6.00
49 Jon Leuer 3.00 8.00
50 Kyle Singler 2.50 6.00
51 Fab Melo 2.50 6.00
52 John Jenkins 2.50 6.00
55 Jared Cunningham 2.50 6.00
56 Miles Plumlee 2.50 6.00
57 Nolan Smith 2.50 6.00
58 Travis Leslie 2.50 6.00
59 Tony Wroten 3.00 8.00
60 Marquis Teague 2.50 6.00
62 Courtney Fortson 2.50 6.00
63 Festus Ezeli 3.00 8.00
64 Jeff Taylor 2.50 6.00
65 Malcolm Lee 2.50 6.00
66 Reggie Jackson 4.00 10.00
67 Jonas Valanciunas 4.00 10.00
68 Bernard James 2.50 6.00
69 E'Twaun Moore 2.50 6.00
70 DeAndre Liggins 3.00 8.00
71 Quincy Acy 2.50 6.00
73 Jimmy Butler 30.00 80.00
74 Josh Selby 2.50 6.00
75 Jae Crowder 3.00 8.00
76 Draymond Green 10.00 25.00
77 Darius Morris 2.50 6.00
78 Trey Thompkins 2.50 6.00
79 Orlando Johnson 2.50 6.00
80 Khris Middleton 4.00 10.00
82 Tyler Honeycutt 2.50 6.00
83 Will Barton 3.00 8.00
85 Chris Singleton 2.50 6.00
88 Mike Scott 2.50 6.00
89 Jeremy Pargo 2.50 6.00
90 Kim English 2.50 6.00
91 Justin Hamilton 3.00 8.00
92 Darius Miller 2.50 6.00
93 Kevin Murphy 2.50 6.00
94 Nikola Vucevic 4.00 10.00
95 Kyle O'Quinn 2.50 6.00
97 Kris Joseph 2.50 6.00
98 Greg Stiemsma 2.50 6.00
100 Justin Harper 2.50 6.00

2012-13 Totally Certified Rookie Roll Call Autographs Blue

*BLUE: .6X TO 1.5X BASE HI
STATED PRINT RUN 49 TO 199 SER.#'d SETS
2 Iman Shumpert/49 20.00 50.00
11 Harrison Barnes/49 12.00 30.00
21 Kemba Walker/49 12.00 30.00
69 E'Twaun Moore/49 10.00 25.00

2012-13 Totally Certified Rookie Roll Call Autographs Gold

*GOLD: 1X TO 2.5X BASE HI
STATED PRINT RUN 15 TO 25 SER.#'d SETS
2 Iman Shumpert/15 20.00 50.00
11 Harrison Barnes/15 25.00 60.00
15 Bradley Beal/15 60.00 120.00
22 Bismack Biyombo/25 12.00 30.00
23 Tyler Zeller/25 20.00 50.00
24 Meyers Leonard/15 25.00 60.00
26 Enes Kanter/15 25.00 60.00
27 Perry Jones/25 EXCH 15.00 40.00
28 Kendall Marshall/25 6.00 15.00
32 John Henson/15 30.00 80.00
34 Norris Cole/25 6.00 15.00
35 Moe Harkless/25 20.00 50.00
36 Dion Waiters/15 10.00 25.00
38 Tristan Thompson/15 25.00 60.00
39 Terrence Ross/15 30.00 80.00
40 Royce White/25 EXCH 6.00 15.00
60 Marquis Teague/25 20.00 50.00
75 Jae Crowder/25 15.00 40.00
86 Tobias Harris/25 EXCH 10.00 25.00

2012-13 Totally Certified Rookie Roll Call Autographs Red

*RED: .5X TO 1.25X BASE HI
STATED PRINT RUN 68 TO 279 SER.#'d SETS
27 Perry Jones/199 EXCH 3.00 8.00

2013-14 Totally Certified

1 Kobe Bryant 3.00 8.00
2 Kevin Durant 2.00 5.00
3 Blake Griffin .75 2.00
4 Kyrie Irving 1.50 4.00
5 Dirk Nowitzki 1.00 2.50
6 LeBron James 3.00 8.00
7 Kevin Love .75 2.00
8 Damian Lillard 1.50 4.00
9 Carmelo Anthony 1.00 2.50
10 Paul Pierce .75 2.00
11 Roy Hibbert .60 1.50
12 James Harden 1.25 3.00
13 Russell Westbrook 2.00 5.00
14 Deron Williams .60 1.50
15 George Hill .60 1.50
16 Stephen Curry 3.00 8.00
17 Carlos Boozer .60 1.50
18 Kenneth Faried .60 1.50
19 Tim Duncan 1.25 3.00

20 DeMarcus Cousins .75 2.00
21 Ersan Ilyasova .50 1.25
22 Kendall Marshall .60 1.50
23 Ben Gordon .60 1.50
24 Jason Richardson .75 2.00
25 DeMar DeRozan .75 2.00
26 David Lee .50 1.25
27 Zach Randolph .60 1.50
28 Jeff Teague .60 1.50
29 Greivis Vasquez .60 1.50
30 Brandon Knight .60 1.50
31 Evan Turner .50 1.25
32 Amar'e Stoudemire .60 1.50
33 Tyreke Evans .50 1.25
34 Bradley Beal .75 2.00
35 Paul Millsap .75 2.00
36 Anderson Varejao .50 1.25
37 Klay Thompson 1.00 2.50
38 LaMarcus Aldridge .75 2.00
39 Dwyane Wade 1.25 3.00
40 Joe Johnson .60 1.50
41 Ricky Rubio .75 2.00
42 Pau Gasol .75 2.00
43 Luol Deng .60 1.50
44 Chris Paul 1.00 2.50
45 Kevin Garnett 1.25 3.00
46 Al Jefferson .60 1.50
47 Andre Iguodala .60 1.50
48 Vince Carter 1.00 2.50
49 Jimmer Fredette .50 1.25
50 Paul George 1.00 2.50
51 DeShawn Stevenson .50 1.25
52 Nick Young .75 2.00
53 Serge Ibaka .60 1.50
54 Glen Davis .50 1.25
55 Harrison Barnes .60 1.50
56 Michael Kidd-Gilchrist .75 2.00
57 Devin Harris .50 1.25
58 Marc Gasol .75 2.00
59 Jeremy Lin .75 2.00
60 Mike Conley .60 1.50
61 Jose Calderon .50 1.25
62 Isaiah Thomas .75 2.00
63 Tony Parker .75 2.00
64 Chris Bosh .75 2.00
65 Wesley Matthews .50 1.25
66 Brandon Jennings .50 1.25
67 Jimmy Butler .75 2.00
68 Anthony Davis 1.50 4.00
69 Shawn Marion .60 1.50
70 Tyson Chandler .60 1.50
71 Brook Lopez .60 1.50
72 Gordon Hayward .75 2.00
73 John Wall 1.00 2.50
74 Rajon Rondo .75 2.00
75 Ty Lawson .50 1.25
76 Andrea Bargnani .60 1.50
77 Marcin Gortat .60 1.50
78 Gary Neal .60 1.50
79 Thabo Sefolosha .50 1.25
80 Kemba Walker .75 2.00
81 Derrick Williams .50 1.25
82 Dwight Howard .60 1.50
83 Al Horford .60 1.50
84 JaVale McGee .60 1.50
85 Draymond Green 1.00 2.50
86 Lance Stephenson .60 1.50
87 Kawhi Leonard 1.25 3.00
88 Chandler Parsons .60 1.50
89 Martell Webster .50 1.25
90 Mario Chalmers .60 1.50
91 Metta World Peace .75 2.00
92 Gerald Wallace .60 1.50
93 Reggie Jackson .60 1.50
94 Austin Rivers .60 1.50
95 Jrue Holiday .75 2.00
96 Joakim Noah .60 1.50
97 Nene .60 1.50
98 Monta Ellis .60 1.50
99 Rudy Gay .75 2.00
100 Danilo Gallinari .50 1.25
101 J.J. Hickson .50 1.25
102 Ramon Sessions .60 1.50
103 Darrell Arthur .50 1.25
104 J.R. Smith .60 1.50
105 Jason Terry .60 1.50
106 Chase Budinger .50 1.25
107 Jameer Nelson .50 1.25
108 Danny Granger .60 1.50
109 Steve Nash .75 2.00
110 Tristan Thompson .60 1.50
111 Derrick Favors .60 1.50
112 Danny Green .60 1.50
113 J.J. Redick .75 2.00
114 DeAndre Jordan .75 2.00
115 Andre Drummond .75 2.00
116 Goran Dragic .60 1.50
117 Louis Williams .60 1.50
118 Chris Kaman .60 1.50
119 Kyle Lowry .60 1.50
120 Eric Gordon .60 1.50
121 Chris Andersen .60 1.50
122 Tayshaun Prince .60 1.50
123 Dion Waiters .60 1.50
124 Thomas Robinson .50 1.25
125 Thaddeus Young .50 1.25
126 Tyler Hansbrough .60 1.50
127 Rodney Stuckey .60 1.50
128 Derrick Rose 1.00 2.50
129 David West .60 1.50
130 Andrew Nicholson .50 1.25
131 Andrew Bogut .60 1.50
132 Arron Afflalo .50 1.25
133 Avery Bradley .60 1.50
134 Bismack Biyombo .50 1.25
135 Carl Landry .50 1.25
136 Carlos Delfino .50 1.25
137 Chris Copeland .50 1.25
138 Corey Brewer .50 1.25
139 Courtney Lee .60 1.50
140 Emeka Okafor .60 1.50
141 Eric Bledsoe .60 1.50
142 Evan Fournier .60 1.50
143 Jae Crowder .60 1.50
144 Jared Dudley .50 1.25
145 Jared Sullinger .50 1.25
146 Jarrett Jack .60 1.50
147 Jeff Green .60 1.50
148 Jeremy Lamb .50 1.25
149 Kevin Martin .60 1.50
150 Larry Sanders .50 1.25
151 Manu Ginobili .75 2.00
152 Matt Barnes .50 1.25
153 Maurice Harkless .50 1.25
154 Nikola Pekovic .50 1.25
155 Nikola Vucevic .60 1.50
156 Norris Cole .50 1.25
157 Richard Jefferson .60 1.50
158 Shane Battier .60 1.50
159 Shannon Brown .50 1.25
160 Tobias Harris .60 1.50
161 Trevor Ariza .50 1.25
162 Tyler Zeller .60 1.50
163 Udonis Haslem .50 1.25
164 Will Bynum .50 1.25
165 Zaza Pachulia .50 1.25
166 Tony Allen .50 1.25
167 Ryan Anderson .60 1.50
168 Steve Novak .50 1.25
169 Jonas Valanciunas .60 1.50
170 Kyle Korver .60 1.50
171 Mike Dunleavy .50 1.25
172 Darren Collison .60 1.50
173 Pablo Prigioni .50 1.25
174 Raymond Felton .60 1.50
175 Tiago Splitter .60 1.50
176 Andray Blatche .50 1.25
177 Gerald Henderson .50 1.25
178 Amir Johnson .50 1.25
179 Robin Lopez .50 1.25
180 Terrence Jones .60 1.50
181 Nicolas Batum .60 1.50
182 Brandon Rush .50 1.25
183 Iman Shumpert .50 1.25
184 Quincy Pondexter .50 1.25
185 Patrick Beverley .50 1.25
186 O.J. Mayo .50 1.25
187 Andre Miller .60 1.50
188 Victor Claver .50 1.25
189 Terrence Ross .60 1.50
190 Wilson Chandler .60 1.50
191 Eric Maynor .50 1.25
192 MarShon Brooks .60 1.50
193 Anthony Morrow .50 1.25
194 Lavoy Allen .50 1.25
195 Andrei Kirilenko .60 1.50
196 Luc Mbah a Moute .50 1.25
197 Jordan Farmar .50 1.25
198 Michael Beasley .50 1.25
199 Dorell Wright .50 1.25
200 Kosta Koufos .50 1.25
201 C.J. Leslie RC .60 1.50
202 Ricky Ledo RC .60 1.50
203 Jeff Withey RC .60 1.50
204 Archie Goodwin RC .75 2.00
205 Dwight Buycks RC .60 1.50
206 Gal Mekel RC .60 1.50
207 Elias Harris RC .75 2.00
208 Peyton Siva RC .60 1.50
209 Romero Osby RC 1.00 2.50
210 Luigi Datome RC .60 1.50
211 Erik Murphy RC .60 1.50
212 Ryan Kelly RC .60 1.50
213 Ian Clark RC .75 2.00
214 Jamaal Franklin RC .60 1.50
215 Grant Jerrett RC .60 1.50
216 Nate Wolters RC .75 2.00
217 Tony Mitchell RC .60 1.50
218 Ray McCallum RC .60 1.50
219 Glen Rice Jr. RC .60 1.50
220 Isaiah Canaan RC .60 1.50
221 Carrick Felix RC .60 1.50
222 Allen Crabbe RC .75 2.00
223 Phil Pressey RC .60 1.50
224 Rudy Gobert RC 1.25 3.00
225 Andre Roberson RC .60 1.50
226 Reggie Bullock RC .75 2.00
227 Tim Hardaway Jr. RC 1.00 2.50
228 Solomon Hill RC .60 1.50
229 Mason Plumlee RC 1.00 2.50
230 Gorgui Dieng RC .75 2.00
231 Tony Snell RC .75 2.00
232 Sergey Karasev RC .60 1.50
233 Shane Larkin RC .60 1.50
234 Dennis Schroder RC 1.00 2.50
235 Robert Covington RC .60 1.50
236 G.Antetokounmpo RC 8.00 20.00
237 Shabazz Muhammad RC .75 2.00
238 Kelly Olynyk RC .75 2.00
239 Steven Adams RC 1.00 2.50
240 M.Carter-Williams RC 1.00 2.50
241 C.J. McCollum RC 1.50 4.00
242 Trey Burke RC .75 2.00
243 Kentavious Caldwell-Pope RC 1.00 2.50
244 Ben McLemore RC .75 2.00
245 Nerlens Noel RC 1.25 3.00
246 Alex Len RC .75 2.00
247 Cody Zeller RC .75 2.00
248 Otto Porter RC 1.00 2.50
249 Victor Oladipo RC 1.25 3.00
250 Anthony Bennett RC .75 2.00
251 Grant Hill 1.25 3.00
252 Larry Bird 2.50 6.00
253 Jerry West 1.25 3.00
254 Rick Barry .75 2.00
255 John Stockton 1.50 4.00
256 Kevin McHale 1.00 2.50
257 Elgin Baylor 1.00 2.50
258 Jason Kidd 1.00 2.50
259 Magic Johnson 2.50 6.00
260 Walt Frazier 1.00 2.50
261 Gary Payton 1.00 2.50
262 Yao Ming 1.25 3.00
263 Allen Iverson 1.25 3.00
264 Kareem Abdul-Jabbar 1.50 4.00
265 Clyde Drexler 1.25 3.00
266 George Mikan 2.00 5.00
267 Pete Maravich 1.50 4.00
268 Hakeem Olajuwon 1.25 3.00
269 Shaquille O'Neal 2.00 5.00
270 Julius Erving 1.50 4.00
271 Scottie Pippen 2.00 5.00
272 Earl Monroe 1.00 2.50
273 Isiah Thomas 1.00 2.50
274 Bill Russell 1.50 4.00
275 Dominique Wilkins 1.25 3.00
276 Wilt Chamberlain 2.00 5.00
277 George Gervin 1.00 2.50
278 Oscar Robertson 1.25 3.00
279 Dennis Rodman 2.00 5.00
280 David Robinson 1.50 4.00
281 John Havlicek 1.25 3.00
282 Bill Laimbeer .75 2.00
283 Calvin Natt .60 1.50
284 Detlef Schrempf 1.00 2.50
285 Len Elmore .60 1.50
286 Gail Goodrich .75 2.00
287 Tim Hardaway 1.00 2.50
288 Moses Malone 1.00 2.50
289 Bill Walton 1.00 2.50
290 Norm Nixon .60 1.50
291 Jim Jackson .60 1.50
292 Phil Jackson 1.25 3.00
293 Rick Fox .75 2.00
294 Spencer Haywood .60 1.50
295 Tom Chambers .75 2.00
296 Toni Kukoc 1.00 2.50
297 Larry Johnson 1.25 3.00
298 Spud Webb .75 2.00
299 Shawn Kemp 1.50 4.00
300 Alonzo Mourning 1.25 3.00

2013-14 Totally Certified Blue

*BLUE: 1.5X TO 4X BASIC
*BLUE RC: 1.2X TO 3X BASIC RC
STATED PRINT RUN 49 SER.#'d SETS
50 Paul George 10.00 25.00
236 Giannis Antetokounmpo 15.00 40.00
239 Steven Adams 30.00 80.00
249 Victor Oladipo 20.00 50.00

2013-14 Totally Certified Gold

*GOLD: 3X TO 8X BASIC
*GOLD RC: 2.5X TO 6X BASIC RC
STATED PRINT RUN 25 SER.#'d SETS
1 Kobe Bryant 40.00 100.00
2 Kevin Durant 30.00 80.00
4 Kyrie Irving 40.00 100.00
6 LeBron James 40.00 100.00
50 Paul George 15.00 40.00
236 Giannis Antetokounmpo 25.00 60.00
239 Steven Adams 50.00 120.00
249 Victor Oladipo 30.00 80.00

2013-14 Totally Certified Red

*RED: 1.2X TO 3X BASIC
*RED RC: 1X TO 2.5X BASIC RC
STATED PRINT RUN 99 SER.#'d SETS

2013-14 Totally Certified Autographs

EXCHANGE DEADLINE 5/27/2015
3 Zydrunas Ilgauskas 3.00 8.00
8 Allan Houston
10 Jim Jackson 2.50 6.00
11 Greg Anthony
13 Kyle Lowry
16 Kenneth Faried 3.00 8.00
17 Brandon Bass
19 Sleepy Floyd 2.50 6.00
20 Iman Shumpert 2.50 6.00
21 Bruce Bowen 2.50 6.00
22 Kobe Bryant 75.00 150.00
23 Kevin Durant EXCH 60.00 120.00
24 Kyrie Irving 20.00 50.00
26 Kareem Abdul-Jabbar 25.00 60.00
27 Kawhi Leonard 25.00 60.00
28 Nikola Pekovic
29 Nikola Vucevic
30 Michael Cooper 3.00 8.00
31 Nick Young
32 David West 3.00 8.00
35 Jeff Malone 2.50 6.00
36 Meyers Leonard
37 Scottie Pippen 90.00 150.00
40 Karl Malone 40.00 80.00
41 John Lucas 4.00 10.00
43 Bob Dandridge 2.50 6.00
44 Bill Cartwright
46 Connie Hawkins
47 Dan Majerle 3.00 8.00
49 A.C. Green 4.00 10.00
51 Ronny Turiaf
52 John Paxson 3.00 8.00
57 David Thompson
58 Kurt Rambis
61 David Robinson 15.00 40.00
62 Horace Grant 10.00 25.00
63 Tom Chambers 3.00 8.00
64 Gary Payton
65 Sidney Moncrief 2.50 6.00
67 Dikembe Mutombo
68 B.J. Armstrong
69 Alonzo Mourning 15.00 40.00
70 Vernon Maxwell 2.50 6.00
71 Jason Kidd
72 Grant Hill 20.00 50.00
73 Corey Brewer 2.50 6.00
74 Sebastian Telfair 2.50 6.00
75 Anthony Mason 3.00 8.00
76 Chuck Person
77 Carl Landry
80 Chris Mullin 8.00 20.00
81 Scott Skiles 3.00 8.00
82 Jo Jo White 3.00 8.00
83 J.R. Smith
84 Ray Williams 2.50 6.00
88 Jarrett Jack 6.00 15.00
90 Ryan Anderson
91 J.J. Redick
96 Kyle Korver
97 Goran Dragic
99 Jeff Teague
100 Danny Green 3.00 8.00
101 Jeff Green
102 Richard Jefferson
103 Bailey Howell
107 Tiago Splitter
108 Boris Diaw
109 Antawn Jamison 3.00 8.00
110 Steve Novak
111 Kendrick Perkins
115 Earl Clark
116 Kris Humphries
119 Nicolas Batum
121 Marcin Gortat
123 Dwyane Wade 60.00 120.00
124 Rodney Stuckey
126 Jerryd Bayless
128 Timofey Mozgov 2.50 6.00
130 Ersan Ilyasova
131 Landry Fields 2.50 6.00
133 Marcus Thornton 2.50 6.00
135 Andray Blatche 2.50 6.00
138 Anderson Varejao 2.50 6.00
140 George Hill
141 Leandro Barbosa
142 Taj Gibson
143 Andrew Bogut
144 Mike Conley 3.00 8.00
147 Vince Carter
148 Jan Vesely
150 Kendall Marshall 3.00 8.00
151 Mel Davis 2.50 6.00
153 MarShon Brooks 3.00 8.00
154 Darryl Dawkins EXCH 2.50 6.00
156 Jack Sikma 3.00 8.00
158 Norris Cole
159 Jonas Valanciunas
161 Enes Kanter
163 Harrison Barnes 12.00 30.00
166 Spud Webb EXCH 3.00 8.00
168 John Henson
169 Isaiah Thomas 10.00 25.00
170 Tyler Zeller
172 Bradley Beal 8.00 20.00
175 Len Elmore 2.50 6.00
176 Tom "Satch" Sanders
181 Ekpe Udoh 2.50 6.00
184 Larry Nance 3.00 8.00
185 Paul Westphal 4.00 10.00
187 Daequan Cook
188 Eric Maynor 2.50 6.00
189 Luis Scola
190 Chase Budinger 2.50 6.00
192 Jared Dudley
193 Mitch Richmond 10.00 25.00
194 Bernard King
195 Thabo Sefolosha
196 Reggie Jackson 3.00 8.00
197 Udonis Haslem 2.50 6.00
199 Kevin Willis 2.50 6.00
200 Kenny Walker
202 Micheal Ray Richardson 3.00 8.00
203 Rolando Blackman 3.00 8.00
205 Jerome Williams 2.50 6.00
206 John Lucas III 2.50 6.00
207 Otis Birdsong 3.00 8.00
208 Mark Aguirre 3.00 8.00
209 Dave Stallworth 4.00 10.00
210 Herb Williams 2.50 6.00
211 Kenny Anderson 3.00 8.00
212 Leonard "Truck" Robinson 2.50 6.00
213 John Salley 2.50 6.00
214 Campy Russell 2.50 6.00
215 Jason Smith 2.50 6.00
216 Norm Nixon 2.50 6.00
217 Bismack Biyombo 2.50 6.00
218 DeMarre Carroll 2.50 6.00
219 Roger Mason Jr. 2.50 6.00
220 Rod Strickland 2.50 6.00
221 Marvin Williams 3.00 8.00
222 Lance Thomas 2.50 6.00
223 Gus Williams 2.50 6.00
224 Reggie Theus 3.00 8.00
225 Bill Laimbeer 3.00 8.00
226 Darrell Armstrong 2.50 6.00
227 Buck Williams 2.50 6.00
228 Spencer Haywood 2.50 6.00
229 Luc Longley 4.00 10.00
230 Kenyon Martin 3.00 8.00
231 Mickael Pietrus 2.50 6.00
232 Jarvis Varnado 2.50 6.00
233 Justin Hamilton 2.50 6.00
234 Lance Stephenson 3.00 8.00
236 Keith Bogans 2.50 6.00
237 Jeremy Evans 2.50 6.00
239 Ronnie Brewer 3.00 8.00
241 Patrick Beverley 2.50 6.00
242 Maurice Harkless 2.50 6.00
243 Justin Holiday 8.00 20.00
244 Darrell Walker 4.00 10.00
246 Darrell Griffith 2.50 6.00
251 Xavier McDaniel 2.50 6.00
254 Robert Horry 3.00 8.00
255 Fat Lever 3.00 8.00
256 Harvey Grant 2.50 6.00
257 Tim Hardaway 5.00 12.00
258 Bobby Jones 3.00 8.00
259 O.J. Mayo 2.50 6.00
260 Bob McAdoo 15.00 40.00

2013-14 Totally Certified Autographs Blue

*BLUE p/r 49: .75X TO 2X BASIC
*BLUE p/r 25: 1X TO 2.5X BASIC
PRINT RUNS B/WN 5-49 COPIES PER
NO PRICING ON QTY 20 OR LESS
EXCHANGE DEADLINE 5/27/2015
33 Cedric Maxwell/49 EXCH 5.00 12.00
34 Chris Wilcox/49 12.00 30.00
129 Luc Mbah a Moute/49 EXCH 5.00 12.00
137 Jonas Jerebko/49 EXCH 5.00 12.00
146 Zaza Pachulia/49 5.00 12.00
157 Jordan Hamilton/49 5.00 12.00
162 Kim English/25 6.00 15.00
164 Jeff Taylor/49 5.00 12.00
204 Julyan Stone/49 5.00 12.00
235 DeSagana Diop/49 5.00 12.00
238 Jon Leuer/49 5.00 12.00
240 Tornike Shengelia/49

2013-14 Totally Certified Autographs Gold

*GOLD p/r 25: 1X TO 2.5X BASIC
PRINT RUNS B/WN 3-25 COPIES PER
NO PRICING ON QTY 20 OR LESS
EXCHANGE DEADLINE 5/27/2015
33 Cedric Maxwell/25 EXCH 6.00 15.00
34 Chris Wilcox/25 15.00 40.00
129 Luc Mbah a Moute/25 EXCH 6.00 15.00
137 Jonas Jerebko/25 EXCH 6.00 15.00
146 Zaza Pachulia/25 6.00 15.00
157 Jordan Hamilton/25 6.00 15.00
164 Jeff Taylor/25 6.00 15.00
204 Julyan Stone/25 6.00 15.00
235 DeSagana Diop/25 6.00 15.00
238 Jon Leuer/25 6.00 15.00
240 Tornike Shengelia/25

2013-14 Totally Certified Autographs Red

*RED p/r 99: .6X TO 1.5X BASIC
*RED p/r 49: .75X TO 2X BASIC
*RED p/r 25: 1X TO 2.5X BASIC
PRINT RUNS B/WN 8-99 COPIES PER
NO PRICING ON QTY 20 OR LESS
EXCHANGE DEADLINE 5/27/2015
33 Cedric Maxwell/99 EXCH 4.00 10.00
34 Chris Wilcox/99 10.00 25.00
129 Luc Mbah a Moute/99 EXCH 4.00 10.00
137 Jonas Jerebko/99 EXCH 4.00 10.00
146 Zaza Pachulia/99 4.00 10.00
157 Jordan Hamilton/99 4.00 10.00
162 Kim English/49 5.00 12.00
164 Jeff Taylor/99 4.00 10.00
204 Julyan Stone/99 4.00 10.00
235 DeSagana Diop/99 4.00 10.00
238 Jon Leuer/99 4.00 10.00
240 Tornike Shengelia/99
245 C.J. Miles/99 EXCH 5.00 12.00
247 Greg Ostertag/99 EXCH 4.00 10.00

2013-14 Totally Certified Ballot Busters Autographs

PRINT RUNS B/WN 10-99 COPIES PER
NO PRICING ON QTY 10
EXCHANGE DEADLINE 5/27/2015
BBAD Adrian Dantley/99 6.00 15.00
BBAE Alex English/99 5.00 12.00
BBAG Artis Gilmore/15 10.00 25.00
BBBH Bailey Howell/99 10.00 25.00
BBBL Bob Lanier/15 5.00 12.00
BBBW Bill Walton/25 8.00 20.00
BBCH Connie Hawkins/49 10.00 25.00
BBCM Calvin Murphy/25 10.00 25.00
BBCM Chris Mullin/49 10.00 25.00
BBDC Dave Cowens/25 4.00 10.00
BBDI Dan Issel/99
BBDR David Robinson/10 10.00 25.00
BBDR Dennis Rodman/25 40.00 100.00
BBDT David Thompson/99 5.00 12.00
BBDW Dominique Wilkins/10 8.00 20.00
BBEH Elvin Hayes/25 12.00 30.00
BBGG Gail Goodrich/25 15.00 40.00
BBIT Isiah Thomas/15 6.00 15.00
BBJD Joe Dumars/25 10.00 25.00
BBJW Jamaal Wilkes/49 15.00 40.00
BBKM Karl Malone/10 8.00 20.00
BBMA Mark Aguirre/50 5.00 12.00
BBMJ Magic Johnson/10 15.00 40.00
BBRP Robert Parish/25 10.00 25.00
BBSS Satch Sanders/99 6.00 15.00

2013-14 Totally Certified Future Stars Autographs

PRINT RUNS B/WN 25-325 COPIES PER
EXCHANGE DEADLINE 5/27/2015
FSAB Anthony Bennett/25 5.00 12.00
FSAG Archie Goodwin/325 5.00 12.00
FSAL Alex Len/25 5.00 12.00
FSBM Ben McLemore/25
FSCM C.J. McCollum/25 60.00 120.00
FSCZ Cody Zeller/25 5.00 12.00
FSGD Gorgui Dieng/299 5.00 12.00
FSGJ Grant Jerrett/299 4.00 10.00
FSJF Jamaal Franklin/325 4.00 10.00
FSKC Kentavious Caldwell-Pope/25 6.00 15.00
FSKO Kelly Olynyk/199 5.00 12.00
FSMC M.Carter-Williams/25 12.00 30.00
FSNN Nerlens Noel/25 12.00 30.00
FSNW Nate Wolters/325 5.00 12.00
FSOP Otto Porter/25 12.00 30.00
FSPS Peyton Siva/325 4.00 10.00
FSRG Rudy Gobert/299 EXCH 8.00 20.00
FSRK Ryan Kelly/299 6.00 15.00
FSRM Ray McCallum/199 4.00 10.00
FSSH Solomon Hill/325 4.00 10.00
FSSM Shabazz Muhammad/25
FSTB Trey Burke/25 75.00 150.00
FSTH Tim Hardaway Jr./299 12.00 30.00
FSTM Tony Mitchell/325 4.00 10.00
FSVO Victor Oladipo/25

2013-14 Totally Certified Materials

COMMON CARD 1.50 4.00
SEMISTARS 2.00 5.00
UNLISTED STARS 2.50 6.00
1 Tim Duncan 4.00 10.00
2 Kevin Martin 2.00 5.00
3 Dee Brown 1.50 4.00
4 Nick Young 2.50 6.00
5 Carl Landry 1.50 4.00
6 Michael Beasley 1.50 4.00
7 Kevin Love 2.50 6.00
8 Louis Williams 2.00 5.00
9 Jason Terry 2.00 5.00
10 Mo Williams 2.00 5.00
11 Manu Ginobili 2.50 6.00
12 Steve Novak 1.50 4.00
13 Luc Mbah a Moute 1.50 4.00
14 Ersan Ilyasova 1.50 4.00
15 David Lee 1.50 4.00
16 Ray Allen 2.50 6.00
17 Brandon Jennings 1.50 4.00
18 Eddie Jones 2.00 5.00
19 Terrence Ross 2.00 5.00
20 Rasheed Wallace 2.50 6.00
21 Joakim Noah 2.00 5.00
22 J.R. Smith 2.00 5.00
23 Monta Ellis 2.00 5.00
24 Bobby Jackson 1.50 4.00
25 Klay Thompson 3.00 8.00
26 David West 2.00 5.00
27 Taj Gibson 2.00 5.00
28 Larry Nance 2.00 5.00
29 Ekpe Udoh 1.50 4.00
30 Deron Williams 2.00 5.00
31 Carlos Boozer 2.00 5.00
32 Karl Malone 3.00 8.00
33 Jrue Holiday 2.50 6.00
34 Spencer Hawes 1.50 4.00
35 Kyrie Irving 5.00 12.00
36 Orlando Johnson 1.50 4.00
37 Alan Anderson 1.50 4.00
38 Will Bynum 1.50 4.00
39 Brook Lopez 2.00 5.00
40 John Wall 3.00 8.00
41 Damian Lillard 5.00 12.00
42 Danny Manning 2.00 5.00
43 Evan Turner 1.50 4.00
44 Jeff Teague 2.00 5.00
45 Kyle Singler 1.50 4.00
46 Rajon Rondo 2.50 6.00
47 Roy Hibbert 2.00 5.00
48 Kobe Bryant 10.00 25.00
49 Jeff Green 2.00 5.00
50 Bradley Beal 2.50 6.00
51 LeBron James
52 Brent Barry 1.50 4.00
53 Carmelo Anthony 3.00 8.00
54 Zaza Pachulia 1.50 4.00
55 Andre Drummond 2.50 6.00
56 Dirk Nowitzki 3.00 8.00
57 DeMarcus Cousins 2.50 6.00
58 Steve Nash 2.50 6.00
59 Bill Laimbeer 2.00 5.00
60 Nene 2.00 5.00
61 Dwyane Wade 4.00 10.00
62 Bob Lanier 2.00 5.00
63 Paul Pierce 2.50 6.00
64 Devin Harris 1.50 4.00
65 Kent Bazemore 2.00 5.00
66 Brandon Bass 1.50 4.00
67 Jonas Jerebko 1.50 4.00
68 Jamal Crawford 2.50 6.00
69 Marcus Camby 2.00 5.00
70 Al Jefferson 2.00 5.00
71 Joel Anthony 1.50 4.00
72 Paul Westphal 2.50 6.00
73 Kevin Garnett 4.00 10.00
74 Pau Gasol 2.50 6.00
75 Chandler Parsons 2.00 5.00
76 Shaquille O'Neal 5.00 12.00
77 Spencer Haywood 1.50 4.00
78 Amar'e Stoudemire 2.00 5.00
79 Lucius Allen 2.50 6.00
80 Derrick Favors 2.00 5.00
81 Shane Battier 2.00 5.00
82 Larry Bird 6.00 15.00
83 Grant Hill 3.00 8.00
84 D.J. Augustin 1.50 4.00
85 LaMarcus Aldridge 2.50 6.00
86 John Lucas 2.50 6.00
87 George Mikan
88 Anthony Davis
89 John Henson 2.00 5.00
90 Gordon Hayward 2.50 6.00
91 Nate Robinson 1.50 4.00
92 Jayson Williams 1.50 4.00
93 Jason Richardson 2.50 6.00
94 Andrew Bogut 2.00 5.00
95 Kendall Marshall 2.00 5.00
96 Cazzie Russell 2.00 5.00
97 Marcin Gortat 2.00 5.00
98 Ryan Anderson 2.00 5.00
99 Draymond Green 3.00 8.00
100 Dominique Wilkins
101 Zydrunas Ilgauskas 2.00 5.00
102 JaVale McGee 2.00 5.00
103 Kemba Walker 2.50 6.00
104 Glen Davis 1.50 4.00
105 Kawhi Leonard 4.00 10.00
106 Rashard Lewis 2.00 5.00
107 Maurice Lucas 2.50 6.00
108 Avery Bradley 2.00 5.00
109 Moses Malone 2.50 6.00
110 Caron Butler 2.00 5.00
111 Shawn Marion 2.00 5.00
112 Jalen Rose 2.50 6.00
113 Gerald Henderson 1.50 4.00
114 Arron Afflalo 1.50 4.00
115 Tony Parker 2.50 6.00
116 Buck Williams 1.50 4.00
117 DeMar DeRozan 2.50 6.00
118 Tristan Thompson 2.00 5.00
119 Serge Ibaka 2.00 5.00
120 Blake Griffin 2.50 6.00
121 Evan Fournier 2.00 5.00
122 Alex English 2.00 5.00
123 Zach Randolph 2.00 5.00
124 J.J. Barea 2.00 5.00
125 Wesley Matthews 1.50 4.00
126 Patrick Ewing
127 Jeff Hornacek 2.00 5.00
128 Derrick Rose 3.00 8.00
129 Cedric Maxwell 1.50 4.00
130 Tyson Chandler 2.00 5.00
131 Ty Lawson 1.50 4.00
132 Robert Parish 2.50 6.00
133 Vince Carter 3.00 8.00
134 Anderson Varejao 1.50 4.00
135 Nicolas Batum 2.00 5.00
136 Kevin Durant 6.00 15.00
137 Emeka Okafor 2.00 5.00
138 Marc Gasol 2.50 6.00
139 Danny Granger 2.00 5.00
140 Raymond Felton 2.00 5.00
141 Kenneth Faried 2.00 5.00
142 Michael Kidd-Gilchrist 2.50 6.00
143 Andrew Nicholson 1.50 4.00
144 Gerald Wallace 2.00 5.00
145 Dwight Howard 2.00 5.00
146 Jimmer Fredette 1.50 4.00
147 DeAndre Jordan 2.50 6.00
148 Chris Paul 3.00 8.00
149 Paul George 3.00 8.00
150 Dion Waiters 2.00 5.00
151 LeBron James 10.00 25.00
152 David West 2.00 5.00
153 Dwight Howard 2.00 5.00
154 Devin Harris 1.50 4.00
155 Rasheed Wallace 2.50 6.00
156 Rashard Lewis 2.00 5.00
157 Nick Young 2.50 6.00
158 Jeff Green 2.00 5.00
159 David Lee 1.50 4.00
160 Jalen Rose 2.50 6.00
161 Al Jefferson 2.00 5.00
162 Carmelo Anthony 3.00 8.00
163 Emeka Okafor 2.00 5.00
164 Marcus Camby 2.00 5.00
165 Steve Nash 2.50 6.00
166 Grant Hill 3.00 8.00
167 Nene 2.00 5.00
168 JaVale McGee 2.00 5.00
169 Chris Paul 3.00 8.00
170 Deron Williams 2.00 5.00
171 Amar'e Stoudemire 2.00 5.00
172 Caron Butler 2.00 5.00
173 Jason Richardson 2.50 6.00
174 Mo Williams 2.00 5.00
175 Vince Carter 3.00 8.00
176 Kevin Martin 2.00 5.00
177 Nate Robinson 1.50 4.00
178 Jason Terry 2.00 5.00
179 Michael Beasley 1.50 4.00
180 Raymond Felton 2.00 5.00
181 Giannis Antetokounmpo 20.00 50.00
182 Shane Larkin 1.50 4.00
183 Andre Roberson 1.50 4.00
184 Tim Hardaway Jr. 2.50 6.00
185 Anthony Bennett 2.00 5.00
186 Kelly Olynyk 2.00 5.00
187 Tony Snell 2.00 5.00
188 Cody Zeller 2.00 5.00
189 Victor Oladipo 3.00 8.00
190 Trey Burke 2.00 5.00
191 Steven Adams 2.50 6.00
192 Michael Carter-Williams 2.50 6.00
193 Nerlens Noel 3.00 8.00
194 Ryan Kelly 1.50 4.00
195 Shabazz Muhammad 2.00 5.00
196 C.J. McCollum 4.00 10.00
197 Ben McLemore 2.00 5.00
198 Otto Porter 2.50 6.00
199 Glen Rice Jr. 1.50 4.00
200 Jamaal Franklin 1.50 4.00

2013-14 Totally Certified Materials Blue

*BLUE p/r 75-99: .5X TO 1.2X BASIC
*BLUE p/r 49: .75X TO 2X BASIC
*BLUE p/r 15-25: 1.2X TO 3X BASIC
PRINT RUN B/WN 5-99 COPIES PER
NO PRICING ON QTY 10 OR LESS
51 LeBron James/99 12.00 30.00
87 George Mikan/15 15.00 40.00
88 Anthony Davis/99 6.00 15.00
100 Dominique Wilkins/25 10.00 25.00
126 Patrick Ewing/99 4.00 10.00

2013-14 Totally Certified Materials Blue Prime

*BLUE PRIME p/r 15-25: 1.2X TO 3X BASIC
PRINT RUN B/WN 2-25 COPIES PER
NO PRICING ON QTY 10 OR LESS
51 LeBron James/25 30.00 80.00
88 Anthony Davis/15 15.00 40.00
126 Patrick Ewing/15 10.00 25.00
151 LeBron James/25 30.00 80.00

2013-14 Totally Certified Materials Gold Prime

*GLD PRIME p/r 15-25: 1.2X TO 3X BASIC
PRINT RUN B/WN 2-25 COPIES PER
NO PRICING ON QTY 10 OR LESS
51 LeBron James/25 30.00 80.00
88 Anthony Davis/25 15.00 40.00

2013-14 Totally Certified Materials Red

*RED p/r 75-99: .5X TO 1.2X BASIC
*RED p/r 49: .75X TO 2X BASIC
*RED p/r 15-25: 1.2X TO 3X BASIC
PRINT RUN B/WN 5-199 COPIES PER
NO PRICING ON QTY 10 OR LESS
51 LeBron James/149 12.00 30.00
87 George Mikan/15 15.00 40.00
88 Anthony Davis/99 6.00 15.00
100 Dominique Wilkins/49 6.00 15.00
126 Patrick Ewing/49 6.00 15.00

2013-14 Totally Certified Materials Red Prime

*RED PREIM p/r 15-25: 1.2X TO 3X BASIC
PRINT RUN B/WN 2-25 COPIES PER
NO PRICING ON QTY 10 OR LESS
51 LeBron James/25 30.00 80.00
126 Patrick Ewing/15 10.00 25.00
151 LeBron James/25 30.00 80.00

2013-14 Totally Certified Present Potential Autographs

PRINT RUNS B/WN 25-299 COPIES PER
NO PRICING ON QTY 10
EXCHANGE DEADLINE 5/27/2015
PPAA Alan Anderson/199 4.00 10.00
PPCB Corey Brewer/125 4.00 10.00
PPDG Danny Green/99 10.00 25.00
PPDG Draymond Green/199 15.00 40.00
PPEC Earl Clark/99 4.00 10.00
PPEI Ersan Ilyasova/75 4.00 10.00
PPEM E'Twaun Moore/199 4.00 10.00
PPEU Ekpe Udoh/199 4.00 10.00
PPGD Goran Dragic/25
PPGV Greivis Vasquez/99 5.00 12.00
PPIS Iman Shumpert/99 4.00 10.00
PPJG Jeff Green/49
PPJH Jrue Holiday/25 6.00 15.00
PPKL Kawhi Leonard/99 40.00 100.00
PPKL Kyle Lowry/49 5.00 12.00
PPLS Lance Stephenson/199 5.00 12.00
PPMC Mike Conley/25 5.00 12.00
PPME Monta Ellis/49 6.00 15.00
PPMH Maurice Harkless/299 4.00 10.00
PPMW Marvin Williams/199 5.00 12.00
PPNB Nicolas Batum/149 5.00 12.00
PPRB Ronnie Brewer/179 5.00 12.00
PPTB Trevor Booker/299 4.00 10.00
PPTH Tobias Harris/99 5.00 12.00
PPTS Tiago Splitter/49

2013-14 Totally Certified Rookie Roll Call Autographs

EXCHANGE DEADLINE 5/27/2015
1 Anthony Bennett 4.00 10.00
2 Victor Oladipo 30.00 80.00
3 Archie Goodwin 4.00 10.00
4 Dennis Schroder 5.00 12.00
5 Glen Rice Jr. 3.00 8.00
6 Isaiah Canaan 3.00 8.00
7 Peyton Siva 3.00 8.00
8 Ryan Kelly 3.00 8.00
9 Phil Pressey 3.00 8.00
10 Shabazz Muhammad
11 Otto Porter 10.00 25.00
12 Trey Burke 4.00 10.00
13 Kelly Olynyk 4.00 10.00
14 Kentavious Caldwell-Pope 5.00 12.00
15 Carrick Felix 3.00 8.00
16 Cody Zeller 4.00 10.00
17 Ray McCallum 3.00 8.00
18 Ben McLemore 4.00 10.00
19 Giannis Antetokounmpo 60.00 150.00
20 Shane Larkin 3.00 8.00
21 Tim Hardaway Jr. 5.00 12.00
22 Andre Roberson 3.00 8.00
23 C.J. McCollum 20.00 50.00
24 Nerlens Noel 6.00 15.00
25 Alex Len 4.00 10.00
26 Michael Carter-Williams 5.00 12.00
27 Erik Murphy 3.00 8.00
28 Gorgui Dieng 4.00 10.00
29 Allen Crabbe 4.00 10.00
30 Reggie Bullock 4.00 10.00
31 Nate Wolters 4.00 10.00
32 Mason Plumlee 5.00 12.00
33 Ricky Ledo 3.00 8.00
34 Tony Mitchell 3.00 8.00
35 C.J. Leslie 3.00 8.00
36 Grant Jerrett 3.00 8.00
37 Solomon Hill 3.00 8.00
38 Tony Snell 4.00 10.00
39 Jamaal Franklin 3.00 8.00
40 Elias Harris 4.00 10.00

2013-14 Totally Certified Rookie Roll Call Autographs Blue

*BLUE p/r 49: .75X TO 2X BASIC
PRINT RUNS B/WN 15-49 COPIES PER
NO PRICING ON QTY 15
EXCHANGE DEADLINE 5/27/2015

2013-14 Totally Certified Rookie Roll Call Autographs Red

*RED p/r 35: .75X TO 2X BASIC
*RED p/r 99: .6X TO 1.5X BASIC
PRINT RUNS B/WN 20-99 COPIES PER
NO PRICING ON QTY 20 OR LESS
EXCHANGE DEADLINE 5/27/2015

2013-14 Totally Certified Select Few Autographs

PRINT RUNS B/WN 10-99 COPIES PER
NO PRICING ON QTY 10
EXCHANGE DEADLINE 5/27/2015
1 Kobe Bryant/99 90.00 150.00
2 Blake Griffin/49 30.00 60.00
3 Kyrie Irving/99 40.00 100.00
4 Kevin Durant/49 60.00 150.00
7 Larry Bird/25 30.00 80.00
8 Magic Johnson/25 30.00 80.00
9 Kareem Abdul-Jabbar/25
12 Gail Goodrich/25 5.00 12.00
13 Scottie Pippen/25
14 George Gervin/25 6.00 15.00
24 Wes Unseld/25 6.00 15.00

2014-15 Totally Certified

1 LaMarcus Aldridge .60 1.50
2 Paul George .75 2.00
3 Kyle Lowry .50 1.25
4 Al Horford .50 1.25
5 Zach Randolph .50 1.25
6 Al Jefferson .50 1.25
7 Anthony Bennett .40 1.00
8 Stephen Curry 2.50 6.00
9 Nicolas Batum .50 1.25
10 Jeff Teague .50 1.25
11A LeBron James 2.50 6.00
11B LeBron James 2.50 6.00
12 Kemba Walker .60 1.50
13 Jrue Holiday .50 1.25
14 Dion Waiters .50 1.25
15 Tobias Harris .50 1.25
16 Andre Iguodala .50 1.25
17 C.J. McCollum .60 1.50
18 Blake Griffin .60 1.50
19 DeMar DeRozan .60 1.50
20 Paul Millsap .60 1.50
21 Dwyane Wade 1.00 2.50
22 Gerald Henderson .40 1.00
23 Ryan Anderson .40 1.00
24 Nikola Vucevic .50 1.25
25 Andrew Bogut .50 1.25
26 DeAndre Jordan .60 1.50
27 Terrence Ross .50 1.25
28 Chris Bosh .60 1.50
29 Shawn Marion .50 1.25
30 Arron Afflalo .40 1.00
31 Klay Thompson .75 2.00
32 Ben McLemore .40 1.00
33A Chris Paul .75 2.00
33B Chris Paul .75 2.00
34 Jonas Valanciunas .50 1.25
35 Jared Sullinger .40 1.00
36 Ray Allen .60 1.50
37 Anthony Davis 1.25 3.00
38 Dirk Nowitzki .75 2.00
39 Victor Oladipo .50 1.25
40 Harrison Barnes .50 1.25
41 Rudy Gay .60 1.50
42 J.J. Redick .60 1.50
43 Enes Kanter .40 1.00
44 Tim Hardaway Jr. .40 1.00

45 Vince Carter .75 2.00
46 Nerlens Noel .50 1.25
47A James Harden 1.00 2.50
47B James Harden 1.00 2.50
48 Trey Burke .40 1.00
49 Jeff Green .50 1.25
50 Brandon Knight .50 1.25
51 Jimmy Butler .60 1.50
52 Amar'e Stoudemire .60 1.50
53 Monta Ellis .50 1.25
54 Michael Carter-Williams .40 1.00
55 Jeremy Lin .60 1.50
56 Isaiah Thomas .60 1.50
57 Nick Young .50 1.25
58 Gordon Hayward .60 1.50
59 Rajon Rondo .60 1.50
60 O.J. Mayo .40 1.00
61 Derrick Rose .75 2.00
62A Carmelo Anthony .75 2.00
62B Carmelo Anthony .75 2.00
63 JaVale McGee .50 1.25
64 Thaddeus Young .40 1.00
65 DeMarcus Cousins .60 1.50
66A Kobe Bryant 2.50 6.00
66B Kobe Bryant 2.50 6.00
67 Derrick Favors .50 1.25
68 Avery Bradley .50 1.25
69 Giannis Antetokounmpo 1.25 3.00
70 Taj Gibson .50 1.25
71 Tyson Chandler .50 1.25
72 Kenneth Faried .50 1.25
73 Eric Bledsoe .50 1.25
74 Dwight Howard .50 1.25
75 Steve Nash .60 1.50
76 Nene .50 1.25
77 Ricky Rubio .60 1.50
78 Joakim Noah .50 1.25
79 Ty Lawson .40 1.00
80 Alex Len .40 1.00
81 Roy Hibbert .50 1.25
82 Tony Parker .60 1.50
83 Pau Gasol .60 1.50
84 Marcin Gortat .50 1.25
85 Deron Williams .50 1.25
86A Kyrie Irving 1.25 3.00
86B Kyrie Irving 1.25 3.00
87 Russell Westbrook 1.50 4.00
88 Josh Smith .50 1.25
89 Lance Stephenson .50 1.25
90A Kawhi Leonard 1.00 2.50
90B Kawhi Leonard 1.00 2.50
91 Marc Gasol .60 1.50
92 John Wall .75 2.00
93 Kevin Garnett 1.00 2.50
94 Nikola Pekovic .40 1.00
95 Luol Deng .50 1.25
96A Kevin Durant 1.50 4.00
96B Kevin Durant 1.50 4.00
97 Brandon Jennings .40 1.00
98 Goran Dragic .50 1.25
99 David West .50 1.25
100 Manu Ginobili .60 1.50
101 Tayshaun Prince .50 1.25
102 Bradley Beal .60 1.50
103 Paul Pierce .60 1.50
104A Kevin Love .60 1.50
104B Kevin Love .60 1.50
105 Anderson Varejao .40 1.00
106 Serge Ibaka .50 1.25
107 Andre Drummond .60 1.50
108 Channing Frye .50 1.25
109A Tim Duncan 1.00 2.50
109B Tim Duncan 1.00 2.50
110 Mike Conley .50 1.25
111 Joe Johnson .50 1.25
112 Kevin Martin .50 1.25
113 Steven Adams .50 1.25
114 Greg Monroe .50 1.25
115A Damian Lillard 1.25 3.00
115B Damian Lillard 1.25 3.00
116 Magic Johnson 1.50 4.00
117 Mitch Richmond .60 1.50
118A Scottie Pippen 1.25 3.00
118B Scottie Pippen 1.25 3.00
119 Bill Russell 1.00 2.50
120 Kareem Abdul-Jabbar 1.00 2.50
121A Shaquille O'Neal 1.25 3.00
121B Shaquille O'Neal 1.25 3.00
122 Larry Bird 1.50 4.00
123 Jason Kidd .60 1.50
124 Clyde Drexler .75 2.00
125 Alonzo Mourning .75 2.00
126A Karl Malone .75 2.00
126B Karl Malone .75 2.00
127 Patrick Ewing .75 2.00
128A Oscar Robertson .75 2.00
128B Oscar Robertson .75 2.00
129 John Stockton 1.00 2.50
130 Isiah Thomas .60 1.50
131 Anfernee Hardaway 1.50 4.00
132A Wilt Chamberlain 1.25 3.00
132B Wilt Chamberlain 1.25 3.00
133 Allen Iverson .75 2.00
134 Julius Erving 1.00 2.50
135 Shawn Kemp 1.00 2.50
136A Pete Maravich 1.00 2.50
136B Pete Maravich 1.00 2.50
137 Yao Ming .75 2.00
138 David Robinson 1.00 2.50
139 Jerry West .75 2.00
140 Elgin Baylor .60 1.50
141A Andrew Wiggins RC 2.50 6.00
141B Andrew Wiggins 2.50 6.00
142A J.Parker RC Grn uni 1.25 3.00
142B Jabari Parker White uni 1.25 3.00
143 Joel Embiid RC 2.50 6.00
144 Aaron Gordon RC 1.25 3.00
145A Dante Exum RC .75 2.00
145B Dante Exum .75 2.00
146 Marcus Smart RC .75 2.00
147 Julius Randle RC 1.25 3.00
148 Nik Stauskas RC .60 1.50
149 Noah Vonleh RC .60 1.50
150 Elfrid Payton RC .75 2.00
151 Doug McDermott RC .75 2.00
152 Zach LaVine RC 1.25 3.00
153 T.J. Warren RC .75 2.00
154 Adreian Payne RC .60 1.50
155 James Young RC .50 1.25
156 Tyler Ennis RC .50 1.25
157 Gary Harris RC .75 2.00
158 Mitch McGary RC .50 1.25
159 Jordan Adams RC .50 1.25
160 Rodney Hood RC .75 2.00
161 Shabazz Napier RC .60 1.50
162 P.J. Hairston RC .50 1.25
163 C.J. Wilcox RC .50 1.25
164 Bruno Caboclo RC .60 1.50
165 Kyle Anderson RC .75 2.00
166 Nikola Mirotic RC 1.00 2.50
167 Joe Harris RC .50 1.25
168 Cleanthony Early RC .50 1.25
169 Jarnell Stokes RC .50 1.25
170 Johnny O'Bryant RC .50 1.25
171 Erick Green RC .50 1.25
172 Spencer Dinwiddie RC .60 1.50
173 Glenn Robinson III RC .50 1.25
174 Nick Johnson RC .50 1.25
175 Damjan Rudez RC .50 1.25
176 Markel Brown RC .50 1.25
177 Cory Jefferson RC .50 1.25
178 Jusuf Nurkic RC .75 2.00
179 Damien Inglis RC .50 1.25
180 Russ Smith RC .50 1.25

2014-15 Totally Certified Platinum Blue

*VETS: .6X TO 1.5X BASE HI
*RC: .6X TO 1.5X BASE HI
RANDOM INSERTS IN PACKS
STATED PRINT RUN 149 SER.#'d SETS

2014-15 Totally Certified Platinum Mirror Blue Die Cuts

*VETS: 1.2X TO 3X BASE HI
*RCs: 1.2X TO 3X BASE HI
RANDOM INSERTS IN PACKS
STATED PRINT RUN 74 SER.#'d SETS
126A Karl Malone 8.00 20.00
141A Andrew Wiggins 25.00 60.00

2014-15 Totally Certified Platinum Mirror Purple Die Cuts

*VETS: 2.5X TO 6X BASE HI
*ROOKIES: 2.5X TO 6X BASE HI
RANDOM INSERTS IN PACKS
STATED PRINT RUN 25 SER.#'d SETS
38 Dirk Nowitzki 12.00 30.00
113 Steven Adams 8.00 20.00

2014-15 Totally Certified Platinum Mirror Red Die Cuts

*VETS: 1X TO 2.5X BASE HI
*RCs: 1X TO 2.5X BASE HI
RANDOM INSERTS IN PACKS
STATED PRINT RUN 135 SER.#'d SETS

2014-15 Totally Certified Platinum Purple

*VETS: 2X TO 5X BASE HI
*RCs: 2X TO 5X BASE HI
RANDOM INSERTS IN PACKS
STATED PRINT RUN 49 SER.#'d SETS
141A Andrew Wiggins 30.00 80.00
152 Zach LaVine 12.00 30.00

2014-15 Totally Certified Platinum Red

*VETS: .5X TO 1.2X BASE HI
*RCs: .5X TO 1.2X BASE HI
RANDOM INSERTS IN PACKS
STATED PRINT RUN 279 SER.#'d SETS

2014-15 Totally Certified Ballot Busters Signatures

RANDOM INSERTS IN PACKS
PRINT RUNS B/WN 12-60 COPIES PER
NO PRICING ON QTY 12
EXCHANGE DEADLINE 5/19/2016
BBAE Alex English/60 5.00 12.00
BBAG Artis Gilmore/49 5.00 12.00
BBAM Alonzo Mourning/12
BBBH Bailey Howell/60 6.00 15.00
BBBK Bernard King/60 5.00 12.00
BBBW Bill Walton/60 8.00 20.00
BBCD Clyde Drexler/49 15.00 40.00
BBCL Clyde Lovellette/60 6.00 15.00
BBCM Calvin Murphy/49 5.00 12.00
BBDC Dave Cowens/25 4.00 10.00
BBDI Dan Issel/60 5.00 12.00
BBDN Don Nelson/60 6.00 15.00
BBDR Dennis Rodman/60 12.00 30.00
BBDT David Thompson/60 5.00 12.00
BBDW Dominique Wilkins/49 10.00 25.00
BBEB Elgin Baylor/35 10.00 25.00
BBEH Elvin Hayes/60 6.00 15.00
BBGG Gail Goodrich/60 5.00 12.00
BBGP Gary Payton/25 10.00 25.00
BBHG Harry Gallatin/60 6.00 15.00
BBJD Joe Dumars/60 6.00 15.00
BBJE Julius Erving/35
BBJH John Havlicek/25 12.00 30.00
BBJL Jerry Lucas/49 8.00 20.00
BBJW Jerry West/35
BBLB Larry Bird/25 40.00 80.00
BBLW Lenny Wilkens/49 6.00 15.00
BBMD Mel Daniels/60 10.00 25.00
BBMJ Magic Johnson/25 20.00 50.00
BBNA Nate Archibald/49 8.00 20.00
BBOR Oscar Robertson/25 30.00 80.00
BBRB Rick Barry/60 5.00 12.00
BBWF Walt Frazier/60 10.00 25.00
BBCHM Chris Mullin/60 12.00 30.00
BBDAR David Robinson/35 20.00 50.00
BBGEG George Gervin/60 8.00 20.00
BBJAW James Worthy/60 10.00 25.00
BBKAJ Kareem Abdul-Jabbar/35 25.00 60.00

2014-15 Totally Certified Clear Cloth Jerseys Red

RANDOM INSERTS IN PACKS
PRINT RUNS B/WN 199-299 COPIES PER
*BLUE/99-199: .6X TO 1.5X BASE HI
1 Al Horford/199 1.50 4.00
2 LeBron James/299 8.00 20.00
3 Kevin Durant/299 5.00 12.00
4 Chris Paul/299 2.50 6.00
5 Damian Lillard/199 4.00 10.00
6 Deron Williams/199 1.50 4.00
7 Kyrie Irving/299 4.00 10.00
8 DeAndre Jordan/299 2.00 5.00
9 DeMarcus Cousins/299 2.00 5.00
10 Dirk Nowitzki/299 2.50 6.00
11 Eric Bledsoe/199 1.50 4.00
12 George Hill/199 1.50 4.00
13 Isaiah Thomas/299 2.00 5.00
14 J.R. Smith/299 1.50 4.00
15 Jamal Crawford/299 2.00 5.00
16 James Harden/299 3.00 8.00
17 Kemba Walker/299 2.00 5.00
18 Kevin Love/299 2.00 5.00
19 Kirk Hinrich/299 1.50 4.00
20 Klay Thompson/299 2.50 6.00
21 Kobe Bryant/299 8.00 20.00
22 LaMarcus Aldridge/299 2.00 5.00
23 Luis Scola/299 1.50 4.00
24 Manu Ginobili/299 2.00 5.00
25 Mike Conley/199 1.50 4.00
26 Nick Young/299 1.50 4.00
27 Dwight Howard/299 1.50 4.00
28 Kevin Garnett/299 3.00 8.00
29 Nikola Vucevic/299 1.50 4.00
30 Pau Gasol/299 2.00 5.00
31 Paul Pierce/299 2.00 5.00
32 Paul George/199 2.50 6.00
33 Paul Millsap/299 2.00 5.00
34 Rajon Rondo/299 2.00 5.00
35 Ray Allen/199 2.00 5.00
36 Russell Westbrook/299 5.00 12.00
37 Ryan Anderson/299 1.25 3.00
38 Serge Ibaka/299 1.50 4.00
39 Stephen Curry/299 8.00 20.00
40 Steve Nash/299 2.00 5.00
41 Terrence Ross/299 1.50 4.00
42 Tiago Splitter/299 1.50 4.00
43 Tim Duncan/299 3.00 8.00
44 Tony Allen/199 1.25 3.00
45 Tony Parker/299 2.00 5.00
46 Ty Lawson/199 1.25 3.00
47 Victor Oladipo/299 1.50 4.00
48 Vince Carter/299 2.50 6.00
49 Zach Randolph/299 1.50 4.00
50 Al Jefferson/299 1.50 4.00
51 Amar'e Stoudemire/299 2.00 5.00
52 Anderson Varejao/299 1.25 3.00
53 Andre Drummond/299 2.00 5.00
54 Andre Iguodala/199 1.50 4.00
55 Anthony Bennett/299 1.25 3.00
56 Carmelo Anthony/199 2.50 6.00
57 Chandler Parsons/299 1.50 4.00
58 Danny Green/299 1.50 4.00
59 David Lee/199 1.25 3.00
60 David West/299 1.50 4.00
61 Dion Waiters/299 1.50 4.00
62 Dwyane Wade/199 3.00 8.00
63 Greg Monroe/299 1.50 4.00
64 Harrison Barnes/299 1.50 4.00
65 Iman Shumpert/199 1.25 3.00
66 Derrick Favors/299 1.50 4.00
67 Goran Dragic/199 1.50 4.00
68 Gordon Hayward/199 2.00 5.00
69 Jeremy Lin/299 2.00 5.00
70 Jimmy Butler/299 2.00 5.00
71 Joe Johnson/299 1.50 4.00
72 John Wall/299 2.50 6.00
73 Jonas Valanciunas/299 1.50 4.00
74 Kawhi Leonard/299 3.00 8.00
75 Kenneth Faried/199 1.50 4.00
76 Kyle Lowry/299 1.50 4.00
77 Marc Gasol/299 2.00 5.00
78 Marco Belinelli/299 1.25 3.00
79 M.Carter-Williams/199 1.25 3.00
80 Michael Kidd-Gilchrist/199 1.50 4.00
81 Monta Ellis/299 1.50 4.00
82 Nene/299 1.50 4.00
83 Nick Collison/299 1.50 4.00
84 Nicolas Batum/299 1.50 4.00
85 Nikola Pekovic/299 1.25 3.00
86 Shawn Marion/299 1.50 4.00
87 Solomon Hill/299 1.25 3.00
88 Taj Gibson/299 1.50 4.00
89 Thaddeus Young/299 1.25 3.00
90 Tyreke Evans/299 1.25 3.00
91 Andrew Wiggins/299 6.00 15.00
92 Jabari Parker/299 3.00 8.00
93 Joel Embiid/299 6.00 15.00
94 Aaron Gordon/299 3.00 8.00
95 Dante Exum/299 2.00 5.00
96 Marcus Smart/299 2.00 5.00
97 Julius Randle/299 3.00 8.00
98 Nik Stauskas/299 1.50 4.00
99 Noah Vonleh/299 1.50 4.00
100 Elfrid Payton/299 2.00 5.00

2014-15 Totally Certified Competitor Autographs

RANDOM INSERTS IN PACKS
PRINT RUNS B/WN 49-99 COPIES PER
EXCHANGE DEADLINE 5/19/2016
CAD Andre Drummond/49 8.00 20.00
CAD A.Davis/49 EXCH 30.00 80.00
CAH Anfernee Hardaway/49 15.00 40.00
CBL Bill Laimbeer/99 5.00 12.00
CBRL Brook Lopez/49 5.00 12.00
CBW Buck Williams/99 4.00 10.00
CCB Caron Butler/49
CCD Clyde Drexler/49 15.00 40.00
CCL Christian Laettner/49 5.00 12.00
CCP Chuck Person/99 5.00 12.00
CCR Cazzie Russell/99 5.00 12.00
CDC Doug Collins/99 6.00 15.00
CDG Danny Green/99 5.00 12.00
CDN Don Nelson/49 10.00 25.00
CGG Gail Goodrich/99 5.00 12.00
CGGH Gerald Henderson/99 4.00 10.00
CGH George Hill/99 5.00 12.00
CGK George Karl/99 6.00 15.00
CGMC George McGinnis/99 4.00 10.00
CGP Gary Payton/49 12.00 30.00
CGRH Grant Hill/49 15.00 40.00
CHB Harrison Barnes/49 12.00 30.00
CHO Hakeem Olajuwon/49 12.00 30.00
CJD Joe Dumars/49 6.00 15.00
CJET Jason Terry/99 5.00 12.00
CJH Jeff Hornacek/99 5.00 12.00
CJJ Jim Jackson/99 4.00 10.00
CJJT John Thompson/99 6.00 15.00
CJMC JaVale McGee/99 5.00 12.00
CJOS John Starks/99 5.00 12.00
CJS John Salley/99 4.00 10.00
CJW Jerry West/49 20.00 50.00
CJW Jo Jo White/99 5.00 12.00
CKB Kobe Bryant/99 75.00 150.00
CKD Kevin Durant/99 40.00 100.00
CKI Kyrie Irving/49 40.00 80.00
CKL Kevin Love/49 10.00 25.00
CKLJ Larry Johnson/99 8.00 20.00
CKM Karl Malone/49 25.00 60.00
CMAJ Mark Jackson/99 5.00 12.00
CMCH Maurice Cheeks/99 4.00 10.00
CMGO Marcin Gortat/99 5.00 12.00
CMJ Marques Johnson/99 5.00 12.00
CPB Patrick Beverley/99 4.00 10.00
CPC Phil Chenier/99 4.00 10.00
CRA Ryan Anderson/99 4.00 10.00
CRB Rolando Blackman/99 5.00 12.00
CRM Rick Mahorn/99 4.00 10.00
CSC Stephen Curry/99 100.00 200.00
CTL Ty Lawson/99 4.00 10.00
CTP Tayshaun Prince/99 5.00 12.00
CTS Thabo Sefolosha/99 4.00 10.00
CTV Tom Van Arsdale/99 5.00 12.00
CWM Wesley Matthews/99 4.00 10.00
CJOW John Wall/49 12.00 30.00

2014-15 Totally Certified Competitor Autographs Mirror

*MIRROR: .5X TO 1.2X BASE HI
RANDOM INSERTS IN PACKS
STATED PRINT RUN 25 SER.#'d SETS
EXCHANGE DEADLINE 5/19/2016

2014-15 Totally Certified EPIX Play Memorabilia Red

RANDOM INSERTS IN PACKS
STATED PRINT RUN 199 SER.#'d SETS
*BLUE/149: .5X TO 1.2X BASE HI
1 LeBron James 8.00 20.00
2 Kevin Durant 5.00 12.00
3 Kobe Bryant 8.00 20.00
4 Dwyane Wade 3.00 8.00
5 Blake Griffin 2.00 5.00
6 Carmelo Anthony 2.50 6.00
7 James Harden 3.00 8.00
8 Stephen Curry 8.00 20.00
9 Chris Paul 2.50 6.00
10 Damian Lillard 4.00 10.00
11 DeMar DeRozan 2.00 5.00
12 Dirk Nowitzki 2.50 6.00
13 Dwight Howard 1.50 4.00
14 Joakim Noah 1.50 4.00
15 Joe Johnson 1.50 4.00
16 John Wall 2.50 6.00
17 Kevin Garnett 3.00 8.00
18 Kevin Love 2.00 5.00
19 Kyrie Irving 4.00 10.00
20 LaMarcus Aldridge 2.00 5.00
21 Marc Gasol 2.00 5.00
22 Rajon Rondo 2.00 5.00
23 Paul George 2.50 6.00
24 Ricky Rubio 2.00 5.00
25 Russell Westbrook 5.00 12.00

2014-15 Totally Certified Excellence

RANDOM INSERTS IN PACKS
STATED PRINT RUN 299 SER.#'d SETS
1 Kobe Bryant 4.00 10.00
2 Kevin Durant 2.50 6.00
3 Kevin Love 1.00 2.50
4 LeBron James 4.00 10.00
5 Tim Duncan 1.50 4.00
6 Chris Paul 1.25 3.00
7 Carmelo Anthony 1.25 3.00
8 James Harden 1.50 4.00
9 Paul George 1.25 3.00
10 Stephen Curry 4.00 10.00
11 Dirk Nowitzki 1.25 3.00
12 Tony Parker 1.00 2.50
13 Blake Griffin 1.00 2.50
14 Dwight Howard .75 2.00
15 Kyrie Irving 2.00 5.00
16 John Wall 1.25 3.00
17 Russell Westbrook 2.50 6.00
18 LaMarcus Aldridge 1.00 2.50
19 DeMar DeRozan 1.00 2.50
20 Joe Johnson .75 2.00
21 DeMarcus Cousins 1.00 2.50
22 Damian Lillard 2.00 5.00
23 Klay Thompson 1.25 3.00
24 Dwyane Wade 1.50 4.00
25 DeAndre Jordan 1.00 2.50
26 Anthony Davis 2.00 5.00
27 Zach Randolph .75 2.00
28 Kenneth Faried .75 2.00
29 Al Jefferson .75 2.00
30 Monta Ellis .75 2.00

2014-15 Totally Certified Excellence Mirror

*MIRROR: 2X TO 5X BASE HI
RANDOM INSERTS IN PACKS
STATED PRINT RUN 25 SER.#'d SETS
4 LeBron James 40.00 80.00

2014-15 Totally Certified Future Stars Signatures

RANDOM INSERTS IN PACKS
STATED PRINT RUN 99 SER.#'d SETS
EXCHANGE DEADLINE 5/19/2016
*MIRROR/25: .5X TO 1.2X BASE HI
FSABE Anthony Bennett 4.00 10.00
FSAC Allen Crabbe 4.00 10.00
FSAD Anthony Davis 25.00 60.00
FSAG Archie Goodwin 4.00 10.00
FSAM Arnett Moultrie 4.00 10.00
FSAP Adreian Payne 5.00 12.00
FSAS Alexey Shved 4.00 10.00
FSAV Anderson Varejao 4.00 10.00
FSBB Bradley Beal 8.00 20.00
FSBC Bruno Caboclo 5.00 12.00
FSCF Carrick Felix 4.00 10.00
FSCJ C.J. Wilcox 4.00 10.00
FSCJM C.J. Miles 5.00 12.00
FSCJW C.J. Watson 4.00 10.00
FSCZ Cody Zeller 4.00 10.00
FSDM Donatas Motiejunas 4.00 10.00
FSDS Dennis Schroder 5.00 12.00
FSEF Evan Fournier 4.00 10.00
FSEK Enes Kanter 4.00 10.00
FSFE Festus Ezeli 4.00 10.00
FSGA Giannis Antetokounmpo 30.00 80.00
FSGD Goran Dragic 5.00 12.00
FSGDI Gorgui Dieng 4.00 10.00
FSGH Gary Harris 6.00 15.00
FSGJ Grant Jerrett 4.00 10.00
FSGM Gal Mekel 4.00 10.00
FSGR Glen Rice Jr. 4.00 10.00
FSHS Henry Sims 4.00 10.00
FSIC Ian Clark 4.00 10.00
FSICA Isaiah Canaan 5.00 12.00
FSIS Iman Shumpert 4.00 10.00
FSIT Isaiah Thomas 6.00 15.00
FSJA Jordan Adams 4.00 10.00
FSJC Jared Cunningham 4.00 10.00
FSJH Justin Hamilton 4.00 10.00
FSJL Jon Leuer 4.00 10.00
FSJLIII John Lucas III 4.00 10.00
FSJM Jamaal Franklin 4.00 10.00
FSJSU Jared Sullinger 4.00 10.00
FSJV Jarvis Varnado 4.00 10.00
FSJVA Jonas Valanciunas 5.00 12.00
FSKJ K.J. McDaniels 5.00 12.00
FSKO Kelly Olynyk 4.00 10.00
FSKOQ Kyle O'Quinn 4.00 10.00
FSLA Lavoy Allen 4.00 10.00
FSLD Luigi Datome 4.00 10.00
FSMCW Michael Carter-Williams 4.00 10.00
FSMD Matthew Dellavedova 5.00 12.00
FSMM Mitch McGary 4.00 10.00
FSMP Mason Plumlee 5.00 12.00
FSMPL Miles Plumlee 4.00 10.00
FSPJ P.J. Hairston 4.00 10.00
FSRH Rodney Hood 6.00 15.00
FSRK Ryan Kelly 4.00 10.00
FSRMC Ray McCallum 4.00 10.00
FSSA Steven Adams 5.00 12.00
FSSN Shabazz Napier 4.00 10.00
FSTB Trey Burke 4.00 10.00
FSTJW T.J. Warren 6.00 15.00
FSTS Tony Snell 4.00 10.00

2014-15 Totally Certified Future Stars Signatures Mirror

*MIRROR: .5X TO 1.2X BASE HI
STATED PRINT RUN 25 SER.#'d SETS
EXCHANGE DEADLINE 5/19/2016
FSAD Anthony Davis 50.00 120.00
FSGA Giannis Antetokounmpo 50.00 120.00

2014-15 Totally Certified Great American Heroes

RANDOM INSERTS IN PACKS
STATED PRINT RUN 299 SER.#'d SETS
1 Kobe Bryant 4.00 10.00
2 Kevin Durant 2.50 6.00
3 LeBron James 4.00 10.00
4 Chris Paul 1.25 3.00
5 Kevin Love 1.00 2.50
6 Paul George 1.25 3.00
7 Derrick Rose 1.25 3.00
8 Stephen Curry 6.00 15.00
9 Carmelo Anthony 1.25 3.00
10 James Harden 1.50 4.00
11 LaMarcus Aldridge 1.00 2.50
12 Russell Westbrook 2.50 6.00
13 Dwyane Wade 1.50 4.00
14 Dwight Howard .75 2.00
15 Kenneth Faried .75 2.00
16 Blake Griffin 1.00 2.50
17 Kyrie Irving 2.00 5.00
18 Anthony Davis 2.00 5.00
19 DeMar DeRozan 1.00 2.50
20 DeMarcus Cousins 1.00 2.50
21 Klay Thompson 1.25 3.00
22 Al Jefferson .75 2.00
23 Rudy Gay 1.00 2.50
24 Joe Johnson .75 2.00
25 Magic Johnson 2.50 6.00
26 Larry Bird 2.50 6.00
27 Pete Maravich 1.50 4.00
28 Jerry West 1.25 3.00
29 Oscar Robertson 1.25 3.00
30 Kareem Abdul-Jabbar 1.50 4.00
31 Bill Russell 1.50 4.00
32 Scottie Pippen 2.00 5.00
33 Shaquille O'Neal 2.00 5.00
34 Wilt Chamberlain 2.00 5.00
35 Allen Iverson 1.25 3.00
36 Clyde Drexler 1.25 3.00
37 David Robinson 1.50 4.00
38 Grant Hill 1.25 3.00
39 Isiah Thomas 1.00 2.50
40 John Havlicek 1.25 3.00
41 Julius Erving 1.50 4.00
42 Karl Malone 1.25 3.00
43 Bill Walton 1.00 2.50
44 Rick Barry .75 2.00
45 Tim Hardaway 1.00 2.50
46 Anfernee Hardaway 6.00 15.00
47 Bob Cousy 1.50 4.00
48 David Thompson .75 2.00
49 Bill Bradley 1.25 3.00
50 John Stockton 1.50 4.00

2014-15 Totally Certified Great American Heroes Mirror

*MIRROR: 2X TO 5X BASE HI
RANDOM INSERTS IN PACKS
STATED PRINT RUN 25 SER.#'d SETS

2014-15 Totally Certified Jerseys Red

*BLUE/99-199: .4X TO 1X BASE HI
*BLUE/25: .4X TO 1X BASE HI
*PURPLE/25-99: .5X TO 1.2X BASE HI
RANDOM INSERTS IN PACKS
PRINT RUNS B/WN 49-249 COPIES PER
1 Al Jefferson/249 1.50 4.00
2 Alex English/149 2.00 5.00
3 Allen Iverson/149 3.00 8.00
4 Amar'e Stoudemire/249 2.50 6.00
5 Anderson Varejao/249 1.50 4.00
6 Andre Drummond/149 2.50 6.00
7 Andre Iguodala/249 2.00 5.00
8 Andrew Bogut/249 2.00 5.00
9 Anfernee Hardaway/249 6.00 15.00
10 Anthony Davis/249 5.00 12.00
11 Blake Griffin/149 2.50 6.00
12 Bradley Beal/149 2.50 6.00
13 Carlos Boozer/249 2.00 5.00
14 Carmelo Anthony/249 3.00 8.00
15 Chandler Parsons/249 2.00 5.00
16 Chris Andersen/249 2.00 5.00
17 Chris Bosh/249 2.50 6.00
18 Chris Paul/249 3.00 8.00
19 Clyde Drexler/249 3.00 8.00
20 Damian Lillard/249 5.00 12.00
21 Dan Majerle/249 2.00 5.00
22 Danny Ainge/49 3.00 8.00
23 David Lee/249 1.50 4.00
24 David Robinson/249 4.00 10.00
25 David West/149 2.00 5.00
26 DeAndre Jordan/249 2.50 6.00
27 DeMar DeRozan/249 2.50 6.00
28 DeMarcus Cousins/249 2.50 6.00
29 Derek Fisher/249 2.00 5.00
30 Dikembe Mutombo/249 2.50 6.00
31 Dirk Nowitzki/249 3.00 8.00
32 Doc Rivers/149 2.50 6.00
33 Dominique Wilkins/149 3.00 8.00
34 Dwight Howard/249 2.00 5.00
35 Dwyane Wade/249 4.00 10.00
36 Gary Payton/149 2.50 6.00
37 Grant Hill/149 3.00 8.00
38 James Harden/249 4.00 10.00
39 Jason Kidd/149 2.50 6.00
40 Jeremy Lin/249 2.50 6.00
41 Jimmy Butler/149 2.50 6.00
42 Joe Dumars/149 2.50 6.00
43 Joe Johnson/249 2.00 5.00
44 John Wall/249 3.00 8.00
45 Julius Erving/149 4.00 10.00
46 Kawhi Leonard/249 4.00 10.00
47 Kenneth Faried/149 2.00 5.00
48 Kevin Durant/249 6.00 15.00
49 Kevin Garnett/249 4.00 10.00
50 Kevin Love/249 2.50 6.00
51 Klay Thompson/149 3.00 8.00
52 Kyrie Irving/249 5.00 12.00
53 LeBron James/249 10.00 25.00
54 Louie Dampier/99 2.50 6.00
55 Manu Ginobili/199 2.50 6.00
56 Marc Gasol/249 2.50 6.00
57 Patrick Ewing/249 3.00 8.00
58 Pau Gasol/249 2.50 6.00
59 Paul George/249 3.00 8.00
60 Paul Millsap/249 2.50 6.00
61 Paul Pierce/249 2.50 6.00
62 Rajon Rondo/249 2.50 6.00
63 Ray Allen/249 2.50 6.00
64 Ricky Rubio/149 2.50 6.00
65 Roy Hibbert/249 2.00 5.00
66 Scottie Pippen/249 5.00 12.00
67 Shaquille O'Neal/149 5.00 12.00
68 Steve Nash/249 2.50 6.00
69 Taj Gibson/249 2.00 5.00
70 Tim Duncan/249 4.00 10.00
71 Tom Chambers/149 2.00 5.00
72 Tracy McGrady/249 2.50 6.00
73 Xavier McDaniel/149 1.50 4.00
74 Yao Ming/149 3.00 8.00
75 Zach Randolph/149 2.00 5.00
76 Andrew Wiggins/249 8.00 20.00
77 Jabari Parker/249 4.00 10.00
78 Joel Embiid/249 8.00 20.00
79 Aaron Gordon/249 4.00 10.00
80 Dante Exum/249 2.50 6.00
81 Marcus Smart/249 2.50 6.00
82 Julius Randle/249 4.00 10.00
83 Nik Stauskas/249 2.00 5.00
84 Noah Vonleh/249 2.00 5.00
85 Elfrid Payton/249 2.50 6.00
86 Doug McDermott/249 2.50 6.00
87 Zach LaVine/249 4.00 10.00
88 T.J. Warren/249 2.50 6.00
89 Adreian Payne/249 2.00 5.00
90 Cory Jefferson/249 1.50 4.00
91 James Young/249 1.50 4.00
92 Tyler Ennis/249 1.50 4.00
93 Gary Harris/249 2.50 6.00
94 Bruno Caboclo/249 2.00 5.00
95 Mitch McGary/249 1.50 4.00
96 Jordan Adams/249 1.50 4.00
97 Rodney Hood/249 2.50 6.00
98 Shabazz Napier/249 2.00 5.00
99 Cleanthony Early/249 1.50 4.00
100 P.J. Hairston/249 1.50 4.00

2014-15 Totally Certified Present Potential Signatures

RANDOM INSERTS IN PACKS
STATED PRINT RUN 99 SER.#'d SETS
EXCHANGE DEADLINE 5/19/2016
*MIRROR/25: .5X TO 1.2X BASE HI
PPSAB Anthony Bennett 4.00 10.00
PPSAD Anthony Davis 50.00 120.00
PPSCJ Cory Joseph 4.00 10.00
PPSDM Donatas Motiejunas 4.00 10.00
PPSGA Giannis Antetokounmpo 30.00 80.00
PPSGJ Grant Jerrett 4.00 10.00
PPSGR Glenn Robinson III 4.00 10.00
PPSIC Ian Clark 4.00 10.00
PPSIT Isaiah Thomas 6.00 15.00
PPSJC Jordan Clarkson 12.00 30.00
PPSJE James Ennis 4.00 10.00
PPSJH Jordan Hamilton 4.00 10.00
PPSJL Jon Leuer 4.00 10.00
PPSJP Jannero Pargo 5.00 12.00
PPSJS Jarnell Stokes 4.00 10.00
PPSJW Jeff Withey 4.00 10.00
PPSKM Khris Middleton 5.00 12.00
PPSKS Kyle Singler 4.00 10.00
PPSLA Lavoy Allen 4.00 10.00
PPSMB Markel Brown 4.00 10.00
PPSMP Mason Plumlee 5.00 12.00
PPSMT Marquis Teague 4.00 10.00
PPSNC Norris Cole 4.00 10.00
PPSNN Nerlens Noel 5.00 12.00
PPSNS Nik Stauskas 5.00 12.00
PPSNV Nikola Vucevic 5.00 12.00
PPSNW Nate Wolters 5.00 12.00
PPSOP Otto Porter 5.00 12.00
PPSPA Pero Antic 4.00 10.00
PPSPP Phil Pressey 4.00 10.00
PPSPS Peyton Siva 5.00 12.00
PPSQA Quincy Acy 4.00 10.00
PPSRB Rasual Butler 4.00 10.00
PPSRG Rudy Gobert 6.00 15.00
PPSRJ Reggie Jackson 4.00 10.00
PPSRK Ryan Kelly 4.00 10.00
PPSRL Ricky Ledo 4.00 10.00
PPSRS Robert Sacre 4.00 10.00
PPSSA Steven Adams 5.00 12.00
PPSSD Spencer Dinwiddie 5.00 12.00
PPSSH Solomon Hill 4.00 10.00
PPSSM Shabazz Muhammad 6.00 15.00
PPSTB Trey Burke 4.00 10.00
PPSTS Tony Snell 4.00 10.00
PPSTT Tristan Thompson 5.00 12.00
PPSVO Victor Oladipo 5.00 12.00
PPSZL Zach LaVine 12.00 30.00
PPSCJE Cory Jefferson 4.00 10.00
PPSICA Isaiah Canaan 5.00 12.00
PPSJFR Jimmer Fredette 4.00 10.00
PPSJHA Joe Harris 8.00 20.00
PPSJSM Jason Smith 4.00 10.00
PPSJUH Justin Hamilton 4.00 10.00
PPSKCP Kentavious Caldwell-Pope 4.00 10.00
PPSMCW Michael Carter-Williams 4.00 10.00
PPSNEN Nemanja Nedovic 4.00 10.00
PPSREB Reggie Bullock 4.00 10.00
PPSRMC Ray McCallum 4.00 10.00
PPSRSM Russ Smith 4.00 10.00
PPSTMI Tony Mitchell 4.00 10.00

2014-15 Totally Certified Rookie Roll Call Autographs

RANDOM INSERTS IN PACKS
PRINT RUN B/WN 249-299 COPIES PER
EXCHANGE DEADLINE 5/19/2016
RRCAG Aaron Gordon/249 10.00 25.00
RRCAP Adreian Payne/249 5.00 12.00
RRCAW Andrew Wiggins/249 60.00 150.00
RRCCE Cleanthony Early/249 4.00 10.00
RRCDE Dante Exum/249 6.00 15.00
RRCDP Dwight Powell/299 4.00 10.00
RRCEP Elfrid Payton/299 6.00 15.00
RRCGH Gary Harris/249 6.00 15.00
RRCGR Glenn Robinson III/299 4.00 10.00
RRCJA Jordan Adams/299 4.00 10.00
RRCJE Joel Embiid/249 40.00 100.00
RRCJG Jerami Grant/249 4.00 10.00
RRCJN Jusuf Nurkic/299 6.00 15.00
RRCJP Jabari Parker/249 20.00 50.00
RRCJR Julius Randle/249 8.00 20.00
RRCJY James Young/249 4.00 10.00
RRCKA Kyle Anderson/249 6.00 15.00
RRCMB Markel Brown/249 4.00 10.00
RRCMM Mitch McGary/299 4.00 10.00
RRCMS Marcus Smart/249 6.00 15.00
RRCNJ Nick Johnson/299
RRCNS Nik Stauskas/249 5.00 12.00
RRCNV Noah Vonleh/249 5.00 12.00
RRCRH Rodney Hood/249 6.00 15.00
RRCRS Russ Smith/299 4.00 10.00
RRCSD Spencer Dinwiddie/299 5.00 12.00
RRCSN Shabazz Napier/299 5.00 12.00
RRCTE Tyler Ennis/249 4.00 10.00
RRCZL Zach LaVine/249 12.00 30.00
RRCCJW C.J. Wilcox/299 4.00 10.00
RRCDMC Doug McDermott/249 6.00 15.00
RRCJHA Joe Harris/249 4.00 10.00
RRCJOB Johnny O'Bryant/299 4.00 10.00
RRCJTS Jarnell Stokes/299 4.00 10.00
RRCKJM K.J. McDaniels/249 5.00 12.00
RRCPJH P.J. Hairston/249 4.00 10.00
RRCTJW T.J. Warren/249 6.00 15.00

2014-15 Totally Certified Rookie Roll Call Autographs Mirror

*MIRROR: .6X TO 1.5X BASE HI
RANDOM INSERTS IN PACKS
STATED PRINT RUN 25 SER.#'d SETS
EXCHANGE DEADLINE 5/19/2016

2014-15 Totally Certified Select Few Signatures

RANDOM INSERTS IN PACKS
PRINT RUNS B/WN 25-60 COPIES PER
EXCHANGE DEADLINE 5/19/2016
SFAG Artis Gilmore/60 5.00 12.00
SFAH Anfernee Hardaway/35 20.00 50.00
SFAS Arvydas Sabonis/60 10.00 25.00
SFBK Bernard King/60 5.00 12.00
SFBS Bill Sharman/49 10.00 25.00
SFCM Calvin Murphy/25 5.00 12.00
SFDS Dolph Schayes/60 6.00 15.00
SFIT Isiah Thomas/60 10.00 25.00
SFJD Joe Dumars/60 6.00 15.00
SFJE Julius Erving/25
SFJH John Havlicek/25 15.00 40.00
SFJMC Jon McGlocklin/60 5.00 12.00
SFJT John Thompson/49 6.00 15.00
SFKAJ Kareem Abdul-Jabbar/25 30.00 80.00
SFKM Karl Malone/25 15.00 40.00
SFKMC Kevin McHale/49 12.00 30.00
SFLB Larry Bird/25 40.00 80.00
SFMJ Magic Johnson/25 25.00 60.00
SFNN Norm Nixon/60 4.00 10.00
SFNT Nate Thurmond/49
SFPR Pat Riley/25 20.00 50.00
SFRB Rick Barry/60 8.00 20.00
SFRC Rick Carlisle/60 6.00 15.00
SFRS Ralph Sampson/49 5.00 12.00
SFSE Sean Elliott/60 6.00 15.00
SFSH Spencer Haywood/60 4.00 10.00
SFSJ Sam Jones/60 6.00 15.00
SFSK Steve Kerr/49 6.00 15.00
SFSO Shaquille O'Neal/25 50.00 100.00
SFSW Spud Webb/60 5.00 12.00
SFTH Tom Heinsohn/45 20.00 50.00
SFTK Toni Kukoc/49 6.00 15.00
SFTMC Tracy McGrady/49 15.00 40.00
SFWB Walt Bellamy/49 5.00 12.00
SFWF Walt Frazier/60 6.00 15.00
SFWR Willis Reed/60 6.00 15.00
SFWU Wes Unseld/60 6.00 15.00
SFXMC Xavier McDaniel/60 4.00 10.00
SFYM Yao Ming/25 15.00 40.00

2014-15 Totally Certified Select Few Signatures Mirror

*MIRROR p/r 25: .4X TO 1X BASIC p/r 25
*MIRROR p/r 25: .5X TO 1.2X BASIC p/r 40-75
RANDOM INSERTS IN PACKS
STATED PRINT RUN 25 SER.#'d SETS
EXCHANGE DEADLINE 5/19/2016
SFBR Bill Russell 60.00 120.00

2014-15 Totally Certified Signatures

RANDOM INSERTS IN PACKS
PRINT RUNS B/WN 25-75 COPIES PER
EXCHANGE DEADLINE 5/19/2016
*MIRROR/25: .5X TO 1.2X BASE HI
TCSAB Anthony Bennett/49 4.00 10.00
TCSAG Artis Gilmore/49 5.00 12.00
TCSAH Allan Houston/75 5.00 12.00
TCSBB Bismack Biyombo/49 4.00 10.00
TCSBBA Brent Barry/49 4.00 10.00
TCSBD Brad Daugherty/49 5.00 12.00
TCSBEG Ben Gordon/49 5.00 12.00
TCSBG Blake Griffin/49 20.00 50.00
TCSBJ Bobby Jones/49 5.00 12.00
TCSBK Bernard King/49 5.00 12.00
TCSBL Bob Lanier/49 5.00 12.00
TCSBRB Bradley Beal/75 6.00 15.00
TCSBRK Brandon Knight/49 5.00 12.00
TCSBS Bill Sharman/49 25.00 60.00
TCSBYS Byron Scott/75 5.00 12.00
TCSCAM Calvin Murphy/25 5.00 12.00
TCSCB Caron Butler/49 5.00 12.00
TCSCC Cedric Ceballos/75 4.00 10.00
TCSCF Chris Ford/49 6.00 15.00
TCSCH Chris Herren/49 4.00 10.00
TCSCHB Chris Bosh/49 6.00 15.00
TCSCJM C.J. McCollum/49 10.00 25.00
TCSCM Chris Mullin/49 8.00 20.00
TCSCW Chet Walker/75 5.00 12.00
TCSDV Dick Van Arsdale/75 5.00 12.00
TCSDW Dominique Wilkins/49 8.00 20.00
TCSDYW Dwyane Wade/49 15.00 40.00
TCSEH Elvin Hayes/49 6.00 15.00
TCSEM Earl Monroe/49 10.00 25.00
TCSFB Fred Brown/49 4.00 10.00
TCSFE Festus Ezeli/49 4.00 10.00
TCSGA G.Antetokounmpo/49 30.00 80.00
TCSGD Goran Dragic/49 5.00 12.00
TCSGG Gail Goodrich/49 5.00 12.00
TCSGH Gordon Hayward/49 6.00 15.00
TCSGK George Karl/49 6.00 15.00
TCSGL Glen Rice/49 5.00 12.00
TCSGM George McGinnis/49 4.00 10.00
TCSGP Gary Payton/49 6.00 15.00
TCSGRA Greg Anthony/49 4.00 10.00
TCSGW Gus Williams/49 4.00 10.00
TCSHB Henry Bibby/49 6.00 15.00
TCSHG Hal Greer/49 5.00 12.00
TCSHO Hakeem Olajuwon/49 15.00 40.00
TCSHOG Horace Grant/49 6.00 15.00
TCSHW Herb Williams/49 6.00 15.00
TCSIT Isiah Thomas/75 10.00 25.00
TCSJC Jose Calderon/49 4.00 10.00
TCSJD Jared Dudley/49 4.00 10.00
TCSJET Jason Terry/60 5.00 12.00
TCSJF Jimmer Fredette/75 4.00 10.00
TCSJG Jeff Green/75 5.00 12.00
TCSJH James Harden/49 20.00 50.00
TCSJJ Jim Jackson/75 4.00 10.00
TCSJK Jason Kidd/49 8.00 20.00
TCSJL Jerry Lucas/49 6.00 15.00
TCSJM Jodie Meeks/49 5.00 12.00
TCSJMC JaVale McGee/49 5.00 12.00
TCSJN Johnny Newman/49 4.00 10.00
TCSJOD Joe Dumars/49 6.00 15.00
TCSJOH Jordan Hill/49 4.00 10.00
TCSJOJ Joe Johnson/49
TCSJOS John Starks/75 5.00 12.00
TCSJP John Paxson/75 5.00 12.00
TCSJR Jalen Rose/49
TCSJS Jared Sullinger/49 4.00 10.00
TCSJT John Thompson/49 6.00 15.00
TCSJW James Worthy/49 10.00 25.00
TCSKB Kobe Bryant/49 75.00 150.00
TCSKD Kevin Durant/49 50.00 120.00
TCSKS Kenny Smith/49 5.00 12.00
TCSKW Kenny Walker/49 4.00 10.00
TCSLD Luol Deng/49 5.00 12.00
TCSLE Len Elmore/49 8.00 20.00
TCSMC Mike Conley/49 5.00 12.00
TCSME Monta Ellis/49 5.00 12.00
TCSMF Michael Finley/49 6.00 15.00
TCSMG Marcin Gortat/49 5.00 12.00
TCSMJ Marques Johnson/75 5.00 12.00
TCSMKG Michael Kidd-Gilchrist/49 5.00 12.00
TCSMT Marquis Teague/75 4.00 10.00
TCSNT Nate Thurmond/49 5.00 12.00
TCSNV Nick Van Exel/49 12.00 30.00
TCSRA Ray Allen/49 25.00 60.00
TCSRH Ron Harper/49 6.00 15.00
TCSRM Rick Mahorn/75 4.00 10.00
TCSRP Robert Parish/49 15.00 40.00
TCSSA Steven Adams/75 5.00 12.00
TCSSB Shane Battier/49 5.00 12.00
TCSSC Stephen Curry/49 100.00 200.00
TCSSE Sean Elliott/49 6.00 15.00
TCSSH Spencer Haywood/75 4.00 10.00
TCSSK Steve Kerr/49 6.00 15.00
TCSSW Scott Wedman/75 5.00 12.00
TCSSWE Spud Webb/75 5.00 12.00
TCSTA Tony Allen/49 4.00 10.00
TCSTB Trey Burke/75 4.00 10.00
TCSTMC Tracy McGrady/75 12.00 30.00
TCSVL Vlade Divac/75 6.00 15.00
TCSZI Zydrunas Ilgauskas/75 5.00 12.00

2014-15 Totally Certified Skills

RANDOM INSERTS IN PACKS
STATED PRINT RUN 299 SER.#'d SETS
*MIRROR/25: 2X TO 5X BASE HI
1 Kevin Durant 2.50 6.00
2 Stephen Curry 4.00 10.00
3 DeAndre Jordan 1.00 2.50
4 James Harden 1.50 4.00
5 Kobe Bryant 4.00 10.00
6 LeBron James 4.00 10.00
7 Chris Paul 1.25 3.00
8 Tim Duncan 1.50 4.00
9 Dirk Nowitzki 1.25 3.00
10 Dwight Howard .75 2.00
11 Dwyane Wade 1.50 4.00
12 Jamal Crawford 1.00 2.50
13 Tony Allen .60 1.50
14 Joakim Noah .75 2.00
15 Paul George 1.25 3.00
16 Carmelo Anthony 1.25 3.00
17 DeMar DeRozan 1.00 2.50
18 John Wall 1.25 3.00
19 Damian Lillard 2.00 5.00
20 Chandler Parsons .75 2.00

2015-16 Totally Certified

1 Kevin Garnett 1.00 2.50
2 DeMar DeRozan .60 1.50
3 Marcin Gortat .50 1.25
4 Evan Turner .50 1.25
5 Noah Vonleh .40 1.00
6 Tobias Harris .50 1.25
7 Rudy Gay .60 1.50
8 Aaron Gordon .50 1.25
9 Jimmy Butler .60 1.50
10 Brandon Jennings .40 1.00
11 Kevin Love .60 1.50
12 DeMarcus Cousins .60 1.50
13 Marcus Smart .50 1.25
14 Gerald Henderson .40 1.00
15 O.J. Mayo .40 1.00
16 Tony Parker .60 1.50
17 Rudy Gobert .60 1.50
18 Al Horford .50 1.25
19 Joakim Noah .50 1.25
20 Brandon Knight .50 1.25
21 Kevin Martin .50 1.25
22 DeMarre Carroll .40 1.00
23 Mario Chalmers .50 1.25
24 Giannis Antetokounmpo 1.25 3.00
25 Omer Asik .50 1.25
26 Tony Wroten .40 1.00
27 Russell Westbrook 1.50 4.00
28 Al Jefferson .50 1.25
29 Jodie Meeks .50 1.25
30 Brook Lopez .50 1.25
31 Khris Middleton .50 1.25
32 Deron Williams .50 1.25
33 Goran Dragic .50 1.25
34 Gordon Hayward .60 1.50
35 P.J. Tucker .40 1.00
36 Trevor Ariza .40 1.00
37 Ryan Anderson .50 1.25
38 Al-Farouq Aminu .50 1.25
39 Joe Johnson .50 1.25
40 Carmelo Anthony .75 2.00
41 Klay Thompson .75 2.00
42 Derrick Favors .50 1.25
43 Markieff Morris .40 1.00
44 Greg Monroe .50 1.25
45 Patrick Beverley .40 1.00
46 Trey Burke .40 1.00
47 Serge Ibaka .50 1.25
48 Amir Johnson .40 1.00
49 John Wall .75 2.00
50 Chandler Parsons .50 1.25
51 Kobe Bryant 2.50 6.00
52 Derrick Rose .75 2.00
53 Mason Plumlee .50 1.25
54 Hassan Whiteside .50 1.25
55 Pau Gasol .60 1.50
56 Tristan Thompson .50 1.25
57 Solomon Hill .40 1.00
58 Andre Drummond .60 1.50
59 Jonas Valanciunas .50 1.25
60 Chase Budinger .40 1.00
61 Kyle Korver .50 1.25
62 Derrick Williams .40 1.00
63 Matt Barnes .40 1.00
64 Hollis Thompson .40 1.00
65 Paul George .75 2.00
66 Ty Lawson .40 1.00
67 Spencer Hawes .40 1.00
68 Andre Iguodala .50 1.25
69 Jordan Clarkson .60 1.50
70 Chris Andersen .50 1.25
71 Kyle Lowry .50 1.25
72 Dirk Nowitzki .75 2.00
73 Michael Carter-Williams .40 1.00
74 J.J. Barea .50 1.25
75 Paul Millsap .60 1.50
76 Tyreke Evans .40 1.00
77 Stephen Curry 2.50 6.00
78 Andre Roberson .40 1.00
79 Jordan Hill .40 1.00
80 Chris Bosh .60 1.50
81 Kyrie Irving 1.25 3.00
82 Donatas Motiejunas .40 1.00
83 Michael Kidd-Gilchrist .50 1.25
84 J.J. Redick .60 1.50
85 Paul Pierce .60 1.50
86 Tyson Chandler .50 1.25
87 Taj Gibson .50 1.25
88 Andrew Wiggins 1.00 2.50
89 Josh Smith .50 1.25
90 Chris Paul .75 2.00
91 LaMarcus Aldridge .60 1.50
92 Draymond Green .75 2.00
93 Mike Conley .60 1.50
94 J.R. Smith .50 1.25
95 Rajon Rondo .60 1.50
96 Victor Oladipo .50 1.25
97 Terrence Ross .50 1.25
98 Anthony Davis 1.25 3.00
99 Jrue Holiday .50 1.25
100 Damian Lillard 1.25 3.00
101 Lance Stephenson .50 1.25
102 Dwight Howard .50 1.25
103 Monta Ellis .50 1.25
104 Jabari Parker .75 2.00
105 Reggie Jackson .50 1.25
106 Vince Carter .75 2.00
107 Thomas Robinson .40 1.00
108 Arron Afflalo .40 1.00
109 Julius Randle .60 1.50
110 Danilo Gallinari .50 1.25
111 Langston Galloway .40 1.00
112 Dwyane Wade 1.00 2.50
113 Nene .50 1.25
114 James Harden 1.00 2.50
115 Ricky Rubio .60 1.50
116 Wesley Matthews .40 1.00
117 Tiago Splitter .50 1.25
118 Avery Bradley .50 1.25
119 Kawhi Leonard 1.00 2.50
120 Danny Green .50 1.25
121 LeBron James 2.50 6.00
122 Elfrid Payton .50 1.25
123 Nerlens Noel .50 1.25
124 Jared Sullinger .40 1.00
125 Robert Covington .40 1.00
126 Wilson Chandler .50 1.25
127 Tim Duncan 1.00 2.50
128 Ben McLemore .40 1.00
129 Kemba Walker .60 1.50
130 Dante Exum .50 1.25
131 Lou Williams .50 1.25
132 Eric Bledsoe .50 1.25
133 Nicolas Batum .50 1.25
134 Jarrett Jack .50 1.25
135 Robin Lopez .40 1.00
136 Zach LaVine .60 1.50
137 Tim Hardaway Jr. .40 1.00
138 Blake Griffin .60 1.50
139 Kenneth Faried .50 1.25
140 Darren Collison .50 1.25
141 Manu Ginobili .60 1.50
142 Eric Gordon .50 1.25
143 Nikola Mirotic .50 1.25
144 Jeff Teague .50 1.25
145 Rodney Stuckey .50 1.25
146 Zach Randolph .50 1.25
147 Timofey Mozgov .40 1.00
148 Bojan Bogdanovic .40 1.00
149 Kentavious Caldwell-Pope .50 1.25
150 David Lee .40 1.00
151 Marc Gasol .60 1.50
152 Ersan Ilyasova .40 1.00
153 Nikola Vucevic .50 1.25
154 Jeremy Lin .60 1.50
155 Roy Hibbert .50 1.25
156 Luol Deng .50 1.25
157 DeAndre Jordan .60 1.50
158 Bradley Beal .60 1.50
159 Kevin Durant 1.50 4.00
160 J.J. Hickson .40 1.00
161 Jarell Martin RC .50 1.25
162 Frank Kaminsky RC .60 1.50
163 Montrezl Harrell RC .50 1.25
164 Devin Booker RC 2.00 5.00
165 Richaun Holmes RC .50 1.25
166 Rashad Vaughn RC .40 1.00
167 Nikola Jokic RC .75 2.00
168 Karl-Anthony Towns RC 3.00 8.00
169 Justin Anderson RC .50 1.25
170 Mario Hezonja RC .50 1.25
171 Larry Nance Jr. RC .60 1.50
172 Justise Winslow RC .60 1.50
173 Jordan Mickey RC .40 1.00
174 Cameron Payne RC .50 1.25
175 Pat Connaughton RC .40 1.00
176 Sam Dekker RC .50 1.25
177 Raul Neto RC .40 1.00
178 D'Angelo Russell RC 1.50 4.00
179 Bobby Portis RC .60 1.50
180 Willie Cauley-Stein RC .60 1.50
181 R.J. Hunter RC .40 1.00
182 Myles Turner RC .60 1.50
183 Anthony Brown RC .40 1.00
184 Kelly Oubre Jr. RC .50 1.25
185 Pierre Jackson RC .40 1.00
186 Jerian Grant RC .40 1.00
187 Tyus Jones RC .60 1.50
188 Jahlil Okafor RC .75 2.00
189 Rondae Hollis-Jefferson RC .50 1.25
190 Emmanuel Mudiay RC .60 1.50
191 Chris McCullough RC .40 1.00
192 Trey Lyles RC .60 1.50
193 Rakeem Christmas RC .40 1.00
194 Terry Rozier RC .50 1.25
195 Nemanja Bjelica RC .50 1.25
196 Delon Wright RC .50 1.25
197 Kevon Looney RC .50 1.25
198 Kristaps Porzingis RC 1.50 4.00
199 Walter Tavares RC .40 1.00
200 Stanley Johnson RC .50 1.25

2015-16 Totally Certified Mirror Blue

*MIRROR BLUE: .6X TO 1.5X BASIC
*MIRROR BLUE RC: .75X TO 2X BASIC
RANDOM INSERTS IN PACKS
STATED PRINT RUN 99 SER.#'d SETS
168 Karl-Anthony Towns 8.00 20.00
198 Kristaps Porzingis 8.00 20.00

2015-16 Totally Certified Mirror Camo

*MIRROR CAMO: 2.5X TO 6X BASIC
*MIRROR CAMO RC: 4X TO 10X BASIC
RANDOM INSERTS IN PACKS
STATED PRINT RUN 25 SER.#'d SETS
168 Karl-Anthony Towns 40.00 100.00
198 Kristaps Porzingis 40.00 100.00

2015-16 Totally Certified Mirror Purple

*MIRROR PURPLE: 1X TO 2.5X BASIC
*MIRROR PURPLE RC: 1.2X TO 3X BASIC
RANDOM INSERTS IN PACKS
STATED PRINT RUN 50 SER.#'d SETS
168 Karl-Anthony Towns 12.00 30.00
198 Kristaps Porzingis 12.00 30.00

2015-16 Totally Certified Mirror Red

*MIRROR RED: .5X TO 1.2X BASIC
*MIRROR RED RC: .6X TO 1.5X BASIC
RANDOM INSERTS IN PACKS
STATED PRINT RUN 149 SER.#'d SETS
168 Karl-Anthony Towns 6.00 15.00
198 Kristaps Porzingis 6.00 15.00

2015-16 Totally Certified Champions

RANDOM INSERTS IN PACKS
STATED PRINT RUN 199 SER.#'d SETS
*MIRROR/25: 1.5X TO 4X BASIC
1 Dirk Nowitzki 1.25 3.00
2 Scottie Pippen 2.00 5.00
3 Tony Parker 1.00 2.50
4 Shaquille O'Neal 2.00 5.00
5 Clyde Drexler 1.25 3.00
6 Larry Bird 2.50 6.00
7 Magic Johnson 2.50 6.00
8 LeBron James 4.00 10.00
9 Kobe Bryant 4.00 10.00
10 Dwyane Wade 1.50 4.00
11 Isiah Thomas 1.00 2.50
12 Tim Duncan 1.50 4.00
13 Bill Russell 1.50 4.00
14 Hakeem Olajuwon 1.25 3.00
15 Stephen Curry 4.00 10.00

2015-16 Totally Certified Competitor Autographs

RANDOM INSERTS IN PACKS
PRINT RUNS B/WN 19-99 COPIES PER
*CAMO/25: .5X TO 1.2X BASIC p/r 99
*CAMO/25: .4X TO 1X BASIC p/r 25
CCAAD Adrian Dantley/25
CCAAD Anthony Davis/25 40.00 100.00
CCAAE Alex English/25 5.00 12.00
CCAAG Artis Gilmore/25 5.00 12.00
CCAAM Antonio McDyess/99 4.00 10.00
CCAAW Antoine Walker/99 4.00 10.00
CCABB Bradley Beal/25 6.00 15.00
CCABD Bob Dandridge/99 3.00 8.00
CCABL Bill Laimbeer/99 4.00 10.00
CCABM Bob McAdoo/25 15.00 40.00
CCACY Carmelo Anthony/25 10.00 25.00
CCADB Dee Brown/99 3.00 8.00
CCADC Dave Cowens/25 4.00 10.00
CCADI Dan Issel/25 5.00 12.00
CCADR Dino Radja/99 12.00 30.00
CCADS Damon Stoudamire/99 4.00 10.00
CCAEJ Eddie Jones/99 4.00 10.00
CCAEK Enes Kanter/25 4.00 10.00
CCAGP Gary Payton/25 8.00 20.00
CCAGR Glen Rice/25
CCAJD Joe Dumars/25 6.00 15.00
CCAJE Julius Erving/25 25.00 60.00
CCAJN Jusuf Nurkic/25 4.00 10.00
CCAJP Jabari Parker/25 15.00 40.00
CCAJR Julius Randle/25 8.00 20.00
CCAJW Jo Jo White/99 4.00 10.00
CCAJW Jerome Williams/99 3.00 8.00
CCAJW John Wall/25 15.00 40.00
CCAKA K. Abdul-Jabbar/25 25.00 60.00
CCAKB Kobe Bryant/25 100.00 200.00
CCAKD Kevin Durant/25 60.00 120.00
CCAKI Kyrie Irving/25
CCALB Larry Bird/25 30.00 80.00
CCAMA Mark Aguirre/25 5.00 12.00
CCAMC Michael Carter-Williams/25 4.00 10.00
CCAMG Marcin Gortat/25 10.00 25.00
CCAMJ Magic Johnson/25 25.00 60.00
CCANY Nick Young/25 5.00 12.00
CCARA Rafer Alston/99 3.00 8.00
CCARG Rudy Gobert/99 5.00 12.00
CCARH Robert Horry/25
CCARL Raef LaFrentz/99 3.00 8.00
CCARP Robert Parish/25 8.00 20.00
CCARS Rony Seikaly/99 3.00 8.00
CCARS Rik Smits/99 4.00 10.00
CCASE Sean Elliott/99 5.00 12.00
CCASO Shaquille O'Neal/25 40.00 100.00
CCASS Steve Smith/99 4.00 10.00
CCATH Tobias Harris/25
CCATH Tim Hardaway/25 6.00 15.00
CCATY Thaddeus Young/99 3.00 8.00
CCAVD Vlade Divac/99 5.00 12.00
CCAZI Zydrunas Ilgauskas/99 4.00 10.00
CCAZR Zach Randolph/25 5.00 12.00

2015-16 Totally Certified EPIX Play Memorabilia

RANDOM INSERTS IN PACKS
PRINT RUNS B/WN 49-99 COPIES PER
*PRIME/25: .75X TO 2X BASIC
*DUAL/49-99: .4X TO 1X BASIC
*TRIPLE/49-99: .4X TO 1X BASIC
*QUAD/49-99: .5X TO 1.2X BASIC
EPIXAD Anthony Davis/99 5.00 12.00
EPIXAM Alonzo Mourning/99 3.00 8.00
EPIXBD Baron Davis/99 2.00 5.00
EPIXCO Charles Oakley/99 2.00 5.00
EPIXCP Chandler Parsons/99 2.00 5.00
EPIXDJ DeAndre Jordan/99 2.50 6.00
EPIXDL Damian Lillard/99 5.00 12.00
EPIXDR Derrick Rose/99 3.00 8.00
EPIXDT David Thompson/49 2.00 5.00
EPIXGH Grant Hill/99 3.00 8.00
EPIXJD Joe Dumars/99 2.50 6.00
EPIXJH James Harden/99 4.00 10.00
EPIXJW John Wall/99 3.00 8.00
EPIXKB Kobe Bryant/99 8.00 20.00
EPIXKD Kevin Durant/99 5.00 12.00
EPIXKW Kemba Walker/99 2.50 6.00
EPIXMA Mark Aguirre/99 2.00 5.00
EPIXPE Patrick Ewing/99 3.00 8.00
EPIXRA Ray Allen/49 2.50 6.00
EPIXRL Reggie Lewis/99 2.50 6.00
EPIXSK Steve Kerr/99 2.50 6.00
EPIXTB Trey Burke/99 1.50 4.00
EPIXTD Tim Duncan/99 4.00 10.00
EPIXYM Yao Ming/49 3.00 8.00
EPIXZR Zach Randolph/99 2.00 5.00

2015-16 Totally Certified Fabric of the Game Materials Red

RANDOM INSERTS IN PACKS
PRINT RUNS B/WN 99-199 COPIES PER
*BLUE/99: .4X TO 1X BASIC
*BLUE/49: .5X TO 1.2X BASIC
*CAMO/20-25: .75X TO 2X BASIC
FGAB Andrew Bogut/199 2.00 5.00
FGAD Anthony Davis/199 5.00 12.00
FGAD Andre Drummond/199 2.50 6.00
FGAE Alex English/199 2.00 5.00
FGAG Aaron Gordon/199 2.00 5.00
FGAH Al Horford/199 2.00 5.00
FGAH Anfernee Hardaway/199 6.00 15.00
FGAI Allen Iverson/199 5.00 12.00
FGAM Alonzo Mourning/199 3.00 8.00
FGBB Bradley Beal/199 2.50 6.00
FGBG Blake Griffin/199 2.50 6.00
FGBK Brandon Knight/199 2.00 5.00
FGBL Brook Lopez/199 2.00 5.00
FGBM Ben McLemore/199 1.50 4.00
FGCA Carmelo Anthony/99 3.00 8.00
FGCA Chris Andersen/199 2.00 5.00
FGCB Chris Bosh/199 2.50 6.00
FGCB Chris Paul/99 3.00 8.00
FGCD Clyde Drexler/99 3.00 8.00
FGDC DeMarcus Cousins/99 2.50 6.00
FGDG Danilo Gallinari/199 2.00 5.00
FGDH Dwight Howard/99 2.00 5.00
FGDJ DeAndre Jordan/199 2.50 6.00
FGDL Damian Lillard/99 5.00 12.00
FGDM Dan Majerle/99 2.00 5.00
FGDM Danny Manning/199 2.00 5.00
FGDM Doug McDermott/99 2.00 5.00
FGDN Dirk Nowitzki/199 3.00 8.00
FGDR David Robinson/99 4.00 10.00
FGDW David West/99 2.50 6.00
FGEP Elfrid Payton/99 2.00 5.00
FGGA Giannis Antetokounmpo/99 5.00 12.00
FGGD Goran Dragic/99 2.00 5.00
FGGH Grant Hill/99 3.00 8.00
FGHO Hakeem Olajuwon/99 3.00 8.00
FGIS Iman Shumpert/99 1.50 4.00
FGJB Jimmy Butler/99 2.50 6.00
FGJD Joe Dumars/199 2.50 6.00
FGJH James Harden/99 4.00 10.00
FGJH Jrue Holiday/99 2.00 5.00
FGJK Jason Kidd/199 2.50 6.00
FGJR J.J. Redick/99 2.50 6.00
FGJS J.R. Smith/199 2.00 5.00
FGJS John Starks/199 2.00 5.00
FGJT Jeff Teague/99 2.00 5.00
FGJV Jonas Valanciunas/99 2.00 5.00
FGJW John Wall/99 3.00 8.00
FGKD Kevin Duckworth/199 1.50 4.00
FGKG Kevin Garnett/99 4.00 10.00
FGKI Kyrie Irving/99 5.00 12.00
FGKK Kyle Korver/99 2.00 5.00
FGKL Kevin Love/199 2.50 6.00
FGKL Kawhi Leonard/199 4.00 10.00
FGKM Karl Malone/99 3.00 8.00
FGKT Klay Thompson/199 3.00 8.00
FGKW Kemba Walker/99 2.50 6.00
FGLA LaMarcus Aldridge/99 2.50 6.00
FGLD Luol Deng/99 2.00 5.00
FGLJ Larry Johnson/199 3.00 8.00
FGLJ LeBron James/199 6.00 15.00
FGLS Lance Stephenson/99 2.00 5.00
FGMA Mark Aguirre/199 2.00 5.00
FGMB Mike Bibby/199 2.00 5.00
FGMC Mike Conley/199 2.50 6.00
FGMC Mario Chalmers/199 2.00 5.00
FGMF Michael Finley/199 2.50 6.00
FGMG Manu Ginobili/99 2.50 6.00
FGMG Marc Gasol/199 2.50 6.00
FGMM Moses Malone/99 2.50 6.00
FGMR Michael Redd/199 2.00 5.00
FGMS Marcus Smart/99 2.00 5.00
FGNS Nik Stauskas/99 1.50 4.00
FGNV Nikola Vucevic/199 2.00 5.00
FGNY Nick Young/99 2.00 5.00
FGOP Otto Porter/99 2.00 5.00
FGPB Patrick Beverley/99 1.50 4.00
FGPP Paul Pierce/99 2.50 6.00
FGRH Roy Hibbert/99 2.00 5.00
FGRJ Reggie Jackson/99 2.00 5.00
FGRR Ricky Rubio/99 2.50 6.00
FGRR Rajon Rondo/199 2.50 6.00
FGRW Russell Westbrook/99 6.00 15.00
FGSC Stephen Curry/99 8.00 20.00
FGSM Shawn Marion/99 2.00 5.00
FGSN Shabazz Napier/199 1.50 4.00
FGSO Shaquille O'Neal/99 5.00 12.00
FGSP Scottie Pippen/199 5.00 12.00
FGTB Trey Burke/99 1.50 4.00
FGTC Tom Chambers/199 2.00 5.00
FGTC Tyson Chandler/99 2.00 5.00
FGTH Tim Hardaway Jr./99 1.50 4.00
FGTJ Terrence Jones/99 2.00 5.00
FGTL Ty Lawson/199 1.50 4.00
FGTM Tracy McGrady/199 2.50 6.00
FGTP Tony Parker/99 2.50 6.00
FGTS Tiago Splitter/199 2.00 5.00
FGTW T.J. Warren/99 2.00 5.00
FGVO Victor Oladipo/99 2.00 5.00
FGWD Walter Davis/199 1.50 4.00
FGZL Zach LaVine/99 2.50 6.00

2015-16 Totally Certified Hall Hopefuls

RANDOM INSERTS IN PACKS
STATED PRINT RUN 199 SER.#'d SETS
*MIRROR/25: 1.5X TO 4X BASIC
1 Kobe Bryant 4.00 10.00
2 Tim Duncan 1.50 4.00
3 Kevin Garnett 1.50 4.00
4 LeBron James 4.00 10.00
5 Shaquille O'Neal 2.00 5.00
6 Dirk Nowitzki 1.25 3.00
7 Dwyane Wade 1.50 4.00
8 Allen Iverson 1.25 3.00
9 Jason Kidd 1.00 2.50
10 Steve Nash 1.00 2.50

2015-16 Totally Certified Hall Hopefuls Signatures

RANDOM INSERTS IN PACKS
PRINT RUNS B/WN 5-49 COPIES PER
NO PRICING ON QTY 5
*CAMO/25: .5X TO 1.2X BASIC p/r 49
*CAMO/25: .4X TO 1X BASIC p/r 19-31
HHAI Allen Iverson/25 40.00 100.00
HHBD Bob Dandridge/49 3.00 8.00
HHCP Chris Paul/25 20.00 50.00
HHCW Chris Webber/25 100.00 200.00
HHDH Dwight Howard/25
HHGM George McGinnis/49 3.00 8.00
HHJK Jason Kidd/22 15.00 40.00
HHJS Jack Sikma/49 4.00 10.00
HHKB Kobe Bryant/25 75.00 150.00
HHLS Latrell Sprewell/49 12.00 30.00
HHMA Mark Aguirre/49 4.00 10.00
HHMC Maurice Cheeks/49 3.00 8.00
HHMJ Mark Jackson/25
HHPW Paul Westphal/49 5.00 12.00
HHRA Ray Allen/25 20.00 50.00
HHRH Robert Horry/31 10.00 25.00
HHSM Sidney Moncrief/19
HHSN Steve Nash/25 15.00 40.00
HHTC Tom Chambers/49 4.00 10.00
HHVC Vince Carter/25 10.00 25.00

2015-16 Totally Certified Imports

RANDOM INSERTS IN PACKS
STATED PRINT RUN 199 SER.#'d SETS
*MIRROR/25: 1.5X TO 4X BASIC
1 Pau Gasol 1.00 2.50
2 Hakeem Olajuwon 1.25 3.00
3 Manu Ginobili 1.00 2.50
4 Steve Nash 1.00 2.50
5 Yao Ming 1.25 3.00
6 Dirk Nowitzki 1.25 3.00
7 Drazen Petrovic 1.00 2.50
8 Tony Parker 1.00 2.50
9 Andrew Wiggins 1.50 4.00
10 Yuta Tabuse 1.00 2.50

2015-16 Totally Certified Materials Red

RANDOM INSERTS IN PACKS
PRINT RUNS B/WN 99-199 COPIES PER
*BLUE/99: .4X TO 1X BASIC
*BLUE/49: .5X TO 1.2X BASIC
*CAMO/25: .75X TO 2X BASIC
TCMAD Adrian Dantley/99 2.00 5.00
TCMAI Andre Iguodala/199 2.00 5.00
TCMAJ Al Jefferson/199 2.00 5.00
TCMAL Alex Len/199 1.50 4.00
TCMAM Alonzo Mourning/99 3.00 8.00
TCMAW Andrew Wiggins/199 4.00 10.00
TCMBD Boris Diaw/199 2.00 5.00
TCMBK Bernard King/99 2.00 5.00
TCMBS Byron Scott/199 2.00 5.00
TCMCD Clyde Drexler/99 3.00 8.00
TCMCP Chandler Parsons/99 2.00 5.00
TCMCR Clifford Robinson/199 1.50 4.00
TCMDD DeMar DeRozan/99 2.50 6.00
TCMDE Dante Exum/199 2.00 5.00
TCMDG Danny Green/199 2.00 5.00
TCMDR Derrick Rose/199 3.00 8.00
TCMDW Dwyane Wade/199 4.00 10.00
TCMEB Eric Bledsoe/199 2.00 5.00
TCMGM Greg Monroe/199 2.00 5.00
TCMHB Harrison Barnes/199 2.00 5.00
TCMJC Jordan Clarkson/99 2.50 6.00
TCMJN Joakim Noah/199 2.00 5.00
TCMJR Jalen Rose/99 2.50 6.00
TCMJS Jared Sullinger/199 1.50 4.00
TCMKA Kareem Abdul-Jabbar/99 4.00 10.00
TCMKB Kobe Bryant/199 8.00 20.00
TCMKD Kevin Durant/199 5.00 12.00
TCMKF Kenneth Faried/99 2.00 5.00
TCMKL Kyle Lowry/99 2.00 5.00
TCMLB Larry Bird/99 6.00 15.00
TCMLJ Larry Johnson/199 3.00 8.00
TCMMB Manute Bol/99 4.00 10.00
TCMMC Michael Carter-Williams/199 1.50 4.00
TCMME Monta Ellis/199 2.00 5.00
TCMMG Marcin Gortat/199 2.00 5.00
TCMMK Michael Kidd-Gilchrist/99 2.00 5.00
TCMNB Nicolas Batum/99 2.00 5.00
TCMNM Nikola Mirotic/99 2.00 5.00
TCMNN Nerlens Noel/99 2.00 5.00
TCMOM O.J. Mayo/99 1.50 4.00
TCMPE Patrick Ewing/199 3.00 8.00
TCMPH P.J. Hairston/199 1.50 4.00
TCMRA Rafer Alston/199 1.50 4.00
TCMRA Ray Allen/199 2.50 6.00
TCMRG Rudy Gay/199 2.50 6.00
TCMRH Richard Hamilton/199 2.00 5.00
TCMRP Robert Parish/199 2.50 6.00
TCMSA Steven Adams/199 2.00 5.00
TCMSB Shane Battier/199 2.00 5.00
TCMSI Serge Ibaka/99 2.00 5.00
TCMSO Shaquille O'Neal/99 5.00 12.00
TCMSP Scottie Pippen/199 5.00 12.00
TCMTA Tony Allen/199 1.50 4.00
TCMTA Trevor Ariza/199 1.50 4.00
TCMTD Tim Duncan/199 4.00 10.00
TCMTE Tyreke Evans/199 1.50 4.00
TCMTG Taj Gibson/199 2.00 5.00
TCMTK Toni Kukoc/199 2.50 6.00
TCMTR Terrence Ross/99 2.00 5.00
TCMTT Tristan Thompson/199 2.00 5.00
TCMYM Yao Ming/99 3.00 8.00
TCMZR Zach Randolph/199 2.00 5.00

2015-16 Totally Certified Potential

RANDOM INSERTS IN PACKS
STATED PRINT RUN 199 SER.#'d SETS
*MIRROR/25: 1.2X TO 3X BASIC
1 Mario Hezonja .75 2.00
2 Sam Dekker .75 2.00
3 Stanley Johnson .75 2.00
4 Justin Anderson .75 2.00
5 Myles Turner 1.00 2.50
6 Tyus Jones 1.00 2.50
7 Cameron Payne .75 2.00
8 Karl-Anthony Towns 5.00 12.00
9 Jahlil Okafor 1.25 3.00
10 Terry Rozier .75 2.00
11 Willie Cauley-Stein 1.00 2.50
12 Jerian Grant .60 1.50
13 Frank Kaminsky 1.00 2.50
14 Bobby Portis 1.00 2.50
15 Trey Lyles 1.00 2.50
16 Larry Nance Jr. 1.00 2.50
17 Kelly Oubre Jr. .75 2.00
18 D'Angelo Russell 2.50 6.00
19 Kristaps Porzingis 2.50 6.00
20 Rashad Vaughn .60 1.50
21 Emmanuel Mudiay 1.00 2.50
22 Delon Wright .75 2.00
23 Justise Winslow 1.00 2.50
24 Rondae Hollis-Jefferson .75 2.00
25 Devin Booker 3.00 8.00

2015-16 Totally Certified Rookie Fabric of the Game Jerseys Red

RANDOM INSERTS IN PACKS
STATED PRINT RUN 199 SER.#'d SETS
*BLUE/99: .4X TO 1X BASIC
FRJAB Anthony Brown 1.50 4.00
FRJBP Bobby Portis 2.50 6.00
FRJCM Chris McCullough 1.50 4.00
FRJCP Cameron Payne 2.00 5.00
FRJDB Devin Booker 8.00 20.00
FRJDR D'Angelo Russell 6.00 15.00
FRJDW Delon Wright 2.00 5.00
FRJEM Emmanuel Mudiay 2.50 6.00
FRJFK Frank Kaminsky 2.50 6.00
FRJJA Justin Anderson 2.00 5.00
FRJJG Jerian Grant 1.50 4.00
FRJJH Josh Huestis 1.50 4.00
FRJJM Jordan Mickey 1.50 4.00
FRJJM Jarell Martin 2.00 5.00
FRJJO Jahlil Okafor 6.00 15.00
FRJJR Josh Richardson 2.50 6.00
FRJJW Justise Winslow 2.50 6.00
FRJJY Joe Young 2.00 5.00
FRJKL Kevon Looney 2.00 5.00
FRJKO Kelly Oubre Jr. 2.00 5.00
FRJKP Kristaps Porzingis 8.00 20.00
FRJKT Karl-Anthony Towns 10.00 25.00
FRJMH Mario Hezonja 2.00 5.00
FRJMH Montrezl Harrell 2.00 5.00
FRJMT Myles Turner 2.50 6.00
FRJPC Pat Connaughton 1.50 4.00
FRJRC Rakeem Christmas 1.50 4.00
FRJRH Richaun Holmes 2.00 5.00
FRJRH R.J. Hunter 1.50 4.00
FRJRH Rondae Hollis-Jefferson 2.00 5.00
FRJRV Rashad Vaughn 1.50 4.00
FRJSD Sam Dekker 2.00 5.00
FRJSJ Stanley Johnson 2.00 5.00
FRJTJ Tyus Jones 2.50 6.00
FRJTL Trey Lyles 2.50 6.00
FRJTR Terry Rozier 2.00 5.00
FRJWC Willie Cauley-Stein 2.50 6.00
FRJWT Walter Tavares 1.50 4.00

2015-16 Totally Certified Rookie Fabric of the Game Jerseys Camo

*CAMO: 1.2X TO 3X BASIC
RANDOM INSERTS IN PACKS
STATED PRINT RUN 25 SER.#'d SETS
FRJKP Kristaps Porzingis 100.00 250.00
FRJKT Karl-Anthony Towns 100.00 250.00

2015-16 Totally Certified Rookie Fabric of the Game Signatures

RANDOM INSERTS IN PACKS
STATED PRINT RUN 49 SER.#'d SETS
*PRIME/25: .75X TO 2X BASIC
RFGAB Anthony Brown 3.00 8.00
RFGBP Bobby Portis 3.00 8.00
RFGCM Chris McCullough 3.00 8.00
RFGCP Cameron Payne 10.00 25.00
RFGDB Devin Booker 20.00 50.00
RFGDR D'Angelo Russell 20.00 50.00
RFGDW Delon Wright 4.00 10.00
RFGEM Emmanuel Mudiay 15.00 40.00
RFGFK Frank Kaminsky 10.00 25.00
RFGJA Justin Anderson 4.00 10.00
RFGJG Jerian Grant 3.00 8.00
RFGJH Josh Huestis 3.00 8.00
RFGJM Jordan Mickey 3.00 8.00
RFGJM Jarell Martin 4.00 10.00
RFGJO Jahlil Okafor 15.00 40.00
RFGJR Josh Richardson 5.00 12.00
RFGJW Justise Winslow 15.00 40.00
RFGJY Joe Young 4.00 10.00
RFGKL Kevon Looney 4.00 10.00
RFGKO Kelly Oubre Jr. 4.00 10.00
RFGKP Kristaps Porzingis 125.00 250.00
RFGKT Karl-Anthony Towns 100.00 200.00
RFGMH Mario Hezonja 15.00 40.00
RFGMH Montrezl Harrell 4.00 10.00
RFGMT Myles Turner 10.00 25.00
RFGPC Pat Connaughton 3.00 8.00
RFGRC Rakeem Christmas 3.00 8.00
RFGRH Richaun Holmes 4.00 10.00
RFGRH R.J. Hunter 3.00 8.00
RFGRH Rondae Hollis-Jefferson 4.00 10.00
RFGRV Rashad Vaughn 3.00 8.00
RFGSD Sam Dekker 4.00 10.00
RFGSJ Stanley Johnson 12.00 30.00
RFGTJ Tyus Jones 5.00 12.00
RFGTL Trey Lyles 5.00 12.00
RFGTR Terry Rozier 4.00 10.00
RFGWC Willie Cauley-Stein 5.00 12.00
RFGWT Walter Tavares 3.00 8.00

2015-16 Totally Certified Rookie Roll Call Autographs

RANDOM INSERTS IN PACKS
STATED PRINT RUN 99 SER.#'d SETS
*CAMO/25: .5X TO 1.2X BASIC p/r 49
RRCAB Anthony Brown 3.00 8.00
RRCBP Bobby Portis 5.00 12.00
RRCCM Chris McCullough 3.00 8.00
RRCCP Cameron Payne 4.00 10.00
RRCDB Devin Booker 40.00 100.00
RRCDR D'Angelo Russell 15.00 40.00
RRCDW Delon Wright 4.00 10.00
RRCEM Emmanuel Mudiay 6.00 15.00
RRCFK Frank Kaminsky 5.00 12.00
RRCJM Jordan Mickey 3.00 8.00
RRCJM Jarell Martin 4.00 10.00
RRCJO Jahlil Okafor 6.00 15.00
RRCJW Justise Winslow
RRCJY Joe Young 4.00 10.00
RRCKO Kelly Oubre Jr. 4.00 10.00
RRCKP Kristaps Porzingis 30.00 80.00
RRCKT Karl-Anthony Towns 100.00 200.00
RRCLN Larry Nance Jr. 5.00 12.00
RRCMH Mario Hezonja 4.00 10.00
RRCMT Myles Turner 15.00 40.00
RRCNB Nemanja Bjelica 4.00 10.00
RRCPC Pat Connaughton 3.00 8.00
RRCRC Rakeem Christmas 3.00 8.00
RRCRH Rondae Hollis-Jefferson 4.00 10.00
RRCRV Rashad Vaughn 3.00 8.00
RRCSD Sam Dekker 4.00 10.00
RRCTL Trey Lyles 5.00 12.00
RRCTR Terry Rozier 4.00 10.00
RRCWT Walter Tavares 3.00 8.00
RRRWC Willie Cauley-Stein

2015-16 Totally Certified Select Few Signatures

RANDOM INSERTS IN PACKS
PRINT RUNS B/WN 19-49 COPIES PER
*CAMO/25: .5X TO 1.2X BASIC p/r 49
*CAMO/25: .4X TO 1X BASIC p/r 19-25
SFAD Adrian Dantley/49 4.00 10.00
SFAE Alex English/49 4.00 10.00
SFAG Artis Gilmore/25 12.00 30.00
SFAM Alonzo Mourning/19
SFAS Arvydas Sabonis/49 8.00 20.00
SFBK Bernard King/25 8.00 20.00
SFBM Bob McAdoo/49
SFBW Bill Walton/25 6.00 15.00
SFCD Clyde Drexler/25 20.00 50.00
SFCH Cliff Hagan/25
SFCM Calvin Murphy/25 5.00 12.00
SFCM Chris Mullin/25 10.00 25.00
SFDC Dave Cowens/25 4.00 10.00
SFDI Dan Issel/49 4.00 10.00
SFDM Dikembe Mutombo/49 6.00 15.00
SFDR Dennis Rodman/25 30.00 80.00
SFDS Dolph Schayes/25 6.00 15.00
SFDT David Thompson/29 5.00 12.00
SFDW Dominique Wilkins/25 8.00 20.00
SFEM Earl Monroe/25 10.00 25.00
SFGG George Gervin/25
SFGG Gail Goodrich/25 5.00 12.00
SFGP Gary Payton/25 8.00 20.00
SFHG Hal Greer/25 5.00 12.00
SFHO Hakeem Olajuwon/25 12.00 30.00
SFJD Joe Dumars/25 6.00 15.00
SFJL Jerry Lucas/25 8.00 20.00
SFJW James Worthy/25 8.00 20.00
SFJW Jamaal Wilkes/49 5.00 12.00
SFJW Jo Jo White/49 4.00 10.00
SFLB Larry Bird/25
SFMJ Magic Johnson/25 25.00 60.00
SFMR Mitch Richmond/49 5.00 12.00
SFNA Nate Archibald/25 5.00 12.00
SFRB Rick Barry/25 5.00 12.00
SFRP Robert Parish/25
SFRS Ralph Sampson/25
SFSH Spencer Haywood/49 3.00 8.00
SFSS Satch Sanders/49 6.00 15.00
SFWF Walt Frazier/25 8.00 20.00

2015-16 Totally Certified Signatures

RANDOM INSERTS IN PACKS
PRINT RUNS B/WN 19-49 COPIES PER
*CAMO/25: .5X TO 1.2X BASIC p/r 49
*CAMO/25: .4X TO 1X BASIC p/r 19-25
TCAD Andre Drummond/25 10.00 25.00
TCAG Aaron Gordon/25 12.00 30.00
TCAG Artis Gilmore/25 5.00 12.00
TCAI Allen Iverson/25 40.00 100.00
TCAL Alex Len/49 3.00 8.00
TCAW Antoine Walker/49 4.00 10.00
TCAW Andrew Wiggins/25 30.00 80.00
TCBB Bojan Bogdanovic/49
TCBD Bob Dandridge/49 3.00 8.00
TCBK Bernard King/25 5.00 12.00
TCBL Bill Laimbeer/49 4.00 10.00
TCBM Ben McLemore/25 4.00 10.00
TCCB Cameron Bairstow/49 3.00 8.00
TCCC Cedric Ceballos/49 3.00 8.00
TCCD Clyde Drexler/25 15.00 40.00
TCCM Chris Mullin/25 6.00 15.00
TCCO Charles Oakley/49 6.00 15.00
TCCR Cazzie Russell/49 4.00 10.00
TCDB Dee Brown/49 3.00 8.00
TCDC DeMarre Carroll/49 3.00 8.00
TCDC Doug Collins/49 5.00 12.00
TCDE Dante Exum/25 5.00 12.00
TCDG Darrell Griffith/49 3.00 8.00
TCDM Donatas Motiejunas/49 3.00 8.00
TCDM Dikembe Mutombo/25 12.00 30.00
TCDR Dennis Rodman/25 20.00 50.00
TCDR Dino Radja/49 20.00 50.00
TCDS Damon Stoudamire/49 4.00 10.00
TCDV Dick Van Arsdale/49 4.00 10.00
TCDW Dominique Wilkins/25 8.00 20.00
TCEB Elgin Baylor/25
TCEJ Eddie Jones/49 4.00 10.00
TCFE Festus Ezeli/49 3.00 8.00
TCFL Fat Lever/49 4.00 10.00
TCGA G. Antetokounmpo/25 30.00 80.00
TCGG George Gervin/25
TCGH Grant Hill/25 15.00 40.00
TCGP Gary Payton/25
TCHB Harrison Barnes/25 8.00 20.00
TCJC Jordan Clarkson/49 6.00 15.00
TCJG Jerami Grant/49 3.00 8.00
TCJH Jrue Holiday/25 5.00 12.00
TCJR Julius Randle/25 6.00 15.00
TCJS Jared Sullinger/25 4.00 10.00
TCJS Josh Smith/25 5.00 12.00
TCJS John Stockton/25 20.00 50.00
TCJSL John Salley/49 3.00 8.00
TCJW Jo Jo White/49 4.00 10.00
TCJW James Worthy/25 8.00 20.00
TCJW Jerome Williams/49 3.00 8.00
TCKA Kenny Anderson/49 4.00 10.00
TCKG Kendall Gill/49 6.00 15.00
TCKV Keith Van Horn/49 4.00 10.00
TCKV Kiki Vandeweghe/49 4.00 10.00
TCLG Langston Galloway/49 3.00 8.00
TCLN Larry Nance/49 4.00 10.00
TCMA Mahmoud Abdul-Rauf/49 8.00 20.00
TCMB Muggsy Bogues/49 4.00 10.00
TCMC Maurice Cheeks/49 3.00 8.00
TCMC Michael Carter-Williams/25 4.00 10.00
TCMD Matthew Dellavedova/49 6.00 15.00
TCMG Manu Ginobili/25 15.00 40.00
TCMP Mark Price/49 5.00 12.00
TCMP Mason Plumlee/49 4.00 10.00
TCMR Mitch Richmond/25 10.00 25.00
TCMS Marcus Smart/25 5.00 12.00
TCNA Nate Archibald/25 15.00 40.00
TCNN Nerlens Noel/25 5.00 12.00
TCNV Nick Van Exel/25 15.00 40.00
TCOR Oscar Robertson/25 25.00 60.00
TCPG Pau Gasol/25 12.00 30.00
TCPS Peja Stojakovic/25 6.00 15.00
TCRA Ray Allen/25 12.00 30.00
TCRC Robert Covington/49 3.00 8.00
TCRG Rudy Gobert/49 10.00 25.00
TCRH Richard Hamilton/25 5.00 12.00
TCRM Ray McCallum/49 3.00 8.00
TCRR Ricky Rubio/25 6.00 15.00
TCRS Rik Smits/49 4.00 10.00
TCRS Rony Seikaly/49 3.00 8.00
TCRT Rudy Tomjanovich/49 4.00 10.00
TCSE Sean Elliott/49 5.00 12.00
TCSH Solomon Hill/49 3.00 8.00
TCSH Spencer Haywood/49 3.00 8.00
TCSM Sidney Moncrief/49 3.00 8.00
TCSS Scott Skiles/49 4.00 10.00
TCSW Sonny Weems/49 3.00 8.00
TCTE Tyreke Evans/25 4.00 10.00
TCTH Tim Hardaway Jr./49 3.00 8.00
TCTH Tim Hardaway/25 6.00 15.00
TCTM Tracy McGrady/25 12.00 30.00
TCTM Timofey Mozgov/49 3.00 8.00
TCTP Terry Porter/49 3.00 8.00
TCTT Tristan Thompson/19 5.00 12.00
TCVB Vin Baker/49 3.00 8.00
TCVD Vlade Divac/49 5.00 12.00
TCVO Victor Oladipo/25 5.00 12.00
TCWF Walt Frazier/25 6.00 15.00
TCWM Wesley Matthews/25 4.00 10.00
TCWU Wes Unseld/25 6.00 15.00

2015-16 Totally Certified Skills

RANDOM INSERTS IN PACKS
STATED PRINT RUN 199 SER.#'d SETS
*MIRROR/25: 1.5X TO 4X BASIC
1 Klay Thompson 1.25 3.00
2 Joakim Noah .75 2.00
3 LaMarcus Aldridge 1.00 2.50
4 Andrew Wiggins 1.50 4.00
5 Pau Gasol 1.00 2.50
6 Carmelo Anthony 1.25 3.00
7 Tim Duncan 1.50 4.00
8 DeMarcus Cousins 1.00 2.50
9 Kenneth Faried .75 2.00
10 Dwyane Wade 1.50 4.00
11 Kobe Bryant 4.00 10.00
12 John Wall 1.25 3.00
13 LeBron James 4.00 10.00
14 Anthony Davis 2.00 5.00
15 Paul George 1.25 3.00
16 Chris Bosh 1.00 2.50
17 Tony Parker 1.00 2.50
18 Derrick Rose 1.25 3.00
19 Kevin Durant 2.50 6.00
20 Jabari Parker 1.25 3.00
21 Kyle Korver .75 2.00
22 Kawhi Leonard 1.50 4.00
23 Blake Griffin 1.00 2.50
24 Manu Ginobili 1.00 2.50
25 Russell Westbrook 2.50 6.00
26 Chris Paul 1.25 3.00
27 Victor Oladipo .75 2.00
28 Dirk Nowitzki 1.25 3.00
29 Kevin Garnett 1.50 4.00
30 James Harden 1.50 4.00
31 Kyrie Irving 2.00 5.00
32 Kemba Walker 1.00 2.50
33 DeAndre Jordan 1.00 2.50
34 Bradley Beal 1.00 2.50
35 Stephen Curry 4.00 10.00
36 Damian Lillard 2.00 5.00
37 Zach LaVine 1.00 2.50
38 Dwight Howard .75 2.00
39 Kevin Love 1.00 2.50
40 Jimmy Butler 1.00 2.50

2016-17 Totally Certified

COMP.SET w/o RCs (100) 15.00 40.00
1 Anthony Davis .75 2.00
2 James Harden .60 1.50
3 Chris Paul .50 1.25
4 Draymond Green .50 1.25
5 Dwyane Wade .60 1.50
6 Michael Kidd-Gilchrist .30 .75
7 Trevor Ariza .25 .60
8 Karl-Anthony Towns 1.00 2.50
9 Zach LaVine .40 1.00
10 Allen Crabbe .25 .60
11 Avery Bradley .30 .75
12 Markieff Morris .25 .60
13 Mason Plumlee .30 .75
14 Stephen Curry 1.50 4.00
15 Jimmy Butler .40 1.00
16 Kemba Walker .40 1.00
17 Jeff Teague .30 .75
18 Andrew Wiggins .60 1.50
19 Jrue Holiday .30 .75
20 Ben McLemore .25 .60
21 Nik Stauskas .25 .60
22 Marcin Gortat .30 .75
23 Damian Lillard .75 2.00
24 Klay Thompson .50 1.25
25 Nikola Mirotic .30 .75
26 Nicolas Batum .30 .75
27 Monta Ellis .30 .75
28 Khris Middleton .30 .75
29 Carmelo Anthony .50 1.25
30 DeMarcus Cousins .40 1.00
31 Bobby Portis .25 .60
32 John Wall .50 1.25
33 C.J. McCollum .30 .75
34 Kevin Durant 1.00 2.50
35 Chris Andersen .30 .75
36 Jeremy Lin .40 1.00
37 Paul George .50 1.25
38 Jabari Parker .50 1.25

39 Derrick Rose .50 1.25
40 Rudy Gay .40 1.00
41 Mario Hezonja .25 .60
42 Rudy Gobert .40 1.00
43 Eric Bledsoe .30 .75
44 Tobias Harris .30 .75
45 Kevin Love .40 1.00
46 Brook Lopez .30 .75
47 Blake Griffin .40 1.00
48 Giannis Antetokounmpo .75 2.00
49 Kristaps Porzingis .75 2.00
50 Kawhi Leonard .60 1.50
51 Willie Cauley-Stein .30 .75
52 Rodney Hood .30 .75
53 Devin Booker .60 1.50
54 Reggie Jackson .30 .75
55 Kyrie Irving .75 2.00
56 Jae Crowder .30 .75
57 Dennis Schroder .30 .75
58 Tyler Johnson .25 .60
59 Russell Westbrook 1.00 2.50
60 Tony Parker .40 1.00
61 Tyreke Evans .25 .60
62 Gordon Hayward .40 1.00
63 Brandon Knight .30 .75
64 Andre Drummond .40 1.00
65 LeBron James 1.50 4.00
66 Isaiah Thomas .40 1.00
67 DeAndre Jordan .40 1.00
68 Hassan Whiteside .30 .75
69 Steven Adams .30 .75
70 LaMarcus Aldridge .40 1.00
71 Justise Winslow .30 .75
72 Dante Exum .30 .75
73 Joel Embiid .60 1.50
74 Nikola Jokic .40 1.00
75 Deron Williams .30 .75
76 Al Horford .30 .75
77 D'Angelo Russell .50 1.25
78 Goran Dragic .30 .75
79 Aaron Gordon .30 .75
80 Manu Ginobili .40 1.00
81 Myles Turner .30 .75
82 Kyle Lowry .30 .75
83 Jahlil Okafor .30 .75
84 Jusuf Nurkic .25 .60
85 Dirk Nowitzki .50 1.25
86 Dwight Howard .30 .75
87 Jordan Clarkson .30 .75
88 Mike Conley .30 .75
89 DeMar DeRozan .40 1.00
90 Clint Capela .25 .60
91 Jonas Valanciunas .30 .75
92 Evan Fournier .30 .75
93 Emmanuel Mudiay .30 .75
94 Harrison Barnes .30 .75
95 Paul Millsap .40 1.00
96 Julius Randle .40 1.00
97 Chandler Parsons .30 .75
98 Elfrid Payton .30 .75
99 DeMarre Carroll .25 .60
100 Bradley Beal .40 1.00
101 Brandon Ingram RC 3.00 8.00
102 Jaylen Brown RC 2.00 5.00
103 Dragan Bender RC .60 1.50
104 Kris Dunn RC 1.50 4.00
105 Buddy Hield RC 1.25 3.00
106 Jamal Murray RC 1.50 4.00
107 Marquese Chriss RC 1.25 3.00
108 Jakob Poeltl RC .60 1.50
109 Thon Maker RC 1.50 4.00
110 Taurean Prince RC .75 2.00
111 Denzel Valentine RC .60 1.50
112 Wade Baldwin IV RC .50 1.25
113 Henry Ellenson RC .60 1.50
114 Malik Beasley RC .50 1.25
115 DeAndre' Bembry RC .50 1.25
116 Malachi Richardson RC .60 1.50
117 T. Luwawu-Cabarrot RC 1.00 2.50
118 Brice Johnson RC .50 1.25
119 Pascal Siakam RC .50 1.25
120 Skal Labissiere RC .75 2.00
121 Damian Jones RC .50 1.25
122 Deyonta Davis RC .50 1.25
123 Cheick Diallo RC .50 1.25
124 Tyler Ulis RC 1.50 4.00
125 Patrick McCaw RC 1.00 2.50
126 Isaiah Whitehead RC .50 1.25
127 Demetrius Jackson RC .50 1.25
128 Ivica Zubac RC .75 2.00
129 Malcolm Brogdon RC 1.25 3.00
130 A.J. Hammons RC .50 1.25
131 Diamond Stone RC .50 1.25
132 Caris LeVert RC .60 1.50
133 Michael Gbinije RC .50 1.25
134 Jake Layman RC .60 1.50
135 Chinanu Onuaku RC .50 1.25
136 Stephen Zimmerman RC .50 1.25
137 Georges Niang RC .50 1.25
138 Dario Saric RC 1.50 4.00
139 Tomas Satoransky RC .50 1.25
140 Ben Simmons RC 6.00 15.00

2016-17 Totally Certified Blue

*BLUE VET: 1.2X TO 3X BASIC VET
*BLUE RC: .6X TO 1.5X BASIC RC
RANDOM INSERTS IN PACKS
STATED PRINT 99 SER. #'d SETS
140 Ben Simmons 25.00 60.00

2016-17 Totally Certified Camo

*CAMO VET: 4X TO 10X BASIC VET
*CAMO RC: 2X TO 5X BASIC RC
RANDOM INSERTS IN PACKS
STATED PRINT 25 SER. #'d SETS
140 Ben Simmons 75.00 200.00

2016-17 Totally Certified Orange

*ORANGE VET: 1.5X TO 4X BASIC VET
*ORANGE RC: .75X TO 2X BASIC RC
RANDOM INSERTS IN PACKS
STATED PRINT RUN 60 SER. #'d SETS
140 Ben Simmons 30.00 80.00

2016-17 Totally Certified Red

*RED VET: 1X TO 2.5X BASIC VET
*RED RC: .5X TO 1.2X BASIC RC
RANDOM INSERTS IN PACKS
STATED PRINT RUN 199 SER. #'d SETS
140 Ben Simmons 20.00 50.00

2016-17 Totally Certified Calling Cards

RANDOM INSERTS IN PACKS
*MIRROR/25: 1.5X TO 4X BASIC
1 Damian Lillard 1.25 3.00
2 Dirk Nowitzki .75 2.00
3 Kyrie Irving 1.25 3.00
4 LeBron James 2.50 6.00
5 Hassan Whiteside .50 1.25
6 Stephen Curry 2.50 6.00
7 Andre Drummond .60 1.50
8 DeAndre Jordan .60 1.50
9 DeMarcus Cousins .60 1.50
10 James Harden 1.00 2.50
11 Russell Westbrook 1.50 4.00
12 Karl-Anthony Towns 1.50 4.00
13 John Wall .75 2.00
14 Wilt Chamberlain 1.25 3.00
15 Bill Russell 1.00 2.50
16 Dennis Rodman 1.25 3.00
17 Hakeem Olajuwon .75 2.00
18 Kevin Durant 1.50 4.00
19 Carmelo Anthony .75 2.00
20 Magic Johnson 1.50 4.00
21 John Stockton 1.00 2.50
22 Chris Paul .75 2.00
23 Allen Iverson .75 2.00
24 Kobe Bryant 2.50 6.00
25 Karl Malone .75 2.00
26 Shaquille O'Neal 1.50 4.00
27 Steve Nash .60 1.50
28 Larry Bird 1.50 4.00
29 J.J. Redick .60 1.50
30 Robert Parish .60 1.50
31 Anthony Davis 1.25 3.00
32 Ricky Rubio .60 1.50
33 Manute Bol .60 1.50
34 Kobe Bryant 2.50 6.00
35 Kendall Gill .40 1.00
36 Scott Skiles .50 1.25
37 Bill Russell 1.00 2.50
38 Charles Oakley .50 1.25
39 Stephen Curry 2.50 6.00
40 David Robinson 1.00 2.50
41 Wilt Chamberlain 1.25 3.00
42 Shaquille O'Neal 1.50 4.00
43 Scottie Pippen 1.25 3.00
44 George Mikan 1.25 3.00

2016-17 Totally Certified Energizers

RANDOM INSERTS IN PACKS
*RED/199: .5X TO 1.2X BASIC
*BLUE/99: .6X TO 1.5X BASIC
*ORANGE/60: .75X TO 2X BASIC
*CAMO/25: 1.2X TO 3X BASIC
1 Elfrid Payton .60 1.50
2 John Wall 1.00 2.50
3 Chris Paul 1.00 2.50
4 Isaiah Thomas .75 2.00
5 Dennis Schroder .60 1.50
6 Damian Lillard 1.50 4.00
7 Leandro Barbosa .50 1.25
8 Stephen Curry 3.00 8.00
9 Nate Archibald .60 1.50
10 Allen Iverson 1.00 2.50
11 Isiah Thomas .75 2.00
12 Kenny Smith .60 1.50
13 Muggsy Bogues .60 1.50
14 Spud Webb .60 1.50
15 John Starks .60 1.50
16 Eddie Johnson .50 1.25

2016-17 Totally Certified Fabric of the Game Jerseys

RANDOM INSERTS IN PACKS
*BLUE/99: .5X TO 1.2X BASIC
*CAMO/25: .75X TO 2X BASIC
1 Jeremy Lamb 1.50 4.00
2 Tim Duncan 3.00 8.00
3 Spencer Hawes 1.50 4.00
4 Chris Andersen 2.00 5.00
5 Hassan Whiteside 2.00 5.00
6 Andre Iguodala 2.00 5.00
7 Russell Westbrook 4.00 10.00
8 LeBron James 8.00 20.00
9 Justise Winslow 2.00 5.00
10 Goran Dragic 2.00 5.00
11 Robin Lopez 1.50 4.00
12 Carmelo Anthony 3.00 8.00
13 Andrew Wiggins 3.00 8.00
14 Serge Ibaka 2.00 5.00
15 Enes Kanter 1.50 4.00
16 Dwight Powell 1.50 4.00
17 Greg Monroe 2.00 5.00
18 Timofey Mozgov 1.50 4.00
19 Zach Randolph 2.00 5.00
20 R.J. Hunter 1.50 4.00
21 Kemba Walker 2.50 6.00
22 Jeff Green 2.00 5.00
23 Mike Conley 2.00 5.00
24 Noah Vonleh 1.50 4.00
25 Gerald Henderson 1.50 4.00
26 Vince Carter 4.00 10.00
27 Jrue Holiday 2.00 5.00
28 Tyreke Evans 1.50 4.00
29 Ryan Anderson 2.00 5.00
30 Chandler Parsons 2.00 5.00
31 Austin Rivers 2.00 5.00
32 Jimmy Butler 2.50 6.00
33 Nik Stauskas 1.50 4.00
34 Jahlil Okafor 2.00 5.00
35 Jeff Teague 2.00 5.00
36 Tim Hardaway Jr. 1.50 4.00
37 Tyus Jones 1.50 4.00
38 Kawhi Leonard 4.00 10.00
39 Manu Ginobili 2.50 6.00
40 Rodney Stuckey 1.50 4.00
41 Kelly Oubre Jr. 1.50 4.00
42 Tobias Harris 2.00 5.00
43 Kris Humphries 1.50 4.00
44 Nikola Mirotic 2.00 5.00
45 Brandon Knight 2.00 5.00
46 Cory Joseph 1.50 4.00
47 Mason Plumlee 2.00 5.00
48 Jerian Grant 1.50 4.00
49 Rudy Gobert 2.50 6.00
50 Derrick Favors 2.00 5.00

2016-17 Totally Certified Fabric of the Game Rookie Jerseys

RANDOM INSERTS IN PACKS
*BLUE/99: .5X TO 1.2X BASIC
*CAMO/25: .75X TO 2X BASIC
1 Tyler Ulis 5.00 12.00
2 T. Luwawu-Cabarrot 3.00 8.00
3 Malachi Richardson 2.00 5.00
4 Brice Johnson 1.50 4.00
5 Brandon Ingram 4.00 10.00
6 Patrick McCaw 3.00 8.00
7 Marquese Chriss 4.00 10.00
8 DeAndre' Bembry 1.50 4.00
9 Pascal Siakam 1.50 4.00
10 Jaylen Brown 3.00 8.00
11 Isaiah Whitehead 1.50 4.00
12 Jakob Poeltl 2.00 5.00
13 Malik Beasley 1.50 4.00
14 Skal Labissiere 2.50 6.00
15 Dragan Bender 2.00 5.00
16 Demetrius Jackson 1.50 4.00
17 Thon Maker 3.00 8.00
18 Henry Ellenson 2.00 5.00
19 Damian Jones 1.50 4.00
20 Kris Dunn 3.00 8.00
21 Wade Baldwin IV 1.50 4.00
22 Deyonta Davis 1.50 4.00
23 Buddy Hield 3.00 8.00
24 Ivica Zubac 2.50 6.00
25 Taurean Prince 2.50 6.00
26 Denzel Valentine 3.00 8.00
27 Cheick Diallo 1.50 4.00
28 Jamal Murray 3.00 8.00
29 A.J. Hammons 1.50 4.00
30 Diamond Stone 1.50 4.00

2016-17 Totally Certified Franchise Foundations

RANDOM INSERTS IN PACKS
1 Anthony Davis 1.50 4.00
2 James Harden 1.25 3.00
3 Chris Paul 1.00 2.50
4 Karl-Anthony Towns 2.00 5.00
5 Stephen Curry 3.00 8.00
6 Jimmy Butler .75 2.00
7 Kemba Walker .75 2.00
8 Damian Lillard 1.50 4.00
9 DeMarcus Cousins .75 2.00
10 John Wall 1.00 2.50
11 Paul George 1.00 2.50
12 Brook Lopez .60 1.50
13 Kristaps Porzingis 1.50 4.00
14 Kawhi Leonard 1.25 3.00
15 Devin Booker 1.25 3.00
16 Kyrie Irving 1.50 4.00
17 Dennis Schroder .60 1.50
18 Russell Westbrook 2.00 5.00
19 Gordon Hayward .75 2.00
20 Andre Drummond .75 2.00
21 Isaiah Thomas .75 2.00
22 Justise Winslow .60 1.50
23 Dirk Nowitzki 1.00 2.50
24 Mike Conley .60 1.50
25 DeMar DeRozan .75 2.00
26 Elfrid Payton .60 1.50
27 Kenneth Faried .60 1.50
28 Giannis Antetokounmpo 1.50 4.00
29 Brandon Ingram 3.00 8.00
30 Ben Simmons 3.00 8.00

2016-17 Totally Certified Franchise Foundations Blue

*BLUE: .6X TO 1.5X BASIC
RANDOM INSERTS PER PACK
STATED PRINT RUN 99 SER. #'d SETS
30 Ben Simmons 15.00 40.00

2016-17 Totally Certified Franchise Foundations Camo

*CAMO: 1.2X TO 3X BASIC
RANDOM INSERTS PER PACK
STATED PRINT RUN 25 SER. #'d SETS
30 Ben Simmons 60.00 150.00

2016-17 Totally Certified Franchise Foundations Orange

*ORANGE: .75X TO 2X BASIC
RANDOM INSERTS PER PACK
STATED PRINT RUN 60 SER. #'d SETS
30 Ben Simmons 20.00 50.00

2016-17 Totally Certified Franchise Foundations Red

*RED: .5X TO 1.2X BASIC
RANDOM INSERTS PER PACK
STATED PRINT RUN 199 SER. #'d SETS
30 Ben Simmons 12.00 30.00

2016-17 Totally Certified Materials

RANDOM INSERTS IN PACK
*BLUE/99: .5X TO 1.2X BASIC
*CAMO/25: .75X TO 2X BASIC
1 Carmelo Anthony 3.00 8.00
2 Kenneth Faried 2.00 5.00
3 Ricky Rubio 2.50 6.00
4 Richard Jefferson 2.00 5.00
5 Kevin Love 2.50 6.00
6 Karl-Anthony Towns 4.00 10.00
7 Cody Zeller 1.50 4.00
8 Rudy Gay 2.50 6.00
9 Paul Millsap 2.50 6.00
10 Stanley Johnson 1.50 4.00
11 Jusuf Nurkic 1.50 4.00
12 Eric Gordon 2.00 5.00
13 Tony Parker 2.50 6.00
14 Tim Duncan 3.00 8.00
15 Clint Capela 1.50 4.00
16 Monta Ellis 2.00 5.00
17 T.J. Warren 2.00 5.00
18 George Hill 2.00 5.00
19 Paul George 3.00 8.00
20 Andre Iguodala 2.00 5.00

2016-17 Totally Certified Representatives Autographs

RANDOM INSERTS IN PACKS
PRINT RUN B/WN 14-100 COPIES PER
EXCHANGE DEADLINE 6/14/2018
*MIRROR/25: .6X TO 1.5X BASIC
1 Dikembe Mutombo/100 8.00 20.00
2 Larry Bird/30 30.00 80.00
3 Brook Lopez/25
4 Michael Kidd-Gilchrist/50
5 Scottie Pippen/50 40.00 100.00
6 Kyrie Irving/35 30.00 80.00
7 Dirk Nowitzki/50 40.00 100.00
8 Alex English/100 3.00 8.00
9 Reggie Jackson/100 3.00 8.00
10 Kevin Durant/35 EXCH 40.00 100.00
11 Hakeem Olajuwon/35 10.00 25.00
12 Myles Turner/50 8.00 20.00
13 Blake Griffin/35
14 Kobe Bryant/50
15 Zach Randolph/65 3.00 8.00
16 Glen Rice/100 3.00 8.00
17 Michael Carter-Williams/75
18 Karl-Anthony Towns/50 30.00 80.00
19 Anthony Davis/35 25.00 60.00
20 Carmelo Anthony/50 20.00 50.00
21 Steven Adams/35 3.00 8.00
23 Allen Iverson/25 30.00 80.00
24 Dan Majerle/100 3.00 8.00
25 C.J. McCollum/75 3.00 8.00
26 Vlade Divac/100 4.00 10.00
27 David Robinson/50 12.00 30.00
28 Jonas Valanciunas/100 3.00 8.00
29 John Stockton/50 15.00 40.00
30 John Wall/35 EXCH 20.00 50.00

2016-17 Totally Certified Return to Sender

RANDOM INSERTS IN PACK
*RED/199: .5X TO 1.2X BASIC
*BLUE/99: .6X TO 1.5X BASIC
*ORANGE/60: .75X TO 2X BASIC
*CAMO/25: 1.2X TO 3X BASIC
1 DeAndre Jordan .75 2.00
2 Anthony Davis 1.50 4.00
3 Myles Turner .60 1.50
4 Jonas Valanciunas .60 1.50
5 Rudy Gobert .75 2.00
6 LeBron James 3.00 8.00
7 Hassan Whiteside .60 1.50
8 Willie Cauley-Stein .60 1.50
9 Hakeem Olajuwon 1.00 2.50
10 David Robinson 1.25 3.00
11 Manute Bol .75 2.00
12 Shawn Marion .60 1.50
13 Ben Wallace .60 1.50
14 Dikembe Mutombo .75 2.00

2016-17 Totally Certified Rookie Roll Call Autographs

RANDOM INSERTS IN PACKS
EXCHANGE DEADLINE 6/14/2018
*BLUE/99: .5X TO 1.2X BASIC
*CAMO/25: .6X TO 1.5X BASIC
1 Brandon Ingram 30.00 80.00
2 Jaylen Brown 15.00 40.00
3 Dragan Bender 4.00 10.00
4 Kris Dunn 15.00 40.00
5 Buddy Hield 12.00 30.00
6 Jamal Murray 10.00 25.00
7 Marquese Chriss 10.00 25.00
8 Jakob Poeltl 4.00 10.00
9 Thon Maker 10.00 25.00
10 Domantas Sabonis 5.00 12.00
11 Taurean Prince 5.00 12.00
12 Denzel Valentine 4.00 10.00
13 Wade Baldwin IV 3.00 8.00
14 Henry Ellenson 4.00 10.00
15 Malik Beasley 3.00 8.00
16 DeAndre' Bembry 3.00 8.00
17 Malachi Richardson 4.00 10.00
18 T. Luwawu-Cabarrot 6.00 15.00
19 Brice Johnson 3.00 8.00
20 Pascal Siakam 3.00 8.00
21 Skal Labissiere 12.00 30.00
22 Damian Jones 3.00 8.00
23 Deyonta Davis 3.00 8.00
24 Cheick Diallo 3.00 8.00
25 Tyler Ulis 10.00 25.00
26 Patrick McCaw 10.00 25.00
27 Isaiah Whitehead 3.00 8.00
28 Demetrius Jackson 3.00 8.00
29 Kay Felder 3.00 8.00
30 Ivica Zubac 10.00 25.00
31 Malcolm Brogdon 12.00 30.00
32 A.J. Hammons 3.00 8.00
33 Diamond Stone 3.00 8.00
34 Gary Payton II 4.00 10.00
35 Caris LeVert 4.00 10.00
36 Michael Gbinije 3.00 8.00
37 Jake Layman 4.00 10.00
38 Ben Bentil 3.00 8.00
39 Chinanu Onuaku 3.00 8.00
40 Stephen Zimmerman 3.00 8.00
41 Georges Niang 3.00 8.00
42 Marcus Paige 3.00 8.00
43 Daniel Hamilton 3.00 8.00
44 Tyrone Wallace 3.00 8.00
45 Isaiah Cousins 3.00 8.00
47 Abdel Nader 3.00 8.00
48 Joel Bolomboy 3.00 8.00
49 Dario Saric 12.00 30.00
50 Tomas Satoransky 3.00 8.00

2016-17 Totally Certified Signed Sealed Delivered Autographs

RANDOM INSERTS IN PACKS
PRINT RUNS B/WN 35-99 COPIES PER
EXCHANGE DEADLINE 6/14/2018
*MIRROR/25: .6X TO 1.5X BASIC
1 John Stockton/75 12.00 30.00
2 Kobe Bryant/75 75.00 200.00
3 Grant Hill/35 12.00 30.00
4 C.J. McCollum/75 5.00 12.00
5 Dikembe Mutombo/99 10.00 25.00
6 Spud Webb/99 3.00 8.00
7 Cody Zeller/75 2.50 6.00
8 Artis Gilmore/99 3.00 8.00
9 Jerry West/35 15.00 40.00
10 Pau Gasol/75 6.00 15.00
11 Oscar Robertson/75 20.00 50.00
12 Tristan Thompson/75 3.00 8.00
13 Dirk Nowitzki/75 40.00 100.00
14 Reggie Jackson/99 3.00 8.00
15 Draymond Green/35 12.00 30.00
16 Tim Hardaway/75 4.00 10.00
17 Hakeem Olajuwon/75 8.00 20.00
18 Chris Paul/35
19 Patrick Ewing/75 60.00 150.00
20 Dwyane Wade/35 40.00 100.00

2016-17 Totally Certified The Mighty

RANDOM INSERTS IN PACKS
1 Stephen Curry 20.00 50.00
2 LeBron James 30.00 80.00
3 Ben Simmons 40.00 100.00
4 Damian Lillard 10.00 25.00
5 Kawhi Leonard 10.00 25.00
6 James Harden 6.00 15.00

1984-85 Trail Blazers Ball Boy

This one card set features Trail Blazer star Kiki Vandewedge posing with a Trail Blazer ball boy.
1 Kiki Vandeweghe 4.00 10.00

1990-91 Trail Blazers British Petroleum

These large (approximately 8 1/2" by 11") high-gloss action player photos were taken by Bryan Drake. The photos are printed on thin paper and have white, red, and white borders (in that order), on a black background. The player's name appears below the picture, between the team and the sponsor's logos. The backs are blank. The set features members of the Portland Trail Blazers. These unnumbered cards were ordered alphabetically by player in the checklist below.
COMPLETE SET (6) 6.00 15.00
1 Danny Ainge 1.50 4.00
2 Clyde Drexler 3.00 8.00
3 Kevin Duckworth .75 2.00
4 Jerome Kersey .75 2.00
5 Terry Porter .75 2.00
6 Buck Williams .75 2.00

1991-92 Trail Blazers Dairy Queen Glasses

Dairy Queen produced this six-glass set to commemorate the Portland Trail Blazers. These glasses show the players in their uniforms. The glasses are not numbered and are checklisted below in alphabetical order.
COMPLETE SET (6) 6.00 15.00
1 Clyde Drexler 2.00 5.00
2 Kevin Duckworth .75 2.00
3 Jerome Kersey .75 2.00
4 Terry Porter .75 2.00
5 Clifford Robinson 1.25 3.00
6 Buck Williams .75 2.00

1992-93 Trail Blazers Dairy Queen Glasses

Dairy Queen produced this six-glass set to commemorate the Portland Trail Blazers. These glasses show the players in casual settings - doing their hobbies. The glasses are not numbered and are checklisted below in alphabetical order.
COMPLETE SET (6) 6.00 15.00
1 Clyde Drexler 2.00 5.00
2 Kevin Duckworth .75 2.00
3 Jerome Kersey .75 2.00
4 Terry Porter .75 2.00
5 Clifford Robinson 1.25 3.00
6 Buck Williams .75 2.00

1984-85 Trail Blazers Franz/Star

This 13-card standard-size set was produced for the Franz Bakery in Portland, Oregon by the Star Company. One card was placed in each loaf of Franz Bread as a promotional giveaway. Cards were printed with FDA approved vegetable ink. The cards have a red border around the fronts of the cards and red printing on the backs. Cards feature the Franz logo on the fronts. These numbered cards were ordered alphabetically by player. The set features one of the first professional cards of Jerome Kersey.
COMPLETE SET (13) 20.00 50.00
1 Jack Ramsay CO 1.50 4.00
2 Sam Bowie 2.50 6.00
3 Kenny Carr .75 2.00
4 Steve Colter .75 2.00
5 Clyde Drexler 12.50 30.00
6 Jerome Kersey 2.50 6.00
7 Audie Norris .75 2.00
8 Jim Paxson 1.25 3.00
9 Tom Scheffler 1.00 2.50
10 Bernard Thompson .75 2.00
11 Mychal Thompson 1.25 3.00
12 Darnell Valentine 1.00 2.50
13 Kiki Vandeweghe 1.50 4.00

1985-86 Trail Blazers Franz/Star

The 1985-86 Franz Portland Trail Blazers standard-size set was produced by The Star Company for Franz Bread. There are 12 player cards and one coach card. The front borders are reddish orange, and the backs feature statistics and biographical information. The set features the first professional card of Terry Porter.
COMPLETE SET (13) 15.00 40.00
1 Jack Ramsay CO 1.50 4.00
2 Sam Bowie 1.50 4.00
3 Kenny Carr .75 2.00
4 Steve Colter .75 2.00
5 Clyde Drexler 6.00 15.00
6 Ken Johnson .75 2.00
7 Caldwell Jones .75 2.00
8 Jerome Kersey 1.25 3.00
9 Jim Paxson 1.25 3.00
10 Terry Porter 4.00 10.00
11 Mychal Thompson 1.25 3.00
12 Darnell Valentine .75 2.00
13 Kiki Vandeweghe 1.25 3.00

1986-87 Trail Blazers Franz

The 1986-87 Franz Portland Trail Blazers set was produced by Fleer for Franz Bread. There are 12 player standard-size cards and one coach card. The front borders are reddish-orange, and the backs feature statistics and biographical information. Card backs are printed in pink and red on white card stock. These numbered cards were ordered alphabetically by player.
COMPLETE SET (13) 40.00 80.00
1 Walter Berry 1.50 4.00
2 Sam Bowie 2.50 6.00
3 Kenny Carr 1.50 4.00
4 Clyde Drexler 15.00 40.00
5 Michael Holton 1.50 4.00
6 Steve Johnson 1.50 4.00
7 Caldwell Jones 1.50 4.00
8 Jerome Kersey 2.00 5.00
9 Fernando Martin 1.50 4.00
10 Jim Paxson 2.00 5.00
11 Terry Porter 3.00 8.00
12 Kiki Vandeweghe 3.00 8.00
13 Mike Schuler CO 1.50 4.00

1987-88 Trail Blazers Franz

This 13 card standard-size card set was produced by Fleer as a promotion for Franz Bread. The cards were distributed in loaves of Franz Bread. The backs have biographical and statistical information. The cards are numbered on the back and are ordered alphabetically by player. The set includes Kevin Duckworth's first professional card.
COMPLETE SET (13) 50.00 100.00
1 Clyde Drexler 20.00 50.00
2 Kevin Duckworth 2.50 6.00
3 Michael Holton 2.00 5.00
4 Steve Johnson 1.50 4.00
5 Caldwell Jones 2.00 5.00
6 Jerome Kersey 3.00 8.00
7 Maurice Lucas 4.00 10.00
8 Jim Paxson 2.50 6.00
9 Terry Porter 4.00 10.00
10 Mike Schuler CO 1.50 4.00
11 Kiki Vandeweghe 3.00 8.00
12 Steve Johnson 1.50 4.00
13 Kiki Vandeweghe 4.00 10.00

1988-89 Trail Blazers Franz

The 1988-89 Franz Portland Trail Blazers set was produced by The Fleer Corporation for Franz Bread. There are 12 player standard-size cards and one coach card. The front borders are white with red bars and the backs feature statistics and biographical information. Card backs are printed in pink and red on white card stock. These numbered cards were ordered alphabetically by player.
COMPLETE SET (13) 30.00 60.00
1 Richard Anderson 1.50 4.00
2 Sam Bowie 2.00 5.00
3 Mark Bryant 1.50 4.00
4 Clyde Drexler 15.00 40.00
5 Kevin Duckworth 1.50 4.00
6 Rolando Ferreira 1.00 2.50
7 Steve Johnson 1.00 2.50
8 Caldwell Jones 1.50 4.00
9 Jerome Kersey 1.50 4.00
10 Terry Porter 2.50 6.00
11 Mike Schuler CO 1.00 2.50
12 Jerry Sichting 1.50 4.00
13 Kiki Vandeweghe 2.50 6.00

1989-90 Trail Blazers Franz

This 20-card standard-size set was produced by the Fleer Corporation for Franz Bread. The set commemorates the 20th anniversary season of the Trail Blazers and showcases current players as well as some "Blazer Greats" from past teams. The front features color action photos on white card stock, with orange border stripes on the left side and black border stripes on the right side and bottom of the picture. The Franz Bread logo appears in the upper right corner. The horizontally oriented back has biographical and statistical information, printed in pink and red on white card stock. The cards are numbered on the back. The set ordering is alphabetical within each group of current (1-11) and past (12-20) Trail Blazers. The set features the first professional card of Drazen Petrovic and Cliff Robinson.
COMPLETE SET (20) 30.00 60.00
1 Rick Adelman CO 1.00 2.50
2 Mark Bryant .75 2.00
3 Wayne Cooper .75 2.00
4 Kevin Duckworth .75 2.00
5 Clyde Drexler 8.00 20.00
6 Byron Irvin .75 2.00
7 Jerome Kersey 1.00 2.50
8 Drazen Petrovic 6.00 15.00
9 Terry Porter 1.25 3.00
10 Cliff Robinson 4.00 10.00
11 Buck Williams 2.00 5.00
12 Lionel Hollins 1.00 2.50
13 Maurice Lucas 1.00 2.50
14 Calvin Natt .75 2.00
15 Lloyd Neal .75 2.00
16 Jim Paxson 1.00 2.50
17 Geoff Petrie 1.00 2.50
18 Larry Steele .75 2.00
19 Mychal Thompson 1.00 2.50
20 Bill Walton 4.00 10.00

1990-91 Trail Blazers Franz

This 20-card standard-size set was produced by the Fleer Corporation for Franz Bread for distribution in the Portland area. The fronts feature color action player photos on a white card face, with black borders on the left side and red borders on the right. The Franz logo appears in a blue oval in the upper left corner, with the words "1991 Collector's Issue" to the right. The player's name, position, and team name appear below the picture. The back has biographical information and player statistics printed in pink and red on white. The team card can be found with and without the notation, 1989-90 Western Conference Champions, at the bottom of the (horizontally oriented) obverse. The set features an early professional card of Cliff Robinson.
COMPLETE SET (20) 15.00 30.00
1 Team Card .75 2.00
2 1989-90 Playoffs .30 .75
3 1989-90 Playoffs .30 .75
4 1989-90 Playoffs .30 .75
5 1989-90 Playoffs 2.50 6.00
Clyde Drexler
6 Bill Walton 2.00 5.00
7 Rick Adelman CO .40 1.00
8 John Schalow ACO and .30 .75
John Wetzel ACO
9 Alaa Abdelnaby .30 .75
10 Danny Ainge 1.25 3.00
11 Mark Bryant .30 .75
12 Wayne Cooper .30 .75
13 Clyde Drexler 5.00 12.00
14 Kevin Duckworth .40 1.00
15 Jerome Kersey .40 1.00
16 Drazen Petrovic 3.00 8.00
17 Terry Porter 1.25 3.00
18 Cliff Robinson 2.00 5.00
19 Buck Williams 1.25 3.00
20 Danny Young .30 .75

1991-92 Trail Blazers Franz

This 17-card standard size set was produced by Hoops for Franz Bread. The print run was 150,000 of each card. Beginning in November, one card per week was issued in a plastic sleeve in loaves of Franz Premium White Bread and Franz 100 Percent Wheat Bread. Robert Pack made the roster in October, and his card (17) was added to the rotation for distribution in February. After the 17-week promotion, Franz repeated each card statewide for one day each to allow collectors who might have missed one or more cards to complete their sets. The front features a full-bleed gold border with a color action photo at a slight angle within a three-sided black border and a red border at the bottom. The player's name appears in a black border beneath the picture. The horizontally oriented backs display a head shot, biography, statistics (by season and career), and career highlights. The cards are numbered in a basketball icon at the upper right corner. The set features the first professional card of Robert Pack.
COMPLETE SET (17) 10.00 25.00
1 Team Photo .75 2.00
2 Blazers All-Star Weekend .40 1.00
3 Buck Williams .75 2.00
4 Rick Adelman CO .60 1.50
5 Alaa Abdelnaby .30 .75
6 Danny Ainge 1.25 3.00
7 Mark Bryant .30 .75
8 Wayne Cooper .30 .75
9 Walter Davis 1.25 3.00
10 Clyde Drexler 5.00 12.00
11 Kevin Duckworth .40 1.00
12 Jerome Kersey .60 1.50
13 Terry Porter .75 2.00
14 Cliff Robinson 1.50 4.00
15 Buck Williams .75 2.00
16 Danny Young .30 .75
17 Robert Pack 1.25 3.00

1992-93 Trail Blazers Franz

This 20-card standard-size set was manufactured by SkyBox for the Trailblazers and distributed by Franz Bread. One card per week was inserted into loaves of Franz Premium White and Roman Meal Sandwich breads, with each card repeated for one day at the end of 20 weeks. The first card was in stores Monday, December 7, and the final card was issued the week of April 19th. Production was limited to 165,000 of each card. The set features color player photos that are full-bleed except at the bottom where a royal blue border stripe carries the player's name. The horizontal backs display close-up color player photos on a white background. A black stripe at the top stretches from the photo to a basketball icon that holds the card number. The black stripe also contains the player's name. Below are statistics and season highlights. The team logo and sponsor logo appear at the bottom.
COMPLETE SET (20) 10.00 25.00
1 Team Photo .75 2.00
2 Buck Williams .75 2.00
1991-92 NBA Playoffs
3 Clifford Robinson .75 2.00
1991-92 NBA Playoffs
4 Terry Porter .40 1.00
1991-92 NBA Playoffs
5 Jerome Kersey 1.25 3.00
Clyde Drexler
1991-92 NBA Playoffs
6 Clyde Drexler AS 1.50 4.00
7 Rick Adelman CO .40 1.00
8 Mark Bryant .20 .50
9 Clyde Drexler 3.00 8.00
10 Kevin Duckworth .30 .75
11 Jerome Kersey UER .40 1.00
(Card back has bio and stats for Tracy Murray)
12 Terry Porter .60 1.50
13 Cliff Robinson .75 2.00
14 Rod Strickland .60 1.50
15 Buck Williams .75 2.00
16 Mario Elie .40 1.00
17 Lamont Strothers .20 .50
18 Dave Johnson .20 .50
19 Tracy Murray .60 1.50
20 Reggie Smith .20 .50

1993-94 Trail Blazers Franz

As with the previous year's set, this 20-card standard-size set was produced by SkyBox. Beginning on December 6, one card per week was inserted in loaves of Franz and Williams Premium White and 100 Percent Wheat Bread. Based in Portland, United States Bakery owns both Franz and Williams. In 1993, the Oregon territory was divided into two regions, with Franz supplying the northern half of the state and Williams (which is based in Eugene) the southern half. As a result of this extended distribution, the production run was increased to 250,000 of each card. The fronts display color action player photos inside a silver frame with a black outer border. The horizontal backs carry a color head shot, biography, statistics, and career summary. Also this is the first year that the set includes Trail Blazers Walk of Fame Charter Member cards, which honor past players and other important individuals; these cards sport black-and-white portraits by S. Katagiri.
COMPLETE SET (20) 10.00 25.00
1 Team Photo .75 2.00
2 Jack Schalow ACO .40 1.00
Rick Adelman CO
John Wetzel ACO
3 Harry Glickman .40 1.00
Trail Blazers Walk of Fame Charter Member
4 Mark Bryant .20 .50
5 Clyde Drexler 4.00 10.00
6 Maurice Lucas .75 2.00
Trail Blazers Walk of Fame Charter Member
7 Chris Dudley .20 .50
8 Harvey Grant .20 .50
9 Geoff Petrie .40 1.00
Trail Blazers Walk of Fame Charter Member
10 Reggie Smith .20 .50
11 Jerome Kersey UER .40 1.00
(Bio& stats& and career summary are Murray's)
12 Jack Ramsay CO .60 1.50
Trail Blazers Walk of Fame Charter Member
13 Tracy Murray .40 1.00
14 Terry Porter .60 1.50
15 Bill Walton 2.00 5.00
Trail Blazers Walk of Fame Charter Member
16 Cliff Robinson 1.25 3.00
17 James Robinson .40 1.00
18 Larry Weinberg .40 1.00
Trail Blazers Walk of Fame Charter Member
19 Rod Strickland .60 1.50
20 Buck Williams .75 2.00

1994-95 Trail Blazers Franz

Produced by SkyBox, this 20-card standard-size set commemorates the Trail Blazers 25th anniversary as an NBA franchise. One card per week was inserted in loaves of Franz and Williams Premium White and 100% White Bread. Both Franz and Williams are owned by United States Bakery, a family-owned business based in Portland. Distribution began on December 5, with the final card being issued the week of April 17th. Following the weekly release of the individual cards, the cards were repeated chronologically over a four- week period, beginning Monday, April 24. This year's set includes a 5-card subset honoring Blazers president emeritus Harry Glickman and the team's first 25 years. Glickman chose an all-time Blazer squad of the players who had the greatest influence on the franchise. The fronts feature full-bleed color action player photos, with the player's name printed in a black bar at the bottom. The backs carry a small color player portrait, along with biography, season highlights and stats.
COMPLETE SET (20) 10.00 25.00
1 Team Photo .75 2.00
2 P.J. Carlesimo CO .75 2.00
3 Bill Walton 1.50 4.00
Glickman's All-Time Team
4 Mark Bryant .20 .50
5 Clyde Drexler 2.50 6.00
6 Chris Dudley .20 .50
7 Buck Williams .75 2.00
Glickman's All-Time Team
8 James Edwards .20 .50
9 Harvey Grant .30 .75
10 Jerome Kersey .30 .75
11 Clyde Drexler 1.50 4.00
Glickman's All-Time Team
12 Aaron McKie .50 1.25
13 Tracy Murray .20 .50
14 Terry Porter .40 1.00
15 Geoff Petrie .40 1.00
Glickman's All-Time Team
16 Clifford Robinson .75 2.00
17 James Robinson .20 .50
18 Rod Strickland .50 1.25
19 Maurice Lucas .60 1.50
Glickman's All-Time Team
20 Buck Williams .75 2.00

1995-96 Trail Blazers Franz

Produced by SkyBox, this 13-card standard-size set continues the long run of regional team sets from the Franz bread company. One card per week was inserted in loaves of Franz and Williams bread. The promotion ran from late 1995 through Spring, 1996. Unlike previous years, the 1995-96 set contained no extraneous playoff or commemorative cards.
COMPLETE SET (13) 4.00 10.00
1 Clifford Robinson .60 1.50
2 Randolph Childress .20 .50
3 Chris Dudley .20 .50
4 Aaron McKie .40 1.00
5 Harvey Grant .30 .75
6 Gary Trent .60 1.50
7 P.J. Carlesimo CO .20 .50
8 Dontonio Wingfield .20 .50
9 Arvydas Sabonis 1.50 4.00
10 James Robinson .20 .50
11 Rod Strickland .40 1.00
12 Bill Curley .20 .50
13 Buck Williams .60 1.50

1996-97 Trail Blazers Franz

Produced by SkyBox, this 7-card standard-size set replicates the cards from the 1996-97 SkyBox set. Cards are numbered "x of 7" on the back. Franz and the Blazers also issued a 6-card sticker/tatoo set. Those were not numbered. The only tatoos with a player photo is Arvydas Sabonis, who is pictured on two of them.

COMPLETE SET (7) 6.00 15.00
1 Jermaine O'Neal 3.00 8.00
2 Clifford Robinson .40 1.00
3 Gary Trent .20 .50
4 Kenny Anderson .20 .50
5 Arvydas Sabonis .75 2.00
6 Isaiah Rider .50 1.25
7 Rasheed Wallace 2.00 5.00
NNO Arvydas Sabonis Tatoo 2.00 5.00
In Black Uniform
NNO Arvydas Sabonis Tatoo 2.00 5.00
Passing behind back

1975-76 Trail Blazers Iron Ons

Sponsored by PayLess Drug Store, this is a set of seven iron ons. Printed on very thin paper and measuring 5" by 7 7/8", they feature black-and-white player portraits. The players' jerseys are outlined in red. A facsimile autograph, also in red, is printed on the bottom. The iron ons are unnumbered and checklisted below in alphabetical order.

COMPLETE SET (7) 20.00 40.00
1 Dan Anderson 1.25 3.00
2 Barry Clemens 1.25 3.00
3 Bob Gross 1.50 4.00
4 LaRue Martin 1.25 3.00
5 Larry Steele 1.50 4.00
6 Bill Walton 12.50 25.00
7 Sidney Wicks 3.00 8.00

1984 Trail Blazers Mr. Z's/Star 5x7

This five-card set was produced by Star Co. as a promotion for Mr. Z's frozen pizzas. Reportedly 10,000 cards of each player were produced. The cards were issued beginning in January 1984. The cards measure approximately 5" by 7" and feature on the fronts glossy color action player photos, with rounded corners as well as white and black borders on a dark red background. The team logo is superimposed over the picture at the intersection of the left side and bottom borders. The sponsor logo "Mr. Z's" appears in the upper right corner of the front, and player information is given below the picture. The backs have an advertisement for Blazer merchandise. The cards are unnumbered and are checklisted below in alphabetical order. Originally the set was planned to feature the whole team (12 players) but only five players were issued. Individual cards were given out in Mr. Z's frozen pizzas.

COMPLETE SET (5) 100.00 200.00
1 Kenny Carr 8.00 20.00
2 Clyde Drexler 60.00 120.00
3 Audie Norris 20.00 40.00
4 Mychal Thompson 8.00 20.00
5 Darnell Valentine 8.00 20.00

1981-82 Trail Blazers Playoff Tickets

These tickets are the actual tickets used in the Portland Trailblazers playoff games for the 1981-82 season. Each ticket was produced with different color backgrounds with black lettering. In addition, some other NBA stars were also featured on these tickets. They are listed after the Trail Blazers.

COMPLETE SET 40.00 100.00
1A Billy Ray Bates 1.50 4.00
White
1B Billy Ray Bates 1.50 4.00
Blue
2A Bob Gross 2.00 5.00
Orange
2B Bob Gross 2.00 5.00
Yellow
3A Michael Harper 1.50 4.00
Orange
3B Michael Harper 1.50 4.00
Yellow
4A Kevin Kunnert 1.50 4.00
Yellow
4B Kevin Kunnert 1.50 4.00
Orange
4C Kevin Kunnert 1.50 4.00
Pink
5A Calvin Natt 1.50 4.00
Yellow
5B Calvin Natt 1.50 4.00
Blue
6A Jim Paxson 2.00 5.00
Orange
6B Jim Paxson 2.00 5.00
Yellow
7A Kelvin Ransey 1.50 4.00
Blue
7B Kelvin Ransey 1.50 4.00
Pink
8A Larry Steele 1.50 4.00
Pink
8B Larry Steele 1.50 4.00
Yellow
9 Mychal Thompson 2.00 5.00
Yellow
10 Dave Twardzik 1.50 4.00
11A Marvin Webster 1.50 4.00
Yellow
11B Marvin Webster 1.50 4.00
White
12 George Gervin 3.00 8.00
13 Julius Erving 6.00 15.00
14 Moses Malone 3.00 8.00

1982-83 Trail Blazers Playoff Tickets

These tickets are the actual tickets used in the Portland Trailblazers playoff games for the 1981-82 season. Each ticket was produced with different color backgrounds with black lettering.

COMPLETE SET (10) 30.00 75.00
1 Wayne Cooper 1.50 4.00
White
1 Wayne Cooper 1.50 4.00
Blue
2 Jeff Judkins 1.50 4.00
White
2 Jeff Judkins 1.50 4.00
Blue
3 Jeff Lamp 1.50 4.00
Blue
3 Jeff Lamp 1.50 4.00
White
4 Lafayette Lever 2.00 5.00
Blue
4 Lafayette Lever 2.00 5.00
White
5 Audie Norris 1.50 4.00
White
5 Audie Norris 1.50 4.00
Blue
6 Larry Steele 1.50 4.00
Blue
6 Larry Steele 1.50 4.00
White
7 Linton Townes 1.50 4.00
Blue
7 Linton Townes 1.50 4.00
White
8 Dave Twardzik 1.50 4.00
Blue UER
Spelled Twarzik
8 Dave Twardzik 1.50 4.00
White UER
Spelled Twarzik
9 Darnell Valentine 1.50 4.00
White
9 Darnell Valentine 1.50 4.00
Blue
10 Pete Verhoeven 1.50 4.00
Blue
10 Pete Verhoeven 1.50 4.00
White

1983-84 Trail Blazers Playoff Tickets

These tickets are the actual tickets used in the Portland Trailblazers playoff games for the 1981-82 season. Each ticket was produced with different color backgrounds with black lettering.

COMPLETE SET (2) 4.00 10.00
1 Jim Paxson 2.00 5.00
Blue
2 Mychal Thompson 2.00 5.00
White

1984-85 Trail Blazers Playoff Tickets

These tickets are the actual tickets used in the Portland Trailblazers playoff games for the 1981-82 season. Each ticket was produced with different color backgrounds with black lettering.

COMPLETE SET (7) 15.00 30.00
1 Rick Adelman ACO 2.00 5.00
2 Bucky Buckwalter ACO 1.50 4.00
3 Audie Norris 1.50 4.00
4 Jim Paxson 2.00 5.00
5 Jack Ramsay CO 3.00 8.00
6 Tom Scheffler 1.50 4.00
7 Kiki Vandeweghe 3.00 8.00

1977-78 Trail Blazers Police

is set contains 14 cards measuring approximately 2 5/8" by 4 1/8" featuring the Portland Trail Blazers. The cards are unnumbered except for uniform number. Backs contain safety tips ("Tips from the Blazers") and are written in black ink with red accent. The set was sponsored by the Kiwanis and the Police Department. According to informed sources, 26, 000 sets were produced.

COMPLETE SET (14) 25.00 50.00
10 Corky Calhoun 1.25 3.00
13 Dave Twardzik 2.00 5.00
14 Lionel Hollins 2.00 5.00
15 Larry Steele 2.00 5.00
16 Johnny Davis 1.50 4.00
20 Maurice Lucas 3.00 8.00
23 T.R. Dunn 1.50 4.00
25 Tom Owens 1.25 3.00
30 Bob Gross 1.50 4.00
32 Bill Walton 10.00 20.00
36 Lloyd Neal 1.25 3.00
NNO Jack Ramsay CO 2.50 6.00
NNO Jack McKinney ACO 2.00 5.00
NNO Ron Culp TR 1.25 3.00

1979-80 Trail Blazers Police

This set contains 16 cards measuring 2 5/8" by 4 1/8" featuring the Portland Trail Blazers. Backs contain safety tips and are available with either light red or maroon printing on the backs. The year of issue and a facsimile autograph are printed on the front of the cards. The set was sponsored by 7-Up, Safeway, Kiwanis, KEX-1190AM, and the Police Departments. The cards are ordered below according to uniform number. The set features an early professional card of Mychal Thompson.

COMPLETE SET (16) 4.00 10.00
4 Jim Paxson .75 2.00
9 Lionel Hollins .60 1.50
10 Ron Brewer .30 .75
11 Abdul Jeelani .30 .75
13 Dave Twardzik .60 1.50
15 Larry Steele .50 1.25
20 Maurice Lucas .75 2.00
23 T.R. Dunn .40 1.00
25 Tom Owens .30 .75
30 Bob Gross .40 1.00
42 Kermit Washington .50 1.25
43 Mychal Thompson .75 2.00
44 Kevin Kunnert .30 .75
xx Jack Ramsay CO .60 1.50
xx Bucky Buckwalter ACO .30 .75
xx Bill Schonely ANN .30 .75

1981-82 Trail Blazers Police

This set contains 16 cards measuring 2 5/8" by 4 1/8" featuring the Portland Trail Blazers. Backs contain safety tips and are written in black ink with red accent. Cards are unnumbered except for uniform number. The year of issue is indicated on the card front. The set was produced courtesy of Kiwanis, the Trail Blazers, the NBA, and the Portland Police Bureau.

COMPLETE SET (16) 4.00 10.00
3 Jeff Lamp .75 2.00
4 Jim Paxson .60 1.50
10 Darnell Valentine .40 1.00
12 Billy Ray Bates .40 1.00
14 Kelvin Ransey .30 .75
30 Bob Gross .40 1.00
31 Peter Verhoeven .40 1.00
32 Mike Harper .30 .75
33 Calvin Natt .40 1.00
40 Petur Gudmundsson .40 1.00
42 Kermit Washington .40 1.00
43 Mychal Thompson .60 1.50
44 Kevin Kunnert .40 1.00
NNO Jack Ramsay CO .60 1.50
NNO Bucky Buckwalter ACO .30 .75
NNO Jimmy Lynam ACO .40 1.00

1982-83 Trail Blazers Police

This set contains 16 cards measuring approximately 2 5/8" by 4 1/8" featuring the Portland Trail Blazers. Backs contain safety tips and are written in black ink with red accent. The year of issue and a facsimile autograph are given on the front. The cards are ordered below according to uniform number. The set features the first professional card of Lafayette "Fat" Lever.

COMPLETE SET (16) 4.00 10.00
2 Linton Townes .30 .75
3 Jeff Lamp .40 1.00
4 Jim Paxson .40 1.00
12 Lafayette Lever .75 2.00
14 Darnell Valentine .40 1.00
22 Jeff Judkins .30 .75
24 Audie Norris .30 .75
31 Peter Verhoeven .30 .75
33 Calvin Natt .40 1.00
34 Kenny Carr .40 1.00
42 Wayne Cooper .40 1.00
43 Mychal Thompson .60 1.50
NNO Jack Ramsay CO .75 2.00
NNO Bucky Buckwalter ACO .30 .75
NNO Jim Lynam ACO .40 1.00

1983-84 Trail Blazers Police

This set contains 16 cards measuring approximately 2 5/8" by 4 1/8" featuring the Portland Trail Blazers. Backs contain safety tips ("Blazer Tips") and are written in black ink with red accent. Drexler and the coaches are the only cards without a small inset photo. The year of issue is indicated on the front of the card. A facsimile autograph is printed on the back of the card. The cards are ordered below according to uniform number. This set features one of Clyde Drexler's first cards.

COMPLETE SET (16) 10.00 25.00
3 Jeff Lamp .40 1.00
4 Jim Paxson .40 1.00
12 Lafayette Lever .40 1.00
14 Darnell Valentine .40 1.00
22 Clyde Drexler 6.00 15.00
24 Audie Norris .30 .75
31 Peter Verhoeven .30 .75
33 Calvin Natt .40 1.00
34 Kenny Carr .30 .75
42 Wayne Cooper .30 .75
43 Mychal Thompson .60 1.50
54 Tom Piotrowski .30 .75
NNO Jack Ramsay CO .60 1.50
NNO Morris Buckwalter ACO .50 1.25
Rick Adelman ACO
NNO Ron Culp TR .30 .75
NNO Dave Twardzik ANN .30 .75
and Bill Schonely ANN

1984-85 Trail Blazers Police

This set contains 16 cards measuring approximately 2 5/8" by 4 1/8" featuring the Portland Trail Blazers. Backs contain safety tips ("Blazer Tips") and are written in black ink with red accent. The cards are numbered in the upper left corner of the obverse; the year of issue is indicated in the lower right corner. The set features one of the first professional cards of Jerome Kersey.

COMPLETE SET (16) 6.00 15.00
1 Portland Team .75 2.00
2 Jim Paxson .40 1.00
3 Bernard Thompson .30 .75
4 Darnell Valentine .30 .75
5 Jack Ramsay CO .75 2.00
Rick Adelman ACO
Bucky Buckwalter ACO
6 Steve Colter .30 .75
7 Clyde Drexler 3.00 8.00
8 Audie Norris .30 .75
9 Jerome Kersey 1.25 3.00
10 Sam Bowie 1.25 3.00
11 Kenny Carr .30 .75
12 Lloyd Neal .30 .75
13 Mychal Thompson .40 1.00
14 Geoff Petrie .40 1.00
15 Tom Scheffler .30 .75
16 Kiki Vandeweghe .75 2.00

1978-79 Trail Blazers Portfolio

These collector prints of Portland Trail Blazers were sponsored by The Benj. Franklin Federal Savings and Loan Association in Portland as a special gift to Blazer-Savers. They were produced by artist Michael Lundy and measure approximately 11" by 14". The Lucas print is in color, while the rest of the prints are in black and white. Two Trail Blazers are depicted together on two of the prints. The backs are blank. The prints are unnumbered and checklisted below in alphabetical order.

COMPLETE SET (10) 20.00 40.00
1 Kim Anderson and 1.25 3.00
Clemon Johnson
2 T.R. Dunn 1.50 4.00
3 Bob Gross 1.50 4.00
4 Lionel Hollins 2.50 6.00
5 Maurice Lucas 3.00 8.00
6 Lloyd Neal 1.25 3.00
7 Tom Owens 1.25 3.00
8 Willie Smith and 1.25 3.00
Ron Brewer
9 Larry Steele 2.50 6.00
10 Dave Twardzik 2.50 6.00

1991-92 Trail Blazers Posters

Produced by Line-Up Productions Inc. (Minnetonka, Minnesota), these six posters are part of "The PlayMakers Collection" print series. Each set was accompanied by a certificate of authenticity. Each poster measures 7" by 18" and is printed on slick cardboard stock. The color action painting on the fronts extends partially outside the inner black picture frame into the wider white border. The player's name is reversed out at the bottom of the picture frame. Various logos are printed across the bottom of the front. The backs are blank. The posters are unnumbered and checklisted below in alphabetical order.

COMPLETE SET (5) 8.00 20.00
1 Clyde Drexler 6.00 15.00
2 Kevin Duckworth 1.25 3.00
3 Jerome Kersey 1.25 3.00
4 Terry Porter 1.50 4.00
5 Buck Williams 1.50 4.00

1977-78 Trail Blazers RC Glasses

These appoximately 6 3/8" tall glasses were produced to celebrate the Portland Trailblazers 1976-77 NBA Championship. The glasses have a head shot with the players name, height and position, a facsimile signature, and other personal data below the player. The back of the glass has the "Me and my RC" slogan, and the glass is ringed with "RC Salutes the Champs-Portland Players" in black type over the blue ring. The checklist below may be incomplete, and any additions would be welcomed.

COMPLETE SET (8) 50.00 100.00
1 Johnny Davis 5.00 10.00
2 Bob Gross 5.00 10.00
3 Lionel Hollins 5.00 10.00
4 Maurice Lucas 7.50 15.00
5 Lloyd Neal 5.00 10.00
6 Larry Steele 5.00 10.00
7 Dave Twardzik 5.00 10.00
8 Bill Walton 20.00 40.00

1972-73 Trail Blazers Team Issue

Measuring 8" x 10", this 25-photo set features members from the 1972-73 Portland Trail Blazers. Each photo features either a close-up posed shot and an in action shot of each player in black and white. The player's name, height and college are listed on the front, as well as the team logo. The backs are blank. The photos are not numbered and listed below alphabetically.

COMPLETE SET (25) 65.00 125.00
1 Rick Adelman 3.00 8.00
2 Rick Adelman IA 2.50 6.00
3 Bob Davis 2.00 5.00
4 Bob Davis IA 2.00 5.00
5 Bobby Fields 2.00 5.00
6 Bobby Fields IA 2.00 5.00
7 Stu Inman VP 2.00 5.00
8 Neil Johnston ACO 3.00 8.00
9 Ollie Johnson 2.00 5.00
10 Ollie Johnson IA 2.00 5.00
11 LaRue Martin 2.00 5.00
12 LaRue Martin IA 2.00 5.00
13 Leo Marty TR 2.00 5.00
14 Jack McCloskey CO 2.00 5.00
15 Stan McKenzie 2.00 5.00
16 Stan McKenzie IA 2.00 5.00
17 Lloyd Neal 2.00 5.00
18 Lloyd Neal IA 2.00 5.00
19 Geoffrey Petrie 5.00 10.00
20 Geoffrey Petrie IA 3.00 8.00
21 Dale Schlueter 2.00 5.00
22 Dale Schlueter IA 2.00 5.00
23 Larry Steele 3.00 8.00
24 Larry Steele IA 2.50 6.00
25 Sidney Wicks IA 7.50 15.00

1976-77 Trail Blazers Team Issue

This 8" x10" set was produced for the Portland Trailblazers during the 1976-77 season. The set features 15 black and white cards of the team's players and coaches.

COMPLETE SET (15) 20.00 40.00
1 Dan Anderson 1.25 3.00
2 Barry Clemens 1.25 3.00
3 Bob Gross 1.25 3.00
4 Steve Hawes 1.25 3.00
5 Lionel Hollins 1.50 4.00
6 Maurice Lucas 2.50 6.00
7 Lloyd Neal 1.25 3.00
8 Larry Steele 1.25 3.00
9 Dave Twardzik 1.25 3.00
10 Wally Walker 1.25 3.00
11 Stu Inman VP 1.25 3.00
12 Ron Culp TR 1.25 3.00
13 Jack McKinney CO 1.25 3.00
14 Harry Glickman EVP 1.25 3.00
15 Larry Weinberg PRES 1.25 3.00

1977-78 Trail Blazers Team Issue

These color photos, which measure 5 7/8" by 9" and are blank-backed, feature members of the Portland Trail Blazers who were the defending NBA champs. Since these photos are unnumbered, we have sequenced them in alphabetical order.

COMPLETE SET (13) 17.50 35.00
1 Corky Calhoun .75 2.00
2 Johnny Davis .75 2.00
3 T.R. Dunn .75 2.00
4 Bob Gross .75 2.00
5 Lionel Hollins .75 2.00
6 Maurice Lucas 1.50 4.00
7 Lloyd Neal .75 2.00
8 Tom Owens .75 2.00
9 Jack Ramsey CO 1.50 4.00
10 Larry Steele .75 2.00
11 Dave Twardzik .75 2.00
12 Bill Walton 3.00 8.00
13 Portland Trail Blazers 1.50 4.00
Team Composite

1971-72 Trail Blazers Texaco

This 12-card set was sponsored by Texaco. The cards measure approximately 8" by 9 5/8" and feature full-bleed, posed player photos. The player's name is printed in white script lettering in the upper right corner. The card backs have biographical information and career statistics. The Texaco logo is printed at the bottom of the card. The cards are unnumbered and checklisted below in alphabetical order.

COMPLETE SET (12) 30.00 60.00
1 Rick Adelman 5.00 12.00
2 Gary Gregor 3.00 8.00
3 Ron Knight 3.00 8.00
4 Jim Marsh 3.00 8.00
5 Willie McCarter 3.00 8.00
6 Stan McKenzie 3.00 8.00
7 Geoff Petrie 5.00 12.00
8 Dale Schlueter 3.00 8.00
9 Bill Smith 3.00 8.00
10 Larry Steele 3.00 8.00
11 Sidney Wicks 6.00 15.00
12 Charles Yelverton 3.00 8.00

2010 TRISTAR Obak

COMMON CARD (1-109) .20 .50
COMMON VAR (1-109) .40 1.00
COMMON SP (110-120) 1.50 4.00
THREE SPs PER BOX
102 Dave Debusschere .20 .50

2010 TRISTAR Obak Black

*BLACK: 2.5X TO 6X BASIC
*BLACK VAR: 1.2X TO 3X BASIC VAR
*BLACK SP: .5X TO 1.2X BASIC SP
OVERALL PARALLEL ODDS 1:10
STATED PRINT RUN 50 SER.#'d SETS

1996-97 UD3

The 1996-97 Upper Deck UD3 set was issued in one series totalling 60 cards. The set breaks down into three different technologies: Light F/X, Cel Chrome and Electric Wood-Cel. The Hardwood prospect cards (1-20) use the Wood-Cel technology, the NBA StarFocus cards (21-40) use the Cel Chrome technology and the Aerial Artists (41-60) use the Light F/X technology. Cards were issued in 3-card packs with a suggested retail price of $3.99.

COMPLETE SET (60) 12.00 30.00
1 Kerry Kittles RC .25 .60
2 Stephon Marbury RC .60 1.50
3 Jermaine O'Neal RC .40 1.00
4 Shareef Abdur-Rahim RC .40 1.00
5 Ray Allen RC 1.00 2.50
6 Antoine Walker RC .40 1.00
7 Erick Dampier RC .25 .60
8 Walter McCarty RC .25 .60
9 Todd Fuller RC .15 .40
10 Tony Delk RC .25 .60
11 Marcus Camby RC .40 1.00
12 John Wallace RC .25 .60
13 Vitaly Potapenko RC .20 .50
14 Allen Iverson RC 1.25 3.00
15 Steve Nash RC 2.50 6.00
16 Derek Fisher RC .30 .75
17 Samaki Walker RC .20 .50
18 Roy Rogers RC .20 .50
19 Kobe Bryant RC 5.00 12.00
20 Lorenzen Wright RC .20 .50
21 Kevin Garnett 1.00 2.50
22 Hakeem Olajuwon .50 1.25
23 Michael Jordan 3.00 8.00
24 John Stockton .50 1.25
25 Terrell Brandon .25 .60
26 Damon Stoudamire .30 .75
27 Charles Barkley .60 1.50
28 Dikembe Mutombo .40 1.00
29 Gary Payton .40 1.00
30 Patrick Ewing .50 1.25
31 Dennis Rodman .75 2.00
32 Joe Smith .30 .75
33 Grant Hill .60 1.50
34 Shaquille O'Neal 1.00 2.50
35 Kevin Johnson .40 1.00
36 David Robinson .60 1.50
37 Juwan Howard .30 .75
38 Mitch Richmond .40 1.00
39 Alonzo Mourning .50 1.25
40 Reggie Miller .50 1.25
41 Shawn Kemp .40 1.00
42 Scottie Pippen .60 1.50
43 Kobe Bryant 3.00 8.00
44 Anfernee Hardaway .60 1.50
45 Brent Barry .30 .75
46 Glenn Robinson .30 .75
47 Karl Malone .50 1.25
48 Chris Webber .50 1.25
49 Danny Manning .30 .75
50 Antonio McDyess .40 1.00
51 Dominique Wilkins .50 1.25
52 Vin Baker .30 .75
53 Isaiah Rider .30 .75
54 Eddie Jones .40 1.00
55 Glen Rice .40 1.00
56 Larry Johnson .40 1.00
57 Latrell Sprewell .40 1.00
58 Sean Elliott .40 1.00
59 Clyde Drexler .50 1.25
60 Jerry Stackhouse .50 1.25

1996-97 UD3 Court Commemorative Autographs

Randomly inserted in packs at a rate of one in 1500, this four-card set features autographed cards of the Upper Deck spokesmen.

STATED ODDS 1:1500
C1 Michael Jordan 2000.00 2500.00
C2 Damon Stoudamire 20.00 50.00
C3 Anfernee Hardaway 125.00 250.00
C4 Shawn Kemp 125.00 250.00

1996-97 UD3 Superstar Spotlight

Randomly inserted in packs at a rate of one in 144, this 10-card set utilizes Cel-Chrome technology and focuses on NBA All-Stars.

COMPLETE SET (10) 50.00 100.00
STATED ODDS 1:144
S1 Shaquille O'Neal 8.00 20.00
S2 Alonzo Mourning 5.00 12.00
S3 Anfernee Hardaway 6.00 15.00
S4 Karl Malone 5.00 12.00
S5 Michael Jordan 25.00 60.00
S6 Hakeem Olajuwon 5.00 12.00
S7 Shawn Kemp 4.00 10.00
S8 Allen Iverson 10.00 25.00
S9 Dennis Rodman 8.00 20.00
S10 Charles Barkley 6.00 15.00

1996-97 UD3 The Winning Edge

Randomly inserted in packs at a rate of one in 11, this 20-card set utilizes the Light F/X technology, and each card focuses on a specific trait that makes these players a success in the NBA.

COMPLETE SET (20) 12.00 30.00
STATED ODDS 1:11
W1 Michael Jordan 6.00 15.00
W2 Charles Barkley 1.25 3.00
W3 Reggie Miller 1.00 2.50
W4 Grant Hill 1.25 3.00
W5 Larry Johnson .75 2.00
W6 Hakeem Olajuwon 1.00 2.50
W7 Anfernee Hardaway 1.25 3.00
W8 Shaquille O'Neal 2.00 5.00
W9 Vin Baker .60 1.50
W10 Kevin Garnett 2.00 5.00
W11 Juwan Howard .60 1.50
W12 John Stockton 1.00 2.50
W13 Mookie Blaylock .50 1.25
W14 Shawn Kemp .75 2.00
W15 David Robinson 1.25 3.00
W16 Kevin Johnson .75 2.00
W17 Joe Dumars .75 2.00
W18 Marcus Camby 1.25 3.00
W19 Clyde Drexler 1.00 2.50
W20 Chris Webber 1.00 2.50

1997-98 UD3

Released in three-card packs that carried a suggested retail price of $3.99, this 60 card set is broken up into three different "subset" themes. The first 20 cards are Jam Masters, the next 20 are All-Stars and the final 20 are The Big Picture. A Michael Jordan promo card was also released with the word "Sample" in white letters on the card front. Since the card is numbered the same as the basic Jordan card (#45), the promo is listed as a "NNO" at the end of the set.

COMPLETE SET (60) 15.00 40.00
1 Anfernee Hardaway JM .50 1.25
2 Alonzo Mourning JM .40 1.00
3 Grant Hill JM .50 1.25
4 Kerry Kittles JM .20 .50
5 Latrell Sprewell JM .30 .75
6 Rasheed Wallace JM .30 .75
7 Jerry Stackhouse JM .30 .75
8 Glen Rice JM .30 .75
9 Marcus Camby JM .30 .75
10 Scottie Pippen JM .50 1.25
11 Patrick Ewing JM .40 1.00
12 Michael Finley JM .30 .75
13 Karl Malone JM .40 1.00
14 Antonio McDyess JM .25 .60
15 Michael Jordan JM 3.00 8.00
16 Clyde Drexler JM .40 1.00
17 Brent Barry JM .25 .60
18 Glenn Robinson JM .25 .60
19 Kobe Bryant JM 1.50 4.00
20 Reggie Miller JM .40 1.00
21 John Stockton AS .40 1.00
22 Gary Payton AS .30 .75
23 Michael Jordan AS 3.00 8.00
24 Vin Baker AS .25 .60
25 Karl Malone AS .40 1.00
26 Juwan Howard AS .25 .60
27 Charles Barkley AS .50 1.25
28 Jason Kidd AS .50 1.25
29 Joe Dumars AS .30 .75
30 Anfernee Hardaway AS .50 1.25
31 Mitch Richmond AS .30 .75
32 Alonzo Mourning AS .40 1.00
33 Grant Hill AS .50 1.25
34 Shaquille O'Neal AS .75 2.00
35 Scottie Pippen AS .50 1.25
36 Reggie Miller AS .40 1.00
37 Hakeem Olajuwon AS .40 1.00
38 Tim Hardaway AS .30 .75
39 David Robinson AS .50 1.25
40 Shawn Kemp AS .30 .75
41 Allen Iverson BP .60 1.50
42 Stephon Marbury BP .40 1.00
43 Dennis Rodman BP .60 1.50
44 Terrell Brandon BP .20 .50
45 Michael Jordan BP 3.00 8.00
46 Kerry Kittles BP .20 .50
47 Hakeem Olajuwon BP .40 1.00
48 Loy Vaught BP .20 .50
49 Antoine Walker BP .30 .75
50 Gary Payton BP .30 .75
51 Kevin Johnson BP .30 .75
52 Kevin Garnett BP .50 1.25
53 Shareef Abdur-Rahim BP .30 .75
54 Larry Johnson BP .30 .75
55 Dikembe Mutombo BP .30 .75
56 Chris Webber BP .30 .75
57 Joe Smith BP .25 .60
58 Kendall Gill BP .20 .50
59 Kenny Anderson BP .25 .60
60 Damon Stoudamire BP .25 .60
NNO Michael Jordan PROMO 2.00 5.00

1997-98 UD3 Awesome Action

Randomly inserted in packs at one in 11, this 20-card set features great action shots of the NBA's best. Card backs carry an "A" prefix.

COMPLETE SET (20) 50.00 120.00
STATED ODDS 1:11
A1 Michael Jordan 15.00 40.00
A2 Nick Van Exel 1.50 4.00
A3 Jerry Stackhouse 2.00 5.00
A4 Shawn Kemp 2.00 5.00
A5 Hakeem Olajuwon 2.50 6.00
A6 Grant Hill 3.00 8.00
A7 Scottie Pippen 3.00 8.00
A8 Alonzo Mourning 2.50 6.00
A9 Damon Stoudamire 1.50 4.00
A10 Kevin Garnett 3.00 8.00
A11 Anfernee Hardaway 3.00 8.00
A12 Shareef Abdur-Rahim 2.00 5.00
A13 Allen Iverson 4.00 10.00
A14 Dennis Rodman 4.00 10.00
A15 Shaquille O'Neal 5.00 12.00
A16 Jason Kidd 3.00 8.00
A17 Gary Payton 2.00 5.00
A18 Dikembe Mutombo 2.00 5.00
A19 Karl Malone 2.50 6.00
A20 Stephon Marbury 2.50 6.00

1997-98 UD3 MJ3

Randomly inserted into packs, this three-card set features a three time tribute to Michael Jordan. The first card was inserted at one in 45, the second at one in 119 and the last at one in 167. When put together, the three cards from one big card. Card backs carry a "MJ3" prefix.

MJ3-1 STATED ODDS 1:45
MJ3-2 STATED ODDS 1:119
MJ3-3 STATED ODDS 1:167
MJ31 Michael Jordan 8.00 20.00
MJ32 Michael Jordan 10.00 25.00
MJ33 Michael Jordan 12.00 30.00

1997-98 UD3 Rookie Portfolio

Randomly inserted into packs at one in 144, this 10-card set features a still shot of some of the top rookies from the 1997 class. The cards feature a portrait front against a see-through back. Card backs carry a "R" prefix.

COMPLETE SET (10) 25.00 60.00
STATED ODDS 1:144
R1 Tim Duncan 8.00 20.00
R2 Keith Van Horn 2.50 6.00
R3 Chauncey Billups 5.00 12.00
R4 Antonio Daniels 1.50 4.00
R5 Tony Battie 1.50 4.00
R6 Ron Mercer 2.00 5.00
R7 Tim Thomas 2.00 5.00
R8 Adonal Foyle 1.25 3.00
R9 Tracy McGrady 6.00 15.00
R10 Danny Fortson 1.50 4.00

1997-98 UD3 Season Ticket Autographs

Randomly inserted in packs at a rate of one in 1,800, this 4-card set features autographs against a facsimile ticket stub. Card backs carry a congratulatory message from Upper Deck.

STATED ODDS 1:1,800
AH Anfernee Hardaway 100.00 200.00
JH Juwan Howard 30.00 80.00
MJ Michael Jordan 1250.00 2000.00
TH Tim Hardaway 40.00 100.00

1997-98 UD3 Season Ticket Trade

These cards are the original trade cards for the Season Ticket Autographs. These cards are still traded on the secondary market due to both the player photo on the card and the toughness of the original trade cards. The checklist also includes some players that were not actually made for the autograph set.

AMT Alonzo Mourning 100.00 200.00
JHT Juwan Howard 4.00 10.00
MJT Michael Jordan 300.00 500.00

2000 UDA The Jordan Experience Printer's Proofs

This 12-proof set was released by UDA in 2000, the set features 22kt gold cards that highlight Michael Jordan's career. There were 23,000 of each proof produced. Each proofed was sold exclusively through UDA's direct marketing channel, and carried a suggested retail price of $29.95.

COMMON CARD (1-12) 40.00 100.00

2002-03 UD Authentics

Issued in November 2002, UD Authentics boasts a 132-card set divided up into 90 veteran player cards and 42 rookie player cards. The base cards borrow their design from 1989 Upper Deck Basebaeball. Cards have full color player photos with white borders and the trademark Upper Deck hologram on the back of the card. Rookie players have red borders instead of the base white and are serially numbered as follows: Cards 91-123 are numbered to 799, and cards 124-132 are numbered to 499. Also inserted within the product were Upper Deck Authenticated redemption cards which were good for autographs, photos, jerseys and other memorabilia-inserted at the rate of one in 216. As with all of UD's new exchange cards, these items were redeemable via UD's website as an e-redemption. UD Authentics was packaged in 18-pack boxes where packs contained five cards and carried a suggested retail price of $6.99.

COMPLETE SET (132) 150.00 300.00
COMP.SET w/o SP's (90) 15.00 40.00
91-123 PRINT RUN 799 SER.#'d SETS
124-132 PRINT RUN 499 SER.#'d SETS
1 Shareef Abdur-Rahim .25 .60
2 Jason Terry .25 .60
3 Glenn Robinson .25 .60
4 Paul Pierce .30 .75
5 Antoine Walker .25 .60
6 Eric Williams .20 .50
7 Kedrick Brown .20 .50
8 Jalen Rose .25 .60
9 Tyson Chandler .30 .75
10 Eddy Curry .20 .50
11 Darius Miles .20 .50
12 Lamond Murray .20 .50
13 Chris Mihm .20 .50
14 Dirk Nowitzki .50 1.25
15 Steve Nash .40 1.00
16 Michael Finley .30 .75
17 Raef LaFrentz .20 .50
18 James Posey .20 .50
19 Juwan Howard .25 .60
20 Jerry Stackhouse .25 .60
21 Ben Wallace .25 .60
22 Clifford Robinson .20 .50
23 Jason Richardson .30 .75
24 Antawn Jamison .30 .75
25 Gilbert Arenas .30 .75
26 Steve Francis .25 .60
27 Eddie Griffin .20 .50
28 Cuttino Mobley .20 .50
29 Reggie Miller .30 .75
30 Jamaal Tinsley .20 .50
31 Jermaine O'Neal .25 .60
32 Elton Brand .30 .75
33 Lamar Odom .25 .60
34 Andre Miller .25 .60
35 Kobe Bryant 1.25 3.00
36 Shaquille O'Neal .75 2.00
37 Derek Fisher .25 .60
38 Devean George .20 .50
39 Pau Gasol .40 1.00
40 Shane Battier .30 .75
41 Alonzo Mourning .40 1.00
42 Brian Grant .20 .50
43 Eddie Jones .25 .60
44 Ray Allen .30 .75
45 Tim Thomas .20 .50
46 Kevin Garnett .50 1.25
47 Wally Szczerbiak .25 .60
48 Terrell Brandon .20 .50
49 Jason Kidd .50 1.25
50 Dikembe Mutombo .30 .75
51 Richard Jefferson .30 .75
52 Baron Davis .25 .60
53 Jamal Mashburn .25 .60
54 David Wesley .20 .50
55 P.J. Brown .20 .50
56 Latrell Sprewell .25 .60
57 Allan Houston .25 .60
58 Antonio McDyess .25 .60
59 Tracy McGrady .50 1.25
60 Mike Miller .25 .60
61 Darrell Armstrong .20 .50
62 Allen Iverson .50 1.25
63 Keith Van Horn .25 .60
64 Stephon Marbury .25 .60
65 Shawn Marion .25 .60
66 Anfernee Hardaway .50 1.25
67 Rasheed Wallace .30 .75
68 Bonzi Wells .20 .50
69 Scottie Pippen .50 1.25
70 Chris Webber .30 .75
71 Peja Stojakovic .30 .75
72 Mike Bibby .30 .75
73 Hedo Turkoglu .25 .60
74 Tim Duncan .60 1.50
75 David Robinson .50 1.25
76 Tony Parker .40 1.00
77 Malik Rose .20 .50
78 Gary Payton .30 .75
79 Rashard Lewis .30 .75
80 Desmond Mason .25 .60
81 Brent Barry .20 .50
82 Vince Carter .50 1.25
83 Morris Peterson .20 .50
84 Antonio Davis .20 .50
85 Karl Malone .40 1.00
86 John Stockton .40 1.00
87 Andrei Kirilenko .30 .75
88 Michael Jordan 2.50 6.00
89 Richard Hamilton .25 .60
90 Kwame Brown .20 .50
91 Efthimios Rentzias RC 1.25 3.00
92 Darius Songaila RC 2.00 5.00
93 Matt Barnes RC 2.50 6.00
94 Sam Clancy RC 1.50 4.00
95 Lonny Baxter RC 1.25 3.00
96 Manu Ginobili RC 5.00 12.00
97 Rod Grizzard RC 1.25 3.00
98 Tito Maddox RC 1.25 3.00
99 Predrag Savovic RC 1.50 4.00
100 Carlos Boozer RC 2.00 5.00
101 Dan Gadzuric RC 1.50 4.00
102 Vincent Yarbrough RC 1.25 3.00
103 Robert Archibald RC 1.25 3.00
104 Roger Mason RC 1.50 4.00
105 Steve Logan RC 2.00 5.00
106 Dan Dickau RC 1.50 4.00
107 Chris Jefferies RC 1.25 3.00
108 John Salmons RC 2.00 5.00
109 Frank Williams RC 1.25 3.00
110 Tayshaun Prince RC 2.50 6.00
111 Casey Jacobsen RC 1.50 4.00
112 Qyntel Woods RC 1.50 4.00
113 Kareem Rush RC 1.50 4.00
114 Ryan Humphrey RC 1.50 4.00
115 Curtis Borchardt RC 1.25 3.00
116 Juan Dixon RC 2.00 5.00
117 Jiri Welsch RC 1.50 4.00
118 Bostjan Nachbar RC 1.50 4.00
119 Fred Jones RC 1.50 4.00
120 Marcus Haislip RC 1.50 4.00
121 Melvin Ely RC 1.50 4.00
122 Jared Jeffries RC 1.50 4.00
123 Caron Butler RC 2.00 5.00
124 Amare Stoudemire RC 3.00 8.00
125 Chris Wilcox RC 2.00 5.00
126 Nene Hilario RC 2.50 6.00
127 DaJuan Wagner RC 2.00 5.00
128 Nikoloz Tskitishvili RC 1.50 4.00
129 Drew Gooden RC 2.50 6.00
130 Mike Dunleavy RC 2.50 6.00
131 Jay Williams RC 2.50 6.00
132 Yao Ming RC 5.00 12.00

2002-03 UD Authentics Gold

*1-90 STARS: 4X TO 10X BASE CARD HI
1-90 PRINT RUN 250 SER.#'d SETS
*91-123 RCs: 1.25X TO 3X BASE RC HI
*124-132 RCs: 1X TO 2.5X BASE HI
91-132 PRINT RUN 100 SER.#'d SETS
88 Michael Jordan 30.00 80.00

2002-03 UD Authentics Rainbow

*STARS: 8X TO 20X BASE CARD HI
1-90 PRINT RUN 50 SER.#'d SETS
*RCs 91-123: 2.5X TO 6X HI
*RCs 124-132: 2X TO 5X HI
91-132 PRINT RUN 25 SER.#'d SETS
88 Michael Jordan 100.00 250.00

2002-03 UD Authentics 100% Amazing

Randomly inserted in packs, this eight card set features some of the NBA's brightest stars. The cards are horizontally designed with a full color player action photo on the left and a swatch of game used memorabilia on the right. Orange borders are present

long the top and bottom of the card and the words 100% Amazing make the border along the left side of the card.
PRINT RUN 100 SER.#'d SETS
AI Allen Iverson 8.00 20.00
AM Alonzo Mourning 6.00 15.00
CW Chris Webber 5.00 12.00
JK Jason Kidd 8.00 20.00
KB Kobe Bryant 20.00 50.00
KG Kevin Garnett 8.00 20.00
MJ Michael Jordan 75.00 150.00
TM Tracy McGrady 8.00 20.00

2002-03 UD Authentics Awesome Authentics

Randomly seeded in packs, this 16-card set places full-color player action photography on a colored background on the right and an "A" shaped swatch of game worn memorabilia on the left set against a different colored background. The background colors are set to match the featured player's team colors. Each card is sequentially numbered to 250.
PRINT RUN 250 SER.#'d SETS
AWA Antoine Walker 2.50 6.00
CWA Chris Webber 3.00 8.00
DMA Darius Miles 2.00 5.00
DNA Dirk Nowitzki 5.00 12.00
EBA Elton Brand 3.00 8.00
JMA Jamal Mashburn 2.50 6.00
KBA Kobe Bryant 12.00 30.00
KGA Kevin Garnett 5.00 12.00
MJA Michael Jordan 40.00 100.00
MPA Morris Peterson 2.00 5.00
QRA Quentin Richardson 2.50 6.00
RWA Rasheed Wallace 3.00 8.00
SFA Steve Francis 2.50 6.00
SMA Stephon Marbury 2.50 6.00
SSA Stromile Swift 2.00 5.00
WSA Wally Szczerbiak 2.50 6.00

2002-03 UD Authentics Court Quality

Randomly inserted in packs, this 15-card set features a horizontal design with player photos on the left and a square swatch of game-worn memorabilia on the right. Each card is sequentially numbered to 300.
PRINT RUN 350 SER.#'d SETS
AMQ Alonzo Mourning 4.00 10.00
CMQ Chris Mihm 2.00 5.00
DJQ DerMarr Johnson 2.00 5.00
DMQ Darius Miles 2.00 5.00
DWQ David Wesley 2.00 5.00
ECQ Eddy Curry 2.00 5.00
GHQ Grant Hill 4.00 10.00
GRQ Glenn Robinson 2.50 6.00
KBQ Kobe Bryant 12.00 30.00
KGQ Kevin Garnett 5.00 12.00
KMQ Kenyon Martin 2.50 6.00
KVQ Keith Van Horn 2.50 6.00
PEQ Patrick Ewing 4.00 10.00
TBQ Terrell Brandon 2.00 5.00
TCQ Tyson Chandler 3.00 8.00

2002-03 UD Authentics Kevin Garnett Heroes of Basketball

Randomly inserted in packs, this 10-card set pays tribute to Kevin Garnett. Cards are white bordered with full-color player action photos. Each card is sequentially numbered to 1989. An Autographed parallel of this set was also inserted with cards sequentially numbered to 10.
COMPLETE SET (10) 15.00 40.00
COMMON CARD (KG1-KG10) 2.50 6.00
PRINT RUN 1989 SER.#'d SETS

2002-03 UD Authentics Kobe Bryant Heroes of Basketball

Randomly inserted in packs, this 10-card set pays tribute to Kobe Bryant. Cards are white bordered with full-color player action photos. Each card is sequentially numbered to 989. An Autographed parallel of this set was also inserted with each card sequentially numbered to eight.
COMPLETE SET (10) 25.00 60.00
COMMON CARD (KB1-KB10) 5.00 12.00
PRINT RUN 989 SER.#'d SETS

2002-03 UD Authentics Michael Jordan Heroes of Basketball

Randomly inserted in packs, this 10-card set pays tribute to Michael Jordan. Cards are white bordered with full-color player action photos. Each card is sequentially numbered to 198. An Autographed parallel of this set was also inserted where each card is a one of one.
COMPLETE SET (10) 175.00 350.00
COMMON CARD (1-10) 20.00 50.00
PRINT RUN 198 SER.#'d SETS

2002-03 UD Authentics Signatures

Seeded in packs at the rate of one in 108, this 23-card set places full color player photographs at the top of the card and an authentic player autograph above the player's printed name on the bottom.
STATED ODDS 1:108
BA Brandon Armstrong 4.00 10.00
BR Brian Scalabrine 4.00 10.00
CM Corey Maggette 4.00 10.00
EC Eddy Curry 5.00 12.00
EG Eddie Griffin 4.00 10.00
EW Earl Watson 4.00 10.00
JA Jarron Collins 4.00 10.00
JC Jason Collins 4.00 10.00
JR Jason Richardson 6.00 15.00
JS Jeryl Sasser 4.00 10.00
KE Kedrick Brown 4.00 10.00
KH Kirk Haston 4.00 10.00
KS Kenny Satterfield 4.00 10.00
KW Kwame Brown 5.00 12.00
MB Michael Bradley 4.00 10.00
RB Ruben Boumtje-Boumtje 4.00 10.00
RJ Richard Jefferson 5.00 12.00
RW Rodney White 4.00 10.00
SD Samuel Dalembert 4.00 10.00
SH Steven Hunter 4.00 10.00
TC Tyson Chandler 6.00 15.00
TM Troy Murphy 4.00 10.00
ZR Zeljko Rebraca 4.00 10.00

2002-03 UD Authentics Stat Patterns

Inserted in packs, this 18-card set features a horzontal design with a blue background. Swatches of game-worn memorabilia appear on the right side of the card and full color player photos appear on the left. Each card is sequentially numbered to 500.
PRINT RUN 500 SER.#'d SETS
AIS Allen Iverson 5.00 12.00
AMS Andre Miller 2.50 6.00
CMS Corey Maggette 2.50 6.00
CWS Chris Webber 3.00 8.00
DMS Dikembe Mutombo 3.00 8.00
EBS Elton Brand 3.00 8.00
ESS Eric Snow 2.00 5.00
GPS Gary Payton 3.00 8.00
JOS Jermaine O'Neal 2.50 6.00
KAS Kenny Anderson 2.50 6.00
KBS Kobe Bryant 12.50 30.00
KGS Kevin Garnett 5.00 12.00
MOS Michael Olowokandi 2.00 5.00
PSS Peja Stojakovic 3.00 8.00
RLS Rashard Lewis 3.00 8.00
SMS Joe Smith 2.50 6.00
TMS Tracy McGrady 5.00 12.00
WSS Wally Szczerbiak 2.50 6.00

2002-03 UD Authentics Uniform Greatness

Inserted in packs at the rate of one in ten, this 21-card set utilizes a horizontal design with full-color player action photographs on the right side of the card and a star swatch of game-used memorabilia on the left side. Background colors on the right are set to match the featured player's team jersey while the background on the left is white with a peach-colored stripe through the middle.
STATED ODDS 1:10
AHU Anfernee Hardaway 5.00 12.00
ALU Allan Houston 2.50 6.00
BRU Bryon Russell 2.00 5.00
DFU Derek Fisher 2.50 6.00
DGU Devean George 2.00 5.00
DMU Desmond Mason 2.50 6.00
JSU Joe Smith 2.50 6.00
JTU Jason Terry 2.50 6.00
KBU Kobe Bryant 10.00 25.00
KGU Kevin Garnett 5.00 12.00
LSU Latrell Sprewell 2.50 6.00
MAU Marcus Fizer 2.00 5.00
MJU Michael Jordan 30.00 80.00
RHU Robert Horry 2.50 6.00
SHU Shawn Marion 2.50 6.00
SMU Stephon Marbury 2.50 6.00
SNU Steve Nash 4.00 10.00
SSU Stromile Swift 2.00 5.00
TBU Terrell Brandon 2.00 5.00
TGU Tom Gugliotta 2.00 5.00
WSU Wally Szczerbiak 2.50 6.00

2006-07 UD Black

STATED PRINT RUN 99 SER.#'d SETS
2 Jerry West 10.00 25.00
3 Michael Jordan 60.00 150.00
4 Kevin McHale 10.00 25.00
5 Ben Wallace 6.00 15.00
6 Antawn Jamison 6.00 15.00
7 Andrei Kirilenko 6.00 15.00
8 Ray Allen 8.00 20.00
9 Tony Parker 8.00 20.00
12 Chris Webber 8.00 20.00
15 Antoine Walker 6.00 15.00
16 Gary Payton 8.00 20.00
19 Josh Smith 6.00 15.00
20 Peja Stojakovic 8.00 20.00

2006-07 UD Black 25

*BLACK: .75X TO 2X BASE HI
STATED PRINT RUN 25 SER.#'d SETS

2006-07 UD Black Autographs Dual

STATED PRINT RUN 25 SER.#'d SETS
UNPRICED DUAL PRINT RUN 10 SETS
BB Dee Brown/Dee Brown 8.00 20.00
CI R.Carney/A.Iguodala 15.00 40.00
GG P.Gasol/R.Gay 8.00 20.00
JH L.James/D.Howard 150.00 300.00
JR M.Jordan/D.Rodman 300.00 500.00
KA B.J.Armstrong/S.Kerr 25.00 60.00
NW P.Westphal/S.Nash 25.00 60.00
PS C.Paul/C.Simmons 15.00 40.00
RF W.Frazier/N.Robinson 25.00 60.00
WJ Sd.Williams/Sol.Jones 10.00 25.00

2006-07 UD Black Autographs Flags

STATED PRINT RUN 25 SER.#'d SETS
AB Andrea Bargnani 15.00 40.00
AI Andre Iguodala 20.00 50.00
EH Elvin Hayes 10.00 25.00
LA LaMarcus Aldridge 30.00 80.00
RG Rudy Gay 15.00 40.00
RO Brandon Roy 15.00 40.00
TT Tyrus Thomas 12.00 30.00
YM Yao Ming 50.00 120.00

2006-07 UD Black Autographs Legends

STATED PRINT RUN 25 SER.#'d SETS
UNPRICED PARALLEL PRINT RUN 5 SETS
AD Adrian Dantley 10.00 25.00
BD Brad Daugherty 10.00 25.00
BL Bill Laimbeer 10.00 25.00
WF Walt Frazier 10.00 25.00

2006-07 UD Black Autographs Nameplates

STATED PRINT RUN 50 SER.#'d SETS
UNPRICED PARALLEL PRINT RUN 5 SETS
BR Brandon Roy 10.00 25.00
GG George Gervin 20.00 50.00
JB Josh Boone 6.00 15.00
JF Jordan Farmar 10.00 25.00
KL Kyle Lowry 12.00 30.00
LA LaMarcus Aldridge 25.00 60.00
LJ LeBron James 125.00 250.00
QD Quincy Douby 6.00 15.00
RC Rodney Carney 6.00 15.00
RF Randy Foye 10.00 25.00
RG Rudy Gay 12.00 30.00
RR Rajon Rondo 50.00 120.00
SW Shawne Williams 6.00 15.00
TT Tyrus Thomas 8.00 20.00

2006-07 UD Black Autographs Rookie Materials

STATED PRINT RUN 50 SER.#'d SETS
UNPRICED PARALLEL PRINT RUN 15 SETS
BR Brandon Roy 10.00 25.00
HA Hilton Armstrong 6.00 15.00
JF Jordan Farmar 10.00 25.00
KL Kyle Lowry 12.00 30.00
KP Kevin Pittsnogle 8.00 20.00
LA LaMarcus Aldridge 25.00 60.00
MC Mardy Collins 6.00 15.00
PT P.J. Tucker 8.00 20.00
RG Rudy Gay 12.00 30.00
RR Rajon Rondo 40.00 100.00
TT Tyrus Thomas 8.00 20.00

2006-07 UD Black Autographs Rookies

STATED PRINT RUN 99 SER.#'d SETS
UNPRICED PARALLEL PRINT RUN 15 SETS
AB Andrea Bargnani 8.00 20.00
BA Renaldo Balkman 6.00 15.00
BR Brandon Roy 8.00 20.00
CS Cedric Simmons 5.00 12.00
HA Hilton Armstrong 5.00 12.00
JB Josh Boone 5.00 12.00
JF Jordan Farmar 8.00 20.00
KL Kyle Lowry 10.00 25.00
MW Marcus Williams 5.00 12.00
PO Patrick O'Bryant 5.00 12.00
RB Ronnie Brewer 8.00 20.00
RC Rodney Carney 5.00 12.00
RR Rajon Rondo 25.00 60.00
SB Shannon Brown 5.00 12.00
SW Shelden Williams 6.00 15.00
TS Thabo Sefolosha 8.00 20.00

2006-07 UD Black Autographs Tickets

STATED PRINT RUN 50 SER.#'d SETS
UNPRICED PARALLEL PRINT RUN 10 SETS
DN David Noel 5.00 12.00
FO Randy Foye 8.00 20.00
JF Jordan Farmar 8.00 20.00
JS J.R. Smith 8.00 20.00
LA LaMarcus Aldridge 20.00 50.00
LB Leandro Barbosa 8.00 20.00
LJ LeBron James 200.00 400.00
MA Maurice Ager 5.00 12.00
NR Nate Robinson 15.00 40.00
RF Raymond Felton 6.00 15.00
SC Craig Smith 6.00 15.00
SN Steve Novak 6.00 15.00
TT Tyrus Thomas 6.00 15.00

2006-07 UD Black Autographs Veteran Materials

STATED PRINT RUN 25 SER.#'d SETS
UNPRICED PARALLEL PRINT RUN 5 SETS
BD Baron Davis 10.00 25.00
BG Ben Gordon 12.50 30.00
CF Channing Frye 10.00 25.00
CM Corey Maggette 12.50 30.00
DH Dwight Howard 30.00 80.00
PP Paul Pierce 25.00 60.00
PS Peja Stojakovic 20.00 50.00
RF Raymond Felton 10.00 25.00
VC Vince Carter 20.00 50.00

2006-07 UD Black Autographs Veterans

UNPRICED PARALLEL PRINT RUN 15 SETS
CV Charlie Villanueva 8.00 20.00
NR Nate Robinson 8.00 20.00
RM Rashad McCants/99 8.00 20.00
RT Ronny Turiaf/99 10.00 25.00
TF T.J. Ford/89 8.00 20.00

2006-07 UD Black Dual Materials

STATED PRINT RUN 99 SER.#'d SETS
*DUAL 25: .5X TO 1.25X BASE HI
DUAL PRINT RUN 25 SER.#'d SETS
AI Allen Iverson 5.00 12.00
CA Carmelo Anthony 5.00 12.00
CM Corey Maggette 3.00 8.00
CP Chris Paul 5.00 12.00
DG Drew Gooden 3.00 8.00
DR David Robinson 6.00 15.00
JE Julius Erving 6.00 15.00
JR Jason Richardson 4.00 10.00
KK Kyle Korver 3.00 8.00
LA LaMarcus Aldridge 10.00 25.00
LD Luol Deng 3.00 8.00
LJ LeBron James 25.00 60.00
MG Manu Ginobili 4.00 10.00
MJ Michael Jordan 100.00 200.00
RA Ray Allen 4.00 10.00
RE J.J. Redick 5.00 12.00
RF Randy Foye 4.00 10.00
RH Richard Hamilton 3.00 8.00
RO Brandon Roy 4.00 10.00
RW Rasheed Wallace 4.00 10.00
SM Shawn Marion 3.00 8.00
SW Shelden Williams 3.00 8.00
TD Tim Duncan 6.00 15.00
TM Tracy McGrady 5.00 12.00
TP Tony Parker 4.00 10.00
WC Wilt Chamberlain 50.00 120.00
WF Walt Frazier 4.00 10.00

2006-07 UD Black Dual Materials Autographs

STATED PRINT RUN 25 SER.#'d SETS
UNPRICED PARALLEL PRINT RUN 15 SETS
BR Brandon Roy 25.00 60.00
CD Clyde Drexler 15.00 40.00
CP Chris Paul 40.00 100.00
EB Elton Brand 8.00 20.00
LA LaMarcus Aldridge 30.00 80.00
LJ LeBron James 200.00 450.00
NR Nate Robinson 15.00 40.00
PP Paul Pierce 15.00 40.00
PS Peja Stojakovic 20.00 50.00
RB Renaldo Balkman 8.00 20.00
RF Raymond Felton 10.00 25.00
RG Rudy Gay 25.00 60.00
RR Rajon Rondo 75.00 150.00

2006-07 UD Black Jerseys Autographs

STATED PRINT RUN 50 SER.#'d SETS
UNPRICED PARALLEL PRINT RUN 10 SETS
AI Andre Iguodala 6.00 15.00
BM Brad Miller 6.00 15.00
DH Dwight Howard 20.00 50.00
DR Dennis Rodman 40.00 100.00
FO Randy Foye 6.00 15.00
JF Jordan Farmar 8.00 20.00
KK Kyle Korver 6.00 15.00
LA LaMarcus Aldridge 20.00 50.00
PG Pau Gasol 10.00 25.00
TC Tyson Chandler 6.00 15.00
TT Tyrus Thomas 10.00 25.00

2006-07 UD Black Jerseys Dual

STATED PRINT RUN 50 SER.#'d SETS
UNPRICED PARALLEL PRINT RUN 15 SETS
BJ K.Bryant/M.Johnson 20.00 50.00
BM L.Bird/K.McHale 15.00 40.00
BT I.Thomas/C.Billups 10.00 25.00
CA T.Chandler/H.Armstrong 6.00 15.00
DM P.Davis/C.Maggette 6.00 15.00
GJ K.Garnett/M.James 10.00 25.00
GL P.Gasol/K.Lowry 10.00 25.00
50 L.James/S.Brown 20.00 50.00
KW J.Kidd/Marc.Williams 10.00 25.00
OW S.O'Neal/A.Walker 12.50 30.00
RT Ty.Thomas/D.Rodman 10.00 25.00
SW J.Stockton/D.Williams 10.00 25.00

2006-07 UD Black Jerseys Dual Autographs

STATED PRINT RUN 25 SER.#'d SETS
AM S.Abdur-Rahim/T.McGrady 30.00 80.00
CJ L.James/V.Carter 175.00 350.00
EC M.Eaton/T.Chambers 10.00 25.00
KB C.Billups/J.Kidd 20.00 50.00
KD J.Kidd/B.Davis 40.00 100.00
LT B.Laimbeer/R.Theus 10.00 25.00
MY B.Miller/Y.Ming 50.00 125.00

2006-07 UD Black Legends Materials Autographs

STATED PRINT RUN 25 SER.#'d SETS
UNPRICED PARALLEL PRINT RUN 5 SETS
BW Bill Walton 12.50 30.00
MJ Michael Jordan 350.00 650.00

2006-07 UD Black Patches

STATED PRINT RUN 50 SER.#'d SETS
*PATCH 25: .5X TO 1.25X BASE HI
PATCH 25 PRINT RUN 25 SETS
UNPRICED PARALLEL PRINT RUN 15 SETS
AI Allen Iverson 60.00 150.00
AM Alonzo Mourning 40.00 100.00
AS Amare Stoudemire 10.00 25.00
DH Devin Harris 8.00 20.00
JN Jameer Nelson 8.00 20.00
JO Jermaine O'Neal 8.00 20.00
JR Jason Richardson 8.00 20.00
KB Kobe Bryant 75.00 150.00
KG Kevin Garnett 25.00 60.00
KM Kevin McHale 20.00 50.00
LJ LeBron James 100.00 200.00
MK Karl Malone 25.00 60.00
MM Moses Malone 20.00 50.00
MR Michael Redd 8.00 20.00
MW Marvin Williams 8.00 20.00
RL Rashard Lewis 8.00 20.00
RW Rasheed Wallace 10.00 25.00
SO Shaquille O'Neal 25.00 60.00
TD Tim Duncan 25.00 60.00
ZI Zydrunas Ilgauskas 8.00 20.00

2006-07 UD Black Patches Autographs

STATED PRINT RUN 25 SER.#'d SETS
UNPRICED PARALLEL PRINT RUN 10 SETS
CS Cedric Simmons 5.00 12.00
DE Dee Brown 5.00 12.00
DN David Noel 5.00 12.00
PD Paul Davis 5.00 12.00
RB Renaldo Balkman 6.00 15.00
RF Randy Foye 8.00 20.00
RR Rajon Rondo 90.00 150.00
SB Shannon Brown 25.00 60.00
SW Shawne Williams 5.00 12.00

2006-07 UD Black Patches Dual

STATED PRINT RUN 25 SER.#'d SETS
UNPRICED COLLEGE PRINT RUN 10 SETS
JM A.Jamison/S.May 8.00 20.00
MI A.Iverson/A.Mourning 50.00 120.00
OA E.Okafor/R.Allen 8.00 20.00
OT S.O'Neal/Ty.Thomas 20.00 50.00
PH P.Pierce/K.Hinrich 12.00 30.00
WH L.Head/D.Williams 8.00 20.00

2006-07 UD Black Patches Numbers

STATED PRINT RUN 25 SER.#'d SETS
BD Baron Davis 12.00 30.00
BW Ben Wallace 15.00 40.00
JK Jason Kidd 15.00 40.00
JR Jason Richardson 12.00 30.00
KB Kobe Bryant 60.00 150.00
TP Tayshaun Prince 8.00 20.00

2007-08 UD Black

Released in March 2008, UD Black was packaged in two-pack boxes with one card per pack where the intial pack SRP was $125. The complete 126-card set is divided up as follows: cards 1-84 are sequentially numbered to 25 and feature a horizontal design which places a player photo on the right next to four swatches of jersey patch, cards 85-120 are sequentially numbered to 99 and feature rookies along with both autographs and jersey swatches, and cards 121-126 feature rookie players sequentially numbered to 99.
1-84 JSY PRINT RUN 25 SER.#'d SETS
85-126 PRINT RUN 99 SER.#'d SETS
UNPRICED GOLD PRINT RUN 5 TO 10 SETS
UNPRICED WHITE PRINT RUN ONE SET
1 Clyde Drexler JSY 15.00 40.00
2 Al Jefferson JSY 8.00 20.00
3 Allen Iverson JSY 25.00 60.00
4 Alonzo Mourning JSY 25.00 50.00
5 Amare Stoudemire JSY 15.00 40.00
6 Andre Iguodala JSY 8.00 20.00
7 Andrea Bargnani JSY 10.00 25.00
8 Andrew Bogut JSY 8.00 20.00
9 Antawn Jamison JSY 8.00 20.00
10 Baron Davis JSY 8.00 20.00
11 Ben Gordon JSY 8.00 20.00
12 Bernard King JSY 8.00 20.00
13 Bill Laimbeer JSY 8.00 20.00
14 Bill Russell JSY 30.00 80.00
15 Dwyane Wade JSY 15.00 40.00
16 Brandon Roy JSY 15.00 40.00
17 Carlos Arroyo JSY 10.00 25.00
18 Carlos Boozer JSY 8.00 20.00
19 Carmelo Anthony JSY 20.00 50.00
20 Chris Bosh JSY 20.00 50.00
21 Chris Mullin JSY 20.00 40.00
22 Chris Paul JSY 40.00 75.00
23 Corey Maggette JSY 10.00 25.00
24 Adrian Dantley JSY 8.00 20.00
25 Dennis Rodman JSY 25.00 60.00
26 Deron Williams JSY 20.00 40.00
27 Dirk Nowitzki JSY 20.00 50.00
28 Dominique Wilkins JSY 15.00 40.00
29 Dwight Howard JSY 20.00 50.00
30 Eddy Curry JSY 10.00 25.00
31 Elton Brand JSY 10.00 25.00
32 Emeka Okafor JSY 8.00 20.00
33 George Gervin JSY 12.50 30.00
34 Gilbert Arenas JSY 12.50 30.00
35 Hakeem Olajuwon JSY 20.00 40.00
36 Jamaal Tinsley JSY 10.00 25.00
37 James Worthy JSY 20.00 40.00
38 Jason Kidd JSY 15.00 40.00
39 Jason Richardson JSY 10.00 25.00
40 Jermaine O'Neal JSY 8.00 20.00
41 Jerry West JSY 40.00 75.00
42 Joe Dumars JSY 15.00 40.00
43 John Stockton JSY 20.00 40.00
44 Josh Howard JSY 10.00 25.00
45 Julius Erving JSY 25.00 60.00
46 Kareem Abdul-Jabbar JSY 30.00 60.00
47 Karl Malone JSY 20.00 40.00
48 Kevin Garnett JSY 40.00 70.00
49 Kevin McHale JSY 12.00 30.00
50 Kirk Hinrich JSY 8.00 20.00
51 Kobe Bryant JSY 100.00 200.00
52 Kyle Korver JSY 10.00 25.00
53 Lamar Odom JSY 8.00 20.00
54 LaMarcus Aldridge JSY 12.00 30.00
55 Larry Bird JSY 25.00 60.00
56 Larry Hughes JSY 10.00 25.00
57 LeBron James JSY 125.00 225.00
58 Magic Johnson JSY 40.00 75.00
59 Marvin Williams JSY 10.00 25.00
60 Michael Jordan JSY 300.00 600.00
61 Michael Redd JSY 8.00 20.00
62 Mike Bibby JSY 10.00 25.00
63 Oscar Robertson JSY 35.00 70.00
64 Pau Gasol JSY 10.00 25.00
65 Paul Pierce JSY 10.00 25.00
66 Pete Maravich JSY 60.00 120.00
67 Randy Foye JSY 10.00 25.00
68 Rashard Lewis JSY 10.00 25.00
69 Rasheed Wallace JSY 12.50 30.00
70 Ray Allen JSY 15.00 40.00
71 Ron Artest JSY 10.00 25.00
72 Rudy Gay JSY 10.00 25.00
73 Shaquille O'Neal JSY 20.00 50.00
74 Shelden Williams JSY 10.00 25.00
75 Stephon Marbury JSY 10.00 25.00
76 Steve Nash JSY 20.00 40.00
77 Tayshaun Prince JSY 10.00 25.00
78 Tim Duncan JSY 30.00 60.00
79 Tony Parker JSY 10.00 25.00
80 Tracy McGrady JSY 10.00 25.00
81 Vince Carter JSY 25.00 50.00
82 Walt Frazier JSY 10.00 25.00
83 Wilt Chamberlain JSY 50.00 120.00
84 Yao Ming JSY 20.00 50.00
85 Carl Landry JSY AU RC 6.00 15.00
86 Gabe Pruitt JSY AU RC 6.00 15.00
87 Marcus Williams JSY AU RC 6.00 15.00
88 Nick Fazekas JSY AU RC 6.00 15.00
89 Glen Davis JSY AU RC 8.00 20.00
90 Jermareo Davidson JSY AU RC 6.00 15.00
91 Josh McRoberts JSY AU RC 8.00 20.00
92 Chris Richard JSY AU RC 6.00 15.00
93 Derrick Byars JSY AU RC 6.00 15.00
94 Adam Haluska JSY AU RC 6.00 15.00
95 Reyshawn Terry JSY AU RC 6.00 15.00
96 Jared Jordan JSY AU RC 6.00 15.00
97 Stephane Lasme JSY AU RC 6.00 15.00
98 Dominic McGuire JSY AU RC 6.00 15.00
99 Al Horford JSY AU RC 12.00 30.00
100 Mike Conley Jr. JSY AU RC 12.00 30.00
101 Jeff Green JSY AU RC 10.00 25.00
102 Corey Brewer JSY AU RC 10.00 25.00
103 Joakim Noah JSY AU RC 10.00 25.00
104 Spencer Hawes JSY AU RC 8.00 20.00
105 Acie Law JSY AU RC 6.00 15.00
106 Kevin Durant JSY AU RC 350.00 700.00
107 Julian Wright JSY AU RC 6.00 15.00
108 Al Thornton JSY AU RC 8.00 20.00
109 Rodney Stuckey JSY AU RC 8.00 20.00
110 Sean Williams JSY AU RC 6.00 15.00
111 Marco Belinelli JSY AU RC 10.00 25.00
112 Javaris Crittenton JSY AU RC 6.00 15.00
113 Jason Smith JSY AU RC 8.00 20.00
114 Daequan Cook JSY AU RC 8.00 20.00
115 Aaron Brooks JSY AU RC 8.00 20.00
116 Arron Afflalo JSY AU RC 10.00 25.00
117 Alando Tucker JSY AU RC 6.00 15.00
118 Jared Dudley JSY AU RC 8.00 20.00
119 Wilson Chandler JSY AU RC 8.00 20.00
120 Morris Almond JSY AU RC 6.00 15.00
121 Greg Oden RC 8.00 20.00
122 Nick Young RC 10.00 25.00
123 Yi Jianlian RC 10.00 25.00
124 Brandan Wright RC 8.00 20.00
125 Sun Yue RC 8.00 20.00
126 Thaddeus Young RC 8.00 20.00

2007-08 UD Black 50th Anniversary Autographs

PRINT RUN 50 SER.#'d SETS
UNPRICED GOLD PRINT RUN 10 SER.#'d SETS
UNPRICED WHITE PRINT RUN ONE SET
BR Bill Russell 125.00 250.00
BS Bill Sharman 30.00 80.00
BW Bill Walton 30.00 70.00
CD Clyde Drexler 125.00 225.00
DC Dave Cowens 25.00 60.00
DR David Robinson 75.00 150.00
DS Dolph Schayes 25.00 60.00
EB Elgin Baylor 35.00 70.00
HG Hal Greer 35.00 70.00
HO Hakeem Olajuwon 40.00 75.00
JE Julius Erving 100.00 200.00
JH John Havlicek 40.00 80.00
JL Jerry Lucas 30.00 80.00
JO Michael Jordan 800.00 1200.00
JS John Stockton 50.00 120.00
JW Jerry West 100.00 200.00
KA Kareem Abdul-Jabbar 100.00 200.00
LB Larry Bird 100.00 200.00
LW Lenny Wilkens 30.00 80.00
MJ Magic Johnson 80.00 200.00
NA Nate Tiny Archibald 25.00 60.00
NT Nate Thurmond 25.00 60.00
RB Rick Barry 25.00 60.00
RP Robert Parish 25.00 60.00
SJ Sam Jones 30.00 80.00
WF Walt Frazier 25.00 60.00
WO James Worthy 40.00 100.00
WU Wes Unseld 35.00 70.00

2007-08 UD Black All-Star Autographs

PRINT RUN 25 SER.#'d SETS
*GOLD: .5X TO 1.25X BASE HI
GOLD PRINT RUN 15 SER.#'d SETS
UNPRICED WHITE PRINT RUN ONE SET
UAJ Antawn Jamison 20.00 40.00
UBD Brad Daugherty 20.00 40.00
UCD Clyde Drexler 50.00 125.00
UDR David Robinson 75.00 150.00
UDT David Thompson 20.00 40.00
UDW Dominique Wilkins 40.00 80.00
UGR Glen Rice 20.00 40.00
UHG Horace Grant 20.00 40.00
UJE Julius Erving 100.00 200.00
UJK Jason Kidd 40.00 100.00
UJS John Stockton 75.00 150.00
UKB Kobe Bryant 400.00 600.00
UKG Kevin Garnett 75.00 150.00
ULJ LeBron James 300.00 500.00
UMJ Michael Jordan 500.00 1000.00
UNA Nate Archibald 20.00 40.00
UPP Paul Pierce 20.00 40.00
URB Rick Barry 30.00 60.00

2007-08 UD Black Autographs

PRINT RUN 25 OR 50 SER.#'d SETS
*GOLD/25: .5X TO 1.25X BASE HI
GOLD/10 UNPRICED DUE TO SCARCITY
UNPRICED WHITE PRINT RUN ONE SET
AUAD Adrian Dantley/50 10.00 25.00
AUAH Al Horford/25 10.00 25.00
AUAJ Antawn Jamison/50 10.00 25.00
AUAL Acie Law/50 10.00 25.00
AUAM Alonzo Mourning/25 25.00 60.00
AUAT Al Thornton/50 10.00 25.00
AUBA Leandro Barbosa/50 10.00 25.00
AUBE Marco Belinelli/50 10.00 25.00
AUBG Ben Gordon/50 10.00 25.00
AUBL Bill Laimbeer/50 10.00 25.00
AUBR Brandon Roy/50 12.00 30.00
AUBW Bill Walton/25 10.00 25.00
AUCA Carmelo Anthony/25 30.00 80.00
AUCB Chris Bosh/25 10.00 25.00
AUCD Chuck Daly/50 20.00 50.00
AUCH Connie Hawkins/25 10.00 25.00
AUCR Javaris Crittenton/50 10.00 25.00
AUCY Corey Brewer/25 10.00 25.00
AUDC Daequan Cook/50 10.00 25.00
AUDH Dwight Howard/25 30.00 80.00
AUDT David Thompson/50 10.00 25.00
AUDW Dominique Wilkins/25 20.00 40.00
AUHO Hakeem Olajuwon/25 20.00 40.00
AUJA James Worthy/25 15.00 40.00
AUJG Jeff Green/50 10.00 25.00
AUJK Jason Kidd/25 30.00 60.00
AUJM Josh McRoberts/50 10.00 25.00
AUJN Joakim Noah/25 10.00 25.00
AUJO Michael Jordan/25 600.00 1000.00
AUJS Jason Smith/50 10.00 25.00
AUJS John Stockton/25 40.00 80.00
AUJW Julian Wright/25 10.00 25.00
AUKH Kirk Hinrich/25 10.00 25.00
AULA LaMarcus Aldridge/25 10.00 25.00
AULJ LeBron James/25 400.00 800.00
AUMB Mike Bibby/25 10.00 25.00
AUMC Mike Conley Jr./25 15.00 40.00
AUMJ Magic Johnson/25 50.00 120.00
AUPP Pat Riley/50 12.00 30.00
AUPP Paul Pierce/25 30.00 80.00
AUPR Pat Riley/25 15.00 40.00
AURB Rick Barry/25 10.00 25.00
AURG Rudy Gay/50 12.00 30.00
AURR Rajon Rondo/50 25.00 60.00
AURS Rodney Stuckey/50 10.00 25.00
AUSH Spencer Hawes/50 10.00 25.00
AUSP Sam Perkins/50 10.00 25.00
AUSW Sean Williams/25 10.00 25.00
AUTP Tayshaun Prince/25 10.00 25.00
AUWF Walt Frazier/50 15.00 40.00
AUWI Deron Williams/50 10.00 25.00
AUWU Wes Unseld/50 10.00 25.00
AUYM Yao Ming/25 20.00 40.00

2007-08 UD Black Autographs Dual

PRINT RUN 25 SER.#'d SETS
*GOLD: .5X TO 1.25X BASE HI
GOLD PRINT RUN 15 SER.#'d SETS
UNPRICED WHITE PRINT RUN ONE SET
BL E.Banks/A.Law 15.00 40.00
BW K.Bryant/J.West 200.00 300.00
CB M.Conley/C.Brewer 15.00 40.00
CC M.Conley Jr./M.Conley Sr. 15.00 40.00
CM V.Carter/T.McGrady 40.00 80.00
DA K.Durant/L.Aldridge 150.00 250.00
DC D.Cook/M.Conley 15.00 40.00
GB C.Brewer/T.Green 15.00 40.00
GN B.Gordon/J.Noah 35.00 75.00
HH A.Horford/A.Horford 25.00 50.00
HR S.Hawes/B.Roy 15.00 40.00
JA C.Anthony/L.James 200.00 350.00
JB M.Johnson/L.Bird 150.00 275.00
JJ L.James/M.Jordan 900.00 1500.00
JR M.Jordan/D.Rodman 400.00 600.00
LD B.Laimbeer/A.Dantley 15.00 40.00
NK S.Nash/J.Kidd 60.00 150.00
OD H.Olajuwon/C.Drexler 30.00 80.00
OG E.Okafor/B.Gordon 15.00 40.00
PM P.Riley/M.Johnson 60.00 120.00
RH B.Russell/T.Heinsohn 75.00 150.00
RJ S.Jones/B.Russell 100.00 200.00
WS D.Williams/J.Stockton 60.00 120.00
WW D.Wilkins/S.Webb 25.00 50.00
YD K.Durant/V.Young 150.00 300.00

2007-08 UD Black Autographs Triple

PRINT RUN 15 SER.#'d SETS
UNPRICED GOLD PRINT RUN TEN SETS
UNPRICED WHITE PRINT RUN ONE SET
ECW Erving/Wilkins/Carter 75.00 150.00
GBM Garnett/Bryant/Malone 200.00 350.00
HBN Horford/Brewer/Noah 50.00 100.00
JBJ Bryant/James/Jordan 2500.00 3000.00
NKS Stockton/Nash/Kidd 200.00 400.00
OSM Samp/Olajuwon/Ming 100.00 200.00
PRB Russell/Bird/Pierce 300.00 450.00
WJA Kareem/Johnson/Worthy 250.00 500.00

2007-08 UD Black Flags Autographs

PRINT RUN 25 SER.#'d SETS
UNPRICED GOLD PRINT RUN 10 SER.#'d SETS
UNPRICED WHITE PRINT RUN ONE SET
FAAB Andrea Bargnani 12.00 30.00
FAAH Al Horford 20.00 40.00
FABG Ben Gordon 20.00 40.00
FACB Corey Brewer 20.00 40.00
FADW Dominique Wilkins 25.00 60.00
FAGR Jeff Green 12.00 30.00
FAHO Hakeem Olajuwon 40.00 80.00
FAJN Joakim Noah 40.00 75.00
FAJW Julian Wright 12.00 30.00
FAKB Kobe Bryant 350.00 550.00
FAKD Kevin Durant 350.00 550.00
FALB Leandro Barbosa 20.00 40.00
FARB Rolando Blackman 20.00 40.00
FASK Steve Kerr 25.00 60.00
FASN Steve Nash 60.00 120.00
FATP Tony Parker 25.00 50.00

2007-08 UD Black Framed Autographs

PRINT RUN 25 SER.#'d SETS
UNPRICED GOLD PRINT RUN 5 SETS
UNPRICED WHITE PRINT RUN ONE SET
AD Adrian Dantley 10.00 25.00
AH Al Horford 25.00 50.00
AL Acie Law 10.00 25.00
BR Brandon Roy 15.00 40.00
CB Corey Brewer 12.50 30.00
CP Chris Paul 40.00 100.00
DW Dominique Wilkins 15.00 40.00
JG Jeff Green 15.00 30.00
JL Jerry Lucas 10.00 25.00
JN Joakim Noah 25.00 60.00
JO Magic Johnson 40.00 80.00
JS John Stockton 40.00 80.00
JW Julian Wright 15.00 30.00
LA LaMarcus Aldridge 15.00 40.00
MC Mike Conley Jr. 15.00 30.00
PP Paul Pierce 15.00 40.00
RG Rudy Gay 15.00 30.00
RR Rajon Rondo 20.00 50.00
SN Steve Nash 40.00 100.00
TT Tyrus Thomas 10.00 25.00
VC Vince Carter 25.00 60.00
WI Deron Williams 20.00 40.00
WO James Worthy 25.00 50.00

2007-08 UD Black Letters Autographs

PRINT RUN 25 SER.#'d SETS
UNPRICED GOLD PRINT RUN 10 SETS
UNPRICED WHITE PRINT RUN ONE SET
LAAD Adrian Dantley 20.00 40.00
LAAE Alex English 20.00 40.00
LAAI Andre Iguodala 20.00 40.00
LAAJ Antawn Jamison 20.00 40.00
LAAM Alonzo Mourning 50.00 100.00
LAAR Arnie Risen 20.00 40.00
LABG Ben Gordon 20.00 40.00
LABL Bill Laimbeer 20.00 40.00
LABS Bill Sharman 25.00 50.00
LABW Bill Walton 20.00 40.00
LADH Dwight Howard 30.00 60.00
LADM Danny Manning 20.00 40.00
LADR David Robinson 50.00 100.00
LADS Dolph Schayes 20.00 40.00
LADW Deron Williams 40.00 75.00
LAJE Julius Erving 100.00 200.00
LAJK Jason Kidd 50.00 100.00
LAJS John Stockton 40.00 80.00
LAKB Kobe Bryant 250.00 400.00
LAPP Paul Pierce 25.00 50.00
LARO Dennis Rodman 50.00 120.00
LASN Steve Nash 60.00 120.00
LASP Sam Perkins 20.00 40.00
LATP Tony Parker 30.00 60.00
LAWE Jerry West 75.00 150.00

2007-08 UD Black Numbers Autographs

PRINT RUNS LISTED IN CHECKLIST
UNPRICED GOLD PRINT RUN 10 SER.#'d SETS
UNPRICED WHITE PRINT RUN ONE SET
NAAA Al Attles/16 25.00 50.00
NAAJ Al Jefferson/25 25.00 60.00
NABW Bill Walton/32 10.00 25.00
NACD Clyde Drexler/22 40.00 75.00
NACH Connie Hawkins/42 15.00 40.00
NADC Dave Cowens/18 10.00 25.00
NADH Dwight Howard/12 50.00 120.00
NADN Don Nelson/19 20.00 40.00
NAEB Elgin Baylor/22 25.00 50.00
NAEO Emeka Okafor/50 10.00 25.00
NAHG Hal Greer/15 20.00 40.00
NAHO Hakeem Olajuwon/34 30.00 80.00
NAJS Jack Sikma/43 10.00 25.00
NAKB Kobe Bryant/24 200.00 400.00
NAKD Kevin Durant/35 150.00 300.00
NAKV Kiki Vandeweghe/55 10.00 25.00
NALA LaMarcus Aldridge/12 25.00 50.00
NALB Larry Bird/33 100.00 200.00
NANT Nate Thurmond/42 15.00 40.00
NARG Rudy Gay/22 20.00 40.00
NART Rudy Tomjanovich/45 20.00 40.00
NASN Steve Nash/13 75.00 150.00
NAVC Vince Carter/15 30.00 60.00

2007-08 UD Black Patch Material Autographs

PRINT RUN 25 OR 50 SER.#'d SETS
UNPRICED GOLD PRINT RUN 10 SER.#'d SETS
UNPRICED BLUE PRINT RUN ONE SET
AA Al Attles/50 10.00 25.00
AC Al Cervi/50 10.00 25.00
AE Alex English/50 10.00 25.00
AH Al Horford/25 10.00 25.00
AM Alonzo Mourning/25 40.00 80.00
AR Arnie Risen/50 10.00 25.00
AT Al Thornton/50 10.00 25.00
BD Baron Davis/50 12.50 30.00
BG Ben Gordon/50 10.00 25.00
BL Bill Laimbeer/50 10.00 25.00
BR Brandon Roy/50 20.00 40.00
CB Chris Bosh/25 20.00 50.00
CD Clyde Drexler/50 25.00 50.00
CL Walt Frazier/50 10.00 25.00
CO Corey Brewer/25 10.00 25.00
CP Chris Paul/25 50.00 100.00
DC Daequan Cook/50 10.00 25.00
DL David Lee/50 10.00 25.00
DO Dominique Wilkins/25 12.00 30.00
DR Dennis Rodman/25 40.00 80.00
DW Deron Williams/50 20.00 50.00
EB Elgin Baylor/50 12.00 30.00
GG Gail Goodrich/50 15.00 40.00
GR Jeff Green/25 10.00 25.00
HG Hal Greer/25 20.00 40.00
JC Javaris Crittenton/50 10.00 25.00
JE Julius Erving/25 75.00 150.00
JL Jerry Lucas/25 30.00 80.00
JN Joakim Noah/25 10.00 25.00
JO Magic Johnson/25 75.00 150.00
JS John Stockton/25 60.00 120.00
JW Julian Wright/25 10.00 25.00
KB Kobe Bryant/25 200.00 400.00
KD Kevin Durant/50 200.00 400.00
KH Kirk Hinrich/25 12.00 30.00
LA LaMarcus Aldridge/50 10.00 25.00
LB Larry Bird/25 75.00 150.00
LJ LeBron James/25 400.00 800.00
MC Dick McGuire/50 10.00 25.00
MI Mike Conley Jr./25 20.00 40.00
MJ Michael Jordan/25 800.00 1200.00
PP Paul Pierce/50 25.00 60.00
RB Renaldo Balkman/50 10.00 25.00
RG Rudy Gay/50 10.00 25.00
RI Rick Barry/25 10.00 25.00
RO David Robinson/25 60.00 120.00
RP Robert Parish/50 15.00 30.00
SH Spencer Hawes/50 10.00 25.00
SN Steve Nash/25 40.00 100.00
TG Taurean Green/50 10.00 25.00
TH Tom Heinsohn/50 10.00 25.00
TY Acie Law/50 10.00 25.00
VC Vince Carter/25 15.00 40.00
WO James Worthy/25 30.00 60.00

2007-08 UD Black Patch Material Autographs Dual

PRINT RUN 15 SER.#'d SETS
UNPRICED GOLD PRINT RUN 5 SETS
UNPRICED WHITE PRINT RUN ONE SET
AE C.Anthony/A.English 30.00 80.00
AR L.Aldridge/B.Roy 25.00 60.00
BG E.Baylor/G.Goodrich 25.00 60.00
BN K.Bryant/S.Nash 300.00 500.00
CR A.Risen/A.Cervi 25.00 60.00
DA B.Davis/A.Attles 25.00 60.00
EW J.Erving/D.Wilkins 100.00 200.00
FD W.Frazier/C.Drexler 60.00 120.00
JB M.Jordan/L.Bird 500.00 800.00
JD K.Durant/L.James 400.00 800.00
LC A.Law/J.Crittenton 25.00 60.00
LM J.Lucas/D.McGuire 25.00 60.00
LR B.Laimbeer/D.Rodman 50.00 100.00
MR A.Mourning/D.Robinson 100.00 200.00
NG J.Noah/T.Greeg 40.00 80.00
OG R.Gay/E.Okafor 25.00 60.00
WJ M.Johnson/J.Worthy 200.00 300.00
WS J.Stockton/D.Williams 75.00 150.00

2007-08 UD Black Patches Dual

PRINT RUN 15 SER.#'d SETS
UNPRICED GOLD PRINT RUN 10 SER.#'d SETS
UNPRICED WHITE PRINT RUN ONE SET
DPAJ G.Arenas/A.Jamison 12.00 30.00
DPAR L.Aldridge/B.Roy 12.00 30.00
DPBO K.Bryant/L.Odom 40.00 80.00
DPBP C.Billups/T.Prince 12.00 30.00
DPDG K.Durant/J.Green 30.00 80.00
DPDR T.Duncan/D.Robinson 25.00 50.00
DPHR D.Howard/J.Redick 12.00 30.00
DPIA A.Iverson/C.Anthony 20.00 50.00
DPJF A.Jefferson/R.Foye 12.00 30.00
DPJR M.Jordan/D.Rodman 100.00 200.00
DPKC V.Carter/J.Kidd 20.00 50.00
DPMB L.Bird/K.McHale 25.00 50.00
DPMM Y.Ming/T.McGrady 12.00 30.00
DPMS K.Malone/J.Stockton 25.00 50.00
DPNS S.Nash/A.Stoudemire 20.00 40.00
DPOD H.Olajuwon/C.Drexler 25.00 50.00
DPPG M.Ginobili/T.Parker 15.00 40.00
DPRF W.Frazier/W.Reed 12.00 30.00
DPSP C.Paul/P.Stojakovic 12.00 30.00

2007-08 UD Black Ticket Autographs

PRINT RUN 50 SER.#'d SETS
*GOLD: .5X TO 1.25X BASE HI
GOLD PRINT RUN 15 SER.#'d SETS
UNPRICED WHITE PRINT RUN ONE SET
TAAB Aaron Brooks 8.00 20.00
TAAH Al Horford 8.00 20.00
TAAI Andre Iguodala 8.00 20.00
TAAJ Antawn Jamison 8.00 20.00
TAAL Acie Law 8.00 20.00
TAAM Alonzo Mourning 20.00 50.00
TAAT Al Thornton 8.00 20.00
TABD Baron Davis 10.00 25.00
TABG Ben Gordon 8.00 20.00
TABI Mike Bibby 8.00 20.00
TABR Brandon Roy 10.00 25.00
TACA Carmelo Anthony 25.00 60.00
TACB Corey Brewer 8.00 20.00
TACH Chris Mihm 8.00 20.00
TACL Carl Landry 8.00 20.00
TACM Corey Maggette 8.00 20.00
TACP Chris Paul 30.00 80.00
TADC Daequan Cook 8.00 20.00
TADG Danny Granger 8.00 20.00
TADH Dwight Howard 25.00 60.00
TADL David Lee 8.00 20.00
TADW Deron Williams 8.00 20.00
TAEO Emeka Okafor 8.00 20.00
TAGD Glen Davis 8.00 20.00
TAGP Gabe Pruitt 8.00 20.00
TAJC Javaris Crittenton 8.00 20.00
TAJD Jared Dudley 8.00 20.00
TAJG Jeff Green 8.00 20.00
TAJM Josh McRoberts 8.00 20.00
TAJN Joakim Noah 8.00 20.00
TAJS Jason Smith 8.00 20.00
TAJW Julian Wright 8.00 20.00
TAKB Kobe Bryant 150.00 300.00
TAKD Kevin Durant 200.00 400.00
TAKG Kevin Garnett 60.00 150.00
TALA LaMarcus Aldridge 10.00 25.00
TALJ LeBron James 200.00 300.00
TAMA Morris Almond 8.00 20.00
TAMB Marco Belinelli 8.00 20.00
TAMC Mike Conley Jr. 10.00 25.00
TANF Nick Fazekas 8.00 20.00
TAPP Paul Pierce 15.00 30.00
TAPR Tayshaun Prince 8.00 20.00
TARF Randy Foye 8.00 20.00
TARG Rudy Gay 10.00 25.00
TARS Rodney Stuckey 8.00 20.00
TASE Shawne Williams 8.00 20.00
TASH Spencer Hawes 8.00 20.00
TASN Steve Nash 25.00 60.00
TASW Sean Williams 8.00 20.00
TATP Tony Parker 10.00 25.00
TATU Alando Tucker 8.00 20.00
TAVC Vince Carter 25.00 60.00
TAWC Wilson Chandler 8.00 20.00
TAWS Shelden Williams 8.00 20.00
TAYM Yao Ming 25.00 50.00

2007-08 UD Black Ticket Autographs Dual

PRINT RUN 15 SER.#'d SETS
UNPRICED GOLD PRINT RUN 5 SETS
UNPRICED WHITE PRINT RUN ONE SET
AD K.Durant/C.Anthony 150.00 300.00
BH M.Bibby/S.Hawes 20.00 40.00
BM Y.Ming/K.Bryant 400.00 600.00
BP M.Bibby/C.Paul 40.00 80.00
DG K.Durant/J.Green 125.00 250.00
DW D.Williams/B.Davis 30.00 60.00
FB C.Brewer/R.Foye 25.00 50.00
GC M.Conley/R.Gay 20.00 50.00
GN B.Gordon/J.Noah 30.00 60.00
HL A.Law/A.Horford 20.00 40.00
HW S.Hawes/J.Wright 20.00 40.00
JG A.Jamison/D.Granger 20.00 40.00
MP T.Prince/A.Mourning 25.00 60.00
MT A.Thornton/C.Maggette 20.00 40.00
NT S.Nash/A.Tucker 40.00 80.00
NW J.Noah/S.Williams 25.00 50.00
OD E.Okafor/J.Dudley 20.00 40.00
PD G.Davis/G.Pruitt 20.00 50.00
PG P.Pierce/K.Garnett 200.00 300.00
PR B.Roy/T.Parker 30.00 60.00
PW C.Paul/J.Wright 40.00 80.00
RM B.Roy/J.McRoberts 20.00 50.00
SC R.Stuckey/D.Cook 25.00 50.00

2007-08 UD Black Trophy Autographs

PRINT RUN 25 SER.#'d SETS
UNPRICED GOLD PRINT RUN ONE TO 11 SETS
UNPRICED WHITE PRINT RUN ONE SET
BL Bill Laimbeer 25.00 50.00
BR Bill Russell 250.00 500.00
BW Bill Walton 40.00 80.00
DR Dennis Rodman 100.00 200.00
GR Hal Greer 25.00 50.00
HO Hakeem Olajuwon 50.00 100.00
JO Michael Jordan 700.00 1200.00
JS Jack Sikma 25.00 50.00
JW James Worthy 50.00 100.00
KA Kareem Abdul-Jabbar 100.00 200.00
KB Kobe Bryant 500.00 800.00
LB Larry Bird 150.00 300.00
MJ Magic Johnson 150.00 300.00
TH Tom Heinsohn 30.00 60.00
TP Tony Parker 50.00 120.00
VM Vern Mikkelsen 30.00 60.00
WF Walt Frazier 30.00 60.00

2008-09 UD Black

1-42 PRINT RUN 25 SER.#'d SETS
JSY AU RC PRINT RUN 99 SER.#'d SETS
UNPRICED WHITE PRINT RUN ONE SET
1 Al Horford 12.00 30.00
2 Allen Iverson 25.00 60.00
3 Amare Stoudemire 10.00 25.00
4 Baron Davis 10.00 25.00
5 Kirk Hinrich 10.00 25.00
6 Brandon Roy 12.00 30.00
7 Carmelo Anthony 30.00 80.00
8 Chauncey Billups 12.00 30.00
9 Chris Bosh 12.00 30.00
10 Peja Stojakovic 12.00 30.00
11 Corey Maggette 10.00 25.00
12 Danny Granger 10.00 25.00
13 Andrei Kirilenko 10.00 25.00
14 Dirk Nowitzki 15.00 40.00
15 Dwight Howard 10.00 25.00
16 Elton Brand 12.00 30.00
17 Gerald Wallace 10.00 25.00
18 Gilbert Arenas 10.00 25.00
19 Jason Kidd 15.00 40.00
20 Kevin Durant 30.00 80.00
21 Kevin Garnett 40.00 100.00
22 Kevin Martin 10.00 25.00
23 Kobe Bryant 60.00 150.00
24 LeBron James 60.00 150.00
25 Michael Redd 10.00 25.00
26 Mike Miller 10.00 25.00
27 Pau Gasol 12.00 30.00
28 Paul Pierce 12.00 30.00
29 Rudy Gay 12.00 30.00
30 Shawn Marion 10.00 25.00
31 Steve Nash 12.00 30.00
32 Tim Duncan 25.00 60.00
33 Tracy McGrady 12.00 30.00
34 Vince Carter 15.00 40.00
35 Yao Ming 20.00 50.00
36 Zach Randolph 10.00 25.00
37 Julius Erving 20.00 50.00
38 Larry Bird 30.00 80.00
39 Magic Johnson 30.00 80.00
40 Michael Jordan 300.00 600.00
41 Oscar Robertson 25.00 50.00
42 Patrick Ewing 30.00 80.00
43 Derrick Rose JSY AU RC 100.00 250.00
44 M.Beasley JSY AU RC 8.00 20.00
45 O.J. Mayo JSY AU RC 8.00 20.00
46 R.Westbrook JSY AU RC 200.00 500.00
47 Kevin Love JSY AU RC 40.00 100.00
48 Eric Gordon JSY AU RC 15.00 40.00
49 Joe Alexander JSY AU RC 5.00 12.00
50 D.J. Augustin JSY AU RC 6.00 15.00
51 Brook Lopez JSY AU RC 10.00 25.00
52 Jerryd Bayless JSY AU RC 6.00 15.00
53 Jason Thompson JSY AU RC 5.00 12.00
54 Brandon Rush JSY AU RC 6.00 15.00
55 A.Randolph JSY AU RC 5.00 12.00
56 Robin Lopez JSY AU RC 8.00 20.00
57 Marreese Speights JSY AU RC 6.00 15.00
58 Roy Hibbert JSY AU RC 15.00 40.00
59 Javale McGee JSY AU RC 15.00 40.00
60 J.J. Hickson JSY AU RC 6.00 15.00
61 Ryan Anderson JSY AU RC 6.00 15.00
62 Kosta Koufos JSY AU RC 6.00 15.00
63 George Hill JSY AU RC 8.00 20.00
64 Darrell Arthur JSY AU RC 6.00 15.00
65 Donte Greene JSY AU RC 5.00 12.00
66 J.R. Giddens JSY AU RC 5.00 12.00
67 Walter Sharpe JSY AU RC 5.00 12.00
68 Joey Dorsey JSY AU RC 5.00 12.00
69 M.Chalmers JSY AU RC 8.00 20.00
70 Sonny Weems JSY AU RC 5.00 12.00
71 R.Fernandez JSY AU RC 6.00 15.00
72 Patrick Ewing Jr. JSY AU RC 5.00 12.00

2008-09 UD Black Gold

*GOLD 1-42: .5X TO 1.25X BASE HI
STATED PRINT RUN 15 SER.#'d SETS
*GOLD 43-72: .6X TO 1.5X BASE HI
STATED PRINT RUN 30 SER.#'d SETS
28 Paul Pierce 25.00 60.00
44 Michael Beasley JSY AU 30.00 80.00
51 Brook Lopez JSY AU 40.00 100.00

2008-09 UD Black 50 Greatest Autographs

PRINT RUN 50 SER.#'d SETS
*GOLD: .5X TO 1.25X BASE HI
GOLD PRINT RUN 15 SER.#'d SETS
50AUBP Bob Pettit 30.00 60.00
50AUBR Bill Russell 80.00 200.00
50AUBS Bill Sharman 20.00 50.00
50AUBW Bill Walton 20.00 50.00
50AUCD Clyde Drexler 30.00 80.00
50AUDC Dave Cowens 20.00 50.00
50AUDR David Robinson 40.00 80.00
50AUDS Dolph Schayes 20.00 50.00
50AUHO Hakeem Olajuwon 30.00 80.00
50AUJE Julius Erving 50.00 125.00
50AUJH John Havlicek 25.00 60.00
50AUJO Michael Jordan 600.00 1200.00
50AUJS John Stockton 50.00 120.00
50AUJW Jerry West 50.00 120.00
50AUKA Kareem Abdul-Jabbar 50.00 120.00
50AULB Larry Bird 60.00 150.00
50AULW Lenny Wilkens 20.00 50.00
50AUMJ Magic Johnson 50.00 120.00
50AUNT Nate Thurmond 20.00 50.00
50AUOR Oscar Robertson 50.00 100.00
50AURB Rick Barry 20.00 50.00
50AURP Robert Parish 20.00 50.00
50AUWF Walt Frazier 20.00 50.00
50AUWO James Worthy 30.00 60.00

2008-09 UD Black ABA Autographs

STATED PRINT RUN 25 SER.#'d SETS
*GOLD: .5X TO 1.25X BASE HI
GOLD PRINT RUN 10 SER.#'d SETS
UNPRICED WHITE PRINT RUN ONE SET
ABAAG Artis Gilmore 8.00 20.00
ABACS Charlie Scott 10.00 25.00
ABADB Don Buse 8.00 20.00
ABAFL Freddie Lewis 8.00 20.00
ABAJE Julius Erving 60.00 120.00
ABALD Louie Dampier 8.00 20.00

2008-09 UD Black ABA/NBA 30th Anniversary Autographs

PRINT RUN 20 TO 30 SER.#'d SETS
UNPRICED GOLD PRINT RUN 5 SER.#'d SETS
UNPRICED WHITE PRINT RUN ONE SET
30DB Don Buse/30 8.00 20.00
30DT David Thompson/30 8.00 20.00
30FL Freddie Lewis/30 8.00 20.00
30GK George Karl/29 12.00 30.00
30GM George McGinnis/20 8.00 20.00
30JE Julius Erving/30 60.00 120.00
30JS James Silas/30 8.00 20.00
30RB Rick Barry/30 15.00 30.00

2008-09 UD Black All-Star Autographs

STATED PRINT RUN 24 TO 25 SER.#'d SETS
UNPRICED GOLD PRINT RUN ONE TO 11 SETS
UNPRICED WHITE PRINT RUN ONE SET
ASAJ Antawn Jamison/25 15.00 30.00
ASAS Amare Stoudemire/25 20.00 40.00
ASBM Brad Miller/25 8.00 20.00
ASCP Chris Paul/25 50.00 100.00
ASDW David West/25 8.00 20.00
ASJK Jason Kidd/24 25.00 60.00
ASKB Kobe Bryant/25 200.00 350.00
ASKG Kevin Garnett/25 50.00 100.00
ASLJ LeBron James/25 200.00 350.00
ASPP Paul Pierce/25 20.00 40.00
ASRA Ray Allen/25 30.00 80.00
ASTM Tracy McGrady/24 15.00 30.00
ASYM Yao Ming/25 20.00 50.00

2008-09 UD Black Autographs

STATED PRINT RUN 23 TO 50 SER.#'d SETS
UNPRICED AUTO OCTO PRINT RUN 5 SETS
UNPRICED AUTO OCTO GOLD PRINT RUN 3 SETS
UNPRICED AUTO OCTO WHITE PRINT RUN ONE SET
UNPRICED AUTO SIX PRINT RUN 5 SETS
UNPRICED AUTO SIX GOLD PRINT RUN 3 SETS
UNPRICED AUTO SIX WHITE PRINT RUN ONE SET
A1AJ Antawn Jamison/35 10.00 25.00
A1AM Alonzo Mourning/35 30.00 80.00
A1BL Bob Lanier/35 8.00 20.00
A1BR Brandon Roy/35 12.00 30.00
A1BW Bill Walton/35 12.50 30.00
A1CP Chris Paul/35 40.00 75.00
A1HO Hakeem Olajuwon/35 25.00 60.00
A1JE Julius Erving/32 60.00 120.00
A1JO Magic Johnson/32 40.00 100.00
A1JS J.R. Smith/35 10.00 25.00
A1KA Kareem Abdul-Jabbar/33 50.00 100.00
A1KD Kevin Durant/35 75.00 150.00
A1KG Kevin Garnett/35 50.00 100.00
A1LB Larry Bird/33 40.00 80.00
A1LJ LeBron James/23 250.00 500.00
A1MJ Michael Jordan/23 400.00 700.00
A1MP Mark Price/35 25.00 60.00
A1PP Paul Pierce/35 30.00 80.00
A1RA Ray Allen/35 30.00 80.00
A1ST John Stockton/35 30.00 80.00
A1TM Tracy McGrady/35 15.00 40.00
A2AB Andrew Bynum/50 25.00 50.00
A2AE Alex English/50 8.00 20.00
A2AJ Al Jefferson/50 8.00 20.00
A2AT Al Thornton/50 8.00 20.00
A2BB Bruce Bowen/50 8.00 20.00
A2BD Brad Daugherty/50 10.00 25.00
A2BS Bill Sharman/50 8.00 20.00
A2CL Carl Landry/50 8.00 20.00
A2FL Freddie Lewis/50 8.00 20.00
A2RR Rajon Rondo/50 25.00 60.00

2008-09 UD Black Autographs Jerseys Quad

STATED PRINT RUN 10 SER.#'d SETS
UNPRICED JERSEY SIX PRINT RUN 5 SETS
UNPRICED PATCH QUAD GOLD PRINT RUN 5 SETS
UNPRICED PATCH QUAD WHITE PRINT RUN 1 SET
UNPRICED PATCH SIX GOLD PRINT RUN 5 SETS
UNPRICED PATCH SIX WHITE PRINT RUN 1 SET
QAJ08RK 2008-09 Rookies 200.00 450.00
QAJBSTN Boston Celtics 150.00 325.00
QAJBULL Chicago Bulls 150.00 300.00
QAJCAVS Cleveland Cavaliers 150.00 300.00
QAJEVSW Celtics/Lakers 350.00 600.00
QAJHAWK Atlanta Hawks 50.00 120.00
QAJLAKR Los Angeles Lakers 300.00 550.00
QAJROCK Houston Rockets 50.00 120.00
QAJROOK 2008-09 Rookies 2 50.00 120.00
QAJUDEX LeBron/Kobe/MJ/KG 1000.00 1500.00

2008-09 UD Black Commemorative Logo Autographs

STATED PRINT RUN 19 TO 25 SER.#'d SETS
*GOLD: .6X TO 1.5X BASE HI
GOLD PRINT RUN 10 SER.#'d SETS
UNPRICED WHITE PRINT RUN ONE SET
CBB Bruce Bowen/25 8.00 20.00
CBG Ben Gordon/25 15.00 40.00
CBR Bill Russell/20 60.00 150.00
CBS Bill Sharman/25 10.00 25.00
CCH Chuck Daly/25 30.00 60.00
CDH Dwight Howard/23 50.00 100.00
CHO Hakeem Olajuwon/25 20.00 50.00
CJO M.Jordan Finals/19 800.00 1200.00
CJW Jerry West/25 30.00 60.00
CKB Kobe Bryant/24 225.00 350.00
CKG Kevin Garnett/25 60.00 120.00
CKV Kiki Vandeweghe/25 8.00 20.00
CLO Lamar Odom/25 20.00 50.00
CMI Michael Jordan/23 350.00 700.00
CMJ Magic Johnson/25 40.00 100.00
CPP Paul Pierce/25 40.00 80.00
CPR Tayshaun Prince/25 8.00 20.00
CRA Ray Allen/25 40.00 100.00
CRR Rajon Rondo/24 25.00 60.00
CRS Rodney Stuckey/25 12.00 30.00
CSK Steve Kerr/25 20.00 50.00
CST John Stockton/25 40.00 100.00
CTP Tony Parker/25 15.00 30.00
CYM Yao Ming/24 20.00 50.00

2008-09 UD Black Dual Autographs

STATED PRINT RUN 15 SER.#'d SETS
UNPRICED GOLD PRINT RUN 5 SETS
UNPRICED WHITE PRINT RUN ONE SET
DAAS M.Almond/D.Strawberry 25.00 60.00
DABG K.Bryant/K.Garnett 200.00 400.00
DABL S.Battier/C.Landry 25.00 60.00
DABW C.Boozer/D.Williams 20.00 50.00
DACW V.Carter/D.Wilkins 40.00 80.00
DADH K.Durant/A.Horford 75.00 150.00
DAEJ J.Erving/L.James 250.00 400.00
DAJA Kareem/Magic 100.00 200.00
DAJB K.Bryant/M.Jordan 1000.00 1400.00
DALT B.Laimbeer/I.Thomas 40.00 100.00
DAMS Y.Ming/L.Scola 30.00 80.00
DAPG Garnett/Pierce 50.00 125.00
DAPR C.Paul/R.Rondo 50.00 125.00
DAPS T.Prince/R.Stuckey 25.00 60.00
DARA Kareem/Robertson 100.00 200.00
DARJ B.Russell/S.Jones 75.00 200.00
DAVF J.Farmar/S.Vujacic 25.00 60.00
DAWP C.Paul/D.West 40.00 80.00
DAWW L.Walton/B.Walton 25.00 60.00

2008-09 UD Black Dual Inscriptions

STATED PRINT RUN 10 SER.#'d SETS
UNPRICED GOLD PRINT RUN 5 SER.#'d SETS
DIBW K.Bryant/L.Walton
DIDE H.Olajuwon/P.Ewing
DIDG K.Durant/J.Green 125.00 225.00
DIMB S.Battier/T.McGrady 75.00 150.00
DIPG P.Pierce/K.Garnett 60.00 150.00
DIRA Abdul-Jabbar/D.Robinson 250.00 350.00
DIWB C.Billups/J.West
DIWR J.Wilkes/D.Rodman 100.00 200.00

2008-09 UD Black Dual Patch Autographs

STATED PRINT RUN 15 SER.#'d SETS
UNPRICED GOLD PRINT RUN 5 SETS
UNPRICED WHITE PRINT RUN ONE SET
DPAAF R.Fernandez/L.Aldridge 40.00 80.00
DPABC D.Cook/M.Beasley 40.00 80.00
DPABF J.Farmar/A.Bynum 25.00 60.00
DPABH M.Bibby/A.Horford 40.00 80.00
DPABJ K.Bryant/L.James 500.00 750.00
DPADG K.Durant/J.Green 125.00 250.00
DPAGC Mike Conley/Rudy Gay 25.00 60.00
DPAJB A.Bogut/R.Jefferson 25.00 60.00
DPAJJ M.Jordan/L.James 1500.00 2200.00
DPALB C.Brewer/K.Love 50.00 125.00
DPAMB T.McGrady/S.Battier 40.00 100.00
DPAMH A.Harrington/C.Maggette 25.00 60.00
DPAMS Y.Ming/A.Stoudemire 40.00 100.00
DPANK J.Kidd/S.Nash 50.00 100.00
DPAOF E.Okafor/R.Felton 25.00 60.00
DPAPG P.Pierce/K.Garnett 100.00 200.00
DPAPS T.Prince/R.Stuckey 25.00 60.00
DPATN T.Thomas/J.Noah 40.00 80.00

2008-09 UD Black Dual Rookie Autographs

STATED PRINT RUN 10 SER.#'d SETS
UNPRICED GOLD PRINT RUN 5 SETS
DRAAB D.Augustin/J.Bayless 25.00 50.00
DRABR D.Rose/Beasley 100.00 200.00
DRAFG Gallinari/Fernandez 40.00 80.00
DRAGL C.Lee/E.Gordon 25.00 60.00
DRAHS J.Hickson/M.Speights 25.00 50.00
DRALG K.Love/M.Gasol 40.00 80.00
DRALL R.Lopez/B.Lopez 25.00 50.00
DRAMW Westbrook/Mayo 60.00 150.00
DRART A.Randolph/J.Thompson 25.00 50.00

2008-09 UD Black Dual Rookie Jersey Autographs

STATED PRINT RUN 25 SER.#'d SETS
*GOLD: .75X TO 2X BASE HI
GOLD PRINT RUN 10 SER.#'d SETS
UNPRICED WHITE PRINT RUN ONE SET
DRBR M.Beasley/D.Rose 40.00 100.00
DRDE P.Ewing Jr/J.Dorsey 8.00 20.00
DRGL E.Gordon/K.Love 20.00 50.00
DRGS W.Sharpe/J.Giddens 8.00 20.00
DRHM J.McGee/R.Hibbert 8.00 20.00
DRHS J.Hickson/M.Speights 12.50 30.00
DRLL R.Lopez/B.Lopez 20.00 50.00
DRMW R.Westbrook/O.Mayo 40.00 100.00
DRRB B.Rush/J.Bayless 15.00 30.00
DRRT Thompson/Randolph 20.00 40.00

2008-09 UD Black Flag Autographs

STATED PRINT RUN 23 TO 50 SER.#'d SETS
*GOLD: .5X TO 1.25X BASE HI
GOLD PRINT RUN 10 TO 25 SER.#'d SETS
UNPRICED WHITE PRINT RUN ONE SET
USAA Arron Afflalo/50 10.00 25.00
USAG Artis Gilmore/50 10.00 25.00
USAJ Al Jefferson/50 10.00 25.00
USAM Alonzo Mourning/50 20.00 50.00
USAT Al Thornton/50 10.00 25.00
USAU D.J. Augustin/50 10.00 25.00
USBL Bill Laimbeer/50 10.00 25.00
USBM Brad Miller/50 10.00 25.00
USBR Brandon Roy/50 20.00 50.00
USBW Bill Walton/50 15.00 40.00
USCB Corey Brewer/50 10.00 25.00
USCH Tom Chambers/50 10.00 25.00
USCL Carl Landry/50 10.00 25.00
USCP Chris Paul/50 40.00 100.00
USDT David Thompson/50 10.00 25.00
USDW David West/50 10.00 25.00
USGI Daniel Gibson/50 10.00 25.00
USGR Donte Greene/50 10.00 25.00
USJB Jerryd Bayless/50 10.00 25.00
USJF Jordan Farmar/50 10.00 25.00
USJG Joey Graham/50 10.00 25.00
USJJ Jarrett Jack/50 10.00 25.00
USJK Jason Kidd/50 30.00 80.00
USKB Kobe Bryant/24 200.00 400.00
USKD Kevin Durant/50 50.00 125.00
USKG Kevin Garnett/25 50.00 100.00
USLB Larry Bird/33 100.00 175.00
USLJ LeBron James/23 300.00 500.00
USMJ Michael Jordan/23 400.00 800.00
USMP Mark Price/50 20.00 40.00
USRP Robert Parish/50 10.00 25.00
USSB Shane Battier/50 15.00 30.00
USTC Tyson Chandler/50 10.00 25.00

2008-09 UD Black Flag Autographs Dual

STATED PRINT RUN 10 SER.#'d SETS
UNPRICED GOLD PRINT RUN 5 SER.#'d SETS
UNPRICED WHITE PRINT RUN ONE SET
DUSBR A.Bynum/D.Rodman 100.00 200.00
DUSDD A.Dantley/K.Durant 100.00 200.00
DUSGE K.Garnett/A.English 75.00 150.00
DUSGJ M.Johnson/G.Gervin 100.00 200.00
DUSHF W.Frazier/D.Howard 50.00 100.00
DUSJE J.Erving/M.Jordan 500.00 800.00
DUSRH O.Robertson/B.Howell 50.00 100.00
DUSRP R.Parish/B.Russell 100.00 200.00
DUSSR D.Robinson/A.Stoudemire 100.00 200.00
DUSTP C.Paul/D.Thompson 50.00 100.00
DUSWW J.West/D.Williams 100.00 200.00

2008-09 UD Black HOF Letters Autographs

TOTAL PRINT RUNS LISTED IN CHECKLIST
HOFAD Adrian Dantley/84* 15.00 40.00
HOFAE Alex English/98* 15.00 40.00
HOFAR Arnie Risen/98* 15.00 40.00
HOFBH Bailey Howell/98* 15.00 40.00
HOFBI Larry Bird/56* 75.00 150.00
HOFBL Bob Lanier/70* 15.00 40.00
HOFBR Bill Russell/56* 100.00 200.00
HOFBS Bill Sharman/70* 15.00 40.00
HOFBW Bill Walton/84* 15.00 40.00
HOFCD Clyde Drexler/70* 40.00 80.00
HOFDC Dave Cowens/70* 20.00 50.00
HOFDT David Thompson/84* 15.00 40.00
HOFDW D.Wilkins/70* 30.00 80.00
HOFEB Elgin Baylor/70* 20.00 50.00
HOFGO Gail Goodrich/70* 15.00 40.00
HOFHG Hal Greer/70* 15.00 40.00
HOFHO Hakeem Olajuwon/70* 30.00 80.00
HOFJH John Havlicek/70* 40.00 100.00
HOFJW James Worthy/70* 25.00 60.00
HOFKA K.Abdul-Jabbar/70* 40.00 100.00
HOFLW Lenny Wilkens/84* 15.00 40.00
HOFMJ Magic Johnson/56* 60.00 150.00
HOFOR Oscar Robertson/70* 30.00 80.00
HOFPR Pat Riley/70* 40.00 70.00
HOFRB Rick Barry/70* 15.00 40.00
HOFRP Robert Parish/98* 15.00 40.00
HOFWE Jerry West/70* 40.00 80.00
HOFWF Walt Frazier/84* 15.00 40.00

2008-09 UD Black Inscriptions Autographs

STATED PRINT RUN 25 SER.#'d SETS
*GOLD: .6X TO 1.5X BASE HI
GOLD PRINT RUN 10 SER.#'d SETS
AIJO L.Johnson Grandmama 50.00 120.00
AICB3 Corey Brewer C-Brew 8.00 20.00
AIDH1 D.Howard Manchild 75.00 150.00
AIDR1 Dennis Rodman Worm 75.00 150.00
AIDW1 Deron Williams Slick 50.00 100.00
AIKD1 Kevin Durant 100.00 250.00
AIKG1 Kevin Garnett None 75.00 150.00
AILJ1 LeBron James None 200.00 400.00
AIPP1 P.Pierce Go Jayhawks 75.00 150.00

2008-09 UD Black Legend Signed Jersey Pieces

STATED PRINT RUN 23 TO 25 SER.#'d SETS
UNPRICED GOLD PRINT RUN 5 SER.#'d SETS
UNPRICED WHITE PRINT RUN ONE SET
SPLBK Bernard King 10.00 25.00
SPLDR David Robinson 40.00 100.00
SPLJO Magic Johnson 50.00 120.00
SPLJS John Stockton 40.00 100.00
SPLLB Larry Bird 50.00 120.00
SPLMJ Michael Jordan 500.00 700.00
SPLRO Dennis Rodman 60.00 120.00
SPLSA Stacey Augmon 10.00 25.00
SPLSK Steve Kerr 25.00 50.00

2008-09 UD Black Legend Signed Jersey Pieces Dual

STATED PRINT RUN 10 SER.#'d SETS
UNPRICED GOLD PRINT RUN 5 SER.#'d SETS
UNPRICED WHITE PRINT RUN ONE SET
DJLEG J.Erving/G.Gervin 60.00 120.00
DJLJB M.Johnson/L.Bird 200.00 400.00
DJLJJ M.Johnson/M.Jordan 600.00 1000.00
DJLKR S.Kerr/D.Rodman 80.00 160.00
DJLOR H.Olajuwon/D.Robinson 60.00 120.00
DJLSK J.Stockton/S.Kerr 60.00 120.00

2008-09 UD Black Michael Jordan Signed Floor

STATED PRINT RUN 23 SER.#'d SETS
UNPRICED GOLD PRINT RUN 5 SER.#'d SETS
UNPRICED WHITE PRINT RUN ONE SET
MJ Michael Jordan/23 600.00 1200.00

2008-09 UD Black MJ Induction

MJHOF Michael Jordan 25.00 60.00
MJHOFG Michael Jordan Gold/23 75.00 200.00

2008-09 UD Black Quad Autographs

STATED PRINT RUN 10 SER.#'d SETS
UNPRICED GOLD PRINT RUN 5 SER.#'d SETS
UNPRICED WHITE PRINT RUN ONE SET
QA2007 Thornton/Horford/Green/Scola 50.00 100.00
QA2008 Myo/Rse/Bsly/Wstbrk 200.00 500.00
QADUNK Hwrd/Spud/VC/Nique 100.00 200.00
QAPGDS Stktn/Isiah/Deron/Paul 125.00 250.00
QAROOK Love/Alxndr/Grdn/Glinri 60.00 150.00
QASTUD LeBron/KG/Kobe/MJ 900.00 1500.00

2008-09 UD Black Rookie Signed Jersey Pieces

STATED PRINT RUN 50 SER.#'d SETS
*GOLD: .75X TO 2X BASE HI
GOLD PRINT RUN 15 SER.#'d SETS
UNPRICED WHITE PRINT RUN ONE SET
SJRAR Anthony Randolph 5.00 12.00
SJRBL Brook Lopez 10.00 25.00
SJRBR Brandon Rush 6.00 15.00
SJRCD Chris Douglas-Roberts 5.00 12.00
SJRCL Courtney Lee 6.00 15.00
SJRDA D.J. Augustin 6.00 15.00
SJRDG Donte Greene 5.00 12.00
SJRDR Derrick Rose 100.00 200.00
SJRDW D.J. White 6.00 15.00
SJREG Eric Gordon 12.00 30.00
SJRGH George Hill 8.00 20.00
SJRJA Joe Alexander 5.00 12.00
SJRJB Jerryd Bayless 6.00 15.00
SJRJD Joey Dorsey 5.00 12.00
SJRJG J.R. Giddens 5.00 12.00
SJRJH J.J. Hickson 6.00 15.00
SJRJM Javale McGee 10.00 25.00
SJRJT Jason Thompson 5.00 12.00
SJRKK Kosta Koufos 6.00 15.00
SJRKL Kevin Love 20.00 50.00
SJRMB Michael Beasley 15.00 40.00
SJRMC Mario Chalmers 8.00 20.00
SJRMS Marreese Speights 6.00 15.00
SJROM O.J. Mayo 10.00 25.00
SJRRA Ryan Anderson 6.00 15.00
SJRRF Rudy Fernandez 6.00 15.00
SJRRH Roy Hibbert 8.00 20.00
SJRRL Robin Lopez 8.00 20.00
SJRRW Russell Westbrook 50.00 120.00
SJRSW Sonny Weems 5.00 12.00
SJRWS Walter Sharpe 5.00 12.00

2008-09 UD Black Rookie Signed Jersey Pieces Dual

STATED PRINT RUN 10 SER.#'d SETS
UNPRICED GOLD PRINT RUN 5 SER.#'d SETS
UNPRICED WHITE PRINT RUN ONE SET
DJRAL R.Anderson/B.Lopez 20.00 40.00
DJRAM D.Arthur/O.Mayo 25.00 50.00
DJRAR B.Rush/D.Augustin 10.00 25.00
DJRBC M.Chalmers/M.Beasley 30.00 80.00
DJRBR M.Beasley/D.Rose 250.00 500.00
DJRDD C.-Roberts/J.Dorsey 10.00 25.00
DJRDH G.Hill/C.D-Roberts 20.00 40.00
DJRGB E.Gordon/J.Bayless 10.00 25.00
DJRGJ Jordan/Gordon 15.00 40.00
DJRGS J.Giddens/W.Sharpe 10.00 25.00
DJRGW S.Weems/J.Giddens 10.00 25.00
DJRHR R.Hibbert/B.Rush 12.00 30.00
DJRHS J.Hickson/W.Sharpe 10.00 25.00
DJRLA J.Alexander/K.Love 25.00 60.00
DJRLL R.Lopez/B.Lopez 15.00 30.00
DJRML R.Lopez/J.McGee 12.00 30.00
DJRRA Randolph/Alexander 20.00 40.00
DJRRH Randolph/Hickson 10.00 25.00
DJRSK K.Koufos/M.Speights 10.00 25.00
DJRTL K.Love/J.Thompson 25.00 60.00
DJRTS Thompson/Speights 10.00 25.00
DJRWG S.Weems/D.Greene 10.00 25.00
DJRWW R.Westbrook/D.White 30.00 80.00

2008-09 UD Black Team Logo Autographs

STATED PRINT RUN 21 TO 49 SER.#'d SETS
*GOLD: .6X TO 1.5X BASE HI
GOLD PRINT RUN 9 TO 20 SETS
UNPRICED WHITE PRINT RUN ONE SET
TLAH Al Horford/25 6.00 15.00
TLAJ Antawn Jamison/24 6.00 15.00
TLAT Al Thornton/21 6.00 15.00
TLBG Ben Gordon/25 10.00 25.00
TLBR Brandon Roy/25 25.00 60.00
TLCB Corey Brewer/25 6.00 15.00
TLCP Chris Paul/25 40.00 80.00
TLDC Daequan Cook/49 8.00 20.00
TLDH Dwight Howard/25 30.00 80.00
TLDL David Lee/25 6.00 15.00
TLJC Javaris Crittenton/24 6.00 15.00
TLJD Jared Dudley/25 6.00 15.00
TLJK Jason Kidd/25 25.00 60.00
TLJS Jason Smith/25 6.00 15.00
TLKG Kevin Garnett/25 50.00 120.00
TLLJ LeBron James/25 200.00 400.00
TLRA Ramon Sessions/25 6.00 15.00
TLRJ Richard Jefferson/25 6.00 15.00
TLRS Rodney Stuckey/25 10.00 25.00
TLSM J.R. Smith/25 10.00 25.00

2008-09 UD Black Trophy Patch Autographs

STATED PRINT RUN 5 TO 25 SER.#'d SETS
UNPRICED GOLD PRINT RUN ONE TO 6 SETS
UNPRICED WHITE PRINT RUN ONE SET
TPDR David Robinson/25 100.00 200.00
TPJO Michael Jordan/25 800.00 1200.00
TPKG Kevin Garnett/25 60.00 150.00
TPLB Larry Bird/25 60.00 150.00
TPMJ Magic Johnson/25 100.00 200.00
TPOR Oscar Robertson/25 125.00 250.00

2008-09 UD Black Veteran Signed Jersey Pieces

STATED PRINT RUN 5 TO 50 SER.#'d SETS
UNPRICED GOLD PRINT RUN 4 TO 15 SETS
UNPRICED WHITE PRINT RUN ONE SET
SPVAB Andrew Bynum/50 20.00 50.00
SPVAH Al Horford/50 8.00 20.00
SPVAM Alonzo Mourning/50 25.00 50.00
SPVAS Amare Stoudemire/50 10.00 25.00
SPVBE Marco Belinelli/50 8.00 20.00
SPVDH Dwight Howard/50 25.00 60.00
SPVGI Daniel Gibson/50 10.00 25.00
SPVJF Jordan Farmar/50 10.00 25.00
SPVJJ Jarrett Jack/50 8.00 20.00
SPVKB Kobe Bryant/50 150.00 300.00
SPVKD Kevin Durant/50 75.00 150.00
SPVKG Kevin Garnett/50 30.00 80.00
SPVLJ LeBron James/50 175.00 300.00
SPVMB Mike Bibby/50 10.00 25.00
SPVMC Mike Conley Jr./50 8.00 20.00
SPVPP Paul Pierce/50 20.00 50.00
SPVRF Randy Foye/50 8.00 20.00
SPVRJ Richard Jefferson/50 8.00 20.00
SPVSN Steve Nash/50 30.00 80.00
SPVTC Tyson Chandler/50 8.00 20.00
SPVYM Yao Ming/50 25.00 60.00

2008-09 UD Black Veteran Signed Jersey Pieces Dual

STATED PRINT RUN 10 SER.#'d SETS
DJVAP R.Allen/P.Pierce 125.00 250.00
DJVBG K.Garnett/K.Bryant 300.00 450.00
DJVBJ M.Bibby/J.Jack 25.00 50.00
DJVBP M.Bibby/C.Paul 40.00 80.00
DJVGJ R.Jefferson/R.Gay 15.00 40.00
DJVGS D.Gibson/R.Stuckey 15.00 40.00
DJVHC D.Howard/T.Chandler 30.00 60.00
DJVJD L.James/K.Durant 250.00 500.00
DJVNS A.Stoudemire/S.Nash 75.00 150.00
DJVPJ L.James/P.Pierce 200.00 350.00

2008-09 UD Black Veteran Signed Patch Pieces

STATED PRINT RUN 15 SER.#'d SETS
UNPRICED GOLD PRINT RUN 4 TO 12 SETS
UNPRICED WHITE PRINT RUN ONE SET
AB Andrew Bynum 12.50 30.00
DC Daequan Cook 12.50 30.00
DG Danny Granger 20.00 50.00
JF Jordan Farmar 15.00 40.00
KD Kevin Durant 100.00 200.00
KG Kevin Garnett 75.00 200.00
LJ LeBron James 300.00 500.00
MB Mike Bibby 15.00 40.00
PP Paul Pierce 40.00 80.00
RF Randy Foye 12.50 30.00
RJ Richard Jefferson 12.50 30.00
SN Steve Nash 50.00 120.00
TC Tyson Chandler 12.50 30.00
YM Yao Ming 50.00 120.00
AH2 Al Harrington 12.50 30.00

2013-14 UD Black

45 PRINT RUN 175 SER.#'d SETS
46-67 PRINT RUNS 199 SER.#'d SETS
68-72 PRINT RUNS 99 SER.#'d SETS
EXCHANGE DEADLINE 2/24/2016
1 Michael Jordan/175 6.00 15.00
2 LeBron James/175 6.00 15.00
3 Clyde Drexler/175 2.50 6.00
4 Julius Erving/175 3.00 8.00
5 Joe Smith/175 1.50 4.00
6 Antoine Walker/175 1.50 4.00
7 Jerry Lucas/175 2.00 5.00
8 Elvin Hayes/175 2.00 5.00
9 Tony Gwynn/175 2.00 5.00
10 Magic Johnson/175 5.00 12.00
11 Allan Houston/175 1.50 4.00
12 Dave Cowens/175 1.25 3.00
13 David Thompson/175 1.50 4.00
14 Jamal Mashburn/175 2.00 5.00
15 Danny Manning/175 1.50 4.00
16 John Havlicek/175 2.50 6.00
17 Larry Bird/175 5.00 12.00
18 Toni Kukoc/175 2.00 5.00
19 Tim Hardaway Sr./175 2.00 5.00
20 Anfernee Hardaway/175 5.00 12.00
21 Alonzo Mourning/175 2.50 6.00
22 Larry Johnson/175 2.50 6.00
23 David Robinson/175 3.00 8.00
24 Sam Perkins/175 1.25 3.00
25 Reggie Miller/175 2.00 5.00
26 Dennis Rodman/175 4.00 10.00
27 Isiah Thomas/175 2.00 5.00
28 Hakeem Olajuwon/175 2.50 6.00
29 Grant Hill/175 2.50 6.00
30 Allen Iverson/175 2.50 6.00
31 Bill Walton/175 2.00 5.00
32 Karl Malone/175 2.50 6.00
33 Dominique Wilkins/175 2.50 6.00
34 Cheryl Miller/175 2.00 5.00
35 Corliss Williamson/175 1.25 3.00
36 Kenny Anderson/175 1.50 4.00
37 Donyell Marshall/175 1.25 3.00
38 Glenn Robinson/175 1.50 4.00
39 Jason Kidd/175 2.00 5.00
40 Jay Williams/175 1.25 3.00
41 Glen Rice/175 1.50 4.00
42 Paul George/175 2.50 6.00
43 Keith Smart/175 2.00 5.00
44 Rajon Rondo/175 2.00 5.00
45 Chris Paul/175 2.50 6.00
46 Grant Jerrett AU/199 4.00 10.00
47 Sergey Karasev AU/199 EXCH 4.00 10.00
48 Allen Crabbe AU/199 5.00 12.00
49 Nemanja Nedovic AU/199 4.00 10.00
50 Peyton Siva AU/199 4.00 10.00
51 Andre Roberson AU/199 4.00 10.00
52 Isaiah Canaan AU/199 4.00 10.00
53 Lorenzo Brown AU/199 4.00 10.00
54 Erick Green AU/199 5.00 12.00
55 Jamaal Franklin AU/199 4.00 10.00
56 Tony Snell AU/199 5.00 12.00
57 Deshaun Thomas AU/199 4.00 10.00
58 Reggie Bullock AU/199 5.00 12.00
59 Pierre Jackson AU/199 4.00 10.00
60 Ryan Kelly AU/199 4.00 10.00
61 R.Gobert AU/199 EXCH 10.00 25.00
62 Archie Goodwin AU/199 5.00 12.00
63 G.Antetokounmpo AU/199 50.00 120.00
64 Livio Jean-Charles AU/199 4.00 10.00
65 Mike Muscala AU/199 6.00 15.00
67 Solomon Hill AU/199 4.00 10.00
68 Shane Larkin AU/99 6.00 15.00
69 Lucas Nogueira AU/99 6.00 15.00
70 Skylar Diggins AU/99 10.00 25.00
71 Tim Hardaway Jr. AU/99 10.00 25.00
72 Mason Plumlee AU/99 10.00 25.00
73 D.Schroeder AU/99 EXCH 12.00 30.00

2013-14 UD Black Gold Spectrum

1-44 PRINT RUN 1 SER.#'d SET
NO 1-44 PRICING DUE TO SCARCITY
*GOLD 46-67: .75X TO 2X BASIC
*GOLD 68-73: .75X TO 2X BASIC
46-73 PRINT RUN 25 SER.#'d SETS
EXCHANGE DEADLINE 2/24/2016
50 Peyton Siva/25 10.00 25.00

2013-14 UD Black Arena Art

PRINT RUNS B/WN 23-65 COPIES PER
EXCHANGE DEADLINE 2/24/2016
AAC A.C. Green/65 6.00 15.00
AAE Alex English/65 5.00 12.00
AAH Allan Houston/65 5.00 12.00
ABD Brad Daugherty/65 8.00 20.00
ABL Bill Laimbeer/65 12.00 30.00
ABM Bob McAdoo/65 5.00 12.00
ABR Bryant Reeves/65 6.00 15.00
ABW Bill Walton/65 6.00 15.00
ACL Christian Laettner/65 12.00 30.00
ADM Danny Manning/65 12.00 30.00
ADS Detlef Schrempf/65 10.00 25.00
ADW D.Wilkins/65 EXCH 10.00 25.00
AGH Grant Hill/65 30.00 60.00
AHI Grant Hill/65 25.00 60.00
AHO Hakeem Olajuwon/65 20.00 50.00
AIT Isiah Thomas/65 10.00 25.00
AJH Jeff Hornacek/65 5.00 12.00
AJO Michael Jordan/23 350.00 450.00
AJW Jay Williams/65 12.00 30.00
AKA Kenny Anderson/65 10.00 25.00
AKG Kendall Gill/65 10.00 25.00
AKM Karl Malone/30 50.00 100.00
AKS Keith Smart/65 10.00 25.00
ALA Larry Johnson/65 12.00 30.00
ALB Larry Bird/30 60.00 150.00
ALS Lonnie Shelton/65 4.00 10.00
AMI Michael Jordan/23 350.00 500.00
AMJ Michael Jordan/23 350.00 500.00
AMR M.Ray Richardson/65 10.00 25.00
ANV Nick Van Exel/65 10.00 25.00
APG Paul George/65 20.00 50.00
ARH Robert Horry/65 10.00 25.00
ASB Shawn Bradley/65 4.00 10.00
ASE Sean Elliott/65 20.00 50.00
ASN Swen Nater/65 10.00 25.00

2013-14 UD Black Chalk Signatures

PRINT RUNS B/WN 23-40 COPIES PER
EXCHANGE DEADLINE 2/24/2016
CSAH Anfernee Hardaway/40 20.00 50.00
CSAW Antoine Walker/40 12.00 30.00
CSCM Cheryl Miller/40 6.00 15.00
CSDM Danny Manning/40 10.00 25.00
CSDR David Robinson/25 20.00 50.00
CSDT David Thompson/40 10.00 25.00
CSGH Grant Hill/40 12.00 30.00
CSHM Harold Miner/40
CSHO Hakeem Olajuwon/40 20.00 50.00
CSJO Magic Johnson/25 EXCH 15.00 40.00
CSJW Jay Williams/40 4.00 10.00
CSKA Kenny Anderson/40 5.00 12.00
CSKM Karl Malone/25 25.00 60.00
CSLB Larry Bird/25 50.00 100.00
CSLJ LeBron James/40 EXCH 150.00 250.00
CSMJ Michael Jordan/23 350.00 450.00
CSRR Rajon Rondo/40

2013-14 UD Black Jordan Brand Classic Dual Autographs

PRINT RUNS B/WN 10-99 COPIES PER
NO PRICING ON QTY 13 OR LESS
EXCHANGE DEADLINE 2/24/2016
JBC21 J.Sullinger/A.Bradley/40 15.00 40.00
JBC24 R.Sidney/R.White/40 8.00 20.00
JBC25 D.Lamb/R.Sidney/40 8.00 20.00
JBC27 P.Jones/Q.Miller/40 6.00 15.00
JBC28 K.Irving/A.Rivers/40 25.00 60.00
JBC29 B.Knight/T.Jones/35 15.00 40.00
JBC210 J.Holiday/M.Teague/45 8.00 20.00
JBC212 H.Barnes/E.Davis/35 15.00 40.00
JBC213 H.Barnes/J.Sullinger/40 20.00 50.00
JBC215 P.Jones/T.Jones/40 10.00 25.00
JBC216 R.Sidney/T.Wroten/99 8.00 20.00
JBC218 D.Lamb/T.Griffin/20
JBC219 B.Knight/J.Holiday/40 10.00 25.00
JBC220 M.Gilchrist/Q.Miller/30 10.00 25.00
JBC221 B.Beal/X.Henry/40 12.00 30.00
JBC222 D.Waiters/A.Bradley/40 15.00 40.00

2013-14 UD Black Jordan Brand Classic Triple Autographs

PRINT RUNS B/WN 10-99 COPIES PER
NO PRICING ON QTY 15 OR LESS
EXCHANGE DEADLINE 2/24/2016
JBC35 Bradley/White/Griffin/90 5.00 12.00
JBC36 Holiday/White/Griffin/50 6.00 15.00
JBC39 Noel/Bennett/Muhammad/99 30.00 60.00

2013-14 UD Black Legendary Lustrous Signatures

STATED PRINT RUN 25 SER.#'d SETS
EXCHANGE DEADLINE 2/24/2016
LLAH Anfernee Hardaway 30.00 60.00
LLAM Alonzo Mourning 20.00 50.00
LLBR Bill Russell
LLDR David Robinson 20.00 50.00
LLGH Grant Hill 20.00 50.00
LLJE Julius Erving 30.00 60.00
LLJO Magic Johnson EXCH 40.00 100.00
LLKM Karl Malone 12.00 30.00
LLLB Larry Bird 25.00 60.00
LLLJ LeBron James
LLMI Michael Jordan 250.00 400.00
LLMJ Michael Jordan 250.00 400.00
LLTG Tony Gwynn 30.00 60.00

2013-14 UD Black Logo Signatures

STATED PRINT RUN 40 SER.#'d SETS
EXCHANGE DEADLINE 2/24/2016
LSAE Alex English 6.00 15.00
LSAG A.C. Green 10.00 25.00
LSAH Anfernee Hardaway 30.00 60.00
LSAL Allan Houston 6.00 15.00
LSAM Alonzo Mourning 12.00 30.00
LSAW Antoine Walker 10.00 25.00
LSBD Brad Daugherty 10.00 25.00
LSBR Bryant Reeves 10.00 25.00
LSBU Buck Williams 10.00 25.00
LSBW Bill Walton 10.00 25.00
LSCL Christian Laettner 12.00 30.00
LSCM Cheryl Miller 8.00 20.00
LSCO Dave Cowens 5.00 12.00
LSCW Corliss Williamson 10.00 25.00
LSDA Danny Manning 12.00 30.00

LSDM Donyell Marshall 5.00 12.00
LSDS Detlef Schrempf 12.00 30.00
LSDT David Thompson 12.00 30.00
LSDW Dominique Wilkins EXCH 20.00 50.00
LSEH Elvin Hayes
LSGH Grant Hill 40.00 100.00
LSGL Glenn Robinson EXCH 12.00 30.00
LSGR Glen Rice 12.00 30.00
LSHM Harold Miner 5.00 12.00
LSHO Hakeem Olajuwon 10.00 25.00
LSIT Isiah Thomas 12.00 30.00
LSJA Mark A. Jackson 6.00 15.00
LSJE Julius Erving 40.00 80.00
LSJH Jeff Hornacek 15.00 40.00
LSJL Jerry Lucas 15.00 40.00
LSJM Jamal Mashburn 12.00 30.00
LSJO Larry Johnson 12.00 30.00
LSJW Jay Williams 10.00 25.00
LSKA Kenny Anderson 6.00 15.00
LSKK Kerry Kittles 10.00 25.00
LSKM Karl Malone 20.00 50.00
LSKS Keith Smart 8.00 20.00
LSLB Larry Bird 60.00 120.00
LSLJ LeBron James EXCH 150.00 250.00
LSLS Lonnie Shelton 5.00 12.00
LSMB Muggsy Bogues 8.00 20.00
LSMC Michael Cooper 6.00 15.00
LSME Ron Mercer
LSMJ Michael Jordan 150.00 300.00
LSPG Paul George 20.00 50.00
LSRO David Robinson 20.00 50.00
LSRR Rajon Rondo 15.00 40.00
LSRS Rod Strickland 5.00 12.00
LSRT Reggie Theus 6.00 15.00
LSRU Bill Russell 60.00 120.00
LSSB Shawn Bradley 5.00 12.00
LSSE Sean Elliott 15.00 40.00
LSTB Terrell Brandon 5.00 12.00
LSTG Tony Gwynn 20.00 50.00
LSTH Tim Hardaway 8.00 20.00
LSVN Vinny Del Negro 5.00 12.00

2013-14 UD Black Old School Signatures

INT RUNS B/WN 23-75 COPIES PER
EXCHANGE DEADLINE 2/24/2016
OSAE Alex English/75 5.00 12.00
OSAG A.C. Green/75 6.00 15.00
OSAM Alonzo Mourning/75 10.00 25.00
OSCC Calbert Cheaney/75 10.00 25.00
OSCW Corliss Williamson/75 4.00 10.00
OSDM Danny Manning/75 5.00 12.00
OSDT David Thompson/75 8.00 20.00
OSEH Elvin Hayes/75 10.00 25.00
OSHA Anfernee Hardaway/75 20.00 50.00
OSHO Hakeem Olajuwon/75 15.00 40.00
OSIT Isiah Thomas/75
OSJE Julius Erving/25 40.00 80.00
OSJL Jerry Lucas/75 6.00 15.00
OSJO Magic Johnson/25 EXCH 40.00 80.00
OSKK Kerry Kittles/75 4.00 10.00
OSKS Keith Smart/75 6.00 15.00
OSLB Larry Bird/25 40.00 80.00
OSLJ LeBron James/75 EXCH 125.00 250.00
OSMJ Michael Jordan/23
OSRI Glen Rice/75 5.00 12.00
OSRU Bill Russell/25 50.00 120.00
OSTG Tony Gwynn/75 20.00 50.00

2013-14 UD Black Scenes Booklet Signatures

PRINT RUNS B/WN 23-35 COPIES PER
EXCHANGE DEADLINE 2/24/2016
SCAH Anfernee Hardaway/35 20.00 50.00
SCAM Alonzo Mourning/35 20.00 50.00
SCAW Antoine Walker/35 20.00 50.00
SCCC Calbert Cheaney/35 25.00 60.00
SCGH Grant Hill/35 25.00 60.00
SCGR Glenn Robinson/35 EXCH 15.00 40.00
SCHA Hakeem Olajuwon/35 25.00 60.00
SCIT Isiah Thomas/35 20.00 50.00
SCJO Michael Jordan/35 350.00 500.00
SCKG Kendall Gill/35 20.00 50.00
SCLB Larry Bird/35
SCLJ LeBron James/35 EXCH 175.00 350.00
SCMA Magic Johnson/35 EXCH 40.00 100.00
SCMI Michael Jordan/23 350.00 500.00
SCMJ Michael Jordan/23 350.00 500.00
SCRR Rajon Rondo/35 20.00 50.00
SCTH Tim Hardaway/35 10.00 25.00

2013-14 UD Black Signatures

PRINT RUNS B/WN 23-75 COPIES PER
EXCHANGE DEADLINE 2/24/2016
SAE Alex English/75 5.00 12.00
SAG A.C. Green/75 10.00 25.00
SAH Allan Houston/75 8.00 20.00
SAI Allen Iverson/25 60.00 120.00
SAW Antoine Walker/75 8.00 20.00
SBR Bill Russell/25 50.00 120.00
SBW Bill Walton/75 6.00 15.00
SCC Calbert Cheaney/75 10.00 25.00
SCW Corliss Williamson/75 15.00 40.00
SDR David Robinson/75 20.00 50.00
SEH Elvin Hayes/75 6.00 15.00
SGH Grant Hill/75 20.00 50.00
SGR Glenn Robinson/75 EXCH 10.00 25.00
SHA Anfernee Hardaway/75 20.00 50.00
SJA LeBron James/75 EXCH 125.00 250.00
SJE Julius Erving/75 30.00 80.00
SJL Jerry Lucas/75 10.00 25.00
SJM Jamal Mashburn/75 10.00 25.00
SJO Michael Jordan/23 350.00 600.00
SJW Jay Williams/75 4.00 10.00
SKA Kenny Anderson/75 5.00 12.00
SKK Kerry Kittles/75 4.00 10.00
SKM Karl Malone/75 20.00 50.00
SKS Keith Smart/75 6.00 15.00
SLB Larry Bird/25 50.00 100.00
SLJ Larry Johnson/75 8.00 20.00
SMA Mark A. Jackson/75 5.00 12.00
SMJ Magic Johnson/75 EXCH 40.00 80.00
SOB Otis Birdsong/75 5.00 12.00
SPG Paul George/75 25.00 60.00
SRR Rajon Rondo/75 12.00 30.00
STC Toni Kukoc/75 8.00 20.00
STG Tony Gwynn/75 20.00 50.00

2014 UD Black Autographs

STATED PRINT RUN 10-65
UNPRICED PRINT RUN 10
27 Michael Jordan/25 250.00 400.00

2014 UD Black Pride of a Nation Patches Autographs

STATED PRINT RUN 10-35
UNPRICED PRINT RUN 10

1998-99 UD Choice Preview

The 1998-99 Upper Deck UD Choice Preview set was issued in one series totalling 55 cards. The 6-card packs retail for $.88 each. The set is skip-numbered and features the word "Preview" in gold foil letters across the front of the card. The set previews the upcoming 1998-99 Upper Deck UD Choice release.
COMPLETE SET (55) 3.00 8.00
1 Dikembe Mutombo .10 .25
3 Mookie Blaylock .05 .15
7 Ron Mercer .07 .20
9 Walter McCarty .05 .15
13 Anthony Mason .05 .15
14 Glen Rice .10 .25
18 Toni Kukoc .10 .25
23 Michael Jordan .75 2.00
26 Zydrunas Ilgauskas .10 .25
27 Cedric Henderson .05 .15
29 Michael Finley .10 .25
32 Hubert Davis .05 .15
34 Bobby Jackson .05 .15
37 Danny Fortson .05 .15
41 Grant Hill .15 .40
43 Jerome Williams .05 .15
45 Erick Dampier .05 .15
48 Donyell Marshall .05 .15
50 Charles Barkley .15 .40
51 Hakeem Olajuwon .12 .30
56 Reggie Miller .12 .30
60 Chris Mullin .10 .25
64 Eric Piatkowski .07 .20
65 Maurice Taylor .05 .15
68 Shaquille O'Neal .25 .60
69 Kobe Bryant .40 1.00
74 Alonzo Mourning .12 .30
75 Tim Hardaway .10 .25
79 Ray Allen .12 .30
80 Terrell Brandon .05 .15
84 Stephon Marbury .12 .30
85 Kevin Garnett .15 .40
89 Keith Van Horn .10 .25
90 Sam Cassell .07 .20
95 Patrick Ewing .12 .30
97 John Starks .07 .20
100 Anfernee Hardaway .15 .40
101 Nick Anderson .05 .15
105 Allen Iverson .20 .50
110 Jason Kidd .15 .40
117 Isaiah Rider .07 .20
118 Rasheed Wallace .10 .25
121 Corliss Williamson .05 .15
123 Billy Owens .05 .15
126 Tim Duncan .20 .50
127 Sean Elliott .10 .25
131 Vin Baker .07 .20
135 Gary Payton .10 .25
137 Chauncey Billups .12 .30
142 John Stockton .12 .30
143 Karl Malone .12 .30
148 Bryant Reeves .05 .15
149 Shareef Abdur-Rahim .10 .25
152 Harvey Grant .05 .15
153 Juwan Howard .07 .20

1998-99 UD Choice Preview Michael Jordan NBA Finals Shots

Inserted one per special retail pack or tin, this 10-card set features memorable shots from Michael Jordan during the 1998 NBA Finals. The card fronts feature a red and black background with "Michael Jordan" in gold foil. The card backs remember a moment from the NBA Finals.
COMMON CARD (1-10) 2.00 5.00

1998-99 UD Choice

e 1998-99 Upper Deck UD Choice Series One was issued with a total of 200 cards. Each pack contained 12 cards with a suggested retail price of $1.29. The fronts feature a color action photo surrounded by a white border. The series two release was cancelled due to the NBA lockout.
COMPLETE SET (200) 8.00 20.00
1 Dikembe Mutombo .12 .30
2 Alan Henderson .07 .20
3 Mookie Blaylock .07 .20
4 Ed Gray .07 .20
5 Eldridge Recasner .07 .20
6 Kenny Anderson .10 .25
7 Ron Mercer .10 .25
8 Dana Barros .07 .20
9 Walter McCarty .07 .20
10 Travis Knight .07 .20
11 Andrew DeClercq .07 .20
12 David Wesley .07 .20
13 Anthony Mason .07 .20
14 Glen Rice .12 .30
15 J.R. Reid .07 .20
16 Bobby Phills .07 .20
17 Dell Curry .07 .20
18 Toni Kukoc .12 .30
19 Randy Brown .07 .20
20 Ron Harper .10 .25
21 Keith Booth .07 .20
22 Scott Burrell .07 .20
23 Michael Jordan 1.00 2.50
24 Derek Anderson .07 .20
25 Brevin Knight .07 .20
26 Zydrunas Ilgauskas .12 .30
27 Cedric Henderson .07 .20
28 Vitaly Potapenko .07 .20
29 Michael Finley .12 .30
30 Erick Strickland .07 .20
31 Shawn Bradley .07 .20
32 Hubert Davis .07 .20
33 Khalid Reeves .07 .20
34 Bobby Jackson .07 .20
35 Tony Battie .10 .25
36 Bryant Stith .07 .20
37 Danny Fortson .07 .20
38 Dean Garrett .07 .20
39 Eric Williams .07 .20
40 Brian Williams .07 .20
41 Grant Hill .20 .50
42 Lindsey Hunter .07 .20
43 Jerome Williams .07 .20
44 Eric Montross .07 .20
45 Erick Dampier .07 .20
46 Muggsy Bogues .10 .25
47 Tony Delk .07 .20
48 Donyell Marshall .07 .20
49 Bimbo Coles .07 .20
50 Charles Barkley .20 .50
51 Hakeem Olajuwon .15 .40
52 Brent Price .07 .20
53 Mario Elie .07 .20
54 Rodrick Rhodes .07 .20
55 Kevin Willis .07 .20
56 Reggie Miller .15 .40
57 Jalen Rose .10 .25
58 Mark Jackson .10 .25
59 Dale Davis .07 .20
60 Chris Mullin .12 .30
61 Derrick McKey .07 .20
62 Lorenzen Wright .07 .20
63 Rodney Rogers .07 .20
64 Eric Piatkowski .10 .25
65 Maurice Taylor .07 .20
66 Isaac Austin .07 .20
67 Corie Blount .07 .20
68 Shaquille O'Neal .30 .75
69 Kobe Bryant .50 1.25
70 Robert Horry .10 .25
71 Sean Rooks .07 .20
72 Derek Fisher .12 .30
73 P.J. Brown .07 .20
74 Alonzo Mourning .15 .40
75 Tim Hardaway .12 .30
76 Voshon Lenard .07 .20
77 Dan Majerle .12 .30
78 Ervin Johnson .07 .20
79 Ray Allen .15 .40
80 Terrell Brandon .07 .20
81 Tyrone Hill .07 .20
82 Elliot Perry .07 .20
83 Anthony Peeler .07 .20
84 Stephon Marbury .15 .40
85 Kevin Garnett .20 .50
86 Paul Grant .07 .20
87 Chris Carr .07 .20
88 Micheal Williams UER .07 .20
89 Keith Van Horn .12 .30
90 Sam Cassell .10 .25
91 Kendall Gill .07 .20
92 Chris Gatling .07 .20
93 Kerry Kittles .07 .20
94 Allan Houston .10 .25
95 Patrick Ewing UER .15 .40
96 Charles Oakley .10 .25
97 John Starks .10 .25
98 Charlie Ward .07 .20
99 Chris Mills .07 .20
100 Anfernee Hardaway .20 .50
101 Nick Anderson .07 .20
102 Mark Price .12 .30
103 Horace Grant .10 .25
104 David Benoit .07 .20
105 Allen Iverson .25 .60
106 Joe Smith .10 .25
107 Tim Thomas .12 .30
108 Brian Shaw .07 .20
109 Aaron McKie .07 .20
110 Jason Kidd .20 .50
111 Danny Manning .10 .25
112 Steve Nash .20 .50
113 Rex Chapman .07 .20
114 Dennis Scott .07 .20
115 Antonio McDyess .10 .25
116 Damon Stoudamire .10 .25
117 Isaiah Rider .10 .25
118 Rasheed Wallace .12 .30
119 Kelvin Cato .07 .20
120 Jermaine O'Neal .12 .30
121 Corliss Williamson .07 .20
122 Olden Polynice .07 .20
123 Billy Owens .07 .20
124 Lawrence Funderburke .07 .20
125 Anthony Johnson .07 .20
126 Tim Duncan .25 .60
127 Sean Elliott .12 .30
128 Avery Johnson .10 .25
129 Vinny Del Negro .07 .20
130 Monty Williams .07 .20
131 Vin Baker .10 .25
132 Hersey Hawkins .07 .20
133 Nate McMillan .07 .20
134 Detlef Schrempf .12 .30
135 Gary Payton .12 .30
136 Jim McIlvaine .07 .20
137 Chauncey Billups .15 .40
138 Doug Christie .07 .20
139 John Wallace .07 .20
140 Tracy McGrady .20 .50
141 Dee Brown .07 .20
142 John Stockton .15 .40
143 Karl Malone .15 .40
144 Shandon Anderson .07 .20
145 Jacque Vaughn .07 .20
146 Bryon Russell .07 .20
147 Lee Mayberry .07 .20
148 Bryant Reeves .07 .20
149 Shareef Abdur-Rahim .12 .30
150 Michael Smith .07 .20
151 Pete Chilcutt .07 .20
152 Harvey Grant .07 .20
153 Juwan Howard .10 .25
154 Calbert Cheaney .07 .20
155 Tracy Murray .07 .20
156 Dikembe Mutombo FS .12 .30
157 Antoine Walker FS .12 .30
158 Glen Rice FS .12 .30
159 Michael Jordan FS 1.00 2.50
160 Wesley Person FS .07 .20
161 Shawn Bradley FS .07 .20
162 Dean Garrett FS .07 .20
163 Jerry Stackhouse FS .12 .30
164 Donyell Marshall FS .07 .20
165 Hakeem Olajuwon FS .15 .40
166 Chris Mullin FS .12 .30
167 Isaac Austin FS .07 .20
168 Shaquille O'Neal FS .30 .75
169 Tim Hardaway FS .12 .30
170 Glenn Robinson FS .10 .25
171 Kevin Garnett FS .20 .50
172 Keith Van Horn FS .12 .30
173 Larry Johnson FS .12 .30
174 Horace Grant FS .10 .25
175 Derrick Coleman FS .10 .25
176 Steve Nash FS .20 .50
177 Arvydas Sabonis FS UER .10 .25
178 Corliss Williamson FS .07 .20
179 David Robinson FS .20 .50
180 Vin Baker FS .10 .25
181 Marcus Camby FS .10 .25
182 John Stockton FS .15 .40
183 Antonio Daniels FS .07 .20
184 Rod Strickland FS .07 .20
185 Michael Jordan FS 1.00 2.50
186 Kobe Bryant YIR .50 1.25
187 Clyde Drexler YIR .15 .40
188 Gary Payton YIR .12 .30
189 Michael Jordan YIR 1.00 2.50
190 D.Robinson/T.Duncan YIR .25 .60
191 Attendance Record YIR .07 .20
192 Karl Malone YIR .15 .40
193 Dikembe Mutombo YIR .12 .30
194 New Jersey Nets YIR .12 .30
195 Ray Allen YIR .15 .40
196 Michael Jordan YIR 1.00 2.50
197 Los Angeles Lakers YIR .50 1.25
198 Michael Jordan YIR 1.00 2.50
199 Michael Jordan CL .40 1.00
200 Michael Jordan CL .40 1.00

1998-99 UD Choice Reserve

*STARS: 3X TO 8X BASE CARD HI
STATED ODDS 1:6 HOB/RET

1998-99 UD Choice Premium Choice Reserve

*STARS: 40X TO 100X BASE CARD HI
STATED PRINT RUN 100 SERIAL #'d SETS
23 Michael Jordan 250.00 350.00
69 Kobe Bryant 75.00 200.00

1998-99 UD Choice Mini Bobbing Heads

ndomly inserted into packs at a rate of one in four, this 30-card set features cards that can be popped-up and displayed similar to a "bobbing" head.
COMPLETE SET (30) 4.00 10.00
STATED ODDS 1:4 HOB/RET
1 Dikembe Mutombo .15 .40
2 Antoine Walker .15 .40
3 Anthony Mason .10 .25
4 Toni Kukoc .15 .40
5 Shawn Kemp .15 .40
6 Shawn Bradley .10 .25
7 Danny Fortson .10 .25
8 Brian Williams .10 .25
9 Muggsy Bogues .12 .30
10 Charles Barkley .25 .60
11 Mark Jackson .12 .30
12 Rodney Rogers .10 .25
13 Kobe Bryant .60 1.50
14 Tim Hardaway .15 .40
15 Ray Allen .20 .50
16 Kevin Garnett .25 .60
17 Sam Cassell .12 .30
18 John Starks .12 .30
19 Anfernee Hardaway .25 .60
20 Allen Iverson .30 .75
21 Danny Manning .12 .30
22 Rasheed Wallace .15 .40
23 Chris Webber .15 .40
24 David Robinson .25 .60
25 Gary Payton .15 .40
26 Marcus Camby .12 .30
27 John Stockton .20 .50
28 Bryant Reeves .10 .25
29 Juwan Howard .12 .30
30 Michael Jordan 1.25 3.00

1998-99 UD Choice StarQuest Blue

Randomly inserted into packs at a rate of one per pack, this 30-card set features some of the best players in the NBA. The card front features blue borders with a photo of the player in the middle. The card backs feature one star to denote the first tier of the insert. Card backs are also numbered with a "SQ" prefix.
STATED ODDS 1:1 HOB/RET
*GREEN STARS: 1.25X TO 3X HI COLUMN
GREEN: STATED ODDS 1:8 H/R
*RED STARS: 3X TO 8X HI COLUMN
RED: STATED ODDS 1:23 H/R
SQ1 Steve Smith .15 .40
SQ2 Kenny Anderson .15 .40
SQ3 Glen Rice .20 .50
SQ4 Toni Kukoc .20 .50
SQ5 Shawn Kemp .20 .50
SQ6 Michael Finley .20 .50
SQ7 Bobby Jackson .12 .30
SQ8 Grant Hill .30 .75
SQ9 Donyell Marshall .12 .30
SQ10 Hakeem Olajuwon .25 .60
SQ11 Reggie Miller .25 .60
SQ12 Maurice Taylor .12 .30
SQ13 Kobe Bryant .75 2.00
SQ14 Alonzo Mourning .25 .60
SQ15 Terrell Brandon .12 .30
SQ16 Stephon Marbury .25 .60
SQ17 Keith Van Horn .20 .50
SQ18 Patrick Ewing .25 .60
SQ19 Anfernee Hardaway .30 .75
SQ20 Allen Iverson .40 1.00
SQ21 Jason Kidd .30 .75
SQ22 Damon Stoudamire .15 .40
SQ23 Corliss Williamson .12 .30
SQ24 Tim Duncan .40 1.00
SQ25 Gary Payton .20 .50
SQ26 Chauncey Billups .25 .60
SQ27 Karl Malone .25 .60
SQ28 Shareef Abdur-Rahim .20 .50
SQ29 Juwan Howard .15 .40
SQ30 Michael Jordan 1.50 4.00

1998-99 UD Choice StarQuest Gold

*STARS: 60X TO 150X BASE INSERT
STATED PRINT RUN 100 SERIAL #'d SETS
SQ8 Grant Hill 100.00 200.00
SQ13 Kobe Bryant 250.00 500.00
SQ19 Anfernee Hardaway 100.00 200.00
SQ30 Michael Jordan 1000.00 2000.00

2002-03 UD Glass

Released in April 2003, UD Glass consists of 150 cards and is divided up as follows: Cards 1-90 feature veteran player base cards, 91-110 are Clear Winner subset cards printed on Upper Deck's Plexi-Glass card stock (1/8" thick clear plastic) inserted at 1:15 packs, 111-120 are also printed on the Plexi-Glass but feature rookies and are sequentially numbered to 250, 121-130 on glass with rookies and sequentially numbered to 500, and 131-150 on glass with rookies and sequentially numbered to 900. Every glass card's face is covered with a masking tape like peel so cards are priced in out-of-pack unpeeled condition. Peeled Glass cards sell for up to 25% less than unpeeled. UD Glass boxes also had one Magnifying Jumbo Glass box-topper. Packaging was three mini-boxes per box which contained eight packs of five cards and packs carried a suggested retail price of $5.99.
COMP.SET w/o SP's (90) 15.00 40.00
91-110 CW STATED ODDS 1:15
111-120 PRINT RUN 250 SERIAL #'d SETS
121-130 PRINT RUN 500 SERIAL #'d SETS
131-150 PRINT RUN 900 SERIAL #'d SETS
**91-150 PRINTED ON GLASS
1 Shareef Abdur-Rahim .30 .75
2 Glenn Robinson .30 .75
3 Jason Terry .30 .75
4 Paul Pierce .40 1.00
5 Antoine Walker .30 .75
6 Vin Baker .30 .75
7 Jalen Rose .30 .75
8 Eddy Curry .25 .60
9 Tyson Chandler .40 1.00
10 Darius Miles .25 .60
11 Ricky Davis .30 .75
12 Zydrunas Ilgauskas .30 .75
13 Dirk Nowitzki .60 1.50
14 Michael Finley .40 1.00
15 Steve Nash .50 1.25
16 Raef LaFrentz .25 .60
17 Rodney White .25 .60
18 Marcus Camby .30 .75
19 Juwan Howard .30 .75
20 Richard Hamilton .30 .75
21 Ben Wallace .30 .75
22 Chauncey Billups .40 1.00
23 Jason Richardson .40 1.00
24 Antawn Jamison .40 1.00
25 Steve Francis .30 .75
26 Cuttino Mobley .25 .60
27 Eddie Griffin .25 .60
28 Jermaine O'Neal .30 .75
29 Reggie Miller .40 1.00
30 Jamaal Tinsley .25 .60
31 Andre Miller .30 .75
32 Elton Brand .40 1.00
33 Quentin Richardson .30 .75
34 Kobe Bryant 1.50 4.00
35 Shaquille O'Neal 1.00 2.50
36 Robert Horry .30 .75
37 Pau Gasol .50 1.25
38 Shane Battier .40 1.00
39 Jason Williams .30 .75
40 Eddie Jones .30 .75
41 Brian Grant .25 .60
42 Malik Allen .25 .60
43 Ray Allen .40 1.00
44 Tim Thomas .25 .60
45 Sam Cassell .30 .75
46 Kevin Garnett .60 1.50
47 Wally Szczerbiak .30 .75
48 Troy Hudson .25 .60
49 Loren Woods .25 .60
50 Jason Kidd .60 1.50
51 Richard Jefferson .40 1.00
52 Kenyon Martin .30 .75
53 Baron Davis .30 .75
54 Jamal Mashburn .30 .75
55 David Wesley .25 .60
56 P.J. Brown .25 .60
57 Allan Houston .30 .75
58 Kurt Thomas .25 .60
59 Latrell Sprewell .30 .75
60 Tracy McGrady .60 1.50
61 Mike Miller .30 .75
62 Grant Hill .50 1.25
63 Allen Iverson .60 1.50
64 Keith Van Horn .30 .75
65 Aaron McKie .25 .60
66 Stephon Marbury .30 .75
67 Shawn Marion .30 .75
68 Anfernee Hardaway .60 1.50
69 Rasheed Wallace .40 1.00
70 Damon Stoudamire .30 .75
71 Bonzi Wells .25 .60
72 Chris Webber .40 1.00
73 Mike Bibby .40 1.00
74 Peja Stojakovic .40 1.00
75 Hedo Turkoglu .30 .75
76 Tim Duncan .75 2.00
77 David Robinson .60 1.50
78 Tony Parker .50 1.25
79 Gary Payton .40 1.00
80 Rashard Lewis .40 1.00
81 Desmond Mason .30 .75
82 Vince Carter .60 1.50
83 Antonio Davis .25 .60
84 Morris Peterson .25 .60
85 John Stockton .50 1.25
86 Karl Malone .50 1.25
87 Andrei Kirilenko .40 1.00
88 Jerry Stackhouse .30 .75
89 Larry Hughes .30 .75
90 Michael Jordan 3.00 8.00
91 Kobe Bryant CW 10.00 25.00
92 Paul Pierce CW 2.50 6.00
93 Chris Webber CW 2.50 6.00
94 Vince Carter CW 4.00 10.00
95 Tracy McGrady CW 4.00 10.00
96 Allen Iverson CW 4.00 10.00
97 Pau Gasol CW 3.00 8.00
98 Steve Francis CW 2.00 5.00
99 Jason Kidd CW 4.00 10.00
100 Dirk Nowitzki CW 4.00 10.00
101 Antoine Walker CW 2.00 5.00
102 Jason Richardson CW 2.50 6.00
103 Baron Davis CW 2.00 5.00
104 Elton Brand CW 2.50 6.00
105 Stephon Marbury CW 2.00 5.00
106 Ray Allen CW 2.50 6.00
107 Shaquille O'Neal CW 6.00 15.00
108 Kevin Garnett CW 4.00 10.00
109 Tim Duncan CW 5.00 12.00
110 Mike Bibby CW 2.50 6.00
111 Jay Williams RC 6.00 15.00
112 Yao Ming RC 12.00 30.00
113 Mike Dunleavy RC 6.00 15.00
114 Drew Gooden RC 6.00 15.00
115 Nikoloz Tskitishvili RC 4.00 10.00
116 DaJuan Wagner RC 5.00 12.00
117 Nene Hilario RC 6.00 15.00
118 Amare Stoudemire RC 8.00 20.00
119 Caron Butler RC 6.00 15.00
120 Manu Ginobili RC 15.00 40.00
121 Juaquin Hawkins RC 2.50 6.00
122 Kareem Rush RC 3.00 8.00
123 Jiri Welsch RC 3.00 8.00
124 Chris Wilcox RC 3.00 8.00
125 Tayshaun Prince RC 5.00 12.00
126 Qyntel Woods RC 3.00 8.00
127 Jared Jeffries RC 3.00 8.00
128 Gordan Giricek RC 4.00 10.00
129 Ryan Humphrey RC 3.00 8.00
130 Marko Jaric 4.00 10.00
131 Casey Jacobsen RC 2.00 5.00
132 Dan Dickau RC 2.00 5.00
133 Juan Dixon RC 2.50 6.00
134 Melvin Ely RC 2.00 5.00
135 Fred Jones RC 2.00 5.00
136 John Salmons RC 2.50 6.00
137 Marcus Haislip RC 2.00 5.00
138 Carlos Boozer RC 2.50 6.00
139 Chris Jefferies RC 1.50 4.00
140 Smush Parker RC 2.50 6.00
141 Vincent Yarbrough RC 1.50 4.00
142 Pat Burke RC 1.50 4.00
143 Lonny Baxter RC 1.50 4.00
144 Bostjan Nachbar RC 2.00 5.00
145 Rasual Butler RC 2.50 6.00
146 Ronald Murray RC 2.50 6.00
147 J.R. Bremer RC 1.50 4.00
148 Reggie Evans RC 2.50 6.00
149 Sam Clancy RC 2.00 5.00
150 Tamar Slay RC 1.50 4.00
NNO Kobe Bryant AF PROMO 4.00 10.00

2002-03 UD Glass UD Promos

*PROMOS: .6X TO 1.5X BASIC

2002-03 UD Glass Auto Focus

Inserted in packs at the rate of one in 72, this 20-card set is printed on Upper Deck's Plexi-Glass and uses a horizontal design. Player photos appear on the left and player autographs appear on the right. Jamaal Magloire was issued with some live versions and some EXCH versions
STATED ODDS 1:72
AW Antoine Walker 6.00 15.00
CB Chauncey Billups 8.00 20.00
DS DeShawn Stevenson 4.00 10.00
DW Dominique Wilkins 15.00 40.00
ET Etan Thomas 4.00 10.00
GW Gerald Wallace 6.00 15.00
JK Jason Kidd 20.00 50.00
JM Jamaal Magloire 4.00 10.00
JO Jermaine O'Neal 10.00 25.00
JR Jason Richardson 6.00 15.00
JW Jay Williams 6.00 15.00
KA Kareem Abdul-Jabbar/20 75.00 150.00
KB Kobe Bryant/50 125.00 250.00
KG Kevin Garnett/50 50.00 120.00
MB Mike Bibby 10.00 25.00
MJ Michael Jordan/23 400.00 700.00
MM Mike Miller 6.00 15.00
PP Paul Pierce 12.50 30.00
TC Tyson Chandler 6.00 15.00
YM Yao Ming 25.00 50.00

2002-03 UD Glass One Two Combo Jerseys

ndomly inserted in packs, this 13-card set is horizontally designed with a white area in the middle separating full-bleed full-color player action photos on each side. Within each photo is a swatch of game-worn memorabilia. Cards are sequentially numbered to 125. An autographed parallel of this set was also inserted with cards sequentially numbered to 25.
PRINT RUN 125 SERIAL #'d SETS
ASCJ A.Stoudemire/C.Jacobsen 10.00 25.00
CWME C.Wilcox/M.Ely 6.00 15.00
DWCB D.Wagner/C.Boozer 6.00 15.00
JJDC J.Jeffries/J.Dixon 6.00 15.00
JOFJ J.O'Neal/F.Jones 6.00 15.00
JWJR J.Williams/J.Richardson 6.00 15.00
JWTC J.Williams/T.Chandler 6.00 15.00
KBKR K.Bryant/K.Rush 15.00 40.00
MJKB M.Jordan/K.Bryant 60.00 150.00
MMRH M.Miller/R.Humphrey 6.00 15.00
MPCJ M.Peterson/C.Jefferies 6.00 15.00
NHNT N.Hilario/N.Tskitishvili 6.00 15.00
SMAS S.Marion/A.Stoudemire 12.50 30.00

2002-03 UD Glass One Two Combo Jerseys Autographs

PRINT RUN 25 SERIAL #'d SETS
ASCJ Stoudemire/Jacobsen 75.00 150.00
CWME C.Wilcox/M.Ely 15.00 40.00
DWCB D.Wagner/C.Boozer 60.00 120.00
JJJD J.Jeffries/J.Dixon 15.00 40.00
JWTC J.Williams/Chandler 15.00 40.00
KBKR K.Bryant/K.Rush 200.00 400.00
MBGW M.Bibby/G.Wallace 50.00 100.00
MJKB M.Jordan/K.Bryant 700.00 1200.00
MMRH M.Miller/Humphrey 20.00 50.00
MPCJ M.Peterson/Jefferies 15.00 40.00
NHNT N.Hilario/Tskitishvili 40.00 100.00
SMAS Marion/Stoudemire 80.00 200.00

2002-03 UD Glass 2 Exciting Dual Jersey

Randomly inserted in packs, this seven card set utilizes a horizontal design with one player photo on the left and one on the right. Each player is coupled with a swatch of game worn memorabilia. The swatch on the left is in the shape of the number two and the swatch on the right is in the shape of the letter X. Each card is sequentially numbered to 50. An Autographed parallel of this set was also inserted with cards sequentially numbered to 10.
PRINT RUN 50 SERIAL #'d SETS
JKKM J.Kidd/K.Martin 20.00 40.00
KBJK K.Bryant/J.Kidd 30.00 80.00
KBKG K.Bryant/K.Garnett 20.00 50.00
MJKB M.Jordan/K.Bryant 75.00 150.00
PPAW P.Pierce/A.Walker 20.00 40.00
SMAS S.Marion/A.Stoudemire 12.50 30.00
YMJW Y.Ming/J.Williams 15.00 40.00

2002-03 UD Glass Game Gear

Inserted in packs at the rate of one in 24, this 14-card set is horizontally designed with full-color player action photos on the left and a swatch of game-worn memorabilia on the right.
STATED ODDS 1:24
DMGG Darius Miles 2.00 5.00
DNGG Dirk Nowitzki 5.00 12.00
DWGG David Wesley 2.00 5.00
EBGG Elton Brand 3.00 8.00
JMGG Jamal Mashburn 2.50 6.00
JTGG Jamaal Tinsley 2.00 5.00
LSGG Latrell Sprewell 2.50 6.00
RAGG Ray Allen 3.00 8.00
RLGG Rashard Lewis 3.00 8.00
RWGG Rasheed Wallace 3.00 8.00
SAGG Shareef Abdur-Rahim 2.50 6.00
SBGG Shane Battier 3.00 8.00
SMGG Shawn Marion 2.50 6.00
WZGG Wang Zhizhi 2.00 5.00

2002-03 UD Glass Get Real Jersey

Seeded in packs randomly at the rate of one in 48, this six-card set places full color player action photos on a white card with a colored V-shape behind them. Below the photo is a swatch of game-worn memorabilia in the shape of an exclamation point.
STATED ODDS 1:48
JKR Jason Kidd 6.00 15.00
KBR Kobe Bryant SP 10.00 25.00
KGR Kevin Garnett 6.00 15.00
MBR Mike Bibby 4.00 10.00
PPR Paul Pierce 4.00 10.00
SPR Scottie Pippen 6.00 15.00

2002-03 UD Glass Magnifying Glass

Inserted as a box-topper at the rate of one per box, these jumbo cards are printed on Upper Deck's Plexi-Glass. The Magnifying Glass cards are horizontally designed with a color player photo on the left and a red stripe running through the middle from left to right.
ONE PER BOX TOPPER
AIM Allen Iverson 3.00 8.00
BDM Baron Davis 1.50 4.00
CWM Chris Webber 2.00 5.00
DGM Drew Gooden 2.00 5.00
DMM Darius Miles 1.25 3.00
JRM Jason Richardson 2.00 5.00
JSM Jerry Stackhouse 1.50 4.00
JWM Jay Williams 2.00 5.00
KBM Kobe Bryant 8.00 20.00
KMM Karl Malone 2.50 6.00
MJM Michael Jordan 15.00 40.00
PSM Peja Stojakovic 2.00 5.00
RAM Ray Allen 2.00 5.00
RLM Rashard Lewis 2.00 5.00
SAM Shareef Abdur-Rahim 1.50 4.00
SBM Shane Battier 2.00 5.00
SFM Steve Francis 1.50 4.00
SHM Shawn Marion 1.50 4.00
SMM Stephon Marbury 1.50 4.00
YMM Yao Ming 4.00 10.00

2002-03 UD Glass Magnifying Glass Autographs

STATED ODDS 1:6 BOX TOPPER
AWA Antoine Walker/84 12.50 30.00
CBA Chauncey Billups 8.00 20.00
DSA DeShawn Stevenson 5.00 12.00
ETA Etan Thomas 5.00 12.00
GWA Gerald Wallace 10.00 25.00
JKA Jason Kidd 25.00 60.00
JMA Jamaal Magloire 5.00 12.00
JOA Jermaine O'Neal 12.50 30.00
JRA Jason Richardson 10.00 25.00
JWA Jay Williams 8.00 20.00
KBA Kobe Bryant/50 200.00 400.00
KGA Kevin Garnett/21 75.00 150.00
KMA Kenyon Martin 6.00 15.00
MBA Mike Bibby 8.00 20.00
MFA Marcus Fizer 5.00 12.00
MJA Michael Jordan/23 400.00 700.00
MMA Mike Miller 10.00 25.00
PPA Paul Pierce 15.00 40.00
TCA Tyson Chandler 10.00 25.00
YMA Yao Ming 25.00 60.00

2002-03 UD Glass Premiere Issues Jersey

Inserted in packs at the rate of one in 48, this six card set features rookie players in posed portrait-style photos. The top of the card is white and the bottom of the card contains a jersey swatch with a background set to match the player's jersey colors.
STATED ODDS 1:48
CBP Carlos Boozer 3.00 8.00
CJP Chris Jefferies 2.00 5.00
JDP Juan Dixon 3.00 8.00
JWP Jay Williams SP 3.00 8.00
SCP Sam Clancy 2.50 6.00
VYP Vincent Yarbrough 2.00 5.00

2002-03 UD Glass Superlative Swatch

Inserted in packs at the rate of one in 36, this 10-card set uses a horizontal design with full-color player photos on the right and a circular swatch of game-worn memorabilia on the left.
STATED ODDS 1:36
AMS Andre Miller 2.50 6.00
AWS Antoine Walker 2.50 6.00
BDS Baron Davis 2.50 6.00
CWS Chris Webber 3.00 8.00
DMS Darius Miles 2.00 5.00
KBS Kobe Bryant SP 12.00 30.00
KMS Karl Malone 4.00 10.00
MFS Michael Finley 3.00 8.00
PGS Pau Gasol 4.00 10.00
SMS Stephon Marbury 2.50 6.00

2002-03 UD Glass VIP Access Jersey

Seeded in packs at the rate of one in 72, this six card set has white borders around a rectangular centered portrait-style photo of the featured player. Under this photo there is a swatch of game-worn memorabilia in the shape of the letter V.
STATED ODDS 1:72
AI Allen Iverson 6.00 15.00
JW Jay Williams 4.00 10.00
KB Kobe Bryant SP 15.00 40.00
MJ Michael Jordan SP 30.00 80.00
SF Steve Francis 3.00 8.00
TM Tracy McGrady 6.00 15.00

2003-04 UD Glass

Released in January 2004, UD Glass is a 100-card set comprised of 60 base veteran cards with centered full color player action photos on a white background with color highlights to match the player's jersey, Level Three Rookies (cards 61-80) sequentially numbered to 1100, Level Two Rookies (cards 81-90) sequentially numbered to 750 and Level One Rookies (cards 91-100) sequentially numbered to 250. UD Glass was packaged in eight-pack mini boxes where packs contained five cards and carried a suggested retail price of $5.99.
COMP.SET w/o SP's (60) 17.50 35.00
61-80 RC 3 PRINT RUN 1100 SER.#'d SETS
81-90 RC 2 PRINT RUN 750 SER.#'d SETS
91-100 RC 1 PRINT RUN 250 SER.#'d SETS
1 Shareef Abdur-Rahim .40 1.00
2 Jason Terry .40 1.00
3 Paul Pierce .50 1.25
4 Antoine Walker .50 1.25
5 Scottie Pippen .75 2.00
6 Jalen Rose .40 1.00
7 Darius Miles .30 .75
8 Dajuan Wagner .30 .75
9 Dirk Nowitzki .75 2.00
10 Steve Nash .60 1.50
11 Michael Finley .50 1.25
12 Andre Miller .40 1.00
13 Nene .40 1.00
14 Richard Hamilton .40 1.00
15 Ben Wallace .40 1.00
16 Jason Richardson .50 1.25
17 Nick Van Exel .40 1.00
18 Steve Francis .40 1.00
19 Yao Ming 1.00 2.50
20 Jermaine O'Neal .40 1.00
21 Reggie Miller .50 1.25
22 Elton Brand .50 1.25
23 Corey Maggette .40 1.00
24 Kobe Bryant 2.00 5.00
25 Shaquille O'Neal 1.25 3.00
26 Gary Payton .50 1.25
27 Pau Gasol .50 1.25
28 Shane Battier .40 1.00
29 Caron Butler .40 1.00
30 Eddie Jones .40 1.00
31 Desmond Mason .40 1.00
32 Michael Redd .50 1.25
33 Kevin Garnett .75 2.00
34 Latrell Sprewell .40 1.00
35 Jason Kidd .75 2.00
36 Richard Jefferson .40 1.00
37 Baron Davis .40 1.00
38 Jamal Mashburn .40 1.00
39 Allan Houston .40 1.00
40 Keith Van Horn .40 1.00
41 Tracy McGrady .60 1.50
42 Juwan Howard .40 1.00
43 Allen Iverson .75 2.00
44 Glenn Robinson .40 1.00
45 Amare Stoudemire .60 1.50
46 Stephon Marbury .40 1.00
47 Rasheed Wallace .50 1.25
48 Bonzi Wells .30 .75
49 Chris Webber .50 1.25
50 Mike Bibby .50 1.25
51 Tim Duncan .75 2.00
52 Tony Parker .50 1.25
53 Ray Allen .50 1.25
54 Rashard Lewis .50 1.25
55 Vince Carter .75 2.00
56 Antonio Davis .30 .75
57 Andrei Kirilenko .50 1.25
58 Jarron Collins .30 .75
59 Gilbert Arenas .40 1.00
60 Jerry Stackhouse .40 1.00
61 Kyle Korver RC 2.50 6.00
62 Travis Hansen RC 1.25 3.00
63 Willie Green RC 1.25 3.00
64 Keith Bogans RC 1.25 3.00
65 Theron Smith RC 1.25 3.00
66 Zaur Pachulia RC 2.00 5.00
67 Derrick Zimmerman RC 2.00 5.00
68 Jason Kapono RC 1.25 3.00
69 Steve Blake RC 1.50 4.00
70 Slavko Vranes RC 1.25 3.00
71 Jerome Beasley RC 1.25 3.00
72 Aleksandar Pavlovic RC 1.50 4.00
73 Boris Diaw RC 2.00 5.00
74 Kendrick Perkins RC 1.50 4.00
75 Leandro Barbosa RC 2.00 5.00

76 Josh Howard RC 2.00 5.00
77 Luke Walton RC 2.00 5.00
78 Maciej Lampe RC 1.25 3.00
79 Brian Cook RC 1.25 3.00
80 Zarko Cabarkapa RC 1.25 3.00
81 Travis Outlaw RC 2.50 6.00
82 Ndudi Ebi RC 2.00 5.00
83 David West RC 3.00 8.00
84 Reece Gaines RC 2.00 5.00
85 Dahntay Jones RC 2.50 6.00
86 Marcus Banks RC 2.00 5.00
87 Troy Bell RC 2.00 5.00
88 Luke Ridnour RC 2.50 6.00
89 Mickael Pietrus RC 2.50 6.00
90 Chris Kaman RC 3.00 8.00
91 Nick Collison RC 6.00 15.00
92 Mike Sweetney RC 5.00 12.00
93 Jarvis Hayes RC 5.00 12.00
94 T.J. Ford RC 6.00 15.00
95 Kirk Hinrich RC 8.00 20.00
96 Chris Bosh RC 12.00 30.00
97 Dwyane Wade RC 20.00 50.00
98 Carmelo Anthony RC 25.00 60.00
99 Darko Milicic RC 6.00 15.00
100 LeBron James RC 150.00 400.00

2003-04 UD Glass Crystal

*1-60 SINGLES: 4X TO 10X BASE HI
*61-80 RCs: 2X TO 5X BASE HI
*81-90 RCs: 1.25X TO 3X BASE HI
*91-100 RCs: .5X TO 1.25X BASE HI
1-60 PRINT RUN 100 SER.#'d SETS
61-100 PRINT RUN 25 SER.#'d SETS
CRYSTAL PRINTED ON PLEXI-GLASS
96 Chris Bosh 20.00 50.00
97 Dwyane Wade 150.00 300.00
98 Carmelo Anthony 75.00 150.00
100 LeBron James 300.00 600.00

2003-04 UD Glass Gold

*1-60 SINGLES: 2.5X TO 6X BASE HI
PRINT RUN 100 SER.#'d SETS
24 Kobe Bryant 25.00 60.00

2003-04 UD Glass Plexi-Glass

*GLASS SINGLES: 1.5X TO 4X BASE HI
STATED ODDS 1:20

2003-04 UD Glass Auto Focus

Randomly seeded at one in 48, this 22-card set is printed on UD's plexi-glass clear cards with player photos on the left and the set logo and autograph on the right. A crystal parallel of this set was also issued and is sequentially numbered to 25.
STATED ODDS 1:48
BC Brian Cook 3.00 8.00
CA Carmelo Anthony 25.00 60.00
CB Caron Butler 5.00 12.00
CK Chris Kaman 5.00 12.00
DA Darius Miles 5.00 12.00
DJ DerMarr Johnson 5.00 12.00
DM Darko Milicic 4.00 10.00
GA Gilbert Arenas 6.00 15.00
GG Gordan Giricek 5.00 12.00
GP Gary Payton 12.50 30.00
KB Kobe Bryant SP 100.00 200.00
LJ LeBron James/100 800.00 1200.00
MC Antonio McDyess 5.00 12.00
MJ Michael Jordan SP 800.00 1300.00
PI Mickael Pietrus 4.00 10.00
PS Peja Stojakovic 6.00 15.00
RG Reece Gaines 3.00 8.00
SB Shane Battier 5.00 12.00
TB Troy Bell 3.00 8.00
TM Tracy McGrady 15.00 40.00
YM Yao Ming 25.00 60.00

2003-04 UD Glass Auto Focus Crystal

*CRYSTAL: 1X TO 2.5X BASE HI
PRINT RUN 25 SER.#'d SETS

2003-04 UD Glass Clear Cut Winners Jerseys

Randomly inserted in packs, this 14-card set places a full-color player photo on the left side of the card and a "W" shaped swatch of jersey on the right. Each card is sequentially numbered to 350.
PRINT RUN 350 SER.#'d SETS
CWAH Allan Houston 2.00 5.00
CWAJ Antawn Jamison 2.00 5.00
CWDN Dirk Nowitzki 4.00 10.00
CWDR David Robinson 6.00 15.00
CWJK Jason Kidd 4.00 10.00
CWKB Kobe Bryant 10.00 25.00
CWKG Kevin Garnett 4.00 10.00
CWKM Kenyon Martin 2.00 5.00
CWLJ LeBron James 40.00 100.00
CWMJ Michael Jordan 30.00 80.00
CWSF Steve Francis 2.00 5.00
CWSM Stephon Marbury 2.00 5.00
CWSO Shaquille O'Neal 6.00 15.00
CWTD Tim Duncan 4.00 10.00

2003-04 UD Glass Cutting Edge Jerseys

Randomly inserted in packs, this 14-card set places full-color player action photos on a white background with colored highlights and a semi-circle swatch of jersey towards the bottom. Each card is sequentially numbered to 100.
PRINT RUN 100 SER.#'d SETS
CEAS Amare Stoudemire 5.00 12.00
CEDR David Robinson 10.00 25.00
CEDW Dajuan Wagner 2.50 6.00
CEGH Grant Hill 5.00 12.00
CEJK Jason Kidd 6.00 15.00
CEKB Kobe Bryant 25.00 60.00
CEKG Kevin Garnett 6.00 15.00
CELJ LeBron James 60.00 150.00
CELS Latrell Sprewell 3.00 8.00
CEMJ Michael Jordan 30.00 80.00
CERW Rasheed Wallace 4.00 10.00
CESF Steve Francis 3.00 8.00
CESN Steve Nash 5.00 12.00
CESO Shaquille O'Neal 10.00 25.00

2003-04 UD Glass Game Gear

Inserted in packs at the rate of one in 24, this 30-card set places full-color player action photos on the left and a semi-circle white border on the right. A swatch of game worn memorabilia appears in the lower right-hand corner of the card.
STATED ODDS 1:24
GGAI Allen Iverson 4.00 10.00
GGAM Alonzo Mourning 4.00 10.00
GGAN Andre Miller 2.00 5.00
GGAS Amare Stoudemire 3.00 8.00
GGAW Antoine Walker 2.50 6.00
GGCB Caron Butler SP 2.00 5.00
GGCW Chris Webber 2.50 6.00
GGDM Darius Miles 2.00 5.00
GGDN Dirk Nowitzki 4.00 10.00
GGDW Dajuan Wagner 2.00 5.00
GGEB Elton Brand 2.50 6.00
GGEG Manu Ginobili 3.00 8.00
GGGH Grant Hill 4.00 10.00
GGKB Kobe Bryant SP 10.00 25.00
GGKG Kevin Garnett 4.00 10.00
GGLJ LeBron James SP 50.00 120.00
GGLO Lamar Odom 2.00 5.00
GGLS Latrell Sprewell 2.00 5.00
GGMB Mike Bibby 2.50 6.00
GGMJ Michael Jordan SP 30.00 80.00
GGPP Paul Pierce 2.50 6.00
GGSA Shareef Abdur-Rahim 2.00 5.00
GGSF Steve Francis 2.00 5.00
GGSM Stephon Marbury SP 2.00 5.00
GGSN Steve Nash 3.00 8.00
GGTD Tim Duncan 4.00 10.00
GGTM Tracy McGrady 3.00 8.00
GGTP Tony Parker 2.50 6.00
GGWS Wally Szczerbiak 2.00 5.00
GGYM Yao Ming 5.00 12.00

2003-04 UD Glass Monumental Marks

Randomly seeded at the rate of one in 144, this 20-card set places a full-color player head shot in the upper left hand corner of the card with an "M" shaped swatch of jersey below it. The right side of the card contains an authentic player autograph.
STATED ODDS 1:144
AMJ Andre Miller 6.00 15.00
DAJ Darius Miles 6.00 15.00
DMJ Darko Milicic 5.00 12.00
JKJ Jason Kidd 20.00 50.00
JRJ Jason Richardson 6.00 15.00
KBJ Kobe Bryant/100 125.00 250.00
LJJ LeBron James/100 1000.00 1500.00
LOJ Lamar Odom 10.00 25.00
LRJ Luke Ridnour 5.00 12.00
MBJ Mike Bibby 6.00 15.00
MJJ Michael Jordan/50 1200.00 1700.00
MPJ Morris Peterson 6.00 15.00
MSJ Mike Sweetney 4.00 10.00
PIJ Mickael Pietrus 5.00 12.00
PPJ Paul Pierce 30.00 80.00
PSJ Peja Stojakovic 10.00 25.00
RHJ Richard Hamilton 8.00 20.00
RJJ Richard Jefferson 8.00 20.00
RMJ Reggie Miller 60.00 150.00
SFJ Steve Francis 8.00 20.00

2003-04 UD Glass Premier Issue Jerseys

Seeded in packs at the rate of one in 96, this 21-card set is horizontally designed where full-color player photos appear on the left side and jersey swatches in the shape of a "P" appear on the right. The focus of the set is this year's new rookies.
STATED ODDS 1:96
PIBC Brian Cook 1.50 4.00
PICA Carmelo Anthony 8.00 20.00
PICB Chris Bosh 4.00 10.00
PICK Chris Kaman 2.50 6.00
PIDE David West 2.50 6.00
PIDJ Dahntay Jones 2.00 5.00
PIDM Darko Milicic 2.00 5.00
PIDY Dwyane Wade 8.00 20.00
PIHO Josh Howard 2.50 6.00
PIJH Jarvis Hayes 1.50 4.00
PILJ LeBron James SP 60.00 120.00
PILR Luke Ridnour 2.00 5.00
PILW Luke Walton 2.50 6.00
PIMB Marcus Banks 1.50 4.00
PIMP Mickael Pietrus 2.00 5.00
PIMS Mike Sweetney 1.50 4.00
PIRG Reece Gaines 1.50 4.00
PISB Steve Blake 2.00 5.00
PITB Troy Bell 1.50 4.00
PITO Travis Outlaw 2.00 5.00
PIZC Zarko Cabarkapa 1.50 4.00

2003-04 UD Glass Superlative Swatches

Inserted at the rate of one in 24, this 21-card set is horizontally designed and player photos on the left of the card appear in black and white while an "S" shaped swatch of memorabilia appears on the right.
STATED ODDS 1:24
SSAH Allan Houston 2.00 5.00
SSAI Allen Iverson 4.00 10.00
SSCB Caron Butler 2.00 5.00
SSCW Charlie Ward 2.00 5.00
SSDN Dirk Nowitzki 4.00 10.00
SSEC Eddy Curry 1.50 4.00
SSGA Gilbert Arenas 2.00 5.00
SSJJ Joe Johnson 2.00 5.00
SSJK Jason Kidd 4.00 10.00
SSJR Jason Richardson 2.50 6.00
SSKB Kobe Bryant SP 10.00 25.00
SSLO Lamar Odom 2.00 5.00
SSMJ Michael Jordan SP 40.00 100.00
SSMM Mark Madsen 2.00 5.00
SSRS Radoslav Nesterovic 2.00 5.00
SSTB Terrell Brandon 2.00 5.00
SSTC Tyson Chandler 2.00 5.00
SSTD Tim Duncan 4.00 10.00
SSTM Tracy McGrady 3.00 8.00
SSWS Wally Szczerbiak 2.00 5.00
SSYM Yao Ming 5.00 12.00

2003-04 UD Glass Swatch of Class

Inserted in packs at the rate of one in 96, this 21-card set is horizontally designed with full-color player photos appearing on the left, a blue-scale light photo centered in the background and a swatch of memorabilia on the right.
STATED ODDS 1:96
SCAJ Antawn Jamison 2.00 5.00
SCEB Elton Brand 2.50 6.00
SCJO Jermaine O'Neal 2.00 5.00
SCJS Jerry Stackhouse 2.00 5.00
SCKB Kobe Bryant SP 20.00 50.00
SCKE Kenyon Martin 2.00 5.00
SCKM Karl Malone 3.00 8.00
SCLJ LeBron James SP 60.00 150.00
SCLO Lamar Odom 2.00 5.00
SCMC Marcus Camby 2.00 5.00
SCMF Michael Finley 2.50 6.00
SCMJ Michael Jordan SP 75.00 150.00
SCPG Pau Gasol 2.50 6.00
SCPP Paul Pierce 2.50 6.00
SCPS Peja Stojakovic 2.50 6.00
SCRA Ray Allen 2.50 6.00
SCRL Rashard Lewis 2.50 6.00
SCRM Reggie Miller 2.50 6.00
SCSH Shawn Marion 2.00 5.00
SCSM Stephon Marbury 2.00 5.00
SCTP Tony Parker 2.50 6.00

2003-04 UD Glass VIP Access Jerseys

Sequentially numbered to 25, this 14-card set is horizontally designed with a player portrait style photo to the left of the card and a memorabilia swatch to the lower right.
PRINT RUN 25 SER.#'d SETS
AI Allen Iverson 15.00 40.00
BW Ben Wallace 8.00 20.00
CA Carmelo Anthony 30.00 80.00
CW Chris Webber 10.00 25.00
DM Darko Milicic 8.00 20.00
DW Dajuan Wagner 6.00 15.00
JO Jermaine O'Neal 8.00 20.00
KB Kobe Bryant 40.00 100.00
LJ LeBron James 400.00 800.00
MJ Michael Jordan 80.00 200.00
PP Paul Pierce 10.00 25.00
SO Shaquille O'Neal 25.00 60.00
TM Tracy McGrady 12.00 30.00
YM Yao Ming 20.00 50.00

2002-03 UD Glass Beckett.com Samples

*SINGLES: .75X TO 2X BASE UD GLASS HI

2013 UD Infinite

1 Michael Jordan
2 Larry Johnson
3 Clyde Drexler
4 LeBron James
5 Bill Walton
6 David Robinson
7 Michael Jordan
8 Walt Frazier
9 Karl Malone
10 Alonzo Mourning
11 Dennis Rodman
12 Michael Jordan
13 Julius Erving
14 Isiah Thomas
15 Larry Bird
16 Michael Jordan
17 Anfernee Hardaway
18 Hakeem Olajuwon
19 Chris Paul
20 Gary Payton
21 Grant Hill
22 Michael Jordan
23 Paul Pierce
24 Dominique Wilkins
25 John Havlicek
26 LeBron James
27 Allen Iverson
28 Ray Allen
29 Magic Johnson
30 Bill Russell

2013 UD Infinite Industry Summit Exclusives

STATED PRINT RUN 150 SER. #'d SETS
EX1 LeBron James 8.00 20.00

1998-99 UD Ionix

This 80-card set was issued in four card packs that carried a suggested retail price of $4.99. It was the debut issue for Ionix. The rookie card subset, Electrix, was inserted at one in four packs and featured 20 of the top rookies from the 1998 NBA Draft.
COMPLETE SET (80) 25.00 60.00
COMPLETE SET w/o RC (60) 10.00 25.00
ELECTRIX RC SUBSET STATED ODDS 1:4
1 Michael Jordan 1.50 4.00
2 Michael Jordan 1.50 4.00
3 Michael Jordan 1.50 4.00
4 Michael Jordan 1.50 4.00
5 Michael Jordan 1.50 4.00
6 Michael Jordan 1.50 4.00
7 Steve Smith .20 .50
8 Dikembe Mutombo .25 .60
9 Ron Mercer .20 .50
10 Antoine Walker .25 .60
11 Derrick Coleman .20 .50
12 Glen Rice .25 .60
13 Michael Jordan 1.50 4.00
14 Toni Kukoc .25 .60
15 Derek Anderson .15 .40
16 Shawn Kemp .25 .60
17 Michael Finley .25 .60
18 Steve Nash .40 1.00
19 Antonio McDyess .20 .50
20 Nick Van Exel .20 .50
21 Grant Hill .40 1.00
22 Jerry Stackhouse .25 .60
23 Donyell Marshall .15 .40
24 John Starks .20 .50
25 Charles Barkley .40 1.00
26 Hakeem Olajuwon .30 .75
27 Scottie Pippen .40 1.00
28 Reggie Miller .30 .75
29 Rik Smits .20 .50
30 Maurice Taylor .15 .40
31 Kobe Bryant 1.00 2.50
32 Shaquille O'Neal .60 1.50
33 Tim Hardaway .25 .60
34 Alonzo Mourning .30 .75
35 Ray Allen .30 .75
36 Glenn Robinson .20 .50
37 Stephon Marbury .30 .75
38 Kevin Garnett .40 1.00
39 Jayson Williams .15 .40
40 Keith Van Horn .25 .60
41 Patrick Ewing .30 .75
42 Allan Houston .20 .50
43 Anfernee Hardaway .40 1.00
44 Isaac Austin .15 .40
45 Tim Thomas .25 .60
46 Allen Iverson .50 1.25
47 Tom Gugliotta .15 .40
48 Jason Kidd .40 1.00
49 Damon Stoudamire .20 .50
50 Chris Webber .25 .60
51 Tim Duncan .50 1.25
52 David Robinson .40 1.00
53 Gary Payton .25 .60
54 Vin Baker .20 .50
55 Tracy McGrady .40 1.00
56 John Stockton .30 .75
57 Karl Malone .30 .75
58 Shareef Abdur-Rahim .25 .60
59 Juwan Howard .20 .50
60 Mitch Richmond .25 .60
61 Michael Olowokandi RC .75 2.00
62 Mike Bibby RC 1.00 2.50
63 Raef LaFrentz RC .75 2.00
64 Antawn Jamison RC 1.00 2.50
65 Vince Carter RC 3.00 8.00
66 Robert Traylor RC .60 1.50
67 Jason Williams RC 1.50 4.00
68 Larry Hughes RC 1.25 3.00
69 Dirk Nowitzki RC 4.00 10.00
70 Paul Pierce RC 2.50 6.00
71 Cuttino Mobley RC 1.25 3.00
72 Corey Benjamin RC .40 1.00
73 Peja Stojakovic RC 1.50 4.00
74 Michael Dickerson RC .60 1.50
75 Matt Harpring RC .60 1.50
76 Rashard Lewis RC 1.50 4.00
77 Pat Garrity RC .50 1.25
78 Roshown McLeod RC .40 1.00
79 Ricky Davis RC 1.00 2.50
80 Felipe Lopez RC .40 1.00
J1A Michael Jordan AU/23 2500.00 4500.00

1998-99 UD Ionix Reciprocal

COMMON MJ (R1-R6/13) 15.00 40.00
*STARS: 5X TO 12X BASE CARD HI
*RCs: 4X TO 10X BASE HI
STARS: PRINT RUN 750 SERIAL #'d SETS
RCs: PRINT RUN 100 SERIAL #'d SETS
R65 Vince Carter 75.00 150.00
R69 Dirk Nowitzki 100.00 200.00

1998-99 UD Ionix Area 23

Randomly inserted in packs at one in 18, this 10-card set features Michael Jordan on cards using rainbow Ionix technology. Card backs carry an "A" prefix.
COMPLETE SET (10) 20.00 50.00
COMMON CARD (A1-A10) 4.00 10.00
STATED ODDS 1:18

1998-99 UD Ionix Kinetix

Randomly inserted into packs at one in nine, this 20-card set focuses on players with lightning quick moves. The card backs carry a "K" prefix.
COMPLETE SET (20) 12.00 30.00
STATED ODDS 1:9
K1 Michael Jordan 6.00 15.00
K2 Michael Olowokandi .60 1.50
K3 Keith Van Horn .75 2.00
K4 Grant Hill 1.25 3.00
K5 Stephon Marbury 1.00 2.50
K6 Larry Hughes 1.00 2.50
K7 Vince Carter 2.50 6.00
K8 Jason Kidd 1.25 3.00
K9 Robert Traylor .50 1.25
K10 Ron Mercer .60 1.50
K11 Dirk Nowitzki 3.00 8.00
K12 Antawn Jamison .75 2.00
K13 Kobe Bryant 3.00 8.00
K14 Jason Williams 1.25 3.00
K15 Raef LaFrentz .60 1.50
K16 Gary Payton .75 2.00
K17 Tim Duncan 1.50 4.00
K18 Paul Pierce 2.00 5.00
K19 Mike Bibby .75 2.00
K20 Scottie Pippen 1.25 3.00

1998-99 UD Ionix MJ HoloGrFX

Randomly inserted in packs at one in 1500, this 10-card set features new technology - and takes trading cards to a new level. Card backs carry a "MJ" prefix.
COMMON CARD (MJ1-10) 60.00 150.00
STATED ODDS 1:1500

1998-99 UD Ionix Skyonix

Randomly inserted in packs at one in 53, this 25-card set features players who can fly through the air like no others. Card backs carry a "S" prefix.
COMPLETE SET (25) 100.00 200.00
STATED ODDS 1:53
S1 Michael Jordan 30.00 80.00
S2 Scottie Pippen 5.00 12.00
S3 Derek Anderson 2.00 5.00
S4 Jason Kidd 5.00 12.00
S5 Damon Stoudamire 2.50 6.00
S6 Antoine Walker 3.00 8.00
S7 Shaquille O'Neal 8.00 20.00
S8 Tim Thomas 3.00 8.00
S9 Reggie Miller 4.00 10.00
S10 Allen Iverson 6.00 15.00
S11 Antonio McDyess 2.50 6.00
S12 Michael Finley 3.00 8.00
S13 Charles Barkley 5.00 12.00
S14 Shareef Abdur-Rahim 3.00 8.00
S15 Gary Payton 3.00 8.00
S16 David Robinson 5.00 12.00
S17 Anfernee Hardaway 5.00 12.00
S18 Ray Allen 4.00 10.00
S19 Ron Mercer 2.50 6.00
S20 Tim Hardaway 3.00 8.00
S21 Chris Webber 3.00 8.00
S22 Kevin Garnett 5.00 12.00
S23 Juwan Howard 2.50 6.00
S24 Karl Malone 4.00 10.00
S25 Keith Van Horn 3.00 8.00

1998-99 UD Ionix UD Authentics

Randomly inserted in packs, this 5-card set features autographs from rookies. Each card is serially numbered out of 475. The card are numbered by the player's initials.
STATED PRINT RUN 475 SETS
AH Anfernee Hardaway No Ser. #
CB Corey Benjamin 2.50 6.00
DO Michael Doleac 3.00 8.00
JW Jason Williams 12.00 30.00
RL Raef LaFrentz 5.00 12.00
RM Roshown McLeod 2.50 6.00

1998-99 UD Ionix Warp Zone

Randomly inserted in packs at one in 216, this 15-card set utilizes a special holographic foil enhancement. Card backs carry a "Z" prefix.
COMPLETE SET (15) 200.00 400.00
Z1 Michael Jordan 100.00 250.00
Z2 Tim Duncan 15.00 40.00
Z3 Robert Traylor 2.50 6.00
Z4 Michael Olowokandi 3.00 8.00
Z5 Vince Carter 20.00 50.00
Z6 Dirk Nowitzki 15.00 40.00
Z7 Antawn Jamison 4.00 10.00
Z8 Jason Williams 8.00 20.00
Z9 Larry Hughes 5.00 12.00
Z10 Raef LaFrentz 3.00 8.00
Z11 Allen Iverson 15.00 40.00
Z12 Kobe Bryant 40.00 100.00
Z13 Grant Hill 12.00 30.00
Z14 Mike Bibby 4.00 10.00
Z15 Paul Pierce 12.00 30.00

1999-00 UD Ionix

The 1999-00 UD Ionix set was released in March,2000 as a 90-card set, containing 60 veterans and 30 rookies. The rookie subset was inserted at one in six packs. Each pack contained 4-cards and carried a suggested retail price of 3.99.
COMPLETE SET (90) 30.00 80.00
COMPLETE SET w/o SP (60) 10.00 25.00
61-90 PRINT RUN 3500 SERIAL #'d SETS
MJ FINAL FLOOR LISTED UNDER 99-00 UD
1 Dikembe Mutombo .30 .75
2 Isaiah Rider .25 .60
3 Antoine Walker .30 .75
4 Paul Pierce .40 1.00
5 Eddie Jones .30 .75
6 Anthony Mason .20 .50
7 Toni Kukoc .30 .75
8 Hersey Hawkins .20 .50
9 Shawn Kemp .30 .75
10 Lamond Murray .20 .50
11 Michael Finley .30 .75
12 Cedric Ceballos .20 .50
13 Antonio McDyess .25 .60
14 Ron Mercer .25 .60
15 Grant Hill .40 1.00
16 Jerry Stackhouse .30 .75
17 Antawn Jamison .30 .75
18 Mookie Blaylock .20 .50
19 Charles Barkley .50 1.25
20 Hakeem Olajuwon .40 1.00
21 Reggie Miller .30 .75
22 Rik Smits .30 .75
23 Maurice Taylor .20 .50
24 Derek Anderson .20 .50
25 Kobe Bryant 1.25 3.00
26 Shaquille O'Neal .75 2.00
27 Tim Hardaway .30 .75
28 Alonzo Mourning .40 1.00
29 Ray Allen .30 .75
30 Glenn Robinson .25 .60
31 Kevin Garnett .50 1.25
32 Terrell Brandon .20 .50
33 Stephon Marbury .25 .60
34 Keith Van Horn .25 .60
35 Allan Houston .25 .60
36 Latrell Sprewell .30 .75
37 Darrell Armstrong .20 .50
38 Tariq Abdul-Wahad .20 .50
39 Allen Iverson .60 1.50
40 Larry Hughes .25 .60
41 Anfernee Hardaway .50 1.25
42 Jason Kidd .50 1.25
43 Tom Gugliotta .20 .50
44 Scottie Pippen .50 1.25
45 Damon Stoudamire .25 .60
46 Rasheed Wallace .30 .75
47 Jason Williams .40 1.00
48 Chris Webber .30 .75
49 Tim Duncan .60 1.50
50 David Robinson .50 1.25
51 Gary Payton .30 .75
52 Vin Baker .25 .60
53 Vince Carter .60 1.50
54 Tracy McGrady .50 1.25
55 Karl Malone .40 1.00
56 John Stockton .40 1.00
57 Mike Bibby .30 .75
58 Shareef Abdur-Rahim .25 .60
59 Mitch Richmond .30 .75
60 Juwan Howard .25 .60
61 Elton Brand RC 2.00 5.00
62 Steve Francis RC 2.00 5.00
63 Baron Davis RC 2.00 5.00
64 Lamar Odom RC 2.00 5.00
65 Jonathan Bender RC .75 2.00
66 Wally Szczerbiak RC 1.50 4.00
67 Richard Hamilton RC 1.50 4.00
68 Andre Miller RC 1.50 4.00
69 Shawn Marion RC 1.50 4.00
70 Jason Terry RC 1.25 3.00
71 Trajan Langdon RC .75 2.00
72 A.Radojevic RC .50 1.25
73 Corey Maggette RC 1.25 3.00
74 William Avery RC .60 1.50
75 Ron Artest RC 1.50 4.00
76 Cal Bowdler RC .50 1.25
77 James Posey RC .75 2.00
78 Quincy Lewis RC .50 1.25
79 Dion Glover RC .60 1.50
80 Jeff Foster RC .75 2.00
81 Kenny Thomas RC .75 2.00
82 Devean George RC .75 2.00
83 Tim James RC .50 1.25
84 Vonteego Cummings RC .50 1.25
85 Jumaine Jones RC .60 1.50
86 Scott Padgett RC .60 1.50
87 Chucky Atkins RC .75 2.00
88 Adrian Griffin RC .75 2.00
89 Todd MacCulloch RC .75 2.00
90 Anthony Carter RC .60 1.50

1999-00 UD Ionix Reciprocal

*STARS: 1.5X TO 4X BASE CARD HI
*RCs: 1.25X TO 3X BASE HI
STARS: STATED ODDS 1:4
RCs: PRINT RUN 100 SERIAL #'d SETS

1999-00 UD Ionix Awesome Powers

Randomly inserted in packs at one in 23, this 15-card set takes a look at the league's greatest powers. Card backs carry an "AP" prefix.
COMPLETE SET (15) 6.00 15.00
STATED ODDS 1:23
AP1 Elton Brand 1.00 2.50
AP2 Corey Maggette .60 1.50
AP3 Wally Szczerbiak .75 2.00
AP4 Charles Barkley 1.25 3.00
AP5 Shawn Marion .75 2.00
AP6 Jason Terry .60 1.50
AP7 Keith Van Horn .60 1.50
AP8 Steve Francis 1.00 2.50
AP9 Trajan Langdon .40 1.00
AP10 Reggie Miller .75 2.00
AP11 Richard Hamilton .75 2.00
AP12 Jonathan Bender .40 1.00
AP13 Baron Davis 1.00 2.50
AP14 Paul Pierce 1.00 2.50
AP15 Andre Miller .75 2.00

1999-00 UD Ionix BIOrhythm

Randomly inserted in packs at one in seven, this 15-card set features key stats and facts on the most thrilling players in the game. Card backs carry a "B" prefix.
COMPLETE SET (15) 5.00 12.00
STATED ODDS 1:7
B1 Grant Hill .75 2.00
B2 Antawn Jamison .60 1.50
B3 Shaquille O'Neal 1.50 4.00
B4 Stephon Marbury .50 1.25
B5 Michael Finley .60 1.50
B6 Hakeem Olajuwon .75 2.00
B7 Ron Mercer .50 1.25
B8 Tim Hardaway .60 1.50
B9 Jason Kidd 1.00 2.50
B10 Allan Houston .50 1.25
B11 Ray Allen .60 1.50
B12 Shawn Kemp .60 1.50
B13 Alonzo Mourning .75 2.00
B14 Tim Duncan 1.25 3.00
B15 Eddie Jones .60 1.50

1999-00 UD Ionix Pyrotechnics

Randomly inserted in packs at one in 72, this 15-card set focuses on the NBA's most electrifying performers. Card backs carry a "P" prefix.
COMPLETE SET (15) 40.00 80.00
STATED ODDS 1:72
P1 Kevin Garnett 4.00 10.00
P2 Shareef Abdur-Rahim 2.00 5.00
P3 Jason Kidd 4.00 10.00
P4 Antonio McDyess 2.00 5.00
P5 Karl Malone 3.00 8.00
P6 Eddie Jones 2.50 6.00
P7 Antoine Walker 2.50 6.00
P8 Kobe Bryant 10.00 25.00
P9 Anfernee Hardaway 4.00 10.00
P10 Antawn Jamison 2.50 6.00
P11 Keith Van Horn 2.00 5.00
P12 Grant Hill 3.00 8.00
P13 Gary Payton 2.50 6.00
P14 Allen Iverson 5.00 12.00
P15 Vince Carter 5.00 12.00

1999-00 UD Ionix UD Authentics

Randomly inserted in packs at one in 144, this 22-card set features autographs of top NBA stars and rookies. Card backs carry the player's initials.
STATED ODDS 1:144
AH Anfernee Hardaway 100.00 250.00
AJ Antawn Jamison 5.00 12.00
AM Andre Miller 5.00 12.00
BD Baron Davis 8.00 20.00
BG Brian Grant 3.00 8.00
CM Corey Maggette 5.00 12.00
JB Jonathan Bender 3.00 8.00
JP James Posey 3.00 8.00
JT Jason Terry 5.00 12.00
KB Kobe Bryant 125.00 300.00
MJ Michael Jordan/23 750.00 1500.00
MT Maurice Taylor 3.00 8.00
RA Ron Artest 8.00 20.00
RH Richard Hamilton 6.00 15.00
RT Robert Traylor 3.00 8.00
SF Steve Francis 8.00 20.00
SM Shawn Marion 6.00 15.00
TG Tom Gugliotta 3.00 8.00
TL Trajan Langdon 3.00 8.00
WA William Avery 2.50 6.00
WS Wally Szczerbiak 4.00 10.00

1999-00 UD Ionix Warp Zone

Randomly inserted in packs at one in 144, this 15-card set features the hottest players in the NBA on rainbow foil. Card backs carry a "WZ" prefix.
COMPLETE SET (15) 150.00 300.00
STATED ODDS 1:144
WZ1 Kobe Bryant 20.00 50.00
WZ2 Kevin Garnett 8.00 20.00
WZ3 Tim Duncan 10.00 25.00
WZ4 Elton Brand 12.00 30.00
WZ5 Wally Szczerbiak 10.00 25.00
WZ6 Stephon Marbury 4.00 10.00
WZ7 Allen Iverson 10.00 25.00
WZ8 Anfernee Hardaway 8.00 20.00
WZ9 Shaquille O'Neal 12.00 30.00
WZ10 Baron Davis 12.00 30.00
WZ11 Scottie Pippen 8.00 20.00
WZ12 Jason Williams 6.00 15.00
WZ13 Steve Francis 12.00 30.00
WZ14 Vince Carter 10.00 25.00
WZ15 Lamar Odom 12.00 30.00

2005-06 UD Portraits

Released in January 2006, this 142-card set features 100 cards where cards 1-100 picture veterans, cards 101-136 picture rookies serially numbered to 399 and cards 137-142 picture rookies serially numbered to 99. Base cards have borders along the bottom with player names, positions and logos and full color player action shots. Portraits was packaged in boxes which contain six cards, one 8x10 autograph and carried a SRP of $125.
COMP.SET w/o SP's (100) 50.00 125.00
137-142 RC PRINT RUN 99 SER.#'d SETS
UNPRICED PARALLEL PRINT RUN 10 SETS
1 Al Harrington .60 1.50
2 Al Jefferson .60 1.50
3 Allen Iverson 1.25 3.00
4 Amare Stoudemire .60 1.50
5 Andre Iguodala .60 1.50
6 Andre Miller .60 1.50
7 Andrei Kirilenko .60 1.50
8 Antawn Jamison .60 1.50
9 Antoine Walker .60 1.50
10 Baron Davis .60 1.50
11 Ben Gordon .60 1.50
12 Ben Wallace .60 1.50
13 Bob Sura .50 1.25
14 Brevin Knight .50 1.25
15 Carlos Boozer .60 1.50
16 Carmelo Anthony 1.50 4.00
17 Caron Butler .60 1.50
18 Chauncey Billups .75 2.00
19 Chris Bosh .75 2.00
20 Chris Webber .75 2.00
21 Corey Maggette .60 1.50
22 Cuttino Mobley .50 1.25
23 Damon Jones .50 1.25
24 Dan Dickau .50 1.25
25 Desmond Mason .50 1.25
26 Dirk Nowitzki 1.25 3.00
27 Donyell Marshall .50 1.25
28 Drew Gooden .60 1.50
29 Dwight Howard .60 1.50
30 Dwyane Wade 1.25 3.00
31 Elton Brand .75 2.00
32 Emeka Okafor .60 1.50
33 Gary Payton .75 2.00
34 Gerald Wallace .60 1.50
35 Gilbert Arenas .60 1.50
36 Grant Hill 1.00 2.50
37 J.R. Smith .60 1.50
38 Jalen Rose .75 2.00
39 Jamaal Magloire .50 1.25
40 Jamaal Tinsley .50 1.25
41 Jamal Crawford .75 2.00
42 Jameer Nelson .50 1.25
43 Jason Kidd 1.25 3.00
44 Jason Richardson .75 2.00
45 Jason Terry .60 1.50
46 Jason Williams .60 1.50
47 Jermaine O'Neal .60 1.50
48 Joe Johnson .60 1.50
49 Josh Childress .60 1.50
50 Josh Howard .75 2.00
51 Josh Smith .60 1.50
52 Kenyon Martin .60 1.50
53 Kevin Garnett 1.25 3.00
54 Kirk Hinrich .60 1.50
55 Kobe Bryant 3.00 8.00
56 Kurt Thomas .50 1.25
57 Kyle Korver .60 1.50
58 Lamar Odom .60 1.50
59 Larry Hughes .60 1.50
60 Eddie Griffin .50 1.25
61 LeBron James 3.00 8.00
62 Luke Ridnour .60 1.50
63 Luol Deng .60 1.50
64 Manu Ginobili .75 2.00
65 Marcus Camby .60 1.50
66 Maurice Williams .60 1.50
67 Michael Finley .75 2.00
68 Michael Jordan 6.00 15.00
69 Michael Redd .60 1.50
70 Mike Bibby .75 2.00
71 Pau Gasol .75 2.00
72 Paul Pierce .75 2.00
73 Peja Stojakovic .75 2.00
74 Raja Bell .60 1.50
75 Rashard Lewis .75 2.00
76 Rasheed Wallace .75 2.00
77 Ray Allen .75 2.00
78 Richard Hamilton .60 1.50
79 Richard Jefferson .60 1.50
80 Ron Artest .75 2.00
81 Sam Cassell .60 1.50
82 Sebastian Telfair .60 1.50
83 Shaquille O'Neal 1.50 4.00
84 Shareef Abdur-Rahim .60 1.50
85 Shaun Livingston .50 1.25
86 Shawn Marion .60 1.50
87 Stephon Marbury .60 1.50
88 Steve Francis .60 1.50
89 Steve Nash 1.00 2.50
90 Stromile Swift .50 1.25
91 Tim Duncan 1.25 3.00
92 Tony Parker .75 2.00
93 Tracy McGrady 1.00 2.50
94 Troy Murphy .50 1.25
95 Tyronn Lue .50 1.25
96 Vince Carter 1.25 3.00
97 Vladimir Radmanovic .50 1.25
98 Yao Ming 1.00 2.50
99 Zach Randolph .60 1.50
100 Zydrunas Ilgauskas .60 1.50
101 Andray Blatche RC 2.00 5.00
102 Andrew Bynum RC 1.50 4.00
103 Antoine Wright RC 1.50 4.00
104 Brandon Bass RC 1.50 4.00
105 C.J. Miles RC 2.00 5.00
106 Channing Frye RC 2.00 5.00
107 Charlie Villanueva RC 2.00 5.00
108 Chris Taft RC 1.50 4.00
109 Daniel Ewing RC 1.50 4.00
110 Danny Granger RC 2.50 6.00
111 David Lee RC 2.00 5.00
112 Dijon Thompson RC 1.25 3.00
113 Ersan Ilyasova RC 2.00 5.00
114 Sarunas Jasikevicius RC 2.00 5.00
115 Francisco Garcia RC 1.50 4.00
116 Gerald Green RC 2.00 5.00
117 Hakim Warrick RC 1.50 4.00
118 Jose Calderon RC 2.00 5.00
119 Ike Diogu RC 1.25 3.00
120 Jarrett Jack RC 2.00 5.00
121 Jason Maxiell RC 1.50 4.00
122 Joey Graham RC 1.50 4.00
123 Julius Hodge RC 1.25 3.00
124 Linas Kleiza RC 1.25 3.00
125 Louis Williams RC 2.00 5.00
126 Luther Head RC 1.50 4.00
127 Martell Webster RC 1.50 4.00
128 Monta Ellis RC 2.50 6.00
129 Nate Robinson RC 2.00 5.00
130 Rashad McCants RC 1.50 4.00
131 James Singleton RC 1.25 3.00
132 Ryan Gomes RC 1.50 4.00
133 Salim Stoudamire RC 1.50 4.00
134 Travis Diener RC 1.25 3.00
135 Wayne Simien RC 1.25 3.00
136 Yaroslav Korolev RC 1.25 3.00
137 Andrew Bogut RC 4.00 10.00
138 Chris Paul RC 12.00 30.00
139 Deron Williams RC 4.00 10.00
140 Raymond Felton RC 3.00 8.00
141 Marvin Williams RC 3.00 8.00
142 Sean May RC 2.00 5.00

2005-06 UD Portraits 75

*1-100 PORT.75: .75X TO 2X BASE HI
*101-136 PORT.75: .6X TO 1.5X BASE HI
*137-142 PORT.75: .4X TO 1X BASE HI
PORT.75 PRINT RUN 75 SER.#'d SETS
68 Michael Jordan 15.00 40.00

2005-06 UD Portraits 30

*1-100 PORT.30: 1.5X TO 4X BASE HI
*101-136 PORT.30: 1X TO 2.5X BASE HI
*137-142 PORT.30: .6X TO 1.5X BASE HI
PORT.30 PRINT RUN 30 SER.#'d SETS
68 Michael Jordan 30.00 80.00

2005-06 UD Portraits Material Moments

Inserted at the rate of one per pack, this 42-card set features framed color photos along the top of the card and a square swatch of memorabilia along the bottom. Borders are brown along the sides and top with a red strip through the middle and white along the bottom.
STATED ODDS ONE PER PACK
AB Andrew Bogut 3.00 8.00
AM Aaron McKie 2.00 5.00
AS Amare Stoudemire 2.00 5.00
AW Antoine Wright 2.00 5.00
CB Caron Butler 2.00 5.00
CF Channing Frye 2.50 6.00
CM C.J. Miles 2.50 6.00
CP Chris Paul 8.00 20.00
CW Chris Webber 2.50 6.00
DA David Wesley 2.00 5.00
DE Deron Williams 3.00 8.00
DF Derek Fisher 2.00 5.00
DG Danny Granger 3.00 8.00
DH Dwight Howard 2.00 5.00
DN Dirk Nowitzki 4.00 10.00
EB Elton Brand 2.50 6.00
ES Eric Snow 2.00 5.00
GG Gerald Green 2.50 6.00
HW Hakim Warrick 2.00 5.00
JA Jason Terry 2.00 5.00
JK Jason Kidd 4.00 10.00
JM Jamaal Magloire 2.00 5.00
JO Jermaine O'Neal 2.00 5.00
JR Jason Richardson 2.50 6.00
JT Jamaal Tinsley 2.00 5.00
KB Kobe Bryant 10.00 25.00
KD Keyon Dooling 2.00 5.00
KG Kevin Garnett 4.00 10.00
KM Kenyon Martin 2.00 5.00
LJ LeBron James 12.50 30.00
LW Luke Walton 2.00 5.00
MA Marvin Williams 2.50 6.00
MJ Michael Jordan SP 40.00 80.00
MW Martell Webster 2.00 5.00
QR Quentin Richardson 2.00 5.00
RF Raymond Felton 2.50 6.00
RW Rasheed Wallace 2.50 6.00
SH Shawn Marion 2.00 5.00
SM Sean May 1.50 4.00
SO Shaquille O'Neal 5.00 12.00
TD Tim Duncan 4.00 10.00
YM Yao Ming 3.00 8.00

2005-06 UD Portraits Scrapbook Signatures

Inserted randomly in packs, this 37-card set features framed player photos with brown borders and player autographs. Each card is sequentially numbered to 25.
PRINT RUN 25 SER.#'d SETS
AB Andrew Bogut 10.00 25.00
AN Andrew Bynum 6.00 15.00
BB Brandon Bass 6.00 15.00
CA Carmelo Anthony 30.00 80.00
CJ C.J. Miles 8.00 20.00
CP Chris Paul 80.00 200.00
DE Daniel Ewing 6.00 15.00

DG Danny Granger 10.00 25.00
DH Dwight Howard 25.00 60.00
DL David Lee 8.00 20.00
DT Dijon Thompson 5.00 12.00
DW Deron Williams 10.00 25.00
EI Ersan Ilyasova 8.00 20.00
FG Francisco Garcia 6.00 15.00
GA Gilbert Arenas 12.50 30.00
GG Gerald Green 8.00 20.00
ID Ike Diogu 5.00 12.00
JG Joey Graham 6.00 15.00
JH Julius Hodge 5.00 12.00
JM Jason Maxiell 6.00 15.00
JP Johan Petro 5.00 12.00
LH Luther Head 6.00 15.00
LJ LeBron James 200.00 400.00
LW Louis Williams 8.00 20.00
MA Marvin Williams 8.00 20.00
MB Mike Bibby 15.00 40.00
MJ Michael Jordan 400.00 600.00
PP Paul Pierce 20.00 50.00
RF Raymond Felton 8.00 20.00
RJ Richard Jefferson 8.00 20.00
SM Sean May 5.00 12.00
SN Steve Nash 30.00 80.00
ST Stephon Marbury 12.50 30.00
WS Wayne Simien 5.00 12.00

2005-06 UD Portraits Scrapbook Swatches

Inserted at the rate of one per pack, this 42-card set is horizontally designed with framed player photos on the left side of the card and a square swatch of memorabilia on the right.
STATED ODDS ONE PER PACK
AB Andrew Bogut 3.00 8.00
AI Andre Iguodala 2.00 5.00
AW Antoine Wright 2.00 5.00
BG Ben Gordon 2.00 5.00
CA Carmelo Anthony 5.00 12.00
CF Channing Frye 2.50 6.00
CM Corey Maggette 2.00 5.00
CP Chris Paul 8.00 20.00
CT Chris Taft 2.00 5.00
CV Charlie Villanueva 2.50 6.00
DE Daniel Ewing 2.00 5.00
DG Danny Granger 3.00 8.00
DH Dwight Howard 2.00 5.00
DW Deron Williams 3.00 8.00
FG Francisco Garcia 2.00 5.00
GA Gilbert Arenas 2.00 5.00
GG Gerald Green 2.50 6.00
GP Gary Payton 2.50 6.00
HK Hakim Warrick 2.00 5.00
JA Jason Maxiell 2.00 5.00
JC Josh Childress 2.00 5.00
JG Joey Graham 2.00 5.00
JH Julius Hodge 1.50 4.00
JJ Jarrett Jack 2.50 6.00
JK Jason Kidd 4.00 10.00
JM Jamaal Magloire 2.00 5.00
JR J.R. Smith 2.00 5.00
LJ LeBron James 12.50 30.00
LW Louis Williams 2.50 6.00
MA Marvin Williams 2.50 6.00
ME Monta Ellis 3.00 8.00
MJ Michael Jordan SP 40.00 80.00
MW Martell Webster 2.00 5.00
QR Quentin Richardson 2.00 5.00
RF Raymond Felton 2.50 6.00
RM Rashad McCants 2.00 5.00
SH Shawn Marion 2.00 5.00
SM Sean May 1.50 4.00
TM Tracy McGrady 3.00 8.00
UH Udonis Haslem 1.50 4.00
WS Wayne Simien 1.50 4.00
YM Yao Ming 3.00 8.00

2005-06 UD Portraits Scrapbook Swatches Autographs

This 31-card set parallels the design of the Scrapbook Swatches set enhanced with authentic player autographs. Most cards are serially numbered to either 40 or 10, but there are a few exceptions in the set. See checklist for details.
PRINT RUN 10 TO 49 SER.#'d SETS
SOME UNPRICED DUE TO SCARCITY
CM Corey Maggette/49 8.00 20.00
DE Daniel Ewing/40 6.00 15.00
DG Danny Granger/40 10.00 25.00
FG Francisco Garcia/40 6.00 15.00
GA Gilbert Arenas/40 12.50 30.00
GG Gerald Green/40 8.00 20.00
GP Gary Payton/40 12.50 30.00
JA Jason Maxiell/40 6.00 15.00
JG Joey Graham/40 6.00 15.00
JH Julius Hodge/40 5.00 12.00
JJ Jarrett Jack/40 8.00 20.00
JR J.R. Smith/40 6.00 15.00
LW Louis Williams/40 8.00 20.00
MW Martell Webster/40 6.00 15.00
RF Raymond Felton/40 8.00 20.00
RM Rashad McCants/40 6.00 15.00
SH Shawn Marion/40 12.50 30.00
WS Wayne Simien/40 5.00 12.00

2005-06 UD Portraits Signature Portraits 8x10

Inserted at about one per box (unless a parallel or other 8x10 autograph is present), this 47-card set places full color player photos at the top of the card and a colored strip along the bottom to match player team colors along with a large autograph sticker.
STATED ODDS ONE PER BOX
*BLACK/WHITE: .5X TO 1.25X BASE HI
BLACK/WHITE RANDOM INSERTS IN PACKS
AB Andrew Bogut 8.00 20.00
AI Andre Iguodala 12.50 30.00
AN Andrew Bynum 5.00 12.00
BK Bernard King 8.00 20.00
CA Carmelo Anthony SP 25.00 50.00
CB Chauncey Billups 12.50 30.00
CP Chris Paul 40.00 100.00
DE Dennis Rodman SP 40.00 100.00
DG Danny Granger 8.00 20.00
DH Dwight Howard 15.00 40.00
DR David Robinson SP 40.00 80.00
DW Deron Williams 8.00 20.00
EH Elvin Hayes 10.00 25.00
HO Hakeem Olajuwon SP 20.00 50.00
ID Ike Diogu 4.00 10.00
IT Isiah Thomas SP 20.00 50.00
JC Josh Childress 6.00 15.00
JG Joey Graham 5.00 12.00
JH Julius Hodge 4.00 10.00
JJ Jarrett Jack 6.00 15.00
JK Jason Kidd SP 20.00 50.00
JN Jameer Nelson 8.00 20.00
JS John Stockton SP 75.00 150.00
JW John Wooden SP 50.00 120.00
KA Kareem Abdul-Jabbar 40.00 100.00
KN Bob Knight SP 30.00 75.00
LJ1 LeBron James 125.00 250.00
LJ2 LeBron James 125.00 250.00
MJ1 Michael Jordan SP 300.00 500.00
MJ2 Michael Jordan SP 300.00 500.00
MW Martell Webster 5.00 12.00
PP Paul Pierce 15.00 40.00
RF Raymond Felton 6.00 15.00
RH Richard Hamilton 8.00 20.00
RJ Richard Jefferson 6.00 15.00
RM Rashad McCants 5.00 12.00
SE Sebastian Telfair 6.00 15.00
SH Shawn Marion 15.00 40.00
SM Sean May 4.00 10.00
SN Steve Nash SP 40.00 100.00
SP Scottie Pippen SP 80.00 200.00
ST Stephon Marbury SP 15.00 40.00
WF Walt Frazier 10.00 25.00
WI Marvin Williams SP 6.00 15.00
WR Willis Reed 15.00 40.00
YM Yao Ming SP 15.00 40.00

2005-06 UD Portraits Signature Portraits 8x10 Dual

Inserted in packs randomly, this 22-card set is horizontally designed with two players and/or coaches, side by side, and two large autograph stickers. Each card is serially numbered to 40.
PRINT RUN 40 SER.#'d SETS
DSP1 M.Jordan/L.James 600.00 1000.00
DSP2 L.James/D.Howard 200.00 350.00
DSP3 M.Jordan/L.Bird 350.00 600.00
DSP4 Mv.Williams/C.Paul 50.00 100.00
DSP5 D.Howard/A.Bogut 30.00 80.00
DSP6 T.McGrady/G.Green 25.00 60.00
DSP7 R.Felton/R.McCants 25.00 60.00
DSP9 Magic/J.Stockton 125.00 250.00
DSP10 C.Anthony/H.Warrick 30.00 80.00
DSP11 S.May/A.Jamison 20.00 50.00
DSP12 W.Frazier/W.Reed 40.00 100.00
DSP14 K.Hinrich/W.Simien 20.00 50.00
DSP16 Y.Ming/A.Bogut 40.00 80.00
DSP17 B.Knight/J.Wooden 75.00 150.00
DSP19 J.Jack/M.Webster 20.00 50.00
DSP20 E.Hayes/G.Arenas 20.00 50.00
DSP21 H.Olajuwon/Y.Ming 50.00 120.00
DSP22 J.R.Smith/M.Webster 20.00 50.00
DSP23 D.Williams/L.Head 40.00 75.00
DSP24 M.Bibby/S.Stoudamire 20.00 50.00
DSP26 S.Pippen/D.Rodman 175.00 350.00

2005-06 UD Portraits Signature Portraits 8x10 Triple

Randomly seeded in packs and limited to 20 copies, this six card set features a horizontal design with three player photos and three sticker autographs.
PRINT RUN 20 SER.#'d SETS
UNPRICED TEN PRINT RUN 3 SETS
TSP2 LeBron/Carmelo/Bosh 200.00 350.00
TSP3 Bogut/MvWilliams/Paul 75.00 150.00
TSP4 May/Felton/McCants 40.00 80.00
TSP6 Pierce/A.Jefferson/Green 40.00 80.00
TSP7 Nash/Marion/D.Thompson 60.00 120.00
TSP8 Arenas/Bibby/Salim 60.00 120.00

2000-01 UD Reserve

COMP.SET w/o SP's (90) 8.00 20.00
91-120 STATED ODDS 1:2
1 Dikembe Mutombo .30 .75
2 Jason Terry .30 .75
3 Alan Henderson .20 .50
4 Paul Pierce .30 .75
5 Antoine Walker .25 .60
6 Kenny Anderson .25 .60
7 Derrick Coleman .25 .60
8 Baron Davis .30 .75
9 Jamal Mashburn .25 .60
10 Elton Brand .30 .75
11 Ron Mercer .20 .50
12 Ron Artest .30 .75
13 Lamond Murray .20 .50
14 Andre Miller .25 .60
15 Matt Harpring .20 .50
16 Michael Finley .30 .75
17 Dirk Nowitzki .50 1.25
18 Steve Nash .50 1.25
19 Antonio McDyess .25 .60
20 James Posey .20 .50
21 Nick Van Exel .25 .60
22 Jerry Stackhouse .25 .60
23 Jerome Williams .20 .50
24 Chucky Atkins .20 .50
25 Antawn Jamison .30 .75
26 Larry Hughes .25 .60
27 Chris Mills .20 .50
28 Steve Francis .25 .60
29 Hakeem Olajuwon .40 1.00
30 Cuttino Mobley .20 .50
31 Reggie Miller .30 .75
32 Jalen Rose .25 .60
33 Austin Croshere .20 .50
34 Lamar Odom .25 .60
35 Jeff McInnis .20 .50
36 Corey Maggette .25 .60
37 Shaquille O'Neal .75 2.00
38 Kobe Bryant 1.25 3.00
39 Isaiah Rider .25 .60
40 Horace Grant .25 .60
41 Eddie Jones .30 .75
42 Tim Hardaway .30 .75
43 Brian Grant .20 .50
44 Ray Allen .30 .75
45 Tim Thomas .20 .50
46 Glenn Robinson .25 .60
47 Sam Cassell .25 .60
48 Kevin Garnett .50 1.25
49 Wally Szczerbiak .25 .60
50 Terrell Brandon .20 .50
51 Chauncey Billups .30 .75
52 Stephon Marbury .25 .60
53 Keith Van Horn .25 .60
54 Kendall Gill .20 .50
55 Latrell Sprewell .25 .60
56 Marcus Camby .25 .60
57 Allan Houston .25 .60
58 Grant Hill .40 1.00
59 Tracy McGrady .50 1.25
60 Darrell Armstrong .20 .50
61 Allen Iverson .60 1.50
62 Theo Ratliff .20 .50
63 Toni Kukoc .30 .75
64 Jason Kidd .50 1.25
65 Clifford Robinson .20 .50
66 Shawn Marion .25 .60
67 Rasheed Wallace .30 .75
68 Scottie Pippen .50 1.25
69 Damon Stoudamire .25 .60
70 Chris Webber .30 .75
71 Jason Williams .30 .75
72 Vlade Divac .25 .60
73 Tim Duncan .60 1.50
74 David Robinson .50 1.25
75 Derek Anderson .20 .50
76 Gary Payton .30 .75
77 Patrick Ewing .40 1.00
78 Rashard Lewis .30 .75
79 Vince Carter .60 1.50
80 Mark Jackson .25 .60
81 Antonio Davis .20 .50
82 Karl Malone .40 1.00
83 John Stockton .40 1.00
84 John Starks .25 .60
85 Shareef Abdur-Rahim .25 .60
86 Mike Bibby .30 .75
87 Michael Dickerson .20 .50
88 Mitch Richmond .25 .60
89 Richard Hamilton .25 .60
90 Juwan Howard .25 .60
91 Kenyon Martin RC 1.00 2.50
92 Stromile Swift RC .40 1.00
93 Darius Miles RC .40 1.00
94 Marcus Fizer RC .40 1.00
95 Mike Miller RC .60 1.50
96 DerMarr Johnson RC .30 .75
97 Chris Mihm RC .30 .75
98 Jamal Crawford RC 1.00 2.50
99 Joel Przybilla RC .30 .75
100 Keyon Dooling RC .40 1.00
101 Jerome Moiso RC .25 .60
102 Etan Thomas RC .40 1.00
103 Courtney Alexander RC .30 .75
104 Mateen Cleaves RC .30 .75
105 Hedo Turkoglu RC .60 1.50
106 Desmond Mason RC .50 1.25
107 Quentin Richardson RC .40 1.00
108 Jamaal Magloire RC .40 1.00
109 Speedy Claxton RC .40 1.00
110 Morris Peterson RC .40 1.00
111 Donnell Harvey RC .30 .75
112 DeShawn Stevenson RC .40 1.00
113 Mamadou N'Diaye RC .25 .60
114 Erick Barkley RC .25 .60
115 Mark Madsen RC .40 1.00
116 Eduardo Najera RC .40 1.00
117 Lavor Postell RC .25 .60
118 Hanno Mottola RC .25 .60
119 Stephen Jackson RC .60 1.50
120 Marc Jackson RC .30 .75

2000-01 UD Reserve Bank Shots

COMPLETE SET (10) 4.00 10.00
STATED ODDS 1:14
BK1 Kevin Garnett .75 2.00
BK2 Lamar Odom .40 1.00
BK3 Grant Hill .60 1.50
BK4 Rashard Lewis .50 1.25
BK5 Reggie Miller .50 1.25
BK6 Ray Allen .50 1.25
BK7 Eddie Jones .50 1.25
BK8 Kobe Bryant 2.00 5.00
BK9 Michael Finley .50 1.25
BK10 Jerry Stackhouse .40 1.00

2000-01 UD Reserve BuyBacks

STATED ODDS 1:239
SOME AU's NOT PRICED DUE TO SCARCITY
1 C.Alexander 00-1P&PPM/98 10.00 25.00
6 S.Claxton 00-1UD/190 10.00 25.00
7 M.Cleaves 00-1UD/74 10.00 25.00
8 M.Cleaves 00-1P&PSF/25 12.50 30.00
9 J.Crawford 00-1UD/120 15.00 40.00
10 K.El-Amin 00-1UD/95 10.00 25.00
11 M.Fizer 00-1UD/50 10.00 25.00
12 M.Fizer 00-1P&PPM/48 10.00 25.00
13 M.Fizer 00-1P&PSF/100 10.00 25.00
15 K.Garnett 95-96UD/21 100.00 200.00
16 D.Harvey 00-1UD/98 10.00 25.00
17 D.Johnson 00-1P&PPM/48 10.00 25.00
18 D.Johnson 00-1P&PSF/95 10.00 25.00
22 M.Madsen 00-1UD/95 10.00 25.00
23 J.Magloire 00-1UD/98 10.00 25.00
24 K.Martin P&PPM/50 20.00 40.00
25 C.Mihm 00-1UD/95 10.00 25.00
26 D.Miles 00-1UD/50 15.00 40.00
27 D.Miles 00-1P&PM/48 15.00 40.00
28 D.Miles 00-1P&PSF/48 15.00 40.00
29 M.Miller 00-1P&PPM/24 10.00 25.00
30 M.Miller 00-1P&PSF/23 10.00 25.00
31 M.Miller 99-0UD/48 20.00 50.00
32 J.Moiso 00-1UD/95 10.00 25.00
33 H.Mottola 00-1UD/95 10.00 25.00
34 M.N'diaye 00-1UD/95 10.00 25.00
35 M.Peterson 00-1UD/95 12.50 30.00
36 J.Przybilla 00-1UD/238 10.00 25.00
37 Q.Richardson 00-1UD/95 20.00 50.00
38 D.Stevenson 00-1UD/95 12.50 30.00
39 S.Swift 00-1UD/50 10.00 25.00
40 S.Swift 00-1P&PPM/50 10.00 25.00
41 S.Swift 00-1P&PSF/50 10.00 25.00

2000-01 UD Reserve Fast Company

COMPLETE SET (10) 4.00 10.00
STATED ODDS 1:14
FC1 Steve Francis .40 1.00
FC2 Kobe Bryant 2.00 5.00
FC3 Allen Iverson 1.00 2.50
FC4 Jason Kidd .75 2.00
FC5 Larry Hughes .40 1.00
FC6 Stephon Marbury .40 1.00
FC7 Jason Williams .50 1.25
FC8 Andre Miller .40 1.00
FC9 Gary Payton .50 1.25
FC10 Paul Pierce .50 1.25

2000-01 UD Reserve NBA Start-Ups

STATED ODDS 1:120
DA Darius Miles 2.50 6.00
DJ DerMarr Johnson 2.00 5.00
JC Jamal Crawford 6.00 15.00
KB Kobe Bryant 15.00 40.00
KG Kevin Garnett 4.00 10.00
KM Kenyon Martin 6.00 15.00
MC Mateen Cleaves 2.00 5.00
MF Marcus Fizer 2.50 6.00
QR Quentin Richardson 2.50 6.00

2000-01 UD Reserve NBA Start-Ups Autographs

STATED ODDS 1:479
DAA Darius Miles 3.00 8.00
DJA DerMarr Johnson 2.50 6.00
JCA Jamal Crawford 12.00 30.00
KGA Kevin Garnett/21 75.00 150.00
KMA Kenyon Martin 8.00 20.00
MFA Marcus Fizer 3.00 8.00
QRA Quentin Richardson 3.00 8.00

2000-01 UD Reserve Power Portfolios

COMPLETE SET (6) 3.00 8.00
STATED ODDS 1:23
PW1 Tim Duncan 1.00 2.50
PW2 Chris Webber .50 1.25
PW3 Grant Hill .60 1.50
PW4 Elton Brand .50 1.25
PW5 Kevin Garnett .75 2.00
PW6 Kobe Bryant 2.00 5.00

2000-01 UD Reserve Principal Powers

COMPLETE SET (10) 6.00 15.00
STATED ODDS 1:14
PP1 Shaquille O'Neal 1.25 3.00
PP2 Tim Duncan 1.00 2.50
PP3 Vince Carter 1.00 2.50
PP4 Elton Brand .50 1.25
PP5 Kevin Garnett .75 2.00
PP6 Tracy McGrady .75 2.00
PP7 Karl Malone .60 1.50
PP8 Kobe Bryant 2.00 5.00
PP9 Shareef Abdur-Rahim .40 1.00
PP10 Antonio McDyess .40 1.00

2000-01 UD Reserve Setting the Standard

COMPLETE SET (6) 4.00 10.00
STATED ODDS 1:23
SS1 Steve Francis .40 1.00
SS2 Vince Carter 1.00 2.50
SS3 Kobe Bryant 2.00 5.00
SS4 Kevin Garnett .75 2.00
SS5 Allen Iverson 1.00 2.50
SS6 Shaquille O'Neal 1.25 3.00

2006-07 UD Reserve

Released in mid May 2007, UD Reserve features a chromium card stock-enhanced version of the base Upper Deck set design. The 240 card-set pictures veteran players on cards 1-200 and rookies, inserted at the approximate rate of one in four packs, on cards 201-240. UD Reserve is packaged in 10-pack boxes of four cards each and carried an initial suggested retail price of $10.00 per pack.
COMP.SET w/o SP's (200) 30.00 60.00
RC APPROXIMATE ODDS 1:4
1 Josh Childress .50 1.25
2 Al Harrington .50 1.25
3 Joe Johnson .50 1.25
4 Josh Smith .50 1.25
5 Salim Stoudamire .40 1.00
6 Marvin Williams .50 1.25
7 Tony Allen .40 1.00
8 Dan Dickau .40 1.00
9 Al Jefferson .50 1.25
10 Raef LaFrentz .40 1.00
11 Michael Olowokandi .40 1.00
12 Paul Pierce .60 1.50
13 Wally Szczerbiak .50 1.25
14 Brevin Knight .40 1.00
15 Raymond Felton .50 1.25
16 Othella Harrington .40 1.00
17 Sean May .40 1.00
18 Emeka Okafor .50 1.25
19 Primoz Brezec .40 1.00
20 Gerald Wallace .50 1.25
21 Tyson Chandler .50 1.25
22 Michael Jordan 5.00 12.00
23 Luol Deng .50 1.25
24 Chris Duhon .40 1.00
25 Ben Gordon .50 1.25
26 Kirk Hinrich .50 1.25
27 Mike Sweetney .40 1.00
28 Drew Gooden .50 1.25
29 Larry Hughes .50 1.25
30 Zydrunas Ilgauskas .50 1.25
31 LeBron James 2.50 6.00
32 Damon Jones .40 1.00
33 Donyell Marshall .40 1.00
34 Anderson Varejao .40 1.00
35 Erick Dampier .40 1.00
36 Marquis Daniels .40 1.00
37 Devin Harris .40 1.00
38 Josh Howard .50 1.25
39 Dirk Nowitzki 1.00 2.50
40 Jerry Stackhouse .50 1.25
41 Jason Terry .50 1.25
42 Carmelo Anthony .75 2.00
43 Earl Boykins .40 1.00
44 Marcus Camby .50 1.25
45 Kenyon Martin .50 1.25
46 Andre Miller .50 1.25
47 Eduardo Najera .40 1.00
48 Nene .50 1.25
49 Chauncey Billups .60 1.50
50 Richard Hamilton .50 1.25
51 Lindsey Hunter .40 1.00
52 Antonio McDyess .50 1.25
53 Tayshaun Prince .50 1.25
54 Ben Wallace .50 1.25
55 Rasheed Wallace .60 1.50
56 Baron Davis .50 1.25
57 Ike Diogu .40 1.00
58 Mike Dunleavy .50 1.25
59 Derek Fisher .50 1.25
60 Troy Murphy .40 1.00
61 Mickael Pietrus .50 1.25
62 Jason Richardson .60 1.50
63 Rafer Alston .40 1.00
64 Luther Head .50 1.25
65 Juwan Howard .50 1.25
66 Tracy McGrady .75 2.00
67 Dikembe Mutombo .60 1.50
68 Stromile Swift .40 1.00
69 Yao Ming .75 2.00
70 Austin Croshere .40 1.00
71 Stephen Jackson .50 1.25
72 Sarunas Jasikevicius .50 1.25
73 Jermaine O'Neal .50 1.25
74 Peja Stojakovic .60 1.50
75 Jamaal Tinsley .40 1.00
76 Elton Brand .60 1.50
77 Sam Cassell .50 1.25
78 Chris Kaman .50 1.25
79 Shaun Livingston .40 1.00
80 Corey Maggette .50 1.25
81 Cuttino Mobley .40 1.00
82 Vladimir Radmanovic .40 1.00
83 Kwame Brown .40 1.00
84 Kobe Bryant 2.50 6.00
85 Devean George .40 1.00
86 Lamar Odom .50 1.25
87 Ronny Turiaf .50 1.25
88 Sasha Vujacic .40 1.00
89 Luke Walton .40 1.00
90 Shane Battier .50 1.25
91 Pau Gasol .60 1.50
92 Bobby Jackson .40 1.00
93 Eddie Jones .50 1.25
94 Mike Miller .50 1.25
95 Damon Stoudamire .50 1.25
96 Hakim Warrick .50 1.25
97 Alonzo Mourning .75 2.00
98 Shaquille O'Neal 1.25 3.00
99 Gary Payton .60 1.50
100 Wayne Simien .40 1.00
101 Dwyane Wade 1.00 2.50
102 Antoine Walker .50 1.25
103 Jason Williams .50 1.25
104 Andrew Bogut .50 1.25
105 T.J. Ford .40 1.00
106 Jamaal Magloire .40 1.00
107 Michael Redd .50 1.25
108 Bobby Simmons .40 1.00
109 Maurice Williams .50 1.25
110 Ricky Davis .50 1.25
111 Kevin Garnett 1.00 2.50
112 Kelenna Azubuike .75 2.00
113 Trenton Hassell .40 1.00
114 Troy Hudson .40 1.00
115 Rashad McCants .40 1.00
116 Vince Carter .75 2.00
117 Jason Collins .40 1.00
118 Richard Jefferson .50 1.25
119 Jason Kidd 1.00 2.50
120 Nenad Krstic .40 1.00
121 Jeff McInnis .40 1.00
122 Antoine Wright .40 1.00
123 P.J. Brown .40 1.00
124 Speedy Claxton .40 1.00
125 Desmond Mason .40 1.00
126 Chris Paul .75 2.00
127 J.R. Smith .50 1.25
128 Kirk Snyder .40 1.00
129 David West .50 1.25
130 Jamal Crawford .60 1.50
131 Eddy Curry .50 1.25
132 Channing Frye .50 1.25
133 Stephon Marbury .50 1.25
134 Quentin Richardson .50 1.25
135 Nate Robinson .40 1.00
136 David Lee .40 1.00
137 Carlos Arroyo .40 1.00
138 Tony Battie .40 1.00
139 Keyon Dooling .40 1.00
140 Grant Hill .75 2.00
141 Dwight Howard .50 1.25
142 Darko Milicic .40 1.00
143 Jameer Nelson .40 1.00
144 Samuel Dalembert .40 1.00
145 Steven Hunter .40 1.00
146 Andre Iguodala .50 1.25
147 Allen Iverson .75 2.00
148 Kyle Korver .50 1.25
149 Shavlik Randolph .40 1.00
150 Chris Webber .60 1.50
151 Raja Bell .50 1.25
152 Boris Diaw .50 1.25
153 Shawn Marion .50 1.25
154 Steve Nash .75 2.00
155 Amare Stoudemire .50 1.25
156 Kurt Thomas .40 1.00
157 Tim Thomas .40 1.00
158 Steve Blake .40 1.00
159 Juan Dixon .40 1.00
160 Zach Randolph .50 1.25
161 Joel Przybilla .40 1.00
162 Sebastian Telfair .40 1.00
163 Martell Webster .50 1.25
164 Shareef Abdur-Rahim .50 1.25
165 Ron Artest .60 1.50
166 Mike Bibby .60 1.50
167 Brad Miller .50 1.25
168 Kenny Thomas .40 1.00
169 Bonzi Wells .40 1.00
170 Bruce Bowen .40 1.00
171 Tim Duncan 1.00 2.50
172 Michael Finley .60 1.50
173 Manu Ginobili .60 1.50
174 Nazr Mohammed .40 1.00
175 Tony Parker .60 1.50
176 Ray Allen .60 1.50
177 Danny Fortson .40 1.00
178 Rashard Lewis .60 1.50
179 Luke Ridnour .50 1.25
180 Earl Watson .40 1.00
181 Chris Wilcox .40 1.00
182 Rafael Araujo .40 1.00
183 Chris Bosh .60 1.50
184 Joey Graham .40 1.00
185 Mike James .40 1.00
186 Morris Peterson .40 1.00
187 Charlie Villanueva .40 1.00
188 Carlos Boozer .50 1.25
189 Matt Harpring .40 1.00
190 Kris Humphries .40 1.00
191 Andrei Kirilenko .50 1.25
192 C.J. Miles .50 1.25
193 Paul Millsap .75 2.00
194 Deron Williams .50 1.25
195 Gilbert Arenas .50 1.25
196 Andray Blatche .40 1.00
197 Caron Butler .50 1.25
198 Antonio Daniels .40 1.00
199 Brendan Haywood .40 1.00
200 Antawn Jamison .50 1.25
201 Andrea Bargnani RC 1.25 3.00
202 LaMarcus Aldridge RC 3.00 8.00
203 Adam Morrison RC 1.25 3.00
204 Tyrus Thomas RC 1.00 2.50
205 Shelden Williams RC 1.00 2.50
206 Brandon Roy RC 1.25 3.00
207 Randy Foye RC 1.25 3.00
208 Rudy Gay RC 1.50 4.00
209 Patrick O'Bryant RC .75 2.00
210 Saer Sene RC .75 2.00
211 J.J. Redick RC 1.50 4.00
212 Hilton Armstrong RC .75 2.00
213 Thabo Sefolosha RC 1.25 3.00
214 Ronnie Brewer RC 1.25 3.00
215 Cedric Simmons RC .75 2.00
216 Rodney Carney RC .75 2.00
217 Shawne Williams RC .75 2.00
218 Quincy Douby RC .75 2.00
219 Renaldo Balkman RC 1.00 2.50
220 Rajon Rondo RC 2.00 5.00
221 Marcus Williams RC .75 2.00
222 Josh Boone RC .75 2.00
223 Kyle Lowry RC 1.50 4.00
224 Shannon Brown RC .75 2.00
225 Jordan Farmar RC 1.25 3.00
226 Maurice Ager RC .75 2.00
227 Mardy Collins RC .75 2.00
228 Jorge Garbajosa RC 1.00 2.50
229 James White RC .75 2.00
230 Steve Novak RC 1.00 2.50
231 Solomon Jones RC .75 2.00
232 Paul Davis RC .75 2.00
233 P.J. Tucker RC 1.00 2.50
234 Craig Smith RC 1.00 2.50
235 Bobby Jones RC .75 2.00
236 David Noel RC .75 2.00
237 Vassilis Spanoulis RC .75 2.00
238 James Augustine RC .75 2.00
239 Daniel Gibson RC 1.00 2.50
240 Alexander Johnson RC .75 2.00

2006-07 UD Reserve Gold

GOLD: 1.25X TO 3X BASE HI
APPROXIMATE ODDS ONE PER BOX

2006-07 UD Reserve Flight Team

COMPLETE SET (30) 15.00 40.00
APPROXIMATE ODDS 1:4
*GOLD: 1X TO 2.5X BASE HI
APPROXIMATE GOLD ODDS 1:20
AI Andre Iguodala .60 1.50
AS Amare Stoudemire .60 1.50
BB Brent Barry .50 1.25
BD Boris Diaw .60 1.50
CA Carmelo Anthony 1.00 2.50
CB Chris Bosh .75 2.00
CM Corey Maggette .60 1.50
DH Dwight Howard .60 1.50
DM Desmond Mason .50 1.25
DW Dwyane Wade 1.25 3.00
EJ Eddie Jones .60 1.50
FJ Fred Jones .50 1.25
GA Gilbert Arenas .60 1.50
JR Jason Richardson .75 2.00
JS J.R. Smith .60 1.50
KB Kobe Bryant 3.00 8.00
KM Kenyon Martin .60 1.50
LJ LeBron James 3.00 8.00
MA Shawn Marion .60 1.50
MG Manu Ginobili .75 2.00
MI Darius Miles .50 1.25
MJ Michael Jordan 6.00 15.00
NR Nate Robinson .50 1.25
RD Ricky Davis .60 1.50
RJ Richard Jefferson .60 1.50
SM Josh Smith .60 1.50
SS Stromile Swift .50 1.25
TM Tracy McGrady 1.00 2.50
TP Tayshaun Prince .60 1.50
VC Vince Carter 1.00 2.50

2006-07 UD Reserve Game Jerseys

APPROXIMATE ODDS ONE PER BOX
*PATCHES: .75X TO 2X BASE HI
APPROXIMATE ODDS 1:12
AB Andrew Bogut 2.50 6.00
AC Carlos Arroyo 2.00 5.00
AI Allen Iverson 4.00 10.00
AJ Al Jefferson 2.50 6.00
AK Andrei Kirilenko 2.50 6.00
AL Rafer Alston 2.50 6.00
AN Antawn Jamison 2.50 6.00
AR Ron Artest 3.00 8.00
AS Amare Stoudemire 2.50 6.00
AW Antoine Walker 2.50 6.00
BB Bruce Bowen 2.50 6.00
BD Baron Davis 2.50 6.00
BG Ben Gordon 2.50 6.00
BM Brad Miller 2.50 6.00
BW Ben Wallace 2.50 6.00
CB Chauncey Billups 3.00 8.00
CF Channing Frye 2.50 6.00
CM Corey Maggette 2.50 6.00
CP Chris Paul 4.00 10.00
CW Chris Webber 3.00 8.00
DG Drew Gooden 2.50 6.00
DH Devin Harris 2.00 5.00
DM Donyell Marshall 2.50 6.00
DN Dirk Nowitzki 5.00 12.00
DW Deron Williams 2.50 6.00
EO Emeka Okafor 2.50 6.00
GA Gilbert Arenas 2.50 6.00
GE Devean George 2.50 6.00
GH Grant Hill 6.00 15.00
HE Luther Head 2.50 6.00
HO Dwight Howard 2.50 6.00
ID Ike Diogu 2.00 5.00
IG Andre Iguodala 2.50 6.00
JC Jamal Crawford 3.00 8.00
JD Juan Dixon 2.50 6.00
JH Josh Howard 2.50 6.00
JJ Joe Johnson 2.50 6.00
JK Jason Kidd 5.00 12.00
JN Jameer Nelson 2.00 5.00
JO Jermaine O'Neal 2.50 6.00
JR Jason Richardson 3.00 8.00
JS J.R. Smith 2.50 6.00
JT Jason Terry 2.50 6.00
JW Jason Williams 2.50 6.00
KB Kwame Brown 2.50 6.00
KG Kevin Garnett 5.00 12.00
KH Kirk Hinrich 2.50 6.00
KK Kyle Korver 2.50 6.00
KM Kenyon Martin 2.50 6.00
LB Leandro Barbosa 2.50 6.00
LD Luol Deng 2.50 6.00
LH Larry Hughes 2.50 6.00
LJ LeBron James 15.00 40.00
LO Lamar Odom 2.50 6.00
LW Luke Walton 2.00 5.00
MA Stephon Marbury 2.50 6.00
MB Mike Bibby 3.00 8.00
MD Marquis Daniels 2.50 6.00
MG Manu Ginobili 3.00 8.00
MJ Michael Jordan 25.00 60.00
MR Michael Redd 2.50 6.00
MW Marvin Williams 2.50 6.00
NR Nate Robinson 2.00 5.00
PA Tony Parker 3.00 8.00
PG Pau Gasol 3.00 8.00
PS Peja Stojakovic 3.00 8.00
QR Quentin Richardson 2.50 6.00
RA Ray Allen 3.00 8.00
RF Raymond Felton 2.50 6.00
RH Richard Hamilton 2.50 6.00
RL Rashard Lewis 3.00 8.00
RM Rashad McCants 2.00 5.00
RW Rasheed Wallace 3.00 8.00
SD Samuel Dalembert 2.50 6.00
SF Steve Francis 2.50 6.00
SH Shawn Marion 2.50 6.00
SJ Sarunas Jasikevicius 2.50 6.00
SL Shaun Livingston 2.50 6.00
SM Sean May 2.00 5.00
SO Shaquille O'Neal 6.00 15.00
ST Sebastian Telfair 2.00 5.00
TC Tyson Chandler 2.50 6.00
TF T.J. Ford 2.00 5.00
TP Tayshaun Prince 2.50 6.00
VC Vince Carter 4.00 10.00
WE Martell Webster 2.50 6.00
WS Wally Szczerbiak 2.50 6.00
ZI Zydrunas Ilgauskas 2.50 6.00

2006-07 UD Reserve Legendary Signatures

APPROXIMATE ODDS ONE PER BOX
BK Bernard King 6.00 15.00
BM Bob McAdoo 6.00 15.00
CD Clyde Drexler 12.50 30.00
CH Connie Hawkins 6.00 15.00
CM Cedric Maxwell 6.00 15.00
DD Darryl Dawkins 8.00 20.00
DR David Robinson 40.00 80.00
HO Hakeem Olajuwon 15.00 40.00
JE Julius Erving 40.00 80.00
JO Michael Jordan 300.00 550.00
JS John Stockton 60.00 120.00
KV Kiki Vandeweghe 6.00 15.00
LB Larry Bird 75.00 150.00
MC Maurice Cheeks 6.00 15.00
MJ Magic Johnson 60.00 120.00
ML Maurice Lucas 6.00 15.00
NA Nate Archibald 6.00 15.00
RO Dennis Rodman 40.00 75.00
SP Sam Perkins 6.00 15.00
SW Spud Webb 8.00 20.00

2006-07 UD Reserve Materials

STATED PRINT RUN 100 SER.#'d SETS
*PATCHES: .75X TO 2X BASE HI
PRINT RUN 35 SER.#'d SETS
AB Andray Blatche 3.00 8.00
AI Allen Iverson 5.00 12.00
AJ Antawn Jamison 3.00 8.00
AK Andrei Kirilenko 3.00 8.00
BD Baron Davis 3.00 8.00
BG Ben Gordon 3.00 8.00
BM Brad Miller 3.00 8.00
BO Chris Bosh 4.00 10.00
BW Ben Wallace 3.00 8.00
CA Carmelo Anthony 5.00 12.00
CB Carlos Boozer 3.00 8.00
CM Corey Maggette 3.00 8.00
CP Chris Paul 5.00 12.00
DG Danny Granger 3.00 8.00
DH Dwight Howard 3.00 8.00
DN Dirk Nowitzki 6.00 15.00
DW David West 3.00 8.00
EB Elton Brand 4.00 10.00
EO Emeka Okafor 3.00 8.00
GH Grant Hill 8.00 20.00
HW Hakim Warrick 3.00 8.00
JC Josh Childress 3.00 8.00
JG Joey Graham 2.50 6.00
JK Jason Kidd 6.00 15.00
JN Jameer Nelson 2.50 6.00
JO Jermaine O'Neal 3.00 8.00
JS Josh Smith 3.00 8.00
KB Kobe Bryant 12.50 30.00
KG Kevin Garnett 6.00 15.00
LH Luther Head 3.00 8.00
LJ LeBron James 12.50 30.00
LW Luke Walton 2.50 6.00
MB Mike Bibby 4.00 10.00
MG Manu Ginobili 4.00 10.00
MJ Michael Jordan 30.00 80.00
MR Michael Redd 3.00 8.00
MW Marvin Williams 3.00 8.00
NE Nene 3.00 8.00
PP Paul Pierce 4.00 10.00
PS Peja Stojakovic 4.00 10.00
RA Ray Allen 4.00 10.00
RB Raja Bell 3.00 8.00
RF Raymond Felton 3.00 8.00
RH Richard Hamilton 3.00 8.00
RJ Richard Jefferson 3.00 8.00
RM Rashad McCants 2.50 6.00
RW Rasheed Wallace 4.00 10.00
SM Stephon Marbury 3.00 8.00
SN Steve Nash 5.00 12.00
TD Tim Duncan 6.00 15.00
TP Tony Parker 4.00 10.00
WI Deron Williams 3.00 8.00
WS Wally Szczerbiak 3.00 8.00
YM Yao Ming 5.00 12.00
ZI Zydrunas Ilgauskas 3.00 8.00

2006-07 UD Reserve Materials Dual

PRINT RUN 50 SER.#'d SETS
*PATCHES: .75X TO 2X BASE HI
PATCH PRINT RUN 15 SER.#'d SETS
AR L.Aldridge/B.Roy 10.00 25.00
BG C.Bosh/J.Graham 6.00 15.00
BM E.Brand/C.Maggette 5.00 12.00
BO K.Brown/L.Odom 5.00 12.00
CJ J.Childress/J.Johnson 5.00 12.00
FM R.Foye/R.McCants 5.00 12.00
GW P.Gasol/H.Warrick 5.00 12.00
HB R.Hamilton/C.Billups 8.00 20.00
HH D.Harris/J.Howard 5.00 12.00
HN G.Hill/J.Nelson 6.00 15.00
JB A.Jamison/A.Blatche 5.00 12.00
JJ L.James/M.Jordan 60.00 150.00
KB A.Kirilenko/C.Boozer 5.00 12.00
MB B.Miller/M.Bibby 5.00 12.00
MF C.Frye/S.Marbury 5.00 12.00
MM Y.Ming/T.McGrady 10.00 25.00
MO Y.Ming/S.O'Neal 20.00 40.00
OG J.O'Neal/D.Granger 5.00 12.00
PD T.Parker/T.Duncan 10.00 25.00
PJ P.Pierce/A.Jefferson 5.00 12.00
PW C.Paul/D.West 6.00 15.00
RD J.Richardson/B.Davis 5.00 12.00
VR C.Villanueva/M.Redd 5.00 12.00
WB M.Williams/J.Boone 5.00 12.00
PAN C.Anthony/Nene 6.00 15.00

2006-07 UD Reserve Materials Triple

PRINT RUN 25 SER.#'d SETS
UNPRICED PATCH PRINT RUN 5 SETS
ARW Aldridge/Roy/Webster 20.00 40.00
BSS Bargnani/Sene/Sefolosha 10.00 25.00
CWS Childress/Williams/Smith 8.00 20.00
GST Gordon/Sefolosha/Thomas 8.00 20.00
GWB Gay/Williams/Boone 8.00 20.00
GWG Gasol/Warrick/Gay 8.00 20.00
ICK Iguodala/Carney/Korver 8.00 20.00
KCJ Kidd/Carter/Jefferson 20.00 40.00
SNM Stoudemire/Nash/Marion 20.00 40.00
SRR Szczerbiak/Rondo/Ray 8.00 20.00

2006-07 UD Reserve MVP Watch

COMPLETE SET (15) 15.00 40.00
APPROXIMATE ODDS 1:6
*GOLD: .75X TO 2X BASE HI
APPROXIMATE GOLD ODDS 1:24
AI Allen Iverson 1.25 3.00
BW Ben Wallace .75 2.00
CB Chauncey Billups 1.00 2.50
DN Dirk Nowitzki 1.50 4.00
DW Dwyane Wade 1.50 4.00
EB Elton Brand 1.00 2.50
GA Gilbert Arenas .75 2.00
KB Kobe Bryant 4.00 10.00
KG Kevin Garnett 1.50 4.00
LJ LeBron James 4.00 10.00
PP Paul Pierce 1.00 2.50
SN Steve Nash 1.25 3.00
SO Shaquille O'Neal 2.00 5.00
TD Tim Duncan 1.50 4.00
TM Tracy McGrady 1.25 3.00

2006-07 UD Reserve Signatures

APPROXIMATE ODDS ONE PER BOX
AI Andre Iguodala 5.00 12.00
AJ Al Jefferson 4.00 10.00
AN Antawn Jamison 4.00 10.00
AR Hilton Armstrong 3.00 8.00

BA Andrea Bargnani 5.00 12.00
BB Brent Barry 6.00 15.00
BD Baron Davis 5.00 12.00
BE Raja Bell 4.00 10.00
BG Ben Gordon 4.00 10.00
BJ Bobby Jackson 3.00 8.00
BO Bruce Bowen 3.00 8.00
BS Bobby Simmons 3.00 8.00
CA Carmelo Anthony 15.00 40.00
CB Chauncey Billups 8.00 20.00
CD Chris Duhon 3.00 8.00
CH Charlie Bell 3.00 8.00
CM Corey Maggette 4.00 10.00
CS Cedric Simmons 3.00 8.00
DB Dee Brown 3.00 8.00
DE Daniel Ewing 3.00 8.00
DG Danny Granger 4.00 10.00
DI Boris Diaw 4.00 10.00
DM Damir Markota 3.00 8.00
DN David Noel 3.00 8.00
DW Deron Williams 4.00 10.00
EC Eddy Curry 4.00 10.00
EO Emeka Okafor 4.00 10.00
FE Raymond Felton 4.00 10.00
GG Gerald Green 4.00 10.00
GI Daniel Gibson 4.00 10.00
GR Joey Graham 3.00 8.00
HA Hassan Adams 3.00 8.00
HW Hakim Warrick 4.00 10.00
IU Ime Udoka 3.00 8.00
JA James Augustine 3.00 8.00
JB Josh Boone 3.00 8.00
JC Josh Childress 4.00 10.00
JF Jordan Farmar 5.00 12.00
JG Jorge Garbajosa 4.00 10.00
JJ Jarrett Jack 4.00 10.00
JO Bobby Jones 3.00 8.00
JS J.R. Smith 4.00 10.00
KD Keyon Dooling 3.00 8.00
KH Kirk Hinrich 4.00 10.00
KK Kyle Korver 4.00 10.00
KL Kyle Lowry 6.00 15.00
LA LaMarcus Aldridge 15.00 40.00
LB Leandro Barbosa 4.00 10.00
LH Larry Hughes 4.00 10.00
LJ LeBron James 125.00 300.00
LR Luke Ridnour 4.00 10.00
MA Maurice Ager 3.00 8.00
MC Mardy Collins 3.00 8.00
MI Mile Ilic 3.00 8.00
MM Chris Mihm 3.00 8.00
MO Cuttino Mobley 3.00 8.00
MW Marvin Williams 4.00 10.00
NO Steve Novak 4.00 10.00
PD Paul Davis 3.00 8.00
PM Paul Millsap 5.00 12.00
PO Patrick O'Bryant 3.00 8.00
PP Paul Pierce 8.00 20.00
PS Peja Stojakovic 5.00 12.00
PT P.J. Tucker 4.00 10.00
QD Quincy Douby 3.00 8.00
QR Quentin Richardson 4.00 10.00
RB Ronnie Brewer 5.00 12.00
RC Rodney Carney 3.00 8.00
RE Renaldo Balkman 4.00 10.00
RF Randy Foye 5.00 12.00
RG Rudy Gay 6.00 15.00
RH Ryan Hollins 4.00 10.00
RM Rashad McCants 3.00 8.00
RO Brandon Roy 5.00 12.00
RR Rajon Rondo 8.00 20.00
SA Shareef Abdur-Rahim 4.00 10.00
SB Shannon Brown 3.00 8.00
SH Shawne Williams 3.00 8.00
SJ Solomon Jones 3.00 8.00
SM Craig Smith 4.00 10.00
SN Steve Nash 15.00 40.00
SR Sergio Rodriguez 5.00 12.00
SS Saer Sene 3.00 8.00
ST Sebastian Telfair 3.00 8.00
SW Shelden Williams 4.00 10.00
TA Tony Allen 5.00 12.00
TF T.J. Ford 3.00 8.00
TM Tracy McGrady 12.00 30.00
TS Thabo Sefolosha 5.00 12.00
TT Tyrus Thomas 4.00 10.00
VC Vince Carter 30.00 60.00
VS Vassilis Spanoulis 3.00 8.00
WB Will Blalock 3.00 8.00
WE Martell Webster 4.00 10.00
WH James White 3.00 8.00
WM Marcus Williams 3.00 8.00
YM Yao Ming 15.00 40.00

2006-07 UD Reserve Signatures Dual

PRINT RUN 50 SER.#'d SETS
AB H.Armstrong/J.Boone 6.00 15.00
AM C.Anthony/T.McGrady 25.00 60.00
AP M.Ager/S.Perkins 6.00 15.00
AR L.Aldridge/B.Roy 20.00 50.00
AW J.Augustine/D.Williams 15.00 40.00
BB C.Billups/W.Blalock 8.00 20.00
BG S.Brown/D.Gibson 8.00 20.00
CB R.Balkman/M.Collins 6.00 15.00
CW R.Carney/S.Williams 6.00 15.00
DA Q.Douby/S.Abdur-Rahim 6.00 15.00
DO B.Davis/P.O'Bryant 8.00 20.00
FS R.Foye/C.Smith 8.00 20.00
GF T.Ford/J.Graham 6.00 15.00
HD K.Hinrich/C.Duhon 12.50 30.00
HF R.Felton/R.Hollins 6.00 15.00
IK A.Iguodala/K.Korver 8.00 20.00
JD J.Augustine/D.Brown 6.00 15.00
JJ L.James/M.Jordan 400.00 700.00
LR D.Lee/Q.Richardson 6.00 15.00
MD C.Maggette/P.Davis 6.00 15.00
OF E.Okafor/R.Felton 15.00 30.00
OM H.Olajuwon/Y.Ming 40.00 80.00
RB D.Robinson/B.Barry 40.00 80.00
RD R.Brewer/D.Brown 6.00 15.00
RF A.Ray/R.Foye 10.00 25.00
SM S.Williams/M.Williams 6.00 15.00
TJ S.Telfair/A.Jefferson 6.00 15.00
TR T.Allen/R.Rondo 15.00 40.00
TS T.Thomas/T.Sefolosha 15.00 40.00
VS K.Vandeweghe/J.Smith 6.00 15.00
WC J.Childress/S.Webb 6.00 15.00
WG S.Williams/D.Granger 6.00 15.00
WS D.Wilkins/S.Sene 6.00 15.00
WW J.White/B.Barry 6.00 15.00

2006-07 UD Reserve Signatures Triple

PRINT RUN 25 SER.#'d SETS
UNPRICED QUAD PRINT RUN 5 SETS
AWB Adams/Williams/Boone 12.00 30.00
BAT Bargnani/Aldridge/Thomas 25.00 60.00
BCR Balkman/Collins/Richardson 12.00 30.00
FSM Foye/Smith/McCants 12.00 30.00
GBH Gibson/Brown/Hughes 12.00 30.00
RGR Rondo/Green/Ray 25.00 60.00
RWS Ridnour/Wilkins/Sene 12.00 30.00
SSA Stojakovic/Simmons/Armstrong 12.00 30.00
WLG Warrick/Lowry/Gay 25.00 50.00

2006-07 UD Reserve The LeBrons

COMPLETE SET (15) 20.00 50.00
APPROXIMATE ODDS 1:12
COMMON GOLD 15.00 30.00
COMMON MEMORABILIA 10.00 25.00
COMMON DUAL/TRIP.MEM. 15.00 40.00

2002-03 UD SuperStars

This 300 card set was released in March, 2003. This set was issued in five card packs with an $3 SRP. The packs were issued in 24 pack boxes which came 12 boxes to a case. The final 50 cards of the set featured two rookies from different sports.

COMPLETE SET (300) 30.00 80.00
12 Stephon Marbury .30 .75
13 Shawn Marion .25 .60
20 Shareef Abdur-Rahim .25 .60
34 Paul Pierce .50 1.25
35 Antoine Walker .40 1.00
97 Ray Allen .30 .75
103 Steve Francis .40 1.00
104 Reggie Miller .40 1.00
119 Kobe Bryant 1.25 3.00
120 Shaquille O'Neal .60 1.50
121 Wilt Chamberlain .60 1.50
122 Andre Miller .25 .60
124 Pau Gasol .30 .75
132 Kevin Garnett .60 1.50
139 Baron Davis .40 1.00
143 Jason Kidd .50 1.25
178 Jason Richardson .40 1.00
179 Grant Hill .40 1.00
180 Tracy McGrady .60 1.50
187 Allen Iverson .60 1.50
188 Julius Erving .60 1.50
198 Rasheed Wallace .30 .75
199 Chris Webber .40 1.00
200 Mike Bibby .30 .75
201 Tim Duncan .60 1.50
222 Rashard Lewis .15 .40
223 Gary Payton .40 1.00
243 Vince Carter .50 1.25
245 Karl Malone .40 1.00
246 Jerry Stackhouse .25 .60
247 Michael Jordan 2.00 5.00
254 S.Chistov M.Ely .40 1.00
258 J.Williams F.Beltran .50 1.25
262 D.Wagner W.Green .60 1.50
264 C.Hutchinson C.Jacobsen .50 1.25
266 N.Hilario N.Rolovich .40 1.00
267 J.Harrington T.Prince 1.25 3.00
269 J.Bouwmeester C.Butler 1.00 2.50
270 M.Dunleavy P.Buchanon .40 1.00
272 B.Nachbar J.Wells .20 .50
273 D.Carr Y.Ming 4.00 10.00
276 D.Gooden S.Upshall .75 2.00
278 M.Haislip J.Walker .60 1.50
283 P.Bouchard I.Rakocevic .20 .50
284 A.Machado J.Salmons .40 1.00
285 A.Stoudemire J.Ward 1.50 4.00
295 R.Johnson C.Jefferies .20 .50
296 P.Ramsey J.Dixon .60 1.50
297 J.Jeffries S.Bechler .20 .50

2002-03 UD SuperStars Gold

*GOLD 1-250: 2.5X TO 6X BASIC
*GOLD MATSUI: 6X TO 12X BASIC
*GOLD 251-300: 2X TO 5X BASIC

2002-03 UD SuperStars Benchmarks

Inserted at a stated rate of one in 20, these 10 cards feature two athletes from different sports with something in common. It could be being a legendary figure in the sport or playing in the same city.

B4 B.Russell M.Mantle 4.00 10.00
B5 A.Iverson D.McNabb 1.00 2.50
B7 K.Garnett R.Moss 1.50 4.00
B10 K.Bryant D.Jeter 3.00 8.00

2002-03 UD SuperStars City All-Stars Dual Jersey

Inserted at a stated rate of one in 32, these 43 cards featured two jersey swatches from star athletes from the same city. Some cards were issued in smaller quantities and we have notated that information with an SP in our database.

ABBD A.Brooks/B.Davis 6.00 15.00
ADDM A.Davis/D.Miles 5.00 12.00
EJJO E.James/J.O'Neal 5.00 12.00
GSSA G.Sheffield/S.Abdur-Rahim 4.00 10.00
IRMF I.Rodriguez/M.Finley 6.00 15.00
MRPP M.Ramirez/P.Pierce 6.00 15.00
RJSM R.Johnson/S.Marbury 6.00 15.00
SDJS S.Davis/J.Stackhouse SP 6.00 15.00
SMPG S.McNair/P.Gasol 10.00 25.00
SSAW S.Samsonov/A.Walker 5.00 12.00
TCMO T.Chandler/M.Ordonez 6.00 15.00
WSMB W.Szczerbiak/M.Bennett 5.00 12.00

2002-03 UD SuperStars City All-Stars Triple Jersey

Randomly inserted in packs, these cards featured three game-used jersey swatches from all-stars from the same city. These cards were issued to a stated print run of 250 serial numbered sets.

CVT Chipper Vick Terry 12.00 30.00
DPE Erstad Kariya Brand 10.00 25.00
IGS Ichiro Payton Alexander 10.00 25.00
IMD I.Rod Modano Nowitzki 15.00 40.00
JCK Griffey Dillon K.Martin 10.00 25.00
JDW Jacque Culp Szczerbiak 10.00 25.00
JDY Bagwell Carr Ming 15.00 40.00
JLP Giambi Sprewell Bure 6.00 15.00
JSB Harrington Yzer Wallace 25.00 50.00
MJA Prior J.Will A.Thomas 5.00 12.00
MJC Piazza Kidd C.Martin 10.00 25.00
MJJ Tejada J.Rich Rice 10.00 25.00
OTD Vizquel Couch D.Wag 10.00 25.00
PTP Pedro Brady Pierce 10.00 25.00
REA Clemens Lind Houston 15.00 30.00
RSS R.Johnson Marion Doan 6.00 15.00
SWK Green Gretzky Kobe 40.00 80.00

2002-03 UD SuperStars Keys to the City

Inserted at a stated rate of one in six. These 10 cards feature two star athletes from the same city.

COMPLETE SET (10) 10.00 25.00
K1 C.Delgado V.Carter .75 2.00
K2 K.Bryant K.Ishii 2.00 5.00

2002-03 UD SuperStars Legendary Leaders Dual Jersey

Inserted at a stated rate of one in 96, these 20 cards feature game-worn jersey pieces from two star athletes from the same city.

AIDM A.Iverson/D.McNabb 10.00 25.00
EJJO E.James/J.O'Neal 6.00 15.00
JKCP J.Kidd/C.Pennington 8.00 20.00
JRJR J.Rice/J.Richardson 10.00 25.00
JWAT J.Williams/A.Thomas 6.00 15.00
KGRM K.Garnett/R.Moss 15.00 30.00
RMPM R.Miller/P.Manning 15.00 30.00
SMRJ S.Marion/R.Johnson 6.00 15.00

2002-03 UD SuperStars Legendary Leaders Triple Jersey

Randomly inserted in packs, these 18 cards feature game-used jersey swatches from three athletes. This set is significant by the usage of game-worn swatches of soccer great David Beckham. Each card was issued to a stated print run of 250 serial numbered sets.

ADJ Iverson McNabb Roenick 20.00 50.00
GMS Maddux Vick A-Rahim 12.50 30.00
IDK Ichiro Beckham Bryant 75.00 150.00
IKD Ichiro Garnett Beckham 40.00 80.00
JWL DiMaggio Gretzky Bird 60.00 120.00
KJT Malone Rice Gwynn 10.00 25.00
PPT Pedro Pierce Brady 20.00 50.00
SKM Sosa Kobe Faulk 15.00 40.00
SWK Green Gretzky Kobe 40.00 80.00

2002-03 UD SuperStars Magic Moments

Inserted at a stated rate of one in five, this 20 card set featured a mix of active and retired players along with history about key moments in their career.

COMPLETE SET (20) 10.00 25.00
MM14 Michael Jordan 2.50 6.00
MM15 Kobe Bryant 1.50 4.00
MM16 Jay Williams .50 1.25

2002-03 UD SuperStars Rookie Review

Inserted at a stated rate of one in 20, these 10 cards feature two athletes who made their American professional debut in the same year.

R3 J.Beckett S.Francis 1.00 2.50
R4 V.Carter P.Manning 1.25 3.00
R7 J.Kidd A.Rodriguez 1.00 2.50
R8 A.Soriano S.Marion 1.00 2.50
R9 K.Griffey Jr. D.Robinson 1.50 4.00

2002-03 UD SuperStars Spokesmen

Issued as a three-card pack topper, these 30 cards feature a mix of players who were also serving as spokesmen for Upper Deck.

*BLACK: 1.25X TO 3X BASIC SPOKESMEN
BLACK/GOLD INSERTS IN SPOKESMEN PACKS
BLACK PRINT RUN 250 SERIAL #'d SETS
*GOLD/25: 3X TO 8X BASIC INSERTS
GOLD PRINT RUN 25 SERIAL #'d SETS
UD8 Michael Jordan 4.00 10.00
UD9 Kobe Bryant 2.00 5.00
UD10 Jay Williams 1.25 3.00
UD23 Michael Jordan 4.00 10.00
UD24 Kobe Bryant 2.00 5.00
UD25 Jay Williams 1.25 3.00

1996 UDA 22kt Gold Michael Jordan Slam Dunk Champion

NNO Michael Jordan 75.00 150.00

2003 UDA LeBron James

Releaed by Upper Deck Authenticated during the 2003-04, this one-card set commemorates LBJ's first NBA game-October 29th, 2003. The cards have a gold border along the left side, a UDA authentication hologram on the front of the card below which, the words, "first game" are printed. The Upper Deck Collectibles logo appears in the upper right-hand corner of the card and each card is accompaned by a UDA tri-fold certificate of authenticity. Also, Released was a LeBron James Rookie of the Month card. This release has a red border along the left side of the card and is also signed and limited to 23 copies.

NNO LeBron James First Game/2323 4.00 10.00
NNO LeBron James First Game AU/23 200.00 500.00
NNO LeBron James ROM AU/23 200.00 500.00
NNO LeBron James Youngest to 1000/5000 3.00 8.00

1995-98 UDA Michael Jordan Commemorative Cards

The cards listed below are not numbered and have been given abbreviations for ease of listing.

AS1 1996 10-Time All-Star/5000 10.00 25.00
AS2 1997 11-Time All-Star/5000 10.00 25.00
AS3 1996 All-Star First Team/2500 12.50 30.00
CE1 Celebration of Excellence 8.00 20.00
CH1 1997 4-Time Champs AU/50
FM1 1996 4-Time Finals MVP/2500 12.50 30.00
FM2 1997 5-Time NBA Finals MVP/5000 10.0025.00
HE1 1981-84 A Higher Education (no serial #)
MM1 1996 Magic Memories MTS 8.00 20.00
NC1 1995 UNC 1st Champ.gold foil/5000 10.00 25.00
NC2 1995 UNC 1st Champ.blue foil/5000 10.00 25.00
NH1 1996 National Hero/5000 10.00 25.00
OG1 Olympic Gold '84 and '92 8.00 20.00
PT1 1996 25,000 Points (no serial #) 8.00 20.00
RM1 1996 Reg.season MVP/2500 12.50 30.00
SC1 1996 8-Time Scoring Champ/5000 10.00 25.00
SC2 1997 9-Time Scoring Champ/5000 10.00 25.00
SJ1 1996 Space Jam w/Porky/5000 10.00 25.00
SJ2 1996 Space Jam w/Bugs/5000 10.00 25.00
SJ3 1996 Space Jam w/ball/5000 10.00 25.00
MJ15 1997 25,000 Career Point 22kt/10000 8.00 20.00

2000 UDA Michael Jordan Final Shot

This 3.5x5 card was released by Upper Deck in 2000, and features a piece of the Delta Center floor upon which Michael Jordan took his final shot. There were 1000 total cards produced, and Michael Jordan signed the first 100. These cards were sold exclusively through Upper Deck's direct marketing channel. The unsigned version retailed at $395, while the signed version retailed at $3999.95.

1A Michael Jordan Floor AU/100 2000.00 4000.00
1B Michael Jordan Floor/900 150.00 400.00

1996 UDA SPx Record Breaker Michael Jordan

Released as a special product through Upper Deck Authenticated, this card is serially numbered to 250 and features a UDA Authentication hologram with the lettered prefix BAD.

R1 Michael Jordan AU/250 600.00 900.00

2000-01 Ultimate Collection

e 2000-01 Upper Deck Ultimate Collection product shipped in February, 2001 and featured a 60-card base veteran set. The full set was broken into tiers as follows: 60 Veterans, and 14 Rookies and 6 Autographed Rookies - the rookies are listed seperately since they were graded. Each pack contained four cards, and carried a suggested retail price of $100 per pack.

RCs STATED PRINT RUN 750 SERIAL #'d SETS
1 Dikembe Mutombo 2.50 6.00
2 Hanno Mottola RC 2.00 5.00
3 Paul Pierce 2.50 6.00
4 Antoine Walker 2.00 5.00
5 Derrick Coleman 2.00 5.00
6 Baron Davis 2.50 6.00
7 Elton Brand 2.50 6.00
8 Michael Jordan 20.00 50.00
9 Andre Miller 2.00 5.00
10 Chris Mihm RC 2.50 6.00
11 Michael Finley 2.50 6.00
12 Donnell Harvey RC 2.50 6.00
13 Antonio McDyess 2.00 5.00
14 Nick Van Exel 2.00 5.00
15 Jerry Stackhouse 2.00 5.00
16 Jerome Williams 1.50 4.00
17 Larry Hughes 2.00 5.00
18 Antawn Jamison 2.50 6.00
19 Steve Francis 2.00 5.00
20 Hakeem Olajuwon 3.00 8.00
21 Reggie Miller 2.50 6.00
22 Jalen Rose 2.00 5.00
23 Lamar Odom 2.00 5.00
24 Michael Olowokandi 1.50 4.00
25 Shaquille O'Neal 6.00 15.00
26 Kobe Bryant 10.00 25.00
27 Ron Harper 2.00 5.00
28 Alonzo Mourning 3.00 8.00
29 Eddie House RC 2.50 6.00
30 Glenn Robinson 2.00 5.00
31 Ray Allen 2.50 6.00
32 Kevin Garnett 4.00 10.00
33 Wally Szczerbiak 2.00 5.00
34 Terrell Brandon 1.50 4.00
35 Stephon Marbury 2.00 5.00
36 Keith Van Horn 2.00 5.00
37 Allan Houston 2.00 5.00
38 Latrell Sprewell 2.00 5.00
39 Grant Hill 3.00 8.00
40 Tracy McGrady 4.00 10.00
41 Allen Iverson 5.00 12.00
42 Toni Kukoc 2.50 6.00
43 Jason Kidd 4.00 10.00
44 Anfernee Hardaway 4.00 10.00
45 Scottie Pippen 4.00 10.00
46 Rasheed Wallace 2.50 6.00
47 Chris Webber 2.50 6.00
48 Jason Williams 2.50 6.00
49 Tim Duncan 5.00 12.00
50 David Robinson 4.00 10.00
51 Gary Payton 2.50 6.00
52 Rashard Lewis 2.50 6.00
53 Vince Carter 5.00 12.00
54 Morris Peterson RC 3.00 8.00
55 Karl Malone 3.00 8.00
56 John Stockton 3.00 8.00
57 Shareef Abdur-Rahim 2.00 5.00
58 Mike Bibby 2.50 6.00
59 Mike Smith RC 2.00 5.00
60 Richard Hamilton 2.00 5.00
P1 Kenyon Martin SAMPLE 1.00 2.50

2000-01 Ultimate Collection Rookies

Randomly inserted into packs, this 20-card set features the rookies from the 2000-01 season. Please note that there were only 250 of each card produced.

STATED PRINT RUN 250 SERIAL #'d SETS
61 Mamadou N'Diaye RC 4.00 10.00
62 Erick Barkley RC 4.00 10.00
63 Desmond Mason RC 8.00 20.00
64 Speedy Claxton RC 6.00 15.00
65 Jamaal Magloire RC 6.00 15.00
66 DeShawn Stevenson RC 6.00 15.00
67 Etan Thomas RC 6.00 15.00
68 Jamal Crawford RC 15.00 40.00
69 Joel Przybilla RC 5.00 12.00
70 Keyon Dooling RC 6.00 15.00
71 Jerome Moiso RC 4.00 10.00
72 Quentin Richardson RC 6.00 15.00
73 Courtney Alexander RC 5.00 12.00
74 Mateen Cleaves RC 5.00 12.00
75 Mike Miller AU RC 10.00 25.00
76 DerMarr Johnson AU RC 5.00 12.00
77 Darius Miles AU RC 6.00 15.00
78 Marcus Fizer AU RC 6.00 15.00
79 Kenyon Martin AU RC 15.00 40.00
80 Stromile Swift AU RC 6.00 15.00

2000-01 Ultimate Collection Game Jerseys Bronze

ndomly inserted into packs at one in three, this nine-card insert features swatches from actual game-used NBA jerseys. Please note that there are three different tiers (Gold, Silver, and Bronze). Card backs carry the players initials as numbering followed by a "J".

STATED ODDS 1:3
*GOLD: .6X TO 1.5X BRONZE HI
GOLD STATED ODDS 1:17
*SILVER: .5X TO 1.25X BRONZE HI
SILVER STATED ODDS 1:6
DSJ Damon Stoudamire 4.00 10.00
JKJ Jason Kidd 8.00 20.00
JSJ John Stockton 8.00 20.00
KBJ Kobe Bryant 15.00 40.00
KGJ Kevin Garnett 8.00 20.00
KMJ Kenyon Martin 12.00 30.00
MFJ Marcus Fizer 5.00 12.00
MJJ Michael Jordan 50.00 120.00
WSJ Wally Szczerbiak 4.00 10.00

2000-01 Ultimate Collection Game Jerseys Patches

Randomly inserted into packs at one in 11, this 25-card insert features swatches from actual game-used NBA jersey patches. Card backs carry the players initials as numbering followed by a "P".

STATED ODDS 1:11
SOME AUTOS UNPRICED DUE TO SCARCITY
STATED PRINT RUN 8 TO 100 SETS
AHP Anfernee Hardaway/75 75.00 150.00
AIP Allen Iverson/75 80.00 200.00
AMP Alonzo Mourning/100 30.00 80.00
DRP David Robinson/100 40.00 100.00
DSP Damon Stoudamire/75 20.00 50.00
GPP Gary Payton/100 20.00 50.00
JKP Jason Kidd/75 50.00 120.00
JSP John Stockton/100 50.00 120.00
JWP Jason Williams/25 50.00 100.00
KGA Kevin Garnett AU/21 150.00 300.00
KGP Kevin Garnett/21 75.00 150.00
KMP Karl Malone/100 40.00 100.00
KVP Keith Van Horn/100 20.00 50.00
MFP Michael Finley/75 25.00 60.00
MJA Michael Jordan AU/23 1500.00 2500.00
PPP Paul Pierce/50 40.00 100.00
RAP Ray Allen/100 40.00 100.00
RMP Reggie Miller/100 50.00 120.00
SAP Shareef Abdur-Rahim/100 20.00 50.00
SHP Shawn Marion/25 40.00 100.00
SMP Stephon Marbury/75 20.00 50.00
SOP Shaquille O'Neal/75 60.00 150.00
WSP Wally Szczerbiak/100 20.00 50.00

2000-01 Ultimate Collection Signatures Bronze

Randomly inserted into packs, this 15-card insert features authenticated autographs of some of the NBA's top players. The checklist includes Kobe Bryant, Kevin Garnett and Michael Jordan. Please note that there were only 200 serial numbered sets produced. Card backs carry the player's initials as numbering followed by a "B". A gold version was also produced and is sequentially numbered to 25.

STATED PRINT RUN 200 SERIAL #'d SETS
UNPRICED SUPER PRINT RUN ONE SET
AHB Anfernee Hardaway 40.00 100.00
AJB Antawn Jamison 6.00 15.00
AMB Andre Miller 6.00 15.00
CAB Courtney Alexander 6.00 15.00
DJB DerMarr Johnson 6.00 15.00
JMB Jerome Moiso 6.00 15.00
JRB Jalen Rose 6.00 15.00
KBB Kobe Bryant 125.00 250.00
KGB Kevin Garnett 30.00 80.00
LHB Larry Hughes 6.00 15.00
MFB Marcus Fizer 6.00 15.00
QRB Quentin Richardson 10.00 25.00
SAB Shareef Abdur-Rahim 6.00 15.00
SMB Shawn Marion 6.00 15.00
TMB Tracy McGrady 20.00 50.00

2000-01 Ultimate Collection Signatures Gold

Randomly inserted into packs, this 15-card insert features authenticated autographs of some of the NBA's top players. The checklist includes Kobe Bryant, Kevin Garnett and Michael Jordan. Please note that there were only 25 serial numbered sets produced. Card backs carry the player's initials as numbering followed by a "G".

STATED PRINT RUN 25 SERIAL #'d SETS
AHG Anfernee Hardaway 200.00 350.00
BRG Bill Russell 150.00 300.00
DMG Darius Miles 15.00 40.00
GPG Gary Payton 30.00 80.00
JRG Jalen Rose 40.00 100.00
KBG Kobe Bryant 200.00 400.00
KGG Kevin Garnett 75.00 200.00
KMG Kenyon Martin 30.00 80.00
LHG Larry Hughes 15.00 40.00
MJG Michael Jordan 750.00 1500.00
SAG Shareef Abdur-Rahim 15.00 40.00
SFG Steve Francis 15.00 40.00
SSG Stromile Swift 15.00 40.00
TMG Tracy McGrady 40.00 100.00

2000-01 Ultimate Collection Signatures Silver

Randomly inserted into packs, this 15-card insert features authenticated autographs of some of the NBA's top players. The checklist includes Kobe Bryant, Kevin Garnett and Michael Jordan. Please note that there were only 75 serial numbered sets produced. Card backs carry the player's initials as numbering followed by a "SI".

STATED PRINT RUN 75 SERIAL #'d SETS
AHSI Anfernee Hardaway 50.00 125.00
AMSI Antonio McDyess 10.00 25.00
DSSI DeShawn Stevenson 8.00 20.00
GPSI Gary Payton 20.00 50.00
JCSI Jamal Crawford 10.00 25.00
KBSI Kobe Bryant 100.00 200.00
KGSI Kevin Garnett 40.00 100.00
MCSI Mateen Cleaves 8.00 20.00
MMSI Mike Miller 15.00 40.00
MPSI Morris Peterson 8.00 20.00
PPSI Paul Pierce 20.00 50.00
SFSI Steve Francis 8.00 20.00
SMSI Shawn Marion 8.00 20.00
THSI Tim Hardaway 10.00 25.00

2001-02 Ultimate Collection

Released in January of 2002, Upper Deck Ultimate Collection boasts a 90-card set broken down into 60 veteran cards and 30 rookie cards. Base cards feature full color player action photos with silver foil and block highlights. Each card is sequentially numbered to 750. The rookies are divided up as follows: card numbers 61-70 have a full color player photo with a bronze stripe centered across the card horizontally and white both above and below this line. These cards have silver foil highlights are are sequentially numbered to 750. Card numbers 71-84 feature the same design except the bronze line is shifted to a silver line and these cards are sequentially numbered to 250. Card numbers 85-90 feature authentic player autographs are sequentailly numbered to 250 as well. Upper Deck Ultimate Collection was packaged in four box cases where boxes contained four packs each, and packs contained four cards and carried a suggested retail price of $100.

COMP.SET w/o SP's (60) 60.00 120.00
1-70 PRINT RUN 750 SER.#'d SETS
71-84 PRINT RUN 250 SER.#'d SETS
85-90 PRINT RUN 250 SER.#'d SETS
1 Jason Terry 2.50 6.00
2 Shareef Abdur-Rahim 2.00 5.00
3 Paul Pierce 2.50 6.00
4 Antoine Walker 2.00 5.00
5 Baron Davis 2.50 6.00
6 Jamal Mashburn 2.00 5.00
7 Ron Mercer 1.50 4.00
8 Marcus Fizer 1.50 4.00
9 Andre Miller 2.00 5.00
10 Lamond Murray 1.50 4.00
11 Dirk Nowitzki 4.00 10.00
12 Michael Finley 2.50 6.00
13 Antonio McDyess 2.00 5.00
14 Nick Van Exel 2.00 5.00
15 Jerry Stackhouse 2.00 5.00
16 Zeljko Rebraca RC 3.00 8.00
17 Antawn Jamison 2.50 6.00
18 Larry Hughes 2.00 5.00
19 Steve Francis 2.00 5.00
20 Cuttino Mobley 1.50 4.00
21 Reggie Miller 2.50 6.00
22 Jalen Rose 2.00 5.00
23 Darius Miles 1.50 4.00
24 Quentin Richardson 2.00 5.00
25 Kobe Bryant 10.00 25.00
26 Shaquille O'Neal 6.00 15.00
27 Mitch Richmond 2.00 5.00
28 Stromile Swift 1.50 4.00
29 Jason Williams 2.00 5.00
30 Alonzo Mourning 3.00 8.00
31 Eddie Jones 2.00 5.00
32 Ray Allen 2.50 6.00
33 Glenn Robinson 2.00 5.00
34 Kevin Garnett 4.00 10.00
35 Terrell Brandon 1.50 4.00
36 Wally Szczerbiak 2.00 5.00
37 Jason Kidd 4.00 10.00
38 Kenyon Martin 2.50 6.00
39 Latrell Sprewell 2.00 5.00
40 Allan Houston 2.00 5.00
41 Tracy McGrady 4.00 10.00
42 Grant Hill 3.00 8.00
43 Allen Iverson 5.00 12.00
44 Dikembe Mutombo 2.50 6.00
45 Stephon Marbury 2.00 5.00
46 Anfernee Hardaway 4.00 10.00
47 Rasheed Wallace 2.50 6.00
48 Derek Anderson 1.50 4.00
49 Chris Webber 2.50 6.00
50 Peja Stojakovic 2.50 6.00
51 Tim Duncan 5.00 12.00
52 David Robinson 4.00 10.00
53 Rashard Lewis 2.50 6.00
54 Desmond Mason 2.00 5.00
55 Vince Carter 4.00 10.00
56 Morris Peterson 1.50 4.00
57 Karl Malone 3.00 8.00
58 John Stockton 3.00 8.00
59 Richard Hamilton 2.00 5.00
60 Michael Jordan 20.00 50.00
61 Andrei Kirilenko RC 5.00 12.00
62 Gilbert Arenas RC 8.00 20.00
63 Trenton Hassell RC 2.50 6.00
64 Tony Parker RC 12.00 30.00
65 Jamaal Tinsley RC 3.00 8.00
66 Samuel Dalembert RC 3.00 8.00
67 Gerald Wallace RC 4.00 10.00
68 Brandon Armstrong RC 2.00 5.00
69 Jeryl Sasser RC 2.00 5.00
70 Joseph Forte RC 2.00 5.00
71 Pau Gasol RC 40.00 100.00
72 Brendan Haywood RC 6.00 15.00
73 Zach Randolph RC 10.00 25.00
74 Jason Collins RC 5.00 12.00
75 Michael Bradley RC 4.00 10.00
76 Kirk Haston RC 4.00 10.00
77 Steven Hunter RC 5.00 12.00
78 Troy Murphy RC 6.00 15.00
79 Richard Jefferson RC 10.00 25.00
80 Vladimir Radmanovic RC 6.00 15.00
81 Kedrick Brown RC 4.00 10.00
82 Joe Johnson RC 8.00 20.00
83 DeSagana Diop RC 5.00 12.00
84 Shane Battier RC 12.00 30.00
85 Rodney White AU RC 4.00 10.00
86 Eddie Griffin AU RC 5.00 12.00
87 Jason Richardson AU RC 10.00 25.00
88 Eddy Curry AU RC 6.00 15.00
89 Tyson Chandler AU RC 10.00 25.00
90 Kwame Brown AU RC 6.00 15.00

2001-02 Ultimate Collection Platinum

*STARS: 3X TO 8X BASE CARD HI
*ROOKIES 16/61-70: 4X TO 10X HI
*ROOKIES 71-84: 2X TO 5X HI
*ROOKIES 85-90: 2X TO 5X HI
PRINT RUN 25 SERIAL #'d SETS
60 Michael Jordan 200.00 500.00
71 Pau Gasol JSY 100.00 250.00

2001-02 Ultimate Collection BuyBacks

Randomly inserted in packs at the rate of one in 16, this set features cards from some of Upper Decks's past releases enhanced with authentic player autographs and hand numbering. Each card was accompanied in the pack with a certificate of authenticity which like the card itself, contained a UDA hologram of authenticity. These holograms carried an "AAA" prefix before the rest of the serial number.

STATED ODDS 1:16
MOST UNPRICED DUE TO SCARCITY
4 A.Walker 98-9SPA/18 25.00 60.00
7 A.Walker 00-1BlaDia/26 10.00 25.00
12 C.Alexandr 00-1SPGamF/30 10.00 25.00
35 J.Kidd 00-1UltColJsyBrnz/31 75.00 150.00
45 K.Bryant 00-1BlaDiaDia/40 150.00 300.00
47 K.Bryant 00-1SPA/31 200.00 400.00
52 K.Bryant 00-1SPGameFlr/24 200.00 400.00
56 K.Bryant 00-1UltColJsyBrz/27 300.00 600.00
59 K.Bryant 00-1UltVic/15 200.00 400.00
75 K.Grntt 00-1SPxWM#KG1/32 100.00 200.00
81 K.Garnett 00-1UltColJsyBz/21 125.00 250.00
84 K.Martin 00-1SPGFlrAFlr/39 40.00 100.00
86 K.Martin 00-1UppDeck/97 10.00 25.00
90 K.Martin 00-1UltColJsyBrz/19 75.00 150.00
108 L.Odom 99-0UD/37 40.00 80.00
110 L.Odom 99-0UDOvat/48 30.00 80.00
120 M.Jordan 98-9SPA#7/25 600.00 1000.00
138 M.Jordan 00-1UltColJsyB/20 700.00 1200.00
156 W.Szcz 00-1UltColJsySilv/22 25.00 60.00

2001-02 Ultimate Collection BuyBacks Unsigned

Randomly inserted in packs, this 16-card set features unsigned buyback cards from previously released Upper Deck products. Each card is sequentially numbered.

MOST UNPRICED DUE TO SCARCITY
4 S.O'Neal 92-3UD#1B/38 40.00 100.00

2001-02 Ultimate Collection Jerseys

Randomly seeded in packs, this 30-card set features several different block backgrounds in blue, one containing a full color player photo, one containing a blue-scale player portrait photo, the player's initials, the set name, and a swatch of a game worn jersey. Each card is sequentially numbered to 250.

PRINT RUN 250 SERIAL #'d SETS
*GOLD: 1X TO 2.5X BASE HI
GOLD PRINT RUN 50 SER.#'d SETS
*SILVER: .6X TO 1.5X BASE HI
SILVER PRINT RUN 125 SER.#'d SETS
AI Allen Iverson 10.00 25.00
BR Kedrick Brown 3.00 8.00
CW Chris Webber 5.00 12.00
DM Darius Miles 3.00 8.00
EC Eddy Curry 5.00 12.00
EG Eddie Griffin 4.00 10.00
JJ Joe Johnson 6.00 15.00
JR Jason Richardson 6.00 15.00
JS John Stockton 6.00 15.00
JT Jamaal Tinsley 5.00 12.00
KB Kobe Bryant 15.00 40.00
KB2 Kobe Bryant 15.00 40.00
KE Kenyon Martin 5.00 12.00
KG Kevin Garnett 8.00 20.00
KG2 Kevin Garnett 8.00 20.00
KM Karl Malone 6.00 15.00
KW Kwame Brown 5.00 12.00
MF Michael Finley 5.00 12.00
MJ Michael Jordan 60.00 120.00
MJ2 Michael Jordan 60.00 120.00
MM Mike Miller 4.00 10.00
NO Dirk Nowitzki 8.00 20.00
PP Paul Pierce 5.00 12.00
RA Ray Allen 5.00 12.00
RJ Richard Jefferson 8.00 20.00
RW Rodney White 3.00 8.00
SF Steve Francis 4.00 10.00
TC Tyson Chandler 8.00 20.00
TM Tracy McGrady 8.00 20.00
TP Tony Parker 20.00 50.00

2001-02 Ultimate Collection Jerseys Patches

PRINT RUN 100 SERIAL #'d SETS
*SILVER: .75X TO 2X HI
SILVER PRINT RUN 25 SETS
KB2P Kobe Bryant 75.00 150.00
KG2P Kevin Garnett 20.00 50.00
MJ2P Michael Jordan 250.00 500.00
AIP Allen Iverson 30.00 80.00
BDP Baron Davis 10.00 25.00
BRP Kedrick Brown 8.00 20.00
CWP Chris Webber 20.00 50.00
DMP Darius Miles 10.00 25.00
ECP Eddy Curry 12.00 30.00
EGP Eddie Griffin 10.00 25.00
JJP Joe Johnson 10.00 25.00
JRP Jason Richardson 10.00 25.00
JSP John Stockton 25.00 60.00
JTP Jason Terry 15.00 40.00
JTP Jamaal Tinsley 15.00 40.00
KBP Kobe Bryant 75.00 200.00
KEP Kenyon Martin 15.00 40.00
KGP Kevin Garnett 25.00 60.00
KMP Karl Malone 15.00 40.00
KWP Kwame Brown 12.00 30.00
MFP Michael Finley 15.00 40.00
MJP Michael Jordan 250.00 500.00
MMP Mike Miller 12.00 30.00
NOP Dirk Nowitzki 25.00 60.00
PPP Paul Pierce 10.00 25.00
RWP Rodney White 8.00 20.00
SFP Steve Francis 12.00 30.00
TCP Tyson Chandler 10.00 25.00
TMP Tracy McGrady 25.00 60.00
TPP Tony Parker 20.00 50.00

2001-02 Ultimate Collection Signatures

Randomly inserted in packs at the rate of one in four, this 15-card set features centered full color player action photo, a gray-scale portrait photo on the left, and an open area with white background on the right for authentic player autographs.

STATED ODDS 1:4
DMA Darius Miles 6.00 15.00
DRA Julius Erving 50.00 120.00
ECA Eddy Curry 8.00 20.00
EGA Eddie Griffin 8.00 20.00
JJA Joe Johnson 6.00 15.00
JKA Jason Kidd 20.00 40.00
JRA Jason Richardson 10.00 25.00
KBA Kobe Bryant 125.00 250.00
KGA Kevin Garnett 40.00 80.00
KWA Kwame Brown 6.00 15.00
LBA Larry Bird 75.00 150.00
MGA Magic Johnson 60.00 120.00
MJA Michael Jordan 400.00 800.00
RWA Rodney White 6.00 15.00
TCA Tyson Chandler 6.00 15.00

2001-02 Ultimate Collection Signatures Gold

STATED PRINT RUN 2 TO 33 SER.#'d SETS
DMA Darius Miles/21 25.00 60.00
EGA Eddie Griffin/33 15.00 40.00
JJA Joe Johnson/31 30.00 80.00
JRA Jason Richardson/23 40.00 100.00
KGA Kevin Garnett/21 150.00 300.00
LBA Larry Bird/33 150.00 300.00
MGA Magic Johnson/32 75.00 150.00
MJA Michael Jordan/23 600.00 1200.00

2002-03 Ultimate Collection

Issued in March 2003, this 120-card set is divided up into four tiers as follows: cards 1-67 feature veteran players and are sequentially numbered to 750, cards 68-79 feature rookies and autographs and are sequentially numbered to 250, cards 80-103 feature rookies and are sequentially numbered to 250, and cards 104-120 feature rookies and are sequentially numbered to 750. Base cards have a white border along the left side and the right side contains a full-color player action photo with background to match the player's team colors and the team name along the right edge. Ultimate Collection was packaged in four pack boxes with four cards per pack and carried a suggested retail price of $100 per pack.

COMP.SET w/o SP's (67) 150.00 300.00
1-67 PRINT RUN 750 SER.#'d SETS
68-79 PRINT RUN 250 SER.#'d SETS
80-103 PRINT RUN 250 SER.#'d SETS
104-120 PRINT RUN 750 SER.#'d SETS
1 Shareef Abdur-Rahim 1.50 4.00
2 Glenn Robinson 1.50 4.00
3 Jason Terry 1.50 4.00
4 Paul Pierce 2.00 5.00
5 Antoine Walker 1.50 4.00
6 Vin Baker 1.50 4.00
7 Jalen Rose 1.50 4.00
8 Darius Miles 1.25 3.00
9 Dirk Nowitzki 3.00 8.00
10 Michael Finley 2.00 5.00
11 Steve Nash 2.50 6.00
12 Raef LaFrentz 1.25 3.00
13 Juwan Howard 1.50 4.00
14 Richard Hamilton 1.50 4.00
15 Chauncey Billups 2.00 5.00
16 Ben Wallace 1.50 4.00
17 Jason Richardson 2.00 5.00
18 Gilbert Arenas 2.00 5.00
19 Antawn Jamison 2.00 5.00
20 Steve Francis 1.50 4.00
21 Reggie Miller 2.00 5.00
22 Jamaal Tinsley 1.25 3.00
23 Jermaine O'Neal 1.50 4.00
24 Elton Brand 2.00 5.00
25 Andre Miller 1.50 4.00
26 Kobe Bryant 8.00 20.00
27 Shaquille O'Neal 5.00 12.00
28 Pau Gasol 2.50 6.00
29 Shane Battier 2.00 5.00
30 Eddie Jones 1.50 4.00
31 Brian Grant 1.25 3.00
32 Ray Allen 2.00 5.00
33 Kevin Garnett 3.00 8.00
34 Wally Szczerbiak 1.50 4.00
35 Troy Hudson 1.25 3.00
36 Jason Kidd 3.00 8.00
37 Richard Jefferson 2.00 5.00
38 Kenyon Martin 1.50 4.00
39 Baron Davis 1.50 4.00
40 Jamal Mashburn 1.50 4.00
41 David Wesley 1.25 3.00
42 P.J. Brown 1.25 3.00
43 Allan Houston 1.50 4.00
44 Latrell Sprewell 1.50 4.00
45 Kurt Thomas 1.25 3.00
46 Tracy McGrady 3.00 8.00
47 Grant Hill 2.50 6.00
48 Allen Iverson 3.00 8.00
49 Stephon Marbury 1.50 4.00
50 Shawn Marion 1.50 4.00
51 Rasheed Wallace 2.00 5.00
52 Derek Anderson 1.25 3.00
53 Bonzi Wells 1.25 3.00
54 Chris Webber 2.00 5.00
55 Mike Bibby 2.00 5.00
56 Peja Stojakovic 2.00 5.00
57 Tim Duncan 4.00 10.00
58 David Robinson 3.00 8.00
59 Tony Parker 3.00 8.00
60 Gary Payton 2.00 5.00
61 Rashard Lewis 2.00 5.00
62 Desmond Mason 1.50 4.00
63 Vince Carter 3.00 8.00
64 Morris Peterson 1.25 3.00
65 Karl Malone 2.50 6.00
66 John Stockton 2.50 6.00
67 Michael Jordan 12.00 30.00
68 Chris Wilcox AU RC 5.00 12.00
69 Drew Gooden AU RC 6.00 15.00
70 Marcus Haislip AU RC 5.00 12.00
71 Melvin Ely AU RC 5.00 12.00
72 Jared Jeffries AU RC 5.00 12.00
73 Caron Butler AU RC 6.00 15.00
74 Amare Stoudemire AU RC 8.00 20.00
75 Nene Hilario AU RC 6.00 15.00
76 DaJuan Wagner AU RC 5.00 12.00
77 Nikoloz Tskitishvili AU RC 4.00 10.00
78 Jay Williams AU RC 6.00 15.00
79 Yao Ming AU RC 75.00 200.00
80 Predrag Savovic RC 4.00 10.00
81 Igor Rakocevic RC 3.00 8.00
82 Sam Clancy RC 4.00 10.00
83 Ronald Murray RC 5.00 12.00
84 Tito Maddox RC 3.00 8.00
85 Carlos Boozer RC 5.00 12.00
86 Dan Gadzuric RC 4.00 10.00
87 Vincent Yarbrough RC 3.00 8.00
88 Robert Archibald RC 3.00 8.00
89 Roger Mason RC 4.00 10.00
90 Juaquin Hawkins RC 3.00 8.00
91 Chris Jefferies RC 3.00 8.00
92 John Salmons RC 5.00 12.00
93 Manu Ginobili RC 12.00 30.00
94 Tayshaun Prince RC 6.00 15.00
95 Casey Jacobsen RC 4.00 10.00
96 Qyntel Woods RC 4.00 10.00
97 Kareem Rush RC 4.00 10.00
98 Ryan Humphrey RC 4.00 10.00
99 Juan Dixon RC 5.00 12.00
100 Fred Jones RC 4.00 10.00
101 Jiri Welsch RC 4.00 10.00
102 Bostjan Nachbar RC 4.00 10.00
103 Marko Jaric 5.00 12.00
104 Gordan Giricek RC 3.00 8.00
105 Frank Williams RC 2.00 5.00
106 Pat Burke RC 2.00 5.00
107 Junior Harrington RC 2.00 5.00
108 Rasual Butler RC 3.00 8.00
109 Raul Lopez RC 3.00 8.00
110 Cezary Trybanski RC 3.00 8.00
111 Dan Dickau RC 2.50 6.00
112 Efthimios Rentzias RC 2.00 5.00
113 Mehmet Okur RC 3.00 8.00
114 Curtis Borchardt RC 2.00 5.00
115 J.R. Bremer RC 2.00 5.00
116 Lonny Baxter RC 2.00 5.00
117 Jamal Sampson RC 3.00 8.00
118 Tamar Slay RC 2.00 5.00
119 Jannero Pargo RC 2.00 5.00
120 Smush Parker RC 3.00 8.00

2002-03 Ultimate Collection Ultimate Parallel

*STARS: 3X TO 8X BASE CARD HI
*RCs 68-79: 1.5X TO 4X HI
*RCs 80-103: 1.5X TO 4X HI
*RCs 104-120: 2X TO 5X HI
68-79 FEATURE PATCH AND AUTO
PRINT RUN 25 SER.#'d SETS
68 Chris Wilcox JSY AU 30.00 80.00
74 Amare Stoudemire JSY AU 300.00 600.00
75 Nene Hilario JSY AU 40.00 100.00
79 Yao Ming JSY AU 400.00 800.00

2002-03 Ultimate Collection Buybacks

Randomly inserted in packs, this set features older upper deck issues re-inserted with player autographs. Most cards are hand numbered and the UDA authenticity hologram sticker begins with an AAA prefix for the registration number.

MOST UNPRICED DUE TO SCARCITY
17 K.Bryant 01-2SPAuth/38 150.00 300.00
18 K.Bryant 01-2SPx/32 150.00 300.00
21 K.Bryant 01-2UDFlightTm/24 150.00 300.00
27 K.Garnett 95-6SPAuth/23 50.00 120.00
32 K.Garnett 01-2SPAuth/23 50.00 120.00
34 K.Garnett 01-2SPx/46 50.00 120.00
35 Garntt 00-1SPGFAF#KG2/18 50.00 120.00
36 Garnett 01-2UDFlightTm/18 50.00 120.00
42 MJ 00-1UDMJMater#MJ1/24 500.00 800.00
47 J.Kidd 01-2 UDLegLFloor/22 25.00 60.00
54 K.Martin 00-1UD/97 15.00 40.00
70 T.Parker 01-2UD#185/155 20.00 50.00
72 P.Pierce 01-2UDGJPatch/20 75.00 150.00
78 P.Stojakovic 01-2SPAuth/23 20.00 50.00
79 P.Stojakovic 01-2SPx/17 20.00 50.00
80 P.Stojak 01-2UDInspir/26 20.00 50.00
84 A.Walk 00-1UDHardGF/54 20.00 50.00
87 A.Walk 01-2UDOvSSWU/26 20.00 50.00
94 J.Kidd 94-5SP/33 25.00 60.00

2002-03 Ultimate Collection Jerseys

Randomly inserted in packs, this 30-card set places a full color player action photo on the card with a swatch of game worn jersey. Each card is sequentially numbered to 250.

STATED PRINT RUN 250 SER.#'d SETS
AI Allen Iverson 10.00 25.00
AM Andre Miller 3.00 8.00
AW Antoine Walker 3.00 8.00
BD Baron Davis 3.00 8.00
CB Caron Butler 4.00 10.00
CW Chris Webber 4.00 10.00
DG Drew Gooden 4.00 10.00
DM Darius Miles 2.50 6.00
DN Dirk Nowitzki 6.00 15.00
DW DaJuan Wagner 3.00 8.00
JK Jason Kidd 6.00 15.00
JR Jason Richardson 4.00 10.00
JW Jay Williams 4.00 10.00
KB Kobe Bryant 12.00 30.00
KG Kevin Garnett 6.00 15.00
KR Kareem Rush 3.00 8.00
MB Mike Bibby 4.00 10.00
MJ Michael Jordan 30.00 80.00
NH Nene Hilario 4.00 10.00
PG Pau Gasol 5.00 12.00
PP Paul Pierce 4.00 10.00
PS Peja Stojakovic 4.00 10.00
RJ Richard Jefferson 4.00 10.00
RL Rashard Lewis 4.00 10.00
SB Shane Battier 4.00 10.00
SF Steve Francis 3.00 8.00
SM Stephon Marbury 3.00 8.00
TM Tracy McGrady 6.00 15.00
WI Chris Wilcox 3.00 8.00
YM Yao Ming 8.00 20.00

2002-03 Ultimate Collection Jerseys Gold

ndomly inserted, this 12-card set parallels the Game Jerseys insert set enhanced with gold highlights and sequential numbering to 50.

STATED PRINT RUN 50 SER.#'d SETS
AI Allen Iverson 20.00 50.00
BD Baron Davis 6.00 15.00
CW Chris Webber 30.00 80.00
DN Dirk Nowitzki 12.00 30.00
DW DaJuan Wagner 6.00 15.00
JK Jason Kidd 12.00 30.00
JR Jason Richardson 8.00 20.00
JW Jay Williams 8.00 20.00
KB Kobe Bryant 40.00 100.00
KG Kevin Garnett 12.00 30.00
MJ Michael Jordan 60.00 150.00
PP Paul Pierce 8.00 20.00
SF Steve Francis 6.00 15.00
TM Tracy McGrady 12.00 30.00
YM Yao Ming 15.00 40.00

2002-03 Ultimate Collection Jerseys Silver

Randomly inserted, this 12-card set parallels the Game Jerseys insert set enhanced with silver highlights and sequential numbering to 125.

STATED PRINT RUN 125 SER.#'d SETS
AM Andre Miller 4.00 10.00
AW Antoine Walker 4.00 10.00
CB Caron Butler 5.00 12.00
DG Drew Gooden 5.00 12.00
DM Darius Miles 3.00 8.00
KR Kareem Rush 4.00 10.00
MB Mike Bibby 5.00 12.00
NH Nene Hilario 5.00 12.00
PG Pau Gasol 6.00 15.00
PS Peja Stojakovic 5.00 12.00
RJ Richard Jefferson 5.00 12.00
RL Rashard Lewis 5.00 12.00
SB Shane Battier 5.00 12.00
SM Stephon Marbury 4.00 10.00
WI Chris Wilcox 4.00 10.00

2002-03 Ultimate Collection Jerseys Dual

Inserted in packs, this 12-card set places two players and two swatches of game worn jersey on each card. Cards are sequentially numbered to 125. Gold and Silver Parallel versions were also inserted and are sequentially numbered to 10 and 25 respectively.

STATED PRINT RUN 125 SER.#'d SETS
*SILVER: .75X TO 2X BASE HI
SILVER PRINT RUN 25 SER.#'d SETS
UNPRICED GOLD PRINT RUN 10 SETS
AISF A.Iverson/S.Francis 12.50 30.00
AMEB A.Miller/E.Brand 10.00 25.00
CWMB C.Webber/M.Bibby 10.00 25.00
DNSN D.Nowitzki/S.Nash 10.00 25.00
JKBD J.Kidd/B.Davis 10.00 25.00
KBJW K.Bryant/J.Williams 12.00 30.00
MJKB M.Jordan/K.Bryant 75.00 200.00
PPAW P.Pierce/A.Walker 10.00 25.00
SBPG S.Battier/P.Gasol 10.00 25.00
SMSM S.Marbury/S.Marion 10.00 25.00
TMKG T.McGrady/K.Garnett 12.50 30.00
YMJW Y.Ming/J.Williams 20.00 50.00

2002-03 Ultimate Collection Jerseys Patches

Inserted in packs, this 30-card set places a player and a patch from a game worn jersey on each card. Cards are sequentially numbered to 50. Gold and Silver parallels were also inserted in packs and are sequentially numbered to 10 and 25 respectively.

STATED PRINT RUN 50 SER.#'d SETS
ASP Amare Stoudemire 60.00 120.00
AWP Antoine Walker 10.00 25.00
BZP Carlos Boozer 12.00 30.00
CAP Casey Jacobsen 10.00 25.00
CBP Caron Butler 12.00 30.00
CJP Chris Jefferies 8.00 20.00
CWP Chris Wilcox 10.00 25.00
DGP Drew Gooden 12.00 30.00
FJP Fred Jones 10.00 25.00
GAP Dan Gadzuric 10.00 25.00
JJP Jared Jeffries 10.00 25.00
JRP Jason Richardson 12.00 30.00
JSP John Salmons 12.00 30.00
JWP Jay Williams 12.00 30.00
KBP Kobe Bryant 100.00 250.00
KMP Karl Malone 15.00 40.00
KRP Kareem Rush 10.00 25.00
MEP Melvin Ely 10.00 25.00
MHP Marcus Haislip 10.00 25.00
NHP Nene Hilario 12.00 30.00
NTP Nikoloz Tskitishvili 8.00 20.00
PPP Paul Pierce 12.00 30.00
QWP Qyntel Woods 10.00 25.00
RHP Ryan Humphrey 10.00 25.00
RLP Rashard Lewis 12.00 30.00
RMP Roger Mason 10.00 25.00
SHP Shareef Abdur-Rahim 10.00 25.00
TPP Tayshaun Prince 12.00 30.00
VYP Vincent Yarbrough 8.00 20.00
YMP Yao Ming 60.00 120.00

2002-03 Ultimate Collection Jerseys Patches Dual

serted randomly, this 12-card set pairs up players with premium swatches of each of their jerseys (one player on the left and one on the right). Cards are sequentially numbered to 25. A Platinum version was also inserted where cards are sequentially numbered to five.

STATED PRINT RUN 25 SER.#'d SETS
BDJMP B.Davis/J.Mashburn 25.00 60.00
CWMBP C.Webber/M.Bibby 50.00 120.00
DMDWP D.Miles/D.Wagner 25.00 60.00
DNSNP D.Nowitzki/S.Nash 60.00 150.00
KBAIP K.Bryant/A.Iverson 150.00 300.00
KBJWP K.Bryant/J.Williams 125.00 250.00
MJKBP M.Jordan/K.Bryant 400.00 700.00
PGDGP P.Gasol/D.Gooden 25.00 60.00
SFJDP S.Francis/J.Dixon 25.00 60.00
SMSMP S.Marbury/S.Marion 40.00 100.00
TMJKP T.McGrady/J.Kidd 60.00 150.00
YMJWP Y.Ming/J.Williams 150.00 300.00

2002-03 Ultimate Collection Signatures

Randomly seeded in packs, this 15-card set places a small circular portrait photo of a player towards the top and leaves the bottom of the card open for authentic player autographs.

RANDOM INSERTS IN PACKS
ASS Amare Stoudemire 12.00 30.00
BRS Bill Russell 60.00 150.00
CBS Caron Butler 8.00 20.00
DRS Julius Erving 25.00 60.00
DWS DaJuan Wagner 6.00 15.00
JKS Jason Kidd 15.00 40.00
JWS Jay Williams 10.00 25.00
KAS Kareem Abdul-Jabbar 50.00 120.00
KBS Kobe Bryant 75.00 200.00
KGS Kevin Garnett 60.00 150.00
KRS Kareem Rush 6.00 15.00
LBS Larry Bird 60.00 150.00
MJS Michael Jordan 400.00 800.00
NTS Nikoloz Tskitishvili 6.00 15.00
YMS Yao Ming 40.00 100.00

2002-03 Ultimate Collection Signatures Gold

Randomly inserted in packs, this 15-card set parallels the base Signatures insert set enhanced with gold highlights and sequential numbering to the featured player's jersey number.

MOST UNPRICED DUE TO SCARCITY
ASS Amare Stoudemire/32 100.00 200.00
JWS Jay Williams/22 30.00 80.00
KAS Kareem Abdul-Jabbar/33 150.00 300.00
KGS Kevin Garnett/21 100.00 200.00
KRS Kareem Rush/21 20.00 50.00
LBS Larry Bird/33 125.00 300.00
MJS Michael Jordan/23 500.00 800.00
NTS Nikoloz Tskitishvili/22 20.00 50.00

2003-04 Ultimate Collection

Released in April 2004, Ultimate Collection is a 190-card set comprised of 116 base cards of mixed veterans and retired players sequentially numbered to 750, 10 base rookie cards (numbers 117-126) sequentially numbered to 750, 37 autographed rookie cards (numbers 127-164) sequentially numbered to 250, and 25 Ultimate Stars cards (numbers 165-190) sequentially numbered to 500. A Limited Parallel set was also inserted into packs and these cards are sequentialy numbered to 25; and a Limited Black set where cards are serially numbered one of one. Ultimate Collection was packaged in four-pack boxes where packs contained four cards and carried a suggested retail price of $100.

1-116 PRINT RUN 750 SER.#'d SETS
165-190 PRINT RUN 500 SER.#'d SETS
UNPRICED LIMITED BLACK PRINT RUN ONE SET
1 Dominique Wilkins 2.50 6.00
2 Jason Terry 1.50 4.00
3 Dion Glover 1.25 3.00
4 Stephen Jackson 1.50 4.00
5 Bill Russell 3.00 8.00
6 Paul Pierce 2.00 5.00
7 Larry Bird 5.00 12.00
8 Ricky Davis 1.50 4.00
9 Antonio Davis 1.25 3.00
10 Michael Jordan 15.00 40.00
11 Scottie Pippen 3.00 8.00
12 Tyson Chandler 1.50 4.00
13 Jeff McInnis 1.25 3.00
14 Dajuan Wagner 1.25 3.00
15 Carlos Boozer 1.50 4.00
16 Zydrunas Ilgauskas 1.50 4.00
17 Dirk Nowitzki 3.00 8.00
18 Steve Nash 2.50 6.00
19 Antoine Walker 2.00 5.00
20 Michael Finley 2.00 5.00
21 Andre Miller 1.50 4.00
22 Nene 1.50 4.00
23 Nikoloz Tskitishvili 1.25 3.00
24 Marcus Camby 1.50 4.00
25 Richard Hamilton 1.50 4.00
26 Ben Wallace 1.50 4.00
27 Chauncey Billups 2.00 5.00
28 Rasheed Wallace 2.00 5.00
29 Jason Richardson 2.00 5.00
30 Nick Van Exel 1.50 4.00
31 Speedy Claxton 1.25 3.00
32 Mike Dunleavy 1.50 4.00
33 Yao Ming 4.00 10.00
34 Steve Francis 1.50 4.00
35 Cuttino Mobley 1.25 3.00
36 Jim Jackson 1.25 3.00
37 Reggie Miller 2.00 5.00
38 Jermaine O'Neal 1.50 4.00
39 Ron Artest 2.00 5.00
40 Al Harrington 1.50 4.00
41 Elton Brand 2.00 5.00
42 Corey Maggette 1.50 4.00
43 Quentin Richardson 1.50 4.00
44 Chris Wilcox 1.25 3.00
45 Kobe Bryant 8.00 20.00
46 Shaquille O'Neal 5.00 12.00
47 Gary Payton 2.00 5.00
48 Karl Malone 2.50 6.00
49 Pau Gasol 2.00 5.00
50 Bonzi Wells 1.25 3.00
51 Mike Miller 1.50 4.00
52 Jason Williams 1.50 4.00
53 Caron Butler 1.50 4.00
54 Lamar Odom 1.50 4.00
55 Eddie Jones 1.50 4.00
56 Brian Grant 1.25 3.00
57 Desmond Mason 1.50 4.00
58 Oscar Robertson 2.00 5.00
59 Michael Redd 2.00 5.00
60 Toni Kukoc 2.00 5.00
61 Latrell Sprewell 1.50 4.00
62 Kevin Garnett 3.00 8.00
63 Wally Szczerbiak 1.50 4.00
64 Sam Cassell 1.50 4.00
65 Kenyon Martin 1.50 4.00
66 Jason Kidd 3.00 8.00
67 Richard Jefferson 1.50 4.00
68 Alonzo Mourning 2.50 6.00
69 Jamal Mashburn 1.50 4.00
70 David Wesley 1.25 3.00
71 Baron Davis 1.50 4.00
72 Jamaal Magloire 1.25 3.00
73 Allan Houston 1.50 4.00
74 Patrick Ewing 2.50 6.00
75 Stephon Marbury 1.50 4.00
76 Dikembe Mutombo 2.00 5.00
77 Tracy McGrady 2.50 6.00
78 Drew Gooden 1.50 4.00
79 Juwan Howard 1.50 4.00
80 DeShawn Stevenson 1.25 3.00
81 Julius Erving 3.00 8.00
82 Allen Iverson 3.00 8.00
83 Glenn Robinson 1.50 4.00
84 Eric Snow 1.25 3.00
85 Amare Stoudemire 2.50 6.00
86 Shawn Marion 1.50 4.00
87 Antonio McDyess 1.50 4.00
88 Joe Johnson 1.50 4.00
89 Shareef Abdur-Rahim 1.50 4.00
90 Derek Anderson 1.25 3.00
91 Damon Stoudamire 1.50 4.00
92 Zach Randolph 1.50 4.00
93 Mike Bibby 2.00 5.00
94 Chris Webber 2.00 5.00
95 Peja Stojakovic 2.00 5.00
96 Bobby Jackson 1.25 3.00
97 Manu Ginobili 2.50 6.00
98 Tim Duncan 3.00 8.00
99 Tony Parker 2.00 5.00
100 Radoslav Nesterovic 1.25 3.00
101 Rashard Lewis 2.00 5.00
102 Ray Allen 2.00 5.00
103 Vladimir Radmanovic 1.25 3.00
104 Brent Barry 1.25 3.00
105 Vince Carter 3.00 8.00
106 Morris Peterson 1.25 3.00
107 Jalen Rose 1.50 4.00
108 Donyell Marshall 1.25 3.00
109 John Stockton 2.50 6.00
110 Andrei Kirilenko 2.00 5.00
111 Matt Harpring 1.25 3.00
112 Carlos Arroyo 1.50 4.00
113 Gilbert Arenas 1.50 4.00
114 Jerry Stackhouse 1.50 4.00
115 Kwame Brown 1.25 3.00
116 Larry Hughes 1.50 4.00
117 T.J. Ford RC 3.00 8.00
118 Kirk Hinrich RC 4.00 10.00
119 Nick Collison RC 3.00 8.00
120 James Jones RC 2.50 6.00
121 Travis Hansen RC 2.50 6.00
122 Alex Garcia RC 2.50 6.00
123 Theron Smith RC 2.50 6.00
124 Francisco Elson RC 2.50 6.00
125 Jon Stefansson RC 2.50 6.00
126 Ronald Dupree RC 2.50 6.00
127 LeBron James AU RC 4000.00 5000.00
128 Darko Milicic AU RC 5.00 12.00
129 Carmelo Anthony AU RC 60.00 150.00
130 Chris Bosh AU RC 40.00 100.00
131 Dwyane Wade AU RC 175.00 300.00
132 Chris Kaman AU RC 6.00 15.00
133 Jarvis Hayes AU RC 4.00 10.00
134 Mickael Pietrus AU RC 5.00 12.00
135 Dahntay Jones AU RC 5.00 12.00
136 Marcus Banks AU RC 4.00 10.00
137 Luke Ridnour AU RC 5.00 12.00
138 Reece Gaines AU RC 4.00 10.00
139 Troy Bell AU RC 4.00 10.00
140 Mike Sweetney AU RC 4.00 10.00
141 David West AU RC 6.00 15.00
142 Aleksandar Pavlovic AU RC 5.00 12.00
143 Steve Blake AU RC 5.00 12.00
144 Boris Diaw AU RC 6.00 15.00
145 Zoran Planinic AU RC 4.00 10.00
146 Travis Outlaw AU RC 5.00 12.00
147 Brian Cook AU RC 4.00 10.00
148 Jerome Beasley AU RC 4.00 10.00
149 Ndudi Ebi AU RC 4.00 10.00
150 Kendrick Perkins AU RC 5.00 12.00
151 Leandro Barbosa AU RC 6.00 15.00
152 Josh Howard AU RC 6.00 15.00
153 Maciej Lampe AU RC 4.00 10.00
154 Jason Kapono AU RC 4.00 10.00
155 Luke Walton AU RC 6.00 15.00
156 Kyle Korver AU RC 8.00 20.00
157 Zarko Cabarkapa AU RC 4.00 10.00
158 Zaur Pachulia AU RC 6.00 15.00
159 Maurice Williams AU RC 6.00 15.00
160 Brandon Hunter AU RC 4.00 10.00
161 Keith Bogans AU RC 4.00 10.00
162 Marquis Daniels AU RC 5.00 12.00
163 Willie Green AU RC 4.00 10.00
164 Udonis Haslem AU RC 5.00 12.00
165 Larry Bird US 6.00 15.00
166 Bill Russell US 4.00 10.00
167 Michael Jordan US 12.00 30.00
168 Steve Nash US 3.00 8.00
169 Michael Finley US 2.50 6.00
170 Ben Wallace US 2.00 5.00
171 Jason Richardson US 2.50 6.00
172 Yao Ming US 5.00 12.00
173 Reggie Miller US 2.50 6.00
174 Kobe Bryant US 10.00 25.00
175 Shaquille O'Neal US 6.00 15.00
176 Gary Payton US 2.50 6.00
177 Magic Johnson US 6.00 15.00
178 Pau Gasol US 2.50 6.00
179 Lamar Odom US 2.00 5.00
180 Oscar Robertson US 2.50 6.00
181 Kenyon Martin US 2.00 5.00
182 Baron Davis US 2.00 5.00
183 Julius Erving US 4.00 10.00
184 Amare Stoudemire US 3.00 8.00
185 Mike Bibby US 2.50 6.00
186 Tony Parker US 2.50 6.00
187 Rashard Lewis US 2.50 6.00
188 Vince Carter US 4.00 10.00
189 Andrei Kirilenko US 2.50 6.00
190 Gilbert Arenas US 2.00 5.00

2003-04 Ultimate Collection Limited

*SINGLES 1-116: 2X TO 5X BASE HI
*RCs 117-126: .75X TO 2X BASE HI
*AUTO RCs: 2X TO 5X BASE HI
*US 165-190: 1.5X TO 4X BASE HI
PRINT RUN 25 SER.#'d SETS
127-158 HAVE BOTH JERSEY AND AUTO
11 Scottie Pippen 25.00 60.00
127 LeBron James JSY AU 2000.00 3200.00
129 Carmelo Anthony JSY AU 600.00 1200.00

2003-04 Ultimate Collection BuyBacks

Randomly seeded, this set is made up of cards from previous year's products that are signed and numbered by the featured player. Each card comes with a certificate of authenticity and UD's Authenticated Hologram. The serial number on the holograms for this set begins with an AAA prefix

RANDOM INSERTS IN PACKS
SOME UNPRICED DUE TO SCARCITY
5 S.Battier02-3UDSwtSht/33 12.50 30.00
6 M.Bibby02-3SPGameUse/19 20.00 50.00
9 M.Bibby02-3MVPMatShirt/17 20.00 50.00
10 M.Bibby02-3UDSwtSht/35 20.00 50.00
12 C.Billups02-3UDSwtSht/27 12.50 30.00
21 Kobe02-3UDSwtShtGlass/15 125.00 250.00
23 Ewing01-2UD15000Jsy/32 150.00 300.00
25 Garnett02-3SPxWinMat/33 50.00 120.00
29 Garnett02-3UDSwtSht/22 50.00 120.00
30 Garnett02-3UDSwtShtJsy/21 50.00 120.00
33 Hamilton02-3SPxWinMat/32 15.00 40.00
34 Hamilton02-3UDSeaPrmJsy/19 20.00 50.00
35 Hamilton02-3UDSwtSht/39 15.00 40.00
36 Hamilton02-3UDSwtShtJsy/18 20.00 50.00
37 Jamison02-3UDAll-AccJsy/18 15.00 40.00
38 Jamison02-3UDSwtSht/28 12.50 30.00
39 Jamison02-3UDSwtShtJsy/16 15.00 40.00
40 Jefferson02-3SPxWinMat/17 15.00 40.00
41 Jefferson02-3UDSwtSht/31 12.50 30.00
43 Jordan03-4UDSEDieCut/24 600.00 1000.00
44 Jordan03-4UDHardcourt/21 400.00 800.00
45 Kidd02-3SPGU#60 SP/16 30.00 80.00
46 KiddSPxWinMat/16 30.00 80.00
48 Kidd02-3UDSwtSht/40 20.00 50.00
49 Kidd02-3UDSwtShtGlass/15 30.00 80.00
50 Maggette02-3UDAll-AccJsy/16 12.50 30.00
51 Marion02-3SPx/31 20.00 50.00
52 Marion02-3SPxWinMat/20 20.00 50.00
55 Marion02-3UDSweetShot/36 15.00 40.00
56 Marion02-3UDSwtShtSwSw/20 20.00 50.00
57 McDyess02-3SPxWinMat/19 20.00 50.00
58 McDyess02-3MVPMatWarm/15 20.00 50.00
62 McGrady02-3UDGenRTJsy/19 60.00 150.00
63 McGrady02-3SwtSht/26 60.00 150.00
64 McGrady02-3SwtShtSwSw/20 60.00 150.00
65 Miles02-3SPGU/21 15.00 40.00
66 Miles02-3UDAirAppJsy/17 15.00 40.00
67 Miles02-3UDSwtSht/34 12.50 30.00
68 Miles02-3UDSwtShtSwSw/19 15.00 40.00
70 A.Miller02-3SPGU/19 12.50 30.00
71 A.Miller02-3UDSwtSht/38 12.50 30.00
72 A.Miller02-3UDSwtShtSSw/20 12.50 30.00
75 Mobley02-3UDSwtSht/30 12.50 30.00
77 Odom02-3MVPMatComb/17 15.00 40.00
78 Odom02-3UDAirAppJsy/19 15.00 40.00
79 Odom02-3UDSwtShot/20 15.00 40.00
80 Odom02-3UDSwtShtSSw/32 12.50 30.00
81 Parker02-3SPGU/18 40.00 100.00
82 Parker02-3UDAll-SAShort/19 40.00 100.00
84 Parker02-3UDSwtSht/22 40.00 100.00
85 Payton02-3SPGUA-Sapp/19 50.00 120.00
86 Pierce02-3SPxWinMat/27 40.00 80.00
90 Pierce02-3UDSwtSht/37 20.00 50.00
91 Pierce02-3UDSwtShtGlass/16 40.00 80.00
92 Robinson02-3SPxWinMat/16 100.00 200.00
93 Robinson02-3UDSwtSht/24 75.00 150.00
94 Rose02-3UDSwtSht/20 20.00 50.00
95 Stack02-3UDAll-AuthJsy/16 20.00 50.00
96 Stack02-3UDGmJsy2/14 20.00 50.00
97 Stack02-3UDSwtSht/37 15.00 40.00
100 Stockton02-3UDSwtSht/32 125.00 250.00
102 Peja02-3UDAll-StAuth/16 40.00 100.00
103 Peja02-3UDInspirations/26 20.00 50.00
104 Peja02-3UDSwtSht/37 20.00 50.00

2003-04 Ultimate Collection Jerseys

Randomly inserted, this 42-card set features a black and white photo of the player along with a swatch (divided into two swatches by design) on the right side of the card. Each card is sequentially numbered to 200. Jerseys Dual and Jerseys Triple parallels of this set were also inserted. Dual jerseys are sequentially numbered to 100, while triple jerseys are sequentially numbered to 25.

PRINT RUN 200 SER.#'d SETS
*DUAL: .6X TO 1.5X BASE JSY HI
DUAL PRINT RUN 100 SER.#'d SETS
*TRIPLE: 1.25X TO 3X BASE HI
TRIPLE PRINT RUN 25 SER.#'d SETS
AI Allen Iverson 6.00 15.00
AS Amare Stoudemire 5.00 12.00
AW Antoine Walker 4.00 10.00
BR Bill Russell 15.00 40.00
BW Ben Wallace 3.00 8.00
CA Carmelo Anthony 12.00 30.00
CB Caron Butler 3.00 8.00
CH Chris Bosh 6.00 15.00
CW Chris Webber 4.00 10.00
DM Darko Milicic 3.00 8.00
DN Dirk Nowitzki 6.00 15.00
DR David Robinson 6.00 15.00
DW Dajuan Wagner 2.50 6.00
DY Dwyane Wade 12.00 30.00
EB Elton Brand 4.00 10.00
EG Manu Ginobili 5.00 12.00
GP Gary Payton 4.00 10.00
JE Julius Erving 8.00 20.00
JK Jason Kidd 6.00 15.00
JO Jermaine O'Neal 3.00 8.00
JR Jason Richardson 4.00 10.00
JS John Stockton 5.00 12.00
KB Kobe Bryant 25.00 60.00
KG Kevin Garnett 6.00 15.00
KM Karl Malone 5.00 12.00
LB Larry Bird 10.00 25.00
LJ LeBron James 50.00 125.00
MA Magic Johnson 10.00 25.00
MJ Michael Jordan 60.00 150.00
OR Oscar Robertson 8.00 20.00
PE Patrick Ewing 8.00 20.00
PP Paul Pierce 4.00 10.00
RA Ray Allen 4.00 10.00
RJ Richard Jefferson 3.00 8.00
SF Steve Francis 3.00 8.00
SH Shawn Marion 3.00 8.00
SM Stephon Marbury 3.00 8.00
SN Steve Nash 5.00 12.00
SO Shaquille O'Neal 10.00 25.00
TD Tim Duncan 6.00 15.00
TM Tracy McGrady 5.00 12.00
YM Yao Ming 8.00 20.00

2003-04 Ultimate Collection Patches

Randomly seeded, this 72-card set parallels the design of the Jerseys set enhanced with premium patch swatches. Each card is squentially numbered to 100. Patches Dual and Patches Triple versions were also inserted and are numbered to 50 and 15 respectively.

AH Allan Houston 6.00 15.00
AI Allen Iverson 12.00 30.00
AJ Antawn Jamison 6.00 15.00
AK Andrei Kirilenko 8.00 20.00
AL Alonzo Mourning 15.00 40.00
AM Andre Miller 6.00 15.00
AP Aleksandar Pavlovic 6.00 15.00
AS Amare Stoudemire 5.00 12.00
BD Baron Davis 6.00 15.00
BG Keith Bogans 5.00 12.00
BO Boris Diaw 8.00 20.00
CA Carmelo Anthony 40.00 80.00
CH Chris Bosh 12.00 30.00
CK Chris Kaman 8.00 20.00
CM Corey Maggette 6.00 15.00
CW Chris Webber 8.00 20.00
DA Darius Miles 5.00 12.00
DE Desmond Mason 6.00 15.00
DJ Dahntay Jones 6.00 15.00
DM Darko Milicic 6.00 15.00
DN Dirk Nowitzki 12.00 30.00
DR David Robinson 25.00 60.00
DW David West 8.00 20.00
DY Dwyane Wade 50.00 120.00
EB Elton Brand 8.00 20.00
GA Gilbert Arenas 6.00 15.00
GH Grant Hill 15.00 40.00
GP Gary Payton 8.00 20.00
JA Jalen Rose 6.00 15.00
JD Josh Howard 8.00 20.00
JE Jerry Stackhouse 6.00 15.00
JH Jarvis Hayes 5.00 12.00
JK Jason Kidd 12.00 30.00
JM Jamal Mashburn 6.00 15.00
JO Jermaine O'Neal 6.00 15.00
JR Jason Richardson 8.00 20.00
JS John Stockton 10.00 25.00
JT Jason Terry 6.00 15.00
KE Kenyon Martin 6.00 15.00
KG Kevin Garnett 12.00 30.00
KM Karl Malone 12.00 30.00
LJ LeBron James 125.00 300.00
LO Lamar Odom 6.00 15.00
LR Luke Ridnour 6.00 15.00
LS Latrell Sprewell 8.00 20.00
MB Mike Bibby 8.00 20.00
MF Michael Finley 8.00 20.00
MO Morris Peterson 5.00 12.00
MP Mickael Pietrus 6.00 15.00
MR Marcus Banks 5.00 12.00
MS Mike Sweetney 5.00 12.00
PG Pau Gasol 8.00 20.00
PP Paul Pierce 8.00 20.00
PS Peja Stojakovic 8.00 20.00
QR Quentin Richardson 6.00 15.00
RA Ray Allen 15.00 40.00
RG Reece Gaines 5.00 12.00
RJ Richard Jefferson 6.00 15.00
RM Reggie Miller 15.00 40.00
SA Shareef Abdur-Rahim 6.00 15.00
SB Steve Blake 6.00 15.00
SF Steve Francis 6.00 15.00
SH Shawn Marion 6.00 15.00
SM Stephon Marbury 6.00 15.00
SN Steve Nash 10.00 25.00
SO Shaquille O'Neal 20.00 50.00
SP Scottie Pippen 40.00 100.00
TB Troy Bell 8.00 20.00
TD Tim Duncan 12.00 30.00
TM Tracy McGrady 10.00 25.00
TP Tony Parker 8.00 20.00
YM Yao Ming 25.00 60.00

2003-04 Ultimate Collection Patches Dual

*DUAL: .6X TO 1.5X BASE PATCH HI
PRINT RUN 50 SER.#'d SETS
AW Antoine Walker 12.00 30.00
JS John Stockton 40.00 100.00
KB Kobe Bryant 150.00 300.00
MJ Michael Jordan 400.00 800.00
PE Patrick Ewing 75.00 150.00

2003-04 Ultimate Collection Patches Triple

Randomly inserted, this 42-card set is a partial parallel the the Patches insert set with three swatches and each card is sequentially numbered to 15.

TRIPLE PRINT RUN 15 SER.#'d SETS
AI3 Allen Iverson 125.00 250.00
CA3 Carmelo Anthony 150.00 300.00
DM3 Darko Milicic 25.00 60.00
DU3 Dajuan Wagner 20.00 50.00
DY3 Dwyane Wade 200.00 400.00
KB3 Kobe Bryant 250.00 500.00
LB3 Larry Bird 80.00 200.00
LJ3 LeBron James 300.00 800.00
MA3 Magic Johnson 200.00 400.00
MJ3 Michael Jordan 1000.00 1600.00
TD3 Tim Duncan 50.00 125.00

2003-04 Ultimate Collection Signatures

Inserted in packs at the overall rate of one in four for autographs, this 21-card set places a full color player portrait style photo in the upper left hand corner of the card and an autograph in the lower right.

AUTOGRAPH ODDS 1:4
AS Amare Stoudemire 6.00 15.00
CA Carmelo Anthony 30.00 60.00
DM Darko Milicic 5.00 12.00
DY Dwyane Wade 50.00 120.00
GP Gary Payton 12.00 30.00
JE Julius Erving 40.00 100.00
JH Jarvis Hayes 4.00 10.00
JK Jason Kidd 15.00 40.00
JS John Stockton 50.00 125.00
KB Kobe Bryant 100.00 200.00
KG Kevin Garnett SP 50.00 120.00
LB Larry Bird SP 60.00 150.00
LJ LeBron James 1500.00 2200.00
MA Magic Johnson SP 50.00 120.00
MJ Michael Jordan 800.00 1200.00
MS Mike Sweetney 4.00 10.00
PE Patrick Ewing 150.00 300.00
RM Reggie Miller 50.00 120.00
RO Dennis Rodman 40.00 100.00
TM Tracy McGrady 20.00 50.00
YM Yao Ming 30.00 80.00

2003-04 Ultimate Collection Signatures Gold

PRINT RUNS LISTED BELOW
SOME NOT PRICED DUE TO SCARCITY
UNPRICED LOGOS SER.#'d TO ONE
AS Amare Stoudemire/32 30.00 80.00
CA Carmelo Anthony/15 150.00 300.00
DM Darko Milicic/31 20.00 50.00
GP Gary Payton/20 30.00 80.00
JH Jarvis Hayes/24 15.00 40.00
KG Kevin Garnett/21 75.00 150.00
LB Larry Bird/33 150.00 300.00
LJ LeBron James/23 1500.00 3000.00
MA Magic Johnson/32 100.00 200.00
MJ Michael Jordan/23 700.00 1000.00
MS Mike Sweetney/50 15.00 40.00
PE Patrick Ewing/33 300.00 600.00
RM Reggie Miller/31 100.00 200.00
RO Dennis Rodman/91 40.00 100.00

2004-05 Ultimate Collection

Released in June 2005, Ultimate Collection boasts a 168-card set divided up to where cards 1-116 feature veteran players serially numbered to 750, cards 117-126 feature rookies serially numbered to 750 and cards 127-168 feature autographed rookies serially numbered to 250. Ultimate Collection was packaged in four-pack boxes that contained four cards each that carried a SRP of $100.

1-116 PRINT RUN 750 SER.#'d SETS
127-168 PRINT RUN 250 SER.#'d SETS
UNPRICED SPECTRUM PRINT RUN ONE SET
1 Tyronn Lue 1.00 2.50
2 Tony Delk 1.00 2.50
3 Al Harrington 1.25 3.00
4 Paul Pierce 1.50 4.00
5 Antoine Walker 1.50 4.00
6 Bill Russell 2.50 6.00
7 Larry Bird 4.00 10.00
8 Gerald Wallace 1.25 3.00
9 Jason Kapono 1.00 2.50
10 Primoz Brezec 1.00 2.50
11 Kirk Hinrich 1.25 3.00
12 Eddy Curry 1.00 2.50
13 Tyson Chandler 1.25 3.00
14 Michael Jordan 12.00 30.00
15 LeBron James 10.00 25.00
16 Drew Gooden 1.00 2.50
17 Jeff McInnis 1.00 2.50
18 Zydrunas Ilgauskas 1.25 3.00
19 Dirk Nowitzki 2.50 6.00
20 Michael Finley 1.50 4.00
21 Josh Howard 1.50 4.00
22 Marquis Daniels 1.00 2.50
23 Carmelo Anthony 3.00 8.00
24 Kenyon Martin 1.25 3.00
25 Andre Miller 1.25 3.00
26 Nene 1.25 3.00
27 Ben Wallace 1.25 3.00
28 Richard Hamilton 1.25 3.00
29 Isiah Thomas 1.50 4.00
30 Chauncey Billups 1.50 4.00
31 Jason Richardson 1.50 4.00
32 Baron Davis 1.25 3.00
33 Derek Fisher 1.25 3.00
34 Tracy McGrady 2.00 5.00
35 Yao Ming 3.00 8.00
36 Hakeem Olajuwon 2.00 5.00
37 Jermaine O'Neal 1.50 4.00
38 Reggie Miller 1.50 4.00
39 Ron Artest 1.50 4.00
40 Stephen Jackson 1.25 3.00
41 Elton Brand 1.50 4.00
42 Chris Kaman 1.25 3.00
43 Corey Maggette 1.25 3.00
44 Bobby Simmons 1.00 2.50
45 Kobe Bryant 6.00 15.00
46 Magic Johnson 4.00 10.00
47 Wilt Chamberlain 3.00 8.00
48 Lamar Odom 1.25 3.00
49 Pau Gasol 1.50 4.00
50 Bonzi Wells 1.00 2.50
51 Jason Williams 1.25 3.00
52 Mike Miller 1.25 3.00
53 Shaquille O'Neal 4.00 10.00
54 Dwyane Wade 2.50 6.00
55 Eddie Jones 1.25 3.00
56 Udonis Haslem 1.00 2.50
57 Oscar Robertson 1.50 4.00
58 Michael Redd 1.25 3.00
59 Desmond Mason 1.25 3.00
60 T.J. Ford 1.00 2.50
61 Kevin Garnett 2.50 6.00
62 Latrell Sprewell 1.25 3.00
63 Sam Cassell 1.25 3.00
64 Michael Olowokandi 1.00 2.50
65 Jason Kidd 2.50 6.00
66 Richard Jefferson 1.25 3.00
67 Vince Carter 2.50 6.00
68 Ron Mercer 1.00 2.50
69 Dan Dickau 1.00 2.50

70 Jamaal Magloire 1.00 2.50
71 P.J. Brown 1.00 2.50
72 Lee Nailon 1.00 2.50
73 Stephon Marbury 1.25 3.00
74 Allan Houston 1.25 3.00
75 Jamal Crawford 1.50 4.00
76 Bernard King 1.25 3.00
77 Steve Francis 1.25 3.00
78 Doug Christie 1.00 2.50
79 Grant Hill 2.00 5.00
80 Hedo Turkoglu 1.25 3.00
81 Allen Iverson 2.50 6.00
82 Julius Erving 2.50 6.00
83 Chris Webber 1.50 4.00
84 Kyle Korver 1.25 3.00
85 Amare Stoudemire 1.25 3.00
86 Steve Nash 2.00 5.00
87 Shawn Marion 1.25 3.00
88 Quentin Richardson 1.25 3.00
89 Shareef Abdur-Rahim 1.25 3.00
90 Darius Miles 1.00 2.50
91 Zach Randolph 1.25 3.00
92 Damon Stoudamire 1.25 3.00
93 Peja Stojakovic 1.50 4.00
94 Mike Bibby 1.50 4.00
95 Cuttino Mobley 1.00 2.50
96 Brad Miller 1.25 3.00
97 Tim Duncan 2.50 6.00
98 Manu Ginobili 2.00 5.00
99 Tony Parker 1.50 4.00
100 David Robinson 2.50 6.00
101 Ray Allen 1.50 4.00
102 Rashard Lewis 1.50 4.00
103 Ronald Murray 1.00 2.50
104 Luke Ridnour 1.25 3.00
105 Rafer Alston 1.00 2.50
106 Jalen Rose 1.25 3.00
107 Chris Bosh 1.50 4.00
108 Morris Peterson 1.00 2.50
109 Andrei Kirilenko 1.25 3.00
110 Carlos Boozer 1.25 3.00
111 John Stockton 2.50 6.00
112 Matt Harpring 1.00 2.50
113 Gilbert Arenas 1.25 3.00
114 Antawn Jamison 1.25 3.00
115 Jarvis Hayes 1.00 2.50
116 Larry Hughes 1.25 3.00
117 D.J. Mbenga RC 2.50 6.00
118 Damien Wilkins RC 2.50 6.00
119 Billy Thomas RC 2.00 5.00
120 Andre Barrett RC 3.00 8.00
121 Erik Daniels RC 2.50 6.00
122 Justin Reed RC 2.00 5.00
123 Viktor Khryapa RC 2.00 5.00
124 Mario Kasun RC 2.50 6.00
125 Luis Flores RC 2.50 6.00
126 Emeka Okafor RC 2.50 6.00
127 Dwight Howard AU RC 25.00 60.00
128 Ben Gordon AU RC 6.00 15.00
129 Shaun Livingston AU RC 6.00 15.00
130 Devin Harris AU RC 5.00 12.00
131 Josh Childress AU RC 5.00 12.00
132 Luol Deng AU RC 6.00 15.00
133 Rafael Araujo AU RC 4.00 10.00
134 Andre Iguodala AU RC 8.00 20.00
135 Luke Jackson AU RC 4.00 10.00
136 Andris Biedrins AU RC 4.00 10.00
137 Robert Swift AU RC 4.00 10.00
138 Sebastian Telfair AU RC 5.00 12.00
139 Kris Humphries AU RC 6.00 15.00
140 Al Jefferson AU RC 8.00 20.00
141 Kirk Snyder AU RC 4.00 10.00
142 Josh Smith AU RC 6.00 15.00
143 J.R. Smith AU RC 6.00 15.00
144 Dorell Wright AU RC 4.00 10.00
145 Jameer Nelson AU RC 6.00 15.00
146 Pavel Podkolzin AU RC 4.00 10.00
147 Delonte West AU RC 6.00 15.00
148 Tony Allen AU RC 6.00 15.00
149 Kevin Martin AU RC 10.00 25.00
150 Sasha Vujacic AU RC 6.00 15.00
151 Beno Udrih AU RC 5.00 12.00
152 David Harrison AU RC 4.00 10.00
153 Anderson Varejao AU RC 5.00 12.00
154 Jackson Vroman AU RC 4.00 10.00
155 Peter John Ramos AU RC 4.00 10.00
156 Lionel Chalmers AU RC 6.00 15.00
157 Donta Smith AU RC 4.00 10.00
158 Andre Emmett AU RC 4.00 10.00
159 Antonio Burks AU RC 5.00 12.00
160 Royal Ivey AU RC 5.00 12.00
161 Chris Duhon AU RC 6.00 15.00
162 Nenad Krstic AU RC 6.00 15.00
163 Trevor Ariza AU RC 6.00 15.00
164 Matt Freije AU RC 5.00 12.00
165 Bernard Robinson AU RC 5.00 12.00
166 Andres Nocioni AU RC 4.00 10.00
167 Pape Sow AU RC 4.00 10.00
168 Ha Seung-Jin AU RC 8.00 20.00

2004-05 Ultimate Collection Limited

*1-116: 1.5X TO 4X BASE HI
*117-126: 1X TO 2.5X BASE HI
*127-168: 1.25X TO 3X BASE HI
STATED PRINT RUN 25 SER.#'d SETS
127-168 HAVE JSY's AND AU's
14 Michael Jordan 60.00 150.00
45 Kobe Bryant 40.00 100.00
127 Dwight Howard JSY AU 200.00 400.00
134 Andre Iguodala JSY AU 100.00 200.00
143 J.R. Smith JSY AU 40.00 100.00

2004-05 Ultimate Collection Achievements Signatures

ndomly seeded in packs, this 13-card set is horizontally designed with a player photo on the right and an autograph on the left. Each card is sequentially numbered, see checklist for print runs.
STATED PRINT RUN 24 TO 71 SER.#'d SETS
BK Bernard King/60 12.00 30.00
CA Carmelo Anthony/41 30.00 80.00
CD Clyde Drexler/50 40.00 80.00
DR David Robinson/71 40.00 100.00
HO Hakeem Olajuwon/52 40.00 100.00
JS John Stockton/28 125.00 250.00
KB Kobe Bryant/56 125.00 250.00
KG Kevin Garnett/40 75.00 150.00
LB Larry Bird/60 75.00 150.00
LJ LeBron James/43 400.00 800.00
MA Magic Johnson/24 75.00 150.00
MJ Michael Jordan/69 800.00 1200.00
TM Tracy McGrady/62 30.00 80.00

2004-05 Ultimate Collection Buybacks

Randomly seeded in packs, this 163-card set features autographed cards and COA's from previous year's Upper Deck products.
MOST UNPRICED DUE TO SCARCITY
1 Abdur-R 03-4SPGUFab/18 10.00 25.00
2 Ray Allen EXCH 10.00 25.00
3 Melo 03-4FntElmJsy/16 40.00 100.00
6 Gilbert Arenas SwtShJsy/18 10.00 25.00
7 Bibby 02-3OvatShtSht/14 10.00 25.00
8 Bibby 02-3OvatWrmUp/21 10.00 25.00
10 Bibby 03-4GlasGamGr/15 20.00 50.00
13 Billups 04-5ASLUWkTh/28 10.00 25.00
14 Billups03-4SPGUAtFab/17 20.00 50.00
15 Kobe 02-3HardCrtGmFlr/14 100.00 200.00
16 Kobe 02-3HrdCrtGmFlrFm/17 100.00 200.00
22 B.Davis 03-4SwtShtJsy/20 10.00 25.00
23 B.Davis 01-2FltTmPtrn/34 10.00 25.00
24 B.Davis 01-2UDAirApp/17 10.00 25.00
25 B.Davis 02-3FinteEleJsy/20 10.00 25.00
26 B.Davis 02-3OvatAthUni/20 10.00 25.00
27 B.Davis 02-3SPxWinMat/19 10.00 25.00
28 B.Davis 02-3SwtShtSS/19 10.00 25.00
29 B.Davis 02-3UDGamPlnJsy/19 10.00 25.00
30 B.Davis 03-4SPGUAuthFab/19 10.00 25.00
31 B.Davis 03-4SPxWinMat/22 10.00 25.00
32 Drexler 02-3GenATAth/18 30.00 80.00
33 Dr.J 02-3GenAllTmAth/15 75.00 150.00
35 Garnett 02-3OvtAthWU/15 50.00 120.00
36 Garnett 03-4SPxWinMat/18 50.00 120.00
37 Garnett 03-4SwtShtJsy/20 50.00 120.00
39 Gasol 02-3ChpDrvPropJsy/14 10.00 25.00
41 Gasol 03-4SPxWinMat/22 10.00 25.00
42 Gasol 03-4UDAllStWkAth/18 10.00 25.00
45 Hamilton 03-4UDSPGUAthFb/18 10.00 25.00
46 Harrngtn 01-2UDAirApp/26 10.00 25.00
47 D.Harris 04-5SwtShtJsy/16 40.00 100.00
48 Hinrich 03-4UpperDeck/28 40.00 80.00
49 D.Howard 04-5SwtShtJsy/18 50.00 120.00
50 LeBron 03-4FinElemJsy/19 600.00 1000.00
53 Jamison 02-3UDPractJsy/24 10.00 25.00
55 Jamison 03-4SPxWinMat/23 10.00 25.00
57 Jefferson 03-4SPxWinMat/15 10.00 25.00
58 Magic 02-3GenATAWht/16 75.00 150.00
59 Magic 02-3GenATAYel/19 75.00 150.00
60 Kidd 02-3HardFlr/15 25.00 60.00
61 Kidd 02-3HardFlrFilm/14 25.00 60.00
62 Kidd 02-3OvatWarUp/16 25.00 60.00
64 Kidd 03-4SPxWinMat/21 25.00 60.00
65 Kidd 03-4SwtShtJsy/19 25.00 60.00
66 Kidd 03-4UDGlsSupSw/20 25.00 60.00
67 AK-47 02-3UDASAuth/21 10.00 25.00
68 AK-47 03-4UDASWkAth/18 10.00 25.00
69 AK-47 04-5HardMat/21 10.00 25.00
70 AK-47 04-5HardMatCom/21 10.00 25.00
71 AK-47 04-5SwtShtSwt/14 10.00 25.00
72 AK-47 04-5UDASWkAth/17 10.00 25.00
73 C.Magg 01-2FltTmPatrn/28 10.00 25.00
74 C.Magg 02-3UDGamPln/19 10.00 25.00
76 C.Magg 04-5SPGUAthFab/19 10.00 25.00
77 C.Magg 04-5SwtShtSw/17 10.00 25.00
78 Marbury 01-2FltTmJmJsy/22 10.00 25.00
81 Marbury 02-3SPxWinMat/17 10.00 25.00
82 Marbury 03-4FinEleWU/20 10.00 25.00
83 Marion 02-3SwtShot/36 10.00 25.00
84 Marion 02-3UDPractice/16 10.00 25.00
86 Marion 03-4SwtShtJsy/18 10.00 25.00
89 Mason 02-3UDAllStrAuth/15 10.00 25.00
95 T-Mac 03-4SPxWinMat/23 40.00 100.00
96 T-Mac 40.00 100.00
Amare 03-4SPxWMC/18
98 A.Miller 02-3SwtSht/38 10.00 25.00
99 A.Miller 03-4SPxWinMat/22 10.00 25.00
100 A.Miller 04-5SPGUAuthFab/20 10.00 25.00
103 Ming 03-4FiniteElemJsy/15 40.00 100.00
104 Ming 03-4GlasSupSw/18 40.00 100.00
109 Zo 03-4GlasGamGr/17 100.00 200.00
110 Zo 03-4SPGUAuthFab/15 100.00 200.00
111 Nash 03-4SPGUAuthFab/20 50.00 120.00
112 Nash 03-4SPxWinMat/20 50.00 120.00
113 Nash 03-4UDSwtShtJsy/15 50.00 120.00
114 Nash 04-5HardMat/19 50.00 120.00
115 Nash 04-5HardMatCom/21 50.00 120.00
116 Odom 02-3MVPMatComb/17 10.00 25.00
117 Odom 03-4GlasGamGr/19 10.00 25.00
118 Odom 04-5HardMatCom/21 10.00 25.00
119 Odom 04-5HrdMatCom/21 10.00 25.00
120 Odom 04-5SPGUAthFab/23 10.00 25.00
123 Parker 03-4SPxWinMat/21 25.00 60.00
124 Parker 04-5HardMat/19 25.00 60.00
125 Parker 04-5HardMatCom/21 25.00 60.00
126 Parker 04-5SwtShtSwt/14 25.00 60.00
127 Payton 02-3GenATAth/20 25.00 60.00
128 Payton 03-4HardFloor/14 20.00 50.00
129 Payton 03-4SPxWinMat/21 20.00 50.00
130 Payton 04-5SwtShtSwt/18 20.00 50.00
131 Paul Pierce Jsy/17 10.00 25.00
132 Scottie Pippen Jsy/19 150.00 300.00
135 J-Rich 03-4SwtShtSwt/17 10.00 25.00
138 D-Rob 03-4SPGUAthFab/18 100.00 200.00
139 D-Rob 03-4SPxWinMat/17 100.00 200.00
141 Stockton 02-3OvatAthShrt/14 100.00 200.00
142 Stockton 03-4SwtShtSwt/20 100.00 200.00
145 Peja 03-4BlkDiamJsy/14 20.00 50.00
147 Peja 03-4SPGUAuthFab/16 20.00 50.00
148 Peja 03-4UDAllStWkAth/14 20.00 50.00
149 Amare 03-4GlasGamGr/17 20.00 50.00
150 Amare 03-4SPxWinMat/20 20.00 50.00
151 Amare 03-4SwtShtJsy/20 20.00 50.00
152 Amare 03-4SwtShtSwt/17 20.00 50.00
153 Amare 04-5HardMatCom/21 20.00 50.00
154 Amare 04-5HardMater/20 20.00 50.00
155 Amare 04-5SPGUAuthFab/16 20.00 50.00
156 Amare 04-5SwtShtSwt/16 20.00 50.00
159 B.Wallace 03-4BlaDiaJsy/14 25.00 60.00
160 B.Wallace 03-4SPGUFab/20 25.00 60.00
161 B.Wallace 03-4UDAsWAth/21 25.00 60.00
163 Kidd 40.00 100.00
Jeff 03-4SPxWinMat/18

2004-05 Ultimate Collection Debuts

Serially numbered to 350, this 30-card set focuses on rookies and places them on colored backgrounds set to match their team's colors.
PRINT RUN 350 SER.#'d SETS
UD1 Dwight Howard 5.00 12.00
UD2 Emeka Okafor 2.00 5.00
UD3 Ben Gordon 2.50 6.00
UD4 Shaun Livingston 2.50 6.00
UD5 Devin Harris 2.00 5.00
UD6 Josh Childress 2.00 5.00
UD7 Luol Deng 2.50 6.00
UD8 Rafael Araujo 1.50 4.00
UD9 Andre Iguodala 3.00 8.00
UD10 Luke Jackson 1.50 4.00
UD11 Andris Biedrins 1.50 4.00
UD12 Robert Swift 1.50 4.00
UD13 Sebastian Telfair 2.00 5.00
UD14 Kris Humphries 2.50 6.00
UD15 Al Jefferson 3.00 8.00
UD16 Kirk Snyder 1.50 4.00
UD17 Josh Smith 2.50 6.00
UD18 J.R. Smith 2.50 6.00
UD19 Dorell Wright 2.50 6.00
UD20 Jameer Nelson 2.50 6.00
UD21 Nenad Krstic 2.50 6.00
UD22 Anderson Varejao 2.00 5.00
UD23 Jackson Vroman 1.50 4.00
UD24 Delonte West 2.50 6.00
UD25 Tony Allen 2.50 6.00
UD26 Kevin Martin 3.00 8.00
UD27 Sasha Vujacic 2.50 6.00
UD28 Beno Udrih 2.00 5.00
UD29 Ha Seung-Jin 2.50 6.00
UD30 Andres Nocioni 2.50 6.00

2004-05 Ultimate Collection Game Jerseys

Randomly seeded in packs and serially numbered to 175 copies, this 42-card set places a player photo on the left and a swatch of game jersey on the right. A Limited parallel serially numbered to 75 and a Limited Extra parallel serially numbered to 25 were also produced.
PRINT RUN 175 SER.#'d SETS
*EXTRA: 1X TO 2.5X BASE HI
EXTRA PRINT RUN 25 SER.#'d SETS
*LIMITED: .5X TO 1.25X BASE JSY HI
LIMITED PRINT RUN 75 SER.#'d SETS
AI Allen Iverson 5.00 12.00
AK Andrei Kirilenko 2.50 6.00
AS Amare Stoudemire 2.50 6.00
BD Baron Davis 2.50 6.00
BG Ben Gordon 3.00 8.00
BK Bernard King 2.50 6.00
BW Ben Wallace 2.50 6.00
CA Carmelo Anthony 6.00 15.00
CD Clyde Drexler 4.00 10.00
DE Dennis Rodman 8.00 20.00
DH Dwight Howard 6.00 15.00
DN Dirk Nowitzki 6.00 15.00
DR David Robinson 5.00 12.00
EG Manu Ginobili 4.00 10.00
HO Hakeem Olajuwon 4.00 10.00
IT Isiah Thomas 3.00 8.00
JE Julius Erving 5.00 12.00
JK Jason Kidd 5.00 12.00
JO Jermaine O'Neal 2.50 6.00
JR Jason Richardson 3.00 8.00
JS John Stockton 5.00 12.00
KB Kobe Bryant 10.00 25.00
KG Kevin Garnett 5.00 12.00
LB Larry Bird 8.00 20.00
LD Luol Deng 3.00 8.00
LJ LeBron James 12.50 30.00
MA Magic Johnson 8.00 20.00
MB Mike Bibby 3.00 8.00
MJ Michael Jordan 40.00 100.00
OR Oscar Robertson 8.00 20.00
PG Pau Gasol 3.00 8.00
PP Paul Pierce 3.00 8.00
PS Peja Stojakovic 3.00 8.00
RM Reggie Miller 6.00 15.00
SF Steve Francis 2.50 6.00
SM Stephon Marbury 2.50 6.00
SN Steve Nash 4.00 10.00
SO Shaquille O'Neal 8.00 20.00
TD Tim Duncan 5.00 12.00
TM Tracy McGrady 4.00 10.00
WC Wilt Chamberlain 20.00 50.00
YM Yao Ming 6.00 15.00

2004-05 Ultimate Collection Game Patches

ndomly seeded in packs, this 42-card set parallels the Game Jerseys insert enhanced with a patch swatch and sequential numbering to 100. A Patches Limited parallel sequentially numbered to 25 and a Patches Limited Extra parallel sequentially numbered to 10 were also produced and inserted.
PRINT RUN 50 TO 100 SER.#'d SETS
*LIMITED: .5X TO 1.25X BASE JSY HI
LIMITED PRINT RUN 25 SER.#'d SETS
AI Allen Iverson/100 25.00 60.00
AK Andrei Kirilenko/100 6.00 15.00
AS Amare Stoudemire/100 6.00 15.00
BD Baron Davis/100 6.00 15.00
BG Ben Gordon/100 8.00 20.00
BK Bernard King/100 6.00 15.00
BW Ben Wallace/100 6.00 15.00
CA Carmelo Anthony/100 15.00 40.00
CD Clyde Drexler/100 15.00 40.00
DE Dennis Rodman/100 25.00 60.00
DH Dwight Howard/100 20.00 50.00
DN Dirk Nowitzki/100 12.00 30.00
DR David Robinson/100 12.00 30.00
EG Manu Ginobili/100 10.00 25.00
HO Hakeem Olajuwon/100 10.00 25.00
IT Isiah Thomas/100 8.00 20.00
JE Julius Erving/100 12.00 30.00
JK Jason Kidd/100 12.00 30.00
JO Jermaine O'Neal/100 6.00 15.00
JR Jason Richardson/100 8.00 20.00
JS John Stockton/100 20.00 50.00
KB Kobe Bryant/100 40.00 100.00
KG Kevin Garnett/100 12.00 30.00
LB Larry Bird/50 40.00 100.00
LD Luol Deng/100 8.00 20.00
LJ LeBron James/100 40.00 100.00
MA Magic Johnson/100 20.00 50.00
MB Mike Bibby/100 8.00 20.00
MJ Michael Jordan/100 125.00 250.00
OR Oscar Robertson/50 20.00 50.00
PG Pau Gasol/100 8.00 20.00
PP Paul Pierce/100 8.00 20.00
PS Peja Stojakovic/100 8.00 20.00
RM Reggie Miller/100 12.00 30.00
SF Steve Francis/100 6.00 15.00
SM Stephon Marbury/100 6.00 15.00
SN Steve Nash/100 15.00 40.00
SO Shaquille O'Neal/100 20.00 50.00
TD Tim Duncan/100 15.00 40.00
TM Tracy McGrady/100 10.00 25.00
WC Wilt Chamberlain/100 50.00 120.00
YM Yao Ming/100 15.00 40.00

2004-05 Ultimate Collection MVP Autographs

Randomly seeded, this seven card set is horizontally designed with a photo on the left and an autograph on the right. Cards are sequentially numbered to either total number of league MVP's won or the year the player received the award.
STATED PRINT RUN 3 TO 94 SER.#'d SETS
MOST NOT PRICED DUE TO SCARCITY
HO Hakeem Olajuwon/94 25.00 60.00
JE Julius Erving/81 40.00 80.00

2004-05 Ultimate Collection Premium Patches

Randomly seeded, this 42-card set is horizontally designed and places player photos on the left of the card and an oversized patch swatch on the right. Each card is sequentially numbered to 75.
PRINT RUN 25 TO 75 SER.#'d SETS
AI Allen Iverson/75 60.00 150.00
AK Andrei Kirilenko/75 20.00 50.00
AS Amare Stoudemire/50 20.00 50.00
BD Baron Davis/75 20.00 50.00
BG Ben Gordon/75 25.00 60.00
BW Ben Wallace/75 20.00 50.00
CA Carmelo Anthony/75 60.00 150.00
CW Chris Webber/75 125.00 300.00
DE Devin Harris/75 20.00 50.00
DH Dwight Howard/50 100.00 250.00
DN Dirk Nowitzki/75 60.00 150.00
EB Elton Brand/75 25.00 60.00
JC Josh Childress/75 20.00 50.00
JK Jason Kidd/75 40.00 100.00
JN Jameer Nelson/75 25.00 60.00
JO Jermaine O'Neal/75 20.00 50.00
JR Jason Richardson/75 25.00 60.00
KB Kobe Bryant/75 250.00 500.00
KG Kevin Garnett/75 200.00 500.00
LD Luol Deng/75 25.00 60.00
LJ LeBron James/50 300.00 600.00
LO Lamar Odom/50 20.00 50.00
MJ Michael Jordan/25 400.00 800.00
PG Pau Gasol/75 30.00 80.00
PP Paul Pierce/75 60.00 150.00
PS Peja Stojakovic/50 25.00 60.00
RA Ray Allen/75 75.00 200.00
RH Richard Hamilton/75 30.00 80.00
RJ Richard Jefferson/75 20.00 50.00
RM Reggie Miller/75 125.00 300.00
SA Shareef Abdur-Rahim/75 20.00 50.00
SF Steve Francis/75 20.00 50.00
SH Shawn Marion/75 20.00 50.00
SL Shaun Livingston/75 25.00 60.00
SM Stephon Marbury/50 25.00 60.00
SN Steve Nash/75 75.00 200.00
SO Shaquille O'Neal/75 100.00 250.00
ST Sebastian Telfair/75 20.00 50.00
TD Tim Duncan/75 100.00 250.00
TM Tracy McGrady/50 125.00 300.00
TP Tony Parker/75 60.00 150.00
YM Yao Ming/75 125.00 300.00

2004-05 Ultimate Collection Rookie Jerseys

Limited to 275 serially numbered copies, this 29-card set places rookie player photos on the left and a swatch of jersey on the right. A Parallel version of this set was also produced and is sequentially numbered to 75.
PRINT RUN 275 SER.#'d SETS
*PARALLEL: .5X TO 1.25X BASE HI
PARALLEL PRINT RUN 75 SER.#'d SETS
AB Andris Biedrins 2.00 5.00
AE Andre Emmett 2.00 5.00
AI Andre Iguodala 4.00 10.00
AJ Al Jefferson 4.00 10.00
AV Anderson Varejao 2.50 6.00
BG Ben Gordon 3.00 8.00
DA David Harrison 2.00 5.00
DE Devin Harris 2.50 6.00
DH Dwight Howard 6.00 15.00
DW Dorell Wright 3.00 8.00
HS Ha Seung-Jin 3.00 8.00
JC Josh Childress 2.50 6.00
JN Jameer Nelson 3.00 8.00
JR J.R. Smith 3.00 8.00
JS Josh Smith 3.00 8.00
JV Jackson Vroman 2.00 5.00
KH Kris Humphries 3.00 8.00
KM Kevin Martin 4.00 10.00
KS Kirk Snyder 2.00 5.00
LC Lionel Chalmers 3.00 8.00
LD Luol Deng 3.00 8.00
LU Luke Jackson 2.00 5.00
PR Peter John Ramos 2.00 5.00
RA Rafael Araujo 2.00 5.00
SL Shaun Livingston 3.00 8.00
ST Sebastian Telfair 2.50 6.00
SV Sasha Vujacic 3.00 8.00
TA Tony Allen 3.00 8.00
WE Delonte West 3.00 8.00

2004-05 Ultimate Collection Signature Patches

Inserted randomly and limited to 25 copies, this 27-card set features a player photo and an autographed jersey patch. Please note a version of the Michael Jordan card may exist as a UDA version from his Flight School Camp.
PRINT RUN 25 SER.#'d SETS
AI Andre Iguodala 60.00 150.00
AS Amare Stoudemire 50.00 120.00
BG Ben Gordon 40.00 100.00
BK Bernard King 40.00 100.00
BW Ben Wallace 50.00 120.00
CA Carmelo Anthony 100.00 200.00
CD Clyde Drexler 150.00 300.00
DE Dennis Rodman 150.00 300.00
DH Dwight Howard 175.00 350.00
DR David Robinson 100.00 200.00
IT Isiah Thomas 20.00 50.00
JC Josh Childress 20.00 50.00
JE Julius Erving 100.00 200.00
JK Jason Kidd 75.00 150.00
JS John Stockton 150.00 300.00
KB Kobe Bryant 400.00 800.00
KG Kevin Garnett 150.00 300.00
LB Larry Bird 150.00 300.00
LD Luol Deng 25.00 60.00
LJ LeBron James 400.00 800.00
MA Magic Johnson 125.00 250.00
MJ Michael Jordan 600.00 1000.00
PG Pau Gasol 25.00 60.00
PP Paul Pierce 50.00 100.00
PS Peja Stojakovic 50.00 100.00
TM Tracy McGrady 100.00 200.00
YM Yao Ming 100.00 200.00

2004-05 Ultimate Collection Signatures

Randomly inserted in packs as no odds are given, this 31-card set is horizontally designed with player photos on the left and autographs on the right.
RANDOM INSERTS IN PACKS
AM Alonzo Mourning 25.00 60.00
AS Amare Stoudemire 12.00 30.00
BG Ben Gordon 6.00 15.00
BK Bernard King 8.00 20.00
BR Bill Russell 75.00 150.00
BW Ben Wallace 15.00 40.00
CA Carmelo Anthony 20.00 50.00
CD Clyde Drexler 20.00 50.00
DE Devin Harris 5.00 12.00
DH Dwight Howard 15.00 40.00
DR David Robinson 30.00 60.00
HO Hakeem Olajuwon 20.00 50.00
IT Isiah Thomas 15.00 40.00
JE Julius Erving 40.00 100.00
JK Jason Kidd 12.00 30.00
JS John Stockton 50.00 120.00
KB Kobe Bryant SP 100.00 200.00
KG Kevin Garnett SP 75.00 150.00
KH Kirk Hinrich 5.00 12.00
LB Larry Bird 50.00 120.00
LD Luol Deng 6.00 15.00
LJ LeBron James 400.00 800.00
MA Magic Johnson 40.00 100.00
MJ Michael Jordan 400.00 800.00
PS Peja Stojakovic 6.00 15.00
RA Ray Allen 15.00 40.00
RO Dennis Rodman 30.00 80.00
SL Shaun Livingston 6.00 15.00
SM Stephon Marbury 12.00 30.00
TM Tracy McGrady 25.00 60.00
YM Yao Ming 30.00 80.00

2004-05 Ultimate Collection Signatures Gold

Randomly seeded, this 31-card set parallels the Signatures set enhanced with gold foil and sequential numbering to the featured player's jersey number.
STATED PRINT RUN ONE TO 91 SETS
SOME UNPRICED DUE TO SCARCITY
AM Alonzo Mourning/33 30.00 80.00
AS Amare Stoudemire/32 30.00 80.00
BK Bernard King/30 12.00 30.00
CA Carmelo Anthony/15 50.00 120.00
CD Clyde Drexler/22 40.00 100.00
DE Devin Harris/34 15.00 40.00
DR David Robinson/50 40.00 100.00
HO Hakeem Olajuwon/34 40.00 80.00
KG Kevin Garnett/21 150.00 250.00
KH Kirk Hinrich/31 25.00 60.00
LB Larry Bird/33 60.00 150.00
LJ LeBron James/23 700.00 1200.00
MA Magic Johnson/32 60.00 150.00
MJ Michael Jordan/23 700.00 1200.00
RA Ray Allen/34 20.00 50.00
RO Dennis Rodman/91 40.00 100.00

2005-06 Ultimate Collection

Released in April 2006, Ultimate Collection boasts a 183-card set where cards 1-130 feature veteran players serially numbered to 750, cards 131-142 feature rookie players serially numbered to 750, cards 143-183 feature rookie autographs serially numbered to 250. Base veteran cards have black backgrounds and white borders on the left and right side of the card. Ultimate was packaged in four-pack boxes where packs contain four cards and carried an initial suggested retail price of $100.
1-130 PRINT RUN 750 SER.#'d SETS
143-183 AU RC PRINT RUN 250 SER.#'d SETS
1 Josh Smith .75 2.00
2 Josh Childress .75 2.00
3 Joe Johnson .75 2.00
4 Al Harrington .75 2.00
5 Tony Allen .60 1.50
6 Ricky Davis .75 2.00
7 Al Jefferson .75 2.00
8 Paul Pierce 1.00 2.50
9 Delonte West .60 1.50
10 Brevin Knight .60 1.50
11 Emeka Okafor .75 2.00
12 Kareem Rush .60 1.50
13 Gerald Wallace .75 2.00
14 Tyson Chandler .75 2.00
15 Luol Deng .75 2.00
16 Michael Jordan 15.00 40.00
17 Ben Gordon .75 2.00
18 Kirk Hinrich .75 2.00
19 LeBron James 4.00 10.00
20 Drew Gooden .75 2.00
21 Larry Hughes .75 2.00
22 Donyell Marshall .60 1.50
23 Zydrunas Ilgauskas .75 2.00
24 Marquis Daniels .60 1.50
25 Josh Howard 1.00 2.50
26 Dirk Nowitzki 1.50 4.00
27 Jason Terry .75 2.00
28 Devin Harris .60 1.50
29 Carmelo Anthony 2.00 5.00
30 Marcus Camby .75 2.00
31 Nene .75 2.00
32 Kenyon Martin .75 2.00
33 Andre Miller .75 2.00
34 Ben Wallace .75 2.00
35 Richard Hamilton .75 2.00
36 Tayshaun Prince .75 2.00
37 Chauncey Billups 1.00 2.50
38 Rasheed Wallace 1.00 2.50
39 Baron Davis .75 2.00
40 Mike Dunleavy .75 2.00
41 Troy Murphy .60 1.50
42 Jason Richardson 1.00 2.50
43 Tracy McGrady 1.25 3.00
44 Yao Ming 1.25 3.00
45 Stromile Swift .60 1.50
46 Juwan Howard .75 2.00
47 Bob Sura .60 1.50
48 Ron Artest 1.00 2.50
49 Stephen Jackson .75 2.00
50 Jermaine O'Neal .75 2.00
51 Jamaal Tinsley .60 1.50
52 Elton Brand 1.00 2.50
53 Corey Maggette .75 2.00
54 Sam Cassell .75 2.00
55 Shaun Livingston .60 1.50
56 Cuttino Mobley .60 1.50
57 Kobe Bryant 4.00 10.00
58 Kwame Brown .60 1.50
59 Lamar Odom .75 2.00
60 Devean George .60 1.50
61 Pau Gasol 1.00 2.50
62 Damon Stoudamire .75 2.00
63 Eddie Jones .75 2.00
64 Bobby Jackson .60 1.50
65 Shaquille O'Neal 2.00 5.00
66 Gary Payton 1.00 2.50
67 Antoine Walker .75 2.00
68 Dwyane Wade 1.50 4.00
69 Jason Williams .75 2.00
70 Jamaal Magloire .60 1.50
71 Michael Redd .75 2.00
72 Bobby Simmons .60 1.50
73 Maurice Williams .75 2.00
74 Kevin Garnett 1.50 4.00
75 Marko Jaric .60 1.50
76 Wally Szczerbiak .75 2.00
77 Michael Olowokandi .60 1.50
78 Vince Carter 1.50 4.00
79 Richard Jefferson .75 2.00
80 Jason Kidd 1.50 4.00
81 Jeff McInnis .60 1.50
82 J.R. Smith .75 2.00
83 Desmond Mason .60 1.50
84 Speedy Claxton .60 1.50
85 David West .75 2.00
86 Stephon Marbury .75 2.00
87 Jamal Crawford 1.00 2.50
88 Quentin Richardson .75 2.00
89 Eddy Curry .60 1.50
90 Steve Francis .75 2.00
91 Grant Hill 1.25 3.00
92 Dwight Howard .75 2.00
93 Jameer Nelson .60 1.50
94 Hedo Turkoglu .75 2.00
95 Allen Iverson 1.50 4.00
96 Andre Iguodala .75 2.00
97 Kyle Korver .75 2.00
98 Chris Webber 1.00 2.50
99 Steve Nash 1.25 3.00
100 Shawn Marion .75 2.00
101 Amare Stoudemire .75 2.00
102 Kurt Thomas .60 1.50
103 Juan Dixon .60 1.50
104 Darius Miles .60 1.50
105 Zach Randolph .75 2.00
106 Sebastian Telfair .75 2.00
107 Shareef Abdur-Rahim .75 2.00
108 Mike Bibby 1.00 2.50
109 Brad Miller .75 2.00
110 Peja Stojakovic 1.00 2.50
111 Tim Duncan 1.50 4.00
112 Manu Ginobili 1.00 2.50
113 Tony Parker 1.00 2.50
114 Michael Finley 1.00 2.50
115 Ray Allen 1.00 2.50
116 Rashard Lewis 1.00 2.50
117 Vladimir Radmanovic .60 1.50
118 Luke Ridnour .75 2.00
119 Chris Bosh 1.00 2.50
120 Morris Peterson .60 1.50
121 Jalen Rose 1.00 2.50
122 Alvin Williams .60 1.50
123 Carlos Boozer .75 2.00
124 Matt Harpring .60 1.50
125 Andrei Kirilenko .75 2.00
126 Mehmet Okur .60 1.50
127 Gilbert Arenas .75 2.00
128 Caron Butler .75 2.00
129 Antawn Jamison .75 2.00
130 Brendan Haywood .60 1.50
131 Von Wafer RC 1.50 4.00
132 Bracey Wright RC 1.50 4.00
133 Ryan Gomes RC 2.00 5.00
134 Robert Whaley RC 1.50 4.00
135 Orien Greene RC 2.00 5.00
136 Dijon Thompson RC 1.50 4.00
137 Lawrence Roberts RC 1.50 4.00
138 Amir Johnson RC 2.50 6.00
139 John Lucas III RC 2.00 5.00
140 Chuck Hayes RC 2.50 6.00
141 Alex Acker RC 1.50 4.00
142 Fabricio Oberto RC 2.00 5.00
143 Andrew Bogut AU RC 6.00 15.00
144 Marvin Williams AU RC 5.00 12.00
145 Deron Williams AU RC 6.00 15.00
146 Chris Paul AU RC 75.00 150.00
147 Raymond Felton AU RC 5.00 12.00
148 Martell Webster AU RC 4.00 10.00
149 Charlie Villanueva AU RC 5.00 12.00
150 Channing Frye AU RC 5.00 12.00
151 Ike Diogu AU RC 3.00 8.00
152 Andrew Bynum AU RC 30.00 80.00
153 Yaroslav Korolev AU RC 3.00 8.00
154 Sean May AU RC 3.00 8.00
155 Rashad McCants AU RC 4.00 10.00
156 Antoine Wright AU RC 4.00 10.00
157 Joey Graham AU RC 4.00 10.00
158 Danny Granger AU RC 6.00 15.00
159 Gerald Green AU RC 5.00 12.00
160 Hakim Warrick AU RC 4.00 10.00
161 Julius Hodge AU RC 3.00 8.00
162 Nate Robinson AU RC 5.00 12.00
163 Jarrett Jack AU RC 5.00 12.00
164 Francisco Garcia AU RC 4.00 10.00
165 Luther Head AU RC 4.00 10.00
166 Johan Petro AU RC 3.00 8.00
167 Jason Maxiell AU RC 4.00 10.00
168 Linas Kleiza AU RC 3.00 8.00
169 Wayne Simien AU RC 3.00 8.00
170 David Lee AU RC 5.00 12.00
171 Salim Stoudamire AU RC 4.00 10.00
172 Daniel Ewing AU RC 4.00 10.00
173 Brandon Bass AU RC 4.00 10.00
174 C.J. Miles AU RC 5.00 12.00
175 Ersan Ilyasova AU RC 5.00 12.00
176 Travis Diener AU RC 3.00 8.00
177 Chris Taft AU RC 4.00 10.00
178 M.Andriuskevicius AU RC 3.00 8.00
179 Louis Williams AU RC 5.00 12.00
180 Monta Ellis AU RC 6.00 15.00
181 Andray Blatche AU RC 5.00 12.00
182 Sarunas Jasikevicius AU RC 5.00 12.00
183 James Singleton AU RC 3.00 8.00

2005-06 Ultimate Collection Blue

*1-130 BLUE: .75X TO 2X BASE HI
*131-142 RC BLUE: .6X TO 1.5X BASE HI
PRINT RUN 125 SER.#'d SETS
19 LeBron James 12.00 30.00
57 Kobe Bryant 12.00 30.00

2005-06 Ultimate Collection Red

*1-130 RED: 1.25X TO 3X BASE HI
*131-142 RC REC: .75X TO 2X BASE HI
RED PRINT RUN 50 SER.#'d SETS

2005-06 Ultimate Collection Silver

*1-130 SILV: 2.5X TO 6X BASE HI
*131-142 SILV.RC: 1X TO 2.5X BASE HI
SILVER PRINT RUN 25 SER.#'d SETS
68 Dwyane Wade 20.00 50.00

2005-06 Ultimate Collection Achievements Signatures

Randomly seeded in packs, this 20-card set is horizontally designed with a player image on the left, a tan stripe through the midde, white borders along the top and bottom and a centered player autograph. Each card is serially numbered to an achievement significant to the player on the card.
PRINT RUNS LISTED IN CHECKLIST
UABG Ben Gordon/35 15.00 40.00
UABK Bernard King/85 10.00 25.00
UADH Dwight Howard/20 40.00 80.00
UADR Dennis Rodman/34 40.00 100.00
UAEB Elton Brand/44 12.00 30.00
UAHO Hakeem Olajuwon/89 20.00 50.00
UAKA K.Abdul-Jabbar/76 50.00 120.00
UAKG Kevin Garnett/47 40.00 80.00
UALB Larry Bird/84 60.00 120.00
UALJ LeBron James/56 400.00 800.00
UAMA Magic Johnson/46 60.00 120.00
UAMJ Michael Jordan/63 1000.00 1500.00
UAPG Pau Gasol/37 10.00 25.00
UAPP Paul Pierce/48 20.00 50.00
UASM Stephon Marbury/50 40.00 100.00
UASN Steve Nash/19 75.00 150.00
UATM Tracy McGrady/17 60.00 150.00
UAVC Vince Carter/51 25.00 60.00
UAYM Yao Ming/41 60.00 150.00

2005-06 Ultimate Collection All-Stars Signatures

ndomly seeded in packs, this 20-card set is horizontally designed with a player image on the left, a tan stripe through the midde, white borders along the top and bottom and a centered player autograph. Cards are serially numbered to the total All-Star Game appearances by player.
PRINT RUNS LISTED IN CHECKLIST
MOST NOT PRICED DUE TO SCARCITY
ASBR Bill Russell/12 125.00 250.00
ASGG George Gervin/12 50.00 100.00
ASHO Hakeem Olajuwon/12 50.00 100.00
ASKA K.Abdul-Jabbar/19 60.00 120.00
ASLB Larry Bird/12 150.00 250.00
ASMJ Michael Jordan/14 450.00 650.00

2005-06 Ultimate Collection Honors Signatures

ndomly seeded in packs, this 20-card set is horizontally designed with a player image on the left, a tan stripe through the midde, white borders along the top and bottom and a centered player autograph. Cards are serially numbered to a significant statistic in the featured player's career.
PRINT RUNS LISTED IN CHECKLIST
MOST NOT PRICED DUE TO SCARCITY
HSHO Hakeem Olajuwon/93 25.00 60.00
HSJK Jason Kidd/95 20.00 50.00
HSPP Paul Pierce/99 30.00 80.00
HSWF Walt Frazier/68 15.00 40.00

2005-06 Ultimate Collection Jerseys

Randomly seeded in packs, this 60-card set is horizontally designed with a player photo on the right and a jersey swatch on the left. Each card is serially numbered to 99.
PRINT RUN 99 SER.#'d SETS
*GOLD: .75X TO 2X BASE JSY HI
GOLD PRINT RUN 25 SER.#'d SETS
UJAB Andrew Bogut 4.00 10.00
UJAN Andrew Bynum 2.50 6.00
UJAS Amare Stoudemire 2.50 6.00
UJAW Antoine Wright 2.50 6.00
UJBG Ben Gordon 2.50 6.00
UJBK Bernard King 2.50 6.00
UJCA Carmelo Anthony 6.00 15.00
UJCB Chauncey Billups 3.00 8.00
UJCD Clyde Drexler 4.00 10.00
UJCF Channing Frye 3.00 8.00
UJCP Chris Paul 8.00 20.00
UJCV Charlie Villanueva 3.00 8.00
UJDA David Robinson 5.00 12.00
UJDG Danny Granger 4.00 10.00
UJDH Dwight Howard 2.50 6.00
UJDN Dirk Nowitzki 5.00 12.00
UJDR Dennis Rodman 6.00 15.00
UJDW Deron Williams 4.00 10.00
UJEO Emeka Okafor 2.50 6.00
UJFG Francisco Garcia 2.50 6.00
UJGG Gerald Green 3.00 8.00
UJHO Hakeem Olajuwon 4.00 10.00
UJHW Hakim Warrick 2.50 6.00
UJID Ike Diogu 2.00 5.00
UJIT Isiah Thomas 3.00 8.00
UJJA Jason Richardson 3.00 8.00
UJJG Joey Graham 2.50 6.00
UJJH Julius Hodge 2.00 5.00
UJJJ Jarrett Jack 3.00 8.00
UJJR J.R. Smith 2.50 6.00
UJJS John Stockton 6.00 15.00
UJJW James Worthy 3.00 8.00
UJKB Kobe Bryant 12.50 30.00
UJKE Kevin McHale 4.00 10.00
UJKG Kevin Garnett 5.00 12.00
UJKM Karl Malone 4.00 10.00
UJLB Larry Bird 8.00 20.00
UJLJ LeBron James 12.50 30.00
UJMA Magic Johnson 8.00 20.00
UJMG Manu Ginobili 3.00 8.00
UJMJ Michael Jordan 40.00 80.00
UJMR Martell Webster 2.50 6.00
UJMW Marvin Williams 3.00 8.00
UJNR Nate Robinson 3.00 8.00
UJOR Oscar Robertson/35 20.00 50.00
UJPP Paul Pierce 3.00 8.00
UJRA Ray Allen 3.00 8.00
UJRF Raymond Felton 3.00 8.00
UJRM Rashad McCants 2.50 6.00
UJSE Sean May 2.00 5.00
UJSF Steve Francis 2.50 6.00
UJSM Shawn Marion 2.50 6.00
UJSN Steve Nash 4.00 10.00
UJSO Shaquille O'Neal 8.00 20.00
UJST Stephon Marbury 2.50 6.00
UJTD Tim Duncan 5.00 12.00
UJTM Tracy McGrady 4.00 10.00
UJTP Tony Parker 3.00 8.00
UJVC Vince Carter 5.00 12.00
UJYM Yao Ming 4.00 10.00

2005-06 Ultimate Collection Jerseys Dual

Randomly inserted in packs, this 40-card set is horizontally designed with player photos on the right and left side and centered swatches of jersey. Cards are serially numbered to 50.
PRINT RUN 50 SER.#'d SETS
UNPRICED DUAL GOLD PRINT RUN 10 SETS
DJAO R.Artest/J.O'Neal 4.00 10.00
DJAS A.Stoudemire/S.Marion 3.00 8.00
DJBA C.Bosh/C.Anthony 8.00 20.00
DJBS M.Bibby/P.Stojakovic 4.00 10.00
DJBW A.Bogut/M.Williams 5.00 12.00
DJCL C.Anthony/L.James 15.00 40.00
DJDG T.Duncan/M.Ginobili 6.00 15.00
DJDL D.Williams/L.Head 5.00 12.00
DJFB C.Frye/A.Bynum 4.00 10.00
DJGV J.Graham/C.Villanueva 4.00 10.00
DJGW G.Green/M.Webster 4.00 10.00
DJHF D.Howard/S.Francis 3.00 8.00
DJJB M.Johnson/L.Bird 30.00 80.00
DJJJ M.Jordan/L.James 60.00 150.00
DJKJ A.Kirilenko/A.Jamison 3.00 8.00
DJLK L.James/K.Bryant 40.00 100.00
DJMF R.McCants/R.Felton 4.00 10.00
DJMG T.McGrady/K.Garnett 6.00 15.00
DJMK S.Marbury/J.Kidd 6.00 15.00
DJMM M.Jordan/M.Johnson 50.00 120.00
DJNH D.Nowitzki/J.Howard 6.00 15.00
DJNK S.Nash/J.Kidd 6.00 15.00
DJOG E.Okafor/B.Gordon 3.00 8.00
DJOM S.O'Neal/Y.Ming 8.00 20.00
DJPG T.Parker/M.Ginobili 10.00 25.00
DJPW C.Paul/D.Williams 15.00 40.00
DJRA M.Redd/R.Allen 4.00 10.00
DJRD J.Richardson/B.Davis 4.00 10.00
DJRJ N.Robinson/J.Jack 4.00 10.00
DJRO D.Robinson/H.Olajuwon 6.00 15.00
DJSM J.Stockton/K.Malone 8.00 20.00
DJSR S.May/R.Felton 4.00 10.00
DJSS J.Smith/J.Smith 3.00 8.00
DJTL S.Telfair/S.Livingston 3.00 8.00
DJTS I.Thomas/J.Stockton 8.00 20.00
DJWD H.Warrick/I.Diogu 3.00 8.00
DJWH B.Wallace/R.Hamilton 3.00 8.00
DJWS M.Williams/S.Stoudamire 4.00 10.00
DJWW M.Webster/A.Wright 3.00 8.00

2005-06 Ultimate Collection Loyalty Signatures

Randomly seeded in packs, this 20-card set is horizontally designed with a player image on the left, a tan stripe through the midde, white borders along the top and bottom and a centered player autograph. Cards are serially numbered to the number of years each player spent with a single team.
PRINT RUNS LISTED IN CHECKLIST
SOME NOT PRICED DUE TO SCARCITY
UNPRICED MVP SIG PRINT RUN ONE TO 6 SETS
LSBL Bill Laimbeer/13 60.00 120.00
LSBR Bill Russell/13 125.00 250.00
LSDR David Robinson/14 75.00 150.00
LSGG George Gervin/11 25.00 60.00
LSHO Hakeem Olajuwon/17 25.00 60.00
LSJE Julius Erving/11 75.00 200.00
LSJS John Stockton/19 100.00 250.00
LSKA Kareem Abdul-Jabbar/14 75.00 150.00

LSLB Larry Bird/13 125.00 250.00
LSMA Magic Johnson/13 100.00 200.00
LSMJ Michael Jordan/13 500.00 700.00

2005-06 Ultimate Collection Patches

Randomly inserted, this 59-card set parallels the design of the jerseys set enhanced with a premium swatch of patch and sequential numbering to 75.
PRINT RUN 75 SER.#'d SETS
GOLD: .75X TO 2X BASE PAT.HI
GOLD PRINT RUN 20 SER.#'d SETS

UJPAB Andrew Bogut 8.00 20.00
UJPAN Andrew Bynum 5.00 12.00
UJPAS Amare Stoudemire 5.00 12.00
UJPAW Antoine Wright 5.00 12.00
UJPBG Ben Gordon 5.00 12.00
UJPBK Bernard King 5.00 12.00
UJPCA Carmelo Anthony 12.00 30.00
UJPCB Chauncey Billups 6.00 15.00
UJPCD Clyde Drexler 10.00 25.00
UJPCF Channing Frye 6.00 15.00
UJPCP Chris Paul 20.00 50.00
UJPCV Charlie Villanueva 6.00 15.00
UJPDA David Robinson 10.00 25.00
UJPDG Danny Granger 8.00 20.00
UJPDH Dwight Howard 5.00 12.00
UJPDN Dirk Nowitzki 10.00 25.00
UJPDR Dennis Rodman 15.00 40.00
UJPDW Deron Williams 12.00 30.00
UJPEO Emeka Okafor 5.00 12.00
UJPFG Francisco Garcia 5.00 12.00
UJPGG Gerald Green 6.00 15.00
UJPHO Hakeem Olajuwon 8.00 20.00
UJPHW Hakim Warrick 5.00 12.00
UJPID Ike Diogu 4.00 10.00
UJPIT Isiah Thomas 6.00 15.00
UJPJA Jason Richardson 6.00 15.00
UJPJG Joey Graham 5.00 12.00
UJPJH Julius Hodge 4.00 10.00
UJPJJ Jarrett Jack 6.00 15.00
UJPJR J.R. Smith 5.00 12.00
UJPJS John Stockton 12.00 30.00
UJPJW James Worthy 12.00 30.00
UJPKB Kobe Bryant 40.00 100.00
UJPKE Kevin McHale 8.00 20.00
UJPKG Kevin Garnett 10.00 25.00
UJPKM Karl Malone 12.50 30.00
UJPLB Larry Bird 15.00 40.00
UJPLJ LeBron James 40.00 100.00
UJPMA Magic Johnson 15.00 40.00
UJPMG Manu Ginobili 6.00 15.00
UJPMJ Michael Jordan 100.00 200.00
UJPMR Martell Webster 5.00 12.00
UJPMW Marvin Williams 6.00 15.00
UJPNR Nate Robinson 6.00 15.00
UJPOR Oscar Robertson/20 25.00 60.00
UJPPP Paul Pierce 6.00 15.00
UJPRA Ray Allen 6.00 15.00
UJPRF Raymond Felton 6.00 15.00
UJPRM Rashad McCants 5.00 12.00
UJPSE Sean May 4.00 10.00
UJPSF Steve Francis 5.00 12.00
UJPSM Shawn Marion 5.00 12.00
UJPSO Shaquille O'Neal 12.00 30.00
UJPST Stephon Marbury 5.00 12.00
UJPTD Tim Duncan 10.00 25.00
UJPTM Tracy McGrady 12.00 30.00
UJPTP Tony Parker 8.00 20.00
UJPVC Vince Carter 10.00 25.00
UJPYM Yao Ming 12.00 30.00

2005-06 Ultimate Collection Patches Dual

Randomly seeded, this 39-card set parallels the design of the Jerseys Dual set enhanced with premium patch swatches and sequential numbering to 40.
PRINT RUN 40 SER.#'d SETS
UNPRICED GOLD PRINT RUN 10 SETS

DPAO R.Artest/J.O'Neal 12.50 30.00
DPAS A.Stoudemire/S.Marion 12.50 30.00
DPBA C.Bosh/C.Anthony 20.00 50.00
DPBS M.Bibby/P.Stojakovic 12.50 30.00
DPBW A.Bogut/M.Williams 12.50 30.00
DPCL C.Anthony/L.James 50.00 125.00
DPDG T.Duncan/M.Ginobili 25.00 60.00
DPDL D.Williams/L.Head 15.00 40.00
DPFB C.Frye/A.Bynum 25.00 50.00
DPGV J.Graham/C.Villanueva 12.50 30.00
DPGW G.Green/M.Webster 12.50 30.00
DPHF D.Howard/S.Francis 12.00 30.00
DPJB M.Johnson/L.Bird 60.00 120.00
DPJJ M.Jordan/L.James 100.00 250.00
DPKJ A.Kirilenko/A.Jamison 15.00 40.00
DPLK L.James/K.Bryant 125.00 250.00
DPMF R.McCants/R.Felton 12.50 30.00
DPMG T.McGrady/K.Garnett 20.00 50.00
DPMK S.Marbury/J.Kidd 25.00 60.00
DPMM M.Jordan/M.Johnson 80.00 160.00
DPNH D.Nowitzki/J.Howard 12.00 30.00
DPOG E.Okafor/B.Gordon 15.00 40.00
DPOM S.O'Neal/Y.Ming 30.00 80.00
DPPG T.Parker/M.Ginobili 20.00 50.00
DPPW C.Paul/D.Williams 25.00 60.00
DPRA M.Redd/R.Allen 12.50 30.00
DPRD J.Richardon/B.Davis 12.50 30.00
DPRJ N.Robinson/J.Jack 12.50 30.00
DPRO D.Robinson/H.Olajuwon 20.00 50.00
DPSM J.Stockton/K.Malone 40.00 80.00
DPSR S.May/R.Felton 12.50 30.00
DPSS J.R. Smith/Josh Smith 12.50 30.00
DPTL S.Telfair/S.Livingston 12.50 30.00
DPTS I.Thomas/J.Stockton 15.00 40.00
DPVJ V.Carter/R.Jefferson 15.00 40.00
DPWD H.Warrick/I.Diogu 12.50 30.00
DPWH B.Wallace/R.Hamilton 20.00 50.00
DPWS M.Williams/S.Stoudamire 12.50 30.00
DPWW M.Webster/A.Wright 12.50 30.00

2005-06 Ultimate Collection Premium Patches

Seeded randomly in packs, this 42-card set places player photos on the left side of the card and premium patch swatches on the right side of the card. Cards are serially numbered to either 25 or 50.
PRINT RUN 25 TO 50 SER.#'d SETS

PPAB Andrew Bogut/50 12.00 30.00
PPAK Andrei Kirilenko/50 8.00 20.00
PPAS Amare Stoudemire/50 8.00 20.00
PPBD Baron Davis/50 8.00 20.00
PPBG Ben Gordon/50 8.00 20.00
PPCB Chris Bosh/50 10.00 25.00
PPCF Channing Frye/50 10.00 25.00
PPCM Corey Maggette/50 8.00 20.00
PPCP Chris Paul/50 40.00 100.00
PPCV Charlie Villanueva/50 10.00 25.00
PPDH Dwight Howard/25 8.00 20.00
PPDN Dirk Nowitzki/25 30.00 80.00
PPDW Deron Williams/50 12.00 30.00
PPEB Elton Brand/50 10.00 25.00
PPEO Emeka Okafor/50 8.00 20.00
PPID Ike Diogu/50 6.00 15.00
PPJK Jason Kidd/50 15.00 40.00
PPJR Jason Richardson/50 10.00 25.00
PPJS J.R. Smith/50 8.00 20.00
PPKB Kobe Bryant/25 100.00 250.00
PPKG Kevin Garnett/25 30.00 80.00
PPLJ LeBron James/25 125.00 300.00
PPMA Marvin Williams/50 10.00 25.00
PPMB Mike Bibby/50 10.00 25.00
PPMJ Michael Jordan/25 350.00 700.00
PPMR Michael Redd/50 8.00 20.00
PPMW Martell Webster/50 8.00 20.00
PPPP Paul Pierce/50 10.00 25.00
PPPP Peja Stojakovic/50 10.00 25.00
PPRF Raymond Felton/50 10.00 25.00
PPRM Rashad McCants/50 8.00 20.00
PPSE Sean May/50 6.00 15.00
PPSF Steve Francis/50 8.00 20.00
PPSH Shawn Marion/50 8.00 20.00
PPSM Stephon Marbury/50 8.00 20.00
PPSN Steve Nash/25 30.00 80.00
PPSO Shaquille O'Neal/25 30.00 80.00
PPTD Tim Duncan/25 30.00 80.00
PPTM Tracy McGrady/25 25.00 60.00
PPTP Tony Parker/50 10.00 25.00
PPVC Vince Carter/25 40.00 100.00
PPYM Yao Ming/25 25.00 60.00

2005-06 Ultimate Collection Premium Swatches

Inserted in packs randomly, this 41-card set places player photos on the left and large jersey swatches on the right. Cards are serially numbered to 100.
PRINT RUN 100 SER.#'d SETS

PSAB Andrew Bogut 5.00 12.00
PSAK Andrei Kirilenko 3.00 8.00
PSAS Amare Stoudemire 3.00 8.00
PSBD Baron Davis 3.00 8.00
PSBG Ben Gordon 3.00 8.00
PSCB Chris Bosh 4.00 10.00
PSCF Channing Frye 4.00 10.00
PSCM Corey Maggette 3.00 8.00
PSCP Chris Paul 15.00 40.00
PSCV Charlie Villanueva 4.00 10.00
PSDH Dwight Howard 3.00 8.00
PSDN Dirk Nowitzki 6.00 15.00
PSDW Deron Williams 5.00 12.00
PSEB Elton Brand 4.00 10.00
PSEO Emeka Okafor 3.00 8.00
PSID Ike Diogu 2.50 6.00
PSJK Jason Kidd 6.00 15.00
PSJR Jason Richardson 4.00 10.00
PSJS J.R. Smith 3.00 8.00
PSKB Kobe Bryant 20.00 50.00
PSKG Kevin Garnett 6.00 15.00
PSLJ LeBron James 25.00 60.00
PSMA Marvin Williams 4.00 10.00
PSMB Mike Bibby 4.00 10.00
PSMJ Michael Jordan 100.00 200.00
PSMR Michael Redd 3.00 8.00
PSMW Martell Webster 3.00 8.00
PSPP Paul Pierce 4.00 10.00
PSPS Peja Stojakovic 4.00 10.00
PSRF Raymond Felton 4.00 10.00
PSRM Rashad McCants 3.00 8.00
PSSE Sean May 2.50 6.00
PSSF Steve Francis 3.00 8.00
PSSH Shawn Marion 3.00 8.00
PSSM Stephon Marbury 3.00 8.00
PSSO Shaquille O'Neal 8.00 20.00
PSTD Tim Duncan 6.00 15.00
PSTM Tracy McGrady 5.00 12.00
PSTP Tony Parker 4.00 10.00
PSVC Vince Carter 6.00 15.00
PSYM Yao Ming 5.00 12.00

2005-06 Ultimate Collection Rookie Autographs Gold

PRINT RUN 25 SER.#'d SETS

143 Andrew Bogut 40.00 100.00
144 Marvin Williams 15.00 40.00
145 Deron Williams 100.00 200.00
146 Chris Paul 250.00 400.00
147 Raymond Felton 15.00 40.00
148 Martell Webster 12.00 30.00
149 Charlie Villanueva 15.00 40.00
150 Channing Frye 15.00 40.00
151 Ike Diogu 10.00 25.00
152 Andrew Bynum 60.00 150.00
153 Yaroslav Korolev 10.00 25.00
154 Sean May 10.00 25.00
155 Rashad McCants 12.00 30.00
156 Antoine Wright 12.00 30.00
157 Joey Graham 12.00 30.00
158 Danny Granger 20.00 50.00
159 Gerald Green 15.00 40.00
160 Hakim Warrick 12.00 30.00
161 Julius Hodge 10.00 25.00
162 Nate Robinson 15.00 40.00
163 Jarrett Jack 15.00 40.00
164 Francisco Garcia 12.00 30.00
165 Luther Head 12.00 30.00
166 Johan Petro 10.00 25.00
167 Jason Maxiell 12.00 30.00
168 Linas Kleiza 10.00 25.00
169 Wayne Simien 10.00 25.00
170 David Lee 15.00 40.00
171 Salim Stoudamire 12.00 30.00
172 Daniel Ewing 12.00 30.00
173 Brandon Bass 12.00 30.00
174 C.J. Miles 15.00 40.00
175 Ersan Ilyasova 15.00 40.00
176 Travis Diener 10.00 25.00
177 Chris Taft 12.00 30.00
178 Martynas Andriuskevicius 10.00 25.00
179 Louis Williams 15.00 40.00
180 Monta Ellis 50.00 100.00
181 Andray Blatche 15.00 40.00
182 Sarunas Jasikevicius 15.00 40.00
183 James Singleton 10.00 25.00

2005-06 Ultimate Collection Rookie Autographs Patches

Randomly inserted in packs, this 40-card set is horizontally designed with player photos on the left and a premium patch swatch on the right. Each card is serially numbered to 25.
PRINT RUN 25 SER.#'d SETS
UNPRICED LOGO PRINT RUN ONE SET

RPAB Andrew Bogut 100.00 200.00
RPAN Andrew Bynum 75.00 150.00
RPAW Antoine Wright 15.00 40.00
RPBB Brandon Bass 15.00 40.00
RPBL Andray Blatche 20.00 50.00
RPCF Channing Frye 20.00 50.00
RPCJ C.J. Miles 20.00 50.00
RPCP Chris Paul 300.00 550.00
RPCT Chris Taft 15.00 40.00
RPCV Charlie Villanueva 20.00 50.00
RPDE Daniel Ewing 15.00 40.00
RPDG Danny Granger 25.00 60.00
RPDL David Lee 20.00 50.00
RPDW Deron Williams 125.00 250.00
RPEI Ersan Ilyasova 20.00 50.00
RPFG Francisco Garcia 15.00 40.00
RPGG Gerald Green 20.00 50.00
RPHW Hakim Warrick 15.00 40.00
RPID Ike Diogu 12.00 30.00
RPJG Joey Graham 15.00 40.00
RPJH Julius Hodge 12.00 30.00
RPJJ Jarrett Jack 20.00 50.00
RPJM Jason Maxiell 15.00 40.00
RPJP Johan Petro 12.00 30.00
RPLH Luther Head 15.00 40.00
RPLK Linas Kleiza 12.00 30.00
RPLW Louis Williams 20.00 50.00
RPMA Martynas Andriuskevicius 12.00 30.00
RPME Monta Ellis 100.00 200.00
RPMW Marvin Williams 20.00 50.00
RPNR Nate Robinson 15.00 40.00
RPRF Raymond Felton 20.00 50.00
RPRG Ryan Gomes 15.00 40.00
RPRM Rashad McCants 15.00 40.00
RPSJ Sarunas Jasikevicius 20.00 50.00
RPSM Sean May 12.00 30.00
RPSS Salim Stoudamire 15.00 40.00
RPTD Travis Diener 12.00 30.00
RPWE Martell Webster 15.00 40.00
RPWS Wayne Simien 12.00 30.00

2005-06 Ultimate Collection Signatures

Found in packs at random, this 42-card set is horizontally designed with player photos on the left, white borders along the top and the bottom, a gray stripe through the midde and a player autograph on the right.
RANDOM INSERTS IN PACKS

USAB Andrew Bogut 6.00 15.00
USAN Andrew Bynum 4.00 10.00
USBD Baron Davis 5.00 12.00
USBK Bernard King 5.00 12.00
USBR Bill Russell SP 75.00 200.00
USCA Carmelo Anthony SP 20.00 50.00
USCF Channing Frye 5.00 12.00
USCP Chris Paul 40.00 100.00
USCV Charlie Villanueva 5.00 12.00
USDE Dennis Rodman 30.00 80.00
USDG Danny Granger 6.00 15.00
USDH Dwight Howard 10.00 25.00
USDR David Robinson 25.00 60.00
USDW Deron Williams 6.00 15.00
USEB Elton Brand 6.00 15.00
USEO Emeka Okafor 6.00 15.00
USGG Gerald Green 5.00 12.00
USHO Hakeem Olajuwon 25.00 60.00
USHW Hakim Warrick 4.00 10.00
USID Ike Diogu 3.00 8.00
USJE Julius Erving SP 50.00 120.00
USJK Jason Kidd 10.00 25.00
USKA Kareem Abdul-Jabbar SP 40.00 80.00
USKG Kevin Garnett 60.00 150.00
USLB Larry Bird SP 60.00 120.00
USLH Larry Hughes 5.00 12.00
USLJ LeBron James 300.00 600.00
USLR Luke Ridnour 5.00 12.00
USMA Magic Johnson SP 50.00 100.00
USMJ Michael Jordan SP 500.00 1000.00
USMR Martell Webster 4.00 10.00
USMW Marvin Williams 5.00 12.00
USRF Raymond Felton 5.00 12.00
USRM Rashad McCants 4.00 10.00
USSM Sean May 3.00 8.00
USSN Steve Nash 30.00 75.00
USSP Scottie Pippen 100.00 200.00
USST Stephon Marbury 8.00 20.00
USTM Tracy McGrady 15.00 40.00
USTP Tayshaun Prince 5.00 12.00
USVC Vince Carter 15.00 40.00
USYM Yao Ming 30.00 80.00

2005-06 Ultimate Collection Signatures Dual

Inserted in packs, this 30-card set utilizes the design of the base Signatures set but with two players. Each card is serially numbered to 25.
PRINT RUN 25 SER.#'d SETS
UNPRICED TRIPLE PRINT RUN 10 SETS
UNPRICED QUAD PRINT RUN 5 SETS

DSAR R.Artest/D.Rodman 75.00 150.00
DSAW C.Anthony/H.Warrick 30.00 80.00
DSBF A.Bogut/C.Frye 25.00 60.00
DSBJ L.Bird/M.Johnson 200.00 400.00
DSBR A.Bogut/M.Redd 25.00 60.00
DSCK V.Carter/J.Kidd 75.00 150.00
DSDD B.Davis/I.Diogu 20.00 50.00
DSFO R.Felton/E.Okafor 20.00 50.00
DSGM K.Garnett/R.McCants 40.00 80.00
DSGV J.Graham/C.Villanueva 20.00 50.00
DSHB R.Hamilton/C.Billups 50.00 100.00
DSHM D.Howard/T.McGrady 30.00 80.00
DSHO D.Howard/E.Okafor 40.00 80.00
DSJA Magic/Abdul-Jabbar 200.00 350.00
DSJG Al Jefferson/G.Green 20.00 50.00
DSJH L.James/D.Howard 200.00 400.00
DSJJ L.James/M.Jordan 600.00 1100.00
DSJP M.Jordan/S.Pippen 2500.00 3500.00
DSLB L.Bird/B.Russell 200.00 300.00
DSMF S.Marbury/C.Frye 20.00 50.00
DSMH Y.Ming/D.Howard 40.00 80.00
DSMM S.May/R.McCants 20.00 50.00
DSMS T.McGrady/S.Swift 25.00 60.00
DSPS Chris Paul/J.R. Smith 60.00 150.00
DSWF M.Williams/R.Felton 20.00 50.00
DSWJ M.Williams/J.Johnson 20.00 50.00
DSWM D.Williams/C.J.Miles 30.00 80.00
DSWP D.Williams/C.Paul 100.00 200.00
DSWT M.Webster/S.Telfair 20.00 50.00

2006-07 Ultimate Collection

Released in late June 2007, Ultimate Collection features a 243-card set where cards 1-140 picture NBA veterans sequentially numbered to 499, cards 141-180 picture retired NBA stars sequentially numbered to 99, cards 181-228 picture NBA rookies, which are sequentially numbered to 350 and contain an on-card player autograph, and cards 236-243 picture NBA rookies sequentially numbered to 499. Ultimate Collection is packaged in four-pack boxes of four packs each and carried an initial suggested retail price of $100.00 per pack.
1-140 PRINT RUN 450 SER.#'d SETS
AU RC PRINT RUN 350 SER.#'d SETS
225-243 RC PRINT RUN 499 SER.#'d SETS

1 Josh Childress 1.25 3.00
2 Joe Johnson 1.25 3.00
3 Salim Stoudamire 1.00 2.50
4 Marvin Williams 1.25 3.00
5 Tony Allen 1.00 2.50
6 Al Jefferson 1.25 3.00
7 Paul Pierce 1.50 4.00
8 Wally Szczerbiak 1.25 3.00
9 Sebastian Telfair 1.00 2.50
10 Raymond Felton 1.25 3.00
11 Sean May 1.00 2.50
12 Emeka Okafor 1.25 3.00
13 Gerald Wallace 1.25 3.00
14 Luol Deng 1.25 3.00
15 Chris Duhon 1.00 2.50
16 Ben Gordon 1.25 3.00
17 Kirk Hinrich 1.25 3.00
18 Ben Wallace 1.25 3.00
19 Drew Gooden 1.25 3.00
20 Larry Hughes 1.25 3.00
21 Zydrunas Ilgauskas 1.25 3.00
22 LeBron James 6.00 15.00
23 Donyell Marshall 1.00 2.50
24 Devin Harris 1.00 2.50
25 Josh Howard 1.25 3.00
26 Dirk Nowitzki 2.50 6.00
27 Jerry Stackhouse 1.25 3.00
28 Jason Terry 1.25 3.00
29 Carmelo Anthony 2.00 5.00
30 Marcus Camby 1.25 3.00
31 Kenyon Martin 1.25 3.00
32 Andre Miller 1.25 3.00
33 J.R. Smith 1.25 3.00
34 Chauncey Billups 1.50 4.00
35 Richard Hamilton 1.25 3.00
36 Antonio McDyess 1.25 3.00
37 Tayshaun Prince 1.25 3.00
38 Rasheed Wallace 1.50 4.00
39 Baron Davis 1.25 3.00
40 Mike Dunleavy 1.25 3.00
41 Troy Murphy 1.00 2.50
42 Jason Richardson 1.50 4.00
43 Rafer Alston 1.00 2.50
44 Shane Battier 1.25 3.00
45 Tracy McGrady 2.00 5.00
46 Bonzi Wells 1.00 2.50
47 Yao Ming 2.00 5.00
48 Marquis Daniels 1.00 2.50
49 Al Harrington 1.25 3.00
50 Sarunas Jasikevicius 1.25 3.00
51 Jermaine O'Neal 1.25 3.00
52 Elton Brand 1.50 4.00
53 Sam Cassell 1.25 3.00
54 Chris Kaman 1.25 3.00
55 Shaun Livingston 1.00 2.50
56 Corey Maggette 1.25 3.00
57 Kobe Bryant 6.00 15.00
58 Andrew Bynum 1.00 2.50
59 Lamar Odom 1.25 3.00
60 Vladimir Radmanovic 1.00 2.50
61 Kwame Brown 1.00 2.50
62 Eddie Jones 1.25 3.00
63 Mike Miller 1.25 3.00
64 Hakim Warrick 1.25 3.00
65 Pau Gasol 1.50 4.00
66 Stromile Swift 1.00 2.50
67 Alonzo Mourning 2.00 5.00
68 Shaquille O'Neal 3.00 8.00
69 Gary Payton 1.50 4.00
70 Dwyane Wade 2.50 6.00
71 Jason Williams 1.25 3.00
72 Andrew Bogut 1.25 3.00
73 Michael Redd 1.25 3.00
74 Charlie Villanueva 1.00 2.50
75 Bobby Simmons 1.00 2.50
76 Ricky Davis 1.25 3.00
77 Kevin Garnett 2.50 6.00
78 Troy Hudson 1.00 2.50
79 Mike James 1.00 2.50
80 Rashad McCants 1.00 2.50
81 Vince Carter 2.00 5.00
82 Richard Jefferson 1.25 3.00
83 Jason Kidd 2.50 6.00
84 Nenad Krstic 1.00 2.50
85 Tyson Chandler 1.25 3.00
86 Bobby Jackson 1.00 2.50
87 Desmond Mason 1.00 2.50
88 Chris Paul 2.00 5.00
89 Peja Stojakovic 1.50 4.00
90 Steve Francis 1.25 3.00
91 Channing Frye 1.25 3.00
92 Stephon Marbury 1.25 3.00
93 Quentin Richardson 1.25 3.00
94 Nate Robinson 1.00 2.50
95 Carlos Arroyo 1.00 2.50
96 Grant Hill 2.00 5.00
97 Dwight Howard 1.25 3.00
98 Darko Milicic 1.00 2.50
99 Jameer Nelson 1.00 2.50
100 Samuel Dalembert 1.00 2.50
101 Andre Iguodala 1.25 3.00
102 Allen Iverson 2.00 5.00
103 Kyle Korver 1.25 3.00
104 Chris Webber 1.50 4.00
105 Leandro Barbosa 1.25 3.00
106 Boris Diaw 1.25 3.00
107 Shawn Marion 1.25 3.00
108 Steve Nash 2.00 5.00
109 Amare Stoudemire 1.25 3.00
110 Juan Dixon 1.00 2.50
111 Jarrett Jack 1.25 3.00
112 Jamaal Magloire 1.00 2.50
113 Zach Randolph 1.25 3.00
114 Martell Webster 1.25 3.00
115 Shareef Abdur-Rahim 1.25 3.00
116 Ron Artest 1.50 4.00
117 Brad Miller 1.25 3.00
118 Mike Bibby 1.50 4.00
119 Tim Duncan 2.50 6.00
120 Michael Finley 1.50 4.00
121 Manu Ginobili 1.50 4.00
122 Robert Horry 1.25 3.00
123 Tony Parker 1.50 4.00
124 Ray Allen 1.50 4.00
125 Rashard Lewis 1.50 4.00
126 Luke Ridnour 1.25 3.00
127 Chris Wilcox 1.00 2.50
128 Chris Bosh 1.50 4.00
129 T.J. Ford 1.00 2.50
130 Joey Graham 1.00 2.50
131 Morris Peterson 1.00 2.50
132 Carlos Boozer 1.25 3.00
133 Andrei Kirilenko 1.25 3.00
134 C.J. Miles 1.25 3.00
135 Mehmet Okur 1.00 2.50
136 Deron Williams 1.25 3.00
137 Gilbert Arenas 1.25 3.00
138 Caron Butler 1.25 3.00
139 Antonio Daniels 1.00 2.50
140 Antawn Jamison 1.25 3.00
141 David Robinson 6.00 15.00
142 Hakeem Olajuwon 5.00 12.00
143 Bill Russell 8.00 20.00
144 Walt Frazier 4.00 10.00
145 Nate Archibald 3.00 8.00
146 Spud Webb 3.00 8.00
147 Larry Bird 10.00 25.00
148 Michael Jordan 40.00 100.00
149 Magic Johnson 10.00 25.00
150 Julius Erving 6.00 15.00
151 Alvin Robertson 4.00 10.00
152 Bill Laimbeer 3.00 8.00
153 Bill Walton 4.00 10.00
154 Bob McAdoo 3.00 8.00
155 Clyde Drexler 5.00 12.00
156 Connie Hawkins 4.00 10.00
157 Dennis Rodman 8.00 20.00
158 Earl Monroe 4.00 10.00
159 Elvin Hayes 4.00 10.00
160 George Gervin 4.00 10.00
161 Kareem Abdul-Jabbar 6.00 15.00
162 Elgin Baylor 4.00 10.00
163 Rolando Blackman 3.00 8.00
164 Maurice Cheeks 2.50 6.00
165 Adrian Dantley 3.00 8.00
166 Joe Dumars 4.00 10.00
167 World B. Free 3.00 8.00
168 Robert Parish 4.00 10.00
169 Kevin McHale 5.00 12.00
170 Kevin Johnson 4.00 10.00
171 Bernard King 3.00 8.00
172 Moses Malone 4.00 10.00
173 Chris Mullin 4.00 10.00
174 Calvin Murphy 3.00 8.00
175 Oscar Robertson 4.00 10.00
176 Isiah Thomas 4.00 10.00
177 Reggie Theus 3.00 8.00
178 Rudy Tomjanovich 3.00 8.00
179 Wes Unseld 4.00 10.00
180 John Starks 3.00 8.00
181 Allan Ray AU RC 3.00 8.00
182 Andrea Bargnani AU RC 10.00 25.00
183 Bobby Jones AU RC 3.00 8.00
184 Brandon Roy AU RC 5.00 12.00
185 Cedric Simmons AU RC 3.00 8.00
186 Craig Smith AU RC 4.00 10.00
187 Damir Markota AU RC 3.00 8.00
188 Daniel Gibson AU RC 4.00 10.00
189 David Noel AU RC 3.00 8.00
190 Dee Brown AU RC 3.00 8.00
191 Hassan Adams AU RC 3.00 8.00
192 Hilton Armstrong AU RC 3.00 8.00
193 James Augustine AU RC 3.00 8.00
194 James White AU RC 3.00 8.00
195 Jordan Farmar AU RC 5.00 12.00
196 Jorge Garbajosa AU RC 4.00 10.00
197 Josh Boone AU RC 3.00 8.00
198 Kyle Lowry AU RC 6.00 15.00
199 LaMarcus Aldridge AU RC 30.00 80.00
200 Marcus Williams AU RC 3.00 8.00
201 Mardy Collins AU RC 3.00 8.00
202 Maurice Ager AU RC 3.00 8.00
203 Patrick O'Bryant AU RC 3.00 8.00
204 Paul Davis AU RC 3.00 8.00
205 Paul Millsap AU RC 6.00 15.00
206 P.J. Tucker AU RC 4.00 10.00
207 Pops Mensah-Bonsu AU RC 3.00 8.00
208 Quincy Douby AU RC 3.00 8.00
209 Rajon Rondo AU RC 8.00 20.00
210 Randy Foye AU RC 5.00 12.00
211 Renaldo Balkman AU RC 4.00 10.00
212 Rodney Carney AU RC 3.00 8.00
213 Ronnie Brewer AU RC 5.00 12.00
214 Rudy Gay AU RC 6.00 15.00
215 Yakhouba Diawara AU 3.00 8.00
216 Saer Sene AU RC 3.00 8.00
217 Sergio Rodriguez AU RC 5.00 12.00
218 Shannon Brown AU RC 3.00 8.00
219 Shawne Williams AU RC 3.00 8.00
220 Shelden Williams AU RC 4.00 10.00
221 Solomon Jones AU RC 3.00 8.00
222 Steve Novak AU RC 4.00 10.00
223 Thabo Sefolosha AU RC 5.00 12.00
224 Tyrus Thomas AU RC 4.00 10.00
225 Will Blalock AU RC 3.00 8.00
226 Robert Hite AU RC 3.00 8.00
227 Vassilis Spanoulis AU RC 3.00 8.00
228 Leon Powe AU RC 4.00 10.00
236 Adam Morrison RC 3.00 8.00
237 Alexander Johnson RC 2.00 5.00
238 J.J. Redick RC 4.00 10.00
239 Kelenna Azubuike RC 4.00 10.00
240 Chris Quinn RC 2.00 5.00
241 Tarence Kinsey RC 2.00 5.00
242 Vassilis Spanoulis RC 2.00 5.00
243 Yakhouba Diawara RC 2.00 5.00
244 Mike Hall RC 2.00 5.00
245 Randolph Morris RC 2.50 6.00
246 Walter Herrmann RC 2.00 5.00
247 Mickael Gelabale RC 2.00 5.00
248 Andre Brown RC 2.00 5.00
249 Justin Williams RC 2.00 5.00
250 Lynn Greer RC 2.00 5.00

2006-07 Ultimate Collection Achievements Signatures

STATED PRINT RUN ONE TO 51 SER.#'d SETS
SOME UNPRICED DUE TO SCARCITY

UAAI Andre Iguodala/27 12.00 30.00
UAAJ Antawn Jamison/51 10.00 25.00
UABG Ben Gordon/39 6.00 15.00
UABJ Bobby Jackson/31 10.00 25.00
UABL Bill Laimbeer/14 100.00 200.00
UABM Bob McAdoo/14 100.00 200.00
UABO Chris Bosh/22 15.00 40.00
UABS Byron Scott/14 50.00 100.00
UACK Chris Kaman/23 10.00 25.00
UACM Corey Maggette/13 20.00 40.00
UACS Cedric Simmons/15 10.00 25.00
UADM Desmond Mason/17 10.00 25.00
UADO Dennis Rodman/34 50.00 125.00
UADU Chris Duhon/38 10.00 25.00
UAGG George Gervin/33 30.00 60.00
UAHO Hakeem Olajuwon/18 40.00 70.00
UAHW Hakim Warrick/19 12.00 30.00
UAJJ Jarrett Jack/22 10.00 25.00
UAJS J.R. Smith/33 10.00 25.00
UALE Leandro Barbosa/28 10.00 25.00
UAMA Magic Johnson/13 80.00 160.00
UAMO Cuffino Mobley/41 10.00 25.00
UAPS Peja Stojakovic/41 10.00 25.00
UARP Robert Parish/21 20.00 40.00
UASE Sean Elliott/12 75.00 150.00
UASK Steve Kerr/15 30.00 60.00
UASN Steve Nash/22 100.00 175.00
UASW Spud Webb/12 10.00 25.00
UATE Sebastian Telfair/13 10.00 25.00

2006-07 Ultimate Collection Autographs Jerseys

PRINT RUN 75 SER.#'d SETS

AUAH Al Harrington 6.00 15.00
AUAI Andre Iguodala 8.00 20.00
AUAJ Al Jefferson 6.00 15.00
AUAM Andre Miller 6.00 15.00
AUBD Baron Davis 8.00 20.00
AUBG Ben Gordon 8.00 20.00
AUBJ Bobby Jackson 6.00 15.00
AUBM Brad Miller 6.00 15.00
AUBO Chris Bosh 12.00 30.00
AUCA Carmelo Anthony 15.00 40.00
AUCB Chauncey Billups 10.00 25.00
AUCD Chris Duhon 6.00 15.00
AUCF Channing Frye 6.00 15.00
AUCM Corey Maggette 6.00 15.00
AUCP Chris Paul 35.00 75.00
AUDM Donyell Marshall 6.00 15.00
AUDR Clyde Drexler 30.00 60.00
AUDW Deron Williams 20.00 50.00
AUEO Emeka Okafor 6.00 15.00
AUHO Hakeem Olajuwon 30.00 80.00
AUID Ike Diogu 6.00 15.00
AUJA Antawn Jamison 6.00 15.00
AUJC Josh Childress 6.00 15.00
AUJG Joey Graham 6.00 15.00
AUJJ Jarrett Jack 6.00 15.00
AUJM Jamaal Magloire 6.00 15.00
AUJO Jermaine O'Neal 10.00 25.00
AUJS J.R. Smith 6.00 15.00
AUKB Kobe Bryant 125.00 250.00
AUKH Kirk Hinrich 6.00 15.00
AUKK Kyle Korver 8.00 20.00
AULB Larry Bird 50.00 120.00
AULH Larry Hughes 8.00 20.00
AULJ LeBron James 150.00 300.00
AULR Luke Ridnour 6.00 15.00
AUMA Magic Johnson 60.00 120.00
AUMB Mike Bibby 6.00 15.00
AUMD Marquis Daniels 6.00 15.00
AUMJ Michael Jordan 800.00 1200.00
AUMO Alonzo Mourning 25.00 60.00
AUMR Michael Ray Richardson 8.00 20.00
AUMW Marvin Williams 6.00 15.00
AUPP Paul Pierce 12.00 30.00
AUQR Quentin Richardson 6.00 15.00
AURF Raymond Felton 8.00 20.00
AURJ Richard Jefferson 6.00 15.00
AURM Rashad McCants 6.00 15.00
AURO David Robinson 30.00 80.00
AUSK Steve Kerr 10.00 25.00
AUSL Shaun Livingston 6.00 15.00
AUSS Stromile Swift 6.00 15.00
AUST Sebastian Telfair 6.00 15.00
AUTC Tyson Chandler 8.00 20.00
AUTM Tracy McGrady 15.00 40.00
AUTP Tony Parker 20.00 50.00
AUVC Vince Carter 20.00 50.00
AUWF Walt Frazier 15.00 40.00
AUYM Yao Ming 40.00 100.00

2006-07 Ultimate Collection Autographs Patches

*PATCHES: .75X TO 2X BASE HI
PRINT RUN 15 SER.#'d SETS

AULB Larry Bird 100.00 250.00
AULJ LeBron James 300.00 500.00
AUMA Magic Johnson 100.00 200.00

2006-07 Ultimate Collection Combos Jerseys Dual

PRINT RUN 75 SER.#'d SETS
*PATCHES: .75X TO 2X BASE HI
PATCH PRINT RUN 25 SER.#'d SETS

AB S.Brown/M.Ager 4.00 10.00
AN J.Nelson/C.Arroyo 4.00 10.00
AR L.Aldridge/B.Roy 8.00 20.00
BB L.Barbosa/R.Bell 4.00 10.00
BD M.Bibby/Q.Douby 4.00 10.00
BV C.Villanueva/A.Bogut 5.00 12.00
CB R.Balkman/M.Collins 4.00 10.00
CS T.Chandler/C.Simmons 4.00 10.00
CW S.Williams/R.Carney 4.00 10.00
DO I.Diogu/J.O'Neal 4.00 10.00
DR B.Davis/J.Richardson 4.00 10.00
GH B.Gordon/K.Hinrich 4.00 10.00
GW P.Gasol/H.Warrick 4.00 10.00
HB C.Billups/R.Hamilton 5.00 12.00
HG D.Gooden/L.Hughes 4.00 10.00
IK Z.Ilgauskas/C.Kaman 4.00 10.00
JC R.Carney/B.Jones 4.00 10.00
JJ M.Jordan/L.James 50.00 100.00
JL A.Johnson/K.Lowry 4.00 10.00
JR A.Jefferson/A.Ray 4.00 10.00
JW S.Jones/M.Williams 4.00 10.00
MJ D.Mason/B.Jackson 4.00 10.00
ML S.Livingston/C.Maggette 4.00 10.00
MO S.O'Neal/A.Mourning 20.00 50.00
MS R.McCants/C.Smith 4.00 10.00
OH E.Okafor/D.Howard 6.00 15.00
OS P.O'Bryant/S.Sene 4.00 10.00
PA P.Pierce/C.Anthony 8.00 20.00
PW G.Payton/J.Williams 8.00 20.00
RM J.Magloire/Z.Randolph 4.00 10.00
RN M.Redd/D.Noel 4.00 10.00
SN P.Stojakovic/S.Novak 5.00 12.00
TG P.Tucker/J.Garbajosa 4.00 10.00
TH D.Harris/J.Terry 4.00 10.00
TR A.Ray/S.Telfair 4.00 10.00
TS T.Thomas/T.Sefolosha 5.00 12.00
WB M.Williams/J.Boone 4.00 10.00
WI C.Webber/A.Iverson 10.00 25.00
WP R.Wallace/T.Prince 4.00 10.00
WR J.Redick/S.Williams 4.00 10.00

2006-07 Ultimate Collection Combos Jerseys Triple

PRINT RUN 25 SER.#'d SETS
UNPRICED QUAD PRINT RUN 5 SETS
UNPRICED TRIPLE PATCH PRINT RUN 10 SETS
UNPRICED QUAD PATCH PRINT RUN ONE SET

ADB Brown/Ager/Davis 8.00 20.00
AKS Allen/Stojakovic/Korver 12.00 30.00
BBB Brand/Boozer/Battier 8.00 20.00
BBS Bosh/Boozer/Stoudemire 12.00 30.00
DPG Duncan/Ginobili/Parker 25.00 50.00
FMR Marbury/Francis/Robinson 12.00 30.00
FRF Richardson/Frye/Francis 8.00 20.00
GDF Garnett/Foye/Davis 25.00 50.00
LRS Lewis/Ridnour/Sene 8.00 20.00
NKB Kirilenko/Bargnani/Nowitzki 15.00 30.00
WBB Williams/Brewer/Brown 8.00 20.00

2006-07 Ultimate Collection Debut Jerseys

PRINT RUN 50 SER.#'d SETS
*PATCHES: .75X TO 2X BASE HI
PATCH PRINT RUN 25 SER.#'d SETS

UDAB Andrea Bargnani 3.00 8.00
UDAR Allan Ray 2.00 5.00
UDBA Renaldo Balkman 2.50 6.00
UDBJ Bobby Jones 2.00 5.00
UDBR Brandon Roy 3.00 8.00
UDCS Cedric Simmons 2.00 5.00
UDDB Dee Brown 2.00 5.00
UDDG Daniel Gibson 2.50 6.00
UDDN David Noel 2.00 5.00
UDHA Hilton Armstrong 2.00 5.00
UDJB Josh Boone 2.00 5.00
UDJF Jordan Farmar 3.00 8.00
UDJG Jorge Garbajosa 2.50 6.00
UDJR J.J. Redick 4.00 10.00
UDJW James White 2.00 5.00
UDKL Kyle Lowry 4.00 10.00
UDLA LaMarcus Aldridge 8.00 20.00
UDMA Maurice Ager 2.00 5.00
UDMC Mardy Collins 2.00 5.00
UDMW Marcus Williams 2.00 5.00
UDPD Paul Davis 2.00 5.00
UDPO Patrick O'Bryant 2.00 5.00
UDPT P.J. Tucker 2.50 6.00
UDQD Quincy Douby 2.00 5.00
UDRB Ronnie Brewer 3.00 8.00
UDRC Rodney Carney 2.00 5.00
UDRF Randy Foye 3.00 8.00
UDRG Rudy Gay 4.00 10.00
UDRR Rajon Rondo 5.00 12.00
UDSB Shannon Brown 2.00 5.00
UDSJ Solomon Jones 2.00 5.00
UDSM Craig Smith 2.50 6.00
UDSN Steve Novak 2.50 6.00
UDSS Saer Sene 2.00 5.00
UDSW Shelden Williams 2.50 6.00
UDTS Thabo Sefolosha 3.00 8.00
UDTT Tyrus Thomas 2.50 6.00
UDWB Will Blalock 2.00 5.00
UDWI Shawne Williams 2.00 5.00

2006-07 Ultimate Collection Debut Jerseys Autographs

PRINT RUN 35 SER.#'d SETS
UNPRICED PATCH AUTO PRINT RUN 10 SETS

UDAB Andrea Bargnani 12.00 30.00
UDAR Allan Ray 5.00 12.00
UDBA Renaldo Balkman 6.00 15.00
UDBJ Bobby Jones 5.00 12.00
UDBR Brandon Roy 8.00 20.00
UDCS Cedric Simmons 5.00 12.00
UDDB Dee Brown 5.00 12.00
UDDN David Noel 5.00 12.00
UDHA Hilton Armstrong 5.00 12.00
UDJB Josh Boone 5.00 12.00
UDJF Jordan Farmar 8.00 20.00
UDJG Jorge Garbajosa 6.00 15.00
UDJW James White 5.00 12.00
UDKL Kyle Lowry 10.00 25.00
UDLA LaMarcus Aldridge 20.00 50.00
UDMA Maurice Ager 5.00 12.00
UDMC Mardy Collins 5.00 12.00
UDMW Marcus Williams 5.00 12.00
UDPO Patrick O'Bryant 5.00 12.00
UDPT P.J. Tucker 6.00 15.00
UDQD Quincy Douby 5.00 12.00
UDRB Ronnie Brewer 8.00 20.00
UDRF Randy Foye 8.00 20.00
UDRG Rudy Gay 10.00 25.00
UDRR Rajon Rondo 12.00 30.00
UDSB Shannon Brown 5.00 12.00
UDSJ Solomon Jones 5.00 12.00
UDSM Craig Smith 6.00 15.00
UDSN Steve Novak 6.00 15.00
UDSS Saer Sene 5.00 12.00
UDSW Shelden Williams 6.00 15.00
UDTS Thabo Sefolosha 8.00 20.00
UDTT Tyrus Thomas 6.00 15.00
UDWB Will Blalock 5.00 12.00
UDWI Shawne Williams 5.00 12.00

2006-07 Ultimate Collection Jerseys Dual

PRINT RUN 25 SER.#'d SETS
*PATCH DUAL: 1X TO 2.5X BASE HI
PATCH DUAL PRINT RUN 25 SETS
UNPRICED TRIPLE PRINT RUN 10 SETS
UNPRICED PAT.TRIPLE PRINT RUN TEN SETS

UJAB Andrea Bargnani 5.00 12.00
UJAI Andre Iguodala 4.00 10.00
UJAS Amare Stoudemire 4.00 10.00
UJBC Carlos Boozer 4.00 10.00
UJBD Baron Davis 4.00 10.00
UJBJ Bobby Jones 3.00 8.00
UJBO Chris Bosh 5.00 12.00
UJBW Ben Wallace 4.00 10.00
UJCA Carmelo Anthony 6.00 15.00
UJCB Chauncey Billups 5.00 12.00
UJCP Chris Paul 6.00 15.00
UJCW Chris Webber 6.00 15.00
UJDB Dee Brown 3.00 8.00
UJDG Drew Gooden 4.00 10.00
UJDH Dwight Howard 4.00 10.00
UJDN Dirk Nowitzki 8.00 20.00
UJDW Deron Williams 4.00 10.00
UJEB Elton Brand 5.00 12.00
UJEO Emeka Okafor 4.00 10.00
UJFE Raymond Felton 4.00 10.00
UJHA Hilton Armstrong 3.00 8.00
UJJF Jordan Farmar 5.00 12.00
UJJK Jason Kidd 8.00 20.00
UJJO Jermaine O'Neal 4.00 10.00
UJJR J.J. Redick 6.00 15.00
UJKB Kobe Bryant 20.00 50.00
UJKG Kevin Garnett 8.00 20.00
UJKH Kirk Hinrich 4.00 10.00
UJKL Kyle Lowry 6.00 15.00
UJLA LaMarcus Aldridge 12.00 30.00
UJLD Luol Deng 4.00 10.00
UJLJ LeBron James 30.00 80.00
UJLO Lamar Odom 4.00 10.00
UJMA Shawn Marion 4.00 10.00
UJMJ Michael Jordan 100.00 200.00
UJMR Michael Redd 4.00 10.00
UJMW Marvin Williams 4.00 10.00
UJNA Steve Nash 6.00 15.00
UJPG Pau Gasol 5.00 12.00
UJPO Patrick O'Bryant 3.00 8.00
UJPP Paul Pierce 5.00 12.00
UJRB Ronnie Brewer 5.00 12.00
UJRC Rodney Carney 3.00 8.00
UJRF Randy Foye 5.00 12.00
UJRG Rudy Gay 6.00 15.00
UJRH Richard Hamilton 4.00 10.00
UJRO Brandon Roy 5.00 12.00
UJSJ Solomon Jones 3.00 8.00
UJSM Stephon Marbury 4.00 10.00
UJSN Steve Novak 4.00 10.00
UJSO Shaquille O'Neal 10.00 25.00
UJSW Shelden Williams 4.00 10.00
UJTD Tim Duncan 8.00 20.00
UJTM Tracy McGrady 6.00 15.00
UJTP Tony Parker 5.00 12.00
UJTT Tyrus Thomas 4.00 10.00
UJVC Vince Carter 8.00 20.00
UJWI Shawne Williams 3.00 8.00
UJYM Yao Ming 6.00 15.00
UJZI Zydrunas Ilgauskas 4.00 10.00

2006-07 Ultimate Collection Numbers

STATED PRINT RUN ONE TO 40 SER.#'d SETS
SOME UNPRICED DUE TO SCARCITY

UNBL Bill Laimbeer/40 10.00 25.00
UNCA Carmelo Anthony/15 50.00 120.00
UNCD Clyde Drexler/22 50.00 120.00
UNDM Desmond Mason/24 10.00 25.00
UNGO Sebastian Telfair/30 10.00 25.00
UNMW Marvin Williams/24 12.00 30.00
UNPP Paul Pierce/34 20.00 50.00
UNPS Peja Stojakovic/16 15.00 40.00
UNRJ Richard Jefferson/24 10.00 25.00
UNST John Stockton/12 100.00 200.00
UNVC Vince Carter/15 60.00 120.00
UNWI Maurice Williams/25 10.00 25.00
UNYM Yao Ming/11 50.00 100.00

2006-07 Ultimate Collection Premium Swatches

PRINT RUN 75 SER.#'d SETS

PRAB Andrea Bargnani 4.00 10.00
PRAI Allen Iverson 8.00 20.00
PRAJ Antawn Jamison 5.00 12.00
PRBA Renaldo Balkman 3.00 8.00
PRBD Baron Davis 5.00 12.00
PRBG Ben Gordon 5.00 12.00
PRBJ Bobby Jones 2.50 6.00
PRBR Brandon Roy 4.00 10.00
PRCA Carlos Arroyo 4.00 10.00
PRCP Chris Paul 8.00 20.00
PRCS Cedric Simmons 2.50 6.00
PRDB Dee Brown 2.50 6.00
PRDG Drew Gooden 5.00 12.00
PRDH Dwight Howard 5.00 12.00

PRDN Dirk Nowitzki 10.00 25.00
PRDW Deron Williams 5.00 12.00
PREB Elton Brand 6.00 15.00
PRHA Hilton Armstrong 2.50 6.00
PRJB Josh Boone 2.50 6.00
PRJF Jordan Farmar 4.00 10.00
PRJK Jason Kidd 10.00 25.00
PRJN Jameer Nelson 4.00 10.00
PRKB Kobe Bryant 20.00 50.00
PRKG Kevin Garnett 10.00 25.00
PRKL Kyle Lowry 5.00 12.00
PRLA LaMarcus Aldridge 10.00 25.00
PRLB Leandro Barbosa 5.00 12.00
PRLJ LeBron James 25.00 60.00
PRMA Maurice Ager 2.50 6.00
PRMB Mike Bibby 6.00 15.00
PRMC Mardy Collins 2.50 6.00
PRMG Manu Ginobili 6.00 15.00
PRMR Michael Redd 5.00 12.00
PRMW Marcus Williams 2.50 6.00
PRNA Steve Nash 8.00 20.00
PRPD Paul Davis 2.50 6.00
PRPG Pau Gasol 6.00 15.00
PRPO Patrick O'Bryant 2.50 6.00
PRPP Paul Pierce 6.00 15.00
PRPT P.J. Tucker 3.00 8.00
PRQD Quincy Douby 2.50 6.00
PRRA Rafer Alston 4.00 10.00
PRRB Ronnie Brewer 4.00 10.00
PRRF Randy Foye 4.00 10.00
PRRG Rudy Gay 5.00 12.00
PRRR Rajon Rondo 10.00 25.00
PRSB Shannon Brown 2.50 6.00
PRSJ Solomon Jones 2.50 6.00
PRSM Craig Smith 3.00 8.00
PRSN Steve Novak 3.00 8.00
PRSO Shaquille O'Neal 12.00 30.00
PRSS Saer Sene 2.50 6.00
PRST Stephon Marbury 5.00 12.00
PRSW Shelden Williams 3.00 8.00
PRTM Tracy McGrady 8.00 20.00
PRTP Tayshaun Prince 5.00 12.00
PRTT Tyrus Thomas 3.00 8.00
PRVC Vince Carter 8.00 20.00
PRWI Shawne Williams 2.50 6.00
PRZI Zydrunas Ilgauskas 5.00 12.00

2006-07 Ultimate Collection Premium Swatches Patch

PRINT RUN 50 SER.#'d SETS
PRAB Andrea Bargnani 15.00 40.00
PRAI Allen Iverson 50.00 100.00
PRAJ Antawn Jamison 12.00 30.00
PRBA Renaldo Balkman 12.00 30.00
PRBD Baron Davis 12.00 30.00
PRBG Ben Gordon 12.00 30.00
PRBJ Bobby Jones 10.00 25.00
PRBR Brandon Roy 12.00 30.00
PRCA Carlos Arroyo 15.00 40.00
PRCP Chris Paul 20.00 50.00
PRCS Cedric Simmons 10.00 25.00
PRDB Dee Brown 10.00 25.00
PRDG Drew Gooden 12.00 30.00
PRDH Dwight Howard 40.00 80.00
PRDN Dirk Nowitzki 75.00 150.00
PREB Elton Brand 12.00 30.00
PRHA Hilton Armstrong 10.00 25.00
PRJB Josh Boone 10.00 25.00
PRJK Jason Kidd 35.00 75.00
PRJN Jameer Nelson 10.00 25.00
PRKB Kobe Bryant 125.00 250.00
PRKG Kevin Garnett 50.00 120.00
PRKL Kyle Lowry 20.00 50.00
PRLA LaMarcus Aldridge 15.00 40.00
PRLJ LeBron James 125.00 250.00
PRMA Maurice Ager 10.00 25.00
PRMB Mike Bibby 15.00 40.00
PRMC Mardy Collins 10.00 25.00
PRMG Manu Ginobili 30.00 60.00
PRMR Michael Redd 12.00 30.00
PRMW Marcus Williams 10.00 25.00
PRPD Paul Davis 10.00 25.00
PRPG Pau Gasol 15.00 40.00
PRPO Patrick O'Bryant 10.00 25.00
PRQD Quincy Douby 10.00 25.00
PRRA Rafer Alston 10.00 25.00
PRRB Ronnie Brewer 15.00 40.00
PRRF Randy Foye 15.00 40.00
PRRG Rudy Gay 20.00 50.00
PRRR Rajon Rondo 40.00 100.00
PRSB Shannon Brown 20.00 50.00
PRSJ Solomon Jones 10.00 25.00
PRSM Craig Smith 12.00 30.00
PRSN Steve Novak 12.00 30.00
PRSO Shaquille O'Neal 40.00 100.00
PRSS Saer Sene 10.00 25.00
PRST Stephon Marbury 12.50 30.00
PRSW Shelden Williams 12.00 30.00
PRTM Tracy McGrady 25.00 60.00
PRTP Tayshaun Prince 12.00 30.00
PRTT Tyrus Thomas 12.00 30.00
PRVC Vince Carter 50.00 100.00
PRWI Shawne Williams 10.00 25.00
PRZI Zydrunas Ilgauskas 12.50 30.00

2006-07 Ultimate Collection Rookie Patches Autographs

PRINT RUN 25 SER.#'d SETS
UNPRICED LOGOMAN PRINT RUN ONE SET
AB Andrea Bargnani 15.00 40.00
AR Allan Ray 10.00 25.00
BJ Bobby Jones 10.00 25.00
BR Brandon Roy 75.00 200.00
CS Cedric Simmons 10.00 25.00
DB Dee Brown 10.00 25.00
DN David Noel 10.00 25.00
HA Hilton Armstrong 10.00 25.00
JB Josh Boone 10.00 25.00
JF Jordan Farmar 15.00 40.00
JG Jorge Garbajosa 12.00 30.00
JW James White 10.00 25.00
KL Kyle Lowry 20.00 50.00
LA LaMarcus Aldridge 100.00 250.00
MA Maurice Ager 10.00 25.00
MC Mardy Collins 10.00 25.00
MW Marcus Williams 10.00 25.00
PT P.J. Tucker 12.00 30.00
QD Quincy Douby 10.00 25.00
RB Renaldo Balkman 12.00 30.00
RC Rodney Carney 10.00 25.00
RF Randy Foye 15.00 40.00
RG Rudy Gay 75.00 150.00
RO Ronnie Brewer 15.00 40.00
RR Rajon Rondo 125.00 300.00
SB Shannon Brown 10.00 25.00
SJ Solomon Jones 10.00 25.00
SM Craig Smith 12.00 30.00
SN Steve Novak 12.00 30.00
SW Shawne Williams 10.00 25.00
TS Thabo Sefolosha 15.00 40.00
TT Tyrus Thomas 12.00 30.00
WB Will Blalock 10.00 25.00
WI Shelden Williams 12.00 30.00

2006-07 Ultimate Collection Signatures

APPROXIMATE ODDS ONE PER BOX
USAB Andrea Bargnani 6.00 15.00
USBL Bill Laimbeer 6.00 15.00
USBO Chris Bosh 6.00 15.00
USBR Brandon Roy 6.00 15.00
USCA Carmelo Anthony 20.00 50.00
USCP Chris Paul 25.00 60.00
USDW Deron Williams 6.00 15.00
USHO Hakeem Olajuwon 15.00 40.00
USHW Hakim Warrick 6.00 15.00
USJE Julius Erving 50.00 120.00
USJF Jordan Farmar 6.00 15.00
USJK Jason Kidd 12.00 30.00
USJO Jermaine O'Neal 6.00 15.00
USJS J.R. Smith 6.00 15.00
USKB Kobe Bryant 125.00 250.00
USLJ LeBron James 300.00 600.00
USMB Mike Bibby 6.00 15.00
USMG Magic Johnson 40.00 100.00
USMJ Michael Jordan 800.00 1200.00
USNA Steve Nash 20.00 50.00
USRG Rudy Gay 6.00 15.00
USRO Dennis Rodman 30.00 80.00
USRU Bill Russell 100.00 200.00
USSW Shelden Williams 6.00 15.00

2007-08 Ultimate Collection

This set was released on May 14, 2008. The base set consists of 150 cards. Cards 1-100 feature veterans serial numbered of 199, and cards 101-144 are autographed rookies serial numbered of either 99 or 150. Cards 145-150 are non-autographed rookies serial numbered of 99. Ultimate Collection is packaged in four-pack boxes of four cards each and packs carried an initial SRP of $125.

1-100 PRINT RUN 199 SER.#'d SETS
145-150 RC PRINT RUN 50 SER.#'d SETS
1 LaMarcus Aldridge 1.50 4.00
2 Ray Allen 1.25 3.00
3 Carmelo Anthony 1.50 4.00
4 Gilbert Arenas 1.00 2.50
5 Ron Artest 1.25 3.00
6 Andrea Bargnani 1.25 3.00
7 Mike Bibby 1.25 3.00
8 Chauncey Billups 1.25 3.00
9 Andrew Bogut 1.00 2.50
10 Carlos Boozer 1.00 2.50
11 Chris Bosh 1.25 3.00
12 Elton Brand 1.25 3.00
13 Kobe Bryant 5.00 12.00
14 Caron Butler 1.00 2.50
15 Jorge Garbajosa 1.00 2.50
16 Marcus Camby .75 2.00
17 Rodney Carney .75 2.00
18 Vince Carter 1.50 4.00
19 Tyson Chandler 1.00 2.50
20 Damien Wilkins .75 2.00
21 Eddy Curry .75 2.00
22 Baron Davis 1.00 2.50
23 Ricky Davis 1.00 2.50
24 Luol Deng 1.00 2.50
25 Tim Duncan 2.00 5.00
26 Shawne Williams .75 2.00
27 Monta Ellis 1.00 2.50
28 Jordan Farmar .75 2.00
29 T.J. Ford .75 2.00
30 Randy Foye 1.25 3.00
31 Channing Frye 1.00 2.50
32 Al Jefferson 1.00 2.50
33 Pau Gasol 1.25 3.00
34 Rudy Gay 1.25 3.00
35 Manu Ginobili 1.25 3.00
36 Ben Gordon 1.00 2.50
37 Richard Hamilton 1.00 2.50
38 Luther Head 1.00 2.50
39 Grant Hill 1.50 4.00
40 Kirk Hinrich 1.00 2.50
41 Dwight Howard 1.00 2.50
42 Josh Howard 1.00 2.50
43 Larry Hughes 1.00 2.50
44 Andre Iguodala 1.00 2.50
45 Daniel Gibson 1.00 2.50
46 Allen Iverson 1.50 4.00
47 Morris Peterson .75 2.00
48 Stephen Jackson 1.00 2.50
49 LeBron James 5.00 12.00
50 Antawn Jamison 1.00 2.50
51 Kevin Garnett 2.00 5.00
52 Richard Jefferson 1.00 2.50
53 Joe Johnson 1.00 2.50
54 Jason Kidd 1.25 3.00
55 Andrei Kirilenko 1.00 2.50
56 David Lee .75 2.00
57 Rashard Lewis 1.00 2.50
58 Corey Maggette 1.00 2.50
59 Stephon Marbury 1.00 2.50
60 Shawn Marion 1.00 2.50
61 Kevin Martin 1.00 2.50
62 Tracy McGrady 1.25 3.00
63 Al Harrington 1.00 2.50
64 Andre Miller 1.00 2.50
65 Francisco Garcia .75 2.00
66 Yao Ming 1.50 4.00
67 Cuttino Mobley 1.00 2.50
68 Alonzo Mourning 1.50 4.00
69 Steve Nash 1.50 4.00
70 Dirk Nowitzki 1.50 4.00
71 Jermaine O`Neal 1.00 2.50
72 Shaquille O`Neal 2.50 6.00
73 Lamar Odom 1.00 2.50
74 Adam Morrison .75 2.00
75 Mehmet Okur .75 2.00
76 Tony Parker 1.25 3.00
77 Chris Paul 1.50 4.00
78 Johan Petro .75 2.00
79 Paul Pierce 1.25 3.00
80 Tayshaun Prince 1.00 2.50
81 Zach Randolph 1.00 2.50
82 Michael Redd 1.00 2.50
83 Jason Richardson 1.25 3.00
84 Brandon Roy 1.25 3.00
85 Josh Smith 1.00 2.50
86 Amare Stoudemire 1.00 2.50
87 Jason Terry 1.00 2.50
88 Jamaal Tinsley .75 2.00
89 Hedo Turkoglu 1.00 2.50
90 Desmond Mason .75 2.00
91 Dwyane Wade 2.00 5.00
92 Ben Wallace 1.00 2.50
93 Gerald Wallace 1.00 2.50
94 Rasheed Wallace 1.25 3.00
95 Mike Miller 1.00 2.50
96 David West 1.00 2.50
97 Delonte West .75 2.00
98 Deron Williams 1.00 2.50
99 Marvin Williams 1.00 2.50
100 Raymond Felton 1.25 3.00
101 Arron Affalo AU/99 RC 6.00 15.00
102 Morris Almond AU/99 RC 4.00 10.00
103 Marco Belinelli AU/99 RC 6.00 15.00
104 Corey Brewer AU/150 RC 6.00 15.00
105 Aaron Brooks AU/99 RC 5.00 12.00
106 Julian Wright AU/150 RC 4.00 10.00
107 Wilson Chandler AU/99 RC 5.00 12.00
108 Mike Conley Jr. AU/150 RC 8.00 20.00
109 Daequan Cook AU/99 RC 5.00 12.00
110 Javaris Crittenton AU/150 RC 4.00 10.00
111 JamesOn Curry AU/99 RC 4.00 10.00
112 Jermareo Davidson AU/99 RC 4.00 10.00
113 Glen Davis AU/150 RC 5.00 12.00
114 Jared Dudley AU/99 RC 5.00 12.00
115 Kevin Durant AU/150 RC 400.00 800.00
116 Nick Fazekas AU/99 RC 4.00 10.00
117 Aaron Gray AU/99 RC 4.00 10.00
118 Jeff Green AU/150 RC 6.00 15.00
119 Taurean Green AU/99 RC 4.00 10.00
120 Adam Haluska AU/99 RC 4.00 10.00
121 Spencer Hawes AU/99 RC 5.00 12.00
122 Herbert Hill AU/99 RC 4.00 10.00
123 Al Horford AU/150 RC 8.00 20.00
124 Louis Amundson AU/99 RC 4.00 10.00
125 Carl Landry AU/99 RC 4.00 10.00
126 Jamario Moon AU/150 RC 5.00 12.00
127 Acie Law AU/150 RC 4.00 10.00
128 Dominic McGuire AU/99 RC 4.00 10.00
129 Josh McRoberts AU/99 RC 5.00 12.00
130 Oleksiy Pecherov AU/99 RC 6.00 15.00
131 Coby Karl AU/99 RC 4.00 10.00
132 Joakim Noah AU/150 RC 6.00 15.00
133 Gabe Pruitt AU/99 RC 4.00 10.00
134 Chris Richard AU/99 RC 4.00 10.00
135 Juan Navarro AU/150 RC 5.00 12.00
136 Ramon Sessions AU/99 RC 6.00 15.00
137 Jason Smith AU/99 RC 5.00 12.00
138 D.J. Strawberry AU/99 RC 4.00 10.00
139 Rodney Stuckey AU/150 RC 5.00 12.00
140 Luis Scola AU/150 RC 8.00 20.00
141 Al Thornton AU/150 RC 5.00 12.00
142 Alando Tucker AU/99 RC 4.00 10.00
143 Sean Williams AU/99 RC 4.00 10.00
144 Cheikh Samb AU/99 RC 4.00 10.00
145 Yi Jianlian RC 5.00 12.00
146 Thaddeus Young RC 4.00 10.00
147 Nick Young RC 5.00 12.00
148 Kyrylo Fesenko RC 2.50 6.00
149 Greg Oden RC 4.00 10.00
150 Brandan Wright RC 4.00 10.00

2007-08 Ultimate Collection Foil

*1-100 FOIL: 2.5X TO 6X BASE HI
101-144 UNPRICED DUE TO SCARCITY
PRINT RUN 10 SER.#'d SETS

2007-08 Ultimate Collection Rookies Gold

*GOLD: .4X TO 1X BASE HI
PRINT RUN 50 SER.#'d SETS
UNPRICED LOGO PRINT RUN ONE SET
115 Kevin Durant AU 400.00 800.00

2007-08 Ultimate Collection Rookies Signature Patches

PRINT RUN 25 SER.#'d SETS
AL Acie Law 12.00 30.00
AT Al Thornton 15.00 40.00
CB Corey Brewer 20.00 50.00
DC Daequan Cook 15.00 40.00
DS D.J. Strawberry 12.00 30.00
GD Glen Davis 15.00 40.00
HO Al Horford 20.00 50.00
JC Javaris Crittenton 12.00 30.00
JG Jeff Green 20.00 50.00
JN Joakim Noah 20.00 50.00
JS Jason Smith 15.00 40.00
JW Julian Wright 12.00 30.00
KD Kevin Durant 1200.00 2000.00
MC Mike Conley Jr. 25.00 60.00
RS Rodney Stuckey 15.00 40.00
SW Sean Williams 12.00 30.00

2007-08 Ultimate Collection Archetypal Autographs

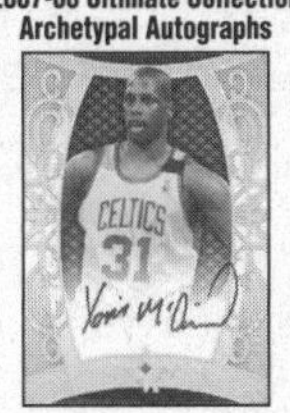

PRINT RUN 25 SER.#'d SETS
AD Adrian Dantley 10.00 25.00
BL Bill Laimbeer 15.00 30.00
DH Dwight Howard 35.00 75.00
HO Hakeem Olajuwon 20.00 40.00
JW Jerry West 30.00 60.00
LB Larry Bird 75.00 150.00
RB Rick Barry 10.00 25.00
RP Robert Parish 10.00 25.00
TC Tom Chambers 8.00 20.00
TY Tyson Chandler 8.00 20.00
WF Walt Frazier 15.00 30.00
XM Xavier McDaniel 8.00 20.00

2007-08 Ultimate Collection Commitment

PRINT RUN 25 SER.#'d SETS
UNPRICED PATCH PRINT RUN 10 SETS
CA Carmelo Anthony 50.00 120.00
CD Clyde Drexler 25.00 60.00
CH Chris Mullin 25.00 60.00
DH Dwight Howard 30.00 60.00
DR David Robinson 40.00 80.00
DW Deron Williams 20.00 40.00
JE Julius Erving 60.00 120.00
JS John Stockton 50.00 100.00
KB Kobe Bryant 200.00 500.00
LJ LeBron James 400.00 800.00
MJ Michael Jordan 800.00 1200.00
SN Steve Nash 30.00 60.00
VC Vince Carter 25.00 50.00
YM Yao Ming 25.00 50.00

2007-08 Ultimate Collection Leadership

PRINT RUN 99 SER.#'d SETS
*GOLD: .5X TO 1.25X BASE HI
GOLD PRINT RUN 50 SER.#'d SETS
BO Chris Bosh 5.00 12.00
BR Brandon Roy 5.00 12.00
CA Carmelo Anthony 6.00 15.00
CB Chauncey Billups 5.00 12.00
CP Chris Paul 6.00 15.00
DH Dwight Howard 4.00 10.00
DR David Robinson 8.00 20.00
DW Deron Williams 4.00 10.00
JE Julius Erving 8.00 20.00
JK Jason Kidd 5.00 12.00
JO Michael Jordan 50.00 125.00
JS John Stockton 8.00 20.00
KA Kareem Abdul-Jabbar 8.00 20.00
KB Kobe Bryant 20.00 50.00
KG Kevin Garnett 8.00 20.00
KH Kirk Hinrich 4.00 10.00
LA LaMarcus Aldridge 6.00 15.00
LB Larry Bird 12.00 30.00
LJ LeBron James 20.00 50.00
MJ Magic Johnson 12.00 30.00
PP Paul Pierce 5.00 12.00
RO Dennis Rodman 10.00 25.00
SN Steve Nash 6.00 15.00
TM Tracy McGrady 5.00 12.00
TP Tony Parker 5.00 12.00
VC Vince Carter 6.00 15.00
WI Dominique Wilkins 6.00 15.00

2007-08 Ultimate Collection Leadership Patches

*PRIME: .75X TO 2X HI COLUMN
PRINT RUN 25 SER.#'d SETS
CA Carmelo Anthony 15.00 30.00
WI Dominique Wilkins 12.00 30.00

2007-08 Ultimate Collection Leadership Autographs

PRINT RUN 25 SER.#'d SETS
CA Carmelo Anthony 30.00 60.00
CP Chris Paul 40.00 80.00
DR David Robinson 50.00 100.00
JE Julius Erving 100.00 200.00
JK Jason Kidd 25.00 60.00
JO Michael Jordan 500.00 750.00
JS John Stockton 30.00 80.00
KA Kareem Abdul-Jabbar 40.00 80.00
KB Kobe Bryant 175.00 350.00
KG Kevin Garnett 75.00 150.00
KH Kirk Hinrich 20.00 50.00
LA LaMarcus Aldridge 20.00 50.00
LB Larry Bird 50.00 100.00
LJ LeBron James 200.00 400.00
MJ Magic Johnson 100.00 200.00
PP Paul Pierce 30.00 80.00
RO Dennis Rodman 60.00 120.00
VC Vince Carter 20.00 50.00

2007-08 Ultimate Collection Matchups

PRINT RUN 99 SER.#'d SETS
*GOLD: .5X TO 1.25X BASE HI
GOLD PRINT RUN 50 SER.#'d SETS
BG K.Bryant/G.Gervin 10.00 25.00
CM V.Carter/T.McGrady 5.00 12.00
DA L.Aldridge/K.Durant 12.00 30.00
DR D.Marshall/R.Brewer 5.00 12.00
EA J.Erving/C.Anthony 10.00 25.00
FF R.Felton/R.Foye 5.00 12.00
GH H.Grant/D.Howard 5.00 12.00
GI B.Gordon/A.Iguodala 5.00 12.00
GR K.Garnett/D.Rodman 10.00 25.00
HG K.Hinrich/D.Gibson 5.00 12.00
JB M.Johnson/L.Bird 20.00 50.00
JJ M.Jordan/L.James 50.00 125.00
JP P.Pierce/R.Jefferson 6.00 15.00
MR Y.Ming/D.Robinson 6.00 15.00
OM H.Olajuwon/A.Mourning 15.00 40.00
PJ T.Prince/A.Jefferson 5.00 12.00
PR C.Paul/B.Roy 6.00 15.00
PW T.Parker/D.Williams 5.00 12.00

2007-08 Ultimate Collection Matchups Patches

PRINT RUN 25 SER.#'d SETS
BG K.Bryant/G.Gervin 50.00 125.00
CM V.Carter/T.McGrady 15.00 40.00
DA L.Aldridge/K.Durant 40.00 80.00
EA J.Erving/C.Anthony 30.00 80.00
GH H.Grant/D.Howard 25.00 50.00
GR K.Garnett/D.Rodman 30.00 80.00
JB M.Johnson/L.Bird 20.00 50.00
JJ M.Jordan/L.James 150.00 300.00
MR Y.Ming/D.Robinson 20.00 50.00
OM H.Olajuwon/A.Mourning 30.00 80.00
PR C.Paul/B.Roy 15.00 40.00
PW T.Parker/D.Williams 15.00 40.00

2007-08 Ultimate Collection Matchups Autographs

PRINT RUN 25 SER.#'d SETS
BG K.Bryant/G.Gervin 175.00 275.00
CM V.Carter/T.McGrady 40.00 80.00
DA L.Aldridge/K.Durant 150.00 300.00
EA J.Erving/C.Anthony 60.00 120.00
GR K.Garnett/D.Rodman 50.00 120.00
JB M.Johnson/L.Bird 175.00 275.00
JJ M.Jordan/L.James 700.00 1100.00
MR Y.Ming/D.Robinson 60.00 120.00
OM H.Olajuwon/A.Mourning 40.00 80.00
PR C.Paul/B.Roy 50.00 100.00
PW T.Parker/D.Williams 40.00 80.00

2007-08 Ultimate Collection Materials

RANDOM INSERTS IN PACKS
*GOLD: .5X TO 1.25X BASE HI
GOLD PRINT RUN 50 SER.#'d SETS
AL Al Jefferson 2.00 5.00
BD Baron Davis 2.00 5.00
BG Ben Gordon 2.00 5.00
BR Brandon Roy 2.50 6.00
CA Carmelo Anthony 3.00 8.00
CP Chris Paul 3.00 8.00
DR David Robinson 4.00 10.00
DW Deron Williams 2.00 5.00
GG George Gervin 2.50 6.00
HG Horace Grant 2.50 6.00
HO Hakeem Olajuwon 3.00 8.00
JE Julius Erving 4.00 10.00
JK Jason Kidd 2.50 6.00
KA Kareem Abdul-Jabbar 4.00 10.00
KB Kobe Bryant 10.00 25.00
KG Kevin Garnett 4.00 10.00
KH Kirk Hinrich 2.00 5.00
LA LaMarcus Aldridge 3.00 8.00
LB Larry Bird 6.00 15.00
LD Luol Deng 2.00 5.00
LE LeBron James 8.00 20.00
LJ LeBron James 8.00 20.00
MJ Magic Johnson 6.00 15.00
MW Marvin Williams 2.00 5.00
PA Tony Parker 2.50 6.00
PG Pau Gasol 2.50 6.00
PP Paul Pierce 2.50 6.00
RG Rudy Gay 2.50 6.00
RH Richard Hamilton 2.00 5.00
RJ Richard Jefferson 2.00 5.00
RO Dennis Rodman 5.00 12.00
RR Rajon Rondo 2.50 6.00
SN Steve Nash 3.00 8.00
ST John Stockton 4.00 10.00
TM Tracy McGrady 2.50 6.00
TT Tyrus Thomas 1.50 4.00
VC Vince Carter 3.00 8.00
WF Walt Frazier 2.50 6.00
YM Yao Ming 3.00 8.00

2007-08 Ultimate Collection Materials Autographs

RANDOM INSERTS IN PACKS
AL Al Jefferson 8.00 20.00
BD Baron Davis 8.00 20.00
BG Ben Gordon 8.00 20.00
BR Brandon Roy 10.00 25.00
CA Carmelo Anthony 20.00 40.00
CP Chris Paul 30.00 60.00
DR David Robinson 30.00 60.00
DW Deron Williams 10.00 25.00
GG George Gervin 15.00 30.00
HG Horace Grant 25.00 60.00
HO Hakeem Olajuwon 30.00 60.00
JE Julius Erving 40.00 80.00
JK Jason Kidd 25.00 60.00
JW Julian Wright 8.00 20.00
KA Kareem Abdul-Jabbar 40.00 80.00
KB Kobe Bryant 125.00 250.00
KH Kirk Hinrich 8.00 20.00
LA LaMarcus Aldridge 10.00 25.00
LJ LeBron James 400.00 800.00
PA Tony Parker 15.00 30.00
PP Paul Pierce 25.00 60.00
RG Rudy Gay 8.00 20.00
RJ Richard Jefferson 8.00 20.00
RO Dennis Rodman 75.00 150.00
RR Rajon Rondo 20.00 50.00
SN Steve Nash 30.00 60.00
ST John Stockton 30.00 80.00
TM Tracy McGrady 10.00 25.00
TT Tyrus Thomas 8.00 20.00
VC Vince Carter 15.00 40.00
WF Walt Frazier 20.00 40.00

2007-08 Ultimate Collection Materials Patches

PRINT RUN 25 SER.#'d SETS
AL Al Jefferson 6.00 15.00
BG Ben Gordon 6.00 15.00
BR Brandon Roy 8.00 20.00
CA Carmelo Anthony 10.00 25.00
CP Chris Paul 15.00 30.00
DR David Robinson 15.00 40.00
DW Deron Williams 6.00 15.00
GG George Gervin 8.00 20.00
HO Hakeem Olajuwon 8.00 20.00
JE Julius Erving 10.00 25.00
JK Jason Kidd 6.00 15.00
KA Kareem Abdul-Jabbar 20.00 40.00
KB Kobe Bryant 50.00 120.00
KG Kevin Garnett 20.00 40.00
KH Kirk Hinrich 8.00 20.00
LA LaMarcus Aldridge 8.00 20.00
LB Larry Bird 20.00 50.00
LD Luol Deng 6.00 15.00
LJ LeBron James 30.00 80.00
MJ Magic Johnson 15.00 30.00
MW Marvin Williams 6.00 15.00
PA Tony Parker 6.00 15.00
PG Pau Gasol 6.00 15.00
PP Paul Pierce 8.00 20.00
RG Rudy Gay 8.00 20.00
RH Richard Hamilton 6.00 15.00
RJ Richard Jefferson 6.00 15.00
RO Dennis Rodman 10.00 25.00
SN Steve Nash 10.00 25.00
ST John Stockton 15.00 30.00
TM Tracy McGrady 8.00 20.00
TT Tyrus Thomas 6.00 15.00
VC Vince Carter 12.00 30.00
WF Walt Frazier 10.00 25.00
YM Yao Ming 10.00 25.00

2007-08 Ultimate Collection Materials Dual

PRINT RUN 99 SER#'d SETS
DBJ K.Bryant/L.James 25.00 60.00
DDP T.Duncan/T.Parker 5.00 12.00
DGB K.Bryant/K.Garnett 15.00 30.00
DGJ K.Garnett/L.James 15.00 30.00
DHB R.Hamilton/C.Billups 5.00 12.00
DIA A.Iverson/C.Anthony 6.00 15.00
DJW L.James/D.Wade 15.00 30.00
DKW A.Kirilenko/D.Williams 5.00 12.00
DMD T.Duncan/Y.Ming 6.00 15.00
DMM T.McGrady/Y.Ming 5.00 12.00
DNH D.Nowitzki/J.Howard 5.00 12.00
DNS S.Nash/A.Stoudemire 5.00 12.00
DSH A.Stoudemire/D.Howard 6.00 15.00

2007-08 Ultimate Collection Materials Dual Patches

PRINT RUN 25 SER.#'d SETS
DBJ K.Bryant/L.James 50.00 125.00
DDS T.Duncan/A.Stoudemire 15.00 30.00
DGB K.Bryant/K.Garnett 30.00 80.00
DGJ K.Garnett/L.James 30.00 80.00
DHB R.Hamilton/C.Billups 8.00 20.00
DIA A.Iverson/C.Anthony 20.00 40.00
DJW L.James/D.Wade 30.00 80.00
DMD T.Duncan/Y.Ming 15.00 30.00
DMM T.McGrady/Y.Ming 10.00 25.00
DNH D.Nowitzki/J.Howard 12.00 30.00
DNS S.Nash/A.Stoudemire 15.00 30.00
DSH A.Stoudemire/D.Howard 20.00 40.00

2007-08 Ultimate Collection Materials Triple

PRINT RUN 50 SER.#'d SETS
UNPRICED PATCH PRINT RUN 10 SETS
TCCM Milicic/Crittenton/Conley 4.00 10.00
TDGT Deng/Gordon/Thomas 4.00 10.00
TDPG Duncan/Parker/Ginobili 5.00 12.00
TDRG Ridnour/Durant/Green 8.00 20.00
THSB Stevenson/Haywood/Butler 4.00 10.00
THWP Hamilton/Wallace/Prince 5.00 12.00
TJMF Jefferson/McCants/Foye 5.00 12.00
TLHN Lewis/Howard/Nelson 4.00 10.00
TMBM McGrady/Battier/Ming 4.00 10.00
TMRB Mason/Redd/Bogut 4.00 10.00
TMRR Marbury/Richardson/Randolph 4.00 10.00
TPAG Pierce/Allen/Garnett 20.00 40.00
TPWP Peterson/West/Paul 8.00 20.00
TWRM Marion/Davis/Wade 5.00 12.00

2007-08 Ultimate Collection Materials Quad

PRINT RUN 25 SER.#'d SETS
UNPRICED PATCH PRINT RUN FIVE SETS
BGJW Kobe/KG/LJ/Wade 40.00 80.00
BPPW Bibby/Parker/Paul/Will 15.00 30.00
BRJA Kobe/Redd/LJ/Anthony 40.00 80.00
CGBH Camby/KG/Bzer/Hwrd 15.00 30.00
DPGR Dncn/Prkr/Manu/D-Rob 25.00 50.00
DSHJ Dncn/Amare/Hwrd/Jffrsn 10.00 25.00
GMMW KG/McG/Marion/Wllce 10.00 25.00
HRSG Hamilton/Redd/Peja/Gibson 10.00 25.00
HWBP Hamilton/Wallace/Billups/Prince 10.00 25.00
JDGT MJ/Deng/Gordon/Thomas 60.00 120.00
JEJB MJ/Erving/Johnson/Bird 100.00 200.00
JIPG James/Iggy/Paul/Green 30.00 60.00
JWHR LJ/Wade/Howard/Roy 25.00 50.00
NKPW Nash/Kidd/Paul/Williams 15.00 30.00
OMMO Olaj/Zo/Yao/Shaq 30.00 60.00
PAGB Pierce/Allen/KG/Bird 40.00 80.00

2007-08 Ultimate Collection Materials Rookies

RANDOM INSERTS IN PACKS
*GOLD: .5X TO 1.25X BASE HI
GOLD PRINT RUN 99 SER.#'d SETS
*PATCH: .75X TO 2X BASE HI
PATCH PRINT RUN 25 SER.#'d SETS
AA Arron Afflalo 2.00 5.00
AB Aaron Brooks 1.50 4.00
AG Aaron Gray 1.25 3.00
AH Al Horford 2.50 6.00
AL Acie Law 1.25 3.00
AT Al Thornton 1.50 4.00
CB Corey Brewer 2.00 5.00
CL Carl Landry 1.25 3.00
DA Jermareo Davidson 1.25 3.00
DC Daequan Cook 1.50 4.00
DM Dominic McGuire 1.25 3.00
GD Glen Davis 1.50 4.00
GP Gabe Pruitt 1.25 3.00
HA Adam Haluska 1.25 3.00
HH Herbert Hill 1.25 3.00
JC Javaris Crittenton 1.25 3.00
JD Jared Dudley 1.50 4.00
JG Jeff Green 2.00 5.00
JN Joakim Noah 2.00 5.00
JS Jason Smith 1.50 4.00
JW Julian Wright 1.25 3.00
KD Kevin Durant 12.00 30.00
MA Morris Almond 1.25 3.00
MC Mike Conley Jr. 2.50 6.00
NF Nick Fazekas 1.25 3.00
RS Rodney Stuckey 1.50 4.00
SH Spencer Hawes 1.50 4.00
SW Sean Williams 1.25 3.00
TU Alando Tucker 1.25 3.00
WC Wilson Chandler 1.50 4.00

2007-08 Ultimate Collection Materials Rookies Autographs

RANDOM INSERTS IN PACKS
AA Arron Afflalo 4.00 10.00
AB Aaron Brooks 3.00 8.00
AH Al Horford 5.00 12.00
AL Acie Law 2.50 6.00
AT Al Thornton 3.00 8.00
CB Corey Brewer 4.00 10.00
CL Carl Landry 2.50 6.00
DC Daequan Cook 3.00 8.00
GD Glen Davis 3.00 8.00
JC Javaris Crittenton 2.50 6.00
JD Jared Dudley 3.00 8.00
JG Jeff Green 4.00 10.00
JN Joakim Noah 12.00 30.00
JS Jason Smith 3.00 8.00
JW Julian Wright 2.50 6.00
KD Kevin Durant 150.00 400.00
MC Mike Conley Jr. 25.00 60.00
RS Rodney Stuckey 3.00 8.00
SH Spencer Hawes 3.00 8.00
SW Sean Williams 2.50 6.00

2007-08 Ultimate Collection Rookie Matchups

PRINT RUN 99 SER.#'d SETS
*GOLD: .5X TO 1.25X HI COLUMN
GOLD PRINT RUN 50 SER.#'d SETS
BC C.Brewer/M.Conley 3.00 8.00
CD G.Davis/W.Chandler 3.00 8.00
DC J.Dudley/W.Chandler 3.00 8.00
DH K.Durant/A.Horford 10.00 25.00
DW K.Durant/J.Wright 10.00 25.00
GS T.Green/D.Strawberry 3.00 8.00
GW J.Green/J.Wright 3.00 8.00
HD G.Davis/S.Hawes 3.00 8.00
HN J.Noah/A.Horford 5.00 12.00
LA M.Almond/A.Law 3.00 8.00
SC R.Stuckey/D.Cook 3.00 8.00
ST A.Tucker/D.Strawberry 3.00 8.00
TC A.Thornton/J.Crittenton 3.00 8.00
TL A.Tucker/C.Landry 3.00 8.00

2007-08 Ultimate Collection Rookie Matchups Patches

PRINT RUN 25 SER.#'d SETS
BC C.Brewer/M.Conley 8.00 20.00
CD G.Davis/W.Chandler 8.00 20.00
DH K.Durant/A.Horford 40.00 80.00
DW K.Durant/J.Wright 40.00 80.00
GS T.Green/D.Strawberry 8.00 20.00
GW J.Green/J.Wright 8.00 20.00
HN J.Noah/A.Horford 12.00 30.00
LA M.Almond/A.Law 8.00 20.00
SC R.Stuckey/D.Cook 8.00 20.00
TC A.Thornton/J.Crittenton 8.00 20.00

2007-08 Ultimate Collection Rookie Matchups Autographs

PRINT RUN 25 SER.#'d SETS
BC C.Brewer/M.Conley 20.00 40.00
CD G.Davis/W.Chandler 12.00 30.00
DH K.Durant/A.Horford 150.00 300.00
DW K.Durant/J.Wright 75.00 200.00
GW J.Green/J.Wright 12.00 30.00
LA M.Almond/A.Law 12.00 30.00

2007-08 Ultimate Collection Signatures

STATED PRINT RUN 20 TO 75 SER.#'d SETS
UNPRICED GOLD PRINT RUN 10 SETS
UNPRICED QUAD PRINT RUN 10 SETS
UNPRICED SIX PRINT RUN 5 SETS
AD Adrian Dantley/50 6.00 15.00
AM Alonzo Mourning/50 30.00 80.00
BA B.J. Armstrong/75 10.00 25.00
BD Baron Davis/75 8.00 20.00
BR Brandon Roy/50 8.00 20.00
BW Bill Walton/25 15.00 30.00
CA Carmelo Anthony/20 30.00 60.00
DA Brad Daugherty/75 6.00 15.00
DF Derek Fisher/50 8.00 20.00
DG Daniel Gibson/75 6.00 15.00
DH Dwight Howard/50 15.00 40.00
DM Donyell Marshall/75 6.00 15.00
DO Dominique Wilkins/50 15.00 40.00
DR David Robinson/20 50.00 100.00
DY Danny Manning/25 15.00 30.00
EC Eddy Curry/25 6.00 15.00
GG George Gervin/50 10.00 25.00
GH Horace Grant/25 20.00 40.00
HA Hilton Armstrong/75 6.00 15.00
HE Luther Head/75 6.00 15.00
HO Hakeem Olajuwon/20 30.00 60.00
JE Al Jefferson/50 6.00 15.00
JJ Jarrett Jack/75 6.00 15.00
JK Jason Kidd/20 20.00 40.00
JW James Worthy/20 30.00 60.00
KH Kirk Hinrich/50 6.00 15.00
KV Kiki Vandeweghe/75 6.00 15.00
LA LaMarcus Aldridge/25 10.00 25.00
LJ LeBron James/20 300.00 600.00
MJ Magic Johnson/20 50.00 100.00
PA Tony Parker/25 15.00 40.00
PR Pat Riley/25 15.00 30.00
RA Randolph Morris/75 6.00 15.00
RF Randy Foye/50 6.00 15.00
RG Rudy Gay/50 6.00 15.00
RO Dennis Rodman/25 30.00 60.00
SJ Solomon Jones/75 6.00 15.00
SM Craig Smith/75 6.00 15.00
SP Sam Perkins/50 6.00 15.00
TC Terry Cummings/75 6.00 15.00
TM Tracy McGrady/20 15.00 40.00
TO Tom Chambers/50 10.00 25.00
TT Tyrus Thomas/25 6.00 15.00
TY Tyson Chandler/75 6.00 15.00
VC Vince Carter/20 25.00 50.00
WE Jerry West/20 30.00 80.00
WF Walt Frazier/50 15.00 30.00
WI Deron Williams/50 10.00 25.00

2007-08 Ultimate Collection Signatures Dual

PRINT RUN 25 SER.#'d SETS
AM H.Armstrong/P.Millsap 10.00 25.00
AW L.Aldridge/S.Williams 10.00 25.00
BD B.Davis/M.Belinelli 10.00 25.00
BH C.Bosh/D.Howard 40.00 80.00
BJ R.Jefferson/B.Bowen 30.00 60.00
CJ V.Carter/A.Jamison 20.00 50.00
CL K.Lowry/M.Conley 10.00 25.00
CM V.Carter/T.McGrady 25.00 50.00
CP T.Chandler/T.Prince 15.00 30.00
CS R.Carney/C.Smith 10.00 25.00
CW T.Chandler/J.Wright 10.00 25.00
DB B.Diaw/L.Barbosa 10.00 25.00
DL K.Dooling/K.Lowry 10.00 25.00
FR R.Foye/R.Rondo 15.00 30.00
FS D.Fisher/J.Stockton 40.00 80.00
GA B.Gordon/M.Ager 10.00 25.00
GB D.Gibson/S.Brown 10.00 25.00
GD K.Garnett/K.Durant 150.00 300.00
GH H.Grant/D.Howard 30.00 60.00
GP A.Gilmore/R.Parish 15.00 30.00
HP A.Harrington/L.Powe 10.00 25.00
HW A.Harrington/M.Williams 10.00 25.00
JG A.Jefferson/R.Gay 10.00 25.00
JP R.Jefferson/T.Prince 10.00 25.00
KA S.Kerr/B.Armstrong 20.00 40.00
LC D.Lee/R.Carney 10.00 25.00
LG D.Lee/R.Gay 10.00 25.00
MB R.Barry/C.Mullin 20.00 50.00
MJ P.Millsap/S.Jones 10.00 25.00
MW Y.Ming/B.Walton 25.00 50.00
OM P.O'Bryant/P.Millsap 10.00 25.00
OR H.Olajuwon/D.Robinson 50.00 100.00
PD P.Pierce/A.Dantley 20.00 40.00
PW C.Paul/D.Williams 25.00 60.00
RF R.Foye/B.Roy 15.00 30.00
RP R.Rondo/G.Pruitt 15.00 40.00
WH D.Wilkins/A.Horford 30.00 60.00

2007-08 Ultimate Collection Signatures Triple

PRINT RUN 15 SER.#'d SETS
BMG Bibby/Miller/Garcia 25.00 50.00
CPW Chandler/Paul/Wright 60.00 120.00
DAE Davis/Anthony/English 25.00 50.00
DAR Drexler/Aldridge/Roy 60.00 120.00
DHB Davis/Harrington/Belinelli 20.00 40.00
FSB Foye/Smith/Brewer 15.00 30.00
GLC Gay/Lowry/Conley 15.00 30.00
GTN Gordon/Thomas/Noah 40.00 80.00
KCJ Kidd/Carter/Jefferson 40.00 100.00
LPR Laimbeer/Prince/Rodman 60.00 120.00
MLT Maggette/Livingston/Thornton 15.00 30.00
OMM Olajuwon/McGrady/Ming 75.00 200.00
PRB Bowen/Parker/Robinson 50.00 100.00
WDG Wilkins/Durant/Green 100.00 200.00
WHL Wilkins/Horford/Law 12.00 30.00

2007-08 Ultimate Collection Virtuoso

PRINT RUN 25 SER.#'d SETS
UNPRICED PATCH PRINT RUN 10 SETS
AM Alonzo Mourning 40.00 100.00
BG Ben Gordon 10.00 25.00
CB Carlos Boozer 10.00 25.00
CM Chris Mullin 20.00 50.00
CP Chris Paul 40.00 100.00
DH Dwight Howard 25.00 60.00
GG George Gervin 12.00 30.00
KB Kobe Bryant 150.00 300.00
KH Kirk Hinrich 10.00 25.00
LA LaMarcus Aldridge 15.00 40.00
600 LeBron James 300.00 600.00
YM Yao Ming 25.00 50.00

2007-08 Ultimate Collection Write of Passage Autographs Dual

INT RUN 25 SER.#'d SETS
CC D.Cook/M.Conley 12.00 30.00
DG K.Durant/J.Green 100.00 225.00
DH K.Durant/A.Horford 100.00 225.00
HL A.Horford/A.Law 20.00 40.00
PD G.Pruitt/G.Davis 12.00 30.00
SC J.Crittenton/L.Scola 12.00 30.00

2008-09 Ultimate Collection

1-80 PRINT RUN 499 SER.#'d SETS
81-100 PRINT RUN 499 SER.#'d SETS
101-120 PRINT RUN 499 SER.#'d SETS
121-141 PRINT RUN 150 SER.#'d SETS
1 LaMarcus Aldridge 2.00 5.00
2 Ray Allen 2.00 5.00
3 Carmelo Anthony 2.50 6.00
4 Gilbert Arenas 1.50 4.00
5 Ron Artest 2.00 5.00
6 Chauncey Billups 2.00 5.00
7 Carlos Boozer 1.50 4.00
8 Chris Bosh 2.00 5.00
9 Elton Brand 2.00 5.00
10 Kobe Bryant 8.00 20.00
11 Caron Butler 1.50 4.00
12 Andrew Bynum 1.25 3.00
13 Jose Calderon 1.25 3.00
14 Vince Carter 2.50 6.00
15 Tyson Chandler 1.50 4.00
16 Mike Conley Jr. 1.50 4.00
17 Jamal Crawford 2.00 5.00
18 Baron Davis 1.50 4.00
19 Luol Deng 1.50 4.00
20 Chris Duhon 1.25 3.00
21 Tim Duncan 3.00 8.00
22 Kevin Durant 5.00 12.00
23 Raymond Felton 1.50 4.00
24 T.J. Ford 1.25 3.00
25 Kevin Garnett 3.00 8.00
26 Pau Gasol 2.00 5.00

27 Rudy Gay 2.00 5.00
28 Manu Ginobili 2.00 5.00
29 Ben Gordon 1.50 4.00
30 Danny Granger 1.50 4.00
31 Jeff Green 1.50 4.00
32 Al Harrington 1.50 4.00
33 Devin Harris 1.25 3.00
34 Kirk Hinrich 1.50 4.00
35 Al Horford 2.00 5.00
36 Dwight Howard 1.50 4.00
37 Josh Howard 1.50 4.00
38 Andre Iguodala 1.50 4.00
39 Allen Iverson 2.50 6.00
40 Stephen Jackson 1.50 4.00
41 LeBron James 8.00 20.00
42 Antawn Jamison 1.50 4.00
43 Al Jefferson 1.50 4.00
44 Richard Jefferson 1.50 4.00
45 Yi Jianlian 2.00 5.00
46 Joe Johnson 1.50 4.00
47 Jason Kidd 2.00 5.00
48 David Lee 1.25 3.00
49 Rashard Lewis 1.50 4.00
50 Corey Maggette 1.50 4.00
51 Shawn Marion 1.50 4.00
52 Kevin Martin 1.50 4.00
53 Tracy McGrady 2.00 5.00
54 Andre Miller 1.50 4.00
55 Mike Miller 1.50 4.00
56 Paul Millsap 1.50 4.00
57 Yao Ming 2.50 6.00
58 Steve Nash 2.00 5.00
59 Jameer Nelson 1.25 3.00
60 Dirk Nowitzki 2.50 6.00
61 Greg Oden 1.50 4.00
62 Tony Parker 2.00 5.00
63 Chris Paul 2.50 6.00
64 Paul Pierce 2.00 5.00
65 Tayshaun Prince 1.50 4.00
66 Zach Randolph 1.50 4.00
67 Michael Redd 1.50 4.00
68 Jason Richardson 2.00 5.00
69 Brandon Roy 2.00 5.00
70 John Salmons 1.50 4.00
71 Josh Smith 1.50 4.00
72 Amare Stoudemire 1.50 4.00
73 Rodney Stuckey 1.50 4.00
74 Al Thornton 1.50 4.00
75 Dwyane Wade 3.00 8.00
76 Gerald Wallace 1.50 4.00
77 David West 1.50 4.00
78 Deron Williams 1.50 4.00
79 Mo Williams 1.50 4.00
80 Thaddeus Young 1.50 4.00
81 Sean Singletary RC 1.50 4.00
82 Luc Mbah A Moute RC 2.00 5.00
83 Darnell Jackson/491 RC 1.50 4.00
84 Nathan Jawai RC 2.50 6.00
85 Jawad Williams RC 2.50 6.00
86 Joey Dorsey RC 1.50 4.00
87 Alexis Ajinca RC 1.50 4.00
88 DeAndre Jordan/491 RC 3.00 8.00
89 Javale McGee RC 3.00 8.00
90 Hamed Haddadi RC 2.50 6.00
91 Roko Ukic RC 2.50 6.00
92 Kosta Koufos RC 2.00 5.00
93 Nicolas Batum RC 3.00 8.00
94 Ryan Anderson/491 RC 2.00 5.00
95 Joe Alexander RC 1.50 4.00
96 Chris Douglas-Roberts RC 1.50 4.00
97 Anthony Morrow RC 6.00 15.00
98 Darrell Arthur RC 2.00 5.00
99 Danilo Gallinari RC 4.00 10.00
100 Marc Gasol RC 5.00 12.00
101 Michael Jordan 15.00 40.00
102 Larry Bird 5.00 12.00
103 Magic Johnson 5.00 12.00
104 Oscar Robertson 2.00 5.00
105 John Stockton 3.00 8.00
106 Julius Erving 3.00 8.00
107 Manute Bol 2.00 5.00
108 Dee Brown 1.25 3.00
109 Joe Dumars 2.00 5.00
110 James Edwards 2.00 5.00
111 A.C. Green 2.00 5.00
112 Tim Hardaway 2.00 5.00
113 Kevin Johnson 2.00 5.00
114 Karl Malone 2.50 6.00
115 Danny Ainge 2.00 5.00
116 Kurt Rambis 1.25 3.00
117 Willis Reed 2.00 5.00
118 Scottie Pippen 3.00 8.00
119 Wilt Chamberlain 4.00 10.00
120 Drazen Petrovic 3.00 8.00
121 Kevin Love JSY AU RC 25.00 60.00
122 Michael Beasley JSY AU RC 8.00 20.00
123 Rudy Fernandez JSY AU RC 6.00 15.00
124 O.J. Mayo JSY AU RC 8.00 20.00
125 Derrick Rose JSY AU RC 75.00 200.00
126 Brook Lopez JSY AU RC 10.00 25.00
127 R.Westbrook JSY AU RC 150.00 400.00
128 Courtney Lee JSY AU RC 6.00 15.00
129 Jerryd Bayless JSY AU RC 6.00 15.00
130 Marreese Speights JSY AU RC 6.00 15.00
131 Donte Greene JSY AU RC 5.00 12.00
132 J.J. Hickson JSY AU RC 6.00 15.00
133 D.J. Augustin JSY AU RC 6.00 15.00
134 J.Thompson JSY AU RC 5.00 12.00
135 Robin Lopez JSY AU RC 8.00 20.00
136 A.Randolph JSY AU RC 5.00 12.00
137 Eric Gordon JSY AU RC 12.00 30.00
138 Brandon Rush JSY AU RC 6.00 15.00
139 Roy Hibbert JSY AU RC 8.00 20.00
140 Mario Chalmers JSY AU RC 8.00 20.00
141 George Hill JSY AU RC 8.00 20.00

2008-09 Ultimate Collection Rookies Patches

STATED PRINT RUN 10 SER.#'d SETS
121 Kevin Love JSY AU 150.00 400.00
122 Michael Beasley JSY AU 75.00 200.00
123 Rudy Fernandez JSY AU 25.00 60.00
124 O.J. Mayo JSY AU 75.00 200.00
125 Derrick Rose JSY AU 1000.00 2000.00
126 Brook Lopez JSY AU 40.00 100.00
127 Russell Westbrook JSY AU 400.00 700.00
128 Courtney Lee JSY AU 25.00 60.00
129 Jerryd Bayless JSY AU 50.00 125.00
130 Marreese Speights JSY AU 25.00 60.00
131 Donte Greene JSY AU 20.00 50.00
132 J.J. Hickson JSY AU 25.00 60.00
133 D.J. Augustin JSY AU 25.00 60.00
134 Jason Thompson JSY AU 20.00 50.00
135 Robin Lopez JSY AU 30.00 80.00
136 Anthony Randolph JSY AU 20.00 50.00
137 Eric Gordon JSY AU 75.00 150.00
138 Brandon Rush JSY AU 25.00 60.00
139 Roy Hibbert JSY AU 30.00 80.00
140 Mario Chalmers JSY AU 30.00 80.00
141 George Hill JSY AU 30.00 80.00

2008-09 Ultimate Collection Rookies Silver

*SILVER: .5X TO 1.25X BASE HI
SILVER PRINT RUN 60 SER.#'d SETS

2008-09 Ultimate Collection Century Legends Epic Signature Update

COMBINED AUTO ODDS 1:3
CLAA Adrian Dantley 8.00 20.00
CLAG Artis Gilmore 8.00 20.00
CLAM Alonzo Mourning 30.00 60.00
CLBK Bernard King 8.00 20.00
CLBL Bill Laimbeer 8.00 20.00
CLBM Bob McAdoo 15.00 30.00
CLBR Brandon Roy 15.00 30.00
CLBS Bill Sharman 8.00 20.00
CLCP Chris Paul SP 200.00 400.00
CLDE Derrick Rose 175.00 325.00
CLDF Derek Fisher 10.00 25.00
CLDG Darrell Griffith 8.00 20.00
CLDH Dwight Howard 40.00 80.00
CLDR David Robinson 60.00 120.00
CLDW Deron Williams 12.00 30.00
CLHG Horace Grant 25.00 60.00
CLJK Jason Kidd 40.00 80.00
CLJS John Stockton 50.00 125.00
CLKB Kobe Bryant 200.00 300.00
CLKD Kevin Durant 50.00 125.00
CLLJ LeBron James 200.00 300.00
CLLW Lenny Wilkens 15.00 30.00
CLMB Michael Beasley 20.00 50.00
CLMJ Magic Johnson 100.00 200.00
CLOJ O.J. Mayo 25.00 60.00
CLPP Paul Pierce 20.00 50.00
CLRB Rick Barry 15.00 30.00
CLRO Dennis Rodman 50.00 100.00
CLRP Robert Parish 8.00 20.00
CLRS Ralph Sampson 8.00 20.00
CLSJ Sam Jones 15.00 40.00
CLSN Steve Nash 60.00 120.00
CLSW Spud Webb 8.00 20.00
CLTM Tracy McGrady 30.00 60.00
CLVC Vince Carter 25.00 50.00

2008-09 Ultimate Collection Entry

STATED PRINT RUN 10 SER.#'d SETS
UEAD Adrian Dantley 15.00 30.00
UEAE Alex English 15.00 30.00
UEBD Brad Daugherty 15.00 30.00
UEBL Bob Lanier 15.00 30.00
UEBS Bill Sharman 15.00 30.00
UEBW Bill Walton 25.00 50.00
UECL Clyde Lovellette 15.00 30.00
UEDC Dave Cowens 25.00 50.00
UEDW Dominique Wilkins 25.00 50.00
UEGE George Gervin 20.00 50.00
UEGG Gail Goodrich 20.00 40.00
UEHG Hal Greer 20.00 40.00
UEJH John Havlicek 25.00 50.00
UEJK Jason Kidd 40.00 80.00
UEJS Jack Sikma 15.00 30.00
UEKG Kevin Garnett 50.00 100.00
UELW Lenny Wilkens 15.00 30.00
UEMJ Michael Jordan 600.00 1000.00
UENT Nate Thurmond 20.00 40.00
UERB Rick Barry 15.00 30.00
UERP Robert Parish 20.00 40.00
UESJ Sam Jones 30.00 60.00
UEVC Vince Carter 40.00 100.00

2008-09 Ultimate Collection Initiation Writes

STATED PRINT RUN 25 SER.#'d SETS
IWAA Alexis Ajinca 4.00 10.00
IWAR Anthony Randolph 12.00 30.00
IWBL Brook Lopez 8.00 20.00
IWBR Brandon Rush 5.00 12.00
IWCL Courtney Lee 15.00 40.00
IWDA D.J. Augustin 10.00 25.00
IWDG Danilo Gallinari 10.00 25.00
IWDR Derrick Rose 200.00 400.00
IWDW D.J. White 5.00 12.00
IWEG Eric Gordon 10.00 25.00
IWGH George Hill 6.00 15.00
IWJA Joe Alexander 4.00 10.00
IWJB Jerryd Bayless 10.00 25.00
IWJH J.J. Hickson 5.00 12.00
IWJM Javale McGee 8.00 20.00
IWJT Jason Thompson 10.00 25.00
IWKK Kosta Koufos 5.00 12.00
IWKL Kevin Love 40.00 100.00
IWMB Michael Beasley 6.00 15.00
IWMG Marc Gasol 12.00 30.00
IWMS Marreese Speights 5.00 12.00
IWNB Nicolas Batum 25.00 60.00
IWOM O.J. Mayo 15.00 40.00
IWRA Ryan Anderson 5.00 12.00
IWRF Rudy Fernandez 10.00 25.00
IWRH Roy Hibbert 6.00 15.00
IWRL Robin Lopez 10.00 25.00
IWRW Russell Westbrook 60.00 120.00

2008-09 Ultimate Collection Jerseys Eight

STATED PRINT RUN 25 SER.#'d SETS
UNPRICED PATCH PRINT RUN 6 SER.#'d SETS
76ERS Philadelphia 76ers 30.00 60.00
BULLS Chicago Bulls 40.00 80.00
HAWKS Atlanta Hawks 15.00 40.00
KNICK New York Knicks 30.00 80.00
SPURS San Antonio Spurs 50.00 100.00
CELTIC Boston Celtics 60.00 120.00
LACLIP Los Angeles Clippers 15.00 40.00
LAKERS LA Lakers 30.00 80.00
PISTON Detroit Pistons 40.00 100.00
ROCKET Houston Rockets 20.00 50.00
UTAHJZ Utah Jazz 15.00 40.00
ROOKIE08 08-09 Rookies 25.00 50.00

2008-09 Ultimate Collection Jerseys Foursome Combos

STATED PRINT RUN 35 SER.#'d SETS
*PATCHES: .75X TO 2X BASE HI
PATCH PRINT RUN 10 SER.#'d SETS
UFCOKC Oklahom.City Thndr 12.00 30.00
UFC3PTS ThreePoint Shooters 15.00 30.00
UFC76ER Philadelphia 76ers 10.00 25.00
UFCBLAZ Portland Trail Blzrs 20.00 50.00
UFCBSTN Boston Celtics 12.00 30.00
UFCBULL Chicago Bulls 30.00 60.00
UFCCHMP Point Guards 15.00 30.00
UFCCLIP LA Clippers 8.00 20.00
UFCDETP Detroit Pistons 10.00 25.00
UFCEVSW Mgic/Kobe/KG/Bird 40.00 80.00
UFCGRDS Point Guards 20.00 40.00
UFCGRIZ Memphis Grizzlies 8.00 20.00
UFCHAWK Atlanta Hawks 8.00 20.00
UFCHEAT Miami Heat 20.00 40.00
UFCJAZG Utah Jazz 10.00 25.00
UFCJAZZ Utah Jazz 10.00 25.00
UFCKNIC New York Knicks 8.00 20.00
UFCLAKR Los Angeles Lakers 40.00 80.00
UFCLEGS Prsh/Rssll/Reed/Karm 20.00 40.00
UFCLGND Riley/Dntly/Olaj/Ewing 15.00 30.00
UFCNETS New Jersey Nets 8.00 20.00
UFCNICK New York Knicks 10.00 25.00
UFCPSTN Detroit Pistons 8.00 20.00
UFCROCK Houston Rockets 10.00 25.00
UFCSCOR Kareem/Kobe/Wilt/Ice 30.00 80.00
UFCSGRD Kobe/Pearl/AI/Pistol 40.00 80.00
UFCTWLV Minnesota Tmbrwlvs 8.00 20.00
UFCUDEX LBJ/Kobe/KG/Jordan 75.00 200.00
UFCWARS Golden State Warriors 10.00 25.00

2008-09 Ultimate Collection Jerseys Foursome Legends

STATED PRINT RUN 25 SER.#'d SETS
*PATCHES: 1X TO 2.5X BASE HI
PATCH PRINT RUN 10 SER.#'d SETS
UFL76ER Philadelphia 76ers 30.00 60.00
UFLBIGS Reed/Olaj/Rssll/DR 30.00 60.00
UFLBULL Chicago Bulls 80.00 200.00
UFLCELT Boston Celtics 40.00 80.00
UFLCLSC Prsh/Wilt/JoJo/PM 30.00 80.00
UFLDUNK Grffth/DW/MM/Grvn 20.00 40.00
UFLEGRD Mo/Spud/Strk/Isah 10.00 25.00
UFLGRDS Coop/JW/Agmn/AD 15.00 30.00
UFLGSTB JoJo/Mulln/Drxl/Pip 30.00 60.00
UFLHRSA Olaj/Drx/DR/Gevn 30.00 60.00
UFLJAZZ Horn/Mail/Etn/Stck 15.00 40.00
UFLLABC McH/Brd/Mgic/KAJ 30.00 80.00
UFLLAKR Wilt/Rdmn/Mail/KG 50.00 120.00
UFLLGND Magic/Bird/Rssll/MJ 60.00 150.00
UFLMBBC McH/Prsh/Oscr/KAJ 20.00 40.00
UFLNYKK Reed/Pearl/King/Fraz 15.00 30.00
UFLNYUJ Ewing/Strk/Stck/Mail 20.00 50.00
UFLUJCB Mail/Stock/MJ/Pip 75.00 150.00
UFLWGRD Kerr/Mgic/Stck/Drex 20.00 50.00

2008-09 Ultimate Collection Jerseys Foursome Rookies

STATED PRINT RUN 50 SER.#'d SETS
*PATCHES: 1X TO 2.5X BASE HI
PATCH PRINT RUN 15 SER.#'d SETS
UFR1234 Rse/Bsly/Myo/Wstbrk 12.00 30.00
UFRBGEA McG/Grn/Alxndr/Hbbrt 6.00 15.00
UFRCNTR Hbbrt/Lpz/Thmpsn/Lpz 6.00 15.00
UFRCUSA Rbrts/Drsy/Shrp/Rose 10.00 25.00
UFREACE Shrp/Hbbrt/Alxndr/Hick 6.00 15.00
UFREASE Mario/Lee/McG/D.J. 8.00 20.00
UFRLASK Grdn/Jrdn/Thmpsn/Grn 6.00 15.00
UFRMGOC Wstbrk/Whte/O.J./Arthr 6.00 15.00
UFRMHIP Rush/Hibrt/Mario/Bsly 6.00 15.00
UFRNCAA Mario/Rose/Rbrts/Arthur 12.00 30.00
UFRPC10 Jerryd/Wvr/Andrsn/Lpz 8.00 20.00
UFRPFWD Love/Hcksn/Spghts/Bsly 8.00 20.00
UFRPGRD Rose/Wstbrk/D.J./Jerryd 15.00 40.00
UFRROOK Frnndz/Alxndr/Love/Grdn 8.00 20.00
UFRSGRD Grdn/Lee/Frnndz/O.J. 6.00 15.00
UFRWEAT Gddns/Spghts/Rbrts/Lpz 6.00 15.00
UFRWENW Kfs/Wems/Jerryd/Wvr 6.00 15.00
UFRWEPA Grn/Rndlph/Jrdn/Lpz 8.00 20.00
UFRWESW Drsy/Hill/O.J./Arthur 6.00 15.00

2008-09 Ultimate Collection Jerseys Foursome Veterans

PRINT RUN 50 SER.#'d SETS
UFV05AS Centers/PF 10.00 25.00
UFV06AS Pau/Rip/Sheed/Arns 10.00 25.00
UFV07AS Two Guards 10.00 25.00
UFV76ER Philadelphia 76ers 6.00 15.00
UFVA06S Prkr/Pierce/Allen/LBJ 12.50 30.00
UFVA07S Three Point Shooters 12.50 30.00
UFVAS03 Al/Duncan/Prce/Kidd 15.00 30.00
UFVAS05 Kobe/Nash/LBJ/TMac 35.00 75.00
UFVAS06 Centers/PF2 10.00 25.00
UFVAS07 Melo/Jrmain/Okr/Booz 10.00 25.00
UFVBUCK Milwaukee Bucks 6.00 15.00
UFVBULL Chicago Bulls 8.00 20.00
UFVCAVS Cleveland Cavaliers 20.00 40.00
UFVCBOB Charlotte Bobcats 6.00 15.00
UFVCELT Boston Celtics 15.00 40.00
UFVDETP Detroit Pistons 10.00 25.00
UFVDNUG Denver Nuggets 8.00 20.00
UFVHAWK Atlanta Hawks 6.00 15.00
UFVKING Sacramento Kings 10.00 25.00
UFVLACP Los Angeles Clippers 6.00 15.00
UFVMAVS Dallas Mavericks 8.00 20.00
UFVNOHO New Orleans Hornets 8.00 20.00
UFVNYKK New York Knicks 6.00 15.00
UFVOMAG Orlando Magic 8.00 20.00
UFVRG03 Pau/Parker/Jeff/Tinsley 6.00 15.00
UFVRG04 Dnlvy/Hayes/Nene/Hslm 6.00 15.00
UFVRG05 Dng/Smth/J-Ho/Hrris 8.00 20.00
UFVSPUR San Antonio Spurs 10.00 25.00
UFVSUNS Phoenix Suns 10.00 25.00
UFVUDEX LJ/Kobe/KG/Drnt 60.00 150.00

2008-09 Ultimate Collection Jerseys Six

STATED PRINT RUN 35 SER.#'d SETS
US05AS Rckts/Spurs/Heat/Magic 10.00 25.00
US06AS Celt/Sun/Cav/Pistn/Wiz 12.00 30.00
US76ER Philadelphia 76ers 10.00 25.00
USBLAZ Portland Trail Blazers 20.00 40.00
USBULL Chicago Bulls 40.00 100.00
USCAVS Cleveland Cavaliers 40.00 80.00
USCELT Boston Celtics 40.00 80.00
USCLIP Los Angeles Clippers 10.00 25.00
USDNUG Denver Nuggets 10.00 25.00
USGSWR Goldein State Warriors 10.00 25.00
USHAWK Atlanta Hawks 10.00 25.00
USHEAT Miami Heat 12.00 30.00
USJAZZ Utah Jazz 30.00 50.00
USLSHO Los Angeles Lakers 40.00 80.00
USNETS New Jersey Nets 15.00 30.00
USNICK New York Knicks 15.00 30.00
USPSTN Detroit Pistons 15.00 30.00
USROCK Houston Rockets 15.00 30.00
USSPUR San Antonio Spurs 15.00 30.00
USSUNS Phoenix Suns 15.00 30.00

2008-09 Ultimate Collection Jerseys Ten

STATED PRINT RUN 15 SER.#'d SETS
UNPRICED PATCH PRINT RUN 3 SER.#'d SETS
UTAH Utah Jazz 25.00 60.00
PHILY Philadelphia 76ers 40.00 80.00
SPURS San Antonio Spurs 75.00 150.00
08ROOKIE 2008-09 Rookies 25.00 60.00
BOSTON Boston Celtics 75.00 150.00
LAKERS Los Angeles Lakers 75.00 150.00
CHICAGO Chicago Bulls 60.00 150.00
DETROIT Detroit Pistons 50.00 100.00
NEW YORK New York Knicks 40.00 80.00
ROOKIE08 2008-09 Rookies 2 50.00 100.00

2008-09 Ultimate Collection Legendary Signatures

STATED PRINT RUN 10 SER.#'d SETS
LSAD Adrian Dantley 15.00 30.00
LSAG Artis Gilmore 15.00 30.00
LSBA B.J. Armstrong 25.00 50.00
LSBD Brad Daugherty 15.00 30.00
LSBK Bernard King 15.00 40.00
LSBL Bill Laimbeer 15.00 30.00
LSBR Bill Russell 100.00 200.00
LSCD Clyde Drexler 40.00 80.00
LSDW Dominique Wilkins 25.00 50.00
LSGG George Gervin 25.00 50.00
LSHO Hakeem Olajuwon 30.00 80.00
LSJE Julius Erving 75.00 150.00
LSJO Magic Johnson 100.00 200.00
LSKV Kiki Vandeweghe 15.00 30.00
LSLB Larry Bird 100.00 200.00
LSLJ Larry Johnson 100.00 200.00
LSMJ Michael Jordan 2000.00 2500.00
LSMP Mark Price 50.00 120.00
LSRO Dennis Rodman 50.00 120.00
LSRP Robert Parish 50.00 120.00
LSRS Ralph Sampson 15.00 30.00
LSSI Jack Sikma 15.00 30.00
LSSJ Sam Jones 30.00 80.00
LSTC Tom Chambers 15.00 30.00

2008-09 Ultimate Collection Memories

STATED PRINT RUN 10 SER.#'d SETS
UMDF Derek Fisher Draft 225.00 325.00
UMDW D.Wilkins GM7 100.00 200.00
UMJP John Paxson 20.00 50.00
UMJS John Stockton 50.00 100.00
UMJW Jerry West Gold Med 225.00 325.00
UMKG Kevin Garnett 75.00 150.00
UMMJ M.Johnson AS MVP 300.00 600.00

2008-09 Ultimate Collection Patches Foursome Veterans

*PATCHES: 1X TO 2.5X BASE HI
PATCH PRINT RUN 20 SER.#'d SETS
UFVAS05 Kobe/Nash/LBJ/T-Mac 125.00 300.00

2008-09 Ultimate Collection Patches Six

STATED PRINT RUN 10 SER.#'d SETS
US05AS Mrn/Mnu/Dunc/Stat/Yao 60.00 120.00
US76ER Philadelphia 76ers 40.00 80.00
USBLAZ Portland Trail Blazers 50.00 100.00
USBULL Chicago Bulls 100.00 200.00
USCAVS Cleveland Cavaliers 80.00 160.00
USCELT Boston Celtics 100.00 200.00
USCLIP Los Angeles Clippers 20.00 40.00
USGSWR Golden State Warriors 20.00 40.00
USHAWK Atlanta Hawks 40.00 80.00
USHEAT Miami Heat 60.00 150.00
USJAZZ Utah Jazz 50.00 120.00
USLSHO Los Angeles Lakers 150.00 300.00
USNETS New Jersey Nets 50.00 100.00
USNICK New York Nets 75.00 150.00
USPSTN Detroit Pistons 60.00 120.00
USROCK Houston Rockets 60.00 120.00
USSPUR San Antonio Spurs 75.00 150.00

2008-09 Ultimate Collection Prototypical Portraits

STATED PRINT RUN 25 SER.#'d SETS
PPBL Bill Laimbeer 10.00 25.00
PPBM Bob McAdoo 20.00 40.00
PPCD Chris Douglas-Roberts 10.00 25.00
PPCK Chris Kaman 10.00 25.00
PPCM Corey Maggette 10.00 25.00
PPDF Derek Fisher 15.00 30.00
PPDJ DeAndre Jordan 20.00 50.00
PPDR Dennis Rodman 25.00 60.00
PPFE Rudy Fernandez 10.00 25.00
PPJD Joey Dorsey 10.00 25.00
PPJK Jason Kidd 25.00 50.00
PPJS Jack Sikma 10.00 25.00
PPLJ LeBron James 200.00 400.00
PPMJ Michael Jordan 600.00 900.00
PPRF Raymond Felton 10.00 25.00
PPRS Ramon Sessions 12.00 30.00
PPSA Ralph Sampson 12.00 30.00
PPTC Tom Chambers 10.00 25.00

2008-09 Ultimate Collection Signature Materials Combos

STATED PRINT RUN 10 SER.#'d SETS
UNPRICED PATCH PRINT RUN 5 SER.#'d SETS
UMCBJ L.James/K.Bryant 500.00 800.00
UMCBR M.Beasley/D.Rose 150.00 300.00
UMCFM O.Mayo/R.Fernandez 60.00 120.00
UMCGL K.Love/K.Garnett 75.00 150.00
UMCHH A.Horford/D.Howard 40.00 80.00

2008-09 Ultimate Collection Signature Materials Legends

STATED PRINT RUN 10 SER.#'d SETS
UNPRICED PATCH PRINT RUN 5 SER.#'d SETS
UMLBK Bernard King 30.00 60.00
UMLDR David Robinson 60.00 120.00
UMLGG George Gervin 30.00 60.00
UMLIT Isiah Thomas 40.00 80.00
UMLLB Larry Bird 75.00 150.00
UMLMJ Michael Jordan 500.00 650.00
UMLSK Steve Kerr 30.00 60.00

2008-09 Ultimate Collection Signature Materials Rookies

STATED PRINT RUN 25 SER.#'d SETS
UNPRICED PATCH PRINT RUN 5 SER.#'d SETS
UMRCD Chris Douglas-Roberts 5.00 12.00
UMRDA Darrell Arthur 6.00 15.00
UMRDJ DeAndre Jordan 10.00 25.00
UMRDR Derrick Rose 250.00 500.00
UMRGH George Hill 25.00 50.00
UMRJA Joe Alexander 5.00 12.00
UMRJB Jerryd Bayless 25.00 50.00
UMRJD Joey Dorsey 5.00 12.00
UMRJG J.R. Giddens 5.00 12.00
UMRJM Javale McGee 10.00 25.00
UMRKK Kosta Koufos 6.00 15.00
UMRKL Kevin Love 50.00 125.00
UMRMB Michael Beasley 8.00 20.00
UMROM O.J. Mayo 25.00 60.00
UMRRA Ryan Anderson 6.00 15.00
UMRRF Rudy Fernandez 6.00 15.00
UMRWS Walter Sharpe 5.00 12.00

2008-09 Ultimate Collection Signature Materials Veterans

STATED PRINT RUN 10 SER.#'d SETS
UNPRICED PATCH PRINT RUN 5 SER.#'d SETS
UMVAM Alonzo Mourning 75.00 150.00
UMVAS Amare Stoudemire 25.00 50.00
UMVBD Baron Davis 15.00 30.00
UMVJJ Jarrett Jack 15.00 30.00
UMVJO Jermaine O'Neal 15.00 30.00
UMVKB Kobe Bryant 300.00 400.00
UMVKG Kevin Garnett 100.00 200.00
UMVMB Mike Bibby 15.00 30.00
UMVYM Yao Ming 25.00 60.00

2008-09 Ultimate Collection Signatures

STATED PRINT RUN 23 TO 25 SER.#'d SETS
UNPRICED OCTO PRINT RUN 4 SER.#'d SETS
UNPRICED QUAD PRINT RUN 8 SER.#'d SETS
UNPRICED SIX PRINT RUN 6 SER.#'d SETS
UAB Aaron Brooks/25 6.00 15.00
UAT Al Thornton/25 6.00 15.00
UBB Bobby Brown/25 6.00 15.00
UBO Josh Boone/25 6.00 15.00
UBR Brandon Roy/25 15.00 30.00
UCB Corey Brewer/25 6.00 15.00
UCL Carl Landry/25 10.00 25.00
UDC Daequan Cook/25 6.00 15.00
UDF Derek Fisher/25 12.00 30.00
UDW Deron Williams/25 20.00 40.00
UEC Eddy Curry/25 6.00 15.00
UGD Glen Davis/25 8.00 20.00
UJB Jose Barea/25 25.00 60.00
UJF Jordan Farmar/25 6.00 15.00
UJG Jeff Green/25 10.00 25.00
UJN Joakim Noah/25 15.00 30.00
UJW Julian Wright/25 6.00 15.00
UKG Kevin Garnett/25 50.00 100.00
ULJ LeBron James/23 125.00 250.00
ULO Lamar Odom/25 8.00 20.00
UMC Mike Conley Jr./25 6.00 15.00
URR Rajon Rondo/25 10.00 25.00
URS Rodney Stuckey/25 6.00 15.00

2008-09 Ultimate Collection Signatures Dual

STATED PRINT RUN 25 SER.#'d SETS
SD76 A.Iguodala/A.Miller 10.00 25.00
SDAH M.Bibby/A.Horford 15.00 30.00
SDBC P.Pierce/K.Garnett 75.00 150.00
SDCB R.Felton/S.Singletary 10.00 25.00
SDCC L.James/M.Williams 125.00 300.00
SDCH J.Noah/T.Thomas 15.00 30.00
SDDM J.Barea/J.Kidd 30.00 80.00
SDDN C.Anthony/J.Smith 40.00 80.00
SDDP R.Stuckey/T.Prince 10.00 25.00
SDGS M.Belinelli/C.Maggette 10.00 25.00
SDHR J.Dorsey/C.Landry 10.00 25.00
SDIP T.Ford/D.Granger 10.00 25.00
SDLA D.Fisher/J.Farmar 20.00 40.00
SDLC A.Thornton/D.Jordan 12.00 30.00
SDMB R.Sessions/R.Jefferson 10.00 25.00
SDMG M.Conley/R.Gay 10.00 25.00
SDMH D.Cook/S.Livingston 10.00 25.00
SDMT R.Foye/C.Brewer 10.00 25.00
SDNJ J.Boone/R.Anderson 10.00 25.00
SDNO D.West/J.Wright 10.00 25.00
SDNY W.Chandler/Richardson 10.00 25.00
SDOC J.Green/K.Durant 40.00 100.00
SDOM C.Lee/D.Howard 30.00 80.00
SDPS J.Dudley/R.Lopez 10.00 25.00
SDSA B.Bowen/T.Parker 20.00 50.00
SDTB L.Aldridge/B.Roy 25.00 50.00
SDUJ D.Williams/C.Boozer 15.00 30.00

2008-09 Ultimate Collection Signatures Rookie

STATED PRINT RUN 25 SER.#'d SETS
URAR Anthony Randolph 5.00 12.00
URBR Brandon Rush 6.00 15.00
URCD Chris Douglas-Roberts 5.00 12.00
URDA D.J. Augustin 6.00 15.00
URDG Danilo Gallinari 12.00 30.00
URDR Derrick Rose 200.00 400.00
UREG Eric Gordon 20.00 50.00
URGH George Hill 20.00 40.00
URGR Donte Greene 5.00 12.00
URJA Joe Alexander 5.00 12.00
URJB Jerryd Bayless 6.00 15.00
URJJ J.J. Hickson 6.00 15.00
URKL Kevin Love 25.00 60.00
URMB Michael Beasley 8.00 20.00
URMC Mario Chalmers 8.00 20.00
URMS Marreese Speights 6.00 15.00
UROM O.J. Mayo 25.00 60.00
URRF Rudy Fernandez 6.00 15.00
URRW Russell Westbrook 75.00 150.00

2008-09 Ultimate Collection Signatures Triple

STATED PRINT RUN 10 SER.#'d SETS
STBOS Giddens/Allen/Rondo 25.00 50.00
STCAV Daughrty/LeBron/Hcksn 125.00 250.00
STCHI Rose/Grdn/Armstrng 100.00 225.00
STHOU Lndry/Drsy/Bttr 20.00 40.00
STLAL Frmr/Odm/Coopr 30.00 60.00
STMIA Cook/Beasley/Zo 75.00 150.00
STMIN Love/BigAl/Brwr 30.00 60.00
STNJN CarterWilliams/Lopez 40.00 80.00
STNYK Q-Rich/Gallinari/Rich 20.00 40.00
STPTB Roy/Drexler/Bylss 50.00 100.00
STSAS Hill/Prkr/Gervin 40.00 80.00
STUTA Dantley/Boozer/Koufos 20.00 40.00

2008-09 Ultimate Collection Validation

STATED PRINT RUN 25 SER.#'d SETS
VAI Andre Iguodala 6.00 15.00
VAM Alonzo Mourning 50.00 100.00
VBK Bernard King 10.00 25.00
VCB Carlos Boozer 10.00 25.00
VCD Chris Duhon 6.00 15.00
VCL Carl Landry 20.00 40.00
VGW Gerald Wallace 8.00 20.00
VMR Micheal Ray Richardson 6.00 15.00
VPW Paul Westphal 6.00 15.00
VRR Rajon Rondo 12.00 30.00
VRS Ramon Sessions 10.00 25.00
VSK Steve Kerr 10.00 25.00
VSV Sasha Vujacic 10.00 25.00
VSW Spud Webb 10.00 25.00

2010-11 Ultimate Collection

COMP.SET w/o AUs (60) 20.00 50.00
AU PRINT RUN 99 SER.#'d SETS
1 Michael Jordan 6.00 15.00
2 James Harden 1.25 3.00
3 Bill Russell 1.25 3.00
4 Larry Bird 2.00 5.00
5 Magic Johnson 2.00 5.00
6 Jerry West 1.00 2.50
7 Hakeem Olajuwon 1.00 2.50
8 David Robinson 1.25 3.00
9 Dennis Rodman 1.50 4.00
10 Rick Fox .60 1.50
11 LeBron James 3.00 8.00
12 Julius Erving 1.25 3.00
13 Roy Williams .75 2.00
14 Clyde Drexler 1.00 2.50
15 George Gervin .75 2.00
16 Dominique Wilkins 1.00 2.50
17 Tracy McGrady .75 2.00
18 Hal Greer .60 1.50
19 Cazzie Russell .60 1.50
20 George Lynch .75 2.00
21 Alonzo Mourning 1.00 2.50
22 Adrian Dantley .60 1.50
23 John Stockton 1.25 3.00
24 Tim Hardaway .75 2.00
25 James Worthy 1.00 2.50
26 Rudy Tomjanovich .60 1.50
27 Gail Goodrich .60 1.50
28 Jack Sikma .60 1.50
29 Hubert Davis .50 1.25
30 David Thompson .60 1.50
31 Bill Walton .75 2.00
32 Sam Cassell .60 1.50
33 Walter Davis .50 1.25
34 Jerry Sloan .75 2.00
35 Yao Ming 1.00 2.50
36 Bill Laimbeer .60 1.50
37 Glen Rice .60 1.50
38 Anfernee Hardaway 2.00 5.00
39 B.J. Armstrong .75 2.00
40 Robert Horry .75 2.00
41 Mike Krzyzewski 1.00 2.50
42 Michael Cooper .60 1.50
43 Elgin Baylor .75 2.00
44 Tom Izzo 1.00 2.50
45 Brandon Roy .75 2.00
46 Christian Laettner .60 1.50
47 Larry Johnson 1.00 2.50
48 Mark Jackson .60 1.50
49 Ricky Rubio .75 2.00
50 Darrell Griffith .50 1.25
51 John Calipari .75 2.00
52 Sam Perkins .50 1.25
53 Bobby Hurley .75 2.00
54 Mateen Cleaves .50 1.25
55 Derrick Rose 1.00 2.50
56 Steve Alford .75 2.00
57 Kenny Smith .60 1.50
58 Avery Johnson .60 1.50
59 Danny Manning .60 1.50
60 Calbert Cheaney .75 2.00
61 Paul George AU 40.00 100.00
62 Deon Thompson AU 8.00 20.00
63 Derrick Favors AU 8.00 20.00
64 DeMarcus Cousins AU 15.00 40.00
65 Jordan Crawford AU 5.00 12.00
66 Cole Aldrich AU 5.00 12.00
67 Ed Davis AU 8.00 20.00
68 Al-Farouq Aminu AU 6.00 15.00
69 Greg Monroe AU 8.00 20.00
70 Ekpe Udoh AU 4.00 10.00
71 Daniel Orton AU 4.00 10.00
72 Gani Lawal AU 4.00 10.00
73 Hassan Whiteside AU 12.00 30.00
74 Xavier Henry AU 10.00 25.00
75 James Anderson AU 8.00 20.00
76 Eric Bledsoe AU 8.00 20.00
77 Damion James AU 4.00 10.00
78 Solomon Alabi AU 4.00 10.00
79 Gordon Hayward AU 10.00 25.00
80 Quincy Pondexter AU 4.00 10.00
81 Patrick Patterson AU 10.00 25.00

2010-11 Ultimate Collection 1997 Legends Autographs

RANDOM INSERTS IN PACKS
AL1 Michael Jordan 400.00 750.00
AL2 LeBron James 175.00 300.00
AL3 Magic Johnson 125.00 250.00
AL4 Larry Bird 50.00 150.00
AL5 Julius Erving 50.00 100.00
AL6 Yao Ming 15.00 40.00
AL7 Brandon Roy 5.00 12.00
AL8 Derrick Rose 40.00 100.00
AL9 Tracy McGrady 30.00 80.00
AL11 Gail Goodrich 5.00 12.00
AL12 Dominique Wilkins 15.00 40.00
AL13 George Gervin 5.00 12.00
AL15 David Robinson 40.00 100.00
AL16 Alonzo Mourning 25.00 60.00
AL17 Bill Walton 5.00 12.00
AL18 Mark Jackson 5.00 12.00
AL19 Bobby Hurley 5.00 12.00
AL20 Jerry West 30.00 60.00
AL21 Christian Laettner 6.00 15.00

2010-11 Ultimate Collection All-Time Draft Signatures Gold

STATED PRINT RUN 25 TO 75 SER.#'d SETS
UNPRICED SILVER PRINT RUN 5 SETS
1 Michael Jordan/25 400.00 700.00
2 LeBron James/25 175.00 350.00
3 Bill Russell/25 50.00 120.00
4 Julius Erving/25 40.00 100.00
5 Magic Johnson/25 40.00 100.00
6 Jerry West/25 25.00 60.00
7 Larry Bird/25 50.00 100.00
8 Chris Mullin/25 15.00 40.00
9 Bill Walton/75 10.00 25.00
10 Bob Lanier/25 10.00 25.00
11 David Robinson/25 25.00 60.00
12 Elgin Baylor/75 8.00 20.00
13 George Gervin/25 12.00 30.00
14 Hakeem Olajuwon/25 20.00 50.00
15 Moses Malone/75 8.00 20.00
16 Yao Ming/25 15.00 40.00
17 Alonzo Mourning/25 30.00 80.00
18 Bobby Hurley/75 6.00 15.00
19 Bill Sharman/75 6.00 15.00
20 Calbert Cheaney/75 6.00 15.00
21 Christian Laettner/75 10.00 25.00
22 Cazzie Russell/75 6.00 15.00
23 Derrick Rose/75 30.00 80.00
24 Danny Ferry/75 6.00 15.00
25 Darrell Griffith/75 6.00 15.00
26 Danny Manning/75 8.00 20.00
27 David Thompson/75 6.00 15.00
28 Gail Goodrich/75 6.00 15.00
29 Hal Greer/75 6.00 15.00
30 Lennie Rosenbluth/75 12.00 30.00
31 Mateen Cleaves/75 6.00 15.00
32 Phil Ford/75 8.00 20.00
33 Brandon Roy/75 8.00 20.00
35 Steve Alford/75 6.00 15.00
36 Tim Hardaway/75 6.00 15.00
37 Tracy McGrady/75 10.00 25.00
38 Adrian Dantley/75 6.00 15.00

2010-11 Ultimate Collection All-Time Team Signatures Gold

STATED PRINT RUN 23 TO 25 SER.#'d SETS
UNPRICED SILVER PRINT RUN 5SETS
ATAH Anfernee Hardaway/25 25.00 60.00
ATAM Alonzo Mourning/25 30.00 80.00
ATBR Brandon Roy/25 8.00 20.00
ATBW Bill Walton/25 10.00 25.00
ATCC Calbert Cheaney/25 8.00 20.00
ATCL Christian Laettner/25 25.00 60.00
ATDF Danny Ferry/25 8.00 20.00
ATDR Derrick Rose/25 30.00 80.00
ATHO Hakeem Olajuwon/25 20.00 50.00
ATKS Kenny Smith/25 12.00 30.00
ATLB Larry Bird/25 50.00 120.00
ATLJ Larry Johnson/25 30.00 80.00
ATMC Mateen Cleaves/25 8.00 20.00
ATMJ Michael Jordan/23 400.00 700.00
ATRO David Robinson/25 20.00 50.00
ATRU Bill Russell/25 50.00 100.00
ATSA Steve Alford/25 8.00 20.00

2010-11 Ultimate Collection Base Autographs

STATED PRINT RUN 25 TO 99 SER.#'d SETS
1 Michael Jordan/25 300.00 600.00
2 James Harden/99 40.00 100.00
3 Bill Russell/25 75.00 150.00
4 Larry Bird/25 50.00 100.00
5 Magic Johnson/25 40.00 100.00
6 Jerry West/25 30.00 80.00
7 Hakeem Olajuwon/75 15.00 40.00
8 David Robinson/75 12.00 30.00
9 Dennis Rodman/75 15.00 40.00
10 Rick Fox/99 10.00 25.00
11 LeBron James/25 150.00 300.00
14 Clyde Drexler/25 20.00 50.00
15 George Gervin/99 6.00 15.00
16 Dominique Wilkins/25 8.00 20.00
17 Tracy McGrady/25 15.00 40.00
18 Hal Greer/75 4.00 10.00
19 Cazzie Russell/25 6.00 15.00
20 George Lynch/75 6.00 15.00
21 Alonzo Mourning/25 30.00 80.00
22 Adrian Dantley/99 6.00 15.00
24 Tim Hardaway/99 6.00 15.00
25 James Worthy/75 15.00 40.00
26 Rudy Tomjanovich/99 6.00 15.00
27 Gail Goodrich/75 4.00 10.00
28 Jack Sikma/75 4.00 10.00
29 Hubert Davis/75 6.00 15.00
30 David Thompson/99 4.00 10.00
31 Bill Walton/99 6.00 15.00
32 Sam Cassell/99 6.00 15.00
33 Walter Davis/75 8.00 20.00
34 Jerry Sloan/99 6.00 15.00
35 Yao Ming/75 15.00 40.00
36 Bill Laimbeer/75 6.00 15.00
37 Glen Rice/75 6.00 15.00
38 Anfernee Hardaway/99 30.00 80.00
39 B.J. Armstrong/99 4.00 10.00
40 Robert Horry/75 6.00 15.00
42 Michael Cooper/75 4.00 10.00
43 Elgin Baylor/75 6.00 15.00
45 Brandon Roy/99 8.00 20.00
46 Christian Laettner/75 10.00 25.00
47 Larry Johnson/25 30.00 80.00
48 Mark Jackson/99 4.00 10.00
49 Ricky Rubio/75 20.00 50.00
50 Darrell Griffith/99 4.00 10.00
52 Sam Perkins/75 6.00 15.00
53 Bobby Hurley/75 6.00 15.00
54 Mateen Cleaves/99 4.00 10.00
55 Derrick Rose/99 15.00 40.00
56 Steve Alford/99 4.00 10.00
57 Kenny Smith/99 6.00 15.00
58 Avery Johnson/99 6.00 15.00
59 Danny Manning/75 6.00 15.00
60 Calbert Cheaney/75 6.00 15.00

2010-11 Ultimate Collection Big Game Signatures Gold

STATED PRINT RUN 23 TO 75 SER.#'d SETS
SILVER UNPRICED SILVER PRINT RUN 5 SETS
BGAJ Avery Johnson/75 4.00 10.00
BGAL Al-Farouq Aminu/75 6.00 15.00
BGAW Al Wood/75 10.00 25.00
BGBH Bobby Hurley/75 6.00 15.00
BGBR Bill Russell/25 50.00 120.00
BGBW Bill Walton/75 8.00 20.00
BGCL Christian Laettner/75 20.00 50.00
BGCS Charlie Scott/75 10.00 25.00
BGDF Derrick Favors/75 12.00 30.00
BGDG Darrell Griffith/75 4.00 10.00
BGDM Danny Manning/75 8.00 20.00
BGDR Derrick Rose/75 30.00 80.00
BGDT David Thompson/75 4.00 10.00
BGEB Elgin Baylor/75 8.00 20.00
BGGR Glen Rice/75 6.00 15.00
BGHO Hakeem Olajuwon/25 15.00 40.00
BGJE Julius Erving/25 30.00 80.00
BGJH James Harden/25 60.00 150.00
BGJO Magic Johnson/25 40.00 100.00
BGJW James Worthy/25 40.00 100.00
BGLB Larry Bird/25 50.00 100.00
BGMC Mateen Cleaves/75 6.00 15.00
BGMJ Michael Jordan/23 400.00 700.00
BGRO Brandon Roy/75 8.00 20.00
BGSA Steve Alford/75 8.00 20.00
BGWD Walter Davis/75 6.00 15.00
BGWE Jerry West/75 25.00 60.00
BGYM Yao Ming/75 12.00 30.00

2010-11 Ultimate Collection College Shout Out Signatures

STATED PRINT RUN 25 TO 35 SER.#'d SETS
SOBA B.J. Armstrong/35 12.00 30.00
SOBL Bill Laimbeer/35 6.00 15.00
SOBR Brandon Roy/35 10.00 25.00
SOBW Bill Walton/35 12.00 30.00
SOCL Christian Laettner/35 12.00 30.00
SOCP Candace Parker/35 30.00 80.00
SODM Danny Manning/35 25.00 60.00
SODR Derrick Rose/35 50.00 120.00
SOJE Julius Erving/35 40.00 100.00
SOJR J.R. Reid/35 15.00 40.00
SOJW James Worthy/35 25.00 60.00
SOLB Larry Bird/35 50.00 120.00
SOLJ Larry Johnson/35 12.00 30.00
SOMC Mateen Cleaves/35 6.00 15.00
SOMJ Michael Jordan/35 350.00 600.00
SOPW Paul Westphal/25 10.00 25.00
SORF Rick Fox/35 12.00 30.00
SOTM Tracy McGrady/35 12.00 30.00

2010-11 Ultimate Collection Personal Touch Hero Autographs

STATED PRINT RUN 25 SER.#'d SETS
HAH Anfernee Hardaway 20.00 50.00
HAM Alonzo Mourning 25.00 60.00
HBR Brandon Roy 8.00 20.00
HCD Clyde Drexler 25.00 60.00
HCL Christian Laettner 25.00 60.00
HDR David Robinson 25.00 60.00
HDW Dominique Wilkins 20.00 50.00
HFA Derrick Favors 10.00 25.00
HHO Hakeem Olajuwon/25 25.00 60.00
HJE Julius Erving 40.00 80.00
HJR J.R. Reid 5.00 12.00
HLB Larry Brown 20.00 50.00
HLJ LeBron James 200.00 400.00
HMA Mark Jackson 6.00 15.00
HMJ Magic Johnson 50.00 125.00
HPP Patrick Patterson 6.00 15.00
HPR Pat Riley 20.00 50.00
HPW Paul Westphal 8.00 20.00
HRF Rick Fox 6.00 15.00
HRH Robert Horry 10.00 25.00
HRR Ricky Rubio 30.00 80.00
HRT Rudy Tomjanovich 8.00 20.00
HSL Jerry Sloan 10.00 25.00
HTM Tracy McGrady 15.00 40.00
HYM Yao Ming 40.00 100.00

2010-11 Ultimate Collection Personal Touch Movie Autographs

STATED PRINT RUN 25 SER.#'d SETS
MAF Al-Farouq Aminu 8.00 20.00
MAH Anfernee Hardaway 50.00 120.00
MAM Alonzo Mourning 15.00 40.00
MBR Brandon Roy 8.00 20.00
MBW Bill Walton 10.00 25.00
MCL Christian Laettner 30.00 60.00

MDO Donald Williams 5.00 12.00
MDR Derrick Rose 30.00 80.00
MDW Dominique Wilkins 20.00 50.00
MED Ed Davis 5.00 12.00
MFA Derrick Favors 10.00 25.00
MGL George Lynch 8.00 20.00
MJC Jordan Crawford 6.00 15.00
MJE Julius Erving 40.00 100.00
MJR J.R. Reid 5.00 12.00
MKS Kenny Smith 15.00 40.00
MLJ LeBron James 200.00 400.00
MMJ Magic Johnson 50.00 120.00
MRH Robert Horry 40.00 100.00
MRO David Robinson 50.00 100.00
MRR Ricky Rubio 30.00 80.00
MRT Rudy Tomjanovich 10.00 25.00
MTM Tracy McGrady 15.00 40.00
MYM Yao Ming 40.00 100.00

2010-11 Ultimate Collection Rivalries Signatures

STATED PRINT RUN 25 SER.#'d SETS
RAS S.Alford/K.Smith 10.00 25.00
RBJ M.Johnson/L.Bird 100.00 200.00
RCR C.Cheaney/G.Rice 20.00 40.00
RFA D.Favors/A.Aminu 30.00 80.00
RFJ W.Frazier/L.James 125.00 300.00
RHH A.Hardaway/T.Hard 50.00 120.00
RHW B.Hurley/D.Williams 10.00 25.00
RJB M.Jordan/L.Bird 400.00 800.00
RJE M.Jordan/J.Erving 400.00 800.00
RJG M.Jackson/D.Griffith 10.00 25.00
RJR M.Jordan/Russell 450.00 750.00
RJU D.James/E.Udoh 15.00 30.00
RLD C.Laettner/E.Davis 15.00 40.00
RLJ C.Laettner/L.Johnson 30.00 80.00
RMJ L.James/T.McGrady 100.00 200.00
RRC M.Cleaves/G.Rice 30.00 80.00
RRM D.Manning/D.Rose 50.00 120.00
RRR B.Roy/D.Rose 40.00 80.00
RTW D.Thompson/B.Walton 20.00 40.00
RWG P.Westphal/G.Goodrich 15.00 40.00

2010-11 Ultimate Collection Signatures

STATED PRINT RUN 23 TO 99 SER.#'d SETS
SAF Al-Farouq Aminu/99 6.00 15.00
SAH Anfernee Hardaway/99 12.00 30.00
SAM Alonzo Mourning/99 12.00 30.00
SBL Bob Lanier/99 6.00 15.00
SBR Brandon Roy/99 6.00 15.00
SCL Christian Laettner/99 10.00 25.00
SDC DeMarcus Cousins/99 15.00 40.00
SDF Derrick Favors/99 8.00 20.00
SDR Derrick Rose/99 15.00 40.00
SDW Dominique Wilkins/99 10.00 25.00
SFL Freddie Lewis/99 5.00 12.00
SGL George Lynch/99 6.00 15.00
SGO Gail Goodrich/99 5.00 12.00
SHW Hassan Whiteside/99 15.00 40.00
SJA James Anderson/99 4.00 10.00
SJC Jordan Crawford/99 5.00 12.00
SJE Julius Erving/25 40.00 80.00
SLA Larry Johnson/99 10.00 25.00
SLB Larry Bird/25 50.00 100.00
SLJ LeBron James/23 200.00 400.00
SMA Mark Jackson/99 5.00 12.00
SMJ Michael Jordan/23 400.00 700.00
SMM Moses Malone/99 10.00 25.00
SRF Rick Fox/25 15.00 40.00
SRR Ricky Rubio/99 15.00 40.00
STH Tim Hardaway/99 6.00 15.00
STM Tracy McGrady/99 10.00 25.00
SXH Xavier Henry/99 4.00 10.00
SYM Yao Ming/99 20.00 50.00

2010-11 Ultimate Collection Signatures Dual

STATED PRINT RUN 10 TO 50 SER.#'d SETS
SOME UNPRICED DUE TO SCARCITY
DBJ M.Jordan/L.Bird/25 350.00 600.00
DBM L.Bird/C.Mullin/25 60.00 150.00
DEM J.Erving/T.McGrady/50 40.00 80.00
DHH A.Hardaway/T.Hard/50 20.00 50.00
DJB M.Johnson/L.Bird/25 150.00 300.00
DJR Jordan/Russell/25 400.00 700.00
DKD B.Knight/B.Donovan/50 30.00 60.00
DKJ S.Kemp/L.Johnson/50 50.00 100.00
DLD L.James/Rose/23 200.00 400.00
DMH T.Hard/A.Mourning/50 25.00 60.00
DMJ L.Johnson/Mourning/50 30.00 60.00
DML F.Lewis/C.Mullin/50 10.00 25.00
DOB D.Orton/E.Bledsoe/50 12.00 30.00
DOM Olajuwon/Ming/50 30.00 80.00
DOR D.Rob/Olajuwon/50 30.00 80.00
DPP D.Cousins/Patterson/50 25.00 60.00
DRJ L.James/R.Rubio/25 175.00 350.00
DRR B.Roy/D.Rose/50 15.00 40.00

2010-11 Ultimate Collection Signatures Quad

STATED PRINT RUN 15 SER.#'d SETS
UNC Perk/Ford/Lynch/Mont 40.00 100.00
1987 Rbnsn/Smith/Jksn/Dnvn 75.00 150.00
1993 Lynch/Hard/Cassell/Chny 50.00 120.00
2010 Davis/Hay/Fav/Cousins 40.00 100.00
9192 Laettner/Mourning/LJ/Davis 50.00 120.00
09HOF Jordan/Rob/Stock/Sloan 600.00 1000.00
JHRR James/Hard/Rubio/Rose 250.00 500.00
JJJB Erving/James/Johnson/Bird 300.00 600.00
JREA Jordan/Russell/Erving/Bird 600.00 1000.00
ROCK Ming/Olaj/McG/Smith 75.00 150.00
RRBE Roy/Rose/Bird/Erving 175.00 350.00
RRRM Rose/Rubio/McG/Roy 150.00 300.00
TSRS Tomj/Sloan/Riley/Shrmn 40.00 100.00

2010-11 Ultimate Collection Signatures Triple

STATED PRINT RUN 25 SER.#'d SETS
TDET Laimbeer/Dantley/Rod 25.00 60.00
TEML Lewis/Erving/Malone 50.00 100.00
THOU Drex/Smith/Olajuwon 50.00 120.00
TJBE Bird/Erving/Johnson 200.00 400.00
TJJJ Jordan/Erving/Johnson 500.00 800.00
TJRB Bird/Russell/James 250.00 400.00
TJRR Rose/James/Roy 150.00 300.00
TLAL Good/Johnson/West 75.00 200.00
TLCH Cheaney/Hurley/Lynch 15.00 40.00
TMHL Lynch/Hardaway/McG 40.00 100.00
TNYK Frazier/Jack/Johnson 60.00 150.00
TSAS Johnson/Rob/Wilkins 40.00 100.00
TUOM Rice/Tomj/Russell 20.00 50.00

2010-11 Ultimate Collection Ultimate Inscriptions

STATED PRINT RUN 25 SER.#'d SETS
NAH Anfernee Hardaway 75.00 200.00
NBR Brandon Roy 15.00 40.00
NBW Bill Walton 15.00 30.00
NCD Clyde Drexler 40.00 100.00
NDR Derrick Rose 75.00 200.00
NDT David Thompson 10.00 25.00
NHO Hakeem Olajuwon 25.00 60.00
NJA LeBron James 200.00 400.00
NJE Julius Erving 40.00 80.00
NJS Jerry Sloan 10.00 25.00
NLJ Larry Johnson 20.00 50.00
NMA Mark Jackson 5.00 12.00
NSP Sam Perkins 20.00 40.00
NYM Yao Ming 150.00 300.00

2013-14 Ultimate Collection Ultimate Legendary Booklets Signatures

OVERALL ULTIMATE ODDS 1:96 HOBBY
PRINT RUNS B/WN 10-60 COPIES PER
NO PRICING ON QTY 10
ISSUED IN 13-14 SP AUTHENTIC
EXCHANGE DEADLINE 3/13/2016
USCW Corliss Williamson/60 6.00 15.00
USDM Donyell Marshall/60 4.00 10.00
USEJ Eddie Jones/60 EXCH 10.00 25.00
USGR Glenn Robinson/60 10.00 25.00
USJL Jerry Lucas/60 6.00 15.00
USJS Joe Smith/60 15.00 40.00
USJW Jay Williams/60 4.00 10.00
USKA Kenny Anderson/60 6.00 15.00
USKK Kerry Kittles/60 4.00 10.00
USKM Karl Malone/60
USKS Keith Smart/60 10.00 25.00
USLJ LeBron James/60 150.00 300.00
USRI Glen Rice/60 6.00 15.00
USSP Sam Perkins/60 6.00 15.00

2013-14 Ultimate Collection Ultimate Rookie Booklets Signatures

OVERALL ULTIMATE ODDS 1:96 HOBBY
PRINT RUNS B/WN 150-250 COPIES PER
ISSUED IN 13-14 SP AUTHENTIC
EXCHANGE DEADLINE 3/13/2016
URS1 G.Antetokounmpo/250 40.00 100.00
URS2 Lucas Nogueira/250 3.00 8.00
URS3 Dennis Schroeder/250 EXCH 5.00 12.00
URS4 Tony Snell/250 4.00 10.00
URS5 Mason Plumlee/250 10.00 25.00
URS6 Solomon Hill/250 3.00 8.00
URS7 Reggie Bullock/250 6.00 15.00
URS8 Andre Roberson/250 3.00 8.00
URS9 Archie Goodwin/250 4.00 10.00
URS10 Skylar Diggins/150 10.00 25.00
URS11 Shane Larkin/150 3.00 8.00
URS12 Tim Hardaway Jr./150 5.00 12.00

1992-93 Ultimate USBL Promo Sheet

The United States Basketball League in conjunction with The Ultimate Trading Card Company released this approximately 7 1/2" by 10 1/2" sheet as a promotion for the planned 1992-93 USBL set. The sheet features nine standard size cards with action color player photos. The upper right corners of the picture appears to be peeled back to reveal The Ultimate Trading Card Company logo. Yellow-orange stripes across the bottom of each photo contain the players' names. The USBL logo overlaps the stripe and photo at the lower right corner. The cards have white borders. The backs display biographies, career highlights, statistics, and a small player photo against a medium gray and white pinstriped background. The card backs are shown on just the two outside columns of cards on the sheet. The center column is printed with promotional information. The players pictured are checklisted below as they appear on the sheet, beginning in the upper left corner and moving toward the lower right.

NNO USBL Promo Sheet 2.00 5.00
Norris Coleman
Dallas Comegys
Kermit Holmes
Anthony Mason
Anthony Pullard
Lloyd Daniels
Michael Anderson
Darrell Armstrong
Roy Tarpley

1999-00 Ultimate Victory

Released in one series as a 150 card set each pack contained five cards and carried a suggested retail price of $2.99. The set breakdown includes 90 regular player cards, 30 MJ's Greatest Hits subset cards (inserted one in two) and 30 Ultimate Rookie cards (inserted one in four).

COMPLETE SET (150) 50.00 100.00
COMP. SET w/o RC (120) 20.00 50.00
MJ HITS SUBSET STATED ODDS 1:2
121-150 SUBSET STATED ODDS 1:4
UNPRICED PARALLEL SERIAL #'d TO 1
1 Dikembe Mutombo .40 1.00
2 Alan Henderson .25 .60
3 LaPhonso Ellis .25 .60
4 Kenny Anderson .30 .75
5 Antoine Walker .40 1.00
6 Paul Pierce .50 1.25
7 Elden Campbell .25 .60
8 Eddie Jones .40 1.00
9 David Wesley .25 .60
10 Michael Jordan 3.00 8.00
11 Kornell David RC .30 .75
12 Toni Kukoc .40 1.00
13 Shawn Kemp .40 1.00
14 Brevin Knight .25 .60
15 Zydrunas Ilgauskas .30 .75
16 Michael Finley .40 1.00
17 Shawn Bradley .25 .60
18 Dirk Nowitzki .75 2.00
19 Antonio McDyess .30 .75
20 Nick Van Exel .30 .75
21 Ron Mercer .30 .75
22 Grant Hill .50 1.25
23 Lindsey Hunter .25 .60
24 Jerry Stackhouse .40 1.00
25 John Starks .30 .75
26 Antawn Jamison .40 1.00
27 Mookie Blaylock .25 .60
28 Hakeem Olajuwon .50 1.25
29 Cuttino Mobley .25 .60
30 Charles Barkley .60 1.50
31 Reggie Miller .40 1.00
32 Rik Smits .40 1.00
33 Jalen Rose .30 .75
34 Maurice Taylor .25 .60
35 Tyrone Nesby RC .30 .75
36 Michael Olowokandi .25 .60
37 Kobe Bryant 1.50 4.00
38 Shaquille O'Neal 1.00 2.50
39 Glen Rice .40 1.00
40 Robert Horry .30 .75
41 Tim Hardaway .40 1.00
42 Alonzo Mourning .50 1.25
43 Jamal Mashburn .30 .75
44 Ray Allen .40 1.00
45 Glenn Robinson .30 .75
46 Robert Traylor .25 .60
47 Kevin Garnett .60 1.50
48 Joe Smith .30 .75
49 Bobby Jackson .25 .60
50 Keith Van Horn .30 .75
51 Stephon Marbury .30 .75
52 Jayson Williams .25 .60
53 Patrick Ewing .50 1.25
54 Allan Houston .30 .75
55 Latrell Sprewell .40 1.00
56 Marcus Camby .30 .75
57 Darrell Armstrong .25 .60
58 Matt Harpring .25 .60
59 Bo Outlaw .25 .60
60 Allen Iverson .75 2.00
61 Theo Ratliff .30 .75
62 Larry Hughes .30 .75
63 Jason Kidd .60 1.50
64 Tom Gugliotta .25 .60
65 Anfernee Hardaway .60 1.50
66 Scottie Pippen .60 1.50
67 Damon Stoudamire .30 .75
68 Brian Grant .25 .60
69 Jason Williams .50 1.25
70 Vlade Divac .40 1.00
71 Chris Webber .40 1.00
72 Tim Duncan .75 2.00
73 Sean Elliott .40 1.00
74 David Robinson .60 1.50
75 Avery Johnson .30 .75
76 Gary Payton .40 1.00
77 Vin Baker .30 .75
78 Brent Barry .30 .75
79 Vince Carter .75 2.00
80 Doug Christie .30 .75
81 Tracy McGrady .60 1.50
82 Karl Malone .50 1.25
83 John Stockton .50 1.25
84 Bryon Russell .25 .60
85 Shareef Abdur-Rahim .30 .75
86 Mike Bibby .40 1.00
87 Felipe Lopez .25 .60
88 Juwan Howard .30 .75
89 Rod Strickland .25 .60
90 Mitch Richmond .40 1.00
121 Elton Brand RC 1.50 4.00
122 Steve Francis RC 1.50 4.00
123 Baron Davis RC 1.50 4.00
124 Lamar Odom RC 1.50 4.00
125 Jonathan Bender RC .60 1.50
126 Wally Szczerbiak RC 1.25 3.00
127 Richard Hamilton RC 1.25 3.00
128 Andre Miller RC 1.25 3.00
129 Shawn Marion RC 1.25 3.00
130 Jason Terry RC 1.00 2.50
131 Trajan Langdon RC .60 1.50
132 A.Radojevic RC .40 1.00
133 Corey Maggette RC 1.00 2.50
134 William Avery RC .50 1.25
135 Ron Artest RC 1.25 3.00
136 Cal Bowdler RC .40 1.00
137 James Posey RC .60 1.50
138 Quincy Lewis RC .40 1.00
139 Dion Glover RC .50 1.25
140 Jeff Foster RC .60 1.50
141 Kenny Thomas RC .60 1.50
142 Devean George RC .60 1.50
143 Tim James RC .40 1.00
144 Vonteego Cummings RC .40 1.00
145 Jumaine Jones RC .50 1.25
146 Scott Padgett RC .50 1.25
147 John Celestand RC .40 1.00
148 Adrian Griffin RC .60 1.50
149 Chris Herren RC .50 1.25
150 Anthony Carter RC .50 1.25

1999-00 Ultimate Victory Victory Collection

COMMON MJ GH (91-120) 2.00 5.00
*STARS: 1.25X TO 3X BASE CARD HI
*RCs: .6X TO 1.5X BASE HI
STARS: STATED ODDS 1:12
RCs: STATED ODDS 1:24

1999-00 Ultimate Victory Parallel 100

COMMON MJ GH (91-120) 25.00 60.00
*STARS: 8X TO 20X BASE CARD HI
*RCs: 2.5X TO 6X BASE HI
STATED PRINT RUN 100 SERIAL #'d SETS
37 Kobe Bryant 75.00 200.00
44 Ray Allen 10.00 25.00

1999-00 Ultimate Victory Court Impact

Randomly inserted in packs at one in 24, this 10-card set contains players who draw the biggest crowds in the league. Card backs carry a "C" prefix.

COMPLETE SET (10) 15.00 40.00
STATED ODDS 1:24
C1 Michael Jordan 10.00 25.00
C2 Vince Carter 2.50 6.00
C3 Kobe Bryant 5.00 12.00
C4 Kevin Garnett 2.00 5.00
C5 Tim Duncan 2.50 6.00
C6 Jason Williams 1.50 4.00
C7 Grant Hill 1.50 4.00
C8 Keith Van Horn 1.00 2.50
C9 Allen Iverson 2.50 6.00
C10 Karl Malone 1.50 4.00

1999-00 Ultimate Victory Dr. J Glory Days

Randomly inserted in packs at one in 24, this eight-card set revisits some of the most memorable moments in NBA history from Dr. J. Card backs carry a "DR" prefix.

COMPLETE SET (8) 12.50 30.00
COMMON CARD (DR1-DR8) 2.00 5.00
STATED ODDS 1:24

1999-00 Ultimate Victory Got Skills?

Randomly inserted in packs at one in 24, this eight-card set highlights the game's flashiest performers. Card backs carry a "GS" prefix.

COMPLETE SET (8) 4.00 10.00
STATED ODDS 1:24
GS1 Kevin Garnett 1.25 3.00
GS2 Tim Hardaway .75 2.00
GS3 Mike Bibby .75 2.00
GS4 Stephon Marbury .60 1.50
GS5 Reggie Miller .75 2.00
GS6 Jason Williams 1.00 2.50
GS7 Antoine Walker .75 2.00
GS8 Jason Kidd 1.25 3.00

1999-00 Ultimate Victory MJ's World Famous

Randomly inserted in packs at one in 24, this 12-card set focuses on some of Jordan's most spectacular feats. Card backs carry a "MJ" prefix.

COMPLETE SET (12) 25.00 50.00
COMMON CARD (MJ1-MJ12) 2.50 6.00
STATED ODDS 1:24

1999-00 Ultimate Victory Scorin' Legion

Randomly inserted in packs at one in 12, this 10-card set features the NBA's top scorers. Card backs carry a "SL" prefix.

COMPLETE SET (10) 4.00 10.00
STATED ODDS 1:12
SL1 Tim Duncan 1.25 3.00
SL2 Karl Malone .75 2.00
SL3 Stephon Marbury .50 1.25
SL4 Shaquille O'Neal 1.50 4.00
SL5 Antonio McDyess .50 1.25
SL6 Gary Payton .60 1.50
SL7 Allen Iverson 1.25 3.00
SL8 Keith Van Horn .50 1.25
SL9 Shareef Abdur-Rahim .50 1.25
SL10 Grant Hill .75 2.00

1999-00 Ultimate Victory Surface to Air

Randomly inserted in packs at one in six, this 12-card set features some of the most dynamic aerial performers. Card backs carry a "SA" prefix.

COMPLETE SET (12) 5.00 12.00
STATED ODDS 1:6
SA1 Vince Carter 1.00 2.50
SA2 Antawn Jamison .50 1.25
SA3 Eddie Jones .50 1.25
SA4 Anfernee Hardaway .75 2.00
SA5 Latrell Sprewell .50 1.25
SA6 Antonio McDyess .40 1.00
SA7 Michael Finley .50 1.25
SA8 Kobe Bryant 2.00 5.00
SA9 Chris Webber .50 1.25
SA10 Shawn Kemp .50 1.25
SA11 Ray Allen .50 1.25
SA12 Shaquille O'Neal 1.25 3.00

1999-00 Ultimate Victory Ultimate Fabrics

Randomly inserted in packs, this three-card set features a swatch of a game-used jersey card. The cards were serially numbered with Erving numbered to 300, Chamberlain to 100, Erving/Kobe to 25 and the special Erving autographed jersey to six.

PRINT RUNS LISTED BELOW
UF1 Julius Erving/300 10.00 25.00
UF2 Wilt Chamberlain/100 200.00 500.00
UF3 J.Erving/K.Bryant/25 125.00 250.00

2000-01 Ultimate Victory

The 2000-01 Upper Deck Ultimate Victory product was released in February, 2001 and features a 120-card base set. The base set was broken into tiers as follows: 60 Base Veterans (1-60), 30 FLY cards featuring Kobe Bryant and Kevin Garnett, and finally 30 Rookie Cards (individually serial numbered to 1500). Each pack contained 5 cards, and carried a suggested retail price of $2.99.

COMP.SET w/o SP (60) 10.00 25.00
FLY2K: STATED ODDS 1:6
RCs: STATED PRINT RUN 1500 SERIAL #'d SETS
1 Dikembe Mutombo .30 .75
2 Jim Jackson .20 .50
3 Paul Pierce .30 .75
4 Antoine Walker .25 .60
5 Jamal Mashburn .25 .60
6 Baron Davis .30 .75
7 Elton Brand .30 .75
8 Ron Artest .30 .75
9 Lamond Murray .20 .50
10 Andre Miller .25 .60
11 Michael Finley .30 .75
12 Dirk Nowitzki .50 1.25
13 Antonio McDyess .25 .60
14 Nick Van Exel .25 .60
15 Jerry Stackhouse .25 .60
16 Chucky Atkins .20 .50
17 Antawn Jamison .30 .75
18 Larry Hughes .25 .60
19 Steve Francis .25 .60
20 Hakeem Olajuwon .40 1.00
21 Reggie Miller .30 .75
22 Jalen Rose .25 .60
23 Lamar Odom .25 .60
24 Corey Maggette .25 .60
25 Shaquille O'Neal .75 2.00
26 Kobe Bryant 1.25 3.00
27 Ron Harper .25 .60
28 Tim Hardaway .30 .75
29 Eddie Jones .30 .75
30 Ray Allen .30 .75
31 Tim Thomas .20 .50
32 Kevin Garnett .50 1.25
33 Wally Szczerbiak .25 .60
34 Terrell Brandon .20 .50
35 Stephon Marbury .25 .60
36 Keith Van Horn .25 .60
37 Allan Houston .25 .60
38 Latrell Sprewell .25 .60
39 Grant Hill .40 1.00
40 Tracy McGrady .50 1.25
41 Allen Iverson .60 1.50
42 Toni Kukoc .30 .75
43 Jason Kidd .50 1.25
44 Anfernee Hardaway .50 1.25
45 Scottie Pippen .50 1.25
46 Rasheed Wallace .30 .75
47 Jason Williams .30 .75
48 Chris Webber .30 .75
49 Tim Duncan .60 1.50
50 David Robinson .50 1.25
51 Gary Payton .30 .75
52 Rashard Lewis .30 .75
53 Vince Carter .60 1.50
54 Mark Jackson .25 .60
55 Karl Malone .40 1.00
56 John Stockton .40 1.00
57 Shareef Abdur-Rahim .25 .60
58 Mike Bibby .30 .75
59 Mitch Richmond .25 .60
60 Richard Hamilton .25 .60
61 Kobe Bryant FLY 1.25 3.00
62 Kobe Bryant FLY 1.25 3.00
63 Kobe Bryant FLY 1.25 3.00
64 Kobe Bryant FLY 1.25 3.00
65 Kobe Bryant FLY 1.25 3.00
66 Kobe Bryant FLY 1.25 3.00
67 Kobe Bryant FLY 1.25 3.00
68 Kobe Bryant FLY 1.25 3.00
69 Kobe Bryant FLY 1.25 3.00
70 Kobe Bryant FLY 1.25 3.00
71 Kobe Bryant FLY 1.25 3.00
72 Kobe Bryant FLY 1.25 3.00
73 Kobe Bryant FLY 1.25 3.00
74 Kobe Bryant FLY 1.25 3.00
75 Kobe Bryant FLY 1.25 3.00
76 Kevin Garnett FLY .75 2.00
77 Kevin Garnett FLY .75 2.00
78 Kevin Garnett FLY .75 2.00
79 Kevin Garnett FLY .75 2.00
80 Kevin Garnett FLY .75 2.00
81 Kevin Garnett FLY .75 2.00
82 Kevin Garnett FLY .75 2.00
83 Kevin Garnett FLY .75 2.00
84 Kevin Garnett FLY .75 2.00
85 Kevin Garnett FLY .75 2.00
86 Kevin Garnett FLY .75 2.00
87 Kevin Garnett FLY .75 2.00
88 Kevin Garnett FLY .75 2.00
89 Kevin Garnett FLY .75 2.00
90 Kevin Garnett FLY .75 2.00
91 Kenyon Martin RC 3.00 8.00
92 Stromile Swift RC 1.25 3.00
93 Darius Miles RC 1.25 3.00
94 Marcus Fizer RC 1.25 3.00
95 Mike Miller RC 2.00 5.00
96 DerMarr Johnson RC 1.00 2.50
97 Chris Mihm RC 1.00 2.50
98 Jamal Crawford RC 3.00 8.00
99 Joel Przybilla RC 1.00 2.50
100 Keyon Dooling RC 1.25 3.00
101 Jerome Moiso RC .75 2.00
102 Etan Thomas RC 1.25 3.00
103 Courtney Alexander RC 1.00 2.50
104 Mateen Cleaves RC 1.00 2.50
105 Jason Collier RC 1.25 3.00
106 Hedo Turkoglu RC 2.00 5.00
107 Desmond Mason RC 1.50 4.00
108 Quentin Richardson RC 1.25 3.00
109 Jamaal Magloire RC 1.25 3.00
110 Speedy Claxton RC 1.25 3.00
111 Morris Peterson RC 1.25 3.00
112 Donnell Harvey RC 1.00 2.50
113 DeShawn Stevenson RC 1.25 3.00
114 Mamadou N'Diaye RC .75 2.00
115 Erick Barkley RC .75 2.00
116 Mike Smith RC .75 2.00
117 Eddie House RC 1.00 2.50
118 Eduardo Najera RC 1.25 3.00
119 Jason Hart RC 1.25 3.00
120 Chris Porter RC .75 2.00

2000-01 Ultimate Victory Victory Collection

COMMON KOBE (61-75) 8.00 20.00
COMMON KG (76-90) 5.00 12.00
*STARS: 2.5X TO 6X BASE CARD HI
*RCs: .6X TO 1.5X BASE CARD HI
STATED PRINT RUN 350 SERIAL #'d SETS

2000-01 Ultimate Victory Ultimate Collection

COMMON KOBE (61-75) 15.00 40.00
COMMON KG (76-90) 12.50 30.00
*STARS: 6X TO 15X BASE CARD HI
*RCs: 1X TO 2.5X BASE CARD HI
STATED PRINT RUN 100 SERIAL #'d SETS

2000-01 Ultimate Victory Ultimate Victory

COMMON KOBE (61-75) 75.00 200.00
COMMON KG (76-90) 30.00 80.00
*STARS: 30X TO 80X BASE CARD HI
*RCs: 3X TO 8X BASE HI
STATED PRINT RUN 25 SERIAL #'d SETS

2000-01 Ultimate Victory Championship Fabrics

Randomly inserted into packs at one in 480, this 8-card insert set features swatches of actual game-used jerseys. Card backs carry a "CF" prefix.

STATED ODDS 1:480
CF1 Kobe Bryant 10.00 25.00
CF2 Shaquille O'Neal 12.50 30.00
CF3 Michael Jordan 60.00 150.00
CF4 Julius Erving 15.00 40.00
CF5 Larry Bird 12.00 30.00
CF6 Isiah Thomas 10.00 25.00
CFC1 K.Bryant/L.Bird/25 125.00 250.00

2000-01 Ultimate Victory Starstruck

Randomly inserted into packs at one in 11, this 10-card insert set features NBA players that have been starstruck from their abilities to play the game. Card backs carry a "S" prefix.

COMPLETE SET (10) 5.00 12.00
STATED ODDS 1:11
S1 Kobe Bryant 2.00 5.00
S2 Gary Payton .50 1.25
S3 Chris Webber .50 1.25
S4 Kevin Garnett .75 2.00
S5 Stephon Marbury .40 1.00
S6 Shareef Abdur-Rahim .40 1.00
S7 Steve Francis .40 1.00
S8 Tim Duncan 1.00 2.50
S9 Anfernee Hardaway .75 2.00
S10 Vince Carter 1.00 2.50

2000-01 Ultimate Victory The Reel World

Randomly inserted into packs at one in 11, this 10-card insert features players that make the highlight reels night in night out. Card backs carry a "RW" prefix.

COMPLETE SET (10) 7.50 15.00
STATED ODDS 1:11
RW1 Kobe Bryant 2.00 5.00
RW2 Vince Carter 1.00 2.50
RW3 Tim Duncan 1.00 2.50
RW4 Allen Iverson 1.00 2.50
RW5 Elton Brand .50 1.25
RW6 Jason Kidd .75 2.00
RW7 Kevin Garnett .75 2.00
RW8 Lamar Odom .40 1.00
RW9 Scottie Pippen .75 2.00
RW10 Karl Malone .60 1.50

2000-01 Ultimate Victory Ultimate Fabrics

Randomly inserted into packs at one in 240, this 5-card insert set features swatches of actual game-used jerseys. Card backs carry a "UFC" prefix. Please note that there is also an autographed version of the Martin/Swift card that is serial numbered to 25.

STATED ODDS 1:240
AU: PRINT RUN 25 SERIAL #'d SETS
UFC1 K.Martin/S.Swift 5.00 12.00
UFC2 K.Martin/D.Miles 5.00 12.00
UFC3 K.Martin/D.Johnson 5.00 12.00
UFC4 K.Martin/M.Fizer 5.00 12.00
UFCA1 K.Martin/S.Swift AU 20.00 40.00

2000-01 Ultimate Victory Ultimate Powers

Randomly inserted into packs at one in 23, this 10-card insert set features players that have incredible skills. Card backs carry a "U" prefix.

COMPLETE SET (10) 12.50 25.00
STATED ODDS 1:23
U1 Shaquille O'Neal 2.00 5.00
U2 Grant Hill 1.00 2.50
U3 Vince Carter 1.50 4.00
U4 Allen Iverson 1.50 4.00
U5 Kevin Garnett 1.25 3.00
U6 Tim Duncan 1.50 4.00
U7 Gary Payton .75 2.00
U8 Kobe Bryant 3.00 8.00
U9 Steve Francis .60 1.50
U10 Elton Brand .75 2.00

1992-93 Ultra Promo Sheet

Measuring approximately 11" by 11 1/2", this promo sheet displays ten cards on one side and nine on the other. Both sides combine to present the top 20 dunkers in the NBA, with the exception that number 16 is omitted. The glossy 2 1/2" by 3 1/2" action photos sport the characteristic Ultra design, with a gold foil stripe separating the bottom of the picture from a black marbleized border. The player's name appears in a gray bar, while his team name and position are printed in a jade bar. Though the cards are unnumbered, they are listed below according to their dunk ranking.

NNO Ultra Panel 2.00 5.00

1992-93 Ultra

The complete premier 1992-93 Ultra basketball set (made by Fleer) consists of 375 standard-size cards. The set was released in two series of 200 and 175 cards, respectively. Both series packs contained 14 cards each with 36 packs to a box. Suggested retail pack price was 1.79. The glossy color action player photos on the fronts are full-bleed except at the bottom where a diagonal gold-foil stripe edges a pale green variegated border. The player's name and team appear on two team color-coded bars that overlay the bottom border. The horizontal backs display action and close-up cut-out player photos against a basketball court background. The team logo and biographical information appear in a pale green bar like that on the front that edges the right side, while the player's name and statistics are given in bars running across the card bottom. The cards are numbered on the back and grouped alphabetically within team order. The first series closes with an NBA Draft Picks subset (193-198) and both series close with checklists (199-200/373-375). The second series contains more than 40 rookies, 30 trade cards, free agent signings, and other veterans omitted from the first series. The second series opens with an NBA Jam Session (201-220) subset. Three players from this Jam Session subset, Duane Causwell, Pervis Ellison, and Stacey Augmon, autographed a total of more than 2,500 cards that were randomly inserted in second series foil packs. These cards were embossed with Fleer logos for authenticity. On each series two pack, a mail-in offer provided the opportunity to acquire two more exclusive Jam Session cards, showing all 20 players in the set, for ten wrappers and 1.00 for postage and handling. According to Fleer, they anticipated about 100,000 requests. Key Rookie Cards include Tom Gugliotta, Robert Horry, Christian Laettner, Alonzo Mourning, Shaquille O'Neal, Latrell Sprewell and Clarence Weatherspoon.

COMPLETE SET (375) 15.00 30.00
COMPLETE SERIES 1 (200) 7.50 15.00
COMPLETE SERIES 2 (175) 7.50 15.00
1 Stacey Augmon .08 .25
2 Duane Ferrell .02 .10
3 Paul Graham .02 .10
4 Blair Rasmussen .02 .10
5 Rumeal Robinson .02 .10
6 Dominique Wilkins .20 .50
7 Kevin Willis .02 .10
8 John Bagley .02 .10
9 Dee Brown .02 .10
10 Rick Fox .08 .25
11 Kevin Gamble .02 .10
12 Joe Kleine .02 .10
13 Reggie Lewis .08 .25
14 Kevin McHale .20 .50
15 Robert Parish .08 .25
16 Ed Pinckney .02 .10
17 Muggsy Bogues .08 .25
18 Dell Curry .02 .10
19 Kenny Gattison .02 .10
20 Kendall Gill .08 .25
21 Larry Johnson .25 .60
22 Johnny Newman .02 .10
23 J.R. Reid .02 .10
24 B.J. Armstrong .02 .10
25 Bill Cartwright .02 .10
26 Horace Grant .08 .25
27 Michael Jordan 2.50 6.00
28 Stacey King .02 .10
29 John Paxson .02 .10
30 Will Perdue .02 .10
31 Scottie Pippen .60 1.50
32 Scott Williams .02 .10
33 John Battle .02 .10
34 Terrell Brandon .20 .50
35 Brad Daugherty .02 .10
36 Craig Ehlo .02 .10
37 Larry Nance .02 .10
38 Mark Price .02 .10
39 Mike Sanders .02 .10
40 John Williams .02 .10
41 Terry Davis .02 .10
42 Derek Harper .08 .25
43 Donald Hodge .02 .10
44 Mike Iuzzolino .02 .10
45 Fat Lever .02 .10
46 Doug Smith .02 .10
47 Randy White .02 .10
48 Winston Garland .02 .10
49 Chris Jackson .02 .10
50 Marcus Liberty .02 .10
51 Todd Lichti .02 .10
52 Mark Macon .02 .10
53 Dikembe Mutombo .25 .60
54 Reggie Williams .02 .10
55 Mark Aguirre .02 .10
56 Joe Dumars .20 .50
57 Bill Laimbeer .08 .25
58 Dennis Rodman .40 1.00
59 Isiah Thomas .20 .50
60 Darrell Walker .02 .10
61 Orlando Woolridge .02 .10
62 Victor Alexander .02 .10
63 Chris Gatling .02 .10
64 Tim Hardaway .25 .60
65 Tyrone Hill .02 .10
66 Sarunas Marciulionis .02 .10
67 Chris Mullin .20 .50
68 Billy Owens .08 .25
69 Sleepy Floyd .02 .10
70 Avery Johnson .02 .10
71 Vernon Maxwell .02 .10
72 Hakeem Olajuwon .30 .75
73 Kenny Smith .02 .10
74 Otis Thorpe .08 .25
75 Dale Davis .02 .10
76 Vern Fleming .02 .10
77 George McCloud .02 .10
78 Reggie Miller .20 .50
79 Detlef Schrempf .08 .25
80 Rik Smits .08 .25
81 LaSalle Thompson .02 .10
82 Gary Grant .02 .10
83 Ron Harper .08 .25
84 Mark Jackson .08 .25
85 Danny Manning .08 .25
86 Ken Norman .02 .10
87 Stanley Roberts .02 .10
88 Loy Vaught .02 .10
89 Elden Campbell .08 .25
90 Vlade Divac .08 .25
91 A.C. Green .08 .25
92 Sam Perkins .08 .25
93 Byron Scott .08 .25
94 Tony Smith .02 .10
95 Sedale Threatt .02 .10
96 James Worthy .20 .50
97 Willie Burton .02 .10
98 Bimbo Coles .02 .10
99 Kevin Edwards .02 .10
100 Grant Long .02 .10
101 Glen Rice .20 .50
102 Rony Seikaly .02 .10
103 Brian Shaw .02 .10
104 Steve Smith .25 .60
105 Frank Brickowski .02 .10
106 Moses Malone .20 .50
107 Fred Roberts .02 .10
108 Alvin Robertson .02 .10
109 Thurl Bailey .02 .10
110 Gerald Glass .02 .10
111 Luc Longley .08 .25
112 Felton Spencer .02 .10
113 Doug West .02 .10
114 Kenny Anderson .20 .50
115 Mookie Blaylock .08 .25
116 Sam Bowie .02 .10
117 Derrick Coleman .08 .25
118 Chris Dudley .02 .10
119 Chris Morris .02 .10
120 Drazen Petrovic .02 .10
121 Greg Anthony .02 .10
122 Patrick Ewing .20 .50
123 Anthony Mason .20 .50
124 Charles Oakley .08 .25
125 Doc Rivers .08 .25
126 Charles Smith .02 .10
127 John Starks .08 .25
128 Nick Anderson .08 .25
129 Anthony Bowie .02 .10
130 Terry Catledge .02 .10
131 Jerry Reynolds .02 .10
132 Dennis Scott .08 .25
133 Scott Skiles .02 .10
134 Brian Williams .02 .10
135 Ron Anderson .02 .10
136 Manute Bol .02 .10
137 Johnny Dawkins .02 .10
138 Armon Gilliam .02 .10
139 Hersey Hawkins .08 .25
140 Jeff Ruland .02 .10
141 Charles Shackleford .02 .10
142 Cedric Ceballos .08 .25
143 Tom Chambers .02 .10
144 Kevin Johnson .20 .50
145 Negele Knight .02 .10
146 Dan Majerle .08 .25
147 Mark West .02 .10
148 Mark Bryant .02 .10
149 Clyde Drexler .20 .50
150 Kevin Duckworth .02 .10
151 Jerome Kersey .02 .10
152 Robert Pack .02 .10
153 Terry Porter .02 .10
154 Clifford Robinson .08 .25
155 Buck Williams .08 .25
156 Anthony Bonner .02 .10
157 Duane Causwell .02 .10
158 Mitch Richmond .20 .50
159 Lionel Simmons .02 .10
160 Wayman Tisdale .02 .10
161 Spud Webb .08 .25
162 Willie Anderson .02 .10
163 Antoine Carr .02 .10
164 Terry Cummings .08 .25
165 Sean Elliott .08 .25
166 Sidney Green .02 .10
167 David Robinson .30 .75
168 Dana Barros .02 .10
169 Benoit Benjamin .02 .10
170 Michael Cage .02 .10
171 Eddie Johnson .02 .10
172 Shawn Kemp .40 1.00
173 Derrick McKey .02 .10
174 Nate McMillan .02 .10
175 Gary Payton .40 1.00
176 Ricky Pierce .02 .10
177 David Benoit .02 .10
178 Mike Brown .02 .10
179 Tyrone Corbin .02 .10
180 Mark Eaton .02 .10
181 Jeff Malone .02 .10
182 Karl Malone .30 .75
183 John Stockton .20 .50
184 Michael Adams .02 .10
185 Ledell Eackles .02 .10
186 Pervis Ellison .02 .10
187 A.J. English .02 .10
188 Harvey Grant .02 .10
189 Buck Johnson .02 .10
190 LaBradford Smith .02 .10
191 Larry Stewart .02 .10
192 David Wingate .02 .10
193 Alonzo Mourning RC .75 2.00
194 Adam Keefe RC .02 .10
195 Robert Horry RC .20 .50
196 Anthony Peeler RC .08 .25
197 Tracy Murray RC .08 .25
198 Dave Johnson RC .02 .10
199 Checklist 1-104 .02 .10
200 Checklist 105-200 .02 .10
201 David Robinson JS .10 .30
202 Dikembe Mutombo JS .10 .30
203 Otis Thorpe JS .01 .05
204 Hakeem Olajuwon JS .10 .30
205 Shawn Kemp JS .20 .50
206 Charles Barkley JS .10 .30
207 Pervis Ellison JS .01 .05
208 Chris Morris JS .01 .05
209 Brad Daugherty JS .01 .05
210 Derrick Coleman JS .01 .05
211 Tim Perry JS .01 .05
212 Duane Causwell JS .01 .05
213 Scottie Pippen JS .20 .50
214 Robert Parish JS .01 .05
215 Stacey Augmon JS .01 .05
216 Michael Jordan JS .75 2.00
217 Karl Malone JS .10 .30
218 John Williams JS .01 .05
219 Horace Grant JS .01 .05
220 Orlando Woolridge JS .01 .05
221 Mookie Blaylock .05 .15
222 Greg Foster .01 .05
223 Steve Henson .01 .05
224 Adam Keefe .01 .05
225 Jon Koncak .01 .05
226 Travis Mays .01 .05
227 Alaa Abdelnaby .01 .05
228 Sherman Douglas .01 .05
229 Xavier McDaniel .01 .05
230 Marcus Webb RC .01 .05
231 Tony Bennett RC .01 .05
232 Mike Gminski .01 .05
233 Kevin Lynch .01 .05
234 Alonzo Mourning .30 .75
235 David Wingate .01 .05
236 Rodney McCray .01 .05
237 Trent Tucker .01 .05
238 Corey Williams RC .01 .05
239 Danny Ferry .01 .05
240 Jay Guidinger RC .01 .05

241 Jerome Lane .01 .05
242 Bobby Phills RC .10 .30
243 Gerald Wilkins .01 .05
244 Walter Bond RC .01 .05
245 Dexter Cambridge RC .01 .05
246 Radisav Curcic UER RC .01 .05
247 Brian Howard RC .01 .05
248 Tracy Moore RC .01 .05
249 Sean Rooks RC .01 .05
250 Kevin Brooks .01 .05
251 LaPhonso Ellis RC .10 .30
252 Scott Hastings .01 .05
253 Robert Pack .01 .05
254 Gary Plummer RC .01 .05
255 Bryant Stith RC .05 .15
256 Robert Werdann RC .01 .05
257 Gerald Glass .01 .05
258 Terry Mills .01 .05
259 Olden Polynice .01 .05
260 Danny Young .01 .05
261 Jud Buechler .01 .05
262 Jeff Grayer .01 .05
263 Byron Houston RC .01 .05
264 Keith Jennings RC .01 .05
265 Ed Nealy .01 .05
266 Latrell Sprewell RC 1.00 2.50
267 Scott Brooks .01 .05
268 Matt Bullard .01 .05
269 Winston Garland .01 .05
270 Carl Herrera .01 .05
271 Robert Horry .10 .30
272 Tree Rollins .01 .05
273 Greg Dreiling .01 .05
274 Sean Green .01 .05
275 Sam Mitchell .01 .05
276 Pooh Richardson .01 .05
277 Malik Sealy RC .05 .15
278 Kenny Williams .01 .05
279 Mark Jackson .05 .15
280 Stanley Roberts .01 .05
281 Elmore Spencer RC .01 .05
282 Kiki Vandeweghe .01 .05
283 John S. Williams .01 .05
284 Randy Woods RC .01 .05
285 Alex Blackwell RC .01 .05
286 Duane Cooper RC .01 .05
287 James Edwards .01 .05
288 Jack Haley .01 .05
289 Anthony Peeler .05 .15
290 Keith Askins .01 .05
291 Matt Geiger RC .05 .15
292 Alec Kessler .01 .05
293 Harold Miner w/M.Jordan RC .10 .30
294 John Salley .01 .05
295 Anthony Avent RC .01 .05
296 Jon Barry RC .05 .15
297 Todd Day RC .05 .15
298 Blue Edwards .01 .05
299 Brad Lohaus .01 .05
300 Lee Mayberry RC .01 .05
301 Eric Murdock .01 .05
302 Danny Schayes .01 .05
303 Lance Blanks .01 .05
304 Christian Laettner RC .25 .60
305 Marlon Maxey RC .01 .05
306 Bob McCann RC .01 .05
307 Chuck Person .01 .05
308 Brad Sellers .01 .05
309 Chris Smith RC .01 .05
310 Gundars Vetra RC .01 .05
311 Micheal Williams .01 .05
312 Rafael Addison .01 .05
313 Chucky Brown .01 .05
314 Maurice Cheeks .01 .05
315 Tate George .01 .05
316 Rick Mahorn .01 .05
317 Rumeal Robinson .01 .05
318 Eric Anderson RC .01 .05
319 Rolando Blackman .01 .05
320 Tony Campbell .01 .05
321 Hubert Davis RC .05 .15
322 Doc Rivers .05 .15
323 Charles Smith .01 .05
324 Herb Williams .01 .05
325 Litterial Green RC .01 .05
326 Steve Kerr .05 .15
327 Greg Kite .01 .05
328 Shaquille O'Neal RC 3.00 8.00
329 Tom Tolbert .01 .05
330 Jeff Turner .01 .05
331 Greg Grant .01 .05
332 Jeff Hornacek .05 .15
333 Andrew Lang .01 .05
334 Tim Perry .01 .05
335 C.Weatherspoon RC .10 .30
336 Danny Ainge .05 .15
337 Charles Barkley .20 .50
338 Richard Dumas RC .01 .05
339 Frank Johnson .01 .05
340 Tim Kempton .01 .05
341 Oliver Miller RC .05 .15
342 Jerrod Mustaf .01 .05
343 Mario Elie .05 .15
344 Dave Johnson .01 .05
345 Tracy Murray .05 .15
346 Rod Strickland .10 .30
347 Randy Brown .01 .05
348 Pete Chilcutt .01 .05
349 Marty Conlon .01 .05
350 Jim Les .01 .05
351 Kurt Rambis .01 .05
352 Walt Williams RC .10 .30
353 Lloyd Daniels RC .01 .05
354 Vinny Del Negro .01 .05
355 Dale Ellis .01 .05
356 Avery Johnson .01 .05
357 Sam Mack RC .05 .15
358 J.R. Reid .01 .05
359 David Wood .01 .05
360 Vincent Askew .01 .05
361 Isaac Austin RC .05 .15
362 John Crotty RC .01 .05
363 Stephen Howard RC .01 .05
364 Jay Humphries .01 .05
365 Larry Krystkowiak .01 .05
366 Rex Chapman .01 .05
367 Tom Gugliotta RC .40 1.00
368 Buck Johnson .01 .05
369 Charles Jones .01 .05
370 Don MacLean RC .01 .05
371 Doug Overton .01 .05
372 Brent Price RC .05 .15
373 Checklist 201-266 .01 .05
374 Checklist 267-330 .01 .05
375 Checklist 331-375 .01 .05
JS207 Pervis Ellison AU 10.00 25.00
JS212 Duane Causwell AU 10.00 25.00
JS215 Stacey Augmon AU 15.00 30.00
NNO Jam Session Rank 1-10 1.00 2.50
NNO Jam Session Rank 11-20 1.00 2.50

1992-93 Ultra All-NBA

This set features 15 standard-size cards, one for each All-NBA first, second, and third-team player. The cards were randomly inserted into approximately one out of every 14 first series foil packs. The fronts feature color action player photos which are full-bleed except at the bottom, where a gold foil stripe separates a marbleized diagonal bottom border. A crest showing which All-NBA team the player was on overlaps the border and picture. The player's name is gold-foil stamped at the bottom. The horizontal backs carry a cut-out player close-up and career highlights on a marbleized background.

COMPLETE SET (15) 12.00 30.00
SER.1 STATED ODDS 1:14
1 Karl Malone 1.00 2.50
2 Chris Mullin .60 1.50
3 David Robinson 1.00 2.50
4 Michael Jordan 6.00 15.00
5 Clyde Drexler .60 1.50
6 Scottie Pippen 2.00 5.00
7 Charles Barkley 1.00 2.50
8 Patrick Ewing .60 1.50
9 Tim Hardaway .75 2.00
10 John Stockton .60 1.50
11 Dennis Rodman 1.25 3.00
12 Kevin Willis .20 .50
13 Brad Daugherty .20 .50
14 Mark Price .20 .50
15 Kevin Johnson .60 1.50

1992-93 Ultra All-Rookies

Randomly inserted in second series foil packs at a reported rate of approximately one card per nine packs, this ten-card standard-size set focuses on the 1992-93 class of outstanding rookies. A color action shot on the front has been cut out and superimposed on grid of identical close-up shots of the player, which resemble the effect produced by a wall of TV sets displaying the same image. The "All-Rookie" logo and the player's name are gold-foil stamped across the bottom of the picture. On the backs, a wheat-colored panel carrying a player profile overlays a second full-bleed color action photo. The set is sequenced in alphabetical order.

COMPLETE SET (10) 6.00 15.00
SER.2 STATED ODDS 1:13
1 LaPhonso Ellis .25 .60
2 Tom Gugliotta .75 2.00
3 Robert Horry .40 1.00
4 Christian Laettner .50 1.25
5 Harold Miner .25 .60
6 Alonzo Mourning 1.50 4.00
7 Shaquille O'Neal 4.00 10.00
8 Latrell Sprewell 2.00 5.00
9 Clarence Weatherspoon .25 .60
10 Walt Williams .25 .60

1992-93 Ultra Award Winners

This five-card standard-size Ultra Award Winners insert set spotlights the 1991-92 MVP, Rookie of the Year, Defensive Player of the Year, top "6th Man" and Most Improved Player. These cards were randomly inserted into first series packs at a rate of one card in every 42 packs according to information printed on the wrappers. Card fronts feature an action photo with the player's name and Award Winners logo at the bottom. Backs have career highlights and a photo.

COMPLETE SET (5) 6.00 15.00
SER.1 STATED ODDS 1:42
1 Michael Jordan 4.00 10.00
2 David Robinson 1.00 2.50
3 Larry Johnson .75 2.00
4 Detlef Schrempf .30 .75
5 Pervis Ellison .10 .30

1992-93 Ultra Scottie Pippen

This 12-card standard-size "Career Highlights" set chronicles Scottie Pippen's rise to NBA stardom. The cards were inserted at a rate of one card per 21 first series packs according to information printed on the wrappers. Pippen autographed more than 2,000 of these cards for random insertion in first series packs. These autograph cards have embossed Fleer logos for authenticity. Through a special mail-in offer only, two additional Pippen cards were made available to collectors who sent in ten wrappers and 1.00 for postage and handling. On the front, the cards feature color action player photos with brownish-green marbleized borders. The player's name and the words "Career Highlights" are stamped in gold foil below the picture. On the same marbleized background, the backs carry a color head shot as well as biography and career summary.

COMPLETE SET (10) 7.50 15.00
COMMON PIPPEN (1-10) .60 1.50
SER.1 STATED ODDS 1:21
CERTIFIED AUTOGRAPH (AU) 30.00 80.00
PIPPEN AU: SER.1 STATED ODDS 1:9,000
COMMON SEND-OFF (11-12) .60 1.50
TWO CARDS PER 10 SER.1 WRAPPERS

1992-93 Ultra Playmakers

Randomly inserted in second series foil packs at a reported rate of one card per 13 packs, this ten-card standard-size set features the NBA's top point guards. The glossy color action photos on the fronts are full-bleed except at the bottom where a lavender stripe edges the picture. The "Playmaker" logo and the player's name are gold-foil stamped across the bottom of the picture. On the backs, a wheat-colored panel carrying a player profile overlays a second full-bleed color action photo. The cards are numbered in the lower left corner of the panel.

COMPLETE SET (10) 1.50 4.00
SER.2 STATED ODDS 1:13
1 Kenny Anderson .50 1.25
2 Muggsy Bogues .25 .60
3 Tim Hardaway .60 1.50
4 Mark Jackson .25 .60
5 Kevin Johnson .50 1.25
6 Mark Price .15 .40
7 Terry Porter .15 .40
8 Scott Skiles .15 .40
9 John Stockton .50 1.25
10 Isiah Thomas .50 1.25

1992-93 Ultra Rejectors

Randomly inserted in second series foil packs at a reported rate of one in 26, this five-card standard-size set showcases defensive big men who are aptly dubbed "Rejectors." The glossy color action photos on the fronts are full-bleed except at the bottom where a gold stripe edges the picture. The player's name and the "Rejector" logo are gold-foil stamped across the bottom of the picture. On a black panel inside gold borders, the horizontal backs carry text describing the player's defensive accomplishments and a color close-up photo. The set is sequenced in alphabetical order.

COMPLETE SET (5) 4.00 10.00
SER.2 STATED ODDS 1:26
1 Alonzo Mourning .50 1.25
2 Dikembe Mutombo .40 1.00
3 Hakeem Olajuwon .50 1.25
4 Shaquille O'Neal 3.00 8.00
5 David Robinson .50 1.25

1993-94 Ultra

The complete 1993-94 Ultra basketball set consists of 375 standard-size cards that were issued in series of 200 and 175 respectively. Cards were issued in 14 and 19-card packs. There are 36 packs per box. The glossy color action player photos on the fronts are full-bleed except at the bottom. The bottom of the front consists of player name, team name and a peach colored border. The horizontal backs feature a player photos against a basketball court background. The team logo and biographical information appear a pale peach bar, while the player's name and statistics are printed in team color-coded bars running across the card bottom. The cards are alphabetically arranged by team and are numbered alphabetically within team order. A USA Basketball subset contains cards 361-372. Ten second series wrappers and $1.50 could be redeemed for USA cards of Reggie Miller (M1), Shaquille O'Neal (M2) and a team photo (M3). The offer was good through June 10, 1994. These cards are not considered part of the basic set. Rookie Cards of note in this set include Vin Baker, Anfernee Hardaway, Allan Houston, Toni Kukoc, Jamal Mashburn, Nick Van Exel and Chris Webber.

COMPLETE SET (375) 15.00 30.00
COMPLETE SERIES 1 (200) 7.50 15.00
COMPLETE SERIES 2 (175) 8.00 20.00
SUBSET CARDS SAME VALUE AS BASE CARDS
1 Stacey Augmon .12 .30
2 Mookie Blaylock .10 .25
3 Doug Edwards RC .20 .50
4 Duane Ferrell .10 .25
5 Paul Graham .10 .25
6 Adam Keefe .10 .25
7 Dominique Wilkins .20 .50
8 Kevin Willis .10 .25
9 Alaa Abdelnaby .10 .25
10 Dee Brown .10 .25
11 Sherman Douglas .10 .25
12 Rick Fox .10 .25
13 Kevin Gamble .10 .25
14 Xavier McDaniel .10 .25
15 Robert Parish .15 .40
16 Muggsy Bogues .12 .30
17 Scott Burrell RC .20 .50
18 Dell Curry .10 .25
19 Kenny Gattison .10 .25
20 Hersey Hawkins .10 .25
21 Eddie Johnson .10 .25
22 Larry Johnson .15 .40
23 Alonzo Mourning .25 .60
24 Johnny Newman .10 .25
25 David Wingate .10 .25
26 B.J. Armstrong .10 .25
27 Corie Blount RC .20 .50
28 Bill Cartwright .12 .30
29 Horace Grant .12 .30
30 Michael Jordan 1.50 4.00
31 Stacey King .10 .25
32 John Paxson .12 .30
33 Will Perdue .10 .25
34 Scottie Pippen .30 .75
35 Terrell Brandon .12 .30
36 Brad Daugherty .12 .30
37 Danny Ferry .10 .25
38 Chris Mills RC .20 .50
39 Larry Nance .12 .30
40 Mark Price .15 .40
41 Gerald Wilkins .10 .25
42 John Williams .10 .25
43 Terry Davis .10 .25
44 Derek Harper .12 .30
45 Donald Hodge .10 .25
46 Jim Jackson .12 .30
47 Sean Rooks .10 .25
48 Doug Smith .10 .25
49 Mahmoud Abdul-Rauf .10 .25
50 LaPhonso Ellis .10 .25
51 Mark Macon .10 .25
52 Dikembe Mutombo .15 .40
53 Bryant Stith .10 .25
54 Reggie Williams .10 .25
55 Mark Aguirre .12 .30
56 Joe Dumars .15 .40
57 Bill Laimbeer .12 .30
58 Terry Mills .10 .25
59 Olden Polynice .10 .25
60 Alvin Robertson .10 .25
61 Sean Elliott .15 .40
62 Isiah Thomas .15 .40
63 Victor Alexander .10 .25
64 Chris Gatling .10 .25
65 Tim Hardaway .15 .40
66 Byron Houston .10 .25
67 Sarunas Marciulionis .10 .25
68 Chris Mullin .15 .40
69 Billy Owens .10 .25
70 Latrell Sprewell .25 .60
71 Matt Bullard .10 .25
72 Sam Cassell RC .40 1.00
73 Carl Herrera .10 .25
74 Robert Horry .15 .40
75 Vernon Maxwell .10 .25
76 Hakeem Olajuwon .20 .50
77 Kenny Smith .12 .30
78 Otis Thorpe .10 .25
79 Dale Davis .10 .25
80 Vern Fleming .10 .25
81 Reggie Miller .20 .50
82 Sam Mitchell .10 .25
83 Pooh Richardson .10 .25
84 Detlef Schrempf .15 .40
85 Rik Smits .12 .30
86 Ron Harper .12 .30
87 Mark Jackson .12 .30
88 Danny Manning .12 .30
89 Stanley Roberts .10 .25
90 Loy Vaught .10 .25
91 John Williams .10 .25
92 Sam Bowie .10 .25
93 Doug Christie .10 .25
94 Vlade Divac .15 .40
95 George Lynch RC .20 .50
96 Anthony Peeler .10 .25
97 James Worthy .20 .50
98 Bimbo Coles .10 .25
99 Grant Long .10 .25
100 Harold Miner .10 .25
101 Glen Rice .15 .40
102 Rony Seikaly .10 .25
103 Brian Shaw .10 .25
104 Steve Smith .12 .30
105 Anthony Avent .10 .25
106 Vin Baker RC .30 .75
107 Frank Brickowski .10 .25
108 Todd Day .10 .25
109 Blue Edwards .10 .25
110 Lee Mayberry .10 .25
111 Eric Murdock .10 .25
112 Orlando Woolridge .10 .25
113 Thurl Bailey .10 .25
114 Christian Laettner .12 .30
115 Chuck Person .12 .30
116 Doug West .10 .25
117 Micheal Williams .10 .25
118 Kenny Anderson .12 .30
119 Derrick Coleman .12 .30
120 Rick Mahorn .10 .25
121 Chris Morris .10 .25
122 Rumeal Robinson .10 .25
123 Rex Walters RC .20 .50
124 Greg Anthony .10 .25
125 Rolando Blackman .12 .30
126 Hubert Davis .10 .25
127 Patrick Ewing .20 .50
128 Anthony Mason .10 .25
129 Charles Oakley .12 .30
130 Doc Rivers .12 .30
131 Charles Smith .10 .25
132 John Starks .12 .30
133 Nick Anderson .10 .25
134 Anthony Bowie .10 .25
135 Shaquille O'Neal .60 1.50
136 Dennis Scott .10 .25
137 Scott Skiles .10 .25
138 Jeff Turner .10 .25
139 Shawn Bradley RC .20 .50
140 Johnny Dawkins .10 .25
141 Jeff Hornacek .12 .30
142 Tim Perry .10 .25
143 Clarence Weatherspoon .10 .25
144 Danny Ainge .15 .40
145 Charles Barkley .25 .60
146 Cedric Ceballos .12 .30
147 Kevin Johnson .15 .40
148 Negele Knight .10 .25
149 Malcolm Mackey RC .20 .50
150 Dan Majerle .15 .40
151 Oliver Miller .10 .25
152 Mark West .10 .25
153 Mark Bryant .10 .25
154 Clyde Drexler .20 .50
155 Jerome Kersey .10 .25
156 Terry Porter .10 .25
157 Clifford Robinson .10 .25
158 Rod Strickland .10 .25
159 Buck Williams .10 .25
160 Duane Causwell .10 .25
161 Bobby Hurley RC .20 .50
162 Mitch Richmond .15 .40
163 Lionel Simmons .10 .25
164 Wayman Tisdale .10 .25
165 Spud Webb .12 .30
166 Walt Williams .10 .25
167 Willie Anderson .10 .25
168 Antoine Carr .10 .25
169 Lloyd Daniels .10 .25
170 Dennis Rodman .30 .75
171 Dale Ellis .10 .25
172 Avery Johnson .12 .30
173 J.R. Reid .10 .25
174 David Robinson .25 .60
175 Michael Cage .10 .25
176 Kendall Gill .10 .25
177 Ervin Johnson RC .20 .50
178 Shawn Kemp .20 .50
179 Derrick McKey .10 .25
180 Nate McMillan .10 .25
181 Gary Payton .20 .50
182 Sam Perkins .10 .25
183 Ricky Pierce .10 .25
184 David Benoit .10 .25
185 Tyrone Corbin .10 .25
186 Mark Eaton .10 .25
187 Jay Humphries .10 .25
188 Jeff Malone .10 .25
189 Karl Malone .20 .50
190 John Stockton .20 .50
191 Luther Wright RC .20 .50
192 Michael Adams .10 .25
193 Calbert Cheaney RC .20 .50
194 Pervis Ellison .10 .25
195 Tom Gugliotta .12 .30
196 Buck Johnson .10 .25
197 LaBradford Smith .10 .25
198 Larry Stewart .10 .25
199 Checklist .10 .25
200 Checklist .10 .25
201 Doug Edwards .10 .25
202 Craig Ehlo .10 .25
203 Jon Koncak .10 .25
204 Andrew Lang .10 .25
205 Ennis Whatley .10 .25
206 Chris Corchiani .10 .25
207 Acie Earl RC .20 .50
208 Jimmy Oliver .10 .25
209 Ed Pinckney .10 .25
210 Dino Radja RC .20 .50
211 Matt Wenstrom RC .20 .50
212 Tony Bennett .10 .25
213 Scott Burrell .10 .25
214 LeRon Ellis .10 .25
215 Hersey Hawkins .10 .25
216 Eddie Johnson .10 .25
217 Rumeal Robinson .10 .25
218 Corie Blount .10 .25
219 Dave Johnson .10 .25
220 Steve Kerr .12 .30
221 Toni Kukoc RC .50 1.25
222 Pete Myers .10 .25
223 Bill Wennington .10 .25
224 Scott Williams .10 .25
225 John Battle .10 .25
226 Tyrone Hill .10 .25
227 Gerald Madkins RC .20 .50
228 Chris Mills .10 .25
229 Bobby Phills .10 .25
230 Greg Dreiling .10 .25
231 Lucious Harris RC .20 .50
232 Popeye Jones RC .20 .50
233 Tim Legler RC .20 .50
234 Fat Lever .12 .30
235 Jamal Mashburn RC .30 .75
236 Tom Hammonds .10 .25
237 Darnell Mee RC .20 .50
238 Robert Pack .10 .25
239 Rodney Rogers RC .20 .50
240 Brian Williams .10 .25
241 Greg Anderson .10 .25
242 Sean Elliott .15 .40
243 Allan Houston RC .40 1.00
244 Lindsey Hunter RC .20 .50
245 Mark Macon .10 .25
246 David Wood .10 .25
247 Jud Buechler .10 .25
248 Josh Grant RC .20 .50
249 Jeff Grayer .10 .25
250 Keith Jennings .10 .25
251 Avery Johnson .12 .30
252 Chris Webber RC 1.00 2.50
253 Scott Brooks .10 .25
254 Sam Cassell .20 .50
255 Mario Elie .10 .25
256 Richard Petruska RC .20 .50
257 Eric Riley RC .20 .50
258 Antonio Davis RC .25 .60
259 Scott Haskin RC .20 .50
260 Derrick McKey .10 .25
261 Byron Scott .15 .40
262 Malik Sealy .10 .25
263 Kenny Williams .10 .25
264 Haywoode Workman .10 .25
265 Mark Aguirre .12 .30
266 Terry Dehere RC .20 .50
267 Harold Ellis RC .20 .50
268 Gary Grant .10 .25
269 Bob Martin RC .20 .50
270 Elmore Spencer .10 .25
271 Tom Tolbert .10 .25
272 Sam Bowie .10 .25
273 Elden Campbell .10 .25
274 Antonio Harvey RC .20 .50
275 George Lynch .10 .25
276 Tony Smith .10 .25
277 Sedale Threatt .10 .25
278 Nick Van Exel RC .40 1.00
279 Willie Burton .10 .25
280 Matt Geiger .10 .25
281 John Salley .10 .25
282 Vin Baker .15 .40
283 Jon Barry .10 .25
284 Brad Lohaus .10 .25
285 Ken Norman .10 .25
286 Derek Strong RC .20 .50
287 Mike Brown .10 .25
288 Brian Davis RC .20 .50
289 Tellis Frank .10 .25
290 Luc Longley .12 .30
291 Marlon Maxey .10 .25
292 Isaiah Rider RC .30 .75
293 Chris Smith .10 .25
294 P.J. Brown RC .20 .50
295 Kevin Edwards .10 .25
296 Armon Gilliam .10 .25
297 Johnny Newman .10 .25
298 Rex Walters .10 .25
299 David Wesley RC .20 .50
300 Jayson Williams .10 .25
301 Anthony Bonner .10 .25
302 Derek Harper .12 .30
303 Herb Williams .10 .25
304 Litterial Green .10 .25
305 Anfernee Hardaway RC 1.00 2.50
306 Greg Kite .10 .25
307 Larry Krystkowiak .10 .25
308 Keith Tower RC .20 .50
309 Dana Barros .10 .25
310 Shawn Bradley .10 .25
311 Greg Graham RC .20 .50
312 Sean Green .10 .25
313 Warren Kidd RC .20 .50
314 Eric Leckner .10 .25
315 Moses Malone .15 .40
316 Orlando Woolridge .10 .25
317 Duane Cooper .10 .25
318 Joe Courtney RC .20 .50
319 A.C. Green .12 .30
320 Frank Johnson .10 .25
321 Joe Kleine .10 .25
322 Chris Dudley .10 .25
323 Harvey Grant .10 .25
324 Jaren Jackson .10 .25
325 Tracy Murray .10 .25
326 James Robinson RC .20 .50
327 Reggie Smith .10 .25
328 Kevin Thompson RC .20 .50
329 Randy Brown .10 .25
330 Evers Burns RC .20 .50
331 Pete Chilcutt .10 .25
332 Bobby Hurley .10 .25
333 Mike Peplowski RC .20 .50
334 LaBradford Smith .10 .25
335 Trevor Wilson .10 .25
336 Terry Cummings .12 .30
337 Vinny Del Negro .10 .25
338 Sleepy Floyd .10 .25
339 Negele Knight .10 .25
340 Dennis Rodman .30 .75
341 Chris Whitney RC .20 .50
342 Vincent Askew .10 .25
343 Kendall Gill .10 .25
344 Ervin Johnson .10 .25
345 Chris King RC .20 .50
346 Detlef Schrempf .15 .40
347 Walter Bond .10 .25
348 Tom Chambers .12 .30
349 John Crotty .10 .25
350 Bryon Russell RC .20 .50
351 Felton Spencer .10 .25
352 Mitchell Butler RC .20 .50
353 Rex Chapman .10 .25
354 Calbert Cheaney .10 .25
355 Kevin Duckworth .10 .25
356 Don MacLean .10 .25
357 Gheorghe Muresan RC .20 .50
358 Doug Overton .10 .25
359 Brent Price .10 .25
360 Kenny Walker .10 .25
361 Derrick Coleman USA .12 .30
362 Joe Dumars USA .15 .40
363 Tim Hardaway USA .15 .40
364 Larry Johnson USA .15 .40
365 Shawn Kemp USA .20 .50
366 Dan Majerle USA .15 .40
367 Alonzo Mourning USA .25 .60
368 Mark Price USA .15 .40
369 Steve Smith USA .12 .30
370 Isiah Thomas USA .15 .40
371 Dominique Wilkins USA .20 .50
372 Don Nelson .15 .40
Don Chaney
373 Jamal Mashburn CL .15 .40
374 Checklist .10 .25
375 Checklist .10 .25
M1 Reggie Miller USA .40 1.00
M2 Shaquille O'Neal USA 2.50 6.00
M3 Team Checklist USA .75 2.00

1993-94 Ultra All-Defensive

Randomly inserted in 1 of 24 first series 19-card jumbo packs, this standard-size ten-card set features members of the first (1-5) and second (6-10) All-NBA defensive teams. The design features a borderless front and color player action cutout set against a background of an enlarged and ghosted version of the same photo. The player's name appears in gold-foil lettering at the bottom. The back features a color player photo at the lower left, along with his career highlights set against the same ghosted photo background. The cards are numbered on the back as "X of 10."

COMPLETE SET (10) 30.00 80.00
SER.1 STATED ODDS 1:24 JUMBO
1 Joe Dumars 2.50 6.00
2 Michael Jordan 30.00 80.00
3 Hakeem Olajuwon 3.00 8.00
4 Scottie Pippen 5.00 12.00
5 Dennis Rodman 5.00 12.00
6 Horace Grant 2.00 5.00
7 Dan Majerle 2.50 6.00
8 Larry Nance 2.00 5.00
9 David Robinson 4.00 10.00
10 John Starks 2.00 5.00

1993-94 Ultra All-NBA

Randomly inserted in 14-card first series packs at a rate of approximately one in 16, this 14-card standard-size set features one card for each All-NBA first (1-5), second (6-10) and third (11-14) team player from the 1992-93 season. Drazen Petrovic was named to the third team. Due to his death following the '92-93 season, a card was not produced. The fronts display full-bleed glossy color action photos with a series of three smaller photos along the left side. The player's name appears in gold-foil lettering at the lower right. The back carries a hardwood floor-design background with three small photos along the left side that progressively zoom in on the player. Career highlights appear alongside. The cards are numbered on the back as "X of 14."

COMPLETE SET (14) 12.00 30.00
SER.1 STATED ODDS 1:16
1 Charles Barkley 1.50 4.00
2 Michael Jordan 5.00 12.00
3 Karl Malone 1.25 3.00
4 Hakeem Olajuwon 1.25 3.00
5 Mark Price 1.00 2.50
6 Joe Dumars 1.00 2.50
7 Patrick Ewing 1.25 3.00
8 Larry Johnson 1.00 2.50
9 John Stockton 1.25 3.00
10 Dominique Wilkins 1.25 3.00
11 Derrick Coleman .75 2.00
12 Tim Hardaway 1.00 2.50
13 Scottie Pippen 2.00 5.00
14 David Robinson 1.50 4.00

1993-94 Ultra All-Rookie Series

Randomly inserted in 14-card second series packs at an approximate rate of one in seven, this 15-card standard-size set features some of the NBA's top draft picks of 1993-94. Each borderless front features a color action photo. The player's name appears in silver foil near the bottom. The horizontal borderless back carries a color player action shot on one side and career highlights on the other. The cards are numbered on the back as "X of 15" and are sequenced in alphabetical order.

COMPLETE SET (15) 8.00 20.00
SER.2 STATED ODDS 1:7
1 Vin Baker .75 2.00
2 Shawn Bradley .50 1.25
3 Calbert Cheaney .50 1.25
4 Anfernee Hardaway 2.50 6.00
5 Lindsey Hunter .50 1.25
6 Bobby Hurley .50 1.25
7 Popeye Jones .50 1.25
8 Toni Kukoc 1.25 3.00
9 Jamal Mashburn .75 2.00
10 Chris Mills .50 1.25
11 Dino Radja .50 1.25
12 Isaiah Rider .75 2.00
13 Rodney Rogers .50 1.25
14 Nick Van Exel 1.00 2.50
15 Chris Webber 2.50 6.00

1993-94 Ultra All-Rookie Team

Randomly inserted in series one 14-card packs at an approximate rate of one in 24, this five-card standard-size set features the NBA's 1992-93 All-Rookie Team. Fronts feature borderless fronts with color player action cutouts breaking out of hardwood floor backgrounds. The player's name appears in gold-foil lettering at the bottom. The horizontal borderless back carries a color player cutout and career highlights on a hardwood floor background. The cards are numbered on the back as "X of 5" and are sequenced in alphabetical order.

COMPLETE SET (5) 2.50 6.00
SER.1 STATED ODDS 1:24
1 LaPhonso Ellis .30 .75
2 Tom Gugliotta w/Jordan .40 1.00
3 Christian Laettner .40 1.00
4 Alonzo Mourning .75 2.00
5 Shaquille O'Neal 2.00 5.00

1993-94 Ultra Award Winners

Randomly inserted in first series 19-card jumbo packs at a rate of one in 36, this five-card standard-size set features NBA award winners from the 1992-93 season. Borderless fronts feature color player action cutouts on metallic backgrounds. The player's name appears in silver-foil lettering at the bottom. The back carries a color player close-up and career highlights. The cards are numbered on the back as "X of 5." and are sequenced in alphabetical order.

COMPLETE SET (5) 6.00 15.00
SER.1 STATED ODDS 1:36 JUMBO
1 Mahmoud Abdul-Rauf .75 2.00
2 Charles Barkley 2.00 5.00
3 Hakeem Olajuwon 1.50 4.00
4 Shaquille O'Neal 5.00 12.00
5 Clifford Robinson .75 2.00

1993-94 Ultra Famous Nicknames

Randomly inserted into 14-card second series packs at a rate of one in five, this 15-card standard-size set features popular nicknames of today's stars. Borderless fronts feature color action cutouts on hardwood-floor and basket-net backgrounds. The player's nickname appears in silver-foil lettering on the right. The borderless back carries a color player photo on one side. On the other, the shot's game background blends into a hardwood-floor background for the player's name in vertical silver-foil lettering and his career highlights. The cards are numbered on the back as "X of 15" and are sequenced in alphabetical order.

COMPLETE SET (15) 15.00 40.00
SER.2 STATED ODDS 1:5
1 Charles Barkley 1.00 2.50
2 Muggsy Bogues .50 1.25
3 Derrick Coleman .50 1.25
4 Clyde Drexler .75 2.00
5 Anfernee Hardaway 5.00 12.00
6 Larry Johnson .60 1.50
7 Michael Jordan 5.00 12.00
8 Toni Kukoc 2.50 6.00
9 Karl Malone .75 2.00
10 Harold Miner .40 1.00
11 Alonzo Mourning 1.00 2.50
12 Hakeem Olajuwon .75 2.00
13 Shaquille O'Neal 2.50 6.00
14 David Robinson 1.00 2.50
15 Dominique Wilkins .75 2.00

1993-94 Ultra Inside/Outside

Randomly inserted in 14-card second series packs, this 10-card standard-size set features on each borderless front a color player action cutout over a shot of a comet like basketball going through the basket, all on a black background. The player's name appears in gold foil near the bottom. This design, but with a different action cutout, is mirrored somewhat on the borderless back, which also carries to the left of the player photo his career highlights within a ghosted box framed by a purple line. The cards are numbered on the back as "X of 10" and are sequenced in alphabetical order.

COMPLETE SET (10) 2.50 6.00
RANDOM INSERTS IN ALL SER.2 PACKS
1 Patrick Ewing .25 .60
2 Jim Jackson .15 .40
3 Larry Johnson .20 .50
4 Michael Jordan 1.50 4.00
5 Dan Majerle .20 .50
6 Hakeem Olajuwon .25 .60
7 Scottie Pippen .40 1.00
8 Latrell Sprewell .30 .75
9 John Starks .15 .40
10 Walt Williams .12 .30

1993-94 Ultra Jam City

Randomly inserted in 19-card second series jumbo packs at a rate of one in 37, this 9-card standard-size set features borderless fronts with color player action cutouts on black and purple metallic cityscape backgrounds. The player's name appears in gold foil in a lower corner. The borderless back carries a color player action cutout on a non-metallic cityscape background otherwise similar to the front. The player's name and career highlights appear in a ghosted box to the left of the photo. The cards are numbered on the back as "X of 10" and are sequenced in alphabetical order.

COMPLETE SET (9) 30.00 60.00
SER.2 STATED ODDS 1:37 JUMBO
1 Charles Barkley 3.00 8.00
2 Derrick Coleman 1.50 4.00
3 Clyde Drexler 2.50 6.00
4 Patrick Ewing 2.50 6.00
5 Shawn Kemp 2.50 6.00
6 Harold Miner 1.25 3.00
7 Shaquille O'Neal 8.00 20.00
8 David Robinson 3.00 8.00
9 Dominique Wilkins 2.50 6.00

1993-94 Ultra Karl Malone

This ten-card standard-size set of Career Highlights spotlights Utah Jazz forward Karl Malone. The cards were randomly inserted in 14-card first series packs at a rate of approximately one in 16. The full-bleed color fronts have purple tinted ghosted backgrounds with Malone portrayed in normal color action and posed photos. Across the bottom edge is a marbleized border with the subset title "Career Highlights", above the lower border is a silver and black box containing Malone's name. The backs carry information about Malone within a purple tinted ghosted box that is superimposed over a color photo. More than 2,000 autographed cards were randomly inserted in packs. These card have embossed Fleer logos for authenticity. An additional two cards (Nos.11 and 12) were available through a mail-in offer. Prior to June 10, 1994, collectors had to send 10 first series Ultra wrappers and $1.50 to receive the cards. The set is considered complete without these cards.

COMPLETE SET (10) 5.00 10.00
COMMON MALONE (1-10) .50 1.25
SER.1 STATED ODDS 1:16
CERTIFIED AUTOGRAPH (AU) 25.00 60.00
COMMON SEND-OFF (11-12) .75 2.00
TWO CARDS PER 10 SER.1 WRAPPERS

1993-94 Ultra Power In The Key

Randomly inserted in 14-card second series packs at a rate of one in 37, this nine-card standard-size features some of the NBA's top power players. Card fronts feature borderless color player action cutouts on multicolored metallic court illustration backgrounds. The player's name appears in gold-foil lettering at the lower right. The borderless horizontal back carries on its right side a color player close-up on a nonmetallic background otherwise similar to the front. The player's name and career highlights appear in a ghosted box to the left of the photo. The cards are numbered on the back as "X of 9" and are sequenced in alphabetical order.

COMPLETE SET (9) 12.00 30.00
SER.2 STATED ODDS 1:37 HOBBY
1 Larry Johnson 1.00 2.50
2 Michael Jordan 20.00 50.00
3 Karl Malone 1.25 3.00
4 Oliver Miller .60 1.50
5 Alonzo Mourning 1.50 4.00
6 Hakeem Olajuwon 1.25 3.00
7 Shaquille O'Neal 4.00 10.00
8 Otis Thorpe .60 1.50
9 Chris Webber 5.00 12.00

1993-94 Ultra Rebound Kings

Randomly inserted in 14-card second series packs at a rate of one in four, this 10-card standard-size set features some of the NBA's top rebounders. Borderless fronts feature color player action shots on backgrounds that blend from the actual action background at the bottom to a ghosted and color-screened player close-up at the top. The player's name appears vertically in gold foil on one side. The borderless horizontal back carries a color player cutout on one side and the player's name in gold foil and career highlights on the other, all on a ghosted and color-screened background. The cards are numbered on the back as "X of 10" and are sequenced in alphabetical order.

COMPLETE SET (10) 1.50 4.00
SER.2 STATED ODDS 1:4
1 Charles Barkley .30 .75
2 Derrick Coleman .15 .40
3 Shawn Kemp .25 .60
4 Karl Malone .25 .60
5 Alonzo Mourning .30 .75
6 Dikembe Mutombo .20 .50
7 Charles Oakley .15 .40
8 Hakeem Olajuwon .25 .60
9 Shaquille O'Neal .75 2.00
10 Dennis Rodman .40 1.00

1993-94 Ultra Scoring Kings

Randomly inserted in first series hobby packs at a rate of one in 36, this 10-card standard-size set features some of the NBA's top scorers. Card fronts feature color player action cutouts on borderless metallic backgrounds highlighted by lightning filaments. The player's name appears in silver-foil lettering in a lower corner. The horizontal back carries a color player close-up on the right, with the player's name appearing in silver-foil lettering at the upper left, followed below by career highlights, all on a dark borderless background again highlighted by lightning filaments. The cards are numbered on the back as "X of 10" and are sequenced in alphabetical order.

COMPLETE SET (10) 125.00 300.00
SER.1 STATED ODDS 1:36 HOBBY
1 Charles Barkley 6.00 15.00

2 Joe Dumars 4.00 10.00
3 Patrick Ewing 5.00 12.00
4 Larry Johnson 4.00 10.00
5 Michael Jordan 100.00 250.00
6 Karl Malone 5.00 12.00
7 Alonzo Mourning 6.00 15.00
8 Shaquille O'Neal 10.00 25.00
9 David Robinson 6.00 15.00
10 Dominique Wilkins 5.00 12.00

1994-95 Ultra

The 350 standard-size cards comprising the 1994-95 Ultra set were issued in two separate series of 200 and 150 cards each. Cards were distributed in 14-card ($1.99) and 17-card ($2.69) retail packs. Borderless fronts feature color player action shots. The player's name, team name, and position appear in vertical silver-foil lettering in an upper corner. The borderless back carries multiple player images, with the player's name and team logo appearing in gold foil, followed by biography and statistics near the bottom. The cards are numbered on the back and grouped alphabetically within team order. Unlike previous years, there are no subset cards in this set. Rookie Cards of note include Grant Hill, Juwan Howard, Jason Kidd, Eddie Jones, and Glenn Robinson. There is an insert in every pack. Every 72nd pack is a Hot Pack that contains inserts only.

COMPLETE SET (350) 17.50 35.00
COMPLETE SERIES 1 (200) 10.00 20.00
COMPLETE SERIES 2 (150) 7.50 15.00
1 Stacey Augmon .15 .40
2 Mookie Blaylock .12 .30
3 Craig Ehlo .12 .30
4 Adam Keefe .12 .30
5 Andrew Lang .12 .30
6 Ken Norman .12 .30
7 Kevin Willis .12 .30
8 Dee Brown .12 .30
9 Sherman Douglas .12 .30
10 Acie Earl .12 .30
11 Pervis Ellison .12 .30
12 Rick Fox .12 .30
13 Xavier McDaniel .12 .30
14 Eric Montross RC .15 .40
15 Dino Radja .12 .30
16 Dominique Wilkins .25 .60
17 Michael Adams .12 .30
18 Muggsy Bogues .15 .40
19 Dell Curry .12 .30
20 Kenny Gattison .12 .30
21 Hersey Hawkins .12 .30
22 Larry Johnson .20 .50
23 Alonzo Mourning .25 .60
24 Robert Parish .20 .50
25 B.J. Armstrong .12 .30
26 Steve Kerr .15 .40
27 Toni Kukoc .25 .60
28 Luc Longley .15 .40
29 Pete Myers .12 .30
30 Will Perdue .12 .30
31 Scottie Pippen .40 1.00
32 Terrell Brandon .12 .30
33 Brad Daugherty .15 .40
34 Tyrone Hill .12 .30
35 Chris Mills .15 .40
36 Bobby Phills .12 .30
37 Mark Price .20 .50
38 Gerald Wilkins .12 .30
39 John Williams .12 .30
40 Terry Davis .12 .30
41 Jim Jackson .12 .30
42 Popeye Jones .12 .30
43 Jason Kidd RC 1.00 2.50
44 Jamal Mashburn .20 .50
45 Sean Rooks .12 .30
46 Doug Smith .12 .30
47 Mahmoud Abdul-Rauf .12 .30
48 LaPhonso Ellis .12 .30
49 Dikembe Mutombo .20 .50
50 Robert Pack .12 .30
51 Rodney Rogers .12 .30
52 Bryant Stith .12 .30
53 Brian Williams .12 .30
54 Reggie Williams .12 .30
55 Greg Anderson .12 .30
56 Joe Dumars .20 .50
57 Allan Houston .20 .50
58 Lindsey Hunter .12 .30
59 Terry Mills .12 .30
60 Tim Hardaway .20 .50
61 Chris Mullin .20 .50
62 Billy Owens .12 .30
63 Latrell Sprewell .25 .60
64 Chris Webber .30 .75
65 Sam Cassell .20 .50
66 Carl Herrera .12 .30
67 Robert Horry .20 .50
68 Vernon Maxwell .12 .30
69 Hakeem Olajuwon .25 .60
70 Kenny Smith .15 .40
71 Otis Thorpe .12 .30
72 Antonio Davis .12 .30
73 Dale Davis .12 .30
74 Mark Jackson .15 .40
75 Derrick McKey .12 .30
76 Reggie Miller .25 .60
77 Byron Scott .15 .40
78 Rik Smits .12 .30
79 Haywoode Workman .12 .30
80 Gary Grant .12 .30
81 Ron Harper .12 .30
82 Elmore Spencer .12 .30
83 Loy Vaught .12 .30
84 Elden Campbell .12 .30
85 Doug Christie .12 .30
86 Vlade Divac .20 .50
87 Eddie Jones RC .60 1.50
88 George Lynch .12 .30
89 Anthony Peeler .12 .30
90 Sedale Threatt .12 .30
91 Nick Van Exel .20 .50
92 James Worthy .25 .60
93 Bimbo Coles .12 .30
94 Matt Geiger .12 .30
95 Grant Long .12 .30
96 Harold Miner .12 .30
97 Glen Rice .20 .50
98 John Salley .12 .30
99 Rony Seikaly .12 .30
100 Brian Shaw .12 .30
101 Steve Smith .15 .40
102 Vin Baker .20 .50
103 Jon Barry .12 .30
104 Todd Day .12 .30
105 Lee Mayberry .12 .30
106 Eric Murdock .12 .30
107 Thurl Bailey .12 .30
108 Stacey King .12 .30
109 Christian Laettner .15 .40
110 Isaiah Rider .20 .50
111 Chris Smith .12 .30
112 Doug West .12 .30
113 Micheal Williams .12 .30
114 Kenny Anderson .15 .40
115 Benoit Benjamin .12 .30
116 P.J. Brown .12 .30
117 Derrick Coleman .15 .40
118 Yinka Dare RC .12 .30
119 Kevin Edwards .12 .30
120 Armon Gilliam .12 .30
121 Chris Morris .12 .30
122 Greg Anthony .12 .30
123 Anthony Bonner .12 .30
124 Hubert Davis .12 .30
125 Patrick Ewing .25 .60
126 Derek Harper .15 .40
127 Anthony Mason .15 .40
128 Charles Oakley .15 .40
129 Doc Rivers .15 .40
130 John Starks .15 .40
131 Nick Anderson .12 .30
132 Anthony Avent .12 .30
133 Anthony Bowie .12 .30
134 Anfernee Hardaway .30 .75
135 Shaquille O'Neal .50 1.25
136 Dennis Scott .12 .30
137 Jeff Turner .12 .30
138 Dana Barros .12 .30
139 Shawn Bradley .12 .30
140 Greg Graham .12 .30
141 Jeff Malone .12 .30
142 Tim Perry .12 .30
143 Clarence Weatherspoon .12 .30
144 Scott Williams .12 .30
145 Danny Ainge .20 .50
146 Charles Barkley .30 .75
147 Cedric Ceballos .12 .30
148 A.C. Green .15 .40
149 Frank Johnson .12 .30
150 Kevin Johnson .20 .50
151 Dan Majerle .20 .50
152 Oliver Miller .12 .30
153 Wesley Person RC .20 .50
154 Mark Bryant .12 .30
155 Clyde Drexler .25 .60
156 Harvey Grant .12 .30
157 Jerome Kersey .12 .30
158 Tracy Murray .12 .30
159 Terry Porter .12 .30
160 Clifford Robinson .12 .30
161 James Robinson .12 .30
162 Rod Strickland .12 .30
163 Buck Williams .12 .30
164 Duane Causwell .12 .30
165 Olden Polynice .12 .30
166 Mitch Richmond .20 .50
167 Lionel Simmons .12 .30
168 Walt Williams .12 .30
169 Willie Anderson .12 .30
170 Terry Cummings .15 .40
171 Sean Elliott .20 .50
172 Avery Johnson .15 .40
173 J.R. Reid .12 .30
174 David Robinson .30 .75
175 Dennis Rodman .40 1.00
176 Kendall Gill .12 .30
177 Shawn Kemp .20 .50
178 Nate McMillan .12 .30
179 Gary Payton .20 .50
180 Sam Perkins .15 .40
181 Detlef Schrempf .20 .50
182 David Benoit .12 .30
183 Tyrone Corbin .12 .30
184 Jeff Hornacek .15 .40
185 Jay Humphries .12 .30
186 Karl Malone .25 .60
187 Bryon Russell .12 .30
188 Felton Spencer .12 .30
189 John Stockton .25 .60
190 Mitchell Butler .12 .30
191 Rex Chapman .12 .30
192 Calbert Cheaney .12 .30
193 Kevin Duckworth .12 .30
194 Tom Gugliotta .12 .30
195 Don MacLean .12 .30
196 Gheorghe Muresan .12 .30
197 Scott Skiles .12 .30
198 Checklist .12 .30
199 Checklist .12 .30
200 Checklist .12 .30
201 Tyrone Corbin .12 .30
202 Doug Edwards .12 .30
203 Jim Les .12 .30
204 Grant Long .12 .30
205 Ken Norman .12 .30
206 Steve Smith .15 .40
207 Blue Edwards .12 .30
208 Greg Minor RC .20 .50
209 Eric Montross .10 .25
210 Derek Strong .12 .30
211 David Wesley .12 .30
212 Tony Bennett .12 .30
213 Scott Burrell .12 .30
214 Darrin Hancock .15 .40
215 Greg Sutton .12 .30
216 Corie Blount .12 .30
217 Jud Buechler .12 .30
218 Ron Harper .15 .40
219 Larry Krystkowiak .12 .30
220 Dickey Simpkins RC .15 .40
221 Bill Wennington .12 .30
222 Michael Cage .12 .30
223 Tony Campbell .12 .30
224 Steve Colter .12 .30
225 Greg Dreiling .12 .30
226 Danny Ferry .12 .30
227 Tony Dumas RC .20 .50
228 Lucious Harris .12 .30
229 Donald Hodge .12 .30
230 Jason Kidd .60 1.50
231 Lorenzo Williams .12 .30
232 Dale Ellis .12 .30
233 Tom Hammonds .12 .30
234 Jalen Rose RC .50 1.25
235 Reggie Slater .12 .30
236 Rafael Addison .12 .30
237 Bill Curley RC .12 .30
238 Johnny Dawkins .12 .30
239 Grant Hill RC 1.00 2.50
240 Eric Leckner .12 .30
241 Mark Macon .12 .30
242 Oliver Miller .12 .30
243 Mark West .12 .30
244 Victor Alexander .12 .30
245 Chris Gatling .12 .30
246 Tom Gugliotta .12 .30
247 Keith Jennings .12 .30
248 Ricky Pierce .12 .30
249 Carlos Rogers RC .15 .40
250 Clifford Rozier RC .12 .30
251 Rony Seikaly .12 .30
252 David Wood .12 .30
253 Tim Breaux .12 .30
254 Scott Brooks .12 .30
255 Zan Tabak .12 .30
256 Duane Ferrell .12 .30
257 Mark Jackson .15 .40
258 Sam Mitchell .12 .30
259 John Williams .12 .30
260 Terry Dehere .12 .30
261 Harold Ellis .12 .30
262 Matt Fish .12 .30
263 Tony Massenburg .12 .30
264 Lamond Murray RC .20 .50
265 Bo Outlaw RC .12 .30
266 Eric Piatkowski RC .25 .60
267 Pooh Richardson .12 .30
268 Malik Sealy .12 .30
269 Randy Woods .12 .30
270 Sam Bowie .12 .30
271 Cedric Ceballos .12 .30
272 Antonio Harvey .12 .30
273 Eddie Jones .40 1.00
274 Anthony Miller RC .12 .30
275 Tony Smith .12 .30
276 Ledell Eackles .12 .30
277 Kevin Gamble .12 .30
278 Brad Lohaus .12 .30
279 Billy Owens .12 .30
280 Khalid Reeves RC .15 .40
281 Kevin Willis .12 .30
282 Marty Conlon .12 .30
283 Alton Lister .12 .30
284 Eric Mobley RC .12 .30
285 Johnny Newman .12 .30
286 Ed Pinckney .12 .30
287 Glenn Robinson RC .40 1.00
288 Howard Eisley .20 .50
289 Winston Garland .12 .30
290 Andres Guibert .12 .30
291 Donyell Marshall RC .20 .50
292 Sean Rooks .12 .30
293 Yinka Dare .07 .20
294 Sleepy Floyd .12 .30
295 Sean Higgins .12 .30
296 Rex Walters .12 .30
297 Jayson Williams .15 .40
298 Charles Smith .12 .30
299 Charlie Ward RC .20 .50
300 Herb Williams .12 .30
301 Monty Williams RC .15 .40
302 Horace Grant .15 .40
303 Geert Hammink .12 .30
304 Tree Rollins .12 .30
305 Donald Royal .12 .30
306 Brian Shaw .12 .30
307 Brooks Thompson RC .15 .40
308 Derrick Alston RC .12 .30
309 Willie Burton .12 .30
310 Jaren Jackson .12 .30
311 B.J. Tyler RC .12 .30
312 Scott Williams .12 .30
313 Sharone Wright RC .15 .40
314 Joe Kleine .12 .30
315 Danny Manning .15 .40
316 Elliot Perry .12 .30
317 Wesley Person .15 .40
318 Trevor Ruffin RC .12 .30
319 Danny Schayes .12 .30
320 Wayman Tisdale .12 .30
321 Chris Dudley .12 .30
322 James Edwards .12 .30
323 Alaa Abdelnaby .12 .30
324 Randy Brown .12 .30
325 Brian Grant RC .30 .75
326 Bobby Hurley .12 .30
327 Michael Smith RC .12 .30
328 Henry Turner .12 .30
329 Trevor Wilson .12 .30
330 Vinny Del Negro .12 .30
331 Moses Malone .20 .50
332 Julius Nwosu .12 .30
333 Chuck Person .15 .40
334 Chris Whitney .12 .30
335 Vincent Askew .12 .30
336 Bill Cartwright .15 .40
337 Ervin Johnson .12 .30
338 Sarunas Marciulionis .12 .30
339 Antoine Carr .12 .30
340 Tom Chambers .15 .40
341 John Crotty .12 .30
342 Jamie Watson RC .12 .30
343 Juwan Howard RC .30 .75
344 Jim McIlvaine RC .15 .40
345 Doug Overton .12 .30
346 Scott Skiles .12 .30
347 Anthony Tucker RC .12 .30
348 Chris Webber .30 .75
349 Checklist .12 .30
350 Checklist .12 .30

1994-95 Ultra All-NBA

Randomly inserted into approximately one in every three first series packs, cards from this 15-card standard-size set feature members of the All-NBA first (1-5), second (6-10), and third (11-15) teams. The fronts are laid out horizontally and have a color action photo and three photos that look like they were taken in a room with a black light. On the right side is the player's first name in white behind his last name in the color of his team. At the bottom in gold-foil are the words "ALL-NBA" and the corresponding team he made. On the backs are a color photo in front of the same photo with the black light look. Their is also player information and the cards are numbered "X of 15."

COMPLETE SET (15) 4.00 10.00
SER.1 STATED ODDS 1:3 HOBBY/RETAIL
1 Karl Malone .50 1.25
2 Hakeem Olajuwon .50 1.25
3 Scottie Pippen .75 2.00
4 Latrell Sprewell .50 1.25
5 John Stockton .50 1.25
6 Charles Barkley .60 1.50
7 Kevin Johnson .40 1.00
8 Shawn Kemp .40 1.00
9 Mitch Richmond .40 1.00
10 David Robinson .60 1.50
11 Derrick Coleman .30 .75
12 Shaquille O'Neal 1.00 2.50
13 Gary Payton .40 1.00
14 Mark Price .40 1.00
15 Dominique Wilkins .50 1.25

1994-95 Ultra All-Rookie Team

Randomly inserted exclusively into first series jumbo packs at a rate of one in 36, cards from this 10-card standard-size set feature some of the top rookies from the 1993-94 season. Fronts feature a full-color action shot aside a bold, gold-foil All-Rookie logo with the player's name.

COMPLETE SET (10) 20.00 50.00
SER.1 STATED ODDS 1:36 JUMBO
1 Vin Baker 3.00 8.00
2 Anfernee Hardaway 8.00 20.00
3 Jamal Mashburn 3.00 8.00
4 Isaiah Rider 3.00 8.00
5 Chris Webber 8.00 20.00
6 Shawn Bradley 2.00 5.00
7 Lindsey Hunter 2.00 5.00
8 Toni Kukoc 4.00 10.00
9 Dino Radja 2.00 5.00
10 Nick Van Exel 3.00 8.00

1994-95 Ultra All-Rookies

Randomly inserted at a rate of one in every five second series packs, this 15-card standard-size set captures the best first-year players from the 1994-95 season. The fronts have a full-color photo with a hardwood floor background. The words "All-Rookie" and the player's name are on the left side in gold-foil. The backs a full-color photo with his name and a hardwood floor in the background. There is also player information and the cards are numbered "X of 15." The set is sequenced in alphabetical order.

COMPLETE SET (15) 5.00 12.00
SER.2 STATED ODDS 1:5 HOBBY/RETAIL
1 Brian Grant .50 1.25
2 Grant Hill 1.50 4.00
3 Juwan Howard .50 1.25
4 Eddie Jones 1.00 2.50
5 Jason Kidd 1.50 4.00
6 Donyell Marshall .30 .75
7 Eric Montross .25 .60
8 Lamond Murray .30 .75
9 Wesley Person .30 .75
10 Khalid Reeves .25 .60
11 Glenn Robinson .60 1.50
12 Carlos Rogers .25 .60
13 Jalen Rose .75 2.00
14 B.J. Tyler .20 .50
15 Sharone Wright .25 .60

1994-95 Ultra Award Winners

Randomly inserted into approximately one in every four first series packs, cards from this four-card standard-size set feature players who won individual awards during the 1993-94 season. The fronts are laid out horizontally and have a color-action photo with the backgrounds having a black and white head shot with horizontal white lines across the card. At on of the bottom corners are the words "NBA Award Winner" with a basketball in gold-foil. The backs have a color photo from the chest up with a similar background to the front. There is also player information and the cards are numbered "X of 4." The set is sequenced in alphabetical order.

COMPLETE SET (4) .60 1.50
SER.1 STATED ODDS 1:4 HOBBY/RETAIL
1 Dell Curry .12 .30
2 Don MacLean .12 .30
3 Hakeem Olajuwon .25 .60
4 Chris Webber .30 .75

1994-95 Ultra Defensive Gems

Randomly inserted at a rate of one in every 37 second-series packs, this 6-card standard-size set focuses on six NBA stars who play standout defense. The borderless fronts feature 100% etched-foil backgrounds. The player's name is located at the bottom while the words "Defensive Gems" surrounding a diamond are in the lower right. The backs are split between another player photo and some information about the player's defensive prowess. The cards are numbered in the lower left as "X" of 6. The set is sequenced in alphabetical order.

COMPLETE SET (6) 6.00 15.00
SER.2 STATED ODDS 1:37 HOBBY/RETAIL
1 Mookie Blaylock 1.00 2.50
2 Hakeem Olajuwon 2.00 5.00
3 Gary Payton 1.50 4.00
4 Scottie Pippen 3.00 8.00
5 David Robinson 2.50 6.00
6 Latrell Sprewell 2.00 5.00

1994-95 Ultra Double Trouble

Randomly inserted into approximately one in every five first series packs, cards from this 10-card standard-size set feature a selection of multi-skilled NBA stars. The fronts feature two photos of the player in a split player design. The words "Double Trouble" and player's name are printed in silver foil on the bottom. The borderless backs are split between an explanation of the the player's skills as well as a photo. The cards are numbered "X" of 10 in the lower left corner. The set is sequenced in alphabetical order.

COMPLETE SET (10) 2.00 5.00
SER.1 STATED ODDS 1:5 HOBBY/RETAIL
1 Derrick Coleman .25 .60
2 Patrick Ewing .40 1.00
3 Anfernee Hardaway .50 1.25
4 Jamal Mashburn .30 .75
5 Reggie Miller .40 1.00
6 Alonzo Mourning .40 1.00
7 Scottie Pippen .60 1.50
8 David Robinson .50 1.25
9 Latrell Sprewell .40 1.00
10 John Stockton .40 1.00

1994-95 Ultra Inside/Outside

Randomly inserted exclusively into one in every seven second series hobby packs, cards from this 10-card standard-size set focus on players who can score from anywhere on the court. The borderless fronts feature dual player photos against a gray background. The player's name is in the lower left corner while the words "Inside/Outside" are in the lower right corner. The backs describe the player's shooting ability and have a small photo as well. The cards are numbered in the lower right as "X" of 10. The set is sequenced in alphabetical order.

COMPLETE SET (10) 2.00 5.00
SER.2 STATED ODDS 1:7 HOBBY
1 Sam Cassell .40 1.00
2 Cedric Ceballos .25 .60
3 Calbert Cheaney .25 .60
4 Anfernee Hardaway .60 1.50
5 Jim Jackson .25 .60
6 Dan Majerle .40 1.00
7 Robert Pack .25 .60
8 Scottie Pippen .75 2.00
9 Mitch Richmond .40 1.00
10 Latrell Sprewell .50 1.25

1994-95 Ultra Jam City

Randomly inserted exclusively into one in every seven second series jumbo packs, cards from this 10-card standard size set spotlight ten well known dunkers. The borderless fronts feature color player action cutouts on a multi colored metallic cityscape background. The words "Jam City" and the player's name are printed in gold foil on the bottom of the card. The backs feature another cutout photo against a different skyscraper background with the player's name in the middle in gold foil. A brief blurb about the player is inset at the bottom. The cards are numbered "X" of 10 in the bottom right. The set is sequenced in alphabetical order.

COMPLETE SET (10) 8.00 20.00
SER.2 STATED ODDS 1:7 JUMBO
1 Vin Baker .75 2.00
2 Grant Hill 4.00 10.00
3 Robert Horry .75 2.00
4 Shawn Kemp .75 2.00
5 Jamal Mashburn .75 2.00
6 Alonzo Mourning 1.00 2.50
7 Dikembe Mutombo .75 2.00
8 Shaquille O'Neal 2.00 5.00
9 Glenn Robinson 1.50 4.00
10 Dominique Wilkins 1.00 2.50

1994-95 Ultra Power

Randomly inserted in all first series packs at an approximate rate of one in three, cards from this 10-card standard-size set feature a selection of the NBA's most powerful stars. This set features color player action cutouts set on a colorful and sparkly starburst background design. The player's name appears in vertical gold lettering in a lower corner. The colorful starburst design continues on the borderless horizontal back, which carries a color player head shot on one side, and career highlights on the other. The cards are numbered on the back as "X of 10." The set is sequenced in alphabetical order.

COMPLETE SET (10) 2.00 5.00
SER.1 STATED ODDS 1:3 HOBBY/RETAIL
1 Charles Barkley .40 1.00
2 Derrick Coleman .20 .50
3 Larry Johnson .25 .60
4 Shawn Kemp .25 .60
5 Karl Malone .30 .75
6 Dikembe Mutombo .25 .60
7 Charles Oakley .25 .60
8 Shaquille O'Neal .60 1.50
9 Dennis Rodman .50 1.25
10 Chris Webber .40 1.00

1994-95 Ultra Power In The Key

Randomly inserted exclusively into one in every seven second series retail packs, cards from this 10-card standard-size set feature ten players who are effective playing near the basket. The front feature a player cutout against a multicolored basketball court design. The words "Power in the Key" are on either side, with the player's name directly underneath those words. The backs contain biographical information along with an inset photo of the player. The cards are numbered in the lower right as "X" of 10. The set is sequenced in alphabetical order.

COMPLETE SET (10) 2.00 5.00
SER.2 STATED ODDS 1:7 RETAIL
1 Charles Barkley .40 1.00
2 Patrick Ewing .30 .75
3 Horace Grant .20 .50
4 Larry Johnson .25 .60
5 Karl Malone .30 .75
6 Hakeem Olajuwon .30 .75
7 Shaquille O'Neal .60 1.50
8 David Robinson .40 1.00
9 Chris Webber .40 1.00
10 Kevin Willis .15 .40

1994-95 Ultra Rebound Kings

Randomly inserted at a rate of one in every two second-series packs, cards from this 10-card standard-size set focus on league's top rebounders. The fronts have a color-action photo and a color picture of his head at the bottom along with a gold-foil crown. The words "Rebound King" are at the top and side with rebound behind king at the top and vice-versa on the side, each card uses different colors for the words. The backs have a color photo with his name in gold-foil and information on why he is a top rebounder. The cards are numbered "X of 10." The set is sequenced in alphabetical order.

COMPLETE SET (10) 1.25 3.00
SER.2 STATED ODDS 1:2 HOBBY/RETAIL
1 Derrick Coleman .15 .40
2 A.C. Green .15 .40
3 Alonzo Mourning .25 .60
4 Dikembe Mutombo .20 .50
5 Charles Oakley .15 .40
6 Hakeem Olajuwon .25 .60
7 Shaquille O'Neal .50 1.25
8 David Robinson .30 .75
9 Chris Webber .30 .75
10 Kevin Willis .12 .30

1994-95 Ultra Scoring Kings

Randomly inserted exclusively into one in every 37 first series hobby packs, cards from this 10-card standard-size set feature a selection of perennial NBA scoring leaders. Fronts feature full-color player action shots cut out against 100% etched-foil backgrounds. The set is sequenced in alphabetical order.

COMPLETE SET (10) 10.00 25.00
SER.1 STATED ODDS 1:37 HOBBY
1 Charles Barkley 3.00 8.00
2 Patrick Ewing 2.50 6.00
3 Karl Malone 2.50 6.00
4 Hakeem Olajuwon 2.50 6.00
5 Shaquille O'Neal 5.00 12.00
6 Scottie Pippen 4.00 10.00
7 Mitch Richmond 2.00 5.00
8 David Robinson 3.00 8.00
9 Latrell Sprewell 2.50 6.00
10 Dominique Wilkins 2.50 6.00

1995-96 Ultra Promo Sheet

Measuring 10" by 10", this promo sheet was issued to preview the second series of the 1995-96 Ultra set. The sheet consists of six cards, with an advertisement at the top of the sheet. The cards, unfortunately, are identical their regular issue counterparts with card numbers being left the same. Some people went on to cut out cards like the Antonio McDyess and Damon Stoudamire All-Rookie cards, which caused a fluctuation in price of their regular issue insert cards.

COMPLETE SET (6) 2.00 5.00
4 Antonio McDyess 1.25 3.00
8 Damon Stoudamire 2.50 6.00
202 Mookie Blaylock .15 .40
219 Hakeem Olajuwon .30 .75
344 Nick Van Exel .25 .60
S3 Jerry Stackhouse 1.25 3.00

1995-96 Ultra

The 1995-96 Ultra set was issued in two series of 200 and 150 for a total of 350 standard-size cards. They were issued in 12-card hobby and retail packs (SRP $2.49) in addition to 17-card pre-priced packs (SRP $2.99). Each 12-card pack contains two insert cards and one in every 72 packs contains nothing but insert cards (referred to as a "Hot Pack"). Fleer upgraded the stock of the 1995-96 cards by making them 40% thicker than the previous year's Ultra release. The fronts have a full-color action photo with the player's name and team at the bottom in gold-foil. The backs have two-color photos and one full black-and-white with statistics at the bottom. The basic issue cards are grouped alphabetically within teams and checklisted below alphabetically according to city. Subsets featured are Rookies (263-298) and Encore (299-348). Rookie Cards of note in this set include Michael Finley, Kevin Garnett, Antonio McDyess, Joe Smith, Jerry Stackhouse and Damon Stoudamire.

COMPLETE SET (350) 20.00 40.00
COMPLETE SERIES 1 (200) 10.00 20.00
COMPLETE SERIES 2 (150) 10.00 20.00
1 Stacey Augmon .20 .50
2 Mookie Blaylock .15 .40
3 Craig Ehlo .15 .40
4 Andrew Lang .15 .40
5 Grant Long .15 .40
6 Ken Norman .15 .40
7 Steve Smith .20 .50
8 Spud Webb .20 .50
9 Dee Brown .15 .40
10 Sherman Douglas .15 .40
11 Pervis Ellison .15 .40
12 Eric Montross .15 .40
13 Eric Montross .15 .40
14 Dino Radja .15 .40
15 David Wesley .15 .40
16 Dominique Wilkins .30 .75
17 Muggsy Bogues .20 .50
18 Scott Burrell .15 .40
19 Dell Curry .15 .40
20 Kendall Gill .15 .40
21 Larry Johnson .25 .60
22 Alonzo Mourning .30 .75
23 Robert Parish .25 .60
24 Ron Harper .20 .50
25 Michael Jordan 2.00 5.00
26 Toni Kukoc .25 .60
27 Will Perdue .15 .40
28 Scottie Pippen .40 1.00
29 Terrell Brandon .15 .40
30 Michael Cage .15 .40
31 Tyrone Hill .15 .40
32 Chris Mills .15 .40
33 Bobby Phills .15 .40
34 Mark Price .25 .60
35 John Williams .15 .40
36 Lucious Harris .15 .40
37 Jim Jackson .15 .40
38 Popeye Jones .15 .40
39 Jason Kidd .40 1.00
40 Jamal Mashburn .25 .60
41 George McCloud .15 .40
42 Roy Tarpley .15 .40
43 Lorenzo Williams .15 .40
44 Mahmoud Abdul-Rauf .15 .40
45 Dikembe Mutombo .25 .60
46 Robert Pack .15 .40
47 Jalen Rose .30 .75
48 Bryant Stith .15 .40
49 Brian Williams .15 .40
50 Reggie Williams .15 .40
51 Joe Dumars .25 .60
52 Grant Hill .40 1.00
53 Allan Houston .20 .50
54 Lindsey Hunter .15 .40
55 Terry Mills .15 .40
56 Mark West .15 .40
57 Chris Gatling .15 .40
58 Tim Hardaway .25 .60
59 Donyell Marshall .15 .40
60 Chris Mullin .25 .60
61 Carlos Rogers .15 .40
62 Clifford Rozier .15 .40
63 Rony Seikaly .15 .40
64 Latrell Sprewell .25 .60
65 Sam Cassell .25 .60
66 Clyde Drexler .30 .75
67 Mario Elie .15 .40
68 Carl Herrera .15 .40
69 Robert Horry .20 .50
70 Hakeem Olajuwon .30 .75
71 Kenny Smith .20 .50
72 Antonio Davis .15 .40
73 Dale Davis .15 .40
74 Mark Jackson .15 .40
75 Derrick McKey .15 .40
76 Reggie Miller .25 .60
77 Rik Smits .20 .50
78 Terry Dehere .15 .40
79 Lamond Murray .15 .40
80 Bo Outlaw .15 .40
81 Pooh Richardson .15 .40
82 Rodney Rogers .15 .40
83 Malik Sealy .15 .40
84 Loy Vaught .15 .40
85 Sam Bowie .15 .40
86 Elden Campbell .15 .40
87 Cedric Ceballos .15 .40
88 Vlade Divac .25 .60
89 Eddie Jones .25 .60
90 Anthony Peeler .15 .40
91 Sedale Threatt .15 .40
92 Nick Van Exel .25 .60
93 Rex Chapman .15 .40
94 Bimbo Coles .15 .40
95 Matt Geiger .15 .40
96 Billy Owens .15 .40
97 Khalid Reeves .15 .40
98 Glen Rice .25 .60
99 Kevin Willis .15 .40
100 Vin Baker .20 .50
101 Marty Conlon .15 .40
102 Todd Day .15 .40
103 Eric Murdock .15 .40
104 Glenn Robinson .20 .50
105 Winston Garland .15 .40
106 Tom Gugliotta .15 .40
107 Christian Laettner .20 .50
108 Isaiah Rider .25 .60
109 Sean Rooks .15 .40
110 Doug West .15 .40
111 Kenny Anderson .20 .50
112 P.J. Brown .15 .40
113 Derrick Coleman .15 .40
114 Armon Gilliam .15 .40
115 Chris Morris .15 .40
116 Anthony Bonner .15 .40
117 Patrick Ewing .30 .75
118 Derek Harper .20 .50
119 Anthony Mason .15 .40
120 Charles Oakley .20 .50
121 Charles Smith .15 .40
122 John Starks .20 .50
123 Nick Anderson .15 .40
124 Horace Grant .20 .50
125 Anfernee Hardaway .40 1.00
126 Shaquille O'Neal .60 1.50
127 Donald Royal .15 .40
128 Dennis Scott .15 .40
129 Brian Shaw .15 .40
130 Derrick Alston .15 .40
131 Dana Barros .15 .40
132 Shawn Bradley .15 .40
133 Willie Burton .15 .40
134 Jeff Malone .15 .40
135 Clarence Weatherspoon .15 .40
136 Scott Williams .15 .40
137 Sharone Wright .15 .40
138 Danny Ainge .20 .50
139 Charles Barkley .40 1.00
140 A.C. Green .20 .50
141 Kevin Johnson .20 .50
142 Dan Majerle .20 .50
143 Danny Manning .20 .50
144 Elliot Perry .15 .40
145 Wesley Person .15 .40
146 Wayman Tisdale .15 .40
147 Chris Dudley .15 .40
148 Harvey Grant .15 .40
149 Aaron McKie .15 .40
150 Terry Porter .15 .40
151 Clifford Robinson .15 .40
152 Rod Strickland .15 .40
153 Otis Thorpe .15 .40
154 Buck Williams .15 .40
155 Brian Grant .20 .50
156 Bobby Hurley .15 .40
157 Olden Polynice .15 .40
158 Mitch Richmond .25 .60
159 Michael Smith .15 .40
160 Walt Williams .15 .40
161 Vinny Del Negro .15 .40
162 Sean Elliott .25 .60
163 Avery Johnson .20 .50
164 Chuck Person .20 .50
165 J.R. Reid .15 .40
166 Doc Rivers .20 .50
167 David Robinson .40 1.00
168 Dennis Rodman .50 1.25
169 Vincent Askew .15 .40
170 Hersey Hawkins .15 .40
171 Shawn Kemp .25 .60
172 Sarunas Marciulionis .15 .40
173 Nate McMillan .15 .40
174 Gary Payton .25 .60
175 Sam Perkins .15 .40
176 Detlef Schrempf .25 .60
177 B.J. Armstrong .15 .40
178 Jerome Kersey .15 .40
179 Tony Massenburg .15 .40
180 Oliver Miller .15 .40
181 John Salley .15 .40
182 David Benoit .15 .40
183 Antoine Carr .15 .40
184 Jeff Hornacek .20 .50
185 Karl Malone .30 .75
186 Felton Spencer .15 .40
187 John Stockton .30 .75
188 Greg Anthony .15 .40
189 Benoit Benjamin .15 .40
190 Byron Scott .20 .50
191 Calbert Cheaney .15 .40
192 Juwan Howard .25 .60
193 Don MacLean .15 .40
194 Gheorghe Muresan .15 .40
195 Doug Overton .15 .40
196 Scott Skiles .15 .40
197 Chris Webber .30 .75
198 Checklist (1-94) .15 .40
199 Checklist (95-190) .15 .40
200 Checklist (191-200) .15 .40
201 Stacey Augmon .20 .50
202 Mookie Blaylock .15 .40
203 Grant Long .15 .40
204 Steve Smith .20 .50
205 Dana Barros .15 .40
206 Kendall Gill .15 .40
207 Khalid Reeves .15 .40
208 Glen Rice .25 .60
209 Luc Longley .15 .40
210 Dennis Rodman .50 1.25
211 Dan Majerle .25 .60
212 Tony Dumas .15 .40
213 Elmore Spencer .15 .40
214 Otis Thorpe .15 .40
215 B.J. Armstrong .15 .40
216 Sam Cassell .25 .60
217 Clyde Drexler .30 .75
218 Robert Horry .20 .50
219 Hakeem Olajuwon .30 .75
220 Eddie Johnson .15 .40
221 Ricky Pierce .15 .40
222 Eric Piatkowski .20 .50
223 Rodney Rogers .15 .40
224 Brian Williams .15 .40
225 George Lynch .15 .40
226 Alonzo Mourning .30 .75
227 Benoit Benjamin .15 .40
228 Terry Porter .15 .40
229 Shawn Bradley .15 .40
230 Kevin Edwards .15 .40
231 Jayson Williams .15 .40
232 Charlie Ward .15 .40
233 Jon Koncak .15 .40
234 Derrick Coleman .20 .50
235 Richard Dumas .15 .40
236 Vernon Maxwell .15 .40
237 John Williams .15 .40
238 Dontonio Wingfield .15 .40
239 Tyrone Corbin .15 .40
240 Will Perdue .15 .40
241 Shawn Kemp .25 .60
242 Gary Payton .25 .60
243 Sam Perkins .15 .40
244 Detlef Schrempf .25 .60
245 Chris Morris .15 .40
246 Robert Pack .15 .40
247 Willie Anderson EXP .15 .40
248 Oliver Miller EXP .15 .40
249 Tracy Murray EXP .15 .40
250 Alvin Robertson EXP .15 .40
251 Carlos Rogers EXP .15 .40
252 John Salley EXP .15 .40
253 Damon Stoudamire EXP .40 1.00
254 Zan Tabak EXP .15 .40
255 Greg Anthony EXP .15 .40
256 Blue Edwards EXP .15 .40
257 Kenny Gattison EXP .15 .40
258 Chris King EXP .15 .40
259 Lawrence Moten EXP .15 .40
260 Eric Murdock EXP .15 .40
261 Bryant Reeves EXP .12 .30
262 Byron Scott EXP .20 .50
263 Cory Alexander RC .20 .50
264 Brent Barry RC .40 1.00
265 Mario Bennett RC .20 .50
266 Travis Best RC .25 .60
267 Junior Burrough RC .20 .50
268 Jason Caffey RC .25 .60
269 Randolph Childress RC .20 .50
270 Sasha Danilovic RC .20 .50
271 Tyus Edney RC .20 .50
272 Michael Finley RC .75 2.00
273 Sherrell Ford RC .20 .50
274 Kevin Garnett RC 2.00 5.00
275 Alan Henderson RC .25 .60
276 Donny Marshall RC .20 .50
277 Antonio McDyess RC .30 .75
278 Loren Meyer RC .20 .50
279 Lawrence Moten RC .25 .60
280 Ed O'Bannon RC .20 .50
281 Greg Ostertag RC .25 .60
282 Cherokee Parks RC .20 .50
283 Theo Ratliff RC .40 1.00
284 Bryant Reeves RC .20 .50
285 Shawn Respert RC .20 .50
286 Lou Roe RC .20 .50
287 Arvydas Sabonis RC .50 1.25
288 Joe Smith RC .30 .75
289 Jerry Stackhouse RC .75 2.00
290 Damon Stoudamire RC .60 1.50
291 Bob Sura RC .20 .50
292 Kurt Thomas RC .25 .60
293 Gary Trent RC .20 .50
294 David Vaughn RC .20 .50
295 Rasheed Wallace RC .75 2.00
296 Eric Williams RC .25 .60
297 Corliss Williamson RC .25 .60

1995-96 Ultra

298 George Zidek RC .20 .50
299 Mahmoud Abdul-Rauf ENC .15 .40
300 Kenny Anderson ENC .20 .50
301 Vin Baker ENC .20 .50
302 Charles Barkley ENC .40 1.00
303 Mookie Blaylock ENC .15 .40
304 Cedric Ceballos ENC .15 .40
305 Vlade Divac ENC .25 .60
306 Clyde Drexler ENC .30 .75
307 Joe Dumars ENC .25 .60
308 Sean Elliott ENC .25 .60
309 Patrick Ewing ENC .30 .75
310 Anfernee Hardaway ENC .40 1.00
311 Tim Hardaway ENC .25 .60
312 Grant Hill ENC .40 1.00
313 Tyrone Hill ENC .15 .40
314 Robert Horry ENC .20 .50
315 Juwan Howard ENC .25 .60
316 Jim Jackson ENC .15 .40
317 Kevin Johnson ENC .25 .60
318 Larry Johnson ENC .25 .60
319 Eddie Jones ENC .25 .60
320 Shawn Kemp ENC .25 .60
321 Jason Kidd ENC .40 1.00
322 Christian Laettner ENC .20 .50
323 Karl Malone ENC .30 .75
324 Jamal Mashburn ENC .25 .60
325 Reggie Miller ENC .30 .75
326 Alonzo Mourning ENC .30 .75
327 Dikembe Mutombo ENC .25 .60
328 Hakeem Olajuwon ENC .30 .75
329 Gary Payton ENC .25 .60
330 Scottie Pippen ENC .40 1.00
331 Dino Radja ENC .15 .40
332 Glen Rice ENC .25 .60
333 Mitch Richmond ENC .25 .60
334 Clifford Robinson ENC .15 .40
335 David Robinson ENC .40 1.00
336 Glenn Robinson ENC .20 .50
337 Dennis Rodman ENC .50 1.25
338 Carlos Rogers ENC .15 .40
339 Detlef Schrempf ENC .25 .60
340 Byron Scott ENC .20 .50
341 Rik Smits ENC .20 .50
342 Latrell Sprewell ENC .25 .60
343 John Stockton ENC .30 .75
344 Nick Van Exel ENC .25 .60
345 Loy Vaught ENC .15 .40
346 Clarence Weatherspoon ENC .15 .40
347 Chris Webber ENC .30 .75
348 Kevin Willis ENC .15 .40
349 Checklist (201-298) .15 .40
350 Checklist (299-350/inserts) .15 .40

1995-96 Ultra Gold Medallion

COMPLETE SET (200) 60.00 120.00
*STARS: 2.5X TO 6X BASE CARD HI
ONE PER SERIES 1 PACK

1995-96 Ultra All-NBA

Randomly inserted in all series one packs at a rate of one in five, this 15-card set features the league's best and is divided into three standard-size sets of five (first, second and third team NBA All-Stars). Borderless fronts picture the player in a full-color action cutout with a black and gold metallic streak background. The "All NBA" box is printed in reverse-type metallic foil on the bottom left with the player's name printed in gold foil across the bottom right. Full-bleed backs continue with the black and gold metallic streaks and another full-color action player cutout. A screened box highlights the player's accomplishments and includes his name in gold foil.

COMPLETE SET (15) 6.00 15.00
SER.1 STATED ODDS 1:5 HOBBY/RETAIL
*GOLD MEDALLION: 1.25X TO 3X HI COLUMN
GOLD: SER.1 STATED ODDS 1:50 HOB/RET
1 Anfernee Hardaway 1.00 2.50
2 Karl Malone .75 2.00
3 Scottie Pippen 1.00 2.50
4 David Robinson 1.00 2.50
5 John Stockton .75 2.00
6 Charles Barkley 1.00 2.50
7 Shawn Kemp .60 1.50
8 Shaquille O'Neal 1.50 4.00
9 Gary Payton .60 1.50
10 Mitch Richmond .60 1.50
11 Clyde Drexler .75 2.00
12 Reggie Miller .75 2.00
13 Hakeem Olajuwon .75 2.00
14 Dennis Rodman 1.25 3.00
15 Detlef Schrempf .60 1.50

1995-96 Ultra All-Rookie Team

Randomly inserted in first series retail cello packs at a rate of one in seven, this 10-card set is divided into first team rookies (1-5) and second team rookies (6-10). Borderless fronts feature a full-color action player cutout set against a dark background with multicolored basketballs. All-Rookie team and the player's name are printed in gold foil across the bottom. Borderless backs continue with the multicolored basketball backgrounds and a full-color cutout of the player. A tan-screened box profiles the player and his name is printed in gold foil script across the top of the screen.

COMPLETE SET (10) 12.00 30.00
SER.1 STATED ODDS 1:7 RETAIL
*GOLD MEDALLION: 1.5X TO 4X HI COLUMN
GOLD: SER.1 STATED ODDS 1:70 RETAIL
1 Brian Grant 1.50 4.00
2 Grant Hill 3.00 8.00
3 Eddie Jones 2.00 5.00
4 Jason Kidd 3.00 8.00
5 Glenn Robinson 1.50 4.00
6 Juwan Howard 2.00 5.00
7 D.Marshall/S.Wright 1.25 3.00
8 Eric Montross 1.25 3.00
9 Wesley Person 1.25 3.00
10 Jalen Rose 2.50 6.00

1995-96 Ultra All-Rookies

Randomly inserted in all second series packs at a rate of one in 30, this set of 10 standard-size cards focuses on the play of the hot rookies of the '95 draft. Borderless fronts have a team color spectrum background with a full-color action cutout. The player's name and position are printed in gold foil near the bottom and "All Rookies" appears at the top. Backs have another full-color action cutout set against a color spectrum background. A screened box holds the player's name and a player profile. Card #'s 4 and 8 (McDyess and Stoudamire) were featured on an unperforated promo sheet of Ultra cards saluting card stores across America. The sheets were distributed to shop owners nationwide. Unfortunately, some unscrupulous parties cut up a number of the sheets and distributed the cut cards into the hobby market under false pretenses. The cut up cards are identical to the real inserts, thus supply has been altered and we've applied a "DP" designation to signify a double-print on this card.

COMPLETE SET (10) 12.00 30.00
SER.2 STATED ODDS 1:30 HOBBY/RETAIL
1 Tyus Edney .75 2.00
2 Michael Finley 2.50 6.00
3 Kevin Garnett 6.00 15.00
4 Antonio McDyess DP 1.00 2.50
5 Ed O'Bannon .60 1.50
6 Joe Smith 1.00 2.50
7 Jerry Stackhouse 2.50 6.00
8 Damon Stoudamire DP 2.00 5.00
9 Rasheed Wallace 2.50 6.00
10 Eric Williams .75 2.00

1995-96 Ultra Double Trouble

Randomly inserted in all first series packs at a rate of one in five, this 10-card standard-size set celebrates the players who perform well in more than one category. Full-bleed fronts feature a full-color action player cutout and a one-color action shot that serves as a background. "Double Trouble" is repeatedly printed in the background with a shadow effect. The player's name and "Double Trouble" are printed in alternating black and gold foil at the bottom. Another full-color action cutout appears on the back against the repeating "Double Trouble" colored background. A light screened box appears on the back with the player's abilities and accomplishments printed in black type. The player's name is printed in gold foil above the screened box. The set is sequenced in alphabetical order.

COMPLETE SET (10) 5.00 12.00
SER.1 STATED ODDS 1:5 HOBBY/RETAIL
*GOLD MEDALLION: 1.25X TO 3X HI COLUMN
GOLD: SER.1 STATED ODDS 1:50 HOB/RET
1 Charles Barkley .60 1.50
2 Anfernee Hardaway .60 1.50
3 Michael Jordan 3.00 8.00
4 Alonzo Mourning .50 1.25
5 Hakeem Olajuwon .50 1.25
6 Shaquille O'Neal 1.00 2.50
7 Gary Payton .40 1.00
8 Scottie Pippen .60 1.50
9 David Robinson .60 1.50
10 John Stockton .50 1.25

1995-96 Ultra Fabulous Fifties

Randomly inserted in first series hobby packs at a rate of one in 12, this seven-card standard-size set spotlights players who scored 50 or more points in a 94/95 NBA single game. The horizontal fronts feature a full-color action player cutout set against a two-color background with basketball nets and "Fabulous 50's" printed in alternating red boxes. Player's name and "Fabulous 50's" are printed in silver foil across the bottom left. A one-color picture of a basketball net serves as a backdrop on the back with the player's name and team printed in silver foil on the top. A full-color action cutout appears with a story of how and when the player reached his 50-point scoring mark. The set is sequenced in alphabetical order.

COMPLETE SET (7) 5.00 12.00
SER.1 STATED ODDS 1:12 HOBBY
*GOLD MEDALLION: 1.25X TO 3X HI COLUMN
GOLD: SER.1 STATED ODDS 1:120 HOBBY
1 Dana Barros .30 .75
2 Willie Burton .30 .75
3 Cedric Ceballos .30 .75
4 Jim Jackson .30 .75
5 Michael Jordan 4.00 10.00
6 Jamal Mashburn .50 1.25
7 Glen Rice .50 1.25

1995-96 Ultra Jam City

Randomly inserted exclusively in second series retail packs at a rate of one in 12, cards from this 12-card standard-size set focus on the NBA's most powerful dunkers. Borderless fronts have full-color action cutouts set against a one-color etched foil background. "Jam City" is printed in gold foil vertically along one side and the player's name is printed in silver foil vertically. Borderless backs feature a full-color player cutout with a halo effect set against a skyline background and a player profile. The set is sequenced in alphabetical order.

COMPLETE SET (12) 15.00 40.00
SER.2 STATED ODDS 1:12 RETAIL
HP: SER.2 STATED ODDS 1:72 RETAIL
1 Grant Hill 2.00 5.00
2 Robert Horry .75 2.00
3 Michael Jordan 12.00 30.00
4 Shawn Kemp 1.00 2.50
5 Jamal Mashburn 1.00 2.50
6 Antonio McDyess 1.25 3.00
7 Alonzo Mourning 1.25 3.00
8 Hakeem Olajuwon 1.25 3.00
9 Shaquille O'Neal 2.50 6.00
10 David Robinson 1.50 4.00
11 Joe Smith 1.25 3.00
12 Jerry Stackhouse 3.00 8.00

1995-96 Ultra Power

Randomly inserted in all first series packs at a rate of one in four, this 10-card standard-size set features the big rebounders and strong inside men of the NBA. A multicolored kaleidoscopic front serves as a background for a full-color action shot. The "Ultra Power" logo and player's name are stamped at the bottom left in gold foil. Backs continue with the kaleidoscopic background and another full-color action cutout. A screened box holds the player's name in gold foil along with a synopsis of the player's abilities and accomplishments. Gold Medallion editions were seeded in packs at 10 percent the rate of regular cards. Backs are identical to regular inserts.

COMPLETE SET (10) 2.00 5.00
SER.1 STATED ODDS 1:4 HOBBY/RETAIL
*GOLD MEDALLION: 1.5X TO 4X HI COLUMN
GOLD: SER.1 STATED ODDS 1:40 HOB/RET
1 Charles Barkley .50 1.25
2 Patrick Ewing .40 1.00
3 Larry Johnson .30 .75
4 Shawn Kemp .30 .75
5 Karl Malone .40 1.00
6 Alonzo Mourning .40 1.00
7 Dikembe Mutombo .30 .75
8 Hakeem Olajuwon .40 1.00
9 Shaquille O'Neal .75 2.00
10 David Robinson .50 1.25

1995-96 Ultra Rising Stars

Randomly inserted in all first series packs at a rate of one in 37, this nine-card standard-size set features promising youngsters of the NBA. Etched foil fronts feature multicolored basketballs and a full-color action cutout. The "Rising Star" logo and player's name are printed in silver foil on the fronts. Backs include a screened player information box and a full-color action cutout set against a multicolored basketball background. The set is sequenced in alphabetical order.

COMPLETE SET (9) 12.00 30.00
SER.1 STATED ODDS 1:37 HOBBY/RETAIL
*GOLD MEDALLION: 1.5X TO 4X HI COLUMN
GOLD: SER.1 STATED ODDS 1:370 HOB/RET
1 Vin Baker 1.25 3.00
2 Anfernee Hardaway 2.50 6.00
3 Grant Hill 2.50 6.00
4 Jason Kidd 2.50 6.00
5 Jamal Mashburn 1.50 4.00
6 Shaquille O'Neal 4.00 10.00
7 Glenn Robinson 1.25 3.00
8 Nick Van Exel 1.50 4.00
9 Chris Webber 2.00 5.00

1995-96 Ultra Scoring Kings

Randomly inserted at a rate of one in 24 hobby packs only, this 12-card standard-size set spotlights the number crunchers of the NBA. Borderless fronts have full color player action shots and are stamped with gold foil. Backs have another full-color action shot and include a player profile. The set is sequenced in alphabetical order.

COMPLETE SET (12) 15.00 40.00
SER.2 STATED ODDS 1:24 HOBBY
1 Patrick Ewing 1.25 3.00
2 Grant Hill 1.50 4.00
3 Jim Jackson .60 1.50
4 Michael Jordan 10.00 25.00
5 Karl Malone 1.25 3.00
6 Reggie Miller 1.25 3.00
7 Hakeem Olajuwon 1.25 3.00
8 Shaquille O'Neal 2.50 6.00
9 Scottie Pippen 1.50 4.00
10 David Robinson 1.50 4.00
11 Glenn Robinson .75 2.00
12 Jerry Stackhouse 3.00 8.00

1995-96 Ultra Scoring Kings Hot Pack

COMPLETE SET (12) 12.00 30.00
*HOT PACK CARDS: .15X TO .4X HI COLUMN
STATED ODDS 1:72 HOBBY
4 Michael Jordan 8.00 20.00

1995-96 Ultra Stackhouse's Scrapbook

Randomly inserted into one in every 24 second series packs, these two cards continue the eight-card, cross-brand set devoted to Fleer spokesperson Jerry Stackhouse. Card #S3 was featured on an unperforated promo sheet of Ultra cards saluting card stores across America. The sheets were distributed to shop owners nationwide. Unfortunately, some unscrupulous parties cut up a number of the sheets and distributed the cut cards into the hobby market which are identical to the real inserts, thus supply has been altered and we've applied a "DP" designation to signify a double-print on this card.

COMPLETE SET (2) 1.50 4.00
COMMON CARD (S3-S4) 1.00 2.50
STATED ODDS 1:24

1995-96 Ultra USA Basketball

Randomly inserted into all second series packs at a rate of one in 54, cards from this 10-card standard-size set capture the first 10 members named to the USA Olympic team in their new red, white and blue jerseys. Borderless fronts feature the player in full-color action set against an American flag backdrop. The player's name, position and the USA basketball logo are stamped in gold foil at the bottom. Backs have a full-color action shot on one side and a player profile set against a red and white stripe background with blue stars on the other side. The set is sequenced in alphabetical order.

COMPLETE SET (10) 25.00 60.00
SER.2 STATED ODDS 1:54 HOBBY/RETAIL
1 Anfernee Hardaway 4.00 10.00
2 Grant Hill 4.00 10.00
3 Karl Malone 3.00 8.00
4 Reggie Miller 3.00 8.00
5 Hakeem Olajuwon 3.00 8.00
6 Shaquille O'Neal 6.00 15.00
7 Scottie Pippen 4.00 10.00
8 David Robinson 4.00 10.00
9 Glenn Robinson 2.00 5.00
10 John Stockton 3.00 8.00

1996-97 Ultra

The 300-card Ultra set from Fleer/SkyBox was issued in two series in 12-card packs with a suggested retail price of $2.49. Each basic player card front features full-bleed photography with the player's name written in script at the bottom of the card in silver holofoil, with the team name printed on the "tail" of the script. Card backs contain two photos of the player with biographical information and career statistics. Subsets include On the Block, Ultra Effort, Maximum Effort, Rookie Encore, Step It Up and Play of the Game. Rookie cards include Shareef Abdur-Rahim, Ray Allen, Kobe Bryant, Marcus Camby, Allen Iverson, Stephon Marbury and Antoine Walker, among others. A Jerry Stackhouse promo was released before the cards went live. It looks exactly like the regular issue card except it does not bear a card number. It is listed below at the end of the set.

COMPLETE SET (300) 25.00 50.00
COMPLETE SERIES 1 (150) 17.50 35.00
COMPLETE SERIES 2 (150) 7.50 15.00
1 Mookie Blaylock .15 .40
2 Alan Henderson .15 .40
3 Christian Laettner .20 .50
4 Dikembe Mutombo .25 .60
5 Steve Smith .20 .50
6 Dana Barros .15 .40
7 Rick Fox .15 .40
8 Dino Radja .15 .40
9 Antoine Walker RC .40 1.00
10 Eric Williams .15 .40
11 Dell Curry .15 .40
12 Tony Delk RC .25 .60
13 Matt Geiger .15 .40
14 Glen Rice .25 .60
15 Ron Harper .20 .50
16 Michael Jordan 2.00 5.00
17 Toni Kukoc .25 .60
18 Scottie Pippen .40 1.00
19 Dennis Rodman .50 1.25
20 Terrell Brandon .15 .40
21 Chris Mills .15 .40
22 Bobby Phills .15 .40
23 Bob Sura .15 .40
24 Jim Jackson .15 .40
25 Jason Kidd .40 1.00
26 Jamal Mashburn .20 .50
27 George McCloud .15 .40
28 Samaki Walker RC .20 .50
29 LaPhonso Ellis .15 .40
30 Antonio McDyess .25 .60
31 Bryant Stith .15 .40
32 Joe Dumars .25 .60
33 Grant Hill .40 1.00
34 Theo Ratliff .15 .40
35 Otis Thorpe .15 .40
36 Chris Mullin .25 .60
37 Joe Smith .20 .50
38 Latrell Sprewell .25 .60
39 Charles Barkley .40 1.00
40 Clyde Drexler .30 .75
41 Mario Elie .15 .40
42 Hakeem Olajuwon .30 .75
43 Erick Dampier RC .25 .60
44 Dale Davis .15 .40
45 Derrick McKey .15 .40
46 Reggie Miller .30 .75
47 Rik Smits .20 .50
48 Brent Barry .20 .50
49 Malik Sealy .15 .40
50 Loy Vaught .15 .40
51 Lorenzen Wright RC .20 .50
52 Kobe Bryant RC 5.00 12.00
53 Cedric Ceballos .15 .40
54 Eddie Jones .25 .60
55 Shaquille O'Neal .60 1.50
56 Nick Van Exel .25 .60
57 Tim Hardaway .25 .60
58 Alonzo Mourning .30 .75
59 Kurt Thomas .15 .40
60 Ray Allen RC 1.00 2.50
61 Vin Baker .20 .50
62 Sherman Douglas .15 .40
63 Glenn Robinson .20 .50
64 Kevin Garnett .60 1.50
65 Tom Gugliotta .15 .40
66 Stephon Marbury RC .60 1.50
67 Doug West .15 .40
68 Shawn Bradley .15 .40
69 Kendall Gill .15 .40
70 Kerry Kittles RC .25 .60
71 Ed O'Bannon .15 .40
72 Patrick Ewing .30 .75
73 Larry Johnson .25 .60
74 Charles Oakley .20 .50
75 John Starks .20 .50
76 John Wallace RC .25 .60
77 Nick Anderson .15 .40
78 Horace Grant .20 .50
79 Anfernee Hardaway .40 1.00
80 Dennis Scott .15 .40
81 Derrick Coleman .20 .50
82 Allen Iverson RC 2.00 5.00
83 Jerry Stackhouse .30 .75
84 Clarence Weatherspoon .15 .40
85 Michael Finley .30 .75
86 Kevin Johnson .25 .60
87 Steve Nash RC 2.00 5.00
88 Wesley Person .15 .40
89 Jermaine O'Neal RC .40 1.00
90 Clifford Robinson .15 .40
91 Arvydas Sabonis .20 .50
92 Gary Trent .15 .40
93 Tyus Edney .15 .40
94 Brian Grant .20 .50
95 Olden Polynice .15 .40
96 Mitch Richmond .25 .60
97 Corliss Williamson .15 .40
98 Vinny Del Negro .15 .40
99 Sean Elliott .25 .60
100 Avery Johnson .20 .50
101 David Robinson .40 1.00
102 Hersey Hawkins .15 .40
103 Shawn Kemp .25 .60
104 Gary Payton .25 .60
105 Sam Perkins .15 .40
106 Detlef Schrempf .25 .60
107 Marcus Camby RC .40 1.00
108 Doug Christie .15 .40
109 Damon Stoudamire .20 .50
110 Sharone Wright .15 .40
111 Jeff Hornacek .20 .50
112 Karl Malone .30 .75
113 Chris Morris .15 .40
114 Bryon Russell .15 .40
115 John Stockton .30 .75
116 Shareef Abdur-Rahim RC .40 1.00
117 Greg Anthony .15 .40
118 Blue Edwards .15 .40
119 Bryant Reeves .15 .40
120 Calbert Cheaney .15 .40
121 Juwan Howard .20 .50
122 Gheorghe Muresan .15 .40
123 Chris Webber .30 .75
124 Vin Baker OTB .20 .50
125 Charles Barkley OTB .40 1.00
126 Kevin Garnett OTB .60 1.50
127 Juwan Howard OTB .20 .50
128 Larry Johnson OTB .25 .60
129 Shawn Kemp OTB .25 .60
130 Karl Malone OTB .30 .75
131 Anthony Mason OTB .15 .40
132 Antonio McDyess OTB .25 .60
133 Alonzo Mourning OTB .30 .75
134 Hakeem Olajuwon OTB .30 .75
135 Shaquille O'Neal OTB .60 1.50
136 David Robinson OTB .40 1.00
137 Dennis Rodman OTB .50 1.25
138 Joe Smith OTB .20 .50
139 Mookie Blaylock UE .15 .40
140 Terrell Brandon UE .15 .40
141 Anfernee Hardaway UE .40 1.00
142 Grant Hill UE .40 1.00
143 Michael Jordan UE 2.00 5.00
144 Jason Kidd UE .40 1.00
145 Gary Payton UE .25 .60
146 Jerry Stackhouse UE .30 .75
147 Damon Stoudamire UE .20 .50
148 H.Olajuwon/D.Robinson ME .40 1.00
149 Checklist .15 .40
150 Checklist .15 .40
151 Tyrone Corbin .08 .25
152 Priest Lauderdale RC .15 .40
153 Dikembe Mutombo .25 .60
154 Eldridge Recasner RC .25 .60
155 Todd Day .15 .40
156 Greg Minor .15 .40
157 David Wesley .15 .40
158 Vlade Divac .25 .60
159 Anthony Mason .15 .40
160 Malik Rose RC .30 .75
161 Jason Caffey .15 .40
162 Steve Kerr .20 .50
163 Luc Longley .20 .50
164 Danny Ferry .15 .40
165 Tyrone Hill .15 .40
166 Vitaly Potapenko RC .20 .50
167 Sam Cassell .20 .50
168 Michael Finley .30 .75
169 Chris Gatling .15 .40
170 A.C. Green .20 .50
171 Oliver Miller .15 .40
172 Eric Montross .15 .40
173 Dale Ellis .15 .40
174 Mark Jackson .20 .50
175 Ervin Johnson .15 .40
176 Sarunas Marciulionis .15 .40
177 Stacey Augmon .20 .50
178 Joe Dumars .25 .60
179 Grant Hill .40 1.00
180 Lindsey Hunter .15 .40
181 Grant Long .15 .40
182 Terry Mills .15 .40
183 Otis Thorpe .15 .40
184 Jerome Williams RC .20 .50
185 Todd Fuller RC .15 .40
186 Ray Owes RC .25 .60
187 Mark Price .25 .60
188 Felton Spencer .15 .40
189 Charles Barkley .40 1.00
190 Emanual Davis RC .25 .60
191 Othella Harrington RC .25 .60
192 Matt Maloney RC .20 .50
193 Brent Price .15 .40
194 Kevin Willis .15 .40
195 Travis Best .15 .40
196 Antonio Davis .15 .40
197 Jalen Rose .20 .50
198 Pooh Richardson .15 .40
199 Stanley Roberts .15 .40
200 Rodney Rogers .15 .40
201 Elden Campbell .15 .40
202 Derek Fisher RC .30 .75
203 Travis Knight RC .25 .60
204 Shaquille O'Neal .60 1.50
205 Byron Scott .20 .50
206 Sasha Danilovic .15 .40
207 Dan Majerle .25 .60
208 Martin Muursepp RC .15 .40
209 Armon Gilliam .15 .40
210 Andrew Lang .15 .40
211 Johnny Newman .15 .40
212 Kevin Garnett .60 1.50
213 Tom Gugliotta .15 .40
214 Shane Heal RC .25 .60
215 Stojko Vrankovic .15 .40
216 Robert Pack .15 .40
217 Khalid Reeves .15 .40
218 Jayson Williams .15 .40
219 Chris Childs .15 .40
220 Allan Houston .20 .50
221 Larry Johnson .25 .60
222 Walter McCarty RC .25 .60
223 Charlie Ward .15 .40
224 Brian Evans RC .25 .60
225 Amal McCaskill RC .25 .60
226 Rony Seikaly .15 .40
227 Gerald Wilkins .15 .40
228 Mark Davis .15 .40
229 Lucious Harris .15 .40
230 Don MacLean .15 .40
231 Cedric Ceballos .15 .40
232 Rex Chapman .15 .40
233 Jason Kidd .40 1.00
234 Danny Manning .20 .50
235 Kenny Anderson .20 .50
236 Aaron McKie .15 .40
237 Isaiah Rider .20 .50
238 Rasheed Wallace .30 .75
239 Mahmoud Abdul-Rauf .15 .40
240 Billy Owens .15 .40
241 Michael Smith .15 .40
242 Vernon Maxwell .15 .40
243 Charles Smith .15 .40
244 Dominique Wilkins .30 .75
245 Craig Ehlo .15 .40
246 Jim McIlvaine .15 .40
247 Nate McMillan .15 .40
248 Hubert Davis .15 .40
249 Carlos Rogers .15 .40
250 Zan Tabak .15 .40
251 Walt Williams .15 .40
252 Jeff Hornacek .20 .50
253 Karl Malone .30 .75
254 Greg Ostertag .15 .40
255 Bryon Russell .15 .40
256 John Stockton .30 .75
257 George Lynch .15 .40
258 Lawrence Moten .15 .40
259 Anthony Peeler .15 .40
260 Roy Rogers RC .20 .50
261 Tracy Murray .15 .40
262 Rod Strickland .15 .40
263 Ben Wallace RC 1.50 4.00
264 Shareef Abdur-Rahim RE .20 .50
265 Ray Allen RE .50 1.25
266 Kobe Bryant RE 3.00 8.00
267 Marcus Camby RE .20 .50
268 Erick Dampier RE .12 .30
269 Tony Delk RE .12 .30
270 Allen Iverson RE 1.00 2.50
271 Kerry Kittles RE .12 .30
272 Stephon Marbury RE .30 .75
273 Steve Nash RE 1.00 2.50
274 Jermaine O'Neal RE .20 .50
275 Antoine Walker RE .20 .50
276 Samaki Walker RE .10 .25
277 John Wallace RE .12 .30
278 Lorenzen Wright RE .10 .25
279 Anfernee Hardaway SU .40 1.00
280 Michael Jordan SU 2.00 5.00
281 Jason Kidd SU .40 1.00
282 Hakeem Olajuwon SU .30 .75
283 Gary Payton SU .25 .60
284 Mitch Richmond SU .25 .60
285 David Robinson SU .40 1.00
286 John Stockton SU .30 .75
287 Damon Stoudamire SU .20 .50
288 Chris Webber SU .30 .75
289 Clyde Drexler PG .30 .75
290 Kevin Garnett PG .60 1.50
291 Grant Hill PG .40 1.00
292 Shawn Kemp PG .25 .60
293 Karl Malone PG .30 .75
294 Antonio McDyess PG .25 .60
295 Alonzo Mourning PG .30 .75
296 Shaquille O'Neal PG .60 1.50
297 Scottie Pippen PG .40 1.00
298 Jerry Stackhouse PG .30 .75
299 Checklist (151-263) .15 .40
300 Checklist (264-300/inserts) .15 .40
NNO Jerry Stackhouse Promo 1.25 3.00

1996-97 Ultra Gold Medallion

*SER.1 STARS: 2X TO 5X BASE CARD HI
*SER.1 RCs: 1.5X TO 4X BASE HI
*SER.2 STARS: .6X TO 1.5X BASE HI
*SER.2 RCs: .5X TO 1.25X BASE HI
*SER.2 SUBSET: .4X TO 1X BASE HI
SER.1 STATED ODDS 1:12 H/R
SER.2 STATED ODDS ONE PER PACK
G52 Kobe Bryant 15.00 40.00
G266 Kobe Bryant RE 10.00 25.00

1996-97 Ultra Platinum Medallion

*STARS: 15X TO 40X BASE CARD HI
*RCs: 10X TO 25X BASE HI
SER.1 STATED ODDS 1:180 HOB/RET
SER.2 STATED ODDS 1:100 HOB/RET
STATED PRINT RUN LESS THAN 250 SETS
SER.1 PLAT.SUB.CARDS HAVE NO "P" PREFIX
P16 Michael Jordan 125.00 300.00
P18 Scottie Pippen 20.00 50.00
P52 Kobe Bryant 500.00 800.00
P82 Allen Iverson 60.00 150.00
P266 Kobe Bryant RE 150.00 300.00

1996-97 Ultra All-Rookies

Randomly inserted in series two packs at a rate of one in 4, this 15-card set focuses on some of the top players from the 1996-97 rookie class. The cards feature gold foil-stamping, glossy UV coating and embossing of the spotlight in the background.

COMPLETE SET (15) 12.00 30.00
SER.2 STATED ODDS 1:4 HOBBY/RETAIL
1 Shareef Abdur-Rahim 1.00 2.50
2 Ray Allen 2.50 6.00
3 Kobe Bryant 6.00 15.00
4 Marcus Camby 1.00 2.50
5 Tony Delk .60 1.50
6 Derek Fisher .75 2.00
7 Allen Iverson 3.00 8.00
8 Kerry Kittles .60 1.50
9 Matt Maloney .50 1.25
10 Stephon Marbury 1.50 4.00
11 Vitaly Potapenko .50 1.25
12 Roy Rogers .50 1.25
13 Antoine Walker 1.00 2.50
14 Samaki Walker .50 1.25
15 John Wallace .60 1.50

1996-97 Ultra Board Game

ndomly inserted in series two packs at a rate of one in 9, this 20-card set features some of the top rebounders in the NBA featured against a "checkerboard" pattern on the front of the cards.

COMPLETE SET (20) 15.00 40.00
SER.2 STATED ODDS 1:9 HOBBY/RETAIL
1 Vin Baker .75 2.00
2 Charles Barkley 1.50 4.00
3 Dale Davis .60 1.50
4 Clyde Drexler 1.25 3.00
5 Patrick Ewing 1.25 3.00
6 Grant Hill 1.50 4.00
7 Michael Jordan 8.00 20.00
8 Shawn Kemp 1.00 2.50
9 Jason Kidd 1.50 4.00
10 Karl Malone 1.25 3.00
11 Alonzo Mourning 1.25 3.00
12 Dikembe Mutombo 1.00 2.50
13 Hakeem Olajuwon 1.25 3.00
14 Shaquille O'Neal 2.50 6.00
15 Scottie Pippen 1.50 4.00
16 David Robinson 1.50 4.00
17 Dennis Rodman 2.00 5.00
18 Loy Vaught .60 1.50
19 Chris Webber 1.25 3.00
20 Jayson Williams .60 1.50

1996-97 Ultra Court Masters

This 15-card set was randomly inserted into series one retail packs only at a rate of one in 180. The cards are made with a plastic stock and features members of the 1st, 2nd and 3rd 1995-96 All-NBA teams.

COMPLETE SET (15) 200.00 400.00
SER.1 STATED ODDS 1:180 RETAIL
1 Anfernee Hardaway 20.00 50.00
2 Michael Jordan 200.00 400.00
3 Karl Malone 8.00 20.00
4 Scottie Pippen 12.00 30.00
5 David Robinson 15.00 40.00
6 Grant Hill 10.00 25.00
7 Shawn Kemp 15.00 40.00
8 Hakeem Olajuwon 8.00 20.00
9 Gary Payton 6.00 15.00
10 John Stockton 20.00 50.00
11 Charles Barkley 10.00 25.00
12 Juwan Howard 5.00 12.00
13 Reggie Miller 10.00 25.00
14 Shaquille O'Neal 12.00 30.00
15 Mitch Richmond 6.00 15.00

1996-97 Ultra Decade of Excellence

Randomly inserted in both series packs at a rate of one in 100, this 20-card set salutes twenty of the players who were included in the 1986-87 Fleer set. Each card features the 1986-87 design, with gold-foil trim and the words "Ultra Decade 1986-1996" in gold foil. Card backs are numbered with a "U" prefix.

COMPLETE SET (20) 25.00 60.00
COMPLETE SERIES 1 (10) 15.00 40.00
COMPLETE SERIES 2 (10) 12.50 25.00
SER.1/2 STATED ODDS 1:100 HOBBY/RETAIL
U1 Clyde Drexler 2.50 6.00
U2 Joe Dumars 2.00 5.00
U3 Derek Harper 1.50 4.00
U4 Michael Jordan 12.00 30.00
U5 Karl Malone 2.50 6.00
U6 Chris Mullin 2.00 5.00
U7 Charles Oakley 1.50 4.00
U8 Sam Perkins 1.25 3.00
U9 Ricky Pierce 1.25 3.00
U10 Buck Williams 1.25 3.00
U11 Charles Barkley 5.00 12.00
U12 Patrick Ewing 2.50 6.00
U13 Eddie Johnson 1.25 3.00
U14 Hakeem Olajuwon 2.50 6.00
U15 Robert Parish 2.00 5.00
U16 Byron Scott 1.50 4.00
U17 Wayman Tisdale 1.25 3.00
U18 Gerald Wilkins 1.25 3.00
U19 Herb Williams 1.25 3.00
U20 Kevin Willis 1.25 3.00

1996-97 Ultra Fresh Faces

Randomly inserted in series one packs at a rate of one in 72, this 9-card set focuses on top players from the 1996 NBA Draft. Each card is die cut featuring an action photo of the player printed against a backdrop of a die cut team jersey. The design was submitted by Shinto Imai, who submitted the winning entry in the 1995-96 Fleer "Design Your Own NBA Card" contest.

COMPLETE SET (9) 40.00 80.00
SER.1 STATED ODDS 1:72 HOBBY/RETAIL
1 Shareef Abdur-Rahim 2.50 6.00
2 Ray Allen 6.00 15.00
3 Kobe Bryant 30.00 80.00
4 Marcus Camby 2.50 6.00
5 Allen Iverson 10.00 25.00
6 Kerry Kittles 1.50 4.00
7 Stephon Marbury 4.00 10.00
8 Steve Nash 8.00 20.00
9 Antoine Walker 2.50 6.00

1996-97 Ultra Full Court Trap

Randomly inserted in series one packs at a rate of one in 15, this 10-card set showcases the players selected to the NBA 1st and 2nd All-Defensive Teams. Card fronts have a foil-etched colored background.

COMPLETE SET (10) 8.00 20.00
SER.1 STATED ODDS 1:15 HOBBY/RETAIL
*GOLD: 2.5X TO 6X HI COLUMN
GOLD: SER.1 STATED ODDS 1:180 HOB/RET
1 Michael Jordan 5.00 12.00
2 Gary Payton .60 1.50
3 Scottie Pippen 1.00 2.50
4 David Robinson 1.00 2.50
5 Dennis Rodman 1.25 3.00
6 Mookie Blaylock .40 1.00
7 Horace Grant .50 1.25
8 Derrick McKey .40 1.00
9 Hakeem Olajuwon .75 2.00
10 Bobby Phills .40 1.00

1996-97 Ultra Give and Take

Randomly inserted in series two retail packs only at a rate of one in 18, this 10-card set focuses on players who can not only dish out the assist, but make the key steals. The cards have a full foil background that is divided into a gold and silver tone split equally from top to bottom.

COMPLETE SET (10) 15.00 40.00
SER.2 STATED ODDS 1:18 RETAIL
1 Mookie Blaylock .75 2.00
2 Anfernee Hardaway 2.00 5.00
3 Tim Hardaway 1.25 3.00
4 Allen Iverson 6.00 15.00
5 Michael Jordan 10.00 25.00
6 Jason Kidd 2.00 5.00
7 Gary Payton 1.25 3.00
8 Scottie Pippen 2.00 5.00
9 John Stockton 1.50 4.00
10 Damon Stoudamire 1.00 2.50

1996-97 Ultra Rising Stars

ndomly inserted in series one hobby packs only at a rate of one in 180, this 10-card set focuses on young stars and rookies. Each card front features a full photo shot of the player against a matted background.

COMPLETE SET (10) 50.00 120.00
SER.1 STATED ODDS 1:180 HOBBY
1 Shareef Abdur-Rahim 2.50 6.00
2 Kobe Bryant 15.00 40.00
3 Anfernee Hardaway 8.00 20.00
4 Grant Hill 8.00 20.00
5 Juwan Howard 4.00 10.00
6 Allen Iverson 10.00 25.00
7 Jason Kidd 8.00 20.00
8 Stephon Marbury 4.00 10.00
9 Joe Smith 4.00 10.00
10 Damon Stoudamire 4.00 10.00

1996-97 Ultra Rookie Flashback

Randomly inserted in series one packs at a rate of one in 45, this 11-card set features the members of the 1995-96 NBA All-Rookie Team, printed against an etched-foil design.

COMPLETE SET (11) 20.00 40.00
SER.1 STATED ODDS 1:45 HOBBY/RETAIL
1 Michael Finley 3.00 8.00
2 Antonio McDyess 2.50 6.00
3 Arvydas Sabonis 2.00 5.00
4 Joe Smith 2.00 5.00
5 Jerry Stackhouse 3.00 8.00
6 Damon Stoudamire 2.00 5.00
7 Brent Barry 2.00 5.00
8 Tyus Edney 1.50 4.00
9 Kevin Garnett 6.00 15.00
10 Bryant Reeves 1.50 4.00
11 Rasheed Wallace 3.00 8.00

1996-97 Ultra Scoring Kings

Randomly inserted in series two hobby packs only at a rate of one in 24, this 29-card set returns for the fourth straight year focusing on some of the NBA's top scoreres. The cards feature a metallic ink background.

COMPLETE SET (29) 75.00 200.00
SER.2 STATED ODDS 1:24 HOBBY
*PLUS STARS: 1.25X TO 3X HI COLUMN
PLUS: SER.2 STATED ODDS 1:96 HOBBY
1 Steve Smith 2.00 5.00
2 Dino Radja 1.50 4.00
3 Glen Rice 2.50 6.00
4 Michael Jordan 60.00 150.00
5 Terrell Brandon 1.50 4.00
6 Jim Jackson 1.50 4.00
7 Antonio McDyess 2.50 6.00
8 Grant Hill 4.00 10.00
9 Latrell Sprewell 2.50 6.00
10 Hakeem Olajuwon 3.00 8.00
11 Reggie Miller 3.00 8.00
12 Loy Vaught 1.50 4.00
13 Shaquille O'Neal 6.00 15.00
14 Alonzo Mourning 3.00 8.00
15 Vin Baker 2.00 5.00
16 Tom Gugliotta 1.50 4.00
17 Kendall Gill 1.50 4.00
18 Patrick Ewing 3.00 8.00
19 Anfernee Hardaway 5.00 12.00
20 Allen Iverson 10.00 25.00
21 Danny Manning 2.00 5.00
22 Kenny Anderson 2.00 5.00
23 Mitch Richmond 2.50 6.00
24 David Robinson 4.00 10.00
25 Shawn Kemp 2.50 6.00
26 Damon Stoudamire 2.00 5.00
27 Karl Malone 3.00 8.00
28 Shareef Abdur-Rahim 2.00 5.00
29 Chris Webber 3.00 8.00

1996-97 Ultra Starring Role

Randomly inserted in series two packs at a rate of one in 288, this 10-card set focuses on players who are spotlighted on their teams. The card design is plastic with silver foil.

COMPLETE SET (10) 200.00 500.00
SER.2 STATED ODDS 1:288 HOBBY/RETAIL
1 Kevin Garnett 12.00 30.00
2 Anfernee Hardaway 20.00 50.00
3 Grant Hill 15.00 40.00
4 Michael Jordan 150.00 300.00
5 Shawn Kemp 15.00 40.00
6 Karl Malone 15.00 40.00
7 Hakeem Olajuwon 6.00 15.00
8 Shaquille O'Neal 12.00 30.00
9 David Robinson 12.00 30.00
10 Damon Stoudamire 4.00 10.00

1997-98 Ultra

The 1997-98 Ultra set, produced by Fleer/SkyBox, was issued in two series with the first containing 150 cards and the second 125 and were packaged in 10-card packs that carried a suggested retail price of $2.49. The first series feature most of the 1997-98 rookie class including Derek Anderson, Tony Battie, Chauncey Billups, Antonio Daniels, Tim Duncan, Brevin Knight, Ron Mercer, Tim Thomas and Keith Van Horn. Those cards were seeded into packs at a rate of one in four. The second series featured the subset "98 Greats" and were inserted at a rate of one in four. A Jerry Stackhouse promo card was also issued. Since that card shares the same number as the regular Stackhouse in the base set (#105), we have made it a "NNO" and listed it at the bottom of the set.

COMPLETE SET (275) 20.00 50.00
COMPLETE SERIES 1 (150) 10.00 25.00
COMPLETE SERIES 2 (125) 10.00 25.00
SER.1 ROOKIE SUBSET ODDS 1:4 H/R
GREATS SUBSET ODDS 1:4 H/R
UNPRICED MASTERPIECES SERIAL #'d TO 1
1 Kobe Bryant 1.25 3.00
2 Charles Barkley .40 1.00
3 Joe Dumars .25 .60
4 Wesley Person .15 .40
5 Walt Williams .15 .40
6 Vlade Divac .25 .60
7 Mookie Blaylock .15 .40
8 Jason Kidd .40 1.00
9 Ron Harper .20 .50
10 Sherman Douglas .15 .40
11 Cedric Ceballos .15 .40
12 Karl Malone .30 .75
13 Antonio McDyess .20 .50
14 Steve Kerr .20 .50
15 Matt Maloney .15 .40
16 Glenn Robinson .20 .50
17 Rony Seikaly .15 .40
18 Derrick Coleman .20 .50
19 Jermaine O'Neal .20 .50
20 Scott Burrell .15 .40
21 Glen Rice .25 .60
22 Dale Ellis .15 .40
23 Michael Jordan 2.00 5.00
24 Anfernee Hardaway .40 1.00
25 Bryon Russell .15 .40
26 Toni Kukoc .25 .60
27 Theo Ratliff .20 .50
28 Tom Gugliotta .15 .40
29 Dennis Rodman .50 1.25
30 John Stockton .30 .75
31 Priest Lauderdale .15 .40
32 Luc Longley .20 .50
33 Grant Hill .40 1.00
34 Antonio Davis .15 .40
35 Eddie Jones .25 .60
36 Nick Anderson .15 .40
37 Shareef Abdur-Rahim .25 .60
38 Stephon Marbury .30 .75
39 Todd Day .15 .40
40 Tim Hardaway .25 .60
41 Larry Johnson .25 .60
42 Sam Perkins .15 .40
43 Dikembe Mutombo .25 .60
44 Bo Outlaw .15 .40
45 Mitch Richmond .25 .60
46 Bryant Reeves .15 .40
47 P.J. Brown .15 .40
48 Steve Smith .20 .50
49 Martin Muursepp .15 .40
50 Jamal Mashburn .20 .50
51 Kendall Gill .15 .40
52 Vinny Del Negro .15 .40
53 Roy Rogers .15 .40
54 Khalid Reeves .15 .40
55 Scottie Pippen .40 1.00
56 Joe Smith .20 .50
57 Mark Jackson .20 .50
58 Voshon Lenard .15 .40
59 Dan Majerle .25 .60
60 Alonzo Mourning .30 .75
61 Kerry Kittles .15 .40
62 Chris Childs .15 .40
63 Patrick Ewing .30 .75
64 Allan Houston .20 .50
65 Marcus Camby .25 .60
66 Christian Laettner .20 .50
67 Loy Vaught .15 .40
68 Jayson Williams .15 .40
69 Avery Johnson .20 .50
70 Damon Stoudamire .20 .50
71 Kevin Johnson .25 .60
72 Gheorghe Muresan .15 .40
73 Reggie Miller .30 .75
74 John Wallace .15 .40
75 Terrell Brandon .15 .40
76 Dale Davis .15 .40
77 Latrell Sprewell .25 .60
78 Lorenzen Wright .15 .40
79 Rod Strickland .15 .40
80 Kenny Anderson .20 .50
81 Anthony Mason .15 .40
82 Hakeem Olajuwon .30 .75
83 Kevin Garnett .40 1.00
84 Isaiah Rider .20 .50
85 Mark Price .25 .60
86 Shawn Bradley .15 .40
87 Vin Baker .20 .50
88 Steve Nash .50 1.25
89 Jeff Hornacek .20 .50
90 Tony Delk .15 .40
91 Horace Grant .20 .50
92 Othella Harrington .15 .40
93 Arvydas Sabonis .20 .50
94 Antoine Walker .25 .60
95 Todd Fuller .15 .40
96 John Starks .20 .50
97 Olden Polynice .15 .40
98 Sean Elliott .25 .60
99 Travis Best .15 .40
100 Chris Gatling .15 .40
101 Derek Harper .20 .50
102 LaPhonso Ellis .15 .40
103 Dean Garrett .15 .40
104 Hersey Hawkins .15 .40
105 Jerry Stackhouse .25 .60
106 Ray Allen .30 .75
107 Allen Iverson .50 1.25
108 Chris Webber .25 .60
109 Robert Pack .15 .40
110 Gary Payton .25 .60
111 Mario Elie .15 .40
112 Dell Curry .15 .40
113 Lindsey Hunter .15 .40
114 Robert Horry .20 .50
115 David Robinson .40 1.00
116 Kevin Willis .15 .40
117 Tyrone Hill .15 .40
118 Vitaly Potapenko .15 .40
119 Clyde Drexler .30 .75
120 Derek Fisher .25 .60
121 Detlef Schrempf .25 .60
122 Gary Trent .15 .40
123 Danny Ferry .15 .40
124 Derek Anderson RC .75 2.00
125 Chris Anstey RC .50 1.25
126 Tony Battie RC .75 2.00
127 Chauncey Billups RC 2.50 6.00
128 Kelvin Cato RC .60 1.50
129 Austin Croshere RC .60 1.50
130 Antonio Daniels RC .75 2.00
131 Tim Duncan RC 4.00 10.00
132 Danny Fortson RC .75 2.00
133 Adonal Foyle RC .60 1.50
134 Paul Grant RC .50 1.25
135 Ed Gray RC .75 2.00
136 Bobby Jackson RC 1.00 2.50
137 Brevin Knight RC .75 2.00
138 Tracy McGrady RC 3.00 8.00
139 Ron Mercer RC 1.00 2.50
140 Anthony Parker RC .75 2.00
141 Scot Pollard RC .75 2.00
142 Rodrick Rhodes RC .60 1.50
143 Olivier Saint-Jean RC .60 1.50
144 Maurice Taylor RC .75 2.00
145 Johnny Taylor RC .60 1.50
146 Tim Thomas RC 1.00 2.50
147 Keith Van Horn RC 1.25 3.00
148 Jacque Vaughn RC .60 1.50
149 Checklist .15 .40
150 Checklist .15 .40
151 Scott Burrell .15 .40
152 Brian Williams .15 .40
153 Terry Mills .15 .40
154 Jim Jackson .15 .40
155 Michael Finley .25 .60
156 Jeff Nordgaard RC .25 .60
157 Carl Herrera .15 .40
158 Otis Thorpe .15 .40
159 Wesley Person .15 .40
160 Tyrone Hill .15 .40
161 Charles O'Bannon RC .25 .60
162 Greg Anthony .15 .40
163 Rusty LaRue RC .25 .60
164 David Wesley .15 .40
165 Chris Garner RC .25 .60
166 George McCloud .15 .40
167 Mark Price .25 .60
168 God Shammgod RC .25 .60
169 Isaac Austin .15 .40
170 Alan Henderson .15 .40
171 Eric Washington RC .25 .60
172 Darrell Armstrong .15 .40
173 Calbert Cheaney .15 .40
174 Cedric Henderson RC .25 .60
175 Bryant Stith .15 .40
176 Sean Rooks .15 .40
177 Chris Mills .15 .40
178 Eldridge Recasner .15 .40
179 Priest Lauderdale .15 .40
180 Rick Fox .15 .40
181 Keith Closs RC .25 .60
182 Chris Dudley .15 .40
183 Lawrence Funderburke RC .25 .60
184 Michael Stewart RC .25 .60
185 Alvin Williams RC .25 .60
186 Adam Keefe .15 .40
187 Chauncey Billups .75 2.00
188 Jon Barry .15 .40
189 Bobby Jackson .30 .75
190 Sam Cassell .20 .50
191 Dee Brown .15 .40
192 Travis Knight .15 .40
193 Dean Garrett .15 .40
194 David Benoit .15 .40
195 Chris Morris .15 .40
196 Bubba Wells RC .25 .60
197 James Robinson .15 .40
198 Anthony Johnson RC .25 .60
199 Dennis Scott .15 .40
200 DeJuan Wheat RC .25 .60
201 Rodney Rogers .15 .40
202 Tariq Abdul-Wahad .20 .50
203 Cherokee Parks .15 .40
204 Jacque Vaughn .20 .50
205 Cory Alexander .15 .40
206 Kevin Ollie RC .25 .60
207 George Lynch .15 .40
208 Lamond Murray .15 .40
209 Jud Buechler .15 .40
210 Erick Dampier .15 .40
211 Malcolm Huckaby RC .25 .60
212 Chris Webber .25 .60
213 Chris Crawford RC .25 .60
214 J.R. Reid .15 .40
215 Eddie Johnson .15 .40
216 Nick Van Exel .20 .50
217 Antonio McDyess .20 .50
218 David Wingate .15 .40
219 Malik Sealy .15 .40
220 Bo Outlaw .15 .40
221 Serge Zwikker RC .25 .60
222 Bobby Phills .15 .40
223 Shea Seals RC .25 .60
224 Clifford Robinson .15 .40
225 Zydrunas Ilgauskas .25 .60
226 John Thomas RC .15 .40
227 Rik Smits .20 .50
228 Rasheed Wallace .25 .60
229 John Wallace .15 .40
230 Bob Sura .15 .40
231 Ervin Johnson .15 .40
232 Keith Booth RC .20 .50
233 Chuck Person .20 .50
234 Brian Shaw .15 .40
235 Todd Day .15 .40
236 Clarence Weatherspoon .15 .40
237 Charlie Ward .15 .40
238 Rod Strickland .15 .40
239 Shawn Kemp .25 .60
240 Terrell Brandon .15 .40
241 Corey Beck RC .25 .60
242 Vin Baker .20 .50
243 Fred Hoiberg .15 .40
244 Chris Mullin .25 .60
245 Brian Grant .15 .40
246 Derek Anderson .25 .60
247 Zan Tabak .15 .40
248 Charles Smith RC .20 .50
249 Shareef Abdur-Rahim GRE .50 1.25
250 Ray Allen GRE .60 1.50
251 Charles Barkley GRE .75 2.00
252 Kobe Bryant GRE 2.50 6.00
253 Marcus Camby GRE .50 1.25
254 Kevin Garnett GRE .75 2.00
255 Anfernee Hardaway GRE .75 2.00
256 Grant Hill GRE .75 2.00
257 Juwan Howard GRE .40 1.00
258 Allen Iverson GRE 1.00 2.50
259 Michael Jordan GRE 4.00 10.00
260 Shawn Kemp GRE .50 1.25
261 Kerry Kittles GRE .30 .75
262 Karl Malone GRE .60 1.50
263 Stephon Marbury GRE .60 1.50
264 Hakeem Olajuwon GRE .60 1.50
265 Shaquille O'Neal GRE 1.25 3.00
266 Gary Payton GRE .50 1.25
267 Scottie Pippen GRE .75 2.00
268 David Robinson GRE .75 2.00
269 Dennis Rodman GRE 1.00 2.50
270 Joe Smith GRE .40 1.00
271 Jerry Stackhouse GRE .50 1.25
272 Damon Stoudamire GRE .40 1.00
273 Antoine Walker GRE .50 1.25
274 Checklist .15 .40
275 Checklist .15 .40
NNO Jerry Stackhouse PROMO .75 2.00

1997-98 Ultra Gold Medallion

*SER.1 STARS: 1X TO 2.5X BASE CARD HI
*SER.1 RCs: .4X TO 1X BASE HI
*SER.2 STARS/RCs: 1X TO 2.5X BASE HI
*SER.2 98 GREATS: .5X TO 1.25X BASE HI
ONE PER SER.1/2 HOBBY PACK
SUBSETS ARE NOT SP's

1997-98 Ultra Platinum Medallion

*STARS: 25X TO 60X BASE CARD HI
*RCs: 3X TO 8X BASE HI
*GREATS: SAME VALUE AS BASE PLATINUM
*SER.2 RCs: 6X TO 15X BASE HI
RANDOM INSERTS SER.1/2 HOBBY PACKS
STATED PRINT RUN 100 SERIAL #'d SETS
LAST 10 SETS AVAILABLE VIA RED.CARDS
1 Kobe Bryant 400.00 800.00
2 Charles Barkley 40.00 100.00
8 Jason Kidd 75.00 150.00
23 Michael Jordan 900.00 1500.00
24 Anfernee Hardaway 75.00 150.00
29 Dennis Rodman 125.00 250.00
33 Grant Hill 75.00 150.00
55 Scottie Pippen 40.00 100.00
60 Alonzo Mourning 40.00 100.00
73 Reggie Miller 30.00 80.00
88 Steve Nash 50.00 125.00
131 Tim Duncan 700.00 900.00
138 Tracy McGrady 75.00 150.00
265 Shaquille O'Neal GRE 75.00 200.00

1997-98 Ultra All-Rookies

Randomly inserted into series two packs at one in four, this 15-card set features the top players from the 1997 Draft. Card backs carry an "AR" prefix.

COMPLETE SET (15) 5.00 12.00
SER.2 STATED ODDS 1:4 HOB/RET
AR1 Tim Duncan 2.00 5.00
AR2 Tony Battie .40 1.00
AR3 Keith Van Horn .60 1.50
AR4 Antonio Daniels .40 1.00
AR5 Chauncey Billups 1.25 3.00
AR6 Ron Mercer .50 1.25
AR7 Tracy McGrady 1.50 4.00
AR8 Danny Fortson .40 1.00
AR9 Brevin Knight .40 1.00
AR10 Derek Anderson .40 1.00
AR11 Cedric Henderson .40 1.00
AR12 Jacque Vaughn .30 .75
AR13 Tim Thomas .50 1.25
AR14 Austin Croshere .30 .75
AR15 Kelvin Cato .30 .75

1997-98 Ultra Big Shots

Randomly inserted into series one packs at a rate of one in four, this 15-card set focuses on some of the best clutch shots from the 1996-97 season.

COMPLETE SET (15) 8.00 20.00
SER.1 STATED ODDS 1:4 HOB/RET
1 Michael Jordan 5.00 12.00
2 Allen Iverson .60 1.50
3 Shaquille O'Neal .75 2.00
4 Anfernee Hardaway .50 1.25
5 Dennis Rodman .60 1.50
6 Grant Hill .50 1.25
7 Juwan Howard .25 .60
8 David Robinson .50 1.25
9 Gary Payton .30 .75
10 Joe Smith .25 .60
11 Charles Barkley .50 1.25
12 Terrell Brandon .20 .50
13 John Stockton .40 1.00
14 Mitch Richmond .30 .75
15 Vin Baker .25 .60

1997-98 Ultra Court Masters

ndomly inserted into series two packs at one in 144, this 20-card set features double images of players who have mastered the game. Each player is shown in both his home and away uniform. The background of the card fronts mimic a hardwood court. Card backs carry a "CM" prefix.

COMPLETE SET (20) 500.00 1000.00
SER.2 STATED ODDS 1:144 HOB/RET
CM1 Michael Jordan 300.00 600.00
CM2 Allen Iverson 30.00 80.00
CM3 Kobe Bryant 75.00 200.00
CM4 Shaquille O'Neal 30.00 80.00
CM5 Stephon Marbury 25.00 60.00
CM6 Shawn Kemp 25.00 60.00
CM7 Anfernee Hardaway 30.00 80.00
CM8 Kevin Garnett 25.00 60.00
CM9 Shareef Abdur-Rahim 10.00 25.00
CM10 Dennis Rodman 40.00 100.00
CM11 Grant Hill 25.00 60.00
CM12 Kerry Kittles 6.00 15.00
CM13 Antoine Walker 10.00 25.00
CM14 Scottie Pippen 30.00 80.00
CM15 Damon Stoudamire 8.00 20.00
CM16 Marcus Camby 10.00 25.00
CM17 Hakeem Olajuwon 20.00 50.00
CM18 Tim Duncan 50.00 120.00
CM19 Keith Van Horn 8.00 20.00
CM20 Chauncey Billups 20.00 50.00

1997-98 Ultra Heir to the Throne

Randomly inserted in series one packs at a rate of one in 18, this 15-card set focuses on some of the best rookies from the 1997-98 class. The cards feature each rookie sitting in a chair that is made up of basketballs.

COMPLETE SET (15) 12.00 30.00
SER.1 STATED ODDS 1:18 HOB/RET
1 Derek Anderson .60 1.50
2 Tony Battie .60 1.50
3 Chauncey Billups 2.00 5.00
4 Kelvin Cato .50 1.25
5 Austin Croshere .50 1.25
6 Antonio Daniels .60 1.50
7 Tim Duncan 5.00 12.00
8 Danny Fortson .60 1.50
9 Jacque Vaughn .50 1.25
10 Tracy McGrady 2.50 6.00
11 Ron Mercer .75 2.00
12 Olivier Saint-Jean .50 1.25
13 Maurice Taylor .60 1.50
14 Tim Thomas .75 2.00
15 Keith Van Horn 1.00 2.50

1997-98 Ultra Inside/Outside

Randomly inserted in series one packs at a rate of one in six, this 15-card set focuses on players who can get the job done with both their inside and outside games.

COMPLETE SET (15) 3.00 8.00
SER.1 STATED ODDS 1:6 HOB/RET
1 Shareef Abdur-Rahim .50 1.25
2 Juwan Howard .40 1.00
3 David Robinson .75 2.00
4 Joe Smith .40 1.00
5 Charles Barkley .75 2.00
6 Tom Gugliotta .30 .75
7 Glenn Robinson .40 1.00
8 Patrick Ewing .60 1.50
9 Chris Webber .50 1.25
10 Glen Rice .50 1.25
11 Shawn Kemp .50 1.25
12 Antonio McDyess .40 1.00
13 Clyde Drexler .60 1.50
14 Eddie Jones .50 1.25
15 Jason Kidd .75 2.00

1997-98 Ultra Jam City

Randomly inserted in series one packs at a rate of one in eight, this 18-card set features some of the NBA's high flying players.

COMPLETE SET (18) 10.00 20.00
SER.1 STATED ODDS 1:8 HOB/RET
1 Kevin Garnett 1.00 2.50
2 Antoine Walker .60 1.50
3 Scottie Pippen 1.00 2.50
4 Shawn Kemp .60 1.50
5 Hakeem Olajuwon .75 2.00
6 Jerry Stackhouse .60 1.50
7 Karl Malone .75 2.00
8 Shaquille O'Neal 1.50 4.00
9 John Wallace .40 1.00
10 Marcus Camby .60 1.50
11 Juwan Howard .50 1.25
12 David Robinson 1.00 2.50
13 Gary Payton .60 1.50
14 Dennis Rodman 1.25 3.00
15 Joe Smith .50 1.25
16 Charles Barkley 1.00 2.50
17 Terrell Brandon .40 1.00
18 Kobe Bryant 4.00 10.00

1997-98 Ultra Neat Feats

Randomly inserted into series two packs at one in eight, this 18-card set focuses on player's career highlights. The card fronts features UV coated player photos on a matte finish background. Card backs are numbered with a "NF" prefix.

COMPLETE SET (18) 5.00 12.00
SER.2 STATED ODDS 1:8 HOB/RET
NF1 Michael Finley .60 1.50
NF2 Jason Kidd 1.00 2.50
NF3 Rasheed Wallace .60 1.50
NF4 Shaquille O'Neal 1.50 4.00
NF5 Tom Gugliotta .40 1.00
NF6 Marcus Camby .60 1.50
NF7 Jerry Stackhouse .60 1.50
NF8 John Wallace .40 1.00
NF9 Juwan Howard .50 1.25
NF10 David Robinson 1.00 2.50
NF11 Gary Payton .60 1.50
NF12 Joe Smith .50 1.25
NF13 Charles Barkley 1.00 2.50
NF14 Terrell Brandon .40 1.00
NF15 John Stockton .75 2.00
NF16 Vin Baker .50 1.25
NF17 Antonio McDyess .50 1.25
NF18 Antonio Daniels .60 1.50

1997-98 Ultra Quick Picks

Randomly inserted in series one packs at a rate of one in eight, this 12-card set focuses on the young defensive wizards of the NBA.

COMPLETE SET (12) 4.00 10.00
SER.1 STATED ODDS 1:8 HOB/RET
1 Stephon Marbury .75 2.00
2 Ray Allen .75 2.00
3 Damon Stoudamire .50 1.25
4 Kerry Kittles .40 1.00
5 Gary Payton .60 1.50
6 Terrell Brandon .40 1.00
7 John Stockton .75 2.00
8 Mookie Blaylock .40 1.00
9 Eddie Jones .60 1.50
10 Nick Van Exel .50 1.25
11 Kenny Anderson .50 1.25
12 Tim Hardaway .60 1.50

1997-98 Ultra Rim Rocker

Randomly inserted into series two packs at one in eight, this 12-card set features color photos of some of the best dunkers in the game printed on custom die-cut silver holofoil cards. Card backs are numbered with a "RR" prefix.

COMPLETE SET (12) 3.00 8.00
SER.2 STATED ODDS 1:8 HOB/RET
RR1 Ron Mercer .50 1.25
RR2 Juwan Howard .50 1.25
RR3 David Robinson 1.00 2.50
RR4 Gary Payton .60 1.50
RR5 Joe Smith .50 1.25
RR6 Charles Barkley 1.00 2.50
RR7 Terrell Brandon .40 1.00
RR8 John Stockton .75 2.00
RR9 Adonal Foyle .30 .75
RR10 Tim Thomas .50 1.25
RR11 Tony Battie .40 1.00
RR12 Antonio McDyess .50 1.25

1997-98 Ultra Star Power

Randomly inserted into series two packs at one in four, this 20-card set chronicles the path of some notable NBA players. These cards in particular focus on early to mid-career highlights. Card backs carry a "SP" prefix.

COMPLETE SET (20) 12.00 30.00
SER.2 STATED ODDS 1:4 HOB/RET
*PLUS: 2X TO 5X BASE STAR POWER
PLUS: SER.2 STATED ODDS 1:36 H/R
SP1 Michael Jordan 4.00 10.00
SP2 Allen Iverson 1.00 2.50
SP3 Kobe Bryant 2.50 6.00
SP4 Shaquille O'Neal 1.25 3.00
SP5 Stephon Marbury .60 1.50
SP6 Shawn Kemp .50 1.25
SP7 Anfernee Hardaway .75 2.00
SP8 Kevin Garnett .75 2.00
SP9 Shareef Abdur-Rahim .50 1.25
SP10 Dennis Rodman 1.00 2.50
SP11 Grant Hill .75 2.00
SP12 Gary Payton .50 1.25
SP13 Antoine Walker .50 1.25
SP14 Scottie Pippen .75 2.00
SP15 Damon Stoudamire .40 1.00
SP16 Marcus Camby .50 1.25
SP17 Hakeem Olajuwon .60 1.50
SP18 Tim Duncan 1.25 3.00
SP19 Keith Van Horn .40 1.00
SP20 Jerry Stackhouse .50 1.25

1997-98 Ultra Star Power Supreme

*SUPREME: 15X TO 40X VALUE
SPS1 Michael Jordan 800.00 1200.00
SPS2 Allen Iverson 50.00 120.00
SPS3 Kobe Bryant 300.00 600.00
SPS7 Anfernee Hardaway 60.00 150.00
SPS10 Dennis Rodman 50.00 120.00
SPS18 Tim Duncan 75.00 200.00

1997-98 Ultra Stars

Randomly inserted in series one packs at a rate of one in 288, this 20-card set features some of the NBA's top stars. Ten percent of the print run was done in gold foil as opposed to the more common silver foil.

SER.1 STATED ODDS 1:144 HOB/RET
1 Michael Jordan 200.00 500.00
2 Allen Iverson 20.00 50.00
3 Kobe Bryant 60.00 150.00
4 Shaquille O'Neal 25.00 60.00
5 Stephon Marbury 12.00 30.00
6 Marcus Camby 10.00 25.00
7 Anfernee Hardaway 15.00 40.00
8 Kevin Garnett 15.00 40.00
9 Shareef Abdur-Rahim 10.00 25.00
10 Dennis Rodman 20.00 50.00
11 Ray Allen 12.00 30.00
12 Grant Hill 15.00 40.00
13 Kerry Kittles 6.00 15.00
14 Antoine Walker 10.00 25.00
15 Scottie Pippen 20.00 50.00
16 Damon Stoudamire 8.00 20.00
17 Shawn Kemp 10.00 25.00
18 Hakeem Olajuwon 12.00 30.00
19 Jerry Stackhouse 10.00 25.00
20 John Wallace 6.00 15.00

1997-98 Ultra Stars Gold

*GOLD: 2X TO 5X HI COLUMN
FIRST TEN PERCENT OF PRINT RUN IN GOLD
1 Michael Jordan 2000.00 4000.00
3 Kobe Bryant 900.00 1500.00
4 Shaquille O'Neal 150.00 400.00
7 Anfernee Hardaway 150.00 400.00
10 Dennis Rodman 150.00 300.00
15 Scottie Pippen 125.00 250.00

1997-98 Ultra Sweet Deal

ndomly inserted into series two packs at one in six, this 12-card set gives insight to some of the best players in the game. Card backs carry a "SD" prefix.

COMPLETE SET (12) 2.50 6.00
SER.2 STATED ODDS 1:6 HOB/RET
SD1 Ray Allen .50 1.25
SD2 Chauncey Billups 1.25 3.00
SD3 Ron Mercer .50 1.25
SD4 Hakeem Olajuwon .50 1.25
SD5 Jerry Stackhouse .40 1.00
SD6 John Wallace .25 .60
SD7 Juwan Howard .30 .75
SD8 David Robinson .60 1.50
SD9 Bobby Jackson .50 1.25
SD10 Joe Smith .30 .75
SD11 Charles Barkley .60 1.50
SD12 Terrell Brandon .25 .60

1997-98 Ultra Ultrabilities

Randomly inserted in series one packs at a rate of one in four, this 20-card set features NBA players that have many different abilities.

COMPLETE SET (20) 12.00 30.00
SER.1 STATED ODDS 1:4 HOB/RET
*ALL-STAR: 2X TO 5X BASE ULTRABIL.
ALL-STAR: SER.1 STATED ODDS 1:36 H/R
1 Michael Jordan 4.00 10.00
2 Allen Iverson 1.00 2.50
3 Kobe Bryant 2.50 6.00
4 Shaquille O'Neal 1.25 3.00
5 Stephon Marbury .60 1.50
6 Gary Payton .50 1.25
7 Anfernee Hardaway .75 2.00
8 Kevin Garnett .75 2.00
9 Scottie Pippen .75 2.00
10 Grant Hill .75 2.00
11 Marcus Camby .50 1.25
12 Ray Allen .60 1.50
13 Kerry Kittles .30 .75
14 Antoine Walker .50 1.25
15 Shareef Abdur-Rahim .50 1.25
16 Damon Stoudamire .40 1.00
17 Shawn Kemp .50 1.25
18 Hakeem Olajuwon .60 1.50
19 Jerry Stackhouse .50 1.25
20 Juwan Howard .40 1.00

1997-98 Ultra Ultrabilities Superstar

*SUPERSTAR: 6X TO 15X VALUE
SER.1 STATED ODDS 1:288 HOBBY/RETAIL
1 Michael Jordan 400.00 700.00
2 Allen Iverson 25.00 60.00
3 Kobe Bryant 100.00 250.00
6 Gary Payton 12.00 30.00
7 Anfernee Hardaway 30.00 80.00
8 Kevin Garnett 25.00 60.00
9 Scottie Pippen 25.00 60.00
10 Grant Hill 20.00 50.00
12 Ray Allen 15.00 40.00
17 Shawn Kemp 15.00 40.00

1997-98 Ultra View to a Thrill

Randomly inserted into series two packs at one in 18, this 15-card set features colorful profiles of players that make the game a thrill to watch. Card backs carry a "VT" prefix.

COMPLETE SET (15) 20.00 50.00
SER.2 STATED ODDS 1:18 HOB/RET
VT1 Michael Jordan 8.00 20.00
VT2 Allen Iverson 2.00 5.00
VT3 Kobe Bryant 5.00 12.00
VT4 Tracy McGrady 2.00 5.00
VT5 Stephon Marbury 1.25 3.00
VT6 Shawn Kemp 1.00 2.50
VT7 Anfernee Hardaway 1.50 4.00
VT8 Kevin Garnett 1.50 4.00
VT9 Shareef Abdur-Rahim 1.00 2.50
VT10 Dennis Rodman 2.00 5.00
VT11 Grant Hill 1.50 4.00
VT12 Kerry Kittles .60 1.50
VT13 Antoine Walker 1.00 2.50
VT14 Scottie Pippen 1.50 4.00
VT15 Damon Stoudamire .75 2.00

1998-99 Ultra

Due to the NBA lockout early in the season, the 1998-99 Ultra product was released in early 1999, and featured a 125-card base set. The set features 100 Veterans (1-100), and 25 Rookies (101-125). Each pack contained 10 cards and carried a suggested retail price of $2.69.

COMPLETE SET (125) 50.00 100.00
COMPLETE SET w/o SP (100) 12.50 25.00
ROOKIE SUBSET ODDS 1:4 H/R
UNPRICED MASTERPIECES SERIAL #'d TO 1
1 Keith Van Horn .25 .60
1B Keith Van Horn PROMO .40 1.00
2 Antonio Daniels .15 .40
3 Patrick Ewing .30 .75
4 Alonzo Mourning .30 .75
5 Isaac Austin .15 .40
6 Bryant Reeves .15 .40
7 Dennis Scott .15 .40
8 Damon Stoudamire .20 .50
9 Kenny Anderson .20 .50
10 Mookie Blaylock .15 .40
11 Mitch Richmond .25 .60
12 Jalen Rose .20 .50
13 Vin Baker .20 .50
14 Donyell Marshall .15 .40
15 Bryon Russell .15 .40
16 Rasheed Wallace .25 .60
17 Allan Houston .20 .50
18 Shawn Kemp .25 .60
19 Nick Van Exel .20 .50
20 Theo Ratliff .20 .50
21 Jayson Williams .15 .40
22 Chauncey Billups .30 .75
23 Brent Barry .20 .50
24 David Wesley .15 .40
25 Joe Dumars .25 .60
26 Marcus Camby .20 .50
27 Juwan Howard .20 .50
28 Brevin Knight .15 .40
29 Reggie Miller .30 .75
30 Ray Allen .30 .75
31 Michael Finley .25 .60
32 Tom Gugliotta .15 .40
33 Allen Iverson .50 1.25
34 Toni Kukoc .25 .60
35 Tim Thomas .25 .60
36 Jeff Hornacek .20 .50
37 Bobby Jackson .15 .40
38 Bo Outlaw .15 .40
39 Steve Smith .20 .50
40 Terrell Brandon .15 .40
41 Glen Rice .25 .60
42 Rik Smits .20 .50
43 Calbert Cheaney .15 .40
44 Stephon Marbury .30 .75
45 Glenn Robinson .20 .50
46 Corliss Williamson .15 .40
47 Larry Johnson .25 .60
48 Antonio McDyess .20 .50
49 Detlef Schrempf .25 .60
50 Jerry Stackhouse .25 .60
51 Doug Christie .15 .40
52 Eddie Jones .25 .60
53 Karl Malone .30 .75
54 Anthony Mason .15 .40
55 Tim Duncan .50 1.25
56 Christian Laettner .20 .50
57 Isaiah Rider .20 .50
58 Shawn Bradley .15 .40
59 Jim Jackson .15 .40
60 Mark Jackson .20 .50
61 Kobe Bryant 1.00 2.50
62 Zydrunas Ilgauskas .25 .60
63 Ron Mercer .20 .50
64 Hersey Hawkins .15 .40
65 John Wallace .15 .40
66 Avery Johnson .20 .50
67 Dikembe Mutombo .25 .60
68 Hakeem Olajuwon .30 .75
69 Tony Battie .20 .50
70 Jason Kidd .40 1.00
71 Latrell Sprewell .25 .60
72 Kevin Garnett .40 1.00
73 Voshon Lenard .15 .40
74 Gary Payton .25 .60
75 Cherokee Parks .15 .40
76 Antoine Walker .25 .60
77 Anthony Johnson .15 .40
78 Danny Fortson .15 .40
79 Grant Hill .40 1.00
80 Dennis Rodman .50 1.25
81 Arvydas Sabonis .20 .50
82 Tracy McGrady .40 1.00
83 David Robinson .40 1.00
84 Tariq Abdul-Wahad .15 .40
85 Michael Jordan 2.00 5.00
86 Kerry Kittles .15 .40
87 Maurice Taylor .15 .40
88 Cedric Ceballos .15 .40
89 Anfernee Hardaway .40 1.00
90 John Stockton .30 .75
91 Shareef Abdur-Rahim .25 .60
92 Tim Hardaway .25 .60
93 Shaquille O'Neal .60 1.50
94 Rodney Rogers .15 .40
95 Derek Anderson .15 .40
96 Kendall Gill .15 .40
97 Rod Strickland .15 .40
98 Charles Barkley .40 1.00
99 Chris Webber .25 .60
100 Scottie Pippen .40 1.00
101 Raef LaFrentz RC .75 2.00
102 Ricky Davis RC 1.00 2.50
103 Robert Traylor RC .60 1.50
104 Roshown McLeod RC .40 1.00
105 Tyronn Lue RC .60 1.50
106 Vince Carter RC 3.00 8.00
107 Miles Simon RC .60 1.50
108 Paul Pierce RC 2.50 6.00
109 Pat Garrity RC .50 1.25
110 Nazr Mohammed RC .60 1.50
111 Mike Bibby RC 1.00 2.50
112 Michael Dickerson RC .60 1.50
113 Michael Doleac RC .50 1.25
114 Matt Harpring RC .60 1.50
115 Larry Hughes RC 1.25 3.00
116 Keon Clark RC .60 1.50
117 Felipe Lopez RC .40 1.00
118 Dirk Nowitzki RC 5.00 12.00
119 Corey Benjamin RC .40 1.00
120 Bryce Drew RC .40 1.00
121 Brian Skinner RC .60 1.50
122 Bonzi Wells RC .60 1.50
123 Antawn Jamison RC 1.00 2.50
124 Al Harrington RC 1.00 2.50
125 Michael Olowokandi RC .75 2.00

1998-99 Ultra Gold Medallion

*STARS: 1X TO 2.5X BASE CARD HI
*RCs: .6X TO 1.5X BASE HI
RCs: STATED ODDS 1:35 HOBBY

1998-99 Ultra Platinum Medallion

*STARS: 20X TO 50X BASE CARD HI
*RCs: 8X TO 20X HI
STARS: PRINT RUN 99 SERIAL #'d SETS
RCs: STATED PRINT RUN 66 SERIAL #'d SETS
16 Rasheed Wallace 25.00 60.00
18 Shawn Kemp 25.00 60.00
55 Tim Duncan 50.00 120.00
61 Kobe Bryant 250.00 500.00
79 Grant Hill 40.00 100.00
80 Dennis Rodman 75.00 200.00
85 Michael Jordan 500.00 1000.00
89 Anfernee Hardaway 30.00 80.00
93 Shaquille O'Neal 60.00 150.00
99 Chris Webber 75.00 200.00
106 Vince Carter 175.00 350.00
108 Paul Pierce 125.00 250.00
118 Dirk Nowitzki 175.00 350.00

1998-99 Ultra Exclamation Points

Randomly inserted into packs at one in 288, this 15-card set features players that have a knack for slam-dunking the basketball.

COMPLETE SET (15) 700.00 1000.00
STATED ODDS 1:288 HOB/RET
1 Vince Carter 30.00 80.00
2 Tim Duncan 30.00 80.00
3 Shawn Kemp 8.00 20.00
4 Shaquille O'Neal 15.00 40.00
5 Mike Bibby 4.00 10.00
6 Michael Jordan 400.00 800.00
7 Michael Olowokandi 4.00 10.00
8 Larry Hughes 5.00 12.00
9 Kobe Bryant 50.00 120.00
10 Kevin Garnett 20.00 50.00
11 Keith Van Horn 6.00 15.00
12 Grant Hill 10.00 25.00
13 Gary Payton 12.00 30.00
14 Antoine Walker 6.00 15.00
15 Antawn Jamison 10.00 25.00

1998-99 Ultra Give and Take

Randomly inserted into retail packs at one in 18, this 10-card set features players that have a knack for stealing the ball.

COMPLETE SET (10) 6.00 15.00
STATED ODDS 1:18 RETAIL
1 Gary Payton 1.00 2.50
2 Shawn Kemp 1.00 2.50
3 Kerry Kittles .60 1.50
4 Ron Mercer .75 2.00
5 Scottie Pippen 1.50 4.00
6 Ray Allen 1.25 3.00
7 Anfernee Hardaway 1.50 4.00
8 Maurice Taylor .60 1.50
9 Brevin Knight .60 1.50
10 Karl Malone 1.25 3.00

1998-99 Ultra Leading Performers

Randomly inserted into packs at one in 72, this 15-card insert features players that are always among the league leaders in the NBA.

COMPLETE SET (15) 25.00 60.00
STATED ODDS 1:72 HOB/RET
1 Allen Iverson 2.50 6.00
2 Anfernee Hardaway 2.00 5.00
3 Kobe Bryant 5.00 12.00
4 Michael Jordan 10.00 25.00
5 Ron Mercer 1.00 2.50
6 Stephon Marbury 1.50 4.00
7 Tim Duncan 2.50 6.00
8 Shareef Abdur-Rahim 1.25 3.00
9 Kevin Garnett 2.00 5.00
10 Grant Hill 2.00 5.00
11 Damon Stoudamire 1.00 2.50
12 Dennis Rodman 2.50 6.00
13 Keith Van Horn 1.25 3.00
14 Scottie Pippen 2.00 5.00
15 Shaquille O'Neal 3.00 8.00

1998-99 Ultra NBAttitude

Randomly inserted into packs at one in six, this 20-card insert features NBA players that have award-winning attitudes.

COMPLETE SET (20) 3.00 8.00
STATED ODDS 1:6 HOB/RET
1 Allen Iverson .75 2.00
2 Chauncey Billups .50 1.25
3 Keith Van Horn .40 1.00
4 Ray Allen .50 1.25
5 Shareef Abdur-Rahim .40 1.00
6 Stephon Marbury .50 1.25
7 Kerry Kittles .25 .60
8 Tim Thomas .40 1.00
9 Damon Stoudamire .30 .75
10 Antoine Walker .40 1.00
11 Brevin Knight .25 .60
12 Maurice Taylor .25 .60
13 Ron Mercer .30 .75
14 Tim Duncan .75 2.00
15 Zydrunas Ilgauskas .40 1.00
16 Michael Finley .40 1.00
17 Bobby Jackson .25 .60
18 Tim Hardaway .40 1.00
19 David Robinson .60 1.50
20 Vin Baker .30 .75

1998-99 Ultra Unstoppable

Randomly inserted into packs at one in 36, this 15-card set features players that are purely unstoppable on the court.

COMPLETE SET (15) 25.00 60.00
STATED ODDS 1:36 HOB/RET
1 Michael Jordan 10.00 25.00
2 Scottie Pippen 2.00 5.00
3 Grant Hill 2.00 5.00
4 Dennis Rodman 2.50 6.00
5 Stephon Marbury 1.50 4.00
6 Antoine Walker 1.25 3.00
7 Shareef Abdur-Rahim 1.25 3.00
8 Shaquille O'Neal 3.00 8.00
9 Damon Stoudamire 1.00 2.50
10 Kerry Kittles .75 2.00
11 Maurice Taylor .75 2.00
12 Kobe Bryant 5.00 12.00
13 Kevin Garnett 2.00 5.00
14 Anfernee Hardaway 2.00 5.00
15 Allen Iverson 2.50 6.00

1998-99 Ultra World Premiere

Randomly inserted into packs at one in 20, this 15-card set features players that have come from all over the world to play in the NBA.

COMPLETE SET (15) 10.00 25.00
STATED ODDS 1:20 HOB/RET
1 Robert Traylor .60 1.50
2 Paul Pierce 2.50 6.00
3 Michael Olowokandi .75 2.00
4 Felipe Lopez .40 1.00
5 Raef LaFrentz .75 2.00
6 Antawn Jamison 1.00 2.50
7 Larry Hughes 1.25 3.00
8 Al Harrington 1.00 2.50
9 Pat Garrity .50 1.25
10 Bryce Drew .40 1.00
11 Michael Doleac .50 1.25
12 Michael Dickerson .60 1.50
13 Keon Clark .60 1.50
14 Vince Carter 3.00 8.00
15 Mike Bibby 1.00 2.50

1999-00 Ultra

Produced by Fleer/SkyBox, the 1999-00 Ultra set contained 150 cards, featuring 125 veterans and 25 rookies. Each pack contained 10 cards and carried a suggested retail price of $2.69. The rookie subset was inserted at one in four packs. Two checklist were also inserted in packs at one in six.

COMPLETE SET (150) 30.00 80.00
COMPLETE SET w/o RC (125) 12.50 25.00
126-150 SUBSET ODDS 1:4 HOB/RET
UNPRICED MASTERPIECES SERIAL #'d TO 1
1 Vince Carter .60 1.50
2 Randell Jackson .20 .50
3 Ray Allen .30 .75
4 Corliss Williamson .20 .50
5 Darrell Armstrong .20 .50
6 Charles Oakley .25 .60
7 Tyrone Nesby RC .25 .60
8 Eddie Jones .30 .75
9 Kerry Kittles .20 .50
10 Jason Williams .40 1.00
11 Elden Campbell .20 .50
12 Mookie Blaylock .20 .50
13 Brent Barry .25 .60
14 Mark Jackson .25 .60
15 Tim Hardaway .30 .75
16 Kendall Gill .20 .50
17 Larry Johnson .30 .75
18 Eric Snow .25 .60
19 Raef LaFrentz .25 .60
20 Allen Iverson .60 1.50
21 Kenny Anderson .25 .60
22 John Starks .25 .60

23 Isaiah Rider .25 .60
24 Tariq Abdul-Wahad .20 .50
25 Vitaly Potapenko .20 .50
26 Patrick Ewing .40 1.00
27 Mitch Richmond .30 .75
28 Steve Nash .50 1.25
29 Dickey Simpkins .20 .50
30 Grant Hill .40 1.00
31 Matt Geiger .20 .50
32 John Stockton .40 1.00
33 Jayson Williams .20 .50
34 Reggie Miller .30 .75
35 Eric Piatkowski .25 .60
36 Jason Kidd .50 1.25
37 Allan Houston .25 .60
38 Christian Laettner .25 .60
39 Marcus Camby .25 .60
40 Shaquille O'Neal .75 2.00
41 Derek Anderson .20 .50
42 Gary Trent .20 .50
43 Vin Baker .25 .60
44 Alonzo Mourning .40 1.00
45 Latrell Sprewell .30 .75
46 Rod Strickland .20 .50
47 Bobby Jackson .20 .50
48 Karl Malone .40 1.00
49 Mario Elie .20 .50
50 Kobe Bryant 1.25 3.00
51 Clifford Robinson .20 .50
52 Jamal Mashburn .25 .60
53 Dirk Nowitzki .60 1.50
54 Rik Smits .30 .75
55 Doug Christie .25 .60
56 Ricky Davis .30 .75
57 Jalen Rose .25 .60
58 Michael Olowokandi .20 .50
59 Cedric Ceballos .20 .50
60 Ron Mercer .25 .60
61 Brevin Knight .20 .50
62 Rashard Lewis .30 .75
63 Detlef Schrempf .25 .60
64 Keith Van Horn .25 .60
64B Keith Van Horn PROMO .25 .60
65 Nick Anderson .20 .50
66 Larry Hughes .25 .60
67 Antonio McDyess .25 .60
68 Terrell Brandon .20 .50
69 Felipe Lopez .20 .50
70 Scottie Pippen .50 1.25
71 Erick Dampier .20 .50
72 Arvydas Sabonis .25 .60
73 Brian Grant .20 .50
74 Nick Van Exel .25 .60
75 Bryon Russell .20 .50
76 Danny Fortson .20 .50
77 Avery Johnson .25 .60
78 Jerry Stackhouse .30 .75
79 Robert Traylor .20 .50
80 Tim Duncan .60 1.50
81 Lindsey Hunter .20 .50
82 Tyronn Lue .20 .50
83 Michael Finley .30 .75
84 Dikembe Mutombo .30 .75
85 Zydrunas Ilgauskas .25 .60
86 Pat Garrity .20 .50
87 Damon Stoudamire .25 .60
88 Shareef Abdur-Rahim .25 .60
89 Matt Harpring .20 .50
90 Michael Dickerson .20 .50
91 Steve Smith .25 .60
92 Bison Dele .20 .50
93 Glenn Robinson .25 .60
94 Antawn Jamison .30 .75
95 Glen Rice .30 .75
96 Vlade Divac .30 .75
97 Vladimir Stepania .20 .50
98 Kornell David RC .25 .60
99 Shawn Kemp .30 .75
100 Kevin Garnett .50 1.25
101 Tim Thomas .25 .60
102 Mike Bibby .30 .75
103 Maurice Taylor .20 .50
104 Gary Payton .30 .75
105 Voshon Lenard .20 .50
106 Theo Ratliff .25 .60
107 Hakeem Olajuwon .40 1.00
108 Joe Smith .25 .60
109 Toni Kukoc .30 .75
110 Stephon Marbury .25 .60
111 Anthony Mason .20 .50
112 Anfernee Hardaway .50 1.25
113 Juwan Howard .25 .60
114 Charles Barkley .50 1.25
115 Antoine Walker .30 .75
116 Donyell Marshall .20 .50
117 Tom Gugliotta .20 .50
118 Rasheed Wallace .30 .75
119 Tracy McGrady .50 1.25
120 Paul Pierce .40 1.00
121 Sean Elliott .30 .75
122 Bryant Reeves .20 .50
123 Michael Doleac .20 .50
124 Chris Webber .30 .75
125 David Robinson .50 1.25
126 Steve Francis RC 1.50 4.00
127 Elton Brand RC 1.50 4.00
128 Wally Szczerbiak RC 1.25 3.00
129 Richard Hamilton RC 1.25 3.00
130 Shawn Marion RC 1.25 3.00
131 Trajan Langdon RC .60 1.50
132 Corey Maggette RC 1.00 2.50
133 Dion Glover RC .50 1.25
134 James Posey RC .60 1.50
135 Lamar Odom RC 1.50 4.00
136 A.Radojevic RC .40 1.00
137 Cal Bowdler RC .40 1.00
138 Scott Padgett RC .50 1.25
139 Jumaine Jones RC .50 1.25
140 Jonathan Bender RC .60 1.50
141 Tim James RC .40 1.00
142 Jason Terry RC 1.00 2.50
143 Quincy Lewis RC .40 1.00
144 William Avery RC .50 1.25
145 Galen Young RC .60 1.50
146 Ron Artest RC 1.25 3.00
147 Kenny Thomas RC .60 1.50
148 Devean George RC .60 1.50
149 Andre Miller RC 1.25 3.00
150 Baron Davis RC 1.50 4.00

1999-00 Ultra Gold Medallion

*STARS: .75X TO 2X BASE CARD HI
*RCs: .6X TO 1.5X BASE HI
RCs: STATED ODDS 1:35 HOBBY

1999-00 Ultra Platinum Medallion

*STARS: 20X TO 50X BASE CARD HI
*RCs: 10X TO 25X BASE HI
STARS: PRINT RUN 50 SERIAL #'d SETS
RCs: PRINT RUN 25 SERIAL #'d SETS
40 Shaquille O'Neal 75.00 150.00
50 Kobe Bryant 200.00 500.00

1999-00 Ultra Feel the Game

Randomly inserted in packs, this 15-card set featues cards with pieces of player worn memorabilia from the top rookies in the NBA. The cards are not numbered and listed below in alphabetical order. Each player contains a different print run and those are noted below next to the player's name.
RANDOM INSERTS IN HOB/RET PACKS
1 Steve Francis 4.00 10.00
2 Richard Hamilton 3.00 8.00
3 Jonathan Bender 2.00 5.00
4 Baron Davis 4.00 10.00
5 Wally Szczerbiak 3.00 8.00
6 Lamar Odom 4.00 10.00
7 Andre Miller 3.00 8.00
8 Jason Terry 2.50 6.00
9 Trajan Langdon 2.00 5.00
10 Corey Maggette 2.50 6.00
11 Cal Bowdler 2.00 5.00
12 James Posey 2.00 5.00
13 Tim James 2.00 5.00
14 Scott Padgett 2.00 5.00
15 Jumaine Jones 2.00 5.00

1999-00 Ultra Fresh Ink

Randomly inserted in packs, this 56-card set features autographs from top NBA stars and rookies. The cards are not numbered, so they are listed below alphabetically. Individual print runs are listed after each card.
PRINT RUNS LISTED BELOW
1 Ray Allen/300 20.00 50.00
2 Ron Artest/1000 5.00 12.00
3 William Avery/1000 2.00 5.00
4 Jonathan Bender/500 2.50 6.00
5 Mike Bibby/550 5.00 12.00
6 Calvin Booth/975 2.50 6.00
7 Cal Bowdler/1000 1.50 4.00
8 Bruce Bowen/1000 4.00 10.00
9 Marcus Camby/750 5.00 12.00
10 John Celestand/1000 1.50 4.00
11 Baron Davis/475 6.00 15.00
12 Michael Dickerson/975 2.50 6.00
13 Michael Doleac/1000 2.50 6.00
14 Bryce Drew/1000 2.50 6.00
15 Evan Eschmeyer/1000 2.00 5.00
16 Steve Francis/500 6.00 15.00
17 Pat Garrity/600 2.50 6.00
18 Devean George/1000 2.50 6.00
19 Dion Glover/875 2.00 5.00
20 Brian Grant/500 2.50 6.00
21 Richard Hamilton/750 5.00 12.00
22 Juwan Howard/225 4.00 10.00
23 Larry Hughes/750 5.00 12.00
24 Jumaine Jones/1000 2.00 5.00
25 Eddie Jones/250 10.00 25.00
26 Raef LaFrentz/500 2.50 6.00
27 Quincy Lewis/1000 1.50 4.00
28 Felipe Lopez/1000 2.50 6.00
29 Corey Maggette/250 8.00 20.00
30 Stephon Marbury/400 5.00 12.00
31 Shawn Marion/1000 5.00 12.00
32 Lamar Odom/350 6.00 15.00
33 Shaquille O'Neal/200 75.00 200.00
34 Scottie Pippen/130 100.00 200.00
35 James Posey/1000 2.50 6.00
36 A.Radojevic/1000 1.50 4.00
37 David Robinson/155 100.00 200.00
38 Jalen Rose/500 8.00 20.00
39 Wally Szczerbiak/500 5.00 12.00
40 Jerry Stackhouse/650 6.00 15.00
41 Maurice Taylor/400 2.50 6.00
42 Jason Terry/1000 4.00 10.00
43 Robert Traylor/1000 2.50 6.00
44 Keith Van Horn/500 6.00 15.00
45 Antoine Walker/245 8.00 20.00
46 Chris Webber/200 125.00 300.00

1999-00 Ultra Good Looks

Randomly inserted in packs at one in six, this 15-card set feature players who put themselves in a position to take over the game at any time. Card fronts feature all-foil.
COMPLETE SET (15) 5.00 12.00
STATED ODDS 1:6 HOB/RET
1 Grant Hill .50 1.25
2 Kevin Garnett .60 1.50
3 Richard Hamilton .50 1.25
4 Larry Hughes .30 .75
5 Shaquille O'Neal 1.00 2.50
6 Kobe Bryant 1.50 4.00
7 Antoine Walker .40 1.00
8 Lamar Odom .60 1.50
9 Allen Iverson .75 2.00
10 Scottie Pippen .60 1.50
11 Ron Mercer .30 .75
12 Anfernee Hardaway .60 1.50
13 Chris Webber .40 1.00
14 Jason Williams .50 1.25
15 Baron Davis .60 1.50

1999-00 Ultra Heir to the Throne

ndomly inserted in packs at one in 24, this 10-card set features the best young players in the NBA on a clear holo-pattern crown background with silver foil stamping.
COMPLETE SET (10) 5.00 12.00
STATED ODDS 1:24 HOB/RET
1 Allen Iverson 1.25 3.00
2 Keith Van Horn .50 1.25
3 Paul Pierce .75 2.00
4 Stephon Marbury .50 1.25
5 Vince Carter 1.25 3.00
6 Tim Duncan 1.25 3.00
7 Ron Mercer .50 1.25
8 Antawn Jamison .60 1.50
9 Shaquille O'Neal 1.50 4.00
10 Grant Hill .75 2.00

1999-00 Ultra Millennium Men

Randomly inserted in hobby packs, this 15-card set features young stars who will take the league to new levels in the next millennium. Card fronts feature a translucent lenticular patterned plastic with silver foil stamping. The cards are serially numbered to 100.
PRINT RUN 100 SERIAL #'d SETS
1 Allen Iverson 300.00 600.00
2 Paul Pierce 150.00 400.00
3 Steve Francis 100.00 250.00
4 Kobe Bryant 800.00 1200.00
5 Vince Carter 200.00 500.00
6 Ron Mercer 60.00 150.00
7 Jason Williams 400.00 800.00
8 Elton Brand 75.00 200.00
9 Grant Hill 200.00 500.00
10 Tim Duncan 300.00 600.00
11 Stephon Marbury 75.00 200.00
12 Keith Van Horn 75.00 200.00
13 Kevin Garnett 400.00 800.00
14 Antawn Jamison 75.00 200.00
15 Antoine Walker 100.00 250.00

1999-00 Ultra Parquet Players

ndomly inserted in packs at one in 72, this 15-card set features players you want on the court when the game is on the line. The fronts feature a debossed parquet pattern floor background with gold foil stamping.
COMPLETE SET (15) 50.00 100.00
STATED ODDS 1:72 HOB/RET
1 Kobe Bryant 10.00 25.00
2 Keith Van Horn 2.00 5.00
3 Tim Duncan 5.00 12.00
4 Shaquille O'Neal 6.00 15.00
5 Kevin Garnett 4.00 10.00
6 Jason Williams 3.00 8.00
7 Vince Carter 5.00 12.00
8 Stephon Marbury 2.00 5.00
9 Paul Pierce 3.00 8.00
10 Scottie Pippen 4.00 10.00
11 Baron Davis 4.00 10.00
12 Antoine Walker 2.50 6.00
13 Larry Hughes 2.00 5.00
14 Antawn Jamison 2.50 6.00
15 Elton Brand 4.00 10.00

1999-00 Ultra World Premiere

Randomly inserted in packs at one in 12, this 10-card set highlights the top rookies from the 99-00 season. The cards feature die cutting and foil etching.
COMPLETE SET (10) 4.00 10.00
STATED ODDS 1:12 HOB/RET
1 Elton Brand .75 2.00
2 Andre Miller .60 1.50
3 Baron Davis .75 2.00
4 Steve Francis .75 2.00
5 Richard Hamilton .60 1.50
6 Jason Terry .50 1.25
7 Jonathan Bender .30 .75
8 Trajan Langdon .30 .75
9 Wally Szczerbiak .60 1.50
10 Lamar Odom .75 2.00

2000-01 Ultra

The 2000-01 Ultra product was released in November,2000 as a 225-card set. The set features 200 veterans, and 25 rookies (serial numbered to 2999). Each pack contained ten cards and carried a suggested retail price of $2.99.
COMPLETE SET w/o RC (200) 15.00 40.00
RCs: STATED PRINT RUN 2999 SERIAL #'d SETS
1 Vince Carter .60 1.50
2 Antawn Jamison .30 .75
3 Shaquille O'Neal .75 2.00
4 Paul Pierce .30 .75
5 Antonio McDyess .25 .60
6 Scott Burrell .20 .50
7 Elton Brand .30 .75
8 Lamar Odom .25 .60
9 Nick Van Exel .25 .60
10 Kobe Bryant 1.25 3.00
11 Reggie Miller .30 .75
12 Sam Cassell .25 .60
13 Darrell Armstrong .20 .50
14 Rasheed Wallace .30 .75
15 Charles Oakley .25 .60
16 David Wesley .20 .50
17 Al Harrington .25 .60
18 Latrell Sprewell .25 .60
19 Rick Brunson .20 .50
20 Steve Smith .25 .60
21 Antonio Davis .20 .50
22 Michael Finley .30 .75
23 Shandon Anderson .20 .50
24 Danny Fortson .20 .50
25 Kerry Kittles .20 .50
26 Anfernee Hardaway .50 1.25
27 Vin Baker .25 .60
28 Calvin Booth .20 .50
29 Haywoode Workman .20 .50
30 Dickey Simpkins .20 .50
31 Jerome Williams .20 .50
32 Ron Artest .30 .75
33 Dennis Scott .20 .50
34 Ron Mercer .20 .50
35 Chris Webber .30 .75
36 Bryon Russell .20 .50
37 Dale Davis .20 .50
38 Dirk Nowitzki .50 1.25
39 Steve Francis .25 .60
40 Glen Rice .25 .60
41 Stephon Marbury .25 .60
42 Jason Kidd .50 1.25
43 Brent Barry .20 .50
44 Richard Hamilton .25 .60
45 Antoine Walker .25 .60
46 Gary Trent .20 .50
47 Cuttino Mobley .20 .50
48 P.J. Brown .20 .50
49 Elliot Perry .20 .50
50 Shawn Marion .25 .60
51 Horace Grant .25 .60
52 Juwan Howard .25 .60
53 Elden Campbell .20 .50
54 Erick Strickland .20 .50
55 Hakeem Olajuwon .40 1.00
56 Anthony Carter .20 .50
57 Keith Van Horn .25 .60
58 Clifford Robinson .20 .50
59 Ruben Patterson .20 .50
60 Mitch Richmond .25 .60
61 Jason Terry .30 .75
62 Andre Miller .25 .60
63 Vonteego Cummings .20 .50
64 Joe Smith .25 .60
65 Toni Kukoc .30 .75
66 Sean Elliott .30 .75
67 Michael Dickerson .20 .50
68 Derrick Coleman .25 .60
69 Shawn Bradley .20 .50
70 Kenny Thomas .20 .50
71 Tim Hardaway .30 .75
72 Rex Chapman .20 .50
73 Gary Payton .30 .75
74 Jahidi White .20 .50
75 Baron Davis .30 .75
76 Chauncey Billups .30 .75
77 Moochie Norris .20 .50
78 Dan Majerle .30 .75
79 Marcus Camby .25 .60
80 Rodney Rogers .20 .50
81 Rashard Lewis .30 .75
82 Laron Profit .20 .50
83 Ricky Davis .25 .60
84 Keon Clark .20 .50
85 Anthony Miller .20 .50
86 Jamal Mashburn .25 .60
87 Chris Childs .20 .50
88 Brian Grant .20 .50
89 Muggsy Bogues .25 .60
90 Randy Brown .20 .50
91 Tariq Abdul-Wahad .20 .50
92 Lindsey Hunter .20 .50
93 Rik Smits .20 .50
94 Glenn Robinson .25 .60
95 Michael Doleac .20 .50
96 Quincy Lewis .20 .50
97 Grant Hill .40 1.00
98 Jalen Rose .25 .60
99 Ervin Johnson .20 .50
100 Chucky Atkins .20 .50
101 Jermaine O'Neal .25 .60
102 Howard Eisley .20 .50
103 Kenny Anderson .25 .60
104 Lamond Murray .20 .50
105 Adonal Foyle .20 .50
106 Derek Fisher .30 .75
107 Wally Szczerbiak .25 .60
108 Todd MacCulloch .20 .50
109 Avery Johnson .25 .60
110 Othella Harrington .20 .50
111 Tony Battie .20 .50
112 Bob Sura .20 .50
113 Larry Hughes .25 .60
114 Rick Fox .20 .50
115 Travis Best .20 .50
116 Theo Ratliff .20 .50
117 David Robinson .50 1.25
118 Felipe Lopez .20 .50
119 John Amaechi .20 .50
120 George Lynch .20 .50
121 Christian Laettner .25 .60
122 Derek Anderson .20 .50
123 Tim Thomas .20 .50
124 Matt Harpring .20 .50
125 Nick Anderson .20 .50
126 Karl Malone .40 1.00
127 Dion Glover .20 .50
128 Wesley Person .20 .50
129 Mikki Moore RC .30 .75
130 Michael Olowokandi .20 .50
131 William Avery .20 .50
132 Bo Outlaw .20 .50
133 Jason Williams .30 .75
134 John Stockton .40 1.00
135 Adrian Griffin .20 .50
136 Hubert Davis .20 .50
137 Donyell Marshall .20 .50
138 Travis Knight .20 .50
139 Kendall Gill .20 .50
140 Tom Gugliotta .20 .50
141 Malik Rose .20 .50
142 Isaac Austin .20 .50
143 Alan Henderson .20 .50
144 Shawn Kemp .30 .75
145 Terry Mills .20 .50
146 Maurice Taylor .20 .50
147 Terrell Brandon .20 .50
148 Matt Geiger .20 .50
149 Corliss Williamson .20 .50
150 Jacque Vaughn .20 .50
151 Dikembe Mutombo .30 .75
152 Trajan Langdon .20 .50
153 Jason Caffey .20 .50
154 Tyrone Nesby .30 .75
155 Bobby Jackson .20 .50
156 Allen Iverson .60 1.50
157 Mario Elie .20 .50
158 Mike Bibby .30 .75
159 Robert Horry .25 .60
160 James Posey .20 .50
161 Mark Jackson .25 .60
162 Ray Allen .30 .75
163 Charlie Ward .20 .50
164 Damon Stoudamire .25 .60
165 Tracy McGrady .50 1.25
166 Bimbo Coles .20 .50
167 Chucky Brown .20 .50
168 Jerry Stackhouse .25 .60
169 Greg Ostertag .20 .50
170 Radoslav Nesterovic .20 .50
171 Corey Maggette .25 .60
172 Vlade Divac .25 .60
173 Scott Padgett .20 .50
174 Anthony Mason .20 .50
175 Raef LaFrentz .20 .50
176 Austin Croshere .20 .50
177 Mark Strickland .20 .50
178 Allan Houston .25 .60
179 Arvydas Sabonis .25 .60
180 Doug Christie .20 .50
181 Jim Jackson .20 .50
182 Brevin Knight .20 .50
183 Mookie Blaylock .20 .50
184 Chris Herren .20 .50
185 Kevin Garnett .50 1.25
186 Tyrone Hill .20 .50
187 Tim Duncan .60 1.50
188 Shareef Abdur-Rahim .25 .60
189 Eddie Jones .30 .75
190 Jonathan Bender .20 .50
191 Alonzo Mourning .40 1.00
192 Patrick Ewing .40 1.00
193 Scottie Pippen .50 1.25
194 Scot Pollard .20 .50
195 Cedric Ceballos .20 .50
196 Clarence Weatherspoon .20 .50
197 Jamie Feick .20 .50
198 Eric Snow .20 .50
199 Ron Harper .25 .60
200 Bryant Reeves .20 .50
201 Chris Mihm RC .60 1.50
202 Joel Przybilla RC .60 1.50
203 Kenyon Martin RC 2.00 5.00
204 Stromile Swift RC .75 2.00
205 Etan Thomas RC .75 2.00
206 Jason Collier RC .75 2.00
207 Marcus Fizer RC .75 2.00
208 Mateen Cleaves RC .60 1.50
209 Dan Langhi RC .50 1.25
210 Mike Miller RC 1.25 3.00
211 Jabari Smith RC .50 1.25
212 Hanno Mottola RC .50 1.25
213 Chris Porter RC .50 1.25
214 Desmond Mason RC 1.00 2.50
215 Erick Barkley RC .50 1.25
216 Donnell Harvey RC .60 1.50
217 DerMarr Johnson RC .60 1.50
218 Jerome Moiso RC .50 1.25
219 Quentin Richardson RC .75 2.00
220 Courtney Alexander RC .60 1.50
221 Michael Redd RC 2.00 5.00
222 Morris Peterson RC .75 2.00
223 Darius Miles RC .75 2.00
224 Jamal Crawford RC 2.00 5.00
225 Keyon Dooling RC .75 2.00

2000-01 Ultra Gold Medallion

STARS: ONE PER PACK
RCs: STATED ODDS 1:24

2000-01 Ultra Platinum Medallion

*STARS: 20X TO 50X BASE CARD HI
STARS: PRINT RUN 50 SERIAL #'d SETS
RCs: PRINT RUN 25 SERIAL #'d SETS
10 Kobe Bryant 250.00 450.00
26 Anfernee Hardaway 75.00 200.00
35 Chris Webber 20.00 50.00

2000-01 Ultra Air Club for Men

Randomly inserted in packs at one in six, this 15-card set features aeriel artists whose play changes the game. Card backs carry an "AC" prefix.
COMPLETE SET (15) 7.50 15.00
STATED ODDS 1:6
*PLATINUM: 12X TO 30X AIR CLUB HI
PLATINUM: PRINT RUN 100 SERIAL #'d SETS
AC1 Kobe Bryant 4.00 10.00
AC2 Lamar Odom .30 .75
AC3 Vince Carter .75 2.00
AC4 Tim Duncan .75 2.00
AC5 Grant Hill .50 1.25
AC6 Tracy McGrady .60 1.50
AC7 Kevin Garnett .60 1.50
AC8 Steve Francis .30 .75
AC9 Allen Iverson .75 2.00
AC10 Jason Williams .40 1.00
AC11 Shaquille O'Neal 1.00 2.50
AC12 Jason Kidd .60 1.50
AC13 Elton Brand .40 1.00
AC14 Eddie Jones .40 1.00
AC15 Stephon Marbury .30 .75

2000-01 Ultra Vince Carter Rookie Remnants

This three-card insert was randomly inserted into 2000-01 Fleer products. The set includes a Vince Carter floor card (numbered to 100), a Vince Carter floor/jersey card (numbered to 15), and finally an autographed Vince Carter floor/jersey card (numbered 1/1).
RANDOM INSERTS IN PACKS
NNO Vince Carter FLR JSY/15 30.00 80.00
NNO Vince Carter FLR/100 12.50 30.00

2000-01 Ultra Slam Show

Randomly inserted in packs at one in 24, this 10-card set features shots from the 1999-2000 NBA Slam Dunk contest. Card backs carry a "SS" prefix.
COMPLETE SET (10) 7.50 15.00
STATED ODDS 1:24
*PLATINUM: 3X TO 8X SLAM SHOW HI
PLATINUM: PRINT RUN 100 SERIAL #'d SETS
SS1 Steve Francis .60 1.50
SS2 Tracy McGrady 1.25 3.00
SS3 Jerry Stackhouse .60 1.50
SS4 Larry Hughes .60 1.50
SS5 Ricky Davis .60 1.50
SS6 Vince Carter 1.50 4.00
SS7 Vince Carter 1.50 4.00
SS8 Vince Carter 1.50 4.00
SS9 Vince Carter 1.50 4.00
SS10 Vince Carter 1.50 4.00

2000-01 Ultra Thrillinium

Randomly inserted in packs at one in 48 packs, this 10-card set features players leading the NBA in the new millennium. Card backs carry a "T" prefix.
COMPLETE SET (10) 25.00 50.00
STATED ODDS 1:48
*PLATINUM: 4X TO 10X THRILLINIUM HI
PLATINUM: PRINT RUN 100 SERIAL #'d SETS
T1 Vince Carter 3.00 8.00
T2 Kobe Bryant 10.00 25.00
T3 Tim Duncan 3.00 8.00
T4 Kevin Garnett 2.50 6.00
T5 Allen Iverson 3.00 8.00
T6 Jason Williams 1.50 4.00
T7 Shaquille O'Neal 4.00 10.00
T8 Lamar Odom 1.25 3.00
T9 Eddie Jones 1.50 4.00
T10 Stephon Marbury 1.25 3.00

2000-01 Ultra Two Ball

Randomly inserted in packs at one in three, this 15-card set focuses on second year players. Card backs carry a "TB" prefix.
COMPLETE SET (15) 2.00 5.00
STATED ODDS 1:3
*PLATINUM: 8X TO 20X TWO BALL HI
PLATINUM: PRINT RUN 100 SERIAL #'d SETS
TB1 Lamar Odom .25 .60
TB2 Elton Brand .30 .75
TB3 Steve Francis .25 .60
TB4 Adrian Griffin .20 .50
TB5 Todd MacCulloch .20 .50
TB6 Andre Miller .25 .60
TB7 James Posey .20 .50
TB8 Wally Szczerbiak .25 .60
TB9 Ron Artest .30 .75
TB10 Corey Maggette .25 .60
TB11 Shawn Marion .25 .60
TB12 Chucky Atkins .20 .50
TB13 Vonteego Cummings .20 .50
TB14 Kenny Thomas .20 .50
TB15 Richard Hamilton .25 .60

2000-01 Ultra Year 3

Randomly inserted in packs at one in 12, this 10-card set showcases players in their third year, from the class of 1998-99. Card backs carry a "YT" prefix.
COMPLETE SET (10) 2.50 6.00
STATED ODDS 1:12
*PLATINUM: 6X TO 15X YEAR 3 HI
PLATINUM: PRINT RUN 100 SERIAL #'d SETS
YT1 Mike Bibby .50 1.25
YT2 Michael Dickerson .30 .75
YT3 Larry Hughes .40 1.00
YT4 Raef LaFrentz .30 .75
YT5 Dirk Nowitzki .75 2.00
YT6 Michael Olowokandi .30 .75
YT7 Paul Pierce .50 1.25
YT8 Jason Williams .50 1.25
YT9 Vince Carter 1.00 2.50
YT10 Antawn Jamison .50 1.25

2001-02 Ultra

sued in mid-November of 2001, Ultra boasts a 181-card base set divided up into 150 base veteran cards and 31 short printed rookie cards sequentially numbered to 2222. The last six cards in the set were inserted in Fleer Focus as Ultra update and are numbered 1U to 6U-these cards are also sequentially numbered to 2222. The card design places full color player action photos on a borderless card design with a foil box centered at the bottom containing the player's name and team logo in silver foil. Ultra was issued in both 16 and six box cases where boxes contained 24 packs of ten cards each.
COMP.SET w/o SP's (150) 10.00 25.00
COMP.UPDATE SET (6) 8.00 20.00
151-181 PRINT RUN 2222 SERIAL #'d SETS
1 Vince Carter .50 1.25
2 Allen Iverson .60 1.50
3 Jerry Stackhouse .25 .60
4 Travis Best .20 .50
5 Eddie Jones .25 .60
6 Felipe Lopez .20 .50
7 Antonio Daniels .20 .50
8 A.J. Guyton .20 .50
9 Quentin Richardson .25 .60
10 Charlie Ward .20 .50
11 Ron Mercer .20 .50
12 Shandon Anderson .20 .50
13 Antawn Jamison .30 .75
14 Darius Miles .20 .50
15 Anthony Mason .20 .50
16 Latrell Sprewell .25 .60
17 Scottie Pippen .50 1.25
18 Shammond Williams .20 .50
19 P.J. Brown .20 .50
20 Dirk Nowitzki .50 1.25
21 Mateen Cleaves .20 .50
22 Tim Hardaway .30 .75
23 Christian Laettner .25 .60
24 Toni Kukoc .30 .75
25 Bob Sura .20 .50
26 Kobe Bryant 1.25 3.00
27 Wally Szczerbiak .25 .60
28 Darrell Armstrong .20 .50
29 Chris Webber .30 .75
30 David Wesley .20 .50
31 Michael Finley .30 .75
32 Jermaine O'Neal .25 .60
33 Jason Kidd .50 1.25
34 Tony Delk .20 .50
35 Avery Johnson .25 .60
36 Elden Campbell .20 .50
37 Lamond Murray .20 .50
38 Ben Wallace .25 .60
39 Jalen Rose .25 .60
40 Michael Dickerson .20 .50
41 Shawn Marion .25 .60
42 Jahidi White .20 .50
43 Jamal Mashburn .25 .60
44 Trajan Langdon .20 .50
45 Reggie Miller .30 .75
46 Stromile Swift .20 .50
47 Keith Van Horn .25 .60
48 Tom Gugliotta .20 .50
49 Brent Barry .20 .50
50 Courtney Alexander .20 .50
51 Antonio McDyess .25 .60
52 Robert Horry .25 .60
53 Ervin Johnson .20 .50
54 Speedy Claxton .20 .50
55 Bryon Russell .20 .50
56 Baron Davis .30 .75
57 Robert Traylor .20 .50
58 Chucky Atkins .20 .50
59 Stephon Marbury .25 .60
60 Desmond Mason .25 .60
61 Tyrone Nesby .20 .50
62 Brevin Knight .20 .50
63 Kenyon Martin .30 .75
64 Jumaine Jones .20 .50
65 Rashard Lewis .30 .75
66 Kenny Anderson .25 .60
67 Andre Miller .25 .60
68 Joe Smith .25 .60
69 Kelvin Cato .20 .50
70 Jason Williams .25 .60
71 Marcus Camby .25 .60
72 Eric Snow .20 .50
73 Gary Payton .30 .75
74 Robert Pack .20 .50
75 Brian Cardinal .20 .50
76 Sam Cassell .25 .60
77 Allan Houston .25 .60
78 Anfernee Hardaway .50 1.25
79 Morris Peterson .20 .50
80 Chris Mihm .20 .50
81 Elton Brand .30 .75
82 Glenn Robinson .25 .60
83 Damon Stoudamire .25 .60
84 Alvin Williams .20 .50
85 Paul Pierce .30 .75
86 James Posey .20 .50
87 Cuttino Mobley .20 .50
88 Tim Thomas .20 .50
89 Dikembe Mutombo .30 .75
90 Tim Duncan .60 1.50
91 John Starks .20 .50
92 Antoine Walker .25 .60
93 Moochie Norris .20 .50
94 Dalibor Bagaric .20 .50
95 Ray Allen .30 .75
96 David Robinson .50 1.25
97 Shareef Abdur-Rahim .25 .60
98 Wang Zhizhi .25 .60
99 Chris Porter .20 .50
100 Chauncey Billups .30 .75
101 Tracy McGrady .50 1.25
102 Michael Jordan 2.50 6.00
103 Jerome Williams .20 .50
104 Jason Terry .30 .75
105 Calvin Booth .20 .50
106 Shaquille O'Neal .75 2.00
107 Kevin Garnett .50 1.25
108 Doug Christie .20 .50
109 Karl Malone .40 1.00
110 Steve Nash .50 1.25
111 Austin Croshere .20 .50
112 Alonzo Mourning .40 1.00
113 Dan Majerle .30 .75
114 Malik Rose .20 .50
115 Richard Hamilton .25 .60
116 DerMarr Johnson .20 .50
117 Raef LaFrentz .20 .50
118 Derek Fisher .25 .60
119 Vlade Divac .25 .60
120 John Stockton .40 1.00
121 Dion Glover .20 .50
122 Voshon Lenard .20 .50
123 Steve Francis .25 .60
124 Darvin Ham .20 .50
125 Aaron McKie .20 .50
126 Peja Stojakovic .30 .75
127 Ron Artest .30 .75
128 Keyon Dooling .20 .50
129 Anthony Carter .20 .50
130 Kurt Thomas .20 .50
131 Rasheed Wallace .30 .75
132 Theo Ratliff .20 .50
133 Eric Piatkowski .20 .50
134 Terrell Brandon .20 .50
135 Mike Miller .25 .60
136 Mike Bibby .30 .75
137 Antonio Davis .20 .50
138 Lamar Odom .25 .60
139 Eddie House .20 .50
140 Nick Van Exel .25 .60
141 Rick Fox .20 .50
142 Juwan Howard .25 .60
143 Hedo Turkoglu .25 .60
144 Donyell Marshall .20 .50
145 Marcus Fizer .20 .50
146 Larry Hughes .25 .60
147 Steve Smith .25 .60
148 Brian Grant .20 .50
149 Grant Hill .40 1.00
150 Derek Anderson .20 .50
151 Kwame Brown RC 1.25 3.00
152 Eddie Griffin RC 1.00 2.50
153 Eddy Curry RC 1.25 3.00
154 Jamaal Tinsley RC 1.25 3.00
155 Jason Richardson RC 1.50 4.00
156 Shane Battier RC 2.50 6.00
157 Troy Murphy RC 1.25 3.00
158 Richard Jefferson RC 2.00 5.00
159 DeSagana Diop RC 1.00 2.50
160 Tyson Chandler RC 2.00 5.00
161 Joe Johnson RC 1.50 4.00
162 Zach Randolph RC 2.00 5.00
163 Andrei Kirilenko RC 2.00 5.00
164 Loren Woods RC .75 2.00
165 Jason Collins RC 1.00 2.50
166 Rodney White RC .75 2.00
167 Jeryl Sasser RC .75 2.00
168 Kirk Haston RC .75 2.00
169 Pau Gasol RC 4.00 10.00
170 Kedrick Brown RC .75 2.00
171 Steven Hunter RC 1.00 2.50
172 Michael Bradley RC .75 2.00
173 Joseph Forte RC .75 2.00
174 Brandon Armstrong RC .75 2.00
175 Primoz Brezec RC 1.25 3.00
176U Gerald Wallace RC 1.50 4.00
177U Tony Parker RC 5.00 12.00
178U Vladimir Radmanovic RC 1.25 3.00
179U Trenton Hassell RC 1.00 2.50
180U Zeljko Rebraca RC 1.25 3.00
181U Oscar Torres RC 1.25 3.00

2001-02 Ultra Gold Medallion

*GOLD STARS: .6X TO 1.5X BASE CARD HI
*GOLD RC's: 1.5X TO 4X BASE CARD HI

2001-02 Ultra 02 Good

Inserted in packs at the rate of one in 20, this 20-card set places player action photos on the left side of the card with a colored background that extends two thirds of the way across the card. The right side features "02 Good" in bronze foil.
COMPLETE SET (20) 10.00 20.00
STATED ODDS 1:20
1 Vince Carter 1.25 3.00
1A Vince Carter AU 25.00 50.00
2 Allen Iverson 1.50 4.00
3 Shawn Marion .60 1.50
4 Jalen Rose .60 1.50
5 Steve Francis .60 1.50
6 Kenyon Martin .75 2.00
7 Sam Cassell .60 1.50
8 Darius Miles .50 1.25
9 Mike Miller .60 1.50
10 Jason Terry .75 2.00
11 Baron Davis .75 2.00
12 Lamar Odom .60 1.50
13 Latrell Sprewell .60 1.50
14 Morris Peterson .50 1.25
15 Antonio Davis .50 1.25
16 Ray Allen .75 2.00
17 Rashard Lewis .75 2.00
18 Desmond Mason .60 1.50
19 Antonio McDyess .60 1.50
20 Keith Van Horn .60 1.50

2001-02 Ultra 02 Good Game Worn

STATED ODDS 1:157
1 Vince Carter 6.00 15.00
2 Allen Iverson 12.00 30.00
3 Shawn Marion 3.00 8.00
4 Jalen Rose 3.00 8.00
5 Steve Francis 3.00 8.00
6 Kenyon Martin 4.00 10.00
7 Sam Cassell 3.00 8.00
8 Darius Miles 2.50 6.00
9 Mike Miller 3.00 8.00
10 Jason Terry 4.00 10.00
11 Baron Davis 4.00 10.00
12 Lamar Odom 3.00 8.00
13 Latrell Sprewell 3.00 8.00
14 Morris Peterson 2.50 6.00
15 Antonio Davis 2.50 6.00
16 Ray Allen 4.00 10.00
17 Rashard Lewis 4.00 10.00
18 Desmond Mason 3.00 8.00
19 Antonio McDyess 3.00 8.00
20 Keith Van Horn 3.00 8.00

2001-02 Ultra League Leaders

Randomly seeded in packs at the rate of one in 20, this 20-card set places two photos of each player on the card. The photo on the right is a full color action photo, and the photo of the left is a portrait style photo of the player's head. The cards have each player's team logo centered towards the left and bronze foil highlights. A Platinum medallion versions sequentially numbered to 25 was also inserted in packs.
COMPLETE SET (20) 10.00 20.00
STATED ODDS 1:20
*PLATINUM: 12X TO 30X HI
PLATINUM PRINT RUN 25 SER.#'d SETS
1 Vince Carter 1.25 3.00
2 Allen Iverson 1.50 4.00
3 Ray Allen .75 2.00
4 Reggie Miller .75 2.00
5 Karl Malone 1.00 2.50
6 Jalen Rose .60 1.50
7 Baron Davis .75 2.00
8 Tracy McGrady 1.25 3.00
9 Chris Webber .75 2.00
10 John Stockton 1.00 2.50
11 Dikembe Mutombo .75 2.00
12 Steve Francis .60 1.50
13 Andre Miller .60 1.50
14 Kenyon Martin .75 2.00
15 Mike Miller .60 1.50
16 Antonio Davis .50 1.25
17 Darius Miles .50 1.25
18 Latrell Sprewell .60 1.50
19 Cuttino Mobley .50 1.25
20 Lamar Odom .60 1.50

2001-02 Ultra League Leaders Game Worn

PRINT RUN 450 SERIAL #'d SETS
1 Vince Carter 6.00 15.00
2 Allen Iverson 8.00 20.00
3 Ray Allen 4.00 10.00
4 Reggie Miller 4.00 10.00
5 Karl Malone 5.00 12.00
6 Jalen Rose 3.00 8.00
7 Baron Davis 4.00 10.00
8 Tracy McGrady 6.00 15.00
9 Chris Webber 4.00 10.00
10 John Stockton 5.00 12.00
11 Dikembe Mutombo 4.00 10.00
12 Steve Francis 3.00 8.00
13 Andre Miller 3.00 8.00
14 Kenyon Martin 4.00 10.00
15 Mike Miller 3.00 8.00
16 Antonio Davis 2.50 6.00
17 Darius Miles 2.50 6.00
18 Latrell Sprewell 3.00 8.00
19 Cuttino Mobley 2.50 6.00
20 Lamar Odom 3.00 8.00

2001-02 Ultra On the Road Game Worn

STATED ODDS 1:156
*PLATINUM: 2.5X TO 6X HI

NUM PRINT RUN 25 SER.#'d SETS
nce Carter 6.00 15.00
Morris Peterson 2.50 6.00
Rashard Lewis 4.00 10.00
4 Keith Van Horn 3.00 8.00
5 Cuttino Mobley 2.50 6.00
6 Tracy McGrady 6.00 15.00
7 Tom Gugliotta 2.50 6.00
8 Dikembe Mutombo 4.00 10.00
9 Stromile Swift 2.50 6.00
10 Mike Miller 3.00 8.00

2001-02 Ultra Triple Double Trouble

Randomly seeded in packs at the rate of one in 72, this 15-card set places a full color player action phot on the right of this horizontal design and the set name and player's name on the left in silver foil. A Platinum medallion versions sequentially numbered to 25 was also inserted in packs.

COMPLETE SET (15) 25.00 60.00
STATED ODDS 1:72
*PLATINUM: 4X TO 10X HI
PLATINUM PRINT RUN 25 SER.#'d SETS
1 Vince Carter 4.00 10.00
2 Steve Francis 2.00 5.00
3 Ray Allen 2.50 6.00
4 Chris Webber 2.50 6.00
5 Kobe Bryant 10.00 25.00
6 Kenyon Martin 2.50 6.00
7 Shaquille O'Neal 6.00 15.00
8 Kevin Garnett 4.00 10.00
9 Tracy McGrady 4.00 10.00
10 Baron Davis 2.50 6.00
11 Lamar Odom 2.00 5.00
12 Allen Iverson 5.00 12.00
13 Antoine Walker 2.00 5.00
14 Reggie Miller 2.50 6.00
15 Terrell Brandon 1.50 4.00

2001-02 Ultra Triple Double Trouble Game Worn

STATED ODDS 1:156
1 Vince Carter 8.00 20.00
2 Steve Francis 4.00 10.00
3 Ray Allen 5.00 12.00
4 Chris Webber 5.00 12.00
6 Kenyon Martin 5.00 12.00
9 Tracy McGrady 8.00 20.00
10 Baron Davis 5.00 12.00
11 Lamar Odom 4.00 10.00
12 Allen Iverson 10.00 25.00
13 Antoine Walker 4.00 10.00
14 Reggie Miller 5.00 12.00
15 Terrell Brandon 3.00 8.00

2002-03 Ultra

Released in late August 2002, Ultra was packaged in 24-pack boxes with 10 cards per pack and carried a suggested retail price of $2.99. Base cards are borderless with the Fleer Ultra logo in the upper right hand corner and silver foil highlights at the bottom of the card including the player's name, position, team name and jersey number.

COMPLETE SET (210) 75.00 150.00
COMP.SET w/o RC's (180) 20.00 50.00
1 Vince Carter .50 1.25
2 Ben Wallace .25 .60
3 Tim Thomas .20 .50
4 Eric Snow .20 .50
5 Peja Stojakovic .30 .75
6 Andrei Kirilenko .30 .75
7 Dion Glover .20 .50
8 James Posey .20 .50
9 Kenny Thomas .20 .50
10 Michael Dickerson .20 .50
11 Charlie Ward .20 .50
12 Gary Payton .30 .75
13 Eddy Curry .20 .50
14 Rick Fox .20 .50
15 Joel Przybilla .20 .50
16 Aaron McKie .20 .50
17 Hedo Turkoglu .25 .60
18 Jarron Collins .20 .50
19 Jason Collins .20 .50
20 Nick Van Exel .25 .60
21 Reggie Miller .30 .75
22 Devean George .20 .50
23 Michael Jordan 2.50 6.00
24 Tony Parker .40 1.00
25 Robert Horry .25 .60
26 Wally Szczerbiak .25 .60
27 Dikembe Mutombo .30 .75
28 Scot Pollard .20 .50
29 Darrell Armstrong .20 .50
30 Jalen Rose .25 .60
31 Antawn Jamison .30 .75
32 Anfernee Hardaway .50 1.25
33 Paul Pierce .30 .75
34 Juwan Howard .25 .60
35 Eddie Griffin .20 .50
36 Shane Battier .30 .75
37 Shandon Anderson .20 .50
38 Vladimir Radmanovic .20 .50
39 DerMarr Johnson .20 .50
40 Antonio McDyess .25 .60
41 Cuttino Mobley .20 .50
42 Stromile Swift .20 .50
43 Tracy McGrady .50 1.25
44 Charles Smith .20 .50
45 Shawn Marion .25 .60
46 P.J. Brown .20 .50
47 Wang Zhizhi .20 .50
48 Austin Croshere .20 .50
49 Ervin Johnson .20 .50
50 Jason Kidd .50 1.25
51 Tom Gugliotta .20 .50
52 Jamal Crawford .30 .75
53 Toni Kukoc .30 .75
54 Mengke Bateer .20 .50
55 Moochie Norris .20 .50
56 Jason Williams .25 .60
57 Mike Miller .25 .60
58 Steve Smith .25 .60
59 Shareef Abdur-Rahim .25 .60
60 Michael Finley .30 .75
61 Jermaine O'Neal .25 .60
62 Mark Madsen .20 .50
63 Troy Hudson .20 .50
64 David Robinson .50 1.25
65 Corliss Williamson .20 .50
66 Rodney Rogers .20 .50
67 Derek Fisher .25 .60
68 Anthony Carter .20 .50
69 Allan Houston .25 .60
70 Desmond Mason .25 .60
71 Brendan Haywood .20 .50
72 Tony Delk .20 .50
73 Ryan Bowen .20 .50
74 Danny Fortson .20 .50
75 Alonzo Mourning .40 1.00
76 Latrell Sprewell .25 .60
77 Rashard Lewis .30 .75
78 Courtney Alexander .20 .50
79 Marcus Fizer .20 .50
80 Jason Richardson .30 .75
81 Terrell Brandon .20 .50
82 Allen Iverson .50 1.25
83 Vlade Divac .25 .60
84 Jahidi White .20 .50
85 Eric Piatkowski .20 .50
86 Marc Jackson .20 .50
87 Pat Garrity .20 .50
88 Tim Duncan .60 1.50
89 Kwame Brown .20 .50
90 Andre Miller .25 .60
91 Troy Murphy .25 .60
92 John Stockton .40 1.00
93 Kenny Anderson .25 .60
94 Chris Mihm .20 .50
95 Larry Hughes .25 .60
96 Lamar Odom .25 .60
97 Brian Grant .20 .50
98 Marcus Camby .25 .60
99 Mike Bibby .30 .75
100 Joseph Forte .20 .50
101 Lamond Murray .20 .50
102 Darius Miles .20 .50
103 Eddie Jones .25 .60
104 Aaron Williams .20 .50
105 Derek Anderson .20 .50
106 Karl Malone .40 1.00
107 Jon Barry .20 .50
108 Tony Battie .20 .50
109 Jumaine Jones .20 .50
110 Corey Maggette .25 .60
111 Eddie House .20 .50
112 Theo Ratliff .20 .50
113 Scottie Pippen .50 1.25
114 Hakeem Olajuwon .40 1.00
115 Antoine Walker .25 .60
116 Tim Hardaway .30 .75
117 Steve Francis .25 .60
118 Lorenzen Wright .20 .50
119 Howard Eisley .20 .50
120 Brent Barry .20 .50
121 Baron Davis .25 .60
122 Michael Doleac .20 .50
123 Quentin Richardson .25 .60
124 LaPhonso Ellis .25 .60
125 Richard Jefferson .30 .75
126 Damon Stoudamire .25 .60
127 Alvin Williams .20 .50
128 Chucky Atkins .20 .50
129 Jamal Mashburn .25 .60
130 Wesley Person .20 .50
131 Elton Brand .30 .75
132 Ray Allen .30 .75
133 Kerry Kittles .20 .50
134 Rasheed Wallace .30 .75
135 Antonio Davis .20 .50
136 David Wesley .20 .50
137 Dirk Nowitzki .50 1.25
138 Rodney White .20 .50
139 Jamaal Tinsley .20 .50
140 Sam Cassell .25 .60
141 Keith Van Horn .25 .60
142 Ruben Patterson .20 .50
143 Jerome Williams .20 .50
144 Jason Terry .25 .60
145 Eduardo Najera .20 .50
146 Maurice Taylor .20 .50
147 Pau Gasol .40 1.00
148 Grant Hill .40 1.00
149 Antonio Daniels .20 .50
150 George Lynch .20 .50
151 Steve Nash .40 1.00
152 Al Harrington .25 .60
153 Anthony Mason .20 .50
154 Kenyon Martin .25 .60
155 Bonzi Wells .20 .50
156 Morris Peterson .20 .50
157 Eddie Robinson .20 .50
158 Kevin Garnett .50 1.25
159 Chris Webber .30 .75
160 John Amaechi .20 .50
161 Kobe Bryant 1.25 3.00
162 Joe Smith .25 .60
163 Speedy Claxton .20 .50
164 Doug Christie .20 .50
165 Richard Hamilton .25 .60
166 Tyson Chandler .30 .75
167 Gilbert Arenas .30 .75
168 Stephon Marbury .25 .60
169 Jamaal Magloire .20 .50
170 Raef LaFrentz .20 .50
171 Ron Mercer .20 .50
172 Glenn Robinson .25 .60
173 Chauncey Billups .30 .75
174 Iakovos Tsakalidis .20 .50
175 Vin Baker .25 .60
176 Joe Johnson .25 .60
177 Jerry Stackhouse .25 .60
178 Shaquille O'Neal .75 2.00
179 Derrick Coleman .25 .60
180 Bryon Russell .20 .50
181 Yao Ming RC 2.50 6.00
182 Jay Williams RC 1.25 3.00
183 Drew Gooden RC 1.25 3.00
184 DaJuan Wagner RC 1.00 2.50
185 Qyntel Woods RC 1.00 2.50
186 Chris Wilcox RC 1.00 2.50
187 Curtis Borchardt RC .75 2.00
188 Nikoloz Tskitishvili RC .75 2.00
189 Caron Butler RC 1.25 3.00
190 Nene Hilario RC 1.25 3.00
191 Jared Jeffries RC 1.00 2.50
192 Mike Dunleavy RC 1.25 3.00
193 Kareem Rush RC 1.00 2.50
194 Amare Stoudemire RC 1.50 4.00
195 Melvin Ely RC 1.00 2.50
196 Marcus Haislip RC 1.00 2.50
197 Jiri Welsch RC 1.00 2.50
198 Frank Williams RC .75 2.00
199 John Salmons RC 1.25 3.00
200 Gordan Giricek RC 1.25 3.00
201 Ryan Humphrey RC 1.00 2.50
202 Casey Jacobsen RC 1.00 2.50
203 Carlos Boozer RC 1.25 3.00
204 Manu Ginobili RC 3.00 8.00
205 Bostjan Nachbar RC 1.00 2.50
206 Fred Jones RC 1.00 2.50
207 Dan Dickau RC 1.00 2.50
208 Tayshaun Prince RC 1.50 4.00
209 Memo Okur RC 1.25 3.00
210 Juan Dixon RC 1.25 3.00

2002-03 Ultra Gold Medallion

*GOLD STARS: .6X TO 1.5X BASE CARD HI
*GOLD RCs: 1.25X TO 3X BASE CARD HI
1-180 STATED ODDS 1:1
181-210 PRINT RUN 100 SER.#'d SETS

2002-03 Ultra Back 2 Back

Randomly inserted in packs, this 18-card set features full color player action photography and borderless cards. The left side of the card has a box that runs from top to bottom and contains the player's name, and the bottom left hand corner of the card has the Back 2 Back logo. Each card is sequentially numbered to 1000. Game Used and Game Used Gold parallels were inserted and are numbered to 500 and 50 respectively.

COMPLETE SET (18) 20.00 50.00
STATED PRINT RUN 1000 SERIAL #'D SETS
1 Vince Carter 2.50 6.00
2 Tracy McGrady 2.50 6.00
3 Allen Iverson 2.50 6.00
4 Baron Davis 1.25 3.00
5 Chris Webber 1.50 4.00
6 Michael Finley 1.50 4.00
7 Steve Francis 1.25 3.00
8 Elton Brand 1.50 4.00
9 Mike Miller 1.25 3.00
10 Morris Peterson 1.00 2.50
11 Dikembe Mutombo 1.50 4.00
12 Alonzo Mourning 2.00 5.00
13 Darius Miles 1.00 2.50
14 Quentin Richardson 1.25 3.00
15 John Stockton 2.00 5.00
16 Karl Malone 2.00 5.00
17 Stephon Marbury 1.25 3.00
18 Jerry Stackhouse 1.25 3.00

2002-03 Ultra Back 2 Back Game Used

ndomly seeded in packs, this 18-card set parallels the base Back 2 Back insert set enhanced with a swatch of game used memorabilia. Each card is sequentially numbered to 500.

STATED PRINT RUN 500 SERIAL #'D SETS
*GOLD: 1X TO 2.5X BASE HI
GOLD PRINT RUN 50 SER.#'d SETS
1 Vince Carter 6.00 15.00
2 Tracy McGrady 6.00 15.00
3 Allen Iverson 6.00 15.00
4 Baron Davis 3.00 8.00
5 Chris Webber 4.00 10.00
6 Michael Finley 4.00 10.00
7 Steve Francis 3.00 8.00
8 Elton Brand 4.00 10.00
9 Mike Miller 3.00 8.00
10 Morris Peterson 2.50 6.00
11 Dikembe Mutombo 4.00 10.00
12 Alonzo Mourning 8.00 20.00
13 Darius Miles 2.50 6.00
14 Quentin Richardson 3.00 8.00
15 John Stockton 5.00 12.00
16 Karl Malone 5.00 12.00
17 Stephon Marbury 3.00 8.00
18 Jerry Stackhouse 3.00 8.00

2002-03 Ultra O!

serted in packs at the rate of one in 12, this 20-card set places full color player action photos on a borderless card with a box running from top to bottom on the right side. This box contains the players name and team name. The O! logo appears in the upper right hand corner.

COMPLETE SET (20) 8.00 20.00
STATED ODDS 1:12
1 Vince Carter 1.00 2.50
2 Shareef Abdur-Rahim .50 1.25
3 Baron Davis .50 1.25
4 Quentin Richardson .50 1.25
5 John Stockton .75 2.00
6 Morris Peterson .40 1.00
7 Elton Brand .60 1.50
8 Glenn Robinson .50 1.25
9 Latrell Sprewell .50 1.25
10 Darius Miles .40 1.00
11 Jason Terry .50 1.25
12 Keith Van Horn .50 1.25
13 Karl Malone .75 2.00
14 Antoine Walker .50 1.25
15 Jason Williams .50 1.25
16 Rasheed Wallace .60 1.50
17 Gary Payton .60 1.50
18 Lamar Odom .50 1.25
19 Cuttino Mobley .40 1.00
20 Desmond Mason .50 1.25

2002-03 Ultra O! Game Used

STATED ODDS 1:30
1 Vince Carter 5.00 12.00
2 Shareef Abdur-Rahim 2.50 6.00
3 Baron Davis 2.50 6.00
4 Quentin Richardson 2.50 6.00
5 John Stockton 4.00 10.00
6 Morris Peterson 2.00 5.00
7 Elton Brand 3.00 8.00
8 Glenn Robinson 2.50 6.00
9 Latrell Sprewell 2.50 6.00
10 Darius Miles 2.00 5.00
11 Jason Terry 2.50 6.00
12 Keith Van Horn 2.50 6.00
13 Karl Malone 4.00 10.00
14 Antoine Walker 2.50 6.00
15 Jason Williams 2.50 6.00
16 Rasheed Wallace 3.00 8.00
17 Gary Payton 3.00 8.00
18 Lamar Odom 2.50 6.00
19 Cuttino Mobley 2.00 5.00

2002-03 Ultra One on One

Randomly seeded in packs at the rate of one in eight, this 10-card set places a player on the front and a player on the back. The right side of the card has "One on One" running from top to bottom, and the left side has a white box from top to bottom which contains the player's name in silver foil and his team logo.

COMPLETE SET (10) 10.00 25.00
STATED ODDS 1:8
1 V.Carter/T.McGrady 3.00 8.00
2 A.Iverson/B.Davis 1.25 3.00
3 C.Webber/M.Finley 1.25 3.00
4 S.Francis/E.Brand 1.25 3.00
5 M.Miller/M.Peterson 1.25 3.00
6 D.Mutombo/A.Mourning 1.25 3.00
7 D.Miles/Q.Richardson 1.25 3.00
8 J.Stockton/K.Malone 1.25 3.00
9 S.Marbury/J.Kidd 1.25 3.00
10 V.Carter/J.Stackhouse 1.50 4.00

2002-03 Ultra One on One Game Used

PRINT RUN 100 SER.#'d SETS
1 V.Carter/T.McGrady 30.00 80.00
2 A.Iverson/B.Davis 20.00 50.00
3 C.Webber/M.Finley 12.00 30.00
4 S.Francis/E.Brand 12.00 30.00
5 M.Miller/M.Peterson 12.00 30.00
6 D.Mutombo/A.Mourning 12.00 30.00
7 D.Miles/Q.Richardson 12.00 30.00
8 J.Stockton/K.Malone 12.00 30.00
9 S.Marbury/J.Kidd 20.00 50.00
10 V.Carter/J.Stackhouse 25.00 60.00

2002-03 Ultra Photo Effex

Randomly inserted in packs at the rate of one in 12, this 20-card set is white bordered and features a portrait style photograph of the featured player. The Fleer Ultra logo appears in the upper left hand corner of the card, and the player's name, team name, and "Photo Effex" appear along the bottom. A Masterpiece version sequentially numbered to 25 was also produced.

COMPLETE SET (20) 12.50 30.00
STATED ODDS 1:12
*MASTERPIECE: 8X TO 20X BASE HI
MASTERPIECE PRINT RUN 25 SETS
1 Vince Carter 1.00 2.50
2 Kobe Bryant 2.50 6.00
3 Michael Jordan 5.00 12.00
4 Peja Stojakovic .60 1.50
5 Allen Iverson 1.00 2.50
6 Shaquille O'Neal 1.50 4.00
7 Tracy McGrady 1.00 2.50
8 Mike Bibby .60 1.50
9 Dirk Nowitzki 1.00 2.50
10 Pau Gasol .75 2.00
11 Jason Kidd 1.00 2.50
12 Ben Wallace .50 1.25
13 Andrei Kirilenko .60 1.50
14 Paul Pierce .60 1.50
15 Antoine Walker .50 1.25
16 Kevin Garnett 1.00 2.50
17 Tony Parker .75 2.00
18 Ray Allen .60 1.50
19 Kenyon Martin .50 1.25
20 Tim Duncan 1.25 3.00

2003-04 Ultra

Released in August 2003, this 195-card set is the first to feature a live out-of-pack LeBron James RC. Base cards are borderless with a player name box along the bottom and as with recent years, the photography is incredible. Ultra was divided up into three different parts, veteran player cards 1-170, Lucky 13 Rookie Cards 171-183 sequentially numbered to 500, and Rookie Cards 184-195 inserted at one in four packs. Ultra was packaged in 24-pack boxes where packs contained eight cards and carried a suggested retail price of $2.99.

COMP. SET w/o SP's 12.50 30.00
171-183 PRINT RUN 500 SER.#'d SETS
184-195 STATED ODDS 1:4
1 Yao Ming .75 2.00
2 DeShawn Stevenson .25 .60
3 Malik Rose .25 .60
4 DaJuan Wagner .25 .60
5 Troy Murphy .25 .60
6 Caron Butler .30 .75
7 Radoslav Nesterovic .25 .60
8 Joe Johnson .30 .75
9 Al Harrington .30 .75
10 Carlos Boozer .30 .75
11 Morris Peterson .25 .60
12 Malik Allen .25 .60
13 Kurt Thomas .25 .60
14 Derek Anderson .25 .60
15 Zydrunas Ilgauskas .30 .75
16 Jason Richardson .40 1.00
17 Brian Grant .25 .60
18 Allan Houston .30 .75
19 Bonzi Wells .25 .60
20 Stephen Jackson .30 .75
21 Eddy Curry .25 .60
22 Tayshaun Prince .30 .75
23 Brad Miller .30 .75
24 Stromile Swift .25 .60
25 Kendall Gill .25 .60
26 Vladimir Radmanovic .25 .60
27 Theo Ratliff .25 .60
28 Nick Van Exel .30 .75
29 Marko Jaric .25 .60
30 Jason Collins .25 .60
31 Darrell Armstrong .25 .60
32 Vlade Divac .30 .75
33 Juan Dixon .25 .60
34 Calbert Cheaney .25 .60
35 Tyson Chandler .30 .75
36 Chauncey Billups .40 1.00
37 Reggie Miller .40 1.00
38 Mike Miller .30 .75
39 Marc Jackson .25 .60
40 Casey Jacobsen .25 .60
41 Ray Allen .40 1.00
42 Mehmet Okur .30 .75
43 Jermaine O'Neal .30 .75
44 Lorenzen Wright .25 .60
45 Wally Szczerbiak .30 .75
46 Anfernee Hardaway .60 1.50
47 Matt Harpring .25 .60
48 Jay Williams .25 .60
49 Corliss Williamson .25 .60
50 Jamaal Tinsley .25 .60
51 Shane Battier .30 .75
52 Kevin Garnett .60 1.50
53 Shawn Marion .30 .75
54 Alvin Williams .25 .60
55 Juwan Howard .30 .75
56 Shaquille O'Neal 1.00 2.50
57 Jamal Mashburn .30 .75
58 Kenny Thomas .25 .60
59 Tim Duncan .60 1.50
60 Predrag Drobnjak .25 .60
61 Jalen Rose .30 .75
62 Ben Wallace .30 .75
63 James Posey .25 .60
64 Pau Gasol .40 1.00
65 Michael Redd .40 1.00
66 Amare Stoudemire .50 1.25
67 Karl Malone .50 1.25
68 Richard Hamilton .30 .75
69 Eddie Griffin .25 .60
70 Robert Horry .30 .75
71 Tim Thomas .25 .60
72 Eric Snow .25 .60
73 Brent Barry .25 .60
74 Jamal Crawford .40 1.00
75 Nikoloz Tskitishvili .25 .60
76 Bostjan Nachbar .25 .60
77 Devean George .25 .60
78 Dan Gadzuric .25 .60
79 Brian Skinner .25 .60
80 Cuttino Mobley .25 .60
81 Desmond Mason .30 .75
82 Othella Harrington .25 .60
83 Chris Webber .40 1.00
84 Dirk Nowitzki .60 1.50
85 Steve Francis .30 .75
86 Gary Payton .40 1.00
87 Howard Eisley .25 .60
88 Zach Randolph .30 .75
89 Sam Cassell .30 .75
90 Tony Battie .25 .60
91 Shammond Williams .25 .60
92 Rick Fox .25 .60
93 David Wesley .25 .60
94 Frank Williams .25 .60
95 Tony Delk .25 .60
96 Troy Hudson .25 .60
97 Donnell Harvey .25 .60
98 Derek Fisher .30 .75
99 Jamaal Magloire .25 .60
100 Keith Van Horn .30 .75
101 Tony Parker .40 1.00
102 Rashard Lewis .40 1.00
103 Shareef Abdur-Rahim .30 .75
104 Michael Finley .40 1.00
105 Jason Kidd .60 1.50
106 Drew Gooden .30 .75
107 Mike Bibby .40 1.00
108 Jerry Stackhouse .30 .75
109 Chris Jefferies .25 .60
110 Glenn Robinson .30 .75
111 Shawn Bradley .25 .60
112 Corey Maggette .30 .75
113 Richard Jefferson .30 .75
114 Gordan Giricek .25 .60
115 Bobby Jackson .25 .60
116 Larry Hughes .30 .75
117 Scott Padgett .25 .60
118 Gilbert Arenas .30 .75
119 Ron Artest .40 1.00
120 Jason Williams .30 .75
121 Eric Williams .25 .60
122 Stephon Marbury .30 .75
123 Vince Carter .60 1.50
124 Jason Terry .30 .75
125 Raef LaFrentz .25 .60
126 Michael Olowokandi .25 .60
127 Kerry Kittles .25 .60
128 Pat Garrity .25 .60
129 Peja Stojakovic .40 1.00
130 Jared Jeffries .25 .60
131 Antonio Davis .25 .60
132 Rodney White .25 .60
133 Kobe Bryant 1.50 4.00
134 Baron Davis .30 .75
135 Derrick Coleman .30 .75
136 Walter McCarty .25 .60
137 Bruce Bowen .25 .60
138 Mike Dunleavy .30 .75
139 Rasual Butler .25 .60
140 Latrell Sprewell .30 .75
141 Rasheed Wallace .40 1.00
142 Andrei Kirilenko .40 1.00
143 Dan Dickau .25 .60
144 Steve Nash .50 1.25
145 Elton Brand .40 1.00
146 Kenyon Martin .30 .75
147 Jeryl Sasser .25 .60
148 Doug Christie .25 .60
149 Kwame Brown .25 .60
150 Ricky Davis .30 .75
151 Antawn Jamison .30 .75
152 Travis Best .25 .60
153 Courtney Alexander .25 .60
154 Scottie Pippen .60 1.50
155 Jerome Williams .25 .60
156 Quentin Richardson .30 .75
157 Lucious Harris .25 .60
158 Allen Iverson .60 1.50
159 Manu Ginobili .50 1.25
160 Bryon Russell .25 .60
161 Paul Pierce .40 1.00
162 Nene .30 .75
163 Darius Miles .25 .60
164 Earl Boykins .25 .60
165 Eddie Jones .30 .75
166 P.J. Brown .25 .60
167 Qyntel Woods .25 .60
168 Andre Miller .30 .75
169 Tracy McGrady .50 1.25
170 Antoine Walker .40 1.00
171 LeBron James L13 RC 100.00 250.00
172 Darko Milicic L13 RC 2.50 6.00
173 Carmelo Anthony L13 RC 10.00 25.00
174 Chris Bosh L13 RC 5.00 12.00
175 Dwyane Wade L13 RC 10.00 25.00
176 Chris Kaman L13 RC 3.00 8.00
177 Kirk Hinrich L13 RC 3.00 8.00
178 T.J. Ford L13 RC 2.50 6.00
179 Mike Sweetney L13 RC 2.00 5.00
180 Jarvis Hayes L13 RC 2.00 5.00
181 Mickael Pietrus L13 RC 2.50 6.00
182 Nick Collison L13 RC 2.50 6.00
183 Marcus Banks L13 RC 2.00 5.00
184 Luke Ridnour RC 1.00 2.50
185 Troy Bell RC .75 2.00
186 Zarko Cabarkapa RC .75 2.00
187 David West RC 1.25 3.00
188 Sofoklis Schortsanitis RC .75 2.00
189 Travis Outlaw RC 1.00 2.50
190 Leandro Barbosa RC 1.25 3.00
191 Josh Howard RC 1.25 3.00
192 Maciej Lampe RC .75 2.00
193 Luke Walton RC 1.25 3.00
194 Travis Hansen RC .75 2.00
195 Rick Rickert RC .75 2.00

2003-04 Ultra Gold Medallion

*STARS: .6X TO 1.5X BASE CARD HI
*171-182 L13s: .25X TO .6X BASE CARD HI
*183-195 RCs: .6X TO 1.5X BASE CARD HI
STATED ODDS 1:1
171-195 ROOKIE STATED ODDS 1:8
171 LeBron James L13 40.00 100.00

2003-04 Ultra Platinum Medallion

*1-170 STARS: 4X TO 10X BASE CARD HI
*171-182 L13s: 1X TO 2.5X BASE CARD HI
*183-195 RCs: 2.5X TO 6X BASE CARD HI
PRINT RUN 100 SER.#'d SETS
41 Ray Allen 6.00 15.00
133 Kobe Bryant 30.00 80.00

2003-04 Ultra Leaps and Bounds

Randomly inserted in packs, this 15-card set profiles dominating scorers and defenders who use their hops to get above the rim. Each card is bordered on the top and the bottom and is sequentially numbered to 500.

COMPLETE SET (15) 15.00 30.00
PRINT RUN 500 SER.#'d SETS
1 Ben Wallace .75 2.00
2 Amare Stoudemire 1.25 3.00
3 Tracy McGrady 1.25 3.00
4 Dirk Nowitzki 1.50 4.00
5 Vince Carter 1.50 4.00
6 Ricky Davis .75 2.00
7 Shawn Marion .75 2.00
8 Steve Francis .75 2.00
9 Jason Richardson 1.00 2.50
10 Nene .75 2.00
11 Richard Jefferson .75 2.00
12 Yao Ming 2.00 5.00
13 Tim Duncan 1.50 4.00
14 Kobe Bryant 4.00 10.00
15 Kevin Garnett 1.50 4.00

2003-04 Ultra Leaps and Bounds Game Used

ndomly inserted in packs at the rate of one in 36, this 10-card set parallels the design of the Leaps and Bounds set enhanced with a square swatch of game used memorabilia.

STATED ODDS 1:36
LBN Nene 2.00 5.00
LBAS Amare Stoudemire 3.00 8.00
LBBW Ben Wallace 2.00 5.00
LBDN Dirk Nowitzki 4.00 10.00
LBJR Jason Richardson 2.50 6.00
LBKG Kevin Garnett 4.00 10.00
LBRJ Richard Jefferson 2.00 5.00
LBSF Steve Francis 2.00 5.00
LBSM Shawn Marion 2.00 5.00
LBTM Tracy McGrady 3.00 8.00
LBVC Vince Carter 4.00 10.00
LBYM Yao Ming 5.00 12.00

2003-04 Ultra Leaps and Bounds Ultra Swatch

SERIAL #'d TO PLAYER JERSEY NUMBER
MOST UNPRICED DUE TO SCARCITY
LBN Nene/31 8.00 20.00
LBAS Amare Stoudemire/32 12.00 30.00
LBDN Dirk Nowitzki/41 15.00 40.00
LBJR Jason Richardson/23 10.00 25.00
LBKG Kevin Garnett/21 15.00 40.00
LBSM Shawn Marion/31 8.00 20.00

2003-04 Ultra Roundball Discs

Randomly inserted in packs at the rate of one in eight, this 36-Disc set is circular and about the width of a normal sized card. Player portrait photos are set against a white background with a dark border color.

COMPLETE SET (36) 25.00 50.00
STATED ODDS 1:8
1 Vince Carter 1.00 2.50
2 Tracy McGrady .75 2.00
3 Allen Iverson 1.00 2.50
4 Yao Ming 1.25 3.00
5 Dirk Nowitzki 1.00 2.50
6 Ben Wallace .50 1.25
7 Paul Pierce .60 1.50
8 Jason Kidd 1.00 2.50
9 Baron Davis .50 1.25
10 Gilbert Arenas .50 1.25
11 DaJuan Wagner .40 1.00
12 Pau Gasol .60 1.50
13 Chris Webber .60 1.50
14 Jermaine O'Neal .50 1.25
15 Steve Francis .50 1.25
16 Ray Allen .60 1.50
17 Steve Nash .75 2.00
18 Gary Payton .60 1.50
19 Caron Butler .50 1.25
20 Karl Malone .75 2.00
21 Mike Bibby .60 1.50
22 Allan Houston .50 1.25
23 Amare Stoudemire .75 2.00
24 Scottie Pippen 1.00 2.50
25 Kevin Garnett 1.00 2.50
26 Michael Finley .60 1.50
27 Richard Hamilton .50 1.25
28 Shaquille O'Neal 1.50 4.00
29 Tim Duncan 1.00 2.50
30 Kobe Bryant 2.50 6.00
31 LeBron James 10.00 25.00
32 Mike Sweetney .40 1.00
33 Carmelo Anthony 2.00 5.00
34 Chris Bosh 1.00 2.50
35 Dwyane Wade 2.00 5.00
36 Chris Kaman .60 1.50

2003-04 Ultra Roundball Discs Game Used

Randomly inserted in packs at the rate of one in 24, this 26-card set parallels the design of the base Roundball Discs insert set enhanced with a swatch of game used memorabilia.

STATED ODDS 1:24
RDAH Allan Houston 2.00 5.00
RDAI Allen Iverson 4.00 10.00
RDAS Amare Stoudemire 3.00 8.00
RDBD Baron Davis 2.00 5.00
RDBW Ben Wallace 2.00 5.00
RDCB Caron Butler 2.00 5.00
RDCW Chris Webber 2.50 6.00
RDDN Dirk Nowitzki 4.00 10.00
RDDW0 DaJuan Wagner 2.00 5.00
RDGP Gary Payton 2.50 6.00
RDJK Jason Kidd 4.00 10.00
RDJO Jermaine O'Neal 2.00 5.00
RDKG Kevin Garnett 4.00 10.00
RDKM Karl Malone 3.00 8.00
RDMB Mike Bibby 2.50 6.00
RDMF Michael Finley 2.50 6.00
RDPG Pau Gasol 2.50 6.00
RDPP Paul Pierce 2.50 6.00
RDRA Ray Allen 2.50 6.00
RDRH Richard Hamilton 2.00 5.00
RDSF Steve Francis 2.00 5.00
RDSN Steve Nash 3.00 8.00
RDSP Scottie Pippen 4.00 10.00
RDTM Tracy McGrady 3.00 8.00
RDVC Vince Carter 4.00 10.00
RDYM Yao Ming 5.00 12.00

2003-04 Ultra Roundball Discs Ultra Swatch

SERIAL #'d TO PLAYER JERSEY NUMBER
MOST UNPRICED DUE TO SCARCITY
RDAH Allan Houston/20 8.00 20.00
RDAS Amare Stoudemire/32 12.00 30.00
RDDN Dirk Nowitzki/41 15.00 40.00
RDKG Karl Malone/32 12.00 30.00
RDKG Kevin Garnett/21 15.00 40.00
RDPG Pau Gasol/16 12.50 30.00
RDPP Paul Pierce/34 10.00 25.00
RDRA Ray Allen/34 15.00 40.00
RDRH Richard Hamilton/32 8.00 20.00
RDSP Scottie Pippen/33 30.00 80.00

2003-04 Ultra Scoring Kings

Randomly inserted in packs at the rate of one in 24, this 10-card set places player action photos on the top of the card with a gray-scale background on the bottom.

COMPLETE SET (10) 6.00 15.00
STATED ODDS 1:24
1 Vince Carter 1.25 3.00
2 Allen Iverson 1.25 3.00
3 Tracy McGrady 1.00 2.50
4 Dirk Nowitzki 1.25 3.00
5 Kevin Garnett 1.25 3.00
6 Steve Francis .60 1.50
7 Chris Webber .75 2.00
8 Ray Allen .75 2.00
9 Paul Pierce .75 2.00
10 Yao Ming 1.50 4.00

2003-04 Ultra Scoring Kings Game Used

Randomly inserted in packs at the rate of one in 100, this 10-card set parallels the look of the base Scoring Kings insert set enhanced with a swatch of game worn memorabilia.

STATED ODDS 1:100
1 Vince Carter 5.00 12.00
2 Allen Iverson 5.00 12.00
3 Tracy McGrady 4.00 10.00
4 Dirk Nowitzki 5.00 12.00
5 Kevin Garnett 5.00 12.00
6 Steve Francis 2.50 6.00
7 Chris Webber 3.00 8.00
8 Ray Allen 3.00 8.00
9 Paul Pierce 3.00 8.00
10 Yao Ming 6.00 15.00

2003-04 Ultra Scoring Kings PPG

PRINT RUNS LISTED BELOW
SOME NOT PRICED DUE TO SCARCITY
AI Allen Iverson/27 15.00 40.00
DN Dirk Nowitzki/25 15.00 40.00
KG Kevin Garnett/25 15.00 40.00
RA Ray Allen/22 10.00 25.00
SF Steve Francis/21 8.00 20.00
TM Tracy McGrady/32 12.00 30.00

2003-04 Ultra Scoring Kings Ultra Swatch

SERIAL #'d TO PLAYER JERSEY NUMBER
MOST UNPRICED DUE TO SCARCITY
4 Dirk Nowitzki/41 15.00 40.00
5 Kevin Garnett/21 15.00 40.00
8 Ray Allen/34 15.00 40.00

2003-04 Ultra Signatures

Randomly inserted in packs, this 20-card set features the base card with an embedded cut signature. Each card is sequentially numbered to 350.

PRINT RUN 350 SER.#'d SETS
1 Carmelo Anthony 25.00 60.00
2 Leandro Barbosa 4.00 10.00
3 Mike Bibby 4.00 10.00
4 Chris Bosh 12.00 30.00
5 Earl Boykins 4.00 10.00
6 Vince Carter 12.00 30.00
7 Manu Ginobili 8.00 20.00
8 Richard Jefferson 4.00 10.00
9 Mike Sweetney 2.50 6.00
11 Jermaine O'Neal 6.00 15.00
12 Tracy McGrady 12.00 30.00
13 Tayshaun Prince 5.00 12.00
14 Luke Ridnour 3.00 8.00
15 Amare Stoudemire 15.00 40.00
16A Dwyane Wade 40.00 100.00
16B Dwyane Wade/250 25.00 60.00
17 DaJuan Wagner 4.00 10.00
18 Ben Wallace 8.00 20.00
19 Luke Walton 4.00 10.00
20 David West 4.00 10.00

2004-05 Ultra

Released in August 2004, Ultra consists of a 219-card set where cards 1-175 feature veteran players, cards 176-188 feature the first 13 lottery picks on a Lucky 13 rookie card sequentially numbered to 500, 189-199 feature rookies inserted at the rate of one in four and cards 200-219 feature Update rookies that were inserted at two per box in Fleer Tradition. Ultra was offered in both Hobby and Retail formats where both contained 24 packs of eight cards each, but Hobby carried a $2.99 SRP and Retail carried a $1.99 SRP.

COMP.SET w/o RC's (175) 15.00 40.00
176-188 PRINT RUN 500 SER.#'d SETS
189-199 STATED ODDS 1:4
UPDATE INSERTED IN TWO PER TRADITION BOX
1 Ben Wallace .25 .60
2 Chris Kaman .25 .60
3 Steve Nash .40 1.00
4 Al Harrington .25 .60
5 T.J. Ford .20 .50
6 Jason Collins .20 .50
7 Theo Ratliff .20 .50
8 Kobe Bryant 1.25 3.00
9 Kirk Hinrich .25 .60
10 Darko Milicic .20 .50
11 Karl Malone .40 1.00
12 Michael Olowokandi .20 .50
13 Frank Williams .20 .50
14 Vlade Divac .25 .60
15 Vince Carter .50 1.25
16 Eddy Curry .20 .50
17 Keith Van Horn .25 .60
18 Chris Wilcox .20 .50
19 Tim Thomas .20 .50
20 Shareef Abdur-Rahim .25 .60
21 Carlos Arroyo .20 .50
22 Jason Collier .20 .50
23 Voshon Lenard .20 .50
24 Reggie Miller .30 .75
25 Dan Gadzuric .20 .50
26 David Wesley .20 .50
27 Vladimir Radmanovic .20 .50
28 Derek Anderson .20 .50
29 Zydrunas Ilgauskas .25 .60
30 Nick Van Exel .25 .60
31 Stromile Swift .20 .50
32 Kerry Kittles .20 .50
33 Zaza Pachulia .20 .50
34 Brad Miller .25 .60
35 Jerry Stackhouse .25 .60
36 Jason Terry .25 .60
37 Earl Boykins .20 .50
38 Jermaine O'Neal .25 .60
39 Joe Smith .25 .60
40 Jamaal Magloire .20 .50
41 Zarko Cabarkapa .20 .50
42 Ronald Murray .20 .50
43 Bob Sura .20 .50
44 Andre Miller .25 .60
45 Jamaal Tinsley .20 .50
46 Michael Redd .25 .60
47 Baron Davis .25 .60
48 Amare Stoudemire .25 .60
49 Rashard Lewis .30 .75
50 Jiri Welsch .20 .50
51 Marcus Camby .25 .60
52 Ron Artest .30 .75
53 Eddie Jones .25 .60
54 Darrell Armstrong .20 .50
55 Shawn Marion .25 .60
56 Brent Barry .20 .50
57 Michael Finley .30 .75
58 Jim Jackson .20 .50
59 Jason Williams .25 .60
60 Kenyon Martin .25 .60
61 Kyle Korver .25 .60
62 Marquis Daniels .20 .50
63 Chucky Atkins .20 .50
64 Nene .25 .60
65 Marko Jaric .20 .50
66 Dwyane Wade .50 1.25

67 P.J. Brown .20 .50
68 Casey Jacobsen .20 .50
69 Morris Peterson .20 .50
70 Ricky Davis .25 .60
71 Tayshaun Prince .25 .60
72 Corey Maggette .25 .60
73 Udonis Haslem .20 .50
74 Kurt Thomas .20 .50
75 Leandro Barbosa .30 .75
76 Alvin Williams .20 .50
77 Mark Blount .20 .50
78 Chauncey Billups .30 .75
79 Boris Diaw .25 .60
80 Brian Grant .20 .50
81 Allan Houston .25 .60
82 Joe Johnson .25 .60
83 Donyell Marshall .20 .50
84 Jamal Crawford .30 .75
85 Jason Richardson .30 .75
86 Gary Payton .30 .75
87 Nazr Mohammed .20 .50
88 Mike Bibby .30 .75
89 Jalen Rose .25 .60
90 Scottie Pippen .50 1.25
91 Speedy Claxton .20 .50
92 Devean George .20 .50
93 Sam Cassell .25 .60
94 Mike Sweetney .20 .50
95 Chris Webber .30 .75
96 Chris Bosh .30 .75
97 Antoine Walker .30 .75
98 Cuttino Mobley .20 .50
99 Caron Butler .25 .60
100 John Salmons .25 .60
101 Bruce Bowen .20 .50
102 Josh Howard .30 .75
103 Steve Francis .25 .60
104 Lamar Odom .25 .60
105 Troy Hudson .20 .50
106 Allen Iverson .50 1.25
107 Dajuan Wagner .20 .50
108 Erick Dampier .20 .50
109 Luke Walton .20 .50
110 Aaron Williams .20 .50
111 Juwan Howard .25 .60
112 Bobby Jackson .20 .50
113 Andrei Kirilenko .25 .60
114 LeBron James 2.00 5.00
115 Brian Cardinal .20 .50
116 Mike Miller .25 .60
117 Tracy McGrady .40 1.00
118 Doug Christie .20 .50
119 Larry Hughes .25 .60
120 Stephen Jackson .25 .60
121 Carmelo Anthony .60 1.50
122 Fred Jones .20 .50
123 Desmond Mason .25 .60
124 Jamal Mashburn .25 .60
125 Ray Allen .30 .75
126 Jeff McInnis .20 .50
127 Yao Ming .60 1.50
128 Bonzi Wells .20 .50
129 Richard Jefferson .25 .60
130 Kenny Thomas .20 .50
131 Hedo Turkoglu .25 .60
132 Kwame Brown .20 .50
133 Dirk Nowitzki .50 1.25
134 Maurice Taylor .20 .50
135 Pau Gasol .30 .75
136 Jason Kidd .50 1.25
137 Samuel Dalembert .20 .50
138 Tim Duncan .50 1.25
139 Gilbert Arenas .25 .60
140 Tony Parker .30 .75
141 Tyson Chandler .25 .60
142 Richard Hamilton .25 .60
143 Shaquille O'Neal .75 2.00
144 Stephon Marbury .25 .60
145 Damon Stoudamire .25 .60
146 Gordan Giricek .20 .50
147 Latrell Sprewell .25 .60
148 Carlos Boozer .25 .60
149 Mike Dunleavy .25 .60
150 Luke Ridnour .25 .60
151 Reece Gaines .20 .50
152 Peja Stojakovic .30 .75
153 Juan Dixon .20 .50
154 Marcus Banks .20 .50
155 Rasheed Wallace .30 .75
156 Quentin Richardson .25 .60
157 Wally Szczerbiak .25 .60
158 Keith Bogans .20 .50
159 Darius Miles .20 .50
160 Matt Harpring .20 .50
161 Antawn Jamison .25 .60
162 Kelvin Cato .20 .50
163 James Posey .20 .50
164 Willie Green .20 .50
165 Rasho Nesterovic .20 .50
166 Jarvis Hayes .20 .50
167 Paul Pierce .30 .75
168 Mehmet Okur .25 .60
169 Elton Brand .30 .75
170 Kevin Garnett .50 1.25
171 Drew Gooden .20 .50
172 Zach Randolph .25 .60
173 Raul Lopez .20 .50
174 Manu Ginobili .40 1.00
175 Raja Bell .25 .60
176 Dwight Howard L13 RC 6.00 15.00
177 Emeka Okafor L13 RC 2.50 6.00
178 Ben Gordon L13 RC 3.00 8.00
179 Shaun Livingston L13 RC 3.00 8.00
180 Devin Harris L13 RC 2.50 6.00
181 Josh Childress L13 RC 2.50 6.00
182 Luol Deng L13 RC 3.00 8.00
183 Rafael Araujo L13 RC 2.00 5.00
184 Andre Iguodala L13 RC 4.00 10.00
185 Luke Jackson L13 RC 2.00 5.00
186 Andris Biedrins L13 RC 2.00 5.00
187 Robert Swift L13 RC 2.00 5.00
188 Sebastian Telfair L13 RC 2.50 6.00
189 Kris Humphries RC 1.50 4.00
190 Al Jefferson RC 2.00 5.00
191 Kirk Snyder RC 1.00 2.50
192 Josh Smith RC 1.50 4.00
193 J.R. Smith RC 1.50 4.00
194 Dorell Wright RC 1.50 4.00
195 Jameer Nelson RC 1.50 4.00
196 Pavel Podkolzin RC 1.00 2.50
197 Ha Seung-Jin RC 1.50 4.00
198 Sasha Vujacic RC 1.50 4.00
199 Anderson Varejao RC 1.25 3.00
200U Bernard Robinson RC 1.50 4.00
201U Andres Nocioni RC 2.00 5.00
202U Delonte West RC 2.00 5.00
203U Tony Allen RC 2.00 5.00
204U Kevin Martin RC 2.50 6.00
205U Beno Udrih RC 1.50 4.00
206U David Harrison RC 1.25 3.00
207U Jackson Vroman RC 1.25 3.00
208U Peter John Ramos RC 1.25 3.00
209U Lionel Chalmers RC 2.00 5.00
210U Donta Smith RC 1.25 3.00
211U Andre Emmett RC 1.25 3.00
212U Antonio Burks RC 1.50 4.00
213U Royal Ivey RC 1.50 4.00
214U Chris Duhon RC 2.00 5.00
215U Damien Wilkins RC 1.50 4.00
216U Justin Reed RC 1.25 3.00
217U Trevor Ariza RC 2.00 5.00
218U Tim Pickett RC 2.00 5.00
219U Yuta Tabuse RC 2.00 5.00

2004-05 Ultra Gold Medallion

*1-175 GOLD: .6X TO 1.5X BASE HI
1-175 STATED ODDS ONE PER PACK
*176-188 GOLD: .25X TO .6X BASE HI
*189-199 GOLD: .5X TO 1.25X BASE HI
176-199 STATED ODDS 1:8

2004-05 Ultra Platinum Medallion

*1-175 SINGLES: 6X TO 15X BASE HI
*189-199 SINGLES: 1.5X TO 4X BASE HI
1-175 PRINT RUN 100 SER.#'d SETS
189-199 PRINT RUN 100 SER.#'d SETS
8 Kobe Bryant 75.00 200.00
106 Allen Iverson 25.00 60.00
114 LeBron James 30.00 80.00
125 Ray Allen 6.00 15.00

2004-05 Ultra Hoop Nation

Randomly inserted in Excel/MVP Retail boxes as three per, this 15-card set features borders along the top and the bottom to match team colors and player photos.
COMPLETE SET (15) 6.00 15.00
THREE PER EXCEL/MVP RETAIL BOX
1 LeBron James 2.00 5.00
2 Kobe Bryant 1.25 3.00
3 Tim Duncan .50 1.25
4 Vince Carter .50 1.25
5 Allen Iverson .50 1.25
6 Shaquille O'Neal .75 2.00
7 Tracy McGrady .40 1.00
8 Carmelo Anthony .60 1.50
9 Yao Ming .60 1.50
10 Dwyane Wade .50 1.25
11 Dirk Nowitzki .50 1.25
12 Jason Kidd .50 1.25
13 Kevin Garnett .50 1.25
14 Jermaine O'Neal .25 .60
15 Paul Pierce .30 .75

2004-05 Ultra Point Gods

Inserted in packs at the rate of one in 36, this 15-card set features the league's premier point guards on a tan background.
COMPLETE SET (15) 10.00 25.00
STATED ODDS 1:36
1 Jason Kidd 1.25 3.00
2 Stephon Marbury .60 1.50
3 Allen Iverson 1.25 3.00
4 Chauncey Billups .75 2.00
5 Vince Carter 1.25 3.00
6 Steve Nash 1.00 2.50
7 Michael Redd .60 1.50
8 Baron Davis .60 1.50
9 Mike Bibby .75 2.00
10 Reggie Miller .75 2.00
11 LeBron James 5.00 12.00
12 Tracy McGrady 1.00 2.50
13 Kirk Hinrich .60 1.50
14 Kobe Bryant 3.00 8.00
15 Dwyane Wade 1.25 3.00

2004-05 Ultra Point Gods Game Used

Randomly inserted in packs, this 12-card set parallels the design of the Point Gods insert set but is enhanced with a swatch of memorabilia and is sequentially numbered to 250. A Ultra Swatch version was also issued and features premium patch swatches and sequential numbering to 25.
PRINT RUN 250 SER.#'d SETS
*ULTRA SWATCH: 1X TO 2.5X BASE HI
AI Allen Iverson 4.00 10.00
BD Baron Davis 2.00 5.00
CB Chauncey Billups 2.50 6.00
DW Dwyane Wade 4.00 10.00
JK Jason Kidd 4.00 10.00
MB Mike Bibby 2.50 6.00
SM Stephon Marbury 2.00 5.00
TM Tracy McGrady 3.00 8.00
VC Vince Carter 4.00 10.00

2004-05 Ultra Scoring Kings

Inserted in packs at the rate of one in six, this 25-card set places full color player photos on a gray background with a profile of the players face.
COMPLETE SET (25) 12.50 30.00
STATED ODDS 1:6
1 Vince Carter .75 2.00
2 Tracy McGrady .60 1.50
3 Peja Stojakovic .50 1.25
4 Kevin Garnett .75 2.00
5 Paul Pierce .50 1.25
6 Baron Davis .40 1.00
7 Tim Duncan .75 2.00
8 Dirk Nowitzki .75 2.00
9 Michael Redd .40 1.00
10 Shaquille O'Neal 1.25 3.00
11 Carmelo Anthony 1.00 2.50
12 Stephon Marbury .40 1.00
13 Corey Maggette .40 1.00
14 Zach Randolph .40 1.00
15 Jermaine O'Neal .40 1.00
16 Yao Ming 1.00 2.50
17 Andrei Kirilenko .40 1.00
18 Rashard Lewis .50 1.25
19 Latrell Sprewell .40 1.00
20 Pau Gasol .50 1.25
21 Kobe Bryant 2.00 5.00
22 LeBron James 3.00 8.00
23 Michael Finley .50 1.25
24 Jason Richardson .50 1.25
25 Richard Hamilton .40 1.00

2004-05 Ultra Scoring Kings Game Used

Randomly inserted in packs at the rate of one in 72, this 23-card set parallels the design of the Scoring Kings insert set but is enhanced with a swatch of memorabilia.. A Ultra Swatch version was also issued and features premium patch swatches and sequential numbering to 50.
STATED ODDS 1:72
*ULTRA SWATCH: .75X TO 2X BASE HI
AK Andrei Kirilenko 2.00 5.00
BD Baron Davis 2.00 5.00
CA Carmelo Anthony 5.00 12.00
CM Corey Maggette 2.00 5.00
JO Jermaine O'Neal 2.00 5.00
JR Jason Richardson 2.50 6.00
KG Kevin Garnett 4.00 10.00
LS Latrell Sprewell 2.00 5.00
MR Michael Redd 2.00 5.00
PG Pau Gasol 2.50 6.00
PP Paul Pierce 2.50 6.00
PS Peja Stojakovic 2.50 6.00
RH Richard Hamilton 2.00 5.00
SM Stephon Marbury 2.00 5.00
SO Shaquille O'Neal 6.00 15.00
TD Tim Duncan 4.00 10.00
TM Tracy McGrady 3.00 8.00
VC Vince Carter 4.00 10.00
YM Yao Ming 5.00 12.00
ZR Zach Randolph 2.00 5.00

2004-05 Ultra Season Crowns Autographs

Inserted in packs at the rate of one in 75, this 33-card set is horizontally designed with a player photo on the left and an autograph on the right.
STATED ODDS 1:75
AK Andrei Kirilenko/74 10.00 25.00
AS Amare Stoudemire/238 8.00 20.00
BG Ben Gordon 6.00 15.00
DM Darius Miles/386 4.00 10.00
DW Dwyane Wade 30.00 80.00
EC Eddy Curry/86 4.00 10.00
GA Gilbert Arenas/86 6.00 15.00
JJ Joe Johnson/222 4.00 10.00
JN Jameer Nelson 4.00 10.00
JS J.R. Smith 5.00 12.00
KB Kwame Brown/86 4.00 10.00
KK Kyle Korver 5.00 12.00
KM Kenyon Martin/50 6.00 15.00
MS Mike Sweetney/86 4.00 10.00
PP Paul Pierce 10.00 25.00
PS Peja Stojakovic/390 6.00 15.00
RG Reece Gaines/386 4.00 10.00
RM Ronald Murray/286 4.00 10.00
SM Shawn Marion/86 8.00 20.00
ST Sebastian Telfair/182 6.00 15.00
TM Tracy McGrady/278 12.00 30.00
VC Vince Carter/286 15.00 40.00

2004-05 Ultra Season Crowns Autographs Gold

PRINT RUN 15 SER.#'d SETS
N Nene 12.00 30.00
AS Amare Stoudemire 20.00 50.00
DW Dwyane Wade 60.00 150.00
EC Eddy Curry 12.00 30.00
JN Jameer Nelson 12.00 30.00
KM Kenyon Martin 12.00 30.00
RM Ronald Murray 12.00 30.00
ST Sebastian Telfair 12.00 30.00
TM Tracy McGrady 30.00 80.00

2004-05 Ultra Season Crowns Autographs Silver

PRINT RUN 99 SER.#'d SETS
N Nene 6.00 15.00
AK Andrei Kirilenko 10.00 25.00
AS Amare Stoudemire 10.00 25.00
AW Antoine Walker 6.00 15.00
BG Ben Gordon 8.00 20.00
DM Darius Miles 6.00 15.00
DW Dwyane Wade 30.00 80.00
EC Eddy Curry 6.00 15.00
GA Gilbert Arenas 6.00 15.00
JJ Joe Johnson 6.00 15.00
JS J.R. Smith 6.00 15.00
JW Jason Williams 15.00 40.00
KB Kwame Brown 6.00 15.00
KK Kyle Korver 6.00 15.00
KM Kenyon Martin 6.00 15.00
MS Mike Sweetney 6.00 15.00
PP Paul Pierce 10.00 25.00
PS Peja Stojakovic 10.00 25.00
RG Reece Gaines 6.00 15.00
RM Ronald Murray 6.00 15.00
SM Shawn Marion 8.00 20.00
ST Sebastian Telfair 6.00 15.00
TM Tracy McGrady 15.00 40.00
VC Vince Carter 25.00 50.00

2004-05 Ultra Season Crowns Game Used

Inserted in packs randomly, this 40-card set utilizes the design from the Season Crowns Autographs but replaced the auto with a swatch of memorabilia. Several parallel versions of this set were inserted and they are numbered to 149, 99 and 29.
PRINT RUN 349 SER.#'d SETS
*149 JSY SINGLES: .5X TO 1.25X BASE JSY HI
*99 JSY SINGLES: .6X TO 1.5X BASE JSY HI
*29 JSY SINGLES: 1.25X TO 3X BASE JSY HI
N Nene 2.00 5.00
AI Allen Iverson 4.00 10.00
AK Andrei Kirilenko 2.00 5.00
AS Amare Stoudemire 2.00 5.00
BD Boris Diaw 2.00 5.00
BW Ben Wallace 2.00 5.00
CA Carmelo Anthony 5.00 12.00
CB Chris Bosh 2.50 6.00
CB Carlos Boozer 2.00 5.00
CK Chris Kaman 2.00 5.00
CM Corey Maggette 2.00 5.00
DM Darius Miles 2.00 5.00
DW Dwyane Wade 4.00 10.00
EB Elton Brand 2.50 6.00
EC Eddy Curry 1.50 4.00
GP Gary Payton 2.50 6.00
JC Jamal Crawford 2.50 6.00
JJ Joe Johnson 2.00 5.00
JK Jason Kidd 4.00 10.00
JO Jermaine O'Neal 2.00 5.00
JW Jason Williams 2.00 5.00
KM Kenyon Martin 2.00 5.00
LO Lamar Odom 2.00 5.00
MG Manu Ginobili 3.00 8.00
MS Mike Sweetney 2.00 5.00
RA Ron Artest 2.50 6.00
RA Ray Allen 2.50 6.00
RJ Richard Jefferson 2.00 5.00
RL Rashard Lewis 2.50 6.00
RM Reggie Miller 2.50 6.00
SM Stephon Marbury 2.00 5.00
SM Shawn Marion 2.00 5.00
SN Steve Nash 3.00 8.00
SP Scottie Pippen 4.00 10.00
TD Tim Duncan 4.00 10.00
TM Tracy McGrady 3.00 8.00
TP Tayshaun Prince 2.00 5.00
TP Tony Parker 2.50 6.00
VC Vince Carter 4.00 10.00
YM Yao Ming 5.00 12.00

2004-05 Ultra Ten for Ten

Inserted in packs at the rate of one in 100, this 10-card set places player images on the right and a portrait photo on the left.
COMPLETE SET (10) 15.00 35.00
STATED ODDS 1:100
1 Kevin Garnett 2.00 5.00
2 Vince Carter 2.00 5.00
3 Shaquille O'Neal 3.00 8.00
4 Tim Duncan 2.00 5.00
5 Dirk Nowitzki 2.00 5.00
6 Yao Ming 2.50 6.00
7 Carmelo Anthony 2.50 6.00
8 Allen Iverson 2.00 5.00
9 Tracy McGrady 1.50 4.00
10 Ben Wallace 1.00 2.50

2004-05 Ultra Ten for Ten Game Used

Randomly seeded in packs, this 10-card set paralells the Ten for Ten set enhanced with a swatch of memorabilia and sequential numbering to 100. An Ultra Swatch parallel set was also issued and is sequentially numbered to 10.
PRINT RUN 100 SER.#'d SETS
UNPRICED ULTRA SWATCH PRINT RUN 10 SETS
AI Allen Iverson 6.00 15.00
BW Ben Wallace 3.00 8.00
DA Carmelo Anthony 8.00 20.00
DN Dirk Nowitzki 6.00 15.00
KG Kevin Garnett 6.00 15.00
SO Shaquille O'Neal 10.00 25.00
TD Tim Duncan 6.00 15.00
TM Tracy McGrady 5.00 12.00
VC Vince Carter 6.00 15.00
YM Yao Ming 8.00 20.00

2006-07 Ultra

Released in mid September 2006, Ultra employs a slightly tweaked version of previous year's minimally designed full-bleed photo card fronts. The 244-card set pictures veteran players on cards 1-170, 2005-06 rookie players in a Lucky 14 Retro subset on cards 171-184 (since no Fleer or Ultra products were issued during the 2005-06 season), 2005-06 rookie players in a World Premier Retro subset on cards 185-200, Lucky 14 rookies serially numbered to 500 on cards 201-214 and World Premier rookies on cards 215-244. Ultra is packaged in 24-pack boxes of eight cards each and carried an initial suggested retail price of $2.99.
COMP.SET w/o SP's (170) 20.00 50.00
L14 RC PRINT RUN 500 SER.#'d SETS
1 Josh Childress .25 .60
2 Al Harrington .25 .60
3 Joe Johnson .25 .60
4 Tyronn Lue .20 .50
5 Josh Smith .25 .60
6 Tony Allen .20 .50
7 Dan Dickau .20 .50
8 Al Jefferson .25 .60
9 Paul Pierce .30 .75
10 Wally Szczerbiak .25 .60
11 Raef LaFrentz .20 .50
12 Primoz Brezec .20 .50
13 Brevin Knight .20 .50
14 Emeka Okafor .25 .60
15 Kareem Rush .20 .50
16 Gerald Wallace .25 .60
17 Bernard Robinson .20 .50
18 Tyson Chandler .25 .60
19 Luol Deng .25 .60
20 Chris Duhon .20 .50
21 Ben Gordon .25 .60
22 Kirk Hinrich .25 .60
23 Drew Gooden .25 .60
24 Larry Hughes .25 .60
25 Zydrunas Ilgauskas .25 .60
26 LeBron James 1.25 3.00
27 Luke Jackson .20 .50
28 Anderson Varejao .20 .50
29 Erick Dampier .20 .50
30 Marquis Daniels .20 .50
31 Devin Harris .20 .50
32 Josh Howard .25 .60
33 Dirk Nowitzki .50 1.25
34 Jason Terry .25 .60
35 Carmelo Anthony .40 1.00
36 Earl Boykins .20 .50
37 Marcus Camby .25 .60
38 Kenyon Martin .25 .60
39 Andre Miller .25 .60
40 Eduardo Najera .20 .50
41 Chauncey Billups .30 .75
42 Richard Hamilton .25 .60
43 Antonio McDyess .25 .60
44 Tayshaun Prince .25 .60
45 Ben Wallace .25 .60
46 Rasheed Wallace .30 .75
47 Baron Davis .25 .60
48 Mike Dunleavy .25 .60
49 Derek Fisher .25 .60
50 Troy Murphy .20 .50
51 Jason Richardson .30 .75
52 Rafer Alston .20 .50
53 Juwan Howard .25 .60
54 Tracy McGrady .40 1.00
55 Stromile Swift .20 .50
56 David Wesley .20 .50
57 Yao Ming .40 1.00
58 Austin Croshere .20 .50
59 Stephen Jackson .25 .60
60 Jermaine O'Neal .25 .60
61 Peja Stojakovic .30 .75
62 Jamaal Tinsley .20 .50
63 Elton Brand .30 .75
64 Sam Cassell .25 .60
65 Chris Kaman .25 .60
66 Shaun Livingston .20 .50
67 Corey Maggette .25 .60
68 Cuttino Mobley .20 .50
69 Kwame Brown .20 .50
70 Kobe Bryant 1.25 3.00
71 Devean George .20 .50
72 Lamar Odom .25 .60
73 Smush Parker .20 .50
74 Luke Walton .20 .50
75 Shane Battier .25 .60
76 Pau Gasol .30 .75
77 Bobby Jackson .20 .50
78 Mike Miller .25 .60
79 Damon Stoudamire .25 .60
80 Alonzo Mourning .40 1.00
81 Shaquille O'Neal .60 1.50
82 Gary Payton .30 .75
83 Dwyane Wade .50 1.25
84 Antoine Walker .25 .60
85 Jason Williams .25 .60
86 T.J. Ford .20 .50
87 Jamaal Magloire .20 .50
88 Michael Redd .25 .60
89 Bobby Simmons .20 .50
90 Maurice Williams .25 .60
91 Mark Blount .20 .50
92 Ricky Davis .25 .60
93 Kevin Garnett .50 1.25
94 Eddie Griffin .20 .50
95 Trenton Hassell .20 .50
96 Troy Hudson .20 .50
97 Vince Carter .40 1.00
98 Jason Collins .20 .50
99 Richard Jefferson .25 .60
100 Jason Kidd .50 1.25
101 Jeff McInnis .20 .50
102 Antoine Wright .20 .50
103 P.J. Brown .20 .50
104 Speedy Claxton .20 .50
105 Marc Jackson .20 .50
106 Desmond Mason .20 .50
107 J.R. Smith .25 .60
108 Eddy Curry .25 .60
109 Steve Francis .25 .60
110 Stephon Marbury .25 .60
111 Quentin Richardson .25 .60
112 Jalen Rose .25 .60
113 Maurice Taylor .20 .50
114 Carlos Arroyo .20 .50
115 Grant Hill .40 1.00
116 Dwight Howard .25 .60
117 Darko Milicic .20 .50
118 Jameer Nelson .20 .50
119 DeShawn Stevenson .20 .50
120 Samuel Dalembert .20 .50
121 Steven Hunter .20 .50
122 Andre Iguodala .25 .60
123 Allen Iverson .40 1.00
124 Kyle Korver .25 .60
125 Chris Webber .30 .75
126 Raja Bell .25 .60
127 Boris Diaw .25 .60
128 Shawn Marion .25 .60
129 Steve Nash .40 1.00
130 Amare Stoudemire .25 .60
131 Kurt Thomas .20 .50
132 Darius Miles .20 .50
133 Joel Przybilla .20 .50
134 Zach Randolph .25 .60
135 Ha Seung-Jin .20 .50
136 Sebastian Telfair .20 .50
137 Shareef Abdur-Rahim .25 .60
138 Ron Artest .30 .75
139 Mike Bibby .30 .75
140 Brad Miller .25 .60
141 Vitaly Potapenko .20 .50
142 Bruce Bowen .20 .50
143 Tim Duncan .50 1.25
144 Michael Finley .30 .75
145 Manu Ginobili .30 .75
146 Robert Horry .25 .60
147 Tony Parker .30 .75
148 Ray Allen .30 .75
149 Rashard Lewis .30 .75
150 Luke Ridnour .25 .60
151 Robert Swift .20 .50
152 Earl Watson .20 .50
153 Chris Wilcox .20 .50
154 Rafael Araujo .20 .50
155 Chris Bosh .30 .75
156 Jose Calderon .20 .50
157 Mike James .20 .50
158 Morris Peterson .20 .50
159 Pape Sow .20 .50
160 Carlos Boozer .25 .60
161 Gordan Giricek .20 .50
162 Kris Humphries .20 .50
163 Andrei Kirilenko .25 .60
164 Mehmet Okur .20 .50
165 Greg Ostertag .20 .50
166 Gilbert Arenas .25 .60
167 Calvin Booth .20 .50
168 Caron Butler .25 .60
169 Antonio Daniels .20 .50
170 Antawn Jamison .25 .60
171 Andrew Bogut L14 Ret 1.00 2.50
172 Marvin Williams L14 Ret 1.00 2.50
173 Deron Williams L14 Ret 1.00 2.50
174 Chris Paul L14 Ret 1.50 4.00
175 Raymond Felton L14 Ret 1.00 2.50
176 Martell Webster L14 Ret 1.00 2.50
177 Charlie Villanueva L14 Ret .75 2.00
178 Channing Frye L14 Ret 1.00 2.50
179 Ike Diogu L14 Ret .75 2.00
180 Andrew Bynum L14 Ret .75 2.00
181 Yaroslav Korolev L14 Ret .75 2.00
182 Sean May L14 Ret .75 2.00
183 Rashad McCants L14 Ret .75 2.00
184 Antoine Wright L14 Ret .75 2.00
185 Nate Robinson WP Ret .75 2.00
186 Luther Head WP Ret 1.00 2.50
187 Joey Graham WP Ret .75 2.00
188 Johan Petro WP Ret .75 2.00
189 Wayne Simien WP Ret .75 2.00
190 David Lee WP Ret .75 2.00
191 Salim Stoudamire WP Ret .75 2.00
192 Travis Diener WP Ret .75 2.00
193 Monta Ellis WP Ret 1.00 2.50
194 Martynas Andriuskevicius WP Ret .75 2.00
195 Chuck Hayes WP Ret .75 2.00
196 Danny Granger WP Ret 1.00 2.50
197 Sarunas Jasikevicius WP Ret 1.00 2.50
198 Francisco Garcia WP Ret .75 2.00
199 Jarrett Jack WP Ret 1.00 2.50
200 Jose Calderon WP Ret .75 2.00
201 Andrea Bargnani L14/500 RC 4.00 10.00
202 LaMarcus Aldridge L14/500 RC 10.00 25.00
203 Adam Morrison L14/500 RC 4.00 10.00
204 Tyrus Thomas L14/500 RC 3.00 8.00
205 Shelden Williams L14/500 RC 3.00 8.00
206 Brandon Roy L14/500 RC 4.00 10.00
207 Randy Foye L14/500 RC 4.00 10.00
208 Rudy Gay L14/500 RC 5.00 12.00
209 Patrick O'Bryant L14/500 RC 2.50 6.00
210 Saer Sene L14/500 RC 2.50 6.00
211 J.J. Redick L14/500 RC 5.00 12.00
212 Hilton Armstrong L14/500 RC 2.50 6.00
213 Thabo Sefolosha L14/500 RC 4.00 10.00
214 Ronnie Brewer L14/500 RC 4.00 10.00
215 Allan Ray WP RC .60 1.50
216 Leon Powe WP RC .75 2.00
217 Joel Freeland WP RC .60 1.50
218 Shawne Williams WP RC .60 1.50
219 Kevin Pittsnogle WP RC .75 2.00
220 Shannon Brown WP RC .60 1.50
221 Kyle Lowry WP RC 1.25 3.00
222 Mardy Collins WP RC .60 1.50
223 Rodney Carney WP RC .60 1.50
224 Maurice Ager WP RC .60 1.50
225 Quincy Douby WP RC .60 1.50
226 Rajon Rondo WP RC 1.50 4.00
227 Jordan Farmar WP RC 1.00 2.50
228 Marcus Williams WP RC .60 1.50
229 Josh Boone WP RC .60 1.50
230 Solomon Jones WP RC .60 1.50
231 Denham Brown WP RC .60 1.50
232 Renaldo Balkman WP RC .75 2.00
233 Will Blalock WP RC .60 1.50
234 Bobby Jones WP RC .60 1.50
235 Steve Novak WP RC .75 2.00
236 James Augustine WP RC .60 1.50
237 Dee Brown WP RC .60 1.50
238 Hassan Adams WP RC .60 1.50
239 Alexander Johnson WP RC .60 1.50
240 Cedric Simmons WP RC .60 1.50
241 James White WP RC .60 1.50
242 Paul Davis WP RC .60 1.50
243 P.J. Tucker WP RC .75 2.00
244 Ryan Hollins WP RC .75 2.00

2006-07 Ultra Gold Medallion

*1-200 GOLD: .75X TO 2X BASE HI
*201-214 GOLD: HALF VALUE OF BASE
*215-244 GOLD: .75X TO 2X BASE HI
ONE PER PACK

2006-07 Ultra Platinum Medallion

*1-170 PLATINUM: 5X TO 12X BASE HI
*171-200 PLATINUM: 1X TO 2.5X BASE HI
1-200 PLAT.PRINT RUN 100 SER.#'d SETS
201-214 NOT PRICED DUE TO SCARCITY
201-214 PRINT RUN 14 SER.#'d SETS
*215-244 PLATINUM: 4X TO 10X BASE HI
215-244 PLAT.PRINT RUN 25 SER.#'d SETS
26 LeBron James 30.00 80.00
70 Kobe Bryant 125.00 250.00
80 Alonzo Mourning 6.00 15.00

2006-07 Ultra Red

*201-214 RED: .3X TO .75X BASE HI
*215-244 RED: 1.25X TO 3X BASE HI
RED APPROXIMATELY ONE PER BOX

2006-07 Ultra Fresh Ink

RANDOM INSERTS IN PACKS
FIBB Brent Barry 6.00 15.00
FIDH Dwight Howard 8.00 20.00
FIHW Hakim Warrick 6.00 15.00
FIKM Kevin Martin 5.00 12.00
FILJ LeBron James SP 75.00 150.00
FIRF Raymond Felton 6.00 15.00
FIRT Ronny Turiaf 6.00 15.00

2006-07 Ultra Kings of the Court

APPROXIMATE ODDS 1:24
KKAI Andre Iguodala 2.50 6.00
KKAJ Antawn Jamison 2.50 6.00
KKAL Al Jefferson 2.50 6.00
KKBD Baron Davis 2.50 6.00
KKBH Brendan Haywood 2.00 5.00
KKBW Ben Wallace 2.50 6.00
KKCM Corey Maggette 2.50 6.00
KKDG Drew Gooden 2.50 6.00
KKDN Dirk Nowitzki 5.00 12.00
KKJM Jeff McInnis 2.00 5.00
KKJO Jermaine O'Neal 2.50 6.00
KKJR Jason Richardson 3.00 8.00
KKKB Kobe Bryant 8.00 20.00
KKKG Kevin Garnett 5.00 12.00
KKLD Luol Deng 2.50 6.00
KKLJ LeBron James 8.00 20.00
KKMG Manu Ginobili 3.00 8.00
KKPS Peja Stojakovic 3.00 8.00
KKSM Stephon Marbury 2.50 6.00
KKYM Yao Ming 4.00 10.00

2006-07 Ultra One on One

PRINT RUN 100 SER.#'d SETS
OOBN C.Billups/S.Nash 6.00 15.00
OOFM S.Francis/S.Marbury 5.00 12.00
OOHD R.Hamilton/R.Davis 5.00 12.00
OOMB S.Marion/C.Bosh 6.00 15.00
OOMO Y.Ming/S.O'Neal 10.00 25.00
OOMP K.Martin/T.Prince 5.00 12.00
OOSH A.Stoudemire/D.Howard 6.00 15.00

2006-07 Ultra Scoring Kings

MPLETE SET 10.00 25.00
APPROXIMATE ODDS 1:6
SKAI Allen Iverson .75 2.00
SKCA Carmelo Anthony .75 2.00
SKDN Dirk Nowitzki 1.00 2.50
SKDW Dwyane Wade 1.00 2.50
SKEB Elton Brand .60 1.50
SKGA Gilbert Arenas .50 1.25
SKJR Jason Richardson .60 1.50
SKKB Kobe Bryant 2.50 6.00
SKKG Kevin Garnett 1.00 2.50
SKLJ LeBron James 2.50 6.00
SKPP Paul Pierce .60 1.50
SKRA Ray Allen .60 1.50
SKRH Richard Hamilton .50 1.25
SKRJ Richard Jefferson .50 1.25
SKSM Shawn Marion .50 1.25
SKSN Steve Nash .75 2.00
SKTD Tim Duncan 1.00 2.50
SKTM Tracy McGrady .75 2.00
SKTP Tony Parker .60 1.50
SKVC Vince Carter .75 2.00

2006-07 Ultra Season Crowns

COMPLETE SET 8.00 20.00
APPROXIMATE ODDS 1:12
SCAI Allen Iverson 1.00 2.50
SCAS Amare Stoudemire .60 1.50
SCCP Chris Paul 1.00 2.50
SCGA Gilbert Arenas .60 1.50
SCJK Jason Kidd 1.25 3.00
SCKG Kevin Garnett 1.25 3.00
SCSO Shaquille O'Neal 1.50 4.00
SCTD Tim Duncan 1.25 3.00
SCTP Tony Parker .75 2.00
SCVC Vince Carter 1.00 2.50

2006-07 Ultra Three Kings

PRINT RUN 50 SER.#'d SETS
TKBMJ Kobe/McGrady/LeBron 30.00 80.00
TKDMO Duncan/Yao/Shaq 15.00 40.00
TKJHB LeBron/Howard/Bogut 15.00 40.00
TKJWD Jamison/Wallace/Deng 6.00 15.00
TKKMN Kidd/Marbury/Nash 12.50 30.00
TKPFV Paul/Frye/Villanueva 12.00 30.00

2007-08 Ultra SE

This 273-card set was released in September, 2007. The set was issued into the hobby in five-card packs with an $20 SRP which came 15 packs to a box. Cards numbered 1-200 feature veterans in team alphabetical order while cards numbered 201-243 feature 2007-08 NBA rookies. The set concludes with retired greats from cards 244-256. The final 13 cards in the rookie subset and the retired greats were all issued as Lucky 13 cards. A few of the players from 201-256 were released in a blank back version. We have notated those cards with an BB notation in our data base.
COMP.SET w/o SP's (200) 25.00 50.00
1 Joe Johnson .30 .75
2 Josh Smith .30 .75
3 Josh Childress .30 .75
4 Marvin Williams .30 .75
5 Anthony Johnson .25 .60
6 Shelden Williams .25 .60
7 Tyronn Lue .25 .60
8 Al Jefferson .30 .75
9 Paul Pierce .40 1.00
10 Wally Szczerbiak .30 .75
11 Sebastian Telfair .25 .60
12 Gerald Green .30 .75
13 Rajon Rondo .40 1.00
14 Delonte West .25 .60
15 Adam Morrison .25 .60
16 Emeka Okafor .30 .75
17 Gerald Wallace .30 .75
18 Raymond Felton .40 1.00
19 Sean May .25 .60
20 Matt Carroll .25 .60
21 Ben Wallace .30 .75
22 Ben Gordon .30 .75
23 Tyrus Thomas .25 .60
24 Luol Deng .30 .75
25 Kirk Hinrich .30 .75
26 Andres Nocioni .25 .60
27 Thabo Sefolosha .25 .60
28 LeBron James 1.50 4[illegible]
29 Larry Hughes .30 .75
30 Zydrunas Ilgauskas .30 .75
31 Drew Gooden .30 .75
32 Daniel Gibson .30 .75
33 Shannon Brown .25 .60
34 Dirk Nowitzki .50 1.25
35 Josh Howard .30 .75
36 Jason Terry .30 .75
37 Jerry Stackhouse .30 .75
38 Devin Harris .25 .60
39 Erick Dampier .25 .60
40 Jose Barea .60 1.50
41 Carmelo Anthony .50 1.25
42 Allen Iverson .50 1.25
43 J.R. Smith .30 .75
44 Yakhouba Diawara .25 .60
45 Marcus Camby .25 .60
46 Eduardo Najera .25 .60
47 Chauncey Billups .40 1.00
48 Richard Hamilton .30 .75
49 Tayshaun Prince .30 .75
50 Chris Webber .40 1.00
51 Rasheed Wallace .40 1.00
52 Will Blalock .25 .60
53 Nazr Mohammed .25 .60
54 Baron Davis .30 .75
55 Al Harrington .30 .75
56 Stephen Jackson .30 .75
57 Jason Richardson .40 1.00
58 Monta Ellis .30 .75
59 Mickael Pietrus .25 .60
60 Kelenna Azubuike .25 .60
61 Yao Ming .50 1.25
62 Tracy McGrady .40 1.00
63 Rafer Alston .25 .60
64 Luther Head .30 .75
65 Shane Battier .30 .75
66 Juwan Howard .30 .75
67 Bonzi Wells .25 .60
68 Jermaine O'Neal .30 .75
69 Danny Granger .30 .75
70 Jamaal Tinsley .25 .60
71 Mike Dunleavy .30 .75
72 Troy Murphy .25 .60
73 Shawne Williams .25 .60
74 Elton Brand .40 1.00
75 Corey Maggette .30 .75
76 Sam Cassell .30 .75
77 Cuttino Mobley .30 .75
78 Tim Thomas .25 .60
79 Chris Kaman .30 .75
80 Kobe Bryant 1.50 4.00
81 Jordan Farmar .25 .60
82 Lamar Odom .30 .75
83 Andrew Bynum .25 .60
84 Smush Parker .25 .60
85 Luke Walton .25 .60
86 Maurice Evans .25 .60
87 Rudy Gay .40 1.00
88 Pau Gasol .40 1.00
89 Mike Miller .30 .75
90 Hakim Warrick .30 .75
91 Kyle Lowry .40 1.00
92 Damon Stoudamire .30 .75
93 Shaquille O'Neal .75 2.00
94 Dwyane Wade .60 1.50
95 Jason Williams .30 .75
96 Jason Kapono .25 .60
97 Alonzo Mourning .50 1.25
98 Udonis Haslem .25 .60
99 Gary Payton .40 1.00
100 Michael Redd .30 .75
101 Maurice Williams .30 .75
102 Andrew Bogut .30 .75
103 Charlie Villanueva .25 .60
104 Ruben Patterson .25 .60
105 Charlie Bell .25 .60
106 Kevin Garnett .60 1.50
107 Rashad McCants .25 .60
108 Ricky Davis .30 .75
109 Randy Foye .40 1.00
110 Craig Smith .25 .60
111 Mike James .25 .60
112 Jason Kidd .40 1.00
113 Vince Carter .50 1.25
114 Richard Jefferson .30 .75
115 Nenad Krstic .25 .60
116 Bernard Robinson .25 .60
117 Marcus Williams .25 .60
118 Josh Boone .25 .60
119 Chris Paul .50 1.25
120 Peja Stojakovic .40 1.00
121 David West .30 .75
122 Desmond Mason .25 .60
123 Cedric Simmons .30 .75
124 Hilton Armstrong .25 .60
125 Devin Brown .25 .60
126 Nate Robinson .25 .60
127 Eddy Curry .25 .60
128 Jamal Crawford .40 1.00
129 Stephon Marbury .30 .75
130 Quentin Richardson .30 .75
131 David Lee .25 .60
132 Channing Frye .30 .75
133 Dwight Howard .30 .75
134 J.J. Redick .40 1.00
135 Grant Hill .50 1.25
136 Jameer Nelson .25 .60
137 Hedo Turkoglu .30 .75
138 Tony Battie .25 .60
139 Darko Milicic .25 .60
140 Carlos Arroyo .25 .60
141 Andre Iguodala .30 .75
142 Kyle Korver .30 .75
143 Samuel Dalembert .25 .60
144 Rodney Carney .25 .60
145 Willie Green .25 .60
146 Andre Miller .30 .75
147 Bobby Jones .25 .60
148 Steve Nash .50 1.25
149 Amare Stoudemire .30 .75
150 Shawn Marion .30 .75
151 Leandro Barbosa .30 .75
152 Raja Bell .30 .75
153 Boris Diaw .30 .75
154 LaMarcus Aldridge .50 1.25
155 Zach Randolph .30 .75
156 Brandon Roy .40 1.00
157 Jarrett Jack .30 .75
158 Ime Udoka .25 .60
159 Martell Webster .30 .75
160 Sergio Rodriguez .25 .60
161 Fred Jones .25 .60
162 Kevin Martin .30 .75
163 Ron Artest .40 1.00
164 Mike Bibby .40 1.00
165 Brad Miller .30 .75
166 Quincy Douby .25 .60
167 Shareef Abdur-Rahim .30 .75
168 Radoslav Nesterovic .25 .60
169 Tony Parker .40 1.00
170 Tim Duncan .60 1.50
171 Manu Ginobili .40 1.00

172 Michael Finley .40 1.00
173 Brent Barry .25 .60
174 Bruce Bowen .25 .60
175 Ray Allen .40 1.00
176 Rashard Lewis .30 .75
177 Chris Wilcox .25 .60
178 Luke Ridnour .30 .75
179 Nick Collison .30 .75
180 Earl Watson .25 .60
181 Mickael Gelabale .25 .60
182 Chris Bosh .40 1.00
183 Andrea Bargnani .40 1.00
184 T.J. Ford .25 .60
185 Anthony Parker .25 .60
186 Jorge Garbajosa .30 .75
187 Morris Peterson .25 .60
188 Jose Calderon .25 .60
189 Carlos Boozer .30 .75
190 Mehmet Okur .25 .60
191 Deron Williams .30 .75
192 Paul Millsap .30 .75
193 Ronnie Brewer .30 .75
194 Andrei Kirilenko .30 .75
195 Gilbert Arenas .30 .75
196 Caron Butler .30 .75
197 Antawn Jamison .30 .75
198 DeShawn Stevenson .25 .60
199 Brendan Haywood .25 .60
200 Etan Thomas .25 .60
201 Al Thornton RC 1.50 4.00
201B Al Thornton BB 1.50 4.00
202 Rodney Stuckey RC 1.50 4.00
203 Nick Young RC 2.50 6.00
204 Sean Williams RC 1.25 3.00
205 Marco Belinelli RC 2.00 5.00
206 Javaris Crittenton RC 1.25 3.00
206B Javaris Crittenton BB 1.25 3.00
207 Jason Smith RC 1.50 4.00
208 Daequan Cook RC 1.50 4.00
209 Jared Dudley RC 1.50 4.00
210 Wilson Chandler RC 1.50 4.00
211 Morris Almond RC 1.25 3.00
212 Aaron Brooks RC 1.50 4.00
213 Arron Afflalo RC 2.00 5.00
214 Alando Tucker RC 1.25 3.00
215 Petteri Koponen RC 2.00 5.00
216 Carl Landry RC 1.25 3.00
217 Gabe Pruitt RC 1.25 3.00
217B Gabe Pruitt BB 1.25 3.00
218 Marcus Williams RC 1.25 3.00
219 Nick Fazekas RC 1.25 3.00
220 Glen Davis RC 1.50 4.00
220B Glen Davis BB 1.50 4.00
221 Jermareo Davidson RC 1.25 3.00
222 Josh McRoberts RC 1.50 4.00
223 Kyrylo Fesenko RC 1.25 3.00
224 Stanko Barac RC 2.00 5.00
225 Sun Yue RC 2.00 5.00
225B Sun Yue BB 2.00 5.00
226 Chris Richard RC 1.25 3.00
227 Derrick Byars RC 1.25 3.00
227B Derrick Byars BB 1.25 3.00
228 Adam Haluska RC 1.25 3.00
229 Reyshawn Terry RC 1.25 3.00
230 Taurean Green RC 1.25 3.00
231 Greg Oden L13 RC 2.50 6.00
231B Greg Oden BB 2.50 6.00
232 Kevin Durant L13 RC 20.00 50.00
233 Al Horford L13 RC 3.00 8.00
233B Al Horford BB 3.00 8.00
234 Mike Conley Jr. L13 RC 3.00 8.00
235 Jeff Green L13 RC 2.50 6.00
236 Yi Jianlian L13 RC 3.00 8.00
236B Yi Jianlian BB 3.00 8.00
237 Corey Brewer L13 RC 2.50 6.00
238 Brandan Wright L13 RC 2.50 6.00
239 Joakim Noah L13 RC 2.50 6.00
239B Joakim Noah BB 2.50 6.00
240 Spencer Hawes L13 RC 2.00 5.00
241 Acie Law L13 RC 1.50 4.00
242 Thaddeus Young L13 RC 2.50 6.00
242B Thaddeus Young BB 2.50 6.00
243 Julian Wright L13 RC 1.50 4.00
243B Julian Wright BB 1.50 4.00
244 Michael Jordan L13 12.00 30.00
244B Michael Jordan BB 12.00 30.00
245 Larry Bird L13 4.00 10.00
246 Magic Johnson L13 4.00 10.00
246B Magic Johnson BB 4.00 10.00
247 Bill Russell L13 2.50 6.00
248 Dennis Rodman L13 3.00 8.00
248B Dennis Rodman BB 3.00 8.00
249 Kareem Abdul-Jabbar L13 2.50 6.00
249B Kareem Abdul-Jabbar BB 2.50 6.00
250 Clyde Drexler L13 2.00 5.00
251 Hakeem Olajuwon L13 2.00 5.00
252 John Havlicek L13 1.50 4.00
253 David Robinson L13 2.50 6.00
254 John Stockton L13 2.50 6.00
254B John Stockton BB 2.50 6.00
255 Jerry West L13 2.00 5.00
256 Julius Erving L13 2.50 6.00

2007-08 Ultra SE Gold Medallion

*1-200 GOLD: .75X TO 2X BASE HI
*201-230 GOLD: .6X TO 1.5X BASE HI
*231-243 GOLD: .5X TO 1.25X BASE HI
*243-256 GOLD: .6X TO 1.5X BASE
GOLD ODDS ONE PER PACK
232 Kevin Durant L13 40.00 100.00

2007-08 Ultra SE Platinum Medallion

*1-200 PLAT: 6X TO 15X BASE HI
*201-230 PLAT: 2X TO 5X BASE
*231-243 PLAT: 1.5X TO 4X BASE
*244-256 PLAT: 2X TO 5X BASE HI
PRINT RUN 25 SER.#'d SETS
28 LeBron James 40.00 100.00
80 Kobe Bryant 175.00 350.00
232 Kevin Durant L13 300.00 600.00
244 Michael Jordan L13 250.00 500.00

2007-08 Ultra SE Autographics Black

ONE AUTO CARD PER HOBBY BOX
CARDS WITH (F) INSERTED IN FLEER
AUAB Andrea Bargnani 3.00 8.00
AUAH Al Harrington 3.00 8.00
AUAI Andre Iguodala 6.00 15.00
AUAJ Antawn Jamison 4.00 10.00
AUAR Allan Ray 3.00 8.00
AUAU James Augustine 3.00 8.00
AUBB Bruce Bowen Ultra, F 3.00 8.00
AUBD Boris Diaw F 3.00 8.00
AUBJ Bobby Jackson 3.00 8.00
AUBJ2 Bobby Jones 3.00 8.00
AUBM Brad Miller F 3.00 8.00
AUBR Ronnie Brewer 3.00 8.00
AUCB Charlie Bell 3.00 8.00
AUCM Chris Mihm 3.00 8.00
AUCS Cedric Simmons 3.00 8.00
AUDB Dee Brown 3.00 8.00
AUDE Daniel Ewing 3.00 8.00
AUDL David Lee F 3.00 8.00
AUDM Donyell Marshall 3.00 8.00
AUDN David Noel 3.00 8.00
AUDW Damien Wilkens F 3.00 8.00
AUFE Raymond Felton Ultra, F 3.00 8.00
AUGK George Karl 8.00 20.00
AUHW Hakim Warrick 3.00 8.00
AUJB Josh Boone 3.00 8.00
AUJJ Jarrett Jack 3.00 8.00
AUJK Jason Kapono 3.00 8.00
AUJO Bobby Jones 4.00 10.00
AUJS J.R. Smith 3.00 8.00
AUJW James White 3.00 8.00
AUKD Keyon Dooling 3.00 8.00
AUKH Kirk Hinrich 3.00 8.00
AUKK Kyle Korver 3.00 8.00
AULA Larry Hughes 3.00 8.00
AULP Leon Powe 3.00 8.00
AUMA Mardy Collins 3.00 8.00
AUMD Marquis Daniels Ultra, F 3.00 8.00
AUMG Corey Maggette 3.00 8.00
AUMI Andre Miller 3.00 8.00
AUMP Morris Peterson 3.00 8.00
AUPD Paul Davis 3.00 8.00
AUPM Paul Millsap 3.00 8.00
AUQR Quentin Richardson 3.00 8.00
AURB Raja Bell F 3.00 8.00
AURC Rodney Carney Ultra, F 3.00 8.00
AURF Randy Foye 3.00 8.00
AURH Ryan Hollins Ultra, F 3.00 8.00
AURM Rashad McCants 3.00 8.00
AURR Rajon Rondo 12.00 30.00
AURT Ronny Turiaf F 3.00 8.00
AUSA Shareef Abdur-Rahim F 3.00 8.00
AUSB Shannon Brown Ultra, F 3.00 8.00
AUSE Sean May F 3.00 8.00
AUSI James Singleton 3.00 8.00
AUSJ Solomon Jones 3.00 8.00
AUSM Craig Smith 3.00 8.00
AUSN Steve Novak 3.00 8.00
AUST DeShawn Stevenson 3.00 8.00
AUTA Tony Allen 3.00 8.00
AUTC Tyson Chandler 3.00 8.00
AUTF T.J. Ford 3.00 8.00
AUWB Will Blalock 3.00 8.00
AUWI Deron Williams F 6.00 15.00

2007-08 Ultra SE Autographics Blue

ONE AUTO CARD PER HOBBY BOX
CARDS WITH (F) INSERTED IN FLEER
RED AU UNPRICED DUE TO SCARCITY
AUAB Andrea Bargnani 3.00 8.00
AUAH Al Harrington 3.00 8.00
AUAI Andre Iguodala 10.00 25.00
AUAJ Antawn Jamison 6.00 15.00
AUAM Alonzo Mourning 50.00 100.00
AUAU James Augustine 3.00 8.00
AUBB Bruce Bowen Ultra, F 3.00 8.00
AUBG Ben Gordon 8.00 20.00
AUBJ Bobby Jackson 6.00 15.00
AUCA Carmelo Anthony Ultra, F 30.00 80.00
AUCB Charlie Bell 3.00 8.00
AUCM Chris Mihm 3.00 8.00
AUCP Chris Paul 15.00 40.00
AUCS Cedric Simmons 3.00 8.00
AUDB Dee Brown 3.00 8.00
AUDE Daniel Ewing 3.00 8.00
AUDM Donyell Marshall 3.00 8.00
AUDN David Noel 3.00 8.00
AUDS Dean Smith 30.00 80.00
AUEO Emeka Okafor 3.00 8.00
AUHW Hakim Warrick 3.00 8.00
AUJB Josh Boone 3.00 8.00
AUJE Julius Erving Ultra, F 30.00 80.00
AUJG Joey Graham 3.00 8.00
AUJJ Jarrett Jack 3.00 8.00
AUJK Jason Kapono 3.00 8.00
AUJO Bobby Jones 3.00 8.00
AUJW James White 3.00 8.00
AUKB Kobe Bryant 125.00 300.00
AUKH Kirk Hinrich 3.00 8.00
AUKI Jason Kidd 15.00 40.00
AUKK Kyle Korver 4.00 10.00
AULA LaMarcus Aldridge Ultra, F 15.00 30.00
AULB Larry Bird 60.00 120.00
AULH Larry Hughes 3.00 8.00
AULJ LeBron James 300.00 600.00
AULP Leon Powe 3.00 8.00
AUMA Magic Johnson 60.00 120.00
AUMC Mardy Collins 3.00 8.00
AUMD Marquis Daniels Ultra, F 3.00 8.00
AUMG Corey Maggette 3.00 8.00
AUMI Andre Miller 3.00 8.00
AUMJ Michael Jordan 400.00 800.00
AUMP Morris Peterson 3.00 8.00
AUNO Steve Novak 3.00 8.00
AUON Jermaine O'Neal 6.00 15.00
AUPM Paul Millsap 5.00 12.00
AUPP Paul Pierce 10.00 25.00
AUPR Pat Riley 15.00 30.00
AUQR Quentin Richardson 3.00 8.00
AURB Raja Bell F 3.00 8.00
AURF Randy Foye 3.00 8.00
AURH Ryan Hollins 3.00 8.00
AURT Ronny Turiaf Ultra, F 3.00 8.00
AUSB Shannon Brown 3.00 8.00
AUSJ Solomon Jones Ultra, F 3.00 8.00
AUSN Steve Nash 30.00 60.00
AUST DeShawn Stevenson 3.00 8.00
AUTA Tony Allen 3.00 8.00
AUTC Tyson Chandler 3.00 8.00
AUTF T.J. Ford 3.00 8.00
AUTM Tracy McGrady 15.00 30.00
AUTP Tony Parker F 15.00 40.00
AUTT Tyrus Thomas 3.00 8.00
AUWB Will Blalock 3.00 8.00
AUWI Deron Williams 6.00 15.00
AUYM Yao Ming 20.00 40.00

2007-08 Ultra SE Award Winners Jersey

PRINT RUN 199 SER.#'d SETS
*PATCH: 1.25X TO 3X BASE HI
PATCH PRINT RUN 25 SER.#'d SETS
AWAI Allen Iverson 4.00 10.00
AWAJ Antawn Jamison 2.50 6.00
AWAM Alonzo Mourning 5.00 12.00
AWAS Amare Stoudemire 2.50 6.00
AWBD Boris Diaw 2.50 6.00
AWBR Brandon Roy 3.00 8.00
AWBW Ben Wallace 2.50 6.00
AWCB Chauncey Billups 3.00 8.00
AWCW Chris Webber 3.00 8.00
AWDM Dikembe Mutombo 3.00 8.00
AWDN Dirk Nowitzki 4.00 10.00
AWDS Damon Stoudamire 2.50 6.00
AWEB Elton Brand 3.00 8.00
AWEO Emeka Okafor 2.50 6.00
AWGA Gilbert Arenas 2.50 6.00
AWGH Grant Hill 4.00 10.00
AWGP Gary Payton 3.00 8.00
AWJK Jason Kidd 3.00 8.00
AWJN Jameer Nelson 2.00 5.00
AWJO Jermaine O'Neal 2.50 6.00
AWKB Kobe Bryant 8.00 20.00
AWKG Kevin Garnett 5.00 12.00
AWLJ LeBron James 8.00 20.00
AWMC Marcus Camby 2.00 5.00
AWNR Nate Robinson 2.00 5.00
AWPG Pau Gasol 3.00 8.00
AWRA Ron Artest 3.00 8.00
AWSN Steve Nash 4.00 10.00
AWTD Tim Duncan 5.00 12.00
AWVC Vince Carter 4.00 10.00

2007-08 Ultra SE Call to the Hall

COMPLETE SET (10) 8.00 20.00
RANDOM INSERTS IN PACKS
CH1 Kobe Bryant 2.50 6.00
CH2 LeBron James 2.50 6.00
CH3 Paul Pierce .60 1.50
CH4 Shaquille O'Neal 1.25 3.00
CH5 Kevin Garnett 1.00 2.50
CH6 Yao Ming .75 2.00
CH7 Michael Jordan 5.00 12.00
CH8 Gary Payton .60 1.50
CH9 Tim Duncan 1.00 2.50
CH10 Allen Iverson .75 2.00

2007-08 Ultra SE Call to the Hall Memorabilia

RANDOM INSERTS IN PACKS
CHAI Allen Iverson 3.00 8.00
CHGP Gary Payton 2.50 6.00
CHKB Kobe Bryant 8.00 20.00
CHKG Kevin Garnett 4.00 10.00
CHLJ LeBron James 8.00 20.00
CHMJ Michael Jordan 20.00 50.00
CHPP Paul Pierce 2.50 6.00
CHSO Shaquille O'Neal 5.00 12.00
CHTD Tim Duncan 4.00 10.00
CHYM Yao Ming 3.00 8.00

2007-08 Ultra SE Court Masters

COMPLETE SET (15) 10.00 25.00
RANDOM INSERTS IN PACKS
CM1 Steve Nash 1.25 3.00
CM2 Jason Williams .75 2.00
CM3 John Stockton 1.50 4.00
CM4 Gary Payton 1.00 2.50
CM5 Stephon Marbury .75 2.00
CM6 Damon Stoudamire .75 2.00
CM7 Jason Kidd 1.00 2.50
CM8 Deron Williams .75 2.00
CM9 Chris Paul 1.25 3.00
CM10 Baron Davis .75 2.00
CM11 Kevin Garnett 1.50 4.00
CM12 Chauncey Billups 1.00 2.50
CM13 Jamaal Tinsley .60 1.50
CM14 Grant Hill 1.25 3.00
CM15 Jarrett Jack .75 2.00

2007-08 Ultra SE Court Masters Memorabilia

RANDOM INSERTS IN PACKS
CMBD Baron Davis 2.00 5.00
CMCB Chauncey Billups 2.50 6.00
CMCP Chris Paul 3.00 8.00
CMDS Damon Stoudamire 2.00 5.00
CMDW Deron Williams 2.00 5.00
CMGH Grant Hill 3.00 8.00
CMGP Gary Payton 2.50 6.00
CMJJ Jarrett Jack 2.00 5.00
CMJK Jason Kidd 2.50 6.00
CMJS John Stockton 4.00 10.00
CMJT Jamaal Tinsley 2.00 5.00
CMJW Jason Williams 2.00 5.00
CMKG Kevin Garnett 4.00 10.00
CMSM Stephon Marbury 2.00 5.00
CMSN Steve Nash 3.00 8.00

2007-08 Ultra SE Heir to the Throne Jersey

PRINT RUN 199 SER.#'d SETS
*PATCHES: 1.25X TO 3X BASE HI
PATCH PRINT RUN 25 SER.#'d SETS
HTAB Andrea Bargnani 3.00 8.00
HTAI Andre Iguodala 2.50 6.00
HTAJ Al Jefferson 2.50 6.00
HTAS Amare Stoudemire 2.50 6.00
HTBL Andray Blatche 2.00 5.00
HTBO Andrew Bogut 2.50 6.00
HTBR Brandon Roy 3.00 8.00
HTCA Carmelo Anthony 4.00 10.00
HTCB Caron Butler 2.50 6.00
HTCP Chris Paul 4.00 10.00
HTDH Dwight Howard 2.50 6.00
HTDW David West 2.50 6.00
HTEO Emeka Okafor 2.50 6.00
HTFE Raymond Felton 3.00 8.00
HTGW Gerald Wallace 2.50 6.00
HTHW Hakim Warrick 2.50 6.00
HTJC Josh Childress 2.50 6.00
HTJF Jordan Farmar 2.00 5.00
HTJH Josh Howard 2.50 6.00
HTJR J.J. Redick 3.00 8.00
HTJS J.R. Smith 2.50 6.00
HTKH Kirk Hinrich 2.50 6.00
HTLA LaMarcus Aldridge 4.00 10.00
HTLD Luol Deng 2.50 6.00
HTLH Luther Head 2.50 6.00
HTLJ LeBron James 8.00 20.00
HTMW Marvin Williams 2.50 6.00
HTPA Tony Parker 3.00 8.00
HTPD Paul Davis 2.00 5.00
HTQD Quincy Douby 2.00 5.00
HTRF Randy Foye 3.00 8.00
HTRG Rudy Gay 3.00 8.00
HTRJ Richard Jefferson 2.50 6.00
HTRM Rashad McCants 2.00 5.00
HTSB Shannon Brown 2.00 5.00
HTSJ Josh Smith 2.50 6.00
HTSM Sean May 2.00 5.00
HTTP Tayshaun Prince 2.50 6.00
HTTS Thabo Sefolosha 2.00 5.00
HTWI Deron Williams 2.50 6.00

2007-08 Ultra SE Jam City

NDOM INSERTS IN PACKS
JC1 Baron Davis .75 2.00
JC2 Clyde Drexler 1.25 3.00
JC3 Dee Brown .60 1.50
JC4 Dwight Howard .75 2.00
JC5 Desmond Mason .60 1.50
JC6 DeShawn Stevenson .60 1.50
JC7 Fred Jones .60 1.50
JC8 Gerald Green .75 2.00
JC9 Julius Erving 1.50 4.00
JC10 Michael Jordan 20.00 50.00
JC11 Jason Richardson 1.00 2.50
JC12 Josh Smith .75 2.00
JC13 Kobe Bryant 4.00 10.00
JC14 Larry Nance .75 2.00
JC15 Michael Finley 1.00 2.50
JC16 Michael Jordan 20.00 50.00
JC17 Nate Robinson .60 1.50
JC18 Tom Chambers .75 2.00
JC19 Tyrus Thomas .60 1.50
JC20 Vince Carter 1.25 3.00

2007-08 Ultra SE Jersey

PRINT RUN 50 SER.#'d SETS
UJAJ Al Jefferson 3.00 8.00
UJBJ Bobby Jones 2.50 6.00
UJCF Channing Frye 3.00 8.00
UJCM Corey Maggette 3.00 8.00
UJCS Cedric Simmons 3.00 8.00
UJDS DeShawn Stevenson 2.50 6.00
UJGW Gerald Wallace 3.00 8.00
UJHA Hilton Armstrong 2.50 6.00
UJJC Jose Calderon 2.50 6.00
UJJO Jermaine O'Neal 3.00 8.00
UJJT Jamaal Tinsley 2.50 6.00
UJKB Kwame Brown 2.50 6.00
UJLJ LeBron James 12.00 30.00
UJMA Maurice Ager 2.50 6.00
UJMB Mike Bibby 4.00 10.00
UJMD Mike Dunleavy 3.00 8.00
UJMP Morris Peterson 2.50 6.00
UJQR Quentin Richardson 3.00 8.00
UJRA Ray Allen 4.00 10.00
UJRD Ricky Davis 3.00 8.00
UJRH Richard Hamilton 3.00 8.00
UJRW Rasheed Wallace 4.00 10.00
UJSD Samuel Dalembert 2.50 6.00
UJSF Steve Francis 3.00 8.00
UJSN Steve Novak 2.50 6.00
UJTP Tayshaun Prince 3.00 8.00
UJUH Udonis Haslem 2.50 6.00
UJWB Will Blalock 2.50 6.00
UJWS Wally Szczerbiak 3.00 8.00
UJZI Zydrunas Ilgauskas 3.00 8.00

2007-08 Ultra SE Mini Jerseys

RANDOM INSERTS IN PACKS
1 LeBron James 6.00 15.00
2 Kobe Bryant 8.00 20.00
3 Allen Iverson 4.00 10.00
4 Shaquille O'Neal 5.00 12.00
5 Paul Pierce 4.00 10.00
6 Dirk Nowitzki 4.00 10.00
7 Tim Duncan 4.00 10.00
8 Kevin Garnett 4.00 10.00
9 Dwight Howard 4.00 10.00
10 Yao Ming 4.00 10.00
11 Steve Nash 4.00 10.00
12 Chris Bosh 4.00 10.00
13 Michael Jordan 12.00 30.00

2007-08 Ultra SE Mini Jerseys Autographs

MOST UNPRICED DUE TO SCARCITY
13 Michael Jordan 400.00 650.00

2007-08 Ultra SE One on One Jersey

PRINT RUN 99 SER.#'d SETS
*PATCHES: 1.25X TO 3X BASE HI
PATCH PRINT RUN 25 SER.#'d SETS
OOAH R.Allen/R.Hamilton 4.00 10.00
OOBA M.Bibby/G.Arenas 4.00 10.00
OOBB C.Boozer/S.Battier 4.00 10.00
OOBH E.Brand/G.Hill 6.00 15.00
OOBJ K.Bryant/L.James 15.00 30.00
OOCB C.Butler/C.Bosh 4.00 10.00
OOCC J.Collins/J.Collins 4.00 10.00
OOCM A.Jamison/S.May 4.00 10.00
OOGO B.Gordon/E.Okafor 4.00 10.00
OOGS P.Gasol/W.Szczerbiak 4.00 10.00
OOHC L.Head/B.Cook 4.00 10.00
OOHP K.Hinrich/P.Pierce 5.00 12.00
OOHW J.Howard/C.Webber 5.00 12.00
OOIW A.Iguodala/L.Walton 4.00 10.00
OOJC B.Jones/M.Collins 4.00 10.00
OOJJ M.Jordan/L.James 40.00 100.00
OOJR F.Jones/L.Ridnour 4.00 10.00
OOJW J.Magloire/A.Walker 4.00 10.00
OOKF J.Kapono/J.Farmar 4.00 10.00
OOMB Y.Ming/A.Bargnani 5.00 12.00
OOMD C.Maggette/L.Deng 4.00 10.00
OOMK D.Milicic/N.Krstic 4.00 10.00
OOML L.Bird/M.Johnson 10.00 25.00
OOMW J.Nelson/J.McInnis 4.00 10.00
OOOL L.Odom/S.Livingston 4.00 10.00
OOOM S.O'Neal/D.Mutombo 5.00 12.00
OORR Z.Randolph/J.Richardson 4.00 10.00
OOSR J.Smith/N.Robinson 4.00 10.00
OOWT J.Williams/J.Terry 4.00 10.00
OOWW B.Wallace/R.Wallace 4.00 10.00

2007-08 Ultra SE Rising Stars

COMPLETE SET (19) 15.00 40.00
RANDOM INSERTS IN PACKS
RS1 Kevin Durant 10.00 25.00
RS2 Al Horford 1.25 3.00
RS3 Mike Conley Jr. 1.25 3.00
RS4 Jeff Green 1.00 2.50
RS5 Corey Brewer 1.00 2.50
RS6 Greg Oden 1.00 2.50
RS8 Brandan Wright 1.00 2.50
RS9 Joakim Noah 1.00 2.50
RS10 Spencer Hawes .75 2.00
RS11 Acie Law .60 1.50
RS12 Thaddeus Young 1.00 2.50
RS13 Julian Wright .60 1.50
RS14 Al Thornton .75 2.00
RS15 Rodney Stuckey .75 2.00
RS16 Nick Young 1.25 3.00
RS17 Sean Williams .60 1.50
RS18 Marco Belinelli 1.00 2.50
RS19 Javaris Crittenton .60 1.50
RS20 Jason Smith .75 2.00

2007-08 Ultra SE Scoring Kings

COMPLETE SET (20) 8.00 20.00
RANDOM INSERTS IN PACKS
SK1 Carmelo Anthony .75 2.00
SK2 Gilbert Arenas .50 1.25
SK3 LeBron James 2.50 6.00
SK4 Mehmet Okur .40 1.00
SK5 Michael Redd .50 1.25
SK6 Joe Johnson .50 1.25
SK7 Ray Allen .60 1.50
SK8 Vince Carter .75 2.00
SK9 Tracy McGrady .60 1.50
SK10 Carlos Boozer .50 1.25
SK11 Kevin Martin .50 1.25
SK12 Ben Gordon .50 1.25
SK13 Elton Brand .60 1.50
SK14 Jermaine O'Neal .50 1.25
SK15 Josh Howard .50 1.25
SK16 Zach Randolph .50 1.25
SK17 Luol Deng .50 1.25
SK18 Ron Artest .60 1.50
SK19 Shawn Marion .50 1.25
SK20 Peja Stojakovic .60 1.50

2007-08 Ultra SE Scoring Kings Memorabilia

RANDOM INSERTS IN PACKS
SKAR Ron Artest 2.50 6.00
SKBG Ben Gordon 2.00 5.00
SKCA Carmelo Anthony 3.00 8.00
SKCB Carlos Boozer 2.00 5.00
SKEB Elton Brand 2.50 6.00
SKGA Gilbert Arenas 2.00 5.00
SKJH Josh Howard 2.00 5.00
SKJJ Joe Johnson 2.00 5.00
SKJO Jermaine O'Neal 2.00 5.00
SKKM Kevin Martin 2.00 5.00
SKLD Luol Deng 2.00 5.00
SKLJ LeBron James 8.00 20.00
SKME Mehmet Okur 2.00 5.00
SKMR Michael Redd 2.00 5.00
SKPS Peja Stojakovic 2.50 6.00
SKRA Ray Allen 2.50 6.00
SKSM Shawn Marion 2.00 5.00
SKTM Tracy McGrady 2.50 6.00
SKVC Vince Carter 3.00 8.00
SKZR Zach Randolph 2.00 5.00

2007-08 Ultra SE Season Crowns

COMPLETE SET (25) 20.00 40.00
RANDOM INSERTS IN PACKS
SC1 Tim Duncan 1.00 2.50
SC2 Michael Jordan 6.00 15.00
SC3 Chauncey Billups .60 1.50
SC4 Shaquille O'Neal 1.25 3.00
SC5 Kareem Abdul-Jabbar 1.00 2.50
SC6 Hakeem Olajuwon .75 2.00
SC7 Alonzo Mourning .75 2.00
SC8 Horace Grant .60 1.50
SC9 Tony Parker .60 1.50
SC10 Manu Ginobili .60 1.50
SC11 David Robinson 1.00 2.50
SC12 Richard Hamilton .50 1.25
SC13 Tayshaun Prince .50 1.25
SC14 Clyde Drexler .75 2.00
SC15 Dennis Rodman 1.25 3.00
SC16 Larry Bird 1.50 4.00
SC17 Julius Erving 1.00 2.50
SC18 Magic Johnson 1.50 4.00
SC19 Sean Elliott .60 1.50
SC20 Jason Williams .50 1.25
SC21 Ben Wallace .50 1.25
SC22 Michael Jordan 6.00 15.00
SC23 Bruce Bowen .40 1.00
SC24 Devean George .40 1.00
SC25 Bill Laimbeer .50 1.25

2007-08 Ultra SE Season Crowns Memorabilia

RANDOM INSERTS IN PACKS
SC1 Tim Duncan 4.00 10.00
SC2 Michael Jordan 20.00 50.00
SC3 Chauncey Billups 2.50 6.00
SC4 Shaquille O'Neal 5.00 12.00
SC5 Kareem Abdul-Jabbar 4.00 10.00
SC6 Hakeem Olajuwon 3.00 8.00
SC7 Alonzo Mourning 3.00 8.00
SC8 Horace Grant 2.50 6.00
SC9 Tony Parker 2.50 6.00
SC10 Manu Ginobili 2.50 6.00
SC11 David Robinson 4.00 10.00
SC12 Richard Hamilton 2.00 5.00
SC13 Tayshaun Prince 2.00 5.00
SC14 Clyde Drexler 3.00 8.00
SC15 Dennis Rodman 5.00 12.00
SC16 Larry Bird 6.00 15.00
SC17 Julius Erving 4.00 10.00
SC18 Magic Johnson 6.00 15.00
SC19 Sean Elliott 2.50 6.00
SC20 Jason Williams 2.00 5.00
SC21 Ben Wallace 2.00 5.00
SC22 Michael Jordan 20.00 50.00
SC23 Bruce Bowen 2.00 5.00
SC24 Devean George 1.50 4.00
SC25 Bill Laimbeer 2.00 5.00

2007-08 Ultra SE Signature Class

PRINT RUN 50 SER.#'d SETS
SCAA Arron Afflalo 6.00 15.00
SCAG Aaron Gray
SCAH Al Horford 8.00 20.00
SCAL Acie Law 4.00 10.00
SCAT Al Thornton
SCCB Corey Brewer 6.00 15.00
SCCL Carl Landry 4.00 10.00
SCDA Jermareo Davidson 4.00 10.00
SCDJ D.J. Strawberry 4.00 10.00
SCGD Glen Davis 5.00 12.00
SCGP Gabe Pruitt 4.00 10.00
SCHH Herbert Hill 4.00 10.00
SCJC Javaris Crittenton 4.00 10.00
SCJD Jared Dudley 5.00 12.00
SCJG Jeff Green 6.00 15.00
SCJJ Jared Jordan 4.00 10.00
SCJN Joakim Noah 30.00 80.00
SCJO JamesOn Curry 4.00 10.00
SCJS Jason Smith 5.00 12.00
SCKD Kevin Durant 200.00 400.00
SCMC Mike Conley Jr. 8.00 20.00
SCMW Marcus Williams 6.00 15.00
SCNF Nick Fazekas 4.00 10.00
SCRT Reyshawn Terry 4.00 10.00
SCSB Stanko Barac 6.00 15.00
SCSH Spencer Hawes 5.00 12.00
SCSL Stephane Lasme 4.00 10.00
SCSM Sammy Mejia 4.00 10.00
SCSW Sean Williams 4.00 10.00
SCTG Taurean Green 4.00 10.00
SCWC Wilson Chandler 5.00 12.00

2007-08 Ultra SE Snap Shots

MPLETE SET (40) 30.00 60.00
RANDOM INSERTS IN PACKS
SS1 Marvin Williams .60 1.50
SS2 Larry Bird 2.00 5.00
SS3 John Havlicek .75 2.00
SS4 Bill Russell 1.25 3.00
SS5 Adam Morrison .50 1.25
SS6 Raymond Felton .75 2.00
SS7 Michael Jordan 6.00 15.00
SS8 Ben Gordon .60 1.50
SS9 Dennis Rodman 1.50 4.00
SS10 LeBron James 3.00 8.00
SS11 Dirk Nowitzki 1.00 2.50
SS12 Carmelo Anthony 1.00 2.50
SS13 Allen Iverson 1.00 2.50
SS14 Tracy McGrady .75 2.00
SS15 Stephon Marbury .60 1.50
SS16 Clyde Drexler 1.00 2.50
SS17 Hakeem Olajuwon 1.00 2.50
SS18 Kobe Bryant 3.00 8.00
SS19 Magic Johnson 2.00 5.00
SS20 Kareem Abdul-Jabbar 1.25 3.00
SS21 Shaquille O'Neal 1.50 4.00
SS22 Dwyane Wade 1.25 3.00
SS23 Andrew Bogut .60 1.50
SS24 Kevin Garnett 1.25 3.00
SS25 Peja Stojakovic .75 2.00
SS26 Jason Kidd .75 2.00
SS27 Chris Paul 1.00 2.50
SS28 Dwight Howard .60 1.50
SS29 J.J. Redick .75 2.00
SS30 Julius Erving 1.25 3.00
SS31 Andre Iguodala .60 1.50
SS32 Steve Nash 1.00 2.50
SS33 LaMarcus Aldridge 1.00 2.50
SS34 Brandon Roy .75 2.00
SS35 Paul Pierce .75 2.00
SS36 David Robinson 1.25 3.00
SS37 Lenny Wilkens .75 2.00
SS38 Kevin Martin .60 1.50
SS39 Lamar Odom .60 1.50
SS40 John Stockton 1.25 3.00

2007-08 Ultra SE Stars

COMPLETE SET (30) 10.00 25.00
RANDOM INSERTS IN PACKS
US1 LeBron James 2.00 5.00
US2 Kevin Martin .40 1.00
US3 Kobe Bryant 2.00 5.00
US4 Jason Richardson .50 1.25
US5 Alonzo Mourning .60 1.50
US6 Brad Miller .40 1.00
US7 Carlos Boozer .40 1.00
US8 Amare Stoudemire .40 1.00
US9 Andrei Kirilenko .40 1.00
US10 Baron Davis .40 1.00
US11 Corey Maggette .40 1.00
US12 Brandon Roy .50 1.25
US13 Lamar Odom .40 1.00
US14 Larry Hughes .40 1.00
US15 Chris Bosh .50 1.25
US16 Tracy McGrady .50 1.25
US17 Yao Ming .60 1.50
US18 Richard Jefferson .40 1.00
US19 Andrea Bargnani .50 1.25
US20 Jordan Farmar .30 .75
US21 Raymond Felton .50 1.25
US22 Drew Gooden .40 1.00
US23 Dirk Nowitzki .60 1.50
US24 Pau Gasol .50 1.25
US25 Mike Bibby .50 1.25
US26 Zach Randolph .40 1.00
US27 Michael Redd .40 1.00
US28 Marvin Williams .40 1.00
US29 Deron Williams .40 1.00
US30 Antoine Walker .40 1.00

2007-08 Ultra SE Stars Memorabilia

RANDOM INSERTS IN PACKS
USAB Andrea Bargnani 2.50 6.00
USAK Andrei Kirilenko 2.00 5.00
USAM Alonzo Mourning 3.00 8.00
USAS Amare Stoudemire 2.00 5.00
USAW Antoine Walker 2.00 5.00
USBD Baron Davis 2.00 5.00
USBM Brad Miller 2.00 5.00
USBO Chris Bosh 2.50 6.00
USBR Brandon Roy 2.50 6.00
USCB Carlos Boozer 2.00 5.00
USCM Corey Maggette 2.00 5.00
USDG Drew Gooden 2.00 5.00
USDN Dirk Nowitzki 3.00 8.00
USDW Deron Williams 2.00 5.00
USJF Jordan Farmar 1.50 4.00
USJR Jason Richardson 2.50 6.00
USKB Kobe Bryant 6.00 15.00
USKM Kevin Martin 2.00 5.00
USLH Larry Hughes 2.00 5.00
USLJ LeBron James 8.00 20.00
USLO Lamar Odom 2.00 5.00
USMB Mike Bibby 2.50 6.00
USMR Michael Redd 2.00 5.00
USMW Marvin Williams 2.00 5.00
USPG Pau Gasol 2.50 6.00
USRF Raymond Felton 2.50 6.00
USRJ Richard Jefferson 2.00 5.00
USTM Tracy McGrady 2.50 6.00
USYM Yao Ming 3.00 8.00
USZR Zach Randolph 2.00 5.00

1992-93 Ultra Jam Session Cassette Insert

Measuring the standard size, this card was included in NBA Jam Session "Gangsta Rap" cassette. On a gray marbleized background, this card display small color action photos of the top five NBA jammers. Their "dunk rank" (from one to five) is reflected in the listing below.

1 David Robinson 1.25 3.00
Dikembe Mutombo
Otis Thorpe
Hakeem Olajuwon
Shawn Kemp

1999 Ultra WNBA

The debut issue of Ultra WNBA, produced by Fleer/SkyBox, was issued as a 125 card set. The packs contained 10 cards that carried a suggested retail price of $2.49. The rookie subset, cards 101-125, was shortprinted at one in two packs.

COMPLETE SET (125) 40.00 100.00
COMPLETE SET w/o SP (100) 8.00 20.00
CARDS 101-125: STATED ODDS 1:2 H/R
SUBSET CARDS HALF VALUE OF BASE CARDS
UNPRICED MASTERPIECES SERIAL #'d TO 1
1 Sheryl Swoopes 1.25 3.00
2 Christy Smith .20 .50
3 Nikki McCray .60 1.50
4 Coquese Washington RC .40 1.00
5 Vickie Johnson .30 .75
6 Toni Foster .30 .75
7 Allison Feaster RC .50 1.25
8 Penny Toler .30 .75
9 Brandy Reed RC .60 1.50
10 Yolanda Moore .20 .50
11 Lisa Leslie 1.00 2.50
12 Kisha Ford .20 .50
13 Merlakia Jones .30 .75
14 Umeki Webb .20 .50
15 Tora Suber .30 .75
16 Octavia Blue RC .20 .50
17 Bridget Pettis .20 .50
18 LaTonya Johnson RC .30 .75
19 A.Santos de Oliveria RC .30 .75
20 Tia Paschal RC .20 .50
21 Jennifer Gillom .50 1.25
22 Wanda Guyton .20 .50
23 Franthea Price RC .20 .50
24 Andrea Kuklova .20 .50
25 Vicky Bullett .30 .75
26 Dena Head .20 .50
27 Isabelle Fijalkowski .20 .50
28 Michelle Edwards .40 1.00
29 Pamela McGee .30 .75
30 Elisabeth Cebrian RC .20 .50
31 Olympia Scott-Richardson .20 .50
32 Murriel Page .30 .75
33 Korie Hlede RC .60 1.50
34 Andrea Stinson .40 1.00
35 Kristie Harrower RC .30 .75
36 Kym Hampton .30 .75
37 Gergana Branzova RC .20 .50
38 Teresa Weatherspoon .75 2.00
39 Rebecca Lobo .60 1.50
40 Michele Timms .60 1.50
41 Tamecka Dixon .30 .75
42 Tina Thompson .75 2.00
43 Janice Braxton .20 .50
44 Elena Baranova .50 1.25
45 Adrienne Johnson RC .60 1.50
46 Adia Barnes RC .30 .75
47 Elaine Powell RC .30 .75
48 Lady Hardmon .20 .50
49 Kim Perrot .60 1.50
50 Marlies Askamp RC .30 .75
51 Deborah Carter .20 .50
52 Sandy Brondello RC .75 2.00
53 Heidi Burge .20 .50
54 Janeth Arcain .20 .50
55 Rushia Brown .20 .50
56 Suzie McConnell-Serio .50 1.25
57 Penny Moore .30 .75
58 Margo Dydek RC .75 2.00
59 Angie Potthoff RC .20 .50
60 Monica Lamb RC .30 .75
61 Jamila Wideman .30 .75
62 Ticha Penicheiro RC 1.00 2.50
63 Andrea Congreaves .20 .50
64 Rachael Sporn RC .30 .75
65 Chantel Tremitiere .20 .50
66 Carla McGhee RC .30 .75
67 Kim Williams .20 .50
68 Tangela Smith .20 .50
69 Quacy Barnes .20 .50
70 Sue Wicks .30 .75
71 Tracy Reid RC .40 1.00
72 Linda Burgess .20 .50
73 Razija Brcaninovic RC .30 .75
74 Sharon Manning .20 .50
75 Tammy Jackson .20 .50
76 Rita Williams .25 .60
77 Carla Porter RC .30 .75
78 Michelle Griffiths RC .40 1.00
79 Eva Nemcova .30 .75
80 Sophia Witherspoon .30 .75
81 Sonja Tate RC .30 .75
82 Cynthia Cooper 1.25 3.00
83 Wendy Palmer .50 1.25
84 Ruthie Bolton-Holifield .60 1.50
85 Tammi Reiss .30 .75
86 Katrina Colleton RC .20 .50
87 Cindy Brown .40 1.00
88 Latasha Byears .30 .75
89 Mwadi Mabika .20 .50
90 Rhonda Mapp .25 .60
91 Tina Thompson AW .40 1.00
92 Sheryl Swoopes AW .60 1.50
93 Jennifer Gillom AW .25 .60
94 Cynthia Cooper AW .60 1.50
95 Suzie McConnell Serio AW .25 .60
96 Cindy Brown AW .20 .50
97 Eva Nemcova AW .15 .40
98 Lisa Leslie AW .50 1.25
99 Andrea Stinson AW .20 .50
100 Teresa Weatherspoon AW .40 1.00
101 Dawn Staley RC 2.50 6.00
102 Chamique Holdsclaw RC 6.00 15.00
103 Kristin Folkl RC 1.50 4.00
104 Nykesha Sales RC 2.00 5.00
105 Natalie Williams RC 2.00 5.00
106 Yolanda Griffith RC 4.00 10.00
107 Crystal Robinson RC 1.25 3.00
108 Edna Campbell RC 1.50 4.00
109 Tari Phillips RC 1.25 3.00
110 Tonya Edwards RC 1.00 2.50
111 Debbie Black RC 1.50 4.00
112 Kate Starbird RC 1.50 4.00
113 Adrienne Goodson RC 1.25 3.00
114 Sheri Sam RC 1.00 2.50
115 DeLisha Milton RC 1.00 2.50
116 Shannon Johnson RC 1.00 2.50
117 Katie Smith RC 2.50 6.00
118 Kara Wolters RC 1.50 4.00
119 Jennifer Azzi RC 2.50 6.00
120 Michele VanGorp RC 1.25 3.00
121 Stephanie White-McCarty RC 1.50 4.00
122 Ukari Figgs RC 1.25 3.00
123 Val Whiting RC 1.00 2.50
124 Mery Andrade RC 1.00 2.50
125 Charlotte Smith RC 1.00 2.50

1999 Ultra WNBA Gold Medallion

COMPLETE SET (125) 75.00 150.00
*GOLD 1-100: .75X TO 2X BASE HI
ONE PER HOBBY PACK

1999 Ultra WNBA Platinum Medallion

*PLATINUM 1-100: 10X TO 25X HI COL.
*PLATINUM 101-125: 6X TO 15X HI COL.
1-100: PRINT RUN 99 SERIAL #'d SETS
101-125: PRINT RUN 66 SERIAL #'d SETS
SUBSET CARDS SAME VALUE

1999 Ultra WNBA Fresh Ink

Randomly inserted in packs, this 13-card set features autographs from the WNBA. The cards feature the Fleer/SkyBox authentication logo in the center with a certificate as the card back. The cards were hand-numbered to 400. They are not numbered and listed below alphabetically.

COMPLETE SET (13) 175.00 350.00
STATED PRINT RUN 400 SERIAL #'d SETS
1 Elena Baranova 12.00 30.00
2 Cynthia Cooper 30.00 80.00
3 Kristin Folkl 10.00 25.00
4 Lisa Leslie 25.00 60.00
5 Suzie McConnell-Serio 12.00 30.00
6 Nikki McCray 6.00 15.00
7 Nykesha Sales 12.00 30.00
8 Dawn Staley 15.00 40.00
9 Andrea Stinson 10.00 25.00
10 Sheryl Swoopes 30.00 80.00
11 Michele Timms 15.00 40.00
12 Penny Toler 8.00 20.00
13 Teresa Weatherspoon 8.00 20.00

1999 Ultra WNBA Rock Talk

Randomly inserted in packs at one in 24, this set features players who leave opponents talking to themselves.

COMPLETE SET (10) 15.00 40.00
1 Eva Nemcova 1.25 3.00
2 Cynthia Cooper 5.00 12.00
3 Ruthie Bolton-Holifield 2.50 6.00
4 Michele Timms 2.50 6.00
5 Jennifer Gillom 2.00 5.00
6 Cindy Brown 1.50 4.00
7 Lisa Leslie 4.00 10.00
8 Andrea Stinson 1.50 4.00
9 Teresa Weatherspoon 3.00 8.00
10 Rebecca Lobo 2.50 6.00

1999 Ultra WNBA WNBAttitude

Randomly inserted in packs at one in six, this 10-card set features some of the league's most high profile personalities.

COMPLETE SET (10) 5.00 12.00

1 Lisa Leslie 1.25 3.00
2 Cynthia Cooper 1.50 4.00
3 Ruthie Bolton-Holifield .75 2.00
4 Rebecca Lobo .75 2.00
5 Sheryl Swoopes 1.50 4.00
6 Nikki McCray .75 2.00
7 Cindy Brown .50 1.25
8 Jennifer Gillom .60 1.50
9 Wendy Palmer .60 1.50
10 Michele Timms .75 2.00

1999 Ultra WNBA World Premiere

Randomly inserted at one in 12, this 10-card set features the newcomers to the WNBA.

COMPLETE SET (10) 8.00 20.00
1 Chamique Holdsclaw 4.00 10.00
2 Dawn Staley 1.50 4.00
3 Nykesha Sales 1.25 3.00
4 Kristin Folkl 1.00 2.50
5 Natalie Williams 1.25 3.00
6 Yolanda Griffith 2.50 6.00
7 Crystal Robinson .75 2.00
8 Edna Campbell 1.00 2.50
9 DeLisha Milton .60 1.50
10 Debbie Black 1.00 2.50

2000 Ultra WNBA Promo

This card was sent out to dealers for promotional purposes. It features Cynthia Cooper.

1 Cynthia Cooper 1.50 4.00

2000 Ultra WNBA

Released in August 2000, this 150-card set features players from the WNBA. The cards came in 10-card packs that carried a suggested retail price of $2.99. The set features 125 regular player cards (with rookies) and a special 25 card rookie subset, inserted at one in two.

COMPLETE SET (150) 35.00 70.00
COMPLETE SET w/o SP (125) 15.00 40.00
RC SUBSET: STATED ODDS 1:2
UNPRICED MASTERPIECES SERIAL #'d TO 1
1 Cynthia Cooper 1.50 4.00
2 Chamique Holdsclaw 1.50 4.00
3 Lisa Leslie 1.25 3.00
4 Anna DeForge RC .25 .60
5 Stephanie McCarty .50 1.25
6 Katrina Colleton .25 .60
7 Clarisse Machanguana RC .25 .60
8 Adrienne Goodson .25 .60
9 Charlotte Smith .25 .60
10 DeLisha Milton .25 .60
11 Janeth Arcain .25 .60
12 Donna Harrington RC .25 .60
13 Michele Timms .75 2.00
14 Charmin Smith RC .60 1.50
15 Tricia Bader RC .25 .60
16 Vickie Johnson .40 1.00
17 Monica Lamb .25 .60
18 Dawn Staley .60 1.50
19 Ruthie Bolton-Holifield .75 2.00
20 Jennifer Azzi .75 2.00
21 Becky Hammon RC 3.00 8.00
22 Latasha Byears .40 1.00
23 Lisa Harrison RC .60 1.50
24 Jennifer Rizzotti RC 1.25 3.00
25 Yolanda Griffith .75 2.00
26 Tracy Henderson RC .25 .60
27 Sophia Witherspoon .40 1.00
28 Sheryl Swoopes 1.50 4.00
29 Korie Hlede .40 1.00
30 Shannon Johnson .25 .60
31 Chasity Melvin RC .25 .60
32 Tamika Whitmore RC .40 1.00
33 Tina Thompson .75 2.00
34 Kedra Holland-Corn RC .40 1.00
35 Markita Aldridge RC .25 .60
36 Dalma Ivanyi RC .25 .60
37 Ticha Penicheiro .60 1.50
38 Quacy Barnes .25 .60
39 Ukari Figgs .25 .60
40 Andrea Lloyd Curry RC .40 1.00
41 Tammy Jackson .25 .60
42 Nikki McCray .60 1.50
43 Kate Starbird .40 1.00
44 Andrea Nagy RC .60 1.50
45 Bridget Pettis .25 .60
46 Eva Nemcova .40 1.00
47 Tangela Smith .25 .60
48 Astou Ndiaye-Diatta RC .75 2.00
49 Tamecka Dixon .40 1.00
50 Taj McWilliams RC .40 1.00
51 Kristin Folkl .40 1.00
52 Amanda Wilson RC .75 2.00
53 Chantel Tremitiere .25 .60
54 Dominique Canty RC .75 2.00
55 Allison Feaster .30 .75
56 Angie Potthoff .25 .60
57 Nykesha Sales .40 1.00
58 Rhonda Mapp .30 .75
59 Murriel Page .30 .75
60 Maria Stepanova .25 .60
61 Katie Smith .75 2.00
62 Michelle Edwards .50 1.25
63 Venus Lacy RC .25 .60
64 Adrienne Johnson .40 1.00
65 Rita Williams .30 .75
66 Andrea Stinson .50 1.25
67 La'Keshia Frett RC .25 .60
68 Jennifer Gillom .60 1.50
69 LaTonya Johnson .25 .60
70 Joy Holmes-Harris RC .25 .60
71 Rushia Brown .25 .60
72 Michelle Campbell RC .25 .60
73 Angie Braziel RC .50 1.25
74 Crystal Robinson .25 .60
75 Alicia Thompson .25 .60
76 Suzie McConnell-Serio .50 1.25
77 Tanja Kostic RC .25 .60
78 Amaya Valdemoro RC .40 1.00
79 Sue Wicks .40 1.00
80 Sonja Tate .25 .60
81 Natalie Williams .50 1.25
82 Mery Andrade .25 .60
83 Tracy Reid .40 1.00
84 Olympia Scott-Richardson .25 .60
85 Rebecca Lobo .75 2.00
86 Margo Dydek .50 1.25
87 Sonja Henning RC .40 1.00
88 Vicky Bullett .40 1.00
89 Mwadi Mabika .25 .60
90 Linda Burgess .25 .60
91 Merlakia Jones .40 1.00
92 Umeki Webb .25 .60
93 Niesa Johnson RC .25 .60
94 Texlan Quinney RC .25 .60
95 Teresa Weatherspoon 1.00 2.50
96 Wendy Palmer .60 1.50
97 Brandy Reed .40 1.00
98 Oksana Zakaluzhnaya RC .25 .60
99 Sharon Manning .25 .60
100 Kara Wolters .30 .75
101 Keisha Anderson RC .40 1.00
102 Edna Campbell .30 .75
103 DeMya Walker RC .25 .60
104 Michele VanGorp .30 .75
105 Coquese Washington .25 .60
106 Marlies Askamp .25 .60
107 Michelle Marciniak RC .60 1.50
108 Angela Aycock RC .40 1.00
109 Tari Phillips .25 .60
110 Sylvia Crawley RC .40 1.00
111 Tonya Edwards .25 .60
112 Monica Maxwell RC .25 .60
113 Beth Cunningham RC .25 .60
114 Debbie Black .40 1.00
115 Shalonda Enis RC .25 .60
116 Naomi Mulitauaopele RC .40 1.00
117 Jamila Wideman .40 1.00
118 Shanele Stires RC .40 1.00
119 Alisa Burras RC .40 1.00
120 Gordana Grubin RC .25 .60
121 Elaine Powell .25 .60
122 Tausha Mills RC .40 1.00
123 Katy Steding RC .25 .60
124 Jannon Roland RC .25 .60
125 Jessie Hicks .25 .60
126 Ann Wauters RC 1.00 2.50
127 Edwina Brown RC 1.00 2.50
128 Grace Daley RC 1.00 2.50
129 Helen Darling RC 1.00 2.50
130 Summer Erb RC 1.00 2.50
131 Kamila Vodichkova RC 1.00 2.50
132 Tamicha Jackson RC 1.00 2.50
133 Betty Lennox RC 4.00 10.00
134 Maylana Martin RC 1.00 2.50
135 Lynn Pride RC 1.00 2.50
136 Paige Sauer RC 1.00 2.50
137 Madinah Slaise RC 1.00 2.50
138 Stacey Thomas RC 1.00 2.50
139 Cintia Dos Santos RC 1.00 2.50
140 Milena Flores RC 1.00 2.50
141 Rhonda Banchero RC 1.00 2.50
142 Jameka Jones RC 1.00 2.50
143 Jessica Bibby RC 1.00 2.50
144 Adrain Williams RC 1.00 2.50
145 Olga Firsova RC 1.00 2.50
146 Usha Gilmore RC 1.00 2.50
147 Shantia Owens RC 1.00 2.50
148 Jurgita Streimikyte RC 1.00 2.50
149 Katrina Hibbert RC 1.00 2.50
150 Tonya Washington RC 1.00 2.50

2000 Ultra WNBA Gold Medallion

COMPLETE SET (150) 80.00 200.00
*GOLD 1-125: .75X TO 2X BASE CARD HI
*GOLD 126-150: 1.25X TO 3X BASE HI
GOLD 126-150: STATED ODDS 1:24

2000 Ultra WNBA Platinum Medallion

*PLAT 1-125: 12X TO 30X BASE CARD HI
*PLAT 126-150: 8X TO 20X HI COL.
1-125: PRINT RUN 50 SERIAL #'d SETS
126-150: PRINT RUN 25 SERIAL #'d SETS

2000 Ultra WNBA Feel the Game

Randomly inserted in packs at one in 144, this 16-card set features swatches of game-worn sneakers. The cards are not numbered and listed below in alphabetical order. Two of the cards also feature numbered autographs: Cynthia Cooper to 14 and Sheryl Swoopes to 22. Those cards are not included in the set price.

STATED ODDS 1:144
1 Debbie Black 10.00 25.00
2 Ruthie Bolton-Holifield 20.00 50.00
3 Cynthia Cooper 15.00 40.00
3A C.Cooper AU/14 400.00 600.00
4 Tonya Edwards 6.00 15.00
5 Jennifer Gillom 15.00 40.00
6 Yolanda Griffith 20.00 50.00
7 Kedra Holland-Corn 10.00 25.00
8 Lisa Leslie 30.00 80.00
9 Suzie McConnell-Serio 12.00 30.00
10 Taj McWilliams 10.00 25.00
11 DeLisha Milton 6.00 15.00
12 Ticha Penicheiro 15.00 40.00
13 Dawn Staley 15.00 40.00
14 Kate Starbird 12.00 30.00
15 Sheryl Swoopes 40.00 100.00
15A S.Swoopes AU/22 300.00 500.00
16 Natalie Williams 12.00 30.00

2000 Ultra WNBA Feminine Adrenaline

Randomly inserted in packs at one in four, this 10-card set features players who always provide a jump-start for their team.

COMPLETE SET (10) 6.00 15.00
1 Nikki McCray 1.00 2.50
2 Ticha Penicheiro 1.00 2.50
3 Teresa Weatherspoon 1.50 4.00
4 Jennifer Azzi 1.25 3.00
5 Lisa Leslie 2.00 5.00
6 Sheryl Swoopes 2.50 6.00
7 Tina Thompson 1.25 3.00
8 Jennifer Gillom 1.00 2.50
9 Suzie McConnell-Serio .75 2.00
10 Dawn Staley 1.00 2.50

2000 Ultra WNBA Fresh Ink

Randomly inserted in packs at one in 72, this 18-card set features autographs from some of the top players in the WNBA. The cards are not numbered on the back, and listed below alphabetically.

COMPLETE SET (18) 75.00 150.00
STATED ODDS 1:72
NNO CARDS LISTED BELOW ALPHABETICALLY
*GOLD: 1.25X TO 3X BASE HI
GOLD PRINT RUN 50 SER.#'d SETS
1 Debbie Black 4.00 10.00
2 Ruthie Bolton-Holifield 8.00 20.00
3 Cynthia Cooper 15.00 40.00
4 Tonya Edwards 2.50 6.00
5 Jennifer Gillom 6.00 15.00
6 Yolanda Griffith 8.00 20.00
7 Vickie Johnson 4.00 10.00
8 Carolyn Jones-Young 4.00 10.00
9 Lisa Leslie 12.00 30.00
10 Suzie McConnell-Serio 5.00 12.00
11 DeLisha Milton 2.50 6.00
12 Eva Nemcova 4.00 10.00
13 Ticha Penicheiro 6.00 15.00
14 Nykesha Sales 4.00 10.00
15 Dawn Staley 6.00 15.00
16 Sheryl Swoopes 15.00 40.00
17 T.Weatherspoon/500 10.00 25.00
18 Natalie Williams 5.00 12.00

2000 Ultra WNBA Trophy Case

ndomly inserted in packs at one in 12, this 10-card set features players named to the WNBA's First or Second All-WNBA team in 1999. The cards feature a die cut design in the shape of a court.

COMPLETE SET (10) 15.00 40.00
1 Sheryl Swoopes 4.00 10.00
2 Natalie Williams 1.25 3.00
3 Yolanda Griffith 2.00 5.00
4 Cynthia Cooper 4.00 10.00
5 Ticha Penicheiro 1.50 4.00
6 Chamique Holdsclaw 4.00 10.00
7 Tina Thompson 2.00 5.00
8 Lisa Leslie 3.00 8.00
9 Teresa Weatherspoon 2.50 6.00
10 Shannon Johnson .60 1.50

2000 Ultra WNBA WNBAttitude

Randomly inserted in packs at one in eight, this 10-card set features the players who play with extreme emotion every night.

COMPLETE SET (10) 8.00 20.00
1 Andrea Stinson 1.00 2.50
2 Eva Nemcova .75 2.00
3 Wendy Palmer 1.25 3.00
4 Shannon Johnson .50 1.25
5 Jennifer Gillom 1.25 3.00
6 Yolanda Griffith 1.50 4.00
7 Natalie Williams 1.00 2.50
8 Chamique Holdsclaw 3.00 8.00
9 Cynthia Cooper 3.00 8.00
10 Vickie Johnson .75 2.00

2001 Ultra WNBA

Released in late August 2001, this 150-card set features a full color borderless card design with a floating box towards the bottom with the player's name and her team logo. A coach subset was printed for cards 110-123, and rookies 124-150 were inserted at 1:2 packs. A special Cynthia Cooper autograph was also inserted with the set and is sequentially numbered to 350. Ultra WNBA was packaged in 24-pack boxes where packs contained eight cards each.

COMPLETE SET (150) 80.00 160.00
RC SUBSET STATED ODDS 1:2
1 Betty Lennox .75 2.00
2 Ukari Figgs .25 .60
3 Tangela Smith .25 .60
4 Sue Wicks .40 1.00
5 Marla Brumfield RC .25 .60
6 Maria Stepanova .25 .60
7 Murriel Page .30 .75
8 Michele Timms .75 2.00
9 Janeth Arcain .25 .60
10 Lisa Harrison .40 1.00
11 Tausha Mills .25 .60
12 Sheri Sam .25 .60
13 Sonja Henning .25 .60
14 Adrienne Johnson .40 1.00
15 Mwadi Mabika .25 .60
16 Chasity Melvin .25 .60
17 Allison Feaster .30 .75
18 Monica Maxwell .25 .60
19 Katie Smith .75 2.00
20 Stacey Thomas .25 .60
21 Robin Threatt-Elliott RC .25 .60
22 Jennifer Azzi .75 2.00
23 Shannon Johnson .25 .60
24 Rhonda Mapp .30 .75
25 Eva Nemcova .40 1.00
26 Edwina Brown .30 .75
27 Margo Dydek .40 1.00
28 Ann Wauters .30 .75
29 Nicky McCrimmon RC .25 .60
30 Dominique Canty .40 1.00
31 Adrienne Goodson .25 .60
32 Taj McWilliams-Franklin .25 .60
33 DeLisha Milton .25 .60
34 Mery Andrade .25 .60
35 Yolanda Griffith .75 2.00
36 Tari Phillips .25 .60
37 Rita Williams .30 .75
38 Marlies Askamp .25 .60
39 Korie Hlede .40 1.00
40 Tamicha Jackson .25 .60
41 Elaine Powell .25 .60
42 Elena Baranova .60 1.50
43 Astou Ndiaye-Diatta .40 1.00
44 Nykesha Sales .40 1.00
45 Natalie Williams .50 1.25
46 Debbie Black .40 1.00
47 Vicky Bullett .40 1.00
48 Michelle Cleary RC .25 .60
49 Wendy Palmer .60 1.50
50 Tully Bevilaqua RC .40 1.00
51 Helen Darling .30 .75
52 Katy Steding .25 .60
53 Sheryl Swoopes 1.50 4.00
54 Kristin Folkl .40 1.00
55 Lady Hardmon .25 .60
56 Jennifer Rizzotti .60 1.50
57 Adrain Williams .25 .60
58 Tricia Bader Binford .25 .60
59 Kedra Holland-Corn .25 .60
60 Crystal Robinson .25 .60
61 Kara Wolters .30 .75
62 Rushia Brown .25 .60
63 Tamecka Dixon .40 1.00
64 Ticha Penicheiro .60 1.50
65 Teresa Weatherspoon 1.00 2.50
66 Edna Campbell .30 .75
67 Sylvia Crawley .25 .60
68 Shalonda Enis .25 .60
69 Andrea Lloyd-Curry .25 .60
70 Tina Thompson .75 2.00
71 Michelle Edwards .50 1.25
72 Stephanie McCarty .50 1.25
73 Shantia Owens .25 .60
74 Shanele Stires .25 .60
75 DeMya Walker .25 .60
76 Quacy Barnes .25 .60
77 Cintia Dos Santos .25 .60
78 Merlakia Jones .40 1.00
79 Lisa Leslie 1.25 3.00
80 Grace Daley .25 .60
81 Jamie Redd RC .25 .60
82 Charlotte Smith .25 .60
83 Jurgita Streimikyte .25 .60
84 Sophia Witherspoon .40 1.00
85 Ruthie Bolton-Holifield .75 2.00
86 Vickie Johnson .40 1.00
87 Andrea Stinson .50 1.25
88 Texlan Quinney .25 .60
89 Tammy Jackson .25 .60
90 Andrea Nagy .40 1.00
91 Brandy Reed .40 1.00
92 Umeki Webb .25 .60
93 Andrea Garner RC .25 .60
94 Maylana Martin .30 .75
95 Vanessa Nygaard RC .25 .60
96 Kamila Vodichkova .25 .60
97 Coquese Washington .25 .60
98 Jennifer Gillom .60 1.50
99 Nikki McCray .60 1.50
100 Tracy Reid .40 1.00
101 Elena Tornikidou RC .25 .60
102 Becky Hammon 1.50 4.00
103 Dawn Staley .60 1.50
104 Alicia Thompson .25 .60
105 Tiffany Travis RC .40 1.00
106 Sandy Brondello .60 1.50
107 Tonya Edwards .25 .60
108 Chamique Holdsclaw 1.50 4.00
109 Olympia Scott-Richardson .25 .60
110 Anne Donovan CO .75 2.00
111 Brian Alger CO .75 2.00
112 Lin Dunn CO .75 2.00
113 Van Chancellor CO .75 2.00
114 Nell Fortner CO .75 2.00
115 Michael Cooper CO .75 2.00
116 Ron Rothstein CO .75 2.00
117 Richie Adubato CO .75 2.00
118 Cynthia Cooper CO 1.50 4.00
119 Linda Hargrove CO .75 2.00
120 Fred Williams CO .75 2.00
121 Dan Hughes CO .75 2.00
122 Carolyn Peck CO .75 2.00
123 Sonny Allen CO .75 2.00
124 Brooke Wyckoff RC 6.00 15.00
125 Jackie Stiles RC 10.00 25.00
126 Svetlana Abrosimova RC 2.50 6.00
127 Tamika Catchings RC 4.00 10.00
128 Katie Douglas RC 4.00 10.00
129 Lauren Jackson RC 10.00 25.00
130 Shea Ralph RC 2.50 6.00
131 Ruth Riley RC 3.00 8.00
132 Kelly Miller RC 2.50 6.00
133 Marie Ferdinand RC 2.50 6.00
134 Tammy Sutton-Brown RC 2.50 6.00
135 Camille Cooper RC 2.50 6.00
136 Janell Burse RC 2.50 6.00
137 LaQuanda Barksdale RC 2.50 6.00
138 Niele Ivey RC 2.50 6.00
139 Coco Miller RC 2.50 6.00
140 Deanna Nolan RC 2.50 6.00
141 Penny Taylor RC 4.00 10.00
142 Kristen Veal RC 2.50 6.00
143 Kelly Schumacher RC 2.50 6.00
144 Amanda Lassiter RC 2.50 6.00
145 Semeka Randall RC 2.50 6.00
146 Jenny Mowe RC 2.50 6.00
147 Georgia Schweitzer RC 2.50 6.00
148 Jae Kingi RC 2.50 6.00
149 Erin Buescher RC 2.50 6.00
150 Michaela Pavlickova RC 2.50 6.00
NNO Cynthia Cooper AU/350 10.00 25.00

2001 Ultra WNBA Autographics

Randomly inserted in packs, this two card set features Cynthia Cooper and Ticha Penicheire. Each card contains an authentic player autograph.

1 Cynthia Cooper 5.00 12.00
2 Ticha Penicheiro 8.00 20.00

2001 Ultra WNBA Feel the Game

Randomly inserted in packs at the rate of one in six, this six card set features player photos, a facsimile autograph, and a swatch of a game worn jersey.

COMPLETE SET (6) 20.00 50.00
STATED ODDS 1:6
1 Jennifer Azzi 6.00 15.00
2 Cynthia Cooper 6.00 15.00
3 Yolanda Griffith 3.00 8.00
4 Chamique Holdsclaw 6.00 15.00
5 Lisa Leslie 5.00 12.00
6 Natalie Williams 2.00 5.00

2002 Ultra WNBA

Released in April 2002, this 120-card set is divided up into 100 veteran player cards and 20 Rookie exchange cards. Base cards are borderless and feature full color player action photos with a foil name box towards the bottom. Ultra WNBA was packaged in 24 pack boxes where packs contained eight cards each.

COMPLETE SET (120) 75.00 200.00
COMP.SET w/o SP's (100) 15.00 40.00
RC STATED ODDS 1:4
1 Jackie Stiles 1.00 2.50
2 Sheryl Swoopes 1.50 4.00
3 Katie Smith .75 2.00
4 Sophia Witherspoon .40 1.00
5 Natalie Williams .50 1.25
6 Trisha Stafford-Odom .25 .60
7 Lynn Pride .25 .60
8 Ruthie Bolton-Holifield .75 2.00
9 Coquese Washington .25 .60
10 Erin Buescher .25 .60
11 Tully Bevilaqua .25 .60
12 Deanna Nolan .25 .60
13 Kristen Rasmussen .25 .60
14 Bridget Pettis .25 .60
15 Marie Ferdinand .25 .60
16 Andrea Stinson .50 1.25
17 Olympia Scott-Richardson .25 .60
18 Teresa Weatherspoon 1.00 2.50
19 Edna Campbell .30 .75
20 Elena Tornikidou .25 .60
21 Elena Baranova .60 1.50
22 Kristen Veal .25 .60
23 Margo Dydek .40 1.00
24 Wendy Palmer .60 1.50
25 Sandy Brondello .60 1.50
26 Lisa Harrison .40 1.00
27 Korie Hlede .40 1.00
28 Astou Ndiaye-Diatta .40 1.00
29 Sheri Sam .25 .60
30 Trisha Fallon RC .25 .60
31 Chamique Holdsclaw 1.50 4.00
32 Chasity Melvin .25 .60
33 Mwadi Mabika .25 .60
34 Shannon Johnson .25 .60
35 Kamila Vodichkova .25 .60
36 Edwina Brown .30 .75
37 Ruth Riley .40 1.00
38 Maria Stepanova .25 .60
39 Coco Miller .25 .60
40 Eva Nemcova .40 1.00
41 DeLisha Milton .25 .60
42 Jennifer Gillom .60 1.50
43 Vicky Bullett .40 1.00
44 Penny Taylor .40 1.00
45 Rhonda Mapp .30 .75
46 Tawona Alehaleem .25 .60
47 Murriel Page .30 .75
48 Tamika Catchings .40 1.00
49 Sue Wicks .40 1.00
50 Ticha Penicheiro .60 1.50
51 Tammy Jackson .25 .60
52 Rebecca Lobo .75 2.00
53 Yolanda Griffith .75 2.00
54 Ann Wauters .30 .75
55 Latasha Byears .40 1.00
56 Katie Douglas .40 1.00
57 Sonja Henning .25 .60
58 Rushia Brown .25 .60
59 Ukari Figgs .25 .60
60 Elaine Powell .25 .60
61 Jennifer Azzi .75 2.00
62 Allison Feaster .30 .75
63 Rita Williams .30 .75
64 Tangela Smith .25 .60
65 Tari Phillips .25 .60
66 Shalonda Enis .25 .60
67 Alicia Thompson .25 .60
68 Crystal Robinson .25 .60
69 Lauren Jackson 1.25 3.00
70 Jae Kingi .25 .60
71 Marla Brumfield .25 .60
72 Dawn Staley .60 1.50
73 Adrienne Goodson .25 .60
74 Clarisse Machanguana .25 .60
75 Nikki McCray .60 1.50
76 Becky Hammon 1.50 4.00
77 Semeka Randall .25 .60
78 Merlakia Jones .40 1.00
79 Tamecka Dixon .40 1.00
80 Taj McWilliams-Franklin .25 .60
81 Jamie Redd .25 .60
82 Amanda Lassiter .25 .60
83 Maylana Martin .30 .75
84 Tamicha Jackson .25 .60
85 Tammy Sutton-Brown .25 .60
86 Jurgita Streimikyte .25 .60
87 Vickie Johnson .40 1.00
88 Kedra Holland-Corn .25 .60
89 Janeth Arcain .25 .60
90 Betty Lennox .60 1.50
91 Kristin Folkl .40 1.00
92 Helen Luz .25 .60
93 Kelly Miller .25 .60
94 Lisa Leslie 1.25 3.00
95 Nykesha Sales .40 1.00
96 Simone Edwards RC .25 .60
97 Tina Thompson .75 2.00
98 Svetlana Abrosimova .25 .60
99 Sylvia Crawley .25 .60
100 Annie Burgess RC .25 .60
101 Sue Bird RC 15.00 40.00
102 Swin Cash RC 3.00 8.00
103 Stacey Dales-Schuman RC 3.00 8.00
104 Asjha Jones RC 3.00 8.00
105 Nikki Teasley RC 2.00 5.00
106 Tamika Williams RC 3.00 8.00
107 Shiela Lambert RC 2.00 5.00
108 Lindsay Yamasaki RC 2.00 5.00
109 Shaunzinski Gortman RC 2.00 5.00
110 Michelle Snow RC 4.00 10.00
111 Danielle Crockrom RC 2.50 6.00
112 Hamchetou Maiga RC 2.00 5.00
113 Towana McDonald RC 2.00 5.00
114 Laneisha Caufield RC 2.00 5.00
115 Tamara Moore RC 2.00 5.00
116 Rosalind Ross RC 2.00 5.00
117 Zuzi Klimesova RC 2.00 5.00
118 Lanae Williams RC 2.00 5.00
119 Iziane Castro-Marques RC 2.00 5.00
120 Ayana Walker RC 2.50 6.00

2002 Ultra WNBA Gold Medallion

*STARS: .6X TO 1.5X BASE CARD HI
STATED ODDS 1:1
101-120 PRINT RUN 25 SER.#'d SETS
101-120 NOT PRICED DUE TO SCARCITY

2002 Ultra WNBA House of Stiles

Randomly seeded in packs at the rate of one in 24, this five card set pays homage to rookie of the year Jackie Stiles. Also inserted with this set is an autographed jersey card sequentially numbered to 50 and a jersey card numbered to 110.

COMPLETE SET (5) 6.00 15.00
COMMON CARD (HS1-HS5) 2.50 6.00
STATED ODDS 1:24
NNO J.Stiles JSY AU/50 100.00 200.00
NNO Jackie Stiles JSY/110 40.00 100.00

2002 Ultra WNBA Summer Love

Inserted in packs at the rate of one in six, this 18-card set showcases a retro-seventies design that places full color action player photos on the left side of the card and a yellow and pink design with gold foil highlights on the right side.

COMPLETE SET (18) 15.00 40.00
SL1 Sheryl Swoopes 3.00 8.00
SL2 Ruthie Bolton-Holifield 1.50 4.00
SL3 Natalie Williams 1.00 2.50
SL4 Jennifer Gillom 1.25 3.00
SL5 Becky Hammon 3.00 8.00
SL6 Dawn Staley 1.25 3.00
SL7 Nikki McCray 1.25 3.00
SL8 Eva Nemcova .75 2.00
SL9 Nykesha Sales .75 2.00
SL10 Jennifer Azzi 1.50 4.00
SL11 Chamique Holdsclaw 3.00 8.00
SL12 Yolanda Griffith 1.50 4.00
SL13 Lisa Leslie 2.50 6.00
SL14 Jackie Stiles 2.00 5.00
SL15 Lauren Jackson 2.50 6.00
SL16 Katie Smith 1.50 4.00
SL17 Deanna Nolan .50 1.25
SL18 Ruth Riley .75 2.00

2002 Ultra WNBA Summer Love Memorabilia

STATED ODDS 1:12
SL1 Sheryl Swoopes 6.00 15.00
SL2 Ruthie Bolton-Holifield 4.00 10.00
SL3 Natalie Williams 2.50 6.00
SL4 Jennifer Gillom 3.00 8.00
SL5 Becky Hammon 8.00 20.00
SL6 Dawn Staley 3.00 8.00
SL7 Nikki McCray 3.00 8.00
SL8 Eva Nemcova 2.00 5.00
SL9 Nykesha Sales 2.00 5.00
SL10 Jennifer Azzi 4.00 10.00
SL11 Chamique Holdsclaw 8.00 20.00
SL12 Yolanda Griffith 4.00 10.00
SL13 Lisa Leslie 6.00 15.00
SL14 Jackie Stiles 5.00 12.00

2003 Ultra WNBA

Released in August 2003, Ultra WNBA boasts a 120-card base set divided up into 105 veteran player cards and 15 rookie cards inserted at the rate of one in three. Base cards are borderless with the Ultra logo in the upper right hand corner and player's names along the bottom. Ultra WNBA was packaged in 24-pack boxes where packs contained eight cards and carried a suggested retail price of $2.99.

COMP.SET w/o SP's (105) 12.50 30.00
106-120 STATED ODDS 1:3
1 Sue Bird 1.25 3.00
2 Kelly Schumacher .25 .60
3 Tamika Williams .30 .75
4 Rebecca Lobo .75 2.00
5 Stacey Thomas .25 .60
6 Lisa Leslie 1.25 3.00
7 Adrain Williams .25 .60
8 Helen Luz .25 .60
9 Rushia Brown .25 .60
10 Bridget Pettis .25 .60
11 Annie Burgess .25 .60
12 Allison Feaster .30 .75
13 Sylvia Crawley .25 .60
14 Svetlana Abrosimova .25 .60
15 Jessie Hicks .25 .60
16 Dominique Canty .40 1.00
17 Michele VanGorp .25 .60
18 Yolanda Griffith .75 2.00
19 Dawn Staley .60 1.50
20 Shalonda Enis .25 .60
21 Katie Smith .75 2.00
22 Brooke Wyckoff .40 1.00
23 Adrienne Goodson .25 .60
24 Erin Buescher .25 .60
25 Sonja Henning .25 .60
26 Betty Lennox .50 1.25
27 Wendy Palmer .60 1.50
28 Semeka Randall .25 .60
29 Charlotte Smith-Taylor .25 .60
30 Tully Bevilaqua .25 .60
31 DeLisha Milton .25 .60
32 Katie Douglas .40 1.00
33 Natalie Williams .50 1.25
34 Kayte Christensen RC .40 1.00
35 Janeth Arcain .25 .60
36 Vickie Johnson .40 1.00
37 Kamila Vodichkova .25 .60
38 Kelly Miller .25 .60
39 Grace Daley .25 .60
40 Nicky McCrimmon .25 .60
41 Taj McWilliams-Franklin .25 .60
42 LaTonya Johnson .25 .60
43 Jackie Stiles 1.00 2.50
44 Rita Williams .30 .75
45 Tamecka Dixon .40 1.00
46 Nykesha Sales .40 1.00
47 Murriel Page .30 .75
48 Marie Ferdinand .25 .60
49 Penny Taylor .40 1.00
50 Tina Thompson .75 2.00
51 Anna DeForge .25 .60
52 Ruth Riley .40 1.00
53 Stacey Dales-Schuman .40 1.00
54 Merlakia Jones .40 1.00
55 Nikki Teasley .25 .60
56 Ticha Penicheiro .60 1.50
57 Lindsey Yamasaki .25 .60
58 Chasity Melvin .25 .60
59 Mwadi Mabika .25 .60
60 Alisa Burras .25 .60
61 Tonya Washington .25 .60
62 Michelle Snow .30 .75
63 Tari Phillips .25 .60
64 Simone Edwards .25 .60
65 Sheryl Swoopes 1.50 4.00
66 Crystal Robinson .25 .60
67 Adia Barnes .25 .60
68 DeMya Walker .25 .60
69 Lynn Pride .25 .60
70 Ruthie Bolton-Holifield .75 2.00
71 Sandy Brondello .60 1.50
72 Debbie Black .40 1.00
73 Sheri Sam .25 .60
74 Kedra Holland-Corn .25 .60
75 Andrea Stinson .50 1.25
76 Tamika Catchings .40 1.00
77 Georgia Schweitzer .25 .60
78 Shannon Johnson .25 .60
79 Jennifer Azzi .75 2.00
80 Deanna Nolan .25 .60
81 Teresa Weatherspoon 1.00 2.50
82 Tangela Smith .25 .60
83 Ukari Figgs .25 .60
84 Becky Hammon 1.50 4.00
85 Lauren Jackson 1.25 3.00
86 LaQuanda Quick RC .25 .60
87 Jennifer Rizzotti .60 1.50
88 Tamicha Jackson .25 .60
89 Asjha Jones .30 .75
90 Margo Dydek .40 1.00
91 Swintayla Cash .40 1.00
92 Kristi Harrower .25 .60
93 Edna Campbell .30 .75
94 Deanna Jackson RC .25 .60
95 Nikki McCray .60 1.50
96 Cynthia Cooper 1.50 4.00
97 Jennifer Gillom .60 1.50
98 Coco Miller .25 .60
99 Ayana Walker .25 .60
100 Tamika Whitmore .25 .60
101 Tammy Sutton-Brown .25 .60
102 Edwina Brown .25 .60
103 Coquese Washington .25 .60
104 Lisa Harrison .40 1.00
105 Chamique Holdsclaw 1.50 4.00
106 LaToya Thomas RC 2.00 5.00
107 Plenette Pierson RC 4.00 10.00
108 Coretta Brown RC 2.00 5.00
109 Sun-Min Jung RC 2.00 5.00
110 Kara Lawson RC 6.00 15.00
111 Gwen Jackson RC 2.00 5.00
112 Cheryl Ford RC 5.00 12.00
113 Courtney Coleman RC 2.00 5.00
114 Chantelle Anderson RC 2.00 5.00
115 Shaquala Williams RC 2.50 6.00
116 Tamara Bowie RC 2.00 5.00
117 Teresa Edwards RC 6.00 15.00
118 Aiysha Smith RC 2.50 6.00
119 Petra Ujhelyi RC 2.00 5.00
120 Allison Curtin RC 2.50 6.00

2003 Ultra WNBA Gold Medallion

*1-105: .6X TO 1.5X BASE CARD HI
*106-120: 5X TO 12X BASE HI
1-105 STATED ODDS ONE PER PACK
106-120 PRINT RUN 25 SER.#'d SETS

2003 Ultra WNBA All-Star Review

Inserted in packs at the rate of one in 12, this 20-card set utilizes a horizontal design with white borders a yellow and orage background and full-color player photos on the left side.

COMPLETE SET (20) 12.00 30.00
1 Tamecka Dixon .60 1.50
2 Katie Smith 1.25 3.00
3 Ticha Penicheiro 1.00 2.50
4 Tari Phillips .40 1.00
5 Teresa Weatherspoon 1.50 4.00
6 Andrea Stinson .75 2.00
7 Lauren Jackson 2.00 5.00
8 Nykesha Sales .60 1.50
9 Tina Thompson 1.25 3.00
10 Lisa Leslie 2.00 5.00
11 Yolanda Griffith 1.25 3.00
12 Janeth Arcain .40 1.00
13 Vickie Johnson .60 1.50
14 Mwadi Mabika .40 1.00
15 Chamique Holdsclaw 2.50 6.00
16 Tamika Catchings .60 1.50
17 Sheryl Swoopes 2.50 6.00
18 Penny Taylor .60 1.50
19 Stacey Dales-Schuman .60 1.50
20 Sue Bird 2.00 5.00

2003 Ultra WNBA All-Star Review Material

MMON CARD 2.00 5.00
STATED ODDS 1:18
*PATCHES: 1.5X TO 4X BASE HI
PATCH PRINT RUN 100 SER.#'d SETS
1 Tamecka Dixon 2.00 5.00
2 Katie Smith 4.00 10.00
3 Ticha Penicheiro 3.00 8.00
4 Tari Phillips 2.00 5.00
5 Teresa Weatherspoon 5.00 12.00
6 Andrea Stinson 2.50 6.00
7 Lauren Jackson 6.00 15.00
8 Nykesha Sales 2.00 5.00
9 Tina Thompson 4.00 10.00
10 Lisa Leslie 6.00 15.00
11 Yolanda Griffith 4.00 10.00
12 Janeth Arcain 2.00 5.00
13 Vickie Johnson 2.00 5.00
14 Mwadi Mabika 2.00 5.00
15 Chamique Holdsclaw 6.00 15.00
16 Tamika Catchings 2.00 5.00
17 Sheryl Swoopes 6.00 15.00
18 Penny Taylor 2.00 5.00
19 Stacey Dales-Schuman 2.00 5.00
20 Sue Bird 6.00 15.00

2003 Ultra WNBA Nameplates

Randomly inserted in packs, this 20-card set places player's on a license plate-shaped card where a full-color player action photo appears on the left and a premium swatch of game-worn memorabilia appears on the right. Each card is sequentially numbered to 50.

PRINT RUN 50 SERIAL #'d SETS
1 Tamecka Dixon 30.00 80.00
3 Ticha Penicheiro 50.00 125.00
4 Tari Phillips 30.00 80.00
5 Teresa Weatherspoon 80.00 200.00
7 Lauren Jackson 100.00 250.00
8 Nykesha Sales 30.00 80.00
9 Tina Thompson 60.00 150.00
10 Lisa Leslie 100.00 250.00
13 Vickie Johnson 30.00 80.00
14 Mwadi Mabika 30.00 80.00
15 Chamique Holdsclaw 100.00 250.00
16 Tamika Catchings 30.00 80.00
17 Sheryl Swoopes 75.00 200.00
18 Penny Taylor 30.00 80.00
19 Stacey Dales-Schuman 30.00 80.00
20 Sue Bird 100.00 250.00

2003 Ultra WNBA Who I AM

Inserted in packs at the rate of one in eight, this 14-card set shows the ladies of the WNBA in their home scene and home lives.

COMPLETE SET (14) 8.00 20.00
1 Chamique Holdsclaw 1.50 4.00
2 Tamika Catchings .40 1.00
3 Tina Thompson .75 2.00
4 Dawn Staley .60 1.50
5 Nykesha Sales .40 1.00
6 Teresa Weatherspoon 1.00 2.50
7 Lisa Leslie 1.25 3.00
8 Sheryl Swoopes 1.50 4.00
9 Swintayla Cash .40 1.00
10 Tamika Williams .30 .75
11 Jennifer Azzi .75 2.00
12 Ticha Penicheiro .60 1.50
13 Sue Bird 1.25 3.00
14 Lisa Harrison .40 1.00

2003 Ultra WNBA Who I AM Game Used

STATED ODDS 1:9
1 Chamique Holdsclaw 6.00 15.00
2 Tamika Catchings 2.00 5.00
3 Tina Thompson 4.00 10.00
4 Dawn Staley 3.00 8.00
5 Nykesha Sales 2.00 5.00
6 Teresa Weatherspoon 5.00 12.00
7 Lisa Leslie 6.00 15.00
8 Sheryl Swoopes 6.00 15.00
9 Ticha Penicheiro 3.00 8.00
10 Sue Bird 6.00 15.00

2004 Ultra WNBA

Released in late July 2004, Ultra WNBA consists of a 110-card set where cards 1-90 feature veteran players and cards 91-110 feature rookies inserted at the rate of one in four packs. All cards are borderless with the Ultra logo in the upper right hand corner and the player's name centered along the bottom. Rookie cards feature a bronze background and full color player images. Ultra was packaged in 24-pack boxes with packs containing eight cards and an SRP of $2.99.

COMPLETE SET (110) 25.00 60.00
COMP.SET w/o SP's (90) 8.00 20.00
91-110 STATED ODDS 1:4
1 Tamika Catchings .30 .75
2 Sheri Sam .20 .50
3 Ruthie Bolton .60 1.50
4 Chamique Holdsclaw 1.25 3.00
5 Michelle Snow .25 .60
6 Crystal Robinson .20 .50
7 Betty Lennox .40 1.00
8 Dominique Canty .30 .75
9 Vickie Johnson .30 .75
10 Margo Dydek .30 .75
11 Charlotte Smith-Taylor .20 .50
12 Katie Smith .60 1.50
13 Shannon Johnson .20 .50
14 Teresa Weatherspoon .75 2.00
15 Natalie Williams .40 1.00
16 Yolanda Griffith .60 1.50
17 Adia Barnes .20 .50
18 Andrea Stinson .40 1.00
19 Michele VanGorp .20 .50
20 Kara Lawson .50 1.25
21 Tammy Sutton-Brown .20 .50
22 Svetlana Abrosimova .20 .50
23 Chantelle Anderson .20 .50
24 Tynesha Lewis .20 .50
25 Tamika Williams .25 .60
26 LaToya Thomas .20 .50
27 Edna Campbell .25 .60
28 Lisa Leslie 1.00 2.50
29 Kayte Christensen .20 .50
30 Stacey Dales-Schuman .30 .75
31 Wendy Palmer .50 1.25
32 Swin Cash .30 .75
33 Jessie Hicks .20 .50
34 Katie Douglas .30 .75
35 Mwadi Mabika .20 .50
36 Adrienne Goodson .20 .50
37 Taj McWilliams-Franklin .20 .50

38 Slobodanka Tuvic RC .30 .75
39 Semeka Randall .20 .50
40 Kelly Miller .20 .50
41 Tamika Whitmore .20 .50
42 Tully Bevilaqua .20 .50
43 Sheryl Swoopes 1.25 3.00
44 Becky Hammon 1.25 3.00
45 Sue Bird 1.00 2.50
46 Debbie Black .30 .75
47 DeLisha Milton-Jones .20 .50
48 Adrain Williams .20 .50
49 Asjha Jones .25 .60
50 Janell Burse .20 .50
51 Tamecka Dixon .30 .75
52 Penny Taylor .30 .75
53 Coco Miller .20 .50
54 Cheryl Ford .40 1.00
55 Deanna Jackson .20 .50
56 DeMya Walker .20 .50
57 Kamila Vodichkova .20 .50
58 Deanna Nolan .20 .50
59 Allison Feaster .25 .60
60 Plenette Pierson .30 .75
61 Lauren Jackson 1.00 2.50
62 Dawn Staley .50 1.25
63 Nykesha Sales .30 .75
64 Tangela Smith .20 .50
65 Aiysha Smith .20 .50
66 Ruth Riley .30 .75
67 Nikki McCray .50 1.25
68 Nikki Teasley .20 .50
69 Chasity Melvin .20 .50
70 Merlakia Jones .30 .75
71 Coretta Brown .20 .50
72 Anna DeForge .20 .50
73 Murriel Page .25 .60
74 Tina Thompson .60 1.50
75 Tari Phillips .20 .50
76 Gwen Jackson .20 .50
77 Ayana Walker .20 .50
78 Kelly Schumacher .20 .50
79 Ticha Penicheiro .50 1.25
80 Simone Edwards .20 .50
81 Kedra Holland-Corn .20 .50
82 K.B. Sharp RC .30 .75
83 LaQuanda Quick .20 .50
84 Barbara Farris RC .30 .75
85 Stephanie White .40 1.00
86 Tamicha Jackson .20 .50
87 Elena Baranova .50 1.25
88 Elaine Powell .20 .50
89 Teresa Edwards .50 1.25
90 Marie Ferdinand .20 .50
91 Diana Taurasi RC 8.00 20.00
92 Alana Beard RC 2.00 5.00
93 Nicole Powell RC 2.50 6.00
94 Lindsay Whalen RC 4.00 10.00
95 Shameka Christon RC 2.00 5.00
96 Nicole Ohlde RC 2.00 5.00
97 Vanessa Hayden RC 2.00 5.00
98 Chandi Jones RC 1.50 4.00
99 Ebony Hoffman RC 2.50 6.00
100 Rebekkah Brunson RC 1.50 4.00
101 Iciss Tillis RC 1.50 4.00
102 Christi Thomas RC 1.50 4.00
103 Shereka Wright RC 1.50 4.00
104 Ashley Robinson RC 1.50 4.00
105 Kaayla Chones RC 1.50 4.00
106 Jessica Brungo RC 1.50 4.00
107 Kelly Mazzante RC 2.50 6.00
108 Catrina Frierson RC 1.50 4.00
109 Bethany Donaphin RC 1.50 4.00
110 Agnieszka Bibrzycka RC 1.50 4.00

2004 Ultra WNBA Gold Medallion

*1-90 GOLD SINGLES: .75X TO 2X BASE HI
1-90 STATED ODDS 1:1
*91-110 GOLD RC: 1.5X TO 4X BASE HI
91-110 PRINT RUN 100 SER.#'d SETS

2004 Ultra WNBA Platinum Medallion

*PLATINUM 1-90: 10X TO 25X HI
*PLATINUM 91-110: 4X TO 10X HI
STATED PRINT RUN 25 SER.#'d SETS
45 Sue Bird 50.00 125.00

2004 Ultra WNBA All-Star Review

Inserted in packs at the rate of one in six, this 20-card set showcases WNBA all-stars on a horizontal card design with a player photo on the left and a facsimile signature on the right. All the wording on the card is printed in red and blue and the background is white.

COMPLETE SET (20) 12.50 30.00
1 Lauren Jackson 2.00 5.00
2 Chamique Holdsclaw 2.50 6.00
3 Tamika Catchings .60 1.50
4 Lisa Leslie 2.00 5.00
5 Katie Smith 1.25 3.00
6 Nikki Teasley .40 1.00
7 Swin Cash .60 1.50
8 Tari Phillips .40 1.00
9 Sheryl Swoopes 2.50 6.00
10 Marie Ferdinand .40 1.00
11 Yolanda Griffith 1.25 3.00
12 Tamecka Dixon .60 1.50
13 Natalie Williams .75 2.00
14 Deanna Nolan .40 1.00
15 Sue Bird 2.00 5.00
16 Dawn Staley 1.00 2.50
17 Cheryl Ford .75 2.00
18 Margo Dydek .60 1.50
19 Adrain Williams .40 1.00
20 Teresa Weatherspoon 1.50 4.00

2004 Ultra WNBA All-Star Review Jerseys

Seeded in packs at the rate of one in 24, this 20-card set parallels the base All-Star Review set enhanced with a square swatch of game-worn jersey. There is also a parallel version available with patch swatches that is sequentially numbered to 100.

STATED ODDS 1:24
*PATCHES: 2X TO 5X BASE JSY HI
PATCH PRINT RUN 100 SER.#'d SETS
1 Lauren Jackson 5.00 12.00
2 Chamique Holdsclaw 6.00 15.00
3 Tamika Catchings 1.50 4.00
4 Lisa Leslie 5.00 12.00
5 Katie Smith 3.00 8.00
6 Nikki Teasley 1.50 4.00
7 Swin Cash 1.50 4.00
8 Tari Phillips 1.50 4.00
9 Sheryl Swoopes 6.00 15.00
10 Marie Ferdinand 1.50 4.00
11 Yolanda Griffith 3.00 8.00
12 Tamecka Dixon 1.50 4.00
13 Natalie Williams 2.00 5.00
14 Deanna Nolan 1.50 4.00
15 Sue Bird 5.00 12.00
16 Dawn Staley 2.50 6.00
17 Cheryl Ford 2.00 5.00
18 Margo Dydek 2.00 5.00
19 Adrain Williams 1.50 4.00
20 Teresa Weatherspoon 4.00 10.00

2004 Ultra WNBA Scoring Stars

Inserted in packs at the rate of one in three, this 15-card set is horizontally designed with a full silver background. On the left side a gray-scale portrait is set behind an action photo of the player and on the right, lettering appears in bronze ink.

COMPLETE SET (15) 8.00 20.00
1 Lauren Jackson 1.25 3.00
2 Chamique Holdsclaw 1.50 4.00
3 Tamika Catchings .40 1.00
4 Lisa Leslie 1.25 3.00
5 Katie Smith .75 2.00
6 Tina Thompson .75 2.00
7 Swin Cash .40 1.00
8 Cheryl Ford .50 1.25
9 Sheryl Swoopes 1.50 4.00
10 Marie Ferdinand .25 .60
11 Yolanda Griffith .75 2.00
12 Tamecka Dixon .40 1.00
13 Natalie Williams .50 1.25
14 Deanna Nolan .25 .60
15 Sue Bird 1.25 3.00

2004 Ultra WNBA Scoring Stars Jerseys

serted in packs at one in 24, this set parallels the Scoring Stars set enhanced with a circular swatch of jersey on the right.

STATED ODDS 1:24
1 Lauren Jackson 5.00 12.00
2 Chamique Holdsclaw 6.00 15.00
3 Tamika Catchings 1.50 4.00
4 Lisa Leslie 5.00 12.00
5 Katie Smith 3.00 8.00
6 Tina Thompson 3.00 8.00
7 Swin Cash 1.50 4.00
8 Cheryl Ford 2.00 5.00
9 Sheryl Swoopes 6.00 15.00
10 Marie Ferdinand 1.50 4.00
11 Yolanda Griffith 3.00 8.00
12 Tamecka Dixon 1.50 4.00
13 Natalie Williams 2.00 5.00
14 Deanna Nolan 1.50 4.00
15 Sue Bird 5.00 12.00

2004 Ultra WNBA Season Crowns Autographs

Sequentially numbered to 100, this 13-card set employs a horizontal design with player action photos on the left and an embedded cut signature on the right.

STATED PRINT RUN 100 SER.#'d SETS
1 Tamika Catchings 60.00 150.00
2 Chamique Holdsclaw 20.00 50.00
3 Swin Cash 8.00 20.00
4 Alana Beard 10.00 25.00
5 Becky Hammon 50.00 120.00
6 Cheryl Ford 10.00 25.00
7 Tangela Smith 5.00 12.00
8 Delisha Milton-Jones 5.00 12.00
9 Deanna Nolan 5.00 12.00
10 Elaine Powell 5.00 12.00
11 Taj McWilliams-Franklin 5.00 12.00
12 Vanessa Hayden 10.00 25.00
13 Ruth Riley 8.00 20.00

2004 Ultra WNBA Season Crowns Rookie Jerseys

Sequentially numbered to 500, this two card set utilizes the same Season Crowns design with a swatch of game-worn jersey.

PRINT RUN 500 SER.#'d SETS
1 Alana Beard 5.00 12.00
2 Diana Taurasi 20.00 50.00

1957-59 Union Oil Booklets

These booklets were distributed by Union Oil. The front cover of each booklet features a drawing of the subject player. The booklets are numbered and were issued over several years beginning in 1957. These are 12-page pamphlets and are approximately 4" by 5 1/2". The set is subtitled "Family Sports Fun." This was apparently primarily a Southern California promotion.

COMPLETE SET (44) 200.00 400.00
5 Bill Russell BK 57 20.00 40.00
6 Forrest Twogood BK57 6.00 12.00
8 Phil Woolpert BK 58 6.00 12.00
9 Bill Sharman BK 58 10.00 20.00
31 George Yardley BK 58 7.50 15.00
32 John Wooden BK 58 20.00 40.00
34 Bob Cousy BK 59 17.50 35.00
36 Slats Gill BK 59 7.50 15.00

1961 Union Oil Chiefs

The 1961 Union Oil basketball card set contains 10 oversized (3" by 3 15/16"), attractive, brown-tinted cards. The cards feature players from the Hawaii Chiefs of the American Basketball League. The backs, printed in dark blue ink, feature a short biography of the player, an ad for KGU radio and the Union Oil circle 76 logo. The catalog number for this set is UO-17. These unnumbered cards are ordered alphabetically by player in the checklist below. Rick Herrscher would go on to have a short career with the 1962 New York Mets baseball team.

COMPLETE SET (10) 125.00 250.00
1 Frank Burgess 12.50 25.00
2 Jeff Cohen 12.50 25.00
3 Lee Harman 12.50 25.00
4 Rick Herrscher 15.00 40.00
5 Lowery Kirk 12.50 25.00
6 Dave Mills 12.50 25.00
7 Max Perry 12.50 25.00
8 George Price 12.50 25.00
9 Fred Sawyer 12.50 25.00
10 Dale Wise 12.50 25.00

1990-91 Upper Deck Prototypes

These standard-size promo cards were issued when Upper Deck applied for a basketball card license with the NBA. The card numbers on the back correspond to the the players' uniform numbers.

COMPLETE SET (2) 700.00 1000.00
32 Magic Johnson 250.00 500.00
33 Larry Bird 300.00 600.00

1991-92 Upper Deck Promos

These standard-size promo cards displayed different pictures of each player from their regular series cards.

COMPLETE SET (2) 8.00 20.00
1 Michael Jordan 4.00 10.00
400 David Robinson 2.00 5.00

1991-92 Upper Deck

The 1991-92 set marks Upper Deck's debut in the basketball card industry. The set contains 500 standard-size cards. The set was released in two series of 400 and 100 cards, respectively. High series cards are in relatively shorter supply because high series packs contained a mix of both high and low series cards. High series lockers contained seven 12-card packs of cards 1-500 and a special "Rookie Standouts" card. Both low and high series were offered in a 500-card factory set. The fronts feature glossy color player photos, bordered below and on the right by a hardwood basketball floor design. The player's name appears beneath the picture, while the team name is printed vertically alongside the picture. The backs display a second color player photo as well as biographical and statistical information. Special subsets featured include Draft Choices (1-21), Classic Confrontations (30-34), All-Rookie Team (35-39), All-Stars (49-72), and Team Checklists (73-99). The fronts feature glossy color player photos, bordered below and on the right by a hardwood basketball floor design. The player's name appears beneath the picture, while the team name is printed vertically alongside the picture. The backs display a second color player photo as well as biographical and statistical information. In addition to rookie and traded players, the high series includes the following topical subsets: Top Prospects (438-448), All-Star Skills (476-484), capturing players who participated in the slam dunk competition as well as the three-point shootout winner, Eastern All-Star Team (449, 451-462), and Western All-Star Team (450, 463-475). Rookie Cards of note include Kenny Anderson, Stacey Augmon, Terrell Brandon, Larry Johnson, Anthony Mason, Dikembe Mutombo, Steve Smith, and John Starks.

COMPLETE SET (500) 10.00 25.00
COMPLETE FACT.SET (500) 10.00 25.00
COMPLETE SERIES 1 (400) 5.00 12.00
COMPLETE SERIES 2 (100) 4.00 8.00
1 S.Augmon/R.Monroe CL .02 .10
2 Larry Johnson UER RC .40 1.00
3 Dikembe Mutombo RC .40 1.00
4 Steve Smith RC .40 1.00
5 Stacey Augmon RC .08 .25
6 Terrell Brandon RC .30 .75
7 Greg Anthony RC .08 .25
8 Rich King RC .02 .10
9 Chris Gatling RC .08 .25
10 Victor Alexander RC .02 .10
11 John Turner RC .02 .10
12 Eric Murdock RC .02 .10
13 Mark Randall RC .02 .10
14 Rodney Monroe RC .02 .10
15 Myron Brown RC .02 .10
16 Mike Iuzzolino RC .02 .10
17 Chris Corchiani RC .02 .10
18 Elliot Perry RC .02 .10
19 Jimmy Oliver RC .02 .10
20 Doug Overton RC .02 .10
21 Steve Hood UER RC .02 .10
22 Michael Jordan SCHOOL .30 .75
23 Kevin Johnson SCHOOL .02 .10
24 Kurk Lee .02 .10
25 Sean Higgins RC .02 .10
26 Morlon Wiley .02 .10
27 Derek Smith .02 .10
28 Kenny Payne .02 .10
29 Magic Johnson SPEC .15 .40
30 L.Bird/C.Person CC .08 .25
31 K.Malone/C.Barkley CC .08 .25
32 K.Johnson/Stockton CC .02 .10
33 H.Olajuwon/P.Ewing CC .08 .25
34 M.Johnson/M.Jordan CC .40 1.00
35 Derrick Coleman ART .02 .10
36 Lionel Simmons ART .02 .10
37 Dee Brown ART .02 .10
38 Dennis Scott ART .02 .10
39 Kendall Gill ART .02 .10
40 Winston Garland .02 .10
41 Danny Young .02 .10
42 Rick Mahorn .02 .10
43 Michael Adams .02 .10
44 Michael Jordan 1.25 3.00
45 Magic Johnson .30 .75
46 Doc Rivers .02 .10
47 Moses Malone .08 .25
48 Michael Jordan AS CL .60 1.50
49 James Worthy AS .02 .10
50 Tim Hardaway AS .08 .25
51 Karl Malone AS .08 .25
52 John Stockton AS .02 .10
53 Clyde Drexler AS .02 .10
54 Terry Porter AS .02 .10
55 Kevin Duckworth AS .02 .10
56 Tom Chambers AS .02 .10
57 Magic Johnson AS .15 .40
58 David Robinson AS .08 .25
59 Kevin Johnson AS .02 .10
60 Chris Mullin AS .02 .10
61 Joe Dumars AS .02 .10
62 Kevin McHale AS .02 .10
63 Brad Daugherty AS .02 .10
64 Alvin Robertson AS .02 .10
65 Bernard King AS .02 .10
66 Dominique Wilkins AS .02 .10
67 Ricky Pierce AS .02 .10
68 Patrick Ewing AS .02 .10
69 Michael Jordan AS .60 1.50
70 Charles Barkley AS .08 .25
71 Hersey Hawkins AS .02 .10
72 Robert Parish AS .02 .10
73 Alvin Robertson TC .02 .10
74 Bernard King TC .02 .10
75 Michael Jordan TC .60 1.50
76 Brad Daugherty TC .02 .10
77 Larry Bird TC .20 .50
78 Ron Harper TC .02 .10
79 Dominique Wilkins TC .02 .10
80 Rony Seikaly TC .02 .10
81 Rex Chapman TC .02 .10
82 Mark Eaton TC .02 .10
83 Lionel Simmons TC .02 .10
84 Gerald Wilkins TC .02 .10
85 James Worthy TC .02 .10
86 Scott Skiles TC .02 .10
87 Rolando Blackman TC .02 .10
88 Derrick Coleman TC .02 .10
89 Chris Jackson TC .02 .10
90 Reggie Miller TC .02 .10
91 Isiah Thomas TC .02 .10
92 Hakeem Olajuwon TC .08 .25
93 Hersey Hawkins TC .02 .10
94 David Robinson TC .08 .25
95 Tom Chambers TC .02 .10
96 Shawn Kemp TC .08 .25
97 Pooh Richardson TC .02 .10
98 Clyde Drexler TC .02 .10
99 Chris Mullin TC .02 .10
100 Checklist 1-100 .02 .10
101 John Shasky .02 .10
102 Dana Barros .02 .10
103 Stojko Vrankovic .02 .10
104 Larry Drew .02 .10
105 Randy White .02 .10
106 Dave Corzine .02 .10
107 Joe Kleine .02 .10
108 Lance Blanks .02 .10
109 Rodney McCray .02 .10
110 Sedale Threatt .02 .10
111 Ken Norman .02 .10
112 Rickey Green .02 .10
113 Andy Toolson .02 .10
114 Bo Kimble .02 .10
115 Mark West .02 .10
116 Mark Eaton .02 .10
117 John Paxson .02 .10
118 Mike Brown .02 .10
119 Brian Oliver .02 .10
120 Will Perdue .02 .10
121 Michael Smith .02 .10
122 Sherman Douglas .02 .10
123 Reggie Lewis .02 .10
124 James Donaldson .02 .10
125 Scottie Pippen .30 .75
126 Elden Campbell .02 .10
127 Michael Cage .02 .10
128 Tony Smith .02 .10
129 Ed Pinckney .02 .10
130 Keith Askins RC .02 .10
131 Darrell Griffith .02 .10
132 Vinnie Johnson .02 .10
133 Ron Harper .02 .10
134 Andre Turner .02 .10
135 Jeff Hornacek .02 .10
136 John Stockton .08 .25
137 Derek Harper .02 .10
138 Loy Vaught .02 .10
139 Thurl Bailey .02 .10
140 Olden Polynice .02 .10
141 Kevin Edwards .02 .10
142 Byron Scott .02 .10
143 Dee Brown .02 .10
144 Sam Perkins .02 .10
145 Rony Seikaly .02 .10
146 James Worthy .08 .25
147 Glen Rice .08 .25
148 Craig Hodges .02 .10
149 Bimbo Coles .02 .10
150 Mychal Thompson .02 .10
151 Xavier McDaniel .02 .10
152 Roy Tarpley .02 .10
153 Gary Payton .25 .60
154 Rolando Blackman .02 .10
155 Hersey Hawkins .02 .10
156 Ricky Pierce .02 .10
157 Fat Lever .02 .10
158 Andrew Lang .02 .10
159 Benoit Benjamin .02 .10
160 Cedric Ceballos .02 .10
161 Charles Smith .02 .10
162 Jeff Martin .02 .10
163 Robert Parish .02 .10
164 Danny Manning .02 .10
165 Mark Aguirre .02 .10
166 Jeff Malone .02 .10
167 Bill Laimbeer .02 .10
168 Willie Burton .02 .10
169 Dennis Hopson .02 .10
170 Kevin Gamble .02 .10
171 Terry Teagle .02 .10
172 Dan Majerle .02 .10
173 Shawn Kemp .25 .60
174 Tom Chambers .02 .10
175 Vlade Divac .02 .10
176 Johnny Dawkins .02 .10
177 A.C. Green .02 .10
178 Manute Bol .02 .10
179 Terry Davis .02 .10
180 Ron Anderson .02 .10
181 Horace Grant .02 .10
182 Stacey King .02 .10
183 William Bedford .02 .10
184 B.J. Armstrong .02 .10
185 Dennis Rodman .20 .50
186 Nate McMillan .02 .10
187 Cliff Levingston .02 .10
188 Quintin Dailey .02 .10
189 Bill Cartwright .02 .10
190 John Salley .02 .10
191 Jayson Williams .08 .25
192 Grant Long .02 .10
193 Negele Knight .02 .10
194 Alec Kessler .02 .10
195 Gary Grant .02 .10
196 Billy Thompson .02 .10
197 Delaney Rudd .02 .10
198 Alan Ogg .02 .10
199 Blue Edwards .02 .10
200 Checklist 101-200 .02 .10
201 Mark Acres .02 .10
202 Craig Ehlo .02 .10
203 Anthony Cook .02 .10
204 Eric Leckner .02 .10
205 Terry Catledge .02 .10
206 Reggie Williams .02 .10
207 Greg Kite .02 .10
208 Steve Kerr .02 .10
209 Kenny Battle .02 .10
210 John Morton .02 .10
211 Kenny Williams .02 .10
212 Mark Jackson .02 .10
213 Alaa Abdelnaby .02 .10
214 Rod Strickland .08 .25
215 Micheal Williams .02 .10
216 Kevin Duckworth .02 .10
217 David Wingate .02 .10
218 LaSalle Thompson .02 .10
219 John Starks RC .08 .25
220 Clifford Robinson .02 .10
221 Jeff Grayer .02 .10
222 Marcus Liberty .02 .10
223 Larry Nance .02 .10
224 Michael Ansley .02 .10
225 Kevin McHale .02 .10
226 Scott Skiles .02 .10
227 Darnell Valentine .02 .10
228 Nick Anderson .02 .10
229 Brad Davis .02 .10
230 Gerald Paddio .02 .10
231 Sam Bowie .02 .10
232 Sam Vincent .02 .10
233 George McCloud .02 .10
234 Gerald Wilkins .02 .10
235 Mookie Blaylock .02 .10
236 Jon Koncak .02 .10
237 Danny Ferry .02 .10
238 Vern Fleming .02 .10
239 Mark Price .02 .10
240 Sidney Moncrief .02 .10
241 Jay Humphries .02 .10
242 Muggsy Bogues .02 .10
243 Tim Hardaway .15 .40
244 Alvin Robertson .02 .10
245 Chris Mullin .08 .25
246 Pooh Richardson .02 .10
247 Winston Bennett .02 .10
248 Kelvin Upshaw .02 .10
249 John Williams .02 .10
250 Steve Alford .02 .10
251 Spud Webb .02 .10
252 Sleepy Floyd .02 .10
253 Chuck Person .02 .10
254 Hakeem Olajuwon .15 .40
255 Dominique Wilkins .08 .25
256 Reggie Miller .08 .25
257 Dennis Scott .02 .10
258 Charles Oakley .02 .10
259 Sidney Green .02 .10
260 Detlef Schrempf .02 .10
261 Rod Higgins .02 .10
262 J.R. Reid .02 .10
263 Tyrone Hill .02 .10
264 Reggie Theus .02 .10
265 Mitch Richmond .08 .25
266 Dale Ellis .02 .10
267 Terry Cummings .02 .10
268 Johnny Newman .02 .10
269 Doug West .02 .10
270 Jim Petersen .02 .10
271 Otis Thorpe .02 .10
272 John Williams .02 .10
273 Kennard Winchester RC .02 .10
274 Duane Ferrell .02 .10
275 Vernon Maxwell .02 .10
276 Kenny Smith .02 .10
277 Jerome Kersey .02 .10
278 Kevin Willis .02 .10
279 Danny Ainge .02 .10
280 Larry Smith .02 .10
281 Maurice Cheeks .02 .10
282 Willie Anderson .02 .10
283 Tom Tolbert .02 .10
284 Jerrod Mustaf .02 .10
285 Randolph Keys .02 .10
286 Jerry Reynolds .02 .10
287 Sean Elliott .02 .10
288 Otis Smith .02 .10
289 Terry Mills RC .08 .25
290 Kelly Tripucka .02 .10
291 Jon Sundvold .02 .10
292 Rumeal Robinson .02 .10
293 Fred Roberts .02 .10
294 Rik Smits .02 .10
295 Jerome Lane .02 .10
296 Dave Jamerson .02 .10
297 Joe Wolf .02 .10
298 David Wood RC .02 .10
299 Todd Lichti .02 .10
300 Checklist 201-300 .02 .10
301 Randy Breuer .02 .10
302 Buck Johnson .02 .10
303 Scott Brooks .02 .10
304 Jeff Turner .02 .10
305 Felton Spencer .02 .10
306 Greg Dreiling .02 .10
307 Gerald Glass .02 .10
308 Tony Brown .02 .10
309 Sam Mitchell .02 .10
310 Adrian Caldwell .02 .10
311 Chris Dudley .02 .10
312 Blair Rasmussen .02 .10
313 Antoine Carr .02 .10
314 Greg Anderson .02 .10
315 Drazen Petrovic .02 .10
316 Alton Lister .02 .10
317 Jack Haley .02 .10
318 Bobby Hansen .02 .10
319 Chris Jackson .02 .10
320 Herb Williams .02 .10
321 Kendall Gill .02 .10
322 Tyrone Corbin .02 .10
323 Kiki Vandeweghe .02 .10
324 David Robinson .20 .50
325 Rex Chapman .02 .10
326 Tony Campbell .02 .10
327 Dell Curry .02 .10
328 Charles Jones .02 .10
329 Kenny Gattison .02 .10
330 Haywoode Workman RC .02 .10
331 Travis Mays .02 .10
332 Derrick Coleman .02 .10
333 Isiah Thomas .08 .25
334 Jud Buechler .02 .10
335 Joe Dumars .08 .25
336 Tate George .02 .10
337 Mike Sanders .02 .10
338 James Edwards .02 .10
339 Chris Morris .02 .10
340 Scott Hastings .02 .10
341 Trent Tucker .02 .10
342 Harvey Grant .02 .10
343 Patrick Ewing .08 .25
344 Larry Bird .40 1.00
345 Charles Barkley .15 .40
346 Brian Shaw .02 .10
347 Kenny Walker .02 .10
348 Danny Schayes .02 .10
349 Tom Hammonds .02 .10
350 Frank Brickowski .02 .10
351 Terry Porter .02 .10
352 Orlando Woolridge .02 .10
353 Buck Williams .02 .10
354 Sarunas Marciulionis .02 .10
355 Karl Malone .15 .40
356 Kevin Johnson .08 .25
357 Clyde Drexler .08 .25
358 Duane Causwell .02 .10
359 Paul Pressey .02 .10
360 Jim Les RC .02 .10
361 Derrick McKey .02 .10
362 Scott Williams RC .02 .10
363 Mark Alarie .02 .10
364 Brad Daugherty .02 .10
365 Bernard King .02 .10
366 Steve Henson .02 .10
367 Darrell Walker .02 .10
368 Larry Krystkowiak .02 .10
369 Henry James UER .02 .10
370 Jack Sikma .02 .10
371 Eddie Johnson .02 .10
372 Wayman Tisdale .02 .10
373 Joe Barry Carroll .02 .10
374 David Greenwood .02 .10
375 Lionel Simmons .02 .10
376 Dwayne Schintzius .02 .10
377 Tod Murphy .02 .10
378 Wayne Cooper .02 .10
379 Anthony Bonner .02 .10
380 Walter Davis .02 .10
381 Lester Conner .02 .10
382 Ledell Eackles .02 .10
383 Brad Lohaus .02 .10
384 Derrick Gervin .02 .10
385 Pervis Ellison .02 .10
386 Tim McCormick .02 .10
387 A.J. English .02 .10
388 John Battle .02 .10
389 Roy Hinson .02 .10
390 Armon Gilliam .02 .10
391 Kurt Rambis .02 .10
392 Mark Bryant .02 .10
393 Chucky Brown .02 .10
394 Avery Johnson .02 .10
395 Rory Sparrow .02 .10
396 Mario Elie RC .08 .25
397 Ralph Sampson .02 .10
398 Mike Gminski .02 .10
399 Bill Wennington .02 .10
400 Checklist 301-400 .02 .10
401 David Wingate .02 .10
402 Moses Malone .20 .50
403 Darrell Walker .02 .10
404 Antoine Carr .02 .10
405 Charles Shackleford .02 .10
406 Orlando Woolridge .02 .10
407 Robert Pack RC .08 .25
408 Bobby Hansen .02 .10
409 Dale Davis RC .20 .50
410 Vincent Askew RC .02 .10
411 Alexander Volkov .02 .10
412 Dwayne Schintzius .02 .10
413 Tim Perry .02 .10
414 Tyrone Corbin .02 .10
415 Pete Chilcutt RC .02 .10
416 James Edwards .02 .10
417 Jerrod Mustaf .02 .10
418 Thurl Bailey .02 .10
419 Spud Webb .08 .25
420 Doc Rivers .08 .25
421 Sean Green RC .02 .10
422 Walter Davis .02 .10
423 Terry Davis .02 .10
424 John Battle .02 .10
425 Vinnie Johnson .02 .10
426 Sherman Douglas .02 .10
427 Kevin Brooks RC .02 .10
428 Greg Sutton RC .02 .10
429 Rafael Addison RC .02 .10
430 Anthony Mason RC .40 1.00
431 Paul Graham RC .02 .10
432 Anthony Frederick RC .02 .10
433 Dennis Hopson .02 .10
434 Rory Sparrow .02 .10
435 Michael Adams .02 .10
436 Kevin Lynch RC .02 .10
437 Randy Brown RC .02 .10
438 L.Johnson/B.Owens TP CL .08 .25
439 Stacey Augmon TP .02 .10
440 Larry Stewart TP RC .02 .10
441 Terrell Brandon TP .20 .50
442 Billy Owens TP RC .02 .10
443 Rick Fox TP RC .08 .25
444 Kenny Anderson TP RC .40 1.00
445 Larry Johnson TP .20 .50
446 Dikembe Mutombo TP .20 .50
447 Steve Smith TP .20 .50
448 Greg Anthony TP .08 .25
449 East All-Star CL .08 .25
450 West All-Star CL .08 .25
451 Isiah Thomas AS w/Magic .20 .50
452 Michael Jordan AS 1.25 3.00
453 Scottie Pippen AS .30 .75
454 Charles Barkley AS .20 .50
455 Patrick Ewing AS .08 .25
456 Michael Adams AS .02 .10
457 Dennis Rodman AS .20 .50
458 Reggie Lewis AS .02 .10
459 Joe Dumars AS .08 .25
460 Mark Price AS .02 .10
461 Brad Daugherty AS .02 .10
462 Kevin Willis AS .02 .10
463 Clyde Drexler AS .08 .25
464 Magic Johnson AS .30 .75
465 Chris Mullin AS .08 .25
466 Karl Malone AS .20 .50
467 David Robinson AS .20 .50
468 Tim Hardaway AS .20 .50
469 Jeff Hornacek AS .02 .10
470 John Stockton AS .08 .25
471 Dikembe Mutombo AS UER .08 .25
472 Hakeem Olajuwon AS .20 .50
473 James Worthy AS .08 .25
474 Otis Thorpe AS .02 .10
475 Dan Majerle AS .02 .10
476 Cedric Ceballos SD CL .02 .10
477 Nick Anderson SD .02 .10
478 Stacey Augmon SD .08 .25
479 Cedric Ceballos SD .02 .10
480 Larry Johnson SD .20 .50
481 Shawn Kemp SD .25 .60
482 John Starks SD .08 .25
483 Doug West SD .02 .10
484 Craig Hodges LD .02 .10
485 LaBradford Smith RC .02 .10
486 Winston Garland .02 .10
487 David Benoit RC .08 .25
488 John Bagley .02 .10
489 Mark Macon RC .02 .10
490 Mitch Richmond .08 .25
491 Luc Longley RC .08 .25
492 Sedale Threatt .02 .10
493 Doug Smith RC .02 .10
494 Travis Mays .02 .10
495 Xavier McDaniel .02 .10
496 Brian Shaw .02 .10
497 Stanley Roberts RC .02 .10
498 Blair Rasmussen .02 .10
499 Brian Williams RC .20 .50
500 Checklist Card .02 .10

1991-92 Upper Deck Award Winner Holograms

These holograms feature NBA statistical leaders in nine different categories. The first six holograms were random inserts in 1991-92 Upper Deck low series foil and jumbo packs, while the last three were inserted in high series foil and jumbo packs. The standard-size holograms have the player's name and award received in the lower right corner on the front. The back has a color player photo and a summary of the player's performance. The cards are numbered on the back with an "AW" prefix before the number.

COMPLETE SET (9) 5.00 12.00
RANDOM INSERTS IN BOTH SERIES PACKS
AW1 Michael Jordan 3.00 8.00
AW2 Alvin Robertson .10 .25
AW3 John Stockton .30 .75
AW4 Michael Jordan 3.00 8.00
AW5 Detlef Schrempf .15 .40
AW6 David Robinson .60 1.50
AW7 Derrick Coleman .15 .40
AW8 Hakeem Olajuwon .50 1.25
AW9 Dennis Rodman .60 1.50

1991-92 Upper Deck Rookie Standouts

Inserted one per jumbo and locker pack in both the low and high series, fronts of this standard-size 40-card set feature color action player photos, bordered on the right and below by a hardwood basketball court and with the "'91-92 Rookie Standouts" emblem in the lower right corner. The back features a second color player photo and player profile.

COMPLETE SET (40) 7.50 15.00
COMPLETE SERIES 1 (20) 2.50 5.00
COMPLETE SERIES 2 (20) 5.00 10.00
R1 Gary Payton 1.00 2.50
R2 Dennis Scott .15 .40
R3 Kendall Gill .25 .60
R4 Felton Spencer .08 .25
R5 Bo Kimble .08 .25
R6 Willie Burton .08 .25
R7 Tyrone Hill .15 .40
R8 Loy Vaught .15 .40
R9 Travis Mays .08 .25
R10 Derrick Coleman .25 .60
R11 Duane Causwell .08 .25
R12 Dee Brown .08 .25
R13 Gerald Glass .08 .25
R14 Jayson Williams .25 .60
R15 Elden Campbell .15 .40
R16 Negele Knight .08 .25
R17 Chris Jackson .08 .25
R18 Danny Ferry .08 .25
R19 Tony Smith .08 .25
R20 Cedric Ceballos .25 .60
R21 Victor Alexander .08 .25
R22 Terrell Brandon .75 2.00
R23 Rick Fox .25 .60
R24 Stacey Augmon .25 .60
R25 Mark Macon .08 .25
R26 Larry Johnson 1.00 2.50
R27 Paul Graham .08 .25
R28 Stanley Roberts UER .08 .25
R29 Dikembe Mutombo 1.00 2.50
R30 Robert Pack .08 .25
R31 Doug Smith .08 .25
R32 Steve Smith 1.00 2.50
R33 Billy Owens .25 .60
R34 David Benoit .15 .40
R35 Brian Williams .25 .60
R36 Kenny Anderson .50 1.25
R37 Greg Anthony .25 .60
R38 Dale Davis .25 .60
R39 Larry Stewart .08 .25
R40 Mike Iuzzolino .08 .25

1991-92 Upper Deck Jerry West Heroes

This ten-card insert set was randomly inserted in Upper Deck's high series basketball foil packs. Also included in the packs were 2,500 checklist cards autographed by West. The fronts of the standard-size cards capture memorable moments from his college and professional career. The player photos are cut out and superimposed over a jump ball circle on a hardwood basketball floor design. The card backs present commentary.

COMMON WEST (1-9) .50 1.25
RANDOM INSERTS IN HI SERIES PACKS
AU Jerry West AU/2500 20.00 50.00
NNO Jerry West Cover .75 2.00

1991-92 Upper Deck Jerry West Box Bottoms

These oversized cards, measuring approximately 5" by 7", are actually the bottom panel of the 1991-92 Upper Deck high number series basketball wax/foil boxes. Except for the size and the blank backs, these waxbox bottoms are identical to the first eight cards in the Jerry West Basketball Heroes insert set.

COMPLETE SET (8) 2.00 5.00
COMMON CARD (1-8) .30 .75

1992-93 Upper Deck

The complete 1992-93 Upper Deck basketball set consists of 510 standard-size cards issued in two series of 310 and 200 cards, respectively. High series cards are slightly tougher to find (compared to the low numbers) because high series packs contained a mix of high and low series cards. For both series, cards were issued in 15-card hobby and retail foil packs, 27-card locker packs and 27-card jumbo packs. No factory sets were produced by Upper Deck for this issue. Both series were also distributed through 27-card Locker packs. Card number 1A (available only in low series packs) is a "Trade Upper Deck" card that the collector could trade to Upper Deck for a Shaquille O'Neal mail-away trade card beginning on Jan. 1, 1993. The offer expired June 30, 1993. The fronts feature color action player photos with white borders. The team name is gold-foil stamped across the top of the picture. The border design at the bottom consists of a team colored stripe that shades from one team color to the other with diagonal stripes within the larger stripe that add texture. The entire design is edged in gold foil. The right end is off-set slightly by the Upper Deck logo. The backs show an action player photo that runs down the left side of the card. The right side displays statistics printed on a ghosted NBA logo. Topical subsets featured include NBA Draft (2-21), Team Checklists (35-61), and Scoring Threats (62-66). The set also includes two art cards (67-68) and one Stay in School card (69). Second series subsets featured are Team Fact Cards (350-376), NBA East All-Star Game (421-433), NBA West All-Star Game (434-445), In Your Face (446-454), Top Prospects (455-482), NBA Game Faces (483-497), Scoring Threats (498-505), and Fanimation (506-510). The cards are numbered on the back. Rookie Cards of note include Doug Christie (second series SP), Tom Gugliotta, Jim Jackson (second series SP), Christian Laettner, Alonzo Mourning, Shaquille O'Neal (second series SP), Latrell Sprewell and Clarence Weatherspoon. A card commemorating the retirement of Larry Bird and Magic Johnson (SP1) and the 20,000th point scored by Dominique Wilkins and Michael Jordan (SP2) were first and second series inserts, respectively. There were inserted at a rate of one in 72 packs. The basic card numbers of Jordan (23), Magic (32) and Bird (33) represent their uniform numbers.

COMPLETE SET (514) 40.00 80.00
COMPLETE LO SERIES (311) 10.00 20.00
COMPLETE HI SERIES (203) 20.00 40.00
SP1: SER.1 STATED ODDS 1:72
SP2: SER.2 STATED ODDS 1:72
1 Shaquille O'Neal SP RC 6.00 15.00
1A Draft Trade Card .10 .30
1B Shaquille O'Neal TRADE 6.00 15.00
1AX Draft Trade Stamped .10 .30
2 Alonzo Mourning RC .75 2.00
3 Christian Laettner RC .25 .60
4 LaPhonso Ellis RC .10 .30
5 Clarence Weatherspoon RC .10 .30
6 Adam Keefe RC .02 .10
7 Robert Horry RC .15 .40
8 Harold Miner RC .10 .30
9 Bryant Stith RC .05 .15
10 Malik Sealy RC .05 .15
11 Anthony Peeler RC .05 .15
12 Randy Woods RC .02 .10
13 Tracy Murray RC .05 .15
14 Tom Gugliotta RC .40 1.00
15 Hubert Davis RC .05 .15
16 Don MacLean RC .02 .10
17 Lee Mayberry RC .02 .10
18 Corey Williams RC .02 .10
19 Sean Rooks RC .02 .10
20 Todd Day RC .05 .15
21 B.Stith/L.Ellis CL .10 .30
22 Jeff Hornacek .05 .15
23 Michael Jordan 1.50 4.00
24 John Salley .02 .10
25 Andre Turner .02 .10
26 Charles Barkley .20 .50
27 Anthony Frederick .02 .10
28 Mario Elie .05 .15
29 Olden Polynice .02 .10
30 Rodney Monroe .02 .10
31 Tim Perry .02 .10
32 Doug Christie SP RC .40 1.00
32A Magic Johnson SP .75 2.00
33 Jim Jackson SP RC 1.00 2.50

33A Larry Bird SP 1.00 2.50
34 Randy White .02 .10
35 Frank Brickowski TC .02 .10
36 Michael Adams TC .02 .10
37 Scottie Pippen TC .20 .50
38 Mark Price TC .02 .10
39 Robert Parish TC .02 .10
40 Danny Manning TC .02 .10
41 Kevin Willis TC .02 .10
42 Glen Rice TC .05 .15
43 Kendall Gill TC .02 .10
44 Karl Malone TC .10 .30
45 Mitch Richmond TC .10 .30
46 Patrick Ewing TC .10 .30
47 Sam Perkins TC .02 .10
48 Dennis Scott TC .02 .10
49 Derek Harper TC .02 .10
50 Drazen Petrovic TC .02 .10
51 Reggie Williams TC .02 .10
52 Rik Smits TC .02 .10
53 Joe Dumars TC .05 .15
54 Otis Thorpe TC .02 .10
55 Johnny Dawkins TC .02 .10
56 Sean Elliott TC .02 .10
57 Kevin Johnson TC .05 .15
58 Ricky Pierce TC .02 .10
59 Doug West TC .02 .10
60 Terry Porter TC .02 .10
61 Tim Hardaway TC .10 .30
62 M.Jordan/S.Pippen ST .40 1.00
63 K.Gill/L.Johnson ST .10 .30
64 T.Chambers/K.Johnson ST .05 .15
65 T.Hardaway/C.Mullin ST .05 .15
66 K.Malone/J.Stockton ST .10 .30
67 Michael Jordan MVP .75 2.00
68 Stacey Augmon 6 MIL .02 .10
69 Bob Lanier .05 .15
70 Alaa Abdelnaby .02 .10
71 Andrew Lang .02 .10
72 Larry Krystkowiak .02 .10
73 Gerald Wilkins .02 .10
74 Rod Strickland .10 .30
75 Danny Ainge .05 .15
76 Chris Corchiani .02 .10
77 Jeff Grayer .02 .10
78 Eric Murdock .02 .10
79 Rex Chapman .02 .10
80 LaBradford Smith .02 .10
81 Jay Humphries .02 .10
82 David Robinson .20 .50
83 William Bedford .02 .10
84 James Edwards .02 .10
85 Danny Schayes .02 .10
86 Lloyd Daniels RC .02 .10
87 Blue Edwards .02 .10
88 Dale Ellis .02 .10
89 Rolando Blackman .02 .10
90 Michael Jordan CL .10 .30
91 Rik Smits .05 .15
92 Terry Davis .02 .10
93 Bill Cartwright .02 .10
94 Avery Johnson .02 .10
95 Micheal Williams .02 .10
96 Spud Webb .05 .15
97 Benoit Benjamin .02 .10
98 Derek Harper .05 .15
99 Matt Bullard .02 .10
100A Tyrone Corbin ERR Heat .40 1.00
100B Tyrone Corbin COR Jazz .02 .10
101 Doc Rivers .05 .15
102 Tony Smith .02 .10
103 Doug West .02 .10
104 Kevin Duckworth .02 .10
105 Luc Longley .05 .15
106 Antoine Carr .02 .10
107 Clifford Robinson .05 .15
108 Grant Long .02 .10
109 Terry Porter .02 .10
110A Steve Smith ERR Jazz 4.00 10.00
110B Steve Smith COR .15 .40
111 Brian Williams .02 .10
112 Karl Malone .20 .50
113 Reggie Williams .02 .10
114 Tom Chambers .02 .10
115 Winston Garland .02 .10
116 John Stockton .10 .30
117 Chris Jackson .02 .10
118 Mike Brown .02 .10
119 Kevin Johnson .10 .30
120 Reggie Lewis .05 .15
121 Bimbo Coles .02 .10
122 Drazen Petrovic .02 .10
123 Reggie Miller .10 .30
124 Derrick Coleman .05 .15
125 Chuck Person .02 .10
126 Glen Rice .10 .30
127 Kenny Anderson .10 .30
128 Willie Burton .02 .10
129 Chris Morris .02 .10
130 Patrick Ewing .10 .30
131 Sean Elliott .05 .15
132 Clyde Drexler .10 .30
133 Scottie Pippen .40 1.00
134 Pooh Richardson .02 .10
135 Horace Grant .05 .15
136 Hakeem Olajuwon .20 .50
137 John Paxson .02 .10
138 Kendall Gill .05 .15
139 Michael Adams .02 .10
140 Otis Thorpe .05 .15
141 Dennis Scott .05 .15
142 Stacey Augmon .05 .15
143 Robert Pack .02 .10
144 Kevin Willis .02 .10
145 Jerome Kersey .02 .10
146 Paul Graham .02 .10
147 Stanley Roberts .02 .10
148 Dominique Wilkins .10 .30
149 Scott Skiles .02 .10
150 Rumeal Robinson .02 .10
151 Mookie Blaylock .05 .15
152 Elden Campbell .05 .15
153 Chris Dudley .02 .10
154 Sedale Threatt .02 .10
155 Tate George .02 .10
156 James Worthy .10 .30
157 B.J. Armstrong .02 .10
158 Gary Payton .25 .60
159 Ledell Eackles .02 .10
160 Sam Perkins .05 .15
161 Nick Anderson .05 .15
162 Mitch Richmond .10 .30
163 Buck Williams .05 .15
164 Blair Rasmussen .02 .10
165 Vern Fleming .02 .10
166 Duane Ferrell .02 .10
167 George McCloud .02 .10
168 Terry Cummings .05 .15
169 Detlef Schrempf .05 .15
170 Willie Anderson .02 .10
171 Scott Williams .02 .10
172 Vernon Maxwell .02 .10
173 Todd Lichti .02 .10
174 David Benoit .02 .10
175 Marcus Liberty .02 .10
176 Kenny Smith .02 .10
177 Dan Majerle .05 .15
178 Jeff Malone .02 .10
179 Robert Parish .05 .15
180 Mark Eaton .02 .10
181 Rony Seikaly .02 .10
182 Tony Campbell .02 .10
183 Kevin McHale .10 .30
184 Thurl Bailey .02 .10
185 Kevin Edwards .02 .10
186 Gerald Glass .02 .10
187 Hersey Hawkins .05 .15
188 Sam Mitchell .02 .10
189 Brian Shaw .02 .10
190 Felton Spencer .02 .10
191 Mark Macon .02 .10
192 Jerry Reynolds .02 .10
193 Dale Davis .02 .10
194 Sleepy Floyd .02 .10
195 A.C. Green .05 .15
196 Terry Catledge .02 .10
197 Byron Scott .05 .15
198 Sam Bowie .02 .10
199 Vlade Divac .05 .15
200 Michael Jordan CL .10 .30
201 Brad Lohaus .02 .10
202 Johnny Newman .02 .10
203 Gary Grant .02 .10
204 Sidney Green .02 .10
205 Frank Brickowski .02 .10
206 Anthony Bowie .02 .10
207 Duane Causwell .02 .10
208 A.J. English .02 .10
209 Mark Aguirre .02 .10
210 Jon Koncak .02 .10
211 Kevin Gamble .02 .10
212 Craig Ehlo .02 .10
213 Herb Williams .05 .15
214 Cedric Ceballos .05 .15
215 Mark Jackson .05 .15
216 John Bagley .02 .10
217 Ron Anderson .02 .10
218 John Battle .02 .10
219 Kevin Lynch .02 .10
220 Donald Hodge .02 .10
221 Chris Gatling .02 .10
222 Muggsy Bogues .05 .15
223 Bill Laimbeer .05 .15
224 Anthony Bonner .02 .10
225 Fred Roberts .02 .10
226 Larry Stewart .02 .10
227 Darrell Walker .02 .10
228 Larry Smith .02 .10
229 Billy Owens .05 .15
230 Vinnie Johnson .02 .10
231 Johnny Dawkins .02 .10
232 Rick Fox .05 .15
233 Travis Mays .02 .10
234 Mark Price .02 .10
235 Derrick McKey .02 .10
236 Greg Anthony .02 .10
237 Doug Smith .02 .10
238 Alec Kessler .02 .10
239 Anthony Mason .10 .30
240 Shawn Kemp .25 .60
241 Jim Les .02 .10
242 Dennis Rodman .25 .60
243 Lionel Simmons .02 .10
244 Pervis Ellison .02 .10
245 Terrell Brandon .10 .30
246 Mark Bryant .02 .10
247 Brad Daugherty .02 .10
248 Scott Brooks .02 .10
249 Sarunas Marciulionis .02 .10
250 Danny Ferry .02 .10
251 Loy Vaught .02 .10
252 Dee Brown .02 .10
253 Alvin Robertson .02 .10
254 Charles Smith .02 .10
255 Dikembe Mutombo .15 .40
256 Greg Kite .02 .10
257 Ed Pinckney .02 .10
258 Ron Harper .05 .15
259 Elliot Perry .02 .10
260 Rafael Addison .02 .10
261 Tim Hardaway .15 .40
262 Randy Brown .02 .10
263 Isiah Thomas .10 .30
264 Victor Alexander .02 .10
265 Wayman Tisdale .02 .10
266 Harvey Grant .02 .10
267 Mike Iuzzolino .02 .10
268 J.Dumars/M.Jordan .10 .30
269 Xavier McDaniel .02 .10
270 Jeff Sanders .02 .10
271 Danny Manning .05 .15
272 Jayson Williams .05 .15
273 Ricky Pierce .02 .10
274 Will Perdue .02 .10
275 Dana Barros .02 .10
276 Randy Breuer .02 .10
277 Manute Bol .02 .10
278 Negele Knight .02 .10
279 Rodney McCray .02 .10
280 Greg Sutton .02 .10
281 L.Nance/M.Jordan .02 .10
282 John Starks .05 .15
283 Pete Chilcutt .02 .10
284 Kenny Gattison .02 .10
285 S.King/M.Jordan .02 .10
286 Bernard King .02 .10
287 Larry Johnson .15 .40
288 John Williams .02 .10
289 Dell Curry .02 .10
290 Orlando Woolridge .02 .10
291 Nate McMillan .02 .10
292 Terry Mills .02 .10
293 Sherman Douglas .02 .10
294 Charles Shackleford .02 .10
295 Ken Norman .02 .10
296 LaSalle Thompson .02 .10
297 Chris Mullin .10 .30
298 Eddie Johnson .02 .10
299 Armon Gilliam .02 .10
300 Michael Cage .02 .10
301 Moses Malone .10 .30
302 Charles Oakley .05 .15
303 David Wingate .02 .10
304 Steve Kerr .05 .15
305 Tyrone Hill .02 .10
306 Mark West .02 .10
307 Fat Lever .02 .10
308 J.R. Reid .02 .10
309 Ed Nealy .02 .10
310 Michael Jordan CL .10 .30
311 Alaa Abdelnaby .02 .10
312 Stacey Augmon .05 .15
313 Anthony Avent RC .02 .10
314 Walter Bond RC .02 .10
315 Byron Houston RC .02 .10
316 Rick Mahorn .02 .10
317 Sam Mitchell .02 .10
318 Mookie Blaylock .05 .15
319 Lance Blanks .02 .10
320 John Williams .02 .10
321 Rolando Blackman .02 .10
322 Danny Ainge .05 .15
323 Gerald Glass .02 .10
324 Robert Pack .02 .10
325 Oliver Miller RC .05 .15
326 Charles Smith .02 .10
327 Duane Ferrell .02 .10
328 Pooh Richardson .02 .10
329 Scott Brooks .02 .10
330 Walt Williams RC .10 .30
331 Andrew Lang .02 .10
332 Eric Murdock .02 .10
333 Vinny Del Negro .02 .10
334 Charles Barkley .20 .50
335 James Edwards .02 .10
336 Xavier McDaniel .02 .10
337 Paul Graham .02 .10
338 David Wingate .02 .10
339 Richard Dumas RC .02 .10
340 Jay Humphries .02 .10
341 Mark Jackson .05 .15
342 John Salley .02 .10
343 Jon Koncak .02 .10
344 Rodney McCray .02 .10
345 Chuck Person .02 .10
346 Mario Elie .05 .15
347 Frank Johnson .02 .10
348 Rumeal Robinson .02 .10
349 Terry Mills .02 .10
350 Kevin Willis TFC .02 .10
351 Dee Brown TFC .02 .10
352 Muggsy Bogues TFC .02 .10
353 B.J. Armstrong TFC .02 .10
354 Larry Nance TFC .02 .10
355 Doug Smith TFC .02 .10
356 Robert Pack TFC .02 .10
357 Joe Dumars TFC .05 .15
358 Sarunas Marciulionis TFC .02 .10
359 Kenny Smith TFC .02 .10
360 Pooh Richardson TFC .02 .10
361 Mark Jackson TFC .02 .10
362 Sedale Threatt TFC .02 .10
363 Grant Long TFC .02 .10
364 Eric Murdock TFC .02 .10
365 Doug West TFC .02 .10
366 Kenny Anderson TFC .05 .15
367 Anthony Mason TFC .05 .15
368 Nick Anderson TFC .02 .10
369 Jeff Hornacek TFC .02 .10
370 Dan Majerle TFC .02 .10
371 Clifford Robinson TFC .02 .10
372 Lionel Simmons TFC .02 .10
373 Dale Ellis TFC .02 .10
374 Gary Payton TFC .10 .30
375 David Benoit TFC .02 .10
376 Harvey Grant TFC .02 .10
377 Buck Johnson .02 .10
378 Brian Howard RC .02 .10
379 Travis Mays .02 .10
380 Jud Buechler .02 .10
381 Matt Geiger RC .05 .15
382 Bob McCann RC .02 .10
383 Cedric Ceballos .05 .15
384 Rod Strickland .10 .30
385 Kiki Vandeweghe .02 .10
386 Latrell Sprewell RC 1.00 2.50
387 Larry Krystkowiak .02 .10
388 Dale Ellis .02 .10
389 Trent Tucker .02 .10
390 Negele Knight .02 .10
391 Stanley Roberts .02 .10
392 Tony Campbell .02 .10
393 Tim Perry .02 .10
394 Doug Overton .02 .10
395 Dan Majerle .05 .15
396 Duane Cooper RC .02 .10
397 Kevin Willis .02 .10
398 Micheal Williams .02 .10
399 Avery Johnson .02 .10
400 Dominique Wilkins .10 .30
401 Chris Smith RC .02 .10
402 Blair Rasmussen .02 .10
403 Jeff Hornacek .05 .15
404 Blue Edwards .02 .10
405 Olden Polynice .02 .10
406 Jeff Grayer .02 .10
407 Tony Bennett RC .02 .10
408 Don MacLean .02 .10
409 Tom Chambers .02 .10
410 Keith Jennings RC .02 .10
411 Gerald Wilkins .02 .10
412 Kennard Winchester .02 .10
413 Doc Rivers .05 .15
414 Brent Price RC .05 .15
415 Mark West .02 .10
416 J.R. Reid .02 .10
417 Jon Barry RC .05 .15
418 Kevin Johnson .10 .30
419 Michael Jordan CL .10 .30
420 Michael Jordan CL .10 .30
421 Daugh/Price/Nance AS CL .02 .10
422 Scottie Pippen AS .20 .50
423 Larry Johnson AS .10 .30
424 Shaquille O'Neal AS 1.00 2.50
425 Michael Jordan AS .75 2.00
426 Isiah Thomas AS .05 .15
427 Brad Daugherty AS .02 .10
428 Joe Dumars AS .05 .15
429 Patrick Ewing AS .05 .15
430 Larry Nance AS .02 .10
431 Mark Price AS .02 .10
432 Detlef Schrempf AS .02 .10
433 Dominique Wilkins AS .05 .15
434 Karl Malone AS .10 .30
435 Charles Barkley AS .10 .30
436 David Robinson AS .10 .30
437 John Stockton AS .05 .15
438 Clyde Drexler AS .05 .15
439 Sean Elliott AS .02 .10
440 Tim Hardaway AS .10 .30
441 Shawn Kemp AS .10 .30
442 Dan Majerle AS .02 .10
443 Danny Manning AS .02 .10
444 Hakeem Olajuwon AS .10 .30
445 Terry Porter AS .02 .10
446 Harold Miner FACE .05 .15
447 David Benoit FACE .02 .10
448 Cedric Ceballos FACE .02 .10
449 Chris Jackson FACE .02 .10
450 Tim Perry FACE .02 .10
451 Kenny Smith FACE .02 .10
452 Clar.Weatherspoon FACE .10 .30
453A M.Jordan FACE 85 ERR 6.00 15.00
453B M.Jordan FACE 87 COR .75 2.00
454A D.Wilkins FACE 87 ERR 1.00 2.50
454B D.Wilkins FACE 85 COR .10 .30
455 D.Cooper/A.Peeler TP CL .02 .10
456 Adam Keefe TP .02 .10
457 Alonzo Mourning TP .20 .50
458 Jim Jackson TP .10 .30
459 Sean Rooks TP .02 .10
460 LaPhonso Ellis TP .05 .15
461 Bryant Stith TP .02 .10
462 Byron Houston TP .02 .10
463 Latrell Sprewell TP .10 .30
464 Robert Horry TP .05 .15
465 Malik Sealy TP .02 .10
466 Doug Christie TP .10 .30
467 Duane Cooper TP .02 .10
468 Anthony Peeler TP .02 .10
469 Harold Miner TP .02 .10
470 Todd Day TP .02 .10
471 Lee Mayberry TP .02 .10
472 Christian Laettner TP .10 .30
473 Hubert Davis TP .02 .10
474 Shaquille O'Neal TP 1.00 2.50
475 Clarence Weatherspoon TP .10 .30
476 Richard Dumas TP .02 .10
477 Oliver Miller TP .02 .10
478 Tracy Murray TP .02 .10
479 Walt Williams TP .05 .15
480 Lloyd Daniels TP .02 .10
481 Tom Gugliotta TP .10 .30
482 Brent Price TP .02 .10
483 Mark Aguirre GF .02 .10
484 Frank Brickowski GF .02 .10
485 Derrick Coleman GF .02 .10
486 Clyde Drexler GF .05 .15
487 Harvey Grant GF .02 .10
488 Michael Jordan GF .75 2.00
489 Karl Malone GF .10 .30
490 Xavier McDaniel GF .02 .10
491 Drazen Petrovic GF .02 .10
492 John Starks GF .02 .10
493 Robert Parish GF .02 .10
494 Christian Laettner GF .10 .30
495 Ron Harper GF .02 .10
496 David Robinson GF .10 .30
497 John Salley GF .02 .10
498 B.Daugherty/M.Price ST .02 .10
499 D.Mutombo/C.Jackson ST .10 .30
500 I.Thomas/J.Dumars ST .10 .30
501 H.Olajuwon/Thorpe ST .10 .30
502 D.Coleman/D.Petrovic ST .05 .15
503 T.Porter/C.Drexler ST .10 .30
504 L.Simmons/M.Richmond ST .05 .15
505 D.Robinson/S.Elliott ST .10 .30
506 Michael Jordan FAN .75 2.00
507 Larry Bird FAN .25 .60
508 Karl Malone FAN .10 .30
509 Dikembe Mutombo FAN .10 .30
510 L.Bird/M.Jordan FAN .40 1.00
SP1 L.Bird/M.Johnson Retire 1.25 3.00
SP2 D.Wilkins/M.Jordan 20K 2.50 6.00

1992-93 Upper Deck All-Division

Inserted one per second series red or gray jumbo pack, this 20-card standard-size set consists of Upper Deck's selection of the top five players in each of the NBA's four divisions. There is a special logo representing each division. The cards are arranged according to division as follows: Atlantic (1-5), Central (6-10), Midwest (11-15), and Pacific (16-20). The cards are numbered with an "AD" prefix. The fronts feature full-bleed, color, action player photos. A black and team color-coded bar outlined with gold foil carries the player's name and position. These cards can be distinguished by an All-Division Team icon in the lower left corner above the player's name. The backs display career highlights against a light blue panel. A U.S. map shows the player's division.

COMPLETE SET (20) 6.00 15.00
ONE PER HI SERIES JUMBO PACK
AD1 Shaquille O'Neal 3.00 8.00
AD2 Derrick Coleman .15 .40
AD3 Glen Rice .30 .75
AD4 Reggie Lewis .15 .40
AD5 Kenny Anderson .30 .75
AD6 Brad Daugherty .08 .20
AD7 Dominique Wilkins .30 .75
AD8 Larry Johnson .40 1.00
AD9 Michael Jordan 4.00 10.00
AD10 Mark Price .08 .20
AD11 David Robinson .50 1.25
AD12 Karl Malone .50 1.25
AD13 Sean Elliott .15 .40
AD14 John Stockton .30 .75
AD15 Derek Harper .15 .40
AD16 Kevin Duckworth .08 .20
AD17 Chris Mullin .30 .75
AD18 Charles Barkley .50 1.25
AD19 Tim Hardaway .40 1.00
AD20 Clyde Drexler .30 .75

1992-93 Upper Deck All-NBA

This ten-card standard-size set featuring the 1991-92 All-NBA team was issued one per 27-card low series Locker pack. Each plastic locker box contained four specially wrapped. The fronts feature full-bleed color action player photos with black bottom borders. The player's name is foil-stamped in the border, and the words "All-NBA Team" are foil-stamped at the top. Gold and silver foil stamping are used to designate the First (1-5) and Second Teams (6-10) respectively. The backs carry a close-up player photo and career summary. The cards are numbered on the back with an "AN" prefix.

COMPLETE SET (10) 6.00 15.00
ONE PER LO SERIES LOCKER PACK
AN1 Michael Jordan ! 4.00 10.00
AN2 Clyde Drexler .75 2.00
AN3 David Robinson 1.25 3.00
AN4 Karl Malone 1.25 3.00
AN5 Chris Mullin .75 2.00
AN6 John Stockton .75 2.00
AN7 Tim Hardaway 1.00 2.50
AN8 Patrick Ewing .75 2.00
AN9 Scottie Pippen 2.50 6.00
AN10 Charles Barkley 1.25 3.00

1992-93 Upper Deck All-Rookies

Randomly inserted in low series 15-card retail foil packs at a reported rate of one card for every twelve packs, this ten-card standard-size insert set features the top first-year players of the 1991-92 season. Card numbers 1-5 present the first team and card numbers 6-10 the second team. The cards are numbered with an "AR" prefix. The fronts feature full-bleed, color, action player photos. A gold and red bottom border design carries the player's name, position, the number team (first or second), and an NBA All-Rookie Team icon. The backs carry player profiles.

COMPLETE SET (10) 5.00 10.00
LO SERIES STATED ODDS 1:12 RETAIL
AR1 Larry Johnson 1.00 2.50
AR2 Dikembe Mutombo 1.00 2.50
AR3 Billy Owens .40 1.00
AR4 Steve Smith 1.00 2.50
AR5 Stacey Augmon .40 1.00
AR6 Rick Fox .40 1.00
AR7 Terrell Brandon .75 2.00
AR8 Larry Stewart .10 .30
AR9 Stanley Roberts .10 .30
AR10 Mark Macon .10 .30

1992-93 Upper Deck Award Winner Holograms

The 1992-93 Upper Deck Award Winner Holograms set features nine holograms depicting league leaders in various statistical categories. The set also honors 1991-92 award winners such as top Sixth Man, Rookie of the Year, Defensive Player of the Year and Most Valuable Player. Card numbers 1-6 were randomly inserted in all forms of low series packs while card numbers 7-9 were included in all forms of high series packs. The card numbers have an "AW" prefix. The fronts feature holographic cut-out images of the player against a game-action photo of the player. The player's name and award are displayed at the bottom. The backs carry vertical, color player photos. A light blue plaque-style panel contains information about the player and the award won.

COMPLETE SET (9) 8.00 20.00
COMPLETE LO SERIES (6) 5.00 12.00
COMPLETE HI SERIES (3) 3.00 8.00
LO/HI SERIES STATED ODDS 1:18 HOB/RET
AW1 Michael Jordan 4.00 10.00
AW2 John Stockton .30 .75
AW3 Dennis Rodman .60 1.50
AW4 Detlef Schrempf .20 .50
AW5 Larry Johnson .40 1.00
AW6 David Robinson .50 1.25
AW7 David Robinson .50 1.25
AW8 John Stockton .30 .75
AW9 Michael Jordan 4.00 10.00

1992-93 Upper Deck Larry Bird Heroes

Randomly inserted into all forms of high series packs, this ten-card standard-size set chronicles the career of Larry Bird from his college days at Indiana State University to pro stardom with the Boston Celtics. The color action player photos on the fronts are bordered on the left and bottom by black borders that carry the card subtitle and "Basketball Heroes, Larry Bird" respectively. On a background shading from white to green, brief summaries of Bird's career are presented on a center panel. The cards are numbered on the back in continuation of the Upper Deck Basketball Heroes.

COMMON BIRD (19-27) .30 .75
HI SERIES STATED ODDS 1:9
NNO Larry Bird .75 2.00

1992-93 Upper Deck Wilt Chamberlain Heroes

Randomly inserted in all types of low series packs, this ten-card standard-size set honors Wilt Chamberlain by highlighting various points in his career. Circular photos on the fronts depict Wilt from college, to the Globetrotter's to pro basketball. Information on the back corresponds to the portion of his career that is represented on front. The set is numbered in continuation of Upper Deck's Hero series.

COMMON CHAMBER. (10-18) .30 .75
LO SERIES STATED ODDS 1:9
NNO Wilt Chamberlain .50 1.25

1992-93 Upper Deck Wilt Chamberlain Box Bottom

Measuring approximately 5" by 7", this box bottom displays a color painting by artist Alan Studt. Four different images of Chamberlain are presented, each showing Wilt at a different stage of his career according to uniform (Kansas, Harlem Globetrotters, Philadelphia 76ers, and Los Angeles Lakers). The back is blank. The box bottom is unnumbered.

NNO Wilt Chamberlain .30 .75

1992-93 Upper Deck 15000 Point Club

Randomly inserted in 15-card high series hobby packs at a reported rate of one card per nine packs, this 20-card standard-size set spotlights then-active NBA players who had scored more than 15,000 points in their career. The fronts feature full-bleed color action player photos accented at the top and bottom by team color-coded stripes carrying the phrase "15,000 Point Club" and the player's name respectively. A gold 15,000-Point club logo at the lower left corner carries the season the player joined this elite club. The backs display a small player photo and year-by-year scoring totals. The cards are numbered with an "PC" prefix.

COMPLETE SET (20) 15.00 40.00
HI SERIES STATED ODDS 1:9 HOBBY
PC1 Dominique Wilkins 1.00 2.50
PC2 Kevin McHale 1.00 2.50
PC3 Robert Parish .50 1.25
PC4 Michael Jordan 10.00 25.00
PC5 Isiah Thomas 1.00 2.50
PC6 Mark Aguirre .30 .75
PC7 Kiki Vandeweghe .30 .75
PC8 James Worthy 1.00 2.50
PC9 Rolando Blackman .30 .75
PC10 Moses Malone 1.00 2.50
PC11 Charles Barkley 1.50 4.00
PC12 Tom Chambers .30 .75
PC13 Clyde Drexler 1.00 2.50
PC14 Terry Cummings .50 1.25
PC15 Eddie Johnson .30 .75
PC16 Karl Malone 1.50 4.00
PC17 Bernard King .30 .75
PC18 Larry Nance .30 .75
PC19 Jeff Malone .30 .75
PC20 Hakeem Olajuwon 1.50 4.00

1992-93 Upper Deck Foreign Exchange

Inserted one card per pack in second series 4-pack locker boxes, this ten-card standard-size set showcases foreign born players who are stars in the NBA. Each card uses the colors of the flag from the player's homeland as well as a "Foreign Exchange" logo. The cards are numbered with an "FE" prefix. The fronts carry full-bleed, color, action player photos. The player's name, position, and place of birth appear in border stripes at the bottom. The backs display either an action or close-up player photo on a pale beige panel along with a player profile. A small representation of the player's home flag appears at the lower right corner of the picture. The set is sequenced in alphabetical order.

COMPLETE SET (10) 7.50 15.00
ONE PER HI SERIES LOCKER PACK
FE1 Manute Bol .25 .60
FE2 Vlade Divac .75 2.00
FE3 Patrick Ewing 1.50 4.00
FE4 Sarunas Marciulionis .25 .60
FE5 Dikembe Mutombo 2.00 5.00
FE6 Hakeem Olajuwon 2.50 6.00
FE7 Drazen Petrovic .75 2.00
FE8 Detlef Schrempf .75 2.00
FE9 Rik Smits .75 2.00
FE10 Dominique Wilkins 1.50 4.00

1992-93 Upper Deck Rookie Standouts

Randomly inserted in high series retail and high series red jumbo packs at a reported rate of one card per nine packs, this 20-card standard-size set honors top rookies who made the most impact during the 1992-93 NBA season. The cards are numbered on the back with an "RS" prefix. The fronts feature full-bleed, color, action player photos. The player's name and position appear in a teal stripe across the bottom. A "Rookie Standouts" icon overlaps the stripe and the picture at the lower right corner. The backs have a vertical action photo and career highlights within a gold box. A red banner over a gold basketball icon accent the top of the box.

COMPLETE SET (20) 10.00 25.00
HI SERIES STATED ODDS 1:9 RET/JUM
RS1 Adam Keefe .05 .15
RS2 Alonzo Mourning 2.00 5.00
RS3 Sean Rooks .05 .15
RS4 LaPhonso Ellis .30 .75
RS5 Latrell Sprewell 1.25 3.00
RS6 Robert Horry .30 .75
RS7 Malik Sealy .15 .40
RS8 Anthony Peeler .15 .40
RS9 Harold Miner .15 .40
RS10 Anthony Avent .05 .15
RS11 Todd Day .15 .40
RS12 Lee Mayberry .05 .15
RS13 Christian Laettner .60 1.50
RS14 Hubert Davis .15 .40
RS15 Shaquille O'Neal 6.00 15.00
RS16 Clarence Weatherspoon .30 .75
RS17 Richard Dumas .05 .15
RS18 Walt Williams .30 .75
RS19 Lloyd Daniels .05 .15
RS20 Tom Gugliotta 1.00 2.50

1992-93 Upper Deck Team MVPs

This 28-card standard-size set honors a top player from each NBA team. One "Team MVP" card was inserted into each 1992-93 Upper Deck low series 27-card jumbo pack. Card fronts feature a photo that takes up most of the front. The only other feature on front is the player's name within a bottom border. Backs contain a photo with highlights. These cards are numbered on the back with a "TM" prefix.

COMPLETE SET (28) 15.00 40.00
ONE PER LO SERIES JUMBO PACK
TM1 Michael Jordan CL 8.00 20.00
TM2 Dominique Wilkins .75 2.00
TM3 Reggie Lewis .40 1.00
TM4 Kendall Gill .40 1.00
TM5 Michael Jordan 8.00 20.00
TM6 Brad Daugherty .10 .30
TM7 Derek Harper .40 1.00
TM8 Dikembe Mutombo 1.00 2.50
TM9 Isiah Thomas .75 2.00
TM10 Chris Mullin .75 2.00
TM11 Hakeem Olajuwon 1.25 3.00
TM12 Reggie Miller .75 2.00
TM13 Ron Harper .40 1.00
TM14 James Worthy .75 2.00
TM15 Rony Seikaly .10 .30
TM16 Alvin Robertson .10 .30
TM17 Pooh Richardson .10 .30
TM18 Derrick Coleman .40 1.00
TM19 Patrick Ewing .75 2.00
TM20 Scott Skiles .10 .30
TM21 Hersey Hawkins .40 1.00
TM22 Kevin Johnson .75 2.00
TM23 Clyde Drexler .75 2.00
TM24 Mitch Richmond .75 2.00
TM25 David Robinson 1.25 3.00
TM26 Ricky Pierce .10 .30
TM27 John Stockton .75 2.00
TM28 Pervis Ellison .10 .30

1992-93 Upper Deck Jerry West Selects

Randomly inserted in 15-card low series hobby packs at a reported rate of one card per nine packs, this 20-card standard-size set pays tribute to Jerry West's selection of NBA players who are the most dominant (or projected to be) in ten different basketball skills. The cards feature color action player photos bordered on the right edge by a white stripe containing the player's name. Two stripes border the bottom of the cards, a black stripe containing a gold foil facsimile autograph of Jerry West and the word "Select," and a gradated team-colored stripe. This second stripe contains the player's specific achievement. The backs show a smaller color action shot of the player above a pale gray panel containing comments by West. The right edge of the card has a 1/2" white border containing the player's name. A small cut-out action image of Jerry West appears at the lower right corner. Card numbers 1-10 feature his present selections for best in ten different categories while card numbers 11-20 are his future selections. The cards are numbered on the back with a "JW" prefix. The set includes four cards of Michael Jordan.

COMPLETE SET (20) 15.00 40.00
LO SERIES STATED ODDS 1:9 HOBBY
JW1 Michael Jordan 4.00 10.00
JW2 Dennis Rodman 1.50 4.00
JW3 David Robinson 1.25 3.00
JW4 Michael Jordan 4.00 10.00
JW5 Magic Johnson 2.50 6.00
JW6 Detlef Schrempf .40 1.00
JW7 Magic Johnson 4.00 10.00
JW8A Michael Jordan 4.00 10.00
JW8B Michael Jordan 4.00 10.00
Best All-Around Player
Jumbo/5000
JW9 Michael Jordan 4.00 10.00
JW10 Magic Johnson 4.00 10.00
JW11 Glen Rice .75 2.00
JW12 Dikembe Mutombo 1.00 2.50
JW13 Dikembe Mutombo 1.00 2.50
JW14 Stacey Augmon .40 1.00
JW15 Tim Hardaway 1.00 2.50
JW16 Shawn Kemp 1.50 4.00
JW17 Danny Manning .40 1.00
JW18 Larry Johnson 1.00 2.50
JW19 Reggie Lewis .40 1.00
JW20 Tim Hardaway 1.00 2.50

1993-94 Upper Deck

This 510-card standard-size UV-coated set was issued in two series of 255. The cards were issued in 12-card hobby and retail packs (36 per box), 22-card green and blue retail jumbo packs (first series only), 22-card red and purple retail jumbo packs (second series only) and 22-card hobby locker packs for both series. Card fronts feature glossy color player action photos on the fronts. The left and bottom borders (team colors) contain the team and player's name respectively. The backs feature another color action player photo at the top. At bottom, player stats are shaded in team colors. Topical subsets featured are the following: Season Leaders (166-177), NBA Playoffs Highlights (178-197), NBA Finals Highlights (198-209), Schedules (210-236), Signature Moves (237-251), Executive Board (421-435), Breakaway Threats (436-455), Game Images (456-465), Skylights (467-480), Top Prospects (482-497) and McDonald's Open (498-507). The cards are numbered on the back. The SP3 card was inserted randomly in all forms of first series packaging with the SP4 in the second series. Both cards were inserted at a rate of 1 in 72 packs. Rookie Cards of note include Vin Baker, Anfernee Hardaway, Allan Houston, Toni Kukoc, Jamal Mashburn, Nick Van Exel and Chris Webber.

COMPLETE SET (510) 15.00 30.00
COMPLETE SERIES 1 (255) 7.50 15.00
COMPLETE SERIES 2 (255) 7.50 15.00
SP3: SER.1 STATED ODDS 1:72
SP4: SER.2 STATED ODDS 1:72
1 Muggsy Bogues .05 .15
2 Kenny Anderson .05 .15
3 Dell Curry .01 .05
4 Charles Smith .01 .05
5 Chuck Person .01 .05
6 Chucky Brown .01 .05
7 Kevin Johnson .05 .15
8 Winston Garland .01 .05
9 John Salley .01 .05
10 Dale Ellis .01 .05
11 Otis Thorpe .05 .15
12 John Stockton .10 .30
13 Kendall Gill .05 .15
14 Randy White .01 .05
15 Mark Jackson .05 .15
16 Vlade Divac .05 .15
17 Scott Skiles .01 .05
18 Xavier McDaniel .01 .05
19 Jeff Hornacek .05 .15
20 Stanley Roberts .01 .05
21 Harold Miner .01 .05
22 Terrell Brandon .05 .15
23 Michael Jordan 1.50 4.00
24 Jim Jackson .05 .15
25 Keith Askins .01 .05
26 Corey Williams .01 .05
27 David Benoit .01 .05
28 Charles Oakley .05 .15
29 Michael Adams .01 .05
30 Clarence Weatherspoon .01 .05
31 Jon Koncak .01 .05
32 Gerald Wilkins .01 .05
33 Anthony Bowie .01 .05
34 Willie Burton .01 .05
35 Stacey Augmon .01 .05
36 Doc Rivers .05 .15
37 Luc Longley .05 .15
38 Dee Brown .01 .05
39 Litterial Green .01 .05
40 Dan Majerle .05 .15
41 Doug West .01 .05
42 Joe Dumars .10 .30
43 Dennis Scott .01 .05
44 Mahmoud Abdul-Rauf .01 .05
45 Mark Eaton .01 .05
46 Danny Ferry .01 .05
47 Kenny Smith .01 .05
48 Ron Harper .05 .15
49 Adam Keefe .01 .05
50 David Robinson .20 .50
51 John Starks .05 .15
52 Jeff Malone .01 .05
53 Vern Fleming .01 .05
54 Olden Polynice .01 .05
55 Dikembe Mutombo .10 .30
56 Chris Morris .01 .05
57 Paul Graham .01 .05
58 Richard Dumas .01 .05
59 J.R. Reid .01 .05
60 Brad Daugherty .01 .05
61 Blue Edwards .01 .05
62 Mark Macon .01 .05
63 Latrell Sprewell .30 .75
64 Mitch Richmond .10 .30
65 David Wingate .01 .05
66 LaSalle Thompson .01 .05
67 Sedale Threatt .01 .05
68 Larry Krystkowiak .01 .05
69 John Paxson .01 .05
70 Frank Brickowski .01 .05
71 Duane Causwell .01 .05
72 Fred Roberts .01 .05
73 Rod Strickland .05 .15
74 Willie Anderson .01 .05
75 Thurl Bailey .01 .05
76 Ricky Pierce .01 .05
77 Todd Day .01 .05
78 Hot Rod Williams .01 .05
79 Danny Ainge .05 .15
80 Mark West .01 .05
81 Marcus Liberty .01 .05
82 Keith Jennings .01 .05
83 Derrick Coleman .05 .15
84 Larry Stewart .01 .05
85 Tracy Murray .01 .05
86 Robert Horry .05 .15
87 Derek Harper .05 .15
88 Scott Hastings .01 .05
89 Sam Perkins .05 .15
90 Clyde Drexler .10 .30
91 Brent Price .01 .05
92 Chris Mullin .10 .30
93 Rafael Addison .01 .05
94 Tyrone Corbin .01 .05
95 Sarunas Marciulionis .01 .05
96 Antoine Carr .01 .05
97 Tony Bennett .01 .05
98 Sam Mitchell .01 .05
99 Lionel Simmons .01 .05
100 Tim Perry .01 .05
101 Horace Grant .05 .15
102 Tom Hammonds .01 .05
103 Walter Bond .01 .05
104 Detlef Schrempf .05 .15
105 Terry Porter .01 .05
106 Danny Schayes .01 .05
107 Rumeal Robinson .01 .05
108 Gerald Glass .01 .05
109 Mike Gminski .01 .05
110 Terry Mills .01 .05
111 Loy Vaught .01 .05
112 Jim Les .01 .05
113 Byron Houston .01 .05
114 Randy Brown .01 .05
115 Anthony Avent .01 .05
116 Donald Hodge .01 .05
117 Kevin Willis .01 .05
118 Robert Pack .01 .05
119 Dale Davis .01 .05
120 Grant Long .01 .05
121 Anthony Bonner .01 .05
122 Chris Smith .01 .05
123 Elden Campbell .01 .05
124 Clifford Robinson .05 .15
125 Sherman Douglas .01 .05
126 Alvin Robertson .01 .05
127 Rolando Blackman .01 .05
128 Malik Sealy .01 .05
129 Ed Pinckney .01 .05
130 Anthony Peeler .01 .05
131 Scott Brooks .01 .05
132 Rik Smits .05 .15
133 Derrick McKey .01 .05
134 Alaa Abdelnaby .01 .05
135 Rex Chapman .01 .05
136 Tony Campbell .01 .05
137 John Williams .01 .05
138 Vincent Askew .01 .05

Card	Low	High
139 LaBradford Smith	.01	.05
140 Vinny Del Negro	.01	.05
141 Darrell Walker	.01	.05
142 James Worthy	.10	.30
143 Jeff Turner	.01	.05
144 Duane Ferrell	.01	.05
145 Larry Smith	.01	.05
146 Eddie Johnson	.01	.05
147 Chris Gatling	.01	.05
148 Buck Williams	.01	.05
149 Donald Royal	.01	.05
150 Dino Radja RC	.01	.05
151 Johnny Dawkins	.01	.05
152 Tim Legler RC	.01	.05
153 Bill Laimbeer	.01	.05
154 Glen Rice	.05	.15
155 Bill Cartwright	.01	.05
156 Luther Wright RC	.01	.05
157 Rex Walters RC	.01	.05
158 Doug Edwards RC	.01	.05
159 George Lynch RC	.01	.05
160 Chris Mills RC	.10	.30
161 Sam Cassell RC	.50	1.25
162 Nick Van Exel RC	.40	1.00
163 Shawn Bradley RC	.10	.30
164 Calbert Cheaney RC	.05	.15
165 Corie Blount RC	.01	.05
166 Michael Jordan SL	.75	2.00
167 Dennis Rodman SL	.10	.30
168 John Stockton SL	.05	.15
169 B.J. Armstrong SL	.01	.05
170 Hakeem Olajuwon SL	.10	.30
171 Michael Jordan SL	.75	2.00
172 Cedric Ceballos SL	.01	.05
173 Mark Price SL	.01	.05
174 Charles Barkley SL	.10	.30
175 Clifford Robinson SL	.01	.05
176 Hakeem Olajuwon SL	.10	.30
177 Shaquille O'Neal SL	.25	.60
178 R.Miller/C.Oakley PO	.05	.15
179 R.Fox/K.Gattison PO	.01	.05
180 M.Jordan/S.Augmon PO	.40	1.00
181 Brad Daugherty PO	.01	.05
182 O.Miller/B.Scott PO	.01	.05
183 D.Robinson/S.Elliott PO	.10	.30
184 K.Smith/M.Jackson PO	.01	.05
185 Eddie Johnson PO	.01	.05
186 A.Mason/P.Ewing/Zo PO	.10	.30
187 M.Jordan/G.Wilkins PO	.40	1.00
188 Oliver Miller PO	.01	.05
189 S.Perkins/H.Olajuwon PO	.10	.30
190 Bill Cartwright PO	.01	.05
191 Kevin Johnson PO	.05	.15
192 Dan Majerle PO	.01	.05
193 Michael Jordan PO	.75	2.00
194 L.Johnson/Bogues PO	.01	.05
195 Reggie Miller PO	.05	.15
196 J.Starks/S.Pippen PO	.10	.30
197 Charles Barkley PO	.10	.30
198 Michael Jordan FIN	.75	2.00
199 Scottie Pippen FIN	.20	.50
200 Kevin Johnson FIN	.01	.05
201 Michael Jordan FIN	.75	2.00
202 Richard Dumas FIN	.01	.05
203 Horace Grant FIN	.01	.05
204 Michael Jordan FIN	.75	2.00
205 S.Pippen/C.Barkley FIN	.10	.30
206 John Paxson FIN	.01	.05
207 B.J. Armstrong FIN	.01	.05
208 1992-93 Bulls FIN	.10	.30
209 1992-93 Suns FIN	.01	.05
210 K.Willis SKED	.01	.05
211 B.Shaw SKED	.01	.05
212 Charlotte Hornets SKED	.01	.05
213 M.Jordan/Group SKED	.40	1.00
214 M.Price SKED	.01	.05
215 J.Jackson/S.Rooks SKED	.01	.05
216 D.Mutombo SKED	.05	.15
217 Detroit Pistons SKED	.05	.15
218 Golden State Warriors SKED	.01	.05
219 H.Olajuwon SKED	.10	.30
220 Indiana Pacers SKED	.01	.05
221 L.A. Clippers SKED	.01	.05
222 L.A. Lakers SKED	.01	.05
223 Miami Heat SKED	.05	.15
224 Milwaukee Bucks SKED	.01	.05
225 Minnesota Timberwolves SKED	.01	.05
226 New Jersey Nets SKED	.01	.05
227 New York Knicks SKED	.01	.05
228 S.O'Neal/Group SKED	.15	.40
229 Philadelphia 76ers SKED	.01	.05
230 C.Barkley/Group SKED	.10	.30
231 Portland Trail Blazers SKED	.01	.05
232 Sacramento Kings SKED	.01	.05
233 D.Robinson/Group SKED	.10	.30
234 S.Kemp/G.Payton SKED	.05	.15
235 Utah Jazz SKED	.01	.05
236 Gugliotta/Adams SKED	.05	.15
237 Michael Jordan SM	.75	2.00
238 Clyde Drexler SM	.05	.15
239 Tim Hardaway SM	.05	.15
240 Dominique Wilkins SM	.05	.15
241 Brad Daugherty SM	.01	.05
242 Chris Mullin SM	.05	.15
243 Kenny Anderson SM	.01	.05
244 Patrick Ewing SM	.05	.15
245 Isiah Thomas SM	.05	.15
246 Dikembe Mutombo SM	.05	.15
247 Danny Manning SM	.01	.05
248 David Robinson SM	.10	.30
249 Karl Malone SM	.10	.30
250 James Worthy SM	.05	.15
251 Shawn Kemp SM	.10	.30
252 Checklist 1-64	.01	.05
253 Checklist 65-128	.01	.05
254 Checklist 129-192	.01	.05
255 Checklist 193-255	.01	.05
256 Patrick Ewing	.10	.30
257 B.J. Armstrong	.01	.05
258 Oliver Miller	.01	.05
259 Jud Buechler	.01	.05
260 Pooh Richardson	.01	.05
261 Victor Alexander	.01	.05
262 Kevin Gamble	.01	.05
263 Doug Smith	.01	.05
264 Isiah Thomas	.10	.30
265 Doug Christie	.05	.15
266 Mark Bryant	.01	.05
267 Lloyd Daniels	.01	.05
268 Micheal Williams	.01	.05
269 Nick Anderson	.05	.15
270 Tom Gugliotta	.10	.30
271 Kenny Gattison	.01	.05
272 Vernon Maxwell	.01	.05
273 Terry Cummings	.01	.05
274 Karl Malone	.20	.50
275 Rick Fox	.01	.05
276 Matt Bullard	.01	.05
277 Johnny Newman	.01	.05
278 Mark Price	.01	.05
279 Mookie Blaylock	.05	.15
280 Charles Barkley	.20	.50
281 Larry Nance	.01	.05
282 Walt Williams	.01	.05
283 Brian Shaw	.01	.05
284 Robert Parish	.05	.15
285 Pervis Ellison	.01	.05
286 Spud Webb	.05	.15
287 Hakeem Olajuwon	.20	.50
288 Jerome Kersey	.01	.05
289 Carl Herrera	.01	.05
290 Dominique Wilkins	.10	.30
291 Billy Owens	.01	.05
292 Greg Anthony	.01	.05
293 Nate McMillan	.01	.05
294 Christian Laettner	.05	.15
295 Gary Payton	.20	.50
296 Steve Smith	.10	.30
297 Anthony Mason	.05	.15
298 Sean Rooks	.01	.05
299 Toni Kukoc RC	.50	1.25
300 Shaquille O'Neal	.60	1.50
301 Jay Humphries	.01	.05
302 Sleepy Floyd	.01	.05
303 Bimbo Coles	.01	.05
304 John Battle	.01	.05
305 Shawn Kemp	.20	.50
306 Scott Williams	.01	.05
307 Wayman Tisdale	.01	.05
308 Rony Seikaly	.01	.05
309 Reggie Miller	.10	.30
310 Scottie Pippen	.40	1.00
311 Chris Webber RC	1.25	3.00
312 Trevor Wilson	.01	.05
313 Derek Strong RC	.01	.05
314 Bobby Hurley RC	.05	.15
315 Herb Williams	.01	.05
316 Rex Walters	.01	.05
317 Doug Edwards	.01	.05
318 Ken Williams	.01	.05
319 Jon Barry	.01	.05
320 Joe Courtney RC	.01	.05
321 Ervin Johnson RC	.05	.15
322 Sam Cassell	.10	.30
323 Tim Hardaway	.10	.30
324 Steve Kerr	.01	.05
325 Pete Chilcutt	.05	.15
326 Doug Overton	.01	.05
327 Reggie Williams	.01	.05
328 Avery Johnson	.01	.05
329 Stacey King	.01	.05
330 Vin Baker RC	.30	.75
331 Greg Kite	.01	.05
332 Michael Cage	.01	.05
333 Alonzo Mourning	.20	.50
334 Acie Earl RC	.01	.05
335 Terry Dehere RC	.01	.05
336 Negele Knight	.01	.05
337 Gerald Madkins RC	.01	.05
338 Lindsey Hunter RC	.10	.30
339 Luther Wright	.01	.05
340 Mike Peplowski RC	.01	.05
341 Dino Radja	.01	.05
342 Danny Manning	.05	.15
343 Chris Mills	.10	.30
344 Hubert Davis	.01	.05
345 Shawn Bradley	.10	.30
346 Evers Burns RC	.01	.05
347 Rodney Rogers RC	.10	.30
348 Cedric Ceballos	.05	.15
349 Warren Kidd RC	.01	.05
350 Darnell Mee RC	.01	.05
351 Matt Geiger	.01	.05
352 Jamal Mashburn RC	.30	.75
353 Antonio Davis RC	.15	.40
354 Calbert Cheaney	.05	.15
355 George Lynch	.01	.05
356 Derrick McKey	.01	.05
357 Jerry Reynolds	.01	.05
358 Don MacLean	.01	.05
359 Scott Haskin RC	.01	.05
360 Malcolm Mackey RC	.01	.05
361 Isaiah Rider RC	.25	.60
362 Detlef Schrempf	.05	.15
363 Josh Grant RC	.01	.05
364 Kurt Rambis	.01	.05
365 Larry Johnson	.10	.30
366 Richard Petruska RC	.01	.05
367 Ken Norman	.01	.05
368 Kenny Walker	.01	.05
369 James Robinson RC	.01	.05
370 Kevin Duckworth	.01	.05
371 Chris Whitney RC	.01	.05
372 Moses Malone	.10	.30
373 Nick Van Exel	.20	.50
374 Scott Burrell RC	.10	.30
375 Harvey Grant	.01	.05
376 Benoit Benjamin	.01	.05
377 Henry James	.01	.05
378 Pete Myers	.01	.05
379 Dwayne Schintzius	.01	.05
380 Sean Green	.01	.05
381 Eric Murdock	.01	.05
382 Anfernee Hardaway RC	1.00	2.50
383 Gheorghe Muresan RC	.10	.30
384 Kendall Gill	.05	.15
385 David Wood	.01	.05
386 Mario Elie	.01	.05
387 Chris Corchiani	.01	.05
388 Greg Graham RC	.01	.05
389 Hersey Hawkins	.05	.15
390 Mark Aguirre	.01	.05
391 LaPhonso Ellis	.01	.05
392 Anthony Bonner	.01	.05
393 Lucious Harris RC	.01	.05
394 Andrew Lang	.01	.05
395 Chris Dudley	.01	.05
396 Dennis Rodman	.25	.60
397 Larry Krystkowiak	.01	.05
398 A.C. Green	.05	.15
399 Eddie Johnson	.01	.05
400 Kevin Edwards	.01	.05
401 Tyrone Hill	.01	.05
402 Greg Anderson	.01	.05
403 P.J. Brown RC	.25	.60
404 Dana Barros	.01	.05
405 Allan Houston RC	.50	1.25
406 Mike Brown	.01	.05
407 Lee Mayberry	.01	.05
408 Fat Lever	.01	.05
409 Tony Smith	.01	.05
410 Tom Chambers	.01	.05
411 Manute Bol	.01	.05
412 Joe Kleine	.01	.05
413 Bryant Stith	.01	.05
414 Chuck Nevitt	.01	.05
415 Jo Jo English RC	.01	.05
416 Sean Elliott	.05	.15
417 Sam Bowie	.01	.05
418 Armon Gilliam	.01	.05
419 Brian Williams	.01	.05
420 Popeye Jones RC	.01	.05
421 Dennis Rodman EB	.10	.30
422 Karl Malone EB	.10	.30
423 Tom Gugliotta EB	.05	.15
424 Kevin Willis EB	.01	.05
425 Hakeem Olajuwon EB	.10	.30
426 Charles Oakley EB	.01	.05
427 Clarence Weatherspoon EB	.01	.05
428 Derrick Coleman EB	.01	.05
429 Buck Williams EB	.01	.05
430 Christian Laettner EB	.01	.05
431 Dikembe Mutombo EB	.05	.15
432 Rony Seikaly EB	.01	.05
433 Brad Daugherty EB	.01	.05
434 Horace Grant EB	.01	.05
435 Larry Johnson EB	.05	.15
436 Dee Brown BT	.01	.05
437 Muggsy Bogues BT	.01	.05
438 Michael Jordan BT	.75	2.00
439 Tim Hardaway BT	.05	.15
440 Micheal Williams BT	.01	.05
441 Gary Payton BT	.10	.30
442 Mookie Blaylock BT	.01	.05
443 Doc Rivers BT	.01	.05
444 Kenny Smith BT	.01	.05
445 John Stockton BT	.05	.15
446 Alvin Robertson BT	.01	.05
447 Mark Jackson BT	.01	.05
448 Kenny Anderson BT	.01	.05
449 Scottie Pippen BT	.20	.50
450 Isiah Thomas BT	.05	.15
451 Mark Price BT	.01	.05
452 Latrell Sprewell BT	.10	.30
453 Sedale Threatt BT	.01	.05
454 Nick Anderson BT	.01	.05
455 Rod Strickland BT	.01	.05
456 Oliver Miller GI	.01	.05
457 J.Worthy/V.Divac GI	.01	.05
458 Robert Horry GI	.01	.05
459 Rockets Shoot-Around GI	.01	.05
460 Rooks/Jackson/Legler GI	.01	.05
461 Mitch Richmond GI	.05	.15
462 Chris Morris GI	.01	.05
463 M.Jackson/G.Grant GI	.01	.05
464 David Robinson GI	.10	.30
465 Danny Ainge GI	.01	.05
466 Michael Jordan SKL	.75	2.00
467 Dominique Wilkins SKL	.05	.15
468 Alonzo Mourning SKL	.10	.30
469 Shaquille O'Neal SKL	.25	.60
470 Tim Hardaway SL	.05	.15
471 Patrick Ewing SKL	.05	.15
472 Kevin Johnson SL	.01	.05
473 Clyde Drexler SKL	.05	.15
474 David Robinson SKL	.10	.30
475 Shawn Kemp SKL	.10	.30
476 Dee Brown SL	.01	.05
477 Jim Jackson SKL	.01	.05
478 John Stockton SKL	.05	.15
479 Robert Horry SL	.01	.05
480 Glen Rice SL	.01	.05
481 Micheal Williams SIS	.01	.05
482 G.Lynch/T.Dehere CL	.01	.05
483 Chris Webber TP	.60	1.50
484 Anfernee Hardaway TP	.50	1.25
485 Shawn Bradley TP	.05	.15
486 Jamal Mashburn TP	.10	.30
487 Calbert Cheaney TP	.01	.05
488 Isaiah Rider TP	.10	.30
489 Bobby Hurley TP	.01	.05
490 Vin Baker TP	.10	.30
491 Rodney Rogers TP	.05	.15
492 Lindsey Hunter TP	.05	.15
493 Allan Houston TP	.10	.30
494 Terry Dehere TP	.01	.05
495 George Lynch TP	.01	.05
496 Toni Kukoc TP	.10	.30
497 Nick Van Exel TP	.10	.30
498 Charles Barkley MO	.10	.30
499 A.C. Green MO	.01	.05
500 Dan Majerle MO	.01	.05
501 Jerrod Mustaf MO	.01	.05
502 Kevin Johnson MO	.01	.05
503 Joe Kleine MO	.01	.05
504 Danny Ainge MO	.01	.05
505 Oliver Miller MO	.01	.05
506 Joe Courtney MO	.01	.05
507 Checklist	.01	.05
508 Checklist	.01	.05
509 Checklist	.01	.05
510 Checklist	.01	.05
SP3 M.Jordan/W.Chamberlain	3.00	8.00
SP4 Bulls 3rd Champ	3.00	8.00

1993-94 Upper Deck All-NBA

Inserted one per blue and green first series retail 22-card jumbo packs, this 15-card standard-size set spotlights All-NBA first, second and third teams. The cards feature a borderless front with a color action photo set against a game-crowd background. The player's name appears in a red vertical stripe along the right side. The All NBA Team appears in a blue vertical stripe along the right side. The back features a color action photo along the left side with player's statistics along the right side.

Card	Low	High
COMPLETE SET (15)	6.00	12.00
ONE PER SER.1 RETAIL/GREEN JUMBO PACK		
AN1 Charles Barkley	.40	1.00
AN2 Karl Malone	.40	1.00
AN3 Hakeem Olajuwon	.40	1.00
AN4 Michael Jordan	3.00	8.00
AN5 Mark Price	.02	.10
AN6 Dominique Wilkins	.25	.60
AN7 Larry Johnson	.25	.60
AN8 Patrick Ewing	.25	.60
AN9 John Stockton	.25	.60
AN10 Joe Dumars	.25	.60
AN11 Scottie Pippen	.60	1.50
AN12 Derrick Coleman	.10	.30
AN13 David Robinson	.40	1.00
AN14 Tim Hardaway	.25	.60
AN15 Michael Jordan CL	3.00	8.00

1993-94 Upper Deck All-Rookies

Randomly inserted in first series 12-card retail packs at a rate of one in 30, this 10-card standard-size set features the NBA All-Rookie first (1-5) and second (6-10) teams from 1992-93. The cards feature color game-action player photos on their fronts. They are borderless, except at the top, where a red stripe edges the cards of the first team and a blue one edges those of the second. The player's name appears in white lettering within a red or blue stripe near the bottom. The back carries a color player action photo on the left and career highlights on the right.

Card	Low	High
COMPLETE SET (10)	7.50	15.00
SER.1 STATED ODDS 1:30 RETAIL		
AR1 Shaquille O'Neal	4.00	10.00
AR2 Alonzo Mourning	1.25	3.00
AR3 Christian Laettner	.40	1.00
AR4 Tom Gugliotta	.75	2.00
AR5 LaPhonso Ellis	.10	.30
AR6 Walt Williams	.10	.30
AR7 Robert Horry	.40	1.00
AR8 Latrell Sprewell	2.00	5.00
AR9 Clarence Weatherspoon	.10	.30
AR10 Richard Dumas	.10	.30

1993-94 Upper Deck Box Bottoms

Measuring approximately 5" by 7", these box bottoms display enlarged versions of the fronts of regular series cards. The backs are blank. The box bottoms are unnumbered and checklisted below in alphabetical order.

Card	Low	High
COMPLETE SET (2)	.75	2.00
1 Bobby Hurley	.08	.25
2 Michael Jordan	.75	2.00

1993-94 Upper Deck Flight Team

Michael Jordan selected the league's best dunkers for this 20-card insert set. The cards are randomly inserted in first series 12-card hobby packs at a rate of one in 30. The standard-size cards feature on their fronts full-bleed color action player photos. The words "Michael Jordan's Flight Team" appear in ghosted block lettering over the background. The player's name is gold-foil stamped at the bottom, with the Flight Team insignia displayed immediately above carrying his team's city name and the his uniform number. On a background consisting of blue sky and clouds, the back carries a color player action cutout and an evaluative quote by Jordan. The set is sequenced in alphabetical order.

Card	Low	High
COMPLETE SET (20)	30.00	80.00
SER.1 STATED ODDS 1:30 HOBBY		
FT1 Stacey Augmon	.40	1.00
FT2 Charles Barkley	4.00	10.00
FT3 David Benoit	.40	1.00
FT4 Dee Brown	.40	1.00
FT5 Cedric Ceballos	1.25	3.00
FT6 Derrick Coleman	1.25	3.00
FT7 Clyde Drexler	2.50	6.00
FT8 Sean Elliott	1.25	3.00
FT9 LaPhonso Ellis	.40	1.00
FT10 Kendall Gill	1.25	3.00
FT11 Larry Johnson	2.50	6.00
FT12 Shawn Kemp	4.00	10.00
FT13 Karl Malone	4.00	10.00
FT14 Harold Miner	.40	1.00
FT15 Alonzo Mourning	4.00	10.00
FT16 Shaquille O'Neal	8.00	20.00
FT17 Scottie Pippen	8.00	20.00
FT18 Clarence Weatherspoon	.40	1.00
FT19 Spud Webb	1.25	3.00
FT20 Dominique Wilkins	2.50	6.00

1993-94 Upper Deck Future Heroes

Inserted one per first series locker pack, this set continues Upper Deck's year-by-year basketball Heroes program. Unlike previous sets devoted to individual players, the 1993-94 set features a selection of young phenoms destined to be stars. This 10-card standard-size set features color player action shots on its fronts. The photos are bordered on the left and bottom by gray and team color-coded stripes. The player's name and position appear in white lettering in the color-coded stripe at the bottom. An embossed silver-foil basketball appears at the lower left. The white back carries the player's career highlights. The set is numbered in continuation of Upper Deck's Hero Series and is sequenced in alphabetical order.

Card	Low	High
COMPLETE SET (10)	10.00	25.00
ONE PER SER.1 LOCKER PACK		
28 Derrick Coleman	.50	1.25
29 LaPhonso Ellis	.15	.40
30 Jim Jackson	.50	1.25
31 Larry Johnson	1.00	2.50
32 Shawn Kemp	1.50	4.00
33 Christian Laettner	.50	1.25
34 Alonzo Mourning	1.50	4.00
35 Shaquille O'Neal	4.00	10.00
36 Walt Williams	.15	.40
NNO L.Ellis/C.Laettner CL	.50	1.25

1993-94 Upper Deck Locker Talk

Inserted one per Series II locker pack, this 15-card standard-size set features color player action photos on their fronts. The player's name appears in white lettering within the gold stripe that edges the left side. A personal player quote appears in white lettering within the photo's "torn" lower right corner. The back carries the same quote at the upper right, within a shot of a locker that has a print of the front's action shot taped to the door. Another player photo and more personal player quotes round out the back.

Card	Low	High
COMPLETE SET (15)	10.00	25.00
ONE PER SER.2 LOCKER PACK		
LT1 Michael Jordan	6.00	15.00
LT2 Stacey Augmon	.60	1.50
LT3 Shaquille O'Neal	3.00	8.00
LT4 Alonzo Mourning	1.25	3.00
LT5 Harold Miner	.50	1.25
LT6 Clarence Weatherspoon	.50	1.25
LT7 Derrick Coleman	.60	1.50
LT8 Charles Barkley	1.25	3.00
LT9 David Robinson	1.25	3.00
LT10 Chuck Person	.60	1.50
LT11 Karl Malone	1.00	2.50
LT12 Muggsy Bogues	.60	1.50
LT13 Latrell Sprewell	1.25	3.00
LT14 John Starks	.60	1.50
LT15 Jim Jackson	.60	1.50

1993-94 Upper Deck Mr. June

Randomly inserted in series two 12-card hobby packs at a rate of one in 30, this 10-card standard-size set focuses on Michael Jordan's performance while leading his team to three consecutive NBA Championships. The front features a color action shot of Michael Jordan with his name, accomplishment, and year thereof printed in the team-colored (Chicago Bulls) stripe at bottom. The back features a color action photo at the upper right with a description of his accomplishments printed alongside and below.

Card	Low	High
COMPLETE SET (10)	15.00	40.00
COMMON JORDAN (1-10)	2.50	6.00
SER.2 STATED ODDS 1:30 HOBBY		

1993-94 Upper Deck Rookie Exchange

This 10-card standard-size set features the top ten players from the 1993 NBA Draft. The set could only be obtained by mail in exchange for the Silver Trade card that was randomly inserted in first series 12-card packs at a rate of one in 72. The Silver Exchange expiration date was 12/31/93. The borderless front features a color player action photo with the his name printed in white lettering within a red stripe near the bottom. The word "Exchange" runs vertically along the left side in silver-foil lettering. The white and gray back carries a color player photo at the upper left and career highlights and statistics alongside and below. The set is sequenced in draft order.

Card	Low	High
COMPLETE SILVER SET (10)	4.00	8.00
*GOLD CARDS: 1X TO 2X HI COLUMN		
SIL.EXCH: SER.1 STATED ODDS 1:72		
GOLD EXCH: SER.1 STATED ODDS 1:288		
RE1 Chris Webber	1.25	3.00
RE2 Shawn Bradley	.10	.30
RE3 Anfernee Hardaway	1.00	2.50
RE4 Jamal Mashburn	.30	.75
RE5 Isaiah Rider	.25	.60
RE6 Calbert Cheaney	.05	.15
RE7 Bobby Hurley	.05	.15
RE8 Vin Baker	.30	.75
RE9 Rodney Rogers	.10	.30
RE10 Lindsey Hunter	.10	.30
TC2 Expired Silver Trade	.08	.25
TC2 Redeemed Silver Trade	.02	.10

1993-94 Upper Deck Rookie Standouts

Randomly inserted at a rate of one in 30 second series 12-card retail packs and inserted one per second series 22-card purple jumbo pack, this 20-card standard-size set showcases top rookies of the 1993-94 NBA season. The borderless front features a color player action photo with his name printed in a gold-foil banner beneath the silver-foil set logo in a lower corner. The gray back carries a color player photo on one side and career highlights on the other.

Card	Low	High
COMPLETE SET (20)	12.00	30.00
SER.2 STATED ODDS 1:30 RETAIL		
RS1 Chris Webber	5.00	12.00
RS2 Bobby Hurley	.25	.60
RS3 Isaiah Rider	1.00	2.50
RS4 Terry Dehere	.07	.20
RS5 Toni Kukoc	2.00	5.00
RS6 Shawn Bradley	.50	1.25
RS7 Allan Houston	2.00	5.00
RS8 Chris Mills	.50	1.25
RS9 Jamal Mashburn	1.25	3.00
RS10 Acie Earl	.07	.20
RS11 George Lynch	.07	.20
RS12 Scott Burrell	.50	1.25
RS13 Calbert Cheaney	.25	.60
RS14 Lindsey Hunter	.50	1.25
RS15 Nick Van Exel	1.50	4.00
RS16 Rex Walters	.07	.20
RS17 Anfernee Hardaway	4.00	10.00
RS18 Sam Cassell	2.00	5.00
RS19 Vin Baker	1.25	3.00
RS20 Rodney Rogers	.50	1.25

1993-94 Upper Deck Team MVPs

Cards from this 27-card standard-size set were issued one per second series red and purple 22-card jumbo packs. The set highlights one key "Team MVP" from each of the 27 NBA teams. The white and prismatic team-colored foil-bordered front features a color player action shot, with the player's name printed vertically in the foil border at the upper right. The horizontal back is bordered in white and a team color and carries a color action shot on the left with career highlights appearing in a gray panel alongside on the right. The set is sequenced in team alphabetical order.

Card	Low	High
COMPLETE SET (27)	6.00	12.00
ONE PER SER.2 RETAIL/PURPLE JUM.PACK		
TM1 Dominique Wilkins	.30	.75
TM2 Robert Parish	.15	.40
TM3 Larry Johnson	.30	.75
TM4 Scottie Pippen	1.00	2.50
TM5 Mark Price	.05	.15
TM6 Jim Jackson	.15	.40
TM7 Mahmoud Abdul-Rauf	.05	.15
TM8 Joe Dumars	.30	.75
TM9 Chris Mullin	.30	.75
TM10 Hakeem Olajuwon	.50	1.25
TM11 Reggie Miller	.30	.75
TM12 Danny Manning	.15	.40
TM13 James Worthy	.30	.75
TM14 Glen Rice	.15	.40
TM15 Blue Edwards	.05	.15
TM16 Christian Laettner	.15	.40
TM17 Derrick Coleman	.15	.40
TM18 Patrick Ewing	.30	.75
TM19 Shaquille O'Neal	1.50	4.00
TM20 Clarence Weatherspoon	.05	.15
TM21 Charles Barkley	.50	1.25
TM22 Clyde Drexler	.30	.75
TM23 Mitch Richmond	.30	.75
TM24 David Robinson	.50	1.25
TM25 Shawn Kemp	.50	1.25
TM26 John Stockton	.30	.75
TM27 Tom Gugliotta	.30	.75

1993-94 Upper Deck Triple Double

This 10-card standard-size set features the NBA leaders in triple-doubles from the 1992-93 season. Cards were randomly inserted at a rate of 1 in 20 first series 12-card hobby and retail packs, 1 in 20 first series 22-card blue jumbo packs, one per first series 22-card green jumbo pack and approximately 1 in every 11 first series 22-card locker packs. The standard-size horizontal hologram cards feature one color player action cutout and two hologram action shots on their fronts. Each of the three images show the player performing three different skills (scoring, rebounding, passing or blocking) necessary to achieve a triple-double. The words "Triple Double" appear vertically on the left. The player's name appears at the upper right of the hologram. The horizontal back displays another color player action shot on the left, with a story of the player's triple-double feat on the right. The player's name appears in a team-colored bar at the bottom.

Card	Low	High
COMPLETE SET (10)	10.00	20.00
SER.1 STATED ODDS 1:20		
TD1 Charles Barkley	.75	2.00
TD2 Michael Jordan	5.00	12.00
TD3 Scottie Pippen	1.50	4.00
TD4 Detlef Schrempf	.25	.60
TD5 Mark Jackson	.25	.60
TD6 Kenny Anderson	.25	.60
TD7 Larry Johnson	.50	1.25
TD8 Dikembe Mutombo	.50	1.25
TD9 Rumeal Robinson	.07	.20
TD10 Micheal Williams	.07	.20

1994-95 Upper Deck

The 1994-95 Upper Deck basketball set consists of 360 standard-size cards, released in two separate 180-card series. Cards were primarily distributed in 12-card packs, each of which carried a suggested retail price of $1.99. Fronts feature full-color action photos with player's name and team running in color-coded bars along the side. Topical subsets featured are All-Rookie Team (1-10), All-NBA (11-25), USA Basketball (167-180), Draft Analysis (181-198), and Then and Now (352-360). Rookie Cards of note include Grant Hill, Juwan Howard, Eddie Jones, Jason Kidd and Glenn Robinson.

Card	Low	High
COMPLETE SET (360)	17.50	35.00
COMPLETE SERIES 1 (180)	10.00	20.00
COMPLETE SERIES 2 (180)	7.50	15.00
1 Chris Webber ART	.25	.60
2 Anfernee Hardaway ART	.25	.60
3 Vin Baker ART	.15	.40
4 Jamal Mashburn ART	.15	.40
5 Isaiah Rider ART	.15	.40
6 Dino Radja ART	.10	.25
7 Nick Van Exel ART	.15	.40
8 Shawn Bradley ART	.10	.25
9 Toni Kukoc ART	.20	.50
10 Lindsey Hunter ART	.10	.25
11 Scottie Pippen AN	.30	.75
12 Karl Malone AN	.20	.50
13 Hakeem Olajuwon AN	.20	.50
14 John Stockton AN	.20	.50
15 Latrell Sprewell AN	.20	.50
16 Shawn Kemp AN	.15	.40
17 Charles Barkley AN	.25	.60
18 David Robinson AN	.25	.60
19 Mitch Richmond AN	.15	.40
20 Kevin Johnson AN	.15	.40
21 Derrick Coleman AN	.12	.30
22 Dominique Wilkins AN	.20	.50
23 Shaquille O'Neal AN	.40	1.00
24 Mark Price AN	.15	.40
25 Gary Payton AN	.15	.40
26 Dan Majerle	.15	.40
27 Vernon Maxwell	.10	.25
28 Matt Geiger	.10	.25
29 Jeff Turner	.10	.25
30 Vinny Del Negro	.10	.25
31 B.J. Armstrong	.10	.25
32 Chris Gatling	.10	.25
33 Tony Smith	.10	.25
34 Doug West	.10	.25
35 Clyde Drexler	.20	.50
36 Keith Jennings	.10	.25
37 Steve Smith	.12	.30
38 Kendall Gill	.10	.25
39 Bob Martin	.10	.25
40 Calbert Cheaney	.10	.25
41 Terrell Brandon	.10	.25
42 Pete Chilcutt	.10	.25
43 Avery Johnson	.12	.30
44 Tom Gugliotta	.10	.25
45 LaBradford Smith	.10	.25
46 Sedale Threatt	.10	.25
47 Chris Smith	.10	.25
48 Kevin Edwards	.10	.25
49 Lucious Harris	.10	.25
50 Tim Perry	.10	.25
51 Lloyd Daniels	.10	.25
52 Dee Brown	.10	.25
53 Sean Elliott	.15	.40
54 Tim Hardaway	.15	.40
55 Christian Laettner	.12	.30
56 Bo Outlaw RC	.20	.50
57 Kevin Johnson	.15	.40
58 Duane Ferrell	.10	.25
59 Jo Jo English	.10	.25
60 Stanley Roberts	.10	.25
61 Kevin Willis	.10	.25
62 Dana Barros	.10	.25
63 Gheorghe Muresan	.10	.25
64 Vern Fleming	.10	.25
65 Anthony Peeler	.10	.25
66 Negele Knight	.10	.25
67 Harold Ellis	.10	.25
68 Vincent Askew	.10	.25
69 Ennis Whatley	.10	.25
70 Elden Campbell	.10	.25
71 Sherman Douglas	.10	.25
72 Luc Longley	.12	.30
73 Lorenzo Williams	.10	.25
74 Jay Humphries	.10	.25
75 Chris King	.10	.25
76 Tyrone Corbin	.10	.25
77 Bobby Hurley	.10	.25
78 Dell Curry	.10	.25
79 Dino Radja	.10	.25
80 A.C. Green	.12	.30
81 Craig Ehlo	.10	.25
82 Gary Payton	.15	.40
83 Sleepy Floyd	.10	.25
84 Rodney Rogers	.10	.25
85 Brian Shaw	.10	.25
86 Kevin Gamble	.10	.25
87 John Stockton	.20	.50
88 Hersey Hawkins	.10	.25
89 Johnny Newman	.10	.25
90 Larry Johnson	.15	.40
91 Robert Pack	.10	.25
92 Willie Burton	.10	.25
93 Bobby Phills	.10	.25
94 David Benoit	.10	.25
95 Harold Miner	.10	.25
96 David Robinson	.25	.60
97 Nate McMillan	.10	.25
98 Chris Mills	.10	.25
99 Hubert Davis	.10	.25
100 Shaquille O'Neal	.40	1.00
101 Loy Vaught	.10	.25
102 Kenny Smith	.12	.30
103 Terry Dehere	.10	.25
104 Carl Herrera	.10	.25
105 LaPhonso Ellis	.10	.25
106 Armon Gilliam	.10	.25
107 Greg Graham	.10	.25
108 Eric Murdock	.10	.25
109 Ron Harper	.12	.30
110 Andrew Lang	.10	.25
111 Johnny Dawkins	.10	.25
112 David Wingate	.10	.25
113 Tom Hammonds	.10	.25
114 Brad Daugherty	.12	.30
115 Charles Smith	.10	.25
116 Dale Ellis	.10	.25
117 Bryant Stith	.10	.25
118 Lindsey Hunter	.10	.25
119 Patrick Ewing	.20	.50
120 Kenny Anderson	.12	.30
121 Charles Barkley	.25	.60
122 Harvey Grant	.10	.25
123 Anthony Bowie	.10	.25
124 Shawn Kemp	.15	.40
125 Lee Mayberry	.10	.25
126 Reggie Miller	.20	.50
127 Scottie Pippen	.30	.75
128 Spud Webb	.12	.30
129 Antonio Davis	.10	.25
130 Greg Anderson	.10	.25
131 Jim Jackson	.10	.25
132 Dikembe Mutombo	.15	.40
133 Terry Porter	.10	.25
134 Mario Elie	.10	.25
135 Vlade Divac	.15	.40
136 Robert Horry	.15	.40
137 Popeye Jones	.10	.25
138 Brad Lohaus	.10	.25
139 Anthony Bonner	.10	.25
140 Doug Christie	.10	.25
141 Rony Seikaly	.10	.25
142 Allan Houston	.15	.40
143 Tyrone Hill	.10	.25
144 Latrell Sprewell	.20	.50
145 Andres Guibert	.10	.25
146 Dominique Wilkins	.20	.50
147 Jon Barry	.10	.25
148 Tracy Murray	.10	.25
149 Mike Peplowski	.10	.25
150 Mike Brown	.10	.25
151 Cedric Ceballos	.10	.25
152 Stacey King	.10	.25
153 Trevor Wilson	.10	.25
154 Anthony Avent	.10	.25
155 Horace Grant	.12	.30
156 Bill Curley RC	.12	.30
157 Grant Hill RC	1.00	2.50
158 Charlie Ward RC	.20	.50
159 Jalen Rose RC	.50	1.25
160 Jason Kidd RC	1.00	2.50
161 Yinka Dare RC	.12	.30
162 Eric Montross RC	.15	.40
163 Donyell Marshall RC	.20	.50
164 Tony Dumas RC	.20	.50
165 Wesley Person RC	.20	.50
166 Eddie Jones RC	.60	1.50
167 Tim Hardaway USA	.15	.40
168 Isiah Thomas USA	.15	.40
169 Joe Dumars USA	.15	.40
170 Mark Price USA	.15	.40
171 Derrick Coleman USA	.12	.30
172 Shawn Kemp USA	.15	.40
173 Steve Smith USA	.12	.30
174 Dan Majerle USA	.15	.40
175 Reggie Miller USA	.20	.50
176 Kevin Johnson USA	.15	.40
177 Dominique Wilkins USA	.20	.50
178 Shaquille O'Neal USA	.40	1.00
179 Alonzo Mourning USA	.20	.50
180 Larry Johnson USA	.15	.40
181 Brian Grant DA	.15	.40
182 Darrin Hancock DA	.07	.20
183 Grant Hill DA	.50	1.25
184 Jalen Rose DA	.25	.60
185 Lamond Murray DA	.10	.25
186 Jason Kidd DA	.50	1.25
187 Donyell Marshall DA	.10	.25
188 Eddie Jones DA	.30	.75
189 Eric Montross DA	.07	.20
190 Khalid Reeves DA	.07	.20
191 Sharone Wright DA	.07	.20
192 Wesley Person DA	.10	.25
193 Glenn Robinson DA	.20	.50
194 Carlos Rogers DA	.07	.20
195 Aaron McKie DA	.10	.25
196 Juwan Howard DA	.25	.60
197 Charlie Ward DA	.10	.25
198 Brooks Thompson DA	.07	.20
199 Tony Massenburg	.10	.25
200 James Robinson	.10	.25
201 Dickey Simpkins RC	.15	.40
202 Johnny Dawkins	.10	.25
203 Joe Kleine	.10	.25
204 Bill Wennington	.10	.25
205 Sean Higgins	.10	.25
206 Larry Krystkowiak	.10	.25
207 Winston Garland	.10	.25
208 Muggsy Bogues	.12	.30
209 Charles Oakley	.12	.30
210 Vin Baker	.15	.40
211 Malik Sealy	.10	.25
212 Willie Anderson	.10	.25
213 Dale Davis	.10	.25
214 Grant Long	.10	.25
215 Danny Ainge	.15	.40
216 Toni Kukoc	.20	.50
217 Doug Smith	.10	.25
218 Danny Manning	.12	.30
219 Otis Thorpe	.10	.25
220 Mark Price	.15	.40
221 Victor Alexander	.10	.25
222 Brent Price	.10	.25
223 Howard Eisley RC	.20	.50
224 Chris Mullin	.15	.40
225 Nick Van Exel	.15	.40
226 Xavier McDaniel	.10	.25
227 Khalid Reeves RC	.15	.40
228 Anfernee Hardaway	.25	.60
229 B.J. Tyler RC	.12	.30
230 Elmore Spencer	.10	.25
231 Rick Fox	.10	.25
232 Alonzo Mourning	.20	.50
233 Hakeem Olajuwon	.20	.50
234 Blue Edwards	.10	.25
235 P.J. Brown	.10	.25
236 Ron Harper	.12	.30
237 Isaiah Rider	.15	.40
238 Eric Mobley RC	.12	.30
239 Brian Williams	.10	.25
240 Eric Piatkowski RC	.25	.60
241 Karl Malone	.20	.50
242 Wayman Tisdale	.10	.25
243 Sarunas Marciulionis	.10	.25
244 Sean Rooks	.10	.25
245 Ricky Pierce	.10	.25
246 Don MacLean	.10	.25
247 Aaron McKie RC	.20	.50
248 Kenny Gattison	.10	.25
249 Derek Harper	.12	.30
250 Michael Smith RC	.12	.30
251 John Williams	.15	.40
252 Pooh Richardson	.10	.25
253 Sergei Bazarevich RC	.20	.50
254 Brian Grant RC	.30	.75
255 Ed Pinckney	.10	.25
256 Ken Norman	.10	.25
257 Marty Conlon	.10	.25
258 Matt Fish	.10	.25
259 Darrin Hancock RC	.15	.40
260 Mahmoud Abdul-Rauf	.10	.25
261 Roy Tarpley	.10	.25
262 Chris Morris	.10	.25
263 Sharone Wright RC	.15	.40
264 Jamal Mashburn	.15	.40
265 John Starks	.12	.30
266 Rod Strickland	.10	.25
267 Adam Keefe	.10	.25
268 Scott Burrell	.10	.25
269 Eric Riley	.10	.25
270 Sam Perkins	.10	.25
271 Stacey Augmon	.12	.30
272 Kevin Willis	.10	.25
273 Lamond Murray RC	.20	.50
274 Derrick Coleman	.12	.30
275 Scott Skiles	.10	.25
276 Buck Williams	.10	.25
277 Sam Cassell	.15	.40
278 Rik Smits	.12	.30
279 Dennis Rodman	.30	.75
280 Olden Polynice	.10	.25
281 Glenn Robinson RC	.40	1.00
282 Clarence Weatherspoon	.10	.25
283 Monty Williams RC	.15	.40
284 Terry Mills	.10	.25
285 Oliver Miller	.10	.25
286 Dennis Scott	.10	.25
287 Micheal Williams	.10	.25
288 Moses Malone	.15	.40
289 Donald Royal	.10	.25

290 Mark Jackson .12 .30
291 Walt Williams .10 .25
292 Bimbo Coles .10 .25
293 Derrick Alston RC .12 .30
294 Scott Williams .10 .25
295 Acie Earl .10 .25
296 Jeff Hornacek .12 .30
297 Kevin Duckworth .10 .25
298 Dontonio Wingfield RC .20 .50
299 Danny Ferry .10 .25
300 Mark West .10 .25
301 Jayson Williams .10 .25
302 David Wesley .10 .25
303 Jim McIlvaine RC .15 .40
304 Michael Adams .10 .25
305 Greg Minor RC .20 .50
306 Jeff Malone .10 .25
307 Pervis Ellison .10 .25
308 Clifford Rozier RC .12 .30
309 Billy Owens .10 .25
310 Duane Causwell .10 .25
311 Rex Chapman .10 .25
312 Detlef Schrempf .15 .40
313 Mitch Richmond .15 .40
314 Carlos Rogers RC .15 .40
315 Byron Scott .12 .30
316 Dwayne Morton .10 .25
317 Bill Cartwright .12 .30
318 J.R. Reid .10 .25
319 Derrick McKey .10 .25
320 Jamie Watson RC .12 .30
321 Mookie Blaylock .10 .25
322 Chris Webber .25 .60
323 Joe Dumars .15 .40
324 Shawn Bradley .10 .25
325 Chuck Person .12 .30
326 Haywoode Workman .10 .25
327 Benoit Benjamin .10 .25
328 Will Perdue .10 .25
329 Sam Mitchell .10 .25
330 George Lynch .10 .25
331 Juwan Howard RC .30 .75
332 Robert Parish .15 .40
333 Glen Rice .15 .40
334 Michael Cage .10 .25
335 Brooks Thompson RC .15 .40
336 Rony Seikaly .10 .25
337 Steve Kerr .12 .30
338 Anthony Miller RC .20 .50
339 Nick Anderson .10 .25
340 Clifford Robinson .10 .25
341 Todd Day .10 .25
342 Jon Koncak .10 .25
343 Felton Spencer .10 .25
344 Willie Burton .10 .25
345 Ledell Eackles .10 .25
346 Anthony Mason .10 .25
347 Derek Strong .10 .25
348 Reggie Williams .10 .25
349 Johnny Newman .10 .25
350 Terry Cummings .12 .30
351 Anthony Tucker RC .12 .30
352 Junior Bridgeman TN .10 .25
353 Jerry West TN .20 .50
354 Harvey Catchings TN .15 .40
355 John Lucas TN .15 .40
356 Bill Bradley TN .20 .50
357 Bill Walton TN .15 .40
358 Don Nelson TN .15 .40
359 Michael Jordan TN 1.25 3.00
360 Tom (Satch) Sanders TN .15 .40

1994-95 Upper Deck Draft Trade

This set was available exclusively by redeeming the Upper Deck Draft Trade card before the June 30th, 1995 deadline. Draft Trade cards were randomly seeded into one in every 240 first series Upper Deck packs. The first ten players selected in the 1994 NBA Draft are featured within this set. The fronts feature the words NBA Draft Lottery Picks 1994 on the top of the card with the player vertically identified on the front left. The NBA draft logo is in the lower left corner. All of this surrounds a playerr cutout photo against a shaded background. The backs contain player information as well as a player photo. The cards are numbered with a "D" prefix in the upper left corner.

COMPLETE SET (10) 5.00 12.00
TRADE: SER.1 STATED ODDS 1:240
D1 Glenn Robinson .75 2.00
D2 Jason Kidd 2.00 5.00
D3 Grant Hill 2.00 5.00
D4 Donyell Marshall .40 1.00
D5 Juwan Howard .60 1.50
D6 Sharone Wright .30 .75
D7 Lamond Murray .40 1.00
D8 Brian Grant .60 1.50
D9 Eric Montross .30 .75
D10 Eddie Jones 1.25 3.00
NNO Expired Exchange Card .07 .20

1994-95 Upper Deck Jordan He's Back Reprints

The ten standard-size cards were reissued to celebrate the return of Michael Jordan. These cards parallel earlier Upper Deck Michael Jordan cards, the difference being that each is stamped with a foil "He's Back" logo on front. The cards were distributed one per second series rack pack. Jumbo versions of these cards were also released. They are priced in the header.

COMPLETE SET (10) 6.00 12.00
COMMON CARD (1-10) .60 1.50
COMPLETE JUMBO SET (3) 5.00 12.00
COMMON JUMBO (1-3) 2.00 5.00

1994-95 Upper Deck Jordan Heroes

Randomly inserted in 12-card first series hobby and retail packs at a rate of one in 30, these 10 (nine numbered cards and one unnumbered header card) standard-size cards spotlight Michael Jordan's outstanding career. The fronts feature color action shots of Jordan from different stages in his career. His name appears in gold-foil lettering in the bottom margin and also as a facsimile autograph in gold foil in the upper margin. The card's subtitle appears in vertical gold-foil lettering in the left margin. The right side is full-bleed. The back carries a color action shot of Jordan on a ghosted background. A small color action shot appears at the lower left. Career highlights appear in a colored panel set off to one side. The cards are numbered on the back 37-45, a continuation of previous Heroes sets which included Jerry West, Wilt Chamberlain, Larry Bird, and Future Heroes. A 3" by 5" jumbo version of the entire set was also issued one card per blister pack sold at retail outlets. These cards are valued at approximately 50% of the values of the standard-size cards.

COMPLETE SET (10) 12.00 30.00
COMMON JORDAN 3.00 8.00
SER.1 STATED ODDS 1:30 HOB/RET

1994-95 Upper Deck Predictor Award Winners

Randomly inserted exclusively into one in every 25 first and second series hobby packs, cards from this 40-card standard-size set are subdivided into All-Star MVP (H1-H10), Defensive Player of the Year (H11-H20), MVP (H21-H30) and ROY (H31-H40) subsets. If the featured player placed first or second in his respective category, the card was redeemable before the June 30th, 1995 deadline for a special Predictors exchange set (of which mailing was delayed until late October, 1995). Winner cards have been designated below with a "W1" (good for a 20-card exchange set) or "W2" (good for a 10-card exchange set) listing. The fronts feature the player photo for most of the card. The award that the card is good for is vertically on the left side of the card. The player's name, team and position is in the lower right corner and is printed in white. The backs of the card contain contest information. The cards are numbered with an "H" prefix.

COMPLETE SET (40) 25.00 60.00
COMPLETE SERIES 1 (20) 12.00 30.00
COMPLETE SERIES 2 (20) 12.00 30.00
SER.1 STATED ODDS 1:25 HOBBY
SER.2 STATED ODDS 1:30 HOBBY
*RED.CARDS: .2X TO .5X HI COLUMN
TWO RED.SETS PER W1 CARD BY MAIL
ONE RED.SET PER W2 CARD BY MAIL
H1 Charles Barkley 1.25 3.00
H2 Hakeem Olajuwon 1.00 2.50
H3 Shaquille O'Neal 2.00 5.00
H4 Scottie Pippen 1.50 4.00
H5 David Robinson 1.25 3.00
H6 Shawn Kemp W2 .75 2.00
H7 Alonzo Mourning 1.00 2.50
H8 Larry Johnson .75 2.00
H9 Patrick Ewing 1.00 2.50
H10 AS-MVP Wild Card W1 .50 1.25
H11 Hakeem Olajuwon 1.00 2.50
H12 Dikembe Mutombo W1 .75 2.00
H13 Nate McMillan .50 1.25
H14 Dennis Rodman 1.50 4.00
H15 Alonzo Mourning 1.00 2.50
H16 Patrick Ewing 1.00 2.50
H17 Charles Barkley 1.25 3.00
H18 David Robinson 1.25 3.00
H19 John Stockton 1.00 2.50
H20 DEF-POY Wild Card W2 .50 1.25
H21 Shaquille O'Neal W2 2.00 5.00
H22 Hakeem Olajuwon 1.00 2.50
H23 David Robinson W1 1.25 3.00
H24 Scottie Pippen 1.50 4.00
H25 Alonzo Mourning 1.00 2.50
H26 Shawn Kemp .75 2.00
H27 Charles Barkley 1.25 3.00
H28 Patrick Ewing 1.00 2.50
H29 Larry Johnson .75 2.00
H30 MVP Wild Card .50 1.25
H31 Jason Kidd W1 2.50 6.00
H32 Grant Hill W1 2.50 6.00
H33 Glenn Robinson 1.00 2.50
H34 Eddie Jones 1.50 4.00
H35 Donyell Marshall .50 1.25
H36 Eric Montross .40 1.00
H37 Sharone Wright .40 1.00
H38 Juwan Howard .75 2.00
H39 Carlos Rogers .40 1.00
H40 ROY Wild Card W1 .50 1.25

1994-95 Upper Deck Predictor League Leaders

ndomly inserted exclusively into one in every 25 first and second series retail packs, cards from this 40-card standard-size set are subdivided into Scoring (R1-R10), Assists (R11-R20), Rebounds (R21-R30) and Blocks (R31-R40) subsets. If the featured player placed first or second in his respective category, the card was redeemable before the June 30th, 1995 deadline for a special Predictors exchange set (of which mailing was delayed until late October, 1995). Winner cards have been designated below with a "W1" (good for a 20-card exchange set) or "W2" (good for a 10-card exchange set) listing.

COMPLETE SET (40) 20.00 50.00
COMPLETE SERIES 1 (20) 10.00 25.00
COMPLETE SERIES 2 (20) 10.00 25.00
SER.1 STATED ODDS 1:25 RETAIL
SER.2 STATED ODDS 1:30 RETAIL
*RED.CARDS: .2X TO .5X HI COLUMN
TWO RED.SETS PER W1 CARD BY MAIL
ONE EXCH.SET PER W2 CARD BY MAIL
R1 David Robinson 1.25 3.00
R2 Shaquille O'Neal W1 2.00 5.00
R3 Hakeem Olajuwon W2 1.00 2.50
R4 Scottie Pippen 1.50 4.00
R5 Chris Webber 1.25 3.00
R6 Karl Malone 1.00 2.50
R7 Patrick Ewing 1.00 2.50
R8 Mitch Richmond .75 2.00
R9 Charles Barkley 1.25 3.00
R10 Scorers Wild Card .50 1.25
R11 John Stockton W1 1.00 2.50
R12 Mookie Blaylock .50 1.25
R13 Kenny Anderson W2 .60 1.50
R14 Kevin Johnson .75 2.00
R15 Muggsy Bogues .60 1.50
R16 Tim Hardaway .75 2.00
R17 Anfernee Hardaway 1.25 3.00
R18 Rod Strickland .50 1.25
R19 Sherman Douglas .50 1.25
R20 Assists Wild Card .50 1.25
R21 Shaquille O'Neal 2.00 5.00
R22 Hakeem Olajuwon 1.00 2.50
R23 Dennis Rodman W1 1.50 4.00
R24 Dikembe Mutombo W2 .75 2.00
R25 Karl Malone 1.00 2.50
R26 Kevin Willis .50 1.25
R27 Chris Webber 1.25 3.00
R28 Alonzo Mourning 1.00 2.50
R29 Derrick Coleman .60 1.50
R30 Rebounds Wild Card .50 1.25
R31 Dikembe Mutombo W1 .75 2.00
R32 Hakeem Olajuwon W2 1.00 2.50
R33 David Robinson 1.25 3.00
R34 Shawn Bradley .50 1.25
R35 Shaquille O'Neal 2.00 5.00
R36 Patrick Ewing 1.00 2.50
R37 Alonzo Mourning 1.00 2.50
R38 Shawn Kemp .75 2.00
R39 Derrick Coleman .60 1.50
R40 Blocks Wild Card .50 1.25

1994-95 Upper Deck Rookie Standouts

ndomly inserted into one in every 30 second series packs, cards from this 20-card standard size set feature a selection of the top rookies from the 1994-95 season. The borderless fronts feature a color photo in the middle. The words "Rookie Standouts" are in gold foil in the bottom left corner. The hard to read player's names are in the upper left corner. The backs have player information and are numbered with a RS prefix in the upper left corner. The set is sequenced in 1994 NBA draft order.

COMPLETE SET (20) 10.00 25.00
SER.2 STATED ODDS 1:30 HOBBY/RETAIL
RS1 Glenn Robinson 1.25 3.00
RS2 Jason Kidd 3.00 8.00
RS3 Grant Hill 3.00 8.00
RS4 Donyell Marshall .60 1.50
RS5 Juwan Howard 1.00 2.50
RS6 Sharone Wright .50 1.25
RS7 Lamond Murray .60 1.50
RS8 Brian Grant 1.00 2.50
RS9 Eric Montross .50 1.25
RS10 Eddie Jones 2.00 5.00
RS11 Carlos Rogers .50 1.25
RS12 Khalid Reeves .50 1.25
RS13 Jalen Rose 1.50 4.00
RS14 Michael Smith .40 1.00
RS15 Eric Piatkowski .75 2.00
RS16 Clifford Rozier .40 1.00
RS17 Aaron McKie .60 1.50
RS18 Eric Mobley .40 1.00
RS19 Bill Curley .40 1.00
RS20 Wesley Person .60 1.50

1994-95 Upper Deck Slam Dunk Stars

Randomly inserted into one in every 30 second series packs, cards from this 20-card standard-size set feature Upper Deck spokesperson Shawn Kemp's selections of the top dunkers. The fronts feature the words "Kemp Slam Dunk Stars" as well as a sculpture of Kemp in gold foil on the left. The rest of the card is dedicated to a photo of the player dunking. The back has Kemp's opinion of each player. There is also a small inset photo of Kemp as well as a cutout of the featured player. The set is sequenced in alphabetical order.

COMPLETE SET (20) 20.00 50.00
SER.2 STATED ODDS 1:30 HOBBY/RETAIL
S1 Vin Baker 1.50 4.00
S2 Charles Barkley 2.50 6.00
S3 Derrick Coleman 1.25 3.00
S4 Clyde Drexler 2.00 5.00
S5 LaPhonso Ellis 1.00 2.50
S6 Larry Johnson 1.50 4.00
S7 Shawn Kemp 1.50 4.00
S8 Donyell Marshall 1.50 4.00
S9 Jamal Mashburn 1.50 4.00
S10 Gheorghe Muresan 1.00 2.50
S11 Alonzo Mourning 2.00 5.00
S12 Shaquille O'Neal 4.00 10.00
S13 Hakeem Olajuwon 2.00 5.00
S14 Scottie Pippen 3.00 8.00
S15 Isaiah Rider 1.50 4.00
S16 David Robinson 2.50 6.00
S17 Clarence Weatherspoon 1.00 2.50
S18 Chris Webber 2.50 6.00
S19 Dominique Wilkins 2.00 5.00
S20 Rik Smits 1.25 3.00

1994-95 Upper Deck Special Edition

COMPLETE SET (180) 20.00 40.00
COMPLETE SERIES 1 (90) 7.50 15.00
COMPLETE SERIES 2 (90) 15.00 30.00
ONE PER PACK
1 Stacey Augmon .25 .60
2 Kevin Willis .20 .50
3 Mookie Blaylock .20 .50
4 Rick Fox .20 .50
5 Xavier McDaniel .20 .50
6 Dee Brown .20 .50
7 Muggsy Bogues .25 .60
8 Kenny Gattison .20 .50
9 Alonzo Mourning .40 1.00
10 B.J. Armstrong .20 .50
11 Bill Cartwright .25 .60
12 Toni Kukoc .40 1.00
13 Mark Price .30 .75
14 Gerald Wilkins .20 .50
15 John Williams .20 .50
16 Jamal Mashburn .30 .75
17 Sean Rooks .20 .50
18 Doug Smith .20 .50
19 Jim Jackson .20 .50
20 Mahmoud Abdul-Rauf .20 .50
21 Rodney Rogers .20 .50
22 Reggie Williams .20 .50
23 LaPhonso Ellis .20 .50
24 Allan Houston .30 .75
25 Terry Mills .20 .50
26 Joe Dumars .30 .75
27 Chris Mullin .30 .75
28 Billy Owens .20 .50
29 Latrell Sprewell .40 1.00
30 Chris Webber .50 1.25
31 Sam Cassell .30 .75
32 Vernon Maxwell .20 .50
33 Hakeem Olajuwon .40 1.00
34 Otis Thorpe .20 .50
35 Rik Smits .25 .60
36 Derrick McKey .20 .50
37 Haywoode Workman .20 .50
38 Bo Outlaw .30 .75
39 Elmore Spencer .20 .50
40 Loy Vaught .20 .50
41 George Lynch .20 .50
42 Nick Van Exel .30 .75
43 James Worthy .40 1.00
44 Elden Campbell .20 .50
45 Grant Long .20 .50
46 Harold Miner .20 .50
47 Glen Rice .30 .75
48 Steve Smith .25 .60
49 Todd Day .20 .50
50 Eric Murdock .20 .50
51 Vin Baker .30 .75
52 Christian Laettner .25 .60
53 Isaiah Rider .30 .75
54 Micheal Williams .20 .50
55 Benoit Benjamin .20 .50
56 Derrick Coleman .25 .60
57 Chris Morris .20 .50
58 Charles Smith .20 .50
59 Greg Anthony .20 .50
60 Doc Rivers .25 .60
61 Derek Harper .25 .60
62 John Starks .25 .60
63 Anfernee Hardaway .50 1.25
64 Dennis Scott .20 .50
65 Nick Anderson .20 .50
66 Shawn Bradley .20 .50
67 Clarence Weatherspoon .20 .50
68 Jeff Malone .20 .50
69 Cedric Ceballos .20 .50
70 Kevin Johnson .30 .75
71 Oliver Miller .20 .50
72 Clifford Robinson .20 .50
73 Rod Strickland .20 .50
74 Buck Williams .20 .50
75 Mitch Richmond .30 .75
76 Walt Williams .20 .50
77 Lionel Simmons .20 .50
78 Willie Anderson .20 .50
79 Terry Cummings .25 .60
80 J.R. Reid .20 .50
81 Dennis Rodman .60 1.50
82 Kendall Gill .20 .50
83 Sam Perkins .20 .50
84 Detlef Schrempf .30 .75
85 Jeff Hornacek .25 .60
86 Karl Malone .40 1.00
87 Felton Spencer .20 .50
88 Calbert Cheaney .20 .50
89 Don MacLean .20 .50
90 Brent Price .20 .50
91 Tyrone Corbin .20 .50
92 Rex Chapman .20 .50
93 Ken Norman .20 .50
94 Steve Smith .25 .60
95 Eric Montross .25 .60
96 Dino Radja .20 .50
97 Dominique Wilkins .40 1.00
98 Scott Burrell .20 .50
99 Hersey Hawkins .20 .50
100 Larry Johnson .30 .75
101 Ron Harper .25 .60
102 Scottie Pippen .60 1.50
103 Dickey Simpkins .25 .60
104 Tyrone Hill .20 .50
105 Chris Mills .20 .50
106 Bobby Phills .20 .50
107 Lorenzo Williams .20 .50
108 Popeye Jones .20 .50
109 Jason Kidd 1.50 4.00
110 Dikembe Mutombo .30 .75
111 Robert Pack .20 .50
112 Jalen Rose .75 2.00
113 Bill Curley .20 .50
114 Grant Hill 1.50 4.00
115 Lindsey Hunter .20 .50
116 Roy Tarpley .20 .50
117 Tim Hardaway .30 .75
118 Ricky Pierce .20 .50
119 Carlos Rogers .25 .60
120 Clifford Rozier .20 .50
121 Rony Seikaly .20 .50
122 Mario Elie .20 .50
123 Robert Horry .30 .75
124 Kenny Smith .25 .60
125 Antonio Davis .20 .50
126 Dale Davis .20 .50
127 Reggie Miller .40 1.00
128 Lamond Murray .30 .75
129 Eric Piatkowski .40 1.00
130 Pooh Richardson .20 .50
131 Cedric Ceballos .20 .50
132 Vlade Divac .30 .75
133 Eddie Jones 1.00 2.50
134 Mark Jackson .25 .60
135 Matt Geiger .20 .50
136 Khalid Reeves .25 .60
137 Kevin Willis .20 .50
138 Lee Mayberry .20 .50
139 Eric Mobley .20 .50
140 Glenn Robinson .60 1.50
141 Doug West .20 .50
142 Donyell Marshall .30 .75
143 Chris Smith .20 .50
144 Kenny Anderson .25 .60
145 Chris Morris .20 .50
146 Armon Gilliam .20 .50
147 Dana Barros .20 .50
148 Patrick Ewing .40 1.00
149 Charles Oakley .25 .60
150 Charlie Ward .30 .75
151 Horace Grant .25 .60
152 Shaquille O'Neal .75 2.00
153 Brian Shaw .20 .50
154 Brooks Thompson .25 .60
155 B.J. Tyler .20 .50
156 Scott Williams .20 .50
157 Sharone Wright .25 .60
158 Charles Barkley .50 1.25
159 Dan Majerle .30 .75
160 Danny Manning .25 .60
161 Wesley Person .30 .75
162 Clyde Drexler .40 1.00
163 Harvey Grant .20 .50
164 Terry Porter .20 .50
165 Brian Grant .50 1.25
166 Bobby Hurley .20 .50
167 Olden Polynice .20 .50
168 Sean Elliott .30 .75
169 Chuck Person .25 .60
170 David Robinson .50 1.25
171 Shawn Kemp .30 .75
172 Nate McMillan .20 .50
173 Gary Payton .30 .75
174 Michael Smith .20 .50
175 David Benoit .20 .50
176 Jay Humphries .20 .50
177 John Stockton .40 1.00
178 Juwan Howard .50 1.25
179 Chris Webber .50 1.25
180 Scott Skiles .20 .50

1994-95 Upper Deck Special Edition Gold

*STARS: 3X TO 8X HI COLUMN
*RCs: 2.5X TO 6X HI
SER.1/2 STATED ODDS 1:35 HOB/RET

1994-95 Upper Deck Special Edition Jumbos

COMPLETE SET (27) 15.00 40.00
1 Steve Smith .60 1.50
2 Dominique Wilkins 1.00 2.50
3 Larry Johnson .75 2.00
4 Scottie Pippen 1.50 4.00
5 Chris Mills .50 1.25
6 Jason Kidd 4.00 10.00
7 Jalen Rose 2.00 5.00
8 Lindsey Hunter .50 1.25
9 Tim Hardaway .75 2.00
10 Kenny Smith .60 1.50
11 Mark Jackson .60 1.50
12 Lamond Murray .75 2.00
13 Cedric Ceballos .50 1.25
14 Kevin Willis .50 1.25
15 Glenn Robinson 1.50 4.00
16 Doug West .50 1.25
17 Kenny Anderson .60 1.50
18 Patrick Ewing 1.00 2.50
19 Horace Grant .60 1.50
20 Sharone Wright .60 1.50
21 Charles Barkley 1.25 3.00
22 Clyde Drexler 1.00 2.50
23 Brian Grant 1.25 3.00
24 Sean Elliott .75 2.00
25 Shawn Kemp .75 2.00
26 John Stockton 1.00 2.50
27 Juwan Howard 1.25 3.00

1995 Upper Deck

Issued in two series over the first half of 1995, Upper Deck released both products through 10-card packs with 36-packs per box. Both series included several insert sets including the popular Predictor redemption cards and one Silver or Gold parallel card in every pack. Series one hobby packs featured a Jeff Gordon Salute card randomly inserted (1:108 packs) and the retail version a Sterling Marlin Salute (1:108 packs). A special Sterling Marlin Back-to-Back Salute card was randomly seeded in series two retail packs (1:108). As with most Upper Deck issues, subsets abound. Series one included Championship Pit Crew, Star Rookies, Images of '95 and Next in Line. Series two featured New for '95, Did You Know, Speedway Legends and more Star Rookies.

COMPLETE SET (300) 12.50 30.00
COMP.SERIES 1 SET (150) 8.00 20.00
COMP.SERIES 2 SET (150) 6.00 15.00
WAX BOX HOBBY SER.1 20.00 50.00
WAX BOX HOBBY SER.2 20.00 50.00
133 Michael Jordan CPC 2.50 6.00

1995 Upper Deck Gold Signature/Electric Gold

COMPLETE GOLD SET (300) 350.00 700.00
COMP.GOLD SIG.SET (150) 200.00 400.00
COMP. ELE.GOLD SET (150) 150.00 300.00
*GOLD STARS: 8X TO 20X BASE CARDS

1995-96 Upper Deck

The 1995-96 Upper Deck set was issued in two separate series of 180 cards each, for a total of 360 cards. Twelve-card packs carried a suggested retail price of $1.99. The fronts are borderless full-color player action shots with the player's name printed in gold foil at the bottom. The backs feature another player color action shot with a graph of the player's career stats. The player's name and biography are printed vertically on the left side of the back in white type. The set features the following topical subsets: The Rookie Years (136-154), All-Rookie team (155-165), All NBA Team (166-180), USA '96 (316-325), Images of '95 (326-335), Major Attractions (336-346) and Slams and Jams (347-360). Rookie Cards of note include Michael Finley, Kevin Garnett, Antonio McDyess, Jerry Stackhouse and Damon Stoudamire.

COMPLETE SET (360) 25.00 50.00
COMPLETE SERIES 1 (180) 10.00 20.00
COMPLETE SERIES 2 (180) 15.00 30.00
1 Eddie Jones .25 .60
2 Hubert Davis .15 .40
3 Latrell Sprewell .25 .60
4 Stacey Augmon .20 .50
5 Mario Elie .15 .40
6 Tyrone Hill .15 .40
7 Dikembe Mutombo .25 .60
8 Antonio Davis .15 .40
9 Horace Grant .20 .50
10 Ken Norman .15 .40
11 Aaron McKie .15 .40
12 Vinny Del Negro .15 .40
13 Glenn Robinson .20 .50
14 Allan Houston .20 .50
15 Bryon Russell .15 .40
16 Tony Dumas .15 .40
17 Gary Payton .25 .60
18 Rik Smits .20 .50
19 Dino Radja .15 .40
20 Robert Pack .15 .40
21 Calbert Cheaney .15 .40
22 Clarence Weatherspoon .15 .40
23 Michael Jordan 2.00 5.00
24 Felton Spencer .15 .40
25 J.R. Reid .15 .40
26 Cedric Ceballos .15 .40
27 Dan Majerle .25 .60
28 Donald Hodge .15 .40
29 Nate McMillan .15 .40
30 Bimbo Coles .15 .40
31 Mitch Richmond .25 .60
32 Scott Brooks .15 .40
33 Patrick Ewing .30 .75
34 Carl Herrera .15 .40
35 Rick Fox .15 .40
36 James Robinson .15 .40
37 Donald Royal .15 .40
38 Joe Dumars .25 .60
39 Rony Seikaly .15 .40
40 Dennis Rodman .50 1.25
41 Muggsy Bogues .20 .50
42 Gheorghe Muresan .15 .40
43 Ervin Johnson .15 .40
44 Todd Day .15 .40
45 Rex Walters .15 .40
46 Terrell Brandon .15 .40
47 Wesley Person .15 .40
48 Terry Dehere .15 .40
49 Steve Smith .20 .50
50 Brian Grant .20 .50
51 Eric Piatkowski .20 .50
52 Lindsey Hunter .15 .40
53 Chris Webber .30 .75
54 Antoine Carr .15 .40
55 Chris Dudley .15 .40
56 Clyde Drexler .30 .75
57 P.J. Brown .15 .40
58 Kevin Willis .15 .40
59 Jeff Turner .15 .40
60 Sean Elliott .25 .60
61 Kevin Johnson .25 .60
62 Scott Skiles .15 .40
63 Charles Smith .15 .40
64 Derrick McKey .15 .40
65 Danny Ferry .15 .40
66 Detlef Schrempf .25 .60
67 Shawn Bradley .15 .40
68 Isaiah Rider .25 .60
69 Karl Malone .30 .75
70 Will Perdue .15 .40
71 Terry Mills .15 .40
72 Glen Rice .25 .60
73 Tim Breaux .15 .40
74 Malik Sealy .15 .40
75 Walt Williams .15 .40
76 Bobby Phills .15 .40
77 Anthony Avent .15 .40
78 Jamal Mashburn UER .25 .60
79 Vlade Divac .25 .60
80 Reggie Williams .15 .40
81 Xavier McDaniel .15 .40
82 Avery Johnson .20 .50
83 Derek Harper .20 .50
84 Don MacLean .15 .40
85 Tom Gugliotta .15 .40
86 Craig Ehlo .15 .40
87 Robert Horry .20 .50
88 Kevin Edwards .15 .40
89 Chuck Person .20 .50
90 Sharone Wright .15 .40
91 Steve Kerr .20 .50
92 Marty Conlon .15 .40
93 Jalen Rose .30 .75
94 Bryant Reeves RC .20 .50
95 Shaquille O'Neal .60 1.50
96 David Wesley .15 .40
97 Chris Mills .15 .40
98 Rod Strickland .15 .40
99 Pooh Richardson .15 .40
100 Sam Perkins .15 .40
101 Dell Curry .15 .40
102 David Benoit .15 .40
103 Christian Laettner .20 .50
104 Duane Causwell .15 .40
105 Jason Kidd .40 1.00
106 Mark West .15 .40
107 Lee Mayberry .15 .40
108 John Salley .15 .40
109 Jeff Malone .15 .40
110 George Zidek RC .20 .50
111 Kenny Smith .20 .50
112 George Lynch .15 .40
113 Toni Kukoc .25 .60
114 A.C. Green .20 .50
115 Kenny Anderson .20 .50
116 Robert Parish .25 .60
117 Chris Mullin .25 .60
118 Loy Vaught .15 .40
119 Olden Polynice .15 .40
120 Clifford Robinson .15 .40
121 Eric Mobley .15 .40
122 Doug West .15 .40
123 Sam Cassell .25 .60
124 Nick Anderson .15 .40
125 Matt Geiger .15 .40
126 Elden Campbell .15 .40
127 Alonzo Mourning .30 .75
128 Bryant Stith .15 .40
129 Mark Jackson .20 .50
130 Cherokee Parks RC .20 .50
131 Shawn Respert RC .20 .50
132 Alan Henderson RC .25 .60
133 Jerry Stackhouse RC .75 2.00
134 Rasheed Wallace RC .75 2.00
135 Antonio McDyess RC .30 .75
136 Charles Barkley ROO .40 1.00
137 Michael Jordan ROO 1.00 2.50
138 Hakeem Olajuwon ROO .30 .75
139 Joe Dumars ROO .25 .60
140 Patrick Ewing ROO .30 .75
141 A.C. Green ROO .20 .50
142 Karl Malone ROO .30 .75
143 Detlef Schrempf ROO .25 .60
144 Chuck Person ROO .20 .50
145 Muggsy Bogues ROO .20 .50
146 Horace Grant ROO .20 .50
147 Mark Jackson ROO .20 .50
148 Kevin Johnson ROO .25 .60
149 Mitch Richmond ROO .25 .60
150 Rik Smits ROO .20 .50
151 Nick Anderson ROO .15 .40
152 Tim Hardaway ROO .25 .60
153 Shawn Kemp ROO .25 .60
154 David Robinson ROO .40 1.00
155 Jason Kidd ART .40 1.00
156 Grant Hill ART .40 1.00
157 Glenn Robinson ART .20 .50
158 Eddie Jones ART .25 .60
159 Brian Grant ART .20 .50
160 Juwan Howard ART .25 .60
161 Eric Montross ART .15 .40
162 Wesley Person ART .15 .40
163 Jalen Rose ART .30 .75
164 Donyell Marshall ART .15 .40
165 Sharone Wright ART .15 .40
166 Karl Malone AN .30 .75
167 Scottie Pippen AN .40 1.00
168 David Robinson AN .40 1.00
169 John Stockton AN .30 .75
170 Anfernee Hardaway AN .40 1.00
171 Charles Barkley AN .40 1.00
172 Shawn Kemp AN .25 .60
173 Shaquille O'Neal AN .60 1.50
174 Gary Payton AN .25 .60
175 Mitch Richmond AN .25 .60
176 Dennis Rodman AN .50 1.25
177 Detlef Schrempf AN .25 .60
178 Hakeem Olajuwon AN .30 .75
179 Reggie Miller AN .30 .75
180 Clyde Drexler AN .30 .75
181 Hakeem Olajuwon .30 .75
182 Vin Baker .20 .50
183 Jeff Hornacek .20 .50
184 Popeye Jones .15 .40
185 Sedale Threatt .15 .40
186 Scottie Pippen .40 1.00
187 Terry Porter .15 .40
188 Dan Majerle .25 .60
189 Clifford Rozier .15 .40
190 Greg Minor .15 .40
191 Dennis Scott .15 .40
192 Hersey Hawkins .15 .40
193 Chris Gatling .15 .40
194 Charles Oakley .20 .50
195 Dale Davis .15 .40
196 Robert Pack .15 .40
197 Lamond Murray .15 .40
198 Mookie Blaylock .15 .40
199 Dickey Simpkins .15 .40
200 Kevin Gamble .15 .40
201 Lorenzo Williams .15 .40
202 Scott Burrell .15 .40
203 Armon Gilliam .15 .40
204 Doc Rivers .20 .50
205 Blue Edwards .15 .40
206 Billy Owens .15 .40
207 Juwan Howard .25 .60
208 Harvey Grant .15 .40
209 Richard Dumas .15 .40
210 Anthony Peeler .15 .40
211 Matt Geiger .15 .40
212 Lucious Harris .15 .40
213 Grant Long .15 .40
214 Sasha Danilovic RC .25 .60
215 Chris Morris .15 .40
216 Donyell Marshall .15 .40
217 Alonzo Mourning .30 .75
218 John Stockton .30 .75
219 Khalid Reeves .15 .40
220 Mahmoud Abdul-Rauf .15 .40
221 Sean Rooks .15 .40
222 Shawn Kemp .25 .60
223 John Williams .15 .40
224 Dee Brown .15 .40
225 Jim Jackson .15 .40
226 Harold Miner .15 .40
227 B.J. Armstrong .15 .40
228 Elliot Perry .15 .40
229 Anthony Miller .15 .40
230 Donny Marshall RC .25 .60
231 Tyrone Corbin .15 .40
232 Anthony Mason .15 .40
233 Grant Hill .40 1.00
234 Buck Williams .15 .40
235 Brian Shaw .15 .40
236 Dale Ellis .15 .40
237 Magic Johnson .60 1.50
238 Eric Montross .15 .40
239 Rex Chapman .15 .40
240 Otis Thorpe .15 .40
241 Tracy Murray .15 .40
242 Sarunas Marciulionis .15 .40
243 Luc Longley .20 .50
244 Elmore Spencer .15 .40
245 Terry Cummings .20 .50
246 Sam Mitchell .15 .40
247 Terrence Rencher RC .25 .60
248 Byron Houston .15 .40
249 Pervis Ellison .15 .40
250 Carlos Rogers .15 .40
251 Kendall Gill .15 .40
252 Sherrell Ford RC .20 .50
253 Michael Finley RC .75 2.00
254 Kurt Thomas RC .25 .60
255 Joe Smith RC .30 .75
256 Bobby Hurley .15 .40
257 Greg Anthony .15 .40
258 Willie Anderson .15 .40
259 Theo Ratliff RC .40 1.00
260 Duane Ferrell .15 .40
261 Antonio Harvey .15 .40
262 Gary Grant .15 .40
263 Brian Williams .15 .40
264 Danny Manning .20 .50
265 Micheal Williams .15 .40
266 Dennis Rodman .50 1.25
267 Arvydas Sabonis RC .50 1.25
268 Don MacLean .15 .40
269 Keith Askins .15 .40
270 Reggie Miller .30 .75
271 Ed Pinckney .15 .40
272 Bob Sura RC .20 .50
273 Kevin Garnett RC 2.50 6.00
274 Byron Scott .20 .50
275 Mario Bennett RC .20 .50
276 Junior Burrough RC .25 .60
277 Anfernee Hardaway .40 1.00
278 George McCloud .15 .40
279 Loren Meyer RC .15 .40
280 Ed O'Bannon RC .20 .50
281 Lawrence Moten RC .25 .60
282 Dana Barros .15 .40
283 Damon Stoudamire RC .60 1.50
284 Eric Williams RC .25 .60
285 Wayman Tisdale .15 .40
286 Rodney Rogers .15 .40
287 Sherman Douglas .15 .40
288 Greg Ostertag RC .25 .60
289 Alvin Robertson .15 .40
290 Tim Legler .15 .40
291 Zan Tabak .15 .40
292 Gary Trent RC .25 .60
293 Haywoode Workman .15 .40
294 Charles Barkley .40 1.00
295 Derrick Coleman .20 .50
296 Ricky Pierce .15 .40
297 Benoit Benjamin .15 .40
298 Larry Johnson .25 .60
299 Travis Best RC .25 .60
300 Jason Caffey RC .25 .60
301 Cory Alexander RC .25 .60
302 Nick Van Exel .25 .60
303 Corliss Williamson RC .25 .60
304 Eric Murdock .15 .40
305 Tyus Edney RC .25 .60
306 Lou Roe RC .25 .60
307 John Salley .15 .40
308 Spud Webb .20 .50
309 Brent Barry RC .40 1.00
310 David Robinson .40 1.00
311 Glen Rice .25 .60
312 Chris King .15 .40
313 David Vaughn RC .25 .60
314 Kenny Gattison .15 .40
315 Randolph Childress RC .20 .50
316 Anfernee Hardaway USA .40 1.00
317 Grant Hill USA .40 1.00
318 Karl Malone USA .30 .75
319 Reggie Miller USA .30 .75
320 Hakeem Olajuwon USA .30 .75
321 Shaquille O'Neal USA .60 1.50
322 Scottie Pippen USA .40 1.00
323 David Robinson USA .40 1.00
324 Glenn Robinson USA .20 .50
325 John Stockton USA .30 .75
326 Cedric Ceballos I95 .15 .40
327 Shaquille O'Neal I95 .60 1.50
328 Glenn Robinson I95 .20 .50
329 Shawn Kemp I95 .25 .60
330 Nick Anderson I95 .15 .40
331 Shawn Bradley I95 .15 .40
332 H.Grant/B.Thomp I95 .20 .50
333 Robert Horry I95 .20 .50
334 NBA Expansion I95 .15 .40
335 Michael Jordan I95 1.00 2.50
336 N.Van Exel/D.Cannon MA .25 .60
337 M.Jordan/D.Hanson MA 1.00 2.50
338 S.Pippen/J.Von Oy MA .40 1.00
339 M.Jordan/C.Sheen MA 1.00 2.50
340 J.Kidd/C.Reid MA .40 1.00
341 M.Jordan/Q.Latifah MA 1.00 2.50
342 C.Barkley/D.Johnson MA .40 1.00
343 Olajuwon/C.Bernsen MA .30 .75
344 Ahmad Rashad MA .15 .40
345 Willow Bay MA .15 .40
346 G.Payton/M.Curry MA .25 .60
347 Horace Grant SJ .20 .50
348 Juwan Howard SJ .25 .60
349 David Robinson SJ .40 1.00
350 Reggie Miller SJ .30 .75
351 Brian Grant SJ .20 .50
352 Michael Jordan SJ 1.00 2.50
353 Cedric Ceballos SJ .15 .40
354 Blue Edwards SJ .15 .40
355 Acie Earl SJ .15 .40
356 Dennis Rodman SJ .50 1.25
357 Shawn Kemp SJ .25 .60
358 Jerry Stackhouse SJ .50 1.25
359 Jamal Mashburn SJ .25 .60
360 Antonio McDyess SJ .20 .50

1995-96 Upper Deck Electric Court

COMPLETE SET (360) 50.00 100.00
COMPLETE SERIES 1 (180) 25.00 50.00
COMPLETE SERIES 2 (180) 25.00 50.00
*STARS: 1X TO 2.5X BASE CARD HI
*SUBSETS/RCs: .75X TO 2X BASE HI
ONE PER RETAIL PACK

1995-96 Upper Deck Electric Court Gold

*STARS: 8X TO 20X BASE CARD HI
*SUBSETS/RCs: 5X TO 12X BASE HI
SER.1/2 STATED ODDS 1:35 RETAIL
23 Michael Jordan 60.00 150.00
137 Michael Jordan ROO 40.00 100.00
335 Michael Jordan I95 40.00 100.00
337 M.Jordan/D.Hansen MA 40.00 100.00
339 M.Jordan/C.Sheen MA 40.00 100.00
341 M.Jordan/Q.Latifah MA 40.00 100.00
352 Michael Jordan SJ 40.00 100.00

1995-96 Upper Deck All Star Class

ndomly inserted in first series packs at a rate of one in 17, this 25-card standard-size set highlights the play of the NBA's best in the 1995 All Star Game. Borderless foil fronts feature the player in full-color action and include the Upper Deck logo stamped in blue foil on the upper right. "1995 NBA All Star Class" is printed in blue foil and centered at the bottom. On either side of the logo are gold pyramids which feature the player's name, team and position printed in black type. Blue backs have a copper bordered posed player shot with game highlights. The Phoenix All Star Weekend logo is printed at the top of the picture and the player's name, team and position are printed over the logo.

COMPLETE SET (25)	60.00	120.00
SER.1 STATED ODDS 1:17 HOBBY/RETAIL		
AS1 Anfernee Hardaway	4.00	10.00
AS2 Reggie Miller	3.00	8.00
AS3 Grant Hill	4.00	10.00
AS4 Scottie Pippen	4.00	10.00
AS5 Shaquille O'Neal	6.00	15.00
AS6 Larry Johnson	2.50	6.00
AS7 Dana Barros	1.50	4.00
AS8 Vin Baker	2.00	5.00
AS9 Alonzo Mourning	3.00	8.00
AS10 Joe Dumars	2.50	6.00
AS11 Patrick Ewing	3.00	8.00
AS12 Tyrone Hill	1.50	4.00
AS13 Latrell Sprewell	2.50	6.00
AS14 Dan Majerle	2.50	6.00
AS15 Shawn Kemp	2.50	6.00
AS16 Karl Malone	3.00	8.00
AS17 Hakeem Olajuwon	3.00	8.00
AS18 Gary Payton	2.50	6.00
AS19 Mitch Richmond	2.50	6.00
AS20 David Robinson	4.00	10.00
AS21 Detlef Schrempf	2.50	6.00
AS22 Cedric Ceballos	1.50	4.00
AS23 John Stockton	3.00	8.00
AS24 Dikembe Mutombo	2.50	6.00
AS25 Charles Barkley	4.00	10.00

1995-96 Upper Deck Jordan Collection

Upper Deck spokesperson and NBA legend Michael Jordan is featured on these eight, multi-series insert cards. Cards JC5-JC8 were randomly inserted into one in every 29 first series packs. Cards JC13-JC16 were randomly inserted into one in every 29 second series packs. The eight cards actually represent two segments of a twenty-four card set issued in six different series across all of Upper Deck's 1995-96 products (except SPx). Full-bleed, silver-foil fronts feature Jordan in full color in both posed and action shots. Backs feature Jordan in a spectacular action shot with alternating boxes of separated colors. A "Jordan Collection" box appears at the mid-left of the card with an explanation of the award that was featured on the front.

COMPLETE SER.1 (4)	10.00	25.00
COMPLETE SER.2 (4)	10.00	25.00
COMMON UD 1 (JC5-JC8)	3.00	8.00
COMMON UD 2 (JC13-JC16)	3.00	8.00
SER.1/2 UD STATED ODDS 1:29 HOB/RET		

1995-96 Upper Deck Jordan Collection Jumbos

COMPLETE SET (25)	12.00	30.00
COMMON CARD	2.00	5.00

1995-96 Upper Deck Predictor MVP

Randomly inserted exclusively into second series retail packs at a rate of one in 30, this 10-card standard-size set features five Michael Jordan cards, four top NBA stars and a Long Shot card (representing all other NBA players). In addition, Upper Deck offered dealers a 5-card Predictor pack with the purchase of one case (20 boxes) of second series product. Dealers were given all 20 second series Predictor cards (retail MVP and hobby Scoring) with the purchase of two cases. Black and red basketball court fronts frame a full-color action player cutout. A black border surrounds the player's name, team and the month of the predicted award, all of which are stamped in gold foil. The outer border of the front is a black marble texture. Numbered backs are printed on white, have the prefix "R" and explain the rules of the game. Those holding a winning Predictor card redeemed the cards through a mail-in offer for a full set of the Predictor MVP cards. The expiration date to redeem winning cards was July 8, 1996.

COMPLETE SET (10)	10.00	25.00
SER.2 STATED ODDS 1:30 RETAIL		
*RED.CARDS: .20X TO .50X HI COLUMN		
ONE RED.SET PER "W" CARD BY MAIL		
R1 Michael Jordan	3.00	8.00
R2 Michael Jordan	3.00	8.00
R3 Michael Jordan	3.00	8.00
R4 Michael Jordan	3.00	8.00
R5 Michael Jordan	3.00	8.00
R6 Hakeem Olajuwon	1.00	2.50
R7 Charles Barkley	1.25	3.00
R8 Karl Malone	1.00	2.50
R9 Anfernee Hardaway	1.25	3.00
R10 Long Shot Card	.75	2.00

1995-96 Upper Deck Predictor Player of the Month

Randomly inserted exclusively into first series retail packs at a rate of one in 30, this 10-card standard-size set features five Michael Jordan cards, four top NBA stars and a Long Shot card (representing all other NBA players). In addition, Upper Deck offered dealers a 5-card Predictor pack with the purchase of one case (20 boxes) of first series product. Dealers were given all 20 first series Predictor cards (retail Player of the Month and hobby Player of the Week) with the purchase of two cases. Each card lists months that the featured player might win Player of the Month honors. Black and red basketball court fronts frame a full-color action player cutout. A black border surrounds the player's name, team and the month of the predicted award, all of which are stamped in gold foil. The outer border of the front is a black marble texture. Numbered backs are printed on white, have the prefix "R" and explain the rules of the game. Those holding a winning Predictor card redeemed the cards through a mail-in offer for a full set of the Predictor Player of the Month cards. The expiration date to redeem winning cards was July 1, 1996.

COMPLETE SET (10)	10.00	25.00
SER.1 STATED ODDS 1:30 RETAIL		
*RED.CARDS: .20X TO .50X HI COLUMN		
ONE RED.SET PER "W" CARD BY MAIL		
R1 Michael Jordan	3.00	8.00
R2 Michael Jordan	3.00	8.00
R3 Michael Jordan	3.00	8.00
R4 Michael Jordan	3.00	8.00
R5 Michael Jordan	3.00	8.00
R6 Jamal Mashburn	.75	2.00
R7 David Robinson	1.25	3.00
R8 Latrell Sprewell	.75	2.00
R9 Chris Webber	1.00	2.50
R10 Long Shot Card	.75	2.00

1995-96 Upper Deck Predictor Player of the Week

Randomly inserted exclusively into first series hobby packs at a rate of one in 30, this 10-card standard-sized set features five Michael Jordan cards, four top NBA stars and a Long Shot card (representing all other NBA players). In addition, Upper Deck offered dealers a 5-card Predictor pack with the purchase of one case (20 boxes) of first series product. Dealers were given all 20 first series Predictor cards (retail Player of the Month and hobby Player of the Week) with the purchase of two cases. Each card lists weeks that the featured player might win Player of the Week honors. The fronts feature the player in a full color cutout set against a red court background and a black border surrounding the red. The player's name, team name and predictor category are printed in gold foil. Card edges are trimmed with a black marble texture. Those holding a winning Predictor card redeemed the cards through a mail-in offer for a full set of the Predictor Player of the Week cards. The expiration date to redeem winning cards was July 1, 1996.

SER.1 STATED ODDS 1:30 HOBBY		
*RED.CARDS: .20X TO .50X HI COLUMN		
ONE RED.SET PER "W" CARD BY MAIL		
H1 Michael Jordan	3.00	8.00
H2 Michael Jordan	3.00	8.00
H3 Michael Jordan	3.00	8.00
H4 Michael Jordan	3.00	8.00
H5 Michael Jordan	3.00	8.00
H6 Anfernee Hardaway	1.25	3.00
H7 Hakeem Olajuwon	1.00	2.50
H8 Scottie Pippen	1.25	3.00
H9 Glenn Robinson	.60	1.50
H10 Long Shot Card	.75	2.00

1995-96 Upper Deck Predictor Scoring

Randomly inserted in second series hobby packs at a rate of one in 30, cards from this 10-card insert set feature five Michael Jordan cards, four top NBA stars and a Long Shot card (representing all other NBA players). In addition, Upper Deck offered dealers a 5-card Predictor pack with the purchase of one case (20 boxes) of second series product. Dealers were given all 20 second series Predictor cards (retail MVP and hobby Scoring) with the purchase of two cases. Card fronts feature the player in a full color cutout set against a red court background and a black border surrounding the red. The player's name, team name and predictor category are printed in gold foil. Card edges are trimmed with a black marble texture. If the player pictured won the NBA scoring title, the card was redeemable for a special version of the hobby Predictor Scoring set. The expiration date to redeem winning cards was July 8, 1996.

SER.2 STATED ODDS 1:30 HOBBY		
*RED.CARDS: .20X TO .50X HI COLUMN		
ONE RED.SET PER "W" CARD BY MAIL		
H1 Michael Jordan	3.00	8.00
H2 Michael Jordan	3.00	8.00
H3 Michael Jordan	3.00	8.00
H4 Michael Jordan	3.00	8.00
H5 Michael Jordan	3.00	8.00
H6 David Robinson	1.25	3.00
H7 Scottie Pippen	1.25	3.00
H8 Jerry Stackhouse	1.25	3.00
H9 Glenn Robinson	.60	1.50
H10 Long Shot Card	.75	2.00

1995-96 Upper Deck Special Edition

These 180 standard-size cards were inserted at a rate of one per hobby pack only and were printed on a silver foil front. The cards were issued in two separate series of 90 (1-90 in first series packs and 91-180 in second series). Only the top veterans and rookies were selected for inclusion in this set. The player is featured in an action shot but only he is singled out for color. The rest of the shot is faded out to black and white. The player's name is stamped in silver foil at the bottom and the Special Edition logo is stamped in silver foil at the top right. "SE" is stamped in silver foil and runs vertically down the left side of the front. Backs are printed on a white and gray background and include a player biography, career statistics and player highlights. A color player action shot appears on the upper left side and includes the card number.

COMPLETE SET (180)	40.00	80.00
COMPLETE SERIES 1 (90)	15.00	30.00
COMPLETE SERIES 2 (90)	20.00	50.00
ONE PER BOTH SERIES HOBBY PACK		
1 Mookie Blaylock	.40	1.00
2 Tyrone Corbin	.40	1.00
3 Grant Long	.40	1.00
4 Dee Brown	.40	1.00
5 Sherman Douglas	.40	1.00
6 Eric Montross	.40	1.00
7 Scott Burrell	.40	1.00
8 Dell Curry	.40	1.00
9 Larry Johnson	.60	1.50
10 Will Perdue	.40	1.00
11 Scottie Pippen	1.00	2.50
12 Dickey Simpkins	.40	1.00
13 Michael Cage	.40	1.00
14 Mark Price	.60	1.50
15 John Williams	.40	1.00
16 Lucious Harris	.40	1.00
17 Jim Jackson	.40	1.00
18 Popeye Jones	.40	1.00
19 Mahmoud Abdul-Rauf	.40	1.00
20 LaPhonso Ellis	.40	1.00
21 Robert Pack	.40	1.00
22 Bill Curley	.40	1.00
23 Grant Hill	1.00	2.50
24 Allan Houston	.50	1.25
25 Chris Gatling	.40	1.00
26 Tim Hardaway	.60	1.50
27 Donyell Marshall	.40	1.00
28 Clifford Rozier	.40	1.00
29 Mario Elie	.40	1.00
30 Robert Horry	.50	1.25
31 Hakeem Olajuwon	.75	2.00
32 Kenny Smith	.50	1.25
33 Dale Davis	.40	1.00
34 Duane Ferrell	.40	1.00
35 Derrick McKey	.40	1.00
36 Reggie Miller	.75	2.00
37 Lamond Murray	.40	1.00
38 Bo Outlaw	.40	1.00
39 Eric Piatkowski	.50	1.25
40 Anthony Peeler	.40	1.00
41 Sedale Threatt	.40	1.00
42 Nick Van Exel	.60	1.50
43 Kevin Gamble	.40	1.00
44 Matt Geiger	.40	1.00
45 Billy Owens	.40	1.00
46 Khalid Reeves	.40	1.00
47 Vin Baker	.50	1.25
48 Eric Murdock	.40	1.00
49 Lee Mayberry	.40	1.00
50 Christian Laettner	.50	1.25
51 Sean Rooks	.40	1.00
52 Doug West	.40	1.00
53 P.J. Brown	.40	1.00
54 Derrick Coleman	.50	1.25
55 Armon Gilliam	.40	1.00
56 Hubert Davis	.40	1.00
57 Charles Oakley	.50	1.25
58 John Starks	.50	1.25
59 Monty Williams	.40	1.00
60 Anfernee Hardaway	1.00	2.50
61 Donald Royal	.40	1.00
62 Dennis Scott	.40	1.00
63 Jeff Turner	.40	1.00
64 Clarence Weatherspoon	.40	1.00
65 Jeff Malone	.40	1.00
66 Scott Williams	.40	1.00
67 A.C. Green	.50	1.25
68 Kevin Johnson	.60	1.50
69 Elliot Perry	.40	1.00
70 Wesley Person	.40	1.00
71 Harvey Grant	.40	1.00
72 Aaron McKie	.40	1.00
73 Rod Strickland	.40	1.00
74 Buck Williams	.40	1.00
75 Randy Brown	.40	1.00
76 Bobby Hurley	.40	1.00
77 Lionel Simmons	.40	1.00
78 Terry Cummings	.50	1.25
79 Vinny Del Negro	.40	1.00
80 Avery Johnson	.50	1.25
81 David Robinson	1.00	2.50
82 Vincent Askew	.40	1.00
83 Shawn Kemp	.60	1.50
84 Nate McMillan	.40	1.00
85 David Benoit	.40	1.00
86 Jeff Hornacek	.50	1.25
87 John Stockton	.75	2.00
88 Juwan Howard	.60	1.50
89 Gheorghe Muresan	.40	1.00
90 Doug Overton	.40	1.00
91 Stacey Augmon	.50	1.25
92 Alan Henderson	.60	1.50
93 Steve Smith	.50	1.25
94 Rick Fox	.40	1.00
95 Dino Radja	.40	1.00
96 Eric Williams	.60	1.50
97 Muggsy Bogues	.50	1.25
98 Kendall Gill	.40	1.00
99 Glen Rice	.60	1.50
100 Michael Jordan	12.00	30.00
101 Toni Kukoc	.60	1.50
102 Dennis Rodman	1.25	3.00
103 Terrell Brandon	.40	1.00
104 Tyrone Hill	.40	1.00
105 Dan Majerle	.60	1.50
106 Jason Kidd	1.00	2.50
107 Jamal Mashburn	.60	1.50
108 Cherokee Parks	.50	1.25
109 Antonio McDyess	.75	2.00
110 Dikembe Mutombo	.60	1.50
111 Reggie Williams	.40	1.00
112 Joe Dumars	.60	1.50
113 Lindsey Hunter	.40	1.00
114 Otis Thorpe	.40	1.00
115 Chris Mullin	.60	1.50
116 Joe Smith	.75	2.00
117 Latrell Sprewell	.60	1.50
118 Chucky Brown	.40	1.00
119 Sam Cassell	.60	1.50
120 Clyde Drexler	.75	2.00
121 Travis Best	.60	1.50
122 Mark Jackson	.50	1.25
123 Rik Smits	.50	1.25
124 Brent Barry	1.00	2.50
125 Rodney Rogers	.40	1.00
126 Loy Vaught	.40	1.00
127 Cedric Ceballos	.40	1.00
128 Magic Johnson	1.50	4.00
129 Eddie Jones	.60	1.50
130 Alonzo Mourning	.75	2.00
131 Kurt Thomas	.60	1.50
132 Kevin Willis	.40	1.00
133 Sherman Douglas	.40	1.00
134 Shawn Respert	.50	1.25
135 Glenn Robinson	.50	1.25
136 Kevin Garnett	5.00	12.00
137 Tom Gugliotta	.40	1.00
138 Isaiah Rider	.60	1.50
139 Kenny Anderson	.50	1.25
140 Ed O'Bannon	.50	1.25
141 Jayson Williams	.40	1.00
142 Patrick Ewing	.75	2.00
143 Derek Harper	.50	1.25
144 Charles Smith	.40	1.00
145 Nick Anderson	.40	1.00
146 Horace Grant	.50	1.25
147 Shaquille O'Neal	1.50	4.00
148 Vernon Maxwell	.40	1.00
149 Jerry Stackhouse	2.00	5.00
150 Sharone Wright	.40	1.00
151 Charles Barkley	1.00	2.50
152 Michael Finley	2.00	5.00
153 Danny Manning	.50	1.25
154 John Williams	.40	1.00
155 Clifford Robinson	.40	1.00
156 Arvydas Sabonis	1.25	3.00
157 Gary Trent	.60	1.50
158 Brian Grant	.50	1.25
159 Mitch Richmond	.60	1.50
160 Corliss Williamson	.60	1.50
161 Sean Elliott	.60	1.50
162 Will Perdue	.40	1.00
163 Doc Rivers	.50	1.25
164 Gary Payton	.60	1.50
165 Sam Perkins	.40	1.00
166 Detlef Schrempf	.60	1.50
167 Tracy Murray	.40	1.00
168 Ed Pinckney	.40	1.00
169 Carlos Rogers	.40	1.00
170 Damon Stoudamire	1.50	4.00
171 Karl Malone	.75	2.00
172 Chris Morris	.40	1.00
173 Greg Ostertag	.60	1.50
174 Greg Anthony	.40	1.00
175 Lawrence Moten	.60	1.50
176 Bryant Reeves	.50	1.25
177 Byron Scott	.50	1.25
178 Calbert Cheaney	.40	1.00
179 Rasheed Wallace	2.00	5.00
180 Chris Webber	.75	2.00

1995-96 Upper Deck Special Edition Gold

*STARS: 2.5X TO 6X HI COLUMN
*RCs: 1.5X TO 4X HI
SER.1/2 STATED ODDS 1:35 HOBBY

1996-97 Upper Deck

This 360-card Upper Deck set was distributed in two series with packs of 12 cards each at the suggested retail price of $2.49. The fronts feature color action player photos with the date stamped in foil indicating the actual game of the photo featured on each card. The backs carry player information. Rookies from both series include Kobe Bryant, Marcus Camby, Allen Iverson, Stephon Marbury, Shareef Abdur-Rahim and Antoine Walker, among others. Randomly inserted in packs at the rate of one in three were "Meet the Stars" trivia game cards which gave the collector a chance to answer questions for prizes including a chance to meet a star player. Inserted one in 56 packs were instant win cards which entitled the holder to prizes without answering questions. One in seven series one packs contained "NBA Pick Up Game" cards which featured stickers representing players' jersey numbers in which the collector affixed to a "3-in-a-Row" game board and sent in for a chance to win a trip to All-Star Weekend.

COMPLETE SET (360)	25.00	60.00
COMPLETE SERIES 1 (180)	15.00	30.00
COMPLETE SERIES 2 (180)	10.00	20.00
1 Mookie Blaylock	.15	.40
2 Alan Henderson	.15	.40
3 Christian Laettner	.20	.50
4 Ken Norman	.15	.40
5 Dee Brown	.15	.40
6 Todd Day	.15	.40
7 Rick Fox	.15	.40
8 Dino Radja	.15	.40
9 Dana Barros	.15	.40
10 Eric Williams	.15	.40
11 Scott Burrell	.15	.40
12 Dell Curry	.15	.40
13 Matt Geiger	.15	.40
14 Glen Rice	.25	.60
15 Ron Harper	.20	.50
16 Michael Jordan	2.00	5.00
17 Luc Longley	.20	.50
18 Toni Kukoc	.25	.60
19 Dennis Rodman	.50	1.25
20 Danny Ferry	.15	.40
21 Tyrone Hill	.15	.40
22 Bobby Phills	.15	.40
23 Bob Sura	.15	.40
24 Tony Dumas	.15	.40
25 George McCloud	.15	.40
26 Jim Jackson	.15	.40
27 Jamal Mashburn	.20	.50
28 Loren Meyer	.15	.40
29 Dale Ellis	.15	.40
30 LaPhonso Ellis	.15	.40
31 Tom Hammonds	.15	.40
32 Antonio McDyess	.25	.60
33 Joe Dumars	.25	.60
34 Grant Hill	.40	1.00
35 Lindsey Hunter	.15	.40
36 Terry Mills	.15	.40
37 Theo Ratliff	.15	.40
38 B.J. Armstrong	.15	.40
39 Donyell Marshall	.15	.40
40 Chris Mullin	.25	.60
41 Rony Seikaly	.15	.40
42 Joe Smith	.20	.50
43 Sam Cassell	.20	.50
44 Clyde Drexler	.30	.75
45 Mario Elie	.15	.40
46 Robert Horry	.20	.50
47 Travis Best	.15	.40
48 Antonio Davis	.15	.40
49 Dale Davis	.15	.40
50 Eddie Johnson	.15	.40
51 Derrick McKey	.15	.40
52 Reggie Miller	.30	.75
53 Brent Barry	.20	.50
54 Lamond Murray	.15	.40
55 Eric Piatkowski	.20	.50
56 Rodney Rogers	.15	.40
57 Loy Vaught	.15	.40
58 Kobe Bryant RC	5.00	12.00
59 Eddie Jones	.25	.60
60 Elden Campbell	.15	.40
61 Shaquille O'Neal	.60	1.50
62 Nick Van Exel	.25	.60
63 Keith Askins	.15	.40
64 Rex Chapman	.15	.40
65 Sasha Danilovic	.15	.40
66 Alonzo Mourning	.30	.75
67 Kurt Thomas	.15	.40
68 Tim Hardaway	.25	.60
69 Ray Allen RC	1.00	2.50
70 Johnny Newman	.15	.40
71 Shawn Respert	.15	.40
72 Glenn Robinson	.20	.50
73 Tom Gugliotta	.15	.40
74 Stephon Marbury RC	.60	1.50
75 Terry Porter	.15	.40
76 Doug West	.15	.40
77 Shawn Bradley	.15	.40
78 Kevin Edwards	.15	.40
79 Vern Fleming	.15	.40
80 Ed O'Bannon	.15	.40
81 Jayson Williams	.15	.40
82 John Starks	.20	.50
83 Patrick Ewing	.30	.75
84 Charlie Ward	.15	.40
85 Nick Anderson	.15	.40
86 Anfernee Hardaway	.40	1.00
87 Jon Koncak	.15	.40
88 Donald Royal	.15	.40
89 Brian Shaw	.15	.40
90 Derrick Coleman	.20	.50
91 Allen Iverson RC	1.25	3.00
92 Jerry Stackhouse	.30	.75
93 Clarence Weatherspoon	.15	.40
94 Charles Barkley	.40	1.00
95 Kevin Johnson	.25	.60
96 Danny Manning	.20	.50
97 Elliot Perry	.15	.40
98 Wayman Tisdale	.15	.40
99 Randolph Childress	.15	.40
100 Aaron McKie	.15	.40
101 Arvydas Sabonis	.20	.50
102 Gary Trent	.15	.40
103 Chris Dudley	.15	.40
104 Tyus Edney	.15	.40
105 Brian Grant	.20	.50
106 Bobby Hurley	.15	.40
107 Olden Polynice	.15	.40
108 Corliss Williamson	.15	.40
109 Vinny Del Negro	.15	.40
110 Avery Johnson	.20	.50
111 Will Perdue	.15	.40
112 David Robinson	.40	1.00
113 Hersey Hawkins	.15	.40
114 Shawn Kemp	.25	.60
115 Nate McMillan	.15	.40
116 Detlef Schrempf	.25	.60
117 Gary Payton	.25	.60
118 Marcus Camby RC	.40	1.00
119 Zan Tabak	.15	.40
120 Damon Stoudamire	.20	.50
121 Carlos Rogers	.15	.40
122 Sharone Wright	.15	.40
123 Antoine Carr	.15	.40
124 Jeff Hornacek	.20	.50
125 Adam Keefe	.15	.40
126 Chris Morris	.15	.40
127 John Stockton	.30	.75
128 Blue Edwards	.15	.40
129 Shareef Abdur-Rahim RC	.40	1.00
130 Bryant Reeves	.15	.40
131 Roy Rogers RC	.20	.50
132 Calbert Cheaney	.15	.40
133 Tim Legler	.15	.40
134 Gheorghe Muresan	.15	.40
135 Chris Webber	.30	.75
136 Mutombo/Blaylock/Smith BW	.25	.60
137 Barros/Radja/Williams BW	.15	.40
138 Rice/Geiger/Divac BW	.25	.60
139 Jordan/Pip/Rodman BW	1.00	2.50
140 Brandon/Ferry/Hill BW	.15	.40
141 Kidd/Mash/Jackson BW	.40	1.00
142 L.Ellis/McDyess/Jackson BW	.25	.60
143 Dumars/Hill/Augmon BW	.40	1.00
144 Smith/Sprewell/Mullin BW	.25	.60
145 Olaj/Drexler/Barkley BW	.40	1.00
146 R.Miller/Best/Smits BW	.30	.75
147 B.Barry/Murray/Rogers BW	.20	.50
148 O'Neal/Jones/Bryant BW	1.25	3.00
149 Zo/Hardaway/Danilovic BW	.30	.75
150 Baker/Robinson/Douglas BW	.20	.50
151 Garnett/Gug/Parks BW	.60	1.50
152 Bradley/Gill/O'Bannon BW	.15	.40
153 Ewing/Houston/L.Johnson BW	.30	.75
154 Hardaway/Scott/Grant BW	.40	1.00
155 Stack/W'spoon/Cole BW	.30	.75
156 K.Johnson/Manning/Finley BW	.30	.75
157 Robinson/Rider/Sabonis BW	.30	.75
158 Richmond/Grant/Owens BW	.25	.60
159 D.Rob/Elliott/Johnson BW	.40	1.00
160 Kemp/Payton/Schrem BW	.25	.60
161 Stoud/Tabak/Wright BW	.20	.50
162 Stockton/Malone/Hornacek BW	.30	.75
163 Reeves/Rahim/Edwards BW	.40	1.00
164 Howard/Muresan/Web BW	.30	.75
165 Michael Jordan GP	2.00	5.00
166 Corliss Williamson GP	.15	.40
167 Dell Curry GP	.15	.40
168 John Starks GP	.20	.50
169 Dennis Rodman GP	.50	1.25
170 C.Webber/L.Sprewell GP	.30	.75
171 Cedric Ceballos GP	.15	.40
172 Theo Ratliff GP	.15	.40
173 Anfernee Hardaway GP	.40	1.00
174 Grant Hill GP	.40	1.00
175 Alonzo Mourning GP	.30	.75
176 Shawn Kemp GP	.25	.60
177 Jason Kidd GP	.40	1.00
178 Avery Johnson GP	.20	.50
179 Gary Payton GP	.25	.60
180 Michael Jordan CL	1.00	2.50
181 Priest Lauderdale RC	.15	.40
182 Dikembe Mutombo	.25	.60
183 Eldridge Recasner RC	.25	.60
184 Steve Smith	.20	.50
185 Pervis Ellison	.15	.40
186 Greg Minor	.15	.40
187 Antoine Walker RC	.40	1.00
188 David Wesley	.15	.40
189 Muggsy Bogues	.20	.50
190 Tony Delk RC	.25	.60
191 Vlade Divac	.25	.60
192 Anthony Mason	.15	.40
193 George Zidek	.15	.40
194 Jason Caffey	.15	.40
195 Steve Kerr	.20	.50
196 Robert Parish	.25	.60
197 Scottie Pippen	.40	1.00
198 Terrell Brandon	.15	.40
199 Antonio Lang	.15	.40
200 Chris Mills	.15	.40
201 Vitaly Potapenko RC	.20	.50
202 Mark West	.15	.40
203 Chris Gatling	.15	.40
204 Derek Harper	.20	.50
205 Sam Cassell	.20	.50
206 Eric Montross	.15	.40
207 Samaki Walker RC	.20	.50
208 Mark Jackson	.20	.50
209 Ervin Johnson	.15	.40
210 Sarunas Marciulionis	.15	.40
211 Ricky Pierce	.15	.40
212 Bryant Stith	.15	.40
213 Stacey Augmon	.20	.50
214 Grant Long	.15	.40
215 Rick Mahorn	.15	.40
216 Otis Thorpe	.15	.40
217 Jerome Williams RC	.20	.50
218 Bimbo Coles	.15	.40
219 Todd Fuller RC	.15	.40
220 Mark Price	.25	.60
221 Felton Spencer	.15	.40
222 Latrell Sprewell	.25	.60
223 Charles Barkley	.40	1.00
224 Othella Harrington RC	.25	.60
225 Hakeem Olajuwon	.30	.75
226 Matt Maloney RC	.20	.50
227 Kevin Willis	.15	.40
228 Erick Dampier RC	.25	.60
229 Duane Ferrell	.15	.40
230 Jalen Rose	.20	.50
231 Rik Smits	.20	.50
232 Terry Dehere	.15	.40
233 Bo Outlaw	.15	.40
234 Pooh Richardson	.15	.40
235 Malik Sealy	.15	.40
236 Lorenzen Wright RC	.20	.50
237 Cedric Ceballos	.15	.40
238 Derek Fisher RC	.30	.75
239 Travis Knight RC	.25	.60
240 Sean Rooks	.15	.40
241 Byron Scott	.20	.50
242 P.J. Brown	.15	.40
243 Voshon Lenard RC	.25	.60
244 Dan Majerle	.25	.60
245 Martin Muursepp RC	.15	.40
246 Gary Grant	.15	.40
247 Vin Baker	.20	.50
248 Armon Gilliam	.15	.40
249 Andrew Lang	.15	.40
250 Elliot Perry	.15	.40
251 Kevin Garnett	.60	1.50
252 Shane Heal RC	.25	.60
253 Cherokee Parks	.15	.40
254 Stojko Vrankovic	.15	.40
255 Kendall Gill	.15	.40
256 Kerry Kittles RC	.25	.60
257 Xavier McDaniel	.15	.40
258 Robert Pack	.15	.40
259 Chris Childs	.15	.40
260 Allan Houston	.20	.50
261 Larry Johnson	.25	.60
262 Dontae' Jones RC	.25	.60
263 Walter McCarty RC	.25	.60
264 Charles Oakley	.20	.50
265 John Wallace RC	.25	.60
266 Buck Williams	.15	.40
267 Brian Evans RC	.25	.60
268 Horace Grant	.20	.50
269 Dennis Scott	.15	.40
270 Rony Seikaly	.15	.40
271 David Vaughn	.15	.40
272 Michael Cage	.15	.40
273 Lucious Harris	.15	.40
274 Don MacLean	.15	.40
275 Mark Davis	.15	.40
276 Jason Kidd	.40	1.00
277 Michael Finley	.30	.75
278 A.C. Green	.20	.50
279 Robert Horry	.20	.50
280 Steve Nash RC	2.00	5.00
281 Wesley Person	.15	.40
282 Kenny Anderson	.20	.50
283 Aleksandar Djordjevic RC	.25	.60
284 Jermaine O'Neal RC	.40	1.00
285 Isaiah Rider	.20	.50
286 Clifford Robinson	.15	.40
287 Rasheed Wallace	.30	.75
288 Mahmoud Abdul-Rauf	.15	.40
289 Billy Owens	.15	.40
290 Mitch Richmond	.25	.60
291 Michael Smith	.15	.40
292 Cory Alexander	.15	.40
293 Sean Elliott	.25	.60
294 Vernon Maxwell	.15	.40
295 Dominique Wilkins	.30	.75
296 Craig Ehlo	.15	.40
297 Jim McIlvaine	.15	.40
298 Sam Perkins	.15	.40
299 Steve Scheffler	.25	.60
300 Hubert Davis	.15	.40
301 Popeye Jones	.15	.40
302 Donald Whiteside RC	.25	.60
303 Walt Williams	.15	.40
304 Karl Malone	.30	.75
305 Greg Ostertag	.15	.40
306 Bryon Russell	.15	.40
307 Jamie Watson	.15	.40
308 Greg Anthony	.15	.40
309 George Lynch	.15	.40
310 Lawrence Moten	.15	.40
311 Anthony Peeler	.15	.40
312 Juwan Howard	.20	.50
313 Tracy Murray	.15	.40
314 Rod Strickland	.15	.40
315 Harvey Grant	.15	.40
316 Charles Barkley DN	.40	1.00
317 Clyde Drexler DN	.30	.75
318 Dikembe Mutombo DN	.25	.60
319 Larry Johnson DN	.25	.60
320 Shaquille O'Neal DN	.60	1.50
321 Mookie Blaylock DN	.15	.40
322 Tim Hardaway DN	.25	.60
323 Dennis Rodman DN	.50	1.25
324 Dan Majerle DN	.25	.60
325 Stacey Augmon DN	.20	.50
326 Anthony Mason DN	.15	.40
327 Kenny Anderson DN	.20	.50
328 Mahmoud Abdul-Rauf DN	.15	.40
329 Chris Webber DN	.30	.75
330 Dominique Wilkins DN	.30	.75
331 Dikembe Mutombo WD	.25	.60
332 Dana Barros WD	.15	.40
333 Glen Rice WD	.25	.60
334 Dennis Rodman WD	.50	1.25
335 Terrell Brandon WD	.15	.40
336 Jason Kidd WD	.40	1.00
337 Antonio McDyess WD	.25	.60
338 Grant Hill WD	.40	1.00
339 Joe Smith WD	.20	.50
340 Charles Barkley WD	.40	1.00
341 Reggie Miller WD	.30	.75
342 Brent Barry WD	.20	.50
343 Shaquille O'Neal WD	.60	1.50
344 Alonzo Mourning WD	.30	.75
345 Glenn Robinson WD	.20	.50
346 Stephon Marbury WD	.30	.75
347 Kerry Kittles WD	.12	.30
348 Patrick Ewing WD	.30	.75
349 Anfernee Hardaway WD	.40	1.00
350 Allen Iverson WD	.60	1.50
351 Danny Manning WD	.20	.50
352 Arvydas Sabonis WD	.20	.50
353 Mitch Richmond WD	.25	.60
354 David Robinson WD	.40	1.00
355 Shawn Kemp WD	.25	.60
356 Marcus Camby WD	.20	.50
357 Karl Malone WD	.30	.75
358 Shareef Abdur-Rahim WD	.20	.50
359 Gheorghe Muresan WD	.15	.40
360 Checklist 181-360	.15	.40

1996-97 Upper Deck Autographs

Hand-numbered to 500, these autographed cards were randomly inserted into packs of series 2 Upper Deck. The cards feature the autograph on the card front, with a congratulatory message on the back. The backs are also numbered with an "A" prefix.

HAND NUMBERED TO 500		
A1 Anfernee Hardaway	25.00	60.00
A2 Shawn Kemp	30.00	80.00
A3 Antonio McDyess	20.00	50.00
A4 Damon Stoudamire	20.00	50.00

1996-97 Upper Deck Fast Break Connections

Randomly inserted in series one packs at a rate of one in eight, this set features color photos of 30 players. Each card features three different players from the same team on special die-cut designs that are combined into one over-sized card. Each card is numbered with a "FB" prefix.

COMPLETE SET (30)	15.00	40.00
SER.1 STATED ODDS 1:8		
FB1 Jim Jackson	.40	1.00
FB2 Jason Kidd	1.00	2.50
FB3 Jamal Mashburn	.50	1.25
FB4 Mario Elie	.40	1.00
FB5 Hakeem Olajuwon	.75	2.00
FB6 Clyde Drexler	.75	2.00
FB7 Cedric Ceballos	.40	1.00
FB8 Nick Van Exel	.60	1.50
FB9 Eddie Jones	.60	1.50
FB10 Danny Manning	.50	1.25
FB11 Michael Finley	.75	2.00
FB12 Kevin Johnson	.60	1.50
FB13 Tyus Edney	.40	1.00
FB14 Brian Grant	.50	1.25
FB15 Mitch Richmond	.60	1.50
FB16 Sean Elliott	.60	1.50
FB17 David Robinson	1.00	2.50
FB18 Avery Johnson	.50	1.25
FB19 Shawn Kemp	.60	1.50
FB20 Gary Payton	.60	1.50
FB21 Detlef Schrempf	.60	1.50
FB22 Scottie Pippen	1.00	2.50
FB23 Michael Jordan	5.00	12.00
FB24 Toni Kukoc	.60	1.50
FB25 Sherman Douglas	.40	1.00
FB26 Glenn Robinson	.50	1.25
FB27 Vin Baker	.50	1.25
FB28 Jeff Hornacek	.50	1.25
FB29 John Stockton	.75	2.00
FB30 Karl Malone	.75	2.00

1996-97 Upper Deck Generation Excitement

Randomly inserted in series one packs at a rate of one in 33, this 30-card set features some of the biggest young stars of the 1990's who willl take the game into the next century. The fronts display color action player images on a background with a head photo of the player on a unique die cut card. Each card is numbered with a "G" prefix.

COMPLETE SET (20)	30.00	80.00
SER.1 STATED ODDS 1:33		
G1 Steve Smith	2.00	5.00
G2 Eric Williams	1.50	4.00
G3 Jason Kidd	4.00	10.00
G4 Antonio McDyess	2.50	6.00
G5 Grant Hill	4.00	10.00
G6 Joe Smith	2.00	5.00
G7 Brent Barry	2.00	5.00
G8 Eddie Jones	2.50	6.00
G9 Vin Baker	2.00	5.00
G10 Kevin Garnett	6.00	15.00
G11 Ed O'Bannon	1.50	4.00
G12 Anfernee Hardaway	4.00	10.00
G13 Jerry Stackhouse	3.00	8.00
G14 Michael Finley	3.00	8.00
G15 Gary Trent	1.50	4.00
G16 Tyus Edney	1.50	4.00
G17 Sean Elliott	2.50	6.00
G18 Shawn Kemp	2.50	6.00
G19 Damon Stoudamire	2.00	5.00
G20 Gheorghe Muresan	1.50	4.00

1996-97 Upper Deck Jordan Greater Heights

Randomly inserted in series one packs at a rate of one in 71, this 10-card set features highlights of Michael Jordan's many trips to the basket. Each card focuses on an area of the game including shooting, dunking, rebounding and defense. Each card is numbered with a "GH" prefix.

COMPLETE SET (10)	20.00	50.00
COMMON JORDAN (1-10)	6.00	15.00
SER.1 STATED ODDS 1:66 HOB/RET		

1996-97 Upper Deck Jordan Greater Heights Jumbos

Sold as a box set in retail outlets, this 10-card set is a jumbo parallel to the Jordan Greater Heights inserted in series one 96-97 Upper Deck packs.

COMPLETE SET (10)	10.00	25.00
COMMON CARD (GH1-GH10)	1.25	3.00

1996-97 Upper Deck Jordan's Viewpoints

Randomly inserted in series two packs at a rate of one in 34, this 10-card die cut set focuses on Michael Jordan's preparation for a full game. Some of the card themes include practice, talking to the media and winning. Each card is numbered with a "VP" prefix.

COMPLETE SET (10)	25.00	60.00
COMMON JORDAN (1-10)	5.00	12.00
SER.2 STATED ODDS 1:34 HOB/RET		

1996-97 Upper Deck Michael's Viewpoints Jumbos

Available as a set through retail outlets for around $10, this 10-card set is a jumbo parallel to the same set that was issued in 1996-97 Upper Deck focusing on Michael Jordan's preparation for a full game. Measuring 3 1/2" x 5", some of the card themes include practice, talking to the media and winning. These cards do not have the shadow of MJ cut-out nor is their any foil treatment on the card fronts like its standard-sized counterparts. Each card is numbered with a "VP" prefix.

COMPLETE SET (10)	10.00	25.00
COMMON CARD (VP1-VP10)	1.25	3.00

1996-97 Upper Deck Predictor Scoring 1

Randomly inserted in series one packs at a rate of one in 23, this 30-card set featured interactive cards based on the above-average game output of 30 players in the scoring category. If the player reached the performance goal printed on the front of the card, the card could be traded for a SP-quality replacement. Each card is numbered with a "P" prefix.

COMPLETE SET (20)	15.00	40.00
SER.1 STATED ODDS 1:23		
PREDICTOR EXPIRATION: 5/1/97		
*TV CEL RED.CARDS: .6X TO 1.5X HI COL.		
P1 Mookie Blaylock	.60	1.50
P2 Dino Radja	.60	1.50
P3 Michael Jordan	8.00	20.00
P4 Terrell Brandon	.60	1.50
P5 Jason Kidd	1.50	4.00
P6 Joe Dumars	1.00	2.50
P7 Joe Smith	.75	2.00
P8 Hakeem Olajuwon	1.25	3.00
P9 Rik Smits	.75	2.00
P10 Brent Barry	.75	2.00
P11 Kurt Thomas	.60	1.50
P12 Anfernee Hardaway	1.50	4.00
P13 Clarence Weatherspoon	.60	1.50
P14 Clifford Robinson	.60	1.50
P15 Mitch Richmond	1.00	2.50
P16 David Robinson	1.50	4.00
P17 Shawn Kemp	1.00	2.50
P18 Damon Stoudamire	.75	2.00
P19 Karl Malone	1.25	3.00
P20 Bryant Reeves	.60	1.50

1996-97 Upper Deck Predictor Scoring 2

Randomly inserted in series two packs at a rate of one in 23, this 20-card set featured interactive cards based on the above-average game output of 30 players in the scoring category. If the player reached the performance goal printed on the front of the card, the card could be traded for a SP-quality replacement. Each card is numbered with a "P" prefix.

COMPLETE SET (20)	20.00	50.00
SER.2 STATED ODDS 1:23		
*TV CEL RED.CARDS: .6X TO 1.5X HI COL.		
P1 Glen Rice	1.00	2.50
P2 Michael Jordan	8.00	20.00
P3 Jamal Mashburn	.75	2.00
P4 Antonio McDyess	1.00	2.50
P5 Charles Barkley	1.50	4.00
P6 Reggie Miller	1.25	3.00
P7 Shaquille O'Neal	2.50	6.00
P8 Alonzo Mourning	1.25	3.00
P9 Vin Baker	.75	2.00
P10 Kevin Garnett	2.50	6.00
P11 Kerry Kittles	.60	1.50
P12 Patrick Ewing	1.25	3.00
P13 Anfernee Hardaway	1.50	4.00
P14 Allen Iverson	4.00	10.00
P15 Robert Horry	.75	2.00
P16 Shawn Kemp	1.00	2.50
P17 Marcus Camby	1.00	2.50
P18 John Stockton	1.25	3.00
P19 Shareef Abdur-Rahim	1.00	2.50
P20 Juwan Howard	.75	2.00

1996-97 Upper Deck Rookie Exclusives

Randomly inserted in series two packs at a rate of one in 4, this 20-card set focuses on the 1996-97 rookie class and features quotes from selected NBA stars on each rookie. Card fronts have a basketball textured background. Each card is numbered with a "R" prefix.

COMPLETE SET (20)	15.00	40.00
SER.2 STATED ODDS 1:4 HOB/RET, 1:2 JUM		
R1 Allen Iverson	2.50	6.00
R2 John Wallace	.50	1.25
R3 Kerry Kittles	.50	1.25
R4 Roy Rogers	.40	1.00
R5 Marcus Camby	.75	2.00
R6 Antoine Walker	.75	2.00
R7 Ray Allen	2.00	5.00
R8 Samaki Walker	.40	1.00
R9 Walter McCarty	.50	1.25

R10 Kobe Bryant 5.00 12.00
R11 Shareef Abdur-Rahim .75 2.00
R12 Dontae' Jones .50 1.25
R13 Todd Fuller .30 .75
R14 Lorenzen Wright .40 1.00
R15 Stephon Marbury 1.25 3.00
R16 Vitaly Potapenko .40 1.00
R17 Tony Delk .50 1.25
R18 Steve Nash 2.50 6.00
R19 Jermaine O'Neal .75 2.00
R20 Erick Dampier .50 1.25
R1P Allen Iverson PROMO 1.00 2.50
R10P Kobe Bryant PROMO 2.00 5.00

1996-97 Upper Deck Rookie of the Year Collection

Randomly inserted in series two packs at a rate of one in 138, this 14-card set spotlight current NBA players who have been named NBA Rookie of the Year. Each card is die cut and features a shot of the player in a rectangle in the middle of the card. Card backs are numbered with a "RC" prefix.

COMPLETE SET (14) 75.00 150.00
SER.2 STATED ODDS 1:138
RC1 Damon Stoudamire 3.00 8.00
RC2 Grant Hill 6.00 15.00
RC3 Jason Kidd 5.00 12.00
RC4 Chris Webber 5.00 12.00
RC5 Shaquille O'Neal 10.00 25.00
RC6 Larry Johnson 4.00 10.00
RC7 Derrick Coleman 3.00 8.00
RC8 David Robinson 6.00 15.00
RC9 Mitch Richmond 4.00 10.00
RC10 Mark Jackson 3.00 8.00
RC11 Chuck Person 3.00 8.00
RC12 Patrick Ewing 5.00 12.00
RC13 Michael Jordan 25.00 60.00
RC14 Buck Williams 2.50 6.00

1996-97 Upper Deck Smooth Grooves

Randomly inserted in series two packs at a rate of one in 72, the 15-card set focuses on players whose slick moves are reminiscent of the great players of the 60's and 70's. Card fronts are full-bleed and feature a shot of the player "swirled" in the background. Card backs are numbered with a "SG" prefix.

COMPLETE SET (15) 50.00 120.00
SER.2 STATED ODDS 1:72
SG1 Dennis Rodman 4.00 10.00
SG2 Jason Kidd 3.00 8.00
SG3 Grant Hill 3.00 8.00
SG4 Damon Stoudamire 1.50 4.00
SG5 Shaquille O'Neal 5.00 12.00
SG6 Clyde Drexler 2.50 6.00
SG7 Shareef Abdur-Rahim 3.00 8.00
SG8 Michael Jordan 15.00 40.00
SG9 Alonzo Mourning 2.50 6.00
SG10 Allen Iverson 5.00 12.00
SG11 Vin Baker 1.50 4.00
SG12 Kevin Garnett 5.00 12.00
SG13 Anfernee Hardaway 3.00 8.00
SG14 Jerry Stackhouse 2.50 6.00
SG15 Shawn Kemp 2.00 5.00

1997-98 Upper Deck

The 1997-98 Upper Deck set was issued in two series totaling 360 cards and was distributed in 12-card packs with a suggested retail price of $2.49. The fronts feature color action player photos while the backs carry player information. The set contains the topical subsets: Jams '97 (136-164), Court Perspectives (165-179), Overtime (316-330) and Defining Moments (331-359).

COMPLETE SET (360) 25.00 50.00
COMPLETE SERIES 1 (180) 12.50 25.00
COMPLETE SERIES 2 (180) 12.50 25.00
BLACK POWER AUDIO 1:23 HOBBY
RED POWER AUDIO 1:72 HOBBY
UNPRICED WHITE AUDIO SERIAL #'d TO 1
1 Steve Smith .20 .50
2 Christian Laettner .20 .50
3 Alan Henderson .15 .40
4 Dikembe Mutombo .25 .60
5 Dana Barros .15 .40
6 Antoine Walker .25 .60
7 Dee Brown .15 .40
8 Eric Williams .15 .40
9 Muggsy Bogues .20 .50
10 Dell Curry .15 .40
11 Vlade Divac .25 .60
12 Anthony Mason .15 .40
13 Glen Rice .25 .60
14 Jason Caffey .15 .40
15 Steve Kerr .20 .50
16 Toni Kukoc .25 .60
17 Luc Longley .20 .50
18 Michael Jordan 2.00 5.00
19 Terrell Brandon .15 .40
20 Danny Ferry .15 .40
21 Tyrone Hill .15 .40
22 Derek Anderson RC .25 .60
23 Bob Sura .15 .40
24 Shawn Bradley .15 .40
25 Michael Finley .25 .60
26 Ed O'Bannon .15 .40
27 Robert Pack .15 .40
28 Samaki Walker .15 .40
29 LaPhonso Ellis .15 .40
30 Tony Battie RC .25 .60
31 Antonio McDyess .20 .50
32 Bryant Stith .15 .40
33 Randolph Childress .15 .40
34 Grant Hill .40 1.00
35 Lindsey Hunter .15 .40
36 Grant Long .15 .40
37 Theo Ratliff .20 .50
38 B.J. Armstrong .15 .40
39 Adonal Foyle RC .20 .50
40 Mark Price .25 .60
41 Felton Spencer .15 .40
42 Latrell Sprewell .25 .60
43 Clyde Drexler .30 .75
44 Mario Elie .15 .40
45 Hakeem Olajuwon .30 .75
46 Brent Price .15 .40
47 Kevin Willis .15 .40
48 Erick Dampier .15 .40
49 Antonio Davis .15 .40
50 Dale Davis .15 .40
51 Mark Jackson .20 .50
52 Rik Smits .20 .50
53 Brent Barry .20 .50
54 Lamond Murray .15 .40
55 Eric Piatkowski .20 .50
56 Loy Vaught .15 .40
57 Lorenzen Wright .15 .40
58 Kobe Bryant 1.25 3.00
59 Elden Campbell .15 .40
60 Derek Fisher .25 .60
61 Eddie Jones .25 .60
62 Nick Van Exel .20 .50
63 Keith Askins .15 .40
64 Isaac Austin .15 .40
65 P.J. Brown .15 .40
66 Tim Hardaway .25 .60
67 Alonzo Mourning .30 .75
68 Ray Allen .30 .75
69 Vin Baker .20 .50
70 Sherman Douglas .15 .40
71 Armon Gilliam .15 .40
72 Elliot Perry .15 .40
73 Chris Carr .15 .40
74 Tom Gugliotta .15 .40
75 Kevin Garnett .40 1.00
76 Doug West .15 .40
77 Keith Van Horn RC .40 1.00
78 Chris Gatling .15 .40
79 Kendall Gill .15 .40
80 Kerry Kittles .15 .40
81 Jayson Williams .15 .40
82 Chris Childs .15 .40
83 Allan Houston .20 .50
84 Larry Johnson .25 .60
85 Charles Oakley .20 .50
86 John Starks .20 .50
87 Horace Grant .20 .50
88 Anfernee Hardaway .40 1.00
89 Dennis Scott .15 .40
90 Rony Seikaly .15 .40
91 Brian Shaw .15 .40
92 Derrick Coleman .20 .50
93 Allen Iverson .50 1.25
94 Tim Thomas RC .30 .75
95 Scott Williams .15 .40
96 Cedric Ceballos .15 .40
97 Kevin Johnson .25 .60
98 Loren Meyer .15 .40
99 Steve Nash .50 1.25
100 Wesley Person .15 .40
101 Kenny Anderson .20 .50
102 Jermaine O'Neal .20 .50
103 Isaiah Rider .20 .50
104 Arvydas Sabonis .20 .50
105 Gary Trent .15 .40
106 Mahmoud Abdul-Rauf .15 .40
107 Billy Owens .15 .40
108 Olden Polynice .15 .40
109 Mitch Richmond .25 .60
110 Michael Smith .15 .40
111 Cory Alexander .15 .40
112 Vinny Del Negro .15 .40
113 Carl Herrera .15 .40
114 Tim Duncan RC 1.25 3.00
115 Hersey Hawkins .15 .40
116 Shawn Kemp .25 .60
117 Nate McMillan .15 .40
118 Sam Perkins .15 .40
119 Detlef Schrempf .25 .60
120 Doug Christie .15 .40
121 Popeye Jones .15 .40
122 Carlos Rogers .15 .40
123 Damon Stoudamire .20 .50
124 Adam Keefe .15 .40
125 Chris Morris .15 .40
126 Greg Ostertag .15 .40
127 John Stockton .30 .75
128 Shareef Abdur-Rahim .25 .60
129 George Lynch .15 .40
130 Lee Mayberry .15 .40
131 Anthony Peeler .15 .40
132 Calbert Cheaney .15 .40
133 Tracy Murray .15 .40
134 Rod Strickland .15 .40
135 Chris Webber .25 .60
136 Christian Laettner JAM .20 .50
137 Eric Williams JAM .15 .40
138 Vlade Divac JAM .25 .60
139 Michael Jordan JAM 2.00 5.00
140 Tyrone Hill JAM .15 .40
141 Michael Finley JAM .25 .60
142 Tom Hammonds JAM .15 .40
143 Theo Ratliff JAM .20 .50
144 Latrell Sprewell JAM .25 .60
145 Hakeem Olajuwon JAM .30 .75
146 Reggie Miller JAM .30 .75
147 Rodney Rogers JAM .15 .40
148 Eddie Jones JAM .25 .60
149 Jamal Mashburn JAM .20 .50
150 Glenn Robinson JAM .20 .50
151 Chris Carr JAM .15 .40
152 Kendall Gill JAM .15 .40
153 John Starks JAM .20 .50
154 Anfernee Hardaway JAM .40 1.00
155 Derrick Coleman JAM .20 .50
156 Cedric Ceballos JAM .15 .40
157 Rasheed Wallace JAM .25 .60
158 Corliss Williamson JAM .15 .40
159 Sean Elliott JAM .25 .60
160 Shawn Kemp JAM .25 .60
161 Doug Christie JAM .15 .40
162 Karl Malone JAM .30 .75
163 Bryant Reeves JAM .15 .40
164 Gheorghe Muresan JAM .15 .40
165 Michael Jordan CP 2.00 5.00
166 Dikembe Mutombo CP .25 .60
167 Glen Rice CP .25 .60
168 Mitch Richmond CP .25 .60
169 Juwan Howard CP .20 .50
170 Clyde Drexler CP .30 .75
171 Terrell Brandon CP .15 .40
172 Jerry Stackhouse CP .25 .60
173 Damon Stoudamire CP .20 .50
174 Jayson Williams CP .15 .40
175 P.J. Brown CP .15 .40
176 Anfernee Hardaway CP .40 1.00
177 Vin Baker CP .20 .50
178 LaPhonso Ellis CP .15 .40
179 Shawn Kemp CP .25 .60
180 Checklist .15 .40
181 Mookie Blaylock .15 .40
182 Tyrone Corbin .15 .40
183 Chucky Brown .15 .40
184 Ed Gray RC .25 .60
185 Chauncey Billups RC .75 2.00
186 Tyus Edney .15 .40
187 Travis Knight .15 .40
188 Ron Mercer RC .30 .75
189 Walter McCarty .15 .40
190 B.J. Armstrong .15 .40
191 Matt Geiger .15 .40
192 Bobby Phills .15 .40
193 David Wesley .15 .40
194 Keith Booth RC .20 .50
195 Randy Brown .15 .40
196 Ron Harper .20 .50
197 Scottie Pippen .40 1.00
198 Dennis Rodman .50 1.25
199 Zydrunas Ilgauskas .25 .60
200 Brevin Knight RC .25 .60
201 Shawn Kemp .25 .60
202 Vitaly Potapenko .15 .40
203 Wesley Person .15 .40
204 Erick Strickland RC .20 .50
205 A.C. Green .20 .50
206 Khalid Reeves .15 .40
207 Hubert Davis .15 .40
208 Dennis Scott .15 .40
209 Danny Fortson RC .25 .60
210 Bobby Jackson RC .30 .75
211 Eric Williams .15 .40
212 Dean Garrett .15 .40
213 Priest Lauderdale .15 .40
214 Joe Dumars .25 .60
215 Aaron McKie .15 .40
216 Scot Pollard RC .25 .60
217 Brian Williams .15 .40
218 Malik Sealy .15 .40
219 Duane Ferrell .15 .40
220 Erick Dampier .15 .40
221 Todd Fuller .15 .40
222 Donyell Marshall .15 .40
223 Joe Smith .20 .50
224 Charles Barkley .40 1.00
225 Matt Bullard .15 .40
226 Othella Harrington .15 .40
227 Rodrick Rhodes RC .20 .50
228 Eddie Johnson .15 .40
229 Matt Maloney .15 .40
230 Travis Best .15 .40
231 Reggie Miller .30 .75
232 Chris Mullin .25 .60
233 Fred Hoiberg .15 .40
234 Austin Croshere RC .20 .50
235 Keith Closs RC .25 .60
236 Darrick Martin .15 .40
237 Pooh Richardson .15 .40
238 Rodney Rogers .15 .40
239 Maurice Taylor RC .25 .60
240 Robert Horry .20 .50
241 Rick Fox .15 .40
242 Shaquille O'Neal .60 1.50
243 Corie Blount .15 .40
244 Charles Smith RC .20 .50
245 Voshon Lenard .15 .40
246 Eric Murdock .15 .40
247 Dan Majerle .25 .60
248 Terry Mills .15 .40
249 Terrell Brandon .15 .40
250 Tyrone Hill .15 .40
251 Ervin Johnson .15 .40
252 Glenn Robinson .20 .50
253 Terry Porter .15 .40
254 Paul Grant RC .15 .40
255 Stephon Marbury .30 .75
256 Sam Mitchell .15 .40
257 Cherokee Parks .15 .40
258 Sam Cassell .20 .50
259 David Benoit .15 .40
260 Kevin Edwards .15 .40
261 Don MacLean .15 .40
262 Patrick Ewing .30 .75
263 Herb Williams .15 .40
264 John Starks .20 .50
265 Chris Mills .15 .40
266 Chris Dudley .15 .40
267 Darrell Armstrong .15 .40
268 Nick Anderson .15 .40
269 Derek Harper .20 .50
270 Johnny Taylor RC .20 .50
271 Mark Price .25 .60
272 Clarence Weatherspoon .15 .40
273 Jerry Stackhouse .25 .60
274 Eric Montross .15 .40
275 Anthony Parker RC .25 .60
276 Antonio McDyess .20 .50
277 Clifford Robinson .15 .40
278 Jason Kidd .40 1.00
279 Danny Manning .20 .50
280 Rex Chapman .15 .40
281 Stacey Augmon .20 .50
282 Kelvin Cato RC .20 .50
283 Brian Grant .15 .40
284 Rasheed Wallace .25 .60
285 Lawrence Funderburke RC .25 .60
286 Anthony Johnson .25 .60
287 Tariq Abdul-Wahad RC .20 .50
288 Corliss Williamson .15 .40
289 Sean Elliott .25 .60
290 Avery Johnson .20 .50
291 David Robinson .40 1.00
292 Will Perdue .15 .40
293 Greg Anthony .15 .40
294 Jim McIlvaine .15 .40
295 Dale Ellis .15 .40
296 Gary Payton .25 .60
297 Aaron Williams .15 .40
298 Marcus Camby .25 .60
299 John Wallace .15 .40
300 Tracy McGrady RC 1.00 2.50
301 Walt Williams .15 .40
302 Shandon Anderson .15 .40
303 Antoine Carr .15 .40
304 Jeff Hornacek .20 .50
305 Karl Malone .30 .75
306 Bryon Russell .15 .40
307 Jacque Vaughn RC .20 .50
308 Antonio Daniels RC .25 .60
309 Blue Edwards .15 .40
310 Bryant Reeves .15 .40
311 Otis Thorpe .15 .40
312 Harvey Grant .15 .40
313 Terry Davis .15 .40
314 Juwan Howard .20 .50
315 Gheorghe Muresan .15 .40
316 Michael Jordan OT 2.00 5.00
317 Allen Iverson OT .50 1.25
318 Karl Malone OT .30 .75
319 Glen Rice OT .25 .60
320 Dikembe Mutombo OT .25 .60
321 Grant Hill OT .40 1.00
322 Hakeem Olajuwon OT .30 .75
323 Stephon Marbury OT .30 .75
324 Anfernee Hardaway OT .40 1.00
325 Eddie Jones OT .25 .60
326 Mitch Richmond OT .25 .60
327 Kevin Johnson OT .25 .60
328 Kevin Garnett OT .40 1.00
329 Shareef Abdur-Rahim OT .25 .60
330 Damon Stoudamire OT .20 .50
331 Atlanta Hawks DM .20 .50
332 Boston Celtics DM .20 .50
333 Charlotte Hornets DM .20 .50
334 Chicago Bulls DM .40 1.00
335 Cleveland Cavaliers DM .20 .50
336 Dallas Mavericks DM .20 .50
337 Denver Nuggets DM .25 .60
338 Detroit Pistons DM .25 .60
339 Golden State Warriors DM .25 .60
340 Houston Rockets DM .30 .75
341 Indiana Pacers DM .20 .50
342 Los Angeles Clippers DM .20 .50
343 Los Angeles Lakers DM .40 1.00
344 Miami Heat DM .25 .60
345 Milwaukee Bucks DM .20 .50
346 Minnesota Timberwolves DM .20 .50
347 New Jersey Nets DM .20 .50
348 New York Knicks DM .20 .50
349 Orlando Magic DM .25 .60
350 Philadelphia 76ers DM .20 .50
351 Phoenix Suns DM .20 .50
352 Portland Trail Blazers DM .20 .50
353 Sacramento Kings DM .20 .50
354 San Antonio Spurs DM .40 1.00
355 Seattle Sonics DM .25 .60
356 Toronto Raptors DM .40 1.00
357 Utah Jazz DM .25 .60
358 Vancouver Grizzlies DM .20 .50
359 Washington Wizards DM .20 .50
360 Checklist .15 .40
NNO Michael Jordan Red Audio 10.00 25.00
NNO Michael Jordan Black Audio 4.00 10.00

1997-98 Upper Deck Game Dated Memorable Moments

*STARS: 12.5X TO 30X BASE CARD HI
SER.1 STATED ODDS 1:1500
18 Michael Jordan 150.00 300.00
61 Eddie Jones 10.00 25.00

1997-98 Upper Deck AIRlines

Randomly inserted in series two packs at a rate of one in 230 packs, this 12-card die cut set chronicles each year in Michael Jordan's career. Card backs are numbered with an "AL" prefix.

COMPLETE SET (12) 250.00 450.00
COMMON JORDAN (AL1-12) 15.00 40.00
SER.2 STATED ODDS 1:230 HOB/RET

1997-98 Upper Deck Game Jerseys

Randomly inserted in both series packs at the rate of one in 2,500, this 22-card set features color player images on a jersey print background with an actual piece of an NBA game worn jersey embedded in the card. Series two packs also contained a special Michael Jordan autographed Game Jersey, which was hand-numbered to 23.

SER.1/2 STATED ODDS 1:2500
JORDAN AU: RANDOM INS.IN SER.2 HOB
GJ1 Charles Barkley 400.00 800.00
GJ2 Clyde Drexler 100.00 250.00
GJ3 Kevin Garnett 200.00 400.00
GJ4 Anfernee Hardaway HOME 400.00 800.00
GJ5 Grant Hill HOME 175.00 350.00
GJ6 Allen Iverson 350.00 700.00
GJ7 Kerry Kittles 60.00 150.00
GJ8 Toni Kukoc 150.00 300.00
GJ9 Reggie Miller 175.00 350.00
GJ10 Hakeem Olajuwon 125.00 250.00
GJ11 Glen Rice 75.00 200.00
GJ12 David Robinson 200.00 400.00
GJ13 Michael Jordan 3000.00 4000.00
GJ14 Alonzo Mourning 100.00 200.00
GJ15 Tim Hardaway 100.00 250.00
GJ16 Marcus Camby 100.00 250.00
GJ17 Antoine Walker 60.00 150.00
GJ18 Kevin Johnson 60.00 150.00
GJ19 Glenn Robinson 50.00 120.00
GJ20 Patrick Ewing 125.00 300.00
GJ21 Anfernee Hardaway AWAY 400.00 800.00
GJ22 Grant Hill AWAY 175.00 350.00

1997-98 Upper Deck Great Eight

Randomly inserted into series two packs, this 8-card set features eight of the best veterans in the NBA. The card backs are serially numbered to 800 and carry a "G" prefix.

STATED PRINT RUN 800 SERIAL #'d SETS
G1 Charles Barkley 10.00 25.00
G2 Clyde Drexler 8.00 20.00
G3 Joe Dumars 6.00 15.00
G4 Patrick Ewing 8.00 20.00
G5 Michael Jordan 100.00 250.00
G6 Karl Malone 8.00 20.00
G7 Hakeem Olajuwon 8.00 20.00
G8 John Stockton 8.00 20.00

1997-98 Upper Deck High Dimensions

Randomly inserted in series one packs, this 30-card set is parallel to the Diamond Dimensions insert set. Only 2,000 of each card was produced and are sequentially numbered.

STATED PRINT RUN 2000 SERIAL #'d SETS
D1 Anfernee Hardaway 8.00 20.00
D2 Gary Payton 5.00 12.00
D3 Marcus Camby 5.00 12.00
D4 Charles Barkley 8.00 20.00
D5 Jason Kidd 8.00 20.00
D6 Alonzo Mourning 6.00 15.00
D7 Kenny Anderson 4.00 10.00
D8 Kobe Bryant 25.00 60.00
D9 Dennis Rodman 10.00 25.00
D10 Kerry Kittles 3.00 8.00
D11 Dikembe Mutombo 5.00 12.00
D12 Shaquille O'Neal 12.00 30.00
D13 Glenn Robinson 4.00 10.00
D14 Tony Delk 3.00 8.00
D15 Larry Johnson 5.00 12.00
D16 Brent Barry 4.00 10.00
D17 Scottie Pippen 8.00 20.00
D18 Shareef Abdur-Rahim 5.00 12.00
D19 Sean Elliott 5.00 12.00
D20 Damon Stoudamire 4.00 10.00
D21 Kevin Garnett 8.00 20.00
D22 Bob Sura 3.00 8.00
D23 Michael Jordan 40.00 100.00
D24 Latrell Sprewell 5.00 12.00
D25 Karl Malone 6.00 15.00
D26 Antonio McDyess 4.00 10.00
D27 Allen Iverson 10.00 25.00
D28 Dale Davis 3.00 8.00
D29 Antoine Walker 5.00 12.00
D30 Chris Webber 5.00 12.00

1997-98 Upper Deck Diamond Dimensions

*STARS: 4X TO 10X HIGH DIMEN. HI
STATED PRINT RUN 100 SERIAL #'d SETS
D1 Anfernee Hardaway 125.00 250.00
D4 Charles Barkley 200.00 300.00
D9 Dennis Rodman 175.00 350.00
D12 Shaquille O'Neal 200.00 400.00
D21 Kevin Garnett 150.00 400.00
D23 Michael Jordan 400.00 800.00
D24 Latrell Sprewell 60.00 150.00
D25 Karl Malone 75.00 200.00

1997-98 Upper Deck Jordan Air Time

Randomly inserted in series one packs at the rate of one in 12, this 10-card set features color action photos of Michael Jordan printed on double-front style cards. The set is comprised of three different fronts, or "Departures," and three different backs, or "Arrivals." The first nine cards combine to create a Jordan "Flight" to the basket. The tenth card features front and back photos and is tougher to find than the first nine, thus commanding a premium.

COMPLETE SET (10) 25.00 60.00
COMMON JORDAN (AT1-9) 2.50 6.00
COMMON JORDAN (AT10) 15.00 40.00
SER.1 STATED ODDS 1:12

1997-98 Upper Deck Records Collection

Randomly inserted into series two packs at a rate of one in 23, this 30-card set features a special look at the outstanding achievements of great NBA performers. The card fronts are similar to a record with a black etched background. Card backs carry a "RC" prefix.

COMPLETE SET (30) 40.00 100.00
SER.2 STATED ODDS 1:23
RC1 Dikembe Mutombo 1.50 4.00
RC2 Dana Barros 1.00 2.50
RC3 Glen Rice 1.50 4.00
RC4 Dennis Rodman 3.00 8.00
RC5 Shawn Kemp 1.50 4.00
RC6 A.C. Green 1.25 3.00
RC7 LaPhonso Ellis 1.00 2.50
RC8 Grant Hill 2.50 6.00
RC9 Joe Smith 1.25 3.00
RC10 Charles Barkley 2.50 6.00
RC11 Reggie Miller 2.00 5.00
RC12 Loy Vaught 1.00 2.50
RC13 Shaquille O'Neal 4.00 10.00
RC14 Tim Hardaway 1.50 4.00
RC15 Glenn Robinson 1.25 3.00
RC16 Stephon Marbury 2.00 5.00
RC17 Sam Cassell 1.25 3.00
RC18 Patrick Ewing 2.00 5.00
RC19 Anfernee Hardaway 2.50 6.00
RC20 Allen Iverson 3.00 8.00
RC21 Kevin Johnson 1.50 4.00
RC22 Kenny Anderson 1.25 3.00
RC23 Mitch Richmond 1.50 4.00
RC24 David Robinson 2.50 6.00
RC25 Gary Payton 1.50 4.00
RC26 Damon Stoudamire 1.25 3.00
RC27 John Stockton 2.00 5.00
RC28 Bryant Reeves 1.00 2.50
RC29 Chris Webber 1.50 4.00
RC30 Michael Jordan 12.00 30.00

1997-98 Upper Deck Rookie Discovery 1

Randomly inserted into packs at a rate of one in four, this 15-card set focuses on the 1997 Rookie Class, and their thoughts and secrets on the game. Card backs are numbered with a "R" prefix.

COMPLETE SET (15) 6.00 15.00
SER.2 STATED ODDS 1:4
*RD2: 2.5X TO 6X HI COLUMN
RD2: SER.2 STATED ODDS 1:108
R1 Tim Duncan 1.50 4.00
R2 Keith Van Horn .50 1.25
R3 Chauncey Billups 1.00 2.50
R4 Antonio Daniels .30 .75
R5 Tony Battie .30 .75
R6 Ron Mercer .40 1.00
R7 Tim Thomas .40 1.00
R8 Adonal Foyle .25 .60
R9 Tracy McGrady 1.25 3.00
R10 Danny Fortson .30 .75
R11 Tariq Abdul-Wahad .25 .60
R12 Austin Croshere .25 .60
R13 Derek Anderson .30 .75
R14 Maurice Taylor .30 .75
R15 Kelvin Cato .25 .60

1997-98 Upper Deck Teammates

Randomly inserted in series one packs at the rate of one in four, this 60-card set features color action photos of players who are the top tandems for each team in the league printed on die-cut, embossed cards.. When the teammates are placed together, the cards spell out the team name.

COMPLETE SET (60) 15.00 40.00
SER.1 STATED ODDS 1:4
T1 Mookie Blaylock .30 .75
T2 Steve Smith .40 1.00
T3 Antoine Walker .50 1.25
T4 Dana Barros .30 .75
T5 Anthony Mason .30 .75
T6 Glen Rice .50 1.25
T7 Michael Jordan 4.00 10.00
T8 Scottie Pippen .75 2.00
T9 Terrell Brandon .30 .75
T10 Tyrone Hill .30 .75
T11 Shawn Bradley .30 .75
T12 Robert Pack .30 .75
T13 LaPhonso Ellis .30 .75
T14 Antonio McDyess .40 1.00
T15 Grant Hill .75 2.00
T16 Lindsey Hunter .30 .75
T17 Latrell Sprewell .50 1.25
T18 Joe Smith .40 1.00
T19 Hakeem Olajuwon .60 1.50
T20 Charles Barkley .75 2.00
T21 Mark Jackson .40 1.00
T22 Reggie Miller .60 1.50
T23 Brent Barry .40 1.00
T24 Loy Vaught .30 .75
T25 Shaquille O'Neal 1.25 3.00
T26 Nick Van Exel .40 1.00
T27 Tim Hardaway .50 1.25
T28 Alonzo Mourning .60 1.50
T29 Vin Baker .40 1.00
T30 Glenn Robinson .40 1.00
T31 Kevin Garnett .75 2.00
T32 Stephon Marbury .60 1.50
T33 Kendall Gill .30 .75
T34 Kerry Kittles .30 .75
T35 Patrick Ewing .60 1.50
T36 John Starks .40 1.00
T37 Horace Grant .40 1.00
T38 Anfernee Hardaway .75 2.00
T39 Allen Iverson 1.00 2.50
T40 Jerry Stackhouse .50 1.25
T41 Jason Kidd .75 2.00
T42 Kevin Johnson .50 1.25
T43 Kenny Anderson .40 1.00
T44 Isaiah Rider .40 1.00
T45 Billy Owens .30 .75
T46 Mitch Richmond .50 1.25
T47 Sean Elliott .50 1.25
T48 David Robinson .75 2.00
T49 Gary Payton .50 1.25
T50 Shawn Kemp .50 1.25
T51 Marcus Camby .50 1.25
T52 Damon Stoudamire .40 1.00
T53 John Stockton .60 1.50
T54 Karl Malone .60 1.50
T55 Shareef Abdur-Rahim .50 1.25
T56 Bryant Reeves .30 .75
T57 Juwan Howard .40 1.00
T58 Chris Webber .50 1.25
T59 Michael Jordan 4.00 10.00
T60 Anfernee Hardaway .75 2.00

1997-98 Upper Deck Ultimates

Randomly inserted in series one packs at the rate of one in 23, this 30-card set features color action player images on Light F/X cards with some of the player's abilities printed across the background.

COMPLETE SET (30) 15.00 40.00
SER.1 STATED ODDS 1:23
U1 Michael Jordan 8.00 20.00
U2 Grant Hill 1.50 4.00
U3 Charles Barkley 1.50 4.00
U4 Tom Gugliotta .60 1.50
U5 Dennis Rodman 2.00 5.00
U6 Reggie Miller 1.25 3.00
U7 Jason Kidd 1.50 4.00
U8 Loy Vaught .60 1.50
U9 Mookie Blaylock .60 1.50
U10 Tim Hardaway 1.00 2.50
U11 Juwan Howard .75 2.00
U12 Shawn Kemp 1.00 2.50
U13 Mitch Richmond 1.00 2.50
U14 Patrick Ewing 1.25 3.00
U15 Marcus Camby 1.00 2.50
U16 Bryant Stith .60 1.50
U17 Bryant Reeves .60 1.50
U18 Joe Smith .75 2.00
U19 Jerry Stackhouse 1.00 2.50
U20 Arvydas Sabonis .75 2.00
U21 John Stockton 1.25 3.00
U22 Eddie Jones 1.00 2.50
U23 Anfernee Hardaway 1.50 4.00
U24 Ray Allen 1.25 3.00
U25 Terrell Brandon .60 1.50
U26 David Robinson 1.50 4.00
U27 Anthony Mason .60 1.50
U28 Robert Pack .60 1.50
U29 Dana Barros .60 1.50
U30 Kendall Gill .60 1.50

1998-99 Upper Deck

The 1998 Upper Deck series one product contained 175 cards featuring two inserted subsets: Heart and Soul (1:4) and To the Net (1:9). The ten card packs carried a suggested retail price of $3.00. The fronts feature color game-action photography. The series two set (also known as MJ Access) features 180 cards with two subsets - Michael Jordan (1:4) and Rookies (1:4). A special card commemorating Michael Jordan's retirement was inserted at one in 11 packs. That card is numbered "UDX".

COMPLETE SET (355) 60.00 150.00
COMPLETE SERIES 1 (175) 30.00 75.00
COMPLETE SERIES 2 (180) 30.00 75.00
HS SUBSET STATED ODDS 1:4 HOB, 1:2 RET
TN SUBSET STATED ODDS 1:9 H/R
JORDAN SUBSET STATED ODDS 1:4 H/R
ROOKIE SUBSET STATED ODDS 1:4 H/R
UNPRICED GOLD PARALLEL SERIAL #'d TO 1
1 Mookie Blaylock .15 .40
2 Ed Gray .15 .40
3 Dikembe Mutombo .25 .60
4 Steve Smith .20 .50
5 D.Mutombo/S.Smith HS .40 1.00
6 Kenny Anderson .20 .50
7 Dana Barros .15 .40
8 Travis Knight .15 .40
9 Walter McCarty .15 .40
10 Ron Mercer .20 .50
11 Greg Minor .15 .40
12 A.Walker/R.Mercer HS .40 1.00
13 B.J. Armstrong .15 .40
14 David Wesley .15 .40
15 Anthony Mason .15 .40
16 Glen Rice .25 .60
17 J.R. Reid .15 .40
18 Bobby Phills .15 .40
19 G.Rice/A.Mason HS .40 1.00
20 Ron Harper .20 .50
21 Toni Kukoc .25 .60
22 Scottie Pippen .40 1.00
23 Michael Jordan 2.00 5.00
24 Dennis Rodman .50 1.25
25 M.Jordan/S.Pippen HS 3.00 8.00
26 M.Jordan/M.Jordan HS 4.00 10.00
27 Shawn Kemp .25 .60
28 Zydrunas Ilgauskas .25 .60
29 Cedric Henderson .15 .40
30 Vitaly Potapenko .15 .40
31 Derek Anderson .15 .40
32 S.Kemp/Z.Ilgauskas HS .40 1.00
33 Shawn Bradley .15 .40
34 Khalid Reeves .15 .40
35 Robert Pack .15 .40
36 Michael Finley .25 .60
37 Erick Strickland .15 .40
38 M.Finley/S.Bradley HS .40 1.00
39 Bryant Stith .15 .40
40 Dean Garrett .15 .40
41 Eric Williams .15 .40
42 Bobby Jackson .15 .40
43 Danny Fortson .15 .40
44 L.Ellis/B.Stith HS .25 .60
45 Grant Hill .40 1.00
46 Lindsey Hunter .15 .40
47 Brian Williams .15 .40
48 Scot Pollard .15 .40
49 G.Hill/B.Williams HS .60 1.50
50 Donyell Marshall .15 .40
51 Tony Delk .15 .40
52 Erick Dampier .15 .40
53 Felton Spencer .15 .40
54 Bimbo Coles .15 .40
55 Muggsy Bogues .20 .50
56 D.Marshall/M.Bogues HS .30 .75
57 Charles Barkley .40 1.00
58 Brent Price .15 .40
59 Hakeem Olajuwon .30 .75
60 Rodrick Rhodes .15 .40
61 C.Barkley/H.Olajuwon HS .60 1.50
62 Dale Davis .15 .40
63 Antonio Davis .15 .40
64 Chris Mullin .25 .60
65 Jalen Rose .20 .50
66 Reggie Miller .30 .75
67 Mark Jackson .20 .50
68 R.Miller/M.Jackson HS .50 1.25
69 Rodney Rogers .15 .40
70 Lamond Murray .15 .40
71 Eric Piatkowski .20 .50
72 Lorenzen Wright .15 .40
73 Maurice Taylor .15 .40
74 M.Taylor/L.Murray HS .25 .60
75 Kobe Bryant 1.00 2.50
76 Shaquille O'Neal .60 1.50
77 Derek Fisher .25 .60
78 Elden Campbell .15 .40
79 Corie Blount .15 .40
80 S.O'Neal/K.Bryant HS 1.50 4.00
81 Jamal Mashburn .20 .50
82 Alonzo Mourning .30 .75
83 Tim Hardaway .25 .60
84 Voshon Lenard .15 .40
85 A.Mourning/T.Hardaway HS .50 1.25
86 Ray Allen .30 .75
87 Terrell Brandon .15 .40
88 Elliot Perry .15 .40
89 Ervin Johnson .15 .40
90 R.Allen/G.Robinson HS .50 1.25
91 Micheal Williams .15 .40
92 Anthony Peeler .15 .40
93 Chris Carr .15 .40
94 Kevin Garnett .40 1.00
95 K.Garnett/S.Marbury HS .60 1.50
96 Keith Van Horn .25 .60
97 Kerry Kittles .15 .40
98 Kendall Gill .15 .40
99 Sam Cassell .20 .50
100 Chris Gatling .15 .40
101 K.Van Horn/Cassell HS .40 1.00
102 Patrick Ewing .30 .75
103 John Starks .20 .50
104 Allan Houston .20 .50
105 Chris Mills .15 .40
106 Chris Childs .15 .40
107 Charlie Ward .15 .40
108 P.Ewing/J.Starks HS .50 1.25
109 Anfernee Hardaway .40 1.00
110 Horace Grant .20 .50
111 Nick Anderson .15 .40
112 Johnny Taylor .15 .40
113 A.Hardaway/H.Grant HS .60 1.50
114 Allen Iverson .50 1.25
115 Scott Williams .15 .40
116 Tim Thomas .25 .60
117 Brian Shaw .15 .40
118 Anthony Parker .15 .40
119 A.Iverson/T.Thomas HS .75 2.00
120 Jason Kidd .40 1.00
121 Rex Chapman .15 .40
122 Danny Manning .20 .50
123 J.Kidd/D.Manning HS .60 1.50
124 Rasheed Wallace .25 .60
125 Walt Williams .15 .40
126 Kelvin Cato .15 .40
127 Arvydas Sabonis .20 .50
128 Brian Grant .15 .40
129 R.Wallace/I.Rider HS .40 1.00
130 Tariq Abdul-Wahad .15 .40
131 Corliss Williamson .15 .40
132 Olden Polynice .15 .40
133 Chris Robinson .15 .40
134 T.Abdul-Wahad/O.Polynice HS .25 .60
135 Tim Duncan .50 1.25
136 Avery Johnson .20 .50
137 David Robinson .40 1.00
138 Monty Williams .15 .40
139 T.Duncan/D.Rob HS .75 2.00
140 Vin Baker .20 .50
141 Hersey Hawkins .15 .40
142 Detlef Schrempf .25 .60
143 Jim McIlvaine .15 .40
144 G.Payton/V.Baker HS .40 1.00
145 Chauncey Billups .30 .75
146 Tracy McGrady .40 1.00
147 John Wallace .15 .40
148 Doug Christie .15 .40
149 Dee Brown .15 .40
150 T.McGrady/C.Billups HS .60 1.50
151 Karl Malone .30 .75
152 John Stockton .30 .75
153 Adam Keefe .15 .40
154 Howard Eisley .15 .40
155 K.Malone/J.Stockton HS .50 1.25
156 Bryant Reeves .15 .40
157 Lee Mayberry .15 .40
158 Michael Smith .15 .40
159 Abdur-Rahim/Reeves HS .40 1.00
160 Juwan Howard .20 .50
161 Calbert Cheaney .15 .40
162 Tracy Murray .15 .40
163 J.Howard/C.Cheaney HS .30 .75
164 Shaquille O'Neal TN 1.25 3.00
165 Maurice Taylor TN .30 .75
166 Stephon Marbury TN .60 1.50
167 Tracy McGrady TN .75 2.00
168 Antoine Walker TN .50 1.25
169 Michael Jordan TN 4.00 10.00
170 Keith Van Horn TN .50 1.25
171 S.Abdur-Rahim TN .50 1.25
172 Kobe Bryant TN 2.00 5.00
173 Gary Payton TN .50 1.25
174 Michael Jordan CL .40 1.00
175 Michael Jordan CL .40 1.00
176 Kevin Johnson .25 .60
177 Glenn Robinson .20 .50
178 Antoine Walker .25 .60
179 Jerry Stackhouse .25 .60
180 Mark Price .25 .60
181 Stephon Marbury .30 .75
182 Shareef Abdur-Rahim .25 .60
183 Wesley Person .15 .40
184 Keith Booth .15 .40
185 Sean Elliott .25 .60
186 Alan Henderson .15 .40
187 Bryon Russell .15 .40
188 Jermaine O'Neal .25 .60
189 Steve Nash .40 1.00
190 Eldridge Recasner .15 .40
191 Damon Stoudamire .20 .50
192 Dell Curry .15 .40
193 Michael Stewart .15 .40
194 Bruce Bowen RC .30 .75
195 Steve Kerr .20 .50
196 Dale Ellis .15 .40
197 Shandon Anderson .15 .40
198 Larry Johnson .25 .60
199 Chris Webber .25 .60
200 Matt Geiger .15 .40
201 Chris Anstey .15 .40
202 Loy Vaught .15 .40
203 Aaron McKie .15 .40
204 A.C. Green .20 .50
205 Bo Outlaw .15 .40
206 Antonio McDyess .20 .50
207 Priest Lauderdale .15 .40
208 Greg Ostertag .15 .40
209 Dan Majerle .25 .60
210 Johnny Newman .15 .40
211 Tyrone Corbin .15 .40
212 Pervis Ellison .15 .40
213 Shawnelle Scott .15 .40
214 Travis Best .15 .40
215 Stacey Augmon .20 .50
216 Brevin Knight .15 .40
217 Jerome Williams .15 .40
218 Terry Mills .15 .40
219 Matt Maloney .15 .40
220 Dennis Scott .15 .40
221 John Thomas .15 .40
222 Nick Van Exel .20 .50
223 Duane Ferrell .15 .40
224 Chris Whitney .15 .40
225 Luc Longley .20 .50
226 Robert Horry .20 .50
227 Clifford Robinson .15 .40
228 Samaki Walker .15 .40
229 Derrick McKey .15 .40
230A Michael Jordan 1.25 3.00
230B Michael Jordan 1.25 3.00
230C Michael Jordan 1.25 3.00
230D Michael Jordan 1.25 3.00
230E Michael Jordan 1.25 3.00
230F Michael Jordan 1.25 3.00
230G Michael Jordan 1.25 3.00
230H Michael Jordan 1.25 3.00
230I Michael Jordan 1.25 3.00
230J Michael Jordan 1.25 3.00
230K Michael Jordan 1.25 3.00
230L Michael Jordan 1.25 3.00
230M Michael Jordan 1.25 3.00
230N Michael Jordan 1.25 3.00
230O Michael Jordan 1.25 3.00
230P Michael Jordan 1.25 3.00
230Q Michael Jordan 1.25 3.00

230R Michael Jordan 1.25 3.00
230S Michael Jordan 1.25 3.00
230T Michael Jordan 1.25 3.00
230U Michael Jordan 1.25 3.00
230V Michael Jordan 1.25 3.00
230W Michael Jordan 1.25 3.00
231 Armon Gilliam .15 .40
232 Andrew DeClercq .15 .40
233 Stojko Vrankovic .15 .40
234 Jayson Williams .15 .40
235 Vinny Del Negro .15 .40
236 Theo Ratliff .20 .50
237 Othella Harrington .15 .40
238 Mitch Richmond .25 .60
239 Vlade Divac .25 .60
240 Duane Causwell .15 .40
241 Todd Fuller .15 .40
242 Tom Gugliotta .15 .40
243 LaPhonso Ellis .15 .40
244 Brian Evans .15 .40
245 Jason Caffey .15 .40
246 Pooh Richardson .15 .40
247 George Lynch .15 .40
248 Bill Wennington .15 .40
249 Rik Smits .20 .50
250 Kevin Willis .15 .40
251 Mario Elie .15 .40
252 Austin Croshere .15 .40
253 Sharone Wright .15 .40
254 Danny Ferry .15 .40
255 Jacque Vaughn .15 .40
256 Adonal Foyle .15 .40
257 Billy Owens .15 .40
258 Randy Brown .15 .40
259 Joe Smith .20 .50
260 Joe Dumars .25 .60
261 Sean Rooks .15 .40
262 Eric Montross .15 .40
263 Hubert Davis .15 .40
264 Gary Payton .25 .60
265 Tyrone Hill .15 .40
266 John Crotty .15 .40
267 P.J. Brown .15 .40
268 Michael Cage .15 .40
269 Scott Burrell .15 .40
270 Marcus Camby .20 .50
271 Rod Strickland .15 .40
272 Jim Jackson .15 .40
273 Corey Beck .15 .40
274 James Robinson .15 .40
275 Cedric Ceballos .15 .40
276 Charles Oakley .20 .50
277 Anthony Johnson .15 .40
278 Bob Sura .15 .40
279 Isaiah Rider .20 .50
280 Jeff Hornacek .20 .50
281 Rony Seikaly .15 .40
282 Charles Smith .15 .40
283 Eddie Jones .25 .60
284 Lucious Harris .15 .40
285 Andrew Lang .15 .40
286 Terry Cummings .20 .50
287 Keith Closs .15 .40
288 Chris Anstey .15 .40
289 Clarence Weatherspoon .15 .40
290 Michael Jordan H99 2.00 5.00
291 Shawn Kemp H99 .25 .60
292 Tracy McGrady H99 .40 1.00
293 Glen Rice H99 .25 .60
294 David Robinson H99 .40 1.00
295 Antonio McDyess H99 .20 .50
296 Vin Baker H99 .20 .50
297 Juwan Howard H99 .20 .50
298 Ron Mercer H99 .20 .50
299 Michael Finley H99 .25 .60
300 Scottie Pippen H99 .40 1.00
301 Tim Thomas H99 .25 .60
302 Rasheed Wallace H99 .25 .60
303 Alonzo Mourning H99 .30 .75
304 Dikembe Mutombo H99 .25 .60
305 Derek Anderson H99 .15 .40
306 Ray Allen H99 .30 .75
307 Patrick Ewing H99 .30 .75
308 Sean Elliott H99 .25 .60
309 Shaquille O'Neal H99 .60 1.50
310 Michael Jordan CL .40 1.00
311 Michael Jordan CL .40 1.00
312 Michael Olowokandi RC 1.00 2.50
313 Mike Bibby RC 1.25 3.00
314 Raef LaFrentz RC 1.00 2.50
315 Antawn Jamison RC 1.25 3.00
316 Vince Carter RC 4.00 10.00
317 Robert Traylor RC .75 2.00
318 Jason Williams RC 2.00 5.00
319 Larry Hughes RC 1.50 4.00
320 Dirk Nowitzki RC 6.00 15.00
321 Paul Pierce RC 3.00 8.00
322 Bonzi Wells RC .75 2.00
323 Michael Doleac RC .60 1.50
324 Keon Clark RC .75 2.00
325 Michael Dickerson RC .75 2.00
326 Matt Harpring RC .75 2.00
327 Bryce Drew RC .50 1.25
328 Pat Garrity RC .60 1.50
329 Roshown McLeod RC .50 1.25
330 Ricky Davis RC 1.25 3.00
331 Peja Stojakovic RC 2.00 5.00
332 Felipe Lopez RC .50 1.25
333 Al Harrington RC 1.25 3.00
UDX M.Jordan Retires 1.00 2.50
P123 Michael Jordan PROMO 2.00 5.00

1998-99 Upper Deck Bronze

COMMON MJ (230A-230W) 25.00 60.00
*STARS: 15X TO 40X BASE CARD HI
*HS SUBSET: 10X TO 25X BASE HI
*TN SUBSET: 8X TO 20X BASE HI
*RCs: 3X TO 8X BASE HI
STATED PRINT RUN 100 SERIAL #'d SETS
NUMBER 230 HAS 23 DIFFERENT CARDS
24 Dennis Rodman 30.00 80.00
26 M.Jordan/M.Jordan HS 125.00 300.00
174 Michael Jordan CL 30.00 80.00
175 Michael Jordan CL 30.00 80.00
310 Michael Jordan CL 30.00 80.00
311 Michael Jordan CL 30.00 80.00
316 Vince Carter 80.00 160.00
320 Dirk Nowitzki 100.00 250.00

1998-99 Upper Deck AeroDynamics

Randomly inserted in series one packs at a rate of seven, this 30-set features the hottest athletes who's talents are best displayed above the rim. The card backs are numbered with an "A" prefix.

COMPLETE SET (30) 15.00 40.00
SER.1 STATED ODDS 1:7 HOB/RET
*BRONZE: 1.25X TO 3X HI COLUMN
STATED PRINT RUN 2000 SERIAL #'d SETS
*SILVER: 10X TO 25X HI
STATED PRINT RUN 100 SERIAL #'d SETS
A1 Michael Jordan 5.00 12.00
A2 Shawn Kemp .60 1.50
A3 Anfernee Hardaway 1.00 2.50
A4 Tracy McGrady 1.00 2.50
A5 Glen Rice .60 1.50
A6 Maurice Taylor .40 1.00
A7 Kevin Garnett 1.00 2.50
A8 Jason Kidd 1.00 2.50
A9 Grant Hill 1.00 2.50
A10 Kendall Gill .40 1.00
A11 Hakeem Olajuwon .75 2.00
A12 Mookie Blaylock .40 1.00
A13 Toni Kukoc .60 1.50
A14 Kobe Bryant 2.50 6.00
A15 Corliss Williamson .40 1.00
A16 Ray Allen .75 2.00
A17 Vin Baker .50 1.25
A18 Reggie Miller .75 2.00
A19 Allan Houston .50 1.25
A20 Shareef Abdur-Rahim .60 1.50
A21 Tim Duncan 1.25 3.00
A22 Michael Finley .60 1.50
A23 Damon Stoudamire .50 1.25
A24 Juwan Howard .50 1.25
A25 Antoine Walker .60 1.50
A26 Donyell Marshall .40 1.00
A27 Allen Iverson 1.25 3.00
A28 Karl Malone .75 2.00
A29 Bobby Jackson .40 1.00
A30 Tim Hardaway .60 1.50

1998-99 Upper Deck AeroDynamics Gold

*STARS: 30X TO 80X BASE INSERT
STATED PRINT RUN 25 SERIAL #'d SETS
A1 Michael Jordan 900.00 1500.00
A14 Kobe Bryant 500.00 900.00

1998-99 Upper Deck Forces

Randomly inserted in series one packs at a rate of one in 23, this 30-card set features high-impact players who dominate the court. The card backs are numbered with a "F" prefix.

COMPLETE SET (30) 30.00 80.00
SER.1 STATED ODDS 1:23 HOB/RET
*BRONZE: 1X TO 2.5X HI COLUMN
STATED PRINT RUN 1000 SERIAL #'d SETS
*GOLD: 15X TO 40X HI
STATED PRINT RUN 25 SER.#'d SETS
*SILVER: 6X TO 15X HI
STATED PRINT RUN 50 SERIAL #'d SETS
F1 Michael Jordan 10.00 25.00
F2 Shareef Abdur-Rahim 1.25 3.00
F3 Shaquille O'Neal 3.00 8.00
F4 Gary Payton 1.25 3.00
F5 Allen Iverson 2.50 6.00
F6 Allan Houston 1.00 2.50
F7 LaPhonso Ellis .75 2.00
F8 Kevin Garnett 2.00 5.00
F9 Chauncey Billups 1.50 4.00
F10 Tim Hardaway 1.25 3.00
F11 Reggie Miller 1.50 4.00
F12 Glen Rice 1.25 3.00
F13 Damon Stoudamire 1.00 2.50
F14 Lamond Murray .75 2.00
F15 Shawn Kemp 1.25 3.00
F16 Steve Smith 1.00 2.50
F17 Tim Duncan 2.50 6.00
F18 Hakeem Olajuwon 1.50 4.00
F19 Karl Malone 1.50 4.00
F20 Donyell Marshall .75 2.00
F21 Anfernee Hardaway 2.00 5.00
F22 Grant Hill 2.00 5.00
F23 Antoine Walker 1.25 3.00
F24 Toni Kukoc 1.25 3.00
F25 Corliss Williamson .75 2.00
F26 Glenn Robinson 1.00 2.50
F27 Keith Van Horn 1.25 3.00
F28 Jason Kidd 2.00 5.00
F29 Juwan Howard 1.00 2.50
F30 Michael Finley 1.25 3.00

1998-99 Upper Deck Game Jerseys

Randomly inserted into packs, this 49-card set features cards with pieces cut from actual game-worn jerseys. The 49-card set is divided into several tiers: GJ1-GJ10 and GJ21-30 were inserted in both hobby and retail packs at a rate of one in 2500. GJ11-GJ20 and GJ31-40 were inserted in hobby packs only at a rate of one in 288. Rookie Game Jerseys were also added in the series two product (GJ41-50) and inserted in both hobby and retail packs at one in 2500. Card GJ38 was not produced.

1-10/21-30/41-50: STATED ODDS 1:2500
11-20/31-40: STATED ODDS 1:288 HOBBY
GJ1 Glen Rice 15.00 40.00
GJ2 Shawn Kemp 40.00 100.00
GJ3 Reggie Miller 25.00 60.00
GJ4 Shaquille O'Neal 60.00 150.00
GJ5 Ray Allen 40.00 100.00
GJ6 Keith Van Horn 10.00 25.00
GJ7 Allen Iverson 40.00 100.00
GJ8 David Robinson 30.00 80.00
GJ9 Karl Malone 15.00 40.00
GJ10 Shareef Abdur-Rahim 15.00 40.00
GJ11 Grant Hill 40.00 100.00
GJ12 Hakeem Olajuwon 20.00 50.00
GJ13 Kevin Garnett 40.00 100.00
GJ14 Jayson Williams 10.00 25.00
GJ15 Tim Duncan 50.00 120.00
GJ16 Gary Payton 25.00 60.00
GJ17 John Stockton 20.00 50.00
GJ18 Bryant Reeves 10.00 25.00
GJ19 Kobe Bryant 125.00 300.00
GJ20 Michael Jordan 400.00 800.00
GJ21 Kobe Bryant 175.00 350.00
GJ22 Grant Hill 40.00 100.00
GJ23 Anfernee Hardaway 100.00 200.00
GJ24 Tim Thomas 12.00 30.00
GJ25 Hakeem Olajuwon 20.00 50.00
GJ26 Damon Stoudamire 30.00 80.00
GJ27 Gary Payton 25.00 60.00
GJ28 Jason Kidd 30.00 80.00
GJ29 Reggie Miller 25.00 60.00
GJ30 Kevin Garnett 40.00 100.00
GJ31 Tim Duncan 30.00 80.00
GJ32 Keith Van Horn 10.00 25.00
GJ33 Stephon Marbury 15.00 40.00
GJ34 Shaquille O'Neal 40.00 100.00
GJ35 Allen Iverson 60.00 150.00
GJ36 Antoine Walker 15.00 40.00
GJ37 Karl Malone 25.00 60.00
GJ39 Shareef Abdur-Rahim 10.00 25.00
GJ40 David Robinson 30.00 80.00
GJ41 Corey Benjamin 10.00 25.00
GJ42 Mike Bibby 15.00 40.00
GJ43 Vince Carter 300.00 600.00
GJ44 Michael Doleac 10.00 25.00
GJ45 Larry Hughes 15.00 40.00
GJ46 Antawn Jamison 30.00 60.00
GJ47 Raef LaFrentz 10.00 25.00
GJ48 Robert Traylor 15.00 40.00
GJ49 Bonzi Wells 15.00 40.00
GJ50 Jason Williams 40.00 100.00

1998-99 Upper Deck Intensity

Randomly inserted in series one packs at a rate of one in 12, this 30-card set features the NBA's most emotionally intense players. The card backs are numbered with an "I" prefix.

COMPLETE SET (30) 15.00 40.00
SER.1 STATED ODDS 1:12 HOB/RET
*BRONZE: 1X TO 2.5X HI COLUMN
STATED PRINT RUN 1500 SERIAL #'d SETS
*GOLD: 20X TO 50X HI
STATED PRINT RUN 25 SER.#'d SETS
*SILVER: 6X TO 15X HI
STATED PRINT RUN 75 SERIAL #'d SETS
I1 Michael Jordan 8.00 20.00
I2 Tracy Murray .60 1.50
I3 Ron Mercer .75 2.00
I4 Terrell Brandon .60 1.50
I5 Brevin Knight .60 1.50
I6 Rasheed Wallace 1.00 2.50
I7 Sam Cassell .75 2.00
I8 Erick Dampier .60 1.50
I9 LaPhonso Ellis .60 1.50
I10 Tim Thomas 1.00 2.50
I11 Anfernee Hardaway 1.50 4.00
I12 Tariq Abdul-Wahad .60 1.50
I13 Lorenzen Wright .60 1.50
I14 Bryant Reeves .60 1.50
I15 Charles Barkley 1.50 4.00
I16 Chauncey Billups 1.25 3.00
I17 John Starks .75 2.00
I18 Jerry Stackhouse 1.00 2.50
I19 Vlade Divac 1.00 2.50
I20 Detlef Schrempf 1.00 2.50
I21 John Stockton 1.25 3.00
I22 Nick Anderson .60 1.50
I23 Alonzo Mourning 1.25 3.00
I24 Dikembe Mutombo 1.00 2.50
I25 Jalen Rose .75 2.00
I26 Robert Pack .60 1.50
I27 Antonio McDyess .75 2.00
I28 Eddie Jones 1.00 2.50
I29 Stephon Marbury 1.25 3.00
I30 David Robinson 1.50 4.00

1998-99 Upper Deck MJ23

Randomly inserted in series two packs at a rate of one in 23, this 30-card set focuses on Michael Jordan and is a tribute to his mastery of the game. Card backs feature a "M" prefix.

COMMON CARD (M1-M30) 3.00 8.00
SER.2 STATED ODDS 1:23 HOB/RET
*BRONZE: .5X TO 1.25X HI COLUMN
BRONZE PRINT RUN 2300 SETS
*SILVER: 12X TO 30X HI COLUMN
SILVER PRINT RUN 23 SETS
UNPRICED GOLD PARALLEL SERIAL #'d TO 1

1998-99 Upper Deck Michael Jordan Game Jersey Autographs

This six-card set was randomly inserted into packs of series one SPx Finite, Michael Jordan - Living Legend, series one Upper Deck, series two Upper Deck, Ovation, and MJx. Each product had 23 of these cards available. The cards feature an actual swatch from a Michael Jordan game worn red Bulls jersey. Each card is autographed by Jordan and hand numbered to 23.

COMMON CARD 3500.00 7000.00
RANDOM INSERTS IN VARIOUS UD PRODUCTS

1998-99 Upper Deck Next Wave

Randomly inserted in series two packs at a rate of one in 11, this 30-card set takes a look at some of the likely candidates who may carry the NBA's torch into the next milennium. Card backs carry a "NW" prefix.

SER.2 STATED ODDS 1:11 HOB/RET
*BRONZE: 1X TO 2.5X HI COLUMN
STATED PRINT RUN 1500 SERIAL #'d SETS
*GOLD: 6X TO 15X HI
STATED PRINT RUN 75 SERIAL #'d SETS
*SILVER: 4X TO 10X HI
STATED PRINT RUN 200 SERIAL #'d SETS
NW1 Kobe Bryant 6.00 15.00
NW2 John Wallace .60 1.50
NW3 Kerry Kittles .60 1.50
NW4 Tim Thomas 1.00 2.50
NW5 Maurice Taylor .60 1.50
NW6 Antonio McDyess .75 2.00
NW7 Jermaine O'Neal 1.00 2.50
NW8 Zydrunas Ilgauskas 1.00 2.50
NW9 Danny Fortson .60 1.50
NW10 Tim Duncan 2.00 5.00
NW11 Derek Anderson .60 1.50
NW12 Ron Mercer .75 2.00
NW13 Joe Smith .75 2.00
NW14 Eddie Jones 1.00 2.50
NW15 Rodrick Rhodes .60 1.50
NW16 Kevin Garnett 1.50 4.00
NW17 Ed Gray .60 1.50
NW18 Bobby Jackson .60 1.50
NW19 Allan Houston .75 2.00
NW20 Chauncey Billups 1.25 3.00
NW21 Keith Booth .60 1.50
NW22 Brevin Knight .60 1.50
NW23 Othella Harrington .60 1.50
NW24 Keith Van Horn 1.00 2.50
NW25 Michael Finley 1.00 2.50
NW26 Tracy McGrady 1.50 4.00
NW27 Derek Fisher 1.00 2.50
NW28 Ray Allen 1.25 3.00
NW29 Anthony Johnson .60 1.50
NW30 Vin Baker .75 2.00

1998-99 Upper Deck Super Powers

Randomly inserted in series two packs at one in five, this 30-card set focuses on NBA players who are considered franchise players. Card backs carry a "PS" prefix.

COMPLETE SET (30) 15.00 40.00
SER.2 STATED ODDS 1:5 HOB/RET
*BRONZE: 2X TO 5X HI COLUMN
STATED PRINT RUN 1000 SERIAL #'d SETS
*GOLD: 15X TO 40X HI
STATED PRINT RUN 50 SERIAL #'d SETS
*SILVER: 10X TO 25X HI
STATED PRINT RUN 100 SERIAL #'d SETS
S1 Dikembe Mutombo .60 1.50
S2 Ron Mercer .50 1.25
S3 Glen Rice .60 1.50
S4 Scottie Pippen 1.00 2.50
S5 Shawn Kemp .60 1.50
S6 Michael Finley .60 1.50
S7 Bobby Jackson .40 1.00
S8 Grant Hill 1.00 2.50
S9 Jim Jackson .40 1.00
S10 Hakeem Olajuwon .75 2.00
S11 Reggie Miller .75 2.00
S12 Maurice Taylor .40 1.00
S13 Kobe Bryant 2.50 6.00
S14 Tim Hardaway .60 1.50
S15 Ray Allen .75 2.00
S16 Stephon Marbury .75 2.00
S17 Keith Van Horn .60 1.50
S18 Allan Houston .50 1.25
S19 Anfernee Hardaway 1.00 2.50
S20 Allen Iverson 1.25 3.00
S21 Jason Kidd 1.00 2.50
S22 Damon Stoudamire .50 1.25
S23 Corliss Williamson .40 1.00
S24 Tim Duncan 1.25 3.00
S25 Gary Payton .60 1.50
S26 Tracy McGrady 1.00 2.50
S27 Karl Malone .75 2.00
S28 Shareef Abdur-Rahim .60 1.50
S29 Juwan Howard .50 1.25
S30 Michael Jordan 5.00 12.00

1999-00 Upper Deck

The 1999-00 Upper Deck set was released in two series, with both containing 180 cards. Each pack contained 10 cards and carried a suggested retail price of $2.99. The base set was made up of 266 regular cards and three subsets: Air of Greatness (20 cards focusing on Michael Jordan), Rookie Class, which features rookie cards inserted one in four series one packs and Rookie Action, which features first year players and rookies inserted one in four series two packs. Also avaible in packs, but unpriced, were five redemption cards for the Michael Jordan Master Collection set.

COMPLETE SET (360) 60.00 150.00
COMPLETE SERIES 1 (180) 40.00 100.00
COMPLETE SERIES 2 (180) 20.00 50.00
COMP.SERIES 1 w/o RC (155) 15.00 40.00
COMP.SERIES 2 w/o SP (133) 4.00 10.00
ROOKIE SUBSET STATED ODDS 1:4 H/R
MJ SUBSET STATED ODDS 1:4 H/R
UNPRICED GOLD PARALLEL SERIAL #'d TO 1
1 Roshown McLeod .20 .50
2 Dikembe Mutombo .30 .75
3 Alan Henderson .20 .50
4 LaPhonso Ellis .20 .50
5 Chris Crawford .20 .50
6 Kenny Anderson .25 .60
7 Antoine Walker .30 .75
8 Paul Pierce .40 1.00
9 Vitaly Potapenko .20 .50
10 Dana Barros .20 .50
11 Elden Campbell .20 .50
12 Eddie Jones .30 .75
13 David Wesley .20 .50
14 Derrick Coleman .25 .60
15 Ricky Davis .30 .75
16 Corey Benjamin .20 .50
17 Randy Brown .20 .50
18 Kornel David RC .25 .60
19 Toni Kukoc .30 .75
20 Keith Booth .20 .50
21 Shawn Kemp .30 .75
22 Wesley Person .20 .50
23 Brevin Knight .20 .50
24 Bob Sura .20 .50
25 Zydrunas Ilgauskas .25 .60
26 Michael Finley .30 .75
27 Shawn Bradley .20 .50
28 Dirk Nowitzki .60 1.50
29 Steve Nash .50 1.25
30 Antonio McDyess .25 .60
31 Nick Van Exel .25 .60
32 Chauncey Billups .30 .75
33 Bryant Stith .20 .50
34 Raef LaFrentz .25 .60
35 Grant Hill .40 1.00
36 Lindsey Hunter .20 .50
37 Bison Dele .20 .50
38 Jerry Stackhouse .30 .75
39 John Starks .25 .60
40 Antawn Jamison .30 .75
41 Erick Dampier .20 .50
42 Jason Caffey .20 .50
43 Hakeem Olajuwon .40 1.00
44 Scottie Pippen .50 1.25
45 Cuttino Mobley .20 .50
46 Charles Barkley .50 1.25
47 Bryce Drew .20 .50
48 Reggie Miller .30 .75
49 Jalen Rose .25 .60
50 Mark Jackson .25 .60
51 Dale Davis .20 .50
52 Chris Mullin .30 .75
53 Maurice Taylor .20 .50
54 Tyrone Nesby RC .25 .60
55 Michael Olowokandi .20 .50
56 Eric Piatkowski .25 .60
57 Troy Hudson RC .30 .75
58 Kobe Bryant 1.25 3.00
59 Shaquille O'Neal .75 2.00
60 Glen Rice .30 .75
61 Robert Horry .25 .60
62 Tim Hardaway .30 .75
63 Alonzo Mourning .40 1.00
64 P.J. Brown .20 .50
65 Dan Majerle .30 .75
66 Ray Allen .30 .75
67 Glenn Robinson .25 .60
68 Sam Cassell .25 .60
69 Robert Traylor .20 .50
70 Kevin Garnett .50 1.25
71 Sam Mitchell .20 .50
72 Dean Garrett .20 .50
73 Bobby Jackson .20 .50
74 Radoslav Nesterovic RC .30 .75
75 Keith Van Horn .25 .60
76 Stephon Marbury .25 .60
77 Kendall Gill .20 .50
78 Scott Burrell .20 .50
79 Patrick Ewing .40 1.00
80 Allan Houston .25 .60
81 Latrell Sprewell .30 .75
82 Larry Johnson .30 .75
83 Marcus Camby .25 .60
84 Darrell Armstrong .20 .50
85 Derek Strong .20 .50
86 Matt Harpring .20 .50
87 Michael Doleac .20 .50
88 Bo Outlaw .20 .50
89 Allen Iverson .60 1.50
90 Theo Ratliff .25 .60
91 Larry Hughes .25 .60
92 Eric Snow .25 .60
93 Jason Kidd .50 1.25
94 Clifford Robinson .20 .50
95 Tom Gugliotta .20 .50
96 Luc Longley .25 .60
97 Rasheed Wallace .30 .75
98 Arvydas Sabonis .25 .60
99 Damon Stoudamire .25 .60
100 Brian Grant .20 .50
101 Jason Williams .40 1.00
102 Vlade Divac .30 .75
103 Peja Stojakovic .30 .75
104 Lawrence Funderburke .20 .50
105 Tim Duncan .60 1.50
106 Sean Elliott .30 .75
107 David Robinson .50 1.25
108 Mario Elie .20 .50
109 Avery Johnson .25 .60
110 Gary Payton .30 .75
111 Vin Baker .25 .60
112 Rashard Lewis .30 .75
113 Jelani McCoy .20 .50
114 Vladimir Stepania .20 .50
115 Vince Carter .60 1.50
116 Doug Christie .25 .60
117 Kevin Willis .20 .50
118 Dee Brown .20 .50
119 John Thomas .20 .50
120 Karl Malone .40 1.00
121 John Stockton .40 1.00
122 Howard Eisley .20 .50
123 Bryon Russell .20 .50
124 Greg Ostertag .20 .50
125 Shareef Abdur-Rahim .25 .60
126 Mike Bibby .30 .75
127 Felipe Lopez .20 .50
128 Cherokee Parks .20 .50
129 Juwan Howard .25 .60
130 Rod Strickland .20 .50
131 Chris Whitney .20 .50
132 Tracy Murray .20 .50
133 Jahidi White .20 .50
134 Michael Jordan AIR 1.25 3.00
135 Michael Jordan AIR 1.25 3.00
136 Michael Jordan AIR 1.25 3.00
137 Michael Jordan AIR 1.25 3.00
138 Michael Jordan AIR 1.25 3.00
139 Michael Jordan AIR 1.25 3.00
140 Michael Jordan AIR 1.25 3.00
141 Michael Jordan AIR 1.25 3.00
142 Michael Jordan AIR 1.25 3.00
143 Michael Jordan AIR 1.25 3.00
144 Michael Jordan AIR 1.25 3.00
145 Michael Jordan AIR 1.25 3.00
146 Michael Jordan AIR 1.25 3.00
147 Michael Jordan AIR 1.25 3.00
148 Michael Jordan AIR 1.25 3.00
149 Michael Jordan AIR 1.25 3.00
150 Michael Jordan AIR 1.25 3.00
151 Michael Jordan AIR 1.25 3.00
152 Michael Jordan AIR 1.25 3.00
153 Michael Jordan AIR 1.25 3.00
154 Michael Jordan CL .75 2.00
155 Michael Jordan CL .75 2.00
156 Elton Brand RC 1.50 4.00
157 Steve Francis RC 1.50 4.00
158 Baron Davis RC 1.50 4.00
159 Lamar Odom RC 1.50 4.00
160 Jonathan Bender RC .60 1.50
161 Wally Szczerbiak RC 1.25 3.00
162 Richard Hamilton RC 1.25 3.00
163 Andre Miller RC 1.25 3.00
164 Shawn Marion RC 1.25 3.00
165 Jason Terry RC 1.00 2.50
166 Trajan Langdon RC .60 1.50
167 Kenny Thomas RC .60 1.50
168 Corey Maggette RC 1.00 2.50
169 William Avery RC .50 1.25
170 Jumaine Jones RC .50 1.25
171 Ron Artest RC 1.25 3.00
172 Cal Bowdler RC .40 1.00
173 James Posey RC .60 1.50
174 Quincy Lewis RC .40 1.00
175 Vonteego Cummings RC .40 1.00
176 Jeff Foster RC .60 1.50
177 Dion Glover RC .50 1.25
178 Devean George RC .60 1.50
179 Evan Eschmeyer RC .50 1.25
180 Tim James RC .40 1.00
181 Jim Jackson .20 .50
182 Isaiah Rider .25 .60
183 Lorenzen Wright .20 .50
184 Bimbo Coles .20 .50
185 Anthony Johnson .20 .50
186 Calbert Cheaney .20 .50
187 Pervis Ellison .20 .50
188 Walter McCarty .20 .50
189 Eric Williams .20 .50
190 Tony Battie .25 .60
191 Anthony Mason .20 .50
192 Bobby Phills .20 .50
193 Todd Fuller .20 .50
194 Brad Miller .25 .60
195 Eldridge Recasner .20 .50
196 Chris Anstey .20 .50
197 Fred Hoiberg .20 .50
198 Hersey Hawkins .20 .50
199 Will Perdue .20 .50
200 Mark Bryant .20 .50
201 Lamond Murray .20 .50
202 Cedric Henderson .20 .50
203 Andrew DeClercq .20 .50
204 Danny Ferry .20 .50
205 Erick Strickland .20 .50
206 Cedric Ceballos .20 .50
207 Hubert Davis .20 .50
208 Robert Pack .20 .50
209 Gary Trent .20 .50
210 Ron Mercer .25 .60
211 George McCloud .20 .50
212 Roy Rogers .20 .50
213 Keon Clark .20 .50
214 Terry Mills .20 .50
215 Michael Curry .20 .50
216 Christian Laettner .25 .60
217 Jerome Williams .20 .50
218 Loy Vaught .20 .50
219 Jud Buechler .20 .50
220 Mookie Blaylock .20 .50
221 Terry Cummings .25 .60
222 Donyell Marshall .20 .50
223 Chris Mills .20 .50
224 Adonal Foyle .20 .50
225 Shandon Anderson .20 .50
226 Kelvin Cato .20 .50
227 Walt Williams .20 .50
228 Al Harrington .30 .75
229 Rik Smits .30 .75
230 Derrick McKey .20 .50
231 Sam Perkins .20 .50
232 Austin Croshere .20 .50
233 Derek Anderson .20 .50
234 Keith Closs .20 .50
235 Eric Murdock .20 .50
236 Brian Skinner .20 .50
237 Charles Jones RC .20 .50
238 Ron Harper .20 .50
239 Derek Fisher .30 .75
240 Rick Fox .20 .50
241 A.C. Green .25 .60
242 Jamal Mashburn .25 .60
243 Mark Strickland .20 .50
244 Rex Walters .20 .50
245 Clarence Weatherspoon .20 .50
246 Ervin Johnson .20 .50
247 J.R. Reid .20 .50
248 Dale Ellis .20 .50
249 Danny Manning .25 .60
250 Tim Thomas .25 .60
251 Terrell Brandon .20 .50
252 Malik Sealy .20 .50
253 Joe Smith .25 .60
254 Anthony Peeler .20 .50
255 Jayson Williams .20 .50
256 Jamie Feick RC .25 .60
257 Kerry Kittles .20 .50
258 Johnny Newman .20 .50
259 Chris Childs .20 .50
260 Kurt Thomas .20 .50
261 Charlie Ward .20 .50
262 Chris Dudley .20 .50
263 John Wallace .20 .50
264 Tariq Abdul-Wahad .20 .50
265 John Amaechi RC .30 .75
266 Chris Gatling .20 .50
267 Monty Williams .20 .50
268 Ben Wallace .25 .60
269 George Lynch .20 .50
270 Tyrone Hill .20 .50
271 Billy Owens .20 .50
272 Anfernee Hardaway .50 1.25
273 Rex Chapman .20 .50
274 Oliver Miller .20 .50
275 Rodney Rogers .20 .50
276 Randy Livingston .20 .50
277 Scottie Pippen .50 1.25
278 Detlef Schrempf .25 .60
279 Steve Smith .25 .60
280 Jermaine O'Neal .25 .60
281 Bonzi Wells .20 .50
282 Chris Webber .30 .75
283 Nick Anderson .20 .50
284 Darrick Martin .20 .50
285 Corliss Williamson .20 .50
286 Samaki Walker .20 .50
287 Terry Porter .20 .50
288 Malik Rose .20 .50
289 Jaren Jackson .20 .50
290 Antonio Daniels .20 .50
291 Steve Kerr .25 .60
292 Brent Barry .25 .60
293 Horace Grant .25 .60
294 Vernon Maxwell .20 .50
295 Ruben Patterson .20 .50
296 Shammond Williams .20 .50
297 Antonio Davis .20 .50
298 Tracy McGrady .50 1.25
299 Dell Curry .20 .50
300 Charles Oakley .25 .60
301 Muggsy Bogues .25 .60
302 Jeff Hornacek .25 .60
303 Adam Keefe .20 .50
304 Olden Polynice .20 .50
305 Doug West .20 .50
306 Michael Dickerson .20 .50
307 Othella Harrington .20 .50
308 Bryant Reeves .20 .50
309 Brent Price .20 .50
310 Mitch Richmond .30 .75
311 Aaron Williams .20 .50
312 Isaac Austin .20 .50
313 Michael Smith .20 .50
314 Michael Jordan CL .75 2.00
315 Kevin Garnett CL .15 .40
316 Elton Brand .75 2.00
317 Steve Francis .75 2.00
318 Baron Davis .75 2.00
319 Lamar Odom .75 2.00
320 Jonathan Bender .30 .75
321 Wally Szczerbiak .60 1.50
322 Richard Hamilton .60 1.50
323 Andre Miller .60 1.50
324 Shawn Marion .60 1.50
325 Jason Terry .50 1.25
326 Trajan Langdon .30 .75
327 A.Radojevic RC .40 1.00
328 Corey Maggette .50 1.25
329 William Avery .25 .60
330 Ron Artest .60 1.50
331 Cal Bowdler .20 .50
332 James Posey .30 .75
333 Quincy Lewis .20 .50
334 Dion Glover .25 .60
335 Jeff Foster .30 .75
336 Kenny Thomas .30 .75
337 Devean George .30 .75
338 Tim James .20 .50
339 Vonteego Cummings .20 .50
340 Jumaine Jones .25 .60
341 Scott Padgett RC .50 1.25
342 John Celestand RC .40 1.00
343 Adrian Griffin RC .60 1.50
344 Michael Ruffin RC .50 1.25
345 Chris Herren RC .50 1.25
346 Evan Eschmeyer .50 1.25
347 Eddie Robinson RC .60 1.50
348 Obinna Ekezie RC .50 1.25
349 Laron Profit RC .50 1.25
350 Jermaine Jackson RC .60 1.50
351 Lazaro Borrell RC .60 1.50
352 Chucky Atkins RC .60 1.50
353 Ryan Robertson RC .40 1.00
354 Todd MacCulloch RC .60 1.50
355 Rafer Alston RC .75 2.00
356 Mirsad Turkcan RC .60 1.50
357 Anthony Carter RC .50 1.25
358 Ryan Bowen RC .60 1.50
359 Rodney Buford RC .60 1.50
360 Tim Young RC .60 1.50

1999-00 Upper Deck Bronze

COMMON MJ (134-153) 30.00 80.00
*STARS: 12.5X TO 30X BASE CARD HI
*RCs: 2.5X TO 6X BASE HI
*SER.2 DRAFT PICKS: 5X TO 12X BASE HI
STATED PRINT RUN 100 SERIAL #'d SETS

1999-00 Upper Deck BioGraphics

Randomly inserted in series two packs at one in four, this 30-card set focuses on NBA stars and their on the court achievements. Card backs carry a "B" prefix.

COMPLETE SET (30) 10.00 25.00
SER.2 STATED ODDS 1:4 HOB/RET
*LEVEL 1: 6X TO 15X VALUE
LEVEL 1: PRINT RUN 100 SERIAL #'d SETS
*LEVEL 2: 15X TO 40X VALUE
LEVEL 2: PRINT RUN 25 SERIAL #'d SETS
B1 Antawn Jamison .60 1.50
B2 Mike Bibby .60 1.50
B3 Antoine Walker .60 1.50
B4 Ray Allen .60 1.50
B5 Anfernee Hardaway 1.00 2.50
B6 Hakeem Olajuwon .75 2.00
B7 Jason Williams .75 2.00
B8 Keith Van Horn .50 1.25
B9 Jason Kidd 1.00 2.50
B10 Reggie Miller .60 1.50
B11 Eddie Jones .60 1.50
B12 Jim Jackson .40 1.00
B13 Jerry Stackhouse .60 1.50
B14 Tim Duncan 1.25 3.00
B15 Kevin Garnett 1.00 2.50
B16 Mitch Richmond .60 1.50
B17 Steve Smith .50 1.25
B18 Charles Barkley 1.00 2.50
B19 Glen Rice .60 1.50
B20 Paul Pierce .75 2.00
B21 Alonzo Mourning .75 2.00
B22 Karl Malone .75 2.00
B23 Stephon Marbury .50 1.25
B24 Chris Webber .60 1.50
B25 Michael Finley .60 1.50
B26 Shawn Kemp .60 1.50
B27 John Stockton .75 2.00
B28 Ron Mercer .50 1.25
B29 Tim Hardaway .60 1.50
B30 Allan Houston .50 1.25

1999-00 Upper Deck Cool Air

Randomly inserted in packs at one in 72, this eight-card set focuses on Michael Jordan's "cool" moves on the court. Card backs carry a "MJ" prefix.

COMPLETE SET (8) 35.00 70.00
COMMON CARD (MJ1-MJ8) 4.00 10.00
SER.2 STATED ODDS 1:72 HOB/RET
*LEVEL 1: 2.5X TO 6X HI
LEVEL 1: PRINT RUN 100 SERIAL #'d SETS
UNPRICED LEVEL 2 SERIAL #'d TO 1

1999-00 Upper Deck Julius Erving Heroes

Randomly inserted in series one packs at one in 23, this 10-card set relives the career of Dr. J. Card backs feature a "H" prefix. The cards are numbered 46-55, which is a continuation of the Basketball Heroes series from earlier Upper Deck releases.

COMMON CARD (H46-H55) 2.00 5.00
SER.1 STATED ODDS 1:23
*LEVEL 1: 2X TO 5X HI COLUMN
LEVEL 1: PRINT RUN 100 SERIAL #'d SETS
UNPRICED LEVEL 2 SERIAL #'d TO 1

1999-00 Upper Deck Future Charge

Randomly inserted in series one packs at one in eight, this 15-card set highlights the current youth movement in the NBA. Card backs carry a "FC" prefix.

COMPLETE SET (15) 4.00 10.00
SER.1 STATED ODDS 1:8 HOB/RET
*LEVEL 1: 6X TO 15X HI COLUMN
LEVEL 1: PRINT RUN 100 SERIAL #'d SETS
*LEVEL 2: 15X TO 40X HI
LEVEL 2: PRINT RUN 25 SERIAL #'d SETS
FC1 Antawn Jamison .50 1.25
FC2 Mike Bibby .50 1.25
FC3 Antoine Walker .50 1.25
FC4 Baron Davis .75 2.00
FC5 Jason Terry .50 1.25
FC6 Andre Miller .60 1.50
FC7 Ray Allen .50 1.25
FC8 Wally Szczerbiak .60 1.50
FC9 Raef LaFrentz .40 1.00
FC10 William Avery .25 .60
FC11 Jason Williams .60 1.50
FC12 Michael Olowokandi .30 .75
FC13 Stephon Marbury .40 1.00
FC14 Quincy Lewis .20 .50
FC15 Shawn Marion .60 1.50

1999-00 Upper Deck Game Jerseys

These cards were inserted at different ratios in both series packs. Cards GJ1-GJ10 and GJ21-GJ42 were inserted at 1:2500 in both hobby and retail packs. Cards GJ11-GJ20 were inserted at one in 287 hobby packs and cards GJ43-GJ64 were inserted at one in 288 hobby packs. Also inserted were Game Jersey autographs. For the hobby and retail market, Charles Barkley (numbered to four), Kevin Garnett (numbered to 21), Michael Jordan (numbered to 23) and Kobe Bryant (numbered to 8) were inserted. For the hobby only market, Karl Malone (numbered to 32) and Baron Davis (numbered to 1) was inserted. Card backs carry a "GJ" prefix.

GJ1-GJ10 STATED ODDS 1:2500 HOB/RET
GJ21-GJ42 STATED ODDS 1:288 H/1:2500 R
GJ11-GJ20 STATED ODDS 1:287 HOBBY
GJ43-GJ64 STATED ODDS 1:288 HOBBY
SOME AU's NOT PRICED DUE TO SCARCITY
*CENT.CLUB: .6X TO 1.5X HI COLUMN
CENT.CLUB: PRINT RUN 100 SERIAL #'d SETS
GJ1 Jason Kidd 35.00 70.00
GJ2 Shaquille O'Neal 20.00 50.00
GJ3 Tim Duncan 40.00 100.00
GJ4 Charles Barkley 75.00 150.00
GJ5 Kevin Garnett 25.00 60.00
GJ5A Kevin Garnett AU/21 100.00 200.00
GJ6 John Stockton 25.00 60.00
GJ7 Keith Van Horn 10.00 25.00
GJ8 Hakeem Olajuwon 15.00 40.00
GJ9 Paul Pierce 20.00 40.00
GJ10 Michael Jordan 250.00 500.00
GJ10A Michael Jordan AU/23 2500.00 4000.00
GJ11 Kobe Bryant 40.00 80.00
GJ12 Scottie Pippen 25.00 60.00
GJ13 Grant Hill 20.00 50.00
GJ14 Gary Payton 15.00 40.00
GJ15 Vince Carter 30.00 60.00
GJ16 Reggie Miller 20.00 50.00
GJ17 Allen Iverson 25.00 60.00
GJ18 David Robinson 25.00 60.00
GJ19 Antoine Walker 8.00 20.00
GJ20 Karl Malone 15.00 40.00
GJ20A Karl Malone AU/32 500.00 1000.00
GJ21 Kobe Bryant 60.00 150.00
GJ22 Wally Szczerbiak 8.00 20.00
GJ23 Richard Hamilton 8.00 20.00
GJ24 Shawn Marion 10.00 25.00
GJ25 Trajan Langdon 8.00 20.00
GJ26 Aleksandar Radojevic 8.00 20.00
GJ27 Corey Maggette 8.00 20.00
GJ28 William Avery 8.00 20.00
GJ29 Quincy Lewis 8.00 20.00
GJ30 Dion Glover 8.00 20.00
GJ31 Jeff Foster 8.00 20.00
GJ32 Devean George 8.00 20.00
GJ33 Shareef Abdur-Rahim 12.50 30.00
GJ34 John Stockton 25.00 60.00
GJ35 Allen Iverson 30.00 80.00
GJ36 Kevin Garnett 25.00 60.00
GJ36A Kevin Garnett AU/21 600.00 900.00
GJ37 Grant Hill 20.00 50.00
GJ38 Vin Baker 8.00 20.00
GJ39 Keith Van Horn 10.00 25.00
GJ40 Reggie Miller 20.00 50.00
GJ41 Tim Hardaway 10.00 25.00
GJ42 Hakeem Olajuwon 10.00 25.00
GJ43 Steve Francis 20.00 50.00
GJ44 Jonathan Bender 8.00 20.00
GJ45 Andre Miller 10.00 25.00
GJ46 Jason Terry 8.00 20.00
GJ47 Alonzo Mourning 15.00 40.00
GJ48 Cal Bowdler 8.00 20.00
GJ49 James Posey 8.00 20.00
GJ50 Kenny Thomas 8.00 20.00
GJ51 Tim James 8.00 20.00
GJ52 Vonteego Cummings 8.00 20.00
GJ53 Jumaine Jones 8.00 20.00
GJ54 Scott Padgett 8.00 20.00
GJ55 Baron Davis 15.00 40.00
GJ56 Karl Malone 15.00 40.00
GJ56A Karl Malone AU/32 500.00 1000.00
GJ57 Gary Payton 15.00 40.00
GJ58 Michael Finley 8.00 20.00
GJ59 Bryon Russell 10.00 25.00
GJ60 Antoine Walker 8.00 20.00
GJ61 Shaquille O'Neal 25.00 60.00

GJ62 Jason Kidd 35.00 70.00
GJ63 Jason Williams 25.00 60.00
GJ64 Antonio McDyess 12.00 30.00

1999-00 Upper Deck Game Jerseys Patch

Randomly inserted in both series packs at one in 7,000, this 30-card set features a higher level of Game Jersey cards by featuring swatches from the names, numbers and team patches from the player's actual game-worn jerseys. Card backs carry a "GJP" prefix.
SER.1/2 STATED ODDS 1:7500 HOB/RET
GJP1 Jason Kidd 150.00 300.00
GJP2 Shaquille O'Neal 150.00 300.00
GJP3 Tim Duncan 250.00 450.00
GJP4 Charles Barkley 200.00 400.00
GJP5 Kevin Garnett 150.00 300.00
GJP6 John Stockton 200.00 400.00
GJP7 Keith Van Horn 75.00 150.00
GJP8 Hakeem Olajuwon 150.00 300.00
GJP9 Paul Pierce 150.00 300.00
GJP10 Michael Jordan 700.00 1200.00
GJP11 Kobe Bryant 300.00 600.00
GJP12 Scottie Pippen 175.00 350.00
GJP13 Grant Hill 150.00 300.00
GJP14 Gary Payton 200.00 400.00
GJP15 Vince Carter 200.00 400.00
GJP16 Reggie Miller 200.00 400.00
GJP17 Allen Iverson 150.00 300.00
GJP18 David Robinson 150.00 300.00
GJP19 Antoine Walker 100.00 200.00
GJP20 Karl Malone 150.00 300.00
GJP21 Baron Davis 150.00 300.00
GJP22 Shaquille O'Neal 175.00 350.00
GJP23 Grant Hill 150.00 300.00
GJP24 Allen Iverson 150.00 300.00
GJP25 Steve Francis 100.00 200.00
GJP26 Jonathan Bender 75.00 150.00
GJP27 Kobe Bryant 300.00 600.00
GJP28 Kevin Garnett 200.00 400.00
GJP29 Jason Williams 100.00 200.00
GJP30 Jason Kidd 125.00 250.00

1999-00 Upper Deck Game Jerseys Patch Super

Randomly inserted in both series packs, this 20-card set is a parallel of the base insert. The cards are serially numbered to 25. Card backs are numbered by the player's initials.
STATED PRINT RUN 25 SERIAL #'d SETS
AI Allen Iverson 1 250.00 500.00
AI Allen Iverson 2 250.00 500.00
AW Antoine Walker 125.00 250.00
BD Baron Davis 150.00 300.00
GH Grant Hill 1 300.00 600.00
GH Grant Hill 2 300.00 600.00
JB Jonathan Bender 125.00 250.00
JK Jason Kidd 250.00 500.00
JW Jason Williams 200.00 400.00
KB Kobe Bryant 1 600.00 1200.00
KB Kobe Bryant 2 600.00 1200.00
KG Kevin Garnett 1 175.00 350.00
KG Kevin Garnett 2 175.00 350.00
KV Keith Van Horn 100.00 200.00
MJ Michael Jordan 1400.00 2200.00
SF Steve Francis 125.00 250.00
SO Shaquille O'Neal 1 300.00 600.00
SO Shaquille O'Neal 2 300.00 600.00
TD Tim Duncan 400.00 700.00
VC Vince Carter 350.00 650.00

1999-00 Upper Deck High Definition

Randomly inserted in series two packs at one in 11, this 20-card set features spectacular dunk shots. Card backs carry a "HD" prefix.
COMPLETE SET (20) 12.00 30.00
SER.2 STATED ODDS 1:11 HOB/RET
*LEVEL 1: 4X TO 10X HI COLUMN
LEVEL 1: PRINT RUN 100 SERIAL #'d SETS
*LEVEL 2: 10X TO 25X HI
LEVEL 2: PRINT RUN 25 SERIAL #'d SETS
HD1 Antonio McDyess .75 2.00
HD2 Kevin Garnett 1.50 4.00
HD3 Vince Carter 2.00 5.00
HD4 Shareef Abdur-Rahim .75 2.00
HD5 Patrick Ewing 1.25 3.00
HD6 Gary Payton 1.00 2.50
HD7 Glenn Robinson .75 2.00
HD8 Kobe Bryant 4.00 10.00
HD9 Antawn Jamison 1.00 2.50
HD10 Chris Webber 1.00 2.50
HD11 Corey Maggette 1.50 4.00
HD12 Shawn Kemp 1.00 2.50
HD13 Derek Anderson .60 1.50
HD14 Michael Finley 1.00 2.50
HD15 Allan Houston .75 2.00
HD16 Anfernee Hardaway 1.50 4.00
HD17 Grant Hill 1.25 3.00
HD18 Shaquille O'Neal 2.50 6.00
HD19 Paul Pierce 1.25 3.00
HD20 Scottie Pippen 1.50 4.00

1999-00 Upper Deck History Class

Randomly inserted in series one packs at one in 11, this 20-card set featues some of the NBA's top legends using Rainbox Light F/X technology. Card backs carry a "HC" prefix.
COMPLETE SET (20) 15.00 40.00
SER.1 STATED ODDS 1:11 HOB/RET
*LEVEL 1: 5X TO 12X HI COLUMN
LEVEL 1: PRINT RUN 100 SER.#'d SETS
*LEVEL 2: 10X TO 25X HI COLUMN
LEVEL 2: PRINT RUN 25 SER.#'d SETS
HC1 Michael Jordan 8.00 20.00
HC2 Julius Erving 1.25 3.00
HC3 Jamaal Wilkes .75 2.00
HC4 John Havlicek 1.00 2.50
HC5 Moses Malone .75 2.00
HC6 Nate Archibald .60 1.50
HC7 Jerry West 1.00 2.50
HC8 Dave DeBusschere .75 2.00
HC9 Bob Cousy 1.25 3.00
HC10 Kevin McHale 1.00 2.50
HC11 Dave Bing .75 2.00
HC12 Walt Frazier .75 2.00
HC13 Bob Lanier .60 1.50
HC14 George Gervin .75 2.00
HC15 Hal Greer .60 1.50
HC16 Earl Monroe .75 2.00
HC17 David Thompson .60 1.50
HC18 Wes Unseld .75 2.00
HC19 Bill Walton .75 2.00
HC20 Larry Bird 2.00 5.00

1999-00 Upper Deck Jamboree

Randomly inserted in series one packs at one in 11, this 15-card set features some of the most electrifying slam-dunkers in the business. Card backs carry a "J" prefix.
COMPLETE SET (15) 8.00 20.00
SER.1 STATED ODDS 1:11 HOB/RET
*LEVEL 1: 6X TO 15X HI COLUMN
LEVEL 1: PRINT RUN 100 SERIAL #'d SETS
*LEVEL 2: 15X TO 40X VALUE
LEVEL 2: PRINT RUN 25 SERIAL #'d SETS
J1 Michael Jordan 5.00 12.00
J2 Karl Malone .75 2.00
J3 Kevin Garnett 1.00 2.50
J4 Antonio McDyess .50 1.25
J5 Shareef Abdur-Rahim .50 1.25
J6 David Robinson 1.00 2.50
J7 Marcus Camby .50 1.25
J8 Kobe Bryant 2.50 6.00
J9 Jason Kidd 1.00 2.50
J10 Scottie Pippen 1.00 2.50
J11 Keith Van Horn .50 1.25
J12 Glenn Robinson .50 1.25
J13 Grant Hill .75 2.00
J14 Michael Finley .60 1.50
J15 Alonzo Mourning .75 2.00

1999-00 Upper Deck MJ - A Higher Power

Randomly inserted in series one packs at one in 23, this 12-card set relives Jordan's high-flying career. Card backs carry a "MJ" prefix.
COMPLETE SET (12) 25.00 60.00
COMMON CARD (MJ1-MJ12) 2.50 6.00
SER.1 STATED ODDS 1:23 HOB/RET
LEVEL 1: PRINT RUN 100 SERIAL #'d SETS
UNPRICED LEVEL 2 SERIAL #'d TO 1

1999-00 Upper Deck MJ Final Floor

Randomly inserted in the following Upper Deck products: SPx, Hardcourt, Ovation, Black Diamond, SP Authentic, UD Ionix, Upper Deck Encore, Upper Deck HoloGrFX, 2000 Century Legends, 2000/01 Upper Deck MVP and Upper Deck 2, this set features pieces of the floor from MJ's final game. The base card is just a piece of the floor and was inserted at one in 2500 packs in each product. The second level features an autograph and those were hand numbered to 23. The final tier features a hand-built wood card that includes the Jordan auto. Only one of these cards were available in each product.
COMMON CARD (FF1-FF12) 12.00 30.00
COMMON AU (FF1A-FF12A) 400.00 800.00
STATED ODDS 1:2500 IN EACH RELEASE
AU PRINT RUN 23 SERIAL #'d SETS
RANDOM INS.IN UD PRODUCTS
UNPRICED WOOD SERIAL NUMBERED TO 1

1999-00 Upper Deck Now Showing

Randomly inserted in series one packs at one in four, this 30-card set captures the top NBA talent. Card backs carry a "NS" prefix.
COMPLETE SET (30) 12.50 30.00
SER.1 STATED ODDS 1:4 HOB/RET
*LEVEL 1: 6X TO 15X HI COLUMN
LEVEL 1: PRINT RUN 100 SERIAL #'d SETS
*LEVEL 2: 15X TO 40X VALUE
LEVEL 2: PRINT RUN 25 SERIAL #'d SETS
NS1 Dikembe Mutombo .60 1.50
NS2 Antoine Walker .60 1.50
NS3 Eddie Jones .60 1.50
NS4 Toni Kukoc .60 1.50
NS5 Shawn Kemp .60 1.50
NS6 Michael Finley .60 1.50
NS7 Antonio McDyess .50 1.25
NS8 Grant Hill .75 2.00
NS9 Antawn Jamison .60 1.50
NS10 Scottie Pippen 1.00 2.50
NS11 Reggie Miller .60 1.50
NS12 Maurice Taylor .40 1.00
NS13 Shaquille O'Neal 1.50 4.00
NS14 Tim Hardaway .60 1.50
NS15 Ray Allen .60 1.50
NS16 Kevin Garnett 1.00 2.50
NS17 Stephon Marbury .50 1.25
NS18 Marcus Camby .50 1.25
NS19 Darrell Armstrong .40 1.00
NS20 Allen Iverson 1.25 3.00
NS21 Jason Kidd 1.00 2.50
NS22 Damon Stoudamire .50 1.25
NS23 Jason Williams .75 2.00
NS24 Tim Duncan 1.25 3.00
NS25 Gary Payton .60 1.50
NS26 Vince Carter 1.25 3.00
NS27 Karl Malone .75 2.00
NS28 Shareef Abdur-Rahim .50 1.25
NS29 Juwan Howard .50 1.25
NS30 Michael Jordan 5.00 12.00

1999-00 Upper Deck PowerDeck

Randomly inserted in both series hobby packs, this 14-card set features Upper Deck's interactive digital technology that focus on one retired NBA star and other current standouts. The series one cards were inserted at one in 23 hobby packs, while the series two cards were inserted at one in 72 hobby packs. Also, randomly inserted in series one packs at one in 288, were two additional Jordan cards - MJPD1 and MJPD2. Each of the three Jordan series one cards were offered as one of ones. In series two, two additonal cards were inserted at one in 2500 packs - PDX1 (Michael Jordan) and PDX2 (Kevin Garnett). None of the special cards are included in the set price.

SER.1 STATED ODDS 1:23 HOBBY
SER.2 STATED ODDS 1:72 HOBBY
MJPD1/2: SER.1 STATED ODDS 1:288 HOB
PDX1/2: SER.2 STATED ODDS 1:2500 HOB
PD1 Michael Jordan 8.00 20.00
PD2 Kobe Bryant 4.00 10.00
PD3 Tim Duncan 2.00 5.00
PD4 Allen Iverson 2.00 5.00
PD5 Vince Carter 2.00 5.00
PD6 Jason Kidd 1.50 4.00
PD7 Scottie Pippen 1.50 4.00
PD8 Elton Brand 2.50 6.00
PD9 Steve Francis 2.50 6.00
PD10 Baron Davis 2.50 6.00
PD11 Lamar Odom 2.50 6.00
PD12 Wally Szczerbiak 2.00 5.00
PD13 Richard Hamilton 2.00 5.00
PD14 Shawn Marion 2.00 5.00
PDX1 Michael Jordan 30.00 80.00
PDX2 Kevin Garnett 8.00 20.00
MJPD1 Michael Jordan 8.00 20.00
MJPD2 Michael Jordan 8.00 20.00

1999-00 Upper Deck Rookies Illustrated

Randomly inserted in series two packs at one in 11, this 10-card set focuses on the top ten rookies from the 1999 Draft Class. Card backs carry a "RI" prefix.
COMPLETE SET (10) 4.00 10.00
SER.2 STATED ODDS 1:11 HOB/RET
*LEVEL 1: 6X TO 15X HI COLUMN
LEVEL 1: PRINT RUN 100 SERIAL #'d SETS
*LEVEL 2: 15X TO 40X HI
LEVEL 2: PRINT RUN 25 SERIAL #'d SETS
RI1 Elton Brand .75 2.00
RI2 Shawn Marion .60 1.50
RI3 Trajan Langdon .30 .75
RI4 Adrian Griffin .30 .75
RI5 Baron Davis .75 2.00
RI6 Richard Hamilton .60 1.50
RI7 Lamar Odom .75 2.00
RI8 Corey Maggette .50 1.25
RI9 Steve Francis .75 2.00
RI10 Wally Szczerbiak .60 1.50

1999-00 Upper Deck Star Surge

Randomly inserted in series two packs at one in 23, this 15-card set salutes the most skilled players in the NBA. Card backs carry a "S" prefix.
COMPLETE SET (15) 15.00 40.00
SER.2 STATED ODDS 1:23 HOB/RET
*LEVEL 1: 3X TO 8X HI COLUMN
LEVEL 1: PRINT RUN 100 SERIAL #'d SETS
*LEVEL 2: 8X TO 20X HI
LEVEL 2: PRINT RUN 25 SERIAL #'d SETS
S1 Michael Jordan 10.00 25.00
S2 Kevin Garnett 2.00 5.00
S3 Allen Iverson 2.50 6.00
S4 Vince Carter 2.50 6.00
S5 Karl Malone 1.50 4.00
S6 Tim Duncan 2.50 6.00
S7 Grant Hill 1.50 4.00
S8 Scottie Pippen 2.00 5.00
S9 Shaquille O'Neal 3.00 8.00
S10 Antoine Walker 1.25 3.00
S11 Shareef Abdur-Rahim 1.00 2.50
S12 Keith Van Horn 1.00 2.50
S13 Gary Payton 1.25 3.00
S14 John Stockton 1.50 4.00
S15 Stephon Marbury 1.00 2.50

1999-00 Upper Deck Wild!

Randomly inserted in packs at one in 23, this 19-card set features some of the NBA's most entertaining talent. Card backs carry a "W" prefix.
COMPLETE SET (19) 20.00 50.00
SER.2 STATED ODDS 1:23 HOB/RET
*LEVEL 1: 3X TO 8X HI COLUMN
LEVEL 1: PRINT RUN 100 SERIAL #'d SETS
*LEVEL 2: 8X TO 20X HI
LEVEL 2: PRINT RUN 25 SERIAL #'d SETS
W1 Kobe Bryant 5.00 12.00
W2 Kevin Garnett 2.00 5.00
W3 Shareef Abdur-Rahim 1.00 2.50
W4 Tim Hardaway 1.25 3.00
W5 Jason Williams 1.50 4.00
W6 Grant Hill 1.50 4.00
W7 Vince Carter 2.50 6.00
W8 Ron Mercer 1.00 2.50
W9 Charles Barkley 2.00 5.00
W10 Eddie Jones 1.25 3.00
W11 Tim Duncan 2.50 6.00
W12 Antonio McDyess 1.00 2.50
W13 Allen Iverson 2.50 6.00
W14 Anfernee Hardaway 2.00 5.00
W15 Michael Jordan 10.00 25.00
W16 Stephon Marbury 1.00 2.50
W17 Paul Pierce 1.50 4.00
W18 Elton Brand 2.00 5.00
W19 Jason Terry 1.25 3.00

2000-01 Upper Deck

The 2000-01 Upper Deck product was released in late November,2000. The product features a 245-card base set that is broken into tiers as follows: 200 veterans (1-200), and 45 Rookies (201-245) that are seeded at one in four packs. Each pack contained 10 cards, and carried a suggested retail price of 2.99. Series two cards all say "Game Jersey Edition" below the Upper Deck logo in the top right hand corner.
COMPLETE SET (445) 100.00 200.00
COMPLETE SERIES 1 (245) 60.00 120.00
COMPLETE SER.1 w/o RC (200) 20.00 40.00
COMPLETE SERIES 2 (200) 40.00 80.00
COMMON MARTIN (196-200) .25 .60
RC: SER.1 STATED ODDS 1:4 H/R
SER.2 CARDS SAY GAME JSY EDITION
SUBSET CARDS SAME VALUE AS BASE
1 Dikembe Mutombo .30 .75
2 Jim Jackson .20 .50
3 Alan Henderson .20 .50
4 Jason Terry .30 .75
5 Roshown McLeod .20 .50
6 Lorenzen Wright .20 .50
7 Paul Pierce .30 .75
8 Antoine Walker .25 .60
9 Vitaly Potapenko .20 .50
10 Kenny Anderson .25 .60
11 Tony Battie .20 .50
12 Adrian Griffin .20 .50
13 Eric Williams .20 .50
14 Derrick Coleman .25 .60
15 David Wesley .20 .50
16 Baron Davis .30 .75
17 Elden Campbell .20 .50
18 Jamal Mashburn .25 .60
19 Eddie Robinson .20 .50
20 Elton Brand .30 .75
21 Chris Carr .20 .50
22 Ron Artest .30 .75
23 Michael Ruffin .20 .50
24 Fred Hoiberg .20 .50
25 Corey Benjamin .20 .50
26 Shawn Kemp .30 .75
27 Lamond Murray .20 .50
28 Andre Miller .25 .60
29 Cedric Henderson .20 .50
30 Wesley Person .20 .50
31 Brevin Knight .20 .50
32 Mark Bryant .20 .50
33 Michael Finley .30 .75
34 Cedric Ceballos .20 .50
35 Dirk Nowitzki .50 1.25
36 Hubert Davis .20 .50
37 Steve Nash .50 1.25
38 Gary Trent .20 .50
39 Antonio McDyess .25 .60
40 James Posey .20 .50
41 Nick Van Exel .25 .60
42 Raef LaFrentz .20 .50
43 George McCloud .20 .50
44 Keon Clark .20 .50
45 Jerry Stackhouse .25 .60
46 Christian Laettner .25 .60
47 Loy Vaught .20 .50
48 Jerome Williams .20 .50
49 Michael Curry .20 .50
50 Lindsey Hunter .20 .50
51 Antawn Jamison .30 .75
52 Larry Hughes .25 .60
53 Chris Mills .20 .50
54 Donyell Marshall .20 .50
55 Mookie Blaylock .20 .50
56 Vonteego Cummings .20 .50
57 Erick Dampier .20 .50
58 Steve Francis .25 .60
59 Shandon Anderson .20 .50
60 Hakeem Olajuwon .40 1.00
61 Walt Williams .20 .50
62 Kenny Thomas .20 .50
63 Kelvin Cato .20 .50
64 Cuttino Mobley .20 .50
65 Reggie Miller .30 .75
66 Jalen Rose .25 .60
67 Austin Croshere .20 .50
68 Dale Davis .20 .50
69 Travis Best .20 .50
70 Jonathan Bender .20 .50
71 Al Harrington .25 .60
72 Lamar Odom .25 .60
73 Tyrone Nesby .30 .75
74 Michael Olowokandi .20 .50
75 Brian Skinner .20 .50
76 Eric Piatkowski .20 .50
77 Keith Closs .20 .50
78 Shaquille O'Neal .75 2.00
79 Ron Harper .25 .60
80 Kobe Bryant 1.25 3.00
81 Rick Fox .20 .50
82 Robert Horry .25 .60
83 Derek Fisher .30 .75
84 Devean George .20 .50
85 Alonzo Mourning .40 1.00
86 Eddie Jones .30 .75
87 Anthony Carter .20 .50
88 Bruce Bowen .20 .50
89 Clarence Weatherspoon .20 .50
90 Tim Hardaway .30 .75
91 Ray Allen .30 .75
92 Tim Thomas .20 .50
93 Glenn Robinson .25 .60
94 Scott Williams .20 .50
95 Sam Cassell .25 .60
96 Ervin Johnson .20 .50
97 Darvin Ham .20 .50
98 Kevin Garnett .50 1.25
99 Wally Szczerbiak .25 .60
100 Terrell Brandon .20 .50
101 Joe Smith .25 .60
102 Radoslav Nesterovic .20 .50
103 William Avery .20 .50
104 Stephon Marbury .25 .60
105 Kerry Kittles .20 .50
106 Keith Van Horn .25 .60
107 Lucious Harris .20 .50
108 Jamie Feick .20 .50
109 Johnny Newman .20 .50
110 Patrick Ewing .40 1.00
111 Latrell Sprewell .25 .60
112 Marcus Camby .25 .60
113 Larry Johnson .30 .75
114 Charlie Ward .20 .50
115 Allan Houston .25 .60
116 Chris Childs .20 .50
117 Grant Hill .40 1.00
118 John Amaechi .20 .50
119 Tracy McGrady .50 1.25
120 Michael Doleac .20 .50
121 Darrell Armstrong .20 .50
122 Bo Outlaw .20 .50
123 Allen Iverson .60 1.50
124 Theo Ratliff .20 .50
125 Matt Geiger .20 .50
126 Tyrone Hill .20 .50
127 George Lynch .20 .50
128 Toni Kukoc .30 .75
129 Jason Kidd .50 1.25
130 Rodney Rogers .20 .50
131 Anfernee Hardaway .50 1.25
132 Clifford Robinson .20 .50
133 Tom Gugliotta .20 .50
134 Shawn Marion .25 .60
135 Luc Longley .25 .60
136 Rasheed Wallace .30 .75
137 Scottie Pippen .50 1.25
138 Arvydas Sabonis .25 .60
139 Steve Smith .25 .60
140 Damon Stoudamire .25 .60
141 Bonzi Wells .20 .50
142 Jermaine O'Neal .25 .60
143 Chris Webber .30 .75
144 Jason Williams .30 .75
145 Nick Anderson .20 .50
146 Vlade Divac .25 .60
147 Peja Stojakovic .30 .75
148 Jon Barry .20 .50
149 Corliss Williamson .20 .50
150 Tim Duncan .60 1.50
151 David Robinson .50 1.25
152 Terry Porter .20 .50
153 Malik Rose .20 .50
154 Steve Kerr .20 .50
155 Avery Johnson .25 .60
156 Gary Payton .30 .75
157 Brent Barry .20 .50
158 Vin Baker .25 .60
159 Rashard Lewis .30 .75
160 Ruben Patterson .20 .50
161 Shammond Williams .20 .50
162 Vince Carter .60 1.50
163 Dell Curry .20 .50
164 Doug Christie .20 .50
165 Antonio Davis .20 .50
166 Kevin Willis .20 .50
167 Charles Oakley .25 .60
168 Karl Malone .40 1.00
169 John Stockton .40 1.00
170 Bryon Russell .20 .50
171 Olden Polynice .20 .50
172 Quincy Lewis .20 .50
173 Scott Padgett .20 .50
174 Shareef Abdur-Rahim .25 .60
175 Mike Bibby .30 .75
176 Michael Dickerson .20 .50
177 Bryant Reeves .20 .50
178 Othella Harrington .20 .50
179 Grant Long .20 .50
180 Mitch Richmond .25 .60
181 Richard Hamilton .25 .60
182 Juwan Howard .25 .60
183 Rod Strickland .20 .50
184 Tracy Murray .20 .50
185 Chris Whitney .20 .50
186 Kobe Bryant Y3K .40 1.00
187 Kobe Bryant Y3K .40 1.00
188 Kobe Bryant Y3K .40 1.00
189 Kobe Bryant Y3K .40 1.00
190 Kobe Bryant Y3K .40 1.00
191 Kevin Garnett Y3K .15 .40
192 Kevin Garnett Y3K .15 .40
193 Kevin Garnett Y3K .15 .40
194 Kevin Garnett Y3K .15 .40
195 Kevin Garnett Y3K .15 .40
196 Kenyon Martin Y3K .25 .60
197 Kenyon Martin Y3K .25 .60
198 Kenyon Martin Y3K .25 .60
199 Kenyon Martin Y3K .25 .60
200 Kenyon Martin Y3K .25 .60
201 Kenyon Martin RC 1.00 2.50
202 Stromile Swift RC .40 1.00
203 Chris Mihm RC .30 .75
204 Marcus Fizer RC .40 1.00
205 Darius Miles RC .40 1.00
206 Joel Przybilla RC .30 .75
207 Mike Miller RC .60 1.50
208 Courtney Alexander RC .30 .75
209 DerMarr Johnson RC .30 .75
210 Iakovos Tsakalidis RC .25 .60
211 Jerome Moiso RC .25 .60
212 Keyon Dooling RC .40 1.00
213 Erick Barkley RC .25 .60
214 Jason Collier RC .40 1.00
215 Jamaal Magloire RC .40 1.00
216 DeShawn Stevenson RC .40 1.00
217 Hedo Turkoglu RC .60 1.50
218 Morris Peterson RC .40 1.00
219 Jamal Crawford RC 1.00 2.50
220 Etan Thomas RC .40 1.00
221 Quentin Richardson RC .40 1.00
222 Mateen Cleaves RC .30 .75
223 Chris Carrawell RC .40 1.00
224 Corey Hightower RC .40 1.00
225 Donnell Harvey RC .30 .75
226 Mark Madsen RC .40 1.00
227 Jake Voskuhl RC .25 .60
228 Soumaila Samake RC .25 .60
229 Mamadou N'Diaye RC .25 .60
230 Dan Langhi RC .25 .60
231 Hanno Mottola RC .25 .60
232 Olumide Oyedeji RC .25 .60
233 Jason Hart RC .40 1.00
234 Mike Smith RC .25 .60
235 Chris Porter RC .25 .60
236 Jabari Smith RC .25 .60
237 Desmond Mason RC .50 1.25
238 Eddie House RC .30 .75
239 A.J. Guyton RC .25 .60
240 Speedy Claxton RC .40 1.00
241 Lavor Postell RC .25 .60
242 Khalid El-Amin RC .25 .60
243 Pepe Sanchez RC .40 1.00
244 Eduardo Najera RC .40 1.00
245 Michael Redd RC 1.00 2.50
246 DerMarr Johnson .25 .60
247 Hanno Mottola .20 .50
248 Dion Glover .20 .50
249 Matt Maloney .20 .50
250 Jason Terry .30 .75
251 Jerome Moiso .20 .50
252 Bryant Stith .20 .50
253 Randy Brown .20 .50
254 Mark Blount .30 .75
255 Chris Herren .20 .50
256 Jamal Mashburn .25 .60
257 P.J. Brown .20 .50
258 Lee Nailon .30 .75
259 Jamaal Magloire .30 .75
260 Otis Thorpe .25 .60
261 Ron Mercer .20 .50
262 Marcus Fizer .30 .75
263 Jamal Crawford .75 2.00
264 A.J. Guyton .20 .50
265 Dalibor Bagaric RC .30 .75
266 Chris Mihm .25 .60
267 Robert Traylor .20 .50
268 Matt Harpring .20 .50
269 Clarence Weatherspoon .20 .50
270 Bimbo Coles .20 .50
271 Etan Thomas .30 .75
272 Courtney Alexander .25 .60
273 Donnell Harvey .25 .60
274 Eduardo Najera .30 .75
275 Christian Laettner .25 .60
276 Mamadou N'Diaye .20 .50
277 Tariq Abdul-Wahad .20 .50
278 Voshon Lenard .20 .50
279 Robert Pack .20 .50
280 Tracy Murray .20 .50
281 Mateen Cleaves .25 .60
282 Ben Wallace .25 .60
283 Chucky Atkins .20 .50
284 Billy Owens .20 .50
285 Brian Cardinal RC .30 .75
286 Chris Porter .20 .50
287 Bob Sura .20 .50
288 Vinny Del Negro .20 .50
289 Marc Jackson RC .30 .75
290 Danny Fortson .20 .50
291 Jason Collier .30 .75
292 Maurice Taylor .20 .50
293 Dan Langhi .20 .50
294 Carlos Rogers .20 .50
295 Moochie Norris .20 .50
296 Jermaine O'Neal .25 .60
297 Derrick McKey .20 .50
298 Sam Perkins .20 .50
299 Zan Tabak .20 .50
300 Jeff Foster .20 .50
301 Corey Maggette .25 .60
302 Darius Miles .30 .75
303 Keyon Dooling .30 .75
304 Quentin Richardson .30 .75
305 Jeff McInnis .20 .50
306 Isaiah Rider .25 .60
307 Mark Madsen .30 .75
308 Mike Penberthy RC .40 1.00
309 Brian Shaw .20 .50
310 Horace Grant .25 .60
311 Eddie Jones .30 .75
312 Brian Grant .20 .50
313 Anthony Mason .20 .50
314 Duane Causwell .20 .50
315 Eddie House .25 .60
316 Lindsey Hunter .20 .50
317 Jason Caffey .20 .50
318 Joel Przybilla .25 .60
319 Michael Redd .75 2.00
320 Rafer Alston .20 .50
321 Chauncey Billups .30 .75
322 LaPhonso Ellis .25 .60
323 Sam Mitchell .20 .50
324 Dean Garrett .20 .50
325 Tom Hammonds .20 .50
326 Kenyon Martin .75 2.00
327 Soumaila Samake .20 .50
328 Aaron Williams .20 .50
329 Kendall Gill .20 .50
330 Stephen Jackson RC .60 1.50
331 Lavor Postell .20 .50
332 Pete Mickeal RC .40 1.00
333 Kurt Thomas .20 .50
334 Erick Strickland .20 .50
335 Glen Rice .25 .60
336 Grant Hill .40 1.00
337 Tracy McGrady .50 1.25
338 Pat Garrity .20 .50
339 Troy Hudson .20 .50
340 Mike Miller .50 1.25
341 Speedy Claxton .30 .75
342 Eric Snow .20 .50
343 Pepe Sanchez .30 .75
344 Aaron McKie .20 .50
345 Nazr Mohammed .20 .50
346 Ruben Garces RC .40 1.00
347 Daniel Santiago RC .40 1.00
348 Tony Delk .20 .50
349 Paul McPherson RC .25 .60
350 Iakovos Tsakalidis .20 .50
351 Dale Davis .20 .50
352 Shawn Kemp .30 .75
353 Erick Barkley .20 .50
354 Greg Anthony .20 .50
355 Stacey Augmon .20 .50
356 Bobby Jackson .20 .50
357 Hedo Turkoglu .50 1.25
358 Jabari Smith .20 .50
359 Doug Christie .20 .50
360 Darrick Martin .20 .50
361 Sean Elliott .30 .75
362 Jaren Jackson .20 .50
363 Samaki Walker .20 .50
364 Derek Anderson .20 .50
365 Antonio Daniels .20 .50
366 Patrick Ewing .40 1.00
367 Desmond Mason .40 1.00
368 Jelani McCoy .20 .50
369 Ruben Wolkowyski RC .25 .60
370 Emanual Davis .20 .50
371 Mark Jackson .25 .60
372 Morris Peterson .30 .75
373 Muggsy Bogues .25 .60
374 Alvin Williams .20 .50
375 Corliss Williamson .20 .50
376 John Starks .25 .60
377 Danny Manning .20 .50
378 DeShawn Stevenson .30 .75
379 Donyell Marshall .20 .50
380 David Benoit .20 .50
381 Isaac Austin .20 .50
382 Mahmoud Abdul-Rauf .20 .50
383 Stromile Swift .30 .75
384 Kevin Edwards .20 .50
385 Brent Price .20 .50
386 Popeye Jones .20 .50
387 Mike Smith .20 .50
388 Jahidi White .20 .50
389 Laron Profit .20 .50
390 Felipe Lopez .20 .50
391 Dikembe Mutombo MVP .30 .75
392 Paul Pierce MVP .30 .75
393 Derrick Coleman MVP .25 .60
394 Elton Brand MVP .30 .75
395 Andre Miller MVP .30 .75
396 Michael Finley MVP .30 .75
397 Antonio McDyess MVP .25 .60
398 Jerry Stackhouse MVP .25 .60
399 Larry Hughes MVP .25 .60
400 Steve Francis MVP .25 .60
401 Reggie Miller MVP .30 .75
402 Lamar Odom MVP .25 .60
403 Shaquille O'Neal MVP .75 2.00
404 Tim Hardaway MVP .30 .75
405 Ray Allen MVP .30 .75
406 Kevin Garnett MVP .50 1.25
407 Stephon Marbury MVP .25 .60
408 Allan Houston MVP .25 .60
409 Grant Hill MVP .40 1.00
410 Allen Iverson MVP .60 1.50
411 Jason Kidd MVP .50 1.25
412 Rasheed Wallace MVP .30 .75
413 Chris Webber MVP .30 .75
414 Tim Duncan MVP .60 1.50
415 Gary Payton MVP .30 .75
416 Vince Carter MVP .60 1.50
417 Karl Malone MVP .40 1.00
418 Shareef Abdur-Rahim MVP .25 .60
419 Mitch Richmond MVP .25 .60
420 Kobe Bryant MVP 1.25 3.00
421 Mateen Cleaves ROC .25 .60
422 Speedy Claxton ROC .30 .75
423 Courtney Alexander ROC .25 .60
424 Desmond Mason ROC .40 1.00
425 Mike Miller ROC .50 1.25
426 DerMarr Johnson ROC .25 .60
427 Chris Mihm ROC .25 .60
428 Jamal Crawford ROC .75 2.00
429 Joel Przybilla ROC .25 .60
430 Keyon Dooling ROC .30 .75
431 Kobe Bryant PR .40 1.00
432 Kobe Bryant PR .40 1.00
433 Kobe Bryant PR .40 1.00
434 Kobe Bryant PR .40 1.00
435 Kobe Bryant PR .40 1.00
436 Kobe Bryant PR .40 1.00
437 Kobe Bryant PR .40 1.00
438 Kobe Bryant PR .40 1.00
439 Kobe Bryant PR .40 1.00
440 Kobe Bryant PR .40 1.00
441 Kobe Bryant PR .40 1.00
442 Kobe Bryant PR .40 1.00
443 Kobe Bryant PR .40 1.00
444 Kobe Bryant PR .40 1.00
445 Kobe Bryant PR .40 1.00
CL1 Checklist .08 .25
CL1 Checklist .08 .25
CL2 Checklist .08 .25
CL2 Checklist .08 .25
CL3 Checklist .08 .25
CL3 Checklist .08 .25

2000-01 Upper Deck Gold

*SER.1 STARS: 6X TO 15X BASE CARD HI
*SER.2 STARS: 12X TO 30X BASE CARD HI
*RCs: 10X TO 25X BASE CARD HI
*SER.2 DP: 12X TO 30X BASE CARD HI
SER.1 STARS: PRINT RUN 100 SERIAL #'d SETS
SER.2 STARS: PRINT RUN 25 SERIAL #'d SETS
RCs: PRINT RUN 25 SERIAL #'d SETS

2000-01 Upper Deck Silver

*SER.1 STARS: 2.5X TO 6X BASE CARD HI
*SER.2 STARS: 8X TO 20X BASE CARD HI
*RCs: 2X TO 5X BASE CARD HI
*SER.2 DP: 6X TO 15X BASE CARD HI
SER.1 STARS: PRINT RUN 500 SERIAL #'d SETS
SER.2 STARS: PRINT RUN 100 SERIAL #'d SETS
RCs: PRINT RUN 100 SERIAL #'d SETS

2000-01 Upper Deck All Star Class

Randomly inserted into series 2 packs at one in 23 hobby/retail, this 10-card insert features players that are usually among the top vote-getters in the All-Star game. Card backs carry a "AS" prefix.
COMPLETE SET (10) 12.50 25.00
SER.2 STATED ODDS 1:23
AS1 Tim Duncan 1.50 4.00
AS2 Shaquille O'Neal 2.00 5.00
AS3 Chris Webber .75 2.00
AS4 Allan Houston .60 1.50
AS5 Kobe Bryant 3.00 8.00
AS6 Ray Allen .75 2.00
AS7 Karl Malone 1.00 2.50
AS8 Rasheed Wallace .75 2.00
AS9 Kevin Garnett 1.25 3.00
AS10 Vince Carter 1.50 4.00

2000-01 Upper Deck Combo Materials

Randomly inserted into series two packs at one in 144, this 7-card insert features patch swatches from actual game-used materials. Card backs are numbered using the players' initials.
SER.2 STATED ODDS 1:144
AMCM Andre Miller 3.00 8.00
DMCM Darius Miles 4.00 10.00
JKCM Jason Kidd 6.00 15.00
JSCM Jerry Stackhouse 3.00 8.00
MCCM Mateen Cleaves 3.00 8.00
QRCM Quentin Richardson 4.00 10.00
SMCM Shawn Marion 3.00 8.00

2000-01 Upper Deck e-Card 1

Inserted as a two-pack box-topper in Upper Deck Series one, this six-card insert features cards that can be viewed over the Upper Deck website. Cards feature a serial number that is to be typed in at the Upper Deck website to reveal that card. Card backs carry an "EC" prefix.
COMPLETE SET (6) 4.00 10.00
SER.1 STATED ODDS 1:12 HOB/RET
EC1 Kobe Bryant 2.50 6.00
EC1A Kobe Bryant JSY AU/50 150.00 300.00
EC1J Kobe Bryant JSY/300 12.00 30.00
EC1S Kobe Bryant AU/200 100.00 200.00
EC2 Kevin Garnett 1.00 2.50
EC2A Kevin Garnett JSY AU/50 40.00 100.00
EC2J Kevin Garnett JSY/300 10.00 25.00
EC2S Kevin Garnett AU/200 25.00 60.00
EC3 Anfernee Hardaway 1.00 2.50
EC3A A.Hardaway JSY AU/50 75.00 150.00
EC3J A.Hardaway JSY/300 10.00 25.00
EC3S A.Hardaway AU/200 20.00 50.00
EC4 Shareef Abdur-Rahim .50 1.25
EC4J S.Abdur-Rahim JSY/300 8.00 20.00
EC4S S.Abdur-Rahim AU/200 20.00 50.00
EC5 Reggie Miller .60 1.50
EC5A Reggie Miller JSY AU/50 75.00 150.00
EC5J Reggie Miller JSY/300 12.00 30.00
EC5S Reggie Miller AU/200 60.00 120.00
EC6 Karl Malone .75 2.00
EC6A Karl Malone JSY AU/50 125.00 225.00
EC6J Karl Malone JSY/300 10.00 25.00
EC6S Karl Malone AU/200 40.00 100.00

2000-01 Upper Deck e-Card 2

Inserted as a two-pack box-topper in Upper Deck Series two, this six-card insert features cards that can be viewed over the Upper Deck website. Cards feature a serial number that is to be typed in at the Upper Deck website to reveal that card. Card backs carry an "EC" prefix.
COMPLETE SET (6) 5.00 12.00
SER.2 STATED ODDS 1:12 HOB/RET
EC1 Kobe Bryant 2.50 6.00
EC1A Kobe Bryant JSY AU/50 125.00 250.00
EC1J Kobe Bryant JSY/300 20.00 50.00
EC1S Kobe Bryant AU/200 100.00 200.00
EC2 Kevin Garnett 1.00 2.50
EC2A Kevin Garnett JSY AU/50 40.00 100.00
EC2J Kevin Garnett JSY/300 10.00 25.00
EC2S Kevin Garnett AU/200 25.00 60.00
EC3 Kenyon Martin 1.50 4.00
EC3A Kenyon Martin JSY AU/50 15.00 40.00
EC3J Kenyon Martin JSY/300 8.00 20.00
EC3S Kenyon Martin AU/200 10.00 25.00
EC4 Stromile Swift .60 1.50
EC4J Stromile Swift JSY/300 5.00 12.00
EC4S Stromile Swift AU/200 8.00 20.00
EC5 Darius Miles .60 1.50
EC5J Darius Miles JSY/300 8.00 20.00
EC5S Darius Miles AU/200 12.50 30.00
EC6 Marcus Fizer .60 1.50
EC6J Marcus Fizer JSY/300 6.00 15.00
EC6S Marcus Fizer AU/200 8.00 20.00

2000-01 Upper Deck Game Jerseys 1

Randomly inserted into series one hobby/retail packs at one in 287, this 20-card insert features swatches from actual game-worn jerseys. Card backs are numbered using the players initials. Please note that autographed game-jerseys were only inserted into hobby packs.
SER.1 GJ: STATED ODDS 1:287
SER.1 AU GJ: STATED ODDS 1:287 H/R
SOME AUTOS UNPRICED DUE TO SCARCITY
AGH Adrian Griffin AU 5.00 12.00
AHH Anfernee Hardaway AU 25.00 60.00
AIC Allen Iverson 8.00 20.00
AMC Alonzo Mourning 8.00 20.00
AWC Antoine Walker 3.00 8.00
BDH Baron Davis AU 12.00 30.00
DRC David Robinson 10.00 25.00
EJH Eddie Jones AU 6.00 15.00
GPC Gary Payton 4.00 10.00
GRH Glenn Robinson AU 8.00 20.00
JKC Jason Kidd 6.00 15.00
JSC Joe Smith 3.00 8.00
KBC Kobe Bryant 15.00 40.00
KBH Kobe Bryant AU 100.00 200.00
KGA Kevin Garnett AU/21 250.00 500.00
KGC Kevin Garnett 6.00 15.00
KGH Kevin Garnett AU 50.00 120.00
KVC Keith Van Horn 3.00 8.00
MBH Mike Bibby AU 6.00 15.00
PPH Paul Pierce AU 15.00 40.00
RMA Reggie Miller AU/31 250.00 500.00
RMC Reggie Miller 4.00 10.00
SAC Shareef Abdur-Rahim 3.00 8.00
SMC Stephon Marbury 3.00 8.00
SOC Shaquille O'Neal 6.00 15.00
STC John Stockton 8.00 20.00
TBH Terrell Brandon AU 8.00 20.00
VBA Vin Baker AU/42 8.00 20.00
VBC Vin Baker 3.00 8.00
WAH William Avery AU 5.00 12.00
WSH Wally Szczerbiak AU 5.00 12.00

2000-01 Upper Deck Game Jerseys 2

Randomly inserted into series two hobby/retail packs at one in 287, this 43-card insert features swatches from actual game-worn jerseys. Card backs carry an "AH" prefix followed by the players initials. Please note that autographed game-jerseys were only inserted into hobby packs.
SER.2 GJ HOB: STATED ODDS 1:72 H
SER.2 AU GJ: STATED ODDS 1:287 HOB
SOME AUTOS UNPRICED DUE TO SCARCITY
AAG Adrian Griffin AU 5.00 12.00
AAH Anfernee Hardaway AU 30.00 80.00
ACM Chris Mihm AU 5.00 12.00
ADM Darius Miles AU 6.00 15.00
AJC Jamal Crawford AU 8.00 20.00
AJM Jamaal Magloire AU 5.00 12.00
AKB Kobe Bryant AU 100.00 200.00
AKG Kevin Garnett AU 30.00 80.00
ASS Stromile Swift AU 4.00 10.00
AHC Allan Houston 3.00 8.00
AHH Anfernee Hardaway 8.00 20.00
AMC Andre Miller 3.00 8.00
CMH Chris Mihm 3.00 8.00

DAH Darrell Armstrong 2.50 6.00
DBC Dalibor Bagaric 3.00 8.00
DMH Darius Miles 4.00 10.00
GHH Grant Hill 8.00 20.00
JCH Jamal Crawford 10.00 25.00
JKC Jason Kidd 6.00 15.00
JKH Jason Kidd 6.00 15.00
JMH Jamaal Magloire 4.00 10.00
JSC Jerry Stackhouse 3.00 8.00
KBC Kobe Bryant 15.00 40.00
KBH Kobe Bryant 15.00 40.00
KDC Keyon Dooling 4.00 10.00
KDH Keyon Dooling 4.00 10.00
KGA Kevin Garnett AU/21 100.00 200.00
KGC Kevin Garnett 6.00 15.00
KGH Kevin Garnett 6.00 15.00
KMC Kenyon Martin 10.00 25.00
LSC Latrell Sprewell 3.00 8.00
LSH Latrell Sprewell 3.00 8.00
MAH Marcus Camby 3.00 8.00
MCC Mateen Cleaves 3.00 8.00
MFC Marcus Fizer 4.00 10.00
QRC Quentin Richardson 4.00 10.00
SMC Shawn Marion 3.00 8.00
SMH Shawn Marion 3.00 8.00
SSH Stromile Swift 4.00 10.00
TGC Tom Gugliotta 2.50 6.00
TMH Tracy McGrady 6.00 15.00

2000-01 Upper Deck Game Jerseys Combo 1

Randomly inserted into series one hobby/retail packs, this 10-card insert features combo swatches from actual game-worn jerseys. Card backs are numbered using the players' initials. Each card is serial numbered to 50. Please note that the two autographed combo game-jerseys were only inserted into hobby packs, and are serial numbered to 10.

STATED PRINT RUN 50 SERIAL #'d SETS
DRLB J.Erving/L.Bird 75.00 150.00
JKAH J.Kidd/A.Hardaway 75.00 150.00
KBDR K.Bryant/J.Erving 50.00 100.00
KBKG K.Bryant/K.Garnett 40.00 80.00
KBSO K.Bryant/S.O'Neal 50.00 100.00
KMJS K.Malone/J.Stockton 20.00 50.00
MJLB M.Johnson/L.Bird 75.00 150.00
WCBR W.Chamb/B.Russell 200.00 400.00

2000-01 Upper Deck Game Jerseys Combo 2

Randomly inserted into series two hobby/retail packs, this 12-card insert features combo swatches from actual game-worn jerseys. Card backs are numbered using the players' initials. Each card is serial numbered to 50. Please note that the autographed combo game-jerseys were only inserted into hobby packs, and are serial numbered to 10.

STATED PRINT RUN 50 SERIAL #'d SETS
AHLS A.Houston/L.Sprewell 25.00 60.00
KBDM K.Bryant/D.Miles 25.00 60.00
KBKG K.Bryant/K.Garnett 30.00 80.00
KBKM K.Bryant/K.Martin 25.00 60.00
KBSO K.Bryant/S.O'Neal 75.00 150.00
MJKB M.Jordan/K.Bryant 125.00 250.00
SASS S.A-Rahim/S.Swift 25.00 60.00

2000-01 Upper Deck Game Jerseys Patch 1

Randomly inserted into series one packs at one in 7500, this 17-card insert features patch swatches from actual game-worn jerseys. Card backs are numbered using the players' initials. Please note that the five autographed patch cards are serial numbered to the player's jersey number.

SER.1 STATED ODDS 1:7500
SOME AUTOS UNPRICED DUE TO SCARCITY
AHP Anfernee Hardaway 50.00 120.00
AIP Allen Iverson 50.00 125.00
GPP Gary Payton 40.00 100.00
GPPA Gary Payton AU/20 350.00 700.00
JKP Jason Kidd 40.00 100.00
KBP Kobe Bryant 200.00 500.00
KGP Kevin Garnett 60.00 150.00
KGPA Kevin Garnett AU/21 800.00 1200.00
MJP Michael Jordan 300.00 600.00
MJPA Michael Jordan AU/23 1500.00 2500.00
RMP Reggie Miller 75.00 150.00
SAP Shareef Abdur-Rahim 20.00 50.00
SMP Stephon Marbury 20.00 50.00
SOP Shaquille O'Neal 60.00 150.00
STP John Stockton 30.00 80.00

2000-01 Upper Deck Game Jerseys Patch 2

Randomly inserted into series two packs at one in 5000, this 18-card insert features patch swatches from actual game-worn jerseys. Card backs are numbered using the players' initials. Please note that the five autographed patch cards are serial numbered to the player's jersey number.

SER.2 STATED ODDS 1:5000
SOME AUTOS UNPRICED DUE TO SCARCITY
AIP Allen Iverson 50.00 125.00
DJP DerMarr Johnson 10.00 25.00
DMP Darius Miles 12.00 30.00
DMPA Darius Miles AU/21 75.00 150.00
JCP Jamal Crawford 30.00 80.00
KBP Kobe Bryant 100.00 200.00
KDP Keyon Dooling 12.00 30.00
KGP Kevin Garnett 40.00 100.00
KGPA Kevin Garnett AU/21 200.00 400.00
KMP Kenyon Martin 30.00 80.00
MFP Marcus Fizer 12.00 30.00
MJP Michael Jordan 200.00 400.00
MJPA Michael Jordan AU/23 1500.00 2200.00
MMP Mike Miller 15.00 40.00
SOP Shaquille O'Neal 60.00 150.00
SSP Stromile Swift 12.00 30.00

2000-01 Upper Deck Game Jerseys Patch Gold 1

*GOLD: .75X TO 2X BASE HI
STATED PRINT RUN 25 SERIAL #'d SETS
AIG Allen Iverson 200.00 400.00
GHG Grant Hill 200.00 400.00
KBG Kobe Bryant 250.00 500.00
KGG Kevin Garnett 100.00 200.00

2000-01 Upper Deck Game Jerseys Patch Gold 2

*GOLD: .75X TO 2X BASE HI
STATED PRINT RUN 25 SERIAL #'d SETS
AIG Allen Iverson 200.00 400.00
KBG Kobe Bryant 250.00 500.00
MJG Michael Jordan 300.00 600.00
SOG Shaquille O'Neal 150.00 300.00

2000-01 Upper Deck Graphic Jam

Randomly inserted into series one packs at one in 14, this 12-card insert features players that have mastered the slam dunk. Card backs carry a "G" prefix.

COMPLETE SET (12) 6.00 15.00
SER.1 STATED ODDS 1:14 HOB/RET
G1 Kobe Bryant 2.50 6.00
G2 Kevin Garnett 1.00 2.50
G3 Chris Webber .60 1.50
G4 Larry Hughes .50 1.25
G5 Tim Duncan 1.25 3.00
G6 Latrell Sprewell .50 1.25
G7 Vince Carter 1.25 3.00
G8 Shareef Abdur-Rahim .50 1.25
G9 Elton Brand .60 1.50
G10 Antonio McDyess .50 1.25
G11 Lamar Odom .50 1.25
G12 Rasheed Wallace .60 1.50

2000-01 Upper Deck Highlight Zone

Randomly inserted into series 2 packs at one in 23 hobby/retail, this 10-card insert features players that usually make the nightly highlight reels. Card backs carry a "HZ" prefix.

COMPLETE SET (10) 8.00 20.00
SER.2 STATED ODDS 1:23 HOB/RET
HZ1 Kobe Bryant 3.00 8.00
HZ2 Eddie Jones .75 2.00
HZ3 Lamar Odom .60 1.50
HZ4 Steve Francis .60 1.50
HZ5 Stephon Marbury .60 1.50
HZ6 Scottie Pippen 1.25 3.00
HZ7 Kevin Garnett 1.25 3.00
HZ8 Chris Webber .75 2.00
HZ9 Anfernee Hardaway 1.25 3.00
HZ10 Shareef Abdur-Rahim .60 1.50

2000-01 Upper Deck Lightning Strikes

Randomly inserted into series one packs at one in 12, this 15-card insert features players that light it up on the court. Card backs carry a "LS" prefix.

COMPLETE SET (15) 7.50 15.00
SER.1 STATED ODDS 1:12 HOB/RET
LS1 Allen Iverson 1.00 2.50
LS2 Stephon Marbury .40 1.00
LS3 Ray Allen .50 1.25
LS4 Allan Houston .40 1.00
LS5 Kevin Garnett .75 2.00
LS6 Gary Payton .50 1.25
LS7 Shawn Marion .40 1.00
LS8 Kobe Bryant 2.00 5.00
LS9 Tim Duncan 1.00 2.50
LS10 Scottie Pippen .75 2.00
LS11 Andre Miller .40 1.00
LS12 Steve Francis .40 1.00
LS13 Jalen Rose .40 1.00
LS14 Jason Williams .50 1.25
LS15 Larry Hughes .40 1.00

2000-01 Upper Deck Live Action

Randomly inserted into series 2 packs at one in 12 hobby/retail, this 8-card insert features players that supply plenty of action on the court. Card backs carry a "LA" prefix.

COMPLETE SET (8) 2.50 6.00
SER.2 STATED ODDS 1:12 HOB/RET
LA1 Kevin Garnett .60 1.50
LA2 Lamar Odom .30 .75
LA3 Jalen Rose .30 .75
LA4 Larry Hughes .30 .75
LA5 Tim Thomas .25 .60
LA6 Kobe Bryant 1.50 4.00
LA7 Wally Szczerbiak .30 .75
LA8 Anfernee Hardaway .60 1.50

2000-01 Upper Deck Masters of Arts

Randomly inserted into series one packs at one in six, this 10-card insert features players that have mastered life in the NBA. Card backs carry a "MA" prefix.

COMPLETE SET (10) 2.00 5.00
SER.1 STATED ODDS 1:6 HOB/RET
MA1 Vince Carter .50 1.25
MA2 Ray Allen .25 .60
MA3 Larry Hughes .20 .50
MA4 Kevin Garnett .40 1.00
MA5 Antonio McDyess .20 .50
MA6 Steve Francis .20 .50
MA7 Stephon Marbury .20 .50
MA8 Kobe Bryant 1.00 2.50
MA9 Paul Pierce .25 .60
MA10 Reggie Miller .25 .60

2000-01 Upper Deck MJ Materials

Randomly inserted into series one packs, this seven-card insert features memorabilia cards of Michael Jordan. Card backs carry a "MJ" prefix. Cards in the set include game-used jerseys,shoes,shorts, and even a suit that Jordan wore.

STATED ODDS ONE PER CASE
MJ1 M.Jordan Suit 15.00 40.00
MJ2 M.Jordan Jersey 50.00 120.00
MJ3 M.Jordan Shoe 125.00 250.00
MJ4 M.Jordan/Suit-Jsy/25 100.00 200.00
MJ5 M.Jordan/Shrt-Shoe/100 175.00 350.00
MJ6 M.Jordan/Jsy-Shrt/100 250.00 500.00
MJ7 M.Jordan/S-J-S-P/23 900.00 1500.00

2000-01 Upper Deck Pure Basketball

Randomly inserted into series 2 packs at one in 12 hobby/retail, this 8-card insert features only the purest of basketball players. Card backs carry a "PB" prefix.

COMPLETE SET (8) 2.50 6.00
SER.2 STATED ODDS 1:12 HOB/RET
PB1 Elton Brand .40 1.00
PB2 Andre Miller .30 .75
PB3 Mitch Richmond .30 .75
PB4 Kobe Bryant 1.50 4.00
PB5 John Stockton .50 1.25
PB6 Antawn Jamison .40 1.00
PB7 Kevin Garnett .60 1.50
PB8 Reggie Miller .40 1.00

2000-01 Upper Deck Rookie Focus

Randomly inserted into series 2 packs at one in 10 hobby/retail, this 9-card insert set focuses on this year's rookie crop. Card backs carry a "RF" prefix.

COMPLETE SET (9) 2.00 5.00
SER.2 STATED ODDS 1:10 HOB/RET
RF1 Kenyon Martin .75 2.00
RF2 Jamal Crawford .75 2.00
RF3 Keyon Dooling .30 .75
RF4 Mike Miller .50 1.25
RF5 Morris Peterson .30 .75
RF6 DerMarr Johnson .25 .60
RF7 Marcus Fizer .30 .75
RF8 DeShawn Stevenson .30 .75
RF9 Chris Mihm .25 .60

2000-01 Upper Deck Super Powers

Randomly inserted into series 2 packs at one in 72 hobby/retail, this 10-card insert features players that have super powers. Card backs carry a "SP" prefix.

COMPLETE SET (10) 25.00 50.00
SER.2 STATED ODDS 1:72 HOB/RET
SP1 Kobe Bryant 6.00 15.00
SP2 Vince Carter 3.00 8.00
SP3 Tim Duncan 3.00 8.00
SP4 Steve Francis 1.25 3.00
SP5 Gary Payton 1.50 4.00
SP6 Chris Webber 1.50 4.00
SP7 Kevin Garnett 2.50 6.00
SP8 Allen Iverson 3.00 8.00
SP9 Jason Kidd 2.50 6.00
SP10 Elton Brand 1.50 4.00

2000-01 Upper Deck Total Dominance

Randomly inserted into series one packs at one in 12, this 15-card insert features players that are truly dominanting on the court. Card backs carry a "TD" prefix.

COMPLETE SET (15) 10.00 25.00
SER.1 STATED ODDS 1:12 HOB/RET
TD1 Shaquille O'Neal 1.50 4.00
TD2 Gary Payton .60 1.50
TD3 Kevin Garnett 1.00 2.50
TD4 Elton Brand .60 1.50
TD5 Jalen Rose .50 1.25
TD6 Allen Iverson 1.25 3.00
TD7 Vince Carter 1.25 3.00
TD8 Kobe Bryant 2.50 6.00
TD9 Lamar Odom .50 1.25
TD10 Jason Kidd 1.00 2.50
TD11 Rasheed Wallace .60 1.50
TD12 Chris Webber .60 1.50
TD13 Ray Allen .60 1.50
TD14 Alonzo Mourning .75 2.00
TD15 Tim Duncan 1.25 3.00

2000-01 Upper Deck Touch the Sky

Randomly inserted into series 2 packs at one in 10 hobby/retail, this 9-card insert features players that can jump so high, you might believe that they could touch the sky. Card backs carry a "T" prefix.

COMPLETE SET (9) 2.50 6.00
SER.2 STATED ODDS 1:10 HOB/RET
T1 Kobe Bryant 1.25 3.00
T2 Kevin Garnett .50 1.25
T3 Michael Finley .30 .75
T4 Anfernee Hardaway .50 1.25
T5 Scottie Pippen .50 1.25
T6 Antonio McDyess .25 .60
T7 Larry Hughes .25 .60
T8 Latrell Sprewell .25 .60
T9 Rashard Lewis .30 .75

2000-01 Upper Deck True Talents

Randomly inserted into series one packs at one in three, this 20-card insert features players that are the true talents of the NBA. Card backs carry a "TT" prefix.

COMPLETE SET (20) 4.00 10.00
SER.1 STATED ODDS 1:3 HOB/RET
TT1 Kobe Bryant 1.25 3.00
TT2 Jalen Rose .25 .60
TT3 Chris Webber .30 .75
TT4 Alonzo Mourning .40 1.00
TT5 Paul Pierce .30 .75
TT6 Allan Houston .25 .60
TT7 Keith Van Horn .25 .60
TT8 Andre Miller .25 .60
TT9 Dirk Nowitzki .50 1.25
TT10 Richard Hamilton .25 .60
TT11 Jason Williams .30 .75
TT12 Antonio McDyess .25 .60
TT13 Antoine Walker .25 .60
TT14 Antawn Jamison .30 .75
TT15 Glenn Robinson .25 .60
TT16 Lamar Odom .25 .60
TT17 Scottie Pippen .50 1.25
TT18 Mike Bibby .30 .75
TT19 Elton Brand .30 .75
TT20 Kevin Garnett .50 1.25

2000-01 Upper Deck Unleashed

Randomly inserted into series 2 packs at one in 12 hobby/retail, this 8-card insert features players that unleash their extreme talent on a daily basis. Card backs carry a "U" prefix.

COMPLETE SET (8) 3.00 8.00
SER.2 STATED ODDS 1:12 HOB/RET
U1 Vince Carter .75 2.00
U2 Lamar Odom .30 .75
U3 Jason Williams .40 1.00
U4 Kevin Garnett .60 1.50
U5 Paul Pierce .40 1.00
U6 Shareef Abdur-Rahim .30 .75
U7 Elton Brand .40 1.00
U8 Kobe Bryant 1.50 4.00

2001-02 Upper Deck

This 450-card base set includes both Series 1 and Series 2. Each series includes 180 veterans and 45 rookies. This commemorative set celebrates Upper Deck Basketball's 10th anniversary! The cards are standard sized and borderless. The card fronts feature the type of quality action shots that have made Upper Deck Basketball so successful. The recurring theme in this product is the blonde court-wood design found in either the background of the cards or somewhere else on the card, as in this case, it acts as borders on two sides of the player's photo. One border carries the player's name and the other carries his team name. The Upper Deck logo is found in the upper right-hand corner with the featured player's team logo and position found in the lower right-hand corner. Cards 406-450 feature two versions - one inserted into Hobby (A) and one inserted into Retail (B). The difference is in the photos, but both are valued equally and were inserted 1:4 packs.

COMP.SET w/o SP's (360) 45.00 90.00
COMPLETE SER.1 (225) 75.00 150.00
COMP.SER 1 w/o SP's (180) 12.00 30.00
COMPLETE SER.2 (225) 75.00 150.00
COMP.SER 2 w/o SP's (180) 30.00 60.00
TWO VERSIONS FOR 406-450 SAME VALUE
406B-450B NOT INCLUDED IN SET PRICES
*SER.2 RCs HALF VALUE SER.1
151-225 STATED ODDS 1:4
MJ BUYBACK EXCH 100 TOTAL CARDS
1 Jason Terry .30 .75
2 Toni Kukoc .30 .75
3 Alan Henderson .20 .50
4 Theo Ratliff .20 .50
5 Shareef Abdur-Rahim .25 .60
6 DerMarr Johnson .20 .50
7 Paul Pierce .30 .75
8 Antoine Walker .25 .60
9 Kenny Anderson .25 .60
10 Vitaly Potapenko .20 .50
11 Eric Williams .20 .50
12 Jamal Mashburn .25 .60
13 Baron Davis .30 .75
14 David Wesley .20 .50
15 P.J. Brown .20 .50
16 Elden Campbell .20 .50
17 Jamaal Magloire .20 .50
18 Lee Nailon .20 .50
19 A.J. Guyton .20 .50
20 Ron Mercer .20 .50
21 Jamal Crawford .30 .75
22 Fred Hoiberg .20 .50
23 Marcus Fizer .20 .50
24 Ron Artest .30 .75
25 Lamond Murray .20 .50
26 Andre Miller .25 .60
27 Jim Jackson .20 .50
28 Chris Mihm .20 .50
29 Trajan Langdon .20 .50
30 Chris Gatling .20 .50
31 Michael Finley .30 .75
32 Dirk Nowitzki .50 1.25
33 Steve Nash .50 1.25
34 Juwan Howard .25 .60
35 Wang Zhizhi .25 .60
36 Eduardo Najera .20 .50
37 Shawn Bradley .20 .50
38 Antonio McDyess .25 .60
39 Nick Van Exel .25 .60
40 Raef LaFrentz .20 .50
41 James Posey .20 .50
42 Voshon Lenard .20 .50
43 Ben Wallace .25 .60
44 Jerry Stackhouse .25 .60
45 Corliss Williamson .20 .50
46 Chucky Atkins .20 .50
47 Michael Curry .20 .50
48 Dana Barros .20 .50
49 Antawn Jamison .30 .75
50 Larry Hughes .25 .60
51 Bob Sura .20 .50
52 Marc Jackson .20 .50
53 Chris Porter .20 .50
54 Vonteego Cummings .20 .50
55 Steve Francis .25 .60
56 Cuttino Mobley .20 .50
57 Maurice Taylor .20 .50
58 Kenny Thomas .20 .50
59 Moochie Norris .20 .50
60 Walt Williams .20 .50
61 Reggie Miller .30 .75
62 Jalen Rose .25 .60
63 Jermaine O'Neal .25 .60
64 Austin Croshere .20 .50
65 Travis Best .20 .50
66 Jonathan Bender .20 .50
67 Eric Piatkowski .20 .50
68 Darius Miles .20 .50
69 Lamar Odom .25 .60
70 Quentin Richardson .25 .60
71 Corey Maggette .25 .60
72 Elton Brand .30 .75
73 Jeff McInnis .20 .50
74 Kobe Bryant 1.25 3.00
75 Shaquille O'Neal .75 2.00
76 Derek Fisher .25 .60
77 Rick Fox .20 .50
78 Mitch Richmond .25 .60
79 Ron Harper .25 .60
80 Brian Shaw .20 .50
81 Stromile Swift .20 .50
82 Michael Dickerson .20 .50
83 Jason Williams .25 .60
84 Grant Long .20 .50
85 Bryant Reeves .20 .50
86 Alonzo Mourning .40 1.00
87 Eddie Jones .25 .60
88 Brian Grant .20 .50
89 Anthony Mason .20 .50
90 LaPhonso Ellis .25 .60
91 Anthony Carter .20 .50
92 Jason Caffey .20 .50
93 Ray Allen .30 .75
94 Glenn Robinson .25 .60
95 Sam Cassell .25 .60
96 Tim Thomas .20 .50
97 Ervin Johnson .20 .50
98 Joel Przybilla .20 .50
99 Kevin Garnett .50 1.25
100 Terrell Brandon .20 .50
101 Wally Szczerbiak .25 .60
102 Felipe Lopez .20 .50
103 Chauncey Billups .30 .75
104 Anthony Peeler .20 .50
105 Kenyon Martin .30 .75
106 Keith Van Horn .25 .60
107 Jamie Feick .20 .50
108 Aaron Williams .20 .50
109 Lucious Harris .20 .50
110 Jason Kidd .50 1.25
111 Latrell Sprewell .25 .60
112 Allan Houston .25 .60
113 Marcus Camby .25 .60
114 Mark Jackson .25 .60
115 Othella Harrington .20 .50
116 Kurt Thomas .20 .50
117 Tracy McGrady .50 1.25
118 Mike Miller .25 .60
119 Darrell Armstrong .20 .50
120 Grant Hill .40 1.00
121 Pat Garrity .20 .50
122 Bo Outlaw .20 .50
123 Allen Iverson .60 1.50
124 Dikembe Mutombo .30 .75
125 Aaron McKie .20 .50
126 Matt Geiger .20 .50
127 Eric Snow .20 .50
128 George Lynch .20 .50
129 Raja Bell RC .75 2.00
130 Shawn Marion .25 .60
131 Tom Gugliotta .20 .50
132 Rodney Rogers .20 .50
133 Anfernee Hardaway .50 1.25
134 Tony Delk .20 .50
135 Stephon Marbury .25 .60
136 Rasheed Wallace .30 .75
137 Damon Stoudamire .25 .60
138 Rod Strickland .20 .50
139 Dale Davis .20 .50
140 Scottie Pippen .50 1.25
141 Bonzi Wells .20 .50
142 Peja Stojakovic .30 .75
143 Chris Webber .30 .75
144 Doug Christie .20 .50
145 Mike Bibby .30 .75
146 Hedo Turkoglu .25 .60
147 Scot Pollard .20 .50
148 Vlade Divac .25 .60
149 Tim Duncan .60 1.50
150 David Robinson .50 1.25
151 Antonio Daniels .20 .50
152 Danny Ferry .20 .50
153 Malik Rose .20 .50
154 Terry Porter .20 .50
155 Rashard Lewis .30 .75
156 Gary Payton .30 .75
157 Brent Barry .20 .50
158 Vin Baker .25 .60
159 Desmond Mason .25 .60
160 Shammond Williams .20 .50
161 Vince Carter .50 1.25
162 Antonio Davis .20 .50
163 Morris Peterson .20 .50
164 Keon Clark .20 .50
165 Chris Childs .20 .50
166 Alvin Williams .20 .50
167 Karl Malone .40 1.00
168 John Stockton .40 1.00
169 Donyell Marshall .20 .50
170 John Starks .20 .50
171 Bryon Russell .20 .50
172 David Benoit .20 .50
173 DeShawn Stevenson .20 .50
174 Richard Hamilton .25 .60
175 Jahidi White .20 .50
176 Courtney Alexander .20 .50
177 Chris Whitney .20 .50
178 Michael Jordan 4.00 10.00
179 Kobe Bryant CL .60 1.50
180 Kevin Garnett CL .25 .60
181 Sean Lampley RC 1.00 2.50
182 Andrei Kirilenko RC 1.50 4.00
183 Brandon Armstrong RC .60 1.50
184 Gerald Wallace RC 1.25 3.00
185 Tony Parker RC 4.00 10.00
186 Jeryl Sasser RC .60 1.50
187 Alton Ford RC 1.00 2.50
188 Kenny Satterfield RC .60 1.50
189 Will Solomon RC 1.00 2.50
190 Earl Watson RC 1.00 2.50
191 Michael Wright RC 1.00 2.50
192 Samuel Dalembert RC 1.00 2.50
193 Ousmane Cisse RC 1.00 2.50
194 Ruben Boumtje-Boumtje RC 1.00 2.50
195 Damone Brown RC .60 1.50
196 Jarron Collins RC 1.00 2.50
197 Terence Morris RC 1.00 2.50
198 Pau Gasol RC 3.00 8.00
199 Trenton Hassell RC .75 2.00
200 Kirk Haston RC .60 1.50
201 Brian Scalabrine RC 1.00 2.50
202 Gilbert Arenas RC 1.50 4.00
203 Jeff Trepagnier RC .60 1.50
204 Joseph Forte RC .60 1.50
205 Steven Hunter RC .75 2.00
206 Omar Cook RC 1.00 2.50
207 Jason Collins RC .75 2.00
208 Kedrick Brown RC .60 1.50
209 Michael Bradley RC .60 1.50
210 Zach Randolph RC 1.50 4.00
211 Richard Jefferson RC 1.50 4.00
212 Jamaal Tinsley RC 1.00 2.50
213 Vladimir Radmanovic RC 1.00 2.50
214 Brendan Haywood RC 1.00 2.50
215 Troy Murphy RC 1.00 2.50
216 DeSagana Diop RC .75 2.00
217 Jason Richardson RC 1.25 3.00
218 Joe Johnson RC 1.25 3.00
219 Rodney White RC .60 1.50
220 Loren Woods RC .60 1.50
221 Tyson Chandler RC 1.50 4.00
222 Eddy Curry RC 1.00 2.50
223 Shane Battier RC 2.00 5.00
224 Eddie Griffin RC .75 2.00
225 Kwame Brown RC 1.00 2.50
226 Shareef Abdur-Rahim .25 .60
227 Nazr Mohammed .20 .50
228 Hanno Mottola .20 .50
229 Emanual Davis .20 .50
230 Dion Glover .20 .50
231 Chris Crawford .20 .50
232 Mark Blount .20 .50
233 Joe Johnson .60 1.50
234 Milt Palacio .20 .50
235 Kedrick Brown .30 .75
236 Tony Battie .20 .50
237 Erick Strickland .20 .50
238 Kirk Haston .30 .75
239 Stacey Augmon .20 .50
240 Matt Bullard .20 .50
241 Bryce Drew .20 .50
242 Jerome Moiso .20 .50
243 Robert Traylor .20 .50
244 Tyson Chandler .75 2.00
245 Eddy Curry .50 1.25
246 Charles Oakley .25 .60
247 Brad Miller .30 .75
248 Kevin Ollie .20 .50
249 Trenton Hassell .40 1.00
250 Ricky Davis .25 .60
251 Jumaine Jones .20 .50
252 DeSagana Diop .40 1.00
253 Bryant Stith .20 .50
254 Jeff Trepagnier .30 .75
255 Michael Doleac .20 .50
256 Tim Hardaway .30 .75
257 Danny Manning .25 .60
258 Johnny Newman .20 .50
259 Adrian Griffin .20 .50
260 Greg Buckner .20 .50
261 Donnell Harvey .20 .50
262 Evan Eschmeyer .20 .50
263 Avery Johnson .25 .60
264 Kenny Satterfield .30 .75
265 Scott Williams .20 .50
266 Tariq Abdul-Wahad .20 .50
267 George McCloud .20 .50
268 Clifford Robinson .20 .50
269 Jon Barry .20 .50
270 Brian Cardinal .20 .50
271 Rodney White .30 .75
272 Mikki Moore .20 .50
273 Victor Alexander .20 .50
274 Jason Richardson .60 1.50
275 Adonal Foyle .20 .50
276 Troy Murphy .50 1.25
277 Chris Mills .20 .50
278 Gilbert Arenas .75 2.00
279 Erick Dampier .20 .50
280 Glen Rice .25 .60
281 Eddie Griffin .40 1.00
282 Kevin Willis .20 .50
283 Terence Morris .50 1.25
284 Kelvin Cato .20 .50
285 Dan Langhi .20 .50
286 Jason Collier .20 .50
287 Jamaal Tinsley .50 1.25
288 Carlos Rogers .20 .50
289 Jeff Foster .20 .50
290 Al Harrington .25 .60
291 Bruno Sundov .20 .50
292 Elton Brand .30 .75
293 Keyon Dooling .20 .50
294 Michael Olowokandi .20 .50
295 Obinna Ekezie .20 .50
296 Earl Boykins .25 .60
297 Harold Jamison .20 .50
298 Sean Rooks .20 .50
299 Lindsey Hunter .20 .50
300 Samaki Walker .20 .50
301 Mitch Richmond .25 .60
302 Stanislav Medvedenko .20 .50
303 Devean George .20 .50
304 Robert Horry .25 .60
305 Jelani McCoy .20 .50
306 Pau Gasol 1.50 4.00
307 Shane Battier 1.00 2.50
308 Jason Williams .25 .60
309 Isaac Austin .20 .50
310 Will Solomon .50 1.25
311 Lorenzen Wright .20 .50
312 Kendall Gill .20 .50
313 LaPhonso Ellis .25 .60
314 Sean Marks .20 .50
315 Rod Strickland .20 .50
316 Jim Jackson .20 .50
317 Eddie House .20 .50
318 Jason Caffey .20 .50
319 Rafer Alston .20 .50
320 Anthony Mason .20 .50
321 Mark Pope .20 .50
322 Michael Redd .30 .75
323 Darvin Ham .20 .50
324 Joe Smith .25 .60
325 William Avery .20 .50
326 Sam Mitchell .20 .50
327 Loren Woods .30 .75
328 Dean Garrett .20 .50
329 Gary Trent .20 .50
330 Jason Kidd .50 1.25
331 Todd MacCulloch .20 .50
332 Richard Jefferson .75 2.00
333 Brandon Armstrong .30 .75
334 Jason Collins .40 1.00
335 Kerry Kittles .20 .50
336 Shandon Anderson .20 .50
337 Howard Eisley .20 .50
338 Charlie Ward .20 .50
339 Lavor Postell .20 .50
340 Clarence Weatherspoon .20 .50
341 Travis Knight .20 .50
342 Horace Grant .25 .60
343 Steven Hunter .40 1.00
344 Patrick Ewing .40 1.00
345 Jeryl Sasser .30 .75
346 Don Reid .20 .50
347 Troy Hudson .20 .50
348 Speedy Claxton .20 .50
349 Derrick Coleman .25 .60
350 Damone Brown .30 .75
351 Samuel Dalembert .50 1.25
352 Vonteego Cummings .20 .50
353 Matt Harpring .20 .50
354 Corie Blount .20 .50
355 Stephon Marbury .25 .60
356 Dan Majerle .30 .75
357 Jake Voskuhl .20 .50
358 Alton Ford .50 1.25
359 Iakovos Tsakalidis .20 .50
360 John Wallace .20 .50
361 Derek Anderson .20 .50
362 Erick Barkley .20 .50
363 Ruben Boumtje-Boumtje .50 1.25
364 Zach Randolph .75 2.00
365 Steve Kerr .20 .50
366 Shawn Kemp .30 .75
367 Mateen Cleaves .20 .50
368 Bobby Jackson .20 .50
369 Mike Bibby .30 .75
370 Gerald Wallace .60 1.50
371 Jabari Smith .20 .50
372 Lawrence Funderburke .20 .50
373 Brent Price .20 .50
374 Bruce Bowen .20 .50
375 Stephen Jackson .25 .60
376 Tony Parker 2.00 5.00
377 Steve Smith .25 .60
378 Cherokee Parks .20 .50
379 Mark Bryant .20 .50
380 Jerome James .20 .50
381 Earl Watson .30 .75
382 Vladimir Radmanovic .50 1.25
383 Art Long .20 .50
384 Calvin Booth .20 .50
385 Olumide Oyedeji .20 .50
386 Jerome Williams .20 .50
387 Hakeem Olajuwon .40 1.00
388 Dell Curry .20 .50
389 Michael Bradley .30 .75
390 Tracy Murray .20 .50
391 Eric Montross .20 .50
392 John Amaechi .20 .50
393 John Crotty .20 .50
394 Scott Padgett .20 .50
395 Andrei Kirilenko .75 2.00
396 Jarron Collins .50 1.25
397 Quincy Lewis .20 .50
398 Kwame Brown .50 1.25
399 Christian Laettner .25 .60
400 Tyrone Nesby .20 .50
401 Brendan Haywood .50 1.25
402 Tyronn Lue .20 .50
403 Michael Jordan 4.00 10.00
404 Kobe Bryant CL .60 1.50
405 Michael Jordan CL 2.00 5.00
406A Zeljko Rebraca RC 1.00 2.50
406B Zeljko Rebraca RC 1.00 2.50
407A Jamison Brewer RC 1.00 2.50
407B Jamison Brewer RC 1.00 2.50
408A Shawn Marion .50 1.25
408B Shawn Marion .50 1.25
409A Primoz Brezec RC 1.00 2.50
409B Primoz Brezec RC 1.00 2.50
410A Antonis Fotsis RC .60 1.50
410B Antonis Fotsis RC .60 1.50
411A Bobby Simmons RC 1.00 2.50
411B Bobby Simmons RC 1.00 2.50
412A Malik Allen RC 1.00 2.50
412B Malik Allen RC 1.00 2.50
413A Ratko Varda RC 1.00 2.50
413B Ratko Varda RC 1.00 2.50
414A Tierre Brown RC 1.00 2.50
414B Tierre Brown RC 1.00 2.50
415A Norm Richardson RC 1.00 2.50
415B Norm Richardson RC 1.00 2.50
416A Oscar Torres RC 1.00 2.50
416B Oscar Torres RC 1.00 2.50
417A Chris Andersen RC 5.00 12.00
417B Chris Andersen RC 5.00 12.00
418A Predrag Drobnjak RC 1.00 2.50
418B Predrag Drobnjak RC 1.00 2.50
419A Dirk Nowitzki 1.00 2.50
419B Dirk Nowitzki 1.00 2.50
420A Shareef Abdur-Rahim .50 1.25
420B Shareef Abdur-Rahim .50 1.25
421A Kenny Anderson .50 1.25
421B Kenny Anderson .50 1.25
422A Jamal Mashburn .50 1.25
422B Jamal Mashburn .50 1.25
423A Charles Oakley .50 1.25
423B Charles Oakley .50 1.25
424A Andre Miller .50 1.25
424B Andre Miller .50 1.25
425A Michael Finley .60 1.50
425B Michael Finley .60 1.50
426A Tim Hardaway .60 1.50
426B Tim Hardaway .60 1.50
427A Nick Van Exel .50 1.25
427B Nick Van Exel .50 1.25
428A Jerry Stackhouse .50 1.25
428B Jerry Stackhouse .50 1.25
429A Mookie Blaylock .40 1.00
429B Mookie Blaylock .40 1.00
430A Glen Rice .50 1.25
430B Glen Rice .50 1.25
431A Reggie Miller .60 1.50
431B Reggie Miller .60 1.50
432A Elton Brand .60 1.50
432B Elton Brand .60 1.50
433A Kobe Bryant Driving 2.50 6.00
433B Kobe Bryant Looking to pass 2.50 6.00
434A Jason Williams .50 1.25
434B Jason Williams .50 1.25
435A Eddie Jones .50 1.25
435B Eddie Jones .50 1.25
436A Alonzo Mourning .75 2.00
436B Alonzo Mourning .75 2.00
437A Glenn Robinson .50 1.25
437B Glenn Robinson .50 1.25
438A Kevin Garnett 1.00 2.50
438B Kevin Garnett 1.00 2.50
439A Jason Kidd 1.00 2.50
439B Jason Kidd 1.00 2.50
440A Latrell Sprewell .50 1.25
440B Latrell Sprewell .50 1.25
441A Grant Hill .75 2.00
441B Grant Hill .75 2.00
442A Dikembe Mutombo .60 1.50
442B Dikembe Mutombo .60 1.50
443A Anfernee Hardaway 1.00 2.50
443B Anfernee Hardaway 1.00 2.50
444A Scottie Pippen 1.00 2.50
444B Scottie Pippen 1.00 2.50
445A Mike Bibby .60 1.50
445B Mike Bibby .60 1.50
446A David Robinson 1.00 2.50
446B David Robinson 1.00 2.50
447A Gary Payton .60 1.50
447B Gary Payton .60 1.50
448A Vince Carter 1.00 2.50
448B Vince Carter 1.00 2.50
449A John Stockton .75 2.00
449B John Stockton .75 2.00
450A Jordan Shooting 6.00 15.00
450B Jordan Dribbling 6.00 15.00

2001-02 Upper Deck UDX

*UDX STARS: 6X TO 15X BASE CARD HI
*UDX RCs: 3X TO 8X BASE CARD HI
*UDX CLs: 12X TO 30X BASE CARD HI
STARS STATED PRINT RUN 100 SETS
RC STATED PRINT RUN 50 SETS
301 Mitch Richmond 10.00 25.00

2001-02 Upper Deck 10th Power Game Jerseys

Randomly inserted in series one packs at a rate of 1:144, this 11-card insert set celebrates the brand's 10th anniversary with a game jersey set. The standard sized cards are borderless and feature swatches of the featured player's game worn jerseys. They also offer a UD Decade Milestone written in the lower right-hand corner of each card. The player's name is in the lower left-hand corner.

STATED ODDS 1:144 SER.1
AWX Antoine Walker 3.00 8.00
DRX David Robinson 6.00 15.00
KBX Kobe Bryant 15.00 40.00
KGX Kevin Garnett 6.00 15.00
KVX Keith Van Horn 3.00 8.00
MJX Michael Jordan 60.00 120.00
MTX Dikembe Mutombo 4.00 10.00
NVX Nick Van Exel 3.00 8.00
RAX Ray Allen 4.00 10.00
RHH Richard Hamilton 3.00 8.00
WSX Wally Szczerbiak 3.00 8.00

2001-02 Upper Deck 15000 Point Club Jerseys

Randomly inserted in series 2 packs at the rate of one in 120, this nine card set showcases the elite members of the NBA's 15000 point club with a swatch of game worn jersey.

STATED ODDS 1:120 SER.2
GR15K Glen Rice 3.00 8.00
IT15K Isiah Thomas 8.00 20.00
JH15K John Havlicek 8.00 20.00
JW15K Jerry West 10.00 25.00
KM15K Karl Malone 5.00 12.00
LB15K Larry Bird 10.00 25.00
MJ15K Michael Jordan 60.00 120.00
MM15K Moses Malone 4.00 10.00
PE15K Patrick Ewing 5.00 12.00

2001-02 Upper Deck Breakout Performers

Randomly inserted in series two packs at the rate of one in 12, this 15-card set showcases players that came straight out into the league and proved they belong. Full color player action photos are surrounded on both the top and the bottom by the words "Breakout Performers" and look as if they're jumping straight out of the card.

COMPLETE SET (15) 7.50 15.00
STATED ODDS 1:12 SER.2
BP1 Kenyon Martin .60 1.50
BP2 Steve Francis .50 1.25
BP3 Stromile Swift .40 1.00
BP4 Baron Davis .60 1.50
BP5 Rashard Lewis .60 1.50
BP6 Vince Carter 1.00 2.50
BP7 Richard Hamilton .50 1.25
BP8 Kobe Bryant 2.50 6.00
BP9 DerMarr Johnson .40 1.00
BP10 Andre Miller .50 1.25
BP11 Kevin Garnett 1.00 2.50
BP12 Morris Peterson .40 1.00
BP13 Dirk Nowitzki 1.00 2.50
BP14 Mike Miller .50 1.25
BP15 Shawn Marion .50 1.25

2001-02 Upper Deck BuyBacks

PRINT RUNS LISTED BELOW
MOST UNPRICED DUE TO SCARCITY
2 K.Bryant 00-1UD#80/88 125.00 300.00
12 J.Stackhouse 00-1 SPA/21 25.00 60.00

2001-02 Upper Deck Class

Randomly inserted in series one packs at a rate of 1:24, this 7-card insert celebrates the best photos from Upper Deck's first ten years in basketball. Player photos appear on the right side of the card, and an irredescent strip with gold foil highlights appears on the left.

COMPLETE SET (7) 8.00 20.00
STATED ODDS 1:24 SER.1
C1 Michael Jordan 6.00 15.00
C2 Shaquille O'Neal 2.00 5.00
C3 Alonzo Mourning 1.00 2.50

C4 Steve Francis .60 1.50
C5 Kobe Bryant 3.00 8.00
C6 Tim Duncan 1.50 4.00
C7 Kevin Garnett 1.25 3.00

2001-02 Upper Deck Classic Duals Jerseys

Seeded in series two packs at the rate of one in 240, this nine card set pairs two players together on the card front of this horizontal design. Player action photos are set on both the left and the right side, and semi-circular swatch of jerseys appear below.

STATED ODDS 1:240 SER.2
JS/GP J.Stockton/G.Payton 5.00 12.00
JT/TP J.Tinsley/T.Parker 6.00 15.00
KB/AI K.Bryant/A.Iverson 15.00 40.00
KB/DM K.Bryant/D.Miles 12.00 30.00
KB/TM K.Bryant/T.McGrady 15.00 40.00
KM/KG K.Malone/K.Garnett 6.00 15.00

2001-02 Upper Deck Cool Cats Jerseys

Randomly inserted in series two packs at the rate of one in 288, this eight card set showcases some of the University of Kentucky Wildcats best players. Car backgrounds are blue on the top and black on the bottom. The top of the card has a swatch in the shape of a Wildcat paw, and the bottom has a portrait style photo of the featured player.

STATED ODDS 1:288 SER.2
AWC Antoine Walker 4.00 10.00
BRC Michael Bradley 3.00 8.00
DJC DerMarr Johnson 3.00 8.00
JMC Jamal Mashburn 4.00 10.00
KMC Kenyon Martin 5.00 12.00
RJC Richard Jefferson 8.00 20.00
RMC Ron Mercer 3.00 8.00
TDC Tony Delk 3.00 8.00

2001-02 Upper Deck Game Jerseys

Randomly inserted in series one packs at a rate of 1:144, this 10-card insert features full color player photos on the right and a rectangular swatch of a game jersey in the lower right hand corner.

STATED ODDS 1:144 SER.1
BR Bryon Russell 1.50 4.00
CM Cuttino Mobley 1.50 4.00
GP Gary Payton 2.50 6.00
JS Joe Smith 2.00 5.00
JT Jason Terry 2.50 6.00
KB Kobe Bryant 10.00 25.00
KG Kevin Garnett 4.00 10.00
KM Karl Malone 3.00 8.00
MC Marc Jackson 1.50 4.00
RA Ron Artest 2.50 6.00

2001-02 Upper Deck Game Jerseys Autographs 1

PRINT RUN 100 SERIAL #'d SETS
CHA Chris Mihm 6.00 15.00
KBA Kobe Bryant 150.00 300.00
KGA Kevin Garnett 50.00 100.00
KMA Kenyon Martin 15.00 40.00
LHA Larry Hughes 20.00 50.00
MAA Marcus Fizer 10.00 25.00
MMA Mike Miller 8.00 20.00
MPA Morris Peterson 10.00 25.00
WZA Wang Zhizhi 30.00 80.00

2001-02 Upper Deck Game Jerseys Autographs 2

Randomly inserted in series two hobby packs, this 11-card set features both a swatch of a game worn jersey as well as an authentic player autographs.

PRINT RUN 100 SER.#'d SETS
DJA DerMarr Johnson 12.00 30.00
DMA Desmond Mason 12.00 30.00
EGA Eddie Griffin 12.00 30.00
JRA Jason Richardson 30.00 80.00
KBA Kobe Bryant 150.00 300.00
KGA Kevin Garnett 40.00 80.00
RMA Ron Mercer 12.00 30.00
RWA Rodney White 12.00 30.00

2001-02 Upper Deck Game Jerseys Combos

Randomly inserted in hobby packs only at a rate of 1:144, this 10-card insert set includes two swatches of a game-worn jersey from two different players on one card.

STATED ODDS 1:144 SER.1
AJLH A.Jamison/L.Hughes 6.00 15.00
AMLM A.Miller/L.Murray 6.00 15.00
DMCM D.Miles/C.Maggette 6.00 15.00
DMQR D.Miles/Q.Richardson 6.00 15.00
JCRM J.Crawford/R.Mercer 6.00 15.00
JMBD J.Mashburn/B.Davis 6.00 15.00
JTTK J.Terry/T.Kukoc 6.00 15.00
KBKG K.Bryant/K.Garnett 10.00 25.00
KMJS K.Malone/J.Stockton 12.50 30.00
MFDN M.Finley/D.Nowitzki 8.00 20.00

2001-02 Upper Deck Game Jerseys Logos

Randomly seeded in series two packs at the rate of one in 5000, this nine card set utilizes the same design as the Game Jerseys insert set enhanced with premium jersey swatches from uniform logos.

STATED ODDS 1:5000 SER.2
AHPL Allan Houston 20.00 50.00
KBPL Kobe Bryant 100.00 250.00
MMPL Mike Miller 20.00 50.00

2001-02 Upper Deck Game Jerseys Names

Randomly seeded in series two packs at the rate of one in 7500, this nine card set utilizes the same design as the Game Jerseys insert set enhanced with premium jersey swatches from uniform names.

STATED ODDS 1:7500 SER.2
MJ2PN Michael Jordan 300.00 600.00
KGPN Kevin Garnett 30.00 80.00

2001-02 Upper Deck Game Jerseys Numbers

Randomly seeded in series two packs at the rate of one in 2500, this nine card set utilizes the same design as the Game Jerseys insert set enhanced with premium jersey swatches from uniform numbers.

STATED ODDS 1:2500 SER.2
AMP Antonio McDyess 15.00 40.00
JMP Jamal Mashburn 15.00 40.00
KBP Kobe Bryant 80.00 200.00
KMP Karl Malone 25.00 60.00
MFP Michael Finley 20.00 50.00

2001-02 Upper Deck Game Jerseys Patches

Randomly seeded in series one packs at the rate of one in 2500, this nine card set utilizes the same design as the Game Jerseys insert set enhanced with premium jersey swatches from uniform patches.

STATED ODDS 1:2500 SER.1
AIP Allen Iverson 40.00 100.00
AMP Andre Miller 15.00 40.00
JMP Jamal Mashburn 15.00 40.00
JTP Jason Terry 20.00 50.00
KBP Kobe Bryant 80.00 200.00
KGP Kevin Garnett 30.00 80.00
KMP Kenyon Martin 20.00 50.00
MAP Marc Jackson 12.00 30.00
MFP Michael Finley 20.00 50.00
MMP Mike Miller 15.00 40.00
QRP Quentin Richardson 15.00 40.00
RAP Ray Allen 20.00 50.00
RWP Rasheed Wallace 20.00 50.00
SMP Shawn Marion 15.00 40.00

2001-02 Upper Deck Higher Ground

Randomly inserted in series one packs at the rate of one in 18, this 10-card set places full color player action photos on a white background with a colored strip to match the player jersey and irridescent foil highlights throught the center of the card. The top and bottom of the card are colored to resemble the three point arc on a basketball court.

COMPLETE SET (10) 7.50 15.00
STATED ODDS 1:18 SER.1
HG1 Vince Carter 1.25 3.00
HG2 Kevin Garnett 1.25 3.00
HG3 Paul Pierce .75 2.00
HG4 Mike Miller .60 1.50
HG5 Jamal Mashburn .60 1.50
HG6 Steve Francis .60 1.50
HG7 Jerry Stackhouse .60 1.50
HG8 Kobe Bryant 3.00 8.00
HG9 Eddie Jones .60 1.50
HG10 Shawn Marion .60 1.50

2001-02 Upper Deck MJ Jersey Collection

Randomly inserted in packs of Upper Deck, this 19 card set features Michael Jordan with different swatches from the different jerseys he's worn throughout the years. Cards MJC1-MJC10 were inserted in series one packs, and cards MJC11-MJC19 were inserted in series two packs. The jerseys are cut in the shape of the letter "M," and each card is sequentailly numbered to 50.

COMMON CARD 150.00 300.00
MJC1-MJC10 SER.1/MJC11-MJC19 SER.2
PRINT RUN 50 SERIAL #'d SETS

2001-02 Upper Deck MJ's Back

This 90-card set was inserted in with the majority of Upper Deck's 2001-02 Basketball releases. Cards were issued in special three-card bonus packs which were found at the top of UD's product boxes. Each card features a photo of Michael Jordan with a border along the left side of the card, and "MJ's Back" in silver foil highlights. Full color action photos are set against a silver and white backdrop. Packs were inserted chronologically in these brands: Upper Deck Hardcourt, Upper Deck Series 1, Upper Deck Ovation, Upper Deck Sweet Shot, and Upper Deck Series 2.

COMMON CARD (MJ1-MJ90) 2.00 5.00
ONE PACK INSERTED IN THE FOLLOWING BRANDS: HARDCOURT, UD 1, UD 2, OVATION, AND SWEET SHOT

2001-02 Upper Deck MJ's Back 23 Karat Gold

COMMON CARD 40.00 100.00
STATED PRINT RUN 23 SER.#'d SETS

2001-02 Upper Deck MJ's Back Jerseys

Randomly inserted in MJ's Back bonus packs, this five card set features a photo of Michael Jordan and traces his way from college to the pros to his comeback with the Wizards with commemorative swatches of each of these jerseys. Each card is sequentially numbered to 100. Dual Jerseys were also issued and feature two jersey swatches and sequential numbering to 50.

COMMON CARD (CC1-CC5) 150.00 300.00
STATED PRINT RUN 100 SER.#'d SETS
DUAL PRINT RUN 50 SER.#'d SETS

2001-02 Upper Deck MJ's Back Jerseys Autographs

COMMON CARD (1-5) 500.00 900.00
PRINT RUN 23 SER.#'d SETS

2001-02 Upper Deck MJ's Back Jerseys Dual

Randomly inserted in Upper Deck MJ's Back Bonus Packs, this five card set feautes a small picture of Michael Jordan in the upper right hand corner of the card with two swatches of jerseys beneath which, the logos of the teams those jerseys are from appear. Each card is sequentially numbered to 50.

COMMON CARD (CCD1-CCD5) 200.00 400.00

2001-02 Upper Deck MJ's Back Jerseys Dual Autographs

COMMON CARD (1-5) 500.00 1000.00
STATED PRINT RUN 23 SER.#'d SETS

2001-02 Upper Deck MJ's Back Jerseys Triple

Randomly inserted in Upper Deck MJ's Back Bonus Packs, this set features a single card with three swatches of jersey on it. Design is similar to the Jerseys Dual set, and the card sequentially numbered to 25.

STATED PRINT RUN 25 SER.#'d SETS
UNPRICED TRIPLE AU PRINT RUN 10 SETS
CCT1 M.Jordan UNC/Bulls/Wiz 300.00 600.00

2001-02 Upper Deck MJ's Back Jerseys Quad

Randomly inserted in Upper Deck MJ's Back Bonus Packs, this set features a single card with four swatches of jersey on it. Design is similar to the Jerseys Dual set, and the card sequentially numbered to 23.

STATED PRINT RUN 23 SER.#'d SETS
UNPRICED QUAD AU PRINT RUN 5 SETS
CCQ1 Jordan NC/Bull/Bull/Wiz 500.00 800.00

2001-02 Upper Deck MJ Tributes MJ Milestones

Randomly inserted in late season UD products, MJ Tributes MJ Milestones featuers photos of Michael Jordan coupled with a swatch of jersey and an authentic autograph. Each card is squentially numbered to 30. These cards were originally issued as exchanges, and were inserted in the following products: Card number M1 in Upper Deck Honor Roll, M2 and M3 in Upper Deck Playmakers, M4 and M5 in SP Authentic, M6 and M7 in Upper Deck Flight Team, and M8 and M9 in Upper Deck Inspirations.

COMMON CARD (M1-M7) 400.00 700.00
PRINT RUN 30 SER.#'d SETS
CARDS ISSUED AS EXCHANGES

2001-02 Upper Deck MJ Tributes Portrait of a Champion

Randomly insereted in the following brands, Upper Deck Honor Roll, Upper Deck Playmakers, SP Authentic, Upper Deck Flight Team, and Upper Deck Inspirations, this set features jerseys from different points in Michael Jordan's career along with autographs. These cards were initially issued as exchanges, and each card is squentially numbered to 23.

COMMON CARD 400.00 700.00
PRINT RUN 23 SER.#'d SETS
CARDS ISSUED AS EXCHANGES

2001-02 Upper Deck Motion Pictures

Randomly seeded in series two packs at the rate of one in 18, this 10-card set pictures players in action set on a "film strip" backdrop on the right side of the card. The left side contains the set name and the player's name in gold foil.

COMPLETE SET (10) 12.50 25.00
STATED ODDS 1:18 SER.2
MP1 Kobe Bryant 3.00 8.00
MP2 Tim Duncan 1.50 4.00
MP3 Michael Jordan 6.00 15.00
MP4 Elton Brand .75 2.00
MP5 Vince Carter 1.25 3.00
MP6 Eddie Jones .60 1.50
MP7 Kevin Garnett 1.25 3.00
MP8 Michael Finley .75 2.00
MP9 Paul Pierce .75 2.00
MP10 Shaquille O'Neal 2.00 5.00

2001-02 Upper Deck NBA All-Star Authentics

Randomly inserted in series one packs at the rate of one in 96, this five card set features NBA All-Stars in full color action coupled with a swatch of game worn memorabilia.

STATED ODDS 1:96 SER.1
BDAS Baron Davis 5.00 12.00
DMAS Desmond Mason 4.00 10.00
PSAS Peja Stojakovic 5.00 12.00
RLAS Rashard Lewis 5.00 12.00
SSAS Stromile Swift 3.00 8.00

2001-02 Upper Deck NBA Finals Fabrics

Randomly inserted in series two packs at the rate of one in 120, this 20-card set features players from the 2000-01 finals in action and swatches of the jerseys they wore in those games.

STATED ODDS 1:120 SER.2
AIF Allen Iverson 12.00 30.00
AMF Aaron McKie 4.00 10.00
BSF Brian Shaw 4.00 10.00
DFF Derek Fisher 5.00 12.00
DGF Devean George 4.00 10.00
DMF Dikembe Mutombo 6.00 15.00
ESF Eric Snow 4.00 10.00
GFF Greg Foster 4.00 10.00
HGF Horace Grant 5.00 12.00
JJF Jumaine Jones 4.00 10.00
KBF Kobe Bryant 100.00 200.00
KOF Kevin Ollie 4.00 10.00
MMF Mark Madsen 4.00 10.00
RBF Rodney Buford 4.00 10.00
RFF Rick Fox 4.00 10.00
RJF Raja Bell 8.00 20.00
ROF Robert Horry 8.00 20.00
THF Tyrone Hill 4.00 10.00
TLF Tyronn Lue 4.00 10.00
TMF Todd MacCulloch 4.00 10.00

2001-02 Upper Deck Rookie Threads

Randomly inserted in series two hobby packs at the rate of one in 144, this 10-card set features full color photos of rookie players on the right side of this horizontal card design with a swatch of a jersey that is cut in the shape of the letter R.

STATED ODDS 1:144 SER.2 HOBBY
ECT Eddy Curry 2.50 6.00
EGT Eddie Griffin 2.00 5.00
GWT Gerald Wallace 3.00 8.00
JJT Joe Johnson 3.00 8.00
JRT Jason Richardson 3.00 8.00
KET Kedrick Brown 1.50 4.00
KWT Kwame Brown 2.50 6.00
RJT Richard Jefferson 4.00 10.00
RWT Rodney White 1.50 4.00
TCT Tyson Chandler 4.00 10.00

2001-02 Upper Deck Sky High

Randomly inserted in series two packs at the rate of one in 24, this seven card set showcases high flyers of the NBA with full color aciton photos. The photos are centered on the card and along the right side, each of the letters in the words, "Sky High" are surrounded with a gold foil circle.

COMPLETE SET (7) 7.50 15.00
STATED ODDS 1:24 SER.2
SH1 Kobe Bryant 3.00 8.00
SH2 Kevin Garnett 1.25 3.00
SH3 Darius Miles .50 1.25
SH4 Tracy McGrady 1.25 3.00
SH5 Kwame Brown .75 2.00
SH6 Eddy Curry .75 2.00
SH7 Tyson Chandler 1.25 3.00

2001-02 Upper Deck SlamCenter

Randomly inserted in series one packs at the rate of one in 12, this 15-card set features in action player photos set on a square irridescent background with white borders. Cards are highlighted with gold foil and the word Slam along the right side and the word Center across the player photo.

COMPLETE SET (15) 7.50 15.00
STATED ODDS 1:12 SER.1
SC1 Kobe Bryant 2.50 6.00
SC2 Desmond Mason .50 1.25
SC3 Vince Carter 1.00 2.50
SC4 Antonio McDyess .50 1.25
SC5 Lamar Odom .50 1.25
SC6 Rashard Lewis .60 1.50
SC7 Chris Webber .60 1.50
SC8 Latrell Sprewell .50 1.25
SC9 Antoine Walker .50 1.25
SC10 Stromile Swift .40 1.00
SC11 Glenn Robinson .50 1.25
SC12 Kevin Garnett 1.00 2.50
SC13 Antawn Jamison .60 1.50
SC14 Jerry Stackhouse .50 1.25
SC15 Shaquille O'Neal 1.50 4.00

2001-02 Upper Deck Superstar Summit

Inserted in series two packs at the rate of one in 18, this 10-card set places full color player action photos on an all foil backdrop. The background is shaped like the letter "X" and has gold foil highlights.

COMPLETE SET (10) 12.50 25.00
STATED ODDS 1:18 SER.2
SS1 Kobe Bryant 3.00 8.00
SS2 Vince Carter 1.25 3.00
SS3 Kevin Garnett 1.25 3.00
SS4 Chris Webber .75 2.00
SS5 Shaquille O'Neal 2.00 5.00
SS6 Tim Duncan 1.50 4.00
SS7 Allen Iverson 1.50 4.00
SS8 Ray Allen .75 2.00
SS9 Steve Francis .60 1.50
SS10 Michael Jordan 6.00 15.00

2001-02 Upper Deck Triple Jump Jerseys

Inserted in hobby packs, this 10-card set featues three small in action photos of the showcased players on the right set against a white background and three swatches of game jersey on the left. Each card is sequentially numbered to 25.

STATED PRINT RUN 25 SER.#'d SETS
JTJRTP Tinsley/J.Rich/Parker 30.00 80.00
KBTMCW Bryant/T-Mac/Webber 75.00 150.00
MJDRKB Jordan/J.Erving/Kobe 250.00 500.00
MJKBKG Jordan/Kobe/Garnett 200.00 400.00
MJMJMJ Jordan/Jordan/Jordan 300.00 600.00

2001-02 Upper Deck UD Originals Jerseys

Seeded in series two packs at the rate of one in 120, this 10-card set focuses on some of the younger players of the NBA. The card design resembles that of the base Upper Deck cards with a swatch of jersey in the lower right hand corner.

STATED ODDS 1:120 SER.2
BDO Baron Davis 5.00 12.00
CWO Chris Webber 5.00 12.00
DMO Darius Miles 3.00 8.00
KBO Kobe Bryant 20.00 50.00
KGO Kevin Garnett 8.00 20.00
MMO Mike Miller 4.00 10.00
RAO Ray Allen 5.00 12.00
SHO Shawn Marion 4.00 10.00
SMO Stephon Marbury 4.00 10.00
SSO Stromile Swift 3.00 8.00

2001-02 Upper Deck Upper Decade Team

Seeded in series one packs at the rate of one in 18, this 10-card set features a colored border on the left side of the card, a full color player action photo in the center on a white background, and an irridescent player portrait style photo along the right side.

COMPLETE SET (10) 12.50 30.00
STATED ODDS 1:18 SER.1
UD1 Michael Jordan 6.00 15.00
UD2 Kobe Bryant 3.00 8.00
UD3 Vince Carter 1.25 3.00
UD4 Kevin Garnett 1.25 3.00
UD5 Shaquille O'Neal 2.00 5.00
UD6 Tim Hardaway .75 2.00
UD7 Gary Payton .75 2.00
UD8 Scottie Pippen 1.25 3.00
UD9 Tim Duncan 1.50 4.00
UD10 David Robinson 1.25 3.00

2001-02 Upper Deck Winning Touch Game Jerseys

Seeded in series one packs at the rate of one in 144, this 11-card set places players in action along the right side of the card, a colored border on the left side, and a "wood grain" center with a swatch of a game jersey.

STATED ODDS 1:144 SER.1
AIWT Allen Iverson 8.00 20.00
DRWT David Robinson 6.00 15.00
JSWT John Stockton 5.00 12.00
KMWT Karl Malone 5.00 12.00
PEWT Patrick Ewing 5.00 12.00
RFWT Rick Fox 2.50 6.00
RPWT Robert Parish 4.00 10.00
SEWT Sean Elliott 4.00 10.00
SKWT Steve Kerr 5.00 12.00

2001-02 Upper Deck World Piece Game Jerseys

Inserted in series one hobby packs at the rate of one in 288, this 10-card set features some of the NBA's most prominent foreign players and a swatch of a game worn jersey.

STATED ODDS 1:288 SER.1 HOBBY
DBWP Dalibor Bagaric 2.50 6.00
DNWP Dirk Nowitzki 6.00 15.00
FLWP Felipe Lopez 2.50 6.00
HMWP Hanno Mottola 2.50 6.00
MOWP Michael Olowokandi 2.50 6.00
MTWP Dikembe Mutombo 4.00 10.00
SNWP Steve Nash 6.00 15.00
TKWP Toni Kukoc 4.00 10.00
VLWP Vlade Divac 3.00 8.00
ZWWP Wang Zhizhi 3.00 8.00

2002-03 Upper Deck

Upper Deck was issued as a 420-card set divided up into two series. Series one contains 210 cards and was released in November 2002, and Series two contains 220 cards and was released in February 2003. Base cards are borderless with a name box at the bottom and silver foil highlights. The breakdown is as follows: Numbers 1-180 feature veteran players, numbers 181-210 feature rookies, numbers 211-390 feature both veterans and rookies, however, the rookie players in this section have rookie cards in series one so these are not RC cards, and numbers 391-419 again feature rookies. The last card in the set features Michael Jordan. Upper Deck was packaged in 24-pack boxes where packs contained eight cards and carried a suggested retail price of $2.99.

COMPLETE SER.1 (210) 80.00 160.00
COMPLETE SER. 2 (210) 20.00 40.00
COMP.SER.1 w/o SP's (180) 15.00 40.00
RC STATED ODDS 1:4
1 Shareef Abdur-Rahim .25 .60
2 Jason Terry .25 .60
3 Glenn Robinson .25 .60
4 Nazr Mohammed .20 .50
5 DerMarr Johnson .20 .50
6 Dion Glover .20 .50
7 Paul Pierce .30 .75
8 Antoine Walker .25 .60
9 Vin Baker .25 .60
10 Eric Williams .20 .50
11 Tony Delk .20 .50
12 Kedrick Brown .20 .50
13 Jalen Rose .25 .60
14 Eddy Curry .20 .50
15 Tyson Chandler .30 .75
16 Jamal Crawford .30 .75
17 Marcus Fizer .20 .50
18 Trenton Hassell .20 .50
19 Zydrunas Ilgauskas .25 .60
20 Tyrone Hill .20 .50
21 Darius Miles .20 .50
22 Chris Mihm .20 .50
23 Ricky Davis .25 .60
24 Jumaine Jones .20 .50
25 Dirk Nowitzki .50 1.25
26 Michael Finley .30 .75
27 Steve Nash .40 1.00
28 Raef LaFrentz .20 .50
29 Nick Van Exel .25 .60
30 Adrian Griffin .20 .50
31 Wang Zhizhi .20 .50
32 Marcus Camby .25 .60
33 Juwan Howard .25 .60
34 James Posey .20 .50
35 Donnell Harvey .20 .50
36 Ryan Bowen .20 .50
37 Zeljko Rebraca .20 .50
38 Ben Wallace .25 .60
39 Clifford Robinson .20 .50
40 Corliss Williamson .20 .50
41 Chucky Atkins .20 .50
42 Michael Curry .20 .50
43 Jason Richardson .30 .75
44 Antawn Jamison .30 .75
45 Troy Murphy .25 .60
46 Gilbert Arenas .30 .75
47 Danny Fortson .20 .50
48 Steve Francis .25 .60
49 Eddie Griffin .20 .50
50 Cuttino Mobley .20 .50
51 Kenny Thomas .20 .50
52 Moochie Norris .20 .50
53 Kelvin Cato .20 .50
54 Reggie Miller .30 .75
55 Jermaine O'Neal .25 .60
56 Ron Mercer .20 .50
57 Austin Croshere .20 .50
58 Ron Artest .30 .75
59 Jamaal Tinsley .20 .50
60 Elton Brand .30 .75
61 Andre Miller .25 .60
62 Lamar Odom .25 .60
63 Michael Olowokandi .20 .50
64 Quentin Richardson .25 .60
65 Corey Maggette .25 .60
66 Kobe Bryant 1.25 3.00
67 Shaquille O'Neal .75 2.00
68 Rick Fox .20 .50
69 Robert Horry .25 .60
70 Devean George .20 .50
71 Samaki Walker .20 .50
72 Brian Shaw .20 .50
73 Pau Gasol .40 1.00
74 Jason Williams .25 .60
75 Shane Battier .30 .75
76 Stromile Swift .20 .50
77 Lorenzen Wright .20 .50
78 LaPhonso Ellis .25 .60
79 Eddie Jones .25 .60
80 Brian Grant .20 .50
81 Vladimir Stepania .20 .50
82 Eddie House .20 .50
83 Anthony Carter .20 .50
84 Ray Allen .30 .75
85 Sam Cassell .25 .60
86 Tim Thomas .20 .50
87 Toni Kukoc .30 .75
88 Jason Caffey .20 .50
89 Anthony Mason .20 .50
90 Joel Przybilla .20 .50
91 Kevin Garnett .50 1.25
92 Wally Szczerbiak .25 .60
93 Terrell Brandon .20 .50
94 Joe Smith .25 .60
95 Felipe Lopez .20 .50
96 Anthony Peeler .20 .50
97 Radoslav Nesterovic .20 .50
98 Jason Kidd .50 1.25
99 Kenyon Martin .25 .60
100 Dikembe Mutombo .30 .75
101 Richard Jefferson .30 .75
102 Kerry Kittles .20 .50
103 Lucious Harris .20 .50
104 Jason Collins .20 .50
105 Baron Davis .25 .60
106 Jamal Mashburn .25 .60
107 Elden Campbell .20 .50
108 David Wesley .20 .50
109 P.J. Brown .20 .50
110 Lee Nailon .20 .50
111 Latrell Sprewell .25 .60
112 Allan Houston .25 .60
113 Kurt Thomas .20 .50
114 Antonio McDyess .25 .60
115 Othella Harrington .20 .50
116 Clarence Weatherspoon .20 .50
117 Tracy McGrady .50 1.25
118 Mike Miller .25 .60
119 Darrell Armstrong .20 .50
120 Grant Hill .40 1.00
121 Pat Garrity .20 .50
122 Steven Hunter .20 .50
123 Allen Iverson .50 1.25
124 Keith Van Horn .25 .60
125 Aaron McKie .20 .50
126 Eric Snow .20 .50
127 Derrick Coleman .25 .60
128 Samuel Dalembert .20 .50
129 Stephon Marbury .25 .60
130 Shawn Marion .25 .60
131 Joe Johnson .25 .60
132 Tom Gugliotta .20 .50
133 Anfernee Hardaway .50 1.25
134 Iakovos Tsakalidis .20 .50
135 Rasheed Wallace .30 .75
136 Bonzi Wells .20 .50
137 Damon Stoudamire .25 .60
138 Scottie Pippen .50 1.25
139 Derek Anderson .20 .50
140 Ruben Patterson .20 .50
141 Dale Davis .20 .50
142 Mike Bibby .30 .75
143 Chris Webber .30 .75
144 Peja Stojakovic .30 .75
145 Doug Christie .20 .50
146 Hedo Turkoglu .25 .60
147 Vlade Divac .25 .60
148 Scot Pollard .20 .50
149 Tim Duncan .60 1.50
150 David Robinson .50 1.25
151 Tony Parker .40 1.00
152 Malik Rose .20 .50
153 Steve Smith .25 .60
154 Bruce Bowen .20 .50
155 Danny Ferry .20 .50
156 Gary Payton .30 .75
157 Rashard Lewis .30 .75
158 Brent Barry .20 .50
159 Kenny Anderson .25 .60
160 Desmond Mason .25 .60
161 Predrag Drobnjak .20 .50
162 Vince Carter .50 1.25
163 Morris Peterson .20 .50
164 Antonio Davis .20 .50
165 Alvin Williams .20 .50
166 Jerome Williams .20 .50
167 Michael Bradley .20 .50
168 Karl Malone .40 1.00
169 John Stockton .40 1.00
170 John Amaechi .20 .50
171 Andrei Kirilenko .30 .75
172 Greg Ostertag .20 .50
173 Jarron Collins .20 .50
174 DeShawn Stevenson .20 .50
175 Christian Laettner .25 .60
176 Brendan Haywood .20 .50
177 Chris Whitney .20 .50
178 Tyronn Lue .20 .50
179 Kwame Brown .20 .50
180 Michael Jordan 2.50 6.00
181 Jay Williams RC 1.25 3.00
182 Juan Dixon RC 1.25 3.00
183 Vincent Yarbrough RC .75 2.00
184 Casey Jacobsen RC 1.00 2.50
185 Chris Wilcox RC 1.00 2.50
186 John Salmons RC 1.25 3.00
187 Marcus Haislip RC 1.00 2.50
188 Robert Archibald RC .75 2.00
189 Jared Jeffries RC 1.00 2.50
190 Nikoloz Tskitishvili RC .75 2.00
191 Kareem Rush RC 1.00 2.50
192 Fred Jones RC 1.00 2.50
193 Caron Butler RC 1.25 3.00
194 Chris Jefferies RC .75 2.00
195 Ryan Humphrey RC 1.00 2.50
196 Frank Williams RC .75 2.00
197 DaJuan Wagner RC 1.00 2.50
198 Bostjan Nachbar RC 1.00 2.50
199 Mike Dunleavy RC 1.25 3.00
200 Roger Mason RC 1.00 2.50
201 Nene Hilario RC 1.25 3.00
202 Melvin Ely RC 1.00 2.50
203 Tayshaun Prince RC 1.50 4.00
204 Jiri Welsch RC 1.00 2.50
205 Dan Dickau RC 1.00 2.50
206 Qyntel Woods RC 1.00 2.50
207 Curtis Borchardt RC .75 2.00
208 Amare Stoudemire RC 1.50 4.00
209 Drew Gooden RC 1.25 3.00
210 Yao Ming RC 2.50 6.00
211 Glenn Robinson .25 .60
212 Theo Ratliff .20 .50
213 Emanual Davis .20 .50
214 Dan Dickau .50 1.25
215 Alan Henderson .20 .50
216 Chris Crawford .20 .50
217 Darvin Ham .20 .50
218 Ira Newble .20 .50
219 Vin Baker .25 .60
220 Shammond Williams .20 .50
221 Tony Battie .20 .50
222 Walter McCarty .20 .50
223 Bruno Sundov .20 .50
224 Ruben Wolkowyski .20 .50
225 Eddie Robinson .20 .50
226 Jay Williams .60 1.50
227 Fred Hoiberg .20 .50
228 Donyell Marshall .20 .50
229 Roger Mason .50 1.25
230 Darius Miles .20 .50
231 Michael Stewart .20 .50
232 Tyrone Hill .20 .50
233 DaJuan Wagner .50 1.25
234 DeSagana Diop .20 .50
235 Bimbo Coles .20 .50
236 Milt Palacio .20 .50
237 Avery Johnson .25 .60
238 Evan Eschmeyer .20 .50
239 Raja Bell .25 .60
240 Shawn Bradley .20 .50
241 Walt Williams .20 .50
242 Eduardo Najera .20 .50
243 Marcus Camby .25 .60
244 Chris Whitney .20 .50
245 Nikoloz Tskitishvili .40 1.00
246 Kenny Satterfield .20 .50
247 Nene Hilario .60 1.50
248 Mark Blount .20 .50
249 Richard Hamilton .25 .60
250 Chauncey Billups .30 .75
251 Tayshaun Prince .75 2.00
252 Don Reid .20 .50
253 Jon Barry .20 .50
254 Hubert Davis .20 .50
255 Pepe Sanchez .20 .50
256 Chris Mills .20 .50
257 Bob Sura .20 .50
258 Mike Dunleavy .60 1.50
259 Jiri Welsch .50 1.25
260 Adonal Foyle .20 .50
261 Erick Dampier .20 .50
262 Maurice Taylor .20 .50
263 Glen Rice .25 .60
264 Yao Ming 1.25 3.00
265 Bostjan Nachbar .50 1.25
266 Jason Collier .20 .50
267 Terence Morris .20 .50
268 Jonathan Bender .20 .50
269 Jeff Foster .20 .50
270 Fred Jones .50 1.25
271 Al Harrington .25 .60
272 Brad Miller .25 .60
273 Jamison Brewer .20 .50
274 Erick Strickland .20 .50
275 Andre Miller .25 .60
276 Melvin Ely .50 1.25
277 Keyon Dooling .20 .50
278 Chris Wilcox .50 1.25
279 Eric Piatkowski .20 .50
280 Sean Rooks .20 .50
281 Wang Zhi Zhi .20 .50
282 Mark Madsen .20 .50
283 Kareem Rush .50 1.25
284 Stanislav Medvedenko .20 .50
285 Derek Fisher .25 .60
286 Tracy Murray .20 .50
287 Michael Dickerson .20 .50
288 Wesley Person .20 .50
289 Drew Gooden .60 1.50
290 Robert Archibald .40 1.00
291 Brevin Knight .20 .50
292 Mike James .20 .50
293 LaPhonso Ellis .25 .60
294 Caron Butler .60 1.50
295 Malik Allen .20 .50
296 Travis Best .20 .50
297 Alonzo Mourning .40 1.00
298 Toni Kukoc .30 .75
299 Michael Redd .25 .60
300 Marcus Haislip .50 1.25
301 Ervin Johnson .20 .50
302 Kevin Ollie .20 .50
303 Troy Hudson .20 .50
304 Marc Jackson .20 .50
305 Gary Trent .20 .50
306 Kendall Gill .20 .50
307 Loren Woods .20 .50
308 Dikembe Mutombo .30 .75
309 Anthony Johnson .20 .50
310 Rodney Rogers .20 .50
311 Brandon Armstrong .20 .50
312 Brian Scalabrine .20 .50
313 Aaron Williams .20 .50
314 Courtney Alexander .20 .50
315 Kirk Haston .20 .50
316 George Lynch .20 .50
317 Stacey Augmon .20 .50
318 Robert Traylor .20 .50
319 Jamaal Magloire .20 .50
320 Lee Nailon .20 .50
321 Frank Williams .40 1.00
322 Michael Doleac .20 .50
323 Shandon Anderson .20 .50
324 Howard Eisley .20 .50
325 Travis Knight .20 .50
326 Lavor Postell .20 .50
327 Charlie Ward .20 .50
328 Mark Pope .20 .50
329 Olumide Oyedeji .20 .50
330 Shawn Kemp .30 .75
331 Jacque Vaughn .20 .50
332 Ryan Humphrey .50 1.25
333 Andrew DeClercq .20 .50
334 Jeryl Sasser .20 .50
335 Keith Van Horn .25 .60
336 Todd MacCulloch .20 .50
337 Monty Williams .20 .50
338 John Salmons .60 1.50
339 Brian Skinner .20 .50
340 Mark Bryant .20 .50
341 Greg Buckner .20 .50
342 Bo Outlaw .20 .50
343 Amare Stoudemire .75 2.00
344 Casey Jacobsen .50 1.25
345 Alton Ford .20 .50
346 Scott Williams .20 .50
347 Dan Langhi .20 .50
348 Arvydas Sabonis .25 .60
349 Antonio Daniels .20 .50
350 Jeff McInnis .20 .50
351 Qyntel Woods .50 1.25
352 Zach Randolph .25 .60
353 Ruben Boumtje-Boumtje .20 .50
354 Chris Dudley .20 .50
355 Charles Smith .20 .50
356 Keon Clark .20 .50
357 Bobby Jackson .20 .50
358 Mateen Cleaves .20 .50
359 Gerald Wallace .25 .60
360 Lawrence Funderburke .20 .50
361 Speedy Claxton .20 .50
362 Stephen Jackson .25 .60
363 Kevin Willis .20 .50
364 Steve Kerr .20 .50
365 Mengke Bateer .20 .50
366 Kenny Anderson .25 .60
367 Vladimir Radmanovic .20 .50
368 Joseph Forte .20 .50
369 Jerome James .20 .50
370 Vitaly Potapenko .20 .50
371 Calvin Booth .20 .50
372 Ansu Sesay .20 .50
373 Voshon Lenard .20 .50
374 Lindsey Hunter .20 .50
375 Mamadou N'Diaye .20 .50
376 Chris Jefferies .40 1.00
377 Jelani McCoy .20 .50
378 Lamond Murray .20 .50
379 Eric Montross .20 .50
380 Matt Harpring .20 .50
381 Calbert Cheaney .20 .50
382 Curtis Borchardt .40 1.00
383 Mark Jackson .25 .60
384 Scott Padgett .20 .50
385 Jerry Stackhouse .25 .60
386 Jared Jeffries .50 1.25
387 Larry Hughes .25 .60
388 Juan Dixon .60 1.50
389 Bryon Russell .20 .50
390 Etan Thomas .20 .50
391 Efthimios Rentzias RC .75 2.00
392 Manu Ginobili RC 3.00 8.00
393 Juaquin Hawkins RC .75 2.00
394 Rasual Butler RC 1.25 3.00
395 Ronald Murray RC 1.25 3.00
396 Igor Rakocevic RC .75 2.00
397 Tito Maddox RC .75 2.00
398 Mike Batiste RC .75 2.00
399 Sam Clancy RC 1.00 2.50
400 Tamar Slay RC .75 2.00
401 Lonny Baxter RC .75 2.00
402 Marko Jaric 1.25 3.00
403 Dan Gadzuric RC 1.00 2.50
404 Jannero Pargo RC .75 2.00
405 Pat Burke RC .75 2.00
406 Smush Parker RC 1.25 3.00
407 Reggie Evans RC 1.25 3.00
408 Gordan Giricek RC 1.25 3.00
409 Mehmet Okur RC 1.25 3.00
410 Jamal Sampson RC 1.25 3.00
411 Raul Lopez RC 1.25 3.00
412 Predrag Savovic RC 1.00 2.50
413 Carlos Boozer RC 1.25 3.00
414 Ken Johnson 1.25 3.00
415 Cezary Trybanski RC 1.25 3.00
416 Mike Wilks RC 1.25 3.00
417 J.R. Bremer RC .75 2.00
418 Junior Harrington RC .75 2.00
419 Nate Huffman RC .75 2.00
420 Michael Jordan 2.50 6.00

2002-03 Upper Deck Exclusives

*STARS: 5X TO 12X BASE CARD HI
STARS PRINT RUN 100 SER.#'d SETS
*RCs: 2.5X TO 6X BASE CARD HI
RC PRINT RUN 50 SER.#'d SETS
*NON RC ROOKIES: 4X TO 10X BASE CARD HI
NON RC ROOKIES PRINT RUN 100 SETS

2002-03 Upper Deck Air Apparel

Randomly inserted in Series One packs at the rate of one in 72, this 12-card set places full color player photos on the right of a blue and white background. The left side of the card has a swatch of game-worn memorabilia and the words, Air Apparel appear along the bottom.

STATED ODDS 1:72 SER 1
BDAA Baron Davis 2.50 6.00
DJAA DerMarr Johnson 2.00 5.00
DMAA Darius Miles 2.00 5.00
JMAA Jamal Mashburn 2.50 6.00
JPAA James Posey 2.00 5.00
KMAA Kenyon Martin 2.50 6.00
KWAA Kwame Brown 2.00 5.00
LOAA Lamar Odom 2.50 6.00
LSAA Latrell Sprewell 2.50 6.00
RHAA Richard Hamilton 2.50 6.00
SAAA Shareef Abdur-Rahim SP 2.50 6.00
TCAA Tyson Chandler 3.00 8.00

2002-03 Upper Deck All-ACCess Jerseys

Randomly inserted in Series Two packs at the rate of one in 96, this 12-card set utilizes a horizontal design where color player action photos are on the right and a swatch of game-worn jersey is on the left. The

backgrounds are different shades of blue and the shape of the background on the left side of the card is the same shape as the jersey swatch.
STATED ODDS 1:96 SER.2
AAJ Antawn Jamison 3.00 8.00
ABH Brendan Haywood 2.00 5.00
ACM Corey Maggette 2.50 6.00
AEB Elton Brand 3.00 8.00
AJS Joe Smith 2.50 6.00
AMJ Michael Jordan SP 75.00 150.00
ARF Rick Fox 2.00 5.00
ARM Roger Mason 2.50 6.00
ASB Shane Battier 3.00 8.00
ASF Steve Francis SP 2.50 6.00
ASM Stephon Marbury 2.50 6.00
AST Jerry Stackhouse 2.50 6.00

2002-03 Upper Deck All-Star Authentics Jerseys

Randomly inserted in Series One packs, this 13-card set is designed horizontally with a full color player action photo on the left side and a star-shaped swatch of game-used jersey. Some cards were issued as short prints and some of a known limited quantity-those numbers appear below.
STATED ODDS 1:288 SER 1
AIAJ Allen Iverson 8.00 20.00
AMAJ Alonzo Mourning SP 6.00 15.00
BHAJ Brendan Haywood SP 3.00 8.00
CWAJ Chris Webber 5.00 12.00
GAAJ Gilbert Arenas SP 5.00 12.00
KMAJ Kenyon Martin/61* 5.00 12.00
MFAJ Marcus Fizer SP 3.00 8.00
PGAJ Pau Gasol/80* 6.00 15.00
PPAJ Paul Pierce 5.00 12.00
PSAJ Peja Stojakovic 5.00 12.00

2002-03 Upper Deck All-Star Authentics Jerseys Autographs

Randomly inserted in Series one packs, this six-card set parallels the base design of the All-Star Authentics Jerseys set enhanced with player autographs. Each card is sequentially numbered to 25.
PRINT RUN 25 SER.#'d SETS
KGAAA Kevin Garnett 40.00 100.00
KMAAA Kenyon Martin 12.50 30.00
PPAAJ Paul Pierce 20.00 50.00

2002-03 Upper Deck All-Star Authentics Shorts

Inserted in Series one packs at the rate of one in 96, this 14-card set parallels the design of the All-Star Authentics Jerseys set with a swatch of game-used shorts.
STATED ODDS 1:96 SER 1
AKAS Andrei Kirilenko 3.00 8.00
BHAS Brendan Haywood 2.00 5.00
CMAS Chris Mihm 2.00 5.00
DMAS Desmond Mason 2.50 6.00
DNAS Dirk Nowitzki 5.00 12.00
KBAS Kobe Bryant 12.50 30.00
LNAS Lee Nailon 2.00 5.00
MJAS Michael Jordan SP 60.00 150.00
QRAS Quentin Richardson 2.50 6.00
SNAS Steve Nash 4.00 10.00
SSAS Steve Smith 2.50 6.00
TPAS Tony Parker 4.00 10.00
WSAS Wally Szczerbiak SP 2.50 6.00
ZRAS Zeljko Rebraca 2.00 5.00

2002-03 Upper Deck All-Star Authentics Warm-Ups

Inserted in Series one packs at the rate of one in 48, this 14-card set parallels the design of the All-Star Authentics Jerseys set with a swatch of game-used warmups.
STATED ODDS 1:48 SER 1
AKAW Andrei Kirilenko 2.50 6.00
AMAW Alonzo Mourning 3.00 8.00
CMAW Chris Mihm 2.00 5.00
DFAW Derek Fisher 2.00 5.00
DMAW Desmond Mason 2.00 5.00
KBAW Kobe Bryant 10.00 25.00
KGAW Kevin Garnett 4.00 10.00
MFAW Marcus Fizer 2.00 5.00
MJAW Michael Jordan SP 30.00 80.00
RAAW Ray Allen 2.50 6.00
SBAW Shane Battier 2.50 6.00
TMAW Tracy McGrady 4.00 10.00
WPAW Wesley Person 2.00 5.00
ZRAW Zeljko Rebraca 2.00 5.00

2002-03 Upper Deck BuyBacks

Randomly inserted in Series two packs, this set is made up of previous year's Upper Deck cards with player autographs. Each card was accompanied out of the pack with a certificate of authenticity.
RANDOMLY INSERTED IN SERIES 2 PACKS
2 M.Bibby 01-2UD#369/29 30.00 80.00
13 T.Chandler 01-2UD#244/54 25.00 60.00
14 M.Fizer 00-1UDEncWup/28 20.00 50.00
18 K.Garnett 01-2UDBrPerf/25 100.00 200.00
22 J.Kidd 00-1UD#129/32 20.00 50.00
29 K.Martin 01-2UDHnRoll/50 40.00 100.00
31 M.Miller 01-2UD#207/95 10.00 25.00
33 M.Miller 01-2UDHRoll/26 40.00 100.00
36 J.Moiso 01-2UD#242/113 8.00 20.00
38 T.Parker 01-2UD#376/155 25.00 60.00
39 Parker 01-2UDHRollFFR/46 30.00 80.00
41 J-Rich 01-2UDHRFFR/41 60.00 120.00
42 D.Stvnson 00-1SPGFAFlr/35 25.00 60.00
45 E.Thomas 00-1UD#220/84 8.00 20.00
46 G.Wallace 01-2UD#370/63 20.00 50.00

2002-03 Upper Deck Combo All-Star Authentics

Randomly inserted in Series one packs, this ten card set teams up players along with swatches of game-worn memorabilia and authentic autographs. Each card is sequentially numbered to 300.
PRINT RUN 300 SER.#'d SETS
DNSN D.Nowitzki/S.Nash 10.00 25.00
EBQR E.Brand/Q.Richardson 6.00 15.00
JRGA J.Richardson/G.Arenas 6.00 15.00
JTMF J.Tinsley/M.Fizer 6.00 15.00
KBKG K.Garnett/K.Bryant 20.00 50.00
KGWS Garnett/Szczerbiak 10.00 25.00
MJKB M.Jordan/K.Bryant 40.00 100.00
RATM T.McGrady/R.Allen 10.00 25.00
SAJK Abdur-Rahim/J.Kidd 10.00 25.00
WPSB W.Person/S.Battier 6.00 15.00

2002-03 Upper Deck Double Team Dual Jerseys

Inserted in Series Two Retail packs at the rate of one in 960, this six-card set pairs up teammates with one guy on the left and one on the right and two swatches of game-worn jersey. The jersey swatches are flat on one side and rounded on the other with one on the top of the card and another on the bottom.
STATED ODDS 1:960 SER.2 RET.
CWMBD C.Webber/M.Bibby 15.00 40.00
JWJRD J.Williams/J.Rose 6.00 15.00
PGDGD P.Gasol/D.Gooden 6.00 15.00
PPAWD P.Pierce/A.Walker 15.00 40.00
TMRHD T.McGrady/R.Humphrey 12.50 30.00

2002-03 Upper Deck Dual Shooting Shirts

Randomly seeded in Series two packs at the rate of one in 288, this nine card set pairs up players, one on the top and one on the bottom, with a small square portrait style photo and an hour-glass shaped shooting shirt swatch. The borders along the top and bottom are made to look like wood and the background is white.
STATED ODDS 1:288 SER.2
BDDWS B.Davis/D.Wesley 1.50 4.00
CWPJS C.Webber/P.Stojakovic 2.00 5.00
DRTPS D.Robinson/T.Parker 3.00 8.00
ECJCS E.Curry/J.Crawford 2.00 5.00
JPJHS J.Posey/J.Howard 1.50 4.00
KBJWS K.Bryant/J.Williams 8.00 20.00
MJKBS M.Jordan/K.Bryant SP 50.00 120.00
SBDGS S.Battier/D.Gooden 2.00 5.00
SMSMS S.Marbury/S.Marion 1.50 4.00

2002-03 Upper Deck Dunkvision

Randomly inserted in Series one packs at the rate of one in 24, this seven card set places full color player action photos on a blue background set to look like a television.
COMPLETE SET (7) 10.00 25.00
STATED ODDS 1:24 SER 1
DV1 Michael Jordan 6.00 15.00
DV2 Kobe Bryant 3.00 8.00
DV3 Tim Duncan 1.50 4.00
DV4 Vince Carter 1.25 3.00
DV5 Shaquille O'Neal 2.00 5.00
DV6 Jason Richardson .75 2.00
DV7 Steve Francis .60 1.50

2002-03 Upper Deck Electric Company

Randomly inserted in Series two packs at the rate of one in 24, this seven card set places a full color player action photo on a greenish blue background with gray lines coming out from the center.
COMPLETE SET (7) 6.00 15.00
STATED ODDS 1:24 SER.2
EC1 Jay Williams .75 2.00
EC2 Paul Pierce .75 2.00
EC3 Tracy McGrady 1.25 3.00
EC4 Nene Hilario .75 2.00
EC5 Caron Butler .75 2.00
EC6 Kareem Rush .60 1.50
EC7 Kobe Bryant 3.00 8.00

2002-03 Upper Deck Electric Company Jerseys

STATED ODDS 1:480 SER.2 RET.
ECCB Caron Butler 4.00 10.00
ECJW Jay Williams 4.00 10.00
ECKR Kareem Rush 3.00 8.00
ECNH Nene Hilario 4.00 10.00
ECPP Paul Pierce 4.00 10.00
ECTM Tracy McGrady 6.00 15.00

2002-03 Upper Deck Game Night

Randomly inserted in Series two packs at the rate of one in 12, this 14-card set uses a horizontal design which places a full color player action photo on the left and a dark colored scale photo of the player's team city on the right.
COMPLETE SET (14) 10.00 25.00
STATED ODDS 1:12 SER.2
GN1 Kobe Bryant 2.50 6.00
GN2 Ray Allen .60 1.50
GN3 Michael Finley .60 1.50
GN4 Karl Malone .75 2.00
GN5 Kevin Garnett 1.00 2.50
GN6 Jason Richardson .60 1.50
GN7 Shawn Marion .50 1.25
GN8 Mike Miller .50 1.25
GN9 Jamaal Tinsley .40 1.00
GN10 Jay Williams .60 1.50
GN11 Rashard Lewis .60 1.50
GN12 Michael Jordan 5.00 12.00
GN13 Tim Duncan 1.25 3.00
GN14 Vince Carter 1.00 2.50

2002-03 Upper Deck Game Night Jerseys

STATED ODDS 1:72 SER.2 H
GNJR Jason Richardson 3.00 8.00
GNJT Jamaal Tinsley 2.00 5.00
GNKB Kobe Bryant SP 15.00 40.00
GNKG Kevin Garnett 5.00 12.00
GNKM Karl Malone 4.00 10.00
GNMF Michael Finley 3.00 8.00
GNMM Mike Miller 2.50 6.00
GNRA Ray Allen 3.00 8.00
GNSM Shawn Marion 2.50 6.00

2002-03 Upper Deck Game Plan Jerseys

Randomly inserted in series one packs at the rate of one in 144, this seven card set features full color player action photography on the left side, white borders on a horizontal design, and a swatch of game-worn jersey on the right.
STATED ODDS 1:144 SER 1
BDGP Baron Davis 2.50 6.00
CMGP Corey Maggette 2.50 6.00
EBGP Elton Brand 3.00 8.00
ECGP Eddy Curry 2.00 5.00
GHGP Grant Hill 4.00 10.00
KMGP Karl Malone 4.00 10.00
SAGP Shareef Abdur-Rahim 2.50 6.00

2002-03 Upper Deck I Love L.A.

Randomly inserted in Series one packs at the rate of one in 12, this 14-card set features members of the 2002 NBA Championship winning Lakers. Each card showcases full-color player photos and yellow and purple borders.
COMPLETE SET (14) 15.00 40.00
STATED ODDS 1:12 SER 1
LA1 Kobe Bryant 3.00 8.00
LA2 Shaquille O'Neal 2.00 5.00
LA3 Rick Fox 1.25 3.00
LA4 Robert Horry 1.25 3.00
LA5 Brian Shaw 1.25 3.00
LA6 Derek Fisher 1.25 3.00
LA7 Devean George 1.25 3.00
LA8 Stanislav Medvedenko 1.25 3.00
LA9 Mark Madsen 1.25 3.00
LA10 Samaki Walker 1.25 3.00
LA11 Shaquille O'Neal 2.00 5.00
LA12 Mitch Richmond 1.25 3.00
LA13 Kobe Bryant 3.00 8.00
LA14 Kobe Bryant 3.00 8.00

2002-03 Upper Deck MJ The Comeback

Randomly inserted in Series one packs, this seven card set pays tribute to Michael Jordan's second comeback to the NBA. The cards are horizontally desiged with full-color photos on the left and a black box on the right with silver foil highlights.
COMPLETE SET (7) 20.00 50.00
COMMON CARD (J1-J7) 4.00 10.00
STATED ODDS 1:24 SER 1

2002-03 Upper Deck New Wave

Randomly seeded in Series one packs at the rate of one in 12, this 14-card set places emerging young stars on a green, purple and blue foil background with silver foil highlights.
COMPLETE SET (14) 6.00 15.00
STATED ODDS 1:12 SER 1
NW1 Dirk Nowitzki 1.25 3.00
NW2 Wally Szczerbiak .60 1.50
NW3 Richard Jefferson .75 2.00
NW4 Mike Miller .60 1.50
NW5 Shawn Marion .60 1.50
NW6 Tyson Chandler .75 2.00
NW7 Baron Davis .60 1.50
NW8 Jamaal Tinsley .50 1.25
NW9 Rashard Lewis .75 2.00
NW10 Eddy Curry .50 1.25
NW11 Vince Carter 1.25 3.00
NW12 Shane Battier .75 2.00
NW13 Tony Parker 1.00 2.50
NW14 Eddie Griffin .50 1.25

2002-03 Upper Deck Practice Session Jerseys

Randomly inserted in Series one packs at the rate of one in 72, this seven card set places full color player photos on a black and gray background with a swatch of a practice jersey.
STATED ODDS 1:72 SER 1
AJPS Antawn Jamison 3.00 8.00
AWPS Antoine Walker 2.50 6.00
CAPS Courtney Alexander 2.00 5.00
DAPS Darrell Armstrong 2.00 5.00
JTPS Jason Terry 2.50 6.00
KWPS Kwame Brown 2.00 5.00
SMPS Shawn Marion 2.50 6.00

2002-03 Upper Deck Rated PG

Randomly inserted in Series two packs at the rate of one in 24, this seven card set is designed to look like a move poster. Full color player photos are accented with silver foil highlights.
COMPLETE SET (7) 5.00 12.00
STATED ODDS 1:24 SER.2
PG1 Jay Williams .75 2.00
PG2 Tony Parker 1.00 2.50
PG3 Jason Kidd 1.25 3.00
PG4 Baron Davis .60 1.50
PG5 DaJuan Wagner .60 1.50
PG6 Steve Francis .60 1.50
PG7 Allen Iverson 1.25 3.00

2002-03 Upper Deck Rated PG Jerseys

ATED ODDS 1:960 SER.2 RET.
PGBD Baron Davis 3.00 8.00
PGDW DaJuan Wagner 3.00 8.00
PGJK Jason Kidd 6.00 15.00
PGJW Jay Williams 4.00 10.00
PGSM Stephon Marbury 3.00 8.00
PGTP Tony Parker 5.00 12.00

2002-03 Upper Deck Rookie Portfolio Jerseys

Inserted in Series two packs at the rate of one in 72, this 16-card set uses a horizontal design where two color portrait style photos appear on the left and right of the card with a centered swatch of a jersey.
STATED ODDS 1:72 SER.2
RPAS Amare Stoudemire 4.00 10.00
RPCA Carlos Boozer 3.00 8.00
RPCB Caron Butler SP 3.00 8.00
RPCW Chris Wilcox 2.50 6.00
RPDG Drew Gooden 3.00 8.00
RPDW DaJuan Wagner 2.50 6.00
RPJD Juan Dixon 3.00 8.00
RPJJ Jared Jeffries 2.50 6.00
RPKR Kareem Rush 2.50 6.00
RPMH Marcus Haislip 2.50 6.00
RPNH Nene Hilario 3.00 8.00
RPNT Nikoloz Tskitishvili 2.00 5.00
RPPS Peja Stojakovic 3.00 8.00
RPQW Qyntel Woods 2.50 6.00
RPRH Ryan Humphrey 2.50 6.00
RPYM Yao Ming SP 6.00 15.00

2002-03 Upper Deck Scoring Threads

Randomly inserted in Series one Hobby and Retail packs at the rate of one in 288, this 13-card set is horizontally desiged with a white background on the right side of the card and a swatch of memorabilia and a photo of the player on the left side with border's to match team colors.
STATED ODDS 1:288
CARDS WITH "H" HOBBY, "R" RETAIL
AHST Allan Houston H 2.50 6.00
AWST Antoine Walker H 2.50 6.00
CWST Chris Webber H 3.00 8.00
SCAM Andre Miller R SP 2.50 6.00
SCJM Jamal Mashburn R 2.50 6.00
SCKB Kobe Bryant R SP 12.50 30.00
SCPP Paul Pierce R SP 3.00 8.00
SCRM Ron Mercer R 2.00 5.00
SCSM Shawn Marion R 2.50 6.00
SCTP Tony Parker R 4.00 10.00
SMST Stephon Marbury H 2.50 6.00

2002-03 Upper Deck Season Premier Jerseys

Randomly inserted in Series two packs at the rate of one in 144, this seven card set places close up player mug shots on the right side of the card with a white border and a swatch of jersey on the left.
STATED ODDS 1:144 SER.2
CAP Caron Butler 3.00 8.00
CJP Casey Jacobsen 2.50 6.00
JEP Chris Jefferies 2.00 5.00
MTP Dikembe Mutombo 3.00 8.00
NTP Nikoloz Tskitishvili 2.00 5.00
RHP Richard Hamilton 2.50 6.00
TPP Tayshaun Prince 4.00 10.00

2002-03 Upper Deck Star Imports

Randomly inserted in Series two packs at the rate of one in 12, this 14-card set showcases foreign NBA player photos set against a globe, a blue and white background, and the player's home country flag in the upper right hand corner.
COMPLETE SET (14) 10.00 25.00
STATED ODDS 1:12 SER.2
SI1 Yao Ming 1.50 4.00
SI2 Dirk Nowitzki 1.25 3.00
SI3 Pau Gasol 1.00 2.50
SI4 Peja Stojakovic .75 2.00
SI5 Nene Hilario .75 2.00
SI6 Tony Parker 1.00 2.50
SI7 Hedo Turkoglu .60 1.50
SI8 Nikoloz Tskitishvili .50 1.25
SI9 Andrei Kirilenko .75 2.00
SI10 Manu Ginobili 2.00 5.00
SI11 Steve Nash 1.00 2.50
SI12 Dikembe Mutombo .75 2.00
SI13 Marko Jaric .75 2.00
SI14 Tim Duncan 1.50 4.00

2002-03 Upper Deck Star Imports Jerseys

STATED ODDS 1:72 SER.2 HOB.
AKSI Andrei Kirilenko 3.00 8.00
DNSI Dirk Nowitzki 5.00 12.00
NHSI Nene Hilario 3.00 8.00
NTSI Nikoloz Tskitishvili 2.00 5.00
PGSI Pau Gasol 4.00 10.00
RFSI Rick Fox 2.00 5.00
TPSI Tony Parker SP 4.00 10.00
VDSI Vlade Divac 2.50 6.00
YMSI Yao Ming SP 6.00 15.00

2002-03 Upper Deck Super Swatches Jerseys

Randomly inserted in Series two packs, this 16-card set places a full color player photo on the left side of the card and and oversized swatch of jersey on the right in the shape of the letter S.
PRINT RUN 200 SERIAL #'d SETS
AIS Allen Iverson 12.00 30.00
ASS Amare Stoudemire 8.00 20.00
AWS Antoine Walker 5.00 12.00
CJS Casey Jacobsen 5.00 12.00
DWS DaJuan Wagner 5.00 12.00
FJS Fred Jones 5.00 12.00
JJS Jared Jeffries 5.00 12.00
JWS Jay Williams 6.00 15.00
KBS Kobe Bryant 25.00 60.00
KGS Kevin Garnett 10.00 25.00
MES Melvin Ely 5.00 12.00
MHS Marcus Haislip 5.00 12.00
QWS Qyntel Woods 5.00 12.00
RHS Ryan Humphrey 5.00 12.00
TMS Tracy McGrady 10.00 25.00
TPS Tayshaun Prince 8.00 20.00

2002-03 Upper Deck Triple Shooting Shirts

Inserted in Series two packs, this six-card set ties three players together from top to bottom, each with a small square mug shot and a swatch of a shooting shirt. Each card is sequentially numbered to 25.
PRINT RUN 25 SERIAL #'d SETS
1 K.Bryant/M.Jordan/J.Williams 100.00 250.00
4 D.Wesley/B.Davis/J.Mashburn 20.00 50.00

2002-03 Upper Deck UD Game Jerseys 1

Randomly inserted in Series one Hobby and Retail packs, this twelve-card set places full color player photos on the left, a jersey swatch in the middle and silver background on the right. Patch Logo 1 and Patch Names 1 parallels exist and were inserted at the rate of one in 5000 and one in 7500 respectively.
CARDS WITH "H" HOBBY, "R" RETAIL
RANDOM INSERTS IN PACKS
AH Allan Houston H 2.50 6.00
KB Kobe Bryant H SP 15.00 40.00
MB Mike Bibby H 3.00 8.00
MC Antonio McDyess H 2.50 6.00
PG Pau Gasol H 4.00 10.00
RA Ron Artest H 3.00 8.00
AMRJ Aaron McKie R 2.00 5.00
JSRJ Joe Smith R 2.50 6.00
KBRJ Kobe Bryant R SP 20.00 50.00
MJRJ Michael Jordan R SP 100.00 200.00
RFRJ Rick Fox R 2.00 5.00
TBRJ Terrell Brandon R 2.00 5.00

2002-03 Upper Deck UD Game Jerseys 2

Randomly inserted in Series two packs, this seven-card set places full color player photos on the left, a jersey swatch in the middle and silver background on the right. Patch Logo 1 and Patch Names 1 parallels exist and were inserted at the rate of one in 5000 and one in 7500 respectively.
STATED ODDS 1:144 SER.2
GJAW Antoine Walker 2.50 6.00
GJCW Chris Wilcox 2.50 6.00
GJJR Jason Richardson 3.00 8.00
GJJS Jerry Stackhouse 2.50 6.00
GJJW Jay Williams SP 3.00 8.00
GJKB Kobe Bryant SP 15.00 40.00
GJWS Wally Szczerbiak 2.50 6.00

2002-03 Upper Deck UD Game Jerseys Autographs 1

Randomly inserted in Series one packs, this 11-card set parallels the design of the UD Game Jerseys set enhanced with player autographs. Each card is sequentially numbered to 275.
PRINT RUN 275 SER.#'d SETS
AUCB Chauncey Billups 8.00 20.00
AUDS DeShawn Stevenson 6.00 15.00
AUJR Jason Richardson 8.00 20.00
AUKM Kenyon Martin 6.00 15.00
AUMB Mike Bibby 10.00 25.00
AUMB2 Mike Bibby 10.00 25.00
AUMM Mike Miller 12.00 30.00
AUPP Paul Pierce 15.00 40.00
AUQR Quentin Richardson 6.00 15.00
AURM Ron Mercer 6.00 15.00
AUTB Terrell Brandon 8.00 20.00
AUTC Tyson Chandler 12.00 30.00

2002-03 Upper Deck UD Game Jerseys Autographs 2

Randomly inserted in Series two packs, this 16-card set parallels the design of the UD Game Jerseys set enhanced with player autographs. Each card is sequentially numbered to 100.
PRINT RUN 100 SERIAL #'d SETS
AUAW Antoine Walker 8.00 20.00
AUDG Drew Gooden 12.00 30.00
AUDS DeShawn Stevenson 8.00 20.00
AUDW DaJuan Wagner 8.00 20.00
AUET Etan Thomas 8.00 20.00
AUJK Jason Kidd 30.00 80.00
AUJM Jerome Moiso 8.00 20.00
AUJW Jay Williams 12.50 30.00
AUKB Kobe Bryant 100.00 250.00
AUKG Kevin Garnett 40.00 100.00
AUKM Kenyon Martin 12.00 30.00
AUMB Mike Bibby 12.50 30.00
AUMF Marcus Fizer 10.00 25.00
AUMM Mike Miller 10.00 25.00
AUPP Paul Pierce 25.00 60.00
AUTC Tyson Chandler 12.00 30.00

2002-03 Upper Deck UD Game Jerseys Combos 2

Randomly inserted in Series two Hobby packs at the rate of one in 72, this nine-card set features two player photos and two swatches of game worn jersey. An Autographed parallel was also inserted and is sequentially numbered to 10.
STATED ODDS 1:72 SER.2 HOB.
AIJR A.Iverson/J.Rose 8.00 20.00
BDJM B.Davis/J.Mashburn 5.00 12.00
DNSN D.Nowitzki/S.Nash 8.00 20.00
JWTC J.Williams/T.Chandler 5.00 12.00
KBJW K.Bryant/J.Williams 12.50 30.00
MBPS M.Bibby/P.Stojakovic 6.00 15.00
PGSB P.Gasol/S.Battier 5.00 12.00
PPAW P.Pierce/A.Walker 6.00 15.00
SMSM S.Marbury/S.Marion 5.00 12.00

2002-03 Upper Deck UD Game Jerseys Patch Logos 1

Randomly inserted in Series one packs at the rate of one in 5000, this 10-card set features both player photos and a swatch from the logo on the player's uniform.
STATED ODDS 1:5000
AIPL Allen Iverson 50.00 120.00
JKPL Jason Kidd 40.00 100.00
JRPL Jason Richardson 25.00 60.00
KBPL Kobe Bryant 100.00 200.00
KGPL Kevin Garnett 50.00 120.00
MMPL Mike Miller 25.00 60.00
PSPL Peja Stojakovic 25.00 60.00
TMPL Tracy McGrady 50.00 120.00

2002-03 Upper Deck UD Game Jerseys Patch Logos 2

STATED ODDS 1:5000
AIPL Allen Iverson 50.00 120.00
JKPL Jason Kidd 40.00 100.00
KBPL Kobe Bryant 75.00 150.00
KGPL Kevin Garnett 50.00 120.00
TMPL Tracy McGrady 50.00 120.00

2002-03 Upper Deck UD Game Jerseys Patch Names 1

Randomly inserted in Series one packs at the rate of one in 7500, this 10-card set features both player photos and a swatch from the name on the player's uniform.
STATED ODDS 1:7500
AIPN Allen Iverson 60.00 150.00
JKPN Jason Kidd 40.00 100.00
KBPN Kobe Bryant 125.00 300.00
KGPN Kevin Garnett 50.00 120.00
MMPN Mike Miller 30.00 80.00
SFPN Steve Francis 30.00 80.00
TMPN Tracy McGrady 50.00 120.00

2002-03 Upper Deck UD Game Jerseys Patch Names 2

STATED ODDS 1:7500
AIPN Allen Iverson 60.00 150.00
CWPN Chris Webber 50.00 120.00
DNPN Dirk Nowitzki 75.00 150.00
KBPN Kobe Bryant 125.00 300.00
MJPN Michael Jordan 300.00 500.00
SFPN Steve Francis 40.00 100.00

2002-03 Upper Deck UD Game Jerseys Patch Numbers 1

Randomly inserted in Series one packs at the rate of one in 2500, this 10-card set features both player photos and a swatch from the logo on the player's uniform.
STATED ODDS 1:2500
AIP Allen Iverson 40.00 100.00
JKP Jason Kidd 40.00 100.00
JRP Jason Richardson 20.00 50.00
KBP Kobe Bryant 75.00 150.00
KGP Kevin Garnett 40.00 100.00
MJP Michael Jordan 150.00 300.00
MMP Mike Miller 20.00 50.00
PSP Peja Stojakovic 20.00 50.00
SFP Steve Francis 20.00 50.00
TMP Tracy McGrady 20.00 50.00

2002-03 Upper Deck UD Game Jerseys Patch Numbers 2

Randomly inserted in Series two packs at the rate of one in 2500, this 10-card set features both player photos and a swatch from the number on the player's uniform.
STATED ODDS 1:2500 SER.2
AIP Allen Iverson 40.00 100.00
CWP Chris Webber 40.00 80.00
DNP Dirk Nowitzki 50.00 120.00
JKP Jason Kidd 40.00 100.00
JWP Jay Williams 20.00 50.00
KBP Kobe Bryant SP 75.00 150.00
KGP Kevin Garnett 40.00 100.00
SFP Steve Francis 20.00 50.00
TMP Tracy McGrady 40.00 100.00

2002-03 Upper Deck UD Playbook Jerseys

Randomly inserted in Series one Hobby packs, this six player set is actually composed of sealed mini-books that open up to reveal a player photo and a swatch of jersey. Only 100 total books were issued and currently actual player print runs are unknown.
PRINT RUN 100 TOTAL SETS
JWH Jay Williams Gold 10.00 25.00
JWR Jay Williams Silver 10.00 25.00
KBH Kobe Bryant Gold 30.00 80.00
KBR Kobe Bryant Silver 30.00 80.00
MJH Michael Jordan Gold 125.00 250.00
MJR Michael Jordan Silver 125.00 250.00

2002-03 Upper Deck UD Playbook Jerseys Combos

Inserted in both hobby and retail packs, this set parallels the design of the base Playbook Jerseys insert set with two players.
KBJWH K.Bryant/J. Williams 40.00 100.00
MJJWH M.Jordan/J.Williams 100.00 250.00
MJKBH M.Jordan/K.Bryant 200.00 400.00

2002-03 Upper Deck Beckett UD Promos

*SINGLES: .75X TO 2X BASE UD HI
*NON RC ROOKIES: .4X TO 1X BASE UD HI

2003-04 Upper Deck

Released in late November 2003, Upper Deck is a 342-card set divided up into 300 veteran cards and 42 rookie cards inserted at the rate of one in four. Base cards are borderless on three sides with the bottom colored to match the featured player's team colors. Upper Deck was packaged in 24-pack boxes where packs contained eight cards and carried a suggested retail price of $2.99.
COMP.SET w/o SP's (300) 25.00 50.00
301-342 STATED ODDS 1:4
1 Shareef Abdur-Rahim .25 .60
2 Alan Henderson .20 .50
3 Dan Dickau .20 .50
4 Theo Ratliff .20 .50
5 Terrell Brandon .20 .50
6 Darvin Ham .20 .50
7 Nazr Mohammed .20 .50
8 Jason Terry .25 .60
9 Dion Glover .20 .50
10 Chris Crawford .20 .50
11 Paul Pierce .30 .75
12 Antoine Walker .30 .75
13 Eric Williams .20 .50
14 Kedrick Brown .20 .50
15 Tony Battie .20 .50
16 Vin Baker .20 .50
17 Mark Blount .20 .50
18 Tony Delk .20 .50
19 Walter McCarty .20 .50
20 Jumaine Jones .20 .50
21 Jalen Rose .25 .60
22 Marcus Fizer .20 .50
23 Jamal Crawford .30 .75
24 Donyell Marshall .20 .50
25 Eddy Curry .20 .50
26 Trenton Hassell .20 .50
27 Michael Jordan 2.50 6.00
28 Tyson Chandler .25 .60
29 Jay Williams .20 .50
30 Scottie Pippen .50 1.25
31 Eddie Robinson .20 .50
32 Lonny Baxter .20 .50
33 Darius Miles .20 .50
34 DeSagana Diop .20 .50
35 Ricky Davis .25 .60
36 Chris Mihm .20 .50
37 Carlos Boozer .25 .60
38 Michael Stewart .20 .50
39 Zydrunas Ilgauskas .25 .60
40 Dajuan Wagner .20 .50
41 J.R. Bremer .20 .50
42 Kevin Ollie .20 .50
43 Dirk Nowitzki .50 1.25
44 Antawn Jamison .25 .60
45 Shawn Bradley .20 .50
46 Raef LaFrentz .20 .50
47 Eduardo Najera .20 .50
48 Travis Best .20 .50
49 Danny Fortson .20 .50
50 Michael Finley .30 .75
51 Jiri Welsch .20 .50
52 Steve Nash .40 1.00
53 Marcus Camby .25 .60
54 Chris Anderson .40 1.00
55 Rodney White .20 .50
56 Vincent Yarbrough .20 .50
57 Nikoloz Tskitishvili .20 .50
58 Nene .25 .60
59 Andre Miller .25 .60
60 Earl Boykins .20 .50
61 Ryan Bowen .20 .50
62 Ben Wallace .25 .60
63 Tayshaun Prince .25 .60
64 Richard Hamilton .25 .60
65 Mehmet Okur .25 .60
66 Bob Sura .20 .50
67 Chucky Atkins .20 .50
68 Chauncey Billups .30 .75
69 Elden Campbell .20 .50
70 Corliss Williamson .20 .50
71 Zeljko Rebraca .20 .50
72 Jason Richardson .30 .75
73 Popeye Jones .20 .50
74 Clifford Robinson .20 .50
75 Mike Dunleavy .25 .60
76 Troy Murphy .20 .50
77 Speedy Claxton .20 .50
78 Erick Dampier .20 .50
79 Nick Van Exel .25 .60
80 Avery Johnson .25 .60
81 Adonal Foyle .20 .50
82 Pepe Sanchez .20 .50
83 Steve Francis .25 .60
84 Glen Rice .20 .50
85 Eddie Griffin .20 .50
86 Moochie Norris .20 .50
87 Maurice Taylor .20 .50
88 Kelvin Cato .20 .50
89 Jason Collier .20 .50
90 Cuttino Mobley .20 .50
91 Yao Ming .60 1.50
92 Eric Piatkowski .20 .50
93 Bostjan Nachbar .20 .50
94 Adrian Griffin .20 .50
95 Reggie Miller .30 .75
96 Fred Jones .25 .60
97 Scot Pollard .20 .50
98 Jamaal Tinsley .20 .50
99 Al Harrington .25 .60
100 Jonathan Bender .20 .50
101 Primoz Brezec .20 .50
102 Ron Artest .30 .75
103 Jermaine O'Neal .25 .60
104 Kenny Anderson .25 .60
105 Jeff Foster .20 .50
106 Austin Croshere .20 .50
107 Elton Brand .30 .75
108 Tremaine Fowlkes .20 .50
109 Quentin Richardson .25 .60
110 Melvin Ely .20 .50
111 Marko Jaric .20 .50
112 Chris Wilcox .20 .50
113 Wang Zhizhi .25 .60
114 Corey Maggette .25 .60
115 Keyon Dooling .20 .50
116 Kobe Bryant 1.25 3.00
117 Shaquille O'Neal .75 2.00
118 Slava Medvedenko .20 .50
119 Gary Payton .30 .75
120 Jannero Pargo .20 .50
121 Kareem Rush .20 .50
122 Karl Malone .40 1.00
123 Derek Fisher .25 .60
124 Rick Fox .20 .50
125 Devean George .20 .50
126 Pau Gasol .30 .75
127 Jason Williams .25 .60
128 Stromile Swift .20 .50
129 Wesley Person .20 .50
130 Michael Dickerson .20 .50
131 Lorenzen Wright .20 .50
132 Earl Watson .20 .50
133 Mike Miller .25 .60
134 Shane Battier .25 .60
135 Eddie Jones .25 .60
136 Rasual Butler .20 .50
137 Caron Butler .25 .60
138 Brian Grant .20 .50
139 Lamar Odom .25 .60
140 Malik Allen .20 .50
141 Ken Johnson .20 .50
142 Samaki Walker .20 .50
143 Sean Lampley .20 .50
144 Vladimir Stepania .20 .50
145 Erick Strickland .20 .50
146 Toni Kukoc .30 .75
147 Joel Przybilla .20 .50
148 Tim Thomas .20 .50
149 Dan Gadzuric .20 .50
150 Joe Smith .25 .60
151 Michael Redd .30 .75
152 Desmond Mason .25 .60
153 Brian Skinner .20 .50
154 Kevin Garnett .50 1.25
155 Michael Olowokandi .20 .50
156 Troy Hudson .20 .50
157 Latrell Sprewell .25 .60
158 Wally Szczerbiak .25 .60
159 Sam Cassell .25 .60
160 Fred Hoiberg .20 .50
161 Ervin Johnson .20 .50
162 Mark Madsen .20 .50
163 Gary Trent .20 .50
164 Jason Kidd .50 1.25
165 Dikembe Mutombo .30 .75
166 Lucious Harris .20 .50
167 Kerry Kittles .20 .50
168 Brandon Armstrong .20 .50
169 Jason Collins .20 .50
170 Alonzo Mourning .40 1.00
171 Kenyon Martin .25 .60
172 Richard Jefferson .25 .60
173 Rodney Rogers .20 .50
174 Aaron Williams .20 .50
175 Jamal Mashburn .25 .60
176 David Wesley .20 .50
177 Kirk Haston .20 .50
178 Courtney Alexander .20 .50
179 Darrell Armstrong .20 .50
180 Robert Traylor .20 .50
181 George Lynch .20 .50
182 Jamaal Magloire .20 .50
183 Baron Davis .25 .60
184 P.J. Brown .20 .50
185 Sean Rooks .20 .50
186 Stacey Augmon .20 .50
187 Allan Houston .25 .60
188 Antonio McDyess .25 .60
189 Clarence Weatherspoon .20 .50
190 Kurt Thomas .20 .50
191 Shandon Anderson .20 .50
192 Keith Van Horn .25 .60
193 Michael Doleac .20 .50
194 Othella Harrington .20 .50
195 Charlie Ward .20 .50
196 Lee Nailon .20 .50
197 Tracy McGrady .40 1.00
198 Pat Garrity .20 .50
199 Grant Hill .40 1.00
200 Gordan Giricek .20 .50
201 Steven Hunter .20 .50
202 Jeryl Sasser .20 .50
203 Andrew DeClercq .20 .50
204 Juwan Howard .25 .60
205 Tyronn Lue .20 .50
206 Drew Gooden .25 .60
207 Marc Jackson .20 .50
208 Aaron McKie .20 .50
209 Derrick Coleman .25 .60
210 Eric Snow .20 .50
211 Glenn Robinson .25 .60
212 Greg Buckner .20 .50
213 Allen Iverson .50 1.25
214 Kenny Thomas .20 .50
215 Sam Clancy .20 .50
216 Monty Williams .20 .50
217 Stephon Marbury .25 .60
218 Shawn Marion .25 .60
219 Joe Johnson .25 .60
220 Bo Outlaw .20 .50
221 Amare Stoudemire .40 1.00
222 Casey Jacobsen .20 .50
223 Tom Gugliotta .20 .50
224 Scott Williams .20 .50
225 Jake Tsakalidis .20 .50
226 Damon Stoudamire .25 .60
227 Arvydas Sabonis .25 .60
228 Zach Randolph .25 .60
229 Ruben Patterson .20 .50
230 Derek Anderson .20 .50
231 Dale Davis .20 .50
232 Bonzi Wells .20 .50
233 Rasheed Wallace .30 .75
234 Jeff McInnis .20 .50
235 Qyntel Woods .20 .50
236 Chris Webber .30 .75
237 Doug Christie .20 .50
238 Vlade Divac .25 .60
239 Bobby Jackson .20 .50
240 Lawrence Funderburke .20 .50
241 Peja Stojakovic .30 .75
242 Gerald Wallace .25 .60
243 Brad Miller .25 .60
244 Mike Bibby .30 .75
245 Anthony Peeler .20 .50
246 Jim Jackson .20 .50
247 David Robinson .50 1.25
248 Ron Mercer .20 .50
249 Tony Parker .30 .75
250 Malik Rose .20 .50
251 Kevin Willis .20 .50
252 Manu Ginobili .40 1.00
253 Bruce Bowen .20 .50
254 Hedo Turkoglu .25 .60
255 Tim Duncan .50 1.25
256 Robert Horry .25 .60
257 Radoslav Nesterovic .20 .50
258 Ray Allen .30 .75
259 Rashard Lewis .30 .75
260 Reggie Evans .20 .50
261 Brent Barry .20 .50
262 Ronald Murray .20 .50
263 Vladimir Radmanovic .20 .50
264 Predrag Drobnjak .20 .50
265 Antonio Daniels .20 .50
266 Vitaly Potapenko .20 .50
267 Calvin Booth .20 .50
268 Vince Carter .50 1.25
269 Chris Jefferies .20 .50
270 Mengke Bateer .20 .50
271 Alvin Williams .20 .50
272 Jerome Williams .20 .50
273 Michael Bradley .20 .50
274 Lamond Murray .20 .50
275 Antonio Davis .20 .50
276 Morris Peterson .20 .50
277 Jerome Moiso .20 .50
278 Carlos Arroyo .25 .60
279 Matt Harpring .20 .50
280 Andrei Kirilenko .30 .75
281 Jarron Collins .20 .50
282 Greg Ostertag .20 .50
283 Curtis Borchardt .30 .75
284 DeShawn Stevenson .20 .50
285 Keon Clark .20 .50
286 John Amaechi .20 .50
287 Raul Lopez .30 .75
288 Jerry Stackhouse .25 .60
289 Kwame Brown .20 .50
290 Larry Hughes .25 .60
291 Brendan Haywood .20 .50
292 Juan Dixon .20 .50

293 Bryon Russell .20 .50
294 Christian Laettner .25 .60
295 Jahidi White .20 .50
296 Jared Jeffries .20 .50
297 Gilbert Arenas .25 .60
298 Kobe Bryant CL .60 1.50
299 Michael Jordan CL 1.25 3.00
300 Michael Jordan CL 1.25 3.00
301 LeBron James RC 25.00 60.00
302 Darko Milicic RC 1.00 2.50
303 Carmelo Anthony RC 4.00 10.00
304 Chris Bosh RC 2.00 5.00
305 Dwyane Wade RC 4.00 10.00
306 Chris Kaman RC 1.25 3.00
307 Kirk Hinrich RC 1.25 3.00
308 T.J. Ford RC 1.00 2.50
309 Mike Sweetney RC .75 2.00
310 Jarvis Hayes RC .75 2.00
311 Mickael Pietrus RC 1.00 2.50
312 Nick Collison RC 1.00 2.50
313 Marcus Banks RC .75 2.00
314 Luke Ridnour RC 1.00 2.50
315 Reece Gaines RC .75 2.00
316 Troy Bell RC .75 2.00
317 Zarko Cabarkapa RC .75 2.00
318 David West RC 1.25 3.00
319 Aleksandar Pavlovic RC 1.00 2.50
320 Dahntay Jones RC 1.00 2.50
321 Boris Diaw RC 1.25 3.00
322 Zoran Planinic RC .75 2.00
323 Travis Outlaw RC 1.00 2.50
324 Brian Cook RC .75 2.00
325 Kirk Penney RC 1.25 3.00
326 Ndudi Ebi RC .75 2.00
327 Kendrick Perkins RC 1.00 2.50
328 Leandro Barbosa RC 1.25 3.00
329 Josh Howard RC 1.25 3.00
330 Maciej Lampe RC .75 2.00
331 Jason Kapono RC .75 2.00
332 Luke Walton RC 1.25 3.00
333 Jerome Beasley RC .75 2.00
334 Brandon Hunter RC .75 2.00
335 Kyle Korver RC 1.50 4.00
336 Travis Hansen RC .75 2.00
337 Steve Blake RC 1.00 2.50
338 Slavko Vranes RC .75 2.00
339 Zaur Pachulia RC 1.25 3.00
340 Keith Bogans RC .75 2.00
341 Willie Green RC .75 2.00
342 Maurice Williams RC 1.25 3.00

2003-04 Upper Deck Gold

*1-297 GOLD SINGLES: 5X TO 12X BASE HI
*298-300 GOLD CL: 10X TO 25X BASE HI
*301-342 GOLD RCs: 2X TO 5X BASE HI
GOLD PRINT RUN 100 SER.#'d SETS
301 LeBron James 150.00 400.00
305 Dwyane Wade 30.00 80.00

2003-04 Upper Deck Rainbow

*1-297 RAINBOW: 8X TO 20X BASE HI
*298-300 RAINBOW: 15X TO 40X BASE HI
*301-342 RAINBOW: 3X TO 8X BASE CARD HI
RAINBOW PRINT RUN 25 SER.#'d SETS
27 Michael Jordan 75.00 150.00
301 LeBron James 300.00 600.00
305 Dwyane Wade 100.00 200.00

2003-04 Upper Deck Air Academy

Inserted at the rate of one in four, this 42-card set centers action photos of players on a white and blue background.
COMPLETE SET (42) 20.00 40.00
STATED ODDS 1:4 H/R SER.1
AA1 Michael Jordan 3.00 8.00
AA2 Kobe Bryant 1.50 4.00
AA3 LeBron James 4.00 10.00
AA4 Vince Carter .60 1.50
AA5 Shaquille O'Neal 1.00 2.50
AA6 Richard Jefferson .30 .75
AA7 Jason Richardson .40 1.00
AA8 Paul Pierce .40 1.00
AA9 Michael Finley .40 1.00
AA10 Steve Francis .30 .75
AA11 Shareef Abdur-Rahim .30 .75
AA12 Desmond Mason .30 .75
AA13 Latrell Sprewell .30 .75
AA14 Baron Davis .30 .75
AA15 Glenn Robinson .30 .75
AA16 Joe Johnson .30 .75
AA17 Rasheed Wallace .40 1.00
AA18 Gerald Wallace .30 .75
AA19 Rashard Lewis .40 1.00
AA20 Jamaal Tinsley .25 .60
AA21 Karl Malone .50 1.25
AA22 Jerry Stackhouse .30 .75
AA23 Gilbert Arenas .30 .75
AA24 Boris Diaw .40 1.00
AA25 Josh Howard .40 1.00
AA26 Antoine Walker .40 1.00
AA27 Darius Miles .25 .60
AA28 Darko Milicic .30 .75
AA29 Carmelo Anthony 1.25 3.00
AA30 Chris Bosh .60 1.50
AA31 Dwyane Wade 1.25 3.00
AA32 Mike Sweetney .25 .60
AA33 Jarvis Hayes .25 .60
AA34 Mickael Pietrus .30 .75
AA35 Nick Collison .30 .75
AA36 Elton Brand .40 1.00
AA37 David West .40 1.00
AA38 Aleksandar Pavlovic .30 .75
AA39 Zarko Cabarkapa .25 .60
AA40 Travis Outlaw .30 .75
AA41 Brian Cook .25 .60
AA42 Ndudi Ebi .25 .60

2003-04 Upper Deck All-Star Weekend Authentics

Horizontally designed, this 29-card set places a gray-scale portrait photo of the player on the left side and a swatch of memorabilia worn on all-star weekend on the right. The set was inserted in packs at the rate of one in 144.
STATED ODDS 1:144 H/R SER.1
ASAK Andrei Kirilenko 2.50 6.00
ASBM Brad Miller 2.00 5.00
ASBW Ben Wallace 2.00 5.00
ASCB Carlos Boozer 2.00 5.00
ASCB Caron Butler 2.00 5.00
ASDG Drew Gooden 2.00 5.00
ASDN Dirk Nowitzki 4.00 10.00
ASGG Gordan Giricek 2.00 5.00
ASGP Gary Payton 2.50 6.00
ASJA Marko Jaric 2.00 5.00
ASJK Jason Kidd 4.00 10.00
ASJM Jamal Mashburn 2.00 5.00
ASJO Jermaine O'Neal 2.00 5.00
ASJT Jamaal Tinsley 2.00 5.00
ASJW Jay Williams 2.00 5.00
ASKB Kobe Bryant 10.00 25.00
ASKG Kevin Garnett 4.00 10.00
ASNH Nene 2.00 5.00
ASPG Pau Gasol 2.50 6.00
ASPS Peja Stojakovic 2.50 6.00
ASSF Steve Francis 2.00 5.00
ASSM Stephon Marbury 2.00 5.00
ASSN Steve Nash 3.00 8.00
ASTC Tyson Chandler 2.00 5.00
ASTD Tim Duncan 4.00 10.00
ASTM Tracy McGrady 3.00 8.00
ASTP Tony Parker 2.50 6.00
ASYM Yao Ming 5.00 12.00
ASZI Zydrunas Ilgauskas 2.00 5.00

2003-04 Upper Deck All-Star Weekend Authentics Dual

Inserted at the rate of one in 144, this 12-card set utilizes the same basic design as the All-Star Weekend Authentics set with two players and two swatches of All-Star Weekend worn memorabilia.
STATED ODDS 1:144 H/R SER.1
BMBW B.Miller/B.Wallace 4.00 10.00
CBDW C.Boozer/D.Wagner 4.00 10.00
DGGG D.Gooden/G.Giricek 4.00 10.00
DMJR D.Mason/J.Richardson 4.00 10.00
JWTC J.Williams/T.Chandler 4.00 10.00
KBKG K.Bryant/K.Garnett 10.00 25.00
KBMJ K.Bryant/M.Jordan 30.00 80.00
NHAK Nene/A.Kirilenko 4.00 10.00
PPAW P.Pierce/A.Walker 4.00 10.00
SFYM S.Francis/Y.Ming 5.00 12.00
SMSM S.Marion/S.Marbury 4.00 10.00
TMJO T.McGrady/J.O'Neal 5.00 12.00

2003-04 Upper Deck Black Diamond Rookies F/X

Inserted at the rate of one in 288, this set places full-color action photos of the 2003-04 draft class with colored borders along the left side and bottom. These cards have a completely different design from the Black Diamond set.
STATED ODDS 1:288 H/R SER.1
BD1 LeBron James 75.00 200.00
BD2 Darko Milicic 5.00 12.00
BD3 Carmelo Anthony 20.00 50.00
BD4 Chris Bosh 10.00 25.00
BD5 Dwyane Wade 20.00 50.00
BD6 Chris Kaman 6.00 15.00
BD7 Kirk Hinrich 6.00 15.00
BD8 T.J. Ford 5.00 12.00
BD9 Mike Sweetney 4.00 10.00
BD10 Jarvis Hayes 4.00 10.00
BD11 Mickael Pietrus 5.00 12.00
BD12 Nick Collison 5.00 12.00
BD13 Marcus Banks 4.00 10.00
BD14 Luke Ridnour 5.00 12.00
BD15 Reece Gaines 4.00 10.00
BD16 Troy Bell 4.00 10.00
BD17 Zarko Cabarkapa 4.00 10.00
BD18 David West 6.00 15.00
BD19 Aleksandar Pavlovic 5.00 12.00
BD20 Dahntay Jones 5.00 12.00
BD21 Boris Diaw 6.00 15.00
BD22 Zoran Planinic 4.00 10.00
BD23 Travis Outlaw 5.00 12.00
BD24 Brian Cook 4.00 10.00
BD25 Kirk Penney 6.00 15.00
BD26 Ndudi Ebi 4.00 10.00
BD27 Kendrick Perkins 5.00 12.00
BD28 Leandro Barbosa 6.00 15.00
BD29 Josh Howard 6.00 15.00
BD30 Maciej Lampe 4.00 10.00
BD31 Jason Kapono 4.00 10.00
BD32 Luke Walton 6.00 15.00
BD33 Jerome Beasley 4.00 10.00
BD34 Brandon Hunter 4.00 10.00
BD35 Kyle Korver 8.00 20.00
BD36 Travis Hansen 4.00 10.00
BD37 Steve Blake 5.00 12.00
BD38 Slavko Vranes 4.00 10.00
BD39 Zaur Pachulia 6.00 15.00
BD40 Keith Bogans 4.00 10.00
BD41 Willie Green 4.00 10.00
BD42 Maurice Williams 6.00 15.00

2003-04 Upper Deck East Coast/West Coast Jerseys

Inserted in hobby packs at the rate of one in 36, this 14-card set pairs players from the eastern and western conference on each card with a half red/half blue background and two circular swatches of jersey.
STATED ODDS 1:36 H SER.1
BATB M.Banks/T.Bell 4.00 10.00
BLAJ S.Blake/A.Jamison 4.00 10.00
DEMF D.Mason/M.Finley 4.00 10.00
JOMC J.O'Neal/M.Olowokandi 4.00 10.00
JTMB J.Terry/M.Bibby 4.00 10.00
KPNE K.Perkins/N.Ebi 4.00 10.00
KVLW K.Van Horn/L.Walton 4.00 10.00
KWHT Kw.Brown/H.Turkoglu 4.00 10.00
MJKB M.Jordan/K.Bryant 30.00 80.00
MPJR M.Peterson/J.Richardson 4.00 10.00
RGCO R.Gaines/B.Cook 4.00 10.00
RHDJ R.Hamilton/D.Jones 4.00 10.00
SAPG S.Abdur-Rahim/P.Gasol 4.00 10.00
TISB J.Tinsely/S.Battier 4.00 10.00

2003-04 Upper Deck LeBron's Diary

Inserted at the rate of one per pack in retail packs only, this 15-card set showcases highlights from young LeBron's High School and brief NBA career.
COMPLETE SET (15) 12.50 30.00
COMMON LEBRON (1-15) 1.25 3.00
ONE PER SER.1 RETAIL

2003-04 Upper Deck Rookie Review Jerseys

Inserted in hobby packs at the rate of one in 96, this 14-card set features the rookies from the 2002-03 season in full color on the right with a swatch of jersey in the lower left hand corner.
STATED ODDS 1:96 H SER.1
RRAS Amare Stoudemire 3.00 8.00
RRCB Caron Butler 2.00 5.00
RRCJ Casey Jacobsen 2.00 5.00
RRCW Chris Wilcox 2.00 5.00
RRDG Dan Gadzuric 2.00 5.00
RRDG Drew Gooden 2.00 5.00
RRDW DaJuan Wagner 2.00 5.00
RRJD Juan Dixon 2.00 5.00
RRJJ Jared Jeffries 2.00 5.00
RRJS John Salmons 2.00 5.00
RRKR Kareem Rush 2.00 5.00
RRQW Qyntel Woods 2.00 5.00
RRRA Robert Archibald 2.00 5.00
RRYM Yao Ming 5.00 12.00

2003-04 Upper Deck SE Die Cut All-Stars

COMPLETE SET (15) 1500.00 3000.00
STATED ODDS 1:288 H SER.1
*BLACK: .5X TO 1.2X BASE HI
BLACK PRINT RUN 25 SER.#'d SETS
SE1 Michael Jordan 1200.00 2200.00
SE2 Kobe Bryant 125.00 250.00
SE3 Shaquille O'Neal 30.00 80.00
SE4 Vince Carter 50.00 120.00
SE5 Ray Allen 30.00 80.00
SE6 Kevin Garnett 30.00 80.00
SE7 Jason Kidd 20.00 50.00
SE8 Paul Pierce 20.00 50.00
SE9 Dirk Nowitzki 30.00 80.00
SE10 Ben Wallace 10.00 25.00
SE11 Tracy McGrady 15.00 40.00
SE12 Allen Iverson 50.00 120.00
SE13 Gary Payton 12.00 30.00
SE14 Elton Brand 12.00 30.00
SE15 Tim Duncan 60.00 150.00

2003-04 Upper Deck SE Die Cut Future All-Stars

Inserted in hobby packs at the rate of one in 24, this 15-card set uses the design for the SE Die Cut All-Stars set but features this year's rookie crop. A black version of the set was also produced with cards sequentially numbered to 25.
COMPLETE SET (15) 100.00 200.00
STATED ODDS 1:24 H SER.1
*BLACK: 1X TO 2.5X BASE HI
BLACK PRINT RUN 25 SER.#'d SETS
E1 Nick Collison 2.50 6.00
E2 Dahntay Jones 2.50 6.00
E3 Zarko Cabarkapa 2.00 5.00
E4 Marcus Banks 2.00 5.00
E5 Mickael Pietrus 2.50 6.00
E6 Jarvis Hayes 2.00 5.00
E7 Mike Sweetney 2.00 5.00
E8 T.J. Ford 2.50 6.00
E9 Kirk Hinrich 3.00 8.00
E10 Chris Kaman 3.00 8.00
E11 Dwyane Wade 10.00 25.00
E12 Chris Bosh 5.00 12.00
E13 Carmelo Anthony 10.00 25.00
E14 Darko Milicic 2.50 6.00
E15 LeBron James 60.00 150.00

2003-04 Upper Deck Shooting Stars Jerseys

Inserted in packs at the rate of one in 96, this 14-card set places some of the NBA's best shooters on a horizontally designed card with full-color player photos and a swatch of jersey.
STATED ODDS 1:96 H/R SER.1
SSDW David Wesley 2.00 5.00
SSGG Gordan Giricek 2.00 5.00
SSJA Jamaal Magloire 2.00 5.00
SSJT Jason Terry 2.00 5.00
SSKV Keith Van Horn 2.00 5.00
SSMM Mike Miller 2.00 5.00
SSPS Peja Stojakovic 2.50 6.00
SSRH Richard Hamilton 2.00 5.00
SSRM Reggie Miller 2.50 6.00
SSSS Steve Smith 2.00 5.00
SSTB Terrell Brandon 2.00 5.00
SSTK Toni Kukoc 2.50 6.00
SSWP Wesley Person 2.00 5.00
SSWS Wally Szczerbiak 2.00 5.00

2003-04 Upper Deck Super Swatches

Randomly seeded in hobby packs, this 18-card set is horizontally designed with a full-color player photo on the right and an oversized swatch of memorabilia on the left.
PRINT RUN 250 SER.#'d SETS
RANDOM INSERTS IN SER.1 HOBBY
AISS Allen Iverson 10.00 25.00
AMSS Antonio McDyess 5.00 12.00
ASSS Amare Stoudemire 8.00 20.00
BDSS Baron Davis 5.00 12.00
CMSS Corey Maggette 5.00 12.00
DMSS Darius Miles 4.00 10.00
DWSS Dajuan Wagner 4.00 10.00
EBSS Elton Brand 6.00 15.00
ECSS Eddy Curry 4.00 10.00
GHSS Grant Hill 8.00 20.00
JMSS Jamal Mashburn 5.00 12.00
JOSS Joe Smith 5.00 12.00
JPSS James Posey 4.00 10.00
KBSS Kobe Bryant 20.00 50.00
LOSS Lamar Odom 5.00 12.00
MJSS Michael Jordan 50.00 120.00
SPSS Scottie Pippen 10.00 25.00
TESS Jason Terry 5.00 12.00

2003-04 Upper Deck UD Game Jerseys

Inserted in packs at the rate of one in 288, this 21-card set places full-color player photos and a swatch of jersey cut to resemble the stitching design of a basketball.
STATED ODDS 1:288 H/R SER.1
GJ1 Caron Butler 2.00 5.00
GJ2 Gilbert Arenas 2.00 5.00
GJ3 Mike Bibby 2.50 6.00
GJ4 Tony Parker 2.50 6.00
GJ5 Manu Ginobili 3.00 8.00
GJ6 Darius Miles 1.50 4.00
GJ7 David Robinson 4.00 10.00
GJ8 Allen Iverson 4.00 10.00
GJ9 Kenyon Martin 2.00 5.00
GJ10 Eddie Jones 2.00 5.00
GJ11 Eddy Curry 1.50 4.00
GJ12 Jalen Rose 2.00 5.00
GJ13 Antawn Jamison 2.00 5.00
GJ14 Lamar Odom 2.00 5.00
GJ15 Karl Malone 3.00 8.00
GJ16 Jamal Mashburn 2.00 5.00
GJ17 Richard Jefferson 2.00 5.00
GJ18 Shaquille O'Neal 6.00 15.00
GJ19 LeBron James 40.00 100.00
GJ20 Kobe Bryant 10.00 25.00
GJ21 Michael Jordan 60.00 150.00
GJ22 Speedy Claxton 1.50 4.00

2003-04 Upper Deck UD Game Jerseys Autographs

Randomly inserted, this set parallels the design of the UD Game Jerseys set enhanced with an authentic player autograph. Each card is sequentially numbered to 100. Card 39, Rashard Lewis, was not produced.
PRINT RUN 100 SER.#'d SETS
RANDOM INSERTS IN SER.1 HOBBY
1 Kobe Bryant 125.00 225.00
2 Paul Pierce 15.00 40.00
3 Jason Kidd 25.00 60.00
4 Etan Thomas 8.00 20.00
5 Jerome Moiso 8.00 20.00
6 Shawn Marion 12.50 30.00
7 Mike Bibby 12.50 30.00
8 Peja Stojakovic 15.00 30.00
9 Chauncey Billups 10.00 25.00
10 Richard Hamilton 8.00 20.00
11 Richard Jefferson 8.00 20.00
12 Jason Richardson 8.00 20.00
13 Tony Parker 20.00 50.00
14 David Robinson 40.00 100.00
15 Jalen Rose 8.00 20.00
16 Corey Maggette 8.00 20.00
17 Jamaal Tinsley 8.00 20.00
18 Yao Ming 25.00 60.00
19 Drew Gooden 8.00 20.00
20 Caron Butler 8.00 20.00
21 Manu Ginobili 20.00 50.00
22 Marko Jaric 8.00 20.00
23 Wang Zhizhi 15.00 40.00
24 Tracy McGrady 30.00 60.00
25 Morris Peterson 8.00 20.00
27 Amare Stoudemire 15.00 40.00
30 Steve Francis 12.00 30.00
31 Andre Miller 10.00 25.00
32 Shane Battier 8.00 20.00
34 Dan Dickau 8.00 20.00
35 Earl Boykins 10.00 25.00
36 Jerry Stackhouse 8.00 20.00
37 Gilbert Arenas 8.00 20.00
38 Lamar Odom 8.00 20.00
40 Antawn Jamison 8.00 20.00
41 Kevin Garnett 30.00 80.00

2003-04 Upper Deck UD Game Jerseys Patches Logo

Inserted at the rate of one in 5000 packs, this 14-card set parallels the look of the UD Game Jerseys set enhanced with a premium patch swatch from the logos on the player's jersey.
STATED ODDS 1:5000 H/R SER.1
SOME UNPRICED DUE TO SCARCITY
ASPL Amare Stoudemire 15.00 40.00
CWPL Chris Webber 12.00 30.00
GHPL Grant Hill 20.00 50.00
KVPL Keith Van Horn 10.00 25.00
TDPL Tim Duncan 20.00 50.00

2003-04 Upper Deck UD Game Jerseys Patches Name

Inserted at the rate of one in 7500 packs, this 14-card set parallels the look of the UD Game Jerseys set enhanced with a premium patch swatch from the name on the player's jersey.
STATED ODDS 1:7500 H/R SER.1
SOME UNPRICED DUE TO SCARCITY
AJPN Antawn Jamison 12.00 30.00
DRPN David Robinson 25.00 60.00
KBPN Kobe Bryant 125.00 300.00
KVPN Keith Van Horn 12.00 30.00
MJPN Michael Jordan 250.00 500.00

2003-04 Upper Deck UD Game Jerseys Patches Numbers

Inserted at the rate of one in 2500 packs, this 14-card set parallels the look of the UD Game Jerseys set enhanced with a premium patch swatch from the numbers on the player's jersey.
STATED ODDS 1:2500 H/R SER.1
SOME UNPRICED DUE TO SCARCITY
AWPN Antoine Walker 10.00 25.00
DRPN David Robinson 15.00 40.00
KBPN Kobe Bryant 40.00 100.00
KMPN Kenyon Martin 8.00 20.00
KVPN Keith Van Horn 8.00 20.00
MJPN Michael Jordan 200.00 350.00
SNPN Steve Nash 12.00 30.00
TDPN Tim Duncan 15.00 40.00

2004-05 Upper Deck

Released in February 2005, Upper Deck features a 230-card set divided up into 200 veteran cards and 20 rookie cards inserted at one in four (cards 201-220) and ten rookie cards inserted at one in 20 (cards 221-230). Upper Deck was packaged for both Hobby and Retail where both boxes contained 24 packs but Hobby packs had eight cards per pack and Retail had nine and packs carried a SRP of $2.99.
COMPLETE SET (230) 60.00 120.00
COMP.SET w/o SP's (200) 20.00 40.00
201-220 RC STATED ODDS 1:4
221-230 RC STATED ODDS 1:20
IMMACULATE UNPRICED DUE TO SCARCITY
1 Antoine Walker .30 .75
2 Boris Diaw .25 .60
3 Al Harrington .25 .60
4 Tony Delk .20 .50
5 Jason Collier .20 .50
6 Chris Crawford .20 .50
7 Ricky Davis .25 .60
8 Paul Pierce .30 .75
9 Jiri Welsch .20 .50
10 Gary Payton .30 .75
11 Rick Fox .20 .50
12 Mark Blount .20 .50
13 Adrian Griffin .20 .50
14 Tyson Chandler .25 .60
15 Eddy Curry .20 .50
16 Kirk Hinrich .25 .60
17 Scottie Pippen .50 1.25
18 Jannero Pargo .20 .50
19 Antonio Davis .20 .50
20 Gerald Wallace .25 .60
21 Eddie House .20 .50
22 Steve Smith .25 .60
23 Brandon Hunter .20 .50
24 Theron Smith .20 .50
25 Jahidi White .20 .50
26 LeBron James 2.00 5.00
27 DeSagana Diop .20 .50
28 Zydrunas Ilgauskas .25 .60
29 Dajuan Wagner .20 .50
30 Jeff McInnis .20 .50
31 Eric Snow .20 .50
32 Dirk Nowitzki .50 1.25
33 Jason Terry .25 .60
34 Michael Finley .30 .75
35 Jerry Stackhouse .25 .60
36 Erick Dampier .20 .50
37 Josh Howard .30 .75
38 Marquis Daniels .20 .50
39 Carmelo Anthony .60 1.50
40 Nene .25 .60
41 Andre Miller .25 .60
42 Earl Boykins .20 .50
43 Marcus Camby .25 .60
44 Voshon Lenard .20 .50
45 Kenyon Martin .25 .60
46 Richard Hamilton .25 .60
47 Chauncey Billups .30 .75
48 Rasheed Wallace .30 .75
49 Tayshaun Prince .25 .60
50 Ben Wallace .25 .60
51 Antonio McDyess .25 .60
52 Carlos Delfino .20 .50
53 Jason Richardson .30 .75
54 Dale Davis .20 .50
55 Adonal Foyle .20 .50
56 Mickael Pietrus .25 .60
57 Mike Dunleavy .25 .60
58 Speedy Claxton .20 .50
59 Derek Fisher .25 .60
60 Yao Ming .60 1.50
61 Jim Jackson .20 .50
62 Tracy McGrady .40 1.00
63 Maurice Taylor .20 .50
64 Juwan Howard .25 .60
65 Tyronn Lue .20 .50
66 Dikembe Mutombo .30 .75
67 Reggie Miller .30 .75
68 Stephen Jackson .25 .60
69 Jermaine O'Neal .25 .60
70 Jamaal Tinsley .20 .50
71 Ron Artest .30 .75
72 Fred Jones .20 .50
73 Jonathan Bender .20 .50
74 Kerry Kittles .20 .50
75 Chris Kaman .25 .60
76 Elton Brand .30 .75
77 Marko Jaric .20 .50
78 Corey Maggette .25 .60
79 Bobby Simmons .20 .50
80 Chris Wilcox .20 .50
81 Lamar Odom .25 .60
82 Karl Malone .40 1.00
83 Kobe Bryant 1.25 3.00
84 Kareem Rush .20 .50
85 Caron Butler .25 .60
86 Devean George .20 .50
87 Vlade Divac .25 .60
88 Pau Gasol .30 .75
89 Bonzi Wells .20 .50
90 Mike Miller .25 .60
91 Jason Williams .25 .60
92 Shane Battier .25 .60
93 James Posey .20 .50
94 Stromile Swift .20 .50
95 Shaquille O'Neal .75 2.00
96 Dwyane Wade .50 1.25
97 Eddie Jones .25 .60
98 Wang Zhizhi .20 .50
99 Rasual Butler .20 .50
100 Malik Allen .20 .50
101 Udonis Haslem .20 .50
102 Michael Redd .25 .60
103 T.J. Ford .20 .50
104 Keith Van Horn .25 .60
105 Toni Kukoc .30 .75
106 Desmond Mason .25 .60
107 Mike James .20 .50
108 Joe Smith .25 .60
109 Kevin Garnett .50 1.25
110 Michael Olowokandi .20 .50
111 Sam Cassell .25 .60
112 Troy Hudson .20 .50
113 Latrell Sprewell .25 .60
114 Fred Hoiberg .20 .50
115 Wally Szczerbiak .25 .60
116 Richard Jefferson .25 .60
117 Alonzo Mourning .40 1.00
118 Jason Kidd .50 1.25
119 Jacque Vaughn .20 .50
120 Jason Collins .20 .50
121 Aaron Williams .20 .50
122 Zoran Planinic .20 .50
123 Jamaal Magloire .20 .50
124 P.J. Brown .20 .50
125 Baron Davis .25 .60
126 Darrell Armstrong .20 .50
127 Jamal Mashburn .25 .60
128 Rodney Rogers .20 .50
129 David Wesley .20 .50
130 Allan Houston .25 .60
131 Jamal Crawford .30 .75
132 Stephon Marbury .25 .60
133 Tim Thomas .20 .50
134 Anfernee Hardaway .75 2.00
135 Kurt Thomas .20 .50
136 Mike Sweetney .20 .50
137 Tony Battie .20 .50
138 DeShawn Stevenson .20 .50
139 Steve Francis .25 .60
140 Cuttino Mobley .20 .50
141 Hedo Turkoglu .25 .60
142 Keith Bogans .20 .50
143 Samuel Dalembert .20 .50
144 Kenny Thomas .20 .50
145 Allen Iverson .50 1.25
146 Aaron McKie .20 .50
147 Glenn Robinson .25 .60
148 Willie Green .20 .50
149 Corliss Williamson .20 .50
150 Shawn Marion .25 .60
151 Leandro Barbosa .30 .75
152 Amare Stoudemire .25 .60
153 Quentin Richardson .25 .60
154 Joe Johnson .25 .60
155 Steve Nash .40 1.00
156 Damon Stoudamire .25 .60
157 Theo Ratliff .20 .50
158 Shareef Abdur-Rahim .25 .60
159 Derek Anderson .20 .50
160 Zach Randolph .25 .60
161 Nick Van Exel .25 .60
162 Darius Miles .20 .50
163 Mike Bibby .30 .75
164 Brad Miller .25 .60
165 Peja Stojakovic .30 .75
166 Bobby Jackson .20 .50
167 Chris Webber .30 .75
168 Darius Songaila .20 .50
169 Doug Christie .20 .50
170 Manu Ginobili .40 1.00
171 Brent Barry .20 .50
172 Tony Parker .30 .75
173 Malik Rose .20 .50
174 Tim Duncan .50 1.25
175 Radoslav Nesterovic .20 .50
176 Bruce Bowen .20 .50
177 Rashard Lewis .30 .75
178 Vladimir Radmanovic .20 .50
179 Ray Allen .30 .75
180 Antonio Daniels .20 .50
181 Ronald Murray .20 .50
182 Luke Ridnour .25 .60
183 Vince Carter .50 1.25
184 Donyell Marshall .20 .50
185 Chris Bosh .30 .75
186 Morris Peterson .20 .50
187 Jalen Rose .25 .60
188 Rafer Alston .20 .50
189 Carlos Arroyo .20 .50
190 Matt Harpring .20 .50
191 Andrei Kirilenko .25 .60
192 Carlos Boozer .25 .60
193 Gordan Giricek .20 .50
194 Mehmet Okur .25 .60
195 Antawn Jamison .25 .60
196 Larry Hughes .25 .60
197 Gilbert Arenas .25 .60
198 Kwame Brown .20 .50
199 Jarvis Hayes .20 .50
200 Juan Dixon .20 .50
201 Rafael Araujo RC .75 2.00
202 Luke Jackson RC .75 2.00
203 Andris Biedrins RC .75 2.00
204 Robert Swift RC .75 2.00
205 Kris Humphries RC 1.25 3.00
206 Al Jefferson RC 1.50 4.00
207 Kirk Snyder RC .75 2.00
208 J.R. Smith RC 1.25 3.00
209 Dorell Wright RC 1.25 3.00
210 Jameer Nelson RC 1.25 3.00
211 Pavel Podkolzin RC .75 2.00
212 Viktor Khryapa RC .75 2.00
213 Sergei Monia RC .75 2.00
214 Delonte West RC 1.25 3.00
215 Tony Allen RC 1.25 3.00
216 Kevin Martin RC 1.50 4.00
217 Sasha Vujacic RC 1.25 3.00
218 Beno Udrih RC 1.00 2.50
219 David Harrison RC .75 2.00
220 Chris Duhon RC 1.25 3.00
221 Josh Smith SP RC 1.50 4.00
222 Sebastian Telfair SP RC 1.25 3.00
223 Andre Iguodala SP RC 2.00 5.00
224 Dwight Howard SP RC 3.00 8.00
225 Emeka Okafor SP RC 1.25 3.00
226 Ben Gordon SP RC 1.50 4.00
227 Shaun Livingston SP RC 1.50 4.00
228 Devin Harris SP RC 1.25 3.00
229 Josh Childress SP RC 1.25 3.00
230 Luol Deng SP RC 1.50 4.00

2004-05 Upper Deck UD Promos

*PROMOS: .75X TO 2X BASIC

2004-05 Upper Deck Exclusives

*1-200: 4X TO 10X BASE HI
*201-220: 1.25X TO 3X BASE HI
*221-230: 1X TO 2.5X BASE HI
PRINT RUN 100 SER.#'d SETS

2004-05 Upper Deck Exclusives Spectrum

*1-200: 10X TO 25X BASE HI
*201-220: 2.5X TO 6X BASE HI
*221-230: 2X TO 5X BASE HI
PRINT RUN 25 SER.#'d SETS

2004-05 Upper Deck All-Star Weekend Authentics

STATED ODDS 1:48
AK Andrei Kirilenko 2.00 5.00
AL Ray Allen 2.50 6.00
AS Amare Stoudemire 2.00 5.00
BD Baron Davis 2.00 5.00
BM Brad Miller 2.00 5.00
BW Ben Wallace 2.00 5.00
CA Carlos Boozer 2.00 5.00
CB Chauncey Billups SP 4.00 10.00
CH Chris Bosh SP 5.00 12.00
CK Chris Kaman 2.00 5.00
CM Cuttino Mobley 1.50 4.00
DF Derek Fisher 2.00 5.00
EB Earl Boykins 2.00 5.00
EG Manu Ginobili 3.00 8.00
FJ Fred Jones 2.00 5.00
JH Jarvis Hayes 2.00 5.00
JM Jamaal Magloire 2.00 5.00
JO Josh Howard 2.50 6.00
JR Jason Richardson 2.50 6.00
KB Kobe Bryant 12.50 30.00
KK Kyle Korver 2.00 5.00
KM Kenyon Martin 2.00 5.00
LJ LeBron James SP 25.00 60.00
MD Mike Dunleavy 2.00 5.00
MJ Marko Jaric SP 2.00 5.00
NH Nene 2.00 5.00
PP Paul Pierce 2.50 6.00
PS Peja Stojakovic 2.50 6.00
RA Ron Artest 2.50 6.00
RL Rashard Lewis 2.50 6.00
RM Ronald Murray 2.00 5.00
SC Sam Cassell 2.00 5.00
SF Steve Francis 2.00 5.00
SM Stephon Marbury 2.00 5.00
TD Tim Duncan 4.00 10.00
UH Udonis Haslem 1.50 4.00
VL Voshon Lenard 2.00 5.00
YM Yao Ming 5.00 12.00

2004-05 Upper Deck All-Star Weekend Authentics Dual

STATED ODDS 1:288 HOBBY
AC R.Allen/S.Cassell 6.00 15.00
FB D.Fisher/C.Billups 5.00 12.00
GN M.Ginobili/Nene 5.00 12.00
HH U.Haslem/J.Howard 5.00 12.00
JR F.Jones/J.Richardson 5.00 12.00
KH K.Korver/J.Hayes 5.00 12.00
LB V.Lenard/E.Boykins 5.00 12.00
ML R.Murray/R.Lewis 5.00 12.00
NL Nene/V.Lenard 5.00 12.00

2004-05 Upper Deck All-Star Weekend Authentics Triple

STATED ODDS 1:288 HOBBY
AI Allen Iverson 8.00 20.00
DN Dirk Nowitzki 8.00 20.00
JK Jason Kidd 8.00 20.00
KB Kobe Bryant 15.00 40.00
KG Kevin Garnett 8.00 20.00
KK Kyle Korver 4.00 10.00
LJ LeBron James SP 20.00 50.00
MD Mike Dunleavy 4.00 10.00
RL Rashard Lewis 5.00 12.00
SO Shaquille O'Neal SP 12.00 30.00
TM Tracy McGrady 3.00 8.00

2004-05 Upper Deck East Coast West Coast

Inserted in Hobby packs at the rate of one in 288, this 12-card set features a horizontal design with a player from the Eastern Conference on the left, a player from the Western Conference on the right and two swatches of jersey between them.
STATED ODDS 1:288 HOBBY
BN C.Billups/S.Nash 6.00 15.00
CR E.Curry/Z.Randolph 5.00 12.00
JB L.James/K.Bryant SP 20.00 50.00
JM R.Jefferson/C.Maggette 5.00 12.00
MB R.Miller/M.Bibby 6.00 15.00
MG D.Mason/M.Ginobili 5.00 12.00
MR K.Martin/Q.Richardson 5.00 12.00
PB P.Pierce/E.Brand 6.00 15.00
WA R.Wallace/S.Abdur-Rahim 5.00 12.00

2004-05 Upper Deck Flight Team

Randomly inserted at the rate of one in four, this 50-card set is printed on foil and places player photos against a blue background.
COMPLETE SET (50) 15.00 40.00
STATED ODDS 1:4
*RAINBOW: 12X TO 30X BASE HI
RAINBOW STATED ODDS 1:1000 PACKS
FT1 Scottie Pippen .60 1.50
FT2 Lamar Odom .30 .75
FT3 Andrei Kirilenko .30 .75
FT4 Dirk Nowitzki .60 1.50
FT5 Michael Redd .30 .75
FT6 Kobe Bryant 1.50 4.00
FT7 Jermaine O'Neal .30 .75
FT8 Shawn Marion .30 .75
FT9 Antawn Jamison .30 .75
FT10 Kevin Garnett .60 1.50
FT11 Michael Finley .40 1.00
FT12 Latrell Sprewell .30 .75
FT13 Richard Hamilton .30 .75
FT14 Al Harrington .30 .75
FT15 Dwyane Wade .60 1.50
FT16 Shaquille O'Neal 1.00 2.50
FT17 Chris Webber .40 1.00
FT18 Rasheed Wallace .40 1.00
FT19 Kenyon Martin .30 .75
FT20 Ben Wallace .30 .75
FT21 Baron Davis .30 .75
FT22 Mickael Pietrus .30 .75
FT23 Stephon Marbury .30 .75
FT24 Ricky Davis .30 .75
FT25 Pau Gasol .40 1.00
FT26 Tim Duncan .60 1.50
FT27 Gilbert Arenas .30 .75
FT28 Bonzi Wells .25 .60
FT29 Chris Bosh .40 1.00
FT30 Carmelo Anthony .75 2.00
FT31 Yao Ming .75 2.00
FT32 Tracy McGrady .50 1.25
FT33 Michael Jordan 3.00 8.00
FT34 Fred Jones .25 .60
FT35 Amare Stoudemire .30 .75
FT36 Dajuan Wagner .25 .60
FT37 Desmond Mason .30 .75
FT38 Jerry Stackhouse .30 .75
FT39 Caron Butler .30 .75
FT40 Quentin Richardson .30 .75
FT41 Shareef Abdur-Rahim .30 .75
FT42 Vince Carter .60 1.50
FT43 Corey Maggette .30 .75
FT44 Peja Stojakovic .40 1.00
FT45 LeBron James 2.50 6.00
FT46 Steve Francis .30 .75
FT47 Allen Iverson .60 1.50
FT48 Ray Allen .40 1.00
FT49 Elton Brand .40 1.00
FT50 Darius Miles .25 .60

2004-05 Upper Deck Flight Team Onyx

CARDS #'d TO PLAYER JERSEY
SOME NOT PRICED DUE TO SCARCITY
FT1 Scottie Pippen/33 15.00 40.00
FT3 Andrei Kirilenko/47 8.00 20.00
FT4 Dirk Nowitzki/41 25.00 60.00
FT5 Michael Redd/22 8.00 20.00
FT26 Tim Duncan/21 50.00 120.00
FT38 Jerry Stackhouse/42 8.00 20.00
FT44 Peja Stojakovic/16 10.00 25.00
FT45 LeBron James/23 400.00 600.00
FT48 Ray Allen/34 10.00 25.00

2004-05 Upper Deck Majestic Materials

Inserted in Hobby packs at the rate of one in 288, this 41-card set is horizontally designed with a player image on the right and a large swatch of memorabilia on the left in the shape of the letter "M."
STATED ODDS 1:288 HOBBY
AH Al Harrington 5.00 12.00
AL Allan Houston 5.00 12.00
AN Anfernee Hardaway 15.00 40.00
BM Brad Miller 5.00 12.00
BW Bonzi Wells 4.00 10.00
CB Caron Butler 5.00 12.00
CM Corey Maggette 5.00 12.00
CU Cuttino Mobley 4.00 10.00
DA Darko Milicic 4.00 10.00
DM Darius Miles 4.00 10.00
DW Dajuan Wagner 4.00 10.00
ES Eric Snow 4.00 10.00
GA Gilbert Arenas 5.00 12.00
GG Gordan Giricek 4.00 10.00
JC Jamal Crawford 6.00 15.00
JH Juwan Howard 5.00 12.00
JJ Joe Johnson 5.00 12.00
JM Jamaal Magloire 4.00 10.00
JP James Posey 4.00 10.00
JS Joe Smith 5.00 12.00
JT Jason Terry 5.00 12.00
KK Kerry Kittles 4.00 10.00
KV Keith Van Horn 5.00 12.00
KW Kwame Brown 4.00 10.00
LO Lamar Odom 5.00 12.00
LS Latrell Sprewell 6.00 15.00
MO Michael Olowokandi 4.00 10.00
MP Morris Peterson 4.00 10.00
QR Quentin Richardson 5.00 12.00
RH Richard Hamilton 5.00 12.00
SB Shane Battier 5.00 12.00
SD Samuel Dalembert 4.00 10.00
SF Steve Francis 5.00 12.00
SM Shawn Marion 5.00 12.00
TC Tyson Chandler 5.00 12.00
TT Tim Thomas 4.00 10.00
WS Wally Szczerbiak 5.00 12.00
ZI Zydrunas Ilgauskas 5.00 12.00
ZR Zach Randolph 5.00 12.00

2004-05 Upper Deck March Memories

Inserted in Hobby packs at the rate of one in 72, this 18-card set features players along with a circular swatch of jersey in honor of the NCAA accomplishments.
STATED ODDS 1:72 HOBBY
AW Antoine Walker 3.00 8.00
BG Ben Gordon 3.00 8.00
CB Carlos Boozer 2.50 6.00
CW Chris Wilcox 2.00 5.00
GH Grant Hill 4.00 10.00
JD Juan Dixon 2.00 5.00
JM Jamaal Magloire 2.00 5.00
JR Jason Richardson 3.00 8.00
JT Jason Terry 2.50 6.00
MA Magic Johnson SP 40.00 100.00
MB Mike Bibby 3.00 8.00
MD Mike Dunleavy 2.50 6.00
MP Morris Peterson 2.00 5.00
RH Richard Hamilton 2.50 6.00
SB Shane Battier 2.50 6.00

2004-05 Upper Deck Rookie Academy

Inserted in packs at the rate of one in 24, this 30-card set is printed on foil, has a gold box along the bottom and shows the 2004-05 rookies in action.
COMPLETE SET (30) 25.00 60.00
STATED ODDS 1:24
UNPRICED RAINBOW STATED ODDS 1:288
RA1 Rafael Araujo .60 1.50
RA2 Luke Jackson .60 1.50
RA3 Andris Biedrins .60 1.50
RA4 Robert Swift .60 1.50
RA5 Kris Humphries 1.00 2.50
RA6 Al Jefferson 1.25 3.00
RA7 Kirk Snyder .60 1.50
RA8 J.R. Smith 1.00 2.50
RA9 Dorell Wright 1.00 2.50
RA10 Jameer Nelson 1.00 2.50

RA11 Pavel Podkolzin .60 1.50
RA12 Viktor Khryapa .60 1.50
RA13 Nenad Krstic 1.00 2.50
RA14 Delonte West 1.00 2.50
RA15 Tony Allen 1.00 2.50
RA16 Kevin Martin 1.25 3.00
RA17 Sasha Vujacic 1.00 2.50
RA18 Beno Udrih .75 2.00
RA19 David Harrison .60 1.50
RA20 Andre Emmett .60 1.50
RA21 Josh Smith 1.00 2.50
RA22 Sebastian Telfair .75 2.00
RA23 Andre Iguodala 1.25 3.00
RA24 Dwight Howard 2.00 5.00
RA25 Emeka Okafor .75 2.00
RA26 Ben Gordon 1.00 2.50
RA27 Shaun Livingston 1.00 2.50
RA28 Devin Harris .75 2.00
RA29 Josh Childress .75 2.00
RA30 Luol Deng 1.00 2.50

2004-05 Upper Deck Rookie Academy Onyx

CARDS #'d TO PLAYER JERSEY
MOST NOT PRICED DUE TO SCARCITY
RA3 Andris Biedrins/15 3.00 8.00
RA16 Kevin Martin/23 6.00 15.00
RA27 Shaun Livingston/14 5.00 12.00

2004-05 Upper Deck Rookie Review

Inserted in packs at the rate of one in 48, this 20-card set features the newest rookie crop in action along with a jersey swatch in the shape of an "R."
STATED ODDS 1:48
BD Boris Diaw 2.00 5.00
CA Carmelo Anthony SP 8.00 20.00
CB Chris Bosh 2.50 6.00
CK Chris Kaman 2.00 5.00
DA David West 2.00 5.00
DJ Dahntay Jones 2.00 5.00
DM Darko Milicic 2.00 5.00
JH Jarvis Hayes 2.00 5.00
JO Josh Howard 2.50 6.00
KB Keith Bogans 2.00 5.00
LB Leandro Barbosa SP 2.50 6.00
LJ LeBron James SP 15.00 40.00
LR Luke Ridnour 2.00 5.00
LW Luke Walton 1.50 4.00
MB Marcus Banks 2.00 5.00
MP Mickael Pietrus 2.00 5.00
MS Mike Sweetney 2.00 5.00
NE Ndudi Ebi 2.00 5.00
RG Reece Gaines 2.00 5.00
SB Steve Blake 2.00 5.00

2004-05 Upper Deck Rookie Scrapbook

Inserted in Retail packs at the rate of one in one, this 30-card set places a rookie portrait photo in the middle of the card and then frames it with the same portrait on all sided.
COMPLETE SET (30) 6.00 15.00
STATED ODDS ONE PER RETAIL PACK
RS1 Rafael Araujo .20 .50
RS2 Luke Jackson .20 .50
RS3 Andris Biedrins .20 .50
RS4 Robert Swift .20 .50
RS5 Kris Humphries .30 .75
RS6 Al Jefferson .40 1.00
RS7 Kirk Snyder .20 .50
RS8 J.R. Smith .30 .75
RS9 Dorell Wright .30 .75
RS10 Jameer Nelson .30 .75
RS11 Pavel Podkolzin .20 .50
RS12 Viktor Khryapa .20 .50
RS13 Nenad Krstic .30 .75
RS14 Delonte West .30 .75
RS15 Tony Allen .30 .75
RS16 Kevin Martin .40 1.00
RS17 Sasha Vujacic .30 .75
RS18 Beno Udrih .25 .60
RS19 David Harrison .20 .50
RS20 Andre Emmett .20 .50
RS21 Josh Smith .30 .75
RS22 Sebastian Telfair .25 .60
RS23 Andre Iguodala .40 1.00
RS24 Dwight Howard .60 1.50
RS25 Emeka Okafor .25 .60
RS26 Ben Gordon .30 .75
RS27 Shaun Livingston .30 .75
RS28 Devin Harris .25 .60
RS29 Josh Childress .25 .60
RS30 Luol Deng .30 .75

2004-05 Upper Deck UD Game Jerseys

Inserted in Hobby packs at the rate of one in 288, this 42-card set is borderless and centers a swatch of jersey along the bottom of the card.
STATED ODDS 1:72 HOBBY
AH Allan Houston 2.50 6.00
AJ Antawn Jamison 2.50 6.00
AK Andrei Kirilenko 2.50 6.00
AM Andre Miller 2.50 6.00
BA Marcus Banks 2.00 5.00
BD Baron Davis 2.50 6.00
BW Ben Wallace 2.50 6.00
CB Caron Butler 2.50 6.00
CW Chris Webber 3.00 8.00
DA Darko Milicic 2.00 5.00
DE Desmond Mason 2.50 6.00
DM Darius Miles 2.00 5.00
DS Damon Stoudamire 2.50 6.00
DW Dajuan Wagner 2.00 5.00
EB Elton Brand 3.00 8.00
GA Gilbert Arenas 2.50 6.00
GP Gary Payton 3.00 8.00
JO Jermaine O'Neal 2.50 6.00
JS Jerry Stackhouse 2.50 6.00
JT Jason Terry 2.50 6.00
KM Karl Malone 4.00 10.00
LJ LeBron James SP 25.00 60.00
LO Lamar Odom 2.50 6.00
LS Latrell Sprewell 2.50 6.00
MB Mike Bibby 3.00 8.00
MF Michael Finley 3.00 8.00
MJ Michael Jordan SP 60.00 150.00
MR Michael Redd 2.50 6.00
PG Pau Gasol 3.00 8.00
PS Peja Stojakovic 3.00 8.00
RJ Richard Jefferson 2.50 6.00
RM Reggie Miller 3.00 8.00
RW Rasheed Wallace 3.00 8.00
SA Shareef Abdur-Rahim 2.50 6.00
SM Shawn Marion 2.50 6.00
SN Steve Nash 4.00 10.00
SP Scottie Pippen 8.00 20.00
TP Tony Parker 3.00 8.00
VD Vlade Divac 2.50 6.00
YM Yao Ming 6.00 15.00

2004-05 Upper Deck UD Game Jerseys Autographs

Randomly seeded in Hobby packs, this 39-card set parallels the look of the UD Game Jerseys set enhanced with player autographs. Each card is sequentially numbered to 100 unless noted in the checklist.
PRINT RUN 25 TO 100 SER.#'d SETS
UNPRICED PROOF AUTO PRINT RUN ONE SET
AJ Antawn Jamison/100 10.00 25.00
BD Baron Davis/100 10.00 25.00
BM Brad Miller/100 8.00 20.00
CB Carlos Boozer/100 10.00 25.00
DF Derek Fisher/100 12.00 30.00
DM Darko Milicic/100 8.00 20.00
JS Jerry Stackhouse/100 10.00 25.00
LJ LeBron James/25 250.00 600.00
MB Mike Bibby/100 8.00 20.00
MJ Michael Jordan/25 400.00 800.00
MR Michael Redd/100 10.00 25.00
PPO Paul Pierce/25 60.00 150.00
RM Reggie Miller/100 75.00 200.00
SC Sam Cassell/100 10.00 25.00
SM Stephon Marbury/25 15.00 40.00
TM Tracy McGrady/25 40.00 100.00
ZR Zach Randolph/100 10.00 25.00

2004-05 Upper Deck UD Game Jerseys Patches Logos

Inserted in packs at the rate of one in 5000, this 14-card set parallels the design of the UD Game Jerseys set but is enhanced with a patch swatch from the jersey's logo.
STATED ODDS 1:5000
SOME UNPRICED DUE TO SCARCITY
CA Carmelo Anthony 25.00 60.00
DN Dirk Nowitzki 20.00 50.00
JK Jason Kidd 20.00 50.00
KB Kobe Bryant 60.00 150.00
KG Kevin Garnett 20.00 50.00
SO Shaquille O'Neal 40.00 100.00

2004-05 Upper Deck UD Game Jerseys Patches Names

Inserted in packs at the rate of one in 7500, this 14-card set parallels the design of the UD Game Jerseys set but is enhanced with a patch swatch from the jersey's name.
STATED ODDS 1:7500
SOME UNPRICED DUE TO SCARCITY
CA Carmelo Anthony 30.00 80.00
JK Jason Kidd 25.00 60.00
MJ Michael Jordan 250.00 400.00
PP Paul Pierce 15.00 40.00
TD Tim Duncan 25.00 60.00
TM Tracy McGrady 20.00 50.00

2004-05 Upper Deck UD Game Jerseys Patches Numbers

Inserted in packs at the rate of one in 2500, this 14-card set parallels the design of the UD Game Jerseys set but is enhanced with a patch swatch from the jersey's numbers.
STATED ODDS 1:2500
SOME UNPRICED DUE TO SCARCITY
AI Allen Iverson 15.00 40.00
JK Jason Kidd 15.00 40.00
KB Kobe Bryant 40.00 100.00
KG Kevin Garnett 15.00 40.00
MJ Michael Jordan SP 150.00 300.00
SO Shaquille O'Neal 25.00 60.00
TD Tim Duncan 15.00 40.00

2005-06 Upper Deck

Released in November 2005, Upper Deck boasts a 230-card set where the first 200 cards in the set picture veterans and cards 201-230 feature rookies inserted at the rate of one in every four packs. Base cards feature a borderless design with a name and position bar along the bottom of the card. Upper Deck was packaged in 24 pack boxes where packs contain eight cards and carry a suggested retail price of $2.99.

COMP.SET w/o SP's (200) 20.00 40.00
210-220 RC STATED ODDS 1:4
221-230 RC STATED ODDS 1:20
1 Josh Childress .25 .60
2 Josh Smith .25 .60
3 Al Harrington .25 .60
4 Tyronn Lue .20 .50
5 Boris Diaw .25 .60
6 Tony Delk .20 .50
7 Paul Pierce .30 .75
8 Antoine Walker .25 .60
9 Gary Payton .30 .75
10 Al Jefferson .25 .60
11 Tony Allen .20 .50
12 Ricky Davis .25 .60
13 Delonte West .20 .50
14 Emeka Okafor .25 .60
15 Primoz Brezec .20 .50
16 Kareem Rush .20 .50
17 Gerald Wallace .25 .60
18 Brevin Knight .20 .50
19 Jason Kapono .20 .50
20 Kirk Hinrich .25 .60
21 Ben Gordon .25 .60
22 Eddy Curry .20 .50
23 Michael Jordan 2.50 6.00
24 Andres Nocioni .20 .50
25 Chris Duhon .20 .50
26 Luol Deng .25 .60
27 LeBron James 1.25 3.00
28 Zydrunas Ilgauskas .25 .60
29 Drew Gooden .25 .60
30 Jeff McInnis .20 .50
31 Dajuan Wagner .20 .50
32 Larry Hughes .25 .60
33 Robert Traylor .20 .50
34 Dirk Nowitzki .50 1.25
35 Michael Finley .30 .75
36 Jerry Stackhouse .25 .60
37 Josh Howard .30 .75
38 Marquis Daniels .20 .50
39 Devin Harris .20 .50
40 Jason Terry .25 .60
41 Carmelo Anthony .60 1.50
42 Kenyon Martin .25 .60
43 Andre Miller .25 .60
44 Earl Boykins .20 .50
45 Nene .25 .60
46 Marcus Camby .25 .60
47 Ben Wallace .25 .60
48 Richard Hamilton .25 .60
49 Chauncey Billups .30 .75
50 Rasheed Wallace .30 .75
51 Tayshaun Prince .25 .60
52 Carlos Arroyo .20 .50
53 Antonio McDyess .25 .60
54 Jason Richardson .30 .75
55 Baron Davis .25 .60
56 Troy Murphy .20 .50
57 Mickael Pietrus .25 .60
58 Derek Fisher .25 .60
59 Mike Dunleavy .25 .60
60 Yao Ming .40 1.00
61 Tracy McGrady .40 1.00
62 David Wesley .20 .50
63 Bob Sura .20 .50
64 Mike James .20 .50
65 Jon Barry .20 .50
66 Jermaine O'Neal .25 .60
67 Ron Artest .30 .75
68 Stephen Jackson .25 .60
69 Jamaal Tinsley .20 .50
70 Dale Davis .20 .50
71 Anthony Johnson .20 .50
72 Elton Brand .30 .75
73 Corey Maggette .25 .60
74 Bobby Simmons .20 .50
75 Marko Jaric .20 .50
76 Shaun Livingston .20 .50
77 Chris Kaman .25 .60
78 Chris Wilcox .20 .50
79 Kobe Bryant 1.25 3.00
80 Caron Butler .25 .60
81 Lamar Odom .25 .60
82 Chucky Atkins .20 .50
83 Brian Cook .20 .50
84 Devean George .20 .50
85 Sasha Vujacic .25 .60
86 Pau Gasol .30 .75
87 Mike Miller .25 .60
88 Jason Williams .25 .60
89 Shane Battier .25 .60
90 Bonzi Wells .20 .50
91 James Posey .20 .50
92 Stromile Swift .20 .50
93 Shaquille O'Neal .60 1.50
94 Dwyane Wade .50 1.25
95 Eddie Jones .25 .60
96 Udonis Haslem .20 .50
97 Damon Jones .20 .50
98 Alonzo Mourning .40 1.00
99 Keyon Dooling .20 .50
100 Michael Redd .25 .60
101 Desmond Mason .20 .50
102 Maurice Williams .25 .60
103 Joe Smith .25 .60
104 Toni Kukoc .30 .75
105 Dan Gadzuric .20 .50
106 T.J. Ford .20 .50
107 Kevin Garnett .50 1.25
108 Sam Cassell .25 .60
109 Latrell Sprewell .25 .60
110 Wally Szczerbiak .25 .60
111 Troy Hudson .20 .50
112 Eddie Griffin .20 .50
113 Jason Kidd .50 1.25
114 Richard Jefferson .25 .60
115 Vince Carter .50 1.25
116 Nenad Krstic .20 .50
117 Scott Padgett .20 .50
118 Jason Collins .20 .50
119 Jamaal Magloire .20 .50
120 J.R. Smith .25 .60
121 Speedy Claxton .20 .50
122 Lee Nailon .20 .50
123 P.J. Brown .20 .50
124 Chris Andersen .30 .75
125 Stephon Marbury .25 .60
126 Jamal Crawford .30 .75
127 Allan Houston .25 .60
128 Trevor Ariza .20 .50
129 Quentin Richardson .25 .60
130 Tim Thomas .20 .50
131 Michael Sweetney .20 .50
132 Dwight Howard .25 .60
133 Steve Francis .25 .60
134 Grant Hill .40 1.00
135 Jameer Nelson .20 .50
136 Hedo Turkoglu .25 .60
137 Doug Christie .20 .50
138 DeShawn Stevenson .20 .50
139 Allen Iverson .50 1.25
140 Chris Webber .30 .75
141 Andre Iguodala .25 .60
142 Samuel Dalembert .20 .50
143 Kyle Korver .25 .60
144 Willie Green .20 .50
145 Marc Jackson .20 .50
146 Steve Nash .40 1.00
147 Amare Stoudemire .25 .60
148 Joe Johnson .25 .60
149 Shawn Marion .25 .60
150 Kurt Thomas .20 .50
151 Jim Jackson .20 .50
152 Leandro Barbosa .25 .60
153 Damon Stoudamire .25 .60
154 Shareef Abdur-Rahim .25 .60
155 Zach Randolph .25 .60
156 Darius Miles .20 .50
157 Sebastian Telfair .25 .60
158 Theo Ratliff .20 .50
159 Nick Van Exel .30 .75
160 Peja Stojakovic .30 .75
161 Mike Bibby .30 .75
162 Brad Miller .25 .60
163 Cuttino Mobley .20 .50
164 Bobby Jackson .20 .50
165 Kenny Thomas .20 .50
166 Corliss Williamson .20 .50
167 Tim Duncan .50 1.25
168 Tony Parker .30 .75
169 Manu Ginobili .30 .75
170 Robert Horry .25 .60
171 Beno Udrih .20 .50
172 Nazr Mohammed .20 .50
173 Brent Barry .20 .50
174 Ray Allen .30 .75
175 Rashard Lewis .30 .75
176 Ronald Murray .20 .50
177 Luke Ridnour .25 .60
178 Vladimir Radmanovic .20 .50
179 Antonio Daniels .20 .50
180 Danny Fortson .20 .50
181 Chris Bosh .30 .75
182 Donyell Marshall .20 .50
183 Jalen Rose .30 .75
184 Morris Peterson .20 .50
185 Rafer Alston .20 .50
186 Matt Bonner .20 .50
187 Aaron Williams .20 .50
188 Andrei Kirilenko .25 .60
189 Carlos Boozer .25 .60
190 Matt Harpring .20 .50
191 Keith McLeod .20 .50
192 Raja Bell .25 .60
193 Raul Lopez .20 .50
194 Gordan Giricek .20 .50
195 Gilbert Arenas .25 .60
196 Antawn Jamison .25 .60
197 Jarvis Hayes .20 .50
198 Brendan Haywood .20 .50
199 Juan Dixon .20 .50
200 Etan Thomas .20 .50
201 Daniel Ewing RC 1.00 2.50
202 Nate Robinson RC 1.25 3.00
203 C.J. Miles RC 1.25 3.00
204 Salim Stoudamire RC 1.00 2.50
205 Francisco Garcia RC 1.00 2.50
206 Julius Hodge RC .75 2.00
207 Andrew Bynum RC 1.00 2.50
208 Joey Graham RC 1.00 2.50
209 Johan Petro RC .75 2.00
210 Luther Head RC 1.00 2.50
211 Channing Frye RC 1.25 3.00
212 Sean May RC .75 2.00
213 Wayne Simien RC .75 2.00
214 Antoine Wright RC 1.00 2.50
215 Ike Diogu RC .75 2.00
216 Jarrett Jack RC 1.25 3.00
217 Jason Maxiell RC 1.00 2.50
218 David Lee RC 1.25 3.00
219 Travis Diener RC .75 2.00
220 Danny Granger RC 1.50 4.00
221 Charlie Villanueva SP RC 2.00 5.00
222 Hakim Warrick SP RC 1.50 4.00
223 Rashad McCants SP RC 1.50 4.00
224 Raymond Felton SP RC 2.00 5.00
225 Martell Webster SP RC 1.50 4.00
226 Gerald Green SP RC 2.00 5.00
227 Deron Williams SP RC 2.50 6.00
228 Andrew Bogut SP RC 2.50 6.00
229 Marvin Williams SP RC 2.00 5.00
230 Chris Paul SP RC 8.00 20.00

2005-06 Upper Deck Gold

*1-200 GOLD: 4X TO 10X BASE HI
201-220 RC GOLD: 1.25X TO 3X BASE HI
221-230 RC GOLD: .75X TO 2X BASE HI
GOLD PRINT RUN 50 SER.#'d SETS

2005-06 Upper Deck Silver

*1-200 SILVER: 2.5X TO 6X BASE HI
201-220 RC SILVER: .75X TO 2X BASE HI
221-230 RC SILVER: .5X TO 1.25X BASE HI
SILVER PRINT RUN 100 SER.#'d SETS

2005-06 Upper Deck All-Star Weekend Authentics

Inserted at approximately one per box, this 40-card set features swatches of memorabilia worn by players at All-Star Weekend. Each card has a full-color player photo, the Denver All-Star Game logo and a swatch of memorabilia.
APPROXIMATELY ONE PER BOX
AJ Antawn Jamison 2.50 6.00
AL Al Jefferson 2.50 6.00
AM Andre Miller 2.50 6.00
AN Andre Iguodala 2.50 6.00
AS Amare Stoudemire 2.50 6.00
BG Ben Gordon 2.50 6.00
BU Beno Udrih 2.00 5.00
BW Ben Wallace 2.50 6.00
CA Carmelo Anthony 6.00 15.00
CB Chris Bosh 3.00 8.00
DE Devin Harris 2.00 5.00
DN Dirk Nowitzki 5.00 12.00
GA Gilbert Arenas 2.50 6.00
GH Grant Hill 4.00 10.00
JH Josh Howard 3.00 8.00
JJ Joe Johnson 2.50 6.00
JO Jermaine O'Neal 2.50 6.00
JR J.R. Smith 2.50 6.00
JS Josh Smith 2.50 6.00
KB Kobe Bryant 8.00 20.00
KG Kevin Garnett 5.00 12.00
KH Kirk Hinrich 2.50 6.00
KK Kyle Korver 2.50 6.00
LD Luol Deng 2.50 6.00
LJ LeBron James 12.50 30.00
LR Luke Ridnour 2.50 6.00
MG Manu Ginobili 3.00 8.00
PP Paul Pierce 3.00 8.00
QR Quentin Richardson 2.50 6.00
RA Ray Allen 3.00 8.00
RL Rashard Lewis 3.00 8.00
SM Shawn Marion 2.50 6.00
SN Steve Nash 4.00 10.00
SO Shaquille O'Neal 6.00 15.00
TA Tony Allen 2.00 5.00
TD Tim Duncan 5.00 12.00
TM Tracy McGrady 4.00 10.00
UH Udonis Haslem 2.00 5.00
YM Yao Ming 4.00 10.00
ZI Zydrunas Ilgauskas 2.50 6.00

2005-06 Upper Deck Game Jerseys

Inserted at the rate of approximately one per box, this 102-card set is horizontally designed with a player photo on the right and a square swatch of memorabilia on the left. The tops and bottoms have gray borders and the middle is colored to match the featured players team colors.
APPROXIMATELY ONE PER BOX
AD Antonio Davis 2.00 5.00
AH Allan Houston 2.00 5.00
AJ Antawn Jamison 2.00 5.00
AK Andrei Kirilenko 2.00 5.00
AM Andre Miller 2.00 5.00
AN Antoine Walker 2.00 5.00
AS Amare Stoudemire 2.00 5.00
AW Aaron Williams 2.00 5.00
BB Bruce Bowen 2.00 5.00
BD Baron Davis 2.00 5.00
BG Ben Gordon 2.00 5.00
BH Brendan Haywood 2.00 5.00
BN Bostjan Nachbar 2.00 5.00
BO Boris Diaw 2.00 5.00
BR Bryon Russell 2.00 5.00
BW Ben Wallace 2.00 5.00
BZ Carlos Boozer 2.00 5.00
CA Carmelo Anthony 5.00 12.00
CA Chris Anderson 2.50 6.00
CB Caron Butler 2.00 5.00
CH Chauncey Billups 2.50 6.00
CJ Andris Biedrins 1.50 4.00
CM Chris Mihm 2.00 5.00
CO Corey Maggette 2.00 5.00
CU Cuttino Mobley 1.50 4.00
CW Charlie Ward 2.00 5.00
DA David Wesley 2.00 5.00
DF Derek Fisher 2.00 5.00
DG Drew Gooden 2.00 5.00
DH Dwight Howard 2.00 5.00
DM Darius Miles 2.00 5.00
DN Dirk Nowitzki 4.00 10.00
DO Donyell Marshall 2.00 5.00
DS DeShawn Stevenson 2.00 5.00
DW Dajuan Wagner 2.00 5.00
EB Elton Brand 2.50 6.00
ES Eric Snow 2.00 5.00
GA Gilbert Arenas 2.00 5.00
GE Devean George 2.00 5.00
GH Grant Hill 3.00 8.00
GP Gary Payton 2.50 6.00
HA Devin Harris 1.50 4.00
JA Jamal Crawford 2.50 6.00
JC Jason Collins 2.00 5.00
JK Jason Kidd 4.00 10.00
JL Jalen Rose 2.50 6.00
JM Jeff McInnis 2.00 5.00
JO Jermaine O'Neal 2.00 5.00
JR Jason Richardson 2.50 6.00
JT Jason Terry 2.00 5.00
KB Kobe Bryant 8.00 20.00
KD Keyon Dooling 2.00 5.00
KG Kevin Garnett 4.00 10.00
KH Kirk Hinrich 2.00 5.00
KK Kerry Kittles 1.50 4.00
KM Kenyon Martin 2.00 5.00
KP Kendrick Perkins 2.00 5.00
KR Kareem Rush 2.00 5.00
KT Kurt Thomas 2.00 5.00
LD Luol Deng 2.00 5.00
LF Luis Flores 2.00 5.00
LJ LeBron James 8.00 20.00
LO Lamar Odom 2.00 5.00
LU Luke Jackson 2.00 5.00
LW Luke Walton 2.00 5.00
LZ Raul Lopez 2.00 5.00
MA Mark Blount 2.00 5.00
MB Mike Bibby 2.50 6.00
MG Manu Ginobili 2.50 6.00
MI Michael Finley 2.50 6.00
MJ Michael Jordan 40.00 100.00
MP Mickael Pietrus 2.00 5.00
MU Troy Murphy 1.50 4.00
NH Nene 2.00 5.00
PG Pau Gasol 2.50 6.00
PP Paul Pierce 2.50 6.00
PS Peja Stojakovic 2.50 6.00
QR Quentin Richardson 2.00 5.00
RA Ray Allen 2.50 6.00
RB Ryan Bowen 2.00 5.00
RH Richard Hamilton 2.00 5.00
RJ Richard Jefferson 2.00 5.00
RL Rashard Lewis 2.50 6.00
RO Ron Artest 2.50 6.00
RW Rasheed Wallace 2.50 6.00
SA Shareef Abdur-Rahim 2.00 5.00
SC Sam Cassell 2.00 5.00
SF Steve Francis 2.00 5.00
SM Shawn Marion 2.00 5.00
SN Steve Nash 3.00 8.00
SO Shaquille O'Neal 5.00 12.00
ST Stephon Marbury 2.00 5.00
TD Tim Duncan 4.00 10.00
TM Tracy McGrady 3.00 8.00
TP Tony Parker 2.50 6.00
TR Theo Ratliff 2.00 5.00
TT Tim Thomas 2.00 5.00
VB Vin Baker 2.00 5.00
WE Chris Webber 2.50 6.00
WI Chris Wilcox 2.00 5.00
YM Yao Ming 3.00 8.00
ZI Zydrunas Ilgauskas 2.00 5.00

2005-06 Upper Deck Game Jerseys Patches

Limited to 25 serially numbered copies, this 102-card set parallels the base Game Jerseys set enhanced with premium patch swatches.
*PATCHES: 1.25X TO 3X BASE HI
PRINT RUN 25 SER.#'d SETS
KB Kobe Bryant 30.00 80.00
WE Chris Webber 12.00 30.00

2005-06 Upper Deck LeBron James

COMPLETE SET (45) 15.00 40.00
COMMON CARD (LJ1-LJ45) 1.25 3.00

2005-06 Upper Deck LeBron James Gold

*GOLD: 6X TO 15X BASE
STATED PRINT RUN 23 SER.#'d SETS
UNPRICED SILVER PRINT RUN 5 SETS

2005-06 Upper Deck Michael Jordan

COMPLETE SET (45) 25.00 60.00
COMMON CARD (MJ1-MJ45) 1.50 4.00

2005-06 Upper Deck Michael Jordan Silver

*SILVER: 6X TO 15X BASE JORDAN HI
PRINT RUN 23 SER.#'d SETS

2005-06 Upper Deck Michael Jordan/LeBron James

COMPLETE SET (10) 15.00 40.00
COMMON CARD 3.00 8.00

2005-06 Upper Deck Michael Jordan/LeBron James Silver

*SILVER: 3X TO 8X BASE MJ/LJ HI

2005-06 Upper Deck Performance Clause Jerseys

STATED PRINT RUN 250 SER.#'d SETS
AK Andrei Kirilenko 2.00 5.00
AN Andre Iguodala 2.00 5.00
BG Ben Gordon 2.00 5.00
BO Carlos Boozer 2.00 5.00
CA Carmelo Anthony 5.00 12.00
CF Channing Frye 2.50 6.00
CP Chris Paul 10.00 25.00
CT Chris Taft 2.00 5.00
CV Charlie Villanueva 2.50 6.00
DG Danny Granger 3.00 8.00
DH Dwight Howard 2.00 5.00
DN Dirk Nowitzki 4.00 10.00
DW Deron Williams 3.00 8.00
FG Francisco Garcia 2.00 5.00
GA Gilbert Arenas 2.00 5.00
JJ Jarrett Jack 2.50 6.00
JO Josh Childress 2.00 5.00
JR J.R. Smith 2.00 5.00
KB Kobe Bryant 10.00 25.00
KG Kevin Garnett 3.00 8.00
KK Kyle Korver 2.00 5.00
LH Luther Head 2.00 5.00
LJ LeBron James 10.00 25.00
LO Lamar Odom 2.00 5.00
MA Marvin Williams 2.50 6.00
MB Mike Bibby 2.50 6.00
MR Michael Redd 2.00 5.00
PG Pau Gasol 2.50 6.00
RF Raymond Felton 2.50 6.00
RG Ryan Gomes 2.00 5.00
RM Rashad McCants 2.00 5.00
SB Shane Battier 2.00 5.00
SF Steve Francis 2.00 5.00
SL Shaun Livingston 2.00 5.00
SM Sean May 1.50 4.00
SO Shaquille O'Neal 5.00 12.00
SS Salim Stoudamire 2.00 5.00
TD Tim Duncan 4.00 10.00
TR Trevor Ariza 2.00 5.00
VC Vince Carter 4.00 10.00
WE Delonte West 1.50 4.00
YM Yao Ming 3.00 8.00

2005-06 Upper Deck Performance Clause Jerseys Autographs

STATED PRINT RUN 50 SER.#'d SETS
MOST UNPRICED DUE TO SCARCITY
CP Chris Paul 25.00 60.00
KB Kobe Bryant 100.00 200.00

2005-06 Upper Deck Rookie Review Materials

Inserted at approximately one per box, this set features a full-color player image towards the top, a bar along the bottom with the player's name and the set name and an "R" shaped swatch of memorabilia in the lower right-hand corner.
APPROXIMATELY ONE PER BOX
AB Andris Biedrins 1.50 4.00
AE Andre Emmett 2.00 5.00
AI Andre Iguodala 2.00 5.00
AJ Al Jefferson 2.00 5.00
AV Anderson Varejao 1.50 4.00
BU Beno Udrih 2.00 5.00
CD Chris Duhon 1.50 4.00
DE Devin Harris 1.50 4.00
DH Dwight Howard 2.00 5.00
DO Dorell Wright 2.00 5.00
DW Delonte West 1.50 4.00
HA David Harrison 2.00 5.00
HS Ha Seung-Jin 2.00 5.00
JC Josh Childress 2.00 5.00
JN Jameer Nelson 1.50 4.00
JR J.R. Smith 2.00 5.00
JS Josh Smith 2.00 5.00
JV Jackson Vroman 2.00 5.00
KH Kris Humphries 2.00 5.00
KM Kevin Martin 2.00 5.00
KS Kirk Snyder 2.00 5.00
LC Lionel Chalmers 2.00 5.00
LD Luol Deng 2.00 5.00
NK Nenad Krstic 2.00 5.00
RA Rafael Araujo 2.00 5.00
SL Shaun Livingston 2.00 5.00
ST Sebastian Telfair 2.00 5.00
SV Sasha Vujacic 2.00 5.00
TA Tony Allen 2.00 5.00
TR Trevor Ariza 2.00 5.00

2005-06 Upper Deck Rookie Scrapbook

Inserted in Retail packs at the rate of one in one, this 30-card set showcases the 2005-06 rookie class with black and white photography and design elements that make the card look like the pages of a spiral notebook.

COMPLETE SET (30) 12.50 30.00
STATED ODDS ONE PER RETAIL PACK
1 Andrew Bogut .60 1.50
2 Andrew Bynum .40 1.00
3 Antoine Wright .40 1.00
4 Channing Frye .50 1.25
5 Charlie Villanueva .50 1.25
6 Chris Paul 2.00 5.00
7 Daniel Ewing .40 1.00
8 Danny Granger .60 1.50
9 David Lee .50 1.25
10 Deron Williams .60 1.50
11 Travis Diener .30 .75
12 Francisco Garcia .40 1.00
13 Gerald Green .50 1.25
14 Hakim Warrick .40 1.00
15 Ike Diogu .30 .75
16 Jarrett Jack .50 1.25
17 Jason Maxiell .40 1.00
18 Joey Graham .40 1.00
19 Julius Hodge .30 .75
20 Luther Head .40 1.00
21 Martell Webster .40 1.00
22 Marvin Williams .50 1.25
23 Monta Ellis .60 1.50
24 Nate Robinson .50 1.25
25 Rashad McCants .40 1.00
26 Raymond Felton .50 1.25
27 C.J. Miles .50 1.25
28 Salim Stoudamire .40 1.00
29 Sean May .30 .75
30 Wayne Simien .30 .75

2005-06 Upper Deck Signature Sensations

Randomly seeded in packs, this 96-card set features player photos on the top of the card and player autographs at the bottom. Each card is sequentially numbered to 25.
PRINT RUN 25 SER.#'d SETS
AL Al Jefferson 8.00 20.00
BG Ben Gordon 12.00 30.00
BW Ben Wallace 12.00 30.00
CA Carmelo Anthony 25.00 60.00
CB Chris Bosh 15.00 40.00
CF Channing Frye 8.00 20.00
CJ C.J. Miles 8.00 20.00
CP Chris Paul 25.00 60.00
CV Charlie Villanueva 8.00 20.00
DE Devin Harris 8.00 20.00
DF Derek Fisher 12.00 30.00
DH Dwight Howard 6.00 15.00
DT Dijon Thompson 5.00 12.00
ID Ike Diogu 5.00 12.00
JK Jason Kidd 10.00 25.00
LH Luther Head 6.00 15.00
LJ LeBron James 300.00 600.00
MD Marquis Daniels 8.00 20.00
ME Monta Ellis 50.00 120.00
MJ Michael Jordan 400.00 800.00
MP Morris Peterson 8.00 20.00
PG Pau Gasol 75.00 150.00
PP Paul Pierce 20.00 50.00
RI Royal Ivey 8.00 20.00
TM Tracy McGrady 12.00 30.00
WI Deron Williams 50.00 120.00
YM Yao Ming 25.00 60.00

2005-06 Upper Deck UD Materials

Inserted in Upper Deck at the rate of approximately one per box, this 30-card set is horizontally designed with full color player photos on the left side of the card and diamond shaped swatches of memorabilia on the right.
APPROXIMATELY ONE PER BOX
AK Andrei Kirilenko 2.00 5.00
AW Antoine Walker 2.00 5.00
BD Baron Davis 2.00 5.00
BO Carlos Boozer 2.00 5.00
CB Caron Butler 2.00 5.00
CH Chris Anderson 2.50 6.00
CM Corey Maggette 2.00 5.00
CW Chris Webber 2.50 6.00
DA David Wesley 2.00 5.00
DW Dajuan Wagner 2.00 5.00
EB Earl Boykins 2.00 5.00
EC Eddy Curry 1.50 4.00
GP Gary Payton 2.50 6.00
JJ Joe Johnson 2.00 5.00
JK Jason Kidd 4.00 10.00
JM Jamaal Magloire 2.00 5.00
JO Jermaine O'Neal 2.00 5.00
JT Jason Terry 2.00 5.00
KB Kobe Bryant 10.00 25.00
KM Kenyon Martin 2.00 5.00
LJ LeBron James 10.00 25.00
MJ Michael Jordan 25.00 60.00
RD Ronald Dupree 2.00 5.00
RJ Richard Jefferson 2.00 5.00
SD Samuel Dalembert 2.00 5.00
SF Steve Francis 2.00 5.00
TP Tony Parker 2.50 6.00
UH Udonis Haslem 1.50 4.00
VL Voshon Lenard 2.00 5.00
VR Vladimir Radmanovic 2.00 5.00

2006-07 Upper Deck

Released in mid Novermber 2006, Upper Deck boasts a 240-card base set where cards 1-200 picture veteran players and cards 201-240 picture rookies inserted at the rate of one in three packs. Base card design consists of full-bleed photos and a box along the bottom containing the player's name, position and team. Upper Deck is packaged in 24-pack boxes of eight cards each and carried an original suggested retail price of $3.00.
COMP.SET w/o SP's (200) 15.00 40.00
ROOKIE ODDS 1:3
1 Josh Childress .25 .60
2 Al Harrington .25 .60
3 Joe Johnson .25 .60
4 Josh Smith .25 .60
5 Salim Stoudamire .20 .50
6 Marvin Williams .25 .60
7 Tony Allen .20 .50
8 Dan Dickau .20 .50
9 Al Jefferson .25 .60
10 Raef LaFrentz .20 .50
11 Michael Olowokandi .20 .50
12 Paul Pierce .30 .75
13 Wally Szczerbiak .25 .60
14 Alan Anderson .20 .50
15 Raymond Felton .25 .60
16 Othella Harrington .20 .50
17 Sean May .20 .50
18 Emeka Okafor .25 .60
19 Primoz Brezec .20 .50
20 Gerald Wallace .25 .60
21 Tyson Chandler .25 .60
22 Michael Jordan 2.50 6.00
23 Luol Deng .25 .60
24 Chris Duhon .20 .50
25 Ben Gordon .25 .60
26 Kirk Hinrich .25 .60
27 Mike Sweetney .20 .50
28 Drew Gooden .25 .60
29 Larry Hughes .25 .60
30 Zydrunas Ilgauskas .25 .60
31 LeBron James 1.25 3.00
32 Damon Jones .20 .50
33 Donyell Marshall .20 .50
34 Anderson Varejao .20 .50
35 Erick Dampier .20 .50
36 Marquis Daniels .20 .50
37 Devin Harris .20 .50
38 Josh Howard .25 .60
39 Dirk Nowitzki .50 1.25
40 Jerry Stackhouse .25 .60
41 Jason Terry .25 .60
42 Carmelo Anthony .40 1.00
43 Earl Boykins .20 .50
44 Marcus Camby .25 .60
45 Kenyon Martin .25 .60
46 Andre Miller .25 .60
47 Eduardo Najera .20 .50
48 Nene .25 .60
49 Chauncey Billups .30 .75
50 Richard Hamilton .25 .60
51 Lindsey Hunter .20 .50
52 Antonio McDyess .25 .60
53 Tayshaun Prince .25 .60
54 Ben Wallace .25 .60
55 Rasheed Wallace .30 .75
56 Baron Davis .25 .60
57 Ike Diogu .20 .50
58 Mike Dunleavy .25 .60
59 Derek Fisher .25 .60
60 Troy Murphy .20 .50
61 Mickael Pietrus .25 .60
62 Jason Richardson .30 .75
63 Rafer Alston .20 .50
64 Luther Head .25 .60
65 Juwan Howard .25 .60
66 Tracy McGrady .40 1.00
67 Dikembe Mutombo .30 .75
68 Stromile Swift .20 .50
69 Yao Ming .40 1.00
70 Austin Croshere .20 .50
71 Stephen Jackson .25 .60
72 Sarunas Jasikevicius .25 .60
73 Jermaine O'Neal .25 .60
74 Peja Stojakovic .30 .75
75 Jamaal Tinsley .20 .50
76 Elton Brand .30 .75
77 Sam Cassell .25 .60
78 Chris Kaman .25 .60
79 Shaun Livingston .20 .50
80 Corey Maggette .25 .60
81 Cuttino Mobley .20 .50
82 Vladimir Radmanovic .20 .50
83 Kwame Brown .20 .50
84 Kobe Bryant 1.25 3.00
85 Devean George .20 .50
86 Lamar Odom .25 .60
87 Ronny Turiaf .25 .60
88 Sasha Vujacic .20 .50
89 Luke Walton .20 .50
90 Shane Battier .25 .60
91 Pau Gasol .30 .75
92 Bobby Jackson .20 .50
93 Eddie Jones .25 .60
94 Mike Miller .25 .60
95 Damon Stoudamire .25 .60
96 Hakim Warrick .25 .60
97 Alonzo Mourning .40 1.00
98 Shaquille O'Neal .60 1.50
99 Gary Payton .30 .75
100 Wayne Simien .20 .50
101 Dwyane Wade .50 1.25
102 Antoine Walker .25 .60
103 Jason Williams .25 .60
104 Andrew Bogut .25 .60
105 T.J. Ford .20 .50
106 Jamaal Magloire .20 .50
107 Michael Redd .25 .60
108 Bobby Simmons .20 .50
109 Maurice Williams .25 .60
110 Ricky Davis .25 .60
111 Kevin Garnett .50 1.25
112 Eddie Griffin .20 .50
113 Trenton Hassell .20 .50
114 Troy Hudson .20 .50
115 Rashad McCants .20 .50
116 Vince Carter .40 1.00
117 Jason Collins .20 .50
118 Richard Jefferson .25 .60
119 Jason Kidd .50 1.25
120 Nenad Krstic .20 .50
121 Jeff McInnis .20 .50
122 Antoine Wright .20 .50
123 P.J. Brown .20 .50
124 Speedy Claxton .20 .50
125 Desmond Mason .20 .50
126 Chris Paul .40 1.00
127 J.R. Smith .25 .60
128 Kirk Snyder .20 .50
129 David West .25 .60
130 Jamal Crawford .30 .75

131 Steve Francis .25 .60
132 Channing Frye .25 .60
133 Stephon Marbury .25 .60
134 Quentin Richardson .25 .60
135 Nate Robinson .20 .50
136 Maurice Taylor .20 .50
137 Carlos Arroyo .20 .50
138 Tony Battie .20 .50
139 Keyon Dooling .20 .50
140 Grant Hill .40 1.00
141 Dwight Howard .25 .60
142 Darko Milicic .20 .50
143 Jameer Nelson .20 .50
144 Samuel Dalembert .20 .50
145 Steven Hunter .20 .50
146 Andre Iguodala .25 .60
147 Allen Iverson .40 1.00
148 Kyle Korver .25 .60
149 Shavlik Randolph .20 .50
150 Chris Webber .30 .75
151 Raja Bell .25 .60
152 Boris Diaw .25 .60
153 Shawn Marion .25 .60
154 Steve Nash .40 1.00
155 Amare Stoudemire .25 .60
156 Kurt Thomas .20 .50
157 Tim Thomas .20 .50
158 Steve Blake .20 .50
159 Juan Dixon .20 .50
160 Zach Randolph .25 .60
161 Ha Seung-Jin .20 .50
162 Sebastian Telfair .20 .50
163 Martell Webster .25 .60
164 Shareef Abdur-Rahim .25 .60
165 Ron Artest .30 .75
166 Mike Bibby .30 .75
167 Brad Miller .25 .60
168 Kenny Thomas .20 .50
169 Bonzi Wells .20 .50
170 Bruce Bowen .20 .50
171 Tim Duncan .50 1.25
172 Michael Finley .30 .75
173 Manu Ginobili .30 .75
174 Nazr Mohammed .20 .50
175 Tony Parker .30 .75
176 Ray Allen .30 .75
177 Danny Fortson .20 .50
178 Rashard Lewis .30 .75
179 Luke Ridnour .25 .60
180 Earl Watson .20 .50
181 Chris Wilcox .20 .50
182 Rafael Araujo .20 .50
183 Chris Bosh .30 .75
184 Joey Graham .20 .50
185 Mike James .20 .50
186 Morris Peterson .20 .50
187 Charlie Villanueva .20 .50
188 Carlos Boozer .25 .60
189 Matt Harpring .20 .50
190 Kris Humphries .20 .50
191 Andrei Kirilenko .25 .60
192 C.J. Miles .25 .60
193 Chris Taft .20 .50
194 Deron Williams .25 .60
195 Gilbert Arenas .25 .60
196 Andray Blatche .20 .50
197 Caron Butler .25 .60
198 Antonio Daniels .20 .50
199 Brendan Haywood .20 .50
200 Antawn Jamison .25 .60
201 Andrea Bargnani RC 1.00 2.50
202 LaMarcus Aldridge RC 2.50 6.00
203 Adam Morrison RC 1.00 2.50
204 Tyrus Thomas RC .75 2.00
205 Shelden Williams RC .75 2.00
206 Brandon Roy RC 1.00 2.50
207 Randy Foye RC 1.00 2.50
208 Rudy Gay RC 1.25 3.00
209 Patrick O'Bryant RC .60 1.50
210 Saer Sene RC .60 1.50
211 J.J. Redick RC 1.25 3.00
212 Hilton Armstrong RC .60 1.50
213 Thabo Sefolosha RC 1.00 2.50
214 Ronnie Brewer RC 1.00 2.50
215 Cedric Simmons RC .60 1.50
216 Rodney Carney RC .60 1.50
217 Shawne Williams RC .60 1.50
218 Quincy Douby RC .60 1.50
219 Renaldo Balkman RC .75 2.00
220 Rajon Rondo RC 1.50 4.00
221 Marcus Williams RC .60 1.50
222 Josh Boone RC .60 1.50
223 Kyle Lowry RC 1.25 3.00
224 Shannon Brown RC .60 1.50
225 Jordan Farmar RC 1.00 2.50
226 Maurice Ager RC .60 1.50
227 Mardy Collins RC .60 1.50
228 Jorge Garbajosa RC .75 2.00
229 James White RC .60 1.50
230 Steve Novak RC .75 2.00
231 Solomon Jones RC .60 1.50
232 Paul Davis RC .60 1.50
233 P.J. Tucker RC .75 2.00
234 Craig Smith RC .75 2.00
235 Bobby Jones RC .60 1.50
236 David Noel RC .60 1.50
237 Denham Brown RC .60 1.50
238 James Augustine RC .60 1.50
239 Daniel Gibson RC .75 2.00
240 Alexander Johnson RC .60 1.50

2006-07 Upper Deck Star Rookies Hot Pack

*HOT PACK: .5X TO 1.25X BASE HI
ONE HOT PACK PER BOX

2006-07 Upper Deck Flight Team

COMPLETE SET (30) 12.50 30.00
*HOT PACK SILVER: .5X TO 1.25X BASE HI
ONE HOT PACK PER BOX
APPROXIMATE ODDS 1:12
AI Andre Iguodala .60 1.50
AS Amare Stoudemire .60 1.50
BB Brent Barry .50 1.25
CA Carmelo Anthony 1.00 2.50
CB Chris Bosh .75 2.00
CM Corey Maggette .60 1.50
DH Dwight Howard .60 1.50
DM Desmond Mason .50 1.25
DW Dwyane Wade 1.25 3.00
FJ Fred Jones .50 1.25
GA Gilbert Arenas .60 1.50
JR Jason Richardson .75 2.00
JS J.R. Smith .60 1.50
KB Kobe Bryant 3.00 8.00
KG Kevin Garnett 1.25 3.00
KM Kenyon Martin .60 1.50
LJ LeBron James 3.00 8.00
MA Shawn Marion .60 1.50
MG Manu Ginobili .75 2.00
MI Darius Miles .50 1.25
MJ Michael Jordan 6.00 15.00
NR Nate Robinson .50 1.25
RJ Richard Jefferson .60 1.50
SF Steve Francis .60 1.50
SM Josh Smith .60 1.50
SO Shaquille O'Neal 1.50 4.00
SS Stromile Swift .50 1.25
TM Tracy McGrady 1.00 2.50
TP Tayshaun Prince .60 1.50
VC Vince Carter 1.00 2.50

2006-07 Upper Deck MVP Watch

MPLETE SET (15) 8.00 20.00
APPROXIMATE ODDS 1:12
*HOT PACK: .5X TO 1.25X BASE HI
ONE HOT PACK PER BOX
AI Allen Iverson .75 2.00
CB Chauncey Billups .60 1.50
DN Dirk Nowitzki 1.00 2.50
DW Dwyane Wade 1.00 2.50
EB Elton Brand .60 1.50
GA Gilbert Arenas .50 1.25
KB Kobe Bryant 2.50 6.00
KG Kevin Garnett 1.00 2.50
LJ LeBron James 2.50 6.00
PP Paul Pierce .60 1.50
SM Shawn Marion .50 1.25
SN Steve Nash .75 2.00
SO Shaquille O'Neal 1.25 3.00
TD Tim Duncan 1.00 2.50
TM Tracy McGrady .75 2.00

2006-07 Upper Deck Signature Sensations

INT RUN 25 SER.#'d SETS
AB Andrew Bogut 8.00 20.00
AI Andre Iguodala 10.00 25.00
BB Bruce Bowen 6.00 15.00
BD Dee Brown 6.00 15.00
BR Brandon Roy 10.00 25.00
CA Carmelo Anthony 30.00 80.00
CP Chris Paul 25.00 60.00
CS Craig Smith 6.00 15.00
DB Denham Brown 6.00 15.00
DM Donyell Marshall 6.00 15.00
DN David Noel 6.00 15.00
HA Hassan Adams 6.00 15.00
ID Ike Diogu 6.00 15.00
JK Jason Kapono 6.00 15.00
KB Kwame Brown 6.00 15.00
KK Kyle Korver 8.00 20.00
LA LaMarcus Aldridge 20.00 50.00
NR Nate Robinson 12.00 30.00
RH Ryan Hollins 6.00 15.00
RT Ronny Turiaf 8.00 20.00
VW Von Wafer 6.00 15.00
WM Maurice Williams 6.00 15.00
YK Yaroslav Korolev 6.00 15.00

2006-07 Upper Deck Signature Sensations Dual

BB B.Barry/B.Bowen 10.00 25.00
GG J.Graham/S.Graham 10.00 25.00
JJ M.Jordan/L.James SP 500.00 800.00
LP S.Livingston/C.Paul 25.00 60.00
PC P.Pierce/V.Carter 20.00 50.00

2006-07 Upper Deck The LeBrons

COMPLETE SET (15) 10.00 25.00
COMMON LEBRON (1-12) 2.50 6.00
*HOT PACK: .5X TO 1.25X BASE HI
ONE HOT PACK PER BOX
APPROXIMATE ODDS 1:3
COMMON MEMORABILIA 12.00 30.00
COMMON DUAL MEM. 40.00 100.00
QUAD UNPRICED DUE TO SCARCITY
RANDOM INSERTS IN PACKS
13 LeBron James Dual 3.00 8.00
14 LeBron James Dual 3.00 8.00
15 LeBron James Triple 3.00 8.00

2006-07 Upper Deck UD Game Jersey

PROXIMATE ODDS ONE PER BOX
AB Andrew Bogut 2.00 5.00
AI Allen Iverson 3.00 8.00
AJ Al Jefferson 2.00 5.00
AK Andrei Kirilenko 2.00 5.00
AL Ray Allen 2.50 6.00
AS Amare Stoudemire 2.00 5.00
AW Antoine Walker 2.00 5.00
BB Bruce Bowen 1.50 4.00
BD Baron Davis 2.00 5.00
BG Ben Gordon 2.00 5.00
BK Kwame Brown 1.50 4.00
BM Brad Miller 2.00 5.00
BW Ben Wallace 2.00 5.00
CA Carmelo Anthony 3.00 8.00
CB Chauncey Billups 2.50 6.00
CF Channing Frye 2.00 5.00
CM Corey Maggette 2.00 5.00
CP Chris Paul 3.00 8.00
CW Chris Webber 2.50 6.00
DG Drew Gooden 2.00 5.00
DH Devin Harris 1.50 4.00
DM Donyell Marshall 1.50 4.00
DN Dirk Nowitzki 4.00 10.00
EB Elton Brand 2.50 6.00
EO Emeka Okafor 2.00 5.00
GA Gilbert Arenas 2.00 5.00
GE Devean George 1.50 4.00
GH Grant Hill 3.00 8.00
HD Dwight Howard 2.00 5.00
HU Larry Hughes 2.00 5.00
IA Andre Iguodala 2.00 5.00
ID Ike Diogu 1.50 4.00
JC Jamal Crawford 2.50 6.00
JD Juan Dixon 1.50 4.00
JH Josh Howard 2.00 5.00
JJ Joe Johnson 2.00 5.00
JK Jason Kidd 4.00 10.00
JM Jeff McInnis 1.50 4.00
JO Jermaine O'Neal 2.00 5.00
JR Jason Richardson 2.50 6.00
JS J.R. Smith 2.00 5.00
JT Jason Terry 2.00 5.00
KB Kobe Bryant 10.00 25.00
KG Kevin Garnett 4.00 10.00
KH Kirk Hinrich 2.00 5.00
KK Kyle Korver 2.00 5.00
LD Luol Deng 2.00 5.00
LH Luther Head 2.00 5.00
LJ LeBron James 10.00 25.00
LO Lamar Odom 2.00 5.00
LW Luke Walton 1.50 4.00
MA Sean May 1.50 4.00
MB Mike Bibby 2.50 6.00
MD Marquis Daniels 1.50 4.00
MG Manu Ginobili 2.50 6.00
MJ Michael Jordan SP 30.00 80.00
MS Stephon Marbury 2.00 5.00
MW Marvin Williams 2.00 5.00
NR Nate Robinson 1.50 4.00
PG Pau Gasol 2.50 6.00
PP Paul Pierce 2.50 6.00
PS Peja Stojakovic 2.50 6.00
PT Tayshaun Prince 2.00 5.00
QR Quentin Richardson 2.00 5.00
RA Ron Artest 2.50 6.00
RF Raymond Felton 2.00 5.00
RH Richard Hamilton 2.00 5.00
RJ Richard Jefferson 2.00 5.00
RL Rashard Lewis 2.50 6.00
RM Rashad McCants 1.50 4.00
RW Rasheed Wallace 2.50 6.00
SD Samuel Dalembert 1.50 4.00
SJ Sarunas Jasikevicius 2.00 5.00
SL Shaun Livingston 1.50 4.00
SM Shawn Marion 2.00 5.00
SN Steve Nash 3.00 8.00
SO Shaquille O'Neal 5.00 12.00
ST Sebastian Telfair 1.50 4.00
TC Tyson Chandler 2.00 5.00
TD Tim Duncan 4.00 10.00
TF T.J. Ford 1.50 4.00
TM Tracy McGrady 3.00 8.00
TP Tony Parker 2.50 6.00
VC Vince Carter 3.00 8.00
WM Martell Webster 2.00 5.00
WS Wally Szczerbiak 2.00 5.00
YM Yao Ming 3.00 8.00
ZI Zydrunas Ilgauskas 2.00 5.00

2006-07 Upper Deck UD Game Patch

*PATCH: .75X TO 2X BASE HI
PRINT RUN 25 SER.#'d SETS
KB Kobe Bryant 25.00 60.00
LJ LeBron James 25.00 60.00

2007-08 Upper Deck

This 242-card set was released in October, 2007. The set was issued into the hobby in two versions (West and East) both versions of which had 15 cards in the pack with 16 packs to a box and 12 boxes to a case and packs carried an initial SRP of $9.99. Cards numbered 1-200 feature NBA veterans while cards numbered 201-242 feature 2007-08 NBA rookies.

COMPLETE SET (242) 75.00 150.00
COMP.SET w/o SP's (200) 15.00 30.00
APPROXIMATE ODDS 1:2
1 Austin Croshere .20 .50
2 Devean George .20 .50
3 Devin Harris .20 .50
4 Josh Howard .25 .60
5 Jerry Stackhouse .25 .60
6 Jason Terry .25 .60
7 Rafer Alston .20 .50
8 Shane Battier .25 .60
9 Luther Head .25 .60
10 Juwan Howard .25 .60
11 Tracy McGrady .30 .75
12 Steve Novak .20 .50
13 Rudy Gay .30 .75
14 Eddie Jones .25 .60
15 Kyle Lowry .30 .75
16 Mike Miller .25 .60
17 Damon Stoudamire .25 .60
18 Hakim Warrick .25 .60
19 Brandon Bass .20 .50
20 Tyson Chandler .25 .60
21 Bobby Jackson .20 .50
22 Desmond Mason .20 .50
23 Cedric Simmons .25 .60
24 Peja Stojakovic .30 .75
25 Bruce Bowen .20 .50
26 Michael Finley .30 .75
27 Manu Ginobili .30 .75
28 Tony Parker .30 .75
29 Beno Udrih .20 .50
30 Monta Ellis .25 .60
31 Al Harrington .25 .60
32 Sarunas Jasikevicius .20 .50
33 Stephen Jackson .25 .60
34 Jason Richardson .30 .75
35 Sam Cassell .25 .60
36 Chris Kaman .25 .60
37 Shaun Livingston .20 .50
38 Corey Maggette .25 .60
39 Cuttino Mobley .25 .60
40 Tim Thomas .20 .50
41 Kwame Brown .20 .50
42 Andrew Bynum .20 .50
43 Jordan Farmar .20 .50
44 Lamar Odom .25 .60
45 Ronny Turiaf .25 .60
46 Luke Walton .20 .50
47 Leandro Barbosa .25 .60
48 Raja Bell .25 .60
49 Boris Diaw .25 .60
50 Shawn Marion .25 .60
51 Amare Stoudemire .25 .60
52 Shareef Abdur-Rahim .25 .60
53 Ron Artest .30 .75
54 Quincy Douby .20 .50
55 Kevin Martin .25 .60
56 Brad Miller .25 .60
57 Allen Iverson .40 1.00
58 Kenyon Martin .25 .60
59 Eduardo Najera .20 .50
60 Nene .25 .60
61 J.R. Smith .25 .60
62 Ricky Davis .25 .60
63 Randy Foye .30 .75
64 Troy Hudson .20 .50
65 Mike James .20 .50
66 Rashad McCants .20 .50
67 Craig Smith .20 .50
68 LaMarcus Aldridge .40 1.00
69 Jarrett Jack .25 .60
70 Jamaal Magloire .20 .50
71 Sergio Rodriguez .20 .50
72 Brandon Roy .30 .75
73 Martell Webster .25 .60
74 Rashard Lewis .25 .60
75 Luke Ridnour .25 .60
76 Danny Fortson .20 .50
77 Chris Wilcox .20 .50
78 Damien Wilkins .20 .50
79 Ronnie Brewer .25 .60
80 Derek Fisher .25 .60
81 Matt Harpring .20 .50
82 Andrei Kirilenko .25 .60
83 Paul Millsap .25 .60
84 Deron Williams .25 .60
85 Tony Allen .20 .50
86 Gerald Green .25 .60
87 Al Jefferson .25 .60
88 Wally Szczerbiak .25 .60
89 Allan Ray .20 .50
90 Delonte West .20 .50
91 Hassan Adams .20 .50
92 Richard Jefferson .25 .60
93 Jason Kidd .30 .75
94 Nenad Krstic .20 .50
95 Marcus Williams .20 .50
96 Renaldo Balkman .20 .50
97 Jamal Crawford .30 .75
98 Eddy Curry .20 .50
99 Channing Frye .25 .60
100 Quentin Richardson .25 .60
101 Nate Robinson .20 .50
102 Rodney Carney .20 .50
103 Samuel Dalembert .20 .50
104 Steven Hunter .20 .50
105 Kyle Korver .25 .60
106 Andre Miller .25 .60
107 Shavlik Randolph .20 .50
108 Andrea Bargnani .30 .75
109 Jose Calderon .20 .50
110 T.J. Ford .20 .50
111 Jorge Garbajosa .25 .60
112 Joey Graham .20 .50
113 Morris Peterson .20 .50
114 Luol Deng .25 .60
115 Ben Gordon .25 .60
116 Kirk Hinrich .25 .60
117 Thabo Sefolosha .20 .50
118 Tyrus Thomas .20 .50
119 Ben Wallace .25 .60
120 Shannon Brown .20 .50
121 Drew Gooden .25 .60
122 Larry Hughes .25 .60
123 Zydrunas Ilgauskas .25 .60
124 Donyell Marshall .20 .50
125 Richard Hamilton .25 .60
126 Amir Johnson .20 .50
127 Antonio McDyess .25 .60
128 Tayshaun Prince .25 .60
129 Rasheed Wallace .30 .75
130 Chris Webber .30 .75
131 Marquis Daniels .20 .50
132 Ike Diogu .20 .50
133 Mike Dunleavy .25 .60
134 Jeff Foster .20 .50
135 Troy Murphy .20 .50
136 Jamaal Tinsley .20 .50
137 Charlie Bell .20 .50
138 Andrew Bogut .25 .60
139 Earl Boykins .20 .50
140 Bobby Simmons .20 .50
141 Charlie Villanueva .20 .50
142 Maurice Williams .25 .60
143 Speedy Claxton .20 .50
144 Solomon Jones .20 .50
145 Tyronn Lue .20 .50
146 Marvin Williams .25 .60
147 Shelden Williams .20 .50
148 Raymond Felton .30 .75
149 Othella Harrington .20 .50
150 Sean May .20 .50
151 Adam Morrison .20 .50
152 Gerald Wallace .25 .60
153 Udonis Haslem .20 .50
154 Alonzo Mourning .40 1.00
155 Shaquille O'Neal .60 1.50
156 Gary Payton .30 .75
157 Antoine Walker .25 .60
158 Jason Williams .25 .60
159 Carlos Arroyo .20 .50
160 Travis Diener .20 .50
161 Grant Hill .40 1.00
162 Darko Milicic .20 .50
163 Jameer Nelson .20 .50
164 J.J. Redick .30 .75
165 Andray Blatche .20 .50
166 Caron Butler .25 .60
167 Antonio Daniels .20 .50
168 Brendan Haywood .20 .50
169 Antawn Jamison .25 .60
170 DeShawn Stevenson .20 .50
171 Dirk Nowitzki .40 1.00
172 Yao Ming .40 1.00
173 Pau Gasol .30 .75
174 Chris Paul .40 1.00
175 Tim Duncan .50 1.25
176 Baron Davis .25 .60
177 Elton Brand .30 .75
178 Kobe Bryant 1.25 3.00
179 Steve Nash .40 1.00
180 Mike Bibby .30 .75
181 Carmelo Anthony .40 1.00
182 Kevin Garnett .50 1.25
183 Zach Randolph .25 .60
184 Ray Allen .30 .75
185 Carlos Boozer .25 .60
186 Paul Pierce .30 .75
187 Vince Carter .40 1.00
188 Stephon Marbury .25 .60
189 Andre Iguodala .25 .60
190 Chris Bosh .30 .75
191 Michael Jordan 2.50 6.00
192 LeBron James 1.25 3.00
193 Chauncey Billups .30 .75
194 Jermaine O'Neal .25 .60
195 Michael Redd .25 .60
196 Joe Johnson .25 .60
197 Emeka Okafor .25 .60
198 Dwyane Wade .50 1.25
199 Dwight Howard .25 .60
200 Gilbert Arenas .25 .60
201 Acie Law RC .60 1.50
202 Thaddeus Young RC 1.00 2.50
203 Julian Wright RC .60 1.50
204 Al Thornton RC .75 2.00
205 Rodney Stuckey RC .75 2.00
206 Nick Young RC 1.25 3.00
207 Sean Williams RC .60 1.50
208 Marco Belinelli RC 1.00 2.50
209 Javaris Crittenton RC .60 1.50
210 Jason Smith RC .75 2.00
211 Daequan Cook RC .75 2.00
212 Jared Dudley RC .75 2.00
213 Wilson Chandler RC .75 2.00
214 Morris Almond RC .60 1.50
215 Aaron Brooks RC .75 2.00
216 Arron Afflalo RC 1.00 2.50
217 Alando Tucker RC .60 1.50
218 Petteri Koponen RC 1.00 2.50
219 Carl Landry RC .60 1.50
220 Gabe Pruitt RC .60 1.50
221 Marcus Williams RC .60 1.50
222 Nick Fazekas RC .60 1.50
223 Glen Davis RC .75 2.00
224 Jermareo Davidson RC .60 1.50
225 Josh McRoberts RC .75 2.00
226 Chris Richard RC .60 1.50
227 Derrick Byars RC .60 1.50
228 Adam Haluska RC .60 1.50
229 Reyshawn Terry RC .60 1.50
230 Jared Jordan RC .60 1.50
231 Stephane Lasme RC .60 1.50
232 Dominic McGuire RC .60 1.50
233 Greg Oden SP RC 1.25 3.00
234 Kevin Durant SP RC 12.00 30.00
235 Al Horford SP RC 1.50 4.00
236 Mike Conley Jr. SP RC 1.50 4.00
237 Jeff Green SP RC 1.25 3.00
238 Taurean Green SP RC .75 2.00
239 Corey Brewer SP RC 1.25 3.00
240 Brandan Wright SP RC 1.25 3.00
241 Joakim Noah SP RC 1.25 3.00
242 Spencer Hawes SP RC 1.00 2.50

2007-08 Upper Deck Championship Court Stamp

*COURT STAMP: 4X TO 10X BASE HI

2007-08 Upper Deck Electric Court Gold

*1-200 GOLD: 1.25X TO 3X BASE HI
*200-242 GOLD RC: .5X TO 1.25X HI
APPROXIMATE ODDS 1:4

2007-08 Upper Deck All-NBA

COMPLETE SET (15) 8.00 20.00
RANDOM INSERTS IN PACKS
1 Dirk Nowitzki .75 2.00
2 Tim Duncan 1.00 2.50
3 Amare Stoudemire .50 1.25
4 Steve Nash .75 2.00
5 Kobe Bryant 2.50 6.00
6 LeBron James 2.50 6.00
7 Chris Bosh .60 1.50
8 Yao Ming .75 2.00
9 Gilbert Arenas .50 1.25
10 Tracy McGrady .60 1.50
11 Kevin Garnett 1.00 2.50
12 Carmelo Anthony .75 2.00
13 Dwight Howard .50 1.25
14 Dwyane Wade 1.00 2.50
15 Chauncey Billups .60 1.50

2007-08 Upper Deck All-Star Die Cuts

NDOM INSERTS IN PACKS
AS1 Antawn Jamison 6.00 15.00
AS2 Ben Wallace 6.00 15.00
AS3 Bill Russell 12.00 30.00
AS4 Chauncey Billups 8.00 20.00
AS5 Jason Kidd 10.00 25.00
AS6 Jermaine O'Neal 6.00 15.00
AS7 John Havlicek 8.00 20.00
AS8 Larry Bird 20.00 50.00
AS9 LeBron James 150.00 300.00
AS10 Michael Jordan 400.00 800.00
AS11 Michael Redd 6.00 15.00
AS12 Paul Pierce 12.00 30.00
AS13 Richard Hamilton 6.00 15.00
AS14 Robert Parish 8.00 20.00
AS15 Walt Frazier 8.00 20.00
AS16 Amare Stoudemire 6.00 15.00
AS17 Bill Walton 8.00 20.00
AS18 Carmelo Anthony 10.00 25.00
AS19 David Robinson 12.00 30.00
AS20 Elton Brand 8.00 20.00
AS21 Hakeem Olajuwon 20.00 50.00
AS22 James Worthy 10.00 25.00
AS23 Jerry West 10.00 25.00
AS24 John Stockton 12.00 30.00
AS25 Josh Howard 6.00 15.00
AS26 Magic Johnson 20.00 50.00
AS27 Manu Ginobili 8.00 20.00
AS28 Yao Ming 10.00 25.00
AS29 Rick Barry 6.00 15.00
AS30 Tony Parker 8.00 20.00

2007-08 Upper Deck Behind the Glass

MPLETE SET (25) 20.00 40.00
RANDOM INSERTS IN PACKS
AI Allen Iverson 1.00 2.50
AS Amare Stoudemire .60 1.50
BO Carlos Boozer .60 1.50
BW Ben Wallace .60 1.50
CA Carmelo Anthony 1.00 2.50
CB Chris Bosh .75 2.00
CP Chris Paul 1.00 2.50
DH Dwight Howard .60 1.50
DN Dirk Nowitzki 1.00 2.50
DW Dwyane Wade 1.25 3.00
GA Gilbert Arenas .60 1.50
JR Jason Richardson .75 2.00
KB Kobe Bryant 3.00 8.00
KG Kevin Garnett 1.25 3.00
LJ LeBron James 3.00 8.00
MA Shawn Marion .60 1.50
MG Manu Ginobili .75 2.00
MJ Michael Jordan 6.00 15.00
PP Paul Pierce .75 2.00
SM Stephon Marbury .60 1.50
SN Steve Nash 1.00 2.50
SO Shaquille O'Neal 1.50 4.00
TD Tim Duncan 1.25 3.00
TM Tracy McGrady .75 2.00
YM Yao Ming 1.00 2.50

2007-08 Upper Deck Champions of the Court

MPLETE SET (25) 15.00 40.00
RANDOM INSERTS IN PACKS
BR Bill Russell 1.25 3.00
BW Bill Walton .75 2.00
CB Chauncey Billups .75 2.00
DR Dennis Rodman 1.50 4.00
DW Dwyane Wade 1.25 3.00
GM George Mikan 1.50 4.00
HO Hakeem Olajuwon 1.00 2.50
JD Joe Dumars .75 2.00
JE Julius Erving 1.25 3.00
JH John Havlicek .75 2.00
JO Magic Johnson 2.00 5.00
JW James Worthy 1.00 2.50
KA Kareem Abdul-Jabbar 1.25 3.00
KB Kobe Bryant 3.00 8.00
LB Larry Bird 2.00 5.00
MG Manu Ginobili .75 2.00
MJ Michael Jordan 6.00 15.00
MM Moses Malone .75 2.00
RH Robert Horry .60 1.50
RO David Robinson 1.25 3.00
SK Steve Kerr .75 2.00
SO Shaquille O'Neal 1.50 4.00
TD Tim Duncan 1.25 3.00
TP Tony Parker .75 2.00
WC Wilt Chamberlain 1.50 4.00

2007-08 Upper Deck Championship Predictor

NDOM INSERTS IN PACKS
CP1 Atlanta Hawks 2.00 5.00
CP2 Boston Celtics 4.00 10.00
CP3 Charlotte Bobcats 2.00 5.00
CP4 Chicago Bulls 2.00 5.00
CP5 Cleveland Cavaliers 4.00 10.00
CP6 Dallas Mavericks 2.00 5.00
CP7 Denver Nuggets 2.00 5.00
CP8 Detroit Pistons 2.00 5.00
CP9 Golden State Warriors 2.00 5.00
CP10 Houston Rockets 2.00 5.00
CP11 Indiana Pacers 2.00 5.00
CP12 Los Angeles Clippers 2.00 5.00
CP13 Los Angeles Lakers 4.00 10.00
CP14 Memphis Grizzlies 2.00 5.00
CP15 Miami Heat 2.00 5.00
CP16 Milwaukee Bucks 2.00 5.00
CP17 Minnesota Timberwolves 2.00 5.00
CP18 New Jersey Nets 2.00 5.00
CP19 New Orleans Hornets 2.00 5.00
CP20 New York Knicks 2.00 5.00
CP21 Orlando Magic 2.00 5.00
CP22 Philadelphia 76ers 2.00 5.00
CP23 Phoenix Suns 2.00 5.00
CP24 Portland Trail Blazers 2.00 5.00
CP25 Sacramento Kings 2.00 5.00
CP26 San Antonio Spurs 2.00 5.00
CP27 Seattle Supersonics 2.00 5.00
CP28 Toronto Raptors 2.00 5.00
CP29 Utah Jazz 2.00 5.00
CP30 Washington Wizards 2.00 5.00

2007-08 Upper Deck Draft Notices

COMPLETE SET (25) 10.00 25.00
RANDOM INSERTS IN PACKS
DN1 Greg Oden .60 1.50
DN2 Kevin Durant 6.00 15.00
DN3 Al Horford .75 2.00
DN4 Mike Conley Jr. .75 2.00
DN5 Jeff Green .60 1.50
DN6 Alando Tucker .40 1.00
DN7 Corey Brewer .60 1.50
DN8 Brandan Wright .60 1.50
DN9 Joakim Noah .60 1.50
DN10 Spencer Hawes .50 1.25
DN11 Acie Law .40 1.00
DN12 Thaddeus Young .60 1.50
DN13 Julian Wright .40 1.00
DN14 Al Thornton .50 1.25
DN15 Rodney Stuckey .50 1.25
DN16 Nick Young .75 2.00
DN17 Sean Williams .40 1.00
DN18 Javaris Crittenton .40 1.00
DN19 Jason Smith .50 1.25
DN20 Daequan Cook .50 1.25
DN21 Jared Dudley .50 1.25
DN22 Wilson Chandler .50 1.25
DN23 Morris Almond .40 1.00
DN24 Aaron Brooks .50 1.25
DN25 Arron Afflalo .60 1.50

2007-08 Upper Deck Jordan Chronicles

COMPLETE SET (20) 40.00 80.00
COMMON JORDAN 4.00 10.00
RANDOM INSERTS IN PACKS
AUTOS UNPRICED DUE TO SCARCITY

2007-08 Upper Deck Legendary All-Stars

COMPLETE SET (20) 15.00 40.00
RANDOM INSERTS IN PACKS
AUTOS NOT PRICED DUE TO SCARCITY
LA1 Michael Jordan 10.00 25.00
LA2 Bill Laimbeer 1.00 2.50
LA3 Isiah Thomas 1.25 3.00
LA4 Larry Bird 3.00 8.00
LA5 Magic Johnson 3.00 8.00
LA6 Bill Russell 2.00 5.00
LA7 Kareem Abdul-Jabbar 2.00 5.00
LA8 David Robinson 2.00 5.00
LA9 Hakeem Olajuwon 1.50 4.00
LA10 James Worthy 1.50 4.00
LA11 Robert Parish 1.25 3.00
LA12 Jerry West 1.50 4.00
LA13 Bill Walton 1.25 3.00
LA14 John Havlicek 1.25 3.00
LA15 Rick Barry 1.00 2.50
LA16 Walt Frazier 1.25 3.00
LA17 Bernard King 1.00 2.50
LA18 Clyde Drexler 1.50 4.00
LA19 Elgin Baylor 1.25 3.00
LA20 Maurice Cheeks .75 2.00

2007-08 Upper Deck Mini Jersey

NDOM INSERTS IN PACKS
1 LeBron James 5.00 12.00
2 Kobe Bryant 5.00 12.00
3 Allen Iverson 2.50 6.00
4 Shaquille O'Neal 3.00 8.00
5 Paul Pierce 2.50 6.00
6 Dirk Nowitzki 2.50 6.00
7 Tim Duncan 2.50 6.00
8 Kevin Garnett 3.00 8.00
9 Dwight Howard 2.50 6.00
10 Yao Ming 3.00 8.00
11 Steve Nash 3.00 8.00
12 Chris Bosh 2.50 6.00
13 Michael Jordan 8.00 20.00

2007-08 Upper Deck MVP Predictor

RANDOM INSERTS IN PACKS
1 Allen Iverson 1.00 2.50
2 Amare Stoudemire .60 1.50
3 Andre Iguodala .60 1.50
4 Baron Davis .60 1.50
5 Ben Gordon .60 1.50
6 Carlos Boozer .60 1.50
7 Carmelo Anthony 1.00 2.50
8 Chauncey Billups .75 2.00
9 Chris Bosh .75 2.00
10 Chris Paul 1.00 2.50
11 Dirk Nowitzki 1.00 2.50
12 Dwight Howard .60 1.50
13 Dwyane Wade 1.25 3.00
14 Eddy Curry .50 1.25
15 Elton Brand .75 2.00
16 Emeka Okafor .60 1.50
17 Gilbert Arenas .60 1.50
18 Jason Kidd .75 2.00
19 Jermaine O'Neal .60 1.50
20 Joe Johnson .60 1.50
21 Kevin Garnett 1.25 3.00
22 Kobe Bryant 3.00 8.00
23 LeBron James 3.00 8.00
24 Michael Redd .60 1.50
25 Mike Bibby .75 2.00
26 Pau Gasol .75 2.00
27 Paul Pierce .75 2.00
28 Ray Allen .75 2.00
29 Tim Duncan 1.25 3.00
30 Tony Parker .75 2.00
31 Tracy McGrady .75 2.00
32 Vince Carter 1.00 2.50
33 Yao Ming 1.00 2.50
34 Zach Randolph .60 1.50
35 Wild Card .60 1.50

2007-08 Upper Deck NBA Heroes

COMMON DURANT 2.50 6.00
COMMON LEBRON 3.00 8.00
COMMON JORDAN 3.00 8.00
APPROXIMATELY TWO PER BOX
UNPRICED AUTO PRINT RUN 5 SETS

2007-08 Upper Deck Rookie Debut Signatures

NDOM INSERTS IN PACKS
AA Arron Afflalo 8.00 20.00
AB Aaron Brooks 6.00 15.00
AG Aaron Gray 5.00 12.00
AH Al Horford 10.00 25.00
AL Acie Law 5.00 12.00
AT Al Thornton 6.00 15.00
CB Corey Brewer 8.00 20.00
CL Carl Landry 5.00 12.00
CR Chris Richard 5.00 12.00
DB Derrick Byars 5.00 12.00
DC Daequan Cook 6.00 15.00
DM Dominic McGuire 5.00 12.00
DN Demetris Nichols 5.00 12.00
DS D.J. Strawberry 5.00 12.00
DU Jared Dudley 6.00 15.00
GD Glen Davis 6.00 15.00
GP Gabe Pruitt 5.00 12.00
HA Adam Haluska 5.00 12.00
JC Javaris Crittenton 5.00 12.00
JD Jermareo Davidson 5.00 12.00
JJ Jared Jordan 5.00 12.00
JM Josh McRoberts 6.00 15.00
JN Joakim Noah 8.00 20.00
JS Jason Smith 6.00 15.00
JW Julian Wright 5.00 12.00
KD Kevin Durant 300.00 600.00
MA Morris Almond 5.00 12.00
MC Mike Conley Jr. 10.00 25.00
MW Marcus Williams 5.00 12.00
NF Nick Fazekas 5.00 12.00
RS Rodney Stuckey 6.00 15.00
RT Reyshawn Terry 5.00 12.00
SH Spencer Hawes 6.00 15.00
SL Stephane Lasme 5.00 12.00
SW Sean Williams 5.00 12.00
TG Taurean Green 5.00 12.00
TU Alando Tucker 5.00 12.00
TY Thaddeus Young 8.00 20.00
WC Wilson Chandler 6.00 15.00

2007-08 Upper Deck ROY Predictor

NDOM INSERTS IN PACKS
1 Greg Oden 2.00 5.00
2 Kevin Durant 20.00 50.00
3 Al Horford 2.50 6.00
4 Mike Conley Jr. 2.50 6.00
5 Jeff Green 2.00 5.00
6 Derrick Byars 1.25 3.00
7 Corey Brewer 2.00 5.00
8 Brandan Wright 2.00 5.00
9 Joakim Noah 2.00 5.00
10 Spencer Hawes 1.50 4.00
11 Acie Law 1.25 3.00
12 Thaddeus Young 2.00 5.00
13 Julian Wright 1.25 3.00
14 Al Thornton 1.50 4.00
15 Rodney Stuckey 1.50 4.00
16 Nick Young 2.50 6.00
17 Sean Williams 1.25 3.00
18 Marco Belinelli 2.00 5.00
19 Javaris Crittenton 1.25 3.00
20 Jason Smith 1.50 4.00
21 Daequan Cook 1.50 4.00
22 Jared Dudley 1.50 4.00
23 Wilson Chandler 1.50 4.00
24 Morris Almond 1.25 3.00
25 Aaron Brooks 1.50 4.00
26 Arron Afflalo 2.00 5.00
27 Alando Tucker 1.25 3.00
28 Reyshawn Terry 1.25 3.00
29 Carl Landry 1.25 3.00
30 Gabe Pruitt 1.25 3.00
31 Marcus Williams 1.25 3.00
32 Nick Fazekas 1.25 3.00
33 Glen Davis 1.50 4.00
34 Jermareo Davidson 1.25 3.00
35 Josh McRoberts 1.50 4.00

2007-08 Upper Deck Santa Hat Rookies

*HAT RCs: .5X TO 1.25X BASE HI
*HAT SP RCs: .4X TO 1X BASE HI
RANDOM INSERTS IN RACK PACKS

2007-08 Upper Deck Star Signings

PROXIMATELY ONE PER BOX
UNPRICED GOLD PRINT RUN 5 TO 20 SETS
AB Andrea Bargnani 8.00 20.00
AI Andre Iguodala 4.00 10.00
AJ Antawn Jamison 4.00 10.00
AM Alonzo Mourning 25.00 60.00
BB Bruce Bowen 4.00 10.00
BG Ben Gordon 6.00 15.00
BM Brad Miller 4.00 10.00
BR Brandon Roy 6.00 15.00
BW Bill Walton 4.00 10.00
CD Chris Duhon 4.00 10.00
CP Chris Paul 20.00 50.00
CS Cedric Simmons 4.00 10.00
DG Daniel Gibson 4.00 10.00
DL David Lee 4.00 10.00
DM Damir Markota 4.00 10.00
DO Keyon Dooling 4.00 10.00
DS DeShawn Stevenson 4.00 10.00
DW Deron Williams 8.00 20.00
FE Raymond Felton 4.00 10.00
GA Jorge Garbajosa 4.00 10.00
GG George Gervin 8.00 20.00
IU Ime Udoka 4.00 10.00
JA James Augustine 4.00 10.00
JG Joey Graham 4.00 10.00
JJ Jarrett Jack 4.00 10.00
JW Julian Wright 6.00 15.00
KB Kobe Bryant 75.00 150.00
KD Kevin Durant 100.00 250.00
KK Kyle Korver 4.00 10.00
LA LaMarcus Aldridge 6.00 15.00
LB Larry Bird 50.00 100.00
LH Larry Hughes 4.00 10.00
LJ LeBron James 75.00 150.00
LL Donyell Marshall 4.00 10.00
MC Mardy Collins 4.00 10.00
MJ Michael Jordan 200.00 400.00
MW Marcus Williams 4.00 10.00
NO Steve Novak 4.00 10.00
PM Paul Millsap 4.00 10.00
PO Patrick O'Bryant 4.00 10.00
RF Randy Foye 4.00 10.00
RG Rudy Gay 4.00 10.00
RJ Richard Jefferson 4.00 10.00
RR Rajon Rondo 6.00 15.00
SB Shannon Brown 4.00 10.00
SJ Solomon Jones 4.00 10.00
SN Steve Nash 15.00 40.00
SW Shawne Williams 4.00 10.00
TA Tony Allen 4.00 10.00
TC Tyson Chandler 4.00 10.00
TF T.J. Ford 4.00 10.00
TM Tracy McGrady 15.00 40.00
TP Tayshaun Prince 4.00 10.00
TT Tyrus Thomas 8.00 20.00
VC Vince Carter 15.00 30.00
WS Wayne Simien 4.00 10.00

2007-08 Upper Deck UD Game Jersey

PROXIMATELY TWO PER BOX
*PATCHES: 1.25X TO 3X BASE HI
PATCHES RANDOM INSERTS IN PACKS
AB Andrew Bogut 2.00 5.00
AI Allen Iverson 3.00 8.00
AJ Al Jefferson 2.00 5.00
AK Andrei Kirilenko 2.00 5.00
AM Alonzo Mourning 4.00 10.00
AW Antoine Walker 2.00 5.00
BC Brian Cook 2.00 5.00
BG Ben Gordon 2.00 5.00
BH Brendan Haywood 2.00 5.00
BO Chris Bosh 2.50 6.00
BR Brandon Roy 2.50 6.00
BW Ben Wallace 2.00 5.00
BY Andrew Bynum 1.50 4.00
CA Carmelo Anthony 3.00 8.00
CB Caron Butler 2.00 5.00
CM Corey Maggette 2.00 5.00
CV Charlie Villanueva 1.50 4.00
DG Danny Granger 2.00 5.00
DH Devin Harris 1.50 4.00
DM Darko Milicic 2.00 5.00
DN Dirk Nowitzki 3.00 8.00
DR Dennis Rodman 5.00 12.00
EB Elton Brand 2.50 6.00
EO Emeka Okafor 2.00 5.00
FG Francisco Garcia 1.50 4.00
GA Gilbert Arenas 2.00 5.00
GH Grant Hill 3.00 8.00
GO Drew Gooden 2.00 5.00
GP Gary Payton 2.50 6.00
HE Luther Head 2.00 5.00
HO Dwight Howard 2.00 5.00
IG Andre Iguodala 2.00 5.00
JA Antawn Jamison 2.00 5.00
JC Josh Childress 2.00 5.00
JE Julius Erving 4.00 10.00
JH Josh Howard 2.00 5.00
JK Jason Kidd 2.50 6.00
JM Michael Jordan 20.00 50.00
JN Jameer Nelson 1.50 4.00
JO Jermaine O'Neal 2.00 5.00
JP Johan Petro 2.00 5.00
JR J.J. Redick 2.50 6.00
JS John Stockton 4.00 10.00
JU Juwan Howard 2.00 5.00
JW Jason Williams 2.00 5.00
KB Kobe Bryant 8.00 20.00
KG Kevin Garnett 4.00 10.00
KH Kirk Hinrich 2.00 5.00
KM Kenyon Martin 2.00 5.00
KT Kevin Garnett 4.00 10.00
KW Kwame Brown 2.00 5.00
LB Larry Bird 10.00 25.00
LD Luol Deng 2.00 5.00
LH Larry Hughes 2.00 5.00
LJ LeBron James 10.00 25.00
LK Linas Kleiza 2.00 5.00
LO Lamar Odom 2.00 5.00
MA Donyell Marshall 2.00 5.00
MB Mike Bibby 2.50 6.00
MD Mike Dunleavy 2.00 5.00
MG Manu Ginobili 2.50 6.00
MI Andre Miller 2.00 5.00
MJ Magic Johnson 8.00 20.00
MO Mehmet Okur 2.00 5.00
MR Michael Redd 2.00 5.00
MW Martell Webster 2.00 5.00
NH Nene 2.00 5.00
PG Pau Gasol 2.50 6.00
PP Paul Pierce 2.50 6.00
RA Ray Allen 2.50 6.00
RI Jason Richardson 2.50 6.00
RJ Richard Jefferson 2.00 5.00
RL Rashard Lewis 2.00 5.00
RO David Robinson 5.00 12.00
RP Robert Parish 2.50 6.00
RW Rasheed Wallace 2.50 6.00
SB Shannon Brown 1.50 4.00
SD Samuel Dalembert 2.00 5.00
SH Shawn Marion 2.00 5.00
SJ Josh Smith 2.00 5.00
SM Sean May 2.00 5.00
SN Steve Nash 3.00 8.00
SO Shaquille O'Neal 5.00 12.00
TD Tim Duncan 4.00 10.00
TM Tracy McGrady 2.50 6.00
TP Tony Parker 2.50 6.00
VC Vince Carter 3.00 8.00
WI Marvin Williams 2.00 5.00
YM Yao Ming 3.00 8.00
ZR Zach Randolph 2.00 5.00

2007-08 Upper Deck UD Top 30

MPLETE SET (30) 12.00 30.00
RANDOM INSERTS IN PACKS
AUTOS NOT PRICED DUE TO SCARCITY
UT1 Al Jefferson .60 1.50
UT2 Baron Davis .60 1.50
UT3 Ben Gordon .60 1.50
UT4 Brandon Roy .75 2.00
UT5 Carlos Boozer .60 1.50
UT6 Chris Paul 1.00 2.50
UT7 Corey Maggette .60 1.50
UT8 Deron Williams .60 1.50
UT9 Dwyane Wade 1.25 3.00
UT10 Eddy Curry .50 1.25
UT11 Emeka Okafor .60 1.50
UT12 Gerald Wallace .60 1.50
UT13 Grant Hill 1.00 2.50
UT14 Jason Richardson .75 2.00
UT15 Jason Terry .60 1.50
UT16 Joe Johnson .60 1.50
UT17 Josh Howard .60 1.50
UT18 Kirk Hinrich .60 1.50
UT19 LeBron James 3.00 8.00
UT20 Luol Deng .60 1.50
UT21 Mike Bibby .75 2.00
UT22 Rashard Lewis .60 1.50
UT23 Raymond Felton .75 2.00
UT24 Richard Hamilton .60 1.50
UT25 Richard Jefferson .60 1.50
UT26 Shaquille O'Neal 1.50 4.00
UT27 Shawn Marion .60 1.50
UT28 Stephon Marbury .60 1.50
UT29 Steve Nash 1.00 2.50
UT30 Tayshaun Prince .60 1.50

2008-09 Upper Deck

This set was released on September 9, 2008. The base set consists of 266 cards. Cards 1-224 feature veterans, and cards 225-266 are rookies. The Legends were inserted at one in two packs and the rookies at one in 4.5.

COMP.SET w/o SPs (200) 10.00 25.00
LEGEND ODDS 1:2
ROOKIE ODDS 1:4.5
1 Mike Bibby .25 .60
2 Al Horford .30 .75
3 Joe Johnson .25 .60
4 Josh Childress .25 .60
5 Josh Smith .25 .60
6 Marvin Williams .25 .60
7 Eddie House .20 .50
8 Glen Davis .20 .50
9 Sam Cassell .25 .60
10 Kevin Garnett .50 1.25
11 Rajon Rondo .30 .75
12 Ray Allen .30 .75
13 Paul Pierce .30 .75
14 Adam Morrison .20 .50
15 Emeka Okafor .25 .60
16 Gerald Wallace .25 .60
17 Jared Dudley .25 .60
18 Jason Richardson .30 .75
19 Nazr Mohammed .20 .50
20 Raymond Felton .25 .60
21 Andres Nocioni .20 .50
22 Ben Gordon .25 .60
23 Larry Hughes .25 .60
24 Joakim Noah .25 .60
25 Kirk Hinrich .25 .60
26 Luol Deng .25 .60
27 Tyrus Thomas .20 .50
28 Aleksandar Pavlovic .20 .50
29 Anderson Varejao .20 .50
30 Daniel Gibson .25 .60
31 Wally Szczerbiak .25 .60
32 Ben Wallace .25 .60
33 LeBron James 1.25 3.00
34 Zydrunas Ilgauskas .25 .60
35 Jason Kidd .30 .75
36 Dirk Nowitzki .40 1.00
37 Jason Terry .25 .60
38 Jerry Stackhouse .25 .60
39 Jose Barea .40 1.00
40 Josh Howard .25 .60
41 Allen Iverson .40 1.00
42 Carmelo Anthony .40 1.00
43 J.R. Smith .25 .60
44 Kenyon Martin .25 .60
45 Linas Kleiza .20 .50
46 Marcus Camby .20 .50
47 Antonio McDyess .25 .60
48 Chauncey Billups .30 .75
49 Jason Maxiell .20 .50
50 Rasheed Wallace .30 .75
51 Richard Hamilton .25 .60
52 Rodney Stuckey .25 .60
53 Tayshaun Prince .25 .60
54 Al Harrington .25 .60
55 Baron Davis .25 .60
56 Kelenna Azubuike .20 .50
57 Matt Barnes .20 .50
58 Monta Ellis .25 .60
59 Stephen Jackson .25 .60
60 Luis Scola .25 .60
61 Luther Head .20 .50
62 Rafer Alston .20 .50
63 Shane Battier .25 .60
64 Tracy McGrady .30 .75
65 Yao Ming .40 1.00
66 Andre Owens .20 .50
67 Danny Granger .25 .60
68 Jamaal Tinsley .20 .50
69 Jermaine O'Neal .25 .60
70 Kareem Rush .20 .50
71 Mike Dunleavy .25 .60
72 Troy Murphy .20 .50
73 Al Thornton .25 .60
74 Chris Kaman .25 .60
75 Corey Maggette .25 .60
76 Cuttino Mobley .20 .50
77 Elton Brand .30 .75
78 Tim Thomas .20 .50
79 Andrew Bynum .20 .50
80 Derek Fisher .25 .60
81 Jordan Farmar .20 .50
82 Kobe Bryant 1.25 3.00
83 Pau Gasol .30 .75
84 Lamar Odom .25 .60
85 Luke Walton .20 .50
86 Darko Milicic .20 .50
87 Javaris Crittenton .20 .50
88 Kyle Lowry .30 .75
89 Mike Conley Jr. .25 .60
90 Mike Miller .25 .60
91 Kwame Brown .20 .50
92 Rudy Gay .30 .75
93 Daequan Cook .20 .50
94 Dorell Wright .20 .50
95 Dwyane Wade .50 1.25
96 Jason Williams .25 .60
97 Ricky Davis .25 .60
98 Shawn Marion .25 .60
99 Udonis Haslem .20 .50
100 Andrew Bogut .25 .60
101 Charlie Villanueva .20 .50
102 Desmond Mason .20 .50
103 Michael Redd .25 .60
104 Mo Williams .25 .60
105 Yi Jianlian .30 .75
106 Al Jefferson .25 .60
107 Corey Brewer .25 .60
108 Craig Smith .20 .50
109 Randy Foye .30 .75
110 Rashad McCants .20 .50
111 Ryan Gomes .20 .50
112 Sebastian Telfair .20 .50
113 Bostjan Nachbar .20 .50
114 Devin Harris .20 .50
115 Josh Boone .20 .50
116 Nenad Krstic .20 .50
117 Richard Jefferson .25 .60
118 Sean Williams .25 .60
119 Vince Carter .40 1.00
120 David Lee .20 .50
121 Eddy Curry .20 .50
122 Jamal Crawford .30 .75
123 Nate Robinson .20 .50
124 Quentin Richardson .25 .60
125 Stephon Marbury .25 .60
126 Zach Randolph .25 .60
127 Chris Paul .40 1.00
128 David West .25 .60
129 Julian Wright .25 .60
130 Morris Peterson .20 .50
131 Peja Stojakovic .30 .75
132 Tyson Chandler .25 .60
133 Carlos Arroyo .20 .50
134 Dwight Howard .25 .60
135 Hedo Turkoglu .25 .60
136 J.J. Redick .30 .75
137 Jameer Nelson .20 .50
138 Maurice Evans .20 .50
139 Rashard Lewis .25 .60
140 Andre Iquodala .25 .60
141 Andre Miller .25 .60
142 Jason Smith .20 .50
143 Louis Williams .25 .60
144 Samuel Dalembert .20 .50
145 Thaddeus Young .25 .60
146 Willie Green .20 .50
147 Amare Stoudemire .25 .60
148 Boris Diaw .25 .60
149 Grant Hill .40 1.00
150 Leandro Barbosa .25 .60
151 Raja Bell .25 .60
152 Shaquille O'Neal .60 1.50
153 Steve Nash .30 .75
154 Brandon Roy .30 .75
155 Channing Frye .25 .60
156 Greg Oden .25 .60
157 LaMarcus Aldridge .30 .75
158 Martell Webster .25 .60
159 Steve Blake .20 .50
160 Beno Udrih .20 .50
161 Brad Miller .25 .60
162 Francisco Garcia .20 .50
163 John Salmons .25 .60
164 Kevin Martin .25 .60
165 Mikki Moore .20 .50
166 Ron Artest .30 .75
167 Brent Barry .20 .50
168 Bruce Bowen .20 .50
169 Manu Ginobili .30 .75
170 Michael Finley .30 .75
171 Robert Horry .25 .60
172 Tim Duncan .50 1.25
173 Tony Parker .30 .75
174 Chris Wilcox .20 .50
175 Damien Wilkins .20 .50
176 Jeff Green .25 .60
177 Kevin Durant .75 2.00
178 Nick Collison .25 .60
179 Earl Watson .20 .50
180 Andrea Bargnani .25 .60
181 Anthony Parker .20 .50
182 Carlos Delfino .20 .50
183 Chris Bosh .30 .75
184 Jamario Moon .20 .50
185 Jose Calderon .20 .50
186 T.J. Ford .20 .50
187 Andrei Kirilenko .25 .60
188 Carlos Boozer .25 .60
189 Deron Williams .25 .60
190 Kyle Korver .25 .60
191 Mehmet Okur .20 .50
192 Paul Millsap .25 .60
193 Ronnie Brewer .25 .60
194 Antawn Jamison .25 .60
195 Antonio Daniels .20 .50
196 Brendan Haywood .20 .50
197 Caron Butler .25 .60
198 DeShawn Stevenson .20 .50
199 Gilbert Arenas .25 .60
200 Nick Young .25 .60
201 Spud Webb .40 1.00
202 Bob Cousy .75 2.00
203 Kevin McHale .60 1.50
204 Larry Bird 1.25 3.00
205 Dennis Rodman 1.00 2.50
206 Michael Jordan 4.00 10.00
207 Isiah Thomas .50 1.25
208 Joe Dumars .50 1.25
209 Nate Thurmond .40 1.00
210 Hakeem Olajuwon .60 1.50
211 Calvin Murphy .40 1.00
212 Kareem Abdul-Jabbar .75 2.00
213 Magic Johnson 1.25 3.00
214 Oscar Robertson .50 1.25
215 Bill Bradley .60 1.50
216 Earl Monroe .50 1.25
217 Willis Reed .50 1.25
218 Julius Erving .75 2.00
219 Clyde Drexler .60 1.50
220 Bill Walton .50 1.25
221 Maurice Lucas .50 1.25
222 David Robinson .75 2.00
223 John Stockton .75 2.00
224 Karl Malone .60 1.50
225 D.J. Augustin RC .75 2.00
226 Brook Lopez RC 1.25 3.00
227 Jerryd Bayless RC .75 2.00
228 Jason Thompson RC .60 1.50
229 Brandon Rush RC .75 2.00
230 Anthony Randolph RC .60 1.50
231 Robin Lopez RC 1.00 2.50
232 Marreese Speights RC .75 2.00
233 Roy Hibbert RC 1.00 2.50
234 Courtney Lee RC .75 2.00
235 J.J. Hickson RC .75 2.00
236 Ryan Anderson RC .75 2.00
237 Kosta Koufos RC .75 2.00
238 James Gist RC .60 1.50
239 Darrell Arthur RC .75 2.00
240 Donte Greene RC .60 1.50
241 D.J. White RC .75 2.00
242 J.R. Giddens RC .60 1.50
243 Deron Washington RC .60 1.50
244 Joey Dorsey RC .60 1.50
245 Mario Chalmers RC 1.00 2.50
246 DeAndre Jordan RC 1.25 3.00
247 Luc Richard Mbah A Moute RC .75 2.00
248 Kyle Weaver RC .60 1.50
249 Sonny Weems RC .60 1.50
250 Chris Douglas-Roberts RC .60 1.50
251 Sean Singletary RC .60 1.50
252 Patrick Ewing Jr. RC .60 1.50
253 Shan Foster RC .60 1.50
254 Bill Walker RC .60 1.50
255 Malik Hairston RC .60 1.50
256 Richard Hendrix RC .60 1.50
257 DeVon Hardin RC .60 1.50
258 Darnell Jackson RC .60 1.50
259 Derrick Rose RC 4.00 10.00
260 Michael Beasley RC 1.00 2.50
261 O.J. Mayo RC 1.00 2.50
262 Russell Westbrook RC 8.00 20.00
263 Kevin Love RC 3.00 8.00
264 Danilo Gallinari RC 1.50 4.00
265 Eric Gordon RC 1.50 4.00
266 Joe Alexander RC .60 1.50

2008-09 Upper Deck Electric Court Gold

*GOLD: .6X TO 1.5X BASE HI
GOLD STATED ODDS 1:5
206 Michael Jordan 10.00 25.00
262 Russell Westbrook 25.00 60.00

2008-09 Upper Deck All Star Class

MPLETE SET (30) 30.00 60.00
RANDOM INSERTS IN PACKS
AUTOS UNPRICED DUE TO SCARCITY
ASAI Allen Iverson 1.25 3.00
ASBL Bill Laimbeer .75 2.00
ASBO Chris Bosh 1.00 2.50
ASCB Chauncey Billups 1.00 2.50
ASDN Dirk Nowitzki 1.25 3.00
ASDR David Robinson 1.50 4.00
ASDW Dominique Wilkins 1.25 3.00
ASGG George Gervin 1.25 3.00
ASJE Julius Erving 1.50 4.00
ASJK Jason Kidd 1.00 2.50
ASJO Magic Johnson 2.50 6.00
ASKA Kareem Abdul-Jabbar 1.50 4.00
ASKB Kobe Bryant 4.00 10.00
ASKG Kevin Garnett 1.50 4.00
ASKM Karl Malone 1.25 3.00
ASLJ LeBron James 4.00 10.00
ASMJ Michael Jordan 8.00 20.00
ASNA Nate Archibald .75 2.00
ASRA Ray Allen 1.00 2.50
ASRB Rick Barry .75 2.00
ASSM Shawn Marion .75 2.00
ASSN Steve Nash 1.00 2.50
ASSO Shaquille O'Neal 2.00 5.00
ASTD Tim Duncan 1.50 4.00
ASTM Tracy McGrady 1.00 2.50
ASTP Tony Parker 1.00 2.50
ASVC Vince Carter 1.25 3.00
ASWA Dwyane Wade 1.50 4.00
ASWF Walt Frazier 1.00 2.50
ASYM Yao Ming 1.25 3.00

2008-09 Upper Deck Bulls Dynasty

COMPLETE SET (30) 25.00 50.00
STATED ODDS 1:8
CHI1 Dennis Rodman 1.50 4.00
CHI2 Horace Grant .75 2.00
CHI3 Toni Kukoc .75 2.00
CHI4 Horace Grant .75 2.00
CHI5 Toni Kukoc .75 2.00
CHI6 Steve Kerr .75 2.00
CHI7 John Paxson .60 1.50
CHI8 Michael Jordan 6.00 15.00
CHI9 Michael Jordan 6.00 15.00
CHI10 Michael Jordan 6.00 15.00
CHI11 Michael Jordan 6.00 15.00
CHI12 Michael Jordan 6.00 15.00
CHI13 Michael Jordan 6.00 15.00
CHI14 Michael Jordan 6.00 15.00
CHI15 Michael Jordan 6.00 15.00
CHI16 Dennis Rodman 1.50 4.00
CHI17 Bill Wennington .75 2.00
CHI18 Bill Cartwright .60 1.50
CHI19 Bill Cartwright .60 1.50
CHI20 Will Perdue .50 1.25
CHI21 Will Perdue .50 1.25
CHI22 Dennis Rodman 1.50 4.00
CHI23 B.J. Armstrong .75 2.00
CHI24 Ron Harper .75 2.00
CHI25 Ron Harper .75 2.00
CHI26 Scottie Pippen 1.25 3.00
CHI27 B.J. Armstrong .75 2.00
CHI28 John Paxson .60 1.50
CHI29 Steve Kerr .75 2.00
CHI30 Scottie Pippen 1.25 3.00

2008-09 Upper Deck Celtics Dynasty

COMPLETE SET (30) 10.00 25.00
STATED ODDS 1:8
BOS1 John Havlicek .75 2.00
BOS2 John Havlicek .75 2.00
BOS3 John Havlicek .75 2.00
BOS4 Sam Jones 1.00 2.50
BOS5 Sam Jones 1.00 2.50
BOS6 Sam Jones 1.00 2.50
BOS7 Bob Cousy 1.25 3.00
BOS8 Don Nelson .75 2.00
BOS9 Don Nelson .75 2.00
BOS10 Tom Sanders .75 2.00
BOS11 Tom Sanders .75 2.00
BOS12 Tom Sanders .75 2.00
BOS13 Gene Conley .75 2.00
BOS14 Bill Russell 1.25 3.00
BOS15 Bill Russell 1.25 3.00
BOS16 Tom Heinsohn .75 2.00
BOS17 Tom Heinsohn .75 2.00
BOS18 Tom Heinsohn .75 2.00
BOS19 Bill Sharman .75 2.00
BOS20 Bill Sharman .75 2.00
BOS21 Bill Sharman .75 2.00
BOS22 Em Bryant .75 2.00
BOS23 Bailey Howell .75 2.00
BOS24 K.C. Jones .75 2.00
BOS25 Clyde Lovellette .75 2.00
BOS26 Bob Cousy 1.25 3.00
BOS27 Wayne Embry .50 1.25
BOS28 Jim Loscutoff .75 2.00
BOS29 Frank Ramsey .75 2.00
BOS30 K.C. Jones .75 2.00

2008-09 Upper Deck Emulation Memorabilia Dual

STATED ODDS 1:32
*PATCHES: .4X TO 1.2X BASE HI
PATCH STATED ODDS 1:600
EAB R.Allen/L.Bird 10.00 25.00
EBW K.Bryant/D.Wilkins 15.00 40.00
EDR T.Duncan/D.Robinson 6.00 15.00
EEJ J.Erving/L.James 15.00 40.00
EGB K.Garnett/A.Bynum 6.00 15.00
EGM G.Gervin/T.McGrady 5.00 12.00
EHO D.Howard/S.O'Neal 8.00 20.00
EIP C.Paul/A.Iverson 5.00 12.00
EKJ J.Kidd/M.Johnson 10.00 25.00
EWR B.Wallace/D.Rodman 8.00 20.00

2008-09 Upper Deck Game Jerseys

STATED ODDS 1:7
*PATCHES: 1.25X TO 3X BASE HI
PATCH STATED ODDS 1:250
GAAB Andrea Bargnani 2.00 5.00
GAAI Allen Iverson 3.00 8.00
GAAJ Al Jefferson 2.00 5.00
GAAK Andrei Kirilenko 2.00 5.00
GAAS Amare Stoudemire 2.00 5.00
GABG Ben Gordon 2.00 5.00
GABI Chauncey Billups 2.50 6.00
GABO Chris Bosh 2.50 6.00
GABU Caron Butler 2.00 5.00
GABW Ben Wallace 2.00 5.00
GACA Carmelo Anthony 3.00 8.00
GACB Carlos Boozer 2.00 5.00
GACP Chris Paul 3.00 8.00
GADG Danny Granger 2.00 5.00
GADH Dwight Howard 2.00 5.00
GADN Dirk Nowitzki 3.00 8.00
GADW Deron Williams 2.00 5.00
GAEB Elton Brand 2.50 6.00
GAEO Emeka Okafor 2.00 5.00
GAIG Andre Iguodala 2.00 5.00
GAJA Antawn Jamison 2.00 5.00
GAJH Josh Howard 2.00 5.00
GAJJ Joe Johnson 2.00 5.00
GAJK Jason Kidd 2.50 6.00
GAJO Jermaine O'Neal 2.00 5.00
GAJR Jason Richardson 2.50 6.00
GAJS Josh Smith 2.00 5.00
GAKB Kobe Bryant 6.00 15.00
GAKG Kevin Garnett 4.00 10.00
GAKH Kirk Hinrich 2.00 5.00
GALJ LeBron James 6.00 15.00
GAMB Mike Bibby 2.00 5.00
GAMG Manu Ginobili 2.50 6.00
GAMR Michael Redd 2.00 5.00
GAMW Marvin Williams 2.00 5.00
GAPA Tony Parker 2.50 6.00
GAPG Pau Gasol 2.50 6.00
GAPP Paul Pierce 2.50 6.00
GARH Richard Hamilton 2.00 5.00
GARJ Richard Jefferson 2.00 5.00
GARL Rashard Lewis 2.00 5.00
GARW Rasheed Wallace 2.50 6.00
GASM Shawn Marion 2.00 5.00
GASO Shaquille O'Neal 5.00 12.00
GATD Tim Duncan 4.00 10.00
GATM Tracy McGrady 2.50 6.00
GATP Tayshaun Prince 2.00 5.00
GAVC Vince Carter 3.00 8.00
GAYM Yao Ming 3.00 8.00
GAZR Zach Randolph 2.00 5.00

2008-09 Upper Deck Kobe Bryant Heroes

MPLETE SET (10) 15.00 40.00
COMMON CARD (KB1-KB10) 2.50 6.00
STATED ODDS 1:25
UNPRICED AUTO PRINT RUN 5 SER.#'d SETS

2008-09 Upper Deck Lakers Dynasty

MPLETE SET (30) 15.00 30.00
STATED ODDS 1:8
LAL1 Kobe Bryant 3.00 8.00
LAL2 Kobe Bryant 3.00 8.00
LAL3 Kobe Bryant 3.00 8.00
LAL4 Derek Fisher .60 1.50
LAL5 Derek Fisher .60 1.50
LAL6 Horace Grant .75 2.00
LAL7 Horace Grant .75 2.00
LAL8 A.C. Green .75 2.00
LAL9 A.C. Green .75 2.00
LAL10 Byron Scott .60 1.50
LAL11 James Worthy .75 2.00
LAL12 James Worthy .75 2.00
LAL13 Magic Johnson 2.00 5.00
LAL14 Magic Johnson 2.00 5.00
LAL15 Magic Johnson 2.00 5.00
LAL16 Kareem Abdul-Jabbar 1.25 3.00
LAL17 Kareem Abdul-Jabbar 1.25 3.00
LAL18 Kareem Abdul-Jabbar 1.25 3.00
LAL19 Michael Cooper .60 1.50
LAL20 Michael Cooper .60 1.50
LAL21 Jamaal Wilkes .75 2.00
LAL22 Jamaal Wilkes .75 2.00
LAL23 Norm Nixon .50 1.25
LAL24 Slater Martin .75 2.00
LAL25 Mitch Richmond .75 2.00
LAL26 Ron Harper .75 2.00
LAL27 George Mikan 1.50 4.00
LAL28 Clyde Lovellette .75 2.00
LAL29 Mitch Kupchak .75 2.00
LAL30 Kurt Rambis .50 1.25

2008-09 Upper Deck Same Day Signatures

RANDOM INSERTS IN PACKS
RPSBR Brandon Rush 8.00 20.00
RPSCD Chris Douglas-Roberts 6.00 15.00
RPSCL Courtney Lee 8.00 20.00
RPSDJ DeAndre Jordan 10.00 25.00
RPSDW D.J. White 8.00 20.00
RPSEG Eric Gordon 15.00 40.00
RPSGH George Hill 10.00 25.00
RPSGR Donte Greene 6.00 15.00
RPSHE Patrick Ewing Jr. 6.00 15.00
RPSJB Jerryd Bayless 8.00 20.00
RPSJG J.R. Giddens 6.00 15.00
RPSJH J.J. Hickson 8.00 20.00
RPSJT Jason Thompson 6.00 15.00
RPSKK Kosta Koufos 8.00 20.00
RPSKL Kevin Love 30.00 80.00
RPSKW Kyle Weaver 6.00 15.00
RPSMC Mario Chalmers 10.00 25.00
RPSMS Marreese Speights 8.00 20.00
RPSOM O.J. Mayo 10.00 25.00
RPSRA Ryan Anderson 8.00 20.00
RPSRH Roy Hibbert 10.00 25.00
RPSSW Sonny Weems 6.00 15.00
RPSWS Walter Sharpe 6.00 15.00

2008-09 Upper Deck Star Signings

ATED ODDS 1:28
GOLD: .6X TO 1.5X BASE HI
GOLD PRINT RUN 25 SER.#'d SETS
SSAH Al Harrington 3.00 8.00
SSAI Andre Iguodala 5.00 12.00
SSAJ Antawn Jamison 3.00 8.00
SSBB Bruce Bowen 3.00 8.00
SSBD Baron Davis 4.00 10.00
SSBG Ben Gordon 5.00 12.00
SSBK Coby Karl 3.00 8.00
SSBM Brad Miller 3.00 8.00
SSBR Brandon Roy 10.00 25.00
SSCA Carmelo Anthony 20.00 40.00
SSCB Corey Brewer 3.00 8.00
SSCM Corey Maggette 3.00 8.00
SSCP Chris Paul 30.00 60.00
SSCS Cedric Simmons 3.00 8.00
SSDA Danny Granger 5.00 12.00
SSDC Daequan Cook 3.00 8.00
SSDG Daniel Gibson 3.00 8.00
SSDM Donyell Marshall 3.00 8.00
SSDO Keyon Dooling 3.00 8.00
SSDS DeShawn Stevenson 3.00 8.00
SSDW Deron Williams 10.00 25.00
SSGD Glen Davis 5.00 12.00
SSGR Jeff Green 4.00 10.00
SSHO Al Horford 5.00 12.00
SSID Ike Diogu 3.00 8.00
SSJB Josh Boone 3.00 8.00
SSJG Joey Graham 3.00 8.00
SSJK Jason Kidd 6.00 15.00
SSJM Jamario Moon 3.00 8.00
SSJO Joakim Noah 10.00 25.00
SSKA Kelenna Azubuike 4.00 10.00
SSKD Kevin Durant 75.00 150.00
SSLA LaMarcus Aldridge 20.00 50.00
SSLH Larry Hughes 4.00 10.00
SSLJ LeBron James 125.00 225.00
SSLP Leon Powe 3.00 8.00
SSLS Luis Scola 3.00 8.00
SSMB Mike Bibby 3.00 8.00
SSMC Mike Conley Jr. 4.00 10.00
SSMW Mo Williams 3.00 8.00
SSNO Steve Novak 3.00 8.00
SSOP Oleksiy Pecherov 3.00 8.00
SSRB Renaldo Balkman 3.00 8.00
SSRF Randy Foye 3.00 8.00
SSRG Rudy Gay 6.00 15.00
SSRJ Richard Jefferson 3.00 8.00
SSSM Craig Smith 3.00 8.00
SSTC Tyson Chandler 3.00 8.00
SSTF T.J. Ford 3.00 8.00
SSTM Tracy McGrady 20.00 40.00
SSTP Tayshaun Prince 3.00 8.00
SSTT Tyrus Thomas 3.00 8.00
SSVC Vince Carter 12.00 30.00
SSWI Marvin Williams 3.00 8.00

2008-09 Upper Deck Starquest

COMPLETE SET (30) 20.00 50.00
APPROXIMATE ODDS 1:8
*BLACK: 1.5X TO 4X BASE HI
BLACK STATED ODDS 1:16
*BLUE: 1X TO 2.5X BASE HI
BLUE: RANDOM INSERTS IN PACKS
*COPPER: .6X TO 1.5X BASE HI
COPPER: RANDOM INSERTS IN PACKS
*CYAN: 1X TO 2.5X BASE HI
CYAN: RANDOM INSERTS IN PACKS
*GOLD: 1X TO 2.5X BASE HI
GOLD: RANDOM INSERTS IN PACKS
SQ1 Carmelo Anthony .75 2.00
SQ2 Chauncey Billups .60 1.50
SQ3 Larry Bird 1.50 4.00
SQ4 Chris Bosh .60 1.50
SQ5 Kobe Bryant 2.50 6.00
SQ6 Vince Carter .75 2.00
SQ7 Baron Davis .50 1.25
SQ8 Tim Duncan 1.00 2.50
SQ9 Kevin Durant 1.50 4.00
SQ10 Julius Erving 1.00 2.50
SQ11 Walt Frazier .60 1.50
SQ12 Kevin Garnett 1.00 2.50
SQ13 Rudy Gay .60 1.50
SQ14 Artis Gilmore .50 1.25
SQ15 Dwight Howard .50 1.25
SQ16 Allen Iverson .75 2.00
SQ17 LeBron James 2.50 6.00
SQ18 Al Jefferson .50 1.25
SQ19 Magic Johnson 1.50 4.00
SQ20 Michael Jordan 5.00 12.00
SQ21 Shawn Marion .50 1.25
SQ22 Tracy McGrady .60 1.50
SQ23 Yao Ming .75 2.00
SQ24 Dirk Nowitzki .75 2.00
SQ25 Shaquille O'Neal 1.25 3.00
SQ26 Greg Oden .50 1.25
SQ27 Chris Paul .75 2.00
SQ28 Brandon Roy .60 1.50
SQ29 Dwyane Wade 1.00 2.50
SQ30 Deron Williams .50 1.25

2008-09 Upper Deck Team MVPs

COMPLETE SET (30) 10.00 25.00
THREE PER RACK PACK
MVP1 Josh Smith .50 1.25
MVP2 Kevin Garnett 1.00 2.50
MVP3 Gerald Wallace .50 1.25
MVP4 Luol Deng .50 1.25
MVP5 LeBron James 2.50 6.00
MVP6 Dirk Nowitzki .75 2.00
MVP7 Carmelo Anthony .75 2.00
MVP8 Chauncey Billups .60 1.50
MVP9 Baron Davis .50 1.25
MVP10 Yao Ming .75 2.00
MVP11 Jermaine O'Neal .50 1.25
MVP12 Chris Kaman .60 1.50
MVP13 Kobe Bryant 2.50 6.00
MVP14 Rudy Gay .60 1.50
MVP15 Dwyane Wade 1.00 2.50
MVP16 Michael Redd .50 1.25
MVP17 Al Jefferson .50 1.25
MVP18 Jason Kidd .60 1.50
MVP19 Chris Paul .75 2.00
MVP20 Zach Randolph .50 1.25
MVP21 Dwight Howard .50 1.25
MVP22 Andre Iguodala .50 1.25
MVP23 Steve Nash .60 1.50
MVP24 Brandon Roy .60 1.50
MVP25 Kevin Martin .50 1.25
MVP26 Tony Parker .60 1.50
MVP27 Kevin Durant 1.50 4.00
MVP28 Chris Bosh .60 1.50
MVP29 Deron Williams .50 1.25
MVP30 Caron Butler .50 1.25

2008-09 Upper Deck True Talents

COMPLETE SET (30) 8.00 20.00
TWO PER RETAIL VALUE PACK
TT1 Thaddeus Young .50 1.25
TT2 Julian Wright .50 1.25
TT3 Sean Williams .50 1.25
TT4 David West .50 1.25
TT5 Luke Walton .40 1.00
TT6 Al Thornton .50 1.25
TT7 Rodney Stuckey .50 1.25
TT8 J.R. Smith .50 1.25
TT9 Luis Scola .50 1.25
TT10 Greg Oden .50 1.25
TT11 Joakim Noah .50 1.25
TT12 Mike Conley Jr. .50 1.25
TT13 Jamario Moon .40 1.00
TT14 Jason Maxiell .40 1.00
TT15 Chris Kaman .50 1.25
TT16 Yi Jianlian .60 1.50
TT17 Al Horford .60 1.50
TT18 Jeff Green .50 1.25
TT19 Daniel Gibson .50 1.25
TT20 Rudy Gay .60 1.50
TT21 Francisco Garcia .40 1.00
TT22 Jordan Farmar .40 1.00
TT23 Monta Ellis .50 1.25
TT24 Kevin Durant 1.50 4.00
TT25 Luol Deng .50 1.25
TT26 Daequan Cook .40 1.00
TT27 Andrew Bynum .40 1.00
TT28 Ronnie Brewer .50 1.25
TT29 Corey Brewer .50 1.25
TT30 Jose Barea .75 2.00

2008-09 Upper Deck Ultimates

COMPLETE SET (30) 25.00 50.00
RANDOM INSERTS IN RETAIL PACKS
UNPRICED AUTOS RANDOM INSERTS IN PACKS
U1 Danny Ainge 1.00 2.50
U2 Dave Bing 1.00 2.50
U3 Larry Bird 2.50 6.00
U4 Muggsy Bogues .75 2.00
U5 Manute Bol 1.00 2.50
U6 Bill Bradley 1.25 3.00
U7 Wilt Chamberlain 2.00 5.00
U8 Vlade Divac 1.00 2.50
U9 Clyde Drexler 1.25 3.00
U10 Joe Dumars 1.00 2.50
U11 Julius Erving 1.50 4.00
U12 Patrick Ewing 1.25 3.00
U13 Kevin Johnson 1.00 2.50
U14 Larry Johnson 1.00 2.50
U15 Magic Johnson 2.50 6.00
U16 Michael Jordan 8.00 20.00
U17 Karl Malone 1.25 3.00
U18 Pete Maravich 1.50 4.00
U19 Gheorghe Muresan 1.00 2.50
U20 Hakeem Olajuwon 1.25 3.00
U21 Scottie Pippen 1.50 4.00
U22 Oscar Robertson 1.00 2.50
U23 David Robinson 1.50 4.00
U24 Bill Russell 1.50 4.00
U25 John Salley .60 1.50
U26 Kenny Smith .75 2.00
U27 John Stockton 1.50 4.00
U28 Isiah Thomas 1.00 2.50
U29 Jerry West 1.25 3.00
U30 Dominique Wilkins 1.25 3.00

2009-10 Upper Deck

COMPLETE SET (295) 40.00 100.00
COMP.SET w/o RCs (200) 15.00 30.00
1 Josh Smith .25 .60
2 Al Horford .30 .75
3 Mike Bibby .25 .60
4 Joe Johnson .25 .60
5 Marvin Williams .25 .60
6 Maurice Evans .20 .50
7 Kevin Garnett .50 1.25
8 Paul Pierce .30 .75
9 Ray Allen .30 .75
10 Rajon Rondo .30 .75
11 Kendrick Perkins .20 .50
12 Bill Walker .20 .50
13 Leon Powe .20 .50
14 Raymond Felton .25 .60
15 Raja Bell .25 .60
16 D.J. Augustin .20 .50
17 Gerald Wallace .25 .60
18 Boris Diaw .25 .60
19 Emeka Okafor .25 .60
20 Vladimir Radmanovic .20 .50
21 Derrick Rose .50 1.25
22 Luol Deng .25 .60
23 Michael Jordan 2.50 6.00
24 John Salmons .25 .60
25 Joakim Noah .25 .60
26 Tyrus Thomas .20 .50
27 Ben Gordon .25 .60
28 LeBron James 1.25 3.00
29 Mo Williams .25 .60
30 Ben Wallace .25 .60
31 Delonte West .20 .50
32 Zydrunas Ilgauskas .25 .60
33 Daniel Gibson .25 .60
34 Wally Szczerbiak .25 .60
35 Josh Howard .25 .60
36 Dirk Nowitzki .40 1.00
37 Jason Kidd .30 .75
38 Antoine Wright .20 .50
39 Erick Dampier .20 .50
40 Jason Terry .25 .60
41 Chauncey Billups .30 .75
42 Carmelo Anthony .40 1.00
43 Kenyon Martin .25 .60
44 Dahntay Jones .20 .50
45 Nene .25 .60
46 J.R. Smith .25 .60
47 Allen Iverson .40 1.00
48 Richard Hamilton .25 .60
49 Tayshaun Prince .25 .60
50 Rodney Stuckey .20 .50
51 Amir Johnson .20 .50
52 Rasheed Wallace .30 .75
53 Monta Ellis .25 .60
54 Stephen Jackson .25 .60
55 Jamal Crawford .30 .75
56 Kelenna Azubuike .20 .50
57 Andris Biedrins .20 .50
58 Anthony Morrow .20 .50
59 Corey Maggette .25 .60
60 Luis Scola .25 .60
61 Tracy McGrady .30 .75
62 Yao Ming .40 1.00
63 Ron Artest .30 .75
64 Aaron Brooks .20 .50
65 Shane Battier .30 .75
66 Von Wafer .20 .50
67 T.J. Ford .20 .50
68 Danny Granger .25 .60
69 Mike Dunleavy .20 .50
70 Troy Murphy .20 .50
71 Jeff Foster .20 .50
72 Jarrett Jack .25 .60
73 Eric Gordon .25 .60
74 Baron Davis .25 .60
75 Al Thornton .25 .60
76 Zach Randolph .25 .60
77 Chris Kaman .25 .60
78 Mardy Collins .20 .50
79 Kobe Bryant 1.25 3.00
80 Pau Gasol .30 .75
81 Lamar Odom .25 .60
82 Derek Fisher .25 .60
83 Adam Morrison .20 .50
84 Andrew Bynum .20 .50
85 Sasha Vujacic .20 .50
86 Trevor Ariza .20 .50
87 O.J. Mayo .20 .50
88 Marc Gasol .30 .75
89 Rudy Gay .30 .75
90 Darrell Arthur .25 .60
91 Marko Jaric .20 .50
92 Mike Conley Jr. .25 .60
93 Michael Beasley .20 .50
94 Mario Chalmers .25 .60
95 Dwyane Wade .50 1.25
96 Jermaine O'Neal .25 .60
97 Udonis Haslem .20 .50
98 Chris Quinn .20 .50
99 Daequan Cook .20 .50
100 Luke Ridnour .25 .60
101 Michael Redd .25 .60
102 Richard Jefferson .25 .60
103 Charlie Villanueva .20 .50
104 Andrew Bogut .25 .60
105 Ramon Sessions .25 .60
106 Joe Alexander .20 .50
107 Kevin Love .30 .75
108 Sebastian Telfair .20 .50
109 Al Jefferson .25 .60
110 Randy Foye .20 .50
111 Ryan Gomes .20 .50
112 Craig Smith .20 .50
113 Mike Miller .25 .60
114 Devin Harris .20 .50
115 Vince Carter .40 1.00
116 Yi Jianlian .25 .60
117 Bobby Simmons .20 .50
118 Brook Lopez .25 .60
119 Chris Douglas-Roberts .20 .50
120 Eduardo Najera .20 .50
121 Chris Paul .40 1.00
122 Peja Stojakovic .30 .75
123 David West .25 .60
124 Tyson Chandler .25 .60
125 Rasual Butler .20 .50
126 James Posey .20 .50
127 Al Harrington .25 .60
128 Chris Duhon .20 .50
129 Quentin Richardson .25 .60
130 David Lee .20 .50
131 Jared Jeffries .20 .50
132 Wilson Chandler .25 .60
133 Danilo Gallinari .25 .60

134 Russell Westbrook .75 2.00
135 Kevin Durant .75 2.00
136 Jeff Green .25 .60
137 Desmond Mason .20 .50
138 Nick Collison .25 .60
139 Earl Watson .20 .50
140 Dwight Howard .25 .60
141 Courtney Lee .25 .60
142 Hedo Turkoglu .25 .60
143 Jameer Nelson .20 .50
144 Rashard Lewis .25 .60
145 Mickael Pietrus .20 .50
146 Elton Brand .30 .75
147 Andre Miller .25 .60
148 Andre Iguodala .25 .60
149 Thaddeus Young .20 .50
150 Willie Green .20 .50
151 Samuel Dalembert .20 .50
152 Jason Richardson .30 .75
153 Shaquille O'Neal .60 1.50
154 Steve Nash .30 .75
155 Grant Hill .40 1.00
156 Amare Stoudemire .25 .60
157 Leandro Barbosa .25 .60
158 Robin Lopez .20 .50
159 Brandon Roy .30 .75
160 LaMarcus Aldridge .30 .75
161 Jerryd Bayless .25 .60
162 Rudy Fernandez .20 .50
163 Steve Blake .20 .50
164 Martell Webster .20 .50
165 Greg Oden .25 .60
166 Spencer Hawes .20 .50
167 Kevin Martin .25 .60
168 Beno Udrih .20 .50
169 Andres Nocioni .20 .50
170 Jason Thompson .20 .50
171 Rashad McCants .20 .50
172 Francisco Garcia .20 .50
173 Tim Duncan .50 1.25
174 Tony Parker .30 .75
175 Manu Ginobili .30 .75
176 Roger Mason .20 .50
177 Michael Finley .30 .75
178 Matt Bonner .20 .50
179 George Hill .30 .75
180 Chris Bosh .30 .75
181 Jose Calderon .20 .50
182 Andrea Bargnani .25 .60
183 Shawn Marion .25 .60
184 Anthony Parker .20 .50
185 Jason Kapono .20 .50
186 Roko Leni Ukic .20 .50
187 Deron Williams .25 .60
188 Carlos Boozer .25 .60
189 Ronnie Brewer .25 .60
190 C.J. Miles .25 .60
191 Mehmet Okur .20 .50
192 Kyle Korver .25 .60
193 Andrei Kirilenko .25 .60
194 Gilbert Arenas .25 .60
195 Antawn Jamison .25 .60
196 DeShawn Stevenson .20 .50
197 Caron Butler .25 .60
198 Brendan Haywood .20 .50
199 Nick Young .25 .60
200 Dominic McGuire .20 .50
201 Toney Douglas RC .50 1.25
202 Taylor Griffin RC .50 1.25
203 DeJuan Blair RC .60 1.50
204 Darren Collison RC .75 2.00
205 Patrick Mills RC 1.50 4.00
206 DaJuan Summers RC .50 1.25
207 Austin Daye RC .50 1.25
208 Eric Maynor RC .50 1.25
209 DeMarre Carroll RC .60 1.50
210 Taj Gibson RC .75 2.00
211 Patrick Beverley RC .75 2.00
212 Dante Cunningham RC .50 1.25
213 Sam Young RC .50 1.25
214 Terrence Williams RC .50 1.25
215 Omri Casspi RC .60 1.50
216 Jeff Pendergraph RC .50 1.25
217 Jrue Holiday RC 1.00 2.50
218 Jeff Teague RC .75 2.00
219 James Johnson RC .60 1.50
220 B.J. Mullens RC .50 1.25
221 Nick Calathes RC .50 1.25
222 A.J. Price RC .50 1.25
223 Danny Green RC 1.00 2.50
224 Marcus Thornton RC .60 1.50
225 Chase Budinger RC .60 1.50
226 Blake Griffin SP RC 4.00 10.00
227 James Harden SP RC 5.00 12.00
228 Tyler Hansbrough SP RC .75 2.00
229 Gerald Henderson SP RC .75 2.00
230 Jordan Hill SP RC .75 2.00
231 Hasheem Thabeet SP RC .60 1.50
232 Earl Clark SP RC .75 2.00
233 Brandon Jennings SP RC 1.00 2.50
234 Stephen Curry SP RC 20.00 50.00
235 Ty Lawson SP RC 1.00 2.50
236 Wayne Ellington SP RC 1.00 2.50
237 Ricky Rubio SP RC 1.50 4.00
238 DeMar DeRozan SP RC 2.50 6.00
239 Jonny Flynn SP RC .60 1.50
240 Tyreke Evans SP RC .75 2.00
241 Michael Jordan 5.00 12.00
242 Larry Bird 1.50 4.00
243 Horace Grant .60 1.50
244 Kiki Vandeweghe .50 1.25
245 Michael Cooper .50 1.25
246 Magic Johnson 1.50 4.00
247 Kareem Abdul-Jabbar 1.00 2.50
248 Julius Erving 1.00 2.50
249 Oscar Robertson .60 1.50
250 Isiah Thomas .60 1.50
251 Patrick Ewing .75 2.00
252 A.C. Green .60 1.50
253 Adrian Dantley .50 1.25
254 Alex English .50 1.25
255 Jerry West .75 2.00
256 Bernard King .50 1.25
257 Bill Laimbeer .50 1.25
258 Bob McAdoo .50 1.25
259 Byron Scott .50 1.25
260 Calvin Murphy .50 1.25
261 Clyde Drexler .75 2.00
262 David Robinson 1.00 2.50
263 Dominique Wilkins .75 2.00
264 Glen Rice .50 1.25
265 Hakeem Olajuwon .75 2.00
266 John Stockton 1.00 2.50
267 Robert Parish .60 1.50
268 Scottie Pippen 1.25 3.00
269 Sean Elliott .60 1.50
270 Bill Walton .60 1.50
271 Chris Mullin .60 1.50
272 Dee Brown .40 1.00
273 Dennis Rodman 1.25 3.00
274 Joe Dumars .60 1.50
275 John Paxson .50 1.25
276 Mark Price .60 1.50
277 Maurice Cheeks .40 1.00
278 Moses Malone .60 1.50
279 Spud Webb .50 1.25
280 Terry Porter .40 1.00
281 Darryl Dawkins .40 1.00
282 Dino Radja .40 1.00
283 Jamaal Wilkes .60 1.50
284 John Salley .40 1.00
285 Larry Johnson .60 1.50
286 Larry Nance .50 1.25
287 Pooh Richardson .40 1.00
288 Reggie Theus .50 1.25
289 Rick Mahorn .40 1.00
290 Rick Barry .50 1.25
291 Ron Harper .60 1.50
292 Steve Kerr .60 1.50
293 Tom Chambers .50 1.25
294 Spencer Haywood .40 1.00
295 Walt Frazier .60 1.50

2009-10 Upper Deck Star Rookies Gold

COMPLETE SET (25) 7.50 15.00
GOLD FOIL RETAIL BLASTER INSERT
201 Toney Douglas .40 1.00
202 Taylor Griffin .40 1.00
203 DeJuan Blair .50 1.25
204 Darren Collison .60 1.50
205 Patrick Mills 1.25 3.00
206 DaJuan Summers .40 1.00
207 Austin Daye .40 1.00
208 Eric Maynor .40 1.00
209 DeMarre Carroll .50 1.25
210 Taj Gibson .60 1.50
211 Patrick Beverley .60 1.50
212 Dante Cunningham .40 1.00
213 Sam Young .40 1.00
214 Terrence Williams .40 1.00
215 Omri Casspi .50 1.25
216 Jeff Pendergraph .40 1.00
217 Jrue Holiday .75 2.00
218 Jeff Teague .60 1.50
219 James Johnson .50 1.25
220 B.J. Mullens .40 1.00
221 Nick Calathes .40 1.00
222 A.J. Price .40 1.00
223 Danny Green .75 2.00
224 Marcus Thornton .50 1.25
225 Chase Budinger .50 1.25

2009-10 Upper Deck 3D NBA Stars

COMPLETE SET (50) 60.00 120.00
STATED ODDS 1:8
3DAI Allen Iverson 1.50 4.00
3DAR B.Roy/L.Aldridge 1.25 3.00
3DAS D.Stevenson/G.Arenas 1.00 2.50
3DAT R.Alston/S.Telfair .75 2.00
3DBA C.Anthony/C.Billups 1.50 4.00
3DBD Baron Davis 1.00 2.50
3DBJ K.Bryant/L.James 5.00 12.00
3DBR D.Rose/M.Beasley 2.00 5.00
3DBW C.Boozer/D.Williams 1.00 2.50
3DCA Carmelo Anthony 1.50 4.00
3DCH D.Harris/V.Carter 1.50 4.00
3DCP C.Paul/T.Chandler 1.50 4.00
3DDE Deron Williams 1.00 2.50
3DDG B.Davis/E.Gordon 1.00 2.50
3DDH Dwight Howard 1.00 2.50
3DDK D.Howard/K.Garnett 2.00 5.00
3DDP T.Duncan/T.Parker 2.00 5.00
3DDR D.Rose/L.Deng 2.00 5.00
3DDW K.Durant/R.Westbrook 3.00 8.00
3DGA Gilbert Arenas 1.00 2.50
3DGG M.Gasol/P.Gasol 1.25 3.00
3DHN D.Howard/J.Nelson 1.00 2.50
3DIB A.Iverson/C.Billups 1.50 4.00
3DIS A.Iverson/R.Stuckey 1.50 4.00
3DJB K.Bryant/M.Jordan 10.00 25.00
3DJJ L.James/M.Jordan 15.00 40.00
3DJR M.Redd/R.Jefferson 1.00 2.50
3DJS J.Johnson/J.Smith 1.00 2.50
3DJW L.James/M.Williams 5.00 12.00
3DKB Kobe Bryant 5.00 12.00
3DKD Kevin Durant 3.00 8.00
3DKN D.Nowitzki/J.Kidd 1.50 4.00
3DLJ LeBron James 5.00 12.00
3DMI A.Iguodala/A.Miller 1.00 2.50
3DMJ Michael Jordan 15.00 40.00
3DMM T.McGrady/Y.Ming 1.50 4.00
3DNK J.Kidd/S.Nash 1.25 3.00
3DNR Nate Robinson .75 2.00
3DNS A.Stoudemire/S.Nash 1.25 3.00
3DPA Chris Paul 1.50 4.00
3DPG K.Garnett/P.Pierce 2.00 5.00
3DPW C.Paul/D.Williams 1.50 4.00
3DRF Rudy Fernandez .75 2.00
3DRO Brandon Roy 1.25 3.00
3DSM Josh Smith 1.00 2.50
3DSN Steve Nash 1.25 3.00
3DTP Tayshaun Prince 1.00 2.50
3DVC Vince Carter 1.50 4.00
3DWA Dwyane Wade 2.00 5.00
3DWC D.Wade/M.Chalmers 2.00 5.00

2009-10 Upper Deck Game Materials

MBINED MEM ODDS 3:16
*GOLD: .5X TO 1.25X BASE HI
GOLD PRINT RUN 150 SER.#'d SETS
GJAA Arron Afflalo/550 2.00 5.00
GJAB Andray Blatche/545 2.00 5.00
GJAH Al Harrington/550 2.50 6.00
GJAI Andre Iguodala/550 2.50 6.00
GJAJ Antawn Jamison/550 2.50 6.00
GJAL Acie Law/550 2.00 5.00
GJAM Alonzo Mourning/400 4.00 10.00
GJAW Antoine Wright/305 2.00 5.00
GJBA Andrea Bargnani/550 2.50 6.00
GJBD Baron Davis/550 2.50 6.00
GJBG Ben Gordon/400 2.50 6.00
GJBH Brendan Haywood/550 2.00 5.00
GJBI Chauncey Billups/550 3.00 8.00
GJBO Andrew Bogut/550 2.50 6.00
GJBR Brandon Roy/400 3.00 8.00
GJBU Beno Udrih/487 2.00 5.00
GJBW Ben Wallace/550 2.50 6.00
GJCA Carmelo Anthony/550 4.00 10.00
GJCB Carlos Boozer/550 2.50 6.00
GJCF Channing Frye/550 2.50 6.00
GJCH Chris Bosh/400 3.00 8.00
GJCK Chris Kaman/550 2.50 6.00
GJCM Chris Mullin/550 4.00 10.00
GJCP Chris Paul/400 4.00 10.00
GJCS Craig Smith/550 2.00 5.00
GJCV Charlie Villanueva/550 2.00 5.00
GJDA Dan Majerle/550 2.50 6.00
GJDG Daniel Gibson/600 2.50 6.00
GJDH Dwight Howard/545 2.50 6.00
GJDI Boris Diaw/545 2.50 6.00
GJDL David Lee/550 2.00 5.00
GJDM Desmond Mason/550 2.00 5.00
GJDN Dirk Nowitzki/400 4.00 10.00
GJDR David Robinson/400 5.00 12.00
GJDS DeShawn Stevenson/550 2.00 5.00
GJDW Dorell Wright/550 2.00 5.00
GJEB Elton Brand/400 3.00 8.00
GJEH Eddie House/400 2.00 5.00
GJEO Emeka Okafor/550 2.50 6.00
GJFE Raymond Felton/550 2.50 6.00
GJGW Gerald Wallace/400 2.50 6.00
GJHE Luther Head 2.00 5.00
GJHO Juwan Howard/550 2.50 6.00
GJJC Jarron Collins/550 2.00 5.00
GJJF Jordan Farmar/400 2.00 5.00
GJJH Josh Howard/550 2.50 6.00
GJJK Jason Kapono/550 2.00 5.00
GJJN Joakim Noah/238 2.50 6.00
GJJO Jermaine O'Neal/545 2.50 6.00
GJJS J.R. Smith/481 2.50 6.00
GJJU Julian Wright/550 2.00 5.00
GJKA Kelenna Azubuike/550 2.00 5.00
GJKB Keith Bogans/400 2.00 5.00
GJKG Kevin Garnett/550 5.00 12.00
GJKO Kobe Bryant/550 8.00 20.00
GJLA LaMarcus Aldridge/550 3.00 8.00
GJLD Luol Deng/550 2.50 6.00
GJLH Larry Hughes/508 2.50 6.00
GJLJ LeBron James/545 8.00 20.00
GJLO Lamar Odom/550 2.50 6.00
GJLS Luis Scola/550 2.50 6.00
GJLU Luke Walton/550 2.00 5.00
GJLW Lorenzen Wright/400 2.00 5.00
GJMA Maurice Ager/550 2.00 5.00
GJMC Mike Conley Jr./397 2.50 6.00
GJMD Marquis Daniels/479 2.00 5.00
GJMJ Mike James/400 2.00 5.00
GJMM Mikki Moore/550 2.00 5.00
GJMO Mehmet Okur/400 2.00 5.00
GJPE Patrick Ewing/400 6.00 15.00
GJPG Pau Gasol/400 3.00 8.00
GJPP Paul Pierce/508 3.00 8.00
GJQD Quincy Douby/550 2.00 5.00
GJRA Ron Artest/550 3.00 8.00
GJRF Randy Foye/545 2.00 5.00
GJRG Rudy Gay/545 3.00 8.00
GJRS Robert Swift/550 2.00 5.00
GJRW Rasheed Wallace/550 3.00 8.00
GJSB Shannon Brown/550 2.00 5.00
GJSI James Singleton/400 2.00 5.00
GJSM Sean May/550 3.00 8.00
GJSN Steve Novak/545 2.00 5.00
GJSO Shaquille O'Neal/550 6.00 15.00
GJSR Sergio Rodriguez/250 2.00 5.00
GJST Stephon Marbury/545 2.50 6.00
GJSW Shawne Williams/550 2.00 5.00
GJTC Tyson Chandler/400 2.50 6.00
GJTF T.J. Ford/550 2.00 5.00
GJTM Tracy McGrady/550 3.00 8.00
GJTP Tayshaun Prince/550 2.50 6.00
GJTT Tyrus Thomas/550 2.00 5.00
GJUH Udonis Haslem/563 2.00 5.00
GJVC Vince Carter/550 4.00 10.00
GJWA Dwyane Wade/550 5.00 12.00
GJWC Wilson Chandler/545 2.50 6.00
GJWE Martell Webster/550 2.00 5.00
GJWI Shelden Williams/563 2.00 5.00
GJWR Brandan Wright/550 2.00 5.00
GJYM Yao Ming/550 4.00 10.00
GJZR Zach Randolph/400 2.50 6.00

2009-10 Upper Deck Game Materials Dual

COMBINED MEM ODDS 3:16
*GOLD: .5X TO 1.25X BASE HI
GOLD PRINT RUN 150 SER.#'d SETS
DGAB L.Bird/R.Allen 6.00 15.00
DGAD G.Davis/R.Allen 2.50 6.00
DGAG A.Iguodala/G.Arenas 2.00 5.00
DGAJ G.Arenas/L.James 10.00 25.00
DGAP M.Price/N.Archibald 2.50 6.00
DGAT C.Anthony/T.McGrady 3.00 8.00
DGBB A.Bargnani/C.Bosh 2.50 6.00
DGBF C.Billups/T.Ford 2.50 6.00
DGBH A.Bynum/D.Howard 2.00 5.00
DGBI A.Iguodala/E.Brand 2.50 6.00
DGBJ C.Billups/J.Johnson 2.50 6.00
DGBO C.Boozer/M.Okur 2.00 5.00
DGBP L.Bird/R.Parish 6.00 15.00
DGBR B.Roy/C.Billups 2.50 6.00
DGCB C.Bosh/V.Carter 3.00 8.00
DGCK C.Bosh/K.Garnett 4.00 10.00
DGCM S.May/V.Carter 3.00 8.00
DGCN D.Nowitzki/V.Carter 3.00 8.00
DGCT C.Drexler/T.McGrady 3.00 8.00
DGDA C.Anthony/T.Duncan 4.00 10.00
DGDL B.Laimbeer/J.Dumars 2.50 6.00
DGDO S.O'Neal/T.Duncan 5.00 12.00
DGDS D.Gibson/S.Brown 2.00 5.00
DGEM J.Erving/M.Malone 4.00 10.00
DGGH D.Gibson/K.Hinrich 2.00 5.00
DGFB R.Foye/S.Brown 1.50 4.00
DGFC M.Conley/R.Felton 2.00 5.00
DGFD C.Drexler/R.Felton 3.00 8.00
DGFF J.Farmar/T.Ford 1.50 4.00
DGFG D.Gibson/J.Farmar 2.00 5.00
DGFJ A.Jefferson/R.Foye 2.00 5.00
DGGA C.Anthony/G.Gervin 3.00 8.00
DGGD B.Davis/B.Gordon 2.00 5.00
DGGG K.Garnett/P.Gasol 4.00 10.00
DGGJ K.Garnett/L.James 10.00 25.00
DGGM K.Garnett/T.McGrady 4.00 10.00
DGGN D.Nowitzki/K.Garnett 4.00 10.00
DGGO J.O'Neal/K.Garnett 4.00 10.00
DGGS A.Stoudemire/K.Garnett 4.00 10.00
DGHB J.Howard/S.Brown 2.00 5.00
DGHC R.Hamilton/V.Carter 3.00 8.00
DGHG B.Gordon/R.Hamilton 2.00 5.00
DGHH J.Howard/L.Hughes 2.00 5.00
DGHT L.Hughes/T.Thomas 2.00 5.00
DGIB A.Iverson/C.Billups 3.00 8.00
DGIP A.Iverson/C.Paul 3.00 8.00
DGJA C.Anthony/L.James 10.00 25.00
DGJD C.Drexler/L.James 10.00 25.00
DGJE J.Erving/M.Jordan 20.00 50.00
DGJG B.Gordon/J.Johnson 2.00 5.00
DGJH A.Horford/J.Johnson 2.50 6.00
DGJJ L.James/M.Johnson 10.00 25.00
DGJP C.Paul/M.Johnson 6.00 15.00
DGJR B.Roy/J.Johnson 2.50 6.00
DGJW D.Wade/L.James 12.00 30.00
DGKL K.Durant/L.Aldridge 6.00 15.00
DGKM Abdul-Jabbar/M.Jordan 20.00 50.00
DGLG K.Garnett/L.Bird 6.00 15.00
DGLK K.Garnett/L.James 10.00 25.00
DGLR B.Laimbeer/D.Rodman 5.00 12.00
DGMA C.Anthony/S.Marion 3.00 8.00
DGMB C.Bosh/C.Maggette 2.50 6.00
DGMD C.Drexler/T.McGrady 3.00 8.00
DGMK K.Abdul-Jabbar/M.Johnson 6.00 15.00
DGML L.James/M.Jordan 40.00 100.00
DGMM A.Mourning/M.Malone 3.00 8.00
DGMN C.Maggette/D.Nowitzki 3.00 8.00
DGMP T.Prince/T.McGrady 2.50 6.00
DGMS A.Stoudemire/S.Marion 2.00 5.00
DGMW C.Maggette/S.Williams 2.00 5.00
DGNB D.Nowitzki/L.Bird 6.00 15.00
DGNH D.Nowitzki/J.Howard 3.00 8.00
DGNK C.Anthony/M.Jordan 20.00 50.00
DGNP C.Paul/S.Nash 3.00 8.00
DGNS A.Stoudemire/D.Nowitzki 3.00 8.00
DGOD C.Drexler/H.Olajuwon 3.00 8.00
DGOM E.Okafor/S.May 2.00 5.00
DGON J.O'Neal/L.Odom 2.00 5.00
DGOO H.Olajuwon/S.O'Neal 5.00 12.00
DGOR D.Robinson/H.Olajuwon 4.00 10.00
DGPS C.Paul/J.Stockton 4.00 10.00
DGRF W.Frazier/W.Reed 2.50 6.00
DGRG D.Robinson/M.Ginobili 4.00 10.00
DGRT D.Rodman/T.Thomas 5.00 12.00
DGRW D.Rodman/S.Williams 5.00 12.00
DGSB A.Stoudemire/C.Bosh 2.50 6.00
DGSM S.Marion/T.McGrady 2.50 6.00
DGST S.Williams/T.McGrady 2.50 6.00
DGSW D.Williams/J.Stockton 4.00 10.00
DGTB B.Roy/T.Parker 2.50 6.00
DGTD D.Robinson/T.Parker 4.00 10.00
DGVT T.McGrady/V.Carter 3.00 8.00
DGWA J.West/K.Abdul-Jabbar 8.00 20.00
DGWB M.Williams/M.Bibby 2.00 5.00
DGWJ J.Worthy/M.Johnson 6.00 15.00
DGWO E.Okafor/R.Wallace 2.50 6.00
DGWS A.Stoudemire/R.Wallace 2.50 6.00
DGYH H.Olajuwon/Y.Ming 3.00 8.00
DGYM M.Malone/Y.Ming 3.00 8.00
DGYS L.Scola/Y.Ming 3.00 8.00

2009-10 Upper Deck Jordan Brand Classic

RANDOM INSERTS IN PACKS
JCBJ Brandon Jennings 3.00 8.00
JCBM B.J. Mullens 2.00 5.00
JCBR Brandon Jennings 3.00 8.00
JCBS B.J. Mullens 2.00 5.00
JCDD DeMar DeRozan 8.00 20.00
JCDM DeMar DeRozan 8.00 20.00
JCDZ DeMar DeRozan 8.00 20.00
JCEV Tyreke Evans 2.50 6.00
JCJE Brandon Jennings 3.00 8.00
JCJH Jrue Holiday 4.00 10.00
JCJR Jrue Holiday 4.00 10.00
JCMU B.J. Mullens 2.00 5.00
JCTE Tyreke Evans 2.50 6.00

2009-10 Upper Deck Masterpieces

COMPLETE SET (35) 25.00 50.00
STATED ODDS 1:8
MAAR Anthony Randolph .60 1.50
MABL Brook Lopez .75 2.00
MABR Brandon Rush .60 1.50
MACL Courtney Lee .75 2.00
MACP Chris Paul 1.25 3.00
MADE Deron Williams .75 2.00
MADG Danilo Gallinari .75 2.00
MADH Dwight Howard .75 2.00
MADR Derrick Rose 1.50 4.00
MADW Dwyane Wade 1.50 4.00
MAGR Donte Greene .60 1.50
MAHI J.J. Hickson .60 1.50
MAJB Jerryd Bayless .75 2.00
MAJE Julius Erving 1.50 4.00
MAJG J.R. Giddens .60 1.50
MAJH John Havlicek 1.00 2.50
MAJO Michael Jordan 8.00 20.00
MAKA Kareem Abdul-Jabbar 1.50 4.00
MAKB Kobe Bryant 4.00 10.00
MAKG Kevin Garnett 1.50 4.00
MAKL Kevin Love 1.00 2.50
MALB Larry Bird 2.50 6.00
MALJ LeBron James 4.00 10.00
MAMB Michael Beasley .60 1.50
MAMJ Michael Jordan 8.00 20.00
MAMS Marreese Speights .75 2.00
MAOM O.J. Mayo .60 1.50
MAPP Paul Pierce 1.00 2.50
MARA Ryan Anderson .75 2.00
MARH Roy Hibbert .75 2.00
MARL Robin Lopez .60 1.50
MASN Steve Nash 1.00 2.50
MATP Tony Parker 1.00 2.50
MAWI Dominique Wilkins 1.25 3.00

2009-10 Upper Deck Now Appearing

COMPLETE SET (20) 8.00 20.00
STATED ODDS 1:8
NA1 Derrick Rose 1.25 3.00
NA2 Michael Beasley .50 1.25
NA3 O.J. Mayo .50 1.25
NA4 Russell Westbrook 2.00 5.00
NA5 Kevin Love .75 2.00
NA6 Michael Jordan 6.00 15.00
NA7 Kevin Durant 2.00 5.00
NA8 LeBron James 3.00 8.00
NA9 Kobe Bryant 3.00 8.00
NA10 Kevin Garnett 1.25 3.00
NA11 Rasheed Wallace .75 2.00
NA12 Tim Duncan 1.25 3.00
NA13 Shaquille O'Neal 1.50 4.00
NA14 Dwight Howard .60 1.50
NA15 Tracy McGrady .75 2.00
NA16 Chris Paul 1.00 2.50
NA17 Dwyane Wade 1.25 3.00
NA18 Dirk Nowitzki 1.00 2.50
NA19 Paul Pierce .75 2.00
NA20 Baron Davis .60 1.50

2009-10 Upper Deck Signature Collection

COMBINED AUTO ODDS 1:19
1 Alexis Ajinca 5.00 12.00
2 Joe Alexander 5.00 12.00
3 Steve Nash 30.00 80.00
4 Clyde Drexler 25.00 60.00
5 Ryan Anderson 5.00 12.00
6 T.J. Ford SP 5.00 12.00
7 D.J. Augustin 5.00 12.00
8 Rajon Rondo 6.00 15.00
9 Chris Paul 20.00 50.00
10 Jerryd Bayless 5.00 12.00
12 Michael Beasley 5.00 12.00
13 Von Wafer 5.00 12.00
14 Stephen Graham 5.00 12.00
15 Josh Boone 5.00 12.00
16 David Robinson 40.00 100.00
17 Bruce Bowen 12.00 30.00
18 Corey Brewer 5.00 12.00
19 Kirk Hinrich 6.00 15.00
20 Bobby Brown 5.00 12.00
21 Hilton Armstrong 5.00 12.00
22 Andrew Bynum 5.00 12.00
23 Louie Dampier 20.00 50.00
25 Mike Conley Jr. 5.00 12.00
26 DaJuan Summers 5.00 12.00
27 Ricky Rubio 50.00 120.00
30 Joey Dorsey 5.00 12.00
31 Jared Dudley 5.00 12.00
32 Hakeem Olajuwon 40.00 100.00
34 Oscar Robertson 50.00 125.00
35 Danilo Gallinari 6.00 15.00
36 Spud Webb 8.00 20.00
37 Kevin Garnett 30.00 80.00
38 Emeka Okafor 6.00 15.00
39 Eric Gordon 6.00 15.00
40 Aaron Gray 5.00 12.00
41 Jeff Green 6.00 15.00
42 Spencer Hawes 5.00 12.00
43 Richard Hendrix 5.00 12.00
44 J.J. Hickson 5.00 12.00
45 Dwight Howard 20.00 50.00
46 Darnell Jackson 5.00 12.00
47 Antawn Jamison 6.00 15.00
48 Al Jefferson 6.00 15.00
49 Bobby Jackson 5.00 12.00
50 DeAndre Jordan 6.00 15.00
51 Kosta Koufos 5.00 12.00
52 Andre Iguodala 6.00 15.00
53 Glen Davis 5.00 12.00
54 Courtney Lee 6.00 15.00
55 Brook Lopez 6.00 15.00
56 Kyle Korver 6.00 15.00
57 Robin Lopez 5.00 12.00
58 Kevin Love 8.00 20.00
59 Walter Herrmann 5.00 12.00
60 Moses Malone 25.00 60.00
61 O.J. Mayo 5.00 12.00
62 Luc Mbah A Moute 5.00 12.00
63 Rashad McCants 5.00 12.00
64 Javale McGee 6.00 15.00
65 Josh McRoberts 5.00 12.00
66 Jerry West 25.00 60.00
67 Larry Hughes 6.00 15.00
68 Yao Ming 20.00 50.00
69 Shannon Brown 5.00 12.00
70 Joakim Noah 6.00 15.00
71 Donte Greene 5.00 12.00
75 Darren Collison 8.00 20.00
76 Tayshaun Prince 6.00 15.00
77 Quentin Richardson 5.00 12.00
78 Derrick Rose 40.00 100.00
79 Brandon Rush 5.00 12.00
81 Walter Sharpe 5.00 12.00
82 Sean Singletary 5.00 12.00
83 Jason Smith 5.00 12.00
84 J.R. Giddens 5.00 12.00
85 Marreese Speights 6.00 15.00
86 A.J. Price 5.00 12.00
87 Rodney Stuckey 5.00 12.00
88 Mike Taylor 5.00 12.00
89 Jason Thompson 5.00 12.00
90 Al Thornton 5.00 12.00
91 Alando Tucker 5.00 12.00
92 Ike Diogu 5.00 12.00
94 Kyle Weaver 5.00 12.00
95 Russell Westbrook 50.00 120.00
97 Deron Williams 6.00 15.00
98 Mo Williams 6.00 15.00
99 Sean Williams 5.00 12.00
100 Shelden Williams 5.00 12.00
101 Kareem Abdul-Jabbar 50.00 120.00
102 Arron Afflalo 5.00 12.00
103 Shane Battier 6.00 15.00
104 LaMarcus Aldridge 12.00 30.00
105 Andre Miller 6.00 15.00
106 Chase Budinger 6.00 15.00
107 James Harden 60.00 150.00
108 Al Harrington 6.00 15.00
109 Alonzo Mourning 75.00 150.00
110 Jack Sikma 6.00 15.00
111 Anthony Randolph 5.00 12.00
112 Patrick Beverley 5.00 12.00
114 Brad Daugherty 6.00 15.00
115 Bailey Howell SP 25.00 60.00
116 Patrick O'Bryant 5.00 12.00
117 James Johnson 6.00 15.00
118 Earl Clark 6.00 15.00
119 Brandon Roy 6.00 15.00
120 Bill Sharman 10.00 25.00
121 Bill Walton 10.00 25.00
122 Jeff Adrien 5.00 12.00
123 Gerald Henderson 6.00 15.00
125 Corey Maggette 5.00 12.00
127 Wayne Ellington 6.00 15.00
128 B.J. Mullens 5.00 12.00
129 Danny Green 6.00 15.00
130 Jonny Flynn 5.00 12.00
131 Joe Crawford 5.00 12.00
132 David Lee 5.00 12.00
133 Donyell Marshall 5.00 12.00
134 Chris Douglas-Roberts 5.00 12.00
135 Damon Stoudamire 20.00 50.00
136 David West 6.00 15.00
137 Eddy Curry 5.00 12.00
138 D.J. White 5.00 12.00
139 Francisco Garcia 5.00 12.00
140 Gail Goodrich 12.00 30.00
141 George Hill 6.00 15.00
142 George Karl 20.00 50.00
143 Gabe Pruitt 5.00 12.00
144 Will Bynum 5.00 12.00
145 Derek Fisher 10.00 25.00
146 Hal Greer 10.00 25.00
147 Horace Grant 15.00 40.00
148 Isiah Thomas 15.00 40.00
149A LeBron James SVSM 200.00 500.00
149B LeBron James Cavs 300.00 600.00
150 Julius Erving SP 75.00 150.00
151 Magic Johnson 40.00 100.00
152 Jason Kidd 75.00 150.00
153 Sonny Weems 5.00 12.00
154 Jeff Pendergraph 5.00 12.00
155 J.R. Smith 6.00 15.00
156 Taj Gibson 6.00 15.00
157 Maurice Ager 5.00 12.00
158 Mike Bibby 5.00 12.00
159 Ronnie Brewer 6.00 15.00
160 Larry Bird SP 100.00 200.00
161 Larry Johnson 25.00 60.00
162 Carmelo Anthony 50.00 120.00
163 Desmond Mason SP 25.00 60.00
164 Mario Chalmers 6.00 15.00
165 Michael Jordan 400.00 800.00
166 Randy Foye 5.00 12.00
168 Cedric Simmons SP 10.00 25.00
169 Mario West SP 40.00 100.00
170 Marvin Williams 5.00 12.00
171 Nicolas Batum 6.00 15.00
172 Jrue Holiday 10.00 25.00
174 Pat Riley 20.00 50.00
175 Stephen Curry 200.00 400.00
176 Ben Gordon 6.00 15.00
177 Joey Graham 5.00 12.00
178 Dionte Christmas 5.00 12.00
179 Raymond Felton 6.00 15.00
180 Rudy Gay 5.00 12.00
181 Roy Hibbert 6.00 15.00
182 George Gervin 12.00 30.00
183 Dennis Rodman SP 40.00 100.00
184 Aaron Brooks 5.00 12.00
185 Robert Parish 8.00 20.00
187 David Noel 5.00 12.00
188 Jamario Moon 5.00 12.00
189 John Stockton SP 150.00 300.00
190 Solomon Jones 5.00 12.00
191 Jermaine Taylor 5.00 12.00
192 Carlos Boozer 6.00 15.00
193 Tracy McGrady 30.00 80.00
194 Tyrus Thomas 5.00 12.00
195 Vince Carter 20.00 50.00
196 Paul Pierce 15.00 40.00
198 Ty Lawson 5.00 12.00
199 Luis Scola 6.00 15.00
200 Julian Wright 5.00 12.00

2009-10 Upper Deck Sophomore Sensations

COMPLETE SET (30) 10.00 25.00
RANDOM INSERTS IN PACKS
SSAA Alexis Ajinca .60 1.50
SSAR Darrell Arthur .75 2.00
SSBB Bobby Brown .60 1.50
SSBL Brook Lopez .75 2.00
SSBR Brandon Rush .60 1.50
SSBW Bill Walker .60 1.50
SSCL Courtney Lee .75 2.00
SSDA D.J. Augustin .60 1.50
SSDG Danilo Gallinari .75 2.00
SSDJ Darnell Jackson .60 1.50
SSDR Derrick Rose 1.50 4.00
SSEG Eric Gordon .75 2.00
SSJB Jerryd Bayless .75 2.00
SSJM Javale McGee .75 2.00
SSJO DeAndre Jordan 1.00 2.50
SSJT Jason Thompson .60 1.50
SSKK Kosta Koufos .60 1.50
SSKL Kevin Love 1.00 2.50
SSLM Luc Mbah A Moute .60 1.50
SSMB Michael Beasley .60 1.50
SSMS Marreese Speights .75 2.00
SSMT Mike Taylor .60 1.50
SSOM O.J. Mayo .60 1.50
SSRA Ryan Anderson .75 2.00
SSRF Rudy Fernandez .60 1.50
SSRH Richard Hendrix .60 1.50
SSRL Robin Lopez .60 1.50
SSRW Russell Westbrook 2.50 6.00
SSSS Sean Singletary .60 1.50
SSWS Walter Sharpe .60 1.50

2009-10 Upper Deck Sophomore Sensations Autographs

MBINED AUTO ODDS 1:16
STATED PRINT RUN 199 SER.#'d SETS
SSAA Alexis Ajinca 5.00 12.00
SSBB Bobby Brown 5.00 12.00
SSBL Brook Lopez 10.00 25.00
SSBR Brandon Rush 6.00 15.00
SSBW Bill Walker 5.00 12.00
SSCL Courtney Lee 8.00 20.00
SSDA D.J. Augustin 5.00 12.00
SSDG Danilo Gallinari 6.00 15.00
SSDJ Darnell Jackson 5.00 12.00
SSDR Derrick Rose 50.00 125.00
SSEG Eric Gordon 10.00 25.00
SSJB Jerryd Bayless 5.00 12.00
SSJM Javale McGee 8.00 20.00
SSJO DeAndre Jordan 10.00 25.00
SSJT Jason Thompson 5.00 12.00
SSKK Kosta Koufos 5.00 12.00
SSKL Kevin Love 8.00 20.00
SSLM Luc Mbah A Moute 5.00 12.00
SSMB Michael Beasley 10.00 25.00
SSMS Marreese Speights 5.00 12.00
SSMT Mike Taylor 5.00 12.00
SSOM O.J. Mayo 10.00 25.00
SSRA Ryan Anderson 5.00 12.00
SSRH Richard Hendrix 5.00 12.00
SSRL Robin Lopez 5.00 12.00
SSRW Russell Westbrook 60.00 150.00
SSSS Sean Singletary 5.00 12.00
SSWS Walter Sharpe 5.00 12.00

2009-10 Upper Deck UD Select Spokesman Signatures

RANDOM INSERTS IN PACKS
SSAH Al Horford 5.00 12.00
SSKG Kevin Garnett 40.00 100.00
SSLJ LeBron James 125.00 250.00
SSMJ Michael Jordan SP 350.00 600.00

2009-10 Upper Deck VS Dual Materials

MBINED MEM ODDS 3:16
STATED PRINT RUN 400 TO 795 SETS
*BRONZE: .5X TO 1.25X BASE HI
BRONZE PRINT RUN 150 SER.#'d SETS
VSAA C.Anthony/R.Artest 5.00 12.00
VSAB C.Billups/R.Allen 5.00 12.00
VSAC A.Stoudemire/C.Bosh 4.00 10.00
VSAM C.Maggette/R.Allen 5.00 12.00
VSAO A.Bargnani/S.O'Neal 5.00 12.00
VSAR N.Robinson/R.Alston 4.00 10.00
VSAS C.Anthony/T.Sefolosha 5.00 12.00
VSAW A.Horford/M.Williams 4.00 10.00
VSBA K.Bryant/R.Artest 8.00 20.00
VSBB K.Bryant/R.Bell 6.00 15.00
VSBJ K.Bryant/L.James 15.00 40.00
VSBK B.King/B.Walton 4.00 10.00
VSBL C.Landry/K.Brown 4.00 10.00
VSBM E.Brand/Y.Ming 5.00 12.00
VSBN K.Bryant/S.Nash 8.00 20.00
VSBR M.Redd/M.Bibby 4.00 10.00
VSBS C.Boozer/L.Scola 4.00 10.00
VSBT A.Tucker/S.Brown/570 4.00 10.00
VSCA C.Anthony/V.Carter 5.00 12.00
VSCD E.Curry/S.Dalembert 4.00 10.00
VSCF J.Farmar/J.Calderon 4.00 10.00
VSCK A.Kirilenko/M.Camby 4.00 10.00
VSCM S.Marion/V.Carter 5.00 12.00
VSCO E.Curry/J.O'Neal 4.00 10.00
VSCS J.Smith/V.Carter 5.00 12.00
VSCW M.Williams/V.Carter 5.00 12.00
VSDB C.Duhon/C.Brewer 4.00 10.00
VSDC G.Davis/W.Chandler 4.00 10.00
VSDF C.Frye/D.Milicic 4.00 10.00
VSDJ D.Williams/J.Kidd 6.00 15.00
VSDL K.Lowry/M.Daniels 4.00 10.00
VSDS B.Davis/D.Stevenson 4.00 10.00
VSEB J.Erving/L.Bird 10.00 25.00
VSEC C.Bosh/E.Brand 4.00 10.00
VSEE M.Eaton/P.Ewing/400 5.00 12.00
VSER D.Robinson/M.Eaton/570 5.00 12.00
VSFG D.Gibson/R.Felton 4.00 10.00
VSFM M.Finley/T.McGrady/570 4.00 10.00
VSFW B.Wright/C.Frye/570 4.00 10.00
VSGA G.Arenas/K.Garnett/570 5.00 12.00
VSGL K.Garnett/R.Lewis 5.00 12.00
VSGN D.Nowitzki/K.Garnett/570 5.00 12.00
VSGO K.Garnett/S.O'Neal/570 6.00 15.00
VSGR D.Robinson/K.Garnett/570 6.00 15.00
VSGW C.Webber/K.Garnett/570 6.00 15.00
VSHB C.Brewer/L.Hughes/795 4.00 10.00
VSHI A.Iguodala/J.Howard/570 4.00 10.00
VSHW A.Horford/J.Wright/570 4.00 10.00
VSIB A.Bogut/Z.Ilgauskas 4.00 10.00
VSIH D.Howard/Z.Ilgauskas 4.00 10.00
VSJS J.Farmar/S.Marbury/776 4.00 10.00
VSJW A.Jefferson/S.Williams/570 4.00 10.00
VSKA A.Jamison/K.Bryant 5.00 12.00
VSKD J.Kidd/K.Durant 6.00 15.00
VSKH J.Kidd/K.Hinrich 4.00 10.00
VSKT K.Martin/T.Ariza 4.00 10.00
VSKU B.Udrih/J.Kidd 4.00 10.00
VSKW C.Kaman/S.Williams 4.00 10.00
VSLA C.Anthony/R.Lewis 4.00 10.00
VSLL A.Law/K.Lowry 4.00 10.00
VSMA C.Anthony/S.Marion/776 5.00 12.00
VSMB C.Bosh/Y.Ming 5.00 12.00
VSMF D.Mason/R.Foye 4.00 10.00
VSMK B.King/K.McHale/551 5.00 12.00
VSMM B.Miller/S.May/570 4.00 10.00
VSMO S.O'Neal/Y.Ming/570 6.00 15.00
VSMP K.Malone/S.Pippen/570 8.00 20.00
VSMR C.Maggette/J.Redick 4.00 10.00
VSMT C.Maggette/T.Thomas/570 4.00 10.00
VSMW D.Marshall/L.Walton 4.00 10.00
VSNB C.Billups/S.Nash 5.00 12.00
VSNK A.Kirilenko/D.Nowitzki/570 4.00 10.00
VSNR D.Robinson/D.Nowitzki/570 6.00 15.00
VSOB A.Bogut/E.Okafor/570 4.00 10.00
VSOD E.Okafor/I.Diogu 4.00 10.00
VSOE H.Olajuwon/P.Ewing/570 5.00 12.00
VSOO H.Olajuwon/S.O'Neal 6.00 15.00
VSOP L.Odom/T.Prince/551 4.00 10.00
VSOW E.Okafor/H.Warrick/570 4.00 10.00
VSPA P.Pierce/T.Ariza/570 4.00 10.00
VSPG D.Granger/T.Prince 4.00 10.00
VSPH M.Peterson/U.Haslem 4.00 10.00
VSPJ L.James/T.Prince 5.00 12.00
VSPK G.Payton/S.Kerr 4.00 10.00
VSRS J.Smith/L.Ridnour 4.00 10.00
VSSB C.Simmons/S.Brown 4.00 10.00
VSSJ J.Starks/M.Johnson 6.00 15.00
VSST R.Sessions/S.Telfair 4.00 10.00
VSTC C.Paul/T.McGrady 4.00 10.00
VSTG D.Gibson/S.Telfair 4.00 10.00
VSTM M.Webster/T.Sefolosha 4.00 10.00
VSVA A.Jamison/V.Carter 4.00 10.00
VSVJ J.Jack/S.Vujacic/570 4.00 10.00
VSVW C.Villanueva/M.Williams 4.00 10.00
VSWH B.Wallace/D.Howard 4.00 10.00
VSWN M.Williams/N. 4.00 10.00
VSWS C.Simmons/H.Warrick 4.00 10.00
VSWY M.Williams/T.Young 4.00 10.00
VSYA A.Bargnani/Y.Ming 4.00 10.00
VSYD D.Mutombo/Y.Ming 6.00 15.00

2008 Upper Deck 20th Anniversary

Upper Deck produced this 80-card set featuring past and present athletes from baseball, football, basketball and hockey and issued them through their Certified Diamond Dealers program. Eight cards were released every month from March through December 2008. By entering in all 80 unique codes from the back of the cards on the company's website by December 31, 2008, collectors had a chance to win a trip to four major sporting events.

UD1 Michael Jordan 2.00 5.00
UD2 LeBron James 1.25 3.00
UD3 Kobe Bryant 1.25 3.00
UD4 Dennis Rodman .75 2.00
UD5 Kevin Durant .60 1.50
UD6 Larry Bird 1.50 4.00
UD7 Magic Johnson 1.50 4.00
UD8 Julius Erving .75 2.00
UD9 Bill Russell .75 2.00
UD10 Al Horford .50 1.25
UD11 David Robinson .75 2.00
UD12 Kareem Abdul-Jabbar .75 2.00
UD13 Jeff Green .30 .75
UD14 Mike Conley Jr. .30 .75
UD15 Steve Nash .60 1.50
UD61 Derrick Rose 1.50 4.00
UD62 O.J. Mayo 1.25 3.00
UD63 Kevin Love .75 2.00
UD64 Michael Beasley 1.25 3.00
UD65 Jerryd Bayless .50 1.25

2009 Upper Deck 20th Anniversary

CARDS ISSUED IN FIVE CARD RUNS
EACH PRICED EQUALLY WITHIN RUNS
36 Michael Jordan 2.50 6.00
37 Michael Jordan 2.50 6.00
38 Michael Jordan 2.50 6.00
39 Michael Jordan 2.50 6.00
40 Michael Jordan 2.50 6.00
56 Kareem Abdul-Jabbar .75 2.00
57 Kareem Abdul-Jabbar .75 2.00
58 Kareem Abdul-Jabbar .75 2.00
59 Kareem Abdul-Jabbar .75 2.00
60 Kareem Abdul-Jabbar .75 2.00
91 Minnesota Timberwolves .20 .50
92 Minnesota Timberwolves .20 .50
93 Minnesota Timberwolves .20 .50
94 Minnesota Timberwolves .20 .50
95 Minnesota Timberwolves .20 .50
96 Orlando Magic .20 .50
97 Orlando Magic .20 .50
98 Orlando Magic .20 .50
99 Orlando Magic .20 .50
100 Orlando Magic .20 .50
176 Michael Jordan 2.50 6.00
177 Michael Jordan 2.50 6.00
178 Michael Jordan 2.50 6.00
179 Michael Jordan 2.50 6.00
180 Michael Jordan 2.50 6.00
216 Detroit Pistons/Thomas .20 .50
217 Detroit Pistons .20 .50
218 Detroit Pistons .20 .50
219 Detroit Pistons .20 .50
220 Detroit Pistons .20 .50
251 David Robinson .75 2.00
252 David Robinson .75 2.00
253 David Robinson .75 2.00
254 David Robinson .75 2.00
255 David Robinson .75 2.00
276 Magic Johnson .75 2.00
277 Magic Johnson .75 2.00
278 Magic Johnson .75 2.00
279 Magic Johnson .75 2.00
280 Magic Johnson .75 2.00
291 Michael Jordan 2.50 6.00
292 Michael Jordan 2.50 6.00
293 Michael Jordan 2.50 6.00
294 Michael Jordan 2.50 6.00
295 Michael Jordan 2.50 6.00
306 Chicago Bulls/Jordan 1.00 2.50
307 Chicago Bulls .20 .50
308 Chicago Bulls .20 .50
309 Chicago Bulls .20 .50
310 Chicago Bulls .20 .50
336 Michael Jordan 2.50 6.00
337 Michael Jordan 2.50 6.00
338 Michael Jordan 2.50 6.00
339 Michael Jordan 2.50 6.00
340 Michael Jordan 2.50 6.00
376 Magic Johnson .75 2.00
377 Magic Johnson .75 2.00
378 Magic Johnson .75 2.00
379 Magic Johnson .75 2.00
380 Magic Johnson .75 2.00
421 Chicago Bulls .20 .50
422 Chicago Bulls .20 .50
423 Chicago Bulls .20 .50
424 Chicago Bulls/Jordan 1.00 2.50
425 Chicago Bulls .20 .50
426 Michael Jordan 2.50 6.00
427 Michael Jordan 2.50 6.00
428 Michael Jordan 2.50 6.00
429 Michael Jordan 2.50 6.00

430 Michael Jordan 2.50 6.00
521 John Paxson .20 .50
522 John Paxson .20 .50
523 John Paxson .20 .50
524 John Paxson .20 .50
525 John Paxson .20 .50
536 Chicago Bulls .20 .50
537 Chicago Bulls .20 .50
538 Chicago Bulls .20 .50
539 Chicago Bulls .20 .50
540 Chicago Bulls .20 .50
Michael Jordan
541 Michael Jordan 2.50 6.00
542 Michael Jordan 2.50 6.00
543 Michael Jordan 2.50 6.00
544 Michael Jordan 2.50 6.00
545 Michael Jordan 2.50 6.00
561 Julius Erving .75 2.00
562 Julius Erving .75 2.00
563 Julius Erving .75 2.00
564 Julius Erving .75 2.00
565 Julius Erving .75 2.00
606 Shaquille O'Neal 1.25 3.00
607 Shaquille O'Neal 1.25 3.00
608 Shaquille O'Neal 1.25 3.00
609 Shaquille O'Neal 1.25 3.00
610 Shaquille O'Neal 1.25 3.00
656 Houston Rockets .20 .50
657 Houston Rockets .20 .50
658 Houston Rockets .20 .50
659 Houston Rockets .20 .50
660 Houston Rockets .20 .50
686 John Stockton .60 1.50
687 John Stockton .60 1.50
688 John Stockton .60 1.50
689 John Stockton .60 1.50
690 John Stockton .60 1.50
691 Jason Kidd .40 1.00
692 Jason Kidd .40 1.00
693 Jason Kidd .40 1.00
694 Jason Kidd .40 1.00
695 Jason Kidd .40 1.00
696 NCAA National Champions/Arizona .20 .50
697 NCAA National Champions/Arizona .20 .50
698 NCAA National Champions/Arizona .20 .50
699 NCAA National Champions/Arizona .20 .50
700 NCAA National Champions/Arizona .20 .50
726 Hakeem Olajuwon .60 1.50
727 Hakeem Olajuwon .60 1.50
728 Hakeem Olajuwon .60 1.50
729 Hakeem Olajuwon .60 1.50
730 Hakeem Olajuwon .60 1.50
751 Michael Jordan 2.50 6.00
752 Michael Jordan 2.50 6.00
753 Michael Jordan 2.50 6.00
754 Michael Jordan 2.50 6.00
755 Michael Jordan 2.50 6.00
771 NCAA National Champions/UCLA .20 .50
772 NCAA National Champions/UCLA .20 .50
773 NCAA National Champions/UCLA .20 .50
774 NCAA National Champions/UCLA .20 .50
775 NCAA National Champions/UCLA .20 .50
781 Final Game at Boston Garden/Bird .75 2.00
782 Final Game at Boston Garden .20 .50
783 Final Game at Boston Garden .60 1.50
784 Final Game at Boston Garden .60 1.50
785 Final Game at Boston Garden .60 1.50
786 Houston Rockets/Olajuwon/Shaq .40 1.00
787 Houston Rockets .20 .50
788 Houston Rockets .20 .50
789 Houston Rockets .20 .50
790 Houston Rockets .20 .50
851 Kareem Abdul-Jabbar .75 2.00
852 Kareem Abdul-Jabbar .75 2.00
853 Kareem Abdul-Jabbar .75 2.00
854 Kareem Abdul-Jabbar .75 2.00
855 Kareem Abdul-Jabbar .75 2.00
881 Chicago Bulls .20 .50
Michael Jordan
882 Chicago Bulls .20 .50
883 Chicago Bulls .20 .50
884 Chicago Bulls .20 .50
885 Chicago Bulls .20 .50
886 Michael Jordan 2.50 6.00
887 Michael Jordan 2.50 6.00
888 Michael Jordan 2.50 6.00
889 Michael Jordan 2.50 6.00
890 Michael Jordan 2.50 6.00
916 NCAA National Champions/Kentucky .20 .50
917 NCAA National Champions/Kentucky .20 .50
918 NCAA National Champions/Kentucky .20 .50
919 NCAA National Champions/Kentucky .20 .50
920 NCAA National Champions/Kentucky .20 .50
931 Bill Russell .75 2.00
932 Bill Russell .75 2.00
933 Bill Russell .75 2.00
934 Bill Russell .75 2.00
935 Bill Russell .75 2.00
981 Tim Duncan .60 1.50
982 Tim Duncan .60 1.50
983 Tim Duncan .60 1.50
984 Tim Duncan .60 1.50
985 Tim Duncan .60 1.50
1006 Michael Jordan 2.50 6.00
1007 Michael Jordan 2.50 6.00
1008 Michael Jordan 2.50 6.00
1009 Michael Jordan 2.50 6.00
1010 Michael Jordan 2.50 6.00
1021 NCAA National Champions .20 .50
1022 NCAA National Champions .20 .50
1023 NCAA National Champions .20 .50
1024 NCAA National Champions .20 .50
1025 NCAA National Champions .20 .50
1106 Julius Erving .75 2.00
1107 Julius Erving .75 2.00
1108 Julius Erving .75 2.00
1109 Julius Erving .75 2.00
1110 Julius Erving .75 2.00
1126 Chicago Bulls .20 .50
Michael Jordan
1127 Chicago Bulls .20 .50
Michael Jordan
1128 Chicago Bulls .20 .50
Michael Jordan
1129 Chicago Bulls .20 .50
1130 Chicago Bulls .20 .50
1131 Michael Jordan 2.50 6.00
1132 Michael Jordan 2.50 6.00
1133 Michael Jordan 2.50 6.00
1134 Michael Jordan 2.50 6.00
1135 Michael Jordan 2.50 6.00
1186 Larry Bird 1.25 3.00
1187 Larry Bird 1.25 3.00
1188 Larry Bird 1.25 3.00
1189 Larry Bird 1.25 3.00
1190 Larry Bird 1.25 3.00
1271 San Antonio Spurs .20 .50
1272 San Antonio Spurs .20 .50
1273 San Antonio Spurs .20 .50
1274 San Antonio Spurs .20 .50
1275 San Antonio Spurs .20 .50
1406 Los Angeles Lakers .30 .75
1407 Los Angeles Lakers .30 .75
1408 Los Angeles Lakers .30 .75
1409 Los Angeles Lakers .30 .75
1410 Los Angeles Lakers .30 .75
1466 Shaquille O'Neal 1.25 3.00
1467 Shaquille O'Neal 1.25 3.00
1468 Shaquille O'Neal 1.25 3.00
1469 Shaquille O'Neal 1.25 3.00
1470 Shaquille O'Neal 1.25 3.00
1526 Los Angeles Lakers .30 .75
1527 Los Angeles Lakers .30 .75
1528 Los Angeles Lakers .30 .75
1529 Los Angeles Lakers .30 .75
1530 Los Angeles Lakers .30 .75
1616 Tony Parker .20 .50
1617 Tony Parker .20 .50
1618 Tony Parker .20 .50
1619 Tony Parker .20 .50
1620 Tony Parker .20 .50
1631 Los Angeles Lakers .30 .75
1632 Los Angeles Lakers .30 .75
1633 Los Angeles Lakers .30 .75
1634 Los Angeles Lakers .30 .75
1635 Los Angeles Lakers .30 .75
1651 Magic Johnson .75 2.00
1652 Magic Johnson .75 2.00
1653 Magic Johnson .75 2.00
1654 Magic Johnson .75 2.00
1655 Magic Johnson .75 2.00
1666 Yao Ming .25 .60
1667 Yao Ming .25 .60
1668 Yao Ming .25 .60
1669 Yao Ming .25 .60
1670 Yao Ming .25 .60
1701 Tim Duncan .60 1.50
1702 Tim Duncan .60 1.50
1703 Tim Duncan .60 1.50
1704 Tim Duncan .60 1.50
1705 Tim Duncan .60 1.50
1741 Kobe Bryant 1.50 4.00
1742 Kobe Bryant 1.50 4.00
1743 Kobe Bryant 1.50 4.00
1744 Kobe Bryant 1.50 4.00
1745 Kobe Bryant 1.50 4.00
1786 San Antonio Spurs .20 .50
1787 San Antonio Spurs .20 .50
1788 San Antonio Spurs .20 .50
1789 San Antonio Spurs .20 .50
1790 San Antonio Spurs .20 .50
1796 Dwyane Wade .60 1.50
1797 Dwyane Wade .60 1.50
1798 Dwyane Wade .60 1.50
1799 Dwyane Wade .60 1.50
1800 Dwyane Wade .60 1.50
1821 LeBron James 2.00 5.00
1822 LeBron James 2.00 5.00
1823 LeBron James 2.00 5.00
1824 LeBron James 2.00 5.00
1825 LeBron James 2.00 5.00
1826 Tim Duncan .60 1.50
1827 Tim Duncan .60 1.50
1828 Tim Duncan .60 1.50
1829 Tim Duncan .60 1.50
1830 Tim Duncan .60 1.50
1871 Chris Bosh .20 .50
1872 Chris Bosh .20 .50
1873 Chris Bosh .20 .50
1874 Chris Bosh .20 .50
1875 Chris Bosh .20 .50
1906 LeBron James 2.00 5.00
1907 LeBron James 2.00 5.00
1908 LeBron James 2.00 5.00
1909 LeBron James 2.00 5.00
1910 LeBron James 2.00 5.00
1926 Detroit Pistons .20 .50
1927 Detroit Pistons .20 .50
1928 Detroit Pistons .20 .50
1929 Detroit Pistons .20 .50
1930 Detroit Pistons .20 .50
1976 Dwight Howard .60 1.50
1977 Dwight Howard .60 1.50
1978 Dwight Howard .60 1.50
1979 Dwight Howard .60 1.50
1980 Dwight Howard .60 1.50
1996 Clyde Drexler .50 1.25
1997 Clyde Drexler .50 1.25
1998 Clyde Drexler .50 1.25
1999 Clyde Drexler .50 1.25
2000 Clyde Drexler .50 1.25
2091 San Antonio Spurs .20 .50
2092 San Antonio Spurs .20 .50
2093 San Antonio Spurs .20 .50
2094 San Antonio Spurs .20 .50
2095 San Antonio Spurs .20 .50
2111 Steve Nash .40 1.00
2112 Steve Nash .40 1.00
2113 Steve Nash .40 1.00
2114 Steve Nash .40 1.00
2115 Steve Nash .40 1.00
2146 Chris Paul .60 1.50
2147 Chris Paul .60 1.50
2148 Chris Paul .60 1.50
2149 Chris Paul .60 1.50
2150 Chris Paul .60 1.50
2166 Kobe Bryant 1.50 4.00
2167 Kobe Bryant 1.50 4.00
2168 Kobe Bryant 1.50 4.00
2169 Kobe Bryant 1.50 4.00
2170 Kobe Bryant 1.50 4.00
2171 Miami Heat .20 .50
2172 Miami Heat .20 .50
2173 Miami Heat .20 .50
2174 Miami Heat .20 .50
2175 Miami Heat .20 .50
2196 Steve Nash .40 1.00
2197 Steve Nash .40 1.00
2198 Steve Nash .40 1.00
2199 Steve Nash .40 1.00
2200 Steve Nash .40 1.00
2211 Dominique Wilkins .50 1.25
2212 Dominique Wilkins .50 1.25
2213 Dominique Wilkins .50 1.25
2214 Dominique Wilkins .50 1.25
2215 Dominique Wilkins .50 1.25
2336 San Antonio Spurs .20 .50
2337 San Antonio Spurs .20 .50
2338 San Antonio Spurs .20 .50
2339 San Antonio Spurs .20 .50
2340 San Antonio Spurs .20 .50
2356 Kevin Durant 1.25 3.00
2357 Kevin Durant 1.25 3.00
2358 Kevin Durant 1.25 3.00
2359 Kevin Durant 1.25 3.00
2360 Kevin Durant 1.25 3.00
2361 Dirk Nowitzki .40 1.00
2362 Dirk Nowitzki .40 1.00
2363 Dirk Nowitzki .40 1.00
2364 Dirk Nowitzki .40 1.00
2365 Dirk Nowitzki .40 1.00
2426 Boston Celtics .40 1.00
2427 Boston Celtics .40 1.00
2428 Boston Celtics .40 1.00
2429 Boston Celtics .40 1.00
2430 Boston Celtics .40 1.00
2436 Kobe Bryant 1.50 4.00
2437 Kobe Bryant 1.50 4.00
2438 Kobe Bryant 1.50 4.00
2439 Kobe Bryant 1.50 4.00
2440 Kobe Bryant 1.50 4.00
2441 Hakeem Olajuwon .60 1.50
2442 Hakeem Olajuwon .60 1.50
2443 Hakeem Olajuwon .60 1.50
2444 Hakeem Olajuwon .60 1.50
2445 Hakeem Olajuwon .60 1.50
2456 Derrick Rose 1.50 4.00
2457 Derrick Rose 1.50 4.00
2458 Derrick Rose 1.50 4.00
2459 Derrick Rose 1.50 4.00
2460 Derrick Rose 1.50 4.00
2471 Michael Beasley 1.25 3.00
2472 Michael Beasley 1.25 3.00
2473 Michael Beasley 1.25 3.00
2474 Michael Beasley 1.25 3.00
2475 Michael Beasley 1.25 3.00

2009 Upper Deck 20th Anniversary Memorabilia

NBABI Chauncey Billups 4.00 10.00
NBACA Carmelo Anthony 4.00 10.00
NBACB Chris Bosh 3.00 8.00
NBACP Chris Paul 3.00 8.00
NBAEO Emeka Okafor 4.00 10.00
NBAKB Kobe Bryant 20.00 40.00
NBAKG Kevin Garnett 4.00 10.00
NBALJ LeBron James 12.50 30.00
NBAMJ Michael Jordan 40.00 80.00
NBASO Shaquille O'Neal 12.50 30.00
NBATD Tim Duncan 5.00 12.00
NBATM Tracy McGrady 4.00 10.00
NBAVC Vince Carter 4.00 10.00
NBAYM Yao Ming 5.00 12.00

1996 Upper Deck 22K Gold Michael Jordan

NNO Michael Jordan 20.00 50.00
4-Time MVP
NNO Michael Jordan 30.00 80.00
ROY/1985
NNO Michael Jordan 20.00 50.00
He's Back
NNO Michael Jordan 20.00 50.00
First Championship

1998 Upper Deck 22K Gold Michael Jordan

COMMON CARD 8.00 20.00

1999 Upper Deck 22K Gold Michael Jordan

Released through Upper Deck and Upper Deck Authenticated, these 5-cards commemorate the retirement of Michael Jordan. Each card is not numbered, but is serially numbered to 9923 on the back.

COMMON CARD 20.00 50.00

2000 Upper Deck 22K Gold Michael Jordan

This 2.5x3.5 sized card was released by Upper Deck in 2000, and features a solid gold card with an actual piece of the Delta Center floor upon which Jordan took his final shot. This card was sold through Upper Deck's direct marketing channel, and carried a suggested retail price of $79.99.

1 Michael Jordan 100.00 200.00

1996 Upper Deck 23 Nights Jordan Experience

Available as both a complete set with or without the interview compact disc, this 23-card set carried a suggested retail price of $19.99. Each set included the oversized (3 1/2" by 5") cards and a circular commemorative card. Each card is specifically dated commemorating each event.

COMPLETE SET w/CD (23) 12.00 30.00
COMPLETE SET (23) 10.00 25.00
COMMON CARD (1-23) .60 1.50
NNO Compact Disc 2.00 5.00
The Jordan Interview
NNO Cardboard Disk .40 1.00
(Michael Jordan)

2014 Upper Deck 25th Anniversary

1 James Harden .60 1.50
6 LeBron James 2.00 5.00
9 Rajon Rondo .50 1.25
11 Elvin Hayes .50 1.25
17 John Havlicek .60 1.50
19 Jamal Mashburn .50 1.25
23 Michael Jordan 2.50 6.00
25 Robert Horry .40 1.00
28 Julius Erving .75 2.00
32 Magic Johnson 1.25 3.00
33 Larry Bird 1.25 3.00
40 Bill Laimbeer .40 1.00
42 James Worthy .60 1.50
50 David Robinson .75 2.00
54 Karl Malone .60 1.50
67 Sam Perkins .30 .75
69 Zydrunas Ilgauskas .30 .75
72 Stacey Augmon .30 .75
73 Allen Iverson .60 1.50
82 Jerry Tarkanian .50 1.25
88 Vinny Del Negro .30 .75
100 Shane Larkin .30 .75
101 Antoine Walker .40 1.00
104 Spud Webb .40 1.00
106 Bill Russell .75 2.00
112 Skylar Diggins 1.00 2.50
127 Giannis Antetokounmpo 1.00 2.50
130 Mason Plumlee .50 1.25
140 Livio Jean-Charles .30 .75

2014 Upper Deck 25th Anniversary Promos

UD25LG Lebron James 5.00 12.00

2014 Upper Deck 25th Anniversary Silver

*SILVER/250: 1.2X TO 3X BASIC CARDS

2014 Upper Deck 25th Anniversary Autographs

6 LeBron James/25
19 Jamal Mashburn/125 6.00 15.00
23 Michael Jordan/25
40 Bill Laimbeer/25
67 Sam Perkins/25
72 Stacey Augmon/25
88 Vinny Del Negro/25
104 Spud Webb/25
112 Skylar Diggins/25
130 Mason Plumlee/125 5.00 12.00

1993 Upper Deck Adventures in Toon World

IT'S WAY COOLER! This new Upper Deck produced set definitely builds the success of the 'Comic Ball' series on. Indeed, nothing creates funnier stories than pairing Looney Tune characters with respected professional athletes. The base set is divided into 9-card subsets: 'Act 1' (A1S1-A1S9) through 'Act 10' (A10S1-A10S9); each of 18 scenes and with each card being double-sided with two different scenes.

COMPLETE SET (91) 10.00 25.00
COMMON CARD (1-90) .20 .50

1993 Upper Deck Adventures in Toon World Bugs Bunny Hare-os

BBH3 Michael Jordan with Bugs
(comic art)
BBH5 Michael Jordan
Wayne Gretzky
Joe Montana
Reggie Jackson with Bugs
(comic art)

1993 Upper Deck Adventures in Toon World Holograms

2 Michael Jordan
Reggie Jackson
with Bugs Bunny
5 Michael Jordan
Wayne Gretzky
Joe Montana
Reggie Jackson
with Bugs and Toonimator

2002 Upper Deck All-Star Game Jordan

Available to collectors at the 2001-02 NBA All-Star game, this 3-card set features Michael Jordan with the Bulls and the Wizards. Each card has and All-Star game stamping on the front, and the card backs are sequentally numbered to 2002.

COMPLETE SET (3) 8.00 20.00
COMMON CARD 3.00 8.00

2003 Upper Deck All-Star Game

Distributed by Upper Deck at the All-Star Jam Session Show in Atlanta, this 4-card set features some of the games greatest slam dunk champion with a full color action photo on a grey background with gold foil highlights. Each card is sequentially numbered to the corresponding year the player won the slam dunk competition.

COMPLETE SET (4) 10.00 25.00
DW1 Dominique Wilkins/1985 1.50 4.00
KB1 Kobe Bryant/1997 4.00 10.00
MJ1 Michael Jordan/1987 6.00 15.00
MJ2 Michael Jordan/1988 6.00 15.00

2004 Upper Deck All-Star Game

Given out by Upper Deck at the 2004 NBA All-Star Jam Session in Los Angeles, this 10-card set was available at the Upper Deck booth as a redemption with 10 packages of any 2003-04 Upper Deck Basketball Product. Cards place players on a purple background with orange trim and holographic highlights. Each card is sequentially numbered to 2004 and the players were available on days as follows: LJ1 LeBron James and Gary Payton on Feb. 12th, LJ2 LeBron James and Carmelo Anthony on Feb. 13th, LJ3 LeBron James and Kobe Bryant on Feb. 14th, LJ4 LeBron James and Michael Jordan on Feb. 15th, and LJ5 LeBron James and Chris Bosh on Feb. 16th. The Star Zone Michael Jordan Sample was also handed out and was not included in the original press material as the set. Rumor has it that these cards were handed out when the initial players with print runs of 2004 ran out.

COMPLETE SET (10) 75.00 150.00
BO Chris Bosh 3.00 8.00
LJ1 LeBron James 12.50 30.00
LJ2 LeBron James 12.50 30.00
LJ3 LeBron James 12.50 30.00
LJ4 LeBron James 12.50 30.00
LJ5 LeBron James 12.50 30.00
CA Carmelo Anthony 4.00 10.00
GP Gary Payton 3.00 8.00
KB Kobe Bryant 5.00 12.00
MJ Michael Jordan 6.00 15.00
SZMJ Michael Jordan 6.00 15.00
Star Zone SAMPLE

2005 Upper Deck All-Star Game

COMPLETE SET 8.00 20.00
LJ LeBron James 2.50 6.00
MJ Michael Jordan 5.00 12.00
KB Kobe Bryant 3.00 8.00

2006-07 Upper Deck All-Star Game

COMPLETE SET (13) 8.00 20.00
AS1 Yao Ming .60 1.50
AS2 Julius Erving .75 2.00
AS3 Larry Bird 1.25 3.00
AS4 Magic Johnson 1.25 3.00
AS5 Steve Nash .60 1.50
AS6 LaMarcus Aldridge 1.25 3.00
AS7 Rudy Gay .60 1.50
AS8 Brandon Roy .50 1.25
AS9 Tyrus Thomas .40 1.00
AS10 Jerry Tarkanian .50 1.25
AS11 LeBron James 2.00 5.00
AS12 Michael Jordan 4.00 10.00
AS13 Kobe Bryant 2.00 5.00

2008-09 Upper Deck All-Star Game

AS1 Amar'e Stoudemire .75 2.00
AS2 Michael Beasley 1.00 2.50
AS3 Derrick Rose 4.00 10.00
AS4 Kobe Bryant 4.00 10.00
AS5 Kevin Garnett 1.50 4.00
AS6 LeBron James 4.00 10.00
AS7 Michael Jordan 8.00 20.00
AS8 O.J. Mayo 1.00 2.50
AS9 Steve Nash 1.00 2.50
AS10 Rudy Fernandez .75 2.00

2004-05 Upper Deck All-Star Lineup

Released in February 2005, this 132-card set features veteran players on cards 1-90 and rookies on cards 91-132. All-Star Lineup was packaged in 24-pack boxes were packs contained six cards and carried a SRP of $2.99.

COMP.SET w/o SP's (90) 12.00 30.00
91-132 STATED ODDS 1:6
1 Jason Terry .25 .60
2 Al Harrington .25 .60
3 Boris Diaw .25 .60
4 Paul Pierce .30 .75
5 Ricky Davis .25 .60
6 Jiri Welsch .20 .50
7 Marcus Fizer .20 .50
8 Gerald Wallace .25 .60
9 Jahidi White .20 .50
10 Eddy Curry .20 .50
11 Kirk Hinrich .25 .60
12 Jamal Crawford .30 .75
13 LeBron James 2.00 5.00
14 Dajuan Wagner .20 .50
15 Jeff McInnis .20 .50
16 Dirk Nowitzki .50 1.25
17 Antoine Walker .30 .75
18 Michael Finley .30 .75
19 Carmelo Anthony .60 1.50
20 Andre Miller .25 .60
21 Kenyon Martin .25 .60
22 Chauncey Billups .30 .75
23 Rasheed Wallace .30 .75
24 Ben Wallace .25 .60
25 Erick Dampier .20 .50
26 Jason Richardson .30 .75
27 Mike Dunleavy .25 .60
28 Yao Ming .60 1.50
29 Tracy McGrady .40 1.00
30 Juwan Howard .25 .60
31 Jermaine O'Neal .25 .60
32 Reggie Miller .30 .75
33 Ron Artest .30 .75
34 Elton Brand .30 .75
35 Corey Maggette .25 .60
36 Quentin Richardson .25 .60
37 Kobe Bryant 1.25 3.00
38 Gary Payton .30 .75
39 Lamar Odom .25 .60
40 Pau Gasol .30 .75
41 Jason Williams .25 .60
42 Bonzi Wells .20 .50
43 Shaquille O'Neal .75 2.00
44 Dwyane Wade .50 1.25
45 Eddie Jones .25 .60
46 Michael Redd .25 .60
47 Desmond Mason .25 .60
48 T.J. Ford .20 .50
49 Latrell Sprewell .25 .60
50 Kevin Garnett .50 1.25
51 Sam Cassell .25 .60
52 Richard Jefferson .25 .60
53 Kerry Kittles .20 .50
54 Jason Kidd .50 1.25
55 Jamal Mashburn .25 .60
56 Baron Davis .25 .60
57 Jamaal Magloire .20 .50
58 Allan Houston .25 .60
59 Kurt Thomas .20 .50
60 Stephon Marbury .25 .60
61 Cuttino Mobley .20 .50
62 Drew Gooden .20 .50
63 Steve Francis .25 .60
64 Glenn Robinson .25 .60
65 Allen Iverson .50 1.25
66 Samuel Dalembert .20 .50
67 Amare Stoudemire .25 .60
68 Steve Nash .40 1.00
69 Shawn Marion .25 .60
70 Shareef Abdur-Rahim .25 .60
71 Damon Stoudamire .25 .60
72 Zach Randolph .25 .60
73 Peja Stojakovic .30 .75
74 Chris Webber .30 .75
75 Mike Bibby .30 .75
76 Tony Parker .30 .75
77 Tim Duncan .50 1.25
78 Manu Ginobili .40 1.00
79 Ronald Murray .20 .50
80 Ray Allen .30 .75
81 Rashard Lewis .30 .75
82 Chris Bosh .30 .75
83 Vince Carter .50 1.25
84 Jalen Rose .25 .60
85 Andrei Kirilenko .25 .60
86 Carlos Boozer .25 .60
87 Carlos Arroyo .20 .50
88 Gilbert Arenas .25 .60
89 Jarvis Hayes .20 .50
90 Antawn Jamison .25 .60
91 Emeka Okafor RC .60 1.50
92 Dwight Howard RC 1.50 4.00
93 Shaun Livingston RC .75 2.00
94 Luol Deng RC .75 2.00
95 Ben Gordon RC .75 2.00
96 Devin Harris RC .60 1.50
97 Andre Iguodala RC 1.00 2.50
98 Andris Biedrins RC .50 1.25
99 Josh Childress RC .60 1.50
100 Josh Smith RC .75 2.00
101 Jameer Nelson RC .75 2.00
102 J.R. Smith RC .75 2.00
103 Sergei Monia RC .50 1.25
104 Sebastian Telfair RC .60 1.50
105 Pavel Podkolzin RC .50 1.25
106 Luke Jackson RC .50 1.25
107 Dorell Wright RC .75 2.00
108 Robert Swift RC .50 1.25
109 Anderson Varejao RC .60 1.50
110 Sasha Vujacic RC .75 2.00
111 Rafael Araujo RC .50 1.25
112 Al Jefferson RC 1.00 2.50
113 Kris Humphries RC .75 2.00
114 Kirk Snyder RC .50 1.25
115 Darius Rice RC .75 2.00
116 Beno Udrih RC .60 1.50
117 Viktor Khryapa RC .50 1.25
118 David Harrison RC .50 1.25
119 Trevor Ariza RC .75 2.00
120 Ha Seung-Jin RC .75 2.00
121 Kevin Martin RC 1.00 2.50
122 Delonte West RC .75 2.00
123 Rickey Paulding RC .50 1.25
124 Chris Duhon RC .75 2.00
125 Tony Allen RC .75 2.00
126 Donta Smith RC .50 1.25
127 Andre Emmett RC .50 1.25
128 Royal Ivey RC .60 1.50
129 Matt Freije RC .60 1.50
130 Romain Sato RC .50 1.25
131 Antonio Burks RC .60 1.50
132 Lionel Chalmers RC .75 2.00

2004-05 Upper Deck All-Star Lineup Gold

*1-90 GOLD: 3X TO 8X BASE HI
1-90 PRINT RUN 100 SER.#'d SETS
*91-132 GOLD RCs: 2X TO 5X BASE HI
91-132 PRINT RUN 25 SER.#'d SETS

2004-05 Upper Deck All-Star Lineup All-Star Staples

Inserted randomly in packs at the rate of one in three, this 14-card set is horizontally designed on gray background with player images on the right and their jersey number on the left. A parallel version serially numbered to 10 was also issued for this set.

COMPLETE SET (14) 6.00 15.00
STATED ODDS 1:3
AI Allen Iverson .75 2.00
BW Ben Wallace .40 1.00
DN Dirk Nowitzki .75 2.00
JK Jason Kidd .75 2.00
JO Jermaine O'Neal .40 1.00
KB Kobe Bryant 2.00 5.00
KG Kevin Garnett .75 2.00
KM Kenyon Martin .40 1.00
PP Paul Pierce .50 1.25
SF Steve Francis .40 1.00
SO Shaquille O'Neal 1.25 3.00
TD Tim Duncan .75 2.00
TM Tracy McGrady .60 1.50
YM Yao Ming 1.00 2.50

2004-05 Upper Deck All-Star Lineup All-Star Staples Threads

Randomly seeded in packs at the rate of one in 12, this 14-card set parallels the base All-Star Staples insert enhanced with a swatch of jersey.

STATED ODDS 1:12
AI Allen Iverson 4.00 10.00
BW Ben Wallace 2.00 5.00
DN Dirk Nowitzki 4.00 10.00
JK Jason Kidd 4.00 10.00
JO Jermaine O'Neal 2.00 5.00
KB Kobe Bryant 6.00 15.00
KG Kevin Garnett 4.00 10.00
KM Kenyon Martin 2.00 5.00
PP Paul Pierce 2.50 6.00
SF Steve Francis 2.00 5.00
SO Shaquille O'Neal 6.00 15.00
TD Tim Duncan 4.00 10.00
TM Tracy McGrady 3.00 8.00
YM Yao Ming 5.00 12.00

2004-05 Upper Deck All-Star Lineup Prominent Futures

Inserted in packs at the rate of one in three, this 14-card set is horizontally designed with a two players, one on each side and gray borders. A parallel version of this set was also inserted in packs and those are sereially numbered to 50.

COMPLETE SET (15) 6.00 15.00
STATED ODDS 1:3
*PARALLEL: 1.5X TO 4X BASE HI
PARALLEL PRINT RUN 50 SER.#'d SETS
BD C.Boozer/M.Dunleavy .60 1.50
HH J.Howard/J.Hayes .60 1.50
HK U.Haslem/C.Kaman .60 1.50
JA L.James/C.Anthony 2.00 5.00
JB M.Jaric/C.Bosh .60 1.50
JS L.James/A.Stoudemire 1.50 4.00
KD C.Kaman/M.Dunleavy .60 1.50
MH R.Murray/J.Hayes .60 1.50
MN Y.Ming/Nene 1.00 2.50
NH Nene/U.Haslem .60 1.50
PH T.Prince/J.Howard .60 1.50
PM T.Prince/R.Murray .60 1.50
SG A.Stoudemire/M.Ginobili 1.00 2.50
WG D.Wade/M.Ginobili 1.25 3.00

2004-05 Upper Deck All-Star Lineup Prominent Futures Threads

Randomly seeded in packs at the rate of one in 12, this 14-card set parallels the base All-Star Staples insert enhanced with two swatches of memorabilia.

STATED ODDS 1:12
BD C.Boozer/M.Dunleavy 4.00 10.00
HH J.Howard/J.Hayes 4.00 10.00
HK U.Haslem/C.Kaman 4.00 10.00
JA L.James/C.Anthony SP 20.00 50.00
JB M.Jaric/C.Bosh 4.00 10.00
JS L.James/A.Stoudemire 10.00 25.00
KD C.Kaman/M.Dunleavy 4.00 10.00
MH R.Murray/J.Hayes 4.00 10.00
MN Y.Ming/Nene 5.00 12.00
NH Nene/U.Haslem 4.00 10.00
PH T.Prince/J.Howard 4.00 10.00
PM T.Prince/R.Murray 4.00 10.00
SG A.Stoudemire/M.Ginobili 5.00 12.00
WG D.Wade/M.Ginobili 8.00 20.00

2004-05 Upper Deck All-Star Lineup Promos/eCards

Inserted in packs at the rate of one in six for the eCards and two per pack on the Promos, these cards were designed to send people to Upper Deck's website and possibly redeem for cool prizes.

eCARD STATED ODDS 1:6
eCARD PRICES FOR UNSCRACHED CARDS
PROMO STATED ODDS 2:1
AS1 Kobe Bryant EC 2.00 5.00
AS2 LeBron James EC 3.00 8.00
AS3 Kevin Garnett EC .75 2.00
AS4 Tracy McGrady EC .60 1.50
AS5 Shaquille O'Neal EC 1.25 3.00
AS6 Allen Iverson EC .75 2.00
AS7 Tim Duncan EC .75 2.00
AS8 Jason Kidd EC .75 2.00
AS9 Paul Pierce .30 .75
AS10 Carmelo Anthony .60 1.50
AS11 Ben Wallace .25 .60
AS12 Yao Ming .60 1.50
AS13 Jermaine O'Neal .25 .60
AS14 Dirk Nowitzki .50 1.25
AS15 Dwyane Wade .50 1.25
AS16 Brad Miller .25 .60
AS17 Kenyon Martin .25 .60
AS18 Jason Richardson .30 .75
AS19 Stephon Marbury .25 .60
AS20 Amare Stoudemire .25 .60
AS21 Baron Davis .25 .60
AS22 Ray Allen .30 .75
AS23 Vince Carter .50 1.25
AS24 Andrei Kirilenko .25 .60
AS25 Jamal Mashburn .25 .60
AS26 Chris Webber .30 .75
AS27 Chris Bosh .30 .75
AS28 Shareef Abdur-Rahim .25 .60
AS29 Michael Redd .25 .60
AS30 Zach Randolph .25 .60
AS31 Rasheed Wallace .30 .75
AS32 Peja Stojakovic .30 .75
AS33 Pau Gasol .30 .75
AS34 Shawn Marion .25 .60
AS35 Jamaal Magloire .20 .50
AS36 Tony Parker .30 .75
AS37 Ron Artest .30 .75
AS38 Elton Brand .30 .75
AS39 Wild Card EC .40 1.00

2004-05 Upper Deck All-Star Lineup Rookie Review

Inserted as a topper in each box, this 30-card set follows LeBron James's rookie season on cards RR-RR21 and some of the more impressive rookies from the class on cards RR22-RR30.

COMPLETE SET (30) 15.00 40.00
STATED ODDS ONE PER BOX TOPPER
RR1 LeBron James 1.50 4.00
RR2 LeBron James 1.50 4.00
RR3 LeBron James 1.50 4.00
RR4 LeBron James 1.50 4.00
RR5 LeBron James 1.50 4.00
RR6 LeBron James 1.50 4.00
RR7 LeBron James 1.50 4.00
RR8 LeBron James 1.50 4.00
RR9 LeBron James 1.50 4.00
RR10 LeBron James 1.50 4.00
RR11 LeBron James 1.50 4.00
RR12 LeBron James 1.50 4.00
RR13 LeBron James 1.50 4.00
RR14 LeBron James 1.50 4.00
RR15 LeBron James 1.50 4.00
RR16 LeBron James 1.50 4.00
RR17 LeBron James 1.50 4.00
RR18 LeBron James 1.50 4.00
RR19 LeBron James 1.50 4.00
RR20 LeBron James 1.50 4.00
RR21 LeBron James 1.50 4.00
RR22 Udonis Haslem .30 .75
RR23 T.J. Ford .30 .75
RR24 Marquis Daniels .30 .75
RR25 Josh Howard .50 1.25
RR26 Kirk Hinrich .40 1.00
RR27 Jarvis Hayes .30 .75
RR28 Carmelo Anthony 1.00 2.50
RR29 Chris Bosh .50 1.25
RR30 Dwyane Wade .75 2.00

2004-05 Upper Deck All-Star Lineup Signature Class

Inserted in packs at the rate of one in 240, this 21-card set is horizontally designed and places player photos on the right and autographs on the left.

COMMON CARD 8.00 20.00
STATED ODDS 1:240
JD Juan Dixon 8.00 20.00
KB Kobe Bryant 125.00 250.00
KG Kevin Garnett 30.00 60.00
LJ LeBron James 150.00 300.00
RM Reggie Miller 40.00 100.00

2004-05 Upper Deck All-Star Lineup Weekend Highlights

Inserted at the rate of one in three, this 14-card set features a full-color image surrounded by red, then gray borders. A parallel version set was printed where cards denoted as L1 are serially numbered to 100 and cards denoted as L2 are serially numbered to 250.

COMPLETE SET (14) 3.00 8.00
STATED ODDS 1:3
*L1 PARALLEL: 2.5X TO 6X BASE HI
L1 PAR.PRINT RUN 100 SER.#'d SETS
*L2 PARALLEL: 1.5X TO 4X BASE HI
L2 PAR.PRINT RUN 250 SER.#'d SETS
AN Chris Anderson L1 .50 1.25
BD Baron Davis L2 .40 1.00
CB Chauncey Billups L2 .50 1.25
CM Cuttino Mobley L2 .30 .75
DF Derek Fisher L1 .40 1.00
EB Earl Boykins L1 .30 .75
FJ Fred Jones L1 .30 .75
JA Marko Jaric L1 .30 .75
JR Jason Richardson L2 .50 1.25
KK Kyle Korver L1 .40 1.00
PS Peja Stojakovic L2 .50 1.25
RD Ricky Davis L2 .40 1.00
SM Stephon Marbury L2 .40 1.00
VL Voshon Lenard L1 .30 .75

2004-05 Upper Deck All-Star Lineup Weekend Highlights Threads

Randomly seeded in packs at the rate of one in 12, this 14-card set parallels the Weekend Highlights insert enhanced with a swatch of memorabilia.

STATED ODDS 1:12
AN Chris Anderson 2.50 6.00
BD Baron Davis 2.00 5.00
CB Chauncey Billups 2.50 6.00
CM Cuttino Mobley 1.50 4.00
DF Derek Fisher 2.00 5.00
EB Earl Boykins 2.00 5.00
FJ Fred Jones 2.00 5.00
JA Marko Jaric 2.00 5.00
JR Jason Richardson 2.50 6.00
KK Kyle Korver 2.00 5.00
PS Peja Stojakovic SP 2.50 6.00
RD Ricky Davis 2.00 5.00
SM Stephon Marbury 2.00 5.00
VL Voshon Lenard 2.00 5.00

1992-93 Upper Deck All-Star Weekend

This 40-card boxed set was originally available only to hobby dealers and to dealers at The Upper Deck Trading Card and Memorabilia Show at the Salt Palace in Salt Lake City, Utah, during February 18-21, 1993. The set captures NBA All-Stars from the past, present, and future, as well as memories of previous NBA All-Star Games. The standard-size cards display full-bleed photos with silver foil highlights on their fronts. At least one set in each case had gold (rather than silver) foil highlights valued at two to four times the prices listed below. The set is comprised of three subsets: NBA All-Star Heroes (1-25), NBA All-Star Recruits (26-35), and NBA All-Star Flashbacks (36-40).

COMP. FACT SET (40) 5.00 12.00
*GOLD: 1.5X TO 4X BASE HI
1 Nate Archibald .08 .25
2 Elgin Baylor .15 .40
3 Wilt Chamberlain .40 1.00
4 Dave Cowens .08 .25
5 Walt Frazier .08 .25
6 George Gervin .15 .40
7 John Havlicek .25 .60
8 Elvin Hayes .10 .30
9 Oscar Robertson .25 .60
10 Jerry West .30 .75
11 Charles Barkley .25 .60
12 Brad Daugherty .08 .25
13 Clyde Drexler .20 .50
14 Patrick Ewing .20 .50
15 Michael Jordan 1.25 3.00
16 Karl Malone .20 .50
17 Moses Malone .08 .25
18 Chris Mullin .08 .25
19 Hakeem Olajuwon .20 .50
20 Robert Parish .08 .25
21 David Robinson .20 .50
22 John Stockton .20 .50
23 Isiah Thomas .08 .25
24 Dominique Wilkins .08 .25
25 James Worthy .10 .30
26 Kenny Anderson .08 .25
27 Stacey Augmon .08 .25
28 Derrick Coleman .08 .25
29 Larry Johnson .10 .30
30 Christian Laettner .25 .60
31 Harold Miner .08 .25
32 Alonzo Mourning .50 1.25
33 Dikembe Mutombo .08 .25
34 Shaquille O'Neal 1.25 3.00
35 Steve Smith .08 .25
36 Larry Nance .08 .25
37 Larry Bird .40 1.00
38 Tom Chambers MVP .08 .25

39 Karl Malone .15 .40
John Stockton
40 Charles Barkley MVP .25 .60

2011 Upper Deck All Time Greats

STATED PRINT RUN 50 TO 80 SER.#'d SETS
UNPRICED GOLD PRINT RUN 5 SETS
ONLY FIRST CARD LISTED PER PLAYER
1 Michael Jordan 1-23/80 12.00 30.00
2 Michael Jordan/80 12.00 30.00
3 Michael Jordan/80 12.00 30.00
4 Michael Jordan/80 12.00 30.00
5 Michael Jordan/80 12.00 30.00
6 Michael Jordan/80 12.00 30.00
7 Michael Jordan/80 12.00 30.00
8 Michael Jordan/80 12.00 30.00
9 Michael Jordan/80 12.00 30.00
10 Michael Jordan/80 12.00 30.00
11 Michael Jordan/80 12.00 30.00
12 Michael Jordan/80 12.00 30.00
13 Michael Jordan/80 12.00 30.00
14 Michael Jordan/80 12.00 30.00
15 Michael Jordan/80 12.00 30.00
16 Michael Jordan/80 12.00 30.00
17 Michael Jordan/80 12.00 30.00
18 Michael Jordan/80 12.00 30.00
19 Michael Jordan/80 12.00 30.00
20 Michael Jordan/80 12.00 30.00
21 Michael Jordan/80 12.00 30.00
22 Michael Jordan/80 12.00 30.00
23 Michael Jordan/80 12.00 30.00
24 Michael Jordan/80 12.00 30.00
25 LeBron James 25-44/50 10.00 25.00
26 LeBron James/50 10.00 25.00
27 LeBron James/50 10.00 25.00
28 LeBron James/50 10.00 25.00
29 LeBron James/50 10.00 25.00
30 LeBron James/50 10.00 25.00
31 LeBron James/50 10.00 25.00
32 LeBron James/50 10.00 25.00
33 LeBron James/50 10.00 25.00
34 LeBron James/50 10.00 25.00
35 LeBron James/50 10.00 25.00
36 LeBron James/50 10.00 25.00
37 LeBron James/50 10.00 25.00
38 LeBron James/50 10.00 25.00
39 LeBron James/50 10.00 25.00
40 LeBron James/50 10.00 25.00
41 LeBron James/50 10.00 25.00
42 LeBron James/50 10.00 25.00
43 LeBron James/50 10.00 25.00
44 LeBron James/50 10.00 25.00
45 Steve Nash 45-48/50 2.50 6.00
46 Steve Nash/50 2.50 6.00
47 Steve Nash/50 2.50 6.00
48 Steve Nash/50 2.50 6.00
49 James Worthy 49-58/50 4.00 10.00
50 James Worthy/50 4.00 10.00
51 James Worthy/50 4.00 10.00
52 James Worthy/50 4.00 10.00
53 James Worthy/50 4.00 10.00
54 James Worthy/50 4.00 10.00
55 James Worthy/50 4.00 10.00
56 James Worthy/50 4.00 10.00
57 James Worthy/50 4.00 10.00
58 James Worthy/50 4.00 10.00
59 John Havlicek 59-61/50 2.50 6.00
60 John Havlicek/50 2.50 6.00
61 John Havlicek/50 2.50 6.00
62 D.Robinson 62-71/50 4.00 10.00
63 David Robinson/50 4.00 10.00
64 David Robinson/50 4.00 10.00
65 David Robinson/50 4.00 10.00
66 David Robinson/50 4.00 10.00
67 David Robinson/50 4.00 10.00
68 David Robinson/50 4.00 10.00
69 David Robinson/50 4.00 10.00
70 David Robinson/50 4.00 10.00
71 David Robinson/50 4.00 10.00
72 Bill Russell 72-76/50 5.00 12.00
73 Bill Russell/50 5.00 12.00
74 Bill Russell/50 5.00 12.00
75 Bill Russell/50 5.00 12.00
76 Bill Russell/50 5.00 12.00
77 A.Mourning 77-91/50 5.00 12.00
78 Alonzo Mourning/50 5.00 12.00
79 Alonzo Mourning/50 5.00 12.00
80 Alonzo Mourning/50 5.00 12.00
81 Alonzo Mourning/50 5.00 12.00
82 Alonzo Mourning/50 5.00 12.00
83 Alonzo Mourning/50 5.00 12.00
84 Alonzo Mourning/50 5.00 12.00
85 Alonzo Mourning/50 5.00 12.00
86 Alonzo Mourning/50 5.00 12.00
87 Alonzo Mourning/50 5.00 12.00
88 Alonzo Mourning/50 5.00 12.00
89 Alonzo Mourning/50 5.00 12.00
90 Alonzo Mourning/50 5.00 12.00
91 Alonzo Mourning/50 5.00 12.00
92 H.Olajuwon 92-98/50 4.00 10.00
93 Hakeem Olajuwon/50 4.00 10.00
94 Hakeem Olajuwon/50 4.00 10.00
95 Hakeem Olajuwon/50 4.00 10.00
96 Hakeem Olajuwon/50 4.00 10.00
97 Hakeem Olajuwon/50 4.00 10.00
98 Hakeem Olajuwon/50 4.00 10.00
99 Walt Frazier 99-103/50 2.50 6.00
100 Walt Frazier/50 2.50 6.00
101 Walt Frazier/50 2.50 6.00
102 Walt Frazier/50 2.50 6.00
103 Walt Frazier/50 2.50 6.00
104 Julius Erving 104-108/50 4.00 10.00
105 Julius Erving/50 4.00 10.00
106 Julius Erving/50 4.00 10.00
107 Julius Erving/50 4.00 10.00
108 Julius Erving/50 4.00 10.00
109 Larry Bird 109-123/50 5.00 12.00
110 Larry Bird/50 5.00 12.00
111 Larry Bird/50 5.00 12.00
112 Larry Bird/50 5.00 12.00
113 Larry Bird/50 5.00 12.00
114 Larry Bird/50 5.00 12.00
115 Larry Bird/50 5.00 12.00
116 Larry Bird/50 5.00 12.00
117 Larry Bird/50 5.00 12.00
118 Larry Bird/50 5.00 12.00
119 Larry Bird/50 5.00 12.00
120 Larry Bird/50 5.00 12.00
121 Larry Bird/50 5.00 12.00
122 Larry Bird/50 5.00 12.00
123 Larry Bird/50 5.00 12.00
124 Derrick Rose 124-128/50 6.00 15.00
125 Derrick Rose/50 6.00 15.00
126 Derrick Rose/50 6.00 15.00
127 Derrick Rose/50 6.00 15.00
128 Derrick Rose/50 6.00 15.00
129 Clyde Drexler 129-136/50 4.00 10.00
130 Clyde Drexler/50 4.00 10.00
131 Clyde Drexler/50 4.00 10.00
132 Clyde Drexler/50 4.00 10.00
133 Clyde Drexler/50 4.00 10.00
134 Clyde Drexler/50 4.00 10.00
135 Clyde Drexler/50 4.00 10.00
136 Clyde Drexler/50 4.00 10.00
137 M.Johnson 137-151/50 5.00 12.00
138 Magic Johnson/50 5.00 12.00
139 Magic Johnson/50 5.00 12.00
140 Magic Johnson/50 5.00 12.00
141 Magic Johnson/50 5.00 12.00
142 Magic Johnson/50 5.00 12.00
143 Magic Johnson/50 5.00 12.00
144 Magic Johnson/50 5.00 12.00
145 Magic Johnson/50 5.00 12.00
146 Magic Johnson/50 5.00 12.00
147 Magic Johnson/50 5.00 12.00
148 Magic Johnson/50 5.00 12.00
149 Magic Johnson/50 5.00 12.00
150 Magic Johnson/50 5.00 12.00
151 Magic Johnson/50 5.00 12.00
152 Larry Johnson 152-161/50 4.00 10.00
153 Larry Johnson/50 4.00 10.00
154 Larry Johnson/50 4.00 10.00
155 Larry Johnson/50 4.00 10.00
156 Larry Johnson/50 4.00 10.00
157 Larry Johnson/50 4.00 10.00
158 Larry Johnson/50 4.00 10.00
159 Larry Johnson/50 4.00 10.00
160 Larry Johnson/50 4.00 10.00
161 Larry Johnson/50 4.00 10.00
162 Grant Hill 162-171/50 10.00 25.00
163 Grant Hill/50 10.00 25.00
164 Grant Hill/50 10.00 25.00
165 Grant Hill/50 10.00 25.00
166 Grant Hill/50 10.00 25.00
167 Grant Hill/50 10.00 25.00
168 Grant Hill/50 10.00 25.00
169 Grant Hill/50 10.00 25.00
170 Grant Hill/50 10.00 25.00
171 Grant Hill/50 10.00 25.00
172 Chris Paul 172-186/50 2.50 6.00
173 Chris Paul/50 2.50 6.00
174 Chris Paul/50 2.50 6.00
175 Chris Paul/50 2.50 6.00
176 Chris Paul/50 2.50 6.00
177 Chris Paul/50 2.50 6.00
178 Chris Paul/50 2.50 6.00
179 Chris Paul/50 2.50 6.00
180 Chris Paul/50 2.50 6.00
181 Chris Paul/50 2.50 6.00
182 Chris Paul/50 2.50 6.00
183 Chris Paul/50 2.50 6.00
184 Chris Paul/50 2.50 6.00
185 Chris Paul/50 2.50 6.00
186 Chris Paul/50 2.50 6.00
187 Jerry West 187-189/50 4.00 10.00
188 Jerry West/50 4.00 10.00
189 Jerry West/50 4.00 10.00
190 A.Hardaway 190-200/50 10.00 25.00
191 Anfernee Hardaway/50 10.00 25.00
192 Anfernee Hardaway/50 10.00 25.00
193 Anfernee Hardaway/50 10.00 25.00
194 Anfernee Hardaway/50 10.00 25.00
195 Anfernee Hardaway/50 10.00 25.00
196 Anfernee Hardaway/50 10.00 25.00
197 Anfernee Hardaway/50 10.00 25.00
198 Anfernee Hardaway/50 10.00 25.00
199 Anfernee Hardaway/50 10.00 25.00
200 Anfernee Hardaway/50 10.00 25.00

2011 Upper Deck All Time Greats Career Book Card Autographs

STATED PRINT RUN ONE TO 15 SER.#'d SETS
SOME UNPRICED DUE TO SCARCITY
SCCP1 Chris Paul/15 40.00 100.00
SCCP2 Chris Paul/15 40.00 100.00
SCMJ1 Michael Jordan/15 400.00 700.00
SCMJ2 Michael Jordan/15 400.00 700.00
SCMJ3 Michael Jordan/15 400.00 700.00
SCRO1 Derrick Rose/15 60.00 150.00

2011 Upper Deck All Time Greats Illustrious Signatures

COMMON CARD
STATED PRINT RUN 3 TO 15 SER.#'d SETS
SOME UNPRICED DUE TO SCARCITY
UNPRICED PARALLEL PRINT RUN ONE SET
ONLY FIRST CARD LISTED PER PLAYER
ISAM1 A.Mourning 1-4/15 40.00 100.00
ISAM2 Alonzo Mourning/15 40.00 100.00
ISAM3 Alonzo Mourning/15 40.00 100.00
ISAM4 Alonzo Mourning/15 40.00 100.00
ISCD1 Clyde Drexler 1-6/10 50.00 120.00
ISCD2 Clyde Drexler/10 50.00 120.00
ISCD3 Clyde Drexler/10 50.00 120.00
ISCD4 Clyde Drexler/10 50.00 120.00
ISCD5 Clyde Drexler/10 50.00 120.00
ISCD6 Clyde Drexler/10 50.00 120.00
ISCP1 Chris Paul 1-7/10 30.00 80.00
ISCP2 Chris Paul/10 30.00 80.00
ISCP3 Chris Paul/10 30.00 80.00
ISCP4 Chris Paul/10 30.00 80.00
ISCP5 Chris Paul/10 30.00 80.00
ISCP6 Chris Paul/10 30.00 80.00
ISCP7 Chris Paul/10 30.00 80.00
ISDR1 D.Robinson 1-6/10 40.00 100.00
ISDR2 David Robinson/10 40.00 100.00
ISDR3 David Robinson/10 40.00 100.00
ISDR4 David Robinson/10 40.00 100.00
ISDR5 David Robinson/10 40.00 100.00
ISDR6 David Robinson/10 40.00 100.00
ISGH1 Grant Hill 1-5/10 60.00 120.00
ISGH2 Grant Hill/10 60.00 120.00
ISGH3 Grant Hill/10 60.00 120.00
ISGH4 Grant Hill/10 60.00 120.00
ISGH5 Grant Hill/10 60.00 120.00
ISJA1 LeBron James 1-8/15 125.00 250.00
ISJA2 LeBron James/15 125.00 250.00
ISJA3 LeBron James/15 125.00 250.00
ISJA4 LeBron James/15 125.00 250.00
ISJA5 LeBron James/15 125.00 250.00
ISJA6 LeBron James/15 125.00 250.00
ISJA7 LeBron James/15 125.00 250.00
ISJA8 LeBron James/15 125.00 250.00
ISJO1 Magic Johnson 1-5/15 30.00 80.00
ISJO2 Magic Johnson/15 30.00 80.00
ISJO3 Magic Johnson/15 30.00 80.00
ISJO4 Magic Johnson/15 30.00 80.00
ISJO5 Magic Johnson/15 30.00 80.00
ISJW1 James Worthy 1-6/10 30.00 80.00
ISJW2 James Worthy/10 30.00 80.00
ISJW3 James Worthy/10 30.00 80.00
ISJW4 James Worthy/10 30.00 80.00
ISJW5 James Worthy/10 30.00 80.00
ISJW6 James Worthy/10 30.00 80.00
ISLB1 Larry Bird 1-6/15 40.00 100.00
ISLB2 Larry Bird/15 40.00 100.00
ISLB3 Larry Bird/15 40.00 100.00
ISLB4 Larry Bird/15 40.00 100.00
ISLB5 Larry Bird/15 40.00 100.00
ISLB6 Larry Bird/15 40.00 100.00
ISLJ1 Larry Johnson 1-5/10 30.00 80.00
ISLJ2 Larry Johnson/10 30.00 80.00
ISLJ3 Larry Johnson/10 30.00 80.00
ISLJ4 Larry Johnson/10 30.00 80.00
ISMJ1 M.Jordan 1-10/15 300.00 600.00
ISMJ2 Michael Jordan/15 300.00 600.00
ISMJ3 Michael Jordan/15 300.00 600.00
ISMJ4 Michael Jordan/15 300.00 600.00
ISMJ5 Michael Jordan/15 300.00 600.00
ISMJ6 Michael Jordan/15 300.00 600.00
ISMJ7 Michael Jordan/15 300.00 600.00
ISMJ8 Michael Jordan/15 300.00 600.00
ISMJ9 Michael Jordan/15 300.00 600.00
ISMJ10 Michael Jordan/15 300.00 600.00

2011 Upper Deck All Time Greats Lettermen Autographs

STATED PRINT RUN 12 TO 80 SER.#'d SETS
PRINT RUNS BASED ON LAST NAME
TOTAL PRINT RUN LISTED WITH ASTERISK
LAH Anfernee Hardaway/80* 75.00 200.00
LAM Alonzo Mourning/80* 40.00 80.00
LBR Bill Russell/21* 100.00 200.00
LCD Clyde Drexler/21* 75.00 150.00
LCP Chris Paul/20* 75.00 150.00
LDR David Robinson/24* 75.00 200.00
LGH Grant Hill/12* 100.00 200.00
LHO Hakeem Olajuwon/32* 30.00 80.00
LJA LeBron James/25* 200.00 400.00
LJE Julius Erving/18* 60.00 120.00
LJH John Havlicek/24* 25.00 60.00
LJO Magic Johnson/21* 75.00 200.00
LJW James Worthy/24* 50.00 125.00
LLB Larry Bird/40* 75.00 200.00
LLJ Larry Johnson/35* 50.00 100.00
LMJ Michael Jordan/30* 400.00 800.00
LRO Derrick Rose/20* 50.00 120.00
LSN Steve Nash/20* 50.00 120.00
LWE Jerry West/12* 50.00 120.00
LWF Walt Frazier/21* 60.00 150.00

2011 Upper Deck All Time Greats Signatures

STATED PRINT RUN 5 TO 25 SER.#'d SETS
SOME UNPRICED DUE TO SCARCITY
UNPRICED GOLD PRINT RUN ONE SET
UNPRICED SILVER PRINT RUN 3 TO 10 SETS
ONLY FIRST CARD LISTED PER PLAYER
AGSAH1 A.Hardaway 1-4/15 30.00 80.00
AGSAH2 Anfernee Hardaway/15 30.00 80.00
AGSAH3 Anfernee Hardaway/15 30.00 80.00
AGSAH4 Anfernee Hardaway/15 30.00 80.00
AGSAM1 A.Mourning 1-6/10 40.00 80.00
AGSAM2 Alonzo Mourning/10 40.00 80.00
AGSAM3 Alonzo Mourning/10 40.00 80.00
AGSAM4 Alonzo Mourning/10 40.00 80.00
AGSAM5 Alonzo Mourning/10 40.00 80.00
AGSAM6 Alonzo Mourning/10 40.00 80.00
AGSCP1 Chris Paul 1-7/10 40.00 100.00
AGSCP2 Chris Paul/10 40.00 100.00
AGSCP3 Chris Paul/10 40.00 100.00
AGSCP4 Chris Paul/10 40.00 100.00
AGSCP5 Chris Paul/10 40.00 100.00
AGSCP6 Chris Paul/10 40.00 100.00
AGSCP7 Chris Paul/10 40.00 100.00
AGSDR1 D.Robinson 1-4/15 50.00 120.00
AGSDR2 David Robinson/15 50.00 120.00
AGSDR3 David Robinson/15 50.00 120.00
AGSDR4 David Robinson/15 50.00 120.00
AGSGH1 Grant Hill 1-5/10 100.00 225.00
AGSGH2 Grant Hill/10 100.00 225.00
AGSGH3 Grant Hill/10 100.00 225.00
AGSGH4 Grant Hill/10 100.00 225.00
AGSGH5 Grant Hill/10 100.00 225.00
AGSHO1 H.Olajuwon 1-4/10 40.00 100.00
AGSHO2 Hakeem Olajuwon/10 40.00 100.00
AGSHO3 Hakeem Olajuwon/10 40.00 100.00
AGSHO4 Hakeem Olajuwon/10 40.00 100.00
AGSJA1 L.James 1-10/15 150.00 300.00
AGSJA2 LeBron James/15 150.00 300.00
AGSJA3 LeBron James/15 150.00 300.00
AGSJA4 LeBron James/15 150.00 300.00
AGSJA5 LeBron James/15 150.00 300.00
AGSJA6 LeBron James/15 150.00 300.00
AGSJA7 LeBron James/15 150.00 300.00
AGSJA8 LeBron James/15 150.00 300.00
AGSJA9 LeBron James/15 150.00 300.00
AGSJO1 M.Johnson 1-7/15 50.00 120.00
AGSJO2 Magic Johnson/15 50.00 120.00
AGSJO3 Magic Johnson/15 50.00 120.00
AGSJO4 Magic Johnson/15 50.00 120.00
AGSJO5 Magic Johnson/15 50.00 120.00
AGSJO6 Magic Johnson/15 50.00 120.00
AGSJO7 Magic Johnson/15 50.00 120.00
AGSJW1 James Worthy 1-4/10 30.00 80.00
AGSJW2 James Worthy/10 30.00 80.00
AGSJW3 James Worthy/10 30.00 80.00
AGSJW4 James Worthy/10 30.00 80.00
AGSLB1 Larry Bird 1-5/15 50.00 120.00
AGSLB2 Larry Bird/15 50.00 120.00
AGSLB3 Larry Bird/15 50.00 120.00
AGSLB4 Larry Bird/15 50.00 120.00
AGSLB5 Larry Bird/15 50.00 120.00
AGSLJ1 L.Johnson 1-4/10 40.00 100.00
AGSLJ2 Larry Johnson/10 40.00 100.00
AGSLJ3 Larry Johnson/10 40.00 100.00
AGSLJ4 Larry Johnson/10 40.00 100.00
AGSMJ1 M.Jordan 1-12/25 300.00 450.00
AGSMJ2 Michael Jordan/25 300.00 450.00
AGSMJ3 Michael Jordan/25 300.00 450.00
AGSMJ4 Michael Jordan/25 300.00 450.00
AGSMJ5 Michael Jordan/25 300.00 450.00
AGSMJ6 Michael Jordan/25 300.00 450.00
AGSMJ7 Michael Jordan/25 300.00 450.00
AGSMJ8 Michael Jordan/25 300.00 450.00
AGSMJ9 Michael Jordan/25 300.00 450.00
AGSJA10 LeBron James/15 125.00 225.00
AGSMJ10 Michael Jordan/25 300.00 550.00
AGSMJ11 Michael Jordan/25 300.00 550.00
AGSMJ12 Michael Jordan/25 300.00 550.00

2012 Upper Deck All-Time Greats

STATED PRINT RUN 99 SER. #'d SETS
1 Michael Jordan 10.00 25.00
2 Michael Jordan 10.00 25.00
3 Michael Jordan 10.00 25.00
4 Michael Jordan 10.00 25.00
5 Michael Jordan 10.00 25.00
6 Michael Jordan 10.00 25.00
7 Michael Jordan 10.00 25.00
38 Larry Bird 6.00 15.00
39 Larry Bird 6.00 15.00
40 Larry Bird 6.00 15.00
41 Larry Bird 6.00 15.00
42 Larry Bird 6.00 15.00
43 LeBron James 8.00 20.00
44 LeBron James 8.00 20.00
45 LeBron James 8.00 20.00
46 LeBron James 8.00 20.00
47 LeBron James 8.00 20.00
48 LeBron James 8.00 20.00

2012 Upper Deck All-Time Greats Bronze

*BRONZE/65: .5X TO 1.2X BASIC CARDS

2012 Upper Deck All-Time Greats Silver

*SILVER/35: .6X TO 1.5X BASIC CARDS

2012 Upper Deck All-Time Greats Athletes of the Century Booklet Autographs

STATED PRINT RUN 5-35
ACLB Larry Bird/25 50.00 100.00
ACLJ LeBron James/25
ACMJ Michael Jordan/5

2012 Upper Deck All-Time Greats Letterman Autographs

PRINT RUN 7-140
LLB Larry Bird/40 60.00 120.00
LLJ LeBron James/25 100.00 200.00
LMJ Michael Jordan/30

2012 Upper Deck All-Time Greats Shining Moments Autographs

PRINT RUN 2-30
SMLB1 Larry Bird/5 60.00 120.00
SMLB2 Larry Bird/5 60.00 120.00
SMLB3 Larry Bird/5 60.00 120.00
SMLB4 Larry Bird/5 60.00 120.00
SMLB5 Larry Bird/5 60.00 120.00
SMLJ1 LeBron James/10 100.00 200.00
SMLJ2 LeBron James/10 100.00 200.00
SMLJ3 LeBron James/10 100.00 200.00
SMLJ4 LeBron James/10 100.00 200.00
SMLJ5 LeBron James/10 100.00 200.00
SMLJ6 LeBron James/5
SMLJ7 LeBron James/5
SMMJ1 Michael Jordan/10
SMMJ2 Michael Jordan/10
SMMJ3 Michael Jordan/10
SMMJ4 Michael Jordan/10
SMMJ5 Michael Jordan/10
SMMJ6 Michael Jordan/10

2012 Upper Deck All-Time Greats Signatures

PRINT RUN 3-70
GALB1 Larry Bird/8
GALB2 Larry Bird/8
GALB3 Larry Bird/8
GALB4 Larry Bird/8
GALJ1 LeBron James/7 150.00 250.00
GALJ2 LeBron James/7 150.00 250.00
GALJ3 LeBron James/7 150.00 250.00
GALJ4 LeBron James/7 150.00 250.00
GALJ5 LeBron James/7 150.00 250.00
GALJ6 LeBron James/7 150.00 250.00
GALJ7 LeBron James/7 150.00 250.00
GAMJ1 Michael Jordan/10 400.00 600.00
GAMJ2 Michael Jordan/10 400.00 600.00
GAMJ3 Michael Jordan/10 400.00 600.00
GAMJ4 Michael Jordan/10 400.00 600.00
GAMJ5 Michael Jordan/40 300.00 500.00
GAMJ6 Michael Jordan/10 400.00 600.00
GAMJ7 Michael Jordan/10 400.00 600.00

2012 Upper Deck All-Time Greats Signatures Silver

*SILVER: X TO X BASIC CARDS
PRINT RUN 2-25

2012 Upper Deck All-Time Greats SPx All-Time Dual Forces Autographs

PRINT RUN 1-25
ATF2BW Larry Bird
Dominique Wilkins/10
ATF2JB Michael Jordan
Larry Bird/10
ATF2JG Michael Jordan
Wayne Gretzky/1
ATF2JJ LeBron James
Michael Jordan/5
ATF2JW Michael Jordan
Tiger Woods/1
ATF2LL Larry Bird
LeBron James/5
ATF2WJ Dominique Wilkins
LeBron James/5

2013 Upper Deck All-Time Greats

STATED PRINT RUN 150 SER.#'d SETS
ALL VERSIONS PRICED EQUALLY
1 Allen Iverson 2.50 6.00
2 Allen Iverson 2.50 6.00
3 Allen Iverson 2.50 6.00
4 Allen Iverson 2.50 6.00
5 Allen Iverson 2.50 6.00
6 Allen Iverson 2.50 6.00
7 Bill Russell 3.00 8.00
8 Bill Russell 3.00 8.00
9 Bill Russell 3.00 8.00
10 David Robinson 3.00 8.00
11 David Robinson 3.00 8.00
12 David Robinson 3.00 8.00
13 David Robinson 3.00 8.00
14 David Robinson 3.00 8.00
15 Dennis Rodman 4.00 10.00
16 Dennis Rodman 4.00 10.00
17 Dennis Rodman 4.00 10.00
18 Grant Hill 2.50 6.00
19 Grant Hill 2.50 6.00
20 Grant Hill 2.50 6.00
21 Grant Hill 2.50 6.00
22 Grant Hill 2.50 6.00
23 Grant Hill 2.50 6.00
24 Grant Hill 2.50 6.00
25 Hakeem Olajuwon 2.50 6.00
26 Hakeem Olajuwon 2.50 6.00
27 Hakeem Olajuwon 2.50 6.00
28 Hakeem Olajuwon 2.50 6.00
29 Isiah Thomas 2.00 5.00
30 Isiah Thomas 2.00 5.00
31 Isiah Thomas 2.00 5.00
32 Isiah Thomas 2.00 5.00
33 Isiah Thomas 2.00 5.00
34 Isiah Thomas 2.00 5.00
35 Jason Kidd 2.00 5.00
36 Jason Kidd 2.00 5.00
37 Jason Kidd 2.00 5.00
38 Jason Kidd 2.00 5.00
39 Jason Kidd 2.00 5.00
40 Jason Kidd 2.00 5.00
41 Julius Erving 3.00 8.00
42 Julius Erving 3.00 8.00
43 Julius Erving 3.00 8.00
44 Karl Malone 2.50 6.00
45 Karl Malone 2.50 6.00
46 Karl Malone 2.50 6.00
47 Karl Malone 2.50 6.00
48 Karl Malone 2.50 6.00
49 Larry Bird 5.00 12.00
50 Larry Bird 5.00 12.00
51 Larry Bird 5.00 12.00
52 Larry Bird 5.00 12.00
53 LeBron James 8.00 20.00
54 LeBron James 8.00 20.00
55 LeBron James 8.00 20.00
56 LeBron James 8.00 20.00
57 LeBron James 8.00 20.00
58 Magic Johnson 5.00 12.00
59 Magic Johnson 5.00 12.00
60 Magic Johnson 5.00 12.00
61 Magic Johnson 5.00 12.00
62 Magic Johnson 5.00 12.00
63 Magic Johnson 5.00 12.00
64 Magic Johnson 3.00 8.00
65 Michael Jordan 10.00 25.00
66 Michael Jordan 10.00 25.00
67 Michael Jordan 10.00 25.00
68 Michael Jordan 10.00 25.00
69 Michael Jordan 10.00 25.00
70 Michael Jordan 10.00 25.00
71 Michael Jordan 10.00 25.00
72 Michael Jordan 10.00 25.00
73 Michael Jordan 10.00 25.00
74 Michael Jordan 10.00 25.00
75 Michael Jordan 10.00 25.00
76 Michael Jordan 10.00 25.00
77 Michael Jordan 10.00 25.00
78 Michael Jordan 10.00 25.00
79 Michael Jordan 10.00 25.00
80 Gary Payton 2.00 5.00
81 Gary Payton 2.00 5.00
82 Gary Payton 2.00 5.00
83 Gary Payton 2.00 5.00
84 Gary Payton 2.00 5.00
85 Paul Pierce 4.00 10.00
86 Paul Pierce 4.00 10.00
87 Paul Pierce 4.00 10.00
88 Paul Pierce 4.00 10.00
89 Paul Pierce 4.00 10.00
90 Ray Allen 2.00 5.00
91 Ray Allen 2.00 5.00
92 Ray Allen 2.00 5.00
93 Ray Allen 2.00 5.00
94 Ray Allen 2.00 5.00
95 Reggie Miller 4.00 10.00
96 Reggie Miller 4.00 10.00
97 Reggie Miller 4.00 10.00
98 Reggie Miller 4.00 10.00
99 Reggie Miller 4.00 10.00
100 Reggie Miller 4.00 10.00

2013 Upper Deck All-Time Greats Silver 10

*GOLD: .75X TO 2X BASIC
STATED PRINT RUN 10 SER.#'d SETS
ALL VERSIONS PRICED EQUALLY
18 Grant Hill 8.00 20.00
85 Paul Pierce 12.00 30.00
90 Ray Allen 8.00 20.00
95 Reggie Miller 12.00 30.00

2013 Upper Deck All-Time Greats Gold

*SILVER: .6X TO 1.5X BASIC
STATED PRINT RUN 50 SER.#'d SETS
ALL VERSIONS PRICED EQUALLY

2013 Upper Deck All-Time Greats All-Time Forces

STATED PRINT RUN 35 SER.#'d SETS
ATFAI Allen Iverson 60.00 120.00
ATFBR Bill Russell 50.00 100.00
ATFDR Dennis Rodman 25.00 60.00
ATFGH Grant Hill 30.00 80.00
ATFGP Gary Payton 12.00 30.00
ATFHO Hakeem Olajuwon 50.00 100.00
ATFIT Isiah Thomas 12.00 30.00
ATFJE Julius Erving 75.00 150.00
ATFJK Jason Kidd 15.00 40.00
ATFJO Magic Johnson 75.00 150.00
ATFKM Karl Malone 40.00 100.00
ATFLB Larry Bird 50.00 100.00
ATFLJ LeBron James 300.00 500.00
ATFMA Karl Malone 75.00 150.00
ATFMI Reggie Miller 75.00 150.00
ATFMJ Michael Jordan 350.00 700.00
ATFOL Hakeem Olajuwon 15.00 40.00
ATFPP Paul Pierce 30.00 80.00
ATFRA Ray Allen 50.00 100.00
ATFRM Reggie Miller 75.00 150.00
ATFRO David Robinson 20.00 50.00

2013 Upper Deck All-Time Greats Banner Season

STATED PRINT RUN 25 SER.#'d SETS
BSAI Allen Iverson 100.00 200.00
BSBR Bill Russell 50.00 120.00
BSDR David Robinson 25.00 60.00
BSGH Grant Hill 15.00 40.00
BSGP Gary Payton 15.00 40.00
BSHO Hakeem Olajuwon 40.00 80.00
BSIT Isiah Thomas 25.00 60.00
BSJE Julius Erving 25.00 60.00
BSJK Jason Kidd 125.00 250.00
BSJO Michael Jordan 250.00 500.00
BSKM Karl Malone 15.00 40.00
BSLB Larry Bird 75.00 150.00
BSLJ LeBron James 200.00 300.00
BSMJ Magic Johnson 100.00 200.00
BSPP Paul Pierce 40.00 100.00
BSRA Ray Allen 75.00 150.00
BSRM Reggie Miller 50.00 100.00
BSRO Dennis Rodman 15.00 40.00

2013 Upper Deck All-Time Greats Jordan Vs.

STATED PRINT RUN 23 SER.#'d SETS
ALL VERSIONS PRICED EQUALLY
JV1 Michael Jordan 40.00 100.00
JV2 Michael Jordan 40.00 100.00
JV3 Michael Jordan 40.00 100.00
JV4 Michael Jordan 40.00 100.00
JV5 Michael Jordan 40.00 100.00
JV6 Michael Jordan 40.00 100.00
JV7 Michael Jordan 40.00 100.00
JV8 Michael Jordan 40.00 100.00
JV9 Michael Jordan 40.00 100.00
JV10 Michael Jordan 40.00 100.00
JV11 Allen Iverson 40.00 100.00
JV12 David Robinson 20.00 50.00
JV13 Julius Erving 20.00 50.00
JV14 Karl Malone 20.00 50.00
JV15 Larry Bird 12.50 30.00
JV16 LeBron James 30.00 80.00
JV17 Magic Johnson 20.00 50.00
JV18 Michael Jordan 40.00 100.00
JV19 Isiah Thomas 20.00 50.00
JV20 Reggie Miller 40.00 100.00

2013 Upper Deck All-Time Greats Jordan Vs. Signatures

STATED PRINT RUN 23 SER.#'d SETS
JVSAI A.Iverson/M.Jordan
JVSDR M.Jordan/D.Robinson 450.00 700.00
JVSJE M.Jordan/J.Erving 300.00 600.00
JVSJO M.Jordan/M.Jordan 450.00 700.00
JVSJT M.Jordan/I.Thomas 400.00 600.00
JVSKM M.Jordan/K.Malone
JVSLB M.Jordan/L.Bird 550.00 800.00
JVSLJ L.James/M.Jordan 800.00 1200.00
JVSMJ M.Jordan/M.Johnson 200.00 400.00
JVSRM M.Jordan/R.Miller 550.00 800.00

2013 Upper Deck All-Time Greats Program of Excellence

PRINT RUNS B/WN 10-23 COPIES PER
PEDR David Robinson/15 60.00 120.00
PEGH Grant Hill/15 60.00 120.00
PEHA Hakeem Olajuwon/15 30.00 80.00
PEHI Grant Hill/15 40.00 80.00
PEHO Hakeem Olajuwon/15 30.00 80.00
PEIT Isiah Thomas/15
PEJO Michael Jordan/23 350.00 700.00
PEMI Michael Jordan/23 350.00 700.00
PEMJ Magic Johnson/15 50.00 120.00
PEOL Hakeem Olajuwon/15 30.00 80.00
PERO David Robinson/15 60.00 120.00

2013 Upper Deck All-Time Greats Signatures

PRINT RUNS B/WN 25-55 COPIES PER
ALL VERSIONS PRICED EQUALLY
ATGAI1 Allen Iverson/35 50.00 100.00
ATGAI2 Allen Iverson/35 50.00 100.00
ATGAI3 Allen Iverson/35 50.00 100.00
ATGAI4 Allen Iverson/35 50.00 100.00
ATGAI5 Allen Iverson/35 50.00 100.00
ATGAI6 Allen Iverson/35 50.00 100.00
ATGAI7 Allen Iverson/35 50.00 100.00
ATGBR1 Bill Russell/50 50.00 120.00
ATGBR2 Bill Russell/55 50.00 120.00
ATGDR1 David Robinson/30 30.00 80.00
ATGDR2 David Robinson/30 30.00 80.00
ATGDR3 David Robinson/30 30.00 80.00
ATGDR4 David Robinson/30 30.00 80.00
ATGDR5 David Robinson/30 30.00 80.00
ATGDR6 David Robinson/30 30.00 80.00
ATGGH1 Grant Hill/35 15.00 40.00
ATGGH2 Grant Hill/35 15.00 40.00
ATGGH3 Grant Hill/35 15.00 40.00
ATGGH4 Grant Hill/35 15.00 40.00
ATGGH5 Grant Hill/35 15.00 40.00
ATGGH6 Grant Hill/35 15.00 40.00
ATGGH7 Grant Hill/35 15.00 40.00
ATGGH8 Grant Hill/35 15.00 40.00
ATGGP1 Gary Payton/30 12.00 30.00
ATGGP2 Gary Payton/30 12.00 30.00
ATGGP3 Gary Payton/30 12.00 30.00
ATGGP4 Gary Payton/30 12.00 30.00
ATGGP5 Gary Payton/30 12.00 30.00
ATGHO1 Hakeem Olajuwon/35 15.00 40.00
ATGHO2 Hakeem Olajuwon/35 15.00 40.00
ATGHO3 Hakeem Olajuwon/35 15.00 40.00
ATGIT1 Isiah Thomas/45 10.00 25.00
ATGIT2 Isiah Thomas/45 10.00 25.00
ATGIT3 Isiah Thomas/45 10.00 25.00
ATGIT4 Isiah Thomas/45 10.00 25.00
ATGIT5 Isiah Thomas/45 10.00 25.00
ATGJE1 Julius Erving/55 30.00 80.00
ATGJE2 Julius Erving/55 30.00 80.00
ATGJK1 Jason Kidd/35 15.00 40.00
ATGJK2 Jason Kidd/35 15.00 40.00
ATGJK3 Jason Kidd/35 15.00 40.00
ATGJK4 Jason Kidd/35 15.00 40.00
ATGJK5 Jason Kidd/35 15.00 40.00
ATGJK6 Jason Kidd/35 15.00 40.00
ATGJK7 Jason Kidd/35 15.00 40.00
ATGJO1 Magic Johnson/50 30.00 80.00
ATGJO2 Magic Johnson/50 30.00 80.00
ATGJO3 Magic Johnson/50 30.00 80.00
ATGJO4 Magic Johnson/50 30.00 80.00
ATGJO5 Magic Johnson/50 30.00 80.00
ATGJO6 Magic Johnson/50 30.00 80.00
ATGJO7 Magic Johnson/50 30.00 80.00
ATGKM1 Karl Malone/35 30.00 60.00
ATGKM2 Karl Malone/35 30.00 60.00
ATGKM3 Karl Malone/35 30.00 60.00
ATGKM4 Karl Malone/35 30.00 60.00
ATGKM5 Karl Malone/35 30.00 60.00
ATGLB1 Larry Bird/33 30.00 80.00
ATGLB2 Larry Bird/33 30.00 80.00
ATGLB3 Larry Bird/33 30.00 80.00
ATGLB4 Larry Bird/33 30.00 80.00
ATGLB5 Larry Bird/33 30.00 80.00
ATGLJ1 LeBron James/30 150.00 300.00
ATGLJ2 LeBron James/30 150.00 300.00
ATGLJ3 LeBron James/30 150.00 300.00
ATGLJ4 LeBron James/30 150.00 300.00
ATGLJ5 LeBron James/30 150.00 300.00
ATGMJ1 Michael Jordan/45 250.00 400.00
ATGMJ2 Michael Jordan/45 250.00 400.00
ATGMJ3 Michael Jordan/45 250.00 400.00
ATGMJ4 Michael Jordan/45 250.00 400.00
ATGMJ5 Michael Jordan/45 250.00 400.00
ATGMJ6 Michael Jordan/45 250.00 400.00
ATGMJ7 Michael Jordan/45 250.00 400.00
ATGMJ8 Michael Jordan/45 250.00 400.00
ATGMJ9 Michael Jordan/45 250.00 400.00
ATGPP1 Paul Pierce/50 20.00 50.00
ATGPP2 Paul Pierce/50 20.00 50.00
ATGPP3 Paul Pierce/50 20.00 50.00
ATGPP4 Paul Pierce/50 20.00 50.00
ATGRA1 Ray Allen/40 20.00 50.00
ATGRA2 Ray Allen/40 20.00 50.00
ATGRA3 Ray Allen/40 20.00 50.00
ATGRA4 Ray Allen/40 20.00 50.00
ATGRA5 Ray Allen/40 20.00 50.00
ATGRM1 Reggie Miller/30 75.00 150.00
ATGRM2 Reggie Miller/30 75.00 150.00
ATGRM3 Reggie Miller/25 75.00 150.00
ATGRM4 Reggie Miller/25 75.00 150.00
ATGRM5 Reggie Miller/25 75.00 150.00
ATGRO1 Dennis Rodman/55 20.00 50.00
ATGRO2 Dennis Rodman/55 20.00 50.00
ATGMJ10 Michael Jordan/45 250.00 400.00
ATGMJ11 Michael Jordan/45 250.00 400.00
ATGMJ12 Michael Jordan/45 250.00 400.00
ATGMJ13 Michael Jordan/45 250.00 400.00
ATGMJ14 Michael Jordan/50 250.00 400.00
ATGMJ15 Michael Jordan/45 250.00 400.00
ATGMJ16 Michael Jordan/45 250.00 400.00
ATGMJ17 Michael Jordan/45 250.00 400.00

1996 Upper Deck Authenticated Space Jam Celcards

Released in two separate matching collections, these celcards were produced by Upper Deck Authenticated and feature pieces from the 1996 Space Jam movie. Set number one contains four-cards with matching numbers 1-5,000. Set number two contains two-cards with matching numbers 5,001-10,000. The cels are not numbered, but listed in order of the sets, with the first four cards representing set one, and the final two representing set two.

COMPLETE SET 1 (4) 30.00 80.00
COMPLETE SET 2 (2) 15.00 40.00
NNO Michael Jordan 8.00 20.00
Bugs Bunny
NNO Michael Jordan 8.00 20.00
Bugs Bunny #2
NNO Michael Jordan 8.00 20.00
Monstar
NNO Michael Jordan 8.00 20.00
The Tune Squad
NNO Michael Jordan 8.00 20.00
Bugs Bunny
NNO Michael Jordan 8.00 20.00
Porky Pig

1995-96 Upper Deck Ball Park Jordan

This 5-card standard size set was available as a mail-in offer from Ball Park hot dogs by sending in two UPCs and one dollar. The card fronts have color action photos (with jersey number and logos airbrushed out) within a U.S. flag border. Michael Jordan's name is below the photo in a transparent font. Ball Park and Upper Deck logos adorn the top. The back has the same U.S. flag background with some biographical information below the same, but smaller, color action photo. His name appears again in the same font vertically on the left side. The traditional Upper Deck hologram resides in the bottom right corner. The cards are numbered with the prefix BP.

COMPLETE SET (5) 15.00 40.00
COMMON CARD (1-5) 4.00 10.00

1995-96 Upper Deck Ball Park Jordan Gold

COMPLETE SET (5) 25.00 60.00
COMMON CARD (1-5) 6.00 15.00

1996-97 Upper Deck Ball Park Jordan

These Michael Jordan tribute cards were available one per limited edition Ball Park hot dog package. The fronts have color action shots or close-ups of Jordan, a Ball Park logo in the top left corner and "Michael" written in large block letters vertically on the right side. The backs contain half of the same photo as the front and a small blurb describing the indescribable player. The Upper Deck logo and hologram are found at the bottom. A gold version, listed separately, was also available as a redemption offer with 4 UPC codes.

COMPLETE SET (5) 10.00 25.00
COMMON CARD (1-5) 2.50 6.00

1996-97 Upper Deck Ball Park Jordan Gold

This set is a gold bordered version of the base set from the same year. The set was available by sending in four UPC's from Ball Park hot dogs. The five Michael Jordan cards are numberd "x/5" on the back.

COMPLETE SET (5) 12.00 30.00
COMMON CARD (1-5) 3.00 8.00

1999 Upper Deck Century Legends

Released as a 89-card set, this set focuses on the best basketball athletes of the century. The cards were released in 5-card packs with a suggested retail price of $4.99. The set featues the top 50 players by The Sporting News, 30 21st Century Phenom cards and 10 Michael Jordan Player of the Century cards. Card number six does not exist. Please note that card "S1" was given out to dealers and members of the hobby press as a promotional card.

COMPLETE SET (89) 20.00 40.00
1 Michael Jordan 2.00 5.00
2 Bill Russell .40 1.00
3 Wilt Chamberlain .50 1.25
4 George Mikan .40 1.00
5 Oscar Robertson .30 .75
7 Larry Bird .60 1.50
8 Karl Malone .30 .75
9 Elgin Baylor .25 .60
10 Kareem Abdul-Jabbar .40 1.00
11 Jerry West .30 .75
12 Bob Cousy .40 1.00
13 Julius Erving .40 1.00
14 Hakeem Olajuwon .30 .75
15 John Havlicek .30 .75
16 John Stockton .30 .75
17 Rick Barry .20 .50
18 Moses Malone .25 .60
19 Nate Thurmond .20 .50
20 Bob Pettit .25 .60
21 Pete Maravich .40 1.00
22 Willis Reed .25 .60
23 Isiah Thomas .25 .60
24 Dolph Schayes .25 .60
25 Walt Frazier .25 .60
26 Wes Unseld .25 .60
27 Bill Sharman .25 .60
28 George Gervin .25 .60
29 Hal Greer .20 .50
30 Dave DeBusschere .25 .60
31 Earl Monroe .25 .60
32 Kevin McHale .30 .75
33 Charles Barkley .30 .75
34 Elvin Hayes .25 .60
35 Scottie Pippen .40 1.00
36 Jerry Lucas .25 .60
37 Dave Bing .25 .60
38 Lenny Wilkens .25 .60
39 Paul Arizin .25 .60
40 Nate Archibald .20 .50
41 James Worthy .30 .75
42 Patrick Ewing .30 .75
43 Billy Cunningham .25 .60
44 Sam Jones .30 .75
45 Dave Cowens .15 .40
46 Robert Parish .25 .60
47 Bill Walton .25 .60
48 Shaquille O'Neal .60 1.50
49 David Robinson .40 1.00
50 Dominique Wilkins .30 .75
51 Kobe Bryant 1.00 2.50
52 Vince Carter .50 1.25
53 Paul Pierce .40 1.00
54 Allen Iverson .50 1.25
55 Stephon Marbury .20 .50
56 Mike Bibby .25 .60
57 Jason Williams .30 .75
58 Kevin Garnett .50 1.25
59 Tim Duncan .50 1.25
60 Antawn Jamison .25 .60
61 Antoine Walker .25 .60
62 Shareef Abdur-Rahim .20 .50
63 Michael Olowokandi .15 .40
64 Robert Traylor .15 .40
65 Keith Van Horn .20 .50
66 Shaquille O'Neal .60 1.50
67 Ray Allen .25 .60
68 Gary Payton .25 .60
69 Raef LaFrentz .15 .40
70 Grant Hill .30 .75
71 Anfernee Hardaway .40 1.00
72 Maurice Taylor .15 .40
73 Ron Mercer .20 .50
74 Michael Finley .25 .60
75 Jason Kidd .40 1.00
76 Allan Houston .20 .50
77 Damon Stoudamire .20 .50
78 Antonio McDyess .20 .50
79 Eddie Jones .25 .60
80 Michael Dickerson .15 .40
81 Michael Jordan 1.25 3.00
82 Michael Jordan 1.25 3.00
83 Michael Jordan 1.25 3.00
84 Michael Jordan 1.25 3.00
85 Michael Jordan 1.25 3.00
86 Michael Jordan 1.25 3.00
87 Michael Jordan 1.25 3.00
88 Michael Jordan 1.25 3.00
89 Michael Jordan 1.25 3.00
90 Michael Jordan 1.25 3.00
S1 Michael Jordan PROMO 2.00 5.00

1999 Upper Deck Century Legends Century Collection

COMMON MJ (81-90) 100.00 250.00
*STARS: 20X TO 50X BASE CARD HI
STATED PRINT RUN 100 SERIAL #'d SETS
CARD NUMBER 6 DOES NOT EXIST
1 Michael Jordan 200.00 400.00
51 Kobe Bryant 200.00 400.00
70 Grant Hill 20.00 50.00
71 Anfernee Hardaway 30.00 80.00

1999 Upper Deck Century Legends All-Century Team

Randomly inserted in packs at one in 11, this set features the top ten player's of all time as selected by Upper Deck. Card backs carry an "A" prefix.
COMPLETE SET (12) 20.00 40.00
STATED ODDS 1:11
A1 Michael Jordan 8.00 20.00
A2 Oscar Robertson 1.25 3.00
A3 Wilt Chamberlain 2.00 5.00
A4 Larry Bird 2.50 6.00
A5 Julius Erving 1.50 4.00
A6 Jerry West 1.25 3.00
A7 Charles Barkley 1.25 3.00
A8 John Stockton 1.25 3.00
A9 Hakeem Olajuwon 1.25 3.00
A10 Karl Malone 1.25 3.00
A11 Scottie Pippen 1.50 4.00
A12 David Robinson 1.50 4.00

1999 Upper Deck Century Legends Epic Milestones

Randomly inserted in packs at one in 11, this 12-card set showcases ten of the most impressive milestones ever achieved in pro basketball history. Card backs carry an "EM" prefix.
COMPLETE SET (12) 20.00 40.00
STATED ODDS 1:11
EM1 Michael Jordan 8.00 20.00
EM2 Jerry West 1.25 3.00
EM3 John Stockton 1.25 3.00
EM4 Wilt Chamberlain 2.00 5.00
EM5 Julius Erving 1.50 4.00
EM6 Reggie Miller 1.00 2.50
EM7 Hakeem Olajuwon 1.25 3.00
EM8 Robert Parish 1.00 2.50
EM9 Kobe Bryant 4.00 10.00
EM10 Rick Barry .75 2.00
EM11 Patrick Ewing 1.25 3.00
EM12 Charles Barkley 1.25 3.00

1999 Upper Deck Century Legends Epic Signatures

Randomly inserted in packs at one in 23, this 32-card set features autographs from some of the greatest stars of the 20th century. The cards are numbered by the player's name initials. Hakeem Olajuwon was issued a trade card, but did not end up signing for the set. Upper Deck sent Allen Iverson cards for Olajuwon.
STATED ODDS 1:23
AE Alex English 6.00 15.00
AI Allen Iverson 200.00 400.00
BC Bob Cousy 50.00 120.00
BL Bob Lanier 6.00 15.00
BP Bob Pettit 15.00 40.00
BR Bill Russell 350.00 700.00
BS Bill Sharman 10.00 25.00
BW Bill Walton 8.00 20.00
CD Clyde Drexler 12.00 30.00
DC Dave Cowens 10.00 25.00
DR Julius Erving 200.00 400.00
DT David Thompson 6.00 15.00
EB Elgin Baylor 10.00 25.00
EH Elvin Hayes 10.00 25.00
EM Earl Monroe 10.00 25.00
GG George Gervin 10.00 25.00
JL Jerry Lucas 12.00 30.00
JW Jerry West 25.00 60.00
KA Kareem Abdul-Jabbar 125.00 250.00
LB Larry Bird 250.00 500.00
MB Mike Bibby 6.00 15.00
MM Moses Malone 30.00 80.00
MO Michael Olowokandi 12.00 30.00
NA Nate Archibald 8.00 20.00
OR Oscar Robertson 40.00 100.00
TH Tim Hardaway 12.00 30.00
WC Wilt Chamberlain 2200.00 3000.00
WF Walt Frazier 8.00 20.00
WR Willis Reed 8.00 20.00
WU Wes Unseld 8.00 20.00
JH John Havlicek 25.00 60.00

1999 Upper Deck Century Legends Epic Signatures Century

*CENTURY: .75X TO 2X HI COLUMN
STATED PRINT RUN 100 SERIAL #'d SETS
EXCEPTIONS NOTED BELOW
BR AND DR NOT PRICED DUE TO SCARCITY
OLAJUWON DID NOT SIGN TRADE CARDS
IVERSON AU REPLACES OLAJUWON
AE Alex English/100 25.00 60.00
AI Allen Iverson/100 400.00 800.00
BC Bob Cousy/100 100.00 250.00
BL Bob Lanier/100 25.00 60.00
BS Bill Sharman/100 75.00 200.00
BW Bill Walton/100 40.00 100.00
EB Elgin Baylor/100 25.00 60.00
EH Elvin Hayes/100 40.00 100.00
KA Kareem Abdul-Jabbar/100 150.00 350.00
LB Larry Bird/33 400.00 800.00
MJ Michael Jordan/23 1500.00 3000.00
WC Wilt Chamberlain/100 3000.00 3800.00
JH John Havlicek/100 100.00 200.00

1999 Upper Deck Century Legends Generations

Randomly inserted in packs at one in four, this 12-card set features double-sided cards of a modern NBA star coupled with an NBA legend. The cards carry a "G" prefix.
COMPLETE SET (12) 12.50 30.00
STATED ODDS 1:4
G1 M.Jordan/J.Erving 5.00 12.00
G2 K.Bryant/M.Jordan 5.00 12.00
G3 S.O'Neal/W.Chamberlain 1.50 4.00
G4 J.Williams/P.Maravich 1.00 2.50
G5 S.Marbury/N.Archibald .50 1.25
G6 A.Walker/K.Malone .75 2.00
G7 G.Hill/G.Gervin .75 2.00
G8 G.Payton/I.Thomas .60 1.50
G9 K.Garnett/D.Wilkins 1.25 3.00
G10 H.Olajuwon/M.Malone .75 2.00
G11 K.Van Horn/L.Bird 1.50 4.00
G12 V.Carter/O.Robertson 1.25 3.00

1999 Upper Deck Century Legends Jerseys of the Century

Randomly inserted in packs at one in 475, this eight-card set features authentic jersey swatches from current and legendary NBA players. In addition, two autographed Game Jersey cards were available, Julius Erving and Kareem Abdul-Jabbar. Those cards are priced at the end of the set.
STATED ODDS 1:475
ERVING AU NOT PRICED DUE TO SCARCITY
CD Clyde Drexler 20.00 50.00
DR Julius Erving 30.00 80.00
JS John Stockton 15.00 40.00
KA Kareem Abdul-Jabbar 40.00 80.00
KM Karl Malone 15.00 40.00
LB Larry Bird 20.00 50.00
MJ Michael Jordan 350.00 700.00
SO Shaquille O'Neal 30.00 80.00
KAA K.Abdul-Jabbar AU/33 150.00 300.00

1999 Upper Deck Century Legends MJ's Most Memorable Shots

Randomly inserted in packs at one in 23, this six-card set features highlights of the most unforgettable shots of Jordan's career. Card backs feature a "MJ" prefix.
COMPLETE SET (6) 20.00 50.00
COMMON CARD (MJ1-MJ6) 4.00 10.00
STATED ODDS 1:23

2000 Upper Deck Century Legends

Released in June 2000, this 90-card set was issued in five-card packs that carried a suggested retail price of $4.99. The base card consisted of 50 regular players plus three subsets that include: History of the Dunk (20 cards), All Upper Deck Team (10 cards) and Jordan - The Best (10 cards).
COMPLETE SET (90) 10.00 25.00
1 Michael Jordan 2.00 5.00
2 Magic Johnson .60 1.50
3 Larry Bird .60 1.50
4 Bob Cousy .40 1.00
5 Bill Russell .40 1.00
6 Julius Erving .40 1.00
7 Nate Archibald .20 .50
8 Oscar Robertson .30 .75
9 Elgin Baylor .25 .60
10 Jo Jo White .20 .50
11 Hal Greer .20 .50
12 Clyde Drexler .30 .75
13 Wilt Chamberlain .50 1.25
14 Walt Bellamy .20 .50
15 Walt Frazier .25 .60
16 Earl Monroe .25 .60
17 John Havlicek .30 .75
18 George Mikan .50 1.25
19 George Karl .25 .60
20 Tom Heinsohn .25 .60
21 Kareem Abdul-Jabbar .40 1.00
22 Bill Sharman .25 .60
23 Elvin Hayes .25 .60
24 Rick Barry .20 .50
25 Paul Silas .25 .60
26 Mitch Kupchak .25 .60
27 Dave Cowens .15 .40
28 Nate Thurmond .20 .50
29 Dave DeBusschere .25 .60
30 Jerry Lucas .25 .60
31 Bill Walton .25 .60
32 Jerry West .30 .75
33 David Thompson .20 .50
34 Spencer Haywood .15 .40
35 Moses Malone .25 .60
36 Alex English .20 .50
37 Willis Reed .25 .60
38 George Gervin .25 .60
39 Dolph Schayes .25 .60
40 Wes Unseld .25 .60
41 Bob Lanier .20 .50
42 James Worthy .30 .75
43 Maurice Lucas .25 .60
44 Pete Maravich .40 1.00
45 Isiah Thomas .25 .60
46 Robert Parish .25 .60
47 Dominique Wilkins .30 .75
48 Walter Davis .25 .60
49 Bob Pettit .25 .60
50 Kevin McHale .30 .75
51 Julius Erving HD .20 .50
52 Dominique Wilkins HD .15 .40
53 George Gervin HD .12 .30
54 Kareem Abdul-Jabbar HD .20 .50
55 Clyde Drexler HD .15 .40
56 David Thompson HD .10 .25
57 Walter Davis HD .12 .30
58 James Worthy HD .15 .40
59 Moses Malone HD .12 .30
60 Bob Lanier HD .10 .25
61 Robert Parish HD .12 .30
62 Maurice Lucas HD .12 .30
63 Wes Unseld HD .12 .30
64 Ron Boone HD .07 .20
65 Larry Nance HD .10 .25
66 Michael Jordan HD 1.00 2.50
67 Michael Jordan HD 1.00 2.50
68 Michael Jordan HD 1.00 2.50
69 Michael Jordan HD 1.00 2.50
70 Michael Jordan HD 1.00 2.50
71 Michael Jordan UDT 1.00 2.50
72 Wilt Chamberlain UDT .25 .60
73 Magic Johnson UDT .30 .75
74 Julius Erving UDT .20 .50
75 Larry Bird UDT .30 .75
76 Bill Russell UDT .20 .50
77 Jerry West UDT .15 .40
78 Oscar Robertson UDT .15 .40
79 John Havlicek UDT .15 .40
80 Elgin Baylor UDT .12 .30
81 Michael Jordan TB 1.00 2.50
82 Michael Jordan TB 1.00 2.50
83 Michael Jordan TB 1.00 2.50
84 Michael Jordan TB 1.00 2.50
85 Michael Jordan TB 1.00 2.50
86 Michael Jordan TB 1.00 2.50
87 Michael Jordan TB 1.00 2.50
88 Michael Jordan TB 1.00 2.50
89 Michael Jordan TB 1.00 2.50
90 Michael Jordan TB 1.00 2.50

2000 Upper Deck Century Legends Commemorative Collection

*STARS: 12.5X TO 30X BASE CARD HI
*SUBSETS: 25X TO 60X BASE HI
STATED PRINT RUN 50 SERIAL #'d SETS

2000 Upper Deck Century Legends History's Heroes

Randomly inserted in packs at one in 12, this nine-card set features some of the greatest heroes in NBA history. Card backs carry a "HH" prefix.
COMPLETE SET (9) 6.00 15.00
STATED ODDS 1:12
HH1 Michael Jordan 5.00 12.00
HH2 Julius Erving 1.00 2.50
HH3 Larry Bird 1.50 4.00
HH4 Clyde Drexler .75 2.00
HH5 Elgin Baylor .60 1.50
HH6 George Gervin .60 1.50
HH7 Oscar Robertson .75 2.00
HH8 Jerry West .75 2.00
HH9 Alex English .50 1.25

2000 Upper Deck Century Legends Legendary Jerseys

Randomly inserted in packs at one in 288, this 10-card set features swatches of game-used jerseys from NBA Legends. Card backs carry the player's initials. Two jerseys were also autographed, Larry Bird to 33 and Michael Jordan to 23.
STATED ODDS 1:288
*GOLD: 1.5X TO 4X HI
GOLD PRINT RUN 25 SER.#'d SETS
BCJ Bob Cousy 15.00 40.00
CDJ Clyde Drexler 10.00 25.00
DRJ Julius Erving 12.00 30.00
DWJ Dominique Wilkins 10.00 25.00
ITJ Isiah Thomas 8.00 20.00
KAJ Kareem Abdul-Jabbar 12.00 30.00
LBA Larry Bird AU/33 300.00 600.00
LBJ Larry Bird 10.00 25.00
MJA Michael Jordan AU/23 2000.00 3000.00
MJJ Michael Jordan 60.00 150.00
MMJ Moses Malone 8.00 20.00
WCJ Wilt Chamberlain 30.00 80.00

2000 Upper Deck Century Legends Legendary Signatures

Randomly inserted in packs at one in 24, this 41-card set features autographs of vintage players. Card backs are numbered with the player's initials.
STATED ODDS 1:24
AE Alex English 6.00 15.00
BC Bob Cousy 40.00 100.00
BL Bob Lanier 6.00 15.00
BP Bob Pettit 12.00 30.00
BR Bill Russell 200.00 400.00
BS Bill Sharman 6.00 15.00
BW Bill Walton 15.00 40.00
CD Clyde Drexler 40.00 100.00
DC Dave Cowens 10.00 25.00
DD Dave DeBusschere 75.00 150.00
DR Julius Erving 125.00 225.00
DS Dolph Schayes 8.00 20.00
DT David Thompson 6.00 15.00
DW Dominique Wilkins 10.00 25.00
EB Elgin Baylor 15.00 40.00
EH Elvin Hayes 8.00 20.00
EM Earl Monroe 10.00 25.00
GA Gail Goodrich 6.00 15.00
GG George Gervin 6.00 15.00
HG Hal Greer 6.00 15.00
IT Isiah Thomas 12.00 30.00
JA Jamaal Wilkes 6.00 15.00
JH John Havlicek 20.00 50.00
JJ Jo Jo White 8.00 20.00
JL Jerry Lucas 12.00 30.00
JW Jerry West 25.00 60.00
KA Kareem Abdul-Jabbar 40.00 100.00
LB Larry Bird 125.00 250.00
MG Magic Johnson 125.00 250.00
MM Moses Malone 15.00 40.00
NA Nate Archibald 8.00 20.00
NT Nate Thurmond 8.00 20.00
OR Oscar Robertson 50.00 100.00
PA Paul Arizin 15.00 40.00
PS Paul Silas 6.00 15.00
RB Rick Barry 20.00 50.00
SH Spencer Haywood 6.00 15.00
WB Walt Bellamy 10.00 25.00
WF Walt Frazier 8.00 20.00
WR Willis Reed 10.00 25.00
WU Wes Unseld 8.00 20.00

2000 Upper Deck Century Legends Legendary Signatures Gold

*GOLD: 1.25X TO 3X HI COLUMN
STATED PRINT RUN 25 SERIAL #'d SETS
BL Bob Lanier 25.00 60.00
BR Bill Russell 300.00 600.00
DR Julius Erving 250.00 500.00
KA Kareem Abdul-Jabbar 150.00 400.00
MG Magic Johnson 250.00 600.00
MJ Michael Jordan 2000.00 3000.00
OR Oscar Robertson 100.00 250.00

2000 Upper Deck Century Legends MJ Final Floor Jumbos

Inserted one per box, this 12-card set features 3" by 5" enlargements of MJ's Final Floor.
COMPLETE SET (12) 150.00 300.00
COMMON CARD (FF1-FF12) 12.00 30.00
ONE PER BOX

2000 Upper Deck Century Legends NBA Originals

Randomly inserted in packs at one in 12, this six-card set features the NBA groundbreakers who invented trademark moves. Card backs carry an "O" prefix.
COMPLETE SET (6) 5.00 12.00
STATED ODDS 1:12
O1 Magic Johnson 1.25 3.00
O2 Julius Erving .75 2.00
O3 Michael Jordan 4.00 10.00
O4 David Thompson .40 1.00
O5 Kareem Abdul-Jabbar .75 2.00
O6 Clyde Drexler .60 1.50

2000 Upper Deck Century Legends Players of the Century

Randomly inserted in packs at one in four, this 20-card set featues the some of the finest NBA performances of the past century. Card backs carry a "P" prefix.
COMPLETE SET (20) 10.00 25.00
STATED ODDS 1:4
P1 Michael Jordan 5.00 12.00
P2 Wilt Chamberlain 1.25 3.00
P3 Magic Johnson 1.50 4.00
P4 Larry Bird 1.50 4.00
P5 Bill Russell 1.00 2.50
P6 Jerry West .75 2.00
P7 Oscar Robertson .75 2.00
P8 John Havlicek .75 2.00
P9 Kareem Abdul-Jabbar 1.00 2.50
P10 Pete Maravich 1.00 2.50
P11 Willis Reed .60 1.50
P12 Bob Lanier .50 1.25
P13 George Gervin .60 1.50
P14 Bill Walton .60 1.50
P15 Elvin Hayes .60 1.50
P16 Julius Erving 1.00 2.50
P17 Rick Barry .50 1.25
P18 Walt Frazier .60 1.50
P19 Nate Thurmond .50 1.25
P20 Moses Malone .60 1.50

2000 Upper Deck Century Legends Recollections

Randomly inserted in packs at one in 24, this seven-card set features memorable moments from former NBA stars. Card backs carry a "R" prefix.
COMPLETE SET (7) 8.00 20.00
STATED ODDS 1:24
R1 Michael Jordan 6.00 15.00
R2 Isiah Thomas .75 2.00
R3 Julius Erving 1.25 3.00
R4 Wilt Chamberlain 1.50 4.00
R5 Clyde Drexler 1.00 2.50
R6 Bill Walton .75 2.00
R7 Dominique Wilkins 1.00 2.50

2002-03 Upper Deck Championship Drive

Released in late January 2003, this 155-card set divided up as follows: Numbers 1-100 are base veteran cards, numbers 101-130 are jersey rookie cards sequentially numbered to 400, and numbers 131-155 are rookies sequentially numbered to 500. Championship drive was packaged in 18-pack boxes with five cards per pack and carried a suggested retail price of $4.99. Also inserted at one per box as it's own mini-box were small gold replica NBA Championship trophies. One version was done for each team and another for each of the NBA Champs from 1978-2002.
COMP.SET w/o SP's (100) 15.00 40.00
101-130 PRINT RUN 400 SER.#'d SETS
131-155 PRINT RUN 500 SER.#'d SETS
1 Shareef Abdur-Rahim .30 .75
2 Glenn Robinson .30 .75
3 Jason Terry .30 .75
4 Dion Glover .25 .60
5 Antoine Walker .30 .75
6 Paul Pierce .40 1.00
7 Vin Baker .30 .75
8 Kedrick Brown .25 .60
9 Jalen Rose .30 .75
10 Tyson Chandler .40 1.00
11 Eddy Curry .25 .60
12 Darius Miles .25 .60
13 Ricky Davis .30 .75
14 Zydrunas Ilgauskas .30 .75
15 Dirk Nowitzki .60 1.50
16 Michael Finley .40 1.00
17 Steve Nash .50 1.25
18 Raef LaFrentz .25 .60
19 Nick Van Exel .30 .75
20 James Posey .25 .60
21 Juwan Howard .30 .75
22 Chauncey Billups .40 1.00
23 Ben Wallace .30 .75
24 Richard Hamilton .30 .75
25 Jason Richardson .40 1.00
26 Antawn Jamison .40 1.00
27 Gilbert Arenas .40 1.00
28 Steve Francis .30 .75
29 Cuttino Mobley .25 .60
30 Eddie Griffin .25 .60
31 Reggie Miller .40 1.00
32 Jermaine O'Neal .30 .75
33 Jamaal Tinsley .25 .60
34 Ron Mercer .25 .60
35 Elton Brand .40 1.00
36 Andre Miller .30 .75
37 Kobe Bryant 1.50 4.00
38 Shaquille O'Neal 1.00 2.50
39 Rick Fox .25 .60
40 Devean George .25 .60
41 Pau Gasol .50 1.25
42 Shane Battier .40 1.00
43 Jason Williams .30 .75
44 Eddie Jones .30 .75
45 Brian Grant .25 .60
46 Anthony Carter .25 .60
47 Ray Allen .40 1.00
48 Tim Thomas .25 .60
49 Kevin Garnett .60 1.50
50 Terrell Brandon .25 .60
51 Wally Szczerbiak .30 .75
52 Joe Smith .30 .75
53 Jason Kidd .60 1.50
54 Richard Jefferson .40 1.00
55 Dikembe Mutombo .40 1.00
56 Kenyon Martin .30 .75
57 Baron Davis .30 .75
58 Jamal Mashburn .30 .75
59 David Wesley .25 .60
60 P.J. Brown .25 .60
61 Courtney Alexander .25 .60
62 Latrell Sprewell .30 .75
63 Allan Houston .30 .75
64 Kurt Thomas .25 .60
65 Antonio McDyess .30 .75
66 Tracy McGrady .60 1.50
67 Mike Miller .30 .75
68 Grant Hill .50 1.25
69 Allen Iverson .60 1.50
70 Keith Van Horn .30 .75
71 Shawn Marion .30 .75
72 Stephon Marbury .30 .75
73 Anfernee Hardaway .60 1.50
74 Rasheed Wallace .40 1.00
75 Bonzi Wells .25 .60
76 Scottie Pippen .60 1.50
77 Mike Bibby .40 1.00
78 Peja Stojakovic .40 1.00
79 Chris Webber .40 1.00
80 Hedo Turkoglu .30 .75
81 Vlade Divac .30 .75
82 Tim Duncan .75 2.00
83 David Robinson .60 1.50
84 Tony Parker .50 1.25
85 Malik Rose .25 .60
86 Gary Payton .40 1.00
87 Rashard Lewis .40 1.00
88 Brent Barry .25 .60
89 Desmond Mason .30 .75
90 Vladimir Radmanovic .25 .60
91 Vince Carter .60 1.50
92 Morris Peterson .25 .60
93 Antonio Davis .25 .60
94 Karl Malone .50 1.25
95 John Stockton .50 1.25
96 Andrei Kirilenko .40 1.00
97 Matt Harpring .25 .60
98 Jerry Stackhouse .30 .75
99 Larry Hughes .30 .75
100 Michael Jordan 3.00 8.00
101 Juan Dixon JSY RC 4.00 10.00
102 Carlos Boozer JSY RC 4.00 10.00
103 Dan Gadzuric JSY RC 3.00 8.00
104 Vincent Yarbrough JSY RC 2.50 6.00
105 Robert Archibald JSY RC 2.50 6.00
106 Roger Mason JSY RC 3.00 8.00
107 Ronald Murray JSY RC 4.00 10.00
108 Chris Jefferies JSY RC 2.50 6.00
109 John Salmons JSY RC 4.00 10.00
110 Predrag Savovic JSY RC 3.00 8.00
111 Tayshaun Prince JSY RC 5.00 12.00
112 Casey Jacobsen JSY RC 3.00 8.00
113 Qyntel Woods JSY RC 3.00 8.00
114 Kareem Rush JSY RC 3.00 8.00
115 Ryan Humphrey JSY RC 3.00 8.00
116 Sam Clancy JSY RC 3.00 8.00
117 Lonny Baxter JSY RC 2.50 6.00
118 Fred Jones JSY RC 3.00 8.00
119 Marcus Haislip JSY RC 3.00 8.00
120 Melvin Ely JSY RC 3.00 8.00
121 Jared Jeffries JSY RC 3.00 8.00
122 Caron Butler JSY RC 4.00 10.00
123 Amare Stoudemire JSY RC 5.00 12.00
124 Chris Wilcox JSY RC 3.00 8.00
125 Nene Hilario JSY RC 4.00 10.00
126 DaJuan Wagner JSY RC 3.00 8.00
127 Nikoloz Tskitishvili JSY RC 2.50 6.00
128 Drew Gooden JSY RC 4.00 10.00
129 Jay Williams JSY RC 4.00 10.00
130 Yao Ming JSY RC 8.00 20.00
131 Manu Ginobili RC 5.00 12.00
132 Efthimios Rentzias RC 1.25 3.00
133 Juaquin Hawkins RC 1.25 3.00
134 Marko Jaric 2.00 5.00
135 Dan Dickau RC 1.50 4.00
136 Frank Williams RC 1.25 3.00
137 Curtis Borchardt RC 1.25 3.00
138 Mike Dunleavy RC 2.00 5.00
139 Smush Parker RC 2.00 5.00
140 Tito Maddox RC 1.25 3.00
141 Jannero Pargo RC 1.25 3.00
142 Jiri Welsch RC 1.50 4.00
143 Bostjan Nachbar RC 1.50 4.00
144 Rasual Butler RC 2.00 5.00
145 Gordan Giricek RC 2.00 5.00
146 Igor Rakocevic RC 1.25 3.00
147 Tamar Slay RC 1.25 3.00
148 Junior Harrington RC 1.25 3.00
149 Nate Huffman RC 1.25 3.00
150 Jamal Sampson RC 2.00 5.00
151 Reggie Evans RC 2.00 5.00
152 Cezary Trybanski RC 2.00 5.00
153 Pat Burke RC 1.25 3.00
154 J.R. Bremer RC 1.25 3.00
155 Mehmet Okur RC 2.00 5.00

2002-03 Upper Deck Championship Drive Parallel

*STARS: 3X TO 8X BASE CARD HI
1-100 PRINT RUN 125 SER.#'d SETS
*RCs 101-130: 1.5X TO 4X HI
*RCs 131-155: 2.5X TO 6X HI
101-155 RC PRINT RUN 25 SER.#'d SETS

2002-03 Upper Deck Championship Drive 2 Amazing Jerseys

Randomly inserted in packs at the rate of one in 144, this eight card set features a horizontal design with one player on each side and two jerseys in the middle in the shape of the number two.
STATED ODDS 1:144
AIJKJ A.Iverson/J.Kidd 10.00 25.00
CWMBJ C.Webber/M.Bibby 8.00 20.00
KBJRJ K.Bryant/J.Richardson 15.00 40.00
KGWSJ K.Garnett/W.Szczerbiak 10.00 25.00
MJKBM M.Jordan/K.Bryant SP 60.00 150.00
PPAWJ P.Pierce/A.Walker 8.00 20.00
SMSFJ S.Marbury/S.Francis 8.00 20.00
TMGHJ T.McGrady/G.Hill 10.00 25.00

2002-03 Upper Deck Championship Drive Best of Seven Jersey

Randomly seeded in packs, this seven card set also features a horizontal design with full color player photos on the right set against a white background and a swatch of a game worn jersey on the left. Each card is sequentially numbered to 50.
PRINT RUN 50 SER.#'d SETS
AIB Allen Iverson 15.00 40.00
JKB Jason Kidd 15.00 40.00
JWB Jay Williams 10.00 25.00
KBB Kobe Bryant 50.00 120.00
MJB Michael Jordan 150.00 300.00
PPB Paul Pierce 10.00 25.00
YMB Yao Ming 20.00 50.00

2002-03 Upper Deck Championship Drive Key Pieces Jersey

Inserted in packs at the rate of one in 96, this 12-card set places a color-scale portrait photo of the player on the far right set to match team colors, a full-color action photo to the left of that and a jersey swatch on the right.
STATED ODDS 1:96
BDKP Baron Davis 2.50 6.00
DNKP Dirk Nowitzki 5.00 12.00
JSKP Jerry Stackhouse 2.50 6.00
KBKP Kobe Bryant SP 12.00 30.00
KGKP Kevin Garnett 5.00 12.00
KMKP Karl Malone 4.00 10.00
MBKP Michael Jordan SP 60.00 150.00
MBKP Mike Bibby 3.00 8.00
PPKP Paul Pierce 3.00 8.00
RAKP Ray Allen 3.00 8.00
SBKP Shane Battier 3.00 8.00
SMKP Stephon Marbury 2.50 6.00

2002-03 Upper Deck Championship Drive Prized Properties Jersey

Inserted in packs at the rate of one in 36, this 12-card set is horizontally designed with player color photos on the left on a colored background to match team colors and a swatch of jersey on the right set to look like the letters PP.
STATED ODDS 1:36
AHPP Allan Houston 2.50 6.00
AWPP Antoine Walker 2.50 6.00
BDPP Baron Davis 2.50 6.00
CWPP Chris Webber 3.00 8.00
EBPP Elton Brand 3.00 8.00
JRPP Jason Richardson 3.00 8.00
KBPP Kobe Bryant 12.00 30.00
KMPP Karl Malone 4.00 10.00
MJPP Michael Jordan 60.00 150.00
PGPP Pau Gasol 4.00 10.00
SAPP Shareef Abdur-Rahim 2.50 6.00
TMPP Tracy McGrady 5.00 12.00

2002-03 Upper Deck Championship Drive Signs of Success Dual Jersey

Randomly seeded in packs, this nine card set centers two small photos of the two featured players, two jersey swatches on the outside of this, and two authentic autographs below the pictures and swatches. Each card is sequentially numbered to 25.
PRINT RUN 25 SER.#'d SETS
CBDG C.Butler/D.Gooden 25.00 60.00
CWME C.Wilcox/M.Ely 25.00 60.00
KBKG K.Bryant/K.Garnett 250.00 500.00
MJKB M.Jordan/K.Bryant 400.00 700.00
PPAW P.Pierce/A.Walker 40.00 100.00
YMJW Y.Ming/J.Williams 100.00 200.00

2002-03 Upper Deck Championship Drive Signs of Success Jersey

Randomly inserted in packs, this set features a swatch of a jersey and an authentic player autograph. Each card is sequentially numbered to 225.
PRINT RUN 225 SER.#'d SETS
AWA Antoine Walker 8.00 20.00
JKA Jason Kidd 25.00 60.00
JWA Jay Williams 12.50 30.00
KMA Kenyon Martin 8.00 20.00
MFA Marcus Fizer 12.50 30.00
YMA Yao Ming 40.00 100.00

2002-03 Upper Deck Championship Drive Superstar Material Jersey

Randomly inserted in packs, this 14-card set places full color player photos on the left side of the card and a swatch of jersey on the right. Each card is sequentially numbered to 100.
PRINT RUN 100 SER.#'d SETS
AIM Allen Iverson 6.00 15.00
AWM Antoine Walker 3.00 8.00
BDM Baron Davis 3.00 8.00
CWM Chris Webber 4.00 10.00
DNM Dirk Nowitzki 6.00 15.00
JRM Jason Richardson 4.00 10.00
JWM Jay Williams 4.00 10.00
KGM Kevin Garnett 6.00 15.00
KMB Kobe Bryant 12.00 30.00
MJM Michael Jordan 60.00 150.00
PGM Pau Gasol 5.00 12.00
RAM Ray Allen 4.00 10.00
SFM Steve Francis 3.00 8.00
YMM Yao Ming 8.00 20.00

2002-03 Upper Deck Championship Drive Then and Now Jersey

Inserted in packs at the rate of one in 108, this nine card set photos recently traded players in their old jerseys on the left and new jerseys on the right. There are also two swatches, one from each of the team's jersey.
STATED ODDS 1:108
TNAM Andre Miller 4.00 10.00
TNJH Juwan Howard 4.00 10.00
TNJK Jason Kidd 8.00 20.00
TNJM Jamal Mashburn 4.00 10.00
TNMB Mike Bibby 5.00 12.00
TNMJ Michael Jordan SP 125.00 250.00
TNSA Shareef Abdur-Rahim 4.00 10.00
TNSM Stephon Marbury 4.00 10.00
TNTM Tracy McGrady 8.00 20.00

2009-10 Upper Deck Champ's Hall of Legends Memorabilia

STATED ODDS 1:160
HLCB Chris Bosh 8.00 20.00
HLJE Julius Erving 12.00 30.00
HLKB Kobe Bryant 25.00 60.00
HLLB Larry Bird 20.00 50.00
HLLJ LeBron James 40.00 80.00
HLMG Magic Johnson 15.00 40.00
HLMJ Michael Jordan 50.00 100.00
HLSN Steve Nash 8.00 20.00

2009-10 Upper Deck Champ's Signatures

STATED ODDS 1:15
CSDR Derrick Rose 50.00 125.00
CSJE Julius Erving SP 200.00 350.00
CSLB Larry Bird 60.00 120.00
CSMJ Michael Jordan 400.00 700.00
CSTM Tracy McGrady 10.00 25.00
CSYM Yao Ming 40.00 80.00

2005 Upper Deck Chicago National

Given away at the 2005 National Sports Collector's Convention, this set features some of the brightest young stars in the game. Each day, in exchage for wrappers from previously released products, Upper Deck handed out a different card. Card fronts feature borders along the left and the bottom, gold foil and sequential numbering to 750.
COMPLETE SET (6) 10.00 25.00
NBA1 Dwight Howard 6.00 15.00
NBA2 Luol Deng 2.50 6.00
NBA3 Ben Gordon 2.50 6.00
NBA4 Chris Duhon 2.00 5.00
NBA5 Josh Smith 3.00 8.00
NBA6 Andre Iguodala 3.00 8.00

1995-96 Upper Deck Chinese Basketball Alliance

Issued only in Taiwan, the 1995-96 Upper Deck Chinese Basketball Alliance set was issued in one series totaling 125 cards. The cards were sold in 10-card packs, and all four teams in the Chinese Basketball Alliance were featured. Each team carries 18 players, with a limit of two foreign players per team. The fronts show white-bordered color action player photos. The backs carry a closeup photo and player information. All text is in Chinese. The four teams represented are Yue Lion (1-16), Hung Kuo (17-34), Tera (35-52), and Luckipar (53-70). Topical subsets or special cards featured are Thousand Times (71-86), 10 Thousand Score (87), Starting Five (88-107), Special Records (108-119), Team Cards (120-123), and Checklists (124-125).
COMPLETE SET (125) 12.00 30.00
1 Chu Chung-Chi .08 .25
2 Lin Chien-Ping .08 .25
3 Roderick James Hannibal .20 .50
4 Tau Song .08 .25
5 Tsi-Fu-Tsi .08 .25
6 Chen Hung-Zung .08 .25
7 Chen Cheng-Sbiun .08 .25
8 Kuo Tien-Lung .08 .25
9 Tungfang Cheieh-Teh .08 .25
10 Li-Yung-Kung .08 .25
11 Hsu Tung-Ching .08 .25
12 Chang Hsien-Ming .08 .25
13 Mark Clark .20 .50
14 Brenton Lloyd Moore .20 .50
15 Arlando F. Bennett .20 .50
16 Christopher Edward Knight .20 .50
17 Tsou Jiunn-San .08 .25
18 Li Chung-Shi .08 .25
19 Liu I-Shang .08 .25
20 Chio Teh-Chih .08 .25
21 Michael Lee Johnson .20 .50
22 Jeng Jyh-Long .08 .25
23 Lo Hsing-Liang .08 .25
24 Huang Chun-Hsiung .08 .25
25 Chang Ya-Tang .08 .25
26 Chu Hao-Ren .08 .25
27 Jye Song .08 .25
28 Stacey Cornilius .20 .50
29 Keith Smith .20 .50
30 Rex Harrison Manu .20 .50
31 Daryl Scott .20 .50
32 Joseph Nathenial Temple .20 .50
33 Laurent Crawford .20 .50
34 David Lewayne Cooke .20 .50
35 Tsou Hai-Zunkg .08 .25
36 Wang Li-Bin .08 .25
37 Bai Ming-Li .08 .25
38 Kofi Kyei .08 .25
39 Lin Chai-Hung .08 .25
40 Chen Chung-Chian .08 .25
41 Li Chi-Chian .08 .25
42 Sun Mao-Shen .08 .25
43 Tzeng Tzeng-Cho .08 .25
44 Cheyenne Durell Gibson .20 .50
45 Chen Jiunn-Chie .08 .25
46 Kelvin Cornell Allen .20 .50
47 Charng Bing-Hsiang .08 .25
48 Kennard Robison .20 .50
49 David Edward Davies .20 .50
50 Todd Alan Rowe .20 .50
51 Mike Sterner .20 .50
52 Robert Zohn Fife .20 .50
53 Carroll Boudreaux .20 .50
54 Chen Cheng-Kwei .08 .25
55 Hung Chang-Ching .08 .25
56 Yen Chao-Chyun .08 .25
57 Lai Kwo-Hong .08 .25
58 Ko Yiing-Yan .08 .25
59 Gerard Arcement .20 .50
60 Jerry Lew .08 .25
61 Tien Su-Chung .08 .25
62 Chris Collier .20 .50
63 Tzeng Yih-Chin .08 .25
64 DWight Myvett .08 .25
65 Anthony Robert Block .20 .50
66 Lan Chih-Ming .08 .25
67 Lin Shin-Hwa .08 .25
68 Derrell Cunegin .20 .50
69 Harold Boudreaux .20 .50
70 Wu Jye-Wei .08 .25
71 Jerry Lew .20 .50
72 Tsou Jiunn-San .08 .25
73 Derrell Cunegin .20 .50
74 Huang Chun-Hsiung .08 .25
75 Christopher Edward Knight .20 .50
76 Huang Chun-Hsiung .08 .25
77 Joseph Nathenial Temple .20 .50
78 Lo Hsing-Liang .08 .25
79 Hung Chang-Ching .08 .25
80 Tsou Jiunn-San .08 .25
81 Christopher Edward Knight .20 .50
82 David Edward Davies .20 .50
83 Christopher Edward Knight .20 .50
84 Harold Boudreaux .20 .50
85 Arlando F. Bennett .20 .50
86 Arlando F. Bennett .20 .50
87 Tungfang Chieh-Teh .08 .25
88 Arlando F. Bennett .20 .50
89 Christopher Edward Knight .20 .50
90 Tungfang Chieh-Teh .08 .25
91 Li Yung-Kung .08 .25
92 Tsi Fu Tsi .08 .25
93 Tsou Jiunn-San .08 .25
94 Jeng Jyh-Long .08 .25
95 Lo Hsing-Liang .08 .25
96 Rex Harrison Manu .20 .50
97 Stacey Cornilius .20 .50
98 Wang Li-Bin .08 .25
99 Chen Chung-Chian .08 .25
100 Tzeng Tzeng-Cho .08 .25
101 Todd Alan Rowe .20 .50
102 Kennard Robison .20 .50
103 Tzeng Yih-Chin .08 .25
104 Jerry Lew .08 .25
105 Chen Cheng-Kwei .08 .25
106 Dwight Myvett .08 .25
107 Harold Boudreaux .20 .50
108 Dwight Myvett .08 .25
109 Harold Boudreaux .20 .50
110 Todd Alan Rowe .20 .50
111 Jeng Jyh-Long .08 .25
112 Li Chi-Chian .08 .25
113 Harold Boudreaux .20 .50
114 Dwight Myvett .08 .25
115 Tsou Jiunn-San .08 .25
116 Christopher Edward Knight .20 .50
117 Anthony Robert Block .20 .50
118 Rex Harrison Manu .20 .50
119 Rex Harrison Manu .20 .50
120 Yue Lon .08 .25
121 Hung Kuo .08 .25
122 Tera .08 .25
123 Luckipar .08 .25
124 Checklist #1 .08 .25
125 Checklist #2 .08 .25

1995-96 Upper Deck Chinese Alliance MVP's

Randomly inserted in packs, this 9-card set spotlights "most valuable players" in the Chinese Basketball Alliance. The fronts show full-bleed color action photos, except on the right edge where a granite stripe carries the player's name. A gold foil "MVP" emblem adorns the upper right corner. With a smaller inset color photo, the backs presents career summary and statistics.
COMPLETE SET (9) 4.00 10.00
M1 Jeng Jyh-Long .40 1.00
M2 Tsou Jiunn-San .40 1.00
M3 Todd Alan Rowe .75 2.00
M4 Tungfang Chieh-Teh .40 1.00
M5 Arlando F. Bennett .75 2.00
M6 Roderick Nathenial Temple .75 2.00
M7 Joseph Nathenial Temple .40 1.00
M8 Tungfang Chieh-Teh .40 1.00
M9 CBA President .40 1.00

2003 Upper Deck City Heights LeBron James

This LeBron James card was returned to collectors along with any 2003-04 Upper Deck redemption card as an added bonus. Early copies of the card were sent out to dealers who provide valuable product input along with a letter from Upper Deck. The card is done in 3-D lenticular style and places James in front of the Cleveland skyline.
NNO LeBron James 6.00 15.00

2004 Upper Deck Collectibles All-Star Game LeBron James

This card was produced by Upper Deck Collectibles. It is not known how this card was distributed, and each is numbered to 5000.
LJAS LeBron James 2.00 5.00

2002 Upper Deck Collector's Club

Released in March 2002, this set was distributed to members of Upper Deck's Collectors Club as part of their starter kit. Each member received a 20-card kit plus one memorabilia card wrapped in a clear cello wrapper along with an Upper Deck baseball cap and a club membership card. Members also received quarterly newsletters with features on upcoming

products and sample cards.
COMPLETE SET (21) 10.00 25.00
NBA1 Kobe Bryant 1.25 3.00
NBA2 Allen Iverson .60 1.50
NBA3 Vince Carter 1.00 2.50
NBA4 Jason Kidd .40 1.00
NBA5 Tracy McGrady .50 1.25
NBA6 Pau Gasol .30 .75
NBA7 Kevin Garnett .60 1.50
NBA8 Steve Francis .40 1.00
NBA9 Chris Webber .40 1.00
NBA10 Ray Allen .25 .60
NBA11 Kwame Brown .25 .60
NBA12 Paul Pierce .25 .60
NBA13 Stephon Marbury .25 .60
NBA14 Tim Duncan .50 1.25
NBA15 Shaquille O'Neal .60 1.50
NBA16 Jerry Stackhouse .25 .60
NBA17 Rashard Lewis .15 .40
NBA18 Darius Miles .40 1.00
NBA19 Jamaal Tinsley .40 1.00
NBA20 Michael Jordan 2.00 5.00
KGU Kevin Garnett JSY 6.00 15.00

2010-11 Upper Deck College Colors

COMPLETE SET (15) 6.00 15.00
1 Michael Jordan 2.00 5.00
2 Bill Walton .40 1.00
3 Magic Johnson .75 2.00
4 Hakeem Olajuwon .60 1.50
5 James Worthy .60 1.50

1994 Upper Deck Commemorative Cards

1 1994 Launch Tour/2000 2.00 5.00
Wayne Gretzky
Reggie Jackson
Michael Jordan
Joe Montana

2008 Upper Deck Diamond Club Autographs

These autographed cards were only available to Upper Deck Diamond Club members in 2008. The cards feature hand-numbering on the front. Some are unpriced due to scarcity.
DC3 LeBron James 300.00 600.00
DC5 Derrick Rose 300.00 600.00
DC6 Michael Beasley 100.00 200.00

2014 Upper Deck Diamond Club Trade Card Autograph

SAUTO Shaquille O'Neal 125.00 300.00

1997-98 Upper Deck Diamond Vision

This 29-card set features color action player photos taken from actual NBA game footage using the latest cutting-edge technology. The set was distributed in one-card packs with a suggested retail price of $7.99.
COMPLETE SET (29) 40.00 100.00
1 Dikembe Mutombo 1.25 3.00
2 Dana Barros .75 2.00
3 Glen Rice 1.25 3.00
4 Michael Jordan 10.00 25.00
5 Terrell Brandon .75 2.00
6 Michael Finley 1.25 3.00
7 Antonio McDyess 1.00 2.50
8 Grant Hill 2.00 5.00
9 Latrell Sprewell 1.25 3.00
10 Hakeem Olajuwon 1.50 4.00
11 Reggie Miller 1.50 4.00
12 Loy Vaught .75 2.00
13 Shaquille O'Neal 3.00 8.00
14 Alonzo Mourning 1.50 4.00
15 Vin Baker 1.00 2.50
16 Kevin Garnett 2.00 5.00
17 Kerry Kittles .75 2.00
18 Patrick Ewing 1.50 4.00
19 Anfernee Hardaway 2.00 5.00
20 Allen Iverson 2.50 6.00
21 Jason Kidd 2.00 5.00
22 Isaiah Rider 1.00 2.50
23 Mitch Richmond 1.25 3.00
24 David Robinson 2.00 5.00
25 Gary Payton 1.25 3.00
26 Damon Stoudamire 1.00 2.50
27 Karl Malone 1.50 4.00
28 Shareef Abdur-Rahim 1.25 3.00
29 Chris Webber 1.25 3.00

1997-98 Upper Deck Diamond Vision Signature Moves

*STARS: .75X TO 2X BASE CARD HI

1997-98 Upper Deck Diamond Vision Dunk Vision

Randomly inserted in packs at the rate of one in 40, this six-card set features borderless color action game photos of spectacular dunks of NBA superstars.
COMPLETE SET (6) 30.00 80.00
D1 Michael Jordan 25.00 60.00
D2 Anfernee Hardaway 5.00 12.00
D3 Shaquille O'Neal 8.00 20.00
D4 Grant Hill 5.00 12.00
D5 Kevin Garnett 5.00 12.00
D6 Hakeem Olajuwon 4.00 10.00

1997-98 Upper Deck Diamond Vision Jordan Highlight Reels

This five-card set was packaged individually with each having an SRP of $9.99. Each 3 1/2" by 5" card features over 20 frames of NBA video footage of various stages of Michael Jordan's career. The cards are numbered on the front - in the upper left-hand corner.
COMPLETE SET (5) 12.00 30.00
COMMON CARD (1-5) 5.00 12.00

1997-98 Upper Deck Diamond Vision Reel Time

Randomly inserted in packs at the rate of one in 500, this one-card set showcases one of Michael Jordan's forays to the hoop in frame-by-frame action imagery during one of the most memorable moments in the NBA.
RT1 Michael Jordan 30.00 80.00

2007-08 Upper Deck Dodge Charger

DC6 Kevin Durant 10.00 25.00

1992 Upper Deck Draft Party Sheets

These 8 1/2" by 11" sheets were given away to attendees of draft day parties hosted by most of the NBA teams. All sheets are dated June 24, 1992, numbered out of 7,000, and feature reproductions of the 1991-92 cards of the top 1992 draft picks: Larry Johnson, Derrick Coleman, Pervis Ellison, Danny Manning, David Robinson and Brad Daugherty. The main differences between the various sheets are the text and logos of the team and corporate sponsor, if any. The sheets are unnumbered and are listed in alphabetical order.
COMPLETE SET (20) 30.00 80.00
COMMON SHEET 2.00 5.00

1993 Upper Deck Draft Party Sheets

These 8 1/2" by 11" sheets were given away to attendees of draft day parties hosted by all 27 NBA teams. All sheets are dated June 30, 1993, numbered out of 7,000, and feature reproductions of the 1992-93 Top Prospect subset cards of the top 1992 draft picks: Shaquille O'Neal, Tom Gugliotta, Alonzo Mourning, Christian Laettner, Jim Jackson and LaPhonso Ellis. The main differences between the various sheets are the text and logos of the team and corporate sponsor, if any. The sheets are unnumbered and are listed in alphabetical order.
COMPLETE SET (27) 60.00 150.00
COMMON SHEET 4.00 10.00

1993-94 Upper Deck Draft Preview Promos

Issued (but never formally released) to promote a new draft picks product, these three draft preview cards measure the standard-size. The fronts feature full-bleed color action photos with the college name airbrushed off the players' jerseys. The player's name appears in a color bar across the bottom of the picture. The backs carry biography, player profile, and statistics.
COMPLETE SET (3) 6.00 15.00
DP1 Shawn Bradley 3.00 8.00
DP2 Calbert Cheaney 3.00 8.00
DP3 Bobby Hurley 1.50 4.00

2007-08 Upper Deck Kevin Durant Promo

KDRC1 Kevin Durant/999 4.00 10.00
KDRC2 Kevin Durant/499 6.00 15.00

1999 Upper Deck Employee Game Jersey

This Michael Jordan card was given to Upper Deck employees as a "Thank You" for the 1999 year. Each card featured a swatch of game-worn jersey. Each card was serially numbered to 275.
NNO Michael Jordan 1000.00 1500.00

2000 Upper Deck Employee Game Jersey

For the second year, Upper Deck gave their employees Game Jerseys as a "Thank You" gift. This year's jersey swatch featured Kobe Bryant, along with Kobe's autograph. The cards were serially numbered out of 300.
KB2000 Kobe Bryant AU/300 400.00 800.00

2003 Upper Deck Employee LeBron James

These LeBron James cards were sent out by Upper Deck to distributors and other members of the collectible card industry in December 2003 as a holiday card. James is featured in a North Pole Winter League jersey on the non memorabilia card.
LBEC L.James JSY/450 100.00 250.00
LBNPL03 LeBron James 4.00 10.00

2006 Upper Deck Employee Quad Jerseys

LJDJSCRB James/Jeter/Crosby/Bush 20.00 40.00

2007 Upper Deck Employee Quad Jerseys

MJKBLJKD Jordan/Bryant/James/Durant 175.00 350.00

1998-99 Upper Deck Encore

Released as a semi-parallel to the 1998-99 Upper Deck set, this 150-card set was issued in six card packs that carried a suggested retail price of $3.99. Each card utilized a special Rainbow Light F/X technology, which differentiated the cards from the regular Upper Deck set. There were several subsets inserted - Michael Jordan cards 91-113 were inserted at one in four, Rookie Watch cards 114-143 were inserted at one in four and Bonus Regular rookie cards 144-150 were inserted at one in eight. A Michael Jordan autograph was also randomly inserted in packs. There were 50 total autographs available.
COMPLETE SET (150) 60.00 120.00
MJ SUBSET STATED ODDS 1:4
ROOKIE SUBSET STATED ODDS 1:4
BONUS SUBSET STATED ODDS 1:8
1 Mookie Blaylock .15 .40
2 Dikembe Mutombo .25 .60
3 Steve Smith .20 .50
4 Kenny Anderson .20 .50
5 Antoine Walker .25 .60
6 Ron Mercer .20 .50
7 David Wesley .15 .40
8 Elden Campbell .15 .40
9 Eddie Jones .25 .60
10 Ron Harper .20 .50
11 Toni Kukoc .25 .60
12 Brent Barry .20 .50
13 Shawn Kemp .25 .60
14 Brevin Knight .15 .40
15 Derek Anderson .15 .40
16 Shawn Bradley .15 .40
17 Robert Pack .15 .40
18 Michael Finley .25 .60
19 Antonio McDyess .20 .50
20 Nick Van Exel .20 .50
21 Danny Fortson .15 .40
22 Grant Hill .40 1.00
23 Jerry Stackhouse .25 .60
24 Bison Dele .15 .40
25 Donyell Marshall .15 .40
26 Tony Delk .15 .40
27 Erick Dampier .15 .40
28 John Starks .20 .50
29 Charles Barkley .40 1.00
30 Hakeem Olajuwon .30 .75
31 Othella Harrington .15 .40
32 Scottie Pippen .40 1.00
33 Rik Smits .20 .50
34 Reggie Miller .30 .75
35 Mark Jackson .20 .50
36 Rodney Rogers .15 .40
37 Lamond Murray .15 .40
38 Maurice Taylor .15 .40
39 Kobe Bryant 1.00 2.50
40 Shaquille O'Neal .60 1.50
41 Derek Fisher .25 .60
42 Glen Rice .25 .60
43 Jamal Mashburn .20 .50
44 Alonzo Mourning .30 .75
45 Tim Hardaway .25 .60
46 Ray Allen .30 .75
47 Vinny Del Negro .15 .40
48 Glenn Robinson .20 .50
49 Joe Smith .20 .50
50 Terrell Brandon .15 .40
51 Kevin Garnett .40 1.00
52 Keith Van Horn .25 .60
53 Stephon Marbury .30 .75
54 Jayson Williams .15 .40
55 Patrick Ewing .30 .75
56 Allan Houston .20 .50
57 Latrell Sprewell .25 .60
58 Anfernee Hardaway .40 1.00
59 Horace Grant .20 .50
60 Nick Anderson .15 .40
61 Allen Iverson .50 1.25
62 Matt Geiger .15 .40
63 Theo Ratliff .20 .50
64 Jason Kidd .40 1.00
65 Rex Chapman .15 .40
66 Tom Gugliotta .15 .40
67 Rasheed Wallace .25 .60
68 Arvydas Sabonis .20 .50
69 Damon Stoudamire .20 .50
70 Vlade Divac .25 .60
71 Corliss Williamson .15 .40
72 Chris Webber .25 .60
73 Tim Duncan .50 1.25
74 Sean Elliott .25 .60
75 David Robinson .40 1.00
76 Vin Baker .20 .50
77 Gary Payton .25 .60
78 Detlef Schrempf .25 .60
79 Tracy McGrady .40 1.00
80 John Wallace .15 .40
81 Doug Christie .15 .40
82 Karl Malone .30 .75
83 John Stockton .30 .75
84 Jeff Hornacek .20 .50
85 Bryant Reeves .15 .40
86 Michael Smith .15 .40
87 Shareef Abdur-Rahim .25 .60
88 Juwan Howard .20 .50
89 Rod Strickland .15 .40
90 Mitch Richmond .25 .60
91 Michael Jordan 1.25 3.00
92 Michael Jordan 1.25 3.00
93 Michael Jordan 1.25 3.00
94 Michael Jordan 1.25 3.00
95 Michael Jordan 1.25 3.00
96 Michael Jordan 1.25 3.00
97 Michael Jordan 1.25 3.00
98 Michael Jordan 1.25 3.00
99 Michael Jordan 1.25 3.00
100 Michael Jordan 1.25 3.00
101 Michael Jordan 1.25 3.00
102 Michael Jordan 1.25 3.00
103 Michael Jordan 1.25 3.00
104 Michael Jordan 1.25 3.00
105 Michael Jordan 1.25 3.00
106 Michael Jordan 1.25 3.00
107 Michael Jordan 1.25 3.00
108 Michael Jordan 1.25 3.00
109 Michael Jordan 1.25 3.00
110 Michael Jordan 1.25 3.00
111 Michael Jordan 1.25 3.00
112 Michael Jordan 1.25 3.00
113 Michael Jordan 1.25 3.00
114 Michael Olowokandi RC 1.00 2.50
115 Mike Bibby RC 1.25 3.00
116 Raef LaFrentz RC 1.00 2.50
117 Antawn Jamison RC 1.25 3.00
118 Vince Carter RC 4.00 10.00
119 Robert Traylor RC .75 2.00
120 Jason Williams RC 2.00 5.00
121 Larry Hughes RC 1.50 4.00
122 Dirk Nowitzki RC 5.00 12.00
123 Paul Pierce RC 3.00 8.00
124 Michael Doleac RC .60 1.50
125 Keon Clark RC .75 2.00
126 Michael Dickerson RC .75 2.00
127 Matt Harpring RC .75 2.00
128 Bryce Drew RC .50 1.25
129 Pat Garrity RC .60 1.50
130 Roshown McLeod RC .50 1.25
131 Ricky Davis RC 1.25 3.00
132 Peja Stojakovic RC 2.00 5.00
133 Felipe Lopez RC .50 1.25
134 Al Harrington RC 1.25 3.00
135 Ruben Patterson RC .75 2.00
136 Cuttino Mobley RC 1.50 4.00
137 Tyronn Lue RC .75 2.00
138 Brian Skinner RC .75 2.00
139 Nazr Mohammed RC .75 2.00
140 Toby Bailey RC .75 2.00
141 Casey Shaw RC .75 2.00
142 Corey Benjamin RC .50 1.25
143 Rashard Lewis RC 2.00 5.00
144 Jason Williams BON 1.25 3.00
145 Paul Pierce BON 2.00 5.00
146 Vince Carter BON 2.50 6.00
147 Antawn Jamison BON .75 2.00
148 Raef LaFrentz BON .60 1.50
149 Mike Bibby BON .75 2.00
150 Michael Olowokandi BON .60 1.50
MJ Michael Jordan AU/50 1500.00 3000.00

1998-99 Upper Deck Encore F/X

COMMON MJ (91-113) 25.00 60.00
*STARS: 12X TO 30X BASE CARD HI
*RCs: 2X TO 5X BASE HI
*BONUS: 3X TO 8X BASE HI
STATED PRINT RUN 125 SERIAL #'d SETS
122 Dirk Nowitzki 30.00 80.00
123 Paul Pierce 25.00 60.00

1998-99 Upper Deck Encore Driving Forces

Randomly inserted in packs at one in 23, this 15-card set focuses on offensive superstars. Card backs are numbered with a "F" prefix.
COMPLETE SET (15) 20.00 50.00
STATED ODDS 1:23
*FX CARDS: 1.5X TO 4X HI COLUMN
FX: STATED PRINT RUN 500 SERIAL #'d SETS
F1 Michael Jordan 15.00 40.00
F2 Kobe Bryant 5.00 12.00
F3 Keith Van Horn 1.25 3.00
F4 Kevin Garnett 2.00 5.00
F5 Tim Duncan 2.50 6.00
F6 Gary Payton 1.25 3.00
F7 Antoine Walker 1.25 3.00
F8 Grant Hill 2.00 5.00
F9 Scottie Pippen 2.00 5.00
F10 Tim Hardaway 1.25 3.00
F11 Reggie Miller 1.50 4.00
F12 Shareef Abdur-Rahim 1.25 3.00
F13 Anfernee Hardaway 2.00 5.00
F14 Allen Iverson 2.50 6.00
F15 Ray Allen 1.50 4.00

1998-99 Upper Deck Encore Intensity

Randomly inserted in packs at one in 11, this 30-card set consists of the league's most intense on-court players. Card backs are numbered with an "I" prefix.
COMPLETE SET (30) 15.00 40.00
STATED ODDS 1:11
I1 Michael Jordan 6.00 15.00
I2 Mitch Richmond .75 2.00
I3 Ron Mercer .60 1.50
I4 Terrell Brandon .50 1.25
I5 Brevin Knight .50 1.25
I6 Rasheed Wallace .75 2.00
I7 Keith Van Horn .75 2.00
I8 Antawn Jamison 1.25 3.00
I9 Antonio McDyess .60 1.50
I10 Allen Iverson 1.50 4.00
I11 Anfernee Hardaway 1.25 3.00
I12 Chris Webber .75 2.00
I13 Lorenzen Wright .50 1.25
I14 Bryant Reeves .50 1.25
I15 Charles Barkley 1.25 3.00
I16 Tracy McGrady 1.25 3.00
I17 Larry Johnson .75 2.00
I18 Jerry Stackhouse .75 2.00
I19 Derrick Coleman .60 1.50
I20 Detlef Schrempf .75 2.00
I21 John Stockton 1.00 2.50
I22 Kobe Bryant 3.00 8.00
I23 Alonzo Mourning 1.00 2.50
I24 Dikembe Mutombo .75 2.00
I25 Jalen Rose .60 1.50
I26 Robert Pack .50 1.25
I27 Tom Gugliotta .50 1.25
I28 Shaquille O'Neal 2.00 5.00
I29 Stephon Marbury 1.00 2.50
I30 David Robinson 1.25 3.00

1998-99 Upper Deck Encore MJ23

Randomly inserted in packs at one in 23, this 20-card set pays tribute to Michael Jordan. Card backs carry a "M" prefix.
COMPLETE SET (20) 60.00 120.00
COMMON CARD (M1-M20) 3.00 8.00
STATED ODDS 1:23
*FX: 10X TO 25X BASE HI
FX: STATED PRINT RUN 23 SERIAL #'d SETS

1998-99 Upper Deck Encore PowerDeck

Randomly inserted in packs at one in 47, this nine-card set features special interactive cards that when loaded in a disk drive, feature game-action footage, sound, photos and career highlights for the players. The cards are not numbered and listed below in alphabetical order.
STATED ODDS 1:47
1 Charles Barkley 5.00 12.00
2 Kobe Bryant 8.00 20.00
3 Vince Carter 6.00 15.00
4 Julius Erving 4.00 10.00
5 Kevin Garnett 4.00 10.00
6 Michael Jordan 15.00 40.00
7 Shaquille O'Neal 4.00 10.00
8 Paul Pierce 4.00 10.00
9 Jason Williams 4.00 10.00

1998-99 Upper Deck Encore Rookie Encore

Randomly inserted into packs at one in 23, this 10-card set features some of the best from the 1998-99 rookie class. Card backs carry a "RE" prefix.
COMPLETE SET (10) 15.00 40.00
STATED ODDS 1:23
*FX: .75X TO 2X HI COLUMN
FX: STATED PRINT RUN 1000 SERIAL #'d SETS
RE1 Jason Williams 2.00 5.00
RE2 Michael Olowokandi 1.00 2.50
RE3 Paul Pierce 3.00 8.00
RE4 Robert Traylor .75 2.00
RE5 Raef LaFrentz 1.00 2.50
RE6 Mike Bibby 1.25 3.00
RE7 Dirk Nowitzki 5.00 12.00
RE8 Antawn Jamison 1.25 3.00
RE9 Larry Hughes 1.50 4.00
RE10 Vince Carter 4.00 10.00

1999-00 Upper Deck Encore

The 1999-00 Upper Deck Encore set was released in late April, 2000 as a 120-card set that featured 90 player cards and 30 rookie cards. The rookies were short printed and serial numbered to 1999. Each pack contained 6-cards and carried a suggested retail price of 3.99.
COMPLETE SET (120) 40.00 100.00
COMPLETE SET w/o RC (90) 10.00 25.00
91-120 PRINT RUN 1999 SERIAL #'d SETS
1 Dikembe Mutombo .30 .75
2 Alan Henderson .20 .50
3 Isaiah Rider .25 .60
4 Kenny Anderson .25 .60
5 Antoine Walker .30 .75
6 Paul Pierce .40 1.00
7 Elden Campbell .20 .50
8 Eddie Jones .30 .75
9 David Wesley .20 .50
10 Hersey Hawkins .20 .50
11 Randy Brown .20 .50
12 Toni Kukoc .30 .75
13 Shawn Kemp .30 .75
14 Bob Sura .20 .50
15 Michael Finley .30 .75
16 Dirk Nowitzki .60 1.50
17 Gary Trent .20 .50
18 Antonio McDyess .25 .60
19 Nick Van Exel .25 .60
20 Raef LaFrentz .25 .60
21 Christian Laettner .25 .60
22 Grant Hill .40 1.00
23 Lindsey Hunter .20 .50
24 Jerry Stackhouse .30 .75
25 John Starks .25 .60
26 Antawn Jamison .30 .75
27 Tony Farmer .20 .50
28 Hakeem Olajuwon .40 1.00
29 Cuttino Mobley .20 .50
30 Charles Barkley .50 1.25
31 Reggie Miller .30 .75
32 Jalen Rose .25 .60
33 Mark Jackson .25 .60
34 Maurice Taylor .20 .50
35 Derek Anderson .20 .50
36 Michael Olowokandi .20 .50
37 Kobe Bryant 1.25 3.00
38 Shaquille O'Neal .75 2.00
39 Glen Rice .30 .75
40 Tim Hardaway .30 .75
41 Alonzo Mourning .40 1.00
42 Ray Allen .30 .75
43 Glenn Robinson .25 .60
44 Sam Cassell .25 .60
45 Tim Thomas .25 .60
46 Kevin Garnett .50 1.25
47 Terrell Brandon .20 .50
48 Keith Van Horn .25 .60
49 Stephon Marbury .25 .60
50 Kendall Gill .20 .50
51 Patrick Ewing .40 1.00
52 Allan Houston .25 .60
53 Latrell Sprewell .30 .75
54 Darrell Armstrong .20 .50
55 John Amaechi RC .30 .75
56 Michael Doleac .20 .50
57 Allen Iverson .60 1.50
58 Theo Ratliff .25 .60
59 Larry Hughes .25 .60
60 Jason Kidd .50 1.25
61 Tom Gugliotta .20 .50
62 Anfernee Hardaway .50 1.25
63 Rasheed Wallace .30 .75
64 Steve Smith .25 .60
65 Damon Stoudamire .25 .60
66 Scottie Pippen .50 1.25
67 Corliss Williamson .20 .50
68 Jason Williams .40 1.00
69 Vlade Divac .30 .75
70 Chris Webber .30 .75
71 Tim Duncan .60 1.50
72 David Robinson .50 1.25
73 Avery Johnson .25 .60
74 Mario Elie .20 .50
75 Gary Payton .30 .75
76 Vin Baker .25 .60
77 Ruben Patterson .20 .50
78 Brent Barry .25 .60
79 Vince Carter .60 1.50
80 Antonio Davis .20 .50
81 Tracy McGrady .50 1.25
82 Karl Malone .40 1.00
83 John Stockton .40 1.00
84 Bryon Russell .20 .50
85 Shareef Abdur-Rahim .25 .60
86 Mike Bibby .30 .75
87 Othella Harrington .20 .50
88 Juwan Howard .25 .60
89 Rod Strickland .20 .50
90 Mitch Richmond .30 .75
91 Elton Brand RC 2.50 6.00
92 Steve Francis RC 2.50 6.00
93 Baron Davis RC 2.50 6.00
94 Lamar Odom RC 2.50 6.00
95 Jonathan Bender RC 1.00 2.50
96 Wally Szczerbiak RC 2.00 5.00
97 Richard Hamilton RC 2.00 5.00
98 Andre Miller RC 2.00 5.00
99 Shawn Marion RC 2.00 5.00
100 Jason Terry RC 1.50 4.00
101 Trajan Langdon RC 1.00 2.50
102 Kenny Thomas RC 1.00 2.50
103 Corey Maggette RC 1.50 4.00
104 William Avery RC .75 2.00
105 Ron Artest RC 2.00 5.00
106 A.Radojevic RC .60 1.50
107 James Posey RC 1.00 2.50
108 Quincy Lewis RC .60 1.50
109 Vonteego Cummings RC .60 1.50
110 Jeff Foster RC 1.00 2.50
111 Dion Glover RC .75 2.00
112 Devean George RC 1.00 2.50
113 Evan Eschmeyer RC .75 2.00
114 Tim James RC .60 1.50
115 Adrian Griffin RC 1.00 2.50
116 Anthony Carter RC .75 2.00
117 Obinna Ekezie RC .75 2.00
118 Todd MacCulloch RC 1.00 2.50
119 Chucky Atkins RC 1.00 2.50
120 Lazaro Borrell RC 1.00 2.50

1999-00 Upper Deck Encore Electric Currents

Randomly inserted in packs at one in three, this insert set features 20 of the leagues most highly recognized scorers. Card backs carry an "EC" prefix.
COMPLETE SET (20) 5.00 12.00
STATED ODDS 1:3
*F/X: 5X TO 12X BASE HI
F/X: PRINT RUN 150 SERIAL #'d SETS
EC1 Kevin Garnett .60 1.50
EC2 Anfernee Hardaway .60 1.50
EC3 Shareef Abdur-Rahim .30 .75
EC4 Allan Houston .30 .75
EC5 Michael Finley .40 1.00
EC6 Tim Duncan .75 2.00
EC7 Gary Payton .40 1.00
EC8 Kobe Bryant 1.50 4.00
EC9 Derek Anderson .25 .60
EC10 Reggie Miller .40 1.00
EC11 Keith Van Horn .30 .75
EC12 Jason Kidd .60 1.50
EC13 Ray Allen .40 1.00
EC14 Tim Hardaway .40 1.00
EC15 Darrell Armstrong .25 .60
EC16 Antonio McDyess .30 .75
EC17 Eddie Jones .40 1.00
EC18 Paul Pierce .50 1.25
EC19 Stephon Marbury .30 .75
EC20 Chris Webber .40 1.00

1999-00 Upper Deck Encore Future Charge

Randomly inserted in packs at one in six, this insert set features 15 of the NBA's next generation of star players. Card backs carry a "FC" prefix.
COMPLETE SET (15) 4.00 10.00
STATED ODDS 1:6
FC1 Antawn Jamison .50 1.25
FC2 Mike Bibby .50 1.25
FC3 Antoine Walker .50 1.25
FC4 Baron Davis .75 2.00
FC5 Jason Terry .50 1.25
FC6 Andre Miller .60 1.50
FC7 Ray Allen .50 1.25
FC8 Wally Szczerbiak .60 1.50
FC9 Raef LaFrentz .40 1.00
FC10 William Avery .25 .60
FC11 Jason Williams .60 1.50
FC12 Michael Olowokandi .30 .75
FC13 Stephon Marbury .40 1.00
FC14 Quincy Lewis .20 .50
FC15 Shawn Marion .60 1.50

1999-00 Upper Deck Encore Game Jerseys

Randomly inserted in packs at one in 300, this insert set features 20-cards that contain pieces of game-worn jerseys of various NBA players. The set also includes autographed game-jersey cards of Michael Jordan, Kevin Garnett, and Kobe Bryant. Card backs are numbered using the players initials. Each autographed card is serial numbered to the specified player's jersey number.
STATED ODDS 1:300
MJ Michael Jordan AU/23 2500.00 4000.00
AIJ Allen Iverson 15.00 40.00
AMJ Andre Miller 8.00 20.00
BDJ Baron Davis 12.00 30.00
GHJ Grant Hill 25.00 60.00
JBJ Jonathan Bender 8.00 20.00
JKJ Jason Kidd 20.00 50.00
JTJ Jason Terry 8.00 20.00
JWJ Jason Williams 25.00 60.00
KBJ Kobe Bryant 75.00 200.00
KGA Kevin Garnett AU/21 300.00 500.00
KGJ Kevin Garnett 20.00 50.00
MCJ Antonio McDyess 8.00 20.00
RHJ Richard Hamilton 8.00 20.00
SFJ Steve Francis 15.00 40.00
SMJ Shawn Marion 10.00 25.00
SOJ Shaquille O'Neal 30.00 80.00
TLJ Trajan Langdon 8.00 20.00
WSJ Wally Szczerbiak 8.00 20.00

1999-00 Upper Deck Encore High Definition

Randomly inserted in packs at one in 15, this insert set features 20 of the most spectacular dunk shots. Card backs carry a "HD" prefix.
COMPLETE SET (20) 15.00 40.00
STATED ODDS 1:15
HD1 Antonio McDyess .75 2.00
HD2 Kevin Garnett 1.50 4.00
HD3 Vince Carter 2.00 5.00
HD4 Shareef Abdur-Rahim .75 2.00
HD5 Stephon Marbury .75 2.00
HD6 Gary Payton 1.00 2.50
HD7 Glenn Robinson .75 2.00
HD8 Kobe Bryant 4.00 10.00
HD9 Antawn Jamison 1.00 2.50
HD10 Chris Webber 1.00 2.50
HD11 Corey Maggette 1.50 4.00
HD12 Shawn Kemp 1.00 2.50
HD13 Derek Anderson .60 1.50
HD14 Michael Finley 1.00 2.50
HD15 Allan Houston .75 2.00
HD16 Anfernee Hardaway 1.50 4.00
HD17 Grant Hill 1.25 3.00
HD18 Shaquille O'Neal 2.50 6.00
HD19 Paul Pierce 1.25 3.00
HD20 Scottie Pippen 1.50 4.00

1999-00 Upper Deck Encore Jamboree

Randomly inserted in packs at one in six, this 15-card insert features some of the most electrifying slam dunkers in the NBA. Card backs carry a "J" prefix.
COMPLETE SET (15) 8.00 20.00
STATED ODDS 1:6
J1 Michael Jordan 5.00 12.00
J2 Karl Malone .75 2.00
J3 Kevin Garnett 1.00 2.50
J4 Antonio McDyess .50 1.25
J5 Shareef Abdur-Rahim .50 1.25
J6 David Robinson 1.00 2.50
J7 Marcus Camby .50 1.25
J8 Kobe Bryant 2.50 6.00
J9 Jason Kidd 1.00 2.50
J10 Tim Duncan 1.25 3.00
J11 Keith Van Horn .50 1.25
J12 Glenn Robinson .50 1.25
J13 Grant Hill .75 2.00
J14 Michael Finley .60 1.50
J15 Vince Carter 1.25 3.00

1999-00 Upper Deck Encore MJ - A Higher Power

Randomly inserted in packs at one in 90, this 10-card insert set honors the greatest player off all time. Card backs carry a "MJ" prefix.
COMPLETE SET (10) 50.00 120.00
COMMON CARD (MJ1-MJ10) 6.00 15.00
STATED ODDS 1:90

1999-00 Upper Deck Encore Upper Realm

Randomly inserted in packs at one in six, this insert set honors 10 of the NBA's most elite players. Card backs carry a "UR" prefix.
COMPLETE SET (10) 4.00 10.00
STATED ODDS 1:6
*F/X: 6X TO 15X HI COLUMN
F/X: PRINT RUN 150 SERIAL #'d SETS
UR1 Kevin Garnett .60 1.50
UR2 Kobe Bryant 1.50 4.00
UR3 Tim Duncan .75 2.00
UR4 Vince Carter .75 2.00
UR5 Gary Payton .40 1.00
UR6 Allen Iverson .75 2.00
UR7 Karl Malone .50 1.25
UR8 Jason Williams .50 1.25
UR9 Scottie Pippen .60 1.50
UR10 Shaquille O'Neal 1.00 2.50

2000-01 Upper Deck Encore

The 2000-01 Upper Deck Encore product was released in May, 2001 and featured a 165-card base set that was broken into tiers as follows: Base Veterans (1-135), and Rookies (136-165) that were serial numbered to 1600. Each pack contained five cards, and carried a suggested retail price of $2.99.
COMPLETE SET w/o RC's 10.00 25.00
136-165 PRINT RUN 1600 SERIAL #'d SETS
1 Brevin Knight .20 .50
2 Lorenzen Wright .20 .50
3 Alan Henderson .20 .50
4 Jason Terry .30 .75
5 Paul Pierce .30 .75
6 Antoine Walker .25 .60
7 Kenny Anderson .25 .60
8 Tony Battie .20 .50
9 Adrian Griffin .20 .50
10 Derrick Coleman .25 .60
11 David Wesley .20 .50
12 Baron Davis .30 .75
13 Elden Campbell .20 .50
14 Jamal Mashburn .25 .60
15 Elton Brand .30 .75
16 Ron Mercer .20 .50
17 Ron Artest .30 .75
18 Michael Ruffin .20 .50
19 Lamond Murray .20 .50
20 Andre Miller .25 .60
21 Matt Harpring .20 .50
22 Jim Jackson .20 .50
23 Michael Finley .30 .75
24 Dirk Nowitzki .50 1.25
25 Steve Nash .50 1.25
26 Howard Eisley .20 .50
27 Antonio McDyess .25 .60
28 James Posey .20 .50
29 Nick Van Exel .25 .60
30 Raef LaFrentz .20 .50
31 Voshon Lenard .20 .50
32 Jerry Stackhouse .25 .60
33 Ben Wallace .25 .60
34 Michael Curry .20 .50
35 Joe Smith .25 .60
36 Chucky Atkins .20 .50
37 Antawn Jamison .30 .75
38 Larry Hughes .25 .60
39 Chris Mills .20 .50
40 Mookie Blaylock .20 .50
41 Vonteego Cummings .20 .50
42 Steve Francis .25 .60
43 Maurice Taylor .20 .50
44 Hakeem Olajuwon .40 1.00
45 Walt Williams .20 .50
46 Cuttino Mobley .20 .50
47 Reggie Miller .30 .75
48 Jalen Rose .25 .60
49 Austin Croshere .20 .50
50 Travis Best .20 .50
51 Jermaine O'Neal .25 .60
52 Lamar Odom .25 .60
53 Jeff McInnis .20 .50
54 Michael Olowokandi .20 .50
55 Brian Skinner .20 .50
56 Corey Maggette .25 .60
57 Shaquille O'Neal .75 2.00
58 Ron Harper .25 .60
59 Kobe Bryant 1.25 3.00
60 Robert Horry .25 .60
61 Isaiah Rider .25 .60
62 Eddie Jones .30 .75
63 Anthony Carter .20 .50
64 Tim Hardaway .30 .75
65 Brian Grant .20 .50
66 Anthony Mason .20 .50
67 Ray Allen .30 .75
68 Tim Thomas .20 .50
69 Glenn Robinson .25 .60
70 Sam Cassell .25 .60
71 Lindsey Hunter .20 .50
72 Kevin Garnett .50 1.25
73 Wally Szczerbiak .25 .60
74 Terrell Brandon .20 .50
75 Chauncey Billups .30 .75
76 Stephon Marbury .25 .60
77 Keith Van Horn .25 .60
78 Lucious Harris .20 .50
79 Kendall Gill .20 .50
80 Latrell Sprewell .25 .60
81 Marcus Camby .25 .60
82 Larry Johnson .30 .75
83 Allan Houston .25 .60
84 Glen Rice .25 .60
85 Grant Hill .40 1.00
86 Tracy McGrady .50 1.25
87 John Amaechi .20 .50
88 Darrell Armstrong .20 .50
89 Allen Iverson .60 1.50
90 Dikembe Mutombo .30 .75
91 George Lynch .20 .50
92 Aaron McKie .20 .50
93 Eric Snow .20 .50
94 Jason Kidd .50 1.25
95 Tony Delk .20 .50
96 Clifford Robinson .20 .50
97 Tom Gugliotta .20 .50
98 Shawn Marion .25 .60
99 Rasheed Wallace .30 .75
100 Scottie Pippen .50 1.25
101 Steve Smith .25 .60
102 Damon Stoudamire .25 .60
103 Bonzi Wells .20 .50
104 Chris Webber .30 .75
105 Jason Williams .30 .75
106 Peja Stojakovic .30 .75
107 Vlade Divac .25 .60
108 Doug Christie .20 .50
109 Tim Duncan .60 1.50
110 David Robinson .50 1.25
111 Derek Anderson .20 .50
112 Antonio Daniels .20 .50
113 Sean Elliott .30 .75
114 Gary Payton .30 .75
115 Patrick Ewing .40 1.00
116 Vin Baker .25 .60
117 Rashard Lewis .30 .75
118 Vince Carter .60 1.50
119 Alvin Williams .20 .50
120 Antonio Davis .20 .50
121 Charles Oakley .25 .60
122 Karl Malone .40 1.00
123 John Stockton .40 1.00
124 Bryon Russell .20 .50
125 John Starks .25 .60
126 Shareef Abdur-Rahim .25 .60
127 Mike Bibby .30 .75
128 Michael Dickerson .20 .50
129 Grant Long .20 .50
130 Mitch Richmond .25 .60
131 Richard Hamilton .25 .60
132 Chris Whitney .20 .50
133 Jahidi White .20 .50
134 Checklist 1 .08 .25
135 Checklist 2 .08 .25
136 Kenyon Martin RC 3.00 8.00
137 Stromile Swift RC 1.25 3.00
138 Chris Mihm RC 1.00 2.50
139 Marcus Fizer RC 1.25 3.00
140 Darius Miles RC 1.25 3.00
141 Joel Przybilla RC 1.00 2.50
142 Mike Miller RC 2.00 5.00
143 Courtney Alexander RC 1.00 2.50
144 DerMarr Johnson RC 1.00 2.50
145 Stephen Jackson RC 2.00 5.00
146 Jerome Moiso RC .75 2.00
147 Keyon Dooling RC 1.25 3.00
148 Erick Barkley RC .75 2.00
149 Jason Collier RC 1.25 3.00
150 Jamaal Magloire RC 1.25 3.00
151 DeShawn Stevenson RC 1.25 3.00
152 Hedo Turkoglu RC 2.00 5.00
153 Morris Peterson RC 1.25 3.00
154 Jamal Crawford RC 3.00 8.00
155 Etan Thomas RC 1.25 3.00
156 Quentin Richardson RC 1.25 3.00
157 Mateen Cleaves RC 1.00 2.50
158 Donnell Harvey RC 1.00 2.50
159 Mark Madsen RC 1.25 3.00
160 Desmond Mason RC 1.50 4.00
161 Speedy Claxton RC 1.25 3.00
162 Hanno Mottola RC .75 2.00
163 Mamadou N'Diaye RC .75 2.00
164 Eduardo Najera RC 1.25 3.00
165 Khalid El-Amin RC .75 2.00

2000-01 Upper Deck Encore High Definition

Randomly inserted in packs at one in 16, this 6-card set features player's that are the cornerstones of their teams. Card backs carry a "HD" prefix.
COMPLETE SET (6) 4.00 10.00
STATED ODDS 1:16
HD1 Stephon Marbury .50 1.25
HD2 Steve Francis .50 1.25
HD3 Shaquille O'Neal 1.50 4.00
HD4 Kevin Garnett 1.00 2.50
HD5 Kobe Bryant 2.50 6.00
HD6 Tracy McGrady 1.00 2.50

2000-01 Upper Deck Encore NBA Warm-Ups

Randomly inserted into packs at one in 8, this 21-card set features swatches of actual game-worn warm-up jerseys. Card backs carry the player's initials followed by the letter "W".
STATED ODDS 1:8
AMW Andre Miller 2.50 6.00
BDW Baron Davis 3.00 8.00
CAW Courtney Alexander 1.50 4.00
CMW Chris Mihm 1.50 4.00

DJW DerMarr Johnson 1.50 4.00
DMW Darius Miles 2.00 5.00
DSW DeShawn Stevenson 2.00 5.00
HMW Hanno Mottola 1.25 3.00
JCW Jamal Crawford 5.00 12.00
JMW Jerome Moiso 1.25 3.00
JSW Jerry Stackhouse 2.50 6.00
KBW Kobe Bryant 10.00 25.00
KDW Keyon Dooling 2.00 5.00
KEW Khalid El-Amin 1.25 3.00
KGW Kevin Garnett 5.00 12.00
KMW Kenyon Martin 5.00 12.00
MAW Corey Maggette 2.50 6.00
MFW Marcus Fizer 2.00 5.00
MMW Mike Miller 3.00 8.00
TMW Tracy McGrady 5.00 12.00
WSW Wally Szczerbiak 2.50 6.00

2000-01 Upper Deck Encore NBA Warm-Ups Autographs

STATED PRINT RUN 8 TO 50 SETS
CMA Chris Mihm/50 6.00 15.00
DJA DerMarr Johnson/50 6.00 15.00
DMA Darius Miles/50 8.00 20.00
DSA DeShawn Stevenson/50 8.00 20.00
JCA Jamal Crawford/50 20.00 50.00
JSA Jerry Stackhouse/50 8.00 20.00
KEA Khalid El-Amin/50 5.00 12.00
KGA Kevin Garnett/21 60.00 120.00
KMA Kenyon Martin/50 20.00 50.00
MFA Marcus Fizer/50 8.00 20.00
MMA Mike Miller/50 12.00 30.00
TMA Tracy McGrady/50 30.00 60.00

2000-01 Upper Deck Encore Performers

Randomly inserted into packs at one in 8, this 12-card set features the league's top performers. Card backs carry a "EP" prefix.
COMPLETE SET (12) 6.00 15.00
STATED ODDS 1:8
EP1 Jason Kidd 1.00 2.50
EP2 Stephon Marbury .50 1.25
EP3 Gary Payton .60 1.50
EP4 Kevin Garnett 1.00 2.50
EP5 Antonio McDyess .50 1.25
EP6 Shareef Abdur-Rahim .50 1.25
EP7 Tim Duncan 1.25 3.00
EP8 Allan Houston .50 1.25
EP9 Kobe Bryant 2.50 6.00
EP10 Andre Miller .50 1.25
EP11 Vince Carter 1.25 3.00
EP12 Ray Allen .60 1.50

2000-01 Upper Deck Encore Powerful Stuff

Randomly inserted in packs at one in 8, this 12-card set highlights some of the more incredible dunks from today's superstars. Card backs carry a "PS" prefix.
COMPLETE SET (12) 8.00 20.00
STATED ODDS 1:8
PS1 Kobe Bryant 2.50 6.00
PS2 Tim Duncan 1.25 3.00
PS3 Allen Iverson 1.25 3.00
PS4 Karl Malone .75 2.00
PS5 Tracy McGrady 1.00 2.50
PS6 Shaquille O'Neal 1.50 4.00
PS7 Vince Carter 1.25 3.00
PS8 Chris Webber .60 1.50
PS9 Eddie Jones .60 1.50
PS10 Kevin Garnett 1.00 2.50
PS11 Elton Brand .60 1.50
PS12 Paul Pierce .60 1.50

2000-01 Upper Deck Encore Star Signatures

Randomly inserted in packs at one in 48, this 37-card insert set features authentic autographs from some of the NBA's elite players. Card backs carry the player's initials as numbering. Please note that a few of the players packed out as exchange cards and must be redeemed no later that 12/05/01.
STATED ODDS 1:48
CA Courtney Alexander 3.00 8.00
CM Chris Mihm 3.00 8.00
CO Corey Maggette 4.00 10.00
CR Jamal Crawford 10.00 25.00
DH Donnell Harvey 3.00 8.00
DJ DerMarr Johnson 3.00 8.00
DM Darius Miles 4.00 10.00
DS DeShawn Stevenson 4.00 10.00
EB Erick Barkley 2.50 6.00
EJ Eddie Jones 12.50 30.00
ET Etan Thomas 4.00 10.00
GP Gary Payton 20.00 50.00
HM Hanno Mottola 2.50 6.00
JA Jamaal Magloire 4.00 10.00
JM Jerome Moiso 2.50 6.00
JO Jermaine O'Neal 6.00 15.00
JP Joel Przybilla 3.00 8.00
JS Jerry Stackhouse 8.00 20.00
KB Kobe Bryant 80.00 160.00
KE Khalid El-Amin 2.50 6.00
KM Kenyon Martin 8.00 20.00
LH Larry Hughes 4.00 10.00
MC Mateen Cleaves 3.00 8.00
MK Mark Madsen 4.00 10.00
MM Mike Miller 6.00 15.00
MN Mamadou N'Diaye 2.50 6.00
MP Morris Peterson 4.00 10.00
RH Richard Hamilton 5.00 12.00
RM Reggie Miller 40.00 100.00
SC Speedy Claxton 4.00 10.00
SF Steve Francis 5.00 12.00
SM Shawn Marion 5.00 12.00
SS Stromile Swift 4.00 10.00
TH Tim Hardaway 8.00 20.00
WS Wally Szczerbiak 5.00 12.00

2000-01 Upper Deck Encore Upper Realm

Randomly inserted in packs at one in 16, this 6-card set features the league's most valuable players. Card backs carry a "UR" prefix.
COMPLETE SET (6) 5.00 12.00
STATED ODDS 1:16
UR1 Shaquille O'Neal 1.50 4.00
UR2 Allen Iverson 1.25 3.00
UR3 Tim Duncan 1.25 3.00
UR4 Kobe Bryant 2.50 6.00
UR5 Chris Webber .60 1.50
UR6 Kevin Garnett 1.00 2.50

2000-01 Upper Deck Encore Vertical Forces

Randomly inserted in packs at one in 16, this 6-card set features the league's most sensational leapers. Card backs carry a "VF" prefix.
COMPLETE SET (6) 4.00 10.00
STATED ODDS 1:16
VF1 Kobe Bryant 2.50 6.00
VF2 Vince Carter 1.25 3.00
VF3 Rashard Lewis .60 1.50
VF4 Chris Webber .60 1.50
VF5 Steve Francis .50 1.25
VF6 Kevin Garnett 1.00 2.50

2005-06 Upper Deck ESPN

Released in September 2005, ESPN consists of 132-cards divided up into 90 veterans and 40 rookies. base cards have borders along the left side and bottom of the card set to match team colors and the ESPN logo and player's name below centered pictures. ESPN was packaged in 24-pack boxes where each pack contains nine cards and carried an initial SRP of $2.99.
COMPLETE SET (132) 15.00 40.00
COMP.SET w/o SP's (90) 6.00 15.00
91-132 RC STATED ODDS 1:4
1 Josh Childress .15 .40
2 Josh Smith .15 .40
3 Al Harrington .15 .40
4 Antoine Walker .15 .40
5 Ricky Davis .15 .40
6 Paul Pierce .20 .50
7 Kareem Rush .12 .30
8 Emeka Okafor .15 .40
9 Gerald Wallace .15 .40
10 Eddy Curry .12 .30
11 Kirk Hinrich .15 .40
12 Ben Gordon .15 .40
13 Drew Gooden .15 .40
14 LeBron James .75 2.00
15 Zydrunas Ilgauskas .15 .40
16 Dirk Nowitzki .30 .75
17 Jason Terry .15 .40
18 Josh Howard .20 .50
19 Carmelo Anthony .40 1.00
20 Kenyon Martin .15 .40
21 Andre Miller .15 .40
22 Ben Wallace .15 .40
23 Chauncey Billups .20 .50
24 Richard Hamilton .15 .40
25 Troy Murphy .12 .30
26 Jason Richardson .20 .50
27 Baron Davis .15 .40
28 Tracy McGrady .25 .60
29 Yao Ming .25 .60
30 Juwan Howard .15 .40
31 Jermaine O'Neal .15 .40
32 Reggie Miller .20 .50
33 Ron Artest .20 .50
34 Corey Maggette .15 .40
35 Elton Brand .20 .50
36 Bobby Simmons .12 .30
37 Caron Butler .15 .40
38 Kobe Bryant .75 2.00
39 Lamar Odom .15 .40
40 Mike Miller .15 .40
41 Jason Williams .15 .40
42 Pau Gasol .20 .50
43 Dwyane Wade .30 .75
44 Eddie Jones .15 .40
45 Shaquille O'Neal .40 1.00
46 Desmond Mason .12 .30
47 Maurice Williams .15 .40
48 Michael Redd .15 .40
49 Kevin Garnett .30 .75
50 Latrell Sprewell .15 .40
51 Sam Cassell .15 .40
52 Vince Carter .30 .75
53 Jason Kidd .30 .75
54 Richard Jefferson .15 .40
55 Dan Dickau .12 .30
56 Jamaal Magloire .12 .30
57 J.R. Smith .15 .40
58 Jamal Crawford .20 .50
59 Stephon Marbury .15 .40
60 Allan Houston .15 .40
61 Dwight Howard .15 .40
62 Grant Hill .25 .60
63 Steve Francis .15 .40
64 Allen Iverson .30 .75
65 Andre Iguodala .15 .40
66 Chris Webber .20 .50
67 Amare Stoudemire .15 .40
68 Shawn Marion .15 .40
69 Steve Nash .25 .60
70 Damon Stoudamire .15 .40
71 Shareef Abdur-Rahim .15 .40
72 Zach Randolph .15 .40
73 Brad Miller .15 .40
74 Mike Bibby .20 .50
75 Peja Stojakovic .20 .50
76 Manu Ginobili .20 .50
77 Tim Duncan .30 .75
78 Tony Parker .20 .50
79 Rashard Lewis .20 .50
80 Ray Allen .20 .50
81 Luke Ridnour .15 .40
82 Rafer Alston .12 .30
83 Jalen Rose .20 .50
84 Chris Bosh .20 .50
85 Andrei Kirilenko .15 .40
86 Carlos Boozer .15 .40
87 Matt Harpring .12 .30
88 Antawn Jamison .15 .40
89 Gilbert Arenas .15 .40
90 Larry Hughes .15 .40
91 Chris Taft RC .60 1.50
92 Marvin Williams RC .75 2.00
93 Chris Paul RC 3.00 8.00
94 Andrew Bogut RC 1.00 2.50
95 Martynas Andriuskevicius RC .50 1.25
96 Louis Williams RC .75 2.00
97 C.J. Miles RC .75 2.00
98 Gerald Green RC .75 2.00
99 Rashad McCants RC .60 1.50
100 Sarunas Jasikevicius RC .75 2.00
101 Andrew Bynum RC .60 1.50
102 Raymond Felton RC .75 2.00
103 Hakim Warrick RC .60 1.50
104 Deron Williams RC 1.00 2.50
105 Daniel Ewing RC .60 1.50
106 Martell Webster RC .60 1.50
107 Johan Petro RC .50 1.25
108 Travis Diener RC .50 1.25
109 Joey Graham RC .60 1.50
110 Antoine Wright RC .60 1.50
111 Ersan Ilyasova RC .75 2.00
112 Jason Maxiell RC .60 1.50
113 Linas Kleiza RC .50 1.25
114 Jarrett Jack RC .75 2.00
115 Danny Granger RC 1.00 2.50
116 Monta Ellis RC 1.00 2.50
117 Francisco Garcia RC .60 1.50
118 Ryan Gomes RC .60 1.50
119 Wayne Simien RC .50 1.25
120 Von Wafer RC .50 1.25
121 Dijon Thompson RC .50 1.25
122 Nate Robinson RC .75 2.00
123 Bracey Wright RC .50 1.25
124 Andray Blatche RC .75 2.00
125 Channing Frye RC .75 2.00
126 Salim Stoudamire RC .60 1.50
127 Luther Head RC .60 1.50
128 Julius Hodge RC .50 1.25
129 David Lee RC .75 2.00
130 Ike Diogu RC .50 1.25
131 Sean May RC .50 1.25
132 Brandon Bass RC .60 1.50

2005-06 Upper Deck ESPN 25th Anniversary

*1-90 25th: 12X TO 30X BASE HI
*91-132 RC 25th: 3X TO 8X BASE HI
PRINT RUN 25 SER.#'d SETS

2005-06 Upper Deck ESPN ESPY Award Winners

Inserted in packs at the rate of one in one along with the Play of the Day, Highlight Reel, Fast Break and ESPN the Mag inserts, this 20-card set is horizontally designed with a player photo on the left and a picture of the ESPY trophy on the right. Several players have multiple versions, see checklist for details.
COMPLETE SET (20) 15.00 40.00
STATED ODDS 1:1 WITH OTHER INSERTS
*25th ANNIV: 6X TO 15X BASE ESPY HI
25th ANNIVERSARY PRINT RUN 25 SETS
AJ Antawn Jamison .30 .75
CA Carmelo Anthony .75 2.00
EB Elton Brand .40 1.00
GH Grant Hill .50 1.25
KG Kevin Garnett .60 1.50
KV Keith Van Horn .30 .75
LJ LeBron James 1.50 4.00
MF Michael Finley .40 1.00
MJ1 Michael Jordan 2.50 6.00
MJ2 Michael Jordan 2.50 6.00
MJ3 Michael Jordan 2.50 6.00
MJ4 Michael Jordan 2.50 6.00
MJ5 Michael Jordan 2.50 6.00
MJ6 Michael Jordan 2.50 6.00
MJ7 Michael Jordan 2.50 6.00
MJ8 Michael Jordan 2.50 6.00
MJ9 Michael Jordan 2.50 6.00
MJ10 Michael Jordan 2.50 6.00
SO Shaquille O'Neal .75 2.00
TD Tim Duncan .60 1.50

2005-06 Upper Deck ESPN Highlight Reel

Inserted in packs at the rate of one in one along with the Play of the Day, ESPY Award Winners, Fast Break and ESPN the Mag inserts, this set features a horizontal design with a black Higlight Reel on the left and a player image on the right.
COMPLETE SET (20) 10.00 25.00
STATED ODDS 1:1 WITH OTHER INSERTS
*25th ANNIV: 6X TO 15X BASE HI
25th ANNIVERSARY PRINT RUN 25 SETS
HR1 Paul Pierce .40 1.00
HR2 Michael Jordan 3.00 8.00
HR3 LeBron James 1.50 4.00
HR4 Dirk Nowitzki .60 1.50
HR5 Ben Wallace .30 .75
HR6 Jason Richardson .40 1.00
HR7 Yao Ming .50 1.25
HR8 Jermaine O'Neal .30 .75
HR9 Kobe Bryant 1.50 4.00
HR10 Dwyane Wade .60 1.50
HR11 Vince Carter .60 1.50
HR12 Richard Jefferson .30 .75
HR13 Baron Davis .30 .75
HR14 Stephon Marbury .30 .75
HR15 Allen Iverson .60 1.50
HR16 Amare Stoudemire .30 .75
HR17 Steve Nash .50 1.25
HR18 Tim Duncan .60 1.50
HR19 Ray Allen .40 1.00
HR20 Chris Bosh .40 1.00

2005-06 Upper Deck ESPN Ink

Inserted in packs at the rate of one in 480, this set features NBA Players along with ESPN Personalities. Cards are horizontally designed with player photos on the right side and an centered autographed sticker on the left. SP information for this set was provided by Upper Deck.
COMBINED AUTO ODDS 1:480
SP INFO PROVIDED BY UPPER DECK
AJ Antawn Jamison SP 8.00 20.00
LC Linda Cohn 8.00 20.00
LJ LeBron James 200.00 300.00

2005-06 Upper Deck ESPN NBA Fast Break

Inserted in packs at the rate of one in one along with the Play of the Day, Highlight Reel, ESPY Award Winners and ESPN the Mag inserts, this 20-card set features a Fast Break logo along the left side of the card in silver foil highlights and full color player action photography.
COMPLETE SET (20) 8.00 20.00
STATED ODDS 1:1 WITH OTHER INSERTS
*25th ANNIV: 6X TO 15X BASE HI
25th ANNIVERSARY PRINT RUN 25 SETS
FB1 Antoine Walker .30 .75
FB2 Gary Payton .40 1.00
FB3 Michael Jordan 3.00 8.00
FB4 LeBron James 1.50 4.00
FB5 Carmelo Anthony .75 2.00
FB6 Chauncey Billups .40 1.00
FB7 Richard Hamilton .30 .75
FB8 Jason Richardson .40 1.00
FB9 Yao Ming .50 1.25
FB10 Kobe Bryant 1.50 4.00
FB11 Dwyane Wade .60 1.50
FB12 Jason Kidd .60 1.50
FB13 Stephon Marbury .30 .75
FB14 Steve Francis .30 .75
FB15 Steve Nash .50 1.25
FB16 Mike Bibby .40 1.00
FB17 Tony Parker .40 1.00
FB18 Rashard Lewis .40 1.00
FB19 Andrei Kirilenko .30 .75
FB20 Gilbert Arenas .30 .75

2005-06 Upper Deck ESPN Plays of the Day

Inserted in packs at the rate of one in one along with the ESPY Award Winners, Highlight Reel, Fast Break and ESPN the Mag inserts, this 20-card set features full color player photos and a border along the bottom of the card with a Plays of the Day logo in silver foil.
COMPLETE SET (20) 6.00 15.00
STATED ODDS 1:1 WITH OTHER INSERTS,
*25th ANNIV: 6X TO 15X BASE HI
25th ANNIVERSARY PRINT RUN 25 SETS
PD1 Paul Pierce .40 1.00
PD2 Michael Jordan 3.00 8.00
PD3 LeBron James 1.50 4.00
PD4 Tracy McGrady .50 1.25
PD5 Kobe Bryant 1.50 4.00
PD6 Corey Maggette .30 .75
PD7 Pau Gasol .40 1.00
PD8 Dwyane Wade .60 1.50
PD9 Michael Redd .30 .75
PD10 Jason Kidd .60 1.50
PD11 Dwight Howard .30 .75
PD12 Amare Stoudemire .30 .75
PD13 Shawn Marion .30 .75
PD14 Damon Stoudamire .30 .75
PD15 Peja Stojakovic .40 1.00
PD16 Manu Ginobili .40 1.00
PD17 Ray Allen .40 1.00
PD18 Andrei Kirilenko .30 .75
PD19 Carlos Boozer .30 .75
PD20 Gilbert Arenas .30 .75

2005-06 Upper Deck ESPN Sports Center Swatches

Found in packs at the rate of one in 12, this 42-card set features an "E" shaped swatch of memorabilia along with color player photos on a card shaded to match the player's team colors.
STATED ODDS 1:12
AM Andre Miller 2.50 6.00
AN Andre Iguodala 2.50 6.00
AS Amare Stoudemire 2.50 6.00
AW Antoine Walker 2.50 6.00
BD Baron Davis 2.50 6.00
BW Ben Wallace 2.50 6.00
CA Carmelo Anthony 6.00 15.00
CB Caron Butler 2.50 6.00
CH Chauncey Billups 3.00 8.00
CM Corey Maggette 2.50 6.00
CW Chris Webber 3.00 8.00
DH Devin Harris 2.00 5.00
DM Desmond Mason 2.00 5.00
DN Dirk Nowitzki 5.00 12.00
EC Eddy Curry 2.00 5.00
ES Eric Snow 2.00 5.00
GA Gilbert Arenas 2.50 6.00
GP Gary Payton 3.00 8.00
JC Josh Childress 2.50 6.00
JH Josh Howard 3.00 8.00
JK Jason Kidd 5.00 12.00
JO Jermaine O'Neal 2.50 6.00
JR Jalen Rose 3.00 8.00
KB Kobe Bryant 10.00 25.00
KG Kevin Garnett 5.00 12.00
KM Kenyon Martin 2.50 6.00
KR Kareem Rush 2.00 5.00
LJ LeBron James 12.50 30.00
LO Lamar Odom 2.50 6.00
LS Latrell Sprewell 2.50 6.00
MJ Michael Jordan 30.00 75.00
PG Pau Gasol 3.00 8.00
PP Paul Pierce 3.00 8.00
RA Ray Allen 3.00 8.00
RM Reggie Miller 3.00 8.00
SF Steve Francis 2.50 6.00
SN Steve Nash 4.00 10.00
SO Shaquille O'Neal 6.00 15.00
ST Sebastian Telfair 2.50 6.00
TD Tim Duncan 5.00 12.00
TM Tracy McGrady 4.00 10.00
YM Yao Ming 4.00 10.00

2005-06 Upper Deck ESPN the Magazine Covers

Inserted in packs at the rate of one in one along with the Play of the Day, Highlight Reel, Fast Break and ESPY Award Winners inserts, this seven card set features colored borders to match the showcased player's team colors along with an image of a memorable ESPN the Magazine cover.
COMPLETE SET (7) 6.00 15.00
STATED ODDS 1:1 WITH OTHER INSERTS
*25th ANNIV: 6X TO 15X MAG COV. HI
25th ANNIVERSARY PRINT RUN 25 SETS
BW Ben Wallace .30 .75
CP Chris Paul 1.50 4.00
DH Dwight Howard .30 .75
LJ1 LeBron James 1.50 4.00
LJ2 LeBron James 1.50 4.00
MJ1 Michael Jordan 3.00 8.00
MJ2 Michael Jordan 3.00 8.00

2006 Upper Deck Finals

LJ1 LeBron James 2.00 5.00
MJ1 Michael Jordan 4.00 10.00

2007 Upper Deck Finals

FLJ1 LeBron James 2.50 6.00
FMJ1 Michael Jordan 4.00 10.00

2002-03 Upper Deck Finite

Released in December 2002, Upper Deck Finite was issued as a 242-card set divided up as follows: numbers 1-100 are veteran base cards, numbers 101-150 are Major Factors cards and are sequentially numbered to 500, numbers 151-180 are Prominent Powers cards and are sequentially numbered to 250, numbers 181-200 are First Class Finite cards and are sequentially numbered to 25, numbers 201-221 feature rookies and are sequentially numbered to 900, numbers 222-233 also feature rookies and are sequentially numbered to 600, and numbers 234-242 are rookie cards sequentially numbered to 200. Finite was packaged in 10 pack boxes with each pack containing three cards and carried a suggested retail price of $9.99.
COMP.SET w/o SP's (100) 15.00 40.00
1-100 PRINT RUN 1999 SER.#'d SETS
101-150 MF PRINT RUN 500 SER.#'d SETS
151-180 PP PRINT RUN 250 SER.#'d SETS
181-200 FC PRINT RUN 25 SER.#'d SETS
201-221 PRINT RUN 900 SER.#'d SETS
222-233 PRINT RUN 600 SER.#'d SETS
234-242 PRINT RUN 200 SER.#'d SETS
1 Shareef Abdur-Rahim .50 1.25
2 Theo Ratliff .40 1.00
3 Glenn Robinson .50 1.25
4 Jason Terry .50 1.25
5 Vin Baker .50 1.25
6 Kedrick Brown .40 1.00
7 Paul Pierce .60 1.50
8 Antoine Walker .50 1.25
9 Tyson Chandler .60 1.50
10 Eddy Curry .40 1.00
11 Jalen Rose .50 1.25
12 Chris Mihm .40 1.00
13 Darius Miles .40 1.00
14 Ricky Davis .50 1.25
15 Michael Finley .60 1.50
16 Raef LaFrentz .40 1.00
17 Steve Nash .75 2.00
18 Dirk Nowitzki 1.00 2.50
19 Nick Van Exel .50 1.25
20 Marcus Camby .50 1.25
21 Juwan Howard .50 1.25
22 James Posey .40 1.00
23 Chauncey Billups .60 1.50
24 Richard Hamilton .50 1.25
25 Ben Wallace .50 1.25
26 Clifford Robinson .40 1.00
27 Gilbert Arenas .60 1.50
28 Antawn Jamison .60 1.50
29 Jason Richardson .60 1.50
30 Eddie Griffin .40 1.00
31 Steve Francis .50 1.25
32 Cuttino Mobley .40 1.00
33 Reggie Miller .60 1.50
34 Jermaine O'Neal .50 1.25
35 Jamaal Tinsley .40 1.00
36 Ron Mercer .40 1.00
37 Elton Brand .60 1.50
38 Andre Miller .50 1.25
39 Lamar Odom .50 1.25
40 Kobe Bryant 2.50 6.00
41 Rick Fox .40 1.00
42 Devean George .40 1.00
43 Shaquille O'Neal 1.50 4.00
44 Shane Battier .60 1.50
45 Pau Gasol .75 2.00
46 Jason Williams .50 1.25
47 LaPhonso Ellis .50 1.25
48 Eddie Jones .50 1.25
49 Brian Grant .40 1.00
50 Ray Allen .60 1.50
51 Tim Thomas .40 1.00
52 Sam Cassell .50 1.25
53 Terrell Brandon .40 1.00
54 Kevin Garnett 1.00 2.50
55 Wally Szczerbiak .50 1.25
56 Marc Jackson .40 1.00
57 Richard Jefferson .60 1.50
58 Jason Kidd 1.00 2.50
59 Kenyon Martin .50 1.25
60 Kerry Kittles .40 1.00
61 Baron Davis .50 1.25
62 Jamal Mashburn .50 1.25
63 David Wesley .40 1.00
64 P.J. Brown .40 1.00
65 Latrell Sprewell .50 1.25
66 Antonio McDyess .50 1.25
67 Allan Houston .50 1.25
68 Tracy McGrady 1.00 2.50
69 Mike Miller .50 1.25
70 Darrell Armstrong .40 1.00
71 Allen Iverson 1.00 2.50
72 Aaron McKie .40 1.00
73 Keith Van Horn .50 1.25
74 Stephon Marbury .50 1.25
75 Shawn Marion .50 1.25
76 Anfernee Hardaway 1.00 2.50
77 Rasheed Wallace .60 1.50
78 Bonzi Wells .40 1.00
79 Scottie Pippen 1.00 2.50
80 Mike Bibby .60 1.50
81 Peja Stojakovic .60 1.50
82 Chris Webber .60 1.50
83 Hedo Turkoglu .50 1.25
84 Tim Duncan 1.25 3.00
85 David Robinson 1.00 2.50
86 Tony Parker .75 2.00
87 Malik Rose .40 1.00
88 Gary Payton .60 1.50
89 Rashard Lewis .60 1.50
90 Brent Barry .40 1.00
91 Desmond Mason .50 1.25
92 Vince Carter 1.00 2.50
93 Morris Peterson .40 1.00
94 Antonio Davis .40 1.00
95 Karl Malone .75 2.00
96 John Stockton .75 2.00
97 Andrei Kirilenko .60 1.50
98 Kwame Brown .40 1.00
99 Jerry Stackhouse .50 1.25
100 Michael Jordan 5.00 12.00
101 Kobe Bryant MF 5.00 12.00
102 Eddie Griffin MF .75 2.00
103 Shawn Marion MF 1.00 2.50
104 Richard Jefferson MF 1.25 3.00
105 Jermaine O'Neal MF 1.00 2.50
106 Allan Houston MF 1.00 2.50
107 Shane Battier MF 1.25 3.00
108 Hedo Turkoglu MF 1.00 2.50
109 Michael Finley MF 1.25 3.00
110 Jamal Mashburn MF 1.00 2.50
111 Rashard Lewis MF 1.25 3.00
112 Tyson Chandler MF 1.25 3.00
113 Terrell Brandon MF .75 2.00
114 Antonio Davis MF .75 2.00
115 Jamaal Tinsley MF .75 2.00
116 Tony Parker MF 1.50 4.00
117 Ray Allen MF 1.25 3.00
118 Rasheed Wallace MF 1.25 3.00
119 Cuttino Mobley MF .75 2.00
120 Jason Terry MF 1.00 2.50
121 Mike Miller MF 1.00 2.50
122 Jalen Rose MF 1.00 2.50
123 Morris Peterson MF .75 2.00
124 Ricky Davis MF 1.00 2.50
125 Peja Stojakovic MF 1.25 3.00
126 Gary Payton MF 1.25 3.00
127 Andrei Kirilenko MF 1.25 3.00
128 Tim Duncan MF 2.50 6.00
129 Anfernee Hardaway MF 2.00 5.00
130 Shaquille O'Neal MF 3.00 8.00
131 Latrell Sprewell MF 1.00 2.50
132 Shareef Abdur-Rahim MF 1.00 2.50
133 Steve Nash MF 1.50 4.00
134 Lamar Odom MF 1.00 2.50
135 Antawn Jamison MF 1.25 3.00
136 Reggie Miller MF 1.25 3.00
137 Tim Thomas MF .75 2.00
138 Eddy Curry MF .75 2.00
139 Jason Williams MF 1.00 2.50
140 John Stockton MF 1.50 4.00
141 Ben Wallace MF 1.00 2.50
142 Bonzi Wells MF .75 2.00
143 David Robinson MF 2.00 5.00
144 Stephon Marbury MF 1.00 2.50
145 Vince Carter MF 2.00 5.00
146 James Posey MF .75 2.00
147 Wally Szczerbiak MF 1.00 2.50
148 Eddie Jones MF 1.00 2.50
149 Scottie Pippen MF 2.00 5.00
150 Michael Jordan MF 10.00 25.00
151 Kobe Bryant PP 10.00 25.00
152 Pau Gasol PP 3.00 8.00
153 Tim Duncan PP 5.00 12.00
154 Karl Malone PP 3.00 8.00
155 Allan Houston PP 2.00 5.00
156 Steve Nash PP 3.00 8.00
157 Shawn Marion PP 2.00 5.00
158 Jamal Mashburn PP 2.00 5.00
159 Shaquille O'Neal PP 6.00 15.00
160 Reggie Miller PP 2.50 6.00
161 Latrell Sprewell PP 2.00 5.00
162 Peja Stojakovic PP 2.50 6.00
163 Jalen Rose PP 2.00 5.00
164 Kenyon Martin PP 2.00 5.00
165 Baron Davis PP 2.00 5.00
166 Ray Allen PP 2.50 6.00
167 Vince Carter PP 4.00 10.00
168 Rashard Lewis PP 2.50 6.00
169 Steve Francis PP 2.00 5.00
170 Jermaine O'Neal PP 2.00 5.00
171 Shane Battier PP 2.50 6.00
172 Shareef Abdur-Rahim PP 2.00 5.00
173 Michael Finley PP 2.50 6.00
174 John Stockton PP 3.00 8.00
175 Jamaal Tinsley PP 1.50 4.00
176 Wally Szczerbiak PP 2.00 5.00
177 Antawn Jamison PP 2.50 6.00
178 Richard Jefferson PP 2.50 6.00
179 Rasheed Wallace PP 2.50 6.00
180 Michael Jordan PP 25.00 60.00
181 Kobe Bryant FC 60.00 150.00
182 Paul Pierce FC 15.00 40.00
183 Nikoloz Tskitishvili FC 10.00 25.00
184 Kareem Rush FC 12.00 30.00
185 Jason Kidd FC 25.00 60.00
186 Dominique Wilkins FC 20.00 50.00
187 Kevin Garnett FC 25.00 60.00
188 Antoine Walker FC 12.00 30.00
189 Jay Williams FC 15.00 40.00
190 DaJuan Wagner FC 12.00 30.00
191 Caron Butler FC 15.00 40.00
192 Mike Bibby FC 15.00 40.00
193 Mike Miller FC 12.00 30.00
194 Tyson Chandler FC 15.00 40.00
195 Drew Gooden FC 15.00 40.00
196 Kenyon Martin FC 12.00 30.00
197 Marcus Fizer FC 10.00 25.00
198 Nene Hilario FC 15.00 40.00
199 Yao Ming FC 30.00 80.00
200 Michael Jordan FC 125.00 300.00
201 Marko Jaric 1.50 4.00
202 Dan Dickau RC 1.25 3.00
203 Tito Maddox RC 1.00 2.50
204 Predrag Savovic RC 1.25 3.00
205 Robert Archibald RC 1.00 2.50
206 Frank Williams RC 1.00 2.50
207 Ronald Murray RC 1.50 4.00
208 Lonny Baxter RC 1.00 2.50
209 Efthimios Rentzias RC 1.00 2.50
210 Vincent Yarbrough RC 1.00 2.50
211 Gordan Giricek RC 1.50 4.00
212 Carlos Boozer RC 1.50 4.00
213 John Salmons RC 1.50 4.00
214 Manu Ginobili RC 5.00 12.00
215 Roger Mason Jr. RC 1.25 3.00
216 Chris Jefferies RC 1.00 2.50
217 Sam Clancy RC 1.25 3.00
218 Rasual Butler RC 1.50 4.00
219 Dan Gadzuric RC 1.25 3.00
220 Tayshaun Prince RC 2.00 5.00
221 Casey Jacobsen RC 1.25 3.00
222 Qyntel Woods RC 1.50 4.00
223 Jiri Welsch RC 1.50 4.00
224 Curtis Borchardt RC 1.25 3.00
225 Marcus Haislip RC 1.50 4.00
226 Kareem Rush RC 1.50 4.00
227 Fred Jones RC 1.50 4.00
228 Caron Butler RC 2.00 5.00
229 Juan Dixon RC 2.00 5.00
230 Ryan Humphrey RC 1.50 4.00
231 Melvin Ely RC 1.50 4.00
232 Bostjan Nachbar RC 1.50 4.00
233 Jared Jeffries RC 1.50 4.00
234 Jay Williams RC 5.00 12.00
235 Nikoloz Tskitishvili RC 3.00 8.00
236 Chris Wilcox RC 4.00 10.00
237 Drew Gooden RC 5.00 12.00
238 Amare Stoudemire RC 6.00 15.00
239 DaJuan Wagner RC 4.00 10.00
240 Nene Hilario RC 5.00 12.00
241 Mike Dunleavy RC 5.00 12.00
242 Yao Ming RC 10.00 25.00

2002-03 Upper Deck Finite Elements Dual Uniforms

Inserted in packs at the rate of one in 20, this eight card set features a horizontal design with a gray background, small square head shots of the players and two swatches of game used uniforms.
STATED ODDS 1:20
AIJKU A.Iverson/J.Kidd 6.00 15.00
JSSFU J.Smith/S.Francis 5.00 12.00
KBJRU K.Bryant/J.Richardson 10.00 25.00
KGTBU K.Garnett/T.Brandon 5.00 12.00
LSCWU L.Sprewell/C.Ward 5.00 12.00
MJKBU M.Jordan/K.Bryant 30.00 80.00
PPAWU P.Pierce/A.Walker 8.00 20.00
TMMMU T.McGrady/M.Miller 6.00 15.00

2002-03 Upper Deck Finite Elements Dual Warm-Ups

Randomly seeded in packs at the rate of one in four, this 20-card set utilizes the same set design as the Elements Dual Uniforms set but contains swatches of warm ups instead.
STATED ODDS 1:4
AHJJ A.Hardaway/J.Johnson 5.00 12.00
AIJK A.Iverson/J.Kidd 5.00 12.00
BDJM B.Davis/J.Mashburn 4.00 10.00
DNSN D.Nowitzki/S.Nash 6.00 15.00
ECTC E.Curry/T.Chandler 4.00 10.00
HTMB H.Turkoglu/M.Bibby 4.00 10.00
JRAJ J.Richardson/A.Jamison 4.00 10.00
KBAI K.Bryant/A.Iverson 10.00 25.00
KBTM K.Bryant/T.McGrady 10.00 25.00
KGWS K.Garnett/W.Szczerbiak 5.00 12.00
KMJS K.Malone/J.Stockton 5.00 12.00
MJKB M.Jordan/K.Bryant 30.00 80.00
PPAW P.Pierce/A.Walker 5.00 12.00
QREB Q.Richardson/E.Brand 4.00 10.00
RHKW R.Hamilton/K.Brown 4.00 10.00
SADJ S.Rahim/D.Johnson 4.00 10.00
SMSM S.Marbury/S.Marion 4.00 10.00

2002-03 Upper Deck Finite Elements Jerseys

Randomly inserted in packs at the rate of one in ten, this 14-card set utilizes a horizontal card design with full color player photos on the right and swatches of jersey on the left.
STATED ODDS 1:10
BDJ Baron Davis 2.50 6.00
DNJ Dirk Nowitzki 5.00 12.00
EBJ Elton Brand 3.00 8.00
JRJ Jason Richardson 3.00 8.00
JWJ Jay Williams 3.00 8.00
KBJ Kobe Bryant 10.00 25.00
KMJ Karl Malone 4.00 10.00
MJJ Michael Jordan 50.00 120.00
SMJ Stephon Marbury 2.50 6.00

2002-03 Upper Deck Finite Signatures

Randomly inserted, this 27-card set features all sequentially numbered cards-print runs are listed below. Color player photos appear on the left and autographs appear on the right. Eleven players signed for a gold parallel set numbered to ten that is unpriced due to scarcity.
PRINT RUNS LISTED BELOW
ASA Amare Stoudemire/80 10.00 25.00
AWA Antoine Walker/50 15.00 40.00
CBA Caron Butler/80 8.00 20.00
CWA Chris Wilcox/80 8.00 20.00
DGA Drew Gooden/80 12.00 30.00
DSA DeShawn Stevenson/100 5.00 12.00
DWA DaJuan Wagner/80 8.00 20.00
ETA Etan Thomas/146 5.00 12.00
JJA Jared Jeffries/80 5.00 12.00
JKA Jason Kidd/128 20.00 50.00
JMA Jamaal Magloire/100 5.00 12.00
JTA Jeff Trepagnier/112 5.00 12.00
JWA Jay Williams/80 5.00 12.00
KBA Kobe Bryant 125.00 250.00
KGA Kevin Garnett/25 60.00 150.00
KMA Kenyon Martin/104 10.00 25.00
KRA Kareem Rush/80 10.00 25.00
MBA Mike Bibby/80 10.00 25.00
MEA Melvin Ely/80 5.00 12.00
MFA Marcus Fizer/104 5.00 12.00
MJA Michael Jordan/23 400.00 800.00
MMA Mike Miller/80 10.00 25.00
MOA Jerome Moiso/146 5.00 12.00
NHA Nene Hilario/80 8.00 20.00
PPA Paul Pierce/104 15.00 40.00
TCA Tyson Chandler/80 10.00 25.00
YMA Yao Ming/80 60.00 150.00

2003-04 Upper Deck Finite

Released in late December/early January, Finite is composed of 342 cards. The breakdown of the set is as follows: cards 1-200 are all sequentially numbered and print runs alternate for odd and even cards. The odd numbered card focus on current NBA players and are sequentially numbered to 2999, while the even numbers focus on retired players and are sequentially numbered to 1999. Base cards have borders and full-color player photos are set against a colored grid pattern set to match the team colors. Card numbers 201-236 feature rookie players and are sequentially numbered to 750. Cards 237-242 also feature rookies and are sequentially numbered to 200. Cards 243-292 are designed differently with borders along the top and the bottom, the words Major Factors and sequential numbering to 1000. Cards 293-322 are part of Prominent Powers subset and are sequentially numbered to 500, and cards 323-342 are part of a First Class subset and are sequentially numbered to 50. Upper Deck Finite was packaged in ten pack boxes where packs contained three cards and carried a suggested retail price of $9.99.
1-200 ODD PRINT RUN 2999 SER.#'d SETS
201-228 PRINT RUN 1500 SER.#'d SETS
201-236 PRINT RUN 750 SER.#'d SETS
237-242 PRINT RUN 200 SER.#'d SETS
MAJ.FACT.PRINT RUN 1000 SER.#'d SETS
PROM.POW.PRINT RUN 500 SER.#'d SETS
FIRST CLASS PRINT RUN 50 SER.#'d SETS
1 Shareef Abdur-Rahim .40 1.00
2 Dominique Wilkins 1.00 2.50
3 Theo Ratliff .30 .75
4 Dan Dickau .50 1.25
5 Jason Terry .40 1.00
6 Dion Glover .50 1.25
7 Alan Henderson .30 .75
8 Paul Pierce .75 2.00
9 Larry Bird 1.25 3.00
10 Raef LaFrentz .50 1.25
11 Robert Parish .60 1.50
12 Jiri Welsch .50 1.25
13 John Havlicek .50 1.25
14 Vin Baker .50 1.25
15 Jamal Crawford .50 1.25
16 Michael Jordan 6.00 15.00
17 Scottie Pippen .75 2.00
18 Reggie Theus .60 1.50
19 Jalen Rose .40 1.00
20 Tyson Chandler .60 1.50
21 Eddy Curry .30 .75
22 Dajuan Wagner .50 1.25
23 Lenny Wilkens .50 1.25
24 Carlos Boozer .60 1.50
25 World B. Free .40 1.00
26 Darius Miles .50 1.25
27 Craig Ehlo .30 .75
28 Ricky Davis .60 1.50
29 Dirk Nowitzki .75 2.00
30 Rolando Blackman .60 1.50
31 Steve Nash .60 1.50
32 Tony Delk .50 1.25
33 Antawn Jamison .40 1.00
34 Antoine Walker .75 2.00
35 Michael Finley .50 1.25
36 Andre Miller .60 1.50
37 David Thompson .40 1.00
38 Nene .60 1.50
39 Dan Issel .40 1.00
40 Nikoloz Tskitishvili .50 1.25
41 Alex English .40 1.00
42 Earl Boykins .50 1.25
43 Richard Hamilton .40 1.00
44 Mehmet Okur .60 1.50
45 Ben Wallace .40 1.00
46 Bob Lanier .60 1.50
47 Chauncey Billups .50 1.25
48 Dave Bing .75 2.00
49 Tayshaun Prince .40 1.00
50 Nick Van Exel .60 1.50
51 Erick Dampier .30 .75
52 Jason Richardson .75 2.00
53 Joe Barry Carroll .30 .75
54 Mike Dunleavy .60 1.50
55 Wilt Chamberlain 1.00 2.50
56 Troy Murphy .50 1.25
57 Steve Francis .40 1.00
58 Maurice Taylor .50 1.25
59 Yao Ming 1.00 2.50
60 Robert Reid .75 2.00
61 Cuttino Mobley .30 .75
62 Moses Malone .75 2.00
63 Eddie Griffin .30 .75
64 Jermaine O'Neal .60 1.50
65 George McGinnis .30 .75
66 Reggie Miller .75 2.00
67 Clark Kellogg .50 1.25
68 Jamaal Tinsley .50 1.25
69 Al Harrington .40 1.00
70 Ron Artest .75 2.00
71 Elton Brand .50 1.25
72 Corey Maggette .60 1.50
73 Chris Wilcox .30 .75
74 Quentin Richardson .60 1.50
75 Bill Walton .50 1.25
76 Marko Jaric .50 1.25
77 Kobe Bryant 2.00 5.00
78 Kareem Abdul-Jabbar 1.25 3.00
79 Shaquille O'Neal 1.25 3.00

80 Michael Cooper .60 1.50
81 Gary Payton .50 1.25
82 James Worthy 1.00 2.50
83 Karl Malone .60 1.50
84 Pau Gasol .75 2.00
85 Michael Dickerson .30 .75
86 Mike Miller .60 1.50
87 Brevin Knight .30 .75
88 Shane Battier .60 1.50
89 Stromile Swift .30 .75
90 Jason Williams .60 1.50
91 Caron Butler .40 1.00
92 Samaki Walker .50 1.25
93 Eddie Jones .40 1.00
94 Rasual Butler .50 1.25
95 Brian Grant .30 .75
96 Loren Woods .50 1.25
97 Lamar Odom .40 1.00
98 Desmond Mason .60 1.50
99 Sidney Moncrief .30 .75
100 Toni Kukoc .75 2.00
101 Oscar Robertson .50 1.25
102 Michael Redd .75 2.00
103 Terry Cummings .40 1.00
104 Tim Thomas .50 1.25
105 Kevin Garnett .75 2.00
106 Troy Hudson .50 1.25
107 Sam Cassell .40 1.00
108 Latrell Sprewell .60 1.50
109 Michael Olowokandi .30 .75
110 Wally Szczerbiak .60 1.50
111 Jason Kidd .75 2.00
112 Otis Birdsong .60 1.50
113 Kenyon Martin .40 1.00
114 Albert King .50 1.25
115 Richard Jefferson .40 1.00
116 Kerry Kittles .50 1.25
117 Alonzo Mourning .60 1.50
118 Baron Davis .60 1.50
119 Darrell Armstrong .30 .75
120 Jamal Mashburn .60 1.50
121 P.J. Brown .30 .75
122 David Wesley .50 1.25
123 Courtney Alexander .30 .75
124 Jamaal Magloire .50 1.25
125 Allan Houston .40 1.00
126 Willis Reed .75 2.00
127 Keith Van Horn .40 1.00
128 Walt Frazier .75 2.00
129 Antonio McDyess .40 1.00
130 Earl Monroe .75 2.00
131 Kurt Thomas .30 .75
132 Tracy McGrady 1.00 2.50
133 Pat Garrity .30 .75
134 Grant Hill 1.00 2.50
135 Tyronn Lue .30 .75
136 Drew Gooden .60 1.50
137 Juwan Howard .40 1.00
138 Gordan Giricek .50 1.25
139 Allen Iverson .75 2.00
140 Julius Erving 1.25 3.00
141 Glenn Robinson .40 1.00
142 Maurice Cheeks .50 1.25
143 Aaron McKie .30 .75
144 Billy Cunningham .75 2.00
145 Eric Snow .30 .75
146 Stephon Marbury .60 1.50
147 Kevin Johnson .50 1.25
148 Amare Stoudemire 1.00 2.50
149 Larry Nance .40 1.00
150 Shawn Marion .60 1.50
151 Walter Davis .50 1.25
152 Anfernee Hardaway 1.25 3.00
153 Rasheed Wallace .50 1.25
154 Zach Randolph .60 1.50
155 Derek Anderson .30 .75
156 Dale Davis .50 1.25
157 Bonzi Wells .30 .75
158 Jim Paxson .75 2.00
159 Damon Stoudamire .40 1.00
160 Chris Webber .75 2.00
161 Vlade Divac .40 1.00
162 Mike Bibby .75 2.00
163 Bobby Jackson .30 .75
164 Peja Stojakovic .75 2.00
165 Doug Christie .30 .75
166 Brad Miller .60 1.50
167 Tim Duncan .75 2.00
168 Radoslav Nesterovic .50 1.25
169 Tony Parker .50 1.25
170 George Gervin .75 2.00
171 Manu Ginobili .60 1.50
172 Artis Gilmore .60 1.50
173 Ron Mercer .30 .75
174 Ray Allen .75 2.00
175 Spencer Haywood .30 .75
176 Rashard Lewis .75 2.00
177 Fred Brown .30 .75
178 Vladimir Radmanovic .50 1.25
179 Jack Sikma .40 1.00
180 Brent Barry .50 1.25
181 Vince Carter .75 2.00
182 Antonio Davis .50 1.25
183 Morris Peterson .30 .75
184 Alvin Williams .50 1.25
185 Chris Jefferies .30 .75
186 Jerome Williams .50 1.25
187 Andrei Kirilenko .50 1.25
188 Pete Maravich 5.00 12.00
189 Matt Harpring .30 .75
190 Mark Eaton .50 1.25
191 Jarron Collins .30 .75
192 Greg Ostertag .50 1.25
193 Carlos Arroyo .40 1.00
194 Jerry Stackhouse .60 1.50
195 Wes Unseld .50 1.25
196 Gilbert Arenas .60 1.50
197 Larry Hughes .40 1.00
198 Kwame Brown .50 1.25
199 Jeff Malone .30 .75
200 Jared Jeffries .50 1.25
201 Aleksandar Pavlovic RC 1.50 4.00
202 James Lang RC 1.25 3.00
203 Jason Kapono RC 1.25 3.00
204 Luke Walton RC 2.00 5.00
205 Jerome Beasley RC 1.25 3.00
206 Willie Green RC 1.25 3.00
207 Steve Blake RC 1.50 4.00
208 Slavko Vranes RC 1.25 3.00
209 Zaur Pachulia RC 2.00 5.00
210 Travis Hansen RC 1.25 3.00
211 Keith Bogans RC 1.25 3.00
212 Kyle Korver RC 2.50 6.00
213 Brandon Hunter RC 1.25 3.00
214 James Jones RC 1.25 3.00
215 Josh Howard RC 2.00 5.00
216 Leandro Barbosa RC 2.00 5.00
217 Kendrick Perkins RC 1.50 4.00
218 Ndudi Ebi RC 1.25 3.00
219 Brian Cook RC 1.25 3.00
220 Travis Outlaw RC 1.50 4.00
221 Zoran Planinic RC 1.25 3.00
222 Dahntay Jones RC 1.50 4.00
223 Boris Diaw RC 2.00 5.00
224 Zarko Cabarkapa RC 1.25 3.00
225 Troy Bell RC 1.25 3.00
226 Reece Gaines RC 1.25 3.00
227 Luke Ridnour RC 1.50 4.00
228 Chris Kaman RC 2.00 5.00
229 Marcus Banks RC 1.50 4.00
230 Maciej Lampe RC 1.50 4.00
231 David West RC 2.50 6.00
232 Mickael Pietrus RC 2.00 5.00
233 Jarvis Hayes RC 1.50 4.00
234 Mike Sweetney RC 1.50 4.00
235 Kirk Hinrich RC 2.50 6.00
236 Chris Bosh RC 4.00 10.00
237 Nick Collison RC 6.00 15.00
238 T.J. Ford RC 6.00 15.00
239 Dwyane Wade RC 15.00 40.00
240 Carmelo Anthony RC 20.00 50.00
241 Darko Milicic RC 6.00 15.00
242 LeBron James RC 400.00 700.00
243 Michael Jordan MF 6.00 15.00
244 Kobe Bryant MF 3.00 8.00
245 Michael Finley MF .75 2.00
246 Andrei Kirilenko MF .75 2.00
247 Desmond Mason MF .60 1.50
248 Kenyon Martin MF .60 1.50
249 Shaquille O'Neal MF 2.00 5.00
250 Jamal Mashburn MF .60 1.50
251 Jason Terry MF .60 1.50
252 Andre Miller MF .60 1.50
253 Keith Van Horn MF .60 1.50
254 Derek Anderson MF .50 1.25
255 Stephon Marbury MF .60 1.50
256 Glenn Robinson MF .60 1.50
257 Richard Hamilton MF .60 1.50
258 Lamar Odom MF .60 1.50
259 Bonzi Wells MF .50 1.25
260 Wally Szczerbiak MF .60 1.50
261 Alonzo Mourning MF 1.00 2.50
262 Gilbert Arenas MF .60 1.50
263 Mike Bibby MF .75 2.00
264 Antawn Jamison MF .60 1.50
265 Tony Parker MF .75 2.00
266 Reggie Miller MF .75 2.00
267 Vince Carter MF 1.25 3.00
268 Richard Jefferson MF .60 1.50
269 Nene MF .60 1.50
270 Grant Hill MF 1.00 2.50
271 Rashard Lewis MF .75 2.00
272 Shawn Marion MF .60 1.50
273 Morris Peterson MF .50 1.25
274 Chauncey Billups MF .75 2.00
275 Eddie Jones MF .60 1.50
276 Raef LaFrentz MF .50 1.25
277 Jerry Stackhouse MF .60 1.50
278 Pau Gasol MF .75 2.00
279 Darius Miles MF .50 1.25
280 Nick Van Exel MF .60 1.50
281 Gary Payton MF .75 2.00
282 Peja Stojakovic MF .75 2.00
283 Karl Malone MF 1.00 2.50
284 Mike Miller MF .60 1.50
285 Caron Butler MF .60 1.50
286 Cuttino Mobley MF .50 1.25
287 Zach Randolph MF .60 1.50
288 Scottie Pippen MF 1.25 3.00
289 Gordan Giricek MF .50 1.25
290 Ben Wallace MF .60 1.50
291 Manu Ginobili MF 1.00 2.50
292 Vladimir Radmanovic MF .50 1.25
293 Michael Jordan PP 12.00 30.00
294 Kobe Bryant PP 6.00 15.00
295 Vince Carter PP 2.50 6.00
296 Steve Nash PP 2.00 5.00
297 Shaquille O'Neal PP 4.00 10.00
298 Amare Stoudemire PP 2.00 5.00
299 Tracy McGrady PP 2.00 5.00
300 Gary Payton PP 1.50 4.00
301 Chris Bosh PP 2.50 6.00
302 Michael Finley PP 1.50 4.00
303 Caron Butler PP 1.25 3.00
304 Jarvis Hayes PP 1.00 2.50
305 Ben Wallace PP 1.25 3.00
306 Allan Houston PP 1.25 3.00
307 Mike Bibby PP 1.50 4.00
308 Antoine Walker PP 1.50 4.00
309 Dajuan Wagner PP 1.00 2.50
310 Kevin Garnett PP 2.50 6.00
311 Mickael Pietrus PP 1.25 3.00
312 Baron Davis PP 1.25 3.00
313 Paul Pierce PP 1.50 4.00
314 Rasheed Wallace PP 1.50 4.00
315 Chris Webber PP 1.50 4.00
316 Jermaine O'Neal PP 1.25 3.00
317 Shareef Abdur-Rahim PP 1.25 3.00
318 Ray Allen PP 1.50 4.00
319 Peja Stojakovic PP 1.50 4.00
320 Tim Duncan PP 2.50 6.00
321 Gilbert Arenas PP 1.25 3.00
322 Jason Richardson PP 1.50 4.00
323 Dwyane Wade FC 20.00 50.00
324 Gary Payton FC 6.00 15.00
325 Karl Malone FC 8.00 20.00
326 Jason Kidd FC 10.00 25.00
327 Darko Milicic FC 5.00 12.00
328 Steve Francis FC 5.00 12.00
329 Vince Carter FC 10.00 25.00
330 Elton Brand FC 6.00 15.00
331 Amare Stoudemire FC 8.00 20.00
332 Shaquille O'Neal FC 15.00 40.00
333 Carmelo Anthony FC 20.00 50.00
334 Tracy McGrady FC 8.00 20.00
335 Tim Duncan FC 10.00 25.00
336 Chris Webber FC 6.00 15.00
337 Allen Iverson FC 10.00 25.00
338 Dirk Nowitzki FC 10.00 25.00
339 Kevin Garnett FC 10.00 25.00
340 Kobe Bryant FC 25.00 60.00
341 LeBron James FC 150.00 300.00
342 Michael Jordan FC 50.00 125.00

2003-04 Upper Deck Finite Gold

*1-200 EVEN SINGLES: 2X TO 5X BASE HI
1-200 EVEN PRINT RUN 100 SER.#'d SETS
*1-200 ODD SINGLES: 2X TO 5X BASE HI
*201-228 RC SINGLES: 1.25X TO 3X BASE HI
201-228 PRINT RUN 100 SER.#'d SETS
*229-236 RC SINGLES: 1X TO 2.5X BASE HI
229-236 PRINT RUN 100 SER.#'d SETS
*237-242 RC SINGLES: .6X TO 1.5X BASE HI
237-242 PRINT RUN 25 SER.#'d SETS
*243-292 SINGLES: 3X TO 8X BASE HI
243-292 PRINT RUN 50 SER.#'d SETS
*293-322 SINGLES: 2X TO 5X BASE HI
293-322 PRINT RUN 25 SER.#'d SETS
323-342 UNPRICED PRINT RUN 10 SETS
239 Dwyane Wade 60.00 150.00
242 LeBron James 700.00 1000.00

2003-04 Upper Deck Finite Elements Warmups

Randomly inserted in packs at the rate of one in four for dual player versions with triple player versions sequentially numbered to 50, this 42-card set utilizes a similar design to its Jerseys counterpart and includes a swatch of game-worn warmup.

STATED ODDS 1:4
FE1 M.Jordan/K.Bryant SP 50.00 100.00
FE2 A.Walker/P.Pierce 4.00 10.00
FE3 V.Divac/G.Wallace 4.00 10.00
FE4 A.Houston/L.Sprewell 4.00 10.00
FE5 Y.Ming/S.Francis 5.00 12.00
FE6 A.Harrington/J.Bender 4.00 10.00
FE7 R.Jefferson/K.Martin 4.00 10.00
FE8 B.Davis/J.Mashburn 4.00 10.00
FE9 J.Richardson/G.Arenas 4.00 10.00
FE10 T.McGrady/K.Garnett 6.00 15.00
FE11 W.Szczerbiak/J.Smith 4.00 10.00
FE12 J.Rose/E.Curry 4.00 10.00
FE13 S.Marion/S.Marbury 4.00 10.00
FE14 M.Sweetney/K.Van Horn 4.00 10.00
FE15 A.Stoudemire/A.Hardaway 5.00 12.00
FE16 T.Ratliff/S.Abdur-Rahim 4.00 10.00
FE17 J.Howard/S.Nash 4.00 10.00
FE18 Magic/Julius Erving SP 15.00 40.00
FE19 J.Stockton/A.Kirilenko 5.00 12.00
FE20 D.Miles/Q.Richardson 4.00 10.00
FE21 L.Odom/E.Brand 4.00 10.00
FE22 J.Tinsley/R.Miller 4.00 10.00
FE23 B.Wallace/R.Hamilton 4.00 10.00
FE24 C.Mihm/D.Wagner 4.00 10.00
FE25 D.Robinson/S.Claxton 5.00 12.00
FE26 T.Chandler/M.Fizer 4.00 10.00
FE27 A.Miller/C.Maggette 4.00 10.00
FE28 S.Battier/P.Gasol 4.00 10.00
FE29 M.Miller/S.Swift 4.00 10.00
FE30 D.Fisher/K.Bryant 10.00 25.00
FE31 Magloire/B.Davis/Wesley 8.00 20.00
FE32 Ratliff/Shareef/Terry 8.00 20.00
FE33 Hard/Marbury/J.Johnson 25.00 60.00
FE34 Chandler/Fizer/Curry 8.00 20.00
FE35 Ming/Mobley/Posey 15.00 40.00
FE36 Iverson/McKie/Snow 12.00 30.00
FE37 Brand/Maggette/Q-Rich 8.00 20.00
FE38 Rose/Webber/Howard 25.00 60.00
FE39 B.Miller/J.O'Neal/Tinisley 8.00 20.00
FE40 Bosh/Sweetney/Hayes 15.00 30.00
FE41 Pietrus/Darko/Wade 15.00 30.00
FE42 Kobe/Jordan/Kidd 100.00 200.00

2003-04 Upper Deck Finite Elements Jerseys

Randomly inserted in packs at the rate of one in 10 for single player jerseys and one in 20 for dual player jerseys, this 42-card set features a horizontal design with full color player photos and a swatch of game-worn jersey.

STATED ODDS 1:10
DUAL STATED ODDS 1:20
FJ1 Michael Jordan SP 50.00 100.00
FJ2 Kobe Bryant SP 12.50 30.00
FJ3 Latrell Sprewell 2.50 6.00
FJ4 Dirk Nowitzki 5.00 12.00
FJ5 Paul Pierce 3.00 8.00
FJ6 John Stockton 4.00 10.00
FJ7 Karl Malone 4.00 10.00
FJ8 Grant Hill 4.00 10.00
FJ9 Shawn Marion 2.50 6.00
FJ10 Ray Allen 3.00 8.00
FJ11 Steve Francis 2.50 6.00
FJ12 Steve Nash 4.00 10.00
FJ13 Antoine Walker 3.00 8.00
FJ14 David Robinson 5.00 12.00
FJ15 Yao Ming 6.00 15.00
FJ16 Allen Iverson 6.00 15.00
FJ17 Carmelo Anthony 10.00 25.00
FJ18 LeBron James 40.00 100.00
FJ19 Darko Milicic 2.50 6.00
FJ20 Chris Bosh 5.00 12.00
FJ21 Mike Sweetney 2.00 5.00
FS1 M.Jordan/K.Bryant SP 25.00 60.00
FS2 A.Houston/C.Ward 5.00 12.00
FS3 L.Sprewell/K.Thomas 5.00 12.00
FS4 D.Stoudamire/R.Wallace 5.00 12.00
FS5 J.Williams/M.Fizer 5.00 12.00
FS6 Nesterovic/Szczerbiak 5.00 12.00
FS7 J.Kidd/T.Parker 6.00 15.00
FS8 R.Miller/J.Bender 5.00 12.00
FS9 A.Jamison/J.Richardson 5.00 12.00
FS10 L.Odom/C.Maggette 5.00 12.00
FS11 J.Rose/E.Curry 5.00 12.00
FS12 J.O'Neal/J.Tinsley 5.00 12.00
FS13 D.Robinson/T.Duncan 10.00 25.00
FS14 D.Miles/D.Wagner 5.00 12.00
FS15 M.Miller/P.Gasol 5.00 12.00
FS16 C.Ward/K.Thomas 5.00 12.00
FS17 K.Martin/R.Jefferson 5.00 12.00
FS18 R.Allen/R.Lewis 5.00 12.00
FS19 M.Ginobili/T.Parker 6.00 15.00
FS20 M.Finley/D.Nowitzki 5.00 12.00
FS21 M.Fizer/T.Chandler 5.00 12.00

2003-04 Upper Deck Finite Signatures

Inserted in packs at the rate of one in 30, this 29-card set features a horizontal design with player photos on the left and a white-out box on the right for a signature. A Gold version was also issued and these cards are sequentially numbered to 10.

STATED ODDS 1:30
AJ Antawn Jamison 5.00 12.00
AM Andre Miller 5.00 12.00
BI Chauncey Billups 6.00 15.00
BO Chris Bosh 20.00 50.00
CA Carmelo Anthony 30.00 80.00
CB Caron Butler 5.00 12.00
CK Chris Kaman 6.00 15.00
DA Darius Miles 5.00 12.00
DJ DerMarr Johnson 5.00 12.00
DM Darko Milicic 6.00 15.00
DW Dwyane Wade 40.00 100.00
GA Gilbert Arenas 8.00 20.00
GP Gary Payton 12.00 30.00
JH Jarvis Hayes 5.00 12.00
JM Jerome Moiso 5.00 12.00
JR Jason Richardson 5.00 12.00
JS Jerry Stackhouse 6.00 15.00
KB Kobe Bryant/100 100.00 200.00
LJ LeBron James/150 400.00 750.00
MB Mike Bibby 6.00 15.00
MJ Michael Jordan/23 300.00 600.00
PP Paul Pierce 12.50 30.00
PS Peja Stojakovic 8.00 20.00
RJ Richard Jefferson 5.00 12.00
SA Shareef Abdur-Rahim 5.00 12.00
SB Shane Battier 5.00 12.00
SF Steve Francis 6.00 15.00
TM Tracy McGrady/100 20.00 50.00
YM Yao Ming 30.00 80.00

2004-05 Upper Deck Finite Dual Signatures Gold

STATED PRINT RUN 25 SER.#'d SETS
NO PRICING DUE TO LACK OF MARKET INFO

2004-05 Upper Deck Finite Signatures

FSJC Jamal Crawford 8.00 20.00
FSJR J.R. Smith 3.00 8.00
FSLU Luke Jackson 3.00 8.00
FSMJ Michael Jordan 500.00 800.00
FSTM Tracy McGrady 10.00 25.00

2007-08 Upper Deck First Edition

This 230-card set was released in October, 2007. The set was issued through Upper Deck's retail channels and the set was released in 10-card packs which came 36 packs to a box where packs carried an inital SRP of $1.25. The first 200 cards in the set feature NBA veterans while cards numbered 201-230 feature 2007-08 NBA rookies.

COMP.SET w/o RC's (200) 10.00 25.00
ROOKIE ODDS ONE PER PACK
1 Austin Croshere .20 .50
2 Devean George .20 .50
3 Devin Harris .20 .50
4 Josh Howard .25 .60
5 Jerry Stackhouse .25 .60
6 Jason Terry .25 .60
7 Rafer Alston .20 .50
8 Shane Battier .25 .60
9 Luther Head .25 .60
10 Juwan Howard .25 .60
11 Tracy McGrady .30 .75
12 Steve Novak .20 .50
13 Rudy Gay .30 .75
14 Eddie Jones .25 .60
15 Kyle Lowry .30 .75
16 Mike Miller .25 .60
17 Damon Stoudamire .25 .60
18 Hakim Warrick .25 .60
19 Brandon Bass .20 .50
20 Tyson Chandler .25 .60
21 Bobby Jackson .20 .50
22 Desmond Mason .20 .50
23 Cedric Simmons .25 .60
24 Peja Stojakovic .30 .75
25 Bruce Bowen .20 .50
26 Michael Finley .30 .75
27 Manu Ginobili .30 .75
28 Tony Parker .30 .75
29 Beno Udrih .20 .50
30 Monta Ellis .25 .60
31 Al Harrington .25 .60
32 Sarunas Jasikevicius .20 .50
33 Stephen Jackson .25 .60
34 Jason Richardson .30 .75
35 Sam Cassell .25 .60
36 Chris Kaman .25 .60
37 Shaun Livingston .20 .50
38 Corey Maggette .25 .60
39 Cuttino Mobley .25 .60
40 Tim Thomas .20 .50
41 Kwame Brown .20 .50
42 Andrew Bynum .20 .50
43 Jordan Farmar .20 .50
44 Lamar Odom .25 .60
45 Ronny Turiaf .25 .60
46 Luke Walton .20 .50
47 Leandro Barbosa .25 .60
48 Raja Bell .25 .60
49 Boris Diaw .25 .60
50 Shawn Marion .25 .60
51 Amare Stoudemire .25 .60
52 Shareef Abdur-Rahim .25 .60
53 Ron Artest .30 .75
54 Quincy Douby .20 .50
55 Kevin Martin .25 .60
56 Brad Miller .25 .60
57 Allen Iverson .40 1.00
58 Kenyon Martin .25 .60
59 Eduardo Najera .20 .50
60 Nene .25 .60
61 J.R. Smith .25 .60
62 Ricky Davis .25 .60
63 Randy Foye .30 .75
64 Troy Hudson .20 .50
65 Mike James .20 .50
66 Rashad McCants .20 .50
67 Craig Smith .20 .50
68 LaMarcus Aldridge .40 1.00
69 Jarrett Jack .25 .60
70 Jamaal Magloire .20 .50
71 Sergio Rodriguez .20 .50
72 Brandon Roy .30 .75
73 Martell Webster .25 .60
74 Rashard Lewis .25 .60
75 Luke Ridnour .25 .60
76 Danny Fortson .20 .50
77 Chris Wilcox .20 .50
78 Damien Wilkins .20 .50
79 Ronnie Brewer .25 .60
80 Derek Fisher .25 .60
81 Matt Harpring .20 .50
82 Andrei Kirilenko .25 .60
83 Paul Millsap .25 .60
84 Deron Williams .25 .60
85 Tony Allen .20 .50
86 Gerald Green .25 .60
87 Al Jefferson .25 .60
88 Wally Szczerbiak .25 .60
89 Allan Ray .20 .50
90 Delonte West .20 .50
91 Hassan Adams .20 .50
92 Richard Jefferson .25 .60
93 Jason Kidd .30 .75
94 Nenad Krstic .20 .50
95 Marcus Williams .20 .50
96 Renaldo Balkman .20 .50
97 Jamal Crawford .30 .75
98 Eddy Curry .20 .50
99 Channing Frye .25 .60
100 Quentin Richardson .25 .60
101 Nate Robinson .20 .50
102 Rodney Carney .20 .50
103 Samuel Dalembert .20 .50
104 Steven Hunter .20 .50
105 Kyle Korver .25 .60
106 Andre Miller .25 .60
107 Shavlik Randolph .20 .50
108 Andrea Bargnani .30 .75
109 Jose Calderon .20 .50
110 T.J. Ford .20 .50
111 Jorge Garbajosa .25 .60
112 Joey Graham .20 .50
113 Morris Peterson .20 .50
114 Luol Deng .25 .60
115 Ben Gordon .25 .60
116 Kirk Hinrich .25 .60
117 Thabo Sefolosha .20 .50
118 Tyrus Thomas .20 .50
119 Ben Wallace .25 .60
120 Shannon Brown .20 .50
121 Drew Gooden .25 .60
122 Larry Hughes .25 .60
123 Zydrunas Ilgauskas .25 .60
124 Donyell Marshall .20 .50
125 Richard Hamilton .25 .60
126 Amir Johnson .20 .50
127 Antonio McDyess .25 .60
128 Tayshaun Prince .25 .60
129 Rasheed Wallace .30 .75
130 Chris Webber .30 .75
131 Marquis Daniels .20 .50
132 Ike Diogu .20 .50
133 Mike Dunleavy .25 .60
134 Jeff Foster .20 .50
135 Troy Murphy .20 .50
136 Jamaal Tinsley .20 .50
137 Charlie Bell .20 .50
138 Andrew Bogut .25 .60
139 Earl Boykins .20 .50
140 Bobby Simmons .20 .50
141 Charlie Villanueva .20 .50
142 Maurice Williams .25 .60
143 Speedy Claxton .20 .50
144 Solomon Jones .20 .50
145 Tyronn Lue .20 .50
146 Marvin Williams .25 .60
147 Shelden Williams .20 .50
148 Raymond Felton .30 .75
149 Othella Harrington .20 .50
150 Sean May .20 .50
151 Adam Morrison .20 .50
152 Gerald Wallace .25 .60
153 Udonis Haslem .25 .60
154 Alonzo Mourning .40 1.00
155 Shaquille O'Neal .60 1.50
156 Gary Payton .30 .75
157 Antoine Walker .25 .60
158 Jason Williams .25 .60
159 Carlos Arroyo .20 .50
160 Travis Diener .20 .50
161 Grant Hill .40 1.00
162 Darko Milicic .20 .50
163 Jameer Nelson .20 .50
164 J.J. Redick .30 .75
165 Andray Blatche .20 .50
166 Caron Butler .25 .60
167 Antonio Daniels .20 .50
168 Brendan Haywood .20 .50
169 Antawn Jamison .25 .60
170 DeShawn Stevenson .20 .50
171 Dirk Nowitzki .40 1.00
172 Yao Ming .40 1.00
173 Pau Gasol .30 .75
174 Chris Paul .40 1.00
175 Tim Duncan .50 1.25
176 Baron Davis .25 .60
177 Elton Brand .25 .60
178 Kobe Bryant 1.25 3.00
179 Steve Nash .40 1.00
180 Mike Bibby .30 .75
181 Carmelo Anthony .40 1.00
182 Kevin Garnett .50 1.25
183 Zach Randolph .25 .60
184 Ray Allen .30 .75
185 Carlos Boozer .25 .60
186 Paul Pierce .30 .75
187 Vince Carter .40 1.00
188 Stephon Marbury .25 .60
189 Andre Iguodala .25 .60
190 Chris Bosh .30 .75
191 Michael Jordan 2.50 6.00
192 LeBron James 1.25 3.00
193 Chauncey Billups .30 .75
194 Jermaine O'Neal .25 .60
195 Michael Redd .25 .60
196 Joe Johnson .25 .60
197 Emeka Okafor .30 .75
198 Dwyane Wade .50 1.25
199 Dwight Howard .25 .60
200 Gilbert Arenas .25 .60
201 Greg Oden RC .50 1.25
202 Kevin Durant RC 5.00 12.00
203 Al Horford RC .60 1.50
204 Mike Conley Jr. RC .60 1.50
205 Jeff Green RC .50 1.25
206 Marcus Williams RC .30 .75
207 Corey Brewer RC .50 1.25
208 Brandan Wright RC .50 1.25
209 Joakim Noah RC .50 1.25
210 Spencer Hawes RC .40 1.00
211 Acie Law RC .30 .75
212 Thaddeus Young RC .50 1.25
213 Julian Wright RC .30 .75
214 Al Thornton RC .40 1.00
215 Rodney Stuckey RC .40 1.00
216 Nick Young RC .60 1.50
217 Sean Williams RC .30 .75
218 Marco Belinelli RC .50 1.25
219 Javaris Crittenton RC .30 .75
220 Jason Smith RC .40 1.00
221 Daequan Cook RC .40 1.00
222 Jared Dudley RC .40 1.00
223 Wilson Chandler RC .40 1.00
224 Morris Almond RC .30 .75
225 Aaron Brooks RC .40 1.00
226 Arron Afflalo RC .50 1.25
227 Alando Tucker RC .40 1.00
228 Petteri Koponen RC .50 1.25
229 Carl Landry RC .30 .75
230 Gabe Pruitt RC .30 .75

2007-08 Upper Deck First Edition Gold

*GOLD: .6X TO 1.5X BASE HI
APPROXIMATE ODDS 1:6

2007-08 Upper Deck First Edition All-NBA

COMPLETE SET (15) 6.00 15.00
APPROXIMATE ODDS 1:8
NBA1 Dirk Nowitzki .75 2.00
NBA2 Tim Duncan 1.00 2.50
NBA3 Amare Stoudemire .50 1.25
NBA4 Steve Nash .75 2.00
NBA5 Kobe Bryant 2.50 6.00
NBA6 LeBron James 2.50 6.00
NBA7 Chris Bosh .60 1.50
NBA8 Yao Ming .75 2.00
NBA9 Gilbert Arenas .50 1.25
NBA10 Tracy McGrady .60 1.50
NBA11 Kevin Garnett 1.00 2.50
NBA12 Carmelo Anthony .75 2.00
NBA13 Dwight Howard .75 2.00
NBA14 Dwyane Wade 1.00 2.50
NBA15 Chauncey Billups .60 1.50

2007-08 Upper Deck First Edition Behind the Glass

COMPLETE SET (25) 8.00 20.00
APPROXIMATE ODDS 1:5
BGAI Allen Iverson .40 1.00
BGAS Amare Stoudemire .25 .60
BGBO Carlos Boozer .25 .60
BGBW Ben Wallace .25 .60
BGCA Carmelo Anthony .40 1.00
BGCB Chris Bosh .30 .75
BGCP Chris Paul .40 1.00
BGDH Dwight Howard .25 .60
BGDN Dirk Nowitzki .40 1.00
BGDW Dwyane Wade .50 1.25
BGGA Gilbert Arenas .25 .60
BGJR Jason Richardson .30 .75
BGKB Kobe Bryant 1.25 3.00
BGKG Kevin Garnett .50 1.25
BGLJ LeBron James 1.25 3.00
BGMA Shawn Marion .25 .60
BGMG Manu Ginobili .30 .75
BGMJ Michael Jordan 2.50 6.00
BGPP Paul Pierce .30 .75
BGSM Stephon Marbury .25 .60
BGSN Steve Nash .40 1.00
BGSO Shaquille O'Neal .60 1.50
BGTD Tim Duncan .50 1.25
BGTM Tracy McGrady .30 .75
BGYM Yao Ming .40 1.00

2007-08 Upper Deck First Edition Champions of the Court

COMPLETE SET (25) 8.00 20.00
APPROXIMATE ODDS 1:5
CCBR Bill Russell .60 1.50
CCBW Bill Walton .40 1.00
CCCB Chauncey Billups .40 1.00
CCDR Dennis Rodman .75 2.00
CCDW Dwyane Wade .60 1.50
CCGM George Mikan .75 2.00
CCHO Hakeem Olajuwon .50 1.25
CCJD Joe Dumars .40 1.00
CCJE Julius Erving .60 1.50
CCJH John Havlicek .40 1.00
CCJO Magic Johnson 1.00 2.50
CCJW James Worthy .50 1.25
CCKA Kareem Abdul-Jabbar .60 1.50
CCKB Kobe Bryant 1.50 4.00
CCLB Larry Bird 1.00 2.50
CCMG Manu Ginobili .40 1.00
CCMJ Michael Jordan 3.00 8.00
CCMM Moses Malone .40 1.00
CCRH Robert Horry .30 .75
CCRO David Robinson .60 1.50
CCSK Steve Kerr .40 1.00
CCSO Shaquille O'Neal .75 2.00
CCTD Tim Duncan .60 1.50
CCTP Tony Parker .40 1.00
CCWC Wilt Chamberlain .75 2.00

2007-08 Upper Deck First Edition Draft Notices

COMPLETE SET (25) 8.00 20.00
APPROXIMATE ODDS 1:5
DN1 Greg Oden .40 1.00
DN2 Kevin Durant 4.00 10.00
DN3 Al Horford .50 1.25
DN4 Mike Conley Jr. .50 1.25
DN5 Jeff Green .40 1.00
DN6 Alando Tucker .25 .60
DN7 Corey Brewer .40 1.00
DN8 Brandan Wright .40 1.00
DN9 Joakim Noah .40 1.00
DN10 Spencer Hawes .30 .75
DN11 Acie Law .25 .60
DN12 Thaddeus Young .40 1.00
DN13 Julian Wright .25 .60
DN14 Al Thornton .30 .75
DN15 Rodney Stuckey .30 .75
DN16 Nick Young .50 1.25
DN17 Sean Williams .25 .60
DN18 Javaris Crittenton .25 .60
DN19 Jason Smith .30 .75
DN20 Daequan Cook .30 .75
DN21 Jared Dudley .30 .75
DN22 Wilson Chandler .30 .75
DN23 Morris Almond .25 .60
DN24 Aaron Brooks .30 .75
DN25 Arron Afflalo .40 1.00

2007-08 Upper Deck First Edition Kevin Durant Exclusive

COMPLETE SET (6) 6.00 15.00
COMMON CARD (KD1-KD6) 1.50 4.00
RANDOM INSERTS IN PACKS
AUTOS NOT PRICED DUE TO SCARCITY

2008-09 Upper Deck First Edition

COMPLETE SET (266) 8.00 20.00
1 Mike Bibby .15 .40
2 Al Horford .20 .50
3 Joe Johnson .15 .40
4 Josh Childress .15 .40
5 Josh Smith .15 .40
6 Marvin Williams .15 .40
7 Eddie House .12 .30
8 Glen Davis .12 .30
9 Sam Cassell .15 .40
10 Kevin Garnett .30 .75
11 Rajon Rondo .20 .50
12 Ray Allen .20 .50
13 Paul Pierce .20 .50
14 Adam Morrison .12 .30
15 Emeka Okafor .15 .40
16 Gerald Wallace .15 .40
17 Jared Dudley .15 .40
18 Jason Richardson .20 .50
19 Nazr Mohammed .12 .30
20 Raymond Felton .15 .40
21 Andres Nocioni .12 .30
22 Ben Gordon .15 .40
23 Larry Hughes .15 .40
24 Joakim Noah .15 .40
25 Kirk Hinrich .15 .40
26 Luol Deng .15 .40
27 Tyrus Thomas .12 .30
28 Aleksandar Pavlovic .12 .30
29 Anderson Varejao .12 .30
30 Daniel Gibson .15 .40
31 Wally Szczerbiak .15 .40
32 Ben Wallace .15 .40
33 LeBron James .75 2.00
34 Zydrunas Ilgauskas .15 .40
35 Jason Kidd .20 .50
36 Dirk Nowitzki .25 .60
37 Jason Terry .15 .40
38 Jerry Stackhouse .15 .40
39 Jose Barea .25 .60
40 Josh Howard .15 .40
41 Allen Iverson .25 .60
42 Carmelo Anthony .25 .60
43 J.R. Smith .15 .40
44 Kenyon Martin .15 .40
45 Linas Kleiza .12 .30
46 Marcus Camby .12 .30
47 Antonio McDyess .15 .40
48 Chauncey Billups .20 .50
49 Jason Maxiell .12 .30
50 Rasheed Wallace .20 .50
51 Richard Hamilton .15 .40
52 Rodney Stuckey .15 .40
53 Tayshaun Prince .15 .40
54 Al Harrington .12 .30
55 Baron Davis .15 .40
56 Kelenna Azubuike .12 .30
57 Matt Barnes .12 .30
58 Monta Ellis .15 .40
59 Stephen Jackson .12 .30
60 Luis Scola .15 .40
61 Luther Head .12 .30
62 Rafer Alston .12 .30
63 Shane Battier .12 .30
64 Tracy McGrady .20 .50
65 Yao Ming .25 .60
66 Andre Owens .12 .30
67 Danny Granger .15 .40
68 Jamaal Tinsley .12 .30
69 Jermaine O'Neal .15 .40
70 Kareem Rush .12 .30
71 Mike Dunleavy .15 .40
72 Troy Murphy .12 .30
73 Al Thornton .15 .40
74 Chris Kaman .15 .40
75 Corey Maggette .15 .40
76 Cuttino Mobley .12 .30
77 Elton Brand .20 .50
78 Tim Thomas .12 .30
79 Andrew Bynum .12 .30
80 Derek Fisher .15 .40
81 Jordan Farmar .12 .30
82 Kobe Bryant .75 2.00
83 Pau Gasol .20 .50
84 Lamar Odom .15 .40
85 Luke Walton .12 .30
86 Darko Milicic .12 .30
87 Javaris Crittenton .12 .30
88 Kyle Lowry .20 .50
89 Mike Conley Jr. .15 .40
90 Mike Miller .15 .40
91 Kwame Brown .12 .30
92 Rudy Gay .20 .50
93 Daequan Cook .12 .30
94 Dorell Wright .12 .30
95 Dwyane Wade .30 .75
96 Jason Williams .15 .40
97 Ricky Davis .15 .40
98 Shawn Marion .15 .40
99 Udonis Haslem .12 .30
100 Andrew Bogut .15 .40
101 Charlie Villanueva .12 .30
102 Desmond Mason .12 .30
103 Michael Redd .15 .40
104 Mo Williams .15 .40
105 Yi Jianlian .20 .50
106 Al Jefferson .15 .40
107 Corey Brewer .15 .40
108 Craig Smith .12 .30
109 Randy Foye .20 .50
110 Rashad McCants .12 .30
111 Ryan Gomes .12 .30
112 Sebastian Telfair .12 .30
113 Bostjan Nachbar .12 .30
114 Devin Harris .12 .30
115 Josh Boone .12 .30
116 Nenad Krstic .12 .30
117 Richard Jefferson .15 .40
118 Sean Williams .12 .30
119 Vince Carter .25 .60
120 David Lee .15 .40
121 Eddy Curry .12 .30
122 Jamal Crawford .20 .50
123 Nate Robinson .12 .30
124 Quentin Richardson .12 .30
125 Stephon Marbury .15 .40
126 Zach Randolph .15 .40
127 Chris Paul .25 .60
128 David West .15 .40
129 Julian Wright .15 .40
130 Morris Peterson .12 .30
131 Peja Stojakovic .20 .50
132 Tyson Chandler .15 .40
133 Carlos Arroyo .12 .30
134 Dwight Howard .15 .40
135 Hedo Turkoglu .15 .40
136 J.J. Redick .20 .50
137 Jameer Nelson .12 .30
138 Maurice Evans .12 .30
139 Rashard Lewis .15 .40
140 Andre Iguodala .15 .40
141 Andre Miller .15 .40
142 Jason Smith .12 .30
143 Louis Williams .15 .40
144 Samuel Dalembert .12 .30
145 Thaddeus Young .15 .40
146 Willie Green .12 .30
147 Amare Stoudemire .15 .40
148 Boris Diaw .12 .30
149 Grant Hill .25 .60
150 Leandro Barbosa .15 .40
151 Raja Bell .15 .40
152 Shaquille O'Neal .40 1.00
153 Steve Nash .20 .50
154 Brandon Roy .20 .50
155 Channing Frye .15 .40
156 Greg Oden .15 .40
157 LaMarcus Aldridge .20 .50
158 Martell Webster .15 .40
159 Steve Blake .12 .30
160 Beno Udrih .12 .30
161 Brad Miller .15 .40
162 Francisco Garcia .12 .30
163 John Salmons .12 .30
164 Kevin Martin .15 .40
165 Mikki Moore .12 .30
166 Ron Artest .20 .50
167 Brent Barry .12 .30
168 Bruce Bowen .12 .30
169 Manu Ginobili .20 .50
170 Michael Finley .20 .50
171 Robert Horry .15 .40
172 Tim Duncan .30 .75
173 Tony Parker .20 .50
174 Chris Wilcox .12 .30
175 Damien Wilkins .12 .30
176 Jeff Green .15 .40
177 Kevin Durant .50 1.25
178 Nick Collison .15 .40
179 Earl Watson .12 .30
180 Andrea Bargnani .15 .40
181 Anthony Parker .12 .30
182 Carlos Delfino .12 .30
183 Chris Bosh .20 .50
184 Jamario Moon .12 .30
185 Jose Calderon .12 .30
186 T.J. Ford .12 .30
187 Andrei Kirilenko .15 .40
188 Carlos Boozer .15 .40
189 Deron Williams .15 .40
190 Kyle Korver .15 .40
191 Mehmet Okur .12 .30
192 Paul Millsap .15 .40
193 Ronnie Brewer .15 .40
194 Antawn Jamison .15 .40
195 Antonio Daniels .12 .30
196 Brendan Haywood .12 .30
197 Caron Butler .15 .40
198 DeShawn Stevenson .12 .30
199 Gilbert Arenas .15 .40
200 Nick Young .15 .40
201 Spud Webb .25 .60
202 Bob Cousy .50 1.25
203 Kevin McHale .40 1.00
204 Larry Bird .75 2.00
205 Dennis Rodman .60 1.50
206 Michael Jordan 2.50 6.00
207 Isiah Thomas .30 .75
208 Joe Dumars .30 .75
209 Nate Thurmond .25 .60
210 Hakeem Olajuwon .40 1.00
211 Calvin Murphy .25 .60
212 Kareem Abdul-Jabbar .50 1.25
213 Magic Johnson .75 2.00
214 Oscar Robertson .30 .75

215 Bill Bradley .40 1.00
216 Earl Monroe .30 .75
217 Willis Reed .30 .75
218 Julius Erving .50 1.25
219 Clyde Drexler .40 1.00
220 Bill Walton .30 .75
221 Maurice Lucas .30 .75
222 David Robinson .50 1.25
223 John Stockton .50 1.25
224 Karl Malone .40 1.00
225 D.J. Augustin .50 1.25
226 Brook Lopez .75 2.00
227 Jerryd Bayless .50 1.25
228 Jason Thompson .40 1.00
229 Brandon Rush .50 1.25
230 Anthony Randolph .40 1.00
231 Robin Lopez .60 1.50
232 Marreese Speights .50 1.25
233 Roy Hibbert .60 1.50
234 Courtney Lee .50 1.25
235 J.J. Hickson .50 1.25
236 Ryan Anderson .50 1.25
237 Kosta Koufos .50 1.25
238 James Gist .40 1.00
239 Darrell Arthur .50 1.25
240 Donte Greene .40 1.00
241 D.J. White .50 1.25
242 J.R. Giddens .40 1.00
243 Deron Washington .40 1.00
244 Joey Dorsey .40 1.00
245 Mario Chalmers .60 1.50
246 DeAndre Jordan .75 2.00
247 Luc Richard Mbah A Moute .50 1.25
248 Kyle Weaver .40 1.00
249 Sonny Weems .40 1.00
250 Chris Douglas-Roberts .40 1.00
251 Sean Singletary .40 1.00
252 Patrick Ewing Jr. .40 1.00
253 Shan Foster .40 1.00
254 Bill Walker .40 1.00
255 Malik Hairston .40 1.00
256 Richard Hendrix .40 1.00
257 DeVon Hardin .40 1.00
258 Darnell Jackson .40 1.00
259 Derrick Rose 2.50 6.00
260 Michael Beasley .60 1.50
261 O.J. Mayo .60 1.50
262 Russell Westbrook 5.00 12.00
263 Kevin Love 2.00 5.00
264 Danilo Gallinari 1.00 2.50
265 Eric Gordon 1.00 2.50
266 Joe Alexander .40 1.00

2008-09 Upper Deck First Edition Gold

*GOLD: .5X TO 1.25X BASE HI
ONE PER PACK

2008-09 Upper Deck First Edition Chalk Talk

COMPLETE SET (30) 4.00 10.00
UNPRICED AUTOS RANDOM INSERTS IN PACKS
APPROXIMATE ODDS 1:2 PACKS
CT1 Joe Johnson .25 .60
CT2 Paul Pierce .30 .75
CT3 Gerald Wallace .25 .60
CT4 Ben Gordon .25 .60
CT5 LeBron James 1.25 3.00
CT6 Josh Howard .25 .60
CT7 Allen Iverson .40 1.00
CT8 Richard Hamilton .25 .60
CT9 Stephen Jackson .25 .60
CT10 Tracy McGrady .30 .75
CT11 Danny Granger .25 .60
CT12 Corey Maggette .25 .60
CT13 Kobe Bryant 1.25 3.00
CT14 Pau Gasol .30 .75
CT15 Dwyane Wade .50 1.25
CT16 Yi Jianlian .30 .75
CT17 Al Jefferson .25 .60
CT18 Richard Jefferson .25 .60
CT19 Chris Paul .40 1.00
CT20 Jamal Crawford .30 .75
CT21 Dwight Howard .25 .60
CT22 Andre Iguodala .25 .60
CT23 Amare Stoudemire .25 .60
CT24 LaMarcus Aldridge .30 .75
CT25 Mike Bibby .25 .60
CT26 Tony Parker .30 .75
CT27 Kevin Durant .75 2.00
CT28 T.J. Ford .20 .50
CT29 Deron Williams .25 .60
CT30 Antawn Jamison .25 .60

2008-09 Upper Deck First Edition Rookie Standouts

COMPLETE SET (30) 30.00 60.00
RANDOM INSERTS IN PACKS
RSAR Anthony Randolph .60 1.50
RSBL Brook Lopez 1.25 3.00
RSBR Brandon Rush .75 2.00
RSBW Bill Walker .60 1.50
RSCD Chris Douglas-Roberts .60 1.50
RSCL Courtney Lee .75 2.00
RSDA D.J. Augustin .75 2.00
RSDG Danilo Gallinari 1.50 4.00
RSDR Derrick Rose 4.00 10.00
RSDW D.J. White .75 2.00
RSEG Eric Gordon 1.50 4.00
RSJA Joe Alexander .60 1.50
RSJB Jerryd Bayless .75 2.00
RSJD Joey Dorsey .60 1.50
RSJG James Gist .60 1.50
RSJH J.J. Hickson .75 2.00
RSJT Jason Thompson .60 1.50
RSKK Kosta Koufos .75 2.00
RSKL Kevin Love 3.00 8.00
RSLM Luc Richard Mbah A Moute .75 2.00
RSMB Michael Beasley 1.00 2.50
RSMC Mario Chalmers 1.00 2.50
RSMS Marreese Speights .75 2.00
RSOM O.J. Mayo 1.00 2.50
RSPE Patrick Ewing Jr. .60 1.50
RSRA Ryan Anderson .75 2.00
RSRH Roy Hibbert 1.00 2.50
RSRL Robin Lopez 1.00 2.50
RSRW Russell Westbrook 8.00 20.00
RSSW Sonny Weems .60 1.50

2008-09 Upper Deck First Edition Starquest Green

COMPLETE SET (30) 8.00 20.00
ONE PER PACK
SQ1 Carmelo Anthony .40 1.00
SQ2 Chauncey Billups .30 .75
SQ3 Larry Bird .75 2.00
SQ4 Chris Bosh .30 .75
SQ5 Kobe Bryant 1.25 3.00
SQ6 Vince Carter .40 1.00
SQ7 Baron Davis .25 .60
SQ8 Tim Duncan .50 1.25
SQ9 Kevin Durant .75 2.00
SQ10 Julius Erving .50 1.25
SQ11 Walt Frazier .30 .75
SQ12 Kevin Garnett .50 1.25
SQ13 Rudy Gay .30 .75
SQ14 Artis Gilmore .25 .60
SQ15 Dwight Howard .25 .60
SQ16 Allen Iverson .40 1.00
SQ17 LeBron James 1.25 3.00
SQ18 Al Jefferson .25 .60
SQ19 Magic Johnson .75 2.00
SQ20 Michael Jordan 2.50 6.00
SQ21 Shawn Marion .25 .60
SQ22 Tracy McGrady .30 .75
SQ23 Yao Ming .40 1.00
SQ24 Dirk Nowitzki .40 1.00
SQ25 Shaquille O'Neal .60 1.50
SQ26 Greg Oden .25 .60
SQ27 Chris Paul .40 1.00
SQ28 Brandon Roy .30 .75
SQ29 Dwyane Wade .50 1.25
SQ30 Deron Williams .25 .60

2009-10 Upper Deck First Edition

COMPLETE SET (200) 20.00 50.00
1 Josh Smith .15 .40
2 Al Horford .20 .50
3 Mike Bibby .15 .40
4 Joe Johnson .15 .40
5 Marvin Williams .15 .40
6 Kevin Garnett .30 .75
7 Paul Pierce .20 .50
8 Ray Allen .20 .50
9 Rajon Rondo .20 .50
10 Kendrick Perkins .12 .30
11 Raymond Felton .15 .40
12 Raja Bell .15 .40
13 D.J. Augustin .12 .30
14 Gerald Wallace .15 .40
15 Boris Diaw .15 .40
16 Emeka Okafor .15 .40
17 Derrick Rose .30 .75
18 Luol Deng .15 .40
19 Ben Gordon .15 .40
20 John Salmons .15 .40
21 Joakim Noah .15 .40
22 Tyrus Thomas .12 .30
23 Michael Jordan 1.50 4.00
24 LeBron James .75 2.00
25 Mo Williams .15 .40
26 Ben Wallace .15 .40
27 Delonte West .12 .30
28 Zydrunas Ilgauskas .15 .40
29 Wally Szczerbiak .15 .40
30 Josh Howard .15 .40
31 Dirk Nowitzki .25 .60
32 Jason Kidd .20 .50
33 Erick Dampier .12 .30
34 Jason Terry .15 .40
35 Chauncey Billups .20 .50
36 Carmelo Anthony .25 .60
37 Kenyon Martin .15 .40
38 Nene .15 .40
39 J.R. Smith .15 .40
40 Allen Iverson .25 .60
41 Richard Hamilton .15 .40
42 Tayshaun Prince .15 .40
43 Rodney Stuckey .12 .30
44 Amir Johnson .12 .30
45 Rasheed Wallace .20 .50
46 Monta Ellis .15 .40
47 Stephen Jackson .15 .40
48 Jamal Crawford .20 .50
49 Kelenna Azubuike .12 .30
50 Andris Biedrins .12 .30
51 Corey Maggette .15 .40
52 Luis Scola .15 .40
53 Tracy McGrady .20 .50
54 Yao Ming .25 .60
55 Ron Artest .20 .50
56 Shane Battier .20 .50
57 Von Wafer .12 .30
58 T.J. Ford .12 .30
59 Danny Granger .15 .40
60 Mike Dunleavy .12 .30
61 Troy Murphy .12 .30
62 Jeff Foster .12 .30
63 Jarrett Jack .15 .40
64 Eric Gordon .15 .40
65 Baron Davis .15 .40
66 Al Thornton .15 .40
67 Zach Randolph .15 .40
68 Chris Kaman .15 .40
69 Kobe Bryant .75 2.00
70 Pau Gasol .20 .50
71 Lamar Odom .15 .40
72 Derek Fisher .15 .40
73 Andrew Bynum .12 .30
74 Sasha Vujacic .12 .30
75 Trevor Ariza .12 .30
76 O.J. Mayo .12 .30
77 Marc Gasol .20 .50
78 Rudy Gay .20 .50
79 Darrell Arthur .15 .40
80 Marko Jaric .12 .30
81 Mike Conley Jr. .15 .40
82 Michael Beasley .12 .30
83 Mario Chalmers .15 .40
84 Dwyane Wade .30 .75
85 Chris Quinn .12 .30
86 Udonis Haslem .12 .30
87 Daequan Cook .12 .30
88 Jermaine O'Neal .15 .40
89 Luke Ridnour .15 .40
90 Michael Redd .15 .40
91 Richard Jefferson .15 .40
92 Charlie Villanueva .12 .30
93 Andrew Bogut .15 .40
94 Ramon Sessions .15 .40
95 Kevin Love .20 .50
96 Sebastian Telfair .12 .30
97 Al Jefferson .15 .40
98 Randy Foye .12 .30
99 Mike Miller .15 .40
100 Devin Harris .12 .30
101 Vince Carter .25 .60
102 Yi Jianlian .15 .40
103 Brook Lopez .15 .40
104 Chris Douglas-Roberts .12 .30
105 Eduardo Najera .12 .30
106 Chris Paul .25 .60
107 Peja Stojakovic .20 .50
108 David West .15 .40
109 Tyson Chandler .15 .40
110 James Posey .12 .30
111 Al Harrington .15 .40
112 Chris Duhon .12 .30
113 Quentin Richardson .15 .40
114 David Lee .12 .30
115 Jared Jeffries .12 .30
116 Wilson Chandler .15 .40
117 Danilo Gallinari .15 .40
118 Russell Westbrook .50 1.25
119 Kevin Durant .50 1.25
120 Jeff Green .15 .40
121 Desmond Mason .12 .30
122 Nick Collison .15 .40
123 Earl Watson .12 .30
124 Dwight Howard .15 .40
125 Courtney Lee .15 .40
126 Hedo Turkoglu .15 .40
127 Jameer Nelson .12 .30
128 Rashard Lewis .15 .40
129 Mickael Pietrus .12 .30
130 Elton Brand .20 .50
131 Andre Miller .15 .40
132 Andre Iguodala .15 .40
133 Thaddeus Young .12 .30
134 Willie Green .12 .30
135 Samuel Dalembert .12 .30
136 Jason Richardson .20 .50
137 Shaquille O'Neal .40 1.00
138 Steve Nash .20 .50
139 Grant Hill .25 .60
140 Amare Stoudemire .15 .40
141 Leandro Barbosa .15 .40
142 Robin Lopez .12 .30
143 Brandon Roy .20 .50
144 LaMarcus Aldridge .20 .50
145 Jerryd Bayless .15 .40
146 Rudy Fernandez .12 .30
147 Steve Blake .12 .30
148 Martell Webster .12 .30
149 Greg Oden .15 .40
150 Kevin Martin .15 .40
151 Beno Udrih .12 .30
152 Francisco Garcia .12 .30
153 Tim Duncan .30 .75
154 Tony Parker .20 .50
155 Manu Ginobili .20 .50
156 Roger Mason .12 .30
157 Michael Finley .20 .50
158 George Hill .20 .50
159 Chris Bosh .20 .50
160 Jose Calderon .12 .30
161 Andrea Bargnani .15 .40
162 Anthony Parker .12 .30
163 Deron Williams .15 .40
164 Carlos Boozer .15 .40
165 Ronnie Brewer .15 .40
166 C.J. Miles .15 .40
167 Mehmet Okur .12 .30
168 Kyle Korver .15 .40
169 Andrei Kirilenko .15 .40
170 Gilbert Arenas .15 .40
171 Antawn Jamison .15 .40
172 DeShawn Stevenson .12 .30
173 Caron Butler .15 .40
174 Brendan Haywood .12 .30
175 Nick Young .15 .40
176 B.J. Mullens RC .40 1.00
177 Blake Griffin RC 2.50 6.00
178 Brandon Jennings RC .60 1.50
179 Chase Budinger RC .50 1.25
180 DaJuan Summers RC .40 1.00
181 Darren Collison RC .60 1.50
182 DeJuan Blair RC .50 1.25
183 Earl Clark RC .50 1.25
184 Eric Maynor RC .40 1.00
185 Gerald Henderson RC .50 1.25
186 Taj Gibson RC .60 1.50
187 Hasheem Thabeet RC .40 1.00
188 James Harden RC 3.00 8.00
189 Jeff Teague RC .60 1.50
190 Jonny Flynn RC .40 1.00
191 Jordan Hill RC .50 1.25
192 Jrue Holiday RC .75 2.00
193 Omri Casspi RC .50 1.25
194 Austin Daye RC .40 1.00
195 Sam Young RC .40 1.00
196 Stephen Curry RC 30.00 80.00
197 Terrence Williams RC .40 1.00
198 Ty Lawson RC .60 1.50
199 Tyler Hansbrough RC .50 1.25
200 Tyreke Evans RC .50 1.25

2009-10 Upper Deck First Edition Gold

*1-175 GOLD: .75X TO 2X BASE HI
*176-200 GOLD: .5X TO 1.25X BASE HI
GOLD CARDS ONE PER PACK
23 Michael Jordan 4.00 10.00
177 Blake Griffin 10.00 25.00

2009-10 Upper Deck First Edition Behind the Arc

COMPLETE SET (25) 5.00 12.00
INSERT ODDS TWO PER PACK
BA1 Rashard Lewis .40 1.00
BA2 Danny Granger .40 1.00
BA3 Ray Allen .50 1.25
BA4 Mike Bibby .40 1.00
BA5 Ben Gordon .40 1.00
BA6 Roger Mason .30 .75
BA7 Peja Stojakovic .50 1.25
BA8 Daequan Cook .30 .75
BA9 Al Harrington .40 1.00
BA10 Rudy Fernandez .30 .75
BA11 Troy Murphy .30 .75
BA12 Chauncey Billups .50 1.25
BA13 Mo Williams .40 1.00
BA14 Jason Terry .40 1.00
BA15 O.J. Mayo .30 .75
BA16 Hedo Turkoglu .40 1.00
BA17 Joe Johnson .40 1.00
BA18 Jamal Crawford .50 1.25
BA19 J.R. Smith .40 1.00
BA20 Ron Artest .50 1.25
BA21 Vince Carter .60 1.50
BA22 Eddie House .30 .75
BA23 Quentin Richardson .40 1.00
BA24 Chris Duhon .30 .75
BA25 Rasual Butler .30 .75

2009-10 Upper Deck First Edition Rejected!

COMPLETE SET (25) 6.00 15.00
INSERT ODDS TWO PER PACK
R1 Dwight Howard .40 1.00
R2 Ronny Turiaf .30 .75
R3 Lamar Odom .40 1.00
R4 Marcus Camby .30 .75
R5 Tim Duncan .75 2.00
R6 Emeka Okafor .40 1.00
R7 Samuel Dalembert .30 .75
R8 Tyrus Thomas .30 .75
R9 Chris Andersen .40 1.00
R10 Yao Ming .60 1.50
R11 Kendrick Perkins .30 .75
R12 Jermaine O'Neal .40 1.00
R13 Andrew Bynum .30 .75
R14 Al Jefferson .40 1.00
R15 Danny Granger .40 1.00
R16 Andris Biedrins .30 .75
R17 Dwyane Wade .75 2.00
R18 Joakim Noah .40 1.00
R19 Spencer Hawes .30 .75
R20 Nene .40 1.00
R21 Erick Dampier .30 .75
R22 Ben Wallace .40 1.00
R23 Shaquille O'Neal 1.00 2.50
R24 Rasheed Wallace .50 1.25
R25 Josh Smith .40 1.00

2009-10 Upper Deck First Edition Slam Dunk

COMPLETE SET 15.00 30.00
INSERT ODDS TWO PER PACK
SD1 Josh Smith .50 1.25
SD2 Dwight Howard .50 1.25
SD3 Nate Robinson .40 1.00
SD4 Gerald Green .50 1.25
SD5 LeBron James 2.50 6.00
SD6 Kobe Bryant 2.50 6.00
SD7 Amare Stoudemire .50 1.25
SD8 Shawn Marion .50 1.25
SD9 Carmelo Anthony .75 2.00
SD10 Dwyane Wade 1.00 2.50
SD11 Pau Gasol .60 1.50
SD12 Andre Iguodala .50 1.25
SD13 Ben Wallace .50 1.25
SD14 Richard Jefferson .50 1.25
SD15 Vince Carter .75 2.00
SD16 Kenyon Martin .50 1.25
SD17 Kevin Garnett 1.00 2.50
SD18 Chris Bosh .60 1.50
SD19 Jason Richardson .60 1.50
SD20 Tim Duncan 1.00 2.50
SD21 Yao Ming .75 2.00
SD22 Shaquille O'Neal 1.25 3.00
SD23 Gerald Wallace .50 1.25
SD24 Tyson Chandler .50 1.25
SD25 Andrew Bynum .40 1.00

2009-10 Upper Deck First Edition Star Attractions

COMPLETE SET (25) 15.00 30.00
INSERT ODDS TWO PER PACK
SA1 Kobe Bryant 2.50 6.00
SA2 LeBron James 2.50 6.00
SA3 Carmelo Anthony .75 2.00
SA4 Kevin Durant 1.50 4.00
SA5 Tim Duncan 1.00 2.50
SA6 Deron Williams .50 1.25
SA7 Steve Nash .60 1.50
SA8 Allen Iverson .75 2.00
SA9 Chauncey Billups .60 1.50
SA10 Kevin Garnett 1.00 2.50
SA11 Paul Pierce .60 1.50
SA12 Jason Kidd .60 1.50
SA13 Dirk Nowitzki .75 2.00
SA14 Chris Bosh .60 1.50
SA15 Vince Carter .75 2.00
SA16 Michael Redd .50 1.25
SA17 Brandon Roy .60 1.50
SA18 Tracy McGrady .60 1.50
SA19 Chris Paul .75 2.00
SA20 Dwight Howard .50 1.25
SA21 Danny Granger .50 1.25
SA22 Kevin Martin .50 1.25
SA23 Devin Harris .40 1.00
SA24 Gilbert Arenas .50 1.25
SA25 Joe Johnson .50 1.25

2001-02 Upper Deck Flight Team

Released in mid-May 2002, this 240-card set is divided up into 90 veteran cards and 50 different rookies with three versions of each card. The rookie "A" version features a portrait style photo and the word "Portrait" along the right edge of the card, the rookie "B" version features and action photo and the word "Action" along the right edge of the card, and the rookie "C" version features an action photo and the words "Hight Performance" along the right edge of the card. The base design places full color player action photos against a colored background that fades to white at both the top and the bottom of the card. Player names are in big letters and silver foil towards the bottom of the card. The rookie print runs are divided up as follows: Card numbers 91-120 are sequentially numberd to 500 on each version with a combined print run of 1500, card numbers 121-134 are sequentially numbered to 375 on each version for a combined print run of 1125, and card numbers 135-140 are sequentially numbered to 250 on each version for a combined print run of 750. Flight Team was packaged in 14 pack boxes with four cards per pack and carried a suggested retail price of $6.99. Also, a PSA graded version of a rookie card was included as a box-topper in each box.

COMPLETE SET (240) 60.00 120.00
COMP.SET w/o SP's (90) 10.00 25.00
91-120 PRINT RUN 1500 PER PLAYER
91-120 THREE VERSIONS SER.#'d TO 500
121-134 PRINT RUN 1125 PER PLAYER
121-134 THREE VERSIONS SER.#'d TO 375
135-140 PRINT RUN 750 PER PLAYER
135-140 THREE VERSIONS SER.#'d TO 250
1 Michael Jordan 2.50 6.00
2 Dirk Nowitzki .50 1.25
3 Antawn Jamison .30 .75
4 Latrell Sprewell .25 .60
5 Peja Stojakovic .30 .75
6 Dikembe Mutombo .30 .75
7 Jason Williams .25 .60
8 Kobe Bryant 1.25 3.00
9 Baron Davis .30 .75
10 Wally Szczerbiak .25 .60
11 Reggie Miller .30 .75
12 Marcus Fizer .20 .50
13 Desmond Mason .25 .60
14 Glenn Robinson .25 .60
15 Vince Carter .50 1.25
16 James Posey .20 .50
17 Darius Miles .20 .50
18 Jason Kidd .50 1.25
19 Anfernee Hardaway .50 1.25
20 Karl Malone .40 1.00
21 Kevin Garnett .50 1.25
22 Shareef Abdur-Rahim .25 .60
23 Steve Francis .25 .60
24 Paul Pierce .30 .75
25 Mike Miller .25 .60
26 Tim Duncan .60 1.50
27 Derek Anderson .20 .50
28 Eddie Jones .25 .60
29 Keith Van Horn .25 .60
30 Chris Mihm .20 .50
31 Clifford Robinson .20 .50
32 Gary Payton .30 .75
33 Courtney Alexander .20 .50
34 Shaquille O'Neal .75 2.00
35 Tim Thomas .20 .50
36 Raef LaFrentz .20 .50
37 Stromile Swift .20 .50
38 Stephon Marbury .25 .60
39 Morris Peterson .20 .50
40 Donyell Marshall .20 .50
41 Kenny Thomas .20 .50
42 Juwan Howard .25 .60
43 Tracy McGrady .50 1.25
44 Kenny Anderson .25 .60
45 Larry Hughes .25 .60
46 Allan Houston .25 .60
47 Chris Webber .30 .75
48 Andre Miller .25 .60
49 Corey Maggette .25 .60
50 Sam Cassell .25 .60
51 Steve Smith .25 .60
52 Jamal Mashburn .25 .60
53 Al Harrington .25 .60
54 Brian Grant .20 .50
55 Rasheed Wallace .30 .75
56 Rick Fox .20 .50
57 Jason Terry .30 .75
58 Rashard Lewis .30 .75
59 Joe Smith .25 .60
60 Michael Dickerson .20 .50
61 Michael Finley .30 .75
62 Danny Fortson .20 .50
63 Allen Iverson .60 1.50
64 Richard Hamilton .25 .60
65 Antonio McDyess .25 .60
66 David Wesley .20 .50
67 Ben Wallace .25 .60
68 Mike Bibby .30 .75
69 Antonio Davis .20 .50
70 Cuttino Mobley .20 .50
71 Lamond Murray .20 .50
72 Antoine Walker .25 .60
73 Jermaine O'Neal .25 .60
74 Alonzo Mourning .40 1.00
75 Shawn Marion .25 .60
76 John Stockton .40 1.00
77 Marcus Camby .25 .60
78 Derek Fisher .25 .60
79 DerMarr Johnson .20 .50
80 Aaron McKie .20 .50
81 David Robinson .50 1.25
82 Steve Nash .50 1.25
83 Ray Allen .30 .75
84 Elton Brand .30 .75
85 Kenyon Martin .30 .75
86 Bonzi Wells .20 .50
87 Grant Hill .40 1.00
88 Terrell Brandon .20 .50
89 Toni Kukoc .30 .75
90 Jerry Stackhouse .25 .60
91A Tierre Brown RC .75 2.00
91B Tierre Brown RC .75 2.00
91C Tierre Brown RC .75 2.00
92A Jamison Brewer RC .75 2.00
92B Jamison Brewer RC .75 2.00
92C Jamison Brewer RC .75 2.00
93A Antonis Fotsis RC .50 1.25
93B Antonis Fotsis RC .50 1.25
93C Antonis Fotsis RC .50 1.25
94A Mike James RC .75 2.00
94B Mike James RC .75 2.00
94C Mike James RC .75 2.00
95A Primoz Brezec RC .75 2.00
95B Primoz Brezec RC .75 2.00
95C Primoz Brezec RC .75 2.00
96A Jeryl Sasser RC .50 1.25
96B Jeryl Sasser RC .50 1.25
96C Jeryl Sasser RC .50 1.25
97A DeSagana Diop RC .60 1.50
97B DeSagana Diop RC .60 1.50
97C DeSagana Diop RC .60 1.50
98A Mengke Bateer RC .75 2.00
98B Mengke Bateer RC .75 2.00
98C Mengke Bateer RC .75 2.00
99A Gerald Wallace RC 1.00 2.50
99B Gerald Wallace RC 1.00 2.50
99C Gerald Wallace RC 1.00 2.50
100A Kenny Satterfield RC .50 1.25
100B Kenny Satterfield RC .50 1.25
100C Kenny Satterfield RC .50 1.25
101A Ruben Boumtje-Boumtje RC .75 2.00
101B Ruben Boumtje-Boumtje RC .75 2.00
101C Ruben Boumtje-Boumtje RC .75 2.00
102A Brian Scalabrine RC .75 2.00
102B Brian Scalabrine RC .75 2.00
102C Brian Scalabrine RC .75 2.00
103A Oscar Torres RC .50 1.25
103B Oscar Torres RC .50 1.25
103C Oscar Torres RC .50 1.25
104A Jarron Collins RC .50 1.25
104B Jarron Collins RC .50 1.25
104C Jarron Collins RC .50 1.25
105A Jeff Trepagnier RC .50 1.25
105B Jeff Trepagnier RC .50 1.25
105C Jeff Trepagnier RC .50 1.25
106A Brendan Haywood RC .75 2.00
106B Brendan Haywood RC .75 2.00
106C Brendan Haywood RC .75 2.00
107A Vladimir Radmanovic RC .75 2.00
107B Vladimir Radmanovic RC .75 2.00
107C Vladimir Radmanovic RC .75 2.00
108A Loren Woods RC .50 1.25
108B Loren Woods RC .50 1.25
108C Loren Woods RC .50 1.25
109A Terence Morris RC .75 2.00
109B Terence Morris RC .75 2.00
109C Terence Morris RC .75 2.00
110A Kirk Haston RC .50 1.25
110B Kirk Haston RC .50 1.25
110C Kirk Haston RC .50 1.25
111A Earl Watson RC .75 2.00
111B Earl Watson RC .75 2.00
111C Earl Watson RC .75 2.00
112A Brandon Armstrong RC .50 1.25
112B Brandon Armstrong RC .50 1.25
112C Brandon Armstrong RC .50 1.25
113A Zach Randolph RC 1.25 3.00
113B Zach Randolph RC 1.25 3.00
113C Zach Randolph RC 1.25 3.00
114A Bobby Simmons RC .50 1.25
114B Bobby Simmons RC .50 1.25
114C Bobby Simmons RC .50 1.25
115A Alton Ford RC .75 2.00
115B Alton Ford RC .75 2.00
115C Alton Ford RC .75 2.00
116A Predrag Drobnjak RC .75 2.00
116B Predrag Drobnjak RC .75 2.00
116C Predrag Drobnjak RC .75 2.00
117A Michael Bradley RC .50 1.25
117B Michael Bradley RC .50 1.25
117C Michael Bradley RC .50 1.25
118A Samuel Dalembert RC .75 2.00
118B Samuel Dalembert RC .75 2.00
118C Samuel Dalembert RC .75 2.00
119A Gilbert Arenas RC 1.25 3.00
119B Gilbert Arenas RC 1.25 3.00
119C Gilbert Arenas RC 1.25 3.00
120A Kedrick Brown RC .50 1.25
120B Kedrick Brown RC .50 1.25
120C Kedrick Brown RC .50 1.25
121A Trenton Hassell RC .75 2.00
121B Trenton Hassell RC .75 2.00
121C Trenton Hassell RC .75 2.00
122A Zeljko Rebraca RC 1.00 2.50
122B Zeljko Rebraca RC 1.00 2.50
122C Zeljko Rebraca RC 1.00 2.50
123A Jason Collins RC .75 2.00
123B Jason Collins RC .75 2.00
123C Jason Collins RC .75 2.00
124A Will Solomon RC 1.00 2.50
124B Will Solomon RC 1.00 2.50
124C Will Solomon RC 1.00 2.50
125A Joseph Forte RC .60 1.50
125B Joseph Forte RC .60 1.50
125C Joseph Forte RC .60 1.50
126A Steven Hunter RC .75 2.00
126B Steven Hunter RC .75 2.00
126C Steven Hunter RC .75 2.00
127A Eddy Curry RC 1.00 2.50
127B Eddy Curry RC 1.00 2.50
127C Eddy Curry RC 1.00 2.50
128A Troy Murphy RC 1.00 2.50
128B Troy Murphy RC 1.00 2.50
128C Troy Murphy RC 1.00 2.50
129A Shane Battier RC 2.00 5.00
129B Shane Battier RC 2.00 5.00
129C Shane Battier RC 2.00 5.00
130A Tyson Chandler RC 1.50 4.00
130B Tyson Chandler RC 1.50 4.00
130C Tyson Chandler RC 1.50 4.00
131A Joe Johnson RC 1.25 3.00
131B Joe Johnson RC 1.25 3.00
131C Joe Johnson RC 1.25 3.00
132A Richard Jefferson RC 1.50 4.00
132B Richard Jefferson RC 1.50 4.00
132C Richard Jefferson RC 1.50 4.00
133A Eddie Griffin RC .75 2.00
133B Eddie Griffin RC .75 2.00
133C Eddie Griffin RC .75 2.00
134A Rodney White RC .60 1.50
134B Rodney White RC .60 1.50
134C Rodney White RC .60 1.50
135A Andrei Kirilenko RC 2.00 5.00
135B Andrei Kirilenko RC 2.00 5.00
135C Andrei Kirilenko RC 2.00 5.00
136A Tony Parker RC 5.00 12.00
136B Tony Parker RC 5.00 12.00
136C Tony Parker RC 5.00 12.00
137A Jamaal Tinsley RC 1.25 3.00
137B Jamaal Tinsley RC 1.25 3.00
137C Jamaal Tinsley RC 1.25 3.00
138A Pau Gasol RC 4.00 10.00
138B Pau Gasol RC 4.00 10.00
138C Pau Gasol RC 4.00 10.00
139A Jason Richardson RC 1.50 4.00
139B Jason Richardson RC 1.50 4.00
139C Jason Richardson RC 1.50 4.00
140A Kwame Brown RC 1.25 3.00
140B Kwame Brown RC 1.25 3.00
140C Kwame Brown RC 1.25 3.00

2001-02 Upper Deck Flight Team Copper

*COPPER STARS: 5X TO 12X BASE CARD HI
*COPPER RC/500: 2X TO 5X BASE CARD HI
*COPPER RC/375: 1.5X TO 4X BASE CARD HI
*COPPER RC/250: 1.25X TO 3X BASE CARD HI
COPPER PRINT RUN 125 SER.#'d SETS
1 Michael Jordan 20.00 50.00

2001-02 Upper Deck Flight Team Gold

*GOLD STARS: 10X TO 25X BASE CARD HI
*GOLD RC/500: 4X TO 10X BASE CARD HI
*GOLD RC/350: 3X TO 8X BASE CARD HI
*GOLD RC/250: 2.5X TO 6X BASE CARD HI
GOLD PRINT RUN 50 SER.#'d SETS
1 Michael Jordan 30.00 80.00

2001-02 Upper Deck Flight Team 2 the Air

Randomly seeded in packs, this six card set features a full color player action photo on the top of the card and a swatch of a game jersey and a swatch of game floor on the bottom of the card. The jersey swatch is embedded in the left side of the floor swatch, and the floor swatch has the player's team logo engraved in it. Each card is sequentially numbered to 100. A gold version sequentially numbered to 10 was also inserted in packs.

PRINT RUN 100 SER.#'d SETS
2AI Allen Iverson 12.00 30.00
2CW Chris Webber 8.00 20.00
2KB Kobe Bryant 25.00 60.00
2KG Kevin Garnett 10.00 25.00
2MC Tracy McGrady 10.00 25.00
2MJ Michael Jordan 100.00 200.00

2001-02 Upper Deck Flight Team Flight Patterns

Randomly inserted in packs at the rate of one in 14, this 24-card set features full color player action photos and an arrow shaped swatch of a game worn jersey where the arrow is pointing to the right. A gold version sequentially numbered to 125 was also issued.

STATED ODDS 1:14
*GOLD: .75X TO 2X FLT.PAT HI
GOLD PRINT RUN 125 SER.#'d SETS
AH Anfernee Hardaway 6.00 15.00
AJ Antawn Jamison 4.00 10.00
AL Al Harrington 3.00 8.00
AM Andre Miller 3.00 8.00
BD Baron Davis 4.00 10.00
BR Bryon Russell 2.50 6.00
CM Corey Maggette 3.00 8.00
DG Devean George 2.50 6.00
DM Desmond Mason 3.00 8.00
DS DeShawn Stevenson 2.50 6.00
GH Grant Hill 5.00 12.00
JK Jason Kidd 6.00 15.00
JM Jamal Mashburn 3.00 8.00
JS Jerry Stackhouse 3.00 8.00
JT Jason Terry 4.00 10.00
KE Kedrick Brown 2.50 6.00
KV Keith Van Horn 3.00 8.00
KW Kwame Brown 4.00 10.00
LO Lamar Odom 3.00 8.00
MF Marcus Fizer 2.50 6.00
MP Morris Peterson 2.50 6.00
QR Quentin Richardson 3.00 8.00
SH Shawn Marion 3.00 8.00
WS Wally Szczerbiak 3.00 8.00

2001-02 Upper Deck Flight Team Key Signatures

Seeded in packs, this 15-card set features a horizontal card design with a colored background to match the featured player's team colors. Each card is sequentially numbered to 100 and has a player photo on the right side of the card and an authentic player signature on the left side.

PRINT RUN 23 TO 100 SER.#'d SETS
BAS Brandon Armstrong/100 4.00 10.00
CWS Kenyon Martin/100 10.00 25.00
ECS Eddy Curry/100 6.00 15.00
JKS Jason Kidd/100 20.00 50.00
JRS Jason Richardson/100 6.00 15.00
JTS Jamaal Tinsley/100 6.00 15.00
KBS Kobe Bryant/100 125.00 250.00
KGS Kevin Garnett/100 30.00 80.00
KWS Kwame Brown/100 6.00 15.00
MJS Michael Jordan/23 400.00 800.00
RJS Richard Jefferson/100 10.00 25.00
SDS Samuel Dalembert/100 6.00 15.00
TCS Tyson Chandler/100 10.00 25.00
TMS Troy Murphy/100 6.00 15.00
TPS Tony Parker/100 25.00 60.00

2001-02 Upper Deck Flight Team Superstar Flight Patterns

Randomly inserted in packs, this 24-card set features full color player action photos and an arrow shaped swatch of a game worn jersey where the arrow is pointing to the left. Each card is sequentially numbered to 100. A Gold version sequentially numbered to 25 was also inserted.

PRINT RUN 100 SER.#'d SETS
*GOLD: 1.25X TO 3X HI
GOLD PRINT RUN 25 SER.#'d SETS
AI Allen Iverson 6.00 15.00
CW Chris Webber 3.00 8.00
KB Kobe Bryant 12.00 30.00
KG Kevin Garnett 5.00 12.00
MC Tracy McGrady 5.00 12.00
MJ Michael Jordan 75.00 150.00

2001-02 Upper Deck Flight Team UD Jersey Jams

Inserted in packs at the rate of one in 19, this 24-card set centers player action photography and a circular swatch of a game jersey. Backgrounds are rainbow colored, and the left and right sides are white. A Gold version sequentially numbered to 50 was also issued.

STATED ODDS 1:19
*GOLD: 1.25X TO 3X JSY JAM HI
GOLD PRINT RUN 50 SER.#'d SETS
AWJ Antoine Walker 3.00 8.00
BDJ Baron Davis 4.00 10.00
DMJ Darius Miles 2.50 6.00
ECJ Eddy Curry 4.00 10.00
EGJ Eddie Griffin 3.00 8.00
GRJ Glenn Robinson 3.00 8.00
JKJ Jason Kidd 6.00 15.00
JRJ Jason Richardson 5.00 12.00
JSJ Jeryl Sasser 2.50 6.00
KBJ Kobe Bryant 15.00 40.00
KGJ Kevin Garnett 6.00 15.00
KMJ Karl Malone 5.00 12.00
LOJ Lamar Odom 3.00 8.00
MJJ Michael Jordan 30.00 80.00
PPJ Paul Pierce 4.00 10.00
RJJ Richard Jefferson 6.00 15.00
RLJ Rashard Lewis 4.00 10.00
SAJ Shareef Abdur-Rahim 3.00 8.00
SFJ Steve Francis 3.00 8.00
SHJ Steven Hunter 3.00 8.00
SMJ Stephon Marbury 3.00 8.00
TCJ Tyson Chandler 6.00 15.00
TMJ Troy Murphy 4.00 10.00
WSJ Wally Szczerbiak 3.00 8.00

1993 Upper Deck French McDonald's

The 1993 Upper Deck McDonald's French set consists of 40 standard-size cards. The three-card foil packs were made available to McDonald's customers in France only, during September and October of 1993. The packs were distributed free to customers who purchased a "Menu Basket Meal", consisting of a Big Mac, large fries and a Coke, and valued at 5.50. Two million packs were produced, with 28,000 randomly inserted cards carrying the words "Slam Dunk". This insert entitled the customer to win an official Spalding basketball. One unique feature of this set is the wrappers were printed in French, while the cards were printed in both French and English. The front design was the same as the regular issue 1991-92 Upper Deck set, with color player photos, bordered below and on the right by a hardwood basketball court design. The player's name appears beneath the photo, while the team name is printed vertically along the right side. The team logo appears in the lower right corner. The backs display a second color player photo as well as biographical and statistical information.

COMPLETE SET (40) 15.00 40.00
1 Charles Barkley 2.00 5.00
2 Muggsy Bogues .60 1.50
3 Derrick Coleman .30 .75
4 Brad Daugherty .20 .50
5 Vlade Divac .40 1.00
6 Clyde Drexler 1.50 4.00
7 Joe Dumars .75 2.00
8 Pervis Ellison .20 .50
9 Patrick Ewing .75 2.00
10 Horace Grant .40 1.00
11 Tim Hardaway .50 1.25
12 Derek Harper .30 .75
13 Hersey Hawkins .30 .75
14 Larry Johnson .40 1.00
15 Michael Jordan 4.00 10.00
16 Shawn Kemp .60 1.50
17 Reggie Lewis .30 .75
18 Karl Malone 2.00 5.00
19 Moses Malone .40 1.00
20 Danny Manning .40 1.00
21 Sarunas Marciulionis .40 1.00
22 Reggie Miller 1.00 2.50
23 Chris Mullin .60 1.50
24 Dikembe Mutombo .75 2.00
25 Hakeem Olajuwon .75 2.00
26 Robert Parish .60 1.50
27 Scottie Pippen 1.50 4.00
28 Mark Price .60 1.50
29 Glen Rice .60 1.50
30 Mitch Richmond .75 2.00
31 David Robinson 2.00 5.00
32 Detlef Schrempf .60 1.50
33 Rony Seikaly .40 1.00
34 Scott Skiles .40 1.00
35 Rik Smits .40 1.00
36 John Stockton 2.50 6.00
37 Isiah Thomas 1.25 3.00
38 Doug West .40 1.00
39 Dominique Wilkins 2.50 6.00
40 James Worthy 1.50 4.00

1994 Upper Deck French McDonald's Team

This 33-card standard-size set was sponsored by McDonald's restaurants and corresponds to the schedule cards (210-236) from the 1993-94 Upper Deck regular series. The cards were available in three-card foil packs, and a six-card hologram set was randomly inserted throughout the packs. The fronts are identical to the regular series cards, while the backs differ insofar as they were redesigned to accommodate bilingual (French and English) text. Two other distinctive features of the back are the card number (1-27) and the holographic anti-counterfeiting mark in the shape of McDonald's golden arches.

COMPLETE SET (33) 60.00 150.00

COMP.TEAM CARD SET (27) 6.00 15.00
COMP.HOLOGRAM SET (6) 50.00 125.00
1 Atlanta Hawks .20 .50
Group
2 Boston Celtics .20 .50
Group
3 Charlotte Hornets .20 .50
Group
4 Chicago Bulls 2.50 6.00
Michael Jordan
5 Cleveland Cavs .30 .75
Mark Price
6 Dallas Mavericks .20 .50
Jim Jackson
7 Denver Nuggets .20 .50
Group
8 Detroit Pistons .30 .75
Isiah Thomas
9 Golden State Warriors .20 .50
Group
10 Houston Rockets .40 1.00
Hakeem Olajuwon
11 Indiana Pacers .25 .60
Rik Smits
12 Los Angeles Clippers .20 .50
Group
13 Los Angeles Lakers .20 .50
Group
14 Miami Heat .20 .50
Group
15 Milwaukee Bucks .20 .50
Group
16 Minnesota Timberwolves .20 .50
Group
17 New Jersey Nets .25 .60
Kenny Anderson
18 New York Knicks .20 .50
Group
19 Orlando Magic .75 2.00
Shaquille O'Neal
20 Philadelphia 76'ers .20 .50
Hersey Hawkins
21 Phoenix Suns .50 1.25
Charles Barkley
Cedric Ceballos
22 Portland Trail Blazers .20 .50
Group
23 Sacramento Kings .30 .75
Mitch Richmond
24 San Antonio Spurs .50 1.25
David Robinson
Sean Elliott
25 Seattle Supersonics .30 .75
Gary Payton
Shawn Kemp
26 Utah Jazz .20 .50
Group
27 Washington Bullets .20 .50
Group
28H Hakeem Olajuwon 6.00 15.00
Hologram
29H Michael Jordan 40.00 100.00
Hologram
30H Charles Barkley 8.00 20.00
Hologram
31H Shawn Kemp 5.00 12.00
Hologram
32H Patrick Ewing 6.00 15.00
Hologram
33H Ron Harper 4.00 10.00
Hologram

1998-99 Upper Deck Game Call

Sold at various retail outlets including Kay-Bee toy stores, this set features a picture of Michael Jordan with a built-in speaker on the back of the card that plays the call of Michael Jordan's 1998 Game 6 and NBA Finals winning shot. While we have five cards checklisted, so far we've only been able to confirm the existance of card number MJ5. If you have any information regarding the first four cards, please email us at basketballmag@beckett.com.

COMMON CARD 4.00 10.00

1999 Upper Deck Kevin Garnett Santa Game Jersey

This one card was sent out as a Christmas card by Upper Deck to various dealers and media outlets. The oversized card features a swatch of a red felt Christmas hat worn by Garnett. The card back features a message from Richard McWilliam and carries a "HH" prefix.

HH2 Kevin Garnett 20.00 50.00

2002-03 Upper Deck Generations

Released in late November 2002, Upper Deck Generations was issued as a 234-card set with UD basketball's first stab at a pack within a pack. Each "pack" actually contained another pack, the outside was the New School pack which features glossy cards and the inside pack was the Old School pack which featured rougher cardboard cards. Generations breaks down as follows: numbers 1-50 were extra glossy veteran cards, numbers 51-92 are glossy RC cards sequentially numbered to 999, numbers 93-192 feature retired players on non-glossy cardboard, and cards 193-234 feature both single and dual player cards, both rookie year players and retired veterans. Cards 193-234 are sequentially numbered to 999. Generations was packaged in 18-pack boxes where packs contained five cards and carried a suggested retail price of $4.99.

COMP.SET w/o SP's (150) 25.00 60.00
51-92 PRINT RUN 999 SER.#'d SETS
1-92 INSERTED IN NEW SCHOOL PACKS
193-234 PRINT RUN 999 SER.#'d SETS
93-192 INSERTED IN NEW SCHOOL PACKS
1 Shareef Abdur-Rahim .25 .60
2 Paul Pierce .30 .75
3 Antoine Walker .25 .60
4 Jalen Rose .25 .60
5 Tyson Chandler .30 .75
6 Darius Miles .20 .50
7 Dirk Nowitzki .50 1.25
8 Steve Nash .40 1.00
9 James Posey .20 .50
10 Richard Hamilton .25 .60
11 Ben Wallace .25 .60
12 Antawn Jamison .30 .75
13 Jason Richardson .30 .75
14 Steve Francis .25 .60
15 Eddie Griffin .20 .50
16 Reggie Miller .30 .75
17 Jamaal Tinsley .20 .50
18 Elton Brand .30 .75
19 Andre Miller .25 .60
20 Kobe Bryant 1.25 3.00
21 Shaquille O'Neal .75 2.00
22 Pau Gasol .40 1.00
23 Shane Battier .30 .75
24 Alonzo Mourning .40 1.00
25 Ray Allen .30 .75
26 Kevin Garnett .50 1.25
27 Wally Szczerbiak .25 .60
28 Jason Kidd .50 1.25
29 Kenyon Martin .25 .60
30 Jamal Mashburn .25 .60
31 Baron Davis .25 .60
32 Latrell Sprewell .25 .60
33 Tracy McGrady .50 1.25
34 Allen Iverson .50 1.25
35 Stephon Marbury .25 .60
36 Shawn Marion .25 .60
37 Rasheed Wallace .30 .75
38 Bonzi Wells .20 .50
39 Chris Webber .30 .75
40 Mike Bibby .30 .75
41 Tim Duncan .60 1.50
42 Tony Parker .40 1.00
43 Gary Payton .30 .75
44 Rashard Lewis .30 .75
45 Vince Carter .50 1.25
46 Morris Peterson .20 .50
47 Karl Malone .40 1.00
48 John Stockton .40 1.00
49 Michael Jordan 3.00 8.00
50 Jerry Stackhouse .25 .60
51 Yao Ming RC 3.00 8.00
52 Jay Williams RC 1.50 4.00
53 Mike Dunleavy RC 1.50 4.00
54 Drew Gooden RC 1.50 4.00
55 Nikoloz Tskitishvili RC 1.00 2.50
56 DaJuan Wagner RC 1.25 3.00
57 Nene Hilario RC 1.50 4.00
58 Chris Wilcox RC 1.25 3.00
59 Amare Stoudemire RC 2.00 5.00
60 Caron Butler RC 1.50 4.00
61 Jared Jeffries RC 1.25 3.00
62 Melvin Ely RC 1.25 3.00
63 Marcus Haislip RC 1.25 3.00
64 Fred Jones RC 1.25 3.00
65 Bostjan Nachbar RC 1.25 3.00
66 Jiri Welsch RC 1.25 3.00
67 Juan Dixon RC 1.50 4.00
68 Curtis Borchardt RC 1.00 2.50
69 Ryan Humphrey RC 1.25 3.00
70 Kareem Rush RC 1.25 3.00
71 Qyntel Woods RC 1.25 3.00
72 Casey Jacobsen RC 1.25 3.00
73 Tayshaun Prince RC 2.00 5.00
74 Predrag Savovic RC 1.25 3.00
75 Frank Williams RC 1.00 2.50
76 John Salmons RC 1.50 4.00
77 Chris Jefferies RC 1.00 2.50
78 Dan Dickau RC 1.25 3.00
79 Marcus Taylor RC 1.50 4.00
80 Roger Mason RC 1.25 3.00
81 Robert Archibald RC 1.00 2.50
82 Vincent Yarbrough RC 1.00 2.50
83 Dan Gadzuric RC 1.25 3.00
84 Carlos Boozer RC 1.50 4.00
85 Tito Maddox RC 1.00 2.50
86 Rod Grizzard RC 1.00 2.50
87 Ronald Murray RC 1.50 4.00
88 Marko Jaric 1.50 4.00
89 Lonny Baxter RC 1.00 2.50
90 Sam Clancy RC 1.25 3.00
91 Matt Barnes RC 2.00 5.00
92 Jamal Sampson RC 1.50 4.00
93 Oscar Robertson .60 1.50
94 Moses Malone .30 .75
95 Earl Monroe .30 .75
96 Pete Maravich .75 2.00
97 Artis Gilmore .25 .60
98 Julius Erving .50 1.25
99 Nate Archibald .25 .60
100 Wes Unseld .30 .75
101 Willis Reed .30 .75
102 Jo Jo White .25 .60
103 Isiah Thomas .30 .75
104 Bill Sharman .30 .75
105 Wilt Chamberlain .60 1.50
106 Bob Cousy .50 1.25
107 Tom Heinsohn .30 .75
108 Terry Cummings .25 .60
109 John Havlicek .40 1.00
110 Bob Pettit .30 .75
111 Drazen Petrovic .30 .75
112 Dan Roundfield .30 .75
113 David Thompson .25 .60
114 Bobby Jones .25 .60
115 Clyde Lovellette .30 .75
116 Rick Barry .25 .60
117 K.C. Jones .30 .75
118 Lionel Hollins .30 .75
119 Bob Lanier .30 .75
120 Al Attles .30 .75
121 Jack Sikma .25 .60
122 George McGinnis .20 .50
123 Quinn Buckner .30 .75
124 Magic Johnson .75 2.00
125 Larry Bird .75 2.00
126 Cliff Hagan .25 .60
127 Jerry Lucas .30 .75
128 Ricky Pierce .20 .50
129 Walter Davis .30 .75
130 Danny Ainge .30 .75
131 Reggie Theus .25 .60
132 Darryl Dawkins .20 .50
133 Tom Chambers .25 .60
134 M.L. Carr .30 .75
135 Kelly Tripucka .20 .50
136 George Gervin .40 1.00
137 Robert Parish .40 1.00
138 Mitch Kupchak .30 .75
139 Lou Hudson .30 .75
140 Bill Cartwright .25 .60
141 Lafayette Lever .25 .60
142 Kevin Loughery .30 .75
143 Hal Greer .30 .75
144 Jamaal Wilkes .30 .75
145 Alvan Adams .20 .50
146 Thomas Sanders .30 .75
147 Cazzie Russell .25 .60
148 Austin Carr .30 .75
149 Gail Goodrich .25 .60
150 Billy Knight .30 .75
151 Dave Bing .30 .75
152 Bill Walton .30 .75
153 Sam Jones .30 .75
154 Swen Nater .30 .75
155 Bobby Dandridge .20 .50
156 Junior Bridgeman .20 .50
157 Paul Silas .30 .75
158 John Kerr .30 .75
159 Phil Chenier .20 .50
160 Alex English .25 .60
161 Geoff Petrie .30 .75
162 Walt Bellamy .25 .60
163 Don Nelson .30 .75
164 Byron Scott .25 .60
165 Harvey Catchings .30 .75
166 Ed Macauley .30 .75
167 John Drew .30 .75
168 Detlef Schrempf .30 .75
169 Rolando Blackman .25 .60
170 Dave DeBusschere .30 .75
171 Marvin Barnes .30 .75
172 Elgin Baylor .30 .75
173 Cedric Maxwell .20 .50
174 Vern Mikkelsen .30 .75
175 Larry Brown .30 .75
176 Rick Mahorn .20 .50
177 Dolph Schayes .30 .75
178 Kevin McHale .40 1.00
179 Clark Kellogg .30 .75
180 Otis Birdsong .25 .60
181 Michael Cooper .25 .60
182 Mike Dunleavy .30 .75
183 Spencer Haywood .20 .50
184 Larry Nance .25 .60
185 Maurice Lucas .30 .75
186 Fred Brown .20 .50
187 Jerry West .40 1.00
188 Joe Barry Carroll .30 .75
189 Dave Cowens .20 .50
190 Sidney Moncrief .20 .50
191 Kiki Vandeweghe .25 .60
192 Walt Frazier .30 .75
193 Y.Ming/W.Chamberlain 4.00 10.00
194 J.Williams/J.Erving 2.50 6.00
195 M.Dunleavy/M.Dunleavy 2.50 6.00
196 D.Gooden/J.Havlicek 3.00 8.00
197 N.Tskitishvili/K.McHale 1.50 4.00
198 D.Wagner/O.Robertson 1.50 4.00
199 N.Hilario/K.Vandeweghe 2.50 6.00
200 Chris Wilcox 1.25 3.00
201 A.Stoudamire/G.McGinnis 5.00 12.00
202 C.Butler/W.Reed 2.50 6.00
203 J.Jeffries/L.Bird 2.00 5.00
204 M.Ely/E.Baylor 1.50 4.00
205 M.Haislip/K.Abdul-Jabbar 1.50 4.00
206 F.Jones/K.C.Jones 1.50 4.00
207 Bostian Nachbar 1.25 3.00
208 Jiri Welsch 1.25 3.00
209 Juan Dixon 1.50 4.00
210 Curtis Borchardt 1.00 2.50
211 R.Humphrey/B.Lanier 1.50 4.00
212 K.Rush/W.Frazier 1.50 4.00
213 Q.Woods/J.Wilkes 1.50 4.00
214 C.Jacobsen/T.Chambers 1.50 4.00
215 T.Prince/B.Scott 2.00 5.00
216 P.Savovic/D.Petrovic 1.50 4.00
217 Frank Williams 1.00 2.50
218 J.Salmons/E.Baylor 1.50 4.00
219 C.Jefferies/W.Davis 1.50 4.00
220 Dan Dickau 1.25 3.00
221 M.Taylor/O.Robertson 1.50 4.00
222 R.Mason/J.White 1.50 4.00
223 R.Archibald/S.Moncrief 1.50 4.00
224 V.Yarbrough/E.Monroe 1.50 4.00
225 D.Gadzuric/B.Walton 1.50 4.00
226 C.Boozer/R.Parish 3.00 8.00
227 Tito Maddox 1.00 2.50
228 R.Grizzard/G.Gervin 1.50 4.00
229 R.Murray/L.Lever 1.50 4.00
230 Marko Jaric 1.50 4.00
231 Lonny Baxter 1.00 2.50
232 S.Clancy/W.Unseld 1.50 4.00
233 Matt Barnes 2.00 5.00
234 Jamal Sampson 1.50 4.00

2002-03 Upper Deck Generations All-Time Authentics

Randomly inserted in packs at the rate of one in 18 Old School, this 27-card set features a horizontal design on which player photos appear on the right and an "A" shaped swatch of game worn material appears on the left.

STATED ODDS 1:18 OLD SCHOOL
AMA Alonzo Mourning 5.00 12.00
BCA Bob Cousy 12.00 30.00
BWA Bill Walton 6.00 15.00
CDA Clyde Drexler 5.00 12.00
DRA David Robinson 6.00 15.00
GPA Gary Payton 4.00 10.00
JEA Julius Erving Blue 15.00 30.00
JE2A Julius Erving White 15.00 30.00
JKA Jason Kidd 6.00 15.00
JSA John Stockton 5.00 12.00
KAA Kareem Abdul-Jabbar 8.00 20.00
KBA Kobe Bryant 12.00 30.00
KMA Karl Malone 5.00 12.00
LBA Larry Bird 10.00 25.00
MCA Kevin McHale 5.00 12.00
MGA Magic Johnson Yellow 8.00 20.00
MG2A Magic Johnson White 8.00 20.00
MJA Michael Jordan Warm 30.00 80.00
MJ2A Michael Jordan Shirt 60.00 150.00
MRA Mitch Richmond 4.00 10.00
ORA Oscar Robertson 10.00 25.00
RBA Rick Barry 5.00 12.00
RMA Reggie Miller 4.00 10.00
SPA Scottie Pippen 10.00 25.00
TAA Nate Archibald Green 3.00 8.00
TA2A Nate Archibald White 3.00 8.00
WCA Wilt Chamberlain 30.00 80.00

2002-03 Upper Deck Generations All-Time Dual Autographs

Inserted randomly in Old School packs, this 10-card set is also horizontally designed with a player in the top left corner and one in the bottom right corner next to authentic player autographs. Each card is sequentially numbered to 25.

PRINT RUN 25 SER.#'d SETS
DT/GG D.Thompson/G.Gervin 25.00 60.00
DW/JR Wilkins/J.Richardson 60.00 120.00
EB/KM E.Baylor/K.Martin 25.00 60.00
KA/TC Abdul-Jabbar/Chandler 100.00 200.00
LB/MM L.Bird/M.Miller 125.00 250.00
MG/JK M.Johnson/J.Kidd 150.00 300.00
MJ/KB M.Jordan/K.Bryant 600.00 1000.00
WF/DJ W.Frazier/D.Johnson 25.00 60.00

2002-03 Upper Deck Generations All-Time Dual Jerseys

Inserted in Old School packs, this seven card set is utilizes the same design as the All-Time Dual Autographs insert set with player photos pushed closer to the middle of the card and two swatches of memorabilia on the left and right side of the card.

PRINT RUN 100 SER.#'d SETS
RANDOM INSERTS IN OLD SCHOOL PACKS
JEAIJ J.Erving/A.Iverson 30.00 60.00
JELBJ J.Erving/L.Bird 60.00 150.00
MGLBJ M.Johnson/L.Bird 40.00 100.00
MJJEJ M.Jordan/J.Erving 50.00 100.00
MJKBJ M.Jordan/K.Bryant 50.00 120.00
MJMGJ M.Jordan/M.Johnson 60.00 150.00
WCBRJ Chamberlain/Russell 75.00 150.00

2002-03 Upper Deck Generations Reel Time Jersey

Inserted in packs at the rate of one in 18 New School, this 20-card set has blueish-silver borders along the top and bottom, a black strip throught the middle of the horozontal design-left to right, full color player photos on the left and a swatch of game worn memorabilia on the right.

STATED ODDS 1:18 NEW SCHOOL
AIJ Allen Iverson 5.00 12.00
AWJ Antoine Walker 2.50 6.00
BDJ Baron Davis 2.50 6.00
CWJ Chris Webber 3.00 8.00
DNJ Dirk Nowitzki 5.00 12.00
EBJ Elton Brand 3.00 8.00
JKJ Jason Kidd 5.00 12.00
JOJ Jermaine O'Neal 2.50 6.00
JSJ Jerry Stackhouse 2.50 6.00
KBJ Kobe Bryant 12.50 30.00
KGJ Kevin Garnett 5.00 12.00
KMJ Kenyon Martin 2.50 6.00
MBJ Mike Bibby 3.00 8.00
MCJ Antonio McDyess 2.50 6.00
MJJ Michael Jordan 30.00 60.00
PPJ Paul Pierce 3.00 8.00
SFJ Steve Francis 2.50 6.00
SMJ Stephon Marbury 2.50 6.00
TCJ Tyson Chandler 3.00 8.00
TMJ Tracy McGrady 5.00 12.00

2002-03 Upper Deck Generations Signature Classics

Inserted in packs at the rate of one in 54 Old School, this 26-card set uses a horizontal design with red borders along the top and bottom of the card, a centered player portrait photo along the top and an authentic player autograph.

STATED ODDS 1:54 OLD SCHOOL
AES Alex English 8.00 20.00
BCS Bob Cousy 30.00 80.00
BWS Bill Walton 8.00 20.00
BYS Byron Scott 8.00 20.00
CDS Clyde Drexler 12.00 30.00
DTS David Thompson 8.00 20.00
DWS Dominique Wilkins 12.00 30.00
EBS Elgin Baylor 12.50 30.00
GGS George Gervin 10.00 25.00
JES Julius Erving 50.00 100.00
JHS John Havlicek 20.00 50.00
JMS Jerome Moiso 4.00 10.00
KAS Kareem Abdul-Jabbar 30.00 80.00
LBS Larry Bird 75.00 150.00
MGS Magic Johnson 60.00 120.00
MJS Michael Jordan 350.00 650.00
MMS Mike Miller 5.00 12.00
NAS Nate Archibald 8.00 20.00
QRS Quentin Richardson 4.00 10.00
RBS Rick Barry 10.00 25.00
RMS Ron Mercer 4.00 10.00
SAS Shareef Abdur-Rahim 6.00 15.00
TBS Terrell Brandon 4.00 10.00
WFS Walt Frazier 8.00 20.00

1996 Upper Deck German Kellogg's

This 40-card set was packaged three per German Kellogg's Frosties or Chocos box. The cards are similar in design to the 1995-96 Upper Deck American cards. The only difference is the cards lack the gold foil on the player's name. Card backs are identical to the American release.

COMPLETE SET (40) 40.00 100.00
CHECKLIST (NNO) .75 2.00
1 Jerry Stackhouse 3.00 8.00
2 Clifford Robinson 1.50 4.00
3 Glenn Robinson 2.00 5.00
4 Chris Webber 3.00 8.00
5 Dennis Rodman 5.00 12.00
6 Scottie Pippen 4.00 10.00
7 Toni Kukoc 2.50 6.00
8 Dan Majerle 2.50 6.00
9 Dino Radja 1.50 4.00
10 Loy Vaught 1.50 4.00
11 Bryant Reeves 1.50 4.00
12 Stacey Augmon 2.00 5.00
13 Kevin Willis 1.50 4.00
14 Muggsy Bogues 2.00 5.00
15 John Stockton 3.00 8.00
16 Karl Malone 3.00 8.00
17 Mitch Richmond 2.50 6.00
18 Charles Oakley 2.00 5.00
19 Nick Van Exel 2.50 6.00
20 Anfernee Hardaway 4.00 10.00
21 Horace Grant 2.00 5.00
22 Jason Kidd 4.00 10.00
23 Ed O'Bannon 1.50 4.00
24 Dikembe Mutombo 2.50 6.00
25 Dale Davis 1.50 4.00
26 Derrick McKey 1.50 4.00
27 Mark Jackson 2.50 6.00
28 Rik Smits 2.00 5.00
29 Grant Hill 4.00 10.00
30 Damon Stoudamire 2.00 5.00
31 Clyde Drexler 3.00 8.00
32 Hakeem Olajuwon 3.00 8.00
33 Detlef Schrempf 2.50 6.00
34 Gary Payton 2.50 6.00
35 Hersey Hawkins 1.50 4.00
36 Sam Perkins 1.50 4.00
37 David Robinson 4.00 10.00
38 Charles Barkley 4.00 10.00
39 Christian Laettner 2.00 5.00
40 B.J. Armstrong 1.50 4.00

1999-00 Upper Deck Gold Reserve

The 1999-00 Upper Deck Gold Reserve product was released as a retail-only product in late March,2000. The 270-card set features 240 player cards and a 30-card rookie subset that is serial numbered to 3500. Each pack contained 10-cards and carried a suggested retail price of 2.99.

COMPLETE SET (270) 60.00 120.00
COMPLETE SET w/o RC (240) 15.00 40.00
241-270 PRINT RUN 3500 SERIAL #'d SETS
MAXWELL CARD #294 SHOULD BE #204
1 Roshown McLeod .20 .50
2 Dikembe Mutombo .30 .75
3 Alan Henderson .20 .50
4 Chris Crawford .20 .50
5 Jim Jackson .20 .50
6 Isaiah Rider .25 .60
7 Lorenzen Wright .20 .50
8 Bimbo Coles .20 .50
9 Kenny Anderson .25 .60
10 Antoine Walker .30 .75
11 Paul Pierce .40 1.00
12 Vitaly Potapenko .20 .50
13 Dana Barros .20 .50
14 Calbert Cheaney .20 .50
15 Pervis Ellison .20 .50
16 Eric Williams .20 .50
17 Tony Battie .25 .60
18 Elden Campbell .20 .50
19 Eddie Jones .30 .75
20 David Wesley .20 .50
21 Derrick Coleman .25 .60
22 Ricky Davis .30 .75
23 Anthony Mason .20 .50
24 Todd Fuller .20 .50
25 Brad Miller .25 .60
26 Corey Benjamin .20 .50
27 Randy Brown .20 .50
28 Dickey Simpkins .20 .50
29 Toni Kukoc .30 .75
30 Fred Hoiberg .20 .50
31 Hersey Hawkins .20 .50
32 Will Perdue .20 .50
33 Chris Anstey .20 .50
34 Shawn Kemp .30 .75
35 Wesley Person .20 .50
36 Brevin Knight .20 .50
37 Bob Sura .20 .50
38 Danny Ferry .20 .50
39 Lamond Murray .20 .50
40 Cedric Henderson .20 .50
41 Andrew DeClercq .20 .50
42 Michael Finley .30 .75
43 Shawn Bradley .20 .50
44 Dirk Nowitzki .60 1.50
45 Erick Strickland .20 .50
46 Cedric Ceballos .20 .50
47 Hubert Davis .20 .50
48 Robert Pack .20 .50
49 Gary Trent .20 .50
50 Antonio McDyess .25 .60
51 Nick Van Exel .25 .60
52 Chauncey Billups .30 .75
53 Bryant Stith .20 .50
54 Raef LaFrentz .25 .60
55 Ron Mercer .25 .60
56 George McCloud .20 .50
57 Roy Rogers .20 .50
58 Keon Clark .20 .50
59 Grant Hill .40 1.00
60 Lindsey Hunter .20 .50
61 Jerry Stackhouse .30 .75
62 Terry Mills .20 .50
63 Michael Curry .20 .50
64 Christian Laettner .25 .60
65 Jerome Williams .20 .50
66 Loy Vaught .20 .50
67 John Starks .25 .60
68 Antawn Jamison .30 .75
69 Erick Dampier .20 .50
70 Jason Caffey .20 .50
71 Terry Cummings .25 .60
72 Donyell Marshall .20 .50
73 Chris Mills .20 .50
74 Tony Farmer .20 .50
75 Adonal Foyle .20 .50
76 Hakeem Olajuwon .40 1.00
77 Cuttino Mobley .20 .50
78 Charles Barkley .50 1.25
79 Bryce Drew .20 .50
80 Shandon Anderson .20 .50
81 Kelvin Cato .20 .50
82 Walt Williams .20 .50
83 Carlos Rogers .20 .50
84 Reggie Miller .30 .75
85 Jalen Rose .25 .60
86 Mark Jackson .25 .60
87 Dale Davis .20 .50
88 Chris Mullin .30 .75
89 Al Harrington .30 .75
90 Rik Smits .30 .75
91 Sam Perkins .20 .50
92 Austin Croshere .20 .50
93 Maurice Taylor .20 .50
94 Tyrone Nesby RC .25 .60
95 Michael Olowokandi .20 .50
96 Eric Piatkowski .25 .60
97 Troy Hudson .30 .75
98 Derek Anderson .20 .50
99 Eric Murdock .20 .50
100 Brian Skinner .20 .50
101 Kobe Bryant 1.25 3.00
102 Shaquille O'Neal .75 2.00
103 Glen Rice .30 .75
104 Robert Horry .25 .60
105 Ron Harper .20 .50
106 Derek Fisher .30 .75
107 Rick Fox .20 .50
108 A.C. Green .25 .60
109 Tim Hardaway .30 .75
110 Alonzo Mourning .40 1.00
111 P.J. Brown .20 .50
112 Dan Majerle .30 .75
113 Jamal Mashburn .25 .60
114 Voshon Lenard .20 .50
115 Clarence Weatherspoon .20 .50
116 Rex Walters .20 .50
117 Ray Allen .30 .75
118 Glenn Robinson .25 .60
119 Sam Cassell .25 .60
120 Robert Traylor .20 .50
121 J.R. Reid .20 .50
122 Ervin Johnson .20 .50
123 Danny Manning .25 .60
124 Tim Thomas .25 .60
125 Kevin Garnett .50 1.25
126 Sam Mitchell .20 .50
127 Dean Garrett .20 .50
128 Bobby Jackson .20 .50
129 Radoslav Nesterovic .30 .75
130 Terrell Brandon .20 .50
131 Joe Smith .25 .60
132 Anthony Peeler .20 .50
133 Keith Van Horn .25 .60
134 Stephon Marbury .25 .60
135 Kendall Gill .20 .50
136 Scott Burrell .20 .50
137 Jayson Williams .20 .50
138 Jamie Feick RC .25 .60
139 Kerry Kittles .20 .50
140 Johnny Newman .20 .50
141 Patrick Ewing .40 1.00
142 Allan Houston .25 .60
143 Latrell Sprewell .30 .75
144 Larry Johnson .30 .75
145 Marcus Camby .25 .60
146 Chris Childs .20 .50
147 Kurt Thomas .20 .50
148 Charlie Ward .20 .50
149 Darrell Armstrong .20 .50
150 Matt Harpring .20 .50
151 Michael Doleac .20 .50
152 Bo Outlaw .20 .50
153 Tariq Abdul-Wahad .20 .50
154 John Amaechi RC .30 .75
155 Ben Wallace .25 .60
156 Monty Williams .20 .50
157 Allen Iverson .60 1.50
158 Theo Ratliff .25 .60
159 Larry Hughes .25 .60
160 Eric Snow .25 .60
161 George Lynch .20 .50
162 Tyrone Hill .20 .50
163 Billy Owens .20 .50
164 Aaron McKie .20 .50
165 Jason Kidd .50 1.25
166 Clifford Robinson .20 .50
167 Tom Gugliotta .20 .50
168 Luc Longley .25 .60
169 Anfernee Hardaway .50 1.25
170 Rex Chapman .20 .50
171 Oliver Miller .20 .50
172 Rodney Rogers .20 .50
173 Rasheed Wallace .30 .75
174 Arvydas Sabonis .25 .60
175 Damon Stoudamire .25 .60
176 Brian Grant .20 .50
177 Scottie Pippen .50 1.25
178 Detlef Schrempf .25 .60
179 Steve Smith .25 .60
180 Jermaine O'Neal .25 .60
181 Bonzi Wells .20 .50
182 Jason Williams .40 1.00
183 Vlade Divac .30 .75
184 Peja Stojakovic .30 .75
185 Lawrence Funderburke .20 .50
186 Chris Webber .30 .75
187 Nick Anderson .20 .50
188 Darrick Martin .20 .50
189 Corliss Williamson .20 .50
190 Tim Duncan .60 1.50
191 Sean Elliott .30 .75
192 David Robinson .50 1.25
193 Mario Elie .20 .50
194 Avery Johnson .25 .60
195 Terry Porter .20 .50
196 Malik Rose .20 .50
197 Jaren Jackson .20 .50
198 Gary Payton .30 .75
199 Vin Baker .25 .60
200 Rashard Lewis .30 .75
201 Jelani McCoy .20 .50
202 Brent Barry .25 .60
203 Horace Grant .25 .60
204 Vernon Maxwell UER .20 .50
205 Ruben Patterson .20 .50
206 Vince Carter .60 1.50
207 Doug Christie .25 .60
208 Kevin Willis .20 .50
209 Dee Brown .20 .50
210 Antonio Davis .20 .50
211 Tracy McGrady .50 1.25
212 Dell Curry .20 .50
213 Charles Oakley .25 .60
214 Karl Malone .40 1.00
215 John Stockton .40 1.00
216 Howard Eisley .20 .50
217 Bryon Russell .20 .50
218 Greg Ostertag .20 .50
219 Jeff Hornacek .25 .60
220 Olden Polynice .20 .50
221 Adam Keefe .20 .50
222 Shareef Abdur-Rahim .25 .60
223 Mike Bibby .30 .75
224 Felipe Lopez .20 .50
225 Cherokee Parks .20 .50
226 Michael Dickerson .20 .50
227 Othella Harrington .20 .50
228 Bryant Reeves .20 .50
229 Brent Price .20 .50
230 Michael Smith .20 .50
231 Juwan Howard .25 .60
232 Rod Strickland .20 .50
233 Chris Whitney .20 .50
234 Tracy Murray .20 .50
235 Mitch Richmond .30 .75
236 Aaron Williams .20 .50
237 Isaac Austin .20 .50
238 Kobe Bryant CL 1.25 3.00
239 Michael Jordan CL 2.50 6.00
240 Kevin Garnett CL .50 1.25
241 Elton Brand RC 2.00 5.00
242 Steve Francis RC 2.00 5.00
243 Baron Davis RC 2.00 5.00
244 Lamar Odom RC 2.00 5.00
245 Jonathan Bender RC .75 2.00
246 Wally Szczerbiak RC 1.50 4.00
247 Richard Hamilton RC 1.50 4.00
248 Andre Miller RC 1.50 4.00
249 Shawn Marion RC 1.50 4.00
250 Jason Terry RC 1.25 3.00
251 Trajan Langdon RC .75 2.00
252 A.Radojevic RC .50 1.25
253 Corey Maggette RC 1.25 3.00
254 William Avery RC .60 1.50
255 Ron Artest RC 1.50 4.00
256 Cal Bowdler RC .50 1.25
257 James Posey RC .75 2.00
258 Quincy Lewis RC .50 1.25
259 Dion Glover RC .60 1.50
260 Jeff Foster RC .75 2.00
261 Kenny Thomas RC .75 2.00
262 Devean George RC .75 2.00
263 Tim James RC .50 1.25
264 Vonteego Cummings RC .50 1.25
265 Jumaine Jones RC .60 1.50
266 Scott Padgett RC .60 1.50
267 Rodney Buford RC .75 2.00
268 Adrian Griffin RC .75 2.00
269 Anthony Carter RC .60 1.50
270 Eddie Robinson RC .75 2.00

1999-00 Upper Deck Gold Reserve Gold Mine

Randomly inserted in packs at one in 11, this 15-card insert set features some of the NBA's greatest players. Card backs carry a "R" prefix.

COMPLETE SET (15) 10.00 25.00
STATED ODDS 1:11
R1 Kobe Bryant 2.50 6.00
R2 Vince Carter 1.25 3.00
R3 Steve Francis 1.50 4.00
R4 Kevin Garnett 1.00 2.50
R5 Elton Brand 1.50 4.00
R6 Gary Payton .60 1.50
R7 Lamar Odom 1.50 4.00
R8 Grant Hill .75 2.00
R9 Jason Williams .75 2.00
R10 Shareef Abdur-Rahim .50 1.25
R11 Tim Duncan 1.25 3.00
R12 Keith Van Horn .50 1.25
R13 Tim Hardaway .60 1.50
R14 Karl Malone .75 2.00
R15 Shaquille O'Neal 1.50 4.00

1999-00 Upper Deck Gold Reserve Gold Strike

Randomly inserted in packs at one in four, this insert set features 15 of the NBA's rising stars. Card backs carry a "GS" prefix.

COMPLETE SET (15) 6.00 15.00
STATED ODDS 1:4
GS1 Kevin Garnett .60 1.50
GS2 Kobe Bryant 1.50 4.00
GS3 Tim Duncan .75 2.00
GS4 Adrian Griffin .40 1.00
GS5 Lamar Odom 1.00 2.50
GS6 Jason Kidd .60 1.50
GS7 Wally Szczerbiak .75 2.00
GS8 Stephon Marbury .30 .75
GS9 Shaquille O'Neal 1.00 2.50
GS10 Elton Brand 1.00 2.50
GS11 Allen Iverson .75 2.00
GS12 Shawn Marion .75 2.00
GS13 Jason Williams .50 1.25
GS14 Antonio McDyess .30 .75
GS15 Vince Carter .75 2.00

1999-00 Upper Deck Gold Reserve UD Authentics

Randomly inserted in packs at one in 480, this 10-card insert set features autographed cards of some of the hottest players in the NBA. Card backs are numbered using the player's initials.

STATED ODDS 1:480
AH Anfernee Hardaway 50.00 120.00
AW Antoine Walker 4.00 10.00
BD Baron Davis 8.00 20.00
JB Jonathan Bender 3.00 8.00
JT Jason Terry 5.00 12.00
KB Kobe Bryant 150.00 325.00
KG Kevin Garnett 100.00 200.00
RH Richard Hamilton 6.00 15.00
SF Steve Francis 8.00 20.00
WS Wally Szczerbiak 6.00 15.00

1993-94 Upper Deck Golden Grahams French

1 Charles Barkley 4.00 10.00
2 Alonzo Mourning 4.00 10.00
3 Billy Owens 1.50 4.00
4 Patrick Ewing 3.00 8.00
5 Toni Kukoc 6.00 15.00
6 Hakeem Olajuwon 3.00 8.00
7 Dan Majerle 2.50 6.00
8 Larry Johnson 2.50 6.00
9 John Stockton 3.00 8.00
10 Christian Laettner 2.00 5.00
11 Dominique Wilkins 3.00 8.00
12 Detlef Schrempf 2.50 6.00
13 Shawn Kemp 3.00 8.00
14 Derrick Coleman 2.00 5.00
15 Shaquille O'Neal 10.00 25.00
16 Clyde Drexler 3.00 8.00
17 David Robinson 4.00 10.00
18 Tom Gugliotta 2.00 5.00
19 Mark Price 2.50 6.00
20 Sean Elliott 2.50 6.00
21 Reggie Miller 3.00 8.00
22 Todd Day 1.50 4.00
23 Mitch Richmond 2.50 6.00
24 Jim Jackson 2.00 5.00
25 Mahmoud Abdul-Rauf 1.50 4.00
26 Danny Manning 2.00 5.00
27 Doug Christie 1.50 4.00
28 Chris Webber 12.00 30.00
29 Anfernee Hardaway 12.00 30.00
30 Karl Malone 3.00 8.00
31 Jamal Mashburn 4.00 10.00
32 Shawn Bradley 2.50 6.00
33 Dino Radja 2.50 6.00
34 Ken Norman 1.50 4.00
35 Harold Miner 1.50 4.00
36 John Starks 2.00 5.00
37 Dale Ellis 1.50 4.00
38 Glen Rice 2.50 6.00
39 Clarence Weatherspoon 1.50 4.00
40 Dee Brown 1.50 4.00

1993-94 Upper Deck Golden Grahams German

1 Charles Barkley 8.00 20.00
2 Alonzo Mourning 8.00 20.00
3 Billy Owens 3.00 8.00
4 Patrick Ewing 6.00 15.00
5 Toni Kukoc 12.00 30.00
6 Hakeem Olajuwon 6.00 15.00
7 Dan Majerle 5.00 12.00
8 Larry Johnson 5.00 12.00
9 John Stockton 6.00 15.00
10 Christian Laettner 4.00 10.00
11 Dominique Wilkins 6.00 15.00
12 Detlef Schrempf 5.00 12.00
13 Shawn Kemp 6.00 15.00
14 Derrick Coleman 4.00 10.00
15 Shaquille O'Neal 20.00 50.00
16 Clyde Drexler 6.00 15.00
17 David Robinson 8.00 20.00
18 Tom Gugliotta 4.00 10.00
19 Mark Price 5.00 12.00
20 Sean Elliott 5.00 12.00
21 Reggie Miller 6.00 15.00
22 Todd Day 3.00 8.00
23 Mitch Richmond 5.00 12.00
24 Jim Jackson 4.00 10.00
25 Mahmoud Abdul-Rauf 3.00 8.00
26 Danny Manning 4.00 10.00
27 Doug Christie 3.00 8.00
28 Chris Webber 25.00 60.00
29 Anfernee Hardaway 25.00 60.00
30 Karl Malone 6.00 15.00
31 Jamal Mashburn 8.00 20.00
32 Shawn Bradley 5.00 12.00
33 Dino Radja 5.00 12.00
34 Ken Norman 3.00 8.00
35 Harold Miner 3.00 8.00
36 John Starks 4.00 10.00
37 Dale Ellis 3.00 8.00
38 Glen Rice 5.00 12.00
39 Clarence Weatherspoon 3.00 8.00
40 Dee Brown 3.00 8.00

1993-94 Upper Deck Golden Grahams Italian

1 Charles Barkley 8.00 20.00
2 Alonzo Mourning 8.00 20.00
3 Billy Owens 3.00 8.00
4 Patrick Ewing 6.00 15.00
5 Toni Kukoc 12.00 30.00
6 Hakeem Olajuwon 6.00 15.00
7 Dan Majerle 5.00 12.00
8 Larry Johnson 5.00 12.00
9 John Stockton 6.00 15.00
10 Christian Laettner 4.00 10.00
11 Dominique Wilkins 6.00 15.00
12 Detlef Schrempf 5.00 12.00
13 Shawn Kemp 6.00 15.00
14 Derrick Coleman 4.00 10.00
15 Shaquille O'Neal 20.00 50.00
16 Clyde Drexler 6.00 15.00
17 David Robinson 8.00 20.00
18 Tom Gugliotta 4.00 10.00
19 Mark Price 5.00 12.00
20 Sean Elliott 5.00 12.00
21 Reggie Miller 6.00 15.00
22 Todd Day 3.00 8.00
23 Mitch Richmond 5.00 12.00
24 Jim Jackson 4.00 10.00
25 Mahmoud Abdul-Rauf 3.00 8.00
26 Danny Manning 4.00 10.00
27 Doug Christie 3.00 8.00
28 Chris Webber 25.00 60.00
29 Anfernee Hardaway 25.00 60.00
30 Karl Malone 6.00 15.00
31 Jamal Mashburn 8.00 20.00
32 Shawn Bradley 5.00 12.00

33 Dino Radja 5.00 12.00
34 Ken Norman 3.00 8.00
35 Harold Miner 3.00 8.00
36 John Starks 4.00 10.00
37 Dale Ellis 3.00 8.00
38 Glen Rice 5.00 12.00
39 Clarence Weatherspoon 3.00 8.00
40 Dee Brown 3.00 8.00

1993-94 Upper Deck Golden Grahams Portuguese

1 Charles Barkley 10.00 25.00
2 Alonzo Mourning 10.00 25.00
3 Billy Owens 4.00 10.00
4 Patrick Ewing 8.00 20.00
5 Toni Kukoc 15.00 40.00
6 Hakeem Olajuwon 8.00 20.00
7 Dan Majerle 6.00 15.00
8 Larry Johnson 6.00 15.00
9 John Stockton 8.00 20.00
10 Christian Laettner 5.00 12.00
11 Dominique Wilkins 8.00 20.00
12 Detlef Schrempf 6.00 15.00
13 Shawn Kemp 8.00 20.00
14 Derrick Coleman 5.00 12.00
15 Shaquille O'Neal 25.00 60.00
16 Clyde Drexler 8.00 20.00
17 David Robinson 10.00 25.00
18 Tom Gugliotta 5.00 12.00
19 Mark Price 6.00 15.00
20 Sean Elliott 6.00 15.00
21 Reggie Miller 8.00 20.00
22 Todd Day 4.00 10.00
23 Mitch Richmond 6.00 15.00
24 Jim Jackson 5.00 12.00
25 Mahmoud Abdul-Rauf 4.00 10.00
26 Danny Manning 5.00 12.00
27 Doug Christie 4.00 10.00
28 Chris Webber 30.00 80.00
29 Anfernee Hardaway 30.00 80.00
30 Karl Malone 8.00 20.00
31 Jamal Mashburn 10.00 25.00
32 Shawn Bradley 6.00 15.00
33 Dino Radja 6.00 15.00
34 Ken Norman 4.00 10.00
35 Harold Miner 4.00 10.00
36 John Starks 5.00 12.00
37 Dale Ellis 4.00 10.00
38 Glen Rice 6.00 15.00
39 Clarence Weatherspoon 4.00 10.00
40 Dee Brown 4.00 10.00

2009 Upper Deck Goodwin Champions Preview

RANDOM INSERTS IN PACKS
GCP8 Michael Jordan 6.00 15.00

2009 Upper Deck Goodwin Champions

COMMON CARD (1-150) .15 .40
COMMON NIGHT 5.00 12.00
COMMON SP (151-190) 1.25 3.00
151-190 STATED ODDS 1:2 HOBBY
COMMON SUPER SP (191-210) 1.50 4.00
SUPER SP MINORS 1.50 4.00
SUPER SP SEMIS 1.50 4.00
SUPER SP UNLISTED 1.50 4.00
191-210 STATED ODDS 1:10 HOBBY
PLATES RANDOMLY INSERTED
PLATE PRINT RUN 1 SET PER COLOR
BLACK-CYAN-MAGENTA-YELLOW ISSUED
NO PLATE PRICING DUE TO SCARCITY
24 O.J. Mayo .20 .50
61 Michael Beasley .40 1.00
73 LeBron James 1.50 4.00
111 Kevin Garnett .60 1.50
114 Michael Jordan 1.00 2.50
143 Derrick Rose .50 1.25

2009 Upper Deck Goodwin Champions Mini

COMPLETE SET (192) 75.00 150.00
*MINI 1-150: 1X TO 2.5X BASIC
APPX.MINI ODDS ONE PER PACK
PLATES RANDOMLY INSERTED
PLATE PRINT RUN 1 SET PER COLOR
BLACK-CYAN-MAGENTA-YELLOW ISSUED
NO PLATE PRICING DUE TO SCARCITY

2009 Upper Deck Goodwin Champions Mini Black Border

*MINI BLK 1-150: 1.5X TO 4X BASE
*MINI BLK 211-252: .75X TO 2X MINI
RANDOM INSERTS IN PACKS

2009 Upper Deck Goodwin Champions Mini Foil

*MINI FOIL 1-150: 3X TO 8X BASE
*MINI FOIL 211-252: 1.5X TO 4X MINI
RANDOM INSERTS IN PACKS
ANNCD PRINT RUN OF 88 TOTAL SETS

2009 Upper Deck Goodwin Champions Autographs

STATED ODDS 1:20 HOBBY
EXCHANGE DEADLINE 8/31/2011
GK Kevin Garnett/25 * 50.00 100.00
MJ Michael Jordan/23 * 500.00 700.00

2009 Upper Deck Goodwin Champions Memorabilia

STATED ODDS 1:10 HOBBY
EXCHANGE DEADLINE 8/31/2011
DR Derrick Rose 5.00 12.00
KG Kevin Garnett 6.00 15.00
LJ LeBron James 15.00 40.00
MB Michael Beasley 4.00 10.00
MJ Michael Jordan/50 * 30.00 60.00
OM O.J. Mayo 2.00 5.00

2011 Upper Deck Goodwin Champions

COMP.SET w/o VAR (210) 40.00 80.00
COMP.SET w/o SP's (150) 10.00 25.00
COMMON SP (151-190) 1.00 2.50
151-190 SP ODDS 1:3 HOBBY
COMMON SP (191-210) 1.50 4.00
191-210 SP ODDS 1:12 HOBBY
COMMON VARIATION SP 4.00 10.00
2 John Havlicek .25 .60
6 LeBron James 1.25 3.00
7 Rick Barry .25 .60
8 Walt Frazier .25 .60
23A Michael Jordan 1.50 4.00
23B Jordan Lightning SP 12.50 30.00
33 Cynthia Cooper .30 .75
35 Hakeem Olajuwon .30 .75
37 Larry Bird .60 1.50
44 Alonzo Mourning .30 .75
45 John Stockton .40 1.00
53 Bill Laimbeer .25 .60
54 Dennis Rodman .40 1.00
55 Bill Walton .25 .60
60 Bill Russell .40 1.00
88 Jerry West .30 .75
90 Magic Johnson .60 1.50
100 Candace Parker .40 1.00
105 David Robinson .40 1.00
106 Tim Hardaway .25 .60
111 Derrick Rose .60 1.50
114 Greg Monroe .40 1.00
115 James Worthy .30 .75
121 Russell Westbrook .30 .75
135 Anfernee Hardaway .60 1.50
137 Chris Paul .40 1.00
138 Julius Erving .50 1.25
143 Derrick Favors .50 1.25
145 Clyde Drexler .30 .75
147A Grant Hill .25 .60
147B G.Hill Lightning SP 4.00 10.00
149 DeMarcus Cousins .75 2.00
207 James Naismith SP 1.50 4.00

2011 Upper Deck Goodwin Champions Mini

*1-150 MINI: 1X TO 2.5X BASIC
1-150 MINI ODDS 1:4 HOBBY
COMMON CARD (211-231) .60 1.50
211-231 MINI ODDS 1:13 HOBBY
PRINTING PLATES RANDOMLY INSERTED
PLATE PRINT RUN 1 SET PER COLOR
BLACK-CYAN-MAGENTA-YELLOW ISSUED
NO PLATE PRICING DUE TO SCARCITY

2011 Upper Deck Goodwin Champions Mini Black

*1-150 MINI BLACK: 1.2X TO 3X BASIC
1-150 MINI BLACK ODDS 1:13 HOBBY
*211-231 MINI BLK: .6X TO 1.5X BASIC MINI
211-231 MINI BLACK ODDS 1:46 HOBBY

2011 Upper Deck Goodwin Champions Mini Foil

*1-150 MINI FOIL: 2.5X TO 6X BASIC
1-150 ANNCD PRINT RUN OF 89
*211-231 MINI FOIL : 1X TO 2.5X BASIC MINI
211-231 ANNCD PRINT RUN OF 178
PRINT RUNS PROVIDED BY UD
23 Michael Jordan 20.00 50.00

2011 Upper Deck Goodwin Champions Autographs

Please note that the Dwayne De Rosario card in this set was issued in the 2014 Upper Deck Goodwin Champions product.
GROUP A ODDS 1:1577 HOBBY
GROUP B ODDS 1:729 HOBBY
GROUP C ODDS 1:339 HOBBY
GROUP D ODDS 1:246 HOBBY
GROUP E ODDS 1:72 HOBBY
GROUP F ODDS 1:35 HOBBY
OVERALL AUTO ODDS 1:20 HOBBY
EXCHANGE DEADLINE 6/7/2013
BL Bill Laimbeer E 4.00 10.00
BW Bill Walton C 10.00 25.00
CP Candace Parker E 6.00 15.00
DR David Robinson A 75.00 150.00
GH Grant Hill A 75.00 150.00
LB Larry Bird A 75.00 150.00
LJ LeBron James C 125.00 250.00
MA Magic Johnson A 75.00 150.00
MJ Michael Jordan C 300.00 600.00
OL Hakeem Olajuwon A 30.00 80.00
PA Chris Paul B 10.00 25.00
RD Derrick Rose A 75.00 150.00
RO Dennis Rodman B 40.00 80.00
TH Tim Hardaway E 8.00 20.00

2011 Upper Deck Goodwin Champions Figures of Sport

COMP.SET. w/o SP's (14) 10.00 25.00
COMMON CARD (1-14) .60 1.50
1-14 STATED ODDS 1:21 HOBBY
15-18 SP ODDS 1:300 HOBBY
FS1 LeBron James 3.00 8.00
FS15 Michael Jordan SP 6.00 15.00

2011 Upper Deck Goodwin Champions Memorabilia

GROUP A ODDS 1:14,613 HOBBY
GROUP B ODDS 1:179 HOBBY
GROUP C ODDS 1:31 HOBBY
GROUP D ODDS 1:22 HOBBY
AM Alonzo Mourning C 4.00 10.00
CD Clyde Drexler B 5.00 12.00
CP Chris Paul D 3.00 8.00
DR David Robinson B 4.00 10.00
GH Grant Hill C 4.00 10.00
JL Julius Erving B 4.00 10.00
JO Magic Johnson C 4.00 10.00
LB Larry Bird C 6.00 15.00
LJ LeBron James C 5.00 12.00
MJ Michael Jordan C 12.00 30.00
OL Hakeem Olajuwon C 4.00 10.00
RD Dennis Rodman B 8.00 20.00
RO Derrick Rose B 4.00 10.00
RW Russell Westbrook D 3.00 8.00

2011 Upper Deck Goodwin Champions Memorabilia Dual

GROUP A ODDS 1:87,680 HOBBY
GROUP B ODDS 1:8768 HOBBY
GROUP C ODDS 1:2923 HOBBY
GROUP D ODDS 1:877 HOBBY
GROUP E ODDS 1:585 HOBBY
NO GROUP A PRICING AVAILABLE
LJ LeBron James E 10.00 25.00
MJ Michael Jordan D 20.00 50.00

2011 Upper Deck Goodwin Champions Sport Royalty Autographs

RANDOM INSERTS IN PACKS
NO PRICING DUE TO SCARCITY
SRAGR Glen Rice
SRAJER Julius Erving

2012 Upper Deck Goodwin Champions

MP.SET w/o VAR (210) 25.00 50.00
COMP.SET w/o SP's (150) 10.00 25.00
151-190 SP ODDS 1:3 HOBBY, BLASTER
191-210 SP ODDS 1:12 HOBBY, BLASTER
4A Hakeem Olajuwon .30 .75
4B Hakeem Olajuwon 6.00 15.00
Bill Clinton SP
5A Magic Johnson .50 1.25
5B Magic/Walton/Bird SP 6.00 15.00
7 Chris Singleton .40 1.00
17 Grant Hill .25 .60
23 Elgin Baylor .30 .75
40 Bill Walton .25 .60
41 Alonzo Mourning .25 .60
44 Chris Paul .40 1.00
47A Karl Malone .30 .75
47B Malone/Hulk/Rodman SP 6.00 15.00
57 Bobby Hurley .15 .40
58 Oscar Robertson .25 .60
63 David Robinson .40 1.00
76 Christian Laettner .20 .50
83 Steve Nash .30 .75
88 Larry Bird .60 1.50
90 Clyde Drexler .30 .75
94 Adrian Dantley .15 .40
106 Jackie Stiles .15 .40
112 Norris Cole .40 1.00
114 Jimmer Fredette .30 .75
116 Jason Kidd .30 .75
118 LeBron James 1.00 2.50
120 Kawhi Leonard .40 1.00
123A Michael Jordan 1.50 4.00
123B Michael Jordan
Julius Erving SP
126 Larry Johnson .20 .50
135 Dominique Wilkins .20 .50
138 Sam Cassell .15 .40
162 Alec Burks SP 1.00 2.50
167 Tristan Thompson SP 1.00 2.50

2012 Upper Deck Goodwin Champions Mini

*1-150 MINI: 1X TO 2.5X BASIC CARDS
1-150 MINI STATED ODDS 1:2 HOBBY, BLASTER
211-231 MINI ODDS 1:2 HOBBY, BLASTER

2012 Upper Deck Goodwin Champions Mini Foil

*1-150 MINI FOIL: 2.5X TO 6X BASIC
1-150 MINI FOIL ANNCD. PRINT RUN 99
*211-231 MINI FOIL: 1X TO 2.5X BASIC MINI
211-231 MINI FOIL ANNCD. PRINT RUN 199

2012 Upper Deck Goodwin Champions Mini Green

*1-150 MINI GREEN: 1.25X TO 3X BASIC
*211-231 MINI GREEN: .6X TO 1.5X BASIC MINI
TWO MINI GREEN PER HOBBY BOX
ONE MINI GREEN PER BLASTER

2012 Upper Deck Goodwin Champions Mini Green Blank Back

UNPRICED DUE TO SCARCITY

2012 Upper Deck Goodwin Champions Autographs

GROUP A ODDS 1:1,977
GROUP B ODDS 1:353
GROUP C ODDS 1:264
GROUP D ODDS 1:185
GROUP E ODDS 1:82
GROUP F ODDS 1:36
OVERALL AUTO ODDS 1:20
EXCHANGE DEADLINE 7/12/2014
ACL Christian Laettner B 10.00 25.00
ACP Chris Paul A 20.00 40.00
ADW Dominique Wilkins B 8.00 20.00
AJF Jimmer Fredette C 12.00 30.00
AJK Jason Kidd B 15.00 40.00
AJS Jackie Stiles F 4.00 10.00
ALJ LeBron James A 150.00 250.00
AMJ Michael Jordan A 350.00 500.00
ASC Sam Cassell C 6.00 15.00

2012 Upper Deck Goodwin Champions Memorabilia

GROUP A ODDS 1:10,631
GROUP B ODDS 1:4,784
GROUP C ODDS 1:302
GROUP D ODDS 1:118
GROUP E ODDS 1:36
GROUP F ODDS 1:23
MAM Alonzo Mourning F 5.00 12.00
MBW Bill Walton D 4.00 10.00
MCP Chris Paul F 3.00 8.00
MDR David Robinson F 3.00 8.00
MHO Hakeem Olajuwon F 4.00 10.00
MJO Magic Johnson E 5.00 12.00
MLB Larry Bird D 6.00 15.00
MLJ LeBron James D 6.00 15.00
MMJ Michael Jordan D 15.00 40.00

2012 Upper Deck Goodwin Champions Memorabilia Dual

GROUP A ODDS 1:95,680
GROUP B ODDS 1:31,893
GROUP C ODDS 1:2,514
GROUP D ODDS 1:1,306
GROUP E ODDS 1:520
NO PRICING ON GROUP A
M2DR David Robinson D 8.00 20.00
M2LJ LeBron James E 10.00 25.00
M2MJ Michael Jordan D 30.00 60.00

2012 Upper Deck Goodwin Champions Sport Royalty Autographs

GROUP A ODDS 1:15,947
GROUP B ODDS 1:7,973
GROUP C ODDS 1:4,932
ABW Bill Walton C 20.00 40.00
AHO Hakeem Olajuwon B 20.00 40.00

2013 Upper Deck Goodwin Champions

COMP. SET w/o VAR (210) 25.00 60.00
COMP. SET w/o SPs (150) 8.00 20.00
151-190 SP ODDS 1:3 HOBBY,BLASTER
191-210 SP ODDS 1:12 HOBBY,BLASTER
OVERALL VARIATION ODDS 1:320 H, 1:1,200 B
GROUP A ODDS 1:4,800
GROUP B ODDS 1:2,400
GROUP C ODDS 1:1,400
4 Michael Jordan 1.50 4.00
5 Clyde Drexler .30 .75
7 Reggie Miller .20 .50
11A Spud Webb .15 .40
11B S.Webb/T.Bogues SP 6.00 15.00
15 Shawn Bradley .15 .40
17 LeBron James 1.00 2.50
23 John Havlicek .30 .75
40 Reggie Theus .15 .40
41 Robert Horry .15 .40
44 Connie Hawkins .15 .40
46 Larry Bird .60 1.50
53 Walt Frazier .25 .60
54 Lonnie Shelton .15 .40
59 Alonzo Mourning .25 .60
72 Dennis Rodman .30 .75
77 Ray Allen .25 .60
82 Glen Rice .15 .40
84 Tim Hardaway .15 .40
86A Bill Laimbeer .15 .40
86B B.Laimbeer/B.Obama SP 6.00 15.00
94 Isiah Thomas .15 .40
100 Meyers Leonard .60 1.50
102 Jeremy Lamb .40 1.00
104 Paul Pierce .25 .60
106 Allen Iverson .25 .60
110 Larry Johnson .20 .50
112 David Robinson .40 1.00
116 Bill Russell .30 .75
118 Adrian Dantley .15 .40
135 Vinny Del Negro .15 .40
139 A.C. Green .20 .50
140 Muggsy Bogues .15 .40
149 Mookie Blaylock .15 .40
154 Kendall Marshall SP 1.00 2.50
160 Moe Harkless SP 1.00 2.50
165 Tyler Zeller SP 1.00 2.50

2013 Upper Deck Goodwin Champions Mini

*1-150 MINI: 1X TO 2.5X BASIC CARDS
7 MINIS PER HOBBY BOX, 4 MINIS PER BLASTER

2013 Upper Deck Goodwin Champions Mini Canvas

*1-150 MINI CANVAS: 2.5X TO 6X BASIC CARDS
1-150 MINI CANVAS ANNCD. PRINT RUN 99
*211-225 MINI CANVAS: 1X TO 2.5 BASIC MINI
211-225 MINI CANVAS ANNCD. PRINT RUN 198

2013 Upper Deck Goodwin Champions Mini Green

STATED ODDS 1:12 HOBBY, 1:15 BLASTER
STATED SP ODDS 1:60 HOBBY, 1:72 BLASTER

2013 Upper Deck Goodwin Champions Autographs

OVERALL ODDS 1:20
GROUP A ODDS 1:7,517
GROUP B ODDS 1:1,224
GROUP C ODDS 1:489
GROUP D ODDS 1:142
GROUP E ODDS 1:206
GROUP F ODDS 1:28
AAG A.C. Green F 4.00 10.00
AAI Allen Iverson B 75.00 150.00
ABO Muggsy Bogues D 5.00 12.00
ACH Connie Hawkins F 5.00 12.00
AIT Isiah Thomas B 10.00 25.00
ALJ LeBron James B 100.00 200.00
AMJ Michael Jordan C 300.00 500.00
AML Meyers Leonard C 8.00 20.00
ARA Ray Allen A
(inserted in 2014 Upper Deck Goodwin Champions)
ASB Shawn Bradley D 4.00 10.00
AVN Vinny Del Negro D 4.00 10.00

2013 Upper Deck Goodwin Champions Memorabilia

OVERALL ODDS 1:12
GROUP A ODDS 1:23,082
GROUP B ODDS 1:5,970
GROUP C ODDS 1:104
GROUP D ODDS 1:22
GROUP E ODDS 1:37
MBL Bill Laimbeer D 3.00 8.00
MLJ LeBron James D 6.00 15.00
MMJ Michael Jordan C 15.00 40.00

2013 Upper Deck Goodwin Champions Sport Royalty Autographs

OVERALL ODDS 1:1,161
GROUP A ODDS 1:7,473
GROUP B ODDS 1:4,171
GROUP C ODDS 1:2,050
SRALJ LeBron James A 150.00 250.00
SRAMJ Michael Jordan A

2013 Upper Deck Goodwin Champions Sport Royalty Memorabilia

OVERALL ODDS 1:350
GROUP A ODDS 1:2,391
GROUP B ODDS 1:957
GROUP C ODDS 1:717
SRMDR David Robinson B 6.00 15.00
SRMLB Larry Bird B 12.00 30.00
SRMLJ LeBron James C 12.00 30.00
SRMMJ Michael Jordan A 20.00 50.00

2013 Upper Deck Goodwin Champions Sport Royalty Memorabilia Dual

OVERALL ODDS 1:3,986
GROUP A ODDS 1:11,957
GROUP B ODDS 1:5,979
SRM2LJ LeBron James B
SRM2MJ Michael Jordan A

2014 Upper Deck Goodwin Champions

COMPLETE SET w/o AU's(180) 40.00 100.00
COMPLETE SET w/o SP's(155) 12.00 30.00
131-155 SP ODDS 1:3 HOBBY,BLAST
156-180 SP ODDS 1:12 HOB/1:12 BLAST
AU ODDS 1:60 HOB/1:720 BLAST
NOLA AU ODDS 1:860 '15 PACKS
NOLA AU ISSUED IN '15 GOODWIN
2 Larry Bird .60 1.50
8 Toni Kukoc .25 .60
15 Skylar Diggins .50 1.25
16 Mason Plumlee .20 .50
21 Lute Olson .25 .60
23 Michael Jordan 1.50 4.00
32 David Robinson .40 1.00
33 Jerry Tarkanian .25 .60
38 Bill Russell .40 1.00
40 Elvin Hayes .25 .60
42 Jerry Stackhouse .20 .50
51 Cheryl Miller .25 .60
60 Paul George .40 1.00
61 T.Hardaway/T.Hardaway Jr. .30 .75
67 LeBron James 1.00 2.50
80A Julius Erving .40 1.00
80B Erving/LeBron SP 20.00 50.00
103 Rajon Rondo .30 .75
113 Hakeem Olajuwon .30 .75
116 Jay Williams .15 .40
117 Bill Walton .25 .60
120A Jason Kidd .25 .60
120B Kidd/Clemens SP 4.00 10.00
121 James Worthy .30 .75
122 Stacey Augmon .15 .40
123 Magic Johnson .60 1.50
125 Giannis Antetokounmpo .50 1.25
127 Isiah Thomas .25 .60
128 Karl Malone .30 .75

2014 Upper Deck Goodwin Champions Mini

*1-130 MINI: .75X TO 2X BASIC
COMMON CARD (131-180) .50 1.25
7 MINIS PER HOBBY 4 PER BLASTER

2014 Upper Deck Goodwin Champions Mini Canvas

*1-130 MINI CANVAS: 2X TO 5X BASIC
COMMON CARD (131-180) 1.25 3.00
RANDOM INSERTS IN PACKS
2 Larry Bird 4.00 10.00
23 Michael Jordan 6.00 15.00
67 LeBron James 6.00 15.00

2014 Upper Deck Goodwin Champions Mini Green

*1-130 MINI GREEN: 1X TO 2.5X BASIC
COMMON CARD (131-180) .60 1.50
STATED ODDS 1:10 HOB/1:12 BLAST

2014 Upper Deck Goodwin Champions Autographs

GROUP A ODDS 1:54,400 HOBBY
GROUP B ODDS 1:6590 HOBBY
GROUP C ODDS 1:17,525 HOBBY
GROUP D ODDS 1:1280 HOBBY
GROUP E ODDS 1:410 HOBBY
GROUP F ODDS 1:135 HOBBY
GROUP G ODDS 1:42 HOBBY
'16 STATED ODDS 1:4352 HOBBY
AHH Hardaway/Hardaway 8.00 20.00
ALJ LeBron James B 100.00 200.00
AMJ Michael Jordan B

2014 Upper Deck Goodwin Champions Goudey

COMPLETE SET (52) 25.00 60.00
BB ODDS 1:13 HOB/1:32 BLAST
BK ODDS 1:25 HOB/1:60 BLAST
FB ODDS 1:25 HOB/1:60 BLAST
HK ODDS 1:33 HOB/1:80 BLAST
GOLF ODDS 1:33 HOB/1:80 BLAST
MISC SPORT ODDS 1:100 HOB/1:240 BLAST
HISTORY ODDS 1:40 HOB/1:96 BLAST
11 Bill Walton .60 1.50
12 Isiah Thomas .60 1.50
13 Hakeem Olajuwon .75 2.00
14 Michael Jordan 5.00 12.00
15 LeBron James 2.50 6.00
16 Larry Bird 1.50 4.00
17 Jason Kidd .60 1.50
18 Karl Malone .75 2.00

2014 Upper Deck Goodwin Champions Goudey Autographs

GROUP A ODDS 1:7200 HOBBY
GROUP B ODDS 1:4800 HOBBY
GROUP C ODDS 1:1650 HOBBY
GROUP D ODDS 1:1200 HOBBY
'16 GROUP A ODDS 1:21,760 HOBBY
'16 GROUP B ODDS 1:8369 HOBBY
13 Hakeem Olajuwon B 12.00 30.00
14 Michael Jordan A
15 LeBron James A
17 Jason Kidd B 25.00 60.00
18 Karl Malone B 25.00 60.00

2014 Upper Deck Goodwin Champions Memorabilia

GROUP A ODDS 1:5140
GROUP B ODDS 1:685
GROUP C ODDS 1:80
GROUP D ODDS 1:18
MLO Lute Olson C 6.00 15.00

2014 Upper Deck Goodwin Champions Memorabilia Premium

*PREMIUM: .75X TO 2X BASIC
RANDOM INSERTS IN PACKS
PRINT RUNS B/WN 10-50 COPIES PER
NO PRICING ON QTY 15 OR LESS
MLO Lute Olson/50 10.00 25.00

2014 Upper Deck Goodwin Champions Sport Royalty Autographs

GROUP A ODDS 1:17,130 HOBBY
GROUP B ODDS 1:4670 HOBBY
GROUP C ODDS 1:2855 HOBBY
GROUP D ODDS 1:1070 HOBBY
'16 GROUP A ODDS 1:21,760 HOBBY
'16 GROUP B ODDS 1:5440 HOBBY
SRALJ LeBron James A
SRAMJ Michael Jordan B

2015 Upper Deck Goodwin Champions

COMPLETE SET w/o AU's(150) 25.00 60.00
COMPLETE SET w/o SP's(100) 6.00 15.00
131-155 SP ODDS APPX. 1:3 PACKS
156-180 SP ODDS 1:8 PACKS
GROUP A AU ODDS 1:755 PACKS
GROUP B AU ODDS 1:65 PACKS
PRINTING PLATES RANDOMLY INSERTED
PLATE PRINT RUN 1 SET PER COLOR
BLACK-CYAN-MAGENTA-YELLOW ISSUED
NO PLATE PRICING DUE TO SCARCITY
EXCHNAGE DEADLINE 6/10/2017
1 David Robinson .40 1.00
4 Larry Bird .60 1.50
9 Yao Ming .30 .75
10 Sam Perkins .15 .40
11 Jerry West .30 .75
13 Danny Manning .25 .60
14 A.C. Green .25 .60
15 Elvin Hayes .25 .60
23 Michael Jordan 1.50 4.00
34 Robert Horry .20 .50
35 Chauncey Billups .25 .60
44 Horace Grant .25 .60
45 John Stockton .40 1.00
49 Shaquille O'Neal .50 1.25
54 John Salley .15 .40
56 Dave Cowens .15 .40
57 Alana Beard .30 .75
58 James Worthy .30 .75
60 LeBron James 1.00 2.50
64 Bill Russell .40 1.00
71 Byron Scott .20 .50
76 Becky Hammon 1.00 2.50
77 Doc Rivers .25 .60
88 Nick Van Exel .25 .60
92 Larry Johnson .30 .75
104 Shaquille O'Neal SP 1.50 4.00
105 Bill Russell SP 1.25 3.00
106 John Stockton SP 1.25 3.00
109 Yao Ming SP 1.00 2.50
114 Grant Hill SP 1.00 2.50
115 John Havlicek SP 1.00 2.50
120 Jerry West SP 1.00 2.50
127 Becky Hammon SP 2.00 5.00
130 Doc Rivers SP 1.00 2.50
133 James Worthy SP 1.25 3.00
139 Michael Jordan SP 4.00 10.00
140 LeBron James SP 4.00 10.00
144 Larry Bird SP 2.50 6.00
145 David Robinson SP 1.50 4.00
146 Bill Walton SP 1.00 2.50
148 Dominique Wilkins SP 1.25 3.00

2015 Upper Deck Goodwin Champions Mini

*MINI 1-100: 1X TO 2.5X BASIC
*MINI 101-125: .3X TO .75X BASIC
*MINI 126-150: .25X TO .6X BASIC
STATED ODDS THREE PER BOX

2015 Upper Deck Goodwin Champions Mini Canvas

*CANVAS 1-100: 2X TO 5X BASIC
*CANVAS 101-125: .6X TO 1.5X BASIC
*CANVAS 126-150: .5X TO 1.2X BASIC
RANDOM INSERTS IN PACKS
ANNCD PRINT RUN OF 99 COPIES PER

2015 Upper Deck Goodwin Champions Mini Cloth Lady Luck

*LUCK 1-100: 2.5X TO 6X BASIC
*LUCK 101-125: .75X TO 2X BASIC
*LUCK 126-150: .6X TO 1.5X BASIC
RANDOM INSERTS IN PACKS
STATED PRINT RUN 50 SER.#'d SETS
23 Michael Jordan 15.00 40.00
139 Michael Jordan 15.00 40.00

2015 Upper Deck Goodwin Champions Mini Leather Magician

*MAGICIAN 1-100: 6X TO 15X BASIC
*MAGICIAN 101-125: 2X TO 5X BASIC
*MAGICIAN 126-150: 1.5X TO 4X BASIC
RANDOM INSERTS IN PACKS
STATED PRINT RUN 15 SER.#'d SETS
23 Michael Jordan 60.00 150.00
139 Michael Jordan 60.00 150.00

2015 Upper Deck Goodwin Champions Autographs

GROUP A ODDS 1:6830 PACKS
GROUP B ODDS 1:780 PACKS
GROUP C ODDS 1:685 PACKS
GROUP D ODDS 1:350 PACKS
GROUP E ODDS 1:150 PACKS
GROUP F ODDS 1:65 PACKS
'16 GROUP A ODDS 1:14,836 PACKS
'16 GROUP B ODDS 1:1106 PACKS
EXCHANGE DEADLINE 6/10/2017
AAB Alana Beard F 2.50 6.00
AEH Elvin Hayes C 4.00 10.00
AHG Horace Grant D 4.00 10.00
AJS John Salley C 4.00 10.00
ALJ LeBron James A EXCH
ANV Nick Van Exel E 2.50 6.00
AWE Jerry West B 40.00 80.00
AWO James Worthy B 10.00 25.00

2015 Upper Deck Goodwin Champions Autographs Black and White

GROUP A ODDS 1:24,800 PACKS
GROUP B ODDS 1:7630 PACKS
GROUP C ODDS 1:5670 PACKS
GROUP D ODDS 1:6615 PACKS
OVERALL B/W ODDS 1:2000 PACKS
EXCHANGE DEADLINE 6/10/2017
140 Becky Hammon D 20.00 50.00
145 LeBron James B EXCH

2015 Upper Deck Goodwin Champions Autographs Inscribed

RANDOM INSERTS IN PACKS
PRINT RUNS B/WN 2-298 COPIES PER
NO PRICING ON QTY 16 OR LESS
EXCHANGE DEADLINE 6/10/2017
AAB Alana Beard 5.00 12.00
4X All Star/30
ABS Byron Scott 6.00 15.00
3X Champion/50

2015 Upper Deck Goodwin Champions Goudey

COMPLETE SET (60) 15.00 40.00
1-40 STATED ODDS 1:5 PACKS
41-60 STATED ODDS 1:20 PACKS
2 Yao Ming .75 2.00
7 John Salley .40 1.00
9 LeBron James 2.50 6.00
14 Bill Russell 1.00 2.50
15 John Havlicek .75 2.00
16 David Robinson 1.00 2.50
20 Jerry West .75 2.00
24 Shaquille O'Neal 1.25 3.00

2015 Upper Deck Goodwin Champions Goudey Autographs

GROUP A ODDS 1:1:16,535 PACKS
GROUP B ODDS 1:15,260 PACKS
GROUP C ODDS 1:1585 PACKS
GROUP D ODDS 1:1340 PACKS
OVERALL GOUDEY ODDS 1:660 PACKS
EXCHANGE DEADLINE 6/10/2017
GAJS John Salley C 4.00 10.00
GALJ LeBron James A EXCH

2015 Upper Deck Goodwin Champions Goudey Memorabilia

GROUP A ODDS 1:750 PACKS
GROUP B ODDS 1:240 PACKS
GROUP C ODDS 1:145 PACKS
OVERALL GOUDEY MEM 1:80 PACKS
GMDR David Robinson Jsy C 2.50 6.00
GMJW Jerry West Jsy B 2.50 6.00

2015 Upper Deck Goodwin Champions Goudey Memorabilia Premium Series

*PREMIUM: .6X TO 1.5X BASIC
RANDOM INSERTS IN PACKS
PRINT RUNS B/WN 10-50 COPIES PER
NO PRICING ON QTY 10
EXCHANGE DEADLINE 6/10/2017

2015 Upper Deck Goodwin Champions Goudey Sport Royalty Autographs

GROUP A ODDS 1:1:24,960 PACKS
GROUP B ODDS 1:9985 PACKS
GROUP C ODDS 1:3995 PACKS
OVERALL GOUDEY ODDS 1:2560 PACKS
'16 STATED ODDS 1:32,640 HOBBY
EXCHANGE DEADLINE 6/10/2017
SRALJ LeBron James A

2015 Upper Deck Goodwin Champions Goudey Sport Royalty Dual Memorabilia

GROUP A ODDS 1:16,215 PACKS
GROUP B ODDS 1:3040 PACKS
OVERAL SR DUAL 1:2560 PACKS
SRM2JR James/Robinson B 15.00 40.00

2015 Upper Deck Goodwin Champions Goudey Sport Royalty Memorabilia

OVERAL SR MEM ODDS 1:320 PACKS
SRMDR David Robinson Jsy 4.00 10.00
SRMLJ LeBron James Jsy 5.00 12.00

2015 Upper Deck Goodwin Champions Goudey Sport Royalty Memorabilia Premium Series

*PREMIUM: .6X TO 1.5X BASIC
RANDOM INSERTS IN PACKS
PRINT RUNS B/WN 5-25 COPIES PER
NO PRICING ON QTY 10 OR LESS

2015 Upper Deck Goodwin Champions Memorabilia

GROUP A ODDS 1:1420 PACKS
GROUP B ODDS 1:175 PACKS
GROUP C ODDS 1:28 PACKS
MDC Dave Cowens Jsy C 2.50 6.00
MEH Elvin Hayes Jsy C 2.50 6.00
MJS John Salley Jsy C 2.50 6.00
MLJ LeBron James Jsy B 5.00 12.00
MMG Danny Manning Jsy C 2.50 6.00
MWE Jerry West Jsy C 3.00 8.00

2015 Upper Deck Goodwin Champions Memorabilia Black and White

GROUP A ODDS 1:3970 PACKS
GROUP B ODDS 1:400 PACKS
OVERAL B/W MEM ODDS 1:360 PACKS
BWMBW Bill Walton Jsy B 3.00 8.00
BWMLJ LeBron James Jsy B 6.00 15.00

2015 Upper Deck Goodwin Champions Memorabilia Black and White Premium Series

*PREMIUM: .6X TO 1.5X BASIC
RANDOM INSERTS IN PACKS
PRINT RUNS B/WN 5-25 COPIES PER
NO PRICING ON QTY 10 OR LESS

2015 Upper Deck Goodwin Champions Memorabilia Premium Series

*PREMIUM: .6X TO 1.5X BASIC
RANDOM INSERTS IN PACKS
PRINT RUNS B/WN 10-75 COPIES PER
NO PRICING ON QTY 15 OR LESS

2007 Upper Deck Goudey Sport Royalty

ONE PER HOBBY BOX LOADER
DS Dean Smith 2.00 5.00
JW John Wooden 3.00 8.00
KB Kobe Bryant 6.00 15.00
KD Kevin Durant 5.00 12.00
LJ LeBron James 15.00 40.00
MJ Michael Jordan 20.00 50.00

2007 Upper Deck Goudey Sport Royalty Autographs

STATED ODDS TWO PER CASE
FOUND IN HOBBY BOX LOADER PACKS
EXCH DEADLINE 8/8/2009
JW John Wooden 100.00 200.00
KD Kevin Durant 150.00 250.00
LJ LeBron James 250.00 400.00

2008 Upper Deck Goudey

COMP.SET w/o HIGH #s (200) 20.00 50.00
COMMON CARD (1-200) .20 .50
COMMON ROOKIE (1-200) .30 .75
COMMON SP (201-230) 2.00 5.00
COMMON SP (231-250) 1.50 4.00
COMMON SP (251-270) 2.00 5.00
COMMON CARD (271-300) 2.00 5.00
COMMON CARD (301-330) 3.00 8.00
279 Cynthia Cooper SR SP 2.00 5.00
288 Julius Erving SR SP 2.50 6.00
299 Magic Johnson SR SP 3.00 8.00
300 Michael Jordan SR SP 3.00 8.00
307 Kobe Bryant SR SP 5.00 12.00
308 Kevin Durant SR SP 5.00 12.00
312 Larry Bird SR SP 6.00 15.00
313 LeBron James SR SP 6.00 15.00

2008 Upper Deck Goudey Mini Black Backs

*BLACK 1-200: .75X TO 2X GRN 1-200
*BLACK RC 1-200: .75X TO 2X GRN RC 1-200
*BLACK SP 201-250: .75X TO 2X GRN 201-250
*BLACK SP 251-270: .5X TO 1.2X GRN 251-270
*BLACK SR 271-330: .5X TO 1.2X GRN 271-330
RANDOM INSERTS IN PACKS
STATED PRINT RUN 34 SER.#'d SETS
300 Michael Jordan SR 20.00 50.00
307 Kobe Bryant 6.00 15.00

2008 Upper Deck Goudey Mini Blue Backs

*BLUE 1-200: 1.5X TO 4X BASIC 1-200
*BLUE RC 1-200: 1X TO 2.5X BASIC RC 1-200
*BLUE 201-270: .6X TO 1.5X BASIC SP 201-270
*BLUE 271-330: .6X TO 1.5X BASIC SR 201-270
RANDOM INSERTS IN PACKS

2008 Upper Deck Goudey Mini Green Backs

RANDOM INSERTS IN PACKS
STATED PRINT RUN 88 SER.#'d SETS
279 Cynthia Cooper SR 2.50 6.00
288 Julius Erving SR 3.00 8.00
299 Magic Johnson SR 4.00 10.00
300 Michael Jordan SR 12.50 30.00
307 Kobe Bryant 4.00 10.00
308 Kevin Durant 4.00 10.00
312 Larry Bird 5.00 12.00
313 LeBron James 10.00 25.00

2008 Upper Deck Goudey Mini Red Backs

*RED 1-200: 1X TO 2.5X BASIC 1-200
*RED RC 1-200: .75X TO 2X BASIC RC 1-200
*RED 201-270: .5X TO 1.2X BASIC SP 201-270
*RED 271-330: .5X to 1.2X BASIC SR 271-330
RANDOM INSERTS IN PACKS

2008 Upper Deck Goudey Hit Parade of Champions

RANDOM INSERTS IN PACKS
4 Bill Russell 1.25 3.00
14 Kobe Bryant 2.50 6.00
16 Larry Bird 2.00 5.00
17 LeBron James 3.00 8.00
18 Magic Johnson 1.25 3.00
21 Michael Jordan 4.00 10.00

2008 Upper Deck Goudey Sport Royalty Autographs

OVERALL AUTO ODDS 1:18 HOBBY
ASTERISK EQUALS PARTIAL EXCHANGE
EXCHANGE DEADLINE 7/17/2010
CC Cynthia Cooper 8.00 20.00

2009 Upper Deck Goudey

COMPLETE SET (300) 200.00 300.00
COMP.SET w/o SP's (200) 20.00 50.00
COMMON CARD (1-200) .20 .50
COMMON RC (1-200) .40 1.00
COMMON SP (201-300) 2.00 5.00
APPX.SP ODDS 201-220 1:9 HOBBY
APPX.SP ODDS 221-260 1:6 HOBBY
APPX.SP ODDS 261-300 1:6 HOBBY
256 Paul Pierce SR SP 3.00 8.00
257 Jerry West SR SP 3.00 8.00
258 Larry Bird SR SP 3.00 8.00
259 John Havlicek SR SP 2.50 6.00
260 Michael Jordan SR SP 5.00 12.00

2009 Upper Deck Goudey Mini Green Back

*GREEN 1-200: 1.2X TO 3X BASIC
*GREEN RC 1-200: .6X TO 1.5X BASIC
COMMON CARD (201-300) .75 2.00
APPROX.ODDS 1:6 HOBBY
256 Paul Pierce SR 2.50 6.00
257 Jerry West SR 3.00 8.00
258 Larry Bird SR 5.00 12.00
259 John Havlicek SR 2.00 5.00
260 Michael Jordan SR 6.00 15.00

2009 Upper Deck Goudey Mini Navy Blue Back

*BLUE 1-200: 1.5X TO 4X BASIC
*BLUE RC 1-200: .75X TO 2X BASIC
*BLUE: 201-300: .6X TO 1.5X MINI GREEN
APPROX.ODDS 1:9 HOBBY

2009 Upper Deck Goudey Sport Royalty Autographs

OVERALL AUTO ODDS 1:18 HOBBY
EXCHANGE DEADLINE 4/1/2011
BS Bill Sharman 15.00 40.00
JH John Havlicek 125.00 250.00
JO Michael Jordan 600.00 900.00
JW Jerry West 75.00 150.00
LB Larry Bird 30.00 60.00

2009 Upper Deck Griffey-Jordan

RANDOM INSERTS IN PACKS
KGMJ K.Griffey Jr./M.Jordan 20.00 50.00

1998 Upper Deck Hardcourt

The 1998 Upper Deck Hardcourt hobby-only set was issued in one series totalling 90 cards. The 4-card packs retail for $5.99 each. The cards feature 32-point stock with a "wood" designed background. The set contains the topical subset: Rookie Experience (71-90). A bonus Michael Jordan card was also included in packs (#23a) at a reported rate of one in every two boxes. Also included, was a 5" by 7" Michael Jordan jumbo card. It was included one per box.
COMPLETE SET (90) 40.00 75.00
JORDAN SPEC. INSERTED EVERY TWO BOXES
ONE JORDAN JUMBO PER BOX
1 Kobe Bryant 2.50 6.00
2 Donyell Marshall .40 1.00
3 Bryant Reeves .40 1.00
4 Keith Van Horn .60 1.50
5 David Robinson 1.00 2.50
6 Nick Anderson .40 1.00
7 Nick Van Exel .50 1.25
8 David Wesley .40 1.00
9 Alonzo Mourning .75 2.00
10 Shawn Kemp .60 1.50
11 Maurice Taylor .40 1.00
12 Kenny Anderson .50 1.25
13 Jason Kidd 1.00 2.50
14 Marcus Camby .50 1.25
15 Tim Hardaway .60 1.50
16 Damon Stoudamire .60 1.50
17 Detlef Schrempf .60 1.50
18 Dikembe Mutombo .60 1.50
19 Charles Barkley 1.00 2.50
20 Ray Allen .75 2.00
21 Ron Mercer .50 1.25
22 Shawn Bradley .40 1.00
23 Michael Jordan 5.00 12.00
23A Michael Jordan Special 8.00 20.00
24 Antonio McDyess .50 1.25
25 Stephon Marbury .75 2.00
26 Rik Smits .50 1.25
27 Michael Stewart .40 1.00
28 Steve Smith .50 1.25
29 Glenn Robinson .50 1.25
30 Chris Webber .60 1.50
31 Antoine Walker .60 1.50
32 Eddie Jones .60 1.50
33 Mitch Richmond .60 1.50
34 Kevin Garnett 1.00 2.50
35 Grant Hill 1.00 2.50
36 John Stockton .75 2.00
37 Allan Houston .50 1.25
38 Bobby Jackson .40 1.00
39 Sam Cassell .50 1.25
40 Allen Iverson 1.25 3.00
41 LaPhonso Ellis .40 1.00
42 Lorenzen Wright .40 1.00
43 Gary Payton .60 1.50
44 Patrick Ewing .75 2.00
45 Scottie Pippen 1.00 2.50
46 Hakeem Olajuwon .75 2.00
47 Glen Rice .60 1.50
48 Antonio Daniels .40 1.00
49 Jayson Williams .40 1.00
50 Juwan Howard .50 1.25
51 Reggie Miller .75 2.00
52 Joe Smith .50 1.25
53 Shaquille O'Neal 1.50 4.00
54 Dennis Rodman 1.25 3.00
55 Vin Baker .50 1.25
56 Rod Strickland .40 1.00
57 Anfernee Hardaway 1.00 2.50
58 Zydrunas Ilgauskas .60 1.50
59 Chris Mullin .60 1.50
60 Rasheed Wallace .60 1.50
61 Shareef Abdur-Rahim .60 1.50
62 Tom Gugliotta .40 1.00
63 Tim Duncan 1.25 3.00
64 Michael Finley .60 1.50
65 Jim Jackson .40 1.00
66 Chauncey Billups .75 2.00
67 Jerry Stackhouse .60 1.50
68 Jeff Hornacek .50 1.25
69 Clyde Drexler .75 2.00
70 Karl Malone .75 2.00
71 Tim Duncan RE 1.25 3.00
72 Keith Van Horn RE .60 1.50
73 Chauncey Billups RE .75 2.00
74 Antonio Daniels RE .40 1.00
75 Tony Battie RE .50 1.25
76 Ron Mercer RE .50 1.25
77 Tim Thomas RE .60 1.50
78 Tracy McGrady RE 1.00 2.50
79 Danny Fortson RE .40 1.00
80 Derek Anderson RE .40 1.00
81 Maurice Taylor RE .40 1.00
82 Kelvin Cato RE .40 1.00
83 Brevin Knight RE .40 1.00
84 Bobby Jackson RE .40 1.00
85 Rodrick Rhodes RE .40 1.00
86 Anthony Johnson RE .40 1.00
87 Cedric Henderson RE .40 1.00
88 Chris Anstey RE .40 1.00
89 Michael Stewart RE .40 1.00
90 Zydrunas Ilgauskas RE .60 1.50
NNO Michael Jordan Jumbo 4.00 10.00

1998 Upper Deck Hardcourt Home Court Advantage

*STARS: .75X TO 2X BASE CARD HI
STATED ODDS 1:4

1998 Upper Deck Hardcourt Home Court Advantage Plus

*STARS: 4X TO 10X BASE CARD HI
STATED PRINT RUN 500 SERIAL #'d SETS

1998 Upper Deck Hardcourt High Court

Randomly inserted into packs, this 30-card set features some of the high-flying performers in the NBA. The cards are producd on wood paper stock with a silver logo titled "High Court" in the lower left corner. The cards are serially numbered to 1300 in gold foil on the card front.
STATED PRINT RUN 1300 SERIAL #'d SETS
H1 Dikembe Mutombo 2.00 5.00
H2 Ron Mercer 1.50 4.00
H3 Glen Rice 2.00 5.00
H4 Scottie Pippen 3.00 8.00
H5 Shawn Kemp 2.00 5.00
H6 Michael Finley 2.00 5.00
H7 LaPhonso Ellis 1.25 3.00
H8 Grant Hill 3.00 8.00
H9 Erick Dampier 1.25 3.00
H10 Hakeem Olajuwon 2.50 6.00
H11 Chris Mullin 2.00 5.00
H12 Lamond Murray 1.25 3.00
H13 Kobe Bryant 8.00 20.00
H14 Tim Hardaway 2.00 5.00
H15 Ray Allen 2.50 6.00
H16 Stephon Marbury 2.50 6.00
H17 Keith Van Horn 2.00 5.00
H18 Allan Houston 1.50 4.00
H19 Anfernee Hardaway 3.00 8.00
H20 Allen Iverson 4.00 10.00
H21 Antonio McDyess 1.50 4.00
H22 Rasheed Wallace 2.00 5.00
H23 Mitch Richmond 2.00 5.00
H24 Tim Duncan 4.00 10.00
H25 Gary Payton 2.00 5.00
H26 Chauncey Billups 2.50 6.00
H27 John Stockton 2.50 6.00
H28 Shareef Abdur-Rahim 2.00 5.00
H29 Juwan Howard 1.50 4.00
H30 Michael Jordan 15.00 40.00

1998 Upper Deck Hardcourt Jordan Holding Court Red

Randomly inserted into packs, this 30-card set features a duel-player, double-wood card. The cards feature 40-point stock. Each card features Michael Jordan on one side and one of 29 other NBA superstars on the other. The base set features the title of the set and the Upper Deck logo in red foil. The cards are serially numbered to 2300.
STATED ODDS 2300 SERIAL #'d SETS
*BRONZE: 1.5X TO 4X HI COLUMN
BRONZE: PRINT RUN 230 SERIAL #'d SETS
UNPRICED GOLD PARALLEL SERIAL #'d TO 1
J1 S.Smith/M.Jordan 2.50 6.00
J2 A.Walker/M.Jordan 3.00 8.00
J3 G.Rice/M.Jordan 3.00 8.00
J4 S.Pippen/M.Jordan 8.00 20.00
J5 S.Kemp/M.Jordan 4.00 10.00
J6 M.Finley/M.Jordan 4.00 10.00
J7 B.Jackson/M.Jordan 2.50 6.00
J8 G.Hill/M.Jordan 6.00 15.00
J9 J.Jackson/M.Jordan 2.00 5.00
J10 C.Barkley/M.Jordan 5.00 12.00
J11 R.Miller/M.Jordan 4.00 10.00
J12 L.Wright/M.Jordan 2.00 5.00
J13 K.Bryant/M.Jordan 15.00 40.00
J14 T.Hardaway/M.Jordan 3.00 8.00
J15 G.Robinson/M.Jordan 2.50 6.00
J16 K.Garnett/M.Jordan 6.00 15.00
J17 K.Van Horn/M.Jordan 3.00 8.00
J18 P.Ewing/M.Jordan 4.00 10.00
J19 A.Hardaway/M.Jordan 6.00 15.00
J20 A.Iverson/M.Jordan 8.00 20.00
J21 J.Kidd/M.Jordan 6.00 15.00
J22 D.Stoudamire/M.Jordan 3.00 8.00
J23 M.Richmond/M.Jordan 3.00 8.00
J24 T.Duncan/M.Jordan 8.00 20.00
J25 G.Payton/M.Jordan 3.00 8.00
J26 C.Billups/M.Jordan 4.00 10.00
J27 K.Malone/M.Jordan 4.00 10.00
J28 S.Abdur-Rahim/M.Jordan 3.00 8.00
J29 C.Webber/M.Jordan 6.00 15.00
J30 M.Jordan/M.Jordan 20.00 50.00

1998 Upper Deck Hardcourt Jordan Holding Court Silver

*SILVER: 5X TO 12X BASE HI
STATED PRINT RUN 23 SETS
J13 K.Bryant/M.Jordan 600.00 1100.00
J20 A.Iverson/M.Jordan 125.00 300.00
J30 M.Jordan/M.Jordan 600.00 1000.00

1999-00 Upper Deck Hardcourt

Released in late 1999, this set consisted of 90 player cards, which included 60 veterans and 30 rookies. The cards came five to a pack with a suggested retail price of $4.99. The 30-card rookie subset was inserted at one in four packs. Also inserted in packs was a Michael Jordan floor card, which was serially numbered to 50 and a Wilt Chamberlain floor card, which was serially numbered to 100. They are listed at the end of the set.
COMPLETE SET (90) 30.00 80.00
COMPLETE SET w/o RC (60) 10.00 25.00
61-90 STATED ODDS 1:4
1 Dikembe Mutombo .40 1.00
2 Alan Henderson .25 .60
3 Antoine Walker .40 1.00
4 Paul Pierce .50 1.25
5 Eddie Jones .40 1.00
6 Elden Campbell .25 .60
7 Toni Kukoc .40 1.00
8 Randy Brown .25 .60
9 Shawn Kemp .40 1.00
10 Brevin Knight .25 .60
11 Michael Finley .40 1.00
12 Dirk Nowitzki .75 2.00
13 Antonio McDyess .30 .75
14 Nick Van Exel .30 .75
15 Grant Hill .50 1.25
16 Jerry Stackhouse .40 1.00
17 Antawn Jamison .40 1.00
18 John Starks .30 .75
19 Hakeem Olajuwon .50 1.25
20 Scottie Pippen .60 1.50
21 Reggie Miller .40 1.00
22 Jalen Rose .30 .75
23 Maurice Taylor .25 .60
24 Michael Olowokandi .25 .60
25 Shaquille O'Neal 1.00 2.50
26 Kobe Bryant 1.50 4.00
27 Tim Hardaway .40 1.00
28 Alonzo Mourning .50 1.25
29 Glenn Robinson .30 .75
30 Ray Allen .40 1.00
31 Kevin Garnett .60 1.50
32 Terrell Brandon .25 .60
33 Stephon Marbury .30 .75
34 Keith Van Horn .30 .75
35 Latrell Sprewell .40 1.00
36 Allan Houston .30 .75
37 Patrick Ewing .50 1.25
38 Darrell Armstrong .25 .60
39 Bo Outlaw .25 .60
40 Allen Iverson .75 2.00
41 Larry Hughes .30 .75
42 Jason Kidd .60 1.50
43 Tom Gugliotta .25 .60
44 Brian Grant .25 .60
45 Damon Stoudamire .30 .75
46 Jason Williams .50 1.25
47 Vlade Divac .40 1.00
48 Tim Duncan .75 2.00
49 David Robinson .60 1.50
50 Avery Johnson .30 .75
51 Gary Payton .40 1.00
52 Vin Baker .30 .75
53 Vince Carter .75 2.00
54 Tracy McGrady .60 1.50
55 Karl Malone .50 1.25
56 John Stockton .50 1.25
57 Shareef Abdur-Rahim .30 .75
58 Mike Bibby .40 1.00
59 Juwan Howard .30 .75
60 Mitch Richmond .40 1.00
61 Elton Brand RC 1.50 4.00
62 Jason Terry RC 1.00 2.50
63 Kenny Thomas RC .60 1.50
64 Jonathan Bender RC .60 1.50
65 A.Radojevic RC .40 1.00
66 Galen Young RC .60 1.50
67 Baron Davis RC 1.50 4.00
68 Corey Maggette RC 1.00 2.50
69 Dion Glover RC .50 1.25
70 Scott Padgett RC .50 1.25
71 Steve Francis RC 1.50 4.00
72 Richard Hamilton RC 1.25 3.00
73 James Posey RC .60 1.50
74 Jumaine Jones RC .50 1.25
75 Chris Herren RC .50 1.25
76 Andre Miller RC 1.25 3.00
77 Lamar Odom RC 1.50 4.00
78 Wally Szczerbiak RC 1.25 3.00
79 William Avery RC .50 1.25
80 Devean George RC .60 1.50
81 Trajan Langdon RC .60 1.50
82 Cal Bowdler RC .40 1.00
83 Kris Clack RC .60 1.50
84 Tim James RC .40 1.00
85 Shawn Marion RC 1.25 3.00
86 Ryan Robertson RC .40 1.00
87 Quincy Lewis RC .40 1.00
88 Vonteego Cummings RC .40 1.00
89 Obinna Ekezie RC .50 1.25
90 Jeff Foster RC .60 1.50
GF1 M.Jordan Floor/50 250.00 500.00
GF6 W.Chamberlain Flr/100 100.00 200.00

1999-00 Upper Deck Hardcourt Baseline Grooves Rainbow

*STARS: 2.5X TO 6X BASE CARD HI
*RCs: .75X TO 2X BASE HI
STATED PRINT RUN 500 SERIAL #'d SETS

1999-00 Upper Deck Hardcourt Baseline Grooves Silver

*STARS: 15X TO 40X BASE CARD HI
*RCs: 5X TO 12X BASE HI
STATED PRINT RUN 50 SERIAL #'d SETS
26 Kobe Bryant 150.00 300.00
48 Tim Duncan 75.00 200.00

1999-00 Upper Deck Hardcourt Court Authority

Randomly inserted in packs at one in 99, this 10-card set captures the players with the most dynamic on court moves in the NBA. Card backs carry an "A" prefix.
COMPLETE SET (10) 40.00 80.00
STATED ODDS 1:99
A1 Tim Duncan 6.00 15.00
A2 Vince Carter 6.00 15.00
A3 Allen Iverson 6.00 15.00
A4 Jason Williams 4.00 10.00
A5 Kevin Garnett 5.00 12.00
A6 Keith Van Horn 2.50 6.00
A7 Jason Kidd 5.00 12.00
A8 Grant Hill 4.00 10.00
A9 Antoine Walker 3.00 8.00
A10 Michael Jordan 10.00 25.00

1999-00 Upper Deck Hardcourt Court Forces

Randomly inserted in packs at one in eight, this 10-card set highlights some of the top newcomers to the NBA. Card backs carry a "CF" prefix.
COMPLETE SET (10) 3.00 8.00
STATED ODDS 1:8
CF1 Shareef Abdur-Rahim .40 1.00
CF2 Scottie Pippen .75 2.00
CF3 Latrell Sprewell .50 1.25
CF4 Tim Hardaway .50 1.25
CF5 Shaquille O'Neal 1.25 3.00
CF6 Mike Bibby .50 1.25
CF7 Allen Iverson 1.00 2.50
CF8 John Stockton .60 1.50
CF9 Michael Finley .50 1.25
CF10 Reggie Miller .50 1.25

1999-00 Upper Deck Hardcourt Legends of the Hardcourt

Randomly inserted in packs at one in 19, this 10-card set takes a look back in time at some of the NBA's all time greatest players. Card backs carry a "L" prefix.
COMPLETE SET (10) 12.50 30.00
STATED ODDS 1:19
L1 Michael Jordan 10.00 25.00
L2 Elgin Baylor 1.25 3.00
L3 Kevin McHale 1.50 4.00
L4 Julius Erving 2.00 5.00
L5 Larry Bird 3.00 8.00
L6 George Gervin 1.25 3.00
L7 Bob Cousy 2.00 5.00
L8 John Havlicek 1.50 4.00
L9 Jerry West 1.50 4.00
L10 Walt Frazier 1.25 3.00

1999-00 Upper Deck Hardcourt MJ Records Almanac

Randomly inserted in packs at one in 19, this 10-card set takes a look inside the numbers at some of the amazing records MJ broke during his career. Card backs carry a "J" prefix.
COMPLETE SET (10) 20.00 50.00
COMMON CARD (J1-J10) 2.50 6.00
STATED ODDS 1:19

1999-00 Upper Deck Hardcourt New Court Order

Randomly inserted in packs at one in three, this 20-card set features current and future NBA stars on 32-point laminated card stock. Card backs carry a "NC" prefix.
COMPLETE SET (20) 5.00 12.00
STATED ODDS 1:3
NC1 Vince Carter .75 2.00
NC2 Allan Houston .30 .75
NC3 Paul Pierce .50 1.25
NC4 Eddie Jones .40 1.00
NC5 Antawn Jamison .40 1.00
NC6 Mike Bibby .40 1.00
NC7 Tim Duncan .75 2.00
NC8 Kobe Bryant 1.50 4.00
NC9 Maurice Taylor .25 .60
NC10 Darrell Armstrong .25 .60
NC11 Stephon Marbury .30 .75
NC12 Gary Payton .40 1.00
NC13 Brian Grant .25 .60
NC14 Jason Williams .50 1.25
NC15 Shareef Abdur-Rahim .30 .75
NC16 Damon Stoudamire .30 .75
NC17 Keith Van Horn .30 .75
NC18 Tom Gugliotta .25 .60
NC19 Antonio McDyess .30 .75
NC20 Ray Allen .40 1.00

1999-00 Upper Deck Hardcourt Power in the Paint

Randomly inserted in packs at one in six, this 12-card set is die cut and features the top big men in the NBA. Card backs carry a "P" prefix.
COMPLETE SET (12) 3.00 8.00
STATED ODDS 1:6
P1 Antoine Walker .50 1.25
P2 Karl Malone .60 1.50
P3 Hakeem Olajuwon .60 1.50
P4 David Robinson .75 2.00
P5 Antonio McDyess .40 1.00
P6 Shawn Kemp .50 1.25
P7 Glenn Robinson .40 1.00
P8 Juwan Howard .40 1.00
P9 Patrick Ewing .60 1.50
P10 Alonzo Mourning .60 1.50
P11 Antawn Jamison .50 1.25
P12 Dikembe Mutombo .50 1.25

2000-01 Upper Deck Hardcourt

The 2000-01 Upper Deck Hardcourt product was released in September,2000 and featured a 102-card base set that was broken into tiers as follows: 60 Base Veterans (1-60), and 42 Rookie cards (61-102) that are individually serial numbered to 900. Each pack contained five cards and carried a suggested retail price of $4.99.
COMPLETE SET w/o RC (60) 10.00 25.00
RCs: PRINT RUN 900 SERIAL #'d SETS
1 Dikembe Mutombo .30 .75
2 Jason Terry .30 .75
3 Antoine Walker .25 .60
4 Paul Pierce .30 .75
5 Eddie Jones .30 .75
6 Baron Davis .30 .75
7 Elton Brand .30 .75
8 Ron Artest .30 .75
9 Andre Miller .25 .60
10 Shawn Kemp .30 .75
11 Dirk Nowitzki .50 1.25
12 Michael Finley .30 .75
13 Antonio McDyess .25 .60
14 Nick Van Exel .25 .60
15 Grant Hill .40 1.00
16 Jerry Stackhouse .25 .60
17 Antawn Jamison .30 .75
18 Larry Hughes .25 .60
19 Steve Francis .25 .60
20 Hakeem Olajuwon .40 1.00
21 Reggie Miller .30 .75
22 Jalen Rose .25 .60
23 Lamar Odom .25 .60
24 Eric Piatkowski .20 .50
25 Shaquille O'Neal .75 2.00
26 Kobe Bryant 1.25 3.00
27 Alonzo Mourning .40 1.00
28 Jamal Mashburn .25 .60
29 Ray Allen .30 .75
30 Glenn Robinson .25 .60
31 Kevin Garnett .50 1.25
32 Wally Szczerbiak .25 .60
33 Keith Van Horn .25 .60
34 Stephon Marbury .25 .60
35 Allan Houston .25 .60
36 Latrell Sprewell .25 .60
37 Darrell Armstrong .20 .50
38 Ron Mercer .20 .50
39 Allen Iverson .60 1.50
40 Toni Kukoc .30 .75
41 Jason Kidd .50 1.25
42 Anfernee Hardaway .50 1.25
43 Shawn Marion .25 .60
44 Scottie Pippen .50 1.25
45 Damon Stoudamire .25 .60
46 Chris Webber .30 .75
47 Jason Williams .30 .75
48 Tim Duncan .60 1.50
49 David Robinson .50 1.25
50 Gary Payton .30 .75
51 Vin Baker .25 .60
52 Rashard Lewis .30 .75
53 Tracy McGrady .50 1.25
54 Vince Carter .60 1.50
55 Karl Malone .40 1.00
56 John Stockton .40 1.00
57 Shareef Abdur-Rahim .25 .60
58 Mike Bibby .30 .75
59 Mitch Richmond .25 .60
60 Richard Hamilton .25 .60
61 Kenyon Martin RC 4.00 10.00
62 Marcus Fizer RC 1.50 4.00
63 Chris Mihm RC 1.25 3.00
64 Chris Porter RC 1.00 2.50
65 Stromile Swift RC 1.50 4.00
66 Morris Peterson RC 1.50 4.00
67 Quentin Richardson RC 1.50 4.00
68 Courtney Alexander RC 1.25 3.00
69 Scoonie Penn RC 1.50 4.00
70 Mateen Cleaves RC 1.25 3.00
71 Erick Barkley RC 1.00 2.50
72 A.J. Guyton RC 1.00 2.50
73 Darius Miles RC 1.50 4.00
74 DerMarr Johnson RC 1.25 3.00
75 Hedo Turkoglu RC 2.50 6.00
76 Hanno Mottola RC 1.00 2.50
77 Mike Miller RC 2.50 6.00
78 Desmond Mason RC 2.00 5.00
79 Mark Madsen RC 1.50 4.00
80 Eduardo Najera RC 1.50 4.00
81 Speedy Claxton RC 1.50 4.00
82 Joel Przybilla RC 1.25 3.00
83 Brian Cardinal RC 1.25 3.00
84 Khalid El-Amin RC 1.00 2.50
85 Etan Thomas RC 1.50 4.00
86 Corey Hightower RC 1.50 4.00
87 Dan Langhi RC 1.00 2.50
88 Michael Redd RC 4.00 10.00
89 Pete Mickeal RC 1.50 4.00
90 Mamadou N'Diaye RC 1.00 2.50
91 Jerome Moiso RC 1.00 2.50
92 Chris Carrawell RC 1.50 4.00
93 Jason Collier RC 1.50 4.00
94 Keyon Dooling RC 1.50 4.00
95 Mark Karcher RC 1.00 2.50
96 Jamaal Magloire RC 1.50 4.00
97 Jason Hart RC 1.50 4.00
98 Jabari Smith RC 1.00 2.50
99 Donnell Harvey RC 1.25 3.00
100 Lavor Postell RC 1.00 2.50
101 Eddie House RC 1.25 3.00
102 Dan McClintock RC 1.50 4.00

2000-01 Upper Deck Hardcourt Court Authority

Randomly inserted in packs at one in 15, this 15-card set features the league's most dominant players. Card backs carry a "CA" prefix.
COMPLETE SET (15) 12.50 30.00
STATED ODDS 1:15
CA1 Kobe Bryant 3.00 8.00
CA2 Allen Iverson 1.50 4.00
CA3 Gary Payton .75 2.00
CA4 Tim Duncan 1.50 4.00
CA5 Kevin Garnett 1.25 3.00
CA6 Steve Francis .60 1.50
CA7 Vince Carter 1.50 4.00
CA8 Shaquille O'Neal 2.00 5.00
CA9 Jason Kidd 1.25 3.00
CA10 Karl Malone 1.00 2.50
CA11 Shareef Abdur-Rahim .60 1.50
CA12 Grant Hill 1.00 2.50
CA13 Reggie Miller .75 2.00
CA14 Keith Van Horn .60 1.50
CA15 John Stockton 1.00 2.50

2000-01 Upper Deck Hardcourt Court Forces

Randomly inserted in packs at one in 12, this 11-card set focuses on players who are the best all-around threats on the floor today. Card backs carry a "C" prefix.
COMPLETE SET (11) 4.00 10.00
STATED ODDS 1:12
C1 Elton Brand .50 1.25
C2 Steve Francis .40 1.00
C3 Allan Houston .40 1.00
C4 Lamar Odom .40 1.00
C5 Andre Miller .40 1.00
C6 Jason Williams .50 1.25
C7 Ron Mercer .30 .75
C8 Kobe Bryant 2.00 5.00
C9 Kevin Garnett .75 2.00
C10 Jerry Stackhouse .40 1.00
C11 Latrell Sprewell .40 1.00

2000-01 Upper Deck Hardcourt Floor Leaders

Randomly inserted in packs at one in seven, this 20-card set showcases the most respected leaders on the NBA hardwood. Card backs carry a "FL" prefix.
COMPLETE SET (20) 6.00 15.00
STATED ODDS 1:7
FL1 Kobe Bryant 2.00 5.00
FL2 Eddie Jones .50 1.25
FL3 Kevin Garnett .75 2.00
FL4 Andre Miller .40 1.00
FL5 Keith Van Horn .40 1.00
FL6 Allan Houston .40 1.00
FL7 Larry Hughes .40 1.00
FL8 Jason Williams .50 1.25
FL9 Tracy McGrady .75 2.00
FL10 Shawn Kemp .50 1.25
FL11 Stephon Marbury .40 1.00
FL12 Glenn Robinson .40 1.00
FL13 Mike Bibby .50 1.25
FL14 Baron Davis .50 1.25
FL15 Scottie Pippen .75 2.00
FL16 David Robinson .75 2.00
FL17 Paul Pierce .50 1.25
FL18 Wally Szczerbiak .40 1.00
FL19 Jalen Rose .40 1.00
FL20 Lamar Odom .40 1.00

2000-01 Upper Deck Hardcourt Game Floor

Randomly inserted in packs at one in 15, this 25-card set features a real piece of the floor that the player played on. Card backs are numbered by the player's initials. Four players also autographed versions of the floor, which were numbered to the player's jersey. Those players were Kobe Bryant, Kevin Garnett, Karl Malone and Michael Jordan.
STATED ODDS 1:15
SOME AU's NOT PRICED DUE TO SCARCITY
AHF Anfernee Hardaway 3.00 8.00
AIF Allen Iverson 4.00 10.00
ALF Allan Houston 1.50 4.00
AMF Alonzo Mourning 2.50 6.00
AWF Antoine Walker 1.50 4.00
CWF Chris Webber 2.00 5.00
DRF David Robinson 3.00 8.00
EJF Eddie Jones 2.00 5.00
GHF Grant Hill 2.50 6.00
GPF Gary Payton 2.00 5.00
JKF Jason Kidd 3.00 8.00
KBF Kobe Bryant 8.00 20.00
KGA Kevin Garnett AU/21 200.00 400.00
KGF Kevin Garnett 3.00 8.00
KMA Karl Malone AU/32 150.00 300.00
KMF Karl Malone 2.50 6.00
MCF Antonio McDyess 1.50 4.00
MFF Michael Finley 2.00 5.00
MJA Michael Jordan AU/23 600.00 1200.00
RAF Ray Allen 2.00 5.00
RGF Reggie Miller 2.00 5.00
RMF Ron Mercer 1.25 3.00
RWF Rasheed Wallace 2.00 5.00
SAF Shareef Abdur-Rahim 1.50 4.00
SMF Stephon Marbury 1.50 4.00
SOF Shaquille O'Neal 5.00 12.00
SPF Scottie Pippen 3.00 8.00
THF Tim Hardaway 2.00 5.00

2000-01 Upper Deck Hardcourt Night Court

Randomly inserted in packs at one in 15, this 15-card set features players who always hold court whenever they are in the game. Card backs carry a "NC" prefix.
COMPLETE SET (15) 10.00 25.00
STATED ODDS 1:15
NC1 Kevin Garnett 1.25 3.00
NC2 Tim Duncan 1.50 4.00
NC3 Larry Hughes .60 1.50
NC4 Elton Brand .75 2.00
NC5 Kobe Bryant 3.00 8.00
NC6 Anfernee Hardaway 1.25 3.00
NC7 Tracy McGrady 1.25 3.00
NC8 Antonio McDyess .60 1.50
NC9 Paul Pierce .75 2.00
NC10 Lamar Odom .60 1.50
NC11 Chris Webber .75 2.00
NC12 Ray Allen .75 2.00
NC13 Allan Houston .60 1.50
NC14 Wally Szczerbiak .60 1.50
NC15 Alonzo Mourning 1.00 2.50

2000-01 Upper Deck Hardcourt Thriller Instinct

Randomly inserted in packs at one in 12, this 11-card set features players who put a scare into opposing coaches on a nightly basis. Card backs carry a "TI" prefix.
COMPLETE SET (11) 4.00 10.00
STATED ODDS 1:12
TI1 Kevin Garnett .75 2.00
TI2 Vince Carter 1.00 2.50
TI3 Shawn Marion .40 1.00
TI4 Stephon Marbury .40 1.00
TI5 Antawn Jamison .50 1.25
TI6 Jason Williams .50 1.25
TI7 Michael Finley .50 1.25
TI8 Kobe Bryant 2.00 5.00
TI9 Richard Hamilton .40 1.00
TI10 Reggie Miller .50 1.25
TI11 Elton Brand .50 1.25

2000-01 Upper Deck Hardcourt UD Authentics

Randomly inserted in packs at one in 100, this 24-card set features authentic autographs from NBA stars. Card backs are numbered using the player's initials.
STATED ODDS 1:100
AH Anfernee Hardaway 25.00 60.00
AI Allen Iverson 30.00 80.00
AM Andre Miller 5.00 12.00
BD Baron Davis 6.00 15.00
DM Darius Miles 5.00 12.00
DS Damon Stoudamire 6.00 15.00
GP Gary Payton 12.00 30.00
JM Jerome Moiso 3.00 8.00
JR Jalen Rose 5.00 12.00
JS Jerry Stackhouse 6.00 15.00
KB Kobe Bryant 100.00 200.00
KG Kevin Garnett 40.00 100.00
KM Karl Malone 80.00 160.00
LH Larry Hughes 5.00 12.00
MC Antonio McDyess 6.00 15.00
MF Marcus Fizer 5.00 12.00
MF Michael Finley 8.00 20.00
PP Paul Pierce 15.00 40.00
QR Quentin Richardson 5.00 12.00
RA Ray Allen 20.00 40.00
SA Shareef Abdur-Rahim 5.00 12.00
SF Steve Francis 6.00 15.00
TH Tim Hardaway 6.00 15.00
WS Wally Szczerbiak 5.00 12.00

2001-02 Upper Deck Hardcourt

Released in late October of 2001, this 121 card set consists of 91 veterans and 30 rookies with three different versions each. The versions are broken down into bronze, silver and gold, with each having: On Court, Off Court, and High Court. Rookies 91-100 are serial #'d to 1000 on each version for a total print run of 3000, 101-110 are serial #'d to 600 on each version for a total print run 1800, and 111-120 are serial #'d 300 on each version for a total print run of 900. Card backgrounds are slightly embossed and resemble the wooden floor of a basketball court, and both player action and portrait photos appear on the fronts. Hardcourt was packaged in 15 pack boxes where packs contained five cards and carried a suggested retail price of $4.99.
COMP.SET w/o SP's (90) 25.00 50.00
91-100 PRINT RUN 3000 PER PLAYER
91-100 THREE VERSIONS SER.#'d TO 1000
101-110 PRINT RUN 1200 PER PLAYER
101-110 THREE VERSIONS SER.#'d TO 600
111-120 PRINT RUN 900 PER PLAYER
111-120 THREE VERSIONS SER.#'d TO 300
ALL RC VERSIONS SAME VALUE
1 Jason Terry .40 1.00
2 DerMarr Johnson .25 .60
3 Toni Kukoc .40 1.00
4 Antoine Walker .30 .75
5 Paul Pierce .40 1.00
6 Kenny Anderson .30 .75
7 Jamal Mashburn .30 .75
8 Baron Davis .40 1.00
9 David Wesley .25 .60
10 Ron Artest .40 1.00
11 Jamal Crawford .40 1.00
12 Ron Mercer .25 .60
13 Andre Miller .30 .75
14 Lamond Murray .25 .60
15 Matt Harpring .25 .60
16 Michael Finley .40 1.00
17 Dirk Nowitzki .60 1.50
18 Steve Nash .60 1.50
19 Antonio McDyess .30 .75
20 Nick Van Exel .30 .75
21 James Posey .25 .60
22 Jerry Stackhouse .30 .75
23 Chucky Atkins .25 .60
24 Mateen Cleaves .25 .60
25 Antawn Jamison .40 1.00
26 Larry Hughes .30 .75
27 Marc Jackson .25 .60
28 Steve Francis .30 .75
29 Maurice Taylor .25 .60
30 Cuttino Mobley .25 .60
31 Reggie Miller .40 1.00
32 Jalen Rose .30 .75
33 Jermaine O'Neal .30 .75
34 Darius Miles .25 .60
35 Lamar Odom .30 .75
36 Elton Brand .40 1.00
37 Kobe Bryant 1.50 4.00
38 Shaquille O'Neal 1.00 2.50
39 Derek Fisher .30 .75
40 Robert Horry .30 .75
41 Alonzo Mourning .50 1.25
42 Eddie Jones .30 .75
43 Brian Grant .25 .60
44 Anthony Mason .25 .60
45 Ray Allen .40 1.00
46 Glenn Robinson .30 .75
47 Tim Thomas .25 .60
48 Kevin Garnett .60 1.50
49 Wally Szczerbiak .30 .75
50 Terrell Brandon .25 .60
51 Anthony Peeler .25 .60
52 Jason Kidd .60 1.50
53 Kenyon Martin .40 1.00
54 Stephen Jackson .30 .75
55 Latrell Sprewell .30 .75
56 Allan Houston .30 .75
57 Glen Rice .30 .75
58 Tracy McGrady .60 1.50
59 Darrell Armstrong .25 .60
60 Mike Miller .30 .75
61 Allen Iverson .75 2.00
62 Dikembe Mutombo .40 1.00
63 Aaron McKie .25 .60
64 Stephon Marbury .30 .75
65 Shawn Marion .30 .75
66 Tom Gugliotta .25 .60
67 Rasheed Wallace .40 1.00
68 Scottie Pippen .60 1.50
69 Damon Stoudamire .30 .75
70 Chris Webber .40 1.00
71 Mike Bibby .40 1.00
72 Peja Stojakovic .40 1.00
73 Tim Duncan .75 2.00
74 David Robinson .60 1.50
75 Derek Anderson .25 .60
76 Gary Payton .40 1.00
77 Rashard Lewis .40 1.00
78 Desmond Mason .30 .75
79 Vince Carter .60 1.50
80 Morris Peterson .25 .60
81 Antonio Davis .25 .60
82 Karl Malone .50 1.25
83 John Stockton .50 1.25
84 Donyell Marshall .25 .60
85 Bryant Reeves .25 .60
86 Jason Williams .30 .75
87 Stromile Swift .25 .60
88 Richard Hamilton .30 .75
89 Courtney Alexander .25 .60
90 Chris Whitney .25 .60
91A Kenny Satterfield ON RC 1.00 2.50
91B Kenny Satterfield OFF RC 1.00 2.50
91C Kenny Satterfield HI RC 1.00 2.50
92A Jeff Trepagnier ON RC 1.00 2.50
92B Jeff Trepagnier OFF RC 1.00 2.50
92C Jeff Trepagnier HI RC 1.00 2.50
93A Michael Wright ON RC 1.50 4.00
93B Michael Wright OFF RC 1.50 4.00
93C Michael Wright HI RC 1.50 4.00
94A Terence Morris ON RC 1.50 4.00
94B Terence Morris OFF RC 1.50 4.00
94C Terence Morris HI RC 1.50 4.00
95A Omar Cook ON RC 1.50 4.00
95B Omar Cook OFF RC 1.50 4.00
95C Omar Cook HI RC 1.50 4.00
96A Gilbert Arenas ON RC 2.50 6.00
96B Gilbert Arenas OFF RC 2.50 6.00
96C Gilbert Arenas HI RC 2.50 6.00
97A Joseph Forte ON RC 1.00 2.50
97B Joseph Forte OFF RC 1.00 2.50
97C Joseph Forte HI RC 1.00 2.50
98A Jamaal Tinsley ON RC 1.50 4.00
98B Jamaal Tinsley OFF RC 1.50 4.00
98C Jamaal Tinsley HI RC 1.50 4.00
99A Samuel Dalembert ON RC 1.50 4.00
99B Samuel Dalembert OFF RC 1.50 4.00
99C Samuel Dalembert HI RC 1.50 4.00
100A Gerald Wallace ON RC 2.00 5.00
100B Gerald Wallace OFF RC 2.00 5.00
100C Gerald Wallace HI RC 2.00 5.00
101A Brendan Haywood ON RC 2.00 5.00
101B Brendan Haywood OFF RC 2.00 5.00
101C Brendan Haywood HI RC 2.00 5.00
102A Richard Jefferson ON RC 3.00 8.00
102B Richard Jefferson OFF RC 3.00 8.00
102C Richard Jefferson HI RC 3.00 8.00
103A Michael Bradley ON RC 1.25 3.00
103B Michael Bradley OFF RC 1.25 3.00
103C Michael Bradley HI RC 1.25 3.00
104A Loren Woods ON RC 1.25 3.00
104B Loren Woods OFF RC 1.25 3.00
104C Loren Woods HI RC 1.25 3.00
105A Jeryl Sasser ON RC 1.25 3.00
105B Jeryl Sasser OFF RC 1.25 3.00
105C Jeryl Sasser HI RC 1.25 3.00
106A Jason Collins ON RC 1.50 4.00
106B Jason Collins OFF RC 1.50 4.00
106C Jason Collins HI RC 1.50 4.00
107A Kirk Haston ON RC 1.25 3.00
107B Kirk Haston OFF RC 1.25 3.00
107C Kirk Haston HI RC 1.25 3.00
108A Steven Hunter ON RC 1.50 4.00
108B Steven Hunter OFF RC 1.50 4.00
108C Steven Hunter HI RC 1.50 4.00
109A Troy Murphy ON RC 2.00 5.00
109B Troy Murphy OFF RC 2.00 5.00
109C Troy Murphy HI RC 2.00 5.00
110A Vladimir Radmanovic ON RC 2.00 5.00
110B Vladimir Radmanovic OFF RC 2.00 5.00
110C Vladimir Radmanovic HI RC 2.00 5.00
111A Rodney White ON RC 2.50 6.00
111B Rodney White OFF RC 2.50 6.00
111C Rodney White HI RC 2.50 6.00
112A Kedrick Brown ON RC 2.50 6.00
112B Kedrick Brown OFF RC 2.50 6.00
112C Kedrick Brown HI RC 2.50 6.00
113A Joe Johnson ON RC 5.00 12.00
113B Joe Johnson OFF RC 5.00 12.00
113C Joe Johnson HI RC 5.00 12.00
114A Eddie Griffin ON RC 3.00 8.00
114B Eddie Griffin OFF RC 3.00 8.00
114C Eddie Griffin HI RC 3.00 8.00
115A Shane Battier ON RC 8.00 20.00
115B Shane Battier OFF RC 8.00 20.00
115C Shane Battier HI RC 8.00 20.00
116A Eddy Curry ON RC 4.00 10.00
116B Eddy Curry OFF RC 4.00 10.00
116C Eddy Curry HI RC 4.00 10.00
117A Jason Richardson ON RC 5.00 12.00
117B Jason Richardson OFF RC 5.00 12.00
117C Jason Richardson HI RC 5.00 12.00
118A DeSagana Diop ON RC 3.00 8.00
118B DeSagana Diop OFF RC 3.00 8.00
118C DeSagana Diop HI RC 3.00 8.00
119A Tyson Chandler ON RC 6.00 15.00
119B Tyson Chandler OFF RC 6.00 15.00
119C Tyson Chandler HI RC 6.00 15.00
120A Kwame Brown ON RC 4.00 10.00
120B Kwame Brown OFF RC 4.00 10.00
120C Kwame Brown HI RC 4.00 10.00
121 Michael Jordan 6.00 15.00

2001-02 Upper Deck Hardcourt Exclusives

*STARS: 20X TO 50X BASE CARD HI
*ROOKIES 91-100: 3X TO 8X BASE CARD HI
*ROOKIES 101-110: 2.5X TO 6X HI
*ROOKIES 111-120: 1.25X TO 3X HI
PRINT RUN 25 SERIAL #'d SETS

2001-02 Upper Deck Hardcourt Fantastic Floor

Randomly inserted in packs, this 22-card set features both player portrait style photos and swatches of NBA court. The court swatches have the respective player's team logo burned into them and each card is sequentially numbered to 100.
PRINT RUN 100 SERIAL #'d SETS
AHLS A.Houston/L.Sprewell 8.00 20.00
AITM A.Iverson/T.McGrady 15.00 40.00
CWPS C.Webber/P.Stojakovic 12.00 30.00
EJTH E.Jones/T.Hardaway 8.00 20.00
GPRLDM Payton/Lewis/Mason 15.00 30.00
JMBD J.Mashburn/B.Davis 8.00 20.00
JSMC J.Stack/M.Cleaves 8.00 20.00

KBAI K.Bryant/A.Iverson 15.00 40.00
KBDM K.Bryant/D.Miles 15.00 40.00
KBKG K.Bryant/K.Garnett 25.00 60.00
KBRL K.Bryant/R.Lewis 12.00 30.00
KBSF K.Bryant/S.Francis 15.00 40.00
KGTBWS Garnett/Brandon/Szcz 15.00 40.00
KMJS K.Malone/J.Stockton 20.00 40.00
MCNV A.McDyess/N.Van Exel 8.00 20.00
MFDNSN Finley/Nowitzki/Nash 15.00 30.00
MJKBKG Jordan/Bryant/KG 100.00 200.00
PPAW P.Pierce/A.Walker 10.00 25.00
RAGR R.Allen/G.Robinson 8.00 20.00
RMJOJB Miller/J.O'Neal/Bender 12.50 30.00
RWSPDS Wallac/Pippn/Stoudm 10.00 25.00
TMMM T.McGrady/M.Miller 10.00 25.00

2001-02 Upper Deck Hardcourt UD Game Film/Floor

Randomly seeded in packs at the rate of one in 15, this 30-card set features player portrait style photos, a swatch of NBA floor with the player's team logo burned into it, and a piece of film with a game photo on it.
STATED ODDS 1:15
AIF Allen Iverson 8.00 20.00
BDF Baron Davis 4.00 10.00
CWF Chris Webber 4.00 10.00
DAF Darius Miles 2.50 6.00
DMF Desmond Mason 3.00 8.00
DRF David Robinson 6.00 15.00
EJF Eddie Jones 3.00 8.00
JMF Jamal Mashburn 3.00 8.00
JSF Jerry Stackhouse 3.00 8.00
JTF Jason Terry 4.00 10.00
KBF Kobe Bryant 12.00 30.00
KEF Kenyon Martin 4.00 10.00
KGF Kevin Garnett 6.00 15.00
KMF Karl Malone 5.00 12.00
LSF Latrell Sprewell 3.00 8.00
MAF Shawn Marion 3.00 8.00
MCF Antonio McDyess 3.00 8.00
MFF Michael Finley 4.00 10.00
MMF Mike Miller 3.00 8.00
MPF Morris Peterson 2.50 6.00
PPF Paul Pierce 4.00 10.00
PSF Peja Stojakovic 4.00 10.00
RAF Ray Allen 4.00 10.00
RMF Reggie Miller 4.00 10.00
SFF Steve Francis 3.00 8.00
SJF Stephen Jackson 3.00 8.00
TMF Tracy McGrady 6.00 15.00

2001-02 Upper Deck Hardcourt UD Game Floor

Randomly inserted in packs at the rate of one in 15, this 27-card set features a "court" background and player portrait style photos. The swatch of NBA court is burned with the featured player's team logo.
STATED ODDS 1:15
AI Allen Iverson 5.00 12.00
BD Baron Davis 2.50 6.00
CW Chris Webber 2.50 6.00
DA Darius Miles 1.50 4.00
DM Desmond Mason 2.00 5.00
DR David Robinson 4.00 10.00
EJ Eddie Jones 2.00 5.00
JM Jamal Mashburn 2.00 5.00
JS Jerry Stackhouse 2.00 5.00
JT Jason Terry 2.50 6.00
KB Kobe Bryant 10.00 25.00
KE Kenyon Martin 2.50 6.00
KG Kevin Garnett 4.00 10.00
KM Karl Malone 3.00 8.00
LS Latrell Sprewell 2.00 5.00
MA Shawn Marion 2.00 5.00
MC Antonio McDyess 2.00 5.00
MF Michael Finley 2.50 6.00
MM Mike Miller 2.00 5.00
MP Morris Peterson 1.50 4.00
PP Paul Pierce 2.50 6.00
PS Peja Stojakovic 2.50 6.00
RA Ray Allen 2.50 6.00
RM Reggie Miller 2.50 6.00
SF Steve Francis 2.00 5.00
SJ Stephen Jackson 2.00 5.00
TM Tracy McGrady 4.00 10.00

2001-02 Upper Deck Hardcourt UD Game Floor Autographs

Inserted one in 150, this 12-card set features two player photos along the right side of the card, one in action, and one portrait; and a piece of game used floor in the upper left hand corner of the card with each player's team logo etched into it. Cards contain authentic player autographs.
STATED ODDS 1:150
DAA Darius Miles 8.00 20.00
DMA Desmond Mason 8.00 20.00
JMA Jamal Mashburn 8.00 20.00
JSA Jerry Stackhouse 10.00 25.00
KBA Kobe Bryant 100.00 250.00
KEA Kenyon Martin 10.00 25.00
KGA Kevin Garnett 60.00 150.00
MCA Antonio McDyess 6.00 15.00
MMA Mike Miller 8.00 20.00
MPA Morris Peterson 6.00 15.00
PPA Paul Pierce 25.00 60.00
RAA Ray Allen 20.00 50.00

2002-03 Upper Deck Hardcourt

Released in late September 2002, Upper Deck Hardcourt boasts a 135-card base set divided up into 90 veteran player cards and 45 rookie cards. The rookie cards were divided up into three tiers as follows: Hardcourt Futures Level III includes card numbers 91-120 where each card is sequentially numbered to 1999, Hardcourt Futures Level II includes card numbers 121-129 where each card is sequentially numbered to 1299, and Hardcourt Futures Level I includes card numbers 130-135 where each card is sequentially numbered to 799. Base card feature full color player action photos set on a true background with a white strip along the right side of the card running from top to bottom. The rookie cards have "wood" borders along the top and bottom of the card and the words, Hardcourt Futures. Each rookie card is sequentially numbered. Upper Deck Hardcourt was issued in 15 pack boxes with packs containing five card and carried a suggested retail price of $4.99.

COMP.SET w/o SP's (90) 20.00 50.00
91-120 PRINT RUN 1999 SER.#'d SETS
121-129 PRINT RUN 1299 SER.#'d SETS
130-135 PRINT RUN 799 SER.#'d SETS
1 Shareef Abdur-Rahim .30 .75
2 Glenn Robinson .30 .75
3 Jason Terry .30 .75
4 Antoine Walker .30 .75
5 Paul Pierce .40 1.00
6 Kedrick Brown .25 .60
7 Jalen Rose .30 .75
8 Eddy Curry .25 .60
9 Tyson Chandler .40 1.00
10 Marcus Fizer .25 .60
11 Lamond Murray .25 .60
12 Darius Miles .25 .60
13 Chris Mihm .25 .60
14 Dirk Nowitzki .60 1.50
15 Michael Finley .40 1.00
16 Steve Nash .50 1.25
17 James Posey .25 .60
18 Juwan Howard .30 .75
19 Kenny Satterfield .25 .60
20 Jerry Stackhouse .30 .75
21 Clifford Robinson .25 .60
22 Ben Wallace .30 .75
23 Antawn Jamison .40 1.00
24 Jason Richardson .40 1.00
25 Gilbert Arenas .40 1.00
26 Steve Francis .30 .75
27 Cuttino Mobley .25 .60
28 Eddie Griffin .25 .60
29 Reggie Miller .40 1.00
30 Jermaine O'Neal .30 .75
31 Jamaal Tinsley .25 .60
32 Elton Brand .40 1.00
33 Andre Miller .30 .75
34 Lamar Odom .30 .75
35 Kobe Bryant 1.50 4.00
36 Shaquille O'Neal 1.00 2.50
37 Derek Fisher .30 .75
38 Devean George .25 .60
39 Pau Gasol .50 1.25
40 Jason Williams .30 .75
41 Shane Battier .40 1.00
42 Alonzo Mourning .50 1.25
43 Eddie Jones .30 .75
44 Brian Grant .25 .60
45 Ray Allen .40 1.00
46 Tim Thomas .25 .60
47 Sam Cassell .30 .75
48 Kevin Garnett .60 1.50
49 Wally Szczerbiak .30 .75
50 Terrell Brandon .25 .60
51 Jason Kidd .60 1.50
52 Richard Jefferson .40 1.00
53 Dikembe Mutombo .40 1.00
54 Jamal Mashburn .30 .75
55 Baron Davis .30 .75
56 David Wesley .25 .60
57 Allan Houston .30 .75
58 Latrell Sprewell .30 .75
59 Antonio McDyess .30 .75
60 Tracy McGrady .60 1.50
61 Mike Miller .30 .75
62 Darrell Armstrong .25 .60
63 Allen Iverson .60 1.50
64 Keith Van Horn .30 .75
65 Aaron McKie .25 .60
66 Stephon Marbury .30 .75
67 Shawn Marion .30 .75
68 Anfernee Hardaway .60 1.50
69 Rasheed Wallace .40 1.00
70 Damon Stoudamire .30 .75
71 Scottie Pippen .60 1.50
72 Chris Webber .40 1.00
73 Mike Bibby .40 1.00
74 Peja Stojakovic .40 1.00
75 Tim Duncan .75 2.00
76 David Robinson .60 1.50
77 Tony Parker .50 1.25
78 Gary Payton .40 1.00
79 Rashard Lewis .40 1.00
80 Desmond Mason .30 .75
81 Vince Carter .60 1.50
82 Morris Peterson .25 .60
83 Antonio Davis .25 .60
84 Karl Malone .50 1.25
85 John Stockton .50 1.25
86 Andrei Kirilenko .40 1.00
87 Richard Hamilton .30 .75
88 Michael Jordan 3.00 8.00
89 Chris Whitney .25 .60
90 Kwame Brown .25 .60
91 Efthimios Rentzias RC .75 2.00
92 Marko Jaric 1.25 3.00
93 Jiri Welsch RC 1.00 2.50
94 Carlos Boozer RC 1.25 3.00
95 Fred Jones RC 1.00 2.50
96 Sam Clancy RC 1.00 2.50
97 Predrag Savovic RC 1.00 2.50
98 Frank Williams RC .75 2.00
99 Rod Grizzard RC .75 2.00
100 Casey Jacobsen RC 1.00 2.50
101 Jamal Sampson RC 1.25 3.00
102 Lonny Baxter RC .75 2.00
103 Darius Songaila RC 1.25 3.00
104 Tito Maddox RC .75 2.00
105 Chris Owens RC .75 2.00
106 Juan Dixon RC 1.25 3.00
107 Chris Jefferies RC .75 2.00
108 Dan Dickau RC 1.00 2.50
109 Manu Ginobili RC 3.00 8.00
110 Tamar Slay RC .75 2.00
111 Matt Barnes RC 1.50 4.00
112 Vincent Yarbrough RC .75 2.00
113 Bostjan Nachbar RC 1.00 2.50
114 Dan Gadzuric RC 1.00 2.50
115 Robert Archibald RC .75 2.00
116 Ryan Humphrey RC 1.00 2.50
117 Tayshaun Prince RC 1.50 4.00
118 John Salmons RC 1.25 3.00
119 Steve Logan RC 1.25 3.00
120 Melvin Ely RC 1.00 2.50
121 Nikoloz Tskitishvili RC 1.00 2.50
122 Qyntel Woods RC 1.25 3.00
123 Marcus Haislip RC 1.25 3.00
124 Nene Hilario RC 1.50 4.00
125 Amare Stoudemire RC 2.00 5.00
126 Jared Jeffries RC 1.25 3.00
127 Kareem Rush RC 1.25 3.00
128 Chris Wilcox RC 1.25 3.00
129 Curtis Borchardt RC 1.00 2.50
130 Drew Gooden RC 2.00 5.00
131 Mike Dunleavy RC 2.00 5.00
132 DaJuan Wagner RC 1.50 4.00
133 Caron Butler RC 2.00 5.00
134 Yao Ming RC 4.00 10.00
135 Jay Williams RC 2.00 5.00

2002-03 Upper Deck Hardcourt Autographs

Randomly seeded in packs at the rate of one in 30, this 21-card set also showcases the base Hardcourt set design with a "cut signature" signed on plastic in place of the white strip from the base set. Information received from Upper Deck suggests the following players are short printed: Jerry Stackhouse, Kobe Bryant, Kevin Garnett, Marcus Fizer, and Wally Szczerbiak. The Michael Jordan card is sequentially numbered to 23.
STATED ODDS 1:30
AJC Alvin Jones 4.00 10.00
CAC Courtney Alexander 4.00 10.00
GAC Gilbert Arenas 8.00 20.00
HMC Hanno Mottola 4.00 10.00
JMC Jamaal Magloire 4.00 10.00
JRC Jason Richardson 6.00 15.00
JSC Jerry Stackhouse SP 10.00 25.00
JTC Jamaal Tinsley 4.00 10.00
KBC Kobe Bryant SP 125.00 250.00
KGC Kevin Garnett SP 40.00 100.00
KMC Kenyon Martin 6.00 15.00
KSC Kenny Satterfield 4.00 10.00
LHC Larry Hughes 4.00 10.00
LMC Lamond Murray 4.00 10.00
MFC Marcus Fizer SP 4.00 10.00
MJC Michael Jordan/23 500.00 800.00
MMC Mike Miller 4.00 10.00
QRC Quentin Richardson 4.00 10.00
RWC Rodney White 4.00 10.00
TCC Tyson Chandler 6.00 15.00
WSC Wally Szczerbiak SP 6.00 15.00

2002-03 Upper Deck Hardcourt UD Game Floor

Randomly inserted in packs at the rate of one in 15, this 11-card set showcases a horizontal design with full color player action photos on the right and a swatch of game used floor on the left. Each floor swatch has the featured player's team logo burned into it. Information received from Upper Deck suggests that the Michael Jordan card is short printed.
STATED ODDS 1:15
JKF Jason Kidd 2.50 6.00
JSF Jerry Stackhouse 1.25 3.00
KBF Kobe Bryant 6.00 15.00
KGF Kevin Garnett 2.50 6.00
MJF Michael Jordan SP 12.00 30.00
MMF Mike Miller 1.25 3.00
PPF Paul Pierce 1.50 4.00
PSF Peja Stojakovic 1.50 4.00
RLF Rashard Lewis 1.50 4.00
SFF Steve Francis 1.25 3.00
SMF Stephon Marbury 1.25 3.00

2002-03 Upper Deck Hardcourt UD Game Floor Metallics

Randomly seeded in packs at the rate of one in 150, this 15-card set parallels the design of the base Hardcourt UD Game Floor insert set enhanced with "metal" surrounding the floor swatch. Information received from Upper Deck suggests the following players are short printed: Kobe Bryant and Michael Jordan.
STATED ODDS 1:150
AIM Allen Iverson 8.00 20.00
AWM Antoine Walker 4.00 10.00
CWM Chris Webber 6.00 15.00
DNM Dirk Nowitzki 8.00 20.00
KBM Kobe Bryant SP 40.00 100.00
KGM Kevin Garnett 8.00 20.00
LSM Latrell Sprewell 4.00 10.00
MFF Michael Finley 5.00 12.00
MJM Michael Jordan SP 100.00 250.00
RAM Ray Allen 5.00 12.00
RLM Rashard Lewis 5.00 12.00
SFM Steve Francis 4.00 10.00
SHM Shawn Marion 4.00 10.00
SMM Stephon Marbury 4.00 10.00
TMN Tracy McGrady 8.00 20.00

2002-03 Upper Deck Hardcourt UD Game Floor/Film

Randomly inserted in packs at the rate of one in 30, this 10-card set features a full color player action photo on the left, and swatch of game used floor in the middle, and a swatch of film with an in-action game photo. Information received from Upper Deck suggests the following players are short printed: Kobe Bryant and Michael Jordan.
STATED ODDS 1:30
AIFF Allen Iverson 5.00 12.00
CWFF Chris Webber 3.00 8.00
DNFF Dirk Nowitzki 5.00 12.00
JKFF Jason Kidd 5.00 12.00
KBFF Kobe Bryant SP 12.50 30.00
KGFF Kevin Garnett 5.00 12.00
MJFF Michael Jordan SP 30.00 80.00
RLFF Rashard Lewis 3.00 8.00
SFFF Steve Francis 2.50 6.00
TMFF Tracy McGrady 5.00 12.00

2002-03 Upper Deck Hardcourt UD Game Jersey Metallics

Randomly inserted in packs at the rate of one in 300, this 15-card set is similar to the Hardcourt UD Game Floor Metallics. The design is opposite, however, placing the player photo on the left and the swatch of jersey surrounded by "metal" on the right. Information from Upper Deck suggests several players are short printed. Those players appear below with print run numbers.
STATED ODDS 1:300
AIJ Allen Iverson/75 25.00 60.00
AMJ Andre Miller 5.00 12.00
CWJ Chris Webber/75 25.00 60.00
DMJ Darius Miles 4.00 10.00
EBJ Elton Brand 6.00 15.00
JKJ Jason Kidd 10.00 25.00
KBJ Kobe Bryant/50 60.00 120.00
KGJ Kevin Garnett 10.00 25.00
KMJ Karl Malone 8.00 20.00
MCJ Antonio McDyess 5.00 12.00
MJJ Michael Jordan/23 175.00 350.00
MMJ Mike Miller 5.00 12.00
PPJ Paul Pierce 6.00 15.00
SMJ Stephon Marbury 5.00 12.00
TMJ Tracy McGrady/75 25.00 60.00

2003-04 Upper Deck Hardcourt

Released in late September 2003, Hardcourt features a 132-card set divided up into 90 base veteran cards, 36 rookie cards sequentially numbered to 1999 (cards 91-126) and six rookie cards sequentially numbered to 799. Base cards have white circles in the upper right and lower left hand corner with player photos in the middle and rookie cards place player photos in the middle of colorful backgrounds set to match the player's team colors. Hardcourt was packaged in 15-pack boxes with five cards per pack which carried a suggested retail price of $4.99.
COMP.SET w/o SP's (90) 15.00 40.00
91-126 PRINT RUN 1999 SER.#'d SETS
1 Shareef Abdur-Rahim .25 .60
2 Jason Terry .25 .60
3 Glenn Robinson .25 .60
4 Paul Pierce .30 .75
5 Antoine Walker .30 .75
6 Vin Baker .20 .50
7 Jalen Rose .25 .60
8 Tyson Chandler .25 .60
9 Michael Jordan 2.50 6.00
10 DaJuan Wagner .20 .50
11 Ricky Davis .25 .60
12 Darius Miles .20 .50
13 Dirk Nowitzki .50 1.25
14 Michael Finley .30 .75
15 Steve Nash .40 1.00
16 Nene .25 .60
17 Marcus Camby .25 .60
18 Nikoloz Tskitishvili .20 .50
19 Richard Hamilton .25 .60
20 Ben Wallace .25 .60
21 Tayshaun Prince .25 .60
22 Antawn Jamison .25 .60
23 Jason Richardson .30 .75
24 Gilbert Arenas .25 .60
25 Steve Francis .25 .60
26 Yao Ming .60 1.50
27 Eddie Griffin .20 .50
28 Reggie Miller .30 .75
29 Jamaal Tinsley .20 .50
30 Jermaine O'Neal .25 .60
31 Elton Brand .30 .75
32 Andre Miller .25 .60
33 Lamar Odom .25 .60
34 Kobe Bryant 1.25 3.00
35 Gary Payton .30 .75
36 Shaquille O'Neal .75 2.00
37 Karl Malone .40 1.00
38 Pau Gasol .30 .75
39 Shane Battier .25 .60
40 Mike Miller .25 .60
41 Eddie Jones .25 .60
42 Rasual Butler .20 .50
43 Caron Butler .25 .60
44 Michael Redd .30 .75
45 Joe Smith .25 .60
46 Desmond Mason .25 .60
47 Kevin Garnett .50 1.25
48 Wally Szczerbiak .25 .60
49 Sam Cassell .25 .60
50 Jason Kidd .50 1.25
51 Richard Jefferson .25 .60
52 Alonzo Mourning .40 1.00
53 Baron Davis .25 .60
54 Jamal Mashburn .25 .60
55 Jamaal Magloire .20 .50
56 Allan Houston .25 .60
57 Antonio McDyess .25 .60
58 Latrell Sprewell .25 .60
59 Tracy McGrady .40 1.00
60 Grant Hill .40 1.00
61 Drew Gooden .25 .60
62 Allen Iverson .50 1.25
63 Keith Van Horn .25 .60
64 Kenny Thomas .20 .50
65 Stephon Marbury .25 .60
66 Shawn Marion .25 .60
67 Amare Stoudemire .40 1.00
68 Rasheed Wallace .30 .75
69 Bonzi Wells .20 .50
70 Damon Stoudamire .25 .60
71 Chris Webber .30 .75
72 Mike Bibby .30 .75
73 Peja Stojakovic .30 .75
74 Bobby Jackson .20 .50
75 Tim Duncan .50 1.25
76 David Robinson .50 1.25
77 Tony Parker .30 .75
78 Manu Ginobili .40 1.00
79 Ray Allen .30 .75
80 Rashard Lewis .30 .75
81 Reggie Evans .20 .50
82 Vince Carter .50 1.25
83 Morris Peterson .20 .50
84 Antonio Davis .20 .50
85 Matt Harpring .20 .50
86 John Stockton .40 1.00
87 Andrei Kirilenko .30 .75
88 Jerry Stackhouse .25 .60
89 Kwame Brown .20 .50
90 Larry Hughes .25 .60
91 Kirk Hinrich RC 2.00 5.00
92 T.J. Ford RC 1.50 4.00
93 Mike Sweetney RC 1.25 3.00
94 Jarvis Hayes RC 1.25 3.00
95 Mickael Pietrus RC 1.50 4.00
96 Nick Collison RC 1.50 4.00
97 Marcus Banks RC 1.25 3.00
98 Luke Ridnour RC 1.50 4.00
99 Reece Gaines RC 1.25 3.00
100 Troy Bell RC 1.25 3.00
101 Zarko Cabarkapa RC 1.25 3.00
102 David West RC 2.00 5.00
103 Aleksandar Pavlovic RC 1.50 4.00
104 Dahntay Jones RC 1.50 4.00
105 Boris Diaw RC 2.00 5.00
106 Zoran Planinic RC 1.25 3.00
107 Travis Outlaw RC 1.50 4.00
108 Brian Cook RC 1.25 3.00
109 Carlos Delfino RC 1.50 4.00
110 Ndudi Ebi RC 1.25 3.00
111 Kendrick Perkins RC 1.50 4.00
112 Leandro Barbosa RC 2.00 5.00
113 Josh Howard RC 2.00 5.00
114 Maciej Lampe RC 1.25 3.00
115 Jason Kapono RC 1.25 3.00
116 Luke Walton RC 2.00 5.00
117 Jerome Beasley RC 1.25 3.00
118 Sofoklis Schortsanitis RC 1.25 3.00
119 Kyle Korver RC 2.50 6.00
120 Travis Hansen RC 1.25 3.00
121 Steve Blake RC 1.50 4.00
122 Slavko Vranes RC 1.25 3.00
123 Zaur Pachulia RC 2.00 5.00
124 Keith Bogans RC 1.25 3.00
125 Matt Bonner RC 2.00 5.00
126 Maurice Williams RC 2.00 5.00
127 Chris Kaman RC 4.00 10.00
128 Dwyane Wade RC 10.00 25.00
129 Chris Bosh RC 6.00 15.00
130 Carmelo Anthony RC 12.00 30.00
131 Darko Milicic RC 3.00 8.00
132 LeBron James RC 60.00 150.00

2003-04 Upper Deck Hardcourt Clear Commemoratives Autographs

Inserted in packs at the rate of one in 60, this 20-card set utilizes a horizontal design with a semi-circular cut in the bottom of the card which is filled with a clear acetate plastic that the player signed.
STATED ODDS 1:60
BIA Chauncey Billups 15.00 40.00
CBA Carlos Boozer 5.00 12.00
EBA Earl Boykins 5.00 12.00
EGA Eddie Griffin 5.00 12.00
ETA Etan Thomas 5.00 12.00
GAA Gilbert Arenas 5.00 12.00
GWA Gerald Wallace 5.00 12.00
JDA Juan Dixon 5.00 12.00
JMA Jerome Moiso 5.00 12.00
JWA Jay Williams 5.00 12.00
KBA Kobe Bryant SP 125.00 250.00
LJA LeBron James 600.00 1000.00
MAA Marko Jaric 5.00 12.00
MBA Mike Bibby 5.00 12.00
MJA Michael Jordan SP 600.00 1000.00
MPA Morris Peterson 5.00 12.00
PSA Peja Stojakovic 6.00 15.00
REA Reggie Evans 5.00 12.00
TMA Tracy McGrady 15.00 40.00
TPA Tony Parker 12.00 30.00

2003-04 Upper Deck Hardcourt Floor

Inserted in packs at the rate of one in 30, this 27-card set places full color player action photos on each card with a star-shaped swatch of game-used floor in the lower right-hand corner.
STATED ODDS 1:30
AIF Allen Iverson 4.00 10.00
CWF Chris Webber 2.50 6.00
DRF David Robinson 4.00 10.00
GHF Grant Hill 4.00 10.00
GPF Gary Payton 2.50 6.00
GRF Glenn Robinson 2.00 5.00
JKF Jason Kidd 4.00 10.00
JMF Jamal Mashburn 2.00 5.00
JOF Jermaine O'Neal 2.00 5.00
JSF Jerry Stackhouse 2.00 5.00
JSF John Stockton 3.00 8.00
KBF Kobe Bryant 12.00 30.00
KGF Kevin Garnett 4.00 10.00
KMF Karl Malone 3.00 8.00
LJF LeBron James 12.00 30.00
LSF Latrell Sprewell 2.00 5.00
MJF Michael Jordan 25.00 60.00
RAF Ray Allen 2.50 6.00
RMF Reggie Miller 2.50 6.00
RWF Rasheed Wallace 2.50 6.00
SAF Shareef Abdur-Rahim 2.00 5.00
SMF Steve Nash 3.00 8.00
SMF Stephon Marbury 2.00 5.00
SOF Shaquille O'Neal 6.00 15.00
SPF Scottie Pippen 4.00 10.00
TDF Tim Duncan 4.00 10.00
TMF Tracy McGrady 3.00 8.00

2003-04 Upper Deck Hardcourt Floor/Fabric Combos

Randomly seeded in packs at the rate of one in 60, this 20-card set is vertically desiged with full-color player action photos. Centered towards the bottom of the card is a swatch of game-used floor with an embedded jersey swatch on the left side.
STATED ODDS 1:60
AIFF Allen Iverson 10.00 25.00
CWFF Chris Webber 6.00 15.00
DRFF David Robinson 10.00 25.00
GHFF Grant Hill 8.00 20.00
GPFF Gary Payton 6.00 15.00
JKFF Jason Kidd 10.00 25.00
JOFF Jermaine O'Neal 5.00 12.00
JSFF John Stockton 8.00 20.00
KBFF Kobe Bryant 20.00 50.00
KMFF Karl Malone 8.00 20.00
LJFF LeBron James 100.00 200.00
LSFF Latrell Sprewell 5.00 12.00
MJFF Michael Jordan 75.00 150.00
RAFF Ray Allen 6.00 15.00
SAFF Shareef Abdur-Rahim 5.00 12.00
SMFF Stephon Marbury 5.00 12.00
SNFF Steve Nash 8.00 20.00
SPFF Scottie Pippen 10.00 25.00
TDFF Tim Duncan 10.00 25.00
TMFF Tracy McGrady 8.00 20.00

2003-04 Upper Deck Hardcourt Hardwood Commemoratives

Inserted at the rate of one in 300, this 14-card set is horizontally desiged with a large swatch of game-used floor appearing centered towards the bottom. A dual swatch version was also produced, featuring two players, and these cards are sequentially numbered to 8. Please note that all SP's in the set were announced by Upper Deck.
STATED ODDS 1:300
STATED ODDS FOR DUAL 1:80000
AMAF Antonio McDyess 8.00 20.00
AWAF Antoine Walker 8.00 20.00
CBAF Chauncey Billups 8.00 20.00
DRAF David Robinson 30.00 80.00
DWAF Dominique Wilkins 6.00 15.00
JBAF LeBron James SP 400.00 600.00
JKAF Jason Kidd 20.00 50.00
JRAF Jalen Rose 8.00 20.00
JSAF Jerry Stackhouse 8.00 20.00
KBAF Kobe Bryant SP 100.00 200.00
KGAF Kevin Garnett SP 50.00 120.00
TMAF Tracy McGrady SP 25.00 60.00

2003-04 Upper Deck Hardcourt Heart of a Champion

Randomly inserted, this 15-card set traces the career of Michael Jordan with a design similar to that of the base Hardcourt cards. Several different versions of this set were inserted in packs. Cards numbers 1-15 were inserted at the rate of one in 23. Silver card numbers 1-15 were inserted at the rate of one in 60, and Gold card numbers 1-15 were inserted at the rate of one in 180.
COMPLETE SET (15) 20.00 50.00
COMMON MJ (1-15) 3.00 8.00
1-15 MJ STATED ODDS 1:23
SILVER STATED ODDS 1:60
COMMON GOLD (1-15) 12.00 30.00
GOLD STATED ODDS 1:180

2003-04 Upper Deck Hardcourt LeBron James Floor

Randomly inserted at the rate of one in 15, this 12-card set features a horizontal design with photos on the right spanning LeBron's High School to the Pros career and a circular swatch of floor on the left.
COMMON CARD (LB1-LB12) 8.00 20.00
STATED ODDS 1:15

2004-05 Upper Deck Hardcourt

Released in October 2004, Upper Deck Hardcourt boasts a 132-card base set where cards 1-90 feature veteran players, cards 91-96 feature rookies serially numbered to 999 and cards 97-132 feature rookies serially numbered to 1999. Hardcourt was packaged in 15-pack boxes where each pack contained five cards and carried a suggested retail price of $4.99.
COMP.SET w/o SP's (90) 15.00 40.00
91-96 RC PRINT RUN 999 SER.#'d SETS
105-132 RC PRINT RUN 1999 SER.#'d SETS
1 Boris Diaw .25 .60
2 Antoine Walker .30 .75
3 Al Harrington .25 .60
4 Jiri Welsch .20 .50
5 Paul Pierce .30 .75
6 Ricky Davis .25 .60
7 Gerald Wallace .25 .60
8 Eddie House .20 .50
9 Jason Kapono .20 .50
10 Tyson Chandler .25 .60
11 Eddy Curry .20 .50
12 Kirk Hinrich .25 .60
13 Jeff McInnis .20 .50
14 Dajuan Wagner .20 .50
15 LeBron James 2.00 5.00
16 Michael Finley .30 .75
17 Dirk Nowitzki .50 1.25
18 Marquis Daniels .20 .50
19 Kenyon Martin .25 .60
20 Carmelo Anthony .60 1.50
21 Nene .25 .60
22 Ben Wallace .25 .60
23 Richard Hamilton .25 .60
24 Rasheed Wallace .30 .75
25 Mike Dunleavy .25 .60
26 Jason Richardson .30 .75
27 Derek Fisher .25 .60
28 Tracy McGrady .40 1.00
29 Tyronn Lue .20 .50
30 Yao Ming .60 1.50
31 Jermaine O'Neal .25 .60
32 Reggie Miller .30 .75
33 Stephen Jackson .25 .60
34 Corey Maggette .25 .60
35 Elton Brand .30 .75
36 Marko Jaric .20 .50
37 Karl Malone .40 1.00
38 Kobe Bryant 1.25 3.00
39 Lamar Odom .25 .60
40 James Posey .20 .50
41 Mike Miller .25 .60
42 Pau Gasol .30 .75
43 Dwyane Wade .50 1.25
44 Eddie Jones .25 .60
45 Shaquille O'Neal .75 2.00
46 Desmond Mason .25 .60
47 Michael Redd .25 .60
48 T.J. Ford .20 .50
49 Kevin Garnett .50 1.25
50 Latrell Sprewell .25 .60
51 Sam Cassell .25 .60
52 Jason Kidd .50 1.25
53 Aaron Williams .20 .50
54 Richard Jefferson .25 .60
55 Baron Davis .25 .60
56 Jamaal Magloire .20 .50
57 Jamal Mashburn .25 .60
58 Allan Houston .25 .60
59 Jamal Crawford .30 .75
60 Stephon Marbury .25 .60
61 Hedo Turkoglu .25 .60
62 Steve Francis .25 .60
63 Cuttino Mobley .20 .50
64 Allen Iverson .50 1.25
65 Glenn Robinson .25 .60
66 Kenny Thomas .20 .50
67 Amare Stoudemire .25 .60
68 Quentin Richardson .25 .60
69 Shawn Marion .25 .60
70 Darius Miles .20 .50
71 Shareef Abdur-Rahim .25 .60
72 Zach Randolph .25 .60
73 Chris Webber .30 .75
74 Mike Bibby .30 .75
75 Peja Stojakovic .30 .75
76 Manu Ginobili .40 1.00
77 Tim Duncan .50 1.25
78 Tony Parker .30 .75
79 Rashard Lewis .30 .75
80 Ray Allen .30 .75
81 Ronald Murray .20 .50
82 Chris Bosh .30 .75
83 Jalen Rose .25 .60
84 Vince Carter .50 1.25
85 Andrei Kirilenko .25 .60
86 Carlos Arroyo .20 .50
87 Carlos Boozer .25 .60
88 Gilbert Arenas .25 .60
89 Jarvis Hayes .20 .50
90 Antawn Jamison .25 .60
91 Dwight Howard RC 5.00 12.00
92 Emeka Okafor RC 2.00 5.00
93 Ben Gordon RC 2.50 6.00
94 Shaun Livingston RC 2.50 6.00
95 Devin Harris RC 2.00 5.00
96 Josh Childress RC 2.00 5.00
97 Luol Deng RC 2.00 5.00
98 Andre Iguodala RC 2.50 6.00
99 Luke Jackson RC 1.25 3.00
100 Andris Biedrins RC 1.25 3.00
101 Sebastian Telfair RC 1.50 4.00
102 Josh Smith RC 2.00 5.00
103 Rafael Araujo RC 1.25 3.00
104 Robert Swift RC 1.25 3.00
105 Kris Humphries RC 2.00 5.00
106 Al Jefferson RC 2.50 6.00
107 Kirk Snyder RC 1.25 3.00
108 J.R. Smith RC 2.00 5.00
109 Dorell Wright RC 2.00 5.00
110 Jameer Nelson RC 2.00 5.00
111 Pavel Podkolzin RC 1.25 3.00
112 Justin Reed RC 1.25 3.00
113 Sergei Monia RC 1.25 3.00
114 Delonte West RC 2.00 5.00
115 Tony Allen RC 2.00 5.00
116 Kevin Martin RC 2.50 6.00
117 Sasha Vujacic RC 2.00 5.00
118 Beno Udrih RC 1.50 4.00
119 David Harrison RC 1.25 3.00
120 Anderson Varejao RC 1.50 4.00
121 Jackson Vroman RC 1.25 3.00
122 Peter John Ramos RC 1.25 3.00
123 Lionel Chalmers RC 2.00 5.00
124 Donta Smith RC 1.25 3.00
125 Andre Emmett RC 1.25 3.00
126 Antonio Burks RC 1.50 4.00
127 Royal Ivey RC 1.50 4.00
128 Chris Duhon RC 2.00 5.00
129 Trevor Ariza RC 2.00 5.00
130 Ha Seung-Jin RC 2.00 5.00
131 Romain Sato RC 1.25 3.00
132 Rickey Paulding RC 1.25 3.00

2005-06 Upper Deck Hardcourt UD Promos

*PROMOS: .75X TO 2X BASIC

2004-05 Upper Deck Hardcourt Clear Commemorative Autographs

Inserted in packs at the rate of one in 60, this 18-card set is horizontally designed and has a die-cut area where a clear piece of plastic was inserted with the featured players autograph.
STATED ODDS 1:60
SP INFO PROVIDED BY UPPER DECK
AH Al Harrington 5.00 12.00
AK Andrei Kirilenko 6.00 15.00
AM Andre Miller 5.00 12.00
CH Chauncey Billups 8.00 20.00
CM Corey Maggette 5.00 12.00
DR Dennis Rodman 40.00 100.00
GA Gilbert Arenas 6.00 15.00
JR Jason Richardson 5.00 12.00
KB Kobe Bryant SP 100.00 200.00
KG Kevin Garnett SP 40.00 100.00
LJ LeBron James SP 200.00 400.00
LO Lamar Odom 8.00 20.00
MJ Michael Jordan SP 400.00 600.00
PS Peja Stojakovic 6.00 15.00
RJ Richard Jefferson 5.00 12.00
TM Tracy McGrady SP 15.00 40.00
ZO Alonzo Mourning 15.00 40.00
ZR Zach Randolph 6.00 15.00

2004-05 Upper Deck Hardcourt Engraved Endorsements

Inserted in packs at the rate of one in 300, this 18-card set features engraved likenesses of the players on a wood card along with an autograph.
STATED ODDS 1:300
SP INFO PROVIDED BY UPPER DECK
AI Andre Iguodala 30.00 80.00
AM Alonzo Mourning 20.00 50.00
AS Amare Stoudemire 15.00 40.00
BD Baron Davis 10.00 25.00
CA Carmelo Anthony 50.00 100.00
CB Carlos Boozer 10.00 25.00
DH Dwight Howard 40.00 100.00
JK Jason Kidd 20.00 50.00
JR Jason Richardson 10.00 25.00
KB Kobe Bryant SP 100.00 200.00
KG Kevin Garnett SP 50.00 120.00
LJ LeBron James SP 200.00 350.00
LO Lamar Odom 10.00 25.00
MJ Michael Jordan SP 1000.00 1500.00
PP Paul Pierce 15.00 40.00
RM Reggie Miller 100.00 200.00
TM Tracy McGrady SP 50.00 100.00
YM Yao Ming 75.00 200.00

2004-05 Upper Deck Hardcourt Hardwood Commemoratives

Randomly inserted in packs at the rate of one in 60, this 21-card set places player photos along with an autographed swatch of wood.
STATED ODDS 1:60
SP INFO PROVIDED BY UPPER DECK
AJ Antawn Jamison 5.00 12.00
AS Amare Stoudemire 10.00 25.00
BD Baron Davis 5.00 12.00
BO Carlos Boozer 5.00 12.00
CA Carmelo Anthony 25.00 60.00
DA Darius Miles 5.00 12.00
DW Dwyane Wade 30.00 80.00
FJ Fred Jones 5.00 12.00
GW Gerald Wallace 5.00 12.00
JA Jalen Rose 5.00 12.00
JK Jason Kidd 15.00 40.00
JS Jerry Stackhouse 5.00 12.00
KB Kobe Bryant SP 125.00 250.00
KG Kevin Garnett SP 40.00 100.00
LJ LeBron James 125.00 250.00
MJ Michael Jordan SP 400.00 700.00
PG Pau Gasol 8.00 20.00
RH Richard Hamilton 5.00 12.00
RJ Richard Jefferson 5.00 12.00
SA Shareef Abdur-Rahim 5.00 12.00
SC Sam Cassell 5.00 12.00

2004-05 Upper Deck Hardcourt Hardwood Commemoratives Dual

Inserted in packs at the rate of one in 300, this 18-card set parallels the design of the Hardwood Commemoratives insert but places two players and two autographs on each card.
STATED ODDS 1:300
SP INFO PROVIDED BY UPPER DECK
AM C.Anthony/A.Miller SP 25.00 60.00
BH C.Billups/R.Hamilton 20.00 50.00
BS M.Bibby/P.Stojakovic 10.00 25.00
GB P.Gasol/S.Battier 20.00 50.00
GC K.Garnett/S.Cassell SP 60.00 150.00
JA A.Jamison/G.Arenas 10.00 25.00
JB L.James/C.Boozer SP 200.00 350.00
JJ L.James/M.Jordan SP 500.00 1000.00
KJ J.Kidd/R.Jefferson 10.00 25.00
KS A.Kirilenko/J.Stockton 50.00 120.00
MH R.Miller/A.Harrington 40.00 100.00
MR D.Mason/M.Redd 10.00 25.00
OW L.Odom/D.Wade 25.00 60.00
PR G.Payton/K.Rush 15.00 40.00
RJ J.Rich/F.Jones 10.00 25.00
RM Z.Randolph/S.Abdur-Rahim 10.00 25.00
SH J.Stackhouse/J.Howard 10.00 25.00
SM A.Stoudemire/S.Marion 10.00 25.00

2004-05 Upper Deck Hardcourt Materials

Inserted in packs at the rate of one in 15, this 42-card set places player images on the top of the card and an "M" shaped swatch of memorabilia on the bottom. A combos version with a swatch of wood was also inserted at the rate of one in 15.
STATED ODDS 1:15
*COMBO SINGLES: .6X TO 1.5X BASE JSY HI
COMBO STATED ODDS 1:15
SP INFO PROVIDED BY UPPER DECK
AI Allen Iverson 4.00 10.00
AJ Antawn Jamison 2.00 5.00
AK Andrei Kirilenko 2.00 5.00
AS Amare Stoudemire 2.00 5.00
BD Baron Davis 2.00 5.00
BW Ben Wallace 2.00 5.00
CA Carmelo Anthony 5.00 12.00
CB Carlos Boozer 2.00 5.00
DN Dirk Nowitzki 4.00 10.00
DW Dwyane Wade 4.00 10.00
EB Elton Brand 2.50 6.00
EG Manu Ginobili 3.00 8.00
GA Gilbert Arenas 2.00 5.00
JC Jamal Crawford 2.50 6.00
JK Jason Kidd 4.00 10.00
JM Jamaal Magloire 2.00 5.00
JO Jermaine O'Neal 2.00 5.00

JR Jason Richardson 2.50 6.00
JT Jason Terry 2.00 5.00
KB Kobe Bryant SP 10.00 25.00
KG Kevin Garnett 4.00 10.00
LJ LeBron James 10.00 25.00
LO Lamar Odom 2.00 5.00
MB Mike Bibby 2.50 6.00
MJ Michael Jordan SP 30.00 80.00
PG Pau Gasol 2.50 6.00
PP Paul Pierce 2.50 6.00
PS Peja Stojakovic 2.50 6.00
RA Ray Allen 2.50 6.00
RJ Richard Jefferson 2.00 5.00
RM Reggie Miller 2.50 6.00
SA Shareef Abdur-Rahim 2.00 5.00
SF Steve Francis 2.00 5.00
SH Shawn Marion 2.00 5.00
SM Stephon Marbury 2.00 5.00
SN Steve Nash 3.00 8.00
SO Shaquille O'Neal 6.00 15.00
TD Tim Duncan 4.00 10.00
TM Tracy McGrady 3.00 8.00
TP Tony Parker 2.50 6.00
YM Yao Ming 5.00 12.00
ZR Zach Randolph 2.00 5.00

2005-06 Upper Deck Hardcourt

Released in late September, Hardcourt boasts a 137 card base set where cards 1-90 feature veterans and 91-140 feature rookies sequentially numbered to 1750. Base cards have wood grain borders on the left and the right, full-color player photos set on backgrounds set to match team colors and silver foil highlights. Hardcourt was packaged in 15-pack boxes of five cards each and carried a SRP of $4.99.

COMP.SET w/o SP's (90) 15.00 40.00
91-140 RC PRINT RUN 1750 SER.#'d SETS
1 Tony Delk .20 .50
2 Josh Smith .25 .60
3 Al Harrington .25 .60
4 Antoine Walker .25 .60
5 Gary Payton .30 .75
6 Paul Pierce .30 .75
7 Kareem Rush .20 .50
8 Emeka Okafor .25 .60
9 Primoz Brezec .20 .50
10 Eddy Curry .20 .50
11 Kirk Hinrich .25 .60
12 Ben Gordon .25 .60
13 Drew Gooden .25 .60
14 LeBron James 1.25 3.00
15 Zydrunas Ilgauskas .25 .60
16 Dirk Nowitzki .50 1.25
17 Jason Terry .25 .60
18 Jerry Stackhouse .25 .60
19 Carmelo Anthony .60 1.50
20 Kenyon Martin .25 .60
21 Earl Boykins .20 .50
22 Ben Wallace .25 .60
23 Chauncey Billups .30 .75
24 Richard Hamilton .25 .60
25 Troy Murphy .20 .50
26 Jason Richardson .30 .75
27 Baron Davis .25 .60
28 Tracy McGrady .40 1.00
29 Yao Ming .40 1.00
30 Juwan Howard .25 .60
31 Jermaine O'Neal .25 .60
32 Stephen Jackson .25 .60
33 Ron Artest .30 .75
34 Corey Maggette .25 .60
35 Elton Brand .30 .75
36 Bobby Simmons .20 .50
37 Caron Butler .25 .60
38 Kobe Bryant 1.25 3.00
39 Lamar Odom .25 .60
40 Mike Miller .25 .60
41 Jason Williams .25 .60
42 Pau Gasol .30 .75
43 Dwyane Wade .50 1.25
44 Eddie Jones .25 .60
45 Shaquille O'Neal .60 1.50
46 Desmond Mason .20 .50
47 Maurice Williams .25 .60
48 Michael Redd .25 .60
49 Kevin Garnett .50 1.25
50 Latrell Sprewell .25 .60
51 Sam Cassell .25 .60
52 Vince Carter .50 1.25
53 Jason Kidd .50 1.25
54 Richard Jefferson .25 .60
55 Dan Dickau .20 .50
56 Jamaal Magloire .20 .50
57 J.R. Smith .25 .60
58 Jamal Crawford .30 .75
59 Stephon Marbury .25 .60
60 Allan Houston .25 .60
61 Dwight Howard .25 .60
62 Grant Hill .40 1.00
63 Steve Francis .25 .60
64 Allen Iverson .50 1.25
65 Andre Iguodala .25 .60
66 Chris Webber .30 .75
67 Amare Stoudemire .25 .60
68 Shawn Marion .25 .60
69 Steve Nash .40 1.00
70 Damon Stoudamire .25 .60
71 Shareef Abdur-Rahim .25 .60
72 Zach Randolph .25 .60
73 Mike Bibby .30 .75
74 Peja Stojakovic .30 .75
75 Brad Miller .25 .60
76 Manu Ginobili .30 .75
77 Tim Duncan .50 1.25
78 Tony Parker .30 .75
79 Rashard Lewis .30 .75
80 Ray Allen .30 .75
81 Ronald Murray .20 .50
82 Rafer Alston .20 .50
83 Jalen Rose .30 .75
84 Chris Bosh .30 .75
85 Andrei Kirilenko .25 .60
86 Carlos Boozer .25 .60
87 Matt Harpring .20 .50
88 Antawn Jamison .25 .60
89 Gilbert Arenas .25 .60
90 Larry Hughes .25 .60
91 Linas Kleiza RC 1.25 3.00
92 Julius Hodge RC 1.25 3.00
93 David Lee RC 2.00 5.00
94 Sarunas Jasikevicius RC 2.00 5.00
95 Jason Maxiell RC 1.50 4.00
96 Luther Head RC 1.50 4.00
97 Brandon Bass RC 1.50 4.00
98 Ricky Sanchez RC 2.00 5.00
99 Ersan Ilyasova RC 2.00 5.00
100 Andray Blatche RC 2.00 5.00
101 Sean May RC 1.25 3.00
102 Ike Diogu RC 1.25 3.00
103 Nate Robinson RC 2.00 5.00
105 Bracey Wright RC 1.25 3.00
106 Daniel Ewing RC 1.50 4.00
107 Salim Stoudamire RC 1.50 4.00
108 Dijon Thompson RC 1.25 3.00
109 Danny Granger RC 2.50 6.00
110 Raymond Felton RC 2.00 5.00
111 Louis Williams RC 2.00 5.00
112 Channing Frye RC 2.00 5.00
113 Francisco Garcia RC 1.50 4.00
114 Ryan Gomes RC 1.50 4.00
115 Travis Diener RC 1.25 3.00
116 Jarrett Jack RC 2.00 5.00
118 Von Wafer RC 1.25 3.00
119 C.J. Miles RC 2.00 5.00
120 Lawrence Roberts RC 1.25 3.00
121 Amir Johnson RC 2.00 5.00
122 Monta Ellis RC 2.50 6.00
123 Martell Webster RC 1.50 4.00
124 Johan Petro RC 1.25 3.00
126 Andrew Bynum RC 1.50 4.00
127 Martynas Andriuskevicius RC 1.25 3.00
128 Charlie Villanueva RC 2.00 5.00
129 Antoine Wright RC 1.50 4.00
130 Joey Graham RC 1.50 4.00
131 Wayne Simien RC 1.25 3.00
132 Hakim Warrick RC 1.50 4.00
133 Gerald Green RC 2.00 5.00
134 Marvin Williams RC 2.00 5.00
135 Deron Williams RC 2.50 6.00
136 Rashad McCants RC 1.50 4.00
137 Yaroslav Korolev RC 1.25 3.00
138 Chris Taft RC 1.50 4.00
139 Chris Paul RC 8.00 20.00
140 Andrew Bogut RC 2.50 6.00

2005-06 Upper Deck Hardcourt Hardwood Signatures

Inserted in packs, this 42-card set is horizontally designed with a wood grain background, player photos on the left and an autograph on a swatch of wood centered on the left. Cards are serially numbered to either 50 or 25.

PRINT RUN 25 TO 50 SER.#'d SETS
UNPRICED DUAL PRINT RUN 10 SETS
AB Andrew Bogut/50 10.00 25.00
AK Andrei Kirilenko/50 8.00 20.00
CA Carmelo Anthony/25 30.00 80.00
CF Channing Frye/50 8.00 20.00
CJ C.J. Miles/50 8.00 20.00
CP Chris Paul/50 100.00 200.00
CV Charlie Villanueva/50 8.00 20.00
DG Danny Granger/50 10.00 25.00
DH Dwight Howard/50 12.00 30.00
DL David Lee/50 8.00 20.00
DT Dijon Thompson/50 5.00 12.00
DW Deron Williams/50 50.00 100.00
GG Gerald Green/50 8.00 20.00
HW Hakim Warrick/50 6.00 15.00
ID Ike Diogu/50 5.00 12.00
JK Jason Kidd/50 20.00 50.00
JR J.R. Smith/50 10.00 25.00
KH Kirk Hinrich/50 8.00 20.00
KK Kyle Korver/50 8.00 20.00
LH Luther Head/50 6.00 15.00
LJ LeBron James/25 125.00 250.00
LO Lamar Odom/50 10.00 25.00
MA Martynas Andriuskevicius/50 5.00 12.00
MD Marquis Daniels/50 8.00 20.00
ME Monta Ellis/50 20.00 50.00
MR Michael Redd/50 15.00 40.00
MW Marvin Williams/50 8.00 20.00
PP Paul Pierce/50 12.00 30.00
RF Raymond Felton/50 8.00 20.00
RM Rashad McCants/50 6.00 15.00
SE Sean May/50 5.00 12.00
SN Steve Nash/25 100.00 200.00
SS Salim Stoudamire/50 6.00 15.00
TA Tony Allen/50 8.00 20.00
WE Martell Webster/50 6.00 15.00
WS Wayne Simien/50 5.00 12.00

2005-06 Upper Deck Hardcourt Materials

Inserted in packs at the rate of one in 15, this horizontally designed set places player photos on the left and an "M" shaped swatch of memorabilia on the right.

STATED ODDS 1:15
*MAT/WOOD: .6X TO 1.5X BASE MAT HI
MAT/WOOD PRINT RUN 99 SER.#'d SETS
AH Al Harrington 2.50 6.00
AK Andrei Kirilenko 2.50 6.00
AN Andre Iguodala 2.50 6.00
BD Baron Davis 2.50 6.00
BG Ben Gordon 2.50 6.00
BM Brad Miller 2.50 6.00
BW Ben Wallace 2.50 6.00
CB Carlos Boozer 2.50 6.00
CH Chris Bosh 3.00 8.00
CM Corey Maggette 2.50 6.00
DF Derek Fisher 2.50 6.00
DG Drew Gooden 2.50 6.00
DH Dwight Howard 2.50 6.00
DM Desmond Mason 2.00 5.00
GA Gilbert Arenas 2.50 6.00
GP Gary Payton 3.00 8.00
GW Gerald Wallace 2.50 6.00
JC Jamal Crawford 3.00 8.00
JH Josh Howard 3.00 8.00
JK Jason Kidd 5.00 12.00
JM Jamaal Magloire 2.00 5.00
JR Jalen Rose 3.00 8.00
KB Kobe Bryant 12.00 30.00
KD Keyon Dooling 2.00 5.00
KG Kevin Garnett 5.00 12.00
KK Kyle Korver 2.50 6.00
LJ LeBron James 12.00 30.00
MB Mike Bibby 3.00 8.00
MJ Michael Jordan 30.00 80.00
PG Pau Gasol 3.00 8.00
PP Paul Pierce 3.00 8.00
PS Peja Stojakovic 3.00 8.00
QR Quentin Richardson 2.50 6.00
RJ Richard Jefferson 2.50 6.00
RM Ronald Murray 2.00 5.00
SB Shane Battier 2.50 6.00
SF Steve Francis 2.50 6.00
SM Stephon Marbury 2.50 6.00
SN Steve Nash 4.00 10.00
TA Tony Allen 2.00 5.00
TM Tracy McGrady 4.00 10.00
YM Yao Ming 4.00 10.00

2005-06 Upper Deck Hardcourt Materials/Wood Autographs

Inserted randomly in packs, this 42-card set parallels the Materials/Wood set enhanced with an autograph sticker and sequential numbering to 50.

PRINT RUN 25 TO 50 SER.#'d SETS
AH Al Harrington/50 8.00 20.00
AK Andrei Kirilenko/50 8.00 20.00
AN Andre Iguodala/50 8.00 20.00
BD Baron Davis/50 10.00 25.00
BG Ben Gordon/50 25.00 60.00
BM Brad Miller/50 8.00 20.00
BW Ben Wallace/50 20.00 50.00
CH Chris Bosh/50 10.00 25.00
CM Corey Maggette/50 8.00 20.00
DF Derek Fisher/50 10.00 25.00
DG Drew Gooden/50 8.00 20.00
DH Dwight Howard/50 20.00 50.00
DM Desmond Mason/50 8.00 20.00
GA Gilbert Arenas/50 12.00 30.00
GP Gary Payton/50 15.00 40.00
JH Josh Howard/50 8.00 20.00
JK Jason Kidd/50 15.00 40.00
JM Jamaal Magloire/50 8.00 20.00
KD Keyon Dooling/50 8.00 20.00
KG Kevin Garnett/50 40.00 100.00
KK Kyle Korver/50 12.00 30.00
LJ LeBron James/25 150.00 300.00
MB Mike Bibby/50 8.00 20.00
MJ Michael Jordan/25 350.00 650.00
PG Pau Gasol/50 12.00 30.00
PP Paul Pierce/50 15.00 40.00
PS Peja Stojakovic/50 12.00 30.00
QR Quentin Richardson/50 8.00 20.00
RJ Richard Jefferson/50 8.00 20.00
RM Ronald Murray/50 8.00 20.00
SB Shane Battier/50 8.00 20.00
SM Stephon Marbury/50 12.00 30.00
SN Steve Nash/50 25.00 60.00
TA Tony Allen/50 8.00 20.00
TM Tracy McGrady/25 30.00 60.00
YM Yao Ming/25 40.00 100.00

2005-06 Upper Deck Hardcourt Rookie Jerseys

PRINT RUN 99 TO 250 SER.#'d SETS
UNPRICED JSY AU PRINT RUN 15 SETS
*JSY/WOOD/250: .6X TO 1.5X BASE JSY HI
*JSY/WOOD/99: .5X TO 1.25X BASE JSY HI
JSY/WOOD PRINT RUN 50 SER.#'d SETS
92J Julius Hodge/250 2.00 5.00
93J David Lee/250 3.00 8.00
95J Jason Maxiell/250 2.50 6.00
96J Luther Head/250 2.50 6.00
97J Brandon Bass/250 2.50 6.00
100J Andray Blatche/250 3.00 8.00
101J Sean May/250 2.00 5.00
103J Nate Robinson/250 3.00 8.00
106J Daniel Ewing/250 2.50 6.00
107J Salim Stoudamire/250 2.50 6.00
109J Danny Granger/250 4.00 10.00
110J Raymond Felton/250 3.00 8.00
111J Louis Williams/250 3.00 8.00
112J Channing Frye/250 3.00 8.00
113J Francisco Garcia/250 2.50 6.00
114J Ryan Gomes/250 2.50 6.00
116J Jarrett Jack/250 3.00 8.00
119J C.J. Miles/250 3.00 8.00
123J Martell Webster/250 2.50 6.00
128J Charlie Villanueva/250 3.00 8.00
129J Antoine Wright/250 2.50 6.00
130J Joey Graham/250 2.50 6.00
131J Wayne Simien/250 2.00 5.00
132J Hakim Warrick/250 2.50 6.00
133J Gerald Green/250 3.00 8.00
134J Marvin Williams/99 3.00 8.00
135J Deron Williams/99 4.00 10.00
136J Rashad McCants/99 2.50 6.00
139J Chris Paul/99 12.00 30.00
140J Andrew Bogut/99 4.00 10.00

2005-06 Upper Deck Hardcourt Signatures

Inserted in packs at the rate of one in 15, this 90-card set features both veteran and rookie players on a card with borders along the left and right, a player photo centered at the top and an autograph sticker centered along the bottom. Short Print information for this set was provided by Upper Deck.

STATED ODDS 1:15
AI Andre Iguodala 6.00 15.00
AK Andrei Kirilenko 4.00 10.00
AM Antonio McDyess 4.00 10.00
AN Andrew Bogut SP 8.00 20.00
AV Anderson Varejao 4.00 10.00
AW Antoine Wright 3.00 8.00
BI Andris Biedrins 4.00 10.00
BU Beno Udrih 4.00 10.00
BY Andrew Bynum 15.00 40.00
CB Chris Bosh SP 10.00 25.00
CD Chris Duhon 4.00 10.00
CF Channing Frye 4.00 10.00
CJ C.J. Miles 4.00 10.00
CM Corey Maggette 4.00 10.00
CP Chris Paul SP 40.00 100.00
CT Chris Taft 3.00 8.00
CU Cuttino Mobley 4.00 10.00
CV Charlie Villanueva 4.00 10.00
DA David Harrison 4.00 10.00
DD Dan Dickau 4.00 10.00
DF Derek Fisher 6.00 15.00
DH Dwight Howard 12.00 30.00
DL David Lee 2.50 6.00
DM Desmond Mason 4.00 10.00
DO Dorell Wright 4.00 10.00
DT Dijon Thompson 2.50 6.00
DW Delonte West 4.00 10.00
FE Raymond Felton 4.00 10.00
FG Francisco Garcia 3.00 8.00
FV Fran Vazquez 2.50 6.00
GA Gilbert Arenas 5.00 12.00
GG Gerald Green 4.00 10.00
GR Danny Granger 5.00 12.00
GW Gerald Wallace 2.50 6.00
HS Ha Seung-Jin 4.00 10.00
HW Hakim Warrick 3.00 8.00
JA Jalen Rose 5.00 12.00
JC Jamal Crawford 4.00 10.00
JM Jamaal Magloire 4.00 10.00
JN Jameer Nelson 6.00 15.00
JO Joey Graham 3.00 8.00
JP Johan Petro 2.50 6.00
JR J.R. Smith 4.00 10.00
JU Justin Reed 4.00 10.00
JW Jason Williams 6.00 15.00
KD Keyon Dooling 4.00 10.00
KH Kirk Hinrich SP 8.00 20.00
KK Kyle Korver 4.00 10.00
KR Kareem Rush 4.00 10.00
KS Kirk Snyder 4.00 10.00
LF Luis Flores 4.00 10.00
LH Luther Head 4.00 10.00
LJ LeBron James 125.00 300.00
LU Luke Jackson 4.00 10.00
MA Martynas Andriuskevicius 2.50 6.00
MC Rashad McCants 3.00 8.00
ME Monta Ellis 10.00 25.00
MJ Michael Jordan SP 300.00 600.00
MP Morris Peterson 4.00 10.00
MW Marvin Williams SP 4.00 10.00
NO Andres Nocioni 4.00 10.00
NR Nate Robinson 6.00 15.00
PA Pavel Podkolzin 4.00 10.00
PB Primoz Brezec 4.00 10.00
QR Quentin Richardson 4.00 10.00
RA Rafael Araujo 4.00 10.00
RG Ryan Gomes 3.00 8.00
RO Robert Traylor 4.00 10.00
RT Ronny Turiaf 6.00 15.00
SM Sean May 2.50 6.00
SN Steve Nash SP 20.00 50.00
SS Salim Stoudamire 3.00 8.00
ST Sebastian Telfair 4.00 10.00
TA Trevor Ariza 4.00 10.00
TK Toni Kukoc 2.50 6.00
TO Travis Outlaw 4.00 10.00
UH Udonis Haslem 4.00 10.00
VK Viktor Khryapa 4.00 10.00
WI Maurice Williams 4.00 10.00
WS Wayne Simien 2.50 6.00
YM Yao Ming SP 20.00 50.00
AU Stacey Augmon 4.00 10.00

2006-07 Upper Deck Hardcourt

Released in mid September 2006, Hardcourt features a 150-card base set where cards 1-100 picture veteran players, cards 101-135 picture rookies sequentially numbered to 1750 and cards 136-150 picture rookies along with an autograph sticker and sequential numbering to 399. Hardcourt is packaged in 15-pack boxes of five cards each and carried an initial suggested retail price of $4.99. Also included in each box is a game floor card of either Michael Jordan or LeBron James.

COMP.SET w/o SP's (100) 15.00 40.00
136-150 AU RC PRINT RUN 399 SER.#'d SETS
UNPRICED GOLD PRINT RUN ONE SET
1 Joe Johnson .25 .60
2 Salim Stoudamire .20 .50
3 Marvin Williams .25 .60
4 Dan Dickau .20 .50
5 Paul Pierce .30 .75
6 Wally Szczerbiak .25 .60
7 Raymond Felton .25 .60
8 Emeka Okafor .25 .60
9 Gerald Wallace .25 .60
10 Tyson Chandler .25 .60
11 Luol Deng .25 .60
12 Ben Gordon .25 .60
13 Michael Jordan 2.50 6.00
14 Drew Gooden .25 .60
15 Larry Hughes .25 .60
16 Zydrunas Ilgauskas .25 .60
17 LeBron James 1.25 3.00
18 Erick Dampier .20 .50
19 Devin Harris .20 .50
20 Dirk Nowitzki .50 1.25
21 Jason Terry .25 .60
22 Carmelo Anthony .40 1.00
23 Earl Boykins .20 .50
24 Marcus Camby .25 .60
25 Kenyon Martin .25 .60
26 Chauncey Billups .30 .75
27 Richard Hamilton .25 .60
28 Antonio McDyess .25 .60
29 Ben Wallace .25 .60
30 Baron Davis .25 .60
31 Derek Fisher .25 .60
32 Troy Murphy .20 .50
33 Jason Richardson .30 .75
34 Luther Head .25 .60
35 Tracy McGrady .40 1.00
36 Yao Ming .40 1.00
37 Danny Granger .25 .60
38 Jermaine O'Neal .25 .60
39 Peja Stojakovic .30 .75
40 Elton Brand .30 .75
41 Sam Cassell .25 .60
42 Chris Kaman .25 .60
43 Shaun Livingston .20 .50
44 Kwame Brown .20 .50
45 Kobe Bryant 1.25 3.00
46 Andrew Bynum .20 .50
47 Shane Battier .25 .60
48 Pau Gasol .30 .75
49 Mike Miller .25 .60
50 Hakim Warrick .25 .60
51 Shaquille O'Neal .60 1.50
52 Dwyane Wade .50 1.25
53 Jason Williams .25 .60
54 Andrew Bogut .25 .60
55 T.J. Ford .20 .50
56 Jamaal Magloire .20 .50
57 Michael Redd .25 .60
58 Ricky Davis .25 .60
59 Kevin Garnett .50 1.25
60 Rashad McCants .20 .50
61 Vince Carter .40 1.00
62 Richard Jefferson .25 .60
63 Jason Kidd .50 1.25
64 Desmond Mason .20 .50
65 Chris Paul .40 1.00
66 J.R. Smith .25 .60
67 Jamal Crawford .30 .75
68 Channing Frye .25 .60
69 Stephon Marbury .25 .60
70 Quentin Richardson .25 .60
71 Dwight Howard .25 .60
72 Darko Milicic .20 .50
73 Jameer Nelson .20 .50
74 Andre Iguodala .25 .60
75 Allen Iverson .40 1.00
76 Chris Webber .30 .75
77 Shawn Marion .25 .60
78 Steve Nash .40 1.00
79 Amare Stoudemire .25 .60
80 Zach Randolph .25 .60
81 Sebastian Telfair .20 .50
82 Martell Webster .25 .60
83 Ron Artest .30 .75
84 Mike Bibby .30 .75
85 Brad Miller .25 .60
86 Tim Duncan .50 1.25
87 Manu Ginobili .30 .75
88 Tony Parker .30 .75
89 Ray Allen .30 .75
90 Danny Fortson .20 .50
91 Rashard Lewis .30 .75
92 Chris Bosh .30 .75
93 Joey Graham .20 .50
94 Charlie Villanueva .20 .50
95 Carlos Boozer .25 .60
96 Andrei Kirilenko .25 .60
97 Deron Williams .25 .60
98 Gilbert Arenas .25 .60
99 Caron Butler .25 .60
100 Antawn Jamison .25 .60
101 Adam Morrison RC 1.50 4.00
102 Randy Foye RC 1.50 4.00
103 Rudy Gay RC 2.00 5.00
104 Patrick O'Bryant RC 1.00 2.50
105 Saer Sene RC 1.00 2.50
106 J.J. Redick RC 2.00 5.00
107 Hilton Armstrong RC 1.00 2.50
108 Thabo Sefolosha RC 1.50 4.00
109 Cedric Simmons RC 1.00 2.50
110 Shawne Williams RC 1.00 2.50
111 Tarence Kinsey RC 1.00 2.50
112 Quincy Douby RC 1.00 2.50
113 Renaldo Balkman RC 1.25 3.00
114 Josh Boone RC 1.00 2.50
115 Kyle Lowry RC 2.00 5.00
116 Shannon Brown RC 1.00 2.50
117 Jordan Farmar RC 1.50 4.00
118 Joel Freeland RC 1.00 2.50
119 Paul Davis RC 1.00 2.50
120 P.J. Tucker RC 1.25 3.00
121 Craig Smith RC 1.25 3.00
122 Bobby Jones RC 1.00 2.50
123 David Noel RC 1.00 2.50
124 Denham Brown RC 1.00 2.50
125 James Augustine RC 1.00 2.50
126 Daniel Gibson RC 1.25 3.00
127 Allan Ray RC 1.00 2.50
128 Alexander Johnson RC 1.00 2.50
129 Dee Brown RC 1.00 2.50
130 Paul Millsap RC 2.00 5.00
131 Leon Powe RC 1.25 3.00
132 Ryan Hollins RC 1.25 3.00
133 Mike Gansey RC 1.00 2.50
134 Hassan Adams RC 1.00 2.50
135 Will Blalock RC 1.00 2.50
136 Andrea Bargnani AU RC 4.00 10.00
137 LaMarcus Aldridge AU RC 15.00 40.00
138 Tyrus Thomas AU RC 3.00 8.00
139 Shelden Williams AU RC 3.00 8.00
140 Brandon Roy AU RC 4.00 10.00
141 Ronnie Brewer AU RC 2.50 6.00
142 Rodney Carney AU RC 2.50 6.00
143 Rajon Rondo AU RC 10.00 25.00
144 Marcus Williams AU RC 2.50 6.00
145 Kevin Pittsnogle AU RC 3.00 8.00
146 Maurice Ager AU RC 2.50 6.00
147 Mardy Collins AU RC 2.50 6.00
148 James White AU RC 2.50 6.00
149 Steve Novak AU RC 3.00 8.00
150 Solomon Jones AU RC 2.50 6.00

2006-07 Upper Deck Hardcourt Copper

*1-100 COPPER: 1X TO 2.5X BASE HI
*101-135 COPPER: .6X TO 1.5X BASE HI
*136-150 COPPER: .25X TO .6X BASE HI
COPPER PRINT RUN 199 SER.#'d SETS
143 Rajon Rondo 4.00 10.00

2006-07 Upper Deck Hardcourt Silver

*1-100 SILVER: 2.5X TO 6X BASE HI
*101-135 SILVER: 1.25X TO 3X BASE HI
*136-150 SILVER: .5X TO 1.25X BASE HI
PRINT RUN 50 SER.#'d SETS
143 Rajon Rondo 20.00 50.00

2006-07 Upper Deck Hardcourt Debut Jerseys

PRINT RUN 199 SER.#'d SETS
AR Allan Ray 2.00 5.00
BA Renaldo Balkman 2.50 6.00
BJ Bobby Jones 2.00 5.00
CS Cedric Simmons 2.00 5.00
DB Dee Brown 2.00 5.00
HA Hilton Armstrong 2.00 5.00
JB Josh Boone 2.00 5.00
JF Jordan Farmar 3.00 8.00
JW James White 2.00 5.00
KL Kyle Lowry 4.00 10.00
MA Maurice Ager 2.00 5.00
MC Mardy Collins 2.00 5.00
MW Marcus Williams 2.00 5.00
PD Paul Davis 2.00 5.00
PO Patrick O'Bryant 2.00 5.00
QD Quincy Douby 2.00 5.00
RB Ronnie Brewer 3.00 8.00
RC Rodney Carney 2.00 5.00
RG Rudy Gay 4.00 10.00
RR Rajon Rondo 8.00 20.00
SB Shannon Brown 2.00 5.00
SJ Solomon Jones 2.00 5.00
SN Steve Novak 2.50 6.00
SW Shawne Williams 2.00 5.00

2006-07 Upper Deck Hardcourt Debut Jerseys 2

PRINT RUN 99 SER.#'d SETS
JR J.J. Redick 5.00 12.00
KP Kevin Pittsnogle 3.00 8.00
LA LaMarcus Aldridge 10.00 25.00
RF Randy Foye 4.00 10.00
TT Tyrus Thomas 3.00 8.00
WS Shelden Williams 3.00 8.00

2006-07 Upper Deck Hardcourt Game Floor

COMMON JORDAN 12.50 30.00
COMMON LEBRON 6.00 15.00
COMMON JORDAN/LEBRON 25.00 60.00
STATED ODDS ONE PER BOX
JORDAN/LEBRON PRINT RUN 99 SER.#'d SETS
AUTO PRINT RUN 23 SER.#'d SETS
1 Michael Jordan 12.50 30.00
25 M.Jordan/L.James 40.00 100.00
26 M.Jordan/L.James 40.00 100.00
27 M.Jordan/L.James 40.00 100.00
28 M.Jordan/L.James AU/23 600.00 1000.00
29 Michael Jordan AU/23 300.00 600.00
30 LeBron James AU/23 150.00 350.00

2006-07 Upper Deck Hardcourt Heart of a Champion Autographs

APPROXIMATE ODDS ONE PER BOX
AA Alex Acker 4.00 10.00
AJ Al Jefferson 4.00 10.00
BB Brent Barry 8.00 20.00
BO Bruce Bowen 5.00 12.00
CA Carmelo Anthony SP 12.00 30.00
CB Chauncey Billups 6.00 15.00
CH Chuck Hayes 4.00 10.00
CM Cuttino Mobley 4.00 10.00
CP Chris Paul 25.00 60.00
DJ Dwayne Jones 4.00 10.00
DW Deron Williams 15.00 40.00
GG George Gervin 8.00 20.00
HW Hakim Warrick 6.00 15.00
JA Jarrett Jack 4.00 10.00
JG Joey Graham 4.00 10.00
KA Kareem Abdul-Jabbar SP 50.00 120.00
KD Keyon Dooling 4.00 10.00
ME Maurice Evans 4.00 10.00
NR Nate Robinson 5.00 12.00
QR Quentin Richardson 4.00 10.00
RF Raymond Felton 8.00 20.00
RT Ronny Turiaf 12.00 30.00
RW Robert Whaley 4.00 10.00
SK Steve Kerr 6.00 15.00
SP Sam Perkins 6.00 15.00
TD Travis Diener 4.00 10.00
TF T.J. Ford 4.00 10.00

2006-07 Upper Deck Hardcourt Materials

APPROXIMATE ODDS ONE PER BOX
AI Andre Iguodala 2.00 5.00
AS Amare Stoudemire 2.00 5.00
BR Kwame Brown 2.00 5.00
CA Carmelo Anthony 3.00 8.00
CB Caron Butler 2.00 5.00
CM Corey Maggette 2.00 5.00
CW Chris Webber 2.50 6.00
DG Drew Gooden 2.00 5.00
DH Dwight Howard SP 2.00 5.00
DM Desmond Mason 1.50 4.00
DN Dirk Nowitzki 4.00 10.00
EB Elton Brand 2.50 6.00
EC Eddy Curry 2.00 5.00
FJ Fred Jones 2.00 5.00
GA Gilbert Arenas 2.00 5.00
JM Jeff McInnis 2.00 5.00
JR Jason Richardson 2.50 6.00
JS J.R. Smith 2.00 5.00
KB Kobe Bryant 8.00 20.00
KG Kevin Garnett 4.00 10.00
KH Kirk Hinrich 2.00 5.00
KK Kyle Korver 2.00 5.00
LH Larry Hughes 2.00 5.00
LJ LeBron James 10.00 25.00
LW Luke Walton 2.00 5.00
MG Manu Ginobili 2.50 6.00
MJ Michael Jordan SP 25.00 60.00
MS Mike Sweetney 2.00 5.00
NE Nene 2.00 5.00
PG Pau Gasol 2.50 6.00
PS Peja Stojakovic 2.50 6.00
QR Quentin Richardson 2.00 5.00
RA Ray Allen 2.50 6.00
RH Richard Hamilton 2.00 5.00
RJ Richard Jefferson 2.00 5.00
SD Samuel Dalembert 2.00 5.00
SN Steve Nash 3.00 8.00
SO Shaquille O'Neal 5.00 12.00
TD Tim Duncan 4.00 10.00
TP Tony Parker 2.50 6.00
WS Wally Szczerbiak 2.00 5.00
ZI Zydrunas Ilgauskas 2.00 5.00

2006-07 Upper Deck Hardcourt Materials Dual

PRINT RUN 50 SER.#'d SETS
BG E.Brand/K.Garnett 4.00 10.00
BH C.Bosh/D.Howard 5.00 12.00
BM K.Bryant/T.McGrady 10.00 25.00
DP T.Duncan/T.Parker 10.00 25.00
DR B.Davis/J.Richardson 4.00 10.00
GN K.Garnett/D.Nowitzki 6.00 15.00
GV D.George/S.Vujacic 4.00 10.00
HW R.Hamilton/B.Wallace 4.00 10.00
JA L.James/C.Anthony 20.00 50.00
JJ M.Jordan/L.James 40.00 100.00
KC J.Kidd/V.Carter 6.00 15.00
MM T.McGrady/Y.Ming 8.00 20.00
MO Y.Ming/S.O'Neal 10.00 25.00
MS S.Marion/A.Stoudemire 5.00 12.00
NM S.Nash/S.Marbury 5.00 12.00
SM W.Szczerbiak/J.McInnis 4.00 10.00
SO P.Stojakovic/J.O'Neal 4.00 10.00
WI C.Webber/A.Iguodala 4.00 10.00

2000 Upper Deck Hawaii

These cards were issued by Upper Deck and given away at the Kit Young annual conference in Hawaii in 2000. These cards feature autographs of four athletes Upper Deck brought over to the conference. Each player signed a card serial numbered to 500. The card featuring all four players signed was not included in the factory set, but 100 cards featuring all four players were also signed and distributed. Two Kit Young cards were also included with the factory sets.

COMPLETE SET (6) 160.00 400.00
DR Julius Erving AU 50.00 120.00
GAU Julius Erving AU/100 200.00 400.00
Gordie Howe AU
Joe Namath AU
Tom Seaver AU

2004 Upper Deck Hawaii Trade Conference LeBron James Room Key

NNO LeBron James 12.00 30.00

2007 Upper Deck Hawaii Trade Conference

COMPLETE SET (13) 15.00 40.00
12 LeBron James 3.00 8.00
13 Michael Jordan 5.00 12.00

1999-00 Upper Deck HoloGrFX

Released for the first time by Upper Deck, this premiere set contained 90 cards. Intended as a retail-only release, each pack contained three-cards and carried a suggested retail price of $1.99.

COMPLETE SET (90) 20.00 50.00
COMPLETE SET w/o RC (60) 8.00 20.00
61-90 SUBSET STATED ODDS 1:2
1 Dikembe Mutombo .30 .75
2 Alan Henderson .20 .50
3 Antoine Walker .30 .75
4 Paul Pierce .40 1.00
5 Eddie Jones .30 .75
6 David Wesley .20 .50
7 Dickey Simpkins .20 .50
8 Toni Kukoc .30 .75
9 Shawn Kemp .30 .75
10 Zydrunas Ilgauskas .25 .60
11 Michael Finley .30 .75
12 Cedric Ceballos .20 .50
13 Antonio McDyess .25 .60
14 Nick Van Exel .25 .60
15 Grant Hill .40 1.00
16 Bison Dele .20 .50
17 Jerry Stackhouse .30 .75
18 Antawn Jamison .30 .75
19 John Starks .25 .60
20 Scottie Pippen .50 1.25
21 Charles Barkley .50 1.25
22 Hakeem Olajuwon .40 1.00
23 Reggie Miller .30 .75
24 Rik Smits .30 .75
25 Michael Olowokandi .20 .50
26 Maurice Taylor .20 .50
27 Shaquille O'Neal .75 2.00
28 Kobe Bryant 1.25 3.00
29 Tim Hardaway .30 .75
30 Alonzo Mourning .40 1.00
31 Ray Allen .30 .75
32 Glenn Robinson .25 .60
33 Kevin Garnett .50 1.25
34 Terrell Brandon .20 .50
35 Stephon Marbury .25 .60
36 Keith Van Horn .25 .60
37 Allan Houston .25 .60
38 Latrell Sprewell .30 .75
39 Bo Outlaw .20 .50
40 Darrell Armstrong .20 .50
41 Allen Iverson .60 1.50
42 Larry Hughes .25 .60
43 Jason Kidd .50 1.25
44 Tom Gugliotta .20 .50
45 Damon Stoudamire .25 .60
46 Rasheed Wallace .30 .75
47 Jason Williams .40 1.00
48 Chris Webber .30 .75
49 Tim Duncan .60 1.50
50 David Robinson .50 1.25
51 Gary Payton .30 .75
52 Vin Baker .25 .60
53 Vince Carter .60 1.50
54 Tracy McGrady .50 1.25
55 John Stockton .40 1.00
56 Karl Malone .40 1.00
57 Mike Bibby .30 .75
58 Shareef Abdur-Rahim .25 .60
59 Juwan Howard .25 .60
60 Mitch Richmond .30 .75
61 Elton Brand RC 1.00 2.50
62 Lamar Odom RC 1.00 2.50
63 Kenny Thomas RC .40 1.00
64 Scott Padgett RC .30 .75
65 Trajan Langdon RC .40 1.00
66 James Posey RC .40 1.00
67 Shawn Marion RC .75 2.00
68 Chris Herren RC .30 .75
69 Tim James RC .25 .60
70 Evan Eschmeyer RC .30 .75
71 Corey Maggette RC .60 1.50
72 Richard Hamilton RC .75 2.00
73 Baron Davis RC 1.00 2.50
74 Galen Young RC .40 1.00
75 Dion Glover RC .30 .75
76 Jumaine Jones RC .30 .75
77 Wally Szczerbiak RC .75 2.00
78 Andre Miller RC .75 2.00
79 Devean George RC .40 1.00
80 Obinna Ekezie RC .30 .75
81 Steve Francis RC 1.00 2.50
82 Jason Terry RC .60 1.50
83 Quincy Lewis RC .25 .60
84 Ryan Robertson RC .25 .60
85 William Avery RC .30 .75
86 A.Radojevic RC .25 .60
87 Jonathan Bender RC .40 1.00
88 Cal Bowdler RC .25 .60
89 Vonteego Cummings RC .25 .60
90 Jeff Foster RC .40 1.00

1999-00 Upper Deck HoloGrFX AUSome

*STARS: 1.5X TO 4X HI COLUMN
*RCs: .75X TO 2X HI
STATED ODDS 1:12

1999-00 Upper Deck HoloGrFX HoloFame

Randomly inserted in packs at one in 17, this nine-card set features NBA standouts already in or bound for the Hall of Fame. Card backs carry a "HF" prefix.

COMPLETE SET (9) 15.00 30.00
STATED ODDS 1:17
*GOLD: 1.5X TO 4X HI COLUMN
GOLD: STATED ODDS 1:210
HF1 Michael Jordan 12.00 30.00
HF2 Julius Erving 1.50 4.00
HF3 Larry Bird 2.50 6.00
HF4 George Gervin 1.00 2.50
HF5 Tim Duncan 2.00 5.00
HF6 Kevin Garnett 1.50 4.00
HF7 Kobe Bryant 8.00 20.00
HF8 Jason Williams 1.25 3.00
HF9 Vince Carter 2.00 5.00

1999-00 Upper Deck HoloGrFX Maximum Jordan

Randomly inserted in packs at one in 34, this six-card set features cards that highlight each one of MJ's six championship seasons. Card backs carry a "MJ" prefix.

COMPLETE SET (6) 12.50 25.00
COMMON CARD (MJ1-MJ6) 2.50 6.00
STATED ODDS 1:34
COMMON GOLD 20.00 50.00
GOLD: STATED ODDS 1:431

1999-00 Upper Deck HoloGrFX NBA 24-7

Randomly inserted in packs at one in three, this 15-card set features the most exciting players in the NBA, 24 hours a day, seven days a week. Card backs carry a "N" prefix.

COMPLETE SET (15) 4.00 10.00
STATED ODDS 1:3
*GOLD: 2.5X TO 6X HI COLUMN
GOLD: STATED ODDS 1:105
N1 Tim Duncan .60 1.50
N2 Allen Iverson .60 1.50
N3 Vince Carter .60 1.50
N4 Kevin Garnett .50 1.25
N5 Shaquille O'Neal .75 2.00
N6 Shareef Abdur-Rahim .25 .60
N7 Jason Williams .40 1.00
N8 Kobe Bryant 1.25 3.00
N9 Grant Hill .40 1.00
N10 Antoine Walker .30 .75
N11 Stephon Marbury .25 .60
N12 Antonio McDyess .25 .60
N13 Jason Kidd .50 1.25
N14 Keith Van Horn .25 .60
N15 Karl Malone .40 1.00

1999-00 Upper Deck HoloGrFX NBA Shoetime

Randomly inserted in packs at one in 431, this 19-card set features pieces of game-used shoes by today's top NBA players. Card backs are numbered by the player's initials.

STATED ODDS 1:431
AIS Allen Iverson 20.00 50.00
BRS Bryon Russell 6.00 15.00
CBS Charles Barkley 30.00 80.00
CWS Chris Webber 30.00 80.00
DMS Dikembe Mutombo 10.00 25.00
DRS David Robinson 10.00 25.00
GHS Grant Hill 20.00 50.00
GPS Gary Payton 15.00 40.00
JKS Jason Kidd 15.00 40.00
JMS Jamal Mashburn 8.00 20.00
JSS John Stockton 12.00 30.00
KBS Kobe Bryant 40.00 100.00
KMA Karl Malone AU/32 300.00 400.00
KMS Karl Malone 12.00 30.00
MJA Michael Jordan AU/23 2500.00 4000.00
MJS Michael Jordan 150.00 400.00
PES Patrick Ewing 12.00 30.00
SMS Stephon Marbury 8.00 20.00
SOS Shaquille O'Neal 20.00 50.00
SPS Scottie Pippen 20.00 50.00
THS Tim Hardaway 10.00 25.00

1999-00 Upper Deck HoloGrFX UD Authentics

Randomly inserted in packs at one in 431, this 21-card set autographs from 21 of the brightest stars in the NBA. Card backs carry the player's initials.

STATED ODDS 1:431

AJ Antawn Jamison 6.00 15.00
BD Baron Davis 10.00 25.00
BG Brian Grant 4.00 10.00
CM Corey Maggette 6.00 15.00
DA Darrell Armstrong 4.00 10.00
JO Michael Jordan 2000.00 3000.00
JS Jerry Stackhouse 6.00 15.00
JT Jason Terry 6.00 15.00
LH Larry Hughes 8.00 20.00
MB Mike Bibby 6.00 15.00
MF Michael Finley 8.00 20.00
MK Mark Jackson 5.00 12.00
MT Maurice Taylor 4.00 10.00
RD Richard Hamilton 8.00 20.00
RH Wally Szczerbiak 8.00 20.00
RL Raef LaFrentz 4.00 10.00
RT Robert Traylor 4.00 10.00
SF Steve Francis 10.00 25.00
SM Sam Mack 4.00 10.00
TG Tom Gugliotta 4.00 10.00
SHM Shawn Marion 8.00 20.00

1993-94 Upper Deck Holojams

This set of 36 standard-size "Lithogram" cards features Upper Deck's picks for the NBA's best slam-dunkers. The boxed set, which was available only at hobby stores at a suggested price of 24.95, includes one player from each NBA team (1-27) plus nine rookies (28-36). A mail-in card for a storage album for the set was included. The checklist card carried the production number out of a total 127,800 sets produced. The borderless fronts feature two pictures of the player, a foreground photo in full-color lithography and a second holographic photo. Cards of the rookies feature a single photo, with the player in full-color and the background printed as a hologram. The player's name and position, along with the Holojam logo, are printed near the bottom. The multicolored back features a small closeup of the player, along with career highlights. The cards are numbered on the back with an "H" prefix.

COMP. FACT SET (38) 10.00 25.00
H1 Dominique Wilkins .20 .50
H2 Dee Brown .08 .25
H3 Alonzo Mourning .40 1.00
H4A Michael Jordan 4.00 10.00
Hologram on right
H4B Michael Jordan 4.00 10.00
Hologram on left
H5 Brad Daugherty .08 .25
H6 Jim Jackson .08 .25
H7 Dikembe Mutombo .08 .25
H8 Terry Mills .08 .25
H9 Billy Owens .08 .25
H10 Hakeem Olajuwon .50 1.25
H11 Reggie Miller .15 .40
H12 Ron Harper .08 .25
H13 James Worthy .15 .40
H14 Harold Miner .08 .25
H15 Blue Edwards .08 .25
H16 Doug West .08 .25
H17 Derrick Coleman .08 .25
H18 Patrick Ewing .20 .50
H19 Shaquille O'Neal 2.00 5.00
H20 Clarence Weatherspoon .08 .25
H21 Charles Barkley .50 1.25
H22 Clyde Drexler .20 .50
H23 Walt Williams .08 .25
H24 David Robinson .50 1.25
H25 Shawn Kemp .40 1.00
H26 Karl Malone .75 2.00
H27 Tom Gugliotta .15 .40
H28 Chris Webber 2.50 6.00
H29 Shawn Bradley .15 .40
H30 Anfernee Hardaway 2.00 5.00
H31 Jamal Mashburn .50 1.25
H32 Isaiah Rider .50 1.25
H33 Rodney Rogers .08 .25
H34 Lindsey Hunter .08 .25
H35 Doug Edwards .08 .25
H36 George Lynch .08 .25
NNO Checklist .08 .25
NNO Album mail-in card .08 .25

1997 Upper Deck Holojams

Singles from this 20-card set were available in an Upper Deck re-pack at Wall-Mart stores towards the end of Summer 1997. A single gold Holojam was issued (visible from inside the packaging) along with two 1996-97 Collector's Choice Series 2 retail packs and two 1996-97 Upper Deck Series 2 retail packs for $9.97. The card fronts contain full bleed holographic in-action player images, and a small color photo of the player. The right side of the card bears the words "Holojam" and "ninety-seven" along with an Upper Deck logo, the player's name, team name, and team logo. The backs contain two more photos and a short description of the player.

COMPLETE SET (20) 125.00 250.00
1 Michael Jordan 40.00 100.00
2 Juwan Howard 2.50 6.00
3 Shaquille O'Neal 8.00 20.00
4 Kevin Garnett 5.00 12.00
5 Allen Iverson 10.00 25.00
6 Glen Rice 3.00 8.00
7 Hakeem Olajuwon 4.00 10.00
8 Patrick Ewing 4.00 10.00
9 Karl Malone 4.00 10.00
10 Reggie Miller 4.00 10.00
11 Shawn Kemp 3.00 8.00
12 Alonzo Mourning 4.00 10.00
13 Grant Hill 5.00 12.00
14 Kobe Bryant 40.00 100.00
15 Stephon Marbury 6.00 15.00
16 Vin Baker 2.50 6.00
17 Latrell Sprewell 3.00 8.00
18 Scottie Pippen 5.00 12.00
19 Shareef Abdur-Rahim 5.00 12.00
20 Anfernee Hardaway 5.00 12.00

2001-02 Upper Deck Honor Roll

Released in late march of 2002, this 130-card set us divided up into 90 veteran cards and 40 rookie cards. Base cards have colored backgrounds to match the featured player's jersey and silver foil highlights. Full color player photos are centered with a semi-circle black and white background. The rookie cards have the same design with a gold background, gold foil highlights, and the word "rookie" centered at the bottom. The rookie print runs are broken down as follows: card numbers 91-120 are sequentially numbered to 2499, and card numbers 121-130 are sequentially numbered to 1000. Honor Roll was packaged in 24-pack boxes where each pack contained five cards and carried a suggested retail price of $2.99.

COMPLETE SET (130) 125.00 250.00
COMP.SET w/o SP's (90) 12.50 30.00
91-120 PRINT RUN 2499 SER.#'d SETS
121-130 PRINT RUN 1000 SER.#'d SETS
1 Shareef Abdur-Rahim .25 .60
2 Jason Terry .30 .75
3 Dion Glover .20 .50
4 Paul Pierce .30 .75
5 Antoine Walker .25 .60
6 Kenny Anderson .25 .60
7 Baron Davis .30 .75
8 Jamal Mashburn .25 .60
9 David Wesley .20 .50
10 Ron Mercer .20 .50
11 Brad Miller .30 .75
12 Andre Miller .25 .60
13 Lamond Murray .20 .50
14 Chris Mihm .20 .50
15 Michael Finley .30 .75
16 Dirk Nowitzki .50 1.25
17 Steve Nash .50 1.25
18 Juwan Howard .25 .60
19 Nick Van Exel .25 .60
20 Raef LaFrentz .20 .50
21 Antonio McDyess .25 .60
22 James Posey .20 .50
23 Jerry Stackhouse .25 .60
24 Clifford Robinson .20 .50
25 Ben Wallace .25 .60
26 Antawn Jamison .30 .75
27 Larry Hughes .25 .60
28 Steve Francis .25 .60
29 Cuttino Mobley .20 .50
30 Glen Rice .25 .60
31 Reggie Miller .30 .75
32 Jalen Rose .25 .60
33 Jermaine O'Neal .25 .60
34 Darius Miles .20 .50
35 Elton Brand .30 .75
36 Lamar Odom .25 .60
37 Corey Maggette .25 .60
38 Kobe Bryant 1.25 3.00
39 Shaquille O'Neal .75 2.00
40 Rick Fox .20 .50
41 Lindsey Hunter .20 .50
42 Stromile Swift .20 .50
43 Jason Williams .25 .60
44 Alonzo Mourning .40 1.00
45 Eddie Jones .25 .60
46 Anthony Carter .20 .50
47 Brian Grant .20 .50
48 Ray Allen .30 .75
49 Glenn Robinson .25 .60
50 Sam Cassell .25 .60
51 Kevin Garnett .50 1.25
52 Terrell Brandon .20 .50
53 Wally Szczerbiak .25 .60
54 Joe Smith .25 .60
55 Jason Kidd .50 1.25
56 Kenyon Martin .30 .75
57 Allan Houston .25 .60
58 Latrell Sprewell .25 .60
59 Marcus Camby .25 .60
60 Mark Jackson .25 .60
61 Tracy McGrady .50 1.25
62 Grant Hill .40 1.00
63 Mike Miller .25 .60
64 Allen Iverson .60 1.50
65 Dikembe Mutombo .30 .75
66 Aaron McKie .20 .50
67 Stephon Marbury .25 .60
68 Shawn Marion .25 .60
69 Anfernee Hardaway .50 1.25
70 Tom Gugliotta .20 .50
71 Rasheed Wallace .30 .75
72 Damon Stoudamire .25 .60
73 Derek Anderson .20 .50
74 Chris Webber .30 .75
75 Mike Bibby .30 .75
76 Peja Stojakovic .30 .75
77 Tim Duncan .60 1.50
78 David Robinson .50 1.25
79 Steve Smith .25 .60
80 Gary Payton .30 .75
81 Rashard Lewis .30 .75
82 Desmond Mason .25 .60
83 Vince Carter .50 1.25
84 Morris Peterson .20 .50
85 Antonio Davis .20 .50
86 Karl Malone .40 1.00
87 John Stockton .40 1.00
88 Donyell Marshall .20 .50
89 Richard Hamilton .25 .60
90 Michael Jordan 2.50 6.00
91 Andrei Kirilenko RC 1.50 4.00
92 Gilbert Arenas RC 1.50 4.00
93 Earl Watson RC 1.00 2.50
94 Terence Morris RC 1.00 2.50
95 Kedrick Brown RC .60 1.50
96 Zach Randolph RC 1.50 4.00
97 Joe Johnson RC 1.25 3.00
98 Brandon Armstrong RC .60 1.50
99 DeSagana Diop RC .75 2.00
100 Joseph Forte RC .60 1.50
101 Brendan Haywood RC 1.00 2.50
102 Samuel Dalembert RC 1.00 2.50
103 Jason Collins RC .75 2.00
104 Michael Bradley RC .60 1.50
105 Gerald Wallace RC 1.25 3.00
106 Tierre Brown RC 1.00 2.50
107 Troy Murphy RC 1.00 2.50
108 Alton Ford RC 1.00 2.50
109 Vladimir Radmanovic RC 1.00 2.50
110 Ruben Boumtje-Boumtje RC 1.00 2.50
111 Bobby Simmons RC 1.00 2.50
112 Oscar Torres RC 1.00 2.50
113 Jeryl Sasser RC .60 1.50
114 Loren Woods RC .60 1.50
115 Shane Battier RC 2.00 5.00
116 Jamison Brewer RC 1.00 2.50
117 Richard Jefferson RC 1.50 4.00
118 Pau Gasol RC 3.00 8.00
119 Damone Brown RC .60 1.50
120 Rodney White RC .60 1.50
121 Kw.Brown RC/Garnett JSY 6.00 15.00
122 Chandler RC/Miles JSY 6.00 15.00
123 Curry RC/Malone JSY 8.00 20.00
124 Richardson RC/Kobe JSY 10.00 25.00
125 Parker RC/Kidd JSY 12.00 30.00
126 Griffin RC/A.Hardaway JSY 5.00 12.00
127 Haston RC/Mash JSY 4.00 10.00
128 Tinsley RC/A.Miller JSY 4.00 10.00
129 Hassell RC/Fizer JSY 4.00 10.00
130 Hunter RC/T-Mac JSY 6.00 15.00

2001-02 Upper Deck Honor Roll All-NBA Authentic Jerseys

Seeded in packs at the rate of one in 88, this 19-card set features a horizontal design with a full color player action photo on the right, and a swatch of a game jersey on the left. The photo and jersey are centered on the card by two silver stripes outside of which are white borders with the brand name, Honor Roll, and the set name running from top to bottom.

STATED ODDS 1:88
1 Kobe Bryant 15.00 40.00
2 Allen Iverson 8.00 20.00
3 Tracy McGrady 6.00 15.00
4 Andre Miller 3.00 8.00
5 Darius Miles 2.50 6.00
6 Baron Davis 4.00 10.00
7 Kevin Garnett 6.00 15.00
8 John Stockton 5.00 12.00
9 Ron Mercer 2.50 6.00
10 Shareef Abdur-Rahim 3.00 8.00
11 Dikembe Mutombo 4.00 10.00
12 Lamar Odom 3.00 8.00
13 Ray Allen 4.00 10.00
14 Mike Miller 3.00 8.00
15 Marcus Fizer 2.50 6.00
16 Toni Kukoc 4.00 10.00
17 Stephon Marbury 3.00 8.00
18 Jason Kidd 6.00 15.00
19 Karl Malone 5.00 12.00

2001-02 Upper Deck Honor Roll All-NBA Authentics Jerseys Combos

Randomly seeded in packs at the rate of one in 240, this nine card set utilizes the same base design as the single jersey version with two players and two swatches of jersey.

STATED ODDS 1:240
1 K.Bryant/K.Garnett 8.00 20.00
2 K.Bryant/A.Iverson 8.00 20.00
3 B.Davis/A.Miller 3.00 8.00
4 J.Kidd/K.Martin 5.00 12.00
5 K.Malone/J.Stockton 4.00 10.00
6 E.Brand/K.Garnett 5.00 12.00
7 G.Hill/M.Miller 4.00 10.00
8 S.Marbury/S.Marion 2.50 6.00
9 S.Abdur-Rahim/J.Terry 3.00 8.00

2001-02 Upper Deck Honor Roll Fab Five All-Stars

Randomly inserted in packs at the rate of one in 24, this 10-card set features color player photos set against a red background with the bottom third of the card contianing a stripe with the player's name and team name. The bottom of the card is in white, and and has the set names in silver foil. All the Fab Five insert sets share the same design.

COMPLETE SET (10) 15.00 30.00
STATED ODDS 1:24
1 Tim Duncan 1.50 4.00
2 Chris Webber .75 2.00
3 Kevin Garnett 1.25 3.00
4 Kobe Bryant 3.00 8.00
5 Shaquille O'Neal 2.00 5.00
6 Vince Carter 1.25 3.00
7 Allen Iverson 1.50 4.00
8 Tracy McGrady 1.25 3.00
9 Latrell Sprewell .60 1.50
10 Michael Jordan 6.00 15.00

2001-02 Upper Deck Honor Roll Fab Five Rookies

Randomly inserted in packs at the rate of one in 24, this 10-card set shares the same set design as the Fab Five All-Stars set with gold backgrounds instead of red.

COMPLETE SET (10) 10.00 25.00
STATED ODDS 1:24
1 Tony Parker 3.00 8.00
2 Jamaal Tinsley .75 2.00
3 Pau Gasol 2.50 6.00
4 Jason Richardson 1.00 2.50
5 Kwame Brown .75 2.00
6 Shane Battier 1.50 4.00
7 Eddie Griffin .60 1.50
8 Eddy Curry .75 2.00
9 Andrei Kirilenko 1.25 3.00
10 Joe Johnson 1.00 2.50

2001-02 Upper Deck Honor Roll Fab Five Scorers

Randomly inserted in packs at the rate of one in 24, this 10-card set shares the same set design as the Fab Five All-Stars set with gold backgrounds instead of red.

COMPLETE SET (10) 15.00 30.00
STATED ODDS 1:24
1 Michael Jordan 6.00 15.00
2 Kobe Bryant 3.00 8.00
3 Vince Carter 1.25 3.00
4 Shaquille O'Neal 2.00 5.00
5 Dirk Nowitzki 1.25 3.00
6 Tim Duncan 1.50 4.00
7 Kevin Garnett 1.25 3.00
8 Paul Pierce .75 2.00
9 Shareef Abdur-Rahim .60 1.50
10 Jerry Stackhouse .60 1.50

2001-02 Upper Deck Honor Roll Fab Floor Autographs

Seeded in packs at the rate of one in 480, this eight card set features full color player action photos on the right side of the card, and an oval swatch of floor on the left containing authentic player autographs. The card backgrounds are gold and cards are highlighted with gold foil.

STATED ODDS 1:480
1 Kobe Bryant 125.00 250.00
2 Michael Jordan 350.00 700.00
3 Kevin Garnett 40.00 80.00
4 Wally Szczerbiak 6.00 15.00
5 Darius Miles 6.00 15.00
6 Antoine Walker 6.00 15.00
7 Andre Miller 6.00 15.00
8 Jason Kidd 25.00 60.00

2001-02 Upper Deck Honor Roll Fab Floor Duos

Randomly seeded in packs at the rate of one in 96, this 17-card set features a horizontal card design with players on both the left and right side of the card and circular swatches of NBA court in the middle. Each swatch is engraved with the respective player's team logo.

STATED ODDS 1:96
1 K.Bryant/M.Jordan 40.00 100.00
2 K.Bryant/K.Garnett 15.00 40.00
3 A.McDyess/S.Marion 4.00 10.00
4 J.Terry/D.Johnson 4.00 10.00
5 K.Garnett/R.Lewis 5.00 12.00
6 K.Garnett/T.Brandon 5.00 12.00
7 K.Garnett/D.Miles 5.00 12.00
8 S.Marbury/S.Marion 4.00 10.00
9 M.Finley/D.Nowitzki 6.00 15.00
10 A.Walker/P.Pierce 6.00 15.00
11 R.Wallace/D.Anderson 4.00 10.00
12 R.Allen/G.Robinson 4.00 10.00
13 J.Stackhouse/R.Wallace 4.00 10.00
14 L.Sprewell/A.Houston 5.00 12.00
15 D.Robinson/D.Mutombo 6.00 15.00
16 B.Davis/J.Mashburn 4.00 10.00
17 G.Payton/D.Mason 4.00 10.00

2001-02 Upper Deck Honor Roll Fab Floor Triples

Randomly inserted in packs at the rate of one in 240, this five card set features three players and three swatches of game used court. Each swatch of court is engraved with the featured player's team logo.

STATED ODDS 1:240
1 Bryant/Garnett/Jordan 40.00 100.00
2 Bryant/Garnett/Martin 10.00 25.00
3 Garnett/Szcz/Brandon 6.00 15.00
4 G.Robnsn/Allen/Thomas 6.00 15.00
5 R.Miller/J.O'Neal/Bender 6.00 15.00

2002-03 Upper Deck Honor Roll

This 135-card standard-size set was issued in five-card packs which were packaged 24 packs to a box. Cards numbered 1 through 90 feature veterans. Cards card 91 through 105 feature rookie cards along with a game-used jersey swatch and those cards were numbered to a stated print run of 499 serial numbered sets. Cards numbered 106 through 135 feature other rookie cards and those cards were issued to a stated print run of 1999 serial numbered sets.

COMP.SET w/o SP's (90) 12.50 30.00
91-105 PRINT RUN 499 SERIAL #'d SETS
106-135 PRINT RUN 1999 SER.#'d SETS
1 Glenn Robinson .25 .60
2 Shareef Abdur-Rahim .25 .60
3 Jason Terry .25 .60
4 Paul Pierce .30 .75
5 Antoine Walker .25 .60
6 Tony Delk .20 .50
7 Jalen Rose .25 .60
8 Tyson Chandler .30 .75
9 Eddy Curry .20 .50
10 Darius Miles .20 .50
11 Zydrunas Ilgauskas .25 .60
12 Ricky Davis .25 .60
13 Dirk Nowitzki .50 1.25
14 Michael Finley .30 .75
15 Steve Nash .40 1.00
16 Raef LaFrentz .20 .50
17 Eduardo Najera .20 .50
18 Rodney White .20 .50
19 Juwan Howard .25 .60
20 Chris Whitney .20 .50
21 Ben Wallace .25 .60
22 Richard Hamilton .25 .60
23 Chauncey Billups .30 .75
24 Chucky Atkins .20 .50
25 Jason Richardson .30 .75
26 Antawn Jamison .30 .75
27 Gilbert Arenas .30 .75
28 Steve Francis .25 .60
29 Cuttino Mobley .20 .50
30 Jermaine O'Neal .25 .60
31 Reggie Miller .30 .75
32 Jamaal Tinsley .20 .50
33 Andre Miller .25 .60
34 Elton Brand .30 .75
35 Quentin Richardson .25 .60
36 Shaquille O'Neal .75 2.00
37 Kobe Bryant 1.25 3.00
38 Robert Horry .25 .60
39 Shane Battier .30 .75
40 Pau Gasol .40 1.00
41 Stromile Swift .20 .50
42 Eddie Jones .25 .60
43 Brian Grant .20 .50
44 Malik Allen .20 .50
45 Ray Allen .30 .75
46 Tim Thomas .20 .50
47 Kevin Garnett .50 1.25
48 Wally Szczerbiak .25 .60
49 Jason Kidd .50 1.25
50 Kenyon Martin .25 .60
51 Richard Jefferson .30 .75
52 Baron Davis .25 .60
53 Jamal Mashburn .25 .60
54 David Wesley .20 .50
55 P.J. Brown .20 .50
56 Allan Houston .25 .60
57 Latrell Sprewell .25 .60
58 Kurt Thomas .20 .50
59 Tracy McGrady .50 1.25
60 Grant Hill .40 1.00
61 Mike Miller .25 .60
62 Allen Iverson .50 1.25
63 Keith Van Horn .25 .60
64 Aaron McKie .20 .50
65 Shawn Marion .25 .60
66 Stephon Marbury .25 .60
67 Rasheed Wallace .30 .75
68 Derek Anderson .20 .50
69 Bonzi Wells .20 .50
70 Mike Bibby .30 .75
71 Chris Webber .30 .75
72 Peja Stojakovic .30 .75
73 Hedo Turkoglu .25 .60
74 Tim Duncan .60 1.50
75 David Robinson .50 1.25
76 Tony Parker .40 1.00
77 Gary Payton .30 .75
78 Rashard Lewis .30 .75
79 Brent Barry .20 .50
80 Desmond Mason .25 .60
81 Vince Carter .50 1.25
82 Antonio Davis .20 .50
83 Morris Peterson .20 .50
84 John Stockton .40 1.00
85 Karl Malone .40 1.00
86 Andrei Kirilenko .30 .75
87 Matt Harpring .20 .50
88 Jerry Stackhouse .25 .60
89 Kwame Brown .20 .50
90 Michael Jordan 2.50 6.00
91 Ryan Humphrey JSY RC 2.50 6.00
92 Juan Dixon JSY RC 3.00 8.00
93 Fred Jones JSY RC 2.50 6.00
94 Marcus Haislip JSY RC 2.50 6.00
95 Melvin Ely JSY RC 2.50 6.00
96 Jared Jeffries JSY RC 2.50 6.00
97 Caron Butler JSY RC 3.00 8.00
98 Amare Stoudemire JSY RC 4.00 10.00
99 Chris Wilcox JSY RC 2.50 6.00
100 Nene Hilario JSY RC 3.00 8.00
101 Dajuan Wagner JSY RC 2.50 6.00
102 Nikoloz Tskitishvili JSY RC 2.00 5.00
103 Drew Gooden JSY RC 3.00 8.00
104 Jay Williams JSY RC 3.00 8.00
105 Yao Ming JSY RC 6.00 15.00
106 Mike Dunleavy RC 1.50 4.00
107 Bostjan Nachbar RC 1.25 3.00
108 Jiri Welsch RC 1.25 3.00
109 Rasual Butler RC 1.50 4.00
110 Kareem Rush RC 1.25 3.00
111 Qyntel Woods RC 1.25 3.00
112 Casey Jacobsen RC 1.25 3.00
113 Tayshaun Prince RC 2.00 5.00
114 Frank Williams RC 1.00 2.50
115 John Salmons RC 1.50 4.00
116 Chris Jefferies RC 1.00 2.50
117 Dan Dickau RC 1.25 3.00
118 Juaquin Hawkins RC 1.00 2.50
119 Roger Mason RC 1.25 3.00
120 Robert Archibald RC 1.00 2.50
121 Vincent Yarbrough RC 1.00 2.50
122 Dan Gadzuric RC 1.25 3.00
123 Carlos Boozer RC 1.50 4.00
124 Tito Maddox RC 1.00 2.50
125 Gordan Giricek RC 1.50 4.00
126 Ronald Murray RC 1.50 4.00
127 Lonny Baxter RC 1.00 2.50
128 Pat Burke RC 1.00 2.50
129 Manu Ginobili RC 4.00 10.00
130 Predrag Savovic RC 1.25 3.00
131 Marko Jaric 1.50 4.00
132 Efthimios Rentzias RC 1.00 2.50
133 J.R. Bremer RC 1.00 2.50
134 Igor Rakocevic RC 1.00 2.50
135 Tamar Slay RC 1.00 2.50

2002-03 Upper Deck Honor Roll Award Performances

Issued at a stated rate of one in 12, this 14 card set features players who are in competition for major NBA awards.

COMPLETE SET (14) 10.00 25.00
STATED ODDS 1:12
AP1 Kobe Bryant 2.50 6.00
AP2 Tim Duncan 1.25 3.00
AP3 Eddie Jones .50 1.25
AP4 Steve Francis .50 1.25
AP5 Shareef Abdur-Rahim .50 1.25
AP6 Rasheed Wallace .60 1.50
AP7 Shaquille O'Neal 1.50 4.00
AP8 Rashard Lewis .60 1.50
AP9 Ray Allen .60 1.50
AP10 Pau Gasol .75 2.00
AP11 Elton Brand .60 1.50
AP12 Ben Wallace .50 1.25
AP13 Andre Miller .50 1.25
AP14 Michael Jordan 5.00 12.00

2002-03 Upper Deck Honor Roll Dual Jerseys

Issued at a stated rate of one in 240, this 12 card set featurs game-used jersey cards from two players (usually from the same team) with something in common.

STATED ODDS 1:240
AWPP A.Walker/P.Pierce 6.00 15.00
BDJM B.Davis/J.Mashburn 6.00 15.00
CWMB C.Webber/M.Bibby 6.00 15.00
DNSN D.Nowitzki/S.Nash 8.00 20.00
JKKM J.Kidd/K.Martin 8.00 20.00
JRAJ J.Richardson/A.Jamison 6.00 15.00
KBAI K.Bryant/A.Iverson 15.00 40.00
KMJS K.Malone/J.Stockton 8.00 20.00
MJKB M.Jordan/K.Bryant SP 40.00 100.00
SMSM S.Marbury/S.Marion 6.00 15.00
TMKG T.McGrady/K.Garnett 12.50 30.00
YMJW Y.Ming/J.Williams 10.00 25.00

2002-03 Upper Deck Honor Roll Dual Warm-ups

Issued at a stated rate of one in 48, these 16 cards feature two swatches of NBA "warm-up" material on them.

STATED ODDS 1:48
AWPP A.Walker/P.Pierce 5.00 12.00
BDJM B.Davis/J.Mashburn 4.00 10.00
CWMB C.Webber/M.Bibby 4.00 10.00
DNSN D.Nowitzki/S.Nash 5.00 12.00
DRTP D.Robinson/T.Parker 6.00 15.00
EBAM E.Brand/A.Miller 4.00 10.00
GPRL G.Payton/R.Lewis 4.00 10.00
JKKM J.Kidd/K.Martin 5.00 12.00
JRAJ J.Richardson/A.Jamison 4.00 10.00
KBKG K.Bryant/K.Garnett 12.00 30.00
KGWS K.Garnett/W.Szczerbiak 5.00 12.00
KMJS K.Malone/J.Stockton 5.00 12.00
MJKB M.Jordan/K.Bryant SP 40.00 100.00
SBSS S.Battier/S.Swift 4.00 10.00
SMSM S.Marbury/S.Marion 4.00 10.00
TMMM T.McGrady/M.Miller 5.00 12.00

2002-03 Upper Deck Honor Roll Popular Acclaim

Issued at a stated rate of one in 12, these 14 cards feature some of the most popular NBA players.

COMPLETE SET (14) 12.50 30.00
STATED ODDS 1:12
PA1 Michael Jordan 5.00 12.00
PA2 Shaquille O'Neal 1.50 4.00
PA3 Shane Battier .60 1.50
PA4 Michael Finley .60 1.50
PA5 Vince Carter 1.00 2.50
PA6 Darius Miles .40 1.00
PA7 Peja Stojakovic .60 1.50
PA8 Kobe Bryant 2.50 6.00
PA9 Yao Ming 1.25 3.00
PA10 Jalen Rose .50 1.25
PA11 Allen Iverson 1.00 2.50
PA12 Jay Williams .60 1.50
PA13 Drew Gooden .60 1.50
PA14 Shawn Marion .50 1.25

2002-03 Upper Deck Honor Roll Principals Autograph Jerseys

Issued at a stated rate of one in 480, these 20 cards feature not only game-used jersey swatches but authentic autographs of the featured players. Some of the players were issued in shorter supply and where noted we have put the announced print run next to the player's name. In addition, some players did not return their signed cards in time for the promotion and those cards were issued as exchange cards.

STATED ODDS 1:480
AWAJ Antoine Walker 10.00 25.00
CJAJ Chris Jefferies 10.00 25.00
DAAJ Dan Gadzuric 10.00 25.00
DGAJ Drew Gooden 15.00 40.00
DSAJ DeShawn Stevenson 10.00 25.00
JKAJ Jason Kidd 40.00 100.00
JWAJ Jay Williams 10.00 25.00
KBAJO Kobe Bryant/25 200.00 400.00
KGAJO Kevin Garnett/21 150.00 300.00
KMAJ Kenyon Martin 10.00 25.00
MFAJ Marcus Fizer 10.00 25.00
MJAJ Michael Jordan/23 400.00 800.00
MMAJ Mike Miller 10.00 25.00
PPAJO Paul Pierce 25.00 60.00
PSAJ Peja Stojakovic 20.00 50.00
SMAJ Shawn Marion 12.00 30.00
TCAJO Tyson Chandler 10.00 25.00
TPAJ Tayshaun Prince 12.00 30.00
YMAJ Yao Ming 75.00 150.00

2002-03 Upper Deck Honor Roll Signature Class

Issued at a stated rate of one in 480, these 12 cards feature authentic autographs from leading NBA players. A few players signed a very limited number of cards and we have put the announced print run next to the player's name in our checklist. In addition, Antoine Walker and Michael Jordan did not return their cards in time for inclusion in this product and those cards were issued as exchange cards.

STATED ODDS 1:480
AWS Antoine Walker 10.00 25.00
ETS Etan Thomas 5.00 12.00
JKS Jason Kidd 30.00 80.00
JMS Jerome Moiso 5.00 12.00
KBS Kobe Bryant/25 150.00 300.00
KMS Kenyon Martin 10.00 25.00
MFS Marcus Fizer 5.00 12.00
MJS Michael Jordan/23 400.00 800.00
MMS Mike Miller 5.00 12.00
SMS Shawn Marion 5.00 12.00

2002-03 Upper Deck Honor Roll Signature Class Duals

PRINT RUN 25 SERIAL#'d SETS
KBJW K.Bryant/J.Williams 75.00 150.00
KBKG K.Bryant/K.Garnett 200.00 400.00
MJKB M.Jordan/K.Bryant 600.00 1200.00
PPAW P.Pierce/A.Walker 75.00 150.00
YMJW Y.Ming/J.Williams 100.00 200.00

2002-03 Upper Deck Honor Roll Superstar Tributes

Issued at a stated rate of one in 24, these seven cards feature tributes to seven of the best NBA players.

COMPLETE SET (7) 10.00 25.00
STATED ODDS 1:24
ST1 Kobe Bryant 3.00 8.00
ST2 Michael Jordan 6.00 15.00
ST3 Steve Francis .60 1.50
ST4 Vince Carter 1.25 3.00
ST5 Allen Iverson 1.25 3.00
ST6 Tim Duncan 1.50 4.00
ST7 Shaquille O'Neal 2.00 5.00

2002-03 Upper Deck Honor Roll Tremendous Talents

Issued at a stated rate of one in 24, these seven cards feature players who have shown more talent than many of their NBA contemporaries during their career.

COMPLETE SET (7) 10.00 25.00
STATED ODDS 1:24
TT1 Jay Williams .75 2.00
TT2 Tim Duncan 1.50 4.00
TT3 Kobe Bryant 3.00 8.00
TT4 Yao Ming 1.50 4.00
TT5 Mike Bibby .75 2.00
TT6 Vince Carter 1.25 3.00
TT7 Michael Jordan 6.00 15.00

2002-03 Upper Deck Honor Roll Triple Warm-ups

ASTERISK CARDS ARE SP's
STATED ODDS 1:120
1 Miller/Brand/Olowkndi 8.00 20.00
2 Webber/Bryant/Pierce 25.00 60.00
3 Nowitzki/Finley/Nash 15.00 40.00
4 Mash/Davis/Wesley 8.00 20.00
5 Stocktn/Malone/Kirilenko 8.00 20.00
6 Martin/Kidd/Jefferson 8.00 20.00
7 McGrady/Bryant/J-Rich 15.00 40.00
8 Szczerb/Smith/Brandon 8.00 20.00

2003-04 Upper Deck Honor Roll

Released in January 2004, Honor Roll boasts a 123-card set divided up into 90 veteran player cards, 15 rookie cards sequentially numbered to 2999 (numbers 91-105) and 24 Rookie Jersey cards sequentially numbered to 499. Base cards feature a split design with color on the right and a centered player photo. Please note that the rookie jerseys are event worn, not game worn. Honor Roll was packaged in 24-pack boxes where packs contained five cards and carried a suggested retail price of $2.99.

COMP.SET w/o SP's (90) 15.00 40.00
JSY RC PRINT RUN 499 SER.#'d SETS
1 Shareef Abdur-Rahim .25 .60
2 Dan Dickau .20 .50
3 Jason Terry .25 .60
4 Raef LaFrentz .20 .50
5 Vin Baker .20 .50
6 Paul Pierce .30 .75
7 Antonio Davis .20 .50
8 Scottie Pippen .50 1.25
9 Jamal Crawford .30 .75
10 Dajuan Wagner .20 .50
11 Ricky Davis .25 .60
12 Darius Miles .20 .50
13 Dirk Nowitzki .50 1.25
14 Antoine Walker .30 .75
15 Steve Nash .40 1.00
16 Michael Finley .30 .75
17 Nikoloz Tskitishvili .20 .50
18 Andre Miller .25 .60
19 Nene .25 .60
20 Chauncey Billups .30 .75
21 Richard Hamilton .25 .60
22 Ben Wallace .25 .60
23 Clifford Robinson .20 .50
24 Jason Richardson .30 .75
25 Mike Dunleavy .25 .60
26 Yao Ming .60 1.50
27 Cuttino Mobley .20 .50
28 Steve Francis .25 .60
29 Jermaine O'Neal .25 .60
30 Reggie Miller .30 .75
31 Al Harrington .25 .60
32 Elton Brand .30 .75
33 Corey Maggette .25 .60
34 Quentin Richardson .25 .60
35 Kobe Bryant 1.25 3.00
36 Karl Malone .40 1.00
37 Gary Payton .30 .75
38 Shaquille O'Neal .75 2.00
39 Pau Gasol .30 .75
40 Jason Williams .25 .60
41 Mike Miller .25 .60
42 Lamar Odom .25 .60
43 Eddie Jones .25 .60
44 Caron Butler .25 .60
45 Michael Redd .30 .75
46 Desmond Mason .25 .60
47 Tim Thomas .20 .50
48 Latrell Sprewell .25 .60
49 Kevin Garnett .50 1.25
50 Wally Szczerbiak .25 .60
51 Richard Jefferson .25 .60
52 Kenyon Martin .25 .60
53 Jason Kidd .50 1.25
54 Jamal Mashburn .25 .60
55 Baron Davis .25 .60
56 Jamaal Magloire .20 .50
57 Allan Houston .25 .60
58 Antonio McDyess .25 .60
59 Keith Van Horn .25 .60
60 Grant Hill .40 1.00
61 Drew Gooden .25 .60
62 Tracy McGrady .40 1.00
63 Glenn Robinson .25 .60
64 Allen Iverson .50 1.25
65 Eric Snow .20 .50
66 Amare Stoudemire .40 1.00
67 Stephon Marbury .25 .60
68 Shawn Marion .25 .60
69 Derek Anderson .20 .50
70 Damon Stoudamire .25 .60
71 Rasheed Wallace .30 .75
72 Peja Stojakovic .30 .75
73 Chris Webber .30 .75
74 Mike Bibby .30 .75
75 Bobby Jackson .20 .50
76 Tony Parker .30 .75
77 Tim Duncan .50 1.25
78 Manu Ginobili .40 1.00
79 Vladimir Radmanovic .20 .50
80 Ray Allen .30 .75
81 Rashard Lewis .30 .75
82 Morris Peterson .20 .50
83 Vince Carter .50 1.25
84 Jalen Rose .25 .60
85 Andrei Kirilenko .30 .75
86 Matt Harpring .20 .50
87 Greg Ostertag .20 .50
88 Gilbert Arenas .25 .60
89 Larry Hughes .25 .60
90 Jerry Stackhouse .25 .60
91 Kirk Hinrich RC 1.50 4.00
92 T.J. Ford RC 1.25 3.00
93 Nick Collison RC 1.25 3.00
94 Kendrick Perkins RC 1.25 3.00
95 Leandro Barbosa RC 1.50 4.00
96 Josh Howard RC 1.50 4.00
97 Jason Kapono RC 1.00 2.50
98 Jerome Beasley RC 1.00 2.50
99 Travis Hansen RC 1.00 2.50
100 Steve Blake RC 1.25 3.00
101 Willie Green RC 1.00 2.50
102 Zaur Pachulia RC 1.50 4.00
103 Keith Bogans RC 1.00 2.50
104 Kyle Korver RC 2.00 5.00
105 Brandon Hunter RC 1.00 2.50
106 LeBron James JSY RC 50.00 120.00
107 Darko Milicic JSY RC 2.50 6.00
108 Carmelo Anthony JSY RC 10.00 25.00
109 Chris Bosh JSY RC 5.00 12.00
110 Dwyane Wade JSY RC 10.00 25.00
111 Chris Kaman JSY RC 3.00 8.00
112 Mike Sweetney JSY RC 2.00 5.00
113 Jarvis Hayes JSY RC 2.00 5.00
114 Mickael Pietrus JSY RC 2.50 6.00
115 Marcus Banks JSY RC 2.00 5.00
116 Luke Ridnour JSY RC 2.50 6.00
117 Reece Gaines JSY RC 2.00 5.00
118 Troy Bell JSY RC 2.00 5.00
119 Z.Cabarkapa JSY RC 2.00 5.00
120 David West JSY RC 3.00 8.00
121 A.Pavlovic JSY RC 2.50 6.00
122 Dahntay Jones JSY RC 2.50 6.00
123 Boris Diaw JSY RC 3.00 8.00
124 Zoran Planinic JSY RC 2.00 5.00
125 Travis Outlaw JSY RC 2.50 6.00
126 Brian Cook JSY RC 2.00 5.00
127 Ndudi Ebi JSY RC 2.00 5.00
128 Maciej Lampe JSY RC 2.00 5.00
129 Slavko Vranes JSY RC 2.00 5.00
130 Luke Walton JSY RC 3.00 8.00

2003-04 Upper Deck Honor Roll Gold

*GOLD 1-90: 4X TO 10X BASE HI
*GOLD 91-105 RCs: 2X TO 5X BASE HI
1-90 PRINT RUN 100 SER.#'d SETS
91-105 PRINT RUN 25 SER.#'d SETS

2003-04 Upper Deck Honor Roll Jersey Autographs Gold

*GOLD: 1.25X TO 3X BASE HI
PRINT RUN 25 SERIAL #'d SETS
106 LeBron James 2500.00 3000.00
108 Carmelo Anthony 100.00 200.00
109 Chris Bosh 50.00 120.00
110 Dwyane Wade 250.00 500.00

2003-04 Upper Deck Honor Roll Award Performers

Randomly inserted at one in 12, this 14-card set features a horizontal design with the player on one side set to a circular background of the team's colors. A gold version of this set was also issued and those cards are sequentially numbered to 100.

COMPLETE SET (14) 10.00 25.00
STATED ODDS 1:12 1.00 2.50
*GOLD SINGLES: 2.5X TO 6X BASE HI
GOLD PRINT RUN 100 SER.#'d SETS
AP1 LeBron James 5.00 12.00
AP2 Peja Stojakovic .40 1.00
AP3 Yao Ming .75 2.00
AP4 Gilbert Arenas .30 .75
AP5 Jermaine O'Neal .30 .75
AP6 Amare Stoudemire .50 1.25
AP7 Kobe Bryant 1.50 4.00
AP8 Jason Kidd .60 1.50
AP9 Vince Carter .60 1.50
AP10 Shaquille O'Neal 1.00 2.50
AP11 Michael Jordan 3.00 8.00
AP12 Caron Butler .30 .75
AP13 Ben Wallace .30 .75
AP14 Elton Brand .40 1.00

2003-04 Upper Deck Honor Roll Dual Warm Ups

Inserted at one in 48, this 21-card set features a horizontal design with two player photos along the top and two swatches of warm up. A Gold version of this set was also issued and those cards are sequentially numbered to 100.

STATED ODDS 1:48
*GOLD SINGLES: .6X TO 1.5X BASE HI
GOLD PRINT RUN 100 SER.#'d SETS
1 A.Iverson/E.Snow 5.00 12.00
2 A.Miller/Nene 4.00 10.00
3 D.Milicic/R.Hamilton 4.00 10.00
4 C.Butler/D.Wade 8.00 20.00
5 E.Curry/T.Chandler 4.00 10.00
6 J.Kidd/K.Martin 4.00 10.00
7 B.Davis/J.Magloire 4.00 10.00
8 J.Tinsley/J.O'Neal 4.00 10.00
9 G.Arenas/J.Richardson 4.00 10.00
10 J.Terry/Abdur-Rahim 4.00 10.00
11 K.Bryant/G.Payton 10.00 25.00
12 K.Garnett/Szczerbiak 5.00 12.00
13 K.Malone/D.George 5.00 12.00
14 J.Stockton/M.Jordan 30.00 80.00
15 D.Wagner/D.Miles 4.00 10.00
16 P.Pierce/A.Walker 4.00 10.00
17 M.Bibby/R.Jefferson 4.00 10.00
18 D.Nowitzki/S.Nash 5.00 12.00
19 T.McGrady/D.Gooden 5.00 12.00
20 T.Duncan/T.Parker 5.00 12.00
21 C.Wilcox/S.Francis 4.00 10.00

2003-04 Upper Deck Honor Roll Popular Acclaim

Inserted at one in 12, this 14-card set is vertically designed with a player photo on the right and a silver bar with the set name along the left. A gold version of this set was issued also, and those cards are sequentially numbered to 50.

COMPLETE SET (14) 8.00 20.00
STATED ODDS 1:12
*GOLD SINGLES: 2.5X TO 6X BASE HI
GOLD PRINT RUN 50 SER.#'d SETS

PA1 Kobe Bryant 1.50 4.00
PA2 Ray Allen .40 1.00
PA3 Shawn Marion .30 .75
PA4 Steve Francis .30 .75
PA5 Dajuan Wagner .25 .60
PA6 Steve Nash .50 1.25
PA7 LeBron James 5.00 12.00
PA8 Carmelo Anthony 1.25 3.00
PA9 Paul Pierce .40 1.00
PA10 Gary Payton .40 1.00
PA11 Richard Jefferson .30 .75
PA12 Michael Jordan 3.00 8.00
PA13 Baron Davis .30 .75
PA14 Shaquille O'Neal 1.00 2.50

2003-04 Upper Deck Honor Roll Principals

Randomly seeded at the rate of one in 480, this 21-card set features a horizontal design with both a player photo and a circular swatch of game used memorabilia.

STATED ODDS 1:480
BA Marcus Banks 5.00 12.00
CA Carmelo Anthony 40.00 100.00
CH Chris Bosh 15.00 40.00
CM Corey Maggette 8.00 20.00
DG Drew Gooden 5.00 12.00
DM Darko Milicic 10.00 25.00
DR David Robinson 20.00 50.00
DW Dajuan Wagner 5.00 12.00
GA Gilbert Arenas 10.00 25.00
JH Jarvis Hayes 5.00 12.00
JK Jason Kidd 25.00 60.00
JM Jerome Moiso 5.00 12.00
LJ LeBron James 400.00 800.00
MB Mike Bibby 12.50 30.00
MJ Michael Jordan/23 400.00 800.00
RJ Richard Jefferson 8.00 20.00
SF Steve Francis 10.00 25.00
TO Travis Outlaw 6.00 15.00
WAO Dwyane Wade 75.00 150.00
YM Yao Ming 30.00 80.00

2003-04 Upper Deck Honor Roll Signature Class

Inserted at one in 480, this 12-card set is horizontally designed with a black and white player portrait on the right and an autograph on the left. Dual signature versions featuring two players were also inserted. Dual cards are sequentially numbered to 15.

STATED ODDS 1:480
SC1 Jerome Moiso 4.00 10.00
SC2 Cuttino Mobley 8.00 20.00
SC3 Richard Hamilton 10.00 25.00
SC4 Andre Miller 8.00 20.00
SC5 Mickael Pietrus 6.00 15.00
SC6 Luke Ridnour 4.00 10.00
SC8 Jarvis Hayes 8.00 20.00
SC9 Ndudi Ebi 8.00 20.00
SC10 LeBron James 500.00 900.00
SC12 Kobe Bryant 200.00 400.00

2003-04 Upper Deck Honor Roll Superstar Tributes

Inserted at one in 24, this seven card set features a "framed" portrait photo of the player centered on a split background where to top of the card is white and the bottom matches the player's team colors. A gold version was inserted as well and these cards are sequentially numbered to five.

COMPLETE SET (7) 10.00 25.00
STATED ODDS 1:24
ST1 Michael Jordan 6.00 15.00
ST2 Dirk Nowitzki 1.25 3.00
ST3 LeBron James 8.00 20.00
ST4 Kobe Bryant 3.00 8.00
ST5 Kevin Garnett 1.25 3.00
ST6 Tracy McGrady 1.00 2.50
ST7 Carmelo Anthony 2.50 6.00

2003-04 Upper Deck Honor Roll Tremendous Talents

Inserted at one in 24, this seven card set places a full-color player action phot on the right and a silver top-to-bottom design on the left. A Gold version of the set was also produced and these cards are sequentially numbered to 25.

COMPLETE SET (7) 8.00 20.00
STATED ODDS 1:24
*GOLD: 3X TO 8X BASE HI
GOLD PRINT RUN 25 SER.#'d SETS
TT1 Tim Duncan 1.25 3.00
TT2 Shaquille O'Neal 2.00 5.00
TT3 Kobe Bryant 3.00 8.00
TT4 Allen Iverson 1.25 3.00
TT5 Vince Carter 1.25 3.00
TT6 Chris Webber .75 2.00
TT7 LeBron James 8.00 20.00

2003-04 Upper Deck Honor Roll Triple Warm Ups

Inserted in packs at the rate of one in 144, this 21-card set places three players and three swatches of warm up on the card front. A Gold version of the set was also produced and those cards are sequentially numbered to 25.

STATED ODDS 1:144
*GOLD: .75X TO 2X BASE HI
GOLD PRINT RUN 25 SER.#'d SETS
1 Iverson/McKie/Snow 8.00 20.00
2 Jamison/Arenas/Richardson 6.00 15.00
3 Wagner/Boozer/Miles 6.00 15.00
4 Nowitzki/Finley/Nash 10.00 25.00
5 Wilcox/Brand/Ely 6.00 15.00
6 Curry/Rose/JayWill 6.00 15.00
7 Kobe/Payton/Malone 25.00 60.00
8 A-Rahim/Terry/G.Robinson 6.00 15.00
9 Kidd/Martin/Jefferson 8.00 20.00
10 Haywood/J-Rich/Hughes 6.00 15.00
11 Houston/Vranes/Mutombo 6.00 15.00
12 Amare/Marion/Marbury 6.00 15.00
13 Jordan/Kobe/Stockton 30.00 80.00
14 Odom/Q-Rich/Maggette 6.00 15.00
15 M.Miller/Gasol/Battier 6.00 15.00
16 G.Wallace/Bibby/Peja 6.00 15.00
17 Mason/J.Smith/R.Allen 6.00 15.00
18 Darko/Billups/Hamilton 6.00 15.00
19 Duncan/Parker/Rasho 12.50 30.00
20 Kobe/Garnett/McGrady 15.00 40.00
21 B.Davis/Francis/Marbury 6.00 15.00

2012 Upper Deck Industry Summit Signature Icons Autographs

LAS VEGAS INDUSTRY SUMMIT EXCLUSIVE
LVLJ LeBron James/25

2001-02 Upper Deck Inspirations

Released in late June of 2002, Upper Deck Inspirations features a 140-card set divided up as follows: cards 1-90 showcase full color player action photos with an orange and black marble background. The left border of the card is a solid orange line, and the right border features orange and black non-embossed basketball texturing. The Upper Deck Inspirations logo appears in the lower left hand corner. Cards 91-106 contain pictures of both a rookie player and a veteran player and are sequentially numbered to 2249. These vertical-style cards have a green backdrop on the right side where a portrait style photo of the veteran player appears along with the corresponding name, while the left side of the card contains a full color action photo of the featured rookie. The rookie name appears along the left hand side of the card. Cards 107-109 feature the same card design as the previous numbers, but are enhanced with player autographs and are sequentially numbered to 275. Cards 104-106 contain veteran player autographs only, and cards 107-109 contain rookie player autographs only. Cards 110-116 once again features the same card design with both rookie and veteran autographs, and are sequentially numbered to 1149. Cards 117-124 have a blue background and showcase a portrait style head shot of both players, the veteran player on the right and the rookie player on the left. These cards feature rookie jerseys only, which are cut in the shape of the letter "R." Each card is sequentially numbered to 1500, and card number 118 is a short print, sequentially numbered to 525. Cards 125-140 feature the same design as the previous rookie jerseys, but have jersey swatches from both rookies and veterans. The rookie jerseys are once again cut in an "R" shape, while the veteran swatches are cut in an "S" shape. Card numbers 141T-180T feature draft picks from the 2002-03 NBA Draft in New York. These cards were originally issued as redemptions, and are sequentially numbered as follows: 141T-152T #'d to 2999, 153T-164T #'d to 2699, 165T to 176T #'d to 1999, and 177T to 182T #'d to 499. Upper Deck inspirations also marks the first draft redemption cards in basketball that were redeemable online at www.upperdeck.com.

COMP.SET w/o SP's (90) 15.00 40.00
91-103 PRINT RUN 2249 SER.#'d SETS
104-109 PRINT RUN 275 SER.#'d SETS
110-116 PRINT RUN 1149 SER.#'d SETS
117-124 PRINT RUN 1500 SER.#'d SETS
CARD 118 PRINT RUN 525 SER.#'d SETS
125-134 PRINT RUN 1100 SER.#'d SETS
125-134 BOTH PLAYERS HAVE JSY
135-140 PRINT RUN 275 SER.#'d SETS
135-140 BOTH PLAYERS HAVE JSY
141-152 PRINT RUN 2999 SER.#'d SETS
153-164 PRINT RUN 2699 SER.#'d SETS
165-176 PRINT RUN 1999 SER.#'d SETS
177-182 PRINT RUN 499 SER.#'d SETS
1 Shareef Abdur-Rahim .25 .60
2 Jason Terry .30 .75
3 Dion Glover .20 .50
4 Antoine Walker .25 .60
5 Paul Pierce .30 .75
6 Larry Bird .75 2.00
7 Baron Davis .30 .75
8 Jamal Mashburn .25 .60
9 David Wesley .20 .50
10 Elden Campbell .20 .50
11 Jalen Rose .25 .60
12 Marcus Fizer .20 .50
13 Andre Miller .25 .60
14 Lamond Murray .20 .50
15 Chris Mihm .20 .50
16 Dirk Nowitzki .50 1.25
17 Steve Nash .50 1.25
18 Michael Finley .30 .75
19 Nick Van Exel .25 .60
20 Raef LaFrentz .20 .50
21 Antonio McDyess .25 .60
22 Juwan Howard .25 .60
23 Tim Hardaway .30 .75
24 James Posey .20 .50
25 Jerry Stackhouse .25 .60
26 Ben Wallace .25 .60
27 Isiah Thomas .30 .75
28 Antawn Jamison .30 .75
29 Larry Hughes .25 .60
30 Steve Francis .25 .60
31 Moses Malone .30 .75
32 Reggie Miller .30 .75
33 Jermaine O'Neal .25 .60
34 Elton Brand .30 .75
35 Darius Miles .20 .50
36 Lamar Odom .25 .60
37 Quentin Richardson .25 .60
38 Kobe Bryant 1.25 3.00
39 Shaquille O'Neal .75 2.00
40 Derek Fisher .25 .60
41 Devean George .20 .50
42 Stromile Swift .20 .50
43 Jason Williams .25 .60
44 Alonzo Mourning .40 1.00
45 Eddie Jones .25 .60
46 Anthony Carter .20 .50
47 Ray Allen .30 .75
48 Sam Cassell .25 .60
49 Glenn Robinson .25 .60
50 Tim Thomas .20 .50
51 Oscar Robertson .40 1.00
52 Kevin Garnett .50 1.25
53 Wally Szczerbiak .25 .60
54 Terrell Brandon .20 .50
55 Chauncey Billups .30 .75
56 Jason Kidd .50 1.25
57 Kenyon Martin .30 .75
58 Latrell Sprewell .25 .60
59 Allan Houston .25 .60
60 Marcus Camby .25 .60
61 Kurt Thomas .20 .50
62 Grant Hill .40 1.00
63 Mike Miller .25 .60
64 Tracy McGrady .50 1.25
65 Allen Iverson .60 1.50
66 Julius Erving .50 1.25
67 Bobby Jones .25 .60
68 Stephon Marbury .25 .60
69 Shawn Marion .25 .60
70 Anfernee Hardaway .50 1.25
71 Rasheed Wallace .30 .75
72 Bill Walton .30 .75
73 Chris Webber .30 .75
74 Peja Stojakovic .30 .75
75 Mike Bibby .30 .75
76 Tim Duncan .60 1.50
77 David Robinson .50 1.25
78 George Gervin .30 .75
79 Gary Payton .30 .75
80 Rashard Lewis .30 .75
81 Desmond Mason .25 .60
82 Vince Carter .50 1.25
83 Morris Peterson .20 .50
84 Antonio Davis .20 .50
85 Hakeem Olajuwon .40 1.00
86 Karl Malone .40 1.00
87 John Stockton .40 1.00
88 Donyell Marshall .20 .50
89 Richard Hamilton .25 .60
90 Michael Jordan 4.00 10.00
91 Z.Rebraca RC/S.O'Neal 2.00 5.00
92 O.Robertson/O.Torres RC 2.00 5.00
93 R.Miller/J.Brewer RC 2.00 5.00
94 P.Stojak/P.Drobnjak RC 2.00 5.00
95 M.Bateer RC/W.Zhi-Zhi 2.00 5.00
96 J.West/W.Solomon RC 2.00 5.00
97 T.Duncan/M.Allen RC 2.00 5.00
98 W.Frazier/D.Brown RC 2.00 5.00
99 S.Marion/A.Ford RC 2.00 5.00
100 T.Kukoc/A.Fotsis RC 2.00 5.00
101 B.Walton/Z.Randolph RC 5.00 12.00
102 S.Marbury/J.Crispin RC 2.00 5.00
103 W.Unseld/B.Simmons RC 2.00 5.00
104 J.Kidd AU/J.Tinsley RC 8.00 20.00
105 K.Garnett AU/P.Gasol RC 15.00 40.00
106 K.Bryant AU/S.Battier RC 50.00 100.00
107 Carter/J.Trepagnier AU RC 6.00 15.00
108 J.Erving/Kw.Brown AU RC 8.00 20.00
109 T.Duncan/E.Curry AU RC 8.00 20.00
110 Odom AU/E.Griffin AU RC 6.00 15.00
111 Alexndr AU/Watson AU RC 6.00 15.00
112 MoPete AU/Arenas AU RC 6.00 15.00
113 Martin AU/Scalabrine AU RC 6.00 15.00
114 Chandler AU RC/Fizer AU 6.00 15.00
115 Mggtte AU/Boumtje AU RC 6.00 15.00
116 Jr.Collins AU RC/Madsen AU 6.00 15.00
117 V.Carter/J.Forte JSY RC 4.00 10.00
118 Jamison/Murphy JSY SP RC 6.00 15.00
119 Martin/Armstrong JSY RC 4.00 10.00
120 Francis/T.Morris JSY RC 4.00 10.00
121 G.Hill/S.Hunter JSY RC 4.00 10.00
122 Mourng/Radmnov JSY RC 4.00 10.00
123 Haywood JSY RC/Shaq 8.00 20.00
124 Dalmbrt JSY RC/M.Malone 5.00 12.00
125 Szczerbiak/P.Brezec RC 5.00 12.00
126 P.Stojakovic/M.Bradley RC 5.00 12.00
127 A.Hardaway/J.Johnson RC 8.00 20.00
128 L.Woods RC/T.Ratliff 5.00 12.00
129 C.Webber/G.Wallace RC 6.00 15.00
130 A.Walker/Ke.Brown RC 5.00 12.00
131 B.Davis/J.Brewer RC 5.00 12.00
132 D.Nowitzki/A.Kirilenko RC 10.00 25.00
133 J.Smith/A.Ford RC 5.00 12.00
134 J.Stockton/J.Crispin RC 6.00 15.00
135 K.Malone/R.White RC 6.00 15.00
136 T.McGrady/J.Sasser RC 6.00 15.00
137 E.Brand/Jas.Collins RC 6.00 15.00
138 K.Bryant/R.Jefferson RC 12.00 30.00
139 A.Iverson/T.Parker RC 10.00 25.00
140 Jordan/J.Richardson RC 25.00 60.00
141 Ronald Murray XRC 2.50 6.00
142 Pat Burke XRC 2.50 6.00
143 Manu Ginobili XRC 6.00 15.00
144 Gordan Giricek XRC 2.50 6.00
145 Tito Maddox XRC 2.50 6.00
146 Tamar Slay XRC 2.50 6.00
147 Rasual Butler XRC 2.50 6.00
148 Carlos Boozer XRC 5.00 12.00
149 Dan Gadzuric XRC 2.00 5.00
150 Vincent Yarbrough XRC 2.50 6.00
151 Robert Archibald XRC 2.50 6.00
152 Roger Mason XRC 2.00 5.00
153 Jamal Sampson XRC 2.50 6.00
154 Sam Clancy XRC 2.50 6.00
155 Dan Dickau XRC 2.50 6.00
156 Chris Jefferies XRC 2.50 6.00
157 John Salmons XRC 3.00 8.00
158 Frank Williams XRC 2.50 6.00
159 Lonny Baxter XRC 2.50 6.00
160 Tayshaun Prince XRC 3.00 8.00
161 Casey Jacobsen XRC 2.50 6.00
162 Qyntel Woods XRC 2.50 6.00
163 Kareem Rush XRC 2.50 6.00
164 Ryan Humphrey XRC 2.50 6.00
165 Curtis Borchardt XRC 3.00 8.00
166 Juan Dixon XRC 3.00 8.00
167 Jiri Welsch XRC 3.00 8.00
168 Bostjan Nachbar XRC 3.00 8.00
169 Fred Jones XRC 3.00 8.00
170 Marcus Haislip XRC 3.00 8.00
171 Melvin Ely XRC 3.00 8.00
172 Jared Jeffries XRC 3.00 8.00
173 Caron Butler XRC 4.00 10.00
174 Amare Stoudemire XRC 8.00 20.00
175 Chris Wilcox XRC 3.00 8.00
176 Nene Hilario XRC 3.00 8.00
177 Dajuan Wagner XRC 6.00 15.00
178 Nikoloz Tskitishvili XRC 6.00 15.00
179 Drew Gooden XRC 6.00 15.00
180 Mike Dunleavy XRC 6.00 15.00
181 Jay Williams XRC 8.00 20.00
182 Yao Ming XRC 20.00 50.00

2001-02 Upper Deck Inspirations Hardwood Imagery

Randomly inserted in packs at the rate of one in 47, this 21-card set features a small color player action photo on a large swatch of floor that takes up approximately 80% of the card front. Engraved in the wood swatch is the featured player's name, number, position, as well as the Upper Deck Inspirations logo. The top and bottom card borders are flat black, and the little bit of cardboard border left exposed by the swatch is printed on to look like wood.

COMPLETE SET (21) 75.00 150.00
STATED ODDS 1:47
AL Allen Iverson 5.00 12.00
AM Andre Miller 2.00 5.00
CW Chris Webber 2.50 6.00
DM Darius Miles 1.50 4.00
DN Dirk Nowitzki 4.00 10.00
JK Jason Kidd 4.00 10.00
JS Jerry Stackhouse 2.00 5.00
KB Kobe Bryant 10.00 25.00
KG Kevin Garnett 4.00 10.00
KM Kenyon Martin 2.50 6.00
MF Michael Finley 2.50 6.00
MJ Michael Jordan 20.00 50.00
MM Mike Miller 2.00 5.00
MP Morris Peterson 1.50 4.00
PP Paul Pierce 2.50 6.00
RA Ray Allen 2.50 6.00
SA Shareef Abdur-Rahim 2.00 5.00
SF Steve Francis 2.00 5.00
SH Shawn Marion 2.00 5.00
SM Stephon Marbury 2.00 5.00
TM Tracy McGrady 4.00 10.00

2001-02 Upper Deck Inspirations Hardwood Imagery Combo

Randomly inserted in packs at the rate of one in 47, this 21-card set features two small color player action photos on a large swatch of floor that takes up approximately 80% of the card front. Engraved in the wood swatch is the featured player's names, numbers, positions, as well as the Upper Deck Inspirations logo. The top and bottom card borders are flat black, and the little bit of cardboard border left exposed by the swatch is printed on to look like wood.

COMPLETE SET (21) 150.00 300.00
STATED ODDS 1:47
AH/LS L.Sprewell/A.Houston 5.00 12.00
AI/SF S.Francis/A.Iverson 6.00 15.00
BD/JM J.Mashburn/B.Davis 4.00 10.00
EJ/BG E.Jones/B.Grant 4.00 10.00
JK/KM J.Kidd/K.Martin 5.00 12.00
KB/JK K.Bryant/J.Kidd 10.00 25.00
KB/JS J.Stackhouse/K.Bryant 10.00 25.00
KB/KG K.Bryant/K.Garnett 12.50 30.00
KG/CW K.Garnett/C.Webber 5.00 12.00
KG/WS W.Szczerbiak/K.Garnett 5.00 12.00
KM/JS K.Malone/J.Stockton 6.00 15.00
LO/QR L.Odom/Q.Richardson 4.00 10.00
MF/DN M.Finley/D.Nowitzki 5.00 12.00
MJ/KB M.Jordan/K.Bryant 40.00 100.00
PP/AW A.Walker/P.Pierce 6.00 15.00
RA/GR R.Allen/G.Robinson 4.00 10.00
RM/JO R.Miller/J.O'Neal 4.00 10.00
RW/SP S.Pippen/R.Wallace 6.00 15.00
SA/DJ S.Rahim/D.Johnson 4.00 10.00
SM/SM S.Marbury/S.Marion 4.00 10.00
TM/DM T.McGrady/D.Miles 6.00 15.00

2001-02 Upper Deck Inspirations Like Mike

Randomly inserted in packs at the rate of one in 576, this 5-card set features the same card design as the double swatch jersey rookies from the base Upper Deck Inspirations. Lil' Bow Wow appears on the left side of the card with an "R" shaped jersey worn in the filming of "Like Mike," and a veteran player appears on the right side of the card with an "S" shaped jersey. Also included in this set is a Lil' Bow Wow autographed card sequentially numbered to 100. This auto'd card features an action photo, a portrait photo, and a cut signature.

STATED ODDS 1:576
LBW Bow Wow AU/100 50.00 100.00
LBWAI A.Iverson/Bow Wow JSY 10.00 25.00
LBWCW C.Webb/Bow Wow JSY 10.00 25.00
LBWGP G.Payton/Bow Wow JSY 10.00 25.00
LBWJK J.Kidd/Bow Wow JSY 10.00 25.00

2002-03 Upper Deck Inspirations

Released in July 2003, this set was Upper Deck's last 2002-03 Product. The 197-card set is divided up as follows: Numbers 1-90 are base veteran cards, numbers 91-104 feature dual player rookie cards with one veteran and one rookie and are inserted at the rate of one in 12, numbers 105-110 are dual player cards as well with a swatch from a rookie player and a swatch from a veteran player, these cards are sequentially numbered to 325, numbers 111-127 are also dual jersey cards with the same format as cards 105-110 and are sequentially numbered to 1500, numbers 128-133 feature one rookie player autograph and one veteran autograph and are sequentially numbered to 275, numbers 134-139 are the same format as cards 128-133 and are sequentially numbered to 1600, numbers 140-149 are autographed by the rookie and sequentially numbered to 1600, and the remaining cards in the set were draft pick redemption cards for the players drawn in the 2003 NBA Draft. The Draft Pick cards breakdown as follows: Cards 156-161 are sequentially numbered to 499, cards 162-167 are sequentially numbered to 799, cards 168-175 are sequentially numbered to 1499, and cards 176-197 are sequentially numbered to 2999. Inspirations was packaged in 24-pack boxes where packs contained five cards and carried a suggested retail price of $4.99.

COMP.SET w/o SP's (90) 12.50 30.00
91-104 STATED ODDS 1:12
105-110 PRINT RUN 325 SER.#'d SETS
105-110 DUAL JERSEY CARDS
111-127 PRINT RUN 1500 SER.#'d SETS
111-127 DUAL JERSEY CARDS
128-133 PRINT RUN 275 SER.#'d SETS
128-133 DUAL AUTOGRAPH CARDS
134-139 PRINT RUN 1600 SER.#'d SETS
134-139 DUAL AUTOGRAPH CARDS
140-149 PRINT RUN 1600 SER.#'d SETS
140-149 ROOKIE AUTOGRAPH ONLY
156-161 PRINT RUN 499 SER.#'d SETS
162-167 PRINT RUN 799 SER.#'d SETS
168-175 PRINT RUN 1499 SER.#'d SETS
176-197 PRINT RUN 2999 SER.#'d SETS
1 Shareef Abdur-Rahim .25 .60
2 Jason Terry .25 .60
3 Glenn Robinson .25 .60
4 Paul Pierce .30 .75
5 Antoine Walker .25 .60
6 Bill Russell .50 1.25
7 Vin Baker .25 .60
8 Jalen Rose .25 .60
9 Tyson Chandler .30 .75
10 Eddy Curry .20 .50
11 Ricky Davis .25 .60
12 Zydrunas Ilgauskas .25 .60
13 Darius Miles .20 .50
14 Dirk Nowitzki .50 1.25
15 Michael Finley .30 .75
16 Steve Nash .40 1.00
17 Nick Van Exel .25 .60
18 Rodney White .20 .50
19 Juwan Howard .25 .60
20 Richard Hamilton .25 .60
21 Ben Wallace .25 .60
22 Isiah Thomas .30 .75
23 Antawn Jamison .30 .75
24 Jason Richardson .30 .75
25 Gilbert Arenas .30 .75
26 Steve Francis .25 .60
27 Eddie Griffin .20 .50
28 Cuttino Mobley .20 .50
29 Reggie Miller .30 .75
30 Jamaal Tinsley .20 .50
31 Jermaine O'Neal .25 .60
32 Elton Brand .30 .75
33 Andre Miller .25 .60
34 Lamar Odom .25 .60
35 Kobe Bryant 1.25 3.00
36 Shaquille O'Neal .75 2.00
37 Wilt Chamberlain .60 1.50
38 Derek Fisher .25 .60
39 Pau Gasol .40 1.00
40 Shane Battier .30 .75
41 Stromile Swift .20 .50
42 Eddie Jones .25 .60
43 Alonzo Mourning .40 1.00
44 Travis Best .20 .50
45 Gary Payton .30 .75
46 Sam Cassell .25 .60
47 Desmond Mason .25 .60
48 Kevin Garnett .50 1.25
49 Wally Szczerbiak .25 .60
50 Joe Smith .25 .60
51 Jason Kidd .50 1.25
52 Richard Jefferson .30 .75
53 Kenyon Martin .25 .60
54 Baron Davis .25 .60
55 Jamal Mashburn .25 .60
56 David Wesley .20 .50
57 Allan Houston .25 .60
58 Antonio McDyess .25 .60
59 Latrell Sprewell .25 .60
60 Tracy McGrady .50 1.25
61 Grant Hill .40 1.00
62 Pat Garrity .20 .50
63 Allen Iverson .50 1.25
64 Julius Erving .50 1.25
65 Stephon Marbury .25 .60
66 Shawn Marion .25 .60
67 Anfernee Hardaway .50 1.25
68 Rasheed Wallace .30 .75
69 Derek Anderson .20 .50
70 Scottie Pippen .50 1.25
71 Chris Webber .30 .75
72 Mike Bibby .30 .75
73 Peja Stojakovic .30 .75
74 Hedo Turkoglu .25 .60
75 Tim Duncan .60 1.50
76 David Robinson .50 1.25
77 Tony Parker .40 1.00
78 Ray Allen .30 .75
79 Rashard Lewis .30 .75
80 Brent Barry .20 .50
81 Voshon Lenard .20 .50
82 Vince Carter .50 1.25
83 Morris Peterson .20 .50
84 Antonio Davis .20 .50
85 Karl Malone .40 1.00
86 John Stockton .40 1.00
87 Andrei Kirilenko .30 .75
88 Jerry Stackhouse .25 .60
89 Michael Jordan 2.50 6.00
90 Kwame Brown .20 .50
91 Mason RC/Jordan 1.50 4.00
92 Harrington RC/English 1.25 3.00
93 Dunleavy RC/R.Barry 1.50 4.00
94 Archibald RC/Swift 1.25 3.00
95 Maddox RC/Francis 1.25 3.00
96 Hawkins RC/M.Malone 1.25 3.00
97 Batiste RC/Jas.Williams 1.25 3.00
98 K.Johnson/Mourning 1.25 3.00
99 S.Parker RC/D.Miles 1.25 3.00
100 P.Burke RC/S.O'Neal 1.25 3.00
101 R.Lopez RC/J.Stockton 1.25 3.00
102 C.Owens RC/S.Battier 1.25 3.00
103 M.Wilks RC/E.Boykins 1.25 3.00
104 Rigadeau RC/Nowitzki 1.25 3.00
105 Butler JSY RC/Garnett JSY 8.00 20.00
106 Wagner JSY RC/Iversn JSY 6.00 15.00
107 Rush JSY RC/Bryant JSY 6.00 15.00
108 Hilario JSY RC/Duncan JSY 8.00 20.00
109 Ely JSY RC/E.Brand JSY 4.00 10.00
110 Hmphry JSY RC/T-Mac JSY 4.00 10.00
111 M.Jaric JSY/A.Miller JSY 3.00 8.00
112 Jones JSY RC/Miller JSY 3.00 8.00
113 Baxter JSY RC/Smith JSY 3.00 8.00
114 Bremer JSY RC/Pierce JSY 3.00 8.00
115 Boozer JSY RC/Hill JSY 6.00 15.00
116 Savovic JSY RC/Divac JSY 3.00 8.00
117 Okur JSY RC/Turkoglu JSY 4.00 10.00
118 Pargo JSY RC/Fisher JSY 3.00 8.00
119 Trybnski JSY RC/Swift JSY 3.00 8.00
120 Murray JSY RC/Lewis JSY 6.00 15.00
121 Evans JSY RC/Allen JSY 3.00 8.00
122 Butler JSY RC/Jones JSY 3.00 8.00
123 Smpsn JSY RC/A-Rahim JSY 3.00 8.00
124 Rakocv JSY RC/Brndn JSY 3.00 8.00
125 Slay JSY RC/Jefferson JSY 3.00 8.00
126 E.Rentz JSY RC/V.Horn JSY 3.00 8.00
127 Yarbr.JSY RC/Howard JSY 3.00 8.00
128A JayWill AU RC/Kobe AU 75.00 150.00
128B JayWill AU RC/Jordan AU 250.00 500.00
129 Gooden AU RC/Garnett AU 20.00 50.00
130 A.Stoud AU RC/Marion AU 20.00 50.00
131 Tskitishv AU RC/Peja AU 6.00 15.00
132 Ming AU RC/Zhizhi AU 100.00 200.00
133 Dixon AU RC/Kidd AU 10.00 25.00
134 Jeffries AU RC/Stack AU 6.00 15.00
135 Haislip AU/K-Mart AU 6.00 15.00
136 Welsch AU RC/J-Rich AU 6.00 15.00
137 Salmons AU RC/Wallace AU 6.00 15.00
138 Ginobili AU RC/Parker AU 50.00 120.00
139 Dickau AU RC/Bibby AU 6.00 15.00
140 Clancy AU RC/J.Erving 3.00 8.00
141 Woods AU RC/Wallace 3.00 8.00
142 F.Williams AU RC/Houston 3.00 8.00
143 Jacobsen AU RC/Hardaway 3.00 8.00
144 Nachbar AU RC/Duncan 3.00 8.00
145 Gadzuric AU RC/S.O'Neal 3.00 8.00
146 Giricek AU RC/McGrady 3.00 8.00
147 Borchardt AU RC/Malone 3.00 8.00
148 Prince AU RC/Walker 3.00 8.00
149 Wilcox AU RC/Carter 3.00 8.00
156 LeBron James XRC 100.00 200.00
157 Darko Milicic XRC 4.00 10.00
158 Carmelo Anthony XRC 12.00 30.00
159 Chris Bosh XRC 8.00 20.00
160 Dwyane Wade XRC 20.00 50.00
161 Chris Kaman XRC 4.00 10.00
162 Kirk Hinrich XRC 4.00 10.00
163 T.J. Ford XRC 3.00 8.00
164 Mike Sweetney XRC 3.00 8.00
165 Jarvis Hayes XRC 3.00 8.00
166 Mickael Pietrus XRC 3.00 8.00
167 Nick Collison XRC 3.00 8.00
168 Marcus Banks XRC 2.50 6.00
169 Luke Ridnour XRC 2.50 6.00
170 Reece Gaines XRC 2.50 6.00
171 Troy Bell XRC 2.50 6.00
172 Zarko Cabarkapa XRC 2.50 6.00
173 David West XRC 3.00 8.00
174 Aleksandar Pavlovic XRC 2.50 6.00
175 Dahntay Jones XRC 2.50 6.00
176 Boris Diaw XRC 1.50 4.00
177 Zoran Planinic XRC 1.50 4.00
178 Travis Outlaw XRC 1.50 4.00
179 Brian Cook XRC 1.50 4.00
180 Udonis Haslem XRC 1.50 4.00
181 Ndudi Ebi XRC 1.50 4.00
182 Kendrick Perkins XRC 1.50 4.00
183 Leandro Barbosa XRC 1.50 4.00
184 Josh Howard XRC 1.50 4.00
185 Maciej Lampe XRC 1.50 4.00
186 Jason Kapono XRC 1.50 4.00
190 Luke Walton XRC 1.50 4.00
191 Jerome Beasley XRC 1.50 4.00
192 Travis Hansen XRC 1.50 4.00
193 Steve Blake XRC 1.50 4.00
194 Slavko Vranes XRC 1.50 4.00
195 Keith Bogans XRC 1.50 4.00
196 Willie Green XRC 1.50 4.00
197 Zaur Pachulia XRC 1.50 4.00

2002-03 Upper Deck Inspirations Rookie Holofoil

These holofoil variations to the XRC Draft Exchange cards were only featured in the first 50 cards printed out of the serial numbering run, for example on LeBron James, cards 1-50 feature holofoil and cards 51-499 feature gold foil. These parallel cards carry the exact same serial numbering as the base XRC exchange cards, but feature holofoil instead of the standard gold foil on the card front and numbering.

*HOLO 156-161: 1X TO 2.5X BASE HI
*HOLO 162-167: 1.25X TO 3X BASE HI
*HOLO 168-175: 1.5X TO 4X BASE HI
*HOLO 176-197: 2.5X TO 6X BASE HI
PRINT RUN FIRST 50 CARDS OF XRC EXCHANGE
156A LeBron James 300.00 600.00
160A Dwyane Wade 125.00 250.00

2002-03 Upper Deck Inspirations UD Promos

*PROMOS: .75X TO 2X BASIC

1991-92 Upper Deck International Award Winner Holograms

The 1991-92 Upper Deck International Hologram set features nine standard-size holograms depicting league leaders in various statistical categories and honoring award winners such as Sixth Man, Rookie of the Year, and Defensive Player of the Year. The cards were randomly inserted into approximately 1:10 packs in both Italian and Spanish packs. The borderless fronts feature holographic cut-out images of the player against a game-action photo of the player. The player's name and award are displayed at the bottom. The backs are blank. The cards are unnumbered and checklisted below in alphabetical order.

COMPLETE SET (9) 5.00 12.00
1 Derrick Coleman .20 .50
2 Michael Jordan MVP 2.00 5.00
3 Michael Jordan Scoring 2.00 5.00
4 Hakeem Olajuwon .60 1.50
5 Alvin Robertson .08 .25
6 David Robinson .60 1.50
7 Dennis Rodman .60 1.50
8 Detlef Schrempf .20 .50
9 John Stockton .60 1.50

1991-92 Upper Deck International Italian

The Italian version of this 200-card standard-size set, which features white-bordered glossy color player action shots on the fronts. The cards were sold in ten-card packs (30 packs per box). Much like the 1991-92 American issues, each card front has the player's name and position displayed below the photo within a simulated hardwood floor strip. This strip continues up the right side and carries the player's team name in a team color. The team logo appears in the bottom right corner. The back is adorned by another player picture that covers the right two-thirds of the back. The horizontal remaining third carries the player's 1991-92 stats, and player highlights in both Italian and English. Card numbers 1 and 2 are East and West All-Star checklists, respectively, and they begin the All-Star subset, comprising the East All-Stars (3-14) and the West All-Stars (15-27). There are three art cards (106-108), cards of the Italian National Team (109-118), the Spanish National Team (119-130), and each NBA team has a logo card (131-157). There are also 1992 NBA Playoffs cards (158-169), NBA Finals (170-177), Cards on Collecting (178-183), and World Stars (184-199), which feature NBA stars born outside the United States. This product has been made available to the U.S. market through closeouts.

COMPLETE SET (200) 10.00 25.00
1 Checklist .50 1.25
East All-Stars
2 Checklist .20 .50
West All-Stars
3 Isiah Thomas AS .25 .60
4 Michael Jordan AS .75 2.00
5 Scottie Pippen AS .25 .60
6 Charles Barkley AS .30 .75
7 Patrick Ewing AS .25 .60
8 Michael Adams AS .07 .20
9 Dennis Rodman AS .25 .60
10 Reggie Lewis AS .07 .20
11 Joe Dumars AS .15 .40
12 Mark Price AS .15 .40
13 Brad Daugherty AS .07 .20
14 Kevin Willis AS .07 .20
15 Clyde Drexler AS .25 .60
16 Magic Johnson AS .30 .75
17 Chris Mullin AS .15 .40
18 Karl Malone AS .25 .60
19 David Robinson AS .25 .60
20 Tim Hardaway AS .20 .50
21 Jeff Hornacek AS .15 .40
22 John Stockton AS .30 .75
23 Dikembe Mutombo AS .20 .50
24 Hakeem Olajuwon AS .20 .50
25 James Worthy AS .20 .50
26 Otis Thorpe AS .07 .20
27 Dan Majerle AS .15 .40
28 Stacey Augmon .15 .40
29 Dominique Wilkins .40 1.00
30 Rumeal Robinson .07 .20
31 Rick Fox .20 .50
32 Reggie Lewis .15 .40
33 Kevin McHale .20 .50
34 Robert Parish .15 .40
35 Muggsy Bogues .15 .40
36 Larry Johnson .20 .50
37 Kendall Gill .20 .50
38 Michael Jordan 1.50 4.00
39 Scottie Pippen .30 .75
40 Horace Grant .15 .40
41 Mark Price .15 .40
42 Brad Daugherty .07 .20
43 Doug Smith .07 .20
44 Derek Harper .15 .40
45 Dikembe Mutombo .25 .60
46 Reggie Williams .07 .20
47 Isiah Thomas .25 .60
48 Joe Dumars .20 .50
49 Bill Laimbeer .15 .40
50 Dennis Rodman .25 .60
51 Chris Mullin .20 .50
52 Tim Hardaway .20 .50
53 Sarunas Marciulionis .07 .20
54 Billy Owens .15 .40
55 Hakeem Olajuwon .20 .50
56 Otis Thorpe .15 .40
57 Reggie Miller .30 .75
58 Vern Fleming .07 .20
59 Detlef Schrempf .15 .40
60 Rik Smits .15 .40
61 Danny Manning .15 .40
62 Ron Harper .15 .40
63 James Worthy .20 .50
64 Vlade Divac .15 .40
65 Byron Scott .15 .40
66 Sam Perkins .15 .40
67 Magic Johnson .40 1.00
68 Rony Seikaly .07 .20
69 Glen Rice .30 .75
70 Alvin Robertson .07 .20
71 Moses Malone .20 .50
72 Doug West .07 .20
73 Felton Spencer .07 .20
74 Derrick Coleman .15 .40
75 Drazen Petrovic .40 1.00
76 Patrick Ewing .30 .75
77 Charles Oakley .07 .20
78 Scott Skiles .15 .40
79 Dennis Scott .15 .40
80 Manute Bol .07 .20
81 Johnny Dawkins .07 .20
82 Hersey Hawkins .15 .40
83 Tom Chambers .15 .40
84 Kevin Johnson .20 .50
85 Dan Majerle .15 .40
86 Clyde Drexler .30 .75
87 Terry Porter .07 .20
88 Kevin Duckworth .07 .20
89 Mitch Richmond .20 .50
90 Spud Webb .15 .40
91 Terry Cummings .15 .40
92 David Robinson .30 .75
93 Sean Elliott .15 .40
94 Shawn Kemp .15 .40
95 Ricky Pierce .07 .20
96 Eddie Johnson .07 .20
97 Gary Payton .20 .50
98 Karl Malone .30 .75
99 John Stockton .30 .75
100 Checklist .07 .20
101 Jeff Malone .07 .20
102 Mark Eaton .07 .20
103 Michael Adams .07 .20
104 Bernard King .15 .40
105 Pervis Ellison .07 .20
106 Magic's Moment ART .20 .50
107 Michael Jordan ART .75 2.00
108 Stacey Augmon ART .07 .20
109 Ferdinando Gentile INT .07 .20
110 Walter Magnifico INT .08 .25
111 Alberto Rossini INT .07 .20
112 Carlton Myers INT .07 .20
113 Riccardo Pittis INT .07 .20
114 Antonello Riva INT .08 .25
115 Ario Costa INT .07 .20
116 Davide Cantarello INT .07 .20
117 Alberto Vianini INT .07 .20
118 Claudio Coldebella INT .07 .20
119 Juan Antonio San SNT .07 .20
120 Javier Fernandez SNT .07 .20
121 Jose A. Arcega SNT .07 .20
122 Juan Antonio SNT .07 .20
123 Jordi Villacampa SNT .07 .20
124 Enrique Andreu SNT .07 .20
125 Jose Antonio Montero SNT .07 .20
126 Rafael Jofresa SNT .07 .20
127 Jose Biriukov SNT .07 .20
128 Santiago Aldama SNT .07 .20
129 Alberto Herreros SNT .07 .20
130 Andres Jimenez SNT .07 .20
131 Hawks Logo .07 .20
132 Celtics Logo .07 .20
133 Hornets Logo .07 .20
134 Bulls Logo .15 .40
135 Cavaliers Logo .07 .20
136 Mavericks Logo .07 .20
137 Nuggets Logo .07 .20
138 Pistons Logo .07 .20
139 Warriors Logo .07 .20
140 Rockets Logo .07 .20
141 Pacers Logo .07 .20
142 Clippers Logo .07 .20
143 Lakers Logo .07 .20
144 Heat Logo .07 .20
145 Bucks Logo .07 .20
146 Timberwolves Logo .07 .20
147 Nets Logo .07 .20
148 Knicks Logo .07 .20
149 Magic Logo .07 .20
150 76ers Logo .07 .20
151 Suns Logo .07 .20
152 Trail Blazers Logo .07 .20
153 Kings Logo .07 .20
154 Spurs Logo .07 .20
155 Supersonics Logo .07 .20
156 Jazz Logo .07 .20
157 Bullets Logo .07 .20
158 Michael Jordan .75 2.00
Rony Seikaly PO
159 Kevin McHale .15 .40
Dale Davis PO
160 Cavaliers .07 .20
Nets PO
161 Patrick Ewing .15 .40
Joe Dumars PO
162 Kevin Duckworth PO .07 .20
163 John Stockton PO .20 .50
164 Tim Hardaway .15 .40
Ricky Pierce PO
165 Kevin Johnson .15 .40
Sean Elliott PO
166 New York Knicks .60 1.50
Scottie Pippen
Michael Jordan PO
167 Brad Daugherty PO .07 .20
168 Terry Porter .07 .20
Kevin Johnson PO
169 Shawn Kemp .20 .50
Karl Malone PO
170 Scottie Pippen .15 .40
Larry Nance PO
171 Clyde Drexler .20 .50
Jeff Malone PO
172 Michael Jordan FIN .75 2.00
173 Clifford Robinson FIN .07 .20
174 Clyde Drexler .60 1.50
Michael Jordan FIN
175 Clyde Drexler FIN .20 .50
176 Michael Jordan FIN .75 2.00
177 Michael Jordan FIN .75 2.00
178 Michael Jordan COC .75 2.00
179 Drazen Petrovic COC .30 .75
180 Magic Johnson COC .30 .75
181 Michael Jordan COC .75 2.00
182 Sarunas Marciulionis COC .07 .20
183 Rik Smits COC .07 .20
184 Rumeal Robinson WS .07 .20
185 Luc Longley WS .15 .40
186 Vlade Divac WS .15 .40
187 Rik Smits WS .07 .20
188 Drazen Petrovic WS .15 .40
189 Detlef Schrempf WS .07 .20
190 Dominique Wilkins WS .15 .40
191 Sarunas Marciulionis WS .07 .20
192 Rick Fox WS .15 .40
193 Patrick Ewing WS .15 .40
194 Manute Bol WS .07 .20
195 Steve Kerr WS .07 .20
196 Dikembe Mutombo WS .15 .40
197 Hakeem Olajuwon WS .20 .50
198 Rony Seikaly WS .07 .20
199 Carl Herrera WS .07 .20
200 Checklist Card .07 .20

1991-92 Upper Deck International Spanish

The Spanish version of this 200-card standard-size set, which features white-bordered glossy color player action shots on the fronts. The cards were sold in ten-card packs (30 packs per box). Much like the 1991-92 American issues, each card front has the player's name and position displayed below the photo within a simulated hardwood floor strip. This strip continues up the right side and carries the player's team name in a team color. The team logo appears in the bottom right corner. The back is adorned by another player picture that covers the right two-thirds of the back. The horizontal remaining third carries the player's 1991-92 stats, and player highlights in both Spanish and English. Card numbers 1 and 2 are East and West All-Star checklists, respectively, and they begin the All-Star subset, comprising the East All-Stars (3-14) and the West All-Stars (15-27). There are three art cards (106-108), cards of the Italian National Team

(109-118), the Spanish National Team (119-130), and each NBA team has a logo card (131-157). There are also 1992 NBA Playoffs cards (158-169), NBA Finals (170-177), Cards on Collecting (178-183), and World Stars (184-199), which feature NBA stars born outside the United States. This product has been made available to the U.S. market through closeouts.

COMPLETE SET (200) 10.00 25.00
SPANISH: SAME VALUE AS ITALIAN

1992-93 Upper Deck International French

The 1992-93 Upper Deck International French basketball set consists of 255 standard-size cards. The fronts feature color action player photos with white borders. The team name is gold-foil stamped across the top of the picture. The border design at the bottom carries the player's name and position, and consists of a team-colored stripe that shades from one team color to the other with diagonal stripes within the larger stripe. The entire design is edged in gold foil. The right end is off-set slightly by the Upper Deck logo. The backs show an action player photo in a vertical layout on the left. The right side is horizontal and displays statistics printed on a ghosted NBA logo. The player's profile is printed in English and French. Within the set are the following subsets: NBA All-Stars (1-25), "In Your Face" 1993 Slam Dunk Competition (26-34), All-Division Team (35-54), Rookie Standouts (55-74), Foreign Exchange (75-85), and Fanimation (86-90). This product has been made available the U.S. market through closeouts.

COMPLETE SET (255) 15.00 40.00
1 All-Star Checklist .07 .20
2 Scottie Pippen AS .40 1.00
3 Larry Johnson AS .15 .40
4 Shaquille O'Neal AS 1.50 4.00
5 Michael Jordan AS 1.00 2.50
6 Isiah Thomas AS .30 .75
7 Brad Daugherty AS .07 .20
8 Joe Dumars AS .25 .60
9 Patrick Ewing AS .40 1.00
10 Larry Nance AS .08 .25
11 Mark Price AS .08 .25
12 Detlef Schrempf AS .07 .20
13 Dominique Wilkins AS .40 1.00
14 Karl Malone AS .40 1.00
15 Charles Barkley AS .40 1.00
16 David Robinson AS .40 1.00
17 John Stockton AS .40 1.00
18 Clyde Drexler AS .40 1.00
19 Sean Elliott AS .10 .30
20 Tim Hardaway AS .08 .25
21 Shawn Kemp AS .30 .75
22 Dan Majerle AS .20 .50
23 Danny Manning AS .07 .20
24 Hakeem Olajuwon AS .40 1.00
25 Terry Porter AS .07 .20
26 Harold Miner FACE .07 .20
27 David Benoit FACE .07 .20
28 Cedric Ceballos FACE .07 .20
29 Mahmoud Abdul-Rauf FACE .07 .20
30 Tim Perry FACE .07 .20
31 Kenny Smith FACE .08 .25
32 Clarence Weatherspoon FACE .07 .20
33 Michael Jordan FACE 1.00 2.50
34 Dominique Wilkins FACE .40 1.00
35 Shaquille O'Neal AD 1.50 4.00
36 Derrick Coleman AD .07 .20
37 Glen Rice AD .20 .50
38 Reggie Lewis AD .08 .25
39 Kenny Anderson AD .07 .20
40 Brad Daugherty AD .07 .20
41 Dominique Wilkins AD .40 1.00
42 Larry Johnson AD .15 .40
43 Michael Jordan AD 1.00 2.50
44 Mark Price AD .08 .25
45 David Robinson AD .40 1.00
46 Karl Malone AD .40 1.00
47 Sean Elliott AD .10 .30
48 John Stockton AD .40 1.00
49 Derek Harper AD .07 .20
50 Kevin Duckworth AD .25 .60
51 Chris Mullin AD .15 .40
52 Charles Barkley AD .40 1.00
53 Tim Hardaway AD .08 .25
54 Clyde Drexler AD .40 1.00
55 Adam Keefe RS .07 .20
56 Alonzo Mourning RS .60 1.50
57 Sean Rooks RS .07 .20
58 LaPhonso Ellis RS .07 .20
59 Latrell Sprewell RS .40 1.00
60 Robert Horry RS .40 1.00
61 Malik Sealy RS .10 .30
62 Anthony Peeler RS .07 .20
63 Harold Miner RS .07 .20
64 Anthony Avent RS .07 .20
65 Todd Day RS .07 .20
66 Lee Mayberry RS .07 .20
67 Christian Laettner RS .30 .75
68 Tom Gugliotta RS .40 1.00
69 Shaquille O'Neal RS 1.50 4.00
70 Clarence Weatherspoon RS .07 .20
71 Richard Dumas RS .07 .20
72 Walt Williams RS .07 .20
73 Lloyd Daniels RS .07 .20
74 Hubert Davis RS .07 .20
75 Manute Bol FE .07 .20
76 Vlade Divac FE .08 .25
77 Patrick Ewing FE .40 1.00
78 Sarunas Marciulionis FE .10 .30
79 Dikembe Mutombo FE .20 .50
80 Hakeem Olajuwon FE .40 1.00
81 Detlef Schrempf FE .07 .20
82 Rony Seikaly FE .07 .20
83 Rik Smits FE .07 .20
84 Kiki Vandeweghe FE .08 .25
85 Dominique Wilkins FE .40 1.00
86 Michael Jordan FAN 1.00 2.50
87 Larry Bird FAN .50 1.25
88 Karl Malone FAN .40 1.00
89 Dikembe Mutombo FAN .20 .50
90 Michael Jordan FAN 1.00 2.50
Larry Bird
91 Stacey Augmon .07 .20
92 Mookie Blaylock .08 .25
93 Duane Ferrell .07 .20
94 Paul Graham .07 .20
95 Adam Keefe .07 .20
96 Jon Koncak .07 .20
97 Dominique Wilkins .40 1.00
98 Kevin Willis .07 .20
99 Alaa Abdelnaby .07 .20
100 Dee Brown .07 .20
101 Sherman Douglas .07 .20
102 Rick Fox .15 .40
103 Reggie Lewis .08 .25
104 Xavier McDaniel .07 .20
105 Robert Parish .15 .40
106 Ed Pinckney .07 .20
107 Muggsy Bogues .15 .40
108 Dell Curry .07 .20
109 Kenny Gattison .07 .20
110 Kendall Gill .08 .25
111 Larry Johnson .15 .40
112 Alonzo Mourning .75 2.00
113 Johnny Newman .07 .20
114 David Wingate .07 .20
115 B.J. Armstrong .15 .40
116 Bill Cartwright .08 .25
117 Horace Grant .15 .40
118 Michael Jordan 2.00 5.00
119 Stacey King .07 .20
120 John Paxson .15 .40
121 Scottie Pippen .60 1.50
122 Scott Williams .07 .20
123 John Battle .07 .20
124 Terrell Brandon .10 .30
125 Brad Daugherty .07 .20
126 Craig Ehlo .07 .20
127 Larry Nance .15 .40
128 Mark Price .20 .50
129 Gerald Wilkins .07 .20
130 Hot Rod Williams .07 .20
131 Walter Bond .07 .20
132 Terry Davis .07 .20
133 Derek Harper .15 .40
134 Donald Hodge .07 .20
135 Brian Howard .07 .20
136 Jim Jackson .75 2.00
137 Sean Rooks .07 .20
138 Doug Smith .07 .20
139 LaPhonso Ellis .20 .50
140 Mahmoud Abdul-Rauf .07 .20
141 Marcus Liberty .07 .20
142 Todd Lichti .07 .20
143 Mark Macon .07 .20
144 Dikembe Mutombo .25 .60
145 Robert Pack .07 .20
146 Reggie Williams .07 .20
147 Mark Aguirre .08 .25
148 Joe Dumars .25 .60
149 Gerald Glass .07 .20
150 Bill Laimbeer .15 .40
151 Terry Mills .07 .20
152 Olden Polynice .07 .20
153 Dennis Rodman .40 1.00
154 Isiah Thomas .30 .75
155 Victor Alexander .07 .20
156 Chris Gatling .07 .20
157 Tim Hardaway .15 .40
158 Tyrone Hill .07 .20
159 Sarunas Marciulionis .10 .30
160 Chris Mullin .25 .60
161 Billy Owens .07 .20
162 Latrell Sprewell .40 1.00
163 Scott Brooks .07 .20
164 Matt Bullard .07 .20
165 Sleepy Floyd .07 .20
166 Robert Horry .40 1.00
167 Vernon Maxwell .07 .20
168 Hakeem Olajuwon .40 1.00
169 Kenny Smith .08 .25
170 Otis Thorpe .08 .25
171 Dale Davis .07 .20
172 Vern Fleming .07 .20
173 Reggie Miller .30 .75
174 Sam Mitchell .07 .20
175 Pooh Richardson .07 .20
176 Detlef Schrempf .08 .25
177 Malik Sealy .10 .30
178 Rik Smits .08 .25
179 Gary Grant .07 .20
180 Ron Harper .30 .75
181 Mark Jackson .30 .75
182 Danny Manning .08 .25
183 Ken Norman .07 .20
184 Stanley Roberts .07 .20
185 Loy Vaught .07 .20
186 John Williams .07 .20
187 Elden Campbell .07 .20
188 Doug Christie .10 .30
189 Vlade Divac .20 .50
190 A.C. Green .20 .50
191 Anthony Peeler .07 .20
192 Byron Scott .20 .50
193 Sedale Threatt .07 .20
194 James Worthy .30 .75
195 Bimbo Coles .07 .20
196 Kevin Edwards .07 .20
197 Grant Long .07 .20
198 Harold Miner .07 .20
199 Glen Rice .30 .75
200 John Salley .08 .25
201 Rony Seikaly .07 .20
202 Brian Shaw .07 .20
203 Frank Brickowski .07 .20
204 Todd Day .07 .20
205 Blue Edwards .07 .20
206 Eric Murdock .07 .20
207 Christian Laettner .30 .75
208 Luc Longley .08 .25
209 Chuck Person .07 .20
210 Doug West .07 .20
211 Kenny Anderson .08 .25
212 Derrick Coleman .08 .25
213 Chris Morris .07 .20
214 Rumeal Robinson .07 .20
215 Patrick Ewing .40 1.00
216 Charles Oakley .08 .25
217 Doc Rivers .15 .40
218 John Starks .08 .25
219 Nick Anderson .08 .25
220 Shaquille O'Neal 5.00 12.00
221 Scott Skiles .25 .60
222 Manute Bol .07 .20
223 Hersey Hawkins .08 .25
224 Jeff Hornacek .25 .60
225 Danny Ainge .15 .40
226 Charles Barkley .40 1.00
227 Richard Dumas .07 .20
228 Kevin Johnson .15 .40
229 Dan Majerle .20 .50
230 Clyde Drexler .40 1.00
231 Terry Porter .07 .20
232 Clifford Robinson .10 .30
233 Buck Williams .08 .25
234 Mitch Richmond .25 .60
235 Lionel Simmons .07 .20
236 Spud Webb .15 .40
237 Walt Williams .07 .20
238 Antoine Carr .07 .20
239 Vinny Del Negro .07 .20
240 Sean Elliott .15 .40
241 David Robinson .40 1.00
242 Eddie Johnson .07 .20
243 Shawn Kemp .30 .75
244 Derrick McKey .07 .20
245 Ricky Pierce .07 .20
246 Mark Eaton .07 .20
247 Jeff Malone .07 .20
248 Karl Malone .40 1.00
249 John Stockton .40 1.00
250 Michael Adams .07 .20
251 Rex Chapman .07 .20
252 Pervis Ellison .07 .20
253 Tom Gugliotta .40 1.00
254 Michael Jordan .40 1.00
Checklist 1-128
255 Michael Jordan .40 1.00
Checklist 129-255

1992-93 Upper Deck International French Award Winner Holograms

The 1992-93 Upper Deck International French Award Winner Hologram standard-size set features nine holograms depicting league leaders in various statistical categories and honoring award winners such as top Sixth Man, Rookie of the Year, Defensive Player of the Year, and Most Valuable Player. The borderless fronts feature holographic cut-out images of the player against a game-action photo of the player. The player's name and award are displayed at the bottom. The backs carry vertical, color player photos. A light blue plaque-style panel contains information about the player and the award won in English and the corresponding foreign language. The cards are numbered on the back with a "EB" prefix.

COMPLETE SET (9) 6.00 15.00
1 Michael Jordan 3.00 8.00
Scoring
2 John Stockton 1.25 3.00
Steals
3 Dennis Rodman 1.25 3.00
Rebounds
4 Detlef Schrempf .20 .50
Sixth Man
5 Larry Johnson .40 1.00
Rookie of the Year
6 David Robinson .75 2.00
Blocked Shots
7 David Robinson .75 2.00
Def. Player of Year
8 John Stockton 1.25 3.00
Assists
9 Michael Jordan 3.00 8.00
Most Valuable Player

1992-93 Upper Deck International Italian

The 1992-93 Upper Deck International Italian basketball set consists of 255 standard-size cards. The fronts feature color action player photos with white borders. The team name is gold-foil stamped across the top of the picture. The border design at the bottom carries the player's name and position, and consists of a team-colored stripe that shades from one team color to the other with diagonal stripes within the larger stripe. The entire design is edged in gold foil. The right end is off-set slightly by the Upper Deck logo. The backs show an action player photo in a vertical layout on the left. The right side is horizontal and displays statistics printed on a ghosted NBA logo. The player's profile is printed in English and Italian. Within the set are the following subsets: NBA All-Stars (1-25), "In Your Face" 1993 Slam Dunk Competition (26-34), All-Division Team (35-54), Rookie Standouts (55-74), Foreign Exchange (75-85), and Fanimation (86-90). This product has been made available the U.S. market through closeouts.

COMPLETE SET (255) 15.00 40.00
*ITALIAN: SAME VALUE AS FRENCH

1992-93 Upper Deck International Italian Award Winner Holograms

The 1992-93 Upper Deck International Italian Award Winner Hologram standard-size set features nine holograms depicting league leaders in various statistical categories and honoring award winners such as top Sixth Man, Rookie of the Year, Defensive Player of the Year, and Most Valuable Player. The borderless fronts feature holographic cut-out images of the player against a game-action photo of the player. The player's name and award are displayed at the bottom. The backs carry vertical, color player photos. A light blue plaque-style panel contains information about the player and the award won in English and the corresponding foreign language. The cards are numbered on the back with a "EB" prefix.

COMPLETE SET (9) 6.00 15.00
*ITALIAN: SAME VALUE AS FRENCH

1992-93 Upper Deck International Spanish

The 1992-93 Upper Deck International Spanish basketball set consists of 255 standard-size cards. The fronts feature color action player photos with white borders. The team name is gold-foil stamped across the top of the picture. The border design at the bottom carries the player's name and position, and consists of a team-colored stripe that shades from one team color to the other with diagonal stripes within the larger stripe. The entire design is edged in gold foil. The right end is off-set slightly by the Upper Deck logo. The backs show an action player photo in a vertical layout on the left. The right side is horizontal and displays statistics printed on a ghosted NBA logo. The player's profile is printed in English and Spanish. Within the set are the following subsets: NBA All-Stars (1-25), "In Your Face" 1993 Slam Dunk Competition (26-34), All-Division Team (35-54), Rookie Standouts (55-74), Foreign Exchange (75-85), and Fanimation (86-90). This product has been made available the U.S. market through closeouts.

COMPLETE SET (255) 15.00 40.00
*SPANISH: SAME VALUE AS FRENCH

1992-93 Upper Deck International Spanish Award Winner Holograms

The 1992-93 Upper Deck International Spanish Award Winner Hologram standard-size set features nine holograms depicting league leaders in various statistical categories and honoring award winners such as top Sixth Man, Rookie of the Year, Defensive Player of the Year, and Most Valuable Player. The borderless fronts feature holographic cut-out images of the player against a game-action photo of the player. The player's name and award are displayed at the bottom. The backs carry vertical, color player photos. A light blue plaque-style panel contains information about the player and the award won in English and the corresponding foreign language. The cards are numbered on the back with a "EB" prefix.

COMPLETE SET (9) 6.00 15.00
*SPANISH: SAME VALUE AS FRENCH

1993-94 Upper Deck International French

This 195-card set is similar in design to the 1993-94 American issue. The cards were distributed in France, Germany, Italy and Spain. Cards were issued in 10-card packs (30 packs per box). Cards 166-175 are Mr. June subset cards. 176-180 are Signature Moves subset cards. 181-192 are Flight Team subset cards. 193-195 are Checklists. Its believed that all of the subset cards are tougher to pull from packs than the regular issue cards. This product was made available to the U.S. market through closeouts.

COMPLETE SET (194) 12.00 30.00
1 Stacey Augmon .05 .15
2 Chris Mills .08 .25
3 Joe Dumars .30 .75
4 Grant Long .05 .15
5 Robert Horry .20 .50
6 Rod Strickland .08 .25
7 Frank Brickowski .05 .15
8 Ricky Pierce .05 .15
9 Dan Majerle .20 .50
10 Dell Curry .05 .15
11 Derek Harper .08 .25
12 Anthony Avent .05 .15
13 Vern Fleming .05 .15
14 Dee Brown .05 .15
15 Kevin Johnson .20 .50
16 Clifford Robinson .08 .25
17 Doc Rivers .15 .40
18 Doug West .05 .15
19 Michael Adams .05 .15
20 Sherman Douglas .05 .15
21 Harold Miner .05 .15
22 John Williams .05 .15
23 Michael Jordan 2.00 5.00
24 Jim Jackson .20 .50
25 Glen Rice .20 .50
26 Jeff Hornacek .25 .60
27 Derrick Coleman .08 .25
28 Sam Perkins .20 .50
29 Willie Anderson .05 .15
30 Rumeal Robinson .05 .15
31 Blue Edwards .05 .15
32 Sarunas Marciulionis .15 .40
33 Clyde Drexler .50 1.25
34 Shawn Bradley .20 .50
35 Ron Harper .20 .50
36 Chris Morris .05 .15
37 Brad Daugherty .05 .15
38 Duane Ferrell .05 .15
39 Chuck Person .05 .15
40 Todd Day .05 .15
41 Sedale Threatt .05 .15
42 Xavier McDaniel .05 .15
43 Kevin Willis .05 .15
44 Chris Mullin .30 .75
45 Terrell Brandon .08 .25
46 Kenny Smith .15 .40
47 Malik Sealy .08 .25
48 John Starks .08 .25
49 Dino Radja .05 .15
50 David Robinson .60 1.50
51 John Salley .08 .25
52 Danny Ainge .25 .60
53 Sam Cassell .40 1.00
54 Latrell Sprewell .25 .60
55 Dikembe Mutombo .20 .50
56 Doug Edwards .05 .15
57 A.C. Green .20 .50
58 Otis Thorpe .05 .15
59 Antoine Carr .05 .15
60 Tim Legler .05 .15
61 Don MacLean .05 .15
62 Horace Grant .15 .40
63 John Stockton .60 1.50
64 Muggsy Bogues .25 .60
65 Rex Chapman .20 .50
66 Stanley Roberts .05 .15
67 Walt Williams .05 .15
68 Dominique Wilkins .30 .75
69 Brent Price .05 .15
70 Lloyd Daniels .05 .15
71 Mark Price .20 .50
72 Sean Elliott .20 .50
73 Scottie Pippen .60 1.50
74 Rodney Rogers .08 .25
75 Charles Barkley .60 1.50
76 Kevin Gamble .05 .15
77 Lionel Simmons .05 .15
78 Dennis Rodman .40 1.00
79 Jeff Malone .05 .15
80 Larry Johnson .25 .60
81 Armon Gilliam .05 .15
82 Chris Dudley .05 .15
83 Bryant Stith .05 .15
84 Mark Jackson .30 .75
85 Paul Graham .05 .15
86 Calbert Cheaney .08 .25
87 Clarence Weatherspoon .05 .15
88 Isiah Thomas .40 1.00
89 Scott Brooks .05 .15
90 Mitch Richmond .30 .75
91 Kendall Gill .15 .40
92 Robert Parish .20 .50
93 Karl Malone .50 1.25
94 Rik Smits .05 .15
95 Rex Walters .05 .15
96 Oliver Miller .05 .15
97 Hersey Hawkins .15 .40
98 Vinny Del Negro .05 .15
99 Spud Webb .20 .50
100 Chris Webber 1.25 3.00
101 Moses Malone .25 .60
102 Hubert Davis .05 .15
103 Gary Payton .40 1.00
104 Mahmoud Abdul-Rauf .05 .15
105 Larry Nance .15 .40
106 Bobby Hurley .15 .40
107 David Benoit .05 .15
108 Danny Manning .08 .25
109 Pervis Ellison .05 .15
110 Anthony Peeler .05 .15
111 Tim Hardaway .20 .50
112 Detlef Schrempf .15 .40
113 Hakeem Olajuwon .40 1.00
114 Elden Campbell .05 .15
115 Charles Smith .05 .15
116 B.J. Armstrong .15 .40
117 Dennis Scott .05 .15
118 LaPhonso Ellis .05 .15
119 Isaiah Rider .08 .25
120 Tim Perry .05 .15
121 Lindsey Hunter .08 .25
122 Anthony Bowie .05 .15
123 Micheal Williams .05 .15
124 Gerald Wilkins .05 .15
125 Tom Chambers .15 .40
126 Vincent Askew .05 .15
127 Vernon Maxwell .05 .15
128 Nick Van Exel .40 1.00
129 Buck Williams .15 .40
130 Alonzo Mourning .30 .75
131 Loy Vaught .05 .15
132 Shaquille O'Neal 1.00 2.50
133 Derrick McKey .05 .15
134 Kenny Anderson .08 .25
135 Bill Cartwright .15 .40
136 Nick Anderson .05 .15
137 Billy Owens .05 .15
138 Anfernee Hardaway .75 2.00
139 Terry Mills .05 .15
140 John Paxson .15 .40
141 Charles Oakley .05 .15
142 Steve Smith .20 .50
143 Johnny Dawkins .05 .15
144 Thurl Bailey .05 .15
145 Jamal Mashburn .75 2.00
146 Terry Porter .08 .25
147 Duane Causwell .05 .15
148 Reggie Miller .40 1.00
149 Shawn Kemp .20 .50
150 James Worthy .30 .75
151 Scott Skiles .20 .50
152 Donald Hodge .05 .15
153 Christian Laettner .20 .50
154 Vin Baker .15 .40
155 Doug Christie .05 .15
156 Tyrone Corbin .05 .15
157 Toni Kukoc .40 1.00
158 Ken Norman .05 .15
159 Randy White .05 .15
160 Rony Seikaly .05 .15
161 Tom Gugliotta .08 .25
162 Vlade Divac .20 .50
163 Eric Murdock .05 .15
164 Pooh Richardson .05 .15
165 Patrick Ewing .40 1.00
166 Michael Jordan 2.00 5.00
A Steal
167 Michael Jordan 2.00 5.00
High Five
168 Michael Jordan 2.00 5.00
Finals MVP
169 Michael Jordan 2.00 5.00
35 Points
170 Michael Jordan 2.00 5.00
Three-Point King
171 Michael Jordan 2.00 5.00
Back-To-Back
172 Michael Jordan 2.00 5.00
55-Point Game
173 Michael Jordan 2.00 5.00
Scoring Avg.
174 Michael Jordan 2.00 5.00
Third Straight MVP
175 Michael Jordan 2.00 5.00
Mr. June Checklist
176 Michael Jordan SM 2.00 5.00
177 Shawn Kemp SM .20 .50
178 Karl Malone SM .50 1.25
179 Clyde Drexler SM .40 1.00
180 Tim Hardaway SM .20 .50
181 Charles Barkley FT .40 1.00
182 Cedric Ceballos FT .05 .15
183 Derrick Coleman FT .05 .15
184 Clyde Drexler FT .40 1.00
185 Larry Johnson FT .15 .40
186 Shawn Kemp FT .20 .50
187 Harold Miner FT .05 .15
188 Alonzo Mourning FT .30 .75
189 Shaquille O'Neal FT .50 1.25
190 Scottie Pippen FT .40 1.00
192 Dominique Wilkins FT .30 .75
193 Kenny Anderson .05 .15
Xavier McDaniel CL
194 Doug West .15 .40
James Worthy CL
195 Reggie Miller .40 1.00
Joe Dumars CL

1993-94 Upper Deck International German

This 195-card set is similar in design to the 1993-94 American issue. The cards were distributed in France, Germany, Italy and Spain. Cards were issued in 10-card packs (30 packs per box). Cards 166-175 are Mr. June subset cards. 176-180 are Signature Moves subset cards. 181-192 are Flight Team subset cards. 193-195 are Checklists. Its believed that all of the subset cards are tougher to pull from packs than the regular issue cards. This product was made available to the U.S. market through closeouts.

COMPLETE SET (195) 12.00 30.00
*GERMAN: SAME VALUE AS FRENCH

1993-94 Upper Deck International German Triple Double

Randomly inserted at a rate of one in five packs, these ten cards parallel the 1993-94 American Triple Double inserts.

COMPLETE SET (10) 5.00 12.00
*GERMAN: SAME VALUE AS FRENCH

1993-94 Upper Deck International Italian

This 195-card set is similar in design to the 1993-94 American issue. The cards were distributed in France, Germany, Italy and Spain. Cards were issued in 10-card packs (30 packs per box). Cards 166-175 are Mr. June subset cards. 176-180 are Signature Moves subset cards. 181-192 are Flight Team subset cards. 193-195 are Checklists. Its believed that all of the subset cards are tougher to pull from packs than the regular issue cards. This product was made available to the U.S. market through closeouts.

COMPLETE SET (195) 12.00 30.00
*ITALIAN: SAME VALUE AS FRENCH

1993-94 Upper Deck International Italian Triple Double

Randomly inserted at a rate of one in five packs, these ten cards parallel the 1993-94 American Triple Double inserts.

COMPLETE SET (10) 5.00 12.00
*ITALIAN: SAME VALUE AS FRENCH

1993-94 Upper Deck International Spanish

This 195-card set is similar in design to the 1993-94 American issue. The cards were distributed in France, Germany, Italy and Spain. Cards were issued in 10-card packs (30 packs per box). Cards 166-175 are Mr. June subset cards. 176-180 are Signature Moves subset cards. 181-192 are Flight Team subset cards. 193-195 are Checklists. Its believed that all of the subset cards are tougher to pull from packs than the regular issue cards. This product was made available to the U.S. market through closeouts.

COMPLETE SET (195) 12.00 30.00
*SPANISH: SAME VALUE AS FRENCH

1993-94 Upper Deck International Spanish Triple Double

Randomly inserted at a rate of one in five packs, these ten cards parallel the 1993-94 American Triple Double inserts.

COMPLETE SET (10) 5.00 12.00
*SPANISH: SAME VALUE AS FRENCH

1993-94 Upper Deck International French Triple Double

Randomly inserted at a rate of one in five packs, these nine cards parallel the 1993-94 American Triple Double inserts, with the only exception being the #TD10 Detlef Schrempf, who exists in the Italian and Spanish parallel, but not the French.

COMPLETE SET (9) 5.00 12.00
TD1 Charles Barkley 1.00 2.50
TD2 Michael Jordan 3.00 8.00
TD3 Scottie Pippen 1.25 3.00
TD4 Micheal Williams .20 .50
TD5 Mark Jackson .40 1.00
TD6 Kenny Anderson .20 .50
TD7 Larry Johnson .30 .75
TD8 Dikembe Mutombo .30 .75
TD9 Rumeal Robinson .20 .50

1996-97 Upper Deck International Japanese Jordan A Cut Above Gold Signature

CC9 Michael Jordan

1996-97 Upper Deck International Japanese Coast to Coast

COMPLETE SET (3)
CC1 Shawn Kemp
CC2 Michael Jordan 40.00 100.00
CC3 Anfernee Hardaway

1996-97 Upper Deck International Japanese Jordan Greater Heights

COMPLETE SET (10)
COMMON JORDAN (1-10)

1996-97 Upper Deck Italian Stickers

This set features a design similar to the American 1996-97 Collector's Choice set. Each sticker measures 2" by 4". In addition to player stickers, each team's logo is featured individually or on a dual-numbered sticker. A sticker album was also available and priced at the end of the set.

COMPLETE SET (186) 15.00 40.00
1 NBA Logo .10 .25
2 Western Conference Logo .10 .25
3 Eastern Conference Logo .10 .25
4 Golden State Warriors Logo .10 .25
5 B.J. Armstrong .10 .25
6 Joe Smith .12 .30
7 Donyell Marshall .10 .25
8 Rony Seikaly .10 .25
9 Chris Mullin .15 .40
10 Los Angeles Clippers Logo .10 .25
11 Rodney Rogers .10 .25
12 Brent Barry .12 .30
13 Lamond Murray .10 .25
14 Pooh Richardson .10 .25
15 Loy Vaught .10 .25
16 Los Angeles Lakers Logo .10 .25
17 Cedric Ceballos .10 .25
18 George Lynch .10 .25
19 Eddie Jones .15 .40
20 Anthony Peeler .10 .25
21 Nick Van Exel .15 .40
22 Phoenix Suns Logo .10 .25
23 Charles Barkley .25 .60
24 Wayman Tisdale .10 .25
25 Wesley Person .10 .25
26 A.C. Green .12 .30
27 Danny Manning .12 .30
28 Portland Trail Blazers Logo .10 .25
29 Harvey Grant .10 .25
30 Aaron McKie .10 .25
31 Gary Trent .10 .25
32 Buck Williams .10 .25
33 Clifford Robinson .10 .25
34 Sacramento Kings Logo .10 .25
35 Billy Owens .10 .25
36 Brian Grant .12 .30
37 Tyus Edney .10 .25
38 Olden Polynice .10 .25
39 Mitch Richmond .15 .40
40 Seattle Supersonics Logo .10 .25
41 Nate McMillan .10 .25
42 Vincent Askew .10 .25
43 Hersey Hawkins .10 .25
44 Detlef Schrempf .15 .40
45 Shawn Kemp .15 .40
46 Dallas Mavericks Logo .10 .25
47 Tony Dumas .10 .25
48 Jim Jackson .10 .25
49 Loren Meyer .10 .25
50 Jamal Mashburn .12 .30
51 Jason Kidd .25 .60
52 Denver Nuggets Logo .10 .25
53 Mahmoud Abdul-Rauf .10 .25
54 Antonio McDyess .15 .40
55 Tom Hammonds .10 .25
56 Dale Ellis .10 .25
57 LaPhonso Ellis .10 .25
58 Houston Rockets Logo .10 .25
59 Hakeem Olajuwon .20 .50
60 Mario Elie .10 .25
61 Robert Horry .12 .30
62 Chucky Brown .10 .25
63 Clyde Drexler .20 .50
64 Minnesota Timberwolves Logo .10 .25
65 Kevin Garnett .40 1.00
66 Terry Porter .10 .25
67 Sam Mitchell .10 .25
68 Tom Gugliotta .10 .25
69 Isaiah Rider .12 .30
70 San Antonio Spurs Logo .10 .25
71 Avery Johnson .12 .30
72 Vinny Del Negro .10 .25
73 Sean Elliott .15 .40
74 Will Perdue .10 .25
75 David Robinson .25 .60
76 Utah Jazz Logo .10 .25
77 Jeff Hornacek .12 .30
78 Chris Morris .10 .25
79 Antoine Carr .10 .25
80 Karl Malone .20 .50
81 John Stockton .20 .50
82 Vancouver Grizzlies Logo .10 .25
83 Shareef Abdur-Rahim .25 .60
84 Blue Edwards .10 .25
85 Bryant Reeves .10 .25
86 Lawrence Moten .10 .25
87 Greg Anthony .10 .25
88 Michael Jordan 1.25 3.00
Bulls Victory Tour
89 Michael Jordan 1.25 3.00
Bulls Victory Tour
90 Michael Jordan 1.25 3.00
Bulls Victory Tour
91 Michael Jordan 1.25 3.00
Bulls Victory Tour
92 Scottie Pippen .25 .60
Bulls Victory Tour
93 Luc Longley .12 .30
Bulls Victory Tour
94 Luc Longley .12 .30
Bulls Victory Tour
95 Toni Kukoc .15 .40
Bulls Victory Tour
96 Toni Kukoc .15 .40
Bulls Victory Tour
97 Atlanta Hawks Logo .10 .25
98 Grant Long .10 .25
99 Mookie Blaylock .10 .25
100 Christian Laettner .12 .30
101 Ken Norman .10 .25
102 Stacey Augmon .12 .30
103 Charlotte Hornets Logo .10 .25
104 Dell Curry .10 .25
105 Scott Burrell .10 .25
106 Matt Geiger .10 .25
107 Muggsy Bogues .12 .30
108 Glen Rice .15 .40
109 Chicago Bulls Logo .10 .25
110 Steve Kerr .12 .30
111 Dennis Rodman .30 .75
112 Scottie Pippen .25 .60
113 Luc Longley .12 .30
114 Michael Jordan 1.25 3.00
115 Cleveland Cavaliers Logo .10 .25
116 Terrell Brandon .10 .25
117 Bobby Phills .10 .25
118 Tyrone Hill .10 .25
119 Bob Sura .10 .25
120 Danny Ferry .10 .25
121 Detroit Pistons Logo .10 .25
122 Joe Dumars .15 .40
123 Theo Ratliff .10 .25
124 Lindsey Hunter .10 .25
125 Terry Mills .10 .25
126 Grant Hill .25 .60
127 Indiana Pacers Logo .10 .25
128 Derrick McKey .10 .25
129 Eddie Johnson .10 .25
130 Travis Best .10 .25
131 Mark Jackson .12 .30
132 Rik Smits .12 .30
133 Milwaukee Bucks Logo .10 .25
134 Vin Baker .12 .30
135 Shawn Respert .10 .25
136 Sherman Douglas .10 .25
137 Johnny Newman .10 .25
138 Glenn Robinson .12 .30
139 Toronto Raptors Logo .10 .25
140 Sharone Wright .10 .25
141 Zan Tabak .10 .25
142 Doug Christie .10 .25
143 Damon Stoudamire .12 .30
144 Oliver Miller .10 .25
145 Boston Celtics Logo .10 .25
146 Dana Barros .10 .25
147 Rick Fox .10 .25
148 David Wesley .10 .25
149 Eric Williams .10 .25
150 Dee Brown .10 .25
151 Miami Heat Logo .10 .25
152 Rex Chapman .10 .25
153 Kurt Thomas .10 .25
154 Keith Askins .10 .25
155 Walt Williams .10 .25
156 Alonzo Mourning .20 .50
157 New Jersey Nets Logo .10 .25
158 Kendall Gill .10 .25
159 Jayson Williams .10 .25
160 Kevin Edwards .10 .25
161 Shawn Bradley .10 .25
162 Ed O'Bannon .10 .25
163 New York Knicks Logo .10 .25
164 Gary Grant .10 .25
165 J.R. Reid .10 .25
166 Charles Oakley .12 .30
167 John Starks .12 .30
168 Patrick Ewing .20 .50
169 Orlando Magic Logo .10 .25
170 Nick Anderson .10 .25
171 Brian Shaw .10 .25
172 Anfernee Hardaway .25 .60
173 Dennis Scott .10 .25
174 Shaquille O'Neal .40 1.00
175 Philadelphia 76ers Logo .10 .25
176 Allen Iverson .75 2.00
177 Rex Walters .10 .25
178 Clarence Weatherspoon .10 .25
179 Jerry Stackhouse .20 .50
180 Derrick Coleman .12 .30
181 Washington Bullets Logo .10 .25
182 Calbert Cheaney .10 .25
183 Chris Webber .20 .50
184 Tim Legler .10 .25
185 Gheorghe Muresan .10 .25
186 Rasheed Wallace .20 .50
NNO Sticker Album 1.50 4.00

1996-97 Upper Deck Italian Stickers Eurostar

This 10-card sticker set was inserted into packs of 1996-97 Upper Deck Italian Stickers. This set focuses on ten European players who made it to the NBA. Card fronts are similar to the basic set except the borders are silver and in the top left of the card contains the word "Eurostar". Card backs are numbered with a "ES" prefix.

COMPLETE SET (10) 1.50 4.00
ES1 Sasha Danilovic .20 .50
ES2 Vlade Divac .30 .75
ES3 Toni Kukoc .30 .75
ES4 Gheorghe Muresan .20 .50
ES5 Dino Radja .20 .50
ES6 Arvydas Sabonis .25 .60
ES7 Detlef Schrempf .30 .75
ES8 Rik Smits .25 .60
ES9 Zan Tabak .20 .50
ES10 George Zidek .20 .50

1996 Upper Deck Jordan Metal

COMPLETE SET (6) 20.00 50.00
COMMON CARD (1-6) 5.00 12.00
*ORANGE: .5X TO 1.25X BASE HI

1994 Upper Deck Jordan Rare Air

The Michael Jordan Rare Air Tribute set consists of 90 standard-size cards, combining Walter Iooss, Jr. photography with other classic shots from Jordan's career. The set was sold exclusively in a factory box with a suggested retail price of $19.99. Each set included two 3 3/8" by 7 7/8" cards featuring black-and-white action shots highlighted by a red tint stripe. In addition, each set had a serial number out of 30,000. One gold foil-stamped set was included in every 12-set case for the hobby only. The fronts feature full- bleed color photos, capturing Jordan both on and off the court. Set subtitles are silver foil-stamped on the fronts. The "Rare Air" cards (1-50) have pictures taken directly from the best-selling book Rare Air, by Michael Jordan and Walter Iooss Jr. The "Out Takes" cards (51-60) feature pictures from Iooss' personal collection that were never released. Finally, the "MJ, Decade of Dominanace" cards (61- 90) highlight Jordan's incredible accomplishments during his NBA career. The backs present personal commentary by Iooss and/or Jordan, or highlights from Jordan's career.

COMPLETE SET (90) 15.00 40.00
1 Michael Jordan .40 1.00
(Close-up with white robe)
2 Michael Jordan .40 1.00
(Close-up profile)
3 Michael Jordan .20 .50
(Michael's shooting form)
4 Michael Jordan .08 .25
(Close-up of his left hand)
5 Michael Jordan .20 .50
(Entering onto court in Orlando)
6 Michael Jordan .20 .50
(Lifting weights)
7 Michael Jordan .20 .50
(Driving car to Chicago Stadium)
8 Michael Jordan .20 .50
(Sitting in visitor's locker room in Miami Arena)
9 Michael Jordan .20 .50
(Relaxing on trainer's table)

10 Michael Jordan .20 .50
(Listening to pre-game instructions)
11 Michael Jordan .20 .50
(Readying himself for action on the floor)
12 Michael Jordan .20 .50
(Greeted by teammates during pre-game introductions)
13 Michael Jordan .08 .25
(Pre-game huddle with Chicago teammates)
14 Michael Jordan .20 .50
(Performing final pre-game rituals)
15 Michael Jordan .08 .25
(Close-up look at his feet)
16 Michael Jordan .40 1.00
(Stealing a pass intended for A.C. Green)
17 Michael Jordan .20 .50
(Guarding James Worthy)
18 Michael Jordan .40 1.00
(Greeted in mid-air by Shaquille O'Neal)
19 Michael Jordan .20 .50
(Slaming another one home during a game in Chicago Stadium)
20 Michael Jordan .20 .50
(Pippen with hand on Michael's head during playoff game)
21 Michael Jordan .08 .25
(Facing reporters in locker room after game)
22 Michael Jordan .40 1.00
(Heading to locker room after game at Chicago Stadium)
23 Michael Jordan .40 1.00
(Listening to questions from reporters)
24 Michael Jordan .20 .50
(Sleeping on the bus)
25 Michael Jordan .20 .50
(Boarding plane after bus ride to airport)
26 Michael Jordan .20 .50
(Settling into seat on team's private airplane)
27 Michael Jordan .08 .25
(Treating sprained ankle in hotel room)
28 Michael Jordan .20 .50
(Getting rest and relaxation on road trip)
29 Michael Jordan .20 .50
(Peering out of car window)
30 Michael Jordan .20 .50
(Enjoying game of cards)
31 Michael Jordan .20 .50
(Shooting pool)
32 Michael Jordan .20 .50
(Caring for golf clubs)
33 Michael Jordan .40 1.00
(Preparing to drive shot onto green)
34 Michael Jordan .40 1.00
(Sizing up a putt)
35 Michael Jordan .08 .25
(Calling home from golf course)
36 Michael Jordan .20 .50
(Sitting by window taking time out)
37 Michael Jordan .40 1.00
(Close-up view, chin resting in hand)
38 Michael Jordan .40 1.00
(Wearing uniform, enjoying 1993 baseball All-Star Game)
39 Michael Jordan .20 .50
(Shaving head)
40 Michael Jordan .20 .50
(Wearing warm-ups, standing outside locker room)
41 Michael Jordan .20 .50
(Passing to Horace Grant in game against Atlanta)
42 Michael Jordan .20 .50
(Preparing to shoot free throw in playoff game against Atlanta)
43 Michael Jordan .20 .50
(Driving lane between New York's John Starks and Doc Rivers)
44 Michael Jordan .20 .50
(Standing next to Charles Barkley during game)
45 Michael Jordan .20 .50
(Celebrating third NBA Championship)
46 Michael Jordan .40 1.00
(Celebrating third NBA Championship, arms outstretched)
47 Michael Jordan .20 .50
(Celebrating with team in locker
48 Michael Jordan .40 1.00
(Holding up three fingers, representing three NBA titles)
49 Michael Jordan .08 .25
(Michael with a special friend)
50 Michael Jordan .40 1.00
(Close-up shot from back)
51 Michael Jordan .08 .25
(Head bowed, hand on brow)
52 Michael Jordan .08 .25
(Palming basketball)
53 Michael Jordan .20 .50
(Lifting weights with curl bar)
54 Michael Jordan .20 .50
(Sitting in weight training room)
55 Michael Jordan .20 .50
(Resting on sofa beside telephone)
56 Michael Jordan .20 .50
(Signing sports cards)
57 Michael Jordan .20 .50
(Boarding team bus)
58 Michael Jordan .20 .50
(In black sports car, outside Chicago Stadium)
59 Michael Jordan .20 .50
(In locker room before game)
60 Michael Jordan .20 .50
(Michael at free throw line, shot from above)
61 Michael Jordan .40 1.00
(Close-up with ball, orange background)
62 Michael Jordan .40 1.00
(Winning NBA Slam Dunk Championship)
63 Michael Jordan .40 1.00
(Cheering on sidelines)
64 Michael Jordan .40 1.00
(Preparing to shoot free throw)
65 Michael Jordan .40 1.00
(Defensive posture)
66 Michael Jordan .20 .50
Efficient Scorer
67 Michael Jordan .20 .50
(In mid-air preparing to dunk)
68 Michael Jordan .20 .50
(Signing autographs for fans)
69 Michael Jordan .20 .50
(A multi-mirror image)
70 Michael Jordan .20 .50
(Playing wheel chair basketball with child)
71 Michael Jordan .20 .50
(Watching a game on TV)
72 Michael Jordan .40 1.00
(Scoring over opponent)
73 Michael Jordan .20 .50
(Jordan defended by
Mark West and Charles Barkley)
74 Michael Jordan .20 .50
(Dunking over Patrick Ewing)
75 Michael Jordan .40 1.00
(Driving baseline)
76 Michael Jordan .40 1.00
(Fighting for rebound position)
77 Michael Jordan .20 .50
(Shooting over Scott Skiles)
78 Michael Jordan .40 1.00
(Defending against Orlando Magic player)
79 Michael Jordan .20 .50
(Driving past Vlade Divac)
80 Michael Jordan .20 .50
(Shooting jump shot over Orlando Magic players)
81 Michael Jordan .20 .50
(Shooting lay up around Patrick Ewing)
82 Michael Jordan .20 .50
(Shooting jump shot over outstretched arms)
83 Michael Jordan .40 1.00
(Driving down court)
84 Michael Jordan .20 .50
(In mid-air during game against Nets)
85 Michael Jordan .40 1.00
(Dribbling past New York defender)
86 Michael Jordan .20 .50
(Positioning for rebound against Phoenix)
87 Michael Jordan .20 .50
(Shooting jump shot over Dan Majerle)
88 Michael Jordan .20 .50
(Fingerroll lay up against Phoenix)
89 Michael Jordan .40 1.00
(Shooting jump shot over Gerald Wilkins)
90 Michael Jordan .20 .50
(In warm-ups shot from above)
NNO Michael Jordan .40 1.00
Passing Ball
NNO Michael Jordan Promo 5.00 12.00
NNO Jordan Under Backboard .40 1.00

2013 Upper Deck Kansas

COMPLETE SET 20.00 50.00
1 James Naismith .50 1.25
2 Phog Allen .50 1.25
3 W.O. Hamilton .50 1.25
4 Dutch Lonborg .50 1.25
5 Paul Endacott .50 1.25
6 Adolph Rupp .50 1.25
7 Tusten Ackerman .50 1.25
8 Skinny Johnson .50 1.25
9 Howard Engleman .30 .75
10 Ray Evans .50 1.25
11 Max Falkenstien .50 1.25
12 Clyde Lovellette .50 1.25
13 Bob Kenney .50 1.25
14 Bill Lienhard .50 1.25
15 Dean Smith .60 1.50
16 Dean Kelley .50 1.25
17 B.H. Born .50 1.25
18 Wilt Chamberlain 1.00 2.50
19 Wilt Chamberlain 1.00 2.50
20 Ron Loneski .40 1.00
21 Jerry Gardner .40 1.00
22 Butch Ellison .50 1.25
23 Nolen Ellison .30 .75
24 Walt Wesley .30 .75
25 Ted Owens .50 1.25
26 Jo Jo White .40 1.00
27 Dave Robisch .50 1.25
28 Bud Stallworth .50 1.25
29 Roger Brown .30 .75
30 Roger Morningstar .50 1.25
31 John Douglas .30 .75
32 Darnell Valentine .40 1.00
33 Paul Mokeski .30 .75
34 Dave Magley .50 1.25
35 Larry Brown .50 1.25
36 Danny Manning .50 1.25
37 Greg Dreiling .30 .75
38 Calvin Thompson .50 1.25
39 Scooter Barry .50 1.25
40 Kevin Pritchard .30 .75
41 Mark Randall .40 1.00
42 Archie Marshall .40 1.00
43 Jeff Gueldner .50 1.25
44 Chris Piper .40 1.00
45 Lincoln Minor .30 .75
46 Roy Williams .50 1.25
47 Terry Brown .40 1.00
48 Alonzo Jamison .40 1.00
49 Adonis Jordan .50 1.25
50 Mike Maddox .40 1.00
51 Steve Woodberry .50 1.25
52 Rex Walters .30 .75
53 Greg Ostertag .30 .75
54 Eric Pauley .50 1.25
55 Scot Pollard .30 .75
56 Scot Pollard .30 .75
57 Jerod Haase .50 1.25
58 Billy Thomas .40 1.00
59 Raef LaFrentz .30 .75
60 Paul Pierce .50 1.25
61 Ryan Robertson .30 .75
62 Eric Chenowith .30 .75
63 Kenny Gregory .50 1.25
64 Jeff Boschee .30 .75
65 Nick Bradford .40 1.00
66 Drew Gooden .40 1.00
67 Nick Collison .40 1.00
68 Kirk Hinrich .50 1.25
69 Wayne Simien .50 1.25
70 Keith Langford .40 1.00
71 Mario Chalmers .40 1.00
72 Sherron Collins .30 .75
73 Brady Morningstar .50 1.25
74 Tyrel Reed .40 1.00
75 Tyshawn Taylor .40 1.00
76 Bill Self .50 1.25
77 Rock Chalk Jayhawk MM .40 1.00
78 Rules of Basketball MM .40 1.00
79 1952 NCAA Champions MM .40 1.00
80 Clyde Lovellette MM .50 1.25
81 Phog Allen MM .50 1.25
82 Allen Fieldhouse MM .40 1.00
83 Wilt Chamberlain MM 1.00 2.50
84 1957 NCAA Championship MM .40 1.00
85 Bud Stallworth MM .50 1.25
86 1988 NCAA Champions MM .40 1.00
87 150-95 MM .40 1.00
88 1991 Final Four MM .40 1.00
89 Danny Manning MM .50 1.25
90 Wilt Chamberlain MM 1.00 2.50
91 Perfect 16-0 MM .40 1.00
92 Nick Collison MM .40 1.00
93 2003 Final Four MM .40 1.00
94 50 Conference Titles MM .40 1.00
95 2008 Final Four MM .40 1.00
96 2008 NCAA Champions MM .40 1.00
97 2000 Wins MM .40 1.00
98 69 in a row MM .40 1.00
99 Border Showdown MM .40 1.00
100 Beware The Phog MM .40 1.00

2013 Upper Deck Kansas Gold

*GOLD: 5X TO 12X BASIC
OVERALL INSERT ODDS 3:1
STATED PRINT RUN 50 SER.#'d SETS
6 Adolph Rupp 10.00 25.00
17 B.H. Born 10.00 25.00
36 Danny Manning 12.00 30.00

2013 Upper Deck Kansas Autographs

OVERALL AUTO ODDS 1:24
11 Max Falkenstien 4.00 10.00
12 Clyde Lovellette 6.00 15.00
13 Bob Kenney 6.00 15.00
14 Bill Lienhard 6.00 15.00
17 B.H. Born 4.00 10.00
20 Ron Loneski 4.00 10.00
21 Jerry Gardner 5.00 12.00
22 Butch Ellison 4.00 10.00
23 Nolen Ellison 4.00 10.00
24 Walt Wesley 4.00 10.00
25 Ted Owens 6.00 15.00
26 Jo Jo White 25.00 60.00
27 Dave Robisch 6.00 15.00
28 Bud Stallworth 4.00 10.00
29 Roger Brown 4.00 10.00
30 Roger Morningstar 4.00 10.00
31 John Douglas 8.00 20.00
32 Darnell Valentine 4.00 10.00
33 Paul Mokeski 4.00 10.00
34 Dave Magley 6.00 15.00
35 Larry Brown 60.00 150.00
36 Danny Manning 150.00 250.00
37 Greg Dreiling 4.00 10.00
38 Calvin Thompson 6.00 15.00
39 Richard Barry 12.00 30.00
40 Kevin Pritchard 10.00 25.00
41 Mark Randall 4.00 10.00
42 Archie Marshall 4.00 10.00
43 Jeff Gueldner 6.00 15.00
44 Chris Piper 4.00 10.00
45 Lincoln Minor 4.00 10.00
46 Roy Williams 30.00 80.00
47 Terry Brown 4.00 10.00
48 Alonzo Jamison 4.00 10.00
49 Adonis Jordan 4.00 10.00
50 Mike Maddox 5.00 12.00
51 Steve Woodberry 4.00 10.00
52 Rex Walters 4.00 10.00
53 Greg Ostertag 10.00 25.00
54 Eric Pauley 6.00 15.00
55 Scot Pollard
56 Scot Pollard 10.00 25.00
57 Jerod Haase 4.00 10.00
58 Billy Thomas 5.00 12.00
59 Raef LaFrentz 10.00 25.00
60 Paul Pierce 25.00 60.00
61 Ryan Robertson 4.00 10.00
62 Eric Chenowith 4.00 10.00
63 Kenny Gregory 6.00 15.00
64 Jeff Boschee 4.00 10.00
65 Nick Bradford 4.00 10.00
66 Drew Gooden 10.00 25.00
67 Nick Collison 10.00 25.00
68 Kirk Hinrich
69 Wayne Simien 8.00 20.00
70 Keith Langford 4.00 10.00
71 Mario Chalmers 15.00 40.00
72 Sherron Collins
73 Brady Morningstar 8.00 20.00
74 Tyrel Reed 4.00 10.00
75 Tyshawn Taylor 5.00 12.00
76 Bill Self 30.00 80.00

2013 Upper Deck Kansas Distinguished Numbers

OVERALL INSERT ODDS 3:1
DN1 Ray Evans .75 2.00
DN2 Clyde Lovellette .75 2.00
DN3 B.H. Born .75 2.00
DN4 Wilt Chamberlain 1.50 4.00
DN5 Jo Jo White .60 1.50
DN6 Dave Robisch .75 2.00
DN7 Bud Stallworth .75 2.00
DN8 Darnell Valentine .60 1.50
DN9 Danny Manning .75 2.00
DN10 Bill Lienhard .75 2.00
DN11 Raef LaFrentz .50 1.25
DN12 Paul Pierce .75 2.00
DN13 Drew Gooden .60 1.50
DN14 Kirk Hinrich .75 2.00
DN15 Nick Collison .60 1.50

2013 Upper Deck Kansas Final 4 Legacy

OVERALL INSERT ODDS 3:1
F41 Phog Allen .75 2.00
F42 Clyde Lovellette .75 2.00
F43 Wilt Chamberlain 1.50 4.00
F44 Larry Brown .75 2.00
F45 Danny Manning .75 2.00
F46 Roy Williams .75 2.00
F47 Drew Gooden .60 1.50
F48 Kirk Hinrich .75 2.00
F49 Nick Collison .60 1.50
F410 Mario Chalmers .60 1.50

2013 Upper Deck Kansas Final 4 Legacy Duos

OVERALL INSERT ODDS 3:1
F4D1 C.Lovellette/B.Born .75 2.00
F4D2 B.Born/D.Kelley .75 2.00
F4D3 L.Brown/D.Manning .75 2.00
F4D4 N.Collison/K.Hinrich .75 2.00
F4D5 M.Chalmers/B.Self .75 2.00

2013 Upper Deck Kansas Icons

STATED ODDS 1:12
BH B.H. Born 5.00 12.00
BL Bill Lienhard 5.00 12.00
BS Bud Stallworth 5.00 12.00
CL Clyde Lovellette 5.00 12.00
DG Drew Gooden 4.00 10.00
DM Danny Manning 5.00 12.00
DR Dave Robisch 5.00 12.00
DV Darnell Valentine 4.00 10.00
JW Jo Jo White 4.00 10.00
KH Kirk Hinrich 5.00 12.00
LB Larry Brown 5.00 12.00
MC Mario Chalmers 4.00 10.00
NC Nick Collison 4.00 10.00
PA Phog Allen 5.00 12.00
PP Paul Pierce 5.00 12.00
RE Ray Evans 5.00 12.00
RL Raef LaFrentz 3.00 8.00
SC Sherron Collins 3.00 8.00
SJ Skinny Johnson 5.00 12.00
WC Wilt Chamberlain 10.00 25.00
WW Walt Wesley 3.00 8.00

2013 Upper Deck Kansas Jayhawk Legacy

OVERALL INSERT ODDS 3:1
JL1 James Naismith .75 2.00
JL2 Phog Allen .75 2.00
JL3 Dutch Lonborg .75 2.00
JL4 Tusten Ackerman .75 2.00
JL5 Skinny Johnson .75 2.00
JL6 Ray Evans .75 2.00
JL7 Bill Lienhard .75 2.00
JL8 Clyde Lovellette .75 2.00
JL9 B.H. Born .75 2.00
JL10 Wilt Chamberlain 1.50 4.00
JL11 Walt Wesley .50 1.25
JL12 Jo Jo White .60 1.50
JL13 Dave Robisch .75 2.00
JL14 Bud Stallworth .75 2.00
JL15 Darnell Valentine .60 1.50
JL16 Larry Brown .75 2.00
JL17 Danny Manning .75 2.00
JL18 Roy Williams .75 2.00
JL19 Greg Ostertag .50 1.25
JL20 Scot Pollard .50 1.25
JL21 Raef LaFrentz .50 1.25
JL22 Paul Pierce .75 2.00
JL23 Drew Gooden .60 1.50
JL24 Nick Collison .60 1.50
JL25 Kirk Hinrich .75 2.00
JL26 Wayne Simien .75 2.00
JL27 Bill Self .75 2.00
JL28 Mario Chalmers .60 1.50
JL29 Sherron Collins .50 1.25
JL30 Tyshawn Taylor .60 1.50

2013 Upper Deck Kansas Jayhawk Legacy Duos

OVERALL INSERT ODDS 3:1
JLD1 P.Allen/J.Naismith .75 2.00
JLD2 J.Naismith/W.Chamberlain 1.50 4.00
JLD3 P.Allen/A.Rupp .75 2.00
JLD4 B.Stallworth/J.White .75 2.00
JLD5 C.Lovellette/D.Manning .75 2.00
JLD6 R.Morningstar/B.Morningstar .75 2.00
JLD7 D.Gooden/N.Collison .60 1.50
JLD8 B.Self/R.Williams .75 2.00
JLD9 M.Chalmers/S.Collins .60 1.50
JLD10 B.Self/T.Taylor .75 2.00

2013 Upper Deck Kansas Jayhawk Legacy Trios

OVERALL INSERT ODDS 3:1
JLT1 Allen/Naismith/Hamilton .75 2.00
JLT2 Lovellette/Chalmers/Manning .75 2.00
JLT3 Williams/Self/Brown .75 2.00
JLT4 Pollard/Pierce/LaFrentz .75 2.00
JLT5 Gooden/Collison/Hinrich .75 2.00

2013 Upper Deck Kansas Jayhawk Hall of Fame

OVERALL INSERT ODDS 3:1
HOF1 James Naismith .75 2.00
HOF2 Phog Allen .75 2.00
HOF3 Tusten Ackerman .75 2.00
HOF4 Bob Kenney .75 2.00
HOF5 Skinny Johnson .75 2.00
HOF6 Larry Brown .75 2.00
HOF7 Howard Engleman .50 1.25
HOF8 Bill Lienhard .75 2.00
HOF9 Ray Evans .75 2.00
HOF10 Clyde Lovellette .75 2.00
HOF11 B.H. Born .75 2.00
HOF12 Wilt Chamberlain 1.50 4.00
HOF13 Dutch Lonborg .75 2.00
HOF14 Walt Wesley .50 1.25
HOF15 Jo Jo White .60 1.50
HOF16 Dave Robisch .75 2.00
HOF17 Bud Stallworth .75 2.00
HOF18 Darnell Valentine .60 1.50
HOF19 Dean Smith 1.00 2.50
HOF20 Danny Manning .75 2.00
HOF21 Raef LaFrentz .50 1.25
HOF22 Paul Pierce .75 2.00
HOF23 Drew Gooden .60 1.50
HOF24 Nick Collison .60 1.50

1996 Upper Deck Kellogg's Space Jam

Inserted into German Kellogg's products, this single card features Michael Jordan and Tweety on the card front.
3 Michael Jordan 6.00 15.00

2007 Upper Deck Kevin Durant Team Upper Deck

This card features Kevin Durant as a Longhorn, dribbling the ball, with a congratulatory message on the card back welcoming him to the Upper Deck Spokesmen family.
KD1 Kevin Durant 8.00 20.00
Pictured as Longhorn w/ball

2000 Upper Deck Lakers Championship Jumbos

This 10-card set was released by Upper Deck shortly after the L.A. Lakers won the NBA Championship during the 1999/00 season. The set features ten postcard sized cards, as well as, two special inserts. The inserts included a Kobe Bryant jersey card (1:100) and a Kobe Bryant autographed game jersey card (1:1250). Each pack contained 4 cards and carried a suggested retail price of $20.00.
COMP. FACT SET (10) 12.00 30.00
1 Shaquille O'Neal 3.20 8.00
2 Kobe Bryant 4.00 10.00
3 Glen Rice .80 2.00
4 A.C. Green .80 2.00
5 Ron Harper .80 2.00
6 Robert Horry .40 1.00
7 Derek Fisher .40 1.00
8 Rick Fox .40 1.00
9 Kobe Bryant 4.80 12.00
10 Team Photo 4.00 10.00
NNO Kobe Bryant JSY/100 100.00 250.00

2000 Upper Deck Lakers Master Collection

The 2000 Upper Deck Lakers Master Collection was released in July,2000, and featured a 25-card base set, one mystery pack, ten game-used jersey cards, one Forum Floor card, and one Wilt Chamberlain warm-up card. The set originally sold for the suggest price of $3000. There were only 300 Master Collections produced.
COMPLETE SET (25) 200.00 400.00
STATED PRINT RUN 300 SERIAL #'d SETS
1 Magic Johnson 15.00 40.00
2 Wilt Chamberlain 20.00 50.00
3 Kareem Abdul-Jabbar 15.00 40.00
4 Jerry West 10.00 25.00
5 Elgin Baylor 6.00 15.00
6 James Worthy 6.00 15.00
7 Byron Scott 5.00 12.00
8 Kurt Rambis 4.00 10.00
9 Michael Cooper 4.00 10.00
10 Norm Nixon 4.00 10.00
11 Gail Goodrich 4.00 10.00
12 Jamaal Wilkes 4.00 10.00
13 A.C. Green 4.00 10.00
14 Kobe Bryant 30.00 80.00
15 Shaquille O'Neal 30.00 80.00
16 Glen Rice 4.00 10.00
17 Derek Fisher 4.00 10.00
18 Robert Horry 4.00 10.00
19 Rick Fox 4.00 10.00
20 Ron Harper 4.00 10.00
21 Chick Hearn 10.00 25.00
22 Phil Jackson 6.00 15.00
23 Pat Riley 5.00 12.00
24 Mitch Kupchak 4.00 10.00
25 L.A. Forum 4.00 10.00

2000 Upper Deck Lakers Master Collection Fabulous Forum Floor Cards

This 6-card set was released in the 2000 Upper Deck Lakers Master Collection. Each Master Collection included one of the six game-used Forum Floor cards. These cards are individually serial numbered to 50. Card backs carry the player's initials as numbering.
STATED PRINT RUN 50 SERIAL #'d SETS
EBJ Elgin Baylor 50.00 100.00
EJF Magic Johnson 150.00 300.00
JWF Jerry West 75.00 150.00
KAF Kareem Abdul-Jabbar 50.00 120.00
WCF Wilt Chamberlain 125.00 250.00
WOJ James Worthy 40.00 80.00

2000 Upper Deck Lakers Master Collection Game Jerseys

This 10-card game-used jersey set was included in the 2000 Upper Deck Laker's Master collection. Each Master Collection incuded all 10-cards, and each card is serial numbered to 300. Card backs carry the player's initials.
COMPLETE SET (10) 250.00 500.00
STATED PRINT RUN 300 SERIAL # 'd SETS
AGJ A.C. Green 20.00 50.00
BSJ Byron Scott 20.00 50.00
EJJ Magic Johnson 25.00 60.00
JWJ Jerry West 20.00 50.00
KAJ Kareem Abdul-Jabbar 20.00 50.00
KBJ Kobe Bryant 30.00 80.00
MCJ Michael Cooper 12.00 30.00
RHJ Robert Horry 12.00 30.00
SOJ Shaquille O'Neal 25.00 60.00
WOJ James Worthy 12.00 30.00

2000 Upper Deck Lakers Master Collection Mystery Pack Inserts

Mystery Packs were inserted at a rate of one per Master Collection. The mystery packs included one autographed game-used memorabilia card from players such as Kobe Bryant, Elgin Baylor, Magic Johnson, Jerry West, Kareem Abdul-Jabbar, and James Worthy. Card backs carry the player's initials as numbering.
SS: SIGNS OF SUCCESS AUTOGRAPHS
ALL ITEMS ARE AUTOGRAPHED
PRINT RUNS LISTED BELOW
EBAF Elgin Baylor FF/22 175.00 350.00
EJAF Magic Johnson FF/32 500.00 1000.00
EJAJ Magic Johnson JSY/32 500.00 1000.00
JWAF Jerry West FF/44 125.00 250.00
JWAJ Jerry West JSY/44 250.00 500.00
KAAF K.Abdul-Jabbar FF/33 250.00 500.00
KAAJ K.Abdul-Jabbar JSY/33 250.00 500.00
WOAJ James Worthy JSY/42 75.00 150.00

2000 Upper Deck Lakers Master Collection Warm-Ups

This card was inserted into Laker Master Collections at a rate of one per set. The card features a swatch from a game-used Wilt Chamberlain warm-up jersey. Card back carries the player's initials.
STATED PRINT RUN 300 SERIAL #'d SETS
WCW Wilt Chamberlain 15.00 40.00

2003 Upper Deck LeBron James Box Set

Released in October 2003, this 32-card box set features an array of photographs of LeBron James ranging from on-court to studio posed. Each card has the Upper Deck logo in the top right corner and a LeBron James Box Set logo with a caption along the bottom in gold foil. Two oversized cards were inserted on top of the three rows of base set cards. Autographs serially numbered to 23 were also randomly inserted in boxes which carried a suggested retail price of $19.99.
COMPLETE SET (30) 15.00 40.00
COMMON JAMES (1-30) .75 2.00
COMMON JUMBO (LJ1-LJ2) .75 2.00
EACH SET INCLUDES TWO JUMBOS
LJA1 LeBron James AU/23 300.00 600.00
LJA2 LeBron James AU

2006 Upper Deck LeBron James Game Giveaway

COMPLETE SET (10) 10.00 25.00
COMMON CARD (1-10) 1.25 3.00

2004 Upper Deck LeBron James Freshman Season

COMPLETE SET (90) 20.00 40.00
COMMON CARD (1-90) .40 1.00

2001-02 Upper Deck Legends

This 132-card base set was issued in July of 2001. The set includes 90 veteran and retired legends and 42 draft pick redemption cards. The redemptions were available starting in September 2001. The standard sized set features both black and white and color photography for players. The left side of the card is white and fades into a gray basketball background then the picture, while the right side has a colored border and the players name. All cards have silver foil highhlights are and rookies break down as follows: card numbers 91-110 are sequentailly numberd to 3250, card numbers 111-125 are sequentially numbered to 1999, and card numbers 126-132 are sequentailly numbered to 500. Legends was packaged in 25-pack boxes with packs containing five cards and carrying a suggested retail price of $4.99. Please notice that these cards read 2000-01 in foil along the top; however, were issued after the 2001 draft with that rookie class inserted as redemptions so is listed with the rest of the 2001-02 sets.
COMP.SET w/o SP's (90) 10.00 25.00
91-110 PRINT RUN 3250 SER.#'d SETS
111-125 PRINT RUN 1999 SER.#'d SETS
126-132 PRINT RUN 500 SER.#'d SETS
NOTE CARDS READ 2000-01
1 Michael Jordan 2.00 5.00
2 Wilt Chamberlain .50 1.25
3 Karl Malone .30 .75
4 Steve Francis .20 .50
5 George McGinnis .15 .40
6 Julius Erving .40 1.00
7 Alonzo Mourning .30 .75
8 Kobe Bryant 1.00 2.50
9 Glen Rice .20 .50
10 Mitch Kupchak .25 .60
11 Isiah Thomas .25 .60
12 Rick Barry .20 .50
13 Moses Malone .25 .60
14 Larry Bird .60 1.50
15 Vince Carter .40 1.00
16 Jamaal Wilkes .25 .60
17 John Havlicek .30 .75
18 Elgin Baylor .25 .60
19 Dave Bing .25 .60
20 Steve Smith .20 .50
21 Kevin Garnett .40 1.00
22 Hakeem Olajuwon .30 .75
23 Walt Bellamy .20 .50
24 Kevin McHale .30 .75
25 Kareem Abdul-Jabbar .40 1.00
26 Chris Webber .25 .60
27 Tom Heinsohn .25 .60
28 Walt Frazier .25 .60
29 Ron Boone .15 .40
30 Gary Payton .25 .60
31 Wes Unseld .25 .60
32 Magic Johnson .75 2.00
33 David Thompson .20 .50
34 Maurice Lucas .25 .60
35 Paul Pierce .25 .60
36 Dikembe Mutombo .25 .60
37 Gail Goodrich .20 .50
38 Bob Lanier .20 .50
39 Chris Mullin .25 .60
40 Allen Iverson .50 1.25
41 Sam Jones .25 .60
42 James Worthy .30 .75
43 Cedric Maxwell .15 .40
44 George Gervin .25 .60
45 Earl Monroe .25 .60
46 Lenny Wilkens .25 .60
47 Tracy McGrady .40 1.00
48 Walter Davis .25 .60
49 Stephon Marbury .20 .50
50 Bob Cousy .40 1.00
51 Spencer Haywood .15 .40
52 Dave Cowens .15 .40
53 Scottie Pippen .40 1.00
54 Hal Greer .20 .50
55 Kiki Vandeweghe .20 .50
56 Paul Silas .25 .60
57 Elton Brand .25 .60
58 John Stockton .30 .75
59 Shareef Abdur-Rahim .20 .50
60 Reggie Miller .25 .60
61 Nate Thurmond .20 .50
62 Billy Cunningham .25 .60
63 Patrick Ewing .30 .75
64 Nate Archibald .20 .50
65 Tim Duncan .50 1.25
66 Lafayette Lever .20 .50
67 Willis Reed .25 .60
68 Ray Allen .25 .60
69 Jo Jo White .20 .50
70 Pete Maravich .40 1.00
71 Grant Hill .30 .75
72 Jerry West .30 .75
73 George Karl .25 .60
74 Bill Sharman .25 .60
75 Dave DeBusschere .25 .60
76 Tim Hardaway .25 .60
77 Bill Walton .25 .60
78 Jerry Lucas .25 .60
79 Antonio McDyess .20 .50
80 Robert Parish .25 .60
81 Shaquille O'Neal .60 1.50
82 Bill Russell .40 1.00
83 Clyde Drexler .30 .75
84 Dolph Schayes .25 .60
85 K.C. Jones .25 .60
86 Bob Pettit .25 .60
87 Jason Kidd .40 1.00
88 Mitch Richmond .20 .50
89 Oscar Robertson .30 .75
90 David Robinson .40 1.00
91 Bobby Simmons RC 1.50 4.00
92 Jamison Brewer RC 1.50 4.00
93 Earl Watson RC 1.50 4.00
94 Kenny Satterfield RC 1.00 2.50
95 Zeljko Rebraca RC 1.50 4.00
96 Damone Brown RC 1.00 2.50
97 Ruben Boumtje-Boumtje RC 1.50 4.00
98 Brian Scalabrine RC 1.50 4.00
99 Terence Morris RC 1.50 4.00
100 Willie Solomon RC 1.50 4.00
101 Primoz Brezec RC 1.50 4.00
102 Gilbert Arenas RC 2.50 6.00
103 Trenton Hassell RC 1.25 3.00
104 Loren Woods RC 1.00 2.50
105 Tony Parker RC 6.00 15.00
106 Jamaal Tinsley RC 1.50 4.00
107 Samuel Dalembert RC 1.50 4.00
108 Gerald Wallace RC 2.00 5.00
109 Andrei Kirilenko RC 2.50 6.00
110 Brandon Armstrong RC 1.00 2.50
111 Jeryl Sasser RC 2.00 5.00
112 Joseph Forte RC 2.00 5.00
113 Brendan Haywood RC 3.00 8.00
114 Zach Randolph RC 5.00 12.00
115 Jason Collins RC 2.50 6.00
116 Michael Bradley RC 2.00 5.00
117 Kirk Haston RC 2.00 5.00
118 Steven Hunter RC 2.50 6.00
119 Troy Murphy RC 3.00 8.00
120 Richard Jefferson RC 5.00 12.00
121 Vladimir Radmanovic RC 3.00 8.00
122 Kedrick Brown RC 2.00 5.00
123 Joe Johnson RC 4.00 10.00
124 Rodney White RC 2.00 5.00
125 DeSagana Diop RC 2.50 6.00
126 Eddie Griffin RC 3.00 8.00
127 Shane Battier RC 8.00 20.00
128 Jason Richardson RC 5.00 12.00
129 Eddy Curry RC 4.00 10.00
130 Pau Gasol RC 12.00 30.00
131 Tyson Chandler RC 6.00 15.00
132 Kwame Brown RC 4.00 10.00

2001-02 Upper Deck Legends Fiorentino Collection

Randomly inserted in packs at a rate of 1:15, this 15-card insert set features portrait paintings of the showcased player by James Fiorentino. Cards are enhanced with silver foil highlights.
COMPLETE SET (15) 15.00 40.00
STATED ODDS 1:15
F1 Michael Jordan 6.00 15.00
F2 Larry Bird 2.00 5.00
F3 Magic Johnson 2.50 6.00
F4 Julius Erving 1.25 3.00
F5 Bill Russell 1.25 3.00
F6 Jerry West 1.00 2.50
F7 Oscar Robertson 1.00 2.50
F8 Wilt Chamberlain 1.50 4.00
F9 Kareem Abdul-Jabbar 1.25 3.00
F10 Isiah Thomas .75 2.00
F11 George Gervin .75 2.00
F12 Elgin Baylor .75 2.00
F13 Bob Cousy 1.25 3.00
F14 Pete Maravich 1.25 3.00
F15 John Havlicek 1.00 2.50

2001-02 Upper Deck Legends Fiorentino Collection Autographs

ANNOUNCED PRINT RUNS LISTED IN CL
JH John Havlicek/17* 15.00 40.00
JW Jerry West/44* 40.00 80.00
KA Kareem Abdul-Jabbar/33* 100.00 200.00
LB Larry Bird/33* 250.00 500.00
MA Magic Johnson/32* 150.00 300.00

2001-02 Upper Deck Legends Generations

This nine-card insert set was randomly inserted in packs at a rate of 1:24, and features two players on the front of each card, one on the left and the other on the right. Each card is enhanced with silver foil highlights.
COMPLETE SET (9) 15.00 40.00
STATED ODDS 1:24
G1 M.Jordan/K.Bryant 6.00 15.00
G2 O.Robertson/J.Kidd 2.50 6.00
G3 W.Frazier/R.Allen 2.50 6.00
G4 E.Hayes/K.Garnett 2.50 6.00
G5 M.Malone/T.Duncan 4.00 10.00
G6 B.Lanier/D.Robinson 2.50 6.00
G7 G.Gervin/T.McGrady 2.50 6.00
G8 N.Archibald/S.Francis 2.50 6.00
G9 M.Jordan/V.Carter 3.00 8.00

2001-02 Upper Deck Legends Legendary Floor

Randomly inserted in packs at a rate of 1:23, this 29-card insert set features a full color player portrait photo on the right and a swatch of court on the left. These cards are horizontally designed and are highlighted with silver foil.
STATED ODDS 1:23
AIF Allen Iverson 8.00 20.00
AMF Alonzo Mourning 5.00 12.00
CWF Chris Webber 4.00 10.00
DAF David Robinson 6.00 15.00
DRF Julius Erving 12.00 30.00
GHF Grant Hill 5.00 12.00
HOF Hakeem Olajuwon 5.00 12.00
ITF Isiah Thomas 4.00 10.00
JHF John Havlicek 10.00 25.00
JKF Jason Kidd 6.00 15.00
JSF John Stockton 5.00 12.00
JWF James Worthy 8.00 20.00
KAF Kareem Abdul-Jabbar 15.00 40.00
KBF Kobe Bryant 12.00 30.00
KGF Kevin Garnett 6.00 15.00
KMF Karl Malone 5.00 12.00
LBF Larry Bird 15.00 40.00
MAF Magic Johnson 15.00 40.00
MJF Michael Jordan 20.00 50.00
MMF Moses Malone 10.00 25.00
PEF Patrick Ewing 5.00 12.00
PMF Pete Maravich 25.00 60.00
RMF Reggie Miller 4.00 10.00
SFF Steve Francis 3.00 8.00
SMF Stephon Marbury 3.00 8.00
SPF Scottie Pippen 6.00 15.00
THF Tim Hardaway 4.00 10.00
TMF Tracy McGrady 6.00 15.00
WCF Wilt Chamberlain 30.00 80.00

2001-02 Upper Deck Legends Legendary Floor Autographs

Seeded in packs, this 10-card set parallels the design of the base Legendary Floor set enhanced with authentic player autographs. Each card is sequentially numbered to 100, except for Michael Jordan who is numbered to 23.
STATED PRINT RUN 23 TO 100 SETS
DRAF Julius Erving/100 60.00 150.00
JHAF John Havlicek/100 50.00 120.00
KAAF Kareem Abdul-Jabbar/100 60.00 150.00
KBAF Kobe Bryant/100 150.00 300.00
KGAF Kevin Garnett/100 100.00 200.00
LBAF Larry Bird/100 100.00 200.00
MAAF Magic Johnson/100 80.00 160.00
MJAF Michael Jordan/23 750.00 1500.00
MMAF Moses Malone/100 30.00 80.00
SFAF Steve Francis/100 30.00 80.00

2001-02 Upper Deck Legends Legendary Jerseys

Randomly inserted in packs at a rate of 1:23, this 28-card set utilizes the same design as the Legendar Floor set and has player jerseys on the left side of the card.
STATED ODDS 1:23
AIJ Allen Iverson 10.00 25.00
BRJ Bill Russell 20.00 50.00
BWJ Bill Walton 6.00 15.00
CDJ Clyde Drexler 10.00 25.00
DAJ David Robinson 8.00 20.00
DDJ Dave DeBusschere 8.00 20.00
DRJ Julius Erving 12.00 30.00
EMJ Earl Monroe 6.00 15.00
GGJ George Gervin 6.00 15.00
GHJ Grant Hill 12.00 30.00
ITJ Isiah Thomas 8.00 20.00
JHJ John Havlicek 10.00 25.00
JSJ John Stockton 6.00 15.00
JWJ Jerry West 10.00 25.00
KAJ Kareem Abdul-Jabbar 15.00 40.00
KBJ Kobe Bryant 10.00 25.00
KGJ Kevin Garnett 8.00 20.00
KMJ Karl Malone 6.00 15.00
LBJ Larry Bird 10.00 25.00
MAJ Magic Johnson 10.00 25.00
MCJ Kevin McHale 6.00 15.00
MJJ Michael Jordan 60.00 120.00
MJ/DRJ M.Jordan/J.Erving 50.00 100.00
MJ/KBJ M.Jordan/K.Bryant 75.00 150.00
MJ/LBJ M.Jordan/L.Bird 80.00 200.00
PEJ Patrick Ewing 6.00 15.00
RPJ Robert Parish 6.00 15.00
SPJ Scottie Pippen 6.00 15.00

2001-02 Upper Deck Legends Legendary Jerseys Autographs

STATED PRINT RUN 10 TO 50 SETS
SOME UNPRICED DUE TO SCARCITY
BRAJ Bill Russell/50 250.00 500.00
DDAJ Dave DeBusschere/50 40.00 100.00
DRAJ Julius Erving/50 150.00 300.00
EMAJ Earl Monroe/50 40.00 100.00
GGAJ George Gervin/50 40.00 100.00
JWAJ Jerry West/50 125.00 250.00
KAAJ Kareem Abdul-Jabbar/50 100.00 200.00
KBAJ Kobe Bryant/50 250.00 500.00
KGAJ Kevin Garnett/50 125.00 250.00
LBAJ Larry Bird/50 200.00 400.00
MAAJ Magic Johnson/50 200.00 400.00
MJAJ Michael Jordan/23 1000.00 2000.00

2001-02 Upper Deck Legends Legendary Signatures

This 31-card insert set was randomly inserted in packs at a rate of 1:71, this 31-card set features authentic player autographs. Full color player photos are set on the top half of the card and are surrounded by a "cloud" background which fades to gold at the card edges. The bottom of the card showcases the autograph. Two dual-player cards were issued with this set featuring Michael Jordan with Julius Erving and Kobe Bryant. Three cards are suspected short prints, Steve Francis, Larry Bird, and Julius Erving.

STATED ODDS 1:71
BR Bill Russell 500.00 700.00
BS Bill Sharman 6.00 15.00
DR Julius Erving SP 100.00 200.00
DT David Thompson 6.00 15.00
EB Elgin Baylor 10.00 25.00
EM Earl Monroe 10.00 25.00
GG George Gervin 6.00 15.00
JH John Havlicek 15.00 40.00
JW Jerry West 25.00 60.00
KA Kareem Abdul-Jabbar 50.00 100.00
KV Kiki Vandeweghe 6.00 15.00
LB Larry Bird SP 250.00 500.00
MA Magic Johnson 75.00 150.00
MM Moses Malone 25.00 60.00
NA Nate Archibald 8.00 20.00
OR Oscar Robertson 40.00 100.00
SF Steve Francis SP 20.00 50.00
WR Willis Reed 10.00 25.00

2001-02 Upper Deck Legends Record Producers

Randomly inserted in packs at a rate of 1:24, this 9-card insert set takes a look at some of the most important milestones on the NBA record books. Base cards contain full color player action photos, gold borders on the left and right, and silver foil highlights.

COMPLETE SET (9) 10.00 25.00
STATED ODDS 1:24
RP1 Michael Jordan 6.00 15.00
RP2 John Stockton 1.00 2.50
RP3 Reggie Miller .75 2.00
RP4 Oscar Robertson 1.00 2.50
RP5 Hakeem Olajuwon 1.00 2.50
RP6 Elgin Baylor .75 2.00
RP7 Karl Malone 1.00 2.50
RP8 Kobe Bryant 3.00 8.00
RP9 Jerry West 1.00 2.50

2001-02 Upper Deck Legends Yearbook

This 9-card insert set was randomly inserted in packs at a rate of 1:24. The retro set captures memorable NBA moments of several NBA stars. Player photos are set agains a silver and black background with white borders.

COMPLETE SET (9) 10.00 25.00
STATED ODDS 1:24
Y1 Michael Jordan 6.00 15.00
Y2 Kobe Bryant 3.00 8.00
Y3 Walt Frazier .75 2.00
Y4 Pete Maravich 1.25 3.00
Y5 Clyde Drexler 1.00 2.50
Y6 Bob Lanier .60 1.50
Y7 Bill Russell 1.25 3.00
Y8 Bill Walton .75 2.00
Y9 Kevin Garnett 1.25 3.00

2003-04 Upper Deck Legends

Released in late June 2004, Upper Deck Legends boasts a 150-card base set divided up into 90 veteran player cards, 35 rookie cards sequentially numbered to 1999 (cards 91-125), 10 rookie cards sequentially numbered to 999 (cards 126-135) and 15 draft pick redemption cards with stated odds of one in 24. Legends was packaged in 24-pack boxes with packs containing five cards and carried a suggested retail price of $4.99. Each box contained an assortment of 16 Legends and eight Legends Retro packs, where Legends came out of the packs with LeBron James on them and Retro out of the Michael Jordan packs

COMP.SET w/o SP's (90) 12.50 30.00
136-150 DRAFT EXCH ODDS 1:24
1 Bob Sura .20 .50
2 Stephen Jackson .25 .60
3 Jason Terry .25 .60
4 Ricky Davis .25 .60
5 Jiri Welsch .20 .50
6 Paul Pierce .30 .75
7 Eddy Curry .20 .50
8 Jamal Crawford .30 .75
9 Tyson Chandler .25 .60
10 Dajuan Wagner .20 .50
11 Carlos Boozer .25 .60
12 Zydrunas Ilgauskas .25 .60
13 Dirk Nowitzki .50 1.25
14 Antoine Walker .30 .75
15 Steve Nash .40 1.00
16 Michael Finley .30 .75
17 Jon Barry .20 .50
18 Andre Miller .25 .60
19 Nene .25 .60
20 Rasheed Wallace .30 .75
21 Richard Hamilton .25 .60
22 Ben Wallace .25 .60
23 Erick Dampier .20 .50
24 Jason Richardson .30 .75
25 Nick Van Exel .25 .60
26 Yao Ming .60 1.50
27 Cuttino Mobley .20 .50
28 Steve Francis .25 .60
29 Jermaine O'Neal .25 .60
30 Reggie Miller .30 .75
31 Ron Artest .30 .75
32 Elton Brand .30 .75
33 Corey Maggette .25 .60
34 Quentin Richardson .25 .60
35 Kobe Bryant 1.25 3.00
36 Karl Malone .40 1.00
37 Gary Payton .30 .75
38 Shaquille O'Neal .75 2.00
39 Pau Gasol .30 .75
40 Bonzi Wells .20 .50
41 Mike Miller .25 .60
42 Lamar Odom .25 .60
43 Eddie Jones .25 .60
44 Caron Butler .25 .60
45 Keith Van Horn .25 .60
46 Desmond Mason .25 .60
47 Michael Redd .30 .75
48 Latrell Sprewell .25 .60
49 Kevin Garnett .50 1.25
50 Sam Cassell .25 .60
51 Richard Jefferson .25 .60
52 Kenyon Martin .25 .60
53 Jason Kidd .50 1.25
54 Jamal Mashburn .25 .60
55 Baron Davis .25 .60
56 David Wesley .20 .50
57 Allan Houston .25 .60
58 Stephon Marbury .25 .60
59 Kurt Thomas .20 .50
60 Juwan Howard .25 .60
61 Drew Gooden .25 .60
62 Tracy McGrady .40 1.00
63 Zendon Hamilton RC .30 .75
64 Allen Iverson .50 1.25
65 Eric Snow .20 .50
66 Amare Stoudemire .40 1.00
67 Joe Johnson .25 .60
68 Shawn Marion .25 .60
69 Zach Randolph .25 .60
70 Darius Miles .20 .50
71 Shareef Abdur-Rahim .25 .60
72 Peja Stojakovic .30 .75
73 Chris Webber .30 .75
74 Mike Bibby .30 .75
75 Brad Miller .25 .60
76 Tony Parker .30 .75
77 Tim Duncan .50 1.25
78 Manu Ginobili .40 1.00
79 Ronald Murray .20 .50
80 Ray Allen .30 .75
81 Rashard Lewis .30 .75
82 Donyell Marshall .20 .50
83 Vince Carter .50 1.25
84 Jalen Rose .25 .60
85 Andrei Kirilenko .30 .75
86 Matt Harpring .20 .50
87 Carlos Arroyo .25 .60
88 Gilbert Arenas .25 .60
89 Larry Hughes .25 .60
90 Jerry Stackhouse .25 .60
91 Devin Brown RC 1.25 3.00
92 Ronald Dupree RC 1.25 3.00
93 Alex Garcia RC 1.25 3.00
94 Udonis Haslem RC 1.50 4.00
95 Maurice Williams RC 2.00 5.00
96 Brandon Hunter RC 1.25 3.00
97 Keith Bogans RC 1.25 3.00
98 Willie Green RC 1.25 3.00
99 Zaza Pachulia RC 2.00 5.00
100 Zarko Cabarkapa RC 1.25 3.00
101 Kyle Korver RC 2.50 6.00
102 Luke Walton RC 2.00 5.00
103 Maciej Lampe RC 1.25 3.00
104 Josh Howard RC 2.00 5.00
105 Kendrick Perkins RC 1.50 4.00
106 Ndudi Ebi RC 1.25 3.00
107 Jerome Beasley RC 1.25 3.00
108 Brian Cook RC 1.25 3.00
109 Travis Outlaw RC 1.50 4.00
110 Zoran Planinic RC 1.25 3.00
111 Boris Diaw RC 2.00 5.00
112 Steve Blake RC 1.50 4.00
113 Aleksandar Pavlovic RC 1.50 4.00
114 David West RC 2.00 5.00
115 Mike Sweetney RC 1.25 3.00
116 Troy Bell RC 1.25 3.00
117 Reece Gaines RC 1.25 3.00
118 Marcus Banks RC 1.25 3.00
119 Dahntay Jones RC 1.50 4.00
120 Chris Kaman RC 2.00 5.00
121 Mickael Pietrus RC 1.50 4.00
122 Luke Ridnour RC 1.50 4.00
123 Jason Kapono RC 1.25 3.00
124 Marquis Daniels RC 1.50 4.00
125 Travis Hansen RC 1.25 3.00
126 Leandro Barbosa RC 2.50 6.00
127 Nick Collison RC 2.00 5.00
128 Kirk Hinrich RC 2.50 6.00
129 T.J. Ford RC 2.00 5.00
130 Jarvis Hayes RC 1.50 4.00
131 Dwyane Wade RC 8.00 20.00
132 Chris Bosh RC 4.00 10.00
133 Carmelo Anthony RC 8.00 20.00
134 Darko Milicic RC 2.00 5.00
135 LeBron James RC 40.00 100.00
136 Dwight Howard XRC 4.00 10.00
137 Emeka Okafor XRC 4.00 10.00
138 Ben Gordon XRC 4.00 10.00
139 Shaun Livingston XRC 3.00 8.00
140 Devin Harris XRC 3.00 8.00
141 Josh Childress XRC 3.00 8.00
142 Luol Deng XRC 5.00 12.00
143 Rafael Araujo XRC 2.00 5.00
144 Andre Iguodala XRC 4.00 10.00
145 Luke Jackson XRC 3.00 8.00
146 Andris Biedrins XRC 2.00 5.00
147 Robert Swift XRC 3.00 8.00
148 Sebastian Telfair XRC 3.00 8.00
149 Kris Humphries XRC 3.00 8.00
150 Al Jefferson XRC 4.00 10.00

2003-04 Upper Deck Legends Throwback

This set breaks down very similarly to the base Upper Deck Legends set but instead features retired players on cards 1-90. Rookie players, numbers 91-135 are sequentially numbered to 100, and draft exchanges were inserted at one in 380.

COMP.SET w/o SP's 15.00 40.00
*TB 91-125: .5X TO 1.25X BASE HI
*TB 126-135: .4X TO 1X BASE HI
91-135 PRINT RUN 100 SER.#'d SETS
*TB 136-150: 1.25X TO 3X BASE HI
136-150 DRAFT EXCH ODDS 1:380
1 Dominique Wilkins .40 1.00
2 Spud Webb .25 .60
3 Danny Ainge .30 .75
4 Larry Bird .75 2.00
5 John Havlicek .30 .75
6 Bob Cousy .50 1.25
7 Bill Russell .50 1.25
8 Kevin McHale .40 1.00
9 Dave Cowens .20 .50
10 Dennis Johnson .25 .60
11 K.C. Jones .30 .75
12 Robert Parish .40 1.00
13 Nate Archibald .25 .60
14 Michael Jordan 2.50 6.00
15 Dennis Rodman .60 1.50
16 Bill Cartwright .25 .60
17 Spencer Haywood .20 .50
18 World B. Free .25 .60
19 Rolando Blackman .25 .60
20 Walt Bellamy .25 .60
21 Dan Issel .25 .60
22 David Thompson .25 .60
23 Alex English .25 .60
24 Dave Bing .30 .75
25 Isiah Thomas .30 .75
26 Bill Laimbeer .25 .60
27 Bob Lanier .25 .60
28 Vinnie Johnson .30 .75
29 M.L. Carr .30 .75
30 Cazzie Russell .25 .60
31 Rick Barry .25 .60
32 Chris Mullin .40 1.00
33 Nate Thurmond .25 .60
34 Gail Goodrich .25 .60
35 Kenny Smith .25 .60
36 George McGinnis .20 .50
37 Clark Kellogg .30 .75
38 Michael Cage .20 .50
39 Wilt Chamberlain .60 1.50
40 Magic Johnson .75 2.00
41 Kurt Rambis .20 .50
42 James Worthy .40 1.00
43 Jamaal Wilkes .30 .75
44 Kareem Abdul-Jabbar .50 1.25
45 George Mikan .60 1.50
46 Elgin Baylor .30 .75
47 Michael Cooper .25 .60
48 Pat Riley .40 1.00
49 Alonzo Mourning .40 1.00
50 Rony Seikaly .20 .50
51 Ricky Pierce .20 .50
52 Terry Cummings .25 .60
53 Oscar Robertson .30 .75
54 Sidney Moncrief .20 .50
55 Darryl Dawkins .20 .50
56 Otis Birdsong .25 .60
57 Jerry Lucas .30 .75
58 Dave DeBusschere .30 .75
59 Patrick Ewing .40 1.00
60 Willis Reed .30 .75
61 Walt Frazier .30 .75
62 Earl Monroe .30 .75
63 Donald Royal .30 .75
64 Moses Malone .30 .75
65 Julius Erving .50 1.25
66 Maurice Cheeks .20 .50
67 Billy Cunningham .30 .75
68 Kevin Johnson .30 .75
69 Tom Chambers .25 .60
70 Larry Nance .25 .60
71 Walter Davis .30 .75
72 Maurice Lucas .30 .75
73 Paul Westphal .40 1.00
74 Bill Walton .30 .75
75 Jim Paxson .30 .75
76 Clyde Drexler .40 1.00
77 Reggie Theus .25 .60
78 Nate McMillan .30 .75
79 David Robinson .50 1.25
80 Artis Gilmore .25 .60
81 George Gervin .30 .75
82 Fred Brown .20 .50
83 Detlef Schrempf .30 .75
84 Jack Sikma .25 .60
85 Lenny Wilkens .30 .75
86 Pete Maravich .50 1.25
87 John Stockton .40 1.00
88 Darrell Griffith .20 .50
89 Wes Unseld .30 .75
90 Elvin Hayes .30 .75
131 Dwyane Wade 15.00 40.00
135 LeBron James 75.00 150.00

2003-04 Upper Deck Legends Championship Numbers Autographs

Randomly seeded, this 35-card set features a picture and an autograph of each player and all cards are sequentially numbered to the jersey number that player wore while winning an NBA Championship.

PRINT RUNS LISTED BELOW
SOME NOT PRICED DUE TO SCARCITY
BL Bill Laimbeer/40 25.00 60.00
BS Bill Sharman/21 15.00 40.00
CD Chuck Daly/80 30.00 60.00
CM Cedric Maxwell/31 15.00 40.00
CO Michael Cooper/21 25.00 60.00
CR Cazzie Russell/33 15.00 40.00
CU Billy Cunningham/80 25.00 60.00
DC Dave Cowens/18 20.00 50.00
DR David Robinson/50 50.00 120.00
GM George Mikan/99 125.00 250.00
JW James Worthy/42 75.00 150.00
KJ K.C. Jones/25 20.00 50.00
KJ K.C. Jones/80 12.50 30.00
KR Kurt Rambis/31 25.00 60.00
LB Larry Bird/33 125.00 250.00
MA Magic Johnson/32 75.00 150.00
MJ Michael Jordan/90 350.00 700.00
PR Pat Riley/80 30.00 80.00
RO Dennis Rodman/91 50.00 100.00
RP Robert Parish/80 20.00 50.00
WI Jamaal Wilkes/52 15.00 40.00
WR Willis Reed/19 40.00 100.00
WU Wes Unseld/41 12.50 30.00

2003-04 Upper Deck Legends Championship Teammates Dual Autographs

Randomly inserted, this 18-card set pairs two players from the same championship team, one on the top and one on the bottom, along with a small head photo and an authentic autograph. Each card is sequentially numbered to 25.

PRINT RUN 25 SER.#'d SETS
UNPRICED TRIPLE PRINT RUN 5 SER.#'d SETS
BT B.Cousy/T.Heinsohn 30.00 80.00
BW L.Bird/B.Walton 125.00 250.00
CC Cunningham/Cheeks 25.00 60.00
CR B.Cousy/B.Russell 200.00 350.00
EC J.Erving/M.Cheeks 50.00 120.00
FR W.Frazier/W.Reed 30.00 80.00
JH K.C.Jones/T.Heinsohn 25.00 60.00
JS K.C.Jones/B.Sharman 40.00 100.00
JW M.Johnson/J.Worthy 150.00 300.00
RF C.Russell/W.Frazier 40.00 100.00
RR P.Riley/K.Rambis 30.00 80.00
TL I.Thomas/B.Laimbeer 30.00 80.00
WJ B.Walton/D.Johnson 25.00 60.00
WP B.Walton/R.Parish 40.00 100.00
WR J.Worthy/K.Rambis 40.00 100.00

2003-04 Upper Deck Legends Hall of Fame Induction Ink

Randomly inserted with all other autographed cards at the combined rate of one in eight, this six-card set features HOF greats, both from the NBA and elsewhere. Each card has a photo on the right and a vertical cut signature on the left.

COMBINED AUTO ODDS 1:8
DM Dino Meneghin 25.00 50.00
EL Earl Lloyd 25.00 60.00
JW James Worthy 30.00 80.00
LB Leon Barmore 15.00 40.00
ML Meadowlark Lemon 40.00 80.00
RP Robert Parish 10.00 25.00

2003-04 Upper Deck Legends Legendary Inscriptions

Limited to 100 copies per, each of these cards is horizontally designed with a small player photo and an autograph along with a special inscription.

PRINT RUN 100 SER.#'d SETS
AG A.Gilmore A-Train 20.00 50.00
BC B.Cousy Cooz 50.00 120.00
BW B.Walton Big Red 25.00 60.00
CM C.Maxwell Cornbread 15.00 40.00
DA D.Robinson Admiral 75.00 150.00
DC D.Cowens Big Red 25.00 60.00
DD Dawkins Chocolate Thunder 20.00 50.00
DD1 D.Dawkins Love Tron 20.00 50.00
DG D.Griffith Dr. Dunkenstein 15.00 40.00
DJ Dennis Johnson DJ 30.00 80.00
DT D.Thompson Skywalker 25.00 60.00
EH E.Hayes The Big E 15.00 40.00
GG G.Gervin The Iceman 25.00 60.00
GM G.Mikan Mr. Basketball 250.00 450.00
IT I.Thomas Zeke 40.00 100.00
JA J.Wilkes Silk 25.00 60.00
JE J.Erving Dr. J 50.00 100.00
JS J.Salley Spider 15.00 40.00
JW J.Worthy Big Game James 60.00 150.00
KR K.Rambis Clark Kent 15.00 40.00
MA Magic Johnson Magic 40.00 100.00
MC Michael Cooper Coop 15.00 40.00
MO Maurice Cheeks Mo 15.00 40.00
RP Robert Parish Chief 30.00 80.00
SW Anthony Webb Spud 15.00 40.00
WF Walt Frazier Clyde 30.00 80.00
WR W.Reed The Captain 30.00 80.00
ZO A.Mourning Zo 30.00 80.00

2003-04 Upper Deck Legends Legendary Signatures

Inserted with all other autographed cards with the combined odds of one in eight, this 40-card set features a photo of each player and an autograph. Please note that SP information was provided by Upper Deck. Michael Cooper has two autograph versions-one is just a signature while the other contains the inscription "Coop."

COMBINED AUTO ODDS 1:8
AG Artis Gilmore 6.00 15.00
AM Alonzo Mourning 20.00 50.00
BC Bob Cousy 50.00 120.00
BL Bill Laimbeer 6.00 15.00
BR Bill Russell SP 125.00 250.00
BS Bill Sharman 8.00 20.00
BW Bill Walton 8.00 20.00
CD Chuck Daly 25.00 60.00
CR Cazzie Russell 6.00 15.00
CU Billy Cunningham 50.00 120.00
DA David Robinson SP 50.00 12.00
DC Dave Cowens 6.00 15.00
DD Darryl Dawkins 6.00 15.00
DG Darrell Griffith 6.00 15.00
DJ Dennis Johnson 25.00 60.00
DR Dennis Rodman 25.00 60.00
DT David Thompson 6.00 15.00
EH Elvin Hayes 6.00 15.00
GG George Gervin 6.00 15.00
GM George Mikan 150.00 400.00
IT Isiah Thomas 10.00 25.00
JA Jamaal Wilkes 6.00 15.00
JE Julius Erving SP 75.00 200.00
JS John Stockton SP 60.00 150.00
JW James Worthy 25.00 60.00
KC K.C. Jones 20.00 50.00
KR Kurt Rambis 6.00 15.00
LB Larry Bird SP 100.00 200.00
MA Magic Johnson SP 60.00 150.00
MC Michael Cooper 6.00 15.00
MC1 Michael Coop Cooper 6.00 15.00
MJ Michael Jordan SP 400.00 700.00
MO Maurice Cheeks 6.00 15.00
PE Patrick Ewing 200.00 400.00
PR Pat Riley 15.00 40.00
RP Robert Parish 6.00 15.00
SW Spud Webb 6.00 15.00
TH Tommy Heinsohn 10.00 25.00
WF Walt Frazier 10.00 25.00
WR Willis Reed 12.00 30.00
WU Wes Unseld 10.00 25.00

2003-04 Upper Deck Legends Rookie Impressions Dual Autographs

Randomly seeded, this 12-card set features a rookie and a veteran on a horizontally designed card with small head-shot photos and authentic autographs. Each card is sequentially numbered to 25.

PRINT RUN 25 SER.#'d SETS
THROWBACKS: SAME PRICE AS BASIC
AJJH A.Jamison/J.Howard 20.00 50.00
GADA G.Arenas/D.West 10.00 25.00
GPTB G.Payton/T.Bell 20.00 50.00
JDSB J.Dixon/S.Blake 20.00 50.00
JKMB J.Kidd/M.Banks 20.00 50.00
JRMP J.Richardson/M.Pietrus 20.00 50.00
KBDW K.Bryant/D.Wade 400.00 700.00
KGCB K.Garnett/C.Bosh 75.00 200.00
LBDM L.Bird/D.Milicic 125.00 250.00
MJLJ M.Jordan/L.James 2500.00 4000.00
TMCA T.McGrady/C.Anthony 30.00 60.00
YMCK Y.Ming/C.Kaman 40.00 100.00

2003-04 Upper Deck Legends Signs of a Future Legend

Inserted along with all other autograph cards at the rate of one in eight, this 36-card set places a photo of the player on the right and a vertical signature on the left.

COMBINED AUTO ODDS 1:8
AK Andrei Kirilenko 6.00 15.00
AM Andre Miller 4.00 10.00
AS Amare Stoudemire 5.00 12.00
BC Brian Cook 2.50 6.00
BD Boris Diaw 4.00 10.00
BO Carlos Boozer 3.00 8.00
CA Carmelo Anthony SP 25.00 60.00
CB Chris Bosh SP 6.00 15.00
CH Chauncey Billups 6.00 15.00
DA David West 4.00 10.00
DM Darko Milicic SP 8.00 20.00
DW Dajuan Wagner 4.00 10.00
DY Dwyane Wade 60.00 150.00
EG Manu Ginobili 30.00 80.00
FJ Fred Jones 4.00 10.00
GA Gilbert Arenas 8.00 20.00
GP Gary Payton SP 15.00 40.00
JA Jalen Rose 5.00 12.00
JH Josh Howard 4.00 10.00
JK Jason Kidd SP 12.00 30.00
JR Jason Richardson 4.00 10.00
KB Keith Bogans 2.50 6.00
KG Kevin Garnett SP 30.00 80.00
KK Kyle Korver 5.00 12.00
KR Kareem Rush 4.00 10.00
LB Leandro Barbosa 4.00 10.00
LJ LeBron James SP 800.00 1200.00
LR Luke Ridnour 3.00 8.00
LW Luke Walton 4.00 10.00
ML Maciej Lampe 2.50 6.00
NH Nene 4.00 10.00
RH Richard Hamilton 4.00 10.00
RJ Richard Jefferson 6.00 15.00
SC Sam Cassell 6.00 15.00
TM Tracy McGrady SP 20.00 50.00
YM Yao Ming SP 25.00 60.00

2000 Upper Deck Legends Master Collection

The 2000 Upper Deck Legends Master Collection was released in late 2000, and featured an 18-card base set, one mystery pack, one Warm-Up card, five Autographs, and one Floor card packaged in a wooden box with a certificate of authenticity. There were only 200 Master Collections produced.

COMPLETE SET (18) 125.00 250.00
STATED PRINT RUN 200 SERIAL #'d SETS
1 Michael Jordan 30.00 80.00
2 Bill Russell 10.00 25.00
3 Magic Johnson 15.00 40.00
4 Larry Bird 15.00 40.00
5 Julius Erving 10.00 25.00
6 Wilt Chamberlain 12.00 30.00
7 Jerry West 8.00 20.00
8 Bill Walton 6.00 15.00
9 Bob Cousy 10.00 25.00
10 John Havlicek 8.00 20.00
11 Elgin Baylor 6.00 15.00
12 Oscar Robertson 8.00 20.00
13 Walt Frazier 6.00 15.00
14 George Gervin 6.00 15.00
15 Pete Maravich 12.00 30.00
16 Isiah Thomas 6.00 15.00
17 Moses Malone 6.00 15.00
18 Rick Barry 5.00 12.00

2000 Upper Deck Legends Master Collection Legendary Floor

This 2-card game-used floor set was included in the 2000 Upper Deck Legends Master collection. Each Master Collection incuded one of the two cards, and each card is serial numbered to 100. Card backs carry the player's initials.

COMPLETE SET (2) 100.00 200.00
COMMON CARD (F1-F2) 60.00 120.00
PRINT RUN 100 SERIAL #'d SETS

2000 Upper Deck Legends Master Collection Living Legends Autographs

This 20-card autograph set was included in the 2000 Upper Deck Legends Master collection. Each Master Collection incuded a set of 5 of these cards, and each card is serial numbered to 50. Card backs carry the player's initials.

PRINT RUN 50 SERIAL #'d SETS
BL1 Bill Russell 125.00 250.00
BL2 Bill Russell 125.00 250.00
BL3 Bill Russell 125.00 250.00
BL4 Bill Russell 75.00 150.00
EL1 Magic Johnson 90.00 150.00
EL2 Magic Johnson 90.00 150.00
EL3 Magic Johnson 90.00 150.00
EL4 Magic Johnson 90.00 150.00
JL1 Julius Erving 75.00 150.00
JL2 Julius Erving 75.00 150.00
JL3 Julius Erving 75.00 150.00
JL4 Julius Erving 75.00 150.00
LL1 Larry Bird 75.00 150.00
LL2 Larry Bird 75.00 150.00
LL3 Larry Bird 75.00 150.00
LL4 Larry Bird 75.00 150.00
ML1 Michael Jordan 600.00 1000.00
ML2 Michael Jordan 600.00 1000.00
ML3 Michael Jordan 600.00 1000.00
ML4 Michael Jordan 600.00 1000.00

2000 Upper Deck Legends Master Collection Mystery Pack Inserts

Mystery Packs were inserted at a rate of one per Master Collection. The mystery packs included one game-used memorabilia card from players such as Michael Jordan, Magic Johnson, Larry Bird, and Bill Russell, and Julius Erving. Card backs carry the player's initials as numbering.

STATED PRINT RUNS LISTED BELOW
EJA Magic Johnson Floor AU/32 80.00 160.00
DREJ Erving/Johnson Jsy/37 30.00 80.00

2000 Upper Deck Legends Master Collection Warm-Ups

This card was inserted into Legends Master Collections at a rate of one per set. The card features a swatch from a game-used Wilt Chamberlain warm-up jersey. Card back carries the player's initials. Stated print run of 200 serial numbered sets.

STATED PRINT RUN 200 SERIAL #'d SETS
WC1 Wilt Chamberlain 40.00 80.00

2003 Upper Deck Lego Sports

Released in eight different packs of three, these cards were produced by Upper Deck in conjunction with Lego. The three packs were issued in the following configurations: #3560 Ray Allen, Tim Duncan, and Pau Gasol. #3561 Antoine Walker, Shaquille O'Neal and Tony Parker. #3562 Gary Payton, Dirk Nowitzki, and Vince Carter. #3563 Toni Kukoc, Jason Kidd, and Kobe Bryant. #3564 Allen Iverson, Steve Francis, and Karl Malone. #3565 Paul Pierce, Jerry Stackhouse, and Steve Nash. #3566 Jalen Rose, Peja Stojakovic and Kevin Garnett. #3567 Tracy McGrady, Chris Webber and Allen Houston. Each package contains three cards, three lego figures and three stands where both the figure and card can be set up. Each three-card pack contained on gold card verson. The gold cards are differentiated by gold foil and embossing on the card front.

COMPLETE SET (24) 6.00 15.00
*GOLD: .75X TO 2X BASE HI
2 Ray Allen .40 1.00
4 Shaquille O'Neal .75 2.00
5 Antoine Walker .40 1.00
6 Tony Parker .40 1.00
7 Vince Carter .40 1.00
8 Dirk Nowitzki .50 1.25
10 Kobe Bryant 2.00 5.00
11 Jason Kidd .50 1.25
12 Toni Kukoc .40 1.00
13 Allen Iverson .50 1.25
14 Tracy McGrady .50 1.25
15 Karl Malone .50 1.25
16 Paul Pierce .40 1.00
17 Jerry Stackhouse .40 1.00
18 Steve Nash .50 1.25
19 Kevin Garnett .60 1.50
21 Jalen Rose .40 1.00
22 Chris Webber .40 1.00
23 Steve Francis .40 1.00
24 Allan Houston .40 1.00

2014-15 Upper Deck Lettermen

COMPLETE SET (80)
51-80 PRINT RUN 999 SER.#'d SETS
1 Allan Houston .30 .75
2 James Worthy .50 1.25
3 Magic Johnson 1.00 2.50
4 Glenn Robinson .30 .75
5 Jerry Lucas .40 1.00
6 Vinny Del Negro .30 .75
7 A.C. Green .40 1.00
8 Elvin Hayes .40 1.00
9 Karl Malone .50 1.25
10 Kendall Gill .25 .60
11 Bo Outlaw .25 .60
12 Christian Laettner .30 .75
13 Hakeem Olajuwon .50 1.25
14 David Robinson .60 1.50
15 James Harden .60 1.50
16 Nick Van Exel .40 1.00
17 Sleepy Floyd .25 .60
18 Stephen Curry 1.50 4.00
19 Sean Elliott .40 1.00
20 LeBron James 1.50 4.00
21 Joe Smith .30 .75
22 Derek Harper .30 .75
23 Julius Erving .60 1.50
24 Jamal Mashburn .40 1.00
25 Larry Bird 1.00 2.50
26 Alex English .30 .75
27 Reggie Theus .30 .75
28 Shane Battier .30 .75
29 Dave Cowens .25 .60
30 Brad Daugherty .30 .75
31 Bo Kimble .25 .60
32 John Salley .25 .60
33 Antoine Walker .30 .75
34 Stacey Augmon .25 .60
35 Danny Manning .30 .75
36 Jerry Stackhouse .30 .75
37 Jay Williams .25 .60
38 Shaquille O'Neal .75 2.00
39 Fat Lever .30 .75
40 Antonio McDyess .30 .75
41 Bobby Hurley .40 1.00
42 Pervis Ellison .25 .60
43 Bill Russell .60 1.50
44 Michael Jordan 3.00 8.00
45 Bill Walton .40 1.00
46 David Thompson .30 .75
47 Harold Miner .25 .60
48 Paul George .50 1.25
49 Keith Smart .40 1.00
50 Jerry West .50 1.25
51 Aaron Gordon 3.00 8.00
52 Adreian Payne 1.50 4.00
53 Sean Kilpatrick 2.50 6.00
54 C.J. Wilcox 1.25 3.00
55 Clint Capela 1.50 4.00
56 Alessandro Gentile 1.25 3.00
57 Dario Saric 3.00 8.00
58 Doug McDermott 2.00 5.00
59 Gary Harris 2.00 5.00
60 Glenn Robinson III 1.25 3.00
61 Jordan Adams 1.25 3.00
62 James Michael McAdoo 1.50 4.00
63 James Young 1.25 3.00
64 Thanasis Antetokounmpo 1.25 3.00
65 Kyle Anderson 2.00 5.00
66 Joe Harris 1.25 3.00
67 Josh Huestis 1.25 3.00
68 Elfrid Payton 2.00 5.00
69 Jusuf Nurkic 2.00 5.00
70 Shabazz Napier 1.50 4.00
71 Mitch McGary 1.25 3.00
72 Nik Stauskas 1.50 4.00
73 Nikola Mirotic 2.50 6.00
74 P.J. Hairston 1.25 3.00
75 Patric Young 1.25 3.00
76 Rodney Hood 2.00 5.00
77 T.J. Warren 2.00 5.00
78 DeAndre Daniels 1.25 3.00
79 Cleanthony Early 1.25 3.00
80 Zach LaVine 3.00 8.00

2014-15 Upper Deck Lettermen Blue

*BLUE 1-50: 1.2X TO 3X BASE HI
*BLUE 51-80: .5X TO 1.2X BASE HI
RANDOM INSERTS IN PACKS
STATED PRINT RUN B/WN 249-499 COPIES PER

2014-15 Upper Deck Lettermen Silver

*SILVER 51-80: .75X TO 2X BASE HI
RANDOM INSERTS IN PACKS
STATED PRINT RUN B/WN 15-99 COPIES PER
1-50 NO PRICING DUE TO SCARCITY

2014-15 Upper Deck Lettermen Autographs Blue

RANDOM INSERTS IN PACKS
EXCHANGE DEADLINE 11/13/2016
LACK OF PRICING DUE TO MARKET INFO
1 Allan Houston
2 James Worthy
3 Magic Johnson
4 Glenn Robinson 4.00 10.00
5 Jerry Lucas 5.00 12.00
6 Vinny Del Negro
7 A.C. Green 5.00 12.00
8 Elvin Hayes
9 Karl Malone 20.00 50.00
10 Kendall Gill 6.00 15.00
12 Christian Laettner 10.00 25.00
13 Hakeem Olajuwon
14 David Robinson
15 James Harden
16 Nick Van Exel 5.00 12.00
17 Sleepy Floyd
18 Stephen Curry
19 Sean Elliott 5.00 12.00
20 LeBron James 125.00 250.00
21 Joe Smith
22 Derek Harper 4.00 10.00
23 Julius Erving 25.00 60.00
24 Jamal Mashburn 5.00 12.00
25 Larry Bird
26 Alex English
27 Reggie Theus
28 Shane Battier 4.00 10.00
29 Dave Cowens
30 Brad Daugherty 8.00 20.00
31 Bo Kimble
32 John Salley
33 Antoine Walker 4.00 10.00
34 Stacey Augmon 15.00 40.00
35 Danny Manning
36 Jerry Stackhouse
37 Jay Williams
38 Shaquille O'Neal
39 Fat Lever
40 Antonio McDyess 4.00 10.00
41 Bobby Hurley 8.00 20.00
43 Bill Russell
44 Michael Jordan
45 Bill Walton 5.00 12.00
46 David Thompson
47 Harold Miner
48 Paul George
49 Keith Smart 5.00 12.00
50 Jerry West 15.00 40.00
51 Aaron Gordon 8.00 20.00
52 Adreian Payne 4.00 10.00
53 Sean Kilpatrick 6.00 15.00
54 C.J. Wilcox
55 Clint Capela
56 Alessandro Gentile 3.00 8.00
57 Dario Saric
58 Doug McDermott 8.00 20.00
59 Gary Harris 5.00 12.00
60 Glenn Robinson III
61 Jordan Adams 3.00 8.00
62 James Michael McAdoo 4.00 10.00
63 James Young
64 Thanasis Antetokounmpo 3.00 8.00
65 Kyle Anderson 12.00 30.00
66 Joe Harris 3.00 8.00
67 Josh Huestis 3.00 8.00
68 Elfrid Payton 5.00 12.00
69 Jusuf Nurkic 5.00 12.00
70 Shabazz Napier 12.00 30.00
71 Mitch McGary 3.00 8.00
72 Nik Stauskas 10.00 25.00
73 Nikola Mirotic 15.00 40.00
74 P.J. Hairston 3.00 8.00
75 Patric Young 3.00 8.00
76 Rodney Hood 5.00 12.00
77 T.J. Warren 4.00 10.00
78 DeAndre Daniels
79 Cleanthony Early
80 Zach LaVine 20.00 50.00

2014-15 Upper Deck Lettermen Championship Banners

RANDOM INSERTS IN PACKS
STATED PRINT RUN 50 SER.#'d SETS
CBBW Bill Walton 5.00 12.00
CBCL Christian Laettner 4.00 10.00
CBCW Corliss Williamson 3.00 8.00
CBDM Danny Manning 4.00 10.00
CBDT David Thompson 4.00 10.00
CBGH Grant Hill 6.00 15.00
CBHI Grant Hill 6.00 15.00
CBJA LeBron James 20.00 50.00
CBJL Jerry Lucas 5.00 12.00
CBJO Larry Johnson 6.00 15.00
CBJW James Worthy 6.00 15.00
CBKS Keith Smart 5.00 12.00
CBLE LeBron James 15.00 50.00
CBLJ LeBron James 15.00 40.00
CBMJ Michael Jordan 150.00 250.00
CBSN Shabazz Napier 12.00 30.00
CBSP Sam Perkins 3.00 8.00

2014-15 Upper Deck Lettermen Championship Banners Autographs

RANDOM INSERTS IN PACKS
STATED PRINT RUN B/WN 23-99 COPIES PER
EXCHANGE DEADLINE 11/13/2016
CBBW Bill Walton/99 8.00 20.00
CBCL Christian Laettner/99 15.00 40.00
CBCW Corliss Williamson/99
CBDM Danny Manning/99 12.00 30.00
CBDT David Thompson/99 15.00 40.00
CBGH Grant Hill/99 25.00 60.00
CBHI Grant Hill/99 25.00 60.00
CBJA LeBron James/23 150.00 250.00
CBJL Jerry Lucas/99 12.00 30.00
CBJO Larry Johnson/99 12.00 30.00
CBJW James Worthy/99 12.00 30.00
CBKS Keith Smart/99 8.00 20.00
CBLE LeBron James/23 150.00 250.00
CBLJ LeBron James/23 150.00 250.00
CBMJ Michael Jordan/23
CBSN Shabazz Napier/99 6.00 15.00
CBSP Sam Perkins/99 8.00 20.00

2014-15 Upper Deck Lettermen Home Court Stars

RANDOM INSERTS IN PACKS
HSAG Aaron Gordon 2.50 6.00
HSAH Anfernee Hardaway 4.00 10.00
HSAL Allan Houston 1.25 3.00
HSBW Bill Walton 1.50 4.00
HSDR David Robinson 2.50 6.00
HSGH Grant Hill 2.00 5.00
HSHO Hakeem Olajuwon 2.00 5.00
HSJA LeBron James 6.00 15.00
HSJE Julius Erving 2.50 6.00
HSJO Magic Johnson 4.00 10.00
HSJW James Worthy 2.00 5.00
HSLB Larry Bird 4.00 10.00
HSLJ Larry Johnson 2.00 5.00
HSMJ Michael Jordan 12.00 30.00
HSNS Nik Stauskas 1.25 3.00
HSSF Sleepy Floyd 1.00 2.50
HSSO Shaquille O'Neal 3.00 8.00
HSZL Zach LaVine 2.50 6.00

2014-15 Upper Deck Lettermen Home Court Stars Autographs

RANDOM INSERTS IN PACKS
LACK OF PRICING DUE TO MARKET INFO
EXCHANGE DEADLINE 11/13/2016
HS-AG Aaron Gordon 12.00 30.00
HSAH Anfernee Hardaway 20.00 50.00
HSAL Allan Houston 5.00 12.00
HSBW Bill Walton 6.00 15.00
HSJA LeBron James 150.00 250.00
HSNS Nik Stauskas 5.00 12.00
HSSF Sleepy Floyd 4.00 10.00
HSZL Zach LaVine 12.00 30.00

2014-15 Upper Deck Lettermen Legendary Letterman Autographs

RANDOM INSERTS IN PACKS
STATED PRINT RUN B/WN 9-245 COPIES PER
NO PRICING ON QTY 15 OR LESS
LACK OF PRICING DUE TO MARKET INFO
EXCHANGE DEADLINE 11/13/2016
LLAH Allan Houston/180 10.00 25.00
LLAM Antonio McDyess/175 8.00 20.00
LLBW Bill Walton/40
LLCL Christian Laettner/40 25.00 60.00
LLDH Derek Harper/200 8.00 20.00
LLDN Vinny Del Negro/70 8.00 20.00
LLDW Dominique Wilkins/21 12.00 30.00
LLEP Eric Piatkowski/200 6.00 15.00
LLHO Hakeem Olajuwon/21
LLJL Jerry Lucas/27 12.00 30.00
LLJO Michael Jordan/195 250.00 350.00
LLJS Jerry Stackhouse/195 12.00 30.00
LLKS Keith Smart/245 6.00 15.00
LLLJ LeBron James/75 200.00 300.00
LLLO Lute Olson/35 100.00 200.00
LLRI Doc Rivers/27 12.00 30.00

LLRT Reggie Theus/40 8.00 20.00
LLSA John Salley/33 12.00 30.00
LLSF Sleepy Floyd/100 6.00 15.00
LLSP Sam Perkins/195 15.00 40.00

2014-15 Upper Deck Lettermen Monumental Logo Patches

STATED PRINT RUN B/WN 210-300 COPIES PER
MLAG Aaron Gordon/15 10.00 25.00
MLBR Bill Russell/30 12.00 30.00
MLDR David Robinson/15 10.00 25.00
MLER Julius Erving/30 10.00 25.00
MLGH Grant Hill/15 12.00 30.00
MLHO Hakeem Olajuwon/15 15.00 40.00
MLJH James Harden/15 15.00 40.00
MLJO Michael Jordan/15 40.00 100.00
MLKM Karl Malone/15 20.00 50.00
MLLA Larry Johnson/15 12.00 30.00
MLLB Larry Bird/30 15.00 40.00
MLLJ LeBron James/15 25.00 60.00
MLSO Shaquille O'Neal/15 12.00 30.00
MLWO James Worthy/15 15.00 40.00

2014-15 Upper Deck Lettermen Retired Numbers

STATED PRINT RUN 72 SER.#'d SETS
RNBR Bill Russell 5.00 12.00
RNJA LeBron James 12.00 30.00
RNJE Julius Erving 5.00 12.00
RNJO Michael Jordan 30.00 80.00
RNKM Karl Malone 4.00 10.00
RNLB Larry Bird 12.00 30.00
RNMJ Magic Johnson 8.00 20.00
RNSO Shaquille O'Neal 10.00 25.00
RNWO James Worthy 4.00 10.00

2014-15 Upper Deck Lettermen Rookie Premier Letterman Autographs

RANDOM INSERTS IN PACKS
STATED PRINT RUN B/WN 120-350 COPIES PER
EXCHANGE DEADLINE 11/13/2016
RLAG Aaron Gordon/25 20.00 50.00
RLAP Adreian Payne/25 15.00 40.00
RLCC Clint Capela/35 15.00 40.00
RLCE Cleanthony Early/25 6.00 15.00
RLCW C.J. Wilcox/35 6.00 15.00
RLDD DeAndre Daniels/65 6.00 15.00
RLDM Doug McDermott/25 20.00 50.00
RLDS Dario Saric/50 30.00 80.00
RLEP Elfrid Payton/10 10.00 25.00
RLGE Alessandro Gentile/50 6.00 15.00
RLGH Gary Harris/10 25.00 60.00
RLGR Glenn Robinson III/35 6.00 15.00
RLHA Joe Harris/50 6.00 15.00
RLJA Jordan Adams/50 6.00 15.00
RLJH Josh Huestis/15 6.00 15.00
RLJM James Michael McAdoo/25 8.00 20.00
RLJN Jusuf Nurkic/35 10.00 25.00
RLJY James Young/35 20.00 50.00
RLKA Kyle Anderson/50 15.00 40.00
RLMC Jordan McRae/35 6.00 15.00
RLMM Mitch McGary/35 15.00 40.00
RLNS Nik Stauskas/35 8.00 20.00
RLPH P.J. Hairston/25 6.00 15.00
RLPY Patric Young/50 6.00 15.00
RLRH Rodney Hood/75 15.00 40.00
RLSK Sean Kilpatrick/35 8.00 20.00
RLSN Shabazz Napier/50 8.00 20.00
RLTA Thanasis Antetokounmpo/50 6.00 15.00
RLTW T.J. Warren/35 10.00 25.00
RLZL Zach LaVine/50 25.00 60.00

2008-09 Upper Deck Lineage

This set was released on April 1, 2009. The base set consists of 233 cards. Cards 1-200 feature veterans, and cards 201-233 are rookies.

COMP.SET w/o RCs (200) 20.00 40.00
1 Bill Russell .50 1.25
2 Sam Jones .40 1.00
3 Oscar Robertson .30 .75
4 Kareem Abdul-Jabbar .50 1.25
5 Julius Erving .50 1.25
6 George Gervin .40 1.00
7 Bill Walton .30 .75
8 Robert Parish .30 .75
9 Larry Bird .75 2.00
10 Magic Johnson .75 2.00
11 Isiah Thomas .30 .75
12 James Worthy .30 .75
13 Dominique Wilkins .40 1.00
14 Clyde Drexler .40 1.00
15 John Stockton .50 1.25
16 Hakeem Olajuwon .40 1.00
17 Michael Jordan 2.50 6.00
18 Tom Chambers .25 .60
19 Adrian Dantley .25 .60
20 David Robinson .50 1.25
21 Shaquille O'Neal .60 1.50
22 Alonzo Mourning .40 1.00
23 Jason Kidd .30 .75
24 Grant Hill .40 1.00
25 Rasheed Wallace .30 .75
26 Kevin Garnett .50 1.25
27 Bruce Bowen .20 .50
28 Steve Nash .30 .75
29 Marcus Camby .20 .50
30 Derek Fisher .25 .60
31 Ben Wallace .25 .60
32 Allen Iverson .40 1.00
33 Ray Allen .30 .75
34 Brad Miller .25 .60
35 Kobe Bryant 1.25 3.00
36 Jermaine O'Neal .25 .60
37 Tim Duncan .50 1.25
38 Chauncey Billups .30 .75
39 Tracy McGrady .30 .75
40 Zydrunas Ilgauskas .25 .60
41 Javaris Crittenton .20 .50
42 Antawn Jamison .25 .60
43 Vince Carter .40 1.00
44 Peja Stojakovic .30 .75
45 Paul Pierce .30 .75
46 Mike Bibby .25 .60
47 Dirk Nowitzki .40 1.00
48 Rashard Lewis .25 .60
49 Al Harrington .25 .60
50 Andre Miller .25 .60
51 Wally Szczerbiak .25 .60
52 Jason Terry .25 .60
53 Richard Hamilton .25 .60
54 Shawn Marion .25 .60
55 Elton Brand .30 .75
56 Baron Davis .25 .60
57 Lamar Odom .25 .60
58 Corey Maggette .25 .60
59 Ron Artest .30 .75
60 Morris Peterson .20 .50
61 Desmond Mason .20 .50
62 Kenyon Martin .25 .60
63 Stephen Jackson .25 .60
64 Hedo Turkoglu .25 .60
65 Michael Redd .25 .60
66 Mike Miller .25 .60
67 Jamal Crawford .30 .75
68 Quentin Richardson .25 .60
69 Keyon Dooling .20 .50
70 DeShawn Stevenson .20 .50
71 Jamaal Tinsley .20 .50
72 Shane Battier .25 .60
73 Earl Watson .20 .50
74 Richard Jefferson .25 .60
75 Pau Gasol .30 .75
76 Jason Richardson .30 .75
77 Andrei Kirilenko .25 .60
78 Joe Johnson .25 .60
79 Zach Randolph .25 .60
80 Gilbert Arenas .25 .60
81 Tony Parker .30 .75
82 Gerald Wallace .25 .60
83 Tyson Chandler .25 .60
84 Eddy Curry .20 .50
85 Manu Ginobili .30 .75
86 Marko Jaric .20 .50
87 Mehmet Okur .20 .50
88 John Salmons .25 .60
89 Tayshaun Prince .25 .60
90 Caron Butler .25 .60
91 Yao Ming .40 1.00
92 Mike Dunleavy .25 .60
93 Samuel Dalembert .20 .50
94 Carlos Boozer .25 .60
95 Chris Wilcox .20 .50
96 Nene .25 .60
97 Amare Stoudemire .25 .60
98 Steve Blake .20 .50
99 Luke Walton .20 .50
100 Josh Howard .25 .60
101 Keith Bogans .20 .50
102 Udonis Haslem .20 .50
103 David West .25 .60
104 Kirk Hinrich .25 .60
105 Kyle Korver .25 .60
106 Willie Green .20 .50
107 Dwyane Wade .50 1.25
108 Boris Diaw .25 .60
109 Chris Kaman .25 .60
110 Leandro Barbosa .25 .60
111 Mo Williams .25 .60
112 Chris Bosh .30 .75
113 Carmelo Anthony .40 1.00
114 Kendrick Perkins .20 .50
115 LeBron James 1.25 3.00
116 Andres Nocioni .20 .50
117 Damien Wilkins .20 .50
118 Jameer Nelson .20 .50
119 Beno Udrih .20 .50
120 Chris Duhon .20 .50
121 Anderson Varejao .20 .50
122 Emeka Okafor .25 .60
123 Kevin Martin .25 .60
124 Devin Harris .20 .50
125 T.J. Ford .20 .50
126 Ben Gordon .25 .60
127 Andre Iguodala .25 .60
128 Sasha Vujacic .20 .50
129 Al Jefferson .25 .60
130 Luol Deng .25 .60
131 J.R. Smith .25 .60
132 Josh Smith .25 .60
133 Dwight Howard .25 .60
134 Fabricio Oberto .20 .50
135 Jose Calderon .20 .50
136 Francisco Garcia .20 .50
137 Hakim Warrick .25 .60
138 Luther Head .20 .50
139 Jason Maxiell .20 .50
140 Danny Granger .25 .60
141 David Lee .20 .50
142 Chuck Hayes .20 .50
143 Jarrett Jack .25 .60
144 Raymond Felton .25 .60
145 Deron Williams .25 .60
146 Rashad McCants .20 .50
147 Andrew Bogut .25 .60
148 Brandon Bass .20 .50
149 Chris Paul .40 1.00
150 Shaun Livingston .20 .50
151 Monta Ellis .25 .60
152 Marvin Williams .25 .60
153 Louis Williams .25 .60
154 Martell Webster .25 .60
155 Andrew Bynum .20 .50
156 Randy Foye .30 .75
157 Shelden Williams .20 .50
158 Leon Powe .20 .50
159 Rodney Carney .20 .50
160 Jose Barea .40 1.00
161 Brandon Roy .30 .75
162 Josh Boone .20 .50
163 Ronnie Brewer .25 .60
164 LaMarcus Aldridge .30 .75
165 Andrea Bargnani .25 .60
166 Rajon Rondo .30 .75
167 Daniel Gibson .25 .60
168 Kyle Lowry .30 .75
169 Sergio Rodriguez .20 .50
170 Tyrus Thomas .20 .50
171 Rudy Gay .30 .75
172 Jordan Farmar .20 .50
173 Luis Scola .25 .60
174 Jamario Moon .20 .50
175 Carl Landry .20 .50
176 Al Thornton .25 .60
177 C.J. Watson .20 .50
178 Adam Morrison .20 .50
179 Acie Law .25 .60
180 Morris Almond .20 .50
181 Joakim Noah .25 .60
182 Nick Young .25 .60
183 Arron Afflalo .20 .50
184 Jared Dudley .25 .60
185 Glen Davis .20 .50
186 Corey Brewer .25 .60
187 Marco Belinelli .20 .50
188 Ramon Sessions .25 .60
189 Rodney Stuckey .25 .60
190 Al Horford .30 .75
191 Jeff Green .25 .60
192 Sean Williams .25 .60
193 Daequan Cook .20 .50
194 Julian Wright .25 .60
195 Brandan Wright .25 .60
196 Mike Conley Jr. .25 .60
197 Yi Jianlian .30 .75
198 Thaddeus Young .25 .60
199 Kevin Durant .75 2.00
200 Greg Oden .25 .60
201 Derrick Rose RC 3.00 8.00
202 Michael Beasley RC .75 2.00
203 O.J. Mayo RC .75 2.00
204 Russell Westbrook RC 8.00 20.00
205 Kevin Love RC 2.50 6.00
206 Danilo Gallinari RC 1.25 3.00
207 Eric Gordon RC 1.25 3.00
208 Joe Alexander RC .50 1.25
209 D.J. Augustin RC .60 1.50
210 Brook Lopez RC 1.00 2.50
211 Jerryd Bayless RC .60 1.50
212 Jason Thompson RC .50 1.25
213 Brandon Rush RC .60 1.50
214 Anthony Randolph RC .50 1.25
215 Robin Lopez RC .75 2.00
216 Marreese Speights RC .60 1.50
217 Roy Hibbert RC .75 2.00
218 J.J. Hickson RC .60 1.50
219 Ryan Anderson RC .60 1.50
220 George Hill RC .75 2.00
221 Darrell Arthur RC .60 1.50
222 Donte Greene RC .50 1.25
223 D.J. White RC .60 1.50
224 J.R. Giddens RC .50 1.25
225 Walter Sharpe RC .50 1.25
226 Mario Chalmers RC .75 2.00
227 Sonny Weems RC .50 1.25
228 Chris Douglas-Roberts RC .50 1.25
229 Sean Singletary RC .50 1.25
230 Luc Richard Mbah A Moute RC .60 1.50
231 Bill Walker RC .50 1.25
232 Marc Gasol RC 1.50 4.00
233 Rudy Fernandez RC .60 1.50

2008-09 Upper Deck Lineage SE

*1-200 VETS: 1.25X TO 3X BASE HI
*201-233 ROOKIES: .6X TO 1.5X BASE HI
RANDOM INSERTS IN PACKS

2008-09 Upper Deck Lineage 15,000 Point Club

COMBINED AUTO ODDS 1:12
15AD Adrian Dantley 6.00 15.00
15AE Alex English 6.00 15.00
15AG Artis Gilmore 6.00 15.00
15BA Rick Barry 10.00 25.00
15GG George Gervin 8.00 20.00
15GR Glen Rice 6.00 15.00
15HO Hakeem Olajuwon 10.00 25.00
15KA Kareem Abdul-Jabbar 40.00 100.00
15KG Kevin Garnett 40.00 75.00
15MJ Michael Jordan 300.00 500.00
15RP Robert Parish 6.00 15.00
15SJ Sam Jones 10.00 25.00
15TC Tom Chambers 6.00 15.00
15VC Vince Carter 30.00 60.00

2008-09 Upper Deck Lineage Collection

COMBINED AUTO ODDS 1:12
LCAD Adrian Dantley 5.00 12.00
LCAM Alonzo Mourning 150.00 300.00
LCBA B.J. Armstrong 6.00 15.00
LCBD Brad Daugherty 6.00 15.00
LCDR David Robinson 40.00 100.00
LCGR Glen Rice 6.00 15.00
LCHG Horace Grant 20.00 50.00
LCHO Hakeem Olajuwon 25.00 60.00
LCIT Isiah Thomas 10.00 25.00
LCJO Michael Jordan 300.00 500.00
LCJS John Stockton 125.00 250.00
LCMB Muggsy Bogues 6.00 15.00
LCME Mark Eaton 5.00 12.00
LCMJ Magic Johnson 30.00 60.00
LCMM Moses Malone 8.00 20.00
LCMP Mark Price 12.00 30.00
LCSA John Salley 6.00 15.00
LCSP Sam Perkins 8.00 20.00
LCSW Spud Webb 6.00 15.00
LCTC Terry Cummings 5.00 12.00
LCTO Tom Chambers 5.00 12.00
LCVD Vlade Divac 6.00 15.00

2008-09 Upper Deck Lineage Flight Team

COMBINED AUTO ODDS 1:12
FTAI Andre Iguodala 6.00 15.00
FTAT Al Thornton 8.00 20.00
FTBD Baron Davis 15.00 30.00
FTDH Dwight Howard 20.00 40.00
FTDM Desmond Mason 5.00 12.00
FTDS DeShawn Stevenson 5.00 12.00
FTGG Gerald Green 5.00 12.00
FTJA Joe Alexander 5.00 12.00
FTJR J.R. Giddens 5.00 12.00
FTKB Kobe Bryant 100.00 200.00
FTLJ LeBron James 125.00 250.00
FTLM Luc Richard Mbah A Moute 5.00 12.00
FTRG Rudy Gay 6.00 15.00
FTRJ Richard Jefferson 5.00 12.00
FTSM J.R. Smith 8.00 20.00
FTSW Sean Williams 5.00 12.00
FTTP Tayshaun Prince 5.00 12.00
FTWE Sonny Weems 5.00 12.00

2008-09 Upper Deck Lineage Mr. June

COMPLETE SET (23) 30.00 60.00
COMMON CARD 1.50 4.00

2008-09 Upper Deck Lineage Rookie Standouts

COMPLETE SET (54) 30.00 60.00
RANDOM INSERTS IN PACKS
RS1 Derrick Rose 3.00 8.00
RS2 Michael Beasley .75 2.00
RS3 O.J. Mayo .75 2.00
RS4 Russell Westbrook 6.00 15.00
RS5 Kevin Love 2.50 6.00
RS6 Danilo Gallinari 1.25 3.00
RS7 Eric Gordon 1.25 3.00
RS8 Joe Alexander .50 1.25
RS9 D.J. Augustin .60 1.50
RS10 Brook Lopez 1.00 2.50
RS11 Jerryd Bayless .60 1.50
RS12 Jason Thompson .50 1.25
RS13 Brandon Rush .60 1.50
RS14 Anthony Randolph .50 1.25
RS15 Robin Lopez .75 2.00
RS16 Marreese Speights .60 1.50
RS17 Roy Hibbert .75 2.00
RS18 Luc Richard Mbah A Moute .60 1.50
RS19 Mario Chalmers .75 2.00
RS20 Javale McGee 1.00 2.50
RS21 Anthony Morrow .75 2.00
RS22 Darrell Arthur .60 1.50
RS23 Nicolas Batum 1.00 2.50
RS24 Ryan Anderson .60 1.50
RS25 Bobby Brown .50 1.25
RS26 J.J. Hickson .60 1.50
RS27 Sun Yue 1.00 2.50
RS28 DeMarcus Nelson .50 1.25
RS29 Courtney Lee .60 1.50
RS30 Kosta Koufos .60 1.50
RS31 Donte Greene .50 1.25
RS32 Mike Taylor .50 1.25
RS33 Roko Leni Ukic .75 2.00
RS34 Anthony Tolliver .50 1.25
RS35 Darnell Jackson .50 1.25
RS36 Alexis Ajinca .50 1.25
RS37 Goran Dragic 20.00 50.00
RS38 Chris Douglas-Roberts .50 1.25
RS39 Sean Singletary .50 1.25
RS40 Kyle Weaver .50 1.25
RS41 Bill Walker .50 1.25
RS42 DeAndre Jordan 1.00 2.50
RS43 Rob Kurz .50 1.25
RS44 Rudy Fernandez .60 1.50
RS45 George Hill .75 2.00
RS46 Greg Oden .60 1.50
RS47 Marc Gasol 1.50 4.00
RS48 Louis Amundson .50 1.25
RS49 Nathan Jawai .75 2.00
RS50 Othello Hunter .75 2.00
RS51 Walter Sharpe .50 1.25
RS52 Joey Dorsey .50 1.25
RS53 J.R. Giddens .50 1.25
RS54 Jawad Williams .75 2.00

2008-09 Upper Deck Lineage SE Die Cut Autographs

COMBINED AUTO ODDS 1:12
2 Sam Jones 15.00 40.00
3 Oscar Robertson 50.00 125.00
4 Kareem Abdul-Jabbar 40.00 80.00
5 Julius Erving 50.00 120.00
6 George Gervin 8.00 20.00
8 Robert Parish 6.00 15.00
10 Magic Johnson 30.00 80.00
12 James Worthy 40.00 80.00
13 Dominique Wilkins 40.00 100.00
17 Michael Jordan 350.00 550.00
18 Tom Chambers 5.00 12.00
19 Adrian Dantley 4.00 10.00
20 David Robinson 50.00 125.00
23 Jason Kidd 20.00 50.00
26 Kevin Garnett 50.00 100.00
27 Bruce Bowen 4.00 10.00
28 Steve Nash 30.00 60.00
30 Derek Fisher 6.00 15.00
33 Ray Allen 20.00 40.00
36 Jermaine O'Neal 12.00 30.00
38 Chauncey Billups 8.00 20.00
41 Javaris Crittenton 4.00 10.00
43 Vince Carter 30.00 60.00
45 Paul Pierce 30.00 60.00
49 Al Harrington 4.00 10.00
57 Lamar Odom 6.00 15.00
58 Corey Maggette 6.00 15.00
59 Ron Artest 6.00 15.00
65 Michael Redd 4.00 10.00
68 Quentin Richardson 4.00 10.00
74 Richard Jefferson 4.00 10.00
78 Joe Johnson 6.00 15.00
84 Eddy Curry 4.00 10.00
89 Tayshaun Prince 4.00 10.00
90 Caron Butler 15.00 40.00
94 Carlos Boozer 5.00 12.00
97 Amare Stoudemire 15.00 30.00
100 Josh Howard 20.00 50.00
103 David West 4.00 10.00
105 Kyle Korver 4.00 10.00
108 Boris Diaw 4.00 10.00
109 Chris Kaman 4.00 10.00
110 Leandro Barbosa 4.00 10.00
112 Chris Bosh 20.00 40.00
115 LeBron James 200.00 325.00
118 Jameer Nelson 4.00 10.00
119 Beno Udrih 4.00 10.00
120 Chris Duhon 4.00 10.00
121 Anderson Varejao 5.00 12.00
126 Ben Gordon 6.00 15.00
127 Andre Iguodala 6.00 15.00
128 Sasha Vujacic 6.00 15.00
129 Al Jefferson 5.00 12.00
130 Luol Deng 4.00 10.00
131 J.R. Smith 6.00 15.00
133 Dwight Howard 20.00 40.00
136 Francisco Garcia 4.00 10.00
139 Jason Maxiell 4.00 10.00
140 Danny Granger 6.00 15.00
141 David Lee 6.00 15.00
143 Jarrett Jack 4.00 10.00
144 Raymond Felton 4.00 10.00
145 Deron Williams 8.00 20.00
148 Brandon Bass 4.00 10.00
149 Chris Paul 40.00 100.00
150 Shaun Livingston 4.00 10.00
152 Marvin Williams 4.00 10.00
153 Louis Williams 4.00 10.00
155 Andrew Bynum 20.00 40.00
156 Randy Foye 4.00 10.00
157 Shelden Williams 4.00 10.00
161 Brandon Roy 10.00 25.00
162 Josh Boone 4.00 10.00
163 Ronnie Brewer 5.00 12.00
165 Andrea Bargnani 5.00 12.00
166 Rajon Rondo 8.00 20.00
167 Daniel Gibson 6.00 15.00
168 Kyle Lowry 4.00 10.00
170 Tyrus Thomas 8.00 20.00
171 Rudy Gay 5.00 12.00
172 Jordan Farmar 6.00 15.00
173 Luis Scola 4.00 10.00
175 Carl Landry 4.00 10.00
176 Al Thornton 6.00 15.00
180 Morris Almond 4.00 10.00
183 Arron Afflalo 4.00 10.00
184 Jared Dudley 4.00 10.00
185 Glen Davis 6.00 15.00
188 Ramon Sessions 5.00 12.00
189 Rodney Stuckey 6.00 15.00
191 Jeff Green 6.00 15.00
192 Sean Williams 4.00 10.00
193 Daequan Cook 4.00 10.00
194 Julian Wright 4.00 10.00
199 Kevin Durant 100.00 200.00
201 Derrick Rose 100.00 200.00
203 O.J. Mayo 10.00 25.00
204 Russell Westbrook 75.00 150.00
205 Kevin Love 40.00 100.00
206 Danilo Gallinari 10.00 25.00
207 Eric Gordon 15.00 40.00
208 Joe Alexander 3.00 8.00
209 D.J. Augustin 4.00 10.00
210 Brook Lopez 6.00 15.00
211 Jerryd Bayless 4.00 10.00
212 Jason Thompson 3.00 8.00
213 Brandon Rush 4.00 10.00
214 Anthony Randolph 10.00 25.00
215 Robin Lopez 5.00 12.00
216 Marreese Speights 4.00 10.00
217 Roy Hibbert 5.00 12.00
218 J.J. Hickson 4.00 10.00
219 Ryan Anderson 4.00 10.00
220 George Hill 5.00 12.00
221 Darrell Arthur 4.00 10.00
222 Donte Greene 3.00 8.00
223 D.J. White 4.00 10.00
224 J.R. Giddens 3.00 8.00
225 Walter Sharpe 3.00 8.00
226 Mario Chalmers 5.00 12.00
227 Sonny Weems 3.00 8.00
228 Chris Douglas-Roberts 3.00 8.00
229 Sean Singletary 5.00 12.00
230 Luc Richard Mbah A Moute 5.00 12.00
231 Bill Walker 10.00 25.00
233 Rudy Fernandez 10.00 25.00

2014-15 Upper Deck March Madness Collection

STATED SP ODDS 1:1 PACK
AC1 A.C. Green 2.00 5.00
AC2 A.C. Green SP 2.00 5.00
AE1 Alex English SP 1.50 4.00
AG1 Aaron Gordon 3.00 8.00
AH1 Anfernee Hardaway 3.00 8.00
AH2 Anfernee Hardaway SP 3.00 8.00
AI1 Allen Iverson 2.50 6.00
AI2 Allen Iverson 2.50 6.00
AI3 Allen Iverson SP 2.50 6.00
AI4 Allen Iverson SP 2.50 6.00
AM1 Alonzo Mourning 2.50 6.00
AM2 Alonzo Mourning SP 2.50 6.00
AN1 Antonio McDyess 1.50 4.00
AN2 Antonio McDyess 1.50 4.00
AP1 Adreian Payne 1.50 4.00
AW1 Antoine Walker 1.50 4.00
AW2 Antoine Walker SP 1.50 4.00
AW3 Antoine Walker SP 1.50 4.00
BD1 Brad Daugherty 1.50 4.00
BD2 Brad Daugherty 1.50 4.00
BD3 Brad Daugherty SP 1.50 4.00
BD4 Brad Daugherty SP 1.50 4.00
BH1 Bobby Hurley 2.00 5.00
BH2 Bobby Hurley SP 2.00 5.00
BH3 Bobby Hurley SP 2.00 5.00
BK1 Bo Kimble 1.25 3.00
BL1 Bill Laimbeer 1.50 4.00
BL2 Bill Laimbeer SP 1.50 4.00
BO1 Bo Outlaw 1.25 3.00
BR1 Bill Russell SP 3.00 8.00
BR2 Bill Russell SP 3.00 8.00
BU1 Buck Williams 1.25 3.00
BW1 Bill Walton 2.00 5.00
BW2 Bill Walton 2.00 5.00
BW3 Bill Walton SP 2.00 5.00
BW4 Bill Walton SP 2.00 5.00
BY1 Byron Scott 1.50 4.00
CC1 Calbert Cheaney 1.25 3.00
CC2 Calbert Cheaney 1.25 3.00
CC3 Calbert Cheaney SP 1.25 3.00
CE1 Cleanthony Early SP 1.25 3.00
CL1 Christian Laettner 1.50 4.00
CL2 Christian Laettner 1.50 4.00
CL3 Christian Laettner 1.50 4.00
CL4 Christian Laettner SP 1.50 4.00
CL5 Christian Laettner SP 1.50 4.00
CL6 Christian Laettner SP 1.50 4.00
CM1 Cheryl Miller 2.00 5.00
CM2 Cheryl Miller SP 2.00 5.00
CW1 Corliss Williamson 1.25 3.00
CW2 Corliss Williamson SP 1.25 3.00
DC1 Dave Cowens SP 1.25 3.00
DD1 DeAndre Daniels 1.25 3.00
DH1 Derek Harper 1.50 4.00
DH2 Derek Harper SP 1.50 4.00
DM1 Danny Manning 1.50 4.00
DM2 Danny Manning 1.50 4.00
DM3 Danny Manning SP 1.50 4.00
DM4 Danny Manning SP 1.50 4.00
DM5 Danny Manning SP 1.50 4.00
DO1 Doc Rivers SP 2.00 5.00
DR1 David Robinson 3.00 8.00
DR2 David Robinson SP 3.00 8.00
DR3 David Robinson SP 3.00 8.00
DS1 Detlef Schrempf 2.00 5.00
DT1 David Thompson 1.50 4.00
DT2 David Thompson 1.50 4.00
DT3 David Thompson SP 1.50 4.00
EH1 Elvin Hayes 2.00 5.00
EH2 Elvin Hayes 2.00 5.00
EP1 Eric Piatkowski 1.25 3.00
FL1 Fat Lever SP 1.50 4.00
GH1 Gary Harris SP 2.00 5.00
GH1 Grant Hill 2.50 6.00
GH2 Grant Hill 2.50 6.00
GH3 Grant Hill SP 2.50 6.00
GH4 Grant Hill SP 2.50 6.00
GH5 Grant Hill SP 2.50 6.00
GH6 Grant Hill SP 2.50 6.00
GH7 Grant Hill SP 2.50 6.00
GL1 Glenn Robinson 1.50 4.00
GL2 Glenn Robinson SP 1.50 4.00
GN1 Glenn Robinson III SP 1.25 3.00
GR1 Glen Rice 1.50 4.00
GR2 Glen Rice SP 1.50 4.00
GR3 Glen Rice SP 1.50 4.00
HA1 James Harden 3.00 8.00
HG1 Horace Grant SP 2.00 5.00
HM1 Harold Miner 1.25 3.00
HM2 Harold Miner SP 1.25 3.00
JA1 Jordan Adams 1.25 3.00
JH1 John Havlicek 2.50 6.00
JH2 John Havlicek SP 2.50 6.00
JH3 John Havlicek SP 2.50 6.00
JK1 Jason Kidd 2.00 5.00
JK2 Jason Kidd SP 2.00 5.00
JL1 Jerry Lucas 2.00 5.00
JL2 Jerry Lucas 2.00 5.00
JL3 Jerry Lucas SP 2.00 5.00
JM1 Jamal Mashburn 2.00 5.00
JM2 Jamal Mashburn 2.00 5.00
JM3 Jamal Mashburn SP 2.00 5.00
JS1 Jerry Stackhouse 1.50 4.00
JS2 Jerry Stackhouse 1.50 4.00
JS3 Jerry Stackhouse SP 1.50 4.00
JT1 Jerry Tarkanian SP 2.00 5.00
JT2 Jerry Tarkanian SP 2.00 5.00
JV1 Jim Valvano SP 1.50 4.00
JV2 Jim Valvano SP 1.50 4.00
JW1 Jerry West 2.50 6.00
JW2 Jerry West 2.50 6.00
JW3 Jerry West SP 2.50 6.00
JY1 James Young 1.25 3.00
KA1 Kenny Anderson 1.50 4.00
KG1 Kendall Gill 1.25 3.00
KG2 Kendall Gill SP 1.25 3.00
KS1 Keith Smart SP 2.00 5.00
KS2 Keith Smart SP 2.00 5.00
KY1 Kyle Anderson 2.00 5.00
LB1 Larry Bird 3.00 8.00
LB2 Larry Bird 3.00 8.00
LB3 Larry Bird SP 3.00 8.00
LE1 LaPhonso Ellis SP 1.25 3.00
LJ1 Larry Johnson 2.50 6.00
LJ2 Larry Johnson 2.50 6.00
LJ3 Larry Johnson SP 2.50 6.00
LO1 Lute Olson 2.00 5.00
LS1 Lonnie Shelton 1.25 3.00
MA1 Donyell Marshall 1.25 3.00
MA2 Donyell Marshall SP 1.25 3.00
MC1 Doug McDermott SP 2.00 5.00
MG1 Magic Johnson 3.00 8.00
MG2 Magic Johnson 3.00 8.00
MG3 Magic Johnson SP 3.00 8.00
MG4 Magic Johnson SP 3.00 8.00
MJ1 Michael Jordan 3.00 8.00
MJ2 Michael Jordan 3.00 8.00
MJ3 Michael Jordan 3.00 8.00
MJ4 Michael Jordan SP 3.00 8.00
MJ5 Michael Jordan SP 3.00 8.00
MJ6 Michael Jordan SP 3.00 8.00
MJ7 Michael Jordan SP 3.00 8.00
MM1 Mitch McGary SP 1.25 3.00
MR1 Micheal Ray Richardson 1.50 4.00
NA1 Swen Nater SP 1.25 3.00
NE1 Nick Van Exel 2.00 5.00
NE2 Nick Van Exel SP 2.00 5.00
NS1 Nik Stauskas SP 1.50 4.00
PA1 Elfrid Payton SP 2.00 5.00
PE1 Pervis Ellison 1.25 3.00
PE2 Pervis Ellison 1.25 3.00
PE3 Pervis Ellison SP 1.25 3.00
PY1 Patric Young 1.25 3.00
RE1 Bryant Reeves SP 1.25 3.00
RH1 Robert Horry 1.50 4.00
RH2 Robert Horry SP 1.50 4.00
RR1 Rajon Rondo 2.00 5.00
RR2 Rajon Rondo SP 2.00 5.00
RT1 Reggie Theus 1.50 4.00
RT2 Reggie Theus SP 1.50 4.00
SA1 John Salley 1.25 3.00
SA2 John Salley SP 1.25 3.00
SB1 Shane Battier 1.50 4.00
SB2 Shane Battier 1.50 4.00
SB3 Shane Battier SP 1.50 4.00
SB4 Shane Battier SP 1.50 4.00
SB5 Shane Battier SP 1.50 4.00
SC1 Stephen Curry 8.00 20.00
SC2 Stephen Curry SP 8.00 20.00
SE1 Sean Elliott 2.00 5.00
SE2 Sean Elliott SP 2.00 5.00
SE3 Sean Elliott SP 2.00 5.00
SF1 Sleepy Floyd SP 1.25 3.00
SK1 Sean Kilpatrick 2.50 6.00
SM1 Joe Smith 1.50 4.00
SM2 Joe Smith 1.50 4.00
SM3 Joe Smith SP 1.50 4.00
SN1 Shabazz Napier 1.50 4.00
SN2 Shabazz Napier SP 1.50 4.00
SO1 Shaquille O'Neal 2.00 5.00
SO2 Shaquille O'Neal 2.00 5.00
SO3 Shaquille O'Neal SP 2.00 5.00
SP1 Sam Perkins 1.25 3.00
SP2 Sam Perkins SP 1.25 3.00
SP3 Sam Perkins SP 1.25 3.00
ST1 Stacey Augmon 1.25 3.00
ST2 Stacey Augmon 1.25 3.00
ST3 Stacey Augmon SP 1.25 3.00
SW1 Spud Webb 1.50 4.00
TH1 Tim Hardaway 2.00 5.00
TW1 T.J. Warren SP 2.00 5.00
VN1 Vinny Del Negro 1.50 4.00
VN2 Vinny Del Negro SP 1.50 4.00
WI1 Jay Williams 1.25 3.00
WI2 Jay Williams 1.25 3.00
WI3 Jay Williams SP 1.25 3.00
WO1 James Worthy 2.50 6.00
WO2 James Worthy 2.50 6.00
WO3 James Worthy SP 2.50 6.00
ZL1 Zach LaVine SP 3.00 8.00

2014-15 Upper Deck March Madness Collection Sepia

*SEPIA: .8X TO 2X BASE HI
STATED ODDS 1:6 PACKS

2014-15 Upper Deck March Madness Collection Autographs Exclusives

OVERALL ODDS 1:144 PACKS
GROUP A ODDS 1:24,192 PACKS
GROUP B ODDS 1:3,456 PACKS
GROUP C ODDS 1:1,613 PACKS
GROUP D ODDS 1:453 PACKS
GROUP E ODDS 1:233 PACKS
EXCHANGE DEADLINE 1/8/2017
KAA Kenny Anderson E 3.00 8.00
SPA Sam Perkins E 12.00 30.00
STA Stacey Augmon D 3.00 8.00

2014-15 Upper Deck March Madness Collection Bracketology

STATED ODDS 1:4 PACKS
AR Arkansas Razorbacks 3.00 8.00
AW Arizona Wildcats 3.00 10.00
AZ Akron Zips 3.00 8.00
BB Belmont Bruins 3.00 8.00
BE Baylor Bears 3.00 8.00
BF Colorado Buffaloes 3.00 8.00
BI Cornell Big Red 3.00 8.00
BU Bulter Bulldogs 3.00 10.00
C4 Charlotte 49ers 3.00 8.00
CB Cincinnati Bearcats 3.00 8.00
CB Creighton Bluejays 3.00 8.00
CH Connecticut Huskies 3.00 10.00
CT Clemson Tigers 3.00 8.00
DD Drexel Dragons 3.00 8.00
DW Davidson Wildcats 3.00 8.00
EC East Carolina Pirates 3.00 8.00
FG Florida Gators 3.00 8.00
GH Georgetown Hoyas 3.00 10.00
GW George Washington Colonials 3.00 8.00
IH Indiana Hoosiers 3.00 8.00
IH Iowa Hawkeyes 3.00 8.00
KJ Kansas Jayhawks 8.00 20.00
KW Kentucky Wildcats 20.00 50.00
LC Louisville Cardinals 3.00 8.00
MH Miami Hurricanes 3.00 8.00
MR Mississippi Rebels 3.00 10.00
MT Memphis Tigers 3.00 8.00
MW Michigan Wolverines 3.00 8.00
ND Notre Dame Fighting Irish 3.00 10.00
NW Northwestern Wildcats 3.00 8.00
OB Ohio Bobcats 3.00 8.00
OD Oregon Ducks 3.00 8.00
OS Oklahoma Sooners 3.00 8.00
PB Purdue Boilermakers 3.00 8.00
PF Providence Friars 3.00 8.00
PP Pittsburgh Panthers 3.00 10.00
RS Richmond Spiders 3.00 8.00
SO Syracuse Orange 3.00 8.00
TL Texas Longhorns 3.00 8.00
TO Temple Owls 3.00 8.00
TV Tennessee Volunteers 3.00 8.00
UB UCLA Bruins 3.00 10.00
UR UNLV Rebels 3.00 10.00
VC Virginia Cavaliers 6.00 15.00
VR VCU Rams 3.00 10.00
VW Villanova Wildcats 6.00 15.00
WB Wisconsin Badgers 10.00 25.00
WC Wildcard 50.00 120.00
WH Washington Huskies 3.00 8.00
ACT Alabama Crimson Tide 3.00 8.00
ASS Arizona State Sun Devils 3.00 8.00
BCE Boston College Eagles 3.00 8.00
BSB Boise State Broncos 3.00 10.00
BYU BYU Cougars 3.00 8.00
CFK Central Florida Knights 3.00 8.00
CGB California Golden Bears 3.00 8.00
DBD Duke Blue Devils 20.00 50.00
FSB Fresno State Bulldogs 3.00 8.00
FSS Florida State Seminoles 3.00 8.00
GB1 Gonzaga Bulldogs 3.00 10.00
GB2 Georgia Bulldogs 3.00 8.00
GMP George Mason Patriots 3.00 8.00
GTY Georgia Tech Yellow Jackets 3.00 8.00
IFI Illinois Fighting Illini 3.00 8.00
ISC Iowa State Cyclones 3.00 10.00
KSW Kansas State Wildcats 3.00 10.00
LSU LSU Tigers 3.00 8.00
MGE Marquette Golden Eagles 3.00 8.00
MGG Minnesota Golden Gophers 3.00 8.00
MSS Michigan State Spartans 3.00 10.00
MTE Maryland Terrapins 3.00 8.00
MTI Missouri Tigers 3.00 8.00
MTS Middle Tennessee State Blue Raiders 3.00 8.00
NCS North Carolina State Wolfpack 3.00 8.00
NCT North Carolina Tar Heels 8.00 20.00
NML New Mexico Lobos 3.00 8.00
NMS New Mexico State Aggies 3.00 8.00
ODM Old Dominion Monarchs 3.00 8.00
OSB Ohio State Buckeyes 3.00 8.00
OSC Oklahoma State Cowboys 3.00 8.00
RIR Rhode Island Rams 3.00 8.00
SCG South Carolina Gamecocks 3.00 8.00
SDS San Diego State Aztecs 3.00 8.00
SJH Saint Joseph's Hawks 3.00 8.00
SJR St. Johns Red Storm 3.00 8.00
SLB Saint Louis Billikens 3.00 8.00
SMG Southern Mississippi Golden Eagles 3.00 8.00
TAM Texas A&M Aggies 3.00 8.00
WSS Wichita State Shockers 3.00 10.00
WVM West Virginia Mountaineers 3.00 8.00

2014-15 Upper Deck March Madness Collection Most Outstanding Player Autographs

OVERALL ODDS 1:288 PACKS
GROUP A ODDS 1:5,498 PACKS
GROUP B ODDS 1:2,372 PACKS
GROUP C ODDS 1:1,234 PACKS
GROUP D ODDS 1:806 PACKS
EXCHANGE DEADLINE 1/8/2017
MOP7 Pervis Ellison D 12.00 30.00
MOP8 Keith Smart D 10.00 25.00
MOP11 Christian Laettner C 6.00 15.00
MOP12 Bobby Hurley C 20.00 50.00
MOP14 Shane Battier B 20.00 50.00
MOP15 S.Napier C EXCH 15.00 40.00

2014-15 Upper Deck March Madness Collection Tournament Champions Autographs

OVERALL ODDS 1:288 PACKS
GROUP A ODDS 1:17,280 PACKS
GROUP B ODDS 1:5,760 PACKS
GROUP C ODDS 1:1,592 PACKS
GROUP D ODDS 1:1,712 PACKS
EXCHANGE DEADLINE 1/8/2017
TC7 Sam Perkins E 6.00 15.00
TC13 Christian Laettner B 20.00 50.00
TC15 C.Williamson D EXCH 12.00 30.00
TC19 DeAndre Daniels E 6.00 15.00
TC20 S.Napier C EXCH 6.00 15.00

2014-15 Upper Deck March Madness Collection Tournament Stars Autographs

OVERALL ODDS 1:1,52 PACKS
GROUP A ODDS 1:30,240 PACKS
GROUP B ODDS 1:3,665 PACKS
GROUP C ODDS 1:2,520 PACKS
EXCHANGE DEADLINE 1/8/2017
DANW V.Del Negro/S.Webb C 6.00 15.00
DAWB J.Williams/S.Battier B 15.00 40.00

1999-00 Upper Deck MJ Master Collection

The 99/00 Upper Deck MJ Master Collection set was released to hobby dealers in late 1999 as a 26-card box set. The set included a 23-card base set that was limited to 500 serial-numbered sets. The box set also included an autographed Michael Jordan card, a jersey card of Michael Jordan, and one mystery pack that contained either an MJ autograph, a MJ game uniform card, a MJ shoe card, a MJ final floor card, or a 1 of 1 Michael Jordan card.

COMP.FACT SET (23) 200.00 500.00
COMMON CARD (1-23) 15.00 40.00
STATED PRINT RUN 500 SERIAL #'d SETS

1999-00 Upper Deck MJ Master Collection Game Jerseys

This insert was randomly inserted into the 99/00 MJ Master Collection box set. The five-card set features swatches from actual game-used Michael Jordan jerseys. The five-card set was limited to 100 serial-numbered sets. Card backs carry a "MJGJ" prefix.

COMMON CARD (MJGJ1-5) 200.00 500.00
STATED PRINT RUN 100 SETS

1999-00 Upper Deck MJ Master Collection Mystery Pack Inserts

This insert was randomly inserted into the 99/00 MJ Master Collection box set. The "mystery packs" were inserted at one per box set, and contained either a 1 of 1 Michael Jordan card, a MJ final floor card, a MJ shoe card, or a MJ game-used uniform card. Several cards are not priced due to scarcity.

PRINT RUNS LISTED BELOW
UNPRICED ONE OF A KIND CARDS EXIST
M1 M.Jordan FLR/54 150.00 300.00
MJGS1 M.Jordan Shoe/223 150.00 300.00
MJGU1 M.Jordan Uniform/200 150.00 300.00

1999-00 Upper Deck MJ Master Collection Signature Performances

This insert was randomly inserted into the 99/00 MJ Master Collection box set. The set features 10 autographed cards of Michael Jordan. This insert was limited to 50 serial-numbered sets. Card backs carry a "MJ" prefix.

COMMON CARD (MJ1-MJ10) 400.00 1000.00
STATED PRINT RUN 50 SERIAL #'d SETS

1998 Upper Deck MJ Sticker Collection

COMPLETE SET (138) 25.00 50.00
COMMON STICKER (1-138) .60 1.50

1998 Upper Deck MJ Sticker Collection Stickers

COMPLETE SET (38) 6.00 15.00
COMMON STICKER (1-38) .60 1.50

1998 Upper Deck MJx

This Michael Jordan only set was released in 5 card packs which carried a suggested retail price of $4.40. The 135 card set was broken up into different themes, with different insertion rates. Cards 1-45 were "MJ Timeline 1st Half" and were inserted at two per pack. Cards 46-55 were "1st Quarter Highlights" and were inserted at one in 17. Cards 56-65 were "2nd Quarter Highlights" and were inserted at one in 12. Cards 66-110 were "MJ Timeline 2nd Half" and were inserted at two per pack. Cards 111-120 were "3rd Quarter Highlights" and inserted at one in 7. Cards 121-130 were "4th Quarter Highlights" and inserted one per pack. The last five cards, 131-135, were "The Best of Times" and inserted one in 23.

COMPLETE SET (135) 100.00 200.00
COMMON CARD (1-45) .20 .50
COMMON CARD (46-55) 5.00 12.00
COMMON CARD (56-65) 4.00 10.00

COMMON CARD (66-110) .20 .50
COMMON CARD (111-120) 2.50 6.00
COMMON CARD (121-130) .40 1.00
COMMON CARD (131-135) 6.00 15.00
A1 Michael Jordan AU/50 1500.00 3000.00
GC1 Michael Jordan Warmups 150.00 300.00
GC2 Michael Jordan Shoes 150.00 300.00

1998 Upper Deck MJx Live

Randomly inserted into packs, this 30-card set features up close and personal interview excerpts from Michael Jordan. The cards are serially numberd to 100.

COMMON CARD (1-30) 40.00 100.00

1998 Upper Deck MJx Timepieces Red

COMPLETE SET (90) 125.00 250.00
COMMON CARD 2.50 5.00

1998 Upper Deck MJx Timepieces Bronze

COMMON CARD 15.00 40.00

1998 Upper Deck MJx Timepieces Gold

COMMON CARD 75.00 200.00

2003 Upper Deck Magazine

As a bonus to buyers of the Upper Deck magazine produced by Krause Publications late in 2003, a nine-card perforated sheet featuring players basically signed to Upper Deck exclusives was included. When the cards were perforated, these cards measured the standard size. Please note that all of these cards have a "UD" prefix.

COMPLETE SET (9) 8.00 20.00
UD1 Lebron James 2.50 6.00
UD3 Darko Milicic .75 2.00
UD8 Michael Jordan 1.25 3.00

1991-92 Upper Deck McDonald's/Paris

This 11-card set was issued by Upper Deck to highlight their involvement in the McDonald's Open held in Paris, France on October 18-19, 1991. The McDonald's Open features four leading international basketball teams, including the Los Angeles Lakers and three European teams. A special 11" by 8 1/2" commemorative sheet (not included in set price) and card packs, containing five Laker player cards and a special hologram card, were distributed to fans attending the event. The front design was the same as the regular issue cards, featuring a full color player photo with a wooden basketball court border on the right and bottom of the picture. The backs have a different color action photo and brief biography of the player in French. The cards are numbered on the back.

COMPLETE SET (11) 3.00 8.00
M1 Elden Campbell .40 1.00
M2 Vlade Divac .40 1.00
M3 A.C. Green .40 1.00
M4 Magic Johnson 2.50 6.00
M5 Sam Perkins .40 1.00
M6 Byron Scott .40 1.00
M7 Tony Smith .20 .50
M8 Terry Teagle .20 .50
M9 James Worthy .60 1.50
M10 Checklist .20 .50
NNO Byron Scott 4.00 10.00
  James Worthy
  A.C. Green
  Magic Johnson
  Sam Perkins
  Vlade Divac
NNO Hologram Card .20 .50

1992-93 Upper Deck McDonald's

Produced by Upper Deck, this 103-card set was issued for McDonald's NBA Fantasy promotion, which began on March 5, 1993 and continued while supplies lasted. Three-card foil packs were available at participating McDonald's restaurants free with the purchase of an Extra Value Meal, or for 59 cents with the purchase of any other menu item. Each three-card pack contained either two player cards and an instant-win NBA fantasy card, or simply three player cards. In the Boston, Chicago, Cleveland, Orlando, and Los Angeles areas, packs featured one special regional player card from the home team. A pack in these areas contained two regular player cards and a local team player card. In addition to meeting Michael Jordan and serving as an honorary ballperson at the 1994 NBA All-Star Game in Minneapolis, many winners received a fantasy NBA contract, special momento jersey, and one-day NBA salary. Over one million other prizes were also available. The cards measure the standard size (2 1/2" by 3 1/2"). The fronts display color action player photos with white borders. The player's name and team name appear in team color-coded bars at the bottom of the picture that intersect a basketball icon that carries the team logo. The Future Force cards, showcasing top rookies, have a special emblem in the upper left corner and the player's name and position on a gray bar. The backs have a second color photo as well as biography and statistics. The Upper Deck foil emblem on the backs takes the shape of the McDonald's golden arches. The cards are numbered on the back and arranged alphabetically according to team names. The set is divided into established NBA stars (P1-P42) and a Future Force subset (P43-P50). The team sets are numbered within themselves and are prefixed with letter abbreviations for the city. A Michael Jordan Hologram was also randomly inserted into all forms of the foil packs. Also, there were some factory sets (master sets containing everything) that were made available for the winner redemption prizes.

COMPLETE SET (103) 25.00 60.00
COMPLETE FACT.SET (103) 25.00 60.00
COMPLETE NAT.SET (50) 5.00 12.00
COMPLETE BOST SET (10) 3.00 8.00
COMPLETE CHI SET (12) 6.00 15.00
COMPLETE CLE SET (10) 1.50 4.00
COMPLETE LA SET (10) 3.00 8.00
COMPLETE ORL SET (10) 5.00 12.00
P1 Dominique Wilkins .20 .50
P2 Reggie Lewis .05 .15
P3 Kevin McHale .10 .30
P4 Larry Johnson .10 .30
P5 Michael Jordan 1.50 4.00
P6 Horace Grant .08 .25
P7 Brad Daugherty .05 .15
P8 Mark Price .08 .25
P9 Derek Harper .08 .25
P10 Dikembe Mutombo .10 .30
P11 Joe Dumars .10 .30
P12 Isiah Thomas .20 .50
P13 Tim Hardaway .10 .30
P14 Chris Mullin .10 .30
P15 Hakeem Olajuwon .15 .40
P16 Otis Thorpe .05 .10
P17 Detlef Schrempf .05 .10
P18 Reggie Miller .20 .50
P19 Ron Harper .08 .25
P20 Danny Manning .08 .25
P21 James Worthy .15 .40
P22 Sam Perkins .08 .25
P23 Rony Seikaly .05 .05
P24 Steve Smith .08 .25
P25 Alvin Robertson .05 .15
P26 Derrick Coleman .05 .10
P27 Drazen Petrovic .25 .60
P28 Patrick Ewing .20 .50
P29 Scott Skiles .08 .25
P30 Hersey Hawkins .05 .10
P31 Dan Majerle .08 .25
P32 Kevin Johnson .08 .25
P33 Clyde Drexler .20 .50
P34 Terry Porter .05 .05
P35 Spud Webb .05 .10
P36 Antoine Carr .05 .05
P37 David Robinson .20 .50
P38 Shawn Kemp .20 .50
P39 Ricky Pierce .05 .05
P40 Karl Malone .20 .50
P41 John Stockton .25 .60
P42 Michael Adams .05 .05
P43 Shaquille O'Neal 1.25 3.00
P44 Alonzo Mourning .50 1.25
P45 Christian Laettner .40 1.00
P46 LaPhonso Ellis .05 .15
P47 Walt Williams .08 .25
P48 Todd Day .05 .15
P49 Clarence Weatherspoon .08 .25
P50 Tom Gugliotta .30 .75
BT1 Dee Brown .20 .50
BT2 Sherman Douglas .20 .50
BT3 Rick Fox .25 .60
BT4 Kevin Gamble .20 .50
BT5 Joe Kleine .20 .50
BT6 Reggie Lewis .40 1.00
BT7 Xavier McDaniel .20 .50
BT8 Kevin McHale 1.00 2.50
BT9 Robert Parish .75 2.00
BT10 Ed Pinckney .20 .50
CH1 B.J. Armstrong .20 .50
CH2 Bill Cartwright .20 .50
CH3 Horace Grant .30 .75
CH4 Michael Jordan 5.00 12.00
CH5 Stacey King .20 .50
CH6 Rodney McCray .20 .50
CH7 John Paxson .20 .50
CH8 Will Perdue .20 .50
CH9 Scottie Pippen 1.50 4.00
CH10 Trent Tucker .20 .50
CH11 Corey Williams .20 .50
CH12 Scott Williams .20 .50
CL1 John Battle .20 .50
CL2 Terrell Brandon .40 1.00
CL3 Brad Daugherty .20 .50
CL4 Craig Ehlo .20 .50
CL5 Danny Ferry .20 .50
CL6 Larry Nance .30 .75
CL7 Mark Price .30 .75
CL8 Mike Sanders .20 .50
CL9 Gerald Wilkins .20 .50
CL10 Hot Rod Williams .20 .50
LA1 Elden Campbell .30 .75
LA2 Duane Cooper .20 .50
LA3 Vlade Divac .40 1.00
LA4 James Edwards .20 .50
LA5 A.C. Green .40 1.00
LA6 Anthony Peeler .40 1.00
LA7 Sam Perkins .40 1.00
LA8 Byron Scott .40 1.00
LA9 Sedale Threatt .20 .50
LA10 James Worthy .75 2.00
OR1 Nick Anderson .40 1.00
OR2 Anthony Bowie .20 .50
OR3 Terry Catledge .20 .50
OR4 Greg Kite .20 .50
OR5 Shaquille O'Neal 4.00 10.00
OR6 Jerry Reynolds .20 .50
OR7 Donald Royal .20 .50
OR8 Dennis Scott .40 1.00
OR9 Scott Skiles .30 .75
OR10 Jeff Turner .20 .50
NNO Michael Jordan Holo 5.00 12.00

1999 Upper Deck Michael Jordan Athlete of the Century

Released as a 90-card set, this Upper Deck product is a Michael Jordan tribute, and only contains images of him. Each pack contained five cards and carried a suggested retail price of $4.99.

COMPLETE SET (90) 12.00 30.00
COMMON CARD (1-90) .40 1.00
MC1 Master Collection .40 1.00
MJSS1 Michael Jordan AU/23 3000.00 6000.00
MJSS2 Michael Jordan AU/23 3000.00 6000.00

1999 Upper Deck Michael Jordan Athlete of the Century Gold

COMMON CARD (1-90) 40.00 100.00

1999 Upper Deck Michael Jordan Athlete of the Century Elevation

Randomly inserted in packs at one in 11, this 16-card set takes the form of a timeline, reliving Jordan's ascension to the 29,277 point plateau. Card backs carry an EL prefix.

COMPLETE SET (16) 20.00 50.00
COMMON CARD (EL1-16) 2.00 5.00

1999 Upper Deck Michael Jordan Athlete of the Century Extreme Air

Randomly inserted in packs at one in 144, this 15-card set uses Ionix technology to bring MJ's aerial moves to live. Card backs carry an EA prefix.

COMPLETE SET (15) 250.00 450.00
COMMON CARD (EA1-15) 15.00 40.00

1999 Upper Deck Michael Jordan Athlete of the Century High Class

Randomly inserted in packs at one in 11, this six-card set highlights Jordan's off-court contributions as a role model. Card backs carry a HC prefix.

COMPLETE SET (6) 7.50 15.00
COMMON CARD (HC1-HC6) 1.50 4.00

1999 Upper Deck Michael Jordan Athlete of the Century MJ Phenomenon

Randomly inserted in packs at one in 72, this 15-card set captures some of Jordan's greatest action shots thoroughout his career. Card backs carry a P prefix.

COMPLETE SET (15) 60.00 150.00
COMMON CARD (P1-P15) 6.00 15.00

1999 Upper Deck Michael Jordan Athlete of the Century The Jordan Era

Randomly inserted in packs at one in five, this 20-card set features each card relating to a specific moment in Jordan's career along with a current world trend at that point in time. Card backs carry a JE prefix.

COMPLETE SET (20) 15.00 40.00
COMMON CARD (JE1-20) 1.50 4.00

1999 Upper Deck Michael Jordan Athlete of the Century Total Dominance

Randomly inserted in packs at one in 23, this 20-card set focuses on how Jordan dominated the NBA during his thirteen year NBA career. Card backs carry a TD prefix.

COMPLETE SET (20) 50.00 120.00
COMMON CARD (TD1-20) 3.00 8.00

1999 Upper Deck Michael Jordan Athlete of the Century Upper Deck Remembers

Randomly inserted in packs at one in 23, this 10-card set features the most memorable MJ cards ever produced by Upper Deck beginning with his first card from the 91-92 season. Card backs carry a UD prefix.

COMPLETE SET (10) 15.00 40.00
COMMON CARD (UD1-10) 2.50 6.00

1999 Upper Deck Michael Jordan Career

Sold exclusively in 60-card box sets, these cards measure the standard size and look at Jordan's career, from the early years, through retirement. Each set also contained one of six blow-up cards. Those are listed at the end of the base set and carry a "CC" prefix.

COMP. FACT SET (60) 12.00 30.00
COMMON CARD (1-60) .40 1.00

1998 Upper Deck Michael Jordan Career Collection

Released as a boxed set, this 60-card set focuses on the early years of Michael Jordan's career - 1984-1993. The set breaks down into several themes: A Michael Jordan Upper Deck rookie card (if they had produced cards at that time), Pictures of Excellence, Spectacular Stats and MJ Retro.

COMP.FACT SET (60) 12.00 30.00
COMMON CARD (1-60) .40 1.00
1 Michael Jordan 1.25 3.00
  Rookie Card
20 Michael Jordan .60 1.50
  Spectacular Stats 90-91
21 Michael Jordan .60 1.50
  Spectacular Stats 1993
22 Michael Jordan .60 1.50
  Spectacular Stats 92-93
23 Michael Jordan .60 1.50
  Spectacular Stats 89-90
24 Michael Jordan .60 1.50
  Spectacular Stats 1991
25 Michael Jordan .60 1.50
  Spectacular Stats 88-89
26 Michael Jordan .60 1.50
  Spectacular Stats 87-88
27 Michael Jordan .60 1.50
  Spectacular Stats 1988
28 Michael Jordan .60 1.50
  Spectacular Stats 86-87

1997 Upper Deck Michael Jordan Championship Journals

This special boxed set features Michael Jordan reviewing his championship seasons. This 24-card set was oversized (3 1/2" by 5") and each card depicted a special moment from Jordan's career with his comments on the card back about that moment. Also included in each set is a special limited edition card of Jordan (to 5,000). Fifty of these cards were autographed and randomly inserted into sets. The suggested retail price for the set was $19.99.

COMP.FACT SET (25) 12.00 30.00
COMMON CARD (1-24) .60 1.50
NNO Michael Jordan 2.00 5.00
  Special Card/5000
NNO Michael Jordan 1000.00 2500.00
  Special Card - AU/50

1998 Upper Deck Michael Jordan Gatorade

This set was released in 1998 as a 12-postcard sized set by Upper Deck. The set was distributed by Gatorade. Each card features a black facimile autograph.

COMPLETE SET (12) 10.00 25.00
COMMON CARD (1-12) 1.20 3.00

1999 Upper Deck Michael Jordan Gatorade

Released by Upper Deck in conjunction with Gatorade, this six card postcard sized set features highlights from each of Michael Jordan's six championships. Card design mirrors that of 1997-98 Upper Deck and each card features a facsimile Michael Jordan autograph along the bottom of the card.

COMPLETE SET (6) 10.00 25.00
COMMON CARD (MJ1-MJ6) 2.50 6.00

2008-09 Upper Deck Michael Jordan Legacy Collection

COMMON CARD 1.50 4.00

2008-09 Upper Deck Michael Jordan Legacy Collection Memorabilia

COMMON CARD (1-100) 60.00 150.00
STATED PRINT RUN 23 SER.#'d SETS

2009-10 Upper Deck Michael Jordan Legacy Collection

COMPLETE SET (50) 10.00 25.00
COMP.FAC.SET (51) 12.00 30.00
COMMON CARD (1-50) .40 1.00

2009-10 Upper Deck Michael Jordan Legacy Collection Gold

This 100-card set was issued in complete box set form, with a limited box run of 30,000 serially numbered boxes.

COMPLETE SET (100) 100.00 200.00
COMMON CARD (1-100) 1.25 3.00
97 Michael Jordan 10.00 25.00
  '86-87 Fleer reprint

2009-10 Upper Deck Michael Jordan Legacy Collection Oversized

COMPLETE SET (10) 25.00 60.00
COMMON CARD (MJ1-MJ10) 4.00 10.00
ONE PER FACTORY SET

1998 Upper Deck Michael Jordan Living Legend

The 1998 Upper Deck Michael Jordan Living Legend product was released during the 1998-99 season and features a 165-card base set that highlights Michael Jordan's NBA career. The product also had Micheal Jordan autographs and game-used jersey cards randomly inserted into packs.

COMPLETE SET (165) 25.00 60.00
COMMON CARD (1-165) .40 1.00
MJ1 Michael Jordan AU/50 3000.00 4000.00

1998 Upper Deck Michael Jordan Living Legend Cover Story

Randomly inserted in packs at a rate of one in 14, this 8-card set features a few of the many magazine covers that Jordan has graced. Each card is numbered with a "C" prefix.

COMPLETE SET (8) 12.50 30.00
COMMON CARD (C1-C8) 2.00 5.00

1998 Upper Deck Michael Jordan Living Legend Game Action Red

Randomly inserted in packs, this 30-card set features several memorable moments of Jordan game action. This first tier features red-foil on the outside of the card and is serially numbered to 2300. Card backs are numbered with a "G" prefix.

COMPLETE SET (30) 100.00 250.00
COMMON CARD (G1-G30) 4.00 10.00

1998 Upper Deck Michael Jordan Living Legend Game Action Silver

COMMON CARD (G1-G30) 25.00 60.00

1998 Upper Deck Michael Jordan Living Legend Game Action Gold

COMMON CARD (G1-G30) 100.00 250.00

1998 Upper Deck Michael Jordan Living Legend In-Flight

Randomly inserted in packs at a rate of one in five, this 15-card set features shots of Jordan in-flight. Each card back carries an "IF" prefix.

COMPLETE SET (15) 10.00 25.00
COMMON CARD (IF1-IF15) .75 2.00

1995 Upper Deck Michael Jordan Milk Caps

COMPLETE SET (54) 15.00 30.00
COMMON POG .40 1.00

1995 Upper Deck Michael Jordan Milk Caps Slammers

COMPLETE SET (45) 25.00 50.00
COMMON SLAMMER (S1-S45) .75 2.00

1999 Upper Deck Michael Jordan Retirement

Released in a 23-card box set, these 3 1/2" by 5" cards commemorate the amazine basketball career of Michael Jordan.

COMP.FACT SET (23) 10.00 25.00
COMMON CARD (1-23) .75 2.00

1997 Upper Deck Michael Jordan Tribute

COMPLETE SET (90) 30.00 75.00
COMP.VISIONS SET (30) 10.00 25.00
COMP.IMPRESSIONS SET (30) 10.00 25.00
COMP.REFLECTIONS SET (30) 10.00 25.00
COMMON CARD (1-90) .40 1.00

1996-97 Upper Deck Folz Minis

This 48-card set features miniature version of the cards used in Collector's Choice sets. The cards were available via Folz Vending Machines at Toys R Us stores and other retailers. The first six cards feature foil and are designated as such in the checklist.

COMPLETE SET (48) 250.00 500.00
1 Michael Jordan FOIL 30.00 80.00
2 Anfernee Hardaway FOIL 12.00 30.00
3 Shawn Kemp FOIL 8.00 20.00
4 Shaquille O'Neal FOIL 20.00 50.00
5 Grant Hill FOIL 12.00 30.00
6 Hakeem Olajuwon FOIL 10.00 25.00
7 Mookie Blaylock 2.00 5.00
8 Antoine Walker 5.00 12.00
9 Anthony Mason 2.00 5.00
10 Scottie Pippen 5.00 12.00
11 Terrell Brandon 2.00 5.00
12 Samaki Walker 2.50 6.00
13 LaPhonso Ellis 2.00 5.00
14 Joe Dumars 3.00 8.00
15 Latrell Sprewell 3.00 8.00
16 Charles Barkley 5.00 12.00
17 Reggie Miller 4.00 10.00
18 Brent Barry 2.50 6.00
19 Eddie Jones 3.00 8.00
20 Tim Hardaway 3.00 8.00
21 Vin Baker 2.50 6.00
22 Stephen Marbury 8.00 20.00
23 Kendall Gill 2.00 5.00
24 Patrick Ewing 4.00 10.00
25 Horace Grant 2.50 6.00
26 Allen Iverson 15.00 40.00
27 Kevin Johnson 3.00 8.00
28 Kenny Anderson 2.50 6.00
29 Olden Polynice 2.00 5.00
30 Sean Elliott 3.00 8.00
31 Gary Payton 3.00 8.00
32 Marcus Camby 5.00 12.00
33 John Stockton 4.00 10.00
34 Shareef Abdur-Rahim 5.00 12.00
35 Juwan Howard 2.50 6.00
36 Dikembe Mutombo 3.00 8.00
37 Glen Rice 3.00 8.00
38 Dennis Rodman 6.00 15.00
39 Antonio McDyess 3.00 8.00
40 Rik Smits 2.50 6.00
41 Nick Van Exel 3.00 8.00
42 Alonzo Mourning 4.00 10.00
43 Glenn Robinson 2.50 6.00
44 Larry Johnson 3.00 8.00
45 Dennis Scott 2.00 5.00
46 Jerry Stackhouse 4.00 10.00
47 Sam Perkins 2.00 5.00
48 Chris Webber 4.00 10.00

1999-00 Upper Deck MVP

The premier set of Upper Deck MVP consisted of 220 cards. The cards came in 10 card packs that carried a suggested retail price of $1.59. The set features 178 base cards, 30 MJ Exclusive cards, 10 rookie cards and two checklists.

COMPLETE SET (220) 20.00 40.00
1 Dikembe Mutombo .20 .50
2 Steve Smith .15 .40
3 Mookie Blaylock .12 .30
4 Alan Henderson .12 .30
5 LaPhonso Ellis .12 .30
6 Grant Long .12 .30
7 Kenny Anderson .15 .40
8 Antoine Walker .20 .50
9 Ron Mercer .15 .40
10 Paul Pierce .25 .60
11 Vitaly Potapenko .12 .30
12 Dana Barros .12 .30
13 Elden Campbell .12 .30
14 Eddie Jones .20 .50
15 David Wesley .12 .30
16 Bobby Phills .12 .30
17 Derrick Coleman .15 .40
18 Ricky Davis .20 .50
19 Toni Kukoc .20 .50
20 Brent Barry .15 .40
21 Ron Harper .12 .30
22 Kornell David RC .15 .40
23 Mark Bryant .12 .30
24 Dickey Simpkins .12 .30
25 Shawn Kemp .20 .50
26 Derek Anderson .12 .30
27 Brevin Knight .12 .30
28 Andrew DeClercq .12 .30
29 Zydrunas Ilgauskas .15 .40
30 Cedric Henderson .12 .30
31 Shawn Bradley .12 .30
32 A.C. Green .15 .40
33 Gary Trent .12 .30
34 Michael Finley .20 .50
35 Dirk Nowitzki .40 1.00
36 Steve Nash .30 .75
37 Antonio McDyess .15 .40
38 Nick Van Exel .15 .40
39 Chauncey Billups .20 .50
40 Danny Fortson .12 .30
41 Eric Washington .12 .30
42 Raef LaFrentz .15 .40
43 Grant Hill .25 .60
44 Bison Dele .12 .30
45 Lindsey Hunter .12 .30
46 Jerry Stackhouse .20 .50
47 Don Reid .12 .30
48 Christian Laettner .15 .40
49 John Starks .15 .40
50 Antawn Jamison .20 .50
51 Erick Dampier .12 .30
52 Donyell Marshall .12 .30
53 Chris Mills .12 .30
54 Bimbo Coles .12 .30
55 Charles Barkley .30 .75
56 Hakeem Olajuwon .25 .60
57 Scottie Pippen .30 .75
58 Othella Harrington .12 .30
59 Bryce Drew .12 .30
60 Michael Dickerson .12 .30
61 Rik Smits .20 .50
62 Reggie Miller .20 .50
63 Mark Jackson .15 .40
64 Antonio Davis .12 .30
65 Jalen Rose .15 .40
66 Dale Davis .12 .30
67 Chris Mullin .20 .50
68 Maurice Taylor .12 .30
69 Lamond Murray .12 .30
70 Rodney Rogers .12 .30
71 Darrick Martin .12 .30
72 Michael Olowokandi .12 .30
73 Tyrone Nesby RC .15 .40
74 Kobe Bryant .75 2.00
75 Shaquille O'Neal .50 1.25
76 Robert Horry .15 .40
77 Glen Rice .20 .50
78 J.R. Reid .12 .30
79 Rick Fox .12 .30
80 Derek Fisher .20 .50
81 Tim Hardaway .20 .50
82 Alonzo Mourning .25 .60
83 Jamal Mashburn .15 .40
84 P.J. Brown .12 .30
85 Terry Porter .12 .30
86 Dan Majerle .20 .50
87 Ray Allen .20 .50
88 Vinny Del Negro .12 .30
89 Glenn Robinson .15 .40
90 Dell Curry .12 .30
91 Sam Cassell .15 .40
92 Robert Traylor .12 .30
93 Kevin Garnett .30 .75
94 Terrell Brandon .12 .30
95 Joe Smith .15 .40
96 Sam Mitchell .12 .30
97 Anthony Peeler .12 .30
98 Bobby Jackson .12 .30
99 Keith Van Horn .15 .40
100 Stephon Marbury .15 .40
101 Jayson Williams .12 .30
102 Kendall Gill .12 .30
103 Kerry Kittles .12 .30
104 Scott Burrell .12 .30
105 Patrick Ewing .25 .60
106 Allan Houston .15 .40
107 Latrell Sprewell .20 .50
108 Larry Johnson .20 .50
109 Marcus Camby .15 .40
110 Charlie Ward .12 .30
111 Anfernee Hardaway .30 .75
112 Darrell Armstrong .12 .30
113 Nick Anderson .12 .30
114 Horace Grant .15 .40
115 Isaac Austin .12 .30
116 Matt Harpring .12 .30
117 Michael Doleac .12 .30
118 Allen Iverson .40 1.00
119 Theo Ratliff .15 .40
120 Matt Geiger .12 .30
121 Larry Hughes .15 .40
122 Tyrone Hill .12 .30
123 George Lynch .12 .30
124 Jason Kidd .30 .75
125 Tom Gugliotta .12 .30
126 Rex Chapman .12 .30
127 Clifford Robinson .12 .30
128 Luc Longley .15 .40
129 Danny Manning .15 .40
130 Rasheed Wallace .20 .50
131 Arvydas Sabonis .15 .40
132 Damon Stoudamire .15 .40
133 Brian Grant .12 .30
134 Isaiah Rider .15 .40
135 Walt Williams .12 .30
136 Jim Jackson .12 .30
137 Jason Williams .25 .60
138 Vlade Divac .20 .50
139 Chris Webber .20 .50
140 Corliss Williamson .12 .30
141 Peja Stojakovic .20 .50
142 Tariq Abdul-Wahad .12 .30
143 Tim Duncan .40 1.00
144 Sean Elliott .20 .50
145 David Robinson .30 .75
146 Mario Elie .12 .30
147 Avery Johnson .15 .40
148 Steve Kerr .15 .40
149 Gary Payton .20 .50
150 Vin Baker .15 .40
151 Detlef Schrempf .15 .40
152 Hersey Hawkins .12 .30
153 Dale Ellis .12 .30
154 Olden Polynice .12 .30
155 Vince Carter .40 1.00
156 John Wallace .12 .30
157 Doug Christie .15 .40
158 Tracy McGrady .30 .75
159 Kevin Willis .12 .30
160 Charles Oakley .15 .40
161 Karl Malone .25 .60
162 John Stockton .25 .60
163 Jeff Hornacek .15 .40
164 Bryon Russell .12 .30
165 Howard Eisley .12 .30
166 Shandon Anderson .12 .30
167 Shareef Abdur-Rahim .15 .40
168 Mike Bibby .20 .50
169 Bryant Reeves .12 .30
170 Felipe Lopez .12 .30
171 Cherokee Parks .12 .30
172 Michael Smith .12 .30
173 Juwan Howard .15 .40
174 Rod Strickland .12 .30
175 Mitch Richmond .20 .50
176 Otis Thorpe .12 .30
177 Calbert Cheaney .12 .30
178 Tracy Murray .12 .30
179 Michael Jordan .75 2.00
180 Michael Jordan .75 2.00
181 Michael Jordan .75 2.00
182 Michael Jordan .75 2.00
183 Michael Jordan .75 2.00
184 Michael Jordan .75 2.00
185 Michael Jordan .75 2.00
186 Michael Jordan .75 2.00
187 Michael Jordan .75 2.00
188 Michael Jordan .75 2.00
189 Michael Jordan .75 2.00
190 Michael Jordan .75 2.00
191 Michael Jordan .75 2.00
192 Michael Jordan .75 2.00
193 Michael Jordan .75 2.00
194 Michael Jordan .75 2.00
195 Michael Jordan .75 2.00
196 Michael Jordan .75 2.00
197 Michael Jordan .75 2.00
198 Michael Jordan .75 2.00
199 Michael Jordan .75 2.00
200 Michael Jordan .75 2.00
201 Michael Jordan .75 2.00
202 Michael Jordan .75 2.00
203 Michael Jordan .75 2.00
204 Michael Jordan .75 2.00
205 Michael Jordan .75 2.00
206 Michael Jordan .75 2.00
207 Michael Jordan .75 2.00
208 Michael Jordan .75 2.00
209 Elton Brand RC .75 2.00
210 Steve Francis RC .75 2.00
211 Baron Davis RC .75 2.00
212 Wally Szczerbiak RC .60 1.50
213 Richard Hamilton RC .60 1.50
214 Andre Miller RC .60 1.50
215 Jason Terry RC .50 1.25
216 Corey Maggette RC .50 1.25
217 Shawn Marion RC .60 1.50
218 Lamar Odom RC .75 2.00
219 M.Jordan CL .75 2.00
220 M.Jordan CL .75 2.00
S1 Michael Jordan PROMO 1.25 3.00

1999-00 Upper Deck MVP Silver Script

COMMON MJ (179-208/CL) 2.00 5.00
*STARS: 1.5X TO 4X BASE CARD HI
*RCs: .75X TO 2X BASE HI
STATED ODDS 1:2 HOB/RET
S1 Michael Jordan PROMO 2.00 5.00

1999-00 Upper Deck MVP Gold Script

COMMON MJ (179-208/CL) 20.00 50.00
*STARS: 15X TO 40X BASE CARD HI
*RCs: 6X TO 15X BASE HI
STATED PRINT RUN 100 SERIAL #'d SETS
161 Karl Malone 12.00 30.00

1999-00 Upper Deck MVP Super Script

COMMON MJ (179-208/CL) 60.00 150.00
*STARS: 50X TO 120X BASE CARD HI
*RCs: 15X TO 40X BASE HI
STATED PRINT RUN 25 SERIAL #'d SETS

1999-00 Upper Deck MVP 21st Century NBA

Randomly inserted in packs at one in 13, this 10-card set features some of the key players in the NBA who are poised to become the next superstars of the league. Card backs carry a "N" prefix.

COMPLETE SET (10) 4.00 10.00
STATED ODDS 1:13 HOB/RET
N1 Jason Williams .60 1.50
N2 Paul Pierce .60 1.50
N3 Antoine Walker .50 1.25
N4 Keith Van Horn .40 1.00
N5 Allen Iverson 1.00 2.50
N6 Antawn Jamison .50 1.25
N7 Kobe Bryant 2.00 5.00
N8 Shareef Abdur-Rahim .40 1.00
N9 Stephon Marbury .40 1.00
N10 Grant Hill .60 1.50

1999-00 Upper Deck MVP Draw Your Own Trading Card

Randomly inserted in packs at one in two, this 26-card set features the winning cards from Upper Deck's Draw Your Own Trading Card contest. The following cards do not exist: W11, W15, W19 and W27. Card backs carry a "W" prefix.

COMPLETE SET (26) 5.00 12.00
W1 Michael Jordan .75 2.00
W2 Grant Hill .12 .30
W3 Kobe Bryant .40 1.00
W4 Michael Jordan .75 2.00
W5 Glen Rice .10 .25
W6 Michael Jordan .75 2.00
W7 David Robinson .15 .40
W8 Grant Hill .12 .30
W9 Stephon Marbury .07 .20
W10 Michael Jordan .75 2.00
W12 Charles Barkley .15 .40
W13 Antoine Walker .10 .25
W14 Shaquille O'Neal .25 .60
W16 Michael Jordan .75 2.00
W17 Stephon Marbury .07 .20
W18 Michael Jordan .75 2.00
W20 Allen Iverson .20 .50
W21 Michael Jordan .75 2.00
W22 Shareef Abdur-Rahim .07 .20
W23 Reggie Miller .10 .25
W24 Karl Malone .12 .30
W25 Christian Laettner .07 .20
W26 John Stockton .12 .30
W28 Michael Jordan .75 2.00
W29 Michael Jordan .75 2.00
W30 Michael Jordan .75 2.00

1999-00 Upper Deck MVP Dynamics

Randomly inserted in packs at one in 27, this six-card set features some of the most collectible players in the NBA. Card backs carry a "D" prefix.

COMPLETE SET (6) 8.00 20.00
STATED ODDS 1:27 HOB/RET
D1 Michael Jordan 6.00 15.00
D2 Kobe Bryant 3.00 8.00
D3 Grant Hill 1.00 2.50
D4 Shareef Abdur-Rahim .60 1.50
D5 Kevin Garnett 1.25 3.00
D6 Vince Carter 1.50 4.00

1999-00 Upper Deck MVP Electrifying

Randomly inserted in packs at one in nine, this 15-card set focuses on players who bring NBA crowds to their feet. Card backs carry an "E" prefix.

COMPLETE SET (15) 4.00 10.00
STATED ODDS 1:9 HOB/RET
E1 Shaquille O'Neal 1.25 3.00
E2 Steve Smith .40 1.00
E3 Toni Kukoc .50 1.25
E4 Ron Mercer .40 1.00
E5 Damon Stoudamire .40 1.00
E6 Tim Hardaway .50 1.25
E7 Paul Pierce .60 1.50
E8 Jason Kidd .75 2.00
E9 Stephon Marbury .40 1.00
E10 Terrell Brandon .30 .75
E11 Reggie Miller .50 1.25
E12 Ray Allen .50 1.25
E13 Maurice Taylor .30 .75
E14 Chris Webber .50 1.25
E15 Charles Barkley .75 2.00

1999-00 Upper Deck MVP Game-Used Souvenirs

Randomly inserted in hobby packs only at one in 131, this 15-card set features a piece of a game-used basketball in each card. The cards are numbered on the back according to the player's initials. Two cards were also autographed: Anfernee Hardaway (card AH-A) and Karl Malone (KM). Those cards are listed below with an "AU" designation.

STATED ODDS 1:131 HOBBY
AHS Anfernee Hardaway 8.00 20.00
AJS Antawn Jamison 4.00 10.00
AMS Antonio McDyess 3.00 8.00
GPS Gary Payton 4.00 10.00
JKS Jason Kidd 6.00 15.00
JWS Jason Williams 10.00 25.00
KBS Kobe Bryant 15.00 40.00
KGS Kevin Garnett 6.00 15.00
KMA Karl Malone AU/32 250.00 500.00
KMS Karl Malone 5.00 12.00
MBS Mike Bibby 4.00 10.00
MFS Michael Finley 4.00 10.00
MOS Michael Olowokandi 2.50 6.00
SOS Shaquille O'Neal 10.00 25.00
SPS Scottie Pippen 6.00 15.00
TDS Tim Duncan 12.00 30.00

1999-00 Upper Deck MVP Jam Time

Randomly inserted in packs at one in six, this 14-card set features some of the best aerial artists of the NBA. Card backs carry a "JT" prefix.

COMPLETE SET (14) 3.00 8.00
STATED ODDS 1:6 HOB/RET
JT1 Michael Jordan 2.00 5.00
JT2 Alonzo Mourning .30 .75
JT3 Shawn Kemp .25 .60
JT4 Juwan Howard .20 .50
JT5 Chris Webber .25 .60
JT6 Tim Duncan .50 1.25
JT7 Keith Van Horn .20 .50
JT8 Eddie Jones .25 .60
JT9 Michael Finley .25 .60
JT10 Anfernee Hardaway .40 1.00
JT11 Antonio McDyess .20 .50
JT12 Charles Barkley .40 1.00
JT13 Latrell Sprewell .25 .60
JT14 Hakeem Olajuwon .30 .75

1999-00 Upper Deck MVP Jordan MVP Moments

Randomly inserted in packs at one in 27, this 14-card set relives all of Michael Jordan's MVP honors from his regular season awards to his All-Star game and post-season highlights. Card backs carry a "MJ" prefix.

COMMON CARD (MJ1-MJ14) 3.00 8.00
STATED ODDS 1:27 HOB/RET

1999-00 Upper Deck MVP MVP Theatre

Randomly inserted in packs at one in nine, this 15-card set takes a look at the players that will be battling it out for the MVP award for years to come. Card backs carry a "M" prefix.

COMPLETE SET (15) 5.00 12.00
STATED ODDS 1:9 HOB/RET
M1 Karl Malone .60 1.50
M2 Tom Gugliotta .30 .75
M3 Shaquille O'Neal 1.25 3.00
M4 Mitch Richmond .50 1.25
M5 David Robinson .75 2.00
M6 Gary Payton .50 1.25
M7 Allen Iverson 1.00 2.50
M8 Glenn Robinson .40 1.00
M9 Antoine Walker .50 1.25
M10 Hakeem Olajuwon .60 1.50
M11 Patrick Ewing .60 1.50
M12 Antonio McDyess .40 1.00
M13 Tim Hardaway .50 1.25
M14 Scottie Pippen .75 2.00
M15 Anfernee Hardaway .75 2.00

1999-00 Upper Deck MVP ProSign

Randomly inserted in retail packs at one in 144, this 16-card set features autographs from NBA players. The cards are numbered on the back by initial.

STATED ODDS 1:144 RETAIL
CH Charlie Ward 4.00 10.00
CW Clarence Weatherspoon 4.00 10.00
DA Darrell Armstrong 4.00 10.00
DF Derek Fisher 8.00 20.00
IA Isaac Austin 4.00 10.00
JJ Jim Jackson 4.00 10.00
JK Jaren Jackson 5.00 12.00

JR Jalen Rose 8.00 20.00
MD Michael Dickerson 4.00 10.00
MJ Michael Jordan/23 600.00 1000.00
NV Nick Van Exel 6.00 15.00
RT Robert Traylor 4.00 10.00
SA Stacey Augmon 4.00 10.00
TC Terry Cummings 4.00 10.00
TR Theo Ratliff 4.00 10.00
VC Vince Carter 15.00 40.00

2000-01 Upper Deck MVP

The 2000-01 Upper Deck MVP product was released in late August, 2000, and featured a 220-card base set that was broken into tiers as follows: Base Veterans (1-188), Checklists (189-190), and Rookies (191-220). Each pack contained 10 cards, and carried a suggested retail price of $1.59.

COMPLETE SET (220) 12.00 30.00
1 Dikembe Mutombo .20 .50
2 Jason Terry .20 .50
3 Jim Jackson .12 .30
4 Alan Henderson .12 .30
5 Roshown McLeod .12 .30
6 Bimbo Coles .12 .30
7 Lorenzen Wright .12 .30
8 Antoine Walker .15 .40
9 Paul Pierce .20 .50
10 Kenny Anderson .15 .40
11 Adrian Griffin .12 .30
12 Vitaly Potapenko .12 .30
13 Dana Barros .12 .30
14 Eric Williams .12 .30
15 Eddie Jones .20 .50
16 Eddie Robinson .12 .30
17 Ricky Davis .15 .40
18 Elden Campbell .12 .30
19 Derrick Coleman .15 .40
20 David Wesley .12 .30
21 Baron Davis .20 .50
22 Elton Brand .20 .50
23 Ron Artest .20 .50
24 Hersey Hawkins .12 .30
25 Chris Carr .12 .30
26 Corey Benjamin .12 .30
27 Will Perdue .12 .30
28 Andre Miller .15 .40
29 Shawn Kemp .20 .50
30 Wesley Person .12 .30
31 Lamond Murray .12 .30
32 Bob Sura .12 .30
33 Andrew DeClercq .12 .30
34 Dirk Nowitzki .30 .75
35 Michael Finley .20 .50
36 Cedric Ceballos .12 .30
37 Shawn Bradley .12 .30
38 Erick Strickland .12 .30
39 Hubert Davis .12 .30
40 Antonio McDyess .15 .40
41 Raef LaFrentz .12 .30
42 Keon Clark .12 .30
43 Nick Van Exel .15 .40
44 James Posey .12 .30
45 Chris Gatling .12 .30
46 George McCloud .12 .30
47 Grant Hill .25 .60
48 Jerry Stackhouse .15 .40
49 Lindsey Hunter .12 .30
50 Christian Laettner .15 .40
51 Jerome Williams .12 .30
52 Terry Mills .12 .30
53 Antawn Jamison .20 .50
54 Donyell Marshall .12 .30
55 Chris Mills .12 .30
56 Larry Hughes .15 .40
57 Mookie Blaylock .12 .30
58 Vonteego Cummings .12 .30
59 Steve Francis .15 .40
60 Shandon Anderson .12 .30
61 Cuttino Mobley .12 .30
62 Hakeem Olajuwon .25 .60
63 Walt Williams .12 .30
64 Kelvin Cato .12 .30
65 Reggie Miller .20 .50
66 Austin Croshere .12 .30
67 Rik Smits .12 .30
68 Jalen Rose .15 .40
69 Dale Davis .12 .30
70 Jonathan Bender .12 .30
71 Michael Olowokandi .12 .30
72 Lamar Odom .15 .40
73 Tyrone Nesby .20 .50
74 Eldrick Bohannon RC .12 .30
75 Eric Piatkowski .12 .30
76 Shaquille O'Neal .50 1.25
77 Kobe Bryant .75 2.00
78 Robert Horry .15 .40
79 Ron Harper .15 .40
80 Rick Fox .12 .30
81 Derek Fisher .20 .50
82 Devean George .12 .30
83 Alonzo Mourning .25 .60
84 Clarence Weatherspoon .12 .30
85 Anthony Carter .12 .30
86 P.J. Brown .12 .30
87 Tim Hardaway .20 .50
88 Jamal Mashburn .15 .40
89 Voshon Lenard .12 .30
90 Ray Allen .20 .50
91 Glenn Robinson .15 .40
92 Tim Thomas .12 .30
93 Sam Cassell .15 .40
94 Robert Traylor .12 .30
95 Ervin Johnson .12 .30
96 Danny Manning .12 .30
97 Kevin Garnett .30 .75
98 Wally Szczerbiak .15 .40
99 Terrell Brandon .12 .30
100 William Avery .12 .30
101 Anthony Peeler .12 .30
102 Radoslav Nesterovic .12 .30
103 Dean Garrett .12 .30
104 Keith Van Horn .15 .40
105 Kerry Kittles .12 .30
106 Stephon Marbury .15 .40
107 Evan Eschmeyer .12 .30
108 Jim McIlvaine .12 .30
109 Lucious Harris .12 .30
110 Jamie Feick .12 .30
111 Allan Houston .15 .40
112 Latrell Sprewell .15 .40
113 Patrick Ewing .25 .60
114 Chris Childs .12 .30
115 Marcus Camby .15 .40
116 Charlie Ward .12 .30
117 Larry Johnson .20 .50
118 Darrell Armstrong .12 .30
119 Corey Maggette .15 .40
120 Ron Mercer .12 .30
121 Pat Garrity .12 .30
122 Chucky Atkins .12 .30
123 Ben Wallace .15 .40
124 Michael Doleac .12 .30
125 Allen Iverson .40 1.00
126 Matt Geiger .12 .30
127 Eric Snow .12 .30
128 Toni Kukoc .20 .50
129 Theo Ratliff .12 .30
130 George Lynch .12 .30
131 Jason Kidd .30 .75
132 Tom Gugliotta .12 .30
133 Rodney Rogers .12 .30
134 Shawn Marion .15 .40
135 Clifford Robinson .12 .30
136 Kevin Johnson .15 .40
137 Anfernee Hardaway .30 .75
138 Scottie Pippen .30 .75
139 Damon Stoudamire .15 .40
140 Arvydas Sabonis .15 .40
141 Jermaine O'Neal .15 .40
142 Bonzi Wells .12 .30
143 Rasheed Wallace .20 .50
144 Detlef Schrempf .15 .40
145 Chris Webber .20 .50
146 Vlade Divac .15 .40
147 Peja Stojakovic .20 .50
148 Jason Williams .20 .50
149 Corliss Williamson .12 .30
150 Nick Anderson .12 .30
151 Jon Barry .12 .30
152 Tim Duncan .40 1.00
153 David Robinson .30 .75
154 Avery Johnson .15 .40
155 Terry Porter .12 .30
156 Mario Elie .12 .30
157 Jaren Jackson .12 .30
158 Steve Kerr .12 .30
159 Gary Payton .20 .50
160 Vin Baker .15 .40
161 Brent Barry .12 .30
162 Horace Grant .15 .40
163 Ruben Patterson .12 .30
164 Rashard Lewis .20 .50
165 Tracy McGrady .30 .75
166 Charles Oakley .15 .40
167 Doug Christie .12 .30
168 Antonio Davis .12 .30
169 Vince Carter .40 1.00
170 Kevin Willis .12 .30
171 Karl Malone .25 .60
172 John Stockton .25 .60
173 Bryon Russell .12 .30
174 Quincy Lewis .12 .30
175 Olden Polynice .12 .30
176 Jacque Vaughn .12 .30
177 Shareef Abdur-Rahim .15 .40
178 Michael Dickerson .12 .30
179 Bryant Reeves .12 .30
180 Mike Bibby .20 .50
181 Othella Harrington .12 .30
182 Felipe Lopez .12 .30
183 Mitch Richmond .15 .40
184 Richard Hamilton .15 .40
185 Jahidi White .12 .30
186 Aaron Williams .12 .30
187 Juwan Howard .15 .40
188 Rod Strickland .12 .30
189 Kobe Bryant CL .75 2.00
190 Kevin Garnett CL .30 .75
191 Kenyon Martin RC .50 1.25
192 Marcus Fizer RC .20 .50
193 Chris Mihm RC .15 .40
194 Stromile Swift RC .20 .50
195 Morris Peterson RC .20 .50
196 Quentin Richardson RC .20 .50
197 Courtney Alexander RC .15 .40
198 Scoonie Penn RC .20 .50
199 Mateen Cleaves RC .15 .40
200 Erick Barkley RC .12 .30
201 A.J. Guyton RC .12 .30
202 Darius Miles RC .20 .50
203 DerMarr Johnson RC .15 .40
204 Jerome Moiso RC .12 .30
205 Jamaal Magloire RC .20 .50
206 Hanno Mottola RC .12 .30
207 Mike Miller RC .30 .75
208 Desmond Mason RC .25 .60
209 Chris Carrawell RC .20 .50
210 Eduardo Najera RC .20 .50
211 Speedy Claxton RC .20 .50
212 Joel Przybilla RC .15 .40
213 Mark Madsen RC .20 .50
214 Khalid El-Amin RC .12 .30
215 Etan Thomas RC .20 .50
216 Jason Collier RC .20 .50
217 Jason Hart RC .20 .50
218 Michael Redd RC .50 1.25
219 Keyon Dooling RC .20 .50
220 Mamadou N'Diaye RC .12 .30

2000-01 Upper Deck MVP Silver Script

*STARS: 1.25X TO 3X BASE CARD HI
*RCs: .75X TO 2X BASE CARD HI
STATED ODDS 1:2 HOB/RET

2000-01 Upper Deck MVP Gold Script

*STARS: 12X TO 30X BASE CARD HI
*RCs: 8X TO 20X BASE CARD HI
STATED PRINT RUN 100 SERIAL #'d SETS
77 Kobe Bryant 40.00 100.00
189 Kobe Bryant CL 40.00 100.00

2000-01 Upper Deck MVP Super Script

*STARS: 50X TO 120X BASE CARD HI
*RCs: 20X TO 50X BASE CARD HI
STATED PRINT RUN 25 SERIAL #'d SETS

2000-01 Upper Deck MVP Dynamics

Randomly inserted into packs at one in 28, this 20-card insert features players that are "dynamic" on the court. Card backs carry a "D" prefix.

COMPLETE SET (20) 15.00 40.00
STATED ODDS 1:28 HOB/RET
D1 Shaquille O'Neal 2.50 6.00
D2 Allen Iverson 2.00 5.00
D3 Paul Pierce 1.00 2.50
D4 Scottie Pippen 1.50 4.00
D5 Lamar Odom .75 2.00
D6 Kobe Bryant 4.00 10.00
D7 Gary Payton 1.00 2.50
D8 Antonio McDyess .75 2.00
D9 Stephon Marbury .75 2.00
D10 Alonzo Mourning 1.25 3.00
D11 Vince Carter 2.00 5.00
D12 Jason Kidd 1.50 4.00
D13 Michael Finley 1.00 2.50
D14 Chris Webber 1.00 2.50
D15 Anfernee Hardaway 1.50 4.00
D16 Kevin Garnett 1.50 4.00
D17 Jason Williams 1.00 2.50
D18 Allan Houston .75 2.00
D19 Elton Brand 1.00 2.50
D20 Karl Malone 1.25 3.00

2000-01 Upper Deck MVP Electrifying

Randomly inserted into packs at one in nine, this 10-card set features players that "electrify" the competition. Card backs carry an "E" prefix.

COMPLETE SET (10) 2.00 5.00
STATED ODDS 1:9 HOB/RET
E1 Kevin Garnett .50 1.25
E2 Stephon Marbury .25 .60
E3 Damon Stoudamire .25 .60
E4 Jalen Rose .25 .60
E5 Eddie Jones .30 .75
E6 Elton Brand .30 .75
E7 Wally Szczerbiak .25 .60
E8 Kobe Bryant 1.25 3.00
E9 Shawn Marion .25 .60
E10 Mike Bibby .30 .75

2000-01 Upper Deck MVP Game-Used Souvenirs

Randomly inserted into hobby packs at one in 130, this 28-card set features game-used basketball cards from some of the best players in the NBA, this set includes names such as Allen Iverson, Kobe Bryant, and Kevin Garnett. Please note that these cards use the player's initials as numbering. Two players that were supposed to be included, did not get produced - Shareef Abdur-Rahim and Shawn Marion. A 12-card autographed set was also produced where each card is sequentially numbered to 25.

STATED ODDS 1:130 HOBBY
AHS Allan Houston 3.00 8.00
AIS Allen Iverson 8.00 20.00
AJS Antawn Jamison 4.00 10.00
AMS Andre Miller 3.00 8.00
ANS Anfernee Hardaway 6.00 15.00
EJS Eddie Jones 4.00 10.00
GPS Gary Payton 4.00 10.00
JKS Jason Kidd 6.00 15.00
JWS Jason Williams 4.00 10.00
KBS Kobe Bryant 12.00 30.00
KGS Kevin Garnett 6.00 15.00
KMS Karl Malone 5.00 12.00
LHS Larry Hughes 3.00 8.00
MBS Mike Bibby 4.00 10.00
MCS Antonio McDyess 3.00 8.00
MFS Michael Finley 4.00 10.00
PPS Paul Pierce 4.00 10.00
RAS Ron Artest 4.00 10.00
RHS Richard Hamilton 3.00 8.00
RMS Reggie Miller 4.00 10.00
RWS Rasheed Wallace 4.00 10.00
RYS Ray Allen 5.00 12.00
SFS Steve Francis 3.00 8.00
SMS Stephon Marbury 3.00 8.00
SOS Shaquille O'Neal 10.00 25.00
SPS Scottie Pippen 6.00 15.00
TMS Tracy McGrady 6.00 15.00
WSS Wally Szczerbiak 3.00 8.00

2000-01 Upper Deck MVP Game-Used Souvenirs Autographs

Randomly inserted into packs, this 12-card set features autographed game-used basketball cards from some of the best players in the NBA, this set includes names such as Allen Iverson, Kobe Bryant, and Kevin Garnett. Please note that these cards use the player's initials as numbering.

STATED PRINT RUN 25 SERIAL #'d SETS
ANA Anfernee Hardaway 75.00 150.00
KBA Kobe Bryant 150.00 300.00
KGA Kevin Garnett 100.00 200.00
KMA Karl Malone 125.00 250.00
LHA Larry Hughes 25.00 60.00
MBA Mike Bibby 25.00 60.00
MCA Antonio McDyess 25.00 60.00
PPA Paul Pierce 40.00 100.00
RHA Richard Hamilton 30.00 80.00
RYA Ray Allen 50.00 120.00
SFA Steve Francis 30.00 80.00
WSA Wally Szczerbiak 25.00 60.00

2000-01 Upper Deck MVP Theatre

Randomly inserted into packs at one in 14, this 10-card set features players that put on a "show" everytime that step onto the court. Card backs carry a "M" prefix.

COMPLETE SET (10) 3.00 8.00
STATED ODDS 1:14 HOB/RET
M1 Kobe Bryant 1.50 4.00
M2 Alonzo Mourning .50 1.25
M3 Reggie Miller .40 1.00
M4 Chris Webber .40 1.00
M5 John Stockton .50 1.25
M6 Vince Carter .75 2.00
M7 Richard Hamilton .30 .75
M8 Hakeem Olajuwon .50 1.25
M9 Kevin Garnett .60 1.50
M10 David Robinson .60 1.50

2000-01 Upper Deck MVP MVPerformers

Randomly inserted into packs at one in 28, this 11-card insert features MVP caliber players. Card backs carry a "P"

COMPLETE SET (11) 5.00 12.00
STATED ODDS 1:28 HOB/RET
P1 Kobe Bryant 2.50 6.00
P2 Antawn Jamison .60 1.50
P3 John Stockton .75 2.00
P4 Andre Miller .50 1.25
P5 Latrell Sprewell .50 1.25
P6 Jason Williams .60 1.50
P7 Kevin Garnett 1.00 2.50
P8 Lamar Odom .50 1.25
P9 Allan Houston .50 1.25
P10 Keith Van Horn .50 1.25
P11 Antoine Walker .50 1.25

2000-01 Upper Deck MVP ProSign

Randomly inserted in retail packs at one in 216, this 18-card set features autographs from NBA players. The cards are numbered on the back by initial. A gold version sequentially numbered to 25 was also issued.

STATED ODDS 1:216 RETAIL
AH Anfernee Hardaway 30.00 80.00
CB Calvin Booth 4.00 10.00
DA Darrell Armstrong 4.00 10.00
DS Damon Stoudamire 10.00 25.00
GP Gary Payton 12.00 30.00
JR Jalen Rose 10.00 25.00
KA Karl Malone 40.00 80.00
KB Kobe Bryant 40.00 100.00
KG Kevin Garnett 50.00 120.00
LH Larry Hughes 6.00 15.00
MB Mike Bibby 6.00 15.00
MD Antonio McDyess 6.00 15.00
PP Paul Pierce 10.00 25.00
RA Ray Allen 10.00 25.00
SA Shareef Abdur-Rahim 6.00 15.00
SF Steve Francis 6.00 15.00
WS Wally Szczerbiak 5.00 12.00

2000-01 Upper Deck MVP ProSign Gold

*GOLD: .75X TO 2X HI
STATED PRINT RUN 25 SERIAL #'d SETS
KB Kobe Bryant 150.00 400.00
MJ Michael Jordan 1000.00 2000.00

2000-01 Upper Deck MVP World Jam

Randomly inserted into packs at one in five, this 20-card insert features players that have mastered the art of the "slam-dunk". Card backs carry a "WJ" prefix.

COMPLETE SET (20) 4.00 10.00
STATED ODDS 1:5 HOB/RET
WJ1 Kobe Bryant 1.25 3.00
WJ2 Vince Carter .60 1.50
WJ3 Steve Francis .25 .60
WJ4 Keith Van Horn .25 .60
WJ5 Rasheed Wallace .30 .75
WJ6 Corey Maggette .25 .60
WJ7 Kevin Garnett .50 1.25
WJ8 Larry Hughes .25 .60
WJ9 Tim Duncan .60 1.50
WJ10 Alonzo Mourning .40 1.00
WJ11 Chris Webber .30 .75
WJ12 Shareef Abdur-Rahim .25 .60
WJ13 Lamar Odom .25 .60
WJ14 Ron Mercer .20 .50
WJ15 Rashard Lewis .30 .75
WJ16 Michael Dickerson .20 .50
WJ17 Jerry Stackhouse .25 .60
WJ18 Latrell Sprewell .25 .60
WJ19 Shawn Kemp .30 .75
WJ20 Elton Brand .30 .75

2001-02 Upper Deck MVP

This 220-card base set includes 188 veterans, 30 rookies and 2 checklist cards. The set was issued in August of 2001. There are 24 packs per box; 8 cards per pack and a SRP of $1.99 per pack. The standard sized card features a color action shot of the featured player set within white borders. Black tags are found on the top and bottom of the card with the player's name on the bottom black tag.

COMPLETE SET (220) 20.00 40.00
1 Jason Terry .20 .50
2 Alan Henderson .12 .30
3 Toni Kukoc .20 .50
4 Hanno Mottola .12 .30
5 Theo Ratliff .12 .30
6 DerMarr Johnson .12 .30
7 Paul Pierce .20 .50
8 Antoine Walker .15 .40
9 Bryant Stith .12 .30
10 Kenny Anderson .15 .40
11 Vitaly Potapenko .12 .30
12 Eric Williams .12 .30
13 Jamal Mashburn .15 .40
14 David Wesley .12 .30
15 Baron Davis .20 .50
16 Elden Campbell .12 .30
17 P.J. Brown .12 .30
18 Jamaal Magloire .12 .30
19 Eddie Robinson .12 .30
20 Elton Brand .20 .50
21 Ron Mercer .12 .30
22 Fred Hoiberg .12 .30
23 Jamal Crawford .20 .50
24 Ron Artest .20 .50
25 Marcus Fizer .12 .30
26 Andre Miller .15 .40
27 Lamond Murray .12 .30
28 Jim Jackson .12 .30
29 Chris Mihm .12 .30
30 Matt Harpring .12 .30
31 Chris Gatling .12 .30
32 Michael Finley .20 .50
33 Steve Nash .30 .75
34 Dirk Nowitzki .30 .75
35 Juwan Howard .15 .40
36 Howard Eisley .12 .30
37 Eduardo Najera .12 .30
38 Wang Zhizhi .15 .40
39 Antonio McDyess .15 .40
40 Nick Van Exel .15 .40
41 Raef LaFrentz .12 .30
42 James Posey .12 .30
43 George McCloud .12 .30
44 Voshon Lenard .12 .30
45 Jerry Stackhouse .15 .40
46 Chucky Atkins .12 .30
47 Corliss Williamson .12 .30
48 Joe Smith .15 .40
49 Mateen Cleaves .12 .30
50 Ben Wallace .15 .40
51 Antawn Jamison .20 .50
52 Marc Jackson .12 .30
53 Larry Hughes .15 .40
54 Bob Sura .12 .30
55 Chris Porter .12 .30
56 Vonteego Cummings .12 .30
57 Steve Francis .15 .40
58 Hakeem Olajuwon .25 .60
59 Cuttino Mobley .12 .30
60 Maurice Taylor .12 .30
61 Shandon Anderson .12 .30
62 Walt Williams .12 .30
63 Moochie Norris .12 .30
64 Reggie Miller .20 .50
65 Jalen Rose .15 .40
66 Jermaine O'Neal .15 .40
67 Austin Croshere .12 .30
68 Travis Best .12 .30
69 Al Harrington .15 .40
70 Jonathan Bender .12 .30
71 Darius Miles .12 .30
72 Corey Maggette .15 .40
73 Lamar Odom .15 .40
74 Quentin Richardson .15 .40
75 Keyon Dooling .12 .30
76 Jeff McInnis .12 .30
77 Eric Piatkowski .12 .30
78 Kobe Bryant .75 2.00
79 Shaquille O'Neal .50 1.25
80 Rick Fox .12 .30
81 Derek Fisher .15 .40
82 Robert Horry .15 .40
83 Ron Harper .15 .40
84 Brian Shaw .12 .30
85 Alonzo Mourning .25 .60
86 Eddie Jones .15 .40
87 Tim Hardaway .20 .50
88 Anthony Mason .12 .30
89 Brian Grant .12 .30
90 Anthony Carter .12 .30
91 Bruce Bowen .12 .30
92 Ray Allen .20 .50
93 Glenn Robinson .15 .40
94 Sam Cassell .15 .40
95 Tim Thomas .12 .30
96 Ervin Johnson .12 .30
97 Joel Przybilla .12 .30
98 Kevin Garnett .30 .75
99 Terrell Brandon .12 .30
100 Wally Szczerbiak .15 .40
101 Chauncey Billups .20 .50
102 LaPhonso Ellis .15 .40
103 Anthony Peeler .12 .30
104 Stephon Marbury .15 .40
105 Keith Van Horn .15 .40
106 Kenyon Martin .20 .50
107 Kendall Gill .12 .30
108 Lucious Harris .12 .30
109 Stephen Jackson .15 .40
110 Latrell Sprewell .15 .40
111 Allan Houston .15 .40
112 Marcus Camby .15 .40
113 Mark Jackson .15 .40
114 Glen Rice .15 .40
115 Kurt Thomas .12 .30
116 Tracy McGrady .30 .75
117 Darrell Armstrong .12 .30
118 Mike Miller .15 .40
119 Grant Hill .25 .60
120 Pat Garrity .12 .30
121 John Amaechi .12 .30
122 Allen Iverson .40 1.00
123 Dikembe Mutombo .20 .50
124 Aaron McKie .12 .30
125 Tyrone Hill .12 .30
126 George Lynch .12 .30
127 Eric Snow .12 .30
128 Matt Geiger .12 .30
129 Jason Kidd .30 .75
130 Shawn Marion .15 .40
131 Tony Delk .12 .30
132 Rodney Rogers .12 .30
133 Tom Gugliotta .12 .30
134 Anfernee Hardaway .30 .75
135 Rasheed Wallace .20 .50
136 Damon Stoudamire .15 .40
137 Arvydas Sabonis .15 .40
138 Scottie Pippen .30 .75
139 Steve Smith .15 .40
140 Stacey Augmon .12 .30
141 Bonzi Wells .12 .30
142 Jason Williams .15 .40
143 Chris Webber .20 .50
144 Peja Stojakovic .20 .50
145 Doug Christie .12 .30
146 Scot Pollard .12 .30
147 Hedo Turkoglu .15 .40
148 Vlade Divac .15 .40
149 Tim Duncan .40 1.00
150 David Robinson .30 .75
151 Antonio Daniels .12 .30
152 Sean Elliott .20 .50
153 Derek Anderson .12 .30
154 Avery Johnson .15 .40
155 Malik Rose .12 .30
156 Gary Payton .20 .50
157 Rashard Lewis .20 .50
158 Patrick Ewing .25 .60
159 Vin Baker .15 .40
160 Emanual Davis .12 .30
161 Desmond Mason .15 .40
162 Vince Carter .30 .75
163 Morris Peterson .12 .30
164 Antonio Davis .12 .30
165 Keon Clark .12 .30
166 Chris Childs .12 .30
167 Charles Oakley .15 .40
168 Alvin Williams .12 .30
169 Dell Curry .12 .30
170 Karl Malone .25 .60
171 John Stockton .25 .60
172 Donyell Marshall .12 .30
173 John Starks .12 .30
174 Bryon Russell .12 .30
175 David Benoit .12 .30
176 Jacque Vaughn .12 .30
177 Shareef Abdur-Rahim .15 .40
178 Mike Bibby .20 .50
179 Michael Dickerson .12 .30
180 Bryant Reeves .12 .30
181 Grant Long .12 .30
182 Stromile Swift .12 .30
183 Richard Hamilton .15 .40
184 Tyrone Nesby .12 .30
185 Jahidi White .12 .30
186 Chris Whitney .12 .30
187 Courtney Alexander .12 .30
188 Christian Laettner .15 .40
189 Kobe Bryant CL .40 1.00
190 Kevin Garnett CL .15 .40
191 Vladimir Radmanovic RC .40 1.00
192 Alvin Jones RC .30 .75
193 Tyson Chandler RC .60 1.50
194 Omar Cook RC .40 1.00
195 Kedrick Brown RC .25 .60
196 DeSagana Diop RC .30 .75
197 Eddie Griffin RC .30 .75
198 Zach Randolph RC .60 1.50
199 Eddy Curry RC .40 1.00
200 Jeryl Sasser RC .25 .60
201 Gerald Wallace RC .50 1.25
202 Jamaal Tinsley RC .40 1.00
203 Kirk Haston RC .25 .60
204 Terence Morris RC .40 1.00
205 Jarron Collins RC .40 1.00
206 Joseph Forte RC .25 .60
207 Kenny Satterfield RC .25 .60
208 Michael Wright RC .40 1.00
209 Jason Richardson RC .50 1.25
210 Michael Bradley RC .25 .60
211 Gilbert Arenas RC .60 1.50
212 Jeff Trepagnier RC .25 .60
213 Samuel Dalembert RC .40 1.00
214 Troy Murphy RC .40 1.00
215 Rodney White RC .25 .60
216 Joe Johnson RC .50 1.25
217 Richard Jefferson RC .60 1.50
218 Kwame Brown RC .40 1.00
219 Jason Collins RC .30 .75
220 Steven Hunter RC .30 .75

2001-02 Upper Deck MVP Airborne

Randomly inserted in packs at a rate of one in 24, this seven card set shows player's in top flight mode set against a purple sky background with silver foil highlights outlining and surround the photo, and gold foil highlights on the Upper Deck MVP Logo, the set name, and the player's name.

COMPLETE SET (7) 5.00 12.00
STATED ODDS 1:24
A1 Kobe Bryant 2.50 6.00
A2 Vince Carter 1.00 2.50
A3 Baron Davis .60 1.50
A4 Kevin Garnett 1.00 2.50
A5 Tracy McGrady 1.00 2.50
A6 Shaquille O'Neal 1.50 4.00
A7 Desmond Mason .50 1.25

2001-02 Upper Deck MVP Authentic Kobe

Randomly inserted in hobby packs only at a rate of one in 288, this insert set showcases Kobe Bryant. The collection is comprised of six different card types: Authentic Kobe Autograph (numbered to 100); Authentic Kobe Warm-up; Authentic Kobe Shooting Shirt, Authentic Kobe Game Floor, Authentic Kobe Autographed Game Floor (numbered to 8), and Authentic Kobe Autograph Gold (numbered to 8).

COMMON AU (KBA1-KBA2) 100.00 200.00
AU PRINT RUN 100 SERIAL #'d SETS
COMMON FLOOR (KBF1-KBF8) 10.00 25.00
OVERALL ODDS 1:288 H, 1:240 R
KBW Kobe Bryant Warm-up 8.00 20.00
KBSS Kobe Bryant Shirt 8.00 20.00

2001-02 Upper Deck MVP Basketball Diary

Randomly inserted in packs at a rate of one in 12, this 14-card set photos players in full color with foil borders on three sides and gold foil highlights.

COMPLETE SET (14) 6.00 15.00
STATED ODDS 1:12
BD1 Alonzo Mourning .60 1.50
BD2 Wang Zhizhi .40 1.00
BD3 Chris Webber .50 1.25
BD4 Paul Pierce .50 1.25
BD5 Kevin Garnett .75 2.00
BD6 Dirk Nowitzki .75 2.00
BD7 Marc Jackson .30 .75
BD8 Kobe Bryant 2.00 5.00
BD9 Ray Allen .50 1.25
BD10 Tracy McGrady .75 2.00
BD11 Jerry Stackhouse .40 1.00
BD12 Kenyon Martin .50 1.25
BD13 Rasheed Wallace .50 1.25
BD14 Steve Francis .40 1.00

2001-02 Upper Deck MVP Game Night Gear

Randomly inserted in hobby packs at a rate of one in 96, this 19-card set features a full color player photo and a swatch of a game used jersey. Jason Kidd appeared on the original checklist but his card was never produced

STATED ODDS 1:96 H, 1:120 R
AIG Allen Iverson 6.00 15.00
AJG A.J. Guyton 2.00 5.00
BCG Brian Cardinal 2.00 5.00
CMG Chris Mihm 2.00 5.00
COG Corey Maggette 2.50 6.00
DAG Darrell Armstrong 2.00 5.00
DGG Dean Garrett 2.00 5.00
DHG Donnell Harvey 2.00 5.00
IRG Isaiah Rider 2.50 6.00
JAG John Amaechi 2.00 5.00
JSG Jerry Stackhouse 2.50 6.00
KBG Kobe Bryant 12.00 30.00
KGG Kevin Garnett 5.00 12.00
KVG Keith Van Horn 2.50 6.00
LMG Lamond Murray 2.00 5.00
MAG Marcus Camby 2.50 6.00
MCG Antonio McDyess 2.50 6.00
RMG Ron Mercer 2.00 5.00
WSG Wally Szczerbiak 2.50 6.00

2001-02 Upper Deck MVP Game Night Gear Autographs

RANDOM INSERTS IN PACKS
STATED PRINT RUN 100 SERIAL #'d SETS
CMA Chris Mihm 8.00 20.00
COA Corey Maggette 8.00 20.00
DAA Darrell Armstrong 8.00 20.00
DHA Donnell Harvey 8.00 20.00
JSA Jerry Stackhouse 12.50 30.00
KBA Kobe Bryant 150.00 300.00
KGA Kevin Garnett 40.00 100.00
LMA Lamond Murray 8.00 20.00
MCA Antonio McDyess 8.00 20.00
WSA Wally Szczerbiak 8.00 20.00

2001-02 Upper Deck MVP Respect the Game

This 14-card insert set was randomly inserted in packs at a rate of one in 12, this 14-card set places full color player action photos on an all holo-foil background. The borders are white except for a square in each corner of holofoil, and cards are enhanced with gold and sliver foil highlights.

COMPLETE SET (14) 8.00 20.00
STATED ODDS 1:12
RG1 Kobe Bryant 2.50 6.00
RG2 Gary Payton .60 1.50
RG3 Tim Duncan 1.25 3.00
RG4 Lamar Odom .50 1.25
RG5 Vince Carter 1.00 2.50
RG6 Eddie Jones .50 1.25
RG7 Kevin Garnett 1.00 2.50
RG8 Jamal Mashburn .50 1.25
RG9 Michael Finley .60 1.50
RG10 Shaquille O'Neal 1.50 4.00
RG11 Latrell Sprewell .50 1.25
RG12 Steve Francis .50 1.25
RG13 Reggie Miller .60 1.50
RG14 Ray Allen .60 1.50

2001-02 Upper Deck MVP Souvenirs

Randomly inserted in hobby packs only at a rate of one in 96, this 19-card set features full color player photography set on a white and silver background. Each card is enhanced with silver foil highlights and a swatch of game used material. A Gold version sequentially numbered to 50 was also issued.

STATED ODDS 1:96 HOBBY
*GOLD: 1.25X TO 3X SOUVENIR HI
GOLD PRINT RUN 50 SER.#'d SETS
AJ Antawn Jamison 4.00 10.00
AM Andre Miller 3.00 8.00
CW Chris Webber 6.00 15.00
DM Darius Miles 2.50 6.00
DR David Robinson 6.00 15.00
JK Jason Kidd 6.00 15.00
JS Jerry Stackhouse 3.00 8.00
JT Jason Terry 4.00 10.00
KB Kobe Bryant 15.00 40.00
KG Kevin Garnett 6.00 15.00
KM Karl Malone 5.00 12.00
MC Antonio McDyess 3.00 8.00
MF Michael Finley 4.00 10.00
RH Richard Hamilton 3.00 8.00
RM Ron Mercer 2.50 6.00
SF Steve Francis 3.00 8.00
SH Shawn Marion 3.00 8.00
SM Stephon Marbury 3.00 8.00
TB Terrell Brandon 2.50 6.00

2001-02 Upper Deck MVP Souvenirs Combos

Randomly inserted in hobby packs only at a rate of one in 288, this nine card set utilizes the same design as the MVP Souvenirs set but switches the card to a horizontal design. Each card features two players and two swatches of game used memorabilia. A Gold version sequentially numbered to 50 was also issued.

STATED ODDS 1:288
*GOLD: 1X TO 2.5X COMBO HI
GOLD PRINT RUN 50 SER.#'d SETS
AWPP A.Walker/P.Pierce 10.00 25.00
BDJM B.Davis/J.Mashburn 8.00 20.00
DMQRCM Miles/Rchrdsn/Mggtte 8.00 20.00
DRDA D.Robinson/D.Anderson 8.00 20.00
JKSM J.Kidd/S.Marion 10.00 25.00
KBDM K.Bryant/D.Miles 12.50 30.00
KBKG K.Bryant/K.Garnett 15.00 40.00
KMJS K.Malone/J.Stockton 15.00 40.00
SMKMKV Mrbury/Mrtn/V.Horn 8.00 20.00

2001-02 Upper Deck MVP Watch

Randomly inserted in packs at a rate of one in 24, this seven card set features full color player photos in holofoil set against a non-foil background. The right side of the card features a one-color player photo and gold foil highlights.

COMPLETE SET (7) 6.00 15.00
STATED ODDS 1:24
M1 Shaquille O'Neal 1.50 4.00
M2 Vince Carter 1.00 2.50
M3 Chris Webber .60 1.50
M4 Karl Malone .75 2.00
M5 Kevin Garnett 1.00 2.50
M6 Kobe Bryant 2.50 6.00
M7 Tim Duncan 1.25 3.00

2002-03 Upper Deck MVP

Released in late August 2002, Upper Deck MVP boasts a 220-card base set divided up into 190 veteran cards and 30 rookie cards. Base card design consists of full-color player action phototgraphy set against a colored background set to match his team's colors. This colored background fades into a white border. MVP was packaged in 24-pack boxes where each pack contained eight cards and carried a suggested retail price of $1.99.

COMPLETE SET (220) 20.00 50.00
1 Shareef Abdur-Rahim .15 .40
2 Jason Terry .15 .40
3 Toni Kukoc .20 .50
4 DerMarr Johnson .12 .30
5 Nazr Mohammed .12 .30
6 Theo Ratliff .12 .30
7 Dion Glover .12 .30
8 Paul Pierce .20 .50
9 Antoine Walker .15 .40
10 Kenny Anderson .15 .40
11 Tony Delk .12 .30
12 Eric Williams .12 .30
13 Rodney Rogers .12 .30
14 Jamal Mashburn .15 .40
15 Baron Davis .15 .40
16 David Wesley .12 .30
17 Elden Campbell .12 .30
18 P.J. Brown .12 .30
19 Jamaal Magloire .12 .30
20 Stacey Augmon .12 .30
21 Jalen Rose .15 .40
22 Marcus Fizer .12 .30
23 Tyson Chandler .20 .50
24 Trenton Hassell .12 .30
25 Eddy Curry .12 .30
26 Travis Best .12 .30
27 Andre Miller .15 .40
28 Lamond Murray .12 .30
29 Ricky Davis .15 .40
30 Zydrunas Ilgauskas .15 .40
31 Jumaine Jones .12 .30
32 Chris Mihm .12 .30
33 Dirk Nowitzki .30 .75
34 Michael Finley .20 .50
35 Steve Nash .25 .60
36 Nick Van Exel .15 .40
37 Raef LaFrentz .12 .30
38 Adrian Griffin .12 .30
39 Avery Johnson .15 .40
40 Marcus Camby .15 .40
41 Juwan Howard .15 .40
42 James Posey .12 .30
43 Ryan Bowen .12 .30
44 Donnell Harvey .12 .30
45 Voshon Lenard .12 .30
46 Jerry Stackhouse .15 .40
47 Clifford Robinson .12 .30
48 Chucky Atkins .12 .30
49 Ben Wallace .15 .40
50 Jon Barry .12 .30
51 Corliss Williamson .12 .30
52 Antawn Jamison .20 .50
53 Jason Richardson .20 .50
54 Danny Fortson .12 .30
55 Gilbert Arenas .20 .50
56 Bob Sura .12 .30
57 Troy Murphy .15 .40
58 Steve Francis .15 .40
59 Cuttino Mobley .12 .30
60 Eddie Griffin .12 .30
61 Kenny Thomas .12 .30
62 Moochie Norris .12 .30
63 Kelvin Cato .12 .30
64 Glen Rice .15 .40
65 Reggie Miller .20 .50
66 Jermaine O'Neal .15 .40
67 Ron Mercer .12 .30
68 Jamaal Tinsley .12 .30
69 Al Harrington .15 .40
70 Ron Artest .20 .50
71 Austin Croshere .12 .30
72 Elton Brand .20 .50
73 Darius Miles .12 .30
74 Lamar Odom .15 .40
75 Quentin Richardson .15 .40
76 Corey Maggette .15 .40
77 Jeff McInnis .12 .30
78 Michael Olowokandi .12 .30
79 Kobe Bryant .75 2.00
80 Shaquille O'Neal .50 1.25
81 Derek Fisher .15 .40
82 Rick Fox .12 .30
83 Robert Horry .15 .40
84 Devean George .12 .30
85 Samaki Walker .12 .30
86 Pau Gasol .25 .60
87 Jason Williams .15 .40
88 Shane Battier .20 .50
89 Stromile Swift .12 .30
90 Lorenzen Wright .12 .30
91 Tony Massenburg .12 .30
92 Eddie Jones .15 .40
93 Alonzo Mourning .25 .60
94 Brian Grant .12 .30
95 Anthony Carter .12 .30
96 LaPhonso Ellis .15 .40
97 Jim Jackson .12 .30
98 Ray Allen .20 .50
99 Glenn Robinson .15 .40
100 Sam Cassell .15 .40
101 Tim Thomas .12 .30
102 Anthony Mason .12 .30
103 Joel Przybilla .12 .30

104 Ervin Johnson .12 .30
105 Kevin Garnett .30 .75
106 Wally Szczerbiak .15 .40
107 Chauncey Billups .20 .50
108 Terrell Brandon .12 .30
109 Marc Jackson .12 .30
110 Joe Smith .15 .40
111 Jason Kidd .30 .75
112 Keith Van Horn .15 .40
113 Kenyon Martin .15 .40
114 Kerry Kittles .12 .30
115 Richard Jefferson .20 .50
116 Jason Collins .12 .30
117 Todd MacCulloch .12 .30
118 Allan Houston .15 .40
119 Latrell Sprewell .15 .40
120 Kurt Thomas .12 .30
121 Antonio McDyess .15 .40
122 Othella Harrington .12 .30
123 Clarence Weatherspoon .12 .30
124 Tracy McGrady .30 .75
125 Mike Miller .15 .40
126 Darrell Armstrong .12 .30
127 Grant Hill .25 .60
128 Horace Grant .15 .40
129 Steven Hunter .12 .30
130 Allen Iverson .30 .75
131 Dikembe Mutombo .20 .50
132 Aaron McKie .12 .30
133 Derrick Coleman .15 .40
134 Eric Snow .12 .30
135 Matt Harpring .12 .30
136 Stephon Marbury .15 .40
137 Shawn Marion .15 .40
138 Joe Johnson .15 .40
139 Anfernee Hardaway .30 .75
140 Iakovos Tsakalidis .12 .30
141 Tom Gugliotta .12 .30
142 Bo Outlaw .12 .30
143 Rasheed Wallace .20 .50
144 Damon Stoudamire .15 .40
145 Scottie Pippen .30 .75
146 Ruben Patterson .12 .30
147 Derek Anderson .12 .30
148 Dale Davis .12 .30
149 Bonzi Wells .12 .30
150 Chris Webber .20 .50
151 Peja Stojakovic .20 .50
152 Mike Bibby .20 .50
153 Doug Christie .12 .30
154 Vlade Divac .15 .40
155 Bobby Jackson .12 .30
156 Hedo Turkoglu .15 .40
157 Tim Duncan .40 1.00
158 David Robinson .30 .75
159 Steve Smith .15 .40
160 Tony Parker .25 .60
161 Antonio Daniels .12 .30
162 Charles Smith .12 .30
163 Bruce Bowen .12 .30
164 Gary Payton .20 .50
165 Rashard Lewis .20 .50
166 Vin Baker .15 .40
167 Brent Barry .12 .30
168 Desmond Mason .15 .40
169 Vladimir Radmanovic .12 .30
170 Vince Carter .30 .75
171 Morris Peterson .12 .30
172 Antonio Davis .12 .30
173 Hakeem Olajuwon .25 .60
174 Alvin Williams .12 .30
175 Jerome Williams .12 .30
176 Keon Clark .12 .30
177 Karl Malone .25 .60
178 John Stockton .25 .60
179 Donyell Marshall .12 .30
180 Andrei Kirilenko .20 .50
181 Bryon Russell .12 .30
182 Jarron Collins .12 .30
183 DeShawn Stevenson .12 .30
184 Michael Jordan 1.50 4.00
185 Richard Hamilton .15 .40
186 Kwame Brown .12 .30
187 Chris Whitney .12 .30
188 Tyronn Lue .12 .30
189 Brendan Haywood .12 .30
190 Jahidi White .12 .30
191 DaJuan Wagner RC .40 1.00
192 Jay Williams RC .50 1.25
193 Yao Ming RC 1.00 2.50
194 Drew Gooden RC .50 1.25
195 Chris Jefferies RC .30 .75
196 Casey Jacobsen RC .40 1.00
197 Juan Dixon RC .50 1.25
198 Melvin Ely RC .40 1.00
199 Curtis Borchardt RC .30 .75
200 John Salmons RC .50 1.25
201 Carlos Boozer RC .50 1.25
202 Fred Jones RC .40 1.00
203 Frank Williams RC .30 .75
204 Jamal Sampson RC .50 1.25
205 Dan Dickau RC .40 1.00
206 Marcus Haislip RC .40 1.00
207 Jared Jeffries RC .40 1.00
208 Amare Stoudemire RC .60 1.50
209 Caron Butler RC .50 1.25
210 Qyntel Woods RC .40 1.00
211 Kareem Rush RC .40 1.00
212 Ryan Humphrey RC .40 1.00
213 Jiri Welsch RC .40 1.00
214 Mike Dunleavy RC .50 1.25
215 Tayshaun Prince RC .60 1.50
216 Nene Hilario RC .50 1.25
217 Nikoloz Tskitishvili RC .30 .75
218 Bostjan Nachbar RC .40 1.00
219 Efthimios Rentzias RC .30 .75
220 Rod Grizzard RC .30 .75

2002-03 Upper Deck MVP Classic

*CLASSIC: .5X TO 1.25X BASE CARD HI
STATED ODDS 1:2

2002-03 Upper Deck MVP Classic Black

*BLACK: 10X TO 25X BASE CARD HI
PRINT RUN 50 SERIAL #'d SETS

2002-03 Upper Deck MVP Gold

*GOLD: 8X TO 20X BASE CARD HI
PRINT RUN 100 SERIAL #'d SETS
79 Kobe Bryant 25.00 60.00

2002-03 Upper Deck MVP Air Apparent

Inserted in packs at the rate of one in 24, this seven card set centers full color player action photography on a card enhanced with silver foil highlights. The Air Apparent logo is centered along the bottom of the card.

COMPLETE SET (7) 5.00 12.00
STATED ODDS 1:24
1 Kobe Bryant 3.00 8.00
2 Kevin Garnett 1.25 3.00
3 Darius Miles .50 1.25
4 Vince Carter 1.25 3.00
5 Tracy McGrady 1.25 3.00
6 Rashard Lewis .75 2.00
7 Jason Richardson .75 2.00

2002-03 Upper Deck MVP Basketball Diary

Inserted in packs at the rate of one 12, this 14-card set showcases a date where the featured player compiled some type of incredible statistic. The top of the card features full color action photo separated towards the bottom third by silver foil and the statistic.

COMPLETE SET (14) 8.00 20.00
STATED ODDS 1:12
1 Michael Jordan 4.00 10.00
2 Kobe Bryant 2.00 5.00
3 Kevin Garnett .75 2.00
4 Dirk Nowitzki .75 2.00
5 Shaquille O'Neal 1.25 3.00
6 Pau Gasol .60 1.50
7 Stephon Marbury .40 1.00
8 Jerry Stackhouse .40 1.00
9 Steve Francis .40 1.00
10 Jason Richardson .50 1.25
11 Elton Brand .50 1.25
12 Vince Carter .75 2.00
13 Jamaal Tinsley .30 .75
14 Tim Duncan 1.00 2.50

2002-03 Upper Deck MVP East Side West Side Shooting Shirt

Inserted in packs, this six card set features a horizontal card design with two players. On the far left side of the card front is a player from the Eastern Conference, and on the far right side is a player from the Western conference. Two swatches of shooting shirt appear towards the middle, and each card is sequentially numbered to 100.

PRINT RUN 100 SERIAL #'d SETS
BD/SM B.Davis/S.Marbury 15.00 40.00
JK/JS J.Kidd/J.Stockton 40.00 80.00
KW/CW K.Martin/C.Webber 25.00 60.00
MJ/KB M.Jordan/K.Bryant 75.00 200.00
PP/SH P.Pierce/S.Marion 25.00 60.00
RH/PS R.Hamilton/P.Stojakovic 15.00 40.00

2002-03 Upper Deck MVP Materials Combo

Inserted in packs at the rate of one in 144, this six card set showcases a player with a swatch of both a shooting shirt and a warm up. The design places players in action in the center of the card with an oval design around him and the swatches on either side of the picture.

STATED ODDS 1:144
1 Chris Webber 4.00 10.00
2 Kobe Bryant 15.00 40.00
3 Kevin Garnett 6.00 15.00
4 Lamar Odom 3.00 8.00
5 Michael Jordan 40.00 80.00
6 Wally Szczerbiak 3.00 8.00

2002-03 Upper Deck MVP Materials Shooting Shirt

Inserted in packs at the rate of one in 72, this 12-card set places a full color player action photo on the left against a background set to match team colors and a square swatch of shooting shirt on the right.

STATED ODDS 1:72
AKS Andrei Kirilenko 4.00 10.00
AWS Antoine Walker 3.00 8.00
DJS DerMarr Johnson 2.50 6.00
EBS Elton Brand 4.00 10.00
JSS Jeryl Sasser 2.50 6.00
KBS Kobe Bryant 15.00 40.00
MBS Mike Bibby 4.00 10.00
MJS Michael Jordan 60.00 150.00
MPS Morris Peterson 2.50 6.00
SHS Shawn Marion 3.00 8.00
SMS Stephon Marbury 3.00 8.00

2002-03 Upper Deck MVP Materials Warm Up

Inserted in packs at the rate of one in 48, this 12-card set places a full color player action photo on the right against a background set to match team colors and a square swatch of shooting shirt on the left.

STATED ODDS 1:48
ADW Antonio Davis 2.00 5.00
BDW Baron Davis 2.50 6.00
BHW Brendan Haywood 2.00 5.00
DNW Dirk Nowitzki 5.00 12.00
GRW Glenn Robinson 2.50 6.00
KBW Kobe Bryant 12.00 30.00
KGW Kevin Garnett 5.00 12.00
KMW Karl Malone 4.00 10.00
KVW Keith Van Horn 2.50 6.00
MCW Antonio McDyess 2.50 6.00
MJW Michael Jordan 40.00 100.00
SAW Shareef Abdur-Rahim 2.50 6.00

2002-03 Upper Deck MVP Moments

Randomly seeded in packs at the rate of one in 24, this seven card set showcases top NBA players on a bordered card. Action photos are centered, and the card front is enhanced with silver foil highlights.

COMPLETE SET (7) 8.00 20.00
STATED ODDS 1:24
1 Shaquille O'Neal 1.50 4.00
2 Jason Kidd 1.00 2.50
3 Allen Iverson 1.00 2.50
4 Tim Duncan 1.25 3.00
5 Michael Jordan 5.00 12.00
6 Kevin Garnett 1.00 2.50
7 Kobe Bryant 2.50 6.00

2002-03 Upper Deck MVP Prosign

Randomly inserted in packs at the rate of one in 288, this 28-card set fatures a player photo on the left, his number on the right over which an authentic player autograph appears.

STATED ODDS 1:288
1 Brandon Armstrong 5.00 12.00
2 Corey Maggette 6.00 15.00
3 DerMarr Johnson 5.00 12.00
4 Eddie Griffin 5.00 12.00
5 Gilbert Arenas 10.00 25.00
6 Hanno Mottola 5.00 12.00
7 Jeff Trepagnier 5.00 12.00
8 Jamaal Magloire 5.00 12.00
9 Jason Richardson 8.00 20.00
12 Kobe Bryant 75.00 150.00
13 Kenyon Martin 15.00 40.00
17 Michael Bradley 5.00 12.00
18 Marcus Fizer 5.00 12.00
20 Terence Morris 5.00 12.00
21 Paul Pierce 20.00 50.00
22 Richard Jefferson 10.00 25.00
25 Samuel Dalembert 5.00 12.00
26 Tyson Chandler 8.00 20.00

2002-03 Upper Deck MVP Rising to the Occasion

Inserted in packs at the rate of one in 12, this 14-card set features a full color player action photo towards the left and a colored background to match team colors containing a player portrait style photo on the right. Each card is enhanced with silver foil higlights.

COMPLETE SET (14) 8.00 20.00
STATED ODDS 1:12
1 Kobe Bryant 2.00 5.00
2 Kevin Garnett .75 2.00
3 Michael Jordan 4.00 10.00
4 Paul Pierce .50 1.25
5 Shawn Marion .40 1.00
6 Jason Kidd .75 2.00
7 Peja Stojakovic .50 1.25
8 Tim Duncan 1.00 2.50
9 Shaquille O'Neal 1.25 3.00
10 Steve Francis .40 1.00
11 Ray Allen .50 1.25
12 Latrell Sprewell .40 1.00
13 Darius Miles .30 .75
14 Vince Carter .75 2.00

2002-03 Upper Deck MVP Triple Dimension

Randomly seeded in packs, this six card set features a horizontal card design with three players on each card, two at the top, and one at the bottom. Each player photo is coupled with a square swatch of game memorabilia, and each card is sequentially numbered to 25.

STATED PRINT RUN 25 SERIAL #'d SETS
KGWSTB Garnett/Szcz/Brandon 25.00 60.00
KMJSAK Malone/Stockton/Kirilenko 30.00 80.00
MJKBKG Jordan/Kobe/Garnett 100.00 200.00
TMMMGH McG/M.Miller/Hill 30.00 80.00

2003-04 Upper Deck MVP

Released as a 230-card set, MVP is divided up into 200 base veteran cards and 30 rookie cards. Base cards feature white borders and colored backgrounds with "MVP" appearing towards the top of the card. Several different parallels were issued for this set. A Gold version is highlighted with gold foil and sequentially numbered to 100. A Silver version was inserted at the rate of one in two for the veterans and one in 24 for the rookies, and a Black version sequentially numbered to 25 exists as well. MVP was packaged in 24-pack boxes where packs contained eight cards and carried a suggested retail price of $1.99.

COMPLETE SET (230) 20.00 50.00
201-230 STATED ODDS 1:1
1 Shareef Abdur-Rahim .15 .40
2 Jason Terry .15 .40
3 Terrell Brandon .12 .30
4 Alan Henderson .12 .30
5 Dan Dickau .12 .30
6 Theo Ratliff .12 .30
7 Dion Glover .12 .30
8 Paul Pierce .20 .50
9 Antoine Walker .20 .50
10 Eric Williams .12 .30
11 Tony Delk .12 .30
12 J.R. Bremer .12 .30
13 Vin Baker .12 .30
14 Jalen Rose .15 .40
15 Marcus Fizer .12 .30
16 Tyson Chandler .15 .40
17 Jamal Crawford .20 .50
18 Eddy Curry .12 .30
19 Scottie Pippen .30 .75
20 Darius Miles .12 .30
21 Dajuan Wagner .12 .30
22 Ricky Davis .15 .40
23 Zydrunas Ilgauskas .15 .40
24 Carlos Boozer .15 .40
25 Chris Mihm .12 .30
26 Dirk Nowitzki .30 .75
27 Michael Finley .20 .50
28 Steve Nash .25 .60
29 Nick Van Exel .15 .40
30 Raef LaFrentz .12 .30
31 Eduardo Najera .12 .30
32 Shawn Bradley .12 .30
33 Marcus Camby .15 .40
34 Vincent Yarbrough .12 .30
35 Rodney White .12 .30
36 Nene Hilario .15 .40
37 Nikoloz Tskitishvili .12 .30
38 Shammond Williams .12 .30
39 Richard Hamilton .15 .40
40 Clifford Robinson .12 .30
41 Chauncey Billups .20 .50
42 Ben Wallace .15 .40
43 Elden Campbell .12 .30
44 Corliss Williamson .12 .30
45 Antawn Jamison .15 .40
46 Jason Richardson .20 .50
47 Danny Fortson .12 .30
48 Speedy Claxton .12 .30
49 Mike Dunleavy .15 .40
50 Troy Murphy .12 .30
51 Steve Francis .15 .40
52 Cuttino Mobley .12 .30
53 Eddie Griffin .12 .30
54 Yao Ming .40 1.00
55 Maurice Taylor .12 .30
56 Kelvin Cato .12 .30
57 Glen Rice .12 .30
58 Reggie Miller .20 .50
59 Jermaine O'Neal .15 .40
60 Scot Pollard .12 .30
61 Jamaal Tinsley .12 .30
62 Al Harrington .15 .40
63 Ron Artest .20 .50
64 Danny Ferry .12 .30
65 Elton Brand .20 .50
66 Andre Miller .15 .40
67 Lamar Odom .15 .40
68 Quentin Richardson .15 .40
69 Corey Maggette .15 .40
70 Chris Wilcox .12 .30
71 Marko Jaric .12 .30
72 Kobe Bryant .75 2.00
73 Shaquille O'Neal .50 1.25
74 Derek Fisher .15 .40
75 Karl Malone .25 .60
76 Gary Payton .20 .50
77 Devean George .12 .30
78 Kareem Rush .12 .30
79 Pau Gasol .20 .50
80 Jason Williams .15 .40
81 Shane Battier .15 .40
82 Stromile Swift .12 .30
83 Lorenzen Wright .12 .30
84 Mike Miller .15 .40
85 Eddie Jones .15 .40
86 Ken Johnson .12 .30
87 Brian Grant .12 .30
88 Anthony Carter .12 .30
89 Rasual Butler .12 .30
90 Caron Butler .15 .40
91 Marcus Haislip .12 .30
92 Toni Kukoc .20 .50
93 Joe Smith .15 .40
94 Tim Thomas .12 .30
95 Anthony Mason .12 .30
96 Joel Przybilla .12 .30
97 Desmond Mason .15 .40
98 Kevin Garnett .30 .75
99 Wally Szczerbiak .15 .40
100 Troy Hudson .12 .30
101 Michael Olowokandi .12 .30
102 Kendall Gill .12 .30
103 Sam Cassell .15 .40
104 Jason Kidd .30 .75
105 Kenyon Martin .15 .40
106 Alonzo Mourning .25 .60
107 Kerry Kittles .12 .30
108 Richard Jefferson .15 .40
109 Jason Collins .12 .30
110 Dikembe Mutombo .20 .50
111 Jamal Mashburn .15 .40
112 Baron Davis .15 .40
113 David Wesley .12 .30
114 Kenny Anderson .15 .40
115 P.J. Brown .12 .30
116 Jamaal Magloire .12 .30
117 George Lynch .12 .30
118 Courtney Alexander .12 .30
119 Allan Houston .15 .40
120 Keith Van Horn .15 .40
121 Kurt Thomas .12 .30
122 Antonio McDyess .15 .40
123 Othella Harrington .12 .30
124 Clarence Weatherspoon .12 .30
125 Tracy McGrady .25 .60
126 Drew Gooden .15 .40
127 Tyronn Lue .12 .30
128 Pat Garrity .12 .30
129 Grant Hill .25 .60
130 Gordan Giricek .12 .30
131 Juwan Howard .15 .40
132 Allen Iverson .30 .75
133 Glenn Robinson .15 .40
134 Aaron McKie .12 .30
135 Derrick Coleman .15 .40
136 Eric Snow .12 .30
137 Kenny Thomas .12 .30
138 Stephon Marbury .15 .40
139 Shawn Marion .15 .40
140 Joe Johnson .15 .40
141 Anfernee Hardaway .30 .75
142 Amare Stoudemire .25 .60
143 Casey Jacobsen .12 .30
144 Tom Gugliotta .12 .30
145 Bo Outlaw .12 .30
146 Rasheed Wallace .20 .50
147 Damon Stoudamire .15 .40
148 Jeff McInnis .12 .30
149 Ruben Patterson .12 .30
150 Derek Anderson .12 .30
151 Dale Davis .12 .30
152 Bonzi Wells .12 .30
153 Chris Webber .20 .50
154 Peja Stojakovic .20 .50
155 Mike Bibby .20 .50
156 Doug Christie .12 .30
157 Vlade Divac .15 .40
158 Bobby Jackson .12 .30
159 Brad Miller .15 .40
160 Keon Clark .12 .30
161 Tim Duncan .30 .75
162 David Robinson .30 .75
163 Steve Smith .15 .40
164 Tony Parker .20 .50
165 Hedo Turkoglu .15 .40
166 Radoslav Nesterovic .12 .30
167 Manu Ginobili .25 .60
168 Ron Mercer .12 .30
169 Ray Allen .20 .50
170 Rashard Lewis .20 .50
171 Antonio Daniels .12 .30
172 Brent Barry .12 .30
173 Predrag Drobnjak .12 .30
174 Vladimir Radmanovic .12 .30
175 Vince Carter .30 .75
176 Morris Peterson .12 .30
177 Antonio Davis .12 .30
178 Chris Jefferies .12 .30
179 Lindsey Hunter .12 .30
180 Alvin Williams .12 .30
181 Jerome Williams .12 .30
182 Jerome Moiso .12 .30
183 Greg Ostertag .12 .30
184 John Stockton .25 .60
185 Matt Harpring .12 .30
186 Andrei Kirilenko .20 .50
187 Calbert Cheaney .12 .30
188 Jarron Collins .12 .30
189 DeShawn Stevenson .12 .30
190 Michael Jordan 1.50 4.00
191 Jerry Stackhouse .15 .40
192 Kwame Brown .12 .30
193 Larry Hughes .15 .40
194 Gilbert Arenas .15 .40
195 Brendan Haywood .12 .30
196 Juan Dixon .12 .30
197 Jahidi White .12 .30
198 Etan Thomas .12 .30
199 Michael Jordan CL 1.00 2.50
200 Michael Jordan CL 1.00 2.50
201 LeBron James RC 12.00 30.00
202 Darko Milicic RC .50 1.25
203 Carmelo Anthony RC 2.00 5.00
204 Chris Bosh RC 1.00 2.50
205 Dwyane Wade RC 2.00 5.00
206 Chris Kaman RC .60 1.50
207 Kirk Hinrich RC .60 1.50
208 T.J. Ford RC .50 1.25
209 Mike Sweetney RC .40 1.00
210 Jarvis Hayes RC .40 1.00
211 Mickael Pietrus RC .50 1.25
212 Nick Collison RC .50 1.25
213 Marcus Banks RC .40 1.00
214 Luke Ridnour RC .50 1.25
215 Reece Gaines RC .40 1.00
216 Troy Bell RC .40 1.00
217 Zarko Cabarkapa RC .40 1.00
218 David West RC .60 1.50
219 Aleksandar Pavlovic RC .50 1.25
220 Dahntay Jones RC .50 1.25
221 Boris Diaw-Riffiod RC .60 1.50
222 Zoran Planinic RC .40 1.00
223 Travis Outlaw RC .50 1.25
224 Brian Cook RC .40 1.00
225 Carlos Delfino RC .50 1.25
226 Ndudi Ebi RC .40 1.00
227 Kendrick Perkins RC .50 1.25
228 Leandro Barbosa RC .60 1.50
229 Josh Howard RC .60 1.50
230 Maciej Lampe RC .40 1.00

2003-04 Upper Deck MVP Black

*BLACK SINGLES: 15X TO 40X BASE HI
*BLACK RCs: 6X TO 15X BASE HI
PRINT RUN 25 SERIAL #'d SETS
190 Michael Jordan 100.00 200.00
199 Michael Jordan CL 100.00 200.00
200 Michael Jordan CL 100.00 200.00

2003-04 Upper Deck MVP Gold

*GOLD SINGLES: 6X TO 15X BASE CARD HI
*GOLD CL: 12X TO 30X BASE CARD HI
*GOLD RCs: 4X TO 10X BASE CARD HI
PRINT RUN 100 SERIAL #'d SETS

2003-04 Upper Deck MVP Silver

*SINGLES: .75X TO 2X BASE CARD HI
1-200 STATED ODDS 1:2
201-230 STATED ODDS 1:24

2003-04 Upper Deck MVP Basketball Diary

Randomly inserted at the rate of one in 12, this 14-card set places a full-color player photo on a card that has a border along the right edge. A Platinum parallel version of this set was also issued where cards are sequentilly numbered to 100.

COMPLETE SET (14) 10.00 25.00
STATED ODDS 1:12
*PLATINUM: 4X TO 10X BASE HI
PLATINUM PRINT RUN 100 SER.#'d SETS
BD1 Yao Ming .75 2.00
BD2 Michael Jordan 3.00 8.00
BD3 Kevin Garnett .60 1.50
BD4 Jason Richardson .40 1.00
BD5 Jason Kidd .60 1.50
BD6 Peja Stojakovic .40 1.00
BD7 Gilbert Arenas .30 .75
BD8 Kobe Bryant 1.50 4.00
BD9 Tim Duncan .60 1.50
BD10 R.Allen/G.Payton .60 1.50
BD11 Vince Carter .60 1.50
BD12 Amare Stoudemire .50 1.25
BD13 LeBron James 4.00 10.00
BD14 T.Duncan/D.Robinson 1.00 2.50

2003-04 Upper Deck MVP Combo Materials

Randomly seeded at the rate of one in 144, this eight card set combines two players on a horizontal design where one player is on the top, the other on the bottom along with a swatch of game used material from each.

STATED ODDS 1:144
DMRJ Mutombo/Jefferson SP 6.00 15.00
DRTP D.Robinson/T.Parker 10.00 25.00
JSKM J.Stockton/K.Malone 10.00 25.00
JSRH Stack/R.Hamilton SP 6.00 15.00
JWEC J.Williams/E.Curry 6.00 15.00
KBMJ Bryant/Jordan SP 75.00 150.00
SHSM S.Marion/S.Marbury 6.00 15.00
WSTB W.Szczerb/T.Brandon 6.00 15.00

2003-04 Upper Deck MVP Materials Shirts

Inserted at the rate of one in 72, this 12-card set places a player action photo on the right side of the card and a star-shaped swatch of memorabilia on the left.

STATED ODDS 1:72
AKSS Andrei Kirilenko SP 2.50 6.00
CWSS Chris Webber 2.50 6.00
DASS Darrell Armstrong 2.00 5.00
EBSS Elton Brand 2.50 6.00
GWSS Gerald Wallace 2.00 5.00
JKSS Jason Kidd SP 4.00 10.00
JOSS Jermaine O'Neal 2.00 5.00
KBSS Kobe Bryant SP 8.00 20.00
MJSS Michael Jordan SP 50.00 120.00
RMSS Reggie Miller 2.50 6.00
SASS Shareef Abdur-Rahim 2.00 5.00
TCSS Tyson Chandler 2.00 5.00

2003-04 Upper Deck MVP Materials Warmups

Inserted in packs at the rate of one in 48, this 11-card set is horizontally designed with a player photo on the right and a swatch of memorabilia on the left.

STATED ODDS 1:48
AMWU Antonio McDyess 2.00 5.00
CMWU Corey Maggette 2.00 5.00
GAWU Gilbert Arenas 2.00 5.00
JFWU Joseph Forte 2.00 5.00
JMWU Jamaal Magloire 2.00 5.00
JWWU Jay Williams 2.00 5.00
KBWU Kobe Bryant SP 8.00 20.00
KGWU Kevin Garnett 4.00 10.00
MJWU Michael Jordan SP 40.00 100.00
RAWU Ray Allen 2.50 6.00
TKWU Toni Kukoc 2.50 6.00

2003-04 Upper Deck MVP Monumental Moments

Inserted at the rate of one in 24, this seven card set places full-color player action photo among gold foil highlights. A Platinum parallel was also produced with cards sequentially numbered to five.

STATED ODDS 1:24
MM1 Kobe Bryant 2.50 6.00
MM2 Michael Jordan 5.00 12.00
MM3 Tim Duncan 1.00 2.50
MM4 Ben Wallace .50 1.25
MM5 Bobby Jackson .40 1.00
MM6 David Robinson 1.00 2.50
MM7 Amare Stoudemire .75 2.00

2003-04 Upper Deck MVP ProSign

Inserted at the rate of one in 288, this 40-card set is horizontally desiged with player photos on the left and a vertically stuck autographed sticker on the right.

STATED ODDS 1:288
AJ Antawn Jamison 8.00 20.00
AS Amare Stoudemire 15.00 40.00
BI Chauncey Billups 6.00 15.00
CB Carlos Boozer 4.00 10.00
CK Chris Kaman SP 10.00 25.00
CM Cuttino Mobley 4.00 10.00
DD Dan Dickau 4.00 10.00
DG Dan Gadzuric 4.00 10.00
DJ DerMarr Johnson 4.00 10.00
DW Dajuan Wagner 4.00 10.00
EB Earl Boykins 4.00 10.00
EG Eddie Griffin 4.00 10.00
ET Etan Thomas 4.00 10.00
GI Manu Ginobili/20 15.00 40.00
GO Drew Gooden 5.00 12.00
HA Richard Hamilton SP 12.50 30.00
JD Juan Dixon 4.00 10.00
JM Jerome Moiso 4.00 10.00
JS Jerry Stackhouse 5.00 12.00
KB Kobe Bryant/25 100.00 200.00
LJ LeBron James/23 600.00 1000.00
MA Corey Maggette 4.00 10.00
MP Morris Peterson 6.00 15.00
PP Paul Pierce/34 12.00 30.00
PS Peja Stojakovic SP 8.00 20.00
RE Reggie Evans 4.00 10.00
RH Ryan Humphrey 4.00 10.00
SB Shane Battier 4.00 10.00
SM Shawn Marion/31 15.00 40.00
TP Tony Parker 12.50 30.00
YM Yao Ming/25 30.00 80.00

2003-04 Upper Deck MVP Rising to the Occasion

Inserted at the rate of one in 12, this 14-card set features full-color player action photos centered between borders on the right and left side of the card. A Gold parallel version of this set was also produced with cards sequentially numbered to 250.

COMPLETE SET (14) 10.00 25.00
STATED ODDS 1:12
*GOLD: 1.5X TO 4X BASE HI
GOLD PRINT RUN 250 SER.#'d SETS
RO1 Kobe Bryant 2.00 5.00
RO2 LeBron James 5.00 12.00
RO3 Michael Jordan 4.00 10.00
RO4 Desmond Mason .40 1.00
RO5 Richard Jefferson .40 1.00
RO6 Vince Carter .75 2.00
RO7 Shaquille O'Neal 1.25 3.00
RO8 Yao Ming 1.00 2.50
RO9 Tracy McGrady .60 1.50
RO10 Jason Richardson .50 1.25
RO11 Rashard Lewis .50 1.25
RO12 Caron Butler .40 1.00
RO13 Baron Davis .40 1.00
RO14 Amare Stoudemire .60 1.50

2003-04 Upper Deck MVP Sportsnut Fantasy

Inserted at the rate of one in three, this 90-card set places full-color player photos on a gray background with borders on both the left and right of the card. Each card has a scratch off box on the front for use at www.upperdeck.com's Sport Nut Fantasy Game website.

COMPLETE SET (90) 20.00 50.00
STATED ODDS 1:3
SN1 Shareef Abdur-Rahim .30 .75
SN2 Jason Terry .30 .75
SN3 Glenn Robinson .30 .75
SN4 Theo Ratliff .25 .60
SN5 Antoine Walker .40 1.00
SN6 Paul Pierce .40 1.00
SN7 Jalen Rose .30 .75
SN8 Eddy Curry .25 .60
SN9 Tyson Chandler .30 .75
SN10 Dajuan Wagner .25 .60
SN11 Darius Miles .25 .60
SN12 Zydrunas Ilgauskas .30 .75
SN13 Michael Finley .40 1.00
SN14 Steve Nash .50 1.25
SN15 Dirk Nowitzki .60 1.50
SN16 Nene Hilario .30 .75
SN17 Juwan Howard .30 .75
SN18 Marcus Camby .30 .75
SN19 Richard Hamilton .30 .75
SN20 Ben Wallace .30 .75
SN21 Chauncey Billups .40 1.00
SN22 Danny Fortson .25 .60
SN23 Antawn Jamison .30 .75
SN24 Jason Richardson .40 1.00
SN25 Gilbert Arenas .30 .75
SN26 Yao Ming .75 2.00
SN27 Steve Francis .30 .75
SN28 Reggie Miller .40 1.00
SN29 Jermaine O'Neal .30 .75
SN30 Brad Miller .30 .75
SN31 Elton Brand .40 1.00
SN32 Michael Olowokandi .25 .60
SN33 Andre Miller .30 .75
SN34 Kobe Bryant 1.50 4.00
SN35 Shaquille O'Neal 1.00 2.50
SN36 Pau Gasol .40 1.00
SN37 Mike Miller .30 .75
SN38 Lorenzen Wright .25 .60
SN39 Alonzo Mourning .50 1.25
SN40 Eddie Jones .30 .75
SN41 Caron Butler .30 .75
SN42 Gary Payton .40 1.00
SN43 Dan Gadzuric .25 .60
SN44 Sam Cassell .30 .75
SN45 Kevin Garnett .60 1.50
SN46 Radoslav Nesterovic .25 .60
SN47 Jason Kidd .60 1.50
SN48 Kenyon Martin .30 .75
SN49 Dikembe Mutombo .40 1.00
SN50 Baron Davis .30 .75
SN51 Jamaal Magloire .25 .60
SN52 Jamal Mashburn .30 .75
SN53 Latrell Sprewell .30 .75
SN54 Allan Houston .30 .75
SN55 Kurt Thomas .25 .60
SN56 Tracy McGrady .50 1.25
SN57 Drew Gooden .30 .75
SN58 Grant Hill .50 1.25
SN59 Allen Iverson .60 1.50
SN60 Todd MacCulloch .25 .60
SN61 Amare Stoudemire .50 1.25
SN62 Stephon Marbury .30 .75
SN63 Shawn Marion .30 .75
SN64 Rasheed Wallace .40 1.00
SN65 Damon Stoudamire .30 .75
SN66 Dale Davis .25 .60
SN67 Vlade Divac .30 .75
SN68 Mike Bibby .40 1.00
SN69 Peja Stojakovic .40 1.00
SN70 Chris Webber .40 1.00
SN71 Tim Duncan .60 1.50
SN72 Tony Parker .40 1.00
SN73 Ray Allen .40 1.00
SN74 Vladimir Radmanovic .25 .60
SN75 Rashard Lewis .40 1.00
SN76 Vince Carter .60 1.50
SN77 Antonio Davis .25 .60
SN78 Karl Malone .50 1.25
SN79 Andrei Kirilenko .40 1.00
SN80 Jerry Stackhouse .30 .75
SN81 Kwame Brown .25 .60
SN82 Nick Collison .30 .75
SN83 Jarvis Hayes .25 .60
SN84 Mike Sweetney .25 .60
SN85 Dwyane Wade 1.25 3.00
SN86 T.J. Ford .30 .75
SN87 Chris Bosh .60 1.50
SN88 Darko Milicic .30 .75
SN89 Carmelo Anthony 1.25 3.00
SN90 LeBron James 4.00 10.00

2003-04 Upper Deck MVP Tribute to Greatness

Randomly inserted in packs, this seven-card set follows the career of Michael Jordan. A Platinum version of the set was issued as well with cards sequentially numbered to 50.

COMMON CARD (MJ1-MJ7) 2.50 6.00
STATED ODDS 1:24
COMMON PLAT. (MJ1-MJ7) 25.00 60.00
PLATINUM PRINT RUN 50 SER.#'d SETS

2008-09 Upper Deck MVP

This set was released on September 30, 2008. The base set consists of 258 cards. Cards 1-200 feature veterans, cards 201-240 are rookies, and cards 241-260 feature legends. Rookies were inserted at one per pack and Legends at one in two packs.

COMPLETE SET (258) 30.00 60.00
COMP.SET w/o SPs (200) 10.00 25.00
ROOKIE STATED ODDS 1:1
LEGEND STATED ODDS 1:2
UNPRICED SUPER SCRIPT PRINT RUN ONE SET
1 Joe Johnson .15 .40
2 Marvin Williams .15 .40
3 Acie Law .15 .40
4 Al Horford .20 .50
5 Mike Bibby .15 .40
6 Josh Smith .15 .40
7 Kendrick Perkins .12 .30
8 Glen Davis .12 .30
9 Rajon Rondo .20 .50
10 Ray Allen .20 .50
11 Paul Pierce .20 .50
12 Kevin Garnett .30 .75
13 Adam Morrison .12 .30
14 Raymond Felton .15 .40
15 Jason Richardson .20 .50
16 Emeka Okafor .15 .40
17 Gerald Wallace .15 .40
18 Tyrus Thomas .12 .30
19 Andres Nocioni .12 .30
20 Joakim Noah .15 .40
21 Luol Deng .15 .40
22 Kirk Hinrich .15 .40
23 Ben Gordon .15 .40
24 Zydrunas Ilgauskas .15 .40
25 Anderson Varejao .12 .30
26 Ben Wallace .15 .40
27 Daniel Gibson .15 .40
28 LeBron James .75 2.00
29 Wally Szczerbiak .15 .40
30 Dirk Nowitzki .25 .60
31 Josh Howard .15 .40
32 Jason Kidd .20 .50
33 Jerry Stackhouse .15 .40
34 Jason Terry .15 .40
35 Brandon Bass .12 .30
36 Allen Iverson .25 .60
37 Carmelo Anthony .25 .60
38 Marcus Camby .12 .30
39 Kenyon Martin .15 .40
40 J.R. Smith .15 .40
41 Linas Kleiza .12 .30
42 Chauncey Billups .20 .50
43 Richard Hamilton .15 .40
44 Tayshaun Prince .15 .40
45 Rasheed Wallace .20 .50
46 Rodney Stuckey .15 .40
47 Jason Maxiell .12 .30
48 Baron Davis .15 .40
49 Monta Ellis .15 .40
50 Al Harrington .15 .40
51 Stephen Jackson .15 .40
52 Marco Belinelli .12 .30
53 Yao Ming .25 .60
54 Tracy McGrady .20 .50
55 Luis Scola .15 .40
56 Rafer Alston .12 .30
57 Shane Battier .15 .40
58 Mike Dunleavy .15 .40
59 Danny Granger .15 .40
60 Jermaine O'Neal .15 .40
61 Jamaal Tinsley .12 .30
62 David Harrison .12 .30
63 Elton Brand .20 .50
64 Chris Kaman .15 .40
65 Corey Maggette .15 .40
66 Al Thornton .15 .40
67 Cuttino Mobley .12 .30
68 Tim Thomas .12 .30
69 Kobe Bryant .75 2.00
70 Pau Gasol .20 .50
71 Andrew Bynum .12 .30
72 Jordan Farmar .12 .30
73 Luke Walton .12 .30
74 Lamar Odom .15 .40
75 Rudy Gay .20 .50
76 Kyle Lowry .20 .50
77 Mike Conley Jr. .15 .40
78 Mike Miller .15 .40
79 Hakim Warrick .15 .40
80 Dwyane Wade .30 .75
81 Shawn Marion .15 .40
82 Ricky Davis .15 .40
83 Jason Williams .15 .40
84 Daequan Cook .12 .30
85 Michael Redd .15 .40
86 Maurice Williams .15 .40
87 Yi Jianlian .20 .50
88 Charlie Villanueva .12 .30
89 Andrew Bogut .15 .40
90 Al Jefferson .15 .40
91 Rashad McCants .12 .30
92 Corey Brewer .15 .40
93 Randy Foye .20 .50
94 Ryan Gomes .12 .30
95 Richard Jefferson .15 .40
96 Vince Carter .25 .60
97 Josh Boone .12 .30
98 Bostjan Nachbar .12 .30
99 Sean Williams .15 .40
100 Chris Paul .25 .60
101 David West .15 .40
102 Peja Stojakovic .20 .50
103 Tyson Chandler .15 .40
104 Morris Peterson .12 .30
105 Julian Wright .15 .40
106 Jamal Crawford .20 .50
107 Zach Randolph .15 .40
108 Stephon Marbury .15 .40
109 Eddy Curry .12 .30
110 Nate Robinson .12 .30
111 David Lee .12 .30
112 Dwight Howard .15 .40
113 Hedo Turkoglu .15 .40
114 Rashard Lewis .15 .40
115 Jameer Nelson .12 .30
116 Keith Bogans .12 .30
117 Carlos Arroyo .12 .30
118 Andre Iguodala .15 .40
119 Andre Miller .15 .40
120 Willie Green .12 .30
121 Samuel Dalembert .12 .30
122 Reggie Evans .12 .30
123 Thaddeus Young .15 .40
124 Amare Stoudemire .15 .40
125 Steve Nash .20 .50
126 Leandro Barbosa .15 .40
127 Shaquille O'Neal .40 1.00
128 Grant Hill .25 .60
129 Raja Bell .15 .40
130 Brandon Roy .20 .50
131 LaMarcus Aldridge .20 .50
132 Travis Outlaw .15 .40
133 Martell Webster .15 .40
134 Greg Oden .15 .40
135 Jarrett Jack .15 .40
136 Kevin Martin .15 .40
137 Ron Artest .20 .50
138 Brad Miller .15 .40
139 John Salmons .15 .40
140 Mikki Moore .12 .30
141 Francisco Garcia .12 .30
142 Manu Ginobili .20 .50
143 Tim Duncan .30 .75
144 Tony Parker .20 .50
145 Michael Finley .20 .50
146 Bruce Bowen .12 .30
147 Damon Stoudamire .15 .40

148 Kevin Durant .50 1.25
149 Chris Wilcox .12 .30
150 Jeff Green .15 .40
151 Damien Wilkins .12 .30
152 Earl Watson .12 .30
153 Chris Bosh .20 .50
154 Jose Calderon .12 .30
155 T.J. Ford .12 .30
156 Andrea Bargnani .15 .40
157 Jamario Moon .12 .30
158 Jason Kapono .12 .30
159 Carlos Boozer .15 .40
160 Deron Williams .15 .40
161 Kyle Korver .15 .40
162 Andrei Kirilenko .15 .40
163 Ronnie Brewer .15 .40
164 Mehmet Okur .12 .30
165 Gilbert Arenas .15 .40
166 Caron Butler .15 .40
167 Antawn Jamison .15 .40
168 DeShawn Stevenson .12 .30
169 Brendan Haywood .12 .30
170 Nick Young .15 .40
171 Joe Johnson .15 .40
172 Kevin Garnett .30 .75
173 Gerald Wallace .15 .40
174 Luol Deng .15 .40
175 LeBron James .75 2.00
176 Dirk Nowitzki .25 .60
177 Carmelo Anthony .25 .60
178 Chauncey Billups .20 .50
179 Monta Ellis .15 .40
180 Tracy McGrady .20 .50
181 Danny Granger .15 .40
182 Chris Kaman .15 .40
183 Kobe Bryant .75 2.00
184 Rudy Gay .20 .50
185 Dwyane Wade .30 .75
186 Michael Redd .15 .40
187 Al Jefferson .15 .40
188 Vince Carter .25 .60
189 Chris Paul .25 .60
190 Zach Randolph .15 .40
191 Dwight Howard .15 .40
192 Andre Iguodala .15 .40
193 Steve Nash .20 .50
194 Brandon Roy .20 .50
195 Kevin Martin .15 .40
196 Tim Duncan .30 .75
197 Kevin Durant .50 1.25
198 Chris Bosh .20 .50
199 Deron Williams .15 .40
200 Antawn Jamison .15 .40
201 Derrick Rose RC 2.50 6.00
202 Michael Beasley RC .60 1.50
203 O.J. Mayo RC .60 1.50
204 Russell Westbrook RC 5.00 12.00
205 Kevin Love RC 2.00 5.00
206 Danilo Gallinari RC 1.00 2.50
207 Eric Gordon RC 1.00 2.50
208 Joe Alexander RC .40 1.00
209 D.J. Augustin RC .50 1.25
210 Brook Lopez RC .75 2.00
211 Jerryd Bayless RC .50 1.25
212 Jason Thompson RC .40 1.00
213 Brandon Rush RC .50 1.25
214 Anthony Randolph RC .40 1.00
215 Robin Lopez RC .60 1.50
216 Marreese Speights RC .50 1.25
217 Roy Hibbert RC .60 1.50
218 Courtney Lee RC .50 1.25
219 J.J. Hickson RC .50 1.25
220 Ryan Anderson RC .50 1.25
221 Kosta Koufos RC .50 1.25
223 Darrell Arthur RC .50 1.25
224 Donte Greene RC .40 1.00
225 D.J. White RC .50 1.25
226 Bill Walker RC .40 1.00
227 James Gist RC .40 1.00
228 Joey Dorsey RC .40 1.00
229 Mario Chalmers RC .60 1.50
230 DeAndre Jordan RC .75 2.00
231 Luc Richard Mbah A Moute RC .50 1.25
232 Kyle Weaver RC .40 1.00
233 Sonny Weems RC .40 1.00
234 Chris Douglas-Roberts RC .40 1.00
235 Sean Singletary RC .40 1.00
236 Patrick Ewing Jr. RC .40 1.00
237 Darnell Jackson RC .40 1.00
238 Maarty Leunen RC .40 1.00
240 Deron Washington RC .40 1.00
241 Spud Webb .75 2.00
242 Larry Bird 2.50 6.00
243 Bill Russell 1.50 4.00
244 Kevin McHale 1.25 3.00
245 Michael Jordan 8.00 20.00
246 Scottie Pippen 1.50 4.00
247 Joe Dumars 1.00 2.50
248 Isiah Thomas 1.00 2.50
249 Hakeem Olajuwon 1.25 3.00
250 Magic Johnson 2.50 6.00
251 Wilt Chamberlain 2.00 5.00
252 Kareem Abdul-Jabbar 1.50 4.00
253 Oscar Robertson 1.00 2.50
254 Pete Maravich 1.50 4.00
255 Patrick Ewing 1.25 3.00
256 Willis Reed 1.00 2.50
257 Julius Erving 1.50 4.00
258 David Robinson 1.50 4.00
259 Karl Malone 1.25 3.00
260 John Stockton 1.50 4.00

2008-09 Upper Deck MVP Gold Script

*GOLD 1-200: 3X TO 8X BASE HI
*GOLD 201-240: 1.25X TO 3X BASE HI
*GOLD 241-260: 1.25X TO 3X BASE
PRINT RUN 100 SER.#'d SET
28 LeBron James 12.00 30.00
69 Kobe Bryant 12.00 30.00
175 LeBron James 12.00 30.00
183 Kobe Bryant 12.00 30.00
245 Michael Jordan 30.00 80.00

2008-09 Upper Deck MVP Silver Script

*SILVER: .6X TO 1.5X BASE HI
OVERALL PARALLEL ODDS 1:4

2008-09 Upper Deck MVP Game Night Souvenirs

STATED ODDS 1:36
*PATCHES: .75X TO 2X BASE HI
PATCH PRINT RUN 25 SER.#'d SETS
GNAB Andris Biedrins 2.00 5.00
GNAI Allen Iverson 4.00 10.00
GNAK Andrei Kirilenko 2.50 6.00
GNAM Adam Morrison 2.00 5.00
GNAW Antoine Walker 2.50 6.00
GNBB Brent Barry 2.00 5.00
GNBC Brian Cook 2.00 5.00
GNBD Boris Diaw 2.50 6.00
GNBO Andrew Bogut 2.50 6.00
GNCM Corey Maggette 2.50 6.00
GNCS Cedric Simmons 2.50 6.00
GNDG Drew Gooden 2.50 6.00
GNDH Devin Harris 2.00 5.00
GNDM Dikembe Mutombo 3.00 8.00
GNDN Dirk Nowitzki 4.00 10.00
GNDW Delonte West 2.00 5.00
GNEB Elton Brand 3.00 8.00
GNGH Grant Hill 6.00 15.00
GNGW Gerald Wallace 2.50 6.00
GNJH Josh Howard 2.50 6.00
GNJJ Joe Johnson 2.50 6.00
GNJK Jason Kidd 3.00 8.00
GNJN Jameer Nelson 2.00 5.00
GNJO Jermaine O'Neal 2.50 6.00
GNJP Johan Petro 2.00 5.00
GNJR Jason Richardson 3.00 8.00
GNJT Jamaal Tinsley 2.00 5.00
GNKG Kevin Garnett 5.00 12.00
GNKM Kenyon Martin 2.50 6.00
GNLJ LeBron James 10.00 25.00
GNMA Donyell Marshall 2.00 5.00
GNMB Mike Bibby 2.50 6.00
GNMG Manu Ginobili 3.00 8.00
GNMR Michael Redd 2.50 6.00
GNPG Pau Gasol 3.00 8.00
GNPS Peja Stojakovic 3.00 8.00
GNRW Rasheed Wallace 3.00 8.00
GNSO Shaquille O'Neal 6.00 15.00
GNZR Zach Randolph 2.50 6.00

2008-09 Upper Deck MVP Kobe MVP

COMMON CARD (KB1-100) 1.50 4.00
STATED ODDS 1:2
COMMON WHITE (KB1-100) 2.50 6.00
WHITE APPROXIMATELY ONE PER BOX

2008-09 Upper Deck MVP Kobe MVP White

COMMON CARD (1-100) 2.50 6.00
INSERTED APPROXIMATELY ONE PER BOX

2008-09 Upper Deck MVP SE

*STARS: 1X TO 2.5X BASE HI
*RCs: .4X TO 1X BASE HI
RANDOM INSERTS IN RETAIL PACKS

2008-09 Upper Deck MVP Signatures Required

STATED ODDS 1:288
SRAO K.Azubuike/P.O'Bryant 5.00 12.00
SRAS A.Afflalo/R.Stuckey 8.00 20.00
SRAT A.Tucker/M.Almond 5.00 12.00
SRAW H.Armstrong/J.Wright 5.00 12.00
SRBA C.Brewer/A.Afflalo 5.00 12.00
SRBJ L.James/K.Bryant 100.00 225.00
SRBL A.Law/M.Bibby 6.00 15.00
SRBP T.Parker/C.Billups 15.00 40.00
SRCW J.Crittenton/M.West 5.00 12.00
SRDD J.Davidson/J.Dudley 6.00 15.00
SRDG K.Durant/J.Green 75.00 150.00
SRDH A.Horford/K.Durant 75.00 150.00
SRDS K.Durant/L.Scola 75.00 150.00
SRGS T.Green/D.Strawberry 5.00 12.00
SRHG L.Hughes/A.Gray 10.00 25.00
SRHH D.Howard/A.Horford 20.00 40.00
SRHW M.Williams/A.Horford 15.00 30.00
SRIS J.Smith/A.Iguodala 6.00 15.00
SRJG T.Green/B.Jones 5.00 12.00
SRJL J.Smith/L.Williams 5.00 12.00
SRJW M.Williams/R.Jefferson 5.00 12.00
SRKB R.Brewer/K.Korver 8.00 20.00
SRKW C.Kaman/S.Williams 6.00 15.00
SRLB C.Landry/A.Brooks 6.00 15.00
SRLS C.Landry/L.Scola 8.00 20.00
SRMS T.McGrady/L.Scola 12.00 30.00
SRNC D.Nichols/J.Curry 5.00 12.00
SRNL S.Novak/C.Landry 6.00 15.00
SRNS A.Stoudemire/S.Nash 40.00 100.00
SROW S.Williams/P.O'Bryant 5.00 12.00
SRPW D.Williams/C.Paul 30.00 80.00
SRRP G.Pruitt/R.Rondo 10.00 25.00
SRSS S.Hawes/S.Williams 8.00 20.00
SRSW S.Williams/C.Samb 5.00 12.00
SRTL C.Landry/A.Tucker 15.00 30.00
SRWH L.Williams/H.Hill 5.00 12.00
SRWS R.Sessions/M.Williams 5.00 12.00

2008-09 Upper Deck MVP Star Combos

STATED ODDS 1:84
*PATCH: 1.25X TO 3X BASE HI
PATCH PRINT RUN 25 SER.#'d SETS
SCBJ J.Johnson/M.Bibby 4.00 10.00
SCBM C.Maggette/E.Brand 4.00 10.00
SCCN B.Cook/J.Nelson 4.00 10.00
SCCR Z.Randolph/E.Curry 4.00 10.00
SCGD D.Gooden/L.Deng 4.00 10.00
SCGK A.Kirilenko/K.Garnett 6.00 15.00
SCGN K.Garnett/D.Nowitzki 6.00 15.00
SCHD G.Hill/B.Diaw 8.00 20.00
SCIA A.Iverson/C.Anthony 6.00 15.00
SCJB L.James/K.Bryant 15.00 40.00
SCKH D.Harris/J.Kidd 4.00 10.00
SCKN D.Nowitzki/J.Kidd 5.00 12.00
SCMB D.Mutombo/S.Battier 4.00 10.00
SCMO S.O'Neal/S.Marion 6.00 15.00
SCOG P.Gasol/L.Odom 8.00 20.00
SCRB A.Bogut/M.Redd 4.00 10.00
SCRM A.Morrison/J.Richardson 4.00 10.00
SCTO J.O'Neal/J.Tinsley 4.00 10.00
SCWP R.Wallace/T.Prince 4.00 10.00
SCWS P.Stojakovic/D.West 4.00 10.00

2008-09 Upper Deck MVP Victory

COMPLETE SET (90) 25.00 50.00
RANDOM INSERTS IN RETAIL PACKS
*ULTIMATE: .6X TO 1.5X VICTORY HI
ULTIMATE STATED ODDS 1:2 HOBBY
1 Joe Johnson .25 .60
2 Al Horford .30 .75
3 Paul Pierce .30 .75
4 Kevin Garnett .50 1.25
5 Jason Richardson .30 .75
6 Gerald Wallace .25 .60
7 Luol Deng .25 .60
8 Ben Gordon .25 .60
9 Ben Wallace .25 .60
10 LeBron James 1.25 3.00
11 Dirk Nowitzki .40 1.00
12 Jason Kidd .30 .75
13 Allen Iverson .40 1.00
14 Carmelo Anthony .40 1.00
15 Chauncey Billups .30 .75
16 Richard Hamilton .25 .60
17 Baron Davis .25 .60
18 Stephen Jackson .25 .60
19 Yao Ming .40 1.00
20 Tracy McGrady .30 .75
21 Danny Granger .25 .60
22 Jermaine O'Neal .25 .60
23 Chris Kaman .25 .60
24 Corey Maggette .25 .60
25 Kobe Bryant 1.25 3.00
26 Pau Gasol .30 .75
27 Rudy Gay .30 .75
28 Mike Conley Jr. .25 .60
29 Dwyane Wade .50 1.25
30 Shawn Marion .25 .60
31 Michael Redd .25 .60
32 Maurice Williams .25 .60
33 Al Jefferson .25 .60
34 Rashad McCants .20 .50
35 Richard Jefferson .25 .60
36 Vince Carter .40 1.00
37 Chris Paul .40 1.00
38 David West .25 .60
39 Jamal Crawford .30 .75
40 Zach Randolph .25 .60
41 Dwight Howard .25 .60
42 Rashard Lewis .25 .60
43 Andre Iguodala .25 .60
44 Andre Miller .25 .60
45 Amare Stoudemire .25 .60
46 Steve Nash .30 .75
47 Brandon Roy .30 .75
48 Greg Oden .25 .60
49 Kevin Martin .25 .60
50 Ron Artest .30 .75
51 Tim Duncan .50 1.25
52 Tony Parker .30 .75
53 Kevin Durant .75 2.00
54 Jeff Green .25 .60
55 Chris Bosh .30 .75
56 Jose Calderon .20 .50
57 Carlos Boozer .25 .60
58 Deron Williams .25 .60
59 Gilbert Arenas .25 .60
60 Antawn Jamison .25 .60
61 Derrick Rose 2.00 5.00
62 Michael Beasley .50 1.25
63 O.J. Mayo .50 1.25
64 Russell Westbrook 4.00 10.00
65 Kevin Love 1.50 4.00
66 Danilo Gallinari .75 2.00
67 Eric Gordon .75 2.00
68 Joe Alexander .30 .75
69 D.J. Augustin .40 1.00
70 Brook Lopez .60 1.50
71 Jerryd Bayless .40 1.00
72 Jason Thompson .30 .75
73 Brandon Rush .40 1.00
74 Anthony Randolph .30 .75
75 Robin Lopez .50 1.25
76 Marreese Speights .40 1.00
77 Roy Hibbert .50 1.25
78 Mario Chalmers .50 1.25
79 J.J. Hickson .40 1.00
80 Ryan Anderson .40 1.00
81 Kosta Koufos .40 1.00
82 Sonny Weems .30 .75
83 Courtney Lee .40 1.00
84 Darrell Arthur .40 1.00
85 Donte Greene .30 .75
86 D.J. White .40 1.00
87 J.R. Giddens .30 .75
88 Darnell Jackson .30 .75
89 Chris Douglas-Roberts .30 .75
90 Patrick Ewing Jr. .30 .75

1992-93 Upper Deck MVP Holograms

This 38-card standard-size hologram set consists of Upper Deck's selection of the MVP on each of the NBA's 27 teams (1-27) plus nine "Future MVPs" (28-36) focusing on player's who could become their team's MVP in the near future. Just 138,000 individually numbered sets were produced, and they were available only through hobby dealers and select retail outlets beginning in mid-May. The fronts display a color, action cut-out photo and a holographic inset photo set against a background of geometric shapes in gray, black, and the team's colors. On team color-coded panels with gray geometric shapes, the backs carry player profiles. Included in the set is a card that carries instructions for ordering a matching display album.

COMP. FACT SET (38) 12.50 30.00
1 Dominique Wilkins .15 .40
2 Reggie Lewis .08 .25
3 Larry Johnson .40 1.00
4 Michael Jordan 4.00 10.00
5 Mark Price .08 .25
6 Derek Harper .08 .25
7 Dikembe Mutombo .15 .40
8 Isiah Thomas .15 .40
9 Chris Mullin .15 .40
10 Hakeem Olajuwon .50 1.25
11 Reggie Miller .30 .75
12 Danny Manning .08 .25
13 James Worthy .15 .40
14 Glen Rice .30 .75
15 Alvin Robertson .08 .25
16 Chuck Person .08 .25
17 Derrick Coleman .08 .25
18 Patrick Ewing .30 .75
19 Scott Skiles .08 .25
20 Hersey Hawkins .08 .25
21 Charles Barkley .50 1.25
22 Clyde Drexler .30 .75
23 Mitch Richmond .30 .75
24 David Robinson .50 1.25
25 Shawn Kemp .75 2.00
26 Karl Malone .50 1.25
27 Pervis Ellison .08 .25
28 Lloyd Daniels .08 .25
29 Todd Day .08 .25
30 Tom Gugliotta 1.00 2.50
31 Robert Horry .50 1.25
32 Christian Laettner .75 2.00
33 Harold Miner .08 .25
34 Alonzo Mourning 1.50 4.00
35 Shaquille O'Neal 4.00 10.00
36 Walt Williams .30 .75
NNO Checklist .08 .25
NNO Album Offer Card .08 .25

2009 Upper Deck Mystery Iconic Cuts Redemption

AUTOS ISSUED VIA EXCH CARD

2000 Upper Deck NBA Card Clips

These minature card clips were released by Upper Deck in early December, 2000. Each card measures 2" wide by 2.75" long. Cards featured are minature versions of the 2000-01 Upper Deck MVP base cards.

COMPLETE SET (58) 25.00 50.00
1 Dikembe Mutombo 1.00 2.50
2 Lorenzen Wright .50 1.25
3 Antoine Walker .50 1.25
4 Kenny Anderson .50 1.25
5 Elden Campbell .50 1.25
6 Baron Davis 1.25 3.00
7 Elton Brand 1.00 2.50
8 Ron Mercer .50 1.25
9 Andre Miller .50 1.25
10 Chris Mihm .50 1.25
11 Michael Finley .60 1.50
12 Dirk Nowitzki 2.00 5.00
13 Antonio McDyess .50 1.25
14 Nick Van Exel .50 1.25
15 Jerry Stackhouse .50 1.25
16 Mateen Cleaves .50 1.25
17 Antawn Jamison .50 1.25
18 Larry Hughes .50 1.25
19 Steve Francis .60 1.50
20 Hakeem Olajuwon 1.00 2.50
21 Reggie Miller 1.25 3.00
22 Jalen Rose .50 1.25
23 Michael Olowokandi .50 1.25
24 Lamar Odom 1.00 2.50
25 Shaquille O'Neal 2.50 6.00
26 Kobe Bryant 4.00 10.00
27 Alonzo Mourning 1.00 2.50
28 Tim Hardaway .50 1.25
29 Ray Allen 1.25 3.00
30 Glenn Robinson .50 1.25
31 Kevin Garnett 2.50 6.00
32 Wally Szczerbiak .50 1.25
33 Keith Van Horn .50 1.25
34 Stephon Marbury .60 1.50
35 Allan Houston .50 1.25
36 Latrell Sprewell .50 1.25
37 Grant Hill 1.25 3.00
38 Tracy McGrady 1.50 4.00
39 Allen Iverson 1.50 4.00
40 Toni Kukoc .50 1.25
41 Jason Kidd 1.50 4.00
42 Anfernee Hardaway .50 1.25
43 Scottie Pippen 1.50 4.00
44 Rasheed Wallace 1.00 2.50
45 Chris Webber 1.25 3.00
46 Jason Williams .50 1.25
47 Tim Duncan 2.00 5.00
48 David Robinson 2.00 5.00
49 Gary Payton .50 1.25
50 Vin Baker .50 1.25
51 Charles Oakley .50 1.25
52 Vince Carter 2.00 5.00
53 Karl Malone 1.50 4.00
54 John Stockton 1.50 4.00
55 Shareef Abdur-Rahim .50 1.26
56 Bryant Reeves .50 1.25
57 Mitch Richmond .50 1.25
58 Juwan Howard .50 1.25

2007-08 Upper Deck NBA Rookie Box Set

COMPLETE SET (30) 10.00 25.00
AUTOS RANDOMLY INSERTED
1 Arron Afflalo .50 1.25
2 Morris Almond .30 .75
3 Corey Brewer .50 1.25
4 Aaron Brooks .40 1.00
5 Wilson Chandler .40 1.00
6 Mike Conley Jr. .60 1.50
7 Daequan Cook .40 1.00
8 Javaris Crittenton .30 .75
9 Glen Davis .40 1.00
10 Jared Dudley .40 1.00
11 Kevin Durant 5.00 12.00
12 Nick Fazekas .30 .75
13 Jeff Green .50 1.25
14 Taurean Green .30 .75
15 Spencer Hawes .40 1.00
16 Al Horford .60 1.50
17 Acie Law .30 .75
18 Josh McRoberts .40 1.00
19 Joakim Noah .50 1.25
20 Greg Oden .50 1.25
21 Gabe Pruitt .30 .75
22 D.J. Strawberry .30 .75
23 Rodney Stuckey .40 1.00
24 Al Thornton .40 1.00
25 Alando Tucker .30 .75
26 Sean Williams .30 .75
27 Brandan Wright .50 1.25
28 Julian Wright .30 .75
29 Nick Young .60 1.50
30 Thaddeus Young .50 1.25

2000 Upper Deck National Kobe Bryant

This 10-card set was sold at the 2000 National Convention in Anaheim, CA in July,2000. The set features 10 Kobe Bryant cards. Card backs carry a "KB" prefix.

COMPLETE SET (10) 12.00 30.00
COMMON CARD (KB1-KB10) 1.00 2.50

2002 Upper Deck National Convention

N13 Kobe Bryant 1.25 3.00
N14 Kevin Garnett .60 1.50
N15 Michael Jordan CL 1.50 4.00

2004 Upper Deck National Convention

STATED PRINT RUN 500 SER.#'d SETS
TN1 LeBron James 4.00 10.00
TN2 Kobe Bryant 4.00 10.00
TN3 Michael Jordan 5.00 12.00
TN18 Kevin Garnett 3.00 8.00
TN19 Carmelo Anthony 2.50 6.00

2004 Upper Deck National Convention LeBron James Fan Favorite

STATED PRINT RUN 100 SER.#'d SETS
FF1 LeBron James 10.00 25.00
FF2 LeBron James 10.00 25.00
FF3 LeBron James 10.00 25.00
FF4 LeBron James 10.00 25.00

2004 Upper Deck National Convention VIP

VIP1 LeBron James 6.00 15.00
VIP2 Michael Jordan 8.00 20.00

2005 Upper Deck National Convention

Upper Deck produced this set and distributed it at the 2005 National Sport Collectors Convention in Chicago. The set includes famous Chicago area athletes from a variety of sports with the title "The National" printed on the cardfronts. The company made the cards available to collectors via a wrapper redemption program at their show booth and each card was serial numbered to 750-copies. Some players also signed just 5-cards which are not priced due to scarcity.

STATED PRINT RUN 750 SER.#'d SETS
UNPRICED AUTO PRINT RUN 5
CL3 Michael Jordan 5.00 12.00

2005 Upper Deck National Convention VIP

Upper Deck produced this set and distributed it to special VIP package members attending the 2005 National Sport Collectors Convention in Chicago. The set includes famous athletes from a variety of sports with the title "The National" printed on the cardfronts along with a "VIP" stamp.

VIP1 Michael Jordan 8.00 20.00
VIP2 LeBron James 8.00 20.00

2006 Upper Deck National NBA

COMPLETE SET (3) 5.00 12.00
PRINT RUN 500 SER.#'d SETS
NBA1 Michael Jordan 3.00 8.00
NBA2 LeBron James 2.50 6.00
NBA3 Chris Paul 1.25 3.00

2006 Upper Deck National Southern California

COMPLETE SET (6) 5.00 12.00
SoCal1 Elton Brand .75 2.00

2006 Upper Deck National NBA VIP

COMPLETE SET (6) 6.00 15.00
1 Michael Jordan 3.00 8.00
2 LeBron James 2.50 6.00
3 Chris Bosh 1.25 3.00
4 Yao Ming 1.25 3.00
5 Tim Duncan 1.25 3.00
6 Chris Paul 1.25 3.00

2007 Upper Deck National Convention

NTL5 Kobe Bryant 1.00 2.50
NTL6 Michael Jordan 1.50 4.00
NTL7 LeBron James 1.25 3.00

2007 Upper Deck National Convention VIP

VIP5 Kobe Bryant 1.50 4.00
VIP6 Michael Jordan 2.50 6.00
VIP7 LeBron James 2.00 5.00

2008 Upper Deck National Convention

NAT4 Kobe Bryant 1.25 3.00
NAT6 Michael Jordan 2.00 5.00
NAT9 LeBron James 1.25 3.00

2008 Upper Deck National Convention VIP

CARDS FEATURE VIP LOGO ON FRONT
NAT4 Kobe Bryant 3.00 8.00
NAT6 Michael Jordan 5.00 12.00
NAT9 LeBron James 3.00 8.00

2009 Upper Deck National Convention

NC6 LeBron James 1.25 3.00
NC7 LeBron James 1.25 3.00
NC8 Mo Williams .40 1.00
NC13 Derrick Rose .75 2.00
NC18 Kobe Bryant 1.25 3.00
NC21 Michael Jordan 2.00 5.00
NC22 Paul Pierce .60 1.50

2009 Upper Deck National Convention VIP

VIP3 LeBron James 2.50 6.00
VIP8 Michael Jordan 4.00 10.00

2010 Upper Deck National Convention

COMPLETE SET (20) 15.00 40.00
NSC1 Michael Jordan 3.00 8.00
NSC5 Julius Erving 2.00 5.00
NSC6 LeBron James 3.00 8.00
NSC14 Alonzo Mourning 1.25 3.00
NSC19 David Robinson 1.25 3.00

2010 Upper Deck National Convention Autographs

STATED PRINT RUN 9-90
NALJ LeBron James/23 125.00 250.00
NAMJ Michael Jordan/23 300.00 600.00

2010 Upper Deck National Convention VIP

COMPLETE SET (6) 6.00 15.00
VIP3 LeBron James 3.00 8.00
VIP5 Michael Jordan 3.00 8.00

2011 Upper Deck National Convention

NSCC1 Michael Jordan 2.00 5.00
NSCC3 Derrick Rose 1.25 3.00
NSCC15 LeBron James 1.25 3.00
NSCC19 B.J. Armstrong .75 2.00

2011 Upper Deck National Convention Autographs

NSCCLJ LeBron James/15 125.00 250.00

2011 Upper Deck National Convention VIP

1 Michael Jordan 1.50 4.00
4 LeBron James 1.00 2.50

2012 Upper Deck National Convention

NSCC1 Michael Jordan 3.00 8.00
NSCC3 Alonzo Mourning 2.00 5.00
NSCC8 David Robinson 1.50 4.00
NSCC16 LeBron James 2.00 5.00

2012 Upper Deck National Convention Autographs

STATED PRINT RUN 1-35
NSCCLJ LeBron James/15 150.00 300.00

2012 Upper Deck National Convention VIP

3 LeBron James 2.00 5.00
5 Michael Jordan 4.00 10.00

2013 Upper Deck National Convention

COMPLETE SET (20) 15.00 40.00
6 LeBron James
16 Michael Jordan

2013 Upper Deck National Convention VIP

COMPLETE SET (6) 3.00 8.00
1 Michael Jordan
6 LeBron James

2015 Upper Deck National Convention

NSCC3 Nikola Mirotic .40 1.00
NSCC9 Horace Grant .30 .75
NSCC14 LeBron James 1.25 3.00
NSCC15 Stephen Curry .60 1.50
NSCC19 Shaquille O'Neal .60 1.50

2015 Upper Deck National Convention Autographs

NSCC3 Horace Grant/30

2015 Upper Deck National Convention VIP

VIP4 Michael Jordan 4.00 10.00

2004 Upper Deck Naxcom LeBron James

Produced by Upper Deck in conjunction with Naxcom, this LeBron James cards was given away to new members of Naxcom's website as a promotion. Each card pictures LeBron in a gray suit and comes sealed in a tamper-proof screw down case.

NNO LeBron James 10.00 25.00

1997 Upper Deck Nestle Crunch Time

Produced by Upper Deck and Nestle, this 40-card set measures the standard size and was inserted in four-card packs in special Nestle Crunch bars. The set focuses on players who either made a clutch shot down the stretch of a 1996-97 NBA game to win the game or seal the victory for his team. Card fronts feature a color action shot of the player against a black and white crowd background. The player's name and team logo are at the bottom. Each card front also features a digital timer. Card backs are numbered with a "CT" prefix.

COMPLETE SET (40) 8.00 20.00
CT1 Kenny Anderson .30 .75
CT2 Arvydas Sabonis .30 .75
CT3 Elliot Perry UER .25 .60
Misp. Elliott
CT4 Chris Webber .40 1.00
CT5 Michael Jordan 4.00 10.00
CT6 Terrell Brandon .25 .60
CT7 Rick Fox .25 .60
CT8 Brent Barry .30 .75
CT9 Bryant Reeves .25 .60
CT10 Steve Smith .30 .75
CT11 Mookie Blaylock .25 .60
CT12 Christian Laettner .30 .75
CT13 Tim Hardaway .40 1.00
CT14 Voshon Lenard .25 .60
CT15 Dan Majerle .40 1.00
CT16 Glen Rice .40 1.00
CT17 Dell Curry .25 .60
CT18 Karl Malone .50 1.25
CT19 John Stockton .50 1.25
CT20 Mitch Richmond .40 1.00
CT21 Patrick Ewing .50 1.25
CT22 Kobe Bryant 3.00 8.00
CT23 Eddie Jones .40 1.00
CT24 Anfernee Hardaway .60 1.50
CT25 Rony Seikaly .30 .75
CT26 Chris Gatling .25 .60
CT27 Kendall Gill .25 .60
CT28 Dale Ellis .25 .60
CT29 Reggie Miller .50 1.25
CT30 Terry Mills .25 .60
CT31 Damon Stoudamire .40 1.00
CT32 Clyde Drexler .50 1.25
CT33 Allen Iverson .75 2.00
CT34 Jerry Stackhouse .40 1.00
CT35 Hersey Hawkins .25 .60
CT36 Gary Payton .40 1.00
CT37 Carl Herrera .25 .60
CT38 Rex Chapman .25 .60
CT39 Tom Gugliotta .25 .60
CT40 Latrell Sprewell .40 1.00

1996 Upper Deck Nestle Slam Dunk

This 40-card set was issued by Upper Deck and inserted with Nestle Crunch bars and features the design of the 1996-97 Collector's Choice series. The exception is card fronts contain the phrase "Slam Dunk Series" in brown-orange at the bottom. Card backs are numbered X of 40.

COMPLETE SET (40) 8.00 20.00
1 Grant Long .25 .60
2 Scott Burrell .25 .60
3 Ron Harper .30 .75
4 Michael Jordan 4.00 10.00
5 Scottie Pippen .60 1.50
6 Bobby Phills .25 .60
7 Tyrone Hill .25 .60
8 Tony Dumas .25 .60
9 LaPhonso Ellis .25 .60
10 Antonio McDyess .40 1.00
11 Theo Ratliff .30 .75
12 Joe Smith .30 .75
13 Rodney Rogers .25 .60
14 Brent Barry .30 .75
15 Cedric Ceballos .25 .60
16 Eddie Jones .40 1.00
17 Vlade Divac .40 1.00
18 Anthony Peeler .25 .60
19 Kurt Thomas .25 .60
20 Vin Baker .30 .75
21 Kevin Garnett 1.00 2.50
22 Shawn Bradley .25 .60
23 Ed O'Bannon .25 .60
24 Nick Anderson .25 .60
25 Clarence Weatherspoon .25 .60
26 Jerry Stackhouse .50 1.25
27 Charles Barkley .60 1.50
28 Gary Trent .25 .60
29 Brian Grant .30 .75
30 Olden Polynice .25 .60
31 Will Perdue .25 .60
32 Vincent Askew .25 .60
33 Doug Christie .25 .60
34 Chris Morris .25 .60
35 Chris Webber .50 1.25
36 Grant Hill .60 1.50
37 Alonzo Mourning .50 1.25
38 Dee Brown .25 .60
39 Shawn Kemp .40 1.00
40 Rasheed Wallace .50 1.25

1997 Upper Deck Nestle Slam Dunk

This 40-card set was issued by Upper Deck and inserted with Nestle Crunch bars. Card fronts contain a borderless action photo with the word "Slam" on the left of the card and the word "Dunk" on the right. The player's name is listed at the bottom. Card backs are numbered X of 40.

COMPLETE SET (40) 8.00 20.00
1 Chris Webber .40 1.00
2 Shawn Kemp .40 1.00
3 Dikembe Mutombo .40 1.00
4 Alonzo Mourning .50 1.25
5 Marcus Camby .40 1.00
6 Otis Thorpe .25 .60
7 Antonio McDyess .30 .75
8 Vin Baker .30 .75
9 Kevin Garnett .60 1.50
10 Patrick Ewing .50 1.25
11 Shareef Abdur-Rahim .40 1.00
12 Antoine Walker .40 1.00
13 Joe Smith .30 .75
14 Glen Rice .40 1.00
15 Juwan Howard .30 .75
16 Eddie Jones .40 1.00
17 Karl Malone .50 1.25
18 Bryant Reeves .25 .60
19 Anfernee Hardaway .60 1.50
20 LaPhonso Ellis .25 .60
21 Kerry Kittles .25 .60
22 Michael Jordan 3.00 8.00
23 Latrell Sprewell .40 1.00
24 Olden Polynice .25 .60
25 Rik Smits .30 .75
26 Glenn Robinson .30 .75
27 Loy Vaught .25 .60
28 Jim Jackson .25 .60
29 Horace Grant .30 .75
30 Allen Iverson .75 2.00
31 Clifford Robinson .25 .60
32 Isaiah Rider .30 .75
33 Clyde Drexler .50 1.25
34 Sean Elliott .40 1.00
35 Eric Williams .25 .60
36 Larry Johnson .40 1.00
37 Anthony Mason .25 .60
38 Terrell Brandon .25 .60
39 Reggie Miller .50 1.25
40 Kevin Johnson .40 1.00

1997 Upper Deck Nestle Slam Dunk Contestants

This set was randomly inserted into packs of special Slam Dunk Nestle Crunch bars and features all of the participants from the 1996-97 Slam Dunk contest at the All-Star game.

COMPLETE SET (6) 25.00 60.00
CC1 Kobe Bryant 15.00 40.00
Champion
CC2 Chris Carr 3.00 8.00
CC3 Michael Finley 5.00 12.00
CC4 Darvin Ham 3.00 8.00
CC5 Bob Sura 3.00 8.00
CC6 Ray Allen 6.00 15.00

1994 Upper Deck Nintendo Chaos in the Windy City

NNO Michael Jordan 25.00 60.00

1994 Upper Deck Nothing But Net

his 15-card standard-size set captures scenes from McDonald's "Nothing but Net" commercials featuring Larry Bird, Michael Jordan, and Charles Barkley. The horizontal fronts feature full-bleed color shots except on the left side, where a gold stripe carries "Upper Deck" in white lettering. A special McDonald's logo appears in the lower left corner. In a film strip design, the back carries four copies of the front picture as well as the dialogue between the players. The cards are numbered on the back "X of 15" in the upper left corner. Also produced was a jumbo-size version of this set distributed only in WalMart. WalMart originally offered complete standard-sized "Nothing But Net" sets along with one jumbo-sized card in a special package for 5.00. Jumbo cards are valued at five times the values listed below.

COMPLETE SET (15) 5.00 12.00
1 Larry Bird 1.00 2.50
Michael Jordan
(I've got an idea)
2 Charles Barkley .40 1.00
(Can I play)
3 Over the Grand Canyon .20 .50
4 Off your face .20 .50
(Mt. Rushmore)
5 Michael Jordan .75 2.00
(Through the window off the floor)
6 Larry Bird .75 2.00
(Nothing but Net)
7 Michael Jordan 1.00 2.50
Larry Bird
(Watch this shot)
8 Charles Barkley .30 .75
(Hey, can I play)
9 Michael Jordan 1.00 2.50
Larry Bird
(No)
10 Charles Barkley .30 .75
(The Shark)
11 Charles Barkley .30 .75
(Please...Pretty Please)
12 Larry Bird .75 2.00
Michael Jordan
Charles Barkley
(No)
13 Michael Jordan .75 2.00
(I'm hungry ...)
14 Larry Bird .60 1.50
(Play ya to see who buys)
15 McDonald's Logo in .08 .25
Outer Space

1998-99 Upper Deck Ovation

The 1998-99 Upper Deck Ovation set was released in in early 1999 as an 80-card set that was broken into tiers as follows: 70 Base Veterans (1-70), 10 Rookies (71-80). Each pack carried a suggested retail of $2.99.

COMPLETE SET (80) 25.00 60.00
COMPLETE SET w/o RC (70) 12.00 30.00
1 Steve Smith .30 .75
2 Dikembe Mutombo .40 1.00
3 Antoine Walker .40 1.00
4 Ron Mercer .30 .75
5 Glen Rice .40 1.00
6 Bobby Phills .25 .60
7 Michael Jordan 3.00 8.00
8 Toni Kukoc .40 1.00
9 Dennis Rodman .75 2.00
10 Scottie Pippen .60 1.50
11 Shawn Kemp .40 1.00
12 Derek Anderson .25 .60
13 Brevin Knight .25 .60
14 Michael Finley .40 1.00
15 Shawn Bradley .25 .60
16 LaPhonso Ellis .25 .60
17 Bobby Jackson .25 .60
18 Grant Hill .60 1.50
19 Jerry Stackhouse .40 1.00
20 Donyell Marshall .25 .60
21 Erick Dampier .25 .60
22 Hakeem Olajuwon .50 1.25
23 Charles Barkley .60 1.50
24 Reggie Miller .50 1.25
25 Chris Mullin .40 1.00
26 Rik Smits .30 .75
27 Maurice Taylor .25 .60
28 Lorenzen Wright .25 .60
29 Kobe Bryant 1.50 4.00
30 Eddie Jones .40 1.00
31 Shaquille O'Neal 1.00 2.50
32 Alonzo Mourning .50 1.25

33 Tim Hardaway .40 1.00
34 Jamal Mashburn .30 .75
35 Ray Allen .50 1.25
36 Terrell Brandon .25 .60
37 Glenn Robinson .30 .75
38 Kevin Garnett .60 1.50
39 Tom Gugliotta .25 .60
40 Stephon Marbury .50 1.25
41 Keith Van Horn .40 1.00
42 Kerry Kittles .25 .60
43 Jayson Williams .25 .60
44 Patrick Ewing .50 1.25
45 Allan Houston .30 .75
46 Larry Johnson .40 1.00
47 Anfernee Hardaway .60 1.50
48 Nick Anderson .25 .60
49 Allen Iverson .75 2.00
50 Joe Smith .30 .75
51 Tim Thomas .40 1.00
52 Jason Kidd .60 1.50
53 Antonio McDyess .30 .75
54 Damon Stoudamire .30 .75
55 Isaiah Rider .30 .75
56 Rasheed Wallace .40 1.00
57 Tariq Abdul-Wahad .25 .60
58 Corliss Williamson .25 .60
59 Tim Duncan .75 2.00
60 David Robinson .60 1.50
61 Vin Baker .30 .75
62 Gary Payton .40 1.00
63 Chauncey Billups .50 1.25
64 Tracy McGrady .60 1.50
65 Karl Malone .50 1.25
66 John Stockton .50 1.25
67 Shareef Abdur-Rahim .40 1.00
68 Bryant Reeves .25 .60
69 Juwan Howard .30 .75
70 Rod Strickland .25 .60
71 Michael Olowokandi RC 1.00 2.50
72 Mike Bibby RC 1.25 3.00
73 Raef LaFrentz RC 1.00 2.50
74 Antawn Jamison RC 1.25 3.00
75 Vince Carter RC 4.00 10.00
76 Robert Traylor RC .75 2.00
77 Jason Williams RC 2.00 5.00
78 Larry Hughes RC 1.50 4.00
79 Dirk Nowitzki RC 5.00 12.00
80 Paul Pierce RC 3.00 8.00
BK1 Michael Jordan Ball/90 750.00 1500.00

1998-99 Upper Deck Ovation Gold

*STARS: 2.5X TO 6X BASE CARD HI
*RCs: .75X TO 2X BASE HI
STATED PRINT RUN 1000 SERIAL #'d SETS
7 Michael Jordan 25.00 60.00
29 Kobe Bryant 15.00 40.00
75 Vince Carter 15.00 40.00
79 Dirk Nowitzki 15.00 40.00

1998-99 Upper Deck Ovation Future Forces

%Randomly inserted into packs at a rate of one in 29, this 20-card set focuses on young players who have the ability to make a high impact. The card fronts feature a silver border, while the card backs are numbered with a "F" prefix.

COMPLETE SET (20) 12.00 30.00
STATED ODDS 1:29
F1 Tim Duncan 2.00 5.00
F2 Keith Van Horn 1.00 2.50
F3 Kobe Bryant 4.00 10.00
F4 Tracy McGrady 1.50 4.00
F5 Maurice Taylor .60 1.50
F6 Shareef Abdur-Rahim 1.00 2.50
F7 Kevin Garnett 1.50 4.00
F8 Brevin Knight .60 1.50
F9 Ron Mercer .75 2.00
F10 Tim Thomas 1.00 2.50
F11 Antoine Walker 1.00 2.50
F12 Michael Finley 1.00 2.50
F13 Grant Hill 1.50 4.00
F14 Jerry Stackhouse 1.00 2.50
F15 Erick Dampier .60 1.50
F16 Lorenzen Wright .60 1.50
F17 Ray Allen 1.25 3.00
F18 Stephon Marbury 1.25 3.00
F19 Allen Iverson 2.00 5.00
F20 Damon Stoudamire .75 2.00

1998-99 Upper Deck Ovation Jordan Rules

Randomly inserted into packs at different levels, this 15-card set focuses on Jordan's dominant play during his NBA career showing why he "rules". The first tier (cards J1-J5) feature a bronze background and were inserted at one in 23. The second tier (cards J6-J10) feature a silver background are were inserted at one in 45. The last tier (cards J11-J15) feature a die cut gold background and were inserted at a rate of one in 99. Card backs feature a "J" prefix.

COMMON CARD (J1-J5) 6.00 15.00
COMMON CARD (J6-J10) 10.00 25.00
COMMON CARD (J11-J15) 12.00 30.00
J1-J5 STATED ODDS 1:23
J6-J10 STATED ODDS 1:45
J11-J15 STATED ODDS 1:99

1998-99 Upper Deck Ovation Superstars of the Court

Randomly inserted in packs at a rate of one in two, this 20-card set features the top stars who dominate the court. The cards feature a holofoil background on the front, and are numbered with a "C" prefix.

COMPLETE SET (20) 10.00 25.00
STATED ODDS 1:2
C1 Michael Jordan 3.00 8.00
C2 Tim Duncan .75 2.00
C3 Grant Hill .60 1.50
C4 Karl Malone .50 1.25
C5 Dennis Rodman .75 2.00
C6 Hakeem Olajuwon .50 1.25
C7 Keith Van Horn .40 1.00
C8 Kobe Bryant 1.50 4.00
C9 Jason Kidd .60 1.50
C10 Stephon Marbury .50 1.25
C11 Reggie Miller .50 1.25
C12 Damon Stoudamire .30 .75
C13 Tracy McGrady .60 1.50
C14 Scottie Pippen .60 1.50
C15 Vin Baker .30 .75
C16 Shaquille O'Neal 1.00 2.50
C17 Anfernee Hardaway .60 1.50
C18 Charles Barkley .60 1.50
C19 Kevin Garnett .60 1.50
C20 Antoine Walker .40 1.00

1999-00 Upper Deck Ovation

The second year for Ovation was released as a 90-card base set, containing 60 veterans and 30 rookies. Each card had the look and feel of an actual basketball, with the color photo in the middle of the front. The rookie subset cards were inserted at one in four packs.

COMPLETE SET (90) 30.00 80.00
COMPLETE SET w/o RC (60) 10.00 25.00
61-90 SUBSET: STATED ODDS 1:4
1 Dikembe Mutombo .40 1.00
2 Alan Henderson .25 .60
3 Antoine Walker .40 1.00
4 Paul Pierce .50 1.25
5 David Wesley .25 .60
6 Eddie Jones .40 1.00
7 Toni Kukoc .40 1.00
8 Randy Brown .25 .60
9 Shawn Kemp .40 1.00
10 Zydrunas Ilgauskas .30 .75
11 Michael Finley .40 1.00
12 Dirk Nowitzki .75 2.00
13 Nick Van Exel .30 .75
14 Antonio McDyess .30 .75
15 Grant Hill .50 1.25
16 Jerry Stackhouse .40 1.00
17 Antawn Jamison .40 1.00
18 John Starks .30 .75
19 Hakeem Olajuwon .50 1.25
20 Charles Barkley .60 1.50
21 Cuttino Mobley .25 .60
22 Reggie Miller .40 1.00
23 Rik Smits .40 1.00
24 Maurice Taylor .25 .60
25 Michael Olowokandi .25 .60
26 Kobe Bryant 1.50 4.00
27 Shaquille O'Neal 1.00 2.50
28 Tim Hardaway .40 1.00
29 Alonzo Mourning .50 1.25
30 Glenn Robinson .30 .75
31 Ray Allen .40 1.00
32 Kevin Garnett .60 1.50
33 Joe Smith .30 .75
34 Stephon Marbury .30 .75
35 Keith Van Horn .30 .75
36 Patrick Ewing .50 1.25
37 Latrell Sprewell .40 1.00
38 Darrell Armstrong .25 .60
39 Bo Outlaw .25 .60
40 Allen Iverson .75 2.00
41 Larry Hughes .30 .75
42 Jason Kidd .60 1.50
43 Anfernee Hardaway .60 1.50
44 Brian Grant .25 .60
45 Damon Stoudamire .30 .75
46 Jason Williams .50 1.25
47 Chris Webber .40 1.00
48 Tim Duncan .75 2.00
49 David Robinson .60 1.50
50 Sean Elliott .40 1.00
51 Gary Payton .40 1.00
52 Vin Baker .30 .75
53 Vince Carter .75 2.00
54 Tracy McGrady .60 1.50
55 Karl Malone .50 1.25
56 John Stockton .50 1.25
57 Shareef Abdur-Rahim .30 .75
58 Mike Bibby .40 1.00
59 Juwan Howard .30 .75
60 Mitch Richmond .40 1.00
61 Elton Brand RC 1.50 4.00
62 Steve Francis RC 1.50 4.00
63 Baron Davis RC 1.50 4.00
64 Lamar Odom RC 1.50 4.00
65 Jonathan Bender RC .60 1.50
66 Wally Szczerbiak RC 1.25 3.00
67 Richard Hamilton RC 1.25 3.00
68 Andre Miller RC 1.25 3.00
69 Shawn Marion RC 1.25 3.00
70 Jason Terry RC 1.00 2.50
71 Trajan Langdon RC .60 1.50
72 A.Radojevic RC .40 1.00
73 Corey Maggette RC 1.00 2.50
74 William Avery RC .50 1.25
75 Galen Young RC .60 1.50
76 Chris Herren RC .50 1.25
77 Cal Bowdler RC .40 1.00
78 James Posey RC .60 1.50
79 Quincy Lewis RC .40 1.00
80 Dion Glover RC .50 1.25
81 Jeff Foster RC .60 1.50
82 Kenny Thomas RC .60 1.50
83 Devean George RC .60 1.50
84 Tim James RC .40 1.00
85 Vonteego Cummings RC .40 1.00
86 Jumaine Jones RC .50 1.25
87 Scott Padgett RC .50 1.25
88 Obinna Ekezie RC .50 1.25
89 Ryan Robertson RC .40 1.00
90 Evan Eschmeyer RC .50 1.25
MJS M.Jordan AU/23 1500.00 2200.00

1999-00 Upper Deck Ovation Standing Ovation

*STARS: 15X TO 40X BASE CARD HI
*RCs: 4X TO 10X BASE HI
STATED PRINT RUN 50 SERIAL #'d SETS

1999-00 Upper Deck Ovation A Piece of History

Randomly inserted in packs at one in 352, this 14-card set features an actual piece of a game-used basketball on the corresponding player's card. There was only 4,560 total cards available. The cards are numbered on the back by the players initials.

STATED ODDS 1:352
STATED PRINT RUN 4560 TOTAL CARDS
AM Andre Miller 6.00 15.00
BD Baron Davis 8.00 20.00
HO Hakeem Olajuwon 12.00 30.00
JB Jonathan Bender 3.00 8.00
JS John Stockton 8.00 20.00
JW Jason Williams 12.00 30.00
KB Kobe Bryant 30.00 80.00
KG Kevin Garnett 10.00 25.00
KM Karl Malone 8.00 20.00
RH Richard Hamilton 6.00 15.00
RM Reggie Miller 15.00 40.00
SF Steve Francis 8.00 20.00
SM Shawn Marion 6.00 15.00
WS Wally Szczerbiak 6.00 15.00

1999-00 Upper Deck Ovation A Piece of History Autographs

PRINT RUN TO PLAYER'S JERSEY #
KGA Kevin Garnett/21 250.00 500.00
KMA Karl Malone/32 200.00 400.00
RHA Richard Hamilton/32 40.00 100.00
SMA Shawn Marion/31 60.00 120.00

1999-00 Upper Deck Ovation Curtain Calls

Randomly inserted in packs at one in nine, this 10-card set focuses on some of the most collectible players in the NBA and their accomplishments during the 98-99 season. Card backs carry a "CC" prefix.

COMPLETE SET (10) 3.00 8.00
STATED ODDS 1:9
CC1 Hakeem Olajuwon .60 1.50
CC2 Karl Malone .60 1.50
CC3 Latrell Sprewell .50 1.25
CC4 Allen Iverson 1.00 2.50
CC5 Tim Hardaway .50 1.25
CC6 Shaquille O'Neal 1.25 3.00
CC7 Jason Kidd .75 2.00
CC8 Charles Barkley .75 2.00
CC9 Antonio McDyess .40 1.00
CC10 Gary Payton .50 1.25

1999-00 Upper Deck Ovation Lead Performers

Randomly inserted in packs at one in nine, this 10-card set highlights players who are known for their leadership skills on the floor. Card backs carry a "LP" prefix.

COMPLETE SET (10) 5.00 12.00
STATED ODDS 1:9
LP1 Tim Duncan 1.00 2.50
LP2 Kevin Garnett .75 2.00
LP3 Keith Van Horn .40 1.00
LP4 Shareef Abdur-Rahim .40 1.00
LP5 Antoine Walker .50 1.25
LP6 Shaquille O'Neal 1.25 3.00
LP7 Grant Hill .60 1.50
LP8 Kobe Bryant 2.00 5.00
LP9 Allen Iverson 1.00 2.50
LP10 Jason Williams .60 1.50

1999-00 Upper Deck Ovation MJ Center Stage

Randomly inserted in packs at varying levels, this 15-card set focuses on Michael Jordan at his best. Cards CS1-CS5 contained silver foil and were inserted at one in nine. Cards CS6-CS10 contained gold foil and were inserted at one in 39. Finally, cards CS11-CS15 contained rainbow foil and were inserted at one in 99. Card backs carry a "CS" prefix.

COMMON CARD (CS1-CS5) 2.00 5.00
COMMON CARD (CS6-CS10) 4.00 10.00
COMMON CARD (CS11-CS15) 8.00 20.00
CS1-CS5: STATED ODDS 1:9
CS6-CS10: STATED ODDS 1:39
CS11-CS15: STATED ODDS 1:99

1999-00 Upper Deck Ovation Premiere Performers

Randomly inserted in packs at one in 19, this 10-card set showcases the top rookies for the 1999-2000 season. Card backs carry a "PP" prefix.

COMPLETE SET (10) 4.00 10.00
STATED ODDS 1:19
PP1 Elton Brand .75 2.00
PP2 Steve Francis .75 2.00
PP3 Baron Davis .75 2.00
PP4 Lamar Odom .75 2.00
PP5 Jonathan Bender .30 .75
PP6 Wally Szczerbiak .60 1.50
PP7 Richard Hamilton .60 1.50
PP8 Andre Miller .60 1.50
PP9 Shawn Marion .60 1.50
PP10 Jason Terry .50 1.25

1999-00 Upper Deck Ovation Spotlight

Randomly inserted in packs at one in three, this 10-card set spotlights some of the top young stars in the NBA. Card backs carry an "OS" prefix.

COMPLETE SET (10) 2.50 6.00
STATED ODDS 1:3
OS1 Kevin Garnett .50 1.25
OS2 Antawn Jamison .30 .75
OS3 Kobe Bryant 1.25 3.00
OS4 Shareef Abdur-Rahim .25 .60
OS5 Keith Van Horn .25 .60
OS6 Vince Carter .60 1.50
OS7 Stephon Marbury .25 .60
OS8 Paul Pierce .40 1.00
OS9 Tim Duncan .60 1.50
OS10 Jason Williams .40 1.00

1999-00 Upper Deck Ovation Superstar Theatre

Randomly inserted in packs at one in 19, this 20-card set features the NBA's best performers. Card backs carry a "ST" prefix.

COMPLETE SET (20) 30.00 60.00
STATED ODDS 1:19
ST1 Michael Jordan 10.00 25.00
ST2 Vince Carter 2.50 6.00
ST3 Kevin Garnett 2.00 5.00
ST4 Paul Pierce 1.50 4.00
ST5 Jason Williams 1.50 4.00
ST6 Tim Duncan 2.50 6.00
ST7 Allen Iverson 2.50 6.00
ST8 Antawn Jamison 1.25 3.00
ST9 Kobe Bryant 5.00 12.00
ST10 Grant Hill 1.50 4.00
ST11 Antoine Walker 1.25 3.00
ST12 Tracy McGrady 2.00 5.00
ST13 Shareef Abdur-Rahim 1.00 2.50
ST14 Stephon Marbury 1.00 2.50
ST15 Jason Kidd 2.00 5.00
ST16 Shaquille O'Neal 3.00 8.00
ST17 Tim Hardaway 1.25 3.00
ST18 Keith Van Horn 1.00 2.50
ST19 Gary Payton 1.25 3.00
ST20 Karl Malone 1.50 4.00

2000-01 Upper Deck Ovation

The 2000-01 Upper Deck Ovation product was released in December,2000. The product featured a 90-card base set that was broken into tiers as follows: 60 Base Veterans (1-60), and 30 Rookies (61-90) that were individually serial numbered to 2000. Each pack contained 5 cards, and carried a suggested retail price of $2.99.

COMPLETE SET w/o RC (60) 10.00 25.00
RCs: STATED PRINT RUN 2000 SERIAL #'d SETS
1 Dikembe Mutombo .30 .75
2 Jim Jackson .20 .50
3 Paul Pierce .30 .75
4 Antoine Walker .25 .60
5 Derrick Coleman .25 .60
6 Baron Davis .30 .75
7 Elton Brand .30 .75
8 Ron Artest .30 .75
9 Lamond Murray .20 .50
10 Andre Miller .25 .60
11 Michael Finley .30 .75
12 Dirk Nowitzki .50 1.25
13 Antonio McDyess .25 .60
14 Nick Van Exel .25 .60
15 Jerry Stackhouse .25 .60
16 Jerome Williams .20 .50
17 Larry Hughes .25 .60
18 Antawn Jamison .30 .75
19 Steve Francis .25 .60
20 Hakeem Olajuwon .40 1.00
21 Reggie Miller .30 .75
22 Jalen Rose .25 .60
23 Lamar Odom .25 .60
24 Michael Olowokandi .20 .50
25 Shaquille O'Neal .75 2.00
26 Kobe Bryant 1.25 3.00
27 Alonzo Mourning .40 1.00
28 Anthony Carter .20 .50
29 Ray Allen .30 .75
30 Tim Thomas .20 .50
31 Kevin Garnett .50 1.25
32 Wally Szczerbiak .25 .60
33 Stephon Marbury .25 .60
34 Keith Van Horn .25 .60
35 Allan Houston .25 .60
36 Latrell Sprewell .25 .60
37 Grant Hill .40 1.00
38 Tracy McGrady .50 1.25
39 Allen Iverson .60 1.50
40 Toni Kukoc .30 .75
41 Jason Kidd .50 1.25
42 Anfernee Hardaway .50 1.25
43 Rasheed Wallace .30 .75
44 Scottie Pippen .50 1.25
45 Damon Stoudamire .25 .60
46 Chris Webber .30 .75
47 Jason Williams .30 .75
48 Tim Duncan .60 1.50
49 David Robinson .50 1.25
50 Gary Payton .30 .75
51 Brent Barry .20 .50
52 Rashard Lewis .30 .75
53 Vince Carter .60 1.50
54 Antonio Davis .20 .50
55 Karl Malone .40 1.00
56 John Stockton .40 1.00
57 Shareef Abdur-Rahim .25 .60
58 Mike Bibby .30 .75
59 Mitch Richmond .25 .60
60 Richard Hamilton .25 .60
61 Kenyon Martin RC 3.00 8.00
62 Stromile Swift RC 1.25 3.00
63 Darius Miles RC 1.25 3.00
64 Marcus Fizer RC 1.25 3.00
65 Mike Miller RC 2.00 5.00
66 DerMarr Johnson RC 1.00 2.50
67 Chris Mihm RC 1.00 2.50
68 Jamal Crawford RC 3.00 8.00
69 Joel Przybilla RC 1.00 2.50
70 Keyon Dooling RC 1.25 3.00
71 Jerome Moiso RC .75 2.00
72 Etan Thomas RC 1.25 3.00
73 Courtney Alexander RC 1.00 2.50
74 Mateen Cleaves RC 1.00 2.50
75 Jason Collier RC 1.25 3.00
76 Hedo Turkoglu RC 2.00 5.00
77 Desmond Mason RC 1.50 4.00
78 Quentin Richardson RC 1.25 3.00
79 Jamaal Magloire RC 1.25 3.00
80 Speedy Claxton RC 1.25 3.00
81 Morris Peterson RC 1.25 3.00
82 Donnell Harvey RC 1.00 2.50
83 DeShawn Stevenson RC 1.25 3.00
84 Mamadou N'Diaye RC .75 2.00
85 Erick Barkley RC .75 2.00
86 Mark Madsen RC 1.25 3.00
87 A.J. Guyton RC .75 2.00
88 Khalid El-Amin RC .75 2.00
89 Eddie House RC 1.00 2.50
90 Chris Porter RC .75 2.00

2000-01 Upper Deck Ovation Standing Ovation

*STARS: 20X TO 50X BASE CARD HI
*RCs: 1.5X TO 4X BASE CARD HI
STATED PRINT RUN 50 SERIAL #'d SETS

2000-01 Upper Deck Ovation A Piece of History

Randomly inserted into packs at one in 120, this 28-card set features game-used ball and shoe cards. Please note that five of these cards are autographed, and are serial numbered to the respective player's jersey number. Card backs are numbered using the player's intials.

STATED ODDS 1:120
PIECES ARE GAME BALLS UNLESS NOTED
AHB Anfernee Hardaway 10.00 25.00
AIB Allen Iverson 12.00 30.00
ALB Alonzo Mourning 8.00 20.00
AMB Andre Miller 5.00 12.00
BDB Baron Davis 6.00 15.00
CWS Chris Webber Shoe 10.00 25.00
GPB Gary Payton 6.00 15.00
JSB Jerry Stackhouse 5.00 12.00
JWB Jason Williams 6.00 15.00
KBB Kobe Bryant 12.00 30.00
KBC Kobe Bryant Combo/25 125.00 250.00
KBS Kobe Bryant Shoe 20.00 50.00
KGA Kevin Garnett AU/21 125.00 250.00
KGB Kevin Garnett 10.00 25.00
KGC Kevin Garnett Combo/25 50.00 100.00
KGS Kevin Garnett Shoe 12.50 30.00
KMS Karl Malone Shoe 12.50 30.00
LHB Larry Hughes 5.00 12.00
MFB Michael Finley 6.00 15.00
MJA Michael Jordan AU/23 900.00 1500.00
MJS Michael Jordan Shoe 100.00 225.00
PPB Paul Pierce 6.00 15.00
RAB Ray Allen 6.00 15.00
SAB Shareef Abdur-Rahim 5.00 12.00
SOS Shaquille O'Neal Shoe 20.00 50.00
SPB Scottie Pippen 10.00 25.00
WSB Wally Szczerbiak 5.00 12.00

2000-01 Upper Deck Ovation Center Stage

Randomly inserted into packs at one in 19, this 10-card insert features players that that take center stage when the game is on the line. Card backs carry a "CS" prefix. Please note that these cards were produced with bronze foil stamping.

COMPLETE SET (10) 6.00 15.00
STATED ODDS 1:19
*SILVER: 2X TO 5X BASE CARD HI
SILVER: PRINT RUN 200 SERIAL #'d SETS
*GOLD: 12X TO 30X BASE CARD HI
GOLD: PRINT RUN 25 SERIAL #'d SETS
CS1 Kevin Garnett 1.00 2.50
CS2 Tim Duncan 1.25 3.00
CS3 Lamar Odom .50 1.25
CS4 Jason Kidd 1.00 2.50
CS5 Vince Carter 1.25 3.00
CS6 Alonzo Mourning .75 2.00
CS7 Elton Brand .60 1.50
CS8 Chris Webber .60 1.50
CS9 Anfernee Hardaway 1.00 2.50
CS10 Kobe Bryant 2.50 6.00

2000-01 Upper Deck Ovation Lead Performers

Randomly inserted into packs at one in 12, this 11-card insert features players that lead their teams to victory. Card backs carry a "LP" prefix.

COMPLETE SET (11) 6.00 15.00
STATED ODDS 1:12
LP1 Shaquille O'Neal 1.25 3.00
LP2 Vince Carter 1.00 2.50
LP3 Kevin Garnett .75 2.00
LP4 Allen Iverson 1.00 2.50
LP5 Jason Kidd .75 2.00
LP6 Elton Brand .50 1.25
LP7 Gary Payton .50 1.25
LP8 Kobe Bryant 2.00 5.00
LP9 Steve Francis .40 1.00
LP10 Stephon Marbury .40 1.00
LP11 Tim Duncan 1.00 2.50

2000-01 Upper Deck Ovation Spotlight

Randomly inserted into packs at one in seven, this 20-card insert spotlights some of the most talented players in the NBA. Card backs carry an "OS" prefix.

COMPLETE SET (20) 6.00 15.00
STATED ODDS 1:7
OS1 Kobe Bryant 2.00 5.00
OS2 Larry Hughes .40 1.00
OS3 Andre Miller .40 1.00
OS4 Michael Finley .50 1.25
OS5 Ray Allen .50 1.25
OS6 Latrell Sprewell .40 1.00
OS7 Jalen Rose .40 1.00
OS8 Antonio McDyess .40 1.00
OS9 Karl Malone .60 1.50
OS10 Paul Pierce .50 1.25
OS11 Shareef Abdur-Rahim .40 1.00
OS12 Chris Webber .50 1.25
OS13 Stephon Marbury .40 1.00
OS14 Scottie Pippen .75 2.00
OS15 Lamar Odom .40 1.00
OS16 Alonzo Mourning .60 1.50
OS17 Kevin Garnett .75 2.00
OS18 Anfernee Hardaway .75 2.00
OS19 Jason Williams .50 1.25
OS20 Rasheed Wallace .50 1.25

2000-01 Upper Deck Ovation Super Signatures

Randomly inserted in packs at one in 200, this 15-card set features signatures from some of the top stars in the NBA. The card backs are numbered by the player's initials.

STATED ODDS 1:200
AH Anfernee Hardaway 30.00 60.00
CA Courtney Alexander 3.00 8.00
CM Chris Mihm 3.00 8.00
DA Darrell Armstrong 4.00 10.00
DM DerMarr Johnson 3.00 8.00
JP Joel Przybilla 3.00 8.00
JR Jalen Rose 6.00 15.00
KB Kobe Bryant 60.00 150.00
KG Kevin Garnett 30.00 80.00
KY Kenyon Martin 6.00 15.00
LH Larry Hughes 8.00 20.00
MF Marcus Fizer 4.00 10.00
SA Shareef Abdur-Rahim 6.00 15.00
SM Shawn Marion 6.00 15.00
SS Stromile Swift 4.00 10.00

2000-01 Upper Deck Ovation Super Signatures Gold

Randomly inserted into packs, this 15-card insert is a complete parallel of the Super Signatures insert. Please note that these cards have gold foil stamping on the card front and are individually serial numbered to the respective player's jersey number.

STATED PRINT RUN ONE TO 31 SETS
SOME UNPRICED DUE TO SCARCITY
KG Kevin Garnett/21 150.00 300.00
LH Larry Hughes/20 30.00 80.00

2000-01 Upper Deck Ovation Superstar Theatre

Randomly inserted into packs at one in 12, this 11-card insert features players that put on a show when they walk onto the court. Card backs carry a "S" prefix.

COMPLETE SET (11) 6.00 15.00
STATED ODDS 1:12
S1 Kobe Bryant 2.00 5.00
S2 Vince Carter 1.00 2.50
S3 Jason Kidd .75 2.00
S4 Steve Francis .40 1.00
S5 Reggie Miller .50 1.25
S6 Tim Duncan 1.00 2.50
S7 Kevin Garnett .75 2.00
S8 Gary Payton .50 1.25
S9 Elton Brand .50 1.25
S10 Allen Iverson 1.00 2.50
S11 Shaquille O'Neal 1.25 3.00

2000-01 Upper Deck Ovation UD Authentics Rookie Exclusives

Randomly inserted in packs, this three-card set features autographs from the 2000-01 rookie class. Each player is numbered with their initials.

RANDOM INSERTS IN PACKS
JP Joel Przybilla 2.50 6.00
MC Mateen Cleaves 2.50 6.00
MP Morris Peterson 3.00 8.00

2001-02 Upper Deck Ovation

This 180-card base set includes 90 veterans and 90 rookies. The rookie players can be found in six different versions. Level 1: 20 Profile cards sequentially #'d to 625; Level 1: 20 Stat cards sequentially #'d to 625; Level 1: 20 Scouting Report cards sequentially #'d to 625; Level 2: 10 Profile cards sequentially #'d to 250; Level 2: 10 Stat cards sequentially #'d to 250; and Level 2: 10 Scouting Report cards sequentially #'d to 250. Base cards feature full color player action photos and bronze highlights. Ovation was packaged in five card packs with boxes containing 20 packs.

COMP.SET w/o SP's (90) 20.00 40.00
91-110 PRINT RUN 1875 PER PLAYER
91-110 THREE VERSIONS SER.#'d TO 625
111-120 PRINT RUN 750 PER PLAYER
111-120 THREE VERSIONS SER.#'d TO 250
1 Jason Terry .30 .75
2 DerMarr Johnson .20 .50
3 Shareef Abdur-Rahim .25 .60
4 Paul Pierce .30 .75
5 Antoine Walker .25 .60
6 Kenny Anderson .25 .60
7 Jamal Mashburn .25 .60
8 David Wesley .20 .50
9 Baron Davis .30 .75
10 Ron Mercer .20 .50
11 Marcus Fizer .20 .50
12 Ron Artest .30 .75
13 Andre Miller .25 .60
14 Lamond Murray .20 .50
15 Chris Mihm .20 .50
16 Michael Finley .30 .75
17 Steve Nash .50 1.25
18 Dirk Nowitzki .50 1.25
19 Antonio McDyess .25 .60
20 Nick Van Exel .25 .60
21 Raef LaFrentz .20 .50
22 Jerry Stackhouse .25 .60
23 Chucky Atkins .20 .50
24 Corliss Williamson .20 .50
25 Antawn Jamison .30 .75
26 Chris Porter .20 .50
27 Larry Hughes .25 .60
28 Steve Francis .25 .60
29 Cuttino Mobley .20 .50
30 Maurice Taylor .20 .50
31 Reggie Miller .30 .75
32 Jalen Rose .25 .60
33 Jermaine O'Neal .25 .60
34 Darius Miles .20 .50
35 Corey Maggette .25 .60
36 Lamar Odom .25 .60
37 Elton Brand .30 .75
38 Kobe Bryant 1.25 3.00
39 Shaquille O'Neal .75 2.00
40 Rick Fox .20 .50
41 Derek Fisher .25 .60
42 Stromile Swift .20 .50
43 Michael Dickerson .20 .50
44 Jason Williams .25 .60
45 Alonzo Mourning .40 1.00
46 Eddie Jones .25 .60
47 Anthony Carter .20 .50
48 Ray Allen .30 .75
49 Glenn Robinson .25 .60
50 Sam Cassell .25 .60
51 Kevin Garnett .50 1.25
52 Terrell Brandon .20 .50
53 Wally Szczerbiak .25 .60
54 Joe Smith .25 .60
55 Kenyon Martin .30 .75
56 Keith Van Horn .25 .60
57 Jason Kidd .50 1.25
58 Latrell Sprewell .25 .60
59 Allan Houston .25 .60
60 Marcus Camby .25 .60
61 Tracy McGrady .50 1.25
62 Mike Miller .25 .60
63 Grant Hill .40 1.00
64 Allen Iverson .60 1.50
65 Dikembe Mutombo .30 .75
66 Aaron McKie .20 .50
67 Stephon Marbury .25 .60
68 Shawn Marion .25 .60
69 Tom Gugliotta .20 .50
70 Rasheed Wallace .30 .75
71 Damon Stoudamire .25 .60
72 Bonzi Wells .20 .50
73 Chris Webber .30 .75
74 Peja Stojakovic .30 .75
75 Mike Bibby .30 .75
76 Tim Duncan .60 1.50
77 David Robinson .50 1.25
78 Antonio Daniels .20 .50
79 Gary Payton .30 .75
80 Rashard Lewis .30 .75
81 Desmond Mason .25 .60
82 Vince Carter .50 1.25
83 Morris Peterson .20 .50
84 Antonio Davis .20 .50
85 Karl Malone .40 1.00
86 John Stockton .40 1.00
87 Donyell Marshall .20 .50
88 Richard Hamilton .25 .60
89 Courtney Alexander .20 .50
90 Michael Jordan 2.50 6.00
91A Jeff Trepagnier P RC .75 2.00
91B Jeff Trepagnier S RC .75 2.00
91C Jeff Trepagnier SR RC .75 2.00
92A Pau Gasol P RC 4.00 10.00
92B Pau Gasol S RC 4.00 10.00
92C Pau Gasol SR RC 4.00 10.00
93A Will Solomon P RC 1.25 3.00
93B Will Solomon S RC 1.25 3.00
93C Will Solomon SP RC 1.25 3.00
94A Gilbert Arenas P RC 2.00 5.00
94B Gilbert Arenas S RC 2.00 5.00
94C Gilbert Arenas SR RC 2.00 5.00
95A Andrei Kirilenko P RC 2.00 5.00
95B Andrei Kirilenko S RC 2.00 5.00
95C Andrei Kirilenko SR RC 2.00 5.00
96A Jamaal Tinsley P RC 1.25 3.00
96B Jamaal Tinsley S RC 1.25 3.00
96C Jamaal Tinsley SR RC 1.25 3.00
97A Samuel Dalembert P RC 1.25 3.00
97B Samuel Dalembert S RC 1.25 3.00
97C Samuel Dalembert SR RC 1.25 3.00
98A Gerald Wallace P RC 1.50 4.00
98B Gerald Wallace S RC 1.50 4.00
98C Gerald Wallace SR RC 1.50 4.00
99A Brandon Armstrong P RC .75 2.00
99B Brandon Armstrong S RC .75 2.00
99C Brandon Armstrong SR RC .75 2.00
100A Jeryl Sasser P RC .75 2.00
100B Jeryl Sasser S RC .75 2.00
100C Jeryl Sasser SR RC .75 2.00
101A Joseph Forte P RC .75 2.00
101B Joseph Forte S RC .75 2.00
101C Joseph Forte SR RC .75 2.00
102A Brendan Haywood P RC 1.25 3.00
102B Brendan Haywood S RC 1.25 3.00
102C Brendan Haywood SR RC 1.25 3.00
103A Zach Randolph P RC 2.00 5.00
103B Zach Randolph S RC 2.00 5.00
103C Zach Randolph SR RC 2.00 5.00
104A Jason Collins P RC 1.00 2.50
104B Jason Collins S RC 1.00 2.50
104C Jason Collins SR RC 1.00 2.50
105A Michael Bradley P RC .75 2.00
105B Michael Bradley S RC .75 2.00
105C Michael Bradley SR RC .75 2.00
106A Kirk Haston P RC .75 2.00
106B Kirk Haston S RC .75 2.00
106C Kirk Haston SR RC .75 2.00
107A Steven Hunter P RC 1.00 2.50
107B Steven Hunter S RC 1.00 2.50
107C Steven Hunter SR RC 1.00 2.50
108A Troy Murphy P RC 1.25 3.00
108B Troy Murphy S RC 1.25 3.00
108C Troy Murphy SR RC 1.25 3.00
109A Richard Jefferson P RC 2.00 5.00
109B Richard Jefferson S RC 2.00 5.00
109C Richard Jefferson SR RC 2.00 5.00
110A V.Radmanovic P RC 1.25 3.00
110B V.Radmanovic S RC 1.25 3.00
110C V.Radmanovic SR RC 1.25 3.00
111A Kedrick Brown P RC 1.50 4.00
111B Kedrick Brown S RC 1.50 4.00
111C Kedrick Brown SR RC 1.50 4.00
112A Joe Johnson P RC 3.00 8.00
112B Joe Johnson S RC 3.00 8.00
112C Joe Johnson SR RC 3.00 8.00
113A Rodney White P RC 1.50 4.00
113B Rodney White S RC 1.50 4.00
113C Rodney White SR RC 1.50 4.00
114A DeSagana Diop P RC 2.00 5.00
114B DeSagana Diop S RC 2.00 5.00
114C DeSagana Diop SR RC 2.00 5.00
115A Eddie Griffin P RC 2.00 5.00
115B Eddie Griffin S RC 2.00 5.00
115C Eddie Griffin SR RC 2.00 5.00
116A Shane Battier P RC 5.00 12.00
116B Shane Battier S RC 5.00 12.00
116C Shane Battier SR RC 5.00 12.00
117A Jason Richardson P RC 3.00 8.00
117B Jason Richardson S RC 3.00 8.00
117C Jason Richardson SR RC 3.00 8.00
118A Eddy Curry P RC 2.50 6.00
118B Eddy Curry S RC 2.50 6.00
118C Eddy Curry SR RC 2.50 6.00
119A Tyson Chandler P RC 4.00 10.00
119B Tyson Chandler S RC 4.00 10.00
119C Tyson Chandler SR RC 4.00 10.00
120A Kwame Brown P RC 2.50 6.00
120B Kwame Brown S RC 2.50 6.00
120C Kwame Brown SR RC 2.50 6.00

2001-02 Upper Deck Ovation MJ UNC Memorabilia

Randomly inserted overall at the rate one in 20, this five card set features a piece of UNC game used memorabilia from Michael Jordan's college days. Several of the cards are sequentially numbered and autographed versions exist also.

MJF1 Michael Jordan Floor 12.00 30.00
MJF2 Michael Jordan Floor 12.00 30.00
MJF3 Michael Jordan Floor 12.00 30.00
MJF4 Michael Jordan Floor 12.00 30.00
MJF5 Michael Jordan Floor 12.00 30.00
MJJ1 Michael Jordan JSY/82 75.00 150.00
MJC1 M.Jordan Floor-JSY/82 75.00 150.00
MJFA M.Jordan Floor AU/23 500.00 800.00
MJJA M.Jordan JSY AU/23 700.00 1200.00
MJCA Jordan Flr-JSY AU/23 1000.00 1500.00

2001-02 Upper Deck Ovation Superstar Warm-Ups

Randomly iinserted in packs at one in 20, this 29 card set features a piece of warm-up jersey on the corresponding player's card. The cards are numbered on back with the player's initials. Photos appear on the left side of the card, while a circular jersey swatch appears on the right.

STATED ODDS 1:10
AM Andre Miller 2.50 6.00
AW Antoine Walker 2.50 6.00
BD Baron Davis 3.00 8.00
CM Corey Maggette 2.50 6.00
DA Darrell Armstrong 2.00 5.00
DJ DerMarr Johnson 2.00 5.00
DM Darius Miles 2.00 5.00
DN Dirk Nowitzki 5.00 12.00
GH Grant Hill 4.00 10.00
HM Hanno Mottola 2.00 5.00
JA Jamaal Magloire 2.00 5.00
JM Jamal Mashburn 2.50 6.00
JS Joe Smith 2.50 6.00
KB Kobe Bryant 12.00 30.00
KD Keyon Dooling 2.00 5.00
KG Kevin Garnett 5.00 12.00
KM Karl Malone 4.00 10.00
MC Antonio McDyess 2.50 6.00
MF Michael Finley 3.00 8.00
MO Michael Olowokandi 2.00 5.00
MP Morris Peterson 2.00 5.00
PP Paul Pierce 3.00 8.00
QR Quentin Richardson 2.50 6.00
RH Richard Hamilton 2.50 6.00
RM Ron Mercer 2.00 5.00
SM Shawn Marion 2.50 6.00
ST John Stockton 4.00 10.00
TB Terrell Brandon 2.00 5.00
WS Wally Szczerbiak 2.50 6.00

2001-02 Upper Deck Ovation Superstar Warm-Ups Autographs

Randomly inserted in packs at one in every 240, this eight card set parallels the base Superstar Warmups set enhanced with authentic player autographs.

STATED ODDS 1:240
DAS Darrell Armstrong 5.00 12.00
DMS Darius Miles 5.00 12.00
HMS Hanno Mottola 5.00 12.00
JMS Jamal Mashburn 6.00 15.00
KBS Kobe Bryant 100.00 200.00
KGS Kevin Garnett 25.00 60.00
MPS Morris Peterson 5.00 12.00
QRS Quentin Richardson 5.00 12.00

2001-02 Upper Deck Ovation Tremendous Trios

Randomly inserted one in 240, this 6 card set features cards with three game-used jersey swatches from three different players. Two player photos appear on both the right and left side of this horizontally designed card with a jersey swatch centered from the single player pictured on the bottom. The two jersey swatches from the top players appear directly below them.

STATED ODDS 1:240
AJLHMA Jamisn/Hughes/Jckson 8.00 20.00
BDJMDW Davis/Mash/Wesley 8.00 20.00
KGTBWS Garnett/Brandon/Szcz 8.00 20.00
MJKBKG Jordan/Kobe/Garnett 60.00 150.00
RMRAJC Mercer/Artest/Fizer 8.00 20.00
TMGHMM T-Mac/Hill/M.Miller 10.00 25.00

2002-03 Upper Deck Ovation

This 134 card standard-size set was issued in five card packs which came 24 to a box. Cards numbered 1-90 feature veterans. Cards 91 through 99 feature 3 cards each of Kevin Garnett, Kobe Bryant and Michael Jordan. The Garnett cards were issued to a stated print run of 2999 cards while the Kobe cards were issued to a stated print run of 1999 cards and the Jordan cards to a stated print run of 499 cards. Cards numbered 100 through 119 feature rookies and were issued to a stated print run of 2999 cards while rookie cards numbered 120 through 134 were issued to a stated print run of 1999 sets.

COMP.SET w/o SP's (90) 20.00 50.00
100-119 PRINT RUN 2999 SER.#'d SETS
120-134 PRINT RUN 1999 SER.#'d SETS
1 Shareef Abdur-Rahim .25 .60
2 Jason Terry .25 .60
3 Glenn Robinson .25 .60
4 Paul Pierce .30 .75
5 Antoine Walker .25 .60
6 Vin Baker .25 .60
7 Jalen Rose .25 .60
8 Tyson Chandler .30 .75
9 Eddy Curry .20 .50
10 Marcus Fizer .20 .50
11 Darius Miles .20 .50
12 Lamond Murray .20 .50
13 Chris Mihm .20 .50
14 Dirk Nowitzki .50 1.25
15 Michael Finley .30 .75
16 Steve Nash .40 1.00
17 Marcus Camby .25 .60
18 Juwan Howard .25 .60
19 James Posey .20 .50
20 Jerry Stackhouse .25 .60
21 Ben Wallace .25 .60
22 Clifford Robinson .20 .50
23 Antawn Jamison .30 .75
24 Jason Richardson .30 .75

25 Gilbert Arenas .30 .75
26 Steve Francis .25 .60
27 Eddie Griffin .20 .50
28 Cuttino Mobley .20 .50
29 Jermaine O'Neal .25 .60
30 Reggie Miller .30 .75
31 Jamaal Tinsley .20 .50
32 Elton Brand .30 .75
33 Andre Miller .25 .60
34 Lamar Odom .25 .60
35 Kobe Bryant 1.25 3.00
36 Shaquille O'Neal .75 2.00
37 Derek Fisher .25 .60
38 Devean George .20 .50
39 Pau Gasol .40 1.00
40 Shane Battier .30 .75
41 Jason Williams .25 .60
42 Alonzo Mourning .40 1.00
43 Eddie Jones .25 .60
44 Brian Grant .20 .50
45 Ray Allen .30 .75
46 Tim Thomas .20 .50
47 Sam Cassell .25 .60
48 Kevin Garnett .50 1.25
49 Wally Szczerbiak .25 .60
50 Terrell Brandon .20 .50
51 Jason Kidd .50 1.25
52 Kenyon Martin .25 .60
53 Richard Jefferson .30 .75
54 Jamal Mashburn .25 .60
55 Baron Davis .25 .60
56 David Wesley .20 .50
57 Latrell Sprewell .25 .60
58 Allan Houston .25 .60
59 Antonio McDyess .25 .60
60 Tracy McGrady .50 1.25
61 Mike Miller .25 .60
62 Darrell Armstrong .20 .50
63 Allen Iverson .50 1.25
64 Eric Snow .20 .50
65 Aaron McKie .20 .50
66 Stephon Marbury .25 .60
67 Shawn Marion .25 .60
68 Anfernee Hardaway .50 1.25
69 Rasheed Wallace .30 .75
70 Bonzi Wells .20 .50
71 Scottie Pippen .50 1.25
72 Chris Webber .30 .75
73 Mike Bibby .30 .75
74 Peja Stojakovic .30 .75
75 Tim Duncan .60 1.50
76 David Robinson .50 1.25
77 Tony Parker .40 1.00
78 Gary Payton .30 .75
79 Rashard Lewis .30 .75
80 Desmond Mason .25 .60
81 Vince Carter .50 1.25
82 Morris Peterson .20 .50
83 Antonio Davis .20 .50
84 Karl Malone .40 1.00
85 John Stockton .40 1.00
86 Andrei Kirilenko .30 .75
87 Michael Jordan 2.50 6.00
88 Richard Hamilton .25 .60
89 Chris Whitney .20 .50
90 Kwame Brown .20 .50
91 Kevin Garnett/2999 2.00 5.00
92 Kevin Garnett/2999 2.00 5.00
93 Kevin Garnett/2999 2.00 5.00
94 Kobe Bryant/1999 4.00 10.00
95 Kobe Bryant/1999 4.00 10.00
96 Kobe Bryant/1999 4.00 10.00
97 Michael Jordan/499 15.00 40.00
98 Michael Jordan/499 15.00 40.00
99 Michael Jordan/499 15.00 40.00
100 Fred Jones RC 2.00 5.00
101 Jamal Sampson RC 2.50 6.00
102 John Salmons RC 2.50 6.00
103 Jiri Welsch RC 2.00 5.00
104 Dan Gadzuric RC 2.00 5.00
105 Vincent Yarbrough RC 1.50 4.00
106 Juan Dixon RC 2.50 6.00
107 Efthimios Rentzias RC 1.50 4.00
108 Predrag Savovic RC 2.00 5.00
109 Rod Grizzard RC 1.50 4.00
110 Bostjan Nachbar RC 2.00 5.00
111 Marko Jaric 2.50 6.00
112 Tayshaun Prince RC 3.00 8.00
113 Chris Jefferies RC 1.50 4.00
114 Casey Jacobsen RC 2.00 5.00
115 Carlos Boozer RC 2.50 6.00
116 Frank Williams RC 1.50 4.00
117 Dan Dickau RC 2.00 5.00
118 Ryan Humphrey RC 2.00 5.00
119 Melvin Ely RC 2.00 5.00
120 Nene Hilario RC 3.00 8.00
121 Nikoloz Tskitishvili RC 2.00 5.00
122 Marcus Haislip RC 2.50 6.00
123 Qyntel Woods RC 2.50 6.00
124 Caron Butler RC 3.00 8.00
125 Amare Stoudemire RC 4.00 10.00
126 Curtis Borchardt RC 2.00 5.00
127 Chris Wilcox RC 2.50 6.00
128 Drew Gooden RC 3.00 8.00
129 Jared Jeffries RC 2.50 6.00
130 Kareem Rush RC 2.50 6.00
131 Mike Dunleavy RC 3.00 8.00
132 Yao Ming RC 6.00 15.00
133 DaJuan Wagner RC 2.50 6.00
134 Jay Williams RC 3.00 8.00

2002-03 Upper Deck Ovation Authentics Shooting Shirt

Issued at a stated rate of one in 144, these 13 cards feature pieces of "shirts" worn by leading NBA players. A Gold parallel sequentially numbered to 15 was also inserted in packs.

STATED ODDS 1:144
AIS Allen Iverson 4.00 10.00
CWS Chris Webber 2.50 6.00
DJS DerMarr Johnson 1.50 4.00
ECS Eddy Curry 1.50 4.00
JES Jerry Stackhouse 2.00 5.00
JSS John Stockton 3.00 8.00
KBS Kobe Bryant 10.00 25.00
KGS Kevin Garnett 4.00 10.00
KWS Kwame Brown 1.50 4.00
MBS Mike Bibby 2.50 6.00
PSS Peja Stojakovic 2.50 6.00
SAS Shareef Abdur-Rahim 2.00 5.00
SMS Stephon Marbury 2.00 5.00

2002-03 Upper Deck Ovation Authentics Uniform

Issued at a stated rate of one in 72, these 13 cards feature swatches of game-worn uniforms. A Gold parallel sequentially numbered to 25 was also inserted in packs.

STATED ODDS 1:72
*GOLD: 1.25X TO 3X BASE HI
GOLD PRINT RUN 25 SER.#'d SETS
AHU Anfernee Hardaway 5.00 12.00
AIU Allen Iverson 5.00 12.00
BDU Baron Davis 2.50 6.00
CMU Corey Maggette 2.50 6.00
DMU Darius Miles 2.00 5.00
DNU Dirk Nowitzki 5.00 12.00
DSU DeShawn Stevenson 2.00 5.00
KBU Kobe Bryant 12.00 30.00
KEU Kenyon Martin 2.50 6.00
KGU Kevin Garnett 5.00 12.00
KMU Karl Malone 4.00 10.00
RFU Rick Fox 2.00 5.00
RLU Rashard Lewis 3.00 8.00

2002-03 Upper Deck Ovation Authentics Warm-Ups

Issued at a stated rate of one in 24, these 18 cards feature authentic swatches of NBA "warm-up" material. A Gold parallel sequentially numbered to 100 was also inserted in packs.

STATED ODDS 1:24
*GOLD: .75X TO 2X WARM UP HI
GOLD PRINT RUN 100 SER.#'d SETS
AWW Antoine Walker 2.50 6.00
BDW Baron Davis 2.50 6.00
CMW Corey Maggette 2.50 6.00
EBW Elton Brand 3.00 8.00
JKW Jason Kidd 5.00 12.00
JMW Jamal Mashburn 2.50 6.00
KBW Kobe Bryant 12.00 30.00
KGW Kevin Garnett 5.00 12.00
KMW Kenyon Martin 2.50 6.00
KWW Kwame Brown 2.00 5.00
LOW Lamar Odom 2.50 6.00
MAW Karl Malone 4.00 10.00
MBW Mike Bibby 3.00 8.00
MJW Michael Jordan 50.00 120.00
MMW Mike Miller 2.50 6.00
QRW Quentin Richardson 2.50 6.00
RJW Richard Jefferson 3.00 8.00
SMW Stephon Marbury 2.50 6.00

2002-03 Upper Deck Ovation Authentics Warm-Ups Dual

Inserted at a stated rate of one in 144, these 18 cards feature two swatches of NBA "Warm-Up" material. In most of the cases the swatches feature teammates but occassionally they feature players who have something in common. A Gold parallel sequentially numbered to 50 was also inserted in packs.

STATED ODDS 1:144
*GOLD: .75X TO 2X WARM UP DUAL HI
GOLD PRINT RUN 50 SER.#'d SETS
AH/LS A.Houston/L.Sprewell 6.00 15.00
AM/LM A.Miller/L.Murray 6.00 15.00
BD/JM B.Davis/J.Mashburn 6.00 15.00
CM/DM C.Maggette/D.Miles 6.00 15.00
CW/PS P.Stojakovic/C.Webber 10.00 25.00
EC/MF E.Curry/M.Fizer 6.00 15.00
KB/KG K.Bryant/K.Garnett 12.00 30.00
KB/MJ K.Bryant/M.Jordan 30.00 80.00
KG/KW K.Garnett/Kw.Brown 10.00 25.00
KG/TB K.Garnett/T.Brandon 10.00 25.00
KG/WS K.Garnett/W.Szczerbiak 10.00 25.00
KM/AK K.Malone/A.Kirilenko 6.00 15.00
KM/RJ K.Martin/R.Jefferson 6.00 15.00
LO/QR L.Odom/Q.Richardson 6.00 15.00
PP/AW P.Pierce/A.Walker 10.00 25.00
SA/JT S.Abdur-Rahim/J.Terry 6.00 15.00
SM/SH S.Marbury/S.Marion 6.00 15.00
WS/TB W.Szczerbiak/T.Brandon 6.00 15.00

2002-03 Upper Deck Ovation Authentics Warm-Ups Triple

Issued at a stated rate of one in 288, these six cards feature three swatches of NBA "Warm-Up" material. Again, the swatches come either from teammates or from players with something in common. A Gold parallel sequentially numbered to 25 was also inserted in packs.

STATED ODDS 1:288
*GOLD: .75X TO 2X BASE HI
GOLD PRINT RUN 25 SER.#'d SETS
BGK Kobe/Garnett/Kidd 30.00 80.00
BJG Kobe/Jordan/Garnett 60.00 150.00
CFC Curry/Fizer/Chandler 10.00 25.00
GSB Garnett/Szcz/T.Brndn 15.00 40.00
MBO Miles/Brand/Odom 10.00 25.00
WSB C.Webb/Peja/Bibby 15.00 40.00

2002-03 Upper Deck Ovation Signatures

Inserted at a stated rate of one in 96, these 16 cards feature authentic autographs from NBA Players. There is one card signed by Michael Jordan, Kobe Bryant and Kevin Garnett and that card was printed to a stated print run of 25 serial numbered sets. Fifteen players signed for a gold parallel set that is sequentially numbered to 10.

STATED ODDS 1:96
CA Courtney Alexander 4.00 10.00
CM Chris Mihm 4.00 10.00
DM Darius Miles 4.00 10.00
GA Gilbert Arenas 4.00 10.00
HM Hanno Mottola 4.00 10.00
JP Joel Przybilla 4.00 10.00
JR Jason Richardson 6.00 15.00
JS Jerry Stackhouse 6.00 15.00
KS Kenny Satterfield 4.00 10.00
LW Loren Woods 4.00 10.00
MF Marcus Fizer 4.00 10.00
QR Quentin Richardson 4.00 10.00
TC Tyson Chandler 6.00 15.00
TM Terence Morris 4.00 10.00
ZZ Wang ZhiZhi 8.00 20.00
OS1 M.Jordan/Kobe/KG/25 700.00 1200.00

2006-07 Upper Deck Ovation

Issued in mid September, Upper Deck Ovation utilizes an embossed card stock and pictures veteran players on cards 1-90 and rookie players on cards 91-132 which are sequentially numbered to 999. On-card rookie autographs are available in the Gold parallel. Ovation is packaged in 18-pack boxes of five cards each and carried an initial suggested retail price of $4.99.

COMP.SET w/o SP's (90) 20.00 50.00
91-132 RC PRINT RUN 999 SER.#'d SETS
1 Joe Johnson .30 .75
2 Marvin Williams .30 .75
3 Paul Pierce .40 1.00
4 Wally Szczerbiak .30 .75
5 Raymond Felton .30 .75
6 Emeka Okafor .30 .75
7 Gerald Wallace .30 .75
8 Tyson Chandler .30 .75
9 Ben Gordon .30 .75
10 Michael Jordan 3.00 8.00
11 Drew Gooden .30 .75
12 Zydrunas Ilgauskas .30 .75
13 LeBron James 1.50 4.00
14 Devin Harris .25 .60
15 Dirk Nowitzki .60 1.50
16 Jason Terry .30 .75
17 Carmelo Anthony .50 1.25
18 Marcus Camby .30 .75
19 Kenyon Martin .30 .75
20 Chauncey Billups .40 1.00
21 Richard Hamilton .30 .75
22 Ben Wallace .30 .75
23 Baron Davis .30 .75
24 Jason Richardson .40 1.00
25 Luther Head .30 .75
26 Tracy McGrady .50 1.25
27 Yao Ming .50 1.25
28 Austin Croshere .25 .60
29 Jermaine O'Neal .30 .75
30 Peja Stojakovic .40 1.00
31 Elton Brand .40 1.00
32 Sam Cassell .30 .75
33 Cuttino Mobley .25 .60
34 Kwame Brown .25 .60
35 Kobe Bryant 1.50 4.00
36 Lamar Odom .30 .75
37 Pau Gasol .40 1.00
38 Mike Miller .30 .75
39 Damon Stoudamire .30 .75
40 Shaquille O'Neal .75 2.00
41 Wayne Simien .25 .60
42 Dwyane Wade .60 1.50
43 Andrew Bogut .30 .75
44 T.J. Ford .25 .60
45 Michael Redd .30 .75
46 Ricky Davis .30 .75
47 Kevin Garnett .60 1.50
48 Rashad McCants .25 .60
49 Vince Carter .50 1.25
50 Richard Jefferson .30 .75
51 Jason Kidd .60 1.50
52 Desmond Mason .25 .60
53 Chris Paul .50 1.25
54 J.R. Smith .30 .75
55 Steve Francis .30 .75
56 Stephon Marbury .30 .75
57 Nate Robinson .25 .60
58 Dwight Howard .30 .75
59 Darko Milicic .25 .60
60 Jameer Nelson .25 .60
61 Andre Iguodala .30 .75
62 Allen Iverson .50 1.25
63 Chris Webber .40 1.00
64 Boris Diaw .30 .75
65 Shawn Marion .30 .75
66 Steve Nash .50 1.25
67 Zach Randolph .30 .75
68 Sebastian Telfair .25 .60
69 Ron Artest .40 1.00
70 Mike Bibby .40 1.00
71 Bonzi Wells .25 .60
72 Tim Duncan .60 1.50
73 Manu Ginobili .40 1.00
74 Tony Parker .40 1.00
75 Ray Allen .40 1.00
76 Rashard Lewis .40 1.00
77 Luke Ridnour .30 .75
78 Chris Bosh .40 1.00
79 Joey Graham .25 .60
80 Charlie Villanueva .25 .60
81 Carlos Boozer .30 .75
82 Andrei Kirilenko .30 .75
83 Gilbert Arenas .30 .75
84 Antawn Jamison .30 .75
85 Josh Childress .30 .75
86 Al Jefferson .30 .75
87 Derek Fisher .30 .75
88 Juan Dixon .25 .60
89 Deron Williams .30 .75
90 Caron Butler .30 .75
91 Tyrus Thomas RC 1.25 3.00
92 Adam Morrison RC 1.50 4.00
93 LaMarcus Aldridge RC 4.00 10.00
94 Rudy Gay RC 2.00 5.00
95 Andrea Bargnani RC 1.50 4.00
96 Rodney Carney RC 1.00 2.50
97 Will Blalock RC 1.00 2.50
98 Brandon Roy RC 1.50 4.00
99 Patrick O'Bryant RC 1.00 2.50
100 Randy Foye RC 1.50 4.00
101 Ronnie Brewer RC 1.50 4.00
102 Mardy Collins RC 1.00 2.50
103 Shelden Williams RC 1.25 3.00
104 J.J. Redick RC 2.00 5.00
105 Hilton Armstrong RC 1.00 2.50
106 Marcus Williams RC 1.00 2.50
107 Rajon Rondo RC 5.00 12.00
108 Cedric Simmons RC 1.00 2.50
109 Alexander Johnson RC 1.00 2.50
110 Jordan Farmar RC 1.50 4.00
111 Maurice Ager RC 1.00 2.50
112 Renaldo Balkman RC 1.25 3.00
113 Leon Powe RC 1.25 3.00
114 Saer Sene RC 1.00 2.50
115 Paul Millsap RC 2.00 5.00
116 Josh Boone RC 1.00 2.50
117 Steve Novak RC 1.25 3.00
118 Daniel Gibson RC 1.25 3.00
119 Hassan Adams RC 1.00 2.50
120 Kyle Lowry RC 2.00 5.00
121 James White RC 1.00 2.50
122 Dee Brown RC 1.00 2.50
123 Shawne Williams RC 1.00 2.50
124 P.J. Tucker RC 1.25 3.00
125 Craig Smith RC 1.25 3.00
126 Paul Davis RC 1.00 2.50
127 Solomon Jones RC 1.00 2.50
128 Denham Brown RC 1.00 2.50
129 Thabo Sefolosha RC 1.50 4.00
130 Quincy Douby RC 1.00 2.50
131 Joel Freeland RC 1.00 2.50
132 Ryan Hollins RC 1.25 3.00

2006-07 Upper Deck Ovation Gold

*1-90 GOLD: 2X TO 5X BASE HI
*91-132 GOLD NON AU: 1.25X TO 3X BASE HI
PRINT RUN 99 SER.#'d SETS
10 Michael Jordan 20.00 50.00
91 Tyrus Thomas AU 6.00 15.00
93 LaMarcus Aldridge AU 20.00 50.00
94 Rudy Gay AU 10.00 25.00
95 Andrea Bargnani AU 8.00 20.00
96 Rodney Carney AU 5.00 12.00
98 Brandon Roy AU 8.00 20.00
99 Patrick O'Bryant AU 5.00 12.00
100 Randy Foye AU 8.00 20.00
101 Ronnie Brewer AU 8.00 20.00
102 Mardy Collins AU 5.00 12.00
103 Shelden Williams AU 6.00 15.00
105 Hilton Armstrong AU 5.00 12.00
106 Marcus Williams AU 5.00 12.00
107 Rajon Rondo AU 20.00 50.00
108 Cedric Simmons AU 5.00 12.00
110 Jordan Farmar AU 8.00 20.00
111 Maurice Ager AU 5.00 12.00
112 Renaldo Balkman AU 6.00 15.00
115 Paul Millsap AU 10.00 25.00
116 Josh Boone AU 5.00 12.00
117 Steve Novak AU 6.00 15.00
119 Hassan Adams AU 5.00 12.00
120 Kyle Lowry AU 10.00 25.00
121 James White AU 5.00 12.00
123 Shawne Williams AU 5.00 12.00
124 P.J. Tucker AU 6.00 15.00
125 Craig Smith AU 6.00 15.00
127 Solomon Jones AU 5.00 12.00
128 Denham Brown AU 5.00 12.00
130 Quincy Douby AU 5.00 12.00
132 Ryan Hollins AU 6.00 15.00

2006-07 Upper Deck Ovation Apparel

APPROXIMATE ODDS 1:18
*GOLD: .6X TO 1.5X BASE JSY HI
GOLD PRINT RUN 50 SER.#'d SETS
AB Andrew Bynum 1.50 4.00
AI Andre Iguodala 2.00 5.00
AK Andrei Kirilenko 2.00 5.00
AS Amare Stoudemire 2.00 5.00
BC Brian Cook 2.00 5.00
BD Baron Davis 2.00 5.00
BH Brendan Haywood 2.00 5.00
BU Beno Udrih 2.00 5.00
CW Chris Wilcox 2.00 5.00
DG Drew Gooden 2.00 5.00
DN Dirk Nowitzki 4.00 10.00
EC Eddy Curry 2.00 5.00
GA Gilbert Arenas 2.00 5.00
HO Julius Hodge 2.00 5.00
JH Josh Howard 2.00 5.00
JM Jeff McInnis 2.00 5.00
JO Jermaine O'Neal 2.00 5.00
JR Jason Richardson 2.50 6.00
JT Jamaal Tinsley 2.00 5.00
KB Kobe Bryant SP 10.00 25.00
KG Kevin Garnett 4.00 10.00
KK Kyle Korver 2.00 5.00
LJ LeBron James SP 10.00 25.00
LK Linas Kleiza 2.00 5.00
LW Luke Walton 2.00 5.00
MG Manu Ginobili 2.50 6.00
MJ Michael Jordan SP 20.00 50.00
MS Mike Sweetney 2.00 5.00
PG Pau Gasol 2.50 6.00
RA Ray Allen 2.50 6.00
RH Richard Hamilton SP 2.00 5.00
RL Rashard Lewis 2.50 6.00
SC Sam Cassell 2.00 5.00
SL Shaun Livingston 2.00 5.00
SM Shawn Marion 2.00 5.00
TC Tyson Chandler 2.00 5.00
TD Tim Duncan 4.00 10.00
TP Tony Parker 2.50 6.00
VC Vince Carter 3.00 8.00
WS Wally Szczerbiak 2.00 5.00
ZI Zydrunas Ilgauskas 2.00 5.00

2006-07 Upper Deck Ovation Center Stage

COMPLETE SET (12) 4.00 10.00
APPROXIMATE ODDS 1:9
AS Amare Stoudemire .50 1.25
BM Brad Miller .50 1.25
BW Ben Wallace .50 1.25
CF Channing Frye .50 1.25
CK Chris Kaman .50 1.25
DH Dwight Howard .50 1.25
MC Marcus Camby .50 1.25
MO Mehmet Okur .40 1.00
SO Shaquille O'Neal 1.25 3.00
YM Yao Ming .75 2.00
ZI Zydrunas Ilgauskas .50 1.25

2006-07 Upper Deck Ovation Leading Performers

COMPLETE SET (20) 10.00 25.00
APPROXIMATE ODDS 1:9
AI Allen Iverson .75 2.00
BG Ben Gordon .50 1.25
CB Chauncey Billups .60 1.50
CP Chris Paul .75 2.00
DH Dwight Howard .50 1.25
DN Dirk Nowitzki 1.00 2.50
DW Dwyane Wade 1.00 2.50
EB Elton Brand .60 1.50
EO Emeka Okafor .50 1.25
KB Kobe Bryant 2.50 6.00
KG Kevin Garnett 1.00 2.50
LJ LeBron James 2.50 6.00
MA Shawn Marion .50 1.25
MJ Michael Jordan 5.00 12.00
PP Paul Pierce .60 1.50
SM Stephon Marbury .50 1.25
SN Steve Nash .75 2.00
SO Shaquille O'Neal 1.25 3.00
TM Tracy McGrady .75 2.00
YM Yao Ming .75 2.00

2006-07 Upper Deck Ovation Spotlight Signature

APPROXIMATE ODDS 1:18
*GOLD: .75X TO 2X BASE HI
GOLD PRINT RUN 25 SER.#'d SETS
AA Alex Acker 4.00 10.00
AB Andrew Bogut SP 5.00 12.00
AJ Al Jefferson 4.00 10.00
AN Andrea Bargnani SP 10.00 25.00
BA Brent Barry 6.00 15.00
BB Brandon Bass 4.00 10.00
BD Baron Davis 4.00 10.00
BJ Bobby Jackson 4.00 10.00
BK Bernard King 8.00 20.00
BO Bruce Bowen 4.00 10.00
BR Brandon Roy 10.00 25.00
BS Bobby Simmons 4.00 10.00
BW Bill Walton 6.00 15.00
CA Carmelo Anthony 12.50 30.00
CB Carlos Boozer 4.00 10.00
CD Chris Duhon 4.00 10.00
CM Cuttino Mobley 4.00 10.00
CP Chris Paul 15.00 40.00
CS Cedric Simmons 4.00 10.00
CT Chris Taft 4.00 10.00
DJ Dwayne Jones 4.00 10.00
DM Desmond Mason 4.00 10.00
DS DeShawn Stevenson 4.00 10.00
DT Dijon Thompson 4.00 10.00
EI Ersan Ilyasova 4.00 10.00
FO Randy Foye 10.00 25.00
HA Hilton Armstrong 4.00 10.00
HW Hakim Warrick 4.00 10.00
ID Ike Diogu SP 4.00 10.00
JK Jarrett Jack 4.00 10.00
JO Amir Johnson 4.00 10.00
JR Jalen Rose 4.00 10.00
JS J.R. Smith 4.00 10.00
KB Kwame Brown 4.00 10.00
KD Keyon Dooling 4.00 10.00
KH Kirk Hinrich 6.00 15.00
LA LaMarcus Aldridge 10.00 25.00
LJ LeBron James SP 150.00 300.00
LR Lawrence Roberts 4.00 10.00
MC Mardy Collins 4.00 10.00
MD Marquis Daniels 4.00 10.00
ME Maurice Evans 4.00 10.00
MJ Michael Jordan SP 250.00 500.00
MW Marvin Williams 4.00 10.00
NR Nate Robinson 4.00 10.00
PO Patrick O'Bryant 4.00 10.00
PP Paul Pierce SP 8.00 20.00
PS Peja Stojakovic 4.00 10.00
QR Quentin Richardson 4.00 10.00
RB Ronnie Brewer 12.00 30.00
RC Rodney Carney 4.00 10.00
RF Raymond Felton 5.00 12.00
RG Rudy Gay 8.00 20.00
RI Luke Ridnour 4.00 10.00
RJ Richard Jefferson 4.00 10.00
RM Rashad McCants 4.00 10.00
RR Rajon Rondo 12.00 30.00
RT Ronny Turiaf 6.00 15.00
SC Speedy Claxton 4.00 10.00
SI James Singleton 4.00 10.00
SK Steve Kerr 4.00 10.00
SL Shaun Livingston 4.00 10.00
SS Stromile Swift 4.00 10.00
SW Shelden Williams 4.00 10.00
TF T.J. Ford 4.00 10.00
TT Tyrus Thomas 5.00 12.00
VC Vince Carter 12.50 30.00
VR Vladimir Radmanovic 4.00 10.00
VW Von Wafer 4.00 10.00
WI Marcus Williams 4.00 10.00
WR Bracey Wright 4.00 10.00
YK Yaroslav Korolev 4.00 10.00
YM Yao Ming SP 12.50 30.00

2006-07 Upper Deck Ovation Superstar Theatre

COMPLETE SET (10) 8.00 20.00
APPROXIMATE ODDS 1:9
BR Bill Russell 1.25 3.00
JE Julius Erving 1.00 2.50
JO Magic Johnson 1.50 4.00
KA Kareem Abdul-Jabbar 1.00 2.50
KB Kobe Bryant 2.50 6.00
LJ LeBron James 2.50 6.00
MJ Michael Jordan 5.00 12.00
SN Steve Nash .75 2.00
SO Shaquille O'Neal 1.25 3.00
TM Tracy McGrady .75 2.00

2001-02 Upper Deck Playmakers

Released in March 2002, this 145-card base set features standard-size cards with full color action shots on the fronts. The set includes 100 veteran cards, 30 rookie red-level cards, numbers 101-130 which are sequentially numbered to 1999, and 15 rookie blue-level cards, numbers 131-145 which are sequentially numbered to 999. Playmakers was packaged in 24-pack boxes with five cards per pack and carried a suggested retai of $2.99. Each Playmaker's box also contained an Upper Deck Bobble Head Doll.

COMPLETE SET (145) 100.00 200.00
COMP.SET w/o SP's (100) 20.00 40.00
101-130 PRINT RUN 1999 SER.#'d SETS
131-145 PRINT RUN 999 SER.#'d SETS
1 Shareef Abdur-Rahim .25 .60
2 Dion Glover .20 .50
3 Jason Terry .30 .75
4 Toni Kukoc .30 .75
5 Theo Ratliff .20 .50
6 Paul Pierce .30 .75
7 Antoine Walker .25 .60
8 Baron Davis .30 .75
9 Jamal Mashburn .25 .60
10 Ron Mercer .20 .50
11 Brad Miller .30 .75
12 Marcus Fizer .20 .50
13 Andre Miller .25 .60
14 Chris Mihm .20 .50
15 Lamond Murray .20 .50
16 Michael Finley .30 .75
17 Dirk Nowitzki .50 1.25
18 Steve Nash .50 1.25
19 Tim Hardaway .30 .75
20 Antonio McDyess .25 .60
21 Nick Van Exel .25 .60
22 Raef LaFrentz .20 .50
23 Jerry Stackhouse .25 .60
24 Clifford Robinson .20 .50
25 Ben Wallace .25 .60
26 Antawn Jamison .30 .75
27 Larry Hughes .25 .60
28 Danny Fortson .20 .50
29 Steve Francis .25 .60
30 Cuttino Mobley .20 .50
31 Kenny Thomas .20 .50
32 Jalen Rose .25 .60
33 Reggie Miller .30 .75
34 Jermaine O'Neal .25 .60
35 Darius Miles .20 .50
36 Elton Brand .30 .75
37 Corey Maggette .25 .60
38 Quentin Richardson .25 .60
39 Kobe Bryant 1.25 3.00
40 Shaquille O'Neal .75 2.00
41 Mitch Richmond .25 .60
42 Derek Fisher .25 .60
43 Lindsey Hunter .20 .50
44 Stromile Swift .20 .50
45 Jason Williams .25 .60
46 Michael Dickerson .20 .50
47 Eddie Jones .25 .60
48 Alonzo Mourning .40 1.00
49 Anthony Carter .20 .50
50 Brian Grant .20 .50
51 Glenn Robinson .25 .60
52 Ray Allen .30 .75
53 Sam Cassell .25 .60
54 Tim Thomas .20 .50
55 Anthony Mason .20 .50
56 Kevin Garnett .50 1.25
57 Wally Szczerbiak .25 .60
58 Terrell Brandon .20 .50
59 Joe Smith .25 .60
60 Jason Kidd .50 1.25
61 Kenyon Martin .30 .75
62 Allan Houston .25 .60
63 Latrell Sprewell .25 .60
64 Marcus Camby .25 .60
65 Mark Jackson .25 .60
66 Kurt Thomas .20 .50
67 Tracy McGrady .50 1.25
68 Grant Hill .40 1.00
69 Mike Miller .25 .60
70 Allen Iverson .60 1.50
71 Dikembe Mutombo .30 .75
72 Aaron McKie .20 .50
73 Stephon Marbury .25 .60
74 Shawn Marion .25 .60
75 Anfernee Hardaway .50 1.25
76 Tom Gugliotta .20 .50
77 Rasheed Wallace .30 .75
78 Derek Anderson .20 .50
79 Bonzi Wells .20 .50
80 Chris Webber .30 .75
81 Peja Stojakovic .30 .75
82 Mike Bibby .30 .75
83 Doug Christie .20 .50
84 Tim Duncan .60 1.50
85 David Robinson .50 1.25
86 Antonio Daniels .20 .50
87 Steve Smith .25 .60
88 Gary Payton .30 .75
89 Rashard Lewis .30 .75
90 Desmond Mason .25 .60
91 Vince Carter .50 1.25
92 Morris Peterson .20 .50
93 Antonio Davis .20 .50
94 Hakeem Olajuwon .40 1.00
95 Karl Malone .40 1.00
96 John Stockton .40 1.00
97 Donyell Marshall .20 .50
98 Michael Jordan 4.00 10.00
99 Courtney Alexander .20 .50
100 Richard Hamilton .25 .60
101 Jeryl Sasser RC .60 1.50
102 DeSagana Diop RC .75 2.00
103 Alvin Jones RC .75 2.00
104 Gerald Wallace RC 1.25 3.00
105 Kenny Satterfield RC .60 1.50
106 Ruben Boumtje-Boumtje RC 1.00 2.50
107 Brian Scalabrine RC 1.00 2.50
108 Oscar Torres RC 1.00 2.50
109 Jarron Collins RC 1.00 2.50
110 Jeff Trepagnier RC .60 1.50
111 Brendan Haywood RC 1.00 2.50
112 Vladimir Radmanovic RC 1.00 2.50
113 Loren Woods RC .60 1.50
114 Terence Morris RC 1.00 2.50
115 Kirk Haston RC .60 1.50
116 Earl Watson RC 1.00 2.50
117 Brandon Armstrong RC .60 1.50
118 Zach Randolph RC 1.50 4.00
119 Bobby Simmons RC 1.00 2.50
120 Alton Ford RC 1.00 2.50
121 Trenton Hassell RC .75 2.00
122 Damone Brown RC .60 1.50
123 Michael Bradley RC .60 1.50
124 Zeljko Rebraca RC 1.00 2.50
125 Jason Collins RC .75 2.00
126 Samuel Dalembert RC 1.00 2.50
127 Gilbert Arenas RC 1.50 4.00
128 Willie Solomon RC 1.00 2.50
129 Joseph Forte RC .60 1.50
130 Steven Hunter RC .75 2.00
131 Andrei Kirilenko RC 2.50 6.00
132 Eddy Curry RC 1.50 4.00
133 Tony Parker RC 6.00 15.00
134 Troy Murphy RC 1.50 4.00
135 Shane Battier RC 3.00 8.00
136 Kedrick Brown RC 1.00 2.50
137 Tyson Chandler RC 2.50 6.00
138 Jamaal Tinsley RC 1.50 4.00
139 Pau Gasol RC 5.00 12.00
140 Joe Johnson RC 2.00 5.00
141 Jason Richardson RC 2.00 5.00
142 Richard Jefferson RC 2.50 6.00
143 Eddie Griffin RC 1.25 3.00
144 Rodney White RC 1.00 2.50
145 Kwame Brown RC 1.50 4.00

2001-02 Upper Deck Playmakers PC Game Jersey

This 27-card insert set comes with pieces of game-used jerseys on standard-size cards. Solid colored player portraits with jagged borders appear on the right side of this horizontally designed card in color's to match the featured player's team, with a matching color stripe along the right side and a swatch of a jersey in the center on a colored "cube" background. Each card is sequentailly numbered to 350. Fourteen players also appear in a parallel Autographed set sequentially numbered to 10 and a Gold version sequentially numbered to 100.

PRINT RUN 350 SER.#'d SETS
*GOLD: .75X TO 2X BASE JSY HI
GOLD PRINT RUN 100 SER.#'d SETS
AIJ Allen Iverson 6.00 15.00
AJJ Antawn Jamison 3.00 8.00
BDJ Baron Davis 3.00 8.00
CWJ Chris Webber 3.00 8.00
DEJ Desmond Mason 2.50 6.00
DMJ Darius Miles 2.00 5.00
DNJ Dirk Nowitzki 5.00 12.00
ECJ Eddy Curry 3.00 8.00
EGJ Eddie Griffin 2.50 6.00
GWJ Gerald Wallace 4.00 10.00
JJJ Joe Johnson 4.00 10.00
JKJ Jason Kidd 5.00 12.00
JRJ Jason Richardson 4.00 10.00
JSJ John Stockton 4.00 10.00
JTJ Jamaal Tinsley 3.00 8.00
KBJ Kobe Bryant 12.00 30.00
KEJ Kedrick Brown 2.00 5.00
KGJ Kevin Garnett 5.00 12.00
KMJ Karl Malone 4.00 10.00
KWJ Kwame Brown 3.00 8.00
LOJ Lamar Odom 2.50 6.00
MAJ Kenyon Martin 3.00 8.00
MMJ Mike Miller 2.50 6.00
PPJ Paul Pierce 3.00 8.00
SHJ Steven Hunter 2.50 6.00
SMJ Stephon Marbury 2.50 6.00
TMJ Tracy McGrady 5.00 12.00

2001-02 Upper Deck Playmakers PC Shooting Shirt

Randomly inserted in packs, this 26-card set uses a similar design to the base Player's Club Game Jerseys set except the player portrait is on the left side of the horizontally designed card in black and white. A matching stripe appears on the right edge of the card and player shooting shirts are centered on the card. Each card is sequentially numbered to 350 and contains silver foil highlights. 10 Players appear in an autographed parallel set sequentially numbered to 25 and 16 players appear in a gold set sequentially numbered to 150.

STATED PRINT RUN 350 SERIAL #'d SETS
*GOLD: .75X TO 2X BASE SHIRT HI
GOLD PRINT RUN 150 SER.#'d SETS
AIS Allen Iverson 5.00 12.00
AKS Andrei Kirilenko 4.00 10.00
DMS Desmond Mason 2.00 5.00
EGS Eddie Griffin 2.00 5.00
JAS Jamaal Magloire 1.50 4.00
JES Jerry Stackhouse 2.00 5.00
JSS Joe Smith 2.00 5.00
JTS Jason Terry 2.50 6.00
KBS Kobe Bryant 10.00 25.00
KDS Keyon Dooling 1.50 4.00
KGS Kevin Garnett 4.00 10.00
KMS Karl Malone 3.00 8.00
KWS Kwame Brown 2.50 6.00
MFS Michael Finley 2.50 6.00
MOS Michael Olowokandi 1.50 4.00
NVS Nick Van Exel 2.00 5.00
PGS Pau Gasol 8.00 20.00
SBS Shane Battier 5.00 12.00
SSS Stromile Swift 1.50 4.00
TBS Terrell Brandon 1.50 4.00
TCS Tyson Chandler 4.00 10.00
TIS Jamaal Tinsley 2.50 6.00
TMS Tracy McGrady 4.00 10.00
VBS Vin Baker 2.00 5.00
WSS Wally Szczerbiak 2.00 5.00
ZRS Zach Randolph 4.00 10.00

2001-02 Upper Deck Playmakers PC Shooting Shirt Autographs

STATED PRINT RUN 25 SERIAL #'d SETS
JEAS Jerry Stackhouse 12.50 30.00
KBAS Kobe Bryant 150.00 300.00
KGAS Kevin Garnett 50.00 120.00
MJAS Michael Jordan 300.00 600.00
TCAS Tyson Chandler 25.00 60.00
TIAS Jamaal Tinsley 15.00 40.00
WSAS Wally Szczerbiak 15.00 40.00

2001-02 Upper Deck Playmakers PC Warm Up

Inserted in packs, this 28-card set features a vertical design with player action photos on the left side and a swatch of jersey on the right. The top and bottom of the card are colored to match the featured player's team colors and are highlighted with silver foil. Each card is sequentially numbered to 350. A Gold version sequentially numbered to 250 was also issued

STATED PRINT RUN 350 SERIAL #'d SETS
*GOLD: .6X TO 1.5X WARMUP HI
WARMUP PRINT RUN 250 SER.#'d SETS
AHW Allan Houston 2.00 5.00
ALW Al Harrington 2.00 5.00
AMW Andre Miller 2.00 5.00
AWW Antoine Walker 2.00 5.00
CMW Corey Maggette 2.00 5.00
DNW Dirk Nowitzki 4.00 10.00
DRW David Robinson 4.00 10.00
ECW Eddy Curry 2.50 6.00
GHW Grant Hill 3.00 8.00
GPW Gary Payton 2.50 6.00
JAW Jamaal Magloire 1.50 4.00
JBW Jonathan Bender 1.50 4.00
JMW Jamal Mashburn 2.00 5.00
JSW Joe Smith 2.00 5.00
KBW Kobe Bryant 10.00 25.00
KGW Kevin Garnett 4.00 10.00
KMW Kenyon Martin 2.50 6.00
LSW Latrell Sprewell 2.00 5.00
MCW Antonio McDyess 2.00 5.00
MFW Michael Finley 2.50 6.00
MPW Morris Peterson 1.50 4.00
PPW Paul Pierce 2.50 6.00
RYW Ray Allen 2.50 6.00
STW John Stockton 3.00 8.00
TBW Terrell Brandon 1.50 4.00
TCW Tyson Chandler 4.00 10.00
TMW Tracy McGrady 4.00 10.00
WSW Wally Szczerbiak 2.00 5.00

2001-02 Upper Deck Playmakers PC Warm Up Autographs

STATED PRINT RUN 50 SERIAL #'d SETS
AMAW Andre Miller 12.50 30.00
CMAW Corey Maggette 12.50 30.00
KBAW Kobe Bryant 125.00 250.00
KGAW Kevin Garnett 40.00 100.00
MPAW Morris Peterson 12.50 30.00
PPAW Paul Pierce 30.00 60.00
TBAW Terrell Brandon 12.50 30.00
WSAW Wally Szczerbiak 12.50 30.00

2001-02 Upper Deck Playmakers Playmaker Dolls

Inserted in boxes as a topper, this 26-card set features plastic bobble head dolls. Both home and away uniform versions are available for each player.

STATED ODDS 1:24
HOME AND AWAY SAME VALUE
APMAIH Allen Iverson H 8.00 20.00
APMAIR Allen Iverson A 8.00 20.00
APMECH Eddy Curry H 6.00 15.00
APMECR Eddy Curry A 6.00 15.00
APMEGH Eddie Griffin H 6.00 15.00
APMEGR Eddie Griffin A 6.00 15.00
APMJEH Julius Erving H 12.50 30.00
APMJER Julius Erving A 12.50 30.00
APMJJH Joe Johnson H 6.00 15.00
APMJJR Joe Johnson A 6.00 15.00
APMJRH Jason Richardson H 6.00 15.00
APMJRR Jason Richardson A 6.00 15.00
APMKBH Kwame Brown H 6.00 15.00
APMKBR Kwame Brown A 6.00 15.00
APMKGH Kevin Garnett H 8.00 20.00
APMKGR Kevin Garnett A 8.00 20.00
APMTCH Tyson Chandler H 6.00 15.00
APMTCR Tyson Chandler A 6.00 15.00
APMTMH Tracy McGrady H 8.00 20.00
APMTMR Tracy McGrady A 8.00 20.00
PMKMH Kenyon Martin H 6.00 15.00
PMKMR Kenyon Martin A 6.00 15.00
PMKOBH Kobe Bryant H 10.00 25.00
PMKOBR Kobe Bryant A 10.00 25.00
PMLSH Latrell Sprewell H 6.00 15.00
PMLSR Latrell Sprewell A 6.00 15.00

2001-02 Upper Deck Playmakers Playmaker Dolls Autographs

STATED ODDS 1:336
HOME VERSIONS SERIALLY #'d BELOW
APMEGR Eddie Griffin 15.00 40.00
APMJJR Joe Johnson 30.00 80.00
APMJRH Jason Richardson/23 75.00 150.00
APMJRR Jason Richardson 25.00 60.00
APMKGA Kevin Garnett 40.00 100.00
APMKMR Kenyon Martin 15.00 40.00
APMKOBR Kobe Bryant 100.00 200.00
APMTCR Tyson Chandler 20.00 50.00

2001-02 Upper Deck Playmakers Triple Overtime

Randomly seeded in packs, this 21-card set has a similar design to the other memorabilia sets. Each card features a swatch of a jersey, a warm-up, and a shooting shirt. Each card is sequentially numbered to 50.

STATED PRINT RUN 50 SER.#'d SETS
AHOT Anfernee Hardaway 30.00 80.00
CMOT Corey Maggette 15.00 40.00
DMOT Darius Miles 12.00 30.00
ECOT Eddy Curry 20.00 50.00
EGOT Eddie Griffin 15.00 40.00
GWOT Gerald Wallace 25.00 60.00
JAOT Jason Terry 20.00 50.00
JKOT Jason Kidd 30.00 80.00
JSOT Joe Smith 15.00 40.00
KBOT Kobe Bryant 80.00 200.00
KGOT Kevin Garnett 30.00 80.00
KMOT Karl Malone 25.00 60.00
KWOT Kwame Brown 20.00 50.00
MMOT Mike Miller 15.00 40.00
NAOT Steve Nash 20.00 50.00
SAOT Shareef Abdur-Rahim 15.00 40.00
SMOT Stephon Marbury 15.00 40.00
SSOT Stromile Swift 12.00 30.00
TBOT Terrell Brandon 12.00 30.00
TCOT Tyson Chandler 30.00 80.00
WSOT Wally Szczerbiak 15.00 40.00

2003-04 Upper Deck Phenomenal Beginning LeBron James

Released by Upper Deck in January 2004, this 20-card set was packaged with all cards, 1-20, and one bonus gold card. The gold cards parallel the design of

the base set enhanced with a gold color shift on the border. The set was issued with a $9.99 SRP.
COMPLETE SET 12.00 30.00
*GOLD: 2X TO 5X BASE HI
GOLD: ONE PER BOX
*GOLD 100: 6X TO 15X BASE HI
LJ L.James AU/23 600.00 1000.00

1999 Upper Deck PowerDeck Athletes of the Century

These CD-Rom cards featuring four of the most prominent athletes of the 20th century were issued by Upper Deck in one boxed set. The cards are inserted into a computer and display various highlights of the player's career and his stats and other information.
COMPLETE SET (4) 8.00 20.00
2 Michael Jordan 3.00 8.00

2013 Upper Deck Precious Metal Gems Employee Exclusive

UD2012 Quad Spokesmen MEM 125.00 250.00
Michael Jordan
LeBron James
Tiger Woods
Wayne Gretzky

2007-08 Upper Deck Premier

Released in April 2008, Upper Deck Premier is packaged in single packs only of five cards each and carried an initial SRP of $300. The base set boasts 136 cards and features veteran and retired players sequentially numbered to 99 on cards 1-94, rookies sequentially numbered to 99 on cards 95-100 and jersey autograph rookies sequentially numbered to 199 on cards 101-136.
1-94 PRINT RUN 99 SER.#'d SETS
95-136 RC PRINT RUN 199 SER.#'d SETS
1 Bill Russell 3.00 8.00
2 Larry Bird 5.00 12.00
3 Paul Pierce 2.00 5.00
4 Ray Allen 2.00 5.00
5 Al Harrington 1.50 4.00
6 Baron Davis 1.50 4.00
7 Rick Barry 1.50 4.00
8 Earl Monroe 2.00 5.00
9 Eddy Curry 1.25 3.00
10 Stephon Marbury 1.50 4.00
11 Chauncey Billups 2.00 5.00
12 Dave Bing 2.00 5.00
13 Richard Hamilton 1.50 4.00
14 Kobe Bryant 8.00 20.00
15 Luke Walton 1.25 3.00
16 Magic Johnson 5.00 12.00
17 Kevin Martin 1.50 4.00
18 Mike Bibby 2.00 5.00
19 Ron Artest 2.00 5.00
20 Bob Pettit 2.50 6.00
21 Joe Johnson 1.50 4.00
22 Josh Smith 1.50 4.00
23 Andre Iguodala 1.50 4.00
24 Andre Miller 1.50 4.00
25 Julius Erving 3.00 8.00
26 Elvin Hayes 2.00 5.00
27 Caron Butler 1.50 4.00
28 Gilbert Arenas 1.50 4.00
29 Ben Gordon 1.50 4.00
30 Ben Wallace 1.50 4.00
31 Michael Jordan 20.00 50.00
32 Allen Iverson 2.50 6.00
33 Carmelo Anthony 2.50 6.00
34 Marcus Camby 1.25 3.00
35 Hakeem Olajuwon 2.50 6.00
36 Tracy McGrady 2.00 5.00
37 Yao Ming 2.50 6.00
38 Jamaal Tinsley 1.25 3.00
39 Jermaine O'Neal 1.50 4.00
40 Mike Dunleavy 1.50 4.00
41 Jason Kidd 2.00 5.00
42 Richard Jefferson 1.50 4.00
43 Vince Carter 2.50 6.00
44 Chris Wilcox 1.25 3.00
45 Delonte West 1.25 3.00
46 Detlef Schrempf 2.00 5.00
47 Andrew Bogut 1.50 4.00
48 Michael Redd 1.50 4.00
49 Oscar Robertson 2.00 5.00
50 Amare Stoudemire 1.50 4.00
51 Grant Hill 2.50 6.00
52 Shawn Marion 1.50 4.00
53 Steve Nash 2.50 6.00
54 Brad Daugherty 1.50 4.00
55 Larry Hughes 1.50 4.00
56 LeBron James 8.00 20.00
57 Cuttino Mobley 1.50 4.00
58 Elton Brand 2.00 5.00
59 Sam Cassell 1.50 4.00
60 Brandon Roy 2.00 5.00
61 Clyde Drexler 2.50 6.00
62 LaMarcus Aldridge 2.50 6.00
63 Sean Elliott 2.00 5.00
64 George Gervin 2.00 5.00
65 Tim Duncan 3.00 8.00
66 Tony Parker 2.00 5.00
67 Carlos Boozer 1.50 4.00
68 Deron Williams 1.50 4.00
69 Karl Malone 2.50 6.00
70 Mehmet Okur 1.25 3.00
71 Dirk Nowitzki 2.50 6.00
72 Jason Terry 1.50 4.00
73 Josh Howard 1.50 4.00
74 Alonzo Mourning 2.50 6.00
75 Dwyane Wade 3.00 8.00
76 Shaquille O'Neal 4.00 10.00
77 Chris Paul 2.50 6.00
78 David West 1.50 4.00
79 Tyson Chandler 1.50 4.00
80 Kevin Garnett 3.00 8.00
81 Randy Foye 2.00 5.00
82 Al Jefferson 1.50 4.00
83 Dwight Howard 1.50 4.00
84 Jameer Nelson 1.25 3.00
85 Rashard Lewis 1.50 4.00
86 Darko Milicic 1.25 3.00
87 Mike Miller 1.50 4.00
88 Pau Gasol 2.00 5.00
89 Andrea Bargnani 2.00 5.00
90 Chris Bosh 2.00 5.00
91 T.J. Ford 1.25 3.00
92 Emeka Okafor 1.50 4.00
93 Gerald Wallace 1.50 4.00
94 Jason Richardson 2.00 5.00
95 Yi Jianlian RC 5.00 12.00
96 Marco Belinelli RC 4.00 10.00
97 Greg Oden RC 4.00 10.00
98 Brandan Wright RC 4.00 10.00
99 Nick Young RC 5.00 12.00
100 Thaddeus Young RC 4.00 10.00
101 Kevin Durant JSY AU RC 200.00 500.00
102 Al Horford JSY AU RC 8.00 20.00
103 Mike Conley Jr. JSY AU RC 8.00 20.00
104 Jeff Green JSY AU RC 6.00 15.00
105 Corey Brewer JSY AU RC 6.00 15.00
106 Joakim Noah JSY AU RC 6.00 15.00
107 Spencer Hawes JSY AU RC 5.00 12.00
108 Acie Law JSY AU RC 4.00 10.00
109 Julian Wright JSY AU RC 4.00 10.00
110 Al Thornton JSY AU RC 5.00 12.00
111 Rodney Stuckey JSY AU RC 5.00 12.00
112 Sean Williams JSY AU RC 4.00 10.00
113 Javaris Crittenton JSY AU RC 4.00 10.00
114 Jason Smith JSY AU RC 5.00 12.00
115 Daequan Cook JSY AU RC 5.00 12.00
116 Jared Dudley JSY AU RC 5.00 12.00
117 Wilson Chandler JSY AU RC 5.00 12.00
118 Morris Almond JSY AU RC 4.00 10.00
119 Arron Afflalo JSY AU RC 6.00 15.00
120 Alando Tucker JSY AU RC 4.00 10.00
121 Carl Landry JSY AU RC 4.00 10.00
122 Gabe Pruitt JSY AU RC 4.00 10.00
124 Nick Fazekas JSY AU RC 4.00 10.00
125 Glen Davis JSY AU RC 5.00 12.00
126 Jermareo Davidson JSY AU RC 4.00 10.00
127 Josh McRoberts JSY AU RC 5.00 12.00
129 Adam Haluska JSY AU RC 4.00 10.00
131 Stephane Lasme JSY AU RC 4.00 10.00
132 Dominic McGuire JSY AU RC 4.00 10.00
133 Aaron Gray JSY AU RC 4.00 10.00
134 Taurean Green JSY AU RC 4.00 10.00
135 Demetris Nichols JSY AU RC 4.00 10.00
136 D.J. Strawberry JSY AU RC 4.00 10.00
137 Aaron Brooks JSY AU RC 5.00 12.00
138 Herbert Hill JSY AU RC 4.00 10.00
139 Chris Richard JSY AU RC 4.00 10.00

2007-08 Upper Deck Premier Attractions Autographs Jerseys

PRINT RUN 50 SER.#'d SETS
PAAD Adrian Dantley 10.00 25.00
PAAI Andre Iguodala 8.00 20.00
PAAJ Al Jefferson 8.00 20.00
PAAM Alonzo Mourning 20.00 50.00
PABD Baron Davis 8.00 20.00
PABG Ben Gordon 8.00 20.00
PACM Corey Maggette 8.00 20.00
PACP Chris Paul 40.00 80.00
PADR Dennis Rodman 30.00 80.00
PADW Deron Williams 8.00 20.00
PAHO Hakeem Olajuwon 20.00 50.00
PAJO Michael Jordan 500.00 1000.00
PAJW James Worthy 20.00 50.00
PAKB Kobe Bryant 125.00 250.00
PALJ LeBron James 400.00 800.00
PAMJ Magic Johnson 50.00 100.00
PAPA Tony Parker 15.00 30.00
PAPR Pat Riley 12.00 30.00
PARG Rudy Gay 10.00 25.00
PASN Steve Nash 30.00 60.00
PATP Tayshaun Prince 8.00 20.00
PAVC Vince Carter 20.00 40.00
PAWE Jerry West 30.00 80.00
PAWF Walt Frazier 12.00 30.00

2007-08 Upper Deck Premier Draft Mates Autographs

PRINT RUN 15 SER.#'d SETS
DMAR B.Roy/L.Aldridge 25.00 60.00
DMBC M.Conley/C.Brewer 25.00 50.00
DMBF C.Bosh/T.Ford 12.00 30.00
DMBN K.Bryant/S.Nash 100.00 250.00
DMBV R.Barry/D.Van Arsdale 25.00 50.00
DMCJ V.Carter/A.Jamison 30.00 60.00
DMDG K.Durant/J.Green 100.00 200.00
DMDH K.Durant/A.Horford 100.00 200.00
DMDR B.Daugherty/D.Rodman 30.00 80.00
DMGI A.Iguodala/B.Gordon 12.00 30.00
DMHJ D.Howard/A.Jefferson 30.00 60.00
DMJA L.James/C.Anthony 125.00 250.00
DMJO M.Jordan/H.Olajuwon 450.00 750.00
DMKM S.Kerr/D.Manning 12.00 30.00
DMNH J.Noah/A.Horford 40.00 75.00
DMPH P.Pierce/A.Harrington 25.00 60.00
DMRS J.Sikma/T.Rollins 12.00 30.00
DMSB R.Stuckey/M.Belinelli 12.00 30.00

2007-08 Upper Deck Premier Exclusivity Autographs

PRINT RUN 25 SER.#'d SETS
EXAH Al Horford 12.50 30.00
EXJG Jeff Green 12.50 30.00
EXJN Joakim Noah 25.00 60.00
EXKB Kobe Bryant 100.00 200.00
EXKD Kevin Durant 150.00 300.00
EXKG Kevin Garnett 40.00 80.00
EXLJ LeBron James 150.00 300.00
EXMC Mike Conley Jr. 12.50 30.00
EXMJ Michael Jordan 300.00 600.00
EXSN Steve Nash 20.00 50.00

2007-08 Upper Deck Premier First Round Phenoms Autographs

PRINT RUN 6 TO 50 SER.#'d SETS
SOME UNPRICED DUE TO SCARCITY
FPAD Adrian Dantley/50 10.00 25.00
FPBI Larry Bird/33 40.00 80.00
FPCA Carmelo Anthony/50 15.00 40.00
FPDA Brad Daugherty/50 10.00 25.00
FPHG Horace Grant/50 15.00 40.00
FPHO Hakeem Olajuwon/34 15.00 40.00
FPJO Magic Johnson/32 40.00 80.00
FPJS John Stockton/12 50.00 100.00
FPKB Kobe Bryant/24 100.00 200.00
FPLJ LeBron James/23 125.00 250.00
FPMJ Michael Jordan/23 300.00 550.00
FPMO Alonzo Mourning/50 15.00 40.00
FPPA Tony Parker/50 10.00 25.00
FPPP Paul Pierce/50 12.00 30.00
FPSN Steve Nash/50 25.00 50.00
FPTM Tracy McGrady/50 12.00 30.00
FPVC Vince Carter/50 15.00 40.00
FPWF Walt Frazier/50 10.00 25.00
FPYM Yao Ming/50 15.00 40.00

2007-08 Upper Deck Premier Franchise Faces Autographs

PRINT RUN 24 TO 50 SER.#'d SETS
FFAM Alonzo Mourning/50 12.00 30.00
FFBG Ben Gordon/50 10.00 25.00
FFBR Brandon Roy/50 10.00 25.00
FFCA Carmelo Anthony/50 25.00 60.00
FFDR David Robinson/50 25.00 50.00
FFDW Deron Williams/50 12.00 30.00
FFHO Hakeem Olajuwon/34 25.00 50.00
FFJE Julius Erving/50 30.00 80.00
FFJO Magic Johnson/32 50.00 100.00
FFJS John Stockton/24 25.00 60.00
FFJW Jerry West/50 25.00 50.00
FFKB Kobe Bryant/24 150.00 300.00
FFLB Larry Bird/33 50.00 100.00
FFLJ LeBron James/23 100.00 200.00
FFMJ Michael Jordan/23 700.00 1000.00
FFPA Tony Parker/50 12.00 30.00
FFPP Paul Pierce/50 10.00 25.00
FFRB Rick Barry/50 10.00 25.00
FFTM Tracy McGrady/50 12.00 30.00
FFWF Walt Frazier/50 10.00 25.00
FFWU Wes Unseld/50 12.00 30.00
FFYM Yao Ming/50 15.00 30.00

2007-08 Upper Deck Premier Impressions

PRINT RUN 50 SER.#'d SETS
UNPRICED COPPER PRINT RUN ONE SET
PIAA Arron Afflalo 5.00 12.00
PIAH Al Horford 6.00 15.00
PICL Carl Landry 3.00 8.00
PIDC Daequan Cook 4.00 10.00
PIGD Glen Davis 4.00 10.00
PIGP Gabe Pruitt 3.00 8.00
PIJN Joakim Noah 8.00 20.00
PIJW Julian Wright 3.00 8.00
PIKD Kevin Durant 100.00 200.00
PIMB Marco Belinelli 5.00 12.00
PIMC Mike Conley Jr. 6.00 15.00
PIRS Rodney Stuckey 4.00 10.00
PISW Sean Williams 3.00 8.00
PIWC Wilson Chandler 4.00 10.00

2007-08 Upper Deck Premier Impressions Gold

PRINT RUN 25 SER.#'d SETS
PIAH Al Horford 10.00 25.00
PIAL Acie Law 5.00 12.00
PICB Corey Brewer 8.00 20.00
PICL Carl Landry 5.00 12.00
PIDC Daequan Cook 6.00 15.00
PIJN Joakim Noah 12.00 30.00
PIKD Kevin Durant 150.00 300.00
PIWC Wilson Chandler 6.00 15.00

2007-08 Upper Deck Premier Noteworthy

PRINT RUNS LISTED IN CHECKLIST
UNPRICED COPPER PRINT RUN ONE SET
NWBG Ben Gordon/48 10.00 25.00
NWBI Larry Bird/60 40.00 100.00
NWBR Brandon Roy/29 15.00 30.00
NWCP Chris Paul/35 40.00 75.00
NWDR David Robinson/71 25.00 60.00
NWDT David Thompson/73 6.00 15.00
NWEB Elgin Baylor/71 15.00 40.00
NWHO Hakeem Olajuwon/51 20.00 40.00
NWJE Al Jefferson/32 6.00 15.00
NWJW Jerry West/63 25.00 60.00
NWKB Kobe Bryant/81 100.00 200.00
NWLA LaMarcus Aldridge/30 12.00 30.00
NWLH Larry Hughes/44 10.00 25.00
NWLJ LeBron James/56 200.00 500.00
NWMJ Michael Jordan/69 250.00 450.00
NWPP Paul Pierce/50 12.00 30.00
NWPR Tayshaun Prince/33 6.00 15.00
NWRB Rick Barry/64 6.00 15.00
NWRG Rudy Gay/31 6.00 15.00
NWSN Steve Nash/42 20.00 50.00
NWTM Tracy McGrady/62 10.00 25.00
NWTP Tony Parker/38 15.00 30.00
NWVC Vince Carter/51 12.00 30.00

2007-08 Upper Deck Premier Noteworthy Gold

PRINT RUN 25 SER.#'d SETS
NWBI Larry Bird 50.00 120.00
NWBR Brandon Roy 15.00 30.00
NWCP Chris Paul 40.00 75.00
NWDR David Robinson 40.00 80.00
NWDT David Thompson 10.00 25.00
NWEB Elgin Baylor 20.00 50.00
NWHO Hakeem Olajuwon 20.00 50.00
NWJW Jerry West 40.00 75.00
NWKB Kobe Bryant 125.00 300.00
NWLJ LeBron James 300.00 600.00
NWMJ Michael Jordan 400.00 600.00
NWPP Paul Pierce 15.00 40.00
NWRG Rudy Gay 10.00 25.00
NWSN Steve Nash 20.00 50.00
NWTM Tracy McGrady 12.00 30.00
NWTP Tony Parker 15.00 40.00
NWVC Vince Carter 15.00 40.00

2007-08 Upper Deck Premier Opening Night Autographs Jerseys

PRINT RUN 25 SER.#'d SETS
ONAD K.Durant/C.Anthony 150.00 300.00
ONAJ A.Jefferson/C.Anthony 20.00 50.00
ONBM K.Bryant/T.McGrady 125.00 225.00
ONBP M.Bibby/C.Paul 40.00 80.00
ONBW M.Bibby/J.Wright 10.00 25.00
ONCG M.Collins/D.Gibson 10.00 25.00
ONCT V.Carter/T.Thomas 30.00 60.00
ONDM B.Davis/C.Maggette 15.00 30.00
ONHN D.Howard/D.Noel 20.00 50.00
ONHT A.Thornton/A.Harrington 10.00 25.00
ONJF L.James/N.Fazekas 80.00 160.00
ONKH K.Hinrich/J.Kidd 25.00 50.00
ONMB B.Bowen/J.McRoberts 25.00 50.00
ONMC Y.Ming/J.Crittenton 25.00 50.00
ONND K.Durant/S.Nash 150.00 250.00
ONNW J.Noah/S.Williams 20.00 40.00
ONPC T.Parker/M.Conley 20.00 40.00
ONPR T.Parker/B.Roy 25.00 50.00
ONSC R.Stuckey/D.Cook 15.00 40.00

2007-08 Upper Deck Premier Pairings Autographs

PRINT RUN 20 SER.#'d SETS
PPAR B.Roy/L.Aldridge 25.00 50.00
PPAS R.Stuckey/A.Afflalo 15.00 30.00
PPBD B.Davis/M.Belinelli 15.00 30.00
PPBN S.Nash/K.Bryant 125.00 225.00
PPCG J.Green/M.Conley 20.00 40.00
PPCM V.Carter/T.McGrady 30.00 80.00
PPDB B.Davis/R.Barry 15.00 30.00
PPDP M.Price/B.Daugherty 20.00 50.00
PPFD W.Frazier/L.Dampier 15.00 30.00
PPGN B.Gordon/J.Noah 15.00 40.00
PPHB A.Horford/C.Brewer 25.00 50.00
PPHG D.Howard/B.Gordon 25.00 50.00
PPJB L.Bird/M.Johnson 100.00 200.00
PPJE M.Jordan/J.Erving 300.00 600.00
PPJJ M.Jordan/L.James 800.00 1200.00
PPKA B.Armstrong/S.Kerr 15.00 30.00
PPKC J.Kidd/V.Carter 40.00 75.00
PPLC M.Conley/K.Lowry 15.00 30.00
PPMO H.Olajuwon/Y.Ming 30.00 60.00
PPND K.Durant/J.Noah 150.00 300.00
PPPP M.Peterson/C.Paul 40.00 75.00
PPRR D.Rodman/D.Robinson 60.00 120.00
PPTN T.Thomas/J.Noah 12.00 30.00
PPWH A.Horford/D.Wilkins 25.00 60.00
PPWP B.Walton/R.Parish 20.00 40.00

2007-08 Upper Deck Premier Patches Dual Gold

PRINT RUN 9 TO 50 SER.#'d SETS
SOME UNPRICED DUE TO SCARCITY
UNPRICED AUTO PRINT RUN 10 TO 23 SETS
UNPRICED SPECTRUM PRINT RUN ONE SET
AA Arron Afflalo/25 6.00 15.00
AT Al Thornton/25 5.00 12.00
CA Carmelo Anthony/25 8.00 20.00
CP Chris Paul/25 8.00 20.00
DC Daequan Cook/25 5.00 12.00
DE Deron Williams/25 5.00 12.00
DN David Noel/25 4.00 10.00
DR David Robinson/25 10.00 25.00
JE Julius Erving/25 10.00 25.00
JS Jason Smith/25 5.00 12.00
JW Jerry West/25 15.00 30.00
KB Kobe Bryant/25 25.00 60.00
LJ LeBron James/25 20.00 50.00
PA Tony Parker/25 6.00 15.00
PP Paul Pierce/25 6.00 15.00
SN Steve Nash/25 8.00 20.00
ST John Stockton/25 10.00 25.00
SW Sean Williams/25 4.00 10.00
VC Vince Carter/25 8.00 20.00

2007-08 Upper Deck Premier Patches Dual Silver

STATED PRINT RUN ONE TO 52 SER.#'d SETS
SOME UNPRICED DUE TO SCARCITY
AT Al Thornton/12 6.00 15.00
DR David Robinson/50 10.00 25.00
JS Jason Smith/14 6.00 15.00
JW Jerry West/44 15.00 30.00
KB Kobe Bryant/24 25.00 60.00
LJ LeBron James/23 25.00 60.00
PP Paul Pierce/34 8.00 20.00
SN Steve Nash/13 10.00 25.00
ST John Stockton/12 12.00 30.00
SW Sean Williams/51 4.00 10.00
TC Tom Chambers/42 5.00 12.00

2007-08 Upper Deck Premier Patches Dual Silver Spectrum

PRINT RUN 15 SER.#'d SETS
AA Arron Afflalo 8.00 20.00
CA Carmelo Anthony 10.00 25.00
DE Deron Williams 6.00 15.00
DR David Robinson 15.00 40.00
JC Javaris Crittenton 5.00 12.00
JS Jason Smith 6.00 15.00
JW Jerry West 20.00 40.00
KB Kobe Bryant 30.00 80.00
LJ LeBron James 25.00 60.00
SB Shannon Brown 5.00 12.00
SN Steve Nash 10.00 25.00
ST John Stockton 12.00 30.00
SW Sean Williams 5.00 12.00
TC Tom Chambers 6.00 15.00
VC Vince Carter 10.00 25.00

2007-08 Upper Deck Premier Patches Triple Silver

PRINT RUN 35 SER.#'d SETS
UNPRICED SILVER SPEC.PRINT RUN 5 SETS
UNPRICED GOLD PRINT RUN 10 SETS
UNPRICED GOLD AUTO PRINT RUN 5 SETS
UNPRICED GOLD SPEC.PRINT RUN ONE SET
AL Acie Law 4.00 10.00
CA Carmelo Anthony 12.00 30.00
CP Chris Paul 8.00 20.00
DR David Robinson 10.00 25.00
DU Kevin Durant 40.00 80.00
GR Jeff Green 6.00 15.00
JE Julius Erving 10.00 25.00
JN Joakim Noah 6.00 15.00
JS John Stockton 10.00 25.00
KB Kobe Bryant 20.00 50.00
KG Kevin Garnett 10.00 25.00
LJ LeBron James 30.00 80.00
MC Mike Conley Jr. 8.00 20.00
PP Paul Pierce 6.00 15.00
PR Tayshaun Prince 5.00 12.00
RS Rodney Stuckey 5.00 12.00
SN Steve Nash 8.00 20.00
TP Tony Parker 6.00 15.00
VC Vince Carter 8.00 20.00
WE Jerry West 15.00 30.00

2007-08 Upper Deck Premier Penmanship Autographs

PRINT RUN 50 SER.#'d SETS
UNPRICED COPPER PRINT RUN ONE SET
AH Al Horford 10.00 25.00
AJ Antawn Jamison 6.00 15.00
AM Alonzo Mourning 25.00 60.00
AT Al Thornton 6.00 15.00
BA B.J. Armstrong 10.00 25.00
BR Brandon Roy 12.00 30.00
BW Bill Walton 8.00 20.00
CA Carmelo Anthony 20.00 50.00
CL Clyde Lovellette 15.00 40.00
CO Corey Brewer 6.00 15.00
CP Chris Paul 30.00 80.00
DR Dennis Rodman 25.00 60.00
DW Deron Williams 20.00 40.00
EO Emeka Okafor 6.00 15.00
GR Glen Rice 15.00 40.00
HO Horace Grant 20.00 40.00
JE Al Jefferson 6.00 15.00
JG Jeff Green 6.00 15.00
JJ Jarrett Jack 6.00 15.00
JN Joakim Noah 15.00 40.00
JO Magic Johnson 30.00 60.00
KB Kobe Bryant 150.00 275.00
KD Kevin Durant 150.00 300.00
LA LaMarcus Aldridge 12.50 30.00
LB Larry Bird 50.00 100.00
LH Larry Hughes 6.00 15.00
LJ LeBron James 300.00 600.00
MJ Michael Jordan 400.00 800.00
OL Hakeem Olajuwon 15.00 40.00
PA Tony Parker 10.00 25.00
PP Paul Pierce 20.00 50.00
RF Randy Foye 6.00 15.00
RG Rudy Gay 6.00 15.00
RO David Robinson 30.00 80.00
RR Rajon Rondo 30.00 60.00
RS Rodney Stuckey 6.00 15.00
RU Bill Russell 125.00 250.00
SK Steve Kerr 8.00 20.00
TM Tracy McGrady 20.00 50.00
TP Tayshaun Prince 6.00 15.00
TT Tyrus Thomas 6.00 15.00
VC Vince Carter 20.00 40.00
WE Jerry West 30.00 80.00
WF Walt Frazier 10.00 25.00
WI Dominique Wilkins 20.00 50.00
WO James Worthy 20.00 50.00
WT Wayman Tisdale 15.00 40.00
WU Wes Unseld 15.00 40.00
YM Yao Ming 20.00 50.00

2007-08 Upper Deck Premier Penmanship Autographs Gold

PRINT RUNS LISTED IN CHECKLIST
SOME UNPRICED DUE TO SCARCITY
AH Al Horford/15 15.00 40.00
AM Alonzo Mourning/33 40.00 80.00
BA B.J. Armstrong/11 60.00 120.00
CA Carmelo Anthony/15 100.00 200.00
CO Corey Brewer/22 8.00 20.00
HO Horace Grant/54 20.00 50.00
JE Al Jefferson/25 8.00 20.00
JO Magic Johnson/32 60.00 120.00
JW Julian Wright/32 10.00 25.00
KB Kobe Bryant/24 300.00 600.00
KD Kevin Durant/35 150.00 300.00
LB Larry Bird/33 75.00 150.00
LJ LeBron James/23 400.00 800.00
MC Mike Conley Jr./11 25.00 50.00
MJ Michael Jordan/23 500.00 1000.00
OL Hakeem Olajuwon/34 25.00 60.00
PP Paul Pierce/34 30.00 60.00
RG Rudy Gay/22 10.00 25.00
RO David Robinson/50 30.00 60.00
SK Steve Kerr/25 12.50 30.00
VC Vince Carter/15 25.00 60.00
WE Jerry West/44 30.00 80.00
WO James Worthy/42 20.00 50.00
YM Yao Ming/11 25.00 50.00

2007-08 Upper Deck Premier Preeminence

PRINT RUN 50 SER.#'d SETS
UNPRICED COPPER PRINT RUN ONE SET
PEAI Andre Iguodala 6.00 15.00
PEBR Brandon Roy 5.00 12.00
PECP Chris Paul 20.00 50.00
PEDG Daniel Gibson 5.00 12.00
PEDW Deron Williams 5.00 12.00
PEJE Al Jefferson 5.00 12.00
PEKB Kobe Bryant 100.00 200.00
PEMJ Magic Johnson 25.00 60.00
PERG Rudy Gay 8.00 20.00
PESK Steve Kerr 8.00 20.00
PETP Tayshaun Prince 5.00 12.00
PEVC Vince Carter 15.00 40.00
PEWT Wayman Tisdale 6.00 15.00
PEYM Yao Ming 15.00 40.00

2007-08 Upper Deck Premier Preeminence Gold

PRINT RUN 25 SER.#'d SETS
PEAI Andre Iguodala 10.00 25.00
PEBR Brandon Roy 15.00 30.00
PECP Chris Paul 40.00 75.00
PEKB Kobe Bryant 150.00 300.00
PEMJ Magic Johnson 40.00 100.00
PERG Rudy Gay 12.50 30.00
PESK Steve Kerr 12.50 30.00
PETC Tyson Chandler 5.00 12.00
PETP Tayshaun Prince 8.00 20.00
PETT Tyrus Thomas 8.00 20.00
PEVC Vince Carter 15.00 40.00

2007-08 Upper Deck Premier Rare Patches Dual Gold

PRINT RUN 15 SER.#'d SETS
UNPRICED SPECTRUM PRINT RUN ONE SET
*SILVER PATCH: .4X TO 1X BASE HI
SILVER PRINT RUN 25 SER.#'d SETS
UNPRICED SILVER SPEC.PRINT RUN 10 SETS
AC A.Horford/C.Brewer 8.00 20.00
AG R.Allen/K.Garnett 25.00 50.00
AH R.Allen/R.Hamilton 8.00 20.00
AS A.Afflalo/R.Stuckey 8.00 20.00
BB S.Battier/C.Boozer 10.00 25.00
BJ K.Bryant/L.James 40.00 100.00
BM D.Mason/A.Bogut 8.00 20.00
BN K.Bryant/S.Nash 20.00 40.00
DG K.Durant/J.Green 40.00 80.00
DJ J.Stockton/D.Williams 15.00 30.00
DM T.Duncan/Y.Ming 15.00 30.00
DR C.Drexler/D.Robinson 20.00 40.00
GI B.Gordon/A.Iguodala 8.00 20.00
GJ K.Garnett/A.Jefferson 20.00 40.00
GN A.Gray/J.Noah 8.00 20.00
HB R.Hamilton/C.Billups 8.00 20.00
HL A.Horford/A.Law 10.00 25.00
IA A.Iverson/C.Anthony 20.00 40.00
IN A.Iverson/D.Nowitzki 15.00 30.00
JB M.Johnson/L.Bird 20.00 40.00
JD L.James/K.Durant 100.00 200.00
JJ M.Jordan/L.James 100.00 250.00
JW A.Jamison/L.Walton 8.00 20.00
KM J.Kidd/S.Marbury 10.00 25.00
PD G.Pruitt/G.Davis 8.00 20.00
PH P.Pierce/K.Hinrich 8.00 20.00
PR C.Paul/B.Roy 10.00 25.00
PW C.Paul/J.Wright 10.00 25.00
SH A.Stoudemire/D.Howard 8.00 20.00
WD G.Wallace/J.Dudley 8.00 20.00
WN B.Wallace/J.Noah 8.00 20.00
WW R.Wallace/B.Wallace 8.00 20.00
YS T.Young/J.Smith 8.00 20.00

2007-08 Upper Deck Premier Rare Patches Triple Silver

PRINT RUN 15 SER.#'d SETS
UNPRICED SILVER SPEC.PRINT RUN 5 SETS
UNPRICED GOLD PRINT RUN 10 SETS
UNPRICED GOLD SPEC.PRINT RUN ONE SET
ASH Afflalo/Stuckey/Hamilton 12.50 30.00
BFC Crittenton/Bryant/Farmar 20.00 50.00
BGJ Bryant/Garnett/James 50.00 100.00
BNI Iverson/Bryant/Nash 30.00 60.00
BPW Paul/Billups/Williams 20.00 50.00
DGC Conley/Durant/Green 40.00 75.00
DGO O'Neal/Garnett/Duncan 25.00 50.00
DPG Parker/Ginobili/Duncan 20.00 50.00
JJB Bird/Jordan/Johnson 100.00 200.00
MRL Lee/Randolph/Marbury 12.50 30.00
NHB Horford/Brewer/Noah 25.00 50.00
NHH Nowitzki/Howard/Harris 15.00 40.00
OGR Robinson/KG/Olajuwon 25.00 50.00
PAG Garnett/Allen/Pierce 50.00 100.00
WSD Stockton/West/Drexler 40.00 100.00

2007-08 Upper Deck Premier Rare Remnants Quad

PRINT RUN 50 SER.#'d SETS
AGDG Durant/Green/Allen/KG 12.00 30.00
AGPD Davis/KG/Pruitt/Allen 8.00 20.00
ARPA Aldridge/Roy/Hilton/Paul 8.00 20.00
DNSA Dirk/Duncan/Melo/Amare 10.00 25.00
GCMM KG/Carter/TMac/Marion 15.00 40.00
GJGB LJ/Gibsn/Goodn/Brwn 12.50 30.00
HDGT Gordon/Kirk/Deng/Tyrus 6.00 15.00
JABW James/Melo/Bosh/Wade 50.00 100.00
JEJB Bird/Magic/Jordan/Erving 60.00 150.00
KCJW RJeff/Vince/Kidd/Williams 6.00 15.00
KJHO LJ/Shaq/Howard/Kidd 25.00 50.00
MWOC Shaq/Wade/Cook/Zo 10.00 25.00
NGHB Noah/Horford/Brewer/Green 8.00 20.00
SDRR DRob/Worm/Stock/Glide 25.00 50.00
YHSI Young/Smith/Iguodala/Hill 6.00 15.00

2007-08 Upper Deck Premier Rare Remnants Quad Gold

PRINT RUN 25 SER.#'d SETS
UNPRICED SPECTRUM PRINT RUN ONE SET
UNPRICED SILVER SPEC.PRINT RUN 10 SETS
AGDG Durant/Green/Allen/KG 20.00 50.00
ARPA Aldridge/Roy/Hilton/Paul 10.00 25.00
DNSA Dirk/Duncan/Melo/Amare 15.00 30.00
GCMM KG/Vince/TMac/Marion 15.00 40.00
GJGB LJ/Gibsn/Goodn/Brwn 20.00 40.00
HDGT Gordo/Hinrich/Deng/Tyrus 10.00 25.00
JABW James/Melo/Bosh/Wade 50.00 120.00
KJHO LJ/Shaq/Howard/Kidd 25.00 60.00
MWOC Shaq/Wade/Cook/Zo 20.00 50.00
YHSI Young/Smith/Iguodala/Hill 10.00 25.00

2007-08 Upper Deck Premier Rare Remnants Triple

PRINT RUN 99 SER.#'d SETS
ASB Afflalo/Stuckey/Billups 4.00 10.00
BAH Artest/Hawes/Bibby 4.00 10.00
BGJ Bryant/Garnett/James 15.00 40.00
BMA Bryant/McGrady/Anthony 10.00 25.00
BNI Iverson/Bryant/Nash 12.00 30.00
BPW Paul/Billups/Williams 6.00 15.00
CBH Carter/Bosh/Howard 6.00 15.00
DGO O'Neal/Garnett/Duncan 8.00 20.00
JAB James/Anthony/Bosh 10.00 25.00
JCS Smith/Johnson/Childress 5.00 12.00
JDM James/Durant/McGrady 20.00 50.00
JEB Jordan/Bird/Erving 30.00 80.00
JHB Harrington/Jamison/Boozer 4.00 10.00
JJJ James/Jordan/Johnson 75.00 200.00
KWS Stockton/Kirilenko/Williams 8.00 20.00
MMB McGrady/Ming/Brooks 6.00 15.00
MNW Williams/Nowitzki/McGrady 6.00 15.00
MSO O'Neal/Stoudemire/Ming 10.00 25.00
NHB Noah/Horford/Brewer 6.00 15.00
NMS Nash/Stoudemire/Marion 6.00 15.00
OGR Robinson/Olajuwon/Garnett 8.00 20.00
TAB Bargnani/Thomas/Aldridge 4.00 10.00

2007-08 Upper Deck Premier Rare Remnants Triple Gold

*GOLD: .5X TO 1.25X HI COLUMN
PRINT RUN 50 SER.#'d SETS
UNPRICED SPECTRUM PRINT RUN ONE SET

2007-08 Upper Deck Premier Rare Remnants Triple Silver Spectrum

*SILVER SPECT: .6X TO 1.5X TRIPLE HI
PRINT RUN 25 SER.#'d SETS
JAB James/Anthony/Bosh 20.00 50.00

2007-08 Upper Deck Premier Remnants Quad

STATED PRINT RUN ONE TO 99 SER.#'d SETS
SOME UNPRICED DUE TO SCARCITY
DR David Robinson/89 8.00 20.00
JE Julius Erving/76 6.00 15.00
JS John Stockton/84 6.00 15.00
KB Kobe Bryant/96 10.00 25.00
KG Kevin Garnett/95 6.00 15.00
SN Steve Nash/96 5.00 12.00
TC Tom Chambers/81 3.00 8.00
VC Vince Carter/98 5.00 12.00
WE Jerry West/60 8.00 20.00

2007-08 Upper Deck Premier Remnants Quad Autographs

PRINT RUN 25 SER.#'d SETS
AH Al Horford 15.00 40.00
AM Andre Miller 8.00 20.00
BD Boris Diaw 8.00 20.00
CA Carmelo Anthony 25.00 60.00
CB Corey Brewer 15.00 30.00
CP Chris Paul 40.00 80.00
DU Kevin Durant 300.00 600.00
JE Julius Erving 50.00 100.00
JN Joakim Noah 25.00 60.00
JS John Stockton 50.00 100.00
KB Kobe Bryant 150.00 250.00
LJ LeBron James 300.00 600.00
MC Mike Conley Jr. 12.00 30.00
PP Paul Pierce 20.00 50.00
RS Rodney Stuckey 15.00 40.00
SN Steve Nash 30.00 80.00
VC Vince Carter 25.00 50.00
WE Jerry West 40.00 80.00

2007-08 Upper Deck Premier Remnants Quad Gold

PRINT RUN 50 SER.#'d SETS
UNPRICED SPECTRUM PRINT RUN ONE SET
UNPRICED SILVER SPEC.PRINT RUN 10 SETS
CA Carmelo Anthony 6.00 15.00
CP Chris Paul 6.00 15.00
DR David Robinson 8.00 20.00
DU Kevin Durant 30.00 80.00
GR Jeff Green 5.00 12.00
JE Julius Erving 8.00 20.00
JN Joakim Noah 5.00 12.00
JS John Stockton 8.00 20.00
JW Julian Wright 3.00 8.00
KB Kobe Bryant 20.00 50.00
LJ LeBron James 15.00 40.00
MC Mike Conley Jr. 6.00 15.00
TC Tom Chambers 4.00 10.00
TP Tony Parker 5.00 12.00
VC Vince Carter 6.00 15.00
WE Jerry West 8.00 20.00

2007-08 Upper Deck Premier Remnants Triple

PRINT RUN 99 SER.#'d SETS
*GOLD: .5X TO 1.25X BASE HI
GOLD PRINT RUN 50 SER.#'d SETS
*SILVER SPEC: .6X TO 1.5X BASE HI
SILVER SPEC.PRINT RUN 25 SETS
UNPRICED GOLD SPEC.PRINT RUN ONE SET
AT Al Thornton 2.50 6.00
CP Chris Paul 4.00 10.00
DC Daequan Cook 2.50 6.00
DE Deron Williams 2.50 6.00
JE Julius Erving 5.00 12.00
KB Kobe Bryant 10.00 25.00
LJ LeBron James 12.00 30.00
SN Steve Nash 4.00 10.00
SW Sean Williams 2.00 5.00
TP Tayshaun Prince 2.50 6.00
VC Vince Carter 4.00 10.00

2007-08 Upper Deck Premier Remnants Triple Autographs

PRINT RUN 50 SER.#'d SETS
AA Arron Afflalo 6.00 15.00
AB Aaron Brooks 6.00 15.00
AM Andre Miller 6.00 15.00
BD Boris Diaw 6.00 15.00
CA Carmelo Anthony 25.00 60.00
CM Corey Maggette 6.00 15.00
CP Chris Paul 30.00 60.00
DC Daequan Cook 6.00 15.00
DE Deron Williams 10.00 25.00
DR David Robinson 30.00 60.00
JE Julius Erving 40.00 80.00
JW Jerry West 30.00 80.00
KB Kobe Bryant 125.00 250.00
LJ LeBron James 300.00 600.00
PA Tony Parker 15.00 40.00
PP Paul Pierce 12.00 30.00
SN Steve Nash 25.00 60.00
ST John Stockton 40.00 75.00
SW Sean Williams 6.00 15.00
TP Tayshaun Prince 8.00 20.00
VC Vince Carter 20.00 40.00
WC Wilson Chandler 10.00 25.00

2007-08 Upper Deck Premier Rookies Autographs Jerseys Copper

PRINT RUN 99 SER.#'d SETS
*BLUE: .6X TO 1.5X COPPER HI
BLUE PRINT RUN 25 SER.#'d SETS
*GREEN: .5X TO 1.25X COPPER
GREEN PRINT RUN 49 SER.#'d SETS
UNPRICED GOLD PRINT RUN ONE SET
UNPRICED RED PRINT RUN 15 SER.#'d SETS
101 Kevin Durant 250.00 500.00
102 Al Horford 15.00 40.00
103 Mike Conley Jr. 12.00 30.00
104 Jeff Green 6.00 15.00
105 Corey Brewer 6.00 15.00
106 Joakim Noah 15.00 40.00
107 Spencer Hawes 5.00 12.00
108 Acie Law 4.00 10.00
109 Julian Wright 4.00 10.00
110 Al Thornton 5.00 12.00
111 Rodney Stuckey 5.00 12.00
112 Sean Williams 4.00 10.00
113 Javaris Crittenton 4.00 10.00
114 Jason Smith 5.00 12.00
115 Daequan Cook 5.00 12.00
116 Jared Dudley 5.00 12.00
117 Wilson Chandler 5.00 12.00
118 Morris Almond 4.00 10.00
119 Arron Afflalo 6.00 15.00
120 Alando Tucker 4.00 10.00
121 Carl Landry 4.00 10.00
122 Gabe Pruitt 4.00 10.00
125 Glen Davis 5.00 12.00
126 Jermareo Davidson 4.00 10.00
129 Adam Haluska 4.00 10.00
133 Aaron Gray 4.00 10.00
134 Taurean Green 4.00 10.00
135 Demetris Nichols 4.00 10.00
136 D.J. Strawberry 4.00 10.00
137 Aaron Brooks 5.00 12.00
138 Herbert Hill 4.00 10.00
139 Chris Richard 4.00 10.00

2007-08 Upper Deck Premier Stitchings Patches

PRINT RUN 50 SER.#'d SETS
STITCHINGS PATCH FEATURE TEAM LOGO
*ALT LOGO: .4X TO 1X BASE HI
ALT LOGO PRINT RUN 50 SETS
*GOLD: .4X TO 1X BASE HI
GOLD PRINT RUN 25 SETS
*GOLD ALT: .4X TO 1X BASE HI
GOLD ALT PRINT RUN 25 SETS
UNPRICED AUTO PRINT RUN 5 SETS
UNPRICED AUTO ALT PRINT RUN ONE SET
UNPRICED COPPER PRINT RUN 10 SETS
UNPRICED COPPER ALT PRINT RUN 10 SETS
PSAB Aaron Brooks 8.00 20.00
PSAH Al Horford 8.00 20.00
PSAI Allen Iverson 10.00 25.00
PSAN Carmelo Anthony 10.00 25.00
PSAS Amare Stoudemire 10.00 25.00
PSAT Al Thornton 8.00 20.00
PSBA Andrea Bargnani 8.00 20.00
PSBB Bill Bradley 8.00 20.00
PSBG Ben Gordon 8.00 20.00
PSBM Bob McAdoo 10.00 25.00
PSBO Chris Bosh 8.00 20.00
PSBR Bill Russell 12.50 30.00
PSBW Bill Walton 8.00 20.00
PSCA Carlos Arroyo 10.00 25.00
PSCB Carlos Boozer 8.00 20.00
PSCD Clyde Drexler 8.00 20.00
PSCH Wilt Chamberlain 10.00 25.00
PSCO Corey Brewer 8.00 20.00
PSCP Chris Paul 10.00 25.00
PSDC Daequan Cook 8.00 20.00
PSDE Dennis Rodman 20.00 40.00
PSDH Dwight Howard 10.00 25.00
PSDN Dirk Nowitzki 10.00 25.00
PSDR David Robinson 12.50 30.00
PSDW Deron Williams 8.00 20.00
PSEJ Magic Johnson 12.50 30.00
PSEM Earl Monroe 8.00 20.00
PSEO Emeka Okafor 8.00 20.00
PSGG George Gervin 10.00 25.00
PSGO Greg Oden 6.00 15.00
PSGR Gerald Green 8.00 20.00
PSHO Hakeem Olajuwon 10.00 25.00
PSIT Isiah Thomas 10.00 25.00
PSJD Jared Dudley 8.00 20.00
PSJG Jeff Green 8.00 20.00
PSJH John Havlicek 10.00 25.00
PSJK Jason Kidd 10.00 25.00
PSJO Jermaine O'Neal 8.00 20.00
PSJS Jason Smith 8.00 20.00
PSJW Jerry West 12.50 30.00
PSKB Kobe Bryant 25.00 60.00
PSKD Kevin Durant 15.00 40.00
PSKG Kevin Garnett 12.50 30.00
PSKH Kirk Hinrich 8.00 20.00
PSKM Karl Malone 8.00 20.00
PSLA LaMarcus Aldridge 8.00 20.00
PSLB Larry Bird 15.00 40.00
PSLD Luol Deng 8.00 20.00
PSLJ LeBron James 15.00 40.00
PSMB Marco Belinelli 8.00 20.00
PSMC Kevin McHale 8.00 20.00
PSMG Manu Ginobili 10.00 25.00
PSMJ Michael Jordan 75.00 200.00
PSMM Moses Malone 8.00 20.00
PSNO Joakim Noah 8.00 20.00
PSNY Nick Young 8.00 20.00
PSOR Oscar Robertson 10.00 25.00
PSPA Tony Parker 12.00 30.00
PSPP Paul Pierce 8.00 20.00
PSPS Peja Stojakovic 8.00 20.00
PSPW Paul Westphal 8.00 20.00
PSRE Willis Reed 10.00 25.00
PSRF Randy Foye 8.00 20.00
PSRG Rudy Gay 8.00 20.00
PSRO Brandon Roy 8.00 20.00
PSRP Robert Parish 10.00 25.00
PSRR Rajon Rondo 10.00 25.00
PSRS Rodney Stuckey 8.00 20.00
PSSH Spencer Hawes 8.00 20.00
PSSN Steve Nash 10.00 25.00
PSSO Shaquille O'Neal 12.50 30.00
PSST John Stockton 8.00 20.00
PSTD Tim Duncan 12.50 30.00
PSTM Tracy McGrady 8.00 20.00
PSTT Tyrus Thomas 8.00 20.00
PSTU Alando Tucker 8.00 20.00
PSTY Thaddeus Young 8.00 20.00
PSVC Vince Carter 10.00 25.00
PSWA Dwyane Wade 12.50 30.00
PSWC Wilson Chandler 8.00 20.00
PSWF Walt Frazier 10.00 25.00

PSWI Dominique Wilkins 10.00 25.00
PSWR Brandan Wright 8.00 20.00
PSYM Yao Ming 10.00 25.00

2007-08 Upper Deck Premier Trios Autographs

PRINT RUN 15 SER.#'d SETS
HGN Hinrich/Noah/Gordon 40.00 75.00
JFB Foye/Jefferson/Brewer 15.00 40.00
JJJ Jordan/James/Johnson 1500.00 2000.00
KCW Williams/Kidd/Carter 50.00 125.00
MLB Landry/Brooks/McGrady 30.00 60.00
OHJ Jefferson/Okafor/Howard 40.00 75.00
PAG Garnett/Pierce/Allen 250.00 500.00
RFD Riley/Frazier/Dampier 40.00 75.00
SDG Durant/Green/Shelton 100.00 200.00
TAG Thomas/Aldridge/Gay 25.00 50.00
WHL Horford/Law/Williams 30.00 60.00

2008-09 Upper Deck Premier

This set was released on March 11, 2009. The base set consists of 130 cards.
1-94 PRINT RUN 99 SER.#'d SETS
95-100 PRINT RUN 99 SER.#'d SETS
95-130 PRINT RUN 199 SER.#'d SETS
1 Kevin Garnett 3.00 8.00
2 Paul Pierce 2.00 5.00
3 Ray Allen 2.00 5.00
4 Larry Bird 5.00 12.00
5 Stephen Jackson 1.50 4.00
6 Monta Ellis 1.50 4.00
7 Mitch Richmond 2.00 5.00
8 Stephon Marbury 1.50 4.00
9 Jamal Crawford 2.00 5.00
10 Patrick Ewing 2.50 6.00
11 Chauncey Billups 2.00 5.00
12 Rasheed Wallace 2.00 5.00
13 Isiah Thomas 2.00 5.00
14 Kobe Bryant 8.00 20.00
15 Pau Gasol 2.00 5.00
16 Magic Johnson 5.00 12.00
17 Elgin Baylor 2.00 5.00
18 Kevin Martin 1.50 4.00
19 Beno Udrih 1.25 3.00
20 Oscar Robertson 2.00 5.00
21 Joe Johnson 1.50 4.00
22 Al Horford 2.00 5.00
23 Dominique Wilkins 2.50 6.00
24 Andre Iguodala 1.50 4.00
25 Elton Brand 2.00 5.00
26 Julius Erving 3.00 8.00
27 Wilt Chamberlain 4.00 10.00
28 Gilbert Arenas 1.50 4.00
29 Antawn Jamison 1.50 4.00
30 Elvin Hayes 2.00 5.00
31 Ben Gordon 1.50 4.00
32 Luol Deng 1.50 4.00
33 Michael Jordan 40.00 100.00
34 Scottie Pippen 3.00 8.00
35 Allen Iverson 2.50 6.00
36 Carmelo Anthony 2.50 6.00
37 Alex English 1.50 4.00
38 Tracy McGrady 2.00 5.00
39 Yao Ming 2.50 6.00
40 Hakeem Olajuwon 2.50 6.00
41 T.J. Ford 1.25 3.00
42 Danny Granger 1.50 4.00
43 Mike Dunleavy 1.50 4.00
44 Yi Jianlian 2.00 5.00
45 Vince Carter 2.50 6.00
46 Buck Williams 1.25 3.00
47 Kevin Durant 5.00 12.00
48 Jeff Green 1.50 4.00
49 Detlef Schrempf 2.00 5.00
50 Richard Jefferson 1.50 4.00
51 Andrew Bogut 1.50 4.00
52 Kareem Abdul-Jabbar 3.00 8.00
53 Steve Nash 2.00 5.00
54 Shaquille O'Neal 4.00 10.00
55 Kevin Johnson 2.00 5.00
56 LeBron James 8.00 20.00
57 Daniel Gibson 1.50 4.00
58 Mark Price 3.00 8.00
59 Baron Davis 1.50 4.00
60 Chris Kaman 1.50 4.00
61 World B. Free 1.50 4.00
62 Brandon Roy 2.00 5.00
63 LaMarcus Aldridge 2.00 5.00
64 Clyde Drexler 2.50 6.00
65 Tim Duncan 3.00 8.00
66 Tony Parker 2.00 5.00
67 David Robinson 3.00 8.00
68 Deron Williams 1.50 4.00
69 Carlos Boozer 1.50 4.00
70 Karl Malone 2.50 6.00
71 John Stockton 3.00 8.00
72 Dirk Nowitzki 2.50 6.00
73 Jason Kidd 2.00 5.00
74 Rolando Blackman 1.50 4.00
75 Dwyane Wade 3.00 8.00
76 Alonzo Mourning 2.50 6.00
77 Tim Hardaway 2.00 5.00
78 Chris Paul 2.50 6.00
79 David West 1.50 4.00
80 Larry Johnson 2.00 5.00
81 Al Jefferson 1.50 4.00
82 Corey Brewer 1.50 4.00
83 Dwight Howard 1.50 4.00
84 Hedo Turkoglu 1.50 4.00
85 Nick Anderson 2.00 5.00
86 Rudy Gay 2.00 5.00
87 Hakim Warrick 1.50 4.00
88 Mike Conley Jr. 1.50 4.00
89 Chris Bosh 2.00 5.00
90 Jermaine O'Neal 1.50 4.00
91 Jose Calderon 1.25 3.00
92 Emeka Okafor 1.50 4.00
93 Gerald Wallace 1.50 4.00
94 Raymond Felton 1.50 4.00
95 Courtney Lee RC 2.00 5.00
96 Chris Douglas-Roberts RC 1.50 4.00
97 Patrick Ewing Jr. RC 1.50 4.00
98 Alexis Ajinca RC 1.50 4.00
99 Bill Walker RC 1.50 4.00
100 Sonny Weems RC 1.50 4.00
101 Derrick Rose JSY AU RC 40.00 100.00
102 Michael Beasley JSY AU RC 5.00 12.00
103 O.J. Mayo JSY AU RC 5.00 12.00
104 R.Westbrook JSY AU RC 125.00 300.00
105 Kevin Love JSY AU RC 30.00 80.00
106 Patrick Ewing Jr. JSY AU RC 3.00 8.00
107 Eric Gordon JSY AU RC 8.00 20.00
108 Joe Alexander JSY AU RC 3.00 8.00
109 D. J. Augustin JSY AU RC 4.00 10.00
110 Brook Lopez JSY AU RC 6.00 15.00
111 Jerryd Bayless JSY AU RC 4.00 10.00
112 Jason Thompson JSY AU RC 3.00 8.00
113 Brandon Rush JSY AU RC 4.00 10.00
114 A.Randolph JSY AU RC 3.00 8.00
115 Robin Lopez JSY AU RC 5.00 12.00
116 Marreese Speights JSY AU RC 4.00 10.00
117 C.Douglas-Roberts JSY AU RC 3.00 8.00
118 Javale McGee JSY AU RC 6.00 15.00
119 J.J. Hickson JSY AU RC 4.00 10.00
120 Ryan Anderson JSY AU RC 4.00 10.00
121 Kosta Koufos JSY AU RC 4.00 10.00
122 George Hill JSY AU RC 5.00 12.00
123 Darrell Arthur JSY AU RC 4.00 10.00
124 Donte Greene JSY AU RC 3.00 8.00
125 Sonny Weems JSY AU RC 3.00 8.00
126 J.R. Giddens JSY AU RC 3.00 8.00
127 Walter Sharpe JSY AU RC 3.00 8.00
128 Joey Dorsey JSY AU RC 3.00 8.00
129 Mario Chalmers JSY AU RC 5.00 12.00
130 DeAndre Jordan JSY AU RC 12.00 30.00

2008-09 Upper Deck Premier Attractions Autographs Jerseys

ATED PRINT RUN 25 SER.#'d SETS
ATAD Adrian Dantley 8.00 20.00
ATAH Al Horford 6.00 15.00
ATAJ Al Jefferson 6.00 15.00
ATAM Louis Amundson 6.00 15.00
ATBG Ben Gordon 10.00 25.00
ATBR Brandon Roy 15.00 30.00
ATBY Andrew Bynum 6.00 15.00
ATCB Carlos Boozer 6.00 15.00
ATCL Carl Landry 6.00 15.00
ATJA Antawn Jamison 6.00 15.00
ATJB Josh Boone 6.00 15.00
ATJE Julius Erving 35.00 75.00
ATJF Jordan Farmar 6.00 15.00
ATJO Michael Jordan 350.00 700.00
ATKB Kobe Bryant 200.00 350.00
ATKD Kevin Durant 125.00 250.00
ATLA LaMarcus Aldridge 10.00 25.00
ATLB Larry Bird 50.00 120.00
ATLJ LeBron James 250.00 500.00
ATMP Mark Price 20.00 50.00
ATMR Micheal Ray Richardson 6.00 15.00
ATPP Paul Pierce 20.00 40.00
ATRB Renaldo Balkman 6.00 15.00
ATRG Rudy Gay 6.00 15.00
ATRJ Richard Jefferson 6.00 15.00
ATRP Robert Parish 10.00 25.00
ATSA Stacey Augmon 6.00 15.00
ATSV Sasha Vujacic 6.00 15.00
ATSW Sean Williams 6.00 15.00
ATTC Tom Chambers 6.00 15.00
ATWE Spud Webb 12.00 30.00

2008-09 Upper Deck Premier Classmates Autographs

STATED PRINT RUN 50 SER.#'d SETS
CLASS01 T.Parker/Jefferson 15.00 30.00
CLASS03 D.West/L.Walton 8.00 20.00
CLASS04 D.Howard/Okafor 10.00 25.00
CLASS07 K.Durant/Horford 50.00 120.00
CLASS70 Lanier/Tomjanovich 10.00 25.00
CLASS86 J.Salley/M.Price 25.00 50.00
CLASS87 K.Smith/M.Bogues 15.00 30.00
CLASS88 T.Horford/S.Kerr 8.00 20.00

2008-09 Upper Deck Premier Consumate Masters Autographs

STATED PRINT RUN 15 SER.#'d SETS
UNPRICED SILVER PRINT RUN ONE SET
CMBP Bob Pettit 20.00 40.00
CMBR Bill Russell 125.00 250.00
CMCA Adrian Dantley 12.00 30.00
CMCP Chris Paul 50.00 100.00
CMDH Dwight Howard 30.00 60.00
CMDR Dennis Rodman 40.00 100.00
CMGR Glen Rice 12.00 30.00
CMHO Hakeem Olajuwon 30.00 60.00
CMJK Jason Kidd 30.00 60.00
CMJO Michael Jordan 450.00 650.00
CMJS John Stockton 50.00 125.00
CMKB Kobe Bryant 200.00 400.00
CMLJ LeBron James 200.00 400.00
CMMB Muggsy Bogues 12.00 30.00
CMMJ Magic Johnson 50.00 100.00
CMMR Micheal Ray Richardson 12.00 30.00
CMRP Robert Parish 15.00 40.00

2008-09 Upper Deck Premier Foursome Autographs

STATED PRINT RUN 10 SER.#'d SETS
P4BOJA Kobe/Odm/Magic/KAJ 250.00 500.00
P4BWWH Bib/Webb/Wlkns/Hrfrd 100.00 200.00
P4PGBP Pierce/KG/Bird/RP 200.00 400.00
P4WBPJ West/Bges/Paul/LJ 150.00 300.00

2008-09 Upper Deck Premier Franchise Faces Autographs

STATED PRINT RUN 25 TO 50 SER.#'d SETS
UNPRICED SILVER PRINT RUN ONE SET
FFAD Adrian Dantley/50 8.00 20.00
FFAH Al Horford/25 6.00 15.00
FFAM Alonzo Mourning/25 30.00 60.00
FFCW Chet Walker/25 6.00 15.00
FFGI Artis Gilmore/50 8.00 20.00
FFJO Michael Jordan/25 300.00 450.00
FFKB Kobe Bryant/25 175.00 300.00
FFKD Kevin Durant/25 125.00 250.00
FFKG Kevin Garnett/25 75.00 150.00
FFLJ LeBron James/25 175.00 350.00
FFSW Spud Webb/25 6.00 15.00
FFTP Tony Parker/25 8.00 20.00
FFWF Walt Frazier/25 10.00 25.00

2008-09 Upper Deck Premier Head to Head Autographs Jerseys

STATED PRINT RUN 25 SER.#'d SETS
H2HBJ L.James/K.Bryant 300.00 600.00
H2HBK A.Bynum/C.Kaman 20.00 40.00
H2HGB R.Gay/S.Battier 15.00 30.00
H2HHH D.Howard/A.Horford 25.00 50.00
H2HJA A.Jefferson/L.Aldridge 20.00 40.00
H2HMC T.Chandler/B.Miller 15.00 30.00
H2HWB L.Walton/B.Bowen 15.00 30.00

2008-09 Upper Deck Premier Impressions Autographs

STATED PRINT RUN 50 SER.#'d SETS
UNPRICED SILVER PRINT RUN ONE SET
PIAA Alexis Ajinca 3.00 8.00
PIAR Anthony Randolph 3.00 8.00
PIBL Brook Lopez 6.00 15.00
PIBR Brandon Rush 4.00 10.00
PIDG Danilo Gallinari 12.50 30.00
PIDW D.J. White 4.00 10.00
PIGH George Hill 5.00 12.00
PIJA Joe Alexander 3.00 8.00
PIJB Jerryd Bayless 4.00 10.00
PIJH J.J. Hickson 4.00 10.00
PIJM Javale McGee 6.00 15.00
PIJT Jason Thompson 3.00 8.00
PIMC Mario Chalmers 5.00 12.00
PIMS Marreese Speights 4.00 10.00
PIRA Ryan Anderson 4.00 10.00
PIRH Roy Hibbert 12.50 30.00
PIRL Robin Lopez 5.00 12.00
PIRW Russell Westbrook 50.00 125.00

2008-09 Upper Deck Premier Pairings Autographs

STATED PRINT RUN 25 SER.#'d SETS
P2AR L.Aldridge/B.Roy 15.00 40.00
P2DJ L.James/K.Durant 300.00 500.00
P2FR W.Frazier/M.Richardson 15.00 30.00
P2GB K.Bryant/K.Garnett 225.00 325.00
P2GC R.Gay/M.Conley 15.00 30.00
P2HH A.Horford/T.Horford 10.00 25.00
P2JJ M.Jordan/L.James 500.00 800.00
P2JW A.Jamison/D.West 10.00 25.00
P2ML M.Bogues/L.Johnson 50.00 100.00
P2PA R.Allen/P.Pierce 50.00 120.00
P2PS J.Salley/T.Prince 15.00 30.00
P2SD K.Smith/C.Drexler 20.00 40.00
P2SV J.Smith/S.Vujacic 10.00 25.00

2008-09 Upper Deck Premier Penmanship Autographs

STATED PRINT RUN 50 SER.#'d SETS
UNPRICED SILVER PRINT RUN ONE SET
PENAE Alex English 5.00 12.00
PENAH Al Harrington 5.00 12.00
PENBD Bob Dandridge 8.00 20.00
PENBL Bob Lanier 6.00 15.00
PENBM Brad Miller 5.00 12.00
PENCH Cliff Hagan 8.00 20.00
PENCK Chris Kaman 5.00 12.00
PENDA Brad Daugherty 5.00 12.00
PENDF Derek Fisher 6.00 15.00
PENDO Don Ohl 8.00 20.00
PENDR Dennis Rodman 40.00 100.00
PENDV Dick Van Arsdale 6.00 15.00
PENEM Ed Macauley 6.00 15.00
PENGI Artis Gilmore 10.00 25.00
PENGR Glen Rice 20.00 40.00
PENHO Tito Horford 5.00 12.00
PENJP Jim Paxson 6.00 15.00
PENKB Kobe Bryant 150.00 400.00
PENLH Lou Hudson 5.00 12.00
PENPA John Paxson 10.00 25.00
PENPF Phil Ford 6.00 15.00
PENRG Richie Guerin 15.00 40.00
PENRH Rod Hundley 25.00 50.00
PENRS Ralph Sampson 6.00 15.00
PENSJ Sam Jones 15.00 30.00
PENSM Slater Martin 10.00 25.00
PENTC Terry Cummings 6.00 15.00
PENTD Terry Dischinger 8.00 20.00
PENTR Tree Rollins 6.00 15.00

2008-09 Upper Deck Premier Preeminence Autographs

STATED PRINT RUN 25 SER.#'d SETS
UNPRICED SILVER PRINT RUN ONE SET
PEAB Andrew Bynum 20.00 40.00
PEAD Adrian Dantley 6.00 15.00
PEAG Artis Gilmore 8.00 20.00
PEAH Al Horford 6.00 15.00
PEAJ Al Jefferson 6.00 15.00
PEAL Joe Alexander 6.00 15.00
PEAT Al Thornton 6.00 15.00
PEBA B.J. Armstrong 8.00 20.00
PEBR Brandon Roy 25.00 50.00
PECW Chet Walker 6.00 15.00
PEDC Daequan Cook 6.00 15.00
PEDW David West 6.00 15.00
PEEG Eric Gordon 20.00 50.00
PEJA Antawn Jamison 6.00 15.00
PEJO Michael Jordan 300.00 550.00
PEKB Kobe Bryant 125.00 250.00
PEKD Kevin Durant 125.00 250.00
PEKG Kevin Garnett 50.00 120.00
PELE LeBron James 150.00 300.00
PELJ Larry Johnson 30.00 60.00
PELW Luke Walton 10.00 25.00
PEMP Mark Price 35.00 70.00
PEMR Micheal Ray Richardson 6.00 15.00
PEPM Paul Millsap 6.00 15.00
PERG Rudy Gay 6.00 15.00
PERJ Richard Jefferson 6.00 15.00
PERS Ramon Sessions 6.00 15.00
PERU Brandon Rush 6.00 15.00
PESK Steve Kerr 10.00 25.00
PESV Sasha Vujacic 8.00 20.00
PESW Spud Webb 8.00 20.00
PETK Toni Kukoc 20.00 40.00
PETP Tayshaun Prince 8.00 20.00

2008-09 Upper Deck Premier Rare Patch Dual

STATED PRINT RUN 15 TO 50 SER.#'d SETS
RP2AW L.James/Anthony/50 30.00 80.00
RP2BD K.Bryant/Durant/50 25.00 60.00
RP2BJ L.James/Bryant/50 50.00 125.00
RP2CM Martin/V.Carter/40 10.00 25.00
RP2DO O'Neal/Duncan/50 10.00 25.00
RP2EW B.Wright/Ellis/50 8.00 20.00
RP2GG Garnett/P.Gasol/50 15.00 40.00
RP2GN Nowitzki/Garnett/50 15.00 40.00
RP2GT Gordon/Thomas/50 8.00 20.00
RP2HW G.Hill/L.Walton/50 25.00 60.00
RP2IA Iverson/Anthony/50 15.00 30.00
RP2IB Iguodala/Brewer/50 8.00 20.00
RP2JA Aldridge/Jefferson/50 8.00 20.00
RP2JD K.Durant/L.James/50 30.00 60.00
RP2LM R.Lewis/S.Marion/15 15.00 30.00
RP2MB A.Bogut/D.Mason/50 8.00 20.00
RP2MP P.Gasol/Ginobili/50 10.00 25.00
RP2MS Zo/Stoudemire/50 15.00 30.00
RP2NG J.Green/J.Noah/50 8.00 20.00
RP2NP S.Nash/C.Paul/30 20.00 40.00
RP2PA P.Pierce/R.Allen/50 15.00 30.00
RP2RB A.Bogut/M.Redd/50 8.00 20.00
RP2RC Q.Rich/E.Curry/50 8.00 20.00
RP2SH Stoudemire/Howard/50 15.00 30.00
RP2TH J.Terry/J.Howard/50 8.00 20.00
RP2WJ Garnett/L.James/50 20.00 50.00
RP2YW B.Wright/T.Young/50 8.00 20.00

2008-09 Upper Deck Premier Rare Patch Rookies Dual

STATED PRINT RUN 25 SER.#'d SETS
R2RAG E.Gordon/D.Augustin 10.00 25.00
R2RAK K.Koufos/D.Arthur 6.00 15.00
R2RAL R.Anderson/C.Lee 15.00 40.00
R2RBL M.Beasley/K.Love 10.00 25.00
R2RBR D.Rose/M.Beasley 25.00 50.00
R2RDS W.Sharpe/J.Dorsey 6.00 15.00
R2RDW K.Weaver/C.D.Roberts 8.00 20.00
R2RGB E.Gordon/J.Bayless 8.00 20.00
R2RGH G.Hill/D.Greene 8.00 20.00
R2RJE D.Jordan/P.Ewing Jr. 6.00 15.00
R2RLL B.Lopez/R.Lopez 10.00 25.00
R2RMR D.Rose/O.Mayo 20.00 50.00
R2RRT J.Thompson/Randolph 10.00 25.00

2008-09 Upper Deck Premier Rare Patch Rookies Triple

STATED PRINT RUN 15 SER.#'d SETS
R3RABJ Beasley/Augustin/Jordan 20.00 40.00
R3RABM Beasley/Augustin/McGee 10.00 25.00
R3RARB Augustin/Bayless/Rush 8.00 20.00
R3RBLK Love/Bayless/Koufos 8.00 20.00
R3RBWW Bayless/Weaver/Weems 8.00 20.00
R3RGEA Alexander/Greene/Ewing Jr. 8.00 20.00
R3RGGT Thompson/Gordon/Greene 8.00 20.00
R3RGLA Love/Gordon/Alexander 15.00 40.00
R3RHAS Alexander/Hickson/Sharpe 8.00 20.00
R3RLDA Lopez/Anderson/Douglas-Roberts 8.00
20.00
R3RMBL Mayo/Love/Bayless 10.00 25.00
R3RMBR Rose/Beasley/Mayo 30.00 60.00
R3RMEH Mayo/Hill/Ewing Jr. 10.00 25.00
R3RRAC Rush/Arthur/Chalmers 10.00 25.00
R3RRDD Rose/Dorsey/D-Roberts 25.00 50.00
R3RRDS Rose/Sharpe/Dorsey 20.00 40.00
R3RRLT Lopez/Thmpsn/Rndlph 15.00 30.00
R3RRWS Speight/Rndlph/Weems 15.00 30.00
R3RWAL Lopez/Anderson/Weaver 10.00 25.00

2008-09 Upper Deck Premier Rare Patch Triple

STATED PRINT RUN 10 TO 15 SER.#'d SETS
RPTBGJ James/Bryant/Garnett 80.00 160.00
RPTBOG Bryant/Gasol/Odom 40.00 80.00
RPTDGR Duncan/Gnbli/D.Rob 60.00 120.00
RPTDLT Thomas/Lmbr/Dmrs 30.00 60.00
RPTHDG Hinrich/Deng/Gordon 15.00 30.00
RPTHMS Stcktn/Malone/Hrnck 40.00 80.00
RPTIMA Ivrsn/Anthony/Martin 20.00 50.00
RPTJAW Bosh/Anthony/LJ/10 40.00 80.00
RPTJBJ James/Jordan/Bryant 125.00 250.00
RPTJPR MJ/Pippen/Rodman 225.00 325.00
RPTKNH Nwtzki/Howard/Kidd 15.00 30.00
RPTNDH Durant/Horford/Noah 20.00 50.00
RPTNSO Stdmre/O'Neal/Nash 60.00 120.00
RPTPAG Allen/Garnett/Pierce 60.00 120.00
RPTWJG Ilgsks/James/Gibson 30.00 80.00
RPTWMW Wilkins/Webb/Malone 15.00 30.00

2008-09 Upper Deck Premier Rare Remnants Quad Patch

STATED PRINT RUN 5 TO 25 SER.#'d SETS
UNPRICED UD LOGO PRINT RUN 10 SETS
RR4AJ L.James/Anthony/25 25.00 50.00
RR4BD K.Bryant/Durant/25 30.00 80.00
RR4BF C.Boozer/Frye/25 8.00 20.00
RR4BJ L.James/Bryant/25 60.00 120.00
RR4BK Kirilenko/Battier/25 6.00 15.00
RR4CM K.Martin/V.Carter/25 15.00 30.00
RR4DD Davidson/Dudley/25 6.00 15.00
RR4GG Garnett/P.Gasol/25 15.00 40.00
RR4GN Nowitzki/Garnett/25 30.00 60.00
RR4GT Gordon/Thomas/25 8.00 20.00
RR4HD Hinrich/L.Deng/25 8.00 20.00
RR4HW G.Hill/L.Walton/15 60.00 120.00
RR4IA Iverson/Anthony/25 15.00 30.00
RR4IB Iguodala/Brewer/25 6.00 15.00
RR4JD Durant/L.James/25 25.00 60.00
RR4JS J.Johnson/J.Smith/25 8.00 20.00
RR4KP T.Parker/J.Kidd/25 10.00 25.00
RR4LM R.Lewis/Marion/25 10.00 25.00
RR4MB Bogut/D.Mason/25 6.00 15.00
RR4MH Mutombo/Howard/25 12.00 30.00
RR4MS Zo/Stoudemire/25 20.00 40.00
RR4MW Maggette/Wright/25 6.00 15.00
RR4NP S.Nash/C.Paul/25 20.00 40.00
RR4NS J.Smith/J.Noah/25 10.00 25.00
RR4PA Pierce/R.Allen/25 15.00 30.00
RR4PM P.Gasol/Ginobili/25 15.00 30.00
RR4RC Q.Rich/E.Curry/25 6.00 15.00
RR4TH J.Terry/J.Howard/25 6.00 15.00
RR4WM Martin/R.Wallace/25 6.00 15.00
RR4YW B.Wright/T.Young/25 6.00 15.00

2008-09 Upper Deck Premier Rare Remnants Triple Patch

STATED PRINT RUN 35 TO 50 SER.#'d SETS
RR3AI Allen Iverson 8.00 20.00
RR3AJ Al Jefferson 5.00 12.00
RR3AK Andrei Kirilenko 5.00 12.00
RR3BG Ben Gordon 5.00 12.00
RR3BR Brandon Roy 6.00 15.00
RR3BU Caron Butler 5.00 12.00
RR3BW Brandan Wright 5.00 12.00
RR3CB Carlos Boozer/35 5.00 12.00
RR3CM Corey Maggette 5.00 12.00
RR3DG Danny Granger 5.00 12.00
RR3DM Dikembe Mutombo 8.00 20.00
RR3DN Dirk Nowitzki 8.00 20.00
RR3EB Elton Brand 6.00 15.00
RR3GH Grant Hill 20.00 40.00
RR3IG Andre Iguodala 5.00 12.00
RR3JA Antawn Jamison 5.00 12.00
RR3JK Jason Kidd 6.00 15.00
RR3JN Joakim Noah 5.00 12.00
RR3JT Jason Terry 5.00 12.00
RR3KA Kelenna Azubuike 4.00 10.00
RR3KB Kobe Bryant 25.00 50.00
RR3KD Kevin Durant 15.00 40.00
RR3KG Kevin Garnett 10.00 25.00
RR3KH Kirk Hinrich 5.00 12.00
RR3KK Kyle Korver 5.00 12.00
RR3KM Kenyon Martin 5.00 12.00
RR3LD Luol Deng 5.00 12.00
RR3LJ LeBron James 25.00 50.00
RR3LW Luke Walton 4.00 10.00
RR3MA Kevin Martin 5.00 12.00
RR3MC Mike Conley Jr. 5.00 12.00
RR3MG Manu Ginobili 6.00 15.00
RR3MR Michael Redd 5.00 12.00
RR3PG Pau Gasol 6.00 15.00
RR3PS Peja Stojakovic 6.00 15.00
RR3RA Ray Allen 8.00 20.00
RR3RL Rashard Lewis 5.00 12.00
RR3RW Rasheed Wallace 6.00 15.00
RR3SM Shawn Marion 5.00 12.00
RR3SN Steve Nash 6.00 15.00
RR3SO Shaquille O'Neal 12.00 30.00
RR3TD Tim Duncan 10.00 25.00
RR3TM Tracy McGrady 6.00 15.00
RR3VC Vince Carter 8.00 20.00

2008-09 Upper Deck Premier Rare Remnants Triple Patch NBA Logo

*NBA LOGO: .5X TO 1.25X BASE HI
STATED PRINT RUN 25 SER.#'d SETS
RR3AB Andrea Bargnani 6.00 15.00
RR3AH Al Harrington 6.00 15.00
RR3AS Amare Stoudemire 6.00 15.00
RR3CA Carmelo Anthony 10.00 25.00
RR3DH Dwight Howard 6.00 15.00
RR3GH Grant Hill 40.00 80.00
RR3GI Daniel Gibson 6.00 15.00
RR3JH Josh Howard 6.00 15.00
RR3JJ Joe Johnson 6.00 15.00
RR3JR Jason Richardson 8.00 20.00
RR3PP Paul Pierce 10.00 25.00
RR3SB Shane Battier 6.00 15.00
RR3TT Tyrus Thomas 5.00 12.00

2008-09 Upper Deck Premier Remnants Quad

STATED PRINT RUN 50 SER.#'d SETS
*CONFERENCE: .4X TO 1X BASE HI
CONFERENCE PRINT RUN 25 SETS
UNPRICED INITIAL PRINT RUN 10 SETS
PR4AR A.Bogut/R.Jefferson 4.00 10.00
PR4BD K.Bryant/K.Durant 25.00 60.00
PR4BF C.Boozer/C.Frye 4.00 10.00
PR4BJ L.James/K.Bryant 30.00 60.00
PR4BP C.Billups/C.Paul 6.00 15.00
PR4BW J.Boone/S.Williams 4.00 10.00
PR4DB B.Davis/C.Billups 4.00 10.00
PR4DD J.Davidson/J.Dudley 4.00 10.00
PR4EC V.Carter/J.Erving 10.00 25.00
PR4FB A.Bynum/J.Farmar 10.00 25.00
PR4FR W.Frazier/M.Richardson 5.00 12.00
PR4GC R.Gay/M.Conley 4.00 10.00
PR4GT B.Gordon/T.Thomas 4.00 10.00
PR4HH D.Howard/A.Horford 5.00 12.00
PR4HL A.Law/A.Horford 4.00 10.00
PR4IB A.Iguodala/C.Brewer 4.00 10.00
PR4JA L.Aldridge/A.Jefferson 4.00 10.00
PR4JB M.Jordan/K.Bryant 50.00 100.00
PR4JD K.Durant/L.James 25.00 50.00
PR4JH A.Jamison/A.Harrington 4.00 10.00
PR4JR O.Robertson/M.Jordan 25.00 60.00
PR4KW B.Walton/C.Kaman 4.00 10.00
PR4LB C.Landry/A.Brooks 6.00 15.00
PR4LM R.Lewis/S.Marion 4.00 10.00
PR4MA T.McGrady/C.Anthony 6.00 15.00
PR4MG C.Mullin/D.Gibson 4.00 10.00
PR4ML M.Johnson/L.Bird 25.00 60.00
PR4MO Y.Ming/E.Okafor 5.00 12.00
PR4MS A.Mourning/Amare 8.00 20.00
PR4MT C.Maggette/A.Thornton 4.00 10.00
PR4ND G.Davis/J.Noah 6.00 15.00
PR4NK S.Nash/J.Kidd 10.00 25.00
PR4NP S.Nash/C.Paul 10.00 25.00
PR4PA P.Pierce/R.Allen 10.00 25.00
PR4RC Q.Richardson/E.Curry 4.00 10.00
PR4RJ O.Robertson/L.James 25.00 50.00
PR4RM D.Rodman/M.Malone 6.00 15.00
PR4WG D.Griffith/D.Williams 4.00 10.00
PR4WR B.Roy/D.Williams 6.00 15.00

2008-09 Upper Deck Premier Remnants Triple

STATED PRINT RUN 99 SER.#'d SETS
PR3AB Andrew Bynum 2.00 5.00
PR3AM Alonzo Mourning 6.00 15.00
PR3AS Amare Stoudemire 2.50 6.00
PR3AT Al Thornton 2.50 6.00
PR3BD Baron Davis 2.50 6.00
PR3BR Brandon Roy 3.00 8.00
PR3CA Carmelo Anthony 4.00 10.00
PR3CB Chauncey Billups 3.00 8.00
PR3CM Corey Maggette 2.50 6.00
PR3CP Chris Paul 4.00 10.00
PR3DG Darrell Griffith 2.00 5.00
PR3DH Dwight Howard 2.50 6.00
PR3DR Dennis Rodman 8.00 20.00
PR3DW Deron Williams 2.50 6.00
PR3HO Hakeem Olajuwon 6.00 15.00
PR3JE Julius Erving 5.00 12.00
PR3JK Jason Kidd 3.00 8.00
PR3JO Michael Jordan 30.00 80.00
PR3KB Kobe Bryant 12.00 30.00
PR3KD Kevin Durant 8.00 20.00
PR3KG Kevin Garnett 5.00 12.00
PR3LB Larry Bird/89 8.00 20.00
PR3LJ LeBron James 12.00 30.00
PR3MJ Magic Johnson 8.00 20.00
PR3MU Chris Mullin 3.00 8.00
PR3ON Jermaine O'Neal 2.50 6.00
PR3OR Oscar Robertson 6.00 15.00
PR3PE Patrick Ewing 6.00 15.00
PR3PP Paul Pierce 3.00 8.00
PR3RA Ray Allen 3.00 8.00
PR3RJ Richard Jefferson 2.50 6.00
PR3RR Rajon Rondo 3.00 8.00
PR3SM Shawn Marion 2.50 6.00
PR3SN Steve Nash 3.00 8.00
PR3TM Tracy McGrady 3.00 8.00
PR3VC Vince Carter 4.00 10.00
PR3WF Walt Frazier 3.00 8.00
PR3YM Yao Ming 4.00 10.00

2008-09 Upper Deck Premier Remnants Triple City

STATED PRINT RUN 50 SER.#'d SETS
PR3AB Andrew Bynum 2.50 6.00
PR3AH Al Horford 4.00 10.00
PR3AI Andre Iguodala 3.00 8.00
PR3AJ Antawn Jamison 3.00 8.00
PR3AL Acie Law 3.00 8.00
PR3AM Alonzo Mourning 8.00 20.00
PR3AS Amare Stoudemire 3.00 8.00
PR3AT Al Thornton 3.00 8.00
PR3BD Baron Davis 3.00 8.00
PR3BG Ben Gordon 3.00 8.00
PR3BO Carlos Boozer 3.00 8.00
PR3BR Brandon Roy 4.00 10.00
PR3CA Carmelo Anthony 5.00 12.00
PR3CB Chauncey Billups 4.00 10.00
PR3CL Carl Landry 2.50 6.00
PR3CM Corey Maggette 3.00 8.00
PR3CP Chris Paul 5.00 12.00
PR3DG Darrell Griffith 2.50 6.00
PR3DH Dwight Howard 3.00 8.00
PR3DR Dennis Rodman 10.00 25.00
PR3DW Deron Williams 3.00 8.00
PR3HO Hakeem Olajuwon 8.00 20.00
PR3JE Julius Erving 6.00 15.00
PR3JF Al Jefferson 3.00 8.00
PR3JK Jason Kidd 4.00 10.00
PR3JO Michael Jordan 40.00 100.00
PR3KB Kobe Bryant 15.00 40.00
PR3KD Kevin Durant 20.00 50.00
PR3KG Kevin Garnett 6.00 15.00
PR3LA LaMarcus Aldridge 4.00 10.00
PR3LB Larry Bird 10.00 25.00
PR3LJ LeBron James 15.00 40.00
PR3MC Mike Conley Jr. 3.00 8.00
PR3MJ Magic Johnson 10.00 25.00
PR3MU Chris Mullin 4.00 10.00
PR3ON Jermaine O'Neal 3.00 8.00
PR3OR Oscar Robertson 8.00 20.00
PR3PE Patrick Ewing 8.00 20.00
PR3PP Paul Pierce 4.00 10.00
PR3QR Quentin Richardson 3.00 8.00
PR3RA Ray Allen 5.00 12.00
PR3RG Rudy Gay 4.00 10.00
PR3RJ Richard Jefferson 3.00 8.00
PR3RR Rajon Rondo 4.00 10.00
PR3SM Shawn Marion 3.00 8.00
PR3SN Steve Nash 4.00 10.00
PR3TM Tracy McGrady 4.00 10.00
PR3VC Vince Carter 5.00 12.00
PR3WF Walt Frazier 4.00 10.00
PR3YM Yao Ming 5.00 12.00

2008-09 Upper Deck Premier Remnants Triple Position

PRINT RUN 25 SER.#'d SETS
PR3AB Andrew Bynum 3.00 8.00
PR3AH Al Horford 5.00 12.00
PR3AI Andre Iguodala 4.00 10.00
PR3AJ Antawn Jamison 4.00 10.00
PR3AL Acie Law 4.00 10.00
PR3AM Alonzo Mourning 15.00 30.00
PR3AS Amare Stoudemire 4.00 10.00
PR3AT Al Thornton 4.00 10.00
PR3BD Baron Davis 4.00 10.00
PR3BG Ben Gordon 4.00 10.00
PR3BO Carlos Boozer 4.00 10.00
PR3BR Brandon Roy 5.00 12.00
PR3CA Carmelo Anthony 6.00 15.00
PR3CB Chauncey Billups 5.00 12.00
PR3CL Carl Landry 3.00 8.00
PR3CM Corey Maggette 4.00 10.00
PR3CP Chris Paul 6.00 15.00
PR3DG Darrell Griffith 3.00 8.00
PR3DH Dwight Howard 4.00 10.00
PR3DR Dennis Rodman 12.00 30.00
PR3DW Deron Williams 4.00 10.00
PR3HO Hakeem Olajuwon 10.00 25.00
PR3JE Julius Erving 8.00 20.00
PR3JF Al Jefferson 4.00 10.00
PR3JK Jason Kidd 5.00 12.00
PR3JO Michael Jordan 60.00 150.00
PR3KB Kobe Bryant 20.00 50.00
PR3KD Kevin Durant 12.00 30.00
PR3KG Kevin Garnett 8.00 20.00
PR3LA LaMarcus Aldridge 5.00 12.00
PR3LB Larry Bird 12.00 30.00
PR3LJ LeBron James 20.00 50.00
PR3MC Mike Conley Jr. 4.00 10.00
PR3MJ Magic Johnson 12.00 30.00
PR3MU Chris Mullin 5.00 12.00
PR3ON Jermaine O'Neal 4.00 10.00
PR3OR Oscar Robertson 10.00 25.00
PR3PE Patrick Ewing 10.00 25.00
PR3PP Paul Pierce 5.00 12.00
PR3QR Quentin Richardson 4.00 10.00
PR3RA Ray Allen 5.00 12.00
PR3RG Rudy Gay 5.00 12.00
PR3RJ Richard Jefferson 4.00 10.00
PR3RR Rajon Rondo 5.00 12.00
PR3SM Shawn Marion 4.00 10.00
PR3SN Steve Nash 5.00 12.00
PR3TM Tracy McGrady 5.00 12.00
PR3VC Vince Carter 6.00 15.00
PR3WF Walt Frazier 5.00 12.00
PR3YM Yao Ming 6.00 15.00

2008-09 Upper Deck Premier Rookies Autographs Jerseys 75

STATED PRINT RUN 75 SER.#'d SETS
UNPRICED JERSEY 15 PRINT RUN 15 SETS
UNPRICED JERSEY 1 PRINT RUN ONE SET
101 Derrick Rose 60.00 150.00
102 Michael Beasley 5.00 12.00
103 O.J. Mayo 5.00 12.00
104 Russell Westbrook 150.00 400.00
105 Kevin Love 50.00 120.00
106 Patrick Ewing Jr. 3.00 8.00
107 Eric Gordon 10.00 25.00
108 Joe Alexander 3.00 8.00
109 D.J. Augustin 4.00 10.00
110 Brook Lopez 6.00 15.00
111 Jerryd Bayless 4.00 10.00
112 Jason Thompson 3.00 8.00
113 Brandon Rush 4.00 10.00
114 Anthony Randolph 3.00 8.00
115 Robin Lopez 5.00 12.00
116 Marreese Speights 4.00 10.00
117 Chris Douglas-Roberts 3.00 8.00
118 Javale McGee 6.00 15.00
119 J.J. Hickson 4.00 10.00
120 Ryan Anderson 4.00 10.00
121 Kosta Koufos 4.00 10.00
122 George Hill 6.00 15.00
123 Darrell Arthur 4.00 10.00
124 Donte Greene 3.00 8.00
125 Sonny Weems 3.00 8.00
126 J.R. Giddens 3.00 8.00
127 Walter Sharpe 3.00 8.00
128 Joey Dorsey 3.00 8.00
129 Mario Chalmers 5.00 12.00
130 DeAndre Jordan 6.00 15.00

2008-09 Upper Deck Premier Stitchings

STATED PRINT RUN 50 SER.#'d SETS
*STITCH 25: .5X TO 1.25X BASE
STITCH 5 UNPRICED DUE TO SCARCITY
STITCH 1 UNPRICED DUE TO SCARCITY
AUTO 5 UNPRICED DUE TO SCARCITY
AUTO 1 UNPRICED DUE TO SCARCITY
PSAC Austin Carr 6.00 15.00
PSAH Al Horford 6.00 15.00
PSAI Allen Iverson 15.00 30.00
PSAM Alonzo Mourning 15.00 30.00
PSAS Amare Stoudemire 6.00 15.00
PSAT Al Thornton 6.00 15.00
PSBB Bill Bradley 6.00 15.00
PSBC Billy Cunningham 15.00 30.00
PSBP Bob Pettit 6.00 15.00
PSBR Bill Russell 20.00 40.00
PSBS Bill Sharman 15.00 30.00
PSBW Bill Walton 8.00 20.00
PSCA Carmelo Anthony 6.00 15.00
PSCD Clyde Drexler 10.00 25.00
PSCM Calvin Murphy 6.00 15.00
PSCO Bob Cousy 8.00 20.00
PSCP Chris Paul 6.00 15.00
PSDA D.J. Augustin 6.00 15.00
PSDB Dave Bing 10.00 25.00
PSDC Dave Cowens 10.00 25.00
PSDD Dave DeBusschere 6.00 15.00
PSDE Dennis Rodman 20.00 50.00
PSDG Darrell Griffith 6.00 15.00
PSDH Dwight Howard 10.00 25.00
PSDN Dirk Nowitzki 10.00 25.00
PSDR David Robinson 10.00 25.00
PSDS Dolph Schayes 10.00 25.00
PSDT David Thompson 10.00 25.00
PSDW Dominique Wilkins 8.00 20.00
PSEB Elgin Baylor 6.00 15.00
PSEG Eric Gordon 8.00 20.00
PSEH Elvin Hayes 6.00 15.00
PSEM Earl Monroe 6.00 15.00
PSGA Danilo Gallinari 6.00 15.00
PSGG George Gervin 8.00 20.00
PSGH Grant Hill 30.00 60.00
PSGM George Mikan 15.00 30.00
PSGO Greg Oden 6.00 15.00
PSHG Hal Greer 6.00 15.00
PSHO Hakeem Olajuwon 8.00 20.00
PSIT Isiah Thomas 6.00 15.00
PSJA LeBron James 25.00 50.00
PSJB Jerryd Bayless 6.00 15.00
PSJD Joe Dumars 8.00 20.00
PSJE Julius Erving 15.00 40.00
PSJH John Havlicek 8.00 20.00
PSJK Jason Kidd 8.00 20.00
PSJL Jerry Lucas 8.00 20.00
PSJO Michael Jordan 60.00 150.00
PSJS John Stockton 15.00 30.00
PSJW James Worthy 6.00 15.00
PSKA Kareem Abdul-Jabbar 10.00 25.00
PSKB Kobe Bryant 25.00 50.00
PSKD Kevin Durant 12.00 30.00
PSKG Kevin Garnett 15.00 30.00
PSKL Kevin Love 8.00 20.00
PSKM Karl Malone 8.00 20.00
PSLB Larry Bird 15.00 30.00
PSLJ Larry Johnson 15.00 40.00
PSLW Lenny Wilkens 6.00 15.00
PSMB Michael Beasley 8.00 20.00
PSMC Kevin McHale 10.00 25.00
PSMJ Magic Johnson 15.00 40.00
PSMM Moses Malone 6.00 15.00
PSMU Chris Mullin 6.00 15.00
PSNA Nate Archibald 10.00 25.00
PSNT Nate Thurmond 8.00 20.00
PSOA Charles Oakley 6.00 15.00
PSOM O.J. Mayo 8.00 20.00
PSOR Oscar Robertson 6.00 15.00
PSPE Patrick Ewing 10.00 25.00
PSPG Pau Gasol 10.00 25.00
PSPM Pete Maravich 20.00 50.00
PSPP Paul Pierce 15.00 30.00
PSPR Pat Riley 8.00 20.00
PSRA Ray Allen 6.00 15.00
PSRB Rick Barry 6.00 15.00
PSRD Derrick Rose 25.00 50.00
PSRO Brandon Roy 6.00 15.00
PSRP Robert Parish 8.00 20.00
PSRS Ralph Sampson 6.00 15.00
PSRW Russell Westbrook 10.00 25.00
PSSJ Sam Jones 10.00 25.00
PSSN Steve Nash 10.00 25.00
PSSO Shaquille O'Neal 15.00 30.00
PSSP Scottie Pippen 20.00 40.00
PSTD Tim Duncan 10.00 25.00
PSTM Tracy McGrady 6.00 15.00
PSVC Vince Carter 10.00 25.00
PSWA Dwyane Wade 8.00 20.00
PSWC Wilt Chamberlain 12.00 30.00
PSWE Jerry West 15.00 30.00
PSWF Walt Frazier 6.00 15.00
PSWR Willis Reed 8.00 20.00
PSWU Wes Unseld 6.00 15.00
PSR08 Rose/Beasley/Mayo 15.00 40.00
PSBBOY Thms/Rod/Lmbr/Dms 8.00 20.00
PSBSTN Bird/Russ/Hav/Csy 20.00 40.00
PSSHOW Magic/KAJ/Wrty/Coop 12.00 30.00

2008-09 Upper Deck Premier Trios Autographs

STATED PRINT RUN 15 SER.#'d SETS
P3TD Westbrk/Drnt/White 175.00 350.00
P3BLA Beasley/Love/Alxndr 10.00 25.00
P3BVB Brynt/Bynum/Vujacic 125.00 250.00
P3HDS Durant/Hrfrd/Scola 75.00 150.00
P3IND Rush/Granger/Hibbrt 30.00 60.00
P3JJJ MJ/Magic/James 500.00 800.00
P3LRD Laimbr/Rdmn/Dntley 50.00 100.00
P3MEM Rose/Dorsey/D.Rbrts 60.00 120.00
P3MTW Brewer/Love/Jffrsn 30.00 60.00
P3PAG Allen/Garnett/Pierce 175.00 350.00
P3RBM Rose/Beasley/Mayo 40.00 80.00
P3SHJ Amare/Hwrd/Jffrsn 40.00 80.00
P3WGA Westbrk/Grdn/D.J. 60.00 150.00
P3BLAZ Byless/Roy/Aldrdg 30.00 80.00
P3GRIZ Conley/Mayo/Gay 12.00 30.00
P3GTWN Zo/Hibbert/Ewing
P3HEAT Beasly/Chlmrs/Cook 40.00 100.00
P3UCLA Wstbrk/Love/Mbah 50.00 120.00

2004-05 Upper Deck Pro Sigs

Released in December 2004, this 120-card set features veteran players on cards 1-90 and rookie players on cards 91-120. This set is also referred to as Diamond Collection and is sometimes difficult to find the listing. Pro Sigs was packaged in 24-pack boxes where packs contained six cards a carried a SRP of $2.99.
COMP.SET w/o SP's 8.00 20.00
91-120 STATED ODDS 1:6
1 Antoine Walker .25 .60
2 Al Harrington .20 .50
3 Boris Diaw .20 .50
4 Paul Pierce .25 .60
5 Ricky Davis .20 .50
6 Gary Payton .25 .60
7 Jahidi White .15 .40
8 Jason Kapono .15 .40
9 Gerald Wallace .20 .50
10 Eddy Curry .15 .40
11 Kirk Hinrich .20 .50
12 Tyson Chandler .20 .50
13 LeBron James 1.50 4.00
14 Dajuan Wagner .15 .40
15 Drew Gooden .15 .40
16 Dirk Nowitzki .40 1.00
17 Michael Finley .25 .60
18 Jerry Stackhouse .25 .60
19 Carmelo Anthony .50 1.25
20 Andre Miller .20 .50
21 Kenyon Martin .20 .50
22 Chauncey Billups .25 .60
23 Rasheed Wallace .25 .60
24 Ben Wallace .25 .60
25 Derek Fisher .20 .50
26 Jason Richardson .20 .50
27 Mike Dunleavy .20 .50
28 Yao Ming .50 1.25
29 Jim Jackson .15 .40
30 Tracy McGrady .30 .75
31 Jermaine O'Neal .25 .60
32 Reggie Miller .25 .60
33 Ron Artest .20 .50
34 Elton Brand .25 .60
35 Corey Maggette .20 .50
36 Kerry Kittles .15 .40
37 Kobe Bryant 1.00 2.50
38 Chris Mihm .15 .40
39 Lamar Odom .20 .50
40 Pau Gasol .25 .60
41 Jason Williams .20 .50
42 Bonzi Wells .15 .40
43 Shaquille O'Neal .60 1.50
44 Dwyane Wade .40 1.00
45 Eddie Jones .20 .50
46 Michael Redd .20 .50
47 Desmond Mason .20 .50
48 T.J. Ford .15 .40
49 Latrell Sprewell .25 .60
50 Kevin Garnett .40 1.00
51 Sam Cassell .20 .50
52 Richard Jefferson .20 .50
53 Aaron Williams .15 .40
54 Jason Kidd .40 1.00
55 Jamal Mashburn .20 .50
56 Baron Davis .25 .60
57 Jamaal Magloire .15 .40
58 Allan Houston .20 .50
59 Jamal Crawford .25 .60
60 Stephon Marbury .25 .60
61 Cuttino Mobley .15 .40
62 Kelvin Cato .15 .40
63 Steve Francis .20 .50
64 Grant Hill .20 .50
65 Allen Iverson .40 1.00
66 Samuel Dalembert .15 .40
67 Amare Stoudemire .40 1.00
68 Steve Nash .30 .75
69 Shawn Marion .20 .50
70 Shareef Abdur-Rahim .20 .50
71 Damon Stoudamire .20 .50
72 Zach Randolph .20 .50
73 Peja Stojakovic .25 .60
74 Chris Webber .25 .60
75 Mike Bibby .25 .60
76 Tony Parker .25 .60
77 Tim Duncan .40 1.00
78 Manu Ginobili .30 .75
79 Ronald Murray .15 .40
80 Ray Allen .25 .60

81 Rashard Lewis .25 .60
82 Chris Bosh .25 .60
83 Vince Carter .40 1.00
84 Jalen Rose .20 .50
85 Andrei Kirilenko .20 .50
86 Carlos Boozer .20 .50
87 Carlos Arroyo .15 .40
88 Gilbert Arenas .20 .50
89 Jarvis Hayes .15 .40
90 Antawn Jamison .20 .50
91 Dwight Howard RC 2.00 5.00
92 Emeka Okafor RC .75 2.00
93 Ben Gordon RC 1.00 2.50
94 Shaun Livingston RC 1.00 2.50
95 Devin Harris RC .75 2.00
96 Josh Childress RC .75 2.00
97 Luol Deng RC 1.00 2.50
98 Rafael Araujo RC .60 1.50
99 Andre Iguodala RC 1.25 3.00
100 Luke Jackson RC .60 1.50
101 Andris Biedrins RC .60 1.50
102 Robert Swift RC .60 1.50
103 Sebastian Telfair RC .75 2.00
104 Kris Humphries RC 1.00 2.50
105 Al Jefferson RC 1.25 3.00
106 Kirk Snyder RC .60 1.50
107 Josh Smith RC 1.00 2.50
108 J.R. Smith RC 1.00 2.50
109 Dorell Wright RC 1.00 2.50
110 Jameer Nelson RC 1.00 2.50
111 Pavel Podkolzin RC .60 1.50
112 Viktor Khryapa RC .60 1.50
113 Sergei Monia RC .60 1.50
114 Delonte West RC 1.00 2.50
115 Tony Allen RC 1.00 2.50
116 Kevin Martin RC 1.25 3.00
117 Sasha Vujacic RC 1.00 2.50
118 Beno Udrih RC .75 2.00
119 David Harrison RC .60 1.50
120 Lionel Chalmers RC 1.00 2.50

2004-05 Upper Deck Pro Sigs Gold

*1-90 GOLD SINGLES: 2X TO 5X BASE HI
1-90 STATED ODDS 1:24
*91-120 GOLD RC's: 1.25X TO 3X BASE HI
91-120 PRINT RUN 100 SER.#'d SETS

2004-05 Upper Deck Pro Sigs Silver

*1-90 SILVER SINGLES: .75X TO 2X BASE HI
1-90 STATED ODDS 1:8
*91-120 SILVER RCs: .6X TO 1.5X BASE HI
91-120 RC STATED ODDS 1:24

2004-05 Upper Deck Pro Sigs Pro Signs

Inserted in packs at the rate of one in 170, this 58-card set is horizontally designed with player images on the left and sticker autographs on the right.
STATED ODDS 1:170
SP INFO PROVIDED BY UPPER DECK
AB Antonio Burks 4.00 10.00
AH Al Harrington 4.00 10.00
AK Andrei Kirilenko 6.00 15.00
AN Antonio McDyess SP 6.00 15.00
BB Brent Barry 5.00 12.00
BH Brandon Hunter 4.00 10.00
CE Cedric Maxwell 6.00 15.00
CL Clyde Drexler SP 20.00 50.00
CM Corey Maggette 4.00 10.00
CR Jamal Crawford 4.00 10.00
DD Dan Dickau 4.00 10.00
DJ Dahntay Jones 4.00 10.00
DY Dwyane Wade SP 50.00 100.00
FE Francisco Elson 4.00 10.00
GA Gilbert Arenas SP 8.00 20.00
GG Gordan Giricek 4.00 10.00
GR Glenn Robinson 4.00 10.00
GW Gerald Wallace 4.00 10.00
JB Jerome Beasley SP 4.00 10.00
JD Juan Dixon 4.00 10.00
JH Josh Howard 4.00 10.00
JJ James Jones 4.00 10.00
JM Jerome Moiso 4.00 10.00
JO Jon Barry 4.00 10.00
JS John Salley 6.00 15.00
JW Jamaal Wilkes 4.00 10.00
KB Kobe Bryant SP 100.00 200.00
KK Kyle Korver 5.00 12.00
KR Kareem Rush 4.00 10.00
LJ LeBron James SP 100.00 200.00
LO Lamar Odom SP 10.00 25.00
LR Luke Ridnour 6.00 15.00
MB Marcus Banks 4.00 10.00
MD Marquis Daniels 4.00 10.00
MI Darko Milicic SP 6.00 15.00
MP Mickael Pietrus 4.00 10.00
MW Maurice Williams 4.00 10.00
NH Nene 4.00 10.00
PB Primoz Brezec 4.00 10.00
RG Reece Gaines 4.00 10.00
RH Richard Hamilton 8.00 20.00
RM Reggie Miller SP 50.00 100.00
SB Steve Blake 4.00 10.00
TO Travis Outlaw 4.00 10.00
TS Theron Smith 4.00 10.00
WG Willie Green 4.00 10.00
WZ Wang Zhizhi 15.00 40.00
ZC Zarko Cabarkapa 4.00 10.00
ZO Zoran Planinic 4.00 10.00
ZP Zaza Pachulia 4.00 10.00

2004-05 Upper Deck Pro Sigs Pro Signs Gold

PRINT RUNS LISTED IN CHECKLIST
SOME NOT PRICED DUE TO SCARCITY
AK Andrei Kirilenko/47 8.00 20.00
BB Brent Barry/32 20.00 50.00
BH Brandon Hunter/56 5.00 12.00
CL Clyde Drexler/22 40.00 100.00
DJ Dahntay Jones/30 5.00 12.00
DM Desmond Mason/24 8.00 20.00
FE Francisco Elson/56 5.00 12.00
GR Glenn Robinson/31 6.00 15.00
JB Jerome Beasley/24 5.00 12.00
JB2 Jon Barry/20 5.00 12.00
JJ James Jones/33 5.00 12.00
JK Jason Kapono/25 5.00 12.00
JS John Salley/22 10.00 25.00
JW Jamaal Wilkes/52 6.00 15.00
KG Kevin Garnett/21 50.00 100.00
KK Kyle Korver/26 12.50 30.00
KR Kareem Rush/21 5.00 12.00
LJ LeBron James/23 250.00 500.00
MA Magic Johnson/32 75.00 150.00
MJ Michael Jordan/23 400.00 700.00
MS Mike Sweetney/50 5.00 12.00
MW Maurice Williams/25 5.00 12.00
NH Nene/31 8.00 20.00
PB Primoz Brezec/27 5.00 12.00
RH Richard Hamilton/32 12.50 30.00
RM Reggie Miller/31 40.00 100.00
WG Willie Green/33 5.00 12.00
ZP Zaza Pachulia/27 6.00 15.00

2004-05 Upper Deck Pro Sigs Pro Signs Rookies

Inserted in packs randomly at the rate of one in 30, this 42-card set parallels the design of the Pro Signs insert set but focuses on the rookies.
STATED ODDS 1:30
*GOLD: 1.25X TO 3X BASE HI
GOLD PRINT RUN 25 SER.#'d SETS
AE Andre Emmett 2.50 6.00
AI Andre Iguodala 5.00 12.00
AL Al Jefferson Big Al 5.00 12.00
AV Anderson Varejao 3.00 8.00
BG Ben Gordon 4.00 10.00
BI Andris Biedrins 2.50 6.00
BS Blake Stepp 4.00 10.00
BU Antonio Burks 3.00 8.00
CD Chris Duhon 4.00 10.00
DA David Harrison 2.50 6.00
DE Delonte West 4.00 10.00
DH Dwight Howard 25.00 60.00
DH Devin Harris 3.00 8.00
DO Dorell Wright 4.00 10.00
DS Donta Smith 2.50 6.00
HS Ha Seung-Jin 4.00 10.00
JC Josh Childress 3.00 8.00
JN Jameer Nelson 4.00 10.00
JR J.R. Smith 4.00 10.00
JR2 Justin Reed 2.50 6.00
JV Jackson Vroman 2.50 6.00
KH Kris Humphries 4.00 10.00
KM Kevin Martin 5.00 12.00
KS Kirk Snyder 2.50 6.00
LC Lionel Chalmers 4.00 10.00
LD Luol Deng 4.00 10.00
LU Luke Jackson 2.50 6.00
MF Matt Freije 3.00 8.00
PP Pavel Podkolzin 2.50 6.00
PR Peter John Ramos 2.50 6.00
PS Pape Sow 3.00 8.00
RA Rafael Araujo 2.50 6.00
RI Royal Ivey 3.00 8.00
RS Robert Swift 2.50 6.00
SL Shaun Livingston 4.00 10.00
ST Sebastian Telfair 3.00 8.00
SV Sasha Vujacic 4.00 10.00
TA Tony Allen 4.00 10.00
TP Tim Pickett 4.00 10.00
TR Trevor Ariza 4.00 10.00
UD Beno Udrih 3.00 8.00
VK Viktor Khryapa 2.50 6.00

2009 Upper Deck Prominent Cuts

COMPLETE SET (60) 30.00 60.00
3 Bill Bradley .40 1.00
4 Jim Bunning .40 1.00
37 Kevin Johnson .40 1.00
43 Kevin Garnett .60 1.50
45 LeBron James 2.00 5.00
47 Michael Jordan 4.00 10.00
60 Dave Bing .40 1.00

2000-01 Upper Deck Pros and Prospects

The 2000-01 Upper Deck Pros & Prospects product was released in September,2000 as a 120-card set. The base set features 90 veterans, and 30 rookies (each serial numbered to 999). Please note that the Kenyon Martin and Marcus Fizer rookies are jersey cards.
COMPLETE SET (120) 40.00 80.00
COMP.SET w/o RC (90) 10.00 25.00
RCs: PRINT RUN 999 SERIAL #'d SETS
1 Dikembe Mutombo .30 .75
2 Alan Henderson .20 .50
3 Jim Jackson .20 .50
4 Paul Pierce .30 .75
5 Kenny Anderson .25 .60
6 Antoine Walker .25 .60
7 Baron Davis .30 .75
8 Derrick Coleman .25 .60
9 David Wesley .20 .50
10 Elton Brand .30 .75
11 Ron Artest .30 .75
12 Hersey Hawkins .20 .50
13 Andre Miller .25 .60
14 Lamond Murray .20 .50
15 Shawn Kemp .30 .75
16 Michael Finley .30 .75
17 Dirk Nowitzki .50 1.25
18 Cedric Ceballos .20 .50
19 Antonio McDyess .25 .60
20 Nick Van Exel .25 .60
21 Raef LaFrentz .20 .50
22 Christian Laettner .25 .60
23 Jerry Stackhouse .25 .60
24 Lindsey Hunter .20 .50
25 Antawn Jamison .30 .75
26 Larry Hughes .25 .60
27 Chris Mills .20 .50
28 Steve Francis .25 .60
29 Hakeem Olajuwon .40 1.00
30 Shandon Anderson .20 .50
31 Reggie Miller .30 .75
32 Jonathan Bender .20 .50
33 Jalen Rose .25 .60
34 Lamar Odom .25 .60
35 Michael Olowokandi .20 .50
36 Tyrone Nesby .30 .75
37 Kobe Bryant 1.25 3.00
38 Shaquille O'Neal .75 2.00
39 Ron Harper .25 .60
40 Robert Horry .25 .60
41 Alonzo Mourning .40 1.00
42 P.J. Brown .20 .50
43 Jamal Mashburn .25 .60
44 Ray Allen .30 .75
45 Glenn Robinson .25 .60
46 Sam Cassell .25 .60
47 Kevin Garnett .50 1.25
48 Wally Szczerbiak .25 .60
49 Terrell Brandon .20 .50
50 William Avery .20 .50
51 Stephon Marbury .25 .60
52 Keith Van Horn .25 .60
53 Kerry Kittles .20 .50
54 Latrell Sprewell .25 .60
55 Allan Houston .25 .60
56 Patrick Ewing .40 1.00
57 Darrell Armstrong .20 .50
58 Pat Garrity .20 .50
59 Michael Doleac .20 .50
60 Allen Iverson .60 1.50
61 Theo Ratliff .20 .50
62 Tyrone Hill .20 .50
63 Jason Kidd .50 1.25
64 Anfernee Hardaway .50 1.25
65 Shawn Marion .25 .60
66 Scottie Pippen .50 1.25
67 Rasheed Wallace .30 .75
68 Damon Stoudamire .25 .60
69 Bonzi Wells .20 .50
70 Chris Webber .30 .75
71 Peja Stojakovic .30 .75
72 Jason Williams .30 .75
73 Tim Duncan .60 1.50
74 David Robinson .50 1.25
75 Terry Porter .20 .50
76 Gary Payton .30 .75
77 Rashard Lewis .30 .75
78 Vin Baker .25 .60
79 Vince Carter .60 1.50
80 Doug Christie .20 .50
81 Antonio Davis .20 .50
82 Karl Malone .40 1.00
83 John Stockton .40 1.00
84 Bryon Russell .20 .50
85 Shareef Abdur-Rahim .25 .60
86 Mike Bibby .30 .75
87 Michael Dickerson .20 .50
88 Mitch Richmond .25 .60
89 Richard Hamilton .25 .60
90 Juwan Howard .25 .60
91 Kenyon Martin JSY RC 12.00 30.00
92 Stromile Swift RC 2.00 5.00
93 Darius Miles RC 2.00 5.00
94 Marcus Fizer JSY RC 4.00 10.00
95 Mike Miller RC 3.00 8.00
96 DerMarr Johnson RC 1.50 4.00
97 Chris Mihm RC 1.50 4.00
98 Chris Porter RC 1.25 3.00
99 Joel Przybilla RC 1.50 4.00
100 Keyon Dooling RC 2.00 5.00
101 Jerome Moiso RC 1.25 3.00
102 Etan Thomas RC 2.00 5.00
103 Courtney Alexander RC 1.50 4.00
104 Mateen Cleaves RC 1.50 4.00
105 Jason Collier RC 2.00 5.00
106 Dan Langhi RC 1.25 3.00
107 Desmond Mason RC 2.50 6.00
108 Quentin Richardson RC 2.00 5.00
109 Jamaal Magloire RC 2.00 5.00
110 Speedy Claxton RC 2.00 5.00
111 Morris Peterson RC 2.00 5.00
112 Donnell Harvey RC 1.50 4.00
113 Hanno Mottola RC 1.25 3.00
114 Mamadou N'Diaye RC 1.25 3.00
115 Erick Barkley RC 1.25 3.00
116 Mark Madsen RC 2.00 5.00
117 A.J. Guyton RC 1.25 3.00
118 Khalid El-Amin RC 1.25 3.00
119 Lavor Postell RC 1.25 3.00
120 Eddie House RC 1.50 4.00

2000-01 Upper Deck Pros and Prospects ProActive

Randomly inserted in packs at one in six, this 10-card set focuses on the best performers in the NBA. Card backs carry a "PA" prefix.
COMPLETE SET (10) 3.00 8.00
STATED ODDS 1:6
PA1 Kobe Bryant 1.25 3.00
PA2 Kevin Garnett .50 1.25
PA3 Vince Carter .60 1.50
PA4 Jason Kidd .50 1.25
PA5 Steve Francis .25 .60
PA6 Chris Webber .30 .75
PA7 Shaquille O'Neal .75 2.00
PA8 Larry Hughes .25 .60
PA9 Gary Payton .30 .75
PA10 Allen Iverson .60 1.50

2000-01 Upper Deck Pros and Prospects ProMotion

Randomly inserted in packs at one in six, this 10-card set features rookie players being "promoted" to the NBA. Card backs carry a "PM" prefix.
COMPLETE SET (10) 2.50 6.00
STATED ODDS 1:6
PM1 Darius Miles .40 1.00
PM2 Stromile Swift .40 1.00
PM3 Marcus Fizer .40 1.00
PM4 Kenyon Martin 1.00 2.50
PM5 Courtney Alexander .30 .75
PM6 Keyon Dooling .40 1.00
PM7 DerMarr Johnson .30 .75
PM8 Chris Mihm .30 .75
PM9 Chris Porter .25 .60
PM10 Mike Miller .60 1.50

2000-01 Upper Deck Pros and Prospects Signature Jerseys

Randomly inserted in packs at one in 96, this 18-card set featured swatches of authentic game-worn jerseys and autographs from top players. Card backs are numbered by the player's initials.
STATED ODDS 1:96
AH Anfernee Hardaway 20.00 50.00
AW Antoine Walker 6.00 15.00
BD Baron Davis 6.00 15.00
CM Corey Maggette 6.00 15.00
DS Damon Stoudamire 8.00 20.00
GP Gary Payton 20.00 50.00
GR Glenn Robinson 6.00 15.00
KB Kobe Bryant 125.00 250.00
KG Kevin Garnett 40.00 100.00
KM Karl Malone 75.00 150.00
MB Mike Bibby 8.00 20.00
MF Michael Finley 15.00 40.00
PP Paul Pierce 15.00 40.00
SA Shareef Abdur-Rahim 8.00 20.00
TB Terrell Brandon 6.00 15.00
VB Vin Baker 6.00 15.00
WA William Avery 6.00 15.00
WS Wally Szczerbiak 6.00 15.00

2000-01 Upper Deck Pros and Prospects Signature Jerseys Level 2

PRINT RUNS TO PLAYERS JERSEY NUMBER
LOWER PRINT RUNS UNPRICED
CM2 Corey Maggette/50 20.00 50.00
KG2 Kevin Garnett/21 125.00 300.00
KM2 Karl Malone/32 300.00 500.00
MJ2 Michael Jordan/23 1200.00 2000.00

2000-01 Upper Deck Pros and Prospects Star Command

Randomly inserted in packs at one in 12, this 12-card set focuses on the most exciting and powerful players in the league. Card backs carry a "SC" prefix.
COMPLETE SET (12) 8.00 20.00
STATED ODDS 1:12
SC1 Kobe Bryant 2.50 6.00
SC2 Vince Carter 1.25 3.00
SC3 Allen Iverson 1.25 3.00
SC4 Shaquille O'Neal 1.50 4.00
SC5 Chris Webber .60 1.50
SC6 Karl Malone .75 2.00
SC7 Lamar Odom .50 1.25
SC8 Jason Kidd 1.00 2.50
SC9 Steve Francis .50 1.25
SC10 Kevin Garnett 1.00 2.50
SC11 Larry Hughes .50 1.25
SC12 Gary Payton .60 1.50

2000-01 Upper Deck Pros and Prospects Star Futures

Randomly inserted in packs at one in 12, this 10-card set focuses on some of the premier prospects from the 2000 Draft. Card backs carry a "SF" prefix.
COMPLETE SET (10) 5.00 12.00
STATED ODDS 1:12
SF1 Kenyon Martin 1.50 4.00
SF2 Keyon Dooling .60 1.50
SF3 Chris Porter .40 1.00
SF4 Courtney Alexander .50 1.25
SF5 Darius Miles .60 1.50
SF6 Mike Miller 1.00 2.50
SF7 Mateen Cleaves .50 1.25
SF8 Stromile Swift .60 1.50
SF9 Marcus Fizer .60 1.50
SF10 DerMarr Johnson .50 1.25

2000-01 Upper Deck Pros and Prospects UD Authentics Rookie Exclusives

Randomly inserted into packs, this 3-card insert features autographs from top draft-packs. Each card is serial numbered to 200. Card backs carry the players initials as numbering.
STATED PRINT RUN 200 SETS
CM Chris Mihm 4.00 10.00
ET Etan Thomas 5.00 12.00
JP Joel Przybilla 4.00 10.00

2001-02 Upper Deck Pros and Prospects

This 131-card base set was issued in August of 2001. The set comes in 24 packs per box; 5 cards per pack; and a SRP of $4.99 per pack. The 131 base cards are broken down as follows: 90 veteran cards where full color action photography is framed by silver foil highlights and white borders, and 31 rookie cards which utilize the same design as the veterans but photos from the NBA draft. Card numbers 91-125 are sequentially numbered to 1000, and card numbers 126-131 are sequentially numbered to 350.
COMP.SET w/o SP's (90) 10.00 25.00
91-125 PRINT RUN 1000 SERIAL #'d SETS
126-131 PRINT RUN 350 SERIAL #'d SETS
1 Jason Terry .30 .75
2 Toni Kukoc .30 .75
3 DerMarr Johnson .20 .50
4 Paul Pierce .30 .75
5 Antoine Walker .25 .60
6 Kenny Anderson .25 .60
7 Jamal Mashburn .25 .60
8 Baron Davis .30 .75
9 David Wesley .20 .50
10 Elton Brand .30 .75
11 Ron Mercer .20 .50
12 Jamal Crawford .30 .75
13 Andre Miller .25 .60
14 Lamond Murray .20 .50
15 Chris Mihm .20 .50
16 Michael Finley .30 .75
17 Wang ZhiZHi .25 .60
18 Dirk Nowitzki .50 1.25
19 Antonio McDyess .25 .60
20 Nick Van Exel .25 .60
21 Raef LaFrentz .20 .50
22 Jerry Stackhouse .25 .60
23 Joe Smith .25 .60
24 Mateen Cleaves .20 .50
25 Antawn Jamison .30 .75
26 Marc Jackson .20 .50
27 Larry Hughes .25 .60
28 Steve Francis .25 .60
29 Maurice Taylor .20 .50
30 Hakeem Olajuwon .40 1.00
31 Reggie Miller .30 .75
32 Jermaine O'Neal .25 .60
33 Jalen Rose .25 .60
34 Lamar Odom .25 .60
35 Darius Miles .20 .50
36 Quentin Richardson .25 .60
37 Kobe Bryant 1.25 3.00
38 Shaquille O'Neal .75 2.00
39 Derek Fisher .25 .60
40 Rick Fox .20 .50
41 Alonzo Mourning .40 1.00
42 Eddie Jones .25 .60
43 Tim Hardaway .30 .75
44 Brian Grant .20 .50
45 Ray Allen .30 .75
46 Glenn Robinson .25 .60
47 Tim Thomas .20 .50
48 Kevin Garnett .50 1.25
49 Terrell Brandon .20 .50
50 Wally Szczerbiak .25 .60
51 Chauncey Billups .30 .75
52 Stephon Marbury .25 .60
53 Kenyon Martin .30 .75
54 Keith Van Horn .25 .60
55 Allan Houston .25 .60
56 Latrell Sprewell .25 .60
57 Glen Rice .25 .60
58 Tracy McGrady .50 1.25
59 Mike Miller .25 .60
60 Darrell Armstrong .20 .50
61 Allen Iverson .60 1.50
62 Dikembe Mutombo .30 .75
63 Aaron McKie .20 .50
64 Jason Kidd .50 1.25
65 Shawn Marion .25 .60
66 Tom Gugliotta .20 .50
67 Rasheed Wallace .30 .75
68 Damon Stoudamire .25 .60
69 Scottie Pippen .50 1.25
70 Peja Stojakovic .30 .75
71 Jason Williams .25 .60
72 Chris Webber .30 .75
73 Tim Duncan .60 1.50
74 Derek Anderson .20 .50
75 David Robinson .50 1.25
76 Gary Payton .30 .75
77 Rashard Lewis .30 .75
78 Desmond Mason .25 .60
79 Vince Carter .50 1.25
80 Morris Peterson .20 .50
81 Antonio Davis .20 .50
82 Karl Malone .40 1.00
83 John Stockton .40 1.00
84 Donyell Marshall .20 .50
85 Shareef Abdur-Rahim .25 .60
86 Mike Bibby .30 .75
87 Stromile Swift .20 .50
88 Richard Hamilton .25 .60
89 Courtney Alexander .20 .50
90 Chris Whitney .20 .50
91 Ruben Boumtje-Boumtje RC 2.00 5.00
92 Sean Lampley RC 2.00 5.00
93 Ken Johnson RC 1.25 3.00
94 Earl Watson RC 2.00 5.00
95 Jamaal Tinsley RC 2.00 5.00
96 Damone Brown RC 1.25 3.00
97 Michael Wright RC 2.00 5.00
98 Alvin Jones RC 1.50 4.00
99 Omar Cook RC 2.00 5.00
100 Jarron Collins RC 2.00 5.00
101 Brian Scalabrine RC 2.00 5.00
102 Jeryl Sasser RC 1.25 3.00
103 Samuel Dalembert RC 2.00 5.00
104 Terence Morris RC 2.00 5.00
105 Will Solomon RC 2.00 5.00
106 Kirk Haston RC 1.25 3.00
107 Richard Jefferson RC 3.00 8.00
108 Jason Collins RC 1.50 4.00
109 Troy Murphy RC 2.00 5.00
110 Gerald Wallace RC 2.50 6.00
111 Shane Battier RC 4.00 10.00
112 Jeff Trepagnier RC 1.25 3.00
113 Brandon Armstrong RC 1.25 3.00
114 Loren Woods RC 1.25 3.00
115 Joseph Forte RC 1.25 3.00
116 Michael Bradley RC 1.25 3.00
117 Joe Johnson RC 2.50 6.00
118 Gilbert Arenas RC 3.00 8.00
119 Ousmane Cisse RC 2.00 5.00
120 Kenny Satterfield RC 1.25 3.00
121 Vladimir Radmanovic RC 2.00 5.00
122 DeSagana Diop RC 1.50 4.00
123 Kedrick Brown RC 1.25 3.00
124 Trenton Hassell RC 1.50 4.00
125 Steven Hunter RC 1.50 4.00
126 Rodney White RC 2.50 6.00
127 Eddy Curry RC 4.00 10.00
128 Jason Richardson RC 5.00 12.00
129 Tyson Chandler RC 6.00 15.00
130 Eddie Griffin RC 3.00 8.00
131 Kwame Brown RC 4.00 10.00

2001-02 Upper Deck Pros and Prospects Rookie Memorabilia

Inserted in packs, this six card set parallels the last six cards in the base Pros and Prospects set. These cards utilize the same design and are enhanced with a swatch of shoe. Each card is sequentially numbered to 350.
RANDOM INSERTS IN PACKS
STATED PRINT RUN 350 SERIAL #'d SETS
126 Rodney White Shoe 3.00 8.00
127 Eddy Curry Shoe 5.00 12.00
128 Jason Richardson Shoe 6.00 15.00
129 Tyson Chandler Shoe 8.00 20.00
130 Eddie Griffin Shoe 4.00 10.00
131 Kwame Brown Shoe 5.00 12.00

2001-02 Upper Deck Pros and Prospects Alley-Oop Team-Ups

This 10-card insert set is sequentially numbered to 100. Each card features two swatches of game-used jersey in the shape of an arrow from some of the league's best alley-oop combinations. Player photos are set on either side of the card on this horizontal design with the two player's team logo in the center. A Gold version sequentially numbered to 25 was also issued.
RANDOM INSERTS IN PACKS
STATED PRINT RUN 100 SERIAL #'d SETS
*GOLD: 1.25X TO 3X BASE HI
GOLD PRINT RUN 25 SER.#'d SETS
BDJM B.Davis/J.Mashburn 8.00 20.00
CPAJ C.Porter/A.Jamison 8.00 20.00
DATM D.Armstrong/T.McGrady 10.00 25.00
GPRL G.Payton/R.Lewis 8.00 20.00
JSKM J.Stockton/K.Malone 25.00 50.00
KGKB K.Garnett/K.Bryant 20.00 50.00
NVAM N.Van Exel/A.McDyess 8.00 20.00
PPAW P.Pierce/A.Walker 10.00 25.00
QRDM Q.Richardson/D.Miles 8.00 20.00
TBKG T.Brandon/K.Garnett 8.00 20.00

2001-02 Upper Deck Pros and Prospects All-Star Team-Ups

Randomly inserted in packs at a rate of one in 192, this 10-card insert set features two swatches of 2001 NBA All-Star Weekend-used memorabilia from two different NBA All-Stars. Each player is pictured on one side of the card on this horizontal design, and centered between them is the 2001 All-Star game logo. A Gold version sequentially numbered to 25 was also issued.
STATED ODDS 1:192
*GOLD: 1.25X TO 3X BASE HI
GOLD PRINT RUN 25 SER.#'d SETS
ADDM A.Davis/D.Mutombo 8.00 20.00
AHLS A.Houston/L.Sprewell 12.50 30.00
AIKB A.Iverson/K.Bryant 20.00 50.00
CWAM C.Webber/A.McDyess 10.00 25.00
DRKG D.Robinson/K.Garnett 10.00 25.00
JKGP J.Kidd/G.Payton 8.00 20.00
JSRW J.Stackhouse/R.Wallace 8.00 20.00
KMMF K.Malone/M.Finley 8.00 20.00
RAGR R.Allen/G.Robinson 8.00 20.00
TMSM T.McGrady/S.Marbury 10.00 25.00

2001-02 Upper Deck Pros and Prospects Game Jerseys

Randomly inserted in packs at a rate of one in 24, this 26-card set features a full color player action photo on the right side of the card and a swatch of jersey on the left. Each card is highlighted with silver foil, and the player's number appears below the swatch on the non-autographed versions rendering counterfeit Autographed versions impossible to make out of base insert versions. A Gold version sequentially numbered to 75 was also issued.
STATED ODDS 1:24
*GOLD: 1X TO 2.5X JSY HI
GOLD PRINT RUN 75 SER.#'d SETS
AI Allen Iverson 8.00 20.00
AJ Antawn Jamison 4.00 10.00
AW Antoine Walker 3.00 8.00
CM Chris Mihm 2.50 6.00
CO Corey Maggette 3.00 8.00
DA Darrell Armstrong 2.50 6.00
DC Derrick Coleman 3.00 8.00
DM Darius Miles 2.50 6.00
GR Glen Rice 3.00 8.00
HM Hanno Mottola 2.50 6.00
JC Jamal Crawford 4.00 10.00
JM Jerome Moiso 2.50 6.00
JS John Stockton 5.00 12.00
KA Kenny Anderson 3.00 8.00
KB Kobe Bryant 12.00 30.00
KG Kevin Garnett 6.00 15.00
KV Keith Van Horn 3.00 8.00
LM Lamond Murray 2.50 6.00
MA Desmond Mason 3.00 8.00
MO Michael Olowokandi 2.50 6.00
MP Morris Peterson 2.50 6.00
RL Raef LaFrentz 2.50 6.00
RM Ron Mercer 2.50 6.00
SS Stromile Swift 2.50 6.00
TB Terrell Brandon 2.50 6.00
WA William Avery 2.50 6.00

2001-02 Upper Deck Pros and Prospects Game Jerseys Autographs

Randomly inserted in packs at a rate of one in 192, this 11-card set features the same design as the base Game Jerseys insert set with a different player photo and gold foil highlights instead of silver foil highlights. Unlike the Non-autographed version, these cards do not have the player's number below the jersey swatch, and this is where the authentic autographs appear. A Gold version of this set was also issued with cards sequentially numbered to 50.
STATED ODDS 1:192
*GOLD: .6X TO 1.5X BASE AU HI
GOLD PRINT RUN 50 SER.#'d SETS
AWA Antoine Walker 8.00 20.00
CMA Chris Mihm 6.00 15.00
COA Corey Maggette 8.00 20.00
DAA Darrell Armstrong 6.00 15.00
DMA Darius Miles 6.00 15.00
KBA Kobe Bryant 150.00 300.00
LMA Lamond Murray 6.00 15.00
MPA Morris Peterson 6.00 15.00
SSA Stromile Swift 6.00 15.00
TBA Terrell Brandon 6.00 15.00
KGA Kevin Garnett 25.00 60.00

2001-02 Upper Deck Pros and Prospects ProActive

Seeded in packs at the rate of one in 23, this 10-card set showcases full color player action photos against a hexagonal color background. Each card has silver foil highlights and white borders along the top, bottom and right side of the card.
COMPLETE SET (10) 8.00 20.00
STATED ODDS 1:23
PA1 Kobe Bryant 3.00 8.00
PA2 Vince Carter 1.25 3.00
PA3 Tim Duncan 1.50 4.00
PA4 Ray Allen .75 2.00
PA5 Michael Finley .75 2.00
PA6 Paul Pierce .75 2.00
PA7 Latrell Sprewell .60 1.50
PA8 Steve Francis .60 1.50
PA9 Kevin Garnett 1.25 3.00
PA10 Eddie Jones .60 1.50

2001-02 Upper Deck Pros and Prospects ProMotion

Randomly inserted in packs at a rate of one in 18, this 12-card set features full color player action photos with brightly colored backgrounds with "shadows" of the player and silver foil highlights.
COMPLETE SET (12) 8.00 20.00
STATED ODDS 1:18
PM1 Kevin Garnett 1.00 2.50
PM2 Chris Webber .60 1.50
PM3 Michael Finley .60 1.50
PM4 Tim Duncan 1.25 3.00
PM5 Ray Allen .60 1.50
PM6 Jamal Mashburn .50 1.25
PM7 Antonio McDyess .50 1.25
PM8 Kobe Bryant 2.50 6.00
PM9 Latrell Sprewell .50 1.25
PM10 Vince Carter 1.00 2.50
PM11 Shaquille O'Neal 1.50 4.00
PM12 Karl Malone .75 2.00

2001-02 Upper Deck Pros and Prospects Star Command

Randomly inserted in packs at a rate of one in 23, this 10-card set shows players in action set against a colorful background. Each card contains silver foil highlights, and the the set name and player name appear on the right side of the card.
COMPLETE SET (10) 10.00 25.00
STATED ODDS 1:23
SC1 Allen Iverson 1.50 4.00
SC2 Steve Francis .60 1.50
SC3 Kevin Garnett 1.25 3.00
SC4 Vince Carter 1.25 3.00
SC5 Kobe Bryant 3.00 8.00
SC6 Tim Duncan 1.50 4.00
SC7 Chris Webber .75 2.00
SC8 Tracy McGrady 1.25 3.00
SC9 Darius Miles .50 1.25
SC10 Shaquille O'Neal 2.00 5.00

2001-02 Upper Deck Pros and Prospects Star Futures

Randomly inserted in packs at the rate of one in 23, this 10-card set focuses on rookie players. Full color player photos are set against a criss-cross colored cubed background.
COMPLETE SET (10) 12.00 30.00
STATED ODDS 1:23
SF1 Eddy Curry 1.25 3.00
SF2 Rodney White .75 2.00
SF3 Tyson Chandler 2.00 5.00
SF4 Steven Hunter 1.00 2.50
SF5 Eddie Griffin 1.00 2.50
SF6 Kwame Brown 1.25 3.00
SF7 DeSagana Diop 1.00 2.50
SF8 Troy Murphy 1.25 3.00
SF9 Joe Johnson 1.50 4.00
SF10 Jason Richardson 1.50 4.00

1993-94 Upper Deck Pro View

This 110-card standard-size set was distributed in 5-card packs (48 per box) that included 3-D glasses with which to see the 3-D effect. Fronts feature white-bordered color player action shots, with the player's name appearing within a vertical ghosted strip on the left. The back carries a color player action shot on the left, with career highlights horizontally printed alongside on the right. The set closes with the following subsets: 3-D Playground Legends (71-79), 3-D Rookie (80-88) and 3-D Jams (89-108). Rookie Cards of note include Vin Baker, Anfernee Hardaway, Jamal Mashburn and Chris Webber.
COMPLETE SET (110) 15.00 30.00
1 Karl Malone .40 1.00
2 Chuck Person .10 .30
3 Latrell Sprewell .40 1.00
4 Dominique Wilkins .15 .40
5 Reggie Miller .15 .40
6 Vlade Divac .12 .30
7 Otis Thorpe .12 .30
8 Patrick Ewing .12 .30
9 Ron Harper .12 .30
10 Brad Daugherty .12 .30
11 Robert Parish .12 .30
12 Glen Rice .12 .30
13 Kevin Johnson .12 .30
14 Christian Laettner .12 .30
15 Ricky Pierce .12 .30
16 Joe Dumars .15 .40
17 James Worthy .20 .50
18 John Stockton .25 .60
19 Robert Horry .12 .30
20 John Starks .12 .30
21 Danny Manning .12 .30
22 Alonzo Mourning .20 .50
23 Michael Jordan 2.00 5.00
24 Hakeem Olajuwon .25 .60
25 Scott Skiles .12 .30
26 Stacey Augmon .12 .30
27 Mitch Richmond .15 .40
28 Derrick Coleman .12 .30
29 Jeff Malone .12 .30
30 Larry Johnson .15 .40
31 Sam Perkins .12 .30
32 Shaquille O'Neal .75 2.00
33 Walt Williams .12 .30
34 Doug West .12 .30
35 Mark Price .12 .30
36 Rony Seikaly .12 .30
37 Michael Adams .12 .30
38 Anthony Peeler .12 .30
39 Larry Nance .12 .30
40 Shawn Kemp .15 .40
41 Terry Porter .12 .30
42 Dan Majerle .12 .30
43 Dennis Rodman .20 .50
44 Isiah Thomas .15 .40
45 Spud Webb .12 .30
46 Pooh Richardson .12 .30
47 Tim Hardaway .15 .40
48 Derek Harper .12 .30
49 Pervis Ellison .12 .30
50 Xavier McDaniel .12 .30
51 Jeff Hornacek .12 .30
52 Ken Norman .12 .30
53 LaPhonso Ellis .12 .30
54 Charles Barkley .25 .60
55 Tom Gugliotta .15 .40
56 Clifford Robinson .12 .30
57 Mark Jackson .12 .30
58 Mahmoud Abdul-Rauf .12 .30
59 Todd Day .12 .30
60 Kenny Anderson .12 .30
61 Jim Jackson .12 .30
62 Chris Mullin .15 .40
63 Scottie Pippen .50 1.25
64 Dikembe Mutombo .12 .30
65 Sean Elliott .12 .30
66 Clarence Weatherspoon .12 .30
67 Chris Morris .12 .30
68 Clyde Drexler .20 .50
69 Dennis Scott .12 .30
70 David Robinson .25 .60
71 Larry Johnson PL .12 .30
72 Chris Webber PL .75 2.00
73 Alonzo Mourning PL .12 .30
74 Lloyd Daniels PL .12 .30
75 Derrick Coleman PL .12 .30
76 Tim Hardaway PL .12 .30
77 Isiah Thomas PL .12 .30
78 Chris Mullin PL .12 .30
79 Shaquille O'Neal PL .40 1.00
80 Shawn Bradley RC .12 .30
81 Chris Webber RC 1.25 3.00
82 Jamal Mashburn RC .30 .75
83 Anfernee Hardaway RC 1.25 3.00
84 Calbert Cheaney RC .12 .30
85 Vin Baker RC .30 .75
86 Isaiah Rider RC .20 .50
87 Lindsey Hunter RC .12 .30
88 Bobby Hurley RC .12 .30
89 Dominique Wilkins 3DJ .12 .30
90 Charles Barkley 3DJ .15 .40
91 Michael Jordan 3DJ 1.00 2.50
92 Derrick Coleman 3DJ .12 .30
93 Scottie Pippen 3DJ .25 .60
94 Karl Malone 3DJ .15 .40
95 Larry Johnson 3DJ .12 .30
96 Cedric Ceballos 3DJ .12 .30
97 David Robinson 3DJ .15 .40
98 Patrick Ewing 3DJ .12 .30
99 Clarence Weatherspoon 3DJ .12 .30
100 Alonzo Mourning 3DJ .12 .30
101 Stacey Augmon 3DJ .12 .30
102 Shaquille O'Neal 3DJ .40 1.00
103 Clyde Drexler 3DJ .12 .30
104 Shawn Kemp 3DJ .12 .30
105 Harold Miner 3DJ .12 .30
106 Chris Webber 3DJ .75 2.00
107 Dikembe Mutombo 3DJ .12 .30
108 Doug West 3DJ .12 .30
109 Michael Jordan CL .12 .30
110 Michael Jordan CL .12 .30

2004-05 Upper Deck R-Class

Released in January 2005, R-Class was a retail product which would seem has replaced the MVP brand. The set consists of veterans for cards 1-90 and rookies for cards 91-132, inserted at the rate of two per pack. R-Class was packaged in 24-pack boxes where packs contained eight cards and carried a SRP of $2.99.
COMPLETE SET (132) 15.00 40.00
COMP.SET w/o RC's (90) 8.00 20.00
91-132 STATED ODDS 2:1
1 Antoine Walker .25 .60
2 Al Harrington .20 .50
3 Boris Diaw .20 .50
4 Paul Pierce .25 .60
5 Gary Payton .25 .60
6 Jiri Welsch .15 .40
7 Gerald Wallace .20 .50
8 Jason Kapono .15 .40
9 Brandon Hunter .15 .40
10 Eddy Curry .15 .40
11 Kirk Hinrich .20 .50
12 Tyson Chandler .20 .50
13 LeBron James 1.50 4.00
14 Dajuan Wagner .15 .40
15 Zydrunas Ilgauskas .20 .50
16 Dirk Nowitzki .40 1.00
17 Michael Finley .25 .60
18 Jason Terry .20 .50
19 Andre Miller .20 .50
20 Carmelo Anthony .50 1.25
21 Kenyon Martin .20 .50
22 Chauncey Billups .25 .60
23 Rasheed Wallace .25 .60
24 Ben Wallace .20 .50
25 Speedy Claxton .15 .40
26 Jason Richardson .25 .60
27 Mike Dunleavy .20 .50
28 Yao Ming .50 1.25
29 Tracy McGrady .30 .75
30 Juwan Howard .20 .50
31 Jermaine O'Neal .20 .50
32 Reggie Miller .25 .60
33 Ron Artest .25 .60
34 Elton Brand .25 .60
35 Corey Maggette .20 .50
36 Marko Jaric .15 .40
37 Kobe Bryant 1.00 2.50
38 Devean George .15 .40
39 Lamar Odom .20 .50
40 Pau Gasol .25 .60
41 Jason Williams .20 .50
42 Bonzi Wells .15 .40
43 Shaquille O'Neal .60 1.50
44 Dwyane Wade .40 1.00
45 Eddie Jones .20 .50
46 Michael Redd .20 .50
47 Desmond Mason .20 .50
48 T.J. Ford .15 .40

49 Latrell Sprewell .20 .50
50 Kevin Garnett .40 1.00
51 Sam Cassell .20 .50
52 Richard Jefferson .20 .50
53 Aaron Williams .15 .40
54 Jason Kidd .40 1.00
55 Jamal Mashburn .20 .50
56 Baron Davis .20 .50
57 Jamaal Magloire .15 .40
58 Allan Houston .20 .50
59 Jamal Crawford .25 .60
60 Stephon Marbury .20 .50
61 Steve Francis .20 .50
62 Kelvin Cato .15 .40
63 Cuttino Mobley .15 .40
64 Glenn Robinson .20 .50
65 Allen Iverson .40 1.00
66 Willie Green .15 .40
67 Amare Stoudemire .20 .50
68 Quentin Richardson .20 .50
69 Steve Nash .30 .75
70 Shareef Abdur-Rahim .20 .50
71 Damon Stoudamire .20 .50
72 Zach Randolph .20 .50
73 Peja Stojakovic .25 .60
74 Chris Webber .25 .60
75 Mike Bibby .25 .60
76 Tony Parker .25 .60
77 Tim Duncan .40 1.00
78 Manu Ginobili .30 .75
79 Ronald Murray .15 .40
80 Ray Allen .25 .60
81 Rashard Lewis .25 .60
82 Chris Bosh .25 .60
83 Vince Carter .40 1.00
84 Jalen Rose .20 .50
85 Andrei Kirilenko .20 .50
86 Carlos Boozer .20 .50
87 Carlos Arroyo .15 .40
88 Gilbert Arenas .20 .50
89 Jarvis Hayes .15 .40
90 Antawn Jamison .20 .50
91 Dwight Howard RC 1.25 3.00
92 Emeka Okafor RC .50 1.25
93 Ben Gordon RC .60 1.50
94 Shaun Livingston RC .60 1.50
95 Devin Harris RC .50 1.25
96 Josh Childress RC .50 1.25
97 Luol Deng RC .60 1.50
98 Andre Iguodala RC .75 2.00
99 Luke Jackson RC .40 1.00
100 Andris Biedrins RC .40 1.00
101 Sebastian Telfair RC .50 1.25
102 Josh Smith RC .60 1.50
103 Rafael Araujo RC .40 1.00
104 Robert Swift RC .40 1.00
105 Kris Humphries RC .60 1.50
106 Al Jefferson RC .75 2.00
107 Kirk Snyder RC .40 1.00
108 J.R. Smith RC .60 1.50
109 Dorell Wright RC .60 1.50
110 Jameer Nelson RC .60 1.50
111 Pavel Podkolzin RC .40 1.00
112 Bernard Robinson RC .50 1.25
113 Yuta Tabuse RC .60 1.50
114 Delonte West RC .60 1.50
115 Tony Allen RC .60 1.50
116 Kevin Martin RC .75 2.00
117 Sasha Vujacic RC .60 1.50
118 Beno Udrih RC .50 1.25
119 David Harrison RC .40 1.00
120 Anderson Varejao RC .50 1.25
121 Jackson Vroman RC .40 1.00
122 Peter John Ramos RC .40 1.00
123 Lionel Chalmers RC .60 1.50
124 Donta Smith RC .40 1.00
125 Andre Emmett RC .40 1.00
126 Antonio Burks RC .50 1.25
127 Royal Ivey RC .50 1.25
128 Chris Duhon RC .60 1.50
129 Trevor Ariza RC .60 1.50
130 Tim Pickett RC .60 1.50
131 Romain Sato RC .40 1.00
132 Nenad Krstic RC .60 1.50

2004-05 Upper Deck R-Class Gold

*1-90 GOLD: 2X TO 5X BASE HI
1-90 PRINT RUN 150 SER.#'d SETS
*91-132 GOLD: 2.5X TO 6X BASE RC HI
91-132 PRINT RUN 50 SER.#'d SETS

2004-05 Upper Deck R-Class Platinum

*1-90 PLATINUM: 8X TO 20X BASE HI
1-90 PRINT RUN 25 SER.#'d SETS

2004-05 Upper Deck R-Class R-Tifacts

Inserted in packs at the rate of one in 18, this 42-card set features a player photo on the right and a swatch of memorabilia on the left.

STATED ODDS 1:18
SP INFO PROVIDED BY UPPER DECK
AH Allan Houston 2.00 5.00
AK Andrei Kirilenko 2.00 5.00
AS Amare Stoudemire 2.00 5.00
BC Brian Cook 2.00 5.00
BD Baron Davis 2.00 5.00
BI Chauncey Billups 2.50 6.00
BM Brad Miller 2.00 5.00
BO Carlos Boozer 2.00 5.00
CA Carmelo Anthony 5.00 12.00
CB Caron Butler 2.00 5.00
CM Corey Maggette 2.00 5.00
DG Drew Gooden 1.50 4.00
DN Dirk Nowitzki 4.00 10.00
DW Dajuan Wagner 2.00 5.00
EC Eddy Curry 1.50 4.00
EG Manu Ginobili 3.00 8.00
ES Eric Snow 2.00 5.00
GA Gilbert Arenas 2.00 5.00
GP Gary Payton 2.50 6.00
JC Jamal Crawford 2.50 6.00
JM Jamaal Magloire 2.00 5.00
JO Jermaine O'Neal 2.00 5.00
JT Jason Terry 2.00 5.00
KB Kobe Bryant 8.00 20.00
KG Kevin Garnett 4.00 10.00
KM Karl Malone 3.00 8.00
LJ LeBron James 6.00 15.00
MF Michael Finley 2.50 6.00
MJ Michael Jordan SP 25.00 60.00
MP Morris Peterson 1.50 4.00
PP Paul Pierce 2.50 6.00
QR Quentin Richardson 2.00 5.00
RJ Richard Jefferson 2.00 5.00
RM Reggie Miller 2.50 6.00
SD Samuel Dalembert 2.00 5.00
SM Shawn Marion 2.00 5.00
SS Steve Smith 2.00 5.00
ST Stephon Marbury 2.00 5.00
TC Tyson Chandler 2.00 5.00
TM Tracy McGrady 3.00 8.00
VD Vlade Divac 2.00 5.00
WS Wally Szczerbiak 2.00 5.00

2004-05 Upper Deck R-Class R-Tifacts Dual

Seeded randomly at the rate of one in 36, this 30-card set places two players along with two swatches of memorabilia on the card front.

STATED ODDS 1:36
SP INFO PROVIDED BY UPPER DECK
AH G.Arenas/B.Haywood 4.00 10.00
AM C.Anthony/A.Miller 5.00 12.00
BJ K.Bryant/L.James SP 12.00 30.00
BM E.Brand/C.Maggette 4.00 10.00
CC E.Curry/T.Chandler 4.00 10.00
CW B.Cook/L.Walton 4.00 10.00
DG T.Duncan/M.Ginobili 10.00 25.00
DM B.Davis/J.Magloire 4.00 10.00
FM S.Francis/C.Mobley 4.00 10.00
GM P.Gasol/M.Miller 4.00 10.00
GS K.Garnett/W.Szczerbiak 6.00 15.00
HB D.Harrision/C.Billups 4.00 10.00
HW A.Harrington/A.Walker 4.00 10.00
JJ L.James/M.Jordan SP 30.00 80.00
KB A.Kirilenko/C.Boozer 4.00 10.00
KJ N.Krstic/R.Jefferson 4.00 10.00
KK K.Bryant/K.Malone 8.00 20.00
MF T.McGrady/S.Francis 6.00 15.00
ML R.Murray/R.Lewis 4.00 10.00
MR S.Marion/Q.Richardson 4.00 10.00
MS S.Marbury/M.Sweetney 4.00 10.00
NF D.Nowitzki/M.Finley 5.00 12.00
OH S.O'Neal/U.Haslem 6.00 15.00
PP P.Pierce/G.Payton 5.00 12.00
PR M.Peterson/J.Richardson 4.00 10.00
RF J.Richardson/D.Fisher 4.00 10.00
RM Q.Richardson/D.Miles 4.00 10.00
SJ A.Stoudemire/J.Johnson 5.00 12.00
TO J.Tinsley/J.O'Neal 4.00 10.00
WS C.Webber/P.Stojakovic 5.00 12.00

2004-05 Upper Deck R-Class R-Tifacts Triple

Randomly inserted in packs, this 12-card set features three players along with three swatches of memorabilia. Each card is sequentially numbered to 25.

PRINT RUN 25 SER.#'d SETS
JJB LeBron/Jordan/Kobe 125.00 250.00
MGB McGrady/Garnett/Kobe 20.00 50.00

2004-05 Upper Deck R-Class R-Tifacts Signatures

Limited to 50 serially numbered copies, this 35-card set includes a player photo, a swatch of memorabilia and an autograph.

PRINT RUN 50 SER.#'d SETS
AB Andris Biedrins 5.00 12.00
AI Andre Iguodala 10.00 25.00
AJ Al Jefferson 10.00 25.00
AV Anderson Varejao 6.00 15.00
BG Ben Gordon 8.00 20.00
DA David Harrison 5.00 12.00
DE Devin Harris 6.00 15.00
DF Derek Fisher 8.00 20.00
DH Dwight Howard 100.00 200.00
DO Dorell Wright 8.00 20.00
DW Delonte West 8.00 20.00
JA Jamal Crawford 10.00 25.00
JN Jameer Nelson 8.00 20.00
JR J.R. Smith 8.00 20.00
JS Josh Smith 8.00 20.00
KB Kobe Bryant 100.00 200.00
KH Kris Humphries 8.00 20.00
KM Kevin Martin 10.00 25.00
KS Kirk Snyder 5.00 12.00
LC Lionel Chalmers 8.00 20.00
LJ LeBron James 150.00 300.00
LU Luke Jackson 5.00 12.00
MJ Michael Jordan 400.00 600.00
NK Nenad Krstic 8.00 20.00
RA Rafael Araujo 5.00 12.00
ST Sebastian Telfair 6.00 15.00
TA Tony Allen 8.00 20.00
YT Yuta Tabuse 8.00 20.00

2004-05 Upper Deck R-Class Signatures

Randomly seeded at the rate of one in 480, this 42-card set features full color player photos on the right of the card and an autograph up the left side.

STATED ODDS 1:480
SP INFO PROVIDED BY UPPER DECK
AI Andre Iguodala 8.00 20.00
JR J.R. Smith 6.00 15.00
KG Kevin Garnett SP 25.00 60.00
LJ LeBron James SP 125.00 250.00

2008-09 Upper Deck Radiance

COMP.SET w/o RCs (90) 125.00 250.00
1-90 PRINT RUN 299 SER.#'d SETS
91-110 RC PRINT RUN 299 SER.#'d SETS
101-120 RC PRINT RUN 99 SER.#'d SETS
1 LaMarcus Aldridge 1.50 4.00
2 Ray Allen 1.50 4.00
3 Carmelo Anthony 2.00 5.00
4 Ron Artest 1.50 4.00
5 Brandon Bass 1.00 2.50
6 Chauncey Billups 1.50 4.00
7 Carlos Boozer 1.25 3.00
8 Chris Bosh 1.50 4.00
9 Elton Brand 1.50 4.00
10 Kobe Bryant 12.00 30.00
11 Caron Butler 1.25 3.00
12 Andrew Bynum 1.00 2.50
13 Jose Calderon 1.00 2.50
14 Marcus Camby 1.00 2.50
15 Vince Carter 2.00 5.00
16 Tyson Chandler 1.25 3.00
17 Wilson Chandler 1.25 3.00
18 Mike Conley Jr. 1.25 3.00
19 Jamal Crawford 1.50 4.00
20 Eddy Curry 1.00 2.50
21 Baron Davis 1.25 3.00
22 Luol Deng 1.25 3.00
23 Michael Jordan 50.00 120.00
24 Tim Duncan 2.50 6.00
25 Kevin Durant 4.00 10.00
26 Monta Ellis 1.25 3.00
27 T.J. Ford 1.00 2.50
28 Francisco Garcia 1.00 2.50
29 Kevin Garnett 2.50 6.00
30 Rudy Gay 1.50 4.00
31 Manu Ginobili 1.50 4.00
32 Ben Gordon 1.25 3.00
33 Danny Granger 1.25 3.00
34 Devin Harris 1.00 2.50
35 Al Horford 1.50 4.00
36 Dwight Howard 1.25 3.00
37 Andre Iguodala 1.25 3.00
38 Allen Iverson 2.00 5.00
39 Stephen Jackson 1.25 3.00
40 LeBron James 15.00 40.00
41 Antawn Jamison 1.25 3.00
42 Al Jefferson 1.25 3.00
43 Richard Jefferson 1.25 3.00
44 Yi Jianlian 1.50 4.00
45 Jason Kidd 1.50 4.00
46 Andrei Kirilenko 1.25 3.00
47 David Lee 1.00 2.50
48 Corey Maggette 1.25 3.00
49 Shawn Marion 1.25 3.00
50 Kenyon Martin 1.25 3.00
51 Kevin Martin 1.25 3.00
52 Desmond Mason 1.00 2.50
53 Tracy McGrady 1.50 4.00
54 Brad Miller 1.25 3.00
55 Mike Miller 1.25 3.00
56 Yao Ming 2.00 5.00
57 Jamario Moon 1.00 2.50
58 Alonzo Mourning 2.00 5.00
59 Steve Nash 1.50 4.00
60 Joakim Noah 1.25 3.00
61 Dirk Nowitzki 2.00 5.00
62 Shaquille O'Neal 3.00 8.00
63 Greg Oden 1.25 3.00
64 Lamar Odom 1.25 3.00
65 Tony Parker 1.50 4.00
66 Chris Paul 2.00 5.00
67 Paul Pierce 1.50 4.00
68 Tayshaun Prince 1.25 3.00
69 Michael Redd 1.25 3.00
70 Jason Richardson 1.50 4.00
71 Brandon Roy 1.50 4.00
72 Luis Scola 1.25 3.00
73 Ramon Sessions 1.25 3.00
74 Josh Smith 1.25 3.00
75 Amare Stoudemire 1.25 3.00
76 Rodney Stuckey 1.25 3.00
77 Al Thornton 1.25 3.00
78 Hedo Turkoglu 1.25 3.00
79 Dwyane Wade 2.50 6.00
80 Ben Wallace 1.25 3.00
81 Gerald Wallace 1.25 3.00
82 Rasheed Wallace 1.50 4.00
83 David West 1.25 3.00
84 Chris Wilcox 1.00 2.50
85 Deron Williams 1.25 3.00
86 Louis Williams 1.25 3.00
87 Marvin Williams 1.25 3.00
88 Mo Williams 1.25 3.00
89 Brandan Wright 1.25 3.00
90 Thaddeus Young 1.25 3.00
91 Joe Alexander AU RC 3.00 8.00
92 Mario Chalmers AU RC 5.00 12.00
93 Joey Dorsey AU RC 3.00 8.00
94 Darrell Arthur AU RC 4.00 10.00
95 Rudy Fernandez AU RC 4.00 10.00
96 Marc Gasol AU RC 10.00 25.00
97 J.R. Giddens AU RC 3.00 8.00
98 Donte Greene AU RC 3.00 8.00
99 Roy Hibbert AU RC 5.00 12.00
100 J.J. Hickson AU RC 4.00 10.00
101 George Hill AU RC 5.00 12.00
102 Robin Lopez AU RC 5.00 12.00
103 A.Randolph AU RC 3.00 8.00
104 Brandon Rush AU RC 4.00 10.00
105 Walter Sharpe AU RC 3.00 8.00
106 Marreese Speights AU RC 4.00 10.00
107 Jason Thompson AU RC 3.00 8.00
108 Kyle Weaver AU RC 3.00 8.00
109 Sonny Weems AU RC 3.00 8.00
110 D.J. White AU RC 4.00 10.00
81RC D.J. Augustin AU RC 8.00 20.00
82RC Jerryd Bayless AU RC 8.00 20.00
83RC Michael Beasley AU RC 10.00 25.00
84RC Danilo Gallinari AU RC 15.00 40.00
85RC Eric Gordon AU RC 15.00 40.00
86RC Brook Lopez AU RC 12.00 30.00
87RC Kevin Love AU RC 75.00 150.00
88RC O.J. Mayo AU RC 10.00 25.00
89RC Derrick Rose AU RC 30.00 80.00
90RC Russell Westbrook AU RC 150.00 400.00

2008-09 Upper Deck Radiance AU Standard

STATED PRINT RUN 10 TO 25 SER.#'d SETS
SOME UNPRICED DUE TO SCARCITY
AUAG Artis Gilmore/25 10.00 25.00
AUAH Al Horford/25 6.00 15.00
AUBR Brandon Roy/25 10.00 25.00
AUCL Carl Landry/25 15.00 30.00
AUCP Chris Paul/25 40.00 80.00
AUDA D.J. Augustin/25 6.00 15.00
AUDH Dwight Howard/25 25.00 50.00
AUDR Derrick Rose/25 150.00 400.00
AUEG Eric Gordon/25 10.00 25.00
AUGG George Gervin/25 12.00 30.00
AUJA Joe Alexander/25 6.00 15.00
AUJB Jerryd Bayless/25 8.00 20.00
AUJG J.R. Giddens/25 6.00 15.00
AULJ LeBron James/23 300.00 600.00
AULW Luke Walton/25 8.00 20.00
AUMA Morris Almond/25 6.00 15.00
AUMB Michael Beasley/25 15.00 40.00
AUMJ Michael Jordan/23 250.00 500.00
AUOM O.J. Mayo/25 15.00 40.00
AUPP Paul Pierce/25 20.00 50.00
AURF Rudy Fernandez/25 10.00 25.00
AURR Rajon Rondo/25 20.00 50.00
AURW Russell Westbrook/25 40.00 100.00
AUSW Sonny Weems/25 6.00 15.00
AUTC Tom Chambers/25 6.00 15.00

2008-09 Upper Deck Radiance Auto Focus

APPROXIMATE ODDS 1:6
AFBE Marco Belinelli 6.00 15.00
AFCL Carl Landry 10.00 25.00
AFDH Dwight Howard SP 20.00 50.00
AFDR Derrick Rose SP 150.00 350.00
AFDW Deron Williams 15.00 40.00
AFGH George Hill 8.00 20.00
AFJG J.R. Giddens 6.00 15.00
AFKB Kobe Bryant SP 125.00 225.00
AFKG Kevin Garnett SP 75.00 150.00
AFLJ LeBron James SP 125.00 250.00
AFMB Michael Beasley 15.00 40.00
AFMC Mario Chalmers 8.00 20.00
AFMJ Michael Jordan 300.00 600.00
AFOM O.J. Mayo SP 15.00 40.00
AFRF Rudy Fernandez 8.00 20.00
AFRR Rajon Rondo 15.00 30.00

2008-09 Upper Deck Radiance Auto Focus Dual

STATED PRINT RUN 10 TO 25 SER.#'d SETS
UNPRICED TRIPLE PRINT RUN 5 TO 10 SETS
AFDBF Farmar/Bynum/25 40.00 100.00
AFDCC Cook/Chalmers/25 15.00 40.00
AFDDH Durant/Horford/25 50.00 120.00
AFDJB Bird/M.Johnson/25 200.00 350.00
AFDJE M.Jordan/Erving/25 300.00 600.00
AFDMB O.J.Mayo/Beasley/25 30.00 60.00
AFDPG K.Garnett/Pierce/25 100.00 200.00
AFDRH Rush/Hibbert/25 15.00 40.00

2008-09 Upper Deck Radiance Diplomatic Autographs

APPROXIMATE ODDS 1:3
DIAD Adrian Dantley 5.00 12.00
DICD Clyde Drexler 20.00 40.00
DIDG Donte Greene 5.00 12.00
DIDH Dwight Howard SP 20.00 50.00
DIDR David Robinson SP 25.00 60.00
DIDW D.J. White 5.00 12.00
DIJC Javaris Crittenton 5.00 12.00
DIJK Jason Kidd SP 20.00 40.00
DIJO Magic Johnson 30.00 80.00
DIKB Kobe Bryant SP 125.00 225.00
DIKG Kevin Garnett 40.00 80.00
DILJ LeBron James 100.00 200.00
DIMB Michael Beasley SP 20.00 40.00
DIMJ Michael Jordan 400.00 700.00
DIMP Mark Price 20.00 40.00
DIRF Randy Foye 5.00 12.00
DIRH Richard Hendrix 5.00 12.00
DIRJ Richard Jefferson 5.00 12.00
DITP Tayshaun Prince 5.00 12.00
DIVC Vince Carter 25.00 50.00

2008-09 Upper Deck Radiance Inked

STATED PRINT RUN 10 TO 99 SER.#'d SETS
IAL Acie Law/99 5.00 12.00
IBE Michael Beasley/99 10.00 25.00
ICW C.J. Watson/99 5.00 12.00
IDE Deron Williams/99 10.00 25.00
IDG Donte Greene/99 5.00 12.00
IEC Eddy Curry/99 5.00 12.00
IGH George Hill/99 10.00 25.00
IJF Jordan Farmar/99 5.00 12.00
IJS Josh Smith/99 5.00 12.00
ILA LaMarcus Aldridge/99 8.00 20.00
ILJ LeBron James/23 200.00 400.00
IMB Mike Bibby/99 5.00 12.00
IMW Mo Williams/99 15.00 30.00
IQR Quentin Richardson/99 5.00 12.00
IRB Ronnie Brewer/99 5.00 12.00
ISM J.R. Smith/99 5.00 12.00
ITT Tyrus Thomas/99 8.00 20.00
IWE David West/99 5.00 12.00

2008-09 Upper Deck Radiance Marks Dual

STATED PRINT RUN 10 TO 50 SER.#'d SETS
SOME UNPRICED DUE TO SCARCITY
DMBW D.Williams/Boozer/50 10.00 25.00
DMCB D.Cook/Beasley/50 15.00 30.00
DMGF Fernandez/Gasol/50 20.00 40.00
DMGM O.J. Mayo/R.Gay/50 10.00 25.00
DMGR Gordon/D.Rose/50 50.00 100.00
DMPG K.Garnett/Pierce/50 50.00 120.00
DMSA W.Sharpe/Afflalo/50 8.00 20.00
DMSW J.R.Smith/Weems/50 8.00 20.00

2008-09 Upper Deck Radiance Name Tag Autographs

APPROXIMATE ODDS 1:3
NTAA Alexis Ajinca 4.00 10.00
NTBW Bill Walker 4.00 10.00
NTDA D.J. Augustin SP 8.00 20.00
NTDR Derrick Rose SP 125.00 250.00
NTDW D.J. White 4.00 10.00
NTGH George Hill 5.00 12.00
NTGR Donte Greene 4.00 10.00
NTJB Jerryd Bayless SP 6.00 15.00
NTJJ J.J. Hickson 5.00 12.00
NTJM Javale McGee 5.00 12.00
NTJT Jason Thompson 4.00 10.00
NTKL Kevin Love SP 25.00 60.00
NTLM Luc Richard Mbah A Moute 4.00 10.00
NTMB Michael Beasley 12.00 30.00
NTMC Mario Chalmers 5.00 12.00
NTMT Mike Taylor 4.00 10.00
NTOM O.J. Mayo SP 20.00 40.00
NTRF Rudy Fernandez 8.00 20.00
NTRH Roy Hibbert 5.00 12.00
NTRW Russell Westbrook SP 25.00 60.00
NTSS Sean Singletary 4.00 10.00
NTSW Sonny Weems 4.00 10.00
NTWS Walter Sharpe 4.00 10.00

2008-09 Upper Deck Radiance Signature Flight

APPROXIMATE ODDS 1:3
SFAB Aaron Brooks 4.00 10.00
SFAT Al Thornton SP 6.00 15.00
SFDH Dwight Howard SP 25.00 50.00
SFDT David Thompson 6.00 15.00
SFDW Dominique Wilkins SP 15.00 30.00
SFJF Jordan Farmar SP 4.00 10.00
SFJG J.R. Giddens 4.00 10.00
SFKB Kobe Bryant SP 100.00 200.00
SFLJ LeBron James 100.00 200.00
SFMJ Michael Jordan 200.00 400.00
SFQR Quentin Richardson SP 4.00 10.00
SFRB Ronnie Brewer 4.00 10.00
SFSS Stromile Swift SP 5.00 12.00
SFSW Sonny Weems 4.00 10.00
SFTM Tracy McGrady 12.00 30.00
SFTP Tayshaun Prince SP 5.00 12.00
SFWE Spud Webb SP 5.00 12.00

2008-09 Upper Deck Radiance Sweet Shot Autographs

APPROXIMATE ODDS 1:6
SSAA Arron Afflalo 4.00 10.00
SSBB Bruce Bowen 15.00 30.00
SSBG Ben Gordon SP 15.00 30.00
SSBM Brad Miller 4.00 10.00
SSBO Andrew Bogut 6.00 15.00
SSCB Carlos Boozer 4.00 10.00
SSCM Corey Maggette SP 6.00 15.00
SSCP Chris Paul 20.00 50.00
SSCS Cedric Simmons 4.00 10.00
SSDG Danny Granger 6.00 15.00
SSDH Dwight Howard SP 25.00 60.00
SSGD Glen Davis 8.00 20.00
SSGI Daniel Gibson SP 5.00 12.00
SSGP Gabe Pruitt 4.00 10.00
SSHA Devin Harris 6.00 15.00
SSJB Josh Boone 4.00 10.00
SSKV Kiki Vandeweghe SP 5.00 12.00
SSLA LaMarcus Aldridge SP 8.00 20.00
SSMA Morris Almond 4.00 10.00
SSMW Marvin Williams 4.00 10.00
SSNR Nate Robinson 8.00 20.00
SSRB Ronnie Brewer SP 6.00 15.00
SSSB Shannon Brown 4.00 10.00
SSSK Steve Kerr 6.00 15.00
SSTP Tony Parker 15.00 30.00

2008-09 Upper Deck Radiance Writing Samples

STATED PRINT RUN 50 SER.#'d SETS
WSAB A.Afflalo/M.Belinelli 10.00 25.00
WSBH S.Battier/D.Howard 25.00 60.00
WSDA K.Durant/D.J.Augustin 50.00 120.00
WSGR G.Hill/R.Hibbert 10.00 25.00
WSGS G.Gervin/R.Stuckey 10.00 25.00
WSJD G.Davis/L.Johnson 12.00 30.00
WSLL B.Lopez/R.Lopez 10.00 25.00
WSLP B.Laimbeer/T.Prince 10.00 25.00
WSLW R.Westbrook/K.Love 100.00 200.00
WSPG K.Garnett/P.Pierce 50.00 120.00
WSRC B.Rush/M.Chalmers 15.00 30.00
WSWR J.Wilkes/D.Rodman 20.00 50.00

1999-00 Upper Deck Retro

The debut release of Retro contained 110-cards, combining legends of the NBA with current NBA stars and new rookies.

COMPLETE SET (110) 20.00 40.00
UNPRICED PLATINUM SERIAL #'d TO 1
1 Michael Jordan 2.00 5.00
2 John Havlicek .30 .75
3 Antawn Jamison .25 .60
4 Chris Webber .25 .60
5 Maurice Taylor .15 .40
6 Kevin Garnett .40 1.00
7 Walter Davis .25 .60
8 Kobe Bryant 1.00 2.50
9 Tim Duncan .50 1.25
10 Karl Malone .30 .75
11 Larry Bird .60 1.50
12 Juwan Howard .20 .50
13 Bill Walton .25 .60
14 Bob Cousy .40 1.00
15 Dave DeBusschere .25 .60
16 Toni Kukoc .25 .60
17 Allan Houston .20 .50
18 Grant Hill .30 .75
19 Rik Smits .25 .60
20 Glenn Robinson .20 .50
21 Dave Cowens .15 .40
22 Isaac Austin .15 .40
23 Derek Anderson .15 .40
24 Tracy McGrady .40 1.00
25 Nate Thurmond .20 .50
26 Dikembe Mutombo .25 .60
27 Oscar Robertson .30 .75
28 Antonio McDyess .20 .50
29 Jamaal Wilkes .25 .60
30 Eddie Jones .25 .60
31 Nick Van Exel .20 .50
32 Reggie Miller .25 .60
33 David Thompson .20 .50
34 Ray Allen .25 .60
35 Anfernee Hardaway .40 1.00
36 Brian Grant .15 .40
37 Allen Iverson .50 1.25
38 Vince Carter .50 1.25
39 Mitch Richmond .25 .60
40 Kareem Abdul-Jabbar .40 1.00
41 Alonzo Mourning .30 .75
42 Jonathan Bender RC .30 .75
43 Scottie Pippen .40 1.00
44 George Gervin .25 .60
45 Shawn Kemp .25 .60
46 Dave Bing .25 .60
47 John Starks .20 .50
48 Earl Monroe .25 .60
49 Stephon Marbury .20 .50
50 Cedric Maxwell .15 .40
51 Tom Gugliotta .15 .40
52 David Robinson .40 1.00
53 Shareef Abdur-Rahim .20 .50
54 Elvin Hayes .25 .60
55 Wilt Chamberlain .50 1.25
56 Willis Reed .25 .60
57 Kevin McHale .30 .75
58 Elden Campbell .15 .40
59 Steve Smith .20 .50
60 Brent Barry .20 .50
61 Jerry Stackhouse .25 .60
62 Otis Birdsong .20 .50
63 Michael Olowokandi .15 .40
64 Joe Smith .20 .50
65 Tim Thomas .20 .50
66 Rick Barry .20 .50
67 Jason Williams .30 .75
68 Julius Erving .40 1.00
69 John Stockton .30 .75
70 Cal Bowdler RC .20 .50
71 Nate Archibald .20 .50
72 Elgin Baylor .25 .60
73 Ron Mercer .20 .50
74 Damon Stoudamire .20 .50
75 Jerry West .30 .75
76 Michael Finley .25 .60
77 Charles Barkley .40 1.00
78 Shaquille O'Neal .60 1.50
79 Paul Pierce .30 .75
80 Keith Van Horn .20 .50
81 Jason Kidd .40 1.00
82 Gary Payton .25 .60
83 James Worthy .30 .75
84 Mike Bibby .25 .60
85 Bill Russell .40 1.00
86 Wes Unseld .25 .60
87 Robert Parish .25 .60
88 Walt Frazier .25 .60
89 Antoine Walker .25 .60
90 Steve Nash .40 1.00
91 Moses Malone .25 .60
92 Hakeem Olajuwon .30 .75
93 Tim Hardaway .25 .60
94 Patrick Ewing .30 .75
95 Vin Baker .20 .50
96 Trajan Langdon RC .30 .75
97 Ron Artest RC .60 1.50
98 James Posey RC .30 .75
99 Shawn Marion RC .60 1.50
100 Jumaine Jones RC .25 .60
101 William Avery RC .25 .60
102 Corey Maggette RC .50 1.25
103 Andre Miller RC .60 1.50
104 Jason Terry RC .50 1.25
105 Wally Szczerbiak RC .60 1.50
106 Richard Hamilton RC .60 1.50
107 Elton Brand RC .75 2.00
108 Baron Davis RC .75 2.00
109 Steve Francis RC .75 2.00
110 Lamar Odom RC .75 2.00

1999-00 Upper Deck Retro Gold

*STARS: 6X TO 15X BASE CARD HI
*RCs: 3X TO 8X BASE HI
STATED PRINT RUN 250 SERIAL #'d SETS

1999-00 Upper Deck Retro Distant Replay

Randomly inserted in packs at one in 11, this 10-card set features some of the early heroes of the NBA and their most memorable accomplishments. Card backs feature a "D" prefix.

COMPLETE SET (10) 12.50 25.00
STATED ODDS 1:11
*PARALLEL: 2.5X TO 6X HI COLUMN
PARALLEL: PRINT RUN 100 SERIAL #'d SETS
D1 Michael Jordan 6.00 15.00
D2 Kareem Abdul-Jabbar 1.25 3.00
D3 Bill Russell 1.25 3.00
D4 Julius Erving 1.25 3.00
D5 George Gervin .75 2.00
D6 Moses Malone .75 2.00
D7 Larry Bird 2.00 5.00
D8 Jerry West 1.00 2.50
D9 Oscar Robertson 1.00 2.50
D10 Elgin Baylor .75 2.00

1999-00 Upper Deck Retro Epic Jordan

Randomly inserted in packs at one in 23, this 10-card set takes you inside Jordan's amazing career. Card backs carry a "J" prefix.

COMPLETE SET (10) 12.00 30.00
COMMON CARD (J1-J10) 2.50 6.00
STATED ODDS 1:23

1999-00 Upper Deck Retro Epic Jordan Parallel

COMMON CARD (J1-J10) 40.00 100.00
STATED PRINT RUN 50 SERIAL #'d SETS

1999-00 Upper Deck Retro Fast Forward

Randomly inserted at one in 23, this 15-card set takes a look into the future of basketball and the next superstars of the NBA. Card backs carry a "F" prefix.

COMPLETE SET (15) 15.00 40.00
STATED ODDS 1:23
F1 Kevin Garnett 1.50 4.00
F2 Kobe Bryant 4.00 10.00
F3 Keith Van Horn .75 2.00
F4 Allen Iverson 2.00 5.00
F5 Vince Carter 2.00 5.00
F6 Paul Pierce 1.25 3.00
F7 Shareef Abdur-Rahim .75 2.00
F8 Jason Williams 1.25 3.00
F9 Tim Duncan 2.00 5.00
F10 Shaquille O'Neal 2.50 6.00
F11 Scottie Pippen 1.50 4.00
F12 Anfernee Hardaway 1.50 4.00
F13 Antawn Jamison 1.00 2.50
F14 Antonio McDyess .75 2.00
F15 Stephon Marbury .75 2.00

1999-00 Upper Deck Retro Inkredible

Randomly inserted in packs at one in 23, this 24-card set features authentic autographs of current and past NBA greats. Card backs are numbered by the player's initial.

STATED ODDS 1:23
AH Anfernee Hardaway 75.00 200.00
AJ Antawn Jamison 6.00 15.00
BC Bob Cousy 25.00 60.00
BG Brian Grant 5.00 12.00
BR Bill Russell 350.00 650.00
CA Cory Alexander 5.00 12.00
DA Darrell Armstrong 5.00 12.00
EH Elvin Hayes 6.00 15.00
ES Eric Snow 5.00 12.00
GG George Gervin 5.00 12.00
GR Glen Rice 40.00 100.00
JH John Havlicek 15.00 40.00
JR Jalen Rose 5.00 12.00
JW Jerry West 20.00 50.00
MB Mookie Blaylock 5.00 12.00
MJ Mark Jackson 5.00 12.00
MT Maurice Taylor 5.00 12.00
NA Nate Archibald 6.00 15.00
RL Raef LaFrentz 5.00 12.00
RT Robert Traylor 5.00 12.00
TK Toni Kukoc 6.00 15.00
VC Vince Carter 15.00 40.00
WC Wilt Chamberlain 2000.00 2500.00
WF Walt Frazier 6.00 15.00

1999-00 Upper Deck Retro Inkredible Level 2

PRINT RUN TO PLAYER'S JERSEY #
BG Brian Grant/44 20.00 50.00
ES Eric Snow/20 20.00 50.00
GG George Gervin/44 20.00 50.00
GR Glen Rice/41 40.00 75.00
JH John Havlicek/17 125.00 250.00
JW Jerry West/44 125.00 300.00
MJ Michael Jordan/23 1700.00 2500.00
MT Maurice Taylor/23 20.00 50.00
RL Raef LaFrentz/45 20.00 50.00
RT Robert Traylor/54 20.00 50.00
VC Vince Carter/15 75.00 150.00

1999-00 Upper Deck Retro Lunchboxes

These 11 lunchboxes served as the boxes in which the 1999-00 Upper Deck Retro product shipped out in. The lunchboxes picture Larry Bird, Michael Jordan, and Julius Erving.

1 Larry Bird 6.00 15.00
2 Julius Erving 6.00 15.00
3 J.Erving/L.Bird 6.00 15.00
4 Michael Jordan #1 6.00 15.00
5 Michael Jordan #2 6.00 15.00
6 Michael Jordan #3 6.00 15.00
7 M.Jordan/L.Bird 6.00 15.00
8 M.Jordan/J.Erving 6.00 15.00
9 M.Jordan #1 6.00 15.00
M.Jordan #2
10 M.Jordan #1 6.00 15.00
M.Jordan #3
11 M.Jordan #2 6.00 15.00
M.Jordan #3

1999-00 Upper Deck Retro Old School/New School

Randomly inserted in packs at one in three, this 30-card set highlights some of the top hoop stars of yesterday and today in two unique card designs. Card backs carry a "S" prefix.

COMPLETE SET (30) 12.50 30.00
STATED ODDS 1:3
*PARALLEL: 2X TO 5X HI COLUMN
PARALLEL: PRINT RUN 500 SERIAL #'d SETS
S1 Michael Jordan 3.00 8.00
S2 Wilt Chamberlain .75 2.00
S3 Oscar Robertson .50 1.25
S4 Julius Erving .60 1.50
S5 George Gervin .40 1.00
S6 John Havlicek .50 1.25
S7 Elgin Baylor .40 1.00
S8 Earl Monroe .40 1.00
S9 Jerry West .50 1.25
S10 Larry Bird 1.00 2.50
S11 Elvin Hayes .40 1.00
S12 Moses Malone .40 1.00
S13 Bill Walton .40 1.00
S14 Kareem Abdul-Jabbar .60 1.50
S15 Bill Russell .60 1.50
S16 Kobe Bryant 1.50 4.00
S17 Allen Iverson .75 2.00
S18 Stephon Marbury .30 .75
S19 Shaquille O'Neal 1.00 2.50
S20 Kevin Garnett .60 1.50
S21 Keith Van Horn .30 .75
S22 Jason Williams .50 1.25
S23 Paul Pierce .50 1.25
S24 Vince Carter .75 2.00
S25 Tim Duncan .75 2.00
S26 Antoine Walker .40 1.00
S27 Shareef Abdur-Rahim .30 .75
S28 Ray Allen .40 1.00
S29 Anfernee Hardaway .60 1.50
S30 Grant Hill .50 1.25

2004-05 Upper Deck Rivals Box Set

COMPLETE SET (30) 8.00 20.00
COMMON LEBRON (1-13) .60 1.50
COMMON CARMELO (14-26) .30 .75
COMMON DUAL (27-30) .40 1.00
AUTO'S NOT PRICED DUE TO SCARCITY
KCLJ LeBron James Jumbo 1.25 3.00

2004-05 Upper Deck Rivals Box Set Gold

*GOLD SINGLES: 1.25X TO 3X BASE HI

2004-05 Upper Deck Rivals Box Set Platinum

LEBRON PRINT RUN 23 SER.#'d SETS
CARMELO PRINT RUN 15 SER.#'d SETS
NOT PRICED DUE TO SCARCITY
COMMON COMBO (27-30) 40.00 100.00
COMBO PRINT RUN 38 SER.#'d SETS

2005-06 Upper Deck Rookie Debut

Released in September of 2005, Rookie Debut features the first live autographs and rookie cards from an NBA licensed products. The base set contains 150 cards where numberes 1-100 picture veterans and numbers 101-150 picture rookies. Base cards have full color action photography on the fronts and a colored line and banner in team colors with the player's name and team logo. Rooki cards employ a slightly different design where the word, "Rookie" is prominently displayed. Rookie Debut was packaged in 28-pack boxes of six cards each and carried a SRP of $2.99.

COMPLETE SET (150) 40.00 80.00
COMP.SET w/o RC's (100) 15.00 40.00
1 Tony Delk .15 .40
2 Josh Smith .20 .50
3 Al Harrington .20 .50
4 Antoine Walker .20 .50
5 Ricky Davis .20 .50
6 Paul Pierce .25 .60
7 Kareem Rush .15 .40
8 Emeka Okafor .20 .50
9 Primoz Brezec .15 .40
10 Eddy Curry .15 .40
11 Kirk Hinrich .20 .50
12 Ben Gordon .20 .50
13 Luol Deng .20 .50
14 Drew Gooden .20 .50
15 LeBron James 1.00 2.50
16 Zydrunas Ilgauskas .20 .50
17 Dirk Nowitzki .40 1.00
18 Jason Terry .20 .50
19 Josh Howard .25 .60
20 Michael Finley .25 .60
21 Carmelo Anthony .50 1.25
22 Kenyon Martin .20 .50
23 Andre Miller .20 .50
24 Earl Boykins .15 .40
25 Ben Wallace .20 .50
26 Chauncey Billups .25 .60
27 Richard Hamilton .20 .50
28 Tayshaun Prince .20 .50
29 Troy Murphy .15 .40
30 Jason Richardson .25 .60
31 Baron Davis .20 .50
32 Tracy McGrady .30 .75
33 Yao Ming .30 .75
34 Juwan Howard .20 .50
35 Jermaine O'Neal .20 .50
36 Stephen Jackson .20 .50
37 Ron Artest .25 .60
38 Corey Maggette .20 .50
39 Elton Brand .25 .60
40 Bobby Simmons .15 .40
41 Caron Butler .20 .50
42 Kobe Bryant 1.00 2.50
43 Lamar Odom .20 .50
44 Mike Miller .20 .50
45 Jason Williams .20 .50
46 Pau Gasol .25 .60
47 Stromile Swift .15 .40
48 Dwyane Wade .40 1.00
49 Eddie Jones .20 .50
50 Shaquille O'Neal .50 1.25
51 Desmond Mason .15 .40
52 Maurice Williams .20 .50
53 Michael Redd .20 .50
54 Kevin Garnett .40 1.00
55 Latrell Sprewell .20 .50
56 Sam Cassell .20 .50
57 Vince Carter .40 1.00
58 Jason Kidd .40 1.00
59 Richard Jefferson .20 .50
60 Dan Dickau .15 .40
61 Jamaal Magloire .15 .40
62 J.R. Smith .20 .50
63 Jamal Crawford .25 .60
64 Stephon Marbury .20 .50
65 Allan Houston .20 .50
66 Dwight Howard .20 .50
67 Grant Hill .30 .75
68 Steve Francis .20 .50
69 Allen Iverson .40 1.00
70 Andre Iguodala .20 .50
71 Chris Webber .25 .60
72 Kyle Korver .20 .50
73 Amare Stoudemire .20 .50
74 Shawn Marion .20 .50
75 Steve Nash .30 .75
76 Quentin Richardson .20 .50
77 Damon Stoudamire .20 .50
78 Shareef Abdur-Rahim .20 .50
79 Zach Randolph .20 .50
80 Brad Miller .20 .50
81 Mike Bibby .25 .60
82 Peja Stojakovic .25 .60
83 Cuttino Mobley .15 .40
84 Manu Ginobili .25 .60
85 Tim Duncan .40 1.00
86 Tony Parker .25 .60
87 Rashard Lewis .25 .60
88 Ray Allen .25 .60
89 Luke Ridnour .20 .50
90 Vladimir Radmanovic .15 .40
91 Rafer Alston .15 .40
92 Jalen Rose .25 .60
93 Chris Bosh .25 .60
94 Andrei Kirilenko .20 .50
95 Carlos Boozer .20 .50
96 Matt Harpring .15 .40

97 Antawn Jamison .20 .50
98 Gilbert Arenas .20 .50
99 Larry Hughes .20 .50
100 Jarvis Hayes .15 .40
101 Andrew Bogut RC 1.00 2.50
102 Chris Taft RC .60 1.50
103 Chris Paul RC 3.00 8.00
104 Martynas Andriuskevicius RC .50 1.25
105 Amir Johnson RC .75 2.00
106 Andrew Bynum RC .60 1.50
107 Gerald Green RC .75 2.00
108 Rashad McCants RC .60 1.50
109 Fran Vazquez RC .50 1.25
110 Ike Diogu RC .50 1.25
111 Raymond Felton RC .75 2.00
112 Hakim Warrick RC .60 1.50
113 Deron Williams RC 1.00 2.50
114 Daniel Ewing RC .60 1.50
115 Sean May RC .50 1.25
116 Johan Petro RC .50 1.25
117 Erazem Lorbek RC .75 2.00
118 Joey Graham RC .60 1.50
119 Antoine Wright RC .60 1.50
120 Ronny Turiaf RC .75 2.00
121 Linas Kleiza RC .50 1.25
122 Alex Acker RC .50 1.25
123 Jarrett Jack RC .75 2.00
124 Danny Granger RC 1.00 2.50
125 Francisco Garcia RC .60 1.50
126 Ryan Gomes RC .60 1.50
127 Wayne Simien RC .50 1.25
128 Robert Whaley RC .50 1.25
129 Dijon Thompson RC .50 1.25
130 Nate Robinson RC .75 2.00
131 Brandon Bass RC .60 1.50
132 Andray Blatche RC .75 2.00
133 Channing Frye RC .75 2.00
134 Salim Stoudamire RC .60 1.50
135 Luther Head RC .60 1.50
136 Julius Hodge RC .50 1.25
137 David Lee RC .75 2.00
138 Travis Diener RC .50 1.25
139 Marvin Williams RC .75 2.00
140 Lawrence Roberts RC .50 1.25
141 C.J. Miles RC .75 2.00
142 Ricky Sanchez RC .75 2.00
143 Bracey Wright RC .50 1.25
144 Jason Maxiell RC .60 1.50
145 Uros Slokar RC .75 2.00
146 Martell Webster RC .60 1.50
147 Orien Greene RC .60 1.50
148 Charlie Villanueva RC .75 2.00
149 Monta Ellis RC 1.00 2.50
150 Von Wafer RC .50 1.25

2005-06 Upper Deck Rookie Debut Blue

*1-100 BLUE: 2X TO 5X BASE HI
*101-150 RC BLUE: .6X TO 1.5X BASE HI
BLUE PRINT RUN 150 SER.#'d SETS

2005-06 Upper Deck Rookie Debut Gold

*1-100 GOLD: 5X TO 12X BASE HI
*101-150 RC GOLD: 1.5X TO 4X BASE HI
PRINT RUN 50 SER.#'d SETS

2005-06 Upper Deck Rookie Debut Silver

*1-100 SILVER: 3X TO 8X BASE HI
*101-150 RC SILVER: 1X TO 2.5X BASE HI
PRINT RUN 100 SER.#'d SETS

2005-06 Upper Deck Rookie Debut Spectrum

*1-100 SPEC: 8X TO 20X BASE HI
101-150 SPEC: 3X TO 6X BASE HI
PRINT RUN 25 SER.#'d SETS

2005-06 Upper Deck Rookie Debut Draft Duos

Randomly inserted in packs, this 24-card set features a horizontal design with two rookie player pictures and two sticker autographs. Each card is sequentially numbered to 75.

PRINT RUN 25 TO 75 SER.#'d SETS
BT A.Bogut/C.Taft/75 10.00 25.00
EB A.Emmett/A.Burks/75 8.00 20.00
EM M.Ellis/C.J.Miles/75 10.00 25.00
FM R.Felton/R.McCants/75 20.00 50.00
FS C.Frye/S.Stoudamire/75 12.50 30.00
GG R.Gomes/D.Granger/75 20.00 50.00
HN D.Howard/J.Nelson/75 30.00 60.00
JA LeBron/Carmelo/25 250.00 500.00
LG D.Lee/F.Garcia/75 15.00 40.00
PU P.Podkolzin/B.Udrih/75 8.00 20.00
PW C.Paul/D.Williams/75 40.00 80.00
RD K.Rush/D.Dickau/75 8.00 20.00
RW J.Reed/Del.West/75 8.00 20.00
TH Thompson/J.Hodge/75 8.00 20.00
TS R.Turiaf/W.Simien/75 12.50 30.00
VD F.Vazquez/T.Diener/75 8.00 20.00
WM M.Williams/S.May/75 8.00 20.00
WV H.Warrick/C.Villanueva/75 25.00 60.00
WW A.Wright/M.Webster/75 8.00 20.00

2005-06 Upper Deck Rookie Debut Hotagraphs

Randomly seeded in packs, this 29-card set places a rookie photo towards the top of the card and an autographed sticker on the bottom, separated by an orange and red bar containing the "HOTAGRAPHS" logo. Hotagraphs were packaged in six-card hot packs available one in 336 packs.

SIX AUTO's PER HOT PACK
HOT PACK STATED ODDS 1:336
ABA Andrew Bogut SP 20.00 50.00
ANA Andres Nocioni 5.00 12.00
AWA Antoine Wright 4.00 10.00
CDA Chris Duhon 5.00 12.00
CPA Chris Paul SP 60.00 120.00
CTA Chris Taft 4.00 10.00
CVA Charlie Villanueva 5.00 12.00
DEA Daniel Ewing 4.00 10.00
DHA Dwight Howard 10.00 25.00
FVA Fran Vazquez 3.00 8.00
GGA Gerald Green SP 8.00 20.00
HWA Hakim Warrick 4.00 10.00
JGA Joey Graham 4.00 10.00
JHA Julius Hodge 3.00 8.00
JNA Jameer Nelson 5.00 12.00
JRA J.R. Smith 5.00 12.00
LHA Luther Head 4.00 10.00
LJA LeBron James SP 150.00 300.00
MAA Martell Webster 4.00 10.00
MWA Marvin Williams SP 5.00 12.00
RFA Raymond Felton 5.00 12.00
RGA Ryan Gomes 4.00 10.00
RMA Rashad McCants 4.00 10.00
RTA Ronny Turiaf 6.00 15.00
SMA Sean May SP 6.00 15.00
SSA Salim Stoudamire 4.00 10.00

2005-06 Upper Deck Rookie Debut Ink

Inserted at the rate of one in 14, this 74-card set employs similar design elements to the base set along with photos and sticker autographs. Several players were shortprinted, information that was provided directly from Upper Deck.

STATED ODDS 1:14
AB Andrew Bogut SP 12.50 30.00
AE Andre Emmett 5.00 12.00
AJ Al Jefferson 5.00 12.00
AN Antonio Burks 5.00 12.00
AV Anderson Varejao 5.00 12.00
AW Antoine Wright 4.00 10.00
BI Andris Biedrins 5.00 12.00
BL Andray Blatche 5.00 12.00
BR Bernard Robinson 5.00 12.00
BU Beno Udrih 5.00 12.00
BW Bracey Wright 3.00 8.00
BY Andrew Bynum 4.00 10.00
CD Chris Duhon 5.00 12.00
CF Channing Frye 5.00 12.00
CJ C.J. Miles 5.00 12.00
CP Chris Paul SP 40.00 100.00
CT Chris Taft 4.00 10.00
CV Charlie Villanueva 5.00 12.00
DA Danny Granger 6.00 15.00
DD Dan Dickau 5.00 12.00
DE Daniel Ewing 4.00 10.00
DH Dwight Howard 12.50 30.00
DL David Lee 5.00 12.00
DT Dijon Thompson 3.00 8.00
DW Deron Williams SP 20.00 40.00
ED Erik Daniels 5.00 12.00
FG Francisco Garcia 4.00 10.00
FV Fran Vazquez 3.00 8.00
GG Gerald Green 5.00 12.00
HS Ha Seung-Jin 5.00 12.00
HW Hakim Warrick 4.00 10.00
ID Ike Diogu 3.00 8.00
JE John Edwards 5.00 12.00
JH Julius Hodge 3.00 8.00
JJ Jarrett Jack 5.00 12.00
JM Jason Maxiell 4.00 10.00
JN Jameer Nelson 5.00 12.00
JP Johan Petro 3.00 8.00
JR J.R. Smith 5.00 12.00
JU Justin Reed 5.00 12.00
KD Keyon Dooling 5.00 12.00
KS Kirk Snyder 5.00 12.00
LC Lionel Chalmers 5.00 12.00
LF Luis Flores 5.00 12.00
LH Luther Head 4.00 10.00
LJ LeBron James SP 150.00 300.00
MA Martynas Andriuskevicius 3.00 8.00
MD Marquis Daniels 5.00 12.00
ME Monta Ellis 6.00 15.00
MG Mickael Gelabale 5.00 12.00
ML Martell Webster 4.00 10.00
MR Michael Redd SP 8.00 20.00
MW Marvin Williams SP 5.00 12.00
NO Andres Nocioni 5.00 12.00
NR Nate Robinson 5.00 12.00
PP Pavel Podkolzin 5.00 12.00
RA Rafael Araujo 5.00 12.00
RF Raymond Felton 5.00 12.00
RG Ryan Gomes 4.00 10.00
RI Royal Ivey 5.00 12.00
RM Rashad McCants 4.00 10.00
RT Ronny Turiaf 5.00 12.00
SM Sean May 3.00 8.00
SS Salim Stoudamire 4.00 10.00
ST Sebastian Telfair 5.00 12.00
TD Travis Diener 3.00 8.00
UH Udonis Haslem 5.00 12.00
VK Viktor Khryapa 5.00 12.00
WE Delonte West 5.00 12.00
WI Maurice Williams 5.00 12.00
WS Wayne Simien 3.00 8.00

2005-06 Upper Deck Rookie Debut Sizzling Swatches

Inserted as four-card memorabilia hot packs at the rate of one in 168, this 42-card set employs a horizontal design with player images on the right and a circle swatch of memorabilia on the left.

FOUR PER MEMORABILIA HOT PACK
HOT PACKS STATED ODDS 1:168
AI Allen Iverson 4.00 10.00
AJ Antawn Jamison 2.00 5.00
AS Amare Stoudemire 2.00 5.00
BG Ben Gordon 2.00 5.00
BW Ben Wallace 2.00 5.00
CA Carmelo Anthony 5.00 12.00
CB Chris Bosh 2.50 6.00
CW Chris Webber 2.50 6.00
DE Devin Harris 1.50 4.00
DH Dwight Howard 2.00 5.00
DN Dirk Nowitzki 4.00 10.00
GA Gilbert Arenas 2.00 5.00
GP Gary Payton 2.50 6.00
IG Andre Iguodala 2.00 5.00
JA Jason Richardson 2.50 6.00
JC Josh Childress 2.00 5.00
JK Jason Kidd 4.00 10.00
JR J.R. Smith 2.00 5.00
JS Josh Smith 2.00 5.00
KB Kobe Bryant 8.00 20.00
KG Kevin Garnett 4.00 10.00
LD Luol Deng 2.00 5.00
LJ LeBron James 10.00 25.00
MF Michael Finley 2.50 6.00
MG Manu Ginobili 2.50 6.00
MJ Michael Jordan 40.00 100.00
PG Pau Gasol 2.50 6.00
PP Paul Pierce 2.50 6.00
PS Peja Stojakovic 2.50 6.00
RA Ray Allen 2.50 6.00
RH Richard Hamilton 2.00 5.00
RJ Richard Jefferson 2.00 5.00
RL Rashard Lewis 2.50 6.00
SF Steve Francis 2.00 5.00
SM Shawn Marion 2.00 5.00
SN Steve Nash 3.00 8.00
SO Shaquille O'Neal 5.00 12.00
ST Stephon Marbury 2.00 5.00
TD Tim Duncan 4.00 10.00
TM Tracy McGrady 3.00 8.00
TP Tony Parker 2.50 6.00
YM Yao Ming 3.00 8.00

2005-06 Upper Deck Rookie Debut Threads

Randomly seeded at one in 28, this 90-card set also utilizes a horizontal design with some similar design attributes to the base set. Player images appear on the right of the card, while a square swatch of memorabilia appears on the left.

STATED ODDS 1:28
AH Allan Houston 2.00 5.00
AI Allen Iverson 4.00 10.00
AK Andrei Kirilenko 2.00 5.00
AL Rafer Alston 2.00 5.00
AM Andre Miller 2.00 5.00
AN Antonio McDyess 2.00 5.00
AR Ron Artest 2.50 6.00
AS Amare Stoudemire 2.00 5.00
AW Antoine Walker 2.00 5.00
BC Brian Cook 2.00 5.00
BD Baron Davis 2.00 5.00
BM Brad Miller 2.00 5.00
BO Chris Bosh 2.50 6.00
BU Caron Butler 2.00 5.00
BW Ben Wallace 2.00 5.00
CA Carmelo Anthony 5.00 12.00
CB Carlos Boozer 2.00 5.00
CH Chauncey Billups 2.50 6.00
CK Chris Kaman 2.00 5.00
CM Corey Maggette 2.00 5.00
CU Cuttino Mobley 1.50 4.00
CW Chris Webber 2.50 6.00
DD Dan Dickau 2.00 5.00
DF Derek Fisher 2.00 5.00
DG Devean George 2.00 5.00
DM Darko Milicic 2.00 5.00
DN Dirk Nowitzki 4.00 10.00
DO Donyell Marshall 2.00 5.00
DR Drew Gooden 2.00 5.00
DS Damon Stoudamire 2.00 5.00
EB Elton Brand 2.50 6.00
EC Eddy Curry 1.50 4.00
GA Gilbert Arenas 2.00 5.00
GH Grant Hill 3.00 8.00
GP Gary Payton 2.50 6.00
GR Glenn Robinson 2.00 5.00
GW Gerald Wallace 2.00 5.00
HA Anfernee Hardaway 6.00 15.00
HO Josh Howard 2.50 6.00
HT Hedo Turkoglu 2.00 5.00
IG Andre Iguodala 2.00 5.00
JA Jason Richardson 2.50 6.00
JC Jamal Crawford 2.50 6.00
JH Jarvis Hayes 2.00 5.00
JJ Joe Johnson 2.00 5.00
JK Jason Kidd 4.00 10.00
JO Jermaine O'Neal 2.00 5.00
JR Jalen Rose 2.50 6.00
JT Jamaal Tinsley 2.00 5.00
KB Kobe Bryant 8.00 20.00
KG Kevin Garnett 4.00 10.00
KK Kyle Korver 2.00 5.00
KM Kenyon Martin 2.00 5.00
KR Kareem Rush 2.00 5.00
KT Kurt Thomas 2.00 5.00
KW Kwame Brown 2.00 5.00
LJ LeBron James 10.00 25.00
LO Lamar Odom 2.00 5.00
LW Luke Walton 2.00 5.00
MA Marko Jaric 2.00 5.00
MB Mike Bibby 2.50 6.00
MF Michael Finley 2.50 6.00
MG Manu Ginobili 2.50 6.00
MJ Michael Jordan 40.00 100.00
MO Morris Peterson 1.50 4.00
MP Mickael Pietrus 2.00 5.00
MR Michael Redd 2.00 5.00
NH Nene 2.00 5.00
NV Nick Van Exel 2.50 6.00
PG Pau Gasol 2.50 6.00
PP Paul Pierce 2.50 6.00
PS Peja Stojakovic 2.50 6.00
QR Quentin Richardson 2.00 5.00
RA Ray Allen 2.50 6.00
RH Richard Hamilton 2.00 5.00
RJ Richard Jefferson 2.00 5.00
RL Rashard Lewis 2.50 6.00
RW Rasheed Wallace 2.50 6.00
SF Steve Francis 2.00 5.00
SM Shawn Marion 2.00 5.00
SN Steve Nash 3.00 8.00
SO Shaquille O'Neal 5.00 12.00
ST Stephon Marbury 2.00 5.00
TC Tyson Chandler 2.00 5.00
TD Tim Duncan 4.00 10.00
TE Jason Terry 2.00 5.00
TM Tracy McGrady 3.00 8.00
TP Tony Parker 2.50 6.00
WE Bonzi Wells 2.00 5.00
WI Chris Wilcox 2.00 5.00

2006-07 Upper Deck Rookie Debut

Released in late September 2006, Rookie Debut base cards place full-color player photos on cards designed with a colored strip along the right side of the card to match team colors and a run sheet of player information along the bottom. Veteran players are pictured on card numbers 1-100 and rookies on cards 101-146. Rookie Debut is packaged in 28-pack boxes of six cards each and carried an initial suggested retail price of $2.99.

COMPLETE SET (146) 40.00 80.00
COMP.SET w/o SP's (100) 12.50 30.00
1 Josh Childress .20 .50
2 Joe Johnson .20 .50
3 Marvin Williams .20 .50
4 Gerald Green .20 .50
5 Al Jefferson .20 .50
6 Paul Pierce .25 .60
7 Raymond Felton .20 .50
8 Emeka Okafor .20 .50
9 Gerald Wallace .20 .50
10 Tyson Chandler .20 .50
11 Luol Deng .20 .50
12 Ben Gordon .20 .50
13 Larry Hughes .20 .50
14 Zydrunas Ilgauskas .20 .50
15 LeBron James 1.00 2.50
16 Devin Harris .15 .40
17 Josh Howard .20 .50
18 Dirk Nowitzki .40 1.00
19 Jason Terry .20 .50
20 Carmelo Anthony .30 .75
21 Marcus Camby .20 .50
22 Kenyon Martin .20 .50
23 Chauncey Billups .25 .60
24 Richard Hamilton .20 .50
25 Tayshaun Prince .20 .50
26 Ben Wallace .20 .50
27 Baron Davis .20 .50
28 Troy Murphy .15 .40
29 Jason Richardson .25 .60
30 Rafer Alston .15 .40
31 Tracy McGrady .30 .75
32 Stromile Swift .15 .40
33 Yao Ming .30 .75
34 Jermaine O'Neal .20 .50
35 Peja Stojakovic .25 .60
36 Jamaal Tinsley .15 .40
37 Elton Brand .25 .60
38 Sam Cassell .20 .50
39 Chris Kaman .20 .50
40 Kobe Bryant 1.00 2.50
41 Devean George .15 .40
42 Ronny Turiaf .20 .50
43 Pau Gasol .25 .60
44 Mike Miller .20 .50
45 Damon Stoudamire .20 .50
46 Shaquille O'Neal .50 1.25
47 Gary Payton .25 .60
48 Dwyane Wade .40 1.00
49 Andrew Bogut .20 .50
50 T.J. Ford .15 .40
51 Jamaal Magloire .15 .40
52 Michael Redd .20 .50
53 Ricky Davis .20 .50
54 Kevin Garnett .40 1.00
55 Rashad McCants .15 .40
56 Vince Carter .30 .75
57 Richard Jefferson .20 .50
58 Jason Kidd .40 1.00
59 P.J. Brown .15 .40
60 Desmond Mason .15 .40
61 Chris Paul .30 .75
62 J.R. Smith .20 .50
63 Steve Francis .20 .50
64 Channing Frye .20 .50
65 Stephon Marbury .20 .50
66 Nate Robinson .15 .40
67 Grant Hill .30 .75
68 Dwight Howard .20 .50
69 Jameer Nelson .15 .40
70 Darko Milicic .15 .40
71 Andre Iguodala .20 .50
72 Allen Iverson .30 .75
73 Kyle Korver .20 .50
74 Chris Webber .25 .60
75 Boris Diaw .20 .50
76 Shawn Marion .20 .50
77 Steve Nash .30 .75
78 Amare Stoudemire .20 .50
79 Juan Dixon .15 .40
80 Joel Przybilla .15 .40
81 Sebastian Telfair .15 .40
82 Shareef Abdur-Rahim .20 .50
83 Ron Artest .25 .60
84 Mike Bibby .25 .60
85 Tim Duncan .40 1.00
86 Manu Ginobili .25 .60
87 Robert Horry .20 .50
88 Tony Parker .25 .60
89 Ray Allen .25 .60
90 Rashard Lewis .25 .60
91 Luke Ridnour .20 .50
92 Chris Bosh .25 .60
93 Jose Calderon .15 .40
94 Charlie Villanueva .15 .40
95 Carlos Boozer .20 .50
96 Andrei Kirilenko .20 .50
97 Deron Williams .20 .50
98 Gilbert Arenas .20 .50
99 Antawn Jamison .20 .50
100 Caron Butler .20 .50
101 Tyrus Thomas RC .50 1.25
102 Adam Morrison RC .60 1.50
103 LaMarcus Aldridge RC 1.50 4.00
104 Rudy Gay RC .75 2.00
105 Andrea Bargnani RC .60 1.50
106 Rodney Carney RC .40 1.00
107 Mike Gansey RC .40 1.00
108 Brandon Roy RC .60 1.50
109 Patrick O'Bryant RC .40 1.00
110 Randy Foye RC .60 1.50
111 Ronnie Brewer RC .60 1.50
112 Mardy Collins RC .40 1.00
113 Shelden Williams RC .50 1.25
114 J.J. Redick RC .75 2.00
115 Hilton Armstrong RC .40 1.00
116 Marcus Williams RC .40 1.00
117 Rajon Rondo RC 1.00 2.50
118 Cedric Simmons RC .40 1.00
119 Ryan Hollins RC .50 1.25
120 Jordan Farmar RC .60 1.50
121 Maurice Ager RC .40 1.00
122 Renaldo Balkman RC .50 1.25
123 Leon Powe RC .50 1.25
124 Solomon Jones RC .40 1.00
125 Bobby Jones RC .40 1.00
126 Josh Boone RC .40 1.00
127 Saer Sene RC .40 1.00
128 Daniel Gibson RC .50 1.25
129 Hassan Adams RC .40 1.00
130 Kyle Lowry RC .75 2.00
131 Shannon Brown RC .40 1.00
132 Dee Brown RC .40 1.00
133 Shawne Williams RC .40 1.00
134 P.J. Tucker RC .50 1.25
135 Craig Smith RC .50 1.25
136 Paul Davis RC .40 1.00
137 Allan Ray RC .40 1.00
138 Denham Brown RC .40 1.00
139 Chris Quinn RC .40 1.00
140 Joel Freeland RC .40 1.00
141 James Augustine RC .40 1.00
142 Thabo Sefolosha RC .60 1.50
143 Quincy Douby RC .40 1.00
144 James White RC .40 1.00
145 David Noel RC .40 1.00
146 Steve Novak RC .50 1.25

2006-07 Upper Deck Rookie Debut Bronze

*1-100 BRONZE: 2.5X TO 6X BASE HI
*101-146 BRONZE: 1.25X TO 3X BASE HI
BRONZE PRINT RUN 100 SER.#'d SETS

2006-07 Upper Deck Rookie Debut Gold

*1-100 GOLD: 10X TO 25X BASE HI
*101-146 GOLD: 6X TO 15X BASE HI
GOLD PRINT RUN 10 SER.#'d SETS

2006-07 Upper Deck Rookie Debut Platinum

*1-100 PLATINUM: 2X TO 5X BASE HI
*101-146 PLATINUM: 1X TO 2.5X BASE HI
STATED PRINT RUN 150 SER.#'d SETS

2006-07 Upper Deck Rookie Debut Silver

*1-100 SILVER: 3X TO 8X BASE HI
*101-146 SILVER: 2X TO 5X BASE HI
SILVER PRINT RUN 50 SER.#'d SETS

2006-07 Upper Deck Rookie Debut Draft Duos

COMPLETE SET (25) 20.00 50.00
APPROXIMATE ODDS 1:20
BA E.Brand/R.Artest 1.50 4.00
BH M.Bibby/L.Hughes 1.50 4.00
BJ C.Billups/B.Jackson 1.50 4.00
BP C.Boozer/T.Prince 1.50 4.00
BW A.Bogut/Mv.Williams 1.50 4.00
CB T.Chandler/Kw.Brown 1.50 4.00
DH B.Davis/R.Hamilton 1.50 4.00
DS K.Dooling/D.Stevenson 1.50 4.00
EK D.Ewing/Y.Korolev 1.50 4.00
FM R.Felton/S.May 1.50 4.00
FV C.Frye/C.Villanueva 1.50 4.00
GD B.Gordon/C.Duhon 1.50 4.00
IC A.Iguodala/J.Childress 2.00 5.00
JA L.James/C.Anthony 4.00 10.00
JJ J.Johnson/R.Jefferson 1.50 4.00
KH K.Korver/K.Hinrich 1.50 4.00
LS S.Livingston/J.R.Smith 1.50 4.00
NJ J.Nelson/A.Jefferson 1.50 4.00
OH E.Okafor/D.Howard 2.00 5.00
PC P.Pierce/V.Carter 2.50 6.00
PW C.Paul/D.Williams 3.00 8.00
RH L.Ridnour/K.Hinrich 1.50 4.00
RS V.Radmanovic/B.Simmons 1.50 4.00
SR Q.Richardson/S.Swift 1.50 4.00
WH H.Warrick/L.Head 1.50 4.00

2006-07 Upper Deck Rookie Debut Draft Duos Autographs

STATED PRINT RUN 5 TO 25 SER.#'d SETS
SOME UNPRICED DUE TO SCARCITY
BH M.Bibby/L.Hughes/25 12.00 30.00
BW A.Bogut/Mv.Williams/25 12.00 30.00
CB T.Chandler/Kw.Brown/25 10.00 25.00
DS K.Dooling/Stevenson/25 10.00 25.00
EK D.Ewing/Y.Korolev/25 10.00 25.00
FM R.Felton/S.May/25 12.00 30.00
JJ J.Johnson/R.Jefferson/25 10.00 25.00
KH K.Korver/K.Hinrich/25 10.00 25.00
LS S.Livingston/J.R.Smith/25 10.00 25.00
PW C.Paul/D.Williams/25 40.00 100.00
RS Radmanovic/Simmons/25 10.00 25.00
SR Q.Richardson/S.Swift/25 10.00 25.00

2006-07 Upper Deck Rookie Debut Ink

APPROXIMATE ODDS 1:20
*GOLD: .75X TO 2X BASE HI
GOLD PRINT RUN 25 SER.#'d SETS
AB Andrea Bargnani 4.00 10.00
AD Hassan Adams 2.50 6.00
BJ Bobby Jones 2.50 6.00
BR Brandon Roy 4.00 10.00
CS Cedric Simmons 2.50 6.00
DB Dee Brown 2.50 6.00
DE Denham Brown 2.50 6.00
DG Daniel Gibson 3.00 8.00
DN David Noel 2.50 6.00
HA Hilton Armstrong 2.50 6.00
JA James Augustine 2.50 6.00
JB Josh Boone 2.50 6.00
JF Jordan Farmar 4.00 10.00
JW James White 2.50 6.00
KL Kyle Lowry 8.00 20.00
LA LaMarcus Aldridge 10.00 25.00
MA Maurice Ager 2.50 6.00
MC Mardy Collins 2.50 6.00
MW Marcus Williams 2.50 6.00
PD Paul Davis 2.50 6.00
PO Patrick O'Bryant 2.50 6.00
PT P.J. Tucker 3.00 8.00
QD Quincy Douby 2.50 6.00
RB Ronnie Brewer 4.00 10.00
RC Rodney Carney 2.50 6.00
RF Randy Foye 4.00 10.00
RG Rudy Gay 5.00 12.00
RH Ryan Hollins 3.00 8.00
RR Rajon Rondo 20.00 50.00
SJ Solomon Jones 2.50 6.00
SM Craig Smith 3.00 8.00
SN Steve Novak 3.00 8.00
SW Shelden Williams 3.00 8.00
TS Thabo Sefolosha 4.00 10.00
TT Tyrus Thomas 3.00 8.00

2006-07 Upper Deck Rookie Debut Materialization

APPROXIMATE ODDS 1:12
AB Andrew Bynum 1.50 4.00
AI Andre Iguodala 2.00 5.00
AS Amare Stoudemire 2.00 5.00
BL Andray Blatche 2.00 5.00
BO Andrew Bogut 2.00 5.00
BR Kobe Bryant 8.00 20.00
CA Carmelo Anthony SP 3.00 8.00
CB Chris Bosh 2.50 6.00
CM Corey Maggette 2.00 5.00
CP Chris Paul 3.00 8.00
CV Charlie Villanueva 1.50 4.00
CW Chris Webber 2.50 6.00
DG Danny Granger 2.00 5.00
DH Dwight Howard 2.00 5.00
DM Donyell Marshall 2.00 5.00
DN Dirk Nowitzki 4.00 10.00
DS Damon Stoudamire 2.00 5.00
EB Elton Brand 2.50 6.00
FG Francisco Garcia 1.50 4.00
GE Devean George 2.00 5.00
GW Gerald Wallace SP 2.00 5.00
HO Julius Hodge 2.00 5.00
ID Ike Diogu 2.00 5.00
JG Joey Graham 2.00 5.00
JJ Joe Johnson 2.00 5.00
JK Jason Kidd 4.00 10.00
JM Jamaal Magloire 2.00 5.00
JO Jermaine O'Neal 2.00 5.00
JP Johan Petro 2.00 5.00
KB Kwame Brown 2.00 5.00
KG Kevin Garnett 4.00 10.00
KM Kenyon Martin 2.00 5.00
KT Kurt Thomas 2.00 5.00
LH Larry Hughes 2.00 5.00
LJ LeBron James 10.00 25.00
MA Desmond Mason 2.00 5.00
MC Jeff McInnis 2.00 5.00
MJ Michael Jordan SP 30.00 80.00
MR Michael Redd 2.00 5.00
MS Mike Sweetney 2.00 5.00
MW Martell Webster 2.00 5.00
PG Pau Gasol 2.50 6.00
PP Paul Pierce 2.50 6.00
PS Peja Stojakovic 2.50 6.00
RJ Richard Jefferson 2.00 5.00
RM Rashad McCants 2.00 5.00
SD Samuel Dalembert 2.00 5.00
SF Steve Francis 2.00 5.00
SH Shawn Marion 2.00 5.00
SM Sean May 1.50 4.00
SO Shaquille O'Neal 5.00 12.00
SS Stromile Swift 2.00 5.00
TC Tyson Chandler 2.00 5.00
TD Tim Duncan 4.00 10.00
TM Tracy McGrady SP 3.00 8.00
TP Tony Parker 2.50 6.00
VC Vince Carter 3.00 8.00
WS Wally Szczerbiak 2.00 5.00
YM Yao Ming 3.00 8.00
ZI Zydrunas Ilgauskas 2.00 5.00

2003-04 Upper Deck Rookie Exclusives

Released in February 2004, Rookie Exclusives boasts a 60-card set where the first 30 are rookie cards and the last 30 are veterans. Each card places a full-color player action photo on a color background with borders on the left right and bottom of the card. Rookie Exclusives was packaged in 28-pack boxes where packs contained six cards and carried a suggested retail price of $2.99.

COMPLETE SET (60) 12.50 30.00
1 LeBron James RC 6.00 15.00
2 Darko Milicic RC .30 .75
3 Carmelo Anthony RC 1.25 3.00
4 Chris Bosh RC .60 1.50
5 Dwyane Wade RC 1.25 3.00
6 Chris Kaman RC .40 1.00
7 Jarvis Hayes RC .25 .60
8 Mickael Pietrus RC .30 .75
9 Marcus Banks RC .25 .60
10 Luke Ridnour RC .30 .75
11 Reece Gaines RC .25 .60
12 Troy Bell RC .25 .60
13 Zarko Cabarkapa RC .25 .60
14 David West RC .40 1.00
15 Aleksandar Pavlovic RC .30 .75
16 Dahntay Jones RC .30 .75
17 Boris Diaw RC .40 1.00
18 Zoran Planinic RC .25 .60
19 Travis Outlaw RC .30 .75
20 Brian Cook RC .25 .60
21 Ndudi Ebi RC .25 .60
22 Kendrick Perkins RC .30 .75
23 Leandro Barbosa RC .40 1.00
24 Josh Howard RC .40 1.00
25 Maciej Lampe RC .25 .60
26 Jason Kapono RC .25 .60
27 Luke Walton RC .40 1.00
28 Travis Hansen RC .25 .60
29 Steve Blake RC .30 .75
30 Slavko Vranes RC .25 .60
31 Darius Miles .12 .30
32 Tony Parker .20 .50
33 Chauncey Billups .20 .50
34 Carlos Boozer .15 .40
35 Richard Hamilton .15 .40
36 Jamaal Tinsley .12 .30
37 Tracy McGrady .25 .60
38 Manu Ginobili .25 .60
39 Andre Miller .15 .40
40 Richard Jefferson .15 .40
41 Paul Pierce .20 .50
42 Peja Stojakovic .20 .50
43 Jason Richardson .20 .50
44 Shawn Marion .15 .40
45 Antawn Jamison .15 .40
46 Reggie Evans .12 .30
47 Earl Boykins .12 .30
48 Corey Maggette .15 .40
49 Cuttino Mobley .12 .30
50 Shane Battier .15 .40
51 Shareef Abdur-Rahim .15 .40
52 Chris Wilcox .12 .30
53 Steve Francis .15 .40
54 Mike Bibby .20 .50
55 Morris Peterson .12 .30
56 Nene .15 .40
57 Juan Dixon .12 .30
58 Yao Ming .40 1.00
59 Kobe Bryant .75 2.00
60 Michael Jordan 1.50 4.00

2003-04 Upper Deck Rookie Exclusives Gold

*1-30 RCs: 3X TO 8X BASE CARD HI
*31-60 SINGLES: 5X TO 12X BASE CARD HI
GOLD PRINT RUN 100 SER.#'d SETS
1 LeBron James 75.00 200.00

2003-04 Upper Deck Rookie Exclusives Variation

*1-30 RCs: 1X TO 2.5X BASE CARD HI
CHECKLIST 31-60 DIFFERENT FROM BASE
31 Allen Iverson .75 2.00
32 Dirk Nowitzki .75 2.00
33 Steve Nash .60 1.50
34 Richard Hamilton .40 1.00
35 Shaquille O'Neal 1.25 3.00
36 Jamaal Tinsley .30 .75
37 Tim Duncan .75 2.00
38 Stephon Marbury .40 1.00
39 Caron Butler .40 1.00
40 Paul Pierce .50 1.25
41 Amare Stoudemire .60 1.50
42 Gary Payton .50 1.25
43 Karl Malone .60 1.50
44 Ben Wallace .40 1.00
45 Antoine Walker .50 1.25
46 Kenyon Martin .40 1.00
47 Latrell Sprewell .40 1.00
48 Rasheed Wallace .50 1.25
49 Chris Webber .50 1.25
50 Ray Allen .50 1.25
51 Jermaine O'Neal .40 1.00
52 Chris Wilcox .30 .75
53 Kevin Garnett .75 2.00
54 Pau Gasol .50 1.25
55 Jason Kidd .75 2.00
56 Jason Terry .40 1.00
57 Dajuan Wagner .30 .75
58 Yao Ming 1.00 2.50
59 Kobe Bryant 2.00 5.00
60 Michael Jordan 4.00 10.00

2003-04 Upper Deck Rookie Exclusives Autographs

AU STATED ODDS 1:28 H, 1:1000 R
A1 LeBron James SP 1000.00 1500.00
A2 Darko Milicic 3.00 8.00
A3 Carmelo Anthony SP 30.00 80.00
A4 Chris Bosh 15.00 40.00
A5 Dwyane Wade 40.00 100.00
A6 Chris Kaman 4.00 10.00
A7 Jarvis Hayes 2.50 6.00
A8 Mickael Pietrus 3.00 8.00
A9 Marcus Banks 2.50 6.00
A10 Luke Ridnour 3.00 8.00
A11 Reece Gaines 2.50 6.00
A12 Troy Bell 2.50 6.00
A13 Zarko Cabarkapa 2.50 6.00
A14 David West 4.00 10.00
A15 Aleksandar Pavlovic 3.00 8.00
A16 Dahntay Jones 3.00 8.00
A17 Boris Diaw 4.00 10.00
A18 Zoran Planinic 2.50 6.00
A19 Travis Outlaw 3.00 8.00
A20 Brian Cook 2.50 6.00
A21 Ndudi Ebi 2.50 6.00
A22 Kendrick Perkins 3.00 8.00
A23 Leandro Barbosa 4.00 10.00
A24 Josh Howard 4.00 10.00
A25 Maciej Lampe 2.50 6.00
A26 Jason Kapono 2.50 6.00
A27 Luke Walton 4.00 10.00
A28 Travis Hansen 2.50 6.00
A29 Steve Blake 3.00 8.00
A30 Slavko Vranes 2.50 6.00
A31 Darius Miles 4.00 10.00
A32 Tony Parker 10.00 25.00
A33 Chauncey Billups 6.00 15.00
A34 Carlos Boozer 5.00 12.00
A35 Richard Hamilton 6.00 15.00
A37 Tracy McGrady 15.00 40.00
A38 Manu Ginobili 10.00 25.00
A39 Andre Miller 4.00 10.00
A40 Richard Jefferson 4.00 10.00
A41 Paul Pierce 12.00 30.00
A42 Peja Stojakovic 8.00 20.00
A43 Jason Richardson 6.00 15.00
A44 Shawn Marion 6.00 15.00
A45 Antawn Jamison 4.00 10.00
A46 Reggie Evans 4.00 10.00
A47 Earl Boykins 4.00 10.00
A48 Corey Maggette 4.00 10.00
A49 Cuttino Mobley 4.00 10.00
A50 Shane Battier 5.00 12.00
A51 Shareef Abdur-Rahim 4.00 10.00
A52 Chris Wilcox 4.00 10.00
A53 Steve Francis 6.00 15.00
A54 Mike Bibby 4.00 10.00
A55 Morris Peterson 4.00 10.00
A56 Nene 4.00 10.00
A57 Juan Dixon 4.00 10.00
A58 Yao Ming 15.00 40.00
A59 Kobe Bryant 100.00 200.00
A60 Michael Jordan 400.00 800.00

2003-04 Upper Deck Rookie Exclusives Jerseys

ALL JSY STATED ODDS 1:28 H, 1:14 R
J1 LeBron James 30.00 80.00
J2 Darko Milicic 2.00 5.00
J3 Carmelo Anthony 8.00 20.00
J4 Chris Bosh 4.00 10.00
J5 Dwyane Wade 8.00 20.00
J6 Chris Kaman 2.50 6.00
J7 Jarvis Hayes 1.50 4.00
J8 Mickael Pietrus 2.00 5.00
J9 Marcus Banks 1.50 4.00
J10 Luke Ridnour 2.00 5.00
J11 Reece Gaines 1.50 4.00
J12 Troy Bell 1.50 4.00
J13 Zarko Cabarkapa 1.50 4.00
J14 David West 2.50 6.00
J15 Aleksandar Pavlovic 2.00 5.00
J16 Dahntay Jones 2.00 5.00
J17 Boris Diaw 2.50 6.00
J18 Zoran Planinic 1.50 4.00
J19 Travis Outlaw 2.00 5.00
J20 Brian Cook 1.50 4.00
J21 Ndudi Ebi 1.50 4.00
J22 Kendrick Perkins 2.00 5.00
J23 Leandro Barbosa 2.50 6.00
J24 Josh Howard 2.50 6.00
J25 Maciej Lampe 1.50 4.00
J26 Jason Kapono 1.50 4.00
J27 Luke Walton 2.50 6.00
J28 Travis Hansen 1.50 4.00
J29 Steve Blake 2.00 5.00
J30 Slavko Vranes 1.50 4.00
J31 Darius Miles 2.00 5.00
J32 Tony Parker 2.50 6.00
J33 Chauncey Billups 2.50 6.00
J34 Carlos Boozer SP 4.00 10.00
J35 Richard Hamilton 2.00 5.00
J36 Jamaal Tinsley 2.00 5.00
J37 Tracy McGrady 3.00 8.00
J38 Manu Ginobili 3.00 8.00
J39 Andre Miller 2.00 5.00
J40 Richard Jefferson 2.00 5.00
J41 Paul Pierce 2.50 6.00
J42 Peja Stojakovic 2.50 6.00
J43 Jason Richardson 2.50 6.00
J44 Shawn Marion 2.00 5.00
J45 Antawn Jamison 2.00 5.00
J46 Reggie Evans 2.00 5.00
J47 Earl Boykins 2.00 5.00
J48 Corey Maggette 2.00 5.00
J50 Shane Battier 2.00 5.00
J51 Shareef Abdur-Rahim 2.00 5.00
J52 Chris Wilcox 2.00 5.00
J53 Steve Francis 2.00 5.00
J54 Mike Bibby 2.50 6.00
J55 Morris Peterson 1.50 4.00
J56 Nene 2.00 5.00
J57 Juan Dixon 2.00 5.00
J58 Yao Ming 5.00 12.00
J59 Kobe Bryant 10.00 25.00
J60 Michael Jordan 40.00 100.00

2003-04 Upper Deck Rookie Exclusives Jerseys Variation

ALL JSY STATED ODDS 1:28 H, 1:14 R
J24 Mike Sweetney 1.50 4.00
J31 Allen Iverson 4.00 10.00
J32 Dirk Nowitzki 4.00 10.00
J33 Steve Nash 3.00 8.00
J35 Shaquille O'Neal 6.00 15.00
J37 Tim Duncan 4.00 10.00
J38 Stephon Marbury 2.00 5.00
J39 Caron Butler 2.00 5.00
J41 Amare Stoudemire 3.00 8.00
J42 Gary Payton 2.50 6.00
J43 Karl Malone 3.00 8.00
J44 Ben Wallace 2.00 5.00
J45 Antoine Walker SP 2.50 6.00
J46 Kenyon Martin 2.00 5.00
J47 Latrell Sprewell 2.00 5.00
J48 Rasheed Wallace SP 2.50 6.00
J49 Chris Webber 2.50 6.00
J50 Ray Allen SP 4.00 10.00
J51 Jermaine O'Neal 2.00 5.00
J53 Kevin Garnett 4.00 10.00
J54 Pau Gasol 2.50 6.00
J55 Jason Kidd 4.00 10.00
J56 Jason Terry 2.00 5.00
J57 Dajuan Wagner 2.00 5.00

2003-04 Upper Deck Rookie Exclusives Superstar Exclusives

Randomly inserted, this 100-card set is designed completely differently than the other inserts. Full-color player photos appear on the right and a the words, Superstar Exclusives, appear in gold foil from top to bottom on the left. Each card is sequentially numbered to 100.

PRINT RUN 100 SER.#'d SETS
EX1 Tracy McGrady 4.00 10.00
EX2 Dajuan Wagner 2.00 5.00
EX3 Allen Iverson 5.00 12.00
EX4 Caron Butler 2.50 6.00
EX5 Jason Kidd 5.00 12.00
EX6 Kenyon Martin 2.50 6.00
EX7 Lamar Odom 2.50 6.00
EX8 Kobe Bryant 12.00 30.00
EX9 T.J. Ford 2.50 6.00
EX10 Wally Szczerbiak 2.50 6.00
EX11 Yao Ming 6.00 15.00
EX12 Kirk Hinrich 3.00 8.00
EX13 Steve Nash 4.00 10.00
EX14 Baron Davis 2.50 6.00
EX15 Carmelo Anthony 10.00 25.00
EX16 Pau Gasol 3.00 8.00
EX17 Amare Stoudemire 4.00 10.00
EX18 Reggie Miller 3.00 8.00
EX19 Sam Cassell 2.50 6.00
EX20 Gary Payton 3.00 8.00
EX21 Kevin Garnett 5.00 12.00
EX22 Reece Gaines 2.00 5.00
EX23 LeBron James 30.00 80.00
EX24 Andre Miller 2.50 6.00
EX25 Rasheed Wallace 3.00 8.00
EX26 Darius Miles 2.00 5.00
EX27 Peja Stojakovic 3.00 8.00
EX28 Paul Pierce 3.00 8.00
EX29 Nick Collison 2.50 6.00
EX30 Dahntay Jones 2.50 6.00
EX31 Darko Milicic 2.50 6.00
EX32 Richard Hamilton 2.50 6.00
EX33 Scottie Pippen 5.00 12.00

EX34 Shaquille O'Neal 8.00 20.00
EX35 Jarvis Hayes 2.00 5.00
EX36 Tony Parker 3.00 8.00
EX37 Nick Van Exel 2.50 6.00
EX38 Maciej Lampe 2.00 5.00
EX39 Jalen Rose 2.50 6.00
EX40 Ray Allen 3.00 8.00
EX41 Dirk Nowitzki 5.00 12.00
EX42 Elton Brand 3.00 8.00
EX43 Jermaine O'Neal 2.50 6.00
EX44 Brian Grant 2.00 5.00
EX45 Jason Richardson 3.00 8.00
EX46 Allan Houston 2.50 6.00
EX47 Tim Thomas 2.00 5.00
EX48 Glenn Robinson 2.50 6.00
EX49 Nene 2.50 6.00
EX50 Corey Maggette 2.50 6.00
EX51 Richard Jefferson 2.50 6.00
EX52 Mickael Pietrus 2.50 6.00
EX53 Stephon Marbury 2.50 6.00
EX54 Mike Miller 2.50 6.00
EX55 Bonzi Wells 2.00 5.00
EX56 Boris Diaw 3.00 8.00
EX57 Manu Ginobili 4.00 10.00
EX58 Steve Francis 2.50 6.00
EX59 Jamal Mashburn 2.50 6.00
EX60 Mike Bibby 3.00 8.00
EX61 Tony Delk 2.00 5.00
EX62 Troy Bell 2.00 5.00
EX63 Dwyane Wade 10.00 25.00
EX64 Karl Malone 4.00 10.00
EX65 Desmond Mason 2.50 6.00
EX66 Antawn Jamison 2.50 6.00
EX67 Vince Carter 5.00 12.00
EX68 Eddie Jones 2.50 6.00
EX69 Gordan Giricek 2.00 5.00
EX70 Ben Wallace 2.50 6.00
EX71 Latrell Sprewell 2.50 6.00
EX72 Leandro Barbosa 3.00 8.00
EX73 Jamaal Tinsley 2.00 5.00
EX74 Travis Outlaw 2.50 6.00
EX75 Jason Terry 2.50 6.00
EX76 Quentin Richardson 2.50 6.00
EX77 Morris Peterson 2.00 5.00
EX78 Cuttino Mobley 2.00 5.00
EX79 Rashard Lewis 3.00 8.00
EX80 Jerry Stackhouse 2.50 6.00
EX81 Michael Finley 3.00 8.00
EX82 Antoine Walker 3.00 8.00
EX83 Shawn Marion 2.50 6.00
EX84 Gilbert Arenas 2.50 6.00
EX85 Marcus Banks 2.00 5.00
EX86 Tim Duncan 5.00 12.00
EX87 Brian Cook 2.00 5.00
EX88 Chauncey Billups 3.00 8.00
EX89 Andrei Kirilenko 3.00 8.00
EX90 Shareef Abdur-Rahim 2.50 6.00
EX91 Antonio McDyess 2.50 6.00
EX92 Chris Bosh 5.00 12.00
EX93 Ron Artest 3.00 8.00
EX94 David West 3.00 8.00
EX95 Chris Webber 3.00 8.00
EX96 Ricky Davis 2.50 6.00
EX97 Vladimir Radmanovic 2.00 5.00
EX98 Nikoloz Tskitishvili 2.00 5.00
EX99 Drew Gooden 2.50 6.00
EX100 Zach Randolph 2.50 6.00

1993-94 Upper Deck SE

This 225-card standard-size set was distributed in 12-card hobby East, hobby West, retail and 10-card magazine retail packs. There are 36 packs per box. Card fronts feature color player action shots that are borderless, except on the left, where a strip carries the player's name in gold foil along with his position and a vertically distorted black-and-white version of the action shot. The player's team name appears in vertical gold-foil lettering near the right edge. The back carries a color player action photo, with his name, position, and brief biography appearing in stripes across the top. Statistics and career highlights are displayed horizontally in a ghosted panel on the left. The set closes with the following topical subsets: NBA All-Star Weekend Highlights (181-198) and Team Headlines (199-225). Two Michael Jordan insert cards are a Kilroy card (JK1) and a retirement tribute card (MJR1). These were inserted at a rate of 1 in 72 packs. Rookie Cards of note in this set include Vin Baker, Anfernee Hardaway, Jamal Mashburn, Nick Van Exel and Chris Webber.

COMPLETE SET (225) 7.50 15.00
JK1/MJR1: STATED ODDS 1:72
1 Scottie Pippen .40 1.00
2 Todd Day .01 .05
3 Detlef Schrempf .05 .15
4 Chris Webber RC 1.25 3.00
5 Michael Adams .01 .05
6 Loy Vaught .01 .05
7 Doug West .01 .05
8 A.C. Green .05 .15
9 Anthony Mason .05 .15
10 Clyde Drexler .10 .30
11 Popeye Jones RC .01 .05
12 Vlade Divac .05 .15
13 Armon Gilliam .01 .05
14 Hersey Hawkins .05 .15
15 Dennis Scott .01 .05
16 Bimbo Coles .01 .05
17 Blue Edwards .01 .05
18 Negele Knight .01 .05
19 Dale Davis .01 .05
20 Isiah Thomas .10 .30
21 Latrell Sprewell .30 .75
22 Kenny Smith .01 .05
23 Bryant Stith .01 .05
24 Terry Porter .01 .05
25 Spud Webb .05 .15
26 John Battle .01 .05
27 Jeff Malone .01 .05
28 Olden Polynice .01 .05
29 Kevin Willis .01 .05
30 Robert Parish .05 .15
31 Kevin Johnson .05 .15
32 Shaquille O'Neal .60 1.50
33 Willie Anderson .01 .05
34 Micheal Williams .01 .05
35 Steve Smith .10 .30
36 Rik Smits .05 .15
37 Pete Myers .01 .05
38 Oliver Miller .01 .05
39 Eddie Johnson .01 .05
40 Calbert Cheaney RC .05 .15
41 Vernon Maxwell .01 .05
42 James Worthy .10 .30
43 Dino Radja RC .05 .15
44 Derrick Coleman .05 .15
45 Reggie Williams .01 .05
46 Dale Ellis .01 .05
47 Clifford Robinson .05 .15
48 Doug Christie .05 .15
49 Ricky Pierce .01 .05
50 Sean Elliott .05 .15
51 Anfernee Hardaway RC 1.00 2.50
52 Dana Barros .01 .05
53 Reggie Miller .10 .30
54 Brian Williams .01 .05
55 Otis Thorpe .05 .15
56 Jerome Kersey .01 .05
57 Larry Johnson .10 .30
58 Rex Chapman .01 .05
59 Kevin Edwards .01 .05
60 Nate McMillan .01 .05
61 Chris Mullin .10 .30
62 Bill Cartwright .01 .05
63 Dennis Rodman .25 .60
64 Pooh Richardson .01 .05
65 Tyrone Hill .01 .05
66 Scott Brooks .01 .05
67 Brad Daugherty .01 .05
68 Joe Dumars .10 .30
69 Vin Baker RC .30 .75
70 Rod Strickland .05 .15
71 Tom Chambers .01 .05
72 Charles Oakley .05 .15
73 Craig Ehlo .01 .05
74 LaPhonso Ellis .01 .05
75 Kevin Gamble .01 .05
76 Shawn Bradley RC .10 .30
77 Kendall Gill .05 .15
78 Hakeem Olajuwon .20 .50
79 Nick Anderson .05 .15
80 Anthony Peeler .01 .05
81 Wayman Tisdale .01 .05
82 Danny Manning .05 .15
83 John Starks .05 .15
84 Jeff Hornacek .05 .15
85 Victor Alexander .01 .05
86 Mitch Richmond .10 .30
87 Mookie Blaylock .05 .15
88 Harvey Grant .01 .05
89 Doug Smith .01 .05
90 John Stockton .10 .30
91 Charles Barkley .20 .50
92 Gerald Wilkins .01 .05
93 Mario Elie .01 .05
94 Ken Norman .01 .05
95 B.J. Armstrong .01 .05
96 John Williams .01 .05
97 Rony Seikaly .01 .05
98 Sean Rooks .01 .05
99 Shawn Kemp .20 .50
100 Danny Ainge .05 .15
101 Terry Mills .01 .05
102 Doc Rivers .05 .15
103 Chuck Person .01 .05
104 Sam Cassell RC .50 1.25
105 Kevin Duckworth .01 .05
106 Dan Majerle .05 .15
107 Mark Jackson .05 .15
108 Steve Kerr .05 .15
109 Sam Perkins .05 .15
110 Clarence Weatherspoon .01 .05
111 Felton Spencer .01 .05
112 Greg Anthony .01 .05
113 Pete Chilcutt .01 .05
114 Malik Sealy .01 .05
115 Horace Grant .05 .15
116 Chris Morris .01 .05
117 Xavier McDaniel .01 .05
118 Lionel Simmons .01 .05
119 Dell Curry .01 .05
120 Moses Malone .10 .30
121 Lindsey Hunter RC .10 .30
122 Buck Williams .01 .05
123 Mahmoud Abdul-Rauf .01 .05
124 Rumeal Robinson .01 .05
125 Chris Mills RC .10 .30
126 Scott Skiles .01 .05
127 Derrick McKey .01 .05
128 Avery Johnson .01 .05
129 Harold Miner .01 .05
130 Frank Brickowski .01 .05
131 Gary Payton .20 .50
132 Don MacLean .01 .05
133 Thurl Bailey .01 .05
134 Nick Van Exel RC .40 1.00
135 Matt Geiger .01 .05
136 Stacey Augmon .01 .05
137 Sedale Threatt .01 .05
138 Patrick Ewing .10 .30
139 Tyrone Corbin .01 .05
140 Jim Jackson .05 .15
141 Christian Laettner .05 .15
142 Robert Horry .05 .15
143 J.R. Reid .01 .05
144 Eric Murdock .01 .05
145 Alonzo Mourning .20 .50
146 Sherman Douglas .01 .05
147 Tom Gugliotta .10 .30
148 Glen Rice .05 .15
149 Mark Price .01 .05
150 Dikembe Mutombo .10 .30
151 Derek Harper .05 .15
152 Karl Malone .20 .50
153 Byron Scott .05 .15
154 Reggie Jordan RC .01 .05
155 Dominique Wilkins .10 .30
156 Bobby Hurley RC .05 .15
157 Ron Harper .05 .15
158 Bryon Russell RC .10 .30
159 Frank Johnson .01 .05
160 Toni Kukoc RC .50 1.25
161 Lloyd Daniels .01 .05
162 Jeff Turner .01 .05
163 Muggsy Bogues .05 .15
164 Chris Gatling .01 .05
165 Kenny Anderson .05 .15
166 Stanley Roberts .01 .05
167 Jamal Mashburn RC .30 .75
168 Tim Perry .01 .05
169 Antonio Davis RC .15 .40
170 Isaiah Rider RC .25 .60
171 Dee Brown .01 .05
172 Walt Williams .01 .05
173 Elden Campbell .01 .05
174 Benoit Benjamin .01 .05
175 Billy Owens .01 .05
176 Andrew Lang .01 .05
177 David Robinson .20 .50
178 Checklist 1 .01 .05
179 Checklist 2 .01 .05
180 Checklist 3 .01 .05
181 Shawn Bradley ASW .01 .05
182 Calbert Cheaney ASW .01 .05
183 Toni Kukoc ASW .10 .30
184 Popeye Jones ASW .01 .05
185 Lindsey Hunter ASW .05 .15
186 Chris Webber ASW .60 1.50
187 Bryon Russell ASW .05 .15
188 A.Hardaway ASW .50 1.25
189 Nick Van Exel ASW .10 .30
190 P.J.Brown ASW .10 .30
191 Isaiah Rider ASW .10 .30
192 Chris Mills ASW .05 .15
193 Antonio Davis ASW .05 .15
194 Jamal Mashburn ASW .10 .30
195 Dino Radja ASW .01 .05
196 Sam Cassell ASW .10 .30
197 Isaiah Rider ASW SD .10 .30
198 Mark Price LDS .01 .05
199 Stacey Augmon TH .01 .05
200 Celtics Team TH .01 .05
201 Eddie Johnson TH .01 .05
202 Scottie Pippen TH .20 .50
203 Brad Daugherty TH .01 .05
204 Jamal Mashburn TH .10 .30
205 Dikembe Mutombo TH .05 .15
206 Lindsey Hunter TH .05 .15
207 Chris Webber TH .40 1.00
208 Rockets Team TH .01 .05
209 Derrick McKey TH .01 .05
210 Danny Manning TH .01 .05
211 Doug Christie TH .05 .15
212 Glen Rice TH .01 .05
213 Day/Norman/Barry/Baker T .01 .05
214 Isaiah Rider TH .10 .30
215 Kenny Anderson TH .01 .05
216 Patrick Ewing TH .05 .15
217 Anfernee Hardaway TH .30 .75
218 Moses Malone TH .05 .15
219 Kevin Johnson TH .01 .05
220 Clifford Robinson TH .01 .05
221 Wayman Tisdale TH .01 .05
222 David Robinson TH .10 .30
223 Sonics Team TH .01 .05
224 John Stockton TH .05 .15
225 Don MacLean TH .01 .05
JK1 Johnny Kilroy 6.00 15.00
MJR1 M.Jordan Retirement 3.00 8.00

1993-94 Upper Deck SE Electric Court

COMPLETE SET (225) 25.00 50.00
*STARS: .75X TO 2X BASE CARD HI
*RCs: .6X TO 1.5X BASE HI
ONE PER PACK

1993-94 Upper Deck SE Electric Court Gold

*STARS: 8X TO 20X BASE CARD HI
*RCs: 5X TO 12X BASE HI
STATED ODDS 1:36 HOB/RET

1993-94 Upper Deck SE Behind the Glass

Randomly inserted in 12-card retail packs at a rate of one in 30, cards from this 15-card standard-size set capture some of the NBA's best dunkers from the unique camera angle behind the backboard glass. A gold-foil "Behind the Glass Trade Card" was randomly inserted in hobby packs at a rate of one in 360. The collector could redeem the card for the complete 15-card "Behind the Glass" set. The redemption deadline was August 31, 1994. The borderless front features a color player action shot on a gold metallic finish. The player's name and position appear vertically along the right side. The back features a color player action shot on the right side with career highlights appearing alongside on the left.

COMPLETE SET (15) 12.00 30.00
STATED ODDS 1:30 RETAIL
BHG TRADE: STATED ODDS 1:360 HOBBY
G1 Shawn Kemp 1.00 2.50
G2 Patrick Ewing .60 1.50
G3 Dikembe Mutombo .60 1.50
G4 Charles Barkley 1.00 2.50
G5 Hakeem Olajuwon 1.00 2.50
G6 Larry Johnson .60 1.50
G7 Chris Webber 4.00 10.00
G8 John Starks .30 .75
G9 Kevin Willis .08 .25
G10 Scottie Pippen 2.00 5.00
G11 Michael Jordan 6.00 15.00
G12 Alonzo Mourning 1.00 2.50
G13 Shaquille O'Neal 3.00 8.00
G14 Shawn Bradley .60 1.50
G15 Ron Harper .30 .75
NNO Expired BHG Trade .60 1.50
NNO Redeemed BHG Trade .20 .50

1993-94 Upper Deck SE Die Cut All-Stars

In these two 15-card insert standard-size sets, Upper Deck saluted a selection of current and potential future all-stars. The cards were available in East hobby and West hobby packs at a rate of one in 30 packs. Hobby dealers in the East received cases containing players from the Eastern conference, while hobby dealers in the West received cases containing players from the Western conference. These die-cut cards were inserted in hobby packs only. This unique card design features a partial gold-foil border at the top only. Centered is a color player action photo. The player's name and team appear in red vertical lettering along the left side. The back features brief statistics. Each set is sequenced in alphabetical team order.

COMPLETE SET (30) 100.00 250.00
COMP.EAST SET (15) 50.00 125.00
COMP.WEST SET (15) 50.00 125.00
STATED ODDS 1:30 HOBBY
E1 Dominique Wilkins 4.00 10.00
E2 Alonzo Mourning 6.00 15.00
E3 B.J. Armstrong 1.50 4.00
E4 Scottie Pippen 10.00 25.00
E5 Mark Price 1.50 4.00
E6 Isiah Thomas 4.00 10.00
E7 Harold Miner 1.50 4.00
E8 Vin Baker 5.00 12.00
E9 Kenny Anderson 2.50 6.00
E10 Derrick Coleman 2.50 6.00
E11 Patrick Ewing 6.00 15.00
E12 Anfernee Hardaway 12.00 30.00
E13 Shaquille O'Neal 10.00 25.00
E14 Shawn Bradley 4.00 10.00
E15 Calbert Cheaney 2.50 6.00
W1 Jim Jackson 3.00 8.00
W2 Jamal Mashburn 8.00 20.00
W3 Dikembe Mutombo 5.00 12.00
W4 Latrell Sprewell 8.00 20.00
W5 Chris Webber 12.00 30.00
W6 Hakeem Olajuwon 8.00 20.00
W7 Danny Manning 3.00 8.00
W8 Nick Van Exel 6.00 15.00
W9 Isaiah Rider 6.00 15.00
W10 Charles Barkley 10.00 25.00
W11 Clyde Drexler 8.00 20.00
W12 Mitch Richmond 8.00 20.00
W13 David Robinson 10.00 25.00
W14 Shawn Kemp 8.00 20.00
W15 Karl Malone 10.00 25.00

1993-94 Upper Deck SE USA Trade

This 24-card standard-size set was only available by exchanging the Upper Deck SE USA Trade card (random insert in one in 360 packs) before August 31, 1994. The set previewed the USA Basketball set that was released in the summer of 1994. The cards depict the 12 players selected by USA Basketball for "Dream Team II" plus Tim Hardaway, who was originally selected to the team was unable to participate due to injury, and 11 from the original Dream Team. Each card features a borderless color player action shot on its front. The player's name and position appear in white lettering within red and blue stripes near the bottom. The words "Exchange Set" in vertical gold-foil lettering and the gold-foil Upper Deck logo appear at the upper left. On a background of the American flag, the back carries a posed color shot of the player in his USA uniform and career highlights. The cards are numbered on the back with a "DSA" prefix.

COMPLETE SET (24) 20.00 40.00
TRADE CARD: STATED ODDS 1:360 HOB/RET
1 Charles Barkley 1.00 2.50
2 Larry Bird 2.50 6.00
3 Clyde Drexler .60 1.50
4 Patrick Ewing .60 1.50
5 Michael Jordan 6.00 15.00
6 Christian Laettner .30 .75
7 Karl Malone 1.00 2.50
8 Chris Mullin .60 1.50
9 Scottie Pippen 2.00 5.00
10 David Robinson 1.00 2.50
11 John Stockton .60 1.50
12 Dominique Wilkins .60 1.50
13 Isiah Thomas .60 1.50
14 Dan Majerle .30 .75
15 Steve Smith .60 1.50
16 Alonzo Mourning 1.00 2.50
17 Shawn Kemp 1.00 2.50
18 Larry Johnson .60 1.50
19 Tim Hardaway .60 1.50
20 Joe Dumars .60 1.50
21 Mark Price .20 .50
22 Derrick Coleman .30 .75
23 Reggie Miller .60 1.50
24 Shaquille O'Neal 3.00 8.00
NNO Expired USA Trade Card .40 1.00
NNO Red. USA Trade Card .08 .25

1991-92 Upper Deck Sheets

Upper Deck produced commemorative sheets that were given away during the 1991-92 season at selected games or events. Each sheet measures approximately 8 1/2" by 11" and is printed on card stock. The sheets have an Upper Deck stamp indicating the production run and an individual number. The design typically features Upper Deck card reproductions or artwork. The backs are blank. The sheets are unnumbered and listed in chronological order.

COMPLETE SET (14) 60.00 150.00
1 Number 1 Draft Choices 4.00 10.00
June 26, 1991 (12,000)
Number One Picks
Patrick Ewing
Brad Daugherty
David Robinson
Danny Manning
Pervis Ellison
Derrick Coleman
2 12th National Sports 2.00 5.00
Collectors Convention
July 4, 1991 (65,000)
Brad Daugherty
David Robinson
Danny Manning
Pervis Ellison
Derrick Coleman
Larry Johnson
3 Philadelphia Sports 4.00 10.00
Heroes
Oct. 17, 1991 (21,500)
Charles Barkley
Mike Schmidt
Rick Tocchet
Reggie White
4 McDonald's Open 4.00 10.00
Paris, France
Oct. 18-19, 1991 (59,000)
James Worthy
Byron Scott
A.C. Green
Magic Johnson
Sam Perkins
Vlade Divac
5 Detroit Pistons vs. 3.00 8.00
Nov. 27, 1991 (38,500)
Joe Dumars
Dennis Rodman
Mark Aguirre
Bill Laimbeer
John Salley
Isiah Thomas
6 All-Star Weekend 8.00 20.00
Orlando, Florida
Feb. 7-9, 1992 (22,000)
7 1971-72 World Champion 8.00 20.00
Feb. 26, 1992 (22,000)(20th Anniversary)
Wilt Chamberlain
Bill Sharman CO
Jerry West
Pat Riley
Jim McMillian
Gail Goodrich
8 New York Knicks 3.00 8.00
vs. Minnesota Timberwolves
Feb. 29, 1992 (19,000)
Kiki Vandeweghe
Patrick Ewing
Charles Oakley
Gerald Wilkins
John Starks
Anthony Mason
Xavier McDaniel
Mark Jackson
9 Detroit Pistons 3.00 8.00
vs. Los Angeles Clippers
March 31, 1992 (38,500)
Bill Laimbeer
John Salley
Isiah Thomas
Orlando Woolridge
Dennis Rodman
Joe Dumars
10 1992 NCAA Final Four 8.00 20.00
Championship Coaches
April 4-6, 1992 (68,000)
John Wooden
Dean Smith
Adolph Rupp
Bob Knight
11 Hoop It Up 4.00 10.00
San Jose, California
June 6-7, 1992 (15,000)
Sarunas Marciulonis
Billy Owens
Tim Hardaway
Victor Alexander
Chris Gatling
Chris Mullin
12 Battle of the 4.00 10.00
Basketball Stars
Undated (10,000)
Reportedly issued 6/20/92
Charles Smith
Dominique Wilkins
Pervis Ellison
Kenny Smith
Isiah Thomas
Mitch Richmond
Pooh Richardson
Tim Hardaway
13 Upper Deck Commemorates 6.00 15.00
the NBA Draft
June 24, 1992 (15,000)
Larry Johnson
Kenny Anderson
Billy Owens
Dikembe Mutombo
Steve Smith
Doug Smith
Luc Longley
Mark Macon
14 1992 USA Basketball 8.00 20.00
Team(80,000)
Issued June 1992

1992-93 Upper Deck Sheets

Upper Deck produced commemorative sheets that were given away during the 1992-93 season at selected events and games. Each sheet measures approximately 8 1/2" by 11" and is printed on card stock. The sheets have an Upper Deck stamp indicating the production run and an individual number. The backs are blank. The sheets are unnumbered and listed in chronological order.

COMPLETE SET (10) 50.00 125.00
1 Utah Jazz 4.00 10.00
Stay in School
Undated (67,000)
Issued Oct. 1992
David Benoit
Karl Malone
Mark Eaton
Jeff Malone
Mike Brown
John Stockton
Jay Humphries
Tyrone Corbin
2 Cleveland Cavaliers 3.00 8.00
Jan. 12, 1993 (30,000)
Larry Nance
Hot Rod Williams
Mark Price
Brad Daugherty
Craig Ehlo
John Battle
3 Larry Bird Salute 10.00 25.00
(Retirement Ceremony,
Boston Garden)
Feb. 4, 1993 (25,000)
(Alan Studt artwork)
4 All-Star Weekend 1.25 3.00
Autograph Sheet/(Upper Deck Trading Card
and Memorabilia Show
Feb. 19-21, 1993 (75,000)
(Picture of Salt Lake
City with mountains in
background)
5 All-Star Heroes 8.00 20.00
Feb. 19-21, 1993 (10,000)
Jerry West
John Havlicek
Elgin Baylor
Dave Cowens
6 Milwaukee Bucks 6.00 15.00
25th Anniversary
Undated (13,000)
Reportedly issued 3/3/93
Jon McGlocklin
Sidney Moncrief
Oscar Robertson
Kareem Abdul-Jabbar
Bob Lanier
Brian Winters
Junior Bridgeman
7 Atlanta Hawks 6.00 15.00
Undated (10,000)
Reportedly issued
March 25, 1993
Stacey Augmon
Mookie Blaylock
Duane Ferrell
Adam Keefe
Dominique Wilkins
Kevin Willis
8 Upper Deck Salutes 10.00 25.00
April 20, 1993 (22,500)
Bill Cartwright
Michael Jordan
John Paxson
Scottie Pippen
B.J. Armstrong
Horace Grant
9 AT and T Long Distance 5.00 12.00
Shootout
Undated (22,500)
Reportedly issued 6/93
Dan Majerle
Mark Price
Terry Porter
Dana Barros
Kenny Smith
B.J. Armstrong
Reggie Miller
10 Upper Deck Commemorates 8.00 20.00
the NBA Draft/(1992 Top Draft Choices)
June 30, 1993 (22,000)
Shaquille O'Neal
Alonzo Mourning
Christian Laettner
Jim Jackson
LaPhonso Ellis
Tom Gugliotta
Walt Williams
Todd Day

1993-94 Upper Deck Sheets

Upper Deck produced commemorative sheets that were given away during the 1993-94 season at selected events and games. Each sheet measures approximately 8 1/2" by 11" and is printed on card stock. The sheets have an Upper Deck stamp indicating the production run and an individual number. The backs are blank. The sheets are unnumbered and listed in chronological order.

COMPLETE SET (8) 25.00 60.00
1 1993 National Conv. 4.00 10.00
Chicago, Illinois
July 20-25, 1993
Michael Jordan
2 1993 McDonald's Open 4.00 10.00
October 21,1993
Danny Ainge
Dan Majerle
Oliver Miller
Charles Barkley
Kevin Johnson
Mark West
Negele Knight
Cedric Ceballos
3 Chicago Bulls 6.00 15.00
Nov.13, 1993 (22,000)
John Paxson
B.J. Armstrong
Corie Blount
Scottie Pippen
Bill Cartwright
Horace Grant
4 Upper Deck Salutes 4.00 10.00
NBA Standouts
All-Star Weekend
Undated (30,000)
Issued Feb. 1994
Harold Miner
Patrick Ewing
Hakeem Olajuwon
Alonzo Mourning
Jim Jackson
Derrick Coleman
5 Upper Deck All-Star 1.25 3.00
Autograph Sheet
All-Star Weekend
Undated (20,000)
Issued Feb. 1994
6 SE Preview 5.00 12.00
Undated (16,000)
Issued March 1994
Shawn Bradley
Shaquille O'Neal
LaPhonso Ellis
Jamal Mashburn
Chris Webber
Calbert Cheaney
7 1994 NBA All-Rookie 4.00 10.00
Team
No Date (40,000)
Chris Webber
Isaiah Rider
Jamal Mashburn
Vin Baker
Anfernee Hardaway
8 Upper Deck Salutes 5.00 12.00
NBA Draft Picks
June 29, 1994 (25,000)
Chris Webber
Shawn Bradley
Anfernee Hardaway
Jamal Mashburn
Isaiah Rider
Calbert Cheaney

1994-95 Upper Deck Sheets

These commemorative sheets were given away during the 1994-95 season at selected events and games. Each sheet measures 8 1/2" by 11" and is printed on card stock. The sheets have an Upper Deck seal indicating the production run and serial number.

COMPLETE SET (4) 12.00 30.00
1 Series Two NBA 3.00 8.00
Basketball Cards/(Promo sheet)
Shawn Kemp (Predictor)
Scottie Pippen
Shaquille O'Neal
Shawn Kemp (Slam Dunk)
Bobby Hurley
Jason Kidd
2 Upper Deck Predictor 4.00 10.00
Series Cards
No date (12,000)
Shawn Kemp
Patrick Ewing
Kevin Willis
Mookie Blaylock
Tim Hardaway
Glenn Robinson
3 Upper Deck Salutes 4.00 10.00
Michael Jordan
Jewel
No date (50,000)
4 1995 NBA Draft 5.00 12.00
Grant Hill
Juwan Howard
Jason Kidd
Donyell Marshall
Glenn Robinson
Sharone Wright
No date(5,000 issued)

1995-96 Upper Deck Sheets

The first commemorative sheet was given away during the 1996 NBA draft. It measures 8 1/2" by 11" and is printed on card stock. It has an Upper Deck seal indicating the production run and serial number. The second sheet commemorates the 1995-96 Chicago Bulls Championship team. The sheet measures 8 1/2" by 11" and is serially numbered out of 7210.

COMPLETE SET (2) 8.00 20.00
1 1996 NBA Draft 6.00 15.00
Kevin Garnett
Antonio McDyess
Bryant Reeves
Joe Smith
Jerry Stackhouse
Rasheed Wallace
2 1996 NBA Champions 6.00 15.00
Randy Brown
Toni Kukoc
Dickey Simpkins
Ron Harper
Luc Longley
John Salley
Michael Jordan
Steve Kerr
Jud Buechler
Scottie Pippen
Bill Wennington
Jason Caffey
James Edwards
Jack Haley
Dennis Rodman

2000-01 Upper Deck Slam

Debuting in November, 2000, this 100-card set featured an all-acetate look. The set contained 60 veterans, 30 rookies serially numbered to 2500 and 10 rookies serially numbered to 900. Please note that a Kevin Garnett promo card was issued to dealers and to members of the media prior to the release of the product. The card is listed below as card "P21".

COMPLETE SET w/o RC (60) 8.00 20.00
RCs: PRINT RUN 900 TO 2500 SERIAL SETS
1 Dikembe Mutombo .30 .75
2 Jim Jackson .20 .50
3 Paul Pierce .30 .75
4 Antoine Walker .25 .60
5 Eddie Jones .30 .75
6 Baron Davis .30 .75
7 Derrick Coleman .25 .60
8 Elton Brand .30 .75
9 Ron Artest .30 .75
10 Andre Miller .25 .60
11 Shawn Kemp .30 .75
12 Michael Finley .30 .75
13 Dirk Nowitzki .50 1.25
14 Antonio McDyess .25 .60
15 James Posey .20 .50
16 Jerry Stackhouse .25 .60
17 Jerome Williams .20 .50
18 Larry Hughes .25 .60
19 Antawn Jamison .30 .75
20 Steve Francis .25 .60
21 Hakeem Olajuwon .40 1.00
22 Reggie Miller .30 .75
23 Jalen Rose .25 .60
24 Lamar Odom .25 .60
25 Michael Olowokandi .20 .50
26 Shaquille O'Neal .75 2.00
27 Kobe Bryant 1.25 3.00
28 Alonzo Mourning .40 1.00
29 Jamal Mashburn .25 .60
30 Ray Allen .30 .75
31 Glenn Robinson .25 .60
32 Kevin Garnett .50 1.25
33 Wally Szczerbiak .25 .60
34 Stephon Marbury .25 .60
35 Keith Van Horn .25 .60
36 Latrell Sprewell .25 .60
37 Allan Houston .25 .60
38 Darrell Armstrong .20 .50
39 Ron Mercer .20 .50
40 Allen Iverson .60 1.50
41 Toni Kukoc .30 .75
42 Jason Kidd .50 1.25
43 Anfernee Hardaway .50 1.25
44 Shawn Marion .25 .60
45 Scottie Pippen .50 1.25
46 Rasheed Wallace .30 .75
47 Chris Webber .30 .75
48 Vlade Divac .25 .60
49 Tim Duncan .60 1.50
50 David Robinson .50 1.25
51 Gary Payton .30 .75
52 Rashard Lewis .30 .75
53 Vince Carter .60 1.50
54 Doug Christie .20 .50
55 Karl Malone .40 1.00
56 Bryon Russell .20 .50
57 Shareef Abdur-Rahim .25 .60
58 Michael Dickerson .20 .50
59 Juwan Howard .25 .60
60 Richard Hamilton .25 .60
61 Jerome Moiso/2500 RC .60 1.50
62 Etan Thomas/2500 RC 1.00 2.50
63 Courtney Alexander/2500 RC .75 2.00
64 Mateen Cleaves/2500 RC .75 2.00
65 Jason Collier/2500 RC 1.00 2.50
66 Hedo Turkoglu/900 RC 3.00 8.00
67 Desmond Mason/2500 RC 1.25 3.00
68 Quentin Richardson/2500 RC 1.00 2.50
69 Jamaal Magloire/2500 RC 1.00 2.50
70 Speedy Claxton/2500 RC 1.00 2.50
71 Morris Peterson/2500 RC 1.00 2.50
72 Donnell Harvey/2500 RC .75 2.00
73 Ira Newble/2500 RC .75 2.00
74 Mamadou N'Diaye/2500 RC .60 1.50
75 Erick Barkley/2500 RC .60 1.50
76 Mark Madsen/2500 RC 1.00 2.50
77 Dan Langhi/2500 RC .60 1.50
78 A.J. Guyton/2500 RC .60 1.50
79 Olumide Oyedeji/900 RC 1.25 3.00
80 Eddie House/900 RC 1.50 4.00
81 Eduardo Najera/900 RC 2.00 5.00
82 Lavor Postell/900 RC 1.25 3.00
83 Hanno Mottola/900 RC 1.25 3.00
84 Chris Carrawell/2500 RC 1.00 2.50
85 Michael Redd/900 RC 5.00 12.00
86 Jabari Smith/900 RC 1.25 3.00
87 Jason Hart/900 RC 2.00 5.00
88 Corey Hightower/2500 RC 1.00 2.50
89 Chris Porter/2500 RC .60 1.50
90 Justin Love/900 RC 2.00 5.00
91 Kenyon Martin/2500 RC 2.50 6.00
92 Stromile Swift/2500 RC 1.00 2.50
93 Darius Miles/2500 RC 1.00 2.50
94 Marcus Fizer/2500 RC 1.00 2.50
95 Mike Miller/2500 RC 1.50 4.00
96 DerMarr Johnson/2500 RC .75 2.00
97 Chris Mihm/2500 RC .75 2.00
98 Jamal Crawford/2500 RC 2.50 6.00
99 Joel Przybilla/2500 RC .75 2.00
100 Keyon Dooling/2500 RC 1.00 2.50
P21 Kevin Garnett 1.00 2.50

2000-01 Upper Deck Slam Extra Strength Silver

*STARS: 3X TO 8X BASE CARD HI
*RCs/2500: .5X TO 1.25X BASE CARD HI
*RCs/900: .25X TO .6X BASE CARD HI
STATED PRINT RUN 500 SERIAL #'d SETS

2000-01 Upper Deck Slam Extra Strength Gold

*STARS: 25X TO 60X BASE CARD HI
*RCs/2500: 4X TO 10X BASE CARD HI
*RCs/900: 2X TO 5X BASE CARD HI
STATED PRINT RUN 25 SERIAL #'d SETS

2000-01 Upper Deck Slam Air Styles

Randomly inserted in packs at one in nine, this nine-card set showcased some of the extraordinary techniques of the top jammers. Card backs carry an "AS" prefix.

COMPLETE SET (9) 4.00 10.00
STATED ODDS 1:9
AS1 Kevin Garnett .75 2.00
AS2 Vince Carter 1.00 2.50
AS3 Gary Payton .50 1.25
AS4 Steve Francis .40 1.00
AS5 Shareef Abdur-Rahim .40 1.00
AS6 Allen Iverson 1.00 2.50
AS7 Elton Brand .50 1.25
AS8 Kobe Bryant 2.00 5.00
AS9 Scottie Pippen .75 2.00

2000-01 Upper Deck Slam Air Supremacy

Randomly inserted in packs at one in 18, this six-card set pays tribute to the top players in the NBA. Card backs carry a "S" prefix.

COMPLETE SET (6) 5.00 12.00
STATED ODDS 1:18
S1 Kobe Bryant 2.50 6.00
S2 Vince Carter 1.25 3.00
S3 Shaquille O'Neal 1.50 4.00
S4 Allen Iverson 1.25 3.00
S5 Steve Francis .50 1.25
S6 Kevin Garnett 1.00 2.50

2000-01 Upper Deck Slam Flight Gear

Randomly inserted in packs at one in 108, this 14-card set features an authentic swatch from a game-used jersey on a see-through card. Card backs are numbered by the player's initials. Two autographed versions were also included, Kobe Bryant numbered to eight and Kevin Garnett numbered to 21. The Kobe Bryant card is not priced due to scarcity.

STATED ODDS 1:108
KB-A NOT PRICED DUE TO SCARCITY
KB2G Kobe Bryant 12.00 30.00
KG2G Kevin Garnett 5.00 12.00
AIG Allen Iverson 6.00 15.00
AMG Alonzo Mourning 4.00 10.00
DRG David Robinson 5.00 12.00
GPG Gary Payton 3.00 8.00

KBG Kobe Bryant 12.00 30.00
KGA Kevin Garnett AU/21 60.00 150.00
KGG Kevin Garnett 5.00 12.00
KMG Karl Malone 4.00 10.00
MJG Michael Jordan/23 250.00 500.00
SAG Shareef Abdur-Rahim 2.50 6.00
SOG Shaquille O'Neal 8.00 20.00
THG Tim Hardaway 3.00 8.00
WSG Wally Szczerbiak 2.50 6.00

2000-01 Upper Deck Slam Power Windows

Randomly inserted in packs at one in 18, this six-card set captures some of the best moves to the hoop, featuring pictures from behind the glass. Card backs carry a "PW" prefix.
COMPLETE SET (6) 5.00 12.00
STATED ODDS 1:18
PW1 Shaquille O'Neal 1.50 4.00
PW2 Kevin Garnett 1.00 2.50
PW3 Karl Malone .75 2.00
PW4 Kobe Bryant 4.00 10.00
PW5 Elton Brand .60 1.50
PW6 Vince Carter 1.25 3.00

2000-01 Upper Deck Slam Signature Slams

Randomly inserted in packs at one in 108, this nine-card set features autographs of some of the top dunkers in the game. The cards are numbered by the player initials.
STATED ODDS 1:108
AH Anfernee Hardaway 25.00 60.00
AJ Antawn Jamison 8.00 20.00
AM Andre Miller 8.00 20.00
BD Baron Davis 8.00 20.00
KB Kobe Bryant 125.00 300.00
KG Kevin Garnett 60.00 150.00
RA Ray Allen 12.50 30.00
TM Tracy McGrady 15.00 40.00
WS Wally Szczerbiak 8.00 20.00

2000-01 Upper Deck Slam Slam Exam

Randomly inserted in packs at one in six, this nine-card set highlights jams by the top NBA stars. Card backs carry a "SE" prefix.
COMPLETE SET (9) 3.00 8.00
STATED ODDS 1:6
SE1 Kobe Bryant 1.50 4.00
SE2 Kevin Garnett .60 1.50
SE3 Anfernee Hardaway .60 1.50
SE4 Lamar Odom .30 .75
SE5 Michael Finley .40 1.00
SE6 Latrell Sprewell .30 .75
SE7 Larry Hughes .30 .75
SE8 Chris Webber .40 1.00
SE9 Antonio McDyess .30 .75

2000-01 Upper Deck Slam UD Authentics

Randomly inserted in packs, this three-card set features autographs from the 2000-01 rookie class. The cards feature a congratulatory message on the back.
RANDOM INSERTS IN PACKS
DH Donnell Harvey 3.00 8.00
JM Jamaal Magloire 4.00 10.00
MN Mamadou N'Diaye 2.50 6.00

2005-06 Upper Deck Slam

Released in September 2005, Upper Deck Slam features a 120 card set where cards 1-90 picture veterans and cards 91-120 picture rookies. Base cards have white borders along the left and right with highlights to match team colors and a Upper Deck Slam logo along the bottom. Slam is packaged in 24-pack boxes where packs contain six cards and upon release, carried a SRP of $1.99.
COMPLETE SET (120) 15.00 40.00
COMP.SET w/o SP's 6.00 15.00
91-120 RC STATED ODDS 1:1
1 Tony Delk .12 .30
2 Josh Smith .15 .40
3 Al Harrington .15 .40
4 Antoine Walker .15 .40
5 Gary Payton .20 .50
6 Paul Pierce .20 .50
7 Kareem Rush .12 .30
8 Emeka Okafor .15 .40
9 Primoz Brezec .12 .30
10 Eddy Curry .12 .30
11 Kirk Hinrich .15 .40
12 Ben Gordon .15 .40
13 Drew Gooden .15 .40
14 LeBron James .75 2.00
15 Zydrunas Ilgauskas .15 .40
16 Dirk Nowitzki .30 .75
17 Jason Terry .15 .40
18 Michael Finley .20 .50
19 Carmelo Anthony .40 1.00
20 Kenyon Martin .15 .40
21 Earl Boykins .12 .30
22 Ben Wallace .15 .40
23 Chauncey Billups .20 .50
24 Richard Hamilton .15 .40
25 Troy Murphy .12 .30
26 Jason Richardson .20 .50
27 Baron Davis .15 .40
28 Tracy McGrady .25 .60
29 Yao Ming .25 .60
30 Juwan Howard .15 .40
31 Jermaine O'Neal .15 .40
32 Stephen Jackson .15 .40
33 Ron Artest .20 .50
34 Corey Maggette .15 .40
35 Elton Brand .20 .50
36 Bobby Simmons .12 .30
37 Caron Butler .15 .40
38 Kobe Bryant .75 2.00
39 Lamar Odom .15 .40
40 Mike Miller .15 .40
41 Jason Williams .15 .40
42 Pau Gasol .20 .50
43 Dwyane Wade .30 .75
44 Eddie Jones .15 .40
45 Shaquille O'Neal .40 1.00
46 Desmond Mason .12 .30
47 Maurice Williams .15 .40
48 Michael Redd .15 .40
49 Kevin Garnett .30 .75
50 Latrell Sprewell .15 .40
51 Sam Cassell .15 .40
52 Vince Carter .30 .75
53 Jason Kidd .30 .75
54 Richard Jefferson .15 .40
55 Dan Dickau .12 .30
56 Jamaal Magloire .12 .30
57 J.R. Smith .15 .40
58 Jamal Crawford .20 .50
59 Stephon Marbury .15 .40
60 Allan Houston .15 .40
61 Dwight Howard .15 .40
62 Grant Hill .25 .60
63 Steve Francis .15 .40
64 Allen Iverson .30 .75
65 Andre Iguodala .15 .40
66 Chris Webber .20 .50
67 Amare Stoudemire .15 .40
68 Shawn Marion .15 .40
69 Steve Nash .25 .60
70 Damon Stoudamire .15 .40
71 Shareef Abdur-Rahim .15 .40
72 Zach Randolph .15 .40
73 Mike Bibby .20 .50
74 Peja Stojakovic .20 .50
75 Brad Miller .15 .40
76 Manu Ginobili .20 .50
77 Tim Duncan .30 .75
78 Tony Parker .20 .50
79 Rashard Lewis .20 .50
80 Ray Allen .20 .50
81 Ronald Murray .12 .30
82 Rafer Alston .12 .30
83 Jalen Rose .20 .50
84 Chris Bosh .20 .50
85 Andrei Kirilenko .15 .40
86 Carlos Boozer .15 .40
87 Matt Harpring .12 .30
88 Antawn Jamison .15 .40
89 Gilbert Arenas .15 .40
90 Larry Hughes .15 .40
91 Andrew Bogut RC .75 2.00
92 Martynas Andriuskevicius RC .40 1.00
93 Chris Paul RC 2.50 6.00
94 Deron Williams RC .75 2.00
95 Luther Head RC .50 1.25
96 Chris Taft RC .50 1.25
97 David Lee RC .60 1.50
98 Gerald Green RC .60 1.50
99 Andrew Bynum RC .50 1.25
100 Rashad McCants RC .50 1.25
101 Raymond Felton RC .60 1.50
102 Danny Granger RC .75 2.00
103 Johan Petro RC .40 1.00
104 Antoine Wright RC .50 1.25
105 Channing Frye RC .60 1.50
106 Joey Graham RC .50 1.25
107 Wayne Simien RC .40 1.00
108 Monta Ellis RC .75 2.00
109 Charlie Villanueva RC .60 1.50
110 Martell Webster RC .50 1.25
111 C.J. Miles RC .60 1.50
112 Hakim Warrick RC .50 1.25
113 Ike Diogu RC .40 1.00
114 Jarrett Jack RC .60 1.50
115 Nate Robinson RC .60 1.50
116 Francisco Garcia RC .50 1.25
117 Sarunas Jasikevicius RC .60 1.50
118 Salim Stoudamire RC .50 1.25
119 Marvin Williams RC .60 1.50
120 Sean May RC .40 1.00

2005-06 Upper Deck Slam Dunk Swatches

Inserted in packs at the rate of one in 24, this 30-card set utilizes a horizontal design where player photos appear on the right and an arrow-shaped swatch of memorabilia appears on the left.
STATED ODDS 1:24
AK Andrei Kirilenko 2.00 5.00
BB Bruce Bowen 2.00 5.00
BR Bryon Russell 2.00 5.00
CB Carlos Boozer 2.00 5.00
CH Chris Bosh 2.50 6.00
DG Devean George 2.00 5.00
DN Dirk Nowitzki 4.00 10.00
DW Dajuan Wagner 2.00 5.00
JK Jason Kidd 4.00 10.00
JO Jermaine O'Neal 2.00 5.00
JR Jason Richardson 2.50 6.00
KB Kobe Bryant 8.00 20.00
KG Kevin Garnett 4.00 10.00
KR Kareem Rush 2.00 5.00
KT Kurt Thomas 2.00 5.00
LJ LeBron James 8.00 20.00
ME Stanislav Medvedenko 2.00 5.00
MJ Michael Jordan SP 25.00 60.00
MR Malik Rose 2.00 5.00
RJ Richard Jefferson 2.00 5.00
SF Steve Francis 2.00 5.00
SM Shawn Marion 2.00 5.00
SN Steve Nash 3.00 8.00
SO Shaquille O'Neal 5.00 12.00
ST Stephon Marbury 2.00 5.00
TD Tim Duncan 4.00 10.00
TM Tracy McGrady 3.00 8.00
UH Udonis Haslem 1.50 4.00
WS Wally Szczerbiak 2.00 5.00
YM Yao Ming 3.00 8.00

2005-06 Upper Deck Slam Signature Slams

Inserted at the rate of one in 480, this 30-card set features a player photo shaded to match team colors on the top and a centered autograph sticker in the middle.
STATED ODDS 1:480
SP INFO PROVIDED BY UPPER DECK
AI Andre Iguodala 8.00 20.00
AJ Antawn Jamison 5.00 12.00
BM Brad Miller 5.00 12.00
BU Beno Udrih 5.00 12.00
CD Chris Duhon 5.00 12.00
CW Chris Wilcox 5.00 12.00
DM Desmond Mason 5.00 12.00
DW Dorell Wright 5.00 12.00
JR J.R. Smith 5.00 12.00
JW Jason Williams 10.00 25.00
LJ LeBron James 150.00 300.00
MJ Michael Jordan SP 350.00 650.00
MP Morris Peterson 5.00 12.00
PP Paul Pierce SP 10.00 25.00
RJ Richard Jefferson 5.00 12.00
SN Steve Nash SP 50.00 120.00

2005-06 Upper Deck Slam Target Jerseys

RANDOM INSERTS IN TARGET PACKS
HC21 Austin Croshere 2.00 5.00
HC22 Brendan Haywood 2.00 5.00
HC23 Darius Songaila 2.00 5.00
HC24 Grant Hill 3.00 8.00
HC25 Jameer Nelson 1.50 4.00
HC26 Jason Richardson 2.50 6.00
HC27 Jason Terry 2.00 5.00
HC28 Josh Howard 2.50 6.00
HC29 Kelvin Cato 2.00 5.00
HC30 Kevin Martin 2.00 5.00
HC31 Lamar Odom 2.00 5.00
HC32 LeBron James 10.00 25.00
HC33 Malik Rose 2.00 5.00
HC34 Marcus Camby 2.00 5.00
HC35 Mike Sweetney 1.50 4.00
HC36 Peja Stojakovic 2.50 6.00
HC37 Reggie Miller 2.50 6.00
HC38 Tayshaun Prince 2.00 5.00
HC39 Yao Ming 3.00 8.00
HC40 Zydrunas Ilgauskas 2.00 5.00

1996-97 Upper Deck Space Jam

COMPLETE SET (106) 4.00 10.00
1 Bugs Bunny .01 .05
2 Lola Bunny .01 .05
3 Daffy Duck .01 .05
4 Porky Pig .01 .05
5 Elmer Fudd .01 .05
6 Tasmanian Devil .01 .05
7 Sylvester .01 .05
8 Tweety .01 .05
9 Granny .01 .05
10 Wile E. Coyote .01 .05
11 Road Runner .01 .05
12 Pepe Le Pew .01 .05
13 Marvin the Martian .01 .05
14 Yosemite Sam .01 .05
15 Speedy Gonzales .01 .05
16 Foghorn Leghorn .01 .05
17 Sniffles .01 .05
18 Witch Hazel .01 .05
19 Michael Jordan w
Stan Podolak 1.25 3.00
20 Minion .01 .05
21 Charles Barkley .25 .60
22 Muggsy Bogues .15 .40
23 Michael Jordan 1.25 3.00
24 Bertie & Hubie .01 .05
25 Swackhammer .01 .05
26 Bang .01 .05
27 Bupkus .01 .05
28 Blanko .01 .05
29 Pound .01 .05
30 Nawt .01 .05
31 Bugs' Latest Creation .01 .05
32 The Ducktor .01 .05
33 Trying to be Terrible .01 .05
34 The Rabbit is Revealed
Michael Jordan .01 .05
35 The Book of Bugs .01 .05
36 Daffy the Demolisher .01 .05
37 An Alien Crash Landing .01 .05
38 The Monstars Meet Their Match .01 .05
39 The Mean Team .01 .05
40 Analyzing the Competition .01 .05
41 Porky Solicits a Souvenir .01 .05
42 A Paranormal Experience .01 .05
43 Michael Jordan 1.25 3.00
44 It's Monstar Time .01 .05
45 Half-Time Heartbreak .01 .05
46 Bang .01 .05
47 Bupkus .01 .05
48 Blanko .01 .05
49 Pound .01 .05
50 Nawt .01 .05
51 Michael Jordan 1.25 3.00
52 Michael Jordan .01 .05
From Golf Clubs to Fan Club
53 Michael Jordan 1.25 3.00
54 Double Agent .01 .05
55 A High-Flyin Monstars-Cryin Jam .01 .05
56 A Scary Stare from Air .01 .05
57 Bugs Bunny Busses a Bull .01 .05
58 Pepe Kisses One off the Glass .01 .05
59 Nice Butt .01 .05
60 Michael Jordan 1.25 3.00
61 Bugs Bunny .01 .05
62 Lola Bunny .01 .05
63 Daffy Duck .01 .05
64 Porky Pig .01 .05
65 Elmer Fudd .01 .05
66 Tasmanian Devil .01 .05
67 Sylvester .01 .05
68 Tweety .01 .05
69 Granny .01 .05
70 Wile E. Coyote .01 .05
71 Road Runner .01 .05
72 Pepe Le Pew .01 .05
73 Marvin the Martian .01 .05
74 Yosemite Sam .01 .05
75 Speedy Gonzales .01 .05
76 Foghorn Leghorn .01 .05
77 Sniffles .01 .05
78 Witch Hazel .01 .05
79 Stan Podolak .01 .05
80 Minion .01 .05
81 Michael Jordan 1.25 3.00
82 Muggsy Bogues .15 .40
83 Michael Jordan 1.25 3.00
84 Hubie & Bertie .01 .05
85 Swackhammer .01 .05
86 Bang .01 .05
87 Bupkus .01 .05
88 Michael Jordan 1.25 3.00
89 Pound .01 .05
90 Nawt .01 .05
91 Pondering Their Plight .01 .05
92 The Monstars Toss An Airball .01 .05
93 Hopping To The Hoop .01 .05
94 Anybody In There? .01 .05
95 Bottom's Up .01 .05
96 Checking Out The Competition .01 .05
97 We're Going To Be Slaves .01 .05
98 Snooping For Some Sneakers .01 .05
99 Looking For Something Looney .01 .05
100 We Gotta Believe In Ourselves .01 .05
101 Naughty Little Nerdlucks .01 .05
102 Boo .01 .05
103 The Ultimate Game .01 .05
104 Taking Back Their Talent .01 .05
105 Love Is In The Hare .01 .05
SJ1 Michael Jordan w
Bugs Bunny PROMO 1.25 3.00

1996-97 Upper Deck Space Jam Scratchers

COMPLETE SET (3) 2.00 5.00
COMMON CARD 1.25 3.00

2004 Upper Deck Sportsfest

These cards were issued in groups of five over the course of three days at the 2004 Sportsfest card show in Chicago. Collectors would receive a group of 5 each day in exchange for 10 Upper Deck card wrappers that carried and SRP valued of $2.99 or higher. A 16th card was issued as an exchange card good for the first pick in the 2004 NBA draft.
STATED PRINT RUN 500 SER.#'d SETS
SF1 LeBron James 5.00 12.00
SF2 Kobe Bryant 5.00 12.00
SF3 Michael Jordan 5.00 12.00

2005 Upper Deck Sportsfest

COMPLETE SET (6) 8.00 20.00
UNPRICED AUTO PRINT RUN 5 SETS
NBA1 LeBron James 2.50 6.00
NBA2 Kobe Bryant 2.50 6.00
NBA3 Michael Jordan 5.00 12.00
NBA4 Kevin Garnett 1.50 4.00
NBA5 Yao Ming 1.25 3.00
NBA6 Steve Nash 1.25 3.00

2006 Upper Deck Sportsfest

COMPLETE SET (3) 7.50 15.00
NBA1 Michael Jordan 4.00 10.00
NBA2 LeBron James 3.00 8.00
NBA3 Chris Paul 2.00 5.00

2007 Upper Deck Sportsfest

UNPRICED AUTO PRINT RUN 3 TO 5 SETS
SF7 Kevin Durant 10.00 25.00
SF8 Michael Jordan 2.50 6.00
SF9 LeBron James 2.00 5.00

2008 Upper Deck Sportsfest

COMPLETE SET (12) 15.00 40.00
UNPRICED AUTO PRINT RUN 5 SETS
SF2 Michael Jordan 2.50 6.00
SF8 Kobe Bryant 2.00 5.00
SF11 LeBron James 2.00 5.00

2003-04 Upper Deck Standing O

Issued in October 2003, Standing O features a 126-card base set where veterans comprise cards 1-84 and rookies are showcased on cards 85-126 and inserted at the rate of one in four. Base cards have white borders and set a full-color player photo against a basketball background. Rookie cards do not have borders, rather a colored background that is set on top of a basketball image and bleeds to the edges. Standing O was packaged in 24-pack boxes where packs contained four cards and carried a suggested retail price of $1.99.
COMP.SET w/o SP's 15.00 40.00
85-126 STATED ODDS 1:4
1 Shareef Abdur-Rahim .25 .60
2 Jason Terry .25 .60
3 Theo Ratliff .20 .50
4 Paul Pierce .30 .75
5 Antoine Walker .30 .75
6 Vin Baker .20 .50
7 Jalen Rose .25 .60
8 Tyson Chandler .25 .60
9 Michael Jordan 2.50 6.00
10 Dajuan Wagner .20 .50
11 Zydrunas Ilgauskas .25 .60
12 Darius Miles .20 .50
13 Dirk Nowitzki .50 1.25
14 Michael Finley .30 .75
15 Steve Nash .40 1.00
16 Nene .25 .60
17 Rodney White .20 .50
18 Richard Hamilton .25 .60
19 Ben Wallace .25 .60
20 Chauncey Billups .30 .75
21 Nick Van Exel .25 .60
22 Jason Richardson .30 .75
23 Mike Dunleavy .25 .60
24 Steve Francis .25 .60
25 Yao Ming .60 1.50
26 Cuttino Mobley .20 .50
27 Reggie Miller .30 .75
28 Jamaal Tinsley .20 .50
29 Jermaine O'Neal .25 .60
30 Elton Brand .30 .75
31 Corey Maggette .25 .60
32 Quentin Richardson .25 .60
33 Kobe Bryant 1.25 3.00
34 Shaquille O'Neal .75 2.00
35 Gary Payton .30 .75
36 Karl Malone .40 1.00
37 Pau Gasol .30 .75
38 Mike Miller .25 .60
39 Eddie Jones .25 .60
40 Brian Grant .20 .50
41 Caron Butler .25 .60
42 Michael Redd .30 .75
43 Joe Smith .25 .60
44 Desmond Mason .25 .60
45 Kevin Garnett .50 1.25
46 Latrell Sprewell .25 .60
47 Sam Cassell .25 .60
48 Jason Kidd .50 1.25
49 Richard Jefferson .25 .60
50 Alonzo Mourning .40 1.00
51 Baron Davis .25 .60
52 Jamal Mashburn .25 .60
53 Jamaal Magloire .20 .50
54 Allan Houston .25 .60
55 Antonio McDyess .25 .60
56 Keith Van Horn .25 .60
57 Tracy McGrady .40 1.00
58 Juwan Howard .25 .60
59 Drew Gooden .25 .60
60 Allen Iverson .50 1.25
61 Glenn Robinson .25 .60
62 Stephon Marbury .25 .60
63 Shawn Marion .25 .60
64 Amare Stoudemire .40 1.00
65 Rasheed Wallace .30 .75
66 Bonzi Wells .20 .50
67 Chris Webber .30 .75
68 Mike Bibby .30 .75
69 Peja Stojakovic .30 .75
70 Tim Duncan .50 1.25
71 David Robinson .50 1.25
72 Tony Parker .30 .75
73 Ray Allen .30 .75
74 Rashard Lewis .30 .75
75 Reggie Evans .20 .50
76 Vince Carter .50 1.25
77 Morris Peterson .20 .50
78 Antonio Davis .20 .50
79 Jarron Collins .20 .50
80 John Stockton .40 1.00
81 Andrei Kirilenko .30 .75
82 Jerry Stackhouse .25 .60
83 Gilbert Arenas .25 .60
84 Larry Hughes .25 .60
85 LeBron James RC 20.00 50.00
86 Darko Milicic RC 1.00 2.50
87 Carmelo Anthony RC 4.00 10.00
88 Chris Bosh RC 2.00 5.00
89 Dwyane Wade RC 4.00 10.00
90 Chris Kaman RC 1.25 3.00
91 Kirk Hinrich RC 1.25 3.00
92 T.J. Ford RC 1.00 2.50
93 Mike Sweetney RC .75 2.00
94 Jarvis Hayes RC .75 2.00
95 Mickael Pietrus RC 1.00 2.50
96 Nick Collison RC 1.00 2.50
97 Marcus Banks RC .75 2.00
98 Luke Ridnour RC 1.00 2.50
99 Reece Gaines RC .75 2.00
100 Troy Bell RC .75 2.00
101 Zarko Cabarkapa RC .75 2.00
102 David West RC 1.25 3.00
103 Aleksandar Pavlovic RC 1.00 2.50
104 Dahntay Jones RC 1.00 2.50
105 Boris Diaw RC 1.25 3.00
106 Zoran Planinic RC .75 2.00
107 Travis Outlaw RC 1.00 2.50
108 Brian Cook RC .75 2.00
109 Carlos Delfino RC 1.00 2.50
110 Ndudi Ebi RC .75 2.00
111 Kendrick Perkins RC 1.00 2.50
112 Leandro Barbosa RC 1.25 3.00
113 Josh Howard RC 1.25 3.00
114 Maciej Lampe RC .75 2.00
115 Jason Kapono RC .75 2.00
116 Luke Walton RC 1.25 3.00
117 Jerome Beasley RC .75 2.00
118 Willie Green RC .75 2.00
119 Kyle Korver RC 1.50 4.00
120 Travis Hansen RC .75 2.00
121 Steve Blake RC 1.00 2.50
122 Slavko Vranes RC .75 2.00
123 Zaur Pachulia RC 1.25 3.00
124 Keith Bogans RC .75 2.00
125 Theron Smith RC .75 2.00
126 Brandon Hunter RC .75 2.00

2003-04 Upper Deck Standing O Die Cuts/Embossed

*SINGLES: .75X TO 2X BASE CARD HI
1-84 STATED ODDS 1:1
*RCs: .4X TO 1X BASE CARD HI
85-126 RC STATED ODDS 1:24
ROOKIES ARE EMBOSSED

2003-04 Upper Deck Standing O Graphs

Randomly inserted, this 21-card set places player action photos on the right and leaves space for the authentic player autograph.
AVAILABLE VIA REDEMPTION CARDS
BI Chauncey Billups SP 10.00 25.00
BO Carlos Boozer 8.00 20.00
DJ DerMarr Johnson 4.00 10.00
ET Etan Thomas 4.00 10.00
GA Gilbert Arenas SP 12.00 30.00
KB Kobe Bryant SP 100.00 225.00
LJ LeBron James SP 400.00 700.00
MJ Michael Jordan/23 400.00 600.00
MP Morris Peterson 4.00 10.00
RE Reggie Evans SP 4.00 10.00
RL Rashard Lewis 6.00 15.00
TM Tracy McGrady/25 20.00 50.00

2003-04 Upper Deck Standing O Swatches

AVAILABLE VIA REDEMPTION CARDS
AIPH Allen Iverson 5.00 12.00
CBPH Caron Butler 2.50 6.00
CWPH Chris Webber 3.00 8.00
DNPH Dirk Nowitzki 5.00 12.00
GHPH Grant Hill 5.00 12.00
JKPH Jason Kidd 5.00 12.00
JOPH Jermaine O'Neal 2.50 6.00
JSPH John Stockton 4.00 10.00
KBPH Kobe Bryant 12.50 30.00
KGPH Kevin Garnett 5.00 12.00
KMPH Kenyon Martin 2.50 6.00
LSPH Latrell Sprewell 2.50 6.00
MJPH Michael Jordan 60.00 120.00
PPPH Paul Pierce 3.00 8.00
SAPH Amare Stoudemire 4.00 10.00
SMPH Stephon Marbury 2.50 6.00
SNPH Steve Nash 4.00 10.00
SPPH Scottie Pippen 5.00 12.00
TDPH Tim Duncan 5.00 12.00
TMPH Tracy McGrady 4.00 10.00
YMPH Yao Ming 6.00 15.00

1991-92 Upper Deck Stay in School Sheets

Upper Deck produced commemorative sheets that were given away at 1991-92 Stay In School events around the country. Orlando was the 1992 All-Star Game city and hosted the nationally televised Stay in School Jam. Each sheet measures approximately 5" by 7" and is printed on card stock. All sheets except Orlando have an Upper Deck stamp indicating the production run of 3,000 and an individual number. The production run for Orlando was 45,000. The design features Stay In School spokesman Bob Lanier and the logo of the team hosting the session, except for Orlando where a photo of Magic player Otis Smith replaces the logo. The backs are blank. The sheets are unnumbered and listed in alphabetical order. Despite the small quantity produced, these sheets do not have much demand because of the lack of subject matter.
COMPLETE SET (10) 15.00 40.00
1 Boston Celtics 2.50 6.00
2 Charlotte Hornets 2.50 6.00
3 Chicago Bulls 2.50 6.00
4 Detroit Pistons 2.50 6.00
5 Houston Rockets 2.50 6.00
6 Miami Heat 2.50 6.00
7 New Jersey Nets 2.50 6.00
8 Orlando Magic DP .75 2.00
9 Portland Trail Blazers 2.50 6.00
10 San Antonio Spurs 2.50 6.00

2003 Upper Deck Superstars LeBron James

COMPLETE SET (6) 20.00 50.00
COMMON CARD (1-6) 5.00 12.00

2013 Upper Deck Tiger Woods Master Collection Legendary Duos Dual Autographs

STATED PRINT RUN 1 SER. #'d SET
UNPRICED DUE TO SCARCITY
LDTJ Tiger Woods
Magic Johnson
LDTL LeBron James
Tiger Woods
LDTR Reggie Miller
Tiger Woods
LDWJ Tiger Woods
Michael Jordan
LDWM Tiger Woods
Karl Malone

2003 Upper Deck Top Prospects LeBron James Promos

Given away in Rosemont, Illinois on June 27-29 at the Collector's Universe Sportsfest show, card number P3 was LeBron James' first issue by a major manufacturer. A total of 4000 LeBron cards were mixed in randomly with other promo cards which were handed out at the Upper Deck show display. Three-packs containing all of the cards were handed out at the National Collector's Convention in Atlantic City, NJ on July 25th, 26th, and 27th. These packages were shrink-wrapped in clear plastic.
COMPLETE SET (3) 10.00 25.00
COMMON CARD (P1-P3) 4.00 10.00

1999 Upper Deck Tribute to Michael Jordan

This set was released in 1999 by Upper Deck, and features 30 cards that highlight Michael Jordan's career.
COMP. FACT SET (30) 10.00 25.00
COMMON CARD (1-30) .40 1.00

2004-05 Upper Deck Trilogy

Released in May 2005, Upper Deck Trilogy boasts a 150-card set where cards 1-100 feature veteran players and cards 101-140 feature rookies serially numbered to 999 and cards 141-150 feature rookies serially numbered to 499. All of the rookies are printed on UD's patented plexi-glass and were covered with a tan tape to avoid scratches. Trilogy was packaged in nine card packs of five cards each and carried a SRP of $29.99.
COMP.SET w/o SP's (100) 30.00 60.00
141-150 RC PRINT RUN 499 SER.#'d SETS
UNPRICED SPECTRUM PRINT RUN 10 SETS
1 Antoine Walker .75 2.00
2 Al Harrington .60 1.50
3 Boris Diaw .60 1.50
4 Paul Pierce .75 2.00
5 Ricky Davis .60 1.50
6 Gary Payton .75 2.00
7 Gerald Wallace .60 1.50
8 Emeka Okafor RC .60 1.50
9 Keith Bogans .50 1.25
10 Eddy Curry .50 1.25
11 Kirk Hinrich .60 1.50
12 Michael Jordan 6.00 15.00
13 LeBron James 5.00 12.00
14 Dajuan Wagner .50 1.25
15 Jeff McInnis .50 1.25
16 Drew Gooden .50 1.25
17 Dirk Nowitzki 1.25 3.00
18 Michael Finley .75 2.00
19 Jerry Stackhouse .60 1.50
20 Jason Terry .60 1.50
21 Kenyon Martin .60 1.50
22 Andre Miller .60 1.50
23 Carmelo Anthony 1.50 4.00
24 Nene .60 1.50
25 Chauncey Billups .75 2.00
26 Rasheed Wallace .75 2.00
27 Ben Wallace .60 1.50
28 Richard Hamilton .60 1.50
29 Derek Fisher .60 1.50
30 Jason Richardson .75 2.00
31 Mike Dunleavy .60 1.50
32 Yao Ming 1.50 4.00
33 Tracy McGrady 1.00 2.50
34 Juwan Howard .60 1.50
35 Jermaine O'Neal .60 1.50
36 Reggie Miller .75 2.00
37 Ron Artest .75 2.00
38 Jamaal Tinsley .50 1.25
39 Elton Brand .75 2.00
40 Corey Maggette .60 1.50
41 Marko Jaric .50 1.25
42 Kerry Kittles .50 1.25
43 Kobe Bryant 3.00 8.00
44 Caron Butler .60 1.50
45 Lamar Odom .60 1.50
46 Brian Cook .50 1.25
47 Pau Gasol .75 2.00
48 Jason Williams .60 1.50
49 Bonzi Wells .50 1.25
50 Shaquille O'Neal 2.00 5.00
51 Dwyane Wade 1.25 3.00
52 Eddie Jones .60 1.50
53 Michael Redd .60 1.50
54 Desmond Mason .60 1.50
55 Maurice Williams .60 1.50
56 Latrell Sprewell .60 1.50
57 Kevin Garnett 1.25 3.00
58 Sam Cassell .60 1.50
59 Troy Hudson .50 1.25
60 Vince Carter 1.25 3.00
61 Richard Jefferson .60 1.50
62 Jason Kidd 1.25 3.00
63 P.J. Brown .50 1.25
64 Baron Davis .60 1.50
65 Jamaal Magloire .50 1.25
66 Allan Houston .60 1.50
67 Jamal Crawford .75 2.00
68 Stephon Marbury .60 1.50
69 Grant Hill 1.00 2.50
70 Cuttino Mobley .50 1.25
71 Steve Francis .60 1.50
72 Glenn Robinson .60 1.50
73 Allen Iverson 1.25 3.00
74 Willie Green .50 1.25
75 Amare Stoudemire .60 1.50
76 Steve Nash 1.00 2.50
77 Quentin Richardson .60 1.50
78 Shawn Marion .60 1.50
79 Shareef Abdur-Rahim .60 1.50
80 Damon Stoudamire .60 1.50
81 Zach Randolph .60 1.50
82 Darius Miles .50 1.25
83 Peja Stojakovic .75 2.00
84 Chris Webber .75 2.00
85 Mike Bibby .75 2.00
86 Tony Parker .75 2.00
87 Tim Duncan 1.25 3.00
88 Manu Ginobili 1.00 2.50
89 Ronald Murray .50 1.25
90 Ray Allen .75 2.00
91 Rashard Lewis .75 2.00
92 Chris Bosh .75 2.00
93 Rafer Alston .50 1.25
94 Jalen Rose .60 1.50
95 Andrei Kirilenko .60 1.50
96 Carlos Arroyo .50 1.25
97 Carlos Boozer .60 1.50
98 Gilbert Arenas .60 1.50
99 Jarvis Hayes .50 1.25
100 Antawn Jamison .60 1.50
101 Rafael Araujo RC 2.00 5.00
102 Luke Jackson RC 2.00 5.00
103 Andris Biedrins RC 2.00 5.00
104 Robert Swift RC 2.00 5.00
105 Kris Humphries RC 3.00 8.00
106 Al Jefferson RC 4.00 10.00
107 Kirk Snyder RC 2.00 5.00
108 Josh Smith RC 3.00 8.00
109 Dorell Wright RC 3.00 8.00
110 Jameer Nelson RC 3.00 8.00
111 Pavel Podkolzin RC 2.00 5.00
112 Andres Nocioni RC 3.00 8.00
113 Luis Flores RC 2.50 6.00
114 Delonte West RC 3.00 8.00
115 Tony Allen RC 3.00 8.00
116 Kevin Martin RC 4.00 10.00
117 Sasha Vujacic RC 3.00 8.00
118 Beno Udrih RC 2.50 6.00
119 David Harrison RC 2.00 5.00
120 Anderson Varejao RC 2.50 6.00
121 Jackson Vroman RC 2.00 5.00
122 Peter John Ramos RC 2.00 5.00
123 Lionel Chalmers RC 3.00 8.00
124 Donta Smith RC 2.00 5.00
125 Andre Emmett RC 2.00 5.00
126 Antonio Burks RC 2.50 6.00
127 Royal Ivey RC 2.50 6.00
128 Chris Duhon RC 3.00 8.00
129 Nenad Krstic RC 3.00 8.00
130 Justin Reed RC 2.00 5.00
131 Pape Sow RC 2.50 6.00
132 Trevor Ariza RC 3.00 8.00
133 Tim Pickett RC 3.00 8.00
134 Bernard Robinson RC 2.50 6.00
135 John Edwards RC 2.00 5.00
136 Damien Wilkins RC 2.50 6.00
137 Romain Sato RC 2.00 5.00
138 Matt Freije RC 2.50 6.00
139 D.J. Mbenga RC 2.50 6.00
140 Yuta Tabuse RC 3.00 8.00
141 Dwight Howard RC 8.00 20.00
142 Emeka Okafor 3.00 8.00
143 Ben Gordon RC 4.00 10.00
144 Shaun Livingston RC 4.00 10.00
145 Devin Harris RC 3.00 8.00
146 Josh Childress RC 3.00 8.00
147 Luol Deng RC 4.00 10.00
148 Andre Iguodala RC 5.00 12.00
149 Sebastian Telfair RC 3.00 8.00
150 J.R. Smith RC 4.00 10.00
P23 Carmelo Anthony PROMO 2.00 5.00

2004-05 Upper Deck Trilogy Gold

*GOLD SINGLES: 1.25X TO 3X BASE HI
GOLD PRINT RUN 100 SER.#'d SETS
12 Michael Jordan 25.00 60.00

2004-05 Upper Deck Trilogy UD Promos

*PROMOS: .6X TO 1.5X BASIC

2004-05 Upper Deck Trilogy Rookie Premiere Crystal

*101-140 RCs: 1X TO 2.5X BASE HI
*141-150 RCs: .75X TO 2X BASE HI
PRINT RUN 25 SER.#'d SETS

2004-05 Upper Deck Trilogy Auto Focus

Inserted in packs at the rate of one in nine, this 40-card set was printed on UD's plexi-glass and contains an autograph of the featured player. A pink Crystal parallel was also inserted and those cards are numbered to 25.
STATED ODDS 1:9
AI Andre Iguodala 6.00 15.00
AJ Al Jefferson 6.00 15.00
AK Andrei Kirilenko 6.00 15.00
AL Ray Allen 20.00 50.00
AS Amare Stoudemire 4.00 10.00
BD Baron Davis 6.00 15.00
BG Ben Gordon 5.00 12.00
CA Carmelo Anthony SP 20.00 40.00
DE Devin Harris 4.00 10.00
DH Dwight Howard SP 12.00 30.00
DW Dorell Wright 5.00 12.00
JC Josh Childress 4.00 10.00
JK Jason Kidd SP 15.00 30.00
JN Jameer Nelson 5.00 12.00
JR J.R. Smith 5.00 12.00
JS Josh Smith 5.00 12.00
KB Kobe Bryant SP 100.00 200.00
KG Kevin Garnett SP 40.00 100.00
KH Kris Humphries 5.00 12.00
KI Kirk Hinrich 8.00 20.00
KS Kirk Snyder 3.00 8.00
LD Luol Deng 10.00 25.00
LJ LeBron James SP 150.00 300.00
LU Luke Jackson 3.00 8.00
MB Mike Bibby 5.00 12.00
MJ Michael Jordan SP 300.00 600.00
PG Pau Gasol 5.00 12.00
PP Paul Pierce 10.00 25.00
PS Peja Stojakovic 6.00 15.00
RA Rafael Araujo 3.00 8.00
RH Richard Hamilton 6.00 15.00
RS Robert Swift 3.00 8.00
SH Shawn Marion 6.00 15.00
SL Shaun Livingston 5.00 12.00
SM Stephon Marbury SP 12.00 30.00
ST Sebastian Telfair 4.00 10.00
TA Tony Allen 5.00 12.00
TM Tracy McGrady SP 12.00 30.00
WE Delonte West 5.00 12.00
YM Yao Ming 30.00 80.00

2004-05 Upper Deck Trilogy Auto Focus Crystal

*CRYSTAL: 1X TO 2.5X BASE HI
PRINT RUN 25 SER.#'d SETS
KB Kobe Bryant 150.00 300.00
KG Kevin Garnett 75.00 200.00
LJ LeBron James 150.00 300.00
MJ Michael Jordan 800.00 1000.00
TM Tracy McGrady 25.00 60.00
YM Yao Ming 50.00 120.00

2004-05 Upper Deck Trilogy One Two Combo Clearcut Autographs

Limited to 25 serially numbered copies, this 14-card set is printed on plastic and features two players along with their autographs.
PRINT RUN 25 SER.#'d SETS
AM C.Anthony/A.Miller 30.00 80.00
CS J.Childress/Josh Smith 20.00 50.00
DG L.Deng/B.Gordon 20.00 50.00
DS B.Davis/J.R.Smith 20.00 50.00
HJ D.Howard/L.James 300.00 500.00
HN D.Howard/J.Nelson 100.00 200.00
JB L.James/K.Bryant 400.00 700.00
JJ M.Jordan/L.James 1000.00 2000.00
KH A.Kirilenko/K.Humphries 20.00 50.00
KJ J.Kidd/R.Jefferson 40.00 100.00
MC S.Marbury/J.Crawford 25.00 60.00
MM Y.Ming/T.McGrady 100.00 200.00
PB P.Pierce/L.Bird 100.00 200.00
SM A.Stoudemire/S.Marion 40.00 100.00

2004-05 Upper Deck Trilogy Signature Swatches

Randomly inserted in packs, this 30-card set is horizontally designed and features a player image on the left, a swatch of memorabilia in the upper-right corner in the shape of "SS", and the player's signature beneath the swatch. Each card is serially numbered to 25.
PRINT RUN 25 SER.#'d SETS
AI Andre Iguodala 15.00 40.00
AJ Al Jefferson 15.00 40.00
AK Andrei Kirilenko 15.00 40.00
AS Amare Stoudemire 30.00 80.00
BD Baron Davis 12.00 30.00
BG Ben Gordon 12.00 30.00
CA Carmelo Anthony 40.00 100.00
DE Devin Harris 10.00 25.00
DH Dwight Howard 125.00 250.00
JC Josh Childress 10.00 25.00
JK Jason Kidd 25.00 60.00
JN Jameer Nelson 12.00 30.00
JR J.R. Smith 12.00 30.00
JS Josh Smith 12.00 30.00
KB Kobe Bryant 175.00 350.00
KG Kevin Garnett 125.00 250.00
KH Kris Humphries 12.00 30.00
KS Kirk Snyder 8.00 20.00
LD Luol Deng 12.00 30.00
LJ LeBron James 175.00 350.00
LO Lamar Odom 10.00 25.00
LU Luke Jackson 8.00 20.00
MB Mike Bibby 12.00 30.00
MJ Michael Jordan 400.00 650.00
PG Pau Gasol 12.00 30.00
PP Paul Pierce 25.00 60.00
SL Shaun Livingston 12.00 30.00
SM Stephon Marbury 25.00 60.00
ST Sebastian Telfair 10.00 25.00
TM Tracy McGrady 40.00 100.00

2004-05 Upper Deck Trilogy Signs of Stardom

Seeded randomly in packs at the rate of one in three, this 50-card set is horizontally designed with gold foil

highlights, player images on the left, and an autograph in a white-out box on the right.
STATED ODDS 1:3
AE Andre Emmett 2.50 6.00
AI Andre Iguodala 5.00 12.00
AJ Al Jefferson 5.00 12.00
AK Andrei Kirilenko 6.00 15.00
AL Ray Allen 15.00 40.00
AS Amare Stoudemire 3.00 8.00
AV Anderson Varejao 3.00 8.00
BD Baron Davis 3.00 8.00
BG Ben Gordon 4.00 10.00
BM Brad Miller 3.00 8.00
BU Beno Udrih 3.00 8.00
CA Carmelo Anthony SP 20.00 50.00
CD Chris Duhon 4.00 10.00
DA David Harrison 2.50 6.00
DE Devin Harris 3.00 8.00
DH Dwight Howard SP 8.00 20.00
DW Dorell Wright 4.00 10.00
JC Josh Childress 3.00 8.00
JK Jason Kidd SP 12.00 30.00
JM Jamaal Magloire 2.50 6.00
JN Jameer Nelson 4.00 10.00
JR J.R. Smith 4.00 10.00
JS Josh Smith 4.00 10.00
JV Jackson Vroman 2.50 6.00
KB Kobe Bryant SP 100.00 200.00
KG Kevin Garnett SP 30.00 80.00
KH Kris Humphries 4.00 10.00
KI Kirk Hinrich 10.00 25.00
KM Kevin Martin 5.00 12.00
KS Kirk Snyder 2.50 6.00
LC Lionel Chalmers 4.00 10.00
LD Luol Deng 4.00 10.00
LJ LeBron James SP 150.00 300.00
LO Lamar Odom 3.00 8.00
LU Luke Jackson 2.50 6.00
MB Mike Bibby 4.00 10.00
MJ Michael Jordan SP 350.00 500.00
PG Pau Gasol 6.00 15.00
PP Paul Pierce 10.00 25.00
RA Rafael Araujo 2.50 6.00
RH Richard Hamilton 6.00 15.00
SH Shawn Marion 6.00 15.00
SL Shaun Livingston 4.00 10.00
SM Stephon Marbury 10.00 25.00
ST Sebastian Telfair 3.00 8.00
SV Sasha Vujacic 4.00 10.00
TA Tony Allen 4.00 10.00
TM Tracy McGrady SP 20.00 40.00
TR Trevor Ariza 4.00 10.00
WE Delonte West 4.00 10.00

2004-05 Upper Deck Trilogy Swatches of Stardom

Randomly seeded in packs and serially numbered to 50, this 42-card set is horizontally designed with a player image on the left and an oversized jersey swatch on the right in the shape of "SS."
PRINT RUN 50 SER.#'d SETS
AI Allen Iverson 8.00 20.00
AK Andrei Kirilenko 4.00 10.00
AS Amare Stoudemire 4.00 10.00
BD Baron Davis 4.00 10.00
BG Ben Gordon 5.00 12.00
BK Bernard King 4.00 10.00
BR Bill Russell 20.00 50.00
BW Ben Wallace 4.00 10.00
CA Carmelo Anthony 10.00 25.00
DE Devin Harris 4.00 10.00
DH Dwight Howard 10.00 25.00
DN Dirk Nowitzki 8.00 20.00
EB Elton Brand 5.00 12.00
JC Josh Childress 4.00 10.00
JE Julius Erving 20.00 50.00
JK Jason Kidd 8.00 20.00
JN Jameer Nelson 5.00 12.00
JO Jermaine O'Neal 4.00 10.00
JR J.R. Smith 5.00 12.00
JS Josh Smith 5.00 12.00
KB Kobe Bryant 25.00 60.00
KG Kevin Garnett 8.00 20.00
LB Larry Bird 35.00 75.00
LD Luol Deng 5.00 12.00
LJ LeBron James 20.00 50.00
MA Magic Johnson 20.00 50.00
MJ Michael Jordan 150.00 300.00
PG Pau Gasol 5.00 12.00
PP Paul Pierce 5.00 12.00
PS Peja Stojakovic 5.00 12.00
RM Reggie Miller 8.00 20.00
SF Steve Francis 4.00 10.00
SH Shawn Marion 4.00 10.00
SL Shaun Livingston 5.00 12.00
SM Stephon Marbury 4.00 10.00
SN Steve Nash 6.00 15.00
SO Shaquille O'Neal 20.00 50.00
ST Sebastian Telfair 4.00 10.00
TD Tim Duncan 8.00 20.00
TM Tracy McGrady 6.00 15.00
WF Walt Frazier 5.00 12.00
YM Yao Ming 10.00 25.00

2004-05 Upper Deck Trilogy The Cutting Edge

Randomly inserted in packs at the rate of one in three, this 42-card set features player photos on the right and a swatch of memorabilia in the lower left.
STATED ODDS 1:3
AE Andre Emmett 1.50 4.00
AI Allen Iverson 4.00 10.00
AJ Al Jefferson 3.00 8.00
AN Andre Iguodala 3.00 8.00
AS Amare Stoudemire 2.00 5.00
BD Baron Davis SP 2.00 5.00
BG Ben Gordon 2.50 6.00
CA Carmelo Anthony 5.00 12.00
CD Chris Duhon 2.50 6.00
DE Devin Harris 2.00 5.00
DH Dwight Howard 5.00 12.00
DN Dirk Nowitzki 4.00 10.00
JA Jason Richardson 2.50 6.00
JC Josh Childress 2.00 5.00
JK Jason Kidd 4.00 10.00
JN Jameer Nelson 2.50 6.00
JR J.R. Smith 2.50 6.00
JS Josh Smith 2.50 6.00
KB Kobe Bryant SP 10.00 25.00
KG Kevin Garnett SP 6.00 15.00
KH Kris Humphries 2.50 6.00
KM Kevin Martin 3.00 8.00
KS Kirk Snyder 1.50 4.00
LD Luol Deng 2.50 6.00
LJ LeBron James SP 75.00 150.00
LU Luke Jackson 1.50 4.00
MB Mike Bibby 2.50 6.00
MJ Michael Jordan SP 40.00 100.00
PP Paul Pierce 2.50 6.00
PS Peja Stojakovic 2.50 6.00
RA Ray Allen 2.50 6.00
RJ Richard Jefferson 2.00 5.00
SA Shareef Abdur-Rahim 2.00 5.00
SL Shaun Livingston 2.50 6.00
SM Stephon Marbury 2.00 5.00
SO Shaquille O'Neal SP 6.00 15.00
ST Sebastian Telfair 2.00 5.00
TA Tony Allen 2.50 6.00
TD Tim Duncan 4.00 10.00
TM Tracy McGrady 3.00 8.00
WE Delonte West 2.50 6.00
YM Yao Ming 5.00 12.00

2004-05 Upper Deck Trilogy TriMarks I

Limited to 35 serially numbered copies, this 29-card set is printed on plastic and features three players along with their autographs.
PRINT RUN 35 SER.#'d SETS
CARDS WITH ASTERISK ISSUED AS EXCH
UNPRICED TRIMARKS II PRINT RUN 10 SETS
AMS R.Allen/Murray/R.Swift* 20.00 50.00
ART Abdur-Rah/Z-BO/Telfair* 20.00 50.00
BMM Bibby/B.Miller/Kv.Martin* 50.00 100.00
BOR Bryant/Odom/Rush 125.00 250.00
CSI Childress/JoshSmith/Ivey* 20.00 50.00
DWK B.Davis/J.Williams/Kidd 125.00 225.00
GDH Gordon/Deng/Hinrich* 125.00 250.00
GEB Gasol/Emmett/Burks 20.00 50.00
HCS Harrington/Childress/Smith 60.00 120.00
HGL Howard/Gordon/Livingston 150.00 300.00
HHD J.Howard/Harris/Daniels 40.00 100.00
HJB Howard/LeBron/Kobe 500.00 900.00
HMB Rip/Chauncey/Darko* 20.00 50.00
IBJ Iguodala/Bibby/Jefferson* 20.00 50.00
JAR Jamison/Arenas/Ramos 20.00 50.00
JJV James/L.Jackson/Varejao* 100.00 200.00
JWA A.Jefferson/West/T.Allen* 60.00 150.00
KHS AK-47/Humphries/Snyder* 20.00 50.00
MCA Marbury/Crawford/Ariza* 20.00 50.00
MLC Magg/Livingstn/Chalmers* 20.00 50.00
MSP Magloire/J.R.Smith/Pickett 20.00 50.00
NTL Nelson/Telfair/Livingston* 20.00 50.00
OVR Odom/Vujacic/Rush 20.00 50.00
PUS Parker/Udrih/Sato 40.00 100.00
RFB J-Rich/Fisher/Biedrins 20.00 50.00
RMK Redd/Mason/Kukoc* 50.00 120.00
RPA Rose/MoPete/Araujo* 20.00 50.00
SBM Peja/Bibby/B.Miller* 60.00 120.00
SMV Amare/Marion/Vroman* 75.00 150.00

2005-06 Upper Deck Trilogy

COMP.SET w/o SP's (90) 25.00 60.00
91-130 RC PRINT RUN 999 SER.#'d SETS
131-140 RC PRINT RUN 599 SER.#'d SETS
1 Josh Smith .75 2.00
2 Josh Childress .75 2.00
3 Al Harrington .75 2.00
4 Paul Pierce 1.00 2.50
5 Ricky Davis .75 2.00
6 Al Jefferson .75 2.00
7 Emeka Okafor .75 2.00
8 Gerald Wallace .75 2.00
9 Kareem Rush .60 1.50
10 Michael Jordan 8.00 20.00
11 Luol Deng .75 2.00
12 Ben Gordon .75 2.00
13 LeBron James 4.00 10.00
14 Larry Hughes .75 2.00
15 Donyell Marshall .60 1.50
16 Dirk Nowitzki 1.50 4.00
17 Josh Howard 1.00 2.50
18 Jason Terry .75 2.00
19 Carmelo Anthony 2.00 5.00
20 Kenyon Martin .75 2.00
21 Andre Miller .75 2.00
22 Chauncey Billups 1.00 2.50
23 Richard Hamilton .75 2.00
24 Ben Wallace .75 2.00
25 Jason Richardson 1.00 2.50
26 Baron Davis .75 2.00
27 Troy Murphy .60 1.50
28 Yao Ming 1.25 3.00
29 Tracy McGrady 1.25 3.00
30 Stromile Swift .60 1.50
31 Ron Artest 1.00 2.50
32 Jermaine O'Neal .75 2.00
33 Fred Jones .60 1.50
34 Elton Brand 1.00 2.50
35 Shaun Livingston .60 1.50
36 Corey Maggette .75 2.00
37 Kobe Bryant 4.00 10.00
38 Kwame Brown .60 1.50
39 Lamar Odom .75 2.00
40 Pau Gasol 1.00 2.50
41 Shane Battier .75 2.00
42 Mike Miller .75 2.00
43 Shaquille O'Neal 2.00 5.00
44 Dwyane Wade 1.50 4.00
45 Udonis Haslem .60 1.50
46 Michael Redd .75 2.00
47 Maurice Williams .75 2.00
48 Desmond Mason .60 1.50
49 Kevin Garnett 1.50 4.00
50 Wally Szczerbiak .75 2.00
51 Marko Jaric .60 1.50
52 Jason Kidd 1.50 4.00
53 Vince Carter 1.50 4.00
54 Richard Jefferson .75 2.00
55 Jamaal Magloire .60 1.50
56 J.R. Smith .75 2.00
57 Speedy Claxton .60 1.50
58 Stephon Marbury .75 2.00
59 Jamal Crawford 1.00 2.50
60 Quentin Richardson .75 2.00
61 Steve Francis .75 2.00
62 Dwight Howard .75 2.00
63 Grant Hill 1.25 3.00
64 Allen Iverson 1.50 4.00
65 Kyle Korver .75 2.00
66 Chris Webber 1.00 2.50
67 Steve Nash 1.25 3.00
68 Amare Stoudemire .75 2.00
69 Shawn Marion .75 2.00
70 Sebastian Telfair .75 2.00
71 Zach Randolph .75 2.00
72 Travis Outlaw .75 2.00
73 Peja Stojakovic 1.00 2.50
74 Mike Bibby 1.00 2.50
75 Brad Miller .75 2.00
76 Tim Duncan 1.50 4.00
77 Manu Ginobili 1.00 2.50
78 Tony Parker 1.00 2.50
79 Ray Allen 1.00 2.50
80 Rashard Lewis 1.00 2.50
81 Luke Ridnour .75 2.00
82 Chris Bosh 1.00 2.50
83 Morris Peterson .60 1.50
84 Jalen Rose 1.00 2.50
85 Carlos Boozer .75 2.00
86 Matt Harpring .60 1.50
87 Andrei Kirilenko .75 2.00
88 Antawn Jamison .75 2.00
89 Gilbert Arenas .75 2.00
90 Caron Butler .75 2.00
91 Sarunas Jasikevicius RC 2.50 6.00
92 Alex Acker RC 1.50 4.00
93 Amir Johnson RC 2.50 6.00
94 Lawrence Roberts RC 1.50 4.00
95 Dijon Thompson RC 1.50 4.00
96 Orien Greene RC 2.00 5.00
97 Robert Whaley RC 1.50 4.00
98 Ryan Gomes RC 2.00 5.00
99 Andray Blatche RC 2.50 6.00
100 Yaroslav Korolev RC 1.50 4.00
101 Bracey Wright RC 1.50 4.00
102 Louis Williams RC 2.50 6.00
103 Martynas Andriuskevicius RC 1.50 4.00
104 Chris Taft RC 2.00 5.00
105 Monta Ellis RC 3.00 8.00
106 Von Wafer RC 1.50 4.00
107 Travis Diener RC 1.50 4.00
108 Ersan Ilyasova RC 2.50 6.00
109 Arvydas Macijauskas RC 1.50 4.00
110 C.J. Miles RC 2.50 6.00
111 Brandon Bass RC 2.00 5.00
112 Daniel Ewing RC 2.00 5.00
113 Salim Stoudamire RC 2.00 5.00
114 David Lee RC 2.50 6.00
115 Wayne Simien RC 1.50 4.00
116 Jason Maxiell RC 2.00 5.00
117 Johan Petro RC 1.50 4.00
118 Luther Head RC 2.00 5.00
119 Francisco Garcia RC 2.00 5.00
120 Jarrett Jack RC 2.50 6.00
121 Nate Robinson RC 2.50 6.00
122 Julius Hodge RC 1.50 4.00
123 Hakim Warrick RC 2.00 5.00
124 Gerald Green RC 2.50 6.00
125 Danny Granger RC 3.00 8.00
126 Joey Graham RC 2.00 5.00
127 Antoine Wright RC 2.00 5.00
128 Rashad McCants RC 2.00 5.00
129 Sean May RC 1.50 4.00
130 Linas Kleiza RC 1.50 4.00
131 Andrew Bynum RC 2.50 6.00
132 Ike Diogu RC 2.00 5.00
133 Channing Frye RC 3.00 8.00
134 Charlie Villanueva RC 3.00 8.00
135 Martell Webster RC 2.50 6.00
136 Raymond Felton RC 3.00 8.00
137 Chris Paul RC 12.00 30.00
138 Deron Williams RC 4.00 10.00
139 Marvin Williams RC 3.00 8.00
140 Andrew Bogut RC 4.00 10.00

2005-06 Upper Deck Trilogy Auto Focus

APPROXIMATELY ONE PER BOX
AB Andrew Bogut 6.00 15.00
AN Andrew Bynum 4.00 10.00
AW Antoine Wright 4.00 10.00
BG Ben Gordon 4.00 10.00
CF Channing Frye 5.00 12.00
CP Chris Paul 30.00 80.00
DG Danny Granger 6.00 15.00
DH Dwight Howard 10.00 25.00
EO Emeka Okafor 4.00 10.00
FG Francisco Garcia 4.00 10.00
GG George Gervin 6.00 15.00
HO Hakeem Olajuwon SP 25.00 60.00
ID Ike Diogu 3.00 8.00
IT Isiah Thomas 8.00 20.00
JA Jarrett Jack 5.00 12.00
JJ Joe Johnson 5.00 12.00
JP Johan Petro 3.00 8.00
JR J.R. Smith SP 8.00 20.00
KB Kwame Brown 5.00 12.00
KD Keyon Dooling 3.00 8.00
LA Larry Bird SP 75.00 150.00
LB LeBron James 200.00 400.00
MA Magic Johnson SP 50.00 120.00
MJ Michael Jordan SP 500.00 800.00
MR Michael Redd 5.00 12.00
MW Marvin Williams 5.00 12.00
NR Nate Robinson 8.00 20.00
PP Paul Pierce 12.00 30.00
RF Raymond Felton 5.00 12.00
RH Richard Hamilton 6.00 15.00
RM Rashad McCants 4.00 10.00
SE Sean May 3.00 8.00
SJ Sarunas Jasikevicius 5.00 12.00
SM Stephon Marbury 10.00 25.00
SP Scottie Pippen SP 100.00 200.00
TM Tracy McGrady SP 15.00 40.00
VR Vladimir Radmanovic 3.00 8.00
WF Walt Frazier 6.00 15.00
WS Wayne Simien 3.00 8.00
YM Yao Ming SP 20.00 50.00

2005-06 Upper Deck Trilogy DuoMarks

INT RUN 25 TO 75 SER.#'d SETS
AW C.Anthony/Warrick/25 25.00 60.00
BF A.Bogut/C.Frye/25 25.00 60.00
BP A.Bynum/J.Petro/75 15.00 40.00
BS B.King/S.Marbury/75 15.00 40.00
CD Cabarkapa/Diogu/75 10.00 25.00
CK V.Carter/J.Kidd/75 60.00 120.00
DR Daniels/Q.Richardson/75 10.00 25.00
GH B.Gordon/Hinrich/75 15.00 40.00
GW D.Granger/Warrick/75 10.00 25.00
HE L.Head/D.Ewing/75 10.00 25.00
HS K.Hinrich/Simien/75 10.00 25.00
HW D.Howard/M.Williams/75 20.00 50.00
IW Iguodala/L.Williams/75 12.50 30.00
JA M.Johnson/Kareem/25 100.00 225.00
JC J.Johnson/Childress/75 10.00 25.00
JG A.Jefferson/O.Greene/75 10.00 25.00
JJ M.Jordan/L.James/25 600.00 1000.00
KH L.Kleiza/J.Hodge/75 10.00 25.00
KM J.Kidd/S.Marbury/25 20.00 50.00
LB D.Lee/B.Bass/75 10.00 25.00
LE Livingston/D.Ewing/75 10.00 25.00
MM S.May/R.McCants/75 10.00 25.00
MS J.Maxiell/W.Simien/75 10.00 25.00
MY T.McGrady/Y.Ming/25 100.00 200.00
NB S.Nash/C.Billups/25 40.00 100.00
ND J.Nelson/T.Diener/75 10.00 25.00
PB T.Prince/C.Billups/75 25.00 60.00
PG P.Pierce/G.Green/75 15.00 40.00
PR S.Pippen/Rodman/25 250.00 450.00
PW C.Paul/M.Williams/25 30.00 80.00
RG D.Robinson/Gervin/25 100.00 200.00
RJ N.Robinson/J.Jack/75 10.00 25.00
SP J.Smith/C.Paul/75 30.00 80.00
SS D.Stoudamire/S.Stoudamire/75 10.00 25.00
SW J.Stockton/D.Williams/25 75.00 200.00
VG C.Villanueva/J.Graham/75 15.00 30.00
WF D.Williams/R.Felton/75 12.00 30.00
WG M.Webster/G.Green/75 12.50 30.00
WH A.Wright/J.Hodge/75 10.00 25.00
WJ M.Webster/J.Jack/75 10.00 25.00

2005-06 Upper Deck Trilogy One Two Combo Clearcut Autographs

PRINT RUN 50 SER.#'d SETS
UNPRICED 1-2-3 AUTO PRINT RUN 10 SETS
BP L.Bird/R.Parish 100.00 250.00
BV C.Bosh/C.Villanueva 40.00 100.00
BW A.Bogut/M.Williams 25.00 60.00
FM R.Felton/S.May 15.00 40.00
GH B.Gordon/K.Hinrich 15.00 40.00
GW P.Gasol/H.Warrick 15.00 40.00
HB R.Hamilton/C.Billups 30.00 75.00
HJ D.Howard/A.Jefferson 25.00 60.00
JJ L.James/M.Jordan 700.00 1000.00
JP A.Jefferson/P.Pierce 20.00 50.00
KW J.Kidd/A.Wright 15.00 40.00
MH T.McGrady/L.Head 25.00 60.00
PW C.Paul/D.Williams 75.00 150.00
RB M.Redd/A.Bogut 30.00 60.00
RM Q.Richardson/S.Marbury 15.00 40.00
SP J.Smith/C.Paul 40.00 75.00
TB I.Thomas/C.Billups 20.00 50.00
TJ S.Telfair/J.Jack 15.00 40.00
VG C.Villanueva/J.Graham 15.00 40.00
WF D.Williams/R.Felton 25.00 60.00

2005-06 Upper Deck Trilogy Signature Swatches

PRINT RUN 25 SER.#'d SETS
UNPRICED PATCH PRINT RUN 15 SETS
UNPRICED DUAL PRINT RUN 15 SETS
UNPRICED DUAL PATCH PRINT RUN 5 SETS
AB Andrew Bogut 20.00 50.00
AW Antoine Wright 12.00 30.00
BG Ben Gordon 25.00 60.00
CF Channing Frye 15.00 40.00
CP Chris Paul 125.00 250.00
CV Charlie Villanueva 15.00 40.00
DG Danny Granger 20.00 50.00
DH Dwight Howard 40.00 80.00
DW Deron Williams 100.00 175.00
FG Francisco Garcia 12.00 30.00
HW Hakim Warrick 12.00 30.00
ID Ike Diogu 10.00 25.00
JG Joey Graham 12.00 30.00
JH Julius Hodge 10.00 25.00
JJ Jarrett Jack 15.00 40.00
JK Jason Kidd 30.00 80.00
JM Jason Maxiell 12.00 30.00
LH Luther Head 12.00 30.00
MA Martell Webster 12.00 30.00
MJ Michael Jordan 500.00 800.00
MW Marvin Williams 15.00 40.00
NR Nate Robinson 15.00 40.00
PG Pau Gasol 15.00 40.00
PP Paul Pierce 20.00 50.00
RF Raymond Felton 15.00 40.00
RM Rashad McCants 12.00 30.00
SM Sean May 10.00 25.00
TM Tracy McGrady 30.00 80.00
YM Yao Ming 40.00 100.00

2005-06 Upper Deck Trilogy Signs of Stardom

APPROXIMATELY TWO PER BOX
AB Andrew Bogut 4.00 10.00
AJ Antawn Jamison 4.00 10.00
AL Al Jefferson 4.00 10.00
AN Andrew Bynum 2.50 6.00
AW Antoine Wright 2.50 6.00
BD Baron Davis 5.00 12.00
BJ Bobby Jackson 4.00 10.00
BM Brad Miller 4.00 10.00
BS Bobby Simmons 4.00 10.00
CA Carmelo Anthony SP 20.00 40.00
CF Channing Frye 3.00 8.00
CH Chauncey Billups 8.00 20.00
CJ C.J. Miles 3.00 8.00
CP Chris Paul 30.00 60.00
CT Chris Taft SP 2.50 6.00
DE Daniel Ewing 2.50 6.00
DG Danny Granger 4.00 10.00
DH Dwight Howard 10.00 25.00
DL David Lee 3.00 8.00
DM Donyell Marshall 4.00 10.00
FG Francisco Garcia 2.50 6.00
GG Gerald Green 3.00 8.00
ID Ike Diogu 2.00 5.00
JA Jamaal Magloire 3.00 8.00
JG Joey Graham 2.50 6.00
JH Julius Hodge 2.00 5.00
JJ Jarrett Jack 3.00 8.00
JK Jason Kidd SP 10.00 25.00
JM Jason Maxiell 2.50 6.00
JP Johan Petro 2.00 5.00
JR J.R. Smith 3.00 8.00
LH Luther Head 2.50 6.00
LJ LeBron James SP 150.00 300.00
LK Linas Kleiza 2.00 5.00
LO Lamar Odom 5.00 12.00
MJ Michael Jordan SP 1200.00 2000.00
MR Michael Redd 5.00 12.00
MW Marvin Williams 3.00 8.00
NR Nate Robinson 3.00 8.00
PP Paul Pierce 15.00 40.00
RF Raymond Felton 3.00 8.00
RH Richard Hamilton 6.00 15.00
RM Rashad McCants 2.50 6.00
SE Sean May 2.00 5.00
SM Stephon Marbury SP 6.00 15.00
SP Speedy Claxton 3.00 8.00
SS Salim Stoudamire 2.50 6.00
ST Stromile Swift 3.00 8.00
TC Tyson Chandler 5.00 12.00
TM Tracy McGrady 10.00 25.00
TP Tayshaun Prince 8.00 20.00
WS Wayne Simien 2.00 5.00
YK Yaroslav Korolev 2.00 5.00

2005-06 Upper Deck Trilogy Swatches of Stardom

PRINT RUN 50 SER.#'d SETS
AB Andrew Bogut 5.00 12.00
AW Antonie Wright 3.00 8.00
BK Bernard King 6.00 15.00
CD Clyde Drexler 12.50 30.00
CF Channing Frye 4.00 10.00
CP Chris Paul 15.00 40.00
CV Charlie Villanueva 4.00 10.00
DG Danny Granger 5.00 12.00
DH Dwight Howard 3.00 8.00
DW Deron Williams 5.00 12.00
FG Francisco Garcia 3.00 8.00
GG Gerald Green 4.00 10.00
HK Hakeem Olajuwon 12.50 30.00
HW Hakim Warrick 3.00 8.00
ID Ike Diogu 2.50 6.00
IT Isiah Thomas 6.00 15.00
JG Joey Graham 3.00 8.00
JH Julius Hodge 2.50 6.00
JJ Jarrett Jack 4.00 10.00
JM Jason Maxiell 3.00 8.00
JO John Stockton 12.50 30.00
JS Jamal Sampson 4.00 10.00
JW James Worthy 15.00 40.00
KB Kobe Bryant 15.00 40.00
KG Kevin Garnett 6.00 15.00
KM Kevin McHale 10.00 25.00
LB Larry Bird 15.00 40.00
LH Luther Head 3.00 8.00
LJ LeBron James 15.00 40.00
MA Magic Johnson 15.00 40.00
MJ Michael Jordan 100.00 200.00
MW Marvin Williams 4.00 10.00
NR Nate Robinson 4.00 10.00
PM Pete Maravich 50.00 120.00
RF Raymond Felton 4.00 10.00
RM Rashad McCants 3.00 8.00
SM Sean May 2.50 6.00
TM Tracy McGrady 5.00 12.00
WE Martell Webster 3.00 8.00
WS Wayne Simien 2.50 6.00
YM Yao Ming 8.00 20.00

2005-06 Upper Deck Trilogy The Cutting Edge

APPROXIMATELY TWO PER BOX
AB Andrew Bogut 3.00 8.00
AI Andre Iguodala 2.00 5.00
AJ Antawn Jamison 2.00 5.00
AS Amare Stoudemire 2.00 5.00
AW Antoine Wright 2.00 5.00
BW Ben Wallace 2.00 5.00
CA Carmelo Anthony 5.00 12.00
CF Channing Frye 2.50 6.00
CP Chris Paul 8.00 20.00
CV Charlie Villanueva 2.50 6.00
CW Chris Webber 2.50 6.00
DE Deron Williams 3.00 8.00
DG Danny Granger 3.00 8.00
DH Dwight Howard 2.00 5.00
DN Dirk Nowitzki 4.00 10.00
EB Elton Brand 2.50 6.00
GA Gilbert Arenas SP 2.00 5.00
ID Ike Diogu 1.50 4.00
JG Joey Graham 2.00 5.00
JK Jason Kidd SP 4.00 10.00
JO Jermaine O'Neal 2.00 5.00
JR Jason Richardson 2.50 6.00
JS J.R. Smith 2.00 5.00
KB Kobe Bryant 8.00 20.00
KG Kevin Garnett 4.00 10.00
KM Kenyon Martin 2.00 5.00
LJ LeBron James 10.00 25.00
MA Martell Webster 2.00 5.00
MJ Michael Jordan SP 30.00 80.00
MW Marvin Williams 2.50 6.00
PP Paul Pierce 2.50 6.00
RF Raymond Felton 2.50 6.00
RJ Richard Jefferson SP 2.00 5.00
RM Rashad McCants 2.00 5.00
SE Sean May 1.50 4.00
SF Steve Francis 2.00 5.00
SH Shawn Marion 2.00 5.00
SM Stephon Marbury 2.00 5.00
SO Shaquille O'Neal 5.00 12.00
TD Tim Duncan 4.00 10.00
TM Tracy McGrady 3.00 8.00
YM Yao Ming 3.00 8.00

2005-06 Upper Deck Trilogy TriMarks

PRINT RUN 10 TO 40 SER.#'d SETS
SOME UNPRICED DUE TO SCARCITY
AGJ Allen/Green/Jefferson 8.00 20.00
BGV Bosh/Graham/Villanueva* 20.00 50.00
DBT I.Diogu/A.Biedrins/C.Taft* 8.00 20.00
DDT B.Davis/I.Diogu/C.Taft 15.00 40.00
DEB C.Duhon/D.Ewing/C.Boozer* 15.00 40.00
FFK W.Frazier/C.Frye/B.King 30.00 80.00
FLR C.Frye/D.Lee/N.Robinson 30.00 60.00
GJA Granger/Sarunas/Artest* 30.00 80.00
GJW Gasol/B.Jackson/Warrick* 25.00 60.00
GOV Gordon/Okafor/Villanueva* 40.00 100.00
JBM J.Jack/C.Bosh/S.Marbury* 25.00 60.00
KJW Kidd/R.Jefferson/Wright 12.00 30.00
MME Maggette/Mobley/D.Ewing* 8.00 20.00
MMF McCants/S.May/Felton 10.00 25.00
MRR Marbury/N.Rob/Q-Rich 25.00 60.00
OBW L.Odom/A.Bynum/V.Wafer* 12.00 30.00
OMF E.Okafor/S.May/R.Felton 20.00 50.00
PSB C.Paul/J.Smith/B.Bass* 50.00 120.00
RSM Redd/Simmons/Mason 8.00 20.00
TRL Isiah/Rodman/Laimbeer* 100.00 200.00
WBG Webster/Bynum/Green* 25.00 60.00
WBP B.Wallace/Billups/Prince 60.00 120.00
WPM Walton/Parish/Maxwell* 40.00 80.00

2006-07 Upper Deck Trilogy

Upper Deck Trilogy was released in mid June 2007 and features a 140-card base set where cards 1-60 picture veteran players, cards 61-90 showcase a horizontal card design with three players from the same team pictured, cards 91-98 picture rookies on a horizontally designed acetate card sequentially numbered to 299 and cards 99-140 picture rookies on the same design and are sequentially numbered to 499. Trilogy is packaged in nine-pack boxes of five cards each and carried an initial suggested retail price of $10.00 per pack. Each box of Trilogy contains three rookies, three autographs and three memorabilia cards.
COMP.SET w/o SP's (90) 20.00 50.00
91-98 PRINT RUN 299 SER.#'d SETS
99-140 PRINT RUN 499 SER.#'d SETS
UNPRICED GOLD PRINT RUN 10 SETS
1 Joe Johnson .60 1.50
2 Marvin Williams .60 1.50
3 Paul Pierce .75 2.00
4 Wally Szczerbiak .60 1.50
5 Emeka Okafor .60 1.50
6 Raymond Felton .60 1.50
7 Ben Wallace .60 1.50
8 Kirk Hinrich .60 1.50
9 Ben Gordon .60 1.50
10 LeBron James 3.00 8.00
11 Larry Hughes .60 1.50
12 Dirk Nowitzki 1.25 3.00
13 Jason Terry .60 1.50
14 Carmelo Anthony 1.00 2.50
15 Andre Miller .60 1.50
16 Chauncey Billups .75 2.00
17 Richard Hamilton .60 1.50
18 Jason Richardson .75 2.00
19 Baron Davis .60 1.50
20 Yao Ming 1.00 2.50
21 Tracy McGrady 1.00 2.50
22 Jermaine O'Neal .60 1.50
23 Al Harrington .60 1.50
24 Elton Brand .75 2.00
25 Sam Cassell .60 1.50
26 Kobe Bryant 3.00 8.00
27 Lamar Odom .60 1.50
28 Pau Gasol .75 2.00
29 Dwyane Wade 1.25 3.00
30 Shaquille O'Neal 1.50 4.00
31 Michael Redd .60 1.50
32 Andrew Bogut .60 1.50
33 Kevin Garnett 1.25 3.00
34 Mike James .50 1.25
35 Vince Carter 1.00 2.50
36 Jason Kidd 1.25 3.00
37 Richard Jefferson .60 1.50
38 Chris Paul 1.00 2.50
39 David West .60 1.50
40 Stephon Marbury .60 1.50
41 Steve Francis .60 1.50
42 Dwight Howard .60 1.50
43 Jameer Nelson .50 1.25
44 Allen Iverson 1.00 2.50
45 Chris Webber .75 2.00
46 Steve Nash 1.00 2.50
47 Shawn Marion .60 1.50
48 Zach Randolph .60 1.50
49 Mike Bibby .75 2.00
50 Ron Artest .75 2.00
51 Tim Duncan 1.25 3.00
52 Tony Parker .75 2.00
53 Ray Allen .75 2.00
54 Rashard Lewis .75 2.00
55 Chris Bosh .75 2.00
56 T.J. Ford .50 1.25
57 Mehmet Okur .50 1.25
58 Andrei Kirilenko .60 1.50
59 Gilbert Arenas .60 1.50
60 Antawn Jamison .60 1.50
61 Childress/Claxton/Smith .75 2.00
62 Jefferson/West/Telfair .75 2.00
63 Wallace/Brezec/Knight .75 2.00
64 Nocioni/Deng/Brown 1.25 3.00
65 Gooden/Ilgauskas/Marshall .75 2.00
66 Howard/Stackhouse/Harris 1.25 3.00
67 Martin/Camby/Smith 1.25 3.00
68 Wallace/Prince/Mohammed 1.25 3.00
69 Murphy/Dunleavy/Diogu .75 2.00
70 Alston/Battier/Wells .75 2.00
71 Granger/Tinsley/Dunleavy .75 2.00
72 Kaman/Maggette/Livingston .75 2.00
73 Parker/Radmanovic/Brown 1.25 3.00
74 Miller/Stoudamire/Warrick .75 2.00
75 Walker/Haslem/Williams 1.25 3.00
76 Villanueva/Patterson/Williams .75 2.00
77 Davis/Hassell/Blount .75 2.00
78 Krstic/Collins/Robinson .75 2.00
79 Chandler/Stojakovic/Mason .75 2.00
80 Curry/Crawford/Frye .75 2.00
81 Milicic/Turkoglu/Hill 1.00 2.50
82 Iguodala/Korver/Dalembert .75 2.00
83 Stoudemire/Diaw/Bell 1.25 3.00
84 Jack/Randolph/Webster .75 2.00
85 Miller/Abdur-Rahim/Martin 1.00 2.50
86 Ginobili/Finley/Bowen 1.50 4.00
87 Ridnour/Wilcox/Collison .75 2.00
88 Peterson/Graham/Calderon .75 2.00
89 Boozer/Williams/Giricek 1.25 3.00
90 Butler/Thomas/Stevenson .75 2.00
91 Shelden Williams RC 2.50 6.00
92 Tyrus Thomas RC 2.50 6.00
93 Rudy Gay RC 4.00 10.00
94 Randy Foye RC 3.00 8.00
95 Rodney Carney RC 2.00 5.00
96 LaMarcus Aldridge RC 8.00 20.00
97 Brandon Roy RC 3.00 8.00
98 Andrea Bargnani RC 3.00 8.00
99 Solomon Jones RC 1.25 3.00
100 Rajon Rondo RC 3.00 8.00
101 Allan Ray RC 1.25 3.00
102 Thabo Sefolosha RC 2.00 5.00
103 Shannon Brown RC 1.25 3.00
104 Maurice Ager RC 1.25 3.00
105 Patrick O'Bryant RC 1.25 3.00
106 Steve Novak RC 1.50 4.00
107 Shawne Williams RC 1.25 3.00
108 Paul Davis RC 1.25 3.00
109 Jordan Farmar RC 2.00 5.00
110 Kyle Lowry RC 2.50 6.00
111 David Noel RC 1.25 3.00
112 Craig Smith RC 1.50 4.00
113 Marcus Williams RC 1.25 3.00
114 Josh Boone RC 1.25 3.00
115 Hilton Armstrong RC 1.25 3.00
116 Cedric Simmons RC 1.25 3.00
117 Renaldo Balkman RC 1.50 4.00
118 Mardy Collins RC 1.25 3.00
119 Bobby Jones RC 1.25 3.00
120 Quincy Douby RC 1.25 3.00
121 Saer Sene RC 1.25 3.00
122 P.J. Tucker RC 1.50 4.00
123 Jorge Garbajosa RC 1.50 4.00
124 Ronnie Brewer RC 2.00 5.00
125 Dee Brown RC 1.25 3.00
126 Leon Powe RC 1.50 4.00
127 Ryan Hollins RC 1.50 4.00
128 Adam Morrison RC 2.00 5.00
129 Daniel Gibson RC 1.50 4.00
130 Pops Mensah-Bonsu RC 1.25 3.00
131 Yakhouba Diawara RC 1.25 3.00
132 Will Blalock RC 1.25 3.00
133 Alexander Johnson RC 1.25 3.00
134 Damir Markota RC 1.25 3.00
135 Hassan Adams RC 1.25 3.00
136 Marcus Vinicius RC 1.25 3.00
137 James Augustine RC 1.25 3.00
138 J.J. Redick RC 2.50 6.00
139 Sergio Rodriguez RC 2.00 5.00
140 Paul Millsap RC 2.50 6.00

2006-07 Upper Deck Trilogy Blue

*1-60 BLUE: .75X TO 2X BASE HI
1-60 BLUE PRINT RUN 66 SER.#'d SETS
*61-90 BLUE: 1.25X TO 3X BASE HI
*91-98 BLUE: .75X TO 2X BASE HI
*99-140 BLUE: 1.25X TO 3X BASE HI
61-140 BLUE PRINT RUN 33 SER.#'d SETS

2006-07 Upper Deck Trilogy Auto Focus

APPROXIMATE ODDS ONE PER BOX
AFAB Andrea Bargnani 5.00 12.00
AFAI Andre Iguodala 6.00 15.00
AFBG Ben Gordon 6.00 15.00
AFBO Chris Bosh 10.00 25.00
AFBR Brandon Roy 5.00 12.00
AFCA Carmelo Anthony 15.00 40.00
AFCP Chris Paul 20.00 50.00
AFCS Cedric Simmons 3.00 8.00
AFJB Josh Boone 3.00 8.00
AFJF Jordan Farmar 5.00 12.00
AFJK Jason Kidd 10.00 25.00
AFJW James White 3.00 8.00
AFLA LaMarcus Aldridge 20.00 50.00
AFLJ LeBron James SP 150.00 300.00
AFMB Mike Bibby 5.00 12.00
AFMC Mardy Collins 3.00 8.00
AFMJ Michael Jordan SP 300.00 600.00
AFMW Marcus Williams 3.00 8.00
AFPP Paul Pierce 12.00 30.00
AFQD Quincy Douby 3.00 8.00
AFRB Renaldo Balkman 4.00 10.00
AFRC Rodney Carney 3.00 8.00
AFRF Randy Foye 5.00 12.00
AFRG Rudy Gay 6.00 15.00
AFRH Richard Hamilton 6.00 15.00
AFRJ Richard Jefferson 5.00 12.00
AFRO Ronnie Brewer 5.00 12.00
AFRR Rajon Rondo 8.00 20.00
AFSB Shannon Brown 3.00 8.00
AFSN Steve Nash SP 60.00 120.00
AFSR Sergio Rodriguez 5.00 12.00
AFSS Saer Sene 3.00 8.00
AFSW Shawne Williams 3.00 8.00
AFTS Thabo Sefolosha 5.00 12.00
AFTT Tyrus Thomas 4.00 10.00
AFWI Shelden Williams 4.00 10.00
AFYM Yao Ming 20.00 50.00

2006-07 Upper Deck Trilogy Generations Future Memorabilia

APPROXIMATE ODDS ONE PER BOX
*PATCHES: .6X TO 1.5X BASE HI
PATCH PRINT RUN 50 SER.#'d SETS
FMAB Andrea Bargnani 2.50 6.00
FMAR Allan Ray 1.50 4.00
FMBJ Bobby Jones 1.50 4.00
FMBR Ronnie Brewer 2.50 6.00
FMCS Cedric Simmons 1.50 4.00
FMHA Hilton Armstrong 1.50 4.00
FMJB Josh Boone 1.50 4.00
FMJG Jorge Garbajosa 2.00 5.00
FMJR J.J. Redick 3.00 8.00
FMJW James White 1.50 4.00
FMKL Kyle Lowry 3.00 8.00
FMLA LaMarcus Aldridge 1.50 4.00
FMMC Mardy Collins 1.50 4.00
FMMW Marcus Williams 1.50 4.00
FMPD Paul Davis 1.50 4.00
FMPO Patrick O'Bryant 1.50 4.00
FMPT P.J. Tucker 2.00 5.00
FMQD Quincy Douby 1.50 4.00
FMRB Renaldo Balkman 2.00 5.00
FMRC Rodney Carney 1.50 4.00
FMRF Randy Foye 2.50 6.00
FMRG Rudy Gay 3.00 8.00
FMRO Brandon Roy 2.50 6.00
FMSB Shannon Brown 1.50 4.00
FMSJ Solomon Jones 1.50 4.00
FMSS Saer Sene 1.50 4.00
FMSW Shawne Williams 1.50 4.00
FMTT Tyrus Thomas 2.00 5.00
FMWB Will Blalock 1.50 4.00
FMWI Shelden Williams 2.00 5.00

2006-07 Upper Deck Trilogy Generations Future Signatures

APPROXIMATE ODDS ONE PER BOX
UNPRICED TRIO PRINT RUN 3 SETS
FSAB Andrea Bargnani 10.00 25.00
FSAR Allan Ray 2.50 6.00
FSBR Brandon Roy 10.00 25.00
FSCS Cedric Simmons 2.50 6.00
FSDN David Noel 2.50 6.00
FSHA Hilton Armstrong 2.50 6.00
FSJB Josh Boone 2.50 6.00
FSJF Jordan Farmar 4.00 10.00
FSKL Kyle Lowry 5.00 12.00
FSLA LaMarcus Aldridge 10.00 25.00
FSMA Maurice Ager 2.50 6.00
FSMC Mardy Collins 2.50 6.00
FSPD Paul Davis 2.50 6.00
FSPO Patrick O'Bryant 2.50 6.00
FSQD Quincy Douby 2.50 6.00
FSRB Renaldo Balkman 3.00 8.00
FSRC Rodney Carney 2.50 6.00
FSRF Randy Foye 4.00 10.00
FSRG Rudy Gay 5.00 12.00
FSRO Ronnie Brewer 4.00 10.00
FSRR Rajon Rondo 12.00 30.00
FSSB Shannon Brown 2.50 6.00
FSSM Craig Smith 3.00 8.00
FSSN Steve Novak 3.00 8.00
FSSS Saer Sene 2.50 6.00
FSSW Shawne Williams 2.50 6.00
FSTS Thabo Sefolosha 4.00 10.00
FSTT Tyrus Thomas 3.00 8.00
FSWI Shelden Williams 3.00 8.00

2006-07 Upper Deck Trilogy Generations Past and Future Memorabilia

PRINT RUN 50 SER.#'d SETS
PFMBB L.Bird/A.Bargnani 15.00 30.00
PFMBE M.Eaton/R.Brewer 5.00 12.00
PFMDA A.Dantley/M.Ager 5.00 12.00
PFMDB C.Drexler/S.Brown 8.00 20.00
PFMDC D.Dawkins/R.Carney 5.00 12.00
PFMEW J.Erving/S.Williams 8.00 20.00
PFMFB W.Frazier/R.Balkman 5.00 12.00
PFMGW G.Gervin/J.White 5.00 12.00
PFMJA J.White/A.Ray 5.00 12.00
PFMJW M.Johnson/M.Williams 8.00 20.00
PFMKB B.King/R.Brewer 5.00 12.00
PFMKC K.Malone/C.Simmons 6.00 15.00
PFMMD K.McHale/P.Davis 5.00 12.00
PFMMF E.Monroe/R.Foye 6.00 15.00
PFMMJ M.Malone/S.Jones 5.00 12.00
PFMMN J.Worthy/D.Noel 6.00 15.00
PFMMR C.Mullin/J.Redick 8.00 20.00
PFMMS K.Malone/C.Smith 8.00 20.00
PFMMT P.Maravich/T.Thomas 30.00 80.00
PFMON H.Olajuwon/S.Novak 5.00 12.00
PFMRJ D.Robinson/S.Jones 6.00 15.00
PFMRS D.Rodman/T.Sefolosha 10.00 25.00
PFMSB J.Stockton/D.Brown 20.00 40.00
PFMTD R.Theus/Q.Douby 5.00 12.00
PFMWE S.Elliott/J.White 8.00 20.00
PFMWF J.West/J.Farmar 10.00 25.00
PFMWG J.Worthy/R.Gay 6.00 15.00
PFMWL S.Webb/K.Lowry 5.00 12.00

2006-07 Upper Deck Trilogy Generations Past and Future Signatures

PRINT RUN 33 SER.#'d SETS
PFSAL N.Archibald/K.Lowry 8.00 20.00
PFSAR A.Robertson/R.Brewer 8.00 20.00
PFSBR D.Brown/R.Rondo 8.00 20.00
PFSDB D.Dawkins/J.Boone 8.00 20.00
PFSEH M.Eaton/R.Hollins 8.00 20.00
PFSEW W.Tisdale/S.Williams 8.00 20.00
PFSFF W.Frazier/R.Foye 10.00 25.00
PFSGG G.Gervin/R.Gay 10.00 25.00
PFSHA E.Hayes/L.Aldridge 15.00 30.00
PFSJC B.Jones/R.Carney 8.00 20.00
PFSKA S.Kerr/H.Adams 10.00 25.00
PFSMM A.Dantley/P.Millsap 15.00 30.00
PFSMN B.McAdoo/D.Noel 10.00 25.00
PFSMR M.Richardson/R.Balkman 8.00 20.00
PFSMS X.McDaniel/S.Sene 8.00 20.00
PFSPA R.Parish/H.Armstrong 10.00 25.00
PFSRB D.Robinson/A.Bargnani 20.00 50.00
PFSRM A.Robertson/D.Markota 15.00 30.00
PFSRT D.Rodman/T.Thomas 30.00 80.00
PFSSF B.Scott/J.Farmar 20.00 40.00
PFSSN R.Sampson/S.Novak 8.00 20.00
PFSTD R.Theus/Q.Douby 8.00 20.00
PFSTO N.Thurmond/P.O'Bryant 8.00 20.00
PFSWR B.Walton/B.Roy 12.00 30.00
PFSWW S.Webb/S.Williams 10.00 25.00

2006-07 Upper Deck Trilogy Generations Past and Present Memorabilia

PRINT RUN 50 SER.#'d SETS
PPMAM E.Monroe/C.Anthony 6.00 15.00
PPMBP L.Bird/P.Pierce 15.00 30.00
PPMCM T.Chambers/S.Marion 15.00 30.00
PPMCO W.Chamberlain/S.O'Neal 15.00 40.00
PPMDM C.Drexler/T.McGrady 20.00 40.00
PPMDR A.Dantley/M.Redd 5.00 12.00
PPMEK M.Eaton/A.Kirilenko 6.00 15.00
PPMFH W.Frazier/R.Hamilton 8.00 20.00
PPMJB M.Johnson/K.Bryant 20.00 40.00
PPMJJ M.Jordan/L.James 60.00 120.00
PPMKA B.King/G.Arenas 5.00 12.00
PPMKE K.McHale/E.Brand 5.00 12.00
PPMKJ S.Kerr/R.Jefferson 5.00 12.00
PPMMA C.Mullin/R.Artest 10.00 25.00
PPMMB K.Malone/C.Boozer 8.00 20.00
PPMMH M.Malone/D.Howard 6.00 15.00
PPMMI P.Maravich/A.Iverson 40.00 80.00
PPMMN P.Maravich/S.Nash 30.00 80.00
PPMOM H.Olajuwon/Y.Ming 6.00 15.00
PPMRB O.Robertson/A.Bogut 12.00 30.00
PPMRD D.Robinson/T.Duncan 20.00 40.00
PPMRK O.Robertson/J.Kidd 15.00 30.00
PPMRO P.Riley/L.Odom 8.00 20.00
PPMRW D.Rodman/B.Wallace 10.00 25.00
PPMTB R.Theus/M.Bibby 5.00 12.00
PPMTG R.Theus/B.Gordon 6.00 15.00
PPMWA J.West/R.Allen 20.00 40.00
PPMWH J.White/K.Hinrich 8.00 20.00
PPMWP S.Webb/C.Paul 8.00 20.00

2006-07 Upper Deck Trilogy Generations Past and Present Signatures

PRINT RUN 33 SER.#'d SETS
PPSAA N.Archibald/G.Arenas 10.00 25.00
PPSAC A.Robertson/C.Bell 10.00 25.00
PPSAG B.Armstrong/B.Gordon 15.00 30.00
PPSBA D.Brown/T.Allen 8.00 20.00
PPSBC M.Cooper/A.Bynum 20.00 40.00
PPSBP M.Bogues/C.Paul 30.00 80.00
PPSDC D.Rodman/C.Billups 30.00 80.00
PPSDH B.Daugherty/L.Hughes 8.00 20.00
PPSDO D.Dawkins/J.O'Neal 15.00 30.00
PPSEB M.Eaton/C.Boozer 15.00 30.00
PPSEJ S.Elliott/R.Jefferson 15.00 30.00
PPSEK M.Eaton/C.Kaman 8.00 20.00
PPSHK C.Hawkins/K.Korver 15.00 40.00
PPSJA M.Jordan/C.Anthony 325.00 550.00
PPSJN M.Richardson/C.Frye 8.00 20.00
PPSJW B.Jones/M.Williams 8.00 20.00
PPSKB S.Kerr/B.Barry 40.00 75.00
PPSLP B.Laimbeer/T.Prince 20.00 40.00
PPSME B.McAdoo/D.Ewing 20.00 40.00
PPSMR X.McDaniel/L.Ridnour 15.00 30.00
PPSMT R.Theus/B.Miller 8.00 20.00
PPSMW X.McDaniel/D.Wilkins 15.00 30.00
PPSPP R.Parish/P.Pierce 20.00 40.00
PPSSM R.Sampson/Y.Ming 30.00 60.00
PPSSV K.Vandeweghe/J.Smith 8.00 20.00
PPSTB R.Theus/M.Bibby 10.00 25.00
PPSTM W.Tisdale/B.Miller 8.00 20.00
PPSWW S.Webb/M.Williams 10.00 25.00

2006-07 Upper Deck Trilogy Generations Past Memorabilia

APPROXIMATE ODDS ONE PER BOX
*PATCHES: .75X TO 2X BASE HI
PATCH PRINT RUN 50 SER.#'d SETS
PMAD Adrian Dantley 3.00 8.00
PMBK Bernard King 3.00 8.00
PMBL Bill Laimbeer 3.00 8.00
PMCD Clyde Drexler 5.00 12.00
PMCM Chris Mullin 4.00 10.00
PMDR Dennis Rodman 8.00 20.00
PMGG George Gervin 4.00 10.00
PMHO Hakeem Olajuwon 5.00 12.00
PMJE Julius Erving 6.00 15.00
PMJH Jeff Hornacek 3.00 8.00
PMJO Magic Johnson 10.00 25.00
PMJS John Stockton 6.00 15.00
PMKA Kareem Abdul-Jabbar 8.00 20.00
PMKM Kevin McHale 5.00 12.00
PMLB Larry Bird 10.00 25.00
PMME Mark Eaton 2.50 6.00
PMMJ Michael Jordan 25.00 60.00
PMMM Moses Malone 4.00 10.00
PMOR Oscar Robertson 6.00 15.00
PMPR Pat Riley 5.00 12.00
PMRO David Robinson 6.00 15.00
PMRT Reggie Theus 3.00 8.00
PMSK Steve Kerr 4.00 10.00
PMSW Spud Webb 3.00 8.00
PMTC Tom Chambers 3.00 8.00
PMWE Jerry West 8.00 20.00
PMWF Walt Frazier 4.00 10.00
PMWH Jo Jo White 3.00 8.00

2006-07 Upper Deck Trilogy Generations Past Present and Future Memorabilia

PRINT RUN 33 SER.#'d SETS
UNPRICED AUTO PRINT RUN 3 SETS
UNPRICED AUTO MEM PRINT RUN 3 SETS
PPFMBAG Bird/Anthony/Gay 15.00 30.00
PPFMCWS Chmbrs/Wkns/Sene 6.00 15.00
PPFMDIC Dwkns/Igdala/Crny 6.00 15.00
PPFMDMB Drxlr/McGrady/Brwn 15.00 40.00
PPFMDMJ Dwkns/Miller/Jones 6.00 15.00
PPFMDNA Dntly/Nwzki/Ager 10.00 25.00
PPFMGJS Gervin/LJ/Seflsha 12.00 30.00
PPFMGLT Gervin/Lewis/Tckr 6.00 15.00
PPFMJBF Magic/Bryant/Farmar 20.00 40.00
PPFMKGS Kerr/Grdn/Seflsha 10.00 25.00
PPFMKMC King/Mrbry/Collins 6.00 15.00
PPFMLOB Laimbr/Okfr/Boone 8.00 20.00
PPFMMBA Mlne/Bosh/Armstng 6.00 15.00
PPFMMDS McHale/Dncn/Smith 10.00 25.00
PPFMMHW Malone/Hwrd/Williams 6.00 15.00
PPFMMIR Monroe/Iverson/Roy 15.00 30.00
PPFMMOT Mrvch/Shaq/Thomas 75.00 150.00
PPFMOMN Olajuwon/Yao/Novak 8.00 20.00
PPFMRGA Robinson/KG/Aldridge 25.00 50.00
PPFMRNR Rbrtsn/Nash/Rondo 20.00 40.00
PPFMRWT Rdmn/Wallace/Thomas 10.00 25.00
PPFMSWB Stock/Williams/Brown 40.00 80.00
PPFMWAR West/Allen/Roy 30.00 60.00
PPFMWBB Walton/Bogut/Brgni 8.00 20.00
PPFMWCN Worthy/Carter/Noel 10.00 25.00
PPFMWJW Wrthy/Jffrsn/Williams 6.00 15.00
PPFMWPL Webb/Paul/Lowry 10.00 25.00
PPFMWPR White/Pierce/Rondo 6.00 15.00

2006-07 Upper Deck Trilogy Generations Past Signatures

APPROXIMATE ODDS ONE PER BOX
UNPRICED TRIO PRINT RUN 3 SETS
PSAD Adrian Dantley 5.00 12.00
PSAJ Avery Johnson 6.00 15.00
PSAR Alvin Robertson 5.00 12.00
PSBA B.J. Armstrong 8.00 20.00
PSBJ Bobby Jones 6.00 15.00
PSBL Bill Laimbeer 10.00 25.00
PSBM Bob McAdoo 10.00 25.00
PSBS Byron Scott 12.00 30.00
PSCH Connie Hawkins 6.00 15.00
PSDB Dee Brown 5.00 12.00
PSDD Darryl Dawkins 10.00 25.00
PSEH Elvin Hayes 8.00 20.00
PSGG George Gervin 10.00 25.00
PSKV Kiki Vandeweghe 5.00 12.00
PSMB Muggsy Bogues 10.00 25.00
PSME Mark Eaton 5.00 12.00
PSMJ Michael Jordan 350.00 700.00
PSML Maurice Lucas 5.00 12.00
PSRP Robert Parish 10.00 25.00
PSRS Ralph Sampson 5.00 12.00
PSRT Reggie Theus 5.00 12.00
PSWT Wayman Tisdale 5.00 12.00
PSXM Xavier McDaniel 5.00 12.00

2006-07 Upper Deck Trilogy Generations Present and Future Memorabilia

PRINT RUN 50 SER.#'d SETS
PRFMAR R.Allen/A.Ray 4.00 10.00
PRFMBD E.Brand/P.Davis 4.00 10.00
PRFMBF A.Bynum/J.Farmar 5.00 12.00
PRFMBG C.Bosh/J.Garbajosa 6.00 15.00
PRFMBN S.Battier/S.Novak 4.00 10.00
PRFMBT C.Bosh/P.Tucker 5.00 12.00
PRFMFB C.Frye/R.Balkman 4.00 10.00
PRFMGS K.Garnett/C.Smith 5.00 12.00
PRFMIJ A.Iguodala/B.Jones 4.00 10.00
PRFMJN A.Jamison/D.Noel 4.00 10.00
PRFMKW J.Kidd/M.Williams 6.00 15.00
PRFMLS R.Lewis/S.Sene 4.00 10.00
PRFMMC S.Marbury/M.Collins 4.00 10.00
PRFMMQ M.Bibby/Q.Douby 4.00 10.00
PRFMNA D.Nowitzki/M.Ager 6.00 15.00
PRFMNR J.Nelson/J.Redick 4.00 10.00
PRFMOA E.Okafor/H.Armstrong 4.00 10.00
PRFMPJ P.Gasol/J.Garbajosa 10.00 25.00
PRFMPR P.Pierce/R.Rondo 8.00 20.00
PRFMPW T.Parker/J.White 5.00 12.00
PRFMRA Z.Randolph/L.Aldridge 5.00 12.00
PRFMRO J.Richardson/P.O'Bryant 4.00 10.00
PRFMWB D.Williams/D.Brown 15.00 30.00
PRFMWT B.Wallace/T.Thomas 10.00 25.00
PRFMWW M.Williams/S.Williams 4.00 10.00

2006-07 Upper Deck Trilogy Generations Present and Future Signatures

PRINT RUN 33 SER.#'d SETS
PRFSAR T.Allen/A.Ray 6.00 15.00
PRFSBB C.Billups/W.Blalock 8.00 20.00
PRFSBD M.Bibby/Q.Douby 8.00 20.00
PRFSBM C.Bell/D.Markota 6.00 15.00
PRFSBS R.Balkman/W.Simien 6.00 15.00
PRFSCA C.Bosh/A.Bargnani 10.00 25.00
PRFSCJ J.Childress/S.Jones 6.00 15.00
PRFSFA L.Aldridge/T.Ford 15.00 40.00
PRFSGS B.Gordon/T.Sefolosha 6.00 15.00
PRFSGT B.Gordon/T.Thomas 15.00 40.00
PRFSIC A.Iguodala/R.Carney 8.00 20.00
PRFSJA R.Jefferson/H.Adams 8.00 20.00
PRFSJF M.James/R.Foye 8.00 20.00
PRFSJR I.Udoka/B.Roy 30.00 60.00
PRFSKD C.Kaman/P.Davis 10.00 25.00
PRFSMB B.Miller/J.Boone 6.00 15.00
PRFSMF C.Mihm/J.Farmar 8.00 20.00
PRFSMN Y.Ming/S.Novak 20.00 40.00
PRFSMS R.McCants/C.Smith 8.00 20.00
PRFSOO J.O'Neal/P.O'Bryant 6.00 15.00
PRFSPA M.Peterson/M.Ager 6.00 15.00
PRFSPR P.Pierce/R.Rondo 25.00 60.00
PRFSRS L.Ridnour/S.Sene 6.00 15.00
PRFSSS P.Stojakovic/C.Simmons 8.00 20.00
PRFSWA D.Williams/J.Augustine 10.00 25.00
PRFSWG H.Warrick/R.Gay 6.00 15.00
PRFSWW M.Williams/S.Williams 6.00 15.00

2006-07 Upper Deck Trilogy Generations Present Memorabilia

APPROXIMATE ODDS ONE PER BOX
*PATCHES: 1X TO 2.5X BASE HI
PATCH PRINT RUN 50 SER.#'d SETS
PRMAI Andre Iguodala 2.00 5.00
PRMAJ Antawn Jamison 2.00 5.00
PRMAK Andrei Kirilenko 2.00 5.00
PRMBD Baron Davis 2.00 5.00
PRMCB Chauncey Billups 2.50 6.00
PRMDH Dwight Howard 2.00 5.00
PRMDN Dirk Nowitzki 4.00 10.00
PRMEO Emeka Okafor 2.00 5.00
PRMGA Gilbert Arenas 2.00 5.00
PRMJK Jason Kidd 4.00 10.00
PRMKB Kobe Bryant 10.00 25.00
PRMKG Kevin Garnett 4.00 10.00
PRMLH Larry Hughes 2.00 5.00
PRMLJ LeBron James 15.00 40.00
PRMLO Lamar Odom 2.00 5.00
PRMMB Mike Bibby 2.50 6.00
PRMMP Morris Peterson 1.50 4.00
PRMMR Michael Redd 2.00 5.00
PRMPG Pau Gasol 2.50 6.00
PRMRH Richard Hamilton 2.00 5.00
PRMRL Rashard Lewis 2.50 6.00
PRMSL Shaun Livingston 2.00 5.00
PRMSM Shawn Marion 2.00 5.00
PRMSN Steve Nash 3.00 8.00
PRMSO Shaquille O'Neal 5.00 12.00
PRMTD Tim Duncan 4.00 10.00
PRMTM Tracy McGrady 3.00 8.00
PRMTP Tayshaun Prince 2.00 5.00
PRMVC Vince Carter 3.00 8.00
PRMYM Yao Ming 3.00 8.00

2006-07 Upper Deck Trilogy Generations Present Signatures

APPROXIMATE ODDS ONE PER BOX
UNPRICED TRIO PRINT RUN 3 SETS
PRSAH Al Harrington 4.00 10.00
PRSBG Ben Gordon 8.00 20.00
PRSBM Brad Miller 4.00 10.00
PRSCD Chris Duhon 4.00 10.00
PRSCK Chris Kaman 4.00 10.00
PRSCM Chris Mihm 4.00 10.00
PRSDW Damien Wilkins 4.00 10.00
PRSGG Gerald Green 4.00 10.00
PRSGW Gerald Wallace 4.00 10.00
PRSJC Josh Childress 4.00 10.00
PRSJH Julius Hodge 4.00 10.00
PRSJS James Singleton 4.00 10.00
PRSLJ LeBron James 125.00 250.00
PRSMJ Mike James 4.00 10.00
PRSMP Morris Peterson 4.00 10.00
PRSMW Marvin Williams 5.00 12.00
PRSRJ Richard Jefferson 4.00 10.00
PRSRM Rashad McCants 4.00 10.00
PRSSL Shaun Livingston 4.00 10.00
PRSTP Tayshaun Prince 6.00 15.00

2006-07 Upper Deck Trilogy Signs of Stardom Dual

PRINT RUN 33 SER.#'d SETS
SOSAR L.Aldridge/B.Roy 20.00 50.00
SOSBB A.Bargnani/C.Bosh 10.00 25.00
SOSBC R.Balkman/M.Collins 8.00 20.00
SOSCM T.McGrady/V.Carter 40.00 100.00
SOSFH J.Farmar/R.Hollins 10.00 25.00
SOSFO R.Felton/E.Okafor 10.00 25.00
SOSGL R.Gay/K.Lowry 12.00 30.00
SOSHB C.Billups/R.Hamilton 20.00 40.00
SOSHG B.Gordon/K.Hinrich 12.00 30.00
SOSJJ M.Jordan/L.James 400.00 800.00
SOSJP R.Jefferson/T.Prince 8.00 20.00
SOSKI A.Iguodala/K.Korver 8.00 20.00
SOSNK J.Kidd/S.Nash 75.00 150.00
SOSOM P.O'Bryant/P.Millsap 8.00 20.00
SOSPA P.Pierce/C.Anthony 30.00 80.00
SOSRD R.Brewer/D.Brown 10.00 25.00
SOSRR R.Rondo/A.Ray 15.00 40.00
SOSSA H.Armstrong/C.Simmons 8.00 20.00
SOSSF C.Smith/R.Foye 10.00 25.00
SOSSP C.Paul/P.Stojakovic 20.00 40.00
SOSSR S.Sene/S.Rodriguez 8.00 20.00
SOSTS T.Thomas/T.Sefolosha 25.00 60.00
SOSWB M.Williams/J.Boone 10.00 25.00
SOSWJ S.Williams/S.Jones 8.00 20.00
SOSWW S.Williams/J.White 8.00 20.00

2003-04 Upper Deck Triple Dimensions

Released in April 2004, Triple Dimensions is a 132-card set divided up into 90 base veteran cards (numbers 1-90), 36 rookie cards sequentially numbered to 1999 (numbers 91-126) and six rookie cards sequentially numbered to 999 (numbers 127-132). Base cards place a full-color player action photo on a card that has a ball background on the top and the bottom. Rookie cards are horizontally desiged with a player photo on the left and a mirror-like hologram image in the shape of an "R" on the right. Triple Dimensions was packaged in 18-pack boxes where packs contained five cards and carried a suggested retail price of $4.99.

COMP.SET w/o SP's (90) 12.50 30.00
91-126 PRINT RUN 1999 SER.#'d SETS
127-132 PRINT RUN 999 SER.#'d SETS
1 Jason Terry .25 .60
2 Theo Ratliff .20 .50
3 Shareef Abdur-Rahim .25 .60
4 Raef LaFrentz .20 .50
5 Vin Baker .20 .50
6 Paul Pierce .30 .75
7 Eddy Curry .20 .50
8 Tyson Chandler .25 .60
9 Antonio Davis .20 .50
10 Dajuan Wagner .20 .50
11 Zydrunas Ilgauskas .25 .60
12 Carlos Boozer .25 .60
13 Steve Nash .40 1.00
14 Antoine Walker .30 .75
15 Dirk Nowitzki .50 1.25
16 Michael Finley .30 .75
17 Andre Miller .25 .60
18 Nene .25 .60
19 Earl Boykins .20 .50
20 Ben Wallace .25 .60
21 Chauncey Billups .30 .75
22 Richard Hamilton .25 .60
23 Mike Dunleavy .25 .60
24 Jason Richardson .30 .75
25 Nick Van Exel .25 .60
26 Cuttino Mobley .20 .50
27 Yao Ming .60 1.50
28 Steve Francis .25 .60
29 Reggie Miller .30 .75
30 Jamaal Tinsley .20 .50
31 Jermaine O'Neal .25 .60
32 Corey Maggette .25 .60
33 Elton Brand .30 .75
34 Quentin Richardson .25 .60
35 Shaquille O'Neal .75 2.00
36 Kobe Bryant 1.25 3.00
37 Karl Malone .40 1.00
38 Gary Payton .30 .75
39 Mike Miller .25 .60
40 Pau Gasol .30 .75
41 Shane Battier .25 .60
42 Eddie Jones .25 .60
43 Caron Butler .25 .60
44 Lamar Odom .25 .60
45 Desmond Mason .25 .60
46 Tim Thomas .20 .50
47 Michael Redd .30 .75
48 Latrell Sprewell .25 .60
49 Kevin Garnett .50 1.25
50 Wally Szczerbiak .25 .60
51 Kenyon Martin .25 .60
52 Jason Kidd .50 1.25
53 Richard Jefferson .25 .60
54 Jamal Mashburn .25 .60
55 Baron Davis .25 .60
56 Jamaal Magloire .20 .50
57 Stephon Marbury .25 .60
58 Allan Houston .25 .60
59 Keith Van Horn .25 .60
60 Drew Gooden .25 .60
61 Tracy McGrady .40 1.00
62 Gordan Giricek .20 .50
63 Glenn Robinson .25 .60
64 Allen Iverson .50 1.25
65 Eric Snow .20 .50
66 Antonio McDyess .25 .60
67 Amare Stoudemire .40 1.00
68 Shawn Marion .25 .60
69 Zach Randolph .25 .60
70 Rasheed Wallace .30 .75
71 Damon Stoudamire .25 .60
72 Mike Bibby .30 .75
73 Chris Webber .30 .75
74 Peja Stojakovic .30 .75
75 Brad Miller .25 .60
76 Tony Parker .30 .75
77 Tim Duncan .50 1.25
78 Manu Ginobili .40 1.00
79 Rashard Lewis .30 .75
80 Ray Allen .30 .75
81 Vladimir Radmanovic .20 .50
82 Morris Peterson .20 .50
83 Vince Carter .50 1.25
84 Jalen Rose .25 .60
85 Andrei Kirilenko .30 .75
86 Matt Harpring .20 .50
87 Carlos Arroyo .25 .60
88 Jerry Stackhouse .25 .60
89 Gilbert Arenas .25 .60
90 Larry Hughes .25 .60
91 Udonis Haslem RC 1.50 4.00
92 Brandon Hunter RC 1.25 3.00
93 Maurice Williams RC 2.00 5.00
94 Keith Bogans RC 1.25 3.00
95 Zaur Pachulia RC 2.00 5.00
96 Willie Green RC 1.25 3.00
97 Kyle Korver RC 2.50 6.00
98 James Jones RC 1.25 3.00
99 Steve Blake RC 1.50 4.00
100 Travis Hansen RC 1.25 3.00
101 Jerome Beasley RC 1.25 3.00
102 Luke Walton RC 2.00 5.00
103 Jason Kapono RC 1.25 3.00
104 Maciej Lampe RC 1.25 3.00
105 Josh Howard RC 2.00 5.00
106 Leandro Barbosa RC 2.00 5.00
107 Kendrick Perkins RC 1.50 4.00
108 Ndudi Ebi RC 1.25 3.00
109 Brian Cook RC 1.25 3.00
110 Travis Outlaw RC 1.50 4.00
111 Zoran Planinic RC 1.25 3.00
112 Boris Diaw RC 2.00 5.00
113 Dahntay Jones RC 1.50 4.00
114 Aleksandar Pavlovic RC 1.50 4.00
115 David West RC 2.00 5.00
116 Zarko Cabarkapa RC 1.25 3.00
117 Troy Bell RC 1.25 3.00
118 Reece Gaines RC 1.25 3.00
119 Luke Ridnour RC 1.50 4.00
120 Marcus Banks RC 1.25 3.00
121 Nick Collison RC 1.50 4.00
122 Mickael Pietrus RC 1.50 4.00
123 Mike Sweetney RC 1.25 3.00
124 Chris Kaman RC 2.00 5.00
125 T.J. Ford RC 1.50 4.00
126 Kirk Hinrich RC 2.00 5.00
127 Jarvis Hayes RC 1.50 4.00
128 Dwyane Wade RC 8.00 20.00
129 Chris Bosh RC 4.00 10.00
130 Carmelo Anthony RC 8.00 20.00
131 Darko Milicic RC 2.00 5.00
132 LeBron James RC 40.00 100.00

2003-04 Upper Deck Triple Dimensions Slam Hologram

*91-132 SLAM HOLO: .75X TO 2X BASE HI
91-132 SLAM HOLO FIRST 100 SER.#'d COPIES

2003-04 Upper Deck Triple Dimensions UD Promos

*PROMOS: .75X TO 2X BASIC

2003-04 Upper Deck Triple Dimensions 3-D Jerseys

All of the memorabilia card designs from Triple Dimensions are similar. Each includes a color photo of the featured player and a swatch of game used jersey. A Patch version was also made and these cards are sequentially numbered to 25.

PRINT RUN 120 TO 249 SER.#'d SETS
*PATCH: 2X TO 5X BASE HI
PATCH PRINT RUN 25 SER.#'d SETS
J1 Ray Allen 3.00 8.00
J2 Allen Iverson 5.00 12.00
J3 Jason Richardson 3.00 8.00
J4 Shareef Abdur-Rahim 2.50 6.00
J5 Jason Kidd 5.00 12.00
J6 Steve Nash 4.00 10.00
J7 Richard Jefferson 2.50 6.00
J8 Manu Ginobili 4.00 10.00
J9 Shaquille O'Neal 8.00 20.00
J10 Shawn Marion 2.50 6.00
J11 Kenyon Martin 2.50 6.00
J12 Gilbert Arenas 2.50 6.00
J13 LeBron James 50.00 120.00
J14 Richard Hamilton 2.50 6.00
J15 Dajuan Wagner 2.00 5.00
J16 Kobe Bryant 10.00 25.00
J17 Tracy McGrady 4.00 10.00
J18 Andrei Kirilenko 3.00 8.00
J19 Reggie Miller 3.00 8.00
J20 Steve Francis 2.50 6.00
J21 Carmelo Anthony 10.00 25.00
J22 Lamar Odom 2.50 6.00
J23 Tim Duncan/120 5.00 12.00
J24 Stephon Marbury 2.50 6.00
J25 Yao Ming 6.00 15.00
J26 Chauncey Billups 3.00 8.00
J27 Chris Webber 3.00 8.00
J28 Baron Davis 2.50 6.00
J29 Elton Brand 3.00 8.00
J30 Bonzi Wells 2.00 5.00
J31 Caron Butler 2.50 6.00
J32 Jermaine O'Neal 2.50 6.00
J33 Paul Pierce 3.00 8.00
J34 Wally Szczerbiak 2.50 6.00
J35 Gary Payton 3.00 8.00
J36 Michael Jordan 50.00 120.00
J37 Tony Parker 3.00 8.00
J38 Michael Finley 3.00 8.00
J39 Rashard Lewis 3.00 8.00
J40 Amare Stoudemire 4.00 10.00
J41 Dirk Nowitzki 5.00 12.00
J42 Kevin Garnett 5.00 12.00

2003-04 Upper Deck Triple Dimensions 3-D Warmups

Randomly seeded in packs, this 47-card set features both a player color photo and a swatch of warmup. Each card is sequentially numbered to 999. Upon release, card number W21 was not issued.

PRINT RUN 999 SER.#'d SETS
*SHOOT.SHIRTS: .5X TO 1.25X WARM HI
SHIRTS PRINT RUN 499 SER.#'d SETS
W1 Ray Allen 2.50 6.00
W2 Allen Iverson 4.00 10.00
W3 Jason Richardson 2.50 6.00
W4 Shareef Abdur-Rahim 2.00 5.00
W5 Jason Kidd 4.00 10.00
W6 Steve Nash 3.00 8.00
W7 Richard Jefferson 2.00 5.00
W8 Manu Ginobili 3.00 8.00
W9 Shaquille O'Neal 6.00 15.00
W10 Shawn Marion 2.00 5.00
W11 Kenyon Martin 2.00 5.00
W12 Gilbert Arenas 2.00 5.00
W13 LeBron James 30.00 80.00
W14 Richard Hamilton 2.00 5.00
W15 Dajuan Wagner 2.00 5.00
W16 Kobe Bryant 8.00 20.00
W17 Tracy McGrady 3.00 8.00
W18 Andrei Kirilenko 2.50 6.00
W19 Reggie Miller 2.50 6.00
W20 Steve Francis 2.00 5.00
W22 Lamar Odom 2.00 5.00
W23 Tim Duncan 4.00 10.00
W24 Stephon Marbury 2.00 5.00
W25 Yao Ming 5.00 12.00
W26 Chauncey Billups 2.50 6.00
W27 Chris Webber 2.50 6.00
W28 Baron Davis 2.00 5.00
W29 Elton Brand 2.50 6.00
W30 Jamal Mashburn 2.00 5.00
W31 Caron Butler 2.00 5.00
W32 Jermaine O'Neal 2.00 5.00
W33 Paul Pierce 2.50 6.00
W34 Wally Szczerbiak 2.00 5.00
W35 Gary Payton 2.50 6.00
W36 Michael Jordan 20.00 50.00
W37 Tony Parker 2.50 6.00
W38 Michael Finley 2.50 6.00
W39 Rashard Lewis 2.50 6.00
W40 Amare Stoudemire 3.00 8.00
W41 Dirk Nowitzki 4.00 10.00
W42 Kevin Garnett 4.00 10.00
W43 Jason Terry 2.00 5.00
W44 Eddy Curry 1.50 4.00
W45 Corey Maggette 2.00 5.00
W46 Quentin Richardson 2.00 5.00
W47 Karl Malone 3.00 8.00
W48 Peja Stojakovic 2.50 6.00

2003-04 Upper Deck Triple Dimensions Reflections

Inserted at the rate of one per pack, this 90-card set places full-color player photos on an all foil background. Several different versions of the set were released as well. An Amethyst foil parallel is sequentially numbered to 300, and Emerald foil parallel is sequentially numbered to 100, a Gold foil parallel is sequentially numbered to 50, a Ruby foil parallel is sequentially numbered to 500, a Sapphire foil parallel is sequentially numbered to 10 and a Titanium foil parallel is sequentially numbered to 1.

ONE PER PACK
*AMETHYST: 1.5X TO 4X BASE REF.HI
AMETH.PRINT RUN 300 SER.#'d SETS
*EMERALD: 2.5X TO 6X BASE REF.HI
EMERALD PRINT RUN 100 SER.#'d SETS
*RUBY: 1X TO 2.5X BASE REF.HI
RUBY PRINT RUN 500 SER.#'d SETS
1 Rasheed Wallace .50 1.25
2 Jason Terry .40 1.00
3 Paul Pierce .50 1.25
4 Ricky Davis .40 1.00
5 Michael Jordan 5.00 12.00
6 Eddy Curry .30 .75
7 Kirk Hinrich .50 1.25
8 Jamal Crawford .50 1.25
9 Scottie Pippen .75 2.00
10 LeBron James 20.00 50.00
11 Carlos Boozer .40 1.00
12 Dajuan Wagner .30 .75
13 Dirk Nowitzki .75 2.00
14 Steve Nash .60 1.50
15 Antoine Walker .50 1.25
16 Josh Howard .50 1.25
17 Carmelo Anthony 1.50 4.00
18 Andre Miller .40 1.00
19 Nene .40 1.00
20 Ben Wallace .40 1.00
21 Darko Milicic .40 1.00
22 Chauncey Billups .50 1.25
23 Jason Richardson .50 1.25
24 Nick Van Exel .40 1.00
25 Steve Francis .40 1.00
26 Yao Ming 1.00 2.50
27 Cuttino Mobley .30 .75
28 Jermaine O'Neal .40 1.00
29 Al Harrington .40 1.00
30 Reggie Miller .50 1.25
31 Kobe Bryant 2.00 5.00
32 Shaquille O'Neal 1.25 3.00
33 Gary Payton .50 1.25
34 Karl Malone .60 1.50
35 Elton Brand .50 1.25
36 Chris Kaman .50 1.25
37 Corey Maggette .40 1.00
38 Pau Gasol .50 1.25
39 Troy Bell .30 .75
40 Jason Williams .40 1.00
41 Dwyane Wade 3.00 8.00
42 Lamar Odom .40 1.00
43 Eddie Jones .40 1.00
44 T.J. Ford .40 1.00
45 Michael Redd .50 1.25
46 Desmond Mason .40 1.00
47 Kevin Garnett .75 2.00
48 Latrell Sprewell .40 1.00
49 Ndudi Ebi .30 .75
50 Kenyon Martin .40 1.00
51 Jason Kidd .75 2.00
52 Richard Jefferson .40 1.00
53 Baron Davis .40 1.00
54 David West .50 1.25
55 Stephon Marbury .40 1.00
56 Allan Houston .40 1.00
57 Kurt Thomas .30 .75
58 Tracy McGrady .60 1.50
59 Keith Bogans .30 .75
60 Drew Gooden .40 1.00
61 Allen Iverson .75 2.00
62 Glenn Robinson .40 1.00
63 Leandro Barbosa .50 1.25
64 Amare Stoudemire .60 1.50
65 Shawn Marion .40 1.00
66 Shareef Abdur-Rahim .40 1.00
67 Zach Randolph .40 1.00
68 Travis Outlaw .40 1.00
69 Darius Miles .30 .75
70 Peja Stojakovic .50 1.25
71 Chris Webber .50 1.25
72 Brad Miller .40 1.00
73 Mike Bibby .50 1.25
74 Bobby Jackson .30 .75
75 Tim Duncan .75 2.00
76 Tony Parker .50 1.25
77 Manu Ginobili .60 1.50
78 Ray Allen .50 1.25
79 Nick Collison .40 1.00
80 Luke Ridnour .40 1.00
81 Chris Bosh .75 2.00
82 Vince Carter .75 2.00
83 Jalen Rose .40 1.00
84 Donyell Marshall .30 .75
85 Andrei Kirilenko .50 1.25
86 Carlos Arroyo .40 1.00
87 Jarvis Hayes .30 .75
88 Jerry Stackhouse .40 1.00
89 Gilbert Arenas .40 1.00
90 Larry Hughes .40 1.00

2003-04 Upper Deck Triple Dimensions Reflections Gold

*GOLD SINGLES: 4X TO 10X BASE REF.HI
PRINT RUN 50 SER.#'d SETS
10 LeBron James 600.00 1000.00
17 Carmelo Anthony 25.00 60.00
31 Kobe Bryant 30.00 80.00
41 Dwyane Wade 60.00 150.00
81 Chris Bosh 15.00 40.00

2003-04 Upper Deck Triple Dimensions Standout Sigs

Randomly inserted in packs, this 69-card set places full-color player photos on a card with green borders along the top and the bottom, gold foil highlights and a white-out oval towards the bottom of the card for an authentic autograph. Unless specified in the checklist, these cards are sequentially numbered to 100. Card 21, Steve Franics, was not produced.

PRINT RUN 25 TO 100 SER.#'d SETS
1 Kobe Bryant/25 125.00 250.00
2 Kevin Garnett/25 75.00 150.00
3 LeBron James/25 600.00 1000.00
4 Carmelo Anthony/25 75.00 200.00
5 Michael Jordan/25 400.00 700.00
6 Patrick Ewing/25 200.00 300.00
7 Tracy McGrady/25 25.00 60.00
8 Amare Stoudemire/25 25.00 60.00
9 Darko Milicic/25 6.00 15.00
12 Luke Walton 6.00 15.00
13 Reggie Evans 6.00 15.00
14 Lamar Odom 10.00 25.00
15 Reggie Miller 60.00 150.00
16 Gerald Wallace 6.00 15.00
17 Dahntay Jones 6.00 15.00
18 Boris Diaw 6.00 15.00
19 Wang ZhiZhi 10.00 25.00
20 Jalen Rose 6.00 15.00
22 Alonzo Mourning 20.00 50.00
23 Dan Dickau 6.00 15.00
24 Antawn Jamison 6.00 15.00
25 Brent Barry 6.00 15.00
26 Cuttino Mobley 6.00 15.00
27 Luke Ridnour 5.00 12.00
28 Chris Wilcox 6.00 15.00
29 Carlos Boozer 6.00 15.00
30 Gordan Giricek 6.00 15.00
31 Chris Kaman 6.00 15.00
32 Josh Howard 6.00 15.00
33 Leandro Barbosa 6.00 15.00
34 Jon Barry 6.00 15.00
35 Shawn Marion 6.00 15.00
36 Kendrick Perkins 5.00 12.00
37 Chris Bosh 10.00 25.00
38 Travis Outlaw 5.00 12.00
39 Antonio McDyess 6.00 15.00
40 Drew Gooden 6.00 15.00
41 Peja Stojakovic 6.00 15.00
42 Chauncey Billups 10.00 25.00
43 Darius Miles 6.00 15.00
44 Marko Jaric 6.00 15.00
45 Corey Maggette 6.00 15.00
46 Dajuan Wagner 6.00 15.00
47 Andre Miller 6.00 15.00
48 Shane Battier 6.00 15.00
49 Reece Gaines 4.00 10.00
50 Troy Bell 4.00 10.00
51 Morris Peterson 6.00 15.00
52 Richard Hamilton 6.00 15.00
53 Mike Sweetney 4.00 10.00
54 Mickael Pietrus 5.00 12.00
55 Tony Parker 12.00 30.00
56 Marcus Banks 4.00 10.00
57 Eddy Curry 6.00 15.00
58 Brian Cook 4.00 10.00
59 Maciej Lampe 4.00 10.00
60 Zoran Planinic 4.00 10.00
61 Paul Pierce 12.00 30.00
62 Jason Kidd 15.00 40.00
63 Richard Jefferson 6.00 15.00
64 Mike Bibby 6.00 15.00
65 Gilbert Arenas 8.00 20.00
66 Earl Boykins 6.00 15.00
67 Dwyane Wade 100.00 200.00
68 David West 6.00 15.00
69 Desmond Mason 6.00 15.00
70 Jerry Stackhouse 8.00 20.00

2015-16 Upper Deck Turkish Airlines Euroleague

E1 Jamel McLean
E2 Cedi Osman
E3 Dario Saric
E4 Marko Arapovic
E5 Roko Leni Ukic
E6 Boban Marjanovic
E7 Marcus Williams
E8 Milos Teodosic
E9 Sonny Weems
E10 David Logan
E11 Allessandro Gentile
E12 Mario Hezonja
E13 Marcus Eriksson
E14 Juan Navarro
E15 Robin Benzing
E16 Nihad Djedovic
E17 Kenan Sipahi
E18 Bogdan Bogdanovic
E19 Carlos Arroyo
E20 Zoran Erceg
E21 Ilimane Diop
E22 Davis Bertans
E23 Leo Westermann
E24 Sofoklis Schortsanitis
E25 Devin Smith
E26 Devidas Gailus
E27 Trey Thompkins
E28 Taylor Rochestie
E29 Ioannis Papaetrou
E30 Vassilis Spanoulis
E31 A.J. Slaughter
E32 Dimitris Diamantidis
E33 Damian Kulig
E34 Rudy Fernandez
E35 Sergio Rodriguez
E36 Mindaugas Kuzminskas
E37 Keith Langford
E38 Guillem Vives
E39 Romain Sato
E40 Tomas Dimsa
E41 Arturas Gudaitis
E42 Moritz Wagner
E43 Nemanja Bjelica
E44 Felipe Reyes
E45 Andrew Goudelock
E46 Furkan Korkmaz
E47 Tomas Satoransky
E48 Dusko Savonvic
E49 Daniel Hackett
E50 Arnas Butkevicius
E51 Bryant Dunston
E52 Marko Tejic
E53 Ludde Hakanson
E54 Andres Nocioni
E55 Thomas Heurtel
E56 Paulius Jankunas
E57 Jayson Granger
E58 Bojan Dubljevic
E59 Pau Ribas
E60 Kostas Kaimakoglou
E61 D'or Fischer
E62 Miro Bilan
E63 Rakim Sanders
E64 Samardo Samuels
E65 James Anderson
E66 Nando De Colo
E67 Emir Preldzic
E68 Esteban Batista
E69 Sasha Kaun
E70 Milko Bjelica
E71 Ender Arslan
E72 Antonis Fotsis
E73 Arturas Milaknis
E74 Stephane Lasme
E75 Sergio Llull
E76 Robertas Javtokas
E77 Ryan Toolson
E78 Georgios Printezis
E79 Fernando San Emerterio
E80 Andrey Vorontsevich
E81 Sinan Guler
E82 Gustavo Ayon
E83 Jan Vesely
E84 Alex Renfroe
E85 Vladmir Stimac
E86 Heiko Schaffartzik
E87 Sylven Landesberg
E88 Jeremy Pargo
E89 Edgar Sosa
E90 Andrei Kirilenko
E91 Trent Plaisted
E92 Nobel Boungou-Colo
E93 Simas Galdikas
E94 Kostas Vasileiadis
E95 Musafa Shakur
E96 Donatas Zavackas
E97 Tarence Kinsey
E98 Artsiom Parakhouski
E99 Filip Dylewicz
E100 Nemanja Jaramaz

2015-16 Upper Deck Turkish Airlines Euroleague Foil

*FOIL: X TO X BASIC
RANDOM INSERTS IN PACKS
STATED PRINT RUN 49 SER.#'d SETS

2015-16 Upper Deck Turkish Airlines Euroleague Autographs

STATED ODDS 1:4.5 PACKS
E1 Jamel McLean
E2 Cedi Osman
E3 Dario Saric
E8 Milos Teodosic
E10 David Logan
E11 Allessandro Gentile
E13 Marcus Eriksson
E14 Juan Navarro
E16 Nihad Djedovic
E18 Bogdan Bogdanovic
E23 Leo Westermann
E24 Sofoklis Schortsanitis
E25 Devin Smith
E27 Trey Thompkins
E28 Taylor Rochestie
E29 Ioannis Papaetrou
E30 Vassilis Spanoulis
E32 Dimitris Diamantidis
E33 Damian Kulig
E36 Mindaugas Kuzminskas
E38 Guillem Vives
E39 Romain Sato
E40 Tomas Dimsa
E41 Arturas Gudaitis
E47 Tomas Satoransky
E49 Daniel Hackett
E55 Thomas Heurtel
E66 Nando De Colo
E67 Emir Preldzic
E74 Stephane Lasme
E80 Andrey Vorontsevich
E91 Trent Plaisted

2002 Upper Deck Twizzlers

5 Alonzo Mourning 1.00 2.50
6 Alonzo Mourning 1.00 2.50

1996 Upper Deck U.S. Olympic

This multisport product was issued in June 1996, prior to the Centennial Olympic Games in Atlanta. Packs of 10 standard-size cards had a suggested retail price of $1.99. The set contains the following subsets: U.S. Olympic Moments (1-90), Future Champions (91-120) and Passing the Torch (121-135).

COMPLETE SET (135) 8.00 20.00
11 Michael Jordan 1.25 3.00
12 Larry Bird .40 1.00
93 Anfernee Hardaway .30 .75
134 Jordan/Hardaway .60 1.50

1996 Upper Deck U.S. Olympic Reflections of Gold

These cards were inserted in packs at a rate of 1:5. The photos are rendered in a bright metallic fashion on the fronts.

COMPLETE SET (10) 8.00 20.00
STATED ODDS 1:5
RG1 Michael Jordan 6.00 15.00

1996 Upper Deck U.S. Olympic Reflections of Gold Signatures

These cards were distributed exclusively via mail-in redemption cards, which were inserted at a rate of 1:79 packs. Each redemption card identified which athlete's signature card it represented. There was an expiration date of Dec. 31, 1996. The Jordan card is extremely scarce; probably 25 or less were signed, and some never were redeemed. Kristi Yamaguchi apparently did not participate in this promotion.

COMPLETE SET (9) 3000.00 5000.00
STATED ODDS 1:79
RG1 Michael Jordan 2500.00 5000.00

1996 Upper Deck U.S. Olympic Reign of Gold Holograms

These hologram cards were inserted at a rate of 1:17 packs. Each of the five athletes in this set have won multiple gold medals.

COMPLETE SET (5) 6.00 15.00
STATED ODDS 1:17
RN1 Michael Jordan 6.00 15.00

1994 Upper Deck USA

These 90 standard-size cards honor the '94 Team USA players. Cards were distributed in 10-card packs. Each foil box contained 36 packs. The borderless fronts feature color posed and action player shots. The player's name and position appear in red, white, and blue bars near the bottom. The card's subtitle appears vertically in gold-foil lettering near the left edge, information for which appears on the back.

COMPLETE SET (90) 10.00 25.00
1 Derrick Coleman .12 .30
2 Derrick Coleman .12 .30
3 Derrick Coleman .12 .30
4 Derrick Coleman .12 .30
5 Derrick Coleman .12 .30
6 Derrick Coleman .12 .30
7 Joe Dumars .15 .40
8 Joe Dumars .15 .40
9 Joe Dumars .15 .40
10 Joe Dumars .15 .40
11 Joe Dumars .15 .40
12 Joe Dumars .15 .40
13 Tim Hardaway .15 .40
14 Tim Hardaway .15 .40
15 Tim Hardaway .15 .40
16 Tim Hardaway .15 .40
17 Tim Hardaway .15 .40
18 Tim Hardaway .15 .40
19 Larry Johnson .15 .40
20 Larry Johnson .15 .40
21 Larry Johnson .15 .40
22 Larry Johnson .15 .40
23 Larry Johnson .15 .40
24 Larry Johnson .15 .40
25 Shawn Kemp .15 .40
26 Shawn Kemp .15 .40
27 Shawn Kemp .15 .40
28 Shawn Kemp .15 .40
29 Shawn Kemp .15 .40
30 Shawn Kemp .15 .40
31 Dan Majerle .15 .40

32 Dan Majerle	.15	.40
33 Dan Majerle	.15	.40
34 Dan Majerle	.15	.40
35 Dan Majerle	.15	.40
36 Dan Majerle	.15	.40
37 Reggie Miller	.20	.50
38 Reggie Miller	.20	.50
39 Reggie Miller	.20	.50
40 Reggie Miller	.20	.50
41 Reggie Miller	.20	.50
42 Reggie Miller	.20	.50
43 Alonzo Mourning	.20	.50
44 Alonzo Mourning	.20	.50
45 Alonzo Mourning	.20	.50
46 Alonzo Mourning	.20	.50
47 Alonzo Mourning	.20	.50
48 Alonzo Mourning	.20	.50
49 Shaquille O'Neal	.40	1.00
50 Shaquille O'Neal	.40	1.00
51 Shaquille O'Neal	.40	1.00
52 Shaquille O'Neal	.40	1.00
53 Shaquille O'Neal	.40	1.00
54 Shaquille O'Neal	.40	1.00
55 Mark Price	.15	.40
56 Mark Price	.15	.40
57 Mark Price	.15	.40
58 Mark Price	.15	.40
59 Mark Price	.15	.40
60 Mark Price	.15	.40
61 Steve Smith	.12	.30
62 Steve Smith	.12	.30
63 Steve Smith	.12	.30
64 Steve Smith	.12	.30
65 Steve Smith	.12	.30
66 Steve Smith	.12	.30
67 Isiah Thomas	.15	.40
68 Isiah Thomas	.15	.40
69 Isiah Thomas	.15	.40
70 Isiah Thomas	.15	.40
71 Isiah Thomas	.15	.40
72 Isiah Thomas	.15	.40
73 Dominique Wilkins	.20	.50
74 Dominique Wilkins	.20	.50
75 Dominique Wilkins	.20	.50
76 Dominique Wilkins	.20	.50
77 Dominique Wilkins	.20	.50
78 Dominique Wilkins	.20	.50
79 Jennifer Azzi	1.25	3.00
80 Daedra Charles	.60	1.50
81 Lisa Leslie	1.50	4.00
82 Katrina McClain	.60	1.50
83 Dawn Staley	1.25	3.00
84 Sheryl Swoopes	1.50	4.00
85 Michael Jordan ATG 85	1.25	3.00
86 Larry Bird ATG 86	.40	1.00
87 Jerry West ATG 87	.20	.50
88 Adrian Dantley ATG 88	.12	.30
89 Cheryl Miller ATG 89	1.50	4.00
90 Henry Iba ATG 90	.12	.30
CK1 Checklist 1	.12	.30
CK2 Checklist 2	.12	.30

1994 Upper Deck USA Gold Medal

Inserted one per '94 Upper Deck USA pack, these gold cards are identical to the regular issues except for the Upper Deck Gold Medal logos appearing on the fronts. The cards are numbered on the back. Please refer to the multipliers provided below (coupled with the prices of the corresponding regular issue cards) to ascertain value.

COMPLETE SET (90)	20.00	50.00

*STARS: .75X TO 2X HI COLUMN

1994 Upper Deck USA Chalk Talk

Randomly inserted in Upper Deck USA packs at a rate of one in 35, the Chalk Talk set consists of 14 standard-size cards. Card fronts include a small hologram of Don Nelson who is also quoted on the back in reference to the player on the card. The card fronts are full-bleed on one side with a gray border on the other that contains the player's name. In addition to Nelson's quote, a small photo of him and a larger photo of the player appear on the back.

COMPLETE SET (14)	6.00	15.00
CT1 Derrick Coleman	.60	1.50
CT2 Joe Dumars	.75	2.00
CT3 Tim Hardaway	.75	2.00
CT4 Larry Johnson	.75	2.00
CT5 Shawn Kemp	.75	2.00
CT6 Dan Majerle	.75	2.00
CT7 Reggie Miller	1.00	2.50
CT8 Alonzo Mourning	1.00	2.50
CT9 Shaquille O'Neal	2.00	5.00
CT10 Mark Price	.75	2.00
CT11 Steve Smith	.60	1.50
CT12 Isiah Thomas	.75	2.00
CT13 Dominique Wilkins	1.00	2.50
CT14 Kevin Johnson	.75	2.00

1994 Upper Deck USA Follow Your Dreams Assists

Randomly inserted at a rate of one in 14 packs, these 42 standard-size game-prize cards feature borderless color player action shots on front. The cards are broken into three 14-card sets that are distinguished by categories: assists, rebounds and scoring. The category appears on gold foil stamping on the front that appears in on one side along with the player's name. The back carries the rules for playing the game. Briefly, each game card depicts one of the 14 players from the '94 USA Dream Team. Each card also designates the player as either a "Top Scorer," "Top Rebounder," or "Top Assists." The player that led Dream Team II in either of these categories could have that specific card redeemed by the collector for a 14-card set of that category. Kevin Johnson's Assists card and Shaquille O'Neal's Rebounds and Scoring cards qualified as the three exchange cards. The redemption deadline for the three cards was November 30, 1994. Card values below are for any of the three sets.

COMPLETE SET (14)	6.00	15.00
*REBOUNDS/SCORING: EQUAL VALUE		
*EXCHANGE SETS: .5X TO 1.25X HI COLUMN		
1 Derrick Coleman	.60	1.50
2 Joe Dumars	.75	2.00
3 Tim Hardaway	.75	2.00
4 Kevin Johnson	.75	2.00
5 Larry Johnson	.75	2.00
6 Shawn Kemp	.75	2.00
7 Dan Majerle	.75	2.00
8 Reggie Miller	1.00	2.50
9 Alonzo Mourning	1.00	2.50
10 Shaquille O'Neal	2.00	5.00
11 Mark Price	.75	2.00
12 Steve Smith	.60	1.50
13 Isiah Thomas	.75	2.00
14 Dominique Wilkins	1.00	2.50

1994 Upper Deck USA Jordan's Highlights

Randomly inserted at a rate of one in 35 packs, the five-card standard-size set features action photos of Michael Jordan representing the United States during international play. A facsimile autograph in gold foil lettering appears near the bottom. On back, the American flag is used as a backdrop to highlights and statistics that pertains to action on the front.

COMPLETE SET (5)	15.00	40.00
COMMON JORDAN (JH1-JH5)	5.00	12.00

1996 Upper Deck USA

This 62-card, skip-numbered set features the first 10 team members of the 1996 men's and complete 1996 USA women's basketball teams. The cards were released during the summer of 1996. Each pack contained twelve cards and sold for a suggested retail price of $2.29. Each box contained 32 packs. The entire set features die-cut cards and gold foil stamping.

COMPLETE SET (62)	8.00	20.00
1 Anfernee Hardaway	.15	.40
2 Anfernee Hardaway	.15	.40
3 Anfernee Hardaway	.15	.40
4 Anfernee Hardaway	.15	.40
5 Grant Hill	.15	.40
6 Grant Hill	.15	.40
7 Grant Hill	.15	.40
8 Grant Hill	.15	.40
9 Karl Malone	.12	.30
10 Karl Malone	.12	.30
11 Karl Malone	.12	.30
12 Karl Malone	.12	.30
13 Reggie Miller	.12	.30
14 Reggie Miller	.12	.30
15 Reggie Miller	.12	.30
16 Reggie Miller	.12	.30
17 Shaquille O'Neal	.25	.60
18 Shaquille O'Neal	.25	.60
19 Shaquille O'Neal	.25	.60
20 Shaquille O'Neal	.25	.60
21 Hakeem Olajuwon	.12	.30
22 Hakeem Olajuwon	.12	.30
23 Hakeem Olajuwon	.12	.30
24 Hakeem Olajuwon	.12	.30
25 Scottie Pippen	.15	.40
26 Scottie Pippen	.15	.40
27 Scottie Pippen	.15	.40
28 Scottie Pippen	.15	.40
29 David Robinson	.15	.40
30 David Robinson	.15	.40
31 David Robinson	.15	.40
32 David Robinson	.15	.40
33 Glenn Robinson	.07	.20
34 Glenn Robinson	.07	.20
35 Glenn Robinson	.07	.20
36 Glenn Robinson	.07	.20
37 John Stockton	.12	.30
38 John Stockton	.12	.30
39 John Stockton	.12	.30
40 John Stockton	.12	.30
49 Anfernee Hardaway	.15	.40
50 Grant Hill	.15	.40
51 Karl Malone	.12	.30
52 Reggie Miller	.12	.30
53 Shaquille O'Neal	.25	.60
54 Hakeem Olajuwon	.12	.30
55 Scottie Pippen	.15	.40
56 David Robinson	.15	.40
57 Glenn Robinson	.07	.20
58 John Stockton	.12	.30
61 Jennifer Azzi	1.00	2.50
62 Ruthie Bolton-Holifield	1.00	2.50
63 Teresa Edwards	.75	2.00
64 Lisa Leslie	1.50	4.00
65 Rebecca Lobo	1.25	3.00
66 Katrina McClain	.40	1.00
67 Nikki McCray	1.00	2.50
68 Carla McGhee	.40	1.00
69 Dawn Staley	1.00	2.50
70 Katy Stedling	.40	1.00
71 Sheryl Swoopes	2.00	5.00
72 Tara VanDerveer CO	.40	1.00
NNO USA Trade Card Expired	.08	.25

1996 Upper Deck USA Exchange Set

This 10-card set was available through a special USA Update Trade card and features Charles Barkley (#'s 41-44 and 59) and Mitch Richmond (#'s 45-48 and 60) to finish off the set. This card was randomly seeded into one in every ten packs. The expiration of the trade card was October 31, 1996.

COMPLETE SET (10)	.75	2.00
41 Charles Barkley	.15	.40
42 Charles Barkley	.15	.40
43 Charles Barkley	.15	.40
44 Charles Barkley	.15	.40
45 Mitch Richmond	.10	.25
46 Mitch Richmond	.10	.25
47 Mitch Richmond	.10	.25
48 Mitch Richmond	.10	.25
59 Charles Barkley	.15	.40
60 Mitch Richmond	.10	.25

1996 Upper Deck USA Follow Your Dreams

Randomly inserted in packs at a rate of one in 6, this 11-card insert set features the first 10 members selected to the team, plus a special "Field Card" representing Charles Barkley, Gary Payton and Mitch Richmond. Card front designs featured a full-color player cut out set against a red and white striped background. If a collector had the card of the USAB 1996 Olympics scoring leader, a 12-card gold commemorative set was awarded; collectors with second place scoring leader cards received a 12-card silver commemorative set. The expiration date for the exchange was October 31, 1996.

COMPLETE SET (11)	5.00	12.00
F1 Anfernee Hardaway	1.00	2.50
F2 Grant Hill	1.00	2.50
F3 Karl Malone	.75	2.00
F4 Reggie Miller W	.75	2.00
F5 Shaquille O'Neal	1.50	4.00
F6 Hakeem Olajuwon	.75	2.00
F7 Scottie Pippen	1.00	2.50
F8 David Robinson W	1.00	2.50
F9 Glenn Robinson	.50	1.25
F10 John Stockton	.75	2.00
F11 Field Card	.20	.50

1996 Upper Deck USA Follow Your Dreams Exchange Set

This 12-card exchange set was redeemable by mailing in winning cards of either Reggie Miller or David Robinson. The set contained cards for Charles Barkley, Mitch Richmond and Gary Payton - who were not available in the regular set. It was Gary Payton's only Olympic card.

COMPLETE SET (12)	8.00	20.00
FD1 Charles Barkley	1.25	3.00
FD2 David Robinson	1.25	3.00
FD3 Reggie Miller	1.00	2.50
FD4 Scottie Pippen	1.25	3.00
FD5 Grant Hill	1.25	3.00
FD6 Mitch Richmond	.75	2.00
FD7 Shaquille O'Neal	2.00	5.00
FD8 Anfernee Hardaway	1.25	3.00
FD9 Karl Malone	1.00	2.50
FD10 Gary Payton	.75	2.00
FD11 Hakeem Olajuwon	1.00	2.50
FD12 John Stockton	1.00	2.50

1996 Upper Deck USA Anfernee Hardaway American Made

Randomly inserted in packs at a rate of one in 56, this 4-card die cut insert set focuses on Orlando guard Penny Hardaway. Each card looks at a particular aspect of Hardaway's abilities - scoring, defense, smoothness and versatility.

COMPLETE SET (4)	10.00	25.00
COMMON CARD (A1-A4)	3.00	8.00

1996 Upper Deck USA Michael Jordan American Made

Randomly inserted in packs at a rate of one in 55, this 4-card die cut insert set looks at basketball legend Michael Jordan. Each card focuses on a particular part of Jordan's game - scoring, defense, desire and leadership.

COMPLETE SET (4)	20.00	50.00
COMMON CARD (M1-M4)	10.00	25.00

1996 Upper Deck USA SP Career Statistics

Inserted one in every pack, this 10-card die cut insert set features a card of each 1996 USAB player outlining their career stats and accomplishments. Each card is printed on premium stock and features Upper Deck's special silver "Light F/X" technology.

COMPLETE SET (10)	2.50	6.00
*GOLD: 3X TO 8X HI COLUMN		
GOLD STATED ODDS 1:27 PACKS		
S1 Anfernee Hardaway	.60	1.50
S2 Grant Hill	.60	1.50
S3 Karl Malone	.50	1.25
S4 Reggie Miller	.50	1.25
S5 Shaquille O'Neal	1.00	2.50
S6 Hakeem Olajuwon	.50	1.25
S7 Scottie Pippen	.60	1.50
S8 David Robinson	.60	1.50
S9 Glenn Robinson	.30	.75
S10 John Stockton	.50	1.25
S11 Charles Barkley	.60	1.50
S12 Mitch Richmond	.40	1.00

1999-00 Upper Deck Victory

Released by Upper Deck, this 440-card set was released as a retail-only product. Each pack contained 12-cards and carried a suggested retail price of $.99. There were no inserts in Victory, but the set contained the following subsets: Check It Out (33 cards), Rookie Flashback (20 cards), Dynamite Dunks (30 cards), Court Catalysts (15 cards), Power Corps (15 cards), Scoring Circle (15 cards), Jordan's Greatest Hits (50 cards) and 10 Rookie Exchange cards.

COMPLETE SET (440)	35.00	60.00
SUBSET CARDS SAME VALUE AS BASE		
1 Dikembe Mutombo CL	.15	.40
2 Steve Smith	.12	.30
3 Dikembe Mutombo	.15	.40
4 Ed Gray	.10	.25
5 Alan Henderson	.10	.25
6 LaPhonso Ellis	.10	.25
7 Roshown McLeod	.10	.25
8 Bimbo Coles	.10	.25
9 Chris Crawford	.10	.25
10 Anthony Johnson	.10	.25
11 Antoine Walker CL	.15	.40
12 Kenny Anderson	.12	.30
13 Antoine Walker	.15	.40
14 Greg Minor	.10	.25
15 Tony Battie	.12	.30
16 Ron Mercer	.12	.30
17 Paul Pierce	.20	.50
18 Vitaly Potapenko	.10	.25
19 Dana Barros	.10	.25
20 Walter McCarty	.10	.25
21 Elden Campbell CL	.10	.25
22 Elden Campbell	.10	.25
23 Eddie Jones	.15	.40
24 David Wesley	.10	.25
25 Bobby Phills	.10	.25
26 Derrick Coleman	.12	.30
27 Anthony Mason	.10	.25
28 Brad Miller	.12	.30
29 Eldridge Recasner	.10	.25
30 Ricky Davis	.15	.40
31 Toni Kukoc CL	.15	.40
32 Michael Jordan	1.25	3.00
33 Brent Barry	.12	.30
34 Randy Brown	.10	.25
35 Keith Booth	.10	.25
36 Kornel David RC	.15	.40
37 Mark Bryant	.10	.25
38 Toni Kukoc	.15	.40
39 Rusty LaRue	.10	.25
40 Brevin Knight CL	.10	.25
41 Shawn Kemp	.15	.40
42 Wesley Person	.10	.25
43 Johnny Newman	.10	.25
44 Derek Anderson	.10	.25
45 Brevin Knight	.10	.25
46 Bob Sura	.10	.25
47 Andrew DeClercq	.10	.25
48 Zydrunas Ilgauskas	.12	.30
49 Danny Ferry	.10	.25
50 Steve Nash CL	.25	.60
51 Michael Finley	.15	.40
52 Robert Pack	.10	.25
53 Shawn Bradley	.10	.25
54 John Williams	.10	.25
55 Hubert Davis	.10	.25
56 Dirk Nowitzki	.30	.75
57 Steve Nash	.25	.60
58 Chris Anstey	.10	.25
59 Erick Strickland	.10	.25
60 Nick Van Exel CL	.12	.30
61 Antonio McDyess	.12	.30
62 Nick Van Exel	.12	.30
63 Bryant Stith	.10	.25
64 Chauncey Billups	.15	.40
65 Danny Fortson	.10	.25
66 Eric Williams	.10	.25
67 Eric Washington	.10	.25
68 Raef LaFrentz	.12	.30
69 Johnny Taylor	.10	.25
70 Jerry Stackhouse CL	.15	.40
71 Grant Hill	.20	.50
72 Lindsey Hunter	.10	.25
73 Bison Dele	.10	.25
74 Loy Vaught	.10	.25
75 Jerome Williams	.10	.25
76 Jerry Stackhouse	.15	.40
77 Christian Laettner	.12	.30
78 Jud Buechler	.10	.25
79 Don Reid	.10	.25
80 Antawn Jamison CL	.15	.40
81 John Starks	.12	.30
82 Antawn Jamison	.15	.40
83 Adonal Foyle	.10	.25
84 Jason Caffey	.10	.25
85 Donyell Marshall	.10	.25
86 Chris Mills	.10	.25
87 Tony Delk	.10	.25
88 Mookie Blaylock	.10	.25
89 Charles Barkley CL	.25	.60
90 Hakeem Olajuwon	.20	.50
91 Scottie Pippen	.25	.60
92 Charles Barkley	.25	.60
93 Bryce Drew	.10	.25
94 Cuttino Mobley	.10	.25
95 Othella Harrington	.10	.25
96 Matt Maloney	.10	.25
97 Michael Dickerson	.10	.25
98 Matt Bullard	.10	.25
99 Jalen Rose CL	.12	.30
100 Reggie Miller	.15	.40
101 Rik Smits	.15	.40
102 Jalen Rose	.12	.30
103 Antonio Davis	.10	.25
104 Mark Jackson	.12	.30
105 Sam Perkins	.10	.25
106 Travis Best	.10	.25
107 Dale Davis	.10	.25
108 Chris Mullin	.15	.40
109 Michael Olowokandi CL	.10	.25
110 Maurice Taylor	.10	.25
111 Tyrone Nesby RC	.15	.40
112 Lamond Murray	.10	.25
113 Darrick Martin	.10	.25
114 Michael Olowokandi	.10	.25
115 Rodney Rogers	.10	.25
116 Eric Piatkowski	.12	.30
117 Lorenzen Wright	.10	.25
118 Brian Skinner	.10	.25
119 Kobe Bryant CL	.60	1.50
120 Kobe Bryant	.60	1.50
121 Shaquille O'Neal	.40	1.00
122 Derek Fisher	.15	.40
123 Tyronn Lue	.10	.25
124 Travis Knight	.10	.25
125 Glen Rice	.15	.40
126 Derek Harper	.12	.30
127 Robert Horry	.12	.30
128 Rick Fox	.10	.25
129 Tim Hardaway CL	.15	.40
130 Tim Hardaway	.15	.40
131 Alonzo Mourning	.20	.50
132 Keith Askins	.10	.25
133 Jamal Mashburn	.12	.30
134 P.J. Brown	.10	.25
135 Clarence Weatherspoon	.10	.25
136 Terry Porter	.10	.25
137 Dan Majerle	.15	.40
138 Voshon Lenard	.10	.25
139 Ray Allen CL	.15	.40
140 Ray Allen	.15	.40
141 Vinny Del Negro	.10	.25
142 Glenn Robinson	.12	.30
143 Dell Curry	.10	.25
144 Sam Cassell	.12	.30
145 Haywoode Workman	.10	.25
146 Armon Gilliam	.10	.25
147 Robert Traylor	.10	.25
148 Chris Gatling	.10	.25
149 Kevin Garnett CL	.25	.60
150 Kevin Garnett	.25	.60
151 Malik Sealy	.10	.25
152 Radoslav Nesterovic	.15	.40
153 Joe Smith	.12	.30
154 Sam Mitchell	.10	.25
155 Dean Garrett	.10	.25
156 Anthony Peeler	.10	.25
157 Tom Hammonds	.10	.25
158 Bobby Jackson	.10	.25
159 Jayson Williams CL	.10	.25
160 Keith Van Horn	.12	.30
161 Stephon Marbury	.12	.30
162 Jayson Williams	.10	.25
163 Kendall Gill	.10	.25
164 Kerry Kittles	.10	.25
165 Jamie Feick RC	.15	.40
166 Scott Burrell	.10	.25
167 Lucious Harris	.10	.25
168 Marcus Camby CL	.12	.30
169 Patrick Ewing	.20	.50
170 Allan Houston	.12	.30
171 Latrell Sprewell	.15	.40
172 Kurt Thomas	.10	.25
173 Larry Johnson	.15	.40
174 Chris Childs	.10	.25
175 Marcus Camby	.12	.30
176 Charlie Ward	.10	.25
177 Chris Dudley	.10	.25
178 Bo Outlaw CL	.10	.25
179 Anfernee Hardaway	.25	.60
180 Darrell Armstrong	.10	.25
181 Nick Anderson	.10	.25
182 Horace Grant	.12	.30
183 Isaac Austin	.10	.25
184 Matt Harpring	.10	.25
185 Michael Doleac	.10	.25
186 Bo Outlaw	.10	.25
187 Allen Iverson CL	.30	.75
188 Allen Iverson	.30	.75
189 Theo Ratliff	.12	.30
190 Matt Geiger	.10	.25
191 Larry Hughes	.12	.30
192 Tyrone Hill	.10	.25
193 George Lynch	.10	.25
194 Eric Snow	.12	.30
195 Aaron McKie	.10	.25
196 Harvey Grant	.10	.25
197 Jason Kidd CL	.25	.60
198 Jason Kidd	.25	.60
199 Tom Gugliotta	.10	.25
200 Rex Chapman	.10	.25
201 Clifford Robinson	.10	.25
202 Luc Longley	.12	.30
203 Danny Manning	.12	.30
204 Pat Garrity	.10	.25
205 George McCloud	.10	.25
206 Toby Bailey	.10	.25
207 Brian Grant CL	.10	.25
208 Rasheed Wallace	.15	.40
209 Arvydas Sabonis	.12	.30
210 Damon Stoudamire	.12	.30
211 Brian Grant	.10	.25
212 Isaiah Rider	.12	.30
213 Walt Williams	.10	.25
214 Jim Jackson	.10	.25
215 Greg Anthony	.10	.25
216 Stacey Augmon	.12	.30
217 Vlade Divac CL	.15	.40
218 Jason Williams	.20	.50
219 Vlade Divac	.15	.40
220 Chris Webber	.15	.40
221 Nick Anderson	.10	.25
222 Peja Stojakovic	.15	.40
223 Tariq Abdul-Wahad	.10	.25
224 Vernon Maxwell	.10	.25
225 Lawrence Funderburke	.10	.25
226 Jon Barry	.10	.25
227 David Robinson CL	.25	.60
228 Tim Duncan	.30	.75
229 Sean Elliott	.15	.40
230 David Robinson	.25	.60
231 Mario Elie	.10	.25
232 Avery Johnson	.12	.30
233 Steve Kerr	.12	.30
234 Malik Rose	.10	.25
235 Jaren Jackson	.10	.25
236 Vin Baker CL	.12	.30
237 Gary Payton	.15	.40
238 Vin Baker	.12	.30
239 Detlef Schrempf	.12	.30
240 Hersey Hawkins	.10	.25
241 Dale Ellis	.10	.25
242 Rashard Lewis	.15	.40
243 Billy Owens	.10	.25
244 Aaron Williams	.10	.25
245 Vince Carter CL	.30	.75
246 Vince Carter	.30	.75
247 John Wallace	.10	.25
248 Doug Christie	.12	.30
249 Tracy McGrady	.25	.60
250 Kevin Willis	.10	.25
251 Michael Stewart	.10	.25
252 Dee Brown	.10	.25
253 John Thomas	.10	.25
254 Alvin Williams	.10	.25
255 Karl Malone CL	.20	.50
256 Karl Malone	.20	.50
257 John Stockton	.20	.50
258 Jacque Vaughn	.10	.25
259 Bryon Russell	.10	.25
260 Howard Eisley	.10	.25
261 Greg Ostertag	.10	.25
262 Adam Keefe	.10	.25
263 Todd Fuller	.10	.25
264 Mike Bibby CL	.15	.40
265 Shareef Abdur-Rahim	.12	.30
266 Mike Bibby	.15	.40
267 Bryant Reeves	.10	.25
268 Felipe Lopez	.10	.25
269 Cherokee Parks	.10	.25
270 Michael Smith	.10	.25
271 Tony Massenburg	.10	.25
272 Rodrick Rhodes	.10	.25
273 Juwan Howard CL	.12	.30
274 Juwan Howard	.12	.30
275 Rod Strickland	.10	.25
276 Mitch Richmond	.15	.40
277 Otis Thorpe	.10	.25
278 Calbert Cheaney	.10	.25
279 Tracy Murray	.10	.25
280 Ben Wallace	.12	.30
281 Terry Davis	.10	.25
282 Michael Jordan RF	1.25	3.00
283 Reggie Miller RF	.15	.40
284 Dikembe Mutombo RF	.15	.40
285 Patrick Ewing RF	.20	.50
286 Allan Houston RF	.12	.30
287 Danny Manning RF	.12	.30
288 Jalen Rose RF	.12	.30
289 Rasheed Wallace RF	.15	.40
290 Jerry Stackhouse RF	.15	.40
291 Damon Stoudamire RF	.12	.30
292 Kenny Anderson RF	.12	.30
293 Shawn Kemp RF	.15	.40
294 Vlade Divac RF	.15	.40
295 Larry Johnson RF	.15	.40
296 Jamal Mashburn RF	.12	.30
297 Ron Harper RF	.10	.25
298 Steve Smith RF	.12	.30
299 Kendall Gill RF	.10	.25
300 Chris Mullin RF	.15	.40
301 Robert Horry RF	.12	.30
302 Dikembe Mutombo DD	.15	.40
303 Ron Mercer DD	.12	.30
304 Eddie Jones DD	.15	.40
305 Toni Kukoc DD	.15	.40
306 Derek Anderson DD	.10	.25
307 Shawn Bradley DD	.10	.25
308 Danny Fortson DD	.10	.25
309 Bison Dele DD	.10	.25
310 Antawn Jamison DD	.15	.40
311 Scottie Pippen DD	.25	.60
312 Reggie Miller DD	.15	.40
313 Maurice Taylor DD	.10	.25
314 Glen Rice DD	.15	.40
315 Alonzo Mourning DD	.20	.50
316 Glenn Robinson DD	.12	.30
317 Anthony Peeler DD	.10	.25
318 Kerry Kittles DD	.10	.25
319 Latrell Sprewell DD	.15	.40
320 Darrell Armstrong DD	.10	.25
321 Larry Hughes DD	.12	.30
322 Tom Gugliotta DD	.10	.25
323 Brian Grant DD	.10	.25
324 Chris Webber DD	.15	.40
325 David Robinson DD	.25	.60
326 Vin Baker DD	.12	.30
327 Vince Carter DD	.30	.75
328 Bryon Russell DD	.10	.25
329 Felipe Lopez DD	.10	.25
330 Juwan Howard DD	.12	.30
331 Michael Jordan DD	1.25	3.00
332 Jason Kidd CC	.25	.60
333 Rod Strickland CC	.10	.25
334 Stephon Marbury CC	.12	.30
335 Gary Payton CC	.15	.40
336 Mark Jackson CC	.12	.30
337 John Stockton CC	.20	.50
338 Brevin Knight CC	.10	.25
339 Bobby Jackson CC	.10	.25
340 Nick Van Exel CC	.12	.30
341 Tim Hardaway CC	.15	.40
342 Darrell Armstrong CC	.10	.25
343 Avery Johnson CC	.12	.30
344 Mike Bibby CC	.15	.40
345 Damon Stoudamire CC	.12	.30
346 Jason Williams CC	.20	.50
347 Allen Iverson PC	.30	.75
348 Kobe Bryant PC	.60	1.50
349 Karl Malone PC	.20	.50
350 Keith Van Horn PC	.12	.30
351 Kevin Garnett PC	.25	.60
352 Antoine Walker PC	.15	.40
353 Tim Duncan PC	.30	.75
354 Scottie Pippen PC	.25	.60
355 Paul Pierce PC	.20	.50
356 Michael Finley PC	.15	.40
357 Shaquille O'Neal PC	.40	1.00
358 Grant Hill PC	.20	.50
359 Jason Williams PC	.20	.50
360 Antonio McDyess PC	.12	.30
361 Shareef Abdur-Rahim PC	.12	.30
362 Allen Iverson SC	.30	.75
363 Shaquille O'Neal SC	.40	1.00
364 Karl Malone SC	.20	.50
365 Shareef Abdur-Rahim SC	.12	.30
366 Keith Van Horn SC	.12	.30
367 Tim Duncan SC	.30	.75
368 Gary Payton SC	.15	.40
369 Stephon Marbury SC	.12	.30
370 Antonio McDyess SC	.12	.30
371 Grant Hill SC	.20	.50
372 Kevin Garnett SC	.25	.60
373 Shawn Kemp SC	.15	.40
374 Kobe Bryant SC	.60	1.50
375 Michael Finley SC	.15	.40
376 Vince Carter SC	.30	.75
377 Checklist	.10	.25
378 Checklist	.10	.25
379 Checklist	.10	.25
380 Checklist	.10	.25
431 Elton Brand RC	.50	1.25
432 Steve Francis RC	.50	1.25
433 Baron Davis RC	.50	1.25
434 Lamar Odom RC	.50	1.25
435 Wally Szczerbiak RC	.40	1.00
436 Richard Hamilton RC	.40	1.00
437 Andre Miller RC	.40	1.00
438 Shawn Marion RC	.40	1.00
439 Jason Terry RC	.30	.75
440 Corey Maggette RC	.30	.75
NNO Michael Jordan Jsy Entry	.75	2.00

2000-01 Upper Deck Victory

Released in October 2000, this 330-card set is the lower-end Upper Deck brand, targeted at kids. The set contained 231 regular player cards, 20 rookies, 29 leader cards and 50 FLY2K cards, featuring Kobe Bryant and Kevin Garnett.

COMPLETE SET (330)	30.00	60.00
FLY2K CARDS INSERTED ONE PER PACK		
1 Dikembe Mutombo	.15	.40
2 Jim Jackson	.10	.25
3 Jason Terry	.15	.40
4 Roshown McLeod	.10	.25
5 Alan Henderson	.10	.25
6 Bimbo Coles	.10	.25
7 Dion Glover	.10	.25
8 Lorenzen Wright	.10	.25
9 Paul Pierce	.15	.40
10 Kenny Anderson	.12	.30
11 Antoine Walker	.12	.30
12 Adrian Griffin	.10	.25
13 Vitaly Potapenko	.10	.25
14 Dana Barros	.10	.25
15 Eric Williams	.10	.25
16 Calbert Cheaney	.10	.25
17 Derrick Coleman	.12	.30
18 Eddie Jones	.15	.40
19 Anthony Mason	.10	.25
20 Elden Campbell	.10	.25
21 Eddie Robinson	.10	.25
22 David Wesley	.10	.25
23 Baron Davis	.15	.40
24 Ricky Davis	.12	.30
25 Elton Brand	.15	.40
26 Ron Artest	.15	.40
27 Chris Carr	.10	.25
28 Fred Hoiberg	.10	.25
29 Hersey Hawkins	.10	.25
30 Dickey Simpkins	.10	.25
31 Corey Benjamin	.10	.25
32 Matt Maloney	.10	.25
33 Shawn Kemp	.15	.40
34 Lamond Murray	.10	.25
35 Wesley Person	.10	.25
36 Andre Miller	.12	.30
37 Bob Sura	.10	.25
38 Andrew DeClercq	.10	.25
39 Brevin Knight	.10	.25
40 Earl Boykins RC	.75	2.00
41 Michael Finley	.15	.40
42 Dirk Nowitzki	.25	.60
43 Cedric Ceballos	.10	.25
44 Robert Pack	.10	.25
45 Erick Strickland	.10	.25
46 Sean Rooks	.10	.25
47 Shawn Bradley	.10	.25
48 Steve Nash	.25	.60
49 Antonio McDyess	.12	.30
50 Nick Van Exel	.12	.30
51 Keon Clark	.10	.25
52 Raef LaFrentz	.10	.25
53 James Posey	.10	.25
54 Chris Gatling	.10	.25
55 George McCloud	.10	.25
56 Bryant Stith	.10	.25
57 Jerry Stackhouse	.12	.30
58 Lindsey Hunter	.10	.25
59 Christian Laettner	.12	.30
60 Jerome Williams	.10	.25
61 Michael Curry	.10	.25
62 Loy Vaught	.10	.25
63 Eric Montross	.10	.25
64 Grant Hill	.20	.50
65 Antawn Jamison	.15	.40
66 Chris Mills	.10	.25
67 Vonteego Cummings	.10	.25
68 Larry Hughes	.12	.30
69 Donyell Marshall	.10	.25
70 Mookie Blaylock	.10	.25
71 Erick Dampier	.10	.25
72 Jason Caffey	.10	.25
73 Steve Francis	.12	.30
74 Shandon Anderson	.10	.25
75 Hakeem Olajuwon	.20	.50
76 Walt Williams	.10	.25
77 Kenny Thomas	.10	.25
78 Carlos Rogers	.10	.25
79 Bryce Drew	.10	.25
80 Kelvin Cato	.10	.25
81 Reggie Miller	.15	.40
82 Austin Croshere	.10	.25
83 Rik Smits	.10	.25
84 Jalen Rose	.12	.30
85 Dale Davis	.10	.25
86 Jonathan Bender	.10	.25
87 Travis Best	.10	.25
88 Chris Mullin	.15	.40
89 Lamar Odom	.12	.30
90 Tyrone Nesby	.15	.40
91 Michael Olowokandi	.10	.25
92 Eric Piatkowski	.10	.25
93 Jeff McInnis	.10	.25
94 Brian Skinner	.10	.25
95 Pete Chilcutt	.10	.25
96 Eric Murdock	.10	.25
97 Shaquille O'Neal	.40	1.00
98 Kobe Bryant	.60	1.50
99 Ron Harper	.12	.30
100 Robert Horry	.12	.30
101 Rick Fox	.10	.25
102 Derek Fisher	.15	.40
103 Tyronn Lue	.10	.25
104 Devean George	.10	.25
105 Alonzo Mourning	.20	.50
106 Jamal Mashburn	.12	.30
107 Anthony Carter	.10	.25
108 P.J. Brown	.10	.25
109 Clarence Weatherspoon	.10	.25
110 Otis Thorpe	.12	.30
111 Voshon Lenard	.10	.25
112 Tim Hardaway	.15	.40
113 Ray Allen	.15	.40
114 Glenn Robinson	.12	.30
115 Sam Cassell	.12	.30
116 Robert Traylor	.10	.25
117 Ervin Johnson	.10	.25
118 Scott Williams	.10	.25
119 Tim Thomas	.10	.25
120 Vinny Del Negro	.10	.25
121 Kevin Garnett	.25	.60
122 Wally Szczerbiak	.12	.30
123 Terrell Brandon	.10	.25
124 Dean Garrett	.10	.25
125 William Avery	.10	.25
126 Sam Mitchell	.10	.25
127 Radoslav Nesterovic	.10	.25
128 Anthony Peeler	.10	.25
129 Stephon Marbury	.12	.30
130 Keith Van Horn	.12	.30
131 Kerry Kittles	.10	.25
132 Lucious Harris	.10	.25
133 Evan Eschmeyer	.10	.25
134 Jamie Feick	.10	.25
135 Jim McIlvaine	.10	.25
136 Kendall Gill	.10	.25
137 Allan Houston	.12	.30
138 Marcus Camby	.12	.30
139 Latrell Sprewell	.12	.30
140 Patrick Ewing	.20	.50
141 Larry Johnson	.15	.40
142 Charlie Ward	.10	.25
143 Chris Childs	.10	.25
144 John Wallace	.10	.25
145 Darrell Armstrong	.10	.25
146 Corey Maggette	.12	.30
147 Pat Garrity	.10	.25
148 John Amaechi	.10	.25
149 Matt Harpring	.10	.25
150 Michael Doleac	.10	.25
151 Ron Mercer	.10	.25
152 Chucky Atkins	.10	.25
153 Allen Iverson	.30	.75
154 Matt Geiger	.10	.25
155 Eric Snow	.10	.25
156 Tyrone Hill	.10	.25
157 Theo Ratliff	.10	.25
158 George Lynch	.10	.25
159 Kevin Ollie	.10	.25
160 Toni Kukoc	.15	.40
161 Jason Kidd	.25	.60
162 Anfernee Hardaway	.25	.60
163 Rodney Rogers	.10	.25
164 Shawn Marion	.12	.30
165 Clifford Robinson	.10	.25
166 Tom Gugliotta	.10	.25
167 Luc Longley	.12	.30
168 Randy Livingston	.10	.25
169 Scottie Pippen	.25	.60
170 Steve Smith	.12	.30
171 Damon Stoudamire	.12	.30
172 Bonzi Wells	.10	.25
173 Jermaine O'Neal	.12	.30
174 Arvydas Sabonis	.12	.30
175 Rasheed Wallace	.15	.40
176 Detlef Schrempf	.12	.30
177 Jason Williams	.15	.40
178 Chris Webber	.15	.40
179 Peja Stojakovic	.15	.40
180 Vlade Divac	.12	.30
181 Lawrence Funderburke	.10	.25
182 Tony Delk	.10	.25
183 Jon Barry	.10	.25
184 Tim Duncan	.30	.75
185 Sean Elliott	.15	.40
186 Terry Porter	.10	.25
187 David Robinson	.25	.60
188 Samaki Walker	.10	.25
189 Malik Rose	.10	.25
190 Jaren Jackson	.10	.25
191 Steve Kerr	.10	.25
192 Gary Payton	.15	.40
193 Brent Barry	.10	.25
194 Vin Baker	.12	.30
195 Horace Grant	.12	.30
196 Ruben Patterson	.10	.25
197 Vernon Maxwell	.10	.25
198 Shammond Williams	.10	.25
199 Rashard Lewis	.15	.40
200 Tracy McGrady	.25	.60
201 Charles Oakley	.12	.30
202 Doug Christie	.10	.25
203 Antonio Davis	.10	.25
204 Vince Carter	.30	.75
205 Kevin Willis	.10	.25
206 Dell Curry	.10	.25
207 Dee Brown	.10	.25
208 Karl Malone	.20	.50
209 John Stockton	.20	.50
210 Bryon Russell	.10	.25
211 Olden Polynice	.10	.25
212 Jacque Vaughn	.10	.25
213 Greg Ostertag	.10	.25
214 Quincy Lewis	.10	.25
215 Armon Gilliam	.10	.25
216 Shareef Abdur-Rahim	.12	.30
217 Michael Dickerson	.10	.25
218 Mike Bibby	.15	.40
219 Bryant Reeves	.10	.25
220 Othella Harrington	.10	.25
221 Grant Long	.10	.25
222 Felipe Lopez	.10	.25
223 Obinna Ekezie	.10	.25
224 Mitch Richmond	.12	.30
225 Richard Hamilton	.12	.30
226 Tracy Murray	.10	.25
227 Jahidi White	.10	.25
228 Aaron Williams	.10	.25
229 Juwan Howard	.12	.30
230 Rod Strickland	.10	.25
231 Isaac Austin	.10	.25
232 Dikembe Mutombo VL	.07	.20
233 Antoine Walker VL	.05	.15
234 Derrick Coleman VL	.05	.15
235 Elton Brand VL	.07	.20
236 Shawn Kemp VL	.07	.20
237 Michael Finley VL	.07	.20
238 Antonio McDyess VL	.05	.15
239 Grant Hill VL	.10	.25
240 Antawn Jamison VL	.07	.20
241 Steve Francis VL	.05	.15
242 Jalen Rose VL	.05	.15
243 Lamar Odom VL	.05	.15
244 Shaquille O'Neal VL	.20	.50
245 Alonzo Mourning VL	.10	.25
246 Ray Allen VL	.07	.20
247 Kevin Garnett VL	.12	.30
248 Stephon Marbury VL	.05	.15
249 Allan Houston VL	.05	.15
250 Darrell Armstrong VL	.05	.15
251 Allen Iverson VL	.15	.40
252 Jason Kidd VL	.12	.30
253 Rasheed Wallace VL	.07	.20
254 Chris Webber VL	.07	.20
255 Tim Duncan VL	.15	.40
256 Gary Payton VL	.07	.20
257 Vince Carter VL	.15	.40
258 Karl Malone VL	.10	.25
259 Shareef Abdur-Rahim VL	.05	.15
260 Mitch Richmond VL	.05	.15
261 Kenyon Martin RC	.60	1.50
262 Marcus Fizer RC	.25	.60
263 Chris Mihm RC	.20	.50
264 Stromile Swift RC	.25	.60
265 Keyon Dooling RC	.25	.60

266 Morris Peterson RC	.25	.60
267 Quentin Richardson RC	.25	.60
268 Courtney Alexander RC	.20	.50
269 Desmond Mason RC	.30	.75
270 Mateen Cleaves RC	.20	.50
271 Erick Barkley RC	.15	.40
272 A.J. Guyton RC	.15	.40
273 Darius Miles RC	.25	.60
274 DerMarr Johnson RC	.20	.50
275 Joel Przybilla RC	.20	.50
276 Hanno Mottola RC	.15	.40
277 Mike Miller RC	.40	1.00
278 Donnell Harvey RC	.20	.50
279 Speedy Claxton RC	.25	.60
280 Khalid El-Amin RC	.15	.40

2003-04 Upper Deck Victory

Released in August 2003, Victory boasts a 230-card set divided up into several different subsets as follows: cards 1-100 feature veteran players and have black borders and full-color action photos, cards 101-130 are Rookie Orientation rookie cards with player photos set on a gold foil background and inserted at the rate of one in two. Cards 131, 132 and 133 were not issued upon release. Cards 134-161 showcase NBA All-Stars on a green background and are inserted at the rate of one in eight. Cards 162-181 feature clutch shooters on a bronze foil background and are inserted at the rate of one in ten. Cards 182-201 are point of difference cards and have a blue foil background are inserted at the rate of one in ten. Cards 202-211 are AKA cards on green foil with the player's nickname and inserted at the rate of one in 20. Cards 212-226 feature Monster Jams from players and are inserted at the rate of one in 35. Cards 227-233 feature Michael Jordan and higlight his career and are inserted at the rate of one in 35. Victory was packaged in 36-pack boxes where packs contained six cards and carried a suggested retail price of $0.99. A Michael Jordan Promotional card was also issued and is card #300. It is not included in the set price and listed at the end.

COMP.SET w/o SP's (100)	6.00	15.00

134-161 AS STATED ODDS 1:8
162-181 CS STATED ODDS 1:10
182-201 POD STATED ODDS 1:10
202-211 AKA STATED ODDS 1:20
212-221 MJ STATED ODDS 1:20
222-226 HR STATED ODDS 1:35

1 Shareef Abdur-Rahim	.12	.30
2 Jason Terry	.12	.30
3 Glenn Robinson	.12	.30
4 Paul Pierce	.15	.40
5 Antoine Walker	.15	.40
6 J.R.Bremer	.10	.25
7 Vin Baker	.10	.25
8 Jalen Rose	.12	.30
9 Tyson Chandler	.12	.30
10 Eddy Curry	.10	.25
11 Jay Williams	.10	.25
12 DaJuan Wagner	.10	.25
13 Ricky Davis	.12	.30
14 Zydrunas Ilgauskas	.12	.30
15 Darius Miles	.10	.25
16 Dirk Nowitzki	.25	.60
17A Michael Finley	.15	.40
17B Jermaine O'Neal	.12	.30
18 Steve Nash	.20	.50
19 Nick Van Exel	.12	.30
20 Rodney White	.10	.25
21 Juwan Howard	.12	.30
22 Marcus Camby	.12	.30
23 Nene Hilario	.12	.30
24 Richard Hamilton	.12	.30
25 Ben Wallace	.12	.30
26 Cliff Robinson	.12	.30
27 Antawn Jamison	.12	.30
28 Jason Richardson	.15	.40
29 Gilbert Arenas	.12	.30
30 Mike Dunleavy	.12	.30
31 Steve Francis	.12	.30
32 Eddie Griffin	.10	.25
33 Cuttino Mobley	.10	.25
34 Yao Ming	.30	.75
35 Reggie Miller	.15	.40
36 Jamaal Tinsley	.10	.25
38 Elton Brand	.15	.40
39 Andre Miller	.12	.30
40 Lamar Odom	.12	.30
41 Kobe Bryant	.60	1.50
42 Shaquille O'Neal	.40	1.00
43 Derek Fisher	.12	.30
44 Pau Gasol	.15	.40
45 Shane Battier	.12	.30
46 Mike Miller	.12	.30
47 Eddie Jones	.12	.30
48 Alonzo Mourning	.20	.50
49 Caron Butler	.12	.30
50 Gary Payton	.15	.40
51 Desmond Mason	.12	.30
52 Sam Cassell	.12	.30
53 Toni Kukoc	.15	.40
54 Kevin Garnett	.25	.60
55 Wally Szczerbiak	.12	.30
56 Joe Smith	.12	.30
57 Jason Kidd	.25	.60
58 Richard Jefferson	.12	.30
59 Kenyon Martin	.12	.30
60 Baron Davis	.12	.30
61 Jamal Mashburn	.12	.30
62 Jamaal Magloire	.10	.25
63 Allan Houston	.12	.30
64 Antonio McDyess	.12	.30
65 Latrell Sprewell	.12	.30
66 Tracy McGrady	.20	.50
67 Grant Hill	.20	.50
68 Drew Gooden	.12	.30
69 Gordan Giricek	.10	.25
70 Allen Iverson	.25	.60
71 Keth Van Horn	.12	.30
72 Aaron McKie	.10	.25
73 Stephon Marbury	.12	.30
74 Shawn Marion	.12	.30
75 Anfernee Hardaway	.25	.60
76 Amare Stoudemire	.20	.50
77 Rasheed Wallace	.15	.40
78 Derek Anderson	.10	.25
79 Scottie Pippen	.25	.60
80 Chris Webber	.15	.40
81 Mike Bibby	.15	.40
82 Peja Stojakovic	.15	.40
83 Hedo Turkoglu	.12	.30
84 Tim Duncan	.25	.60
85 David Robinson	.25	.60
86 Tony Parker	.15	.40
87 Manu Ginobili	.20	.50
88 Ray Allen	.15	.40
89 Rashard Lewis	.15	.40
90 Reggie Evans	.10	.25
91 Alvin Williams	.10	.25
92 Vince Carter	.25	.60
93 Morris Peterson	.10	.25
94 Antonio Davis	.10	.25
95 Karl Malone	.20	.50
96 John Stockton	.20	.50
97 Andrei Kirilenko	.15	.40
98 Jerry Stackhouse	.12	.30
99 Kwame Brown	.10	.25
100 Michael Jordan	1.25	3.00
101 Lebron James SP RC	6.00	15.00
102 Darko Milicic RC	.50	1.25
103 Carmelo Anthony RC	2.00	5.00
104 Chris Bosh RC	1.00	2.50
105 Dwyane Wade RC	2.00	5.00
106 Chris Kaman RC	.60	1.50
107 Kirk Hinrich RC	.60	1.50
108 T.J. Ford RC	.50	1.25
109 Mike Sweetney RC	.40	1.00
110 Jarvis Hayes RC	.40	1.00
111 Mickael Pietrus RC	.50	1.25
112 Nick Collison RC	.50	1.25
113 Marcus Banks RC	.40	1.00
114 Luke Ridnour RC	.50	1.25
115 Reece Gaines RC	.40	1.00
116 Troy Bell RC	.40	1.00
117 Zarko Cabarkapa RC	.40	1.00
118 David West RC	.60	1.50
119 Aleksandar Pavlovic RC	.50	1.25
120 Dahntay Jones RC	.50	1.25
121 Boris Diaw RC	.60	1.50
122 Zoran Planinic RC	.40	1.00
123 Travis Outlaw RC	.50	1.25
124 Brian Cook RC	.40	1.00
125 Carlos Delfino RC	.50	1.25
126 Ndudi Ebi RC	.40	1.00
127 Kendrick Perkins RC	.50	1.25
128 Leandro Barbosa RC	.60	1.50
129 Josh Howard RC	.60	1.50
130 Maciej Lampe RC	.40	1.00
134 Michael Jordan AS	5.00	12.00
135 Kobe Bryant AS	2.50	6.00
136 Kevin Garnett AS	1.00	2.50
137 Yao Ming AS	1.25	3.00
138 Vince Carter AS	1.00	2.50
139 Dirk Nowitzki AS	1.00	2.50
140 Antoine Walker AS	.60	1.50
141 Chris Webber AS	.60	1.50
142 Ben Wallace AS	.50	1.25
143 Tracy McGrady AS	.75	2.00
144 Jason Kidd AS	1.00	2.50
145 Steve Francis AS	.50	1.25
146 Gary Payton AS	.60	1.50
147 Peja Stojakovic AS	.60	1.50
148 Brad Miller AS	.50	1.25
149 Shawn Marion AS	.50	1.25
150 Zydrunas Ilgauskas AS	.50	1.25
151 Stephon Marbury AS	.50	1.25
152 Jermaine O'Neal AS	.50	1.25
153 Desmond Mason AS	.50	1.25
154 Jeson Richardson AS	.60	1.50
155 Tony Parker AS	.60	1.50
156 Tim Duncan AS	1.00	2.50
157 Jamal Mashburn AS	.50	1.25
158 Allen Iverson AS	1.00	2.50
159 Shaquille O'Neal AS	1.50	4.00
160 Paul Pierce AS	.60	1.50
161 Steve Nash AS	.75	2.00
162 Michael Jordan CS	5.00	12.00
163 Mike Bibby CS	.60	1.50
164 Jay Williams CS	.40	1.00
165 Richard Hamilton CS	.50	1.25
166 Jerry Stackhouse CS	.50	1.25
167 Peja Stojakovic CS	.60	1.50
168 Reggie Miller CS	.60	1.50
169 Robert Horry CS	.50	1.25
170 Tim Duncan CS	1.00	2.50
171 Jalen Rose CS	.50	1.25
172 Jason Richardson CS	.60	1.50
173 Allen Iverson CS	1.00	2.50
174 Tracy McGrady CS	.75	2.00
175 Paul Pierce CS	.60	1.50
176 Dirk Nowitzki CS	1.00	2.50
177 Baron Davis CS	.50	1.25
178 Latrell Sprewell CS	.50	1.25
179 John Stockton CS	.75	2.00
180 Ray Allen CS	.60	1.50
181 Kobe Bryant CS	2.50	6.00
182 Mike Bibby POD	.60	1.50
183 Earl Boykins POD	.40	1.00
184 John Stockton POD	.75	2.00
185 Alvin Williams POD	.40	1.00
186 Darrell Armstrong POD	.40	1.00
187 Tony Parker POD	.60	1.50
188 Gary Payton POD	.60	1.50
189 Jalen Rose POD	.50	1.25
190 Jason Williams POD	.50	1.25
191 Derek Fisher POD	.50	1.25
192 Steve Nash POD	.75	2.00
193 Jamaal Tinsley POD	.40	1.00
194 Andre Miller POD	.50	1.25
195 Baron Davis POD	.50	1.25
196 Steve Francis POD	.50	1.25
197 DaJuan Wagner POD	.40	1.00
198 Stephon Marbury POD	.50	1.25
199 Jason Kidd POD	1.00	2.50
200 Chauncey Billups POD	.60	1.50
201 Jay Williams POD	.40	1.00
202 Allen Iverson AKA	1.50	4.00
203 Steve Francis AKA	.75	2.00
204 Kenyon Martin AKA	.75	2.00
205 Vince Carter AKA	1.50	4.00
206 Lebron James AKA	5.00	12.00
207 Julius Erving AKA	1.50	4.00
208 Tracy McGrady AKA	1.25	3.00
209 Jason Richardson AKA	1.00	2.50
210 Earvin Johnson AKA	2.50	6.00
211 Michael Jordan AKA	8.00	20.00
212 Michael Jordan MJ	8.00	20.00
213 Kobe Bryant MJ	4.00	10.00
214 Richard Jefferson MJ	.75	2.00
215 Desmond Mason MJ	.75	2.00
216 Vince Carter MJ	1.50	4.00
217 Amare Stoudemire MJ	1.25	3.00
218 Yao Ming MJ	2.00	5.00
219 Elton Brand MJ	1.00	2.50
220 Kevin Garnett MJ	1.50	4.00
221 Shaquille O'Neal MJ	2.50	6.00
222 Lebron James HR	10.00	25.00
223 Kobe Bryant HR	4.00	10.00
224 Richard Jefferson HR	.75	2.00
225 Yao Ming HR	2.00	5.00
226 Amare Stoudemire HR	1.25	3.00
227 Michael Jordan HR	6.00	15.00
228 Michael Jordan FL	6.00	15.00
229 Michael Jordan FL	6.00	15.00
230 Michael Jordan FL	6.00	15.00
231 Michael Jordan FL	6.00	15.00
232 Michael Jordan FL	6.00	15.00
233 Michael Jordan FL	6.00	15.00
300 Michael Jordan Promotional Card	4.00	10.00

2003-04 Upper Deck Victory Parallel

*101-133 RCs: 5X TO 12X BASE HI
*134-201 SINGLES: 2.5X TO 6X BASE HI
*202-226 SINGLES: 1.5X TO 4X BASE HI

COMMON JORDAN (227-233)	30.00	80.00

134-226 PRINT RUN 100 SER.#'d SETS

101 Lebron James	100.00	250.00

1993-94 Upper Deck Wal-mart Jumbos

These jumbo size (3 1/2" by 5") cards were available in blister packs at Walmart. Each pack consisted of a retail foil pack, a team set (ten team sets in all were offered), and two jumbo cards, one of which was a player from the team set. The advertising insert indicates that only one jumbo card was included per repack, but a gold foil sticker on the blister packs states that each repack "contains 2 jumbo cards." The jumbo cards are oversized versions of the regular cards, and both regular series cards and subset cards are featured. The cards are numbered on the back as they are in the regular series.

COMPLETE SET (28)	30.00	75.00
32 Shawn Kemp	1.00	2.50
48 Ron Harper	.30	.75
64 Mitch Richmond	.75	2.00
154 Glen Rice	.75	2.00
195 Reggie Miller	.75	2.00
243 Kenny Anderson	.30	.75
361 Isaiah Rider	1.00	2.50
382 Anfernee Hardaway	4.00	10.00
391 LaPhonso Ellis	.40	1.00
483 Chris Webber	5.00	12.00
485 Shawn Bradley	.75	2.00
486 Jamal Mashburn	2.00	5.00
487 Calbert Cheaney	.60	1.50
490 Vin Baker	2.50	6.00
492 Lindsey Hunter	.60	1.50
497 Nick Van Exel	2.50	6.00
AN5 Mark Price	.30	.75
AN8 Patrick Ewing	.75	2.00
FT2 Charles Barkley	1.25	3.00
FT4 Dee Brown	.20	.50
FT7 Clyde Drexler	.75	2.00
FT13 Karl Malone	2.00	5.00
FT15 Alonzo Mourning	.60	1.50
LT3 Shaquille O'Neal	3.00	8.00
TM1 Dominique Wilkins	.30	.75
TM4 Scottie Pippen	2.50	6.00
TM10 Hakeem Olajuwon	1.25	3.00
TM24 David Robinson	1.25	3.00

2010 Upper Deck World of Sports

COMPLETE SET (375)	100.00	150.00
COMP.SET w/o SPs (300)	30.00	60.00
1 LeBron James	1.50	4.00
2 Yao Ming	.25	.60
3 Brandon Roy	.15	.40
4 Russell Westbrook	.25	.60
5 Derrick Rose	.40	1.00
6 Bill Russell	.25	.60
7 Bobby Hurley	.15	.40
8 Christian Laettner	.15	.40
9 Danny Ferry	.15	.40
10 Bill Walton	.15	.40
11 Jerry West	.25	.60
12 Rick Barry	.15	.40
13 Steve Alford	.15	.40
14 Calbert Cheaney	.15	.40
15 Larry Johnson	.15	.40
16 John Havlicek	.25	.60
17 Tim Hardaway	.15	.40
18 Dennis Rodman	.25	.60
19 Bill Laimbeer	.15	.40
20 Mateen Cleaves	.15	.40
21 Magic Johnson	.25	.60
22 Larry Bird	.40	1.00
23 Michael Jordan	2.00	5.00
24 Craig Brackins	.15	.40
25 Gani Lawal	.15	.40
26 James Anderson	.15	.40
27 Sherron Collins	.15	.40
28 Stanley Robinson	.15	.40
29 Trevor Booker	.15	.40
30 Devin Ebanks	.15	.40
31 Aubrey Coleman	.15	.40
32 Ekpe Udoh	.25	.60
33 Solomon Alabi	.15	.40
34 Jarvis Varnado	.15	.40
35 Jerome Jordan	.15	.40
36 Luke Babbitt	.15	.40
37 Terrico White	.15	.40
38 DeMarcus Cousins	.75	2.00
39 Hassan Whiteside	.15	.40
40 Da'Sean Butler	.15	.40
41 Derrick Favors	.40	1.00
42 Damion James	.15	.40
43 Gordon Hayward	.25	.60
44 Paul George	.25	.60
45 Dexter Pittman	.15	.40
46 Luke Harangody	.15	.40
47 Jordan Crawford	.15	.40
48 Manny Harris	.25	.60
49 Quincy Pondexter	.15	.40
50 Scottie Reynolds	.15	.40
51 Elliot Williams	.15	.40
52 Brian Zoubek	.15	.40
53 Xavier Henry	.25	.60
54 A.J. Ogilvy	.15	.40
55 Armon Johnson	.15	.40
56 Cole Aldrich	.25	.60
57 Deon Thompson	.15	.40
58 Donald Williams	.15	.40
59 Sam Cassell	.15	.40
60 Toni Kukoc	.15	.40
331 Xavier Henry SP	2.00	5.00
332 DeMarcus Cousins SP	1.00	2.50
333 Derrick Favors SP	1.00	2.50
334 Damion James SP	1.00	2.50
335 Luke Harangody SP	1.00	2.50
336 LeBron James SP	2.00	5.00
337 Michael Jordan SP	3.00	8.00
338 Larry Bird SP	1.50	4.00
339 Magic Johnson SP	1.00	2.50
340 Dennis Rodman SP	1.00	2.50
345 Tubby Smith SP	1.00	2.50
346 Gary Williams SP	1.00	2.50
347 Matt Painter SP	1.00	2.50
348 Jamie Dixon SP	1.00	2.50
349 Mark Few SP	1.00	2.50
350 Steve Alford SP	1.00	2.50
351 Bruce Pearl SP	1.00	2.50
352 Mike Montgomery SP	1.00	2.50
353 Steve Fisher SP	1.00	2.50
354 Bo Ryan SP	1.00	2.50
355 Jeff Capel III SP	1.00	2.50
356 Bobby Cremins SP	1.00	2.50
357 Rick Majerus SP	1.00	2.50
358 Sean Miller SP	1.00	2.50
359 Jim Boeheim SP	1.00	2.50
360 Dana Altman SP	1.00	2.50
361 Tom Crean SP	1.00	2.50
362 Roy Williams SP	1.00	2.50
363 Jim Calhoun SP	1.00	2.50
364 Tom Izzo SP	1.00	2.50
365 Ben Howland SP	1.00	2.50
366 Billy Donovan SP	1.00	2.50
367 Bill Self SP	1.00	2.50
368 Thad Matta SP	1.00	2.50
369 Bob Huggins SP	1.00	2.50
370 John Beilein SP	1.00	2.50
371 Homer Drew SP	1.00	2.50
372 Jay Wright SP	1.00	2.50
373 Bruce Weber SP	1.00	2.50
374 Mike Brey SP	1.00	2.50
375 Seth Greenberg SP	1.00	2.50

2010 Upper Deck World of Sports All-Sport Apparel Memorabilia

STATED ODDS ONE PER BOX

ASA1 LeBron James	8.00	20.00
ASA2 Michael Jordan	25.00	50.00
ASA3 Yao Ming	5.00	12.00
ASA4 Brandon Roy	4.00	10.00
ASA5 Russell Westbrook	5.00	12.00
ASA6 Derrick Rose	6.00	15.00
ASA8 Hakeem Olajuwon	6.00	15.00
ASA9 Julius Erving	5.00	12.00
ASA10 Magic Johnson	6.00	15.00
ASA11 Alonzo Mourning	5.00	12.00
ASA12 Bill Walton	4.00	10.00
ASA13 David Robinson	5.00	12.00
ASA14 Xavier Henry	4.00	10.00

2010 Upper Deck World of Sports All-Sport Apparel Memorabilia Autographs

OVERALL AUTO ODDS TWO PER BOX
STATED PRINT RUN 25 SER.#'d SETS

ASA1 LeBron James	125.00	250.00
ASA2 Michael Jordan	300.00	600.00
ASA3 Yao Ming	20.00	50.00
ASA4 Brandon Roy	12.00	30.00
ASA5 Russell Westbrook	60.00	150.00
ASA6 Derrick Rose	75.00	150.00
ASA7 Clyde Drexler	20.00	50.00
ASA8 Hakeem Olajuwon	25.00	60.00
ASA9 Julius Erving	40.00	80.00
ASA11 Alonzo Mourning	25.00	60.00
ASA13 David Robinson	40.00	100.00
ASA15 Greg Monroe	12.00	30.00

2010 Upper Deck World of Sports Autographs

OVERALL AUTO ODDS TWO PER BOX

1 LeBron James	100.00	200.00
2 Yao Ming	12.00	30.00
3 Brandon Roy	6.00	15.00
4 Russell Westbrook	25.00	60.00
5 Derrick Rose	30.00	60.00
6 Bill Russell	50.00	100.00
7 Bobby Hurley	5.00	12.00
9 Danny Ferry	5.00	12.00
10 Bill Walton	15.00	30.00
11 Jerry West	30.00	60.00
12 Rick Barry	10.00	25.00
13 Steve Alford	6.00	15.00
14 Calbert Cheaney	5.00	12.00
17 Tim Hardaway	6.00	15.00
18 Dennis Rodman	15.00	40.00
19 Bill Laimbeer	5.00	12.00
20 Mateen Cleaves	5.00	12.00
22 Larry Bird	40.00	80.00
23 Michael Jordan	250.00	400.00
24 Craig Brackins	5.00	12.00
26 James Anderson	6.00	15.00
27 Sherron Collins	10.00	25.00
28 Stanley Robinson	5.00	12.00
29 Trevor Booker	5.00	12.00
32 Ekpe Udoh	5.00	12.00
33 Solomon Alabi	5.00	12.00
35 Jerome Jordan	5.00	12.00
36 Luke Babbitt	5.00	12.00
38 DeMarcus Cousins	20.00	50.00
39 Hassan Whiteside	5.00	12.00
40 Da'Sean Butler	6.00	15.00
41 Derrick Favors	10.00	25.00
43 Gordon Hayward	10.00	25.00
44 Paul George	6.00	15.00
45 Dexter Pittman	5.00	12.00
47 Jordan Crawford	5.00	12.00
49 Quincy Pondexter	10.00	25.00
50 Scottie Reynolds	5.00	12.00
51 Elliot Williams	5.00	12.00
52 Brian Zoubek	6.00	15.00
53 Xavier Henry	6.00	15.00
54 A.J. Ogilvy	5.00	12.00
55 Armon Johnson	5.00	12.00
56 Cole Aldrich	10.00	25.00
58 Donald Williams	10.00	25.00
59 Sam Cassell	6.00	15.00
331 Xavier Henry	5.00	12.00
332 DeMarcus Cousins	15.00	40.00
333 Derrick Favors	10.00	25.00
336 LeBron James	100.00	175.00
337 Michael Jordan	250.00	400.00
338 Larry Bird	40.00	80.00
340 Dennis Rodman	12.00	30.00
345 Tubby Smith	10.00	25.00
346 Gary Williams	30.00	60.00
347 Matt Painter	10.00	25.00
348 Jamie Dixon	15.00	30.00
349 Mark Few	10.00	25.00
350 Steve Alford	6.00	15.00
351 Bruce Pearl	10.00	25.00
352 Mike Montgomery	6.00	15.00
354 Bo Ryan	15.00	40.00
355 Jeff Capel III	6.00	15.00
356 Bobby Cremins	10.00	25.00
358 Sean Miller	6.00	15.00
359 Jim Boeheim	10.00	25.00
360 Dana Altman	6.00	15.00
361 Tom Crean	10.00	25.00
362 Roy Williams	25.00	50.00
363 Jim Calhoun	15.00	40.00
364 Tom Izzo	15.00	40.00
365 Ben Howland	6.00	15.00
366 Billy Donovan	10.00	25.00
367 Bill Self	20.00	40.00
368 Thad Matta	25.00	50.00
369 Bob Huggins	15.00	40.00
370 John Beilein	10.00	25.00
372 Jay Wright	15.00	40.00
373 Bruce Weber	6.00	15.00
374 Mike Brey	10.00	25.00
375 Seth Greenberg	6.00	15.00

2010 Upper Deck World of Sports Clear Competitors

STATED ODDS ONE PER BOX
STATED PRINT RUN 550 SER.#'d SETS

CC1 LeBron James	6.00	15.00
CC2 Yao Ming	3.00	8.00
CC3 Magic Johnson	4.00	10.00
CC4 Larry Bird	5.00	12.00
CC5 Derrick Rose	5.00	12.00
CC6 DeMarcus Cousins	5.00	12.00
CC7 Derrick Favors	3.00	8.00
CC8 Xavier Henry	4.00	10.00
CC9 Anfernee Hardaway	4.00	10.00
CC10 Tom Izzo	3.00	8.00
CC11 Roy Williams	5.00	12.00
CC12 Jim Boeheim	3.00	8.00

2011 Upper Deck World of Sports

COMPLETE SET (400)	75.00	150.00
COMP.SET w/o SPs (300)	25.00	60.00
33 LeBron James	1.25	3.00
34 DeMarcus Cousins	.40	1.00
35 Michael Jordan	2.00	5.00
36 Scottie Reynolds	.15	.40
37 Quincy Pondexter	.15	.40
38 Rick Fox	.15	.40
39 Cole Aldrich	.25	.60
40 Al-Farouq Aminu	.15	.40
41 Stanley Robinson	.15	.40
42 Sherron Collins	.25	.60
43 Jerome Jordan	.15	.40
44 Jarvis Varnado	.15	.40
45 James Anderson	.15	.40
46 Gani Lawal	.15	.40
47 Ekpe Udoh	.15	.40
48 Devin Ebanks	.15	.40
49 Craig Brackins	.15	.40
50 Larry Johnson	.15	.40
51 Brook Lopez	.15	.40
52 Eric Bledsoe	.15	.40
53 Mark A. Jackson	.15	.40
54 Steve Nash	.25	.60
55 Manny Harris	.15	.40
56 John Starks	.15	.40
57 John Stockton	.25	.60
58 Bill Walton	.15	.40
59 Anfernee Hardaway	.15	.40
60 Tim Hardaway	.15	.40
61 Jimmer Fredette	.15	.40
62 Toni Kukoc	.25	.60
63 Candace Parker	.15	.40
64 Jackie Stiles	.15	.40
65 Steve Alford	.15	.40
66 Bobby Cremins	.15	.40
67 Bruce Pearl	.15	.40
68 Mike Montgomery	.15	.40
69 Mike Brey	.15	.40
70 Thad Matta	.15	.40
71 Bo Ryan	.15	.40
72 Steve Fisher	.15	.40
73 Bob Huggins	.15	.40
74 Jay Wright	.15	.40
75 Ben Howland	.15	.40
76 Gary Williams	.15	.40
77 Mark Few	.15	.40
78 Jeff Capel III	.15	.40
79 John Beilein	.15	.40
80 Jim Calhoun	.15	.40
81 Sean Miller	.15	.40
82 Dana Altman	.15	.40
83 Seth Greenberg	.15	.40
84 Homer Drew	.15	.40
85 Matt Painter	.15	.40
86 Bruce Weber	.15	.40
87 Tom Crean	.15	.40
88 Rick Majerus	.15	.40
311 Chris Paul SP	1.00	2.50
312 Derrick Rose SP	1.50	4.00
313 Alonzo Mourning SP	1.00	2.50
314 Magic Johnson SP	1.00	2.50
315 David Robinson SP	1.00	2.50
316 Walt Frazier SP	1.00	2.50
317 Hakeem Olajuwon SP	1.00	2.50
318 Clyde Drexler SP	1.00	2.50
319 Christian Laettner SP	1.00	2.50
320 Greg Monroe SP	1.00	2.50
321 LeBron James SP	1.50	4.00
322 Michael Jordan SP	2.00	5.00
323 Julius Erving SP	1.25	3.00
324 Tom Izzo SP	1.00	2.50
325 Billy Donovan SP	1.00	2.50
326 Jamie Dixon SP	1.00	2.50
327 Bill Self SP	1.00	2.50
328 Tubby Smith SP	1.00	2.50
329 Jim Boeheim SP	1.00	2.50

2011 Upper Deck World of Sports Athletes of the World Autographs

OVERALL AUTO/MEM ODDS 3 PER BOX

AWKG Kevin Garnett	20.00	40.00
AWYM Yao Ming	15.00	40.00

2011 Upper Deck World of Sports Autographs

33 LeBron James B	100.00	175.00
34 DeMarcus Cousins B	25.00	60.00
35 Michael Jordan B	350.00	500.00
41 Stanley Robinson C	4.00	10.00
43 Jerome Jordan C	4.00	10.00
45 James Anderson A	4.00	10.00
46 Gani Lawal C	4.00	10.00
47 Ekpe Udoh B	4.00	10.00
49 Craig Brackins C	4.00	10.00
50 Larry Johnson B	15.00	40.00
51 Brook Lopez B	5.00	12.00
52 Eric Bledsoe B	15.00	40.00
54 Steve Nash B	25.00	60.00
57 John Stockton A	40.00	100.00
58 Bill Walton A	10.00	25.00
60 Tim Hardaway B	6.00	15.00
61 Jimmer Fredette B	25.00	60.00
62 Toni Kukoc B	12.00	30.00
64 Jackie Stiles C	6.00	15.00
65 Steve Alford C	5.00	12.00
66 Bobby Cremins C	4.00	10.00
67 Bruce Pearl C	4.00	10.00
68 Mike Montgomery (Coach) C	4.00	10.00
69 Mike Brey C	6.00	15.00
70 Thad Matta C	10.00	25.00
71 Bo Ryan C	8.00	20.00
72 Steve Fisher C	5.00	12.00
73 Bob Huggins C	12.00	30.00
74 Jay Wright B	15.00	40.00
76 Gary Williams C	15.00	40.00
77 Mark Few B	6.00	15.00
78 Jeff Capel III C	5.00	12.00
79 John Beilein C	6.00	15.00
80 Jim Calhoun B	8.00	20.00
81 Sean Miller C	4.00	10.00
82 Dana Altman C	4.00	10.00
83 Seth Greenberg C	6.00	15.00
84 Homer Drew C	4.00	10.00
85 Matt Painter C	5.00	12.00
86 Bruce Weber C	4.00	10.00
87 Tom Crean C	10.00	25.00
88 Rick Majerus C	4.00	10.00
312 Derrick Rose A	75.00	150.00
318 Clyde Drexler A	15.00	40.00
321 LeBron James A	100.00	200.00
322 Michael Jordan B	300.00	450.00
324 Tom Izzo A	15.00	40.00
325 Billy Donovan A	12.00	30.00
326 Jamie Dixon B	4.00	10.00
327 Bill Self B	25.00	50.00
328 Tubby Smith B	4.00	10.00

2011 Upper Deck World of Sports Evolution Video Cards

EVO1 Michael Jordan	150.00	250.00
EVO2 Chris Paul	15.00	40.00
EVO3 Alonzo Mourning	50.00	100.00

2001-02 USBL

COMPLETE SET (44)	6.00	15.00
1 Kwan Johnson	.15	.40
2 Mark Blount	.15	.40
3 Sean Colson	.15	.40
4 Chudney Gray	.15	.40
5 Tariq Kirksay	.15	.40
6 Larry Abney	.15	.40
7 Tyson Patterson	.15	.40
8 Steve Smith	.15	.40
9 Bryan Gates	.15	.40
10 Darryl Dawkins	.30	.75
11 Kent Davison	.15	.40
12 Rick Barry	.30	.75
13 K'Zell Wessoon	.15	.40
14 Tunji Awojobi	.15	.40
15 Artie Griffin	.15	.40
16 Bryant Basemore	.15	.40
17 Andre Perry	.15	.40
18 Willie Burton	.15	.40
19 Raphael Edwards	.15	.40
20 Kelvin Price	.15	.40
21 Ira Newbie	.15	.40
22 Alvin Jefferson	.15	.40
23 LaMarr Greer	.15	.40
24 David Harrison	.15	.40
25 Reggie Slater	.15	.40
26 Michael Lewis	.15	.40
27 Doug Gottlieb	.15	.40
28 Chianti Roberts	.15	.40
29 Mike Lloyd	.15	.40
30 Wayne Copeland	.15	.40
31 Franklin Paul	.15	.40
32 Tom Wideman	.15	.40
33 Marshall Phillips	.15	.40
34 Terrell Baker	.15	.40
35 Jerrod West	.15	.40
36 Billy Thomas	.15	.40
37 Brian Green	.15	.40
38 Martin Lewis	.15	.40
39 Duane Woodward	.15	.40
40 Rashon Turner	.15	.40
41 Fred Herzog	.15	.40
42 Reggie Bassette	.15	.40
43 Adrian Peterson	.15	.40
44 Checklist Card	.15	.40

2001-02 USBL Chase Cards

COMPLETE SET (6)	1.00	2.50
C1 Sean Colson	.20	.50
C2 Artie Griffin	.20	.50
C3 Denny Price	.20	.50
C4 Chudney Gray	.20	.50
C5 Lloyd Daniels	.20	.50
C6 USBL Champions	.20	.50

1988-89 Warriors Smokey

The 1988-89 Smokey Golden State Warriors set contains four 5" by 8" (approximately) cards featuring color action photos. The card backs feature a large fire safety cartoon and minimal player information. The cards are unnumbered and are ordered below alphabetically. The set was sponsored by the California Department of Forestry and Fire Protection and the Bureau of Land Management. The player's name, number, and position are overprinted in the lower right corner of each obverse.

COMPLETE SET (4)	12.00	30.00
1 Winston Garland	2.00	5.00
2 Chris Mullin	10.00	20.00
3 Ralph Sampson	3.00	8.00
4 Larry Smith	2.00	5.00

1971-72 Warriors Team Issue

This 1971-72 Golden State Warriors set consists of 13 team-issued photos, each measuring approximately 10" by 8 1/8". The fronts feature one black-and-white posed action player photograph on the right side, and a smaller black-and-white player portrait in the top left corner. The player's name appears under the photo, with the team logo in the lower left. The backs are blank. The photos are unnumbered and checklisted below in alphabetical order. The set's date is based on the fact that Odis Allison and Vic Bartolome only played in 1971-72.

COMPLETE SET (13)	40.00	80.00
1 Odis Allison	1.50	4.00
2 Al Attles	5.00	10.00
3 Jim Barnett	2.00	5.00
4 Vic Bartolome	1.50	4.00
5 Joe Ellis	2.00	5.00
6 Nick Jones	1.50	4.00
7 Clyde Lee	2.00	5.00
8 Jeff Mullins	5.00	10.00
9 Bob Portman	1.50	4.00
10 Cazzie Russell	6.00	12.00
11 Nate Thurmond	10.00	20.00
12 Bill Turner	1.50	4.00
13 Ron(Fritz) Williams	2.00	5.00

1993-94 Warriors Topps/Safeway

Issued in four perforated five-card strips (the fifth card being the coupon card), these 16 standard-size cards were distributed at Safeway stores in the Bay Area. The white-bordered fronts display color action player photos with a team-color-coded inner border three quarters of the way down the left side and curving along the bottom of the picture. The player's name is printed in white script at the lower left with the team name appearing on a team-color-coded bar at the very bottom. The horizontal backs carry a close-up player photo on one side, with complete NBA statistics, biography, and career highlights on a beige panel on the other side. The cards are numbered on the back with a "GS" prefix. Reportedly there were 162 Safeway stores from Northern California and Nevada involved with the promotion which ran from Jan. 19 through Apr. 12. Shoppers were to obtain a coupon from the store's photo department and redeem it at the customer service window for their free cards. In addition, 8,000 four-card strips were handed out at Warrior games (Jan. 26, Feb 19, Mar. 15, and Apr. 14.) to promote the offer. It has been reported that of the 162 Safeway stores, 100 were given 1,000 of each strip, while the remaining stores recieved 785 of each strip.

COMPLETE SET (16)	3.00	8.00
1 Chris Mullin	.60	1.50
2 Byron Houston	.08	.25
3 Chris Gatling	.20	.50
4 Don Nelson CO	.20	.50
5 Nate Thurmond LEGEND	.40	1.00
6 Chris Webber	1.50	4.00
7 Latrell Sprewell	.60	1.50
8 Jeff Grayer	.08	.25
9 Al Attles LEGEND	.20	.50
10 Tim Hardaway	.60	1.50
11 Jud Buechler	.08	.25
12 Victor Alexander	.08	.25
13 Keith Jennings	.08	.25
14 Sarunas Marciulionis	.30	.75
15 Billy Owens	.20	.50
16 Avery Johnson	.30	.75

1994-95 Warriors Topps/Safeway

Produced by Topps, this sets consists of three 5-card perforated strips that measure 12 1/2" by 3 1/2". After perforation, the cards measure the standard size, and the fifth slot on each strip features either a Kellogg's Pop-Tarts Minis coupon or a Safeway film-developing coupon. Most of the cards are identical to their regular issue counterparts; several cards appear to produced just for this set (Jennings and Lanier). Note also that the cards are numbered as one series with "GS" prefixes, and several of the card numbers (as noted below) are misnumbered.

COMPLETE SET (12)	2.50	6.00
GS1 Tim Hardaway	.60	1.50
GS2 Victor Alexander	.08	.25
GS3 Latrell Sprewell (Numbered GS13 on back)	.40	1.00
GS4 Rod Higgins (Numbered GS16 on back)	.08	.25
GS5 Chris Mullin	.50	1.25
GS6 Clifford Rozier	.08	.25
GS7 Chris Gatling	.20	.50
GS8 Keith Jennings	.08	.25
GS9 Rony Seikaly	.08	.25
GS10 Carlos Rogers	.08	.25
GS11 Ricky Pierce (Numbered 267 on back)	.08	.25
GS12 Bob Lanier CO	.40	1.00

1995-96 Warriors Topps/Safeway

Produced by Topps, this set consists of three 5-card perforated strips that measure 12 1/2" by 3 1/2". After perforation, the cards measure the standard size. Each strip contains four player cards and one Kodak or Kellogg's advertising card. Most of the player cards are identical to their corresponding regular-issue 1995-96 Topps cards, except for the card numbering each of which is a ssigned a GS prefix and numbered as a twelve card series. The cards were regionally distributed in California in early 1996 at participating Safeway stores.

COMPLETE SET (15)	2.00	5.00
GS1 Chris Gatling	.08	.25
GS2 Donyell Marshall	.20	.50
GS3 Tim Hardaway	.50	1.25
GS4 Rick Adelman CO	.20	.50
GS5 B.J. Armstrong	.15	.40
GS6 Jon Barry	.15	.40
GS7 Latrell Sprewell	.40	1.00
GS8 Joe Smith	.75	2.00
GS9 Jerome Kersey	.08	.25
GS10 Rony Seikaly	.08	.25
GS11 Chris Mullin	.50	1.25
GS12 Clifford Rozier	.08	.25
NNO Kellogg's Ad Card 2	.08	.25
NNO Kellogg's Ad Card 1	.08	.25
NNO Kodak Ad Card	.08	.25

1992 Washington Little Sun

Produced by Little Sun and distributed by Snyder's Bakery of Spokane, Washington, this eight-card multi-sport standard-size set features former and current athletes from the state of Washington. The cards were available for eight weeks beginning Sept. 14. One card per week was inserted into loaves of Snyder's Premium White and Roman Meal bread. During the promotion, a total of 80,000 of each card were distributed. The bakery also made a donation to the Scholarship Fund of the Tacoma Athletic Commission in the names of the athletes included in the set. The sports represented in the set are baseball (1, 6), football (2, 8), basketball (3), bowling (4), skiing (5), and mountain climbing (7).

COMPLETE SET (8)	3.00	8.00
3 Doug Christie	.60	1.50

1924 Willard's Chocolates Sports Champions V122

42 Edmonton Grads
Women's Basketball

1996-98 Worldcom Calling Cards

1 Michael Jordan 10 minutes Black Uniform	2.50	6.00
2 Michael Jordan 10 minutes Red Uniform	2.50	6.00
3 Michael Jordan 30 minutes Black Uniform	4.00	10.00
4 Michael Jordan 10 minutes Rayovac	2.50	6.00
5 Michael Jordan 5 minutes Red Uniform	2.00	5.00
6 Michael Jordan 5 minutes Cologne Ad	2.00	5.00
7 Michael Jordan 60 minutes Black Uniform	4.00	10.00
10 Michael Jordan 5 dollars Limited Edition	4.00	10.00

1951 Wheaties

The cards in this six-card set measure approximately 2 1/2" by 3 1/4". Cards of the 1951 Wheaties set are actually the backs of small individual boxes of Wheaties. The cards are waxed and depict three baseball players, one football player, one basketball player, and one golfer. They are occasionally found as complete boxes, which are worth 50 percent more than the prices listed below. The catalog designation for this set is F272-3. The cards are blank-backed and unnumbered; they are numbered below in alphabetical order for convenience.

COMPLETE SET (6)	300.00	600.00
3 George Mikan	100.00	200.00

1952 Wheaties

The cards in this 60-card set measure 2" by 2 3/4". The 1952 Wheaties set of orange, blue and white, unnumbered cards was issued in panels of eight or ten cards on the backs of Wheaties cereal boxes. Each player appears in an action pose, designated in the checklist with an "A", and as a portrait, listed in the checklist with a "B". The catalog designation is F272-4. The cards are blank-backed and unnumbered, but have been assigned numbers below using a sport prefix (BB- baseball, BK- basketball, FB- football, G-Golf, OT- other).

COMPLETE SET (60)	600.00	1000.00
BK1A Bob Davies Action	12.50	20.00
BK1B Bob Davies Portrait	12.50	20.00
BK2A George Mikan Action	75.00	125.00
BK2B George Mikan Portrait	75.00	125.00
BK3A Jim Pollard Action	10.00	25.00
BK3B Jim Pollard Portrait	10.00	25.00

2005 WNBA Promo Sheet

Given out to distributors, this six-card promo sheet debuts the new look of the 2005 WNBA set. The sheet contains six cards, three on top and three on bottom and is perforated.

NNO Promo Sheet	4.00	10.00

2005 WNBA

COMPLETE SET (110)	10.00	25.00
1 Seattle Storm TC	1.25	3.00
2 LaToya Thomas	.15	.40
3 Crystal Robinson	.15	.40
4 Chasity Melvin	.15	.40
5 Dawn Staley	.40	1.00
6 Svetlana Abrosimova	.15	.40
7 Houston Comets TC	.60	1.50

8 Wendy Palmer-Daniel .40 1.00
9 Betty Lennox .30 .75
10 Lisa Leslie .75 2.00
11 Margo Dydek .25 .60
12 Vickie Johnson .25 .60
13 Charlotte Sting TC .60 1.50
14 Ayana Walker .15 .40
15 Shannon Johnson .15 .40
16 Tangela Smith .15 .40
17 Michelle Snow .20 .50
18 Chandi Jones .15 .40
19 Adrienne Goodson .15 .40
20 Lauren Jackson .75 2.00
21 Elaine Powell .15 .40
22 Minnesota Lynx TC .60 1.50
23 La'Keshia Frett .15 .40
24 Allison Feaster .20 .50
25 Lindsay Whalen .40 1.00
26 DeMya Walker .15 .40
27 Tamecka Dixon .25 .60
28 Kelly Miller .15 .40
29 San Antonio Silver Stars TC .60 1.50
30 Tina Thompson .50 1.25
31 Tamika Williams .20 .50
32 Doneeka Hodges RC .25 .60
33 Kelly Mazzante .25 .60
34 Shameka Christon .15 .40
35 Sheryl Swoopes 1.00 2.50
36 Nicole Powell .20 .50
37 Indiana Fever TC .60 1.50
38 Alicia Thompson .15 .40
39 Kristen Rasmussen .15 .40
40 Diana Taurasi .75 2.00
41 Elena Baranova .40 1.00
42 Taj McWilliams-Franklin .15 .40
43 Nakia Sanford RC .30 .75
44 Tamika Whitmore .15 .40
45 Katie Smith .50 1.25
46 Phoenix Mercury TC .60 1.50
47 Tully Bevilaqua .15 .40
48 Tari Phillips .15 .40
49 Charlotte Smith-Taylor .15 .40
50 Sue Bird .75 2.00
51 Natalie Williams .30 .75
52 Connecticut Sun TC .75 2.00
53 Bernadette Ngoyisa RC .30 .75
54 Anna DeForge .15 .40
55 Becky Hammon 1.00 2.50
56 Sacramento Monarchs TC .60 1.50
57 Mwadi Mabika .15 .40
58 Asjha Jones .20 .50
59 Kamila Vodichkova .15 .40
60 Yolanda Griffith .50 1.25
61 Deanna Jackson .15 .40
62 Le'Coe Willingham RC .25 .60
63 Gwen Jackson .15 .40
64 Erin Buescher .15 .40
65 Alana Beard .20 .50
66 New York Liberty TC .60 1.50
67 Helen Darling .15 .40
68 Dominique Canty .25 .60
69 Marie Ferdinand .15 .40
70 Tamika Catchings .25 .60
71 Kara Lawson .30 .75
72 Vanessa Hayden .15 .40
73 Nikki McCray .40 1.00
74 Washington Mystics TC .60 1.50
75 Ruth Riley .25 .60
76 Penny Taylor .25 .60
77 Ticha Penicheiro .40 1.00
78 Katie Douglas .25 .60
79 Janeth Arcain .15 .40
80 Swin Cash .25 .60
81 Kelly Schumacher .15 .40
82 Detroit Shock TC .60 1.50
83 Plenette Pierson .25 .60
84 Sheri Sam .15 .40
85 Chamique Holdsclaw 1.00 2.50
86 Delisha Milton-Jones .15 .40
87 Nicole Ohlde .15 .40
88 Edna Campbell .20 .50
89 Tammy Sutton-Brown .15 .40
90 Nikki Teasley .15 .40
91 Ann Wauters .20 .50
92 Janell Burse .15 .40
93 Kristi Harrower .15 .40
94 Murriel Page .20 .50
95 Cheryl Ford .25 .60
96 Christi Thomas .15 .40
97 Brooke Wyckoff .25 .60
98 Barbara Farris .15 .40
99 Mandisa Stevenson RC .30 .75
100 Nykesha Sales .25 .60
101 Jurgita Streimikyte .15 .40
102 Amber Jacobs RC .25 .60
103 Coco Miller .15 .40
104 Iziane Castro Marques .15 .40
105 Deanna Nolan .15 .40
106 Los Angeles Sparks TC .60 1.50
107 Rebekkah Brunson .15 .40
108 Checklist 1 .15 .40
109 Checklist 2 .15 .40
110 Checklist 3 .15 .40
P1 Diana Taurasi PROMO 2.50 6.00
P1A Becky Hammon Binder 4.00 10.00

2005 WNBA Autographs

STATED ODDS 1:20
AB Adia Barnes Trophy 5.00 12.00
AB1 Alana Beard Posed 4.00 10.00
AB2 Alana Beard Action 4.00 10.00
AD Anne Donovan CO 10.00 25.00
AT Alicia Thompson Trophy 5.00 12.00
BH1 Becky Hammon Posed 12.00 30.00
BH2 Becky Hammon Action 12.00 30.00
BH3 Becky Hammon Dress 12.00 30.00
BL Betty Lennox Trophy 6.00 15.00
CC1 Cynthia Cooper 8.00 20.00
DA1 L.Jackson/S.Bird AU 20.00 50.00
DS1 Dawn Staley Posed 8.00 20.00
DS2 Dawn Staley Action 8.00 20.00
DT1 Diana Taurasi Posed 10.00 25.00
DT2 Diana Taurasi Action 10.00 25.00
DT3 Diana Taurasi Dress 10.00 25.00
JB Janell Burse Trophy 5.00 12.00
KS1 Katie Smith Posed 10.00 25.00
KS2 Katie Smith Action 10.00 25.00
KS3 Katie Smith Dress 10.00 25.00
KV Kamila Vodichkova Trophy 5.00 12.00
LJ1 Lauren Jackson Trophy 12.00 30.00
LJ2 Lauren Jackson Action 12.00 30.00
LL1 Lisa Leslie Yellow 8.00 20.00
LL2 Lisa Leslie Black 8.00 20.00
LL3 Lisa Leslie Dress 8.00 20.00
NS1 Nykesha Sales Action 5.00 12.00
NS2 Nykesha Sales Dress 5.00 12.00
NT1 Nikki Teasley Posed 5.00 12.00
NT2 Nikki Teasley Action 5.00 12.00
NT3 Nikki Teasley Dress 5.00 12.00
SB1 Sue Bird Trophy 15.00 40.00
SB2 Sue Bird Posed 15.00 40.00
SB3 Sue Bird Action 15.00 40.00
SC1 Swin Cash Posed 5.00 12.00
SC2 Swin Cash Action 5.00 12.00
SC3 Swin Cash Dress 5.00 12.00
SE Simone Edwards Trophy 5.00 12.00
SJ1 Shannon Johnson Action 5.00 12.00
SJ2 Shannon Johnson Dress 5.00 12.00
SS Sheri Sam Trophy 5.00 12.00
TB Tully Bevilaqua Trophy 5.00 12.00
TC1 Tamika Catchings Posed 5.00 12.00
TC2 Tamika Catchings Action 5.00 12.00
TC3 Tamika Catchings Dress 5.00 12.00
YG1 Yolanda Griffith Press 6.00 15.00
YG2 Yolanda Griffith Action 6.00 15.00

2005 WNBA Jerseys

Inserted in packs at the rate of one in 80, this 12-card set features numbers R1-R10 in packs, #AR1 and AR2 as autographed and numbered distributor promos, #DR1 Sue Bird/Lauren Jackson as a random case topper, and a Becky Hammon card available through a mail-in offer for the Rittenhouse Archives binder for storing 2005 WNBA cards.

STATED ODDS 1:80
R1 Lisa Leslie 6.00 15.00
R2 Lauren Jackson 20.00 50.00
R3 Tina Thompson 4.00 10.00
R4 Diana Taurasi 10.00 25.00
R5 Sue Bird 6.00 15.00
R6 Yolanda Griffith 4.00 10.00
R7 Tamika Catchings 4.00 10.00
R8 Swin Cash 6.00 15.00
R9 Nikki Teasley 6.00 15.00
R10 Nykesha Sales 4.00 10.00
AR1 Lisa Leslie AU/299 25.00 60.00
AR2 Diana Taurasi AU/99 125.00 250.00
DR1 S.Bird/L.Jackson Topper 20.00 50.00
NNO Becky Hammon Archives 10.00 25.00

2005 WNBA League Leaders

COMPLETE SET (8) 8.00 20.00
STATED ODDS 1:20
LL1 Jackson/Thompson/Leslie 2.00 5.00
LL2 Teasley/Bird/Staley 2.00 5.00
LL3 Leslie/Ford/Snow 2.00 5.00
LL4 Griffith/Sales/Beard 1.25 3.00
LL5 Leslie/Sutton-Brown/Jackson 2.00 5.00
LL6 Smith/Johnson/Miller 1.25 3.00
LL7 Smith-T/Baranova/Jackson 1.00 2.50
LL8 Williams/Griffith/Leslie 2.00 5.00

2005 WNBA Playoffs

STATED ODDS 1:7
P1 Conn. def. Wash 2-1 .75 2.00
P2 NY def. LA 2-1 .75 2.00
P3 Sacram. def. LA 2-1 .75 2.00
P4 Seattle def. Minn. 2-0 .75 2.00
P5 Conn. def. NY 2-0 .75 2.00
P6 Seattle def. Sacram 2-1 1.25 3.00
P7 Conn. Win Game 1 .75 2.00
P8 Seattle Ties it Up 1.25 3.00
P9 Seattle Reigns 1.25 3.00

2005 WNBA Rookies

COMPLETE SET (33) 250.00 450.00
STATED PRINT RUN 333 SER.#'d SETS
RC1 Janel McCarville 8.00 20.00
RC2 Tan White 10.00 25.00
RC3 Sandora Irvin 10.00 25.00
RC4 Kendra Wecker 10.00 25.00
RC5 Sancho Lyttle 8.00 20.00
RC6 Temeka Johnson 8.00 20.00
RC7 Kara Braxton 10.00 25.00
RC8 Katie Feenstra 10.00 25.00
RC9 Kristin Haynie 15.00 40.00
RC10 Loree Moore 8.00 20.00
RC11 Kristen Mann 8.00 20.00
RC12 Tanisha Wright 12.00 30.00
RC13 Shyra Ely 10.00 25.00
RC14 Roneeka Hodges 8.00 20.00
RC15 Yolanda Paige 10.00 25.00
RC16 Jacqueline Batteast 10.00 25.00
RC17 Angelina Williams 8.00 20.00
RC18 Chelsea Newton 12.00 30.00
RC19 Jessica Moore 10.00 25.00
RC20 Ashley Battle 10.00 25.00
RC21 Belinda Snell 8.00 20.00
RC22 Laurie Koehn 8.00 20.00
RC23 Caity Matter 8.00 20.00
RC24 Cathrine Kraayeveld 8.00 20.00
RC25 Edwige Lawson 8.00 20.00
RC26 Francesca Zara 8.00 20.00
RC27 Jamie Carey 8.00 20.00
RC28 Jenni Benningfield 8.00 20.00
RC29 Laura Summerton 8.00 20.00
RC30 Miao Li Jie 8.00 20.00
RC31 Natalia Vodopyanova 8.00 20.00
RC32 Sui Fei Fei 8.00 20.00
RC33 Suzy Batkovic 8.00 20.00

2005 WNBA Team Leaders

COMPLETE SET (13) 8.00 20.00
STATED ODDS 1:8
TL1 Feaster/Staley/Sutton-Brn .75 2.00
TL2 Sales/Whalen/McWilliams-F .75 2.00
TL3 Cash/Powell/Ford .50 1.25
TL4 Thompson/Swoopes/Snow 2.00 5.00
TL5 Tamika Catchings .50 1.25
TL6 Leslie/Teasley/Leslie 1.50 4.00
TL7 Smith/Darling/Williams 1.00 2.50
TL8 Hammon/Hammon/Baranova 2.00 5.00
TL9 Taurasi/Taurasi/Taylor 1.50 4.00
TL10 Griffith/Penicheiro/Griffith 1.00 2.50
TL11 Thomas/Johnson/Goodson .30 .75
TL12 Jackson/Bird/Jackson 1.50 4.00
TL13 Holdsclaw/Beard/Holdsclaw 2.00 5.00

2006 WNBA

COMPLETE SET (1-110) 10.00 25.00
1 Sacramento Monarchs TC .60 1.50
2 Lindsay Whalen .40 1.00
3 Tamika Whitmore .15 .40
4 Tangela Smith .15 .40
5 Alana Beard .20 .50
6 Chicago Sky TC .60 1.50
7 Vickie Johnson .25 .60
8 Kelly Schumacher .15 .40
9 Plenette Pierson .25 .60
10 Sheryl Swoopes 1.00 2.50
11 Los Angeles Sparks TC 1.00 2.50
12 Katie Douglas .25 .60
13 Nicole Ohlde .15 .40
14 Anna DeForge .15 .40
15 Swin Cash .25 .60
16 Kelly Miller .15 .40
17 Kara Lawson .30 .75
18 Shameka Christon .15 .40
19 Dominique Canty .25 .60
20 Sue Bird .75 2.00
21 Detroit Shock TC .75 2.00
22 Margo Dydek .25 .60
23 Shannon Johnson .15 .40
24 Chandi Jones .15 .40
25 Cheryl Ford .25 .60
26 Katie Feenstra .20 .50
27 Ashley Battle .20 .50
28 Tammy Sutton-Brown .15 .40
29 Deanna Jackson .15 .40
30 Yolanda Griffith .50 1.25
31 Minnesota Lynx TC .60 1.50
32 Asjha Jones .20 .50
33 Nicole Powell .20 .50
34 Sancho Lyttle .20 .50
35 Nykesha Sales .25 .60
36 LaToya Thomas .15 .40
37 Nikki Teasley .15 .40
38 Kara Braxton .20 .50
39 Rebekkah Brunson .15 .40
40 Lauren Jackson .75 2.00
41 Phoenix Mercury TC .75 2.00
42 Brooke Wyckoff .25 .60
43 Betty Lennox .30 .75
44 Tan White .20 .50
45 Dawn Staley .40 1.00
46 Washington Mystics TC .60 1.50
47 Svetlana Abrosimova .15 .40
48 Mandisa Stevenson .15 .40
49 Chantelle Anderson .15 .40
50 Deanna Nolan .15 .40
51 Indiana Fever TC .60 1.50
52 Le'coe Willingham .15 .40
53 Stacey Dales .25 .60
54 Tully Bevilaqua .15 .40
55 Ruth Riley .25 .60
56 Janell Burse .15 .40
57 Doneeka Hodges .15 .40
58 Stacey Lovelace .25 .60
59 Hamchetou Maiga-Ba .15 .40
60 Tamika Catchings .25 .60
61 New York Liberty TC 1.00 2.50
62 Jamie Carey .15 .40
63 Delisha Milton-Jones .15 .40
64 Elaine Powell .15 .40
65 Laurie Koehn .15 .40
66 Allison Feaster .20 .50
67 Shyra Ely .20 .50
68 Ticha Penicheiro .40 1.00
69 Laura Summerton .15 .40
70 Diana Taurasi .75 2.00
71 Seattle Storm TC 1.25 3.00
72 Kristin Haynie .25 .60
73 Iziane Castro Marques .15 .40
74 Tamika Williams .20 .50
75 Marie Ferdinand .15 .40
76 Belinda Snell .15 .40
77 Mwadi Mabika .15 .40
78 Loree Moore .15 .40
79 Crystal Robinson .15 .40
80 Taj McWilliams-Franklin .15 .40
81 Houston Comets TC .60 1.50
82 Kendra Wecker .20 .50
83 Janel McCarville .15 .40
84 Kristen Mann .15 .40
85 Chamique Holdsclaw 1.00 2.50
86 Tanisha Wright .20 .50
87 Kamila Vodichkova .15 .40
88 Christi Thomas .15 .40
89 Chasity Melvin .15 .40
90 Lisa Leslie .75 2.00
91 Tina Thompson .50 1.25
92 Connecticut Sun TC .75 2.00
93 Erin Buescher .15 .40
94 Chelsea Newton .25 .60
95 Katie Smith .50 1.25
96 Temeka Johnson .15 .40
97 Sheri Sam .15 .40
98 Wendy Palmer .40 1.00
99 DeMya Walker .15 .40
100 Becky Hammon 1.00 2.50
101 Charlotte Sting TC .60 1.50
102 Charlotte Smith .15 .40
103 Cathrine Kraayeveld .15 .40
104 Tamecka Dixon .25 .60
105 Michelle Snow .20 .50
106 Vanessa Hayden .15 .40
107 San Antonio Silver Stars TC .60 1.50
108 Checklist 1 .15 .40
109 Checklist 2 .15 .40
110 Checklist 3 .15 .40

2006 WNBA All-Star Jerseys

APPROXIMATELY ONE PER BOX
RE1 Alana Beard 2.00 5.00
RE2 Swin Cash 2.50 6.00
RE3 Tamika Catchings 2.50 6.00
RE4 Cheryl Ford 2.50 6.00
RE5 Becky Hammon 10.00 25.00
RE6 Taj McWilliams-Franklin 2.50 6.00
RE7 Deanna Nolan 2.50 6.00
RE8 Ruth Riley 2.50 6.00
RE9 Nykesha Sales 2.50 6.00
RW1 Sue Bird 8.00 20.00
RW2 Marie Ferdinand 2.50 6.00
RW3 Yolanda Griffith 5.00 12.00
RW4 Chamique Holdsclaw 6.00 15.00
RW5 Lauren Jackson 8.00 20.00
RW6 Lisa Leslie 8.00 20.00
RW7 Katie Smith 5.00 12.00
RW8 Michelle Snow 2.50 6.00
RW9 Sheryl Swoopes 6.00 15.00
RE10 Dawn Staley 4.00 10.00
RE11 Ann Wauters 2.50 6.00
RW10 Diana Taurasi 8.00 20.00
RW11 DeMya Walker 2.50 6.00

2006 WNBA Autographs

APPROXIMATELY TWO PER BOX
1 Temeka Johnson Action 5.00 12.00
2 Temeka Johnson ROY 5.00 12.00
3 Chelsea Newton 5.00 12.00
4 Katie Feenstra Action 5.00 12.00
5 Katie Feenstra Close Up 5.00 12.00
6 Tan White 5.00 12.00
7 Janel McCarville 5.00 12.00
8 Kara Braxton 5.00 12.00
9 Yolanda Griffith MVP 8.00 20.00
10 Yolanda Griffith Champs 8.00 20.00
11 Kristin Haynie 5.00 12.00
12 Rebekkah Brunson 5.00 12.00
13 Nicole Powell 5.00 12.00
14 Olympia Scott-Richardson 5.00 12.00
15 Erin Buescher 5.00 12.00
16 DeMya Walker 5.00 12.00
17 Kara Lawson 6.00 15.00
18 Ticha Penicheiro 8.00 20.00
19 Hamchetou Maiga 5.00 12.00
20 Chelsea Newton 5.00 12.00
21 John Whisenant 5.00 12.00
22 Sue Bird Assists 12.00 30.00
23 Sue Bird Action 12.00 30.00
24 Sue Bird Glamour 12.00 30.00
25 Marie Ferdinand Action 5.00 12.00
26 Marie Ferdinand Glamour 5.00 12.00
27 Anna DeForge Action 5.00 12.00
28 Anna DeForge Glamour 5.00 12.00
29 Diana Taurasi Action 10.00 25.00
30 Diana Taurasi Glamour 10.00 25.00
31 Becky Hammon Career 12.00 30.00
32 Becky Hammon Action 12.00 30.00
33 Becky Hammon Glamour 12.00 30.00
34 Nicole Ohlde 5.00 12.00
35 Svetlana Abrosimova 5.00 12.00
36 Chamique Holdsclaw Portrait 8.00 20.00
37 Chamique Holdsclaw Glamour 8.00 20.00
38 Tamika Catchings Defensive 5.00 12.00
39 Tamika Catchings Glamour 5.00 12.00
40 Tamika Catchings 2nd Team 5.00 12.00
41 Michelle Snow Action 5.00 12.00
42 Michelle Snow Glamour 5.00 12.00
43 S.Swoopes AS MVP 8.00 20.00
44 S.Swoopes WNBA 1st Team 8.00 20.00
45 Sheryl Swoopes MVP 8.00 20.00
46 Sheryl Swoopes Glamour 8.00 20.00
47 Deanna Nolan Glamour 5.00 12.00
48 Deanna Nolan Action 5.00 12.00
49 Ruth Riley Glamour 5.00 12.00
50 Ruth Riley Action 5.00 12.00
51 Cheryl Ford Glamour 5.00 12.00
52 Cheryl Ford Action 5.00 12.00
53 Taj McWilliams Award 5.00 12.00
54 Taj McWilliams Action 5.00 12.00
55 Taj McWilliams Glamour 5.00 12.00
56 Lindsey Whalen Album 10.00 25.00

2006 WNBA League Leaders

COMPLETE SET (9) 8.00 20.00
APPROXIMATELY TWO PER BOX
LL1 Swoopes/Jackson/Hldsclw 2.00 5.00
LL2 Bird/Johnson/Whalen 1.50 4.00
LL3 Ford/Jackson/Catchings 1.50 4.00
LL4 Catch/Swoopes/Leslie 2.00 5.00
LL5 Dydek/Layden/Leslie 1.50 4.00
LL6 Hammon/Arcain/Lennx 2.00 5.00
LL7 Koehn/Hodges/Lawson .60 1.50
LL8 Snow/Wauters/Walker .40 1.00
LL9 Ford/Jackson 1.50 4.00

2006 WNBA Patches

PRINT RUN 250 SER.#'d SETS
P1 Sheryl Swoopes 20.00 50.00
P2 Sue Bird 15.00 40.00
P3 Yolanda Griffith 10.00 25.00
P4 Lauren Jackson 15.00 40.00
P5 Deanna Nolan 3.00 8.00
P6 Tamika Catchings 5.00 12.00
P7 Diana Taurasi 15.00 40.00
P8 Taj McWilliams-Franklin 3.00 8.00
P9 Lisa Leslie 15.00 40.00
P10 Becky Hammon 20.00 50.00

2006 WNBA Playoffs

COMPLETE SET (10) 5.00 12.00
APPROXIMATELY SIX PER BOX
P1 Eastern Semi-Finals .75 2.00
P2 Eastern Semi-Finals .75 2.00
P3 Western Semi-Finals .75 2.00
P4 Western Semi-Finals .75 2.00
P5 Eastern Finals .75 2.00
P6 Western Finals .75 2.00
P7 WNBA Finals .75 2.00
P8 WNBA Finals .75 2.00
P9 WNBA Finals .75 2.00
P10 WNBA Finals .75 2.00

2006 WNBA Rookies

PRINT RUN 333 SER.#'d SETS
RC1 Seimone Augustus 5.00 12.00
RC2 Cappie Pondexter 8.00 20.00
RC3 Monique Currie 5.00 12.00
RC4 Sophia Young 5.00 12.00
RC5 Lisa Willis 3.00 8.00
RC6 Candice Dupree 6.00 15.00
RC7 Shona Thorburn 3.00 8.00
RC8 Tamara James 3.00 8.00
RC9 La'Tangela Atkinson 3.00 8.00
RC10 Tye'sha Fluker 3.00 8.00
RC11 Barbara Turner 5.00 12.00
RC12 Sherill Baker 3.00 8.00
RC13 Kim Smith 3.00 8.00
RC14 Ann Strother 8.00 20.00
RC15 Shanna Zolman 8.00 20.00
RC16 Ambrosia Anderson 3.00 8.00
RC17 Liz Shimek 3.00 8.00
RC18 Nikki Blue 4.00 10.00
RC19 Mistie Williams 4.00 10.00
RC20 LaToya Bond 3.00 8.00
RC21 Erin Phillips 3.00 8.00
RC22 Megan Mahoney 10.00 25.00
RC23 Scholanda Dorrell 3.00 8.00
RC24 Jennifer Lacy 3.00 8.00
RC25 Megan Duffy 4.00 10.00
RC26 Crystal Smith 3.00 8.00
RC27 Anastasia Hostaki 3.00 8.00
RC28 Emmeline Ndongue 3.00 8.00
RC29 Yelena Leuchanka 3.00 8.00
RC30 Kasha Terry 3.00 8.00
RC31 Brandi Davis 3.00 8.00
RC32 Christelle N'Garsanet 3.00 8.00
RC33 Brittany Wilkins 3.00 8.00
RC34 Zane Teilane 3.00 8.00

2006 WNBA Team Leaders

COMPLETE SET (13) 5.00 12.00
APPROXIMATELY FIVE PER BOX
L1 Smith/Staley/Sutton .50 1.25
L2 Sales/Whalen/Taj .50 1.25
L3 D.Nolan/C.Ford .30 .75
L4 S.Swoopes/M.Snow 1.25 3.00
L5 Tamika Catchings .30 .75
L6 Holdsclaw/Tsly/Leslie 1.25 3.00
L7 Smith/Harrower/Ohlde .60 1.50
L8 B.Hammon/E.Baranova 1.25 3.00
L9 D.Taurasi/Vodichkova 1.00 2.50
L10 Walker/Pnchro/Griffith .60 1.50
L11 Ferdinand/Jhnsn/Palmer .50 1.25
L12 L.Jackson/S.Bird 1.00 2.50
L13 Beard/Johnson/Melvin .25 .60

2006 WNBA Toppers

RANDOM INSERTS IN BOXES
NNO White JSY/Feenstra JSY 6.00 15.00
NNO Y.Griffith JSY AU/333 12.00 30.00
NNO S.Swoops JSY AU/150 12.00 30.00
NNO T.Johnson JSY AU/150 8.00 20.00

2007 WNBA

COMPLETE SET (90) 8.00 20.00
COMMON CARD (1-90) .20 .50
1 Diana Taurasi 1.00 2.50
2 Marie Ferdinand-Harris .20 .50
3 Megan Mahoney .50 1.25
4 Chasity Melvin .20 .50
5 Lauren Jackson 1.00 2.50
6 Tammy Sutton-Brown .20 .50
7 Nicole Ohlde .20 .50
8 Dominique Canty .30 .75
9 Alana Beard .25 .60
10 Tina Thompson .60 1.50
11 Janell Burse .20 .50
12 Asjha Jones .25 .60
13 Kelly Miller .20 .50
14 Tamika Catchings .30 .75
15 Kara Braxton .25 .60
16 Erika DeSouza RC .30 .75
17 Erin Thorn RC .20 .50
18 Tamika Whitmore .20 .50
19 Seimone Augustus .30 .75
20 Erin Buescher .20 .50
21 Nicole Powell .25 .60
22 Mwadi Mabika .20 .50
23 Cappie Pondexter .30 .75
24 Stacey Dales .30 .75
25 Temeka Johnson .20 .50
26 Nikki Teasley .20 .50
27 Katie Douglas .30 .75
28 Sheryl Swoopes 1.25 3.00
29 Anna DeForge .20 .50
30 Monique Currie .25 .60
31 Kelly Schumacher .20 .50
32 Becky Hammon 1.25 3.00
33 Tangela Smith .20 .50
34 Jia Perkins RC .25 .60
35 DeMya Walker .20 .50
36 DeLisha Milton-Jones .20 .50
37 Chamique Holdsclaw 1.25 3.00
38 Kelly Mazzante .30 .75
39 Tan White .25 .60
40 Penny Taylor .30 .75
41 Cheryl Ford .30 .75
42 Ebony Hoffman .25 .60
43 Vickie Johnson .30 .75
44 Loree Moore .20 .50
45 Candice Dupree .30 .75
46 Deanna Nolan .20 .50
47 Nakia Sanford .25 .60
48 Cathrine Kraayeveld .20 .50
49 Hamchetou Maiga-Ba .20 .50
50 Nykesha Sales .30 .75
51 Amber Jacobs .20 .50
52 Kara Lawson .40 1.00
53 Shannon Johnson .20 .50
54 Taj McWilliams-Franklin .20 .50
55 Sue Bird 1.00 2.50
56 Laurie Koehn .20 .50
57 Barbara Farris .20 .50
58 Tari Phillips .20 .50
59 Swin Cash .30 .75
60 Jamie Carey .20 .50
61 Kristen Mann .20 .50
62 Sherill Baker .20 .50
63 Lindsay Whalen .50 1.25
64 Yolanda Griffith .60 1.50
65 Shanna Zolman Crossley .40 1.00
66 Tully Bevilaqua .20 .50
67 Chelsea Newton .30 .75
68 Katie Smith .60 1.50
69 K.B. Sharp .20 .50
70 Iziane Castro Marques .20 .50
71 Rebekkah Brunson .20 .50
72 Sophia Young .25 .60
73 Shameka Christon .20 .50
74 Christi Thomas .20 .50
75 Coco Miller .20 .50
76 Plenette Pierson .30 .75
77 Ruth Riley .30 .75
78 Scholanda Robinson RC .30 .75
79 Murriel Page .25 .60
80 Ashley Battle .25 .60
81 Michelle Snow .25 .60
82 Betty Lennox .40 1.00
83 LaToya Thomas .20 .50
84 Katie Feenstra .25 .60
85 Kendra Wecker .25 .60
86 Margo Dydek .30 .75
87 Ticha Penicheiro .50 1.25
88 Kayte Christensen .20 .50
89 Lecoe Willingham .20 .50
90 Lisa Leslie 1.00 2.50

2007 WNBA Parallel

*PARALLEL: 2X TO 5X BASE HI
PRINT RUN 333 SER.#'d SETS

2007 WNBA 3-Case Incentive

1 N.Lieberman/A.Meyers AU 6.00 15.00

2007 WNBA All-WNBA Team

PRINT RUN 100 SER.#'d SETS
T01 Lisa Leslie 8.00 20.00
T02 Tamika Catchings 2.00 5.00
T03 Diana Taurasi 6.00 15.00
T04 Lauren Jackson 6.00 15.00
T05 Katie Douglas 2.00 5.00
T06 Alana Beard 1.50 4.00
T07 Cheryl Ford 2.00 5.00
T08 Taj McWilliams-Franklin 1.25 3.00
T09 Seimone Augustus 2.00 5.00
T10 Sheryl Swoopes 8.00 20.00

2007 WNBA Autographs

APPROXIMATE ODDS THREE PER BOX
1 Seimone Augustus 6.00 15.00
2 Cheryl Ford 6.00 15.00
3 Plenette Pierson 6.00 15.00
4 Kara Braxton 5.00 12.00
5 Angelina Williams 4.00 10.00
6 Jacqueline Batteast 5.00 12.00
7 Bill Laimbeer 8.00 20.00
8 Cheryl Miller 10.00 25.00
9 Ann Meyers 10.00 25.00
10 Sherill Baker 4.00 10.00
11 Shanna Zolman Crossley 8.00 20.00
12 Cappie Pondexter 6.00 15.00
13 Barbara Turner 5.00 12.00
14 Scholanda Robinson 6.00 15.00
15 Jennifer Lacy 4.00 10.00
17 Brooke Wyckoff 6.00 15.00
18 Katie Douglas 6.00 15.00
19 Asjha Jones 5.00 12.00
20 Le'coe Willingham 4.00 10.00
21 Margo Dydek 6.00 15.00
22 Tamika Whitmore 4.00 10.00
23 Sophia Young 5.00 12.00
24 Kristen Mann 4.00 10.00
25 Amber Jacobs 4.00 10.00
26 Shameka Christon 4.00 10.00
27 Cathrine Kraayeveld 4.00 10.00
28 Kelly Schumacher 4.00 10.00
29 Kendra Wecker 5.00 12.00
30 Chasity Melvin 4.00 10.00
31 Nakia Sanford 5.00 12.00
32 Jia Perkins 5.00 12.00
33 Dominique Canty 6.00 15.00
34 Candice Dupree 6.00 15.00
35 Mwadi Mabika 4.00 10.00
36 Katie Smith 10.00 25.00
37 Swin Cash 6.00 15.00
38 Ruth Riley 6.00 15.00
39 Elaine Powell 4.00 10.00
40 Deanna Nolan 4.00 10.00
MC Monique Currie 4.00 10.00
MT Mike Thibault 4.00 10.00
DMJ DeLisha Milton-Jones 4.00 10.00

2007 WNBA Highlights

COMPLETE SET (9) 10.00 25.00
RANDOM INSERTS IN PACKS
H1 L.Leslie 5,000th Point 2.50 6.00
H2 2006 All-Star Game .75 2.00
H3 D.Taurasi 47 Points 2.50 6.00
H4 D.Taurasi Scoring Mark 2.50 6.00
H5 S.Augustus RC Scoring .75 2.00
H6 C.Ford Rebound Total .75 2.00
H7 V.Chancellor 200 Wins .75 2.00
H8 Detroit Shock WNBA Title .75 2.00
H9 L.Leslie Ties MVP 2.50 6.00

2007 WNBA League Leaders

COMPLETE SET (9) 8.00 20.00
RANDOM INSERTS IN PACKS
LL1 Taurasi/Agstus/Leslie 1.50 4.00
LL2 Teasley/Temeka/Bird 1.50 4.00
LL3 Ford/Taj/Leslie 1.50 4.00
LL4 Catchings/Tully/Swoopes 2.00 5.00
LL5 Dydek/Suttn-Bwn/Jkson 1.50 4.00
LL6 Hammon/Smith/Whalen 2.00 5.00
LL7 Thorn/DeLisha/Staley .30 .75
LL8 Bschr/Jackson/Ngoyisa 1.50 4.00
LL9 Ford/Leslie/Taj 1.50 4.00

2007 WNBA Rookies

PRINT RUN 444 SER.#'d SETS
RC01 Lindsey Harding 4.00 10.00
RC02 Jessica Davenport 4.00 10.00
RC03 Armintie Price 4.00 10.00
RC04 Noelle Quinn 3.00 8.00
RC05 Tiffany Jackson 6.00 15.00
RC06 Bernice Mosby 5.00 12.00
RC07 Katie Gearlds 6.00 15.00
RC08 Ashley Shields 3.00 8.00
RC09 Alison Bales 6.00 15.00
RC10 Carla Thomas 4.00 10.00
RC11 Ivory Latta 4.00 10.00
RC12 Kamesha Hairston 3.00 8.00
RC13 Dee Davis 3.00 8.00
RC14 Eshaya Murphy 4.00 10.00
RC15 Shay Doron 8.00 20.00
RC16 Camille Little 5.00 12.00
RC17 Stephanie Raymond 3.00 8.00
RC18 Amy Sanders 3.00 8.00
RC19 Kathrin Ress 4.00 10.00
RC20 Sidney Spencer 10.00 25.00
RC21 Cori Chambers 4.00 10.00
RC22 Martina Weber 3.00 8.00
RC23 Gillian Goring 3.00 8.00
RC24 Claire Coggins 5.00 12.00
RC25 Navonda Moore 4.00 10.00
RC26 Marta Fernandez 3.00 8.00
RC27 Lindsay Bowen 3.00 8.00

2008 WNBA

COMPLETE SET (90) 8.00 20.00
COMP.ARCHIVE BOX SET 625.00 825.00
1 Lauren Jackson 1.00 2.50
2 Jia Perkins .25 .60
3 Swin Cash .30 .75
4 Tina Thompson .60 1.50
5 Katie Douglas .30 .75
6 Taj McWilliams-Franklin .20 .50
7 Nicole Ohlde .20 .50
8 Shameka Christon .20 .50
9 Nicole Powell .25 .60
10 Diana Taurasi 1.00 2.50
11 Yolanda Griffith .60 1.50
12 Nikki Blue .25 .60
13 Cathrine Kraayeveld .20 .50
14 Jamie Carey .20 .50
15 Deanna Nolan .20 .50
16 Sidney Spencer .50 1.25
17 Rebekkah Brunson .20 .50
18 Tamecka Dixon .30 .75
19 Becky Hammon 1.25 3.00
20 Tamika Catchings .30 .75
21 Alana Beard .25 .60
22 Betty Lennox .40 1.00
23 Tangela Smith .20 .50
24 Asjha Jones .25 .60
25 Temeka Johnson .20 .50
26 Elaine Powell .20 .50
27 Michelle Snow .25 .60
28 Marie Ferdinand-Harris .20 .50
29 Noelle Quinn .20 .50
30 Candice Dupree .30 .75
31 Kelly Miller .20 .50
32 Kara Lawson .40 1.00
33 Monique Currie .25 .60
34 Barbara Turner .25 .60
35 Katie Smith .60 1.50
36 Janel McCarville .20 .50
37 Katie Feenstra .25 .60
38 Tan White .25 .60
39 Tiffany Jackson .30 .75
40 Stacey Lovelace .30 .75
41 Kristen Rasmussen .20 .50
42 Nakia Sanford .25 .60
43 Murriel Page .25 .60
44 Helen Darling .20 .50
45 Seimone Augustus .30 .75
46 Brooke Wyckoff .30 .75
47 Tammy Sutton-Brown .20 .50
48 Iziane Castro .20 .50
49 Ticha Penicheiro .50 1.25
50 Cappie Pondexter .30 .75
51 Mwadi Mabika .20 .50
52 Erin Thorn .20 .50
53 Kim Smith .20 .50
54 Keisha Brown RC .30 .75
55 Lindsay Whalen .50 1.25
56 Alison Bales .40 1.00
57 Tamika Whitmore .20 .50
58 Sancho Lyttle .25 .60
59 Chasity Melvin .20 .50
60 Cheryl Ford .30 .75
61 Loree Moore .20 .50
62 Camille Little .25 .60
63 Le'coe Willingham .20 .50
64 Jessica Davenport .25 .60
65 DeLisha Milton-Jones .20 .50
66 Katie Gearlds .40 1.00
67 Shanna Crossley RC .40 1.00
68 Tamika Raymond RC .30 .75
69 Kara Braxton .25 .60
70 Sheryl Swoopes 1.25 3.00
71 Erika DeSouza .20 .50
72 Coco Miller .20 .50
73 Ivory Latta .25 .60
74 Ruth Riley .30 .75
75 Armintie Price .25 .60
76 Erin Buescher .20 .50
77 Plenette Pierson .30 .75
78 Chelsea Newton .30 .75
79 Vickie Johnson .30 .75
80 Lisa Leslie 1.00 2.50
81 Tully Bevilaqua .20 .50
82 Nykesha Sales .30 .75
83 Lindsey Harding .25 .60
84 Sophia Young .25 .60
85 Adrian Williams-Strong .20 .50
86 Shannon Johnson .20 .50
87 Dominique Canty .30 .75
88 Anna DeForge .20 .50
89 Kelly Mazzante .30 .75
90 Sue Bird 1.00 2.50
P1 All-Star Team Promo 2.00 5.00
P2 Candace Parker Promo 25.00 50.00

2008 WNBA 3-Case Incentive

TP Taurasi AU/Pondexter AU 20.00 50.00

2008 WNBA Autographs

APPROXIMATE ODDS 1:12
AM Ann Meyers-Drysdale 3.00 8.00
AP Armintie Price 3.00 8.00
AS Ann Strother 5.00 12.00
BH Becky Hammon 10.00 25.00
CL Crystal Langhorne 3.00 8.00
CL Camille Little 3.00 8.00
CP Candace Parker 25.00 60.00
CP Cappie Pondexter 4.00 10.00
CW Candice Wiggins 10.00 25.00
DT Diana Taurasi 12.00 30.00
ET Erin Thorn 2.50 6.00
JD Jessica Davenport 3.00 8.00
JD Jennifer Derevjanik 2.50 6.00
JL Jennifer Lacy 2.50 6.00
KM Kelly Mazzante 4.00 10.00
KM Kelly Miller 2.50 6.00
KS Kelly Schumacher 2.50 6.00
LH Laura Harper 2.50 6.00
LH Lindsey Harding 3.00 8.00
LJ Lauren Jackson 12.00 30.00
LM Loree Moore 2.50 6.00
LW Lindsay Whalen 6.00 15.00
NL Nancy Lieberman 8.00 20.00
NQ Noelle Quinn 2.50 6.00
OS Olympia Scott 2.50 6.00
SF Sylvia Fowles 4.00 10.00
SS Sidney Spencer 6.00 15.00
TJ Tiffany Jackson 4.00 10.00
TS Tangela Smith 2.50 6.00

2008 WNBA Case Topper

BALL PRINT RUN 250 SER.#'d SETS
2Q 2006 AS 2Q Ball/250 8.00 20.00
3Q 2006 AS 3Q Ball/250 8.00 20.00
NNO Kendra Wecker AU 4.00 10.00
NNO Monique Currie AU 4.00 10.00

2008 WNBA Relics

PRINT RUN 444 SER.#'d SETS
AS1 Cheryl Ford 2.50 6.00
AS2 Tamika Catchings 2.50 6.00
AS3 Anna DeForge 2.50 6.00
AS4 Deanna Nolan 2.50 6.00
AS5 Kara Braxton 2.50 6.00
AS6 Katie Douglas 3.00 8.00
AS7 Asjha Jones 2.50 6.00
AS8 Alana Beard 2.00 5.00
AS9 DeLisha Milton-Jones 2.50 6.00
AS10 Candice Dupree 2.50 6.00
AS11 Tammy Sutton-Brown 2.50 6.00
AS12 Diana Taurasi 8.00 20.00
AS13 Becky Hammon 10.00 25.00
AS14 Tina Thompson 4.00 10.00
AS15 Lauren Jackson 8.00 20.00
AS16 Yolanda Griffith 4.00 10.00
AS17 Taj McWilliams-Franklin 2.50 6.00
AS18 Seimone Augustus 8.00 20.00
AS19 Penny Taylor 4.00 10.00
AS20 Sophia Young 2.50 6.00
AS21 Cappie Pondexter 2.50 6.00
AS22 Kara Lawson 3.00 8.00
PM1 Cappie Pondexter 4.00 10.00
PM2 Diana Taurasi 12.00 30.00
PM3 Penny Taylor 4.00 10.00
PM4 Tangela Smith 4.00 10.00
PM5 Kelly Miller 4.00 10.00
PM6 Kelly Schumacher 4.00 10.00
PM7 Kelly Mazzante 4.00 10.00
PM8 Belinda Snell 4.00 10.00
RR1 Candace Parker 25.00 60.00
RR2 Sylvia Fowles 4.00 10.00
RR3 Candice Wiggins 10.00 25.00

2008 WNBA Rookies

PRINT RUN 444 SER.#'d SETS
R01 Candace Parker 12.00 30.00
R02 Sylvia Fowles 5.00 12.00
R03 Candice Wiggins 12.00 30.00
R04 Alexis Hornbuckle 8.00 20.00
R05 Matee Ajavon 4.00 10.00
R06 Crystal Langhorne 4.00 10.00
R07 Essence Carson 5.00 12.00
R08 Tamera Young 5.00 12.00
R09 Amber Holt 5.00 12.00
R10 Laura Harper 3.00 8.00
R11 Tasha Humphrey 3.00 8.00
R12 Ketia Swanier 3.00 8.00
R13 LaToya Pringle 3.00 8.00
R14 Erlana Larkins 5.00 12.00
R15 Charde Houston 5.00 12.00
R16 Nicky Anosike 8.00 20.00
R17 Jolene Anderson 5.00 12.00
R18 Khadijah Whittington 3.00 8.00
R19 Crystal Kelly 3.00 8.00
R20 Sandrine Gruda 3.00 8.00
R21 Shannon Bobbitt 3.00 8.00
R22 Brooke Smith 3.00 8.00
R23 Leilani Mitchell 3.00 8.00
R24 Erica White 3.00 8.00
R25 Kerri Gardin 3.00 8.00
R26 Olayinka Sanni 3.00 8.00
R27 Quianna Chaney 3.00 8.00
R28 Morenike Atunrase 3.00 8.00
R29 A'Quonesia Franklin 3.00 8.00

2008 WNBA USAB Womens National Team

STATED PRINT RUN 667 SER.#'d SETS
STATED PRINT RUN 444 SER.#'d SETS
G1 Seimone Augustus 1.00 2.50
G2 Sue Bird 3.00 8.00
G3 Tamika Catchings 1.00 2.50
G4 Sylvia Fowles 1.50 4.00
G5 Kara Lawson 1.25 3.00
G6 Lisa Leslie 3.00 8.00
G7 DeLisha Milton-Jones .60 1.50
G8 Candace Parker 4.00 10.00
G9 Cappie Pondexter 1.00 2.50
G10 Katie Smith 2.00 5.00
G11 Diana Taurasi 3.00 8.00
G12 Tina Thompson 2.00 5.00
USAB1 Parker/Fowles/Wiggins 3.00 8.00
USAB2 Taurasi/Bird/Cash 2.50 6.00
USAB3 Snow/Catch/Lawson 2.00 5.00
USAB4 Augustus/Ford/Swoopes 3.00 8.00
USAB5 Smith/Davenport/Douglas 2.00 5.00
USAB6 Beard/Milton-Jones/Moore 2.00 5.00
USAB7 McCarville/Jones/Whalen 2.00 5.00
USAB8 Leslie/Thomp/McW-Frank 2.50 6.00
USAB9 Brundon/Harding/Pondexter 2.00 5.00

2009 WNBA 1

COMPLETE BOX SET (17) 45.00 90.00
STATED PRINT RUN 399 SER.#'d SETS
1 Phoenix Mercury 4.00 10.00
4 Atlanta Dream 1.25 3.00
7 Detroit Shock 2.00 5.00
10 Los Angeles Sparks 4.00 10.00
13 Chicago Sky 1.50 4.00
16 Connecticut Sun 1.50 4.00

19 Seattle Storm 5.00 12.00
22 Washington Mystics 1.25 3.00
25 Indiana Fever 1.50 4.00
28 New York Liberty 1.25 3.00
31 Sacramento Monarchs 1.25 3.00
34 Minnesota Lynx 2.00 5.00
37 San Antonio Silver Stars 4.00 10.00
NNO Parker/Leslie Header 4.00 10.00

2009 WNBA 1 Autographs

INSERTED IN SERIES 1 BOX SET
CP Candace Parker 25.00 60.00
MA Matee Ajavon 4.00 10.00
NA Nicky Anosike 4.00 10.00

2009 WNBA 2 Rookies

COMPLETE BOX SET 45.00 90.00
PRINT RUN 499 SER.#'d SETS
BOX SET INCLUDES FIVE AUTOS
1 Angel McCoughtry 6.00 15.00
2 Marissa Coleman 5.00 12.00
3 Kristi Toliver 6.00 15.00
4 Renee Montgomery 5.00 12.00
5 DeWanna Bonner 6.00 15.00
6 Briann January 3.00 8.00
7 Courtney Paris 2.50 6.00
8 Kia Vaughn 3.00 8.00
9 Quanitra Holligsworth 3.00 8.00
10 Chante Black 3.00 8.00
11 Shavonte Zellous 5.00 12.00
12 Ashley Walker 3.00 8.00
13 Lindsay Wisdom-Hylton 4.00 10.00

2009 WNBA 2 Rookies Autographs

INSERTED IN SERIES 2 BOX SET
AM Angel McCoughtry 6.00 15.00
CP Courtney Paris 2.50 6.00
KT Kristi Toliver 6.00 15.00
MC Marissa Coleman 5.00 12.00
RM Renee Montgomery 5.00 12.00

2009 WNBA 3 All-Stars

COMPLETE BOX SET 60.00 120.00
BOX SET INCL. 4 RCs AND 5 AUTOS
AS1 S.Bird/K.Douglas 5.00 12.00
AS2 B.Hammon/A.Beard 5.00 12.00
AS3 T.Thompson/S.Fowles 2.50 6.00
AS4 S.Cash/C.Dupree 1.25 3.00
AS5 L.Jackson/T.Catchings 3.00 8.00
AS6 D.Taurasi/A.Jones 4.00 10.00
AS7 N.Anosike/K.Smith 2.00 5.00
AS8 C.Pondexter/E.DeSouza 1.25 3.00
AS9 N.Powell/S.Christon 1.25 3.00
AS10 S.Young/J.Perkins 1.25 3.00
AS11 C.Houston/S.Lyttle 1.25 3.00

2009 WNBA 3 Rookies

PRINT RUN 499 SER.#'d SETS
RC14 Megan Frazee 4.00 10.00
RC15 Anete Jekobsone 3.00 8.00
RC16 Rashanda McCants 4.00 10.00
RC17 Shalee Lehning 6.00 15.00

2009 WNBA 3 Rookies Autographs

INSERTED IN SERIES 3 BOX SET
BJ Briann January 4.00 10.00
CB Chante Black 4.00 10.00
DB DeWanna Bonner 8.00 20.00
MF Megan Frazee 5.00 12.00
QH Quanitra Hollingsworth 4.00 10.00
SZ Shavonte Zellous 6.00 15.00

2009 WNBA Autographs Three-Set Incentive

ANNOUNCED PRINT RUN 133 SETS
CP Candace Parker MVP 30.00 80.00

2010 WNBA

COMPLETE SET (36) 15.00 40.00
COMPLETE FACT.BOX 45.00 90.00
ANNOUNCED PRINT RUN 675 SETS
1 A.McCoughtry/I.Castro-Marques 1.00 2.50
2 S.Lyttle/A.Bales 1.25 3.00
3 E.deSouza/A.Price .75 2.00
4 S.Christon/D.Canty 1.00 2.50
5 S.Fowles/J.Perkins 1.25 3.00
6 C.Kraayeveld/E.Thorn .60 1.50
7 A.Jones/T.White .75 2.00
8 K.Lawson/S.Gruda 1.25 3.00
9 R.Montgomery/A.Jekabsone-Zogota .60 1.50
10 T.Catchings/E.Hoffman 1.50 4.00
11 K.Douglas/T.Sutton-Brown 1.00 2.50
12 B.January/E.Murphy .75 2.00
13 C.Parker/T.Thompson 4.00 10.00
14 D.Milton-Jones/B.Lennox 1.25 3.00
15 N.Quinn/K.Toliver 1.00 2.50
16 S.Augustus/N.Anosike 2.00 5.00
17 C.Houston/C.Wiggins 2.00 5.00
18 L.Whalen/R.McCants 1.50 4.00
19 C.Pondexter/J.McCarville 1.25 3.00
20 E.Carson/McWilliams-Franklin 1.00 2.50
21 N.Powell/L.Mitchell .75 2.00
22 D.Taurasi/T.Smith 4.00 10.00
23 C.Dupree/P.Taylor 1.00 2.50
24 D.Bonner/T.Johnson .60 1.50
25 S.Young/M.Snow .75 2.00
26 B.Hammon/R.Riley 4.00 10.00
27 E.Lawson-Wade/C.Holdsclaw 4.00 10.00
28 S.Bird/S.Cash 5.00 12.00
29 L.Jackson/T.Wright 3.00 8.00
30 C.Little/L.Willingham .60 1.50
31 K.Braxton/S.Crossley 1.25 3.00
32 C.Black/S.Robinson .60 1.50
33 A.Holt/A.Hornbuckle 1.25 3.00
34 K.Smith/L.Harding 2.00 5.00
35 C.Langhorne/M.Coleman 1.00 2.50
36 M.Currie/N.Sanford .75 2.00

2010 WNBA Autographs

TWO RANDOM AUTOS PER SET
AH Ashley Houts 4.00 10.00
DM Danielle McCray 4.00 10.00
MW Monica Wright 6.00 15.00
TC Tina Charles 12.00 30.00

2010 WNBA Diana Taurasi MVP Bonus

RANDOM INSERTS IN SETS
NNO Diana Taurasi MVP/250 8.00 20.00

2010 WNBA Rookies

COMPLETE SET (12) 60.00 120.00
PRINT RUN 250 SER.#'d SETS
FOUR RANDOM ROOKIES PER SET
R1 Tina Charles 15.00 40.00
R2 Monica Wright 8.00 20.00
R3 Kelsey Griffin 8.00 20.00
R4 Epiphanny Prince 6.00 15.00
R5 Jayne Appel
R6 Jacinta Monroe 5.00 12.00
R7 Andrea Riley 5.00 12.00
R8 Alison Lacey 5.00 12.00
R9 Jene Morris 6.00 15.00
R10 Natasha Lacy 6.00 15.00
R11 Kalana Greene 6.00 15.00
R12 Marion Jones 10.00 25.00

2011 WNBA

STATED PRINT RUN 225 SER.#'d SETS
1 Diana Taurasi 6.00 15.00
2 Cappie Pondexter 2.00 5.00
3 Angel McCoughtry 2.50 6.00
4 Candace Parker 5.00 12.00
5 Lauren Jackson 6.00 15.00
6 Tamika Catchings 2.00 5.00
7 Sylvia Fowles 2.00 5.00
8 Iziane Castro-Marques 1.25 3.00
9 Seimone Augustus 2.00 5.00
10 Tina Thompson 4.00 10.00
11 Crystal Langhorne 1.50 4.00
12 Penny Taylor 2.50 6.00
13 Candice Dupree 2.00 5.00
14 Tina Charles 4.00 10.00
15 DeLisha Milton-Jones 1.25 3.00
16 Sophia Young 1.50 4.00
17 Becky Hammon 8.00 20.00
18 Monique Currie 1.50 4.00
19 Swin Cash 2.00 5.00
20 Candice Wiggins 4.00 10.00
21 Katie Douglas 2.00 5.00
22 Renee Montgomery 1.50 4.00
23 Sancho Lyttle 1.50 4.00
24 Lindsay Whalen 3.00 8.00
25 Ivory Latta 1.50 4.00
26 Erika DeSouza 1.25 3.00
27 Lindsey Harding 1.50 4.00
28 DeWanna Bonner 2.50 6.00
29 Scholanda Robinson 1.25 3.00
30 Charde Houston 2.00 5.00
31 Matee Ajavon 1.50 4.00
32 Rebekkah Brunson 1.25 3.00
33 Monica Wright 2.00 5.00
34 Sue Bird 6.00 15.00
35 Asjha Jones 1.50 4.00
36 Jia Perkins 1.50 4.00
37 Taj McWilliams-Franklin 1.25 3.00
38 Michelle Snow 1.50 4.00
39 Noelle Quinn 1.25 3.00
40 Camille Little 1.50 4.00
41 Tan White 1.50 4.00
42 Kara Braxton 1.50 4.00
43 Epiphanny Prince 1.50 4.00
44 Plenette Pierson 2.00 5.00
45 Kelsey Griffin 2.00 5.00
46 Katie Smith 4.00 10.00
47 Leilani Mitchell 1.25 3.00
48 Nicole Powell 1.50 4.00
49 Tangela Smith 1.25 3.00
50 Temeka Johnson 1.25 3.00
51 Tanisha Wright 1.50 4.00
52 Nicky Anosike 2.00 5.00
53 Dominique Canty 2.00 5.00
54 Marie Ferdinand-Harris 1.25 3.00
55 Essence Carson 1.50 4.00
56 Amber Holt 2.00 5.00
57 Kristi Toliver 2.00 5.00
58 Kelly Miller 1.25 3.00
59 Kara Lawson 2.50 6.00
60 Tammy Sutton-Brown 1.25 3.00
61 Ebony Hoffman 1.50 4.00
62 Ticha Penicheiro 3.00 8.00
63 Sheryl Swoopes 4.00 10.00

2011 WNBA 3-Box Incentive Autographs

NNO Tina Charles/55 50.00 120.00

2011 WNBA Autographs

STATED ODDS THREE PER PACK
NNO CARDS LISTED BY INITIALS
AH Amber Harris 3.00 8.00
AM Angel McCoughtry 6.00 15.00
CP Cappie Pondexter 3.00 8.00
CV Courtney Vandersloot 8.00 20.00
DR Danielle Robinson 4.00 10.00
DT Diana Taurasi 10.00 25.00
JM1 Jene Morris 3.00 8.00
JM2 Jacinta Monroe 3.00 8.00
JP Jeanette Pohlen 5.00 12.00
JT Jasmine Thomas 3.00 8.00
KG1 Kelsey Griffin 5.00 12.00
KG2 Kalana Greene 3.00 8.00
KP Kayla Pedersen 4.00 10.00
MM1 Maya Moore 40.00 100.00
MM2 M.Moore VAR Hold Jsy 100.00 200.00
PT Penny Taylor 8.00 20.00
TP Ta'Shia Phillips 3.00 8.00
VD Victoria Dunlap 3.00 8.00

2011 WNBA Rookies

STATED PRINT RUN 225 SER.#'d SETS
R1 Maya Moore 25.00 60.00
R2 Elizabeth Cambage 8.00 20.00
R3 Courtney Vandersloot 6.00 15.00
R4 Amber Harris 6.00 15.00
R5 Jantel Lavender 8.00 20.00
R6 Danielle Robinson 6.00 15.00
R7 Kayla Pedersen 6.00 15.00
R8 Ta'Shia Phillips 5.00 12.00
R9 Jeanette Pohlen 6.00 15.00
R10 Victoria Dunlap 5.00 12.00
R11 Jasmine Thomas 10.00 25.00
R12 Danielle Adams 6.00 15.00

2012 WNBA

COMPLETE FACT.SET (111) 60.00 150.00
COMPLETE SET (96) 30.00 80.00
ANNOUNCED PRINT RUN 400 SETS
1 Angel McCoughtry 1.50 4.00
2 Armintie Price 1.00 2.50
3 Cathrine Kraayeveld .75 2.00
4 Ketia Swanier .75 2.00
5 Lindsey Harding 1.00 2.50
6 Sancho Lyttle 1.00 2.50
7 Yelena Leuchanka .75 2.00
8 Courtney Vandersloot 1.00 2.50
9 Epiphanny Prince 1.00 2.50
10 Eshaya Murphy 1.00 2.50
11 Le'coe Willingham .75 2.00
12 Ruth Riley 1.25 3.00
13 Swin Cash 1.25 3.00
14 Sylvia Fowles 1.25 3.00
15 Tamera Young 1.00 2.50
16 Ticha Penicheiro 2.00 5.00
17 Allison Hightower RC 2.00 5.00
18 Asjha Jones 1.00 2.50
19 Danielle McCray .75 2.00
20 Kalana Greene 1.00 2.50
21 Kara Lawson 1.50 4.00
22 Mistie Mims RC 2.00 5.00
23 Renee Montgomery 1.00 2.50
24 Tan White 1.00 2.50
25 Tina Charles 2.50 6.00
26 Briann January .75 2.00
27 Erin Phillips .75 2.00
28 Jeanette Pohlen 1.00 2.50
29 Jessica Davenport 1.00 2.50
30 Katie Douglas 1.25 3.00
31 Shavonte Zellous 1.00 2.50
32 Tamika Catchings 1.25 3.00
33 Tammy Sutton-Brown .75 2.00
34 Alana Beard 1.00 2.50
35 Candace Parker 3.00 8.00
36 Delisha Milton-Jones .75 2.00
37 Ebony Hoffman 1.00 2.50
38 Jantel Lavender 1.00 2.50
39 Kristi Toliver 1.25 3.00
40 Marissa Coleman 1.00 2.50
41 Candice Wiggins 2.50 6.00
42 Jessica Adair RC 2.00 5.00
43 Lindsay Whalen 2.00 5.00
44 Maya Moore 4.00 10.00
45 Monica Wright 1.25 3.00
46 Rebekkah Brunson .75 2.00
47 Seimone Augustus 1.25 3.00
48 Taj McWilliams-Franklin .75 2.00
49 Cappie Pondexter 1.25 3.00
50 DeMya Walker .75 2.00
51 Essence Carson 1.00 2.50
52 Kara Braxton 1.00 2.50
53 Kelly Miller .75 2.00
54 Kia Vaughn .75 2.00
55 Leilani Mitchell .75 2.00
56 Nicole Powell 1.00 2.50
57 Plenette Pierson 1.25 3.00
58 Alexis Gray-Lawson RC 2.00 5.00
59 Alexis Hornbuckle 1.50 4.00
60 Candice Dupree 1.25 3.00
61 Charde Houston 1.25 3.00
62 DeWanna Bonner 1.50 4.00
63 Diana Taurasi 4.00 10.00
64 Nakia Sanford 1.00 2.50
65 Becky Hammon 5.00 12.00
66 Danielle Adams 1.00 2.50
67 Danielle Robinson 1.00 2.50
68 Jayne Appel
69 Jia Perkins 1.00 2.50
70 Shameka Christon .75 2.00
71 Sophia Young 1.00 2.50
72 Tangela Smith .75 2.00
73 Ann Wauters 1.00 2.50
74 Camille Little 1.00 2.50
75 Ewelina Kobryn RC 2.00 5.00
76 Katie Smith 2.50 6.00
77 Lauren Jackson 4.00 10.00
78 Sue Bird 4.00 10.00
79 Tanisha Wright 1.00 2.50
80 Tina Thompson 2.50 6.00
81 Chante Black .75 2.00
82 Ivory Latta 1.00 2.50
83 Courtney Paris 1.00 2.50
84 Jennifer Lacy .75 2.00
85 Kayla Pedersen 1.00 2.50
86 Liz Cambage 1.25 3.00
87 Scholanda Dorrell .75 2.00
88 Temeka Johnson .75 2.00
89 Ashley Robinson .75 2.00
90 Crystal Langhorne 1.00 2.50
91 Shannon Bobbitt .75 2.00
92 Jasmine Thomas 1.25 3.00
93 Matee Ajavon 1.00 2.50
94 Michelle Snow 1.00 2.50
95 Monique Currie 1.00 2.50
96 Noelle Quinn .75 2.00
NNO N.Ogwumike AU 10.00 25.00

2012 WNBA Rookies

COMPLETE SET (14) 20.00 50.00
ANNOUNCED PRINT RUN 400 SETS
R1 Nnemkadi Ogwumike 5.00 12.00
R2 Shekinna Stricklen 4.00 10.00
R3 Devereaux Peters 4.00 10.00
R4 Glory Johnson 5.00 12.00
R5 Shenise Johnson 4.00 10.00
R6 Samantha Prahalis 6.00 15.00
R7 Kelley Cain 4.00 10.00
R8 Natalie Novosel 5.00 12.00
R9 Sasha Goodlett 2.50 6.00
R10 Riquna Williams 2.50 6.00
R11 Avery Warley 2.50 6.00
R12 Tiffany Hayes 5.00 12.00
R13 Aneika Henry 2.50 6.00
R14 April Sykes 2.50 6.00

2013 WNBA

COMP.FACT.SET (102) 60.00 150.00
COMP.SET w/o AU's (100) 40.00 100.00
ANNOUNCED PRINT RUN 500 SETS
1 Alex Bentley RC 2.00 5.00
2 Aneika Henry .75 2.00
3 Angel McCoughtry 1.50 4.00
4 Armintie Herrington .75 2.00
5 Erika de Souza .75 2.00
6 Jasmine Thomas 1.25 3.00
7 Sancho Lyttle 1.00 2.50
8 Tiffany Hayes 1.25 3.00
9 Allie Quigley RC 3.00 8.00
10 Carolyn Swords RC 2.00 5.00
11 Courtney Vandersloot 1.00 2.50
12 Elena Delle Donne RC 20.00 50.00
13 Epiphanny Prince 1.00 2.50
14 Swin Cash 1.25 3.00
15 Sylvia Fowles 1.25 3.00
16 Tamera Young 1.00 2.50
17 Allison Hightower .75 2.00
18 Kalana Greene 1.00 2.50
19 Kara Lawson 1.50 4.00
20 Kelsey Griffin 1.00 2.50
21 Mistie Bass .75 2.00
22 Renee Montgomery 1.00 2.50
23 Tan White 1.00 2.50
24 Tina Charles 2.50 6.00
25 Briann January .75 2.00
26 Erlana Larkins 1.00 2.50
27 Jessica Breland .75 2.00
28 Karima Christmas 1.25 3.00
29 Katie Douglas 1.25 3.00
30 Layshia Clarendon RC 2.00 5.00
31 Shavonte Zellous 1.00 2.50
32 Tamika Catchings 1.25 3.00
33 Alana Beard 1.00 2.50
34 Candace Parker 3.00 8.00
35 Ebony Hoffman 1.00 2.50
36 Farhiya Abdi RC 2.00 5.00
37 Jantel Lavender 1.00 2.50
38 Kristi Toliver 1.25 3.00
39 Lindsey Harding 1.00 2.50
40 Marissa Coleman 1.00 2.50
41 Nneka Ogwumike 1.50 4.00
42 Amber Harris .75 2.00
43 Devereaux Peters 1.00 2.50
44 Janel McCarville .75 2.00
45 Lindsay Whalen 2.00 5.00
46 Maya Moore 4.00 10.00
47 Monica Wright 1.25 3.00
48 Rebekkah Brunson .75 2.00
49 Seimone Augustus 1.25 3.00
50 Alex Montgomery .75 2.00
51 Cappie Pondexter 1.25 3.00
52 Essence Carson 1.00 2.50
53 Kamiko Williams RC 2.00 5.00
54 Kara Braxton 1.00 2.50
55 Katie Smith 2.50 6.00
56 Kelsey Bone RC 2.00 5.00
57 Leilani Mitchell .75 2.00
58 Plenette Pierson 1.25 3.00
59 Toni Young RC 2.00 5.00
60 Briana Gilbreath .75 2.00
61 Brittney Griner RC 10.00 25.00
62 Candice Dupree 1.25 3.00
63 Charde Houston 1.25 3.00
64 DeWanna Bonner 1.50 4.00
65 Diana Taurasi 4.00 10.00
66 Lynetta Kizer .75 2.00
67 Penny Taylor 1.25 3.00
68 Becky Hammon 5.00 12.00
69 Danielle Adams 1.00 2.50
70 Danielle Robinson 1.00 2.50
71 Davellyn Whyte RC 2.00 5.00
72 Delisha Milton-Jones .75 2.00
73 Jayne Appel
74 Jia Perkins 1.00 2.50
75 Shameka Christon .75 2.00
76 Shenise Johnson 1.00 2.50
77 Alysha Clark RC 2.50 6.00
78 Camille Little 1.00 2.50
79 Noelle Quinn .75 2.00
80 Shekinna Stricklen .75 2.00
81 Sue Bird 4.00 10.00
82 Tanisha Wright 1.00 2.50
83 Temeka Johnson .75 2.00
84 Tina Thompson 2.50 6.00
85 Angel Goodrich RC 2.00 5.00
86 Candice Wiggins 2.50 6.00
87 Glory Johnson 1.25 3.00
88 Liz Cambage 1.25 3.00
89 Nicole Powell 1.00 2.50
90 Riquna Williams .75 2.00
91 Roneeka Hodges .75 2.00
92 Skylar Diggins RC 8.00 20.00
93 Crystal Langhorne 1.00 2.50
94 Ivory Latta 1.00 2.50
95 Kia Vaughn .75 2.00
96 Matee Ajavon 1.00 2.50
97 Michelle Snow 1.00 2.50
98 Monique Currie 1.00 2.50
99 Tayler Hill RC 4.00 10.00
100 Tierra Ruffin-Pratt RC 2.50 6.00

2013 WNBA Autographs

ANNOUNCED PRINT RUN 500 SETS
BG Brittney Griner 20.00 50.00
EDD Elena Delle Donne 30.00 80.00

2014 WNBA

COMP.FACT.SET (104) 100.00 200.00
COMP.SET w/o AU's (100) 40.00 100.00
ANNOUNCED PRINT RUN 500 SETS
1 Aneika Henry .75 2.00
2 Angel McCoughtry 1.50 4.00
3 Erika de Souza .75 2.00
4 Jasmine Thomas 1.25 3.00
5 Matee Ajavon 1.00 2.50
6 Sancho Lyttle 1.00 2.50
7 Shoni Schimmel RC 8.00 20.00
8 Tiffany Hayes 1.25 3.00
9 Allie Quigley 1.00 2.50
10 Courtney Vandersloot 1.00 2.50
11 Elena Delle Donne 8.00 20.00
12 Jamierra Faulkner RC 3.00 8.00
13 Jessica Breland .75 2.00
14 Markeisha Gatling .75 2.00
15 Sasha Goodlett .75 2.00
16 Sylvia Fowles 1.25 3.00
17 Tamera Young 1.00 2.50
18 Alex Bentley 1.25 3.00
19 Allison Hightower .75 2.00
20 Alyssa Thomas RC 4.00 10.00
21 Chiney Ogwumike RC 4.00 10.00
22 Katie Douglas 1.25 3.00
23 Kelsey Bone .75 2.00
24 Kelsey Griffin 1.00 2.50
25 Renee Montgomery 1.00 2.50
26 Briann January .75 2.00
27 Erlana Larkins 1.00 2.50
28 Karima Christmas 1.25 3.00
29 Maggie Lucas RC 3.00 8.00
30 Marissa Coleman 1.00 2.50
31 Natasha Howard RC 3.00 8.00
32 Shavonte Zellous 1.00 2.50
33 Tamika Catchings 1.25 3.00
34 Alana Beard 1.00 2.50
35 Armintie Herrington .75 2.00
36 Candice Wiggins 2.50 6.00
37 Candace Parker 3.00 8.00
38 Jantel Lavender 1.00 2.50
39 Kristi Toliver 1.25 3.00
40 Lindsey Harding 1.00 2.50
41 Nneka Ogwumike 1.50 4.00
42 Asia Taylor RC 2.00 5.00
43 Damiris Dantas RC 2.00 5.00
44 Janel McCarville .75 2.00
45 Lindsay Whalen 2.00 5.00
46 Lindsey Moore 6.00 15.00
47 Maya Moore 4.00 10.00
48 Seimone Augustus 1.25 3.00
49 Tan White 1.00 2.50
50 Anna Cruz RC 2.00 5.00
51 Alex Montgomery .75 2.00
52 Cappie Pondexter 1.25 3.00
53 Delisha Milton-Jones .75 2.00
54 Essence Carson 1.00 2.50
55 Plenette Pierson 1.25 3.00
56 Sugar Rodgers RC 3.00 8.00
57 Tina Charles 2.50 6.00
58 Anete Jekabsone-Zogota .75 2.00
59 Brittney Griner 4.00 10.00
60 Candice Dupree 1.25 3.00
61 DeWanna Bonner 1.50 4.00
62 Diana Taurasi 4.00 10.00
63 Erin Phillips .75 2.00
64 Mistie Bass .75 2.00
65 Penny Taylor 1.25 3.00
66 Becky Hammon 5.00 12.00
67 Danielle Adams 1.00 2.50
68 Danielle Robinson 1.00 2.50
69 Jayne Appel
70 Jia Perkins 1.00 2.50
71 Kayla McBride RC 4.00 10.00
72 Shameka Christon .75 2.00
73 Shenise Johnson 1.00 2.50
74 Sophia Young-Malcolm 1.00 2.50
75 Alysha Clark 1.00 2.50
76 Angel Robinson RC 1.25 3.00
77 Camille Little 1.00 2.50
78 Crystal Langhorne 1.00 2.50
79 Jenna O'Hea .75 2.00
80 Noelle Quinn .75 2.00
81 Shekinna Stricklen .75 2.00
82 Sue Bird 4.00 10.00
83 Tanisha Wright 1.00 2.50
84 Temeka Johnson .75 2.00
85 Courtney Paris 1.00 2.50
86 Glory Johnson 1.25 3.00
87 Jordan Hooper RC 2.00 5.00
88 Odyssey Sims RC 4.00 10.00
89 Riquna Williams .75 2.00
90 Roneeka Hodges .75 2.00
91 Skylar Diggins 2.50 6.00
92 Bria Hartley RC 2.50 6.00
93 Emma Meesseman RC 4.00 10.00
94 Ivory Latta 1.00 2.50
95 Jelena Milovanovic RC 1.25 3.00
96 Kara Lawson 1.50 4.00
97 Kia Vaughn .75 2.00
98 Monique Currie 1.00 2.50
99 Stefanie Dolson RC 3.00 8.00
100 Tierra Ruffin-Pratt 1.00 2.50

2014 WNBA Autographs

FOUR AUTOS PER FACTORY SET
ANNCD PRINT RUN OF 500 FACTORY SETS
BH Bria Hartley 8.00 20.00
CO Chiney Ogwumike 8.00 20.00
NO Nneka Ogwumike 8.00 20.00
SD Stefanie Dolson 8.00 20.00

2014 WNBA Dual Autographs

THREE SET PURCHASE INCENTIVE
CNO C.Ogwumike/N.Ogwumike 25.00 60.00

2015 WNBA

COMP.FACT.SET (103) 100.00 150.00
COMP.SET w/o AU's (100) 40.00 100.00
ANNOUNCED PRINT RUN 500 SETS
1 Aneika Henry .75 2.00
2 Angel McCoughtry 1.50 4.00
3 Erica Wheeler RC 3.00 8.00
4 Erika de Souza .75 2.00
5 Matee Ajavon 1.00 2.50
6 Sancho Lyttle 1.00 2.50
7 Shoni Schimmel 3.00 8.00
8 Tiffany Hayes 1.25 3.00
9 Allie Quigley 1.00 2.50
10 Betnijah Laney RC 4.00 10.00
11 Cappie Pondexter 1.25 3.00
12 Courtney Vandersloot 1.00 2.50
13 Elena Delle Donne 8.00 20.00
14 Jessica Breland .75 2.00
15 Sasha Goodlett .75 2.00
16 Tamera Young 1.00 2.50
17 Alex Bentley 1.25 3.00
18 Alyssa Thomas 1.25 3.00
19 Camille Little 1.00 2.50
20 Chelsea Gray RC 2.00 5.00
21 Chiney Ogwumike 1.25 3.00
22 Elizabeth Williams RC 3.00 8.00
23 Jasmine Thomas 1.25 3.00
24 Kelsey Bone .75 2.00
25 Shekinna Stricklen .75 2.00
26 Briann January 1.00 2.50
27 Layshia Clarendon 1.25 3.00
28 Lynetta Kizer 1.00 2.50
29 Maggie Lucas 1.25 3.00
30 Marissa Coleman 1.00 2.50
31 Natalie Achonwa RC 4.00 10.00
32 Shavonte Zellous 1.00 2.50
33 Tamika Catchings 1.25 3.00
34 Alana Beard 1.00 2.50
35 Erin Phillips .75 2.00
36 Farhiya Abdi 1.00 2.50
37 Jantel Lavender 1.00 2.50
38 Jennifer Lacy 1.00 2.50
39 Candace Parker 3.00 8.00
40 Marianna Tolo RC 3.00 8.00
41 Nneka Ogwumike 1.50 4.00
42 Asjha Jones 1.25 3.00
43 Damiris Dantas 1.25 3.00
44 Jennifer O'Neill RC 3.00 8.00
45 Lindsay Whalen 2.00 5.00
46 Maya Moore 4.00 10.00
47 Rebekkah Brunson 1.00 2.50
48 Seimone Augustus 1.25 3.00
49 Tricia Liston 1.00 2.50
50 Brittany Boyd RC 2.50 6.00
51 Candice Wiggins 2.50 6.00
52 Carolyn Swords .75 2.00
53 Essence Carson 1.00 2.50
54 Kiah Stokes RC 3.00 8.00
55 Sugar Rodgers 1.25 3.00
56 Swin Cash 1.25 3.00
57 Tanisha Wright 1.00 2.50
58 Tina Charles 2.50 6.00
59 Alex Harden RC 3.00 8.00
60 Brittney Griner 4.00 10.00
61 Candice Dupree 1.25 3.00
62 Cayla Francis RC 3.00 8.00
63 DeWanna Bonner 1.50 4.00
64 Leilani Mitchell .75 2.00
65 Mistie Bass .75 2.00
66 Monique Currie 1.00 2.50
67 Danielle Robinson 1.00 2.50
68 Dearica Hamby RC 2.50 6.00
69 Jayne Appel
70 Jia Perkins 1.00 2.50
71 Kayla Alexander RC 2.50 6.00
72 Kayla McBride 1.50 4.00
73 Sophia Young-Malcolm 1.25 3.00
74 Sydney Colson RC 2.00 5.00
75 Abby Bishop 1.25 3.00
76 Alysha Clark 1.00 2.50
77 Crystal Langhorne 1.00 2.50
78 Jenna O'Hea .75 2.00
79 Jewell Loyd RC 5.00 12.00
80 Kaleena Mosqueda-Lewis RC 2.00 5.00
81 Quanitra Hollingsworth .75 2.00
82 Ramu Tokashiki RC 2.00 5.00
83 Renee Montgomery 1.00 2.50
84 Sue Bird 4.00 10.00
85 Amanda Zahui B. RC 2.50 6.00
86 Courtney Paris 1.00 2.50
87 Jordan Hooper .75 2.00
88 Karima Christmas 1.25 3.00
89 Odyssey Sims 1.25 3.00
90 Plenette Pierson 1.25 3.00
91 Riquna Williams .75 2.00
92 Skylar Diggins 2.50 6.00
93 Armintie Herrington .75 2.00
94 Emma Meesseman 1.50 4.00
95 Ivory Latta 1.00 2.50
96 Kara Lawson 1.50 4.00
97 Natasha Cloud RC 2.00 5.00
98 Stefanie Dolson 3.00 8.00
99 Tayler Hill 1.50 4.00
100 Tierra Ruffin-Pratt 1.00 2.50

2015 WNBA Autographs

THREE AUTOS PER FACTORY SET
ANNCD PRINT RUN OF 500 FACTORY SETS
AZ Amanda Zahui B. 8.00 20.00
JL Jewell Loyd 8.00 20.00
KM Kaleena Mosqueda-Lewis 8.00 20.00

2016 WNBA

COMP.FACT.SET (102) 100.00 150.00
COMP.SET w/o AU's (100) 40.00 100.00
ANNOUNCED PRINT RUN 500 SETS
1 Angel McCoughtry 1.50 4.00
2 Bria Holmes RC 2.00 5.00
3 Carla Cortijo .75 2.00
4 Elizabeth Williams 1.25 3.00
5 Layshia Clarendon 1.25 3.00
6 Meighan Simmons RC 2.00 5.00
7 Rachel Hollivay RC 2.00 5.00
8 Reshanda Gray .75 2.00
9 Sancho Lyttle 1.00 2.50
10 Tiffany Hayes 1.25 3.00
11 Allie Quigley 1.00 2.50
12 Cappie Pondexter 1.25 3.00
13 Courtney Vandersloot 1.00 2.50
14 Elena Delle Donne 5.00 12.00
15 Erika de Souza .75 2.00
16 Imani Boyette RC 2.00 5.00
17 Jamierra Faulkner 1.00 2.50
18 Jessica Breland .75 2.00
19 Tamera Young 1.00 2.50
20 Alex Bentley 1.25 3.00
21 Alyssa Thomas 1.25 3.00
22 Camille Little 1.00 2.50
23 Chiney Ogwumike 1.25 3.00
24 Jasmine Thomas 1.25 3.00
25 Jonquel Jones RC 2.50 6.00
26 Kelsey Bone 1.00 2.50
27 Morgan Tuck RC 5.00 12.00
28 Rachel Banham RC 4.00 10.00
29 Aerial Powers RC 3.00 8.00
30 Courtney Paris 1.00 2.50
31 Erin Phillips .75 2.00
32 Glory Johnson 1.25 3.00
33 Jordan Hooper .75 2.00
34 Karima Christmas 1.25 3.00
35 Odyssey Sims 1.25 3.00
36 Plenette Pierson 1.25 3.00
37 Skylar Diggins 2.50 6.00
38 Theresa Plaisance RC 1.25 3.00
39 Briann January 1.00 2.50
40 Devereaux Peters 1.00 2.50
41 Erica Wheeler 1.00 2.50
42 Erlana Larkins 1.00 2.50
43 Lynetta Kizer 1.00 2.50
44 Maggie Lucas 1.25 3.00
45 Marissa Coleman 1.00 2.50
46 Shenise Johnson 1.00 2.50
47 Tamika Catchings 1.25 3.00
48 Tiffany Mitchell RC 5.00 12.00
49 Alana Beard 1.00 2.50
50 Ana Dabovic RC 1.25 3.00
51 Candace Parker 3.00 8.00
52 Chelsea Gray .75 2.00
53 Essence Carson 1.00 2.50
54 Evgeniia Belyakova RC 1.50 4.00
55 Jantel Lavender 1.00 2.50
56 Kristi Toliver 1.25 3.00
57 Nneka Ogwumike 1.50 4.00
58 Janel McCarville .75 2.00
59 Jia Perkins 1.00 2.50
60 Lindsay Whalen 2.00 5.00
61 Maya Moore 4.00 10.00
62 Natasha Howard 1.00 2.50
63 Rebekkah Brunson 1.00 2.50
64 Renee Montgomery 1.00 2.50
65 Seimone Augustus 1.25 3.00
66 Sylvia Fowles 1.25 3.00
67 Brittany Boyd .75 2.00
68 Carolyn Swords .75 2.00
69 Kiah Stokes 1.00 2.50
70 Amanda Zahui B 1.00 2.50
71 Shavonte Zellous 1.00 2.50
72 Sugar Rodgers 1.25 3.00
73 Swin Cash 1.25 3.00
74 Tanisha Wright 1.00 2.50
75 Tina Charles 2.50 6.00
76 Brittney Griner 4.00 10.00
77 Candice Dupree 1.25 3.00
78 DeWanna Bonner 1.50 4.00
79 Diana Taurasi 4.00 10.00
80 Isabelle Harrison RC 1.50 4.00
81 Mistie Bass .75 2.00
82 Noelle Quinn .75 2.00
83 Penny Taylor 1.25 3.00
84 Sonja Petrovic RC 1.25 3.00
85 Alex Montgomery .75 2.00
86 Dearica Hamby 1.00 2.50
87 Haley Peters RC 1.50 4.00
88 Jayne Appel-Marinelli 1.25 3.00
89 Kayla Alexander 1.00 2.50
90 Kayla McBride 1.50 4.00
91 Monique Currie 1.00 2.50
92 Moriah Jefferson RC 5.00 12.00
93 Sydney Colson .75 2.00
94 Alysha Clark 1.00 2.50
95 Breanna Stewart RC 20.00 50.00
96 Crystal Langhorne 1.00 2.50
97 Jenna O'Hea RC 1.25 3.00
98 Jewell Loyd 1.50 4.00
99 Kaleena Mosqueda-Lewis .75 2.00
100 Ramu Tokashiki .75 2.00
101 Sue Bird 4.00 10.00
102 Bria Hartley 1.00 2.50
103 Emma Meesseman 1.50 4.00
104 Ivory Latta 1.00 2.50
105 Kahleah Copper RC 2.00 5.00
106 Kia Vaughn .75 2.00
107 Stefanie Dolson 1.25 3.00
108 Tayler Hill 1.50 4.00
109 Tierra Ruffin-Pratt 1.00 2.50
110 Natasha Cloud .75 2.00

2016 WNBA Autographs

TWO AUTOS PER FACTORY SET
BS1 Stewart Action 50.00 120.00
BS2 Stewart Draft 50.00 120.00
BS3 Stewart Posed 50.00 120.00
MT1 Tuck Action 15.00 40.00
MT2 Tuck Draft 15.00 40.00
MT3 Tuck Posed 15.00 40.00

1995 Women's Basketball Association

Produced by Fair Play Inc., this set consists of nineteen player cards and eight schedule cards of the Women's Basketball Association. The player cards present the 1994 WBA All-Stars. Measuring the standard size, the player card fronts feature full-bleed color action photos. The player's name is printed in a stripe across the bottom. Either "American Conference" or "National Conference" is printed vertically in red block lettering along the right edge. The backs carry a color closeup photo, biography, and professional and college statistics. The schedule cards show the team logo on the front and the schedule on the back.

COMPLETE SET (27) 4.00 10.00
1 Checklist .20 .50
2 Lightning Mitchell DIR .20 .50
3 Sarah Campbell .20 .50
4 Lisa Carlsen .20 .50
5 Joy Champ .20 .50
6 Cledella Evans .20 .50
7 Crystal Flint .20 .50
8 Robbie Garcia .20 .50
9 Kay Kay Hart .20 .50
10 Petra Jackson .20 .50
11 Patrice Marshall .20 .50
12 Evette Ott .20 .50
13 Lynn Page .20 .50
14 Lisa Sandbothe .20 .50
15 Danielle Shareef .20 .50
16 Lisa Tate .20 .50
17 Diana Vines .20 .50
18 Tammy Williams .20 .50
19 Cynthia Wilson .20 .50
L1 Kansas City Mustangs .08 .25
L2 Chicago Twisters .08 .25
L3 St. Louis River Queens .08 .25
L4 Kentucky Marauders .08 .25
L5 Memphis Blues .08 .25
L6 Minnesota Stars .08 .25
L7 Nebraska Express .08 .25
L8 Oklahoma Flames .08 .25

1993 World University Games

This 10-card set features borderless photos of various sporting events at the World University Games in Buffalo in 1993. The backs display two different ways the collector could win prizes in two different scratch-off games. The cards are unnumbered and checklisted below alphabetically according to the sport pictured on the card front.

COMPLETE SET (10) 1.20 3.00
2 Basketball .10 .25

1993 XXV Jogos Olimpicos

This 84-card set commemorates medal winners from the 1992 XXV Olympics in Barcelona. The cards measure 2 11/16" by 3 7/8", have rounded corners, and are printed on thin cardboard stock. The fronts feature full-bleed color action photos, with the event, player's name, and country in one of the corners. The back is divided into two registers.The top register consists of a 1993 calendar, while the bottom lists the three medal winners' names, countries, and their winning scores or times. All text is in Portuguese. NBA stars Scottie Pippen (77) and Magic Johnson (78) are featured in this set.

COMPLETE SET (84) 25.00 60.00
77 Scottie Pippen 3.00 8.00
78 Magic Johnson 5.00 12.00

1996-97 Z-Force

The inaugural edtion of SkyBox Z-Force has a total of 200 cards. The eight-card hobby and retail packs carry a suggested retail price of $2.49 each. Card fronts contain an action shot of the player against an "explosive-type" background. The player's name is in block letters at the top of the card and the SkyBox Z-Force logo is outlined in gold foil along the bottom right of the card. Card backs contain a hardwood floor design in the background with a player shot over it. Statistical and biographical information is also located on the back. The cards are grouped alphabetically within teams. The series two cards feature the same graphics as series one, but a thicker card stock. A Grant Hill Total Z card was inserted in series two packs at a rate of one in 900 packs. The card is a one-shot leather card. Series two packs also featured a 10-card redemption for a full set of the 1996-97 SkyBox Autographics program. The tough card number was card #5. Also, a non-numbered two-card promo sheet was also issued for the first series which features a basic card of Grant Hill and Jerry Stackhouse. For the second series, a Grant Hill promo was released that mirrored his regular issue card bearing the words "Promotion Sample" on the front and back. The two promos are listed below at the end of the set.

COMPLETE SET (200) 20.00 40.00
COMPLETE SERIES 1 (100) 10.00 20.00
COMPLETE SERIES 2 (100) 10.00 20.00
SUBSET CARDS SAME VALUE AS BASE CARDS
HILL Z: SER.2 STATED ODDS 1:900 HOB/RET
1 Mookie Blaylock .12 .30
2 Alan Henderson .12 .30
3 Christian Laettner .15 .40
4 Steve Smith .15 .40
5 Rick Fox .12 .30
6 Dino Radja .12 .30
7 Eric Williams .12 .30
8 Muggsy Bogues .15 .40
9 Larry Johnson .20 .50
10 Glen Rice .20 .50
11 Michael Jordan 1.50 4.00
12 Toni Kukoc .20 .50
13 Scottie Pippen .30 .75
14 Dennis Rodman .40 1.00
15 Terrell Brandon .12 .30
16 Bobby Phills .12 .30
17 Bob Sura .12 .30
18 Jim Jackson .12 .30
19 Jason Kidd .30 .75
20 Jamal Mashburn .15 .40
21 George McCloud .12 .30
22 Mahmoud Abdul-Rauf .12 .30
23 Antonio McDyess .20 .50
24 Dikembe Mutombo .20 .50
25 Joe Dumars .20 .50
26 Grant Hill .30 .75
27 Allan Houston .15 .40
28 Otis Thorpe .12 .30
29 Chris Mullin .20 .50
30 Joe Smith .15 .40
31 Latrell Sprewell .20 .50
32 Sam Cassell .15 .40
33 Clyde Drexler .25 .60
34 Robert Horry .15 .40
35 Hakeem Olajuwon .25 .60
36 Travis Best .12 .30
37 Dale Davis .12 .30
38 Reggie Miller .25 .60
39 Rik Smits .15 .40
40 Brent Barry .15 .40
41 Loy Vaught .12 .30
42 Brian Williams .12 .30
43 Cedric Ceballos .12 .30
44 Eddie Jones .20 .50
45 Nick Van Exel .20 .50
46 Tim Hardaway .20 .50
47 Alonzo Mourning .25 .60
48 Kurt Thomas .12 .30
49 Walt Williams .12 .30
50 Vin Baker .15 .40
51 Glenn Robinson .15 .40
52 Kevin Garnett .50 1.25
53 Tom Gugliotta .12 .30
54 Isaiah Rider .15 .40
55 Shawn Bradley .12 .30
56 Chris Childs .12 .30
57 Jayson Williams .12 .30
58 Patrick Ewing .25 .60
59 Anthony Mason .12 .30
60 Charles Oakley .15 .40
61 Nick Anderson .12 .30
62 Horace Grant .15 .40
63 Anfernee Hardaway .30 .75
64 Shaquille O'Neal .50 1.25
65 Dennis Scott .12 .30
66 Jerry Stackhouse .25 .60
67 Clarence Weatherspoon .12 .30
68 Charles Barkley .30 .75
69 Michael Finley .25 .60
70 Kevin Johnson .20 .50

71 Clifford Robinson .12 .30
72 Arvydas Sabonis .15 .40
73 Rod Strickland .12 .30
74 Tyus Edney .12 .30
75 Brian Grant .15 .40
76 Billy Owens .12 .30
77 Mitch Richmond .20 .50
78 Vinny Del Negro .12 .30
79 Sean Elliott .20 .50
80 Avery Johnson .15 .40
81 David Robinson .30 .75
82 Hersey Hawkins .12 .30
83 Shawn Kemp .20 .50
84 Gary Payton .20 .50
85 Detlef Schrempf .20 .50
86 Doug Christie .12 .30
87 Damon Stoudamire .15 .40
88 Sharone Wright .12 .30
89 Jeff Hornacek .15 .40
90 Karl Malone .25 .60
91 John Stockton .25 .60
92 Greg Anthony .12 .30
93 Bryant Reeves .12 .30
94 Byron Scott .15 .40
95 Juwan Howard .15 .40
96 Gheorghe Muresan .12 .30
97 Rasheed Wallace .25 .60
98 Chris Webber .25 .60
99 Checklist .12 .30
100 Checklist .12 .30
101 Dikembe Mutombo .20 .50
102 Dee Brown .12 .30
103 Dell Curry .12 .30
104 Vlade Divac .20 .50
105 Anthony Mason .12 .30
106 Robert Parish .20 .50
107 Oliver Miller .12 .30
108 Eric Montross .12 .30
109 Ervin Johnson .12 .30
110 Stacey Augmon .15 .40
111 Charles Barkley .30 .75
112 Jalen Rose .15 .40
113 Rodney Rogers .12 .30
114 Shaquille O'Neal .50 1.25
115 Dan Majerle .20 .50
116 Kendall Gill .12 .30
117 Khalid Reeves .12 .30
118 Allan Houston .15 .40
119 Larry Johnson .20 .50
120 John Starks .15 .40
121 Rony Seikaly .12 .30
122 Gerald Wilkins .12 .30
123 Michael Cage .12 .30
124 Derrick Coleman .15 .40
125 Sam Cassell .15 .40
126 Danny Manning .15 .40
127 Robert Horry .15 .40
128 Kenny Anderson .15 .40
129 Isaiah Rider .15 .40
130 Rasheed Wallace .25 .60
131 Mahmoud Abdul-Rauf .12 .30
132 Vernon Maxwell .12 .30
133 Dominique Wilkins .25 .60
134 Hubert Davis .12 .30
135 Popeye Jones .12 .30
136 Anthony Peeler .12 .30
137 Tracy Murray .12 .30
138 Rod Strickland .12 .30
139 Shareef Abdur-Rahim RC .30 .75
140 Ray Allen RC .75 2.00
141 Shandon Anderson RC .15 .40
142 Kobe Bryant RC 4.00 10.00
143 Marcus Camby RC .30 .75
144 Erick Dampier RC .20 .50
145 Emanual Davis RC .20 .50
146 Tony Delk RC .20 .50
147 Todd Fuller RC .12 .30
148 Darvin Ham RC .20 .50
149 Othella Harrington RC .20 .50
150 Shane Heal RC .12 .30
151 Allen Iverson RC 1.00 2.50
152 Dontae' Jones RC .12 .30
153 Kerry Kittles RC .20 .50
154 Priest Lauderdale RC .12 .30
155 Matt Maloney RC .15 .40
156 Stephon Marbury RC .50 1.25
157 Walter McCarty RC .20 .50
158 Steve Nash RC 1.00 2.50
159 Jermaine O'Neal RC .30 .75
160 Ray Owes RC .12 .30
161 Vitaly Potapenko RC .15 .40
162 Roy Rogers RC .15 .40
163 Antoine Walker RC .30 .75
164 Samaki Walker RC .15 .40
165 Ben Wallace RC 1.00 2.50
166 John Wallace RC .20 .50
167 Jerome Williams RC .15 .40
168 Lorenzen Wright RC .15 .40
169 Vin Baker ZUP .15 .40
170 Charles Barkley ZUP .30 .75
171 Patrick Ewing ZUP .20 .50
172 Michael Finley ZUP .20 .50
173 Kevin Garnett ZUP .50 1.25
174 Anfernee Hardaway ZUP .30 .75
175 Grant Hill ZUP .30 .75
176 Juwan Howard ZUP .15 .40
177 Jim Jackson ZUP .12 .30
178 Eddie Jones ZUP .20 .50
179 Michael Jordan ZUP 1.50 4.00
180 Shawn Kemp ZUP .20 .50
181 Jason Kidd ZUP .30 .75
182 Karl Malone ZUP .25 .60
183 Antonio McDyess ZUP .20 .50
184 Reggie Miller ZUP .25 .60
185 Alonzo Mourning ZUP .20 .50
186 Hakeem Olajuwon ZUP .25 .60
187 Shaquille O'Neal ZUP .50 1.25
188 Gary Payton ZUP .20 .50
189 Mitch Richmond ZUP .20 .50
190 Clifford Robinson ZUP .12 .30
191 David Robinson ZUP .30 .75
192 Glenn Robinson ZUP .20 .50
193 Dennis Rodman ZUP .40 1.00
194 Joe Smith ZUP .15 .40
195 Jerry Stackhouse ZUP .25 .60
196 John Stockton ZUP .25 .60
197 Damon Stoudamire ZUP .15 .40
198 Chris Webber ZUP .25 .60
199 Checklist (1-157) .12 .30
200 Checklist (158-200/ins.) .12 .30
NNO Grant Hill PROMO .75 2.00
NNO Grant Hill Total Z 8.00 20.00
NNO Grant Hill .75 2.00
Jerry Stackhouse PROMO

1996-97 Z-Force Z-Cling

COMPLETE SET (100) 15.00 40.00
*Z-CLING: .75X TO 2X BASIC
64 Shaquille O'Neal Lakers 2.00 5.00
R1 Ray Allen 2.50 6.00
R2 Stephon Marbury 1.50 4.00
R3 Shareef Abdur-Rahim 1.25 3.00

1996-97 Z-Force Big Men on the Court

Randomly inserted in series two packs at a rate of one in 240, this 10-card die-cut set feature some of the leagues top players. The cards are printed with silver foil with the insert set name "Big Men on the Court" in the background.

COMPLETE SET (10) 300.00 600.00
SER.2 STATED ODDS 1:240 HOBBY/RETAIL
1 Charles Barkley 20.00 50.00
2 Anfernee Hardaway 20.00 50.00
3 Grant Hill 15.00 40.00
4 Michael Jordan 200.00 400.00
5 Shawn Kemp 15.00 40.00
6 Alonzo Mourning 12.00 30.00
7 Hakeem Olajuwon 20.00 50.00
8 Shaquille O'Neal 40.00 100.00
9 Scottie Pippen 25.00 60.00
10 David Robinson 20.00 50.00

1996-97 Z-Force Big Men on the Court Z-peat

*STARS: .75X TO 2X HI COLUMN
STATED ODDS 1:1,120 PACKS

1996-97 Z-Force Little Big Men

Randomly inserted in series two retail packs only at a rate of one in 36, this 10-card set focuses on some of the NBA's smaller superstars. Card fronts contain buildings in the background on silver foil.

COMPLETE SET (10) 20.00 40.00
SER.2 STATED ODDS 1:36 RETAIL
1 Kenny Anderson 2.00 5.00
2 Mookie Blaylock 1.50 4.00
3 Muggsy Bogues 2.00 5.00
4 Terrell Brandon 1.50 4.00
5 Allen Iverson 6.00 15.00
6 Avery Johnson 2.00 5.00
7 Kevin Johnson 2.50 6.00
8 Stephon Marbury 3.00 8.00
9 Gary Payton 2.50 6.00
10 Nick Van Exel 2.50 6.00

1996-97 Z-Force Slam Cam

Randomly inserted in series one hobby and retail packs at a rate of one in 240, this nine-card set features some of the top slam dunkers in the game. Card fronts contain a kaleidoscopic color background with an action photo laid on top. The player's name and the set name "Slam Cam" are located above the photo. Card backs are horizontal with the set name in the background with another action shot of the player. The cards are numbered with a "SC" prefix.

COMPLETE SET (9) 350.00 700.00
SER.1 STATED ODDS 1:240 HOBBY/RETAIL
SC1 Clyde Drexler 12.00 30.00
SC2 Michael Finley 12.00 30.00
SC3 Anfernee Hardaway 15.00 40.00
SC4 Grant Hill 15.00 40.00
SC5 Michael Jordan 200.00 500.00
SC6 Shawn Kemp 10.00 25.00
SC7 Karl Malone 12.00 30.00
SC8 Antonio McDyess 10.00 25.00
SC9 Shaquille O'Neal 25.00 60.00

1996-97 Z-Force Swat Team

Randomly inserted in series one hobby packs only at a rate of one in 72, this 9-card set features some of the leagues best blockers. Card front backgrounds are prismatic with the logo "Swat Team" designed into it. An action shot of the player is laid on top with their names directly underneath. Card backs contain the same type background as the front, without the prismatic foil. The cards are numbered with a "ST" prefix.

COMPLETE SET (9) 40.00 80.00
SER.1 STATED ODDS 1:72 HOBBY
ST1 Patrick Ewing 5.00 12.00
ST2 Kevin Garnett 10.00 25.00
ST3 Alonzo Mourning 5.00 12.00
ST4 Dikembe Mutombo 4.00 10.00
ST5 Hakeem Olajuwon 5.00 12.00
ST6 Shaquille O'Neal 10.00 25.00
ST7 David Robinson 6.00 15.00
ST8 Dennis Rodman 8.00 20.00
ST9 Joe Smith 3.00 8.00

1996-97 Z-Force Vortex

Randomly inserted in series one retail packs only at a rate of one in 36, this 15-card set features embossed card fronts with a swirl background. The action shot of the player is located in the middle of the card with the player's name in gold foil block letters directly below. Card backs are horizontal with a similar background and have a brief commentary along with another action shot. The cards are numbered as "Vortex/X".

COMPLETE SET (15) 50.00 120.00
SER.1 STATED ODDS 1:36 RETAIL
V1 Charles Barkley 5.00 12.00
V2 Anfernee Hardaway 5.00 12.00
V3 Grant Hill 5.00 12.00
V4 Juwan Howard 2.50 6.00
V5 Michael Jordan 60.00 150.00
V6 Jason Kidd 5.00 12.00
V7 Reggie Miller 4.00 10.00
V8 Gary Payton 3.00 8.00
V9 Scottie Pippen 5.00 12.00
V10 Mitch Richmond 3.00 8.00
V11 Glenn Robinson 2.50 6.00
V12 Arvydas Sabonis 2.50 6.00
V13 Jerry Stackhouse 4.00 10.00
V14 John Stockton 4.00 10.00
V15 Damon Stoudamire 2.50 6.00

1996-97 Z-Force Zebut

Randomly inserted in series two hobby packs only at a rate of one in 24, this 20-card set is embossed and printed on silver foil. The set focuses on first year players from the 96-97 class.

COMPLETE SET (20) 50.00 100.00
SER.2 STATED ODDS 1:24 HOBBY
1 Shareef Abdur-Rahim 2.50 6.00
2 Ray Allen 6.00 15.00
3 Kobe Bryant 15.00 40.00
4 Marcus Camby 2.50 6.00
5 Erick Dampier 1.50 4.00
6 Todd Fuller 1.00 2.50
7 Othella Harrington 1.50 4.00
8 Allen Iverson 8.00 20.00
9 Kerry Kittles 1.50 4.00
10 Priest Lauderdale 1.00 2.50
11 Stephon Marbury 4.00 10.00
12 Steve Nash 8.00 20.00
13 Jermaine O'Neal 2.50 6.00
14 Ray Owes 1.50 4.00
15 Vitaly Potapenko 1.50 4.00
16 Roy Rogers 1.50 4.00
17 Antoine Walker 2.50 6.00
18 Samaki Walker 1.50 4.00
19 John Wallace 1.50 4.00
20 Lorenzen Wright 1.50 4.00

1996-97 Z-Force Zebut Z-peat

*ZPEAT: 1.5X TO 4X BASE HI
RANDOM INSERTS IN SER.2 HOBBY PACKS
3 Kobe Bryant 175.00 350.00

1996-97 Z-Force Zensations

Randomly inserted in all series two packs at a rate of one in six, this 20-card set features a foil-stamped background and focuses on veterans and rookies. Card fronts feature the player spotlighted.

COMPLETE SET (20) 10.00 25.00
SER.2 STATED ODDS 1:6 HOBBY/RETAIL
1 Shareef Abdur-Rahim .75 2.00
2 Ray Allen 2.00 5.00
3 Nick Anderson .50 1.25
4 Vin Baker .60 1.50
5 Mookie Blaylock .50 1.25
6 Calbert Cheaney .50 1.25
7 Kevin Garnett 2.00 5.00
8 Horace Grant .60 1.50
9 Tim Hardaway .75 2.00
10 Allen Iverson 2.50 6.00
11 Avery Johnson .60 1.50
12 Kevin Johnson .75 2.00
13 Danny Manning .60 1.50
14 Stephon Marbury 1.25 3.00
15 Jamal Mashburn .60 1.50
16 Glen Rice .75 2.00
17 Isaiah Rider .60 1.50
18 Latrell Sprewell .75 2.00
19 Rod Strickland .50 1.25
20 Nick Van Exel .75 2.00

1997-98 Z-Force

This 210-card set was issued in two series, distributed in eight-card packs with a suggested retail price of $1.59. The fronts feature borderless color action player photos printed on 14 pt. card stock with gold foil stamping and UV coating. The player's name is written vertically down the side in different foil colors. The backs carry another player photo and player information.

COMPLETE SET (210) 12.50 25.00
COMPLETE SERIES 1 (110) 5.00 10.00
COMPLETE SERIES 2 (100) 7.50 15.00
CARD NUMBER 143 DOES NOT EXIST
BAKER AND MCGRADY BOTH #'d 172
SUBSET CARDS SAME VALUE AS BASE
1 Anfernee Hardaway .25 .60
2 Mitch Richmond .15 .40
3 Stephon Marbury .20 .50
4 Charles Barkley .25 .60
5 Juwan Howard .12 .30
6 Avery Johnson .12 .30
7 Rex Chapman .10 .25
8 Antoine Walker .25 .60
9 Nick Van Exel .15 .40
10 Tim Hardaway .15 .40
11 Clarence Weatherspoon .10 .25
12 John Stockton .20 .50
13 Glenn Robinson .12 .30
14 Anthony Mason .12 .30
15 Latrell Sprewell .15 .40
16 Kendall Gill .10 .25
17 Terry Mills .10 .25
18 Mookie Blaylock .10 .25
19 Michael Finley .15 .40
20 Gary Payton .15 .40
21 Kevin Garnett .25 .60
22 Clyde Drexler .15 .40
23 Michael Jordan 1.25 3.00
24 Antonio McDyess .12 .30
25 Nick Anderson .10 .25
26 Patrick Ewing .20 .50
27 Anthony Peeler .10 .25
28 Doug Christie .10 .25
29 Bobby Phills .10 .25
30 Kerry Kittles .15 .40
31 Reggie Miller .15 .40
32 Karl Malone .20 .50
33 Grant Hill .20 .50
34 Shaquille O'Neal .40 1.00
35 Loy Vaught .10 .25
36 Kenny Anderson .12 .30
37 Wesley Person .10 .25
38 Jamal Mashburn .12 .30
39 Christian Laettner .12 .30
40 Shawn Kemp .15 .40
41 Glen Rice .15 .40
42 Vin Baker .12 .30
43 Popeye Jones .10 .25
44 Derrick Coleman .12 .30
45 Rik Smits .12 .30
46 Dale Ellis .10 .25
47 Rod Strickland .10 .25
48 Mark Price .10 .25
49 Toni Kukoc .20 .50
50 David Robinson .25 .60
51 John Wallace .10 .25
52 Samaki Walker .10 .25
53 Shareef Abdur-Rahim .20 .50
54 Rodney Rogers .10 .25
55 Dikembe Mutombo .12 .30
56 Rony Seikaly .10 .25
57 Matt Maloney .10 .25
58 Chris Webber .15 .40
59 Robert Horry .15 .40
60 Rasheed Wallace .15 .40
61 Jeff Hornacek .12 .30
62 Walt Williams .10 .25
63 Detlef Schrempf .12 .30
64 Dan Majerle .15 .40
65 Dell Curry .10 .25
66 Scottie Pippen .25 .60
67 Greg Anthony .10 .25
68 Mahmoud Abdul-Rauf .10 .25
69 Cedric Ceballos .10 .25
70 Terrell Brandon .10 .25
71 Arvydas Sabonis .12 .30
72 Malik Sealy .10 .25
73 Dean Garrett .10 .25
74 Joe Dumars .15 .40
75 Joe Smith .12 .30
76 Shawn Bradley .10 .25
77 Gheorghe Muresan .10 .25
78 Dale Davis .10 .25
79 Bryant Stith .10 .25
80 Lorenzen Wright .10 .25
81 Chris Childs .10 .25
82 Bryon Russell .10 .25
83 Steve Smith .12 .30
84 Jerry Stackhouse .15 .40
85 Hersey Hawkins .10 .25
86 Ray Allen .20 .50
87 Dominique Wilkins .20 .50
88 Kobe Bryant .75 2.00
89 Tom Gugliotta .10 .25
90 Dennis Scott .10 .25
91 Dennis Rodman .30 .75
92 Bryant Reeves .10 .25
93 Vlade Divac .12 .30
94 Jason Kidd .25 .60
95 Mario Elie .10 .25
96 Lindsey Hunter .10 .25
97 Olden Polynice .10 .25
98 Allan Houston .12 .30
99 Alonzo Mourning .20 .50
100 Allen Iverson .30 .75
101 LaPhonso Ellis .10 .25
102 Bob Sura .10 .25
103 Chris Mullin .15 .40
104 Sam Cassell .12 .30
105 Eric Williams .10 .25
106 Antonio Davis .10 .25
107 Marcus Camby .15 .40
108 Isaiah Rider .12 .30
109 Checklist .10 .25
110 Checklist .10 .25
111 Tim Duncan RC .75 2.00
112 Joe Smith .12 .30
113 Shawn Kemp .15 .40
114 Terry Mills .10 .25
115 Jacque Vaughn RC .10 .25
116 Ron Mercer RC .20 .50
117 Brian Williams .10 .25
118 Rik Smits .12 .30
119 Eric Williams .10 .25
120 Tim Thomas RC .20 .50
121 Damon Stoudamire .12 .30
122 God Shammgod RC .15 .40
123 Tyrone Hill .10 .25
124 Elden Campbell .10 .25
125 Keith Van Horn RC .25 .60
126 Brian Grant .10 .25
127 Antonio McDyess .12 .30
128 Darrell Armstrong .10 .25
129 Sam Perkins .10 .25
130 Chris Mills .10 .25
131 Reggie Miller .20 .50
132 Chris Gatling .10 .25
133 Ed Gray RC .15 .40
134 Hakeem Olajuwon .20 .50
135 Chris Webber .15 .40
136 Kendall Gill .10 .25
137 Wesley Person .10 .25
138 Derrick Coleman .12 .30
139 Dana Barros .10 .25
140 Dennis Scott .10 .25
141 Paul Grant RC .10 .25
142 Scott Burrell .10 .25
144 Austin Croshere RC .15 .40
145 Maurice Taylor RC .15 .40
146 Kevin Johnson .15 .40
147 Tony Battie RC .15 .40
148 Tariq Abdul-Wahad RC .12 .30
149 Johnny Taylor RC .12 .30
150 Allen Iverson .30 .75
151 Terrell Brandon .10 .25
152 Derek Anderson RC .15 .40
153 Calbert Cheaney .10 .25
154 Jayson Williams .10 .25
155 Rick Fox .10 .25
156 John Thomas RC .10 .25
157 David Wesley .10 .25
158 Bobby Jackson RC .20 .50
159 Kelvin Cato RC .10 .25
160 Vinny Del Negro .10 .25
161 Adonal Foyle RC .12 .30
162 Larry Johnson .15 .40
163 Brevin Knight RC .15 .40
164 Rod Strickland .10 .25
165 Rodrick Rhodes RC .10 .25
166 Scot Pollard RC .15 .40
167 Sam Cassell .12 .30
168 Jerry Stackhouse .15 .40
169 Mark Jackson .12 .30
170 John Wallace .10 .25
171 Horace Grant .12 .30
172A Vin Baker .12 .30
172B Tracy McGrady ERR RC .60 1.50
173 Eddie Jones .10 .25
174 Kerry Kittles .15 .40
175 Antonio Daniels RC .15 .40
176 Alan Henderson .10 .25
177 Sean Elliott .15 .40
178 John Starks .12 .30
179 Chauncey Billups RC .50 1.25
180 Juwan Howard .12 .30
181 Bobby Phills .10 .25
182 Latrell Sprewell .15 .40
183 Jim Jackson .10 .25
184 Danny Fortson RC .15 .40
185 Zydrunas Ilgauskas .15 .40
186 Clifford Robinson .10 .25
187 Chris Mullin .15 .40
188 Greg Ostertag .10 .25
189 Antoine Walker ZUP .15 .40
190 Michael Jordan ZUP 1.25 3.00
191 Scottie Pippen ZUP .25 .60
192 Dennis Rodman ZUP .30 .75
193 Grant Hill ZUP .25 .60
194 Clyde Drexler ZUP .20 .50
195 Kobe Bryant ZUP .75 2.00
196 Shaquille O'Neal ZUP .40 1.00
197 Alonzo Mourning ZUP .20 .50
198 Ray Allen ZUP .20 .50
199 Kevin Garnett ZUP .25 .60
200 Stephon Marbury ZUP .20 .50
201 Anfernee Hardaway ZUP .25 .60
202 Jason Kidd ZUP .25 .60
203 David Robinson ZUP .25 .60
204 Gary Payton ZUP .15 .40
205 Marcus Camby ZUP .15 .40
206 Karl Malone ZUP .20 .50
207 John Stockton ZUP .20 .50
208 Shareef Abdur-Rahim ZUP .20 .50
209 Charles Barkley CL .25 .60
210 Gary Payton CL .15 .40

1997-98 Z-Force Rave

*STARS: 25X TO 60X BASE CARD HI
*RCs: 12X TO 30X BASE HI
STATED PRINT RUN 399 SERIAL #'d SETS
23 Michael Jordan 150.00 400.00
88 Kobe Bryant 100.00 250.00
91 Dennis Rodman 25.00 60.00
111 Tim Duncan 40.00 100.00

1997-98 Z-Force Super Rave

*STARS: 75X TO 200X BASE CARD HI
*RCs: 40X TO 100X BASE HI
STATED PRINT RUN 50 SERIAL #'d SETS
111 Tim Duncan 250.00 500.00
135 Chris Webber 60.00 150.00
190 Michael Jordan ZUP 3000.00 4500.00
192 Dennis Rodman ZUP 175.00 350.00
194 Clyde Drexler ZUP 80.00 200.00
195 Kobe Bryant ZUP 600.00 1000.00

1997-98 Z-Force Big Men on Court

Randomly inserted in series two packs at a rate of one in 288, this 15-card set features some of the best players on the court. The cards are produced on special multi-dimensional thermo-plastic card stock.

COMPLETE SET (15) 1000.00 1500.00
SER.2 STATED ODDS 1:288 HOB/RET
1 Shareef Abdur-Rahim 15.00 40.00
2 Kobe Bryant 150.00 400.00
3 Marcus Camby 20.00 50.00
4 Tim Duncan 75.00 200.00
5 Kevin Garnett 50.00 120.00
6 Anfernee Hardaway 60.00 150.00
7 Grant Hill 40.00 100.00
8 Allen Iverson 75.00 200.00
9 Michael Jordan 800.00 1200.00
10 Shawn Kemp 20.00 50.00
11 Stephon Marbury 25.00 60.00
12 Shaquille O'Neal 60.00 150.00
13 Scottie Pippen 50.00 120.00
14 Dennis Rodman 50.00 120.00
15 Antoine Walker 20.00 50.00

1997-98 Z-Force Boss

Randomly inserted in series one packs at a rate of one in six, this 20-card set features color action player photos of top players on the courts. The card fronts feature a photo of the player embossed against a hardwood floor background. The backs carry player information.

COMPLETE SET (20) 12.00 30.00
SER.1 STATED ODDS 1:6 HOBBY/RETAIL
*SUPER BOSS: 1X TO 2.5X BASE BOSS
SUPER BOSS: SER.1 STATED ODDS 1:36 H/R
1 Shareef Abdur-Rahim .50 1.25
2 Ray Allen .60 1.50
3 Kobe Bryant 3.00 8.00
4 Marcus Camby .50 1.25
5 Kevin Garnett .75 2.00
6 Anfernee Hardaway .75 2.00
7 Grant Hill .75 2.00
8 Allen Iverson 1.00 2.50
9 Eddie Jones .50 1.25
10 Michael Jordan 5.00 12.00
11 Shawn Kemp .50 1.25
12 Kerry Kittles .30 .75
13 Stephon Marbury .60 1.50
14 Shaquille O'Neal 1.25 3.00
15 Hakeem Olajuwon .60 1.50
16 Scottie Pippen .75 2.00
17 Dennis Rodman 1.00 2.50
18 Joe Smith .40 1.00
19 Damon Stoudamire .40 1.00
20 Antoine Walker .50 1.25

1997-98 Z-Force Fast Track

Randomly inserted in series one packs at a rate of one in 24, this 12-card set features color action photos of players who are on the road to NBA stardom. Card fronts contain a yellow background with the title "Fast Track" having a felt-feel. The backs carry player information.

COMPLETE SET (12) 12.00 30.00
SER.1 STATED ODDS 1:24 HOBBY/RETAIL
1 Ray Allen 1.50 4.00
2 Kobe Bryant 6.00 15.00
3 Marcus Camby 1.25 3.00
4 Juwan Howard 1.00 2.50
5 Eddie Jones 1.25 3.00
6 Kerry Kittles .75 2.00
7 Antonio McDyess 1.00 2.50
8 Joe Smith 1.00 2.50
9 Jerry Stackhouse 1.25 3.00
10 Damon Stoudamire 1.00 2.50
11 Antoine Walker 1.25 3.00
12 Chris Webber 1.25 3.00

1997-98 Z-Force Limited Access

Randomly inserted in series one retail packs only at a rate of one in 18, this 10-card set features color player photos on a bi-fold card with in-depth statistical analysis.

COMPLETE SET (10) 10.00 25.00
SER.1 STATED ODDS 1:18 RETAIL
1 Shareef Abdur-Rahim .75 2.00
2 Ray Allen 1.00 2.50
3 Charles Barkley 1.25 3.00
4 Anfernee Hardaway 1.25 3.00
5 Juwan Howard .60 1.50
6 Michael Jordan 6.00 15.00
7 Stephon Marbury 1.00 2.50
8 Shaquille O'Neal 2.00 5.00
9 Dennis Rodman 1.50 4.00
10 Antoine Walker .75 2.00

1997-98 Z-Force Quick Strike

Randomly inserted in series two packs at a rate of one in 96, this 12-card set focuses on players who can light up the scoreboard in the blink of an eye. Card fronts feature holofoil backing on clear plastic stock.

COMPLETE SET (12) 125.00 300.00
SER.2 STATED ODDS 1:96 HOB/RET
1 Shareef Abdur-Rahim 4.00 10.00
2 Anfernee Hardaway 6.00 15.00
3 Grant Hill 6.00 15.00
4 Allen Iverson 8.00 20.00
5 Michael Jordan 100.00 250.00
6 Stephon Marbury 5.00 12.00
7 Hakeem Olajuwon 5.00 12.00
8 Scottie Pippen 6.00 15.00
9 Damon Stoudamire 3.00 8.00
10 Keith Van Horn 3.00 8.00
11 Antoine Walker 4.00 10.00
12 Chris Webber 4.00 10.00

1997-98 Z-Force Rave Reviews

Randomly inserted in series one packs at a rate of one in 288, this 12-card set features color action photos of players who generate incredible numbers on the court and continually make the headlines. The backs carry player information.

COMPLETE SET (12) 400.00 800.00
SER.1 STATED ODDS 1:288 HOBBY/RETAIL
1 Shareef Abdur-Rahim 10.00 25.00
2 Kevin Garnett 30.00 80.00
3 Anfernee Hardaway 25.00 60.00
4 Grant Hill 15.00 40.00
5 Allen Iverson 20.00 50.00
6 Michael Jordan 200.00 500.00
7 Shawn Kemp 12.00 30.00
8 Stephon Marbury 12.00 30.00
9 Shaquille O'Neal 25.00 60.00
10 Hakeem Olajuwon 15.00 40.00
11 Scottie Pippen 15.00 40.00
12 Dennis Rodman 30.00 80.00

1997-98 Z-Force Slam Cam

Randomly inserted in series two packs at a rate of one in 36, this 12-card set featues NBA players who play their game above the rim. The card fronts feature a black and white film footage background on plastic stock.

COMPLETE SET (12) 40.00 70.00
SER.2 STATED ODDS 1:36 HOB/RET
1 Kobe Bryant 8.00 20.00
2 Marcus Camby 1.50 4.00
3 Tim Duncan 4.00 10.00
4 Kevin Garnett 2.50 6.00
5 Michael Jordan 20.00 50.00
6 Shawn Kemp 1.50 4.00
7 Karl Malone 2.00 5.00
8 Antonio McDyess 1.25 3.00
9 Shaquille O'Neal 4.00 10.00
10 Joe Smith 1.25 3.00
11 Jerry Stackhouse 1.50 4.00
12 Chris Webber 1.50 4.00

1997-98 Z-Force Star Gazing

Randomly inserted in series two retail packs at a rate of one in 18, this 15-card set features some of the NBA's best against a dark foil-board background.

COMPLETE SET (15) 30.00 60.00
SER.2 STATED ODDS 1:18 RETAIL
1 Shareef Abdur-Rahim 1.50 4.00
2 Kobe Bryant 8.00 20.00
3 Marcus Camby 1.50 4.00
4 Kevin Garnett 2.50 6.00
5 Anfernee Hardaway 2.50 6.00
6 Grant Hill 2.50 6.00
7 Allen Iverson 3.00 8.00
8 Stephon Marbury 2.00 5.00
9 Hakeem Olajuwon 2.00 5.00
10 Shaquille O'Neal 4.00 10.00
11 Scottie Pippen 2.50 6.00
12 Dennis Rodman 3.00 8.00
13 Damon Stoudamire 1.25 3.00
14 Keith Van Horn 1.25 3.00
15 Antoine Walker 1.50 4.00

1997-98 Z-Force Total Impact

Randomly inserted in series one packs at a rate of one in 48, this 12-card set features color action photos of players who can hurt their opponents with their many skills. Card fronts carry a player shot against a diffracting foil background. The backs carry player information.

COMPLETE SET (12) 20.00 50.00
SER.1 STATED ODDS 1:48 HOBBY/RETAIL
1 Kobe Bryant 8.00 20.00
2 Marcus Camby 1.50 4.00
3 Kevin Garnett 2.50 6.00
4 Grant Hill 2.50 6.00
5 Allen Iverson 3.00 8.00
6 Eddie Jones 1.50 4.00
7 Shawn Kemp 1.50 4.00
8 Kerry Kittles 1.00 2.50
9 Hakeem Olajuwon 2.00 5.00
10 Scottie Pippen 2.50 6.00
11 Joe Smith 1.25 3.00
12 Chris Webber 1.50 4.00

1997-98 Z-Force Zebut

Randomly inserted in series two packs at a rate of one in 24, this 12-card set features rookie phenoms who are destined for the NBA spotlight. Each player is set against a spotlight with a 100% die cut foil background.

COMPLETE SET (12) 6.00 15.00
SER.2 STATED ODDS 1:24 HOB/RET
1 Derek Anderson .40 1.00
2 Tony Battie .40 1.00
3 Chauncey Billups 1.25 3.00
4 Austin Croshere .30 .75
5 Antonio Daniels .40 1.00
6 Tim Duncan 2.00 5.00
7 Danny Fortson .40 1.00
8 Tracy McGrady 1.50 4.00
9 Ron Mercer .50 1.25
10 Tariq Abdul-Wahad .30 .75
11 Tim Thomas .50 1.25
12 Keith Van Horn .60 1.50

1997-98 Z-Force Zensations

Randomly inserted in series two packs at a rate of one in six, this 25-card set features die cut, multi-colored cards showcasing the league's marquee players.

COMPLETE SET (25) 6.00 15.00
SER.2 STATED ODDS 1:6 HOB/RET
1 Ray Allen .60 1.50
2 Vin Baker .40 1.00
3 Charles Barkley .75 2.00
4 Clyde Drexler .60 1.50
5 Patrick Ewing .60 1.50
6 Juwan Howard .40 1.00
7 Eddie Jones .50 1.25
8 Shawn Kemp .50 1.25
9 Jason Kidd .75 2.00
10 Kerry Kittles .50 1.25
11 Karl Malone .60 1.50
12 Antonio McDyess .50 1.25
13 Hakeem Olajuwon .60 1.50
14 Gary Payton .50 1.25
15 Glen Rice .50 1.25
16 Mitch Richmond .50 1.25
17 David Robinson .75 2.00
18 Dennis Rodman 1.00 2.50
19 Joe Smith .40 1.00
20 Latrell Sprewell .50 1.25
21 Jerry Stackhouse .50 1.25
22 John Stockton .60 1.50
23 Damon Stoudamire .40 1.00
24 Rasheed Wallace .50 1.25
25 Chris Webber .50 1.25

1992 ACC Tournament Champs

This 40-card boxed set was offered by the Atlantic Coast Conference in conjunction with Spectator Sports Services. It features 36 championship teams from 1954 to 1989, including 19 NCAA Final Four teams and three national championship teams. Only 10,000 of this first edition set were produced, with the set number indicated on a sequentially numbered gold card of authenticity. Also each set includes a randomly inserted bonus card, which is a duplicate of one of the championship team cards but portrays the official ACC seal in gold foil. The standard-size cards display on the front reproductions of the original black and white or color team photos as taken during the respective ACC championship seasons. The information presented on the backs includes a synopsis of the championship game, the box score, a listing of players and coaches appearing in the team photo, and the winner of the MVP award of the ACC Tournament. There are a number of noteworthy inclusions in the photos that have increased demand somewhat for some of the cards; these are noted parenthetically in the checklist below.

COMPLETE SET (40) 8.00 20.00
1 '54 NC State Wolfpack .20 .50
2 '55 NC State Wolfpack .20 .40
3 '56 NC State Wolfpack .20 .40
4 '57 UNC Tar Heels .20 .40
5 '58 Maryland Terrapins .20 .40
6 '59 NC State Wolfpack .20 .40
7 '60 Duke Blue Devils .20 .40
8 '61 Wake Forest .25 .60
Demon Deacons
(Billy Packer)
9 '62 Wake Forest .25 .60
Demon Deacons
(Billy Packer)
10 '63 Duke Blue Devils .20 .50
11 '64 Duke Blue Devils .20 .40
12 '65 NC State Wolfpack .20 .40
13 '66 Duke Blue Devils .20 .40
14 '67 UNC Tar Heels .20 .40
15 '68 UNC Tar Heels .20 .40
16 '69 UNC Tar Heels .20 .40
17 '70 NC State Wolfpack .20 .40
18 '71 SC Gamecocks .20 .40
19 '72 UNC Tar Heels .20 .40
20 '73 NC State Wolfpack .20 .50
21 '74 NC State Wolfpack .40 1.00
22 '75 UNC Tar Heels .20 .40
23 '76 Virginia Cavaliers .20 .40
24 '77 UNC Tar Heels .20 .40
25 '78 Duke Blue Devils .20 .40
26 '79 UNC Tar Heels .20 .40
27 '80 Duke Blue Devils .20 .40
28 '81 UNC Tar Heels .20 .50
29 '82 UNC Tar Heels 5.00 12.00
(Michael Jordan)
30 '83 NC State Wolfpack .40 1.00
(Coach Jim Valvano)
31 '84 Maryland Terrapins 1.50 4.00
(Len Bias)
32 '85 Georgia Tech .40 1.00
Yellow Jackets
(Mark Price)
33 '86 Duke Blue Devils .40 1.00
34 '87 NC State Wolfpack .20 .50
35 '88 Duke Blue Devils .40 1.00
36 '89 UNC Tar Heels .20 .50
NNO '91 FSU Joins ACC .20 .50
NNO Original ACC Seal .20 .40
NNO Revised ACC Seal .20 .40
(With Florida State)
NNO Certificate of .20 .40
Authenticity

1992 ACC Tournament Champs Gold

1 '54 NC State Wolfpack 1.50 4.00
2 '55 NC State Wolfpack 1.50 4.00
3 '56 NC State Wolfpack 1.50 4.00
4 '57 UNC Tar Heels 1.50 4.00
5 '58 Maryland Terrapins 1.50 4.00
6 '59 NC State Wolfpack 1.50 4.00
7 '60 Duke Blue Devils 1.50 4.00
8 '61 Wake Forest 2.50 6.00
Demon Deacons
(Billy Packer)
9 '62 Wake Forest 2.50 6.00
Demon Deacons
(Billy Packer)
10 '63 Duke Blue Devils 1.50 4.00
11 '64 Duke Blue Devils 1.50 4.00
12 '65 NC State Wolfpack 1.50 4.00
13 '66 Duke Blue Devils 1.50 4.00
14 '67 UNC Tar Heels 2.00 5.00
15 '68 UNC Tar Heels 2.00 5.00
16 '69 UNC Tar Heels 2.00 5.00
17 '70 NC State Wolfpack 1.50 4.00
18 '71 SC Gamecocks 1.50 4.00
19 '72 UNC Tar Heels 3.00 8.00
20 '73 NC State Wolfpack 3.00 8.00
21 '74 NC State Wolfpack 3.00 8.00
22 '75 UNC Tar Heels 2.50 6.00
23 '76 Virginia Cavaliers 1.50 4.00
24 '77 UNC Tar Heels 2.00 5.00
25 '78 Duke Blue Devils 2.00 5.00
26 '79 UNC Tar Heels 2.00 5.00
27 '80 Duke Blue Devils 2.00 5.00
28 '81 UNC Tar Heels 2.00 5.00
29 '82 UNC Tar Heels 25.00 60.00
(Michael Jordan)
30 '83 NC State Wolfpack 3.00 8.00
(Coach Jim Valvano)
31 '84 Maryland Terrapins 6.00 15.00
(Len Bias)
32 '85 Georgia Tech 5.00 12.00
Yellow Jackets
(Mark Price)
33 '86 Duke Blue Devils 3.00 8.00
34 '87 NC State Wolfpack 3.00 8.00
35 '88 Duke Blue Devils 5.00 12.00
36 '89 UNC Tar Heels 3.00 8.00

1993 Air Force Smokey

This set was produced to honor current and past Air Force Academy athletes and athletic traditions. These 16 standard-size cards feature on their fronts color player action shots set within gray borders with white diagonal stripes. The player's name and position appear on the left side underneath the photo. The team name and logo appear above the photo. The plain white back carries the player's name and position at the top, followed by a Smokey safety tip, and the player's career highlights. The cards are unnumbered and checklisted below in alphabetical order.

COMPLETE SET (16) 6.00 15.00
6 Reggie Minton BK CO .30 .75

1994 Air Force Smokey

Similar to the 1993 release, this set was produced to honor current and past Air Force Academy athletes and athletic traditions. These 16 standard-size cards feature on their fronts color player action shots set within gray borders with white diagonal stripes. The player's name and position appear on the left side underneath the photo and the team name and logo above the photo. The cards are unnumbered and checklisted below in alphabetical order.

COMPLETE SET (16) 6.00 15.00
3 Ray Dudley BK .30 .75
6 Reggie Minton BK CO .30 .75

1996-97 Alabama Schedules

This three card set features full color schedules picturing two players plus coach David Hobbs. The schedules were distributed for free at home games and at sponsor businesses like Texaco gas and Winn Dixie super markets.

COMPLETE SET (3) .60 1.50
1 Anthony Brown .20 .50
2 David Hobbs CO .30 .75
3 Wade Kaiser .20 .50

1992-93 Alabama-Birmingham

This 16-card set was issued in two eight-card perforated sheets consisting of standard-size cards. The fronts feature color action and posed player photos on a black card face. Two team color-coded horizontal stripes intersect the black border about one-third of the way from the top. The team logo is printed in golden yellow at the lower left edge. The player's name, team position, and number are printed on a golden yellow bar at the bottom of the picture. The white backs carry a black-and-white head shot of the player in the upper left. A brief biography appears to the right of the head shot while below is a player profile.

COMPLETE SET (16) 4.00 10.00
1 Reginald Allen .20 .50
2 Jeremy Bearden .20 .50
3 Carlos Browning .20 .50
4 Willie Chapman .20 .50
5 Patrick Craft .20 .50
6 Travis Harper .20 .50
7 Frank Haywood .20 .50
8 Nigel Hodges .20 .50
9 Corey Jackson .20 .50
10 Stanley Jackson .75 2.00
11 Carter Long .20 .50
12 Robert Shannon .60 1.50
13 Clarence Thrash .20 .50
14 George Wilkerson .20 .50
15 Gene Bartow CO .75 2.00
16 Willie Chapman .40 1.00
Stanley Jackson
George Wilkerson

1993-94 Alabama-Birmingham

This set consists of 14 standard-size cards. The fronts feature white-bordered color action and posed player photos. The team name appears in yellow and green lettering at the top; the player's name, position, and uniform number appear at the bottom. The white backs have the player's name and position centered at the top, with the career highlights below.

COMPLETE SET (14) 4.00 10.00
1 Gene Bartow CO .75 2.00
2 Frank Haywood .20 .50
3 Reginald Allen .20 .50
4 Carlos Browning .20 .50
5 George Wilkerson .20 .50
6 Clarence Thrash .20 .50
7 Robert Shannon 1.50 4.00
guarded by Anfernee Hardaway
8 Carter Long .20 .50
9 Corey Jackson .20 .50
10 Jeremy Bearden .20 .50
11 Chad Jones .20 .50
12 Travis Harper .20 .50
13 Blazer Seniors .40 1.00
Reginald Allen
Frank Haywood
Carter Long
Robert Shannon
Clarence Thrash
George Wilkerson
14 Checklist .20 .50

1998 AMA Kentucky Legends

This 36-card set was released by AMA in 1998, the set features some of the University of Kentucky's all-time great players.

COMPLETE SET (36) 8.00 20.00
1 Rupp Arena .25 .60
2 Team CL .25 .60
3 Cliff Barker .25 .60
4 Ralph Beard .40 1.00
5 Jerry Bird .25 .60
6 Rex Chapman .50 1.25
7 Johnny Cox .25 .60
8 Louie Dampier .40 1.00
9 John DeMoisey .25 .60
10 Billy Evans .25 .60
11 Richie Farmer .25 .60
12 Jack Givens .40 1.00
13 Phil Grawemeyer .30 .75
14 Kevin Grevey .50 1.25
15 Alex Groza .40 1.00
16 Cliff Hagan .60 1.50
17 Joe Hall .60 1.50
18 Vernon Hatton .25 .60
19 Basil Hayden .25 .60
20 Dan Issel .50 1.25
21 Wallace Jones .25 .60
22 Kyle Macy .40 1.00
23 Jamal Mashburn .75 2.00
24 Cotton Nash .40 1.00
25 Frank Ramsey .40 1.00
26 Pat Riley 1.00 2.50
27 Kenny Rollins .25 .60
28 Gayle Rose .25 .60
29 Layton Rouse .25 .60
30 Adolph Rupp 1.50 3.00
31 Forest Sale .25 .60
32 Jeff Sheppard .25 .60
33 Orlando Smith .25 .60
34 Carey Spicer .25 .60
35 Lou Tsioropoulos .40 1.00
36 Antoine Walker .75 2.00

1980-81 Arizona

This 19-card standard-size set was co-sponsored by Golden Eagle Distributors and the Tucson Police Department. The cards feature on the fronts color posed close-up photos, with the players in uniform and holding a basketball in their hands. The pictures are full-bleed on three sides, with the player's name and number in the bottom white border. The backs have biographical information, a discussion or definition of an aspect of basketball, and a safety message. The cards are unnumbered and checklisted below in alphabetical order. The two SP cards (Cook and Mosebar) are very difficult to find as they were pulled from the set before the set went into general distribution.

COMPLETE SET (19) 75.00 150.00
1 John Belobraydic 1.25 3.00
2 Russell Brown 1.25 3.00
3 Jeff Collins 1.25 3.00
4 Greg Cook SP 40.00 80.00
5 Ron Davis 1.25 3.00
6 Robbie Dosty 1.25 3.00
7 Mike Frink ACO 1.25 3.00
8 Len Gordy ACO 1.50 4.00
9 Mike Green ACO 1.25 3.00
10 Jack Magno 1.25 3.00
11 Donald Mellon 1.25 3.00
12 Charles Miller 1.25 3.00
13 David Mosebar SP 25.00 50.00
14 Frank Smith 1.25 3.00
15 John Smith 1.25 3.00
16 Fred Snowden CO 1.50 4.00
17 Harvey Thompson 1.25 3.00
18 Ernie Valenzuela 1.25 3.00
19 Ricky Walker 1.50 4.00

1981-82 Arizona

This 20-card set measures approximately 2 5/8" by 3 5/8". It is sponsored by Golden Eagle Distributors. A posed color photo appears on the front of the card, with the name and uniform number underneath the picture. The back of the card provides basic biographical information, a discussion or definition of an aspect of basketball, and a safety message. The cards have been arranged and numbered alphabetically in the checklist below.

COMPLETE SET (20) 16.00 40.00
1 Ken Atkins CO 1.00 2.50
2 John Belobraydic 55 1.00 2.50
3 Brock Brunkhorst 10 1.00 2.50
4 Jeff Collins 24 1.00 2.50
5 Greg Cook 22 2.00 5.00
6 Len Gordy CO 1.25 3.00
7 Gary J. Heintz CO 1.00 2.50
8 Keith Jackson 21 1.00 2.50
9 Mark Jung 33 1.00 2.50
10 Jack Magno 41 1.00 2.50
11 Donald Mellon 35 1.00 2.50
12 Charles Miller 52 1.00 2.50
13 Pete Murphy 15 1.00 2.50
14 Kevin Roundfield 44 1.00 2.50
(Misspelled Ronndfield)
15 Frank Smith 31 1.00 2.50
16 Fred Snowden CO 1.50 4.00
17 Ernest Taylor-Harris 32 1.00 2.50
18 Harvey Thompson 34 1.00 2.50
19 John Vlahogeorge 14 1.00 2.50
20 Ricky Walker 12 1.25 3.00

1983-84 Arizona

This 18-card set was cosponsored by the Tucson Police Department and Golden Eagle Distributors. The cards measure approximately 2 1/4" by 3 3/4". The fronts feature borderless posed color player photos, with the player's name and uniform number in the white stripe beneath the picture. The Beard and Haskin cards differ from the others in having the 1983-84 basketball schedule printed on the front. The backs present player profile, a discussion or definition of some aspect of basketball, and a safety message. The cards are unnumbered and checklisted below in alphabetical order, with the uniform number after the player's name. Among the players in the set is Steve Kerr, who would later go on to a career in the NBA.

COMPLETE SET (18) 20.00 35.00
1 Van Beard 54 .60 1.50
2 Ricky Byrdsong ACO 1.50 4.00
3 Brock Brunkhorst 10 .60 1.50
4 Ken Burmeister ACO .60 1.50
5 Troy Cooke 20 .60 1.50
6 Ken Ensor 22 .60 1.50
7 David Haskin 24 .60 1.50
8 Keith Jackson 21 .60 1.50
9 Steve Kerr 25 6.00 15.00
10 Lute Olson CO 5.00 12.00
11 Eddie Smith 14 .60 1.50
12 Michael Tait 11 .60 1.50
13 Greg Taylor 52 .60 1.50
14 Harvey Thompson 34 .60 1.50
15 Scott Thompson ACO .60 1.50
16 Pete Williams 32 1.00 2.50
17 Andy Woodtli 44 .60 1.50
18 Scott Thompson ACO 3.00 8.00
Lute Olson CO
Ricky Byrdsong ACO
Ken Burmeister ACO

1984-85 Arizona

This 16-card set measures approximately 2 1/4" by 3 3/4". It is jointly sponsored by the Tucson Police Department and Golden Eagle Distributors. The front of the card features a posed color photo of the player on the top portion, and the name and uniform number underneath the picture. The back of the card gives basic biographical information (including the player's nickname where appropriate), a discussion or definition of an aspect of basketball, and a safety message. Among the players in the set is Steve Kerr, who would later go on to a career in the NBA.

COMPLETE SET (16) 10.00 25.00
1 Brock Brunkhorst 10 .50 1.25
2 Ken Burmeister ACO 1.00 2.50
3 Ricky Byrdsong ACO .75 2.00
4 John Edgar 50 .50 1.25
5 Bruce Fraser 22 .50 1.25
6 David Haskin 24 .50 1.25
7 Keith Jackson 21 .50 1.25
8 Rolf Jacobs 13 .50 1.25
9 Steve Kerr 25 5.00 12.00
10 Craig McMillan 20 .50 1.25
11 Lute Olson CO 4.00 10.00
12 Eddie Smith 14 .50 1.25
13 Morgan Taylor 34 .50 1.25
14 Scott Thompson CO .50 1.25
15 Joe Turner 33 .50 1.25
16 Pete Williams 32 .50 1.25

1985-86 Arizona

This 14-card set measures approximately 2 1/4" by 3 3/4". It is jointly sponsered by the Tucson Police Department and Golden Eagle Distributors. The front of the card features a posed color photo of the player on the top portion and the name and uniform number underneath the picture. The back of the card gives basic biographical information, a discussion or definition of an aspect of basketball and a safety message. This set includes future NBA players and TV analysts Sean Elliott and Steve Kerr as well as major league star outfielder Kenny Lofton.

COMPLETE SET (14) 30.00 60.00
1 Anthony Cook 00 .75 2.00
2 Eric Cooper 21 .40 1.00
3 Brian David 34 .40 1.00
4 John Edgar 50 .40 1.00
5 Sean Elliott 32 8.00 20.00
6 Bruce Fraser 22 .40 1.00
7 David Haskin 24 .40 1.00
8 Rolf Jacobs 13 .40 1.00
9 Steve Kerr 25 4.00 10.00
10 Kenny Lofton 11 10.00 25.00
11 Craig McMillan 20 .40 1.00
12 Lute Olson CO 3.00 8.00
13 Joe Turner 33 .40 1.00
14 Bruce Wheatley 45 .40 1.00

1986-87 Arizona

COMPLETE SET (12) 25.00 50.00
1 Jud Buechler 2.00 5.00
2 Anthony Cook .60 1.50
3 Brian David .40 1.00
4 Sean Elliott 6.00 15.00
5 Bruce Fraser .40 1.00
6 Steve Kerr 3.00 8.00
7 Kenny Lofton 8.00 20.00
8 Harvey Mason .40 1.00
9 Craig McMillan .40 1.00
10 Lute Olson CO 3.00 8.00
11 Tom Tolbert 3.00 8.00
12 Joe Turner .40 1.00

1987-88 Arizona

COMPLETE SET (14) 20.00 40.00
1 Jud Buechler 35 1.25 3.00
2 Anthony Cook 00 .60 1.50
3 Brian David 34 .40 1.00
4 Sean Elliott 32 5.00 12.00
5 Mark Georgeson 34 .40 1.00
6 Steve Kerr 25 2.50 6.00
7 Kenny Lofton 11 6.00 15.00
8 Harvey Mason 44 .40 1.00
9 Craig McMillan 20 .40 1.00
10 Matt Muehlebach 44 .60 1.50
11 Lute Olson CO 2.00 5.00
12 Sean Rooks 23 1.50 4.00
13 Tom Tolbert 23 2.50 6.00
14 Joe Turner 33 .40 1.00

1988-89 Arizona

This 13-card set measures approximately 2 1/4" by 3 3/4". The set was jointly sponsored by the Tucson Police Department and Golden Eagle Distributors; some sets have been found however without the Golden Eagle logo. The front of the card features a posed color photo of the player on the top portion, and the name and uniform number underneath the picture. The back of the card gives basic biographical information, a discussion or definition of an aspect of basketball, and a safety message. NBA players Jud Buechler, Sean Elliott (misspelled Elliot), and Sean Rooks are included in this set as well as Cleveland Indians star outfielder Kenny Lofton. The cards are unnumbered and are checklisted below in alphabetical order, with the uniform number after the player's name.

COMPLETE SET (13) 12.00 30.00
1 Jud Buechler 35 1.25 3.00
2 Anthony Cook 00 .60 1.50
3 Ron Curry 33 .40 1.00
4 Brian David 34 .40 1.00
5 Sean Elliott 32 UER 4.00 10.00
6 Mark Georgeson 45 .40 1.00
7 Kenny Lofton 11 5.00 12.00
8 Harvey Mason 44 .40 1.00
9 Matt Muehlebach 24 .60 1.50
10 Lute Olson CO 2.00 5.00
11 Matt Othick 12 .60 1.50
12 Sean Rooks 42 1.25 3.00
13 Wayne Womack 30 .60 1.50

1989-90 Arizona

This 14-card set was cosponsored by the Tucson Police Department and Golden Eagle Distributors. The cards measure approximately 2 1/4" by 3 3/4". The fronts feature borderless posed color player photos, with the player's name and uniform number in the white stripe beneath the picture. The backs present player profile, a discussion or definition of some aspect of basketball, and a safety message. The cards are unnumbered and checklisted below in alphabetical order, with the uniform number after the player's name. The key cards in the set are Chris Mills, Sean Rooks, and Brian Williams.

COMPLETE SET (14) 8.00 20.00
1 Jud Buechler 35 1.00 2.50
2 Brian David 34 .40 1.00
3 Kevin Flanagan 51 .40 1.00
4 Deron Johnson 23 .40 1.00
5 Harvey Mason 44 .40 1.00
6 Chris Mills 42 3.00 8.00
7 Matt Muehlebach 24 .60 1.50
8 Lute Olson CO 2.00 5.00
9 Matt Othick 12 .60 1.50
10 Sean Rooks 45 1.25 3.00
11 Casey Schmidt 11 .40 1.00
12 Ed Stokes 41 .60 1.50
13 Brian Williams 21 2.50 6.00
14 Wayne Womack 30 .40 1.00

1990-91 Arizona

This 13-card set was cosponsored by the Tucson Police Department and Golden Eagles Distributors. The cards measure approximately 2 1/4" by 3 5/8". The fronts feature borderless posed color photos shot in front of the basketball goal. Each player is dressed in a dark blue jersey and is holding a basketball at his right side. The backs carry player profile, a discussion or definition of some aspect of basketball, and a safety message. The cards are unnumbered and checklisted below in alphabetical order. The key cards in this set are Chris Mills, Khalid Reeves, Sean Rooks, and Brian Williams.

COMPLETE SET (13) 10.00 25.00
1 Tony Clark .40 1.00
2 Kevin Flanagan .40 1.00
3 Deron Johnson .40 1.00
4 Chris Mills 2.50 6.00
5 Matt Muehlebach .60 1.50
6 Lute Olson CO 1.50 4.00
7 Matt Othick .60 1.50
8 Khalid Reeves 2.00 5.00
9 Sean Rooks 1.00 2.50
10 Casey Schmidt .40 1.00
11 Ed Stokes .60 1.50
12 Brian Williams 2.00 5.00
13 Wayne Womack .40 1.00

1990-91 Arizona Collegiate Collection Promos

This ten-card standard size set was produced by Collegiate Collection and features some of the great players of Arizona over the past few years. This set involves players of different sports and we have added a two-letter abbreviation next to the person's name to indicate what sport is pictured on the card. The back of the card either has statistical or biographical information about the player during their college career.

COMPLETE SET (10) 2.00 5.00
2 Steve Kerr BK .40 1.00
3 Lute Olson CO BK .40 1.00
5 Lute Olson CO BK .40 1.00
9 Sean Elliott BK .75 2.00

1990-91 Arizona Collegiate Collection

This 125-card standard-size was produced by Collegiate Collection. We've included a sport initial (B-baseball, K-basketball, F-football) for players in the top collected sports.

COMPLETE SET (125) 5.00 12.00
1 Steve Kerr K .20 .50
2 Sean Elliott K .40 1.00
4 Lute Olson CO K .20 .50
11 Warren Rustand K .05 .15
13 Steve Strong K .05 .15
17 Fred Snowden CO K .05 .15
21 Larry Demic K .05 .15
28 Steve Kerr K .20 .50
33 Anthony Cook K .05 .15
38 Sean Elliott K .40 1.00
39 Alan Zinter K .05 .15
40 Russell Brown K .05 .15
57 Pete Williams K .05 .15
64 Al Fleming K .05 .15
71 Joe Tofflemire K .05 .15
79 Kenny Lofton K 1.00 2.50
85 Sean Elliott K .40 1.00
88 Morris Udall K .10 .25
92 Eddie Smith K .05 .15
93 Steve Kerr K .20 .50
94 Dwight Taylor K .05 .15
97 Bob Elliott K .05 .15
99 Joe Nehls K .05 .15
103 Lute Olson CO K .30 .75
106 Bob Elliott K .05 .15
110 Sean Elliott K .40 1.00
118 J.F.(Pop) McKale CO K .05 .15
121 Ken Lofton K 1.00 2.50

1990-91 Arizona State Collegiate Collection Promos

This ten-card standard size set was issued by Collegiate Collection to honor some of the leading athletes in all sports played at Arizona State. The front features a full-color photo while the back of the card has information or statistical information about the player featured. To help identify the player there is a two-letter abbreviation of the athlete's sport next to the player's name.

COMPLETE SET (10) 1.50 4.00
2 Fat Lever BK .20 .50
5 Byron Scott BK .30 .75
6 Sam Williams BK .05 .15

1990-91 Arizona State Collegiate Collection

This 200-card standard-size mulit-sport set was produced by Collegiate Collection. We've included a sport initial (B-baseball, K-basketball, F-football, WK-women's basketball) for players in the top collected sports. The key card is one of the few cards featuring all-time Baseball great Barry Bonds in a college uniform.

COMPLETE SET (200) 6.00 15.00
4 Sam Williams K .05 .15
8 Byron Scott K .20 .50
9 Fat Lever K .07 .20
12 Lionel Hollins K .07 .20
15 Kurt Nimphius K .05 .15
18 Scott Lloyd K .05 .15
23 Chris Beasley K .05 .15
26 Steve Beck K .05 .15
31 Alton Lister K .07 .20
33 Fat Lever K .07 .20
41 Mark Landsberger K .05 .15
44 Paul Williams K .05 .15
64 Byron Scott K .15 .40
102 Bobby Winkles CO K .08 .25
128 Ned Wulk CO K .05 .15
154 Joe Caldwell K .05 .15
161 Art Becker K .05 .15
184 Freddie Lewis K .05 .15

1993-94 Arizona

COMPLETE SET (14) 10.00 25.00
1 Marty Barmentioo .50 1.25
2 Joseph Blair .60 1.50
3 Andy Brown .50 1.25
4 Kevin Flanagan .50 1.25
5 Reggie Geary .60 1.50
6 Jarvis Kelley .50 1.25
7 Joe McLean .50 1.25
8 Lute Olson CO 1.50 4.00
9 Ray Owes .60 1.50
10 Khalid Reeves 2.00 5.00
11 Jason Richey .50 1.25
12 Dylan Rigdon .50 1.25
13 Damon Stoudamire 3.00 8.00
14 Corey Williams .50 1.25

1995-96 Arizona

COMPLETE SET (15) 10.00 25.00
1 Marty Barmentioo .50 1.25
2 Joseph Blair .60 1.50
3 Ben Davis .60 1.50
4 Michael Dickerson .50 1.25
5 Kelvin Eafon .50 1.25
6 Reggie Geary .60 1.50
7 Donnell Harris .50 1.25
8 Jarvis Kelley .50 1.25
9 Joe McLean .50 1.25
10 Lute Olson CO 1.50 4.00
11 Ray Owes .60 1.50
12 Jason Richey .50 1.25
13 Miles Simon .60 1.50
14 Damon Stoudamire 2.00 5.00
15 Corey Williams .50 1.25

1987-88 Arizona State

Sponsored by the Valley of the Sun Kiwanis Club and "Our Quest: Their Best", this 22-card standard-size was produced by Sports Marketing Inc. The cards feature Arizona State athletes from various sports. The fronts have action color player photos against a white background. A maroon and wider yellow stripe appear below the picture, with the yellow stripe containing the player's name and sport. The words "Arizona State" are printed in maroon block letters above the photo and are underlined by a yellow stripe printed with the word "University". The Sun Devils mascot in the lower right corner rounds out the front. The backs are white with maroon print and include a player profile and a community service announcement from Sparky, the mascot. Sponsors' logos appear at the bottom. The sports represented are basketball, swimming, baseball, football, softball, track, gymnastics, tennis, and volleyball. The cards are unnumbered and checklisted below in alphabetical order.

COMPLETE SET (22) 8.00 20.00
1 Mark Becker BK .40 1.00
4 Mark Carlino BK .40 1.00
7 Mike Davies BK .40 1.00
15 Shamona Mosley BK .40 1.00
18 Steve Patterson CO BK .75 2.00
21 Arthur Thomas BK .40 1.00

1982-83 Arkansas

This 16-card set measures standard card size, 2 1/2" by 3 1/2". The card set was sponsored by Tom Kamerling's Sports Magazine. The black and white posed photo on the card's front is enclosed by a red border. The Arkansas Razorback logo appears above the photo, and the player's name, position, height, college classification, and hometown below the photo. The back of the card has the 1982-83 game schedule. Future NBA players included in this set are Joe Kleine, Alvin Robertson, and Darrell Walker. The cards are numbered for convenience in the checklist below alphabetically by subject.

COMPLETE SET (16) 25.00 60.00
1 Charles Balentine 1.50 4.00
2 Darryl Bedford 1.25 3.00
3 Robert Brannon 1.25 3.00
4 Willie Cutts 1.25 3.00
5 Keenan DeBose 1.25 3.00
6 Carey Kelly 1.25 3.00
7 Robert Kitchen 1.25 3.00
8 Joe Kleine 6.00 15.00
9 Ricky Norton 1.50 4.00
10 Eric Poerschke 1.25 3.00
11 Mike Ratliff 1.25 3.00
12 Alvin Robertson 6.00 15.00
13 John Snively 1.25 3.00
14 Eddie Sutton CO 6.00 15.00
15 Leroy Sutton 1.25 3.00
16 Darrell Walker 6.00 15.00

1989-90 Arkansas

This 24-card basketball standard-size set commemorates the 1989-90 Arkansas Razorbacks' appearance in the Final Four. The fronts feature action player photos. The player's name appears in a diagonal bar across the lower right corner. The words "1990 Final Four" are printed in a similar diagonal bar at the upper left corner of the picture. The title "Arkansas" is printed in bold lettering across the top of the card. The backs carry biographical information, player profile, and anti-drug messages in the form of "Tips from the Razorbacks."

COMPLETE SET (24) 20.00 50.00
1 Nolan Richardson CO 3.00 8.00
2 Clyde Fletcher .40 1.00
3 Larry Marks .40 1.00
4 Mario Credit .60 1.50
5 Warren Linn .40 1.00
6 Ernie Murry .40 1.00
7 Darrell Hawkins .40 1.00
8 Cannon Whitby .40 1.00
9 Ron Huery .60 1.50
10 Lenzie Howell .60 1.50
11 Lee Mayberry 2.00 5.00
12 Todd Day 2.50 6.00
13 Arlyn Bowers .40 1.00
14 Shawn Davis .40 1.00
15 Lee Mayberry 2.00 5.00
16 Lenzie Howell .60 1.50
17 Lee Mayberry 1.50 4.00
18 Todd Day 2.50 6.00
19 Nolan Richardson CO 3.00 8.00
20 SWC Classic Champs .60 1.50
21 Barnhill Arena .60 1.50
22 Todd Day 2.50 6.00
23 Oliver Miller 2.00 5.00
24 Edgar Anderson ACO 1.50 4.00
Nolan Richardson CO

1991 Arkansas Collegiate Collection

This 100-card multi-sport standard-size set was produced by Collegiate Collection. The fronts features a mixture of black and white or color player photos with black borders. The player's name is included in a black stripe below the picture. In a horizontal format the backs present biographical information, career summary, or statistics on a white background. Unless noted below, all players are from the sport of football.

COMPLETE SET (100) 6.00 15.00
3 Sidney Moncrief BK .20 .50
15 Tony Brown BK .07 .20
20 Keith Wilson BK .07 .20
35 Scott Hastings BK .05 .15
38 Joe Kleine BK .07 .20
44 Marvin Delph BK .07 .20
51 Alvin Robertson BK .07 .20
66 Martin Terry BK .10 .30
67 Andrew Lang BK .08 .25
69 Ron Brewer BK .07 .20
80 Ron Huery BK .07 .20
85 Darrell Walker BK .10 .30

1991-92 Arkansas Collegiate Collection

This 25-card standard-size set was produced by Collegiate Collection. The fronts display either action or posed color player photos, with rounded corners and black borders. The player's name appears in a red stripe below the picture. The horizontally oriented backs have biography, statistics, and career summary, superimposed over a gray razorback. The cards are numbered on the back and generally arranged in alphabetical order. The key cards in the set are Todd Day, Lee Mayberry, and Oliver Miller.

COMPLETE SET (25) 10.00 25.00
1 Nolan Richardson CO 2.50 6.00
2 Ray Biggers .40 1.00
3 Ken Biley .40 1.00
4 Shawn Davis .40 1.00
5 Todd Day 2.00 5.00
6 Clyde Fletcher .40 1.00
7 Darrell Hawkins .60 1.50
8 Warren Linn .40 1.00
9 Elmer Martin .40 1.00
10 Lee Mayberry 1.25 3.00
11 Clint McDaniel 1.00 2.50
12 Oliver Miller 2.00 5.00
13 Isaiah Morris 1.25 3.00
guarded by Larry Johnson
14 Davor Rimac .40 1.00
15 Robert Shepherd .40 1.00
16 Roosevelt Wallace .60 1.50
17 Alfred Warren .40 1.00
18 Barnhill Arena .40 1.00
19 Mike Anderson ACO .40 1.00
20 Brad Dunn ACO .40 1.00
21 Wayne Stehlik ACO .40 1.00
22 Nolan Richardson III .40 1.00
Volunteer Assistant CO
23 Ernie Murry .40 1.00
Graduate Assistant CO
24 Team Photo .75 2.00
25 Director Card .40 1.00
Checklist

1992-93 Arkansas

This 15-card set measures the standard size and features color action player photos bordered on the left or right edge by a gray stripe containing the team name. The player's name appears in red lettering on a white stripe at the bottom. The horizontal backs feature close-up player pictures with shadow box borders. The white background is printed with a profile of the player. The school logo and biographical information appear at the top. The cards are numbered on the back. The set contains the first card of Corliss Williamson.

COMPLETE SET (15) 5.00 12.00
1 Nolan Richardson CO 1.00 2.50
2 Dwight Stewart .60 1.50
3 Ken Biley .30 .75
4 Craig Tyson .30 .75
5 Corey Beck .75 2.00
6 Darrell Hawkins .40 1.00
7 Scotty Thurman 1.25 3.00
8 Warren Linn .30 .75
9 Davor Rimac .30 .75
10 Robert Shepherd .30 .75
11 Roger Crawford .30 .75
12 Corliss Williamson 2.00 5.00
13 Elmer Martin .30 .75
14 Clint McDaniel .60 1.50
15 Ray Biggers .30 .75

1993-94 Arkansas

Issued to commemorate the inaugural season of Arkansas' Walton Arena, these 18 standard-size cards feature on their fronts red-bordered color player action shots of the 1993-94 NCAA champion Razorbacks. The player's name appears in gold-colored lettering within one of the photo's corners. A gray panel on the red-bordered back carries another color player action shot at its upper left, followed by Coach Nolan Richardson's comments on the player, and previous season highlights. The player's name, position, class, and major appear in white lettering within the bottom red margin. The cards are unnumbered and checklisted below in alphabetical order. There were two versions of this set produced. The first printing indicates "Walton Arena Inaugural Season" and the second printing indicates "1994 NCAA Champs". Some premiums have been seen for the slightly more dificult to obtain "Walton" set.

COMPLETE SET (18) 6.00 15.00
1 Corey Beck .60 1.50
2 Ray Biggers .20 .50
3 Ken Biley .20 .50
4 Roger Crawford .20 .50
5 Al Dillard .30 .75
6 Elmer Martin .20 .50
7 Clint McDaniel .40 1.00
8 Nolan Richardson CO 1.00 2.50
9 Davor Rimac .20 .50
10 Darnell Robinson 1.25 3.00
11 Dwight Stewart .40 1.00
12 Scotty Thurman 1.25 3.00
13 Corliss Williamson 2.00 5.00
14 Lee Wilson .60 1.50
15 Mike Anderson ACO .25 .60
Brad Dunn ACO
Wayne Stehlik ACO
Nolan Richardson III ACO
16 Team Card .30 .75
17 Walton Arena .30 .75
18 Title Card .20 .50

1994-95 Arkansas Tickets

This set of 18 tickets features the 1994-95 Arkansas Razorbacks. Each ticket measures 1 1/2" by 5" and shows evidence of perforation on all four sides. (The set is also known to exist as an uncut sheet.) The ickets divide into two portions: the top portion and the bottom 1 3/8" perforated tab. The tabs have the admission price, day of the week, date of game, and are numbered Event 1-18. Inside gold borders, the top portion displays a color photo with a 1994 National Champions banner drapped across the top of the picture. The location of the game ("Bud Walton Arena") and the opponent are printed in the bottom gold border. The back consists of an advertisement from Coca-Cola and Subway and an offer to receive a free medium Coke with the purchase of a sandwich. The tickets are numbered according to the event and are checklisted below accordingly. Ticket #1 shows President Bill Clinton congratulating Nolan Richardson. Ticket #13 features Corliss Williamson, who was drafted by the Sacramento Kings in the 1995 NBA Draft.

COMPLETE SET (18) 4.00 10.00
1 Nolan Richardson CO 1.50 4.00
Bill Clinton PRES
2 John Engskov .20 .50
3 Reggie Merritt .20 .50
4 Nat'l Championship Trophy .20 .50
5 Kareem Reed .40 1.00
6 Lee Wilson .30 .75
7 Elmer Martin .20 .50
8 Landis Williams .20 .50
9 Nolan Richardson CO 1.25 3.00
10 Davor Rimac .20 .50
11 Darnell Robinson .40 1.00
12 Corey Beck .40 1.00
13 Corliss Williamson 1.50 4.00
14 Scotty Thurman .40 1.00
15 Dwight Stewart .30 .75
16 Clint McDaniel .30 .75
17 Reggie Garrett .20 .50
18 Alex Dillard .30 .75

1987-88 Auburn

This 16-card standard-size set was issued by Auburn University and includes members from different sports programs. Reportedly only 5,000 sets were made by McDag Productions, and the cards were distributed by the Opelika, Alabama police department. The cards feature color player photos on white card stock. The backs present safety tips for children. The last three cards of the set feature "Tiger Greats," former Auburn athletes Bo Jackson, Rowdy Gaines, and Chuck Person. The key card in the set is Frank Thomas. The sports represented in this set are football (1, 3, 5, 11-13, 16), basketball (4, 6, 9-10, 14), baseball (2), and swimming (15). A card of Bo Jackson playing Football has been recently discovered. Since very few of these cards are known it is not considered part of the complete set

COMPLETE SET (16) 70.00 175.00
4 Sonny Smith CO BK .60 1.50
6 Joe Ciampi BK .60 1.50
9 Jeff Moore BK .60 1.50
10 Vickie Orr BK .60 1.50
14 Chuck Person BK 4.00 10.00

1992-93 Auburn

This 14-card standard size set was produced by Collegiate Products. The fronts feature a mix of posed and action photos with a dark blue stripe on the left side displaying the school name. Along the bottom edge within a white stripe is the player's name in orange print. The horizontal backs carry a color head shot with black shadow box borders, school logo, biography, career summary and statistics. The set features the frst card of Wesley Person.

COMPLETE SET (14) 4.00 10.00
1 Tommy Joe Eagles CO .30 .75
2 Aubrey Wiley .30 .75
3 Wesley Person 2.50 6.00
4 Aaron Swinson .40 1.00
5 Ronnie Battle .30 .75
6 Cameron Boozer .30 .75
7 Reggie Gallon .20 .50
8 Leonard Smith .20 .50
9 Rod Joyce .20 .50
10 Byron Bell .20 .50
11 Pat Burke .20 .50
12 Mark Hutton .20 .50
13 Shawn Stuart .20 .50
14 Lance Weems .30 .75

1987-88 Baylor

This 17-card standard-size set was sponsored by the Hillcrest Baptist Medical Center, the Waco Police Department, and the Baylor University Department of Public Safety. The cards represent several sports: baseball (1-3), basketball (4-6), track (7-10), and football (11-17). The front feature color action shots of the players on white card stock. At the top the words "Baylor Bears 1987-88" are printed between the Hillcrest and Baylor University logos. Player information is given below the picture. The back has more logos, brief career summaries, and "Bear Briefs," which consist of instructional sports information and an anti-drug or crime message.

COMPLETE SET (17) 12.00 30.00
4 Micheal Williams 3.00 8.00
5 Darryl Middleton .75 2.00
6 Gene Iba CO .75 2.00

1989-90 Baylor

This 15-card standard-size set was issued compliments of the Waco Tribune-Herald. Inside white and green borders, the fronts feature posed color player photos shot against a yellow background. The player's name, position, and number are printed in the wider bottom border. The horizontal backs present biography, player profile, and collegiate statistics. The cards are unnumbered and checklisted below in alphabetical order. The most important card is that of David Wesley, a 1993-94 NBA rookie.

COMPLETE SET (15) 6.00 15.00
1 Kelvin Chalmers .40 1.00
2 Toby Christian .40 1.00
3 Julius Denton .40 1.00
4 Joey Fatta .40 1.00
5 Mitch Fogle .40 1.00
6 Michael Hobbs .40 1.00
7 Alex Holcombe .40 1.00
8 Melvin Hunt .40 1.00
9 Gene Iba CO .75 2.00
10 Ivan Jones .40 1.00
11 Dennis Lindsey .40 1.00
12 Tim Schumacher .40 1.00
13 David Wesley 3.00 8.00
14 Brian Zvonocek .40 1.00
15 Team photo .40 1.00

1990-91 Baylor

This 16-card set, sponsored by the Waco Tribune-Herald, highlights the 1990-91 Baylor Bears basketball team. The fronts have player close-up shots inside a green border. The rest of the card is white and green including the Baylor University logo in the bottom right corner. The backs are green and white as well with "Baylor Basketball 1990-91" inside a green border on the side. The player biographies and statistics are also included horizontally on the back. The cards are unnumbered and checklisted below in alphabetical order.

COMPLETE SET (16) 6.00 15.00
1 Ulises Asprilla .40 1.00
2 Herb Baker .40 1.00
3 Kelvin Chalmers .40 1.00
4 Toby Christian .40 1.00
5 Joey Fatta .40 1.00
6 David Hamilton .40 1.00
7 Alex Holcombe .40 1.00
8 Melvin Hunt .40 1.00
9 Gene Iba CO .75 2.00
10 Anthony Lewis .40 1.00
11 Dennis Lindsey .40 1.00
12 Tim Schumacher .40 1.00
13 Willie Sublett .40 1.00
14 Joe Tanksley .40 1.00
15 David Wesley 2.00 5.00
16 Brian Zvonocek .40 1.00
17 Baylor Bear CL .40 1.00

1972-73 Bradley Schedules

These five schedule cards measure approximately 2 1/2" by 3 3/4" and are printed on heavy cardboard stock. Each card shows a black and white photo of a player on the front with a Bradley schedule for the 1972-73 basketball season on the back. The cards have rounded corners; on the front, the player's name appears on a white stripe beneath the posed black-and-white player photo.

COMPLETE SET (5) 40.00 80.00
1 Sam Allen 10.00 20.00
2 Mark Dohner 10.00 20.00
3 Dave Klobucher 10.00 20.00
4 Seymour Reed 12.50 25.00
5 Doug Shank 10.00 20.00

1982-83 Bradley

This 16 card set measures approximately 3 1/2" by 2 1/8". The full color fronts feature a mix of posed and action shots. The backs have some limited biographical information. A variety of local spornsors helped produce these cards. Some cards do not have sponsor stamping on the back.

COMPLETE SET (16) 6.00 15.00
1 Tony Barrone ACO 1.00 2.50
2 Roosevelt Davison .40 1.00
3 Jay Eck ACO .40 1.00
4 Melvin Harden .40 1.00
5 Rudy Keeling ACO .40 1.00
6 Booker Johnson .40 1.00
7 Pat Marshall .40 1.00
8 Eddie Mathews .40 1.00
9 Barney Mines .40 1.00
10 Willie Scott .40 1.00
11 Franz Smith .40 1.00
12 Dick Versace CO 1.50 4.00
13 Anthony Webster .40 1.00
14 Greg Willie .40 1.00
15 Boise Winters .40 1.00
16 Arena .40 1.00

1985-86 Bradley

This 56-card standard-size set was made as a playing card set, complete with rounded corners and playing-card finish. Most of the fronts feature white-bordered black-and-white photos of great Bradley Braves players from the past. The player's name and distinction appear on the border beneath the photo, and the card number and suit appear in the top left, and again, but inverted, in the bottom right. The back has the Bradley Braves name and logo in a pink field edged in red and bordered in white. Also on the back, "75 Memorable Years" is printed in red. The cards are listed below as they appear on the cards, with suffixes (C, D, H and S) representing the suits (Clubs, Diamonds, Hearts and Spades); the numbers 11, 12 and 13 representing Jacks, Queens and Kings, respectively; and JK denoting Jokers.

COMPLETE SET (56) 16.00 40.00
C1 Chet Walker 2.00 5.00
C2 Al Smith .60 1.50
C3 Mike Owens .40 1.00
C4 Tom Les .40 1.00
C5 1950-51 Team Photo .60 1.50
C6 Jack Brickhouse ANN 1.25 3.00
Mark Holtz ANN
Tom Kelly ANN
Vince Lloyd ANN
Dave Snell ANN
Bob Starr ANN
C7 Levern Tart .60 1.50
C8 Chuck Orsborn CO .40 1.00
C9 Willie Scott .40 1.00
C10 1956-57 Team Photo .60 1.50
C11 Forddy Anderson CO .40 1.00
C12 1963-64 Team Photo .60 1.50
C13 1981-82 Team Photo .60 1.50
D1 Gene Morse .40 1.00
D2 Joe Stowell CO .40 1.00
D3 Steve Kuberski .75 2.00
D4 L.C. Bowen .40 1.00
D5 Bobby Humbles .40 1.00
D6 Joe Allen ACO .75 2.00
Tony Barone ACO
Chuck Buescher ACO
Mark Dohner ACO
Ron Harris ACO
Rudy Keeling ACO
D7 Journal Star Writers .40 1.00
Gary Childs
Kenneth Jones
Paul King
Dick Lien
Max Siebel
Phil Theobald
Lefty Tyler
D8 Harry Wilcoxen .40 1.00
D9 Joe Billy McDade .40 1.00
D10 Ron Ferguson CO .40 1.00
D11 Mitchell Anderson .75 2.00

D12 1979-80 Team Photo	.60	1.50
D13 Joe Allen	.60	1.50
H1 Paul Unruh	.75	2.00
H2 Voise Winters	.40	1.00
H3 PA Announcers	.40	1.00
Frank Busone		
Paul Herzog		
Bob Loy		
H4 Ken Brown ANN	.40	1.00
Lorne Brown ANN		
Frank Busone ANN		
Mort Cantor ANN		
H5 1965-66 Team Photo	.60	1.50
H6 Joe Strawder	.40	1.00
H7 Chiefs Club Presidents	.40	1.00
Grant Bush		
Mort Cantor		
Ed Erhgott		
Henry Holling		
Keith Holloway		
Grant Mathey		
Paul Unruh		
H8 Marcel DeSouza	.75	2.00
H9 1959-60 Team Photo	.60	1.50
H10 Shellie McMillon	.75	2.00
H11 Gene Melchiorre	.60	1.50
H12 Bradley's Famous Five	.60	1.50
H13 A.J. Robertson CO	.40	1.00
S1 Bob Carney	.40	1.00
S2 Ray Ramsey	.40	1.00
S3 Barney Cable	.75	2.00
S4 Dutch Meinen CO	.40	1.00
S5 All-Stars Who	.75	2.00
Toured Brazil		
Jim Caruthers		
Mike Davis		
Mark Dohner		
Tom Les		
Seymour Reed		
S6 Bradley Area	.40	1.00
Automobile Sponsors		
Joe McCarthy		
Dick Miller		
Neil Norton		
John Pearl		
Mickey Smith		
Bill and Ken Schaffnit		
S7 B Club Presidents	.40	1.00
Ron Baurer		
Larry Cowling		
Jack Heintzman		
Glen McCullough		
Bill Ridgely		
William Robertson		
Carl Traficana		
S8 Bobby Joe Mason	1.25	3.00
S9 Dick Versace CO	1.25	3.00
S10 Stan Albeck	1.25	3.00
S11 Roger Phegley	.75	2.00
S12 Jack Brickhouse	1.25	3.00
HOF broadcaster		
S13 1949-50 Team Photo	.60	1.50
JK Peoria Civic Center	.40	1.00
JK 1985-86 Schedule	.40	1.00
NNO Joker	.40	1.00
Peoria Civic Center		
NNO Schedule card	.40	1.00

1987-88 Bradley Schedules

Sponsered by Cheddar's, this 16-card schedule set was produced for the Bradley Braves 1987-88 season. Each schedule (when flat) features a coupon on the front left half and a player photo on the right half. The back features the basketball schedule on the left half and the Chiefs Club Promotional Events on the right. The cards measure 4 1/4" by 5 1/2". The cards are not numbered and listed below alphabetically.

COMPLETE SET (16)	5.00	12.00
1 Stan Albeck CO	1.25	3.00
2 Steve Bayless	.30	.75
3 Scott Beccue	.30	.75
4 Len Bertolini	.30	.75
5 Deon Butler	.30	.75
6 Mike Cash	.30	.75
7 Hersey Hawkins	3.00	8.00
8 Luke Jackson	.30	.75
9 Greg Jones	.30	.75
10 Anthony Manuel	.30	.75
11 Bruce Mordini	.30	.75
12 Donald Powell	.30	.75
13 Jay Schell	.30	.75
14 Jerry Thomas	.30	.75
15 Trevor Trimpe	.30	.75
16 Paul Wilson	.30	.75

1990-91 Bradley

Co-sponsored by Kodacolor and Peoria Camera Shop, this 25-card standard-size set was issued in five five-card perforated strips. One strip was given away at each of five home games. The fronts feature red-bordered color player posed and action shots on the fronts, except for a couple "Brave of the Past" cards, which sport black-and-white photos. The player's name, jersey number, and position appear in black beneath his picture, and the Bradley logo is displayed in the upper left. The plain white back has the player's name, jersey number and position, along with a brief biography and the Bradley logo, at the top. A short section that contains career highlights and stats lies beneath, and the Kodak logo at the bottom rounds out the back. The cards are unnumbered and checklisted below in alphabetical order.

COMPLETE SET (25)	12.00	30.00
1 Stan Albeck CO	1.00	2.50
2 James Bailey	.40	1.00
3 Mark Bailey	.40	1.00
4 Andy Bastock	.40	1.00
5 Scott Behrends	.40	1.00
6 Duane Broussard	.40	1.00
7 Kwame Brown	.40	1.00
8 Adam Carl	.40	1.00
9 Mark Dietrich	.40	1.00
10 Marty Gillespie CO	.40	1.00
11 James Hamilton	.40	1.00
12 Hersey Hawkins	5.00	12.00
13 Xanthus Houston	.60	1.50
14 Paul Lee	.40	1.00
15 Jim Les	1.25	3.00
16 Mo McHone ACO	.60	1.50
17 Roger Phegley	.60	1.50
18 Sean Smith	.40	1.00
19 Maurice Stovall	.40	1.00
20 Curtis Stuckey	.60	1.50
21 Paul Unruh	.60	1.50
22 Chet Walker	2.50	6.00
23 Charles White	.40	1.00
24 Tom Wilson	.40	1.00
25 Tony Wysinger	.40	1.00

1993-94 Bradley

Sponsored by Peoria Downtown Kiwanis Club, this 18-card standard-size set features the 1993-94 Bradley Braves. The fronts feature color player photos with white borders. The player's name and position appear on the bottom of the card on team color-coded stripes. The horizontal backs have another small color player photo, with short biography and accomplishments. Platinum sponsors are printed in a red rectangle, gold sponsors in a gray rectangle.

COMPLETE SET (18)	5.00	12.00
1 Checklist	.20	.50
2 Duane Broussard	.20	.50
3 Jim Molinari	.30	.75
4 Duane Broussard ACO	.20	.50
Pat Donahue ACO		
Rob Judson ACO		
5 Marcus Pollard	.20	.50
6 Roger Suchy	.20	.50
7 David Winslow	.20	.50
8 Dwayne Funches	.20	.50
9 Rick Harris	.20	.50
10 Deon Jackson	.30	.75
11 Chad Kleine	.20	.50
12 Billy Wright	.30	.75
13 James Baptist	.20	.50
14 Kerry Burrell	.20	.50
15 Anthony Parker	1.25	3.00
16 Aaron Zobrist	.20	.50
17 Jim Les	1.25	3.00
Hersey Hawkins		
Bradley Alumni		
in the NBA		
18 Dave Snell ANN	.20	.50
Joe Stowell ANN		
Jim Watson ANN		

1994-95 Bradley

Sponsored by Peoria Downtown Kiwanis Club, this 18-card standard-size set features the 1994-95 Bradley Braves. On a simulated wooden background, the fronts feature tilted color action player photos. The player's name and position appear at the bottom on red stripes. The horizontal backs carry a small black-and-white player photo, along with short biography and accomplishments. Platinum sponsors are printed in a red rectangle, gold sponsors in a gray rectangle.

COMPLETE SET (18)	3.00	8.00
1 Checklist	.20	.50
Bob Carney		
Joe Allen		
2 Jim Molinari CO	.30	.75
3 Duane Broussard ACO	.20	.50
Pat Donahue ACO		
Rob Judson ACO		
4 David Winslow	.20	.50
5 Aaron Zobrist	.20	.50
6 Billy Wright	.30	.75
7 Marcus Samuels	.20	.50
8 Anthony Parker	1.00	2.50
9 Kerry Burrell	.20	.50
10 Chad Kleine	.20	.50
11 Dwayne Funches	.20	.50
12 Deon Jackson	.40	1.00
guarded by Brent Barry		
13 Mbaukwu Nwaogwugwu	.20	.50
14 James Baptist	.20	.50
15 Adebayo Akinkunle	.20	.50
16 Ben Coupet	.20	.50
17 Dave Snell ANN	.20	.50
Joe Stowell ANN		
Jim Watson ANN		
18 Marcus Pollard	.20	.50

1995-96 Bradley

Sponsored by Peoria Downtown Kiwanis Club, this 18-card standard-size set features the 1995-96 Bradley Braves. The fronts have color action player photos set on a red background. The player's name appears in a white oval below the picture, and their postion is listed in white below the oval. The horizontal backs carry a small colored action photo with a short biography and accomplishments. Platinum sponsors are listed with white type in a red oval, and below the oval in red print are gold sponsors.

COMPLETE SET (18)	3.00	8.00
1 Checklist	.60	1.50
Banquet		
Hall of Fame		
Gene Gathers		
Chet Walker		
2 Jim Molinari CO	.30	.75
3 Duane Broussard ACO	.20	.50
Pat Donahue ACO		
Rob Judson ACO		
4 Deon Jackson	.30	.75
5 Chad Kleine	.20	.50
6 Billy Wright	.30	.75
7 Dwayne Funches	.20	.50
8 Mbaukwu Nwaogwugwu	.20	.50
9 Anthony Parker	1.00	2.50
10 Ben Coupet	.20	.50
11 Kerry Burrell	.20	.50
12 Aaron Zobrist	.20	.50
13 James Baptist	.20	.50
14 Adebayo Akinkunle	.20	.50
15 Marcus Samuels	.20	.50
16 Gavin Schairer	.20	.50
17 Jim Watson ANN	.20	.50
Dave Snell ANN		
Joe Stowell ANN		
18 Kiwanis Builder Award	.30	.75
Billy Wright		

1987-88 BYU

This 25-card standard-size set was issued by Brigham Young University. Reportedly only 20,000 sets were produced, and each set was numbered from 1 to 20,000 on the back of every card. The player cards feature color photos, while the team photo card is sepia-toned. The cards have a blue border, with the BYU logo in the lower right corner. Popular players on the team are featured on two cards, one action shot and one portrait. The backs have biographical and statistical information, as well as the card number.

COMPLETE SET (25)	5.00	12.00
1 Michael Smith	.75	2.00
2 BYU Header card	.40	1.00
3 Jim Usevitch	.20	.50
4 Nathan Call	.20	.50
5 Brian Taylor	.20	.50
6 Ladell Andersen CO	.40	1.00
7 Roger Reid	.40	1.00
8 Carl Ingersoll	.20	.50
9 Jeff Chatman	.30	.75
10 Team Photo	.60	1.50
11 Mike Herring	.20	.50
12 Chris Lynch	.20	.50
13 Steve Schreiner	.20	.50
14 Gary Trost	.30	.75
15 David Lynch	.20	.50
16 Brian Taylor	.30	.75
17 Andy Toolson	.60	1.50
18 Jim Usevitch	.20	.50
19 Vince Bryan	.20	.50
20 Mark Clausen	.20	.50
21 Alan Astle	.20	.50
22 Nathan Call	.20	.50
23 Jeff Chatman	.30	.75
24 Marty Haws	.30	.75
25 Michael Smith	.75	2.00

1988-89 BYU

This 25-card set measures the standard size. Five thousand sets were printed, and the set serial number appears on a cardboard tag attached to the clear plastic package. The fronts feature color action and posed player photos with white borders. A light blue bar area below the picture contains the player's name, height, weight, classification, and position. The BYU logo is in the lower right corner. The season year is printed in black and superimposed at the upper left corner of the photo. The horizontal backs of card numbers 1-17 present statistics, and player information under the following categories: personal, high school, BYU, and Coach Ladell Andersen's comments on the player. The content of the backs of card numbers 18-24 is listed below.

COMPLETE SET (25)	4.00	10.00
1 Team Photo	.60	1.50
2 Michael Smith	.75	2.00
3 Alan Framton	.20	.50
4 Alan Astle	.20	.50
5 Mike Herring	.20	.50
6 Mark Heslop	.20	.50
7 Steve Andrus	.20	.50
8 Steve Schreiner	.20	.50
9 Andy Toolson UER	.40	1.00
10 Vince Bryan	.20	.50
11 Marty Haws	.30	.75
12 Kevin Santiago	.20	.50
13 David Wolfe	.20	.50
14 John Fish	.20	.50
15 Carl Ingersoll ACO	.20	.50
16 Roger Reid ACO	.30	.75
17 Ladell Andersen CO	.40	1.00
18 Alan Astle	.20	.50
19 Marty Haws	.30	.75
20 Michael Smith	.40	1.00
(Coaching records on back)		
21 Michael Smith	.40	1.00
22 Marty Haws	.30	.75
23 Andy Toolson UER	.40	1.00
24 Marty Haws	.30	.75
25 Title Card	.30	.75

1990-91 BYU Shawn Bradley

Sponsored by Pizza Hut, this black and white, over-sized card (2 7/8" x 4 1/4") features star center and eventual number two overall draft pick Shawn Bradley. The black and white back features information on Bradley and a basketball tip. The best information known is that there are at least two other cards in this set, but no specifics are known. It may be part of a larger set and it's likely that it was distributed at home games and or with pizza delivery.

1 Shawn Bradley	3.00	8.00

1989-90 California

This 16-card standard-size set was jointly sponsored by the USDA Forest Service, California Dept. of Forestry and Fire Protection, and USDI Bureau of Land Management. On a white card face, the fronts feature either posed or action color player photos. Yellow stripes edge the photo above and below, and a blue shadow border runs along the right side of the picture. The backs carry biography, player profile, and a fire prevention cartoon starring Smokey the Bear. The cards are unnumbered and checklisted below in alphabetical order.

COMPLETE SET (16)	12.00	30.00
1 Rich Branham	.75	2.00
2 Andrew Brigham	.75	2.00
3 DeShon Brown	.75	2.00
4 Lou Campanelli CO	1.50	4.00
5 John Carty	.75	2.00
6 Gary Colson ACO	1.25	3.00
7 Ryan Drew	.75	2.00
8 Bill Elleby	.75	2.00
9 Roy Fisher	1.25	3.00
10 Sean Harrell	.75	2.00
11 Brian Hendrick	1.25	3.00
12 Eric McDonough	.75	2.00
13 Andre Reyes	.75	2.00
14 Keith Smith	.75	2.00
15 Bryant Walton	.75	2.00
16 Jeff Wulburn ACO	.75	2.00

1994-95 California

%This 16 card standard-size set was sponsored by Power Bar. The front features a full bleed, full color action photo with the player's name written vertically on the left side in white letters. There is a yellow "Cal" emblem in the upper-right hand corner. The backs have a blue border with four blue diamonds. Inside the border, the player's biography, player profile, and Power Bar logo are found. The cards are unnumbered and checklisted below in alphabetical order.

COMPLETE SET (16)	8.00	20.00
1 Monty Buckley	.20	.50
2 Randy Duck	.60	1.50
3 Tremaine Fowlkes	1.25	3.00
4 Jelani Gardner	.75	2.00
5 Tony Gonzalez	5.00	12.00
6 Alfred Grigsby	.30	.75
7 Ryan Jamison	.20	.50
8 Sean Marks	.20	.50
9 Anwar McQueen	.20	.50
10 K.J. Roberts	.20	.50
11 Michael Stewart	1.00	2.50
12 Todd Bozeman CO	.60	1.50
13 Billy Kennedy ACO	.20	.50
Kurtis Townsend ACO		
Charles Payne ACO		
14 Oski (Mascot)	.20	.50
15 Team Photo	.30	.75
16 Team Photo	.30	.75

1996-97 California

This 10-card set was released at California during the 1996-97 season. These cards were sponsored by the California Highway Patrol, and feature many of the players from that season's team. The set is not numbered and is listed below in alphabetical order.

COMPLETE SET (10)	6.00	15.00
1 Randy Duck	.40	1.00
2 Tony Gonzalez	3.00	8.00
3 Ed Gray	1.25	3.00
4 Alfred Grigsby	.20	.50
5 Sean Jackson	.20	.50
6 Kenyon Jones	.20	.50
7 Sean Marks	.20	.50
8 Prentice McGruder	.20	.50
9 Anwar McQueen	.20	.50
10 Michael Stewart	.75	2.00

1996-97 California Women

This 10-card set was released at California during the 1996-97 season. These cards were sponsored by the California Highway Patrol, and feature many of the players from that season's team. The set is not numbered and is listed below in alphabetical order.

COMPLETE SET (10)	3.00	8.00
1 Patrycja Czepiec	.30	.75
Tatiana Dmitrieva		
2 Elke Snijder	.30	.75
Lexy Tamony		
3 Sherrise Smith	.30	.75
Kobie Kennon		
4 Geneva McDaniel	.30	.75
Paige Bowie		
5 Mary Scotty	.30	.75
Liz Rizzo		
6 Jamilla Churchill	.30	.75
Jennie Leander		
7 Marie Folsom	.30	.75
Angie Wong		
8 Marianne Stanley	1.25	3.00
Barbara Thaxton		
Marie Christian		
9 Team Photo	.30	.75
10 Team Photo	.30	.75

1990-91 California State Women

This 17-card standard size set was sponsered by Smokey. The cards are unnumbered and checklisted below in alphabetical order.

COMPLETE SET (17)	2.50	6.00
1 Ann Brewster	.20	.50
2 Alice Cole	.20	.50
3 Nicole Coupland	.20	.50
4 Kristy Cox	.20	.50
5 Lori Cox	.20	.50
6 Keli Floyd	.20	.50
7 Melinda Levering	.20	.50
8 Julie Mack	.20	.50
9 Stacy McClelland	.20	.50
10 Lisa Minturn	.20	.50
11 Heather Moulton	.20	.50
12 Nicole Perry	.20	.50
13 Sherri Renfrow	.20	.50
14 Kellie Rhoads	.20	.50
15 Carol Schoenmann	.20	.50
16 Tricia Stilwell	.20	.50
17 Kelly Walund	.20	.50

1994-95 Cassville HS

This 30-card set measures the standard size and features the men's (111-118, 129-135) and women's (112-128) basketball teams. Just 500 sets were produced. The fronts feature color action player shots with the school name on a green stripe at the bottom. The cards are numbered on the back with #111-135 as the team set and #147-151 being special edition singles. In black print on a gray background, the backs carry the player's name, sport, activities, a positive image point, and the slogan "Youth for a Positive Self Image." The team's best player was Sam Okey, who signed with the University of Wisconsin.

COMPLETE SET (30)	8.00	20.00
111 Scott Uppena	.20	.50
112 Chris Koopman	.20	.50
John Koopman		
113 John Koopman	.20	.50
114 Chris Koopman	.20	.50
115 Tim Ackerman	.20	.50
Todd Ackerman		
116 Tim Ackerman	.20	.50
117 Todd Ackerman	.20	.50
118 Marty Riedl	.20	.50
119 Katie Koopman	.20	.50
120 Maureen White	.20	.50
121 Jaime Hochhausen	.20	.50
122 Annie Klein	.20	.50
123 Sara Wunderlin	.20	.50
124 Laura Uppena	.20	.50
125 Jessica Kartman	.20	.50
126 Carolyn Hughes	.20	.50
127 Jane Tennessen	.40	1.00
128 Jason Schulting CO	.20	.50
129 Jeff Adrian	.20	.50
130 Tom Tennessen	.20	.50
131 T. J.-Whyte	.20	.50
132 Kris Willis	.20	.50
133 Dennis Uppena CO	.75	2.00
134 Adam Ploessl	.20	.50
135 Sam Okey	1.25	3.00
147 Sam Okey	1.25	3.00
148 Sam Okey	1.25	3.00
149 Sam Okey	1.25	3.00
150 Sam Okey	1.25	3.00
151 Sam Okey	1.25	3.00

1992-93 Cincinnati

This 14-card standard-size set features full-bleed action color player photos. A diagonal gray stripe across one of the top corners contains the word "Cincinnati". A white bar near the bottom displays the player's name in red print. The horizontal backs feature small, color close-ups, and the player's name and biographical information. The major portion of the back is devoted to a player profile and statistics. The cards are unnumbered and checklisted below in alphabetical order. The set features the first card of Nick Van Exel.

COMPLETE SET (14)	5.00	12.00
1 Corie Blount	1.00	2.50
2 Curtis Bostic	.40	1.00
3 LaZelle Durden	.40	1.00
4 David Evans	.20	.50
5 Darrick Ford	.20	.50
6 Tarrance Gibson	.20	.50
7 Keith Gregor	.30	.75
8 Mike Harris	.20	.50
9 Bob Huggins CO	1.25	3.00
10 Allen Jackson	.20	.50
11 John Jacobs	.20	.50
12 Erick Martin	.30	.75
13 Terry Nelson	.30	.75
14 Nick Van Exel	3.00	8.00

1993-94 Cincinnati

This 18-card standard-size set features the 1993-94 Cincinnati Bearcats. Inside bright red borders, the fronts feature color player cutouts on a screened maroon background. Printed in red lettering at the top in the background is "Cincinnati Bearcats"; the player's name is printed in gold next to the cutout. Inside a bright red border on a gray panel, the horizontal backs carry a color head shot, player profile, and statistics. The cards are unnumbered and checklisted below in alphabetical order.

COMPLETE SET (18)	5.00	12.00
1 Corie Blount	2.00	5.00
Nick Van Exel		
Bearcats in the Pros		
2 Curtis Bostic	.40	1.00
3 Darnell Burton	.40	1.00
4 LaZelle Durden	.40	1.00
5 David Evans	.20	.50
6 Damon Flint	.40	1.00
7 Keith Gregor	.20	.50
8 Mike Harris	.20	.50
9 Larry Harrison ACO	.20	.50
Steve Moeller ACO		
John Loyer ACO		
10 Bob Huggins CO	1.00	2.50
11 John Jacobs	.20	.50
12 Jackson Julson	.20	.50
13 Dontonio Wingfield	1.00	2.50
14 Brian Wolf	.20	.50
15 Marko Wright	.20	.50
16 The Shoemaker Center	.20	.50
17 Cincinnati in the	.20	.50
NCAA Tournament		
18 Title Card	.20	.50

1988-89 Clemson

This 16-card standard-size set was sponsored by Carolina Pride, and its company logo appears in the upper right corner of the card face. The fronts feature color head and shoulders player photos on a white card face. Player identification is given in the border below the picture. The cards are unnumbered and checklisted below in alphabetical order. Key cards in the set include Elden Campbell and Dale Davis.

COMPLETE SET (16)	15.00	40.00
1 Colby Brown	.40	1.00
2 Donnell Bruce	.40	1.00
3 Elden Campbell	5.00	12.00
4 Marion Cash	.40	1.00
5 Dale Davis	5.00	12.00
6 Cliff Ellis CO	1.25	3.00
7 Derrick Forrest	.40	1.00
8 Len Gordy ACO	.40	1.00
9 Eugene Harris ACO	.40	1.00
10 Kirkland Howling	.40	1.00
11 Ricky Jones	.40	1.00
12 Tim Kincaid	.40	1.00
13 Rod Mitchell	.40	1.00
14 Jerry Pryor	.40	1.00
15 David Young	.40	1.00
16 Logo Card	.40	1.00

1989-90 Clemson

This 16-card set was sponsored by Carolina Pride, and its company logo appears in the lower left corner of the card face as well as on the back. The cards were issued on an unperforated sheet with four rows of four cards; after cutting, the cards measure the standard size. The fronts feature color head and shoulders player photos on a white card face. Blue borders on the bottom and right of the picture form a shadow. The school and team names are printed in orange and blue above the picture, with an orange pawprint in the upper right corner. Player identification is given in the blue border below the picture. The backs have biographical information, player evaluation, and basketball advice in the form of "Tips from the Tigers." The cards are unnumbered and checklisted below in alphabetical order, with the uniform number after the player's name. Key cards in the set include Elden Campbell and Dale Davis.

COMPLETE SET (16)	10.00	25.00
1 Colby Brown 44	.40	1.00
2 Donnell Bruce 14	.40	1.00
3 Wayne Buckingham 42	.40	1.00
4 Elden Campbell 41	4.00	10.00
5 Marion Cash 12	.40	1.00
6 Dale Davis 34	4.00	10.00
7 Cliff Ellis CO	.75	2.00
8 Derrick Forrest 13	.40	1.00
9 Len Gordy CO	.40	1.00
10 Eugene Harris CO	.40	1.00
11 Kirkland Howling 4	.40	1.00
12 Ricky Jones 25	.40	1.00
13 Zlatko Josic 32	.40	1.00
14 Shawn Lastinger 15	.40	1.00
15 Sean Tyson 22	.40	1.00
16 David Young 11	.40	1.00

1990-91 Clemson

This 16-card standard-size set was issued by Carolina Pride. The orange color front of the card has an action color photo in the middle, with black text on each of its four sides. The back of each card includes basic biographical information and a basketball tip. The cards are numbered for convenience in the checklist below alphabetically by subject. The key card in the set is Dale Davis.

COMPLETE SET (16)	6.00	15.00
1 Andre Bovain 31	.40	1.00
2 Colby Brown 44	.40	1.00
3 Donnell Bruce 14	.40	1.00
4 Eric Burks 24	.40	1.00
5 Dale Davis 34	3.00	8.00
6 Cliff Ellis CO	.60	1.50
7 Len Gordy ACO	.40	1.00
8 Eugene Harris ACO	.40	1.00
9 Steve Harris 13	.60	1.50
10 Ricky Jones 25	.75	2.00
11 Shawn Lastinger 15	.40	1.00
12 Jimmy Mason 10	.40	1.00
13 Tyrone Paul 32	.40	1.00
14 Sean Tyson 22	.40	1.00
15 Joey Watts 20	.40	1.00
16 David Young 11	.40	1.00

1990-91 Clemson Collegiate Collection Promos

This ten-card standard-size set was issued by Collegiate Collection to honor some of the great athletes who played at Clemson. The front of the card features a full-color photo of the person featured while the back of the card has details about the person pictured. As this set is a multi-sport set we have used a two-letter identification of the sport next to the person's name.

COMPLETE SET (10)	1.50	4.00
C1 Tree Rollins BK	.30	.75

1990-91 Clemson Collegiate Collection

This 200-card standard-size set was produced by Collegiate Collection. We've included a sport initial (B-baseball, K-basketball, F-football, G-Golf, WK-women's basketball) for players in the top collected sports.

COMPLETE SET (200)	6.00	15.00
3 Wayne(Tree) Rollins K	.08	.25
6 Larry Nance K	.20	.50
8 Horace Grant K	.40	1.00
12 Bobby Conrad K	.07	.20
17 Elden Campbell K	.20	.50
24 Vincent Hamilton K	.05	.15
29 Tigers Win Classic K	.05	.15
35 Murray Jarman K	.05	.15
40 Grayson Marshall K	.05	.15
43 Billy Williams K	.05	.15
59 Randy Mazey B	.05	.15
68 Butch Zatezalo K	.05	.15
74 Michael Tait K	.05	.15
76 Horace Wyatt K	.05	.15
80 Tigers with ACC Title K	.05	.15
92 Cliff Ellis CO K	.07	.20
97 Derrick Forrest K	.05	.15
114 Bill Foster CO K	.07	.20
125 Kirk Howling K	.05	.15
135 Littlejohn Coliseum K	.05	.15
148 Jim Davis WK	.05	.15
149 Jim Brennan K	.05	.15
154 Andie Tribble WK	.05	.15
157 Choppy Patterson K	.05	.15
166 Tommy Mahaffey K	.08	.25
168 Bill Yarborough K	.05	.15
172 Jerry Pryor K	.05	.15
177 Richie Mahaffey K	.05	.15
185 Mary Ann Cubelic WK	.05	.15
188 Randy Mahaffey K	.05	.15
191 Karen Ann Jenkins WK	.05	.15
192 Bobbie Mims WK	.05	.15
193 Janet Knight WK	.05	.15
199 Donnie Mahaffey K	.05	.15

1990-91 Clemson Women

This 16-card standard-size set was sponsored by Carolina Pride and features Clemson's Lady Tigers basketball team, who made it to the round of sixteen in the 1990 NCAA tournament. The cards are printed on thin card stock. The fronts feature color action player photos enclosed by full-bleed orange borders. The top has 1990 NCAA Sweet Sixteen in black; the sides display the school and team names; and the bottom carries player information. The backs present biography, career summary, and "Tips from the Lady Tigers" which consist of anti-drug and alcohol messages. The cards are unnumbered and checklisted below in alphabetical order.

COMPLETE SET (16)	2.50	6.00
1 Kerry Boyatt	.20	.50
2 Shandy Bryan	.20	.50
3 Jim Davis CO	.30	.75
4 Jackie Farmer	.20	.50
5 Donna Forrest	.20	.50
6 Shanna Howard	.20	.50
7 Courtney Johnson	.20	.50
8 Jackie Mattress	.20	.50
9 Melissa Miller	.20	.50
10 Angie Peters	.20	.50
11 Dana Puckett	.20	.50
12 Peggy Sells	.20	.50
13 Kim Stephens	.20	.50
14 Cheron Wells	.20	.50
15 Imani Wilson	.20	.50
16 Title Card	.20	.50
The Davis Era		

1992-93 Clemson Schedules

These ten cards measure approximately 2 1/4" by 3 1/2" and feature color action shots on their orange-bordered fronts. The white backs carry the various sport schedules in orange and black lettering. The name of the player depicted on the front appears at the bottom of the back. The cards are unnumbered and checklisted below in alphabetical order.

COMPLETE SET (11)	1.50	4.00
1 Kerry Boyatt-Hall	.20	.50
Women's Basketball		
9 Chris Whitney BK	.30	.75

1910 College Athlete Felts B-33

Issued as a cigarette redemption premium, most prominently by Egyptiene Cigarettes, but other companies also probably offered these as premiums. Many of the backs have a listing on the reverse side listing a factory and district number. Although 10 different sports are included in this series, we are only listing the colleges in which basketball figures are known to exist. Although these are not numbered, we are putting these in alphabetical order for convenience.

COMPLETE SET	2000.00	3300.00
1 Amherst	50.00	100.00
2 Army	75.00	150.00
3 Brown	75.00	150.00
4 Bucknell	50.00	100.00
5 California	50.00	100.00
6 Chicago	50.00	100.00
7 Colgate	50.00	100.00
8 Colorado	50.00	100.00
9 Columbia	75.00	150.00
10 Cornell	75.00	150.00
11 Dartmouth	75.00	150.00
12 Harvard	100.00	200.00
13 Johns Hopkins	60.00	120.00
14 Knox	50.00	100.00
15 Michigan	75.00	150.00
16 Navy	50.00	100.00
17 Oregon	50.00	100.00
18 Pennsylvania	75.00	150.00
19 Princeton	100.00	200.00
20 Rutgers	50.00	100.00
21 St Louis	50.00	100.00
22 Stanford	100.00	200.00
23 Syracuse	50.00	100.00
24 Trinity	50.00	100.00
25 Tufts	50.00	100.00
26 Utah	50.00	100.00
27 Vermont	50.00	100.00
28 Williams	60.00	120.00
29 Wisconsin	50.00	100.00
30 Yale	100.00	200.00

1990 Collegiate Collection Say No to Drugs

This multi-sport set was released by Collegiate Collection for the "Say No To Drugs, Yes to Life" campaign. Each card is essentially a re-issue of a standard card from one of the college team sets along with a different card number and different copyright line.

COMPLETE SET (6)	5.00	12.00
NC1 Michael Jordan	3.00	8.00

1995-96 Colorado

COMPLETE SET (16)	6.00	15.00
3 Martice Moore	.40	1.00
4 Chauncey Billups	5.00	12.00
5 Howard Frier	.40	1.00
11 Leroy Carter	.40	1.00
12 Matt Daniel	.40	1.00
13 Charlie Melvin	.40	1.00
21 Devon Gilchrist	.40	1.00
23 Jamie Miller	.40	1.00
31 Fred Edmonds	.40	1.00
32 Mack Tuck	.40	1.00
40 Ted Kritza	.40	1.00
42 Greg Jensen	.40	1.00
44 Charles Thompson	.40	1.00
45 Dennis Griffin	.40	1.00
NNO Joe Harrington CO	.40	1.00
NNO Colorado Title Card	.40	1.00

1990-91 Connecticut

This 16-card set was sponsored by Petro Pantry food stores, WTIC 1080 radio, and Citgo. The cards were issued in four strips of four cards each; after perforation, they measure the standard size. The front features a color action player photo on a dark blue background. In white lettering the team name appears above the picture. Player information is given below the picture, sandwiched between sponsors' logos. The back has biographical information, career summary, and "Husky Rap," which consists of an anti-drug or alcohol message. A Huskie's logo at the bottom completes the card back. The cards are unnumbered and are checklisted below in alphabetical order, with the uniform number after the player's name. Key cards in the set include Scott Burrell and Chris Smith.

COMPLETE SET (16)	6.00	15.00
1 Scott Burrell 24	1.50	4.00
2 Jim Calhoun CO	3.00	8.00
3 Dan Cyrulik 55	.40	1.00
4 Lyman DePriest 23	.40	1.00
5 Shawn Ellison 32	.40	1.00
guarding Vin Baker		
6 John Gwynn 15	.30	.75
7 Gilad Katz 10	.30	.75
8 Oliver Macklin 11	.30	.75
9 Steve Pikiell 21	.30	.75
10 Tim Pikiell 31	.30	.75
11 Rod Sellers 22	.40	1.00
12 Chris Smith 13	1.25	3.00
13 Marc Suhr 30	.30	.75
14 Toraino Walker 42	.40	1.00
15 Murray Williams 20	.30	.75
16 Jonathan (Mascot)	.30	.75

1991-92 Connecticut Legends

This 16-card standard-size set was sponsored by Petro Pantry Food Stores and WTIC-1080. It was issued in four stripes with four cards each and features outstanding players and coaches from the University of Connecticut. The fronts feature a mix of black, white or color player photos. The pictures are bordered by white on the top and the sides, with the words "Connecticut Basketball Legends" printed in dark blue in these white borders. Sponsor logos and the player's name appear in the bottom dark blue border. In dark blue print on white, the backs present biography, career summary, and "Husky Rap," which consists of anti-drug and alcohol messages. The cards are unnumbered and checklisted below in alphabetical order. The key card in the set is Cliff Robinson.

COMPLETE SET (16)	5.00	12.00
1 Wes Bialosuknia	.20	.50
2 Jim Calhoun CO	1.50	4.00
3 Walt Dropo	.60	1.50
4 Phil Gamble	.20	.50
5 Tate George	.40	1.00
6 Hugh Greer CO	.20	.50
7 Tony Hanson	.20	.50
8 Nadav Henefeld	.40	1.00
9 Toby Kimball	.20	.50
10 Mike McKay	.20	.50
11 Art Quimby	.20	.50
12 Clifford Robinson	2.00	5.00
13 Dee Rowe CO	.20	.50
14 John Thomas	.20	.50
15 Corny Thompson	.40	1.00
16 UConn Field House	.20	.50

1991-92 Connecticut

This 16-card standard-size set was sponsored by Petro Pantry Food Stores and Citgo. The fronts are accented in the team's colors (dark blue and white) and have color action player photos. The top of the pictures is curved to resemble an archway, and the school and team names follow the curve of the arch. In dark blue print on white, the backs have biography, career summary, and "Husky Rap," which consist of anti-drug and alcohol messages. The cards are unnumbered and checklisted below in alphabetical order. The key card in the set is Donyell Marshall's first card.

COMPLETE SET (16)	5.00	12.00
1 Rich Ashmeade	.20	.50
2 Scott Burrell	1.25	3.00
3 Jeff Calhoun	.30	.75
4 Dan Cyrulik	.30	.75
5 Brian Fair	.30	.75
6 Rudy Johnson	.20	.50
7 Gilad Katz	.30	.75
8 Oliver Macklin	.20	.50
9 Donny Marshall	1.25	3.00
10 Donyell Marshall	2.50	6.00
11 Kevin Ollie	.40	1.00
12 Tim Pikiell	.20	.50
13 Rod Sellers	.30	.75
14 Chris Smith	.75	2.00
15 Toraino Walker	.30	.75
16 Nantambu Willingham	.20	.50

1992-93 Connecticut

Issued in a perforated sheet, these 16 standard-size cards feature on their fronts color player action shots that are borderless on the right and bottom, blue-bordered on the left and top. The player's name, position, and class appear in white lettering within the blue border on the left. The white backs carry a black-and-white head shot at the upper left. The player's uniform number, name, class, and position appear alongside; career highlights appear below. The cards are unnumbered and checklisted below in alphabetical order.

COMPLETE SET (16)	12.50	30.00
1 Scott Burrell	1.50	4.00
2 Jeff Calhoun	.60	1.50
3 Jim Calhoun CO	2.00	5.00
4 Covington Cormier	.60	1.50
5 Steve Emt	.60	1.50
6 Brian Fair	.60	1.50
7 Eric Hayward	.60	1.50
8 Rudy Johnson	.60	1.50
9 Travis Knight	2.50	6.00
10 Oliver Macklin	.60	1.50
11 Donny Marshall	1.00	2.50
12 Donyell Marshall	3.00	8.00
13 Kevin Ollie	.60	1.50
14 Nantambu Willingham	.60	1.50
15 Howie Dickenman ACO	.60	1.50
Dave Leitao ACO		
Glen Miller ACO		
16 Cheerleaders	.75	2.00

1993-94 Connecticut

Issued in a perforated sheet, these 16 standard-size cards feature on their fronts color player action shots that are borderless on the right and top, blue-bordered on the left and bottom. The player's name and uniform number appear in white lettering within the blue border on the bottom. The horizontal white backs carry a black-and-white head shot at the upper left and the player's career highlights appear to the right. A ghosted Huskies logo forms the background. The cards are unnumbered and checklisted below in alphabetical order. Ray Allen's first card is in this set.

COMPLETE SET (16)	20.00	50.00
1 Ray Allen	12.00	30.00
2 Jeff Calhoun	.20	.50
3 Jim Calhoun CO	2.00	5.00
4 Brian Fair	.30	.75
5 Eric Hayward	.20	.50
6 Ruslan Inyatkin	.20	.50
7 Rudy Johnson	.20	.50
8 Kirk King	.30	.75

9 Travis Knight 1.25 3.00
10 Donny Marshall .75 2.00
11 Donyell Marshall 2.00 5.00
12 Kevin Ollie .40 1.00
13 Doron Sheffer .75 2.00
14 Marcus Thomas .20 .50
15 Nantambu Willingham .20 .50
16 Howie Dickenman ACO .20 .50
Dave Leitao ACO
Glen Miller ACO

1993-94 Connecticut Women

Issued in a perforated sheet, these 16 standard-size cards feature on their fronts color player action shots that are borderless on the right and top, blue-bordered on the left and bottom. The player's name and uniform number appear in white lettering within the blue border on the bottom. The horizontal white backs carry a black-and-white head shot at the upper left and the player's career highlights appear to the right. A ghosted Huskies logo forms the background. The cards are unnumbered and checklisted below in alphabetical order. This set contains the first card of Rebecca Lobo, who led the Lady Huskies to an undefeated, national championship season, and later played for the gold medal-winning 1996 USA team. Also included in this set are Jennifer Rizzotti and Kara Wolters, key members of the national championship team.

COMPLETE SET (16) 20.00 50.00
1 Geno Auriemma CO 6.00 15.00
2 Carla Berube 1.00 2.50
3 Kim Better .75 2.00
4 Tonya Boone .75 2.00
5 The Connecticut Fans .75 2.00
6 Jamelle Elliott .75 2.00
7 Colleen Healy .75 2.00
8 Jonathan the Husky Dog .75 2.00
(Mascot)
9 Rebecca Lobo 6.00 15.00
10 Shea Matlock .75 2.00
11 Sue Mayo .75 2.00
12 Jennifer Rizzotti 5.00 12.00
13 Missy Rose .75 2.00
14 Pam Webber 1.00 2.50
15 Kara Wolters 5.00 12.00
16 Chris Dailey ACO .75 2.00
Meghan Pattyson ACO
Wendy Davis ACO

1994-95 Connecticut

This 10" by 14" perforated sheet was sponsored by First Fidelity. After perforation, the cards measure the standard size. The fronts feature color action player photos that are superposed over the top dark blue stripes that carry the school and year. Another dark blue stripe cuts across the bottom and provides player information. The horizontal backs show a black-and-white closeup, biography, and player profile. The cards are unnumbered and checklisted below in alphabetical order. Notable players are Donny Marshall and Ray Allen.

COMPLETE SET (16) 12.50 30.00
1 Ray Allen 8.00 20.00
2 Jim Calhoun CO 2.00 5.00
3 Uri Cohen-Mintz .40 1.00
4 Brian Fair .40 1.00
5 Eric Hayward .40 1.00
6 Ruslan Inyatkin .40 1.00
7 Rudy Johnson .40 1.00
8 Kirk King .40 1.00
9 Travis Knight 1.50 4.00
10 Donny Marshall .75 2.00
11 Kevin Ollie .60 1.50
12 Doron Sheffer .75 2.00
13 Justin Srb .40 1.00
14 Marcus Thomas .40 1.00
15 Nantambu Willingham .40 1.00
16 Greg Yeomens .40 1.00

1995-96 Connecticut

Sponsored by First Union Bank, this 16-card set was issued as a perforated sheet. The sheets were given out at Connecticut home games during the 1995-96 season. When broken up, the individual cards measure the standard 2 1/2" by 3 1/2". The fronts display color, action photos surrounded by a dark blue border. The back are black and white, featuring a small player head shot and biographical information. The cards are unnumbered and checklisted below in alphabetical order. Add a 10% premium for complete sets in their original uncut sheet format.

COMPLETE SET (16) 10.00 25.00
1 Ray Allen 6.00 15.00
2 Jim Calhoun CO 2.00 5.00
3 Dion Carson .40 1.00
4 Kyle Chapman .40 1.00
5 Eric Hayward .40 1.00
6 Ruslan Inyatkin .40 1.00
7 Rudy Johnson .40 1.00
8 Rashamel Jones 1.00 2.50
9 Pete Kane .40 1.00
10 Kirk King .50 1.25
11 Antric Klaiber .40 1.00
12 Travis Knight 1.25 3.00
13 Predrag Materic .40 1.00
14 Rickey Moore .50 1.25
15 Doron Sheffer .50 1.25
16 Justin Srb .40 1.00

1996-97 Connecticut

This 16-card set was released at the University of Connecticut during the 1996-97 season. These cards were sponsored by First Union, and feature many of the players from that season's team. The set is not numbered and is listed below in alphabetical order.

COMPLETE SET (16) 15.00 35.00
1 Jim Calhoun CO 1.50 4.00
2 Dion Carson .30 .75
3 Kyle Chapman .30 .75
4 Kevin Freeman .75 2.00
5 Sam Funches .30 .75
6 Richard Hamilton 10.00 25.00
7 Monquencio Hardnett .30 .75
8 Ruslan Inyatkin .30 .75
9 Rashamel Jones .75 2.00
10 Kirk King .30 .75
11 Antric Klaiber .30 .75
12 Michael LeBlanc .30 .75
13 Pete McCann .30 .75
14 Ricky Moore. .75 2.00
15 Mike Smith .30 .75
16 Jake Voskuhl 1.50 4.00

1997-98 Connecticut

This 16-card set was released at the University of Connecticut during the 1997-98 season. These cards were sponsored by First Union, and feature many of the players from that season's team. The set is not numbered and is listed below in alphabetical order.

COMPLETE SET (16) 10.00 25.00
1 Jeff Cybart .20 .50
2 Khalid El-Amin 1.00 2.50
3 Kevin Freeman .75 2.00
4 Richard Hamilton 6.00 15.00
5 Monquencio Hardnett .20 .50
6 E.J. Harrison .20 .50
7 Rashamel Jones .75 2.00
8 Antric Klaiber .20 .50
9 Rickey Moore .60 1.50
10 Albert Mouring .20 .50
11 Jake Voskuhl 1.00 2.50
12 Souleymane Wane .20 .50
13 Jim Calhoun CO 1.25 3.00
14 Karl Hobbs ACO .20 .50
15 Dave Leitao ACO .20 .50
16 Tom Moore ACO .20 .50

1997-98 Connecticut Women

This 16-card set was released at the University of Connecticut during the 1997-98 season. These cards were sponsored by First Union, and feature many of the players from that season's team. The set is not numbered and is listed below in alphabetical order.

COMPLETE SET (16) 8.00 20.00
1 Geno Auriemma CO 3.00 8.00
2 Tihana Abrlic .20 .50
3 Svetlana Abrosimova 2.00 5.00
4 Jean Clark .20 .50
5 Amy Duran .40 1.00
6 Courtney Gaine .20 .50
7 Marci Glenney .20 .50
8 Stacy Hansmeyer .20 .50
9 Kelley Hunt .20 .50
10 Shea Ralph 1.00 2.50
11 Nykesha Sales 3.00 8.00
12 Paige Sauer .60 1.50
13 Kelly Schumacher .20 .50
14 Rita Williams 1.00 2.50
15 Chris Dailey ACO .20 .50
16 Tonya Cartloza .20 .50
Jamelle Elliot CO

1998-99 Connecticut

This 20-card set was released at the University of Connecticut during the 1998-99 season. These cards were sponsored by First Union, and feature many of the players from that-season's team. The set is not numbered and is listed below in alphabetical order.

COMPLETE SET (20) 10.00 25.00
1 Beau Archibald .20 .50
2 Justin Brown .20 .50
3 Ajou Ajou Deng .20 .50
4 Khalid El-Amin .75 2.00
5 Kevin Freeman .75 2.00
6 Richard Hamilton 6.00 15.00
7 E.J. Harrison .20 .50
8 Rashamel Jones .75 2.00
9 Antric Klaiber .20 .50
10 Ricky Moore .60 1.50
11 Albert Mouring .20 .50
12 Edmund Saunders .20 .50
13 Jake Voskuhl .75 2.00
14 Souleymane Wane .20 .50
15 Jim Calhoun CO 1.25 3.00
16 Karl Hobbs ACO .20 .50
17 Dave Leitao ACO .20 .50
18 Tom Moore ACO .20 .50
19 Harry A. Gampel Pavillion .20 .50
20 Hartford Civic Center .20 .50

1998-99 Connecticut Women

This 19-card set was released at the University of Connecticut during the 1998-99 season. These cards were sponsored by First Union, and feature many of the players from that season's team. The set is not numbered and is listed below in alphabetical order. Sue Bird's first ever card is in this set.

COMPLETE SET (19) 8.00 20.00
1 Geno Auriemma CO 2.00 5.00
2 Tihana Abrlic .20 .50
3 Svetlana Abrosimova 2.00 5.00
4 Sue Bird 6.00 15.00
5 Swintayla Cash 2.50 6.00
6 Marci Czel .20 .50
7 Amy Duran .30 .75
8 Courtney Gaine .20 .50
9 Marci Glenney .20 .50
10 Stacy Hansmeyer .20 .50
11 Asjha Jones .20 .50
12 Shea Ralph .75 2.00
13 Kelly Schumacher .20 .50
14 Keirsten Walters .20 .50
15 Tamika Williams .60 1.50
16 Chris Dailey ACO .20 .50
17 Tonya Cardoza ACO .20 .50
18 Jamelle Elliott ACO .20 .50
19 Rita Williams ACO .75 2.00

1999-00 Connecticut

This 18 card standard-size set features members of the then defending National Champion Uconn Huskies. The full-bleed borders feature glossy fronts with the players name on the bottom. The backs have a portrait, some biographical information as well as career highlights. As the cards are not numbered, we have put them in alphabetical order.

COMPLETE SET (18) 6.00 15.00
1 Beau Archibald .20 .50
2 Justin Brown .20 .50
3 Jim Calhoun CO 1.25 3.00
4 Marcus Cox .20 .50
5 Ajou Deng .20 .50
6 Khalid El-Amin .75 2.00
7 Kevin Freeman .60 1.50
8 Karl Hobbs ACO .20 .50
9 Dave Leitao ACO .20 .50
10 Tom Moore ACO .20 .50
11 Albert Mouring .40 1.00
12 Tony Robertson .20 .50
13 Edmund Saunders .20 .50
14 Jake Voskuhl .75 2.00
15 Soulemane Wane .20 .50
16 Brett Watson .20 .50
17 Doug Wrenn .20 .50
18 Big Blue and Johnathan .20 .50
Mascots

1999-00 Connecticut Women

This 18 card standard-size set features members of the then defending National Champion Uconn Huskies. The full-bleed borders feature glossy fronts with the players name on the bottom. The backs have a portrait, some biographical information as well as career highlights. As the cards are not numbered, we have put them in alphabetical order.

COMPLETE SET (18) 8.00 20.00
1 Svetlana Abrosimova 1.25 3.00
2 Geno Auriemma CO 1.50 4.00
3 Sue Bird 4.00 10.00
4 Tonya Cardoza .20 .50
5 Swin Cash 1.50 4.00
6 Marci Czel .20 .50
7 Chris Dailey ACO .20 .50
8 Jamelle Elliott .20 .50
9 Stacy Hansmeyer .20 .50
10 Kennitrya Johnson .20 .50
11 Ashja Jones .75 2.00
12 Shea Ralph .75 2.00
13 Christine Rigby .20 .50
14 Paige Sauer .20 .50
15 Kelly Schumacher .40 1.00
16 Keirsten Walters .20 .50
17 Tamika Williams .20 .50
18 Big Blue and Johnathan .20 .50
Mascots

1991-92 David Lipscomb

This 30-card standard-size set features the David Lipscomb University Bison basketball team. Inside a black border, color player cut-outs are superimposed on a geometric background that fades between pink and purple. The bottom purple bar carries the school logo and the player's name. The backs present a black-and-white head shot, biography, statistics, and player profile in the form of "Coaches Comments."

COMPLETE SET (30) 5.00 12.00
1 Chuck Ross .20 .50
2 Shannon Terry .20 .50
3 Rob Browne .20 .50
4 Greg Eubanks .20 .50
5 Greg Thompson .20 .50
6 Brian Ayers .20 .50
7 Lyndell Goldston .20 .50
8 Jerry Meyer .20 .50
9 Mark Campbell .20 .50
10 Michael Green .20 .50
11 John Pierce .20 .50
12 Daniel Dennison .20 .50
13 Malcolm Montgomery .20 .50
14 Kevin Dixon .20 .50
15 Andy McQueen .20 .50
16 Lee Anderson .20 .50
17 Adam Pierce .20 .50
18 Thomas Lanier .20 .50
19 Paul Rogers ACO .20 .50
20 Gene Barnett ACO .20 .50
21 Robert Sain ACO .20 .50
22 Jon Fouss ACO .20 .50
23 Greg Brown ACO .20 .50
24 Todd Fouss ACO .20 .50
25 Robert Butler ACO .20 .50
26 Chris Snoddy TR .20 .50
27 Jonathan Seamon ADM .20 .50
28 Mike Roller ACO .20 .50
29 Ralph Turner ACO .20 .50
30 Don Meyer CO .20 .50

1992-93 David Lipscomb

This 30-card standard-size set features the David Lipscomb University Bison basketball team. Inside a black border, color player cut-outs are superimposed on a geometric background that fades between pink and purple. The bottom purple bar carries the school logo and the player's name. The backs present a black-and-white head shot, biography, statistics, and player profile in the form of "Coaches Comments."

COMPLETE SET (30) 5.00 12.00
1 Chuck Ross .20 .50
2 Shannon Terry .20 .50
3 Rob Browne .20 .50
4 Greg Eubanks .20 .50
5 Greg Thompson .20 .50
6 Brian Ayers .20 .50
7 Lyndell Goldston .20 .50
8 Jerry Meyer .20 .50
9 Mark Campbell .20 .50
10 Michael Green .20 .50
11 John Pierce .20 .50
12 Daniel Dennison .20 .50
13 Malcolm Montgomery .20 .50
14 Kevin Dixon .20 .50
15 Andy McQueen .20 .50
16 Lee Anderson .20 .50
17 Adam Pierce .20 .50
18 Thomas Lanier .20 .50
19 Paul Rogers ACO .20 .50
20 Gene Barnett ACO .20 .50
21 Robert Sain ACO .20 .50
22 Jon Fouss ACO .20 .50
23 Greg Brown ACO .20 .50
24 Todd Fouss ACO .20 .50
25 Robert Butler ACO .20 .50
26 Chris Snoddy TR .20 .50
27 Jonathan Seamon ADM .20 .50
28 Mike Roller ACO .20 .50
29 Ralph Turner ACO .20 .50
30 Don Meyer CO .20 .50

1983-84 Dayton

This 20-card standard-size set of Dayton Flyers was sponsored by Blue Shield and television Channel 7. The front features borderless blue-tinted posed player photos, with the player's name above and team name below in red lettering on white card stock. The horizontally oriented backs are printed in blue and provide biographical information and the sponsors' logos. The cards are unnumbered and are checklisted below in alphabetical order. There was a 21st card in the set which was pulled from the set just prior to mass distribution due to the fact that the player quit the team.

COMPLETE SET (20) 8.00 20.00
1 Jack Butler ACO and .40 1.00
Dan Hipsher ACO
2 Roosevelt Chapman 2.00 5.00
3 Dan Christie .40 1.00
4 Dave Colbert .40 1.00
5 Rory Dahlinghaus .40 1.00
6 Don Donoher CO .75 2.00
7 Damon Goodwin .40 1.00
8 Anthony Grant .40 1.00
9 Ted Harris .40 1.00
10 Mike Hartsock .40 1.00
11 Paul Hawkins .40 1.00
12 Mick Hubert .40 1.00
13 Don Hughes .40 1.00
14 Larry Schellenberg .40 1.00
15 Jim Shields .40 1.00
16 Sedric Toney 1.25 3.00
17 Jeff Tressler .40 1.00
18 Ed Young .40 1.00
19 Jeff Zern .40 1.00
20 Flyer Fan Card .40 1.00

1986-87 DePaul Playing Cards

This rather unattractive set of playing cards was issued to honor Ray Meyer, who retired fifth on the all-time list of most career victories for Division I coaches. The cards measure the standard size. The fronts feature posed or action black and white photos that span Meyer's career and his teams. The backs are turquoise with a white border and white lettering. At the top is a DePaul Blue Demons logo in white, then the school name, and in the lower half of the card is a head shot of Ray Meyer in a heart-shaped opening. At the bottom the coach's name is given along with the words "42 Memorable Years." Numerical values have been assigned to all the cards (ace equals 1; jack equals 11, etc.). The cards are listed according to suits as follows: hearts (H), clubs (C), diamonds (D), and spades (S). The two jokers are listed at the end.

COMP. FACT SET (54) 20.00 50.00
C1 Coach of the Year 1944 .40 1.00
C2 Frank Blum and .30 .75
Jim Lamkin
C3 Bill Robinzine and .50 1.25
Ron Sobieszcyk
C4 Howie Carl .40 1.00
C5 McKinley Cowsen .30 .75
C6 M.C. Thompson .30 .75
C7 Emmette Bryant .40 1.00
C8 NIT Tournament 1963 .40 1.00
C9 Tom Meyer .30 .75
C10 Starting Five 1965-66 .40 1.00
C11 Dave Mills .30 .75
C12 400th Victory Celebration .40 1.00
C13 Joey Meyer .50 1.25
D1 Basketball Hall of Fame .40 1.00
D2 Jim Mitchem .30 .75
D3 Mark Aguirre 1.25 3.00
D4 Gary Garland .40 1.00
D5 Final Four NCAA 1978-79 .40 1.00
D6 Curtis Watkins .30 .75
D7 Joe Ponsetto .30 .75
D8 Ray and Digger Phelps .75 2.00
D9 Ron Norwood .30 .75
D10 Dave Corzine .50 1.25
D11 Ray and Al McGuire 1.25 3.00
D12 Bill Robinzine Jr. .50 1.25
D13 500th Victory .40 1.00
H1 Ray Meyer 1.50 4.00
H2 1st Team (1942) .40 1.00
H3 Dick Triptow .30 .75
H4 1st NIT Championship 1945 1.25 3.00
H5 George Mikan 5.00 12.00
H6 NIT Starting Five 1945 1.25 3.00
H7 Ed Mikan and .75 2.00
Whitey Kachan
H8 Early Great Team .60 1.50
H9 George Mikan and 2.50 6.00
Bill Donato
H10 Bato Govedarica .30 .75
H11 1948 Team .40 1.00
H12 Ray Meyer .40 1.00
Marge Meyer and Family
H13 Dick Heise .30 .75
S1 700th Victory .40 1.00
S2 Jerry McMillan .40 1.00
S3 Last Home Game .30 .75
S4 Rosemont Horizon .30 .75
S5 Ray and Joey .75 2.00
S6 Terry Cummings turns pro 1.00 2.50
S7 Terry Cummings 1.25 3.00
S8 No. 1 Basketball Family .40 1.00
S9 Last Game at Alumni Hall .40 1.00
S10 Mark Aguirre and .60 1.50
Clyde Bradshaw
S11 Mark Aguirre and 1.25 3.00
Terry Cummings
S12 1979-80 Team .40 1.00
S13 1979-80 Team Clowning .40 1.00
xx Joker Card .30 .75
Year by year record
xx Joker Card Milestones .30 .75

1974-75 Duke Schedules

1 Tate Armstrong 2.00 5.00
2 Kevin Billerman 2.00 5.00
3 Bob Fleischer 2.00 5.00
4 Willie Hodge 2.00 5.00
5 Pete Kramer 2.00 5.00
6 George Moses 2.00 5.00
7 Kenneth Young 2.00 5.00
8 Coaching Staff 2.00 5.00

1975-76 Duke Schedules

1 Tate Armstrong 2.00 5.00
2 Bruce Bell 2.00 5.00
3 Terry Chili 2.00 5.00
4 Rick Gomez 2.00 5.00
5 Scott Goetsch 2.00 5.00
6 Steve Gray 2.00 5.00
7 Cameron Hall 2.00 5.00
8 George Moses 2.00 5.00

1976-77 Duke Schedules

1 Tate Armstrong 2.00 5.00

1978-79 Duke Schedules

1 Gene Banks 2.00 5.00
2 Kenny Dennard 2.00 5.00
3 Mike Gminski 3.00 8.00
4 John Harrell 2.00 5.00
5 Jim Spanarkel 2.00 5.00

1979-80 Duke Schedules

1 Gene Banks 2.00 5.00
2 Kenny Dennard 2.00 5.00

1980-81 Duke Schedules

1 Gene Banks .40 1.00

1981-82 Duke Schedules

1 Vince Taylor .40 1.00

1983-84 Duke Schedules

1 Johnny Dawkins 2.00 5.00

1984-85 Duke Schedules

1 Mark Alarie 1.25 3.00
2 Jay Bilas 1.25 3.00

1985-86 Duke Schedules

1 David Henderson .40 1.00

1986-87 Duke Schedules

1 Tommy Amaker .40 1.00

1987-88 Duke

This 13-card standard-size set features the Duke Blue Devils basketball team. A special logo cover card was also released, but is not considered part of the complete set. This set features members of the semi-finalists of the 1988 NCAA Tournament. The set is sponsored by Adolescent Care Unit and Glaxo and their company names are on the top of the card. Underneath their names is the Blue Devils' identification. The full-color players photo is in the middle of the card and on the bottom of the card is the players name, uniform number, and position. The back has basic biographical information about the players along with both a basketball and a anti-crime or drug message. Some of the key players in the set include NBA players Danny Ferry and Alaa Abdelnaby in addition to the first card of Duke coach Mike Krzyzewski. The set was produced by Sports Marketing of Seattle, Washington. The cards are numbered for convenience in the checklist below according to the player's uniform number.

COMPLETE SET (13) 30.00 60.00
13 Joe Cook .75 2.00
14 Quin Snyder 2.50 6.00
21 Robert Brickey 1.00 2.50
22 Greg Koubek 1.25 3.00
30 Alaa Abdelnaby 1.50 4.00
31 Kevin Strickland .75 2.00
33 John Smith .75 2.00
35 Danny Ferry 3.00 8.00
42 George Burgin .75 2.00
44 Phil Henderson 1.50 4.00
45 Clay Buckley .75 2.00
55 Billy King .75 2.00
xx Mike Krzyzewski CO 12.00 30.00
NNO Logo Cover Card 8.00 20.00

1987-88 Duke Schedules

1 Billy King .40 1.00
2 Kevin Strickland .40 1.00

1988-89 Duke

This 13-card standard-size set featuring the Duke Blue Devils was sponsored by Adolescent CareUnit, Glaxo, and local law enforcement agencies. On a royal blue card face, the fronts show color action player photos enclosed by gray border stripes. Sponsor logos and the team name appear above the picture, while the player's name, jersey number, and position are given below it. In addition to sponsor acknowledgments, the backs carry player profile and "Tips from the Blue Devils," which consist of anti-drug and alcohol messages. The cards are unnumbered and checklisted below in alphabetical order. The key card in the set is the first card of Christian Laettner.

COMPLETE SET (13) 40.00 100.00
1 Alaa Abdelnaby 2.00 5.00
2 Robert Brickey 1.50 4.00
3 Clay Buckley 1.50 4.00
4 George Burgin 1.50 4.00
5 Brian Davis 2.00 5.00
6 Danny Ferry 4.00 10.00
7 Phil Henderson 2.00 5.00
8 Greg Koubek 2.00 5.00
9 Mike Krzyzewski CO 10.00 25.00
10 Christian Laettner 25.00 60.00
11 Crawford Palmer 1.50 4.00
12 John Smith 1.50 4.00
13 Quin Snyder 3.00 8.00

1988-89 Duke Schedules

1 Quin Snyder .40 1.00

1989-90 Duke Schedules

1 Robert Brickey .40 1.00

1990-91 Duke Schedules

1 Christian Laettner 2.00 5.00

1991-92 Duke Schedules

1 Brian Davis .20 .50
2 Christian Laettner 1.00 2.50

1992-93 Duke Schedules

1 Thomas Hill .20 .50

1993-94 Duke Schedules

1 Marty Clark .20 .50
2 Antonio Lang .40 1.00

1994-95 Duke Schedules

1 Cherokee Parks .75 2.00

1995-96 Duke Schedules

1 Chris Collins .20 .50

1996-97 Duke Schedules

1 Jeff Capel .20 .50
2 Greg Newton .20 .50

1997-98 Duke Schedules

1 Roshown McLeod .20 .50
2 Steve Wojciechowski .20 .50

1998-99 Duke Schedules

1 Trajan Langdon .40 1.00

1999-00 Duke Schedules

1 Chris Carrawell .20 .50

2000-01 Duke Schedules

1 Nate James .20 .50

2001-02 Duke Schedules

1 Jason Williams .20 .50

2002-03 Duke Schedules

1 Dahntay Jones .20 .50

2003-04 Duke Schedules

1 Chris Duhon .20 .50

2004-05 Duke Schedules

1 Daniel Ewing .20 .50

2005-06 Duke Schedules

1 Shelden Williams .40 1.00

2006-07 Duke Schedules

1 Josh McRoberts .20 .50
2 DeMarcus Nelson .20 .50
3 Greg Paulus .20 .50

2007-08 Duke Schedules

1 DeMarcus Nelson .20 .50

2008-09 Duke Schedules

1 Greg Paulus .20 .50

2009-10 Duke Schedules

1 Jon Scheyer .20 .50

2010-11 Duke Schedules

1 Kyle Singler .40 1.00
2 Nolan Smith .40 1.00

2011-12 Duke Schedules

1 Seth Curry .75 2.00
2 Miles Plumlee .40 1.00

1988-89 East Carolina

Sponsored by Pizza Hut, this six-card standard-size set features 1988-89 East Carolina Pirates basketball players. On a white card face, the color action photos are bordered on three sides by team color-coded (purple and mustard) borders. Player information appears in the bottom purple border. The backs carry a player profile and "Tips from the Pirates" which consist of anti-drug or alcohol messages. There were four other football cards produced by East Carolina that are sometimes considered part of this set.

COMPLETE SET (6) 6.00 15.00
1 Gus Hill .75 2.00
2 Kenny Murphy .75 2.00
3 Jeff Kelly .75 2.00
4 Mike Steele CO .75 2.00
5 Reed Lose .75 2.00
6 Blue Edwards 3.00 8.00

1989-90 East Tennessee State

Sponsored by Shoney's and East Tennessee State University, this 12-card standard-size set features color action shots of the players. The backs carry biographical information, statistics, and public service messages. The cards are unnumbered and checklisted below in alphabetical order.

COMPLETE SET (12) 6.00 15.00
1 Greg Dennis .75 2.00
2 Major Geer .60 1.50
3 Keith (Mister) Jennings 1.50 4.00
4 Chad Keller .30 .75
5 Avery Marshall .30 .75
6 Jerry Pelphrey .60 1.50
Robert Spears
James Jacobs
Darell Jones
7 Les Robinson CO 1.25 3.00
8 Marty Story .60 1.50
9 Calvin Talford 1.00 2.50
10 Alvin West .30 .75
11 Michael Woods .30 .75
12 East Tennessee State .60 1.50

1990-91 East Tennessee State

Sponsored by Shoney's and East Tennessee State University, this 14-card standard-size set features color shots of the players posed against a blue studio background. The card backs carry biographical information, statistics, and public service messages. The cards are unnumbered and checklisted below in alphabetical order.

COMPLETE SET (14) 5.00 12.00
1 Jeff Lebo ACO .50 1.25
Grafton Young ACO
John Shulman ACO
Ed Howat ACO
2 Eric Palmer .50 1.25
Trazel Silvers
Moe Hayes
3 Greg Dennis .60 1.50
4 Rodney English .50 1.25
5 Major Geer .50 1.25
6 Keith(Mister) Jennings .75 2.00
7 Darell Jones .30 .75
8 Alan LeForce CO .50 1.25
9 Jerry Pelphrey .50 1.25
10 Robert Spears .30 .75
11 Marty Story .50 1.25
12 Calvin Talford .75 2.00
13 Alvin West .30 .75
14 Michael Woods .30 .75

1991-92 East Tennessee State

Sponsored by Shoney's and East Tennessee State University, this 15-card standard-size set features color shots of the players posed against a blue studio background. The card face is orange-yellow and is printed with the player's name, jersey number, and position at the bottom. The year, school, and team names appear at the top. The backs carry biographical information, statistics, and public service messages. The cards are unnumbered and checklisted below in alphabetical order.

COMPLETE SET (15) 4.00 10.00
1 Grafton Young ACO .40 1.00
Ed Howat ACO
John Shulman ACO
Jeff Lebo ACO
2 Greg Dennis .40 1.00
3 Rodney English .40 1.00
4 Moe Hayes .30 .75
Loren Riddick
5 Damien Hodge .30 .75
Justin McClellan
Reece Dudley
Leslie Brunn
6 Darell Jones .30 .75
7 Alan LeForce CO .60 1.50
8 Jason Niblett .40 1.00
9 Eric Palmer .30 .75
10 Jerry Pelphrey .40 1.00
11 Trazel Silvers .40 1.00
12 Southern Conference .40 1.00
Trophy and Ball
13 Robert Spears .30 .75
14 Marty Story .40 1.00
15 Calvin Talford .60 1.50

1992-93 East Tennessee State

Sponsored by Shoney's, the ETSU Department of Public Safety, and East Tennessee State University, this 14-card standard-size set features the 1992-93 East Tennessee State men's basketball team. Ten thousand sets and 500 uncut sheets were reportedly produced. The cards are printed on thin card stock and feature posed color player photos on the fronts. The pictures have irregular edges that make it appear as though they have been revealed by tearing through the blue border. The ETSU letters appear at the top in yellow, and the team name, the Buccaneers, is shown just below in white. The player's name, position, and jersey number are shown in white at the bottom. The white back displays the player's name in white letters within a black bar. A brief biography and stats are placed beneath. At the bottom, safety advice provided by the ETSU Department of Public Safety, and the ETSU and Shoney's logos, round out the card. The cards are unnumbered and checklisted below in alphabetical order.

COMPLETE SET (14) 4.00 10.00
1 Leslie Brunn .30 .75
2 Robert Doggett .40 1.00
Geoff Herman
Tony Patterson
3 Darell Jones .30 .75
4 Alan LeForce CO .60 1.50
5 Alan LeForce CO .60 1.50
(Cutting down net)
6 Justin McClellan .30 .75
7 Jason Niblett .40 1.00
8 Jay Nidiffer ACO .30 .75
John Shulman ACO
Grafton Young ACO
9 Eric Palmer .30 .75
10 Jerry Pelphrey .40 1.00
11 Andy Pennington .30 .75
Phil Powe
12 Trazel Silvers .40 1.00
13 Robert Spears .30 .75
14 Team Photo .40 1.00

1993-94 East Tennessee State

Sponsored by Shoney's, the ETSU Department of Public Safety, and East Tennessee State University, this 15-card standard-size set features the 1993-94 East Tennessee State Men's Basketball team. The cards are printed on thin card stock and the fronts carry posed color player photos. The team logo is in the top left corner with player's name, position, and jersey number at the bottom right below the picture. The backs have biographical information and statistics with an anti-drug message and sponsor logos below. The cards are unnumbered and checklisted below in alphabetical order.

COMPLETE SET (15) 4.00 10.00
1 Leslie Brunn .30 .75
2 Robert Doggett .40 1.00
3 Junior Floyd .30 .75
4 Geoff Herman .30 .75
5 Corrie Johnson .30 .75
Mike Biggs
6 Darell Jones .30 .75
7 Alan LeForce CO .60 1.50
8 Justin McClellan .30 .75
9 Tony Patterson .30 .75
10 Andy Pennington .30 .75
11 Shahid Perkins .30 .75
12 Phil Powe .30 .75
13 Trazel Silvers .30 .75
14 Steve Snell ACO .30 .75
John Shulman ACO
Jay Nidiffer ACO
Jerry Pelphrey ACO
15 Chris Timmerman .30 .75
James Abrams

1992-93 Eastern Illinois

This 12-card standard-size set was sponsored by the Coles County Law Enforcement Agencies and area businesses. The cards feature posed, color player photos with red, white, and blue borders. The player's names are printed at the bottom in the margin, and the school logo appears in the lower right corner. Two players are featured on some of the cards. The backs display public service messages and biographical information within white boxes on a light blue background.

COMPLETE SET (12) 5.00 12.00
1 Rick Samuels CO .40 1.00
and Assistants
2 Team Photo .60 1.50
3 Michael Slaughter .60 1.50
Johnny Hernandez
4 Steve Weemer .40 1.00
Steven Nichols
5 Andre Rodriguez .60 1.50
Louis Jordan
6 Kurt Comer .40 1.00
Walter Graham
7 Troy Collier .60 1.50
Derrick Landrus
8 C.J. Williams .40 1.00
Darrell Young
9 Eric West .60 1.50
10 Curtis Leib .60 1.50
11 Derek Kelley .60 1.50
12 Billy Panther .40 1.00
(Mascot)

1986-87 Emporia State

Sponsored by B and K Nostalgia, this eighteen-card set was issued in two uncut unperforated sheets. If the cards were cut, they would measure the standard size. The fronts feature black-and-white player portraits inside a black frame with white outer borders. The top of the pictures is curved to resemble an archway, and the team name follows the curve of the arch on a yellow background. Player information appears in a yellow stripe below the pictures. The backs carry biography, statistics, or career summary. The cards are unnumbered and checklisted below in alphabetical order.

COMPLETE SET (18) 12.00 30.00
1 Eric Anderson .75 2.00
Bill Pitko
2 Cardell Armstrong .75 2.00
3 Jim Biggs .75 2.00
4 Gary Birch .75 2.00
5 Marvin Chatman .75 2.00
6 Jon Cramer .75 2.00
7 Johnny Craven .75 2.00
8 Dale Cushinberry .75 2.00
9 Dennis Fort .75 2.00
10 Derrick Howse .75 2.00
11 John Hughes .75 2.00
12 Mark Lackey .75 2.00
13 Brian Robinson .75 2.00
14 Ron Slaymaker CO .75 2.00
Hornets Logo
15 Chris Sparks .75 2.00
16 Ryan Sprecker .75 2.00
17 Craig Stromgren .75 2.00
18 Bob Yonke .75 2.00

1993-94 Evansville

The 1993-94 University of Evansville Purple Aces consists of 16 standard-size cards. The cards are printed on thin card stock. The white-bordered fronts carry a mix of posed and action color photos. In the upper left corner within a basketball icon are the school initials and the year of the set. Below the photo on team color-coded bars are the player's name and school name. The backs display a head shot of the player with player profile, biography, and statistics on a purple speckled background. The cards are unnumbered and checklisted below in alphabetical order.

COMPLETE SET (16) 3.00 8.00
1 Jermaine Ball .40 1.00
guarded by Sam Cassell
2 Todd Cochenour .20 .50
3 Jim Crews CO .40 1.00
4 Andy Elkins .60 1.50
5 Mark Hisle .30 .75
6 Reed Jackson .20 .50
7 Brent Kell .20 .50
8 Jeff Layden .20 .50
9 Toby Madison .20 .50
10 Arad McCutchan CO .20 .50
11 Chris Quinn .20 .50
12 Carl Reeder .20 .50
13 Scott Sparks .20 .50
14 Ace Purple (Mascot) .20 .50
15 Ace-Ettes .20 .50
16 Cheerleaders .20 .50

1982-83 Fairfield

This 18-card standard-size set for Fairfield University was produced by Big League Cards. The front features a posed color photo enframed by black and red borders, with the player's name, the university, and a basketball logo below the picture. The back gives biographical information.

COMPLETE SET (18) 6.00 15.00
1 Jay Byrne .40 1.00
2 Vin Cazzetta .60 1.50
3 Pete DeBisschop .40 1.00
4 Joe DeSantis CO .60 1.50
5 Tony George .40 1.00
6 Craig Golden .40 1.00
7 Bobby Hurt .60 1.50
8 Ed Janka CO .40 1.00
9 Jerry Johnson .40 1.00
10 John Leonard .40 1.00
11 Terry O'Connor .60 1.50
12 Tim O'Toole .40 1.00
13 Brendan Potter .60 1.50
14 Ron Ross CO .60 1.50
15 Greg Schwartz .40 1.00
16 Don Wilson .40 1.00
17 Pat Yerina .40 1.00
18 Fairfield Stags .60 1.50

1993 FCA Final Four

This seven-card standard-size set was packaged in a cello pack by the Fellowship of Christian Athletes for distribution at Final Four viewing parties. The color player photos on the fronts are accented on three sides by a thin pink stripe; the card face itself shades from purple to white as one moves toward the bgottom. The FCA logo, featuring a cross with two olive branches, is superimposed in the upper left corner, while the player's name and position are printed beneath the picture. On a purple background, the backs carry a close-up photo, biography, and the player's testimony.

COMPLETE SET (7)	3.00	8.00
1 Steve Alford	.75	2.00
2 John Wooden CO	1.50	4.00
3 Bobby Jones	1.00	2.50
4 Rod Foster	.60	1.50
5 Keith Erickson	.75	2.00
NNO Cover Card	.20	.50
NNO Order Form	.20	.50

1988-89 Florida

This 14-card standard-size set was sponsored by University Athletic Association in conjunction with Burger King. The front features a color action shot of an athlete engaging in the particular sport highlighted on the card. The pictures are outlined by a thin black border on white card stock. The Burger King and the Gators' logo round out the card face. The back provides additional information on the sport as well as an anti-drug or crime message.

COMPLETE SET (14)	6.00	15.00
3 Men's Basketball	2.00	5.00

1990-91 Florida State Collegiate Collection

This 200-card standard-size set by Collegiate Collection features past and current athletes of Florida State University from a variety of sports.

COMPLETE SET (200)	6.00	15.00
107 Jeff Hogan BK	.05	.15
109 Dick Artmeier BK	.05	.15
116 Gary Schull BK	.05	.15
123 Rowland Garrett BK	.05	.15
131 Dave Cowens BK	.20	.50
147 Hugh Durham BK	.07	.20
183 Ron King BK	.05	.15
192 Paul Wernke BK	.05	.15
194 Dave Fedor BK	.05	.15

1992-93 Florida State

This 80-card multi-sport standard-size set features "Seminole Superstars" from various Florida State teams. The sports represented are golf (1-3), tennis (4-8), swimming and diving (9-14), track and field (15-21), softball (22-25), basketball (26-28, 39-42), volleyball (29-31), baseball (32-38), basketball (39-43), and football (44-75).

COMPLETE SET (80)	15.00	30.00
26 Marynell Meadors CO BK	.02	.10
27 Allison Peercy BK	.07	.20
28 Ursula Woods BK	.07	.20
39 Pat Kennedy CO BK	.20	.50
40 Sam Cassell BK	3.20	8.00
41 Rodney Dobard BK	.07	.20
42 Chuck Graham BK	.07	.20
43 Charlie Ward BK	3.20	8.00

1985-86 Fort Hays State

As indicated on the bottom of the reverse, this rather unattractive 18-card standard-size set was sponsored by K-Bob's Steakhouse. Each set was accompanied by a coupon redeemable at K-Bob's Steakhouse. The cards are printed on thin card stock. The fronts feature black and white head shots framed by black borders on a white card face. A yellow diagonal bar in the upper right corner carries the college letters while the player's name appears beneath the photo in a yellow stripe. The backs have a Tiger pawprint in the upper left corner and present biography, statistics, and career summary. The cards are unnumbered and checklisted below in alphabetical order.

COMPLETE SET (18)	3.00	8.00
1 Tyree Allen	.20	.50
2 Joe Anderson	.20	.50
3 Troy Applegate Student Coach	.20	.50
4 Kale Barton	.20	.50
5 Bruce Brawner	.20	.50
6 Fred Campbell	.40	1.00
7 Craig Cox CO	.20	.50
8 Thomas Hardnett	.20	.50
9 Archie Johnson	.20	.50
10 David Lackey	.20	.50
11 Greg Lackey CO	.20	.50
12 Raymond Lee	.20	.50
13 Mike Miller	.20	.50
14 Bill Morse CO	.20	.50
15 Ron Morse	.20	.50
16 Cedric Williams	.20	.50
17 Team Photo	.40	1.00
18 Title Card	.40	1.00

1989 Fresno State Women

This three-card 3" by 5" set was sponsored by Smokey. The cards are not numbered and checklisted below in alphabetical order.

COMPLETE SET (3)	1.25	3.00
1 Ginger Connolly Softball	.40	1.00
2 RaeAnn Pifferini Gina LoPiccolo Basketball	.75	2.00
3 Margie Wright Julie Smith Softball	.40	1.00

1989-90 Fresno State

This 16-card standard-size set was sponsored by the USDA Forest Service, several other federal agencies, and Grandy's restaurants. The fronts feature either posed or action color player photos with a white card face background. The school name appears in red lettering above the picture, with the team name in the blue stripe just below it. Red and blue stripes appear below the picture, overlayed by the Smokey and Grandy's logos. The back has brief biographical information and a fire prevention cartoon starring Smokey the Bear. The cards are unnumbered and are checklisted below in alphabetical order, with the uniform number after the player's name.

COMPLETE SET (16)	4.00	10.00
1 Ron Adams CO	.40	1.00
2 Bijou Baly 15	.40	1.00
3 Dave Barnett 12	.40	1.00
4 Tod Bernard 33	.60	1.50
5 Chris Henderson 25	.40	1.00
6 Wilbert Hooker 30	.60	1.50
7 Pasi Lahtinen 3	.40	1.00
8 Dimitri Lambrecht 32	.40	1.00
9 Sammie Lindsey 50	.40	1.00
10 Joey Paglierani 00	.40	1.00
11 Todd Peebles 23	.40	1.00
12 Pat Riddlesprigger 34	.40	1.00
13 Sammy Taylor 22	.40	1.00
14 Carlo Williams 44	.40	1.00
15 Rey Young 54	.40	1.00
16 Greg Zuffelato 24	.40	1.00

1990-91 Fresno State

This 16-card standard-size set was sponsored by Grandy's. The front features a color action photo enframed by a blue border on red background, with the player's name, position, and years below the photo, as well as a picture of Smokey the Bear in the left hand corner and a Grandy's logo in the right. The back has biographical information and a public service announcement (with cartoon) concerning wildfire prevention. Ron Anderson of the Philadelphia 76ers is included in this set. The cards are numbered for convenience in the checklist below according to alphabetical order of the player's name.

COMPLETE SET (16)	4.00	10.00
1 Ron Anderson	1.00	2.50
2 Dave Barnett 12	.30	.75
3 Tod Bernard 33	.40	1.00
4 Tyrone Bradley	.30	.75
5 Gary Colson CO	.75	2.00
6 Carl Ray Harris 11	.40	1.00
7 Doug Harris 20	.30	.75
8 Wilbert Hooker 30	.40	1.00
9 Dimitri Lambrecht 32	.30	.75
10 Sammie Lindsey 50	.30	.75
11 Michael Pearson 3	.30	.75
12 Pat Riddlesprigger 34	.30	.75
13 Sammy Taylor 22	.30	.75
14 Rey Young 54	.30	.75
15 Fresno State Mascot	.30	.75
16 Selland Arena	.30	.75

1981-82 Georgetown

This set contains 20 cards measuring approximately 2 5/8" by 4 1/8" featuring the Georgetown Hoyas. The fronts of the cards have a blue border. Backs contain safety tips with black print on white card stock. The set was sponsored by the District of Columbia Police Dept. and Safeway. The cards are numbered below by "Tip Number" as listed on the card back. The key card in the set is the first card of NBA superstar Patrick Ewing.

COMPLETE SET (20)	30.00	80.00
1 Jack the Bulldog (Mascot)	.60	1.50
2 Elvado Smith	.60	1.50
3 Eric Smith	.75	2.00
4 Patrick Ewing	30.00	70.00
5 Anthony Jones	.75	2.00
6 Bill Martin	.75	2.00
7 Bill Stein ACO	.60	1.50
8 Norman Washington Grad. Asst. Coach	.60	1.50
9 Ed Spriggs	.75	2.00
10 Eric(Sleepy) Floyd	3.00	8.00
11 Gene Smith	.75	2.00
12 Fred Brown	1.50	4.00
13 Mike Hancock	.60	1.50
14 Kurt Kaull	.60	1.50
15 Ed Meyers	.60	1.50
16 Ron Blaylock	.60	1.50
17 David Blue	.60	1.50
18 John Thompson CO	5.00	12.00
19 Ralph Dalton	.75	2.00
20 Hoyas Team 1981-1982	3.00	8.00

1982-83 Georgetown

This set contains 15 cards measuring approximately 2 5/8" by 4 1/8" featuring the Georgetown Hoyas. The fronts of the cards have a blue border. Backs contain safety tips with black print on white card stock. The cards are numbered below by "Tip Number" as listed on the card back. The set was sponsored by the District of Columbia Police Dept. and Games Production, Inc. The key card in the set is Patrick Ewing.

COMPLETE SET (15)	15.00	35.00
1 John Thompson CO	3.00	7.00
2 Patrick Ewing	10.00	20.00
3 David Dunn	.40	1.00
4 Ralph Dalton	.60	1.50
5 Fred Brown	.75	2.00
6 Horace Broadnax	.60	1.50
7 David Blue	.40	1.00
8 Michael Jackson	.75	2.00
9 David Wingate	2.00	5.00
10 Vadi Smith	.40	1.00
11 Gene Smith	.60	1.50
12 Victor Morris	.40	1.00
13 Bill Martin	.60	1.50
14 Kurt Kaull	.40	1.00
15 Anthony Jones	.60	1.50

1983-84 Georgetown

This set contains 15 cards measuring approximately 2 5/8" by 4 1/8" featuring the Georgetown Hoyas. Backs contain safety tips. The set was sponsored by the District of Columbia Police Dept. and Coca Cola. This set features the Hoya team that won the 1983-84 NCAA Championship. The key cards in the set are Patrick Ewing and the first card of NBA guard Reggie Williams.

COMPLETE SET (15)	10.00	25.00
1 John Thompson CO	2.00	5.00
2 Hoya 1983-84 Team	2.00	5.00
3 Michael Jackson	.60	1.50
4 Bill Martin	.60	1.50
5 Jack the Bulldog Hoya Mascot	.40	1.00
6 Gene Smith	.60	1.50
7 Fred Brown	.60	1.50
8 Horace Broadnax	.60	1.50
9 Victor Morris	.40	1.00
10 Patrick Ewing	6.00	15.00
11 Ralph Dalton	.60	1.50
12 Michael Graham	.60	1.50
13 Clifton Dairsow	.60	1.50
14 David Wingate	1.25	3.00
15 Reggie Williams	1.50	4.00

1984-85 Georgetown

This set contains 14 cards each measuring approximately 2 5/8" by 4 1/8" featuring the Georgetown Hoyas. Fronts of the cards make reference to Georgetown's National Championship the year before. This set was sponsored by the District of Columbia Police Dept. and Coca Cola. Backs contain safety tips and are written in black ink with a red accent. The cards are numbered for convenience in the checklist below according to alphabetical order of the player's name. The key card in the set is Patrick Ewing.

COMPLETE SET (14)	10.00	25.00
1 John Thompson CO	1.50	4.00
2 Horace Broadnax	.60	1.50
3 Ralph Dalton	.60	1.50
4 Patrick Ewing	5.00	12.00
5 Kevin Floyd	.40	1.00
6 Ron Highsmith	.60	1.50
7 Michael Jackson	.60	1.50
8 Bill Martin	.60	1.50
9 Grady Mateen	.40	1.00
10 Perry McDonald	.60	1.50
11 Reggie Williams	1.00	2.50
12 David Wingate	.75	2.00
13 NCAA Championship Trophy	.40	1.00
14 Team Photo	1.50	4.00

1985-86 Georgetown

The 1985-86 Georgetown Hoyas set contains 16 cards measuring approximately 2 1/2" by 4". There are 13 player cards, plus one coach card, one team picture card, and one mascot card. The card fronts feature color photos and fascimile signatures. Each card back has one basketball tip and one safety tip. The cards are numbered for convenience in the checklist below according to alphabetical order of the player's name.

COMPLETE SET (16)	2.50	6.00
1 1985-86 Hoyas Team Photo	.20	.50
2 John Thompson CO	1.25	3.00
3 Horace Broadnax	.30	.75
4 Ralph Dalton	.30	.75
5 Johnathan Edwards	.30	.75
6 Hoyas Mascot	.20	.50
7 Ronnie Highsmith	.20	.50
8 Jaren Jackson	.75	2.00
9 Michael Jackson	.30	.75
10 Grady Mateen	.20	.50
11 Perry McDonald	.30	.75
12 Victor Morris	.20	.50
13 Charles Smith	.40	1.00
14 Reggie Williams	.75	2.00
15 David Wingate	.75	2.00
16 Bobby Winston	.20	.50

1986-87 Georgetown

The 1986-87 Georgetown Hoyas set contains 14 cards measuring approximately 2 1/2" by 4". There are 12 player cards, plus one coach card and one team picture card. The card fronts have color photos, and each card back has one basketball tip and one safety tip. The cards are numbered for convenience in the checklist below according to alphabetical order of the player's name.

COMPLETE SET (14)	2.50	6.00
1 1986-87 Hoyas	.40	1.00
2 John Thompson CO	1.25	3.00
3 Anthony Allen	.20	.50
4 Dwayne Bryant	.20	.50
5 Johnathan Edwards	.30	.75
6 Ben Gillery	.20	.50
7 Ronnie Highsmith	.20	.50
8 Jaren Jackson	.60	1.50
9 Sam Jefferson	.20	.50
10 Perry McDonald	.30	.75
11 Charles Smith	.30	.75
12 Mark Tillmon	.30	.75
13 Reggie Williams	.60	1.50
14 Bobby Winston	.20	.50

1987-88 Georgetown

The 1987-88 Georgetown Hoyas set contains 16 cards measuring approximately 2 1/2" by 4". There are 14 player cards, plus one coach card and one team picture card. The card fronts have color photos, and each card back has one basketball tip and one safety tip. The cards are numbered for convenience in the checklist below according to alphabetical order of the player's name.

COMPLETE SET (16)	2.50	6.00
1 1987-88 Hoyas	.30	.75
2 John Thompson CO	.75	2.00
3 Anthony Allen	.20	.50
4 Dwayne Bryant	.20	.50
5 Johnathan Edwards	.30	.75
6 Ben Gillery	.20	.50
7 Ronnie Highsmith	.20	.50
8 Jaren Jackson	.40	1.00
9 Sam Jefferson	.20	.50
10 Johnny Jones	.20	.50
11 Tom Lang	.20	.50
12 Perry McDonald	.30	.75
13 Charles Smith	.30	.75
14 Mark Tillmon	.30	.75
15 Anthony Tucker	.20	.50
16 Bobby Winston	.20	.50

1988-89 Georgetown

The 1988-89 Georgetown Hoyas set contains 17 cards measuring approximately 2 1/2" by 4". There are 14 player cards, plus one coach card, one team picture card and one mascot card. The card fronts have color photos, and each card back has one safety tip. The cards are numbered for convenience in the checklist below according to alphabetical order of the player's name. The set features the first cards of future NBA Lottery picks and star centers Alonzo Mourning and Dikembe Mutombo.

COMPLETE SET (17)	15.00	40.00
1 1988-89 Hoyas	2.00	5.00
2 John Thompson CO	1.25	3.00
3 Anthony Allen	.20	.50
4 Dwayne Bryant	.20	.50
5 Johnathan Edwards	.30	.75
6 Ronnie Thompson	.20	.50
7 Milton Bell	.40	1.00
8 Jaren Jackson	.40	1.00
9 Sam Jefferson	.20	.50
10 Johnny Jones	.20	.50
11 Alonzo Mourning	8.00	20.00
12 John Turner	.30	.75
13 Charles Smith	.30	.75
14 Mark Tillmon	.30	.75
15 Dikembe Mutombo	6.00	15.00
16 Bobby Winston	.20	.50
17 McGruff The Crime Dog and Jack The Bulldog	.20	.50

1989-90 Georgetown

The 1989-90 Georgetown Hoyas set contains 17 cards measuring approximately 2 1/2" by 4". The front has a posed color photo of the player, enclosed by a blue border on the top and a gray one below. The back is printed in blue and red ink and has a safety tip from McGruff the Crime Dog. The cards are numbered below by "Tip Number" as listed on the card back. The key cards in the set feature Alonzo Mourning and Dikembe Mutombo.

COMPLETE SET (17)	2.50	6.00
1 1989-90 Hoyas	.40	1.00
2 John Thompson CO	.40	1.00
3 Anthony Allen	.08	.25
4 Dwayne Bryant	.08	.25
5 David Edwards	.08	.25
6 Ronny Thompson	.08	.25
7 Milton Bell	.20	.50
8 Kayode Vann	.08	.25
9 Sam Jefferson	.08	.25
10 Johnny Jones	.08	.25
11 Alonzo Mourning	1.25	3.00
12 Mike Sabol	.08	.25
13 Michael Tate	.20	.50
14 Mark Tillmon	.20	.50
15 Dikembe Mutombo	1.00	2.50
16 Antoine Stoudamire	.08	.25
17 McGruff The Crime Dog and Jack the Bulldog	.08	.25

1990-91 Georgetown

The 1990-91 Georgetown Hoyas set contains 15 cards measuring approximately 2 1/2" by 4". The front has a posed color photo of the player, enclosed by gray borders above and below. The back is printed in blue and red ink and has a safety tip from McGruff the Crime Dog. The cards are numbered below by "Tip Number" as listed on the card back. The key cards in the set feature Alonzo Mourning and Dikembe Mutombo.

COMPLETE SET (15)	2.50	6.00
1 1990-91 Hoyas Team Photo	.40	1.00
2 Kayode Vann	.08	.25
4 Antoine Stoudamire	.08	.25
5 Alonzo Mourning	1.00	2.50
6 Ronny Thompson	.08	.25
7 Dikembe Mutombo	.75	2.00
8 Charles Harrison	.08	.25
9 Brian Kelly	.08	.25
10 Robert Churchwell	.20	.50
11 Joey Brown	.20	.50
12 Vladimir Bosanac	.08	.25
13 Lamont Morgan	.08	.25
14 John Thompson CO	.40	1.00
15 McGruff The Crime Dog and Jack The Bulldog	.08	.25

1991 Georgetown Collegiate Collection

This 100-card standard-size set was produced by Collegiate Collection. The fronts feature color player photos, with dark blue borders and the player's name in the gray stripe below the picture. The horizontally oriented backs present biographical information, career summary, or statistics on a white background with dark blue lettering and borders.

COMPLETE SET (100)	6.00	15.00
1 John Thompson CO	.20	.50
2 Patrick Ewing	.40	1.00
3 Eric(Sleepy) Floyd	.10	.30
4 Reggie Williams	.15	.40
5 John Duren	.07	.20
6 Craig Shelton	.10	.30
7 Charles Smith	.10	.30
8 Michael Jackson	.08	.25
9 Jaren Jackson	.10	.30
10 David Wingate	.10	.30
11 Mark Tillmon	.08	.25
12 Fred Brown	.08	.25
13 Kurt Kaull	.07	.15
14 Ron Highsmith	.07	.15
15 Dwayne Bryant	.07	.15
16 Michael Jackson	.08	.25
17 Al Dutch	.07	.15
18 Jim Barry	.07	.15
19 Ralph Dalton	.07	.20
20 1984 NCAA Champs	.15	.40
21 Craig Esherick	.07	.15
22 Bobby Winston	.07	.15
23 Bill Martin	.07	.20
24 Horace Broadnax	.07	.20
25 John Thompson CO	.20	.50
26 Dwayne Bryant	.07	.15
27 Tom Lang	.07	.15
28 Perry McDonald	.07	.20
29 Reggie Williams	.15	.40
30 Patrick Ewing	.40	1.00
31 Patrick Ewing	.40	1.00
32 Perry McDonald	.07	.20
33 Sam Jefferson	.07	.20
34 Michael Jackson	.08	.25
35 Anthony Allen	.07	.15
36 Mike Riley	.07	.15
37 John Duren	.07	.20
38 Mark Tillmon	.08	.25
39 Mike Frazier	.07	.15
40 Eric Smith	.07	.20
41 Ed Spriggs	.07	.20
42 Johnathan Edwards	.07	.20
43 Derrick Jackson	.07	.20
44 Mike Hancock	.07	.15
45 Tom Scales	.07	.15
46 David Blue	.07	.15
47 Charles Smith	.10	.30
48 John Thompson CO	.20	.50
49 Patrick Ewing	.40	1.00
50 Al Dutch	.07	.15
51 Eric (Sleepy) Floyd	.10	.30
52 Craig Shelton	.10	.30
53 Reggie Williams	.15	.40
53 Tom Lang	.07	.15
54 Michael Jackson	.08	.25
55 Patrick Ewing	.40	1.00
56 Bill Thomas	.07	.15
57 Ed Hopkins	.07	.15
58 John Thompson CO	.20	.50
59 Jon Smith	.07	.15
60 Merlin Wilson	.07	.15
61 Gene Smith	.07	.20
62 Johnny Jones	.07	.15
63 Senior Night	.07	.15
64 Eric (Sleepy) Floyd	.10	.30
65 Reggie Williams	.15	.40
66 Steve Martin	.07	.15
67 Mark Gallagher	.07	.15
68 Mike McDermont	.07	.15
69 Greg Brooks	.07	.15
70 Larry Long	.07	.15
71 Felix Yeoman	.07	.15
72 Lonnie Duren	.07	.15
73 Terry Fenlon	.07	.15
74 Steve Martin	.07	.15
75 Fred Brown	.08	.25
76 Bill Lynn	.07	.15
77 Patrick Ewing	.40	1.00
78 Mike Laska	.07	.15
79 Paul Tagliabue	.40	1.00
80 Don Weber	.07	.15
81 Jaren Jackson	.10	.30
82 1982 NCAA Finalists	.10	.30
83 1985 NCAA Finalists	.10	.30
84 Jim Brown	.07	.15
85 Jim Christy	.07	.15
86 Tim Mercier	.07	.15
87 Joe Missett	.07	.20
88 Charlie Adrian	.07	.15
89 John Thompson CO	.20	.50
90 Craig Esherick	.07	.15
91 Dennis Cesar	.07	.15
92 Ken Pichette	.07	.15
93 Charlie Adrian	.07	.15
94 Mike Laughna	.07	.15
95 Tommy O'Keefe	.07	.15
96 Merlin Wilson	.07	.15
97 Craig Shelton	.10	.30
98 Derrick Jackson	.07	.15
99 Mike Riley	.07	.15
100 Director Card	.07	.15

1991-92 Georgetown

The 1991-92 Georgetown Hoyas police set contains 18 cards measuring approximately 2 1/2" by 4". The fronts carry a posed player photo enclosed by a white border. The year and team name appear in a purple stripe above the picture, while player information is printed in a gray stripe beneath the picture. In blue and red ink, the backs carry "Kids and Cops" safety tips (from McGruff the Crime Dog), a list of sponsor names, the McGruff logo, and the Coke logo. The cards are numbered by the safety tips on the back. The key card in the set features Alonzo Mourning.

COMPLETE SET (18)	2.50	6.00
1 Team Photo	.40	1.00
2 Robert Churchwell	.20	.50
3 Charles Harrison	.08	.25
4 Joey Brown	.20	.50
5 Alonzo Mourning	1.25	3.00
6 Ronny Thompson	.08	.25
7 Vladimir Bosanac	.08	.25
8 Pascal Fleury	.08	.25
9 Brian Kelly	.08	.25
10 Lamont Morgan	.08	.25
11 Kevin Millen	.08	.25
12 Don Reid	.40	1.00
13 Derrick Patterson	.08	.25
14 Lonnie Harrell	.08	.25
15 Irvin Church	.20	.50
16 John Jacques	.08	.25
17 McGruff The Crime Dog Jack The Bulldog	.08	.25
18 John Thompson CO	.40	1.00

1992-93 Georgetown

This 16-card set measures approximately 2 1/2" by 4" and was sponsored by the National Crime Prevention Council, Coca-Cola, and local police departments. The cards feature posed color player photos with white borders. A dark purple stripe across the top of the photo contains the words "1992-93 Hoyas" in white lettering. A gray stripe at the bottom displays the player's name and basic biographical information. The backs are white and carry "Kids and Cops" public service tips from the Hoyas. The cards are numbered on the back by the tip number.

COMPLETE SET (16)	2.00	5.00
1 Team Photo	.30	.75
2 John Thompson CO	.40	1.00
3 Duane Spencer	.08	.25
4 Derrick Patterson	.08	.25
5 Vladimir Bosanac	.08	.25
6 Don Reid	.40	1.00
7 Othella Harrington	.75	2.00
8 John Jacques	.08	.25
9 Irvin Church	.20	.50
10 Joey Brown	.20	.50
11 Robert Churchwell	.20	.50
12 Lonnie Harrell	.08	.25
13 Eric Micoud	.08	.25
14 Lamont Morgan	.08	.25
15 Kevin Millen	.08	.25
16 Jack the Bulldog Mascot McGruff the Crime Dog	.08	.25

1993-94 Georgetown

The 1993-94 Georgetown Hoyas set consists of 16 cards measuring approximately 2 1/2" by 4". The cards are printed on thin card stock. The white-bordered fronts carry posed color player photos. Above the photo the team name and year is reversed out of a blue bar. Below the photo the player's name and bio are reversed out of a gray bar. The backs have a Kids and Cops safety tip printed in navy and red. The cards are unnumbered and checklisted below in alphabetical order.

COMPLETE SET (16)	2.00	5.00
1 Team Photo	.30	.75
2 John Thompson CO	.40	1.00
3 Joey Brown	.20	.50
4 John Jacques	.08	.25
5 Vladimir Bosanac	.08	.25
6 Robert Churchwell	.20	.50
7 Eric Micoud	.08	.25
8 Lamont Morgan	.08	.25
9 Kevin Millen	.08	.25
10 George Butler	.20	.50
11 Othella Harrington	.60	1.50
12 Cheikh Dia	.30	.75
13 Duane Spencer	.20	.50
14 Don Reid	.30	.75
15 Irvin Church	.20	.50
16 McGruff Crime Dog Jack the Bulldog	.08	.25

1994-95 Georgetown

The 1994-95 Georgetown Hoyas set was sponsored by the National Crime Prevention Council, various law enforcement agencies, as well as Nissan and Coca-Cola. The cards measure 2 1/2" by 4". Inside white borders, the fronts feature posed player portraits, in which the players are dressed in coat-and-tie. Above the photo the team name and year are reversed out in a blue bar. Below the photo the player's name and bio are reversed on in a gray bar. The backs are printed in navy and red and have Kids & Cops safety tips. The cards are numbered on the back by tip. Allen Iverson's first card is in this set.

COMPLETE SET (16)	12.50	30.00
1 Team Photo	.40	1.00
2 John Thompson CO	.40	1.00
3 John Jacques	.08	.25
4 Boubacar Aw	.30	.75
5 Allen Iverson	10.00	25.00
6 Irvin Church	.20	.50
7 Kevin Millen	.08	.25
8 George Butler	.08	.25
9 Jerry Nichols	.30	.75
10 Othella Harrington	.40	1.00
11 Cheikh Dia	.30	.75
12 Jerome Williams	1.50	4.00
13 Eric Myles	.08	.25
14 Jahidi White	.75	2.00
15 Don Reid	.30	.75
16 McGruff The Crime Dog And Jack The Bulldog	.08	.25

1996-97 Georgetown

This set was sponsored by the National Crime Prevention Council, various law enforcement agencies, as well as Nissan and Coca-Cola. The cards measure 2 1/2" by 4". The fronts feature posed player portraits, in which the players are dressed in coat-and-tie or an action photo . In the top left corner of the photo the team name and year are in white on a black diagonal bar. Below the photo, the player's name and bio are in a gray bar. The backs are printed in navy and red and have Kids & Cops safety tips. The sponsors names and a few logos are represented as well. The cards are numbered on the back by tip.

COMPLETE SET (18)	4.00	10.00
1 Team Photo	.40	1.00
2 Joseph Touomou	.20	.50
3 Daymond Jackson	.20	.50
4 Dean Berry	.20	.50
5 Brendan Gaughan	.20	.50
6 Cheikh Ya-Ya Dia	.30	.75
7 Shernard Long	.20	.50
8 Boubacar Aw	.30	.75
9 Rhese Gibson	.20	.50
10 Jerry Nichols	.20	.50
11 Ed Sheffey	.20	.50
12 Godwin Owinje	.20	.50
13 Jahidi White	.40	1.00
14 Jameel Watkins	.20	.50
15 Victor Page	.75	2.00
16 Shamel Jones	.30	.75
17 John Thompson CO	.40	1.00
18 Law Enforcement Agencies Group Photo	.20	.50

1989-90 Georgia

This 12-card standard-size set was sponsored by the USDA Forest Service and other agencies. The fronts feature color action photos on a white card face. The school name appears in red lettering across the top. The team name and player identification are given in white lettering on a black bar above and below the picture, with the Smokey icon in the lower left corner. The backs carry biographical information as well as a fire prevention cartoon starring Smokey. The cards are unnumbered and checklisted below in alphabetical order.

COMPLETE SET (12)	6.00	15.00
1 Neville Austin	.40	1.00
2 Arlando Bennett	.40	1.00
3 Rod Cole	.40	1.00
4 Hugh Durham CO	1.25	3.00
5 Litterial Green	1.25	3.00
6 Pat Hamilton	.40	1.00
7 Mike Harron	.40	1.00
8 Lemuel Howard	.40	1.00
9 Alec Kessler	1.00	2.50
10 Jody Patton	.40	1.00
11 Elmore Spencer	.75	2.00
12 Marshall Wilson	.40	1.00

1990-91 Georgia

This 16-card standard-size set was sponsored by the USDA Forest Service in conjunction with several other federal agencies. The cards feature on fronts color action photos bordered in red. Inside the border the school name and player identification are given in gray stripes above and below the picture, with the Smokey icon in the lower left corner. The background color outside the red border varies from card to card, ranging from black to gray. The back presents either career statistics or summary, as well as a fire prevention cartoon starring Smokey. The cards are unnumbered and are checklisted below in alphabetical order, with the uniform number after the player's name.

COMPLETE SET (16)	6.00	15.00
1 Neville Austin 35	.40	1.00
2 Arlando Bennett 32	.40	1.00
3 Charles Claxton 33	.75	2.00
4 Rod Cole 22	.40	1.00
5 Bernard Davis 23	.40	1.00
6 Hugh Durham CO	1.00	2.50
7 Shaun Golden 10	.40	1.00
8 Litterial Green 11	1.00	2.50
9 Antonio Harvey 34	1.00	2.50
10 Lem Howard 25	.40	1.00
11 Marcel Kon 51	.40	1.00
12 Jody Patton 12	.40	1.00
13 Kendall Rhine 15	.40	1.00
14 Reggie Tinch 24	.40	1.00
15 Marshall Wilson 44 guarded by Dennis Scott	.60	1.50
16 1990-91 Bulldogs Team Photo	.75	2.00

1992-93 Georgia

Sponsored by the USDA Forest Service and the state forestry agency, this 16-card standard-size set was issued as a perforated sheet consisting of four rows of four cards each. On a red card face, the fronts feature posed and action color player photos. A white frame encloses the pictures as well as player information. A Smokey the Bear logo at the lower left rounds out the front. The backs carry biographical information and a fire prevention cartoon starring Smokey. The cards are unnumbered and checklisted below in alphabetical order.

COMPLETE SET (16)	6.00	15.00
1 Shandon Anderson	2.50	6.00
2 Terrell Bell	.40	1.00
3 Arlando Bennett	.30	.75
4 Dathon Brown	.30	.75
5 Charles Claxton	.75	2.00
6 Bernard Davis	.30	.75
7 Shaun Golden	.30	.75
8 Cleveland Jackson	.30	.75
9 Steve Jones	.30	.75
10 Kris Nordholz	.30	.75
11 Brian Peterson	.30	.75
12 Kendall Rhine	.40	1.00
13 Pertha Robinson	.40	1.00
14 Carlos Strong	.40	1.00
15 Chris Tiger	.30	.75
16 Ty Wilson	.30	.75

1993-94 Georgia

Sponsored by the USDA Forest Service and the state forestry agency, this 16-card standard size set was issued as a perforated sheet consisting of four rows of four cards each. On a red card face, the fronts feature posed and action color player photos. The team name is printed above the photo, with the player's name, number and position below. The team logo and Smokey's 50th year anniversary logo complete the fronts. The backs carry the player's name and number and a fire prevention cartoon starring Smokey. The cards are unnumbered and checklisted below in alphabetical order.

COMPLETE SET (16)	5.00	12.00
1 Shandon Anderson	1.50	4.00
2 Terrell Bell	.40	1.00
3 Dathon Brown	.30	.75
4 Charles Claxton	.60	1.50
5 Bernard Davis	.30	.75
6 Melvin Drake	.30	.75
7 Hugh Durham CO	.60	1.50
8 Cleveland Jackson	.30	.75
9 Steve Jones	.30	.75
10 Kris Nordholz	.30	.75
11 Brian Peterson	.30	.75
12 Pertha Robinson	.40	1.00
13 Carlos Strong	.40	1.00
14 Chris Tiger	.30	.75
15 Ty Wilson	.30	.75
16 Team Photo	.40	1.00

1988-89 Georgia Tech

This 12-card standard-size set was sponsored by Nike, whose company name appears on both sides of the card. Sets were given out to fans attending a certain Georgia Tech home game during the 1988-89 season. The fronts feature either posed or action color photos, with a gold border on the left and dark blue borders on the bottom and right of the picture. The backs have biographical information and a tip from the Yellow Jackets consisting of an anti-drug message. The key cards in the set are Tom Hammonds, Brian Oliver, and Dennis Scott. The cards are numbered for convenience alphabetically by player's name in the checklist below.

COMPLETE SET (12)	8.00	20.00
1 Maurice Brittain 52	.40	1.00
2 Karl Brown 5	.75	2.00
3 Bobby Cremins CO	2.50	6.00
4 Brian Domalik 12	.40	1.00
5 Tom Hammonds 20	1.50	4.00
6 Johnny McNeil 44	.75	2.00
7 James Munlyn 24	.40	1.00
8 Brian Oliver 13	.75	2.00
9 Willie Reese 31	.40	1.00
10 Dennis Scott 4	2.00	5.00
11 Anthony Sherrod 42	.75	2.00
12 David Whitmore 23	.40	1.00

1989-90 Georgia Tech

This 20-card standard-size set was sponsored by the Atlanta City Police Department and produced by Coca-Cola. The cards were distributed in the Atlanta area by the Police Athletic League; reportedly 10,000 sets were distributed. The fronts feature either posed or action color photos on a white card stock. The backs have biographical information and a tip from the Yellow Jackets consisting of an anti-drug message. The cards are numbered for convenience alphabetically by player's name in the checklist below. Key cards in the set include the three Kenny Andersons, two Dennis Scotts, Matt Geiger and Malcolm Mackey's first card.

COMPLETE SET (20)	7.00	14.00
1 Kenny Anderson 12 (Portrait)	1.25	3.00
2 Kenny Anderson 12 (Free Throw)	1.25	3.00
3 Kenny Anderson 12 (Jump Shot)	1.25	3.00
4 Rod Balanis 34	.20	.50
5 Darryl Barnes 15	.20	.50
6 Brian Black 23	.20	.50
7 Karl Brown 5	.30	.75
8 Bobby Cremins CO	.60	1.50
9 Brian Domalik 3	.20	.50
10 Matt Geiger 52	.75	2.00
11 Malcolm Mackey 32	.30	.75
12 Johnny McNeil 44	.30	.75
13 James Munlyn 24	.20	.50
14 Ivano Newbill 33	.30	.75
15 Brian Oliver 13	.40	1.00
16 Dennis Scott 4 (Free Throw)	.75	2.00
17 Dennis Scott 4 (Shooting)	.75	2.00
18 Greg White 14	.20	.50
19 Team Photo	.40	1.00
20 Lethal Weapon 3 Brian Oliver Dennis Scott Kenny Anderson	.60	1.50

1990-91 Georgia Tech

This 20-card standard-size set was sponsored by the Atlanta City Police Department and Coca-Cola, and the latter sponsor's logos appear in the upper right corner of the card face as well as at the bottom of the back. It is reported that 10,000 sets were issued in two lots: the first 5,000 went out to the housing projects and kids in the Atlanta Police Athletic Program, and the second lot was offered to the general public. The front features a borderless color action photo of the player on white card stock. The team name appears in gold lettering above the picture, with player information in black lettering below the picture. The back has brief biographical information and "Tips from the Yellow Jackets," which consist of various public service announcements. The cards are unnumbered and are checklisted below in alphabetical order. Key cards in the set include the three Kenny Andersons, two Malcolm Mackeys, and Jon Barry's first card.

COMPLETE SET (20)	4.00	10.00
1 Kenny Anderson 12 (Shooting lay-up)	1.00	2.50
2 Kenny Anderson 12 (Driving past defender)	1.00	2.50
3 Kenny Anderson 12 (Dribbling)	1.00	2.50
4 Rod Balanis 34	.20	.50
5 Darryl Barnes 15	.20	.50
6 Jon Barry 14	1.00	2.50
7 Brian Black 23	.20	.50
8 Bobby Cremins CO	.60	1.50
9 Brian Domalik 3	.20	.50
10 James Gaddy 10	.20	.50
11 Todd Harlicka 30	.20	.50
12 Bryan Hill 11	.30	.75
13 Matt Geiger 52	.60	1.50
14 Brian Gemberling 41	.20	.50
15 Malcolm Mackey 32	.30	.75
16 Malcolm Mackey 32	.30	.75
17 James Munlyn 24	.20	.50
18 Ivano Newbill 33	.30	.75
19 Greg White 31	.20	.50
20 Team Photo	.40	1.00

1991 Georgia Tech Collegiate Collection

This 200-card set is standard sized. The fronts have a blue border with color action shots on each one. The school name and logo are found across the top border of the card. The featured player's name is found along the bottom border set against a yellow-gold background. The backs carry a small bio of the player and his/her statistics.

COMPLETE SET (200)	4.00	10.00
2 Ida Neal BK	.05	.15
3 Lenny Horton BK	.05	.15
4 Dennis Scott BK	.10	.25
6 Dolores Bootz BK	.05	.15
9 LeeAnn Woodhull BK	.05	.15
15 Tom Hammonds BK	.05	.15
17 Cindy Cochran BK	.05	.15
24 Tory Ehle BK	.05	.15
26 Brook Steppe BK	.07	.20
30 Brian Oliver BK	.05	.15
33 Craig Neal BK	.05	.15
35 Duane Ferrell BK	.05	.15
40 Marielle Walker BK	.05	.15
42 Yvon Joseph BK	.05	.15
46 Karl Brown BK	.05	.15
58 John Salley BK	.20	.50
60 Sheila Wagner BK	.05	.15
91 Bonnie Tafe BK	.05	.15
109 Pete Silas BK	.05	.15
122 Mark Price BK	.20	.50
124 Bobby Cremins BK CO	.07	.20
134 Bruce Dalrymple BK	.05	.15

135 Johnny McNeil BK .05 .15
141 Scott Petway BK .05 .15
158 Kate Brandt BK .05 .15
159 Melvin Dold BK .05 .15
160 Tico Brown BK .05 .15
167 Jim Caldwell BK .05 .15
168 Buddy Blemker BK .05 .15
170 Roger Kaiser BK .05 .15
176 Bobby Kimmel BK .05 .15
177 Phil Wagner BK .05 .15
178 Jim Wood BK .05 .15
179 Rich Yunkus BK .07 .20

1991-92 Georgia Tech

This 15-card standard-size set was sponsored by Coca-Cola in conjunction with Atlanta Police Athletic League. The fronts feature glossy color player photos on a gold card face. The year, Coke logo, jersey number, and team name appear above the picture, while player information is given below it. The backs carry biographical information and "Tips from the Yellow Jackets," which consist of safety tips. The cards are unnumbered and checklisted below in alphabetical order. Key cards in the set include the first cards of Travis Best and James Forrest.

COMPLETE SET (15) 6.00 15.00
1 Rod Balanis .20 .50
2 Darryl Barnes .20 .50
3 Drew Barry 1.25 3.00
4 Jon Barry .75 2.00
5 Travis Best 1.50 4.00
6 Bobby Cremins CO .60 1.50
7 James Forrest .75 2.00
8 James Gaddy .20 .50
9 Matt Geiger .60 1.50
10 Todd Harlicka .20 .50
11 Bryan Hill .30 .75
12 Malcolm Mackey .40 1.00
13 Ivano Newbill .30 .75
14 Fred Vinson .30 .75
15 Greg White .20 .50

1992-93 Georgia Tech

This 15-card standard-size set features color action player photos. A mustard border on one side of the card carries the school name. A white bar at the bottom contains the player's name in mustard print. This bar intersects the mustard border at one of the lower corners. The horizontal backs feature black-and-white portraits with shadow borders in the upper left corner. The player's name, biography, statistics, and a personal profile fills the remainder of the back.

COMPLETE SET (15) 3.00 8.00
1 Bobby Cremins CO .60 1.50
2 Bryan Hill .30 .75
3 James Gaddy .20 .50
4 Ivano Newbill .30 .75
5 Malcolm Mackey .30 .75
6 Rod Balanis .20 .50
7 Travis Best 1.25 3.00
8 Fred Vinson .30 .75
9 Darryl Barnes .20 .50
10 James Forrest .40 1.00
11 Todd Harlicka .20 .50
12 Drew Barry .60 1.50
13 Keith Kenney .20 .50
14 John Kelly .20 .50
15 Martice Moore .40 1.00

1991-92 Hawaii-Hilo

This 15-card set measures 2 1/4" by 3 1/2" and is sponsored by Mauna Loa. The fronts feature posed player shots framed with a thin purple inner border and a thin red outer border on a blue background. The player's name and position run along the right side of the photo. The backs carry the player's name, position and jersey number on a white stripe at the top with biographical information, career summary, and statistics below on a blue background. The cards are unnumbered and checklisted below in alphabetical order.

COMPLETE SET (15) 10.00 25.00
1 Steve Armstrong .75 2.00
2 Darren Buchanan .75 2.00
3 Jason Cabral .75 2.00
4 Chris Dane .75 2.00
5 Jeff Garner .75 2.00
6 Russ Harper .75 2.00
7 Warren Harrell .75 2.00
8 Mike Helm .75 2.00
9 Paul Lee .75 2.00
10 Jim Malinchak .75 2.00
11 Cris Murphy .75 2.00
12 Brett Nesland .75 2.00
13 Mike Pollock .75 2.00
14 Dwayne Sarver .75 2.00
15 Booker Waugh .75 2.00

1992-93 Hawaii-Hilo

This 15-card set measures the standard size. The fronts feature posed color shots with a red border. The player's name and jersey number are listed at the bottom. The backs carry a small black-and-white player's portrait in the upper left corner with biographical information on a white background. The cards are unnumbered and checklisted below in alphabetical order.

COMPLETE SET (15) 8.00 20.00
1 Dan Androff .60 1.50
2 Tyro Banks .60 1.50
3 Fred Crawford .60 1.50
4 Jerome Facione .60 1.50
5 Jeff Garner .60 1.50
6 Eddie Hayward .60 1.50
7 Paul Lee .60 1.50
8 Tim Lovejoy ACO .60 1.50
9 Brett Nesland .60 1.50
10 Mike Redwood .60 1.50
11 Dwayne Sarver .60 1.50
12 Mike Seawright .60 1.50
13 Mike Van Staveren .60 1.50
14 Bob Wilson CO .60 1.50
15 Syrus Yarbrough .60 1.50

1921 Holy Cross

This set was issued around 1922 and features cards of coaches and team captains for various Holy Cross University sports. The six cards measrue roughly 2 1/2" by 3 3/4" and were issued inside a "wrap-around" style folder that included a photo of the football team. Each card is blankbacked and was printed on thick cream colored stock.

COMPLETE SET (7) 100.00 200.00
4 McLaughlin BK 10.00 20.00

1992-93 Houston

This 28-card standard-size set was produced by Motion Sports Inc. The fronts feature posed, color player photos with black borders. A red bar at the top contains the player's name, while the school name appears in a similar red bar at the bottom. The backs carry biographical information and player profiles on white semi-transparent panels. The panels are set against an action photo of the player that is visible through the panel.

COMPLETE SET (29) 10.00 25.00
1 Pat Foster CO .20 .50
(Close up)
2 Bo Outlaw 2.50 6.00
3 Jessie Drain .08 .25
4 Derrick Smith .08 .25
5 Craig Lillie .20 .50
6 Tyrone Evans .08 .25
7 Rafael Carrasco .08 .25
8 Brandon Rollins .08 .25
9 David Diaz .08 .25
10 Jermaine Johnson .08 .25
11 Darrell Grayson .08 .25
12 Anthony Goldwire 1.00 2.50
13 Lloyd Wiles .08 .25
14 Pat Foster CO .20 .50
(Standing)
15 Tommy Jones ACO .08 .25
16 Alvin Brooks ACO .08 .25
17 Team Photo .20 .50
18 Game of Century .40 1.00
Houston vs. UCLA
19 Otis Birdsong .40 1.00
20 Elvin Hayes 2.00 5.00
21 Hakeem Olajuwon 2.50 6.00
22 Clyde Drexler 2.50 6.00
23 Guy V. Lewis .75 2.00
Former CO
24 1968 UPI and AP .20 .50
25 Cougar Pride .08 .25
26 Ad Card Motion Sports .08 .25
NNO Front Card .08 .25
NNO Back Card .08 .25
NNO Checklist .08 .25

1990 Idaho Women

COMPLETE SET (12) 3.00 8.00
1 Julie Balch .40 1.00
2 Jennifer Ballenger .40 1.00
3 Hettie DeJong .40 1.00
4 Sabrina Dial .40 1.00
5 Kortnie Edwards .40 1.00
6 Brenda Kuehlthau .40 1.00
7 Sherri Lathen .40 1.00
8 Andi McCarthy .40 1.00
9 Kelly Moeller .40 1.00
10 Sherry Peterson .40 1.00
11 Erina Queen .40 1.00
12 Krista Smith .40 1.00

1994-95 IHSA Boys A State Tournament

Produced by Roox Limited Corporation, this set presents the final sixteen Boys A teams that participated in the Illinois High School Association March Madness Tournament. Just 1,000 sets of each team was produced at tournament time. Measuring the standard size, the borderless fronts feature a mix of color or black-and-white action or posed player photos. A gold-shaded bar across the top carries the player's name with the words "March Madness '95" in a brighter, thin yellow bar below it. The horizontal backs carry the player's name and high school; in addition, his position, height, weight, and class are printed across a faded picture of a basketball. Each set came with a title card, which is not included in the listing below. The school name is given first, followed by the city or township (where appropriate) in parentheses. Numbering errors or inconsistencies abound--some are not in order, some are out of sequence, some are missing, and some are duplicated. For example, #184-195 (except for #186) are duplicated. Both sets of numbers are used for Tabernacle Christian and Unity High School. #193 is duplicated under Unity High School.

COMPLETE SET (215) 25.00 60.00
1 Neal Cotts .15 .40
2 Richard Douglas .15 .40
3 John Flick .15 .40
4 Chad Kerksick .15 .40
5 Jason Kunz .15 .40
6 Duane Roth .15 .40
7 Parnell Roulds .15 .40
8 Adam Schieppe .15 .40
9 Eric Schwehr .15 .40
10 Justin Tarver .30 .75
11 Steve Walraven .15 .40
12 DeMarcus Walter .15 .40
13 Mike Schaefer .15 .40
14 Steve St. Jules .15 .40
15 Jim Ward .15 .40
16 Matt Becker .15 .40
17 Brad Bryan .15 .40
18 Duane Goebel .15 .40
19 Scott Huegen .15 .40
20 Kurt Kalmer .15 .40
21 Jeff Kehrer .15 .40
22 Nathan Kreke .15 .40
23 Glenn Lammers .15 .40
24 Troy Pingsterhaus .15 .40
25 Brett Schulte .15 .40
26 Bob Tebbe .15 .40
27 Luke Woltering .15 .40
28 Adam Zieren .15 .40
29 Clayton Arnett .15 .40
30 Tyson Bottom .15 .40
31 Andy Brannan .15 .40
32 Brian Clough .15 .40
33 Blake Cunningham .15 .40
34 Derek Freand .15 .40
35 Ben Goetten .15 .40
36 Ryan Graner .15 .40
37 Brian Hires .15 .40
38 Matt Hoots .15 .40
39 Adam Price .15 .40
40 Matt Ruyle .15 .40
41 Daryl Schnelten .15 .40
42 Mark Tepen .15 .40
43 Dan Walker .15 .40
44 Josh Allen .15 .40
45 Eric Glass .15 .40
46 Kyle Herring .15 .40
47 Charlie Holland .15 .40
48 Damon Lampley .15 .40
49 Robert Neal .15 .40
50 Martin Nicholes .15 .40
51 Dale Overstreet UER .15 .40
(Card misnumbered as 581)
52 C.R. Rath .15 .40
53 Brandon Reynolds .15 .40
54 Jared Sperling .15 .40
55 Brad Vineyard .15 .40
56 Daniel Wenzel .15 .40
57 Brock Billings .15 .40
59 Peter Craig .15 .40
61 Heath Hall .15 .40
62 Jimmy Harris .15 .40
63 Marty Hull .15 .40
65 Rusty Lynch .15 .40
67 Kirk Mosley .15 .40
68 Ryan Pulliam .15 .40
70 Jason Stotts .15 .40
71 Joe Wilson .15 .40
72 Neil Banwart .15 .40
73 Brandon Branson .15 .40
74 Kevin Dyer .15 .40
75 Derric Eisenmann .15 .40
76 Chris Fowler .15 .40
77 Ryan Hivley .15 .40
78 Jeff Howard .15 .40
79 Ryan Martin .15 .40
80 Matt Mougey .15 .40
81 Jeff Peterson .15 .40
82 Cory Richmond .15 .40
83 Tim Sinclair .15 .40
84 Dustin Sullivan .15 .40
85 Kendall Welch .15 .40
86 Matt Wills .15 .40
87 Jonah Batambuze .15 .40
88 Jason Graf .15 .40
89 D.J. Hubbard .15 .40
90 Nathan Hubbard .15 .40
91 Kevin Jones .15 .40
92 Andy Matthews .15 .40
93 Matt McClintock .15 .40
94 Jason Naftziger .15 .40
95 Kurt Olson .15 .40
96 Eric Schlipf .15 .40
97 Nitai Spiro .15 .40
98 Jeremy Stanton .15 .40
99 Darrin York .15 .40
100 Bryan Butt .15 .40
101 Mark Churchill .15 .40
102 Nathlan DeBaillie .15 .40
103 Mark Gannon .15 .40
104 Jamie Hixson .15 .40
105 Chris John .15 .40
106 Ryan Jones .15 .40
107 Aaron Kunert .15 .40
108 Jason Larson .15 .40
109 Tim Shields .15 .40
110 Josh Talley .15 .40
111 Brandon Welborn .15 .40
112 Justin Welborn .15 .40
113 Ryan Westlund .15 .40
114 Jarred Wilson .15 .40
115 Scott Cornelis .15 .40
116 Dan Coyne-Logan .15 .40
117 Mike Coyne-Logan .15 .40
118 Tim Dinneen .15 .40
119 Matt Gripp .15 .40
120 Shawn Keeven .15 .40
121 Ryan Kelly .15 .40
122 Charlie Manis .15 .40
123 Brian Moran .15 .40
124 Steve Sottos .15 .40
125 Tony Stock .15 .40
126 Brian Trapkus .15 .40
127 Pat Voss .15 .40
128 Chris Watson .15 .40
129 Pat Watson .15 .40
130 Josh Anderson .15 .40
131 Marc Carlson .15 .40
132 Tyson Erdelac .15 .40
133 Scott Frank .15 .40
134 Erik Frykholm .15 .40
135 Sam Glomp .15 .40
136 Andre Green .15 .40
137 Anthony Harris .15 .40
138 John Harris .15 .40
139 Bret Holmertz .15 .40
140 Dan Jameson .15 .40
141 Neil Kessman .15 .40
142 Bob Lindwall .15 .40
143 Shannon Tripplett .15 .40
144 Rich Beyers .15 .40
145 Jim Brix .15 .40
149 Kevin Herdes .15 .40
150 Roger Jones .15 .40
151 Harlan Kennell .15 .40
152 Alex Miller .15 .40
153 Aaron Rohdemann .15 .40
154 Ryan Shambo .15 .40
155 Ben Short .15 .40
156 Mike Steers .15 .40
157 Todd Wilderman .15 .40
158 Derek Williams .15 .40
159 Eric Roley .15 .40
160 Ryan Cox .15 .40
161 Brock Friese .15 .40
162 Mark Giertz .15 .40
163 Phil Manhart .15 .40
164 Scott Meers .30 .75
165 Christian Merriman .15 .40
166 Patrick Merriman .15 .40
167 Ryan Moomaw .15 .40
168 Craig Ogle .15 .40
170 Brock Vonderheide .15 .40
171 Ben Commare .15 .40
172 Peter Doetschman .15 .40
173 Brian Duffy .15 .40
174 Jake Engler .15 .40
175 Trevor Gartner .15 .40
176 Scott Gengler .15 .40
177 Greg Johnson .15 .40
178 Pat Keller .15 .40
179 Peter Knaub .15 .40
180 Matt Lowry .15 .40
181 Jake Nauman .15 .40
182 Matt Pavesich .15 .40
183 Gary Anderson .15 .40
184 Ricky Brown .15 .40
184 Brian Cardinal .15 .40
185 Kendall Caples .15 .40
185 C.J. Franks .15 .40
186 Sterling Chears .15 .40
187 Vincent Dawkins .15 .40
187 Jacques LeFaivre .15 .40
188 Roosevelt Deanes .15 .40
188 Lyndon Mumm .15 .40
189 Ephraim Eaddy .15 .40
189 Brad Siuts .15 .40
190 Hiawatha Griffin .15 .40
190 Eric Stevens .15 .40
191 Philip Johnson .15 .40
191 Eric Tempel .15 .40
192 Craig Jones .15 .40
192 Zach Trimble .15 .40
193 John Jones .15 .40
193 Brady Allison .15 .40
193 Matt VanNote .15 .40
194 Reginald Jones .15 .40
194 Ryan Rich .15 .40
195 Jamell McLaurin .15 .40
195 John Hausman .15 .40
196 Thaddeus Bates .15 .40
321 Derrick York .15 .40
323 Dustin Rothrock .15 .40
341 Adam Law .15 .40
342 PJ McKinney .15 .40
343 Jed Cryder .15 .40
344 Jabari Harrell .15 .40
345 Brad Punke .15 .40
346 Zeno Weems .15 .40
347 Matt Scott .15 .40
348 Joe Mann .15 .40
349 Steve Becker .15 .40
350 Aaron Sovern .15 .40
351 Nathan Thompson .15 .40
352 Josh Wayne .15 .40
353 Julian Harrell .15 .40
354 Mark Allen .15 .40

1994-95 IHSA Boys A Slam Dunk

This 65-card set features those players who participated in the slam dunk competition at the state tournament. Five hundred of each card were printed. The fronts feature a small color or black-and-white, posed or action player photo in a thin red frame on a blue background. The player's name is printed in white on a purple stripe below the picture. The set title is printed up the right and across the top with a basketball between the words in the top right. The horizontal backs carry the player's name in white on a black stripe with his high school below along with the player's height, class, and what college he would like to attend or career highlights. The March Madness logo appears at the right. Cards are numbered consecutively except the last card is numbered 106 instead of 66 and is a duplicate of card 65.

COMPLETE SET (65) 8.00 20.00
1 Charles Adams .15 .40
2 Ricky Brown .15 .40
3 Jeff Averkamp .15 .40
4 Tim Cavinder .15 .40
5 Phil Durkin .15 .40
6 Robert Hahn .15 .40
7 Mike Hawks .15 .40
8 Jason Peake .15 .40
9 Damiano Scalera .15 .40
10 James Gast .15 .40
11 Bryan Zotz .15 .40
12 Mike Tyler .15 .40
13 Tim West .15 .40
14 Jim Vance .15 .40
15 Tom Pshak .15 .40
16 Tommy Sawyer .15 .40
17 Derek Crabill .15 .40
18 Rick Lawson .15 .40
19 Brian Shaw .15 .40
20 Joel Hubbard .15 .40
21 Josh Born .15 .40
22 Jamie Reel .15 .40
23 Shawn Lade .15 .40
24 Jeff Peterson .15 .40
25 Josh Pistole .15 .40
26 Josh Jones .15 .40
27 A.J. Strum .15 .40
28 Kale Sellers .15 .40
29 Andy Ellet .15 .40
30 Chad Brecunier .15 .40
31 Eric Esker .15 .40
32 Marty Hull .15 .40
33 Matt Alepra .15 .40
34 Mark Rasmussen .15 .40
35 Robert Clark .15 .40
36 Damon Lampley .15 .40
37 Trevor Hiel .15 .40
38 Greg McDanel .15 .40
39 Todd Stewart .15 .40
40 William Newton .15 .40
41 Cory Eshleman .15 .40
42 Jackson Jones .15 .40
43 Tim Volpert .15 .40
44 Tony Zook .15 .40
45 Thomas Robinson .15 .40
46 Matt Gunier .15 .40
47 Ronnie Kammes .15 .40
48 Ryan Ashley .15 .40
49 Michael Glover .15 .40
50 Chris Prather .15 .40
51 Brandon Merchalnt .15 .40
52 Duane Roth .15 .40
53 Dusty Johnson .15 .40
54 Jason Ogorzaly .15 .40
55 Jeremy Browne .15 .40
56 Derrick DeWilde .15 .40
57 Brian Miller .15 .40
58 Alan Loy .15 .40
59 Kris Stoneking .15 .40
60 Michael Klinger .15 .40
61 Shea Banning .15 .40
62 James Gast .15 .40
63 David Cerven .15 .40
64 Alvin Valentine .15 .40
65 Andre Williams .15 .40
106 Andre Williams .15 .40

1994-95 IHSA Boys A 3-Point Showdown

This 52-card features those players who participated in the 3-point showdown at the state tournament. Five hundred of each card were printed. Measuring the standard size, the fronts feature a small color or black-and-white, posed or action player photo in a thin red frame on a blue background. The player's name is printed in white on a purple stripe below the picture. The set title is printed down the left and at the top with a basketball between the words in the top left. The horizontal backs carry the player's name in white on a black stripe with his high school below along with the player's height, class, and what college he would like to attend or some career highlights. The March Madness logo appears at the right. The title card is not included in the listing below. Some card numbers are out of sequence; some numbers are skipped. Two cards are not numbered.

COMPLETE SET (52) 8.00 20.00
1 Mike Abner .15 .40
2 Rob Buckley .15 .40
3 Mike Cox .15 .40
4 Corey Fox .15 .40
5 Ryan Fritch .15 .40
6 Drazen Jozic .15 .40
7 Muamer Karamovic .15 .40
9 Josh Komnick .15 .40
10 Steven Lester .15 .40
11 Mike Martin .15 .40
13 Patrick Presser .15 .40
14 Willie Reinburg .15 .40
15 Torey Rein .15 .40
16 Douglas Scott .15 .40
17 Michael Sommer .15 .40
18 Tom Stirnaman .15 .40
19 Brian Tackitt .15 .40
20 Josh Williams .15 .40
21 Joe Whitmore .15 .40
22 Andy Murray .15 .40
23 Luke Williams .15 .40
24 Michael Torman .15 .40
25 Michael Siegfried .15 .40
26 Aaron Sovern .15 .40
27 Scot Kent .15 .40
31 Guy Kuhn .15 .40
32 Dru McCulley .15 .40
33 Tony Merlie .15 .40
35 Eric Sherrier .15 .40
36 Bill Heisler .15 .40
37 Tony Hartman .15 .40
38 Ryan Hammer .15 .40
39 Chad Hammond .15 .40
40 David Griffiths .15 .40
41 Brent Fowler .15 .40
42 Chad Fulton .15 .40
43 Adam Crenshaw .15 .40
44 Ryan Clark .15 .40
45 Jason Clark .15 .40
46 Brian Ball .15 .40
47 Brent Baker .15 .40
48 Michael Arroyo .15 .40
52 Jeremy Lansaw .15 .40
53 John Harris .15 .40
54 Jacob Mundell .15 .40
55 Josh Menser .15 .40
56 Nick Pestka .15 .40
66 Troy Kemmerling .15 .40
67 Matt Morris .15 .40
302 J.C. Murray .15 .40
NNO Ryan Knuppel .15 .40
NNO Eric Schwehr .15 .40

1994-95 IHSA Boys AA State Tournament

Produced by Roox Limited Corporation, this set presents the final sixteen Boys AA teams that participated in the Illinois High School Association March Madness Tournament. Just 1,000 sets of each team were produced at tournament time. Measuring the standard size, the borderless fronts feature a mix of color or black-and-white, action or posed player photos. A gold-shaded bar across the top carries the player's name with the words "March Madness '95" in a brighter, thin yellow bar below it. The horizontal backs carry the player's name and high school; in addition, his position, height, weight, and class are printed across a faded picture of a basketball. Each set came with a title card, which is not included in the listing below. The set is checklisted below according to school. Some numbers are not used in this set, and there are two of #101 and #106. Some cards have no photos because they were unavailable. This set includes the first cards of Kevin Garnett, drafted by the Minnesota Timberwolves with the fifth pick in the 1995 NBA Draft. His high school teammate, Ronnie Fields (227), was first team all-state in basketball. Other athletes who will play sports at the collegiate level are Antonio "Chico" Brown (64; Illinois football); Tai Streets (106; Michigan football); Gary Bell (108; Notre Dame football); Willie Coleman (139; Bradley basketball); and Monte Jenkins (172; Southern Illinois basketball).

COMPLETE SET (328) 50.00 125.00
1 Mike Becker .20 .50
1 Josh Veith .20 .50
2 Brad Bowsher .20 .50
3 Rob Brynjelsen .20 .50
4 Todd Dahlstrom .20 .50
5 Robert Davis .20 .50
6 Tom Honeycutt .20 .50
7 Chris Jacobs .20 .50
8 Steve Koliopoulos .20 .50
9 Dan Korvas .20 .50
10 Zach Maddox .20 .50
11 Jason McKinney .20 .50
12 Steve Nelson .20 .50
13 Chris Nowinski .20 .50
14 Joe Potocnic .20 .50
15 Brent Prorok .20 .50
16 Michael White .20 .50
17 Paul Wolf .20 .50
18 John Wotal .20 .50
19 Hector Barnes .20 .50
20 Durius Cunningham .20 .50
21 Corey Dagley .20 .50
22 Chuck Garrett .20 .50
23 Rick Garrett .20 .50
24 Mark Hamilton .20 .50
25 Tyrone Jones .20 .50
26 Justin Knolhoff .20 .50
27 Andre Marshall .20 .50
28 Ivan McPhail .20 .50
29 Ewin Meeks .20 .50
30 Ty Moss .20 .50
31 Chad Schnitker .20 .50
32 Luke Sharp .20 .50
33 Brett Skort .20 .50
34 Kimonie Evans .75 2.00
35 Jerry Harris .20 .50
36 Kevin Thornton .20 .50
37 Jason Price .20 .50
38 Nick Irvin .20 .50
39 John Smith .20 .50
40 Marcel O'Neal .20 .50
41 Jason Garcia .20 .50
42 Keith Coley .20 .50
43 Chris Worrell .20 .50
44 Rodderick Thompson .20 .50
45 Artis James .20 .50
46 Alvin Robinson .20 .50
47 Darius Hampton .20 .50
48 Matt Horner .20 .50
49 Mark Wiggins .20 .50
50 Mike Valentine .20 .50
51 Andrew LeCrone .20 .50
52 Eric Norberg .20 .50
53 Milo Moreland .20 .50
54 Harry Beck .20 .50
55 Ed Precht .20 .50
56 Antwan Cuble .20 .50
57 Marty Mulcrone .20 .50
58 Matt Koch .20 .50
59 Doug Meyers .20 .50
60 Steve Rogala .20 .50
61 Andy Mitchell .20 .50
62 Erasmus Baffour .20 .50
63 Mark Allaria .20 .50
64 Antonio Brown .40 1.00
65 Derek Cowan .20 .50
66 Jim Dougherty .20 .50
67 Maurice Douglas .20 .50
68 Eric Ess .20 .50
69 John Harris .20 .50
70 Tom Hofeditz .20 .50
71 Anthony Jumper .20 .50
72 Steffan Nicholson .20 .50
73 Joe Semith .20 .50
74 Mark Thomas .20 .50
75 Stacy Vaughn .20 .50
76 Dwight Woods .20 .50
77 Chris Wright .20 .50
78 Joe Bongratz .20 .50
79 Eric Bradley .20 .50
80 Joel Dangel .20 .50
81 Damion Forrest .20 .50
82 Maurice Foster .20 .50
83 Chris Hayes .20 .50
85 Brian Jaworski .20 .50
86 Ryan Kelver .20 .50
87 Ted Makela .20 .50
88 Joe Merrick .20 .50
89 David Moo .20 .50
90 Luke Moo .20 .50
92 Darnell Smith .20 .50
93 Carlton DeBose .20 .50
94 Denard Eaves .20 .50
95 Melvin Ely 4.00 10.00
96 Corey Harris .20 .50
97 Napoleon Harris .20 .50
98 Erik Herring .20 .50
99 James Johnson .20 .50
100 Chauncey Jones .20 .50
101A Richard King .20 .50
(Running down court)
101B Richard King .20 .50
(In action against other team)
102 Nick Love .20 .50
103 Antwaan Randle El .20 .50
104 Curtis Randle El .20 .50
105 Maurice Scott .20 .50
106A Tai Streets 3.00 8.00
(Crashing the boards)
106B Tai Streets 3.00 8.00
(different shot)
107 Chip Bates .20 .50
108 Gary Bell .40 1.00
109 Eric Breuer .20 .50
110 Dwayne Edmon .20 .50
111 Adrice Edwards .20 .50
112 John Ford .20 .50
113 Paul Forsythe .20 .50
114 Joel House .20 .50
115 Michael Mines .20 .50
116 Blowery Moody .20 .50
117 Rory O'Connell .20 .50
118 Eric Patnoudes .20 .50
119 Paul Purcell .20 .50
120 Kevin Raub .20 .50
121 Oku Satcher .20 .50
122 Erik Walton .20 .50
123 Tim Barrett .20 .50
125 Peter Carroll .20 .50
127 James Dombkiewicz .20 .50
128 Bill Donlon .20 .50
129 Michael Downes .20 .50
130 Sean Eggert .20 .50
131 Gabe Frank .20 .50
132 Joe Hein .20 .50
133 Stu Katz .20 .50
134 Jon Moeller .20 .50
135 Doug Rosen .20 .50
136 Adam Schimel .20 .50
138 Tim Caldwell .20 .50
139 Willie Coleman .75 2.00
140 Kahil Gayton .20 .50
141 Marcus Griffin .20 .50
142 Darrell Ivory .20 .50
143 Dewayne Johnson .20 .50
144 Sergio McClain .20 .50
145 Charles Russell .20 .50
146 Willie Simmons .20 .50
148 Sean Walls .20 .50
149 Jeff Walraven .20 .50
150 Ivan Watson .20 .50
151 Frank Williams .20 .50
152 Willie Williams .20 .50
168 L.T. Boyd .20 .50
169 Josh Elston .20 .50
170 Heith Gadient .20 .50
171 Cory Jenkins .20 .50
172 Monte Jenkins .75 2.00
173 Mike King .20 .50
174 Pete Mickeal .20 .50
175 Andy Milton .20 .50
176 Matt Quinones .20 .50
177 Larry Stevens .20 .50
178 Tymon Vesey .20 .50
179 Marlon White .20 .50
180 Brad Wilson .20 .50
181 Luke Woods .20 .50
183 Ricky Boone .20 .50
184 Dexter Gipson .20 .50
185 Pat Hand .20 .50
187 Walter Hill .20 .50
188 Craig Hopson .20 .50
189 Jon Luchetti .20 .50
190 Ryan Melling .20 .50
192 Charlie Newman .20 .50
193 Ryan Peterson .20 .50
195 Jeremy Warner .20 .50
196 Ali Azim .20 .50
197 Steve Ball .20 .50
198 Garrett Beatty .20 .50
199 Schaun Catey .20 .50
200 Kevin DePiazza .20 .50
201 Cameron Deppe .20 .50
202 Casey Dodson .20 .50
203 Mike Gullickson .20 .50
204 Daryl Kowalski .20 .50
205 Phillip Krahenbuhl .20 .50
206 Chris Levandowski .20 .50
207 Ryan Lindgren .20 .50
208 Lynwood Schambach .20 .50
209 Matt Wasinger .20 .50
210 Chris Wright .20 .50
211 Marcus Betts .20 .50
212 Ron Blanchard .20 .50
213 Gregory Bryant .20 .50
214 Danny Cassell .20 .50
215 Rubin Conway .20 .50
216 Marcus Crump .20 .50
217 Ian Dent .20 .50
218 Jim Devereux .20 .50
219 Mike Gadomski .20 .50
220 Richard James .20 .50
221 Aaron McIntosh .20 .50
222 Derrick Mims .20 .50
223 Ted Moore .20 .50
224 Justin Papuga .20 .50
225 Rob Walls .20 .50
226 Kevin Garnett 25.00 60.00
227 Ronnie Fields 2.00 5.00
228 Michael Wright .40 1.00
229 Jonathon Washington .20 .50
230 Charles Johnson .20 .50
231 Maurice Woodfork .20 .50
233 Jerome McBride .20 .50
234 Daniel Sierra .20 .50
235 Miguel Estrada .20 .50
236 Jamal Rome .20 .50
(Misnumbered 237)
237 Frank Smith .20 .50
(Identical to 238)
238 Frank Smith .20 .50
(Identical to 237)
342 Tory Hickman .20 .50
343 Brandon Douglas .20 .50
344 Brian Trowbridge .20 .50
345 Jim Flynn .20 .50
346 Loren Wallace CO .20 .50
Tim Wallace ACO
Jeff Wallace ACO
347 Brett Douglas .20 .50
348 Kendall Davis .20 .50
349 Mike Reddington .20 .50
350 Cory VonderHaar .20 .50
351 Adam Requet .20 .50
352 Ryan Stanton .20 .50
353 Kyle Cartmill .20 .50
354 Everette Abbey .20 .50

1994-95 IHSA Boys AA State Tournament Garnett Special Edition

Issued after the original 330-card IHSA Boys AA State Tournament set, these two Kevin Garnett cards feature the current NBA wunderkind during his high school days in Chicago.

COMPLETE SET (2) 70.00 130.00
COMMON CARD (239-240) 30.00 65.00

1994-95 IHSA Boys AA 3-Point Showdown

This 60-card set features those players who participated in the 3-point showdown at the state tournament. Five hundred of each card were printed. Measuring the standard size, the fronts feature a small color or black-and-white, posed or action player photo in a thin red frame on a blue background. The player's name is printed in white on a purple stripe below the picture. The set title is printed down the left and at the top with a basketball between the words in the top left. The horizontal backs carry the player's name in white on a black stripe with his high school below along with the player's height, class, and what college he would like to attend or career highlights. The March Madness logo appears at the right. The title card is not included in the listing below. Card number 10, 59, 60, 62, and 63 were not produced. One card was not numbered.

COMPLETE SET (60) 8.00 20.00
1 Marcus Blossom .15 .40
2 Durwood McCoy .15 .40
3 Brad Mann .15 .40
4 Brett Nishibayashi .15 .40
5 Micah Ogburn .15 .40
6 Matt Wasinger .15 .40
7 Ray Hooks .15 .40
8 Charlie McKenna .15 .40
9 Steve Dahl .15 .40
11 Nick Sanchez .15 .40
12 Greg Gilberg .15 .40
13 Brian Sims .15 .40
14 Steven Wennstrom .15 .40
15 Tony Alvarado .15 .40
16 Josh Suter .30 .75
17 Dave Zell .15 .40
18 Ali Ali .15 .40
19 Ryan Naughton .15 .40
20 Frederick Smith .15 .40
21 Greg Moog .15 .40
22 Dominic Catalano .15 .40
23 Brad Fuller .15 .40
24 David Mikes .15 .40
25 Jon Heider .15 .40
26 Korey Coon .15 .40
27 Michael Mines .15 .40
28 Mark Richardson .15 .40
29 Kyle Breden .15 .40
30 Danny Nicholas .15 .40
31 Todd Meggos .15 .40
32 Chris Johnston .15 .40
33 Jasper Mallory .15 .40
34 Cordell Henry .15 .40
35 Adam Riva .15 .40
36 Alfonzo Lewis .15 .40
37 Luke Windy .15 .40
38 Bob Castelli .15 .40
39 Jeff Peterson .15 .40
40 Arthur Stapleton .15 .40
41 Darius Wesley .15 .40
42 Matt Boudeman .15 .40
43 Kevin Casey .15 .40
44 John Lackaff .15 .40
45 Tom Schmidt .15 .40
46 Mike Pryor .15 .40
47 Mike Geurin .15 .40
48 Bob Tolone .15 .40
49 Jonathan Daniels .15 .40
50 John Mackinson .15 .40
51 Tarise Bryson .15 .40
52 Jeremy Lansaw .15 .40
53 John Harris .15 .40
54 Jacob Mundell .15 .40
55 Josh Menser .15 .40
56 Nick Pestka .15 .40
57 Brandon Frerichs .15 .40
58 Donya Jackson .15 .40
61 Adrian Diaz .15 .40
64 Danyell Cresswell .15 .40
NNO Chris Berezniak .15 .40

1994-95 IHSA Girls A State Tournament

Produced by Roox Limited Corporation, this set presents the final sixteen Girls A teams that participated in the Illinois High School Association March Madness Tournament. Just 1,000 sets of each team was produced at tournament time. Measuring the standard size, the borderless fronts feature a mix of color or black-and-white, action or posed player photos. A gold-shaded bar across the top carries the player's name with the words "March Madness '95" in a brighter, thin yellow bar below it. The horizontal backs carry the player's name and high school; in addition, her position, height, weight, and class are printed across a faded picture of a basketball. Each set came with a title card, which is not included in the listing below. The set is checklisted below according to school. Numbering errors abound--some numbering is out of sequence or card numbers are omitted altogether. Some cards have no photos because they were unavailable for the player whose name is on the card.

COMPLETE SET (195) 20.00 50.00
29 Michelle Donahoo .15 .40
30 Leslie Dumstorff .15 .40
31 Sara Evans .15 .40
32 Heather Fruend .15 .40
33 Danielle Funderburk .15 .40
34 Kristin Hustedde .15 .40
35 Tara Kell .15 .40
36 Erin Knuf .15 .40
37 Racheal Nelson .15 .40
38 Shannon Pollmann .15 .40
39 Courtney Smith .15 .40
40 Amy Allison .15 .40
43 Lindsay Fecht .15 .40
45 Cassie Kinnamon .15 .40
46 Andrea Livingston .15 .40
49 Alisha Nagel .15 .40
52 Koula Toubekis .15 .40
53 Sabrina Bannister .15 .40
54 Ladonna Barton .15 .40
55 Lawanda Burras .15 .40

56 Christina Evans .15 .40
57 Sabrina Minter .15 .40
58 Latrice Payne .15 .40
59 Latrice Ray .15 .40
60 Whitney Wells .15 .40
61 Quinlora Smith .15 .40
62 Tondalaya Wilson .15 .40
115 Lindsey Armstrong .15 .40
116 Heather Cassady .15 .40
117 Jacey Cook .15 .40
118 Melissa Cotter .15 .40
119 Jessi Davis .15 .40
120 Stephanie Donovan .15 .40
121 Tracie Gramkow .15 .40
122 Sara Harlan .15 .40
123 Stephanie Marino .15 .40
124 Lisa Nicoll .15 .40
125 Kari Singer .15 .40
126 Jaima Stowell .15 .40
128 Sara Urban .15 .40
172 Corrie Allan .15 .40
173 Randi Anderson .15 .40
174 Theresa Bertolino .15 .40
175 Kami Derganc .15 .40
176 Margo Girardi .15 .40
177 Kara Joyce .15 .40
178 Celia Jubelt .15 .40
179 Laura Mansholt .15 .40
180 Jodi Ottersburg .15 .40
181 Kristine Polo .15 .40
182 Deneisch Reiniesch .15 .40
183 Alisha Saracco .15 .40
184 Angie Thompson .15 .40
185 Wendy Wolff .15 .40
186 Anna Banks .15 .40
187 Kelly Cartwright .15 .40
188 Rachyl Clayton .15 .40
189 Jaylyn Crabb .15 .40
190 Ricki DeArmon .15 .40
191 Amanda Duggins .15 .40
192 Dawn Halverson .15 .40
193 Alisha Logan .15 .40
194 Chrystal Milligan .15 .40
195 Amy Molinarolo .15 .40
196 Audrey Murphy .15 .40
197 Traci Richerson .15 .40
198 Jessica Stafford .15 .40
199 Tory Teckenbrock .15 .40
200 Erin Watson .15 .40
230 Monica Blyenberg .15 .40
231 Kristen Bruinsma .15 .40
232 Linda DeJong .15 .40
233 Suzanne DeJong .15 .40
234 Kim DeYoung .15 .40
235 Karri Hamstra .15 .40
237 Jennifer Huizenga .15 .40
238 Jennifer Kreykes .15 .40
239 Jill Scott .15 .40
240 Nicole Terpstra .15 .40
241 Becky Vugteveen .15 .40
286 Julie Abell .15 .40
287 Kim Beer .15 .40
288 Shanda Cushing .15 .40
289 Laura Dwyer .15 .40
290 Jenelle Halm .15 .40
291 Hilary Hamer .15 .40
292 Lisa Hendrickson .15 .40
293 Meredith Jackson .15 .40
294 Courtney Jones .15 .40
295 Nikki McCleary .15 .40
296 Erin Micheletti .15 .40
297 Christine O'Connor .15 .40
327 Nicki Bradford .15 .40
328 Cali Broege .15 .40
329 Stacy Ditzler .15 .40
330 Stephanie Fransen .15 .40
331 Kara Hillmer .15 .40
332 Kendra Hillmer .15 .40
333 Kelley Hofmaster .15 .40
334 Jody Knoup .15 .40
335 Kim Koehn .15 .40
336 Cari Pacey .15 .40
337 Elaine Smielewski .15 .40
338 Jocelyn Stiefel .15 .40
339 Sara Thompson .15 .40
340 Tiffany Gallamore .15 .40
341 Shannon Hoyt .15 .40
342 Julie Knuffman .15 .40
344 Susan Laws .15 .40
345 Julie Ludwig .15 .40
346 Robyn Martin .15 .40
347 Dana Schutte .15 .40
348 Deanna Schutte .15 .40
349 Becky Smith .15 .40
350 Michelle Sulewski .15 .40
351 Deanna Venvertloh .15 .40
352 Abbey Williams .15 .40
353 Angie Zanger .15 .40
354 Hope Almy .15 .40
355 Jennie Baird .15 .40
356 Cindy Cheney .15 .40
357 Jill Cheney .15 .40
358 Karen Davis .15 .40
359 Brandi Heleine .15 .40
360 Kasi High .15 .40
361 Lisa Hillary .15 .40
363 Laine Kistler .15 .40
364 Angela Pryle .15 .40
365 Billy Reagan .15 .40
366 Amy Thompson .15 .40
367 Jamie Todd .15 .40
368 Lisa Holley .15 .40
369 Amy Johnson .15 .40
370 Trish Kazak .15 .40
371 Lisa Kuppler .15 .40
372 Stephanie Morphey .15 .40
373 Jacqui Powers .15 .40
374 Amy Reiss .15 .40
375 Cori Stahl .15 .40
376 Leanne Stinson .15 .40
377 LeAnne Stout .15 .40
379 Haylie Behmer .15 .40
380 Brianne Bennett .15 .40
381 Michelle Fager .15 .40
382 Jennifer Harms .15 .40
383 Lea Horii .15 .40
384 Mandey Johnson .15 .40
385 Shelley Johnson .15 .40
386 Angie Patzner .15 .40
387 Jill Schwitters .15 .40
388 Elizabeth Stout .15 .40
389 Jill Tyler .15 .40
390 Katie Tyler .15 .40
391 Erin York .15 .40
392 Gina Bloemer .15 .40
393 Karla Campbell .15 .40
394 Sara Gebben .15 .40
395 Karen Kroeger .15 .40
396 Marcia Meyer .15 .40
397 Amy Niebrugge .15 .40
398 Maria Niebrugge .15 .40
399 Sarah Niebrugge .15 .40
400 Elizabeth Ordner .15 .40
401 Emily Probst .15 .40
402 Kari Probst .15 .40
403 Christina Sehy .15 .40
404 Monica Tegeler .15 .40
405 Kim Walk .15 .40
406 Crystal Worman .15 .40
407 Stormy Young .15 .40
408 Sherry Austin .15 .40
409 Jennifer Bales .15 .40
410 Alicia Brown .15 .40
411 Carissa Brown .15 .40
412 Kristy Duncan .15 .40
413 Katie Edgecombe .15 .40
414 Julie Farr .15 .40
415 Amy Friend .15 .40
416 Stacey Garner .15 .40
417 Leslie Harris .15 .40
418 Chrissy Kunz .15 .40
419 Amanda Park .15 .40
420 Carrie Wickline .15 .40
423 Amy Anderson .15 .40
424 Hilary Anderson .15 .40
425 Lynette Carlson .15 .40
427 Laura Curry .15 .40
428 Kindel McLaughlin .15 .40
429 Shanna Metzler .15 .40
430 Tara Miller .15 .40
431 Jodie Peterson .15 .40
432 Rachel Peterson .15 .40
433 April Schultz .15 .40
436 Laura Bearrows .15 .40
443 Corrie Allan .15 .40

1994-95 IHSA Girls A 3-Point Showdown

This 64-card set features those players who participated in the 3-point showdown at the state tournament. Five hundred of each card were printed. The fronts feature a small color or black-and-white, posed or action player photo in a thin red frame on a blue background. The player's name is printed in white on a purple stripe below the picture. The set title is printed down the left and at the top with a basketball between the words in the top left. The horizontal backs carry the player's name in white on a black stripe with his high school below along with the player's height, class, and what college he would like to attend or career highlights. The March Madness logo appears at the right.

COMPLETE SET (64) 6.00 15.00
1 Missy Barrett .15 .40
2 Ami Beck .15 .40
3 Kristi Bosman .15 .40
4 Nicole Brinker .15 .40
5 Trudy Brooks .15 .40
6 Amanda Colgan .15 .40
7 Patty Conover .15 .40
8 Kami Dergane .15 .40
9 Heather Downing .15 .40
10 Bethany Ellis .15 .40
11 Jill Gomric .15 .40
12 Alicia Granger .15 .40
13 Liza Gualandi .15 .40
14 Stacie Hall .15 .40
15 Erin Henderson .15 .40
16 Heather Holsapple .15 .40
17 Shannon Huff .15 .40
18 Kim Jones .15 .40
19 Ning Kongrut .15 .40
20 Kari Koonce .15 .40
21 Megan Linke .15 .40
22 Traci Lloyd .15 .40
23 Kimberly Lowe .15 .40
24 Ashley Mathias .15 .40
25 Paula Meeker .15 .40
26 Kendra Meyer .15 .40
27 Crystal Miller .15 .40
28 Bridget Monahan .15 .40
29 Dobee Oros .15 .40
30 Heidi Ott .15 .40
31 Cari Pacey .15 .40
32 Jenny Pansa .15 .40
33 Melissa Piper .15 .40
34 Michelle Plack .15 .40
35 Stephanie Rolf .15 .40
36 Maggie Ross .15 .40
37 Kelli Ryan .15 .40
38 Mary Saline .15 .40
39 Kimberly Shafer .15 .40
40 Kelly Slaughter .15 .40
41 Mandy Snell .15 .40
42 Shavon Ellen Sork .15 .40
43 Kimberly Stephenson .15 .40
44 Laura Stucker .15 .40
45 Jody Turrell .15 .40
46 Jesse Weber .15 .40
47 Cathy Wells .15 .40
48 Laurie Zawila .15 .40
49 Lisa Dolan .15 .40
50 Amber Grubbs .15 .40
51 Jessica Kittel .15 .40
52 Amanda White .15 .40
53 Sarah Hunt .15 .40
54 Valerie Lepper .15 .40
55 Gina Fisher .15 .40
56 Brooke Moyer .15 .40
57 Addie Ahlemeyer .15 .40
58 Kris Slavin .15 .40
59 Melanie Mueller .15 .40
60 Melissa Signa .15 .40
61 Alisha Logan .15 .40
62 Teara Backens .15 .40
63 Erin Murphy .15 .40
64 Meredith Jackson .15 .40

1994-95 IHSA Girls AA State Tournament

Produced by Roox Limited Corporation, this set presents the final sixteen Girls AA teams that participated in the Illinois High School Association March Madness Tournament. Just 1,000 sets of each team was produced at tournament time. Measuring the standard size, the borderless fronts feature a mix of color or black-and-white, action or posed player photos. A gold-shaded bar across the top carries the player's name with the words "March Madness '95" in a brighter, thin yellow bar below it. The horizontal backs carry the player's name and high school; in addition, her position, height, weight, and class are printed across a faded picture of a basketball. Each set came with a title card, which is not included in the listing below. The set is checklisted below according to school. Numbering errors and inconsistencies abound--some are out of sequence; others are duplicated; and some are omitted. For example, cards 15 and 16 are out of order and so are cards numbered 436, 437, 438, 439, and 445. Cards 162 and 168 are duplicated with different players and pictures on each card. The Jerseyville High School set, numbered 201-214, is duplicated with the second set having the same but better quality photos. Cards numbers 220 and 221 have the same photo, but two different players' names on them. Some cards have no photos because they were unavailable. This set includes the first card of Dominique Canty (102), a high school All-American who signed to play basketball at Univ. of Alabama. Her teammates, Danielle Scott (113; Coppin State) and Jacqui Jones (107; Alabama), have also signed to play college basketball. Finally, the Lincolnshire team, featuring Tamika and Tauja Catchings (245-46), was ranked #3 in the USA Today final national poll.

COMPLETE SET (227) 25.00 60.00
1 Kathy Fioresi .15 .40
2 Dana Hellgren .15 .40
3 Julie Janota .15 .40
4 Anna Johnson .15 .40
5 Mary Beth Johnson .15 .40
6 Karly Kirkpatrick .15 .40
7 Melissa Parker .15 .40
8 Kim Pompa .15 .40
9 Cathy Ptasnik .15 .40
10 Leslie Schock .15 .40
11 Suzy Smith .15 .40
12 Karisa Turek .15 .40
13 Rachel Voss .15 .40
14 Tina Wenckaitis .15 .40
15 Nykisha Barefield .15 .40
16 Samantha Cartwright .15 .40
17 Sheila Ahern .15 .40
18 Tanisha Brewer .15 .40
19 Cherise Compobasso .15 .40
20 Kate Harker .15 .40
21 Lisa Holman .15 .40
22 Christina Jost .15 .40
23 Stacy Kondziolka .15 .40
24 Kelly Ludy .15 .40
25 Kelly Murman .15 .40
26 Anne Sudlow .15 .40
27 Diana Wendell .15 .40
28 Karen Zygowicz .15 .40
63 Cheri Buchanan .15 .40
64 Jill Fagan .15 .40
65 Andrea Gunnell .15 .40
66 Valerie Kobel .15 .40
67 Jenny Linane .15 .40
68 Katie McAlinden .15 .40
69 Anne McDonald .15 .40
70 Mary Moravek .15 .40
71 Katie Morrissey .15 .40
72 Jeanene Novick .15 .40
73 Katie Schumacher .15 .40
75 Karen Siska .15 .40
76 Karen Valentas .15 .40
77 Trish Watson .15 .40
78 Latasha Love .15 .40
79 Lakendra Moffett .15 .40
80 Kilah Moore .15 .40
81 Michelle Roberts .15 .40
82 Virginia Sellers .15 .40
83 Lori Shelby .15 .40
84 Janelle Tabor .15 .40
85 Stephanie Wallace .15 .40
86 Jenny Accardo .15 .40
87 Amy Anderson .15 .40
88 Tara Babich .15 .40
89 Ann Brophy .15 .40
90 Melissa Collins .15 .40
91 Michelle Foley .15 .40
92 Beth Gawlinski .15 .40
93 Jackie Geraci .15 .40
94 Julie Johnson .15 .40
95 Lauren Manczko .15 .40
96 Mfary Ellen O'Grady .15 .40
97 Kristen Rezny .15 .40
98 Sara Shrader .15 .40
99 Erin Stafford .15 .40
100 Krista Thomas .15 .40
101 Marcella Barry .15 .40
102 Dominique Canty .75 2.00
103 Shereena Clarke .15 .40
104 Deon Cooper .15 .40
105 Clarissa Flores .15 .40
106 Yolanda Howard .15 .40
107 Jaqui Jones .60 1.50
108 Terica Keaton .15 .40
109 Lawanda McCants .15 .40
110 Kimberly Moore .15 .40
111 Danielle Pinkston .15 .40
112 Natasha Pointer .15 .40
113 Danielle Scott .60 1.50
129 Sandi Andersen .15 .40
130 Stefanie Boerema .15 .40
131 Kristi Bosman .15 .40
132 Beth Boven .15 .40
133 Anna Christen .15 .40
134 Laurie Decker .15 .40
135 Cheryl Kooima .15 .40
136 Marisa Kottke .15 .40
137 Becky Lanenga .15 .40
138 Heidi Rimpila .15 .40
139 Siira Rimpila .15 .40
140 Lora Vandenberg .15 .40
141 Stephanie Webber .15 .40
142 Nicole Wieringa .15 .40
143 Katie Zeilstra .15 .40
144 Kristine Abramowski .15 .40
145 Kim Brock .15 .40
146 Betsy Byers .15 .40
147 Tracy Clay .15 .40
148 Amy Coleman .15 .40
149 Jenny Crouse .15 .40
150 Emily Dale .15 .40
151 Tanya Deutscher .15 .40
152 Heather Dittmar .15 .40
153 Melissa Meyers .15 .40
154 Emily Stadel .15 .40
155 Colleen Stebbins .15 .40
156 Lindsay Werntz .15 .40
157 Bonny Apsey .15 .40
158 Jennifer Bulkeley .15 .40
160 Angie Galyean .15 .40
161 Heidi Gengenbacher .15 .40
162 Jenny Cirimotich .15 .40
162 Kathy Kelley .15 .40
163 Steph Latham .15 .40
164 Julie Lofing .15 .40
165 Gina Miller .15 .40
167 Ami Pendry .15 .40
168 Stefanie Mitchell .15 .40
168 Mandy Rinker .15 .40
169 Molly Watson .15 .40
170 Sara Wood .15 .40
171 Jen Wright .15 .40
201 Beth Bear .15 .40
202 Lori Breitweiser .15 .40
203 Julie Carroll .15 .40
204 Brieanna Coffman .15 .40
205 Becky Cox .15 .40
206 Paula Hawkins .15 .40
207 Jara Hellrung .15 .40
208 Michelle Jarman .15 .40
209 Karla Krueger .15 .40
210 Amy Mortensen .15 .40
211 Katie Mortensen .15 .40
212 Kristen Norton .15 .40
213 Jana Shortal .15 .40
214 Amanda Vaughn .15 .40
216 Jennifer Buell .15 .40
217 Kelly Byrne .15 .40
218 Lashonda Clay .15 .40
219 Jamie Hankus .15 .40
220 Katie Maley .15 .40
221 Kelly Maley .15 .40
222 Alicia Mesi .15 .40
223 Amanda Miller .15 .40
224 Kim Nischik .15 .40
225 Ellen Sauser .15 .40
226 Aubrey Sekal .15 .40
227 Jamie Selip .15 .40
228 Beth Walse .15 .40
229 Kate Walse .15 .40
242 Aarin Bartelt .15 .40
243 Ashley Campbell .15 .40
244 Kimberly Carter .15 .40
245 Tamika Catchings 5.00 12.00
246 Tauja Catchings 2.00 5.00
247 Amy Chaness .15 .40
248 Kelly Cole .15 .40
249 Katie Coleman .15 .40
250 Tricia DeClark .15 .40
251 Rebekah Ford .15 .40
252 Noelle Mendenwaldt .15 .40
253 Christy Miller .15 .40
254 Felice Rosenzwig .15 .40
255 Carolyn Roth .15 .40
256 Jamie Smith .15 .40
257 Jennifer Warkins .15 .40
258 Laura Boyer .15 .40
259 Amanda Ely .15 .40
260 Kristen Hamman .15 .40
261 Jessica Jackson .15 .40
262 Jennifer Klein .15 .40
263 Kari Kuefler .15 .40
264 Jenny Leigh .15 .40
265 Liz Luthman .15 .40
266 Jamila Minnicks .15 .40
267 Heather Ory .15 .40
268 Suzie Rizek .15 .40
269 Alicia Stewart .15 .40
270 Tjunia(T.J.) Williams .15 .40
271 Sara Eggleston .15 .40
272 Jaime Gray .15 .40
273 Samantha Hardwick .15 .40
274 Missi Keeley .15 .40
275 Jackie Kopp .15 .40
276 Abby Lewis .15 .40
277 Katy McCain .15 .40
278 Jill McDaniel .15 .40
279 Kelly Moore .15 .40
280 Sara Mozingo .15 .40
281 Jenny Reeves .15 .40
282 Jenny Schmidt .15 .40
283 Kristy Schutz .15 .40
284 Sparkle Thornton .15 .40
298 Kim Bugel .15 .40
299 Laura Castelloni .15 .40
300 Maureen Enright .15 .40
301 Becky Gorecki .15 .40
302 Nora Hogueisson .15 .40
303 Tina LaCombe .15 .40
304 Meggan MacFarlane .15 .40
305 Jenny Malone .15 .40
306 Trisha Monahan .15 .40
307 Jean Nagler .15 .40
308 Amy Novak .15 .40
309 Julie Ricci .15 .40
310 Jenny Sosnowski .15 .40
311 Jill Turner .15 .40
312 Jodi Williams .15 .40
313 Kim Anderson .15 .40
314 Dixie Brazelton .15 .40
315 Missi Clark .15 .40
316 Katie Cutright .15 .40
317 Angi Dewitt .15 .40
318 Bessie Fulk .15 .40
319 Erin Hutchinson .15 .40
320 Randi Johnson .15 .40
321 Adrienne Kraemer .15 .40
322 Erin McNary .15 .40
323 Danette Pine .15 .40
324 Denise Pine .15 .40
325 Shelby Strow .15 .40
326 Emily Stuck .15 .40
436 Tammy Cartwright .15 .40
437 Vanessa Harris .15 .40
438 Danyell Humphries .15 .40
439 Quatoya Johnson .15 .40
445 Laurie Schumacher .15 .40

1994-95 IHSA Girls AA 3-Point Showdown

This 56-card features those players who participated in the 3-point showdown at the state tournament. Five hundred of each card were printed. The fronts feature a small colored or black-and-white, posed or action player photo in a thin red frame on a blue background. The player's name is printed in white on a purple stripe below the picture. The set title is printed down the left and at the top with a basketball between the words in the top left. The horizontal backs carry the player's name in white on a black stripe with his high school below along with the player's height, class, and what college he would like to attend or career highlights. The March Madness logo appears at the right. Photos were not available and thus omitted on several cards.

COMPLETE SET (56) 6.00 15.00
65 Stacy Albrecht .15 .40
66 Michelle Allured .15 .40
67 Tamika Coleman .15 .40
68 Latavia Davis .20 .50
69 Manali Doshi .15 .40
70 Bessie Jo Fulk .15 .40
71 Mackenzie Goebel .15 .40
72 Danielle Green .15 .40
73 Andrea Gunnell .15 .40
74 K.C. Hammond .15 .40
75 Esther Henigan .15 .40
76 Keesha Humphrey .15 .40
77 Holly Johnson .15 .40
78 Jaime Johnson .15 .40
79 Yulonda Jones .15 .40
80 GeGe King .15 .40
81 Tammie Krysh .15 .40
82 Maggie Lamb .15 .40
83 Roz Leeck .15 .40
84 Jenny Lindemann .15 .40
85 Karen Niebrugge .15 .40
86 Denise Pavichevich .15 .40
87 Lisa Perales .15 .40
88 Stacey Pohar .15 .40
89 Holly Palombi .15 .40
90 Tania Price .15 .40
91 Michelle Roof .15 .40
92 Daryl Schaffeld .15 .40
93 Jennifer Sciortino .15 .40
94 Anne Sudlow .15 .40
95 Amanda Vaughn .15 .40
96 Beth Walse .15 .40
97 Jodi Williams .15 .40
98 Carly Zilligen .15 .40
99 Kameelah Morgan .15 .40
100 Anne Mucci .15 .40
101 Denise McMillan .15 .40
102 Jaime Maurer .15 .40
103 Anne McDonald .15 .40
104 Jaime Lynn Burandt .15 .40
105 Shannon O'Neill .15 .40
106 Jenny Schmidt .15 .40
107 Jaime Gray .15 .40
108 Amanda Cavitt .15 .40
109 Jill Carpenter .15 .40
110 Trish Ackerman .15 .40
111 Crystal Tarr .15 .40
112 Danielle Moles .15 .40
113 Laura Valente .15 .40
114 Kelly Gilbert .15 .40
115 Monique Daniel .15 .40
116 Erin Backman .15 .40
117 Nicole LaBuhn .15 .40
118 Wakeelah Ross .15 .40
119 Vanessa Johnson .15 .40
120 Melissa Frawley .15 .40

1994-95 IHSA Historic Record Holders

This 30-card set commemorates outstanding performances in Illinois state basketball tournaments. Five hundred of each card were printed. The fronts feature action or posed player photos in hues of brown which blend into the brown background. The player's name is printed on a black nameplate below the year when they set the record. The March Madness logo is at the bottom. The horizontal backs carry the player's name, height, position, school attended, record set, and state tournament statistics. This set includes past NBA star Dave Robisch and current NBA star LaPhonso Ellis.

COMPLETE SET (30) 6.00 15.00
62 Fernando Bunch .20 .50
63 Sandy Braun .20 .50
64 Brent Carmichael .20 .50
65 Walter Downing .20 .50
66 Mike Duff .20 .50
67 Jim Edmondson .20 .50
68 LaPhonso Ellis 1.25 3.00
69 Jo Jo Johnson .20 .50
70 Dale Kelley .20 .50
71 Jim Lazenby .20 .50
72 Nora Lewis .20 .50
73 Matt Maton .20 .50
74 Chris Payne .20 .50
75 Courtney Porter .20 .50
76 Dave Robisch .60 1.50
77 Johnny Selvie .40 1.00
78 Jay Shidler .40 1.00
79 Cathy Shoup .20 .50
80 Marty Simmons .20 .50
81 Gary Tidwell .20 .50
82 Tammy Van Oppen .20 .50
83 Kevin Washington .20 .50
84 Connie Erickson .20 .50
85 Lori Fitzjarrald .20 .50
86 Dee Dee Franklin .20 .50
87 Shannon Hickenbottom .20 .50
88 Cammy Hudson .20 .50
89 Tina Hutchinson .20 .50
90 Cindy Kaufmann .20 .50
91 Jamie Brandon .40 1.00

1980-81 Illinois

This 15-card standard-size set was sponsored by Arby's Restaurants and features players of the 1980-81 Fighting Illini squad. The player's signature and an Arby's advertisement appear below a color posed photo of the player. The horizontally oriented back provides biographical and statistical information. The cards are numbered for convenience alphabetically in the checklist below. Key cards in the set include the first cards of NBA veterans Derek Harper and Eddie Johnson.

COMPLETE SET (15) 15.00 30.00
1 Kevin Bontemps .40 1.00
2 James Griffin .40 1.00
3 Derek Harper 7.50 15.00
4 Lou Henson CO 1.50 4.00
5 Derek Holcomb .75 2.00
6 Eddie Johnson 6.00 12.00
7 Bryan Leonard .40 1.00
8 Dick Nagy ACO .40 1.00
9 Perry Range .40 1.00
10 Quinn Richardson .40 1.00
11 Mark Smith .40 1.00
12 Neale Stoner .40 1.00
13 Craig Tucker .40 1.00
14 Tony Yates ACO .75 2.00
15 Team Photo 1.50 4.00

1981-82 Illinois

This 16-card standard-size set was sponsored by Arby's Restaurants and features players of the 1981-82 Fighting Illini squad. The player's signature and an Arby's advertisement appear below a color posed photo of the player. The horizontally oriented back provides biographical and statistical information. Lou Henson's last name is misspelled on the back of his card (Hensen). The cards are numbered for convenience alphabetically in the checklist below. The key card in the set is Derek Harper.

COMPLETE SET (16) 8.00 20.00
1 Kevin Bontemps .40 1.00
2 Jay Daniels .40 1.00
3 James Griffin .40 1.00
4 Derek Harper 4.00 10.00
5 Lou Henson CO UER 1.25 3.00
6 Dan Klier .40 1.00
7 Bryan Leonard .40 1.00
8 Dee Maras .40 1.00
9 George Montgomery .40 1.00
10 Dick Nagy ACO .40 1.00
11 Perry Range .40 1.00
12 Quinn Richardson .40 1.00
13 Craig Tucker .40 1.00
14 Anthony Welch .60 1.50
15 Tony Yates ACO .60 1.50
16 Team Photo .75 2.00

1992-93 Illinois

Produced by Flying Color Graphics Inc., this 16-card standard-size set was sponsored by Pepsi. This set features both basketball players from the University of Illinois. The fronts display color, action player photos with an orange stripe down the left side and a dark blue stripe across the bottom. The school name is reversed out in dark blue in the orange stripe, while the player's name is printed in orange in the dark blue stripe. The backs are white and carry biographical information, the sponsor logo, and a public service message. The cards are unnumbered and checklisted below alphabetically.

COMPLETE SET (16) 4.00 10.00
1 Robert Bennett .08 .25
2 Rennie Clemons .40 1.00
3 Jimmy Collins ACO .20 .50
4 Mark Coomes ACO .08 .25
5 Marc Davidson .08 .25
6 Chris Gandy .08 .25
7 Lou Henson CO 1.25 3.00
8 Chief Illiniwek .08 .25
(Mascot)
9 Andy Kaufmann .40 1.00
10 Richard Keene .20 .50
11 Tom Michael .60 1.50
guarded by Jalen Rose
12 Dick Nagy ACO .08 .25
13 Brooks Taylor .08 .25
14 Deon Thomas .60 1.50
15 T.J. Wheeler .20 .50
16 Assembly Hall .20 .50

1992-93 Illinois Women's

Produced by Flying Color Graphics Inc., this 16-card standard-size set was sponsored by Pepsi. This set features female basketball players from the University of Illinois. The fronts display color, action player photos with an orange stripe down the left side and a dark blue stripe across the bottom. The school name is reversed out in dark blue in the orange stripe, while the player's name is printed in orange in the dark blue stripe. The backs are white and carry biographical information, the sponsor logo, and a public service message. Though they share similar card front designs, the women's cards have different backs than the men's backs. The cards are unnumbered and checklisted below alphabetically.

COMPLETE SET (16) 1.25 3.00
1 Tonya Booker .08 .25
2 Anita Clinton .08 .25
3 Mandy Cunningham .08 .25
4 Merimartha Cunningham .08 .25
5 Cindy Dilger .08 .25
6 Kris Dupps .08 .25
7 Jill Estey .08 .25
8 Keila Flagg .08 .25
9 Cindi Hanna .08 .25
10 Jackie Hemann .08 .25
11 Bridget Inman .08 .25
12 Vicki Klingler .08 .25
13 Kathy Lindsey CO .08 .25
14 Lolita Platt .08 .25
15 Robbyn Preacely .08 .25
16 Connie Ruholl .08 .25

1986-87 Indiana Greats I

This 42-card standard-size set is the first series of the All-Time Greats of Indiana University. The cards were sponsored by Bank One of Indiana. The fronts present a mixture of black and white or color photos, posed and action. The horizontally-oriented backs have biographical and statistical information on the player, with the card number in the upper right hand corner. The key card in the set is the first card of Indiana coach Bobby Knight.

COMPLETE SET (42) 6.00 15.00
1 Bobby Knight CO 2.00 5.00
2 Walt Bellamy 1.00 2.50
3 Pete Obremskey .08 .25
4 Jim Wisman .08 .25
5 Frank Radovich .08 .25
6 Ted Kitchel .08 .25
7 Don Schlundt .40 1.00
8 Uwe Blab .20 .50
9 Lou Watson .08 .25
10 Bobby Masters .08 .25
11 Steve Redenbaugh .08 .25
12 Bob Wilkerson .25 .60
13 Kent Benson .60 1.50
14 Everett Dean .40 1.00
15 Rick Ford .08 .25
16 Hallie Bryant .08 .25
17 Dan Dakich .20 .50
18 Sam Gee .08 .25
19 George McGinnis 1.00 2.50
20 John Ritter .08 .25
21 Jon McGlocklin .40 1.00
22 Landon Turner .40 1.00
23 Gary Long .08 .25
24 Jim Crews .40 1.00
25 Steve Downing .40 1.00
26 Vern Huffman .20 .50
27 Ernie Andres .08 .25
28 Charles Hodson .08 .25
29 Jerry Thompson .08 .25
30 Tom Abernethy .20 .50
31 Tom Bolyard .08 .25
32 Jimmy Rayl .40 1.00
33 John Laskowski .20 .50
34 Archie Dees .20 .50
35 Joby Wright .40 1.00
36 Gary Greiger .08 .25
37 Randy Wittman .40 1.00
38 Steve Green .08 .25
39 Erv Inniger .08 .25
40 Steve Risley .08 .25
41 Bill DeHeer .08 .25
42 Checklist Card .20 .50

1987-88 Indiana Greats II

This 42-card standard-size set is the second series of the All-Time Greats of Indiana University. The cards were sponsored by Bank One of Indiana. The fronts present a mixture of black and white or color photos, posed and action. The horizontally oriented backs have biographical and statistical information on the player, with the card number in the upper right hand corner. The back of the checklist card contains an offer to buy either Series I or II for 10.00 from the Big Red Gift Center. The key card in the set features NBA superstar Isiah Thomas.

COMPLETE SET (42) 10.00 25.00
1 Steve Alford's .75 2.00
Farewell
2 Bob Dro .08 .25
3 Butch Joyner .08 .25
4 Bobby Leonard .30 .75
5 Branch McCracken CO .40 1.00
with Walt Bellamy
6 Ray Tolbert .40 1.00
7 Wayne Radford .20 .50
8 Earl Schneider .08 .25
9 Jim Strickland .08 .25
10 Al Harden .08 .25
11 Bob Menke .08 .25
12 Steve Alford .75 2.00
13 Mike Woodson .40 1.00
14 Tom Van Arsdale .75 2.00
Dick Van Arsdale
15 Wally Choice .08 .25
16 Charlie Hall .08 .25
17 Indiana Coach Legend .40 1.00
18 Stew Robinson .20 .50
19 Dynamic Duo .40 1.00
20 Steve Alford .75 2.00
21 Quinn Buckner .60 1.50
22 Bob Knight .40 1.00
Everett Dean
23 Winston Morgan .08 .25
24 1975-76 Seniors .40 1.00
25 Jim Thomas .20 .50
26 Vern Payne .08 .25
27 Scott May .60 1.50
28 Dave Porter .08 .25
29 Dick Farley .08 .25
30 Isiah Thomas 3.00 8.00
31 Butch Carter .20 .50
32 Burke Scott .08 .25
33 Jack Johnson .08 .25
34 Charley Kraak .08 .25
35 Marv Huffman .08 .25
36 Steve Bouchie .08 .25
37 Bobby Knight .75 2.00
38 Bill Garrett .08 .25
39 Jerry Bass .08 .25
40 Jay McCreary .08 .25
41 Ken Johnson .08 .25
42 Checklist Card .20 .50
(Send-in offer on back)

1991-92 Indiana Magazine Insert

The premiere issue of Hoosier College Basketball (November, 1991) featured 12 cards (nine on an unperforated sheet and three additional cards on an attached strip). The production run was reportedly 5,000 sets. The sheet is unperforated; if the cards were cut, they would measure approximately the standard size. The glossy color player photos appear on a jet black card face and are framed by narrow gold-foil border stripes. The player's name is printed in gold-foil lettering beneath the picture. The backs carry biographical information, jersey number, and player profile. The cards are unnumbered and checklisted below in alphabetical order. Key cards in the set include Damon Bailey, Calbert Cheaney, Greg Graham, and Alan Henderson. Reportedly an additional 100 sets were made with red borders; these sell at a 3X to 4X multiple of the regular gold-border cards. According to sources in the hobby, due to licensing issues, the NCAA recalled a good deal of these sets after release.

COMPLETE SET (12) 10.00 25.00
1 Eric Anderson 1.50 4.00
2 Damon Bailey 3.00 8.00
3 Calbert Cheaney 3.00 8.00
4 Brian Evans 2.00 5.00
5 Greg Graham 1.50 4.00
6 Pat Graham 1.50 4.00
7 Alan Henderson 2.50 6.00
8 Bobby Knight CO 2.50 6.00
9 Pat Knight 1.50 4.00
10 Jamal Meeks .75 2.00
11 Matt Nover 1.50 4.00
12 Chris Reynolds .75 2.00

1992-93 Indiana

This 18-card standard-size set was produced by Phipps Sports Marketing, Inc. Inside red borders, the fronts display color action player photos against a background of a basketball. The player's name and number are printed vertically in block lettering to the left of the picture. A "1992-1993 Hoosiers" emblem at the lower right corner rounds out the front. On the same basic background, the horizontal backs carry a color headshot, biography, career summary, and statistics on a panel that shades from white to rose. The cards are unnumbered and checklisted below in alphabetical order, with non-player cards listed at the end.

COMPLETE SET (18) 6.00 15.00
1 Damon Bailey .75 2.00
2 Calbert Cheaney 1.50 4.00
3 Brian Evans .75 2.00
4 Greg Graham .30 .75
5 Pat Graham .30 .75
6 Alan Henderson 1.50 4.00
7 Bob Knight CO 1.50 4.00
8 Pat Knight .75 2.00
9 Todd Leary .20 .50
10 Todd Lindeman .30 .75
11 Matt Nover .40 1.00
12 Chris Reynolds .20 .50
13 Malcolm Sims .20 .50
14 Assembly Hall .30 .75
15 Dan Dakich ACO .20 .50
Norm Ellenberger ACO
Ron Felling ACO
16 Team Photo .40 1.00
17 The Knight Era .30 .75
18 Title Card .20 .50

1993-94 Indiana

Produced by Phipps Sports Marketing, Inc., this 18-card standard-size set features the Indiana Hoosiers. Inside red borders, the fronts display color action or posed player photos. The player's name is printed inside the photo, while the words "1993-94 Indiana Hoosiers Basketball" appear under the photo. Printed vertically in block lettering to the left inside the picture is "Indiana". Inside red borders, the backs carry a color player portrait, along with player name, number, biography and statistics, and career summary. The cards are unnumbered and checklisted below in alphabetical order.

COMPLETE SET (18) 5.00 12.00
1 Damon Bailey .60 1.50
2 Robbie Eggers .20 .50
3 Brian Evans .60 1.50
4 Robert Foster .20 .50
5 Pat Graham .30 .75
6 Steve Hart .20 .50
7 Alan Henderson 1.00 2.50
8 Bob Knight CO 1.00 2.50
9 Pat Knight .60 1.50
10 Todd Leary .20 .50
11 Todd Lindeman .30 .75
12 Richard Mandeville .20 .50
13 Sherron Wilkerson .30 .75
14 Team Photo .30 .75
15 Dan Dakich ACO .20 .50
Ron Felling ACO
Norm Ellenberger ACO
Tim Garl ACO
16 Assembly Hall .30 .75
17 Chris Reynolds .60 1.50
Matt Nover
Greg Graham
Calbert Cheaney
The Class of 1993
18 Title Card .20 .50

1994-95 Indiana

14 card set, blank white backs, fronts have a red border and a wood-like rectangle with red streaks and color action photos in them. "Hoosiers" is written vertically on either the right or left side of the card in the wood-like colored font. The players name and personal data are found in white at the bottom of the card.

COMPLETE SET (14) 2.00 5.00
1 Bob Knight CO .60 1.50
Brian Evans
2 Robbie Eggers .20 .50
3 Brian Evans .40 1.00
4 Steve Hart .20 .50
5 Alan Henderson .40 1.00
6 Michael Hermon .20 .50
7 Rob Hodgson .20 .50
8 Pat Knight .40 1.00
9 Todd Lindeman .40 1.00
10 Richard Mandeville .20 .50
11 Charlie Miller .20 .50

12 Andrae Patterson .60 1.50
13 Neil Reed .60 1.50
14 Sherron Wilkerson .40 1.00

1982-83 Indiana State

This multi-sport set was sponsored by the First National Bank of Terre Haute, 7-Up, and WTHI/TV Channel 10. The cards measure approximately 2 5/8" by 4 1/8". On a bright blue card face, the fronts feature black and white player photos enclosed by a white border. A white diagonal stripe appears beneath the picture, with a drawing of the Sycamores' mascot and the words "Sycamore Rampage." The backs have brief biographical information, a quote about the player, a safety tip, and sponsor logos. Sports represented in this set include wrestling (1), basketball (2-3, 4-10, 12), football (11), and gymnastics (13). Olympic athletes included in the set are Bruce Baumgartner and Kurt Thomas. The key card in the set is NBA superstar Larry Bird. The cards are unnumbered and checklisted below in alphabetical order.

9 Larry Bird BK 40.00 100.00
13 Terry Braun BK 1.25 3.00
20 Myron Christian BK 1.25 3.00
22 Al Cole BK 1.25 3.00
29 Rick Fields BK 1.25 3.00
31 Mark Golden BK 1.25 3.00
48 Jeff McComb BK 1.25 3.00
53 Scott Mugg BK 1.25 3.00
61 Dave Schellhase CO BK 1.25 3.00
64 James Smith BK 1.25 3.00

1987-88 Iowa

This 15-card standard-size set features Iowa Hawkeyes and was sponsored by Nike. The cards are unnumbered and are listed below in alphabetical order by subject. The set features the first card of B.J. Armstrong.

COMPLETE SET (15) 8.00 20.00
1 B.J. Armstrong 5.00 12.00
2 Curtis Cuthbert .40 1.00
3 Rodell Davis .60 1.50
4 Brian Garner .40 1.00
5 Kent Hill .40 1.00
6 Ed Horton .60 1.50
7 Les Jepsen 1.25 3.00
8 Mark Jewell .40 1.00
9 Bill Jones .40 1.00
10 Al Lorenzen .40 1.00
11 Roy Marble .75 2.00
12 Jeff Moe .40 1.00
13 Michael Morgan .40 1.00
14 Mike Reaves .40 1.00
15 Brig Tubbs .40 1.00

1990-91 Iowa

This 14-card set was issued by the University of Iowa and sponsored by radio station KCRG Country 1600. The fronts display color portraits of the player within a black border. The players are photographed out of uniform. Below the photo is a basketball icon in the lower left corner with the player's name, team number, and position printed in black on a yellow bar. The horizontal white backs list the 1990-91 Iowa basketball schedule. The KCRG 1600 radio station logo appears in the upper right corner. The cards are unnumbered and checklisted below alphabetically.

COMPLETE SET (14) 6.00 15.00
1 Val Barnes 1.25 3.00
2 Jim Bartels .40 1.00
3 Philip Chime .40 1.00
4 Rodell Davis .75 2.00
5 Acie Earl 2.00 5.00
6 Wade Lookingbill .40 1.00
7 Paul Lusk .40 1.00
8 James Moses .75 2.00
9 Troy Skinner .40 1.00
10 Kevin Smith .40 1.00
11 Chris Street 2.00 5.00
12 Brig Tubbs .40 1.00
13 Jay Webb .40 1.00
14 James Winters .40 1.00

1991-92 Iowa

This 15-card standard-size set is printed on thin card stock. The fronts feature color player photos, with a gold and black parquet floor border. Player information appears in the black stripe at the bottom of the card face, while the school logo appears in an orange basketball at the lower left corner. In a horizontal format, the backs carry a black and white head shot and a player profile. The cards are unnumbered and checklisted below in alphabetical order. The key cards in the set feature Acie Earl and Chris Street.

COMPLETE SET (15) 5.00 12.00
1 Val Barnes .40 1.00
2 Jim Bartels .30 .75
3 Phil Chime .30 .75
4 Rodell Davis .40 1.00
5 Acie Earl 1.50 4.00
6 Wade Lookingbill .30 .75
7 Paul Lusk .30 .75
8 Russ Millard .60 1.50
9 James Moses .40 1.00
10 Troy Skinner .30 .75
11 Kevin Smith .30 .75
12 Chris Street 1.50 4.00
13 Brig Tubbs .30 .75
14 Jay Webb .30 .75
15 James Winters .30 .75

1992-93 Iowa

This 13-card standard-size set features color, action and posed player photos. The pictures are set against a black panel in the upper left corner. The player's first name appears in the lower black margin. A white stripe just below the panel contains the player's last name in reverse type. An orange-yellow border runs along the bottom and up the right side of the card. This border contains the player's classification, school, and the team name. The horizontal backs are white and carry biographical information, statistics, and a public service message from Herky, the mascot. The cards are unnumbered and checklisted below in alphabetical order.

COMPLETE SET (13) 4.00 10.00
1 Val Barnes .40 1.00
2 Jim Bartles .30 .75
3 Fred Brown Jr. .30 .75
4 Acie Earl 1.00 2.50
5 Mon'ter Glasper .40 1.00
6 Wade Lookingbill .30 .75
7 Russ Millard .40 1.00
8 Kenyon Murray .40 1.00
9 Kevin Skillett .30 .75
10 Kevin Smith .30 .75
11 Chris Street 1.25 3.00
12 Jay Webb .30 .75
13 James Winters .30 .75

1992-93 Iowa Women

Sponsored by Wendy's restaurants, this is a 13-card standard-size set. The fronts feature color player portraits tilted slightly the left and resting on a golden background. The player's name and the team name are printed above the picture. The sponsor's logo appears on a white box at the lower left corner, while the uniform number appears in an orange basketball at the lower right corner. In a horizontal format, the backs carry biographical and statistical information. The cards are unnumbered and checklisted below in alphabetical order.

COMPLETE SET (13) 4.00 10.00
1 Laurie Aaron .20 .50
2 Karen Clayton .20 .50
3 Virgie Dillingham .20 .50
4 Toni Foster 1.25 3.00
5 Andrea Harmon .20 .50
6 Tia Jackson 1.25 3.00
7 Antonia Macklin .20 .50
8 Cathy Marx .20 .50
9 Jenny Noll .20 .50
10 C.Vivian Stringer CO 1.50 4.00
11 Molly Tideback .20 .50
12 Necole Tunsil .20 .50
13 Arneda Yarbrough .20 .50

1993-94 Iowa

The 1993-94 University of Iowa basketball set consists of 11 standard-size cards printed on thin card stock. The glossy fronts display color action and posed player photos with a black shadow box border. The player's name and team number are printed within the border below the photo. The picture is placed at an angle over a black-and-white parquet basketball court background. The word "Hawkeyes" is printed across the top in gold lettering. The team logo is printed in the lower right corner. The horizontal light yellow backs have the school name printed in ghosted yellow lettering. The player's biography, profile, statistics, and a black-and-white head shot complete the back. The set includes a card in memory of Chris Street, the Iowa player tragically killed in a car accident during the 1992-93 season. The cards are unnumbered and checklisted below in alphabetical order.

COMPLETE SET (11) 4.00 10.00
1 Jim Bartels .20 .50
2 John Carter .20 .50
3 Mon'ter Glasper .30 .75
4 Chris Kingsbury .75 2.00
5 Russ Millard .40 1.00
6 Kenyon Murray .30 .75
7 Jess Settles .75 2.00
8 Kevin Skillett .20 .50
9 Chris Street MEM 1.25 3.00
10 James Winters .20 .50
11 Andre Woolridge .75 2.00

1993-94 Iowa Women

Sponsored by Wendy's restaurants, this 13-card set measures the standard-size. The fronts feature posed color player portraits tilted slightly to the left and resting on gray and yellow backgrounds. The player's name and uniform number appear below the picture. The yellowish backs carry biographical and statistical information. The cards are unnumbered and checklisted below in alphabetical order.

COMPLETE SET (13) 3.00 8.00
1 Karen Clayton .20 .50
2 Virgie Dillingham .20 .50
3 Simone Edwards .20 .50
4 Andrea Harmon .20 .50
5 Tia Jackson 1.00 2.50
6 Susan Koering .20 .50
7 Antonia Macklin .20 .50
8 Cathy Marx .20 .50
9 Jenny Noll .20 .50
10 Erinn Reed .20 .50
11 C.Vivian Stringer CO 1.50 4.00
12 Necole Tunsil .20 .50
13 Arneda Yarbrough .20 .50

1994-95 Iowa

Sponsored by Norwest Banks, Coca-Cola and 1040 WHO Des Moines, this 13-card set measures the standard size. The fronts feature color, action and posed, player photos framed by white borders. Across the bottom, the player's name, his number and the words "94-95 Iowa Basketball" are printed in team color-coded bars that intersect an orange basketball at the lower right corner. On a white background, the horizontal backs carry a black-and-white player head shot, biography, a player profile in an "Iowa Item" feature, and complete statistics. The cards are unnumbered and checklisted below in alphabetical order.

COMPLETE SET (13) 4.00 10.00
1 Jim Bartels .20 .50
2 Ryan Bowen .20 .50
3 John Carter .20 .50
4 Mon'ter Glasper .30 .75
5 Herky (Mascot) .20 .50
6 Chris Kingsbury .75 2.00
7 Kent McCausland .20 .50
8 Kenyon Murray .30 .75
9 Jess Settles .75 2.00
10 Kevin Skillett .20 .50
11 Andre Woolridge .75 2.00
12 Black and Gold Blowout .20 .50
13 Carver-Hawkeye Arena .30 .75

1995-96 Iowa

This 14-card set was released at the University of Iowa during the 1995-96 season. The set features many of the players from that year's team. This set was produced by Partners In Excellence. Please note that these cards are not numbered and are listed below in alphabetical order.

COMPLETE SET (14) 4.00 10.00
1 Ryan Bowen .30 .75
2 Trey Bullet .30 .75
3 Mon'ter Glasper .30 .75
4 Greg Helmers .30 .75
5 Chris Kingsbury .30 .75
6 J.R. Koch .40 1.00
7 Kent McCausland .30 .75
8 Russ Millard .30 .75
9 Kenyon Murray .30 .75
10 Alvin Robinson .30 .75
11 Guy Rucker .30 .75
12 Jess Settles .75 2.00
13 Andre Woolridge .60 1.50
14 Herky MASCOT .30 .75

1996-97 Iowa

This 13-card set was released at the University of Iowa during the 1996-97 season. The set features many of the players from that season's team. This set was produced by Partners In Excellence. Please note that these cards are not numbered and are listed below in alphabetical order.

COMPLETE SET (13) 4.00 10.00
1 Ryan Bowen .30 .75
2 Marcelo Gomes .30 .75
3 Greg Helmers .30 .75
4 J.R. Koch .40 1.00
5 Ryan Luehrsmann .30 .75
6 Kent McCausland .30 .75
7 Alvin Robinson .30 .75
8 Guy Rucker .30 .75
9 Jess Settles 1.00 2.50
10 Vernon Simmons .30 .75
11 Andre Woolridge .60 1.50
12 Herky MASCOT .30 .75
13 Hawkeye Sports.com .30 .75

1997-98 Iowa

This 13-card set was released at the University of Iowa during the 1997-98 season. The set features many of the players from that season's team. This set was produced by Partners In Excellence. Please note that these cards are not numbered and are listed below in alphabetical order.

COMPLETE SET (13) 5.00 12.00
1 Jason Bauer .20 .50
2 Ryan Bowen .20 .50
3 Ricky Davis 4.00 9.00
4 Marcelo Gomes .20 .50
5 Greg Helmers .20 .50
6 J.R. Koch .20 .50
7 Ryan Luehrsmann .20 .50
8 Kent McCausland .20 .50
9 Darryl Moore .20 .50
10 Dean Oliver .20 .50
11 Guy Rucker .20 .50
12 Jess Settles .75 2.00
13 Vernon Simmons .20 .50

1999-00 Iowa

This 15-card set was released at the University of Iowa during the 1999-2000 season. The set features many of the players from that season's team. Please note that these cards are not numbered and are listed below in alphabetical order.

COMPLETE SET 1.25 3.00
1 Steve Alford CO .75 2.00
2 Joe Fermino .15 .40
3 Kyle Galloway .15 .40
4 Marcelo Gomez .15 .40
5 Rob Griffin .15 .40
6 Duez Henderson .15 .40
7 Ryan Hogan .15 .40
8 Jacob Jaacks .15 .40
9 Ryan Luehrsmann .15 .40
10 Dean Oliver .15 .40
11 Jason Price .15 .40
12 Antonio Ramos .15 .40
13 Jason Smith .15 .40
14 Rod Thompson .15 .40
15 John Carl Williams .15 .40

2000-01 Iowa

This 14-card set was released at the University of Iowa during the 2000-01 season. The set features many of the players from that season's team. Please note that these cards are not numbered and are listed below in alphabetical order.

COMPLETE SET 1.50 4.00
1 Steve Alford CO .75 2.00
2 Brody Boyd .15 .40
3 Reggie Evans .30 .75
4 Joe Fermino .15 .40
5 Ryan Hogan .15 .40
6 Duez Henderson .15 .40
7 Dean Oliver .15 .40
8 Luke Recker .15 .40
9 Jared Reiner .15 .40
10 Cortney Scott .15 .40
11 Jason Smith .15 .40
12 Sean Sonderleiter .15 .40
13 Rod Thompson .15 .40
14 Glen Worley .15 .40

2001-02 Iowa

This 16-card set was released at the University of Iowa during the 2001-02 season. The set features many of the players from that season's team. Please note that these cards are not numbered and are listed below in alphabetical order.

COMPLETE SET 1.50 4.00
1 Steve Alford CO .75 2.00
2 Brody Boyd .15 .40
3 Reggie Evans .30 .75
4 Erek Hansen .15 .40
5 Duez Henderson .15 .40
6 Ryan Hogan .15 .40
7 Chauncey Leslie .15 .40
8 Pierre Pierce .15 .40
9 Luke Recker .25 .60
10 Jared Reiner .15 .40
11 Cortney Scott .15 .40
12 Marcellus Sommerville .15 .40
13 Sean Sonderleiter .15 .40
14 Rod Thompson .15 .40
15 Glen Worley .15 .40
16 Big 10 Tourney Winners .15 .40

2002-03 Iowa

This 12-card set was released at the University of Iowa during the 2002-03 season. The set features many of the players from that season's team. This set was produced by Partners In Excellence. Please note that these cards are not numbered and are listed below in alphabetical order.

COMPLETE SET 1.50 4.00
1 Steve Alford CO .75 2.00
2 Brody Boyd .15 .40
3 Jack Brownlee .15 .40
4 Greg Brunner .15 .40
5 Jeff Horner .15 .40
6 Josh Kimm .15 .40
7 Chauncey Leslie .15 .40
8 Pierre Pierce .15 .40
9 Jared Reiner .15 .40
10 Sean Sonderleiter .15 .40
11 Kurt Spurgeon .15 .40
12 Glen Worley .15 .40

1988-89 Jacksonville

This 15-card set was co-sponsored by Blue Cross and Blue Shield of Florida, The Jacksonville Sheriff's Office, and the Jacksonville Say No To Drugs Coalition. The cards measure approximately 2 1/2" by 4 1/2", and one inch of the length of the card consists of a tab containing a coupon for one free child's admission to a regular season basketball game. The white-bordered fronts feature action color photos with a yellow bar above and below the picture. The player's name, team number, and position are printed below. The white backs are borderless and carry biography, career highlights, and anti-drug messages. The Blue Cross and Blue Shield of Florida logo is printed in the lower left corner. The Dolphins' home schedule appears on the tab portion at the bottom. The cards are unnumbered and checklisted below alphabetically.

COMPLETE SET (15) 10.00 25.00
1 Ken Aldrich .40 1.00
2 Tyrone Boykin .75 2.00
3 Dee Brown 6.00 15.00
4 Sean Byrd .40 1.00
5 Jim Cavanaugh .40 1.00
6 Steve Gilbert .40 1.00
7 Rich Haddad CO .40 1.00
8 Willie Ivery .40 1.00
9 Pat Laguerre .40 1.00
10 Reggie Law .75 2.00
11 Adrian Simmons .75 2.00
12 Chris Slocum .40 1.00
13 Curtis Taylor .40 1.00
14 JU-D2 (Mascot) .40 1.00
15 Team Photo 1.50 4.00

1989-90 Jacksonville Classic

Showcasing the 1969-70 team that was the NCAA runner-up, this eight-card standard-size set was sponsored by Blue Cross and Blue Shield of Florida, the Jacksonville Sheriff's Office, and the Clay County Sheriff's Office. The cards are printed on a thin paper stock. The fronts carry sepia-toned action photos with a green outer border and a gold inner border. On a gold diagonal bar in the upper left corner are the words "Classic Card". The Jacksonville University Dolphins is printed above the photo and the player's name is printed on a gold bar below. The white backs list biographical information and NCAA career highlights. The Blue Cross and Blue Shield of Florida logo is printed in the lower left corner. The cards are unnumbered and checklisted below alphabetically.

COMPLETE SET (8) 8.00 20.00
1 Mike Blevins .75 2.00
2 Pembrook Burrows .75 2.00
3 Chip Dublin .75 2.00
4 Artis Gilmore 4.00 10.00
5 Rod McIntyre .75 2.00
6 Rex Morgan .75 2.00
7 Greg Nelson .75 2.00
8 Vaughn Wedeking .75 2.00

1989-90 Jacksonville

This 13-card standard-size set was sponsored by Blue Cross Blue Shield of Florida in conjunction with the Jacksonville and Clay County Sheriff's Offices. Each card has a perforated coupon at the bottom good for one free child's general admission ticket to any regular season home game when accompanied by a paying adult. The fronts display a mix of action and posed color photos enclosed by a yellow border on a green card face. The team name appears in yellow block lettering at the top while the team logo and player's name appears in the bottom yellow border. The backs feature biography, player profile, and an anti-drug message between black bands. Sponsor logos and names round out the back. The cards are unnumbered and checklisted below in alphabetical order. The key card in the set is Dee Brown.

COMPLETE SET (13) 8.00 20.00
1 Tyrone Boykin .40 1.00
2 Dee Brown 5.00 12.00
3 Sean Byrd .40 1.00
4 Chris Capers .75 2.00
5 Steve Gilbert .40 1.00
6 Rich Haddad .40 1.00
7 Tabarris Hamilton and Alonzo Harris .40 1.00
8 Willie Ivery .40 1.00
9 Reggie Law .40 1.00
10 Jerome McDuffie and Danny Tirado .40 1.00
11 Al Powell and Kent Shafer .40 1.00
12 Curtis Taylor .40 1.00
13 Team Photo 1.50 4.00

1991-92 James Madison

The 1991-92 James Madison basketball set was sponsored by the USDA Forest Service, the state forestry service, and James Madison University. The standard-size cards are printed on thin card stock. The fronts display a mix of color posed and action player photos, enclosed by purple borders and accented by mustard stripes above and below. The school name, player's name, number, and position appear in the mustard stripes. In black print on white card stock, the backs have brief biographical information, a fire prevention cartoon starring Smokey, and sponsor acknowledgments. The cards are unnumbered and checklisted below alphabetically by player's last name.

COMPLETE SET (12) 4.00 10.00
1 Troy Bostic .40 1.00
2 Paul Carter .40 1.00
3 Jeff Chambers .40 1.00
4 Vladimir Cuk .40 1.00
5 Kent Culuko .60 1.50
6 William Davis .40 1.00
7 Lefty Driesell CO 1.50 4.00
8 Bryan Edwards .60 1.50
9 Gerry Lancaster .40 1.00
10 Keith Peoples .40 1.00
11 Clayton Ritter .40 1.00
12 Michael Venson .60 1.50

1992-93 James Madison

This 12-card standard-size set was sponsored by the USDA Forest Service and state forestry agencies. The fronts feature color, action player photos on a purple card face. Above and below the photo are orange-yellow border stripes containing the team name and the player's name and position. The photo and borders are accented by a gray shadow border. The backs are white with black print and carry limited player information and a wildfire prevention cartoon. The cards are unnumbered and checklisted below in alphabetical order.

COMPLETE SET (12) 3.00 8.00
1 Paul Carter .30 .75
2 Jeff Chambers .30 .75
3 Vladimir Cuk .30 .75
4 Kent Culuko .40 1.00
5 William Davis .30 .75
6 Duke Dog (Mascot) .30 .75
7 Lefty Driesell CO 1.25 3.00
8 Bryan Edwards .40 1.00
9 Channing McGuffin .30 .75
10 Clayton Ritter .30 .75
11 Michael Venson .40 1.00
12 Travis Wells .30 .75

1993-94 James Madison

The 1993-94 University of James Madison basketball set consists of 13 standard-size cards. Fronts display color action and posed player photos with a yellow border with white diagonal stripes. The player's name and position are printed below the photo to the right of the Smokey 50th logo. The team name and logo are centered above the photo. The player's biography is centered at the top of the plain back with a Smokey saftey tip below. The cards are unnumbered and checklisted below in alphabetical order.

COMPLETE SET (13) 3.00 8.00
1 Vladimir Cuk .20 .50
2 Ryan Culicerto .20 .50
3 Kent Culuko .30 .75
4 Lefty Driesell CO 1.25 3.00
5 Dennis Leonard .20 .50
6 Charles Lott .20 .50
7 Darren McLinton .20 .50
8 Clayton Ritter .20 .50
9 Kareem Robinson .20 .50
10 Louis Rowe .20 .50
11 Michael Venson .30 .75
12 Emeka Wilson .20 .50
13 Duke Dog (Mascot) .20 .50

1994-95 James Madison

This 16-card set was issued on a 10" by 14" perforated sheet with four rows of four cards. When the cards are separated, they measure the standard size. The set is sponsored by the USDA Forest Service and the state forestry agency. The fronts display color action and posed player photos with player's name, position, jersey number and Smokey logo below the photo in the violet border. The backs carry player information above a Smokey cartoon and a fire prevention safety tip. The cards are unnumbered and checklisted below in alphabetical order.

COMPLETE SET (16) 3.00 8.00
1 Lamont Boozer .20 .50
2 Eric Carpenter .20 .50
3 Cheerleaders .20 .50
4 James Colemano .20 .50
5 Ryan Culicerto .20 .50
6 Kent Culuko .30 .75
7 Charles Driesell CO (Lefty) 1.25 3.00
8 Duke Dog (Mascot) .20 .50
9 Duke Dog (Mascot) Smokey Bear .20 .50
10 Dennis Leonard .20 .50
11 Charles Lott .20 .50
12 Darren McLinton .20 .50
13 James Pelham .20 .50
14 Kareem Robinson .20 .50
15 Louis Rowe .20 .50
16 Heath Smith .20 .50

1987-88 Kansas

This 16-card set was sponsored by Nike and issued on an unperforated sheet with four rows of four cards. After cutting, they measure the standard size. The fronts feature a mix of posed and action color player photos on a white card face. Above the picture appears the team name, year, and the Nike logo. The picture is bordered by red on the left and by dark blue on the right and bottom. The Jayhawk logo appears in the lower left corner, with player identification in the blue border below the picture. The backs have biographical information, player evaluation, and basketball advice in the form of "Tips from the Jayhawks." The cards are unnumbered and checklisted below in alphabetical order, with the uniform number after the player's name. This set features the team that won the 1987-88 NCAA Championship as well as the first card of NBA star Danny Manning.

COMPLETE SET (16) 20.00 40.00
1 Sean Alvarado 52 .40 1.00
2 Scooter Barry 10 2.00 5.00
3 Marvin Branch 54 .40 1.00
4 Larry Brown CO 4.00 10.00
5 Jeff Gueldner 33 .40 1.00
6 Keith Harris 45 .40 1.00
7 Otis Livingston 12 .40 1.00
8 Mike Maddox 32 .40 1.00
9 Danny Manning 25 8.00 20.00
10 Archie Marshall 23 .40 1.00
11 Mike Masucci 44 .40 1.00
12 Lincoln Minor 11 .40 1.00
13 Milt Newton 21 .75 2.00
14 Chris Piper 24 .75 2.00
15 Kevin Pritchard 14 1.25 3.00
16 Mark Randall 42 1.25 3.00

1989-90 Kansas

This 16-card standard-size set was licensed to Leesley by the University of Kansas. The cards feature on the fronts color action player shots, with white and black borders on dark blue background. The player's name is given below the picture, with the Jayhawk team logo on an orange basketball in the lower right corner. The backs present biographical information and a player profile. The cards are numbered on the back in continuation of the Kansas Football card set. The set features the first cards of Adonis Jordan and coach Roy Williams.

COMPLETE SET (16) 8.00 20.00
41 Frequent Flyers Poster .60 1.50
42 Jeff Gueldner .30 .75
43 Freeman West .30 .75
44 Rick Calloway .40 1.00
45 Mark Randall .75 2.00
46 Mike Maddox .40 1.00
47 Alonzo Jamison .60 1.50
48 Kevin Pritchard .75 2.00
49 Terry Brown .30 .75
50 Kirk Wagner .30 .75
51 Pekka Markkanen .30 .75
52 Sean Tunstall .30 .75
53 Macolm Nash .30 .75
54 Todd Alexander .30 .75
55 Adonis Jordan 1.50 4.00
56 Roy Williams CO 4.00 10.00
NNO Title Card .30 .75

1991-92 Kansas

This 18-card standard-size set features on the fronts either posed or action color photos, enclosed by red and blue borders.The player's position appears in a gray stripe on the right side of the picture, while his name is printed in gray stripe beneath the picture. The horizontally oriented backs carry a black and white head shot, biography, and player profile. The cards are unnumbered and checklisted below in alphabetical order. The key cards in the set feature Alonzo Jamison, Adonis Jordan, Greg Ostertag, and Rex Walters.

COMPLETE SET (18) 6.00 15.00
1 Lane Czaplinski .30 .75
2 Ben Davis .75 2.00
3 Greg Gurley .30 .75
4 Alonzo Jamison .60 1.50
5 David Johanning .30 .75
6 Adonis Jordan 1.25 3.00
7 Macolm Nash .30 .75
8 Greg Ostertag 1.50 4.00
9 Eric Pauley .40 1.00
10 Sean Pearson .40 1.00
11 Calvin Rayford .40 1.00
12 Patrick Richey .30 .75
13 Richard Scott .40 1.00
14 Rex Walters 1.50 4.00
15 Roy Williams CO 3.00 8.00
16 Steve Woodberry .75 2.00
17 The O-Zone Alonzo Jamison .40 1.00
18 Team Photo Checklist .40 1.00

1992-93 Kansas

This 16-card standard-size set features color, posed and action player photos with red and blue borders. Also featured in this set is an art card of former Kansas player, Danny Manning. The player's name appears in a light gray bar at the bottom, while his position is contained in a light gray vertical bar running down the right edge. Though the design is identical to the previous year's issue, these cards are easily distinguished by the "92-93" year indication in the upper left corner. The horizontal backs carry biographical information, statistics, and a player profile. The cards are unnumbered and checklisted below in alphabetical order.

COMPLETE SET (16) 5.00 12.00
1 Matt Doherty ACO Steve Robinson ACO Kevin Stallings ACO .40 1.00
2 Greg Gurley .20 .50
3 Darrin Hancock .60 1.50
4 Adonis Jordan .75 2.00
5 Danny Manning Art 1.25 3.00
6 Greg Ostertag 1.00 2.50
7 Eric Pauley .30 .75
8 Sean Pearson .30 .75
9 Calvin Rayford .30 .75
10 Patrick Richey .20 .50
11 Richard Scott .30 .75
12 Rex Walters .75 2.00
13 Rex Walters Eric Pauley Adonis Jordan .75 2.00
14 Roy Williams CO 1.50 4.00
15 Steve Woodberry .40 1.00
16 Team Photo .30 .75

1993-94 Kansas

The 1993-94 Kansas University set consists of 17 standard-size cards. The fronts consist of full color action photos bleeding off the top, right, and left sides. Below the photo is a blue bar with the player's name reversed out and his position in red. The mascot and year is printed to the left. The white backs have a black-and-white player head shot in the upper left. The player's name and bio are printed in blue centered at the top with the team mascot to the right. The player's autograph is centered below the bio with the his career highlights below. The cards are unnumbered and checklisted below in alphabetical order. The set features the first card of Jacque Vaughn.

COMPLETE SET (17) 6.00 15.00
1 Greg Gurley .20 .50
2 Greg Ostertag 1.25 3.00
3 Sean Pearson .30 .75
4 Scot Pollard 1.50 4.00
5 Nick Proud Jason Kidd in background .75 2.00
6 Calvin Rayford .20 .50
7 Patrick Richey .20 .50
8 Richard Scott .30 .75
9 Jacque Vaughn 1.50 4.00
10 Blake Weichbrodt .20 .50
11 T.J. Whatley .20 .50
12 B.J. Williams .60 1.50
13 Roy Williams CO 1.50 4.00
14 Steve Woodberry .30 .75
15 Assistant Coaches Matt Doherty Joe Holladay Steve Robinson .40 1.00

2009-10 Kansas

COMPLETE SET (8) 15.00 40.00
1 Cole Aldrich 4.00 10.00
2 Sherron Collins 4.00 10.00
3 Brady Morningstar 4.00 10.00
4 Marcus Morris 6.00 15.00
5 Markieff Morris 6.00 15.00
6 Thomas Robinson 4.00 10.00
7 Bill Self CO 2.00 5.00
8 Jeff Withey 4.00 10.00

1996-97 Kansas Schedules

Unlike previous seasons where all seniors were pictured together on one schedule, Kansas University decided to honor their talented 1996-97 seniors by featuring each on his own schedule. The set is highlighted by the inclusion of All-American candidate and NBA guard Jacques Vaughn. These schedules were distributed for free at 1996-97 home games. The schedules are unnumbered on back and have been checklisted below alphabetically for convenience.

COMPLETE SET (4) 1.50 4.00
1 Jerod Haase .08 .25
2 Scot Pollard .75 2.00
3 Jacque Vaughn .75 2.00
4 B.J. Williams .08 .25

1987-88 Kansas State

This cards from this set measure 2 1/2" by 3 1/2" and feature posed or game action shots. The set was sponsered by The Saint Mary Hospital. Card backs have the player's biographical information and an anti-drug message. The cards are not numbered and listed below alphabetically.

COMPLETE SET (14) 30.00 80.00
1 Charles Bledsoe 1.25 3.00
2 Fabio de Almedia 1.25 3.00
3 Carlos Diggins 1.25 3.00
4 Mark Dobbins 1.25 3.00
5 Buster Glover 1.25 3.00
6 Steve Henson 2.50 6.00
7 Lon Kruger CO 3.00 8.00
8 Fred McCoy 1.25 3.00
9 Ron Meyer 1.25 3.00
10 Mark Nelson 1.25 3.00
11 John Rettiger 1.25 3.00
12 Mitch Richmond 20.00 50.00
13 William Scott 1.25 3.00
14 Willie the Wildcat Mascot 1.25 3.00

1997-98 Kansas State Legends

This 20-card set was produced by the Blind Tiger Brewery during the 1997-98 season at Kansas State University. This set features some of the greatest players to ever play for Kansas State University.

COMPLETE SET (20) 8.00 20.00
1 Ernie Barrett .30 .75
2 Rolando Blackman 1.00 2.50
3 Bob Boozer .75 2.00
4 Mike Evans .40 1.00
5 Steve Henson .40 1.00
6 Lon Kruger .40 1.00
7 Dick Kuosfman .30 .75
8 Ed Nealy .40 1.00
9 Mitch Richmond 2.00 5.00
10 Howard Shannon .30 .75
11 Willie Murrell .30 .75
12 Jack Gardner .30 .75
13 Jack Hartman .30 .75
14 Tex Winter .60 1.50
15 Elliot Hatcher .30 .75
16 Askia Jones .30 .75
17 Eddie Elder .30 .75
18 Jack Parr .40 1.00
19 Rick Harman .30 .75
20 Team Photo .40 1.00

1998-99 Kansas State

This 16-card set was released at Kansas State University during the 1998-99 season, the set features many of the players from that year's team. Please not that this set is unnumbered and is listed below in alphabetical order.

COMPLETE SET (16) 6.00 15.00
1 Team Photo .40 1.00
2 Willie the Wildcat MASCOT .40 1.00
3 Tom Asbury CO .60 1.50
4 Manny Dies .40 1.00
5 Chris Griffin .40 1.00
6 Cortez Groves .40 1.00
7 Jay Heidrick .40 1.00
8 Josh Kimm .40 1.00
9 Tony Kitt .40 1.00
10 Joe Leonard .40 1.00
11 Ayome May .40 1.00
12 Josh Reid .40 1.00
13 Travis Reynolds .40 1.00
14 Shawn Rhodes .40 1.00
15 David Ries .40 1.00
16 Ty Simms .40 1.00

2010-11 Kansas State

COMPLETE SET (17) 3.00 8.00
1 Freddy Asprilla .40 1.00
2 Jordan Henriquez-Roberts .40 1.00
3 Martavious Irving .40 1.00
4 Wally Judge .40 1.00
5 Curtis Kelly .40 1.00
6 Frank Martin CO .40 1.00
7 Rodney McGruder .40 1.00
8 Juevol Myles .40 1.00
9 Victor Ojeleye .40 1.00
10 Devon Peterson .40 1.00
11 Alex Potuzak .40 1.00
12 Jacob Pullen .40 1.00
13 Nick Russell .40 1.00
14 Jamar Samuels .40 1.00
15 Shane Southwell .40 1.00
16 Will Spradling .40 1.00
17 Nino Williams .40 1.00

2011-12 Kansas State

COMPLETE SET (16) 6.00 15.00
1 Adrian Diaz .60 1.50
2 Thomas Gipson .60 1.50
3 Jordan Henriquez .60 1.50
4 Martavious Irving .60 1.50
5 Jeremy Jones .60 1.50
6 Omari Lawrence .60 1.50
7 Rodney McGruder .60 1.50
8 Shawn Meyer .60 1.50
9 Victor Ojeleye .60 1.50
10 Angel Rodriguez .60 1.50
11 Brian Rohleder .60 1.50
12 Jamar Samuels .60 1.50
13 Shane Southwell .60 1.50
14 Will Spradling .60 1.50
15 James Watson .60 1.50
16 Nino Williams .60 1.50

2011-12 Kansas State Women

COMPLETE SET (13) 4.00 10.00
1 Branshea Brown .40 1.00
2 Heidi Brown .40 1.00
3 Chantay Caron .40 1.00
4 Brittany Chambers .40 1.00
5 Jalana Childs .40 1.00
6 Julianne Chisholm .40 1.00
7 Tasha Dickey .40 1.00
8 Katya Leick .40 1.00
9 Emma Ostermann .40 1.00
10 Haley Texada .40 1.00
11 Mariah White .40 1.00
12 Stephanie Wittman .40 1.00
13 Ashia Woods .40 1.00

1976-77 Kentucky Schedules

This 12-card set features schedule cards each measuring approximately 2 1/4" by 3 3/4". The fronts display borderless dark blue-tinted player photos. Player information is given in the white stripe below the picture. On white backgrounds in dark blue lettering, the backs carry the 1976-77 basketball schedule. The cards are unnumbered and checklisted below in alphabetical order. These schedule cards were passed out individually at games by booster clubs.

COMPLETE SET (12) 15.00 30.00
1 Dwane Casey 2.00 5.00
2 Truman Claytor 1.25 3.00
3 Jack Givens 2.50 6.00
4 Merion Haskins .75 2.00
5 Larry Johnson 1.25 3.00
6 James Lee 1.25 3.00
7 Kyle Macy 3.00 8.00
8 Mike Phillips 1.25 3.00
9 Rick Robey 2.50 6.00
10 Jay Shidler 1.25 3.00
11 Tim Stephens 1.25 3.00
12 LaVon Williams 1.25 3.00

1977-78 Kentucky

This 22-card set measures 2 1/2" by 3 3/4" and was produced by Wildcat News. The front features a black and white action photo with a royal blue border on white card stock. The player cards have the Wildcat logo, year, and the card number (in a basketball) across the top of the card face. The player's name and position appear below the picture. The back has a black and white head shot of the player in the upper right corner, with biographical and statistical information filling in the remainder of the space. This set features early cards of Kyle Macy and Rick Robey, who later played with different NBA teams. This set features the team that won the 1977-78 NCAA Championship.

COMPLETE SET (22) 22.50 45.00
1 The Fabulous Five 2.50 6.00
2 Joe Hall's First UK Team (Team Photo) .75 2.00
3 1975 NCAA Runners-Up (Team photo in plaid blazers) .75 2.00
4 1977-78 Wildcats .75 2.00
5 Leonard Hamilton CO 1.25 3.00
6 Joe Dean CO .75 2.00
7 Joe B. Hall CO 1.25 3.00
8 Dick Parsons CO .75 2.00
9 Scott Courts .40 1.00
10 Chuck Aleksinas .75 2.00
11 LaVon Williams .75 2.00
12 Chris Gettelfinger .40 1.00
13 Dwane Casey 1.25 3.00
14 Fred Cowan .75 2.00
15 Kyle Macy 3.00 8.00
16 Tim Stephens .40 1.00
17 James Lee 1.25 3.00
18 Jay Shidler 1.25 3.00
19 Rick Robey 2.00 5.00
20 Truman Claytor .75 2.00
21 Jack Givens 2.50 6.00
22 Mike Phillips .75 2.00

1977-78 Kentucky Schedules

This 19-card set features schedule cards each measuring approximately 2 1/4" by 3 3/4". These schedule cards were passed out individually at games by booster clubs. The fronts display borderless dark blue-tinted player photos. Player information is given in the white stripe below the picture. On white backgrounds in dark blue lettering, the backs carry the 1977-78 basketball schedule. Included in this set is a second card of head coach Joe B. Hall featuring a full-bleed color photo. The cards are unnumbered and checklisted below in alphabetical order.

COMPLETE SET (19) 20.00 40.00
1 Chuck Aleksinas 1.25 3.00
2 Dwane Casey 1.50 4.00
3 Truman Claytor 1.25 3.00
4 Scott Courts .75 2.00
5 Fred Cowan 1.25 3.00
6 Joe Dean ACO .75 2.00
7 Joe B. Hall CO 1.25 3.00
8 Joe B. Hall CO 1.25 3.00
9 Leonard Hamilton ACO 1.25 3.00
10 Chris Gettelfinger .75 2.00
11 Jack Givens 2.00 5.00
12 James Lee 1.50 4.00
13 Kyle Macy 2.50 6.00
14 Dick Parsons ACO .75 2.00
15 Mike Phillips 1.25 3.00
16 Rick Robey 2.00 5.00
17 Jay Shidler 1.25 3.00
18 Tim Stephens .75 2.00
19 LaVon Williams .75 2.00

1978-79 Kentucky

This 22-card set was produced by Wildcat News and sponsored by Food Town. The cards were originally given out one per week at the participating grocery stores. The cards measure approximately 2 1/2" by 3 3/4". The front features a black and white action photo, with the Wildcat logo, year, and the card number (in a basketball) to the left of the picture. The player's name and position appear below the picture, and a royal blue border outlines the card face. The back has a black and white head shot of the player in the upper right corner, with biographical and statistical information filling in the remainder of the space. This set features an early card of Kyle Macy, who later played in the NBA.

COMPLETE SET (22) 7.50 15.00
1 Homeward Bound .60 1.50
(Joe B. Hall and wife)
2 Jack Givens .60 1.50
Mike Phillips
Rick Robey
James Lee
3 Moment of Glory .75 2.00
(Jack Givens)
4 Cliff Hagan's .75 2.00
Hall of Fame Induction
5 1978-79 Wildcats .60 1.50
Team Photo
6 1978 NCAA Champions .60 1.50
Team Photo
7 Dwight Anderson .75 2.00
8 Clarence Tillman .30 .75
9 Chuck Verderber .60 1.50
10 Dwane Casey .75 2.00
11 Truman Claytor .60 1.50
12 Tim Stephens .30 .75
13 Kyle Macy 1.50 4.00
14 LaVon Williams .60 1.50
15 Jay Shidler .60 1.50
16 Freddie Cowan .60 1.50
17 Chuck Aleksinas .60 1.50
18 Chris Gettelfinger .30 .75
19 Joe B. Hall CO .75 2.00
20 Dick Parsons ACO .60 1.50
21 Leonard Hamilton ACO .60 1.50
22 Joe Dean ACO .30 .75

1978-79 Kentucky Schedules

This 16-card set features schedule cards each measuring approximately 2 1/4" by 3 3/4". These schedule cards were passed out individually at games by booster clubs. The fronts feature borderless dark blue-tinted player photos. Player information is given in the white stripe below the picture. In dark blue lettering on a white background, the backs have the 1978-79 basketball schedule. The cards are unnumbered and checklisted below in alphabetical order.

COMPLETE SET (16) 15.00 30.00
1 Chuck Aleksinas .75 2.00
2 Dwight Anderson 1.25 3.00
3 Dwane Casey 1.25 3.00
4 Truman Claytor 1.25 3.00
5 Fred Cowan .75 2.00
6 Joe Dean ACO .75 2.00
7 Chris Gettelfinger .75 2.00
8 Joe B. Hall CO 1.25 3.00
9 Leonard Hamilton ACO 1.25 3.00
10 Kyle Macy 1.50 4.00
11 Dick Parsons ACO .75 2.00
12 Jay Shidler 1.25 3.00
13 Tim Stephens .75 2.00
14 Clarence Tillman .75 2.00
15 Chuck Verderber 1.25 3.00
16 LaVon Williams .75 2.00

1979-80 Kentucky

This 22-card set was sponsored by Food Town. The cards measures approximately 2 1/2" by 3 3/4". The front features a black and white action photo, with the player's name printed vertically to the right of the picture. The card number (in a basketball), the year, and the Wildcat logo appear at the bottom of the card face. A royal blue border outlines the card face. The back has a black and white head shot of the player in the upper right corner, with biographical information filling in the remainder of the space. This set features cards of Kyle Macy, Sam Bowie, and Dirk Minniefield, who later played with different NBA teams.

COMPLETE SET (22) 10.00 20.00
1 1979-1980 Wildcats .40 1.00
Team Photo
2 Kyle Macy 1.25 3.00
3 Jay Shidler .40 1.00
4 LaVon Williams .40 1.00
5 Chris Gettelfinger .30 .75
6 Fred Cowan .40 1.00
7 Dwight Anderson .60 1.50
8 Bo Lanter .30 .75
9 Chuck Verderber .30 .75
10 Dirk Minniefield 1.00 2.50
11 Sam Bowie 2.50 6.00
12 Charles Hurt .75 2.00
13 Derrick Hord .60 1.50
14 Tom Heitz .30 .75
15 Joe Dean CO .30 .75
16 Leonard Hamilton CO .60 1.50
17 Dick Parsons CO .40 1.00
18 Joe B. Hall CO .60 1.50
19 Rupp Arena .30 .75
20 Kyle Macy .75 2.00
Pan Am Gold Medalist
(Schedule on back)
21 Sam Bowie .75 2.00
Tom Heitz
Derrick Hord
Charles Hurt
Dirk Minniefield
22 Kyle Macy .75 2.00
LaVon Williams
Jay Shidler

1979-80 Kentucky Schedules

This 17-card set features schedule cards each measuring approximately 2 1/4" by 3 3/4". These schedule cards were passed out individually at games by booster clubs. The fronts feature borderless dark blue-tinted player photos. Player information is given in the white stripe below the picture. In dark blue lettering, the backs have the 1979-80 basketball schedule. The cards are unnumbered and checklisted below in alphabetical order.

COMPLETE SET (17) 10.00 20.00
1 Dwight Anderson .75 2.00
2 Sam Bowie 2.00 5.00
3 Fred Cowan .40 1.00
4 Joe Dean ACO .40 1.00
5 Chris Gettelfinger .40 1.00
6 Joe B. Hall CO .60 1.50
7 Leonard Hamilton ACO .60 1.50
8 Tom Heitz .40 1.00
9 Derrick Hord .75 2.00
10 Charles Hurt .75 2.00
11 Bo Lanter .40 1.00
12 Kyle Macy 1.25 3.00
13 Dirk Minniefield 1.25 3.00
14 Dick Parsons ACO .40 1.00
15 Jay Shidler .60 1.50
16 Chuck Verderber .40 1.00
17 LaVon Williams .40 1.00

1980-81 Kentucky Schedules

This 16-card set features schedule cards each measuring approximately 2 1/4" by 3 3/4". These schedule cards were passed out individually at games by booster clubs. The fronts feature borderless dark blue-tinted player photos. Player information is given in the white stripe below the picture. In dark blue lettering, the backs have the 1980-81 basketball schedule. The only color photo in this set is of head coach Joe B. Hall. The cards are unnumbered and checklisted below in alphabetical order.

COMPLETE SET (16) 10.00 20.00
1 Dicky Beal .40 1.00
2 Bret Bearup .40 1.00
3 Sam Bowie 1.50 4.00
4 Fred Cowan .40 1.00
5 Joe Dean ACO .40 1.00
6 Chris Gettelfinger .40 1.00
7 Joe B. Hall CO .60 1.50
8 Leonard Hamilton ACO .60 1.50
9 Tom Heitz .40 1.00
10 Derrick Hord .60 1.50
11 Charles Hurt .60 1.50
12 Bo Lanter .40 1.00
13 Jim Master .75 2.00
14 Dirk Minniefield .75 2.00
15 Melvin Turpin 1.25 3.00
16 Chuck Verderber .40 1.00

1981-82 Kentucky Schedules

This 17-card set features schedule cards each measuring approximately 2 1/4" by 3 3/4". These schedule cards were passed out individually at games by booster clubs. The card fronts feature a borderless black and white player photo with a dark blue tint. Player information is given in the white stripe below the picture. In dark blue lettering the back has the 1981-82 basketball schedule. The only color photo in this set is of head coach Joe B. Hall. These unnumbered cards are ordered below alphabetically by subject's name.

COMPLETE SET (17) 8.00 20.00
1 Mike Ballenger .40 1.00
2 Dicky Beal .40 1.00
3 Butch Bearup .40 1.00
4 Sam Bowie 1.50 4.00
5 Bob Chambers ACO .40 1.00
6 Joe Dean ACO .40 1.00
7 Joe B. Hall CO .60 1.50
8 Leonard Hamilton ACO .40 1.00
9 Tom Heitz .40 1.00
10 Derrick Hord .60 1.50
11 Charles Hurt .60 1.50
12 Bo Lanter .40 1.00
13 Jim Master .60 1.50
14 Troy McKinley .40 1.00
15 Dirk Minniefield .75 2.00
16 Melvin Turpin .75 2.00
17 Chuck Verderber .40 1.00

1981-82 Kentucky Women

This 15-card set was released during the 1981-82 season at the University of Kentucky. The set features all of the members of the Kentucky Women's basketball team. Please note that each card back carries a team schedule for the 1981-82 season.

COMPLETE SET (15) 5.00 12.00
1 Dottie Berry CO .40 1.00
2 Lisa Collins .40 1.00
3 Lori Edgington .40 1.00
4 Tayna Fogle .40 1.00
5 Terry Hall CO .40 1.00
6 Patty Jo Hedges .40 1.00
7 Lynnette Lewis .40 1.00
8 Kathy Lokie .40 1.00
9 Donna Martin .40 1.00
10 Terri Naiser .40 1.00
11 Lynn Norenberg TR .40 1.00
12 Grace Odrick .40 1.00
13 Jody Runge .40 1.00
14 Diane Stephens .40 1.00
15 Lea Wise .40 1.00

1982-83 Kentucky Schedules

This 17-card set features schedule cards each measuring approximately 2 1/4" by 3 1/4". The card fronts feature a borderless black and white player photo with a dark blue tint. Player information is given in the white stripe below the picture. In dark blue lettering the back has the 1982-83 basketball schedule. These unnumbered cards are ordered below alphabetically by player's name.

COMPLETE SET (17) 8.00 20.00
1 Dicky Beal .40 1.00
2 Bret Bearup .40 1.00
3 Sam Bowie 1.25 3.00
4 Bob Chambers ACO .40 1.00
5 Joe Dean ACO .40 1.00
6 Joe B. Hall CO .75 2.00
7 Leonard Hamilton ACO .40 1.00
8 Roger Harden .40 1.00
9 Tom Heitz .40 1.00
10 Derrick Hord .60 1.50
11 Charles Hurt .60 1.50
12 Todd May .40 1.00
13 Jim Master .60 1.50
14 Troy McKinley .40 1.00
15 Dirk Minniefield .75 2.00
16 Melvin Turpin .75 2.00
17 Kenny Walker 1.50 4.00

1983-84 Kentucky Schedules

This 17-card set features schedule cards each measuring approximately 2 1/4" by 3 1/4". The card fronts feature a borderless black and white player photo with a dark blue tint. Player information is given in the white stripe below the picture. In dark blue lettering the back has the 1983-84 basketball schedule. These unnumbered cards are ordered below alphabetically by player's name.

COMPLETE SET (17) 8.00 20.00
1 Paul Andrews .40 1.00
2 Dicky Beal .40 1.00
3 Bret Bearup .40 1.00
4 Winston Bennett .75 2.00
5 James Blackmon .60 1.50
6 Sam Bowie 1.25 3.00
7 Joe B. Hall CO .60 1.50
8 Leonard Hamilton ACO .60 1.50
9 Hatfield .40 1.00
10 Tom Heitz .40 1.00
11 John Kelly .40 1.00
12 Jim Master .60 1.50
13 Todd May .40 1.00
14 Troy McKinley .40 1.00
15 Melvin Turpin .75 2.00
16 Kenny Walker .75 2.00
17 Todd Ziegler .40 1.00

1984-85 Kentucky Schedules

This 16-card set features schedule cards each measuring approximately 2 1/4" by 3 3/4". The card fronts feature a borderless black and white player photo with a dark blue tint. Player information is given in the white stripe below the picture. In dark blue lettering the back has the 1984-85 basketball schedule. These unnumbered cards are ordered below alphabetically by player's name.

COMPLETE SET (16) 6.00 15.00
1 Joe B. Hall CO .60 1.50
2 Leonard Hamilton ACO .60 1.50
3 John Kelly ACO .40 1.00
4 Hatfield .40 1.00
5 Troy McKinley .40 1.00
6 Leroy Byrd .40 1.00
7 Todd Ziegler .40 1.00
8 Rob Lock .40 1.00
9 James Blackmon .40 1.00
10 Cedric Jenkins .60 1.50
11 Richard Madison .40 1.00
12 Butch Bearup .40 1.00
13 Kenny Walker .75 2.00
14 Ed Davender .40 1.00
15 Roger Harden .40 1.00
16 Paul Andrews .40 1.00

1988 Kentucky Soviet Program Insert

This 18-card set was issued as an insert in the U.S. AAU All-Stars vs. Soviet Junior Nationals official program for the game played at Memorial Coliseum in Lexington, KY, May 14, 1988. The set is the only one printed during the Russian Junior team's U.S. tour. The cards were issued in two panels; after perforation, the cards measure approximately 2 1/2" by 3 1/2". The front features a mix of posed or action, black and white player photos, with a light blue background and thin black border on white card stock. A 1888-1988 AAU/USA 100th anniversary emblem is superimposed at the left corner of the photo. Player information appears below the picture in the lower left corner. An AAU/Soviet tour emblem in the lower right corner rounds out the card face. The back has a black and white head shot of the player in the upper left corner. Biographical information appears in a light blue-tinted box, with high school statistics at the bottom. The cards are numbered on the back. The set features the first cards of Damon Bailey, Allan Houston, Shawn Kemp, Don McLean, and Chris Mills.

COMPLETE SET (18) 50.00 100.00
1 Checklist 1.25 3.00
2 Scott Davenport CO .75 2.00
3 Keith Adkins .75 2.00
4 Mike Allen .75 2.00
5 Damon Bailey 4.00 10.00
6 Scott Boley .75 2.00
7 David DeMarcus .75 2.00
8 Richie Farmer 1.50 4.00
9 Travis Ford 2.00 5.00
10 Pat Graham 1.50 4.00
11 Robbie Graham .75 2.00
12 Allan Houston 25.00 50.00
13 Shawn Kemp 20.00 50.00
14 Don MacLean 5.00 12.00
15 Kenneth Martin .75 2.00
16 Chris Mills 6.00 15.00
17 Derrick Miller .75 2.00
18 Sean Woods 1.50 4.00

1988-89 Kentucky Collegiate Collection

The 1988-89 University of Kentucky Wildcats set contains 269 standard-sized cards featuring "Kentucky's Finest" basketball players. This set was issued in eight-card cello packs. The fronts have deep blue and white borders. The backs have various statistical and biographical information.

COMPLETE SET (269) 12.00 30.00
1 Adolph Rupp CO .30 .75
2 Cliff Hagan .20 .50
3 Frank Ramsey .15 .40
4 Ralph Beard .15 .40
5 Alex Groza .15 .40
6 Wallace Jones .15 .40
7 Dan Issel .30 .75
8 Cotton Nash .15 .40
9 Kevin Grevey .15 .40
10 Kyle Macy .15 .40
11 Kenny Walker .15 .40
12 Louie Dampier .15 .40
13 Vernon Hatton .15 .40
14 Johnny Cox .15 .40
15 Jack Givens .15 .40
16 Bill Spivey .15 .40
17 Pat Riley .40 1.00
18 Ellis Johnson .15 .40
19 Forest Sale .15 .40
20 Kenny Rollins .15 .40
21 Sam Bowie .15 .40
22 John DeMoisey .15 .40
23 Leroy Edwards .15 .40
24 Lee Huber .15 .40
25 Rick Robey .15 .40
26 Bob Burrow .15 .40
27 Cliff Barker .15 .40
28 Bernie Opper .15 .40
29 Ralph Carlisle .15 .40
30 Joe B. Hall CO .15 .40
31 Bob Brannum .15 .40
32 Jack Parkinson .15 .40
33 Jack Tingle .15 .40
34 Joe Holland .15 .40
35 Jim Line .15 .40
36 Bobby Watson .15 .40
37 Bill Evans .15 .40
38 Bill Lickert .15 .40
39 Larry Conley .15 .40
40 Eddie Sutton .15 .40
41 Larry Steele .15 .15
42 Tom Parker .15 .10
43 Shelby Linville .15 .10
44 Lou Tsioropoulos .15 .15
45 Gayle Rose .15 .15
46 Jim Andrews .15 .10
47 Ed Davender .15 .15
48 Winston Bennett .15 .20
49 Willie Rouse .15 .10
50 Mike Pratt .15 .15
51 Harry C. Lancaster .15 .15
52 Dirk Minniefield .15 .20
53 Russell Rice .15 .10
54 Carey Spicer .15 .10
55 Paul McBrayer .15 .10
56 Burgess Carey .15 .10
57 Ermal Allen .15 .15
58 Dale Barnstable .15 .10
59 Kenton Campbell .15 .10
60 Guy Strong .15 .10
61 Lucian Whitaker .15 .10
62 Bennie Coffman .15 .10
63 C.M. Newton .15 .30
64 Walt Hirsch .15 .10
65 John Brewer .15 .15
66 Phil Grawemeyer .15 .10
67 John Crigler .15 .10
68 Gerry Calvert .15 .10
69 Ed Beck .15 .10
70 Jerry Bird .15 .10
71 Harold Ross .15 .40
72 Adrian Smith .15 .15
73 Don Mills .15 .10
74 Ned Jennings .15 .10
75 Sid Cohen .15 .10
76 Dickie Parsons .15 .10
77 Larry Pursiful .15 .10
78 Herky Rupp .15 .15
79 Charles Ishmael .15 .10
80 Jim McDonald .15 .10
81 Terry Mobley .15 .10
82 Tommy Kron .15 .15
83 Randy Embry .15 .10
84 Steve Clevenger .15 .10
85 Jim LeMaster .15 .10
86 Basil Hayden .15 .10
87 Cliff Berger .15 .10
88 Jim Dinwiddie .15 .15
89 Randy Pool .15 .10
90 Terry Mills .15 .15
91 Bob McCowan .15 .10
92 Mike Casey .15 .15
93 Kent Hollenbeck .15 .10
94 Scotty Baesler .15 .10
95 Phil Argento .15 .10
96 John R. Adams .15 .10
97 Larry Stamper .15 .10
98 Ray Edelman .15 .10
99 Ronnie Lyons .15 .10
100 G.J. Smith .15 .10
101 Jerry Hale .15 .10
102 Bob Guyette .15 .10
103 Mike Flynn .15 .15
104 Jimmy Dan Connor .15 .15
105 Larry Johnson .15 .15
106 Joey Holland .15 .10
107 Reggie Warford .15 .10
108 Merion Haskins .15 .10
109 James Lee .15 .15
110 Dwane Casey .15 .25
111 Truman Claytor .15 .15
112 LaVon Williams .15 .15
113 Jay Shidler .15 .15
114 Fred Cowan .15 .15
115 Dwight Anderson .15 .25
116 Chuck Verderber .15 .15
117 Bo Lanter .15 .10
118 Charles Hurt .15 .15
119 Derrick Hord .15 .15
120 Tom Heitz .15 .10
121 Dicky Beal .15 .15
122 Bret Bearup .15 .15
123 Melvin Turpin .15 .20
124 Jim Master .15 .15
125 Troy McKinley .15 .10
126 Roger Harden .15 .15
127 James Blackmon .15 .15
128 Leroy Byrd .15 .15
129 Cedric Jenkins .15 .15
130 Rob Lock .15 .15
131 Richard Madison .15 .15
132 Cawood Ledford .15 .20
133 '47-'48 Team .15 .20
134 '48-'49 Team .15 .20
135 '50-'51 Team .15 .20
136 '57-'58 Team .15 .20
137 '77-'78 Team .15 .20
138 Stan Key .15 .10
139 Mike Phillips .15 .15
140 Joe B. Hall CO .15 .25
141 Mike Flynn .15 .15
142 Thad Jaracz .15 .15
143 Larry Conley .15 .30
144 Rex Chapman .20 .50
145 Pat Riley .40 1.00
146 Melvin Turpin .15 .20
147 Kenny Walker .15 .25
148 Wallace Jones .15 .15
149 Alex Groza .15 .40
150 Mike Pratt .15 .15
151 Cliff Barker .15 .15
152 Jim Andrews .15 .10
153 Kenny Walker .15 .25
154 Kevin Grevey .15 .20
155 Kyle Macy .15 .30
156 Jim Line .15 .10
157 Pat Riley .40 1.00
158 Larry Steele .15 .15
159 Jack Givens .15 .25
160 Ed Davender .15 .15
161 Ralph Beard .15 .40
162 Vernon Hatton .15 .10
163 Frank Ramsey .15 .40
164 Bob Burrow .15 .10
165 Sam Bowie .15 .30
166 Dan Issel .30 .75
167 Rick Robey .15 .20
168 Winston Bennett .15 .20
169 Louie Dampier .15 .20
170 Gayle Rose .15 .15
171 Cliff Hagan .20 .50
172 Cotton Nash .15 .25
173 Mike Pratt .15 .15
174 Richard Madison .15 .15
175 Kyle Macy .15 .30
176 Rob Lock .15 .15
177 Larry Johnson .15 .15
178 Cedric Jenkins .15 .15
179 Dan Issel .30 .75
180 Charles Hurt .15 .15
181 Cliff Hagan .20 .50
182 Wallace Jones .15 .15
183 Roger Harden .15 .15
184 Bob Guyette .15 .10
185 Kevin Grevey .15 .20
186 Jack Givens .15 .25
187 Ed Davender .15 .15
188 Jimmy Dan Connor .15 .15
189 Fred Cowan .15 .15
190 Larry Conley .15 .30
191 Leroy Byrd .15 .15
192 Sam Bowie .15 .30
193 James Blackmon .15 .15
194 Winston Bennett .15 .20
195 Dicky Beal .15 .15
196 Jim Andrews .15 .10
197 Kenny Walker .15 .25
198 Pat Riley .40 1.00
199 Frank Ramsey .15 .40
200 Truman Claytor .15 .15
201 Dwane Casey .15 .25
202 Rex Chapman .20 .50
203 Jim Master .15 .15
204 Mike Phillips .15 .15
205 Dirk Minniefield .15 .20
206 Jimmy Dan Connor .15 .15
207 Bill Lickert .15 .10
208 Leroy Byrd .15 .15
209 Mike Pratt .15 .15
210 Rob Lock .15 .40
211 Dickie Parsons .15 .10
212 Frank Ramsey .15 .40
213 Adolph Rupp CO .30 .75
214 G.J. Smith .15 .10
215 Rick Robey .15 .20
216 James Blackmon .15 .15
217 Mike Casey .15 .15
218 LaVon Williams .15 .15
219 Larry Pursiful .15 .10
220 Terry Mobley .15 .10
221 Kyle Macy .15 .30
222 Larry Conley .15 .30
223 Dirk Minniefield .15 .20
224 Jim Master .15 .40
225 Jerry Bird .15 .10
226 Dan Issel .30 .75
227 Larry Johnson .15 .15
228 Bret Bearup .15 .15
229 Ronnie Lyons .15 .10
230 James Lee .15 .15
231 Don Mills .15 .10
232 Truman Claytor .15 .15
233 Rex Chapman .20 .50
234 Fred Cowan .15 .15
235 Truman Claytor .15 .15
236 Dicky Beal .15 .15
237 Larry Johnson .15 .15
238 John R. Adams .15 .10
239 Sam Bowie .15 .30
240 Thad Jaracz .15 .15
241 Phil Argento .15 .10
242 Cedric Jenkins .15 .15
243 Charles Hurt .15 .15
244 Charles Hurt .15 .15
245 Cliff Hagan .20 .50
246 Kent Hollenbeck .15 .10
247 Wallace Jones .15 .15
248 Roger Harden .15 .15
249 Bob Guyette .15 .10
250 Richard Madison .15 .15
251 Kevin Grevey .15 .20
252 Jack Givens .15 .25
253 Tommy Kron .15 .15
254 Derrick Hord .15 .15
255 Tom Heitz .15 .10
256 Cliff Hagan .20 .50
257 Louie Dampier .15 .20
258 Jimmy Dan Connor .15 .15
259 Dwane Casey .15 .25
260 Cliff Hagan .20 .50
261 Walt Hirsch .15 .10
262 Merion Haskins .15 .10
263 Roger Harden .15 .15
264 Bob Guyette .15 .10
265 Phil Grawemeyer .15 .10
266 Jay Shidler .15 .15
267 Jim Dinwiddie .15 .15
268 Fred Cowan .15 .15
269 Leroy Byrd .15 .15

1988-89 Kentucky Big Blue

This 18-card set was issued as an insert in the Summer 1989 Volume 3, Number 2 issue of Oscar Combs' Big Blue Basketball magazine. The cards honor Kentucky players for various outstanding achievements. The cards were issued in two panels; after perforation, the cards measure approximately 2 1/2" by 3 1/2". In a horizontal format, the front features a color action player photo, with blue and black borders on white card stock. The name of the award appears in white lettering in the upper left corner of the photo, with the player's name in a white box in the lower left corner. The back has a black and white head shot of the player in the upper left corner. Biographical information appears in a light blue-tinted box. The cards are numbered on the back, and we have listed the award below after the player's name.

COMPLETE SET (18) 9.00 18.00
1 Sean Sutton .30 .75
Leadership
2 Chris Mills 1.50 4.00
Most Valuable Player
3 Mike Scott .30 .75
Outstanding Senior
4 Richie Farmer .60 1.50
Best Free Throw
Percentage
5 Derrick Miller .30 .75
Fewest Turnovers
6 Chris Mills 1.50 4.00
Freshman Leadership
7 Mike Scott .30 .75
Scholastic
8 Sean Sutton .30 .75
Most Assists
9 Chris Mills 1.50 4.00
Most Rebounds
10 LeRon Ellis .60 1.50
Leading Scorer
11 Reggie Hanson .60 1.50
Best Defender
12 Deron Feldhaus .60 1.50
110 Percent Award
13 Sean Sutton and .60 1.50
Leron Ellis
Sacrifice Award
14 LeRon Ellis .60 1.50
Best Field Goal
Percentage
15 Sean Sutton .30 .75
Best Three-pt. Field
Goal Percentage
16 Reggie Hanson .60 1.50
Most Steals
17 Eddie Sutton CO .75 2.00
18 Checklist Card UER .30 .75
(Misspelled sacrifice
as sacrafice)

1989-90 Kentucky Big Blue

This perforated 18-card set was issued as an insert in the Winter 1990 Volume 3,, Number 4 issue of Oscar Combs' Big Blue Basketball magazine. The cards honor Kentucky players for various outstanding achievements. The cards were issued in two panels; after perforation, the cards measure approximately 2 1/2" by 3 1/2". The front features a color action player photo, with dark blue and black borders on white card stock. The name of the award is written vertically in an orange bar to the left of the picture, while the player's name appears in a gray bar above the picture. The back has a black and white head shot of the player in the upper left corner. Biographical information appears in a blue-tinted box. The cards are numbered on the back, beginning with 19 in continuation of the numbering of the previous year's issue. The award is listed below after the player's name.

COMPLETE SET (18) 8.00 20.00
19 Checklist Card .30 .75
20 Richie Farmer .60 1.50
Best FT Shooter
21 Reggie Hanson .60 1.50
Most Rebounds
22 Deron Feldhaus .60 1.50
Fewest Turnovers
23 Billy Donovan ACO 1.25 3.00
Herb Sendek ACO
Tubby Smith ACO
Ralph Willard ACO
24 Deron Feldhaus .60 1.50
Mr. Hustle Award
25 Reggie Hanson .60 1.50
Leadership
26 John Pelphrey .60 1.50
Student Athlete
27 Derrick Miller .30 .75
Outstanding Senior
28 Deron Feldhaus .60 1.50
Most Improved
29 Happy Chandler 1.25 3.00
Fan of the Year
30 John Pelphrey .60 1.50
Best Playmaker
31 Reggie Hanson .60 1.50
John Pelphrey
Mr. Deflection
32 Reggie Hanson .60 1.50
Most Valuable
33 Deron Feldhaus .60 1.50
Best FG Shooter
34 Sean Woods .30 .75
Most Assists
35 Derrick Miller .30 .75
Leading Scorer
36 Rick Pitino 2.00 5.00
Coach of the Year

1989-90 Kentucky Big Blue Team of the 80's

This perforated 18-card set was issued as an insert in the Spring 1990 Volume 4, Number 1 issue of Oscar Combs' Big Blue Basketball magazine. The cards honor outstanding Kentucky players for the decade of the 1980's. The cards were issued in two panels; after perforation, the cards measure approximately 2 1/2" by 3 1/2". The front features a color action player photo, on a light blue background that washes out as one moves from top to bottom. A thin black border outlines this blue background. The player's name appears in black lettering above the picture. The left lower corner of the photo is cut out, and in the triangular-shaped area appears a basketball icon and the pro team(s) played for. The back is blue tinted, and it has a black and white head shot of the player on the left side, with biographical information around the picture and career college statistics on the bottom. The cards are numbered on the back, beginning with 37 in continuation of the numbering of the previous year's issue.

COMPLETE SET (18) 8.00 20.00
37 Checklist Card .30 .75
38 Kyle Macy .75 2.00
39 Rex Chapman 1.25 3.00
40 Kenny Walker .75 2.00
41 Winston Bennett .50 1.25
42 Melvin Turpin .50 1.25
43 Sam Bowie 1.00 2.50
44 Dicky Beal .30 .75
45 Dirk Minniefield .50 1.25
46 Jim Master .50 1.25
47 Rob Lock .30 .75
48 Chris Mills 1.00 2.50
49 Roger Harden .30 .75
50 Jay Shidler .50 1.25
51 LeRon Ellis .50 1.25
52 Fred Cowan .30 .75
53 Derrick Hord .50 1.25
54 Joe Hall CO 1.25 3.00
Eddie Sutton CO
Rick Pitino CO

1989-90 Kentucky Schedules

This seven-card multi-sport set features schedule cards each measuring approximately 2 1/4" by 3 3/4". These schedule cards were passed out individually at games by booster clubs. The fronts feature full-bleed color action photos, some horizontally, some vertically oriented. The name "Kentucky" appears in either blue or white letters across the top of the card face on most cards. The backs carry the 1989-90 schedules for the respective sports. The cards are unnumbered and checklisted below with the named individuals listed first.

COMPLETE SET (7) 2.50 6.00
2 Rick Pitino CO 1.60 4.00

1990 Kentucky Class A High School All-Stars

This 18-card set was issued as an insert in the Kentucky All "A" Classic official program (produced by Wildcat News) for the state tournament played at Memorial Coliseum in Lexington, KY, February 7-10, 1990. The set consists of a checklist card, a special card honoring current Lexington mayor Scotty Baesler as a "Class A Great" player of the past, and 16 cards honoring the coaches' preseason choices for best players in each of the sixteen regions. The cards were issued in two panels; after perforation, the cards measure approximately 2 1/2" by 3 1/2". The front features a mix of posed or action, black and white player photos, with a peach color background and thin blue border on white card stock. Below the picture, the region number and player's name appears in a gray stripe, with player information further below in the right corner. A Kentucky shaped emblem in the lower left corner rounds out the card face. The back has a black and white head shot of the player in the upper left corner. Biographical information appears in a peach-tinted box, with high school statistics on the bottom. The cards are numbered on the back.

COMPLETE SET (18) 4.00 10.00
1 Checklist Card .40 1.00
2 Scott Baesler .40 1.00
3 Eugene Alexander .30 .75
4 Sergio Luyk .40 1.00
5 Chris Knight .30 .75
6 Chris Huffman .40 1.00
7 Shannon Phillips .30 .75
8 Glen Wathen .30 .75
9 Jason Hagan .30 .75
10 Bryan Milburn .40 1.00
11 Andre McClendon .30 .75
12 Chris Harrison .40 1.00
13 Daniel Swintosky .40 1.00
14 Jamie Cromer .30 .75
15 Mo Hollingsworth .30 .75
16 Jeff Moore .40 1.00
17 Jody Thompson .30 .75
18 Mike Helton .30 .75

1990 Kentucky Soviet Program Insert

This 18-card set was issued in two panels inside the AAU/Soviet Tour program (produced by Wildcat News) for the game played in Memorial Coliseum at Lexington, Kentucky, on May 15, 1990. After perforation, the cards measure approximately 2 1/2" by 3 1/2" and showcase the Kentucky AAU All-Stars. The fronts feature a mix of action or posed, black and white player photos, with red borders on a white and blue diagonally-striped background. The words "Ky. AAU All-Stars" appear in blue lettering in white stripe above the picture; the player's name is presented in the same format below the picture. The backs have black and white head shots of the player in the upper left corners. In a lavender colored box, they present career summaries, with high school statistics appearing at the bottom of the card. The cards are numbered on the back in the upper right corners. The key card in the set is the first card of NBA Lottery Pick Jamal Mashburn.

COMPLETE SET (18) 12.00 30.00
1 Checklist Card .40 1.00
2 Kentucky .40 1.00
USSR rosters
3 Jim Lankster .40 1.00
4 Paul Bingham .40 1.00
5 James Crutcher .40 1.00
6 Jason Eitutis .40 1.00
7 Greg Glass .40 1.00
8 Arlando Johnson .40 1.00
9 Gimel Martinez .60 1.50
10 Jamal Mashburn 10.00 25.00
11 Jeff Moore .40 1.00
12 Dwayne Morton 1.50 4.00
13 Keith Peel .40 1.00
14 Andy Penick .40 1.00
15 Daniel Swintosky .40 1.00
16 Jody Thompson .40 1.00
17 Carlos Toomer .40 1.00
18 Kelly Wells .40 1.00

1990-91 Kentucky Big Blue 18

This rather unattractive perforated 18-card set was issued as an insert in Oscar Combs' Big Blue Basketball magazine. After perforation, the cards measure approximately 2 5/8" by 3 5/8." The fronts display a mix of action and posed color head shots enclosed by a white border. The player's name appears in black lettering in a yellow bar at the top flanked by a basketball to the left. In a horizontal format, the backs have blue and white reverse lettering and carry a black and white head shot, a Fun Fact, and a "Coach Pitino Sez" feature. The cards are numbered on the back. The key card in the set features NBA Lottery Pick Jamal Mashburn.

COMPLETE SET (18) 8.00 20.00
1 Johnathon Davis .30 .75
2 Reggie Hanson .30 .75
3 Richie Farmer .60 1.50
4 Deron Feldhaus .30 .75
5 John Pelphrey .60 1.50
6 Sean Woods .30 .75
7 Todd Bearup .20 .50
8 Junior Braddy .20 .50
9 Jeff Brassow .30 .75
10 Gimel Martinez .30 .75
11 Jamal Mashburn 4.00 10.00
12 Henry Thomas .20 .50
13 Carlos Toomer .20 .50
14 Travis Ford .60 1.50
15 Rick Pitino CO 1.50 4.00
16 UK Cracks Top 10 .20 .50
17 UK 93, U of L 85 .20 .50
18 Checklist Card .20 .50

1990-91 Kentucky Big Blue Dream Team/Award Winners

This perforated 18-card set was issued as an insert in the Spring 1991 Volume 5, Number 1 issue of Oscar Combs' Big Blue Basketball magazine. The cards were issued in two panels of nine cards each. After perforation, the cards measure approximately 2 9/16" by 3 5/8". The cards are numbered 19-36, in continuation of an 18-card insert set of 1990-91 Kentucky players in an earlier issue of Big Blue Basketball. The fronts feature a color action photo enclosed by a white border. A blue box in the upper left corner indicates whether the player belongs to the Dream Team (19-26), which consists the most impressive opponents faced during the season as voted by the captains on the Kentucky squad, or is an Award Winner (28-36). The player's name appears in a color stripe at the bottom of the picture. Within a light blue border, the backs show a black and white head shot and a career summmary presented in the format of a newspaper article. The cards are numbered on the back. Reportedly only 7,500 sets were produced. The key cards in the set are NBA superstar Shaquille O'Neal and NBA stars Allan Houston and Jamal Mashburn. The O'Neal card is his very first trading card and the only card issued of him during his LSU collegiate career. "B" Versions of this set are available also. This version mirrors the cards found in the Big Blue Magazine, but are unperforated and were machine cut with a print run of about 1,200 sets.

COMPLETE SET (18) 40.00 100.00
19 Shaquille O'Neal 10.00 25.00
LSU
19B Shaquille O'Neal 25.00 60.00
Unperforated
20 Allan Houston 2.50 6.00

Tennessee
20B Allan Houston 6.00 15.00
Unperforated
21 Calbert Cheaney 1.50 4.00
Indiana
21B Calbert Cheaney 4.00 10.00
Unperforated
22 Rick Fox 2.00 5.00
North Carolina
22B Rick Fox 4.00 10.00
Unperforated
23 Litterial Green .60 1.50
Georgia
23B Litterial Green 1.25 3.00
Unperforated
24 Bobby Knight CO 1.25 3.00
Indiana
24B Bobby Knight CO 2.00 5.00
Unperforated
25 Dean Smith CO 1.50 4.00
North Carolina
25B Dean Smith CO 3.00 8.00
Unperforated
26 Freedom Hall .30 .75
26B Freedom Hall .60 1.50
Unperforated
27 Checklist .30 .75
27B Checklist .60 1.50
Unperforated
28 Richie Farmer .60 1.50
28B Richie Farmer .75 2.00
Unperforated
29 Jamal Mashburn 2.50 6.00
29B Jamal Mashburn 6.00 15.00
Unperforated
30 Jeff Brassow .30 .75
30B Jeff Brassow .60 1.50
Unperforated
31 Todd Bearup .30 .75
31B Todd Bearup .60 1.50
Unperforated
32 Sean Woods .60 1.50
32B Sean Woods .75 2.00
Unperforated
33 Deron Feldhaus .60 1.50
33B Deron Feldhaus .75 2.00
Unperforated
34 John Pelphrey .60 1.50
34B John Pelphrey .75 2.00
Unperforated
35 Reggie Hanson .60 1.50
35B Reggie Hanson .75 2.00
Unperforated
36 Rick Pitino CO 1.00 2.50
36B Rick Pitino CO 2.00 5.00
Unperforated

1990-91 Kentucky Women Schedules

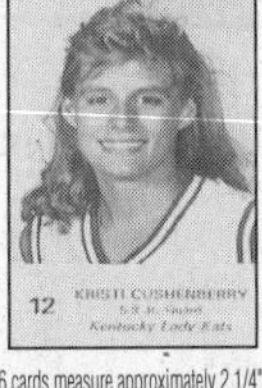

These 16 cards measure approximately 2 1/4" by 3 3/4" and feature blue-screened posed player head shots on their fronts. The player's name, uniform number, height, class, and position appear in the white margin below the photo. Otherwise, the photos are borderless. The white back carries the Lady Kats' 1990-91 game schedule in blue lettering. The cards are unnumbered and checklisted below in alphabetical order.

COMPLETE SET (16) 2.50 6.00
1 Kayla Campbell .20 .50
2 Kristi Cushenberry .20 .50
3 Mia Daniel .20 .50
4 Tracye Davis .20 .50
5 Tedra Eberhart .20 .50
6 Jennifer Gray .20 .50
7 Sharon Fanning CO .20 .50
8 Jamie Hobgood .20 .50
9 Christe Jordan .20 .50
10 Karen Killen .20 .50
11 Pattresa Leonard .20 .50
12 Tiundra Love .20 .50
13 Stacy McIntyre .20 .50
14 Jocelyn Mills .20 .50
15 Cathy Proctor .20 .50
16 Rebekah Reasor .20 .50

1991-92 Kentucky Big Blue 20

This 20-card set was issued as inserts in the Summer 1991 Volume 5, Number 2, and Fall 1991 Volume 5, Number 3 issues of Oscar Combs' Big Blue Basketball magazine. Each issue had two insert sheets: an 8 1/2" by 11" photo and a sheet of player cards. After perforation, the player cards measure 2 9/16" by 3 5/8." The horizontally oriented fronts feature a color head shot to the left of the Wildcats' logo. A blue stripe traverses the top of the card face, while the player's name appears in a short red stripe at the lower right corner. The backs are vertically oriented and display black and white action photos. The cards are numbered on the back. The key card in the set features NBA Lottery Pick Jamal Mashburn.

COMPLETE SET (20) 8.00 20.00
1 John Pelphrey .40 1.00
2 Deron Feldhaus .30 .75
3 Richie Farmer .40 1.00
4 Jeff Brassow .30 .75
5 Junior Braddy .20 .50
6 Sean Woods .30 .75
7 Gimel Martinez .30 .75
8 Travis Ford .40 1.00
9 Dale Brown .30 .75
10 Chris Harrison .20 .50
11 Carlos Toomer .20 .50
12 Jamal Mashburn 4.00 10.00
13 Rick Pitino CO 1.25 3.00
14 Aminu Timberlake .20 .50
15 Andre Riddick .60 1.50
16 Bernadette Locke-Mattox .40 1.00
Asst. CO
17 Billy Donovan ACO 1.50 4.00
18 Herb Sendek ACO .30 .75
NNO Wildcat Seniors 1.00 2.50
NNO Team Photo 1.50 4.00

1992-93 Kentucky Schedules

Sponsored by McDonald's, this ten-card multi-sport schedule features schedule cards each measuring 2 1/4" by 3 1/2". These schedule cards were passed out individually at games by booster clubs. The fronts feature a mix of color and black-and-white action player photos. Card numbers 1 and 2 are folded in the middle. The backs (or the insides) carry the 1992-93 schedules for the respective sports. The sponsor's logo appears either on the front or on the back. The cards are unnumbered and checklisted below in alphabetical order, with the schedule cards not featuring athletes listed at the end.

COMPLETE SET (10) 2.50 6.00
4 Jamal Mashburn BK 1.20 3.00
5 Stacey Reed .10 .25
Women's Basketball
schedule
8 Basketball schedule .20 .50

1993-94 Kentucky

The 1993-94 University of Kentucky set contains 18 standard-size cards. The light blue-bordered fronts feature a mix of posed and action color photos. The team nickname, "Cats," appears across the top of the photo in simulated polished metal. The player's name is printed in blue and white script and appears in a lower corner. The set name is printed in the lower border. The blue-bordered horizontal backs carry a second player photo in a narrow vertical box on the left side. Player profile, statistics, biography, team number, and logo are printed on a ghosted photo of a basketball court. The cards are unnumbered and checklisted below in alphabetical order. The set could originally be purchased through the mail for 9.25 plus 2.00 for shipping and handling.

COMPLETE SET (18) 6.00 15.00
1 Jeff Brassow .20 .50
2 Tony Delk 1.50 4.00
3 Rodney Dent .30 .75
4 Anthony Epps .75 2.00
5 Travis Ford .30 .75
6 Chris Harrison .20 .50
7 Bill Keightley EQ MG .20 .50
8 Gimel Martinez .30 .75
9 Walter McCarty 1.50 4.00
10 Rick Pitino CO 1.00 2.50
11 Jared Prickett .30 .75
12 Rodrick Rhodes 1.00 2.50
13 Andre Riddick .30 .75
14 Jeff Sheppard .30 .75
15 Delray Brooks ACO 1.25 3.00
Shaun Brown ACO
Billy Donovan ACO
Bernadette Locke-Mattox ACO
16 1993 SEC Champions .40 1.00
17 Team Photo Card .30 .75
18 Title Card .20 .50

1993-94 Kentucky Schedules

4 Men's Basketball .20 .50
Gimel Martinez
Rodney Dent
Travis Ford
Jeff Brassow
5 Jennifer Gray .20 .50
Kayla Campbell
Tedra Eberhart
Christe Jordan
Women's Basketball

1997-98 Kentucky Women

This set was released for the University of Kentucky Women's Basketball during the 1997-98 season. The set features cards of all of the players and coaches on a purple bordered card courtesy of Mildred White.

COMPLETE SET (20) 2.50 6.00
1 Leah Berki .20 .50
2 Lisa Byington .20 .50
3 Megan Chawansky .20 .50
4 Mary Connolly .20 .50
5 Amber DeWall .20 .50
6 Kristina Divjak .20 .50
7 Becky Fisher .20 .50
8 Clarissa Flores .20 .50
9 Anne Giblin .20 .50
10 Chala Holland .20 .50
11 Shannon McGarrigle .20 .50
12 Leslie Schock .20 .50
13 Tami Sears .20 .50
14 Candace Wrenn .20 .50
15 Dana Leonard .20 .50
16 Team Photo .20 .50
17 Don Perrelli CO .30 .75
18 Robin Garrett .20 .50
Amy Backus
Jennifer Kiefer
19 Wildcat Seniors .20 .50
20 Wildcat Freshmen .20 .50

1998-99 Kentucky Schedules

This three-card set features the 1998-99 Kentucky team schedule cards that were passed out during Kentucky home games.

COMPLETE SET (3) 1.50 4.00
1 Heshimu Evans .40 1.00
2 Scott Padgett 1.25 3.00
3 Wayne Turner .40 1.00

1987 Kentucky Bluegrass State Games

This 24-card set of standard size cards was co-sponsored by Coca-Cola and Valvoline, and their company logos appear on the bottom of the card face. The card sets were originally given out by the Kentucky county sheriff's departments and the Kentucky Highway Patrol. Reportedly about 350 sets were given to the approximately 120 counties in the state of Kentucky. One card per week was given out from May 25 to October 19, 1987. Once all 22 of the numbered cards were collected, they could be turned in to a local sheriff's department for prizes. The front features a color action player photo, on a blue card face with a white outer border. The player's name and the "Champions Against Drugs" insignia appear below the picture. The back has a anti-drug or alcohol tip on a gray background, with white border. The set commemorates Kentucky's hosting of the 1987 Bluegrass State Games and was endorsed by Governor Martha Layne Collins in Kentucky's Champions Against Drugs Crusade for Youth. The set features stars from a variety of sports as well as public figures. The two cards in the set numbered "SC" for special card were not distributed with the regular cards; they were produced in smaller quantities than the 22 numbered cards. The set features the first card of NBA superstar David Robinson. Reportedly the Robinson cards were distributed at the March 1987 Kentucky Boy's State High School Tournament in Rupp Arena, when David Robinson was in attendance.

COMPLETE SET (24) 25.00 60.00
2 Kenny Walker K .30 .75
4 Dan Issel K 1.60 4.00
7 Melvin Turpin .60 1.50
Sam Bowie K
8 Darrell Griffith K .60 1.50
9 Winston Bennett K .30 .75
15 Jim Master K .30 .75
16 Kyle Macy K .40 1.00
17 Pervis Ellison K .60 1.50
18 Dale Baldwin K .20 .50
21 Rex Chapman K 1.60 4.00
SC Billy Packer SP K 4.00 10.00
SC David Robinson SP K 16.00 40.00

1985-86 LSU

This 16-card standard-size set was sponsored by LSU, Baton Rouge General Medical Center, Chemical Dependency Unit of Baton Rouge, and various law enforcement agencies and produced by McDag Productions. The General and the Chemical Dependency Unit logos adorn the top of the observe and the bottom of the reverse. The cards are unnumbered and we have checklisted them in alphabetical order. Since this set includes athletes from two different sports, we have indicated the sport after the player's name (B for baseball; BK for basketball). The set features Major League Baseball slugger Joey (Albert) Belle and other future Major Leaguers Mark Guthrie and Jeff Reboulet.

COMPLETE SET (16) 10.00 25.00
3 Ricky Blanton BK .40 1.00
4 Dale Brown BK CO 1.20 3.00
5 Ollie Brown BK .20 .50
11 Don Redden BK .20 .50
12 Derrick Taylor BK .20 .50
13 Jose Vargas BK .20 .50
14 John Williams BK 1.00 2.50
15 Nikita Wilson BK .40 1.00
16 Anthony Wilson BK .20 .50

1987-88 LSU

This 16-card standard-size set was sponsored by LSU, Baton Rouge General Medical Center, Chemical Dependency Unit of Baton Rouge, and various law enforcement agencies and was produced by McDag Productions. The General and the Chemical Dependency Unit logos adorn the bottom of both sides of the card. Six thousand sets were printed, and they were distributed by participating police agencies in the Baton Rouge area. The fronts feature borderless action or posed color photos of the players on white card stock. The upper left and right corners give the school name and player information. The backs have additional player information and "Tips from the Tigers", which consist of anti-drug or alcohol messages. This set includes athletes from basketball (1-7, 16) and baseball (8-15). Of special interest is card number 16, issued in memory of the late Pete Maravich, the all-time leading scorer in college basketball history. The set features the first card of Ben McDonald.

COMPLETE SET (16) 15.00 40.00
1 Dale Brown BK CO 1.20 3.00
2 Ricky Blanton BK .60 1.50
3 Jose Vargas BK .40 1.00
4 Fess Irvin BK .60 1.50
5 Darryl Joe BK .40 1.00
6 Bernard Woodside BK .40 1.00
7 Neboisha Bukumirovich BK .40 1.00
16 Pete Maravich BK MEM 12.00 30.00

1988-89 LSU

This 16-card standard-size set was sponsored by LSU, Baton Rouge General Medical Center, Chemical Dependency Unit of Baton Rouge, and various law enforcement agencies and was produced by McDag Productions. The General Medical Center and Chemical Dependency Unit logos adorn the bottom of both sides of the card. The cards were distributed in the Baton Rouge area by participating law enforcement agencies, the Medical Center, and the Chemical Dependency Unit. This set features athletes from basketball (1-8) and baseball (9-16). This set includes early cards of Chris Jackson, who played in the NBA, and of Ben McDonald, who pitched for the USA Olympic Baseball Team and the Baltimore Orioles.

COMPLETE SET (16) 5.00 12.00
1 Ricky Blanton .40 1.00
2 Dale Brown CO 1.25 3.00
3 Wayne Simms .20 .50
4 Chris Jackson 1.60 4.00
5 Kyle McKenzie .20 .50
6 Lyle Mouton .60 1.50
7 Vernel Singleton .40 1.00
8 Russell Grant .20 .50
9 Skip Bertman CO .75 2.00

1990 LSU Collegiate Collection

This 200-card standard-size multi-sport set was produced by Collegiate Collection. Although a few color photos are included, the front features mostly black and white player photos, with borders in the team's colors of gold and purple. Unless noted below, all are football subjects.

COMPLETE SET (200) 6.00 15.00
1 Pete Maravich BK 2.00 5.00
2 Chris Jackson BK .20 .50
4 Ricky Blanton BK .10 .25
6 Joe Dean BK .07 .20
11 Dale Brown CO BK .15 .40
14 John Williams BK .10 .25
18 Chris Jackson BK .10 .25
22 Glenn Hansen BK .05 .15
25 Leonard Mitchell BK .05 .15
32 Ethan Martin BK .05 .15
33 Julie Gross WBK .05 .15
35 Eddie Palubinskas BK .05 .15
37 Frank Brian BK .05 .15
40 Howard Carter BK .07 .20
42 Nikita Wilson BK .07 .20
46 DeWayne Scales BK .05 .15
50 Durand Macklin BK .07 .20
53 Joyce Walker WBK .05 .15
54 Bobby Lowther BK .05 .15
55 Al Sanders BK .05 .15
58 George Nattin BK .05 .15
61 Maree Jackson WBK .05 .15
62 Sparky Wade BK .05 .15
65 Al Green BK .05 .15
71 Dick Maile BK .05 .15
74 Pete Maravich BK 2.00 5.00
91 Chris Jackson BK .20 .50
98 Jerry Reynolds BK .10 .25
136 Kenny Higgs BK .05 .15
138 Bob Pettit BK .30 .75
154 Pete Maravich Center BK .20 .50
165 Buddy Blair BK .05 .15
171 Joe Bill Padcock BK .05 .15
189 Chris Jackson BK .20 .50
190 Chris Jackson BK .20 .50
196 Howard Carter BK .07 .20
197 Glenn Hansen BK .05 .15
198 Durand Macklin BK .07 .20

1993-94 LSU

This 16-card standard-size set was produced by McDag Productions Inc. The fronts feature color action player photos framed by yellowish-orange borders. "LSU Tigers" and "1993-94" are printed in purple in the top border. The player's name, position, and uniform number are printed in purple in the bottom border, immediately to the right of an orange basketball icon. In purple print on a white background, the horizontal backs present biographical information and player profile. This set features the first card of Randy Livingston, a highly-touted two-time Parade magazine Prep All-American who was red-shirted during his first year due to a knee injury. The cards are unnumbered and checklisted below in alphabetical order.

COMPLETE SET (16) 3.00 8.00
1 Doug Annison .20 .50
2 David Bosley .20 .50
3 Dale Brown CO .75 2.00
4 Jamie Brandon .30 .75
5 Lenear Burns .20 .50
6 Clarence Ceasar .30 .75
7 Sean Gipson .20 .50
8 Ronnie Henderson .75 2.00
9 Glover Jackson .20 .50
10 Randy Livingston 1.00 2.50
11 Andre Owens .30 .75
12 Roman Roubtchenko .20 .50
13 Brandon Titus .20 .50
14 Mike the Tiger .20 .50
The Tiger
15 Mike the Tiger .20 .50
The Mascot
16 Cheerleaders .20 .50

1988-89 LSU All-Americas

Produced by McDag Productions, this 16-card standard-size set was sponsored by LSU, Baton Rouge General Medical Center, Chemical Dependency Unit of Baton Rouge, and various law enforcement agencies. The General Medical Center and Chemical Dependency Unit logos adorn the bottom of both sides of the card. This set showcases athletes from basketball (1-2), baseball (3-5), track (6), volleyball (7), football (8-15) and golf (16). This set includes early cards of Chris Jackson, who was selected in the first round of the NBA draft by the Denver Nuggets, and of Ben McDonald, who was selected first by the Baltimore Orioles.

COMPLETE SET (16) 5.00 12.00
1 Chris Jackson 1.60 4.00
2 Durand(Rudy) Macklin .40 1.00

1989-90 Louisiana Tech

This 16-card set measures the standard size and features members of the men's (1-8) and women's (9-16) basketball teams. The fronts feature close-up photos with red and white borders. Above the picture is a gray box containing the school name and year. Below the photo is a sky blue box that displays the player's name, jersey number, and position. The backs carry limited player information and a wildfire prevention cartoon. The cards are unnumbered and checklisted below in alphabetical order within each team. This set features the first card of Venus Lacy, a member of the gold medal-winning 1996 USA team.

COMPLETE SET (16) 6.00 15.00
1 Eldon Bowman .20 .50
2 P.J. Brown 3.00 8.00
3 Dickie Crawford .20 .50
4 Anthony Dade .40 1.00
5 Reggie Gibbs .20 .50
6 Jo Jo Goldsmith .20 .50
7 Brett Guillory .20 .50
8 Roosevelt Powell .20 .50
9 Barbara Bolden .40 1.00
10 Sheila Ethridge .20 .50
11 Cara Gullion .20 .50
12 Shantel Hardison .20 .50
13 Venus Lacy 1.25 3.00
14 Annie Lockett .20 .50
15 Sebrena Smith .20 .50
16 Pam Wells .40 1.00

1981-82 Louisville

This 31-card set was sponsored by Pepsi, the Louisville Area Chamber of Commerce, and Greater Louisville Police Departments. The cards measure approximately 2 5/8" by 4 1/8" and are printed in thin card stock. On a red card face, the fronts show black and white player photos enclosed by a white border. Player information and the words "Cardinal Spirit" appear beneath the picture. The backs include a safety tip, a definition or discussion of an aspect of basketball, and sponsor logos. The cards are numbered on the back by the tip number.

COMPLETE SET (31) 30.00 55.00
1 Charles Jones 1.00 2.50
2 Rodin's The Thinker .60 1.50
3 1981-82 Schedule .60 1.50
4 Bill Olsen ATH DIR .60 1.50
and family
5 Coaching Staff 1.00 2.50
6 Lancaster Gordon 1.25 3.00
7 Donald C. Swain PRES .60 1.50
8 Scooter McCray 1.25 3.00
9 Cheerleaders .60 1.50
10 Marty Pulliam .60 1.50
11 Derek Smith 2.50 6.00
12 Jack Tennant ANN 1.00 2.50
and Van Vance ANN
13 Jerry Eaves 1.00 2.50
14 Greg Deuser .60 1.50
15 Manuel Forrest 1.00 2.50
16 Danny Mitchell .60 1.50
17 Team Photo 2.00 5.00
Men's team
18 Jerry May TR .60 1.50
Rudy Ellis
Dir. Sports Medicine
19 Poncho Wright 1.00 2.50
20 James Jeter .60 1.50
21 Cardinal Bird .60 1.50
Mascot
22 Milt Wagner 2.00 5.00
23 Denny Crum CO 2.00 5.00
and 1981-82 Freshman
24 Team Photo .60 1.50
Women's Team
25 Wiley Brown 1.00 2.50
26 Kent Jones .60 1.50
27 Denny Crum CO 2.00 5.00
and Returning Starters
28 Darrell Griffith 3.00 8.00
U of L Professional
Basketball Players
29 Denny Crum CO 3.00 8.00
30 Rodney McCray 2.00 5.00
NNO Logo Card SP 15.00 30.00

1983-84 Louisville

This 20-card set consists of oversized cards measuring approximately 7" by 5". On the left portion the front features a borderless color action photo, measuring 4" by 5". On the remaining portion, a head shot of the player, player information (in white lettering), and a Cardinal logo appear on a red background. The back of the cards presents biographical information, career summary, and statistics in a two-column format, along with the player's autograph. The cards are unnumbered and checklisted below in alphabetical order.

COMPLETE SET (20) 15.00 40.00
1 Denny Crum CO 4.00 10.00
2 Manuel Forrest .75 2.00
3 Lancaster Gordon 1.50 4.00
4 Darrell Griffith 4.00 10.00
5 Jeff Hall .75 2.00
6 James Jeter .75 2.00
7 Charles Jones .75 2.00
8 Kent Jones .75 2.00
9 Mark McSwain .75 2.00
10 Danny Mitchell 2.50 6.00
11 Will Olliges .75 2.00
12 Barry Sumpter 1.50 4.00
13 Billy Thompson 1.50 4.00
14 Robbie Valentine 1.50 4.00
15 Milt Wagner 2.50 6.00
16 Chris West .75 2.00
17 Bobby Dotson ACO .75 2.00
Wade Houston ACO
Jerry Jones ACO
18 Cheerleaders 1.50 4.00
19 Pep Band .75 2.00
20 Freedom Hall 1.50 4.00
Home of the Cardinals

1988-89 Louisville Collegiate Collection

The 1988-89 University of Louisville Cardinals basketball set contains 194 standard-sized cards featuring "Louisville's Finest" basketball players. The fronts have red and white borders. The backs have various statistical and biographical information. This set was issued in eight-card cello packs.

COMPLETE SET (194) 6.00 15.00
1 Denny Crum CO .15 .40
2 Wes Unseld .20 .50
3 Darrell Griffith .10 .30
4 John Dromo .07 .20
5 Bernard (Peck) Hickman .07 .20
6 Butch Beard .10 .30
7 Herbert Crook .07 .20
8 Milt Wagner .07 .20
9 Lancaster Gordon .07 .20
10 Billy Thompson .07 .20
11 Rodney McCray .08 .25
12 Scooter McCray .07 .15
13 Wade Houston .07 .15
14 Jerry Jones .07 .05
15 Derek Smith .07 .15
16 Tony Branch .07 .10
17 Wesley Cox .07 .10
18 Manuel Forrest .07 .10
19 Jerry Eaves .07 .10
20 1980 NCAA Champs .08 .25
21 Junior Bridgeman .07 .15
22 Jeff Hall .07 .10
23 Charles Jones .07 .10
24 Rick Wilson .07 .05
25 The Cardinal Bird .07 .05
26 Wiley Brown .07 .10
27 Charlie Tyra .07 .10
28 Phil Rollins .07 .05
29 James Jeter .07 .05
30 Poncho Wright .07 .05
31 Vladimir Gastevich .07 .05
32 Terry Howard .07 .05
33 Mark McSwain .07 .10
34 Ricky Gallon .07 .05
35 1975 NCAA Final Four .07 .10
36 1972 NCAA Final Four .07 .10
37 Mike Lawhon .07 .05
38 Bill Bunton .07 .10
39 Roger Burkman .07 .05
40 Henry Bacon .07 .05
41 Larry Williams .07 .05
42 Phil Bond .07 .05
43 Bobby Brown .07 .05
44 Charles Jones .07 .10
45 Mike Grosso .07 .05
46 Freedom Hall .07 .15
47 Fred Holden .07 .05
48 1948 NAIB Champs .07 .10
49 Glen Combs .07 .10
50 Jadie Frazier .07 .05
51 Marty Pulliam .07 .05
52 Eddie Whitehead .07 .05
53 Bobby Turner .07 .05
54 Will Olliges .07 .20
55 Eddie Creamer .07 .05
56 Corky Cox .07 .05
57 Bob Lochmueller .07 .05
58 Jeff Hall .07 .10
59 Al Vilcheck .07 .05
60 Jim Morgan .07 .05
61 Jim Price .07 .10
62 Ron Thomas .07 .10
63 Bobby Dotson .07 .05
64 Jerry Eaves .07 .10
65 1956 NIT Champs .07 .10
66 John Reuther .07 .05
67 Ron Hawley .07 .05
68 Kent Jones .07 .05
69 1983 NCAA Final Four .07 .15
70 1982 NCAA Final Four .07 .15
71 1959 Louisville .07 .10
72 Fred Sawyer .07 .05
73 Kenny Reeves .07 .05
74 Chris West .07 .05
75 Dick Peloff .07 .05
76 Allen Murphy .07 .05
77 John Prudhoe .07 .05
78 Mike Abram .07 .05
79 Bud Olsen .07 .05
80 Ron Rubenstein .07 .05
81 Gerald Moreman .07 .05
82 Chuck Noble .07 .05
83 Bill Darragh .07 .05
84 Jerry Dupont .07 .05
85 Danny Mitchell .07 .05
86 John Turner .07 .05
87 Daryl Cleveland .07 .05
88 Greg Deuser .07 .05
89 Don Goldstein .07 .05
90 Marv Selvy .07 .05
91 Dave Gilbert .07 .05
92 Tommy Finnegan .07 .05
93 Joe Liedtke .07 .05
94 Jack Coleman .07 .05
95 Dennis Clifford .07 .05
96 Robbie Valentine .07 .05
97 Ron Rooks .07 .05
98 The Coaching Staff .07 .15
99 Denny Crum CO .15 .40
100 Manuel Forrest .07 .10
101 Darrell Griffith .10 .30
102 Wesley Cox .07 .10
103 Wes Unseld .20 .50
104 John Dromo .07 .10
105 Peck Hickman .07 .10
106 Butch Beard .10 .30
107 Herbert Crook .07 .15
108 Milt Wagner .07 .20
109 Lancaster Gordon .07 .20
110 Billy Thompson .07 .20
111 Rodney McCray .08 .25
112 Scooter McCray .07 .15
113 Derek Smith .07 .15
114 Tony Branch .07 .10
115 Manuel Forrest .07 .10
116 Jerry Eaves .07 .10
117 Jeff Hall .07 .10
118 Charles Jones .07 .10
119 Rick Wilson .07 .05
120 Wiley Brown .07 .10
121 Charlie Tyra .07 .10
122 Phil Rollins .07 .05
123 Poncho Wright .07 .05
124 Terry Howard .07 .05
125 Mark McSwain .07 .10
126 Ricky Gallon .07 .05
127 Mike Lawhon .07 .05
128 Roger Burkman .07 .05
129 Henry Bacon .07 .05
130 Larry Williams .07 .05
131 Phil Bond .07 .05
132 Stanley Bunton .07 .05
133 Fred Holden .07 .05
134 Marty Pulliam .07 .05
135 Bobby Turner .07 .05
136 Will Olliges .07 .05
137 Al Vilcheck .07 .05
138 Jim Price .07 .10
139 Chris West .07 .05
140 Allen Murphy .07 .05
141 Mike Abram .07 .05
142 Danny Mitchell .07 .05
143 John Turner .07 .05
144 Daryl Cleveland .07 .05
145 Don Goldstein .07 .05
146 Marv Selvy .07 .05
147 Dave Gilbert .07 .05
148 Joe Liedtke .07 .05
149 Robbie Valentine .07 .05
150 Tony Branch .07 .10
151 Manuel Forrest .07 .10
152 Jerry Eaves .07 .10
153 Rick Wilson .07 .05
154 Jeff Hall .07 .10
155 Charles Jones .07 .10
156 Derek Smith .07 .15
157 Scooter McCray .07 .15
158 Robbie Valentine .07 .05
159 Mike Abram .07 .05
160 Rodney McCray .08 .25
161 Roger Burkman .07 .05
162 Henry Bacon .07 .05
163 Mike Lawhon .07 .05
164 Ricky Gallon .07 .05
165 Billy Thompson .08 .20
166 Milt Wagner .07 .20
167 Lancaster Gordon .07 .20
168 Butch Beard .10 .30
169 Herbert Crook .07 .15
170 Wes Unseld .20 .50
171 Wesley Cox .07 .10
172 Darrell Griffith .10 .30
173 Denny Crum CO .15 .40
174 Mark McSwain .07 .10
175 Wiley Brown .07 .10
176 Will Olliges .07 .05
177 Phil Bond .07 .05
178 Phil Bond .07 .05
179 Wiley Brown .07 .10
180 Mark McSwain .07 .10
181 Denny Crum CO .15 .40
182 Darrell Griffith .10 .30
183 Wesley Cox .07 .20
184 Peck Hickman CO .07 .10
185 Lancaster Gordon .07 .20
186 Billy Thompson .07 .20
187 Rodney McCray .08 .25
188 Stanley Bunton .07 .05
189 Henry Bacon .07 .05
190 Scooter McCray .07 .15
191 Derek Smith .07 .15
192 Jerry King .07 .05
193 Van Vance and .07 .05
Jock Sutherland
194 Bill Olsen .07 .05

1991-92 Louisville Schedules

Sponsored by UL/Cellular One, this three-card set features schedule cards each measuring approximately 4 1/2" by 3 1/2". The fronts, which carry a Cellular One advertisement on the left portion and a full-bleed color action player photo on the right, can be folded in the middle. The inside pages carry the 1991-92 basketball schedule and identify the senior pictured. The cards are unnumbered and checklisted below in alphabetical order.

COMPLETE SET (3) .60 1.50
1 Cornelius Holden .20 .50
2 Everick Sullivan .30 .75
3 Jason McClendon .20 .50

1992-93 Louisville

Produced by Motion Sports, this 31-card standard-size set features posed and action color player photos. The top and right edge of the picture is accented by an L-shaped white border design containing the player's name. The bottom and left edge is accented by a red L-shaped border design containing the university name. The entire card front is framed by a thin black border. The backs display career summary on a ghosted panel superimposed on a basketball arena scene. Some sets also included a value coupon that could be redeemed at the Cardinal athletic offices for one free set of basketball trading cards; a total of 50 sets were given away in this manner. Some uncut press sheets were also offered to the public for 20.00 plus 2.00 for shipping and handling.

COMPLETE SET (31) 6.00 15.00
1 Denny Crum CO 1.25 3.00
2 NCAA Championship .20 .50
3 Brian Hopgood .08 .25
4 Clifford Rozier 1.00 2.50
5 Keith LeGree .20 .50
6 Tick Rogers .20 .50
7 Jimmy King .08 .25
8 Brian Kiser .08 .25
9 Doug Calhoun .08 .25
10 Mike Case .08 .25
11 James Brewer .08 .25
12 Dwayne Morton .60 1.50
13 Greg Minor 1.00 2.50
14 Troy Smith .08 .25
15 Robby Wine .08 .25
16 Derwin Webb .08 .25
17 Brian Hopgood .08 .25
18 Keith LeGree .20 .50
19 Mike Case .08 .25
20 James Brewer .08 .25
21 Dwayne Morton .60 1.50
22 Greg Minor 1.00 2.50
23 Troy Smith .08 .25
24 Derwin Webb .08 .25
25 Seniors .08 .25
Mike Case
Troy Smith
Derwin Webb
James Brewer
26 Cardinal Mascot .08 .25
27 Denny Crum CO 1.25 3.00
500th Career
Victory
28 Ad Card Motion Sports .08 .25
DC1 Denny Crum Promo .40 1.00
DC2 Denny Crum Comm 1.25 3.00
4-inch x 9-inch
honoring his 500th win
NNO Title Card .08 .25
NNO Back Card .08 .25
NNO Card Directory .08 .25

1992-93 Louisville Schedules

Sponsored by Storer Cable Communications, this five-card set features schedule cards each measuring approximately 4 1/2" by 3 1/2". The fronts, which carry a Storer Cable Communications advertisement on the left portion and a full-bleed color action player photo on the right, can be folded in the middle. The insides carry the 1992-93 basketball schedule and identify the senior pictured. The cards are unnumbered and checklisted below in alphabetical order.

COMPLETE SET (5) .80 2.00
1 James (Boo) Brewer .20 .50
2 Mike Case .20 .50
3 Neil Knox .20 .50
4 Troy Smith .20 .50
5 Derwin Webb .20 .50

1993-94 Louisville

This 20-card standard-size set was produced by Collect-A-Sport, College Division. The fronts feature color action player photos inside white borders. A red marbleized bar at the bottom of the picture carries the player's name, position, and team logo. On a white back, two red marbleized panels present biography and player profile respectively. The cards are unnumbered and checklisted below in alphabetical order.

COMPLETE SET (20) 6.00 15.00
1 Doug Calhoun .20 .50
2 Denny Crum CO 1.25 3.00
3 Jimmy King .20 .50
4 Brian Kiser .30 .75
5 Greg Minor .75 2.00
6 Dwayne Morton .40 1.00
7 Jason Osborne .20 .50
8 Tick Rogers .30 .75
9 Clifford Rozier .75 2.00
10 Matt Simons .20 .50
11 Alvin Sims .30 .75
12 Beau Zach Smith .20 .50
13 DeJuan Wheat 1.25 3.00
14 Robby Wine .20 .50
15 Larry Gay ACO .30 .75
Jerry Jones ACO
Scooter McCray ACO
16 Greg Minor .60 1.50
Doug Calhoun
Dwayne Morton
17 Mascot .60 1.50
Greg Minor
Doug Calhoun
Dwayne Morton
18 Team Photo .30 .75
19 Freedom Hall .30 .75
20 Title Card .20 .50

1993-94 Louisville Schedules

Sponsored by BellSouth Mobility, this three-card set features schedule cards each measuring approximately 4 1/2" by 3 1/2". The fronts, which carry a BellSouth Mobility advertisement on the left portion and a full-bleed color action player photo on the right, can be folded in the middle. The inside pages carry the 1993-94 basketball schedule and identify the senior pictured. The cards are unnumbered and checklisted below in alphabetical order.

COMPLETE SET (3) .75 2.00
1 Jody Martin .20 .50
2 Greg Minor .40 1.00
3 Dwayne Morton .30 .75

1994-95 Louisville Schedules

Sponsored by BellSouth Mobility, this three-card set features schedule cards each measuring approximately 4 1/2" by 3 1/2". (The cards fold in the middle to measure 2 1/4" by 3 1/2".) The fronts feature full-bleed color action player photos. The inside pages carry the 1994-95 women's (1) or men's (2-3) basketball schedule and identify the player pictured. The backs carry a BellSouth Mobility advertisement. The cards are unnumbered and checklisted below in alphabetical order.

COMPLETE SET (3) .80 2.00
1 Kristin Mattox .20 .50
2 Jason Osborne .30 .75
3 DeJuan Wheat .40 1.00

2011 Lowe's Senior Class

COMPLETE SET (11) 20.00 50.00
1 Shane Battier TRIB 3.00 8.00
2 Devon Beitzel 3.00 8.00
3 Dodie Dunson 3.00 8.00
4 Jimmer Fredette 3.00 8.00
5 Matt Howard 3.00 8.00
6 Cameron Jones 3.00 8.00
7 Jon Leuer 3.00 8.00
8 David Lighty 3.00 8.00
9 E'Twaun Moore 3.00 8.00
10 Tyrel Reed 3.00 8.00
11 Kyle Singler 3.00 8.00

2012 Lowe's Senior Class

COMPLETE SET (11) 20.00 50.00
1 William Buford 3.00 8.00
2 Jimmer Fredette TRIB 3.00 8.00
3 Ashton Gibbs 3.00 8.00
4 Draymond Green 5.00 12.00
5 Mick Hedgepeth 3.00 8.00
6 Robbie Hummel 3.00 8.00
7 Quinn McDowell 3.00 8.00
8 Ronald Nored 3.00 8.00
9 Zach Novak 3.00 8.00
10 Zach Rosen 3.00 8.00
11 Tyler Zeller 3.00 8.00

1986-87 Maine

This 14-card set of Maine Black Bears is part of a "Kids and Kops" promotion, and one card was printed each Saturday in the Bangor Daily News. The cards measure approximately 2 1/2" by 4". The cards were to be collected from any participating plice officer. Once five cards had been collected (including card number 1), they could be turned in at a police station for a University of Maine ID card, which permitted free admission to selected university activities. When all 14 cards had been collected, they could be turned in at a police station to register for the Grand Prize drawing (bicycle) and to pick up a free "Kids and Kops" tee-shirt. The backs have tips in the form of an anti-drug or alcohol message and logos of Burger King, University of Maine and Pepsi across the bottom. With the exception of the rules card, the cards are numbered on the back.

COMPLETE SET (14) 6.00 15.00
3 Amadou Coco Barry BK .40 1.00
9 Jim Boylen BK .40 1.00
13 Matt Rossignoi BK .40 1.00
NNO Matt Rossignol .40 1.00
Kids
Kops

1987-88 Maine

This 14-card set of Maine Black Bears is part of a "Kids and Kops" promotion, and one card was printed each Saturday in the Bangor Daily News. The cards measure approximately 2 1/2" by 4". The cards were to be collected from any participating police officer. Once five cards had been collected (including card number 1), they could be turned in at a police station for a University of Maine ID card, which permitted free admission to selected university activities. When all 14 cards had been collected, they could be turned in at a police station to register for the Grand Prize drawing (bicycle) and to pick up a free "Kids and Kops" tee-shirt. The backs have tips in the form of an anti-drug or alcohol message and logos of Burger King, University of Maine, and Pepsi across the bottom. With the exception of the rules card, the cards are numbered on the back. Sports represented in this set include hockey (2), basketball (3, 9, 13), tennis (4), baseball (5), swimming (6), soccer (7), track (8), football (10), field hockey (11), and softball (12).

COMPLETE SET (14) 6.00 15.00
1 Bananas 2.00 5.00
K.C. Jones CO BK
3 Matt Rossignoi BK .40 1.00
9 Elizabeth(Liz) Coffin BK .40 1.00
13 Amadou Coco Barry BK .40 1.00
NNO Matt Rossignoi BK .40 1.00
Kids and Kops

1982-83 Marquette

This 16-card set measures the standard card size, 2 1/2" by 3 1/2", and was issued in conjunction with Lite Beer. The front of the card features a black and white action photo inside an "arrowhead" against a pale yellow background, surrounded by the player's name, height, and position, with the team name ("Warriors") emblazoned across the bottom. The back has biographical and statistical information. The set also features the first card of NBA veteran Glenn "Doc" Rivers.

COMPLETE SET (16) 8.00 20.00
1 Ric Cobb ACO .50 1.25
2 Dwayne(DJ) Johnson .30 .75
3 Mandy Johnson .30 .75
4 Vic Lazzaretti .30 .75
5 Rick Majerus ACO 3.00 8.00
6 Marc Marotta .30 .75
7 Lloyd Moore .30 .75
8 Paul Newman .30 .75
9 Tom Pipines .30 .75
10 Hank Raymonds CO .75 2.00
11 Terry Reason .30 .75
12 Doc Rivers 4.00 10.00
13 Terrell Schlundt .50 1.25
14 Don Smolinski .30 .75
15 Kerry Trotter .30 .75
xx Title Card .50 1.25

1991-92 Marquette

Sponsored by Cyganiak Planning Inc., this 17-card set measures the standard size. The cards show signs of perforation on their sides and feature color action player photos on their fronts. The photo is framed by a thin yellow line and set on a white card face. The player's name and jersey number appear in black print at the top. His height and classification appear below the picture. An emblem in the lower left corner commemorates the 75th year of Marquette basketball. The backs carry biographical information, high school or college highlights, and statistics. The cards are unnumbered and checklisted below in alphabetical order. This set features the first card of William Gates, one of two players featured in the critically acclaimed 1995 documentary film Hoop Dreams.

COMPLETE SET (17) 6.00 15.00
1 Craig Aamot .40 1.00
2 Ron Curry .40 1.00
3 William Gates 1.50 4.00
star of the movie Hoop Dreams
4 Damon Key .40 1.00
5 Robb Logterman .40 1.00
6 Amal McCaskill .75 2.00
7 Jim McIlvaine 1.25 3.00
8 Tony Miller .20 .50
9 Kevin O'Neill CO .75 2.00
10 Ben Peavy .20 .50
11 Shannon Smith .20 .50
12 Jay Zulauf .40 1.00
13 Team Photo .60 1.50
14 Ron Curry .60 1.50
Jim McIlvaine
Damon Key
15 Building on a Great Tradition/(Team photo at construction site) .40 1.00
16 Bradley Center .20 .50
17 Sponsor Card .20 .50

1992-93 Marquette

This 17-card set was issued on 4 perforated strips. When the cards are separated, they measure the standard size. This set was sponsored by Cyganiak Planning Inc. The fronts feature color action player photos on a white background. The player's name is above the photo and the team and sponsor logos along with the player's position and jersey number are below. The backs carry the player's name, biographical information and career highlights in blue print on a white background. The cards are unnumbered and checklisted below in alphabetical order. Among the players in the set are NBA center Jim McIlvaine and William Gates, star of the acclaimed documentary Hoop Dreams.

COMPLETE SET (17) 5.00 12.00
1 Craig Aamot .40 1.00
2 Ron Curry .40 1.00
3 Roney Eford .40 1.00
4 William Gates 1.00 2.50
5 Damon Key .40 1.00
6 Robb Logterman .40 1.00
7 Amal McCaskill .60 1.50
8 Jim McIlvaine 1.00 2.50
9 Tony Miller .20 .50
10 Kevin O'Neill CO .75 2.00
11 Ben Peavy .20 .50
12 Adam Schabes .20 .50
13 Shannon Smith .20 .50
14 Dwaine Streater .20 .50
15 Jay Zulauf .40 1.00
16 Team Photo .20 .50
Roster
17 Sponsor Card .20 .50

1994-95 Marquette

Sponsored by Cyganiak Planning Inc., this 17-card set was issued on 4 perforated strips. When the cards are separated, they measure the standard size. The fronts feature color action player photos on a gold background. The player's name is above the photo and the team and sponsor logos are below. The backs carry the player's name, jersey number, biographical information and career highlights in blue print on a white background. The cards are unnumbered and checklisted below in alphabetical order. William Gates, featured in the movie Hoop Dreams, is included in this set.

COMPLETE SET (17) 5.00 12.00
1 Faisal Abraham .40 1.00
2 Chris Crawford .40 1.00
3 Mike Deane CO .30 .75
4 Roney Eford .40 1.00
5 William Gates .75 2.00
6 Aaron Hutchins .75 2.00
7 Abel Joseph .30 .75
8 Shane Littles .30 .75
9 Zack McCall .30 .75
10 Amal McCaskill .75 2.00
11 Tony Miller .30 .75
12 Anthony Pieper .40 1.00
13 Richard Shaw .30 .75
14 Dwaine Streater .30 .75
15 1969-70 Team Photo .40 1.00
1970 NIT Champions
16 Team Photo .40 1.00
1994-95 Roster
17 Sponsor Card .20 .50

1995-96 Marquette

Sponsored by Cyganiak Planning Inc., this 20-card set was issued on 4 perforated strips. When the cards are separated, they measure the standard size. The fronts feature color action player photos on a blue background. The player's name is above the photo and the team and sponsor logos are below. The backs carry the player's name, jersey number, biographical information and career highlights in blue print on a white background. The cards are unnumbered and checklisted below in alphabetical order.

COMPLETE SET (20) 5.00 12.00
1 Faisal Abraham .30 .75
2 Mike Bargen .30 .75
3 Chris Crawford .30 .75
4 Mike Deane CO .40 1.00
5 Roney Eford .40 1.00
6 Mark Harris .30 .75
7 Aaron Hutchins .75 2.00
8 Abel Joseph .30 .75
9 Jarrod Lovette .30 .75
10 Zack McCall .30 .75
11 Amal McCaskill .75 2.00
12 Anthony Pieper .40 1.00
13 John Polonowski .30 .75
14 Richard Shaw .30 .75
15 Dwaine Streater .30 .75
16 Team Photo .40 1.00
1995-96 Roster
17 Sponsor Card .20 .50
18 Sponsor Card .20 .50
19 Sponsor Card .20 .50
20 Sponsor Card .20 .50

2009-10 Marquette

COMPLETE SET (4) 4.00 10.00
1 Sheet 1 1.50 4.00
David Cubillan
Robert Frozena
Darius Johnson-Odom
Hank Raymonds
Spirit Card
2 Sheet 2 1.50 4.00
Buzz Williams
Dwight Buycks
Erik Williams
Al McGuire
Sixth Man
3 Sheet 3 2.00 5.00
Lazar Hayward
Jimmy Butler
Chris Otule
Youssoupha Mbao
Team Card
4 Sheet 4 1.50 4.00
Maurice Acker
Joseph Fulce
Junior Cadougan
Marquette Seniors
Pep Band

2011-12 Marquette

COMPLETE SET (4) 4.00 10.00
1 Sheet 1 1.50 4.00
Jae Crowder
Jamil Wilson
Derrick Wilson
Tony Benford
Pep Band
2 Sheet 2 1.50 4.00
Darius Johnson-Odom
Davante Gardner
Jake Thomas
Buzz Williams
Team Card
3 Sheet 3 1.50 4.00
Chris Otule
Jamail Jones
Todd Mayo
Scott Monarch
Sixth Man
4 Sheet 4 1.50 4.00
Junior Cadougan
Vander Blue
Juan Anderson
Aki Collins
Spirit Card

1984 Marshall Playing Cards

Produced by Triangle Productions, Inc., this All-Time Greats boxed-set of playing cards is reported to have been issued in conjunction with old-timer games. The set originally sold for 2.00 and could be purchased at the Marshall University bookstore. The cards measure approximately 2 1/4" by 3 1/2" and have rounded corners. The fronts feature black-and-white posed or action shots, with coach or player identification below the picture. The backs are green on white and display the Marshall University logo and the phrase All Time Greats.~ The cards are checklisted in playing card order by suits and numbers are assigned to Aces (1), Jacks (11), Queens (12), and Kings (13). The jokers are unnumbered and listed at the end.

COMP. FACT SET (54) 12.00 30.00
C1 Stewart Way CO .20 .50
C2 Jim Davidson .20 .50
C3 Tom Langfitt .20 .50
C4 Bill Hall .20 .50
C5 Bill Toothman .20 .50
C6 Gene James .20 .50
C7 Bob Koontz .20 .50
C8 Andy Tonkovich .20 .50
C9 Danny D'Antoni .40 1.00
C10 Paul Underwood .20 .50
C11 Walt Walowac .20 .50
C12 Cebe Price .20 .50
C13 John Milhoan .20 .50
D1 Ellis Johnson CO .20 .50
D2 Walt Walowac .20 .50
D3 George Stone .30 .75
D4 Charlie Slack .20 .50
D5 Mike D'Antoni 2.00 5.00
D6 Jules Rivlin .20 .50
D7 Danny D'Antoni .40 1.00
D8 Greg White .20 .50
D9 Ken Labanowski .20 .50
D10 Bob Burgess .20 .50
D11 Bob Allen .20 .50
D12 Leo Byrd .20 .50
D13 Hal Greer 2.00 5.00
H1 Stu Aberden CO .20 .50
H2 Stu Aberden CO .20 .50
(Same picture as H1)
H3 Bob Daniels CO .20 .50
H4 Bunny Gibson .30 .75
H5 Cebe Price .20 .50
H6 Carl Tacy CO .30 .75
H7 Stewart Way CO .20 .50
H8 Ellis Johnson CO .20 .50
H9 Cam Henderson CO .60 1.50
H10 Mike D'Antoni 2.00 5.00
H11 Bob Daniels CO .20 .50
H12 Jules Rivlin .20 .50
H13 Russell Lee .40 1.00
S1 Cam Henderson CO .60 1.50
S2 Ken Labanowski .20 .50
S3 Greg White .20 .50
S4 Randy Noll .20 .50
S5 Bob Redd .20 .50
S6 George Stone .30 .75
S7 Bunny Gibson .30 .75
S8 Bob Wright .20 .50
S9 Charlie Slack .20 .50
S10 Russell Lee .40 1.00
S11 Carl Tacy CO .30 .75
S12 Leo Byrd .20 .50
S13 Hal Greer 2.00 5.00
NNO Joker .20 .50
Marshall University
NNO Joker .20 .50
Triangle Productions

1988 Marshall Women

Originally a 20-card set sponsored by Ashland Oil, these standard-size cards were made available by Marshall University for a $20 donation to the Lady Herd basketball program. Two seasons later, a twenty-first card was issued, that of Lady Herd coach Judy Southard. The fronts display a mix of black-and-white or color action photos. The pictures are full-bleed and accented by a white picture frame. The Lady Herd logo and the year are printed on each front. On a white background in green print, the backs present a player profile or summary of the event commemorated. The cards are unnumbered and checklisted below in chronological order. The set includes a card of professional lady golfer Tammie Green, who was on the 1994 U.S. Solheim Cup team.

COMPLETE SET (21) 5.00 12.00
1 1907 Team Picture .40 1.00
2 Donna Lawson CO .40 1.00
Judy Southard CO
3 Beverly Duckwyler .20 .50
4 1971-72 Team .20 .50
5 Jody Lambert .20 .50
6 Brenda Dennis .20 .50
7 Agnes Wheeler .20 .50
8 Gullickson Hall Action .20 .50
9 Mary Lopez .20 .50
10 Stephanie Austin .40 1.00
Agnes Wheeler
Mary Lopez
Kim Williams
Kathy Baker
Donna Lawson CO
11 Tammie Green 1.25 3.00
12 Saundra Fullen .40 1.00
Thea Garland
Becky Williamson
Paula Hatten
Deanna Carter
13 Lisa Prunner .20 .50
14 Barb McConnell .20 .50
15 Tywands Abercrombie .40 1.00
Karla May
Karen Pelphrey
Debbie Van Liew
16 Karen Pelphrey .20 .50
17 Tammy Wiggins .20 .50
18 Chris Laslo .20 .50
19 The Challenge .20 .50
20 Kim Lewis .20 .50
21 Judy Southard CO .40 1.00

1988-89 Maryland

This set consists of 12 cards, measuring the standard card size 2 1/2" by 3 1/2". The company name of the sponsor, Group Health Association, appears in the right corner on the front of the card. The action color photo on the front is bordered on three sides by Maryland's colors (red and yellow), with the player's name, uniform number, classification, and position listed below the photo. The Terrapin logo in the lower left hand corner completes the front of the card. The back includes biographical information and a basketball tip. For convenience the cards are ordered and numbered below in alphabetical order. The set features first cards of future NBA players Jerrod Mustaf and Walt Williams.

COMPLETE SET (12) 6.00 15.00
1 Vincent Broadnax .30 .75
2 Dave Dickerson .30 .75
3 John Johnson SP 1.25 3.00
4 Matt Kaluzienski .30 .75
5 Mitch Kasoff .30 .75
6 Cedric Lewis .40 1.00
7 Jesse Martin .30 .75
8 Tony Massenburg 2.00 5.00
9 Jerrod Mustaf .75 2.00
10 Greg Nared SP 1.25 3.00
11 Bob Wade CO .40 1.00
12 Walt Williams 3.00 8.00

1989 McNeese State

This 16-card standard-size set was sponsored by the Behavioral Health Unit of Lake Charles Memorial Hospital, and the sponsor's logo appears at the bottom of both sides of the card. This set was produced by McDag Productions. The front features a color posed player photo, with the McNeese logo and player information in the upper corners. The back presents biographical information and "Tips from The Cowboys," which consist of mental health tips. Sports represented in this set include basketball (1-6, 9-12), softball (7), golf (8), and baseball (13-15). Card number 13 Steve Boulet was missing from a number of sets and is believed to be somewhat tougher to find than other cards in the set.

COMPLETE SET (16) 4.00 10.00
1 Kevin Williams BK .30 .75
2 Terry Griggley BK .20 .50
3 Tab Harris BK .20 .50
4 Chandra Davis BK .40 1.00
5 Tom McGrath BK .20 .50
6 Angie Perry BK .40 1.00
9 Michael Cutright BK .40 1.00
10 Anthony Pullard BK .60 1.50
11 Mark Thompson BK .20 .50
12 Kim Turner BK .20 .50

1992-93 Memphis State

This 15-card standard-size set features color action player photos bordered on the left or right edge by a blue stripe containing the words "Memphis State." The player's name appears in blue lettering on a white stripe at the bottom. The horizontal backs feature close-up player pictures with shadow box borders. The white background is printed with a profile of the player. The school logo and biographical information appear at the top. Reportedly less than 10,000 sets were produced.

COMPLETE SET (15) 5.00 12.00
1 Larry Finch CO .40 1.00
2 Kelvin Allen .20 .50
3 Anthony Douglas .20 .50
4 Anfernee Hardaway 3.00 8.00
5 Chris Haynes .20 .50
6 Leon Mitchell .20 .50
7 Marcus Nolan .20 .50
8 Billy Smith .20 .50
9 David Vaughn .75 2.00
10 Sidney Coles .20 .50
11 Jerrell Horne .20 .50
12 Rodney Newsom .40 1.00
13 Team Photo .75 2.00
14 The Pyramid .20 .50
15 Tom II (Mascot) .20 .50

1993 Memphis Sheriff Anfernee Hardaway

This one standard-size card was issued by the Millington County Police Departement and features Memphis State player Anfernee "Penny" Hardaway. The front features Hardaway in a "keep the dream" uniform and he is identified on the left. The back has vital statistics and a safety tip.

1 Anfernee Hardaway 3.00 8.00

1993-94 Memphis State

This 16-card standard-size set (2 1/2 by 3 1/2") has fronts composed of color action and posed player photos inset in gray borders. Below the photo are the player's name and position with the team logo to the left. The back has a color player head shot in the upper left. The player's number is in the upper right while the team logo, player's name and bio are centered at the top. Career highlights follow below. The cards are unnumbered and checklisted below in alphabetical order.

COMPLETE SET (16) 4.00 10.00
1 Larry Finch CO .40 1.00
2 David Vaughn .75 2.00
3 Jerrell Horne .20 .50
4 Leon Mitchell .20 .50
5 Sidney Coles .20 .50
6 Rob Forrest .20 .50
7 Jason Fox .20 .50
8 Rodney Newsom .40 1.00
9 Marcus Nolan .20 .50
10 Chris Garner .60 1.50
11 Deuce Ford .20 .50
12 Cedric Henderson .60 1.50
13 Johnny Miller .20 .50
14 Michael Simmons .20 .50
15 Jason Smith .20 .50
16 Justin Wimmer .20 .50

1994-95 Memphis State

Produced by The 7th Inning, this 17-card standard-size set features the 1994-95 University of Memphis men's basketball team (formerly Memphis State). The fronts show full-bleed color action photos. The player's name and number are printed vertically in blue on a white bar along the left edge. The bar intersects the school logo at the lower left corner. The horizontal backs carry player profile on the left and a color closeup photo on the right. The cards are unnumbered and checklisted below in alphabetical order. David Vaughn, drafted by the NBA in the first round, is included in this set.

COMPLETE SET (16) 5.00 12.00
1 Larry Finch CO .30 .75
2 Deuce Ford .20 .50
3 Rob Forrest .20 .50
4 Jason Fox .20 .50
5 Chris Garner .40 1.00
6 Cedric Henderson .40 1.00
7 Mingo Johnson .30 .75
8 Leon Mitchell .20 .50
9 Rodney Newsom .30 .75
10 Marcus Nolan .20 .50
11 Jason Smith .20 .50
12 David Vaughn .60 1.50
13 Michael Wilson .30 .75
14 Justin Wimmer .20 .50
15 Lorenzen Wright 2.50 6.00
16 Team Photo .30 .75

1993-94 Miami

Given away in four-card perforated strips at University of Miami games, these 20 cards measure approximately 2 1/2" by 3 5/8". The fronts feature color player action shots with black and green borders highlighted by orange basketballs. The player's name appears in orange lettering above the photo; his position and jersey number appear below the photo. The plain white backs carry the player's name, uniform number, height, weight, and hometown at the top, followed below by a bilingual description of his style of play. The Bumble Bee sponsor logo at the bottom rounds out the card. The cards are unnumbered and checklisted below in alphabetical order.

COMPLETE SET (20) 6.00 15.00
1 Will Davis .40 1.00
2 Adam Dusewicz .40 1.00
Chris Parker
Anthony Rosa
3 Steven Edwards .60 1.50
4 Alex Fraser .40 1.00
5 Steve Frazier .60 1.50
6 Michael Gardner .40 1.00
7 Leonard Hamilton CO .75 2.00
8 Tshombe High .40 1.00
9 Jamal Johnson .40 1.00
10 Pat Lawrence .40 1.00
11 Torey McCormick .40 1.00
12 Lorenzo Pearson .40 1.00
13 Constantin Popa .60 1.50
14 Steve Rich .60 1.50
15 Brad Timpf .40 1.00
16 Thad Fitzpatrick ACO .40 1.00
Scott Howard ACO
Mike Jaskulski ACO
17 Free Ticket Offer .20 .50
18 Free Ticket Offer .20 .50
19 Free Ticket Offer .20 .50
20 Checklist .20 .50

1994-95 Miami

Sponsored by Bumble Bee, this 20-card, unperforated sheet measures 10 1/2" by 18" and consists of five rows of four cards each. The first three cards in each row are player cards, while the fourth card is a "Buy One, Get One Free" ticket offer for a particular game. One row (or strip) of cards was given away at five different University of Miami games. On a black and orange card face, the fronts feature color action player shots with the player's name and uniform number in orange and green stencil lettering. The backs carry biography, player profile (in English and Spanish), and different answers to the question "What advice would you give young basketball players wanting to play at the collegiate level?" The cards are unnumbered and checklisted below in alphabetical order.

COMPLETE SET (20) 3.00 8.00
1 Chuck Barker .20 .50
David Isles
Jaime Waggoner
2 Will Davis .20 .50
3 Mitchell Dunn .20 .50
4 Steven Edwards .30 .75
5 Alex Fraser .20 .50
6 Steve Frazier .30 .75
7 Leonard Hamilton CO .60 1.50
8 Scott Howard ACO .08 .25
Mike Jaskulski ACO
Silas McKinnie ACO
9 Torey McCormick .20 .50
10 Kevin Norris .20 .50
11 Lorenzo Pearson .30 .75
12 Constantin Popa .30 .75
13 Steve Rich .30 .75
14 Anthony Rosa .20 .50
15 Brad Timpf .20 .50
16 Team Photo .30 .75
17 Free Ticket Offer CL .08 .25
18 Free Ticket Offer .08 .25
19 Free Ticket Offer .08 .25
20 Free Ticket Offer .08 .25

1997 Miami (OH) Cradle of Coaches

This set was produced by American Marketing Associates and features coaching greats from the University of Miami in Ohio. Football is the focus of the set although it also contains a few coaches from other sports as noted below. The cards are unnumbered and checklisted below in alphabetical order.

COMPLETE SET (19) 8.00 20.00
7 Wayne Embry BK .80 2.00
11 Darrell Hedric BK .40 1.00
17 Richard Shrider BK .40 1.00

1988-89 Michigan

This 16-card standard-size set was sponsored by Nike and distributed at Michigan Wolverine games during the 1988-89 season. The front features a color action photo, with a yellow border on the left side and purple borders on the right and below. The sponsor logo appears in the upper right corner, and player information is given in the bottom border. The back has biographical information and an anti-drug tip. The cards are unnumbered and are checklisted below in alphabetical order. The set features first cards of NBA players Sean Higgins, Terry Mills, Glen Rice, Rumeal Robinson, and Loy Vaught.

COMPLETE SET (16) 20.00 50.00
1 Demetrius Calip .75 2.00
2 Bill Frieder CO 1.50 4.00
3 Mike Griffin .40 1.00
4 Sean Higgins 1.50 4.00
5 Mark Hughes .40 1.00
6 Marc Koenig .40 1.00
7 Terry Mills 3.00 8.00
8 J.P. Oosterbaan .40 1.00
9 Rob Pelinka 1.50 4.00
10 Glen Rice 10.00 25.00
11 Eric Riley 1.50 4.00
12 Rumeal Robinson 3.00 7.00
13 Chris Seter .40 1.00
14 Kirk Taylor .40 1.00
15 Loy Vaught 4.00 10.00
16 James Voskuil 1.25 3.00

1989 Michigan

This 17-card set measures approximately 2 3/8" by 4" and is numbered on the back. The set features members of the 1989 Michigan Wolverines NCAA Championship basketball team. The front features a color photo, and the school and team name are printed in the school's colors (purple and yellow) on the top of the card. Below the photo appears the team logo (lower left hand corner) and the player's name. The back has biographical information (black lettering on white card stock). Future NBA players Sean Higgins, Terry Mills, Glen Rice, Rumeal Robinson, and Loy Vaught are featured in this set.

COMPLETE SET (17) 10.00 25.00
1 Steve Fisher CO 1.00 2.50
2 Brian Dutcher .30 .75
3 Kirk Taylor .30 .75
4 Chris Seter .30 .75
5 Glen Rice 3.00 8.00
6 Rob Pelinka 1.00 2.50
7 Rumeal Robinson 1.25 3.00
8 Terry Mills 1.25 3.00
9 Demetrius Calip .60 1.50
10 James Voskuil .60 1.50
11 Loy Vaught 1.50 4.00
12 J.P. Oosterbaan .30 .75
13 Sean Higgins .75 2.00
14 Marc Koenig .30 .75
15 Mark Hughes .30 .75
16 Eric Riley .75 2.00
17 Mike Griffin .30 .75

1991 Michigan

This 56-card multi-sport standard-size set was issued by College Classics. The fronts feature a mix of color or black and white player photos. This set features a card of Gerald Ford, center for the Wolverine football squad from 1932-34. Ford autographed 200 of his cards, one of which was to be included in each of the 200 cases of 50 sets. The Ford autographs were printed on linen card stock, feature a hand serial number on the front and have a different player image than card #21. A letter of authenticity (containing a matching serial number) on Gerald Ford stationery accompaned each Ford autographed card. Some Ford autographs, also on the linen stock, surfaced later missing the serial numbering. The cards are unnumbered and we have checklisted them below according to alphabetical order.

COMPLETE SET (56) 6.00 15.00
5 Marty Bodnar BK .02 .10
7 M.C. Burton BK .02 .10
15 Diane Dietz BK .02 .10
27 Phil Hubbard BK .30 .75
36 Tim McCormick BK .08 .25
43 Richard Rellford BK .02 .10
45 Cazzie Russell BK .30 .75
52 Rudy Tomjanovich BK .60 1.50

1992-93 Michigan

This 15-card set measures the standard size (2 1/2" by 3 1/2") and features color action player photos bordered on one side by a navy blue stripe containing the word "Michigan." The cards were produced by College Classics and were originally available from the M Den at Yost and Crisler Arenas for around 7.00. The player's name appears in yellow print on a white bar at the bottom. The horizontal backs are white and display a shadow bordered close-up picture, the player's name, and a player profile. The cards are numbered on the back. This set contains the cards of Michigan's "Fab Five", Juwan Howard, Ray Jackson, Jimmy King, Jalen Rose, and Chris Webber.

COMPLETE SET (15) 5.00 12.00
1 Steve Fisher CO .40 1.00
2 Jason Bossard .20 .50
3 Juwan Howard 1.25 3.00
4 Eric Riley .30 .75
5 Jalen Rose 1.50 4.00
6 Michael Talley .30 .75
7 James Voskuil .30 .75
8 Chris Webber 2.50 6.00
9 Ray Jackson .40 1.00
10 Jimmy King .40 1.00
11 Rob Pelinka .40 1.00
12 Leon Derricks .20 .50
13 Dugan Fife .30 .75
14 Checklist .20 .50
15 Sean Dobbins .20 .50

1990-91 Michigan State Collegiate Collection 20

This 20-card standard-size set was produced by Collegiate Collection and features the 1990-91 Michigan State Spartan basketball team. The fronts display color action player photos, bordered in white and green, and with the corners of the pictures cut off. In green print on a white background, the backs have biography, statistics, and player profile. This set features an early card of NBA guard Steve Smith.

COMPLETE SET (20) 8.00 20.00
1 Jud Heathcote CO 2.00 5.00
2 Matt Hofkamp .30 .75
3 Parish Hickman .60 1.50
4 Matt Steigenga .60 1.50
5 Dwayne Stephens .30 .75
6 Jon Zulauf .30 .75
7 Shawn Respert 2.00 5.00
8 Jeff Casler .30 .75
9 Steve Smith 5.00 12.00
10 Andy Penick .30 .75
11 Mark Montgomery .60 1.50
12 Kris Weshinskey .30 .75
13 Jack Breslin Center .30 .75
14 Spartan Captains 2.00 5.00
Steve Smith
Matt Steigenga
15 Brian Gregory CO .30 .75
16 Jim Boylen CO .30 .75
17 Stan Joplin CO .40 1.00
18 Tom Izzo CO 3.00 8.00
19 Mike Peplowski 1.00 2.50
20 Team Photo 1.00 2.50

1990-91 Michigan State Collegiate Collection Promos

This ten-card standard size set features some of the great athletes from Michigan State History. Most of the cards in the set feature an action photograph on the front of the card along with either statistical or biographical information on the back of the card. Since this set involves more than one sport we have put a two-letter abbreviation to indicate the sport played.

COMPLETE SET (10) 1.50 4.00
4 Magic Johnson BK 1.00 2.50
9 Gregory Kelser BK .20 .50
10 Kip Miller HK .10 .30

1990-91 Michigan State Collegiate Collection 200

This 200-card standard-size set was produced by Collegiate Collection. The fronts feature black and white shots for earlier players or color shots for later players, with borders in the team's colors white and green. Since most cards are football, we've noted below which cards feature other sports. Although some players were famous in others sports, like Kirk Gibson and Steve Garvey, they do have football cards in this set.

COMPLETE SET (200) 6.00 15.00
46 Jerry West .05 .15
62 Amo Bessone CO BK .05 .15
101 Michael Robinson BK .05 .15
102 Jack Quiggle BK .05 .15
103 Robert Anderegg BK .05 .15
112 Gregory Kelser BK .07 .20
119 Kevin Willis BK .08 .25
123 Jay Vincent BK .05 .15
128 Johnny Green BK .08 .25
131 Magic Johnson BK .40 1.00
132 Gregory Kelser BK .07 .20
133 Magic Johnson BK .40 1.00
140 Scott Skiles BK .08 .25
148 Sam Vincent BK .05 .15
152 Scott Skiles BK .08 .25
159 Jud Heathcote CO BK .08 .25
161 Pete Newell CO BK .08 .25
163 Kevin Willis BK .08 .25
170 Ralph Simpson BK .07 .20
171 Terry Furlow BK .05 .15
178 Jud Heathcote CO BK .08 .25
179 Kevin Willis BK .08 .25
182 Magic Johnson BK .40 1.00
186 Magic Johnson BK .40 1.00
189 Magic Johnson BK .40 1.00
191 Gus Ganakas .05 .15
192 Jay Vincent BK .05 .15
194 Magic Johnson BK .40 1.00
198 Sam Vincent BK .05 .15
199 Terry Donnelly BK .05 .15

1998-99 Michigan State Legends

This set, features leading players in Michigan State history. The full bleed cards feature a player's photo on one side with a solid border in Michigan State's colors on the other side. The backs feature player information about the career at Michigan State. Since these cards are unnumbered, we have sequenced them in alphabetical order.

COMPLETE SET (36) 8.00 20.00
1 Bob Anderegg .30 .75
2 Chet Aubuchon .30 .75
3 Rickey Ayala .30 .75
4 Bob Chapman .30 .75
5 Bill Curtis .30 .75
6 Al Ferrari .30 .75
7 Terry Furlow .40 1.00
8 Pete Gent .40 1.00
9 Johnny Green .40 1.00
10 Lindsay Hairston .30 .75
11 Tom Izzo CO 1.25 3.00
12 Darryl Johnson .30 .75
13 Magic Johnson 3.00 8.00
14 Gregory Kelser .75 2.00
15 Bill Kilgore .30 .75
16 Lee Lafayette .30 .75
17 Julius McCoy .30 .75
18 Mark Montgomery .30 .75
19 Lance Olson .30 .75
20 Mike Peplowski .30 .75
21 Jack Quiggle .30 .75
22 Shawn Respert .60 1.50
23 Mike Robinson .30 .75
24 Steve Smith 1.00 2.50
25 Ralph Simpson .40 1.00
26 Scott Skiles .75 2.00
27 Eric Snow .75 2.00
28 Matt Steigenga .30 .75
29 Jay Vincent .40 1.00
30 Sam Vincent .60 1.50
31 Horace Walker .30 .75
32 Stan Washington .30 .75
33 Title Card .30 .75
34 Team CL .30 .75
35 Breslin Center .30 .75
36 Jenison Field House .30 .75

2003 Michigan State TK Legacy

COMPLETE SET (27) 12.00 30.00
B1 Greg Kelser BK .50 1.25
B2 Brad Van Pelt BK .50 1.25
B3 Mike Brkovich BK .40 1.00
B4 Ron Charles BK .50 1.25
B5 Gary Ganakas BK .40 1.00
BC1 Jud Heathcote CO BK .50 1.25
BC2 Gus Ganakas CO BK .40 1.00

2003 Michigan State TK Legacy All-Americans

COMPLETE SET (6) 7.50 15.00
STATED ODDS 1:14
BAA1 Greg Kelser BK .75 2.00

2003 Michigan State TK Legacy Autographs

OVERALL AUTO STATED ODDS 1:1
SB1 Greg Kelser BK 6.00 15.00
SB2 Mike Brkovich BK 6.00 15.00
SB3 Ron Charles BK 6.00 15.00
SB4 Gary Ganakas BK 6.00 15.00
SB5 Jud Heathcote BK 6.00 15.00
SB6 Gus Ganakas BK 6.00 15.00
SB7 Brad Van Pelt BK 6.00 15.00

2003 Michigan State TK Legacy Historical Links Autographs

DOUBLE AUTO STATED ODDS 1:31
TRIPLE AUTO STATED ODDS 1:100
HL3 J.Heathcote 20.00 40.00
G.Kelser BK/200

2003 Michigan State TK Legacy National Champions Autographs

STATED ODDS 1:5
1979A Greg Kelser BK 7.50 15.00
1979B Jud Heathcote BK 7.50 15.00
1979C Mike Brkovich BK 7.50 15.00
1979D Ron Charles BK 7.50 15.00

2003 Michigan State TK Legacy Retired Numbers

STATED ODDS 1:38
STATED PRINT RUN 300 SER.#'d SETS
BRN1 Greg Kelser BK 1.50 4.00

1991-92 Minnesota

Sponsored by Hardee's restaurants, this 17-card standard-size set features posed and action color player photos on an orange-yellow card face. The picture is offset, and the player's name runs down the left edge of the card. The sponsor logo appears at the bottom. The backs carry biographical information and player profile within an orange-yellow outlined box. The cards are unnumbered and checklisted below in alphabetical order.

COMPLETE SET (17) 6.00 15.00
1 Randy Carter .30 .75
2 Chris Clark .20 .50
3 David Grim .30 .75
4 Clem Haskins CO .60 1.50
5 Dana Jackson .20 .50
6 Chad Kolander .30 .75
7 Jon Laster .20 .50
8 Voshon Lenard 3.00 8.00
9 Bob Martin .75 2.00
10 Arriel McDonald .60 1.50
11 Josh Nichols .20 .50
12 Ernest Nzigamasabo .20 .50
13 Townsend Orr .30 .75
14 Robert Roe .20 .50
15 Nate Tubbs .20 .50
16 Jayson Walton .30 .75
17 Ryan Wolf .20 .50

1992-93 Minnesota

Sponsored by the University of Minnesota's Department of Men's Intercollegiate Athletics, this 17-card set measures the standard size and features color action player photos. A gray border stripe at the top contains the words "University of Minnesota" while a bright yellow bar near the bottom is printed in red with the player's name. The horizontal backs display a small, close-up player picture with a yellow shadow border. The card face is white and includes player profile information. The player's name appears at the top right in burgundy lettering.

COMPLETE SET (17) 4.00 10.00
1 Clem Haskins CO .60 1.50
2 Milton Barnes ACO .20 .50
Dan Kosmoski ACO
Dave Thorson ACO
3 Kevin Baker .20 .50
4 Randy Carter .30 .75
5 David Grim .30 .75
6 Dana Jackson .20 .50
7 Chad Kolander .30 .75
8 Voshon Lenard 1.50 4.00
9 Arriel McDonald .30 .75
10 Ernest Nzigamasabo .20 .50
11 Townsend Orr .30 .75
12 Robert Roe .20 .50
13 Nate Tubbs .20 .50
14 Jayson Walton .30 .75
15 David Washington .20 .50
16 Trevor Winter .20 .50
17 Ryan Wolf .20 .50

1993-94 Minnesota

The 1993-94 University of Minnesota set consists of 18 standard-size cards. The set was produced by Phipps Sports Marketing. The team color-bordered fronts feature a mix of posed and action color photos. Along the wider left border are the words "Golden Gophers" in simulated gold lettering. The player's name appears in one corner and the school logo is in another. The horizontal backs are also bordered in team colors and carry a black-and-white head shot at the upper left. The player's biography, profile, and statistics are printed on a ghosted cartoon of the team mascot. The cards are unnumbered and checklisted below in alphabetical order. There have been reports that the Lenard card may have been reprinted.

COMPLETE SET (18) 4.00 10.00
1 Kevin Baker .20 .50
2 Randy Carter .30 .75
3 Hosea Crittenden .20 .50
4 David Grim .30 .75
5 Clem Haskins CO .60 1.50
6 Chad Kolander .30 .75
7 Voshon Lenard 1.25 3.00
8 Arriel McDonald .30 .75
9 Ernest Nzigamasabo .20 .50
10 Townsend Orr .30 .75
11 John Thomas .75 2.00
12 Jayson Walton .30 .75
13 David Washington .20 .50
14 Sean Whitlock .20 .50
15 Trevor Winter .20 .50
16 Ryan Wolf .20 .50
17 1993 NIT Champions .30 .75
Milton Barnes ACO
Dan Kosmoski ACO
Dave Thorson ACO
18 Title Card .20 .50

1994-95 Minnesota

This 17-card set of the University of Minnesota Basketball Team measures the standard size and is sponsored by Hardee's. The fronts feature action color photos with red variegated borders. The team name, player's name, position, and team logo are printed in the wider left border. The backs carry biography, profile, and statistics. The cards are unnumbered and checklisted below in alphabetical order.

COMPLETE SET (17) 3.00 8.00
1 Hosea Crittenden .20 .50
2 David Grim .30 .75
3 Eric Harris .20 .50
4 Clem Haskins CO .60 1.50
5 Sam Jacobson .75 2.00
6 Chad Kolander .30 .75
7 Voshon Lenard 1.00 2.50
8 Townsend Orr .30 .75
9 John Thomas .60 1.50
10 Jayson Walton .30 .75
11 Micah Watkins .20 .50
12 Darrell Whaley .20 .50
13 Trevor Winter .20 .50
14 Ryan Wolf .20 .50
15 Williams Arena/(The Barn) .20 .50
16 Coaching Staff .20 .50
Milton Barnes ACO
Larry Davis ACO
Bill Brown ACO
17 Title Card .20 .50

1996-97 Minnesota

This 17-card standard size set was produced by Collect-A-Sport for the 1996-97 Gophers basketball team and was sponsored by Coca Cola. The fronts have full color player action photographs inside a border that is maroon on the left half, and white on the right. The players name and jersey number appear on the top right hand corner of the card. Minnesota's logo is in maroon and white in the bottom left corner, and a Coca Cola logo is "cut" into the photo in the middle of the right side. The backs give the player's biography, Minnesota statistics and are mostly white with some maroon. A large maroon "M" appears in the middle along with the words "Big Ten Conference." The cards are unnumbered and listed below in alphabetical order.

COMPLETE SET (17) 9.00 18.00
1 Russ Archambault .20 .50
2 Eric Harris .20 .50
3 Bobby Jackson 4.00 10.00
4 Sam Jacobson .60 1.50
5 Courtney James .30 .75
6 Quincy Lewis .75 2.00
7 Kevin Lodge .20 .50
8 Kyle Sanden .20 .50
9 Aaron Stauber .20 .50
10 Jason Stanford .20 .50
11 Jermaine Stanford .20 .50
12 Miles Tarver .20 .50
13 Charles Thomas .30 .75
14 John Thomas .60 1.50
15 Trevor Winter .20 .50
16 Coaching Staff .20 .50
Bill Brown ACO
Hosea Crittenden SACO
Charles Cunningham
Larry Davis ACO
Brent Haskins AIDE
Clem Haskins CO
17 Title Card CL .30 .75

1984-85 Minnesota-Duluth

Measuring 2 1/2" by 3 1/2", this 20-card set features players from the men's basketball team. The fronts feature color photos, with a player action shot, the mascot, and the player's name, number and position. The backs feature vitals and player information. The cards are numbered.

COMPLETE SET (20) 6.00 15.00
1 David Thompson .40 1.00
2 Todd Leyse .40 1.00
3 Rich Hirstein .40 1.00
4 Alan Wimes .40 1.00
5 Todd Lind .40 1.00
6 Kraig Erickson .40 1.00
7 Jerry Brockhaus .40 1.00
8 Jeff Guidinger .40 1.00
9 John Podominick .40 1.00
10 Tom Hutton .40 1.00
11 Kendall Kelly .40 1.00
12 Tod Kowalczyk .40 1.00
13 Robby Peterson .40 1.00
14 David Asplund .40 1.00
15 Bernie Lindner .40 1.00
Student Asst. Coach
16 Dale Race .40 1.00
Head Coach
17 Butch Koronen ACO .40 1.00
Chris Neumann ACO
Bill DeVinney - TR
18 U.M.D. Bulldog Team Photo .40 1.00
19 David Thompson IA .40 1.00
20 Alan Wimes IA .40 1.00

1985-86 Minnesota-Duluth

Measuring 2 1/2" by 3 1/2", this 18-card set features players from the men's basketball team. The fronts feature color photos, with a player action shot, a posed shot in a circle, and the player's name, number and position. The backs feature vitals and player information. The cards are numbered.

COMPLETE SET (18) 6.00 15.00
1 Kendall Kelly .40 1.00
2 Bernie Lindner .40 1.00
3 Jerry Brockhaus .40 1.00
4 Lonnie Schock .40 1.00
5 Tom Hutton .40 1.00
6 Dave Asplund .40 1.00
7 Jeff Vandenberg .40 1.00
8 Tod Kowalczyk .40 1.00
9 Jeff Guidinger .40 1.00
10 Steve Geels .40 1.00
11 Rich Hirstein .40 1.00
12 Jim Olson .40 1.00
13 Alan Wimes .40 1.00
14 David Thompson .40 1.00
15 Jim Hill .40 1.00
16 Dale Race CO .40 1.00
17 Butch Kuronen ACO .40 1.00
18 Cheerleaders .40 1.00

1985-86 Minnesota-Duluth Women

Measuring 2 1/2" by 3 1/2", this 18-card set features players from the women's basketball team. The fronts feature color photos, with a player action shot, a posed shot in a circle, and the player's name, number and position. The backs feature vitals and player information. The cards are numbered.

COMPLETE SET (18) 8.00 20.00
1 85-86 UMD Team Photo .60 1.50
2 Mary Zgonc .60 1.50
3 Brenda Kuczmarski .60 1.50
4 Julie Hay .60 1.50
5 Mary Hannula .60 1.50
6 Lori Ogren .60 1.50
7 Carmen Kuntz .60 1.50
8 Suzanne Peterson .60 1.50
9 Denise Holm .60 1.50
10 Sarah Halsey .60 1.50
11 Laura Lackner .60 1.50
12 Mindy Boorman .60 1.50
13 Lisa Muehlbauer .60 1.50
14 Carolyn Neumann .60 1.50
15 Sue Anderson .60 1.50
16 Chris Beal .60 1.50
17 Lisa Bogatzki .60 1.50
18 Bonnie Jacobon MG .60 1.50
Amy Jaeger - ACO
Dee Dee Schreier - TR
Karen Stromme - CO

1988-89 Missouri

This 16-card standard-size set of Missouri Tigers was sponsored by Kodak, KMIZ-17 TV, and Columbia Photo. The cards were originally issued in four-card sheets. The front features a color photo, with borders above and below in the school's colors (black and yellow). The player's name, uniform number, classification, and position appear below the picture, with a tiger pawprint in the lower left hand corner. Biographical information and "tips for better sports pictures" are provided on the card backs. The first three panels of cards were given out at games between Missouri and Oklahoma State (January 21), Nebraska (February 19), and Colorado. The final panel was available at Columbia Photo and Video sometime after March 4. For convenience the cards are ordered and numbered alphabetically by player's name. The set features the first cards of NBA players Anthony Peeler and Doug Smith.

COMPLETE SET (16) 15.00 40.00
1 Nathan Buntin .75 2.00
2 Derrick Chievous PRO 1.50 4.00
3 Greg Church .75 2.00
4 Jamal Coleman .75 2.00
5 Jim Horton .75 2.00
6 Byron Irvin 1.50 4.00
7 Gary Leonard 1.50 4.00
8 John McIntyre .75 2.00
9 Anthony Peeler 4.00 10.00
10 Mike Sandbothe .75 2.00
11 Doug Smith 1.50 4.00
12 Norm Stewart CO 2.00 5.00
13 Steve Stipanovich 1.50 4.00
14 Jon Sundvold PRO 1.50 4.00
15 Bradd Sutton .75 2.00
16 Mike Wawrzyniak .75 2.00

1989-90 Missouri

This 16-card standard-size set was originally issued on three four-card sheets and sponsored by Kodak, Jiffy Lube, and Columbia Photo and Video. The front has an action color photo, with borders in the school's colors (yellow and black). The player's name, classification, and position appear below the card, with a tiger pawprint in the lower left hand corner. The back has biographical information and a tip for better sports pictures. For convenience the cards are ordered and numbered alphabetically by player's name. The set features cards of NBA players Anthony Peeler and Doug Smith.

COMPLETE SET (16) 10.00 25.00
1 Nathan Buntin 22 .40 1.00
2 John Burns 33 .40 1.00
3 Jamal Coleman 32 .40 1.00
4 Lee Coward 4 .40 1.00
5 Larry Drew 1.25 3.00
6 Travis Ford 5 .75 2.00
7 Chris Heller 41 .75 2.00
8 Jim Horton 13 .40 1.00
9 John McIntyre 23 .40 1.00
10 Anthony Peeler 44 3.00 8.00
11 Todd Satalowich 54 .40 1.00
12 Doug Smith 34 1.25 3.00
13 Norm Stewart CO 1.50 4.00
14 Steve Stipanovich 1.25 3.00
15 Bradd Sutton 35 .40 1.00
16 Jeff Warren 45 .40 1.00

1990-91 Missouri

This 16-card set was issued in four four-card strips and given away at four non-conference games last season. The standard-size cards are similar in design to the previous year's issue, with color action photos bordered in the school's colors (yellow and black). One difference is that "Missouri Tigers" appears in white rather than yellow lettering. The backs contain biographical information and Missouri Basketball Fun Facts. The cards are unnumbered and checklisted below in alphabetical order. The set features cards of NBA players Anthony Peeler and Doug Smith as well as the first cards of Melvin Booker and Jevon Crudup.

COMPLETE SET (16) 8.00 20.00
1 Melvin Booker 1.25 3.00
2 John Brown .75 2.00
Tiger of the Past
3 John Burns .40 1.00
4 Jamal Coleman .40 1.00
5 Jevon Crudup .75 2.00
6 Derek Dunham .40 1.00
7 Lamont Frazier .40 1.00
8 Jed Frost .40 1.00
9 Chris Heller .40 1.00
10 Jim Horton .40 1.00
11 Anthony Peeler 2.50 6.00
12 Doug Smith .75 2.00
13 Reggie Smith .40 1.00
14 Willie Smith .75 2.00
Tiger of the Past
15 Norm Stewart CO 1.25 3.00
16 Jeff Warren .40 1.00

1991-92 Missouri

This 16-card set was sponsored by Coca-Cola, Farm Bureau Insurance, and Columbia Photo. The production run was reportedly limited to 9,000 sets, with eight cards per perforated sheet. One sheet was given away at the February 23 home game against Oklahoma State, while the second sheet was given out at the March 4 game against Oklahoma. In total, 7,000 sets were distributed at home games; the rest of the sets were given to the sponsors. The standard size (2 1/2" by 3 1/2") cards have on the fronts color action photos enclosed by white and black borders, with the words "Mizzou Tigers" inscribed above the picture. The player's name appears beneath the picture, with his jersey number in a basketball at the lower right corner. The backs have biographical information, player profile, and "Tips for Better Sports Pictures." The cards are unnumbered and checklisted below in alphabetical order. The key card in the set is Anthony Peeler.

COMPLETE SET (16) 9.00 18.00
1 Kim Anderson .60 1.50
Tiger of the Past
2 Melvin Booker .75 2.00
3 John Burns .30 .75
4 Jamal Coleman .30 .75
5 Jevon Crudup .60 1.50
6 Derek Dunham .30 .75
7 Lamont Frazier .30 .75
8 Ricky Frazier .60 1.50
Tiger of the Past
9 Jed Frost .30 .75
10 Chris Heller .30 .75
11 Steve Horton .30 .75
12 Anthony Peeler 1.50 4.00
13 Chris Smith .30 .75
14 Reggie Smith .30 .75
15 Norm Stewart CO .75 2.00
16 Jeff Warren .30 .75

1992-93 Missouri

This 16-card set was sponsored by Coca-Cola, KOMU-TV, Columbia Photo, and the University of Missouri-Columbia Hearnes Center. The set was issued in four-card perforated strips. The fronts of these standard-size cards display color action photos framed by white and black borders, with the words "Mizzou Tigers" printed above the picture. The player's name appears beneath the picture with his jersey number in a basketball at the lower right corner. The backs carry biographical information, a player profile, and "Tips for Better Sports Pictures." The card are unnumbered and checklisted below in alphabetical order.

COMPLETE SET (16) 5.00 12.00
1 Mark Atkins .30 .75
2 Melvin Booker .75 2.00
3 John Burns .30 .75
4 Jevon Crudup .60 1.50
5 Derek Dunham .30 .75
6 Marlo Finner .30 .75
7 Lamont Frazier .30 .75
8 Jed Frost .30 .75
9 Chris Heller .30 .75
10 Steve Horton .30 .75
11 Derrick Johnson .30 .75
12 Reggie Smith .30 .75
13 Norm Stewart CO .75 2.00
14 Jon Sundvold .60 1.50
15 Chip Walther .30 .75
16 Jeff Warren .30 .75

1993-94 Missouri

This 16-card set was sponsored by Modern Business Systems, Inc. and Ford. The perforated set was issued in two eight-card strips. The fronts feature color action player photos framed by a thin, yellow, white and black border. The words "Mizzou Tigers" are printed above the picture with the player's name and jersey number below. The white backs carry biographical information and player profile with the sposors' logos at the bottom. The cards are unnumbered and checklisted below in alphabetical order.

COMPLETE SET (16) 5.00 12.00
1 Mark Atkins .30 .75
2 Melvin Booker .75 2.00
3 Jevon Crudup .60 1.50
4 Marlo Finner .30 .75
5 Lamont Frazier .30 .75
6 Jed Frost .30 .75
7 Derek Grimm .30 .75
8 Chris Heller .30 .75
9 Derrick Johnson .30 .75
10 Paul O'Liney .30 .75
11 Reggie Smith .30 .75
12 Norm Stewart CO .60 1.50
13 Jason Sutherland .30 .75
14 Kelly Thames .60 1.50
15 Chip Walther .30 .75
16 Julian Winfield .60 1.50

1995-96 Missouri

This 16-card set was sponsored by Pizza Hut, Subway, and Radio Station 96.7 KCMQ. The perforated set was issued in two six-card sheets and one four-card strip. The fronts feature color action player photos framed by a thin yellow, white, and black borders. The words "Mizzou Tigers" are printed above the picture with the player's name and jersey number below. The white backs carry biographical information and player profile with sponsors' logos at the bottom. The cards are unnumbered and checklisted below in alphabetical order.

COMPLETE SET (16) 4.00 10.00
1 Danny Allouche .30 .75
2 Scott Combs .30 .75
3 Desmond Ferguson .30 .75
4 Derek Grimm .30 .75
5 Sammie Haley .40 1.00
6 Simeon Haley .40 1.00
7 Monte Hardge .30 .75
8 Kendrick Moore .30 .75
9 L. Dee Murdock .30 .75
10 Dustin Reeve .30 .75
11 Norm Stewart CO .60 1.50
12 Jason Sutherland .30 .75
13 Corey Tate .30 .75
14 Kelly Thames .40 1.00
15 Chip Walther .30 .75
16 Julian Winfield .40 1.00

1989-90 Montana Smokey

COMPLETE SET (12) 5.00 10.00
1 Cheryl Brandell .40 1.00
Women's basketball
5 K.C. McGowan .40 1.00
Men's basketball
6 Lisa McLeod .40 1.00
Women's basketball
7 Jean McNulty .40 1.00
Women's basketball
9 John Reckard .40 1.00
Men's basketball
10 Tony Reed .40 1.00
Men's basketball
12 Wayne Tinkle .40 1.00
Men's basketball

1992-93 Montana

Sponsored by Taco Bell, these 20 standard-size cards feature color player action shots on their white-bordered fronts. The player's name, position, and the sponsor logo appear in black lettering within the wide lower margin. The black-and-white backs carry the player's name and uniform number at the top, followed below by his height, position, biography, and college highlights. The cards are unnumbered and checklisted below in alphabetical order.

COMPLETE SET (20) 6.00 15.00
1 Guy Bonner .30 .75
2 Nate Covill .30 .75
3 Brandon Dade .30 .75
4 Travis DeCuire .30 .75
5 Israel Evans .30 .75
6 Don Hedge .30 .75
7 Don Holst ACO .30 .75
8 Gary Kane .30 .75
9 Matt Kempfert .60 1.50
10 Josh Lacheur .30 .75
11 Jeremy Lake .40 1.00
12 Kevin McLeod ACO .30 .75
13 Paul Perkins .30 .75
14 Shawn Samuelson .60 1.50
15 Chris Spoja .40 1.00
16 Blaine Taylor CO .30 .75
17 Scott Tharp .30 .75
18 Kirk Walker .30 .75
19 Leroy Washington ACO .30 .75
20 Title Card .30 .75

1997 Montana

COMPLETE SET (23) 15.00 25.00
18 Brandon Dade BK .50 1.25
19 Brent Smith BK .50 1.25
20 Chris Spoja BK .50 1.25
21 Kirk Walker BK .50 1.25
22 Greta Koss WBK .50 1.25

1990-91 Montana State

This 16-card set was sponsored by the USDA Forest Service and other agencies. The cards measure slightly shorted than standard size (2 1/2" by 3 7/16"). The school name appears above the picture while the player's name appears beneath it. The backs carry player information, biographical data, and cartoons depicting a fire safety message. The cards are unnumbered and checklisted below in alphabetical order within sex; the men's team are listed as card numbers 1-8 and the women's team are listed as card numbers 9-16.

COMPLETE SET (16) 6.00 15.00
1 Willard Dean .75 2.00
2 Todd Dickson .60 1.50
3 Chris Herriford .60 1.50
4 Allen Lightfoot .60 1.50
5 Johnny Mack .75 2.00
6 Dave Moritz .60 1.50
7 Johnny Perkins .75 2.00
8 Greg Powell .60 1.50
9 Alaina Bauer .40 1.00
10 Debbie Cober .40 1.00
11 Sarah Flock .40 1.00
12 Sandy Neiss and .60 1.50
Susan Neiss
13 Terri Ross .40 1.00
14 Judy Spoelstra CO .60 1.50
15 Karen Weeter .40 1.00
16 Anna Wheery .40 1.00

1990-91 Murray State

This 16-card set was sponsored by The Pro Image, a sporting goods store in Paducah, Kentucky. The production run was reportedly limited to 2,000 sets, with only 1,000 of these being distributed as sets. The other 1,000 sets were given away as singles. Moreover, 45 uncut and numbered sheets were produced. The cards measure approximately 2 1/4" by 3 1/4" and are printed on thin card stock. The fronts feature black and white action or posed photos enclosed by full-bleed canary yellow borders. "Murray State Basketball," the player's name, and the sponsor logo appear on the front in blue ink. The horizontally oriented backs have biography, statistics, and player profile. The cards are numbered in the upper right corner.

COMPLETE SET (16) 5.00 12.00
1 Paul King .20 .50
2 Doug Gold .20 .50
3 Donald Overstreet .20 .50
4 Greg Coble .20 .50
5 John Jackson .20 .50
6 Popeye Jones 2.00 5.00
7 Donnie Langhi .20 .50
8 Terry Birdsong .20 .50
9 Scott Adams .20 .50
10 Frank Allen .20 .50
11 Scott Sivills .20 .50
12 Cedric Gumm .40 1.00
13 Jerry Wilson .20 .50
14 Jason Karem .20 .50
15 Coaching Staff .40 1.00
Steve Newton CO
Craig Morris ACO
James Holland ACO
16 Team Photo .60 1.50

1991-92 Murray State

This 17-card set was sponsored by The Pro Image, a sporting goods store in Paducah, Kentucky. The production run was limited to 1,500 sets, with 1,000 of these being distributed as sets and the rest as singles. Moreover, 35 uncut sheets were produced. The cards measure 2 1/2" by 3 1/2" and are printed on thin card stock. The fronts feature black and white action photos enclosed by white borders. The team name "Racers" appears in a blue diagonal toward the bottom of the card; the stripe intersects a basketball icon, which has the player's uniform number. The sponsor logo and player's name round out the card face and are printed on a yellow background immediately below the stripe. The backs have biography and player profile on a white background enclosed by blue borders. The cards are numbered on the back.

COMPLETE SET (17) 4.00 10.00
1 Scott Adams .20 .50
2 Popeye Jones 1.50 4.00
3 Frank Allen .40 1.00
4 Maurice Cannon .40 1.00
5 Jamal Evans .20 .50
6 Darren Hill .20 .50
7 Michael Hunt .20 .50
8 Rafeal Peterson .20 .50
9 Scott Sivills .20 .50
10 Bo Walden .20 .50
11 Craig Gray .20 .50
12 Cedric Gumm .40 1.00
13 Jerry Wilson .20 .50
14 Scott Edgar CO .20 .50
15 Ken Roth ACO .20 .50
16 Eddie Fields ACO .20 .50
17 Team Photo .60 1.50

1992-93 Murray State

Sponsored by The Pro Image (Paducah, Kentucky), this 17-card standard-size set features black-and-white action player photos with thin royal blue borders. The pictures are set on a white card face and are accented by an orange-yellow stripe down the left side. The stripe carries the player's name and the school and team name in royal blue print. The backs display biographical information on a yellow panel and a career summary on the remaining white portion. The cards are unnumbered and checklisted below in alphabetical order.

COMPLETE SET (17) 3.00 8.00
1 Frank Allen .30 .75
2 Tony Bailey .20 .50
3 Marcus Brown .75 2.00
4 Lawrence Bussell .20 .50
5 Maurice Cannon .30 .75
6 Scott Edgar CO .30 .75
7 Cedric Gumm .30 .75
8 Antwan Hoard .20 .50
9 Michael Hunt .20 .50
10 Michael James .20 .50
11 Jeremy Park .20 .50
12 Scott Sivills .20 .50
13 Kenneth Taylor .20 .50
14 Antoine Teague .20 .50
15 Bo Walden .20 .50
16 Jerry Wilson .20 .50
17 Team Photo .60 1.50

1984-85 Nebraska

This 31-card multi-sport set was distributed by the Lincoln Police Department. The cards measure approximately 2 1/4" by 3 5/8" and are printed on thin card stock. The sports represented are football (1-10), volleyball (11-12), gymnastics (13-15), basketball (16-19), baseball (20-24, 26, 28, 30), and track (25, 27, 29, 31).

COMPLETE SET (31) 20.00 40.00
16 Dave Hoppen BK 1.25 3.00
17 Debra Powell BK .40 1.00
18 Ronnie Smith BK .80 2.00
19 Angie Miller BK .40 1.00

1985 Nebraska All Stars Cereal

COMPLETE SET (25) 125.00 250.00
7 Lyle Nannen 6.00 12.00
10 Stuart Lantz 6.00 12.00
11 Ron Simmons 6.00 12.00

1985-86 Nebraska

This 37-card multi-sport set measuring 2 1/2" by 4" has on the fronts color action and posed player photos enclosed by a red border. The sports represented are football (2-11), volleyball (12, 14), gymnastics (13, 15-17), track (18, 20, 29-30), basketball (19, 21, 23, 26), baseball (20-24, 31-37), and swimming (22, 24, 27-28). The cards are numbered on the back. The key cards in the set are NBA draftee Rich King and NFL running back Tom Rathman.

COMPLETE SET (37) 20.00 40.00
23 Dave Hoppen .80 2.00
36 Rich King 1.00 2.50

1986-87 Nebraska

This 30-card multi-sport set was distributed by the Lincoln Police Department. The cards measure approzimately 2 1/2" by 4" and are printed on thin card stock.

COMPLETE SET (30) 20.00 35.00
11 Tisha Delaney .50 1.25
12 Brian Carr .50 1.25
13 Angie Miller .50 1.25
14 Bill Jackman .50 1.25
15 Mauritce Ivy .50 1.25
16 Anthony Bailous .50 1.25

1987-88 Nebraska

This 26-card multi-sport set was distributed by the Lincoln Police Department. The cards measure approximately 2 1/2" by 4" and is printed on this cardboard stock.

COMPLETE SET (26) 20.00 35.00
10 Virginia Stahr .50 1.25
14 Stephanie Bolli .50 1.25
16 Amy Stephens .50 1.25

1988-89 Nebraska

COMPLETE SET (32) 12.50 30.00
16 Eric Johnson .40 1.00
17 Amy Stephens .40 1.00
18 Pete Manning .40 1.00
19 Kim Harris .40 1.00
20 Richard Van Poelgeest .40 1.00
21 Amy Bullock .40 1.00

1989-90 Nebraska

This 33-card multi-sport set measures approximately 2 1/2" by 4" and is printed on thin cardboard stock. The fronts feature color player action photos on a red card face. In black lettering the words "89-90 Huskers" appear over the picture, while the player's name and other information are printed beneath the picture. The backs carry "Husker Tips," which consist of comments about the players combined with crime prevention tips. Sponsor names and logos at the bottom round out the back.

COMPLETE SET (33) 10.00 25.00
20 Ray Richardson .40 1.00
21 Ann Halsne .40 1.00
22 Clifford Scales .60 1.50
23 Kelly Hubert .40 1.00
24 Richard Van Poelgeest .40 1.00
25 Kim Yancey .40 1.00

1990-91 Nebraska

This 28-card set was sponsored by the National Bank of Commerce, the University of Nebraska-Lincoln, and the Lincoln Police Department. Sponsors' logos at the bottom round out the back. The sports represented in this set are football (2-13), volleyball (14-15), wrestling (16), gymnastics (17-20), basketball (21-24), softball (25, 27), and baseball (26, 28). The key cards in the set are these players with NFL experience: Mike Croel, Bruce Pickens, and Kenny Walker.

COMPLETE SET (28) 12.50 30.00
21 Clifford Scales .40 1.00
22 Ann Halsne .40 1.00
23 Carl Hayes .40 1.00
24 Kelly Hubert .40 1.00

1991-92 Nebraska

COMPLETE SET (22) 10.00 25.00
13 Danny Lee CO .40 1.00
14 Carl Hayes .40 1.00
15 Carol Russell .40 1.00
16 Eric Piatkowski 1.25 3.00
17 Karen Jennings .40 1.00
18 DaPreis Owens .40 1.00
19 Sue Hesch .40 1.00

1992-93 Nebraska

This 27-card multisport set was sponsored by the National Bank of Commerce, the University of Nebraska-Lincoln, and the Lincoln Police Department. The cards measure approximately 2 5/8" by 3 1/2" and are printed on thin card stock. Sponsor names and logos round out the back. The sports represented are football (1-9), women's volleyball (10, 11), basketball (12-17), gymnastics (18-20), track and field, (21-22) and baseball (23-27).

COMPLETE SET (27) 10.00 25.00
16 Eric Piatkowski 1.50 4.00

1993-94 Nebraska

This 25-card multisport standard-size set was jointly sponsored by the National Bank of Commerce, the Lincoln Police Department, and the university. The cards are unnumbered and checklisted below alphabetically within sport as follows: football (1-9), basketball (men [10-11]; women [12-13]), gymnastics (14-17), baseball (18-19), women's softball (20-21), volleyball (22-23), and wrestling (24-25).

COMPLETE SET (25) 10.00 25.00
11 Eric Piatkowski 1.25 3.00

1994-95 Nebraska

This 21-card multi-sport set was jointly sponsored by Union Bank, the Lincoln Police Department and the university. The unnumbered, attractive, full color cards are slightly wider than standard size and printed on very thin stock. Several sports are featured and are listed below alphabetically within sport as follows: baseball (1-2), men's basketball (3-4), women's basketball (5-6), football (7-14), men's gymnastics (15-16), women's gymnastics (17-18), softball (19) and women's volleyball (20-21). Future NBA player Erick Strickland has his first card in this set.

COMPLETE SET (21) 10.00 25.00
3 Jaron Boone .75 2.00
4 Erick Strickland 1.50 4.00
5 Emily Thompson .40 1.00
6 Tanya Upthegrove .40 1.00

1995-96 Nebraska

This 21-card multisport set was jointly sponsored by National Bank, Lincoln Police Department and the university. The unnumbered, full-color cards are slightly wider than standard size and feature bold red borders on front. The set contains several sports and is checklisted below alphabetically within sport as follows: men's basketball (1-3), women's basketball (4-6), football (7-13), men's gymnastics (14), women's soccer (15), women's swimming (16), women's volleyball (17-20) and wrestling (21). The set contains early cards of football players Tommy Frazier and Brook Berringer as well as an early card of NBA player Erick Strickland.

COMPLETE SET (21) 15.00 40.00
1 Jaron Boone .60 1.50
2 Erick Strickland 1.20 3.00
3 Tom Wald .30 .75
4 Pyra Aarden .30 .75
5 Anna DeForge .30 .75
6 Kate Galligan .30 .75

1995-96 Nebraska Schedules

Each of these attractive full color schedules features a different senior from the 1995-96 team. The set is highlighted by the inclusion of NBA guard Erick Strickland. The schedules were distributed for free at home games throughout the 1995-96 season.

COMPLETE SET (3) .75 2.00
1 Jaron Boone .20 .50
2 Erick Strickland .60 1.50
3 Tom Wald .08 .25

1996-97 Nebraska

This 21-card standard-size set was produced by Nebraska and features athletes from all sports. The set features primarily football players, but a variety of other sports as well. We've included initials after each player's name that represent the sport in which they played.

COMPLETE SET (21) 10.00 25.00
11 Bernard Garner BK .40 1.00
12 Mikki Moore BK 1.25 3.00
15 Anna DeForge BK 1.00 2.50
16 LaToya Doage BK .40 1.00

1996-97 Nebraska Schedules

Each of these attractive full color schedules features an action photo of one of the three different seniors from the 1996-97 team. The schedules were distributed for free at Nebraska home games throughout the 1996-97 season.

COMPLETE SET (3) .75 2.00
1 Bernard Garner .08 .25
2 Tyronn Lue .60 1.50
3 Mikki Moore .40 1.00

1997-98 Nebraska

This 21-card standard-size set featured players who were seniors at Nebraska. The set features primarily football players, but a variety of other sports as well. We've included initials after each player's name that represent the sport in which they played.

COMPLETE SET (21) 10.00 20.00
11 Tyronn Lue BK 1.00 2.50
12 Venson Hamilton BK .40 1.00
16 Anna DeForge BK 1.00 2.50

1998-99 Nebraska

This 21-card set was sponsored by Union Bank and Trust Co, University of Nebraska-Lincoln and the Lincoln Police Department. Each includes a color photo of the player surrounded by a red and gray border with the the year "98 and '99" printed on the front. The unnumbered backs are a simple black print on white card stock. The set features primarily football players, but a variety of other sports as well. We've included initials after each player's name that represent the sport in which they played.

COMPLETE SET (21) 10.00 20.00
6 Venson Hamilton BK .30 .75
14 Andy Markowski BK .30 .75
15 Cori McDill W-BK .30 .75
21 Monet Williams BK .30 .75

1999-00 Nebraska

This 19-card set was sponsored by Union Bank and Trust Co, University of Nebraska-Lincoln and the Lincoln Police Department. The set features a variety of sports and we have the put an appropriate initial after each player's name.

COMPLETE SET (19) 6.00 15.00
8 Nicole Kubik W-BK .20 .50
14 Charlie Rogers BK .20 .50

2000-01 Nebraska

This 20-card standard-size features star athletes from Nebraska. The set features primarily football players, but a variety of other sports as well. We've included initials after each player's name that represent the sport in which they played.

COMPLETE SET (20) 8.00 20.00
6 Cookie Blecher BK .60 1.50
7 Amanda Went BK .60 1.50

1988-89 New Mexico

This 18-card set was sponsored by Drug Emporium and KGGM-TV (Channel 13). The cards measure the standard size (2 1/2" by 3 1/2"). The fronts feature color posed player photos enclosed by white borders. Sponsor logos and the words "Lobos 88-89" appear above the picture, while player information is given below the picture. The cards are unnumbered and checklisted below in alphabetical order.

COMPLETE SET (18) 12.00 30.00
1 Doug Ash ACO .40 1.00
2 Willie Banks .75 2.00
3 Dave Bliss CO .40 1.00
4 Scott Duncan ACO .40 1.00
5 Rob Loeffel .40 1.00
6 Luc Longley 5.00 12.00
7 Marvin McBurrows .40 1.00
8 John McCullough ACO .75 2.00
9 Darrell McGee .40 1.00
10 Kurt Miller .40 1.00
11 Chriss O'Gorman .40 1.00
12 Rob Robbins .75 2.00
13 Tony Steffen .40 1.00
14 Charlie Thomas .75 2.00
15 Chris Tower .40 1.00
16 Donnie Walker .40 1.00
17 Mike Winters .40 1.00
Graduate Assistant
18 The Pit .75 2.00
University Arena

1989-90 New Mexico

This 18-card set was sponsored by Drug Emporium and KGGM-TV (Channel 13). The cards measure the standard size (2 1/2" by 3 1/2"). The fronts feature color posed player photos enclosed by white borders. Sponsor logos and the words "Lobos 89-90" appear above the picture, while player information is given below the picture. The cards are unnumbered and checklisted below in alphabetical order.

COMPLETE SET (18) 10.00 25.00
1 Doug Ash ACO .40 1.00
2 Willie Banks .75 2.00
3 Dave Bliss CO .40 1.00
4 Scott Duncan ACO .40 1.00
5 J.J. Griego .40 1.00
6 Samie Liberatore .40 1.00
7 Luc Longley 4.00 10.00
8 Marvin McBurrows .40 1.00
9 John McCullough ACO .40 1.00
10 Andre McGee .40 1.00
11 Darrell McGee .40 1.00
12 Kurt Miller .40 1.00
13 Rob Newton .40 1.00
14 Rob Robbins .75 2.00
15 Omar Sierra .40 1.00
16 Tony Steffen .40 1.00
17 Donnie Walker .40 1.00
18 Mike Winters .40 1.00

1990-91 New Mexico

This 17-card standard-size set was sponsored by Arby's restaurants and KGGM-TV (Channel 13). The fronts feature color posed player photos enclosed by white borders. Sponsor logos and the words "Lobos 90-91" appear above the picture, while player information is given below the picture. The cards are unnumbered and checklisted below in alphabetical order.

COMPLETE SET (17) 12.00 30.00
1 Doug Ash ACO .30 .75
2 Willie Banks .60 1.50
3 Dave Bliss CO .30 .75
4 Paul Graham ACO .30 .75
5 Khari Jaxon .60 1.50
6 Luc Longley 2.50 6.00
7 Marvin McBurrows .30 .75
8 Vladimir McCrary .30 .75
9 John McCullough ACO .30 .75
10 Lance Milford .30 .75
11 Kurt Miller .30 .75
12 Rob Newton .30 .75
13 George Powdrill SP 6.00 15.00
14 Rob Robbins .60 1.50
15 Jimmy Taylor .30 .75
16 Ike Williams .60 1.50
17 The Pit .60 1.50
University Arena

1991-92 New Mexico

This 18-card set was sponsored by Arby's restaurants and KGGM-TV (Channel 13). It is reported that 10,000 sets were printed, and two to four cards per week were given away at Arby's restaurants in the Albuquerque area. The cards measure the standard size. The fronts feature color posed player photos enclosed by white borders. Sponsor logos and the words "Lobos 91-92" appear above the picture, while player information is given below the picture. The cards are unnumbered and checklisted below in alphabetical order.

COMPLETE SET (18) 4.00 10.00
1 Doug Ash ACO .20 .50
2 Willie Banks .40 1.00
3 Dave Bliss CO .20 .50
4 Paul Graham ACO .20 .50
5 J.J. Griego .20 .50
6 Brian Hayden .20 .50
7 Trent Heffner .20 .50
8 Khari Jaxon .40 1.00
9 Lewis Lamar .20 .50

10 Steve Logan .40 1.00
11 Vladimir McCrary .20 .50
12 John McCullough ACO .20 .50
13 Andre McGee .20 .50
14 Lance Milford .20 .50
15 Scott Pritchett .20 .50
16 Will Scott .20 .50
17 Eric Thomas .20 .50
18 Ike Williams .40 1.00

1992-93 New Mexico

This 16-card set issued in two-card perforated strips was sponsored by First National Bank in Albuquerque. A total of 15,000 sets were produced according to information on the reverse. The cards measure standard size (2 1/2" by 3 1/2"). The white-bordered fronts feature color action player shots with a red banner superimposed on the upper portion of the photo. Within the red banner in white lettering appears the team name, with the season dates printed in white below. A basketball icon in the lower right corner carries the player's name and across the bottom edge a green stripe contains the set sponsors: First National Bank in Albuquerque and radio station KRQE. The white backs carry biography and college statistics. The cards are unnumbered and checklisted below in alphabetical order.

COMPLETE SET (16) 3.00 8.00
1 Dave Bliss CO .60 1.50
2 Greg Brown .20 .50
3 J.J. Griego .20 .50
4 Brian Hayden .20 .50
5 Trent Heffner .20 .50
6 Khari Jaxon .40 1.00
7 Corey Jenkins .20 .50
8 Lewis LaMar .20 .50
9 Lobo Lucy and Louie (Mascots) .20 .50
10 Steve Logan .20 .50
11 Lance Milford .20 .50
12 Canonchet Neves .20 .50
13 Mike Powers Sports Director .20 .50
14 Eric Thomas .20 .50
15 Ike Williams .40 1.00
16 Frank Willis .20 .50

1992-93 New Mexico State

This 13-card set measures the standard size (2 1/2" by 3 1/2") and features color action player photos bordered on one side by a gray stripe containing the words "New Mexico State." The player's name appears in maroon print on a white bar at the bottom. The horizontal backs are white and display a shadow bordered close-up picture, the player's name, and a player profile. The cards are numbered on the back.

COMPLETE SET (13) 3.00 8.00
1 Neil McCarthy CO .75 2.00
2 Ron Putzi .20 .50
3 Eric Traylor .40 1.00
4 Tracey Ware .30 .75
5 Marc Thompson .30 .75
6 David Lofton .20 .50
7 D.J. Jackson .30 .75
8 Corey Rogers .30 .75
9 Cliff Reed .20 .50
10 Ron Coleman .20 .50
11 Juriad Hughes .20 .50
12 James Dockery .40 1.00
13 Sam Crawford .75 2.00

1993-94 New Mexico State

This 18-card standard size (2 1/2" by 3 1/2") set. The fronts feature full bleed color posed player shots. In the lower right side there is a red color bar with the team name reversed out which overlaps a black color bar whick has the players name reversed out. The white backs have as a color player head shot in the upper left. The player'a player's name and bio are centered at the top. A player profile follow below. The cards numbered and listed below.

COMPLETE SET (18) 4.00 10.00
1 Ron Coleman .20 .50
2 James Dockery .30 .75
3 D.J. Jackson .20 .50
4 Corey Rogers .30 .75
5 Chris Lopez .20 .50
6 Mike Schutz .20 .50
7 Dwain Bradberry .20 .50
8 William Howze .20 .50
9 Lance Jackson .20 .50
10 Paul Jarrett .20 .50
11 Keith Johnson .20 .50
12 Skip McCoy .20 .50
13 Johnny Selvie .30 .75
14 Rodney Walker .30 .75
15 Thomas Wyatt .30 .75
16 Pistol Pete (Mascot) .20 .50
17 Dr. James Halligan PR .20 .50
18 Neil McCarthy CO .75 2.00

1996-97 New Mexico State

This 14-card set was offered at New Mexico State University during the 1996-97 season. The set was produced by White Sands Federal Credit Union.

COMPLETE SET (14) 3.00 8.00
1 Charles Gosa .30 .75
2 Antoine Hubbard .30 .75
3 Chris Lopez .30 .75
4 Louis Richardson .30 .75
5 Carl Laws .30 .75
6 Maurice Lawson .30 .75
7 Aaron Brodt .30 .75
8 Denmark Reid .30 .75
9 Joaquin Chavez .30 .75
10 Bostjan Leban .30 .75
11 Rhoute Davis .30 .75
12 Douminic Ellison .30 .75
13 Neil McCarthy CO .40 1.00
14 Team Card .30 .75

1988 New Mexico State Greats

This 12-card multi-sport set was sponsored by the Charter Hospital of Santa Teresa. The cards measure approximately 2 5/8" by 4" and are printed on thin cardboard stock. On a white background with a dark red border on three sides, the fronts feature black-and-white posed or action player photos and player information. The backs have brief biographical and statistical information, a cartoon of Chum and a public service announcement. The logo and address of the sponsor round out the backs. The cards are unnumbered and checklisted below in alphabetical order.

COMPLETE SET (12) 9.00 18.00
3 Jimmy Collins BK 1.00 2.50
4 Steve Colter BK .75 2.00
7 Sam Lacey BK 1.25 3.00

1970-71 North Carolina Schedules

1 Dean Smith 10.00 20.00

1972-73 North Carolina Schedules

1 Donn Johnston 2.00 5.00
2 George Karl 4.00 10.00

1973-74 North Carolina Playing Cards

This 54-card standard-size set features North Carolina players. The set is designed like a playing card set and has rounded corners. On a white background, the fronts feature black-and-white player photos, with the player's name printed below. The backs are blue on white and carry the team name and logo. The cards are checklisted in playing card order by suits and numbers are assigned to Aces (1), Jacks (11), Queens (12), and Kings (13).

COMP. FACT SET (54) 75.00 150.00
1C 1956-57 National Champs 1.00 2.50
1D Bobby Jones 4.00 10.00
1H Homer Rice DIR 1.00 2.50
1S Dean Smith CO 20.00 35.00
2C Bob Lewis 1.00 2.50
2D Dave Hanners 1.00 2.50
2H Jerry Vayda 1.25 3.00
2S James Smith 1.00 2.50
3C Dennis Wuycik 1.00 2.50
3D Billy Chambers 1.00 2.50
3H Steve Previs 1.00 2.50
3S Bruce Buckley 1.00 2.50
4C Billy Cunningham 5.00 10.00
4D Mickey Bell 1.00 2.50
4H Dick Grubar 1.00 2.50
4S Tommy LaGarde 1.25 3.00
5C Lee Shaffer 1.00 2.50
5D Charles Waddell 1.00 2.50
5H Rusty Clark 1.00 2.50
5S John Kuester 1.00 2.50
6C Hook Dillon 1.00 2.50
6D Brad Hoffman 1.00 2.50
6H Joe Quigg 1.00 2.50
6S Tony Shaver 1.00 2.50
7C York Larese 1.50 4.00
7D Ray Hite 1.00 2.50
7H Tommy Kearns 1.25 3.00
7S Eddie Fogler 2.00 5.00
8C Jim Jorden 1.00 2.50
8D Walter Davis 5.00 12.00
8H Bill Bunting 1.00 2.50
8S Bill Guthridge 5.00 12.00
9C Doug Moe 3.00 8.00
9D Ed Stahl 1.00 2.50
9H Larry Brown 5.00 12.00
9S 1971-72 Third Nationally 1.00 2.50
10C Pete Brennan 1.50 4.00
10D Mitch Kupchak 3.00 8.00
10H Bill Chamberlain 1.00 2.50
10S 1970-71 NIT Champs 1.00 2.50
11C Charlie Scott 3.00 8.00
11D John O'Donnell 1.00 2.50
11H Robert McAdoo 6.00 15.00
11S 1968-69 ACC Champs 1.00 2.50
12C Larry Miller 2.50 6.00
12D Ray Harrison 1.00 2.50
12H Lailee McNair 1.00 2.50
12S 1967-68 Second Nationally 1.25 3.00
13C Lennie Rosenbluth 2.50 6.00
13D Darrell Elston 1.00 2.50
13H George Karl 4.00 10.00
13S 1966-67 ACC Champs 1.25 3.00
JK Bell Tower 1.00 2.50
JK Old Well 1.00 2.50

1973-74 North Carolina Schedules

1 Bobby Jones 3.00 8.00

1974-75 North Carolina Schedules

This three-card set was issued by the University of North Carolina. Each card measures approximately 2 3/8" by 3 1/2". The fronts feature full-bleed close-up color player photos, with the player's name and jersey number at the bottom of the card. The backs list the 1974-75 varsity basketball schedule. The cards are unnumbered and checklisted below in alphabetical order.

COMPLETE SET (3) 7.50 15.00
1 Mickey Bell 2.00 5.00
2 Brad Hoffman 2.00 5.00
3 Ed Stahl 2.00 5.00

1975-76 North Carolina Schedules

This three-card set was issued by the University of North Carolina. Each card measures approximately 2 3/8" by 3 1/2". The fronts feature full-bleed close-up color player photos, with the player's name and jersey number at the bottom of the card. The backs list the 1975-76 varsity basketball schedule. The cards are unnumbered and checklisted below in alphabetical order.

COMPLETE SET (3) 7.50 15.00
1 Bill Chambers 1.50 4.00
2 Dave Hanners 1.50 4.00
3 Mitch Kupchak 5.00 10.00

1976-77 North Carolina Schedules

This five-card set was issued by the University of North Carolina. Each card measures approximately 2 3/8" by 3 1/2". The fronts feature full-bleed close-up color player photos, with the player's name and jersey number at the bottom of the card. The backs list the 1976-77 varsity basketball schedule. The cards are unnumbered and checklisted below in alphabetical order.

COMPLETE SET (5) 12.50 25.00
1 Bruce Buckley 1.25 3.00
2 Woody Coley 1.25 3.00
3 Walter Davis 5.00 10.00
4 John Kuester 1.50 4.00
5 Tommy LaGarde 2.50 6.00

1977-78 North Carolina Schedules

This three-card set was issued by the University of North Carolina. Each card measures approximately 2 3/8" by 3 1/2". The fronts feature full-bleed close-up color player photos, with the player's name and jersey number at the bottom of the card. The backs list the 1977-78 varsity basketball schedule. The cards are unnumbered and checklisted below in alphabetical order.

COMPLETE SET (3) 5.00 10.00
1 Geoff Crompton 1.25 3.00
2 Phil Ford 2.50 6.00
3 Tom Zaliagiris 1.25 3.00

1978-79 North Carolina Schedules

This three-card set was issued by the University of North Carolina. Each card measures approximately 2 3/8" by 3 1/2". The fronts feature full-bleed close-up color player photos, with the player's name and jersey number at the bottom of the card. The backs list the 1978-79 varsity basketball schedule. The cards are unnumbered and checklisted below in alphabetical order.

COMPLETE SET (3) 4.00 8.00
1 Dudley Bradley 1.50 4.00
2 Ged Doughton 1.25 3.00
3 Randy Wiel 1.25 3.00

1979-80 North Carolina Schedules

This five-card set was issued by the University of North Carolina. Each card measures approximately 2 3/8" by 3 1/2". The fronts feature full-bleed close-up color player photos, with the player's name and jersey number at the bottom of the card. The backs list the 1979-80 varsity basketball schedule. The cards are unnumbered and checklisted below in alphabetical order.

COMPLETE SET (5) 6.00 12.00
1 Dave Colescott .75 2.00
2 Mike O'Koren 1.50 4.00
3 John Virgil .75 2.00
4 Jeff Wolf 1.25 3.00
5 Rich Yonakor 1.25 3.00

1980-81 North Carolina Schedules

These four cards were apparently issued by the Athletic Department of the University of North Carolina. Each card measures approximately 2 3/8" by 3 3/8". The fronts feature full-bleed close-up color photos, with the player's name and jersey number at the bottom of the card face. The backs list the 1980-81 varsity basketball schedule. The cards are unnumbered and checklisted below in alphabetical order.

COMPLETE SET (4) 3.00 6.00
1 Pete Budko .60 1.50
2 Eric Kenny .60 1.50
3 Mike Pepper .60 1.50
4 Al Wood 1.25 3.00

1981-82 North Carolina Schedules

These three cards were apparently issued by the Athletic Department of the University of North Carolina. Each card measures approximately 2 3/8" by 3 3/8". The fronts feature full-bleed close-up color photos, with the player's name and jersey number at the bottom of the card face. The backs list the 1981-82 varsity basketball schedule. The cards are unnumbered and checklisted below in alphabetical order.

COMPLETE SET (3) 2.00 5.00
1 Jeb Barlow .60 1.50
2 Jimmy Black .75 2.00
3 Chris Brust .60 1.50

1982-83 North Carolina Schedules

Measuring approximately 2 3/8" by 3 1/2", this card was issued by the University of North Carolina. The front features a full-bleed color portrait with the player's name and jersey number at the bottom of the card. The back lists the 1982-83 varsity basketball schedule. The card is unnumbered.

1 Jimmy Braddock .60 1.50

1983-84 North Carolina Schedules

This three-card set was issued by the University of North Carolina. Each card measures approximately 2 3/8" by 3 1/2". The fronts feature full-bleed close-up color player photos, with the player's name and jersey number at the bottom of the card. The backs list the 1983-84 varsity basketball schedule. The cards are unnumbered and checklisted below in alphabetical order.

COMPLETE SET (3) 3.00 8.00
1 Matt Doherty .75 2.00
2 Cecil Exum .60 1.50
3 Sam Perkins 2.50 6.00

1984-85 North Carolina Schedules

This three-card set was issued by the University of North Carolina. Each card measures approximately 2 3/8" by 3 1/2". The fronts feature full-bleed close-up color player photos, with the player's name and jersey number at the bottom of the card. The backs list the 1984-85 varsity basketball schedule. The cards are unnumbered and checklisted below in alphabetical order.

COMPLETE SET (3) 1.50 4.00
1 Timo Makkonen .40 1.00
2 Cliff Morris .40 1.00
3 Buzz Peterson .75 2.00

1985-86 North Carolina Schedules

This four-card set was issued by the University of North Carolina. Each card measures approximately 2 3/8" by 3 1/2". The fronts feature full-bleed close-up color player photos, with the player's name and jersey number at the bottom of the card. The backs list the 1985-86 varsity basketball schedule. The cards are unnumbered and checklisted below in alphabetical order.

COMPLETE SET (4) 2.50 6.00
1 Brad Daugherty 1.50 4.00
2 Jimmy Daye .40 1.00
3 Steve Hale .40 1.00
4 Warren Martin .40 1.00

1986-87 North Carolina

This 13-card set was sponsored by Adolescent CareUnit, Alamance Health Services, and various police departments. The cards measure the standard size (2 1/2" by 3 1/2"). The front features a posed color head-and-shoulders shot of the player on a white card face. In black lettering, the Adolescent Care Unit logo, the school name, and year appear above the picture. The player's name and number are given below, sandwiched between the team name. The back is printed in black on white card stock and presents biographical information and "Tips from the Tar Heels," which consist of anti-drug and alcohol messages. The cards are unnumbered and checklisted below by uniform number. The set features the first cards of NBA players Kenny Smith, J.R. Reid, and Scott Williams.

COMPLETE SET (13) 9.00 18.00
3 Jeff Denny .40 1.00
14 Jeff Lebo 1.00 2.50
20 Steve Bucknall .60 1.50
21 Michael Norwood .40 1.00
24 Joe Wolf 1.25 3.00
30 Kenny Smith 2.50 6.00
32 Pete Chilcutt 1.25 3.00
33 Ranzino Smith .60 1.50
34 J.R. Reid 1.25 3.00
35 Dave Popson .75 2.00
42 Scott Williams 1.25 3.00
43 Curtis Hunter .60 1.50
45 Marty Hensley .40 1.00

1986-87 North Carolina Schedules

This five-card set was issued by the University of North Carolina. Each card measures approximately 2 3/8" by 3 1/2". The fronts feature full-bleed close-up color player photos, with the player's name and jersey number at the bottom of the card. The backs list the 1986-87 varsity basketball schedule. The cards are unnumbered and checklisted below in alphabetical order.

COMPLETE SET (5) 2.50 6.00
1 Curtis Hunter .40 1.00
2 Mike Norwood .30 .75
3 Dave Popson .60 1.50
4 Kenny Smith 1.25 3.00
5 Joe Wolf .60 1.50

1987-88 North Carolina

This 12-card standard-size set was sponsored by Adolescent CareUnit, Alamance Health Services, and various police departments. The front features a posed color head-and-shoulders shot of the player on a white card face. In black lettering, the Adolescent CareUnit and Blue Cross/Blue Shield logos appear above the picture. In contrast to the previous year's issue, these cards have "Tar Heels" printed in large blue type above the picture. The player's name and number are given below, sandwiched between two blue basketballs. The back is printed in black on white card stock and presents biographical information and "Tips from the Tar Heels," which consist of anti-drug and alcohol messages. The cards are unnumbered and checklisted below by uniform number. The set features the first card of NBA player Rick Fox.

COMPLETE SET (12) 9.00 18.00
34 J.R. Reid 1.25 3.00
42 Scott Williams 1.00 2.50
44 Rick Fox 4.00 9.00

1987-88 North Carolina Schedules

Sponsored by the Meredith-Webb Printing Company, this schedule card measures approximately 2 1/4" by 3 1/2" when folded. The front features a full-bleed close-up color player photo, with the player's name at the bottom of the card face. The inside lists the 1987-88 varsity basketball schedule. The back carries the sponsor's logo and address in gold lettering on a brown background. The card is unnumbered.

1 Ranzino Smith .30 .75

1988-89 North Carolina

This 15-card standard-size set was sponsored by Adolescent CareUnit, Alamance Health Services, and local law enforcement agencies. The fronts feature a color action photo of the player, with black borders on a medium blue card face. In black lettering, the Adolescent CareUnit and Blue Cross/Blue Shield logos appear within the border above the picture. These cards have "Tar Heels" printed in large white type above the picture. The player's name and number are given below, with the letters "NC" superimposed over one another in the lower left corner. The back is printed in black on white card stock and presents biographical information and "Tips from the Tar Heels," which consist of anti-drug and alcohol messages. The cards are unnumbered and checklisted below by uniform number. The Defense card is mysteriously listed on the back as '87 and '88 in the upper corners.

COMPLETE SET (15) 8.00 20.00
3 Jeff Denny .40 1.00
14 Jeff Lebo .60 1.50
20 Steve Bucknall .40 1.00
21 King Rice .60 1.50
22 Kevin Madden .40 1.00
32 Pete Chilcutt 1.25 3.00
34 J.R. Reid 1.00 2.50
42 Scott Williams 1.25 3.00
44 Rick Fox 3.00 7.00
45 Marty Hensley .40 1.00
NNO Dean Smith CO 4.00 10.00
NNO Teamwork .40 1.00
NNO Defense (Scott Williams and Jeff Lebo defending) .60 1.50
NNO The Fast Break (King Rice dribbling) .60 1.50
NNO A Fun Game (bench scene with Rick Fox and Scott Williams) 1.25 3.00

1988-89 North Carolina Schedules

Sponsored by Hardee's, this three-card set features schedule cards that fold in the middle. Each card measures approximately 2 1/4" by 3 1/2" when folded. The fronts feature full-bleed close-up color player photos, with the player's name at the bottom of the card face. The insides list the 1988-89 varsity basketball schedule. The backs carry the sponsor's advertisement showing a color photo of a hamburger, with the Hardee's logo and the slogan "We're out to win you over" below. The cards are unnumbered and checklisted below in alphabetical order.

COMPLETE SET (3) 1.20 3.00
1 Steve Bucknall .40 1.00
2 Jeff Lebo .60 1.50
3 David May .30 .75

1989-90 North Carolina Collegiate Collection

This 200-card standard-size set was produced by Collegiate Collection and sponsored by Coca-Cola, and the Coke logo appears in the lower left corner on the card face. The fronts feature a mix of black and white photos for earlier players and color for later ones, with rounded corners and powder blue borders. The pictures are superimposed over a powder blue and white diagonally striped card face, with a powder blue outer border. The top reads "North Carolina's Finest," and the school logo appears in the upper right corner. The horizontally oriented backs are printed in powder blue on white and present biographical information, career summaries, or statistics. Many numbers can be found without the trademark notation on the card front, i.e., missing the circled R under the Tar heel logo. Collegiate Collection also issued a Gold version of this set in a special binder, with an individually numbered certificate indicating that 1,000 sets were produced. The Gold cards have gold foil trim surrounding the photos.

COMPLETE SET (200) 8.00 20.00
1 Dean Smith .20 .50
2 Dean Smith .20 .50
3 Dean Smith .20 .50
4 Dean Smith .20 .50
5 Dean Smith .20 .50
6 Dean Smith .20 .50
7 Phil Ford .08 .25
8 Phil Ford .08 .25
9 Phil Ford .08 .25
10 Phil Ford .08 .25
11 Phil Ford .08 .25
12 Phil Ford .08 .25
13 Michael Jordan .75 2.00
14 Michael Jordan .75 2.00
15 Michael Jordan .75 2.00
16 Michael Jordan .75 2.00
17 Michael Jordan .75 2.00
18 Michael Jordan .75 2.00
19 James Worthy .10 .30
20 James Worthy .10 .30
21 James Worthy .10 .30
22 James Worthy .10 .30
23 James Worthy .10 .30
24 Larry Miller .08 .25
25 Larry Miller .08 .25
26 Larry Miller .08 .25
27 Larry Miller .08 .25
28 Charlie Scott .08 .25
29 Charlie Scott .08 .25
30 Charlie Scott .08 .25
31 Charlie Scott .08 .25
32 Sam Perkins .08 .25
33 Sam Perkins .08 .25
34 Sam Perkins .08 .25
35 Sam Perkins .08 .25
36 Sam Perkins .08 .25
37 Billy Cunningham .08 .25
38 Billy Cunningham .08 .25
39 Billy Cunningham .08 .25
40 Billy Cunningham .08 .25
41 Lennie Rosenbluth .08 .25
42 Lennie Rosenbluth .08 .25
43 Lennie Rosenbluth .08 .25
44 Bobby Jones .08 .25
45 Bobby Jones .08 .25
46 Bobby Jones .08 .25
47 Mitch Kupchak .08 .25
48 Mitch Kupchak .08 .25
49 Mitch Kupchak .08 .25
50 1980-81 Tar Heels .08 .25
51 Walter Davis .08 .25
52 Walter Davis .08 .25
53 Walter Davis .08 .25
54 Walter Davis .08 .25
55 Mike O'Koren .08 .25
56 Mike O'Koren .08 .25
57 Mike O'Koren .08 .25
58 Mike O'Koren .08 .25
59 The Huddle .08 .25
60 Larry Brown .08 .25
61 Billy Cunningham .08 .25
62 Matt Doherty .08 .25
63 Phil Ford .08 .25
64 Doug Moe .08 .25
65 Michael Jordan 1.00 2.50
66 Kenny Smith .08 .25
67 Kenny Smith .08 .25
68 Kenny Smith .08 .25
69 Bob Lewis .08 .25
70 Bob Lewis .08 .25
71 Bob Lewis .08 .25
72 Charlie Scott .08 .25
73 Sam Perkins .08 .25
74 Doug Moe .08 .25
75 Doug Moe .08 .25
76 Bob McAdoo .08 .25
77 Bob McAdoo .08 .25
78A Pete Brennan ERR .08 .25
78B Pete Brennan COR .08 .25
79 Pete Brennan .08 .25
80 J.R. Reid .08 .25
81 J.R. Reid .08 .25
82 J.R. Reid .08 .25
83 Tommy Kearns .08 .25
84 Tommy Kearns .08 .25
85 John Dillon .08 .25
86 The Smith Center .08 .25
87 Dick Grubar .08 .25
88 Dick Grubar .08 .25
89 Rusty Clark .08 .25
90 Rusty Clark .08 .25
91 Bill Bunting .08 .25
92 Bill Bunting .08 .25
93 Jimmy Black .08 .25
94 Jimmy Black .08 .25
95 Five Tournament Titles .08 .25
96 UNC Cheerleaders .08 .25
97 Bobby Jones .08 .25
98 J.R. Reid .08 .25
99 Frank McGuire .08 .25
100 1957 NCAA Champions .08 .25
101 Bill Guthridge .08 .25
102 York Larese .08 .25
103 York Larese .08 .25
104 Frank McGuire .08 .25
105 Bones McKinney .08 .25
106 Larry Miller .08 .25
107 Kenny Smith .08 .25
108 Steve Previs .08 .25
109 Steve Previs .08 .25
110 Larry Brown .08 .25
111 Larry Brown .08 .25
112 Eddie Fogler .08 .25
113 Eddie Fogler .08 .25
114 James Worthy .10 .30
115 Bob McAdoo .08 .25
116 Checklist 1-100 .08 .25
117 Checklist 101-200 .08 .25
118 Cartwright Carmichael .08 .25
119 Steve Hale .08 .25
120 Steve Hale .08 .25
121 Joe Quigg .08 .25
122 Joe Quigg .08 .25
123 Bob Cunningham .08 .25
124 Bob Cunningham .08 .25
125 Jim Delaney .08 .25
126 Bones McKinney .08 .25
127 Jerry Vayda .08 .25
128 Matt Doherty .08 .25
129 Matt Doherty .08 .25
130 Bob Paxton .08 .25
131 Dave Chadwick .08 .25
132 Dave Hanners .08 .25
133 Jim Jordan .08 .25
134 Jeff Lebo .08 .25
135 Jeff Lebo .08 .25
136 Lee Shaffer .08 .25
137 Lee Shaffer .08 .25
138 Joe Wolf .08 .25
139 Joe Wolf .08 .25
140 Warren Martin .08 .25
141 Warren Martin .08 .25
142 Carmichael Auditorium .08 .25
143 Jim Hudock .08 .25
144 Darrell Elston .08 .25
145 Brad Hoffman .08 .25
146 Harvey Salz .08 .25
147 Dave Colescott .08 .25
148 Ed Stahl .08 .25
149 Joe Brown .08 .25
150 Gerald Tuttle .08 .25
151 Richard Tuttle .08 .25
152 Tony Radovich .08 .25
153 Dave Popson .08 .25
154 Donnie Walsh .08 .25
155 Rich Yonakor .08 .25
156 Jeff Wolf .08 .25
157 Pete Budko .08 .25
158 Randy Wiel .08 .25
159 Tom Gauntlett .08 .25
160 Mike Pepper .08 .25
161 Jim Braddock .08 .25
162 Yogi Poteet .08 .25
163 Charlie Shaffer .08 .25
164 Lee Dedmon .08 .25
165 Bob Bennett .08 .25
166 Ray Hite .08 .25
167 Tom Zaliagiris UER .08 .25
168 Kim Huband .08 .25
169 Ranzino Smith .08 .25
170 Donn Johnston .08 .25
171 Dale Gipple .08 .25
172 Curtis Hunter .08 .25
173 John Yokley .08 .25
174 Bryan McSweeney .08 .25
175 John O'Donnell .08 .25
176 Hugh Donahue .08 .25
177 1968-69 Tar Heels .08 .25
178 Bruce Buckley .08 .25
179 Ray Respess .08 .25
180 Buzz Peterson .08 .25
181 Mike Cooke .08 .25
182 Mickey Bell .08 .25
183 John Virgil .08 .25
184 Charles Waddell .08 .25
185 Mark Mirken .08 .25
186 Ralph Fletcher .08 .25
187 1971-72 ACC Champs .08 .25
188 Ged Doughton .08 .25
189 Bill Chambers .08 .25
190 Bill Chambers .08 .25
191 James Daye .08 .25
192 Jeb Barlow .08 .25
193 Chris Brust .08 .25
194 Eric Kenny .08 .25
195 1970-71 NIT Champs .08 .25
196 Don Eggleston .08 .25
197 Ricky Webb .08 .25
198 Jim Frye .08 .25
199 Timo Makkonen .08 .25
200 1982 NCAA Champions .08 .25

1989-90 North Carolina Collegiate Collection Gold Edition

COMPLETE SET (201) 50.00 120.00
*GOLD: 3X TO 8X BASE HI
ANNCD PRINT RUN 1000

1989-90 North Carolina Schedules

Sponsored by Hardee's, this five-card set features schedule cards that fold in the middle. Each card measures approximately 2 1/4" by 3 1/2" when folded. The fronts feature full-bleed close-up color player photos, with the player's name at the bottom of the card. The insides list the 1989-90 varsity basketball schedule. The backs carry the words "1989-90 UNC Basketball Schedule" in black letters, the sponsor's logo in red letters, and the slogan "We're out to win you over." The cards are unnumbered and checklisted below in alphabetical order.

COMPLETE SET (5) 1.50 4.00
1 Jeff Denny .20 .50
2 John Greene .20 .50
3 Marty Hensley .20 .50
4 Kevin Madden .30 .75
5 Scott Williams .75 2.00

1990-91 North Carolina Collegiate Collection Promos

This ten-card set features various sports stars of North Carolina from recent years. Since this set features athletes from more than one sport we have put a two letter abbreviation next to the player's name which identifies the sport he plays. This set includes a Michael Jordan card. All the cards in the set feature full-color photos of the athletes on the front along with either a biography or statistics of the players pictured on the card.

COMPLETE SET (10) 3.00 8.00
NC1 Michael Jordan BK 2.50 6.00
NC3 Steve Hale BK .08 .25
NC5 Matt Doherty BK .08 .25
NC7 Sam Perkins BK .40 1.00
NC9 Kenny Smith BK .40 1.00

1990-91 North Carolina Schedules

Sponsored by Hardee's, this three-card set features schedule cards that fold in the middle. Each card measures approximately 2 1/4" by 3 1/2" when folded. The fronts feature full-bleed close-up color player photos, with the player's name at the bottom of the card face. The insides list the 1990-91 varsity basketball schedule. The backs carry the words "1990-91 UNC Basketball Schedule" and the sponsor's logo in black letters on a white background. The cards are unnumbered and checklisted below in alphabetical order.

COMPLETE SET (3) 1.50 4.00
1 Pete Chilcutt .30 .75
2 Rick Fox 1.50 4.00
3 King Rice .20 .50

1991-92 North Carolina Schedules

Sponsored by Hardee's, this one-card set is a schedule card that can be folded in the middle. It measures approximately 2 1/8" by 3 1/2" when folded. The front features a full-bleed close-up color player photo, with the player's name at the bottom of the card face. The inside lists the 1991-92 men's basketball schedule. The card is unnumbered. There also exists a Knox card which carries the women's basketball schedule.

COMPLETE SET (1) .80 2.00
1 Hubert Davis .75 2.00

1992-93 North Carolina Schedules

Sponsored by Hardee's, this five-card set features schedule cards each measuring the standard size when folded in the middle. The fronts feature glossy full-bleed color player photos of seniors with their names across the bottom of the picture. The insides carry the 1992-93 men's basketball schedule. On white backgrounds, the backs have the words "1992-93 UNC Basketball Schedule" and the sponsor's logo. The cards are unnumbered and checklisted below in alphabetical order.

COMPLETE SET (5) 1.00 2.50
1 Scott Cherry .20 .50
2 George Lynch .40 1.00
3 Henrik Rodl .20 .50
4 Travis Stephenson .20 .50
5 Matt Wenstrom .20 .50

1993-94 North Carolina Schedules

1 Eric Montross .60 1.50
2 Derrick Phelps .20 .50
3 Brian Reese .20 .50
4 Kevin Salvadori .20 .50
5 Pat Sullivan .20 .50

1994-95 North Carolina Schedules

1 Pearce Landry .20 .50
2 Pat Sullivan .20 .50
3 Donald Williams .20 .50

1995-96 North Carolina Schedules

Continuing the tradition of featuring all of the seniors from each year's team, the 1995-96 UNC schedule set is highlighted by the inclusion of scrappy Dante Calabria. As is typical with UNC skeds, these skeds eature a close-up, full color, posed shot of each player. The skeds were distributed for free at 1996-97 home games. Though they are unnumbered on back, we've checklisted them below alphabetically for convenience.

COMPLETE SET (3) .40 1.00
1 Dante Calabria .30 .75
2 Clyde Lynn .08 .25
3 David Neal .08 .25

1996-97 North Carolina Schedules

The 1996-97 UNC skeds features the typical theme of honoring each senior with his own schedule. This year's set is highlighted by the inclusion of NBA draftee Serge Zwikker. Each schedule features a full color, posed shot. The schedules were distributed for free at 1996-97 home games. Though unnumbered, we've checklisted them below in alphabetical order for convenience.

COMPLETE SET (3) .40 1.00
1 Charlie McNairy .08 .25
2 Webb Tyndall .08 .25
3 Serge Zwikker .40 1.00

1997-98 North Carolina Schedules

The 1997-98 UNC skeds features the typical theme of honoring each senior with his own schedule. Each schedule features a full color, posed shot. The schedules were distributed for free at 1997-98 home games. The schedules were sponsered by Hardee's. Though unnumbered, we've checklisted them below in alphabetical order for convenience.

COMPLETE SET (2) .40 1.00
1 Makhtar Ndiaye .20 .50
2 Shammond Williams .20 .50

1998-99 North Carolina Schedules

1 Brad Frederick .20 .50
2 Ademola Okulaja .20 .50
3 Scott Williams .20 .50

1999-00 North Carolina Schedules

1 Ed Cota .20 .50
2 Terrence Newby .20 .50

2000-01 North Carolina Schedules

1 Michael Brooker .20 .50
2 Jim Everett .20 .50
3 Brendan Haywood .40 1.00
4 Max Owens .20 .50

2001-02 North Carolina Schedules

1 Brian Bersticker .20 .50
2 Jason Capel .20 .50
3 Kris Lang .20 .50
4 Orlando Melendez .20 .50

2002-03 North Carolina Schedules

1 Jonathan Holmes .20 .50
2 Will Johnson .20 .50

2003-04 North Carolina Schedules

1 Jackie Manuel .20 .50
2 Melvin Scott .20 .50
3 Jawad Williams .20 .50

2004-05 North Carolina Schedules

1 Jackie Manuel .20 .50
2 Melvin Scott .20 .50
3 Jawad Williams .20 .50

2005-06 North Carolina Schedules

1 David Noel .20 .50
2 Byron Sanders .20 .50

2006-07 North Carolina Schedules

1 Wes Miller .20 .50
2 Reyshawn Terry .20 .50

2007-08 North Carolina Schedules

1 Quentin Thomas .20 .50
2 Surry Wood .20 .50

2008-09 North Carolina Schedules

1 Mike Copeland .20 .50
2 Bobby Frasor .20 .50
3 Marcus Ginyard .20 .50
4 Danny Green .40 1.00
5 Tyler Hansbrough 1.00 2.50
6 Patrick Moody .20 .50
7 J.B. Tanner .20 .50
8 Jack Wooten .20 .50

2009-10 North Carolina Schedules

1 Marc Campbell .20 .50
2 Marcus Ginyard .20 .50
3 Dion Thompson .20 .50

2010-11 North Carolina Schedules

1 Justin Knox .20 .50

2011-12 North Carolina Schedules

1 Stewart Cooper .20 .50
2 Patrick Crouch .20 .50
3 David Dupont .20 .50
4 Justin Watts .20 .50
5 Tyler Zeller .60 1.50

1972-73 North Carolina State Schedules

1 Tom Burleson 2.00 5.00

1973-74 North Carolina State Playing Cards

This 54-card standard size set features former North Carolina State University All-America players and team photos of ACC champions. The set is designed like a playing card set and has rounded corners and black-and-white photos on white backgrounds. The backs are red on white and display the N.C. State mascot and have the words "Pack Power" printed above the mascot and "Wolfpack Country" printed below in red outlined block letters. Since the set is similar to a playing card deck, it is checklisted below as if it were a playing card set. In the checklist C means Clubs, D means Diamonds, H means Hearts, S means Spades, and JK means Joker. The cards are checklisted in playing card order by suits and numbers are assigned to Aces (1), Jacks (11), Queens (12), and Kings (13). The jokers are unnumbered and listed at the end.

COMPLETE SET (54) 50.00 120.00
C1 Willis Casey AD .40 1.00
C2 Ken Gehring .40 1.00
C3 Steve Smith .75 2.00
C4 Dwight Johnson .40 1.00
C5 Jerry Hunt .40 1.00
C6 Tommy Burleson 2.00 5.00
C7 John Richter .40 1.00
C8 Lou Pucillo .40 1.00
C9 Vic Molodet .40 1.00
C10 Ronnie Shavlik .40 1.00
C11 Bob Speight .40 1.00
C12 Sammy Ranzino .40 1.00
C13 Dick Dickey .40 1.00
D1 Everett Case CO 1.25 3.00
D2 1965 ACC Champs .75 2.00
D3 1959 ACC Champs .75 2.00
D4 1956 ACC Champs .75 2.00

D5 1955 ACC Champs .75 2.00
D6 1954 ACC Champs .75 2.00
D7 1953 Dixie Classic .75 2.00
D8 1952 S.C. Champs .75 2.00
D9 1951 S.C. Champs .75 2.00
D10 1950 S.C. Champs .75 2.00
D11 1949 S.C. Champs .75 2.00
D12 1948 S.C. Champs .75 2.00
D13 1947 S.C. Champs .75 2.00
H1 Tommy Burleson 2.00 5.00
H2 Bruce Dayhuff .40 1.00
H3 Bill Lake .40 1.00
H4 Mike Buurma .40 1.00
H5 Greg Hawkins .40 1.00
H6 Craig Kuszmaul .40 1.00
H7 Mark Moeller .40 1.00
H8 Phil Spence .40 1.00
H9 Steve Nuce .75 2.00
H10 Moe Rivers .75 2.00
H11 Tim Stoddard .75 2.00
H12 Monte Towe 1.50 4.00
H13 David Thompson 12.00 30.00
S1 Norm Sloan CO 4.00 10.00
S2 Vann Williford .75 2.00
S3 Jo Ann Sloan .40 1.00
S4 Everett Case CO 1.25 3.00
S5 Tommy Burleson 2.00 5.00
S6 Three All-Americans 5.00 12.00
S7 David Thompson 10.00 25.00
S8 David Thompson 10.00 25.00
S9 1970 ACC Champs .75 2.00
S10 1973 ACC Champs 1.25 3.00
S11 Sam Esposito ACO .75 2.00
S12 Art Musselman ACO .40 1.00
S13 Eddie Bierderbach ACO .40 1.00
JK Pack Power .75 2.00
JK Reynolds Coliseum .75 2.00

1973-74 North Carolina State Schedules

1 David Thompson 5.00 12.00

1974-75 North Carolina State Schedules

1 David Thompson 3.00 8.00

1975-76 North Carolina State Schedules

1 Kenny Carr 2.00 5.00

1977-78 North Carolina State Schedules

1 Hawkeye Whitney 2.00 5.00

1978-79 North Carolina State Schedules

1 Clyde Austin 2.00 5.00

1979-80 North Carolina State Schedules

1 Hawkeye Whitney 2.00

1980-81 North Carolina State Schedules

1 Sidney Lowe 1.00 2.50

1981-82 North Carolina State Schedules

1 Thurl Bailey 1.50 4.00

1982-83 North Carolina State Schedules

1 Dereck Whittenburg .40 1.00

1983-84 North Carolina State Schedules

1 Lorenzo Charles .40 1.00

1984-85 North Carolina State Schedules

1 Lorenzo Charles .40 1.00

1985-86 North Carolina State Schedules

1 Jim Valvano 2.00 5.00

1986-87 North Carolina State Schedules

1 Benny Bolton .40 1.00

1987-88 North Carolina State

This 15-card standard-size set commemorates the Wolfpack's 1987 ACC title. It was sponsored by Adolescent CareUnit, IBM, and local police agencies. The sets were distributed at a home game and by police officers. Most fans in attendance at the home game only received 14 cards, because Sean Green transferred after the cards were printed and his cards were removed from the set. A small number of his cards still made their way to the general public. The fronts feature either posed or action color photos on a white card face, with a drop border in red on the bottom and right side of picture. The school name in red and ACC Champions in black appear above the picture, while the player's name is printed in white in the bottom red drop border. The backs carry biography, career summary, and "Tips from the Wolfpack," which consist of anti-drug or alcohol messages. The cards are unnumbered and checklisted below in alphabetical order. The set features the first card of coach Jim Valvano.

COMPLETE SET (15) 10.00 25.00
1 Chucky Brown 1.50 4.00
2 Chris Corchiani 1.50 4.00
3 Brian D'Amico .30 .75
4 Vinny Del Negro 2.00 5.00
5 Sean Green SP 1.50 4.00
6 Brian Howard .50 1.25
7 Quinton Jackson .30 .75
8 Avie Lester .50 1.25
9 Rodney Monroe 1.00 2.50
10 Kenny Poston .30 .75
11 Charles Shackleford .50 1.25
12 Bryon Tucker .30 .75
13 Jim Valvano CO 3.00 8.00
14 Kelsey Weems .30 .75
15 Team Photo .75 2.00

1987-88 North Carolina State Schedules

1 Vinny Del Negro 1.00 2.50

1988-89 North Carolina State

This 16-card standard size (2 1/2" by 3 1/2") set was sponsored by Adolescent CareUnit, IBM, and local police agencies. The sets were given away at a home game and by local police officers. On a white card face, the fronts feature action or posed color photos enclosed by a black drop border on the left and red drop borders on the right and bottom of the picture. A Wolfpack logo appears in the lower left corner while player information appears in the bottom red drop border. The backs carry biography, player profile, and "Tips from the Wolfpack," which consist of anti-drug or alcohol messages. The cards are unnumbered and checklisted below in alphabetical order. The set features the first card of NBA player Tom Gugliotta.

COMPLETE SET (16) 8.00 20.00
1 Chucky Brown 52 1.25 3.00
2 Chris Corchiani 13 1.25 3.00
3 Brian D'Amico 54 .30 .75
4 Tom Gugliotta 24 4.00 10.00
5 Mickey Hinnant 3 .30 .75
6 Brian Howard 22 .60 1.50
7 James Knox 23 .30 .75
8 David Lee 25 .30 .75
9 Avie Lester 32 .30 .75
10 Rodney Monroe .60 1.50
11 Kenny Poston 30 1.25 3.00
12 Jim Valvano CO 2.50 6.00
13 Kelsey Weems 11 .60 1.50
14 Mr. and Mrs. Wuf Mascots .30 .75
15 Kay Yow CO Women's Basketball 1.25 3.00
16 Women's Team .60 1.50

1988-89 North Carolina State Schedules

1 Chucky Brown .40 1.00

1989 North Carolina State Collegiate Collection

This 200-card standard-size set was produced by Collegiate Collection and sponsored by Coca-Cola, and the Coke logo appears in the lower left corner on the card face. The fronts feature a mix of black and white photos for earlier players and color for later ones, with rounded corners and red borders. The pictures are superimposed over a red and white diagonally-striped card face, with a red outer border. The top reads "N.C. State's Finest," and the school logo appears in the upper right corner. The horizontally oriented backs are printed in red on white and present biographical information, career summaries, or statistics.

COMPLETE SET (200) 10.00 25.00
1 Rick Anheuser .07 .15
2 Rick Anheuser .07 .15
3 Rick Anheuser .07 .15
4 Pete Auksel .07 .15
5 Pete Auksel .07 .15
6 Pete Auksel .07 .15
7 Clyde Austin .07 .20
8 Clyde Austin .07 .20
9 Clyde Austin .07 .20
10 Thurl Bailey .10 .30
11 Thurl Bailey .10 .30
12 Thurl Bailey .10 .30
13 Eddie Bartels .07 .15
14 Eddie Bartels .07 .15
15 Eddie Bartels .07 .15
16 Alvin Battle .07 .15
17 Alvin Battle .07 .15
18 Alvin Battle .07 .15
19 William Bell .07 .15
20 William Bell .07 .15
21 Eddie Bierderbach .07 .15
22 Eddie Bierderbach .07 .15
23 Eddie Bierderbach .07 .15
24 Dick Braucher .07 .15
25 Dick Braucher .07 .15
26 Dick Braucher .07 .15
27 Chucky Brown .08 .25
28 Chucky Brown .08 .25
29 Chucky Brown .08 .25
30 Vic Bubas .08 .25
31 Vic Bubas .08 .25
32 Tom Burleson .10 .30
33 Tom Burleson .10 .30
34 Tom Burleson .10 .30
35 Charles Shackleford .07 .20
36 Charles Shackleford .07 .20
37 Charles Shackleford .07 .20
38 Terry Shackleford .07 .15
39 Ronnie Shavlik .07 .15
40 Ronnie Shavlik .07 .15
41 Ronnie Shavlik .07 .15
42 Jon Garwood Speaks .07 .15
43 Jon Garwood Speaks .07 .15
44 Jon Garwood Speaks .07 .15
45 Craig Watts .07 .15
46 Phil Spence .07 .15
47 Phil Spence .07 .20
48 Phil Spence .07 .15
49 Tim Stoddard .08 .25
50 Tim Stoddard .08 .25
51 Tim Stoddard .08 .25
52 Glenn Joseph Sudhop .07 .15
53 Glenn Joseph Sudhop .07 .15
54 Glenn Joseph Sudhop .07 .15
55 Joe Cafferky .07 .15
56 Joe Cafferky .07 .15
57 Larry Wosley .07 .15
58 Kenny Carr .08 .25
59 Kenny Carr .08 .25
60 Kenny Carr .08 .25
61 Horace McKinney .10 .30
62 John Richter .07 .15
63 Warren Cartier .07 .15
64 Paul Coder .07 .15
65 Paul Coder .07 .15
66 Paul Coder .07 .15
67 Bill Kretzer .07 .15
68 Darnell Adell .07 .15
69 Gary Stokan .07 .15
70 Pete Coker .07 .15
71 Dereck Whittenburg .08 .25
72 Pete Coker .07 .15
73 Craig Davis .07 .15
74 Smedes York .07 .15
75 Craig Davis .07 .15
76 Dick Dickey .07 .15
77 Dick Dickey .07 .15
78 Dick Dickey .07 .15
79 Tommy Dinardo .07 .15
80 Tommy Dinardo .07 .15
81 Vann Williford .07 .15
82 Bob Distefano .07 .15
83 Dan Englehardt .07 .15
84 Dan Englehardt .07 .15
85 Gary Stokan .07 .15
86 Smedes York .07 .15
87 Vann Williford .07 .15
88 Vinny Del Negro .10 .30
89 Vinny Del Negro .10 .30
90 Vinny Del Negro .10 .30
91 Larry Larkins .07 .15
92 Larry Larkins .07 .15
93 Larry Larkins .07 .15
94 Larry Larkins .07 .15
95 Sidney Lowe .08 .25
96 Sidney Lowe .08 .25
97 Ernest Myers .07 .15
98 Ernest Myers .07 .15
99 Ernest Myers .07 .15
100 Checklist 1-100 .07 .15
101 Hal Blondeau .07 .15
102 Les Robinson .10 .30
103 Nate McMillan .10 .30
104 Nate McMillan .10 .30
105 Nate McMillan .10 .30
106 Charles G. Nevitt .08 .25
107 Charles G. Nevitt .08 .25
108 Charles G. Nevitt .08 .25
109 Quinton Leonard .07 .15
110 Bruce Hoadley .07 .15
111 Les Robinson .10 .30
112 Bruce Hoadley .07 .15
113 Emmett Lay .07 .15
114 Emmett Lay .07 .15
115 Larry Worsley .07 .15
116 Harold Thompson .07 .15
117 Harold Thompson .07 .15
118 Harold Thompson .07 .15
119 Howard Turner .07 .15
120 Mike O'Neal Warren .07 .15
121 Mike O'Neal Warren .07 .15
122 Kenny Matthews .07 .15
123 Anthony Warren .07 .15
124 Anthony Warren .07 .15
125 Vann Williford .07 .15
126 Raymond Walters .07 .15
127 Raymond Walters .07 .15
128 Raymond Walters .07 .15
129 Craig T. Watts .07 .15
130 Larry Worsley .07 .15
131 Craig T. Watts .07 .15
132 Spud Webb .15 .40
133 Spud Webb .15 .40
134 Spud Webb .15 .40
135 Ray Hodgdon .07 .15
136 Herb Applebaum .07 .15
137 Bill Kretzer .07 .15
138 Charles Whitney .07 .20
139 Charles Whitney .07 .20
140 Charles Whitney .07 .20
141 Dereck Whittenburg .08 .25
142 Dereck Whittenburg .08 .25
143 Tom Mattocks .07 .15
144 Tom Mattocks .07 .15
145 Tom Mattocks .07 .15
146 Mark Moeller .07 .15
147 Mark Moeller .07 .15
148 Mark Moeller .07 .15
149 Cheerleader Mascot .07 .15
150 Quentin Jackson .07 .15
151 Quentin Jackson .07 .15
152 Steve Nuce .07 .15
153 Steve Nuce .07 .15
154 Steve Nuce .07 .15
155 Scott Parzych .07 .15
156 Scott Parzych .07 .15
157 Scott Parzych .07 .15
158 Dan Wherry .07 .15
159 Hal Blondeau .07 .15
160 Dan Wherry .07 .15
161 Mascots .07 .15
162 Max Perry .07 .15
163 Max Perry .07 .15
164 David Thompson .30 .75
165 David Thompson .30 .75
166 David Thompson .30 .75
167 Monte Towe .08 .25
168 Monte Towe .08 .25
169 Monte Towe .08 .25
170 Press Maravich .07 .20
171 Terry Gannon .08 .25
172 Nick Pond .07 .15
173 Lou Pucillo .07 .15
174 Ray Hodgdon .07 .15
175 Darnell Adell .07 .15
176 Herb Applebaum .07 .15
177 Max Perry .07 .15
178 John Richter .07 .20
179 Kenny Poston .07 .20
180 Terry Gannon .08 .25
181 Pete Coker .07 .15
182 Quentin Jackson .07 .15
183 Jim Rezinger .07 .15
184 Kenny Poston .07 .20
185 Rick Hoot .07 .15
186 Everett Case .08 .25
187 Everett Case .08 .25
188 Everett Case .08 .25
189 Kenny Matthews .07 .15
190 Reynolds Stadium .07 .20
191 Jim Valvano CO .20 .50
192 Jim Valvano CO .20 .50
193 Jim Valvano CO .20 .50
194 Cheerleaders .07 .20
195 Ray Hodgdon .07 .15
196 Lou Pucillo .07 .15
197 Kenny Poston .07 .20
198 Everett Case .08 .25
199 Reynolds Coliseum .07 .15
200 Checklist 101-200 .07 .15

1989-90 North Carolina State

This 16-card set of standard-size cards was sponsored by Hardee's WPTF/680 AM radio, and IBM; these company logos adorn the top of observe and the bottom of the reverse. The front features a color action player photo, with red borders on the top, right, and for most of the bottom. The school name and player identification is given in the top and bottom borders, with the year "1989-90" in the lower left corner. The back has biographical information and "Tips from the Wolfpack," which consist of anti-drug messages. The cards are unnumbered and are checklisted below in alphabetical order, with the uniform number after the player's name. The set features a card of NBA player Tom Gugliotta.

COMPLETE SET (16) 6.00 15.00
1 Chris Corchiani 13 .60 1.50
2 Brian D'Amico 54 .30 .75
3 Bryant Feggins 34 .60 1.50
4 Tom Gugliotta 24 3.00 8.00
5 Mickey Hinnant 3 .30 .75
6 Brian Howard 22 .60 1.50
7 Jamie Knox 23 .30 .75
8 David Lee 25 .30 .75
9 Avie Lester 32 .30 .75
10 Rodney Monroe 21 .60 1.50
11 Andrea Stinson 32 2.00 5.00
12 Kevin Thompson 42 .60 1.50
13 Jim Valvano CO 2.00 5.00
14 Roland Whitley 15 .30 .75
15 Wuf (Mascot) .30 .75
16 Kay Yow Women's Coach 1.25 3.00

1989-90 North Carolina State Schedules

1 Brian Howard Avie Lester .40 1.00

1990-91 North Carolina State

This 16-card standard size set was cosponsored by IBM and Nabisco Brands. Reportedly 2500 sets were given away at Youth Night before a home game, and an equal number of sets were distributed by local police officers. On a white card face, the fronts feature action or posed color photos enclosed by a red border. The school name appears above the picture, while player information is provided beneath the picture. A Wolfpack logo appears in the lower right corner in a circle. The backs carry biography and player profile, with anti-drug and alcohol messages in a black box. The cards are unnumbered and checklisted below in alphabetical order. The key card in the set features NBA player Tom Gugliotta.

COMPLETE SET (16) 6.00 15.00
1 Migjen Bakalli .30 .75
2 Chris Corchiani .60 1.50
3 Bryant Feggins .30 .75
4 Adam Fletcher .30 .75
5 Tom Gugliotta 3.00 8.00
6 Jamie Knox .30 .75
7 David Lee .30 .75
8 Marc Lewis .30 .75
9 Rodney Monroe .60 1.50
10 Anthony Robinson .30 .75
11 Les Robinson CO .60 1.50
12 Andrea Stinson 1.50 4.00
13 Kevin Thompson .60 1.50
14 Kay Yow CO Women's Basketball 1.25 3.00
15 Celebrating a Victory Paul Campion Chris Ritter Tim Thompson .30 .75
16 Mr. Wuf (Mascot) .30 .75

1990-91 North Carolina State Schedules

1 Chris Corchiani Rodney Monroe Les Robinson 1.25 3.00

1991-92 North Carolina State

This 16-card standard size set was cosponsored by IBM and Nabisco Biscuit Company. The print run was limited to 5,000 sets, and the sets were given away at Youth Night and distributed by the local police department. The fronts feature action color player photos enclosed by a red border. The team name is superimposed in white lettering at the top of the picture, while the player's name, Wolfpack logo, and sponsor names appear at the bottom of the card face. In a horizontal format, the backs carry a black and white mug shot, biography, career highlights, and anti-drug messages in a black box. The cards are unnumbered and checklisted below in alphabetical order. The key card in the set features NBA player Tom Gugliotta.

COMPLETE SET (16) 5.00 12.00
1 Migjen Bakalli .30 .75
2 Mark Davis .60 1.50
3 Bryant Feggins .30 .75
4 Adam Fletcher .30 .75
5 Tom Gugliotta 2.50 6.00
6 Jamie Knox .30 .75
7 Marc Lewis .30 .75
8 Curtis Marshall .30 .75
9 Lakista McCuller .30 .75
10 Victor Newman .30 .75
11 Anthony Robinson .30 .75
12 Les Robinson CO .60 1.50
13 Donnie Seale .30 .75
14 Kevin Thompson .60 1.50
15 Mr. Wuf (Mascot) .30 .75
16 Reynolds Coliseum .60 1.50

1991-92 North Carolina State Schedules

1 Tom Gugliotta Les Robinson 2.00 5.00

1992-93 North Carolina State

This 16-card set features the 1992-93 North Carolina State Wolfpack. The fronts display color action photos with team color-coded borders. The backs provide a closeup shot and player information. The cards are unnumbered and checklisted below in alphabetical order.

COMPLETE SET (16) 4.00 10.00
1 Migjen Bakalli .30 .75
2 Mark Davis .60 1.50
3 Todd Fuller 1.50 4.00
4 Jamie Knox .30 .75
5 Chuck Kornegay .60 1.50
6 Bill Kretzer .30 .75
7 Marc Lewis .30 .75
8 Curtis Marshall .30 .75
9 Lakista McCuller .30 .75
10 Victor Newman .30 .75
11 Les Robinson CO .60 1.50
12 Donnie Seale .30 .75
13 Kevin Thompson .30 .75
14 Marcus Wilson .30 .75
15 Mr. Wuf (Mascot) .30 .75
16 Coaching Staff .30 .75

1992-93 North Carolina State Schedules

1 Kevin Thompson .20 .50

1993-94 North Carolina State

This 16-card set features the 1993-94 North Carolina State Wolfpack. The fronts display color action photos with team color-coded borders. The backs provide a closeup shot and player information. The cards are unnumbered and checklisted below in alphabetical order.

COMPLETE SET (16) 5.00 12.00
1 Greg Clucas .30 .75
2 Ricky Daniels .30 .75
3 Mark Davis .60 1.50
4 Bryant Feggins .30 .75
5 Todd Fuller 1.00 2.50
6 Jeremy Hyatt .60 1.50
7 Bill Kretzer .30 .75
8 Marc Lewis .30 .75
9 Lakista McCuller .30 .75
10 Curtis Marshall .30 .75
11 Les Robinson CO .60 1.50
12 Lewis Sims .30 .75
13 Jason Sutton .30 .75
14 Marcus Wilson .30 .75
15 Mr. Wuf (Mascot) .30 .75
16 Coaching Staff .30 .75

1993-94 North Carolina State Schedules

1 Migjen Bakalli Marc Lewis Les Robinson .40 1.00

1994-95 North Carolina State

This 16-card set features the 1994-95 North Carolina State Wolfpack. The fronts display color action photos with team color-coded borders. The backs provide a closeup shot and player information. The cards are unnumbered and checklisted below in alphabetical order.

COMPLETE SET (16) 4.00 10.00
1 Ishua Benjamin .60 1.50
2 Ricky Daniels .30 .75
3 Mark Davis .40 1.00
4 Bryant Feggins .30 .75
5 Todd Fuller .75 2.00
6 Clint(CC) Harrison .30 .75
7 Jeremy Hyatt .60 1.50
8 Bill Kretzer .30 .75
9 Lakista McCuller .30 .75
10 Curtis Marshall .30 .75
11 Al Pinkins .30 .75
12 Geoff Richards .30 .75
13 Les Robinson CO .60 1.50
14 Jason Sutton .30 .75
15 Marcus Wilson .30 .75
16 Coaching Staff .30 .75

1994-95 North Carolina State Schedules

1 Ricky Daniels .20 .50
2 Mark Davis .20 .50
3 Bryant Feggins .20 .50
4 Curtis Marshall .20 .50
5 Lakista McCuller .20 .50

1995-96 North Carolina State Schedules

1 Todd Fuller .40 1.00

1997-98 North Carolina State

This 17-card standard size set, highlighting the 1996-97 Wolfpack basketball team, was produced by Action Graphics in conjunction with Sears Roebuck and The National Association of Basketball Coaches. The card fronts have color action photos transposed over a red sea of fans background within a black border. "Wolfpack Basketball" is written in cursive at the top and an Action Graphics logo can be found at the bottom. The black and white horizontal backs carry player biographies and career high NC State statistics through January 1997. The right side dawns a close-up photo and anti-drug advice. The cards are numbered out of 16, but there was also a cover card that gives information on how to support the Coaches vs. Cancer Program.

COMPLETE SET (17) 3.00 8.00
1 Team Photo CL .40 1.00
2 Herb Sendek CO .20 .50
3 John Groce ACO Larry Harris ACO Sean Miller ACO .20 .50
4 Ishua Benjamin .40 1.00
5 Luke Buffum .20 .50
6 Justin Gainey .20 .50
7 Clint C.C. Harrison .20 .50
8 Jeremy Hyatt .40 1.00
9 Andre McCullum .60 1.50
10 Steve Norton .20 .50
11 Al Pinkins .20 .50
12 Danny Strong .40 1.00
13 Jason Sutton .20 .50
14 Damon Thornton .40 1.00
15 Tim Wells .20 .50
16 Mr. Wuf (Mascot) .20 .50
NNO Sears Coaches vs. Cancer Cover Card .20 .50

1997-98 North Carolina State Schedules

1 Ishua Benjamin C.C. Harrison .40 1.00

1999-00 North Carolina State Schedules

1 Justin Gainey .20 .50

2000-01 North Carolina State Schedules

1 Kenny Inge Ron Kelley Damon Thornton Cornelius Williams .40 1.00

2001-02 North Carolina State Schedules

1 Archie Miller .20 .50

2002-03 North Carolina State Schedules

1 Clifford Crawford .20 .50

2003-04 North Carolina State Schedules

1 Marcus Melvin Scooter Sherrill .40 1.00

2004-05 North Carolina State Schedules

1 Jordan Collins Julius Hodge Levi Watkins .40 1.00

2005-06 North Carolina State Schedules

1 Cameron Bennerman Tony Bethel Illian Evtimov .40 1.00

2006-07 North Carolina State Schedules

1 Sidney Lowe .40 1.00

2007-08 North Carolina State Schedules

1 Gavin Grant Chad Williams .40 1.00

2008-09 North Carolina State Schedules

1 Brandon Costner Courtney Fells Simon Harris Ben McCauley .40 1.00

2009-10 North Carolina State Schedules

1 Fernold Degand Dennis Horner .40 1.00

2010-11 North Carolina State Schedules

1 Javier Gonzalez Tracy Smith .40 1.00

2011-12 North Carolina State Schedules

1 Richard Howell Mark Gottfried C.J. Williams Scott Wood .40 1.00

1991-92 North Dakota

COMPLETE SET (12) 6.00 12.00
1 Whitney Meier Greg Johnson David Vonesh men's basketball .20 .50
2 Marty McDermott Chris Gardner Scott Guldseth men's basketball .20 .50
3 Ben Jacobson Steve McAndrew David Robertson men's basketball .20 .50
4 Jonathon Marshall Mike Wiskus Broderick Powell men's basketball
5 Todd Johnson Mark Sipple James Baird men's basketball .20 .50
6 Men's Basketball Team Photo .20 .50
7 Women's Basketball Team Photo .20 .50
8 Darcy Deutsch Tracey Pudenz Jenny Walter women's basketball .20 .50
9 Heidi Kasprowicz Misty Langseth Shea Smirl women's basketball .20 .50
10 Maria Oistad Heidi Meyer Emily Shilhanek women's basketball .20 .50

1997-98 Northwestern Women

This 20-card set was released at Northwestern University during the 1997-98 season. The set features player cards from that season's team. These cards are not numbered, and are listed below in alphabetical order. Please note that these cards were issued as singles, and were not distributed as complete team sets.

COMPLETE SET (20) 4.00 10.00
1 Team Photo .20 .50
2 Don Perrelli CO .75 2.00
3 Robin Garrett Amy Backus Jennifer Kiefer CO .20 .50
4 Lisa Byington Mary Connolly Amber DeWall Shannon McGarrigle Candace Wrenn .20 .50
5 Becky Fisher Clarissa Flores Chala Holland Dana Leonard Tami Sears .20 .50
6 Leah Berki .20 .50
7 Lisa Byington .20 .50
8 Megan Chawansky .20 .50
9 Mary Connolly .20 .50
10 Amber DeWall .20 .50
11 Kristina Divjak .20 .50
12 Becky Fisher .20 .50
13 Clarissa Flores .20 .50
14 Anne Giblin .20 .50
15 Chala Holland .20 .50
16 Dana Leonard .20 .50
17 Shannon McGarrigle .20 .50
18 Leslie Schock .20 .50
19 Tami Sears .20 .50
20 Candace Wrenn .20 .50

1998-99 Northwestern Women

Released as a 16-card set, the cards measure standard size and feature photos of the 1998-99 Northwestern Women's basketball team. The cards are not numbered and listed below in alphabetical order.

COMPLETE SET (16) 2.50 6.00
1 Leah Berki .20 .50
2 Megan Chawansky .20 .50
3 Kristina Divjak .20 .50
4 Becky Fisher .20 .50
5 Clarissa Flores .20 .50
6 Anne Giblin .20 .50
7 Chala Holland .20 .50
8 Sara Jurek .20 .50
9 Dana Leonard .20 .50
10 Shannon McGarrigle .20 .50
11 Billee Russell .20 .50
12 Leslie Schock .20 .50
13 Tami Sears .20 .50
14 Team Photo .20 .50
15 Don Perrelli CO .30 .75
16 Robin Garrett ACO Amy Backus ACO Jennifer Kiefer ACO .20 .50

1988 Notre Dame Smokey

This 14-card standard size set was sponsored by the U. S. Forestry Service. The front features a color action photo, with orange and green borders on a purple background. The back has biographical information (or a schedule) and a fire prevention cartoon starring Smokey the Bear. These unnumbered cards are ordered alphabetically within type for convenience. Ricky Watters is featured in this set.

COMPLETE SET (14) 14.00 35.00
15 Women's Basketball .60 1.50

1990-91 Notre Dame

This 58 card standard-size set is a retrospective on famous and outstanding players at Notre Dame. The cards are numbered as "X of 58"; the Anson card is unnumbered and is the only baseball player featured and is not considered part of the set On the front of the cards, older players appear in black and white photos while newer players appear in color. These current players have been highlighted in the checklist below with the word "NEW" after each name. The photos are enframed by a black line on a white background, with the school name and the Notre Dame logo (upper right hand corner) above the photo, and the player's name below. The card backs provide biographical information, including the player's position and the team they played on. Past and present NBA players included are Gary Brokaw, Austin Carr, Adrian Dantley, LaPhonso Ellis (his first card), Bill Hanzlik, Tom Hawkins, Toby Knight, Bill Laimbeer, John Paxson, David Rivers, John Shumate, Kelly Tripucka, and Orlando Woolridge.

COMPLETE SET (59) 10.00 25.00
CAP ANSON NOT INCLUDED IN SET
1 Richard (Digger) Phelps NEW .75 2.00
2 Collis Jones .20 .50
3 Dick Rosenthal .20 .50
4 Tim Singleton NEW .30 .75
5 Austin Carr .40 1.00
6 Kevin O'Shea .20 .50
7 Keith Tower NEW .40 1.00
8 Tom Hawkins .40 1.00
9 Leo Barnhorst .30 .75
10 John Shumate .40 1.00
11 Donald Royal .40 1.00
12 Edward(Moose) Krause .20 .50
13 Bill Laimbeer .75 2.00
14 Adrian Dantley .75 2.00
15 Keith Robinson .20 .50
16 Edward(Monk) Malloy .20 .50
17 Leo Klier .20 .50
18 Rich Branning .20 .50
19 Don(Duck) Williams .20 .50
20 Kevin Ellery NEW .30 .75
21 Eddie Smith .20 .50
22 Ken Barlow .40 1.00
23 LaPhonso Ellis NEW 2.00 5.00
24 John Nyikos .20 .50
25 Daimon Sweet NEW .60 1.50
26 Jack Stephens .20 .50
27 Orlando Woolridge .75 2.00
28 Noble Kizer .20 .50
29 John Smyth .20 .50
30 John Paxson .75 2.00
31 Paul Nowak .20 .50
32 Elmer Bennett NEW .60 1.50
33 Toby Knight .20 .50
34 Dave Batton .20 .50
35 Bob Whitmore .20 .50
36 David Rivers .40 1.00
37 Gary Brokaw .40 1.00
38 Gary Novak .20 .50
39 Lloyd Aubrey .20 .50
40 Robert Faught .20 .50
41 Raymond Scanlan .20 .50
42 Bill Hanzlik .40 1.00
43 Vince Boryla .30 .75
44 Eddie Riska .20 .50
45 Dwight Clay .20 .50
46 Bruce Flowers .25 .60
47 Ray Meyer .75 2.00
48 Monty Williams NEW 1.00 2.50
49 John Moir .20 .50
50 Bill Hassett .20 .50
51 Bob Arnzen .20 .50
52 Robert Rensberger .20 .50
53 Larry Sheffield .20 .50
54 Kelly Tripucka .40 1.00
55 Ron Reed .40 1.00
56 George Ireland .20 .50
57 Tracy Jackson .40 1.00
58 Walt Sahm .20 .50
NNO Adrian(Cap) Anson 1.25 3.00

1996-97 Notre Dame Schedules

Featuring a surprisingly lively design, highlighted by full color action photos framed by gold borders and dark blue text, cards from this schedule set feature all three seniors from the 1996-97 team. The schedules were distributed for free at home games throughout the 1996-97 season. The schedules are unnumbered on back and have been checklisted below alphabetically for convenience.

COMPLETE SET (3) .30 .75
1 Matt Gotsch .08 .25
2 Ardmore White .08 .25
3 Marcus Young .08 .25

1991 Oklahoma State Collegiate Collection

This 100-card multi-sport standard-size set was produced by Collegiate Collection. We've cataloged players from the top three sports using these initials: B-baseball, K-basketball, and F-football.

COMPLETE SET (100) 6.00 15.00
1 Henry Iba K .08 .25
8 1945 NCAA Basketball .05 .15
40 John Starks K .20 .50
49 Jess(Cob) Rennick K .05 .15
80 Gale McArthur K .05 .15
99 Eddie Sutton K .08 .25

1999-00 Oklahoma State

This fifteen-card standard-size set was issued to commemorate the 1999-2000 Oklahoma State care. It was issued in a sheet of 16 cards, which when perforated, measures the standard size for each card. Since these cards are unnumbered, we have sequenced them in alphabetical order. This set was sponsored by Oklahoma Gas and Electric.

COMPLETE SET (15) 6.00 15.00
1 Joe Adkins .20 .50
2 Glendon Alexander .20 .50
3 Zac Cazzelle .20 .50
4 Nate Fleming .20 .50
5 Doug Gottlieb .40 1.00
6 Fredrik Jonzen .20 .50
7 Jason Keep .20 .50
8 Daniel Lawson .20 .50
9 Desmond Mason 4.00 10.00
10 Brian Montonati .20 .50
11 Rodney Sooter .20 .50
12 Eddie Sutton CO 1.25 3.00
13 Alex Webber .20 .50
14 Andre Williams .20 .50
15 Gallagher-Iba Arena .20 .50

1991-92 Ohio State

This 15-card standard-size set was produced by College Classics of Columbus, Ohio. The cards were sold in the university bookstore and at a souvenir shop in St. John Arena. The cards were sold through April 30, and the print run was limited by the number of sets requested by the bookstore. It is reported that more than 10,000 sets were sold in the first four weeks. The fronts features either action or posed color player photos enclosed by red and gray borders. The player's name is printed in a gray stripe beneath the picture, while his position appears in a gray stripe along the right side of the picture. The school logo appears at the top right of the photo. In a horizontal format, the backs carry a color head shot, school logo, biography, career summary, and statistics. The cards are unnumbered and checklisted below in alphabetical order. The key card in the set features NBA player Jim Jackson.

COMPLETE SET (15) 6.00 15.00
1 Randy Ayers CO .40 1.00
2 Mark Baker .40 1.00
3 Tom Brandewie .20 .50
4 Jamaal Brown .20 .50
5 Alex Davis .20 .50
6 Rickey Dudley .75 2.00
7 Doug Etzler .20 .50
8 Lawrence Funderburke 1.25 3.00
9 Steve Hall .20 .50
10 Jim Jackson 3.00 8.00
11 Chris Jent 1.25 3.00
12 Jimmy Ratliff .20 .50
13 Joe Reid .20 .50
14 Bill Robinson .20 .50
15 Jamie Skelton .40 1.00

1992-93 Ohio State

This 15-card set measures the standard size (2 1/2" by 3 1/2") and was available through the Ohio State Department of Athletics, the Arena Shop, and its affiliated bookstores. The fronts feature color action player photos bordered on the left or right edge by a gray stripe containing the school name. The player's name appears in red lettering on a gray stripe at the bottom. The horizontal backs feature close-up player pictures with gray shadow box borders. The white background is printed with a profile of the player. The school logo and biographical information appear at the top. The cards are numbered on the back.

COMPLETE SET (15) 5.00 12.00
1 Randy Ayers CO .40 1.00
2 Derek Anderson 2.50 6.00
3 Tom Brandewie .20 .50
4 Alex Davis .20 .50
5 Rickey Dudley 1.00 2.50
6 Gerald Eaker .20 .50
7 Doug Etzler .20 .50
8 Lawrence Funderburke .75 2.00
9 Charles Macon .20 .50
10 Jimmy Ratliff .20 .50

11 Greg Simpson .40 1.00
12 Jamie Skelton .40 1.00
13 Antonio Watson .20 .50
14 Nate Wilbourne .20 .50
15 Otis Winston .20 .50

1992-93 Ohio State Women

This 16-card set features the 1992-93 Ohio State Lady Buckeyes. The cards measure the standard size. The fronts feature color action photos; the backs provide biography and statistics. The cards are unnumbered and checklisted below in alphabetical order. This set includes the first card of Katie Smith.

COMPLETE SET (16) 5.00 12.00
1 Alysiah Bond .20 .50
2 Audrey Burcy .20 .50
3 Nancy Darsch CO .20 .50
4 Kelly Fergus .20 .50
5 Stacie Howard .20 .50
6 Erin Ingwersen .20 .50
7 Gigi Jackson .20 .50
8 Adrienne Johnson .40 1.00
9 Nikki Keyton .20 .50
10 Lisa Negri .20 .50
11 Averrill Roberts .20 .50
12 Lisa Sebastian .20 .50
13 Katie Smith 3.00 8.00
14 Lavona Turner .20 .50
15 Big Bear .20 .50
(Sponsor card)
16 820 WOSU-AM .20 .50
(Sponsor card)

1993-94 Ohio State

This is a 12-card standard size set. The gray-bordered fronts feature color action player shots with a series of basketballs apearing to bounce along the bottom of the photo. Above the photo is the players name printed in red with a black drop shadow. Below the photo the players number is printed in red and their position is printed on top in black. The white backs carry a player head shot with the biography to the right and the player profile below. The cards are numbered and checklisted below. Card number 2 was never issued.

COMPLETE SET (12) 4.00 10.00
1 Randy Ayers CO .60 1.50
3 Jamie Skelton .40 1.00
4 Jimmy Ratliff .20 .50
5 Derek Anderson 1.50 4.00
6 Doug Etzler .20 .50
7 Charles Macon .20 .50
8 Greg Simpson .40 1.00
9 Antonio Watson .20 .50
10 Rickey Dudley .75 2.00
11 Gerald Eaker .20 .50
12 Nate Wilbourne .20 .50
13 Otis Winston .20 .50

1993-94 Ohio State Women

This 16-card set features the 1993-94 Ohio State Lady Buckeyes. The cards measure the standard size. The fronts feature color action photos; the backs provide biography and statistics. The cards are unnumbered and checklisted below in alphabetical order. This set includes the second card of Katie Smith.

COMPLETE SET (16) 4.00 10.00
1 Marcie Alberts .20 .50
2 Alysiah Bond .20 .50
3 Nancy Darsch CO .20 .50
4 Kelly Fergus .20 .50
5 Stacie Howard .20 .50
6 Erin Ingwersen .20 .50
7 Gigi Jackson .20 .50
8 Adrienne Johnson .30 .75
9 Lisa Negri .20 .50
10 Katie Smith 2.50 6.00
11 Marlene Stollings .20 .50
12 Amy Turner .20 .50
13 Lavona Turner .20 .50
14 Team Photo .30 .75
15 Big Bear .20 .50
(Sponsor card)
16 1460 WBNS-AM .20 .50
(Sponsor card)

1994-95 Ohio State Women

This set consists of 16 standard-size cards. Inside white borders, the fronts feature color action player photos. Player information is printed on a bar that is superposed on a basketball-and-hardwood floor design. On a ghosted version of the school logo, the backs carry biography and player profile. The cards are unnumbered and checklisted below in alphabetical order, with nonplayer cards listed at the end.

COMPLETE SET (16) 3.00 8.00
1 Marcie Alberts .20 .50
2 Alysiah Bond .20 .50
3 Peggy Evans .20 .50
4 Kelly Fergus .20 .50
5 Tiffany Glosson .20 .50
6 Erin Ingwersen .20 .50
7 GiGi Jackson .20 .50
8 Adrienne Johnson .25 .60
9 Lisa Negri .20 .50
10 Katie Smith 2.00 5.00
11 Marlene Stollings .20 .50
12 Amy Turner .20 .50
13 Melissa McFerrin ACO .20 .50
Nancy Darsch CO
Nikita Lowry ACO
14 1994-95 OSU Buckeyes .20 .50
Go Bucks!
15 Big Bear .20 .50
(Sponsor card)
16 1460 WBNS-AM Radio .20 .50
(Sponsor Card)

1997-98 Ohio State

This 22-card set is unnumbered and listed below in alphabetical order. The cards feature top athletes from both men's and women's sports at Ohio State.

COMPLETE SET (22) 4.00 10.00
1 Roslyn Barker BK .20 .50
17 Jason Singleton BK .20 .50

2000-01 Ohio State

Released by Ohio State in conjunction with Honda, this 16-card set was released as a sheet. The card backgrounds are read and feature a basketball design and the card backs showcase player photos and biographies.

COMPLETE SET (16) 1.25 3.00
COMPLETE SHEET 2.00 5.00
3 Sean Connolly .15 .40
4 Brent Darby .15 .40
10 Doylan Robinson .15 .40
13 Brian Brown .15 .40
14 Velimir Radinovic .15 .40
21 Boban Savovic .15 .40
23 Ryan Heflin .15 .40
24 Shaun Smith .15 .40
31 Kel Frazier .15 .40
32 Ken Johnson .15 .40
33 Zach Williams .15 .40
34 Cobe Ocokoljic .15 .40
43 Will Dudley .15 .40
44 Tim Martin .15 .40
NNO Mascot .15 .40
NNO Jim O'Brien .75 2.00

2006-07 Ohio State

Produced by Ohio State and sponsored by Gatorade, this 12-player sheet measures 10x12" and each player's card is standard sized and surrounded by perforation lines.

COMPLETE SHEET 12.00 30.00
NNO Daequan Cook 2.00 5.00
NNO Ivan Harris .75 2.00
NNO Othello Hunter .75 2.00
NNO David Lighty .75 2.00
NNO Kyle Madsen .75 2.00
NNO Matt Terwilliger .75 2.00
NNO Jamar Butler 2.00 5.00
NNO Mike Conley Jr. 5.00 12.00
NNO Ron Lewis .75 2.00
NNO Greg Oden 6.00 15.00
NNO Danny Peters .75 2.00
NNO Mark Titus .75 2.00

1992-93 Ohio Valley Conference ATG

These two perforated sheets were issued as an insert in the 1993 Ohio Valley Conference Basketball Tourney Program and feature stars of the past who played in the Ohio Valley Conference. Each sheet consists of nine cards, each measuring approximately 2 5/8" by 3 1/2". The fronts feature black-and-white action player photos on a white card face. In green, the Ohio Valley Conference logo appears in the left corner above the picture, while the words "Stars of the Past" appear in the right corner on a green panel. The player's name is printed in a white stripe below the picture, and the school he attended in a green stripe immediately below. The backs carry biography, statistics, and career summary. The cards are unnumbered and checklisted below in alphabetical order.

COMPLETE SET (18) 6.00 15.00
1 John (Sonny) Allen .60 1.50
2 Jim Baechtold .40 1.00
3 Jerry Beck .40 1.00
4 Tom Chilton .40 1.00
5 Howard Crittenden .40 1.00
6 Jimmy Hagan .40 1.00
7 Steve Hamilton .60 1.50
8 Clem Haskins 1.00 2.50
9 Joe Jakubick .40 1.00
10 Ronald(Popeye) Jones .75 2.00
11 Tom Marshall .40 1.00
12 Jeff Martin .40 1.00
13 Anthony Mason 1.50 4.00
14 Jim McDonald .60 1.50
15 Brett Roberts .40 1.00
16 Kenny Sidwell .40 1.00
17 James (Fly) Williams .75 2.00
18 Stars of the Past .60 1.50
Checklist Card
(OVC Dream Team)

1991-92 Oklahoma State

Produced by Motion Sports, this 57-card set features the Oklahoma State Cowboys basketball team. Two sets were available: 1) a team-issued set (no more than 5,000 sets produced), and 2) a limited edition "Signature Series" set of 8" by 10" photos autographed by all players and coaches, and encased in an 8" by 10" leather binder (originally sold for 99.95). The regular set was sold to the public at all home games and through the Student Union Bookstore. The cards measure the standard size (2 1/2" by 3 1/2"). The fronts of card numbers 1-25 display a full-color head shot of the player on a screened red background entramed by a black border. The player's name appears in a gray-to-red screened band at the top of the photo while the school name and sponsor's name (Johnsons) appear in a red band at the bottom. Card numbers 28-32 have on the fronts action photos of seniors on the squad. The last major section of the set consists of card numbers 37-54. These cards are similar to SkyBox in design, with color action player photos cut out and superimposed over a background of computer-generated graphics and geometric shapes. The player information on the backs of all cards is superimposed over ghosted OSU campus scenes. The cards are numbered on the back.

COMPLETE SET (57) 10.00 25.00
1 Earl Jones .08 .25
2 Corey Williams .20 .50
3 Jason Turk .08 .25
4 Binky Triplett .08 .25
5 Sean Sutton .20 .50
6 Darwyn Alexander .08 .25
7 Sean Walker .08 .25
8 Terry Collins .08 .25
9 Byron Houston .50 1.25
10 Randy Davis .08 .25
11 Scott Sutton .08 .25
12 Brooks Thompson .75 2.00
13 Mike Philpott .08 .25
14 Cornell Hatcher .08 .25
15 Milton Brown .08 .25
16 Sean Pell .08 .25
17 Von Bennett .08 .25
18 Bryant Reeves 1.50 4.00
19 Steve Anthis ACO .08 .25
20 Scott Streller ACO .08 .25
21 Russ Pennell ACO .08 .25
22 Eddie Sutton CO 1.25 3.00
23 Rob Evans ACO .08 .25
24 Bill Self ACO .08 .25
25 Pistol Pete (Mascot) .08 .25
26 Eddie Sutton CO 1.25 3.00
27 Trophies .08 .25
28 Cornell Hatcher .08 .25
29 Byron Houston .50 1.25
30 Corey Williams .20 .50
31 Sean Sutton .20 .50
32 Darwyn Alexander .08 .25
33 Eddie Sutton CO 1.25 3.00
Henry Iba CO
34 Team Photo .40 1.00
35 Mike Johnson .08 .25
John Johnson
Basketball Sponsors
36 Scott Sutton .40 1.00
Sean Sutton
Eddie Sutton CO
37 Milton Brown .08 .25
38 Earl Jones .08 .25
39 Terry Collins .08 .25
40 Von Bennett .08 .25
41 Byron Houston .50 1.25
42 Darwyn Alexander .08 .25
43 Mike Philpott .08 .25
44 Sean Pell .08 .25
45 Bryant Reeves 1.50 4.00
46 Randy Davis .08 .25
47 Cornell Hatcher .08 .25
48 Jason Turk .08 .25
49 Sean Sutton .20 .50
50 Sean Walker .08 .25
51 Sean Walker .08 .25
52 Binky Triplett .08 .25
53 Corey Williams .20 .50
54 Brooks Thompson .75 2.00
NNO Ad Card Motion Sports .08 .25
NNO Card Directory CL .08 .25
NNO Title Card .08 .25

2002-03 Oregon

These 24 cards feature members of both the men's and women's Oregon basketball team. The cards feature the an action photo with the player's name on the bottom. The back features some personal information as well as some blurbed information. Since these cards are unnumbered, we have sequenced them in alphabetical order by first men's and then the women's team.

COMPLETE SET 6.00 15.00
1 Jay Anderson .30 .75
2 Ian Crosswhite .30 .75
3 Jame Davis .30 .75
4 Brian Helquist .30 .75
5 Luke Jackson 1.25 3.00
6 Robert Johnson .30 .75
7 Andre Joseph .30 .75
8 Brandon Lincoln .30 .75
9 Luke Ridnour 2.50 6.00
10 Matt Short .30 .75
11 Tyler York .30 .75
12 Adam Zahn .30 .75
Jordan Kent
13 Andrea Bills .30 .75
14 Brandi Davis .30 .75
15 Alissa Edwards .30 .75
16 Carolyn Ganes .30 .75
17 Kedzie Gunderson .30 .75
18 Cathrine Kraayeveld .30 .75
19 Corrie Mizusawa .30 .75
20 Yadili Okwumabua .30 .75
21 Kourtney Shreve .30 .75
22 Kayla Sleen .30 .75
23 Amy Taylor .30 .75
24 Chelsea Wagner .30 .75

1996-97 Oregon Women

Sponsored by Pepsi, this 12-card set was issued on a perforated sheet with three columns and four rows. When separated, the cards are standard size with white backgrounds and color action photos on the front. The school name is written in white inside a green rectangle at the top of the card. The backs are white stock with black print stating the players' position, year, and hometown followed by the previous year's highlights. The university and Pepsi logo are found at the bottom of the card. The cards are unnumbered so listed below in alphabetical order.

COMPLETE SET (12) 4.00 10.00
1 Mendy Benson .30 .75
2 Betty Ann Boeving .30 .75
3 Lisa Bowyer .30 .75
4 Adrianne Boyer .60 1.50
5 Sonja Curtis .30 .75
6 Cindie Edamura .30 .75
7 Sandie Edwards .30 .75
8 Renae Fegent .60 1.50
9 Kirsten McKnight .30 .75
10 Jenny Mowe .30 .75
11 Eisa Oliveira .30 .75
12 Jody Runge CO .30 .75

1989-90 Oregon State

This 16-card set was printed on thin cardboard stock and issued in one sheet; after perforation, the cards measure approximately 3" by 4 1/16". The set may also have been issued as single unperforated cards. It is reported that some autographed sets were available in limited quantities. The front features a black and white action player photo, with white borders. The player's name appears in an orange and black basketball superimposed in the upper left corner. The player's name and position appear below the picture in a black stripe. In orange lettering, the team name "Beavers" is printed, with an oversized B--. The backs are printed in orange and black, and present a black and white head shot as well as biographical and statistical information. The cards are unnumbered and are checklisted below in alphabetical order, with the uniform number after the player's name. There are two variations of the Teo Alibegovic card. This set includes the first card of Gary Payton, who was chosen as the second pick by Seattle in the 1990 NBA draft, as well as 1993 NBA draftee Scott Haskin.

COMPLETE SET (16) 12.00 30.00
1 Teo Alibegovic 12 .20 .50
2 Jim Anderson CO .40 1.00
3 Karl Anderson 22 .40 1.00
4 Will Brantley 25 .40 1.00
5 Bob Cavell 4 .20 .50
6 Allan Celestine 40 .20 .50
7 Kevin Grant 11 .20 .50
8 Kevin Harris 14 .20 .50
9 Scott Haskin 44 .75 2.00
10 Earl Martin 24 .20 .50
11 Lamont McIntosh 33 .20 .50
12 Charles McKinney 23 .40 1.00
13 Gary Payton 20 10.00 25.00
14 Chris Rueppell 21 .20 .50
15 Travis Stel 13 .20 .50
16 Rich Wold 35 .40 1.00

1990-91 Oregon State

The 1990-91 Oregon State basketball set was issued on a perforated sheet, with three rows of six cards each. After perforation, the cards measure approximately 2 1/2" by 3 1/2". Reportedly 2,000 perforated sheets were produced. This set includes a card of Brent Barry, son of HOFer Rick Barry. On an orange background enclosed by white and black borders, the fronts feature black and white player photos inside an oval design. Player information appears beneath the picture. In orange and black print, the backs carry biography, career summary, and statistics. The cards are unnumbered and checklisted below in alphabetical order. The key cards in the set feature Brent Barry and Scott Haskin.

COMPLETE SET (18) 6.00 15.00
1 Teo Alibegovic .20 .50
2 Jim Anderson CO .40 1.00
3 Karl Anderson .20 .50
4 Brent Barry 3.00 8.00
5 Will Brantley .20 .50
6 Bob Cavell .20 .50
7 Allan Celestine .20 .50
8 Canaan Chatman .20 .50
9 Kevin Harris .20 .50
10 Scott Haskin .60 1.50
11 Mario Jackson .20 .50
12 Charles McKinney .20 .50
13 Henrik Ringmar .20 .50
14 Tony Ross .20 .50
15 Chris Rueppell .20 .50
16 Chad Scott .40 1.00
17 Travis Stel .20 .50
18 Fred Boyd ACO .20 .50
Andy McClouskey ACO
Jim Shaw ACO
Brent Wilder ACO

1991-92 Oregon State

The 1991-92 Oregon State basketball set was issued on a perforated sheet, with three rows of six cards each. After perforation, the cards measure approximately 2 1/2" by 3 1/2". On a white card face, the fronts feature black and white player photos enclosed by black and orange borders. The player's name appears beneath the picture, while the words "Oregon State 1991-92" are printed in a box at the upper right corner of the picture. The backs present biography and career highlights. The cards are unnumbered and checklisted below in alphabetical order. Reportedly 2,000 perforated sheets were produced. No complete autographed sheets exist; Earnest Killum died two days before the sets were completed.

COMPLETE SET (18) 6.00 15.00
1 Jim Anderson CO .40 1.00
2 Kareem Anderson .60 1.50
3 Karl Anderson .20 .50
4 Brent Barry 2.50 6.00
5 Freddie Boyd ACO .20 .50
6 David Brown .20 .50
7 Canaan Chatman .20 .50
8 Kevin Harris .20 .50
9 Scott Haskin .60 1.50
10 Mario Jackson .20 .50
11 Earnest Killum .60 1.50
12 David Lawson .20 .50
13 Andy McClouskey ACO .20 .50
14 Charles McKinney .20 .50
15 Ray Ross .20 .50
16 Chad Scott .40 1.00
17 Pat Strickland .20 .50
18 Brent Wilder ACO .20 .50

1992-93 Oregon State

These standard-size cards were available in a perforated sheet consisting of three rows with six cards per row. The fronts feature black-and-white action player photos inside a white border. The left and bottom edge of the pictures is edged by black stripes carrying "Oregon State 1992-93" and the player's name. The horizontal backs have a black-and-white head shot, biography, career highlights, and career statistics. The cards are unnumbered and checklisted below in alphabetical order.

COMPLETE SET (18) 5.00 12.00
1 Jim Anderson CO .40 1.00
2 Kareem Anderson .40 1.00
3 Brent Barry 2.50 6.00
4 David Brown .20 .50
5 Jerohn Brown .40 1.00
6 Kevin Harris .20 .50
(Dribbling ball)
7 Kevin Harris .20 .50
(Lay up)
8 Scott Haskin .40 1.00
(Blocking shot)
9 Scott Haskin .40 1.00
(Shooting hook shot)
10 Mustapha Hoff .20 .50
11 David Lawson .20 .50
12 Charles McKinney .20 .50
(Looking down court)
13 Charles McKinney .20 .50
(Looking at ball while dribbling)
14 Brandon Peterson .20 .50
15 Chad Scott .40 1.00
16 Pat Strickland .20 .50
17 Ibou Thioune .20 .50
18 J.D. Vetter .20 .50

1993-94 Oregon State

The 1993-94 Oregon State basketball set was issued on a perforated sheet, with four rows of three cards each. After perforation, the cards measure approximately 3" by 4". The fronts feature color posed and action player photos with white borders. The team name is printed above the photo, with the player's name, number and the team logo below, all in team colors. The backs carry a short biography, career highlights and a fire prevention cartoon starring Smokey. The cards are unnumbered and checklisted below in alphabetical order.

COMPLETE SET (12) 5.00 12.00
1 Kareem Anderson .60 1.50
2 Brent Barry 2.00 5.00
3 Sonny Benjamin .60 1.50
4 Jelani Boline .40 1.00
5 David Brown .40 1.00
6 Jerohn Brown .40 1.00
7 Stephane Brown .60 1.50
8 David Drakeford .40 1.00
9 Dwayne Franklin .40 1.00
10 Mustapha Hoff .40 1.00
11 Brandon Peterson .40 1.00
12 J.D. Vetter .40 1.00

1995-96 Pacific

Produced by High Step, this 2-card set was available at the University of Pacific during the 1995-96 school year.

COMPLETE SET (2) .40 1.00
21 Adam Jacobsen .20 .50
31 Charles Jones RC .20 .50

1996-97 Pacific

Produced by High Step, this card was available through the University of Pacific during the 1996-97 school year.

NNO Bob Thomason CO .25 .60

1997-98 Pacific

55 Michael Olowokandi .40 1.00

1992 Penn State Winter Sports

This 16-card standard-size set was sponsored by The Second Mile, the Jostens Foundation, KMart, and Penn State Intercollegiate Athletics. The cards are printed on thin card stock. A diagonal cuts across the card face, separating the top white portion from the bottom blue portion. The color player photos are superimposed on this background and are tilted slightly to the left. The backs have career summary, Nittany Lion Tips in the form of player quotes, and sponsor logos. The cards are unnumbered and checklisted below.

COMPLETE SET (16) 6.00 15.00
2 Monroe Brown .40 1.00
5 Dave Degitz .40 1.00
7 Dana Eikenberg .40 1.00
9 Kathy Phillips .40 1.00
12 Susan Robinson .40 1.00

1994 Penn State Winter Sports

This 25-card standard-size set was sponsored by The Second Mile, Penn State Intercollegiate Athletics and Keystone Real Estate. The cards are printed on thin card stock. The card fronts feature a thin red border with a light blue border inside. A white triangle at the top of the card features the Penn State name, while another white triangle at the bottom feature the player's name and class or position. The color player photos are featured in the middle of the card. The backs have career summary and Nittany Lion Tips in the form of player quotes. The cards are unnumbered and checklisted below.

COMPLETE SET (25) 5.00 12.00
3 John Amaechi .80 2.00
4 Greg Bartram .20 .50
7 Carla Coleman .20 .50
12 Katina Mack .20 .50
14 Missy Masley .20 .50
16 Tina Nicholson .20 .50
20 Glenn Sekunda .40 1.00
23 Donovan Williams .20 .50

1996 Penn State Winter Sports

This 25-card set was sponsored by The Second Mile and Penn State Intercollegiate Athletics. The set covers men's and women's basketball, men's and women's gymnastics and men's wrestling. Each team is given five cards. The full-color cards measure the standard size and are printed on thin non-coated stock. The cards are unnumbered and checklisted below in alphabetical order.

COMPLETE SET (25) 6.00 15.00
4 Kim Calhoun .30 .75
6 Dan Earl .80 2.00
8 Matt Gaudio .30 .75
14 Pete Lisickey .80 2.00
Calvin Booth
15 Tiffany Longworth .30 .75
16 Katina Mack .30 .75
20 Tina Nicholson .30 .75
21 Angie Potthoff .30 .75
23 Glenn Sekunda .40 1.00
24 Phil Williams .30 .75

2002 Penn State Winter Sports

The set is unnumbered and listed below in alphabetical order.

COMPLETE SET (25) 8.00 20.00
2 Rashana Barnes BK .40 1.00
5 Jennifer Brenden BK .40 1.00
6 Jessica Brungo BK .40 1.00
10 Ndu Egekeze BK .40 1.00
12 Ken Krimell BK .40 1.00
13 Kelly Mazzante BK .40 1.00
18 Tyler Smith BK .40 1.00
20 Jamaal Tate BK .40 1.00
22 Courtney Upshaw BK .40 1.00
25 Brandon Watkins BK .40 1.00

2003 Penn State Winter Sports

COMPLETE SET (25) 8.00 20.00
4 Jenny Brenden BK .40 1.00
5 Jessica Brungo BK .40 1.00
6 Sharif Chambliss BK .40 1.00
9 Ndu Egekeze BK .40 1.00
11 Kelly Mazzante BK .40 1.00
18 Jessica Strom BK .40 1.00
19 Jamaal Tate BK .40 1.00
23 B.J. Vossekul BK .40 1.00
24 Brandon Watkins BK .40 1.00
25 Tanisha Wright BK .40 1.00

2008 Penn State Winter Sports

COMPLETE SET (25) 5.00 10.00
2 Geary Claxton BK .40 1.00
3 Jamelle Cornley BK .40 1.00
6 Kamela Gissendanner WBK .30 .75
7 Tyra Grant WBK .30 .75
9 Brandon Hassell BK .40 1.00
13 Rashida Mark WBK .30 .75
15 Danny Morrissey BK .40 1.00
16 Brianne O'Rourke WBK .30 .75
24 Mike Walker BK .40 1.00
25 Mashea Williams WBK .30 .75

1989-90 Pittsburgh

This 12-card set featuring members of the Pittsburgh Panthers basketball team was sponsored by Foodland; each card measures the standard size. The front features an action color photo enframed by orange border on blue background. Above the photo appears the school's name "Panthers" (in orange print), player's name, jersey number, classification, and position. The sponsor's name is found below the photo. The back is filled with biographical information, a basketball tip from the Panthers, and an anti-drug message. The set is unnumbered and checklisted below in alphabetical order.

COMPLETE SET (12) 2.50 6.00
1 Rod Brookin .30 .75
2 Pat Cavanaugh .20 .50
3 Paul Evans CO .30 .75
4 Gilbert Johnson .30 .75
5 Bobby Martin .30 .75
6 Jason Matthews .20 .50
7 Sean Miller .40 1.00
8 Darren Morningstar .40 1.00
9 Pitt Panther/(team mascot) .20 .50
10 Darelle Porter .20 .50
11 Brian Shorter .40 1.00
12 Travis Ziegler .20 .50

1990-91 Pittsburgh

This 12 card standard-size set was sponsored by Foodland. The front features a borderless color action photo of the player, with "Panthers" written in blue letter on white above the picture. Two color stripes appear below the picture; in the blue one appears the player's name and number, while in the thicker orange one appears the sponsor's logo. A basketball icon superimposed over these two bars at the left completes the card face. The back has biographical information, a tip from the Pittsburgh Panthers in the form of an anti-drug or alcohol message, and the sponsor's logo. The cards are unnumbered and are checklisted them below in alphabetical order, with uniform number after the player's name.

COMPLETE SET (12) 2.50 6.00
1 Antoine Jones 21 .20 .50
2 Gandhi Jordan 4 .30 .75
3 Bobby Martin 55 .30 .75
4 Jason Matthews 22 .20 .50
5 Chris McNeal 24 .20 .50
6 Jermaine Morgan 42 .20 .50
7 Sean Miller 3 .30 .75
8 Darren Morningstar 33 .30 .75
9 Omo Moses 44 .20 .50
10 Darelle Porter 20 .20 .50
11 Ahmad Shareef 13 .20 .50
12 Brian Shorter 00 .30 .75

1991-92 Providence

This 24-card retrospective set features the all-time great basketball players of Providence. The sets were originally available direct from the school for 7.00 postpaid. The set was produced by Ballpark Cards, and each card measures the standard size. The fronts feature a mix of black and white action or posed player photos enclosed by an orange border. The words "Providence Friars" appear at the top superimposed over an orange basketball. In black lettering on a gray background, the horizontally oriented backs have collegiate statistics, pro stints, and awards received. The card numbers appear in a circle at the bottom right.

COMPLETE SET (24) 6.00 15.00
1 Joseph Mullaney CO .40 1.00
2 Dave Gavitt CO .40 1.00
3 Rick Pitino CO 1.00 2.50
4 Rick Barnes CO .30 .75
5 Team Photo .30 .75
1973 Friars
6 Team Photo .30 .75
1987 Friars
7 Lenny Wilkens 1.50 4.00
8 John Egan .20 .50
9 Jim Hadnot .30 .75
10 Vinny Ernst .20 .50
11 Ray Flynn .30 .75
12 John Thompson .75 2.00
13 Mike Riordan .40 1.00
14 Jimmy Walker .30 .75
15 Jim Larranaga .20 .50
16 Ernie DiGregorio .75 2.00
17 Marvin Barnes 1.25 3.00
18 Kevin Stacom .30 .75
19 Joe Hassett .20 .50
20 Bruce Campbell .20 .50
21 Otis Thorpe 1.00 2.50
22 Billy Donovan .40 1.00
23 Eric Murdock .60 1.50
24 Checklist Card .20 .50

1992-93 Purdue

Produced by Phipps Sports Marketing Inc., this 18-card measures the standard size and features color, action player photos with gold and black borders. The player's name and jersey number are superimposed on the photo in the lower right corner. The horizontal backs carry a small, close-up picture along with biographical information, career highlights, and statistics. The backs are pale yellow-orange. The cards are unnumbered and checklisted below in alphabetical order. The set features the first card of Glenn Robinson.

COMPLETE SET (18) 6.00 15.00
1 Brandon Brantley .30 .75
2 Linc Darner .30 .75
3 Herb Dove .30 .75
4 Todd Foster .30 .75
5 Justin Jennings .30 .75
6 Gene Keady CO 2.00 5.00
7 Cuonzo Martin .60 1.50
8 Cornelius McNary .20 .50
9 Matt Painter .40 1.00
10 Porter Roberts .30 .75
11 Glenn Robinson 2.50 6.00
12 Tim Spiker .20 .50
13 Ian Stanback .20 .50
14 Matt Waddell .40 1.00
15 Bruce Weber ACO 1.50 4.00
Frank Kendrick ACO
Gene Keady CO
Gary Johnson TR
Tom Reiter ACO
16 Kenny Williams .20 .50
17 Mackey Arena .30 .75
18 Title Card .20 .50
(Checklist)

1993-94 Purdue

Produced by Phipps Sports Marketing Inc., the funds generated from the sale of this 18-card standard-size set benefitted the Purdue University Athletic Scholarship Fund. It could be ordered from the John Purdue Club for 7.00. The fronts feature a mix of posed and action color player photos inside gold borders. In the wider right margin, the player's name is printed vertically in script and overlays the team name in ghosted block lettering. The bottom border of the picture is formed by the school name in variegated gold lettering. On a ghosted panel featuring a basketball, the back presents a black-and-white head shot, biography, career highlights, and statistics. The cards are unnumbered and checklisted below in alphabetical order.

COMPLETE SET (18) 5.00 12.00
1 Brandon Brantley .40 1.00
2 Matt ten Dam .20 .50
3 Linc Darner .30 .75
4 Herb Dove .30 .75
5 Tim Ervin .20 .50
6 Todd Foster .30 .75
7 Paul Gilvydis .20 .50
8 Justin Jennings .30 .75
9 Gene Keady CO 1.25 3.00
10 Cuonzo Martin .40 1.00
11 Cornelius McNary .20 .50
12 Porter Roberts .30 .75
13 Glenn Robinson 2.00 5.00
14 Ian Stanback .20 .50
15 Matt Waddell .30 .75
16 Kenny Williams .20 .50
17 Larry Leverenz ACO 1.25 3.00
Jay Price ACO
Gene Keady CO
Frank Kendrick ACO
Bruce Weber ACO
18 Title card .20 .50

1993-94 Purdue Women

Produced by Phipps Sports Marketing Inc., the funds generated from the sale of this 18-card standard-size set benefitted the Purdue University Athletic Scholarship Fund. It could be ordered from the John Purdue Club for 7.00. The fronts feature a mix of posed and action color player photos inside gold borders. In the wider right margin, the player's name is printed vertically in script and overlays the team name in ghosted block lettering. The bottom border of the picture is formed by the school name in variegated gold lettering. On a ghosted panel featuring a basketball, the back presents a black-and-white head shot, biography, career highlights, and statistics. The cards are unnumbered and checklisted below in alphabetical order.

COMPLETE SET (17) 5.00 12.00
1 Melina Griffin .30 .75
2 Andrea Hildebrand .30 .75
3 Jennifer Jacoby .40 1.00
4 Leslie Johnson 1.00 2.50
5 Tonya Kirk .30 .75
6 Cindy Lamping .40 1.00
7 Shannon Lindsey .30 .75
8 Stacey Lovelace .40 1.00
9 Danielle McCulley .30 .75
10 Jannon Roland .40 1.00
11 Nicki Taggart .30 .75
12 Lin Dunn CO .60 1.50
13 Tracy Brown MG .30 .75
Tammi Hoffman MG
Angie Brown MG
14 Sarah Sharp ACO .30 .75
Dallas Boychuk ACO
MaCelle Joseph ACO
15 1993-94 Boiler Makers .30 .75
16 Mackey Arena .30 .75
17 Title card .30 .75

2000 Purdue Legends

COMPLETE SET (36) 10.00 25.00
1 Mark Atkinson .25 .60
2 Chad Austin .25 .60
3 Joe Barry Carroll .30 .75
4 Russell Cross .25 .60
5 Terry Dischinger .40 1.00
6 Keith Edmonson .30 .75
7 Bob Ford .25 .60
8 Mel Garland .25 .60
9 John Garrett .25 .60
10 Herman Gilliam .30 .75
11 Paul Hoffman .40 1.00
12 Walter Jordan .25 .60
13 Gene Keady CO .75 2.00
14 Billy Keller .60 1.50
15 Frank Kendrick .25 .60
16 Troy Lewis .25 .60
17 Cuonzo Martin .40 1.00
18 Willie Merriweather .25 .60
19 Brad Miller .75 2.00
20 Todd Mitchell .25 .60
21 Rick Mount .60 1.50
22 Charles Murphy .75 2.00
23 Eugene Parker .25 .60
24 Bruce Parkinson .25 .60
25 Glenn Robinson .75 2.00
26 Jim Rowinski .25 .60
27 Stephen Scheffler .30 .75
28 Dave Schellhase .25 .60
29 Joe Sexson .25 .60
30 Jerry Sichting .40 1.00
31 Everette Stephens .30 .75
32 Matt Waddell .30 .75
33 Brian Walker .25 .60
34 John Wooden 1.25 3.00
35 Jewell Young .25 .60
36 Logo CL .25 .60

1910 Richmond College Silks S23

These colorful silks were issued around 1910 by Richmond Straight Cut Cigarettes. Each measures roughly 4" by 5 1/2" and are often called "College Flag, Seal, Song, and Yell" due to the content found on each one. More importantly to most sports collectors is the image found in the lower right hand bottom corner. A few feature a mainstream sports' subject such as a generic player or piece of equipment, while most include a realistic image of the school's mascot or image of the founder or the school's namesake.

28 Oberlin BK Player 75.00 150.00
32 Rochester Basketball 60.00 120.00

2003-06 Saint Vincent-Saint Mary High School

Released by the Saint Vincent-Saint Mary's high school book store, this oversized post card (3.5" x 5.25") features a team photo on the front and the words, "2002-03 National Champion/State Champion" in green letters along the bottom. It was announced that 10,000 total green versions of the team card were printed. The card back lists the players in the photo and team statistics from the season. Also present is a silver hologram with a background circle and a serial number starting with the letter A. Each card also came with a certificate of authenticity from St.V-St.M bookstore with the corresponding serial number. This green version came with a green COA. Gold and Ruby versions were also printed and the "2002-03 National Champion/State Champion" on the bottom front of the card appears in gold or red depending on the version and a gold serial numbered hologram is attached to the card back along with a separate COA from the school with a matching gold hologram. 2300 copies of the Gold and 2003 copies of the Ruby version were printed. A LeBron James football card and three basketball cards dated 1999 to 2002 showed up on the secondary market sometime during or after 2005.

*GOLD: .5X TO 1.2X BASE HI
*RUBY: .6X TO 1.5X BASE HI
1A Lebron James 1999-00 15.00 40.00
2A LeBron James 2000-01 12.00 30.00
3 LeBron James 2001 Football 12.00 30.00
5 Team Photo 12.00 30.00
Willie McGee
Brandon Weems
Dru Joyce III
Marcus Johnson
Corey Jones
Mike Snowbarger CO
Dru Joyce HCO
Tim Marks
Sian Cotton
LeBron James
Romeo Travis
Preston Sims
Lee Cotton CO
Steve Culp CO
6A LeBron James 2001-02 12.00 30.00

2005-06 San Diego State

Produced by High Step in conjunction with the San Diego State Alumni Association, this 15-card set was available on the campus during the 2005-06 school year.

COMPLETE SET (15) 3.00 8.00
0 Tommy Johnson .20 .50
1 Brandon Heath .60 1.50
3 Chris Walton .30 .75
5 Travis Hanour .20 .50
11 Tyler Smith .20 .50
15 John Sharper .20 .50
20 Trimaine Davis .20 .50
21 Matt Thomas .20 .50
24 Tim McGrath .20 .50
30 Chris Lamb .20 .50
31 Jared Ines .20 .50
33 Chris Manker .20 .50
42 Marcus Slaughter .20 .50
50 Mohamed Camara .20 .50
NNO Steve Fisher CO .50 1.25

2006-07 San Diego State

Produced by High Step, this 13-card set was available through San Diego State during the 2006-07 school year.

COMPLETE SET (13) 3.00 8.00
1 Mohamed Camara .20 .50
2 Trimaine Davis .20 .50
3 Mohamed Abukar .20 .50
4 Brandon Heath .75 2.00
5 Brett Hoerner .20 .50
6 Tim McGrath .20 .50
7 Chris Lamb .20 .50
8 Marcus Slaughter .20 .50
9 John Sharper .20 .50
10 Matt Thomas .20 .50
11 Kyle Spain .20 .50
12 Richie Williams .20 .50
13 Steve Fisher CO .60 1.50

1990-91 San Jose State

This nine-card set was printed in the same style as the 1990 San Jose football set. The cards measure 2 1/2" by 3 1/2" and are printed on thin white stock. The fronts feature color action player photos. The picture is enframed by an orange border on a blue background. The backs provide player information and have a fire prevention cartoon starring Smokey the Bear. The cards are unnumbered and are checklisted below in alphabetical order with non-player cards listed at the end.

COMPLETE SET (9) 2.50 6.00
1 Troy Batiste .40 1.00
2 Terry Cannon .40 1.00
3 Robert Dunlap .40 1.00
4 Kevin Logan .40 1.00
5 Stan Morrison CO .60 1.50
6 Daryl Scott .40 1.00
7 Charles Terrell .60 1.50
8 Event Center .40 1.00
9 Smokey Bear .40 1.00

1991 South Carolina Collegiate Collection

This 200-card set measures standard sized and features cards of all-time great South Carolina athletes. The fronts have a black border with color action shots on each one. The school name and logo are found across the top border of the card. The featured player's name is found along the bottom border set against a red background. The backs carry a small bio of the player and his/her statistics.

COMPLETE SET (200) 5.00 12.00
1 Frank McGuire .20 .50
3 Alex English BK .20 .50
5 Kevin Darmody BK .05 .15
9 Linwood Moye BK .05 .15
24 Karlton Hilton BK .05 .15
26 Zam Fredrick BK .05 .15
35 Alex English BK .20 .50
38 Jimmy Hawthorne BK .05 .15
62 Jack Thompson BK .05 .15
64 Kevin Joyce BK .08 .25
68 Cedrick Hordges BK .05 .15
73 Grady Wallace BK .05 .15
78 Tom Riker BK .08 .25
80 Bobby Cremins BK .20 .50
85 Gary Gregor BK .05 .15
90 Ronnie Collins BK .05 .15
99 Joe Smith BK .05 .15
106 Jack Gilloon BK .05 .15
125 Mike Doyle BK .05 .15
126 Brad Jergenson BK .05 .15
143 John Hudson BK .05 .15
150 Mike Brittain BK .05 .15
156 Art Whisnant BK .05 .15
157 Jim Slaughter BK .05 .15
158 Skip Harlicka BK .05 .15
178 Ray Pericola BK .05 .15

1987-88 Southern

This 16-card standard-size set was sponsored by McDonald's, Southern University, and local law enforcement agencies, and was produced by McDag Productions. The McDonald's logo appears at the bottom of both sides of the card. The front features a mix of action or posed, black and white player photos. The pictures are bordered in turquoise on the sides, yellow above, and white below. The school name and player information appear in black lettering in the yellow border. A picture of the school mascot in the lower right corner rounds out the card face. The back presents biographical information, Jag Facts, and "Tips from The Jaguars" in the form of an anti-drug message. The sports represented in this set are football (1-3, 14-16) and basketball (4-13). The key cards in the set feature the first cards of NBA player Avery Johnson and NFL player Gerald Perry.

COMPLETE SET (16) 5.00 12.00
4 Ben Jobe CO BK .40 1.00
5 Daryl Battles BK .20 .50
6 Patrick Garner BK .20 .50
7 Avery Johnson BK 3.20 8.00
8 Rodney Washington BK .20 .50
9 Kevin Florent BK .20 .50
10 Dervynn Johnson BK .20 .50
11 Claudene Stovall BK .20 .50
12 Michelle Currie BK .20 .50
13 Gibbie Phillips BK .20 .50

1990-91 Southern Cal

This 20-card standard-size set was sponsored by the USDA Forest Service in conjunction with several other agencies. The cards have color action shots, with orange borders on a maroon card face with the words "USC Trojans" above the player's picture and his name, uniform number, school year, and position underneath his picture. The back has two Trojan logos at the top and features a player profile and a fire prevention cartoon starring Smokey. The cards are unnumbered and checklisted below in alphabetical order, with the uniform number after the name. Cards 1-2 and 12 feature basketball rather than football players and are so indicated by BKB. The checklist card in the set lists the football players but not the basketball players. The set features the first cards of NFL running back Ricky Ervins and NBA guard Robert Pack.

COMPLETE SET (20) 8.00 20.00
1 Calvin Banks BKB .60 1.50
2 Ronnie Coleman BKB .30 .75
12 Robert Pack BKB 2.00 5.00

1991 Southern Cal College Classics

Produced by College Classics Inc., this 100-card standard-size set honors former Trojan Athletes of various sports. Most players are football, other sports are designated in the listings below. The complete set comes with a blank-backed white card that carries the set's production number out of a total of 20,000 produced. In addition, 1,400 cards autographed by John Naber, Ron Fairly, Tom Seaver, Charles White, Dave Stockton, Mike Garrett, Anthony Davis, and Fred Lynn were randomly inserted throughout 1,000 of these sets. Since these cards rarely appear in the secondary marketplace, they are not priced.

COMPLETE SET (100) 10.00 25.00
6 Bill Sharman BK .30 .75
20 John Block BK .02 .10
42 Wayne Carlander BK .02 .10
52 Bob Boyd CO BK .02 .10
54 John Lambert BK .02 .10
75 Paul Westphal BK .40 1.00

1987-88 Southern Mississippi

This 14-card set, measuring 2 3/8" by 3 1/2", was co-sponsored by Deposit Guaranty National Bank and Coca-Cola, and their company names appear at the bottom corners on the front. The front has a posed action photo on a yellow background; two cards of the set feature two players. Player's names and team logo surmount the photo. The back presents biographical information and the card number.

COMPLETE SET (14) 8.00 20.00
1 The Freshmen .60 1.50
2 The Coaches .60 1.50
3 Casey Fisher .60 1.50
4 Derrek Hamilton .60 1.50
5 Randolph Keys 1.50 4.00
6 John White .60 1.50
7 D.J. and Allen .60 1.50
D.J. Bowe and
Allen Chapman
8 The Browns .60 1.50
John Brown and
Willie Brown
9 Jurado Hinton .60 1.50
10 Jay Ladner .60 1.50
11 Randy Pettus .60 1.50
12 Jimmy Smith .60 1.50
13 Roger Boyd .60 1.50
14 The Team 1.25 3.00

1994-95 Southwest Missouri St. Women

This 14-card Women's set measures the standard size and was produced by Springfield News-Leader and Southwest Missouri State University Athletic Program. The fronts feature posed color player photos framed by rose-colored borders. The player's name, position, and jersey number are printed in the border below the picture. The backs carry biographical information, statistics, and career highlights. The sponsor logos are at the bottom. The cards are unnumbered and checklisted below in alphabetical order.

COMPLETE SET (14) 5.00 12.00
1 Marsha Burton .40 1.00
2 Lisa Davies .40 1.00
3 Latanya Davis .40 1.00
4 Shannon Gage .40 1.00
5 Kindra Garst .40 1.00
6 Marla Harrison .40 1.00
7 Julie Howard .40 1.00
8 Charitee Longstreth .40 1.00
9 Lisa Moore .40 1.00
10 Courtney Murdock .40 1.00
11 Donease Smith .40 1.00
12 Stephanie Thurman .40 1.00
13 Richelle Winn .40 1.00
14 Team Photo .40 1.00

1996-97 Southwest Missouri State

This 13-card set was released at Southwest Missouri State University during the 1996-97. The set features all of the players from that years team. Each card is unnumbered and is listed below in alphabetical order.

COMPLETE SET (13) 4.00 10.00
1 Steve Alford CO 1.25 3.00
2 Kevin Aull .30 .75
3 Ryan Bettenhausen .30 .75
4 Coleco Buie .30 .75
5 JoJo Dabbs .30 .75
6 Tony Davis .30 .75
7 William Fontleroy .30 .75
8 Josh Hotz .30 .75
9 Ben Kandlbinder .30 .75
10 Omar Lincoln .30 .75
11 Omar Lincoln .30 .75
12 Monte Marsh .30 .75
13 Team Photo .30 .75

1986-87 Southwestern Louisiana

This 16-card standard-size set was sponsored by the Chemical Dependency Unit of Acadiana in Lafayette, the University of Southwest Louisiana, and local law enforcement agencies and was produced by McDag Productions. Only 3,500 sets were produced. The cards were distributed by the CDU adolescent program and by law enforcement officers.The front features borderless color action player photos, on white card stock with black lettering. The CDU logo and the words "USL Ragin' Cajuns" appear on the top of the card, with player information below the picture. The back has biographical information and "Tips from the Ragin' Cajuns" which encourage children to avoid drug use. Sports represented in the set include basketball (1, 4, 9, 11, 15), baseball (2, 5, 8, 16), softball (7, 14), track (3), and tennis (6, 10, 12-13). The cards are unnumbered and we have checklisted them below in alphabetical order. The set includes a card of high jumper Hollis Conway, who competed for the 1992 United States Olympic team at Barcelona.

COMPLETE SET (16) 4.00 10.00
1 Stephen Beene .30 .75
4 Teena Cooper .30 .75
9 Brian Jolivette .30 .75
11 Rodney McNeil .30 .75
15 Randal Smith .30 .75

1987-88 Southwestern Louisiana

This 16-card standard-size set was sponsored by CDU of Acadiana in Lafayette, University of Southwestern Louisiana, and local law enforcement agencies. The fronts display color action player photos on a white card face. The CDU logo, school logo, and year appear above the picture, while player information is given below the picture. The backs carry player profile, advertisements, and "Tips From the Ragin' Cajuns," which consist of anti-drug and alcohol messages. Sports represented in this set include men's basketball (1-4), women's basketball (5-6), tennis (7-8), men's baseball (9-12), women's softball (14-16), and track (13). The set includes a card of high jumper Hollis Conway, who competed for the 1992 United States Olympic team at Barcelona.

COMPLETE SET (16) 5.00 12.00
1 Randal Smith BK .30 .75
2 Earl Watkins BK .30 .75
3 Kevin Brooks BK .60 1.50
4 Stephen Beene BK .30 .75
5 Kim Perrot BK 2.40 6.00
6 Teena Cooper BK .30 .75

1979-80 St. Bonaventure

This 18-card set measures the standard size, 2 1/2" by 3 1/2". The front features a sepia-toned photo with the player's name above and jersey number in a basketball logo at upper right hand corner; the team name "Bonnies" appears below the photo. The photo is also enframed by a thin brown border on white card stock. The back is filled with biographical and statistical information. The set is ordered below alphabetically for convenience. At time of issue, a collector could order this set from St Bonaventure for $1.

COMPLETE SET (18) 20.00 40.00
1 Earl Belcher 25 1.50 4.00
2 Dan Burns 41 1.25 3.00
3 Bruno DeGiglio 24 1.25 3.00
4 Jim Elenz 10 1.25 3.00
5 Lacey Fulmer 20 1.25 3.00
6 Delmar Harrod 52 1.25 3.00
7 Alfonza Jones 12 1.25 3.00
8 Mark Jones 11 1.50 4.00
9 Bill Kalbaugh CO 1.25 3.00
10 Lloyd Praedel 44 1.25 3.00
11 Pat Rodgers 35 1.25 3.00
12 Bob Sassone CO 1.25 3.00
13 Jim Satalin CO 1.25 3.00
14 Mark Spencer 15 1.25 3.00
15 Eric Stover 40 1.25 3.00
16 Shawn Waterman 33 1.25 3.00
17 Brian West 30 1.25 3.00
18 Title Card 2.00 5.00

1985-86 Stanford Schedules

Measuring 3 1/2" by 4 1/2", this 16-card set features schedules for the 1985-86 Stanford basketball team. The schedules are in color (despite the black and white photo above) and the right-half features a player photo with his name, height, weight, position and collegiate status underneath. The left-half features an advertisement from Miller. The back features ticket information and the actual schedule. These are not numbered and listed below in alphabetical order.

COMPLETE SET (16) 1.00 2.50
1 Steve Brown .08 .25
2 Derek Bruton .08 .25
3 Greg Butler .08 .25
4 Andy Fischer .08 .25
5 Neil Johnson .08 .25
6 Earl Koberlein .08 .25
7 Todd Lichti .60 1.50
8 Bryan McSweeney .08 .25
9 Scott Meinert .08 .25
10 John Paye .08 .25
11 Keith Ramee .08 .25
12 Eric Reveno .08 .25
13 Terry Taylor .08 .25
14 Novlan Whitsitt .08 .25
15 John Williams .30 .75
16 Howard Wright .08 .25

1994-95 Stanford Schedules

Mixing elements of traditional trading cards and pocket schedules, cards from this set feature members of the 1994-95 men's and women's Stanford Cardinal. The cards are believed to have been distributed at Cardinal home games during the 1994-95 season. Because they crry no numbers on back, we've listed the set below in the order we discovered them. The set is highlighted by a freshman season card of future NBA guard Brevin Knight.

COMPLETE SET (7) 1.50 4.00
1 Dion Cross .40 1.00
guarded by Jason Kidd
2 David Harbour .40 1.00
guarded by Jason Kidd
3 Brevin Knight .75 2.00
4 Bart Lammerson .08 .25
5 Todd Manley .08 .25
6 Vanessa Nygaard .08 .25
7 Andy Poppink .08 .25
8 Darren Allaway .08 .25
9 Warren Gravely .08 .25
10 David Harbour .08 .25
11 Rich Jackson .08 .25

1995-96 Stanford Women

Issued by High Step, this 12-card set was available through Stanford during the 1995-96 school year.

COMPLETE SET (12) 2.50 6.00
0 Olympia Scott .10 .30
4 Amy Wustefeld .10 .30
10 Jamila Wideman .15 .40
13 Vanessa Nygaard .75 2.00
15 Regan Freuen .10 .30
21 Charmin Smith .15 .40
23 Bobbie Kelsey .10 .30
30 Kate Starbird 1.25 3.00
32 Chandra Benton .10 .30
33 Tara Harrington .10 .30
34 Naome Mulitauaopele .10 .30
44 Heather Owen .10 .30

1996-97 Stanford

This 16-card set, produced by High Step Trading Cards, pays tribute to the 1996-97 Stanford men's basketball team. The card fronts have black backgrounds with a color action photo (except for Madsen in black and white) underneath the school name which is written in large red type at the top. The card backs, in black and white, contain basic player biographies and university statistics. For some unknown reason, two Brevin Knights cards were produced. The backs carry identical information; however, one card front shows him passing, and the other going to the hoop. The cards are unnumbered and listed below in alphabetical order.

COMPLETE SET (16) 8.00 20.00
1 Rich Jackson .20 .50
2 Brevin Knight 1.50 4.00
Charging
3 Brevin Knight 1.50 4.00
Passing
4 Arthur Lee .75 2.00
5 Mark Madsen 2.00 5.00
6 Ryan Mendez .40 1.00
7 Mike Montgomery CO 1.25 3.00
8 David Moseley .20 .50
9 Peter Sauer .40 1.00
10 Mark Seaton .40 1.00
11 Mark Thompson .20 .50
12 Kamba Tshionyi .20 .50
13 Peter Van Elswyk .20 .50
14 Kris Weems .40 1.00
15 Karl Wente .20 .50
16 Tim Young 1.00 2.50

1996-97 Stanford Women

Produced by High Step, this 16-card set was available through Stanford during the 1996-97 school year.

COMPLETE SET (16) 4.00 10.00
0 Olympia Scott .10 .30
4 Melody Peterson .10 .30
5 Christina Batastini .10 .30
10 Jamila Wideman .20 .50
13 Vanessa Nygaard .75 2.00
14 Yvonne Gbalazeh .10 .30
15 Regan Freuen .10 .30
20 Milena Flores .20 .50
21 Charmin Smith .75 2.00
30 Kate Starbird 1.00 2.50
32 Chandra Benton .10 .30
33 Tara Harrington .10 .30
34 Naomi Mulitauaopele .15 .40
44 Heather Owen .15 .40
NNO Tara VanDerveer CO .40 1.00
NNO Team Card .40 1.00
Schedule

1997-98 Stanford

This collegiate set measures the standard-size was sponsered by Pepsi and produced by High Step. Card fronts feature a bordered action photo with the school name in a maroon bar across the top and the player's name in light-yellow at the bottom. Card backs feature the player's bio and statistics. The cards are numbered by jersey on the card back.

COMPLETE SET (14) 8.00 20.00
3 Kris Weems .40 1.00
4 Michael McDonald .20 .50
5 Peter Sauer .40 1.00
21 David Moseley .20 .50
31 Jarron Collins 1.50 4.00
32 Ryan Mendez .20 .50
33 Jason Collins 1.50 4.00
35 Kamba Tshionyi .20 .50
40 Peter Van Elswyk .20 .50
44 Mark Seaton .40 1.00
45 Mark Madsen 1.50 4.00
55 Tim Young .75 2.00
NNO 1997-98 Schedule .20 .50
NNO Mike Montgomery CO .75 2.00

1997-98 Stanford Women

Produced by High Step and sponsored by Pepsi, this 17-card set was available through Stanford during the 1997-98 school year.

COMPLETE SET (17) 4.00 10.00
0 Olympia Scott .10 .30
4 Melody Peterson .10 .30
5 Christina Batastini .10 .30
13 Vanessa Nygaard .75 2.00
14 Yvonne Gbalazeh .10 .30
15 Regan Freuen .10 .30
20 Milena Flores .25 .60
24 Kristin Folkl .75 2.00
31 Karesa Granderson .10 .30
32 Chandra Benton .10 .30
33 Sarah Dimson .10 .30
34 Naomi Mulitauaopele .75 2.00
44 Heather Owen .75 2.00
53 Carolyn Moos .10 .30
55 Naila Moseley .10 .30
NNO Tara VanDerveer CO .40 1.00
NNO Team Card .40 1.00
Schedule

1998-99 Stanford

Produced by High Step, this 16-card set was offered at Stanford University during the 1998-99 season. The set was produced by Pepsi Cola. Please note that the set is not numbered and is listed in alphabetical order below.

COMPLETE SET (16) 9.00 18.00
1 Jarron Collins 1.25 3.00
2 Jason Collins 1.25 3.00
3 Alex Gelbard .20 .50
4 Tony Giovacchini .20 .50
5 Arthur Lee .75 2.00
6 Kyle Logan .20 .50
7 Mark Madsen 1.25 3.00
8 Michael McDonald .20 .50
9 Ryan Mendez .40 1.00
10 Mike Montgomery CO .75 2.00
11 David Moseley .20 .50
12 Peter Sauer .20 .50
13 Mark Seaton .20 .50
14 Kris Weems .20 .50
15 Tim Young .75 2.00
16 The Stanford Tree .20 .50

1998-99 Stanford Women

Produced by High Step and sponsored by Pepsi, this 14-card set was available through Stanford during the 1998-99 school year.

COMPLETE SET (14) 2.00 5.00
1 Christina Batastini .10 .30
2 Sarah Dimson .10 .30
3 Bethany Donaphin .20 .50
4 Cori Enghusen .10 .30
5 Milena Flores .20 .50
6 Regan Freuen .10 .30
7 Yvonne Gbalazeh .10 .30
8 Karesa Granderson .10 .30
9 Enjoli Izidor .10 .30
10 Carolyn Moos .10 .30
11 Naila Moseley .10 .30
12 Lauren St. Clair .10 .30
13 Tara VanDerveer CO .40 1.00
14 Lindsey Yamasaki .10 .30

2000-01 Stanford

This 16 card set was sponsored by Pepsi and featured NCAA championship contender Stanford. Since these cards are unnumbered we have sequenced them in alphabetical order.

COMPLETE SET (16) 9.00 18.00
1 Julius Barnes .20 .50
2 Tyler Besecker .20 .50
3 Curtis Borchardt .20 .50
4 Jarron Collins 1.25 3.00
5 Jason Collins 1.25 3.00
6 Justin Davis .20 .50
7 Tony Giovacchini .20 .50
8 Casey Jacobsen 2.00 5.00
9 Teyo Johnson 1.25 3.00
10 Joe Kirchofer .20 .50
11 Kyle Logan .20 .50
12 Matt Lottich .20 .50
13 Mike McDonald .20 .50
14 Ryan Mendez .20 .50
15 Mike Montgomery CO .75 2.00
16 Nick Robinson .20 .50

2000-01 Stanford Women

Produced by High Step and sponsored by Pepsi, this 14-card set was available through Stanford during the 1996-97 school year.

COMPLETE SET (14) 2.50 6.00
0 Chelsea Trotter .20 .40
10 Becky Bonner .20 .40
11 Jamie Carey .40 1.00
14 Nicole Powell .60 1.50
22 Enjoli Izidor .20 .40
24 Susan King .20 .40
25 Lindsey Yamasaki .40 1.00
32 Katie Denny .20 .40
33 Sarah Dimson .20 .40
41 Bethany Donaphin .40 1.00
42 Lauren St. Clair .20 .40
51 Cori Enghusen .20 .40
53 Carolyn Moos .20 .40
NNO Tara VanDerveer CO .40 1.00

2001-02 Stanford Women

Produced by High Step, this 16-card set was available through Stanford during the 2001-02 school year.

COMPLETE SET (8) 1.50 4.00
5 Kelley Suminski .20 .40
22 Enjoli Izidor .20 .40
25 Lindsey Yamasaki .60 1.50
33 Sebnem Kimyacioglu .20 .40
34 T'Nae Thiel .20 .40
44 Azella Perryman .20 .40
51 Cori Enghusen .20 .40
NNO Karen Middleton ACO .20 .50

2002-03 Stanford Women

COMPLETE SET (13) 3.00 8.00
0 Chelsea Trotter .15 .40
2 Krista Rappahahn .15 .40
4 Clare Bodensteiner .15 .40
5 Kelley Suminski .15 .40
14 Nicole Powell .60 1.50
21 Shelley Nweke .15 .40
22 Eziamaka Okafor .30 .75
24 Susan King .15 .40
32 Katie Denny .15 .40
33 Sebnem Kimyacioglu .15 .40
34 T'Nae Thiel .15 .40
44 Azella Perryman .15 .40
NNO Tara VanDerveer CO .60 1.50

2003-04 Stanford

COMPLETE SET (13) 3.00 8.00
0 Joe Kirchofer .20 .50
1 Josh Childress 1.25 3.00
10 Tim Morris .20 .50
11 Chris Hernandez .20 .50
20 Dan Grunfeld .20 .50
21 Nick Robinson .20 .50
22 Justin Davis .20 .50
32 Jason Haas .20 .50
33 Matt Lottich .20 .50
42 Rob Little .20 .50
44 Fred Washington .20 .50
52 Matt Haryasz .20 .50
NNO Mike Montgomery CO .75 2.00

2003-04 Stanford Women

Produced by High Step in conjunction with Pepsi, this 15-card set was available through the school during the 2003-04 school year.

COMPLETE SET (15) 3.00 8.00
0 Chelsea Trotter .15 .40
2 Krista Rappahahn .15 .40
4 Clare Bodensteiner .15 .40
5 Kelley Suminski .15 .40
14 Nicole Powell .60 1.50
21 Shelley Mweke .15 .40
22 Eziamaka Okafor .30 .75
24 Susan King Borchardt .15 .40
30 Brooke Smith .15 .40
32 Katie Denny .15 .40
33 Sebnem Kimyacioglu .15 .40
34 T'Nae Thiel .15 .40
43 Kristen Newlin .15 .40
44 Azella Perryman .15 .40
NNO Tara VanDerveer CO .60 1.50

2004-05 Stanford

Produced by High Step and sponsored by Pepsi, this 15-card set was available through Stanford during the 2004-05 school year.

COMPLETE SET (15) 2.50 6.00
1 Mark Bradford .20 .50
2 Kenny Brown .20 .50
3 Dan Grunfeld .20 .50
4 Taj Finger .20 .50
5 Jason Haas .20 .50
6 Matt Haryasz .20 .50
7 Chris Hernandez .20 .50
8 Trent Johnson .20 .50
9 Rob Little .20 .50
10 Evan Moore .20 .50
11 Tim Morris .20 .50
12 Peter Prowitt .20 .50
13 Nick Robinson .20 .50
14 Fred Washington .20 .50
15 Carlton Weatherby .20 .50

2004-05 Stanford Women

Produced by High Step in conjunction with Pepsi, this 17-card set was available through Stanford during the 2004-05 school year.

COMPLETE SET (17) 2.50 6.00
2 Krista Rappahahn .15 .40
3 Markisha Coleman .15 .40
4 Clare Bodensteiner .15 .40
5 Kelley Suminski .15 .40
11 Candice Wiggins .15 .40
12 Christy Titchenal .15 .40
13 Cissy Pierce .15 .40
21 Shelley Nweke .15 .40
22 Eziamaka Okafor .30 .75
24 Susan King Borchardt .15 .40
30 Brooke Smith .15 .40
33 Sebnem Kimyacioglu .15 .40
34 T'Nae Thiel .15 .40
42 Jessica Elway .15 .40
43 Kristen Newlin .15 .40
44 Azella Perryman .15 .40
NNO Tara VanDerveer .40 1.00

2005-06 Stanford

Produced by High Step in conjunction with Pepsi, this 14-card set was available through Stanford during the 2005-06 school year.

COMPLETE SET (14) 2.50 6.00
1 Kenny Brown .20 .50
2 Taj Finger .20 .50
3 Anthony Goods .20 .50
4 Dan Grunfeld .20 .50
5 Jason Haas .20 .50
6 Matt Haryasz .20 .50
7 Chris Hernandez .20 .50
8 Lawrence Hill .20 .50
9 Mitch Johnson .20 .50
10 Tim Morris .20 .50
11 Peter Prowitt .20 .50
12 Fred Washington .20 .50
13 Carlton Weatherby .20 .50
14 Trent Johnson .20 .50

2005-06 Stanford Women

Produced by High Step and sponsored by Pepsi, this 14-card set was available through Stanford during the 2005-06 school year.

COMPLETE SET (14) 2.00 5.00
1 Krista Rappahahn .15 .40
2 Markisha Coleman .15 .40
3 Clare Bodensteiner .15 .40
4 Candice Wiggins .15 .40
5 Christy Titchenal .15 .40
6 Cissy Pierce .15 .40
7 Shelley Nweke .15 .40
8 Eziamaka Okafor .15 .40
9 Rosalyn Gold-Onwude .15 .40
10 Brooke Smith .15 .40
11 Morgan Clyburn .15 .40
12 Jillian Harmon .15 .40
13 Kristen Newlin .15 .40
14 Tara VanDerveer .60 1.50

1988-89 Syracuse

This 12-card standard-size set was sponsored by Louis Rich; their company logo appears on the bottom of the reverse. The front features a posed color photo of the player, shot from waist up on a blue background. The lettering and border on the card face are orange on white card stock. The back has biographical information and career summary, and "The Orangemen Say" feature, which consists of an anti-drug or alcohol message. The cards are unnumbered and are checklisted below in alphabetical order. Future NBA players showcased in this set include Derrick Coleman, Sherman Douglas, David Johnson, and Billy Owens.

COMPLETE SET (12) 15.00 40.00
1 Jim Boeheim CO 6.00 15.00
2 Derrick Coleman 5.00 12.00
3 Sherman Douglas 3.00 8.00
4 Herman Harried .75 2.00
5 Dave Johnson 1.50 4.00
6 Rich Manning .75 2.00
7 Billy Owens 3.00 8.00
8 Matt Roe 1.25 3.00
9 Erik Rogers .75 2.00
10 Anthony Scott .75 2.00
11 Dave Siock .75 2.00
12 Stephen Thompson 1.50 4.00

1989-90 Syracuse

This 15-card set was sponsored by Pepsi, Y94FM radio, and Burger King. The cards measure approximately 2 5/8" by 3 1/2" and are numbered on the back. The action color photo on the front is outlined by orange border on white background. Below the photo in an orange bar appears the school's name, year, and the player's name in white lettering. The back has biographical information and a brief anti-drug message. Several players have two cards in this set: Derrick Coleman, Stephen Thompson, and Billy Owens.

COMPLETE SET (15) 2.50 6.00
1 Derrick Coleman 44 1.00 2.50
2 LeRon Ellis 25 .30 .75
3 Rich Manning 34 .20 .50
4 Stephen Thompson 32 .30 .75
5 Michael Edwards 5 .20 .50
6 Dave Johnson 23 .30 .75
7 Billy Owens 30 .75 2.00
8 Conrad McRae 13 .20 .50
9 Jim Boeheim CO .75 2.00
10 Stephen Thompson 32 .30 .75
11 Mike Hopkins 33 .20 .50
12 Tony Scott 40 .20 .50
13 Billy Owens 30 .75 2.00
14 Erik Rogers 41 .20 .50
15 Derrick Coleman 44 1.00 2.50

1988-89 Tennessee

This 12-card set features members of the Tenessee Volunteers basketball team and measures the standard card size, 2 1/2" by 3 1/2". The front features a color action photo; above and below appear orange and gray lettering and borders. The Smokey the Bear logo in the lower left hand corner completes the front. The back gives brief biographical information and a public service announcement (illustrated with cartoon) concerning wildfire prevention. The set is checklisted below according to uniform number.

COMPLETE SET (12) 8.00 20.00
11 Clarence Swearengen 1.25 3.00
23 Greg Bell 1.25 3.00
24 Rickey Clark .40 1.00
25 Travis Henry .40 1.00
31 Dyron Nix 1.25 3.00
33 Mark Griffin .40 1.00
34 Ronnie Reese .40 1.00
50 Doug Roth .40 1.00
51 Ian Lockhart 1.25 3.00
xx Don Devoe CO 1.25 3.00
xx Smokey The Hound .40 1.00
(Mascot)
xx Thompson-Boling Arena 1.25 3.00

1990-91 Tennessee Women

This 16-card standard-size set was sponsored by the USDA Forest Service and the state forestry agency. The fronts feature color action player photos, with a turquoise border on an orange background. Within the border, the team's name is printed above the picture, with the player's name, jersey number, and position below. The Smokey the Bear logo in the lower left corner rounds out the card face. The backs have two Lady Volunteers logos at the top, brief biographical information, and a fire prevention cartoon starring Smokey. The cards are unnumbered and checklisted below in alphabetical order.

COMPLETE SET (16) 10.00 25.00
1 Jody Adams .50 1.25
2 Nikki Caldwell .50 1.25
3 Tamara Carver .50 1.25
4 Kelli Casteel .50 1.25
5 Daedra Charles 1.50 4.00
6 Regina Clark .50 1.25
7 Mickie DeMoss ACO .50 1.25
8 Peggy Evans .50 1.25
9 Lisa Harrison .50 1.25
10 Debbie Hawhee .50 1.25
11 Dena Head 1.00 2.50
12 Marlene Jeter .50 1.25
13 Pat Summitt CO 5.00 12.00
14 Holly Warlick ACO .50 1.25
15 Thompson-Boling Arena .50 1.25
16 Smokey (Mascot) .40 1.00

1991-92 Tennessee Women

COMPLETE SET (18) 15.00 30.00
1 Jody Adams .50 1.25
2 Nikki Caldwell .50 1.25
3 Kelli Casteel .50 1.25
4 Regina Clark .50 1.25
5 Mickie DeMoss ACO .50 1.25
6 Rochone Dilligard .50 1.25
7 Peggy Evans .50 1.25
8 Lisa Harrison .75 2.00
9 Debbie Hawhee .50 1.25
10 Dena Head .50 1.25
11 Marlene Jeter .50 1.25
12 Dana Johnson .50 1.25
13 Nikki McCray 4.00 10.00
14 Pat Summitt CO 4.00 10.00
15 Vonda Ward .50 1.25
16 Holly Warlick ACO .50 1.25
17 Tiffany Woosley .50 1.25
18 Smokey (Mascot) .40 1.00

1992-93 Tennessee Women

This 16-card standard-size set was sponsored by the USDA Forest Service and the state forestry agency. The fronts feature color action player photos, with a turquoise border on an orange background. Within the border, the team's name is printed above the picture, with the player's name, number, and position below. The Smokey the Bear logo in the lower left corner completes the card face. The backs have two Lady Volunteers logos at the top, brief biographical information, and a fire prevention cartoon starring Smokey. The cards are unnumbered and checklisted below in alphabetical order. This set features the first card of Nikki McCray, a member of the gold medal-winning 1996 USA team.

COMPLETE SET (16) 8.00 20.00
1 Jody Adams .30 .75
2 Nikki Caldwell .30 .75
3 Latina Davis .75 2.00
4 Mickie DeMoss ACO .30 .75
5 Rochone Dilligard .30 .75
6 Peggy Evans .30 .75
7 Lisa Harrison .30 .75
8 Dana Johnson .30 .75
9 Michelle Johnson .30 .75
10 Nikki McCray 4.00 10.00
11 Pat Summitt CO 2.00 5.00
12 Pam Tanner ACO .30 .75
13 Vonda Ward .30 .75
14 Holly Warlick ACO .30 .75
15 Tiffany Woosley 1.25 3.00
16 Cheerleaders .30 .75

1993-94 Tennessee Women

This 16-card standard-size set was sponsored by the USDA Forest Service and the state forestry agency. On an orange background with white stripes, the fronts feature color action player photos. The team name is printed above the photo, with the player's name, number and position below. The team logo and Smokey's 50th year anniversary logo complete the fronts. The backs carry two Lady Volunteers logos at the top, the player's name and number, and a fire prevention cartoon starring Smokey. The cards are unnumbered and checklisted below in alphabetical order.

COMPLETE SET (16) 6.00 15.00
1 Nikki Caldwell .20 .50
2 Abby Conklin .40 1.00
3 Latina Davis .40 1.00
4 Mickie DeMoss ACO .20 .50
5 Rochone Dilligard .20 .50
6 Dana Johnson .20 .50
7 Michelle Marciniak .40 1.00
8 Nikki McCray 2.50 6.00
9 Carolyn Peck ACO .20 .50
10 Tanika Smith .20 .50
11 Pat Summitt CO 1.50 4.00
12 Pashen Thompson .40 1.00
13 Vonda Ward .20 .50
14 Holly Warlick ACO .20 .50
15 Tiffany Woosley .75 2.00
16 The Cheerleaders .20 .50

1994-95 Tennessee Women

This 16-card set was issued on a 10" by 14" perforated sheet with four rows of four cards. When the cards are separated, they measure the standard size. The set is sponsored by the USDA Forest Service and the state forestry agency. The fronts display color action and posed player photos with player's name, position, jersey number and Smokey logo below the photo in the orange border. The backs carry the player's name, jersey number, school year, and position at the top above a Smokey cartoon and a fire prevention safety tip. The cards are unnumbered and checklisted below in alphabetical order.

COMPLETE SET (16) 5.00 12.00
1 Abby Conklin .40 1.00
2 Latina Davis .40 1.00
3 Mickie DeMoss ACO .20 .50
4 Dana Johnson .20 .50
5 Tiffani Johnson .60 1.50
6 Brynae Laxton .20 .50
7 Michelle Marciniak .60 1.50
8 Nikki McCray 1.50 4.00
9 Laurie Milligan .20 .50
10 Carolyn Peck ACO .20 .50
11 Tanika Smith .20 .50
12 Pat Summitt CO 1.50 4.00
13 Pashen Thompson .40 1.00
14 Vonda Ward .20 .50
15 Holly Warlick ACO .20 .50
16 Tiffany Woosley .60 1.50

1998-99 Tennessee

This set was released for the University of Tennessee Men's Basketball team during the 1998-99 season. The 16-card set features all of the team's players and coaches.

COMPLETE SET (16) 2.50 6.00
1 Krystal Title Card .20 .50
2 Team Photo .20 .50
3 Del Baker .20 .50
4 C.J. Black .20 .50
5 Vegas Davis .20 .50
6 Aaron Green .20 .50
7 Jerry Green CO .30 .75
8 Tony Harris .20 .50
9 Torrey Harris .20 .50
10 Charles Hathaway .20 .50
11 Rashard Lee .20 .50
12 Isiah Victor .20 .50
13 John Ward .20 .50
14 Brandon Wharton .20 .50
15 Vincent Yarbrough .40 1.00
16 The 6th Man .20 .50

2010-11 Tennessee

COMPLETE SET (18) 6.00 15.00
1 Josh Bone .40 1.00
2 John Fields .40 1.00
3 Melvin Goins .40 1.00
4 Trae Golden .40 1.00
5 Kenny Hall .40 1.00
6 Tobias Harris 2.00 5.00
7 Scotty Hopson .40 1.00
8 Allan Houston HON .60 1.50
9 Michael Hubert .40 1.00
10 Jeronne Maymon .40 1.00
11 Skylar McBee .40 1.00
12 Jordan McRae .40 1.00
13 Bruce Pearl CO .40 1.00
14 Steven Pearl .40 1.00
15 Tyler Summitt .40 1.00
16 Cameron Tatum .40 1.00
17 Brian Williams .40 1.00
18 Renaldo Woolridge .40 1.00

2011-12 Tennessee Women

COMPLETE SET (12) 10.00 25.00
1 Briana Bass .75 2.00
2 Vicki Baugh .75 2.00
3 Cierra Burdick .75 2.00
4 Isabelle Harrison .75 2.00
5 Glory Johnson .75 2.00
6 Alicia Manning 1.25 3.00
7 Ariel Massengale .75 2.00
8 Meighan Simmons .75 2.00
9 Taber Spani .75 2.00
10 Shekinna Stricklen .75 2.00
11 Pat Summitt CO 4.00 10.00
12 Kamiko Williams .75 2.00

1999-00 Tennessee Multi-Ad

COMPLETE SET (16) 4.00 10.00
1 Krystal Card .20 .50
2 Tennessee Volunteers .20 .50
3 Del Baker .20 .50
4 C.J. Black .20 .50
5 Vegas Davis .20 .50
6 Jerry Green CO .40 1.00
7 Jenis Grindstaff .20 .50
8 Marcus Haislip .75 2.00
9 Tony Harris .20 .50

10 Charles Hathaway .20 .50
11 Jon Higgins .20 .50
12 Ron Slay .75 2.00
13 Isiah Victor .20 .50
14 Harris Walker .20 .50
15 Terrence Woods .20 .50
16 Vincent Yarbrough .20 .50

1991-92 Tennessee Tech

This 16-card standard size (2 1/2" by 3 1/2") set was sponsored by Little Caesar's Pizza and features posed color player photos. Within a violet border, a bright yellow frame around the picture contains the player's name and jersey number. The backs are white with violet print and present the player's name, classification, position, hometown, and a player profile. A violet dot-pattern circle at the upper left contains the jersey number. The sponsor's name appears at the top. The cards are unnumbered and checklisted below in alphabetical order.

COMPLETE SET (16) 4.00 10.00
1 John Best .40 1.00
2 Mitch Cupples .40 1.00
3 Damon Davis .40 1.00
4 John Dykstra .40 1.00
5 Charles Edmonson .40 1.00
6 Frank Harrell CO .40 1.00
7 Clyde Hopkins .40 1.00
8 Maurice Houston .40 1.00
9 P.J. Mays .40 1.00
10 Eric Mitchell .40 1.00
11 Jesse Nayadley .40 1.00
12 Donnie Paulk .40 1.00
13 Ronnie Robinson .40 1.00
14 Van Usher .40 1.00
15 Rob West .40 1.00
16 Wade Wester .40 1.00

1992-93 Tennessee Tech

This 18-card standard-size (2 1/2" by 3 1/2") set was sponsored by Little Caesars' Pizza. The fronts feature posed color player photos inside a thin black frame on a purple card face. In yellow lettering, the words "Tennessee Tech" overlay the bottom of the picture. The player's number is printed on the left and his name on the right side below the picture. On a yellow background in black lettering, the backs carry the sponsor's logo at the top, the uniform number in a big circle in the upper life corner, with biographical, statistical, and personal information filling in the remainder of the space. The cards are unnumbered and checklisted below in alphabetical order.

COMPLETE SET (18) 3.00 8.00
1 John Best .30 .75
2 Greg Bibb .30 .75
3 Carlos Carter .30 .75
4 Chad Crouch .30 .75
5 Mitch Cupples .30 .75
6 Charley Dean .30 .75
7 John Dykstra .30 .75
8 Carlos Floyd .30 .75
9 Maurice Houston .30 .75
10 David Ingram .30 .75
11 Trent McCracken .30 .75
12 Eric Mitchell .30 .75
13 Jesse Nayadley .30 .75
14 Brian Riggins .30 .75
15 Earl Smith .30 .75
16 Rob West .30 .75
17 Wade Wester .30 .75
18 Team Leaders .30 .75
Angelo Volpe PRES
Frank Harrell CO

1993-94 Tennessee Tech

This 18-card standard-size set was sponsored by Little Caesars' Pizza. The fronts feature posed color player photos with yellow borders. The player's name and uniform number appear in white lettering within purple bars at the bottom of the photo. The white backs carry the player's uniform number, name, and biography at the top, followed below by his class, position, hometown, statistics, and college highlights, all in purple lettering. The cards are unnumbered and checklisted below in alphabetical order.

COMPLETE SET (18) 3.00 8.00
1 Greg Bibb .30 .75
2 Dennis Buckley .30 .75
3 Marc Burnett .40 1.00
'93 Inductee HOF
4 Carlos Carter .30 .75
5 Lorenzo Coleman .60 1.50
6 Chad Crouch .30 .75
7 Charley Dean .30 .75
8 Carlos Floyd .30 .75
9 Maurice Houston .30 .75
10 David Ingram .30 .75
11 Reggie Mayo .30 .75
12 Eric Mitchell .30 .75
13 Jesse Nayadley .30 .75
14 Earl Smith .30 .75
15 Chris Turner .30 .75
16 Steve Taylor .30 .75
Distinguished Career
17 Rob West .30 .75
18 Eblen Center (Arena) .30 .75

1994-95 Tennessee Tech

This 18-card set measures the standard size. The fronts feature posed color player photos with purple borders. The player's name appears in white lettering at the bottom below the team logo. The lavender backs carry the uniform number, name, biography, class, position, statistics and college highlights all in purple lettering. The cards are unnumbered and checklisted below in alphabetical order.

COMPLETE SET (18) 3.00 8.00
1 Greg Bibb .30 .75
2 Carlos Carter .30 .75
3 Lorenzo Coleman .40 1.00
4 Romain Coleman .30 .75
5 Chad Crouch .30 .75
6 Theron Curry .30 .75
7 Carlos Floyd .30 .75
8 Marc Glanton .30 .75
9 Eric Mitchell .30 .75
10 Jesse Nayadley .30 .75
11 Ricky Norris .30 .75
12 Lance Parr .30 .75
13 Kenneth Smith .30 .75
14 Chris Turner .30 .75
15 Frank Harrell CO .30 .75
Kevin Bray ACO
Bob Eskew ACO
Jason Craighead MG
Susan Fitzpatrick SECY
16 Loyal Fans .30 .75
Johnny Donnelly
17 Gene Davidson ANN .30 .75
Eldon Burgess ANN
18 Chad Smith MG .30 .75
Timmy Rogers MG
Phil Dennis MG

1996-97 Tennessee Tech Schedules

Though they'll certainly win no awards for outstanding achievement in card design, these four unsightly purple pocket schedules nonetheless present part of the collecting universe for die-hard Golden Eagle basketball fans. The set features all of the seniors from the 1996-97 team, including Lorenzo Coleman, one of the nation's more talented big men. These schedules were distributed free at various home games throughout the season. The skeds are unnumbered andhave been checklisted below alphabetically for convenience.

COMPLETE SET (4) .75 2.00
1 Lorenzo Coleman .60 1.50
2 Jason Embry .08 .25
3 Chris Turner .08 .25
4 Curtis Wiggins .08 .25

1990 Texas

Financed by the MOSHANA Foundation and distributed by local law enforcement agencies, this 32-card multi-sport set measures 2 1/2" by 3 1/2" and is printed on thin card stock. The fronts display color action player photos inside a black frame on a white card face. The team name appears in a black bar above the picture, while the player's name and position are printed in the wider bottom border. The backs feature biographical information, player profile, and "A Texas Tip" in the form of anti-drug or alcohol messages. The sports represented are golf (1, 19), basketball (2-4, 8, 25-26, 29, 30), track and field (5-6, 15, 23), tennis (7, 28), baseball (9-10, 16, 32), swimming and diving (11, 13, 20-21), volleyball (12, 14, 18, 31), and football (17, 22, 24, 27). The cards are unnumbered and checklisted below in alphabetical order.

COMPLETE SET (32) 8.00 20.00
2 Susan Anderson BK .30 .75
3 Ellen Bayer BK .30 .75
4 Lance Blanks BK .60 1.50
8 Jody Conradt CO BK .80 2.00
25 Travis Mays BK .60 1.50
26 Lyssa McBride BK .40 1.00
29 George Muller BK .30 .75
30 Tom Penders CO BK .80 2.00

1991 Texas A&M Collegiate Collection

This 100 card standard-size multi-sport set was produced by Collegiate Collection. Although a few color photos are included, the front features mainly black and white player photos with borders in the team's colors. All cards are of football players unless noted.

COMPLETE SET (100) 5.00 10.00
8 John Beasley BK .05 .15
15 Lisa Langston BK .01 .05
30 John Thornton BK .01 .05
49 Barry Davis BK .01 .05
53 Dave Goff BK .01 .05
55 Lynn Hickey CO BK .01 .05
63 James H. Heitmann BK .01 .05
78 Lisa L.J. Jordon BK .01 .05
87 Lisa Herner BK .01 .05
88 Traci Thomas BK .01 .05
97 Yvonne Hill BK .01 .05

1994-95 Texas A&M

Sponsored by Star Tel Long Distance Telephone Service, this 20-card multi-sport set was issued in five 12 1/2" by 3 1/2" strips. The strips are not perforated; however, if the cards were cut, they would measure the standard size. The set is subdivided as follows: men's baseball (1-5), men's basketball (6-10), women's basketball (11-15), and women's volleyball (16-20). The fronts feature posed or action player photos with the sport and sponsor name in the right border. The backs carry a caption on the photo on a maroon background with the sponsor name at the bottom. The cards are unnumbered and checklisted below in alphabetical order within the sport.

6 Tony Barone CO BK .75 2.00
Porter Moser ACO
Mitch Buonaguro ACO
Frank Haith ACO
7 Kyle Kessel BK .40 1.00
Waseem Ali
Quinton James
Chris Oney
John Stevens
Dario Que
8 Jimmy Smith BK .40 1.00
Chris Pulliams
John Stevens
Chris LeBlanc/1994-95 Schedule
9 Roy Wills BK .75 2.00
Damon Johnson
Tony McGinnis
Corey Henderson
Joe Wilbert
John
11 Carey Owens BK .40 1.00
Sutton Helvey
Kim Linder
12 Christy Lake BK .40 1.00
Shanae Ford
Marianne Miller
Lana Tucker/1994-95 Schedule
13 Juniors and Seniors BK .40 1.00
Angel Spinks
Martha McClelland
Kelly Cerny
Debbie B
14 Coaches .40 1.00
Angela Taylor ACO
Kristy Sims ACO
Candi Harvey CO
Lisa Jordon A

1992-93 Texas Tech Women

Sponsored by the Lubbock Avalanche-Journal and other local businesses, this 19-card set measures the standard size and is printed on thin card stock. The fronts display posed, color photos of the Lady Raiders, the 1992-93 Southwest Conference and NCAA Champions. The pictures are framed by a thin black line and set on a card face that is divided diagonally by a black stripe. The upper portion is red, while the lower portion is gray. The player's name is printed above the photo in the black border. The set year is in the upper left corner. The backs carry biographical information, statistics, and sponsor logos. The cards are unnumbered and checklisted below in alphabetical order. The key card in the set is Sheryl Swoopes, who started for the gold medal-winning 1996 USA team and is considered to be among the best female basketball players of all time.

COMPLETE SET (19) 10.00 25.00
1 Michi Atkins .60 1.50
2 Cynthia Clinger .30 .75
3 Nikki Heath .30 .75
4 Noel Johnson .30 .75
5 Diana Kersey .30 .75
6 Krista Kirkland .30 .75
7 Kim Pruitt .30 .75
8 Raider Red (Mascot) .30 .75
9 Roger Reding ACO .30 .75
10 Stephanie Scott .30 .75
11 Marsha Sharp CO 1.00 2.50
12 Sheryl Swoopes 8.00 20.00
13 Michelle Thomas .30 .75
14 Linden Weese ACO .30 .75
15 Terri Weldon .30 .75
Graduate Assistant
16 Melinda White .30 .75
17 Checklist .30 .75
18 Sponsor Card .30 .75
19 Texas Tech Sign .30 .75

1992-93 Texas Tech Women NCAA Champs

Sponsored by United Supermarket, this 25-card standard-size set commemorates the 1993 Lady Raiders National Championship team. The fronts feature color action photos with a red inner border and a black pebble grain outer border. The player's name, position and number appear on a light gray bar at the bottom. The backs carry a black-and-white portrait with biographical information, career summary and statistics on a gray background. This set features several cards of Sheryl Swoopes, who started for the gold medal-winning 1996 USA team and is considered to be among the best female basketball players of all time.

COMPLETE SET (25) 12.00 30.00
1 Trophy Card .40 1.00
2 Diana Kersey .20 .50
3 Nikki Heath .20 .50
4 Stephanie Scott .20 .50
5 Krista Kirkland .20 .50
6 Sheryl Swoopes 6.00 15.00
7 Noel Johnson .20 .50
8 Janice Farris .20 .50
9 Kim Pruitt .20 .50
10 Cynthia Clinger .20 .50
11 Michelle Thomas .20 .50
12 Melinda White .20 .50
13 Michi Atkins .40 1.00
14 Marsha Sharp CO .75 2.00
15 Linden Weese ACO .20 .50
16 Roger Reding ACO .20 .50
17 Terri Weldon .20 .50
Graduate Assistant
18 Jeannine McHaney DIR .20 .50
19 SWC Championship .40 1.00
20 National Semifinals .40 1.00
Michi Atkins
21 National Finals 2.00 5.00
Sheryl Swoopes
22 Emotional Finish 2.00 5.00
Sheryl Swoopes
Krista Kirkland
23 1992-93 Season Record .20 .50
Krista Kirkland
Sheryl Swoopes
Cynthia Clinger
24 Sheryl Swoopes 2.00 5.00
Player of the Year
Records and Accolades
25 Team Photo CL .40 1.00

1990-91 UCLA

This 40-card set was produced by Collegiate Collection and features the men's and women's basketball teams. The standard size (2 1/2" by 3 1/2") cards feature on the fronts a mix of posed or action color player photos (with rounded corners), with a thin black border on royal blue background. While the school name appears above the picture in yellow lettering, the player's name appears in black lettering in a yellow stripe below the picture. The UCLA and Collegiate Collection logos at the top complete the card face. The horizontally oriented backs provide brief biography, statistics, and the card number, all within a royal blue border. Due to a production error, the Keith Owens card incorrectly depicts Destah Owens. A coupon was included in the set to exchange for a free replacement card. Note that the back of the corrected card differs from the regular issue in format and color. Men's basketball is represented by cards 1-15 and 35-39; women's basketball by cards 16-34. The set features first cards of Tracy Murray and Ed O'Bannon in addtion to an early Don MacLean card.

COMPLETE SET (40) 8.00 20.00
1 Team Photo .40 1.00
2 Tracy Murray 1.25 3.00
3 Ed O'Bannon 1.25 3.00
4 Darrick Martin .60 1.50
5 Mitchell Butler .60 1.50
6 Mike Lanier .08 .25
7 Chris Kenny .08 .25
8A Keith Owens ERR .60 1.50
8B Keith Owens COR .75 2.00
9 Dave Paulsell .08 .25
10 Shon Tarver .40 1.00
11 Rodney Zimmerman .08 .25
12 Zan Mason .08 .25
13 Gerald Madkins .75 2.00
14 Don MacLean 1.25 3.00
15 Lou Richie .08 .25
16 Billie Moore CO .30 .75
17 Rehema Stephens .08 .25
18 Nicole Anderson .08 .25
19 Amy Jalewalia .08 .25
20 Pam Walker ACO .08 .25
21 Lynn Kamrath .08 .25
22 Detra Lockhart .08 .25
23 Stacie Gravely .08 .25
24 Laura Collins .08 .25
25 Genevieve Vanoostveen .08 .25
26 Dede Mosman .08 .25
27 Nicole Young .08 .25
28 Dawn Baker .08 .25
29 Melissa Gische .08 .25
30 Rachelle Roulier .08 .25
31 Marcy Tarabochia .08 .25
32 Natalie Williams 2.00 5.00
33 Kathy Olivier ACO .20 .50
34 Mary Hegarty ACO .08 .25
35 Jim Harrick CO .60 1.50
36 Brad Holland ACO .60 1.50
37 Tony Fuller ACO .20 .50
38 Ken Barone ACO .08 .25
39 Mark Gottfried ACO .20 .50
40 Checklist Card .08 .25

1991 UCLA Collegiate Collection

This 144-card standard-size set was produced by Collegiate Collection. The fronts feature a mix of black and white or color player photos, with royal blue borders and the player's name in the yellow stripe below the picture. The horizontally oriented backs present biographical information, career summary, or statistics on a white background with blue lettering and borders.

COMPLETE SET (144) 6.00 15.00
1A John Wooden CO .30 .75
1B John Wooden CO .60 1.50
Prototype
2A Kareem Abdul-Jabbar .30 .75
2B Kareem Abdul-Jabbar .60 1.50
Prototype
3 Bill Walton .20 .50
4 Larry Farmer .07 .20
5 Marques Johnson .10 .30
6 Walt Hazzard .08 .25
7 Henry Bibby .20 .50
8 Gail Goodrich .20 .50
9 Jim Harrick .15 .40
10 Kareem Abdul-Jabbar .30 .75
11 Mike Warren .08 .25
12 Gary Maloncon .07 .20
13 James Wilkes .07 .20
14 Kiki Vandeweghe .08 .25
15 1969 NCAA Champs .07 .20
16 Sidney Wicks .08 .25
17 Andre McCarter .07 .20
18 Michael Holton .07 .20
19 Greg Lee .07 .20
20 John Wooden CO .30 .75
21 Gene Bartow CO .07 .20
22 Richard Washington .07 .20
23 Brad Wright .07 .20
24 Pooh Richardson .07 .20
25 Terry Schofield .07 .20
26 Gig Sims .07 .20
27 Darren Daye .07 .20
28 Dave Immel .07 .20
29 Brad Holland .07 .20
30 Bill Walton .20 .50
31 Larry Brown CO .15 .40
32 Kevin Walker .07 .20
33 Kareem Abdul-Jabbar .30 .75
34 Kenny Heitz .07 .20
35 Gary Cunningham .07 .20
36 Lynn Shackelford .07 .20
37 Keith Wilkes .08 .25
38 1975 NCAA Champs .07 .20
39 Raymond Townsend .07 .20
40 Pete Trgovich .07 .20
41 Kelvin Butler .07 .20
42 Ed Sheldrake .07 .20
43 Larry Hollyfield .07 .20
44 Montel Hatcher .07 .20
45 Denise Curry .08 .25
46 Curtis Rowe .08 .25
47 David Meyers .07 .20
48 Lucius Allen .08 .25
49 Kenny Fields .07 .20
50 John Vallely .07 .20
51 John Wooden .20 .50
Nell Wooden
52 Sidney Wicks .10 .30
53 1973 NCAA Champs .07 .20
54 Jack Haley .07 .20
55 Ralph Drollinger .07 .20
56 Don Johnson .07 .20
57 Bill Ellis .07 .20
58 Willie Naulls .07 .20
59 Ron Livingston .07 .20
60 Bill Putnam .07 .20
61 Rod Foster .07 .20
62 Bill Walton .20 .50
63 Roy Hamilton .07 .20
64 Jim Spillane .07 .20
65 Ralph Jackson .07 .20
66 Morris Taft .07 .20
67 Dick Ridgeway .07 .20
68 Dave Minor .07 .20
69 1965 Champs .07 .20
70 Karl Kraushaar .07 .20
71 Craig Jackson .07 .20
72 Kenny Washington .07 .20
73 Keith Wilkes .08 .25
74 Stuart Gray .07 .20
75 John Green .07 .20
76 Doug McIntosh .07 .20
77 Walt Hazzard .08 .25
78 Frank Lubin .07 .20
79 Don Piper .07 .20
80 1967 Champs .07 .20
81 Kenny Booker .07 .20
82 Marques Johnson .10 .30
83 Bill Walton .20 .50
84 1972 Champs .07 .20
85 Steve Patterson .07 .20
86 1964 NCAA Champs .07 .20
87 Alan Sawyer .07 .20
88 Walt Torrence .07 .20
89 Gail Goodrich .20 .50
90 Ralph Bunche .20 .50
91 Swen Nater .08 .25
92 Larry Farmer .07 .20
93 Kareem Abdul-Jabbar .30 .75
94 Mike Sanders .07 .20
95 Niguel Miguel .07 .20
96 Jackie Robinson .60 1.50
97 Dick West .07 .20
98 Rafer Johnson .15 .40
99 John Berberich .07 .20
100 Director Card .07 .20
101 Richard Linthicum .07 .20
102 Chuck Clustka .07 .20
103 John Wooden CO .20 .50
Denny Crum CO
Gary Cunningham CO
104 Jerry Norman .07 .20
105 John Moore .07 .20
106 Trevor Wilson .08 .25
107 David Greenwood .07 .20
108 John Wooden CO .20 .50
J.D.Morgan AD
109 Kareem Abdul-Jabbar .30 .75
110 Ann Meyers .20 .50
111 Denny Crum .20 .50
112 Pierce Works .07 .20
113 Carl Cozens .07 .20
114 George Stanich .07 .20
115 Don Ashen .07 .20
116 David Greenwood .07 .20
117 1971 Team Photo .07 .20
118 Johns Barksdale .07 .20
119 1978 Champion .07 .20
120 John Stanich .07 .20
121 Don Barksdale .07 .20
122 1968 Champs .07 .20
123 Carl Knowles .07 .20
124 Don Bragg .07 .20
125 Ducky Drake .07 .20
126 John Ball .07 .20
127 Pauley Pavilion .07 .20
128 Sam Balter .07 .20
129 A Caddy Works Team .07 .20
130 John Wooden CO .30 .75
131 Fred Goss .07 .20
132 Keith Erickson .08 .25
133 Pete Blackman .07 .20
134 Gail Goodrich .20 .50
135 Kent Miller .07 .20
136 Jack Ketchum .07 .20
137 1970 Team Photo .07 .20
138 Jim Milhorn .07 .20
139 Bill Rankin .07 .20
140 Gary Cunningham .07 .20
141 Bob (Ace) Caikins .07 .20
142 J.D. Morgan AD .07 .20
143 Fred Slaughter .07 .20
144 Director Card .07 .20

1991-92 UCLA

This 21-card set was produced by Collegiate Collection and measures the standard size (2 1/2" by 3 1/2"). The fronts feature color action player photos, with royal blue borders and the player's name in a yellow stripe beneath the picture. The horizontally oriented backs present biographical information, statistics, and career summary on a white background with blue lettering and borders. The cards are numbered on the back in the upper right corner. The set features early cards of Don MacLean, Tracy Murray, and Ed O'Bannon.

COMPLETE SET (21) 6.00 15.00
1 Mike Lanier .20 .50
2 Don MacLean .75 2.00
3 Rodney Zimmerman .20 .50
4 Pauley Pavilion .30 .75
5 Tyus Edney 1.25 3.00
6 Jiri (George) Zidek .75 2.00
7 Brad Holland CO .40 1.00
8 Ed O'Bannon .75 2.00
9 Richard Petruska .30 .75
10 Darrick Martin .40 1.00
11 Tony Fuller CO .20 .50
12 Tracy Murray .75 2.00
13 Gerald Madkins .40 1.00
14 Mitchell Butler .40 1.00
15 Mark Gottfried .20 .50
16 Jim Harrick CO .40 1.00
17 Jonah Naulls .20 .50
18 Steve Lavin CO .60 1.50
19 Steve Elkind .20 .50
20 Shon Tarver .40 1.00
21 Checklist Card .20 .50

1988-89 UNLV

This 12-card standard-size set was produced by Hall of Fame Cards, Inc. Reportedly there were only 10,000 sets produced. The front features a color action shot of the player, trimmed in red borders on a gray card face. The words "Runnin' Rebels" appears in red lettering above the picture, while the school name, player's name, and his position appear below. The back is printed in red and includes biographical information, career statistics at UNLV, and an anti-drug message titled "Rebel Rap." The cards are numbered on the back and checklisted below accordingly. The set features the first cards of NBA players Greg Anthony and Stacey Augmon.

COMPLETE SET (12) 5.00 12.00
1 Stacey Augmon 2.50 6.00
2 Greg Anthony 2.00 5.00
3 Anderson Hunt .75 2.00
4 George Ackles .40 1.00
5 David Butler .75 2.00
6 Clint Rossum .40 1.00
7 Moses Scurry .40 1.00
8 Barry Young .40 1.00
9 James Jones .40 1.00
10 Stacey Cvijanovich .40 1.00
11 Chris Jeter .40 1.00
12 Bryan Emerzian .40 1.00

1989-90 UNLV 7-Eleven

This 14-card standard-size set was sponsored by 7-Eleven, 98.5 KLUC-FM radio, and Nationwide Communications Inc. The cards are printed on very thin card stock. Reportedly more than 25,000 sets were produced and distributed. The fronts feature color action player photos, with black borders on red card face. The team and player's names appear in red lettering in gray boxes above and below the picture respectively. The backs are printed in black on white card stock and provide biographical information and player profile. The cards are unnumbered and are checklisted below in alphabetical order. The set features an early card of NBA star Larry Johnson as well as the first card of coach Jerry Tarkanian.

COMPLETE SET (14) 5.00 12.00
1 Greg Anthony .75 2.00
2 Stacey Augmon 1.25 3.00
3 Travis Bice .40 1.00
4 David Butler .40 1.00
5 Stacey Cvijanovich .20 .50
6 Bryan Emerzian .20 .50
7 Anderson Hunt .40 1.00
8 Chris Jeter .20 .50
9 Larry Johnson 2.00 5.00
10 James Jones .20 .50
11 David Rice .20 .50
12 Moses Scurry .40 1.00
13 Barry Young .20 .50
14 Jerry Tarkanian CO 1.50 4.00

1989-90 UNLV HOF

This 14-card standard-size set was produced by Hall of Fame Cards, Inc. Reportedly 5000 sets were originally produced but an additional 3000 sets were made after UNLV won the NCAA Championship. The card front features a color action player photo outlined by a thin black border. The school name is superimposed at the right upper corner of the picture. The background is red for the top half of the card face and gray for the bottom half. The player's name is printed in red lettering below the picture. In a horizontal format the back has biographical information and the slogan "Say No to Drugs." The set features an early card of NBA star Larry Johnson.

COMPLETE SET (14) 5.00 12.00
1 Stacey Augmon 1.25 3.00
2 Greg Anthony .75 2.00
3 Larry Johnson 2.50 6.00
4 George Ackles .40 1.00
5 Moses Scurry .40 1.00
6 Anderson Hunt .75 2.00
(Hank Gathers visible in background)
7 Travis Bice .40 1.00
8 David Butler .40 1.00
9 Stacey Cvijanovich .20 .50
10 Chris Jeter .20 .50
11 Bryan Emerzian .20 .50
12 James Jones .75 2.00
(Hank Gathers visible in background)
13 Barry Young .20 .50
14 Dave Rice .20 .50

1990-91 UNLV HOF

This 15-card standard-size set was produced by Hall of Fame Cards, Inc. and features the UNLV Runnin' Rebels, the 1990 NCAA national champions. Reportedly only 15,000 sets were produced; each set is individually numbered on card number 4 Anderson Hunt. The fronts feature color action player photos; cards numbered 11-13 feature "Future Rebels" and have posed color photos. All cards have red borders on the top and bottom and white borders on the sides. A red diagonal cuts across the lower right corner of the picture, with the words "1990 Nat'l Champions" in white lettering. The player's name and position are given in white lettering in the bottom red border. The backs have statistical information and the slogan "Say No to Drugs" in either horizontal or vertical formats. The key cards in the set are the two Larry Johnson cards.

COMPLETE SET (15) 4.00 10.00
1 Larry Johnson 1.25 3.00
2 Stacey Augmon .75 2.00
3 Greg Anthony .60 1.50
4 Anderson Hunt .40 1.00
5 Travis Bice .20 .50
6 George Ackles .40 1.00
7 Bryan Emerzian .20 .50
8 Dave Rice .20 .50
9 Chris Jeter .20 .50
10 Anderson Hunt .40 1.00
11 Evric Gray .40 1.00
12 Bobby Joyce .20 .50
13 H. Waldman .40 1.00
14 Larry Johnson 1.25 3.00
15 Runnin' Rebels .40 1.00

1990-91 UNLV Season to Remember

This 15-card standard-size set features the UNLV Runnin' Rebels, who were runner-ups for the 1991 NCAA championship. The front features a color action photo of the player, with a thin black border on dark red background. The school name is superimposed at the right upper corner of the picture, and the player's name is inscribed across the bottom of the picture. In black lettering the words "A Season to Remember" appear below the photo. The back gives biographical and statistical information in a horizontal format, and repeats the words "A Season to Remember," with the team record "34-1." The key card in the set features NBA star Larry Johnson.

COMPLETE SET (15) 3.00 8.00
1 Larry Johnson .75 2.00
2 Stacey Augmon .40 1.00
3 Greg Anthony .40 1.00
4 Anderson Hunt .20 .50
5 Travis Bice .08 .25
6 George Ackles .20 .50
7 Bryan Emerzian .08 .25
8 Dave Rice .08 .25
9 Chris Jeter .08 .25
10 Elmore Spencer .20 .50
11 Evric Gray .20 .50
12 Bobby Joyce .08 .25
13 H. Waldman .20 .50
14 Melvin Love .08 .25
15 Rebel All-Americans .60 1.50
(Anderson Hunt
Greg Anthony
George Ackles
Larry Johnson
Stacey Augmon)

1990-91 UNLV Smokey

This 15-card set was sponsored by the USDA Forest Service in cooperation with other federal agencies. The standard size cards were issued as a set of single cards or as a sheet consisting of four rows of four cards (the 16th slot is blank). The front features a color action player photo, with gray border on dark red background. In black lettering the words "1990-91 UNLV Runnin' Rebels" are printed above the picture, with the player's name and number below. The Smokey the Bear logo in the lower left corner completes the card face. The back presents biographical information and a fire prevention cartoon starring Smokey. The cards unnumbered and we have checklisted them below in alphabetical order, with the jersey number to the right of the name. The key card in the set features NBA star Larry Johnson.

COMPLETE SET (15) 4.00 10.00
1 George Ackles 44 .40 1.00
2 Greg Anthony 50 .60 1.50
3 Stacey Augmon 32 .75 2.00
4 Travis Bice 3 .30 .75
5 Bryan Emerzian 15 .30 .75
6 Evric Gray 23 .40 1.00
7 Anderson Hunt 12 .40 1.00
8 Chris Jeter 53 .30 .75
9 Larry Johnson 4 1.25 3.00
10 Bobby Joyce 42 .30 .75
11 Melvin Love 40 .30 .75
12 Dave Rice 30 .30 .75
13 Elmore Spencer 24 .40 1.00
14 Jerry Tarkanian CO 1.25 3.00
15 H. Waldman 31 .40 1.00

1992-93 UNLV

Sponsored by KVBC Channel 3 (Las Vegas) and Centel First Source (phone book), this 16-card set was issued as a perforated sheet that features 14 standard-size player cards and two sponsor cards. The fronts display color, action player photos on a red card face. A gray bar at the bottom contains the player's name, jersey number, and position. A red and gray banner design at the top carries the school and team name, as well as the year. The backs have biographical information, a player profile, and a cartoon of the team mascot. Sponsor logos are printed at the bottom. The cards are unnumbered and checklisted below in alphabetical order.

COMPLETE SET (16) 6.00 15.00
1 Derrick Alesevich .30 .75
2 Dexter Boney .60 1.50
3 Jason Brooks .30 .75
4 Clint Clausen .30 .75
5 Ken Gibson .30 .75
6 Evric Gray .60 1.50
7 Fred Haygood .30 .75
8 Sean Loughran .30 .75
9 Reggie Manuel .30 .75
10 Rollie Massimino CO 1.00 2.50
11 Isaiah (J.R.) Rider 2.50 6.00
12 Damian Smith .30 .75
13 Dedan Thomas .30 .75
14 Lawrence Thomas .30 .75
15 Sponsor Card .30 .75
KVBC Channel 3
16 Sponsor Card .30 .75
Centel First Source

2010-11 Upper Deck North Carolina

COMPLETE SET (183) 25.00 60.00
1 Nathaniel Cartmell .30 .75
2 Cartwright Carmichael .30 .75
3 Monk McDonald .30 .75
4 Jack Cobb .30 .75
5 George Glamack .30 .75
6 Horace Bones McKinney .30 .75
7 Skippy Winstead .30 .75
8 Jerry Vayda .30 .75
9 Frank McGuire .30 .75
10 Lennie Rosenbluth .30 .75
11 Pete Brennan .30 .75
12 Joe Quigg .30 .75
13 York Larese .30 .75
14 Doug Moe .30 .75
15 Larry Brown .30 .75
16 Bobby Lewis .30 .75
17 Rusty Clark .30 .75
18 Dick Grubar .30 .75
19 Charlie Scott .30 .75
20 Jim Delany .30 .75
21 Lee Dedmon .30 .75
22 Bill Chamberlain .30 .75
23 Stephen Previs .30 .75
24 Darrell Elston .30 .75
25 Bobby Jones .40 1.00
26 Bob McAdoo .40 1.00
27 Mitch Kupchak .30 .75
28 Walter Davis .30 .75
29 John Kuester .30 .75
30 Tom LaGarde .30 .75
31 Angela Lumpkin .30 .75
32 Phil Ford .30 .75
33 Marsha Mann .30 .75
34 Mike O'Koren .30 .75
35 Bernadette McGlade .30 .75
36 Dave Colescott .30 .75
37 Al Wood .30 .75
38 Rich Yonakor .30 .75
39 Jennifer Alley .40 1.00
40 James Worthy .60 1.50
41 Matt Doherty .30 .75
42 Sam Perkins .30 .75
43 Michael Jordan 2.00 5.00
44 Buzz Peterson .30 .75
45 Brad Daugherty .30 .75
46 Steve Hale .30 .75
47 Pam Leake .30 .75
48 Kenny Smith .40 1.00
49 Joe Wolf .30 .75
50 J.R. Reid .30 .75
51 Sylvia Hatchell .30 .75
52 Steve Bucknall .30 .75
53 Jeff Lebo .30 .75
54 Kevin Madden .30 .75
55 Scott Williams .30 .75
56 Pete Chilcutt .30 .75
57 Rick Fox .30 .75
58 Hubert Davis .30 .75
59 George Lynch .30 .75
60 Henrik Rodl .30 .75
61 Matt Wenstrom .30 .75
62 Sylvia Crawley .30 .75
63 Eric Montross .30 .75
64 Derrick Phelps .30 .75
65 Tonya Sampson .30 .75
66 Charlotte Smith .30 .75
67 Donald Williams .30 .75
68 Dante Calabria .30 .75
69 Kevin Salvadori .30 .75
70 Marion Jones .40 1.00
71 Jerry Stackhouse .60 1.50
72 Serge Zwikker .30 .75
73 Vince Carter .75 2.00
74 Antawn Jamison .40 1.00
75 Makhtar N'diaye .30 .75
76 Jason Capel .30 .75
77 Kris Lang .30 .75
78 Sean May .30 .75
79 David Noel .30 .75
80 Ty Lawson .60 1.50
81 Ed Davis .60 1.50
82 Roy Williams .60 1.50
83 Dean Smith .75 2.00
84 UNC/MSU 1957 RIV 1.00 2.50
85 UNC/Kansas 1957 RIV 1.00 2.50
86 C.Scott/D.Cowens RIV 1.00 2.50
87 UNC/UNLV 1977 RIV 1.00 2.50
88 L.Nance/J.Worthy RIV 1.00 2.50
89 UNC/Georgetown 1982 RIV 1.00 2.50
90 H.Grant/M.Jordan RIV 2.50 6.00
91 UNC/NC State 1985 RIV 1.00 2.50
92 D.Ferry/B.Daugherty RIV 1.00 2.50
93 D.Ferry/J.R.Reid RIV 1.00 2.50
94 UNC/Oklahoma 1990 RIV 1.00 2.50
95 C.Laettner/R.Fox RIV 1.00 2.50
96 C.Laettner/E.Montross RIV 1.00 2.50
97 UNC/Michigan 1993 RIV 1.00 2.50
98 UNC/Duke 1995 RIV 1.00 2.50
99 UNC/Maryland 2005 RIV 1.00 2.50
100 UNC/Duke 2005 RIV 1.00 2.50
101 UNC/Illinois 2005 RIV 1.00 2.50
102 UNC/Duke 2006 RIV 1.00 2.50
103 UNC/MSU 2009 RIV 1.00 2.50
104 George Glamack AA 1.00 2.50
105 Lennie Rosenbluth AA 1.00 2.50
106 Charlie Scott AA 1.00 2.50
107 Phil Ford AA 1.00 2.50
108 James Worthy AA 1.25 3.00
109 Bob McAdoo AA 1.00 2.50
110 Sam Perkins AA 1.00 2.50
111 Michael Jordan AA 2.50 6.00
112 Pam Leake AA 1.00 2.50
113 Kenny Smith AA 1.00 2.50
114 J.R. Reid AA 1.00 2.50
115 Tonya Sampson AA 1.00 2.50
116 Charlotte Smith AA 1.00 2.50
117 Jerry Stackhouse AA 1.25 3.00
118 Antawn Jamison AA 1.00 2.50
119 Sean May AA 1.00 2.50
120 Marion Jones AA 1.00 2.50
121 Vince Carter AA 1.25 3.00
122 Brad Daugherty AA 1.00 2.50
123 Ty Lawson AA 1.00 2.50
124 Michael Jordan BM 2.00 5.00
125 Bob McAdoo BM .75 2.00
126 Bobby Jones BM .75 2.00
127 UNC 1957 Trophy BM .75 2.00
128 UNC Champ Trophies BM .75 2.00
129 Michael Jordan BM 2.00 5.00
130 Joe Quigg BM .75 2.00
131 Dean Smith BM 1.00 2.50
132 Jerry Stackhouse BM .75 2.00
133 James Worthy BM 1.00 2.50
134 Lee Shaffer BM .75 2.00
135 Michael Jordan BM 2.00 5.00
136 UNC Inside Museum BM .75 2.00
137 Phil Ford BM .75 2.00
138 Walter Davis BM .75 2.00
139 Kenny Smith BM .75 2.00
140 Roy Williams BM 1.00 2.50
141 Eric Montross BM .75 2.00

142 Vince Carter BM 1.00 2.50
143 Tyler Hansbrough BM 1.00 2.50
144 Nathaniel Cartmell TL 1.00 2.50
145 UNC/Duke TL 1.00 2.50
146 Cartwright Carmichael TL 1.00 2.50
147 Jack Cobb TL 1.00 2.50
148 Horace Bones McKinney TL 1.00 2.50
149 Frank McGuire TL 1.00 2.50
150 Pete Brennan TL 1.00 2.50
151 Lennie Rosenbluth TL 1.00 2.50
152 Dean Smith TL 1.25 3.00
153 George Karl TL 1.00 2.50
154 Michael Jordan TL 2.50 6.00
155 Sam Perkins TL 1.00 2.50
156 James Worthy TL 1.25 3.00
157 Donald Williams TL 1.00 2.50
158 Charlotte Smith TL 1.00 2.50
159 Dean Smith TL 1.25 3.00
160 Matt Doherty TL 1.00 2.50
161 Roy Williams TL 1.25 3.00
162 Sean May TL 1.00 2.50
163 Ty Lawson TL 1.00 2.50
164 Michael Jordan JY 1.50 4.00
165 Michael Jordan JY 1.50 4.00
166 Michael Jordan JY 1.50 4.00
167 Michael Jordan JY 1.50 4.00
168 Michael Jordan JY 1.50 4.00
169 Michael Jordan JY 1.50 4.00
170 Michael Jordan JY 1.50 4.00
171 Michael Jordan JY 1.50 4.00
172 Michael Jordan JY 1.50 4.00
173 Michael Jordan JY 1.50 4.00
174 Michael Jordan JY 1.50 4.00
175 Michael Jordan JY 1.50 4.00
176 Michael Jordan JY 1.50 4.00
177 Michael Jordan JY 1.50 4.00
178 Michael Jordan JY 1.50 4.00
179 Michael Jordan JY 1.50 4.00
180 Michael Jordan JY 1.50 4.00
181 Michael Jordan JY 1.50 4.00
182 Michael Jordan JY 1.50 4.00
183 Michael Jordan JY 1.50 4.00
NNO M.Jordan Banner AU 400.00 600.00

2010-11 Upper Deck North Carolina Autographs

STATED ODDS 1:24 PACKS
UNPRICED SUBSET PRINT RUN ONE TO 3 SETS
7 Skippy Winstead 6.00 15.00
10 Lennie Rosenbluth 10.00 25.00
11 Pete Brennan 8.00 20.00
12 Joe Quigg 8.00 20.00
13 York Larese 6.00 15.00
14 Doug Moe 6.00 15.00
15 Larry Brown 12.00 30.00
16 Bobby Lewis 6.00 15.00
18 Dick Grubar 6.00 15.00
19 Charlie Scott 6.00 15.00
20 Jim Delany 8.00 20.00
21 Lee Dedmon 6.00 15.00
22 Bill Chamberlain 6.00 15.00
23 Stephen Previs 8.00 20.00
24 Darrell Elston 6.00 15.00
25 Bobby Jones 20.00 50.00
26 Bob McAdoo 20.00 50.00
27 Mitch Kupchak 15.00 40.00
28 Walter Davis 10.00 25.00
29 John Kuester 6.00 15.00
31 Angela Lumpkin 6.00 15.00
32 Phil Ford 15.00 40.00
33 Marsha Mann 6.00 15.00
34 Mike O'Koren 8.00 20.00
35 Bernadette McGlade 6.00 15.00
36 Dave Colescott 6.00 15.00
37 Al Wood 6.00 15.00
38 Rich Yonakor 6.00 15.00
39 Jennifer Alley 6.00 15.00
40 James Worthy 50.00 120.00
41 Matt Doherty 6.00 15.00
42 Sam Perkins 50.00 120.00
43 Michael Jordan 500.00 800.00
44 Buzz Peterson 10.00 25.00
45 Brad Daugherty 20.00 50.00
46 Steve Hale 6.00 15.00
47 Pam Leake 6.00 15.00
48 Kenny Smith 25.00 60.00
49 Joe Wolf 6.00 15.00
50 J.R. Reid 30.00 80.00
51 Sylvia Hatchell 8.00 20.00
52 Steve Bucknall 6.00 15.00
53 Jeff Lebo 6.00 15.00
54 Kevin Madden 6.00 15.00
55 Scott Williams 12.00 30.00
56 Pete Chilcutt 6.00 15.00
57 Rick Fox 20.00 50.00
58 Hubert Davis 10.00 25.00
59 George Lynch 8.00 20.00
60 Henrik Rodl 8.00 20.00
61 Matt Wenstrom 6.00 15.00
62 Sylvia Crawley 6.00 15.00
63 Eric Montross 8.00 20.00
64 Derrick Phelps 6.00 15.00
65 Tonya Sampson 6.00 15.00
66 Charlotte Smith 6.00 15.00
67 Donald Williams 10.00 25.00
68 Dante Calabria 6.00 15.00
69 Kevin Salvadori 8.00 20.00
70 Marion Jones 25.00 60.00
71 Jerry Stackhouse 30.00 80.00
72 Serge Zwikker 6.00 15.00
73 Vince Carter 15.00 40.00
74 Antawn Jamison 10.00 25.00
75 Makhtar N'diaye 6.00 15.00
76 Jason Capel 10.00 25.00
77 Kris Lang 6.00 15.00
78 Sean May 8.00 20.00
79 David Noel 6.00 15.00
80 Ty Lawson 10.00 25.00
81 Ed Davis 6.00 15.00
82 Roy Williams 100.00 200.00

2010-11 Upper Deck North Carolina Dream Team 3D

COMPLETE SET (25) 40.00 70.00
STATED ODDS 1:24 PACKS
DT1 Michael Jordan 8.00 20.00
DT2 Jack Cobb 1.50 4.00
DT3 George Glamack 1.50 4.00
DT4 Lennie Rosenbluth 1.50 4.00
DT5 Walter Davis 2.50 6.00
DT6 Marion Jones 2.50 6.00
DT7 Charlie Scott 1.50 4.00
DT8 Bobby Jones 2.00 5.00
DT9 Phil Ford 2.50 6.00
DT10 Mike O'Koren 2.50 6.00
DT11 Al Wood 1.50 4.00
DT12 James Worthy 2.50 6.00
DT13 Sam Perkins 1.50 4.00
DT14 Cartwright Carmichael 1.50 4.00
DT15 Brad Daugherty 2.50 6.00
DT16 Kenny Smith 2.00 5.00
DT17 J.R. Reid 1.50 4.00
DT18 Eric Montross 1.50 4.00
DT19 Charlotte Smith 2.50 6.00
DT20 Jerry Stackhouse 1.50 4.00
DT21 Vince Carter 2.50 6.00
DT22 Antawn Jamison 2.00 5.00
DT23 Sean May 1.50 4.00
DT24 Ty Lawson 2.00 5.00
DT25 Dean Smith 2.50 6.00

2010-11 Upper Deck North Carolina Legendary Numbers 3D

COMPLETE SET (25) 40.00 70.00
STATED ODDS 1:24 PACKS
LN1 Michael Jordan 12.00 30.00
LN2 Ty Lawson 2.00 5.00
LN3 Lennie Rosenbluth 1.50 4.00
LN4 Larry Brown 1.50 4.00
LN5 Vince Carter 2.50 6.00
LN6 George Glamack 1.50 4.00
LN7 Donald Williams 1.50 4.00
LN8 Phil Ford 2.50 6.00
LN9 Buzz Peterson 1.50 4.00
LN10 Eric Montross 1.50 4.00
LN11 Al Wood 1.50 4.00
LN12 Kenny Smith 2.00 5.00
LN13 Sam Perkins 1.50 4.00
LN14 Jack Cobb 1.50 4.00
LN15 Charlie Scott 1.50 4.00
LN16 Antawn Jamison 2.00 5.00
LN17 Bobby Jones 2.00 5.00
LN18 J.R. Reid 1.50 4.00
LN19 George Lynch 1.50 4.00
LN20 Hubert Davis 1.50 4.00
LN21 Sean May 1.50 4.00
LN22 Matt Doherty 1.50 4.00
LN23 Rick Fox 2.00 5.00
LN24 Charlotte Smith 2.50 6.00
LN25 James Worthy 2.50 6.00

2010-11 Upper Deck North Carolina Parallel 50

*1-83 PARALLEL: 8X TO 20X BASE HI
*84-103 PARALLEL: 5X TO 12X BASE HI
*104-123 PARALLEL: 4X TO 10X BASE HI
*124-143 PARALLEL: 5X TO 12X BASE HI
*144-163 PARALLEL: 4X TO 10X BASE HI
*164-183 PARALLEL: 6X TO 15X BASE HI
STATED PRINT RUN 50 SER.#'d SETS
43 Michael Jordan 25.00 60.00
90 H.Grant/M.Jordan RIV 25.00 60.00
111 Michael Jordan AA 25.00 60.00
124 Michael Jordan BM 25.00 60.00
129 Michael Jordan BM 25.00 60.00
135 Michael Jordan BM 25.00 60.00
154 Michael Jordan TL 25.00 60.00

1989-90 UTEP

This 24-card standard-size set was sponsored by 7-Together and Drug Emporium and their names are on the top of the card. The team name/subtitle ("Star Miners") is given above the photo, and the player's name and position below it, with black and white photos for older players and color for newer players. Biographical information is on the back. Current and past NBA Stars featured in this set are Nate Archibald and Tim Hardaway (in his first card appearance); also note the presence of a card of Nolan Richardson, who went on to coach the Arkansas Razorbacks. The set is not numbered so the subjects are listed below in alphabetical order by name.

COMPLETE SET (24) 10.00 25.00
1 Nate Archibald 2.00 5.00
2 Jim Barnes .40 1.00
3 Rus Bradburd .20 .50
4 Dallas David .20 .50
5 Antonio Davis 2.00 5.00
6 Ralph Davis .30 .75
7 Norm Ellenberger CO .40 1.00
8 Francis Ezenwa .20 .50
9 Greg Foster .40 1.00
10 Joe Griffin .20 .50
11 Henry Hall .30 .75
12 Tim Hardaway 3.00 8.00
13 Don Haskins CO 1.50 4.00
14 Merle Heimer .20 .50
15 Bobby Joe Hill .30 .75
16 Greg Lackey .20 .50
17 David Lattin .75 2.00
18 Marlon Maxey .40 1.00
19 Mark McCall .20 .50
20 Chris Perez .20 .50
21 Nolan Richardson .75 2.00
22 Arlandis Rush .20 .50
23 Alprentice Stewart .20 .50
24 David Van Dyke .20 .50

1992-93 UTEP

This 14-card standard-size set was sponsored by Whataburger, 95.5 KLAQ radio station, and Major Players. The cards feature color action player photos. The top of the card is accented by an orange stripe that contains sponsor logos. Near the bottom, the player's name appears in orange print in a white bar. The horizontal backs are white and display a shadow-bordered picture in the upper left corner. Biographical information, statistics, and a player profile are presented next to the photo. .

COMPLETE SET (14) 3.00 8.00
1 Don Haskins CO 1.00 2.50
2 Gym Bice .20 .50
3 Jeff Deal .20 .50
4 Roy Howard .20 .50
5 Johnny Melvin .30 .75
6 John Portis .20 .50
7 Daryl Christopher .20 .50
8 Eddie Rivera .30 .75
9 Ralph Davis .30 .75
10 Bryan Barnes .20 .50
11 Antoine Gillespie .30 .75
12 Hector Gonzalez .20 .50
13 Phil Crocker .20 .50
14 G.Ray Johnson ACO .20 .50
Gary Brewster ACO
Gilbert Miranda
Restricted Earnings CO

1994 Valparaiso Indiana High School

1 Tim Bishop
2 Mark Burnison
3 Pete Dirindin
4 Bryce Drew
5 Ryan Erdelac
6 Bob Finley
7 Dave Furlin
8 Mike Folis
9 Chris Kaleth
10 Mark Roscoe
11 Justin Schmidt
12 Mark Turek
13 Bob Punter CO

1987-88 Vanderbilt

This 14-card set was sponsored by Vanderbilt University Police and Security. The cards measure approximately 2 1/2" by 4". On a white card face, the fronts feature black and white player photos enclosed by black and yellow borders. Player information and the school logo appear in a box below the picture. The backs have biography, a safety tip, and a list of phone numbers to call for a police response. The cards are numbered on the back. Card number 5, Chip Rupp who transfered, was pulled from the sets although perhaps as many as the first 100 sets released included 14 cards, instead of the more typical 13-card sets that are usually found.

COMPLETE SET (14) 25.00 60.00
1 Team Photo 1.50 4.00
2 C.M. Newton CO 1.50 4.00
3 Fred Benjamin .60 1.50
4 Barry Booker .60 1.50
5 Chip Rupp SP 20.00 50.00
6 Scott Laughinghouse .60 1.50
7 Eric Reid .60 1.50
8 Steve Grant .60 1.50
9 Derrick Wilcox .60 1.50
10 Will Perdue 3.00 8.00
11 Frank Kornet 1.25 3.00
12 Charles Mayes .60 1.50
13 Barry Goheen 1.25 3.00
14 Scott Draud .60 1.50

1991-92 Vanderbilt Schedules

This two-card set features schedule cards each measuring approximately 4 1/2" by 3 1/2" when unfolded. The fronts show a full-bleed color player photo, except on the left where a black stripe carries "Vanderbilt 1991-92" in gold lettering. The backs display sponsor advertisements. The inside pages carry the 1991-92 basketball schedule. The cards are unnumbered and checklisted below in alphabetical order.

COMPLETE SET (2) .40 1.00
1 Jade Huntington .20 .50
2 Todd Milholland .20 .50

1982-83 Victoria

Measuring approximately 2 1/8" by 4", this 15-card was sponsored by Honda City, Weathergard Shop, Factory Sound, CJVI 900 radio, and the Saanich police. On a white card face, the front features posed color action player photos framed by a thin blue border. The wider margin beneath the picture carries the team logo, player identification, and the years (1980, 1981, and 1982) the Vikings won the national championship. The backs present a safety slogan, facsimile autograph, and an offer to see a free game and win a stereo cassette walkman. The sponsor logos at the bottom round out the back. The cards are unnumbered and checklisted below in alphabetical order.

COMPLETE SET (15) 6.00 15.00
1 Dave Bakken .50 1.25
2 Dan Brosseuk .50 1.25
3 Ryan Burles .50 1.25
4 Kelly Dukeshire .50 1.25
5 Quinn Groenhyde .50 1.25
6 Gerald Kazanowski .50 1.25
7 Gregg Kazanowski .50 1.25
8 Tom Narbeshuber .50 1.25
9 Phil Ohl .50 1.25
10 Eli Pasquale .50 1.25
11 Vito Pasquale .50 1.25
12 David Sheehan .50 1.25
13 Ken Shields CO .50 1.25
14 Billy Turney-Loos ACO .50 1.25
15 Craig Higgins ACO .50 1.25

1983-84 Victoria

This 15-card set was sponsored by Sprite, CJVI900 (a radio station), Factory Sound, Sanyo, and the Saanich Police. The cards measure approximately 2 5/8" by 4". On a white card face, the fronts feature posed action photos. The pictures and the player information below them are enclosed by a blue border. The backs have player quotes ("Viking Quotes"), a facsimile autograph, an offer to see a game free and win a stereo cassette walkman, and sponsor logos. The game at which the card holder will be admitted free is noted on the back. The safety slogan "Working together with our youth and the community" rounds out the back. The cards are unnumbered and checklisted below in alphabetical order.

COMPLETE SET (15) 5.00 12.00
1 Cord Clemens .40 1.00
2 Quinn Groenhyde .40 1.00
3 Ian Hyde-Lay ACO .40 1.00
4 Sean Kalinovich .40 1.00
5 Ken Larson .40 1.00
6 John Munro .40 1.00
7 Jamie Newman .40 1.00
8 Phil Ohl .40 1.00
9 Eli Pasquale .40 1.00
10 Dave Sheehan .40 1.00
11 Ken Shields CO .40 1.00
12 Randy Steel .40 1.00
13 Graham Taylor .40 1.00
14 Greg Wiltjer .40 1.00
15 Logo Card .60 1.50
Saanich Police

1984-85 Victoria

This 16-card set was sponsored by Westcoast Savings Credit Union, CJVI-900 (a radio station), Factory Sound and Sanyo, and the Saanich Police. The cards measure approximately 2 5/8" by 4". On a white card face, the fronts feature posed action photos. The pictures and the player information below them are enclosed by a blue border. The backs have player quotes ("Viking Quotes"), a facsimile autograph, an offer to see a game free and win a stereo cassette walkman, and sponsor logos. The game at which the card holder will be admitted free is noted on the back. The safety slogan "Working together with our youth and the community" rounds out the back. The cards are unnumbered and checklisted below in alphabetical order.

COMPLETE SET (16) 5.00 12.00
1 Cord Clemens .40 1.00
2 Jerry Divoky .40 1.00
3 Quinn Groenhyde ACO .40 1.00
4 Shawn Kalinovich .40 1.00
5 Robert Kreke .40 1.00
6 Wade Loukes .40 1.00
7 James Newman .40 1.00
8 Phil Ohl .40 1.00
9 Vito Pasquale .40 1.00
10 Lloyd Scrubb UER .40 1.00
11 David Sheehan .40 1.00
12 Ken Shields CO .40 1.00
13 Randy Steel .40 1.00
14 Graham Taylor .40 1.00
15 Ellis Whalen .40 1.00
16 Logo Card .60 1.50
Saanich Police

1985-86 Victoria

This 17-card set was sponsored by Pacific Coast Savings Credit Union, Converse, 1200-CKDA, and the Saanich Police. The cards measure approximately 2 5/8" by 4". On a white card face, the fronts feature posed action photos. The pictures and the player information below them are enclosed by a blue border. The backs have player quotes ("Viking Quotes"), a facsimile autograph, an offer to see a game free and win a stereo cassette walkman, and sponsor logos. The game at which the card holder will be admitted free is noted on the back. The safety slogan "Crime prevention is everyone's business" rounds out the back. The cards are unnumbered and checklisted below in alphabetical order.

COMPLETE SET (17) 5.00 12.00
1 Maurice Basso .40 1.00
2 Clint Hamilton .40 1.00
3 Fraser Jefferson .40 1.00
4 Tom Johnson .40 1.00
5 Jim Knox .40 1.00
6 David Lescheid .40 1.00
7 Vesa Linnamo .40 1.00
8 David McIntosh .40 1.00
9 Geoff McKay .40 1.00
10 Spencer McKay .40 1.00
11 Rick Mesich .40 1.00
12 Kevin Ottewell .40 1.00
13 Roger Rai .40 1.00
14 Chris Schriek .40 1.00
15 Scott Stinson ACO .40 1.00
16 Guy Vetrie CO .40 1.00
17 Logo Card .60 1.50
Saanich Police

1986-87 Victoria

This set contains 16 cards, each measuring approximately 2 5/8" by 4". The white and blue bordered fronts have posed color player shots. Below the photo are the player's name and biography printed in black. The white backs carry a players quote and copy of their autograph below. The cards are unnumbered and checklisted below in alphabetical order.

COMPLETE SET (16) 5.00 12.00
1 Jerry Divoky .40 1.00
2 Shawn Kalinovich .40 1.00
3 Jay Kenyon .40 1.00
4 Rob Kreke .40 1.00
5 Brian Kruger .40 1.00
6 Wade Loukes .40 1.00
7 Geoff McKay .40 1.00
8 Spencer McKay .40 1.00
9 Steve Mitton .40 1.00
10 Vito Pasquale .40 1.00
11 Alan Phillips .40 1.00
12 Rob Poole .40 1.00
13 Tom Johnson .40 1.00
14 Lloyd Scrubb .40 1.00
15 Ken Shields CO .40 1.00
16 Mark Simpson ACO .40 1.00

1988-89 Victoria

This 16-card set was sponsored by Pacific Coast Savings Credit Union, Converse, 1200-CKDA, and the Saanich Police. The cards were issued on an unperforated sheet; if cut, they would measure approximately 2 5/8" by 4". On a white card face, the fronts feature posed action photos. The pictures and the player information below them are enclosed by a blue border. The backs have player quotes ("Viking Quotes"), a facsimile autograph, an offer to see a game free and win a stereo cassette walkman, and sponsor logos. The game at which the card holder will be admitted free is noted on the back. The safety slogan "Crime prevention is everyone's business" rounds out the back. The cards are unnumbered and checklisted below in alphabetical order.

COMPLETE SET (16) 3.00 8.00
1 Maurice Basso .30 .75
2 Colin Brousson .30 .75
3 Jerry Divoky .30 .75
4 Kevin Harrington .30 .75
5 Tom Johnson .30 .75
6 Daryn Lansdell .30 .75
7 Wade Loukes .30 .75
8 Geoff McKay .30 .75
9 Spencer McKay .30 .75
10 Rick Mesich .30 .75
11 Dale Olson .30 .75
12 Ken Olynyk ACO .30 .75
13 Kevin Ottewell .30 .75
14 Tug Rados .30 .75
15 Ken Shields CO .30 .75
16 Guy Vetrie ACO .30 .75

1988-89 Virginia

This 16-card standard-size set was sponsored by Hardee's Restaurants in conjunction with WINA Radio AM 1070, and their company names appear on the top of the card. The action color photos are surrounded on their sides and bottom by blue and orange thick borders (the school's colors), with the Cavalier logo in the lower left hand corner. The player's name, jersey number, year, and position appear below the photo. The back gives biographical information and Tips from the Cavaliers. The cards are ordered and numbered below according to the alphabetical order of the player's name. The set features a card of Matt Blundin, drafted by the NFL as a quarterback and NBA first-rounder Bryant Stith.

COMPLETE SET (16) 12.50 30.00
1 Brent Bair .75 2.00
2 Matt Blundin 3.00 8.00
3 Mark Cooke .75 2.00
4 John Crotty 3.00 8.00
5 Brent Dabbs .75 2.00
6 Jeff Daniel .75 2.00
7 Terry Holland CO 2.50 6.00
8 Dirk Katstra .75 2.00
9 Richard Morgan .75 2.00
10 Anthony Oliver .75 2.00
11 Bryant Stith 4.00 10.00
12 Kenny Turner .75 2.00
13 Curtis Williams .75 2.00
14 Cheerleaders .75 2.00
15 Coaching Staff .75 2.00
16 Title Card .75 2.00

1991-92 Virginia

This 16-card set was sponsored by Capitol Sports Network, whose logo appears at the top of each card front. The cards are perforated and measure the standard size. The fronts feature posed head and shoulders shots enclosed by white and purple borders. Player identification appears in an orange stripe beneath the picture, and the team logo at the lower left corner rounds out the card face. The backs carry biographical information, career summary, and a player quote. The cards are unnumbered and checklisted below in alphabetical order. Key cards in the set are Chris Havlicek (John's son), NFL running back Terry Kirby, and NBA player Bryant Stith.

COMPLETE SET (16) 10.00 25.00
1 Chris Alexander .40 1.00
2 Cory Alexander 2.50 6.00
3 Yuri Barnes .75 2.00
4 Junior Burrough 1.25 3.00
5 Chris Havlicek .75 2.00
6 Ted Jeffries .75 2.00
7 Derrick Johnson .40 1.00
8 Jeff Jones CO 1.25 3.00
9 Terry Kirby 2.00 5.00
10 Anthony Oliver .75 2.00
11 Cornell Parker .75 2.00
12 Doug Smith .40 1.00
13 Corey Stewart .40 1.00
14 Bryant Stith 2.50 6.00
15 Jason Williford .75 2.00
16 Shawn Wilson .40 1.00

1991-92 Virginia Women

This 16-card set was issued as a perforated sheet and sponsored by McDonald's. After perforation, the cards measure the standard size (2 1/2" by 3 1/2"). On a white card face, the fronts feature a mix of posed or action color player photos enclosed by blue borders. A McDonald's logo with the words "Food Folks and Fun" appears in a bar above the picture, while school logo and player information appear in an orange stripe at the bottom. In black print on white, the backs carry biography, player profile, and an inspirational quote. This set includes the first card of Dawn Staley, who later played point guard for the gold medal-winning 1996 USA team. The cards are unnumbered and checklisted below in alphabetical order.

COMPLETE SET (16) 8.00 20.00
1 Charleata Beale .20 .50
2 Heather Burge .75 2.00
3 Heidi Burge 1.25 3.00
4 Dena Evans 1.25 3.00
5 Chris Lesoravage .20 .50
6 Amy Lofstedt .20 .50
7 Allison Moore .20 .50
8 Tammi Reiss 1.25 3.00
9 Debbie Ryan CO .75 2.00
10 Felicia Santelli .20 .50
11 Audra Smith .20 .50
12 Dawn Staley 3.00 8.00
13 Wendy Toussaint .20 .50
14 Melanee Wagener .20 .50
15 NCAA Midwest Regional .20 .50
16 Virginia vs. NC State .20 .50

1992-93 Virginia

Sponsored by Coca-Cola, this 16-card set was issued as a perforated sheet with four rows of four cards each. After perforation, the cards measure the standard size. On a gradated blue card face, the fronts feature posed or action color player photos. The school name appears above the photo in orange block lettering. The player's name and position appear in a blue bar below the picture. The Coca-Cola emblem is printed at the bottom. The backs carry biographical information and career highlights. The cards are unnumbered and checklisted below in alphabetical order.

COMPLETE SET (16) 5.00 12.00
1 Chris Alexander .20 .50
2 Cory Alexander 1.25 3.00
3 Yuri Barnes .30 .75
4 Junior Burrough .60 1.50
5 Chris Havlicek .30 .75
6 Ted Jeffries .30 .75
7 Cornell Parker .30 .75
8 Doug Smith .20 .50
9 Jason Williford .30 .75
10 Shawn Wilson .20 .50
11 Jeff Jones CO .75 2.00
12 Brian Ellerbe ACO .20 .50
Dennis Wolff ACO
Tom Perrin ACO
13 1980 NIT Champions .30 .75
14 1981 NCAA East .30 .75
Regional Tournament Champions
15 1984 NCAA East .30 .75
Regional Tournament Champions
16 1992 NIT Champions .30 .75

1992-93 Virginia Women

Sponsored by Coca-Cola, this 16-card set was issued as a perforated sheet with four rows of four cards each. After perforation, the cards measure the standard size. On a gradated blue card face, the fronts feature posed or action color player photos. The school name appears above the photo in orange block lettering. The player's name and position appear in a blue bar below the picture. The Coca-Cola emblem is printed at the bottom. The backs carry biographical information and career highlights. The cards are unnumbered and checklisted below in alphabetical order.

COMPLETE SET (16) 5.00 12.00
1 Charleata Beale .20 .50
2 Jenny Boucek .20 .50
3 Heather Burge .60 1.50
4 Heidi Burge .75 2.00
5 Dena Evans 1.00 2.50
6 Jeffra Gausepohl .20 .50
7 Chris Lesoravage .20 .50
8 Amy Lofstedt .20 .50
9 Allison Moore .20 .50
10 Wendy Palmer 2.00 5.00
11 Debbie Ryan CO .75 2.00
12 Kristen Somogyi .20 .50
13 Cheryl Taylor .20 .50
14 Wendy Toussaint .20 .50
15 1992 Atlantic Coast .20 .50
Conference Tournament Champions
16 1992 East Regional .20 .50
Tournament Champions

1993-94 Virginia

These 16 standard-size (2 1/2" by 3 1/2") cards originally were issued in a perforated sheet. The blue-bordered fronts feature color player action and posed photos set within ovals. The player's name and position appear in white lettering at the bottom. The white backs carry the player's name an jersey number in white lettering set on a black stripe at the top. The player's position, height, weight, class, high school, hometown, and career highlights follow below. The cards are unnumbered, but are arranged in alphabetical order on the perforated sheet, except for the coach cards, and are so checklisted below.

COMPLETE SET (16) 5.00 12.00
1 Chris Alexander .20 .50
2 Cory Alexander 1.00 2.50
3 Yuri Barnes .30 .75
4 Mark Bogosh .20 .50
5 Junior Burrough .50 1.25
6 Harold Deane .75 2.00
7 Bobby Graves .20 .50
8 Chris Havlicek .30 .75
9 Cornel Parker .30 .75
10 Mike Powell .20 .50
11 Jamal Robinson .30 .75
12 Maurice Watkins .20 .50
13 Jason Williford .30 .75
14 Shawn Wilson .20 .50
15 Jeff Jones CO .60 1.50
16 Assistant Coaches .20 .50
Brian Ellerbe
Dennis Wolff
Tom Perrin

1993-94 Virginia Women

Sponsored by Cavalier Inn, these 16 standard-size (2 1/2" by 3 1/2") cards originally were issued in a perforated sheet. The blue-bordered fronts feature color player action and posed photos set within ovals. The player's name and position appear in white lettering at the bottom. The white backs carry the player's name an jersey number in white lettering set on a black stripe at the top. The player's position, height, class, hometown, and career highlights follow below. The cards are unnumbered and checklisted below in alphabetical order.

COMPLETE SET (16) 5.00 12.00
1 Charleata Beale .20 .50
2 Jenny Boucek .20 .50
3 Konecka Drakeford .20 .50
4 Tammy Gardner .20 .50
5 Jeffra Gausepohl .20 .50
6 Jackie Glessner .20 .50
7 Chris Lesoravage .20 .50
8 Amy Lofstedt .20 .50
9 Wendy Palmer 1.25 3.00
10 Debbie Ryan CO .75 2.00
11 Tora Suber 1.25 3.00
12 Cheryl Taylor .20 .50
13 Wendy Toussaint .20 .50
14 Dawn Staley's 1.50 4.00
Number Retired
15 NCAA East Regional .20 .50
16 Mascot Day .20 .50

1999-00 Virginia

This set was released for the University of Virginia Men's Basketball during the 1999-00 season. The set features cards of all of the players and coaches on a slightly over-sized white bordered card. The set was produced by Cavalier Sports Cards.

COMPLETE SET (15) 2.00 5.00
1 Willie Dersch .20 .50
2 Stephane Dondon .20 .50
3 Jason Dowling .20 .50
4 Colin Ducharme .20 .50
5 Keith Friel .20 .50
6 Pete Gillen CO .30 .75
7 Adam Hall .20 .50
8 Donald Hand .20 .50
9 Josh Hare .20 .50
10 Cade Lemcke .20 .50
11 Majestic Mapp .20 .50
12 Roger Mason .20 .50
13 Jason Rogers .20 .50
14 Travis Watson .20 .50
15 Chris Williams .20 .50

1999-00 Virginia Women

This set was released for the University of Virginia Women's Basketball during the 1999-00 season. The set features cards of all of the players and coaches on a slightly over-sized white bordered card. The set was produced by Cavalier Sports Cards.

COMPLETE SET (13) 1.50 4.00
1 Anna Crosswhite .20 .50
2 Marcie Dickson .20 .50
3 Lisa Hosac .20 .50
4 Elena Kravchenko .20 .50
5 Schuye Larue .20 .50
6 Chalois Lias .20 .50
7 Dean'na Mitchelson .20 .50
8 Telisha Quarles .20 .50
9 Renee Robinson .20 .50
10 Debbie Ryan CO .30 .75
11 Lauren Swierczek .20 .50
12 Katie Tracy .20 .50
13 Svetlana Volnaya .20 .50

1992-93 Virginia Tech

This 12-card multi-sport set measures the standard size and features full-bleed, color, action player photos. The sports represented in the set are football (1, 2, 5, 10-11), basketball (3, 7-8), baseball (4), soccer (6), and volleyball (9).

COMPLETE SET (12) 5.00 12.00
3 Phyllis Tonkin BK .20 .50
Dayna Sonovick
Tisa Brown
7 Thomas Elliott .20 .50
Jay Purcell
8 Dell Curry 2.40 6.00

1988-89 Wake Forest

This 16-card standard-size set was sponsored by the Adolescent CareUnit of Almanac Health Services, local law enforcement agencies, and Wake Forest University. The cards feature on the front posed color head and shoulders shots, bordered in black on the left and in yellow on the right and below. Player information appears in the bottom yellow border, while the school logo in the lower left corner rounds out the front. The backs present biography, player profile, and "Tips from the Demon Deacons," which consist of anti-drug and alcohol messages. The cards are unnumbered and checklisted below in alphabetical order.

COMPLETE SET (16) 6.00 15.00
1 Tony Black .40 1.00
2 Cal Boyd .40 1.00
3 David Carlyle .40 1.00
4 Darryl Cheeley .40 1.00
5 Sam Ivy .60 1.50
6 Antonio Johnson .60 1.50
7 Daric Keys .40 1.00
8 Chris King 1.00 2.50
9 Ralph Kitley .40 1.00
10 Derrick McQueen .40 1.00
11 Phil Medlin .40 1.00
12 Steve Ray .40 1.00
13 Todd Sanders .40 1.00
14 Robert Siler .40 1.00
15 Bob Staak CO .60 1.50
16 Tom Wise .40 1.00

1991 Washington

This 17-card standard-size (2 1/2" by 3 1/2") set was sponsored by Prime Sports Northwest and TCI Cablevision of Washington. The fronts display color action player photos enframed by purple borders. The school and team name appear above the pictures, while player information is printed in a gold stripe beneath them. The backs have career statistics, an announcement of the Husky KidSports Program, and sponsor logos. The cards are unnumbered and checklisted below in alphabetical order within sex; men's team are given card numbers 1-9 and women's team are numbered 10-17.

COMPLETE SET (17) 5.00 12.00
1 Dion Brown .40 1.00
2 Tim Caviezel .75 2.00
3 James French .40 1.00
4 Mike Hayward .40 1.00
5 Todd Lautenbach .40 1.00
6 Doug Meekins .60 1.50
7 Brent Merritt .40 1.00
8 Lynn Nance CO .60 1.50
9 Quentin Youngblood .40 1.00
10 Tara Davis .30 .75
11 Karen Deden .30 .75
12 Chris Gobrecht CO .30 .75
13 Erika Hardwick .30 .75
14 Jocelyn McIntire .30 .75
15 Laurie Merlino .30 .75
16 Laura Moore .30 .75
17 Dianne Williams .30 .75

1991-92 Washington

This 17-card standard-size basketball set was sponsored by Prime Sports Northwest and Viacom Cable. The fronts are accented in the team's colors (purple and gold) and have color action player photos. The top of the pictures is curved to resemble an archway, and the team name follows the curve of the arch. Sponsor logos and player identification appear in the gold stripe below the picture. The backs carry statistics (or career summary), an announcement of the Husky KidSports Program, and sponsor logos. The cards are unnumbered and checklisted below in alphabetical order as follows: men's basketball (1-9) and women's basketball (10-17).

COMPLETE SET (17) 5.00 12.00
1 Bryant Boston .40 1.00
2 Tim Caviezel .60 1.50
3 Rich Manning .60 1.50
4 Doug Meekins .40 1.00
5 Chandler Nairn .40 1.00
6 Lynn Nance CO .60 1.50
7 Mark Pope .75 2.00
8 Andy Woods .40 1.00
9 Quentin Youngblood .40 1.00
10 Tara Davis .30 .75
11 Katia Foucade .30 .75
12 Shaunda Greene .30 .75
13 Chris Gobrecht CO .30 .75
14 Erika Hardwick .30 .75
15 Laura Moore .30 .75
16 Jo Shafer .30 .75
17 Dianne Williams .30 .75

2003-04 Washington

Produced by High Step and printed in conjunction with Red Robin and Pepsi, this 14-card set was available through Washington during the 2003-04 school year.

COMPLETE SET (14) 4.00 10.00
1 C.J. Massingale .20 .50
2 Nate Robinson 1.50 4.00
4 Jeffrey Day .20 .50
5 Will Conroy .60 1.50
15 Bobby Jones .20 .50
20 Curtis Allen .20 .50
24 Doug Wrenn .20 .50
30 Anthony Washington .20 .50
42 Mike Jensen .20 .50
44 Marlon Shelton .20 .50
52 David Hudson .20 .50
55 Ben Devoe .20 .50
20a Lorenzo Romar .30 .75
NNO Lorenzo Romar CO .30 .75

2003-04 Washington Women

Produced by High Step and sponsored by Red Robin and Pepsi, this 16-card set was available through Washington during the 2003-04 school year.

COMPLETE SET (16) 2.00 5.00
3 Andrea Lalum .15 .40
4 Sarah Keller .15 .40
5 Alicia Heathcote .15 .40
12 Angie Jones .15 .40
13 Giuliana Mendiola .15 .40
15 Nicole Castro .15 .40
20 Kayla Burt .15 .40
21 Erica Schelly .15 .40
22 Loree Payne .15 .40
23 Emily Autrey .15 .40
24 Kellie Dalan .15 .40
25 Jill Bell .15 .40
31 Gioconda Mendiola .15 .40
33 Kristen O'Neill .15 .40
40 Kirsten Brockman .15 .40
44 Cheryl Sorenson .15 .40

1991-92 Washington State

This 12-card standard-size basketball set was sponsored by Prime Sports Northwest and CableVision. The set was issued as an perforated sheet with three rows of four cards each; the first six cards feature the women's basketball team, while the last six cards present the men's team. The fronts are accented in the team's colors (maroon and gray) and have posed and action player photos. The top of the pictures is curved to resemble an archway, and the team name follows the curve of the arch. Sponsor logos and player identification appear in the gray stripe below the picture. The backs carry statistics, player profile, and sponsor advertisements. The cards are unnumbered and checklisted below in alphabetical order as follows: men's basketball (1-6) and women's basketball (7-12).

COMPLETE SET (12) 5.00 12.00
1 Rob Corkrum .60 1.50
2 Ken Critton .60 1.50
3 Eddie Hill .60 1.50
4 Tyrone Maxey .60 1.50
5 Sean Tresvant .60 1.50
6 Joey Warmenhoven .60 1.50
7 Janel Benton .40 1.00
Erika Wheeler
8 Lori Lollis .40 1.00
9 Heather Norman .40 1.00
10 Camille Thompson .40 1.00
Kathy Weber
11 Darla Williamson .40 1.00
12 Team Photo .60 1.50

1996-97 Weber State

This 13-card standard size set was sponsored by Matrix Marketing. The company's logo is found on the bottom of the back of the card. The front features a full color action player photo inside of a black border. The words "Weber Fever" and an orange basketball adorn the top. The bottom has an orange basketball emblem that designates the player's postion. Besides the ball the word "Wildcats" resides in a purple font. The player's name is listed below. The back is black and white, listing the palyer's name at the top within a black box. The player's biography and player profile adorn the back as does the Webber State Logo on the bottom right corner. The cards are unnumbered and listed below in alphabetical order.

COMPLETE SET (13) 2.00 5.00
1 Damien Baskerville .20 .50
2 Ryan Cuff .20 .50
3 Jimmy DeGraffenried .20 .50
4 Bryan Emery .20 .50
5 Joey Haws .20 .50
6 Squirt Hicks .20 .50
7 Eric Ketcham .20 .50
8 Bart McIntire .20 .50
9 Justyn Nielsen .20 .50

10 Andy Smith .20 .50
11 Justin Tebbs .20 .50
12 Women's Basketball Team .20 .50
13 WSU Cheerleaders .20 .50

1977-78 West Virginia Schedules

This set of four schedule cards measures the standard size, 2 1/2" by 3 1/2". Printed on cardboard stock, the fronts show black-and-white action shots or portraits enframed by thick white borders. In team color-coded print, the school name, logo, and "Basketball 1977-78" appear above the pictures, while player information is presented below the pictures. On a white background, the back lists the 1978-78 basketball schedule, again in team color-coded print. The schedule cards are unnumbered and checklisted below in alphabetical order.

COMPLETE SET (4) 4.00 8.00
1 Sid Bostick .75 2.00
2 Dennis Hosey .75 2.00
3 Tommy Roberts .75 2.00
4 Maurice Robinson 1.50 4.00

1978-79 West Virginia Schedules

This set of 15 schedule cards measures approximately 2 5/16" by 3 1/2". Printed on cardboard stock, the fronts show black-and-white closeup player photos enframed by thick white borders. In blue print, the school name and "Basketball '79" appear above the pictures, while player information is presented below the pictures. On a white background, the back lists the 1978-78 basketball schedule, again in blue print. The schedule cards are unnumbered and checklisted below in alphabetical order.

COMPLETE SET (15) 7.50 15.00
1 Gale Catlett CO .75 2.00
2 John Goots .40 1.00
3 Vic Herbert .40 1.00
4 Dennis Hosey .40 1.00
5 Junius Lewis .40 1.00
6 Steve McCune .40 1.00
7 Lowes Moore .75 2.00
8 Noah Moore .40 1.00
9 Greg Nance .40 1.00
10 Dana Perno .40 1.00
11 Mike Richardson .40 1.00
12 Jeff Szczepanski .40 1.00
13 Lanny Van Eman ACO .75 2.00
14 Coaching Staff .40 1.00
15 Eastern Eight Logo .40 1.00

1980-81 Wichita State

This 15-card standard size (2 1/2" by 3 1/2") set was sponsored by Service Auto Glass and the Wichita Police Department. The cards were given away at the Wichita State athletic banquet and also by police officers. The fronts feature a close-up of the player enclosed by a border. The slogan "Love 'Ya Shockers" appears in the upper right corner, while player information is printed beneath the picture. Each card back carries a different safety message and a reminder to call 911. The cards are unnumbered and checklisted below in alphabetical order. Key cards in the set include the first cards of Antoine Carr and Cliff Levingston.

COMPLETE SET (15) 50.00 100.00
1 Antoine Carr 20.00 40.00
2 Mike Denny 1.50 4.00
3 Zarko Djuricic 1.50 4.00
4 James Gibbs 1.50 4.00
5 Jay Jackson 1.50 4.00
6 Mike Jones 1.50 4.00
7 Ozell Jones 4.00 10.00
8 Eric Kuhn 1.50 4.00
9 Cliff Levingston 15.00 30.00
10 Tony Martin 1.50 4.00
11 Karl Papke 1.50 4.00
12 Zoran Rdovic 1.50 4.00
13 Gene Smithson CO 1.50 4.00
14 Randy Smithson 1.50 4.00
15 Team Photo 2.50 6.00

1987-88 Wichita State

This 12-card standard-size set was jointly sponsored by Scholfield Honda, KNSS News Radio (1240 AM), and Riverside Hospital. The fronts show a mix of posed and action color player photos on a white card face. Sponsor logos appear at the top, while player information appears between school logos beneath the picture. The backs carry biography, career summary, "Tips from the Shockers," which consist of anti-drug and alcohol messages. The cards are unnumbered and checklisted below in alphabetical order.

COMPLETE SET (12) 10.00 25.00
1 John Cooper .75 2.00
2 Aaron Davis .75 2.00
3 John Felter .75 2.00
4 Eddie Fogler CO 3.00 8.00
5 Steve Grayer .75 2.00
6 Joe Griffin .75 2.00
7 Paul Guffrovich .75 2.00
8 Tom Kosich .75 2.00
9 Dwayne Praylow .75 2.00
10 Dwight Praylow .75 2.00
11 Sasha Radunovich 2.00 5.00
12 Team Photo 2.00 5.00

1988-89 Wichita State

This 11-card set was jointly sponsored by KWCH TV, KNSS Radio, and Scholfield Auto Dealership, and these sponsors' logos adorn the bottom of the card face. The standard size cards feature posed player photos on the fronts. In the upper left corner the school logo appears inside a circle, while player identification is placed in a rectangle overlaying the bottom edge of the picture. The backs have anti-drug messages. The cards are unnumbered and are checklisted below in alphabetical order. The only player not portrayed in this series is Ricky Bell, who joined the team after the set was composed.

COMPLETE SET (11) 6.00 15.00
1 Keith Bonds .75 2.00
2 John Cooper .75 2.00
3 Aaron Davis .75 2.00
4 Darin Dugger .75 2.00
5 John Felter .75 2.00
6 Steve Grayer .75 2.00
7 Paul Guffrovich .75 2.00
8 Phil Mendelson .75 2.00
9 Dwayne Praylow .75 2.00
10 Dwight Praylow .75 2.00
11 Sasha Radunovich 1.50 4.00

1989-90 Wisconsin

This 14-card set was sponsored by the USDA Forest Service in cooperation with the National Association of State Foresters and BD and A, Inc. The cards were issued on an unperforated sheet with four rows of four cards; two of the cards slots are blacked out where the photo should appear and feature a fire cartoon on their backs. After cutting, the cards measure the standard size (2 1/2" by 3 1/2"). The fronts feature a mix of posed and action color player photos on a white card face. Above the picture appears the school name (in red lettering) and a black stripe. Red and black stripes traverse the card below the picture, with the Smokey logo in the lower left corner and player identification to the right. The backs have biographical information, player evaluation, and a fire prevention cartoon starring Smokey. The cards are unnumbered and checklisted below in alphabetical order.

COMPLETE SET (14) 5.00 12.00
1 Bobby Douglass .40 1.00
2 John Ellenson .40 1.00
3 Brian Good .40 1.00
4 Damon Harrell .40 1.00
5 Larry Hisle Jr. .60 1.50
6 Danny Jones .40 1.00
7 Jason Johnsen .40 1.00
8 Grant Johnson .40 1.00
9 Tim Locum .40 1.00
10 Carlton McGee .40 1.00
11 Kurt Portmann .40 1.00
12 Willie Simms .60 1.50
13 Patrick Tompkins .40 1.00
14 Steve Yoder CO .75 2.00

2005-06 Wisconsin

This 16-card set was originally issued in uncut sheet form. The cards are listed below alphabetically.

COMPLETE SET (16) 3.00 8.00
1 Devin Barry .40 1.00
2 Tanner Bronson .40 1.00
3 Brian Butch .40 1.00
4 Morris Cain .40 1.00
5 Jason Chappell .40 1.00
6 Michael Flowers .40 1.00
7 Kevin Gullikson .40 1.00
8 Joe Krabbenhoft .40 1.00
9 Marcus Landry .60 1.50
10 Ray Nixon .40 1.00
11 Mickey Perry .40 1.00
12 Bo Ryan CO .40 1.00
13 Greg Stiemsma .40 1.00
14 Kammron Taylor .40 1.00
15 Alando Tucker .60 1.50
16 Bucky Badger .40 1.00

2006-07 Wisconsin

This 18-card set was originally issued in uncut sheet form. The cards are listed below alphabetically.

COMPLETE SET (18) 4.00 10.00
1 Jason Bohannon .40 1.00
2 Tanner Bronson .40 1.00
3 Brian Butch .40 1.00
4 Morris Cain .40 1.00
5 Jason Chappell .40 1.00
6 Michael Flowers .40 1.00
7 J.P. Gavinski .40 1.00
8 Kevin Gullikson .40 1.00
9 Trevon Hughes .40 1.00
10 Joe Krabbenhoft .40 1.00
11 Marcus Landry .60 1.50
12 Mickey Perry .40 1.00
13 Bo Ryan CO .40 1.00
14 Greg Stiemsma .40 1.00
15 Kammron Taylor .40 1.00
16 Alando Tucker .60 1.50
17 Brett Valentyn .40 1.00
18 Bucky Badger .40 1.00

2007-08 Wisconsin

This 16-card set was originally issued in uncut sheet form. The cards are listed below alphabetically.

COMPLETE SET (16) 3.00 8.00
1 Jason Bohannon .40 1.00
2 Tanner Bronson .40 1.00
3 Brian Butch .40 1.00
4 Morris Cain .40 1.00
5 Michael Flowers .40 1.00
6 J.P. Gavinski .40 1.00
7 Kevin Gullikson .40 1.00
8 Trevon Hughes .40 1.00
9 Jim Jarmusz .40 1.00
10 Joe Krabbenhoft .40 1.00
11 Marcus Landry .60 1.50
12 Jon Leuer .40 1.00
13 Keaton Nankivil .40 1.00
14 Bo Ryan CO .40 1.00
15 Greg Stiemsma .40 1.00
16 Brett Valentyn .40 1.00

2009-10 Wisconsin

This 16-card set was originally issued in uncut sheet form. The cards are listed below alphabetically.

COMPLETE SET (16) 3.00 8.00
1 Jared Berggren .40 1.00
2 Jason Bohannon .40 1.00
3 Mike Bruesewitz .40 1.00
4 Ryan Evans .40 1.00
5 Dan Fahey .40 1.00
6 J.P. Gavinski .40 1.00
7 Trevon Hughes .40 1.00
8 Tim Jarmusz .40 1.00
9 Jon Leuer .40 1.00
10 Ian Markolf .40 1.00
11 Keaton Nankivil .40 1.00
12 Bo Ryan CO .40 1.00
13 Wquinton Smith .40 1.00
14 Jordan Taylor .40 1.00
15 Brett Valentyn .40 1.00
16 Rob Wilson .40 1.00

2010-11 Wisconsin

This 18-card set was originally issued in uncut sheet form. The cards are listed below alphabetically.

COMPLETE SET (18) 4.00 10.00
1 Evan Anderson .40 1.00
2 Jared Berggren .40 1.00
3 Mike Bruesewitz .40 1.00
4 Ben Brust .40 1.00
5 Duje Dukan .40 1.00
6 Ryan Evans .40 1.00
7 Dan Fahey .40 1.00
8 Josh Gasser .40 1.00
9 J.P. Gavinski .40 1.00
10 Tim Jarmusz .40 1.00
11 Jon Leuer .40 1.00
12 Keaton Nankivil .40 1.00
13 Bo Ryan CO .40 1.00
14 Wquinton Smith .40 1.00
15 Jordan Taylor .40 1.00
16 Brett Valentyn .40 1.00
17 Rob Wilson .40 1.00
18 J.D. Wise .40 1.00

1991 Wooden Award Winners

This 22-card standard-size set was released by Little Sun of Monrovia, California, to commemorate the John R. Wooden Award. Only 28,000 sets were produced, and the set number is given on the certification card. The set is accompanied by a deluxe card album with two-up plastic sheets to house the cards. The cards chronicle the career of John Wooden and feature all 14 winners (in their college uniforms) of college basketball's most prestigious award. With the exception of some early black and white Wooden photos, the fronts feature borderless color player photos. Each picture is bordered on the left side by a gray stripe, with the Little Sun logo superimposed at the top. A lavender stripe traverses the bottom of the card face and gives a title for that card. The backs have biographical information and full close-ups of each player printed in a blue Mezzo-tint process. John Wooden also signed a select number of card number 1. That price is listed at the bottom of the set and is numbered as "AU1" to not confuse the two cards. It is not considered part of the set.

COMP. FACT SET (22) 4.00 10.00
1 John Wooden 1991 .20 .50
2 Wooden Trophy .05 .15
3 John Wooden Purdue .20 .50
4 John Wooden UCLA .20 .50
5 Wooden Summer Camp .05 .15
6 Duke Llewellyn .05 .15
7 Marques Johnson .08 .25
8 Phil Ford .08 .25
9 Larry Bird 1.00 2.50
10 Darrell Griffith .08 .25
11 Danny Ainge .25 .60
12 Ralph Sampson .08 .25
13 Michael Jordan 2.00 5.00
14 Chris Mullin .20 .50
15 Walter Berry .05 .15
16 David Robinson .40 1.00
17 Danny Manning .15 .40
18 Sean Elliott .20 .50
19 Lionel Simmons .05 .15
20 Larry Johnson .20 .50
21 Press Conference 1991 .05 .15
AU1 John Wooden AU 20.00 50.00
NNO Certification of Limited Edition .05 .15

1991-92 Wright State

This 18-card standard size (2 1/2" by 3 1/2") set was sponsored by Synergy Building Systems Inc. The fronts feature color action player photos that are superimposed over black-green-and-lime geometrically shaped backgrounds inside thin white borders on a yellow background. The team logo and player's name appear on a green stripe below the picture. The horizontal backs carry biography, statistics, uniform number, and the sponsor's logo. The cards are unnumbered and checklisted below in alphabetical order.

COMPLETE SET (18) 6.00 15.00
1 Scott Blair .40 1.00
2 Lincoln Bramlage .40 1.00
3 Bill Edwards .75 2.00
4 Mike Haley II .40 1.00
5 Sean Hammonds .60 1.50
6 Rob Haucke .40 1.00
7 Delme Herriman .60 1.50
8 Andy Holderman .60 1.50
9 Chris McGuire .40 1.00
10 Marcus Mumphrey .40 1.00
11 Mike Nahar .60 1.50
12 Renaldo O'Neal .40 1.00
13 Jon Ramey .40 1.00
14 Dan Skeoch .40 1.00
15 Ralph Underhill CO .60 1.50
16 Jeff Unverferth .40 1.00
17 Eric Wills .40 1.00
18 Coaching Staff .40 1.00
Ralph Underhill
Jim Brown
Jack Butler
Jim Ehler

1993-94 Wright State

This is a 18-card standard size (2 1/2" by 3 1/2") set. The green and yellow bordered fronts have color player action shots siloweted on to a 3-D graphic rendition of the team name. Below the photo is the players name and number printed in green and white. The gray bordered backs carry the players name and number at the top with the bio boxed in below. The cards are unnumbered and checklisted below in alphabetical order.

COMPLETE SET (18) 5.00 12.00
1 Scott Blair .20 .50
2 Sterling Collins .20 .50
3 Mike Connor .20 .50
4 Sean Hammonds .40 1.00
5 Delme Herriman .40 1.00
6 Andy Holderman .40 1.00
7 Rick Martinez .60 1.50
8 Mike Nahar .40 1.00
9 Jon Ramey .20 .50
10 Dan Skeoch .20 .50
11 Jason Smith .20 .50
12 Ralph Underhill CO .40 1.00
13 Rob Welch .60 1.50
14 Eric Wills .20 .50
15 Darryl Woods .40 1.00
16 Assistant Coaches .20 .50
Jim Brown
Jack Butler
Jim Ehler
17 Mid-Continent Champs .40 1.00
18 Student Assistants .20 .50
Brad Hess
Brian Kelly
Tom Rhoades
Matt Brown

1994-95 Wright State

Sponsored by Cap'n Bogey's Family Entertainment Center and Fairborn Camera and Video, this 21-card set measures the standard size. The fronts feature borderless color action player photos with the player's name and jersey number printed vertically in a green bar along the left or right side. His position is printed across the bottom of the picture. On a green background, the horizontal backs carry a posed color player photo on the left and player biography and profile on the right. Sponsor logos round out the back.

COMPLETE SET (21) 5.00 12.00
1 Ralph Underhill CO .40 1.00
2 Quincy Brann .20 .50
3 Jon Ramey .20 .50
4 Eric Wills .20 .50
5 Darryl Woods .20 .50
6 Delme Herriman .40 1.00
7 Jason Smith .20 .50
8 Bilaal Neal .20 .50
9 Keith Blankenship .20 .50
10 Mike Conner .20 .50
11 Rick Martinez .40 1.00
12 Vitaly Potapenko 1.25 3.00
13 Rob Welch .40 1.00
14 Thad Burton .20 .50
15 Antuan Johnson .20 .50
16 Derek Watkins .20 .50
17 Jim Brown ACO .20 .50
Jack Butler ACO
Jim Ehler ACO
18 Student Assistants .20 .50
Matt Brown
Skip Carter
Joe Dick
Brad Hess
Dela Angela Mayho
19 Rowdy Raider (Mascot) .20 .50
20 Cap'n Bogey .20 .50
NNO Team Photo .40 1.00

1994-95 Wyoming

This 16-card set was issued on a 10" by 14" perforated sheet with four rows of four cards. When the cards are separated, they measure the standard size. The set is sponsored by the USDA Forest Service and National Association of State Foresters. The fronts display color posed player photos framed in white and black, with player's name and position below the photo in the gold border. The Smokey logo is centered at the bottom of the picture. The backs carry the player's name and position at the top above a Smokey cartoon and a fire prevention safety tip. Biographical information is below the cartoon. The cards are unnumbered and checklisted below in alphabetical order. The key player in this set is Theo Ratliff, a first-round NBA draft pick.

COMPLETE SET (16) 6.00 15.00
1 Jeff Allen .40 1.00
2 H.L. Coleman .40 1.00
3 Chris Haslam .40 1.00
4 Billy Hessel .40 1.00
5 Savalious (Sly) Johnson .40 1.00
6 Pat Kelsey .40 1.00
7 Theo Ratliff 2.50 6.00
8 Jeron Roberts .40 1.00
9 Gregg Sawyer .40 1.00
10 Aaron Smith .40 1.00
11 Bobby Traylor .60 1.50
12 LaDrell Whitehead .40 1.00
13 Alma Mater .40 1.00
14 Cowboy Joe Song .40 1.00
15 Team Logo .40 1.00
16 Team Logo .40 1.00

1994-95 Wyoming Women

This 16-card set was issued on a 10" by 14" perforated sheet with four rows of four cards. When the cards are separated, they measure the standard size. The set is sponsored by the USDA Forest Service and National Association of State Foresters. The fronts display color posed player photos framed in white and black with player's name and position below the photo in the gold border. The Smokey logo is centered at the bottom of the picture. The backs carry the player's name and position at the top above a Smokey cartoon and a fire prevention safety tip. Biographical information is below the cartoon. The cards are unnumbered and checklisted below in alphabetical order.

COMPLETE SET (16) 2.50 6.00
1 Lauren Andrade .20 .50
2 Amy Burnett .20 .50
3 Jesseca Cross .20 .50
4 Casey Crouch .20 .50
5 Heather McAdams .20 .50
6 Laura Pejsa .20 .50
7 Jennifer Rider .20 .50
8 Nichole Rider .20 .50
9 Jennifer Russell .20 .50
10 Courtney Stapp .20 .50
11 Jessica Thompson .20 .50
12 Rebecca Tomlin .20 .50
13 Alma Mater .20 .50
14 Cowboy Joe Song .20 .50
15 Team Logo .20 .50
16 Team Logo .20 .50

1994-95 Assets

Produced by Classic, the 1994 Assets set features stars from basketball, hockey, football, baseball, and auto racing. The set was released in two series of 50 cards each. 1,994 cases were produced of each series. This standard-sized card set features a player photo with his name in silver letters on the lower left corner and the Assets logo on the upper right. The back has a color photo on the left side along with a biography on the right side of the card. A Sprint phone card is randomly inserted in each five-card pack.

COMPLETE SET (100) 6.00 15.00
1 Shaquille O'Neal .20 .50
2 Hakeem Olajuwon .08 .25
6 Glenn Robinson .08 .25
10 Alonzo Mourning .07 .20
14 Jason Kidd .40 1.00
17 Donyell Marshall .05 .15
19 Eric Montross .05 .15
22 Jalen Rose .15 .40
26 Shaquille O'Neal .20 .50
27 Hakeem Olajuwon .08 .25
31 Glenn Robinson .10 .30
35 Alonzo Mourning .07 .20
39 Jason Kidd .40 1.00
42 Donyell Marshall .05 .15
44 Eric Montross .05 .15
47 Jalen Rose .15 .40
50 Glenn Robinson CL .07 .20
51 Dikembe Mutombo .05 .15
53 Anfernee Hardaway .15 .40
54 Isaiah Rider .05 .15
56 Juwan Howard .08 .25
58 Jamal Mashburn .07 .20
69 Eddie Jones .30 .75
73 Shaquille O'Neal .20 .50
75 Grant Hill CL .08 .25
76 Dikembe Mutombo .05 .15
78 Anfernee Hardaway .20 .50
79 Isaiah Rider .05 .15
81 Juwan Howard .07 .20
83 Jamal Mashburn .07 .20
94 Eddie Jones .20 .50
98 Shaquille O'Neal .20 .50

1994-95 Assets Die Cuts

This 25-card standard-size set was randomly inserted into packs. DC1-10 were included in series one while DC11-25 were included in series two packs. These cards feature the player on the card and the ability to separate the player's photo. The back contains information about the player on the section of the card that is separable.

COMPLETE SET (25) 30.00 80.00
DC1 Shaquille O'Neal 4.00 10.00
DC2 Hakeem Olajuwon .75 2.00
DC6 Glenn Robinson 1.25 3.00
DC11 Grant Hill 1.25 3.00
DC12 Jason Kidd 4.00 10.00
DC13 Eddie Jones 2.00 5.00
DC20 Isaiah Rider .60 1.50
DC22 Donyell Marshall .60 1.50

1994-95 Assets Silver Signature

This 48-card standard-size set was randomly inserted at a rate of four per box. The cards are identical to the first twenty-four cards in the each series, except that these show a silver facsimile autograph on their fronts. The first 24 cards correspond to cards 1-24 in the first series while the second 24 cards correspond to cards 51-74 in the second series.

*SILVER SIGS: 1.2X TO 3X BASIC CARDS

1994-95 Assets Phone Cards $100

These 2" by 3 1/4" rounded corner cards were randomly inserted into packs. These cards were placed into series one packs. The front features the player's photo, with "One Hundred Dollars" written in cursive script along the left edge. The Assets logo is in the bottom left corner. The back gives instructions on how to use the phone card. These cards are listed in alphabetical order. These cards expired on December 1, 1995.

COMPLETE SET (5) 15.00 40.00
*PIN NUMBER REVEALED: .2X TO .5X
3 Jason Kidd 4.00 10.00
4 Hakeem Olajuwon 3.00 8.00

1994-95 Assets Phone Cards $200

These rounded corner cards were randomly inserted into second series packs and measure 2" by 3 1/4". The front features the player's photo, with "Two Hundred Dollars" written in cursive script along the left edge. In the bottom left corner is the Assets logo. The back gives instructions on how to use the phone card. These cards are arranged in alphabetical order. These cards expired on March 31, 1996.

COMPLETE SET (5) 25.00 50.00
*PIN NUMBER REVEALED: .2X TO .5X
4 Jason Kidd 6.00 15.00

1994-95 Assets Phone Cards $2000

These rounded-corner cards measuring 2" by 3 1/4" were randomly inserted into second series packs. Just four of each of these cards were produced. The front features the player's photo, with "Two Thousand Dollars" written in cursive script along the left edge. In the bottom left corner is the Assets logo. The back gives instructions on how to use the phone card. Two differnt Emmitt Smith promo cards were also issued to promote the product. The cards are unnumbered and checklisted below in alphabetical order. The cards expired on March 31, 1996.

1994-95 Assets Phone Cards $5

These cards measure 2" by 3 1/4", have rounded corners and were randomly inserted into packs. Cards 1-5 were inserted into first series packs while 6-15 were in second series packs. The front features the player's photo, with "Five Dollars" written in cursive script along the left edge. In the bottom left corner is the Assets logo. The back gives instructions on how to use the phone card. Series one cards expired on December 1, 1995 while second series cards expired on March 31, 1996.

COMPLETE SET (15) 8.00 20.00
*PIN NUMBER REVEALED: .2X TO .5X
3 Jason Kidd .75 2.00
4 Hakeem Olajuwon .50 1.25
10 Jason Kidd .75 2.00
15 Glenn Robinson .30 .75

1994-95 Assets Phone Cards One Minute

Measuring 2" by 3 1/4", these cards have rounded corners and were inserted one per pack. Cards 1-24 were in first series packs while 25-48 were included with second series packs. The front features the player's photo and on the side is how long the card is good for. The Assets logo is in the bottom left corner. The back gives instructions on how to use the phone card. The first series cards expired on December 1, 1995 while the second series cards expired on March 31, 1996. The cards with a $2 logo are worth a mulitple of the regular cards. Please refer to the values below for these cards.

COMPLETE SET (48) 7.50 20.00
*PIN NUMB.REVEALED: .2X TO .5X BASIC INS.
*TWO DOLLAR: .5X TO 1.2X BASIC INSERTS
11 Jason Kidd .50 1.25
13 Donyell Marshall .15 .40
14 Eric Montross .15 .40
15 Alonzo Mourning .20 .50
16 Hakeem Olajuwon .40 1.00
17 Shaquille O'Neal .75 2.00
19 Glenn Robinson .20 .50
20 Jalen Rose .20 .50
31 Anfernee Hardaway .30 .75
32 Juwan Howard .30 .75
33 Eddie Jones .30 .75
34 Jamal Mashburn .20 .50
39 Dikembe Mutombo .20 .50
40 Shaquille O'Neal .75 2.00
44 Isaiah Rider .15 .40

1995 Assets Gold

This 50-card set measures the standard size. The fronts feature borderless player action photos with the player's name printed in gold at the bottom. The backs carry a portrait of the player with his name, career highlights, and statistics. The Dale Earnhardt card was pulled from circulation early in the product's release. It is considered a Short Print (SP) but is not included in the complete set price.

COMPLETE SET (49) 6.00 15.00
32 Rasheed Wallace .20 .50
33 Corliss Williamson .07 .20
34 Tyus Edney .05 .15
35 Ed O'Bannon .05 .15
36 Damon Stoudamire .20 .50
37 Eddie Jones .08 .25
38 Khalid Reeves .05 .15
39 Jason Kidd .30 .75
40 Glenn Robinson .07 .20
41 Juwan Howard .07 .20
42 Jamal Mashburn .07 .20
43 Shaquille O'Neal .40 1.00
44 Alonzo Mourning .08 .25
45 Donyell Marshall .05 .15
46 Jalen Rose .08 .25
47 Wesley Person .05 .15
48 Grant Hill .20 .50
49 Rasheed Wallace CL .08 .25
NNO Jason Kidd 2.00 5.00
Grant Hill
NNO Jason Kidd 5.00 12.00
Grant Hill DC

1995 Assets Gold Die Cuts Silver

This 20-card set was randomly inserted in packs at a rate of one in 18. The fronts feature a borderless player color action photo with a diamond-shaped top and the player's action taking place in front of the card name. The backs carry the card name, player's name and career highlights. The cards are numbered on the backs. Gold versions were inserted at a rate of one in 72 packs.

COMPLETE SET (20) 10.00 25.00
*GOLDS: .8X TO 2X SILVERS
GOLD STATED ODDS 1:72
SDC2 Shaquille O'Neal 1.50 4.00
SDC4 Glenn Robinson .50 1.25
SDC6 Grant Hill .60 1.50
SDC7 Rasheed Wallace .60 1.50
SDC8 Ed O'Bannon .40 1.00
SDC14 Jason Kidd .75 2.00

1995 Assets Gold Printer's Proofs

*PRINT PROOF: 2X TO 5X BASIC CARDS

1995 Assets Gold Silver Signatures

COMP. SILVER SIG SET (50) 15.00 40.00
*SILVER SIGS: .8X TO 2X BASIC CARDS

1995 Assets Gold Phone Cards $100

This five-card set measures 2 1/8" by 3 3/8". The fronts feature color action player photos with the player's name below. The $100 calling value is printed on the left. The backs carry the instructions on how to use the cards which expired on 7/31/96. The cards are unnumbered and checklisted below in alphabetical order.

*PIN NUMBER REVEALED: HALF VALUE
2 Jason Kidd 8.00 20.00
4 Rasheed Wallace 6.00 15.00

1995 Assets Gold Phone Cards $2

This 47-card set was randomly inserted in packs and measures 2 1/8" by 3 3/8". The fronts feature color action player photos with the player's name below. The $2 calling value is printed vertically down the left. The backs carry the instructions on how to use the cards which expired on 7/31/96. The cards are unnumbered.

COMPLETE SET (47) 15.00 40.00
*PIN NUMBER REVEALED: HALF VALUE
32 Rasheed Wallace .60 1.50
33 Corliss Williamson .30 .75
34 Tyus Edney .30 .75
35 Ed O'Bannon .30 .75
36 Damon Stoudamire .60 1.50
37 Eddie Jones .60 1.50
38 Khalid Reeves .30 .75
39 Jason Kidd 1.00 2.50
40 Glenn Robinson .40 1.00
41 Juwan Howard .40 1.00
42 Jamal Mashburn .30 .75
43 Shaquille O'Neal 1.25 3.00
44 Alonzo Mourning .40 1.00
45 Donyell Marshall .30 .75
46 Jalen Rose .60 1.50
47 Wesley Person .30 .75

1995 Assets Gold Phone Cards $25

This 5-card set measures 2 1/8" by 3 3/8" and was randomly inserted in packs. The fronts feature color action player photos of two different players with the player's name in gold below each photo. The $25 calling value is printed vertically in gold separating the two players. The backs carry the instructions on how to use the cards which expired on 7/31/96. The cards are unnumbered.

COMPLETE SET (5) 20.00 50.00
*PIN NUMBER REVEALED: HALF VALUE
3 Glenn Robinson 4.00 10.00
Rasheed Wallace
5 Corliss Williamson 3.00 8.00
Ed O'Bannon

1995 Assets Gold Phone Cards $5

This 16-card set measures 2 1/8" by 3 3/8" and was randomly inserted in packs. The fronts feature color action player photos with the player's name below. The $5 calling value is printed vertically down the left. The backs carry the instructions on how to use the cards which expired on 7/31/96. The cards are unnumbered. The Microlined versions are inserted at a rate of one in 18 packs versus one in six packs for the basic $5 card.

COMPLETE SET (16) 25.00 60.00
*MICROLINED: .6X TO 1.5X BASIC INSERTS
STATED ODDS 1:18
*PIN NUMBER REVEALED: HALF VALUE
7 Damon Stoudamire .75 2.00
13 Jason Kidd 1.00 2.50
14 Ed O'Bannon .50 1.25
15 Shaquille O'Neal 2.00 5.00
16 Glenn Robinson .60 1.50

1996 Assets

The 1996 Classic Assets was issued in one set totalling 50 cards. This 50-card premium set has a tremendous selection of the top athletes in the world headlines. Each card features action photos, up-to-date statistics and is printed on high-quality, foil-stamped stock. Hot Print cards are parallel cards randomly inserted in Hot Packs and are valued at a multiple of the regular cards below.

COMPLETE SET (50) 5.00 10.00
13 Kevin Garnett .75 2.00
15 Juwan Howard .07 .20
16 Eddie Jones .08 .25
19 Jason Kidd .15 .40
20 Rebecca Lobo .08 .25
23 Antonio McDyess .20 .50
26 Alonzo Mourning .05 .15
28 Dikembe Mutombo .07 .20
29 Ed O'Bannon .05 .15
30 Shaquille O'Neal .30 .75
31 Hakeem Olajuwon .08 .25
32 Cherokee Parks .05 .15
34 Scottie Pippen .08 .25
37 Glenn Robinson .05 .15
38 Jalen Rose .07 .20
42 Joe Smith .08 .25
43 Jerry Stackhouse .20 .50
44 Damon Stoudamire .30 .75
46 Rasheed Wallace .20 .50
47 Corliss Williamson .05 .15

1996 Assets A Cut Above

The even cards were randomly inserted in retail packs at a rate of one in eight, and the odd cards were inserted in clear asset packs at a rate of one in 20, this 20-card die-cut set is composed of 10 phone cards and 10 trading cards. The cards have rounded corners except for one which is cut in a straight corner design. The fronts feature a color action player cut-out superimposed over a gray background with the words "cut above" printed throughout and resembled to be cut so it displays a basketball game behind it. The backs carry a color action player photo with the player's name and a short career summary.

COMPLETE SET (20) 20.00 50.00
CA3 Shaquille O'Neal 3.00 8.00
CA5 Scottie Pippen 1.00 2.50
CA9 Jerry Stackhouse .60 1.50
CA12 Rasheed Wallace 1.00 2.50
CA14 Joe Smith .60 1.50
CA15 Kevin Garnett 4.00 10.00
CA16 Jason Kidd 1.25 3.00
CA18 Rebecca Lobo 1.25 3.00
CA20 Glenn Robinson .60 1.50

1996 Assets A Cut Above Phone Cards

This 10-card set, which were inserted at a rate of one in eight, measures approximately 2 1/8" by 3 3/8" have rounded corners except for one corner which is cut out and made straight. The fronts feature a color action player cut-out superimposed over a gray background with the words "cut above" printed throughout and resembled to be cut so that it displays a game going on behind the background. The backs carry the instructions on how to use the card. The cards expired on 1/31/97.

COMPLETE SET (10) 12.50 30.00
*PIN NUMBER REVEALED: HALF VALUE
2 Shaquille O'Neal 2.50 6.00
3 Scottie Pippen 1.00 2.50
5 Jerry Stackhouse 1.00 2.50
8 Kevin Garnett 4.00 10.00
9 Ed O'Bannon .50 1.25

1996 Assets Crystal Phone Cards

Randomly inserted in retail packs at a rate of one in 250, this high-tech, 10-card insert set contains clear holographic phone cards worth five minutes of long distance calling time. The cards measure approximately 2 1/8" by 3 3/8" with rounded corners. The fronts display a color action double-image player cut-out on a clear crystal background with the player's name printed vertically on the side. The backs carry instructions on how to use the card. The cards expired January 31, 1997. Twenty dollar phone cards of these athletes were issued, they are valued as a multiple of the cards below.

COMPLETE SET (10) 20.00 50.00
*PIN NUMBER REVEALED: HALF VALUE
5 Shaquille O'Neal 2.50 6.00
6 Scottie Pippen 1.00 2.50
8 Jason Kidd 1.25 3.00
9 Joe Smith .60 1.50
10 Jerry Stackhouse .75 2.00

1996 Assets Crystal Phone Cards $20

5 Shaquille O'Neal 6.00 15.00
6 Scottie Pippen 2.50 6.00
8 Jason Kidd 3.00 8.00
9 Joe Smith 1.50 4.00
10 Jerry Stackhouse 2.00 5.00

1996 Assets Hot Prints

*HOT PRINTS: .8X TO 2X BASIC CARDS

1996 Assets Phone Cards $10

This 10-card set was randomly inserted in packs at a rate of 1 in 20. The cards measure approximately 2 1/8" by 3 3/8" with rounded corners. The fronts display color action player photos with the player's name in a red bar below. The backs carry the instructions on how to use the cards and the expiration date of 1/31/97.

COMPLETE SET (10) 25.00 60.00
*PIN NUMBER REVEALED: HALF VALUE
5 Shaquille O'Neal 3.00 8.00
6 Scottie Pippen 2.00 5.00
9 Joe Smith 1.50 4.00
10 Jerry Stackhouse 2.00 5.00

1996 Assets Phone Cards $100

This five card set, randomly inserted in packs, measures approximately 2 1/8" by 3 3/8" with rounded corners. The fronts display color action player photos with the player's name. The backs carry the instructions on how to use the cards and the expiration date of 1/31/97.

COMPLETE SET (5) 40.00 80.00
*PIN NUMBER REVEALED: HALF VALUE
3 Shaquille O'Neal 8.00 20.00
4 Scottie Pippen 6.00 15.00

1996 Assets Phone Cards $2

COMPLETE SET (30) 12.50 30.00
*$2 CARDS: .6X TO 1.5X $1 CARDS
*PIN NUMBER REVEALED: HALF VALUE

1996 Assets Phone Cards $20

This five card set measures approximately 2 1/8" by 3 3/8" with rounded corners and were randomly inserted in retail packs. The fronts display color action player photos with the player's name. The backs carry the instructions on how to use the cards and the expiration date of 1/31/97.

COMPLETE SET (5) 25.00 60.00
*PIN NUMBER REVEALED: HALF VALUE
2 Scottie Pippen 3.00 8.00
5 Shaquille O'Neal 6.00 15.00

1996 Assets Phone Cards $5

This 20-card set was randomly inserted in retail packs at a rate of 1 in 5. The cards measure approximately 2 1/8" by 3 3/8" with rounded corners. The fronts display color action player photos with the player's name in a red bar below. The backs carry the instructions on how to use the cards and the expiration date of 1/31/97.

COMPLETE SET (20) 30.00 80.00
*PIN NUMBER REVEALED: HALF VALUE
8 Kevin Garnett 2.00 5.00
9 Jason Kidd 1.00 2.50
11 Shaquille O'Neal 4.00 5.00
12 Hakeem Olajuwon 1.00 2.50
13 Scottie Pippen 1.00 2.50
17 Joe Smith .60 1.50
18 Jerry Stackhouse .60 1.50
19 Rasheed Wallace .40 1.00

1996 Assets Silksations

Randomly inserted in retail packs at a rate of one in 100, this 10-card standard-size set features duplexed fabric-stock with top athletes. The fronts display a color action player cut-out with a two-tone background. The player's name is printed below. The backs carry a head photo of the player made to appear as if it is coming out of a square hole in gold cloth. The player's name and a short career summary are below. The cards are numbered with a "S" prefix and sequenced in alphabetical order.

COMPLETE SET (10) 40.00 80.00
5 Jason Kidd 5.00 12.00
6 Shaquille O'Neal 8.00 20.00
7 Scottie Pippen 4.00 10.00
9 Joe Smith 2.00 5.00
10 Jerry Stackhouse 3.00 8.00

1991 Classic

This 50-card standard-size set of basketball draft picks was produced by Classic Games, Inc. and features 48 players picked in the first two rounds of the 1991 NBA draft. A total of 450,000 sets were issued, and each set is accompanied by a letter of limited edition. The cards were only available for sale in these factory-sealed complete sets with no wax product being produced. The fronts feature a glossy color action photo of each player. The backs have statistics and biographical information. Special cards included in the set are a commemorative number one draft choice card of Larry Johnson and a "One-on-One" card of Billy Owens slam-dunking over Johnson. Three cards were issued as promos for the regular editon set. The player's name appears below the picture in black lettering. The backs are blank, except for the disclaimer "For Promotional Purposes Only." These cards are listed at the end of the regular set.

COMPLETE SET (50) 2.00 5.00
STATED PRINT RUN 450,000 SETS
1 Larry Johnson .40 1.00
2 Billy Owens .15 .40
3 Dikembe Mutombo .40 1.00
4 Mark Macon .05 .15
5 Brian Williams .15 .40
6 Greg Anthony .15 .40
7 Terrell Brandon .30 .75
8 Dale Davis .30 .75
9 Anthony Avent .05 .15
10 Chris Gatling .15 .40
11 Victor Alexander .05 .15
12 Kevin Brooks .05 .15
13 Eric Murdock .05 .15
14 LeRon Ellis .05 .15
15 Stanley Roberts .05 .15
16 Rick Fox .30 .75
17 Pete Chilcutt .05 .15
18 Kevin Lynch .05 .15
19 George Ackles .05 .15
20 Rodney Monroe .05 .15
21 Randy Brown .05 .15
22 Chad Gallagher .05 .15
23 Donald Hodge .05 .15
24 Myron Brown .05 .15
25 Mike Iuzzolino .05 .15
26 Chris Corchiani .05 .15
27 Elliot Perry .05 .15
28 Joe Wylie .05 .15
29 Jimmy Oliver .05 .15
30 Doug Overton .05 .15
31 Sean Green .05 .15
32 Steve Hood .05 .15
33 Lamont Strothers .05 .15
34 Alvaro Teheran .05 .15
35 Bobby Phills .15 .40
36 Richard Dumas .05 .15
37 Keith Hughes .05 .15
38 Isaac Austin .15 .40
39 Greg Sutton .05 .15
40 Joey Wright .05 .15
41 Anthony Jones .05 .15
42 Von McDade .05 .15
43 Marcus Kennedy .05 .15
44 L.Johnson Top Pick .20 .50
45 Johnson vs. Owens .20 .50
46 Anderson Hunt .05 .15
47 Darrin Chancellor .05 .15
48 Damon Lopez .05 .15
49 Thomas Jordan .05 .15
50 Tony Farmer .05 .15
NNO Larry Johnson PROMO .75 2.00
NNO Dikembe Mutombo PROMO .40 1.00
NNO Billy Owens PROMO .40 1.00

1991 Classic Autographs

These six certified autograph cards have the same design as the regular issue, except that inside a black frame, the horizontal backs read "Congratulations on receiving this limited edition autographed Classic Draft Pick Card," with the serial number and total production run (1100) written in blue ink near the bottom. The cards are unnumbered and checklisted below in alphabetical order.

RANDOM INSERTS IN PACKS
STATED PRINT RUN 1100 SERIAL #'d SETS
1 Victor Alexander 1.25 3.00
2 Anderson Hunt 1.25 3.00
3 Dikembe Mutombo 8.00 20.00
4 Billy Owens 2.00 5.00
5 Stanley Roberts 1.25 3.00
6 Brian Williams 1.25 3.00

1992 Classic Previews

These Classic Basketball Draft Picks preview cards were randomly inserted in the 1992 Classic Football Draft Picks 15-card foil packs. Only 10,000 of each card were produced. The standard-size cards feature on the front glossy color action player photos enclosed by white borders. The Classic logo, player's name, and position appear in a silver stripe beneath the picture. The backs read repeatedly "For Promotional Purposes Only" as well as bearing an advertisement and the Classic logo.

COMPLETE SET (5) 20.00 40.00
1 Shaquille O'Neal 15.00 40.00
2 Alonzo Mourning 3.00 8.00
3 Don MacLean .40 1.00
4 Walt Williams .75 2.00
5 Christian Laettner 1.25 3.00

1992 Classic Promos

These standard-size cards feature on the front glossy color action player photos enclosed by white borders. The Classic logo, player's name, and position appear in a silver stripe beneath the picture. The backs have biography, scouting report, and a partially cut out color action photo of the player. Beneath the statistical title line (in the space allotted for statistics), the backs read "For Promotional Purposes Only."

COMPLETE SET (6) 10.00 25.00
1 Shaquille O'Neal 10.00 25.00
2 Alonzo Mourning 2.00 5.00
3 Christian Laettner .75 2.00
4 Walt Williams .40 1.00
5 Don MacLean .20 .50
6 Jimmy Jackson 1.25 3.00

1992 Classic

The 1992 Classic Basketball Draft Picks set contains 100 standard-size cards, including all 54 drafted players. The set features the first nationally distributed 1992 trading card of NBA first overall pick Shaquille O'Neal as well as the only draft cards of second pick Alonzo Mourning and fourth pick Jimmy Jackson. The set also includes a Flashback (95-98) subset. The fronts feature glossy color action photos bordered in white. The player's name appears in a silver stripe beneath the picture, which intersects the Classic logo at the lower left corner. The backs have a second color player photo and present biographical information, complete college statistics, and a scouting report. The cards are numbered on the back. Cards 61-100 were only available in 15-card foil packs as the blister sets contained only cards 1-60. The production run was reportedly 28,000 ten-box cases and 125,000 60-card factory blister sets. The Laettner Bonus Card was inserted one per blister set. Also listed at the end of the set is a Shaquille O'Neal autographed card numbered to 2500. This card was available in a hanging wall plaque from shop at home where it is engraved as Shaquille O'Neal limited edition and the print run of 2500.

COMP.BLISTER SET (61) 6.00 8.00
COMPLETE SET (100) 5.00 10.00
CARDS 61-100 DIST.ONLY IN FOIL PACKS
1 Shaquille O'Neal 1.50 4.00
2 Walt Williams .15 .40
3 Lee Mayberry .05 .15
4 Tony Bennett .05 .15
5 Litterial Green .05 .15
6 Chris Smith .05 .15
7 Henry Williams .05 .15
8 Terrell Lowery .05 .15
9 Radenko Dobras .05 .15
10 Curtis Blair .05 .15
11 Randy Woods .05 .15
12 Todd Day .15 .40
13 Anthony Peeler .15 .40
14 Darin Archbold .05 .15
15 Benford Williams .05 .15
16 Terrence Lewis .05 .15
17 James McCoy .05 .15
18 Damon Patterson .05 .15
19 Bryant Stith .15 .40
20 Doug Christie .15 .40
21 Latrell Sprewell .25 .60
22 Hubert Davis .15 .40
23 David Booth .05 .15
24 David Johnson .05 .15
25 Jon Barry .05 .15
26 Everick Sullivan .05 .15
27 Brian Davis .05 .15
28 Clarence Weatherspoon .15 .40
29 Malik Sealy .15 .40
30 Matt Geiger .15 .40
31 Jimmy Jackson .25 .60
32 Matt Steigenga .05 .15
33 Robert Horry .15 .40
34 Marlon Maxey .05 .15
35 Reggie Slater .05 .15
36 Lucius Davis .05 .15
37 Chris King .05 .15
38 Dexter Cambridge .05 .15
39 Alonzo Jamison .05 .15
40 Anthony Tucker .05 .15
41 Tracy Murray .05 .15
42 Vernel Singleton .05 .15
43 Christian Laettner .15 .40
44 Don MacLean .05 .15
45 Adam Keefe .05 .15
46 Tom Gugliotta .15 .40
47 LaPhonso Ellis .15 .40
48 Byron Houston .05 .15
49 Oliver Miller .05 .15
50 Popeye Jones .05 .15
51 P.J. Brown .15 .40
52 Eric Anderson .05 .15
53 Darren Morningstar .05 .15
54 Isaiah Morris .05 .15
55 Stephen Howard .05 .15
56 Reggie Smith .05 .15
57 Elmore Spencer .05 .15
58 Sean Rooks .05 .15
59 Robert Werdann .05 .15
60 Alonzo Mourning .40 1.00
61 Steve Rogers .05 .15
62 Tim Burroughs .05 .15
63 Ed Book .05 .15
64 Herb Jones .05 .15
65 Mik Kilgore .05 .15
66 Ken Leeks .05 .15
67 Sam Mack .05 .15
68 Sean Miller .05 .15
69 Craig Upchurch .05 .15
70 Van Usher .05 .15
71 Corey Williams .05 .15
72 Duane Cooper .05 .15
73 Brett Roberts .05 .15
74 Elmer Bennett .05 .15
75 Brent Price .05 .15
76 Daimon Sweet .05 .15
77 Darrick Martin .05 .15
78 Gerald Madkins .05 .15
79 Jo Jo English .05 .15
80 Alex Blackwell .05 .15
81 Anthony Dade .05 .15
82 Matt Fish .05 .15
83 Byron Tucker .05 .15
84 Harold Miner .15 .40
85 Greg Dennis .05 .15
86 Jeff Roulston .05 .15
87 Keir Rogers .05 .15
88 Billy Law .05 .15
89 Geoff Lear .05 .15
90 Lambert Shell .05 .15
91 Elbert Rogers .05 .15
92 Ron Ellis .05 .15
93 Predrag Danilovic .05 .15
94 Calvin Talford .05 .15
95 Stacey Augmon FB .05 .15
96 Steve Smith FB .15 .40
97 Billy Owens FB .05 .15
98 Dikembe Mutombo FB .15 .40
99 Checklist 1-50 .05 .15
100 Checklist 51-100 .05 .15
NNO1 Shaquille O'Neal AU/2500 30.00 80.00
NNO2 Christian Laettner BC .40 1.00
NNO3 Shaquille O'Neal AU/500 60.00 150.00
NNO4 Jim Jackson AU/1992

1992 Classic Gold Promo

This card measures the standard size and features an action color player photo with white borders. The player's name and position are gold foil stamped in a black border stripe at the bottom. The Classic Draft Picks Gold logo overlaps the stripe and the photo at the lower left corner. The white background on the backs displays a vertical action color picture and a scouting report, while the player's name (in a gold stripe), biography, and statistics are printed horizontally. This card can be distinguished by the words "For Promotional Purposes Only" on the back. The card is numbered on the back.

2 Alonzo Mourning 4.00 10.00

1992 Classic Gold

COMP.FACT.SET (101) 40.00 80.00
*GOLD: 2.5X TO 6X BASE CARD HI
DISTRIBUTED ONLY IN FACTORY SET FORM
STATED PRINT RUN 8,500 SETS
O'NEAL AUTO ONE PER GOLD FACT.SET
AU Shaquille O'Neal AU/8500 25.00 60.00

1992 Classic LPs

This ten-card set, subtitled "Top Ten Pick", features the top ten picks of the 1992 NBA Draft. These standard size cards were randomly inserted in 1992 Classic Draft Picks 15-card foil packs. The fronts feature glossy color action photos enclosed by white borders. The player's name appears in a silver foil stripe beneath the picture, which intersects the Classic logo at the lower left corner. The production figures "1 of 56,000" and the "Top Ten Pick" emblem at the card top are also silver foil. The horizontally oriented backs have a silver background and feature a second color player photo and player profile. The cards are numbered on the back with an "LP" (limited print) prefix. An 8 1/2" by 11" version of Alonzo Mourning is known to exist.

COMPLETE SET (10) 8.00 20.00
RANDOM INSERTS IN PACKS
LP1 Shaquille O'Neal 8.00 20.00
LP2 Alonzo Mourning 1.50 4.00
LP3 Christian Laettner .60 1.50
LP4 Jimmy Jackson 1.00 2.50
LP5 LaPhonso Ellis .30 .75
LP6 Tom Gugliotta 1.00 2.50
LP7 Walt Williams .30 .75
LP8 Todd Day .20 .50
LP9 Clarence Weatherspoon .20 .50
LP10 Adam Keefe .08 .25

1992 Classic Magicians

Inserted one per jumbo pack, this 20-card standard-size set features white-bordered color action shots on the fronts. Each card displays the player's name in blue lettering inside a silver foil stripe at the bottom of the photo, with the player's position appearing just beneath inside a black bar, and the Classic logo atop the foil to the left. The silver foil Magician logo in the top right rounds out the front. The backs have narrow-cropped color action photos on their right sides and silver stripes down the left with the player's name. Scouting reports and horizontally oriented biography and stats appear between. Cards 2, 4 and 5 have "91 Flashback" printed in white across the tops of the fronts. The cards are numbered on the back with a "BC" prefix.

COMPLETE SET (20) 2.50 6.00
ONE PER JUMBO PACK
BC1 Doug Christie .15 .40
BC2 Billy Owens .05 .15
BC3 Latrell Sprewell 1.25 3.00
BC4 Stacey Augmon .05 .15
BC5 Steve Smith .20 .50
BC6 Jon Barry .05 .15
BC7 Christian Laettner .30 .75
BC8 Jimmy Jackson .50 1.25
BC9 Tracy Murray .05 .15
BC10 Walt Williams .15 .40
BC11 Todd Day .08 .25
BC12 Dave Johnson .05 .15
BC13 Byron Houston .05 .15
BC14 Robert Horry .15 .40
BC15 Harold Miner .05 .15
BC16 Bryant Stith .08 .25
BC17 Malik Sealy .08 .25
BC18 Randy Woods .05 .15
BC19 Anthony Peeler .08 .25
BC20 Lee Mayberry .05 .15

1992 Classic Mutombo Promo

This standard-size card features Dikembe Mutombo. The front has a color action player photo with a bronze-like outer border, and silver and gold inner borders. The player's name appears in a silver bar at the bottom, while the words "Uncirculated - 1 of 5,000" are printed in a silver bar at the top. On a silver background, the back carries information about Dikembe Mutombo and Classic. The card is unnumbered.

1 Dikembe Mutombo .75 2.00

1992 Classic Show Promos 20

This 20-card standard-size set was issued one card at a time at the various shows throughout the year where Classic maintained a presence or booth. Typically the cards were given out free to attendees while supplies lasted. The cards all read "Promo Card x of 20" prominently on the card back. The cards are done in several different styles depending on the Classic issue that was being promoted by that particular card.

COMPLETE SET (20) 15.00 30.00
1 Billy Owens .20 .50
(1992 Sports Spectacular)
2 Dikembe Mutombo .30 .75
(1992 SportsNet National)
9 Jimmy Jackson .40 1.00
(July 1992 Atlanta National)
11 Shaquille O'Neal 2.00 5.00
(July 1992 Atlanta National)
12 Alonzo Mourning .80 2.00
(July 1992 Atlanta National)
13 Christian Laettner .30 .75
(1992 East Coast National)
17 Shaquille O'Neal 2.00 5.00
(1992 Tri-Star St. Louis)
20 Harold Miner .20 .50
(1992 Tri-Star Houston)

1992 Classic World Class Athletes

Packaged in a high impact clam shell, this 60-card standard-size set features current and past world class athletes. The production run was 295,000 sets, and an enclosed certificate of limited edition carries the set serial number. A few athletes had autographs randomly inserted into the factory sets. We have noted those cards at the end of our checklist.

COMP.FACT.SET (60) 1.60 4.00
2 Larry Bird BK .20 .50
47 Jennifer Azzi BK .08 .25
48 Katrina McClain BK .08 .25
49 Scottie Pippen BK .20 .50
50 John Stockton BK .08 .25
51 Patrick Ewing BK .08 .25
52 Charles Barkley BK .20 .50

1993 Classic Previews

These basketball cards were randomly inserted in 1993 Classic Football Draft Picks foil packs as well as 1993 Classic NFL Pro Line Collection packs. Reportedly 17,500 of each standard-size card were produced and randomly inserted an average of two cards per case, evenly distributed through both products. The fronts feature color player action shots with simulated pinewood borders. The player's name and position appear in a colored stripe at the bottom of the photo. The red-bordered back carries a basketball icon and the number of cards produced. The cards are unnumbered and are checklisted below in alphabetical order.

COMPLETE SET (4) 6.00 15.00
BK1 Chris Webber 4.00 10.00
BK2 Jamal Mashburn .75 2.00
BK3 Anfernee Hardaway 4.00 10.00
BK4 Allan Houston UER 1.50 4.00

1993 Classic

The 1993 Classic Draft Picks set consists of 110 standard-size cards.The production run was limited to 32,500 ten-box cases. The fronts feature color action player photos with simulated pinewood borders. The player's name and position, along with the 1993 Classic Draft Picks logo, appears in a white bar across the base of each picture. The simulated pinewood design continues on the horizontal back. The player's name appears at the top in an ellipse that is of a lighter-colored simulated pinewood. Stats are displayed in a lighter-colored rectangle at the bottom. A narrow-cropped pinewood-bordered player color action shot along the left side rounds out the card. Gold factory sets were produced later.

COMPLETE SET (110) 5.00 10.00
1 Chris Webber .40 1.00
2 Anfernee Hardaway .40 1.00
3 Jamal Mashburn .30 .75
4 Isaiah Rider .15 .40
5 Vin Baker .15 .40
6 Rodney Rogers .15 .40
7 Lindsey Hunter .15 .40
8 Allan Houston .15 .40
9 George Lynch .05 .15
10 Toni Kukoc .30 .75
11 Ashraf Amaya .05 .15
12 Mark Bell .05 .15
13 John Best .05 .15
14 Corie Blount .05 .15
15 Dexter Boney .05 .15
16 Tim Brooks .05 .15
17 James Bryson .05 .15
18 Evers Burns .05 .15
19 Scott Burrell .05 .15
20 Sam Cassell .07 .20
21 Derrick Chandler .05 .15
22 Sam Crawford .05 .15
23 Ron Curry .05 .15
24 William Davis .05 .15
25 Rodney Dobard .05 .15
26 Tony Dunkin .05 .15
27 Spencer Dunkley .05 .15
28 Bill Edwards .05 .15
29 Bryan Edwards .05 .15
30 Doug Edwards .05 .15
31 Chuck Evans .05 .15
32 Terry Evans .05 .15
33 Will Flemons .05 .15
34 Alphonso Ford .05 .15
35 Brian Gilgeous .05 .15
36 Josh Grant .05 .15
37 Evric Gray .05 .15
38 Geert Hammink .05 .15
39 Lucious Harris .05 .15
40 Joe Harvell .05 .15
41 Antonio Harvey .05 .15
42 Scott Haskin .05 .15
43 Brian Hendrick .05 .15
44 Sascha Hupmann .05 .15
45 Stanley Jackson .05 .15
46 Ervin Johnson .05 .15
47 Adonis Jordan .05 .15
48 Warren Kidd .05 .15
49 Malcolm Mackey .05 .15
50 Rich Manning .05 .15
51 Chris McNeal .05 .15
52 Conrad McRae .05 .15
53 Lance Miller .05 .15
54 Chris Mills .15 .40
55 Matt Nover .05 .15
56 Bo Outlaw .15 .40
57 Eric Pauley .05 .15
58 Mike Peplowski .05 .15
59 Stacey Poole .05 .15
60 Anthony Reed .05 .15
61 Eric Riley .05 .15
62 Darrin Robinson .05 .15
63 Jackie Robinson .05 .15
64 James Robinson .05 .15
65 Bryon Russell .15 .40
66 Brent Scott .05 .15
67 Bennie Seltzer .05 .15
68 Ed Stokes .05 .15
69 Antoine Stoudamire .05 .15
70 Dirk Surles .05 .15
71 Justus Thigpen .05 .15
72 Kevin Thompson .05 .15
73 Ray Thompson .05 .15
74 Gary Trost .05 .15
75 Nick Van Exel .07 .20
76 Jerry Walker .05 .15
77 Rex Walters .05 .15
78 Leonard White .05 .15
79 Chris Whitney .05 .15
80 Steve Worthy .05 .15
81 Alex Wright .05 .15
82 Luther Wright .05 .15
83 Mark Buford .05 .15
84 Keith Bullock .05 .15
85 Mitchell Butler .05 .15
86 Brian Clifford .05 .15
87 Terry Dehere .05 .15
88 Acie Earl .05 .15
89 Greg Graham .05 .15
90 Angelo Hamilton .05 .15
91 Thomas Hill .05 .15
92 Alex Holcombe .05 .15
93 Khari Jaxon .05 .15
94 Darnell Mee .05 .15
95 Sherron Mills .05 .15
96 Gheorghe Muresan .15 .40
97 Eddie Rivera .05 .15
98 Julius Nwosu .05 .15
99 Richard Petruska .05 .15
100 Bryan Sallier .05 .15
101 Harper Williams .05 .15
102 Ike Williams .05 .15
103 Byron Wilson .05 .15
104 Shaquille O'Neal FLB .15 .40
105 Alonzo Mourning FLB .15 .40
106 Christian Laettner FLB .05 .15
107 Jimmy Jackson FLB .05 .15
108 Harold Miner FLB .05 .15
109 Checklist 1 .05 .15
110 Checklist 2 .05 .15
PF Chris Webber SPEC/60000 1.00 2.50
PR1 Chris Webber PROMO 1.25 3.00
NNO Chris Webber DP AU 15.00 40.00

1993 Classic Gold

COMP.FACT.SET (112) 40.00 80.00
*GOLD: 1.5X TO 4X BASIC CARDS
DIST.ONLY IN FACTORY SET FORM
STATED PRINT RUN 9,500 SETS
NNO Jamal Mashburn AU/9500 6.00 15.00
NNO Chris Webber AU/9500 12.50 30.00

1993 Classic Acetate Draft Stars

These five acetate cards were randomly inserted in foil packs. By visually interlocking these cards, the collector created a "Draft Stars" panoramic image featuring Webber, Hardaway, Mashburn, Rider, and Rogers. These visually interlocking clear plastic acetate cards were inserted on an average of three per ten-box case of 1993 Classic Basketball Draft Picks. The cards are unnumbered and checklisted below in alphabetical order.

COMPLETE SET (5) 3.00 8.00
UNNUMBERED RANDOM INSERTS IN PACKS
AD1 Anfernee Hardaway 2.00 5.00
AD2 Jamal Mashburn .40 1.00
AD3 Isaiah Rider .40 1.00
AD4 Rodney Rogers .20 .50
AD5 Chris Webber 1.50 4.00

1993 Classic Chromium Draft Stars

Inserted one per jumbo pack, these 20 standard-size cards feature on their metallic fronts borderless color player action shots. The player's name and position appear within the silver bar near the bottom. The horizontal simulated pinewood back carries a narrow-cropped color player action shot on the left. The player's name and biography appear at the top, followed below by a congratulatory message and statistics. The cards are numbered on the back with a "DS" prefix.

COMPLETE SET (20) 2.00 5.00
ONE PER JUMBO PACK
DS21 Vin Baker .20 .50
DS22 Terry Dehere .01 .05
DS23 Sam Cassell .25 .60
DS24 Doug Edwards .01 .05
DS25 Greg Graham .01 .05
DS26 Scott Haskin .01 .05
DS27 Allan Houston .30 .75
DS28 Toni Kukoc .30 .75
DS29 George Lynch .01 .05
DS30 Jamal Mashburn .15 .40
DS31 Harold Miner .01 .05
DS32 Rex Walters .01 .05
DS33 James Robinson .01 .05
DS34 Rodney Rogers .02 .10
DS35 Luther Wright .01 .05
DS36 Alonzo Mourning .10 .30
DS37 Anfernee Hardaway .75 2.00
DS38 Isaiah Rider .15 .40
DS39 Lindsey Hunter .07 .20
DS40 Chris Webber .75 2.00

1993 Classic Chromium Jumbos

These eight oversized (3 1/2 by 5 inches) chromium cards were issued by Classic as bonuses for various retail repackaged products. There are four different cards each of top draft picks Anfernee Hardaway and Chris Webber, using four designs from previously issued Classic Draft sets and insert sets.

COMPLETE SET (8) 6.00 15.00
1 Chris Webber BK draft 1.00 2.50
2 A.Hardaway BK draft 1.00 2.50
3 C.Webber BK draft Illust. 1.00 2.50
4 A.Hardaway BK draft Illust. 1.00 2.50
5 C.Webber 4-Sport LPs 1.00 2.50
6 A.Hardaway 4-Sport LPs 1.00 2.50
7 Chris Webber 4-Sport 1.00 2.50
8 A.Hardaway 4-Sport 1.00 2.50

1993 Classic Deathwatch Jumbos

Inserted in Classic Deathwatch comic card boxes, these three oversized cards measure approximately 3 1/2" by 5". The fronts feature color player action shots with simulated pinewood borders. The player's name and position appear in black lettering within a gold-foil stripe near the bottom. His NBA team name appears in white cursive lettering in an upper corner. A gold-foil "Traded" or "Drafted" message appears in the other upper corner. The back carries a congratulatory message. The cards are numbered on the back with an "SE" prefix. On a white screened background with the words "Special Edition", the backs give production figures (25,000).

COMPLETE SET (3) 4.00 10.00
SE1 Chris Webber 2.50 6.00
SE2 Jamal Mashburn .50 1.25
SE3 Anfernee Hardaway 2.50 6.00

1993 Classic Draft Draft Day

This 12-card standard-size set was given away on NBA Draft Day, June 30, 1993. In anticipation of these players being the top draft picks, Classic produced these cards showing the teams (in the upper right corner) who would most likely draft these players. The fronts feature color action player photos with simulated pinewood borders. The player's name and position, along with the 1993 Classic Draft Picks logo, appears in a white bar across the base of each picture. On a white screened background with the words "1993 Draft Day," the backs display the 1993 Classic Draft Picks logo and give the production figures (19,930). The sets were sold through QVC Shopping Network. The cards are unnumbered and checklisted below in alphabetical order.

COMPLETE SET (12) 8.00 20.00
*SILVER: .5X TO 1.2X BASIC
1 Anfernee Hardaway 1.25 3.00
Dallas
2 Anfernee Hardaway 1.25 3.00
Golden State
3 Anfernee Hardaway 1.25 3.00
Orlando
4 Jamal Mashburn .30 .75
Dallas
5 Jamal Mashburn .30 .75
Golden State
6 Jamal Mashburn .30 .75
Orlando
7 Shaquille O'Neal .75 2.00
8 Rodney Rogers .20 .50
Dallas
9 Rodney Rogers .20 .50
Minnesota
10 Chris Webber 1.50 4.00
Golden State
11 Chris Webber 1.50 4.00
Orlando
12 Chris Webber 1.50 4.00
Philadelphia

1993 Classic Draft East Coast National

This standard-size card features a borderless color action shot of Jamal Mashburn on its front. The player's name and position appear within a prismatic foil strip near the bottom. The back carries a message about the '93 East Coast National card show. The card is unnumbered.

1 Jamal Mashburn .75 2.00

1993 Classic Illustrated

Drawn by artist Craig Hamilton, these three standard-size cards display images of basketball superstars and they were reportedly inserted on an average of three per ten-box case. The fronts feature full-bleed artistic portraits of exaggerated action scenes. The player's name and position appear in a white bar across the bottom, and 1993 Classic Draft Picks logo overlays the bar. On a background consisting of a ghosted blow-up of the front portrait, the backs have a narrowly-cropped color player picture and a player profile. The production figures ("1 of 39,000") round out the back. The cards are numbered on the back with an "SS" prefix.

COMPLETE SET (3) 4.00 10.00
RANDOM INSERTS IN PACKS
SS1 Chris Webber 2.50 6.00
SS2 Jamal Mashburn .50 1.25
SS3 Anfernee Hardaway 2.50 6.00

1993 Classic LPs

These ten standard-size cards were randomly inserted on an average of two per box of 1993 Classic Basketball Draft Picks. The fronts feature full-bleed color action player photos. The player's name and position appear in a holographic bar at the bottom, with the production run figures ("1 of 74,500") in holographic lettering immediately above. Also the 1993 Classic Draft Picks logo overlays the holographic bar. On a woodgrain-textured silver background, the horizontal backs carry a narrowly-cropped color player picture on the left and a player profile on the right. The player's name appears in a silver foil oval at the top. The cards are numbered on the back with an "LP" prefix.

COMPLETE SET (10) 5.00 12.00
RANDOM INSERTS IN PACKS
LP1 Chris Webber 2.00 5.00
LP2 Anfernee Hardaway 2.00 5.00
LP3 Jamal Mashburn .40 1.00
LP4 Isaiah Rider .40 1.00
LP5 Vin Baker .50 1.25
LP6 Rodney Rogers .20 .50
LP7 Lindsey Hunter .30 .75
LP8 Toni Kukoc .75 2.00
LP9 Shaquille O'Neal 1.25 3.00
LP10 Alonzo Mourning .40 1.00

1993 Classic Special Bonus

Issued one per jumbo sheet, these 20 standard-size cards feature on their fronts borderless color player action shots. The player's name and position appear within the gold-foil bar near the bottom. The horizontal simulated pinewood back carries a narrow-cropped color player action shot on the left. The player's name and biography appear at the top, followed below by a scouting report and statistics. The cards are numbered on the back with an "SB" prefix. The Webber card is a special random insert in the sheets.

COMPLETE SET (20) 4.00 10.00
ONE PER JUMBO SHEET
WEBBER SPECIAL RANDOM INSERT IN SHEETS
SB1 Chris Webber 1.00 2.50
SB2 Anfernee Hardaway 1.00 2.50
SB3 Jamal Mashburn .20 .50
SB4 Isaiah Rider .20 .50
SB5 Rodney Rogers .05 .15
SB6 Vin Baker .25 .60
SB7 Lindsey Hunter .08 .25
SB8 Allan Houston .40 1.00
SB9 Toni Kukoc .40 1.00
SB10 Acie Earl .02 .10
SB11 George Lynch .02 .10
SB12 Terry Dehere .02 .10
SB13 Rex Walters .02 .10
SB14 Harold Miner .02 .10
SB15 Scott Haskin .02 .10
SB16 Doug Edwards .02 .10
SB17 Greg Graham .02 .10
SB18 Christian Laettner .05 .15
SB19 Alonzo Mourning .15 .40
SB20 Shaquille O'Neal .50 1.25
NNO Chris Webber Special 2.00 5.00

1993 Classic Tri-Star Promos

These two standard-siz promo cards were issued in 1993 by Classic for Tri-Star Productions. The fronts display color action photos. The Tri-Star Productions logo is stamped in gold foil near one corner. The player's name appears at the bottom of the photo. The white back carries promo information and has no number.

COMPLETE SET (2) 1.25 3.00
1 Chris Webber 1.25 3.00
2 Jamal Mashburn .40 1.00

1994 Classic Previews

Randomly inserted in 1994 Classic football and ProLine football packs, these five standard-size cards feature color player action shots on their borderless fronts. The player's name and position appear in a black bar near the bottom. The back carries a congratulatory message. The complete set was also available using a redemption card. This offer expired Oct. 1, 1994.

COMPLETE SET (5) 4.00 10.00
BP1 Eric Montross .60 1.50
BP2 Jason Kidd 3.00 8.00
BP3 Yinka Dare .60 1.50
BP4 Glenn Robinson 1.25 3.00
BP5 Clifford Rozier .60 1.50

1994 Classic

These 105 standard-size cards feature borderless color player action shots on their fronts. The player's name and position appear within a black bar near the bottom. The back carries another borderless color player action shot, which is gradually ghosted toward the bottom. The player's name and position appear at the top; statistics and career highlights appear near the bottom. Dick Vitale's facsimile autograph at the lower right rounds out the card. A promotional card of Glenn Robinson was released before the product was live. It is numbered BP1, and the back gives information about the set and its inserts.

COMPLETE SET (100) 5.00 10.00
1 Glenn Robinson .25 .60
2 Jason Kidd .60 1.50
3 Charlie Ward .12 .30
4 Grant Hill .60 1.50
5 Juwan Howard .20 .50
6 Eric Montross .12 .30
7 Carlos Rogers .12 .30
8 Wesley Person .12 .30
9 Anthony Miller .12 .30
10 Dwayne Morton .12 .30
11 Chris Mills ART .07 .20
12 Jamal Mashburn ART .12 .30
13 Chris Webber ART .20 .50
14 Anfernee Hardaway ART .20 .50
15 Isaiah Rider ART .12 .30
16 Billy McCaffrey .12 .30
17 Steve Woodberry .12 .30
18 Damon Bailey .12 .30
19 Deon Thomas .12 .30
20 Dontonio Wingfield .12 .30
21 Albert Burditt .12 .30
22 Aaron Mckie .12 .30
23 Steve Smith .12 .30
24 Tony Dumas .12 .30
25 Adrian Autry .12 .30
26 Monty Williams .12 .30
27 Askia Jones .12 .30
28 Howard Eisley .12 .30
29 Brian Grant .20 .50
30 Eddie Jones .40 1.00
31 Dickey Simpkins .12 .30
32 Michael Smith .12 .30
33 Clifford Rozier .12 .30
34 Travis Ford .12 .30
35 Jervaughn Scales .12 .30
36 Tracy Webster .12 .30
37 Brooks Thompson .12 .30
38 Jim McIlvaine .12 .30
39 Eric Piatkowski .15 .40
40 Arturas Karnishovas .12 .30
41 Rodney Dent .12 .30
42 Robert Shannon .12 .30
43 Derrick Phelps .12 .30
44 Brian Reese .12 .30
45 Kevin Salvadori .12 .30
46 Shon Tarver .12 .30
47 Anthony Goldwire .12 .30
48 Jamie Watson .12 .30
49 Damon Key .12 .30
50 Kevin Rankin .12 .30
51 Khalid Reeves .12 .30
52 Doremus Benneman .12 .30
53 Sharone Wright .12 .30
54 Melvin Simon .12 .30
55 Andrei Fetisov .12 .30
56 Barry Brown .12 .30
57 B.J. Tyler .12 .30
58 Lawrence Funderburke .12 .30
59 Darrin Hancock .12 .30
60 Gaylon Nickerson .12 .30
61 Jeff Webster .12 .30
62 Derrick Alston .12 .30
63 Kendrick Warren .12 .30
64 Yinka Dare .12 .30
65 Shawnelle Scott .12 .30
66 Patrick Ewing CEN .15 .40
67 Dikembe Mutombo CEN .12 .30
68 Alonzo Mourning CEN .15 .40
69 Shaquille O'Neal CEN .30 .75
70 Hakeem Olajuwon CEN .15 .40
71 Thomas Hamilton .12 .30
72 Joey Brown .12 .30
73 Voshon Lenard .12 .30
74 Donyell Marshall .12 .30
75 Abdul Fox .12 .30
76 Checklist .07 .20
77 Checklist .07 .20
78 Jalen Rose .30 .75
79 Trevor Ruffin .12 .30
80 Sam Mitchell .12 .30
81 Dick Vitale .15 .40
82 Charlie Ward 2-Sport .12 .30
83 Cornell Parker .12 .30
84 Clayton Ritter .12 .30
85 Carl Ray Harris .12 .30
86 Randy Blocker .12 .30
87 Chuck Graham .12 .30
88 Greg Minor .12 .30
89 Bill Curley .12 .30
90 Harry Moore .12 .30
91 Melvin Booker .12 .30
92 Gary Collier .12 .30
93 Myron Walker .12 .30
94 Jamie Brandon .12 .30
95 Eric Mobley .12 .30
96 Byron Starks .12 .30
97 Antonio Lang .12 .30
98 Jevon Crudup .12 .30
99 Robert Churchwell .12 .30
100 Aaron Swinson .12 .30
101 Glenn Robinson COMIC SP 1.25 3.00
102 Jason Kidd COMIC SP 3.00 8.00
103 Juwan Howard COMIC SP 1.00 2.50
104 Charlie Ward COMIC SP .60 1.50
105 Eric Montross COMIC SP .60 1.50
BP1 Glenn Robinson PROMO .40 1.00
PR1 Jason Kidd PROMO 1.00 2.50
AU1 S.O'Neal AU/500 50.00 100.00
NNO S.O'Neal Chrome 4.00 10.00

1994 Classic Gold

*GOLD: 1.25X TO 3X HI COLUMN
*GOLD COMIC: .6X TO 1.5X HI
ONE PER FOIL OR JUMBO PACK

1994 Classic Printer's Proofs

*PROOFS: 3X TO 8X HI COLUMN
*PROOFS COMIC: 1.25X TO 3X HI
RANDOM INSERTS IN EARLY HOBBY PACKS
STATED PRINT RUN 975 SETS

1994 Classic Acetate Shaquille O'Neal

This 2 1/2" by 4 3/4" card shows Shaquille O'Neal holding a basketball. According to hobbyists, this card was only available through Home Shopping Network. This card is numbered out of 24,900.

SO1 Shaquille O'Neal 4.00 10.00

1994 Classic BCs

Inserted one per periodical pack, these 25 standard-size cards feature borderless color player action shots on their metallic fronts. The player's name and position appear within a black bar at the lower right. The back carries another borderless color action shot, with the player's biography appearing at the lower right within a ghosted triangle. The cards are numbered on the back with a "BC" prefix.

COMPLETE SET (25) 4.00 10.00
ONE PER MAGAZINE PACK
BC1 Glenn Robinson .50 1.25
BC2 Jason Kidd 1.25 3.00
BC3 Grant Hill 1.25 3.00
BC4 Donyell Marshall .25 .60
BC5 Juwan Howard .40 1.00
BC6 Sharone Wright .25 .60
BC7 Brian Grant .40 1.00
BC8 Eric Montross .25 .60
BC9 Eddie Jones .75 2.00
BC10 Carlos Rogers .25 .60
BC11 Khalid Reeves .25 .60
BC12 Jalen Rose .60 1.50
BC13 Yinka Dare .25 .60
BC14 Eric Piatkowski .30 .75
BC15 Clifford Rozier .25 .60
BC16 Aaron McKie .25 .60
BC17 Eric Mobley .25 .60
BC18 Tony Dumas .25 .60
BC19 B.J. Tyler .25 .60
BC20 Dickey Simpkins .25 .60
BC21 Bill Curley .25 .60
BC22 Wesley Person .25 .60
BC23 Monty Williams .25 .60
BC24 Greg Minor .25 .60
BC25 Charlie Ward .25 .60
NNO Jason Kidd Chrome 6.00 15.00

1994 Classic Game Cards

Inserted one per jumbo pack, these cards were redeemable for a gold sheet. The cards feature the expression "game card" in red letters down the left side of the front while the rest of the card displays the player's photo and in the bottom right part are the players' name and who drafted them. The back features instructions on how to play and scratch off your cards for the gold sheet prize. Winning cards were redeemable until May 1, 1995.

COMPLETE SET (5) 1.00 2.50
ONE PER JUMBO PACK
GC1 Glenn Robinson .30 .75
GC2 Jason Kidd .75 2.00
GC3 Juwan Howard .25 .60
GC4 Donyell Marshall .15 .40
GC5 Sharone Wright .15 .40

1994 Classic National Party Autographs

Measuring the standard-size, these cards were signed at a party hosted by Classic during the 15th National Collectors Convention in Houston. Attendees were entitled to have one card signed by one of the athletes present. The fronts display full-bleed color action shots. For the rookies, the player's name appears in red print on a black bar near the bottom. The player's signature is inscribed across the front in silver ink. On a dark screened background, the backs carry a congratulatory message. The cards are unnumbered and checklisted below in alphabetical order. The Kidd and Olajuwon cards showed up on the market at a later date.

COMPLETE SET (4) 15.00 40.00
1 Juwan Howard 6.00 15.00
2 Jason Kidd 12.50 30.00
3 Donyell Marshall 3.00 8.00
4 Hakeem Olajuwon
5 Jalen Rose 12.00 30.00

1994 Classic Phone Cards $2

1994 Classic Basketball Jumbo is the first Classic trading card product to include Sprint PrePaid Foncards. Randomly inserted at a rate of one in every seven 12-card jumbo packs, each Sprint card provides $2.00 worth of Sprint long distance service. The packs were sold at selected Walmart, Bookland, Sam's and other major retailers. The potential usage of these cards expired on June 30, 1995. The fronts feature a full-color player photo along with the Sprint logo in the upper left corner and the Scoreboard logo in the upper right corner. The bottom of the card features in red lettering the amount the card is worth along with the player's name. The horizontal back features information on how to use the card. The phone cards are unnumbered and checklisted below in alphabetical order.

COMPLETE SET (6) 2.50 6.00
STATED ODDS 1:7 RETAIL JUMBOS
1 Yinka Dare .40 1.00
2 Jason Kidd 2.00 5.00
3 Donyell Marshall .40 1.00
4 Eric Montross .40 1.00
5 Glenn Robinson .75 2.00
6 Jalen Rose 1.00 2.50

1994 Classic Picks

This five-card standard-size set was randomly inserted in packs. The fronts feature color-action player cutouts superimposed on a metallized background. The player's name appears on the bottom, while the words "Classic Pick" are printed at the top. On a ghosted background, the backs carry a small color player portrait, along with a short biography and a player profile. 20,000 football and hockey sets were produced while 24,900 basketball and four-sport were produced. The football picks (1-5) were found in the football draft picks packs; the basketball picks (6-10) were in the basketball draft pick packs; the hockey picks (11-15) were in the hockey draft pick packs while the four-sport picks (16-25) were in four-sport packs. We are pricing only the basketball cards in this section.

COMPLETE SET (5) 6.00 15.00
STATED ODDS 1:72 HOBBY
6 Glenn Robinson 1.50 4.00
7 Jason Kidd 4.00 10.00
8 Grant Hill 4.00 10.00
9 Eric Montross .75 2.00
10 Juwan Howard 1.25 3.00

1994 Classic ROY Sweepstakes

Randomly inserted in foil and jumbo packs, these 20 standard-size cards feature color action player cutouts on a borderless basketball background. A silhouette of a player appears to the left. The player's name appears within a gold-foil stripe near the bottom. Also in gold foil is the number of cards produced, 6,225. The card of the player selected Rookie of the Year was redeemable for an uncut Vitale's PTPers set sheet as well as a bonus card. This offer expired 7/15/95. The cards are numbered on the back with an "ROY" prefix.

COMPLETE SET (20) 15.00 40.00
STATED ODDS 1:72 HOB/RET
1 Glenn Robinson 2.50 6.00
2 Jason Kidd 6.00 15.00
3 Grant Hill 6.00 15.00
4 Sharone Wright .40 1.00
5 Juwan Howard 2.00 5.00
6 Monty Williams .40 1.00
7 Khalid Reeves .40 1.00
8 Eddie Jones 4.00 10.00
9 Clifford Rozier .40 1.00
10 Aaron McKie .40 1.00
11 Eric Montross .40 1.00
12 Askia Jones .40 1.00
13 Yinka Dare .40 1.00
14 Dontonio Wingfield .40 1.00
15 Carlos Rogers .40 1.00
16 Eric Piatkowski .50 1.25
17 Charlie Ward .40 1.00
18 Deon Thomas .40 1.00
19 Dickey Simpkins .40 1.00
20 Field Card/Vitale .50 1.25

1994 Classic Vitale's PTPers

Randomly inserted in packs, these 15 standard-size cards feature on their borderless metallic fronts color player action cutouts set on multicolored backgrounds. The player's name appears within a colored stripe across the bottom. The back carries a color player action shot on the right and career highlights on a yellow panel on the left. A color cutout of Dick Vitale and his facsimile autograph at the bottom round out the card. The cards are numbered on the back with a "PTP" prefix.

COMPLETE SET (15) 6.00 15.00
STATED ODDS 1:24 HOBBY
1 Glenn Robinson 1.00 2.50
2 Jason Kidd 2.50 6.00
3 Grant Hill 2.50 6.00
4 Sharone Wright .50 1.25
5 Juwan Howard .75 2.00
6 Billy McCaffrey .50 1.25
7 Khalid Reeves .50 1.25
8 Eddie Jones 1.50 4.00
9 Clifford Rozier .50 1.25
10 Charlie Ward .50 1.25
11 Eric Montross .50 1.25
12 Wesley Person .50 1.25
13 Yinka Dare .50 1.25
14 Dontonio Wingfield .50 1.25
15 Carlos Rogers .50 1.25

1994 Classic International Promos

This four-card standard-size set was given away during the International Sportscard and Memorabilia Expo at the Anaheim Convention Center July 19-24, 1994. The fronts display full-bleed color action shots. The player's name appears in red print on a black bar near the bottom. On a dark screened background, the backs carry the logo for the card show. The cards are unnumbered and checklisted below in alphabetical order.

COMPLETE SET (4) 3.00 8.00
4 Grant Hill BK 1.00 2.50

1994 Classic National Promos

This five-card standard-size set was issued to promote the 15th National Sports Collectors Convention in Houston August 4-7, 1994. The fronts display full-bleed color action shots. The player's name appears in red print on a black bar near the bottom. On a dark screened background, the backs carry a gold foil National Convention logo. The Hill card was given out on Exhibitor Preview Night, as noted on its back. The cards are unnumbered and checklisted below in alphabetical order.

COMPLETE SET (5) 6.00 15.00
2 Grant Hill BK 2.00 5.00
3 Jason Kidd BK 1.50 4.00

1995 Classic Previews

This five-card set measures the standard size. Both a hobby and retail set were produced and inserted at a rate of one per box in both the 1995 Classic Assets Gold and 1995 NFL ProLine boxes. This set was also available via a redemption offer in 1995 Images packs. The fronts feature borderless color action player photos with the player's name below. The hobby version has a aqua printer's proof logo while the retail version carries a silver foil signature across the bottom above the player's name. The backs show another player action photo with the player's name, position, biographical information, and career statistics. Sponsors' logos are below. The cards are numbered on the back with prefixes of RP for the retail version and HP for the hobby version.

COMPLETE SET (5) 2.00 5.00
1 Ed O'Bannon .40 1.00
2 Corliss Williamson .40 1.00
3 Joe Smith .50 1.25
4 Rasheed Wallace 1.25 3.00
5 Damon Stoudamire 1.00 2.50

1995 Classic

The 1995 Classic Basketball Rookies set was issued in one series of cards totalling 120 standard-size cards and showcases the best collection of rookie basketball talent. Every card has a unique innovative design with two-color foil stamping. The fronts feature a borderless color action player photo with the player's name across the bottom. The backs carry a color action player shot on the left with the player's name, career highlights, biographical information, and statistics on the right.

COMPLETE SET (120) 4.00 10.00
1 Joe Smith .15 .40
2 Antonio McDyess .15 .40
3 Jerry Stackhouse .40 1.00
4 Rasheed Wallace .40 1.00
5 Kevin Garnett 1.00 2.50
6 Damon Stoudamire .30 .75
7 Shawn Respert .12 .30
8 Ed O'Bannon .12 .30
9 Kurt Thomas .12 .30
10 Gary Trent .12 .30
11 Cherokee Parks .12 .30
12 Corliss Williamson .12 .30
13 Eric Williams .12 .30
14 Brent Barry .20 .50
15 Bob Sura .12 .30
16 Theo Ratliff .20 .50
17 Randolph Childress .12 .30
18 Jason Caffey .12 .30
19 Michael Finley .40 1.00
20 George Zidek .12 .30
21 Travis Best .12 .30
22 Loren Meyer .12 .30
23 David Vaughn .12 .30
24 Sherrell Ford .12 .30
25 Mario Bennett .12 .30
26 Greg Ostertag .12 .30
27 Cory Alexander .12 .30
28 Lou Roe .12 .30
29 Dragan Tarlac .12 .30
30 Terrence Rencher .12 .30
31 Junior Burrough .12 .30
32 Andrew DeClercq .12 .30
33 Jimmy King .12 .30
34 Lawrence Moten .12 .30
35 Frankie King .12 .30
36 Rashard Griffith .12 .30
37 Donny Marshall .12 .30
38 Julius Michalik .12 .30
39 Erik Meeks .12 .30
40 Donnie Boyce .12 .30
41 Eric Snow .12 .30
42 Anthony Pelle .12 .30
43 Troy Brown .12 .30
44 George Banks .12 .30
45 Tyus Edney .12 .30
46 Mark Davis .12 .30
47 Jerome Allen .12 .30
48 Fred Hoiberg .12 .30
49 Constantin Popa .12 .30
50 Erwin Claggett .12 .30
51 Michael McDonald .12 .30
52 Andre Riddick .12 .30
53 Cuonzo Martin .12 .30
54 Don Reid .12 .30
55 James Forrest .12 .30
56 Glen Whisby .12 .30
57 Dwight Stewart .12 .30
58 Jamal Faulkner .12 .30
59 Tom Kleinschmidt .12 .30
60 Donald Williams .12 .30
61 Dan Cross .12 .30
62 Rick Brunson .12 .30
63 Corey Beck .12 .30
64 Lance Hughes .12 .30
65 Bernard Blunt .12 .30
66 Clint McDaniel .12 .30
67 John Amaechi .12 .30
68 Lorenzo Orr .12 .30
69 Randy Rutherford .12 .30
70 Ray Jackson .12 .30
71 Reggie Jackson .12 .30
72 Russell Larson .12 .30
73 Carlin Warley .12 .30
74 James Scott .12 .30
75 Roderick Anderson .12 .30
76 Antoine Gillespie .12 .30
77 Gerald King .12 .30
78 Petey Sessoms .12 .30
79 Steve Payne .12 .30
80 William Gates .12 .30
81 Arthur Agee .12 .30
82 Rebecca Lobo .20 .50
83 Devin Gray .12 .30
84 Scotty Thurman .12 .30
85 Matt Maloney .12 .30
86 Michael Evans .12 .30
87 LaZelle Durden .12 .30
88 Ronnie McMahan .12 .30
89 Ed O'Bannon AW .05 .15
90 Mario Bennett AW .05 .15
91 Randolph Childress AW .05 .15
92 Rasheed Wallace AW .20 .50
93 Lawrence Moten AW .05 .15
94 Shawn Respert AW .05 .15
95 Lou Roe AW .05 .15
96 Damon Stoudamire AW .15 .40
97 Gary Trent AW .05 .15
98 Corliss Williamson AW .05 .15
99 Jerry Stackhouse AW .20 .50
100 Glenn Robinson AR .10 .25
101 Jason Kidd AR .20 .50
102 Juwan Howard AR .12 .30
103 Brian Grant AR .10 .25
104 Eddie Jones AR .15 .40
105 Shaquille O'Neal CA .30 .75
106 Dikembe Mutombo CA .12 .30
107 Alonzo Mourning CA .15 .40
108 Hakeem Olajuwon CA .15 .40
109 Cherokee Parks SS .05 .15
110 Corliss Williamson SS .05 .15
111 Shawn Respert SS .05 .15
112 Bob Sura SS .05 .15
113 Michael Finley SS .20 .50
114 Greg Ostertag SS .05 .15
115 Lou Roe SS .05 .15
116 Loren Meyer SS .05 .15
117 Mario Bennett SS .05 .15
118 Cuonzo Martin SS .05 .15
119 Joe Smith CL .07 .20
120 Jerry Stackhouse CL .20 .50

1995 Classic Gold Foil

*GOLD FOIL: 1.2X TO 3X BASE CARD HI

1995 Classic Printer's Proofs

*PROOFS: 4X TO 10X BASIC CARDS
ANNOUNCED PRINT RUN 949 SETS

1995 Classic Silver Foil

*SILVER FOIL: .75X TO 2X BASE CARD HI

1995 Classic Silver Signatures

*SILVER: 2.5X TO 6X BASIC CARDS
RANDOM INSERTS IN PACKS

1995 Classic Autographs

This set was randomly inserted in boxes of Classic Basketball Rookies at the rate of one to a box. The fronts feature a borderless player action photo with an autograph above the player's printed name. The backs have a congratulations message printed on a background of the bottom view of a basketball net. The Auto Edition autograph cards are not sequentially numbered. They currently have the same value as the cards in the regular rookies packs. Some of the Auto Edition autograph cards are numbered out of 200, these cards were inserted one per box. Ed O'Bannon and Dikembe Mutombo only had Auto Edition cards produced.

ONE PER HOBBY BOX
STATED PRINT RUNS LISTED BELOW
1 Joe Smith/1230 3.00 8.00
2 Antonio McDyess/1270 4.00 10.00
2A Antonio McDyess/1975 4.00 10.00
3 Jerry Stackhouse/2370 6.00 15.00
4 Rasheed Wallace/1275 6.00 15.00
6 Damon Stoudamire/1255 4.00 10.00
7 Shawn Respert/1275 1.25 3.00
8A Ed O'Bannon 2.00 5.00
9 Kurt Thomas/3420 1.25 3.00
10 Gary Trent/3465 1.25 3.00
11 Cherokee Parks/2630 2.00 5.00
12 Corliss Williamson/3355 1.25 3.00
13 Eric Williams/2435 1.25 3.00
14 Brent Barry/2690 2.00 5.00
15 Bob Sura/3410 1.25 3.00
16 Theo Ratliff/3310 2.00 5.00
17 Randolph Childress/1260 1.25 3.00
18 Jason Caffey/2500 1.25 3.00
19 Michael Finley/3695 5.00 12.00
19A Michael Finley/5900 4.00 10.00
20 George Zidek/2650 1.25 3.00
21 Travis Best/1990 1.25 3.00
22 Loren Meyer/2920 1.25 3.00
23 David Vaughn/3320 1.25 3.00
24 Sherrell Ford/3635 1.25 3.00
25 Mario Bennett/2620 1.25 3.00
26 Greg Ostertag/2600 1.25 3.00
27 Cory Alexander/3335 1.25 3.00
28 Lou Roe/2845 1.25 3.00
30 Terrence Rencher/3275 1.25 3.00
31 Junior Burrough/3220 1.25 3.00
32 Andrew DeClercq/4080 2.00 5.00
33 Jimmy King/3740 4.00 10.00
34 Lawrence Moten/1715 1.25 3.00
35 Frankie King/3330 1.25 3.00
37 Donny Marshall/4000 1.25 3.00
38 Julius Michalik/3240 1.25 3.00
39 Erik Meeks/3165 1.25 3.00
40 Donnie Boyce/3100 1.25 3.00
41 Eric Snow/3980 1.25 3.00
43 Troy Brown/3340 1.25 3.00
44 George Banks/3240 1.25 3.00
45 Tyus Edney/3600 1.25 3.00
46 Mark Davis/3475 1.25 3.00
47 Jerome Allen/3700 1.25 3.00
48 Fred Hoiberg/4080 1.25 3.00
49 Constantin Popa/3275 1.25 3.00
50 Erwin Claggett/3300 1.25 3.00
52 Andre Riddick/3215 1.25 3.00
53 Cuonzo Martin/3280 1.25 3.00
54 Don Reid/2700 1.25 3.00
55 James Forrest 1.50 4.00
57 Dwight Stewart/3445 1.25 3.00
58 Jamal Faulkner/3250 1.25 3.00
59 Tom Kleinschmidt/3250 1.25 3.00
60 Donald Williams/2095 1.25 3.00
61 Dan Cross/3320 1.25 3.00
62 Rick Brunson/3780 1.25 3.00
63 Corey Beck/3155 1.25 3.00
64 Lance Hughes/3500 1.25 3.00
65 Bernard Blunt/3230 1.25 3.00
66 Clint McDaniel/3570 1.25 3.00
67 John Amaechi/3375 1.25 3.00
68 Lorenzo Orr/2870 1.25 3.00
69 Randy Rutherford/3180 1.25 3.00
70 Ray Jackson/3430 5.00 12.00
71 Reggie Jackson/2085 1.25 3.00
72 Russell Larson/3430 1.25 3.00
73 Carlin Warley/3215 1.25 3.00
76 Antoine Gillespie/3320 1.25 3.00
77 Gerald King/3945 1.25 3.00
78 Petey Sessoms/2135 1.25 3.00
79 Steve Payne/3170 1.25 3.00
80 William Gates/3290 1.25 3.00
81 Arthur Agee/3285 1.25 3.00
84 Scotty Thurman/3975 3.00 8.00
85 Matt Maloney/2800 1.25 3.00
86 Michael Evans/3310 1.25 3.00
87 LaZelle Durden/2400 1.25 3.00
88 Ronnie McMahan/3490 1.25 3.00
101 Jason Kidd/300 15.00 40.00
101A Jason Kidd/200 15.00 40.00
102 Juwan Howard/285 6.00 15.00
102A Juwan Howard/200 6.00 15.00
105 Shaquille O'Neal/400 30.00 80.00
105A Shaquille O'Neal/200 30.00 80.00
106A Dikembe Mutombo 6.00 15.00
107 Alonzo Mourning/2550 12.50 30.00

1995 Classic Big Time

This 10-card insert set was randomly inserted into specially marked retail packs of 1995 Classic Basketball Rookies. Each of the ten cards highlights an NBA new-comer who is expected to do well in the "Big Time". The cards are numbered with a "BT" prefix on the back.

COMPLETE SET (10) 8.00 20.00
RANDOM INSERTS IN RETAIL PACKS
BT1 Joe Smith .60 1.50
BT2 Antonio McDyess .60 1.50
BT3 Jerry Stackhouse 1.50 4.00
BT4 Rasheed Wallace 1.50 4.00
BT5 Kevin Garnett 4.00 10.00
BT6 Damon Stoudamire 1.25 3.00
BT7 Shawn Respert .50 1.25
BT8 Ed O'Bannon .50 1.25
BT9 Gary Trent .50 1.25
BT10 Cherokee Parks .50 1.25

1995 Classic Center Stage

Randomly inserted in hobby packs, this 10-card standard-size set captures outstanding college players. The fronts display a color action cut out on a metallic background. Each card is hand-numbered out of 1,750 produced. The backs have a second color photo and a player profile. The cards are numbered with a "CS" prefix.

COMPLETE SET (10) 25.00 60.00
STATED PRINT RUN 1750 SETS
CS1 Joe Smith 2.00 5.00
CS2 Antonio McDyess 2.00 5.00
CS3 Rasheed Wallace 5.00 12.00
CS4 Kevin Garnett 12.00 30.00
CS5 Damon Stoudamire 4.00 10.00
CS6 Ed O'Bannon 1.50 4.00
CS7 Gary Trent 1.50 4.00
CS8 Corliss Williamson 1.50 4.00
CS9 Jerry Stackhouse 5.00 12.00
CS10 Randolph Childress 1.50 4.00

1995 Classic Clear Cuts

The first five cards were randomly inserted in hobby "Hot Boxes," while the second five were included in retail "Hot Boxes." These cards have a color player action cutout superposed on a colored transparent stock that is die cut along the right edge. The backs have the mirror image of the fronts. The hobby cards have a "CCH" prefix while the retail cards have a "CCR" prefix.

COMPLETE SET (10) 30.00 60.00
CCR INSERTS IN RETAIL HOT BOXES
CCH1 Shaquille O'Neal 4.00 10.00
CCH2 Joe Smith 2.00 5.00
CCH3 Rasheed Wallace 5.00 12.00
CCH4 Kevin Garnett 12.00 30.00
CCH5 Corliss Williamson 1.50 4.00
CCR1 Jason Kidd 2.50 6.00
CCR2 Ed O'Bannon 1.50 4.00
CCR3 Antonio McDyess 2.00 5.00
CCR4 Damon Stoudamire 4.00 10.00
CCR5 Shawn Respert 1.50 4.00

1995 Classic Draft Day

Randomly inserted in retail jumbo packs, this 14-card standard-size set focuses on top NBA draft choices. The fronts feature color action player photos while the backs carry player information.

COMPLETE SET (14) 1.50 4.00
STATED ODDS 1:16 RETAIL JUMBOS
1 Joe Smith .12 .30
2 Joe Smith-Warriors .12 .30
3 Joe Smith .12 .30
4 Rasheed Wallace .30 .75
5 Rasheed Wallace .30 .75
6 Rasheed Wallace .30 .75
7 Ed O'Bannon .10 .25
8 Ed O'Bannon .10 .25
9 Ed O'Bannon .10 .25
10 Corliss Williamson .10 .25
11 Corliss Williamson .10 .25
12 Corliss Williamson .10 .25
13 Kidd/Hill ROY .40 1.00
14 Checklist .10 .25

1995 Classic Draft Day Autographs

PRINT RUN 1995 SER.#'d SETS
NNO Rasheed Wallace 8.00 20.00

1995 Classic Instant Energy

This 20-card set was randomly inserted at a rate of one per retail jumbo pack. The fronts feature a color action player cut-out on a metallic background of lightning and a basketball court during a game. The player's name, team, and card name appear in an aqua and silver stripe at the bottom. The backs carry another player cut-out on a lightning background with a short career summary.

COMPLETE SET (20) 4.00 10.00
IE1 Joe Smith .30 .75
IE2 Antonio McDyess .30 .75
IE3 Jerry Stackhouse .75 2.00
IE4 Rasheed Wallace .75 2.00
IE5 Kevin Garnett 2.00 5.00
IE6 Damon Stoudamire .60 1.50
IE7 Shawn Respert .25 .60
IE8 Ed O'Bannon .25 .60
IE9 Kurt Thomas .25 .60
IE10 Gary Trent .25 .60
IE11 Cherokee Parks .25 .60
IE12 Corliss Williamson .25 .60
IE13 Eric Williams .25 .60
IE14 Brent Barry .40 1.00
IE15 Bob Sura .25 .60
IE16 Theo Ratliff .40 1.00
IE17 Randolph Childress .25 .60
IE18 Jason Caffey .25 .60
IE19 Michael Finley .75 2.00
IE20 George Zidek .25 .60

1995 Classic Phone Cards $4

This 5-card set, randomly inserted in retail packs, is made up of fully functional phone cards; however, they expired 10/1/96. The fronts contain color photos of the player on a phone-card sized, rounded corner, plastic stock card. The backs contain information on how to use the card. They are individually numbered out of 6334.

COMPLETE SET (5) 8.00 20.00
RANDOM INSERTS IN RETAIL PACKS
1 Joe Smith 1.00 2.50
2 Antonio McDyess 1.00 2.50
3 Jerry Stackhouse 2.50 6.00
4 Kevin Garnett 6.00 15.00
5 Rasheed Wallace 2.50 6.00

1995 Classic ROY Candidates

This 5-card insert set was randomly inserted into retail packs of 1995 Classic Basketball Rookies. Each of the five cards highlights a potential NBA Rookie of the Year for the 1995-96 season. (Damon Stoudamire ended up with the trophy, with Jerry Stackhouse as a not-so-distant runner-up.)

COMPLETE SET (5) 2.00 5.00
STATED ODDS 1:16 RETAIL JUMBOS
1 Joe Smith .40 1.00
2 Antonio McDyess .40 1.00
3 Jerry Stackhouse 1.00 2.50
4 Rasheed Wallace 1.00 2.50
5 Damon Stoudamire .75 2.00

1995 Classic ROY Redemptions

Inserted at a rate of 1 per 72 packs, these 20 standard-size cards feature a borderless color player action photo with the player's name above "Rookie of the Year" in gold on the left. The backs carry the player's name and instructions on how to participate in the redemption program. A checklist is listed below the instructions. The cards are numbered with a "ROY" prefix.

COMPLETE SET (20) 12.00 30.00
STATED ODDS 1:72 HOB/1:108 RET
1 Joe Smith 1.00 2.50
2 Rasheed Wallace 2.50 6.00
3 Ed O'Bannon .75 2.00
4 Antonio McDyess 1.00 2.50
5 Shawn Respert .75 2.00
6 Mario Bennett .75 2.00
7 Jerry Stackhouse 2.50 6.00
8 Cherokee Parks .75 2.00
9 Damon Stoudamire 2.00 5.00
10 Kurt Thomas .75 2.00
11 Randolph Childress .75 2.00
12 Brent Barry 1.25 3.00
13 Corliss Williamson .75 2.00
14 Gary Trent .75 2.00
15 Bob Sura .75 2.00
16 David Vaughn .75 2.00
17 Michael Finley 2.50 6.00
18 Rashard Griffith .75 2.00
19 Lou Roe .75 2.00
20 Field Card .75 2.00

1995 Classic Showtime

Each of these 20 standard-size cards was randomly inserted in retail packs. On a metallic background with color streaks radiating from a row of stage lights, the fronts display a color action player cutout. On a similar design, the backs have a player profile at top and a second color photo at the bottom. Card number S4 was originally going to be Kevin Garnett, but the card does not exist. The cards are numbered with a "S" prefix.

COMPLETE SET (19) 12.00 30.00
STATED ODDS 1:216 RETAIL
S1 Joe Smith 1.00 2.50
S2 Antonio McDyess 1.00 2.50
S3 Rasheed Wallace 2.50 6.00
S5 Shawn Respert .75 2.00
S6 Kurt Thomas .75 2.00
S7 Gary Trent .75 2.00
S8 Cherokee Parks .75 2.00
S9 Eric Williams .75 2.00
S10 Jerry Stackhouse 2.50 6.00
S11 Travis Best .75 2.00
S12 Michael Finley 2.50 6.00
S13 George Zidek .75 2.00
S14 David Vaughn .75 2.00
S15 Mario Bennett .75 2.00
S16 Greg Ostertag .75 2.00
S17 Bob Sura .75 2.00
S18 Lou Roe .75 2.00
S19 Tyus Edney .75 2.00
S20 Jimmy King .75 2.00

1995 Classic Spotlight

Random inserts in auto edition packs, this 10-card set measures the standard size. The fronts display a color action player photo with a blurred background. The player's name and card name round out the front. The backs carry a single player photo with the player's name and a short career summary. The cards are numbered with a "RS" prefix.

COMPLETE SET (10) 5.00 12.00
STATED ODDS 1:5 AUTO EDITION
RS1 Joe Smith .50 1.25
RS2 Antonio McDyess .50 1.25
RS3 Jason Kidd 1.25 3.00
RS4 Rasheed Wallace 1.25 3.00
RS5 Kevin Garnett 3.00 8.00
RS6 Damon Stoudamire 1.00 2.50
RS7 Ed O'Bannon .40 1.00
RS8 Shawn Respert .40 1.00
RS9 Kurt Thomas .40 1.00
RS10 Randolph Childress .40 1.00

1995 Classic Stackhouse Showtime

This 5-card insert set was randomly inserted into specially marked retail packs of 1995 Classic Basketball Rookies. Each of the five cards highlights NBA new-comer and ex-Tar Heel, Jerry Stackhouse. The cards are numbered with an "S" prefix on the back.

COMPLETE SET (5) 6.00 15.00
COMMON CARD (S1-S5) 2.00 5.00
RANDOM INSERTS IN RETAIL PACKS

1995 Classic National

This 20-card multi-sport set was issued by Classic to commemorate the 16th National Sports Collectors Convention in St. Louis. The set included a certificate of limited edition, with the serial number out of 9,995 sets produced. One thousand Sprint 20-minute phone cards featuring Ki-Jana Carter and Nolan Ryan were also distributed.

COMPLETE SET (20) 8.00 20.00
NC1 Shaquille O'Neal 2.00 5.00
NC7 Glenn Robinson .20 .50
NC9 Jason Kidd 1.00 2.50
NC14 Alonzo Mourning .60 1.50
NC16 Joe Smith .20 .50
NC17 Rasheed Wallace .40 1.00
NC18 Ed O'Bannon .20 .50
NC19 Corliss Williamson .20 .50

1992-93 Classic C3

Limited to only 25,000 members, the Classic Collectors Club (also known as C3) featured two types of memberships: 1) the Presidential Charter membership (5,000), and 2) the Charter membership (20,000). As a bonus, the first 10,000 members received three packs of the bilingual edition of the 1991 Classic Draft Picks Collection. Exclusive to Presidential members were the following: a Brien Taylor autograph card (hand numbered "X/5,000"); an uncut sheet of either 1992 baseball, football, or hockey draft picks; and three special promo cards. In addition to other items (promo cards, T-shirt, newsletter, membership card, and posters), all members received a 30-card standard-size multi-sport set featuring tomorrow's future stars. Each set was accompanied by a certificate of limited edition, giving the set serial number and total production run (25,000). The sports represented are baseball (1-7, 25-27), basketball (8-13), football (14-20), hockey (21-24), track and field (28), and swimming (29).

COMP.FACT SET (30) 6.00 15.00
8 Alonzo Mourning 1.25 3.00
9 Christian Laettner .40 1.00
10 Jimmy Jackson .40 1.00
11 Harold Miner .30 .75
12 Billy Owens .40 1.00
13 Dikembe Mutombo .50 1.25

1993 Classic C3 Promos

Members of the Classic Collectors Club received one standard-size promo card with each newsletter. Although these promo cards have different designs, they share having a "C3" gold foil stamped on their fronts. The production run was 25,000 for each card. The O'Neal card is full-bleed on its front, with a gray stripe running near the left edge. Except for a narrowly-cropped photo, the back has a silver background and presents biography and player profile. The Webber card has simulated pinewood borders on the card front. The simulated pinewood design continues on the horizontal back, which carries brief biography and a narrow-cropped color action shot along the left side.

COMPLETE SET (2) 4.00 10.00
PR1 Shaquille O'Neal 3.00 8.00
PR2 Chris Webber 2.00 5.00

1993-94 Classic C3 Gold Crown Cut Lasercut

Along with the 20-card set checklisted below, the 10,000 members of the 1994 Classic Collectors Gold Crown Club received a 1994 C3 T-shirt, a TONX milk caps collectible sheet, a Classic Games magnet, and a 1994 C3 membership card. In later mailings they also received a 1993 Basketball Draft uncut sheet, a Chris Webber poster, and an autographed card of Jamal Mashburn, along with two promo cards. The sports represented are basketball (1-6), football (7-13), baseball (14-17), and hockey (18-20). The unnumbered checklist carries the set's production number out of the 10,000 produced.

COMPLETE SET (21) 10.00 25.00
1 Chris Webber .75 2.00
2 Anfernee Hardaway .60 1.50
3 Jamal Mashburn .40 1.00
4 Isaiah Rider .40 1.00
5 Rodney Rogers .40 1.00
6 Toni Kukoc .40 1.00

1994 Classic C3 Gold Crown Club

Part of a special issue to Classic Collector's Club members, these standard-size cards feature on their fronts color player action shots that are borderless, except at the bottom, where the player's name appears. His first name is shown at the bottom left within a gray rectangle, which is actually a vertically distorted and ghosted black-and-white player action shot. The last name is shown within a black rectangle edging the bottom right. Another vertically distorted black-and-white player action shot forms a stripe that roughly bisects the back. A color player action shot appears on the left side; the player's name and statistics are shown vertically within white and black panels on the right. As part of the 1994 Classic Collectors Gold Crown Club offer, members also received one of 10,000 individually numbered standard-size white bordered autographed card of Jamal Mashburn. His autograph in blue ink appears across the card face. The back carries the C3 logo and a congratulatory message.

COMPLETE SET (4) 6.00 15.00
CC1 Alonzo Mourning 1.25 3.00
CC4 Donyell Marshall .75 2.00
NNO Jamal Mashburn AU/10000 6.00 15.00

1995 Classic Five Sport

The 1995 Classic Five Sport set was issued in one series of 200 standard-size cards. Cards were issued in 10-card regular packs (SRP $1.99). Boxes contained 36 packs. One autographed card was guaranteed in each pack and one certified autographed card (with an embossed logo) appeared in each box. There were also memorabilia redemption cards included in some packs and were guaranteed in at least one pack per box. The cards are numbered and divided into the five sports as follows: Basketball (1-42), Football (43-92), Baseball (93-122), Hockey (123-160), Racing (161-180), Alma Maters (181-190), Picture Perfect (191-200).

COMPLETE SET (200) 6.00 15.00
1 Joe Smith .15 .40
2 Antonio McDyess .20 .50
3 Jerry Stackhouse .30 .75
4 Rasheed Wallace .30 .75
5 Kevin Garnett 1.00 2.50
6 Damon Stoudamire .15 .40
7 Shawn Respert .05 .15
8 Ed O'Bannon .05 .15
9 Kurt Thomas .08 .25
10 Gary Trent .05 .15
11 Cherokee Parks .05 .15
12 Corliss Williamson .08 .25
13 Eric Williams .05 .15
14 Brent Barry .08 .25
15 Bob Sura .07 .20
16 Theo Ratliff .08 .25
17 Randolph Childress .05 .15
18 Jason Caffey .05 .15
19 Michael Finley .20 .50
20 George Zidek .05 .15
21 Travis Best .05 .15
22 Loren Meyer .05 .15
23 David Vaughn .05 .15
24 Sherrell Ford .05 .15
25 Mario Bennett .05 .15
26 Greg Ostertag .15 .40
27 Cory Alexander .05 .15
28 Lou Roe .05 .15
29 Dragan Tarlac .05 .15
30 Terrence Rencher .05 .15
31 Junior Burrough .05 .15
32 Andrew DeClercq .05 .15
33 Jimmy King .05 .15
34 Lawrence Moten .05 .15
35 Donny Marshall .05 .15
36 Eric Snow .15 .40
37 Anthony Pelle .05 .15
38 Tyus Edney .05 .15
39 Jerome Allen .05 .15
40 Fred Hoiberg .05 .15
41 Constantin Popa .05 .15
42 Rebecca Lobo .15 .40
181 Stackhouse Hitchcock .15 .40
182 McDyess Williams .10 .30
183 Garciaparra Best .40 1.00
184 DeClercq K.J.Carter .07 .20
185 Wheatley King .10 .30
186 J.J. Stokes O'Bannon .10 .30
187 Sapp Popa .10 .30
189 E.Williams Breen .05 .15
190 Sura Alexander .05 .15
192 Hakeem Olajuwon .15 .40
198 Jason Kidd .25 .60
199 Shaquille O'Neal .40 1.00
200 Alonzo Mourning .15 .40

1995 Classic Five Sport Silver Die Cuts

COMPLETE SET (200) 12.00 30.00
*SILVER DC: .8X TO 2X BASIC CARDS

1995 Classic Five Sport Autographs

This set was randomly inserted into packs and is a signed version of the basic issue cards. The backs carry a "Congratulations" message stating that it is an autographed 1995 Five Sport Autograph Edition Card with the sport's ball pictured at the bottom. The cards are unnumbered. Many of these autographed cards were later re-issued in 1995-96 Classic Five Sport Signings witha a slightly different cardback that reads "...Received a Limited-Edition Autographed Card." This message is the same one used on the Hot Box Autographs but these Five Sport Signings Autographs are not serial numbered on the back.

*SIGNINGS VERSION: .4X TO 1X
1 Joe Smith 2.00 5.00
2 Antonio McDyess SP 8.00 20.00
4 Rasheed Wallace SP 15.00 30.00
6 Damon Stoudamire SP 8.00 20.00
8 Ed O'Bannon 2.00 5.00
9 Kurt Thomas 2.00 5.00
11 Cherokee Parks 2.00 5.00
14 Brent Barry SP 2.00 5.00
15 Bob Sura 2.00 5.00
16 Theo Ratliff 2.50 6.00
17 Randolph Childress SP 2.00 5.00
19 Michael Finley 3.00 8.00
20 George Zidek 2.00 5.00
24 Sherrell Ford 2.00 5.00
27 Cory Alexander 2.00 5.00
30 Terrence Rencher 2.00 5.00
32 Andrew DeClercq SP 2.00 5.00
35 Donny Marshall 2.00 5.00
36 Eric Snow 2.00 5.00
37 Anthony Pelle 2.00 5.00
38 Tyus Edney 2.00 5.00
39 Jerome Allen 2.00 5.00
40 Fred Hoiberg 2.00 5.00
41 Constantin Popa 2.00 5.00
192 Hakeem Olajuwon SP 10.00 25.00
198 Jason Kidd SP 15.00 30.00
199 Shaquille O'Neal SP 40.00 80.00
200 Alonzo Mourning SP 20.00 40.00

1995 Classic Five Sport Autographs Numbered

Cards in this set were issued primarily in 1995-96 Classic Five Sport Signings packs and are essentially a parallel verson of the basic 1995 Classic Five Sport Autographs insert. The only differences are in the hand serial numbering on the cardbacks (of 225 or 295) and the embossing crimp on the card's corner.

2 Antonio McDyess/225 12.50 30.00
4 Rasheed Wallace/225 30.00 60.00
6 Damon Stoudamire/225 15.00 30.00
14 Brent Barry/225 4.00 10.00
19 Michael Finley/225 20.00 40.00
192 Hakeem Olajuwon/225 25.00 50.00
198 Jason Kidd/225 30.00 60.00
199 Shaquille O'Neal/225 40.00 80.00

1995 Classic Five Sport Classic Standouts

Randomly inserted in regular packs at a rate of one in 216, this 10-card standard-size set features both the hot new stars and the established elite of all five sports. Fronts have full-color action player cutouts set against a gold and black foil background. The player's name is printed in gold foil at the top. Backs contain a full-color action shot with the player's name printed in yellow and a career highlights box. The cards are numbered with a "CS" prefix.

COMPLETE SET (10) 15.00 40.00
CS1 Joe Smith 1.25 3.00
CS2 Rebecca Lobo 1.25 3.00
CS6 Jerry Stackhouse 2.00 5.00
CS8 Rasheed Wallace 1.50 4.00

1995 Classic Five Sport Fast Track

Randomly inserted in retail packs, this 20-card standard-size set spotlights the young stars of sports who are fast becoming major stars. Borderless fronts contain a player in full-color action while the rest of the shot is printed in colored foil. Backs have a color action shot in one box and two color separted boxes with the rest of the photo. A player profile appears underneath the photo. The cards are numbered with a "FT" prefix.

COMPLETE SET (20) 15.00 40.00
FT1 Joe Smith .75 2.00
FT3 Jason Kidd 2.50 6.00
FT6 Jerry Stackhouse 1.25 3.00
FT7 Shawn Respert .40 1.00
FT9 Rasheed Wallace .75 2.00
FT10 Ed O'Bannon .50 1.25
FT12 Kevin Garnett 6.00 15.00
FT16 Antonio McDyess 1.25 3.00
FT18 Damon Stoudamire 1.25 3.00
FT20 Corliss Williamson .60 1.50

1995 Classic Five Sport Hot Box Autographs

This set of six autographed standard-sized cards were randomly inserted in Hobby Hot boxes. The cards are nearly identical to the basic Five Sports Autographs with the exception of the hand written serial number on the backs and the slightly different congratulatory message on the back that reads "...Received a Limited-Edition Autographed Card."

4 Jason Kidd/650 10.00 25.00
6 Shaquille O'Neal/655 40.00 80.00

1995 Classic Five Sport On Fire

Ten of the 20-cards in this set were released in Hobby Hot Packs while the other ten were released in retail Hot packs. Fronts have full-color player cutouts set against a flame background with the On Fire logo printed at the bottom. The player's name is printed vertically in white type on the left side. backs feature biography and players's statistics.

COMPLETE SET (20) 30.00 80.00
H2 Joe Smith 2.50 6.00
H6 Rasheed Wallace 2.00 5.00
H7 Jerry Stackhouse 3.00 8.00
H9 Kevin Garnett 6.00 15.00
H10 Rebecca Lobo 2.50 6.00
R1 Jason Kidd 2.50 6.00
R2 Antonio McDyess 2.50 6.00

R3 Hakeem Olajuwon 2.50 6.00
R6 Ed O'Bannon 2.00 5.00

1995 Classic Five Sport Phone Cards $3

The five-card set of $3 Foncards were found one per 72 retail packs. The credit-card size plastic pieces have a borderless front with a full-color action player photo and the $3 emblem printed on the upper right in blue. The player's name is printed in white type vertically on the lower left. The Sprint logo appears on the bottom also. White backs carry information of how to place calls using the card.

COMPLETE SET (5) 4.00 8.00
5 Joe Smith .60 1.50

1995 Classic Five Sport Phone Cards $4

These cards were inserted randomly into packs at a rate of one in 72 and featured the five top prospects or performers of the individual sports. The borderless fronts feature full-color action photos with the athlete's name printed in white across the bottom. The Sprint logo and $4 are printed along the top. White backs contain information about placing calls using the card.

COMPLETE SET (5) 6.00 15.00
4 Jerry Stackhouse 1.00 2.50

1995 Classic Five Sport Previews

Randomly inserted in Classic hockey packs, this five-card standard-size set salutes the leaders and the up-and-coming rookies of the five sports. Borderless fronts have a full-color action shot with gold foil stamp of "preview" and the player's name, school and position printed vertically on the right side of the card. The player's sport's ball (or tire) is printed in a montage on the right. Backs have another full-color action shot and also a biography, statistics and profile. The cards are numbered with a "SP" prefix.

COMPLETE SET (5) 3.00 8.00
SP2 Joe Smith .40 1.00

1995 Classic Five Sport Printer's Proofs

*PRINTER PROOF/75: 4X TO 10X BASIC CARDS
STATED PRINT RUN 795 SETS

1995 Classic Five Sport Record Setters

This 10-card standard-size set was inserted in retail packs and feature the stars and rookies of the five sports. The fronts display full-bleed color action photos; the set title "Record Setters" iin prismatic block lettering appears toward the bottom. On a sepia-tone photo, the backs carry a player profile. The cards are numbered on the back with an "RS" prefix and hand-numbered out of 1250.

COMPLETE SET (10) 12.00 30.00
RS3 Ed O'Bannon .60 1.50
RS5 Joe Smith .75 2.00
RS6 Jerry Stackhouse .75 2.00
RS9 Kevin Garnett 2.50 6.00
RS10 Shaquille O'Neal 2.50 6.00

1995 Classic Five Sport Red Die Cuts

*RED DIE CUT: 1.2X TO 3X BASIC CARDS
RED DIE CUT STATED ODDS 1:8

1995 Classic Five Sport Strive For Five

This interactive game card set consists of 65 cards to be used like playing cards. Collector's gained a full suit of cards to redeem prizes. The odds of finding the card in packs were one in 10. Fronts are bordered in metallic silver foil and picture the player in full-color action. The cards are numbered on both top and bottom in silver foil and the player's name is printed vertically in silver foil. Backs have green backgrounds with the game rules printed in white type.

COMPLETE SET (65) 12.00 30.00
BK1 Joe Smith .50 1.25
BK2 Gary Trent .20 .50
BK3 Kurt Thomas .20 .50
BK4 Ed O'Bannon .20 .50
BK5 Shawn Respert .20 .50
BK6 Damon Stoudamire .75 2.00
BK7 Kevin Garnett 2.00 5.00
BK8 Rasheed Wallace .60 1.50
BK9 Antonio McDyess .60 1.50
BK10 Hakeem Olajuwon .40 .75
BK11 Jason Kidd .60 1.50
BK12 Rebecca Lobo .50 1.25
BK13 Jerry Stackhouse .50 1.25

1995-96 Classic Five Sport Signings

COMPLETE SET (100) 6.00 15.00
1 Joe Smith .20 .50
2 Antonio McDyess .25 .60
3 Jerry Stackhouse .40 1.00
4 Rasheed Wallace .40 1.00
5 Kevin Garnett 1.25 3.00
6 Damon Stoudamire .20 .50
7 Shawn Respert .07 .20
8 Ed O'Bannon .07 .20
9 Kurt Thomas .10 .30
10 Gary Trent .07 .20
11 Cherokee Parks .07 .20
12 Corliss Williamson .10 .30
13 Eric Williams .07 .20
14 Brent Barry .10 .30
15 Bob Sura .08 .25
16 Randolph Childress .07 .20
17 Michael Finley .25 .60
18 George Zidek .07 .20
19 Travis Best .07 .20
20 David Vaughn .07 .20
21 Mario Bennett .07 .20
22 Greg Ostertag .20 .50
23 Lou Roe .07 .20
24 Junior Burrough .07 .20
25 Andrew DeClercq .07 .20
26 Lawrence Moten .07 .20
27 Donny Marshall .07 .20
28 Tyus Edney .07 .20
29 Jimmy King .07 .20
30 Rebecca Lobo .20 .50
92 Hakeem Olajuwon .20 .50
98 Jason Kidd .30 .75
99 Shaquille O'Neal .50 1.25
100 Alonzo Mourning .20 .50

1995-96 Classic Five Sport Signings Blue Signature

*BLUE SIGN: 1.5X TO 4X BASIC CARDS

1995-96 Classic Five Sport Signings Red Signature

*RED SIGN: 1.5X TO 4X BASIC CARDS

1995-96 Classic Five Sport Signings Die Cuts

*DIE CUT: .8X TO 2X BASIC CARDS
STATED ODDS 1:4

1995-96 Classic Five Sport Signings Etched in Stone

This 10-card set, printed on 16-point foil board, was randomly inserted in Hot boxes only. Hot boxes were distributed at a rate of 1:5 cases.

1 Shaquille O'Neal 3.00 8.00
2 Jason Kidd 2.00 5.00
3 Scottie Pippen 1.50 4.00
4 Alonzo Mourning 1.50 4.00
10 Hakeem Olajuwon 1.50 4.00

1995-96 Classic Five Sport Signings Freshly Inked

This 30-card set was randomly inserted in 1995 Classic Five Sport Signings packs. The fronts features borderless player color action photos with the player's name printed in gold foil across the bottom. The backs carry an artist's drawing of the player with the player's name at the top.

COMPLETE SET (30) 12.00 30.00
STATED ODDS 1:10
FS1 Joe Smith .75 2.00
FS2 Antonio McDyess 1.00 2.50
FS3 George Zidek .40 1.00
FS4 Ed O'Bannon .40 1.00
FS5 Damon Stoudamire .75 2.00
FS6 Jerry Stackhouse 1.25 3.00
FS7 Cherokee Parks .40 1.00
FS8 Bob Sura .50 1.25
FS9 Rasheed Wallace 1.25 3.00
FS10 Shawn Respert .40 1.00

1991 Classic Four Sport

This 230-card multi-sport standard-size set includes all 200 draft picks players from the four Classic Draft Picks sets (football, baseball, basketball, and hockey), plus an additional 30 draft picks not previously found in these other sets. A subset within the 230 cards consists of five cards highlighting the publicized one-on-one game between Billy Owens and Larry Johnson. As an additional incentive to collectors, Classic randomly inserted over 60,000 autographed cards into the 15-card foil packs; it is claimed that each case should contain two or more autographed cards. The autographed cards feature 61 different players, approximately two-thirds of whom were hockey players. The production run for the English version was 25,000 cases, and a bilingual (French) version of the set was also produced at 20 percent of the English production.

COMPLETE SET (230) 5.00 12.00
1 Future Superstars .15 .40
134 Terrell Brandon .05 .15
149 Larry Johnson .40 1.00
150 Billy Owens .15 .40
151 Dikembe Mutombo .40 1.00
152 Mark Macon .07 .20
153 Brian Williams .05 .15
154 Terrell Brandon .15 .40
155 Greg Anthony .07 .20
156 Dale Davis .15 .40
157 Anthony Avent .05 .15
158 Chris Gatling .08 .25
159 Victor Alexander .05 .15
160 Kevin Brooks .05 .15
161 Eric Murdock .08 .25
162 LeRon Ellis .05 .15
163 Stanley Roberts .05 .15
164 Rick Fox .20 .50
165 Pete Chilcutt .08 .25
166 Kevin Lynch .05 .15
167 George Ackles .05 .15
168 Rodney Monroe .05 .15
169 Randy Brown .08 .25
170 Chad Gallagher .05 .15
171 Donald Hodge .05 .15
172 Myron Brown .05 .15
173 Mike Iuzzolino .05 .15
174 Chris Corchiani .05 .15
175 Elliot Perry .08 .25
176 Joe Wylie .05 .15
177 Jimmy Oliver .05 .15
178 Doug Overton .05 .15
179 Sean Green .05 .15
180 Steve Hood .05 .15
181 Lamont Strothers .05 .15
182 Alvaro Teheran .05 .15
183 Bobby Phills .08 .25
184 Richard Dumas .05 .15
185 Keith Hughes .05 .15
186 Isaac Austin .08 .25
187 Greg Sutton .05 .15
188 Joey Wright .05 .15
189 Anthony Jones .05 .15
190 Von McDade .05 .15
191 Marcus Kennedy .05 .15
192 Larry Johnson No. 1 Pick .20 .50
193 Classic One on One II .15 .40
194 Anderson Hunt .05 .15
195 Darrin Chancellor .05 .15
196 Damon Lopez .05 .15
197 Thomas Jordan .05 .15
198 Tony Farmer .05 .15
199 Billy Owens No. 3 Pick .15 .40
200 Owens Takes 4-3 Lead (Billy Owens) .15 .40
201 Johnson Slams for 6-6 Tie (Larry Johnson) .20 .50
202 Score Tied with :49 Left .15 .40
210 Chris Smith .05 .15
216 Dexter Davis .05 .15
219 Marc Kroon .05 .15

1991 Classic Four Sport Autographs

The 1991 Classic Draft Collection Autograph set consists of 61 standard-size cards. They were randomly inserted throughout the foil packs. Listed after the player's name is how many cards were autographed by that player. An "A" suffix after card number is used here for convenience.

150A Billy Owens/2500 2.50 6.00
151A Dikembe Mutombo/1000 8.00 20.00
153A Brian Williams/1500 2.00 5.00
163A Stanley Roberts/2000 2.00 5.00

1991 Classic Four Sport LPs

This ten-card set was randomly inserted in 1991 Classic Draft Picks Collection foil packs. The cards are distinguished from the regular issue in that nine of them have a silver inner border while one has a gold inner border. A five-card Ismail subset is also to be found within the nine silver-bordered cards. The "1991 Classic Draft Picks" emblem appears as a wine-colored wax seal at the upper left corner. The horizontally oriented backs carry brief comments superimposed over a dusted version of Classic's wax seal emblem. There was also a French parallel set produced.

COMPLETE SET (10) 5.00 12.00
*FRENCH: SAME VALUE
RANDOM INSERTS IN PACKS .40 1.00
LP6 Larry Johnson Guns .75 2.00
LP9 Final Shot:Johnson Owens .75 2.00

1991 Classic Four Sport French

COMPLETE SET (230) 6.00 15.00
*FRENCH VERSION: .4X TO 1X

1992 Classic Four Sport

The 1992 Classic Draft Picks Collection consists of 325 standard-size cards, featuring the top picks from football, basketball, baseball, and hockey drafts. According to Classic, 40,000 12-box foil cases were produced. Randomly inserted in the 12-card packs were over 100,000 autograph cards from over 50 of the top draft picks from basketball, football, baseball, and hockey, including cards autographed by Shaquille O'Neal, Desmond Howard, Roman Hamrlik, and Phil Nevin. Also inserted in the packs were "Instant Win Giveway Cards" that entitled the collector to the 500,000.00 sports memorabilia giveway that Classic offered in this contest. There was also a factory set produced with gold parallel cards.

COMPLETE SET (326) 6.00 15.00
1 Shaquille O'Neal 1.50 4.00
2 Walt Williams .15 .40
3 Lee Mayberry .05 .15
4 Tony Bennett .05 .15
5 Litterial Green .05 .15
6 Chris Smith .05 .15
7 Henry Williams .05 .15
8 Terrell Lowery .05 .15
9 Curtis Blair .05 .15
10 Randy Woods .05 .15
11 Todd Day .15 .40
12 Anthony Peeler .15 .40
13 Darin Archbold .05 .15
14 Benford Williams .05 .15
15 Damon Patterson .05 .15
16 Bryant Stith .15 .40
17 Doug Christie .15 .40
18 Latrell Sprewell .50 1.25
19 Hubert Davis .15 .40
20 David Booth .05 .15
21 Dave Johnson .05 .15
22 Jon Barry .05 .15
23 Everick Sullivan .05 .15
24 Brian Davis .05 .15
25 Clarence Weatherspoon .15 .40
26 Malik Sealy .15 .40
27 Matt Geiger .15 .40
28 Jimmy Jackson .15 .40
29 Matt Steigenga .05 .15
30 Robert Horry .15 .40
31 Marlon Maxey .05 .15
32 Chris King .05 .15
33 Dexter Cambridge .05 .15
34 Alonzo Jamison .05 .15
35 Anthony Tucker .05 .15
36 Tracy Murray .15 .40
37 Vernel Singleton .05 .15
38 Christian Laettner .15 .40
39 Don MacLean .15 .40
40 Adam Keefe .05 .15
41 Tom Gugliotta .15 .40
42 LaPhonso Ellis .15 .40
43 Byron Houston .05 .15
44 Oliver Miller .05 .15
45 Popeye Jones .05 .15
46 P.J. Brown .15 .40
47 Eric Anderson .05 .15
48 Darren Morningstar .05 .15
49 Isaiah Morris .05 .15
50 Stephen Howard .05 .15
51 Elmore Spencer .05 .15
52 Sean Rooks .05 .15
53 Robert Werdann .05 .15
54 Alonzo Mourning .40 1.00
55 Steve Rogers .05 .15
56 Tim Burroughs .05 .15
57 Herb Jones .05 .15
58 Sean Miller .05 .15
59 Corey Williams .05 .15
60 Duane Cooper .05 .15
61 Brett Roberts .05 .15
62 Elmer Bennett .05 .15
63 Brent Price .05 .15
64 Daimon Sweet .05 .15
65 Darrick Martin .05 .15
66 Gerald Madkins .05 .15
67 Jo Jo English .05 .15
68 Matt Fish .05 .15
69 Harold Miner .15 .40
70 Greg Dennis .05 .15
71 Jeff Roulston .05 .15
72 Keir Rogers .05 .15
73 Geoff Lear .05 .15
74 Ron Ellis .05 .15
75 Predrag Danilovic .05 .15
258 Chris Smith .05 .15
303 Reggie Smith .05 .15
311 Billy Owens FLB .05 .15
312 Dikembe Mutombo FLB .15 .40
315 Christian Laettner JWA .15 .40
316 Harold Miner JWA .15 .40
317 Jimmy Jackson JWA .15 .40
318A Shaquille O'Neal JWA 1.00 2.50
318B Shaquille O'Neal JWA Promo 1.00 2.50
319 Alonzo Mourning JWA .15 .40

1992 Classic Four Sport Gold

COMP.FACT.SET (326) 60.00 120.00
*GOLD: 1.2X TO 3X BASIC CARDS
AU Future Superstars AU 30.00 60.00

1992 Classic Four Sport Autographs

The 1992 Classic Four Sport Autograph set consists of base cards hand signed by the featured player with a congratulatory message on the backs. They were randomly inserted throughout the foil packs. Each card also included a hand written serial number on the front and the checklist below reflects the quantity of cards each player signed. We've assigned card number according to the player's base card. Jan Caloun and Jan Vopat were not included in the regular set and hence are listed as unnumbered.

1A Shaquille O'Neal/150 150.00 300.00
2 Walt Williams/2550 3.00 8.00
3 Lee Mayberry/2575 2.00 5.00
11 Todd Day/1575 2.50 6.00
25 Clar.Weatherspoon/1575 3.00 8.00
26 Malik Sealy/1575 2.50 6.00
28 Jimmy Jackson/1575 5.00 12.00
36 Tracy Murray/1450 2.50 6.00
38 Christian Laettner/725 10.00 25.00
39 Don MacLean/2575 2.00 5.00
40 Adam Keefe/1575 2.00 5.00
54 Alonzo Mourning/975 10.00 25.00
69 Harold Miner/1475 4.00 10.00

1992 Classic Four Sport BCs

Inserted one per jumbo pack, these 20 bonus cards measure the standard size. The cards are numbered on the dark gray stripe and arranged according to sport as follows: basketball (1-6), hockey (7-12), football (13-17), and baseball (18-20). A randomly inserted Future Superstars card has a picture of all four players on its front, shot against a horizon with dark clouds and lightning; the back indicates that just 10,000 of these cards were produced.

COMPLETE SET (20) 3.00 8.00
BC1 Alonzo Mourning .08 .25
BC2 Christian Laettner .08 .25
BC3 Jimmy Jackson .15 .40
BC4 Tom Gugliotta .20 .50
BC5 Walt Williams .08 .25
BC6 Harold Miner .15 .40

1992 Classic Four Sport LPs

Randomly inserted in foil packs, this 25-card standard-size insert set features full-bleed glossy color action player photos on the fronts. The sports represented are football (1-7, 16), basketball (8-14), baseball (17-21), and hockey (22-25). An 8 1/2" by 11" version of Shaquille O'Neal is known to exist.

LP8 Shaquille O'Neal 3.00 8.00
LP9 Jimmy Jackson .30 .75
LP10 Alonzo Mourning .75 2.00
LP11 Christian Laettner .20 .50
LP12 Harold Miner .20 .50
LP13 Todd Day .20 .50
LP14 The King and His Heir 1.25 3.00
LP15 Future Superstars 1.50 4.00
LP14A Kareem Abdul-Jabbar AU Shaquille O'Neal 25.00 60.00
LP14B Kareem Abdul-Jabbar AU Shaquille O'Neal AU/2500 50.00 120.00
LP15P Phil Nevin Shaquille O'Neal Roman Hamrlik Desmond Howard (Super Bowl Show promo) 2.00 5.00

1992 Classic Four Sport Previews

These five preview standard-size cards were randomly inserted in baseball and hockey draft picks foil packs. According to the backs, just 10,000 of each card were produced. The fronts display the full-bleed glossy color player photos. At the upper right corner, the word "Preview" surmounts the Classic logo. This logo overlays a black stripe that runs down the left side and features the player's name and position. The gray backs have the word "Preview" in red lettering at the top and are accented by short purple diagonal stripes on each side. Between the stripes are a congratulations and an advertisement. The cards are numbered on the back with a "CC" prefix.

COMPLETE SET (5) 6.00 15.00
CC1 Shaquille O'Neal 4.00 10.00
CC5 Alonzo Mourning 1.25 3.00

1992 Classic Four Sport Promos

These five promo cards were packaged in a cello pack and distributed to dealers. The cards measure the standard size (2 1/2" by 3 1/2"). The fronts display the same full-bleed glossy color player photos as the above-mentioned preview cards. They differ in that the Classic logo at the upper left corner is not surmounted by the word Preview." The promo backs have a different design than the preview backs, displaying a second color player photo on the right side as well as biography and player profile in black print on a silver background. The cards are numbered on the back.

COMPLETE SET (5) 6.00 15.00
PR1 Shaquille O'Neal 3.00 8.00
PR5 Alonzo Mourning 1.25 3.00

1993 Classic Four Sport

The 1993 Classic Four-Sport Draft Pick Collection set consists of 325 standard-size cards of the top 1993 draft picks from football, basketball, baseball, and hockey. Just 49,500 sequentially numbered 12-box cases were produced. The set includes two topical subsets: John R. Wooden Award (310-314) and All-Rookie Basketball Team (315-319).

COMPLETE SET (325) 4.00 10.00
1 Chris Webber .40 1.00
2 Anfernee Hardaway .40 1.00
3 Jamal Mashburn .30 .75
4 Isaiah Rider .15 .40
5 Vin Baker .08 .25
6 Rodney Rogers .07 .20
7 Lindsey Hunter .07 .20
8 Allan Houston .20 .50
9 George Lynch .07 .20
10 Toni Kukoc .20 .50
11 Ashraf Amaya .05 .15
12 Mark Bell .05 .15
13 Corie Blount .05 .15
14 Dexter Boney .05 .15
15 Tim Brooks .05 .15
16 James Bryson .05 .15
17 Evers Burns .05 .15
18 Scott Burrell .07 .20
19 Sam Cassell .15 .40
20 Sam Crawford .05 .15
21 Ron Curry .05 .15
22 William Davis .05 .15
23 Rodney Dobard .05 .15
24 Tony Dunkin .05 .15
25 Spencer Dunkley .05 .15
26 Bryan Edwards .05 .15
27 Doug Edwards .05 .15
28 Chuck Evans .05 .15
29 Terry Evans .05 .15
30 Will Flemons .05 .15
31 Alphonso Ford .05 .15
32 Josh Grant .05 .15
33 Eric Gray .05 .15
34 Geert Hammink .05 .15
35 Joe Harvell .05 .15
36 Scott Haskin .05 .15
37 Brian Hendrick .05 .15
38 Sascha Hupmann .05 .15
39 Stanley Jackson .05 .15
40 Ervin Johnson .15 .40
41 Adonis Jordan .05 .15
42 Malcolm Mackey .05 .15
43 Rich Manning .05 .15
44 Chris McNeal .05 .15
45 Conrad McRae .05 .15
46 Lance Miller .05 .15
47 Chris Mills .05 .15
48 Matt Nover .05 .15
49 Charles (Bo) Outlaw .07 .20
50 Eric Pauley .05 .15
51 Mike Peplowski .05 .15
52 Stacey Poole .05 .15
53 Anthony Reed .05 .15
54 Eric Riley .05 .15
55 Darrin Robinson .05 .15
56 James Robinson .05 .15
57 Bryon Russell .07 .20
58 Brent Scott .05 .15
59 Bennie Seitzer .05 .15
60 Ed Stokes .05 .15
61 Antoine Stoudamire .05 .15
62 Dirk Surles .05 .15
63 Justus Thigpen .05 .15
64 Kevin Thompson .05 .15
65 Ray Thompson .05 .15
66 Gary Trost .05 .15
67 Nick Van Exel .20 .50
68 Jerry Walker .05 .15
69 Rex Walters .05 .15
70 Chris Whitney .05 .15
71 Steve Worthy .05 .15
72 Luther Wright .05 .15
73 Mark Buford .05 .15
74 Mitchell Butler .05 .15
75 Brian Clifford .05 .15
76 Terry Dehere .05 .15
77 Acie Earl .05 .15
78 Greg Graham .05 .15
79 Angelo Hamilton .05 .15
80 Thomas Hill .05 .15
81 Khari Jaxon .05 .15
82 Darnell Mee .05 .15
83 Sherron Mills .05 .15
84 Gheorghe Muresan .08 .25
85 Eddie Rivera .05 .15
86 Richard Petruska .05 .15
87 Bryan Sallier .05 .15
88 Harper Williams .05 .15
89 Ike Williams .05 .15
90 Byron Wilson .05 .15
310 John Wooden CO .30 .75
311 Chris Webber JWA .30 .75
312 Jamal Mashburn JWA .15 .40
313 Anfernee Hardaway JWA .10 .30
314 Terry Dehere JWA .05 .15
315 Shaquille O'Neal ART .30 .75
316 Alonzo Mourning ART .10 .30
317 Christian Laettner ART .05 .15
318 Jimmy Jackson ART .05 .15
319 Harold Miner ART .05 .15
NNO Mashburn D.Star Mail-In .75 2.00

1993 Classic Four Sport Gold

COMP.FACT.SET (332) 150.00 250.00
*GOLD: 1.5X TO 4X BASIC CARDS
AU3 Alonzo Mourning AU/3900 15.00 30.00
PR1 Anfernee Hardaway Promo 2.00 5.00

1993 Classic Four Sport Acetates

Randomly inserted throughout the 1993 Classic Four-Sport foil packs, this 12-card standard-size acetate set features on its fronts clear-bordered color player action cutouts set on basketball, football, baseball, or hockey stick backgrounds. The cards are unnumbered but carry letter designations. They are checklisted in the order that spells '93 Rookie Class.

COMPLETE SET (12) 6.00 15.00
1 Chris Webber 1.00 2.50
2 Anfernee Hardaway .75 2.00
3 Jamal Mashburn .40 1.00
4 Isaiah Rider .40 1.00
5 Toni Kukoc .60 1.50

1993 Classic Four Sport Autographs

Randomly inserted in '93 Classic Four-Sport packs, these standard-size cards feature on their fronts borderless color player action shots. The back carries a congratulatory message. The cards are listed below by their corresponding regular card numbers, except for Jennings and Klippenstein, which are shown as unnumbered cards (NNO) at the end of the checklist since they are not in the regular set. The number of cards each player signed is shown. The Rider card may have been autopenned.

1A Chris Webber/550 20.00 50.00
3A Jamal Mashburn/800 12.50 30.00
4A Isaiah Rider/4100 4.00 10.00
6A Rodney Rogers/4000 4.00 10.00
77A Acie Earl/550 1.50 4.00
310A John Wooden/150 75.00 150.00
315A Shaq. O'Neal/500 20.00 50.00
316A Alonzo Mourning/400 15.00 40.00

1993 Classic Four Sport Chromium Draft Stars

Inserted one per jumbo pack, these 20 standard-size cards feature color player action cutouts on their borderless metallic fronts. The player's name, along with the production number (1 of 80,000), appear vertically in gold foil at the lower left. The cards are numbered on the back with a "DS" prefix.

COMPLETE SET (20) 8.00 20.00
DS41 Chris Webber .60 1.50
DS42 Anfernee Hardaway .50 1.25
DS43 Jamal Mashburn .40 1.00
DS44 Isaiah Rider .40 1.00
DS45 Toni Kukoc .30 .75
DS46 Rodney Rogers .30 .75
DS47 Chris Mills .30 .75

1993 Classic Four Sport LP Jumbos

Random inserts in hobby boxes, these five oversized cards measure approximately 3 1/2" by 5" and feature on their fronts borderless color player action shots. The player's name, statistics, biography, and career highlights, along with the card's production number out of 8,000 produced, appear on a gray lithic background to the left. The cards are numbered on the back as "X of 5."

COMPLETE SET (5) 12.00 30.00
4 Chris Webber 2.50 6.00
5 Four in One 2.50 6.00

1993 Classic Four Sport LPs

Randomly inserted throughout the 1993 Classic Four-Sport foil packs, this 25-card standard-size set features the hottest draft pick players in 1993. The borderless fronts feature color player action shots. The player's name appears vertically at the lower left. The production number (1 of 63,400) appears in gold foil at the lower right. The cards are numbered on the back with an "LP" prefix.

COMPLETE SET (25) 20.00 40.00
LP1 Four in One 1.50 4.00
LP2 Chris Webber 1.50 4.00
LP3 Anfernee Hardaway 1.00 2.50
LP4 Jamal Mashburn .75 2.00
LP5 Isaiah Rider .40 1.00
LP6 Shaquille O'Neal 1.50 4.00
LP7 Toni Kukoc .60 1.50
LP8 Rodney Rogers .30 .75
LP9 Lindsey Hunter .40 1.00

1993 Classic Four Sport C3 Promo

This standard-size promo card was issued in 1993 by Classic for its Classic Collectors Club Members. The front features a full-bleed color action player photo. A ghosted strip runs down the card face near the right edge and carries the player's name and the Classic Four Sport logo in gold foil. The C3 gold foil logo is in the upper left corner. On a rock simulated background, the back carries a brief biography on the left, as well as production figures (25,000). A color player photo along the right edge and the Classic Four Sport Logo on the bottom completes the back. The card is unnumbered.

1 Jamal Mashburn 1.00 2.50

1993 Classic Four Sport MBNA Promos

This two-card set uses Classic's designs from its Four-Sport LPs "Four in One" insert number LP1. Card number 1 reproduces the Chris Webber/Alex Rodriguez side of LP1, card number 2 reproduces the Drew Bledsoe/Alexandre Daigle side. This set was issued exclusively to cardholders of the MBNA/ScoreBoard VISA. The backs contain congratulatory messages, information about the players depicted, and a notation than 10,000 sets were issued. Although the design and copyright reads 1993, these cards probably were first issued in 1994.

1 C.Webber A.Rodriguez 4.00 10.00

1993 Classic Four Sport McDonald's

Classic produced this 35-card four-sport standard-size set for a promotion at McDonald's restaurants in central and southeastern Pennsylvania, southern New Jersey, Delaware, and central Florida. The cards were distributed in five-card packs. A five-card "limited production" subset was randomly inserted throughout these packs. The promotion also featured instant win cards awarding 2,000 pieces of autographed Score Board memorabilia. An autographed Chris Webber card was also randomly inserted in the packs on a limited basis. The set is arranged according to sports as follows: football (1-10), baseball (11, 26, 31-35), hockey (12-20), and basketball (21-25, 27-30). The cards are numbered on the back in the upper left, and the McDonald's trademark is gold foil stamped toward the bottom.

COMPLETE SET (35) 4.00 10.00
12 Vyacheslav Butsayev .05 .15
21 Anfernee Hardaway .50 1.25
22 Jimmy Jackson .08 .25
23 Christian Laettner .08 .25
24 Jamal Mashburn .20 .50
25 Harold Miner .05 .15
27 Alonzo Mourning .15 .40
28 Shaquille O'Neal .60 1.50
29 Clarence Weatherspoon .05 .15
30 Chris Webber .50 1.25

1993 Classic Four Sport McDonald's LPs

Measuring the standard size, these five limited production cards were randomly inserted in 1993 Classic McDonald's five-card packs. Chris Webber, the number one pick in the NBA draft, autographed 1,250 of his cards. Printed vertically, and parallel and next to the gold foil band, "1 of 16,750" appears in gold foil. The Classic Four Sport logo appears in the upper right. The cards are numbered on the back in gold foil with an "LP" prefix.

COMPLETE SET (5) 3.00 8.00
LP3 Alonzo Mourning .30 .75
NNO Chris Webber AU/1250 30.00 60.00

1993 Classic Four Sport Power Pick Bonus

Issued one per jumbo sheet, these 20 standard-size cards feature on their borderless fronts color player action shots, the backgrounds for which are faded to black-and-white. The player's name and the sets production number (1 of 80,000) appear in green-foil cursive lettering near the bottom. The cards are numbered on the back with a "PP" prefix.

COMPLETE SET (20) 10.00 25.00
PP1 Chris Webber .75 2.00
PP2 Anfernee Hardaway .60 1.50
PP3 Jamal Mashburn .60 1.50
PP4 Isaiah Rider .40 1.00
PP5 Toni Kukoc .60 1.50
PP6 Rodney Rogers .40 1.00
PP7 Chris Mills .40 1.00
NNO Four in One/60,000 1.50 4.00

1993 Classic Four Sport Previews

Issued as unnumbered inserts in '93 Classic hockey packs, these five cards measure the standard size. The fronts are similar in design to regular 1993 Classic Four-Sport cards. The backs carry a congratulatory message.

COMPLETE SET (5) 2.50 6.00
CC4 Chris Webber 1.50 4.00
CC5 Toni Kukoc .30 .75

1993 Classic Four Sport Tri-Cards

Randomly inserted throughout the 1993 Classic Four-Sport foil packs, this set features five standard-size cards with three players on each card separated by perforations. The cards are numbered on the back with a "TC" prefix.

COMPLETE SET (5) 10.00 25.00
TC1 Hard/6 Shaq/11 Webb 2.50 6.00
TC5 Bleds/10 Web/15 A-Rod 3.00 8.00

1994 Classic Four Sport

Featuring top rookies from basketball, baseball, football and hockey, the 1994 Classic Four-Sport set consists of 200 standard-size cards. No more than 25,000 cases were produced. Over 100 players signed 100,000 cards that were randomly inserted four per case. Collectors who found one of 100 Glenn Robinson Instant Winner Cards received a complete Classic Four-Sport autographed card set. Also inserted on an average of one in every five cases were 4,695 hand-numbered 4-in-1 cards featuring all four number 1 picks. Classic's wrapper redemption program offered four levels of participation: 1) bronze-collect 20 wrappers and receive a 4-card Classic Player of the Year set, featuring Grant Hill, Shaquille O'Neal, Emmitt Smith, and Steve Young; 2) silver-collect 30 wrappers and receive the Classic Player of the Year set and a random autograph card; 3) gold-collect 144 wrappers and receive the Classic Player of the Year set and an autograph card by Muhammad Ali; and 4) platinum-collect 216 wrappers and receive the Classic Player of the Year set plus an autograph card by Shaquille O'Neal. The cards are numbered on the back and checklisted below by sport.

COMPLETE SET (200) 6.00 15.00
1 Glenn Robinson .40 1.00
2 Jason Kidd .75 2.00
3 Grant Hill .50 1.25
4 Donyell Marshall .15 .40
5 Juwan Howard .15 .40
6 Sharone Wright .05 .15
7 Billy McCaffrey .05 .15
8 Brian Grant .15 .40
9 Eric Montross .05 .15
10 Eddie Jones .40 1.00
11 Carlos Rogers .05 .15
12 Khalid Reeves .05 .15
13 Jalen Rose .30 .75
14 Yinka Dare .05 .15
15 Eric Piatkowski .15 .40
16 Clifford Rozier .05 .15
17 Aaron McKie .08 .25
18 Eric Mobley .05 .15
19 Tony Dumas .05 .15
20 B.J. Tyler .05 .15
21 Dickey Simpkins .05 .15
22 Bill Curley .05 .15
23 Wesley Person .08 .25
24 Monty Williams .05 .15
25 Greg Minor .05 .15
26 Charlie Ward .15 .40
27 Brooks Thompson .05 .15
28 Deon Thomas .05 .15
29 Antonio Lang .05 .15
30 Howard Eisley .08 .25
31 Rodney Dent .05 .15
32 Jim McIlvaine .05 .15
33 Derrick Alston .05 .15
34 Gaylon Nickerson .05 .15
35 Michael Smith .05 .15
36 Andrei Fetisov .05 .15
37 Dontonio Wingfield .05 .15
38 Darrin Hancock .05 .15
39 Anthony Miller .05 .15
40 Jeff Webster .05 .15
41 Arturas Karnishovas .05 .15
42 Gary Collier .05 .15
43 Shawnelle Scott .05 .15
44 Damon Bailey .05 .15
45 Dwayne Morton .05 .15
46 Jamie Watson .05 .15
47 Jevon Crudup .05 .15
48 Melvin Booker .05 .15
49 Brian Reese .05 .15
50 Lawrence Funderburke .05 .15
189 Glenn Robinson JWA .15 .40
190 Jason Kidd JWA .30 .75
191 Grant Hill JWA .25 .60
192 Donyell Marshall JWA .05 .15
193 Eric Montross JWA .05 .15
194 Khalid Reeves JWA .05 .15
195 Jalen Rose JWA .15 .40
196 Clifford Rozier JWA .05 .15
197 Damon Bailey JWA .05 .15
F01 4-in-1 Glenn Robinson Dan Wilkinson Paul Wilson Ed Jovanovski Number One Draft Picks 1.00 2.50
PC1 Shaquille O'Neal $25 Phone Card 2.00 5.00

1994 Classic Four Sport Gold

COMPLETE SET (200) 12.00 30.00
*GOLD: .8X TO 2X BASIC CARDS

1994 Classic Four Sport Autographs

Randomly inserted in packs at a rate of one in 103, this standard-size set features players from the 1994 Classic Four-Sport set who autographed cards within the set. The fronts feature full-bleed color action player photos. The player's name is gold-foil stamped across the bottom of the picture. The backs have a congratulatory message about receiving an autographed card. Though the cards are unnumbered, we have assigned them the same number as their four-sport regular issue counterpart.

1A Glenn Robinson/1000 6.00 15.00
2A Jason Kidd/1300 10.00 25.00
5A Juwan Howard/940 5.00 12.00
9A Eric Montross/1000 2.50 6.00
11A Carlos Rogers/660 2.00 5.00
13A Jalen Rose/970 6.00 15.00
15A Eric Piatkowski/1090 2.50 6.00
16A Clifford Rozier/900 2.00 5.00
22A Bill Curley/1120 2.00 5.00
23A Wesley Person/1000 2.00 5.00
24A Monty Williams/1100 2.00 5.00
28A Deon Thomas/1090 2.00 5.00
30A Howard Eisley/970 2.50 6.00
32A Jim McIlvaine/965 2.00 5.00
33A Derrick Alston/1050 2.00 5.00
36A Andrei Fetisov/1080 2.00 5.00
39A Anthony Miller/1000 2.00 5.00
40A Jeff Webster/1070 2.00 5.00
41A Arturas Karnishovas/980 2.00 5.00
42A Gary Collier/1000 2.00 5.00
44A Damon Bailey/1050 2.00 5.00
45A Dwayne Morton/1000 2.00 5.00
46A Jamie Watson/1080 2.00 5.00
47A Jevon Crudup/1180 2.00 5.00
49A Brian Reese/960 2.00 5.00

1994 Classic Four Sport BCs

This 20-card bonus standard-size set was inserted one per '94 Classic Four-Sport jumbo packs. The fronts feature full color player photos. The backs carry biographical and statistical information about the player.

COMPLETE SET (20) 6.00 15.00
BC6 Glenn Robinson .40 1.00
BC7 Jason Kidd .75 2.00
BC8 Grant Hill .50 1.25
BC9 Jalen Rose .30 .75
BC10 Donyell Marshall .20 .50
BC11 Juwan Howard .40 1.00
BC12 Khalid Reeves .20 .50

1994 Classic Four Sport C3 Collector's Club

The cards were issued to members of the 1995 Classic Collectors Club. Each is numbered 1 of 10,000 on the cardbacks and carries a 1995 copyright line. However, the cards are in the design of the 1994 Classic Four Sport set.

C6 Grant Hill 1.50 4.00
C7 Glenn Robinson .75 2.00

1994 Classic Four Sport Classic Picks

This 10-card standard-size set was randomly inserted in packs at rate of one in 72. The fronts feature full-color action player photos with the player's name and card title below. The backs carry a small player photo, the player's name, biographical information, and career highlights printed over a ghosted photo of the same player.

COMPLETE SET (10) 6.00 15.00
23 Khalid Reeves .40 1.00
24 Grant Hill 1.50 4.00

1994 Classic Four Sport High Voltage

This 20-card sequentially-numbered standard-size set features the top draft picks. The cards are printed on holographic foil board with a striking design. 2,995 of each even-numbered card and 5,495 of each odd-numbered cards were produced. The cards were inserted on an average of 3 per case and had stated odds of one in 144 hobby packs. The fronts feature the players against a background of lightning while the backs feature a biography on the left side of the card. The right side shows more lightning and the player's photo.

COMPLETE SET (20) 40.00 100.00
HV2 Glenn Robinson SP 5.00 12.00
HV6 Jason Kidd SP 6.00 15.00
HV10 Grant Hill SP 8.00 20.00
HV14 Donyell Marshall SP 2.00 5.00
HV18 Juwan Howard SP 2.50 6.00

1994 Classic Four Sport Phone Cards $1

This set of eight phone cards was randomly inserted in Four-Sport packs. Printed on hard plastic, each card measures 2 1/8" by 3 3/8" and has rounded corners. The fronts display full-bleed color action photos, with the phone time value ($1, $2, $3, $4 or $5) and the player's name printed vertically in red along the right edge. The horizontal backs carry instructions for use of the cards. The cards are unnumbered and checklisted below in alphabetical order. The $3 and $5 cards were inserted into retail packs. The phone cards could be used until November 30, 1995.

COMPLETE SET (8) 3.00 8.00
*TWO DOLLAR: .5X TO 1.2X $1 CARDS
*THREE DOLLAR: .6X TO 1.5X $1 CARDS
*FOUR DOLLAR: .8X TO 2X $1 CARDS
*FIVE DOLLAR: 1X TO 2.5X $1 CARDS
*PIN NUMBER REVEALED: HALF VALUE
5 Jason Kidd 1.00 2.50
7 Glenn Robinson .40 1.00

1994 Classic Four Sport Previews

Randomly inserted in 1994-95 Classic hockey foil packs at a rate of three per case, these five standard-size preview cards show the design of the 1994-95 Classic Four-Sport series. The full-bleed color action photos are gold-foil stamped with the "4-Sport Preview" emblem and the player's name. The backs feature another full-bleed closeup photo, with biography and statistics displayed on a ghosted panel.

COMPLETE SET (5) 6.00 15.00
P3 Grant Hill 2.00 5.00
P4 Jason Kidd 1.50 4.00

1994 Classic Four Sport Printer's Proofs

*PRINT PROOFS: 2.5X TO 6X BASIC CARDS

1994 Classic Four Sport Shaq-Fu Tip Cards

Inserted one in every 18 packs, this 25-card standard-size set features hints and secret clues to play Shaq-Fu, a new video game for Super Nintendo and Sega systems. The fronts feature the title on the left side along with a computerized photo showing on the right 3/4 of the card. The backs are divided between a computer photo on the left side and a description of what the photo means on the right side of he card. The cards are numbered on the back and checklisted below as follows: Character Profiles (SF1-SF12), Special Moves (SF13-SF24), and Secret Tip (SF25). The cards are also licensed throught Electronic Arts and Dolphine Software International.

COMPLETE SET (25) 3.00 8.00
SF1 Shaq 1.00 2.50

1994 Classic Four Sport Tri-Cards

Inserted one in every three cases, this five-card standard-size set features three top running backs, linebackers, hockey centers, pitchers and basketball guards and compares their individual skills. Every card is sequentially-numbered out of 2,695. The horizontal fronts feature the three players equally while the backs gives a brief biography of why the three players are grouped together.

COMPLETE SET (5) 4.00 10.00
TC3 Rose 1.25 3.00
Kidd
Reeves

1993 Classic Futures Promo

Classic released this promo card in 1993 to spotlight future NBA superstars. The card measures approximately 2 1/2" by 4 3/4". The front features a color action player photo with full-bleed sides. Above and below the photo is a white bar with gold foil lettering. The upper bar carries the set title and the lower bar carries the Classic logo and the player's name and positon. The back has a second action player shot on the left side with a grey panel to the right containing biography and statistics for 1992-93 season. The words "For Promotional Purposes Only" is printed in the middle of the grey panel. The card is unnumbered.

1 Isaiah Rider .40 1.00

1993 Classic Futures

These 100 cards measure approximately 2 1/2" by 4 3/4" and feature on their fronts color player action shots with backgrounds that have been thrown out of focus. The card has white borders at the top and bottom. The player's name and position appear in gold-foil lettering within the bottom white margin. The same border design is duplicated on the back, which carries a narrow-cropped color player action shot on the left, and biography, career highlights and statistics on the right.

COMPLETE SET (100) 5.00 10.00
1 Chris Webber 1.25 3.00
2 Bill Edwards .02 .10
3 Anfernee Hardaway 1.25 3.00
4 Bryan Edwards .02 .10
5 Jamal Mashburn .25 .60
6 Doug Edwards .02 .10
7 Isaiah Rider .25 .60
8 Chuck Evans .02 .10
9 Vin Baker .30 .75
10 Terry Evans .02 .10
11 Rodney Rogers .07 .20
12 Will Flemons .02 .10
13 Lindsey Hunter .10 .30
14 Alphonso Ford .02 .10
15 Allan Houston .50 1.25
16 Josh Grant .02 .10
17 George Lynch .02 .10
18 Evric Gray .02 .10
19 Toni Kukoc .50 1.25
20 Geert Hammink .02 .10
21 Ashraf Amaya .02 .10
22 Lucious Harris .02 .10
23 Mark Bell .02 .10
24 Joe Harvell .02 .10
25 Corie Blount .02 .10
26 Antonio Harvey .02 .10
27 Dexter Boney .02 .10
28 Scott Haskin .02 .10
29 Tim Brooks .02 .10
30 Brian Hendrick .02 .10
31 James Bryson .02 .10
32 Sascha Hupmann .02 .10
33 Evers Burns .02 .10
34 Stanley Jackson .02 .10
35 Scott Burrell .02 .10
36 Ervin Johnson .02 .10
37 Sam Cassell .40 1.00
38 Adonis Jordan .02 .10
39 Sam Crawford .02 .10
40 Warren Kidd .02 .10
41 Ron Curry .02 .10
42 Malcolm Mackey .02 .10
43 William Davis .02 .10
44 Rich Manning .02 .10
45 Rodney Dobard .02 .10
46 Chris McNeal .02 .10
47 Tony Dunkin .02 .10
48 Conrad McRae .02 .10
49 Spencer Dunkley .02 .10
50 Lance Miller .02 .10
51 Chris Mills .10 .30
52 Chris Whitney .02 .10
53 Matt Nover .02 .10
54 Steve Worthy .02 .10
55 Bo Outlaw .07 .20
56 Luther Wright .02 .10
57 Eric Pauley .02 .10
58 Mark Buford .02 .10
59 Mike Peplowski .02 .10
60 Mitchell Butler .02 .10
61 Stacey Poole .02 .10
62 Brian Clifford .02 .10
63 Anthony Reed .02 .10
64 Terry Dehere .02 .10
65 Eric Riley .02 .10
66 Acie Earl .02 .10
67 Darrin Robinson .02 .10
68 Greg Graham .02 .10
69 James Robinson .02 .10
70 Angelo Hamilton .02 .10
71 Bryon Russell .10 .30
72 Thomas Hill .02 .10
73 Brent Scott .02 .10
74 Khari Jaxon .02 .10
75 Bennie Seltzer .02 .10
76 Darnell Mee .02 .10
77 Ed Stokes .02 .10
78 Sherron Mills .02 .10
79 Antoine Stoudamire .02 .10
80 Gheorghe Muresan .10 .30
81 Dirk Surles .02 .10
82 Eddie Vivera .02 .10
83 Justus Thigpen .02 .10
84 Julius Nwosu .02 .10
85 Kevin Thompson .02 .10
86 Richard Petruska .02 .10
87 Ray Thompson .02 .10
88 Bryan Sallier .02 .10
89 Gary Trost .02 .10
90 Harper Williams .02 .10
91 Nick Van Exel .30 .75
92 Ike Williams .02 .10
93 Jerry Walker .02 .10
94 Byron Wilson .02 .10
95 Rex Walters .02 .10
96 Alex Holcombe .02 .10
97 Leonard White .02 .10
98 Alex Wright .02 .10
99 Checklist 1-50 .02 .10
100 Checklist 51-100 .02 .10
NNO S.O'Neal Acetate 12.00 30.00

1993 Classic Futures LPs

This 1993 Classic Futures Limited Edition five-card set had a production of 29,500. The cards measure approximately 2 1/2" by 4 3/4". The fronts contain full-bleed color action player photos. The player's name is printed in bold lettering within a wide white bar across the lower edge. The white backs have the number of cards produced prominently displayed across the top of the card. Below is biography, career summary and statistics. The player's name is printed at the bottom. The cards are unnumbered and checklisted below in draft order.

COMPLETE SET (5) 6.00 15.00
UNNUMBERED RANDOM INSERTS IN PACKS
LP1 Chris Webber 3.00 8.00
LP2 Anfernee Hardaway 3.00 8.00
LP3 Jamal Mashburn .60 1.50
LP4 Isaiah Rider .60 1.50
LP5 Toni Kukoc 1.25 3.00

1993 Classic Futures Team

Randomly inserted in packs, these five cards measure approximately 2 1/2" by 4 3/4" and feature on their fronts elliptical color player action shots set on white backgrounds. The player's name and position appear in gold-foil lettering at the bottom. The back carries a color player action shot at the top and career highlights at the bottom. The cards are numbered on the back with a "CFT" prefix.

COMPLETE SET (5) 8.00 20.00
RANDOM INSERTS IN PACKS
CFT1 Chris Webber 4.00 10.00
CFT2 Anfernee Hardaway 4.00 10.00
CFT3 Jamal Mashburn .75 2.00
CFT4 Isaiah Rider .75 2.00
CFT5 Toni Kukoc 1.50 4.00

1993 Classic Superheroes

This purple-bordered three-card standard-size subset features the art work of Neal Adams, who has produced sports and comics fantasy cards of various athletes. It is one of two insert sets included (randomly inserted) in Classic's Deathwatch 2,000 110-card set. The horizontal backs carry a color action player photo with a player profile on a purple background.

COMPLETE SET (3) 8.00 20.00
SS1 Shaquille O'Neal 3.00 8.00

1996 Clear Assets

The 1996 Clear Assets set was issued in one series totaling 70 cards. The set features 75 upscale acetate cards of the most collectible athletes from baseball, basketball, football, hockey and auto racing. Also included is the debut appearance by many of the top players entering the 1996 football draft. Release date was April 1996.

COMPLETE SET (70) 6.00 15.00
1 Shaquille O'Neal .60 1.50
2 Hakeem Olajuwon .30 .75
3 Scottie Pippen .30 .75
4 Alonzo Mourning .15 .40
5 Damon Stoudamire .25 .60
6 Jerry Stackhouse .30 .75
7 Joe Smith .25 .60
8 Antonio McDyess .30 .75
9 Rasheed Wallace .20 .50
10 Kevin Garnett 1.50 4.00
11 Shawn Respert .08 .25
12 Ed O'Bannon .10 .30
13 Kurt Thomas .08 .25
14 Gary Trent .10 .30
15 Cherokee Parks .08 .25
16 Corliss Williamson .08 .25
17 Eric Williams .08 .25
18 Brent Barry .08 .25
19 Bob Sura .08 .25
20 Michael Finley .40 1.00
21 Jimmy King .08 .25
22 Jason Kidd .30 .75
23 Dikembe Mutombo .15 .40
24 Greg Ostertag .08 .25
25 Cory Alexander .08 .25
26 Glenn Robinson .10 .30
27 Tyus Edney .08 .25
28 Rebecca Lobo .20 .50
CA96 Shaquille O'Neal Promo 2.50 6.00

1996 Clear Assets 3X

Randomly inserted in packs at a rate of one in 100, this 10-card set is another first from Classic. The cards resemble triplexed cards with acetate in the middle and an opaque covering.

COMPLETE SET (10) 40.00 100.00
X2 Rasheed Wallace 4.00 10.00
X3 Rebecca Lobo 5.00 12.00
X6 Joe Smith 3.00 8.00
X7 Damon Stoudamire 6.00 15.00
X9 Jerry Stackhouse 4.00 10.00

1996 Clear Assets A Cut Above

CA3 Shaquille O'Neal
CA9 Jerry Stackhouse
CA15 Kevin Garnett 1.25 3.00

1996 Clear Assets Phone Cards $1

COMPLETE SET (30) 5.00 12.00
*PIN NUMBER REVEALED: HALF VALUE
$1 CARDS ONE PER RETAIL PACK
*$2 CARDS: .6X TO 1.5X $1 CARDS
ONE PER HOBBY PACK
CARDS EXPIRED 10/1/97
1 Shaquille O'Neal .60 1.50
3 Jerry Stackhouse .25 .60
9 Jason Kidd .15 .40
13 Joe Smith .15 .40
15 Damon Stoudamire .20 .50
17 Hakeem Olajuwon .20 .50
20 Dikembe Mutombo .15 .40
25 Alonzo Mourning .20 .50
28 Rasheed Wallace .20 .50
29 Ed O'Bannon .10 .30
30 Michael Finley .30 .75

1996 Clear Assets Phone Cards $10

Inserted at a rate of 1:30 packs, this 10-card set of acetate phone cards features many of the biggest names in sports. The Sprint phone cards carry expiration dates of 10/1/97.

COMPLETE SET (10) 20.00 50.00
*PIN NUMBER REVEALED:HALF VALUE
1 Shaquille O'Neal 3.00 8.00
6 Joe Smith 1.00 2.50
9 Scottie Pippen 1.25 3.00
10 Jason Kidd 1.50 4.00

1996 Clear Assets Phone Cards $5

Inserted at a rate of 1:10 packs, this 20-card set of acetate phone cards features many of the biggest names in sports. The Sprint phone cards carry expiration dates of 10/1/97.

COMPLETE SET (20) 12.00 30.00
*PIN NUMBER REVEALED: HALF VALUE
1 Shaquille O'Neal 2.00 5.00
3 Jerry Stackhouse .60 1.25
8 Jason Kidd 1.00 2.50
9 Brent Barry .30 .75
11 Joe Smith .30 .75
13 Hakeem Olajuwon .75 2.00
14 Dikembe Mutombo .40 1.00
18 Alonzo Mourning .50 1.25

1995 Collect-A-Card

This 100-card standard-size set features fronts with color action player photos. The player's name is printed vertically in gold foil on the side and his position in silver below. The horizontal backs carry the player's name, position, biographical information, career highlights and statistics.

COMPLETE SET (100) 4.00 10.00
1 Cory Alexander .10 .25
2 Mario Bennett .10 .25
3 Travis Best .10 .25
4 Jason Caffey .10 .25
5 Randolph Childress .10 .25
6 Michael Finley .30 .75
7 Sherrell Ford .10 .25
8 Kevin Garnett .75 2.00
9 Alan Henderson .10 .25
10 Antonio McDyess .12 .30
11 Loren Meyer .10 .25
12 Ed O'Bannon .10 .25
13 Greg Ostertag .10 .25
14 Cherokee Parks .10 .25
15 Theo Ratliff .15 .40
16 Bryant Reeves .10 .25
17 Shawn Respert .10 .25
18 Joe Smith .12 .30
19 Jerry Stackhouse .30 .75
20 Damon Stoudamire .25 .60
21 Bob Sura .10 .25
22 Kurt Thomas .10 .25
23 Gary Trent .10 .25
24 Rasheed Wallace .30 .75
25 Eric Williams .10 .25
26 Corliss Williamson .10 .25
27 George Zidek .10 .25
28 Alan Henderson .10 .25
29 Donnie Boyce .10 .25
30 Cuonzo Martin .10 .25
31 Eric Williams .10 .25
32 Junior Burrough .10 .25
33 Bob Sura .10 .25
34 Donny Marshall .10 .25
35 George Zidek .10 .25
36 Jason Caffey .10 .25
37 Cherokee Parks .10 .25
38 Loren Meyer .10 .25
39 Anthony Pelle .10 .25
40 Theo Ratliff .15 .40
41 Randolph Childress .10 .25
42 Lou Roe .10 .25
43 Andrew DeClercq .10 .25
44 Michael McDonald .10 .25
45 Travis Best .10 .25
46 Fred Hoiberg .10 .25
47 Antonio McDyess .12 .30
48 Constantin Popa .10 .25
49 Kurt Thomas .10 .25
50 Gary Trent .10 .25
51 Eric Snow .10 .25
52 Kevin Garnett .75 2.00
53 Larry Sykes .10 .25
54 Jerome Allen .10 .25
55 Ed O'Bannon .10 .25
56 Jerry Stackhouse .30 .75
57 Michael Finley .30 .75
58 Mario Bennett .10 .25
59 Shawn Respert .10 .25
60 Corliss Williamson .10 .25
61 Tyus Edney .10 .25
62 Cory Alexander .10 .25
63 Sherrell Ford .10 .25
64 Damon Stoudamire .25 .60
65 Jimmy King .10 .25
66 Greg Ostertag .10 .25
67 Bryant Reeves .10 .25
68 Lawrence Moten .10 .25
69 Terrence Rencher .10 .25
70 Corey Beck .10 .25
71 Bryan Collins .10 .25
72 Dan Cross .10 .25
73 Joe Smith .12 .30
74 Michael Hawkins .10 .25
75 Scott Highmark .10 .25
76 Ray Jackson .10 .25
77 Tom Kleinschmidt .10 .25
78 Matt Maloney .10 .25
79 Clint McDaniel .10 .25
80 Julius Michalik .10 .25
81 Paul O'Liney .10 .25
82 Randy Rutherford .10 .25
83 James Scott .10 .25
84 Dwight Stewart .10 .25
85 Scotty Thurman .10 .25
86 Rasheed Wallace .30 .75
87 John Amaechi .10 .25
88 Jamal Faulkner .10 .25
89 Jerry Stackhouse .15 .40
Rasheed Wallace
90 Scotty Thurman .05 .15
Corey Beck
Clint McDaniel
91 Loren Meyer .05 .15
Julius Michalik
Fred Hoiberg
92 Ed O'Bannon .05 .15
Tyus Edney
93 Cory Alexander .05 .15
Junior Burrough
94 Antonio McDyess .05 .15
Jason Caffey
95 Bryant Reeves .05 .15
Randy Rutherford
96 Matt Maloney .05 .15
Jerome Allen
97 Ray Jackson .05 .15
Jimmy King
98 Shawn Respert .05 .15
Eric Snow
99 Andrew DeClercq .05 .15
Dan Cross
100 Checklist (1-100) .05 .15

1995 Collect-A-Card 2 on 1

Randomly inserted in packs at a rate of one in 21, this 10-card set measures the standard size. The fronts display a color action cut-out of a player on a metallic patterned background. The player's name and his school logo are below. The card's name is printed vertically in a wide bar at the side. The backs carry a color action cut-out of another player on the same background with his name below. Sponsors' logos are displayed in a wide bar at the side. The cards are numbered with a "T" prefix.

COMPLETE SET (10) 5.00 12.00
T1 Antonio McDyess .50 1.25
Kurt Thomas
T2 Jerry Stackhouse 3.00 8.00
Kevin Garnett
T3 Ed O'Bannon .40 1.00
Corliss Williamson
T4 Michael Finley 1.25 3.00
Mario Bennett
T5 Tyus Edney 1.00 2.50
Damon Stoudamire
T6 Joe Smith 1.25 3.00
Rasheed Wallace
T7 Cherokee Parks .40 1.00
Bryant Reeves
T8 Greg Ostertag .40 1.00
George Zidek
T9 Shawn Respert .40 1.00
Jerome Allen
T10 Sherrell Ford .40 1.00
Randolph Childress

1995 Collect-A-Card 24K Gold

This 4-card set was issued as redemption's at the rate of one per case. Four hundred cards were made of each player. Once redeemed, each card contained 1 gram of .999 pure 24 karat gold.

1 Kevin Garnett 100.00 200.00
2 Ed O'Bannon 40.00 100.00
3 Joe Smith 40.00 100.00
4 Jerry Stackhouse 75.00 150.00

1995 Collect-A-Card Ignition

Randomly inserted in packs at a rate of one in 5, this 15-card set measures the standard size. The fronts feature a color action player cut-out on a metallic marble background with the player's name printed vertically in a gold border on one side. The backs carry a small color action player photo with the player's name and small career summary. Card and sponsor logos are below. The cards are numbered with an "I" prefix.

COMPLETE SET (15) 2.50 6.00
I1 Travis Best .20 .50
I2 Randolph Childress .20 .50
I3 Michael Finley .60 1.50
I4 Sherrell Ford .20 .50
I5 Alan Henderson .20 .50
I6 Shawn Respert .20 .50
I7 Jerry Stackhouse .60 1.50
I8 Damon Stoudamire .50 1.25
I9 Bob Sura .20 .50
I10 Gary Trent .20 .50
I11 Kevin Garnett 1.50 4.00
I12 Lou Roe .20 .50
I13 Tyus Edney .20 .50
I14 Fred Hoiberg .20 .50
I15 Jerome Allen .20 .50

1995 Collect-A-Card Liftoff

Randomly inserted in packs at a rate of one in 5, this 15-card set measures the standard size. The fronts feature a color action player cut-out on a patterned silver background. The player's name runs horizontally and vertically on a colored bar. The school logo and card name round out the front. The backs carry a small player photo with the player's name and short career summary. The cards are numbered with a "L" prefix.

COMPLETE SET (15) 1.50 4.00
L1 Cory Alexander .20 .50
L2 Mario Bennett .20 .50
L3 Joe Smith .25 .60
L4 Constantin Popa .20 .50
L5 Antonio McDyess .25 .60
L6 Loren Meyer .20 .50
L7 Ed O'Bannon .20 .50
L8 Greg Ostertag .20 .50
L9 Cherokee Parks .20 .50
L10 Theo Ratliff .30 .75
L11 Bryant Reeves .20 .50
L12 Kurt Thomas .20 .50
L13 Eric Williams .20 .50
L14 Corliss Williamson .20 .50
L15 Rasheed Wallace .60 1.50

1995 Collect-A-Card Stackhouse

Randomly inserted in packs, this 5-card set measures the standard size. The fronts display a player action photo in a beige frame on a light blue background. The backs carry a short discription of some phase of Jerry Stackhouse's career. The cards are numbered with a "FH" prefix.

COMPLETE SET (5) 4.00 10.00
COMMON CARD (J1-J5) 1.25 3.00

1995 Collect-A-Card Stackhouse Autographs

Randomly inserted in packs, this 5-card set measures the standard size. The fronts display a player action photo in a beige frame on a light blue background. The backs carry a short description of some phase of Jerry Stackhouse's career. The cards are numbered with a "J" prefix.

FH1 Jerry Stackhouse/400 6.00 15.00
FH2 Jerry Stackhouse/275 8.00 20.00
FH3 Jerry Stackhouse/175 10.00 25.00
FH4 Jerry Stackhouse/100 12.50 30.00
FH5 Jerry Stackhouse/50 30.00 60.00

1996 Collector's Edge

The 1996 Collector's Edge Rookie Rage set was issued in one series totaling 50 cards. The card fronts have player photo on a foil, etched background. "Rookie Rage" is written vertically on the left. The backs have a close-up photo and career collegiate statistics. There were two parallel versions to the base set. One die-cut and one gold foil. Both were inserted at the rate of 1 in every 2 retail packs. Also note the prototype card is not included in the number of cards in the complete set or the complete set price.

COMPLETE SET (50) 4.00 10.00
1 Shareef Abdur-Rahim .30 .75
2 Ray Allen .60 1.50
3 Drew Barry .15 .40
4 Terrell Bell .15 .40
5 Joseph Blair .15 .40
6 Kobe Bryant 1.50 4.00
7 Marcus Camby .25 .60
8 Erick Dampier .15 .40
9 Ben Davis .15 .40
10 Tony Delk .15 .40
11 Brian Evans .15 .40
12 Jamie Feick .15 .40
13 Derek Fisher .30 .75
14 Todd Fuller .15 .40
15 Steve Hamer .15 .40
16 Othella Harrington .15 .40
17 Mark Hendrickson .15 .40
18 Reggie Geary .15 .40
19 Allen Iverson .75 2.00
20 Dontae' Jones .15 .40
21 Kerry Kittles .15 .40
22 Travis Knight .15 .40
23 Priest Lauderdale .15 .40
24 Randy Livingston .15 .40
25 Marcus Mann .15 .40
26 Stephon Marbury .40 1.00
27 Walter McCarty .15 .40
28 Amal McCaskill .15 .40
29 Jeff McInnis .15 .40
30 Ryan Minor .20 .50
31 Darnell Robinson .15 .40
32 Steve Nash .75 2.00
33 Moochie Norris .15 .40
34 Jermaine O'Neal .40 1.00
35 Mark Pope .15 .40
36 Vitaly Potapenko .15 .40
37 Shandon Anderson .15 .40
38 Ron Riley .15 .40
39 Roy Rogers .15 .40
40 Malik Rose .20 .50
41 Jason Sasser .15 .40
42 Doron Sheffer .15 .40
43 Ronnie Henderson .15 .40
44 Antoine Walker .30 .75
45 Samaki Walker .15 .40
46 John Wallace .15 .40
47 Jerome Williams .15 .40
48 Lorenzen Wright .15 .40
49 Checklist (1-25) .08 .25
50 Checklist (26-50) .08 .25
P1 Marcus Camby PROMO .60 1.50

1996 Collector's Edge Die Cuts

*STARS: .75X TO 2X BASE CARD HI
STATED ODDS 1:2 RETAIL

1996 Collector's Edge Gold

*STARS: .75X TO 2X BASE CARD HI
STATED ODDS 1:2 RETAIL

1996 Collector's Edge Ice Sculpture

*ICE: 3X TO 8X BASE HI

1996 Collector's Edge Key Kraze

Randomly inserted in packs at a rate of one in 24 and serially numbered to 3,200, this 24 cards are produced with a "metalized rainbow embossed" front.

COMPLETE SET (24) 10.00 25.00
STATED PRINT RUN 3200 SER.#'d SETS
*DIE CUTS: .4X TO 1X BASE HI
DIE CUTS PRINT RUN 3100 SER.#'d SETS
*GOLD: 1X TO 2.5X KEY KRAZE HI
GOLD PRINT RUN 1000 SER.#'d SETS
HOLOFOIL PRINT RUN 2000 SER.#'d SETS
1 Shareef Abdur-Rahim 1.25 3.00
2 Ray Allen 2.50 6.00
3 Kobe Bryant 6.00 15.00
4 Marcus Camby 1.00 2.50
5 Erick Dampier .60 1.50
6 Tony Delk .60 1.50
7 Todd Fuller .60 1.50
8 Reggie Geary .60 1.50
9 Allen Iverson 3.00 8.00
10 Dontae' Jones .60 1.50
11 Kerry Kittles .60 1.50
12 Stephon Marbury 1.50 4.00
13 Walter McCarty .60 1.50
14 Darnell Robinson .60 1.50
15 Steve Nash 3.00 8.00
16 Ben Davis .60 1.50
17 Mark Pope .60 1.50
18 Roy Rogers .60 1.50
19 Ronnie Henderson .60 1.50
20 Antoine Walker 1.25 3.00
21 Samaki Walker .60 1.50
22 John Wallace .60 1.50
23 Jerome Williams .60 1.50
24 Lorenzen Wright .60 1.50
CK Checklist (1-24) .40 1.00
PR1 Kerry Kittles PROMO .40 1.00

1996 Collector's Edge Key Kraze Factory Set

*FACTORY SET: .2X TO .5X BASE HI

1996 Collector's Edge Key Kraze Holofoil

*HOLOFOIL: .5X TO 1.25X VALUE
PR1 Kerry Kittles PROMO .60 1.50

1996 Collector's Edge Radical Recruits

Randomly inserted in packs at a rate of one in 8 and serially numbered to 6,750, this 24-card set were produced with metalized fronts.

COMPLETE SET (24) 12.00 30.00
STATED PRINT RUN 6,750 SER.#'d SETS
*GOLD: 1.25X TO 3X RAD.REC.HI
GOLD PRINT RUN 1,000 SER.#'d SETS
HOLOFOIL PRINT RUN 2,500 SER.#'d SETS
1 Shareef Abdur-Rahim 1.25 3.00
2 Ray Allen 2.50 6.00
3 Kobe Bryant 6.00 15.00
4 Marcus Camby 1.00 2.50
5 Erick Dampier .60 1.50
6 Tony Delk .60 1.50
7 Todd Fuller .60 1.50
8 Allen Iverson 3.00 8.00
9 Dontae' Jones .60 1.50
10 Kerry Kittles .60 1.50
11 Darnell Robinson .60 1.50
12 Stephon Marbury 1.50 4.00
13 Walter McCarty .60 1.50
14 Steve Nash 3.00 8.00
15 Ben Davis .60 1.50
16 Reggie Geary .60 1.50
17 Mark Pope .60 1.50
18 Roy Rogers .60 1.50
19 Ronnie Henderson .60 1.50
20 Antoine Walker 1.25 3.00
21 Samaki Walker .60 1.50
22 John Wallace .60 1.50
23 Jerome Williams .60 1.50
24 Lorenzen Wright .60 1.50
PR1 Allen Iverson PROMO .60 1.50
NNO Checklist (1-24) .20 .50

1996 Collector's Edge Radical Recruits Factory Set

*FACTORY SET: .2X TO .5X BASE HI

1996 Collector's Edge Radical Recruits Holofoil

*HOLOFOIL: 1.25X TO 3X VALUE
PR1 Allen Iverson PROMO 1.00 2.50

1996 Collector's Edge Time Warp

Randomly inserted in packs at a rate of one in 8 and serially numbered to 12,000, this 12-card set puts one pro legend up against the 1996-97 rookie class.

COMPLETE SET (12) 8.00 20.00
STATED PRINT RUN 12,000 SER.#'d SETS
*GOLD: 1.5X TO 4X TIME WARP HI
GOLD STATED PRINT RUN 1,000 SETS
*HOLOFOIL: 1.25X TO 3X TIME WARP HI
HOLOFOIL STATED PRINT RUN 2,500 SETS
1 S.A-Rahim/D.Thompson .75 2.00
2 R.Allen/A.English 1.50 4.00
3 K.Bryant/A.English 4.00 10.00
4 M.Camby/M.Malone .60 1.50
5 E.Dampier/G.Gervin .40 1.00
6 A.Iverson/I.Thomas 2.00 5.00
7 K.Kittles/I.Thomas .40 1.00
8 S.Marbury/D.Thompson 1.00 2.50
9 A.Walker/M.Malone .75 2.00
10 S.Walker/W.Frazier .40 1.00
11 J.Wallace/G.Gervin .40 1.00
12 L.Wright/W.Frazier .40 1.00
P1 Antoine Walker .60 1.50
Moses Malone PROMO
NNO Checklist (1-12) .20 .50

1996 Collector's Edge Time Warp Factory Set

COMPLETE SET (12)
*FACTORY SET: .4X TO 1X BASE HI

1996 Collector's Edge Time Warp Vintage Autographs

The 6 cards in this set are identical to the regular Time Warp cards, except they are signed by the vintage player in black ink. The card backs are serial numbered with an "AU" prefix and are limited to 1,000 of each card. The set is skip-numbered as each player only signed one version of his two cards in the base set. Cards were randomly inserted into packs.

COMPLETE SET (6) 20.00 50.00
STATED PRINT RUN 1,000 SERIAL #'d SETS
SKIP-NUMBERED SET
3 K.Bryant/A.English 3.00 8.00
5 E.Dampier/G.Gervin 6.00 15.00
6 A.Iverson/I.Thomas 5.00 12.00
8 S.Marbury/D.Thompson 3.00 8.00
9 A.Walker/M.Malone 8.00 20.00
10 S.Walker/W.Frazier 4.00 10.00

1997 Collector's Edge Promos

These six cards where issued as promotional cards for the forthcoming 1997 Collector's Edge set. The fronts have player photos and a bronze statue of the player image in the bottom right corner. The backs contain biographical information and 1996-97 statistics. The cards are numbered "PROMO x-6".

COMPLETE SET 3.00 8.00
1 Tim Duncan 2.50 6.00
2 Scottie Pippen .60 1.50
3 Ron Mercer .50 1.25
4 Keith Van Horn .75 2.00
5 Antonio Daniels .40 1.00
6 Kobe Bryant 2.00 5.00

1997 Collector's Edge

This 45-card set features borderless color action photos of both rookies and veterans printed on 16 pt. card stock with gold foil and gloss matte highlights. The backs carry player information.

COMPLETE SET (45) 3.00 8.00
1 Tim Duncan .60 1.50
2 Keith Van Horn .20 .50
3 Kebu Stewart .10 .25
4 Antonio Daniels .10 .25
5 Tony Battie .10 .25
6 Ron Mercer .12 .30
7 Tim Thomas .20 .50
8 Adonal Foyle .10 .25
9 Chauncey Billups .30 .75
10 Danny Fortson .10 .25
11 Austin Croshere .07 .20
12 Derek Anderson .10 .25
13 Antoine Walker .10 .25
14 Kobe Bryant .50 1.25
15 Shareef Abdur-Rahim .10 .25
16 Stephon Marbury .12 .30
17 Scottie Pippen .15 .40
18 Kelvin Cato .10 .25
19 Scot Pollard .10 .25
20 Paul Grant .10 .25
21 Anthony Parker .10 .25
22 Ed Gray .10 .25
23 Bobby Jackson .12 .30
24 John Thomas .10 .25
25 Charles Smith .10 .25
26 Jacque Vaughn .10 .25
27 Keith Booth .10 .25
28 Charles O'Bannon .10 .25
29 James Collins .10 .25
30 Marc Jackson .10 .25
31 Anthony Johnson .10 .25
32 Jason Lawson .10 .25
33 Alvin Williams .10 .25
34 DeJuan Wheat .10 .25
35 Nate Erdmann .10 .25
36 Olivier Saint-Jean .10 .25
37 Serge Zwikker .10 .25
38 Antoine Walker .10 .25
39 Kobe Bryant .50 1.25
40 Shareef Abdur-Rahim .10 .25
41 Stephon Marbury .12 .30
42 Scottie Pippen .15 .40
43 Checklist 1 .10 .25
44 Checklist 2 .10 .25
45 Checklist 3 .10 .25

1997 Collector's Edge Air Apparent

Randomly inserted in packs at the rate of one in 72, this 15-card set features double color action player images printed on double metal 40 mil card stock with a basketball background. One player image is faded while the other is sharp and bright. The backs carry player information.

COMPLETE SET (15) 25.00 60.00
1 T.Duncan/S.Pippen 12.50 30.00
2 K.Van Horn/K.Bryant 12.50 25.00
3 O.St.Jean/S.A-Rahim 2.00 5.00
4 A.Daniels/S.Marbury 2.00 5.00
5 T.Battie/S.Pippen 2.50 6.00
6 R.Mercer/S.Marbury 2.00 5.00
7 T.Thomas/K.Bryant 4.00 10.00
8 A.Foyle/S.A-Rahim 2.00 5.00
9 C.Billups/S.Marbury 2.50 6.00
10 D.Fortson/S.Pippen 2.00 5.00
11 Antoine Walker 2.00 5.00
12 D.Anderson/K.Bryant 5.00 12.00
13 K.Cato/S.A-Rahim 2.00 5.00
14 Antoine Walker 2.00 5.00
15 Antoine Walker 2.00 5.00

1997 Collector's Edge Energy

Randomly inserted in packs at the rate of one in 12, this 12-card set features color action player images on an animation card highlighted by a glass-shattering backboard.

COMPLETE SET (12) 4.00 10.00
1 Antonio Daniels .30 .75
2 Austin Croshere .25 .60
3 Charles O'Bannon .30 .75
4 Scot Pollard .30 .75
5 Paul Grant .30 .75
6 Danny Fortson .30 .75
7 Keith Van Horn .60 1.50
8 Kelvin Cato .30 .75
9 Ron Mercer .40 1.00
10 Tim Duncan 2.00 5.00
11 Tim Thomas .60 1.50
12 Chauncey Billups 1.00 2.50
NNO Checklist .30 .75

1997 Collector's Edge Extra

This 12-card insert set features color action photos of top rookies and veterans printed on textured embossed card stock with a newspaper extra edition background. Only 100 of this set were produced and could be obtained by special redemption cards inserted into packs at the rate of one in 48. Only 100 of these redemption cards were also produced.

COMPLETE SET (12) 75.00 150.00
1 Tim Duncan 20.00 50.00
2 Keith Van Horn 6.00 15.00
3 Olivier Saint-Jean 3.00 8.00
4 Antonio Daniels 3.00 8.00
5 Tony Battie 3.00 8.00
6 Ron Mercer 4.00 10.00
7 Tim Thomas 6.00 15.00
8 Antoine Walker 5.00 12.00
9 Kobe Bryant 25.00 60.00
10 Shareef Abdur-Rahim 5.00 12.00
11 Stephon Marbury 6.00 15.00
12 Scottie Pippen 8.00 20.00

1997 Collector's Edge Game Ball

Randomly inserted in packs at the rate of one in 36, this five-card set features color photos of top players with an actual medallion of an authentic game used basketball embedded in each card.

STATED ODDS 1:36
1 Antoine Walker 1.00 2.50
2 Kobe Bryant 5.00 12.00
3 Shareef Abdur-Rahim 1.00 2.50
4 Stephon Marbury 1.25 3.00
5 Scottie Pippen 1.50 4.00

1997 Collector's Edge Hardcourt Force

Randomly inserted in packs at the rate of one in 36, this 25-card set features color player photos printed using metal holofoil technology and forming a puzzle background.

COMPLETE SET (25) 20.00 50.00
1 Chauncey Billups 3.00 8.00
2 Tony Battie 1.00 2.50
3 Tim Duncan 6.00 15.00
4 Paul Grant 1.00 2.50
5 John Thomas 1.00 2.50
6 Scottie Pippen 1.50 4.00
7 Scot Pollard 1.00 2.50
8 Ron Mercer 1.25 3.00
9 Tim Thomas 2.00 5.00
10 Kobe Bryant 5.00 12.00
11 Antonio Daniels 1.00 2.50
12 Kelvin Cato 1.00 2.50
13 Danny Fortson 1.00 2.50
14 Ed Gray 1.00 2.50
15 Derek Anderson 1.00 2.50
16 Bobby Jackson 1.25 3.00
17 Antoine Walker 1.00 2.50
18 Anthony Parker 1.00 2.50
19 Shareef Abdur-Rahim 1.00 2.50
20 Olivier Saint-Jean 1.00 2.50
21 Stephon Marbury 1.25 3.00
22 Keith Van Horn 2.00 5.00
23 Austin Croshere .75 2.00
24 Adonal Foyle 1.00 2.50
25 Serge Zwikker 1.00 2.50

1997 Collector's Edge Swoosh

Randomly inserted in packs at the rate of one in 24, this 12-card set features color player images printed on clear acetate, foil-stamped cards viewable from both sides.

COMPLETE SET (12) 8.00 20.00
1 Adonal Foyle .60 1.50
2 Keith Booth .60 1.50
3 Danny Fortson .60 1.50
4 Derek Anderson .60 1.50
5 Jacque Vaughn .60 1.50
6 Keith Van Horn 1.25 3.00
7 Kelvin Cato .60 1.50
8 Ron Mercer .75 2.00
9 Tim Duncan 4.00 10.00
10 Tony Battie .60 1.50
11 Chauncey Billups 2.00 5.00
12 Charles O'Bannon .60 1.50
13 Checklist .60 1.50

1997 Collector's Edge Impulse

The 1997 Collector's Edge Impulse product was released in 1997, and featured a 42-card base set. Each card is diecut, and the top of each card is rounded off to resemble a basketball.

1 Tim Duncan .60 1.50
2 Keith Van Horn .20 .50
3 Kebu Stewart .10 .25
4 Antonio Daniels .10 .25

5 Tony Battie .10 .25
6 Ron Mercer .12 .30
7 Tim Thomas .20 .50
8 Adonal Foyle .10 .25
9 Chauncey Billups .30 .75
10 Danny Fortson .10 .25
11 Austin Croshere .07 .20
12 Derek Anderson .10 .25
13 Antoine Walker .10 .25
14 Kobe Bryant .50 1.25
15 Shareef Abdur-Rahim .10 .25
16 Stephon Marbury .12 .30
17 Scottie Pippen .15 .40
18 Kelvin Cato .10 .25
19 Scot Pollard .10 .25
20 Paul Grant .10 .25
21 Anthony Parker .10 .25
22 Ed Gray .10 .25
23 Bobby Jackson .12 .30
24 John Thomas .10 .25
25 Charles Smith .10 .25
26 Jacque Vaughn .10 .25
27 Keith Booth .10 .25
28 Charles O'Bannon .10 .25
29 James Collins .10 .25
30 Marc Jackson .10 .25
31 Anthony Johnson .10 .25
32 Jason Lawson .10 .25
33 Alvin Williams .10 .25
34 DeJuan Wheat .10 .25
35 Nate Erdmann .10 .25
36 Olivier Saint-Jean .10 .25
37 Serge Zwikker .10 .25
38 Antoine Walker .10 .25
39 Kobe Bryant .50 1.25
40 Shareef Abdur-Rahim .10 .25
41 Stephon Marbury .12 .30
42 Scottie Pippen .15 .40
CL1 Checklist .10 .25
CL2 Checklist .10 .25
CL3 Checklist .10 .25

1998 Collector's Edge Impulse

The 1998-99 Collector's Edge Impulse set was issued in one series totalling 100 cards. The set contains the topical subsets: All American (33-42), All Rookie (43-50), and Rookie+Veteran (51-100).

COMPLETE SET (100) 7.50 15.00
1 Michael Olowokandi .12 .30
2 Antawn Jamison .25 .60
3 Vince Carter .50 1.25
4 Robert Traylor .10 .25
5 Jason Williams .25 .60
6 Paul Pierce .40 1.00
7 Bonzi Wells .10 .25
8 Keon Clark .10 .25
9A Kobe Bryant CL .25 .60
9B Radoslav Nesterovic .10 .25
10 Pat Garrity .10 .25
11 Ricky Davis .15 .40
12 Tyronn Lue .10 .25
13 Felipe Lopez .10 .25
14 Al Harrington .15 .40
15 Corey Benjamin .10 .25
16 Rashard Lewis .25 .60
17 Jelani McCoy .10 .25
18 Shammond Williams .10 .25
19 DeMarco Johnson .10 .25
20 Korleone Young .10 .25
21 Miles Simon .10 .25
22 Toby Bailey .10 .25
23 J.R. Henderson .10 .25
24 Zendon Hamilton .10 .25
25 Jeff Sheppard .10 .25
26 Kobe Bryant .40 1.00
27 Stephon Marbury .12 .30
28 Tracy McGrady .15 .40
29 Scottie Pippen .15 .40
30 Tim Thomas .10 .25
31 Michael Olowokandi CL .07 .20
32 Antawn Jamison CL .15 .40
33 Michael Olowokandi AA .07 .20
34 Antawn Jamison AA .15 .40
35 Vince Carter AA .30 .75
36 Robert Traylor AA .05 .15
37 Jason Williams AA .15 .40
38 Paul Pierce AA .25 .60
39 Bonzi Wells AA .05 .15
40 Keon Clark AA .05 .15
41A Radoslav Nesterovic AA .05 .15
41B Kobe Bryant CL 2.50 6.00
42 Pat Garrity AA .05 .15
43 Michael Olowokandi AR .07 .20
44 Antawn Jamison AR .15 .40
45 Vince Carter AR .30 .75
46 Robert Traylor AR .05 .15
47 Jason Williams AR .15 .40
48 Paul Pierce AR .25 .60
49 Bonzi Wells AR .05 .15
50 Keon Clark AR .05 .15
51 P.Pierce/K.Bryant .30 .75
52 P.Pierce/S.Pippen .25 .60
53 A.Jamison/S.Marbury .20 .50
54 A.Jamison/T.McGrady .20 .50
55 M.Olowokandi/T.Thomas .15 .40
56 M.Olowokandi/K.Bryant .30 .75
57 K.Clark/S.Pippen .15 .40
58 K.Clark/S.Marbury .15 .40
59 P.Garrity/T.McGrady .15 .40
60 P.Garrity/T.Thomas .15 .40
61 C.Benjamin/K.Bryant .30 .75
62 C.Benjamin/S.Pippen .15 .40
63 R.Traylor/S.Marbury .15 .40
64 R.Traylor/T.McGrady .15 .40
65 R.Lewis/T.Thomas .15 .40
66 R.Lewis/K.Bryant .30 .75
67 B.Wells/S.Pippen .15 .40
68 B.Wells/S.Marbury .15 .40
69 J.R.Henderson/T.McGrady .15 .40
70 J.R.Henderson/T.Thomas .15 .40
71 T.Bailey/K.Bryant .30 .75
72 T.Bailey/S.Pippen .15 .40
73 T.Lue/S.Marbury .15 .40
74 T.Lue/T.McGrady .15 .40
75 R.Nesterovic/T.Thomas .15 .40
76 R.Nesterovic/K.Bryant .30 .75
77 M.Simon/S.Pippen .15 .40
78 M.Simon/S.Marbury .15 .40
79 J.Sheppard/T.McGrady .15 .40
80 J.Sheppard/T.Thomas .15 .40
81 F.Lopez/K.Bryant .30 .75
82 F.Lopez/S.Pippen .15 .40
83 S.Williams/S.Marbury .15 .40
84 S.Williams/T.McGrady .15 .40
85 Z.Hamilton/T.Thomas .15 .40
86 Z.Hamilton/K.Bryant .30 .75
87 J.Williams/S.Pippen .20 .50
88 J.Williams/S.Marbury .15 .40
89 R.Davis/T.McGrady .15 .40
90 R.Davis/T.Thomas .15 .40
91 K.Young/K.Bryant .30 .75
92 K.Young/S.Pippen .15 .40
93 V.Carter/S.Marbury .25 .60
94 V.Carter/T.McGrady .30 .75
95 A.Harrington/T.Thomas .15 .40
96 A.Harrington/K.Bryant .30 .75
97 J.McCoy/S.Pippen .15 .40
98 J.McCoy/S.Marbury .15 .40
99 D.Johnson/T.McGrady .15 .40
100 D.Johnson/T.Thomas .15 .40

1998 Collector's Edge Impulse Jersey City '99

JSY CITY: .75X TO 2X HI COL.

1998 Collector's Edge Impulse Jersey City '99 Gold

*GOLD: 2X TO 5X HI COL.

1998 Collector's Edge Impulse Jersey City '99 Parallel 50

*SINGLES: 12X TO 30X BASE CARD HI

1998 Collector's Edge Impulse Parallel

*STARS: .75X TO 2X BASE CARD HI

1998 Collector's Edge Impulse KB8

Randomly inserted in packs at one in 36, this five-card set focuses on Kobe Bryant. Cards have a bronze coloring.

COMMON BRONZE (1-5) 2.50 6.00
*SILVER: .6X TO 1.5X BRONZE
SILVER STATED ODDS 1:54
*GOLD: .75X TO 2X BRONZE
GOLD STATED ODDS 1:72
*HOLOFOIL: 1X TO 2.5X BRONZE
HOLOFOIL STATED ODDS 1:90

1998 Collector's Edge Impulse Memorable Moments

Redeemable via an exchange card that was inserted one in 360 packs, this 5-card set features players with a patch of a game-used basketball.

COMPLETE SET (5) 25.00 60.00
STATED ODDS 1:360
1 Kobe Bryant 12.00 30.00
2 Stephon Marbury 4.00 10.00
3 Tracy McGrady 5.00 12.00
4 Scottie Pippen 5.00 12.00
5 Tim Thomas 3.00 8.00

1998 Collector's Edge Impulse Pro Signatures

Randomly inserted in packs at one in 18, this 30-card set features autographs from some of the top rookies from the 1998 NBA Draft, as well as some veterans of the NBA.

STATED ODDS 1:18
1 Antawn Jamison 5.00 12.00
2 Paul Pierce 10.00 25.00
3 Corey Benjamin 2.00 5.00
4 Ricky Davis 3.00 8.00
5 Jason Williams 5.00 12.00
6 Felipe Lopez 2.00 5.00
7 Jelani McCoy 2.00 5.00
8 Vince Carter 8.00 20.00
9 Keon Clark 2.00 5.00
10 Michael Olowokandi 2.50 6.00
11 Robert Traylor 2.00 5.00
12 Bonzi Wells 2.00 5.00
13 Toby Bailey 2.00 5.00
14 Pat Garrity 2.00 5.00
15 Al Harrington 3.00 8.00
16 J.R. Henderson 2.00 5.00
17 DeMarco Johnson 2.00 5.00
18 Zendon Hamilton 2.00 5.00
19 Rashard Lewis 5.00 12.00
20 Tyronn Lue 2.00 5.00
21 Kobe Bryant 30.00 80.00
22 Jeff Sheppard 2.00 5.00
23 Miles Simon 2.00 5.00
24 Shammond Williams 2.00 5.00
25 Korleone Young 2.00 5.00
26 Radoslav Nesterovic 2.00 5.00
27 Stephon Marbury 5.00 12.00
28 Tracy McGrady 8.00 20.00
29 Scottie Pippen 50.00 100.00
30 Tim Thomas 2.00 5.00

1998 Collector's Edge Impulse Swoosh

Randomly inserted at one in 72 packs, this 24-card set featured some of the leading players from the 1998 draft.

COMPLETE SET (24) 25.00 60.00
1L Michael Olowokandi 1.25 3.00
1R Antawn Jamison 2.50 6.00
2L Vince Carter 5.00 12.00
2R Robert Traylor 1.00 2.50
3L Jason Williams 2.50 6.00
3R Paul Pierce 4.00 10.00
4L Keon Clark 1.00 2.50
4R Bonzi Wells 1.00 2.50
5L Kobe Bryant 4.00 10.00
5R Pat Garrity 1.00 2.50
6L Ricky Davis 1.50 4.00
6R Tyronn Lue 1.00 2.50
7L Felipe Lopez 1.00 2.50
7R Al Harrington 1.50 4.00
8L Corey Benjamin 1.00 2.50
8R Rashard Lewis 2.50 6.00
9L Jelani McCoy 1.00 2.50
9R Shammond Williams 1.00 2.50
10L DeMarco Johnson 1.00 2.50
10R Korleone Young 1.00 2.50
11L Miles Simon 1.00 2.50
11R Kobe Bryant 4.00 10.00
12L Stephon Marbury 1.25 3.00
12R Tracy McGrady 1.50 4.00

1998 Collector's Edge Impulse T3

Released as a multi-level set, the first five cards were bronze and inserted at one in 12. The second level, or cards 6-10 were silver and inserted at one in 18. The third level, or cards 11-15 were gold and inserted at one in 36.

COMPLETE SET (15) 10.00 25.00
1 Michael Olowokandi G 1.00 2.50
2 Antawn Jamison G 2.00 5.00
3 Kobe Bryant G 3.00 8.00
4 Scottie Pippen G 1.25 3.00
5 Robert Traylor G .75 2.00
6 Stephon Marbury S .60 1.50
7 Paul Pierce S 2.00 5.00
8 Vince Carter S 2.50 6.00
9 Jason Williams S .50 1.25
10 Tim Thomas S .50 1.25
11 Bonzi Wells B .40 1.00
12 Tracy McGrady B .60 1.50
13 Rashard Lewis B 1.00 2.50
14 Keon Clark B .40 1.00
15 Corey Benjamin B .40 1.00

1999 Collector's Edge Rookie Rage

The 1999 version of Rookie Rage by Collector's Edge was released as a 50-card set. Each pack carried a suggested retail price of $2.19.

COMPLETE SET (50) 3.00 8.00
1 Ron Artest .25 .60
2 William Avery .10 .25
3 Michael Batiste .10 .25
4 Jonathan Bender .10 .25
5 Roberto Bergersen .10 .25
6 Calvin Booth .10 .25
7 Cal Bowdler .10 .25
8 A.J. Bramlett .10 .25
9 Rodney Buford .10 .25
10 John Celestand .10 .25
11 Kris Clack .10 .25
12 Lonnie Cooper .10 .25
13 Vonteego Cummings .10 .25
14 Baron Davis .25 .60
15 Evan Eschmeyer .10 .25
16 Jeff Foster .10 .25
17 Jelani Gardner .10 .25
18 Devean George .10 .25
19 Dion Glover .10 .25
20 Richard Hamilton .25 .60
21 Venson Hamilton .10 .25
22 Rico Hill .10 .25
23 Tim James .10 .25
24 Jumaine Jones .10 .25
25 J.R. Koch .10 .25
26 Trajan Langdon .10 .25
27 Bobby Lazor .10 .25
28 Melvin Levett .10 .25
29 Quincy Lewis .10 .25
30 Corey Maggette .20 .50
31 Shawn Marion .25 .60
32 B.J. McKie .10 .25
33 Andre Miller .25 .60
34 Lee Nailon .10 .25
35 Ademola Okulaja .10 .25
36 Scott Padgett .10 .25
37 James Posey .10 .25
38 Aleksandar Radojevic .10 .25
39 Michael Ruffin .10 .25
40 Leon Smith .10 .25
41 Jason Terry .25 .60
42 Kenny Thomas .10 .25
43 Tyrone Washington .10 .25
44 Frederic Weis .10 .25
45 Alvin Young .10 .25
46 Kobe Bryant .40 1.00
47 Vince Carter .20 .50
48 Antawn Jamison .10 .25
49 Paul Pierce .15 .40
50 Jason Williams .12 .30

1999 Collector's Edge Rookie Rage Gold

*GOLD: .6X TO 1.5X VALUE

1999 Collector's Edge Rookie Rage HoloGold

*HOLO: 15X TO 40X VALUE

1999 Collector's Edge Rookie Rage Future Legends

Randomly inserted in packs at one in eight, this 10-card set features top rookies destined to be legends. Card backs carry a "FL" prefix.

COMPLETE SET (10) 2.00 5.00
FL1 Ron Artest .50 1.25
FL2 William Avery .20 .50
FL3 Jonathan Bender .20 .50
FL4 Baron Davis .50 1.25
FL5 Richard Hamilton .50 1.25
FL6 Trajan Langdon .20 .50
FL7 Corey Maggette .40 1.00
FL8 Andre Miller .50 1.25
FL9 Jason Terry .50 1.25
FL10 Frederic Weis .20 .50

1999 Collector's Edge Rookie Rage Game Ball

Randomly inserted in packs at one in 72, this five-card set features pieces of game-used balls in every card.

STATED ODDS 1:72
GG1 Kobe Bryant 10.00 25.00
GG2 Vince Carter 5.00 12.00
GG3 Antawn Jamison 2.50 6.00
GG4 Paul Pierce 4.00 10.00
GG5 Jason Williams 3.00 8.00
AM Andre Miller 6.00 15.00
BD Baron Davis 6.00 15.00
FW Frederic Weis 2.50 6.00
JB Jonathan Bender 2.50 6.00
JT Jason Terry 6.00 15.00
KB1 Bryant Driving 10.00 25.00
KB2 Bryant Yellow jsy 10.00 25.00
KB3 Bryant Shooting 10.00 25.00
KB4 Bryant Follow through 10.00 25.00
KB5 Bryant Ball at chest 10.00 25.00
RA Ron Artest 6.00 15.00
RH Richard Hamilton 6.00 15.00
TL Trajan Langdon 2.50 6.00
WA William Avery 2.50 6.00
CM Corey Maggette 5.00 12.00

1999 Collector's Edge Rookie Rage Livin' Large

Randomly inserted in packs at one in 16, this five-card set features top pro player at the top of their game. Card backs carry a "LL" prefix.

COMPLETE SET (5) 1.00 2.50
LL1 Kobe Bryant .75 2.00
LL2 Vince Carter .40 1.00
LL3 Antawn Jamison .20 .50
LL4 Paul Pierce .30 .75
LL5 Jason Williams .25 .60

1999 Collector's Edge Rookie Rage Loud and Proud

Randomly inserted in packs at one in 16, this five-card set featues young NBA stars whose game is "loud and proud". Card backs carry a "LP" prefix.

COMPLETE SET (5) 1.00 2.50
LP1 Kobe Bryant .75 2.00
LP2 Vince Carter .40 1.00
LP3 Antawn Jamison .20 .50
LP4 Paul Pierce .30 .75
LP5 Jason Williams .25 .60

1999 Collector's Edge Rookie Rage Pro Signatures

Randomly inserted in packs at one in 12, this 50-card set features autographs of each player in the base set.

STATED ODDS 1:12
1 Ron Artest 4.00 10.00
2 William Avery 1.50 4.00
3 Michael Batiste 1.50 4.00
4 Jonathan Bender 1.50 4.00
5 Roberto Bergersen 1.50 4.00
6 Calvin Booth 1.50 4.00
7 Cal Bowdler 1.50 4.00
8 A.J. Bramlett 1.50 4.00
9 Rodney Buford 1.50 4.00
10 John Celestand 1.50 4.00
11 Kris Clack 1.50 4.00
12 Lonnie Cooper 1.50 4.00
13 Vonteego Cummings 1.50 4.00
14 Baron Davis 4.00 10.00
15 Evan Eschmeyer 1.50 4.00
16 Jeff Foster 1.50 4.00
17 Jelani Gardner 1.50 4.00
18 Devean George 1.50 4.00
19 Dion Glover 1.50 4.00
20 Richard Hamilton 4.00 10.00
21 Venson Hamilton 1.50 4.00
22 Rico Hill 1.50 4.00
23 Tim James 1.50 4.00
24 Jumaine Jones 1.50 4.00
25 J.R. Koch 1.50 4.00
26 Trajan Langdon 1.50 4.00
27 Bobby Lazor 1.50 4.00
28 Melvin Levett 1.50 4.00
29 Quincy Lewis 1.50 4.00
30 Corey Maggette 3.00 8.00
31 Shawn Marion 4.00 10.00
32 B.J. McKie 1.50 4.00
33 Andre Miller 4.00 10.00
34 Lee Nailon 1.50 4.00
35 Ademola Okulaja 1.50 4.00
36 Scott Padgett 1.50 4.00
37 James Posey 1.50 4.00
38 Aleksandar Radojevic 1.50 4.00
39 Michael Ruffin 1.50 4.00
40 Leon Smith 1.50 4.00
41 Jason Terry 4.00 10.00
42 Kenny Thomas 1.50 4.00
43 Tyrone Washington 1.50 4.00
44 Frederic Weis 1.50 4.00
45 Alvin Young 1.50 4.00
46 Kobe Bryant/39 60.00 120.00
48 Antawn Jamison 4.00 10.00
49 Paul Pierce 6.00 15.00

1999 Collector's Edge Rookie Rage Successors

Randomly inserted in packs at one in eight, this 10-card set features top rookie players who will suceed in the NBA. Card backs carry a "S" prefix.

COMPLETE SET (10) 2.00 5.00
S1 Ron Artest .50 1.25
S2 William Avery .20 .50
S3 Jonathan Bender .20 .50
S4 Baron Davis .50 1.25
S5 Richard Hamilton .50 1.25
S6 Trajan Langdon .20 .50
S7 Corey Maggette .40 1.00
S8 Andre Miller .50 1.25
S9 Jason Terry .50 1.25
S10 Frederic Weis .20 .50

1991 Courtside

The 1991 Courtside Draft Pix basketball set consists of 45 standard-size cards. All 198,000 sets produced are numbered and distributed as complete sets in their own custom boxes each accompanied by a certificate with a unique serial number. The card front features a color action player photo. The design of the card fronts features a color rectangle (either pearlized red, blue, or green) on a pearlized white background, with two border stripes in the same color intersecting at the upper right corner. The player's name appears at the upper right corner of the card face, with the words "Courtside 1991" at the bottom. The backs reflect the color on the fronts and present stats (biographical), college record (year by year statistics), and player profile. The unnumbered Larry Johnson sendaway card is not included in the complete set price below. Promo versions of all cards in the set are known to exist; they bear a circle-shaped disclaimer reading "Sample Not For Sale" on their back. Single promo cards were given out at the 1991 San Francisco Labor Day show. These promo versions are valued at four times the regualr issue values.

COMP.FACT.SET (45) 1.50 3.00
STATED PRINT RUN 198,000 SETS
1 Larry Johnson No. 1 Pick .30 .75
2 George Ackles .02 .10
3 Kenny Anderson .20 .50
4 Greg Anthony .05 .15
5 Anthony Avent .02 .10
6 Terrell Brandon .20 .50
7 Kevin Brooks .02 .10
8 Marc Brown .02 .10
9 Myron Brown .02 .10
10 Randy Brown .05 .15
11 Darrin Chancellor .02 .10
12 Pete Chilcutt .05 .15
13 Chris Corchiani .05 .15
14 John Crotty .05 .15
15 Dale Davis .20 .50
16 Marty Dow .02 .10
17 Richard Dumas .02 .10
18 LeRon Ellis .02 .10
19 Tony Farmer .02 .10
20 Roy Fisher .02 .10
21 Rick Fox .20 .50
22 Chad Gallagher .02 .10
23 Chris Gatling .05 .15
24 Sean Green .02 .10
25 Reggie Hanson .02 .10
26 Donald Hodge .02 .10
27 Steve Hood .02 .10
28 Keith Hughes .02 .10
29 Mike Iuzzolino .02 .10
30 Keith Jennings .02 .10
31 Larry Johnson .30 .75
32 Treg Lee .02 .10
33 Cedric Lewis .02 .10
34 Kevin Lynch .02 .10
35 Mark Macon .05 .15
36 Jason Matthews .02 .10
37 Eric Murdock .05 .15
38 Jimmy Oliver .02 .10
39 Doug Overton .02 .10
40 Elliot Perry .05 .15
41 Brian Shorter .02 .10
42 Alvaro Teheran .02 .10
43 Joey Wright .02 .10
44 Joe Wylie .02 .10
45 Larry Johnson POY .30 .75
NNO Larry Johnson Mail-In .75 2.00

1991 Courtside Autographs

Reportedly, 30,000 autographs were randomly inserted in the 9,900 cases. The cards feature autographs of each player.

RANDOM INSERTS IN SETS
STATED PRINT RUN 30,000 TOTAL AU'S
1 Larry Johnson No. 1 Pick 15.00 40.00
2 George Ackles 4.00 10.00
4 Greg Anthony 8.00 20.00
5 Anthony Avent 4.00 10.00
6 Terrell Brandon 6.00 15.00
7 Kevin Brooks 4.00 10.00
8 Marc Brown 4.00 10.00
9 Myron Brown 4.00 10.00
10 Randy Brown 4.00 10.00
11 Darrin Chancellor 4.00 10.00
12 Pete Chilcutt 4.00 10.00
13 Chris Corchiani 4.00 10.00
14 John Crotty 4.00 10.00
15 Dale Davis 6.00 15.00
16 Marty Dow 4.00 10.00
17 Richard Dumas 4.00 10.00
18 LeRon Ellis 4.00 10.00
19 Tony Farmer 4.00 10.00
20 Roy Fisher 4.00 10.00
21 Rick Fox 8.00 20.00
22 Chad Gallagher 4.00 10.00
23 Chris Gatling 4.00 10.00
24 Sean Green 4.00 10.00
25 Reggie Hanson 4.00 10.00
26 Donald Hodge 4.00 10.00
27 Steve Hood 4.00 10.00
28 Keith Hughes 4.00 10.00
29 Mike Iuzzolino 4.00 10.00
30 Keith Jennings 4.00 10.00
31 Larry Johnson 20.00 40.00
32 Treg Lee 4.00 10.00
33 Cedric Lewis 4.00 10.00
34 Kevin Lynch 4.00 10.00
35 Mark Macon 4.00 10.00
36 Jason Matthews 4.00 10.00
37 Eric Murdock 4.00 10.00
38 Jimmy Oliver 4.00 10.00
39 Doug Overton 4.00 10.00
40 Elliot Perry 4.00 10.00
41 Brian Shorter 4.00 10.00
42 Alvaro Teheran 4.00 10.00
43 Joey Wright 4.00 10.00
44 Joe Wylie 4.00 10.00
45 Larry Johnson POY 10.00 25.00

1991 Courtside Holograms

These three holograms were issued in a plastic sleeve within a paper envelope. According to information printed on the envelope, 99,000 sets were produced. Each hologram features the player photo against a parquet basketball floor background, with a subtitle at the bottom of the card face. Framed by turquoise borders above and on the right, the backs present stats (biographical), college record (year by year statistics), and profile. The cards are unnumbered and checklisted below in alphabetical order.

COMPLETE SET (3) 1.00 2.50
1 Greg Anthony .20 .50
2 Larry Johnson .75 2.00
3 Mark Macon .10 .30

1992 Courtside Flashback Promo Sheet

The cards, when cut, are standard size, 2 1/2" by 3 1/2". The players are pictured in their college uniforms. The back of the panel states that only 5,000 were printed. The panel's back congratulates them on their gold medal winning performances as a form of Dream Team tie-in. All the card photos are action shots.

1 Courtside Promo Sheet .75 2.00
Chris Mullin
St. John's
Kareem Abdul-Jabbar
UCLA
David Robinson
Navy
Rick Barry

1992 Courtside Flashback

As a tribute to 100 years of college basketball, Courtside released this 45-card standard-size set, featuring some of the greatest players and coaches of the sport. It is reported that the production run was 199,000 sets, with 20 sets per individually numbered (from 1 to 9,950) case. Ten thousand autographed cards were randomly included with the sets; the exact number of players who signed is not known, but it is suspected that only a few did not sign. In exchange for the Courtside certificate found within each set, the collector received one of 25,000 promotional strips, featuring Larry Bird, David Robinson, and Kareem Abdul-Jabbar. The front features a color player photo cut out and superimposed on a background consisting of white and either red, green, or blue blocks. The backs carry a second color player photo and a brief career summary. The cards are numbered on the back. A promo version of card 41, Bill Walton, is known; its white back reads "The Big 9 Sports Card Show."

COMP.FACT.SET (45) 2.00 4.00
COMMON CARD (1-45) .02 .10
STATED PRINT RUN 199,000 SETS
1 Tommy Amaker .02 .10
2 Charles Barkley .30 .75
3 Rick Barry .20 .50
4 Larry Bird .40 1.00
5 Larry Brown CO .08 .25
6 Quinn Buckner .02 .10
7 Tom Burleson .02 .10
8 Austin Carr .02 .10
9 Phil Ford .02 .10
10 Andrew Gaze .08 .25
11 Artis Gilmore .08 .25
12 Jack Givens .02 .10
13 Gail Goodrich .08 .25
14 Kevin Grevey .02 .10
15 Ernie Grunfeld .02 .10
16 Elvin Hayes .20 .50
17 Walt Hazzard .08 .25
18 Kareem Abdul-Jabbar .30 .75
19 Marques Johnson .08 .25
20 John Lucas .08 .25
21 Kyle Macy .02 .10
22 Rollie Massimino CO .02 .10
23 Cedric Maxwell .02 .10
24 Bob McAdoo .08 .25
25 Al McGuire CO .08 .25
26 George Mikan .30 .75
27 Sidney Moncrief .08 .25
28 Chris Mullin .20 .50
29 Calvin Murphy .08 .25
30 Sam Perkins .08 .25
31 David Robinson .20 .50
32 Curtis Rowe .02 .10
33 Cazzie Russell .08 .25
34 Charlie Scott .08 .25
35 Dean Smith CO .20 .50
36 Jerry Tarkanian CO .08 .25
37 David Thompson .08 .25
38 Nate Thurmond .08 .25
39 Monte Towe .02 .10
40 Jim Valvano CO .20 .50
41 Bill Walton .20 .50
42 Paul Westphal .08 .25
43 Dereck Whittenburg .02 .10
44 Sidney Wicks .02 .10
45 John Wooden CO .20 .50

1992 Courtside Flashback Autographs

RANDOM INSERTS IN SETS
1 Tommy Amaker 10.00 25.00
3 Rick Barry 10.00 25.00
4 Larry Bird 50.00 120.00
5 Larry Brown CO 12.50 30.00
6 Quinn Buckner 5.00 12.00
7 Tom Burleson 5.00 12.00
8 Austin Carr 10.00 25.00
9 Phil Ford 5.00 12.00
10 Andrew Gaze 25.00 60.00
11 Artis Gilmore 6.00 15.00
12 Jack Givens 8.00 20.00
13 Gail Goodrich 8.00 20.00
14 Kevin Grevey 3.00 8.00
15 Ernie Grunfeld 5.00 12.00
16 Elvin Hayes 10.00 25.00
17 Walt Hazzard 5.00 12.00
18 Kareem Abdul-Jabbar 25.00 60.00
19 Marques Johnson 6.00 15.00
20 John Lucas 6.00 15.00
21 Kyle Macy 3.00 8.00
22 Rollie Massimino CO 5.00 12.00
23 Cedric Maxwell 5.00 12.00
24 Bob McAdoo 10.00 25.00
25 Al McGuire CO 15.00 40.00
26 George Mikan 75.00 150.00
27 Sidney Moncrief 5.00 12.00
29 Calvin Murphy 6.00 15.00
30 Sam Perkins 5.00 12.00
32 Curtis Rowe 3.00 8.00
33 Cazzie Russell 5.00 12.00
34 Charlie Scott 5.00 12.00
35 Dean Smith CO 40.00 100.00
37 David Thompson 10.00 25.00
38 Nate Thurmond 10.00 25.00
39 Monte Towe 3.00 8.00
40 Jim Valvano CO 150.00 300.00
41 Bill Walton 8.00 20.00
42 Paul Westphal 10.00 25.00
43 Dereck Whittenburg 3.00 8.00
44 Sidney Wicks 3.00 8.00
45 John Wooden CO 40.00 100.00

1991 Front Row

The 1991 Front Row Italian/English Basketball Draft Pick set contains 100 standard-size cards. Each factory set comes with an official certificate of authenticity that bears a unique serial number. This set is distinguished from the American version by size (100 instead of 50 cards), different production quantities (30,000 factory sets and 3,000 wax cases) and a red stripe on the card front. The front design features glossy color action player photos with white borders. The player's name appears in a red stripe beneath the picture. The backs have different smaller color photos (upper right corner) as well as biography, college statistics and achievements superimposed on a gray background with an orange basketball. This set also includes a second (career highlights) card of some players (39-43), a subset devoted to Larry Johnson (44-49) and two "Retrospect" cards (96-97). Italian and Japanese cards are valued the same. Please refer to the multipliers in the header below for foreign cards.

COMPLETE SET (50) 1.25 3.00
COMPLETE ITALIAN SET (100) 1.25 3.00
*ITALIAN AND JAPANESE: SAME VALUE
1 Larry Johnson .40 1.00
2 Kenny Anderson .20 .50
3 Rick Fox .08 .25
4 Pete Chilcutt .01 .05
5 George Ackles .01 .05
6 Mark Macon .01 .05
7 Greg Anthony .05 .15
8 Mike Iuzzolino .01 .05
9 Anthony Avent .01 .05
10 Terrell Brandon .30 .75
11 Kevin Brooks .01 .05
12 Myron Brown .01 .05
13 Chris Corchiani .01 .05
14 Chris Gatling .05 .15
15 Marcus Kennedy .01 .05
16 Eric Murdock .01 .05
17 Tony Farmer .01 .05
18 Keith Hughes .01 .05
19 Kevin Lynch .01 .05
20 Chad Gallagher .01 .05
21 Darrin Chancellor .01 .05
22 Jimmy Oliver .01 .05
23 Von McDade .01 .05
24 Donald Hodge .01 .05
25 Randy Brown .01 .05
26 Doug Overton .01 .05
27 LeRon Ellis .01 .05
28 Sean Green .01 .05
29 Elliot Perry .01 .05
30 Richard Dumas .01 .05
31 Dale Davis .08 .25
32 Lamont Strothers .01 .05
33 Steve Hood .01 .05
34 Joey Wright .01 .05
35 Patrick Eddie .01 .05
36 Joe Wylie .01 .05
37 Bobby Phills .05 .15
38 Alvaro Teheran .01 .05
39 Dale Davis HL .05 .15
40 Rick Fox HL .05 .15
41 Terrell Brandon HL .15 .40
42 Greg Anthony HL .01 .05
43 Mark Macon HL .01 .05
44 Larry Johnson HL .20 .50
45 Larry Johnson FN .20 .50
46 Larry Johnson POW .20 .50
47 Larry Johnson CA .20 .50
48 Larry Johnson FB .20 .50
49 Larry Johson UC .20 .50
50A Bonus Card .01 .05
50B Marty Conlon .01 .05
51 Mike Goodson .01 .05
52 Drexel Deveaux .01 .05
53 Sean Muto .01 .05
54 Keith Owens .01 .05
55 Joao Viana .01 .05
56 Chancellor Nichols .01 .05
57 Charles Thomas .01 .05
58 Carl Thomas .01 .05
59 Anthony Blakley .01 .05
60 Demetrius Calip .01 .05
61 Dale Turnquist .01 .05
62 Carlos Funchess .01 .05
63 Tharon Mayes .01 .05
64 Andy Kennedy .01 .05
65 Oliver Taylor .01 .05
66 David Benoit .05 .15
67 Gary Waites .01 .05
68 Corey Crowder .01 .05
69 Sydney Grider .01 .05
70 Derek Strong .01 .05
71 Larry Stewart .01 .05
72 Matt Roe .01 .05
73 Cedric Lewis .01 .05
74 Anthony Houston .01 .05
75 Steve Bardo .01 .05
76 Marc Brown .01 .05
77 Michael Cutright .01 .05
78 Emanual Davis .01 .05
79 Paris McCurdy .01 .05
80 Jackie Jones .01 .05
81 Mark Peterson .01 .05
82 Clifford Scales .01 .05
83 Robert Pack .05 .15
84 Doug Lee .01 .05
85 Cameron Burns .01 .05
86 Tom Copa .01 .05
87 Clinton Venable .01 .05
88 Ken Redfield .01 .05
89 Melvin Newbern .01 .05
90 Darren Henrie .01 .05
91 Chris Harris .01 .05
92 John Crotty .01 .05
93 Paul Graham .01 .05
94 Stevie Thompson .01 .05
95 Clifford Martin .01 .05
96 Brian Shaw .05 .15
97 Danny Ferry .05 .15
98 Doug Loescher .01 .05
99 Checklist .01 .05
100 Bonus Card .01 .05

1991 Front Row Gold

*GOLD: 1.5X TO 4X BASE CARD HI

1991 Front Row Silver

*SILVER: .75X TO 2X BASE CARD HI

1991 Front Row Update

Comprising of 50 standard size cards, the update version is a continuation (51-100) of the 50-card Draft Pick set. The checklist to the Draft Pick is identical (with identical values) to the first 50 cards of the Italian/English 100 version. Each set was accompanied by a certificate of authenticity that bears a unique serial number, with the production run reported to be 50,000 sets. The fronts feature glossy color action player photos enclosed by white borders. A basketball backboard and rim with the words "Update 92" appears in the lower left corner, with the player's name and position in a dark green stripe beneath the picture. On a gray background with an orange basketball, the backs carry biography, color close-up photo, statistics, and achievements.

COMPLETE SET (50) 1.25 3.00
51 Billy Owens .08 .25
52 Dikembe Mutombo .30 .75
53 Steve Smith .40 1.00
54 Luc Longley .08 .25
55 Doug Smith .01 .05
56 Stacey Augmon .08 .25
57 Brian Williams .05 .15
58 Stanley Roberts .01 .05
59 Rodney Monroe .01 .05
60 Isaac Austin .05 .15
61 Rich King .01 .05
62 Victor Alexander .01 .05
63 LaBradford Smith .01 .05
64 Greg Sutton .01 .05
65 John Turner .01 .05
66 Joao Viana .01 .05
67 Charles Thomas .01 .05
68 Carl Thomas .01 .05
69 Tharon Mayes .01 .05
70 David Benoit .05 .15
71 Corey Crowder .01 .05
72 Larry Stewart .01 .05
73 Steve Bardo .01 .05
74 Paris McCurdy .01 .05
75 Robert Pack .05 .15
76 Doug Lee .01 .05
77 Tom Copa .01 .05
78 Keith Owens .01 .05
79 Mike Goodson .01 .05
80 John Crotty .01 .05
81 Sean Muto .01 .05
82 Chancellor Nichols .01 .05
83 Stevie Thompson .01 .05
84 Demetrius Calip .01 .05
85 Clifford Martin .01 .05
86 Andy Kennedy .01 .05
87 Oliver Taylor .01 .05
88 Gary Waites .01 .05
89 Matt Roe .01 .05
90 Cedric Lewis .01 .05
91 Emanual Davis .01 .05
92 Jackie Jones .01 .05
93 Clifford Scales .01 .05
94 Cameron Burns .01 .05
95 Clinton Venable .01 .05
96 Ken Redfield .01 .05
97 Melvin Newbern .01 .05
98 Chris Harris .01 .05
99 Bonus Card .01 .05
100 Checklist .01 .05

1991 Front Row Update Gold

*GOLD: 1.25X TO 3X BASE CARD HI

1991 Front Row Update Silver

*SILVER: .75X TO 2X BASE CARD HI

1991 Front Row Stacey Augmon

These seven standard-size cards feature seven different action shots of Stacey Augmon. The glossy color photos are enclosed by white borders, while the player's name appears in a purple stripe beneath the picture. Issued with each set, a certificate of authenticity gives the individual serial number of the set and the total production run (25,000). The words "Limited Edition" are gold-foil stamped across the card top. On a gray background with an orange basketball, the horizontally oriented backs summarize Augmon's career. Only card number 7 includes a second photo on its back.

COMPLETE SET (7) .60 1.50
COMMON CARD (1-7) .10 .25

1991 Front Row Italian Promos

The American version of the 1991 Front Row Draft Pick set (50) included a bonus card that could be redeemed for two Italian promo cards through a mail-in offer. This promo set consists of ten standard-size cards. The color player photos on the front are bordered in white, and the player's name appears in a red stripe beneath the picture. On a gray background with an orange Front Row basketball logo, the backs read "Italian Promo Card" and "20,000 Ten Card Sets Produced" although the back of the Bonus Card says "50,000 Sets Produced". The cards are unnumbered and checklisted below in alphabetical order.

COMPLETE SET (10) 1.00 2.50
1 Steve Bardo .08 .25
2 Corey Crowder .08 .25
3 Danny Ferry .30 .75
4 Doug Lee .08 .25
5 Tharon Mayes .08 .25
6 Robert Pack .30 .75
7 Brian Shaw .30 .75
8 Larry Stewart .08 .25
9 Carl Thomas .08 .25
10 Charles Thomas .08 .25

1991 Front Row Larry Johnson

These ten standard-size cards feature different action shots of Larry Johnson. According to Front Row, there were 50,000 sets produced.

COMPLETE SET (10)	1.60	4.00
COMMON CARD (1-10)	.20	.50

1991 Front Row Dikembe Mutombo

These seven standard-size cards feature seven different action shots of Dikembe Mutombo. The glossy color photos are enclosed by white borders, while the player's name appears in a purple stripe beneath the picture. Issued with each set, a certificate of authenticity gives the individual serial number of the set and the total production run (50,000). The words "Limited Edition" are gold-foil stamped across the card top. On a gray background with an orange basketball, the horizontally oriented backs summarize Mutombo's collegiate career. The same set was produced with the Front Row seal and the words "Charter Member" gold-foil stamped on the backs. Again, the certificate of authenticity carries the set serial number and the total production run (20,000).

COMPLETE SET (7)	1.00	2.50
COMMON CARD (1-7)	.16	.40

1991 Front Row Billy Owens

These seven standard-size cards feature seven different action shots of Billy Owens. The glossy color photos are enclosed by white borders, while the player's name appears in a purple stripe beneath the picture. Issued with each set, a certificate of authenticity gives the individual serial number of the set and the total production run (25,000). The words "Limited Edition" are gold-foil stamped across the card top. On a gray background with an orange basketball, the horizontally oriented backs summarize Owens' collegiate career.

COMPLETE SET (7)	.60	1.50
COMMON CARD (1-7)	.10	.25

1991 Front Row Steve Smith

These seven standard-size cards feature seven different action shots of Steve Smith. The glossy color photos are enclosed by white borders, while the player's name appears in a purple stripe beneath the picture. Issued with each set, a certificate of authenticity gives the individual serial number of the set and the total production run (25,000). The words "Limited Edition" are gold-foil stamped across the card top. On a gray background with an orange basketball, the horizontally oriented backs summarize Smith's collegiate career. Only card number 5 includes a second photo on its back.

COMPLETE SET (7)	1.20	3.00
COMMON CARD (1-7)	.20	.50

1991-92 Front Row Premier

The 1991-92 Front Row Premier set contains 120 standard-size cards. No factory sets were made, and the production run was limited to 2,500 waxbox cases, with 360 cards per box. The set included five bonus cards (86, 88, 90, 91, 93) that were redeemable through a mail-in offer for unnamed player cards. The player's name appears in a silver stripe beneath the picture. The backs have biography, statistics, and achievements superimposed on an orange basketball icon.

COMPLETE SET (120)	2.50	6.00
1 Rich King	.01	.05
2 Kenny Anderson	.20	.50
3 Billy Owens	.08	.25
4 Ken Redfield	.01	.05
5 Robert Pack	.05	.15
6 Clinton Venable	.01	.05
7 Tom Copa	.01	.05
8 Rick Fox HL	.05	.15
9 Cameron Burns	.01	.05
10 Doug Lee	.01	.05
11 LaBradford Smith	.01	.05
12 Clifford Scales	.01	.05
13 Mark Peterson	.01	.05
14 Jackie Jones	.01	.05
15 Paris McCurdy	.01	.05
16 Dikembe Mutombo	.30	.75
17 Emanual Davis	.01	.05
18 Michael Cutright	.01	.05
19 Marc Brown	.01	.05
20 Steve Bardo	.01	.05
21 John Turner	.01	.05
22 Anthony Houston	.01	.05
23 Cedric Lewis	.01	.05
24 Matt Roe	.01	.05
25 Larry Stewart	.01	.05
26 Derek Strong	.01	.05
27 Sydney Grider	.01	.05
28 Corey Crowder	.01	.05
29 Gary Waites	.01	.05
30 David Benoit	.05	.15
31 Larry Johnson	.25	.60
32 Oliver Taylor UER	.01	.05
33 Andy Kennedy	.01	.05
34 Tharon Mayes	.01	.05
35 Carlos Funchess	.01	.05
36 Dale Turnquist	.01	.05
37 Luc Longley	.08	.25
38 Demetrius Calip	.01	.05
39 Anthony Blakley	.01	.05
40 Carl Thomas	.01	.05
41 Charles Thomas	.01	.05
42 Chancellor Nichols	.01	.05
43 Joao Viana	.01	.05
44 Keith Owens	.01	.05
45 Sean Muto	.01	.05
46 Drexel Deveaux	.01	.05
47 Stacey Augmon	.05	.15
48 Mike Goodson	.01	.05
49 Marty Conlon	.01	.05
50 Mark Macon	.01	.05
51 Greg Anthony	.05	.15
52 Dale Davis	.08	.25
53 Isaac Austin	.05	.15
54 Alvaro Teheran	.01	.05
55 Bobby Phills	.05	.15
56 Joe Wylie	.01	.05
57 Patrick Eddie	.01	.05
58 Joey Wright	.01	.05
59 Steve Hood	.01	.05
60 Lamont Strothers	.01	.05
61 Victor Alexander	.01	.05
62 Richard Dumas	.01	.05
63 Elliot Perry	.01	.05
64 Sean Green	.01	.05
65 Rick Fox	.08	.25
66 LeRon Ellis	.01	.05
67 Doug Overton	.01	.05
68 Randy Brown	.01	.05
69 Donald Hodge	.01	.05
70 Von McDade	.01	.05
71 Greg Sutton	.01	.05
72 Jimmy Oliver	.01	.05
73 Terrell Brandon HL	.15	.40
74 Darrin Chancellor	.01	.05
75 Chad Gallagher	.01	.05
76 Kevin Lynch	.01	.05
77 Keith Hughes	.01	.05
78 Tony Farmer	.01	.05
79 Eric Murdock	.01	.05
80 Marcus Kennedy	.01	.05
81 Larry Johnson	.25	.60
82 Stacey Augmon	.08	.25
83 Dikembe Mutombo	.30	.75
84 Steve Smith	.40	1.00
85 Billy Owens UER	.08	.25
86 Bonus Card 1	.01	.05
87 Brian Shaw	.05	.15
88 Bonus Card 2	.01	.05
89 LaBradford Smith HL	.01	.05
90 Bonus Card 3	.01	.05
91 Bonus Card 4	.05	.15
92 Danny Ferry FLB	.05	.15
93 Bonus Card 5	.01	.05
94 Doug Smith HL	.01	.05
95 Luc Longley HL	.05	.15
96 Billy Owens HL	.05	.15
97 Steve Smith HL	.20	.50
98 Dikembe Mutombo HL	.15	.40
99 Stacey Augmon HL	.05	.15
100 Larry Johnson HL	.10	.30
101 Chris Gatling	.05	.15
102 Chris Corchiani	.01	.05
103 Myron Brown	.01	.05
104 Kevin Brooks	.01	.05
105 Anthony Avent	.01	.05
106 Steve Smith	.40	1.00
107 Mike Iuzzolino	.01	.05
108 George Ackles	.01	.05
109 Melvin Newbern	.01	.05
110 Robert Pack HL	.01	.05
111 Darren Henrie	.01	.05
112 Chris Harris	.01	.05
113 John Crotty	.01	.05
114 Terrell Brandon	.30	.75
115 Paul Graham	.01	.05
116 Stevie Thompson	.01	.05
117 Clifford Martin	.01	.05
118 Doug Smith	.01	.05
119 Pete Chilcutt	.01	.05
120 Checklist Card	.01	.05

1992 Front Row

The 1992 Front Row Draft Picks basketball set consists of 100 standard-size cards. The set was sold in a cardboard box, and the back panel carries the set serial number and total production run (150,000). The fronts features color action player photos. Teal borders shading from dark to light surround the pictures. A gradated orange vertical bar containing the player's name is superimposed over one side of the photo. The Front Row Draft Picks logo appears below it. The miniature representation of the team mascot appears in the lower left corner. The horizontal backs display biography, collegiate statistics, and career highlights on a teal background with white borders. An orange bar similar to the one on the front runs down the right edge and contains the words "Draft Picks '92". Four cards (90, 92, 96, and 99) have player photos instead of text on their backs.

COMPLETE SET (100)	2.00	5.00
1 Eric Anderson	.01	.05
2 Darin Archbold	.01	.05
3 Woody Austin	.01	.05
4 Mark Baker	.01	.05
5 Jon Barry	.01	.05
6 Elmer Bennett	.01	.05
7 Tony Bennett	.01	.05
8 Alex Blackwell	.01	.05
9 Curtis Blair	.01	.05
10 Ed Book	.01	.05
11 Marques Bragg	.01	.05
12 P.J. Brown	.02	.10
13 Anthony Buford	.01	.05
14 Dexter Cambridge	.01	.05
15 Brian Davis	.01	.05
16 Lucius Davis	.01	.05
17 Todd Day	.02	.10
18 Greg Dennis	.01	.05
19 Radenko Dobras	.01	.05
20 Harold Ellis	.01	.05
21 Chris King	.01	.05
22 Jo Jo English	.01	.05
23 Deron Feldhaus	.01	.05
24 Matt Geiger	.02	.10
25 Lewis Geter	.01	.05
26 George Gilmore	.01	.05
27 Litterial Green	.01	.05
28 Tom Gugliotta	.25	.60
29 Jim Havrilla	.01	.05
30 Robert Horry	.07	.20
31 Stephen Howard	.01	.05
32 Alonzo Jamison	.01	.05
33 David Johnson	.01	.05
34 Herb Jones	.01	.05
35 Popeye Jones	.01	.05
36 Adam Keefe	.01	.05
37 Dan Cyrulik	.01	.05
38 Ken Leeks	.01	.05
39 Ricardo Leonard	.01	.05
40 Gerald Madkins	.01	.05
41 Eric Manuel	.01	.05
42 Marlon Maxey	.01	.05
43 Jim McCoy	.01	.05
44 Oliver Miller	.01	.05
45 Sean Miller	.01	.05
46 Darren Morningstar	.01	.05
47 Isaiah Morris	.01	.05
48 James Moses	.01	.05
49 Doug Christie	.07	.20
50 Damon Patterson	.01	.05
51 John Pelphrey	.01	.05
52 Brent Price	.01	.05
53 Brett Roberts	.01	.05
54 Steve Rogers	.01	.05
55 Sean Rooks	.01	.05
56 Malik Sealy	.02	.10
57 Tom Schurfranz	.01	.05
58 David Scott	.01	.05
59 Rod Sellers	.01	.05
60 Vernel Singleton	.01	.05
61 Reggie Slater	.01	.05
62 Elmore Spencer	.01	.05
63 Chris Smith	.01	.05
64 Latrell Sprewell	.60	1.50
65 Matt Steigenga	.01	.05
66 Bryant Stith	.02	.10
67 Daimon Sweet	.01	.05
68 Craig Upchurch	.01	.05
69 Van Usher	.01	.05
70 Tony Watts	.01	.05
71 Clarence Weatherspoon	.02	.10
72 Robert Werdann	.01	.05
73 Benford Williams	.01	.05
74 Corey Williams	.01	.05
75 Henry Williams	.01	.05
76 Tim Burroughs	.01	.05
77 Erik Wilson	.01	.05
78 Randy Woods	.01	.05
79 Kendall Youngblood	.01	.05
80 Terry Boyd	.01	.05
81 Tracy Murray	.01	.05
82 Reggie Smith	.01	.05
83 Lee Mayberry	.01	.05
84 Matt Fish	.01	.05
85 Hubert Davis	.02	.10
86 Duane Cooper	.01	.05
87 Anthony Peeler	.02	.10
88 Harold Miner	.01	.05
89 Harold Miner	.01	.05
90 Harold Miner	.01	.05
91 Christian Laettner	.15	.40
92 Christian Laettner Special	.07	.20
93 Christian Laettner Special	.07	.20
94 Walt Williams	.07	.20
95 Walt Williams Special	.02	.10
96 Walt Williams Special	.02	.10
97 LaPhonso Ellis	.07	.20
98 LaPhonso Ellis	.02	.10
99 LaPhonso Ellis	.02	.10
100 Checklist 1-100	.01	.05
100B Larry Johnson Promo	.75	2.00

1992 Front Row Gold

*GOLD: 1.5X TO 4X BASE CARD HI

1992 Front Row Silver

*SILVER: .75X TO 2X BASE CARD HI

1992 Front Row Dream Picks

The 1992 Front Row Dream Picks basketball set contains 100 standard-size cards. The set features five cards each of the top ten players who signed with Front Row from the 1991 NBA Draft and five cards of the top ten from the 1992 draft. The fronts display color action player photos bordered in purple. The player's name appears above the picture in a yellow bar accented by a red shadow border. The Front Row logo appears at the lower right corner in an orange diagonal stripe. The backs are predominantly yellow and present career summary and highlights. The words "Dream Picks" appear in an orange diagonal stripe on the back. The fifth card of each five-card set has a second color player photo on its back.

COMPLETE SET (100)	2.00	5.00
1 Larry Johnson	.08	.25
2 Larry Johnson	.08	.25
3 Larry Johnson	.08	.25
4 Larry Johnson	.08	.25
5 Larry Johnson	.08	.25
6 Dikembe Mutombo	.08	.25
7 Dikembe Mutombo	.08	.25
8 Dikembe Mutombo	.08	.25
9 Dikembe Mutombo	.08	.25
10 Dikembe Mutombo	.08	.25
11 Stacey Augmon	.04	.10
12 Stacey Augmon	.04	.10
13 Stacey Augmon	.04	.10
14 Stacey Augmon	.04	.10
15 Stacey Augmon	.04	.10
16 Billy Owens	.01	.05
17 Billy Owens	.01	.05
18 Billy Owens	.01	.05
19 Billy Owens	.01	.05
20 Billy Owens	.01	.05
21 Clarence Weatherspoon	.01	.05
22 Clarence Weatherspoon	.01	.05
23 Clarence Weatherspoon	.01	.05
24 Clarence Weatherspoon	.01	.05
25 Clarence Weatherspoon	.01	.05
26 Steve Smith	.08	.25
27 Steve Smith	.08	.25
28 Steve Smith	.08	.25
29 Steve Smith	.08	.25
30 Steve Smith	.08	.25
31 Larry Stewart	.01	.05
32 Larry Stewart	.01	.05
33 Larry Stewart	.01	.05
34 Larry Stewart	.01	.05
35 Larry Stewart	.01	.05
36 Rick Fox	.01	.05
37 Rick Fox	.01	.05
38 Rick Fox	.01	.05
39 Rick Fox	.01	.05
40 Rick Fox	.01	.05
41 Christian Laettner	.10	.30
42 Christian Laettner	.10	.30
43 Christian Laettner	.10	.30
44 Christian Laettner	.10	.30
45 Christian Laettner	.10	.30
46 Bryant Stith	.01	.05
47 Bryant Stith	.01	.05
48 Bryant Stith	.01	.05
49 Bryant Stith	.01	.05
50 Bryant Stith	.01	.05
51 Harold Miner	.01	.05
52 Harold Miner	.01	.05
53 Harold Miner	.01	.05
54 Harold Miner	.01	.05
55 Harold Miner	.01	.05
56 Mark Macon	.01	.05
57 Mark Macon	.01	.05
58 Mark Macon	.01	.05
59 Mark Macon	.01	.05
60 Mark Macon	.01	.05
61 Adam Keefe	.01	.05
62 Adam Keefe	.01	.05
63 Adam Keefe	.01	.05
64 Adam Keefe	.01	.05
65 Adam Keefe	.01	.05
66 Tom Gugliotta	.20	.50
67 Tom Gugliotta	.20	.50
68 Tom Gugliotta	.20	.50
69 Tom Gugliotta	.20	.50
70 Tom Gugliotta	.20	.50
71 Todd Day	.01	.05
72 Todd Day	.01	.05
73 Todd Day	.01	.05
74 Todd Day	.01	.05
75 Todd Day	.01	.05
76 Walt Williams	.04	.10
77 Walt Williams	.04	.10
78 Walt Williams	.04	.10
79 Walt Williams	.04	.10
80 Walt Williams	.04	.10
81 Malik Sealy	.01	.05
82 Malik Sealy	.01	.05
83 Malik Sealy	.01	.05
84 Malik Sealy	.01	.05
85 Malik Sealy	.01	.05
86 Stanley Roberts	.01	.05
87 Stanley Roberts	.01	.05
88 Stanley Roberts	.01	.05
89 Stanley Roberts	.01	.05
90 Stanley Roberts	.01	.05
91 LaPhonso Ellis	.04	.10
92 LaPhonso Ellis	.04	.10
93 LaPhonso Ellis	.04	.10
94 LaPhonso Ellis	.04	.10
95 LaPhonso Ellis	.04	.10
96 Terrell Brandon	.04	.10
97 Terrell Brandon	.04	.10
98 Terrell Brandon	.04	.10
99 Terrell Brandon	.04	.10
100 Terrell Brandon	.04	.10

1992 Front Row Dream Picks Gold

*GOLD: 1.5X TO 4X BASE HI
RANDOM INSERTS IN PACKS

1992 Front Row Dream Picks Silver

*SILVER: ..75X TO 2X BASE HI
RANDOM INSERTS IN PACKS

1992 Front Row Holograms

This three-card standard-size hologram set features close-up player images against graphic art backgrounds. The player's name appears at the bottom in large block letters. The backs carry a small, square color photo in the center of a light blue background with white borders. Biographical information and career achievements are printed in black above and below the picture, respectively. Magenta lettering sets off the player's name printed vertically on each side of the photo. The set comes with a signed certificate of authenticity giving the set serial number and the total production run (50,000).

COMPLETE SET (3)	1.25	3.00
1 Larry Johnson	.75	2.00
2 Billy Owens	.30	.75
3 Dikembe Mutombo	.60	1.50

1992 Front Row Christian Laettner

This set consists of four standard-size cards plus an official certificate of authenticity giving the set serial number and the production run figures (15,000). The fronts feature white-bordered glossy color action photos of Laettner in his Duke uniform. His name appears in white lettering within a dark blue stripe that runs vertically down the left side. Three different design layouts adorn the card backs. The top half of the white-bordered first card has a picture of Laettner glancing up, the bottom half contains a brief description of his Olympic exploits. The backs of card numbers two and four feature full-bleed color action photos of Laettner, with statistics shown in a dark blue rectangle near the bottom of each. The third card's layout is split vertically, with a color action photo of Laettner passing the ball on the left side, and a review of his playoff heroics on the right, all within a white border. The cards are numbered on the back.

COMPLETE SET (4)	1.25	3.00
COMMON CARD (1-4)	.40	1.00

1992-93 Front Row Holograms

This 3-card standard size hologram set features close-up player images against an action scene. The horizontal backs contain a color action photo, 1992 collegiate statistics and a Front Row individually numbered holographic strip. The cards are numbered out of 125,000.

COMPLETE SET (3)	.60	1.50
1 Christian Laettner	.40	1.00
2 Harold Miner	.08	.25
3 Walt Williams	.20	.50

1992-93 Front Row LJ Pure Gold

This three-card standard-size set comes with a numbered certificate of authenticity carrying the set serial number. Production was limited to 20,000 sets. The cards feature a 23K gold dust stamped border around color action photos of Larry Johnson. The Front Row logo is stamped into the border, as are the words "Pure Gold" at the bottom. The backs feature a small color photo and player information on a light gray background. The player information is printed on the Front Row basketball icon.

COMPLETE SET (3)	4.00	10.00
COMMON CARD (1-3)	1.60	4.00

1993 Front Row LJ Grandmama

This seven-card standard-size captures Larry Johnson's alter ego, Grandmama, who was created to merchandise the new Converse shoes. The production run was 100,000 sets. Inside black borders, the fronts feature color pictures of Grandmama in action from one of the television commercials. The pictures are accented by a red stripe on top and on the right side. The Converse and Front Row logos in opposite corners round out the front. On a pastel blue background with ghosted photo of Grandmama, the backs carry interesting stories on the life of Grandmama.

COMPLETE SET (7)	1.50	4.00
COMMON CARD (G1-G7)	.30	.75

1993 Front Row LJ Grandmama Gold

Again teaming up with Converse, the ten-card second edition of the 1993 Front Row Larry Johnson Grandmama set is part of the company's new card line called "The Gold Collection." Production was limited to 5,000 standard-sized sets. The cards feature full-bleed color photos on the fronts. The words "The Gold Collection" are printed in gold foil along the left edge, while "Grandmama" is printed in the same way on a black bar toward the bottom of the picture. The backs have a second full-bleed color photo and, printed on a white rectangle, a quote from Grandmama or a statement extolling her extraordinary roundball skills. The Converse logo appears in the upper left corner.

COMPLETE SET (10)	3.00	8.00
COMMON CARD (1-10)	.40	1.00

1997 Genuine Article Previews

This 5-card set was released by Geniune Article to promote their 1997 Genuine Coverage set. The set features some of the NBA's top draft picks of the 1996-97 season. Card backs carry a "BK" prefix.

COMPLETE SET (5)	.75	2.00
BK1 Ray Allen	.40	1.00
BK2 Allen Iverson	.60	1.50
BK3 Kerry Kittles	.20	.50
BK4 Antoine Walker	.30	.75
BK5 Lorenzen Wright	.20	.50

1997 Genuine Article

This 27-card set, produced by The Genuine Article, Inc., came in 7-card packs in 12-pack boxes. The card fronts have color photographs of the player on a hardwood floor background. Under the photo, "Hardwood Signature Series" is written in a gold foil oval. Each pack contained one autograph and one of the following insert sets: Double Cards, Dual Sport Preview, Hometown Heroes, Lottery Connection or Lottery Gems. There is also a Genuine Article "Charlotte Series" product that was produced. Little information is available due to the fact that the company folded around the time this set was printed. Many of these autographed cards have been inexpensively wholesaled via mail order catalogues.

COMPLETE SET (27)	1.50	4.00
1 Derek Anderson UER	.10	.25
2 Keith Booth	.10	.25
3 Bobby Jackson	.12	.30
4 Antonio Daniels	.10	.25
5 Harold Deane	.10	.25
6 Ya-Ya Dia	.05	.15
7 Lee Wilson	.05	.15
8 Kebu Stewart	.10	.25
9 Adonal Foyle	.10	.25
10 Othella Harrington	.05	.15
11 Alvin Sims	.10	.25
12 Brevin Knight	.10	.25
13 Walter McCarty	.05	.15
14 Victor Page	.10	.25
15 Lorenzen Wright	.05	.15
16 Scot Pollard	.10	.25
17 Vitaly Potapenko	.05	.15
18 Jamal Robinson	.05	.15
19 Roy Rogers UER	.05	.15
20 Shea Seals	.10	.25
21 Carmelo Travieso	.05	.15
22 Jacque Vaughn	.10	.25
23 DeJuan Wheat	.10	.25
24 Allen Iverson	.20	.50
25 Damon Stoudamire	.10	.25
26 Ron Mercer	.12	.30
27 Keith Van Horn	.20	.50

1997 Genuine Article Autographs

This 27-card is a parallel of the base set. Each player autographed 7500 hand-numbered cards except for Ron Mercer and Keith Van Horn who signed only 200 each. Each autograph, inserted one per pack, has the same card fronts, but the handnumbered backs say who signed the card in the "presence of a representative of The Genuine Article, Inc."

1 Derek Anderson UER	1.50	4.00
2 Keith Booth	1.50	4.00
3 Bobby Jackson	2.00	5.00
4 Antonio Daniels	1.50	4.00
5 Harold Deane	1.50	4.00
6 Ya-Ya Dia	1.00	2.50
7 Lee Wilson	1.00	2.50
8 Kebu Stewart	1.50	4.00
9 Adonal Foyle	1.50	4.00
10 Othella Harrington	1.00	2.50
11 Alvin Sims	1.50	4.00
12 Brevin Knight	1.50	4.00
13 Walter McCarty	1.00	2.50
14 Victor Page	1.50	4.00
15 Lorenzen Wright	1.00	2.50
16 Scot Pollard	1.50	4.00
17 Vitaly Potapenko	1.00	2.50
18 Jamal Robinson	1.00	2.50
19 Roy Rogers UER	1.00	2.50
20 Shea Seals	1.50	4.00
21 Carmelo Travieso	1.00	2.50
22 Jacque Vaughn	1.50	4.00
23 DeJuan Wheat	1.50	4.00
25 Damon Stoudamire	1.50	4.00
26 Ron Mercer/200	6.00	15.00
27 Keith Van Horn/200	8.00	20.00
B3 DeJuan Wheat BON/2500	1.50	4.00

1997 Genuine Article Charlotte Series

MP1 Antonio Daniels	.15	.40
MP2 Tony Battie	.15	.40
MP3 Adonal Foyle	.15	.40
MP5 Austin Croshere	.12	.30
MP6 Derek Anderson	.15	.40
MP7 Kelvin Cato	.15	.40
MP8 Brevin Knight	.15	.40
MP9 Johnny Taylor	.15	.40
MP11 Scot Pollard	.15	.40
MP12 Anthony Parker	.15	.40
MP14 Bobby Jackson	.20	.50
MP16 Charles Smith	.15	.40
MP17 Jacque Vaughn	.15	.40

1997 Genuine Article Charlotte Series Autographs

MP1 Antonio Daniels/5000	2.50	6.00
MP2 Tony Battie/5000	2.50	6.00
MP3 Adonal Foyle/5000	2.50	6.00
MP5 Austin Croshere/5000	2.00	5.00
MP6 Derek Anderson/5000	2.50	6.00
MP7 Kelvin Cato/5000	2.50	6.00
MP8 Brevin Knight/5000	2.50	6.00
MP9 Johnny Taylor/5000	2.50	6.00
MP11 Scot Pollard/5000	2.50	6.00
MP12 Anthony Parker/5000	2.50	6.00
MP14 Bobby Jackson/5000	3.00	8.00
MP16 Charles Smith/5000	2.50	6.00
MP17 Jacque Vaughn/5000	2.50	6.00

1997 Genuine Article Double Cards

This 3-card randomly inserted set highlights some of the youngest professional players in their college uniforms. Each card has a different design and are numbered D1S-D3S on the back.

COMPLETE SET (3)	1.50	4.00
D1S Walker/Mercer/Anderson	1.00	2.50
D2S Iverson/Stoudamire	1.25	3.00
D3S Mercer/Van Horn	.75	2.00

1997 Genuine Article Double Cards Autographs

D1S A.Walker/Mercer/D.Anderson	40.00	80.00
D3S Ron Mercer	6.00	15.00
D3S Keith Van Horn	8.00	20.00

1997 Genuine Article Hometown Heroes

This 13-card set was randomly inserted and highlights eight different professional players. The card fronts have a photograph of the player in front of a map background of where they are currently playing in the NBA or where they played college ball. Their uniforms have the NBA logos airbrushed out. The card backs are numbered with an "HH" prefix.

COMPLETE SET (13)	3.00	8.00
HH1 Ray Allen	.60	1.50
HH2 Ray Allen	.60	1.50
HH3 Allen Iverson	1.00	2.50
HH4 Kerry Kittles	.30	.75
HH5 Kerry Kittles	.30	.75
HH6 Bryant Reeves	.30	.75
HH7 Glen Rice	.50	1.25
HH8 Damon Stoudamire	.50	1.25
HH9 Damon Stoudamire	.50	1.25
HH10 Antoine Walker	.50	1.25
HH11 Antoine Walker	.50	1.25
HH12 Lorenzen Wright	.30	.75
HH13 Lorenzen Wright	.30	.75

1997 Genuine Article Hometown Heroes Autographs

This 13-card set was randomly inserted and highlights eight different professional players. The card fronts have a photograph of the player in front of a map background of where they are currently playing in the NBA or where they played college ball. Their uniforms have the NBA logos airbrushed out. The card backs are numbered with an "HH" prefix. Each card is autographed and numbered on the back out of 750.

HH1 Ray Allen	8.00	20.00
HH2 Ray Allen	8.00	20.00
HH10 Antoine Walker	6.00	15.00
HH11 Antoine Walker	6.00	15.00

1997 Genuine Article Jumbos

These three jumbo card, measuring 3.5 x 5, are cards that parallel smaller Genuine Article cards except the backs contain a long description of the players pictured on the card fronts. The original distribution of the cards is uncertain; however, they were inexpensively offered through mail order catalogues when Genuine Article disbanded. The back are numbered with a D-prefix.

COMPLETE SET (3)	1.50	4.00
D1 Ron Mercer Antoine Walker Derek Anderson (Kentucky's Finest)	.60	1.50
D2 Allen Iverson Damon Stoudamire (Rookie of the Year)	1.50	4.00
D3 Keith Van Horn Ron Mercer (Legends of Tomorrow)	.40	1.00

1997 Genuine Article Lottery Connection

This randomly inserted, 5-card set highlights some of the younger NBA players in their college uniforms. The fronts have the insert name in the top left corner with a basketball/world icon. Below the full-bleed player photo, the player's last name only appears in a gold foil font. The backs are numbered with a "LC" prefix.

COMPLETE SET (5)	1.50	4.00
LC1 Derek Anderson	.60	1.50
LC2 Bobby Jackson	.75	2.00
LC3 Brevin Knight	.60	1.50
LC4 Jacque Vaughn	.60	1.50
LC5 Lorenzen Wright	.40	1.00

1997 Genuine Article Lottery Connection Autographs

This randomly inserted, 5-card set highlights some of the younger NBA players in their college uniforms. The fronts have the insert name in the top left corner with a basketball/world icon. Below the full-bleed player photo, the player's last name only appears in a gold foil font. The backs are numbered with a "LC" prefix. The cards are autographed on the front, and numbered out of 3500 on the back.

LC1 Derek Anderson	2.00	5.00
LC2 Bobby Jackson	2.50	6.00
LC3 Brevin Knight	2.00	5.00
LC4 Jacque Vaughn	2.00	5.00
LC5 Lorenzen Wright	1.25	3.00

1997 Genuine Article Lottery Gems

This 5-card insert set, randomly inserted in packs, highlights five of the top picks in the 1997 NBA draft. The fronts picture a color photo of the player inside an oval distorted swirl. The player's name is written gold foil at the bottom . The card backs are numbered with a "LG" prefix.

COMPLETE SET (5)	2.00	5.00
LG1 Antonio Daniels	.60	1.50
LG2 Adonal Foyle	.60	1.50
LG3 Danny Fortson	.60	1.50
LG4 Ron Mercer	.75	2.00
LG5 Keith Van Horn	1.25	3.00

1997 Genuine Article Lottery Gems Autographs

This 5-card insert set, randomly inserted in packs, highlights five of the top picks in the 1997 NBA draft. The fronts picture a color photo of the player inside an oval distorted swirl. The player's name is written gold foil at the bottom . The card backs are numbered with a "LG" prefix. The cards are autographed on the front and numbered out of 1500 on the back.

LG2 Adonal Foyle	2.50	6.00
LG3 Danny Fortson	2.50	6.00
LG4 Ron Mercer	3.00	8.00
LG5 Keith Van Horn	5.00	12.00

1993-94 Images Four Sport

These 150 standard-size cards feature on their borderless fronts color player action shots with backgrounds that have been thrown out of focus. On the white background to the left, career highlights, biography and statistics are displayed. Just 6,500 of each card were produced. The set closes with Classic Headlines (128-147) and checklists (148-150). A redemption card inserted one per case entitled the collector to one set of basketball draft preview cards. This offered expired 9/30/94.

COMPLETE SET (150)	6.00	15.00
2 Chris Webber	.40	1.00
6 Anfernee Hardaway	.30	.75
10 Sherron Mills	.08	.25
12 Warren Kidd	.08	.25
13 Bryon Russell	.15	.40
14 Mike Peplowski	.08	.25
18 Doug Edwards	.08	.25
22 Darnell Mee	.08	.25
27 Corie Blount	.08	.25
36 Shaquille O'Neal Rap	.50	1.25
40 George Lynch	.08	.25
41 Gheorghe Muresan	.10	.30
50 Isaiah Rider	.10	.30
59 Vin Baker	.10	.30
60 Rodney Rogers	.08	.25
66 Josh Grant	.08	.25
67 Luther Wright	.08	.25
68 Allan Houston	.25	.60
75 Lindsey Hunter	.08	.25
76 Scott Burrell	.08	.25
79 Sam Cassell	.15	.40
81 Jimmy Jackson	.10	.30
84 Chris Mills	.08	.25
89 Acie Earl	.08	.25
90 Terry Dehere	.08	.25
94 James Robinson	.08	.25
96 Jamal Mashburn	.15	.40
98 Ed Stokes	.08	.25
99 Ervin Johnson	.08	.25
100 Nick Van Exel	.10	.30
109 Rex Walters	.08	.25
110 Chris Whitney	.08	.25
112 Alonzo Mourning	.15	.40
113 Lucious Harris	.08	.25
122 Dino Radja	.08	.25
123 Harold Miner	.08	.25
124 Greg Graham	.08	.25
128 Shaquille O'Neal B/W	.40	1.00
132 Chris Webber B/W	.20	.50
134 Anfernee Hardaway B/W	.15	.40
136 Alonzo Mourning BW	.15	.40
141 Jamal Mashburn B/W	.08	.25
145 Isaiah Rider B/W	.08	.25
146 Harold Miner B/W	.08	.25
NNO Jamal Mashburn PROMO	.75	2.00
NNO BK Preview Redemption	.08	.25

1993-94 Images Four Sport Acetates

Randomly inserted in 1993-94 Classic Images packs (four per case; 6,500 of each), these four standard-size clear acetate cards feature color player action cutouts on their fronts.

COMPLETE SET (4)	12.00	30.00
1 Chris Webber	2.00	5.00
4 Hakeem Olajuwon	2.50	6.00

1993-94 Images Four Sport Chrome

Randomly inserted one in every fourteen 1994 Classic Images packs, these 20 limited print (9,750 of each) cards measure the standard size and feature color player action shots on their borderless metallic fronts. The cards are numbered on the back with a "CC" prefix. This set was also available in uncut sheet form as a redeemed prize for the Marshall Faulk M5 card.

COMPLETE SET (20)	15.00	40.00
CC1 Chris Webber	1.25	3.00
CC2 Anfernee Hardaway	1.00	2.50
CC3 Jimmy Jackson	.50	1.25
CC4 Nick Van Exel	.50	1.25
CC5 Jamal Mashburn	.60	1.50
CC6 Isaiah Rider	.40	1.00
NNO Uncut Sheet	30.00	80.00

1993-94 Images Four Sport Sudden Impact

Inserted one per '94 Classic Images pack, these 20 gold foil-board cards measure the standard-size. The gold metallic fronts feature borderless color player action shots on backgrounds that have been thrown out of focus. The player's name and position appear in vertical lettering within a black strip across the card near the right edge. The back carries a color player action shot at the top, followed below by career highlights on a white panel. The player's name appears in vertical black lettering within a ghosted action strip at the left edge. The cards are numbered on the back with an "SI" prefix.

COMPLETE SET (20)	4.00	10.00
SI2 Vin Baker	.30	.75
SI9 Shaquille O'Neal	.75	2.00
SI10 Alonzo Mourning	.40	1.00
SI11 Harold Miner	.20	.50
SI12 Chris Webber	.40	1.00
SI13 Anfernee Hardaway	.30	.75
SI14 Jamal Mashburn	.30	.75
SI20 Dino Radja	.15	.40

1995 Images Four Sport

Printed on 18-point micro-lined foil board, the 1995 Classic Images set consists of 120 standard-size cards, featuring the top draft picks from the four major sports. Classic produced 1,995 sequentially-numbered 16-box hobby cases. This series also features one "Hot Box" in every four cases; each pack in it included at least one card from five insert sets, plus the special Clear Excitement chase cards not found anywhere else, for a total of 24 inserts per Hot Box. There was a promotional card issued, not inserted into '94-95 Assets packs, for Grant Hill numbered HP1. The front is the same as the card in the set, but the back has an orange background and describes the product's features.

COMPLETE SET (120)	6.00	15.00
1 Glenn Robinson	.20	.50
2 Jason Kidd	.60	1.50
3 Grant Hill	.40	1.00
4 Donyell Marshall	.10	.30
5 Juwan Howard	.20	.50
6 Sharone Wright	.10	.30
7 Brian Grant	.20	.50
8 Eric Montross	.10	.30
9 Eddie Jones	.20	.50
10 Carlos Rogers	.10	.30
11 Khalid Reeves	.10	.30
12 Jalen Rose	.20	.50
13 Yinka Dare	.10	.30
14 Eric Piatkowski	.10	.30
15 Clifford Rozier	.10	.30
16 Aaron McKie	.10	.30
17 Eric Mobley	.10	.30
18 B.J. Tyler	.10	.30
19 Dickey Simpkins	.10	.30
20 Bill Curley	.10	.30
21 Wesley Person	.10	.30
22 Monty Williams	.10	.30
23 Antonio Lang	.10	.30
24 Darrin Hancock	.10	.30
25 Michael Smith	.10	.30
26 Rodney Dent	.10	.30
27 Charlie Ward	.30	.75
28 Jim McIlvaine	.10	.30
29 Brooks Thompson	.10	.30
30 Gaylon Nickerson	.10	.30
31 Jamie Watson	.10	.30
32 Damon Bailey	.10	.30
33 Dontonio Wingfield	.10	.30
34 Trevor Ruffin	.10	.30
35 Greg Minor	.10	.30
36 Dwayne Morton	.10	.30
37 Shaquille O'Neal	.60	1.50
119 Grant Hill CL	.20	.50
HP1 Grant Hill Promo	1.00	2.50

1995 Images Four Sport Classic Performances

Randomly inserted in hobby boxes at a rate of one in every 12 packs, this 20-card standard-size set relives great moments from the careers of 20 top athletes. Each card is numbered out of 4,495. The fronts feature the player against a gold background. The back contains on the left side a description of the great moment and on the right side a color player photo. The cards are numbered with a "CP" prefix.

COMPLETE SET (20)	20.00	50.00
CP1 Glenn Robinson	.75	2.00
CP2 Grant Hill	2.00	5.00
CP3 Jason Kidd	2.00	5.00
CP4 Juwan Howard	.60	1.50
CP5 Shaquille O'Neal	3.00	8.00
CP6 Alonzo Mourning	1.25	3.00
CP7 Jamal Mashburn	.50	1.25

1995 Images Four Sport Clear Excitement

Randomly inserted at a rate of one in every 24 packs in hobby and retail hot boxes (1:1536 over the product run), these two five-card acetate sets each feature five notable athletes from different sports. Cards with the prefix "E" were inserted in hobby hot boxes, while cards with the prefix "C" were found in retail hot boxes. The cards are numbered out of 300.

COMPLETE SET (10)	60.00	150.00
C1 Shaquille O'Neal	12.50	30.00
E1 Grant Hill	6.00	15.00
E4 Hakeem Olajuwon	5.00	12.00

1995 Images Four Sport EP

Randomly inserted in Classic Images boxes these standard-size cards feature a print run of 8000 sets. The fronts feature the player against a silver foil background. The backs contain another player photo and a short bio on the player. The cards are numbered with an "EP" prefix.

EP2 Jason Kidd	1.25	3.00
EP3 Grant Hill	1.00	2.50
EP5 Shaquille O'Neal	2.00	5.00

1995 Images Four Sport Flashbacks

These 10 standard-size cards were randomly inserted into retail boxes at a rate of 1 per 24 packs. The fronts

display color action photos, while the backs carry a second photo and player information.
COMPLETE SET (10) 20.00 50.00
TF1 Glenn Robinson 2.50 6.00
TF2 Jason Kidd 3.00 8.00
TF3 Grant Hill 3.00 8.00
TF4 Donyell Marshall 1.50 4.00
TF5 Jamal Mashburn 1.50 4.00
TF6 Eric Montross 1.25 3.00
TF7 Eddie Jones 2.00 5.00
TF8 Alonzo Mourning 2.50 6.00
TF9 Jalen Rose 1.50 4.00
TF10 Shaquille O'Neal 8.00 20.00

1995 Images Four Sport Player of the Year

This four-card standard-size set was obtained through a mail-in wrapper offer, or one set was also included per retail box. The borderless fronts feature a color action player image on a metalic, starburst-look background. The player's name is printed in a black strip at the bottom with the card logo. The backs carry a small color head photo with the player's name, position, and team name below it. A black-and-white player action photo along with the player's statistics round out the back. The cards are numbered with a "POY" prefix.
COMPLETE SET (4) 4.00 10.00
POY3 Grant Hill 1.00 2.50
POY4 Shaquille O'Neal 1.50 4.00

1995 Images Four Sport Previews

Randomly inserted one per 24 packs in second-series '94-95 Assets packs, this five-card standard-size set was issued to promote the Classic Images series. Just 5,000 of each card were produced. The fronts display the player's photo showcased against a metallic background. The backs are devoted on the left side to the player's identification and a note saying you have received a limited edition preview card. The right side of the reverse has a full-color photo of the player and the card is numbered at the upper right corner. The cards are numbered with an "IP" prefix.
COMPLETE SET (5) 6.00 15.00
IP1 Grant Hill 1.00 2.50
IP2 Shaquille O'Neal 2.00 5.00

1999 Jersey City Basketball

COMPLETE SET (50) 3.00 8.00
COMMON CARD (1-50) .05 .15
SEMISTARS .07 .20
UNLISTED STARS .10 .25
1 Michael Olowokandi .05 .15
2 Antawn Jamison .10 .25
3 Vince Carter .20 .50
4 Robert Traylor .05 .15
5 Jason Williams .12 .30
6 Paul Pierce .15 .40
7 Bonzi Wells .05 .15
8 Keon Clark .05 .15
9 Kobe Bryant CL .40 1.00
10 Pat Garrity .05 .15
11 Ricky Davis .07 .20
12 Tyronn Lue .07 .20
13 Felipe Lopez .05 .15
14 Al Harrington .10 .25
15 Corey Benjamin .05 .15
16 Rashard Lewis .10 .25
17 Jelani McCoy .05 .15
18 Shammond Williams .05 .15
19 DeMarco Johnson .05 .15
20 Korleone Young .05 .15
21 Mile Simon .05 .15
22 Toby Bailey .05 .15
23 J.R. Henderson .05 .15
24 Zendon Hamilton .05 .15
25 Jeff Sheppard .05 .15
26 Kobe Bryant .40 1.00
27 Stephon Marbury .07 .20
28 Tracy McGrady .15 .40
29 Scottie Pippen .15 .40
30 Tim Thomas .05 .15
31 Michael Olowokandi CL .05 .15
32 Antawn Jamison CL .10 .25
33 Michael Olowokandi .05 .15
34 Antawn Jamison .10 .25
35 Vince Carter .20 .50
36 Robert Traylor .05 .15
37 Jason Williams .12 .30
38 Paul Pierce .15 .40
39 Bonzi Wells .05 .15
40 Keon Clark .05 .15
41 Kobe Bryant CL .40 1.00
42 Pat Garrity .05 .15
43 Michael Olowokandi .05 .15
44 Antawn Jamison .10 .25
45 Vince Carter .20 .50
46 Robert Traylor .05 .15
47 Jason Williams .12 .30
48 Paul Pierce .15 .40
49 Bonzi Wells .05 .15
50 Keon Clark .05 .15

1999 Jersey City Basketball Gold

*GOLD: .6X TO 1.5X BASE HI

1999 Jersey City Game Gear

STATED ODDS 1:36
1 Kobe Bryant 10.00 25.00
2 Scottie Pippen 4.00 10.00
3 Stephon Marbury 2.00 5.00
4 Tim Thomas 2.00 5.00
5 Tracy McGrady 4.00 10.00

1999 Jersey City Hard Court Time Warp

COMPLETE SET (12) 6.00 15.00
STATED PRINT RUN 1000 TO 12000 SETS
TW1 S.Abdur-Rahim/D.Thompson .50 1.25
TW2 R.Allen/A.English .60 1.50
TW3 K.Bryant/A.English 2.50 6.00
TW4 M.Camby/M.Malone .60 1.50
TW5 E.Dampier/G.Gervin .60 1.50
TW6 A.Iverson/I.Thomas 1.25 3.00
TW7 K.Kittles/I.Thomas 1.25 3.00
TW8 S.Marbury/D.Thompson .50 1.25
TW9 A.Walker/M.Malone .60 1.50
TW10 S.Walker/W.Frazier .60 1.50
TW11 J.Wallace/G.Gervin .60 1.50
TW12 L.Wright/W.Frazier .60 1.50

1999 Jersey City Hard Court Time Warp Autographs

STATED PRINT RUN 1000 SETS
ONLY RETIRED SIGNED CARDS
TW2 R.Allen/A.English AU 6.00 15.00
TW5 E.Dampier/G.Gervin AU 8.00 20.00
TW6 A.Iverson/I.Thomas AU 10.00 25.00
TW8 S.Marbury/D.Thompson AU 6.00 15.00
TW9 A.Walker/M.Malone AU 8.00 20.00
TW10 S.Walker/W.Frazier AU 8.00 20.00

1999 Jersey City KB8

COMPLETE SET (5) 2.50 6.00
COMMON CARD (1-5) .75 2.00

1999 Jersey City KB8 Special Edition

COMMON CARD (1-5) 4.00 10.00

1999 Jersey City Markers

COMPLETE SET (15) 2.00 5.00
STATED PRINT RUN 1500 SETS
1 Michael Olowokandi .12 .30
2 Antawn Jamison .20 .50
3 Vince Carter .40 1.00
4 Robert Traylor .12 .30
5 Jason Williams .25 .60
6 Paul Pierce .30 .75
7 Keon Clark .12 .30
8 Pat Garrity .12 .30
9 Jelani McCoy .12 .30
10 Tyronn Lue .15 .40
11 Felipe Lopez .12 .30
12 Al Harrington .20 .50
13 Corey Benjamin .12 .30
14 Kobe Bryant .75 2.00
15 Toby Bailey .12 .30

1999 Jersey City Pro Signature Authentics

RANDOM INSERTS IN PACKS
1 Michael Olowokandi 2.00 5.00
2 Antawn Jamison 4.00 10.00
3 Vince Carter 10.00 25.00
4 Robert Traylor 2.00 5.00
5 Jason Williams 3.00 8.00
6 Paul Pierce 6.00 15.00
7 Bonzi Wells 2.00 5.00
8 Keon Clark 2.00 5.00
9 Pat Garrity 2.00 5.00
10 Ricky Davis 2.00 5.00
11 Tyronn Lue 2.00 5.00
12 Felipe Lopez 2.00 5.00
13 Al Harrington 2.00 5.00
14 Corey Benjamin 2.00 5.00
15 Rashard Lewis 3.00 8.00
16 Jelani McCoy 2.00 5.00
17 Shammond Williams 2.00 5.00
18 DeMarco Johnson 2.00 5.00
19 Korleone Young 2.00 5.00
20 Miles Simon 2.00 5.00
21 Toby Bailey 2.00 5.00
22 J.R. Henderson 2.00 5.00
23 Zendon Hamilton 2.00 5.00
24 Jeff Sheppard 2.00 5.00

1996 Pacific Power

This 54-card set highlights 42 draft picks and 12 pre players. Each pack contained three cards. The card fronts have a foil background with player's name written vertically on the left side of the color player photo. The backs have another photo along with a player biography. Also included in the set are a silver (3:37) and platinum (1:721) parallel to the base set. The platinum cards have sky blue foil treament on the card fronts and a PP prefix on the card numbers. Insert sets include Gold Crown Die Cuts, In the Paint and Jump Ball.
COMPLETE SET (54) 8.00 20.00
1 Shareef Abdur-Rahim .50 1.25
2 Ray Allen 1.00 2.50
3 Terrell Bell .25 .60
4 Joseph Blair .25 .60
5 Marcus Brown .25 .60
6 Kobe Bryant 3.00 8.00
7 Marcus Camby .40 1.00
8 Erick Dampier .25 .60
9 Ben Davis .25 .60
10 Tony Delk .25 .60
11 Tyus Edney .15 .40
12 Brian Evans .25 .60
13 Michael Finley .30 .75
14 Derek Fisher .50 1.25
15 Todd Fuller .25 .60
16 Reggie Geary .25 .60
17 Steve Hamer .25 .60
18 Othella Harrington .25 .60
19 Mark Hendrickson .25 .60
20 Allen Iverson 1.25 3.00
21 Dontae' Jones .25 .60
22 Jason Kidd .40 1.00
23 Kerry Kittles .25 .60
24 Randy Livingston .25 .60
25 Stephon Marbury .60 1.50
26 Jamal Mashburn .20 .50
27 Walter McCarty .25 .60
28 Amal McCaskill .25 .60
29 Antonio McDyess .25 .60
30 Jeff McInnis .25 .60
31 Russ Millard .25 .60
32 Ryan Minor .30 .75
33 Alonzo Mourning .30 .75
34 Dikembe Mutombo .25 .60
35 Steve Nash 1.25 3.00
36 Moochie Norris .25 .60
37 Ed O'Bannon .15 .40
38 Jermaine O'Neal .60 1.50
39 Mark Pope .25 .60
40 Vitaly Potapenko .25 .60
41 Ron Riley .25 .60
42 Darnell Robinson .25 .60
43 Glenn Robinson .20 .50
44 Roy Rogers .25 .60
45 Jason Sasser .25 .60
46 Doron Sheffer .25 .60
47 Joe Smith .20 .50
48 Damon Stoudamire .20 .50
49 Antoine Walker .50 1.25
50 Samaki Walker .25 .60
51 John Wallace .25 .60
52 Rasheed Wallace .30 .75
53 Jerome Williams .25 .60
54 Lorenzen Wright .25 .60

1996 Pacific Power Platinum

*PLATINUM: 25X TO 60X BASE CARD HI
STATED ODDS 1:721

1996 Pacific Power Silver

*SILVER: 4X TO 10X BASE CARD HI
STATED ODDS 3:37

1996 Pacific Power Gold Crown Die Cuts

This 15-card insert set, inserted at a rate of 3:37, follows the same basic design of every other Pacific Gold Crown Die Cuts. A gold crown is die-cut out of the top. Below the player photograph is the player's name in gold foil. The backs have another player photo and a small biography. The cards are numbered with a "GC-" prefix.
COMPLETE SET (15) 20.00 50.00
STATED ODDS 3:37
GC1 Shareef Abdur-Rahim 2.00 5.00
GC2 Ray Allen 4.00 10.00
GC3 Kobe Bryant 10.00 25.00
GC4 Marcus Camby 1.50 4.00
GC5 Erick Dampier 1.00 2.50
GC6 Tony Delk 1.00 2.50
GC7 Allen Iverson 5.00 12.00
GC8 Jason Kidd 1.50 4.00
GC9 Stephon Marbury 2.50 6.00
GC10 Steve Nash 5.00 12.00
GC11 Jermaine O'Neal 2.50 6.00
GC12 Joe Smith .75 2.00
GC13 Damon Stoudamire .75 2.00
GC14 Antoine Walker 2.00 5.00
GC15 John Wallace 1.00 2.50

1996 Pacific Power In The Paint

This 20-card insert set was inserted at a rate of 3:37. Each card highlights a pro or college player that spends time in the paint-rebounding or driving. The cards have an action player shot and the player's name is written in a transparent font in large letters behind the player. The backs have another photo and some biographical information. The cards are numbered with a "IP-" prefix.
COMPLETE SET (20) 20.00 50.00
STATED ODDS 3:37
IP1 Shareef Abdur-Rahim 2.00 5.00
IP2 Ray Allen 4.00 10.00
IP3 Kobe Bryant 10.00 25.00
IP4 Marcus Camby 1.50 4.00
IP5 Erick Dampier 1.00 2.50
IP6 Tyus Edney .60 1.50
IP7 Michael Finley 1.25 3.00
IP8 Allen Iverson 5.00 12.00
IP9 Dontae' Jones 1.00 2.50
IP10 Jason Kidd 1.50 4.00
IP11 Stephon Marbury 2.50 6.00
IP12 Antonio McDyess 1.00 2.50
IP13 Dikembe Mutombo 1.00 2.50
IP14 Steve Nash 5.00 12.00
IP15 Ed O'Bannon .60 1.50
IP16 Jermaine O'Neal 2.50 6.00
IP17 Joe Smith .75 2.00
IP18 Damon Stoudamire .75 2.00
IP19 Antoine Walker 2.00 5.00
IP20 John Wallace 1.00 2.50

1996 Pacific Power Jump Ball

This 10-card insert set was inserted at a rate of 1:37. The fronts have a gold foil background and a round see-through plastic center that appears you're looking down into the net. A player photo is imprinted on the plastic center. The words "Jump Ball" appear in the bottom right corner next to a small basketball. The backs have another photo. some biographical information and are numbered with the prefix "JB-".
COMPLETE SET (10) 20.00 50.00
STATED ODDS 1:37
JB1 Shareef Abdur-Rahim 2.50 6.00
JB2 Ray Allen 5.00 12.00
JB3 Kobe Bryant 12.00 30.00
JB4 Marcus Camby 2.00 5.00
JB5 Erick Dampier 1.25 3.00
JB6 Allen Iverson 6.00 15.00
JB7 Dontae' Jones 1.25 3.00
JB8 Stephon Marbury 3.00 8.00
JB9 Antoine Walker 2.50 6.00
JB10 Lorenzen Wright 1.25 3.00

1996 Pacific Power Platinum Crown Die Cuts

This mail-in set of five cards resembles the randomly inserted Gold Crown Die Cuts, but the foil is platinum colored. Collectors could receive a complete set by mailing in 18 wrappers and $4.95 to Pacific by 7/31/97.
COMPLETE SET (5) 10.00 25.00
1 Kobe Bryant 8.00 20.00
2 Marcus Camby 1.25 3.00
3 Erick Dampier .75 2.00
4 Allen Iverson 4.00 10.00
5 Steve Nash 4.00 10.00

1996 Pacific Power Regents of Roundball

*REGENTS: .5X TO 1.25X BASE CARD HI

1994 Pacific Prisms Samples

This six-card standard-size set was issued to preview the 1994 Pacific Prisms Draft Picks series. The cards were available in both silver and gold prism foil. The fronts display a player action cutout on a prism foil background. The player's name and the Pacific logo appear in a bar toward the bottom. On a background displaying colorful rays of light emanating from a central point, the horizontal back carries a color player photo, biography, and player profile. On the backs, the cards have the word "SAMPLE" followed by the card number in the upper right corner.
COMPLETE SET (6) 6.00 15.00
1G Glenn Robinson Gold 1.50 4.00
1S Glenn Robinson Silver .75 2.00
2G Jason Kidd Gold 4.00 10.00
2S Jason Kidd Silver 2.00 5.00
3G Anfernee Hardaway Gold 1.25 3.00
3S Anfernee Hardaway Silver .60 1.50

1994 Pacific Prisms

This 72-card standard-size set was licensed by Classic Games and produced by Pacific. Just 3,999 individually-numbered cases were produced. The cards were available in both silver and gold prism foil and were printed on 18-point card stock with UV coating on both sides. One prism card was inserted per pack, and each pack also had a "backer" card from either the 20-card Dan Majerle set, checklist cards, or a production information card. The fronts display a player action cutout on a prism foil background. The player's name and the Pacific logo appear in a bar toward the bottom. On a background displaying colorful rays of light emanating from a central point, the horizontal back carries a color player photo, biography, and player profile.
COMPLETE SET (75) 6.00 15.00
1 Derrick Alston .20 .50
2 Adrian Autry .20 .50
3 Damon Bailey .20 .50
4 Melvin Booker .20 .50
5 Joey Brown .20 .50
6 Albert Burditt .20 .50
7 Robert Churchwell .20 .50
8 Gary Collier .20 .50
9 Jevon Crudup .20 .50
10 Bill Curley .20 .50
11 Yinka Dare .20 .50
12 Rodney Dent .20 .50
13 Tony Dumas .20 .50
14 Howard Eisley .20 .50
15 Travis Ford .20 .50
16 Lawrence Funderburke .20 .50
17 Anthony Goldwire .20 .50
18 Chuck Graham .20 .50
19 Brian Grant .30 .75
20 Darrin Hancock .20 .50
21 Anfernee Hardaway .30 .75
22 Carl Ray Harris .20 .50
23 Grant Hill 1.00 2.50
24 Askia Jones .20 .50
25 Eddie Jones .60 1.50
26 Arturas Karnishovas .20 .50
27 Damon Key .20 .50
28 Jason Kidd 1.00 2.50
29 Antonio Lang .20 .50
30 Donyell Marshall .20 .50
31 Jamal Mashburn .20 .50
32 Billy McCaffrey .20 .50
33 Jim McIlvaine .20 .50
34 Aaron McKie .20 .50
35 Harold Miner .12 .30
36 Greg Minor .20 .50
37 Eric Mobley .20 .50
38 Eric Montross .20 .50
39 Dwayne Morton .20 .50
40 Alonzo Mourning .25 .60
41 Dikembe Mutombo .20 .50
42 Gaylon Nickerson .20 .50
43 Wesley Person .20 .50
44 Derrick Phelps .20 .50
45 Eric Piatkowski .25 .60
46 Kevin Rankin .20 .50
47 Brian Reese .20 .50
48 Khalid Reeves .20 .50
49 Isaiah Rider .20 .50
50 Glenn Robinson .40 1.00
51 Carlos Rogers .20 .50
52 Jalen Rose .50 1.25
53 Clifford Rozier .20 .50
54 Kevin Salvadori .20 .50
55 Jervaughn Scales .20 .50
56 Shawnelle Scott .20 .50
57 Dickey Simpkins .20 .50
58 Michael Smith .20 .50
59 Shon Tarver .20 .50
60 Deon Thomas .20 .50
61 Brooks Thompson .20 .50
62 B.J. Tyler .20 .50
63 Charlie Ward .20 .50
64 Jamie Watson .20 .50
65 Jeff Webster .20 .50
66 Monty Williams .20 .50
67 Dontonio Wingfield .20 .50
68 Steve Woodberry .20 .50
69 Anfernee Hardaway .30 .75
70 Jamal Mashburn .20 .50
71 Alonzo Mourning .25 .60
72 Dikembe Mutombo .20 .50
NNO Pacific Logo .12 .30
NNO Checklist #1 .12 .30
NNO Checklist #2 .12 .30

1994 Pacific Prisms Gold

*GOLD: 2.5X TO 6X HI COLUMN
RANDOM INSERTS IN PACKS

1994 Pacific Prisms Dan Majerle

This 20-card standard-size insert set highlights Dan Majerle. The fronts feature color action player photos with a white border. Pacific's Crown Collection logo appears in the upper left corner, while the player's name and position are printed in cursive letters in the lower right corner. The white-bordered backs carry another color action player shot with brief player information in the lower right. The cards are numbered on the back as "X of 20".
COMPLETE SET (20) 1.25 3.00
COMMON MAJERLE (1-20) .08 .25
RANDOM INSERTS IN PACKS

1995 Pacific Prisms

This 54-card set, produced by Pacific Trading Cards, features a borderless color action player photo on the front with the player's name printed on a diagonal stripe in the lower right. The backs carry a small color player photo with the player's name, position, biographical and draft information.
COMPLETE SET (54) 4.00 10.00
1 Joe Smith .25 .60
2 David Vaughn .20 .50
3 Anthony Pelle .20 .50
4 Sherrell Ford .20 .50
5 Corliss Williamson .20 .50
6 Mario Bennett .20 .50
7 Jason Caffey .20 .50
8 R.Brunson/E.Claggett .20 .50
9 George Zidek .20 .50
10 Eric Snow .20 .50
11 Travis Best .20 .50
12 Theo Ratliff .30 .75
13 Greg Ostertag .20 .50
14 Lou Roe .20 .50
15 Eric Montross .12 .30
16 Hakeem Olajuwon .25 .60
17 Cherokee Parks .20 .50
18 Glenn Robinson .15 .40
19 Hakeem Olajuwon .25 .60
20 Terrence Rencher .20 .50
21 Cory Alexander .20 .50
22 Tyus Edney .20 .50
23 Damon Stoudamire .50 1.25
24 Junior Burrough .20 .50
25 Donny Marshall UER .20 .50
26 Brent Barry .30 .75
27 Rasheed Wallace .60 1.50
28 LaZelle Durden .20 .50
29 Jimmy King .20 .50
30 Don Reid .20 .50
31 Loren Meyer .20 .50
32 Joe Smith .25 .60
33 Cuonzo Martin .20 .50
34 Eddie Jones .25 .60
35 Ed O'Bannon .20 .50
36 Jason Kidd .30 .75
37 Erik Meeks .20 .50
38 Greg Ostertag .20 .50
39 E.O'Bannon/R.Wallace .60 1.50
40 Eric Williams .20 .50
41 Randolph Childress .20 .50
42 Wesley Person .12 .30
43 Antonio McDyess .25 .60
44 Andrew DeClercq .20 .50
45 Constantin Popa .20 .50
46 Gary Trent .20 .50
47 Jerome Allen .20 .50
48 Michael Finley .60 1.50
49 Mark Davis .20 .50
50 Shawn Respert .20 .50
51 J.Amaechi/C.Beck .20 .50
52 Rashard Griffith .20 .50
53 Kurt Thomas .20 .50
54 Lawrence Moten .20 .50

1995 Pacific Prisms Blue

COMPLETE SET (54) 25.00 60.00
*BLUE: 1.5X TO 4X BASE CARD HI
STATED ODDS 3:37 PACKS

1995 Pacific Prisms Presidential Gold

*GOLD: 20X TO 50X BASE CARD HI
STATED ODDS 2:720

1995 Pacific Prisms Red

COMPLETE SET (54) 25.00 60.00
*RED: 1.5X TO 4X BASE CARD HI
STATED ODDS 3:37

1995 Pacific Prisms Centers of Attention

This 10-card set was randomly inserted in packs and was produced by Pacific Trading Cards with its crystalline technology. The fronts feature a color action player photo with the player's name and a clear backboard in the background. The backs carry the player's name with a discription of the player's ability and a small color player photo.
COMPLETE SET (10) 8.00 20.00
STATED ODDS 3:37
C1 Jason Kidd 1.25 3.00
C2 Antonio McDyess 1.00 2.50
C3 Ed O'Bannon .75 2.00
C4 Hakeem Olajuwon 1.00 2.50
C5 Greg Ostertag .75 2.00
C6 Shawn Respert .75 2.00
C7 Glenn Robinson .60 1.50
C8 Joe Smith 1.00 2.50
C9 Damon Stoudamire 2.00 5.00
C10 Rasheed Wallace 2.50 6.00

1995 Pacific Prisms Gold Crown Die Cuts

This 15-card set was randomly inserted in packs of Draft Pick Prism Basketball Cards. The set features 11 different draft pick players and four current players in their second professional season. The fronts display a color action player photo with the player's name printed in gold foil at the bottom. The top of the card is cut in the shape of a crown with gold foil accents. The backs carry another player photo with the player's name, draft information, and career highlights.
COMPLETE SET (15) 20.00 50.00
STATED ODDS 3:37
DC1 Jason Caffey 1.25 3.00
DC2 Michael Finley 4.00 10.00
DC3 Eddie Jones 1.50 4.00
DC4 Jason Kidd 2.00 5.00
DC5 Antonio McDyess 1.50 4.00
DC6 Ed O'Bannon 1.25 3.00
DC7 Greg Ostertag 1.25 3.00
DC8 Cherokee Parks 1.25 3.00
DC9 Shawn Respert 1.25 3.00
DC10 Glenn Robinson 1.00 2.50
DC11 Joe Smith 1.50 4.00
DC12 Damon Stoudamire 3.00 8.00
DC13 Rasheed Wallace 4.00 10.00
DC14 Eric Williams 1.25 3.00
DC15 Corliss Williamson 1.25 3.00

1995 Pacific Prisms Olajuwon

These cards were randomly inserted in foil packs. Inside an ornate, prismatic gold-foil picture frame, the fronts display color action player photos. Because the set is not licensed by the NBA, team logos have been airbrushed off the pictures. On an orange background displaying a basketball, the backs have "Hakeem Olajuwon The Dream" in large block letters, with a player fact and head shot below.
COMPLETE SET (12) 3.00 8.00
COMMON CARD (1-12) .40 1.00
RANDOM INSERTS IN PACKS

1995 Pacific Prisms Platinum Crown Die Cuts

This five-card set could be obtained by mailing in 18 wrappers of 1995 Pacific Crown Collection Draft Picks Prism Basketball Cards plus shipping and handling charges to Pacific Trading Cards.
COMPLETE SET (5) 6.00 15.00
AVAILABLE VIA WRAPPER REDEMPTION
P1 Antonio McDyess 1.50 4.00
P2 Ed O'Bannon 1.25 3.00
P3 Greg Ostertag 1.25 3.00
P4 Joe Smith 1.50 4.00
P5 Rasheed Wallace 4.00 10.00

1995 Press Pass

The 1995 Press Pass set consists of 36 regular cards and were issued in three-card packs. Packs contained a regular card, a die-cut card and an insert card. Prime Time Phone cards were inserted in one of every five boxes (36 packs per box). Borderless fronts feature a full-color player cutout set against a photo panel with photo boxes. A gold foil ribbon appears across the bottom with the player's name, draft number and his team in black type. Backs continue with the cutout panel background and a full-color player cutout. A white screened box contains a player biography and statistics which are printed vertically. A blue strip runs along the bottom and has the player's name in white print inside.
COMPLETE SET (36) 5.00 10.00
1 Joe Smith .15 .40
2 Antonio McDyess .15 .40
3 Jerry Stackhouse .40 1.00
4 Rasheed Wallace .40 1.00
5 Kevin Garnett 1.00 2.50
6 Bryant Reeves .12 .30
7 Damon Stoudamire .30 .75
8 Shawn Respert .12 .30
9 Ed O'Bannon .12 .30
10 Kurt Thomas .12 .30
11 Gary Trent .12 .30
12 Cherokee Parks .12 .30
13 Corliss Williamson .12 .30
14 Eric Williams .12 .30
15 Brent Barry .20 .50
16 Theo Ratliff .20 .50
17 Randolph Childress .12 .30
18 Jason Caffey .12 .30
19 Michael Finley .40 1.00
20 George Zidek .12 .30
21 Travis Best .12 .30
22 David Vaughn .12 .30
23 Sherrell Ford .12 .30
24 Mario Bennett .12 .30
25 Lou Roe .12 .30
26 Frankie King .12 .30
27 Rashard Griffith .12 .30
28 Donny Marshall .12 .30
29 Tyus Edney .12 .30
30 Antonio McDyess .12 .30
31 Rasheed Wallace .30 .75
32 Eddie Jones .15 .40
33 Jason Kidd .20 .50
34 Glenn Robinson .10 .25
35 Jalen Rose .15 .40
36 Joe Smith CL .12 .30

1995 Press Pass Die Cuts Blue

COMPLETE SET (36) 8.00 20.00
*BLUE: 1X TO 2.5X BASE CARD HI
ONE PER PACK

1995 Press Pass Die Cuts Red

COMPLETE SET (36) 8.00 20.00
*RED: 1X TO 2.5X BASE HI
ONE PER PACK

1995 Press Pass Foil

*FOIL: 4X TO 10X BASE CARD HI
STATED ODDS 1:9

1995 Press Pass Autographs

These autograph cards were randomly seeded in packs. They differ from the regular issue in not having the gold foil across the bottom of the front and bearing an autograph in blue ink.
COMPLETE SET (8) 20.00 50.00
STATED ODDS 1:108
1 Jimmy King 2.00 5.00
2 Antonio McDyess 6.00 15.00
3 Cherokee Parks 2.00 5.00
4 Joe Smith 2.50 6.00
5 Damon Stoudamire 5.00 12.00
6 David Vaughn 2.00 5.00
7 Rasheed Wallace 10.00 25.00
8 Eric Williams 2.00 5.00

1995 Press Pass Pandemonium

Randomly inserted in packs at a rate of one in 18 packs, this nine card standard-size set was printed on Nitrokrome card stock and feature the top nine draft picks. Fronts have colored foil backgrounds and a player action cutout appears in front. The player's last name is printed in a silver foil and his full name is printed in smaller type across the last name. Backs have a full-color action shot and a black strip running vertically down the right side. The player's last name is printed in gray type along the black strip and his full name is printed in smaller white type across that.
COMPLETE SET (9) 6.00 15.00
STATED ODDS 1:18
1 Antonio McDyess 1.00 2.50
2 Ed O'Bannon .75 2.00
3 Shawn Respert .75 2.00
4 Joe Smith 1.00 2.50
5 Damon Stoudamire 2.00 5.00
6 Kurt Thomas .75 2.00
7 Gary Trent .75 2.00
8 Rasheed Wallace 2.50 6.00
9 Corliss Williamson .75 2.00

1995 Press Pass Phone Cards $5

Randomly inserted in packs at one in 36, with the $5 card being the most prevalent, this set of eight cards uses the top draft picks for free phone time. The top three picks, Stackhouse, Smith and McDyess appear on the scarce $1,995 cards. Borderless fronts have two full-color player photos with his name printed vertically on the left side with two stripes on the top and bottom. All printing, including the card value, which appears on the upper right, is gold type. Backs are all white with the rules and instructions for calling printed in black type. $10 and $20 are priced below as multipliers of the $5 cards.
COMPLETE SET (8) 35.00 40.00
*TEN DOLLAR CARDS: .75X TO 2X VALUE
STATED ODDS 1:216
*TWENTY DOLLAR CARDS: 1.5X TO 4X VALUE
STATED ODDS 1:864
1 Kevin Garnett 6.00 15.00
2 Jason Kidd 1.25 3.00
3 Antonio McDyess 1.00 2.50
4 Ed O'Bannon .75 2.00
5 Glenn Robinson .60 1.50
6 Joe Smith 1.00 2.50
7 Jerry Stackhouse 2.50 6.00
8 Rasheed Wallace 2.50 6.00

1995 Press Pass Joe Smith

Randomly inserted in packs at various rates, this set of four standard-size cards focuses on 1995's No. 1 draft pick. The cards were numbered with the prefix "JS" with JS1 being the easiest to find at one in 36 packs. JS2 was inserted in one of 72 packs. JS3 could be found in one of 216 packs and JS4 was scarcest at one in 864. Borderless fronts featured a silver holgraphic foil background with a player action cutout of Smith in his Maryland uniform. Backs carry a montage of Smith action photos.
COMPLETE SET (4) 12.00 30.00
STATED ODDS #1 1:36, #2 1:72
STATED ODDS #3 1:216, #4 1:864
JS1 Joe Smith .60 1.50
JS2 Joe Smith 1.00 2.50
JS3 Joe Smith 4.00 10.00
JS4 Joe Smith 12.00 30.00

1996 Press Pass

The 1996 Press Pass set was issued in one series totaling 45 cards. The 4-card packs were issued with two bases set cards and two inserts. Over 12,000 autographed were inserted into packs. Also included were random inserts: Acetates, Swish and Net Burner parallels, Jersey Cards, Lottos and Pandemonium.
COMPLETE SET (45) 5.00 12.00
1 Allen Iverson .75 2.00
2 Marcus Camby .25 .60
3 Shareef Abdur-Rahim .30 .75
4 Stephon Marbury .40 1.00
5 Ray Allen .60 1.50
6 Antoine Walker .30 .75
7 Lorenzen Wright .15 .40
8 Kerry Kittles .15 .40
9 Samaki Walker .15 .40
10 Erick Dampier .15 .40
11 Todd Fuller .15 .40
12 Vitaly Potapenko .15 .40
13 Kobe Bryant 1.50 4.00
14 Steve Nash .75 2.00
15 Tony Delk .15 .40
16 Jermaine O'Neal .40 1.00
17 John Wallace .15 .40
18 Walter McCarty .15 .40
19 Dontae' Jones .15 .40
20 Roy Rogers .15 .40
21 Jerome Williams .15 .40
22 Brian Evans .15 .40
23 Travis Knight .15 .40
24 Othella Harrington .15 .40
25 Ryan Minor .20 .50
26 Doron Sheffer .15 .40
27 Jeff McInnis .15 .40
28 Jason Sasser .15 .40
29 Randy Livingston .15 .40
30 Malik Rose .20 .50
31 Jamie Feick .15 .40
32 Mark Pope .15 .40
33 Damon Stoudamire .12 .30
34 Jerry Stackhouse .20 .50
35 Joe Smith .12 .30
36 Michael Finley .20 .50
37 Rasheed Wallace .20 .50
38 Antonio McDyess .15 .40
39 R.Allen/Knight/Sheffer .30 .75
40 W.McC/Delk/A.Walk/Pope .15 .40
41 J.Will/Iverson/O.Harr .30 .75
42 E.Dampier/D.Jones .12 .30
43 S.Marbury/B.Barry .15 .40
44 K.Bryant/J.O'Neal .75 2.00
45 Checklist .12 .30

1996 Press Pass Net Burners

COMPLETE SET (45) 12.00 30.00
*STARS: .6X TO 1.5X BASE CARD HI
ONE PER PACK

1996 Press Pass Swisssh

COMPLETE SET (45) 10.00 25.00
*STARS: .6X TO 1.5X BASE CARD HI
ONE PER PACK

1996 Press Pass Acetates

Randomly inserted in hobby packs only at a rate of one in 18, this 9-card set are designed on a see-through plastic card stock. The cards are numbered "F x/9" on the front. Also on the front is a player action shot and the players name written several times in the background. The card backs are blank except for a small copyright notice at the bottom.
COMPLETE SET (9) 10.00 25.00
STATED ODDS 1:18
1 Allen Iverson 5.00 12.00
2 Marcus Camby 1.50 4.00
3 Shareef Abdur-Rahim 2.00 5.00
4 Stephon Marbury 2.50 6.00
5 Ray Allen 4.00 10.00
6 Antoine Walker 2.00 5.00
7 Lorenzen Wright 1.00 2.50
8 Kerry Kittles 1.00 2.50
9 Samaki Walker 1.00 2.50

1996 Press Pass Autographs

This 20-card autograph set were inserted 1:72 packs. The card fronts have the same design as the base set except they bear an autograph of the player. The backs have the player's name and a congratulatory message on receiving the card. The cards are unnumbered and listed below in alphabetical order.
STATED ODDS 1:72
1 Ray Allen 15.00 40.00
2 Kobe Bryant 150.00 300.00
3 Marcus Camby 6.00 15.00
4 Tony Delk 2.00 5.00
5 Brian Evans 2.00 5.00
6 Othella Harrington 2.00 5.00
7 Allen Iverson 40.00 100.00
8 Dontae' Jones 2.00 5.00
9 Travis Knight 2.00 5.00
10 Randy Livingston 2.00 5.00
11 Stephon Marbury 10.00 25.00
12 Walter McCarty 2.00 5.00
13 Steve Nash 20.00 50.00
14 Vitaly Potapenko 2.00 5.00
15 Roy Rogers 2.00 5.00
16 Jason Sasser 2.00 5.00
17 Antoine Walker 8.00 20.00
18 Samaki Walker 2.00 5.00
19 Jerome Williams 2.00 5.00
20 Lorenzen Wright 2.00 5.00

1996 Press Pass Jersey Cards

Randomly inserted in hobby packs at a rate of one in 640 and retail packs at a rate of one in 720, this 4-card set contains actual pieces of a player's game-used jersey. A small piece of the college jersey is in the center of the card above the player's name and the words "Game Used Jersey". The backs have a congratulatory message and are numbered "J x of 4."
STATED ODDS 1:640
J1 Allen Iverson 20.00 50.00
J2 Marcus Camby 6.00 15.00
J3 Ray Allen 10.00 25.00
J4 Shareef Abdur-Rahim 6.00 15.00

1996 Press Pass Lotto

This is a six-card "progressive insert" where each card has a different ratio to be pulled from pack. The cards were available as follows: #1 1:720, #2 1:360, #3 1:180, #4 1:90, #5 1:45, #6 1:36. The cards fronts have silver borders and a picture of the player in front of an orange background. The backs have a picture of the top six picks and are numbers "Lx of 6".
COMPLETE SET (6) 20.00 50.00
STATED ODDS #1 1:720, #2 1:360, #3 1:180
STATED ODDS #4 1:90, #5 1:45, #6 1:36
1 Allen Iverson 20.00 50.00
2 Marcus Camby 8.00 20.00
3 Shareef Abdur-Rahim 6.00 15.00
4 Stephon Marbury 2.50 6.00
5 Ray Allen 2.00 5.00
6 Antoine Walker 1.00 2.50

1996 Press Pass Pandemonium

Randomly inserted in packs at a rate of one in 12, this 12-card set features some of the hottest players in the college game. Press Pass uses what it calls "NitroKrome" all foil cards. The word "Pandemonium" in very hard to make out, but is jumbled up behind the player photograph on the card fronts. The backs have another player photo and some biographical information. They are also numbered "PM x of 12".
COMPLETE SET (12) 10.00 25.00
STATED ODDS 1:12
1 Shareef Abdur-Rahim 1.50 4.00
2 Ray Allen 3.00 8.00
3 Kobe Bryant 8.00 20.00
4 Marcus Camby 1.25 3.00
5 Erick Dampier .75 2.00
6 Othella Harrington .75 2.00
7 Allen Iverson 4.00 10.00
8 Kerry Kittles .75 2.00
9 Stephon Marbury 2.00 5.00
10 Walter McCarty .75 2.00
11 Antoine Walker 1.50 4.00
12 John Wallace .75 2.00

1997 Press Pass

This 45-card set was issued in 4-card packs in 36-pack hobby boxes. The card fronts have full-bleed color player photos and the player's name and Press Pass in gold foil at the bottom. Each hobby box states that is contains on average, two autographs per box. Each pack contained at least two insert cards among the following: All-American, Autographs, Blue Torquers, In Your Face, Jersey Cards, Lotto, Net Burners, One on One and Red Zone.
COMPLETE SET (45) 4.00 10.00
1 Tim Duncan 1.00 2.50
2 Ron Mercer .20 .50
3 Keith Van Horn .30 .75
4 Tony Battie .15 .40
5 Olivier Saint-Jean .15 .40
6 Tim Thomas .30 .75
7 Adonal Foyle .15 .40
8 Tracy McGrady .75 2.00
9 Antonio Daniels .15 .40
10 Kelvin Cato .15 .40
11 Danny Fortson .15 .40
12 Chauncey Billups .50 1.25

13 Brevin Knight .15 .40
14 Jacque Vaughn .15 .40
15 James Collins .15 .40
16 Johnny Taylor .15 .40
17 Derek Anderson .15 .40
18 Austin Croshere .12 .30
19 Reggie Freeman .15 .40
20 Maurice Taylor .15 .40
21 Shea Seals .15 .40
22 Anthony Parker .15 .40
23 John Thomas .15 .40
24 Kebu Stewart .15 .40
25 Dedric Willoughby .15 .40
26 Serge Zwikker .15 .40
27 Paul Grant .15 .40
28 Victor Page .15 .40
29 Bubba Wells .15 .40
30 Ed Gray .15 .40
31 Charles O'Bannon .15 .40
32 Bobby Jackson .20 .50
33 Keith Booth .15 .40
34 Eddie Elisma .15 .40
35 Scot Pollard .15 .40
36 Harold Deane .15 .40
37 Jeff Capel .15 .40
38 Kiwane Garris .15 .40
39 Charles Smith .15 .40
40 Alvin Sims .15 .40
41 Duncan/Zwikker/Elisma .40 1.00
42 A.Croshere/T.Thomas .15 .40
43 T.Battie/J.Vaughn/C.Billups .20 .50
44 R.Mercer/D.Anderson .20 .50
45 Tim Duncan CL .40 1.00

1997 Press Pass Blue Torquers

*STARS: .6X TO 1.5X BASE CARD HI
ONE PER RETAIL PACK

1997 Press Pass Red Zone

*STARS: .6X TO 1.5X BASE CARD HI
ONE PER RETAIL PACK

1997 Press Pass All-American

This 12-card set used Press Pass' "NitroKrome" technology. Each card has a foil based background and two photos of the player on the front. The backs have another photo and some biographical information. The cards are numbered "AX of 12".

COMPLETE SET (12) 10.00 25.00
STATED ODDS 1:12
A1 Tim Duncan 4.00 10.00
A2 Keith Van Horn 1.25 3.00
A3 Ron Mercer .75 2.00
A4 Tracy McGrady 3.00 8.00
A5 Danny Fortson .60 1.50
A6 Brevin Knight .60 1.50
A7 Tony Battie .60 1.50
A8 Jacque Vaughn .60 1.50
A9 Chauncey Billups 2.00 5.00
A10 Bobby Jackson .75 2.00
A11 Adonal Foyle .60 1.50
A12 Shea Seals .60 1.50

1997 Press Pass Autographs

This 30-card set offers autographs from 30 different NBA rookies. The cards parallel their base set card, but the foil on the bottom is in a yellow font, and the card background has an added white shading to it. The packs have a congratulatory message on receiving the autograph. Some cards were inserted as redemption cards that expired July 30, 1998. The cards are unnumbered and listed below in alphabetical order.

STATED ODDS 1:18 HOBBY
1 Derek Anderson 1.50 4.00
2 Tony Battie 1.50 4.00
3 Chauncey Billups 5.00 12.00
4 Jeff Capel 1.50 4.00
5 Kelvin Cato 1.50 4.00
6 James Collins 1.50 4.00
7 Austin Croshere 1.25 3.00
8 Harold Deane 1.50 4.00
9 Tim Duncan 75.00 200.00
10 Eddie Elisma 1.50 4.00
11 Danny Fortson 1.50 4.00
12 Kiwane Garris 1.50 4.00
13 Paul Grant 1.50 4.00
14 Bobby Jackson 2.00 5.00
15 Brevin Knight 1.50 4.00
16 Tracy McGrady 15.00 40.00
17 Charles O'Bannon 1.50 4.00
18 Anthony Parker 1.50 4.00
19 Scot Pollard 1.50 4.00
20 Olivier Saint-Jean 1.50 4.00
21 Alvin Sims 1.50 4.00
22 Charles Smith 1.50 4.00
23 Kebu Stewart 1.50 4.00
24 Johnny Taylor 1.50 4.00
25 Maurice Taylor 1.50 4.00
26 John Thomas 1.50 4.00
27 Tim Thomas 3.00 8.00
28 Jacque Vaughn 1.50 4.00
29 Bubba Wells 1.50 4.00
30 Serge Zwikker 1.50 4.00

1997 Press Pass In Your Face

Inserted at a rate of 1 per 36 hobby packs, these cards highlight nine different players on a clear acetate-stock card. The cards are numbered on the back with a prefix of "IYF"

COMPLETE SET (9) 10.00 25.00
STATED ODDS 1:36 HOBBY
IYF1 Ron Mercer 1.25 3.00
IYF2 Danny Fortson 1.00 2.50
IYF3 Chauncey Billups 3.00 8.00
IYF4 Maurice Taylor 1.00 2.50
IYF5 Keith Van Horn 2.00 5.00
IYF6 Bobby Jackson 1.25 3.00
IYF7 Tony Battie 1.00 2.50
IYF8 Tim Duncan 6.00 15.00
IYF9 Kelvin Cato 1.00 2.50

1997 Press Pass Jersey Cards

Inserted at the rate of 1 in 612 packs, these cards contain actual pieces of game-worn jerseys from top 1997 NBA draft picks. The cards of Ron Mercer, Keith Van Horn, Tony Battie and Tim Duncan were released later in the Double Threat product.

DOUBLE THREAT STATED ODDS 1:612
PRESS PASS STATED ODDS 1:720
PP SUFFIX ON PRESS PASS DISTRIBUTION
JC1 Tim Duncan PP 12.00 30.00
JC2 Ron Mercer DT 10.00 25.00
JC3 Keith Van Horn DT 12.50 30.00
JC4 Jacque Vaughn PP 6.00 15.00
BON Tim Duncan DT 40.00 100.00
BON Tony Battie DT 6.00 15.00
BON Chauncey Billups PP 8.00 20.00

1997 Press Pass Lotto

This 7-card set was inserted into packs with progressive ratios that were tougher the lower the card number. The cards have foil background fronts with a player photo, and all players pictured on the back. Each is numbered "LX of 6". The odds for each is as follows: #1 1:720, #2 1:360, #3 1:180, #4 1:90, #5 1:45, #6 1:36. Chauncey Billups was added at the last minute without a card number and was inserted at a rate of one in 360 packs.

COMPLETE SET (7) 25.00 60.00
STATED ODDS #1 1:720, #2 1:360, #3 1:180
STATED ODDS #4 1:90, #5 1:45, #6 1:36
STATED ODDS NNO 1:360
L1 Tim Duncan 20.00 50.00
L2 Ron Mercer 4.00 10.00
L3 Keith Van Horn 6.00 15.00
L4 Tony Battie 2.50 6.00
L5 Adonal Foyle 2.00 5.00
L6 Tim Thomas 2.50 6.00
NNO Chauncey Billups 5.00 12.00

1997 Press Pass Net Burners

COMPLETE SET (36) 6.00 15.00
ONE PER PACK
NB1 Tim Duncan 1.50 4.00
NB2 Ron Mercer .30 .75
NB3 Keith Van Horn .50 1.25
NB4 Tony Battie .25 .60
NB5 Scot Pollard .25 .60
NB6 Tim Thomas .50 1.25
NB7 Adonal Foyle .25 .60
NB8 Tracy McGrady 1.25 3.00
NB9 Antonio Daniels .25 .60
NB10 Kelvin Cato .25 .60
NB11 Danny Fortson .25 .60
NB12 Chauncey Billups .75 2.00
NB13 Brevin Knight .25 .60
NB14 Jacque Vaughn .25 .60
NB15 James Collins .25 .60
NB16 Alvin Sims .25 .60
NB17 Derek Anderson .25 .60
NB18 Austin Croshere .20 .50
NB19 Reggie Freeman .25 .60
NB20 Maurice Taylor .25 .60
NB21 Shea Seals .25 .60
NB22 Anthony Parker .25 .60
NB23 Johnny Taylor .25 .60
NB24 Kebu Stewart .25 .60
NB25 Dedric Willoughby .25 .60
NB26 Serge Zwikker .25 .60
NB27 Olivier Saint-Jean .25 .60
NB28 Victor Page .25 .60
NB29 Bubba Wells .25 .60
NB30 Ed Gray .25 .60
NB31 Charles O'Bannon .25 .60
NB32 Bobby Jackson .30 .75
NB33 Eddie Elisma .25 .60
NB34 Kiwane Garris .25 .60
NB35 Keith Booth .25 .60
NB36 Tim Duncan CL .60 1.50
NNO Ray Allen Promo .60 1.50

1997 Press Pass One On One

This 9-card set, inserted at a rate of 1 in 18 packs, highlights one-on-one match-ups of NBA players-to-be. The card fronts picture both players on a silver foil background. The backs talk about what the match-up would be like. Cards are numbered "X of 9".

COMPLETE SET (9) 10.00 25.00
STATED ODDS 1:18
1 T.Duncan/T.Battie 4.00 10.00
2 D.Fortson/T.Duncan 4.00 10.00
3 R.Mercer/T.McGrady 3.00 8.00
4 K.Van Horn/T.Thomas 1.25 3.00
5 A.Daniels/C.Billups 2.00 5.00
6 A.Foyle/K.Cato .60 1.50
7 D.Anderson/R.Mercer .75 2.00
8 J.Vaughn/B.Knight .60 1.50
9 A.Croshere/M.Taylor .60 1.50

1997 Press Pass Tim Duncan Draft Set

TD1 Tim Duncan 2.50 6.00
TD1 Tim Duncan 2.50 6.00
TD1 Tim Duncan 2.50 6.00

1998 Press Pass

The 1998 Press Pass set was issued in one series totaling 45 cards and was distributed in four-card packs. The fronts feature full-bleed color player photos. The backs carry player information. Along with the parallel and insert sets that follow this listing, there was a Solo parallel set that was a "One of One" style set where there was only one card produced per base set card. Due to there scarcity, the cards values can not be assessed by our guides.

COMPLETE SET (45) 5.00 10.00
1 Mike Bibby .40 1.00
2 Nazr Mohammed .15 .40
3 Raef LaFrentz .20 .50
4 Vince Carter .75 2.00
5 Paul Pierce .60 1.50
6 Michael Olowokandi .20 .50
7 Larry Hughes .30 .75
8 Keon Clark .15 .40
9 Robert Traylor .15 .40
10 Michael Doleac .15 .40
11 Pat Garrity .15 .40
12 Jason Williams .40 1.00
13 Miles Simon .15 .40
14 Toby Bailey .15 .40
15 Bonzi Wells .15 .40
16 Tyronn Lue .15 .40
17 Matt Harpring .15 .40
18 J.R. Henderson .15 .40
19 Clayton Shields .10 .25
20 Michael Dickerson .15 .40
21 Saddi Washington .15 .40
22 Malcolm Johnson .15 .40
23 Cory Carr .10 .25
24 Brad Miller .40 1.00
25 Mike Jones .15 .40
26 Brian Skinner .15 .40
27 Al Harrington .25 .60
28 Torraye Braggs .15 .40
29 Corey Louis .15 .40
30 DeMarco Johnson .15 .40
31 Anthony Carter .15 .40
32 Earl Boykins .15 .40
33 Roshown McLeod .15 .40
34 Casey Shaw .10 .25
35 Andrae Patterson .15 .40
36 Bryce Drew .15 .40
37 Jeff Sheppard .15 .40
38 Jahidi White .15 .40
39 Shammond Williams .15 .40
40 Ruben Patterson .15 .40
41 S.Williams/V.Carter .40 1.00
42 M.Dickerson/M.Simon .15 .40
43 R.LaFrentz/P.Pierce .40 1.00
44 T.Bailey/J.R.Henderson .15 .40
45 Mike Bibby CL .15 .40

1998 Press Pass Blue

*BLUE .6X TO 1.5X BASE CARD HI

1998 Press Pass In The Zone

*STARS: .6X TO 1.5X BASE CARD HI
STATED ODDS 1:1 HOBBY

1998 Press Pass Reflectors

*STARS: 6X TO 15X BASE CARD HI
STATED ODDS 1:90

1998 Press Pass Torquers

*STARS: .6X TO 1.5X BASE CARD HI
STATED ODDS 1:1 RETAIL

1998 Press Pass Autographs

These autographed cards were inserted 1:18 hobby and 1:36 retail packs. Either an autograph or redemption card was inserted. While some players were available via both packs and redemption cards, nine players were only made available via redemption cards: Keon Clark, Bonzi Wells, Paul Pierce, Brian Skinner, Michael Dickerson, Tyronn Lue, Jeff Sheppard, DeMarco Johnson and Miles Simon.

STATED ODDS 1:18 HOB/1:36 RET
SOME ONLY AVAILABLE VIA REDEMPTION
NNO CARDS LISTED BELOW ALPHABETICALLY
1 Toby Bailey 1.50 4.00
2 Mike Bibby 6.00 15.00
3 Earl Boykins 3.00 8.00
4 Torraye Braggs 1.50 4.00
5 Cory Carr 1.00 2.50
6 Anthony Carter 1.50 4.00
7 Vince Carter 20.00 50.00
8 Keon Clark 1.50 4.00
9 Michael Dickerson 1.50 4.00
10 Michael Doleac 1.50 4.00
11 Bryce Drew 1.50 4.00
12 Pat Garrity 1.50 4.00
13 Matt Harpring 1.50 4.00
14 Al Harrington 2.50 6.00
15 J.R. Henderson 1.50 4.00
16 Larry Hughes 4.00 10.00
17 DeMarco Johnson 1.50 4.00
18 Malcolm Johnson 1.50 4.00
19 Mike Jones 1.50 4.00
20 Raef Lafrentz 2.00 5.00
21 Tyronn Lue 1.50 4.00
22 Roshown McLeod 1.50 4.00
23 Brad Miller 4.00 10.00
24 Nazr Mohammed 1.50 4.00
25 Michael Olowokandi 2.00 5.00
26 Andrae Patterson 1.50 4.00
27 Paul Pierce 10.00 25.00
28 Casey Shaw 1.00 2.50
29 Jeff Sheppard 1.50 4.00
30 Clayton Shields 1.00 2.50
31 Miles Simon 1.50 4.00
32 Brian Skinner 1.50 4.00
33 Robert Traylor 1.50 4.00
34 Saddi Washington 1.50 4.00
35 Bonzi Wells 1.50 4.00
36 Jahidi White 1.50 4.00
37 Jason Williams 15.00 40.00
38 Shammond Williams 1.50 4.00

1998 Press Pass Fastbreak

This 12-card set is produced with micro-etched foil technology. Seeded 1:12 packs, card fronts feature two different photographs of the highlighted player. The backs contain another photo and some biographical information. Cards are numbered with a "FB" prefix.

COMPLETE SET (12) 8.00 20.00
STATED ODDS 1:12
FB1 Raef LaFrentz .75 2.00
FB2 Toby Bailey .60 1.50
FB3 Mike Bibby 1.50 4.00
FB4 Vince Carter 3.00 8.00
FB5 Paul Pierce 2.50 6.00
FB6 Michael Olowokandi .75 2.00
FB7 Keon Clark .60 1.50
FB8 Robert Traylor .60 1.50
FB9 Michael Doleac .60 1.50
FB10 Larry Hughes 1.25 3.00
FB11 Pat Garrity .60 1.50
FB12 Miles Simon .60 1.50

1998 Press Pass In Your Face

These 9 clear acetate cards were inserted in 1:36 hobby packs only. On a see-through plastic card stock, a player action photo graces the card fronts while the backs are bare save for a copyright line and the card number, prefaced with "IYF".

COMPLETE SET (9) 8.00 20.00
STATED ODDS 1:36 HOBBY
IYF1 Raef LaFrentz 1.00 2.50
IYF2 Mike Bibby 2.00 5.00
IYF3 Michael Dickerson .75 2.00
IYF4 Paul Pierce 3.00 8.00
IYF5 Pat Garrity .75 2.00
IYF6 Matt Harpring .75 2.00
IYF7 Robert Traylor .75 2.00
IYF8 Brad Miller 2.00 5.00
IYF9 Vince Carter 4.00 10.00

1998 Press Pass Jersey Cards

Randomly inserted in packs at the rate of one in 720, this five-card set features color player photos with actual game-used jersey pieces from top draft picks embedded in the cards. Card #'s JC1, JC2 and JC3 were only available via redeemed redemption cards inserted into packs at a rate of 1:720 as well. Card JC3, originally Mike Bibby, was replaced by Michael Olowokandi.

STATED ODDS 1:720
STATED PRINT RUN 375 SERIAL #'d SETS
OLOWAKANDI USED AS REDEMPTION ON BIBBY JERSEYS
JC1 M.Olowokandi/600 8.00 20.00
JC2 Vince Carter 12.00 30.00
JC3 M.Bibby/Olowokandi 10.00 25.00
JC4 Robert Traylor 6.00 15.00
JC5 Toby Bailey 6.00 15.00

1998 Press Pass Net Burners

Inserted one per pack, this 36-card set features color action player photos printed on all-foil die-cut cards. The backs carry player information.

COMPLETE SET (36) 6.00 15.00
STATED ODDS 1:1
1 Mike Bibby .60 1.50
2 Nazr Mohammed .25 .60
3 Raef LaFrentz .30 .75
4 Vince Carter 1.25 3.00
5 Paul Pierce 1.00 2.50
6 Michael Olowokandi .30 .75
7 Larry Hughes .50 1.25
8 Keon Clark .25 .60
9 Robert Traylor .25 .60
10 Michael Doleac .25 .60
11 Pat Garrity .25 .60
12 Saddi Washington .25 .60
13 Miles Simon .25 .60
14 Toby Bailey .25 .60
15 Bonzi Wells .25 .60
16 Tyronn Lue .25 .60
17 Matt Harpring .25 .60
18 J.R. Henderson .25 .60
19 Clayton Shields .15 .40
20 Michael Dickerson .25 .60
21 DeMarco Johnson .25 .60
22 Andrae Patterson .25 .60
23 Cory Carr .15 .40
24 Torraye Braggs .25 .60
25 Ruben Patterson .25 .60
26 Brian Skinner .25 .60
27 Bryce Drew .25 .60
28 Shammond Williams .25 .60
29 Corey Louis .25 .60
30 Tim Duncan .50 1.25
31 Keith Van Horn .25 .60
32 Tim Thomas .25 .60
33 Derek Anderson .15 .40
34 Brevin Knight .15 .40
35 Ron Mercer .20 .50
36 Roshown McLeod CL .25 .60
S1 Mike Bibby PROMO .60 1.50

1998 Press Pass Real Deal Rookies

The nine cards that make up this set are representative of NBA rookies from the 1997-98 season. With the NBA team logos air-brushed out, the card fronts contain two player photos, and the backs contain another photo and rookie year statistics. Card were inserted in 1:18 packs and have an "R" prefix on the card numbers.

COMPLETE SET (9) 5.00 12.00
STATED ODDS 1:18
R1 Tim Duncan 2.00 5.00
R2 Keith Van Horn 1.00 2.50
R3 Tim Thomas 1.00 2.50
R4 Derek Anderson .60 1.50
R5 Brevin Knight .60 1.50
R6 Ron Mercer .75 2.00
R7 Tracy McGrady 1.50 4.00
R8 Danny Fortson .60 1.50
R9 Maurice Taylor .60 1.50

1998 Press Pass Super Six

The six players in the set were perceived as six of the best players heading into the 1998 NBA draft. Cards feature dual photo fronts with holofoil technology. The backs contain another player photo and some text that explains why the player made Press Pass' "Superior Six." One card was inserted in every thirty-six packs. Card numbers have a "S" prefix.

COMPLETE SET (6) 6.00 15.00
STATED ODDS 1:36
S1 Raef LaFrentz .75 2.00
S2 Larry Hughes 1.25 3.00
S3 Mike Bibby 1.50 4.00
S4 Vince Carter 3.00 8.00
S5 Paul Pierce 2.50 6.00
S6 Michael Olowokandi .75 2.00

1999 Press Pass

The 1999 Press Pass draft pick set was released as a 45-card set. Each box contained 24 packs with five cards per pack. A special Vince Carter card was randomly inserted in packs at one in 480 hobby and one in 720 retail. It is priced at the end of the base set.

COMPLETE SET (45) 4.00 10.00
1 Elton Brand .30 .75
2 Steve Francis .30 .75
3 Baron Davis .30 .75
4 Lamar Odom .30 .75
5 Jonathan Bender .12 .30
6 Wally Szczerbiak .25 .60
7 Richard Hamilton .30 .75
8 Andre Miller .30 .75
9 Jason Terry .30 .75
10 Trajan Langdon .12 .30
11 William Avery .12 .30
12 Ron Artest .30 .75
13 Cal Bowdler .12 .30
14 James Posey .12 .30
15 Quincy Lewis .12 .30
16 Jeff Foster .12 .30
17 Kenny Thomas .12 .30
18 Devean George .12 .30
19 Tim James .12 .30
20 Vonteego Cummings .12 .30
21 Jumaine Jones .12 .30
22 Scott Padgett .12 .30
23 John Celestand .12 .30
24 Rico Hill .12 .30
25 Michael Ruffin .12 .30
26 Chris Herren .12 .30
27 Evan Eschmeyer .12 .30
28 Calvin Booth .12 .30
29 Obinna Ekezie .12 .30
30 A.J. Bramlett .12 .30
31 Louis Bullock .12 .30
32 Lee Nailon .12 .30
33 Tyrone Washington .12 .30
34 Lari Ketner .12 .30
35 Venson Hamilton .12 .30
36 Roberto Bergersen .12 .30
37 Rodney Buford .12 .30
38 Melvin Levett .12 .30
39 Kris Clack .12 .30
40 Harold Jamison .12 .30
41 Heshimu Evans .12 .30
42 Ademola Okulaja .12 .30
43 Jamel Thomas .12 .30
44 Jason Miskiri .12 .30
45 Elton Brand CL .30 .75
NNO Vince Carter Special 15.00 40.00

1999 Press Pass Gold Zone

*GOLD: .75X TO 2X BASE CARD HI

1999 Press Pass Reflectors

*REFLECTORS: 5X TO 12X BASE CARD HI
STATED PRINT RUN 250 SERIAL #'D SETS
STATED ODDS 1:90

1999 Press Pass Torquers

TORQUERS: .75X TO 2X BASE CARD HI
ONE PER RETAIL PACK

1999 Press Pass Autographs

Randomly inserted in hobby packs at one in eight, and retail packs at one in 36, this 40-card set features autographed cards from some of the top draft picks.

STATED ODDS 1:8 HOB, 1:36 RET
STAND.SIG.STATED ODDS 1:120 HOB
STAND.SIG.PRINT RUN 100 SERIAL #'d SETS
1 Elton Brand 4.00 10.00
2 Steve Francis 4.00 10.00
3 Baron Davis 4.00 10.00
4 Lamar Odom 4.00 10.00
5 Jonathan Bender 1.50 4.00
6 Wally Szczerbiak 3.00 8.00
7 Richard Hamilton 4.00 10.00
8 Andre Miller 4.00 10.00
9 Jason Terry 4.00 10.00
10 Trajan Langdon 1.50 4.00
11 William Avery 1.50 4.00
12 Ron Artest 4.00 10.00
13 Cal Bowdler 1.50 4.00
14 James Posey 1.50 4.00
15 Quincy Lewis 1.50 4.00
16 Kenny Thomas 1.50 4.00
17 Devean George 1.50 4.00
18 Tim James 1.50 4.00
19 Vonteego Cummings 1.50 4.00
20 John Celestand 1.50 4.00
21 Rico Hill 1.50 4.00
22 Michael Ruffin 1.50 4.00
23 Chris Herren 2.50 6.00
24 Evan Eschmeyer 1.50 4.00
25 Calvin Booth 1.50 4.00
26 A.J. Bramlett 1.50 4.00
27 Louis Bullock 1.50 4.00
28 Lee Nailon 1.50 4.00
29 Tyrone Washington 1.50 4.00
30 Lari Ketner 1.50 4.00
31 Venson Hamilton 1.50 4.00
32 Roberto Bergersen 1.50 4.00
33 Rodney Buford 1.50 4.00
34 Melvin Levett 1.50 4.00
35 Kris Clack 1.50 4.00
36 Harold Jamison 1.50 4.00
37 Heshimu Evans 1.50 4.00
38 Ademola Okulaja 1.50 4.00
39 Jamel Thomas 1.50 4.00
40 Jason Miskiri 1.50 4.00

1999 Press Pass Standout Signatures

*STAND.SIG: .6X TO 1.5X VALUE

1999 Press Pass Courtside

Randomly inserted into retail boxes at a ratio of one in six packs, this 5-card insert features some of the top new talent to enter the NBA.

COMPLETE SET (5) 1.25 3.00
STATED ODDS 1:6 RETAIL
1 Steve Francis .50 1.25
2 Elton Brand .50 1.25
3 Lamar Odom .50 1.25
4 Richard Hamilton .50 1.25
5 Wally Szczerbiak .40 1.00

1999 Press Pass Crunch Time

Randomly inserted in packs at one in 18, this nine-card set features players who deliver in "crunch time". The cards feature a silver foil front and a "CT" prefix on the back.

COMPLETE SET (9) 2.50 6.00
STATED ODDS 1:18 HOB/RET
CT1 Elton Brand .60 1.50
CT2 Steve Francis .60 1.50
CT3 Baron Davis .60 1.50
CT4 Lamar Odom .60 1.50
CT5 Wally Szczerbiak .50 1.25
CT6 Richard Hamilton .60 1.50
CT7 Andre Miller .60 1.50
CT8 Jason Terry .60 1.50
CT9 William Avery .25 .60

1999 Press Pass In Your Face

Randomly inserted in hobby packs at one in 24 and retail packs at one in 36, this six-card set features above the rim photos combined with clear acetate. Card backs carry an "IYF" prefix.

COMPLETE SET (6) 2.00 5.00
STATED ODDS 1:24 HOB, 1:36 RET
IYF1 Elton Brand .60 1.50
IYF2 Baron Davis .60 1.50
IYF3 Andre Miller .60 1.50
IYF4 Jason Terry .60 1.50
IYF5 Ron Artest .60 1.50
IYF6 Kenny Thomas .25 .60

1999 Press Pass Jersey Cards

Randomly inserted in hobby packs at one in 480 and retail packs at one in 720, this five-card set features cards that contain an actual pierce of a game-used jersey from top 1999 picks. Card backs carry a "JC" prefix and are serially numbered to 300.

STATED ODDS 1:480 HOB, 1:720 RET
STATED PRINT RUN 300 SERIAL #'d SETS
JC1 Elton Brand 10.00 25.00
JC2 Steve Francis 10.00 25.00
JC3 Lamar Odom 10.00 25.00
JC4 James Posey 4.00 10.00
JC5 Evan Eschmeyer 4.00 10.00

1999 Press Pass Net Burners

Seeded one per pack, this 36-card set features all foil die cut cards.

COMPLETE SET (36) 5.00 12.00
ONE PER PACK
NB1 Steve Francis .50 1.25
NB2 Richard Hamilton .50 1.25
NB3 Baron Davis .50 1.25
NB4 Lamar Odom .50 1.25
NB5 Elton Brand .50 1.25
NB6 Jason Terry .50 1.25
NB7 Andre Miller .50 1.25
NB8 Ron Artest .50 1.25
NB9 William Avery .20 .50
NB10 James Posey .20 .50
NB11 Tim James .20 .50
NB12 Evan Eschmeyer .20 .50
NB13 Quincy Lewis .20 .50
NB14 Scott Padgett .20 .50
NB15 Jamel Thomas .20 .50
NB16 Kenny Thomas .20 .50
NB17 Melvin Levett .20 .50
NB18 A.J. Bramlett .20 .50
NB19 Lari Ketner .20 .50
NB20 Kris Clack .20 .50
NB21 Lee Nailon .20 .50
NB22 Vonteego Cummings .20 .50
NB23 Trajan Langdon .20 .50
NB24 Wally Szczerbiak .40 1.00
NB25 Obinna Ekezie .20 .50
NB26 Rico Hill .20 .50
NB27 Venson Hamilton .20 .50
NB28 Michael Ruffin .20 .50
NB29 Harold Jamison .20 .50
NB30 Ademola Okulaja .20 .50
NB31 Chris Herren .20 .50
NB32 Calvin Booth .20 .50
NB33 Jonathan Bender .20 .50
NB34 Rodney Buford .20 .50
NB35 John Celestand .20 .50
NB36 Steve Francis CL .50 1.25

1999 Press Pass On Fire

Randomly inserted in packs at one in 12, this 12-card set features some of the nation's hottest players. The cards are on all foil, microetched Nitrokrome. Card backs carry an "OF" prefix.

COMPLETE SET (12) 3.00 8.00
STATED ODDS 1:12 HOB/RET
OF1 Elton Brand .60 1.50
OF2 Steve Francis .60 1.50
OF3 Baron Davis .60 1.50
OF4 Lamar Odom .60 1.50
OF5 Wally Szczerbiak .50 1.25
OF6 Richard Hamilton .60 1.50
OF7 Andre Miller .60 1.50
OF8 Jason Terry .60 1.50
OF9 William Avery .25 .60
OF10 Ron Artest .60 1.50
OF11 James Posey .25 .60
OF12 Kenny Thomas .25 .60

1999 Press Pass Y2K

Randomly inserted in hobby packs only at one in 36, this eight-card set features the future stars of the millennium. Card fronts feature a die cut basketball background. Card backs are serially numbered to 2000 and carry a "Y" prefix.

COMPLETE SET (8) 5.00 12.00
STATED PRINT RUN 2000 SERIAL #'d SETS
STATED ODDS 1:36 HOB
Y1 Elton Brand 1.00 2.50
Y2 Steve Francis 1.00 2.50
Y3 Baron Davis 1.00 2.50
Y4 Lamar Odom 1.00 2.50
Y5 Wally Szczerbiak .75 2.00
Y6 Richard Hamilton 1.00 2.50
Y7 Andre Miller 1.00 2.50
Y8 Jason Terry 1.00 2.50

2000 Press Pass

Released in July 2000, this 46-card set features top picks and prospects from the NBA Draft class. Each hobby pack carried five-cards with a suggested retail price of $3.79. Each retail pack carried four-cards with a suggested retail price of $2.99.

COMPLETE SET (46) 10.00 25.00
COMPLETE SET w/o SP (40) 5.00 12.00
PP CARDS STATED ODDS 1:14 HOBBY
UNPRICED SOLOS SERIAL #'d TO 1
1 Chris Mihm CL .25 .60
2 Chris Mihm .25 .60
3 Mike Miller .40 1.00
4 Chris Porter .25 .60
5 Morris Peterson .25 .60
6 Darius Miles .25 .60
7 Jerome Moiso .25 .60
8 Quentin Richardson .30 .75
9 Mateen Cleaves .25 .60
10 Etan Thomas .25 .60
11 Scoonie Penn .25 .60
12 Jason Collier .25 .60
13 Hanno Mottola .25 .60
14 Mark Madsen .25 .60
15 DeShawn Stevenson .25 .60
16 Dan Langhi .25 .60
17 Jamaal Magloire .25 .60
18 Pepe Sanchez .25 .60
19 Khalid El-Amin .25 .60
20 Harold Arceneaux .25 .60
21 Mark Karcher .25 .60
22 Jason Hart .25 .60
23 Eddie House .25 .60
24 Gabe Muoneke .25 .60
25 Jake Voskuhl .25 .60
26 Brad Millard .25 .60
27 Bootsy Thornton .25 .60
28 Eddie Gill .25 .60
29 Shaheen Holloway .25 .60
30 Kevin Freeman .25 .60
31 Jarrett Stephens .25 .60
32 Brian Cardinal .25 .60
33 Brandon Kurtz .25 .60
34 Elton Brand .25 .60
35 Steve Francis .25 .60
36 Lamar Odom .20 .50
37 Wally Szczerbiak .25 .60
38 Baron Davis .25 .60
39 Richard Hamilton .25 .60
40 Chris Carrawell .25 .60
41 Chris Mihm PP .75 2.00
42 Darius Miles PP .75 2.00
43 Mike Miller PP 1.25 3.00
44 Jerome Moiso PP .75 2.00
45 Mateen Cleaves PP .75 2.00
46 Morris Peterson PP .75 2.00

2000 Press Pass Gold Zone

COMPLETE SET (40) 8.00 20.00
*GOLD ZONE: .6X TO 1.5X BASIC CARDS
ONE PER HOBBY PACK

2000 Press Pass Reflectors

*REFLECTORS: 2.5X TO 6X BASE HI
STATED ODDS 1:72 HOBBY/RETAIL
STATED PRINT RUN 500 SERIAL #'d SETS

2000 Press Pass Torquers

COMPLETE SET (40) 8.00 20.00
*TORQUERS: .6X TO 1.5X BASIC CARDS
ONE PER RETAIL PACK

2000 Press Pass Autographs

Randomly inserted in hobby packs at one in nine and retail packs at one in 36, this set features autographs of top draft picks and stars from the NBA. The cards are not numbered and listed below alphabetically. Card numbers 31 and 32 were issued through various retail re-packs after this product was released

STATED ODDS 1:9 HOBBY, 1:36 RETAIL
NNO CARDS LISTED BELOW ALPHABETICALLY
ASTERISK CARDS IN RETAIL RE-PACK
1 Elton Brand 4.00 10.00
2 Brian Cardinal 2.00 5.00
3 Mateen Cleaves 2.00 5.00
4 Jason Collier 2.00 5.00
5 Baron Davis 4.00 10.00
6 Keyon Dooling 2.00 5.00
7 Richie Frahm 2.00 5.00
8 Steve Francis 4.00 10.00
9 Eddie Gill 2.00 5.00
10 Jason Hart 2.00 5.00
11 Eddie House 2.00 5.00
12 Dan Langhi 2.00 5.00
13 Mark Madsen 2.00 5.00
14 Jamaal Magloire 2.00 5.00
15 Dan McClintock 2.00 5.00
16 Chris Mihm 2.00 5.00
17 Darius Miles 2.00 5.00
18 Brad Millard 2.00 5.00
19 Mike Miller 3.00 8.00
20 Jerome Moiso 2.00 5.00
21 Hanno Mottola 2.00 5.00
22 Lamar Odom 4.00 10.00
23 Scoonie Penn 2.00 5.00
24 Morris Peterson 2.00 5.00
25 Chris Porter 2.00 5.00
26 Quentin Richardson 2.50 6.00
27 Jarrett Stephens 2.00 5.00
28 DeShawn Stevenson 2.00 5.00
29 Wally Szczerbiak 2.00 5.00
30 Etan Thomas 2.00 5.00
31 Jake Voskuhl 2.00 5.00
32 Shaheen Halloway* 2.00 5.00
33 Harold Arceneaux* 2.00 5.00

2000 Press Pass Breakaway

Inserted one per pack, this 36-card set semi-parallels the base set. Each card is die cut. To ascertain values on individual cards, please refer to the multiplier in the header, coupled with the value of the base card.

COMPLETE SET (36) 8.00 20.00
ONE PER PACK
BA1 Mateen Cleaves CL .40 1.00
BA2 Chris Mihm .40 1.00
BA3 Mike Miller .60 1.50
BA4 Chris Porter .40 1.00
BA5 Morris Peterson .40 1.00
BA6 Darius Miles .40 1.00
BA7 Jerome Moiso .40 1.00
BA8 Quentin Richardson .50 1.25
BA9 Mateen Cleaves .40 1.00
BA10 Etan Thomas .40 1.00
BA11 Scoonie Penn .40 1.00
BA12 Jason Collier .40 1.00
BA13 Hanno Mottola .40 1.00
BA14 Mark Madsen .40 1.00
BA15 DeShawn Stevenson .40 1.00
BA16 Dan Langhi .40 1.00
BA17 Jamaal Magloire .40 1.00
BA18 Pepe Sanchez .40 1.00
BA19 Mark Karcher .40 1.00
BA20 Khalid El-Amin .40 1.00
BA21 Jason Hart .40 1.00
BA22 Eddie House .40 1.00
BA23 Gabe Muoneke .40 1.00
BA24 Jake Voskuhl .40 1.00
BA25 Brad Millard .40 1.00
BA26 Shaheen Holloway .40 1.00
BA27 Jarrett Stephens .40 1.00
BA28 Elton Brand .40 1.00
BA29 Steve Francis .40 1.00
BA30 Lamar Odom .30 .75
BA31 Wally Szczerbiak .40 1.00
BA32 Baron Davis .40 1.00
BA33 Richard Hamilton .40 1.00
BA34 Bootsy Thornton .40 1.00
BA35 Brian Cardinal .40 1.00
BA36 Chris Carrawell .40 1.00

2000 Press Pass In the Paint

Randomly inserted in packs at one in 12, this eight-card set featured some of the premier draft picks who do their work in the paint. Card backs carry an "IP" prefix.

COMPLETE SET (8) 3.00 8.00
STATED ODDS 1:12 HOB/RET
*DIE CUT: .6X TO 1.5X HI COLUMN
DIE CUT: STATED ODDS 1:24 H/R
IP1 Chris Mihm .60 1.50
IP2 Mateen Cleaves .60 1.50
IP3 Morris Peterson .60 1.50
IP4 Jerome Moiso .60 1.50
IP5 Mike Miller 1.00 2.50
IP6 Darius Miles .60 1.50
IP7 Jason Collier .60 1.50
IP8 Etan Thomas .60 1.50

2000 Press Pass In Your Face

Randomly inserted in packs at one in 28, this six-card set features aerial shots of high-flying draft picks. Card backs carry an "IF" prefix.

COMPLETE SET (6) 3.00 8.00
STATED ODDS 1:28
IF1 Chris Mihm .75 2.00
IF2 Mateen Cleaves .75 2.00
IF3 Morris Peterson .75 2.00
IF4 Jerome Moiso .75 2.00
IF5 Chris Porter .75 2.00
IF6 Quentin Richardson 1.00 2.50

2000 Press Pass Jersey Cards

Randomly inserted in hobby packs at one in 420 and retail packs at one in 720, this four-card set features a game-used jersey swatch of top draft picks. Each card was serially numbered out of 425.

COMPLETE SET (4) 15.00 40.00
STATED ODDS 1:420 H, 1:720 R
STATED PRINT RUN 425 SERIAL #'d SETS
JCCM Chris Mihm 5.00 12.00
JCDM Darius Miles 5.00 12.00
JCMC Mateen Cleaves 5.00 12.00
JCMM Mike Miller 8.00 20.00

2000 Press Pass On Fire

Randomly inseted in packs at one in six, this 11-card set features some of the hottest players on microetched foil. Card backs carry an "OF" prefix.

COMPLETE SET (11) 4.00 10.00
STATED ODDS 1:6
OF1 Mike Miller .75 2.00
OF2 Darius Miles .50 1.25
OF3 Chris Mihm .50 1.25
OF4 Quentin Richardson .60 1.50
OF5 Mateen Cleaves .50 1.25
OF6 Chris Porter .50 1.25
OF7 Morris Peterson .50 1.25
OF8 Khalid El-Amin .50 1.25
OF9 Jerome Moiso .50 1.25
OF10 Hanno Mottola .50 1.25
OF11 Etan Thomas .50 1.25

2000 Press Pass Power Pick Autographs

COMPLETE SET (6) 20.00 50.00
STATED ODDS 1:269 HOBBY
STATED PRINT RUN 250 SERIAL #'d SETS
1 Mateen Cleaves 4.00 10.00
2 Chris Mihm 4.00 10.00
3 Darius Miles 4.00 10.00
4 Mike Miller 6.00 15.00
5 Jerome Moiso 4.00 10.00
6 Morris Peterson/240 4.00 10.00

2002 Press Pass

Released in August, 2002, this 46-card set showcases 2002 draft picks and college coaches. Hobby product SRP was $3.49 per pack where each pack contained five cards, and boxes contained 24 packs while cases contained 20 boxes. Retail product S.R.P. $2.99 per pack contains four cards per pack, 28 packs per box and 20 boxes per case. Base cards contain full color player action photos and silver foil accents on the player name box and the player's name. There are two versions of the Jay Williams checklist #40, and the last five cards in the set are Power Pick short prints. These cards are inserted in packs at the rate of one in 14.

COMPLETE SET (45) 8.00 20.00
41-45 STATED ODDS 1:14
1 Matt Barnes .30 .75
2 Lonny Baxter .25 .60
3 Carlos Boozer .50 1.25
4 Curtis Borchardt .25 .60
5 Chris Christoffersen .25 .60
6 Sam Clancy .25 .60
7 Dan Dickau .25 .60
8 Juan Dixon .25 .60
9 Mike Dunleavy .25 .60
10 Dan Gadzuric .20 .50
11 Drew Gooden .25 .60
12 Ryan Humphrey .25 .60
13 Chris Jefferies .25 .60
14 Jared Jeffries .25 .60
15 Jason Jennings .25 .60
16 Fred Jones .25 .60
17 Steve Logan .25 .60
18 Yao Ming .75 2.00
19 Chris Owens .25 .60
20 Tayshaun Prince .30 .75
21 Kareem Rush .25 .60
22 Predrag Savovic .25 .60
23 Jamal Sampson .25 .60
24 Tamar Slay .25 .60
25 Darius Songaila .25 .60
26 Amare Stoudemire .60 1.50
27 Nikoloz Tskitishvili .25 .60
28 DaJuan Wagner .25 .60
29 Jiri Welsch .25 .60
30 Chris Wilcox .25 .60
31 Jay Williams .30 .75
32 Frank Williams .25 .60
33 Vincent Yarbrough .25 .60
34 Jim Boeheim CO .40 1.00
35 Jim Calhoun CO .40 1.00

36 Lute Olson CO .40 1.00
37 Tubby Smith CO .40 1.00
38 Gary Williams CO .75 2.00
39 Roy Williams CO .40 1.00
40A Jay Williams CL .25 .60
40B Jay Williams CL .25 .60
41 Chris Wilcox PP .75 2.00
42 Kareem Rush PP .75 2.00
43 Drew Gooden PP .75 2.00
44 DaJuan Wagner PP .75 2.00
45 Jay Williams PP 1.00 2.50

2002 Press Pass Gold Zone

*GOLD: .75X TO 2X BASE CARD HI
STATED ODDS 1:1 HOBBY

2002 Press Pass Red

*RED: .75X TO 2X BASE CARD HI
RANDOM INSERTS IN RETAIL PACKS

2002 Press Pass Reflectors

*REF: 2X TO 5X BASE CARD HI
PRINT RUN 500 SERIAL #'d SETS

2002 Press Pass Autographs

Randomly inserted in packs at a rate of 1:6 (hobby) and 1:14 (retail), this set features signed cards from the 2002 draft prospects and college coaches. The card design features full color action photography, gold ink highlights on the Press Pass logo and player's name, and a diagonal white strip on the bottom third of the card for player autographs. Also priced with this set is a special Jay Williams autograph that was given away at the 2002 National Card Collector's Convention in Chicago. Williams autographed 286 total cards and signed both with his jersey number and without. It is rumored that somewhere in the neighborhood of 200 cards were signed with his jersey number.

STATED ODDS 1:6 H/1:14 R
*SILVER: .75X TO 2X BASE HI
SILVER PRINT RUN 100 SER.#'d SETS
1 Matt Barnes 3.00 8.00
2 Jim Boeheim 12.00 30.00
3 Carlos Boozer 5.00 12.00
4 Curtis Borchardt 2.50 6.00
5 Jim Calhoun 6.00 15.00
6 Chris Christoffersen 2.50 6.00
7 Sam Clancy 2.50 6.00
8 Dan Dickau 2.50 6.00
10 Mike Dunleavy 2.50 6.00
11 Andy Ellis 2.50 6.00
12 Dan Gadzuric 2.00 5.00
13 Drew Gooden 2.50 6.00
14 Lynn Greer 2.50 6.00
15 Ryan Humphrey 2.50 6.00
16 Chris Jefferies 2.50 6.00
17 Jared Jeffries 2.50 6.00
18 Jason Jennings 2.50 6.00
19 Fred Jones 2.50 6.00
20 Yao Ming 12.50 30.00
21 Lute Olson 6.00 15.00
22 Chris Owens 2.50 6.00
23 Tayshaun Prince 3.00 8.00
24 Kareem Rush 2.50 6.00
25 Jamal Sampson 2.50 6.00
26 Predrag Savovic 2.50 6.00
27 Tamar Slay 2.50 6.00
28 Tubby Smith 6.00 15.00
29 Darius Songaila 2.50 6.00
30 Amare Stoudemire 5.00 12.00
31 Nikoloz Tskitishvili 2.50 6.00
32 DaJuan Wagner 2.50 6.00
33 Jiri Welsch 2.50 6.00
34 Chris Wilcox 2.50 6.00
35 Frank Williams 2.50 6.00
36 Gary Williams 10.00 25.00
37 Jay Williams 6.00 15.00
38 Roy Williams 15.00 40.00
39 Vincent Yarbrough 2.50 6.00
NNO Jay Williams SPEC Nat'l 30.00 60.00

2002 Press Pass Big Numbers

Randomly seeded in packs at the rate of one in one, this 27-card set features a horizontal design on an all foil card stock. Two player photos appear on the left, one in color, and one in black and white, and the player's jersey number appears on the right side of the card.

COMPLETE SET (27) 6.00 15.00
STATED ODDS 1:1
BN1 Jay Williams CL .50 1.25
BN2 Carlos Boozer .75 2.00
BN3 Curtis Borchardt .40 1.00
BN4 Lonny Baxter .40 1.00
BN5 Sam Clancy .40 1.00
BN6 Dan Dickau .40 1.00
BN7 Juan Dixon .40 1.00
BN8 Kelly Wise .40 1.00
BN9 Andy Ellis .40 1.00
BN10 Dan Gadzuric .30 .75
BN11 Drew Gooden .40 1.00
BN12 Chris Owens .40 1.00
BN13 Chris Jefferies .40 1.00
BN14 Jared Jeffries .40 1.00
BN15 Fred Jones .40 1.00
BN16 Steve Logan .40 1.00
BN17 Tayshaun Prince .50 1.25
BN18 Kareem Rush .40 1.00
BN19 Jamal Sampson .40 1.00
BN20 Darius Songaila .40 1.00
BN21 Nikoloz Tskitishvili .40 1.00
BN22 DaJuan Wagner .40 1.00
BN23 Jiri Welsch .40 1.00
BN24 Chris Wilcox .40 1.00
BN25 Frank Williams .40 1.00
BN26 Jay Williams .50 1.25
BN27 Vincent Yarbrough .40 1.00

2002 Press Pass Cagers

Randomly inserted in packs at a rate of one in 24, this six card set features an all foil design with full color player action photos set in the middle of a silver fence border. Each player's name is printed in a different color foil.

COMPLETE SET (6) 4.00 10.00
STATED ODDS 1:24
C1 Jared Jeffries 1.00 2.50
C2 Frank Williams 1.00 2.50
C3 Drew Gooden 1.00 2.50
C4 DaJuan Wagner 1.00 2.50
C5 Chris Wilcox 1.00 2.50
C6 Jay Williams 1.25 3.00

2002 Press Pass Class of 2002

Randomly inserted in packs at a rate of one in eight, this 12-card set features an all foil card stock with full color player action photos. The top of the card shows about 1/4 of a basketball above the player photo, and the bottom has the same dome shape of the 1/4 basketball but contains a silver embossed portrait of the showcased player along with the player's name.

COMPLETE SET (12) 5.00 12.00
STATED ODDS 1:8
CL1 Carlos Boozer 1.25 3.00
CL2 Curtis Borchardt .60 1.50
CL3 Dan Dickau .60 1.50
CL4 Dan Gadzuric .50 1.25
CL5 Drew Gooden .60 1.50
CL6 Jared Jeffries .60 1.50
CL7 Kareem Rush .60 1.50
CL8 DaJuan Wagner .60 1.50
CL9 Chris Wilcox .60 1.50
CL10 Frank Williams .60 1.50
CL11 Jay Williams .75 2.00
CL12 Mike Dunleavy .60 1.50

2002 Press Pass College Jerseys

Randomly inserted in packs at a rate of 1:120 (hobby) and 1:280 (retail). The set contains genuine game-used jersey from the top draft picks of the 2002 class. Each card features a full color player photo, and the jersey swatches are cut in the shape of a tank-top jersey. Each card is sequentially numbered to 425 except Yao Ming which is a short print and was issued originally as an exchange card.

COMPLETE SET (8) 40.00 80.00
STATED ODDS 1:120 H/1:280 R
PRINT RUN 100 TO 425 SER.#'d SETS
JCCB1 Carlos Boozer/425 6.00 15.00
JCDG1 Drew Gooden/425 3.00 8.00
JCDG2 Dan Gadzuric/425 2.50 6.00
JCDS Darius Songaila/425 3.00 8.00
JCFJ Fred Jones/425 3.00 8.00
JCJW Jay Williams/425 6.00 15.00
JCSC Sam Clancy/425 3.00 8.00
JCYM Yao Ming/100 25.00 60.00

2002 Press Pass Combo Jerseys

This hobby only set features jersey swatches from current pro's college team and pro team on the same card. A college photo appears in the upper left hand corner while the corresponding college jersey swatch appears below. The upper left hand corner contains a swatch of a pro game used jersey with a pro picture below. Each card is sequentially numbered to 100.

PRINT RUN 100 SERIAL #'d SETS
CJCM Chris Mihm 4.00 10.00
CJDM Darius Miles 5.00 12.00
CJDS DeShawn Stevenson 4.00 10.00
CJET Etan Thomas 4.00 10.00
CJJMA Jamaal Magloire 4.00 10.00
CJJMO Jerome Moiso 4.00 10.00
CJMMA Mark Madsen 4.00 10.00
CJMMI Mike Miller 8.00 20.00
CJMP Morris Peterson 5.00 12.00
CJQR Quentin Richardson 6.00 15.00

2002 Press Pass Hang Time

Randomly inserted in packs at a rate of one in 12, this nine card set features all foil card stock with full color player action photos. Each player is framed by a dome border with a box towards the bottom of the card containing the player's name.

COMPLETE SET (9) 4.00 10.00
STATED ODDS 1:12
*DIE CUTS: .75X TO 2X BASE HI
DIE CUTS STATED ODDS 1:24
HT1 Curtis Borchardt .60 1.50
HT2 Kareem Rush .60 1.50
HT3 Carlos Boozer 1.25 3.00
HT4 Juan Dixon .60 1.50
HT5 Drew Gooden .60 1.50
HT6 DaJuan Wagner .60 1.50
HT7 Chris Wilcox .60 1.50
HT8 Jay Williams .75 2.00
HT9 Jared Jeffries .60 1.50

2002 Press Pass Hang Time Die Cuts

HT1 Curtis Borchardt 1.25 3.00
HT2 Kareem Rush 1.25 3.00
HT3 Carlos Boozer 2.50 6.00
HT4 Juan Dixon 1.25 3.00
HT5 Drew Gooden 1.25 3.00
HT6 DaJuan Wagner 1.25 3.00
HT7 Chris Wilcox 1.25 3.00
HT8 Jay Williams 1.50 4.00
HT9 Jared Jeffries 1.25 3.00

2002 Press Pass Power Pick Autographs

Randomly seeded in packs, this 12-card set utilizes the Power Pick design from the base set enhanced by authentic player autographs. Each card is sequentially numbered to 250.

STATED PRINT RUN 250 SERIAL #'d SETS
1 Carlos Boozer 10.00 25.00
2 Curtis Borchardt 4.00 10.00
3 Mike Dunleavy 4.00 10.00
4 Dan Gadzuric 3.00 8.00
5 Drew Gooden 4.00 10.00
6 Jared Jeffries 4.00 10.00
7 Yao Ming 20.00 50.00
8 Tayshaun Prince 5.00 12.00
9 Kareem Rush 4.00 10.00
10 DaJuan Wagner 4.00 10.00
11 Chris Wilcox 4.00 10.00
12 Jay Williams 5.00 12.00

2002 Press Pass Pro Autographs

Randomly inserted in packs at the rate of one in six, this 12-card set features a white background with a square portrait style photo of the showcased player towards the top of the card. Below the photo appears authentic player autographs.

STATED ODDS 1:6
1 Steve Francis 6.00 15.00
2 Mark Madsen 2.50 6.00
3 Jamaal Magloire 2.50 6.00
4 Chris Mihm 2.50 6.00
5 Darius Miles 4.00 10.00
6 Mike Miller 6.00 15.00
7 Jerome Moiso 2.50 6.00
8 Hanno Mottola 2.50 6.00
9 Morris Peterson 2.50 6.00
10 Quentin Richardson 4.00 10.00
11 DeShawn Stevenson 3.00 8.00
12 Etan Thomas 2.50 6.00

2002 Press Pass Pro Jerseys

Randomly inserted in packs at a rate of 1:120 Hobby and 1:280 Retail, this 10-card set features full color player portrait photos on the left side of the card and a swatch of a game worn jersey on the right of the card. Each card is sequentailly numbered to 300.

STATED ODDS 1:120 H/1:280 R
PRINT RUN 300 SER.#'d SETS
PJCCM Chris Mihm 2.00 5.00
PJCDM Darius Miles 3.00 8.00
PJCDS DeShawn Stevenson 2.00 5.00
PJCET Etan Thomas 2.00 5.00
PJCHM Hanno Mottola 2.00 5.00
PJCJM Jamaal Magloire 2.00 5.00
PJCMP Morris Peterson 2.00 5.00
PJCMMA Mark Madsen 2.00 5.00
PJCMMI Mike Miller 5.00 12.00
PJCQR Quentin Richardson 3.00 8.00

2002 Press Pass Pro Shoes

Randomly inserted in Hobby packs, this 10-card set features a full color player portrait photo and a square swatch of a game worn shoe. Each card is sequentially numbered to 40.

PRINT RUN 40 SER.#'d SETS
SHCM Chris Mihm 5.00 12.00
SHDM Darius Miles 8.00 20.00
SHMMA Mark Madsen 5.00 12.00
SHMP Morris Peterson 5.00 12.00

2002 Press Pass Rookie Chase

Randomly inserted in packs at a rate of one in 24, collectors have a chance to win a complete set of autographed cards from every player in the Press Pass autograph program by sending in eligible cards. There are eleven different players plus a "field card" in the set. Two players are named each November as Rookie of the Month, and the corresponding player card is the winner. If no winner is named, the Field card is the winner.

COMPLETE SET (12) 10.00 25.00
STATED ODDS 1:24
RC1 Carlos Boozer 2.50 6.00
RC2 Curtis Borchardt 1.25 3.00
RC3 Nikoloz Tskitishvili 1.25 3.00
RC4 Chris Jefferies 1.25 3.00
RC5 Drew Gooden 1.25 3.00
RC6 Jared Jeffries 1.25 3.00
RC7 Kareem Rush 1.25 3.00
RC8 DaJuan Wagner 1.25 3.00
RC9 Chris Wilcox 1.25 3.00
RC10 Jay Williams 1.50 4.00
RC11 Frank Williams 1.25 3.00
RC12 Field Card 1.25 3.00

2004 Press Pass

Released in late July, Press Pass boasts "the first look at the 2004-05 Rookies" with a 40 card base set. The cards are borderless with the Press Pass logo in the upper right corner, the player's previous team logo in the lower left and the player's name in the lower right. Both Hobby and Retail packaging with both containing 24 packs of four cards each, Hobby carried a SRP of $3.99 and a Retail SRP of $2.99.

COMPLETE SET (40) 10.00 25.00
COMP.SET w/o SP's (33) 6.00 15.00
34-40 PRINT RUN 250 SER.#'d SETS
1 Tony Allen .30 .75
2 Rafael Araujo .20 .50
3 Andris Biedrins .20 .50
4 Andre Brown .30 .75
5 Antonio Burks .25 .60
6 Lionel Chalmers .30 .75
7 Josh Childress .30 .75
8 Luol Deng .40 1.00
9 Chris Duhon .30 .75
10 Andre Emmett .20 .50
11 Desmon Farmer .30 .75
12 Matt Freije .20 .50
13 Ben Gordon .40 1.00
14 Devin Harris .30 .75
15 David Harrison .25 .60
16 Andre Iguodala .40 1.00
17 Luke Jackson .25 .60
18 Shaun Livingston .30 .75
19 Brandon Mouton .20 .50
20 Emeka Okafor .40 1.00
21 Rickey Paulding .30 .75
22 Tim Pickett .20 .50
23 Justin Reed .30 .75
24 Romain Sato .20 .50
25 Ha Seung-Jin .30 .75
26 J.R. Smith .30 .75
27 Kirk Snyder .30 .75
28 Blake Stepp .30 .75
29 Robert Swift .20 .50
30 Sebastian Telfair .30 .75
31 Anderson Varejao .25 .60
32 Damien Wilkins .30 .75
33 Emeka Okafor CL .30 .75
34 Emeka Okafor 1.00 2.50
35 Shaun Livingston .75 2.00
36 Ben Gordon 1.00 2.50
37 Devin Harris .75 2.00
38 Andre Iguodala 1.00 2.50
39 Sebastian Telfair .75 2.00
40 Andris Biedrins .50 1.25

2004 Press Pass Blue

*BLUE SINGLES: .75X TO 2X BASE HI
STATED ODDS ONE PER RETAIL PACK

2004 Press Pass Gold

*GOLD SINGLES: .75X TO 2X BASE HI
STATED ODDS ONE PER HOBBY PACK

2004 Press Pass Reflectors

*REFLECTORS: 1.5X TO 4X BASE HI
PRINT RUN 500 SER.#'d SETS

2004 Press Pass Reflectors Proofs

*REF.PROOF SINGLES: 2.5X TO 6X BASE HI
PRINT RUN 100 SER.#'d SETS

2004 Press Pass Autographs

Randomly inserted at four per box, this horizontally designed card places a player photo on the right side of the card, an autograph on the left, and a background that is printed in bronze. Several parallel versions of this set were also issued: Blue serially numbered to 50, Gold serially numbered to 100 and Silver serially numbered to 200. These sets also differ in that the card's background appears in the set name's color. Several players have red ink versions of their cards, most of these are unpriced due to scarcity. Print numbers were never released.

STATED ODDS FOUR PER BOX
SOME PLAYERS HAVE RED INK VERSIONS
RED NOT PRICED DUE TO SCARCITY
*BLUE AU SINGLES: 1X TO 2.5X BASE AU HI
BLUE PRINT RUN 50 SER.#'d SETS
*GOLD AU SINGLES: .6X TO 1.5X BASE AU HI
*SILVER SINGLES: .5X TO 1.25X BASE AU HI
SILVER PRINT RUN 200 SER.#'d SETS
1 Tony Allen 2.50 6.00
2 Rafael Araujo 1.50 4.00
3 Andris Biedrins 1.50 4.00
4 Brian Boddicker 1.50 4.00
5 Andre Brown 2.50 6.00
6 Antonio Burks 2.00 5.00
7 Lionel Chalmers 2.50 6.00
8 Josh Childress 2.50 6.00
9 Luol Deng 3.00 8.00
10 Chris Duhon 2.50 6.00
11 Andre Emmett 1.50 4.00
12 Desmon Farmer 2.50 6.00
13 Matt Freije 1.50 4.00
14 Ben Gordon 6.00 15.00
15 Devin Harris 2.50 6.00
16 David Harrison 2.00 5.00
17 Kris Humphries 2.50 6.00
18 Andre Iguodala 3.00 8.00
19 Luke Jackson 2.00 5.00
20 Shaun Livingston 2.50 6.00
21 James Moore 2.50 6.00
22 Brandon Mouton 1.50 4.00
23 Emeka Okafor 6.00 15.00
24 Rickey Paulding 2.50 6.00
25 Tim Pickett 1.50 4.00
26 Justin Reed 2.50 6.00
27 Romain Sato 1.50 4.00
28 Ha Seung-Jin 2.50 6.00
29 J.R. Smith 2.50 6.00
30 Kirk Snyder 2.50 6.00
31 Pape Sow 1.50 4.00
32 Blake Stepp 2.50 6.00
33 Robert Swift 1.50 4.00
34 Sebastian Telfair 2.50 6.00
35 Anderson Varejao 2.00 5.00
36 Jackson Vroman 1.50 4.00
37 Damien Wilkens 2.50 6.00
38 Carmelo Anthony 20.00 40.00

2004 Press Pass Big Numbers

Inserted one per pack, this 25-card set is horizontally designed with two die-cut basketballs along the left side. Two images of the player, the left in color, the right in color scale, and the player's jersey number appear on the card front.

COMPLETE SET (25) 5.00 12.00
STATED ODDS ONE PER PACK
1 Blake Stepp .50 1.25
2 Luke Jackson .40 1.00
3 Rafael Araujo .30 .75
4 Tim Pickett .30 .75
5 Tony Allen .50 1.25
6 Robert Swift .30 .75
7 Andris Biedrins .30 .75
8 Sebastian Telfair .50 1.25
9 Josh Childress .50 1.25
10 Shaun Livingston .50 1.25
11 Anderson Varejao .40 1.00
12 James Moore .50 1.25
13 Brandon Mouton .30 .75
14 Andre Emmett .30 .75
15 Ben Gordon .60 1.50
16 Brian Boddicker .30 .75
17 Emeka Okafor .60 1.50
18 Devin Harris .50 1.25
19 Desmon Farmer .50 1.25
20 David Harrison .40 1.00
21 Romain Sato .30 .75
22 J.R. Smith .50 1.25
23 Andre Iguodala .60 1.50
24 Chris Duhon .50 1.25
25 Emeka Okafor CL .60 1.50

2004 Press Pass Game-Used Jerseys

Inserted in packs at the rate of one in 72, this six card memorabilia set places a full-color player image on the left side of the card and a basketball court design on the right containing a rectangular swatch of jersey. Several parallel versions of this set were also released: Gold serially numbered to 200, HoloFoil serially numbered to 50 and Silver seriallly numbered to 350. Each of the different color versions feature the set name's color as the background.

STATED ODDS 1:72
*GOLD SINGLES: .6X TO 1.5X BASE JSY HI
GOLD PRINT RUN 200 SER.#'d SETS
*HOLO.SINGLES: .75X TO 2X BASE JSY HI
HOLO.PRINT RUN 50 SER.#'d SETS
*SILVER SINGLES: .5X TO 1.25X BASE JSY HI
SILVER PRINT RUN 350 SER.#'d SETS
AB Antonio Burks 2.50 6.00
BS Blake Stepp 3.00 8.00
JC Josh Childress 3.00 8.00
LJ Luke Jackson 2.50 6.00
RS Romain Sato 2.00 5.00
SL Shaun Livingston 3.00 8.00

2004 Press Pass Game-Used Shoes

Seeded in packs at the rate of one in 72, this four card set employs the same card design as the jerseys set but has a swatch of game-worn shoe. Several parallels for this set were also produced: Gold featuring gold background highlights is serially numbered to 100 and holofoil features holo background highlights and is sequentially numbered to 50.

STATED ODDS 1:72
*GOLD SINGLES: .75X TO 2X BASE SHOE HI
GOLD PRINT RUN 100 SER.#'d SETS
*HOLO.SINGLES: 1.25X TO 3X BASE SHOE HI
EO Emeka Okafor 5.00 12.00
JS J.R. Smith 4.00 10.00
RS Robert Swift 2.50 6.00
ST Sebastian Telfair 4.00 10.00

2004 Press Pass Hang Time

This nine card foil-board set was inserted one in 12 packs and places a full color player action shot against a shiny circle-dominated themed background. The player's name appears in gold foil.

COMPLETE SET (9) 5.00 12.00
STATED ODDS 1:12
1 Ben Gordon 1.00 2.50
2 Andre Iguodala 1.00 2.50
3 Emeka Okafor 1.00 2.50
4 Shaun Livingston .75 2.00
5 Devin Harris .75 2.00
6 Sebastian Telfair .75 2.00
7 Josh Childress .75 2.00
8 David Harrison .60 1.50
9 Luke Jackson .60 1.50

2004 Press Pass Lottery Club

Full-color player photos appear on this foil-board set that was inserted in packs at the rate of one in eight. The player's name appears in gold foil along the bottom of the card, and the background consists of 13 numbered basketballs to signify the first 13 lottery picks of the NBA draft.

COMPLETE SET (12) 5.00 12.00
STATED ODDS 1:8
1 Sebastian Telfair .60 1.50
2 Emeka Okafor .75 2.00
3 Andre Iguodala .75 2.00
4 Shaun Livingston .60 1.50
5 Ben Gordon .75 2.00
6 Devin Harris .60 1.50
7 Andris Biedrins .40 1.00
8 Josh Childress .60 1.50
9 J.R. Smith .60 1.50
10 Rafael Araujo .40 1.00
11 Luke Jackson .50 1.25
12 Robert Swift .40 1.00

2004 Press Pass Power Pick Autographs

Randomly seeded, this 10-card set places full-color player photos on a background that fades from jersey-matching background color to white. Cards are sequentially numbered to 250 and are autographed.

PRINT RUN 250 SER.#'d SETS
AB Andris Biedrins 3.00 8.00
AI Andre Iguodala 6.00 15.00
AV Anderson Varejao 4.00 10.00
BG Ben Gordon 8.00 20.00
CD Chris Duhon 5.00 12.00
DH Devin Harris 5.00 12.00
EO Emeka Okafor 6.00 15.00
LD Luol Deng 6.00 15.00
SL Shaun Livingston 5.00 12.00
ST Sebastian Telfair 5.00 12.00

2005 Press Pass

COMPLETE SET (45) 8.00 20.00
1 Deji Akindele .30 .75
2 Kelenna Azubuike .30 .75
3 Brandon Bass .25 .60
4 Andrew Bogut .50 1.25
5 Will Bynum .30 .75
6 Taylor Coppenrath .30 .75
7 Drake Diener .30 .75
8 Monta Ellis .60 1.50
9 Daniel Ewing .30 .75
10 Raymond Felton .30 .75
11 Channing Frye .30 .75
12 John Gilchrist .30 .75
13 Ryan Gomes .30 .75
14 Joey Graham .30 .75
15 Stephen Graham .30 .75
16 Danny Granger .40 1.00
17 Gerald Green .30 .75
18 Chuck Hayes .30 .75
19 Luther Head .30 .75
20 Julius Hodge .30 .75
21 Mindaugas Katelynas .30 .75
22 David Lee .30 .75
23 Sean May .30 .75
24 Rashad McCants .30 .75
25 Ellis Myles .30 .75
26 Chris Paul 1.25 3.00
27 Luke Schenscher .30 .75
28 Wayne Simien .30 .75
29 Chris Taft .30 .75
30 Chris Thomas .30 .75
31 Dijon Thompson .30 .75
32 Fran Vazquez .30 .75
33 Charlie Villanueva .30 .75
34 Hakim Warrick .30 .75
35 Martell Webster .30 .75
36 Deron Williams .40 1.00
37 Louis Williams .30 .75
38 Marvin Williams .30 .75
39 Antoine Wright .30 .75
40 Bracey Wright .30 .75
41 S.May/S.May .30 .75
42 E.Okafor/B.Gordon 1.00 2.50
43 Bruce Weber .75 2.00
44 Roy Williams 1.50 4.00
45 Andrew Bogut CL .40 1.00

2005 Press Pass Blue

*BLUE: .75X TO 2X BASE HI
BLUE STATED ODDS 1:1 RETAIL

2005 Press Pass Gold

*GOLD: .75X TO 2X BASE HI
STATED ODDS 1:1 HOBBY

2005 Press Pass Holo Gold

*HOLO GOLD: 3X TO 8X BASE HI
PRINT RUN 100 SER.#'d SETS

2005 Press Pass Holo Green

*HOLO GREEN: 1.5X TO 4X BASE HI
PRINT RUN 500 SER.#'d SETS

2005 Press Pass Autographs

COMBINED JSY/AU ODDS SIX PER BOX
SP INFO PRIVIDED BY PRESS PASS
*BLUE: .75X TO 2X BASE HI
BLUE PRINT RUN 50 SER.#'d SETS
*GOLD: .6X TO 1.5X BASE HI
GOLD PRINT RUN 100 SER.#'d SETS
*SILVER: .5X TO 1.25X BASE HI
SILVER PRINT RUN 200 SER.#'d SETS
AB Andrew Bogut 6.00 15.00
BB Brandon Bass 3.00 8.00
BW Bruce Weber SP 12.50 30.00
CA Carmelo Anthony/100 12.50 30.00
CF Channing Frye 4.00 10.00
CF2 Channing Frye Red 5.00 12.00
CH Chuck Hayes 4.00 10.00
CH2 Chuck Hayes Red 5.00 12.00
CP Chris Paul 20.00 50.00
CT Chris Thomas 4.00 10.00
CT2 Chris Thomas Red CT 5.00 12.00
CT3 Chris Taft 4.00 10.00
CV Charlie Villanueva 4.00 10.00
DA Deji Akindele 4.00 10.00
DA2 Deji Akindele Red 5.00 12.00
DD Drake Diener 4.00 10.00
DE Daniel Ewing 4.00 10.00
DG Danny Granger 5.00 12.00
DG2 Danny Granger Red 6.00 15.00
DL David Lee SP 4.00 10.00
DT Dijon Thompson 4.00 10.00
DW Deron Williams SP 8.00 20.00
EM Ellis Myles 4.00 10.00
FV3 Fran Vazquez FV 4.00 10.00
FV4 Fran Vazquez Red FV 5.00 12.00
GG Gerald Green SP 4.00 10.00
HW Hakim Warrick 4.00 10.00
HW2 Hakim Warrick Red 5.00 12.00
JG Joey Graham 4.00 10.00
JG2 Joey Graham Red 5.00 12.00
JH Julius Hodge 4.00 10.00
JH2 Julius Hodge Red 5.00 12.00
LH Luther Head 4.00 10.00
LH2 Luther Head Red 5.00 12.00
LO Lute Olsen SP 15.00 40.00
LS Luke Schenscher 4.00 10.00
LW Louis Williams 4.00 10.00
MK Mindaugas Katelynas 4.00 10.00
MK2 Mindaugas Katelynas Red 5.00 12.00
MW Marvin Williams 4.00 10.00
RF Raymond Felton 4.00 10.00
RF2 Raymond Felton Red 5.00 12.00
RG Ryan Gomes 4.00 10.00
RM Rashad McCants 4.00 10.00
RW Roy Williams SP 30.00 80.00
SG Stephen Graham 4.00 10.00
SM Sean May 4.00 10.00
TC Taylor Coppenrath 4.00 10.00
WB Will Bynum 4.00 10.00
WS Wayne Simien 4.00 10.00
WS2 Wayne Simien Red 5.00 12.00
MWE Martell Webster 4.00 10.00
MWE2 Martell Webster Red 5.00 12.00
CFAI C.Frye/A.Iguodala/200 10.00 25.00
SMSM S.May/S.May/400 6.00 15.00
AH Axel Hervelle 4.00 10.00

2005 Press Pass Jerseys

INT RUN 600 SER.#'d SETS
*BLUE: .6X TO 1.5X BASE HI
BLUE PRINT RUN 100 SER.#'d SETS
*GOLD: .5X TO 1.25X BASE HI
GOLD PRINT RUN 250 SER.#'d SETS
AB Andrew Bogut 5.00 12.00
CP Chris Paul 12.00 30.00
DE Daniel Ewing 3.00 8.00
DG Danny Granger 4.00 10.00
DL David Lee 3.00 8.00
DT Dijon Thompson 3.00 8.00
SM Sean May 3.00 8.00

2005 Press Pass Old School

COMPLETE SET (25) 8.00 20.00
ONE PER PACK
1 Andrew Bogut .75 2.00
2 Taylor Coppenrath .50 1.25
3 Daniel Ewing .50 1.25
4 Raymond Felton .50 1.25
5 Channing Frye .50 1.25
6 John Gilchrist .50 1.25
7 Ryan Gomes .50 1.25
8 Joey Graham .50 1.25
9 Danny Granger .60 1.50
10 Luther Head .50 1.25
11 Julius Hodge .50 1.25
12 David Lee .50 1.25
13 Sean May .50 1.25
14 Rashad McCants .50 1.25
15 Chris Paul 2.00 5.00
16 Luke Schenscher .50 1.25
17 Wayne Simien .50 1.25
18 Chris Taft .50 1.25
19 Chris Thomas .50 1.25
20 Dijon Thompson .50 1.25
21 Charlie Villanueva .50 1.25
22 Hakim Warrick .50 1.25
23 Deron Williams .60 1.50
24 Marvin Williams .50 1.25
25 Chris Paul CL 2.00 5.00

2005 Press Pass Power Pick Autographs

PRINT RUN 250 SER.#'d SETS
AB Andrew Bogut 8.00 20.00
CF Channing Frye 5.00 12.00
CP Chris Paul 20.00 50.00
CV Charlie Villanueva 5.00 12.00
DG Danny Granger 6.00 15.00
DW Deron Williams 6.00 15.00
HW Hakim Warrick 5.00 12.00
JH Julius Hodge 5.00 12.00
LH Luther Head 5.00 12.00
MW Marvin Williams 5.00 12.00
RF Raymond Felton 5.00 12.00
RM Rashad McCants 5.00 12.00

2006 Press Pass

Released in July 2006, Press Pass features a 45-card base set picturing 2006-07 rookie players on cards 1-33, 2006-07 rookies in a Power Pick subset on cards 34-38, 2005-06 rookie players on cards 39-42, NCAA Coaches Dean Smith and John Wooden on cards 43 and 44 and Adam Morrison on a checklist card at number 45. Press Pass is packaged in 30-pack boxes of four cards each and carried an initial suggested retail price of $3.99 per pack.

COMPLETE SET (45) 8.00 20.00
1 Maurice Ager .20 .50
2 LaMarcus Aldridge .75 2.00
3 Hilton Armstrong .20 .50
4 James Augustine .20 .50
5 Andrea Bargnani .50 1.25
6 Ronnie Brewer .30 .75
7 Dee Brown .30 .75
8 Shannon Brown .25 .60
9 Nick Caner-Medley .30 .75
10 Rodney Carney .30 .75
11 Mardy Collins .20 .50
12 Paul Davis .30 .75
13 Taquan Dean .30 .75
14 Terence Dials .30 .75
15 Randy Foye .40 1.00
16 Mike Gansey .30 .75
17 Rudy Gay .50 1.25
18 Taj Gray .20 .50
19 Kyle Lowry .40 1.00
20 Adam Morrison .30 .75
21 David Noel .30 .75
22 Patrick O'Bryant .30 .75
23 Kevin Pittsnogle .20 .50
24 Allan Ray .20 .50
25 J.J. Redick .40 1.00
26 Rajon Rondo 1.00 2.50
27 Brandon Roy .40 1.00
28 Curtis Stinson .20 .50
29 Tyrus Thomas .25 .60
30 P.J. Tucker .30 .75
31 Marcus Williams .30 .75
32 Shawne Williams .20 .50
33 Shelden Williams .30 .75
34 LaMarcus Aldridge PP .75 2.00
35 Adam Morrison PP .30 .75
36 J.J. Redick PP .40 1.00
37 Brandon Roy PP .40 1.00
38 Tyrus Thomas PP .25 .60
39 Chris Paul .40 1.00
40 Charlie Villanueva .20 .50
41 Andrew Bogut .25 .60
42 Raymond Felton .30 .75
43 Dean Smith .60 1.50
44 John Wooden .60 1.50
45 Adam Morrison CL .30 .75

2006 Press Pass Gold

*GOLD: .5X TO 1.25X BASE HI
ONE PER PACK

2006 Press Pass Autographs

APPROXIMATELY FIVE PER BOX
1 Maurice Ager 2.50 6.00
2 LaMarcus Aldridge 12.00 30.00
3 L.Aldridge Red/92* 8.00 20.00
5 Hilton Armstrong 2.50 6.00
8 James Augustine 2.50 6.00
10 Andrea Bargnani 6.00 15.00
11 A.Bargnani Red/116* 10.00 25.00
12 Ronnie Brewer 4.00 10.00
13 R.Brewer Go Hogs Red/24* 10.00 25.00
14 Dee Brown 4.00 10.00
15 Denham Brown 4.00 10.00
20 Shannon Brown 3.00 8.00
23 Nick Caner-Medley 4.00 10.00
24 N.Caner-Medley Red/74* 4.00 10.00
25 Rodney Carney 4.00 10.00
26 Mardy Collins 2.50 6.00
45 Paul Davis 4.00 10.00
46 Terence Dials 4.00 10.00
47 Terence Dials Red/86* 4.00 10.00
48 Randy Foye 5.00 12.00
49 R.Foye Foye Wonder/12* 15.00 40.00
50 Mike Gansey 4.00 10.00
60 Rudy Gay 6.00 15.00
61 Taj Gray 2.50 6.00
63 Vincent Grier 2.50 6.00
64 Ryan Hollins 3.00 8.00
65 Damir Markota 2.50 6.00
66 D.Markota Svetko Red/23* 5.00 12.00
67 Adam Morrison 4.00 10.00
70 David Noel 4.00 10.00
71 Olexsiy Pecherov 2.50 6.00
72 O.Pecherov Pech Red/14* 5.00 12.00
73 Kevin Pittsnogle 2.50 6.00
75 Chris Quinn 2.50 6.00
76 Chris Quinn Go Irish/23* 5.00 12.00
77 Allan Ray 2.50 6.00
78 Allan Ray Reezy/25* 5.00 12.00
80 Rajon Rondo Blue/Red 12.00 30.00
81 Brandon Roy 5.00 12.00
83 Cedric Simmons 4.00 10.00
84 Dean Smith 75.00 150.00
85 Curtis Stinson 2.50 6.00
87 Tyrus Thomas 3.00 8.00
89 P.J. Tucker 4.00 10.00
90 Shawne Williams 2.50 6.00
91 Shawne Williams Red/143* 5.00 12.00
92 Shelden Williams 4.00 10.00
93 John Wooden 40.00 80.00
94 J.Wooden/D.Smith 125.00 250.00

2006 Press Pass Autographs Blue

*BLUE: .6X TO 1.5X BASE AU HI
PRINT RUN 50 SER.#'d SETS
38 J.J. Redick 8.00 20.00
45 C.Stinson Blue Collar/20* 4.00 10.00

2006 Press Pass Autographs Gold

*GOLD: .5X TO 1.25X BASE AU HI
PRINT RUN 100 SER.#'d SETS
3 LaMarcus Aldridge Blue/40* 15.00 40.00
24 T.Dials Go Bucks Red/25* 6.00 15.00
26 Randy Foye Red/43* 6.00 15.00
40 A.Morrison Go Zags/25* 20.00 40.00
46 J.J. Redick 6.00 15.00

2006 Press Pass Autographs Silver

*SILVER: .5X TO 1.25X BASE AU HI
PRINT RUN 200 SER.#'d SETS
3 L.Aldridge Red/77* 15.00 40.00
28 P.Davis Go State/20* 8.00 20.00
47 A.Morrison Go Zags/35* 12.50 30.00
53 J.J. Redick 6.00 15.00
60 T.Thomas Blue/39* 10.00 25.00
63 Shawne Williams Blue/39* 8.00 20.00

2006 Press Pass Jerseys

APPROXIMATELY ONE PER BOX
*SILVER: .5X TO 1.25X BASE JSY HI
SILVER RANDOM INSERTS IN PACKS
*GOLD: .5X TO 1.25X BASE JSY HI
GOLD PRINT RUN 299 SER.#'d SETS
*HOLOFOIL: .6X TO 1.5X BASE JSY HI
HOLO PRINT RUN 99 SER.#'d SETS
JCBR Brandon Roy 2.50 6.00
JCKL Kyle Lowry 2.50 6.00
JCLA LaMarcus Aldridge 5.00 12.00
JCRB Ronnie Brewer 2.00 5.00
JCRC Rodney Carney 2.00 5.00
JCRG Rudy Gay 3.00 8.00
JCSB Shannon Brown 1.50 4.00

2006 Press Pass Old School

APPROXIMATELY ONE PER PACK
1 Ronnie Brewer .40 1.00
2 Patrick O'Bryant .40 1.00
3 Hilton Armstrong .25 .60
4 Rudy Gay .60 1.50
5 Marcus Williams .40 1.00
6 J.J. Redick .50 1.25
7 Shelden Williams .40 1.00
8 Adam Morrison .40 1.00
9 Dee Brown .40 1.00
10 Rajon Rondo 1.25 3.00
11 Taquan Dean .40 1.00
12 Tyrus Thomas .30 .75
13 Rodney Carney .40 1.00
14 Shawne Williams .25 .60
15 Shannon Brown .30 .75
16 Paul Davis .40 1.00
17 David Noel .40 1.00
18 Taj Gray .25 .60
19 Mardy Collins .25 .60
20 LaMarcus Aldridge 1.00 2.50
21 Randy Foye .50 1.25
22 Kyle Lowry .50 1.25
23 Brandon Roy .50 1.25
24 Kevin Pittsnogle .25 .60
25 J.J. Redick .50 1.25

2006 Press Pass Power Pick Autographs

PRINT RUN 250 SER.#'d SETS
1 LaMarcus Aldridge 12.00 30.00
2 Andrea Bargnani 8.00 20.00
3 Ronnie Brewer 5.00 12.00
4 Rodney Carney 5.00 12.00
5 Randy Foye 6.00 15.00
7 Rudy Gay 8.00 20.00
9 Rudy Gay The Kid/21* 20.00 50.00
10 Adam Morrison 5.00 12.00
12 Brandon Roy 6.00 15.00
13 Tyrus Thomas 4.00 10.00
14 T.Thomas T-Time Red/15* 10.00 25.00
15 Shelden Williams 5.00 12.00
16 S.Williams Red/96* 5.00 12.00
17 S.Williams Landlord/25* 6.00 15.00

2008 Press Pass

MPLETE SET (65) 10.00 25.00
UNPRICED SOLO PRINT RUN ONE SET
1 D.J. Augustin .25 .60
2 Jerryd Bayless .25 .60
3 Michael Beasley .30 .75
4 Mario Chalmers .40 1.00
5 Joey Dorsey .30 .75
6 Chris Douglas-Roberts .30 .75
7 Patrick Ewing Jr. .30 .75
8 Shan Foster .30 .75
9 Danilo Gallinari .50 1.25
10 J.R. Giddens .30 .75
11 Eric Gordon .60 1.50
12 Malik Hairston .30 .75
13 DeVon Hardin .30 .75
14 Roy Hibbert .30 .75
15 J.J. Hickson .30 .75
16 Darnell Jackson .30 .75
17 Davon Jefferson .30 .75
18 DeAndre Jordan .60 1.50
19 Kosta Koufos .30 .75
20 Courtney Lee .40 1.00
21 Chris Lofton .30 .75
22 Brook Lopez .50 1.25
23 Robin Lopez .30 .75
24 Kevin Love 1.25 3.00
25 O.J. Mayo .30 .75
26 Candace Parker 1.25 3.00
27 Trent Plaisted .20 .50
28 Anthony Randolph .30 .75
29 Derrick Rose 1.25 3.00
30 Brandon Rush .25 .60
31 Marreese Speights .30 .75
32 Bryce Taylor .30 .75
33 Sonny Weems .20 .50
34 Russell Westbrook 2.50 6.00

35 D.J. White .30 .75
36 Michael Beasley CL .15 .40
37 Kevin Love CL .60 1.50
38 O.J. Mayo CL .15 .40
39 D.J. Augustin CL .12 .30
40 Jerryd Bayless CL .12 .30
41 Eric Gordon CL .30 .75
42 D.J. White CL .15 .40
43 Courtney Lee CL .20 .50
44 Shan Foster CL .15 .40
45 Derrick Rose AA 1.25 3.00
46 Brandon Rush AA .25 .60
47 Michael Beasley AA .30 .75
48 Kevin Love AA 1.25 3.00
49 D.J. Augustin AA .25 .60
50 Candace Parker AA 1.25 3.00
51 Chris Douglas-Roberts AA .30 .75
52 Eric Gordon AA .60 1.50
53 Roy Hibbert AA .30 .75
54 Brook Lopez AA .50 1.25
55 B.Lopez/R.Lopez 1.00 2.50
56 K.Love/R.Westbrook 1.50 4.00
57 D.Rose/C.Douglas-Roberts 1.25 3.00
58 E.Gordon/D.White 1.00 2.50
59 O.Mayo/D.Jefferson 1.00 2.50
60 B.Rush/M.Chalmers 1.00 2.50
61 Derrick Rose PP 1.25 3.00
62 O.J. Mayo PP .30 .75
63 Michael Beasley PP .30 .75
64 Kevin Love PP 1.25 3.00
65 Russell Westbrook PP 2.50 6.00

2008 Press Pass Reflectors
*REF: .5X TO 1.25X BASE HI
REFLECTOR STATED ODDS 1:1

2008 Press Pass Reflectors Blue
*BLUE: .6X TO 1.5X BASE HI
RANDOM INSERTS IN RETAIL PACKS

2008 Press Pass Reflectors Holofoil
*HOLO: .75X TO 2X BASE HI
STATED PRINT RUN 250 SER.#'d SETS

2008 Press Pass Reflectors Proofs
*PROOF: 1.25X TO 3X BASE HI
HOLO PRINT RUN 100 SER.#'d SETS

2008 Press Pass Class of 2008
COMPLETE SET (10) 5.00 12.00
STATED ODDS 1:5
CL1 Derrick Rose 2.00 5.00
CL2 O.J. Mayo .50 1.25
CL3 Anthony Randolph .50 1.25
CL4 Brandon Rush .40 1.00
CL5 Russell Westbrook 4.00 10.00
CL6 Eric Gordon 1.00 2.50
CL7 Michael Beasley .50 1.25
CL8 Jerryd Bayless .40 1.00
CL9 Kevin Love 2.00 5.00
CL10 D.J. Augustin .40 1.00

2008 Press Pass Class of 2008 Autographs
STATED PRINT RUN 100 TO 199 SER.#'d SETS
CLAR Anthony Randolph/155 5.00 12.00
CLBL Brook Lopez/155 8.00 20.00
CLBR Brandon Rush/199 4.00 10.00
CLDA D.J. Augustin/155 4.00 10.00
CLDJ DeAndre Jordan/100 6.00 15.00
CLDR Derrick Rose/199 15.00 40.00
CLEG Eric Gordon/199 10.00 25.00
CLJB Jerryd Bayless/107 4.00 10.00
CLKK Kosta Koufos/199 5.00 12.00
CLKL Kevin Love/199 15.00 40.00
CLMB Michael Beasley/199 5.00 12.00
CLOM O.J. Mayo/100 5.00 12.00
CLRW Russell Westbrook/155 60.00 150.00
CLCDR Chris Douglas-Roberts/199 5.00 12.00

2008 Press Pass Game Day Gear Jerseys
ATED PRINT RUN 400 SER.#'d SETS
*GOLD: .5X TO 1.25X BASE JSY
GOLD PRINT RUN 99 SER.#'d SETS
*HOLO: .6X TO 1.5X BASE JSY
HOLO PRINT RUN 50 SER.#'d SETS
GDGAR Anthony Randolph 2.00 5.00
GDGBL Brook Lopez 3.00 8.00
GDGBR Brandon Rush 1.50 4.00
GDGDA D.J. Augustin 1.50 4.00
GDGDR Derrick Rose 4.00 10.00
GDGJD Joey Dorsey 2.00 5.00
GDGRH Roy Hibbert 2.00 5.00
GDGRL Robin Lopez 2.00 5.00
GDGRW Russell Westbrook 6.00 15.00

2008 Press Pass Insider Insight
COMPLETE SET (10) 4.00 10.00
STATED ODDS 1:4
*GOLD: .5X TO 1.25X BASE
RANDOM INSERTS IN PACKS
*FOIL: .6X TO 1.5X BASE
FOIL PRINT RUN 199 SER.#'d SETS
*FOIL GOLD: 1X TO 2.5X BASE
FOIL GOLD PRINT RUN 99 SER.#'d SETS
II1 Michael Beasley .40 1.00
II2 Derrick Rose 1.50 4.00
II3 Jerryd Bayless .30 .75
II4 Eric Gordon .75 2.00
II5 Brook Lopez .60 1.50
II6 Russell Westbrook 3.00 8.00
II7 O.J. Mayo .40 1.00
II8 Kevin Love 1.50 4.00
II9 D.J. Augustin .30 .75
II10 Brandon Rush .30 .75

2008 Press Pass Power Pick Autographs
STATED PRINT RUN 100 TO 250 SER.#'d SETS
RED INK: SAME VALUE
PPAR Anthony Randolph/199 6.00 15.00
PPAR1 Anthony Randolph Red 6.00 15.00
PPBL Brook Lopez/199 10.00 25.00
PPBL1 Brook Lopez Red 10.00 25.00
PPBR Brandon Rush/250 5.00 12.00
PPBR1 Brandon Rush Red 5.00 12.00
PPDA D.J. Augustin/199 5.00 12.00
PPDJ DeAndre Jordan/250 12.00 30.00
PPDJ1 DeAndre Jordan Red 12.00 30.00
PPDR Derrick Rose/250 25.00 60.00
PPEG Eric Gordon/250 12.00 30.00
PPJB Jerryd Bayless/250 5.00 12.00
PPKK Kosta Koufos/250 6.00 15.00
PPKK1 Kosta Koufos Red 6.00 15.00
PPKL Kevin Love/250 10.00 25.00
PPKL1 Kevin Love Red 25.00 60.00
PPMB Michael Beasley/250 6.00 15.00
PPOM O.J. Mayo/100 6.00 15.00
PPRW Russell Westbrook/199 60.00 150.00
PPCDR Chris Douglas-Roberts/250 6.00 15.00

2008 Press Pass Primetime Players
COMPLETE SET (10) 5.00 12.00
STATED ODDS 1:5
PT1 Derrick Rose 2.00 5.00
PT2 Brook Lopez .75 2.00
PT3 D.J. Augustin .40 1.00
PT4 Brandon Rush .40 1.00
PT5 Russell Westbrook 4.00 10.00
PT6 Eric Gordon 1.00 2.50
PT7 Michael Beasley .50 1.25
PT8 Jerryd Bayless .40 1.00
PT9 Kevin Love 2.00 5.00
PT10 O.J. Mayo .50 1.25

2008 Press Pass Signings Bronze
FIVE AUTOGRAPHS PER BOX
PPSAR Anthony Randolph 3.00 8.00
PPSBL Brook Lopez 5.00 12.00
PPSBT Brandon Rush 2.50 6.00
PPSBT1 Brandon Rush Red 4.00 10.00
PPSBT2 Bryce Taylor 3.00 8.00
PPSCL Chris Lofton 3.00 8.00
PPSCL Courtney Lee 4.00 10.00
PPSCL1 Courtney Lee Red 6.00 15.00
PPSCP Candace Parker 30.00 60.00
PPSDA D.J. Augustin 2.50 6.00
PPSDG Danilo Gallinari 5.00 12.00
PPSDH DeVon Hardin 3.00 8.00
PPSDJ DeAndre Jordan 6.00 15.00
PPSDR Derrick Rose 20.00 50.00
PPSDW D.J. White 3.00 8.00
PPSEG Eric Gordon 6.00 15.00
PPSEG1 Eric Gordon Red 10.00 25.00
PPSJB Jerryd Bayless 2.50 6.00
PPSJD Joey Dorsey 3.00 8.00
PPSJG J.R. Giddens 3.00 8.00
PPSJG1 J.R. Giddens Red 4.00 10.00
PPSJH J.J. Hickson 3.00 8.00
PPSJM James Mays 3.00 8.00
PPSKK Kosta Koufos 3.00 8.00
PPSKL Kevin Love 6.00 15.00
PPSMB Michael Beasley 3.00 8.00
PPSMC Mario Chalmers 4.00 10.00
PPSMH Malik Hairston 3.00 8.00
PPSML Maarty Leunen 3.00 8.00
PPSMS Marreese Speights 3.00 8.00
PPSMS1 Marreese Speights Red 4.00 10.00
PPSOM O.J. Mayo 3.00 8.00
PPSPE Patrick Ewing Jr. 3.00 8.00
PPSPE1 Patrick Ewing Jr. Red 4.00 10.00
PPSRH Roy Hibbert 3.00 8.00
PPSRL Robin Lopez 3.00 8.00
PPSRW Russell Westbrook 75.00 200.00
PPSSF Shan Foster 3.00 8.00
PPSSW Sonny Weems 2.00 5.00
PPSTP Trent Plaisted 2.00 5.00
PPSCDR Chris Douglas-Roberts 3.00 8.00
PPSDJ2 Darnell Jackson 3.00 8.00
PPSDJ4 Davon Jefferson 3.00 8.00

2008 Press Pass Signings Blue
*BLUE: .75X TO 2X BASE AU
PRINT RUN 50 SER.#'d SETS
PPSRW Russell Westbrook 100.00 250.00
PPSRW1 Russell Westbrook Red 100.00 250.00

2008 Press Pass Signings Gold
*GOLD: .6X TO 1.5X BASE AU
STATED PRINT RUN 75 TO 99 SER.#'d SETS
PPSCP Candace Parker/99 30.00 80.00
PPSRW Russell Westbrook/75 75.00 200.00

2008 Press Pass Signings Silver
*SILVER: .5X TO 1.25X BASE AU
STATED PRINT RUN 67 TO 199 SER.#'d SETS
PPSCP Candace Parker/199 25.00 60.00
PPSDR Derrick Rose/127 60.00 150.00
PPSRW Russell Westbrook/100 75.00 200.00
PPSRW1 Russell Westbrook Red 75.00 200.00

2008 Press Pass Teammates Autographs
STATED PRINT RUN 25 SER.#'d SETS
TABLRL B.Lopez/R.Lopez 20.00 40.00
TAKLRW K.Love/R.Westbrook 40.00 100.00
TADRCDR Rose/Dgls-Roberts 30.00 60.00

1998 Press Pass Authentics
The Press Pass Authentics set was released during the 1998-99 season and featured many of the NBA's top prospects and young stars.
COMPLETE SET (45) 5.00 10.00
1 Michael Olowokandi .20 .50
2 Mike Bibby .40 1.00
3 Raef LaFrentz .20 .50
4 Vince Carter .75 2.00
5 Robert Traylor .15 .40
6 Jason Williams .40 1.00
7 Larry Hughes .30 .75
8 Paul Pierce .60 1.50
9 Bonzi Wells .15 .40
10 Michael Doleac .15 .40
11 Keon Clark .15 .40
12 Michael Dickerson .15 .40
13 Matt Harpring .15 .40
14 Bryce Drew .15 .40
15 Pat Garrity .15 .40
16 Roshown McLeod .15 .40
17 Brian Skinner .15 .40
18 Tyronn Lue .15 .40
19 Al Harrington .25 .60
20 Sam Jacobson .15 .40
21 Nazr Mohammed .15 .40
22 Ruben Patterson .15 .40
23 Shammond Williams .15 .40
24 Casey Shaw .10 .25
25 DeMarco Johnson .15 .40
26 Miles Simon .15 .40
27 Jahidi White .15 .40
28 Sean Marks .15 .40
29 Toby Bailey .15 .40
30 Andrae Patterson .15 .40
31 Tyson Wheeler .15 .40
32 Cory Carr .10 .25
33 J.R. Henderson .15 .40
34 Torraye Braggs .15 .40
35 Tim Duncan .30 .75
36 Keith Van Horn .15 .40
37 Ron Mercer .12 .30
38 Stephon Marbury .20 .50
39 Ray Allen .20 .50
40 Glen Rice .15 .40
41 Brevin Knight .10 .25
42 Antoine Walker .15 .40
43 Kerry Kittles .10 .25
44 Derek Anderson .10 .25
45 Michael Olowokandi .20 .50

1998 Press Pass Authentics Hang Time
*STARS: .6X TO 1.5X BASE CARD HI
STATED ODDS 1:1

1998 Press Pass Authentics Autographs
Randomly inserted in packs at one in eight, this 30-card set features autographs from some of the top stars and rookies of the NBA.
STATED ODDS 1:8
1 Tim Duncan 40.00 80.00
2 Stephon Marbury 5.00 12.00
3 Antoine Walker 5.00 12.00
4 Ray Allen 10.00 25.00
5 Kerry Kittles 1.50 4.00
6 Mike Bibby 6.00 15.00
7 Raef LaFrentz 2.00 5.00
8 Vince Carter 10.00 25.00
9 Robert Traylor 1.50 4.00
10 Jason Williams 6.00 15.00
11 Larry Hughes 4.00 10.00
12 Paul Pierce 10.00 25.00
13 Michael Doleac 1.50 4.00
14 Matt Harpring 1.50 4.00
15 Bryce Drew 1.50 4.00
16 Pat Garrity 1.50 4.00
17 Roshown McLeod 1.50 4.00
18 Brian Skinner 1.50 4.00
19 Tyronn Lue 1.50 4.00
20 Al Harrington 2.50 6.00
21 Sam Jacobson 1.50 4.00
22 Nazr Mohammed 1.50 4.00
23 Ruben Patterson 1.50 4.00
24 Casey Shaw 1.00 2.50
25 DeMarco Johnson 1.50 4.00
26 Sean Marks 1.50 4.00
27 Tyson Wheeler 1.50 4.00
28 Cory Carr 1.00 2.50
29 J.R. Henderson 1.50 4.00
30 Torraye Braggs 1.50 4.00

1998 Press Pass Authentics Full Court Press
Randomly inserted in packs at one in six, this 12-card set features current and future NBA stars who are prominent at both ends of the court. Card backs carry a "FP" prefix.
COMPLETE SET (12) 4.00 10.00
STATED ODDS 1:6
FP1 Paul Pierce 1.50 4.00
FP2 Pat Garrity .40 1.00
FP3 Nazr Mohammed .40 1.00
FP4 Vince Carter 2.00 5.00
FP5 Tim Duncan .75 2.00
FP6 Stephon Marbury .50 1.25
FP7 Ron Mercer .30 .75
FP8 Antoine Walker .40 1.00
FP9 Keith Van Horn .40 1.00
FP10 Michael Olowokandi .50 1.25
FP11 Mike Bibby 1.00 2.50
FP12 Raef LaFrentz .50 1.25

1998 Press Pass Authentics Lottery Club
Randomly inserted at one in 12, this 12-card set features top picks from past NBA Drafts. Card backs carry a "LC" prefix.
COMPLETE SET (12) 8.00 20.00
STATED ODDS 1:12
LC1 Michael Olowokandi .75 2.00
LC2 Tim Duncan 1.25 3.00
LC3 Mike Bibby 1.50 4.00
LC4 Keith Van Horn .60 1.50
LC5 Raef LaFrentz .75 2.00
LC6 Shareef Abdur-Rahim .60 1.50
LC7 Vince Carter 3.00 8.00
LC8 Stephon Marbury .75 2.00
LC9 Ray Allen .75 2.00
LC10 Robert Traylor .60 1.50
LC11 Antoine Walker .60 1.50
LC12 Jason Williams 1.50 4.00

1998 Press Pass Authentics Signed Memorabilia
Randomly inserted in packs at one in 29, this 23-card set features autographed memorabilia from the top rookies of the 1998 NBA Draft, as well as veterans from the NBA. Several items have been too scarce to price, they are listed below for cataloguing purposes.
STATED ODDS 1:29
1B M.Bibby/Mini-BK 15.00 40.00
3 V.Carter/8X10 20.00 40.00
3A V.Carter/IO BK 40.00 100.00
3B V.Carter/Mini-BK 25.00 60.00
4 M.Dickerson/8X10 2.00 5.00
4A M.Dickerson/Plaque 10.00 25.00
5 M.Doleac/8X10 2.00 5.00
6 B.Drew/8X10 2.00 5.00
7 P.Garrity/Plaque 6.00 15.00
8 M.Harpring/8X10 2.00 5.00
9 L.Hughes/8X10 4.00 10.00
10 K.Kittles/8X10 2.00 5.00
11 B.Knight/8X10 2.00 5.00
12 R.LaFrentz/8X10 4.00 10.00
13 T.Lue/8X10 2.00 5.00
14 K.Malone/Plaque 25.00 60.00
15 S.Marbury/8X10 8.00 20.00
16 N.Moham/8X10 2.00 5.00
17 M.Olowo/8X10 2.50 6.00
18 P.Pierce/Plaque 10.00 25.00
19 D.Robinson/Plaque 20.00 50.00
20 B.Skinner/8X10 2.00 5.00
21 R.Traylor/8X10 2.00 5.00
21A R.Traylor/Plaque 6.00 15.00
22 K.Van Horn/Plaque 6.00 15.00
23 A.Walker/8X10 6.00 15.00

1998 Press Pass Authentics Sterling Autographs
Randomly inserted in packs at one in 720, this 21-card set features autographs of some of the top stars and rookies from the NBA.
STATED ODDS 1:720
1 Tim Duncan 60.00 150.00
2 Stephon Marbury 10.00 25.00
3 Mike Bibby 12.00 30.00
4 Raef LaFrentz 4.00 10.00
5 Vince Carter 30.00 80.00
6 Robert Traylor 3.00 8.00
7 Jason Williams 12.00 30.00
8 Larry Hughes 8.00 20.00
9 Paul Pierce 20.00 50.00
10 Michael Doleac 3.00 8.00
11 Matt Harpring 3.00 8.00
12 Bryce Drew 3.00 8.00
13 Pat Garrity 3.00 8.00
14 Roshown Mcleod 3.00 8.00
15 Casey Shaw 2.00 5.00
16 DeMarco Johnson 3.00 8.00
17 Tyronn Lue 3.00 8.00
18 Cory Carr 2.00 5.00
19 J.R. Henderson 3.00 8.00
20 Torraye Braggs 3.00 8.00
21 Al Harrington 5.00 12.00

1999 Press Pass Authentics
Released in four-card packs, this 45-card set features draft picks from the 1999 season.
COMPLETE SET (45) 4.00 10.00
1 Elton Brand .30 .75
2 Steve Francis .30 .75
3 Baron Davis .30 .75
4 Lamar Odom .30 .75
5 Jonathan Bender .12 .30
6 Wally Szczerbiak .25 .60
7 Richard Hamilton .30 .75
8 Andre Miller .30 .75
9 Jason Terry .30 .75
10 Trajan Langdon .12 .30
11 William Avery .12 .30
12 Ron Artest .30 .75
13 Cal Bowdler .12 .30
14 James Posey .12 .30
15 Quincy Lewis .12 .30
16 Jeff Foster .12 .30
17 Kenny Thomas .12 .30
18 Devean George .12 .30
19 Tim James .12 .30
20 Vonteego Cummings .12 .30
21 Jumaine Jones .12 .30
22 John Celestand .12 .30
23 Rico Hill .12 .30
24 Michael Ruffin .12 .30
25 Chris Herren .12 .30
26 Evan Eschmeyer .12 .30
27 Calvin Booth .12 .30
28 Obinna Ekezie .12 .30
29 A.J. Bramlett .12 .30
30 Louis Bullock .12 .30
31 Lee Nailon .12 .30
32 Tyrone Washington .12 .30
33 Venson Hamilton .12 .30
34 Roberto Bergersen .12 .30
35 Rodney Buford .12 .30
36 Melvin Levett .12 .30
37 Kris Clack .12 .30
38 Vince Carter .25 .60
39 Jason Williams .15 .40
40 Paul Pierce .20 .50
41 Mike Bibby .12 .30
42 Michael Olowokandi .07 .20
43 Marcus Camby .10 .25
44 Raef LaFrentz .07 .20
45 Vince Carter CL .25 .60

1999 Press Pass Authentics Hang Time
*HANG TIME: .75X TO 2X VALUE
ONE PER PACK

1999 Press Pass Authentics Autographs
Randomly inserted in packs at one in eight, this 33-card set features autographs of the top draft picks. The backs feature a congratulatory message.
STATED ODDS 1:8 HOB, 1:36 RET
*GOLD: .6X TO 1.5X BASIC CARDS
GOLD RANDOM INSERTS IN PACKS
GOLD PRINT RUN 100 SERIAL #'d SETS
1 Elton Brand 4.00 10.00
2 Steve Francis 4.00 10.00
3 Baron Davis 4.00 10.00
4 Lamar Odom 4.00 10.00
5 Wally Szczerbiak 3.00 8.00
6 Richard Hamilton 4.00 10.00
7 Andre Miller 4.00 10.00
8 Jason Terry 4.00 10.00
9 Trajan Langdon 1.50 4.00
10 Ron Artest 4.00 10.00
11 Cal Bowdler 1.50 4.00
12 James Posey 1.50 4.00
13 Quincy Lewis 1.50 4.00
14 Jeff Foster 1.50 4.00
15 Devean George 1.50 4.00
16 Tim James 1.50 4.00
17 Vonteego Cummings 1.50 4.00
18 Jumaine Jones 1.50 4.00
19 John Celestand 1.50 4.00
20 Michael Ruffin 1.50 4.00
21 Chris Herren 2.50 6.00
22 Evan Eschmeyer 1.50 4.00
23 Calvin Booth 1.50 4.00
24 Obinna Ekezie 1.50 4.00
25 A.J. Bramlett 1.50 4.00
26 Louis Bullock 1.50 4.00
27 Lee Nailon 1.50 4.00
28 Tyrone Washington 1.50 4.00
29 Venson Hamilton 1.50 4.00
30 Roberto Bergersen 1.50 4.00
31 Melvin Levett 1.50 4.00
32 Kris Clack 1.50 4.00
33 William Avery 1.50 4.00

1999 Press Pass Authentics Full Court Press
Randomly inserted in packs at one in 12, this 12-card set features future stars who excel on both ends of the court. Card backs carry a "FC" prefix.
COMPLETE SET (12) 3.00 8.00
STATED ODDS 1:12
FC1 Elton Brand .60 1.50
FC2 Steve Francis .60 1.50
FC3 Baron Davis .60 1.50
FC4 Lamar Odom .60 1.50
FC5 Jonathan Bender .25 .60
FC6 Wally Szczerbiak .50 1.25
FC7 Richard Hamilton .60 1.50
FC8 Andre Miller .60 1.50
FC9 Jason Terry .60 1.50
FC10 Trajan Langdon .25 .60
FC11 William Avery .25 .60
FC12 James Posey .25 .60

1999 Press Pass Authentics Lottery Club
Randomly inserted in packs at one in 23, this six-card set six of the hottest draft picks against Nitrokrome. Card backs carry a "LC" prefix.
COMPLETE SET (6) 2.00 5.00
STATED ODDS 1:23
LC1 Elton Brand .60 1.50
LC2 Steve Francis .60 1.50
LC3 Baron Davis .60 1.50
LC4 Lamar Odom .60 1.50
LC5 Jonathan Bender .25 .60
LC6 Wally Szczerbiak .50 1.25

1999 Press Pass Authentics Signed Memorabilia
Inserted one per box, this 46-card set features autographed memorabilia from the top draft picks and some current stars of the NBA. This includes jerseys, basketballs, 8X10 photos and jersey plaques. The items are not numbered, but numbered below for checklisting purposes.
STATED ODDS 1:24
1 W.Avery/8X10 4.00 10.00
2 M.Bibby/Plaque 15.00 40.00
3 C.Booth/8X10 4.00 10.00
4 C.Bowdler/8X10 4.00 10.00
5 E.Brand/8X10 6.00 15.00
5A E.Brand/IO BK 20.00 50.00
5B E.Brand/Jersey 60.00 150.00
5C E.Brand/Mini-BK 15.00 40.00
5D E.Brand/Plaque 12.00 30.00
6 L.Bullock/8X10 4.00 10.00
7 V.Carter/8X10 30.00 80.00
7A V.Carter/IO BK 50.00 120.00
8 J.Celestand/8X10 4.00 10.00
9 V.Cummings/8X10 4.00 10.00
10 O.Ekezie/8X10 4.00 10.00
11 E.Esch/8X10 4.00 10.00
11A E.Esch/Plaque 6.00 15.00
12 S.Francis/8X10 8.00 20.00
12A S.Francis/IO BK 25.00 60.00
12B S.Francis/Jersey 75.00 150.00
12C S.Francis/Mini-BK 20.00 50.00
12D S.Francis/Plaque 15.00 40.00
13 R.Hamilton/8X10 6.00 15.00
13A R.Hamilton/IO BK 20.00 50.00
14 C.Herren/8X10 4.00 10.00
15 L.Hughes/Plaque 10.00 25.00
16 T.James/8X10 4.00 10.00
17 J.Jones/8X10 4.00 10.00
18 R.LaFrentz/8X10 4.00 10.00
18A R.LaFrentz/Plaque 6.00 15.00
19 Q.Lewis/8X10 4.00 10.00
20 A.Miller/8X10 6.00 15.00
20A A.Miller/Plaque 10.00 25.00
21 L.Nailon/8X10 4.00 10.00
22 L.Odom/IO BK 25.00 60.00
22A L.Odom/Mini-BK 20.00 50.00
22B L.Odom/Plaque 15.00 40.00
23 M.Olowo/IO BK 8.00 20.00
24 J.Posey/8X10 4.00 10.00
24A J.Posey/Plaque 6.00 15.00
25 M.Ruffin/8X10 4.00 10.00
26 W.Szczer/8X10 6.00 15.00
26A W.Szczer/IO BK 15.00 40.00
26B W.Szczer/Mini-BK 12.50 30.00
26C W.Szczer/Plaque 10.00 25.00
27 J.Terry/8X10 6.00 15.00

1999 Press Pass Authentics Team 2000
Randomly inserted in packs at one in five, this 12-card set highlights top draft picks who look to lead their new teams into the new millennium. Card backs carry a "T" prefix.
COMPLETE SET (12) 2.50 6.00
STATED ODDS 1:5
T1 Elton Brand .50 1.25
T2 Steve Francis .50 1.25
T3 Baron Davis .50 1.25
T4 Lamar Odom .50 1.25
T5 Wally Szczerbiak .40 1.00
T6 Richard Hamilton .50 1.25
T7 Andre Miller .50 1.25
T8 Jason Terry .50 1.25
T9 Trajan Langdon .20 .50
T10 Ron Artest .50 1.25
T11 Tim James .20 .50
T12 William Avery .20 .50

1997 Press Pass Double Threat
The 1997 Press Pass Double Threat set was issued in one series totalling 45 cards. The fronts feature borderless color action player photos with foil highlights. The backs carry biographical information and career statistics. Cards 34-45 display a photo of both a top veteran and rookie on the same card. A blue-foil parallel version of this base set was also produced as well as a silver-foil hobby only parallel version.
COMPLETE SET (45) 3.00 8.00
1 Tim Duncan 1.00 2.50
2 Keith Van Horn .30 .75
3 Chauncey Billups .50 1.25
4 Antonio Daniels .15 .40
5 Tony Battie .15 .40
6 Ron Mercer .20 .50
7 Tim Thomas .30 .75
8 Adonal Foyle .15 .40
9 Tracy McGrady .75 2.00
10 Danny Fortson .15 .40
11 Olivier Saint-Jean .15 .40
12 Austin Croshere .12 .30
13 Derek Anderson .15 .40
14 Maurice Taylor .15 .40
15 Kelvin Cato .15 .40
16 Brevin Knight .15 .40
17 Johnny Taylor .15 .40
18 Chris Anstey .15 .40
19 Scot Pollard .15 .40
20 Paul Grant .15 .40
21 Anthony Parker .15 .40
22 Ed Gray .15 .40
23 Bobby Jackson .20 .50
24 John Thomas .15 .40
25 Charles Smith .15 .40
26 Jacque Vaughn .15 .40
27 Keith Booth .15 .40
28 Serge Zwikker .15 .40
29 Charles O'Bannon .15 .40
30 Bubba Wells .15 .40
31 Kebu Stewart .15 .40
32 James Collins .15 .40
33 Eddie Elisma .15 .40
34 T.Duncan/D.Robinson .60 1.50
35 C.Billups/A.Walker .30 .75
36 T.Battie/A.McDyess .10 .25
37 R.Mercer/A.Walker .12 .30
38 A.Daniels/S.A-Rahim .10 .25
39 D.Fortson/A.McDyess .10 .25
40 J.Vaughn/K.Malone .12 .30
41 A.Foyle/J.Smith .10 .25
42 P.Grant/S.Marbury .12 .30
43 K.Booth/S.Pippen .15 .40
44 C.Smith/A.Mourning .12 .30
45 T.Duncan/D.Robinson CL .60 1.50
NNO Tim Duncan 1.00 2.50
David Robinson PROMO

1997 Press Pass Double Threat Blue
*STARS: .6X TO 1.5X BASE CARD HI
ONE PER RETAIL PACK

1997 Press Pass Double Threat Retroactive
COMPLETE SET (36) 6.00 15.00
*STARS: .5X TO 1.25X BASE CARD HI
STATED ODDS 1:1

1997 Press Pass Double Threat Silver
*SILVER: .6X TO 1.5X BASE CARD HI
ONE PER HOBBY PACK

1997 Press Pass Double Threat Autographs
Randomly inserted in hobby packs at the rate of one in 18 and in retail packs at the rate of one in 36, this 30-card set features autographed cards of top players.
STATED ODDS 1:18 HOB, 1:36 RET
1A Tim Duncan 75.00 200.00
2A Keith Van Horn 3.00 8.00
3A Chauncey Billups 5.00 12.00
4A Antonio Daniels 1.50 4.00
5A Tony Battie 1.50 4.00
7A Tim Thomas 3.00 8.00
8A Adonal Foyle 1.50 4.00
9A Tracy McGrady 20.00 50.00
10A Danny Fortson 1.50 4.00
11A Olivier Saint-Jean 1.50 4.00
12A Austin Croshere 1.25 3.00
13A Derek Anderson 1.50 4.00
14A Maurice Taylor 1.50 4.00
15A Kelvin Cato 1.50 4.00
16A Brevin Knight 1.50 4.00
17A Johnny Taylor 1.50 4.00
18A Chris Anstey 1.50 4.00
19A Scot Pollard 1.50 4.00
20A Paul Grant 1.50 4.00
21A Anthony Parker 1.50 4.00
23A Bobby Jackson 2.00 5.00
24A John Thomas 1.50 4.00
25A Charles Smith 1.50 4.00
26A Jacque Vaughn 1.50 4.00
28A Serge Zwikker 1.50 4.00
29A Charles O'Bannon 1.50 4.00
30A Bubba Wells 1.50 4.00
31A Kebu Stewart 1.50 4.00
32A James Collins 1.50 4.00
33A Eddie Elisma 1.50 4.00

1997 Press Pass Double Threat Double Autographs
Randomly inserted in packs, this limited five-card set features autographed color action photos of two top players on the same card. The numbers after the players' names indicate how many of each card were produced and signed.
STATED PRINT RUNS 100 TO 750 SETS
1 T.Duncan/D.Robinson/100 250.00 500.00
2 J.Vaughn/K.Malone/625 30.00 80.00
3 T.Battie/A.McDyess/750 8.00 20.00
4 R.Mercer/A.Walker/250 15.00 40.00
5 C.Billups/A.Walker/500 12.00 30.00

1997 Press Pass Double Threat Double Thread Jerseys
Randomly inserted in packs at the rate of one in 720, this five-card set features color player photos. A different player is pictured on each side with an authentic piece of a game-used jersey of each player embedded in the card beside his picture. Only 325 of each card were produced.
STATED ODDS 1:720
STATED PRINT RUN 325 SETS
DD1 T.Duncan/D.Robinson 60.00 150.00
DD2 C.Billups/A.Walker 15.00 40.00
DD3 R.Mercer/A.Walker 15.00 40.00
DD4 T.Battie/A.McDyess 12.50 30.00
DD5 J.Vaughn/K.Malone 15.00 40.00

1997 Press Pass Double Threat Light It Up
Randomly inserted in packs at the rate of one in nine, this 25-card set features color action photos of top players printed on die-cut cards.
COMPLETE SET (25) 10.00 25.00
STATED ODDS 1:9
LU1 Tim Duncan 3.00 8.00
LU2 Keith Van Horn 1.00 2.50
LU3 Chauncey Billups 1.50 4.00
LU4 Antonio Daniels .50 1.25
LU5 Tony Battie .50 1.25
LU6 Ron Mercer .60 1.50
LU7 Tim Thomas 1.00 2.50
LU8 Adonal Foyle .50 1.25
LU9 Tracy McGrady 2.50 6.00
LU10 Danny Fortson .50 1.25
LU11 Olivier Saint-Jean .50 1.25
LU12 Austin Croshere .40 1.00
LU13 Derek Anderson .50 1.25
LU14 Maurice Taylor .50 1.25
LU15 Kelvin Cato .50 1.25
LU16 Brevin Knight .50 1.25
LU17 Alonzo Mourning .60 1.50
LU18 Joe Smith .40 1.00
LU19 Shareef Abdur-Rahim .50 1.25
LU20 Scottie Pippen .75 2.00
LU21 David Robinson .75 2.00
LU22 Karl Malone .60 1.50
LU23 Stephon Marbury .60 1.50
LU24 Antonio McDyess .40 1.00
LU25 Antoine Walker CL .50 1.25

1997 Press Pass Double Threat Lotto
This eight-card "progressive insert" set features color action photos of top lotto picks through the years printed on holofoil cards. The cards were inserted as follows: #1A 1:720, #1B 1:360, #2A 1:180, #2B 1:90, #3A & 3B 1:45, and #4A & 4B 1:36.
COMPLETE SET (8) 40.00 100.00
STATED ODDS 1A 1:720, 1B 1:360, 2A 1:180
STATED ODDS 2B 1:90, 3 1:45, 4 1:36
LC1A Tim Duncan 20.00 50.00
LC1B David Robinson 15.00 40.00
LC2A Keith Van Horn 6.00 15.00
LC2B Antonio McDyess 6.00 15.00
LC3A Antonio Daniels 1.50 4.00
LC3B Stephon Marbury 2.50 6.00
LC4A Ron Mercer 1.50 4.00
LC4B Antoine Walker 2.50 6.00

1997 Press Pass Double Threat Nitrokrome
Randomly inserted in packs at the rate of one in 18, this nine-card set features color action player photos of top NBA players and rookies printed on all-foil cards
COMPLETE SET (9) 6.00 15.00
STATED ODDS 1:18
DT1 T.Duncan/D.Robinson 4.00 10.00
DT2 J.Vaughn/K.Malone .75 2.00
DT3 T.Battie/A.McDyess .60 1.50
DT4 R.Mercer/A.Walker .75 2.00
DT5 P.Grant/S.Marbury .75 2.00
DT6 C.Billups/A.Walker 2.00 5.00
DT7 A.Daniels/S.A-Rahim .60 1.50
DT8 A.Mourning/C.Smith .75 2.00
DT9 J.Smith/A.Foyle .60 1.50

1997 Press Pass Double Threat Showdown
Randomly inserted in hobby only packs at the rate of one in 36, this six card set features color action photos of a rookie on one side and a veteran on the other printed on canvas card stock.
COMPLETE SET (6) 12.50 30.00
STATED ODDS 1:36 HOBBY
S1 A.Mourning/T.Duncan 10.00 25.00
S2 K.Malone/D.Fortson 2.00 5.00
S3 J.Smith/T.Battie 1.50 4.00
S4 A.McDyess/K.Van Horn 3.00 8.00
S5 S.Pippen/R.Mercer 2.50 6.00
S6 D.Robinson/A.Foyle 2.50 6.00

1998 Press Pass Double Threat
The 1998 Press Pass Double Threat set was issued in one series totalling 45 cards. Special bonus cards were also issued of the top three draft picks. Each card has a special foil treatment and was inserted at one in 180 packs. Those cards are numbered F1 through F3 and are listed at the end of the base set.
COMPLETE SET (45) 5.00 10.00
F1-F3 STATED ODDS 1:180
1 Michael Olowokandi .30 .75
2 Mike Bibby .60 1.50
3 Raef LaFrentz .30 .75
4 Vince Carter 1.25 3.00
5 Robert Traylor .25 .60
6 Jason Williams .60 1.50
7 Larry Hughes .50 1.25
8 Paul Pierce 1.00 2.50
9 Bonzi Wells .25 .60
10 Michael Doleac .25 .60
11 Keon Clark .25 .60
12 Michael Dickerson .25 .60
13 Matt Harpring .25 .60
14 Bryce Drew .25 .60
15 Pat Garrity .25 .60
16 Roshown McLeod .25 .60
17 Brian Skinner .25 .60
18 Tyronn Lue .25 .60
19 Al Harrington .40 1.00
20 Sam Jacobson .25 .60
21 Nazr Mohammed .25 .60
22 Ruben Patterson .25 .60
23 Shammond Williams .25 .60
24 Casey Shaw .15 .40
25 DeMarco Johnson .25 .60
26 Miles Simon .25 .60
27 Jahidi White .25 .60
28 Sean Marks .25 .60
29 Toby Bailey .25 .60
30 Andrae Patterson .25 .60
31 Tyson Wheeler .25 .60
32 Cory Carr .15 .40
33 J.R. Henderson .25 .60
34 Torraye Braggs .25 .60
35 Tim Duncan .50 1.25
36 Keith Van Horn .25 .60
37 Ron Mercer .20 .50
38 Stephon Marbury .30 .75
39 Ray Allen .30 .75
40 Glen Rice .25 .60
41 Tim Thomas .25 .60
42 Antoine Walker .25 .60
43 Kerry Kittles .15 .40
44 Shareef Abdur-Rahim .25 .60
45 Michael Olowokandi CL .30 .75
F1 Michael Olowokandi FOIL 4.00 10.00
F2 Mike Bibby FOIL 8.00 20.00
F3 Raef LaFrentz FOIL 4.00 10.00

1998 Press Pass Double Threat Alley-Oop
*STARS: .6X TO 1.5X BASE CARD HI
STATED ODDS 1:1 HOBBY

1998 Press Pass Double Threat Torquers
*STARS: .6X TO 1.5X BASE CARD HI
STATED ODDS 1:1 RETAIL

1998 Press Pass Double Threat Double Thread Jerseys
Randomly inserted in packs at one in 720, this three-card set featues dual jerseys of current NBA players and draft picks. Card number DT1 was never issued. Cards DT2 and DT4 were only available via trade. Card backs carry a "DT" prefix. Please note that there were only 425 serial numbered sets produced.
STATED ODDS 1:720
DT2 M.Olowokandi/T.Duncan 12.00 30.00
DT3 R.Traylor/K.Van Horn 10.00 25.00
DT4 V.Carter/G.Rice 30.00 80.00

1998 Press Pass Double Threat Dreammates
Inserted in packs at one in 18, this nine-card set features some pairings of "dream" teammates. Each card features a NBA star and a draft pick. Card backs carry a "DM" prefix.
COMPLETE SET (9) 10.00 25.00
STATED ODDS 1:18
DM1 M.Bibby/T.Duncan 2.00 5.00
DM2 M.Olowokandi/S.Marbury 1.00 2.50
DM3 L.Hughes/T.Thomas 1.50 4.00
DM4 V.Carter/G.Rice 4.00 10.00
DM5 R.Traylor/R.Allen 1.00 2.50
DM6 P.Pierce/R.Mercer 3.00 8.00
DM7 R.LaFrentz/K.Van Horn 1.00 2.50
DM8 M.Dickerson/A.Walker .75 2.00
DM9 J.Williams/S.Abdur-Rahim 2.00 5.00
NNO M.Bibby/T.Duncan .75 2.00

1998 Press Pass Double Threat Jackpot
Randomly inserted in packs at multi-levels, this eight-card set featues the top picks of the draft. Card J1A was inserted at one in 720, card J1B was inserted at one in 360, card J2A was inserted at one in 180, and card J2B was inserted at one in 90. Both cards J3A and J3B were inserted at one in 45, while cards J4A and J4B were inserted at one in 36.
COMPLETE SET (8) 15.00 40.00
STATED ODDS 1A 1:720, 1B 1:360, 2A 1:180
STATED ODDS 2B 1:90, 3A-B 1:45, 4A-B 1:36
J1A Michael Olowokandi 3.00 8.00
J1B Mike Bibby 6.00 15.00
J2A Raef LaFrentz 3.00 8.00
J2B Vince Carter 10.00 25.00
J3A Robert Traylor 1.25 3.00
J3B Jason Williams 2.50 6.00
J4A Larry Hughes 2.00 5.00
J4B Paul Pierce 2.50 6.00

1998 Press Pass Double Threat Player's Club Autographs
Randomly inserted in hobby packs only at one in 360, this 13-card set features autographs of the top draft picks. The cards are serially numbered out of 125. Card backs carry a "PC" prefix.
STATED ODDS 1:360 HOBBY
STATED PRINT RUN 125 SERIAL #'d SETS
PC1 Michael Olowokandi 6.00 15.00
PC2 Mike Bibby 12.00 30.00
PC3 Raef LaFrentz 6.00 15.00
PC4 Vince Carter 60.00 150.00
PC5 Robert Traylor 5.00 12.00
PC6 Jason Williams 12.00 30.00
PC7 Larry Hughes 10.00 25.00
PC8 Paul Pierce 20.00 50.00
PC9 Bonzi Wells 5.00 12.00
PC10 Michael Doleac 5.00 12.00
PC11 Keon Clark 5.00 12.00
PC12 Michael Dickerson 5.00 12.00
PC13 Matt Harpring 5.00 12.00

1998 Press Pass Double Threat Retros
Inserted one per pack, this 36-card set is a semi-parallel of the base set. The cards feature a black and white design. Card backs carry a "R" prefix.
COMPLETE SET (36) 8.00 20.00
STATED ODDS 1:1
R1 Michael Olowokandi .30 .75
R2 Mike Bibby .60 1.50
R3 Raef LaFrentz .30 .75
R4 Vince Carter 1.25 3.00
R5 Robert Traylor .25 .60
R6 Jason Williams .60 1.50
R7 Larry Hughes .50 1.25
R8 Paul Pierce 1.00 2.50
R9 Bonzi Wells .25 .60
R10 Michael Doleac .25 .60
R11 Keon Clark .25 .60
R12 Michael Dickerson .25 .60
R13 Matt Harpring .25 .60

R14 Bryce Drew .25 .60
R15 Cory Carr .15 .40
R16 Andrae Patterson .25 .60
R17 Pat Garrity .25 .60
R18 Roshown McLeod .25 .60
R19 Brian Skinner .25 .60
R20 Tyronn Lue .25 .60
R21 Sam Jacobson .25 .60
R22 J.R. Henderson .25 .60
R23 Nazr Mohammed .25 .60
R24 Ruben Patterson .25 .60
R25 Shammond Williams .25 .60
R26 Toby Bailey .25 .60
R27 DeMarco Johnson .25 .60
R28 Miles Simon .25 .60
R29 Jahidi White .25 .60
R30 Tim Duncan .50 1.25
R31 Keith Van Horn .25 .60
R32 Ron Mercer .20 .50
R33 Stephon Marbury .30 .75
R34 Ray Allen .30 .75
R35 Glen Rice .25 .60
R36 Mike Bibby CL .60 1.50

1998 Press Pass Double Threat Rookie Jerseys

Randomly inserted in packs at one in 720, this four-card set featues jersey cards of draft picks. Both the Pierce and Dickerson were available via trade cards. Card backs carry a "JC" prefix.
STATED ODDS 1:720
JC1 Raef LaFrentz 6.00 15.00
JC2 Pat Garrity 5.00 12.00
JC3 Paul Pierce 12.50 30.00

1998 Press Pass Double Threat Rookie Script Autographs

Randomly inserted in hobby packs at one in 18 and retail packs at one in 36, this 34-card set featues autographs of the 1998 NBA Draft class. Michael Olowokandi, Jason Williams, Keon Clark, Bonzi Wells, Michael Dickerson, Roshown McLeod, Paul Pierce, Miles Simon, Toby Baily and Robert Patterson where only made available via redemption cards. The cards are not numbered and listed below alphabetically.
STATED ODDS 1:18 HOB, 1:36 RET
SOME ONLY AVAILABLE VIA REDEMPTION
NNO CARDS LISTED BELOW ALPHABETICALLY
1 Toby Bailey 1.50 4.00
2 Mike Bibby 6.00 15.00
3 Torraye Braggs 1.50 4.00
4 Cory Carr 1.00 2.50
5 Vince Carter 25.00 60.00
6 Keon Clark 1.50 4.00
7 Michael Dickerson 1.50 4.00
8 Michael Doleac 1.50 4.00
9 Bryce Drew 1.50 4.00
10 Pat Garrity 1.50 4.00
11 Matt Harpring 1.50 4.00
12 Al Harrington 2.50 6.00
13 J.R. Henderson 1.50 4.00
14 Larry Hughes 4.00 10.00
15 Sam Jacobson 1.50 4.00
16 DeMarco Johnson 1.50 4.00
17 Raef LaFrentz 2.00 5.00
18 Tyronn Lue 1.50 4.00
19 Sean Marks 1.50 4.00
20 Roshown McLeod 1.50 4.00
21 Nazr Mohammed 1.50 4.00
22 Michael Olowokandi 2.00 5.00
23 Andrae Patterson 1.50 4.00
24 Ruben Patterson 1.50 4.00
25 Paul Pierce 12.00 30.00
26 Casey Shaw 1.00 2.50
27 Miles Simon 1.50 4.00
28 Brian Skinner 1.50 4.00
29 Robert Traylor 1.50 4.00
30 Bonzi Wells 1.50 4.00
31 Tyson Wheeler 1.50 4.00
32 Jahidi White 1.50 4.00
33 Jason Williams 15.00 40.00
34 Shammond Williams 1.50 4.00

1998 Press Pass Double Threat Two-On-One

Randomly inserted in packs at one in 12, this 12-card set features top combos of NBA stars and draft picks. Each player has an individual card and a combo card. Card backs carry a "TO" prefix.
COMPLETE SET (12) 8.00 20.00
STATED ODDS 1:12
TO1 Raef LaFrentz .75 2.00
TO2 R.LaFrentz/K.Van Horn .75 2.00
TO3 Keith Van Horn .60 1.50
TO4 Michael Olowokandi .75 2.00
TO5 M.Olowokandi/T.Duncan 1.25 3.00
TO6 Tim Duncan 1.25 3.00
TO7 Mike Bibby 1.50 4.00
TO8 M.Bibby/S.Marbury 1.50 4.00
TO9 Stephon Marbury .75 2.00
TO10 Vince Carter 3.00 8.00
TO11 V.Carter/A.Walker 3.00 8.00
TO12 Antoine Walker .60 1.50

1998 Press Pass Double Threat Veteran Approved Autographs

Randomly inserted in packs at one in 360, this seven-card set features veteran autographs. The following players were only available via trade: Ray Allen, Kerry Kittles, Ron Mercer and Glen Rice. The set is unnumbered and checklisted below in alphabetical order.
STATED ODDS 1:360
1 Ray Allen 8.00 20.00
2 Tim Duncan 125.00 300.00
3 Kerry Kittles 3.00 8.00
4 Stephon Marbury 5.00 12.00
5 Antoine Walker 6.00 15.00

2009 Press Pass Fusion

MPLETE SET (90) 15.00 40.00
14 Nate Archibald .15 .40
15 DJ Augustin .15 .40
16 Larry Bird .75 2.00
17 Darren Collison .30 .75
18 Stephen Curry 8.00 20.00
19 Joey Dorsey .30 .75
20 Joe Dumars .15 .40
21 Wayne Ellington .30 .75
22 Jonny Flynn .30 .75
23 Gerald Henderson .30 .75
24 Bobby Hurley .15 .40
25 Brook Lopez .15 .40
26 Robin Lopez .15 .40
27 Jerry Lucas .15 .40
28 Kevin McHale .15 .40
29 Anthony Randolph .15 .40
30 Derrick Rose .30 .75
31 Brandon Rush .15 .40
32 Russell Westbrook .20 .50
33 John Wooden .30 .75
34 James Worthy .15 .40
35 Willis Reed .30 .75
36 Ty Lawson .30 .75
WWJW John Wooden AU/100 50.00 120.00

2009 Press Pass Fusion Bronze

*BRONZE: 1X TO 2.5X BASE
STATED PRINT RUN 150 SER. #'d SETS
18 Stephen Curry 20.00 50.00

2009 Press Pass Fusion Gold

*GOLD: 2X TO 5X BASE
STATED PRINT RUN 50 SER. #'d SETS
18 Stephen Curry 40.00 100.00

2009 Press Pass Fusion Green

*GREEN: 3X TO 8X BASE
STATED PRINT RUN 25 SER. #'d SETS
18 Stephen Curry 60.00 150.00

2009 Press Pass Fusion Silver

*SILVER: 1.25X TO 3X BASE
STATED PRINT RUN 99 SER. #'d SETS
18 Stephen Curry 25.00 60.00

2009 Press Pass Fusion Autographs Gold

STATED PRINT RUN 10-199
EXCHANGE DEADLINE 12/1/10
SSBH Bobby Hurley/190 7.50 15.00
SSDC Darren Collison/198 7.50 15.00
SSGH Gerald Henderson/199 7.50 15.00
SSJD Joe Dumars/42 10.00 25.00
SSJF Jonny Flynn/150 10.00 25.00
SSJL Jerry Lucas/75 7.50 15.00
SSKM Kevin McHale/50 15.00 30.00
SSLB Larry Bird/26 30.00 80.00
SSNA Nate Archibald/50 7.50 15.00
SSSC Stephen Curry/75 300.00 500.00
SSWE Wayne Ellington/199 7.50 15.00
SSWR Willis Reed/75 10.00 20.00

2009 Press Pass Fusion Autographs Green

STATED PRINT RUN 5-100
EXCHANGE DEADLINE 12/1/2010
SSBH Bobby Hurley/91 10.00 20.00
SSGH Gerald Henderson/99 10.00 20.00
SSJF Jonny Flynn/96 15.00 30.00
SSJL Jerry Lucas/50 15.00 30.00
SSNA Nate Archibald/25 10.00 20.00
SSSC Stephen Curry/50 300.00 500.00
SSTL Ty Lawson/99 8.00 20.00
SSWE Wayne Ellington/99 10.00 20.00
SSWR Willis Reed/50 15.00 30.00

2009 Press Pass Fusion Autographs Silver

RANDOM INSERT IN PACKS
EXCHANGE DEADLINE 12/1/2010
SSBH Bobby Hurley 7.50 15.00
SSDC Darren Collison 7.50 15.00
SSGH Gerald Henderson 7.50 15.00
SSJF Jonny Flynn 10.00 25.00
SSNA Nate Archibald 7.50 15.00
SSSC Stephen Curry 250.00 400.00
SSTL Ty Lawson 7.50 15.00
SSWE Wayne Ellington 7.50 15.00
SSWR Willis Reed 10.00 20.00

2009 Press Pass Fusion Classic Champions

MPLETE SET (10) 6.00 15.00
STATED ODDS 1:10
CCH3 Larry Bird 2.50 6.00
CCH8 Joe Dumars .60 1.50
CCH9 Wayne Ellington 1.00 2.50

2009 Press Pass Fusion Collegiate Connections

COMPLETE SET (10) 6.00 15.00
STATED ODDS 1:10
CCN1 K.McHale/P.Molitor .60 1.50
CCN3 J.Worthy/T.Lawson 1.00 2.50
CCN5 B.Hurley/G.Henderson 1.00 2.50
CCN6 W.Reed/D.Williams .60 1.50
CCN7 D.Maynard/N.Archibald .60 1.50
CCN10 J.Wooden/K.Kiraly 1.00 2.50

2009 Press Pass Fusion Cross Training

MPLETE SET (10) 6.00 15.00
STATED ODDS 1:10
CT4 D.Gable/K.McHale 1.00 2.50

2009 Press Pass Fusion Renowned Rivals

COMPLETE SET (10) 6.00 15.00
STATED ODDS 1:10
RR2 K.McHale/J.Worthy .60 1.50
RR4 S.Curry/T.Lawson 6.00 15.00
RR6 J.Lucas/W.Reed .60 1.50
RR8 W.Ellington/G.Henderson 1.00 2.50
RR9 J.Dumars/L.Bird 2.50 6.00

2009 Press Pass Fusion Revered Relics Gold

STATED PRINT RUN 5-50
*HOLOFOIL/25: .5X TO 1.2X BASIC RELIC
RRAR Anthony Randolph 6.00 15.00
RRBR Brandon Rush 6.00 15.00
RRDA DJ Augustin 6.00 15.00
RRRW Russell Westbrook 6.00 15.00
RRBLRL B.Lopez/R.Lopez 6.00 15.00
RRDRJD D.Rose/J.Dorsey 6.00 15.00

2009 Press Pass Fusion Revered Relics Silver

STATED PRINT RUN 15-299
RRAR Anthony Randolph/85 4.00 10.00
RRBR Brandon Rush/99 4.00 10.00
RRDA DJ Augustin/99 4.00 10.00
RRRW Russell Westbrook/99 4.00 10.00
RRBLRL B.Lopez/R.Lopez/99 4.00 10.00
RRDRJD D.Rose/J.Dorsey/299 4.00 10.00

2009 Press Pass Fusion Timeless Talent

COMPLETE SET (10) 6.00 15.00
STATED ODDS 1:10
TT2 Joe Dumars .60 1.50
TT4 Jonny Flynn 1.00 2.50
TT5 Stephen Curry 4.00 10.00

2009 Press Pass Fusion Timeless Talent Autographs Gold

STATED PRINT RUN 15-99
TTJD Joe Dumars/48 10.00 20.00
TTJF Jonny Flynn/99 15.00 30.00
TTSC Stephen Curry 250.00 400.00

2009 Press Pass Fusion Timeless Talent Autographs Green

STATED PRINT RUN 10-50
TTJF Jonny Flynn/50 12.00 30.00
TTSC Stephen Curry/50 300.00 500.00

2009 Press Pass Fusion Timeless Talent Autographs Silver

STATED PRINT RUN 26-193
TTJD Joe Dumars/74 10.00 20.00
TTJF Jonny Flynn/193 10.00 20.00
TTSC Stephen Curry/100 250.00 400.00

2006 Press Pass National VIP Promos

COMPLETE SET (25) 6.00 15.00
1 Ronnie Brewer .40 1.00
2 Patrick O'Bryant .40 1.00
3 Hilton Armstrong .25 .60
4 Rudy Gay .60 1.50
5 Marcus Williams .40 1.00
6 J.J. Redick .50 1.25
7 Shelden Williams .40 1.00
8 Adam Morrison .40 1.00
9 Dee Brown .40 1.00
10 Rajon Rondo 1.25 3.00
11 Taquan Dean .40 1.00
12 Tyrus Thomas .30 .75
13 Rodney Carney .40 1.00
14 Shawne Williams .25 .60
15 Shannon Brown .30 .75
16 Paul Davis .40 1.00
17 David Noel .40 1.00
18 Taj Gray .25 .60
19 Mardy Collins .25 .60
20 LaMarcus Aldridge 1.00 2.50
21 Randy Foye .50 1.25
22 Kyle Lowry .50 1.25
23 Brandon Roy .50 1.25
24 Kevin Pittsnogle .25 .60
25 J.J. Redick CL .50 1.25

1999 Press Pass SE

Released in four-card packs, this 45-card set features draft picks from the 1999 season. Each hobby carried one autograph per pack. The cards are also known as Signature Edition.
COMPLETE SET (45) 4.00 10.00
1 Elton Brand .30 .75
2 Steve Francis .30 .75
3 Baron Davis .30 .75
4 Lamar Odom .30 .75
5 Jonathan Bender .12 .30
6 Wally Szczerbiak .25 .60
7 Richard Hamilton .30 .75
8 Andre Miller .30 .75
9 Jason Terry .30 .75
10 Trajan Langdon .12 .30
11 William Avery .12 .30
12 Ron Artest .30 .75
13 Cal Bowdler .12 .30
14 James Posey .12 .30
15 Quincy Lewis .12 .30
16 Jeff Foster .12 .30
17 Kenny Thomas .12 .30
18 Devean George .12 .30
19 Tim James .12 .30
20 Vonteego Cummings .12 .30
21 Jumaine Jones .12 .30
22 John Celestand .12 .30
23 Rico Hill .12 .30
24 Michael Ruffin .12 .30
25 Chris Herren .12 .30
26 Evan Eschmeyer .12 .30
27 Calvin Booth .12 .30
28 Obinna Ekezie .12 .30
29 A.J. Bramlett .12 .30
30 Louis Bullock .12 .30
31 Lee Nailon .12 .30
32 Tyrone Washington .12 .30
33 Venson Hamilton .12 .30
34 Roberto Bergersen .12 .30
35 Rodney Buford .12 .30
36 Melvin Levett .12 .30
37 Kris Clack .12 .30
38 Galen Young .12 .30
39 Lari Ketner .12 .30
40 Eddie Lucas .12 .30
41 Todd MacCulloch .12 .30
42 Francisco Elson .12 .30
43 Vince Carter .25 .60
44 Jason Williams .15 .40
45 Checklist Card .12 .30
Elton Brand
Wally Szczerbiak
Steve Francis
Lamar Odom
1 Elton Brand PROMO 2.00 5.00

1999 Press Pass SE Alley Oop

*ALLEY-OOP: .75X TO 2X VALUE
ONE PER HOBBY PACK

1999 Press Pass SE Torquers

*TORQUERS: .75X TO 2X VALUE
ONE PER RETAIL PACK

1999 Press Pass SE Autographs

Randomly inserted in hobby packs at one per pack, this 38-card set features autographs from the top picks of the 1999 NBA Draft along with several veterans mixed in. The cards are unnumbered and listed below alphabetically.
ONE PER HOBBY PACK
*BLUE: .5X TO 1.25X BASIC CARDS
BLUE PRINT RUN 500 SERIAL #'d SETS
*SILVER: .6X TO 1.5X BASIC CARDS
SILVER PRINT RUN 100 SERIAL #'d SETS
1 Ron Artest 4.00 10.00
2 William Avery 1.50 4.00
3 Roberto Bergersen 1.50 4.00
4 Mike Bibby 2.50 6.00
5 Calvin Booth 1.50 4.00
6 Cal Bowdler 1.50 4.00
7 A.J. Bramlett 1.50 4.00
8 Elton Brand 4.00 10.00
9 Louis Bullock 1.50 4.00
10 Marcus Camby 2.50 6.00
11 Vince Carter 12.50 30.00
12 John Celestand 1.50 4.00
13 Baron Davis 4.00 10.00
14 Obinna Ekezie 1.50 4.00
15 Francisco Elson 1.50 4.00
16 Evan Eschmeyer 1.50 4.00
17 Jeff Foster 1.50 4.00
18 Steve Francis 4.00 10.00
19 Devean George 1.50 4.00
20 Richard Hamilton 4.00 10.00
21 Venson Hamilton 1.50 4.00
22 Chris Herren 2.50 6.00
23 Jumaine Jones 1.50 4.00
24 Lari Ketner 1.50 4.00
25 Raef LaFrentz 2.00 5.00
26 Melvin Levett 1.50 4.00
27 Quincy Lewis 1.50 4.00
28 Eddie Lucas 1.50 4.00
29 Todd MacCulloch 1.50 4.00
30 Andre Miller 4.00 10.00
31 Lee Nailon 1.50 4.00
32 Lamar Odom 4.00 10.00
33 Laron Profit 1.50 4.00
34 Wally Szczerbiak 3.00 8.00
35 Jason Terry 4.00 10.00
36 Kenny Thomas 1.50 4.00
37 Tyrone Washington 1.50 4.00
38 Galen Young 1.50 4.00

1999 Press Pass SE In the Bonus

Randomly inserted in packs at ranging odds from 1:12 to 1:144, this eight-card set features the top picks from the 1999 Draft. Card backs carry an "IB" prefix.
COMPLETE SET (8) 8.00 20.00
STATED ODDS #IB1 1:144, #IB2-IB4 1:72
IB1 Elton Brand 2.00 5.00
IB2 Steve Francis 2.00 5.00
IB3 Baron Davis 2.00 5.00
IB4 Lamar Odom 2.00 5.00
IB5 Wally Szczerbiak 1.50 4.00
IB6 Richard Hamilton 2.00 5.00
IB7 Jason Terry 2.00 5.00
IB8 Trajan Langdon .75 2.00

1999 Press Pass SE Instant Replay

Randomly inserted in packs at one in six, this six-card set features the top players from the draft on microetched foil. Card backs carry an "IR" prefix.
COMPLETE SET (6) 1.50 4.00
STATED ODDS 1:6 HOB/RET
IR1 Elton Brand .50 1.25
IR2 Steve Francis .50 1.25
IR3 Baron Davis .50 1.25
IR4 Lamar Odom .50 1.25
IR5 Wally Szczerbiak .40 1.00
IR6 Andre Miller .50 1.25

1999 Press Pass SE Jersey Cards

Randomly inserted in packs at one in 720, this four-card set features an authentic swatch from a game-used jersey. Card backs carry a "JC" prefix and are serially #'d to 300.
STATED ODDS 1:720 HOB/RET
STATED PRINT RUN 300 SER.#'d SETS
JC1 Elton Brand 10.00 25.00
JC2 Steve Francis 10.00 25.00
JC3 Raef LaFrentz 6.00 15.00
JC3A Lamar Odom 10.00 25.00

1999 Press Pass SE Old School

Inserted one per pack, this 36-card set features the set within a set. The cards carry the design of an old time 70's set.
COMPLETE SET (36) 5.00 12.00
ONE PER PACK
1 Elton Brand .50 1.25
2 Steve Francis .50 1.25
3 Baron Davis .50 1.25
4 Lamar Odom .50 1.25
5 Jonathan Bender .20 .50
6 Wally Szczerbiak .40 1.00
7 Richard Hamilton .50 1.25
8 Andre Miller .50 1.25
9 Jason Terry .50 1.25
10 Trajan Langdon .20 .50
11 William Avery .20 .50
12 Ron Artest .50 1.25
13 Cal Bowdler .20 .50
14 James Posey .20 .50
15 Quincy Lewis .20 .50
16 Kenny Thomas .20 .50
17 Tim James .20 .50
18 Vonteego Cummings .20 .50
19 Jumaine Jones .20 .50
20 John Celestand .20 .50
21 Rico Hill .20 .50
22 Michael Ruffin .20 .50
23 Chris Herren .20 .50
24 Evan Eschmeyer .20 .50
25 Calvin Booth .20 .50
26 Obinna Ekezie .20 .50
27 Laron Profit .20 .50
28 A.J. Bramlett .20 .50
29 Francisco Elson .20 .50
30 Louis Bullock .20 .50
31 Lee Nailon .20 .50
32 Tyrone Washington .20 .50
33 Galen Young .20 .50
34 Venson Hamilton .20 .50
35 Melvin Levett .20 .50
36 Checklist Card .20 .50

1999 Press Pass SE Two on One

Randomly inserted in packs at one in 12, this 12-card set featues die cut cards that interlock to form one larger card. Card backs carry a "TO" prefix.
COMPLETE SET (12) 6.00 15.00
STATED ODDS 1:12 HOB/RET
TO1A Elton Brand 1.00 2.50
TO1B E.Brand/M.Bibby 1.00 2.50
TO1C Mike Bibby .40 1.00
TO2A Steve Francis 1.00 2.50
TO2B S.Francis/V.Carter 1.00 2.50
TO2C Vince Carter .75 2.00
TO3A Wally Szczerbiak .75 2.00
TO3B W.Szczer/J.Williams .75 2.00
TO3C Jason Williams .50 1.25
TO4A Lamar Odom 1.00 2.50
TO4B L.Odom/M.Camby 1.00 2.50
TO4C Marcus Camby .30 .75

2000 Press Pass SE

The 2000 Press Pass SE product was released in late September,2000 and featured a 45-card base set. The set was broken into tiers as follows: 35 Base prospects (1-35), and 10 Rookie Vision (36-45) subset cards. Each pack contained four cards, and each hobby pack carried a $10.99 SRP, while the retail packs carried a $3.49 SRP.
COMPLETE SET (45) 4.00 10.00
1 Mike Miller CL .15 .40
2 Darius Miles .20 .50
3 Mike Miller .30 .75
4 Chris Mihm .20 .50
5 Keyon Dooling .20 .50
6 Jerome Moiso .20 .50
7 Etan Thomas .20 .50
8 Mateen Cleaves .20 .50
9 Jason Collier .20 .50
10 Quentin Richardson .25 .60
11 Jamaal Magloire .20 .50
12 Morris Peterson .20 .50
13 DeShawn Stevenson .20 .50
14 Mark Madsen .20 .50
15 A.J. Guyton .20 .50
16 Dan Langhi .20 .50
17 Jake Voskuhl .20 .50
18 Khalid El-Amin .20 .50
19 Eddie House .20 .50
20 Hanno Mottola .20 .50
21 Chris Carrawell .20 .50
22 Brian Cardinal .20 .50
23 Mark Karcher .20 .50
24 Jason Hart .20 .50
25 Dan McClintock .20 .50
26 Chris Porter .20 .50
27 Jaquay Walls .20 .50
28 Scoonie Penn .20 .50
29 Pete Mickeal .20 .50
30 Elton Brand .20 .50
31 Steve Francis .20 .50
32 Baron Davis .20 .50
33 Lamar Odom .15 .40
34 Wally Szczerbiak .20 .50
35 Richard Hamilton .20 .50
36 Darius Miles RV .10 .25
37 Mike Miller RV .15 .40
38 Chris Mihm RV .10 .25
39 Keyon Dooling RV .10 .25
40 Jerome Moiso RV .10 .25
41 Etan Thomas RV .10 .25
42 Mateen Cleaves RV .10 .25
43 Jason Collier RV .10 .25
44 Quentin Richardson RV .12 .30
45 Morris Peterson RV .10 .25

2000 Press Pass SE Alley Oop

COMPLETE SET (45) 8.00 20.00
*ALLEY OOP: .75X TO 2X BASIC CARDS
ONE PER RETAIL PACK

2000 Press Pass SE Autographs

Randomly inserted into packs at one per pack (hobby), and one in 18 (retail), this 36-card insert features authentic autographs from some of the NBA's top young prospects. The cards are not numbered and listed below alphabetically.
STATED ODDS 1:1 HOB, 1:18 RET
NNO CARDS LISTED BELOW ALPHABETICALLY
*SILVER AU: .5X TO 1.25X HI COLUMN
SILVER AU PRINT RUN 500 SERIAL #'d SETS
1 Elton Brand 4.00 10.00
2 Brian Cardinal 2.00 5.00
3 Chris Carrawell 2.00 5.00
4 Mateen Cleaves 2.00 5.00
5 Jason Collier 2.00 5.00
6 Baron Davis 4.00 10.00
7 Keyon Dooling 2.00 5.00
8 Khalid El-Amin 2.00 5.00
9 Steve Francis 4.00 10.00
10 A.J. Guyton 2.00 5.00
11 Richard Hamilton 5.00 10.00
12 Jason Hart 2.00 5.00
13 Eddie House 2.00 5.00
14 Mark Karcher 2.00 5.00
15 Dan Langhi 2.00 5.00
16 Mark Madsen 2.00 5.00
17 Jamaal Magloire 2.00 5.00
18 Dan McClintock 2.00 5.00
19 Pete Mickeal 2.00 5.00
20 Chris Mihm 2.00 5.00
21 Darius Miles 2.00 5.00
22 Mike Miller 3.00 8.00
23 Jerome Moiso 2.00 5.00
24 Hanno Mottola 2.00 5.00
25 Lamar Odom 4.00 10.00
26 Scoonie Penn 2.00 5.00
27 Morris Peterson 2.00 5.00
28 Chris Porter 2.00 5.00
29 Lavor Postell 2.00 5.00
30 Quentin Richardson 2.50 6.00
31 Jabari Smith 2.00 5.00
32 DeShawn Stevenson 2.00 5.00
33 Wally Szczerbiak 2.00 5.00
34 Etan Thomas 2.00 5.00
35 Jake Voskuhl 2.00 5.00
36 Jaquay Walls 2.00 5.00

2000 Press Pass SE Jersey Cards

Randomly inserted into hobby packs at one in 84 and retail packs at one in 720, this 12-card insert features collegiate level game-used jersey cards of some of the NBA's top prospects. Card backs carry a "JC" prefix.
STATED ODDS 1:84 HOB, 1:720 RET
STATED PRINT RUN 200 SERIAL #'d SETS
*NUMBERS: 1.25X TO 3X BASE HI
NUMBERS PRINT RUN 25 SETS
JC1 Mateen Cleaves 5.00 12.00
JC2 Mark Karcher 5.00 12.00
JC3 Mark Madsen 5.00 12.00
JC4 Jamaal Magloire 5.00 12.00
JC5 Chris Mihm 5.00 12.00
JC6 Darius Miles 5.00 12.00
JC7 Mike Miller 8.00 20.00
JC8 Jerome Moiso 5.00 12.00
JC9 Morris Peterson 5.00 12.00
JC10 Quentin Richardson 6.00 15.00
JC11 DeShawn Stevenson 5.00 12.00
JC12 Etan Thomas 5.00 12.00

2000 Press Pass SE Lottery Club

Randomly inserted into packs at one in six, this 6-card insert features some of the NBA's top first round draft picks. Card backs carry a "LC" prefix.
COMPLETE SET (6) 2.00 5.00
STATED ODDS 1:6 HOB/RET
LC1 Darius Miles .50 1.25
LC2 Mike Miller .75 2.00
LC3 Chris Mihm .50 1.25
LC4 Keyon Dooling .50 1.25
LC5 Jerome Moiso .50 1.25
LC6 Etan Thomas .50 1.25

2000 Press Pass SE Lottery Club Autographs

RANDOM INSERTS IN HOBBY PACKS
STATED PRINT RUN 100 SERIAL #'d SETS
1 Darius Miles 5.00 12.00
2 Mike Miller 8.00 20.00
3 Chris Mihm 5.00 12.00
4 Keyon Dooling 5.00 12.00
5 Jerome Moiso 5.00 12.00
6 Etan Thomas 5.00 12.00

2000 Press Pass SE Old School

Randomly inserted into packs at one per pack, this 27-card insert features young prospects with a 1970's "old school" design. Card backs carry an "OS" prefix. To ascertain values on individual cards, please refer to the multiplier in the header, coupled with the value of the base card.
COMPLETE SET (27) 6.00 15.00
ONE PER PACK
OS1 Darius Miles .40 1.00
OS2 Mike Miller .60 1.50
OS3 Chris Mihm .40 1.00
OS4 Keyon Dooling .40 1.00
OS5 Jerome Moiso .40 1.00
OS6 Etan Thomas .40 1.00
OS7 Mateen Cleaves .40 1.00
OS8 Jason Collier .40 1.00
OS9 Quentin Richardson .50 1.25
OS10 Jamaal Magloire .40 1.00
OS11 Morris Peterson .40 1.00
OS12 DeShawn Stevenson .40 1.00
OS13 Mark Madsen .40 1.00
OS14 Dan Langhi .40 1.00
OS15 Jake Voskuhl .40 1.00
OS16 Khalid El-Amin .40 1.00
OS17 Eddie House .40 1.00
OS18 Hanno Mottola .40 1.00
OS19 Chris Carrawell .40 1.00
OS20 Brian Cardinal .40 1.00
OS21 Mark Karcher .40 1.00
OS22 Jason Hart .40 1.00
OS23 Chris Porter .40 1.00
OS24 Scoonie Penn .40 1.00
OS25 A.J. Guyton .40 1.00
OS26 Jabari Smith .40 1.00
OS27 Mateen Cleaves CL .40 1.00

2000 Press Pass SE Old School Threads

Randomly inserted into packs, this 2-card insert features swatches from college used game jerseys of Elton Brand and Steve Francis. Card backs carry an "OST" prefix, and each card is individually serial numbered to 50.
RANDOM INSERTS IN PACKS
STATED PRINT RUN 50 SERIAL #'d SETS
OST1 Elton Brand 15.00 40.00
OST2 Steve Francis 15.00 40.00

2000 Press Pass SE Sophomore Sensation

Randomly inserted into hobby/retail packs, this 6-card insert features NBA players that are going into their second year of action. Card backs carry a "SS" prefix. Please note that this insert was tiered, SS1-SS2 were inserted at 1:96 hobby, SS3-SS4 were inserted at 1:48 hobby, SS5-SS6 were inserted at 1:24 hobby, while SS1-SS2 were inserted at 1:192 retail, SS3-SS4 were inserted at 1:96 retail, and SS5-SS6 were inserted at 1:48 retail.
COMPLETE SET (6) 6.00 15.00
STATED ODDS SS1-2 1:96 HOB, 1:192 RET
STATED ODDS SS3-4 1:48 HOB, 1:96 RET
STATED ODDS SS5-6 1:24 HOB, 1:48 RET
SS1 Elton Brand 2.50 6.00
SS2 Steve Francis 2.50 6.00
SS3 Baron Davis 1.25 3.00
SS4 Wally Szczerbiak 1.25 3.00
SS5 Lamar Odom .75 2.00
SS6 Richard Hamilton .75 2.00

2000 Press Pass SE Two on One

Randomly inserted into packs at one in 12, this 12-card insert features die-cut cards that interlock to form one card. Card backs carry a "TO" prefix.
COMPLETE SET (12) 5.00 12.00
STATED ODDS 1:12
TO1A Darius Miles .60 1.50
TO1B D.Miles/Q.Richardson .75 2.00
TO1C Quentin Richardson .75 2.00
TO2A Mateen Cleaves .60 1.50
TO2B M.Cleaves/M.Peterson .60 1.50
TO2C Morris Peterson .60 1.50
TO3A Jerome Moiso .60 1.50
TO3B B.Davis/J.Moiso .60 1.50
TO3C Baron Davis .60 1.50
TO4A Steve Francis .60 1.50
TO4B E.Brand/S.Francis .60 1.50
TO4C Elton Brand .60 1.50

1998 SAGE

The 1998 Sage product was released during the 1998-99 season, and featured some of the NBA's top prospects and young superstars. Please note that a 1 of 1 version does exist of the base set.
COMPLETE SET (50) 5.00 12.00
1 Toby Bailey .15 .40
2 Corey Benjamin .15 .40
3 Andrew Betts .15 .40
4 Torraye Braggs .15 .40
5 Corey Brewer .15 .40
6 Kobe Bryant .60 1.50
7 Anthony Carter .15 .40
8 Vince Carter .75 2.00
9 Keon Clark .15 .40
10 Ricky Davis .25 .60
11 Michael Dickerson .15 .40
12 Michael Doleac .15 .40
13 Bryce Drew .15 .40
14 Tremaine Fowlkes .15 .40
15 Pat Garrity .15 .40
16 Zendon Hamilton .15 .40
17 Matt Harpring .15 .40
18 Al Harrington .25 .60
19 J.R. Henderson .15 .40
20 Antawn Jamison .40 1.00
21 DeMarco Johnson .15 .40
22 Charles Jones .15 .40
23 Rashard Lewis .40 1.00
24 Felipe Lopez .15 .40
25 Corey Louis .15 .40
26 Tyronn Lue .15 .40
27 Stephon Marbury .20 .50
28 Sean Marks .15 .40
29 Jelani McCoy .15 .40
30 Tracy McGrady .25 .60
31 Roshown McLeod .15 .40
32 Brad Miller .40 1.00
33 Cuttino Mobley .20 .50
34 Nazr Mohammed .15 .40
35 Makhtar Ndiaye .15 .40
36 Radoslav Nesterovic .15 .40
37 Michael Olowokandi .20 .50
38 Andrae Patterson .15 .40
39 Ruben Patterson .15 .40
40 Paul Pierce .60 1.50
41 Jeff Sheppard .15 .40
42 Miles Simon .15 .40
43 Tim Thomas .15 .40
44 Robert Traylor .15 .40
45 Bonzi Wells .15 .40
46 Tyson Wheeler .15 .40
47 Jahidi White .15 .40
48 Jason Williams .40 1.00
49 Shammond Williams .15 .40
50 Korleone Young .15 .40

1998 SAGE Autographs

Randomly inserted in packs, this 52-card set features autographs from the draft picks in the set. The cards feature a red background. Print runs are listed below.
RANDOM INSERTS IN PACKS
PRINT RUNS LISTED BELOW
A1 Toby Bailey/535 1.50 4.00
A2 Corey Benjamin/999 1.50 4.00
A3 Andrew Betts/475 1.50 4.00
A4 Torraye Braggs/890 1.50 4.00
A5 Corey Brewer/999 1.50 4.00
A6 Kobe Bryant/129 50.00 120.00
A7 Anthony Carter/999 1.50 4.00
A8 Vince Carter/479 15.00 40.00
A9 Keon Clark/999 1.50 4.00
A10 Ricky Davis/860 2.50 6.00
A11 Michael Dickerson/999 1.50 4.00
A12 Michael Doleac/549 1.50 4.00
A13 Bryce Drew/999 1.50 4.00
A14 Tremaine Fowlkes/999 1.50 4.00
A15 Pat Garrity/999 1.50 4.00
A16A Z.Hamilton (Black)/175 1.50 4.00
A16B Z.Hamilton (Blue)/825 1.50 4.00
A17 Matt Harpring/999 1.50 4.00
A18 Al Harrington/999 2.50 6.00
A19 J.R. Henderson/599 1.50 4.00
A20 Antawn Jamison/909 6.00 15.00
A21 DeMarco Johnson/890 1.50 4.00
A22 Charles Jones/999 1.50 4.00
A23 Rashard Lewis/999 4.00 10.00
A24 Felipe Lopez/999 1.50 4.00
A25 Corey Louis/990 1.50 4.00
A26 Tyronn Lue/999 1.50 4.00
A27 Stephon Marbury/149 8.00 20.00
A28 Sean Marks/999 1.50 4.00
A29 Jelani McCoy/125 2.00 5.00
A30 Tracy McGrady/99 30.00 80.00
A31 Roshown McLeod/970 1.50 4.00
A32 Brad Miller/879 4.00 10.00
A33 Cuttino Mobley/999 2.00 5.00
A34 Nazr Mohammed/739 1.50 4.00
A35 Makhtar Ndiaye/999 1.50 4.00
A36 Radoslav Nesterovic/999 1.50 4.00
A37 Michael Olowokandi/999 2.00 5.00
A38 Andrae Patterson/999 1.50 4.00
A39 Ruben Patterson/690 1.50 4.00
A40 Paul Pierce/199 12.50 30.00
A41 Jeff Sheppard/999 1.50 4.00
A42 Miles Simon/475 1.50 4.00
A43A Tim Thomas (Black)/219 1.50 4.00
A43B Tim Thomas (Blue)/819 1.50 4.00
A44 Robert Traylor/999 1.50 4.00
A45 Bonzi Wells/999 1.50 4.00
A46 Tyson Wheeler/999 1.50 4.00
A47 Jahidi White/459 1.50 4.00
A48 Jason Williams/999 6.00 15.00
A49 Shammond Williams/670 1.50 4.00
A50 Korleone Young/999 1.50 4.00

1998 SAGE Autographs Bronze

Randomly inserted in packs, this 52-card set parallels the regular autograph set. The cards feature a bronze background. Print runs are listed below. To ascertain values on individual cards, please refer to the multiplier in the header, coupled with the value of the base autograph.
*BRONZE AU: .5X TO 1.25X BASE AU
RANDOM INSERTS IN PACKS

1998 SAGE Autographs Gold

Randomly inserted in packs, this 52-card set parallels the regular autograph set. The cards feature a gold background. Print runs are listed below. To ascertain values on individual cards, please refer to the multiplier in the header, coupled with the value of the base autograph.
*GOLD AU: .75X TO 2X BASE AU
RANDOM INSERTS IN PACKS

1998 SAGE Autographs Platinum

Randomly inserted in packs, this 52-card set parallels the regular autograph set. The cards feature a platinum background. Print runs are listed below. To ascertain values on individual cards, please refer to the multiplier in the header, coupled with the value of the base autograph. Lower print runs are unpriced.
*PLATINUM AU: 1.5X TO 4X BASE AU
RANDOM INSERTS IN PACKS
A8 Vince Carter/25 75.00 200.00

1998 SAGE Autographs Silver

Randomly inserted in packs, this 52-card set parallels the regular autograph set. The cards feature a silver background. Print runs are listed below. To ascertain values on individual cards, please refer to the multiplier in the header, coupled with the value of the base autograph.
*SILVER AU: .6X TO 1.5X BASE AU
RANDOM INSERTS IN PACKS

1999 SAGE

The 1999 version of SAGE was released in three-card packs, which contained one autograph per pack. All autographs were inserted in packs and there were no redemptions. The base set contained 50 cards. .
COMPLETE SET (50) 8.00 20.00
MASTER AUs: STATED ODDS 1:2000
1 Ron Artest .60 1.50
2 William Avery .25 .60
3 Michael Batiste .25 .60
4 Jonathan Bender .25 .60
5 Roberto Bergersen .25 .60
6 Calvin Booth .25 .60
7 Cal Bowdler .25 .60
8 A.J. Bramlett .25 .60
9 Kobe Bryant 1.00 2.50
10 Rodney Buford .25 .60
11 Vince Carter .50 1.25
12 John Celestand .25 .60
13 Kris Clack .25 .60
14 Lonnie Cooper .25 .60
15 Vonteego Cummings .25 .60
16 Baron Davis .60 1.50
17 Francisco Elson .25 .60
18 Evan Eschmeyer .25 .60
19 Jeff Foster .25 .60
20 Devean George .25 .60
21 Dion Glover .25 .60
22 Richard Hamilton .60 1.50
23 Venson Hamilton .25 .60
24 Rico Hill .25 .60
25 Tim James .25 .60
26 Antawn Jamison .25 .60
27 Jumaine Jones .25 .60
28 J.R. Koch .25 .60
29 Trajan Langdon .25 .60
30 Bobby Lazor .25 .60
31 Melvin Levett .25 .60
32 Quincy Lewis .25 .60
33 Corey Maggette .50 1.25
34 Shawn Marion .60 1.50
35 B.J. McKie .25 .60
36 Andre Miller .60 1.50
37 Lee Nailon .25 .60
38 Ademola Okulaja .25 .60
39 Scott Padgett .25 .60
40 Paul Pierce .40 1.00
41 James Posey .25 .60
42 Aleksandar Radojevic .25 .60
43 David Robinson .40 1.00
44 Michael Ruffin .25 .60
45 Leon Smith .25 .60
46 Jason Terry .60 1.50
47 Kenny Thomas .25 .60
48 Tyrone Washington .25 .60
49 Frederic Weis .25 .60
50 Alvin Young .25 .60

1999 SAGE Autographs

The base, or red, autographs were inserted in packs at one in two. Most players in the 48-card set autographed 999 cards, but some did less. The print runs are listed next to the player's name. Card backs carry an "A" prefix. Cards A24 and A49 do not exist
STATED ODDS 1:2
A1 Ron Artest/699 4.00 10.00
A2 William Avery/999 1.50 4.00
A3 Michael Batiste/999 1.50 4.00
A4 Jonathan Bender/369 1.50 4.00
A5 Roberto Bergersen/999 1.50 4.00
A6 Calvin Booth/999 1.50 4.00
A7 Cal Bowdler/999 1.50 4.00
A8 A.J. Bramlett/999 1.50 4.00
A9 Kobe Bryant/114 40.00 100.00
A10 Rodney Buford/999 1.50 4.00
A11 Vince Carter/39 30.00 80.00
A12 John Celestand/999 1.50 4.00
A13 Kris Clack/999 1.50 4.00
A14 Lonnie Cooper/999 1.50 4.00
A15 Vonteego Cummings/999 1.50 4.00
A16 Baron Davis/339 4.00 10.00
A17 Francisco Elson/999 1.50 4.00
A18 Evan Eschmeyer/999 1.50 4.00

A19 Jeff Foster/999 1.50 4.00
A20 Devean George/999 1.50 4.00
A21 Dion Glover/885 1.50 4.00
A22 Richard Hamilton/899 4.00 10.00
A23 Venson Hamilton/999 1.50 4.00
A25 Tim James/999 1.50 4.00
A26 Antawn Jamison/745 4.00 10.00
A27 Jumaine Jones/999 1.50 4.00
A28 J.R. Koch/999 1.50 4.00
A29 Trajan Langdon/699 1.50 4.00
A30 Bobby Lazor/999 1.50 4.00
A31 Melvin Levett/999 1.50 4.00
A32 Quincy Lewis/999 1.50 4.00
A33 Corey Maggette/464 3.00 8.00
A34 Shawn Marion/789 4.00 10.00
A35 B.J. McKie/999 1.50 4.00
A36 Andre Miller/999 4.00 10.00
A37 Lee Nailon/999 1.50 4.00
A38 Ademola Okulaja/999 1.50 4.00
A39 Scott Padgett/999 1.50 4.00
A41 James Posey/999 1.50 4.00
A42 A.Radojevic/999 1.50 4.00
A43 David Robinson/113 25.00 60.00
A44 Michael Ruffin/999 1.50 4.00
A45 Leon Smith/999 1.50 4.00
A46 Jason Terry/999 4.00 10.00
A47 Kenny Thomas/999 1.50 4.00
A48 Tyrone Washington/999 1.50 4.00
A50 Alvin Young/999 1.50 4.00

1999 SAGE Autographs Bonus White

Randomly inserted in packs, these 24 autographs were inserted as a bonus. The cards feature the design of the 1998 set, but have a white border. The print runs are listed next to the player. Card backs carry an "A" prefix. Lower print runs are not priced.
RANDOM INSERTS IN PACKS
A1 Toby Bailey/45 4.00 10.00
A9 Keon Clark/95 4.00 10.00
A11 Michael Dickerson/100 5.00 12.00
A13 Bryce Drew/75 4.00 10.00
A15 Pat Garrity/25 10.00 25.00
A17 Matt Harpring/60 5.00 12.00
A18 Al Harrington/45 10.00 25.00
A23 Rashard Lewis/95 10.00 25.00
A24 Felipe Lopez/100 4.00 10.00
A26 Tyronn Lue/65 4.00 10.00
A33 Cuttino Mobley/85 4.00 10.00
A36 Radoslav Nesterovic/80 4.00 10.00
A37 Michael Olowokandi/90 4.00 10.00
A43 Tim Thomas Blue/20 12.00 30.00
A44 Robert Traylor/85 4.00 10.00
A45 Bonzi Wells/50 10.00 25.00
A50 Korleone Young/90 4.00 10.00

1999 SAGE Autographs Bronze

*BRONZE AU: .5X TO 1.25X BASIC AU
STATED ODDS 1:4

1999 SAGE Autographs Gold

*GOLD AU: .75X TO 2X BASIC AU
STATED ODDS 1:12
A9 Kobe Bryant/25 200.00 400.00
A43 David Robinson/25 80.00 200.00

1999 SAGE Autographs Platinum

*PLATINUM AU: 1.5X TO 4X BASIC AU
STATED ODDS 1:46

1999 SAGE Autographs Silver

*SILVER AU: .6X TO 1.5X BASIC AU
STATED ODDS 1:6

2000 SAGE

The 2000 Sage product was released at the end of October 2000. This set features 50 draft picks and young stars. Each pack contained five cards and carried a suggested retail price of 2.99.
COMPLETE SET (50) 6.00 15.00
1 Dalibor Bagaric .25 .60
2 Vin Baker .25 .60
3 Jonathan Bender .25 .60
4 Primoz Brezec .25 .60
5 Brian Cardinal .25 .60
6 Chris Carrawell .25 .60
7 Eric Coley .25 .60
8 Jason Collier .25 .60
9 Ed Cota .25 .60
10 Schea Cotton .25 .60
11 Baron Davis .25 .60
12 Kaniel Dickens .25 .60
13 Keyon Dooling .25 .60
14 Khalid El-Amin .25 .60
15 Michael Finley .25 .60
16 Kevin Freeman .25 .60
17 Gee Gervin .25 .60
18 Tom Gugliotta .25 .60
19 A.J. Guyton .25 .60
20 Tim Hardaway .25 .60
21 Jason Hart .25 .60
22 Johnny Hemsley .25 .60
23 Shaheen Holloway .25 .60
24 DeeAndre Hulett .25 .60
25 Antawn Jamison .25 .60
26 Marko Jaric .25 .60
27 Larry Johnson .25 .60
28 Michael Jordan .25 .60
29 Dan Langhi .25 .60
30 Lamont Long .25 .60
31 Justin Love .25 .60
32 T.J. Lux .25 .60
33 Desmond Mason .30 .75
34 Antonio McDyess .25 .60
35 Brad Millard .25 .60
36 Gabe Muoneke .25 .60
37 Alonzo Mourning .30 .75
38 Eduardo Najera .25 .60
39 Olumide Oyedeji .25 .60
40 Scoonie Penn .25 .60
41 Scottie Pippen .40 1.00
42 Rodney Rogers .25 .60
43 Pepe Sanchez .25 .60
44 Josip Sesar .25 .60
45 Steve Smith .20 .50
46 Jerry Stackhouse .25 .60
47 Jarrett Stephens .25 .60
48 Hedo Turkoglu .50 1.25
49 Jaquay Walls .25 .60
50 Corliss Williamson .25 .60

2000 SAGE Autographs

Randomly inserted in packs at one in two, this 48-card set features autographs from NBA stars and draft picks. The cards are also known as "red" autographs. Cards 2 and 26 do not exist. Card backs carry an "A" prefix.
STATED ODDS 1:2
A1 Dalibor Bagaric/999 2.00 5.00
A3 Jonathan Bender/369 2.00 5.00
A4 Primoz Brezec/999 2.00 5.00
A5 Brian Cardinal/999 2.00 5.00
A6 Chris Carrawell/999 2.00 5.00
A7 Eric Coley/999 2.00 5.00
A8 Jason Collier/999 2.00 5.00
A9 Ed Cota/999 2.00 5.00
A10 Schea Cotton/999 2.00 5.00
A11 Baron Davis/499 4.00 10.00
A12 Kaniel Dickens/999 2.00 5.00
A13 Keyon Dooling/999 2.00 5.00
A14 Khalid El-Amin/999 2.00 5.00
A15 Michael Finley/179 6.00 15.00
A16 Kevin Freeman/999 2.00 5.00
A17 Gee Gervin/999 2.00 5.00
A18 Tom Gugliotta/299 3.00 8.00
A19 A.J. Guyton/999 2.00 5.00
A20 Tim Hardaway/189 5.00 12.00
A21 Jason Hart/999 2.00 5.00
A22 Johnny Hemsley/999 2.00 5.00
A23 Shaheen Holloway/999 2.00 5.00
A24 DeeAndre Hulett/999 2.00 5.00
A25 Antawn Jamison/369 4.00 10.00
A27 Larry Johnson/299 5.00 12.00
A28 Michael Jordan/999 2.00 5.00
A29 Dan Langhi/999 2.00 5.00
A30 Lamont Long/999 2.00 5.00
A31 Justin Love/999 2.00 5.00
A32 T.J. Lux/999 2.00 5.00
A33 Desmond Mason/999 2.50 6.00
A34 Antonio McDyess/349 4.00 10.00
A35 Brad Millard/999 2.00 5.00
A36 Gabe Muoneke/999 2.00 5.00
A37 Alonzo Mourning/189 12.50 30.00
A38 Eduardo Najera/999 2.00 5.00
A39 Olumide Oyedeji/999 2.00 5.00
A40 Scoonie Penn/999 2.00 5.00
A41 Scottie Pippen/399 20.00 50.00
A42 Rodney Rogers/149 2.50 6.00
A43 Pepe Sanchez/999 2.00 5.00
A44 Josip Sesar/999 2.00 5.00
A45 Steve Smith/319 3.00 8.00
A46 Jerry Stackhouse/369 4.00 10.00
A47 Jarrett Stephens/999 2.00 5.00
A48 Hedo Turkoglu/999 4.00 10.00
A49 Jaquay Walls/999 2.00 5.00
A50 Corliss Williamson/169 3.00 8.00

2000 SAGE Autographs Bonus White

Randomly inserted in packs at one in 135, this 24-card set features "bonus" autographs in last years "style". The cards feature a white background. Lower print run cards are not priced. Card backs carry an "A" prefix.
STATED ODDS 1:135
STATED PRINT RUNS LISTED BELOW
LOWER PRINT RUNS UNPRICED
SKIP-NUMBERED SET
A1 Ron Artest/40 10.00 25.00
A2 William Avery/40 8.00 20.00
A3 Jonathan Bender/20 8.00 20.00
A7 Cal Bowdler/90 8.00 20.00
A15 Vonteego Cummings/60 8.00 20.00
A20 Devean George/30 8.00 20.00
A27 Jumaine Jones/100 8.00 20.00
A36 Andre Miller/90 10.00 25.00
A39 Scott Padgett/70 8.00 20.00
A41 James Posey/40 8.00 20.00
A42 Aleksandar Radojevic/30 8.00 20.00
A47 Kenny Thomas/40 8.00 20.00

2000 SAGE Autographs Bronze

*BRONZE AU: .5X TO 1.25X BASIC AU
STATED ODDS 1:4

2000 SAGE Autographs Gold

*GOLD AU: .75X TO 2X BASIC AU
STATED ODDS 1:12

2000 SAGE Autographs Platinum

*PLATINUM AU: 1.5X TO 4X BASIC AU
STATED ODDS 1:46
LOWER PRINT RUNS UNPRICED

2000 SAGE Autographs Silver

*SILVER AU: .6X TO 1.5X BASIC AU
STATED ODDS 1:6

2000 SAGE Rookie Limited Autographs

Randomly inserted in packs at one in 18, this 24-card set features serial #'d autographs of selected rookies and stars. The cards are numbered out of 500. Card R15 does not exist.
STATED ODDS 1:18
STATED PRINT RUN 500 SERIAL #'d SETS
R1 Dalibor Bagaric 2.50 6.00
R2 Jonathan Bender 2.50 6.00
R3 Primoz Brezec 2.50 6.00
R4 Brian Cardinal 2.50 6.00
R5 Chris Carrawell 2.50 6.00
R6 Jason Collier 2.50 6.00
R7 Ed Cota 2.50 6.00
R8 Baron Davis 4.00 10.00
R9 Kaniel Dickens 2.50 6.00
R10 Keyon Dooling 2.50 6.00
R11 Khalid El-Amin 2.50 6.00
R12 A.J. Guyton 2.50 6.00
R13 Jason Hart 2.50 6.00
R14 DeeAndre Hulett 2.50 6.00
R16 Dan Langhi 2.50 6.00
R17 Justin Love 2.50 6.00
R18 Desmond Mason 3.00 8.00
R19 Eduardo Najera 2.50 6.00
R20 Olumide Oyedeji 2.50 6.00
R21 Scoonie Penn 2.50 6.00
R22 Pepe Sanchez 2.50 6.00
R23 Josip Sesar 2.50 6.00
R24 Hedo Turkoglu 5.00 12.00
R25 Jaquay Walls 2.50 6.00

2001 SAGE

Released in August 2001, SAGE features a 36-card set of 2001's top draft packs and rookies. Base cards have a white border along the left side of the card, a full color player photo, and a red strip along the bottom of the card with the player's name. SAGE was packaged so each pack contained either a jersey card or an autographed card, where autographed cards came eight per box, and jersey cards came four per box. Each rookie player's card is numbered one of 3200. SAGE was packaged in 12 box cases with 12 packs per box and three cards per pack.
COMPLETE SET (36) 6.00 15.00
1 Gilbert Arenas .30 .75
2 Shane Battier .50 1.25
3 Ruben Boumtje-Boumtje .15 .40
4 Bryan Bracey .15 .40
5 Michael Bradley .25 .60
6 Jamison Brewer .25 .60
7 Damone Brown .25 .60
8 Kwame Brown .25 .60
9 Eric Chenowith .15 .40
10 Eddy Curry .25 .60
11 Samuel Dalembert .25 .60
12 Maurice Evans .25 .60
13 Joseph Forte .25 .60
14 Antonis Fotsis .15 .40
15 Pau Gasol .75 2.00
16 Eddie Griffin .25 .60
17 Trenton Hassell .25 .60
18 Brendan Haywood .25 .60
19 Steven Hunter .25 .60
20 Andre Hutson .25 .60
21 Maurice Jeffers .15 .40
22 Richard Jefferson .40 1.00
23 Ken Johnson .25 .60
24 Alvin Jones .25 .60
25 Sean Lampley .15 .40
26 Troy Murphy .25 .60
27 Zach Randolph .60 1.50
28 Jason Richardson .40 1.00
29 Jeryl Sasser .15 .40
30 Kenny Satterfield .25 .60
31 Will Solomon .25 .60
32 Jamaal Tinsley .25 .60
33 Gerald Wallace .30 .75
34 Rodney White .15 .40
35 Loren Woods .25 .60
36 Michael Wright .25 .60

2001 SAGE Authentic Jerseys Red

Randomly seeded in packs, this 21-card set features red borders along the top and the bottom of the card, a full color player photo and an oval swatch of an authentic jersey towards the bottom of the card. Each card is sequentially numbered to 400. Two versions of the Shane Battier card were issued, a blue jersey swatch and a white jersey swatch. These cards are denoted as "A" and "B" verions of card #J2.
STATED PRINT RUN 400 SERIAL #'d SETS
*BRONZE: .5X TO 1.25X BASE HI
BRONZE PRINT RUN 300 SER.#'d SETS
*GOLD: .6X TO 1.5X BASE HI
GOLD PRINT RUN 99 SER.#'d SETS
*PLATINUM: 1X TO 2.5X BASE HI
PLATINUM PRINT RUN 25 SER.#'d SETS
*SILVER: .5X TO 1.25X BASE HI
SILVER PRINT RUN 200 SER.#'d SETS
UNPRICED MASTER PRINT RUN ONE SET
J1 Gilbert Arenas 4.00 10.00
J2A Shane Battier Blue 6.00 15.00
J2B Shane Battier White 6.00 15.00
J3 Michael Bradley 3.00 8.00
J4 Damone Brown 3.00 8.00
J5 Kwame Brown 3.00 8.00
J6 Eddy Curry 3.00 8.00
J7 Samuel Dalembert 3.00 8.00
J8 Joseph Forte 3.00 8.00
J9 Eddie Griffin 3.00 8.00
J10 Brendan Haywood 3.00 8.00
J11 Steven Hunter 3.00 8.00
J12 Richard Jefferson 5.00 12.00
J13 Troy Murphy 3.00 8.00
J14 Zach Randolph 8.00 20.00
J15 Jason Richardson 5.00 12.00
J16 Jeryl Sasser 2.00 5.00
J17 Jamaal Tinsley 3.00 8.00
J18 Gerald Wallace 4.00 10.00
J19 Rodney White 2.00 5.00
J20 Loren Woods 3.00 8.00

2001 SAGE Autographs Red

Randomly inserted in packs, this 36-card set features player photos on the right side of the card, a red border on the left side of the card, and a foil oval in the lower left hand corner with an authentic player autograph. These cards are horizontally designed, and each card is sequentially numbered. Print runs are listed below.
PRINT RUNS LISTED BELOW
*BRONZE: .5X TO 1.25X BASE HI
*GOLD: .75X TO 2X BASE HI
*PLATINUM: 1.5X TO 4X BASE HI
*SILVER: .6X TO 1.5X BASE HI
UNPRICED MASTER PRINT RUN ONE SET
A1 Gilbert Arenas/349 3.00 8.00
A2 Shane Battier/499 5.00 12.00
A3 R.Boumtje-Boumtje/699 1.50 4.00
A4 Bryan Bracey/849 1.50 4.00
A5 Michael Bradley/349 2.50 6.00
A6 Jamison Brewer/849 2.50 6.00
A7 Damone Brown/159 2.50 6.00
A8 Kwame Brown/325 2.50 6.00
A9 Eric Chenowith/499 1.50 4.00
A10 Eddy Curry/500 2.50 6.00
A11 Samuel Dalembert/349 2.50 6.00
A12 Maurice Evans/849 2.50 6.00
A13 Joseph Forte/349 2.50 6.00
A14 Antonis Fotsis/849 1.50 4.00
A15 Pau Gasol/349 8.00 20.00
A16 Eddie Griffin/500 2.50 6.00
A17 Trenton Hassell/499 2.50 6.00
A18 Brendan Haywood/349 2.50 6.00
A19 Steven Hunter/349 2.50 6.00
A20 Andre Hutson/549 2.50 6.00
A21 Maurice Jeffers/799 1.50 4.00
A22 Richard Jefferson/699 4.00 10.00
A23 Ken Johnson/159 2.50 6.00
A24 Alvin Jones/599 2.50 6.00
A25 Sean Lampley/999 1.50 4.00
A26 Troy Murphy/349 2.50 6.00
A27 Zach Randolph/349 6.00 15.00
A28 Jason Richardson/349 4.00 10.00
A29 Jeryl Sasser/999 1.50 4.00
A30 Kenny Satterfield/249 2.50 6.00
A31 Will Solomon/599 2.50 6.00
A32 Jamaal Tinsley/349 2.50 6.00
A33 Gerald Wallace/349 3.00 8.00
A34 Rodney White/499 1.50 4.00
A35 Loren Woods/699 2.50 6.00
A36 Michael Wright/999 2.50 6.00

2002 SAGE

Released in August of 2002, Sage consists of 36 draft picks. The base cards place full color player action photos on a true to life background at the bottom of the card which fades into white at the top. The player's name and position appear across the middle of the card, as does the print run for the set. SAGE had a total print run of 2900 sets and was packaged in 12 pack boxes where each pack contained three cards.
COMPLETE SET (36) 8.00 20.00
STATED PRINT RUN 2900 SETS
1 David Anderson .30 .75
2 Robert Archibald .30 .75
3 Matt Barnes .40 1.00
4 Carlos Boozer .60 1.50
5 Curtis Borchardt .30 .75
6 Caron Butler .50 1.25
7 Chris Christoffersen .30 .75
8 Ousmane Cisse .30 .75
9 Sam Clancy .30 .75
10 Dan Dickau .30 .75
11 Melvin Ely .30 .75
12 Dan Gadzuric .25 .60
13 Drew Gooden .30 .75
14 Rod Grizzard .20 .50
15 Ryan Humphrey .30 .75
16 Casey Jacobsen .30 .75
17 Chris Jefferies .30 .75
18 Jared Jeffries .30 .75
19 Fred Jones .30 .75
20 Tito Maddox .30 .75
21 Yao Ming 1.00 2.50
22 Bostjan Nachbar .30 .75
23 Smush Parker .30 .75
24 Tayshaun Prince .40 1.00
25 Kareem Rush .30 .75
26 Jamal Sampson .30 .75
27 Predrag Savovic .30 .75
28 Darius Songaila .30 .75
29 Amare Stoudemire .75 2.00
30 Nikoloz Tskitishvili .30 .75
31 DaJuan Wagner .30 .75
32 Jiri Welsch .30 .75
33 Frank Williams .30 .75
34 Jay Williams .40 1.00
35 Kelly Wise .30 .75
36 Vincent Yarbrough .30 .75

2002 SAGE Autographs Red

Randomly inserted in packs at the rate of one in two, this 34-card set features a horizontal design where a full color player photo appears on the right and a silver oval sticker with the player's autograph on it appears in the lower left hand corner. The upper right hand corner has the players name and a portrait. This portrait and the trim on the card are red. Each card is sequentially numbered.
STATED ODDS 1:2
*BRONZE: .5X TO 1.25X BASE HI
BRONZE STATED ODDS 1:4
*GOLD: .75X TO 2X BASE HI
GOLD STATED ODDS 1:12
*PLATINUM: 1.5X TO 4X BASE HI
PLATINUM STATED ODDS 1:48
*SILVER: .6X TO 1.5X BASE HI
SILVER STATED ODDS 1:6
UNPRICED MASTER PRINT RUN ONE SET
A1 David Anderson/125 3.00 8.00
A2 Robert Archibald/550 3.00 8.00
A3 Matt Barnes/500 4.00 10.00
A4 Carlos Boozer/440 6.00 15.00
A5 Curtis Borchardt/440 3.00 8.00
A7 Chris Christoffersen/220 3.00 8.00
A8 Ousmane Cisse/550 3.00 8.00
A9 Sam Clancy/440 3.00 8.00
A10 Dan Dickau/440 3.00 8.00
A12 Dan Gadzuric/500 2.50 6.00
A13 Drew Gooden/300 3.00 8.00
A14 Rod Grizzard/500 2.00 5.00
A15 Ryan Humphrey/550 3.00 8.00
A16 Casey Jacobsen/120 3.00 8.00
A17 Chris Jefferies/440 3.00 8.00
A18 Jared Jeffries/440 3.00 8.00
A19 Fred Jones/440 3.00 8.00
A20 Tito Maddox/550 3.00 8.00
A21 Yao Ming/125 25.00 60.00
A22 Bostjan Nachbar/440 3.00 8.00
A23 Smush Parker/125 3.00 8.00
A24 Tayshaun Prince/440 4.00 10.00
A25 Kareem Rush/300 3.00 8.00
A26 Jamal Sampson/440 3.00 8.00
A27 Predrag Savovic/550 3.00 8.00
A28 Darius Songaila/550 3.00 8.00
A29 Amare Stoudemire/440 5.00 12.00
A30 Nikoloz Tskitishvili/550 3.00 8.00
A31 DaJuan Wagner/250 3.00 8.00
A32 Jiri Welsch/440 3.00 8.00
A33 Frank Williams/300 3.00 8.00
A34 Jay Williams/320 8.00 20.00
A35 Kelly Wise/440 3.00 8.00
A36 Vincent Yarbrough/550 3.00 8.00

2002 SAGE Jerseys Red

Randomly inserted in packs at the rate of one in 53, this 10-card set featuers a horizontal design with a portrait style photo of the player on the right side and an oval cut jersey swatch in the lower left hand corner. Each card is sequentially numbered to 99, and the trim by the borders and background through the center of the card are red.
PRINT RUN 99 SER.#'d SETS
*BRONZE: .5X TO 1.25X BASE HI
BRONZE PRINT RUN 75 SER.#'d SETS
*GOLD: .75X TO 2X BASE HI
GOLD PRINT RUN 25 SER.#'d SETS
*SILVER: .6X TO 1.5X BASE HI
SILVER PRINT RUN 50 SER.#'d SETS
UNPRICED AUTO COMBO PRINT RUN 10 SETS
UNPRICED COMBO PRINT RUN 10 SETS
UNPRICED MASTER PRINT RUN ONE SET
UNPRICED PLATINUM PRINT RUN 10 SETS
ASJ Amare Stoudemire 5.00 12.00
DDJ Dan Dickau 4.00 10.00
DGJ Drew Gooden 4.00 10.00
DWJ DaJuan Wagner 4.00 10.00
FJJ Fred Jones 4.00 10.00
JJJ Jared Jeffries 4.00 10.00
JWJ Jay Williams 5.00 12.00
KRJ Kareem Rush 4.00 10.00
WEJ Jiri Welsch 4.00 10.00
YMJ Yao Ming 12.00 30.00

2004 SAGE

Released late in the summer of 2004, SAGE boasts a 36-card set of the newest draft picks with their slogan, "First cards of the 2004 draft." Base cards have thick white borders framing a player action photo with the player's name centered along the top, the SAGE logo in the lower right and "1 of 2650" appearing in the lower left. Sage was packaged in 12-pack boxes with packs containing three cards each.
COMPLETE SET (36) 6.00 15.00
STATED PRINT RUN 2650 SETS
1 Tony Allen .30 .75
2 Rafael Araujo .20 .50
3 Brian Boddicker .20 .50
4 Taliek Brown .20 .50
5 Antonio Burks .25 .60
6 Josh Childress .30 .75
7 Luol Deng .40 1.00
8 Marcus Douthit .30 .75
9 Chris Duhon .30 .75
10 Andre Emmett .20 .50
11 Matt Freije .20 .50
12 Ben Gordon .40 1.00
13 Devin Harris .30 .75
14 David Harrison .25 .60
15 Kris Humphries .30 .75
16 Andre Iguodala .40 1.00
17 Luke Jackson .25 .60
19 Shaun Livingston .30 .75
20 Marcus Moore .25 .60
21 Michel Morandais .30 .75
22 Brandon Mouton .20 .50
23 Emeka Okafor .40 1.00
24 Julius Page .20 .50
25 Rickey Paulding .30 .75
26 Tim Pickett .20 .50
27 Bernard Robinson .20 .50
28 Romain Sato .20 .50
29 Kirk Snyder .30 .75
30 Pape Sow .20 .50
31 Robert Swift .20 .50
32 Diana Taurasi 1.00 2.50
33 Sebastian Telfair .30 .75
34 Beno Udrih .30 .75
35 Jackson Vroman .20 .50
36 Sasha Vujacic .30 .75

2004 SAGE Autographs

Randomly inserted in packs, this 36-card set is horizontally designed and has red borders along the top and the bottom of the card. Player action photos appear on the left, while the trade mark SAGE silver sticker appears on the right with an autograph. Each card is individually numbered to a varying amount.
PRINT RUNS LISTED IN CHECKLIST
*BRONZE: .5X TO 1.25X BASE HI
*SILVER: .6X TO 1.5X BASE HI
*GOLD: .75X TO 2X BASE HI
UNPRICED PROOF PRINT RUN 20 SETS
UNPRICED MASTER PRINT RUN ONE SET
A1 Tony Allen/550 4.00 10.00
A2 Rafael Araujo/550 2.50 6.00
A3 Brian Boddicker/560 2.50 6.00
A4 Taliek Brown/560 2.50 6.00
A5 Antonio Burks/790 3.00 8.00
A6 Josh Childress/370 4.00 10.00
A7 Luol Deng/400 5.00 12.00
A8 Marcus Douthit/750 4.00 10.00
A9 Chris Duhon/660 4.00 10.00
A10 Andre Emmett/550 2.50 6.00
A11 Matt Freije/770 2.50 6.00
A12 Ben Gordon/400 6.00 15.00
A13 Devin Harris/400 4.00 10.00
A14 David Harrison/300 3.00 8.00
A15 Kris Humphries/400 4.00 10.00
A16 Andre Iguodala/270 5.00 12.00
A17 Luke Jackson/250 3.00 8.00
A19 Shaun Livingston/400 4.00 10.00
A20 Marcus Moore/770 3.00 8.00
A21 Michel Morandais/770 4.00 10.00
A22 Brandon Mouton/530 2.50 6.00
A23 Emeka Okafor/300 5.00 12.00
A24 Julius Page/520 2.50 6.00
A25 Rickey Paulding/750 4.00 10.00
A26 Tim Pickett/330 2.50 6.00
A27 Bernard Robinson/700 2.50 6.00
A28 Romain Sato/740 2.50 6.00
A29 Kirk Snyder/400 4.00 10.00
A30 Pape Sow/510 2.50 6.00
A31 Robert Swift/400 2.50 6.00
A32 Diana Taurasi/400 10.00 25.00
A33 Sebastian Telfair/600 4.00 10.00
A34 Beno Udrih/400 4.00 10.00
A35 Jackson Vroman/750 2.50 6.00
A36 Sasha Vujacic/400 4.00 10.00

2004 SAGE Jerseys

Inserted in packs and sequentially numbered to 99, this 15-card set features a horizontal design with a player photo on the left and an oval swatch of jersey on the right. For the base cards, there are red borders along the top of the card along with the player's last name in red and large block lettering. Several different parallels were produced for this set where the name depicts the color of the borders: Bronze is sequentially numbered to 75, Silver is sequentially numbered to 50, Gold is sequentially numbered to 25, Player's Proof is sequentially numbered to 20, Platinum is seuqentially numbered to 10 and Masterpiece one of one's were also produced.
PRINT RUN 99 SER.#'d SETS
*BRONZE: .5X TO 1.25X JSY HI
BRONZE PRINT RUN 75 SER.#'d SETS
*SILVER: .75X TO 2X JSY HI
SILVER PRINT RUN 50 SER.#'d SETS
*GOLD: 1X TO 2.5X BASE HI
GOLD PRINT RUN 25 SER.#'d SETS
UNPRICED PLAYER PROOF PRINT RUN 20 SETS
UNPRICED AU JSY PRINT RUN 10 SETS
UNPRICED COMBO PRINT RUN 10 SETS
UNPRICED MASTER PRINT RUN ONE SET
UNPRICED PLATINUM PRINT RUN 10 SETS
J1 Rafael Araujo 2.00 5.00
J2 Josh Childress 3.00 8.00
J3 Luol Deng 4.00 10.00
J4 Chris Duhon 3.00 8.00
J5 Ben Gordon 4.00 10.00
J6 Devin Harris 3.00 8.00
J7 Kris Humphries 3.00 8.00
J8 Andre Iguodala 4.00 10.00
J9 Luke Jackson 2.50 6.00
J10 Shaun Livingston 3.00 8.00
J11 Emeka Okafor 4.00 10.00
J12 Kirk Snyder 3.00 8.00
J13 Robert Swift 2.00 5.00
J14 Diana Taurasi 8.00 20.00
J15 Sebastian Telfair 3.00 8.00

2005 SAGE

COMPLETE SET (30) 4.00 10.00
1 Eddie Basden .25 .60
2 Brandon Bass .20 .50
3 Andrew Bogut .40 1.00
4 Will Bynum .25 .60
5 Travis Diener .25 .60
6 Raymond Felton .25 .60
7 Channing Frye .25 .60
8 Angelo Gigli .25 .60
9 Joey Graham .25 .60
10 Stephen Graham .25 .60
11 Julius Hodge .25 .60
12 Matt Jones .25 .60
13 Jackie Manuel .25 .60
14 Jason Maxiell .25 .60
15 Sean May .25 .60
16 Rashad McCants .25 .60
17 Josh Pace .25 .60
18 Johan Petro .25 .60
19 Wayne Simien .25 .60
20 Chris Taft .25 .60
21 Dijon Thompson .25 .60
22 Fran Vazquez .25 .60
23 Charlie Villanueva .25 .60
24 Von Wafer .25 .60
25 Hakim Warrick .25 .60
26 Deron Williams .30 .75
27 Jawad Williams .25 .60
28 Marvin Williams .25 .60
29 Antoine Wright .25 .60
30 Bracey Wright .25 .60

2005 SAGE Autographs Red

PRINT RUNS LISTED IN CHECKLIST
*BRONZE: .5X TO 1.25X BASE HI
*SILVER: .6X TO 1.5X BASE HI
*GOLD: .75X TO 2X BASE HI
PLATINUM NOT PRICED DUE TO SCARCITY
UNPRICED PROOF PRINT RUN 20 SETS
UNPRICED MASTER PRINT RUN ONE SET
A1 Eddie Basden/360 4.00 10.00
A2 Brandon Bass/450 3.00 8.00
A3 Andrew Bogut/250 6.00 15.00
A4 Will Bynum/625 4.00 10.00
A5 Travis Diener/540 4.00 10.00
A6 Raymond Felton/250 4.00 10.00
A7 Channing Frye/300 4.00 10.00
A8 Angelo Gigli/210 4.00 10.00
A9 Joey Graham/300 4.00 10.00
A10 Stephen Graham/210 4.00 10.00
A11 Julius Hodge/500 4.00 10.00
A13 Jackie Manuel/425 4.00 10.00
A14 Jason Maxiell/500 4.00 10.00
A15 Sean May/350 4.00 10.00
A16 Rashad McCants/250 4.00 10.00
A17 Josh Pace/450 4.00 10.00
A18 Johan Petro/300 4.00 10.00
A19 Wayne Simien/300 4.00 10.00
A20 Chris Taft/230 4.00 10.00
A21 Dijon Thompson/440 4.00 10.00
A22 Fran Vazquez/270 4.00 10.00
A23 Charlie Villanueva/270 4.00 10.00
A24 Von Wafer/220 4.00 10.00
A25 Hakim Warrick/300 4.00 10.00
A26 Deron Williams/270 5.00 12.00
A27 Jawad Williams/440 4.00 10.00
A28 Marvin Williams/250 4.00 10.00

2002 SAGE Beckett.com Stoudemire Jerseys

Produced by SAGE, and sold exclusively through Beckett.com, this three card set features three different versions of an Amare Stoudemire Jersey card. The Bronze version is sequentially numbered to 299, this silver is numbered to 199, and the gold is numbered to 99. These cards were originally offered as both singles and as a complete set-if the collector wanted all the same serial numbers on each of the three cards. The retail price as sold on Beckett.com was $19.95 for the bronze card, $29.95 for the silver card, $59.95 for the gold card, or the complete three-card set for $79.95
COMPLETE SET (3) 60.00 120.00
1 A.Stoudemire B/299 2.50 6.00
2 A.Stoudemire S/199 3.00 8.00
3 A.Stoudemire G/99 6.00 15.00

2000 SAGE HIT

The 2000 Sage Hit product was released in October,2000 as a 50-card set. The set features young NBA stars and draft picks. Each pack contained five cards, and carried a suggested retail price of $2.99.
COMPLETE SET (50) 4.00 8.00
1 Baron Davis .20 .50
2 Larry Johnson .20 .50
3 Jerry Stackhouse .20 .50
4 Michael Finley .20 .50
5 Keyon Dooling .20 .50
6 Schea Cotton .20 .50
7 DeeAndre Hulett .20 .50
8 Steve Smith .15 .40
9 Brad Millard .20 .50
10 Tim Hardaway .20 .50
11 Eric Coley .20 .50
12 Scoonie Penn .20 .50
13 Antonio McDyess .20 .50
14 Pepe Sanchez .20 .50
15 Kevin Freeman .20 .50
16 Olumide Oyedeji .20 .50
17 Dan Langhi .20 .50
18 Ed Cota .20 .50
19 Jonathan Bender .20 .50
20 Lamont Long .20 .50
21 Eduardo Najera .20 .50
22 Marko Jaric .20 .50
23 Michael Jordan .20 .50
24 Tom Gugliotta .20 .50
25 A.J. Guyton .20 .50
26 Chris Carrawell .20 .50
27 Jarrett Stephens .20 .50
28 Hedo Turkoglu .40 1.00
29 T.J. Lux .20 .50
30 Jaquay Walls .20 .50
31 Johnny Hemsley .20 .50
32 Alonzo Mourning .25 .60
33 Scottie Pippen .30 .75
34 Desmond Mason .25 .60
35 Brian Cardinal .20 .50
36 Shaheen Holloway .20 .50
37 Khalid El-Amin .20 .50
38 Josip Sesar .20 .50
39 Gabe Muoneke .20 .50
40 Kaniel Dickens .20 .50
41 Antawn Jamison .20 .50
42 Vin Baker .20 .50
43 Justin Love .20 .50
44 Dalibor Bagaric .20 .50
45 Rodney Rogers .20 .50
46 Jason Hart .20 .50
47 Gee Gervin .20 .50
48 Corliss Williamson .20 .50
49 Primoz Brezec .20 .50
50 Jason Collier .20 .50

2000 SAGE HIT NRG

COMPLETE SET (50) 7.50 15.00
*NRG: .6X TO 1.5X BASE CARD HI
STATED ODDS 1:1.5

2000 SAGE HIT Autographs Emerald

Randomly inserted in packs at one in 16, this 48-card set features autographed versions of the base cards. Cards 22 and 42 do not exist.
STATED ODDS 1:16
RANDOM INSERTS IN PACKS
*EMERALD CUT: .6X TO 1.5X HI COLUMN
EMERALD CUT: STATED ODDS 1:53
*DIAMOND: .5X TO 1.25X HI COLUMN
DIAMOND: STATED ODDS 1:27
*DIAMOND CUT: .75X TO 2X HI COLUMN
DIAMOND CUT: STATED ODDS 1:160
1 Baron Davis 3.00 8.00
2 Larry Johnson 5.00 12.00
3 Jerry Stackhouse 4.00 10.00
4 Michael Finley 4.00 10.00
5 Keyon Dooling 2.00 5.00
6 Schea Cotton 2.00 5.00
7 DeeAndre Hulett 2.00 5.00
8 Steve Smith 2.50 6.00
9 Brad Millard 2.00 5.00
10 Tim Hardaway 4.00 10.00
11 Eric Coley 2.00 5.00
12 Scoonie Penn 2.00 5.00
13 Antonio McDyess 4.00 10.00
14 Pepe Sanchez 2.00 5.00
15 Kevin Freeman 2.00 5.00
16 Olumide Oyedeji 2.00 5.00
17 Dan Langhi 2.00 5.00
18 Ed Cota 2.00 5.00
19 Jonathan Bender 2.00 5.00
20 Lamont Long 2.00 5.00
21 Eduardo Najera 2.00 5.00
23 Michael Jordan 2.00 5.00
24 Tom Gugliotta 2.50 6.00
25 A.J. Guyton 2.00 5.00
26 Chris Carrawell 2.00 5.00
27 Jarrett Stephens 2.00 5.00
28 Hedo Turkoglu 4.00 10.00
29 T.J. Lux 2.00 5.00
30 Jaquay Walls 2.00 5.00
31 Johnny Hemsley 2.00 5.00
32 Alonzo Mourning 12.00 30.00
33 Scottie Pippen 25.00 60.00
34 Desmond Mason 2.50 6.00
35 Brian Cardinal 2.00 5.00
36 Shaheen Holloway 2.00 5.00
37 Khalid El-Amin 2.00 5.00
38 Josip Sesar 2.00 5.00
39 Gabe Muoneke 2.00 5.00
40 Kaniel Dickens 2.00 5.00
41 Antawn Jamison 4.00 10.00
43 Justin Love 2.00 5.00
44 Dalibor Bagaric 2.00 5.00
45 Rodney Rogers 2.00 5.00
46 Jason Hart 2.00 5.00
47 Gee Gervin 2.00 5.00
48 Corliss Williamson 2.00 5.00
49 Primoz Brezec 2.00 5.00
50 Jason Collier 2.00 5.00

2000 SAGE HIT Draft Flashbacks Emerald

COMPLETE SET (10) 8.00 20.00
STATED ODDS 1:80
STATED PRINT RUN 500 SERIAL #'s SETS
*EMERALD CUT: 1.25X TO 3X HI COLUMN
EMERALD CUT: STATED ODDS 1:264
EMERALD CUT: PRINT RUN 150 SETS
*DIAMOND: .6X TO 1.5X HI COLUMN
DIAMOND: STATED ODDS 1:132
DIAMOND: PRINT RUN 300 SETS
*DIAMOND CUT: 2.5X TO 6X HI COLUMN
DIAMOND CUT: STATED ODDS 1:800
DIAMOND CUT: PRINT RUN 50 SETS
D1 Scottie Pippen 1.50 4.00
D2 Larry Johnson 1.00 2.50
D3 Steve Smith .75 2.00
D4 Alonzo Mourning 1.25 3.00
D5 Tom Gugliotta 1.00 2.50
D6 Vin Baker 1.00 2.50
D7 Rodney Rogers 1.00 2.50
D8 Jerry Stackhouse 1.00 2.50
D9 Corliss Williamson 1.00 2.50
D10 Antawn Jamison 1.00 2.50

2000 SAGE HIT Prospector Emerald

COMPLETE SET (20) 8.00 20.00
STATED ODDS 1:20
STATED PRINT RUN 999 SERIAL #'s SETS
*EMERALD CUT: .75X TO 2X HI COLUMN
EMERALD CUT: STATED ODDS 1:66
EMERALD CUT: PRINT RUN 300 SETS
*DIAMOND: .5X TO 1.25X HI COLUMN
DIAMOND: STATED ODDS 1:33
DIAMOND: PRINT RUN 600 SETS
*DIAMOND CUT: 2X TO 5X HI COLUMN
DIAMOND CUT: STATED ODDS 1:200
DIAMOND CUT: PRINT RUN 100 SETS
P1 Jonathan Bender .75 2.00
P2 Chris Carrawell .75 2.00
P3 Jason Collier .75 2.00
P4 Baron Davis .75 2.00
P5 Keyon Dooling .75 2.00
P6 Khalid El-Amin .75 2.00
P7 Michael Finley .75 2.00
P8 A.J. Guyton .75 2.00
P9 Tim Hardaway .75 2.00
P10 Jason Hart .75 2.00
P11 Larry Johnson .75 2.00
P12 Dan Langhi .75 2.00
P13 Desmond Mason 1.00 2.50
P14 Antonio McDyess .75 2.00
P15 Alonzo Mourning 1.00 2.50
P16 Eduardo Najera .75 2.00
P17 Scoonie Penn .75 2.00
P18 Scottie Pippen 1.25 3.00
P19 Steve Smith .60 1.50
P20 Jerry Stackhouse .75 2.00

2001 SAGE HIT

Released in August of 2001, this 36-card base set are standard size and set on white bordered cards. The cards feature color action shots of the top 2001 draft picks.. The HIT logo can be found in the upper left-hand corner of the card. On the back of the card there are statistics and in-depth insight on each featured player. SAGE HIT was packaged in 16-box cases with 24-packs per box and four cards per pack. Each pack contained one insert card.
COMPLETE SET (36) 5.00 12.00
1 Kwame Brown .20 .50
2 Michael Wright .20 .50
3 Troy Murphy .20 .50
4 Eddy Curry .20 .50
5 Rodney White .12 .30
6 Loren Woods .20 .50
7 Maurice Jeffers .12 .30
8 Eric Chenowith .12 .30
9 Antonis Fotsis .12 .30
10 Kenny Satterfield .20 .50
11 Jamaal Tinsley .20 .50
12 Sean Lampley .12 .30
13 Richard Jefferson .30 .75
14 Jamison Brewer .20 .50
15 Steven Hunter .20 .50
16 Pau Gasol .60 1.50
17 Michael Bradley .20 .50
18 Bryan Bracey .12 .30
19 Zach Randolph .50 1.25
20 Brendan Haywood .20 .50
21 Joseph Forte .20 .50
22 Jeryl Sasser .12 .30
23 Jason Richardson .30 .75
24 Gerald Wallace .25 .60
25 Damone Brown .20 .50
26 Samuel Dalembert .20 .50
27 Will Solomon .20 .50
28 Maurice Evans .20 .50
29 Trenton Hassell .20 .50
30 Gilbert Arenas .25 .60
31 Shane Battier .40 1.00
32 Ken Johnson .20 .50
33 Eddie Griffin .20 .50
34 Andre Hutson .20 .50
35 Alvin Jones .20 .50
36 Ruben Boumtje-Boumtje .12 .30

2001 SAGE HIT Authentic Jerseys

This 21-card insert set is randomly inserted in packs and cards are sequentially numbered to 175. Swatches of jerseys worn by the top 2001 draft picks are featured on the bottom third of the card in an oval shape, and full color player action photos appear above.
STATED PRINT RUN 175 SERIAL #'d SETS
J1 Gerald Wallace 6.00 15.00
J2 Gilbert Arenas/175 6.00 15.00
J3 Richard Jefferson 8.00 20.00
J4 Loren Woods 5.00 12.00
J5 Rodney White 3.00 8.00
J6 Steven Hunter 5.00 12.00
J7A Shane Battier Blue 10.00 25.00
J7B Shane Battier White 10.00 25.00
J8 Kwame Brown 5.00 12.00
J9 Jamaal Tinsley 5.00 12.00
J10 Zach Randolph 12.00 30.00
J11 Jason Richardson 8.00 20.00
J12 Joseph Forte 5.00 12.00
J13 Brendan Haywood 5.00 12.00
J14 Troy Murphy 5.00 12.00
J15 Jeryl Sasser 3.00 8.00
J16 Samuel Dalembert 5.00 12.00
J17 Eddie Griffin 5.00 12.00
J18 Damone Brown 5.00 12.00
J19 Eddy Curry 5.00 12.00
J20 Michael Bradley 5.00 12.00

2001 SAGE HIT Autographs

This 36-card insert set is randomly inserted in packs at a rate of 1:6. The set features authentic autographs in a foil logo towards the bottom of the card.
RANDOM INSERTS IN PACKS
*DIE CUTS: .5X TO 1.25X BASE HI
DIE CUTS PRINT RUN 250 SER.#'d SETS
*RARE CUTS: .75X TO 2X BASE HI
RARE CUTS PRINT RUN 100 SER.#'d SETS
A1 Kwame Brown 2.50 6.00
A2 Michael Wright 2.50 6.00
A3 Troy Murphy 2.50 6.00
A4 Eddy Curry 2.50 6.00
A5 Rodney White 1.50 4.00
A6 Loren Woods 2.50 6.00
A7 Maurice Jeffers 1.50 4.00
A8 Eric Chenowith 1.50 4.00
A9 Antonis Fotsis 1.50 4.00
A10 Kenny Satterfield 2.50 6.00
A11 Jamaal Tinsley 2.50 6.00
A12 Sean Lampley 1.50 4.00
A13 Richard Jefferson 4.00 10.00
A14 Jamison Brewer 2.50 6.00
A15 Steven Hunter 2.50 6.00
A16 Pau Gasol 8.00 20.00
A17 Michael Bradley 2.50 6.00
A18 Bryan Bracey 1.50 4.00
A19 Zach Randolph 6.00 15.00
A20 Brendan Haywood 2.50 6.00
A21 Joseph Forte 2.50 6.00
A22 Jeryl Sasser 1.50 4.00
A23 Jason Richardson 4.00 10.00
A24 Gerald Wallace 3.00 8.00
A25 Damone Brown 2.50 6.00
A26 Samuel Dalembert 2.50 6.00
A27 Will Solomon 2.50 6.00
A28 Maurice Evans 2.50 6.00
A29 Trenton Hassell 2.50 6.00
A30 Gilbert Arenas 3.00 8.00
A31 Shane Battier 5.00 12.00
A32 Ken Johnson 2.50 6.00
A33 Eddie Griffin 2.50 6.00
A34 Andre Hutson 2.50 6.00
A35 Alvin Jones 2.50 6.00
A36 Ruben Boumtje-Boumtje 1.50 4.00

2001 SAGE HIT Rarefied Bronze

Randomly inserted in packs at the rate of one in two, this 36-card set parallels the base set order with a bronze rarefied logo centered along the bottom of the card. Cards have a blue border along the right edge containing the player's name, and are sequentially numbered to 2001.
COMPLETE SET (36) 8.00 20.00
PRINT RUN 2001 SERIAL #'d SETS
*GOLD: 1.25X TO 3X BASE HI
GOLD PRINT RUN 500 SER.#'d SETS
*SILVER: .6X TO 1.5X BASE HI
SILVER PRINT RUN 999 SER.#'d SETS
R1 Gilbert Arenas .30 .75
R2 Shane Battier .50 1.25
R3 Michael Bradley .25 .60
R4 Kwame Brown .25 .60
R5 Eddy Curry .25 .60
R6 Samuel Dalembert .25 .60
R7 Michael Finley .25 .60
R8 Joseph Forte .25 .60
R9 Antonis Fotsis .15 .40
R10 Pau Gasol .75 2.00
R11 Eddie Griffin .25 .60
R12 Tim Hardaway .25 .60
R13 Trenton Hassell .25 .60
R14 Brendan Haywood .25 .60
R15 Steven Hunter .25 .60
R16 Antawn Jamison .25 .60
R17 Richard Jefferson .40 1.00
R18 Desmond Mason .20 .50
R19 Alonzo Mourning .30 .75
R20 Troy Murphy .25 .60
R21 Scottie Pippen .40 1.00
R22 Zach Randolph .60 1.50
R23 Jason Richardson .40 1.00
R24 Jeryl Sasser .15 .40
R25 Jerry Stackhouse .20 .50
R26 Jamaal Tinsley .25 .60
R27 Gerald Wallace .30 .75
R28 Rodney White .15 .40
R29 Loren Woods .25 .60
R30 Kwame Brown .25 .60
R31 Pau Gasol .75 2.00
R32 Eddy Curry .25 .60
R33 Jason Richardson .40 1.00
R34 Shane Battier .50 1.25
R35 Eddie Griffin .25 .60
R36 Rodney White .15 .40

2002 SAGE HIT

Released in late July of 2002, Sage HIT features a 52-card set comprised of the top draft picks of the 2002 season and and several players from the 2001 draft. Base cards feature a full color player photo and a white line towards the bottom below which the HIT logo appears and the player's name. Along the right edge of the card, a small blue fading to white box is present, where the player's position appears. HIT was packaged in 30-pack boxes with packs containing five cards.
COMPLETE SET (52) 6.00 15.00
1 Jared Jeffries .20 .50
2 DaJuan Wagner .20 .50
3 Caron Butler .30 .75
4 Carlos Boozer .40 1.00
5 Yao Ming .60 1.50
6 Curtis Borchardt .20 .50
7 Tito Maddox .20 .50
8 Ryan Humphrey .20 .50
9 Bostjan Nachbar .20 .50
10 Drew Gooden .20 .50
11 Predrag Savovic .20 .50
12 Dan Dickau .20 .50
13 David Andersen .20 .50
14 Lynn Greer .20 .50
15 Rod Grizzard .12 .30
16 Tayshaun Prince .25 .60
17 Smush Parker .20 .50
18 Robert Archibald .20 .50
19 Nikoloz Tskitishvili .20 .50
20 Fred Jones .20 .50
21 Kareem Rush .20 .50
22 Jay Williams .25 .60
23 Matt Barnes .25 .60
24 Jiri Welsch .20 .50
25 Darius Songaila .20 .50
26 Vincent Yarbrough .20 .50
27 Chris Jefferies .20 .50
28 Casey Jacobsen .20 .50
29 Chris Christoffersen .20 .50
30 Frank Williams .20 .50
31 Jamal Sampson .20 .50
32 Amare Stoudemire .50 1.25
33 Melvin Ely .20 .50
34 Dan Gadzuric .15 .40
35 Kelly Wise .20 .50
36 Sam Clancy .20 .50
37 Ousmane Cisse .20 .50
38 Jason Richardson .25 .60
39 Shane Battier .25 .60
40 Gilbert Arenas .25 .60
41 Jamaal Tinsley .20 .50
42 Eddy Curry .20 .50
43 Gerald Wallace .25 .60
44 Richard Jefferson .25 .60
45 Rodney White .20 .50
46 Pau Gasol .30 .75
47 Brendan Haywood .20 .50
48 Kwame Brown .20 .50
49 Troy Murphy .20 .50
50 Zach Randolph .25 .60
51 Eddie Griffin .20 .50
52 Jay Williams CL .20 .50

2002 SAGE HIT 5th Anniversary

COMPLETE SET (52) 12.50 30.00
*5th ANNIVERSARY: .75X TO 2X BASE CARD HI
HOT PACK STATED ODDS 1:15
THREE ANNIVERSARY CARDS PER HOT PACK

2002 SAGE HIT Authentic Jerseys

Randomly seeded in packs at the rate of one in 45, this six card set contains authentic swatches of player worn jerseys. Each card features a full color player photo enhanced with silver foil highlights. The bottom of the card is separated from the picture by a silver foil line, is colored in green, and the player's name appears in white. The jersey swatch is an oval shape in the lower left hand corner, and is also outlined in silver foil.
STATED ODDS 1:45
*RARE: 1X TO 2.5X BASE HI
RARE PRINT RUN 25 SER.#'d SETS
J1 Jay Williams 4.00 10.00
J3 Kareem Rush 3.00 8.00
J4 DaJuan Wagner 3.00 8.00
J5 Jared Jeffries 3.00 8.00
J6 Drew Gooden 3.00 8.00
J7 Amare Stoudemire 8.00 20.00
J8 Yao Ming 10.00 25.00

2002 SAGE HIT Autographs Emerald

STATED ODDS 1:10
*SILVER: .5X TO 1.25X BASE HI
SILVER STATED ODDS 1:20
H1 Jared Jeffries 3.00 8.00
H2 DaJuan Wagner 3.00 8.00
H4 Carlos Boozer 6.00 15.00
H5 Yao Ming 20.00 50.00
H6 Curtis Borchardt 3.00 8.00
H7 Tito Maddox 3.00 8.00
H8 Ryan Humphrey 3.00 8.00
H9 Bostjan Nachbar 3.00 8.00
H10 Drew Gooden 3.00 8.00
H11 Predrag Savovic 3.00 8.00
H12 Dan Dickau 3.00 8.00
H13 David Andersen 3.00 8.00
H14 Lynn Greer 3.00 8.00
H15 Rod Grizzard 2.00 5.00
H16 Tayshaun Prince 4.00 10.00
H18 Robert Archibald 3.00 8.00
H19 Nikoloz Tskitishvili 3.00 8.00
H20 Fred Jones 3.00 8.00
H21 Kareem Rush 3.00 8.00
H22 Jay Williams 6.00 15.00
H23 Matt Barnes 4.00 10.00
H24 Jiri Welsch 3.00 8.00
H25 Darius Songaila 3.00 8.00
H27 Chris Jefferies 3.00 8.00
H29 Chris Christoffersen 3.00 8.00
H31 Jamal Sampson 3.00 8.00
H32 Amare Stoudemire 8.00 20.00
H34 Dan Gadzuric 2.50 6.00
H35 Kelly Wise 3.00 8.00
H36 Sam Clancy 3.00 8.00
H37 Ousmane Cisse 3.00 8.00

2002 SAGE HIT Autographs Gold

*GOLD: .6X TO 1.5X AUTOS EMER HI
STATED ODDS 1:24
PRINT RUN 250 SER.#'d SETS
H17 Smush Parker 5.00 12.00
H28 Casey Jacobsen 5.00 12.00
H30 Frank Williams 5.00 12.00

2002 SAGE HIT Rarefied Emerald

Randomly seeded in packs at the rate of one in two, this 45-card set pictures players in full color with white borders along the top and the right side of the card. The word "Rarefied" and "2002" appear on the right side of the card in emerald foil highlights, as doe the player's name on the bottom, and the team name on the photo.
*SILVER: .5X TO 1.25X BASE CARD HI
STATED ODDS 1:2
R1 David Andersen .40 1.00
R2 Robert Archibald .40 1.00
R3 Gilbert Arenas .40 1.00
R4 Matt Barnes .50 1.25
R5 Shane Battier .40 1.00
R6 Carlos Boozer .75 2.00
R7 Curtis Borchardt .40 1.00
R8 Kwame Brown .40 1.00
R9 Caron Butler .60 1.50
R10 Ousmane Cisse .40 1.00
R11 Sam Clancy .40 1.00
R12 Eddy Curry .40 1.00
R13 Dan Dickau .40 1.00
R14 Melvin Ely .40 1.00
R15 Dan Gadzuric .30 .75
R16 Pau Gasol .40 1.00
R17 Drew Gooden .40 1.00
R18 Eddie Griffin .40 1.00
R19 Rod Grizzard .25 .60
R20 Brendan Haywood .40 1.00
R21 Ryan Humphrey .40 1.00
R22 Chris Jefferies .40 1.00
R23 Richard Jefferson .40 1.00
R24 Jared Jeffries .40 1.00
R25 Fred Jones .40 1.00
R26 Tito Maddox .40 1.00
R27 Yao Ming 1.25 3.00
R28 Bostjan Nachbar .40 1.00
R29 Tayshaun Prince .50 1.25
R30 Zach Randolph .40 1.00
R31 Jason Richardson .40 1.00
R32 Kareem Rush .40 1.00
R33 Jamal Sampson .40 1.00
R34 Predrag Savovic .40 1.00
R35 Darius Songaila .40 1.00
R36 Amare Stoudemire 1.00 2.50
R37 Jamaal Tinsley .40 1.00
R38 Nikoloz Tskitishvili .40 1.00
R39 DaJuan Wagner .40 1.00
R40 Gerald Wallace .40 1.00
R41 Jiri Welsch .40 1.00
R42 Rodney White .40 1.00
R43 Frank Williams .40 1.00
R44 Jay Williams .50 1.25
R45 Vincent Yarbrough .40 1.00

2002 SAGE HIT Rarefied Gold Autographs

ATED ODDS 1:55
G1 Jared Jeffries 6.00 15.00
G2 DaJuan Wagner 6.00 15.00
G4 Carlos Boozer 12.00 30.00
G5 Yao Ming 40.00 100.00
G6 Curtis Borchardt 6.00 15.00
G7 Tito Maddox 6.00 15.00
G8 Ryan Humphrey 6.00 15.00
G9 Bostjan Nachbar 6.00 15.00
G10 Drew Gooden 6.00 15.00
G11 Predrag Savovic 6.00 15.00
G12 Dan Dickau 6.00 15.00
G13 David Andersen 6.00 15.00
G15 Rod Grizzard 4.00 10.00
G16 Tayshaun Prince 8.00 20.00
G17 Drew Gooden 6.00 15.00
G18 Robert Archibald 6.00 15.00
G19 Nikoloz Tskitishvili 6.00 15.00
G20 Fred Jones 6.00 15.00
G21 Kareem Rush 6.00 15.00
G22 Jay Williams 12.50 30.00
G23 Matt Barnes 8.00 20.00
G24 Jiri Welsch 6.00 15.00
G25 Darius Songaila 6.00 15.00
G27 Chris Jefferies 6.00 15.00
G30 Frank Williams 6.00 15.00
G31 Jamal Sampson 6.00 15.00
G32 Amare Stoudemire 5.00 12.00
G34 Dan Gadzuric 5.00 12.00
G36 Sam Clancy 6.00 15.00
G37 Ousmane Cisse 6.00 15.00
G38 Jason Richardson 8.00 20.00
G39 Shane Battier 8.00 20.00
G43 Gerald Wallace 8.00 20.00
G44 Richard Jefferson 8.00 20.00
G45 Rodney White 6.00 15.00
G47 Brendan Haywood 6.00 15.00
G50 Zach Randolph 8.00 20.00

2002 SAGE HIT The Write Stuff

Sage HIT The Write Stuff singles are found one in each Sage HIT hot packs, inserted at the rate of one in 15. This 15-card set features a brown to gray scale bacground with the featured player's photo and an irridescent foil "The Write Stuff" stamp centered along the bottom. A color player photo appears to the left of the card, and the player's name appears along the left edge of the card.
COMPLETE SET (15) 15.00 40.00
STATED ODDS 1:15
UNPRICED AUTO PRINT RUN 15 SETS
1 Jay Williams 1.50 4.00
2 Drew Gooden 1.25 3.00
3 DaJuan Wagner 1.25 3.00
4 Amare Stoudemire 3.00 8.00
5 Jared Jeffries 1.25 3.00
6 Fred Jones 1.25 3.00
7 Kareem Rush 1.25 3.00
8 Tayshaun Prince 1.50 4.00
9 Dan Dickau 1.25 3.00
10 Caron Butler 2.00 5.00
11 Yao Ming 4.00 10.00
12 Casey Jacobsen 1.25 3.00
13 Melvin Ely 1.25 3.00
14 Nikoloz Tskitishvili 1.25 3.00
15 Carlos Boozer 2.50 6.00

2004 SAGE HIT

Released late in the summer of 2004, SAGE HIT consists of a 50-card base set where the first 36-cards share a similar design that places action photos on a stock that has white and green borders along the right side and bottom, and 19 of the top draft picks on a green bordered Lottery Pick card. SAGE HIT was packaged in 30-pack boxes with packs containing five cards (one insert and four base cards).
COMPLETE SET (50) 6.00 15.00
1 Josh Childress .20 .50
2 Luol Deng .25 .60
3 Diana Taurasi .60 1.50
4 Ben Gordon .25 .60
5 Emeka Okafor .25 .60
6 Brian Boddicker .12 .30
7 Shaun Livingston .20 .50
8 Sasha Vujacic .20 .50
9 Julius Page .12 .30
10 Romain Sato .12 .30
11 Pape Sow .12 .30
12 Robert Swift .12 .30
13 David Harrison .15 .40
14 Andre Emmett .12 .30
15 Beno Udrih .20 .50
16 Kirk Snyder .20 .50
17 Jackson Vroman .12 .30
18 Herve Lamizana .20 .50
19 Antonio Burks .15 .40
20 Marcus Douthit .20 .50
21 Chris Duhon .20 .50
22 Tim Pickett .12 .30
23 Rickey Paulding .20 .50
24 Andre Iguodala .25 .60
25 Tony Allen .20 .50
26 Bernard Robinson .12 .30
27 Brandon Mouton .12 .30
28 Taliek Brown .12 .30
29 Marcus Moore .15 .40
30 Michel Morandais .20 .50
31 Sebastian Telfair .20 .50
32 Kris Humphries .20 .50
33 Luke Jackson .15 .40
34 Devin Harris .20 .50
35 Matt Freije .12 .30
36 Rafael Araujo .12 .30
37 Diana Taurasi LP .60 1.50
38 Emeka Okafor LP .25 .60
39 Ben Gordon LP .25 .60
40 Shaun Livingston LP .20 .50
41 Devin Harris LP .20 .50
42 Josh Childress LP .20 .50
43 Luol Deng LP .25 .60
44 Rafael Araujo LP .12 .30
45 Andre Iguodala LP .25 .60
46 Luke Jackson LP .15 .40
47 Robert Swift LP .12 .30
48 Sebastian Telfair LP .20 .50
49 Kris Humphries LP .20 .50
50 Emeka Okafor CL .20 .50

2004 SAGE HIT Autographs

Inserted at the rate of one in 10, this 36-card set has a green border along the left side of the card, full-color player photos and and signature on SAGE's foil sticker along the bottom of the card. Two different autograph versions were issue of this set, Gold features gold highlights and is sequentially numbered to 250, and Silver features silver highlights and can be found one in every 18 packs.
STATED ODDS 1:10
*GOLD: .6X TO 1.5X BASE AU HI
GOLD PRINT RUN 250 SER.#'d SETS
*SILVER: .5X TO 1.25X BASE AU HI
SILVER STATED ODDS 1:18
1 Josh Childress 2.50 6.00
2 Luol Deng 3.00 8.00
3 Diana Taurasi 8.00 20.00
4 Ben Gordon 3.00 8.00
5 Emeka Okafor 3.00 8.00
6 Brian Boddicker 1.50 4.00
7 Shaun Livingston 2.50 6.00
8 Sasha Vujacic 2.50 6.00
9 Julius Page 1.50 4.00
10 Romain Sato 1.50 4.00
11 Pape Sow 1.50 4.00
12 Robert Swift 1.50 4.00
13 David Harrison 2.00 5.00
14 Andre Emmett 1.50 4.00
15 Beno Udrih 2.50 6.00
16 Kirk Snyder 2.50 6.00
17 Jackson Vroman 1.50 4.00
18 Herve Lamizana 2.50 6.00
19 Antonio Burks 2.00 5.00
20 Marcus Douthit 2.50 6.00
21 Chris Duhon 2.50 6.00
22 Tim Pickett 1.50 4.00
23 Rickey Paulding 2.50 6.00
24 Andre Iguodala 6.00 15.00
25 Tony Allen 2.50 6.00
26 Bernard Robinson 1.50 4.00
27 Brandon Mouton 1.50 4.00
28 Taliek Brown 1.50 4.00
29 Marcus Moore 2.00 5.00
30 Michel Morandais 2.50 6.00
31 Sebastian Telfair 2.50 6.00
32 Kris Humphries 2.50 6.00
33 Luke Jackson 2.00 5.00
34 Devin Harris 2.50 6.00
35 Matt Freije 1.50 4.00
36 Rafael Araujo 1.50 4.00

2004 SAGE HIT Jerseys

Inserted one per box, this 12-card set has white borders along the left side and bottom of the card that change to green where they meet. Player action photos appear as does an oval swatch of jersey. Premium Swatch versions were also inserted and feature just what the name implies and sequential numbering to 50.
STATED ODDS 1:31
*PREMIUM JSY's: .75X TO 2X BASE JSY HI
PREMIUM PRINT RUN 50 SER.#'d SETS
JAI Andre Iguodala 4.00 10.00
JBG Ben Gordon 4.00 10.00
JDH Devin Harris 3.00 8.00
JDT Diana Taurasi 8.00 20.00
JEO Emeka Okafor 4.00 10.00
JJC Josh Childress 3.00 8.00
JKH Kris Humphries 3.00 8.00
JLD Luol Deng 4.00 10.00
JLJ Luke Jackson 2.50 6.00
JRS Robert Swift 2.00 5.00
JSL Shaun Livingston 3.00 8.00
JST Sebastian Telfair 3.00 8.00
JTA Tony Allen 3.00 8.00

2004 SAGE HIT Q&A

Inserted at one in two packs, this 36-card set is bordered only on the bottom where in large green foil, the letters "Q" and "A" appear. A silver foil version of this set was also produced and those cards were inesert at the rate on one in five packs.
COMPLETE SET (36) 8.00 20.00
STATED ODDS 1:2
*SILVER: .6X TO 1.5X BASE HI
SILVER STATED ODDS 1:5
Q1 Josh Childress .40 1.00
Q2 Luol Deng .50 1.25
Q3 Diana Taurasi .75 2.00
Q4 Ben Gordon .50 1.25
Q5 Emeka Okafor .50 1.25
Q6 Brian Boddicker .25 .60
Q7 Shaun Livingston .40 1.00
Q8 Sasha Vujacic .40 1.00
Q9 Julius Page .25 .60
Q10 Romain Sato .25 .60
Q11 Pape Sow .25 .60
Q12 Robert Swift .25 .60
Q13 David Harrison .30 .75
Q14 Andre Emmett .25 .60
Q15 Beno Udrih .40 1.00
Q16 Kirk Snyder .40 1.00
Q17 Jackson Vroman .25 .60
Q18 Herve Lamizana .40 1.00
Q19 Antonio Burks .30 .75
Q20 Marcus Douthit .40 1.00
Q21 Chris Duhon .40 1.00
Q22 Tim Pickett .25 .60
Q23 Rickey Paulding .40 1.00
Q24 Andre Iguodala .50 1.25
Q25 Tony Allen .40 1.00
Q26 Bernard Robinson .25 .60
Q27 Brandon Mouton .25 .60
Q28 Taliek Brown .25 .60
Q29 Marcus Moore .30 .75
Q30 Michel Morandais .40 1.00
Q31 Sebastian Telfair .40 1.00
Q32 Kris Humphries .40 1.00
Q33 Luke Jackson .30 .75
Q34 Devin Harris .40 1.00
Q35 Matt Freije .25 .60
Q36 Rafael Araujo .25 .60

2004 SAGE HIT Q&A Autographs

Sequentially numbered to 100, this 36-card set parallels the Q&A set but also includes player autographs.
PRINT RUN 100 SER.#'d SETS
Q1 Josh Childress 5.00 12.00
Q2 Luol Deng 6.00 15.00
Q3 Diana Taurasi 20.00 50.00
Q4 Ben Gordon 6.00 15.00
Q5 Emeka Okafor 6.00 15.00
Q6 Brian Boddicker 3.00 8.00
Q7 Shaun Livingston 5.00 12.00
Q8 Sasha Vujacic 5.00 12.00
Q9 Julius Page 3.00 8.00
Q10 Romain Sato 3.00 8.00
Q11 Pape Sow 3.00 8.00
Q12 Robert Swift 3.00 8.00
Q13 David Harrison 4.00 10.00
Q14 Andre Emmett 3.00 8.00
Q15 Beno Udrih 5.00 12.00
Q16 Kirk Snyder 5.00 12.00
Q17 Jackson Vroman 3.00 8.00
Q18 Herve Lamizana 5.00 12.00
Q19 Antonio Burks 4.00 10.00
Q20 Marcus Douthit 5.00 12.00
Q21 Chris Duhon 5.00 12.00
Q22 Tim Pickett 3.00 8.00
Q23 Rickey Paulding 5.00 12.00
Q24 Andre Iguodala 6.00 15.00
Q25 Tony Allen 5.00 12.00
Q26 Bernard Robinson 3.00 8.00
Q27 Brandon Mouton 3.00 8.00
Q28 Taliek Brown 3.00 8.00
Q29 Marcus Moore 4.00 10.00
Q30 Michel Morandais 5.00 12.00
Q31 Sebastian Telfair 5.00 12.00
Q32 Kris Humphries 5.00 12.00
Q34 Devin Harris 5.00 12.00
Q35 Matt Freije 3.00 8.00
Q36 Rafael Araujo 3.00 8.00

2004 SAGE HIT The Write Stuff

Inserted in packs at one in 15, this 15-card set is horizontally designed with a brown-scale background, irridescent foil letters and a full color player image on the left. On the back the card shows an expert's analysis of the featured player's autograph. An actual player autographed version of this set was also produced, and those cards are sequentially numbered to 25.
COMPLETE SET (15) 10.00 25.00
STATED ODDS 1:15
1 Diana Taurasi 1.50 4.00
2 Emeka Okafor 1.25 3.00
3 Ben Gordon 1.25 3.00
4 Shaun Livingston 1.00 2.50
5 Devin Harris 1.00 2.50
6 Josh Childress 1.00 2.50
7 Luol Deng 1.25 3.00
8 Rafael Araujo .60 1.50
9 Andre Iguodala 1.25 3.00
10 Luke Jackson .75 2.00
11 Chris Duhon 1.00 2.50
12 Robert Swift .60 1.50
13 Sebastian Telfair 1.00 2.50
14 Kris Humphries 1.00 2.50
15 Kirk Snyder 1.00 2.50

2004 SAGE HIT The Write Stuff Autographs

Randomly inserted, this 15-card set parallels the base Write Stuff insert enahnced with player autographs and sequential numbering to 25.
STATED ODDS 1:845
PRINT RUN 25 SER.#'d SETS
5 Devin Harris 12.00 30.00
7 Luol Deng 15.00 40.00
9 Andre Iguodala 15.00 40.00
10 Luke Jackson 10.00 25.00
13 Sebastian Telfair 12.00 30.00

2005 SAGE HIT

MPLETE SET (53) 6.00 15.00
1 Hakim Warrick .20 .50
2 Raymond Felton .20 .50
3 Charlie Villanueva .20 .50
4 Andrew Bogut .30 .75
5 Deron Williams .25 .60
6 Fran Vazquez .20 .50
7 Ben Gordon .25 .60
8 Andre Iguodala .30 .75
9 Luol Deng .25 .60
10 Mindaugas Katelynas .20 .50
11 Dijon Thompson .20 .50
12 Angelo Gigli .20 .50
13 David Harrison .20 .50
14 Joey Graham .20 .50
15 Johan Petro .20 .50
16 Kirk Snyder .20 .50
17 Eddie Basden .20 .50
18 Sasha Vujacic .20 .50
19 Robert Swift .20 .50
20 Jawad Williams .20 .50
21 Antoine Wright .20 .50
22 Wayne Simien .20 .50
23 Chris Taft .20 .50
24 Marvin Williams .20 .50
25 Tony Allen .25 .60
26 Julius Hodge .20 .50
27 Donell Taylor .20 .50
28 Beno Udrih .20 .50
29 Stephen Graham .20 .50
30 Brandon Bass .15 .40
31 Sebastian Telfair .20 .50
32 Rashad McCants .20 .50
33 Luke Jackson .20 .50
34 Devin Harris .30 .75
35 Jackie Manuel .20 .50
36 Mile Ilic .20 .50
37 Diana Taurasi .60 1.50
38 Will Bynum .20 .50
39 Chris Duhon .20 .50
40 Bracey Wright .20 .50
41 Josh Childress .20 .50
42 Sean May .20 .50
43 Kris Humphries .20 .50
44 Shaun Livingston .20 .50
45 Channing Frye .20 .50
46 Jason Maxiell .20 .50
47 Josh Pace .20 .50
48 Rafael Araujo .20 .50
49 Matt Jones .20 .50
50 Emeka Okafor .30 .75
51 Robert Whaley .20 .50
52 Von Wafer .20 .50
53 Travis Diener .20 .50

2005 SAGE HIT Autographs

RANDOM INSERTS IN PACKS
*GOLD: .5X TO 1.25X BASE HI
GOLD PRINT RUN 250 SETS
*SILVER: .4X TO 1X BASE HI
A1 Hakim Warrick 3.00 8.00
A2 Raymond Felton 3.00 8.00
A3 Charlie Villanueva 3.00 8.00
A4 Andrew Bogut 5.00 12.00
A5 Deron Williams 4.00 10.00
A6 Fran Vazquez 3.00 8.00
A11 Dijon Thompson 3.00 8.00
A12 Angelo Gigli 3.00 8.00
A14 Joey Graham 3.00 8.00
A15 Johan Petro 3.00 8.00
A17 Eddie Basden 3.00 8.00
A20 Jawad Williams 3.00 8.00
A22 Wayne Simien 3.00 8.00
A23 Chris Taft 3.00 8.00
A24 Marvin Williams 3.00 8.00
A26 Julius Hodge 3.00 8.00
A29 Stephen Graham 3.00 8.00
A30 Brandon Bass 2.50 6.00
A32 Rashad McCants 3.00 8.00
A35 Jackie Manuel 3.00 8.00
A38 Will Bynum 3.00 8.00
A42 Sean May 3.00 8.00
A45 Channing Frye 3.00 8.00
A46 Jason Maxiell 3.00 8.00
A47 Josh Pace 3.00 8.00
A52 Von Wafer 3.00 8.00
A53 Travis Diener 3.00 8.00

2005 SAGE HIT Autographs Gold Reflections

*GOLD REF.: .75X TO 2X BASE AU HI
PRINT RUN 50 TO 100 SER.#'d SETS
7 Ben Gordon/50 10.00 25.00
8 Andre Iguodala/50 8.00 20.00
9 Luol Deng/50 6.00 15.00
34 Devin Harris/50 6.00 15.00
37 Diana Taurasi/50 12.50 30.00
41 Josh Childress/50 5.00 12.00
43 Kris Humphries/50 5.00 12.00
44 Shaun Livingston/50 5.00 12.00
50 Emeka Okafor/50 10.00 25.00

2005 SAGE HIT The Write Stuff

COMPLETE SET (15) 5.00 12.00
RANDOM INSERTS IN PACKS
1 Andrew Bogut .75 2.00
2 Raymond Felton .50 1.25
3 Channing Frye .50 1.25
4 Joey Graham .50 1.25
5 Julius Hodge .50 1.25
6 Matt Jones .50 1.25
7 Sean May .50 1.25
8 Rashad McCants .50 1.25
9 Wayne Simien .50 1.25
10 Fran Vazquez .50 1.25
11 Charlie Villanueva .50 1.25
12 Hakim Warrick .50 1.25
13 Deron Williams .60 1.50
14 Marvin Williams .50 1.25
15 Antoine Wright .50 1.25

2005 SAGE HIT The Write Stuff Autographs

STATED PRINT RUN 25 SER.#'d SETS
1 Andrew Bogut 15.00 40.00
2 Raymond Felton 10.00 25.00
3 Channing Frye 10.00 25.00
6 Matt Jones 10.00 25.00
7 Sean May 10.00 25.00
8 Rashad McCants 10.00 25.00
11 Charlie Villanueva 10.00 25.00
13 Deron Williams 10.00 25.00
14 Marvin Williams 10.00 25.00

2005 SAGE HIT Title Series Autographs

PRINT RUN 10 TO 50 SER.#'d SETS
SOME UNPRICED DUE TO SCARCITY
1 Raymond Felton/50 5.00 12.00
2 Jackie Manuel/50 5.00 12.00
5 Jawad Williams/50 5.00 12.00
6 Marvin Williams/50 5.00 12.00
12 Josh Pace/50 5.00 12.00
13 Hakim Warrick/50 5.00 12.00

2005 SAGE HIT Title Trips

COMPLETE SET (36) 15.00 40.00
RANDOM INSERTS IN PACKS
TT1 Felton/McCants/May .75 2.00
TT2 Mv.Willms/Jaw.Willms/Manuel .75 2.00
TT3 Felton/J.Williams/McCants .75 2.00
TT4 Mv.Williams/May/Manuel .75 2.00
TT5 Felton/Manuel/McCants .75 2.00
TT6 Mv.Willms/Jaw.Willms/McCants .75 2.00
TT7 Felton/Manuel/May .75 2.00
TT8 Mv.Williams/Manuel/McCants .75 2.00
TT9 Felton/McCants/Jaw.Williams .75 2.00
TT10 Mv.Willms/Jaw.Willms/May .75 2.00
TT11 Felton/Jaw.Williams/McCants .75 2.00
TT12 Mv.Williams/McCants/May .75 2.00
TT13 Felton/Manuel/Mv.Williams .75 2.00
TT14 McCants/Manuel/May .75 2.00
TT15 Felton/May/Mv.Williams .75 2.00
TT16 McCants/Manuel/Jaw.Williams .75 2.00
TT17 Felton/McCants/Mv.Williams .75 2.00
TT18 May/Manuel/Jaw.Williams .75 2.00
TT19 Felton/Jaw.Willms/Mv.Williams .75 2.00
TT20 May/Jaw.Williams/McCants .75 2.00
TT21 Gordon/Okafor/Taurasi 1.50 4.00
TT22 Villanueva/T.Brown/Okafor 1.00 2.50
TT23 Gordon/Okafor/T.Brown 1.00 2.50
TT24 Villanueva/T.Brown/Taurasi 1.25 3.00
TT25 Gordon/Villanueva/T.Brown 1.00 2.50
TT26 Villanueva/Okafor/Taurasi 1.50 4.00
TT27 Taurasi/Gordon/T.Brown 1.25 3.00
TT28 Gordon/Villanueva/Taurasi 1.50 4.00
TT29 Okafor/Taurasi/T.Brown 1.25 3.00
TT30 Gordon/Okafor/Villanueva 1.25 3.00
TT31 Warrick/Pace/Duhon 1.00 2.50
TT32 Felton/Gordon/Warrick 1.00 2.50
TT33 Mv.Williams/Gordon/Warrick 1.00 2.50
TT34 Gordon/Taurasi/Warrick 1.50 4.00
TT35 Gordon/Warrick/Duhon 1.25 3.00
TT36 Taurasi/Warrick/Duhon 1.25 3.00

2002 SAGE National Jerseys

These cards were issued during the National are are serially numbered to 50.
N1 Jay Williams 10.00 25.00
N4 Amare Stoudemire 20.00 50.00

2002 SAGE Pangos Sheets

Given away at Pauley Pavilion, UCLA, on January 4th 2003, this four sheet set features the first card of high school sensation LeBron James. Each sheet features eight players and the SAGE logo coupled with the Pangos Dream Classic 2003 logo. Two versions of these sheets were printed, a Green version and a Gold version. The Green version features a green background with with gold trim around the player's school and position, and around the.Pangos logo on the card front. The Gold version features a shift where the background is gold, and the green appears around the school/position box and the logo. 5000 green sheets were produced, 1250 of each, for handing out at the game, and 500 gold, 125 of each, were produced for handing out to the players the sheets featured. LeBron James and Wesley Washington received some sheets, but through a mix-up, the rest were never given to the players. SAGE did, however, give these remaining sheets out with product press releases to dealers and sports card distributors.
1 Sheet 1 15.00 40.00
D.J. Strawberry
Sebastian Telfair
Wesley Washington
DeMarcus Nelson
Header Card
Justin Hawkins
Omar Wilkes
LeBron James
Ekene Ibekwe
2 Sheet 2 15.00 40.00
Dru Joyce III
Sebastian Telfair
Justin Hawkins
DeMarcus Nelson
Aaron Afflalo
D.J. Strawberry
LeBron James
Ekene Ibekwe
3 Sheet 3 15.00 40.00
Wesley Washington
Sebastian Telfair
Harrison Schaen
Ekene Ibekwe
Header Card
Aaron Afflalo
Omar Wilkes
LeBron James
Justin Hawkins
4 Sheet 4 15.00 40.00
DeMarcus Nelson
Sebastian Telfair
Dru Joyce III
D.J. Strawberry
Header Card
Aaron Afflalo
Omar Wilkes
LeBron James
Harrison Schaen

2002 SAGE Pangos Sheets Gold

*GOLD: 2X TO 5X HI COLUMN

1994 Score Board Draft Day

Subtitled "Basketball Draft Day," this 13-card standard-size (2 1/2" by 3 1/2") set features some of the top picks in the 1994 NBA draft. Each set included a certificate of limited edition bearing a unique serial number and the production run figures (19,500). The cards are full-bleed except at the bottom, where a color stripe carries the palyer's last name in block lettering. Featuring a player cutout superposed on a background consisting of the appropriate city skyline, the color photos have a metallic sheen to them. The name of the city is printed in a typewriter font and cuts across the middle of the picture in "ticker-tape" fashion. The backs have a player profile and a color headshot. The cards are numbered on the back with a "DD" prefix.
COMPLETE SET (13) 6.00 15.00
DD1 Glenn Robinson .60 1.50
DD2 Glenn Robinson .60 1.50
DD3 Glenn Robinson .60 1.50
DD4 Jason Kidd 1.50 4.00
DD5 Jason Kidd 1.50 4.00
DD6 Jason Kidd 1.50 4.00
DD7 Grant Hill 1.50 4.00
DD8 Grant Hill 1.50 4.00
DD9 Eric Montross .30 .75
DD10 Eric Montross .30 .75
DD11 Juwan Howard .50 1.25
DD12 Juwan Howard .50 1.25
DD13 Checklist .08 .25

1994 Score Board National Promos

Distributed during the 1994 National Sports Collectors Convention, this 20-card standard-size multi-sport set features four subsets: Salute to 1994 Draft Stars (1-5), Centers of Attention (6-9), Texas Heroes (10-13, 20), and Salute to Racing's Greatest (14-18). The borderless fronts feature color action cutouts on multi-colored metallic backgrounds. The players name, position, and team name appear randomly placed on arcs. The borderless backs feature a color head shot on a ghosted backgound. The players name and biography appear at the top with the player's stats and profile at the bottom. The cards are numbered on the back with an "NC" prefix. The sets were given away to attendees at Classic's National Convention Party. Each set included a certificate of authenticity, giving the set serial number out of a total of 9,900 sets produced. There were five different checklist cards created using the fronts of other cards in the set. The complete set price includes only one of the checklist cards.
COMPLETE SET (20) 20.00 40.00
1 Glenn Robinson .40 1.00
2 Jason Kidd 1.25 3.00
3 Donyell Marshall .20 .50
4 Juwan Howard .40 1.00
5 Grant Hill .75 2.00
6 Hakeem Olajuwon .60 1.50
7 Patrick Ewing .60 1.50
8 Dikembe Mutombo .30 .75
9 Alonzo Mourning .60 1.50
13 Hakeem Olajuwon Texas Heroes .60 1.50
20C Hakeem Olajuwon CL .60 1.50

1996 Score Board Draft Day

COMPLETE SET (20) 6.00 15.00
COMMON CARD .12 .30
1A Allen Iverson Philadelphia 1.00 2.50
1B Allen Iverson Vancouver 1.00 2.50
1C Allen Iverson Minnesota 1.00 2.50
2A Marcus Camby Toronto .30 .75
2B Marcus Camby Vancouver .30 .75
2C Marcus Camby Minnesota .30 .75
3A Stephon Marbury Phoenix .50 1.25
3B Stephon Marbury Minnesota .50 1.25
3C Stephon Marbury Denver .50 1.25
4A Ray Allen Milwaukee .75 2.00
4B Ray Allen Minnesota .75 2.00
4C Ray Allen Dallas .75 2.00
5A Antoine Walker Minnesota .40 1.00
5B Antoine Walker New Jersey .40 1.00
5C Antoine Walker Boston .40 1.00
6 Shaquille O'Neal .50 1.25
7 Jason Kidd .30 .75
8 Joe Smith .15 .40
9 Damon Stoudamire .15 .40
10 Checklist .12 .30

1996 Score Board Frontier Phone Cards

9 Kobe Bryant $100 100.00 200.00
4 Allen Iverson $100

1997 Score Board Draft Day

1A Tim Duncan 5.00 12.00
1B Tim Duncan 5.00 12.00
1C Tim Duncan 5.00 12.00
2A Ron Mercer 1.00 2.50

2B Ron Mercer 1.00 2.50
2C Ron Mercer 1.00 2.50
3A Keith Van Horn 1.50 4.00
3B Keith Van Horn 1.50 4.00
3C Keith Van Horn 1.50 4.00

1996-97 Score Board All Sport PPF

The 1996-97 All Sport Past Present and Future set was issued in two series in six-card packs. The product contains original vintage and rookie cards of the top athletes from baseball, basketball, football and hockey as well as new cards of tomorrow's stars from each sport. Release date for series one was October 1996; series two was February 1997. There was also a gold parallel produced for this set. Series one gold cards were inserted 1:10 packs while series two had gold cards inserted at a 1:5 ratio.

COMPLETE SET (200) 6.00 15.00
1 Shaquille O'Neal .30 .75
2 Scottie Pippen .15 .40
3 Dikembe Mutombo .15 .40
4 Damon Stoudamire .15 .40
5 Brent Barry .07 .20
6 Michael Finley .15 .40
7 Allen Iverson .50 1.25
8 Marcus Camby .15 .40
9 Stephon Marbury .25 .60
10 Antonio McDyess .15 .40
11 Kobe Bryant 1.00 2.50
12 Ray Allen .40 1.00
13 Antoine Walker .30 .75
14 Erick Dampier .07 .20
15 Vitaly Potapenko .07 .20
16 Tony Delk .15 .40
17 John Wallace .15 .40
18 Roy Rogers .07 .20
19 Jerome Williams .15 .40
20 Travis Knight .07 .20
21 Ryan Minor .15 .40
22 Shawn Harvey .07 .20
23 Jason Sasser .07 .20
24 Doron Sheffer .07 .20
25 Malik Rose .15 .40
26 Jermaine O'Neal .08 .25
27 Mark Hendrickson .05 .15
28 Dontae' Jones .07 .20
29 Othella Harrington .15 .40
50 Shaquille O'Neal CL .15 .40
80 Allen Iverson .50 1.25
81 Jason Kidd .15 .40
82 Hakeem Olajuwon .15 .40
83 Alonzo Mourning .15 .40
84 Shareef Abdur-Rahim .30 .75
85 Glenn Robinson .15 .40
86 Rasheed Wallace .15 .40
101 Hakeem Olajuwon .15 .40
102 Alonzo Mourning .15 .40
103 Rasheed Wallace .15 .40
104 Glenn Robinson .15 .40
105 Tyus Edney .07 .20
106 Joe Smith .15 .40
107 Jason Kidd .15 .40
108 Shareef Abdur-Rahim .15 .40
109 Kerry Kittles .10 .30
110 Lorenzen Wright .15 .40
111 Samaki Walker .07 .20
112 Todd Fuller .07 .20
113 Steve Nash .30 .75
114 Jamie Feick .07 .20
115 Walter McCarty .07 .20
116 Jeff McInnis .07 .20
117 Derek Fisher .30 .75
118 Moochie Norris .07 .20
119 Joseph Blair .07 .20
120 Steve Hamer .07 .20
121 Randy Livingston .07 .20
122 Ron Riley .07 .20
123 Mark Pope .05 .15
124 Drew Barry .07 .20
125 Brian Evans .07 .20
150 Kobe Bryant CL .50 1.25
179 Allen Iverson .25 .60
180 Antonio McDyess .15 .40
181 Scottie Pippen .15 .40
182 Dikembe Mutombo .15 .40
183 Damon Stoudamire .15 .40
184 Stephon Marbury .15 .40
185 Kobe Bryant .60 1.50
186 Marcus Camby .15 .40

1996-97 Score Board All Sport PPF Gold

*GOLDS: 1.2X TO 3X BASIC CARDS
GOLD STATED ODDS SER.1 1:10/SER.2 1:5

1996-97 Score Board All Sport PPF Retro

Randomly inserted in series one packs at a rate of one in 35, this 10-card set was printed on old-style card stock.

COMPLETE SET (10) 12.00 30.00
R1 Allen Iverson 3.00 8.00
R3 Scottie Pippen 1.50 4.00
R5 Shaquille O'Neal 2.00 5.00
R6 Marcus Camby .60 1.50
R8 Damon Stoudamire .50 1.25

1996-97 Score Board All Sport PPF Revivals

Randomly inserted in series two packs at a rate of one in 35, this 10-card set was printed on old-style card stock.

COMPLETE SET (10) 12.00 30.00
REV1 Allen Iverson 3.00 8.00
REV2 Stephon Marbury 1.50 4.00
REV3 Alonzo Mourning .60 1.50
REV4 Shareef Abdur-Rahim 1.00 2.50
REV5 Kerry Kittles .50 1.25

1996 Score Board Autographed BK

This 50-card set was overshadowed by the autograph (3-4 per box) and memorabilia redemption (I per box) inserts found in this product. Six base cards found their way into each pack in 16-pack boxes. Each 12 box case was to contain one Shaquille O'Neal autographed memorabilia item, an average of one Allen Iverson autographed memorabilia item, and an average of one game or warm-up jersey. The card fronts have a grainy area on the left or right side of the card next to a color photo of a collegiate player. The backs contain another photo accompanied with collegiate statistics and a small biography.

COMPLETE SET (50) 4.00 10.00
1 Allen Iverson .75 2.00
2 Marcus Camby .25 .60
3 Shareef Abdur-Rahim .30 .75
4 Stephon Marbury .40 1.00
5 Ray Allen .60 1.50
6 Erick Dampier .15 .40
7 Antoine Walker .30 .75
8 John Wallace .15 .40
9 Kerry Kittles .15 .40
10 Lorenzen Wright .15 .40
11 Samaki Walker .15 .40
12 Todd Fuller .15 .40
13 Malik Rose .20 .50
14 Roy Rogers .15 .40
15 Kobe Bryant 1.50 4.00
16 Walter McCarty .15 .40
17 Ryan Minor .20 .50
18 Steve Nash .75 2.00
19 Jermaine O'Neal .40 1.00
20 Vitaly Potapenko .15 .40
21 Mark Pope .15 .40
22 Tony Delk .15 .40
23 Brian Evans .15 .40
24 Reggie Geary .15 .40
25 Dontae' Jones .15 .40
26 Travis Knight .15 .40
27 Priest Lauderdale .15 .40
28 Moochie Norris .15 .40
29 Efthmis Retzias .15 .40
30 Jerome Williams .15 .40
31 Jamie Feick .15 .40
32 Othella Harrington .15 .40
33 Mark Hendrickson .15 .40
34 Chris Robinson .15 .40
35 Randy Livingston .15 .40
36 Marcus Mann .15 .40
37 Darnell Robinson .15 .40
38 Jason Sasser .15 .40
39 Doron Sheffer .15 .40
40 Drew Barry .15 .40
41 Ben Davis .15 .40
42 Steve Hamer .15 .40
43 Ronnie Henderson .15 .40
44 Jeff McInnis .15 .40
45 Scottie Pippen .25 .60
46 Jason Kidd .25 .60
47 Alonzo Mourning .20 .50
48 Hakeem Olajuwon .20 .50
49 Damon Stoudamire .12 .30
50 Allen Iverson CL .40 1.00

1996 Score Board Autographed BK Autographs

Found at the rate of 3 to 4 per 16 pack box, these autographs were hand numbered and signed by 35 different players. Each autograph has a red parallel numbered of 400 and a silver parallel numbered of 325. The values for these parallels are listed below. 1A and 3A were made available via redemption cards only. The following cards do not exist: 7, 9, 11, 12, 19, 24, 25, 27, 29, 36, 41, 43, 45, 46, 47, 48, 49 and 50.

STATED ODDS 1:7
*RED AUTOS: .6X TO 1.5X BASE HI
RED PRINT RUN 240 TO 400 SER.#'d SETS
*SILVER AUTOS: .75X TO 2X BASE HI
SILVER PRINT RUN 325 SER.#'d SETS
1 Allen Iverson 50.00 100.00
2 Marcus Camby 6.00 15.00
3 Shareef Abdur-Rahim 8.00 20.00
3 Stephon Marbury 10.00 25.00
5 Ray Allen 8.00 20.00
6 Erick Dampier 1.50 4.00
8 John Wallace 1.50 4.00
10 Lorenzen Wright 1.50 4.00
13 Malik Rose 2.00 5.00
14 Roy Rogers 1.50 4.00
15 Kobe Bryant 50.00 120.00
16 Walter McCarty 1.50 4.00
17 Ryan Minor 2.00 5.00
18 Steve Nash 20.00 50.00
20 Vitaly Potapenko 1.50 4.00
21 Mark Pope 1.50 4.00
22 Tony Delk 1.50 4.00
23 Brian Evans 1.50 4.00
26 Travis Knight 1.50 4.00
28 Moochie Norris 1.50 4.00
30 Jerome Williams 1.50 4.00
31 Jamie Feick 1.50 4.00
32 Othella Harrington 1.50 4.00
33 Mark Hendrickson 1.50 4.00
34 Chris Robinson 1.50 4.00
35 Randy Livingston 1.50 4.00
37 Darnell Robinson 1.50 4.00
38 Jason Sasser 1.50 4.00
39 Doron Sheffer 1.50 4.00
40 Drew Barry 1.50 4.00
42 Steve Hamer 1.50 4.00
44 Jeff McInnis 1.50 4.00
NNO Derek Fisher 12.00 30.00
NNO Jamal Mashburn/1000 6.00 15.00
NNO Antonio McDyess/995 5.00 12.00
NNO Terrell Bell 1.50 4.00
NNO Ron Riley 1.50 4.00
NNO Shawn Harvey 1.50 4.00

1996 Score Board Autographed BK Pure Performance

Inserted at the rate of 1 in 10 packs, this 30-card set highlights thirty pro and collegiate players. The cards have the insert name embossed on the front in a silver metallic background behind a color player photo. The backs have another player photo and some biographical information. The cards are numbered with a "PP" prefix.

COMPLETE SET (30) 30.00 80.00
STATED ODDS 1:10
*GOLD: .75X TO 2X VALUE
STATED ODDS 1:50
PP1 Allen Iverson 5.00 12.00
PP2 Marcus Camby 1.50 4.00
PP3 Shareef Abdur-Rahim 2.00 5.00
PP4 Stephon Marbury 2.50 6.00
PP5 Ray Allen 4.00 10.00
PP6 Erick Dampier 1.00 2.50
PP7 Antoine Walker 2.00 5.00
PP8 John Wallace 1.00 2.50
PP9 Kerry Kittles 1.00 2.50
PP10 Lorenzen Wright 1.00 2.50
PP11 Samaki Walker 1.00 2.50
PP12 Todd Fuller 1.00 2.50
PP13 Roy Rogers 1.00 2.50
PP14 Kobe Bryant 10.00 25.00
PP15 Walter McCarty 1.00 2.50
PP16 Ryan Minor 1.25 3.00
PP17 Steve Nash 5.00 12.00
PP18 Jermaine O'Neal 2.50 6.00
PP19 Vitaly Potapenko 1.00 2.50
PP20 Tony Delk 1.00 2.50
PP21 Brian Evans 1.00 2.50
PP22 Reggie Geary 1.00 2.50
PP23 Dontae' Jones 1.00 2.50
PP24 Travis Knight 1.00 2.50
PP25 Othella Harrington 1.00 2.50
PP26 Alonzo Mourning 1.25 3.00
PP27 Scottie Pippen 1.50 4.00
PP28 Jason Kidd 1.50 4.00
PP29 Damon Stoudamire .75 2.00
PP30 Hakeem Olajuwon 1.25 3.00

1997 Score Board Autographed BK

The 1997-98 Score Board Autographed Basketball set was issued in one series totalling 50 cards and was distributed in five-card packs. The fronts feature color action player photos printed on foil-stamped cards. The backs carry player information.

COMPLETE SET (50) 4.00 10.00
1 Tim Duncan .75 2.00
2 Ron Mercer .15 .40
3 Tracy McGrady .60 1.50
4 Johnny Taylor .12 .30
5 Tim Thomas .25 .60
6 John Thomas .12 .30
7 Scot Pollard .12 .30
8 Brevin Knight .12 .30
9 Keith Booth .12 .30
10 Charles Smith .12 .30
11 Kobe Bryant .60 1.50
12 Kerry Kittles .07 .20
13 Marcus Camby .12 .30
14 Paul Grant .12 .30
15 Damon Stoudamire .12 .30
16 Shareef Abdur-Rahim .12 .30
17 Antonio Daniels .12 .30
18 Stephon Marbury .15 .40
19 Kelvin Cato .12 .30
20 Allen Iverson .25 .60
21 Derek Anderson .12 .30
22 Rasheed Wallace .12 .30
23 Austin Croshere .10 .25
24 Hakeem Olajuwon .15 .40
25 Clyde Drexler .15 .40
26 Adonal Foyle .12 .30
27 Alonzo Mourning .15 .40
28 Ed Gray .12 .30
29 Antonio McDyess .10 .25
30 Ray Allen .15 .40
31 Joe Smith .10 .25
32 Keith Van Horn .25 .60
33 Tony Battie .12 .30
34 Bobby Jackson .15 .40
35 Anthony Parker .12 .30
36 Scottie Pippen .20 .50
37 Chauncey Billups .40 1.00
38 Jacque Vaughn .12 .30
39 Danny Fortson .12 .30
40 Olivier Saint-Jean .12 .30
41 Marc Jackson .12 .30
42 God Shammgod .12 .30
43 Chris Anstey .12 .30
44 DeJuan Wheat .12 .30
45 Serge Zwikker .12 .30
46 Jason Lawson .12 .30
47 Antoine Walker .12 .30
48 Charles O'Bannon .12 .30
49 Kebu Stewart .12 .30
50 Mark Sanford .12 .30

1997 Score Board Autographed BK Tim Duncan

Randomly inserted in packs at one in 18, this 10-card set features a tribute to Tim Duncan, the number one pick of the 1997 NBA Draft.

COMPLETE SET (10) 10.00 25.00
COMMON CARD (SD1-SD10) 1.25 3.00
STATED ODDS 1:18

1997 Score Board Autographed BK Gold Autographs

Randomly inserted one per every 18 hobby only packs, this limited 65-card set features hand-numbered autographed action player photos with gold foil highlights. The numbers after the players' names indicate how many cards they signed.

STATED ODDS 1:18 HOBBY PACKS
PRINT RUNS LISTED BELOW
1 Danya Abrams/266 1.50 4.00
2 Ray Allen/300 10.00 25.00
3 Peter Aluma/300 1.50 4.00
4 Derek Anderson/300 1.50 4.00
5 Chris Anstey/300 1.50 4.00
6 Tunji Awojobi/300 1.50 4.00
7 Tony Battie/291 1.50 4.00
8 Chauncey Billups/300 5.00 12.00
9 Marcus Camby/300 4.00 10.00
10 Kelvin Cato/300 1.50 4.00
11 Lorenzen Coleman/300 1.50 4.00
12 James Collins/300 1.50 4.00
13 Austin Croshere/269 1.25 3.00
14 Erick Dampier/280 1.50 4.00
15 Harold Deane/300 1.50 4.00
16 Tony Delk/295 1.50 4.00
17 Tim Duncan/221 50.00 120.00
18 Eddie Elisma/300 1.50 4.00
19 Nate Erdmann/278 1.50 4.00
20 Derek Fisher/300 3.00 8.00
21 Isaac Fontaine/290 1.50 4.00
22 Danny Fortson/300 1.50 4.00
23 Kiwane Garris/266 1.50 4.00
24 Paul Grant/293 1.50 4.00
25 Steve Hamer/299 1.50 4.00
26 Othella Harrington/300 1.50 4.00
27 Otis Hill/300 1.50 4.00
28 Allen Iverson/45 75.00 150.00
29 Bobby Jackson/288 2.00 5.00
30 Anthony Johnson/300 1.50 4.00
31 Kerry Kittles/300 2.50 6.00
32 Brevin Knight/300 1.50 4.00
33 Travis Knight/300 1.50 4.00
34 Jason Lawson/300 1.50 4.00
35 Quincy Lee/300 1.50 4.00
36 Gordon Malone/296 1.50 4.00
37 Stephon Marbury/300 6.00 15.00
38 Walter McCarty/297 1.50 4.00
39 Antonio McDyess/293 4.00 10.00
40 Tracy McGrady/86 50.00 100.00
40A Tracy McGrady/300 12.00 30.00
41 Alonzo Mourning/300 8.00 20.00
42 Charles O'Bannon/268 1.50 4.00
43 Ed O'Bannon/164 1.50 4.00
44 Anthony Parker/300 1.50 4.00
45 Scot Pollard/300 1.50 4.00
46 Malik Rose/259 1.50 4.00
47 Olivier Saint Jean/300 1.50 4.00
48 Mark Sanford/290 1.50 4.00
49 Shea Seals/300 1.50 4.00
50 God Shammgod/500 1.50 4.00
51 Alvin Sims/300 1.50 4.00
52 Charles Smith/300 1.50 4.00
53 Joe Smith/289 2.50 6.00
54 Kebu Stewart/300 1.50 4.00
55 Damon Stoudamire/284 4.00 10.00
56 John Thomas/300 1.50 4.00
57 Tim Thomas/201 3.00 8.00
58 Jacque Vaughn/300 1.50 4.00
59 Antoine Walker/290 6.00 15.00
60 John Wallace/300 2.50 6.00
61 Rasheed Wallace/300 6.00 15.00
62 Reggie Welch/300 1.50 4.00
63 DeJuan Wheat/300 1.50 4.00
64 Alvin Williams/300 1.50 4.00
65 Jerome Williams/300 1.50 4.00
66 Serge Zwikker/282 1.50 4.00

1997 Score Board Autographed BK Platinum Autographs

Randomly inserted one in every nine retail only packs, this 53-card set features autographed color action player photos with platinum foil highlights. Only 200 of each player's card were signed and produced, except for Othella Harrington with only 197 and Charles O'Bannon and Kebu Stewart with 198 each.

STATED ODDS: 1:9 RETAIL PACKS
STATED PRINT RUN 200 SETS
1 Shareef Abdur-Rahim 6.00 15.00
2 Danya Abrams 2.00 5.00
3 Chris Anstey 2.00 5.00
4 Peter Aluma 2.00 5.00
5 Tunji Awojobi 2.00 5.00
6 Tony Battie 2.00 5.00
7 Chauncey Billups 6.00 15.00
8 Kelvin Cato 2.00 5.00
9 Lorenzo Coleman 2.00 5.00
10 James Collins 2.00 5.00
11 Austin Croshere 1.50 4.00
12 Harold Deane 2.00 5.00
13 Eddie Elisma 2.00 5.00
14 Nate Erdmann 2.00 5.00
15 Derek Fisher 4.00 10.00
16 Isaac Fontaine 2.00 5.00
17 Danny Fortson 2.00 5.00
18 Kiwane Garris 2.00 5.00
19 Paul Grant 2.00 5.00
20 Steve Hamer 2.00 5.00
21 Othella Harrington/197 2.00 5.00
22 Otis Hill 2.00 5.00
23 Bobby Jackson 2.50 6.00
24 Anthony Johnson 2.00 5.00
25 Brevin Knight 2.00 5.00
26 Travis Knight 2.00 5.00
27 Jason Lawson 2.00 5.00
28 Quincy Lee 2.00 5.00
29 Gordon Malone 2.00 5.00
30 Stephon Marbury 10.00 25.00
31 Walter McCarty 2.00 5.00
32 Charles O'Bannon/198 2.00 5.00
33 Ed O'Bannon 2.00 5.00
34 Anthony Parker 2.00 5.00
35 Scot Pollard 2.00 5.00
36 Malik Rose 2.00 5.00
37 Olivier Saint Jean 2.00 5.00
38 Mark Sanford 2.00 5.00
39 Shea Seals 2.00 5.00
40 Alvin Sims 2.00 5.00
41 Charles Smith 2.00 5.00
42 Kebu Stewart/198 2.00 5.00
43 John Thomas 2.00 5.00
44 Tim Thomas 4.00 10.00
45 Jacque Vaughn 2.00 5.00
46 Antoine Walker 8.00 20.00
47 John Wallace 3.00 8.00
48 Rasheed Wallace 8.00 20.00
49 Reggie Welch 2.00 5.00
50 DeJuan Wheat 2.00 5.00
51 Alvin Williams 2.00 5.00
52 Jerome Williams 2.00 5.00
53 Serge Zwikker 2.00 5.00

1997 Score Board Autographed BK Silver Autographs

Randomly inserted in hobby and retail packs at the rate of two in nine, this 23-card set features autographed color action player photos with silver-foil highlights.

STATED ODDS 2:9 HOBBY/RETAIL
LOTTERY/SUPERSTAR HOBBY ONLY
12 CARDS ONLY IN RETAIL PACKS
LP1 Derek Anderson 1.50 4.00
LP2 Danya Abrams 1.50 4.00
LP3 Tony Battie 1.50 4.00
LP4 Chauncey Billups SP 5.00 12.00
LP5 Austin Croshere 1.25 3.00
LP6 Erick Dampier 1.50 4.00
LP7 Danny Fortson 1.50 4.00
LP8 Brevin Knight SP 2.00 5.00
LP9 Tracy McGrady SP 12.00 30.00
LP10 Ed O'Bannon SP 1.50 4.00
LP11 Olivier Saint-Jean 1.50 4.00
LP12 Tim Thomas 3.00 8.00
SS1 Shareef Abdur-Rahim 6.00 15.00
SS2 Ray Allen SP 8.00 20.00
SS3 Kobe Bryant 30.00 80.00
SS4 Marcus Camby SP 4.00 10.00
SS5 Allen Iverson SP 15.00 40.00
SS6 Kerry Kittles SP 2.50 6.00
SS7 Stephon Marbury 8.00 20.00
SS8 Antonio McDyess SP 4.00 10.00
SS9 Alonzo Mourning SP 8.00 20.00
SS10 Damon Stoudamire SP 4.00 10.00
SS11 Antoine Walker 6.00 15.00
SS12 Rasheed Wallace 8.00 20.00

1997 Score Board Autographed BK Trademark Slam

Randomly inserted in packs at the rate of one in eight, this 30-card set features color action player photos representing the greatest dunks in each pictured player's career printed on foil-stamped cards.

COMPLETE SET (30) 10.00 25.00
STATED ODDS 1:8
1 Stephon Marbury .50 1.25
2 Scottie Pippen .60 1.50
3 Antonio McDyess .30 .75
4 Alonzo Mourning .50 1.25
5 Clyde Drexler .50 1.25
6 Joe Smith .30 .75
7 Hakeem Olajuwon .50 1.25
8 Tim Duncan 2.50 6.00
9 Ron Mercer .50 1.25
10 Tracy McGrady 2.00 5.00
11 Paul Grant .40 1.00
12 Tim Thomas .75 2.00
13 John Thomas .40 1.00
14 Scot Pollard .40 1.00
15 Kobe Bryant 2.00 5.00
16 Kerry Kittles .25 .60
17 Marcus Camby .40 1.00
18 Shareef Abdur-Rahim .40 1.00
19 Allen Iverson .75 2.00
20 Derek Anderson .40 1.00
21 Rasheed Wallace .40 1.00
22 Austin Croshere .30 .75
23 Adonal Foyle .40 1.00
24 Danny Fortson .40 1.00
25 Keith Van Horn .75 2.00
26 Tony Battie .40 1.00
27 Olivier Saint-Jean .40 1.00
28 Kelvin Cato .40 1.00
29 Jason Lawson .40 1.00
30 Antoine Walker .40 1.00

1996-97 Score Board Autographed Collection

Each box of Score Board Autographed Collection contains 16 packs containing six cards. The 50-card regular set includes top athletes from all four major team sports. According to Score Board, a total of 1,500 sequentially numbered cases were produced.

COMPLETE SET (50) 5.00 12.00
1 Damon Stoudamire .07 .20
2 Scottie Pippen .15 .40
3 Jason Kidd .15 .40
4 Hakeem Olajuwon .15 .40
5 Alonzo Mourning .15 .40
6 Antonio McDyess .10 .30
7 Allen Iverson .75 2.00
8 Rasheed Wallace .15 .40
9 Glenn Robinson .10 .30
10 Marcus Camby .30 .75
11 Shareef Abdur-Rahim .40 1.00
12 Stephon Marbury .25 .60
13 Kobe Bryant 1.50 4.00
14 Ray Allen .60 1.50
15 Antoine Walker .30 .75
16 Kerry Kittles .10 .30
17 John Wallace .15 .40

1996-97 Score Board Autographed Collection Autographs

Each box of Autographed Collection contains an average of four autographed cards. There are two different varieties: silver foil stamped cards with no individual serial numbering inserted at a rate of 1:7 packs, and Gold foil serial numbered autographs inserted at a rate of 1:16 packs.

2 Shareef Abdur-Rahim 5.00 12.00
3 Ray Allen 6.00 15.00
4 Drew Barry 2.00 5.00
6 Kobe Bryant 50.00 100.00
7 Marcus Camby 3.00 8.00
12 Tony Delk 2.50 6.00
20 Othella Harrington 2.50 6.00
23 Allen Iverson 25.00 50.00
28 Kerry Kittles 2.50 6.00
29 Travis Knight 2.00 5.00
30 Stephon Marbury 8.00 20.00
32 Walter McCarty 2.00 5.00
38 Vitaly Potapenko 2.00 5.00
39 Roy Rogers 2.00 5.00
47 Antoine Walker 4.00 10.00
49 John Wallace 2.50 6.00
50 Jerome Williams 2.50 6.00
52 Lorenzen Wright 2.50 6.00

1996-97 Score Board Autographed Collection Autographs Gold

*UNLISTED GOLD: .6X TO 1.5X BASIC AU
6 Kobe Bryant/300 75.00 150.00
23 Allen Iverson/250 50.00 100.00
47 Antoine Walker/350 8.00 20.00

1996-97 Score Board Autographed Collection Game Breakers

This 30-card insert set was printed on metallic stock and has two versions-- regular and gold. The insertion ratio is 1:10 packs for regular inserts and 1:50 for the gold foil version.

COMPLETE SET (30) 25.00 60.00
*GOLD: .8X TO 2X BASIC INSERTS
GB1 Damon Stoudamire .60 1.50
GB2 Scottie Pippen .75 2.00
GB3 Jason Kidd 1.25 3.00
GB4 Ray Allen 1.25 3.00
GB5 Alonzo Mourning .75 2.00
GB6 Joe Smith .60 1.50
GB7 Allen Iverson 3.00 8.00
GB8 Rasheed Wallace .75 2.00
GB9 Antoine Walker 1.00 2.50
GB10 Marcus Camby 1.50 4.00
GB11 Shareef Abdur-Rahim UER 1.50 4.00
GB12 Stephon Marbury 2.50 3.00
GB13 Kobe Bryant 5.00 12.00

1997-98 Score Board Autographed Collection

The 1998 Autographed Collection set was issued in one series totaling 50 cards with players from baseball, basketball, football and hockey. The product's major draw was an average of five autographed cards and one memorabilia redemption card per 18-pack box. The regular autographs were inserted 1:4.5 packs, the Blue Ribbon autographs were inserted 1:18 packs. The one-per box memorabilia redemption cards were not all redeemed due to the fact that Score Board, Inc. filed for bankruptcy a few months after the product's release. Score Board also released a "Strongbox Collection" that original retailed for around $125. Each Strongbox included a parallel of this 50 card set, one star player autographed baseball with holder, one star player autographed 8" x 10", one Athletic Excellence card and One Sports City USA card.

COMPLETE SET (50) 5.00 12.00
1 Tim Duncan .50 1.25
5 Allen Iverson .40 1.00
7 Scottie Pippen .15 .40
9 Stephon Marbury .20 .50
14 Keith Van Horn .07 .20
15 Tiki Barber .30 .75
16 Kobe Bryant .75 2.00
18 Tim Thomas .07 .20
20 Hakeem Olajuwon .15 .40
22 Clyde Drexler .15 .40
24 Adonal Foyle .07 .20
25 Alonzo Mourning .15 .40
30 Joe Smith .08 .25
32 Tony Battie .07 .20
37 Chauncey Billups .07 .20
39 Tracy McGrady .40 1.00
41 Antoine Walker .30 .75
45 Ron Mercer .15 .40
47 Antonio Daniels .07 .20
50 Kerry Kittles .15 .40

1997-98 Score Board Autographed Collection Athletic Excellence

These 3 1/2" x 5" cards, were inserted one per Score Board "Strongbox Collection" box that originally retailed for around $125. Each Strongbox also included a parallel of the 1998 Autograph Collection 50 card set, one star player autographed baseball with holder, one star player autographed 8" x 10" and one Sports City USA card. Each card is sequentially numbered out of 750.

COMPLETE SET (12) 10.00 25.00
AE1 Chauncey Billups .75 2.00
AE6 Tim Thomas .75 2.00
AE9 Tim Duncan 3.00 8.00
AE11 Tracy McGrady 2.00 5.00
AE12 Keith Van Horn 1.25 3.00

1997-98 Score Board Autographed Collection Autographs

One autographed card was available in one in every 4.5 Score Board Autograph Collection packs. The cards have a circular player photograph in the middle with a white oval below that includes a player's autograph. The card backs read, "Congratulations! You have received an authentic Score Board autographed card." There were also Kerry Wood and Greg Jones cards produced that appear on the marketplace later, although not inserted into packs. The cards are unnumbered and listed below in alphabetical order.

6 Tony Delk BK 2.00 5.00
13 Brevin Knight BK 2.00 5.00
16 Anthony Parker BK 3.00 8.00
21 Charles Smith BK 1.50 4.00
22 John Thomas BK 1.50 4.00
25 Lorenzen Wright BK 1.50 4.00

1997-98 Score Board Autographed Collection Blue Ribbon Autographs

One Blue Ribbon autographed card was available in one in every 18 Score Board Autograph Collection packs. The cards have a circular player photograph with a blue ribbon border in the middle with a white oval below that includes a player's autograph. The cards are hand numbered out of the amounts listed below in the upper right hand corner. The card backs read, "Congratulations! You have received an authentic Score Board autographed card." The cards are unnumbered and listed below in alphabetical order. A Warrick Dunn card was later released through a home shopping network show. Some Kobe Bryant cards have surfaced in un-signed form and can often be found with forged autographs on the front. No authentic Kobe signed and numbered cards are known although the Congratulations Score Board message is included on the cardbacks.

1 Shareef Abdur-Rahim/570 6.00 15.00
2 Tony Battie/650 2.00 5.00
3 Marcus Camby/675 3.00 8.00
4 Austin Croshere/1350 2.00 5.00
6 Tim Duncan/210 75.00 200.00
7 Danny Fortson/1350 2.00 5.00
9 Kerry Kittles/650 2.00 5.00
10 Stephon Marbury/1300 5.00 12.00
11 Tracy McGrady/670 8.00 20.00
12 Scottie Pippen/90 60.00 120.00
P2 Kobe Bryant Unsigned 6.00 15.00

1997-98 Score Board Autographed Collection Sports City USA

These multi-player, city-themed cards were inserted one in nine Autographed Collection packs. There is also a Strongbox parallel found one per Score Board "Strongbox Collection" box that originally retailed for around $125. Each Strongbox also included a parallel of the 1998 Autograph Collection 50 card set, one star player autographed baseball with holder, one star player autographed 8" x 10"and one Athletic Excellence jumbo card..

COMPLETE SET (15) 10.00 25.00
SC1 A.Foyle/J.Smith/S.Young .75 2.00
SC3 Olajuwon/Drexler/Hidalgo .60 1.50
SC4 K.Wood/Pippen/D.Autry .60 1.50
SC5 R.Allen/B.Favre 2.00 5.00
SC6 K.Bryant/A.Beltre 2.00 5.00
SC7 T.Thomas/D.Staley/J.D.Drew 1.00 2.50
SC8 A.Mourning/Y.Green .50 1.25
SC9 J.Thornton/C.Billups .40 1.00
SC12 W.Helms/Hanspard/E.Gray .40 1.00
SC13 S.Marbury/D.Rudd .40 1.00
SC14 J.Payton/Barber/V.Horn .75 2.00
SC15 M.Drews/B.Westbrook/Pollard .75 2.00

1997-98 Score Board Autographed Collection Sports City USA Strongbox

*STRONGBOX/600: .8X TO 2X BASIC INSERTS

1997-98 Score Board Autographed Collection Strongbox

*STRONGBOX: .8X TO 2X BASIC CARDS

1997 Score Board Players Club

The 70 cards that make-up this set are a grouping from baseball, basketball, football and hockey players. Card fronts are full colored action shots, with professional team names air-brushed out. The card backs contain 1997 projected statistics and biographical information. Along with the number 1 Die-Cuts and Play Back inserts, vintage cards were the major draw to this product. One in 32 packs contained a vintage card from 1909-1979 from any of the four sports. An original Honus Wagner T206 card was offered as a redemption in 1:153,600 packs. Also, one vintage wax pack was available via redemption card in one in every 32 packs.

COMPLETE SET (70) 5.00 12.00
4 Shareef Abdur-Rahim .15 .40
8 Ray Allen .15 .40
9 Derek Anderson .07 .20
15 Tony Battie .07 .20
16 Kobe Bryant .50 1.25
18 Marcus Camby .07 .20
19 Keith Van Horn .07 .20
23 Chauncey Billups .10 .30
24 Scottie Pippen .15 .40
29 Jacque Vaughn .07 .20
30 Tim Thomas .07 .20
31 Clyde Drexler .15 .40
35 Joe Smith .07 .20
36 Antoine Walker .15 .40
40 Hakeem Olajuwon .15 .40
41 Alonzo Mourning .15 .40
43 Stephon Marbury .15 .40
45 Kerry Kittles .07 .20
49 Allen Iverson .25 .60
52 Antonio Daniels .10 .30
55 Olivier Saint-Jean .07 .20
58 Tracy McGrady 1.00 2.50
62 Johnny Taylor .07 .20
64 Austin Croshere .08 .25
66 Brevin Knight .08 .25
68 Ron Mercer .15 .40

1997 Score Board Players Club #1 Die-Cuts

Each player in this 20 card set, inserted one in 32 packs, was at one time selected as a first round selection in the professional draft. The cards are die-cut in the shape of a "1" and have gold foil on the left border. The backs contain pre-professional biographical information and (if applicable) statistics from their last college or minor league season. The card numbers have a "D" prefix.

COMPLETE SET (20) 25.00 60.00
D1 Allen Iverson 4.00 10.00
D5 Hakeem Olajuwon 1.50 4.00
D6 Joe Smith 1.25 3.00
D8 Shareef Abdur-Rahim 1.50 4.00
D9 Stephon Marbury 2.00 5.00
D12 Keith Van Horn 1.25 3.00
D13 Kobe Bryant 8.00 20.00
D14 Chauncey Billups 1.25 3.00
D16 Tim Thomas 1.25 3.00
D17 Tony Battie 1.25 3.00
D20 Antonio Daniels 1.25 3.00

1997 Score Board Players Club Play Backs

This 15-card set highlights stars form all four major U.S. sports. The card fronts have a player photo superimposed on a photo of the player's jersey. To the left is a movie reel design with individual action shots. The backs have another player photograph and biographical information. The cards are numbered with a "PB" prefix.

COMPLETE SET (15) 30.00 80.00
STATED ODDS 1:32
PB5 Scottie Pippen 2.50 6.00
PB7 Allen Iverson 4.00 10.00
PB9 Marcus Camby 1.50 4.00
PB10 Kobe Bryant 8.00 20.00
PB11 Hakeem Olajuwon 1.50 4.00
PB12 Stephon Marbury 2.00 5.00
PB14 Joe Smith 1.25 3.00
PB15 John Wallace 1.25 3.00

1996 Score Board Rookies

The 1996 Basketball Rookies set was issued in one series totaling 100 cards. The 10-card packs retailed for $1.99 each. Each box contained two original "vintage" rookie cards (1986-1995) from a list of several players. Also in packs were two randomly inserted insert sets: College Jerseys and Die Cuts.

COMPLETE SET (100) 5.00 12.00
SUBSET CARDS HALF VALUE OF BASE
1 Allen Iverson .75 2.00
2 Marcus Camby .25 .60
3 Stephon Marbury .40 1.00
4 Shareef Abdur-Rahim .30 .75
5 Ray Allen .60 1.50
6 Erick Dampier .15 .40
7 Antoine Walker .30 .75
8 John Wallace .15 .40
9 Kerry Kittles .15 .40
10 Lorenzen Wright .15 .40
11 Samaki Walker .15 .40
12 Todd Fuller .15 .40
13 Jaron Boone .15 .40
14 Roy Rogers .15 .40
15 Kobe Bryant 1.50 4.00
16 Walter McCarty .15 .40
17 Ryan Minor .20 .50
18 Steve Nash .75 2.00
19 Jermaine O'Neal .40 1.00
20 Vitaly Potapenko .15 .40
21 Kwame Evans .15 .40
22 Tony Delk .15 .40
23 Brian Evans .15 .40
24 Dion Cross .15 .40
25 Dontae' Jones .15 .40
26 Travis Knight .15 .40
27 Priest Lauderdale .15 .40
28 Moochie Norris .15 .40
29 Efthmis Retzias .15 .40
30 Jerome Williams .15 .40
31 Jamie Feick .15 .40
32 Othella Harrington .15 .40
33 Mark Hendrickson .15 .40
34 Chris Robinson .15 .40
35 Randy Livingston .15 .40
36 Marcus Mann .15 .40
37 Darnell Robinson .15 .40
38 Jason Sasser .15 .40
39 Doron Sheffer .15 .40
40 Kevin Simpson .15 .40
41 Joseph Blair .15 .40
42 Eric Gingold .15 .40
43 Steve Hamer .15 .40
44 Ronnie Henderson .15 .40
45 Jeff McInnis .15 .40
46 Dante Calabria .15 .40
47 Martin Muursepp .15 .40
48 Mark Pope .15 .40
49 Ron Riley .15 .40
50 Shandon Anderson .15 .40
51 Derrick Battie .15 .40
52 Derek Fisher .30 .75
53 Kevin Granger .15 .40
53AU Kevin Granger AU 2.00 5.00
54 Shawn Harvey .15 .40
55 Bernard Hopkins .15 .40
56 Raimonds Miglinieks .15 .40
57 Tim Moore .15 .40
58 Carlos Strong .15 .40
59 Chucky Atkins .15 .40
60 Drew Barry .15 .40
61 Terrell Bell .15 .40
62 Donta Bright .15 .40
63 Marcus Brown .15 .40
64 William Cunningham .15 .40
65 Katu Davis .15 .40
66 Ben Davis .15 .40
67 Adrian Griffin .15 .40
68 Darvin Ham .15 .40
69 Art Long .15 .40
70 Jerome Lambert .15 .40
71 Amal McCaskill .15 .40
72 Mingo Johnson .15 .40
73 Dametri Hill .15 .40
74 Michael Lloyd .15 .40
75 Malik Rose .20 .50
76 Jeff Nordgaard .15 .40
77 Duane Simpkins .15 .40
78 Russ Millard .15 .40
79 Allen Iverson CL .40 1.00
80 Marcus Camby CL .12 .30
81 Allen Iverson AA .40 1.00
82 Marcus Camby AA .12 .30
83 Stephon Marbury AA .20 .50
84 Ray Allen AA .30 .75
85 Kerry Kittles AA .07 .20
86 Erick Dampier AA .07 .20
87 Shareef Abdur-Rahim AA .15 .40
88 John Wallace AA .07 .20
89 Lorenzen Wright AA .07 .20
90 Tony Delk AA .07 .20
91 Shaquille O'Neal BG .40 1.00
92 Hakeem Olajuwon BG .20 .50

93 Joe Smith BG .12 .30
94 Brent Barry BG .12 .30
95 Jason Kidd BG .25 .60
96 Scottie Pippen BG .25 .60
97 Damon Stoudamire BG .12 .30
98 Alonzo Mourning BG .20 .50
99 Rasheed Wallace BG .20 .50
100 Glenn Robinson BG .12 .30
BR1 Allen Iverson/1996* 6.00 15.00

1996 Score Board Rookies College Jerseys

Randomly inserted in packs at a rate of one in 10, this 30-card set highlights professional and college athletes on a vertical designed card. The fronts have a photo of the player next to a textured college jersey (not an actual jersey). The backs have another photo and some biographical information. The cards are numbered with a "J" prefix. There was also a Shaquille O'Neal Los Angeles card, inserted one in 432 packs, that tributes his move from the east to west coast. The jersey on this card in not textured. That card is not included in the set price.

COMPLETE SET (30) 15.00 40.00
STATED ODDS 1:10
SHAQ LA: STATED ODDS 1:432
J1 Allen Iverson 3.00 8.00
J2 Stephon Marbury 1.50 4.00
J3 Marcus Camby 1.00 2.50
J4 Ray Allen 2.50 6.00
J5 Erick Dampier .60 1.50
J6 John Wallace .60 1.50
J7 Antoine Walker 1.25 3.00
J8 Lorenzen Wright .60 1.50
J9 Kerry Kittles .60 1.50
J10 Todd Fuller .60 1.50
J11 Samaki Walker .60 1.50
J12 Roy Rogers .60 1.50
J13 Walter McCarty .60 1.50
J14 Dontae' Jones .60 1.50
J15 Steve Nash 3.00 8.00
J16 Jerome Williams .60 1.50
J17 Ryan Minor .75 2.00
J18 Shareef Abdur-Rahim 1.25 3.00
J19 Brian Evans .60 1.50
J20 Travis Knight .60 1.50
J21 Mark Hendrickson .60 1.50
J22 Tony Delk .60 1.50
J23 Ronnie Henderson .60 1.50
J24 Drew Barry .60 1.50
J25 Damon Stoudamire .50 1.25
J26 Shaquille O'Neal 1.50 4.00
J27 Joe Smith .50 1.25
J28 Jason Kidd 1.00 2.50
J29 Alonzo Mourning .75 2.00
J30 Rasheed Wallace .75 2.00
LA34 Shaquille O'Neal LA 6.00 15.00

1996 Score Board Rookies Die Cuts

Randomly inserted in packs at a rate of one in 50, this 30-card set highlights, in order, the top 29 picks of the 1997 draft. (In addition, Damon Stoudamire was thrown in at the end for good measure.) Each card is die-cut in the shape of a "one". The players name is vertically written in blue on a gold strip on the left of the card next to his photo. The backs have another photo and some information about his place in the draft. The cards are numbered "X of 30".

COMPLETE SET (30) 25.00 60.00
STATED ODDS 1:50
1 Allen Iverson 5.00 12.00
2 Marcus Camby 1.50 4.00
3 Shareef Abdur-Rahim 2.00 5.00
4 Stephon Marbury 2.50 6.00
5 Ray Allen 4.00 10.00
6 Antoine Walker 2.00 5.00
7 Lorenzen Wright 1.00 2.50
8 Kerry Kittles 1.00 2.50
9 Samaki Walker 1.00 2.50
10 Erick Dampier 1.00 2.50
11 Todd Fuller 1.00 2.50
12 Vitaly Potapenko 1.00 2.50
13 Kobe Bryant 10.00 25.00
14 Shaquille O'Neal 5.00 12.00
15 Steve Nash 5.00 12.00
16 Tony Delk 1.00 2.50
17 Jermaine O'Neal 2.50 6.00
18 John Wallace 1.00 2.50
19 Walter McCarty 1.00 2.50
20 Jason Kidd 3.00 8.00
21 Dontae' Jones 1.00 2.50
22 Roy Rogers 1.00 2.50
23 Efthimis Retzias 1.00 2.50
24 Derek Fisher 2.00 5.00
25 Martin Muursepp 1.00 2.50
26 Jerome Williams 1.00 2.50
27 Brian Evans 1.00 2.50
28 Priest Lauderdale 1.00 2.50
29 Travis Knight 1.00 2.50
30 Damon Stoudamire 1.50 4.00
NNO Damon Stoudamire PROMO .40 1.00

1997 Score Board Rookies

The 1997 Basketball Rookies set was issued in one series totaling 100 cards and was distributed in eight-card packs with a suggested retail price of $2.79. The fronts feature borderless color action player photos. The backs carry player information. Each box of the Hobby-exclusive version contained an average of one vintage card from 50 top players of all time or one original, unopened wax pack from one of the top basketball series ever produced. Redemption cards were inserted for all cards with a book value of more than $200 and for a select few original wax packs. Each box also contained an average of one autographed card signed by a first round pick from the 1994-1997 drafts. These cards were preproduced cards that were signed and stamped with a ScoreBoard seal. The Retail boxes did not contain an autographed card, but contained two vintage cards or packs.

COMPLETE SET (100) 6.00 15.00
1 Tim Duncan .75 2.00
2 Ron Mercer .15 .40
3 Marc Jackson .12 .30
4 Tunji Awojobi .12 .30
5 Reggie Freeman .12 .30
6 John Thomas .12 .30
7 Scot Pollard .12 .30
8 Brevin Knight .12 .30
9 Keith Booth .12 .30
10 Reggie Welch .12 .30
11 Alvin Sims .12 .30
12 Victor Page .12 .30
13 Jason Lawson .12 .30
14 Paul Grant .12 .30
15 Kiwane Garris .12 .30
16 Eddie Elisma .12 .30
17 Antonio Daniels .12 .30
18 James Collins .12 .30
19 Kelvin Cato .12 .30
20 Peter Aluma .12 .30
21 Derek Anderson .12 .30
22 Lorenzo Coleman .12 .30
23 Austin Croshere .10 .25
24 Harold Deane .12 .30
25 Nate Erdmann .12 .30
26 Adonal Foyle .12 .30
27 Tony Gonzalez .12 .30
28 Ed Gray .12 .30
29 Quincy Lee .12 .30
30 Charles O'Bannon .12 .30
31 Shea Seals .12 .30
32 Keith Van Horn .25 .60
33 Tony Battie .12 .30
34 Bobby Jackson .15 .40
35 Anthony Parker .12 .30
36 Kebu Stewart .12 .30
37 Chris Anstey .12 .30
38 Jacque Vaughn .12 .30
39 DeJuan Wheat .12 .30
40 Anthony Johnson .12 .30
41 Danny Fortson .12 .30
42 Mark Sanford .12 .30
43 Jerald Honeycutt .12 .30
44 Olivier Saint-Jean .12 .30
45 Chauncey Billups .40 1.00
46 Isaac Fontaine .12 .30
47 Otis Hill .12 .30
48 Tracy McGrady .60 1.50
49 Johnny Taylor .12 .30
50 God Shammgod .12 .30
51 Dedric Willoughby .12 .30
52 Tim Thomas .25 .60
53 Alvin Williams .12 .30
54 Gordon Malone .12 .30
55 Serge Zwikker .12 .30
56 Charles Smith .12 .30
57 Tim Duncan ROY? .60 1.50
58 Ron Mercer ROY? .12 .30
59 Keith Van Horn ROY? .20 .50
60 Tim Thomas ROY? .20 .50
61 Tim Duncan CL .60 1.50
62 Tim Duncan AA .60 1.50
63 Ron Mercer AA .12 .30
64 Keith Van Horn AA .20 .50
65 Tony Battie AA .10 .25
66 Tracy McGrady AA .50 1.25
67 Danny Fortson AA .10 .25
68 Brevin Knight AA .10 .25
69 DeJuan Wheat AA .10 .25
70 Adonal Foyle AA .10 .25
71 Jacque Vaughn AA .10 .25
72 Tim Duncan AA CL .60 1.50
73 Allen Iverson ART .20 .50
74 Marcus Camby ART .10 .25
75 Shareef Abdur-Rahim ART .10 .25
76 Stephon Marbury ART .12 .30
77 Ray Allen ART .12 .30
78 Antoine Walker ART .10 .25
79 Lorenzen Wright ART .05 .15
80 Kerry Kittles ART .05 .15
81 Erick Dampier ART .05 .15
82 Vitaly Potapenko ART .05 .15
83 Kobe Bryant ART .50 1.25
84 Tony Delk ART .05 .15
85 John Wallace ART .05 .15
86 Walter McCarty ART .05 .15
87 Roy Rogers ART .05 .15
88 Allen Iverson ART CL .20 .50
89 Rasheed Wallace BD .10 .25
90 Damon Stoudamire BD .10 .25
91 Joe Smith BD .07 .20
92 Glenn Robinson BD .07 .20
93 Scottie Pippen BD .15 .40
94 Ed O'Bannon BD .05 .15
95 Antonio McDyess BD .07 .20
96 Alonzo Mourning BD .12 .30
97 Clyde Drexler BD .12 .30
98 Dikembe Mutombo BD .10 .25
99 Hakeem Olajuwon BD .12 .30
100 Scottie Pippen BD CL .15 .40

1997 Score Board Rookies Dean's List

COMPLETE SET (100) 12.00 30.00
*STARS: .75X TO 2X BASE VALUE

1997 Score Board Rookies #1 Die Cuts

Randomly inserted in packs at the rate of one in 36, this 20-card set features color action images of players selected in the first round of the draft and are printed on die-cut foil board around the shape of the number one.

COMPLETE SET (20) 40.00 100.00
1 Tim Duncan 12.00 30.00
2 Tony Battie 2.00 5.00
3 Ron Mercer 2.50 6.00
4 Keith Van Horn 4.00 10.00
5 Antonio Daniels 2.00 5.00
6 Tim Thomas 4.00 10.00
7 Adonal Foyle 2.00 5.00
8 Derek Anderson 2.00 5.00
9 Chauncey Billups 6.00 15.00
10 Tracy McGrady 10.00 25.00
11 Danny Fortson 2.00 5.00
12 Brevin Knight 2.00 5.00
13 Jacque Vaughn 2.00 5.00
14 Austin Croshere 1.50 4.00
15 Stephon Marbury 2.50 6.00
16 Kobe Bryant 10.00 25.00
17 Clyde Drexler 2.50 6.00
18 Scottie Pippen 3.00 8.00
19 Allen Iverson 4.00 10.00
20 Alonzo Mourning 2.50 6.00

1997 Score Board Rookies Traded

Inserted at a rate of 1:36 packs, these cards look identical to the base set cards except they have a glossy finish and have a "Traded to..." stamp on the front. Card numbers are followed by a "T" on the back.

COMPLETE SET (7) 3.00 8.00
19T Kelvin Cato .75 2.00
32T Keith Van Horn 1.50 4.00
34T Bobby Jackson 1.00 2.50
35T Anthony Parker .75 2.00
37T Chris Anstey .75 2.00
41T Danny Fortson .75 2.00
52T Tim Thomas 1.50 4.00

1997 Score Board Rookies Varsity Club

Randomly inserted in packs at the rate of one in 18, this 20-card set features color photos of the brightest basketball stars printed on foil with an authentic pennant look.

COMPLETE SET (20) 15.00 40.00
VC1 Tim Duncan 6.00 15.00
VC2 Ron Mercer 1.25 3.00
VC3 Keith Van Horn 2.00 5.00
VC4 Tim Thomas 2.00 5.00
VC5 Adonal Foyle 1.00 2.50
VC6 Tony Battie 1.00 2.50
VC7 Antonio Daniels 1.00 2.50
VC8 Kelvin Cato 1.00 2.50
VC9 Charles O'Bannon 1.00 2.50
VC10 Brevin Knight 1.00 2.50
VC11 Danny Fortson 1.00 2.50
VC12 Derek Anderson 1.00 2.50
VC13 Austin Croshere .75 2.00
VC14 Tracy McGrady 5.00 12.00
VC15 Jacque Vaughn 1.00 2.50
VC16 God Shammgod 1.00 2.50
VC17 DeJuan Wheat 1.00 2.50
VC18 Danya Abrams 1.00 2.50
VC19 Reggie Freeman 1.00 2.50
VC20 Tony Gonzalez 1.00 2.50

1997 Score Board Talk N' Sports

This product features phone cards with a couple twists, including trivia contests to win memorabilia and to check current sports scores. The 50-card regular set includes stars and prospects from all four major team sports. According to Score Board, a total of 1,500 sequentially numbered cases were produced.

COMPLETE SET (50) 4.00 10.00
24 Clyde Drexler .15 .40
25 Scottie Pippen .15 .40
26 Hakeem Olajuwon .15 .40
27 Alonzo Mourning .10 .30
28 Joe Smith .08 .25
29 Antonio McDyess .07 .20
30 Allen Iverson .50 1.25
31 Kerry Kittles .07 .20
32 Stephon Marbury .15 .40
33 Marcus Camby .07 .20
34 Ray Allen .20 .50
35 Shareef Abdur-Rahim .15 .40
36 Kobe Bryant .75 2.00
37 Antoine Walker .15 .40
38 Glenn Robinson .08 .25
39 Dikembe Mutombo .10 .30

1997 Score Board Talk N' Sports Essentials

These 10 plastic acetate cards were randomly inserted at a rate of 1:24 Talk N' Sports packs.

COMPLETE SET (10) 25.00 60.00
E2 Scottie Pippen 3.00 8.00
E5 Clyde Drexler 2.50 6.00
E6 Kobe Bryant 8.00 20.00

1997 Score Board Talk N' Sports Phone Cards $1

COMPLETE SET (50) 8.00 20.00
*PIN NUMBER REVEALED: HALF VALUE

1997 Score Board Talk N' Sports Phone Cards $10

These $10 phone cards allow users to choose trivia contests to win memorabilia in lieu of the phone time. Entrants who choose the trivia contest forfeit their phone time, but if they answer 9 of 10 questions, they win a baseball bat autographed by one of these six players: Willie Mays, Hank Aaron, Barry Bonds, Ken Griffey Jr., Pete Rose or Chipper Jones. The $10 cards were inserted at a rate of 1:12 packs and expired on 5/20/1998. Each card is sequentially numbered out of 3,960.

COMPLETE SET (10) 12.00 30.00
*PIN NUMBER REVEALED: HALF VALUE
2 Hakeem Olajuwon 1.25 3.00
9 Clyde Drexler 1.25 3.00
10 Scottie Pippen 2.00 5.00

1997 Score Board Talk N' Sports Phone Cards $20

These $20 phone cards allow users to choose sports updates in lieu of the phone time. The time on the card can be used interchangably for either phone calls or sports updates. The $20 cards were inserted at a rate of 1:36 packs and expired on 7/31/1998. Each card is sequentially numbered out of 1,440.

COMPLETE SET (10) 25.00 60.00
*PIN NUMBER REVEALED: HALF VALUE
2 Scottie Pippen 3.00 8.00
5 Clyde Drexler 2.50 6.00
6 Kobe Bryant 8.00 20.00

1995 Signature Rookies Auto-Phonex Promo

This card measures approximately 2 1/4" by 3 1/3" and is on a glossy phone card plastic stock. On a black background, two pictures of Jerry Stackhouse in a North Carolina jersey are shown. His name and "1 of 40,000" are printed on the top of the card while "$1,000 Promo" is printed vertically on the left side. The Signatures Rookies Auto Phonex and Sprint logos adorn the bottom. The back is black and white and has a blurb promoting the forthcoming set that was actually never distributed. The word "Promo" is written at the top. The card is unnumbered.

COMPLETE SET (1) 1.20 3.00
NNO Jerry Stackhouse 1.25 3.00

1995 Signature Rookies Club Promos

S4 Wesley Person .60 1.50

1995 Signature Rookies Sports Slammers Stackers

Printed on 18-point card stock, this set of 40 stackers and 5 slammers POGs combines football and basketball stars in a game. Each pack contained five sports stackers as well as one rule card.

3 Eric Montross BK .15 .40
8 Brian Grant BK .15 .40
9 Monty Williams BK .15 .40
12 Eddie Jones BK .50 1.25
20 Wesley Person BK .15 .40
24 Wesley Person BK .15 .40
27 Eddie Jones BK .50 1.25
28 Monty Williams BK .15 .40
31 Eric Montross BK .15 .40
36 Brian Grant BK .15 .40
S3 Eric Montross BK .30 .75
Masher
S5 Eddie Jones BK .60 1.50
Jammer

1995 Signature Rookies Autobilia

This 30-card set measures the standard size. The fronts feature a small color action player image on a white background with a larger faded duplicate image as a shadow. The player's first name is printed in gold foil down the side with his last name across the bottom. The backs carry the player's name, position, college statistics, biographical information, and player facts on a background of a faded color action player photo. This is a breakdown of memorablia signed: Players signed 1,000 cards, 3,000 photos, 500 pennants, 400 team balls, 350 hats, 24 practice jerseys, and 550 basketballs. Jerry Stackhouse and Kevin Garnett signed 250 Sports Illustrateds.

COMPLETE SET (30) 2.50 6.00
1 Joe Smith .15 .40
2 Antonio McDyess .15 .40
3 Jerry Stackhouse .40 1.00
4 Rasheed Wallace .40 1.00
5 Kevin Garnett 1.00 2.50
6 Bryant Reeves .12 .30
7 Damon Stoudamire .30 .75
8 Shawn Respert .12 .30
9 Ed O'Bannon .12 .30
10 Kurt Thomas .12 .30
11 Gary Trent .12 .30
12 Cherokee Parks .12 .30
13 Corliss Williamson .12 .30
14 Eric Williams .12 .30
15 Brent Barry .20 .50
16 Alan Henderson .12 .30
17 Bob Sura .12 .30
18 Theo Ratliff .20 .50
19 Randolph Childress .12 .30
20 Jason Caffey .12 .30
21 Michael Finley .40 1.00
22 George Zidek .12 .30
23 Travis Best .12 .30
24 Loren Meyer .12 .30
25 David Vaughn .12 .30
26 Sherrell Ford .12 .30
27 Mario Bennett .12 .30
28 Greg Ostertag .12 .30
29 Cory Alexander .12 .30
NNO Checklist .12 .30

1995 Signature Rookies Autobilia Autographs

STATED PRINT RUN 1000 SETS
1 Joe Smith 1.50 4.00
2 Antonio McDyess 5.00 12.00
3 Jerry Stackhouse 8.00 20.00
4 Rasheed Wallace 8.00 20.00
5 Kevin Garnett 20.00 50.00
6 Bryant Reeves 1.25 3.00
7 Damon Stoudamire 4.00 10.00
8 Shawn Respert 1.25 3.00
9 Ed O'Bannon 1.25 3.00
10 Kurt Thomas 1.25 3.00
11 Gary Trent 1.25 3.00
12 Cherokee Parks 1.25 3.00
13 Corliss Williamson 1.25 3.00
14 Eric Williams 1.25 3.00
15 Brent Barry 2.00 5.00
16 Alan Henderson 1.25 3.00
17 Bob Sura 1.25 3.00
18 Theo Ratliff 2.00 5.00
19 Randolph Childress 1.25 3.00
20 Jason Caffey 1.25 3.00
21 Michael Finley 6.00 15.00
22 George Zidek 1.25 3.00
23 Travis Best 1.25 3.00
24 Loren Meyer 1.25 3.00
25 David Vaughn 1.25 3.00
26 Sherrell Ford 1.25 3.00
27 Mario Bennett 1.25 3.00
28 Greg Ostertag 1.25 3.00
29 Cory Alexander 1.25 3.00

1995 Signature Rookies Autobilia Garnett

Randomly inserted in packs, this five-card set measures the standard size. The fronts feature two different color action player images on a black background. The player's name, Kevin Garnett, is printed in gold foil on the left. "AutoBilia" is printed in dark pink across the top. The backs carry the card name, player's name, position, career statistics, and a player fact on a background of a player photo.

COMPLETE SET (5) 6.00 15.00
COMMON GARNETT (G1-G5) 1.50 4.00
G3P Kevin Garnett PROMO 4.00 10.00
G4P Kevin Garnett PROMO 4.00 10.00
G5P Kevin Garnett PROMO 4.00 10.00

1995 Signature Rookies Autobilia Stackhouse

Randomly inserted in packs, this five-card set measures the standard size. The fronts feature two different color action player images on a black background. The player's name, Jerry Stackhouse, is printed in gold foil on the left. "AutoBilia" is printed in dark pink across the top. The backs carry the card name, player's name, position, career statistics, and a player fact on a background of a player photo. There were also autographed promo cards available from this set, hand numbered out of 500.

COMPLETE SET (5) 1.50 4.00
COMMON CARD (S1-S5) .40 1.00
S2AU Jerry Stackhouse 6.00 15.00
Promo Auto/500
S4AU Jerry Stackhouse 6.00 15.00
Promo Auto/500
S5AU Jerry Stackhouse 6.00 15.00
Promo Auto/500

1995 Signature Rookies Draft Day

This 50-card set measures the standard size. The fronts carry a borderless color player action photo with the player's name and a player's silhouette is printed in gold in a faded black stripe at the bottom. The backs carry three small additional action player photos with the player's name, position, biographical information, career highlights, college attended, and statistics. 38,000 of each card was issued.

COMPLETE SET (50) 1.50 4.00
1 Donny Marshall .10 .25
2 Mario Bennett .10 .25
3 Dan Cross .10 .25
4 Devin Gray .10 .25
5 Dwight Stewart .10 .25
6 Jerome Allen .10 .25
7 Travis Best .10 .25
8 Tyus Edney .10 .25
9 Mark Davis .10 .25
10 Michael Finley .30 .75
11 Gary Trent .10 .25
12 Julius Michalik .10 .25
13 Clint McDaniel .10 .25
14 Sherrell Ford .10 .25
15 Junior Burrough .10 .25
16 Bryan Collins .10 .25
17 Andrew DeClercq .10 .25
18 Glen Whisby .10 .25
19 Terrence Rencher .10 .25
20 Eric Snow .10 .25
21 Alan Henderson .10 .25
22 Bob Sura .10 .25
23 James Forrest .10 .25
24 Jimmy King .10 .25
25 Scotty Thurman .10 .25
26 Matt Maloney .10 .25
27 Paul O'Liney .10 .25
28 Lazelle Durden .10 .25
29 Eric Williams .10 .25
30 Tom Kleinschmidt .10 .25
31 Cory Alexander .10 .25
32 James Scott .10 .25
33 Michael McDonald .10 .25
34 Randy Rutherford .10 .25
35 Donald Williams .10 .25
36 Kurt Thomas .10 .25
37 Loren Meyer .10 .25
38 Donnie Boyce .10 .25
39 Michael Hawkins .10 .25
40 Lou Roe .10 .25
41 Larry Skyes .10 .25
42 Cuonzo Martin .10 .25
43 Jason Caffey .10 .25
44 Scott Highmark .10 .25
45 Lawrence Moten .10 .25
46 Anthony Pelle .10 .25
47 Randolph Childress .10 .25
48 Ray Jackson .10 .25
49 Corey Beck .10 .25
50 Fred Hoiberg .10 .25
KG Kevin Garnett AU/260 15.00 40.00
NNO Checklist .10 .25

1995 Signature Rookies Draft Day Signatures

Inserted one per '95 Signature Rookies Draft Day pack, these 50 standard-size cards are the same as 1995 Draft Day only with the player's signature on the front. All 50 players in the set signed 7750 cards. If the cards weren't ready when this product was shipped a "trade coupon" was inserted into the packs. An autograph card or trade coupon was inserted into every pack.

STATED PRINT RUN 7,750 SERIAL #'d SETS
1 Donny Marshall 1.00 2.50
2 Mario Bennett 1.00 2.50
3 Dan Cross 1.00 2.50
4 Devin Gray 1.00 2.50
5 Dwight Stewart 1.00 2.50
6 Jerome Allen 1.00 2.50
7 Travis Best 1.00 2.50
8 Tyus Edney 1.00 2.50
9 Mark Davis 1.00 2.50
10 Michael Finley/1050 4.00 10.00
11 Gary Trent 1.00 2.50
12 Julius Michalik 1.00 2.50
13 Clint McDaniel 1.00 2.50
14 Sherrell Ford 1.00 2.50
15 Junior Burrough 1.00 2.50
16 Bryan Collins 1.00 2.50
17 Andrew DeClercq 1.00 2.50
18 Glen Whisby 1.00 2.50
19 Terrence Rencher 1.00 2.50
20 Eric Snow 1.00 2.50
21 Alan Henderson 1.00 2.50
22 Bob Sura 1.00 2.50
23 James Forrest 1.00 2.50
24 Jimmy King 1.00 2.50
25 Scotty Thurman 1.00 2.50
26 Matt Maloney 1.00 2.50
27 Paul O'Liney 1.00 2.50
28 Lazelle Durden 1.00 2.50
29 Eric Williams 1.00 2.50
30 Tom Kleinschmidt 1.00 2.50
31 Cory Alexander 1.00 2.50
32 James Scott 1.00 2.50
33 Michael McDonald 1.00 2.50
34 Randy Rutherford 1.00 2.50
35 Donald Williams 1.00 2.50
36 Kurt Thomas 1.00 2.50
37 Loren Meyer 1.00 2.50
38 Donnie Boyce 1.00 2.50
39 Michael Hawkins 1.00 2.50
40 Lou Roe 1.00 2.50
41 Larry Skyes 1.00 2.50
42 Cuonzo Martin 1.00 2.50
43 Jason Caffey 1.00 2.50
44 Scott Highmark 1.00 2.50
45 Lawrence Moten 1.00 2.50
46 Anthony Pelle 1.00 2.50
47 Randolph Childress 1.00 2.50
48 Ray Jackson 1.00 2.50
49 Corey Beck 1.00 2.50
50 Fred Hoiberg 1.00 2.50
PROMO Michael Finley/1050 5.00 12.00

1995 Signature Rookies Draft Day Abdul Jabbar

Inserted at a rate of one per 87 packs, these 5 standard-size cards consist of different action portraits of Kareem Abdul Jabbar on the front. All the cards have a black stripe down the left side with his name printed in gold. The backs carry his different career highlights and collegiate stats printed over another color action photo. There is a signed version of each of these cards. Abdul-Jabbar signed 105 of each card.

COMPLETE SET (5) 3.00 8.00
COMMON KAREEM (K1-K5) .75 2.00

1995 Signature Rookies Draft Day Abdul Jabbar Signatures

COMMON CARD (K1-K5) 20.00 50.00
STATED PRINT RUN 105 SERIAL #'d SETS

1995 Signature Rookies Draft Day Draft Gems

Randomly inserted at a rate of 1 per 22 packs, these 10 standard-size cards consist of five player's with two cards each. The fronts feature two different color player action photos. The larger background one is faded while the smaller foreground one is bright. The player's last name is in big gold letters above the bottom of a thin red "L" on the left with his first name printed in red above it. The backs carry the player's name, biographical information, career highlights, statistics, and college printed over a faded player action photo with part of the photo brightly displayed inside a diamond-shaped frame. The cards were announced with a print run of 38,000, are also numbered with a "DG" prefix on the card backs.

COMPLETE SET (10) 4.00 10.00
DG1 Jerry Stackhouse 1.00 2.50
DG2 Jerry Stackhouse 1.00 2.50
DG3 Antonio McDyess .40 1.00
DG4 Antonio McDyess .40 1.00
DG5 Cherokee Parks .30 .75
DG6 Cherokee Parks .30 .75
DG7 Joe Smith .40 1.00
DG8 Joe Smith .40 1.00
DG9 Rasheed Wallace 1.00 2.50
DG10 Rasheed Wallace 1.00 2.50
BP Kevin Garnett PROMO 4.00 10.00
DG2P Jerry Stackhouse PROMO 2.00 5.00

1995 Signature Rookies Draft Day Draft Gems Signatures

STATED ODDS 1:87
STATED PRINT RUN 525 SERIAL #'d SETS
DG1 Jerry Stackhouse 6.00 15.00
DG2 Jerry Stackhouse 6.00 15.00
DG3 Antonio McDyess 6.00 15.00
DG4 Antonio McDyess 6.00 15.00
DG5 Cherokee Parks 2.00 5.00
DG6 Cherokee Parks 2.00 5.00
DG7 Joe Smith 4.00 10.00
DG8 Joe Smith 4.00 10.00
DG9 Rasheed Wallace 10.00 25.00
DG10 Rasheed Wallace 10.00 25.00

1995 Signature Rookies Draft Day Reflections

Inserted at a rate of 1 per 18 packs, these 5 cards measure the standard size. The fronts feature borderless player action photos with the player's name and a player silhouette printed in gold in a vertical black stripe on the left. The backs carry the player's name, college, biographical information, career highlights and statistics along with another action player photo and a narrowly-cropped version of the front photo. The cards are numbered with a "R" prefix and have announced numbering out of 15,250..

COMPLETE SET (5) .75 2.00
R1 Brian Grant .30 .75
R2 Wesley Person .25 .60
R3 Eric Montross .25 .60
R4 Juwan Howard .40 1.00
R5 Eddie Jones .50 1.25

1995 Signature Rookies Draft Day Reflections Signatures

COMPLETE SET (5) 15.00 40.00
STATED ODDS 1:346
STATED PRINT RUN 250 SERIAL #'d SETS
R1 Brian Grant 4.00 10.00
R2 Wesley Person 4.00 10.00
R3 Eric Montross 4.00 10.00
R4 Juwan Howard 6.00 15.00
R5 Eddie Jones 10.00 25.00

1995 Signature Rookies Draft Day Show Stoppers

Inserted at a rate of 1 per 3 packs, these 25 cards measure the standard size. The set consists of five cards each of five different players. The fronts feature color action player photos with a border resembling a roll of film. The player's name is printed in gold in a black bar at the bottom with a gold player silhouette. The backs carry another color action photo, the player's name, position, biographical information, career highlights, college, and statistics over a background of game action. Each card has an announced print run of 11,000.

COMPLETE SET (25) 5.00 12.00
B1 Bryant Reeves .40 1.00
B2 Bryant Reeves .40 1.00
B3 Bryant Reeves .40 1.00
B4 Bryant Reeves .40 1.00
B5 Bryant Reeves .40 1.00
C1 Corliss Williamson .40 1.00
C2 Corliss Williamson .40 1.00
C3 Corliss Williamson .40 1.00
C4 Corliss Williamson .40 1.00
C5 Corliss Williamson .40 1.00
D1 Damon Stoudamire 1.00 2.50
D2 Damon Stoudamire 1.00 2.50
D3 Damon Stoudamire 1.00 2.50
D4 Damon Stoudamire 1.00 2.50
D5 Damon Stoudamire 1.00 2.50
E1 Ed O'Bannon .40 1.00
E2 Ed O'Bannon .40 1.00
E3 Ed O'Bannon .40 1.00
E4 Ed O'Bannon .40 1.00
E5 Ed O'Bannon .40 1.00
S1 Shawn Respert .40 1.00
S2 Shawn Respert .40 1.00
S3 Shawn Respert .40 1.00
S4 Shawn Respert .40 1.00
S5 Shawn Respert .40 1.00
P2 Bryant Reeves .40 1.00
Mail In Promo
P3 Shawn Respert .40 1.00
Mail In Promo

1995 Signature Rookies Draft Day Show Stoppers Signatures

ATED ODDS 1:18
STATED PRINT RUN 1050 SERIAL #'d SETS
B1 Bryant Reeves 2.00 5.00
B2 Bryant Reeves 2.00 5.00
B3 Bryant Reeves 2.00 5.00
B4 Bryant Reeves 2.00 5.00
B5 Bryant Reeves 2.00 5.00
C1 Corliss Williamson 2.00 5.00
C2 Corliss Williamson 2.00 5.00
C3 Corliss Williamson 2.00 5.00
C4 Corliss Williamson 2.00 5.00
C5 Corliss Williamson 2.00 5.00
D1 Damon Stoudamire 5.00 12.00
D2 Damon Stoudamire 5.00 12.00
D3 Damon Stoudamire 5.00 12.00
D4 Damon Stoudamire 5.00 12.00
D5 Damon Stoudamire 5.00 12.00
E1 Ed O'Bannon 2.00 5.00
E2 Ed O'Bannon 2.00 5.00
E3 Ed O'Bannon 2.00 5.00
E4 Ed O'Bannon 2.00 5.00
E5 Ed O'Bannon 2.00 5.00
S1 Shawn Respert 2.00 5.00
S2 Shawn Respert 2.00 5.00
S3 Shawn Respert 2.00 5.00
S4 Shawn Respert 2.00 5.00
S5 Shawn Respert 2.00 5.00

1995 Signature Rookies Draft Day Swat Team

Inserted at a rate of 1 per 3 packs, these 5 cards measure the standard size. The fronts feature borderless color action player photos. The player's name is printed in green above gold sunbeams in the lower right. The backs carry the player's name, position, biographical information, college, career highlights, and statistics. The cards are numbered with a "ST" prefix. Each card has an announced print run of 12,500.

COMPLETE SET (5) .75 2.00
ST1 Tony Maroney .30 .75
ST2 Greg Ostertag .30 .75
ST3 George Zidek .30 .75
ST4 Constantin Popa .30 .75
ST5 Theo Ratliff .50 1.25
P1 Ed O'Bannon PROMO
P5 Corliss Williamson PROMO .60 1.50

1995 Signature Rookies Draft Day Swat Team Signatures

STATED ODDS 1:18
STATED PRINT RUN 5200 SERIAL #'d SETS
ST1 Tony Maroney 1.00 2.50
ST2 Greg Ostertag 1.00 2.50
ST3 George Zidek 1.00 2.50
ST4 Constantin Popa 1.00 2.50
ST5 Theo Ratliff 3.00 8.00

1995 Signature Rookies Fame and Fortune

The 1995 Fame and Fortune set was issued in one series totalling 100 cards and featured NBA and NFL draft picks. Cards were distributed in eight-card packs. Five insert card sets were produced with the set and include Collector's Pick, Top 5, Erstad, Star Squad and #1 Pick. The first 48 cards are basketball draft picks and the remaining 52 are football picks. ronts have full-color action cutout photos with a black background with either a football or basketball. The player's first name is printed in gold foil horizontally while his last name is printed twice vertically in both gold foil and a larger green type on the left side. Backs have another action shot that is seprated with a color screen process. Backs include college statistics, a short biography and a player profile.

COMPLETE SET (100) 5.00 12.00
1 Cory Alexander .07 .20
2 Jerome Allen .07 .20
3 Brent Barry .08 .25
4 Mario Bennett .07 .20
5 Travis Best .08 .25
6 Donie Boyce .07 .20
7 Junior Burrough .07 .20
8 Jason Caffey .08 .25
9 Chris Carr .07 .20
10 Randolph Childress .07 .20
11 Mark Davis .07 .20
12 Andrew DeClerco .07 .20
13 Tyus Edney .08 .25
14 Michael Finley .20 .50
15 Sherell Ford .07 .20
16 Kevin Garnett .60 1.50
17 Alan Henderson .08 .25
18 Fred Hoiberg .07 .20
19 Jimmy King .07 .20
20 Donny Marshall .07 .20
21 Cuonzo Martin .07 .20
22 Michael McDonald .07 .20
23 Anthony McDyess .20 .50
24 Loren Meyer .07 .20
25 Lawrence Moten .07 .20
26 Ed O'Bannon .07 .20
27 Greg Ostertag .08 .25
28 Cherokee Parks .07 .20
29 Anthony Pelle .07 .20
30 Constantin Popa .07 .20
31 Theo Ratliff .08 .25
32 Bryant Reeves .08 .25
33 Don Reid .07 .20
34 Terrance Rencher .07 .20
35 Shawn Respert .07 .20
36 Lou Roe .07 .20
37 Joe Smith .08 .25
38 Eric Snow .08 .25
39 Jerry Stackhouse .30 .75
40 Damon Stoudamire .08 .25
41 Bob Sura .08 .25
42 Kurt Thomas .07 .20
43 Gary Trent .08 .25
44 David Vaughn .07 .20
45 Rasheed Wallace .30 .75
46 Eric Williams .07 .20
47 Corliss Williamson .08 .25
48 George Zidek .07 .20

1995 Signature Rookies Fame and Fortune #1 Pick

Randomly inserted in packs at a rate of three in 16, this five-card set features the No. 1 pick in the NHL, the NFL, The NBA and Major leagues. The No. 5 card pictures all four of the picks. Fronts have a psychedelic background and feature the player in a full-color action cutout. "#1 Pick" appears in a sky blue and green type at the top and the bottom has a gold foil strip that contains the player's name, or names in the case of the #5 card, in raised white letters. Backs continue with the psychedelic background and picture the player or players in action. Player stats and biographies also appear on the back.

COMPLETE SET (5) 1.00 2.50
P4 Joe Smith .20 .50
P5 Berard .30 .75
Carter
Erstad
J.Smith

1995 Signature Rookies Fame and Fortune Collectors Pick

Randomly inserted in packs at a rate of one in 16, this 10-card set highlights the first five NBA picks and the first five NFL picks. Fronts are borderless with white backgrounds with "Collectors" on the top third and "Pick" in a vertically stretched type on the rest of the front. The player is pictured in a full-color action cutout in the foreground. His name is printed vertically in gold foil on the lower left. Backs have a small player head shot, and a faded screen action shot for a background. Player biography, statistics and profile appear on the back.

COMPLETE SET (100) 4.00 10.00
B2 Ed O'Bannon .25 .60
B3 Cherokee Parks .25 .60
B4 Bryant Reeves .30 .75
B7 Joe Smith .30 .75
B8 Jerry Stackhouse 1.00 2.50
B10 Rasheed Wallace 1.00 2.50

1995 Signature Rookies Fame and Fortune Red Hot Rookies

This 10-card set randomly inserted in packs of 1995 Signature Rookies Fame and Fortune. Each card was printed on red foil stock and include a photo of one football or basketball draft pick from 1995.

COMPLTE SET (10) 5.00 12.00
R2 Jerry Stackhouse .60 1.50
R4 Damon Stoudamire .20 .50
R6 Kevin Garnett 1.25 3.00
R8 Michael Finley .40 1.00
R10 Joe Smith .20 .50

1995 Signature Rookies Fame and Fortune Top Five

Randomly inserted in packs at a rate of one in four, this five-card set focuses on basketball's '95 draft. "Top Five" is printed in an "L" pattern in red block type with a blue shadow on the front. A full-color action player shot appears also and his name is printed in a backwards "L" pattern in gold type on the top right. A player biography and profile are printed in gold foil on the back against a purple background. A full-color action shot is placed on the right side of the back.

COMPLETE SET (100) 2.50 6.00
T1 Joe Smith .20 .50
T2 Antonio McDyess .40 1.00
T3 Jerry Stackhouse .60 1.50
T4 Rasheed Wallace .60 1.50
T5 Kevin Garnett 1.25 3.00

1994 Signature Rookies Gold Standard

This multi-sport set consists of 100 standard-size cards. The fronts feature color action players photos with a circular gold foil seal at the upper left corner. The player's name appears on a diagonal black stripe edged by yellow. The horizontal backs carry a narrowly-cropped closeup photo and, on a ghosted panel, biography and player profile. The set is subdivided according to sport as follows: basketball

1-25), football (26-50), baseball (51-75), and hockey (76-100). Each sport is sequenced in alphabetical order.

COMPLETE SET (100) 5.00 12.00
1 Derrick Alston .07 .20
2 Damon Bailey .07 .20
3 Bill Curley .07 .20
4 Yinka Dare .07 .20
5 Rodney Dent .07 .20
6 Brian Grant .10 .30
7 Juwan Howard .30 .75
8 Askia Jones .07 .20
9 Eddie Jones .25 .60
10 Donyell Marshall .15 .40
11 Aaron McKie .10 .30
12 Greg Minor .07 .20
13 Eric Montross .07 .20
14 Wesley Person .10 .30
15 Eric Piatkowski .10 .30
16 Jalen Rose .25 .60
17 Clifford Rozier .07 .20
18 Dickey Simpkins .07 .20
19 Deon Thomas .07 .20
20 Brooks Thompson .07 .20
21 B.J. Tyler .07 .20
22 Charlie Ward .10 .30
23 Monty Williams .07 .20
24 Dontonio Wingfield .07 .20
25 Sharone Wright .07 .20

1994 Signature Rookies Gold Standard Facsimile

This 20-card standard-size set was inserted one per pack. The fronts display full-bleed color player photos. A facsimile autograph, the "Gold Standard" seal, and another emblem are gold-foil stamped on the fronts. Also a diagonal line carrying the player's name (also in gold foil) is edged by gold foil stripes. On the left side, the horizontal backs show a narrowly-cropped closeup of the front photo. The remainder of the backs carry biography, statistics, and player profile, all on a ghosted background. In addition to card number, each back carries a serial number.

COMPLETE SET (20) 5.00 12.00
GS9 Juwan Howard .75 2.00
GS12 Eric Montross .60 1.50
GS14 Donyell Marshall .75 2.00
GS16 Sharone Wright .30 .75
GS19 Clifford Rozier .30 .75
GS20 Jalen Rose .60 1.50

1994 Signature Rookies Gold Standard HOF

COMPLETE SET (24) 8.00 20.00
STATED PRINT RUN 20,000 SETS
ISSUED VIA MAIL REDEMPTION
HOF1 Nate Archibald .50 1.25
HOF2 Rick Barry .60 1.50
HOF4 Bob Cousy 1.00 2.50
HOF5 Dave Cowens .50 1.25
HOF6 Dave DeBusschere .60 1.50
HOF8 Walt Frazier .60 1.50
HOF11 Connie Hawkins .50 1.25
HOF12 Elvin Hayes .60 1.50
HOF19 Bob Pettit .50 1.25
HOF22 Bill Walton .75 2.00

1994 Signature Rookies Gold Standard HOF Autographs

Inserted at a rate of one per box, this 24-card standard-sized set is identical to the regular set except for the signatures inscribed across the front and the expression "Hall of Fame" gold-foil stamped at the upper left. Each card is numbered out of 2500. The collector could obtain unsigned versions by mailing in a redemption card that was randomly inserted in packs. These redemption cards are valued at 1/10 the value of the signed cards. The cards are numbered with an "HOF" prefix.

1 Nate Archibald 6.00 15.00
2 Rick Barry 8.00 20.00
4 Bob Cousy 8.00 20.00
5 Dave Cowens 6.00 15.00
6 Dave DeBusschere 30.00 60.00
8 Walt Frazier 8.00 20.00
11 Connie Hawkins 8.00 20.00
12 Elvin Hayes 8.00 20.00
19 Bob Pettit 8.00 20.00
22 Bill Walton 8.00 20.00

1994 Signature Rookies Gold Standard Legends

This five-card standard size set was randomly inserted into packs. This set has great athletes past and presents from all sports. The fronts have the word "Legends" on the top and the player's name on the bottom printed in silver ink against a black background. Meanwhile, the player's photo is shown against a gold background. The backs contains the player's photo on the left quarter with a biography about that player on the remainder of the card.

COMPLETE SET (5) 3.00 8.00
L1 Isiah Thomas .40 1.00
L2 Larry Bird 1.25 3.00

1994 Signature Rookies Gold Standard Promos

COMPLETE SET (5) .75 2.00
ANNOUNCED PRINT RUN 10000
P1 Donyell Marshall .20 .50
P2 Jalen Rose .20 .50

1995 Signature Rookies Kromax Promos

These standard-size promo cards were given away to preview the design of the Kro-Max series. On a purple and black background, the metallic front features a color player cutout. The player's name is printed parallel to the left edge, while the Kro-Max emblem adorns the bottom of the card. On a brightly neon-colored background, the backs carry a player cutout, biography, player profile, and complete collegiate statistics.

COMPLETE SET (2) .40 1.00
P1 Donyell Marshall .30 .75
P2 Juwan Howard .50 1.25

1995 Signature Rookies Kromax

Signature Rookies produced 1,995 eight-box cases, and every box contained one randomly inserted autographed card of a First Round Pick, a Super Acrylium player, or a Flash From the Past star. (SRP $5). Insert sets include Flash from the Past, available one in every six packs, Super Acrylium, which were inserted in the ratio of one every 12 packs, and First Rounders, which were available one every 19 packs. There were no more than 10,000 Super Acrylium and 2,500 First Rounders and Flash from the Past of each player made. Each box of Kro-max included one autograph from one of the three insert sets. One group of players autographed 1,050 each of their cards (Dumas, Montross, Person, Rose, and Rozier). A second group autographed 2,100 each of their cards (Curley, Dare, Grant, Jones, McKie, Piatkowski, Williams, and Wright). The front features the player's name on the left side and the Kromax logo across the bottom of the card. The player's image is in full color, hwile the rest of the scene is a negative print. Backs contain biographical information, a player profile, and college statistics. Members received one of 1,995 uncut sheets, featuring cards 1-40 and accompanied by a certificate of authenticity.

COMPLETE SET (50) 1.25 3.00
1 Donyell Marshall .05 .15
2 Juwan Howard .10 .25
3 Sharone Wright .05 .15
4 Brian Grant .07 .20
5 Eric Montross .05 .15
6 Eddie Jones .12 .30
7 Jalen Rose .12 .30
8 Yinka Dare .05 .15
9 Eric Piatkowski .07 .20
10 Clifford Rozier .05 .15
11 Aaron McKie .05 .15
12 Eric Mobley .05 .15
13 Tony Dumas .05 .15
14 B.J. Tyler .05 .15
15 Dickey Simpkins .05 .15
16 Bill Curley .05 .15
17 Wesley Person .05 .15
18 Monty Williams .05 .15
19 Greg Minor .05 .15
20 Charlie Ward .05 .15
21 Brooks Thompson .05 .15
22 Deon Thomas .05 .15
23 Howard Eisley .05 .15
24 Rodney Dent .05 .15
25 Jim McIlvaine .05 .15
26 Derrick Alston .05 .15
27 Gaylon Nickerson .05 .15
28 Michael Smith .05 .15
29 Andrei Fetisov .05 .15
30 Dontonio Wingfield .05 .15
31 Anthony Miller .05 .15
32 Jeff Webster .05 .15
33 Shawnelle Scott .05 .15
34 Damon Bailey .05 .15
35 Jevon Crudup .05 .15
36 Lawrence Funderburke .05 .15
37 Anthony Goldwire .05 .15
38 Adrian Autry .05 .15
39 Doremus Benneman .05 .15
40 Melvin Booker .05 .15
41 Dwayne Fontana .05 .15
42 Travis Ford .05 .15
43 Kenny Harris .05 .15
44 Askia Jones .05 .15
45 Jason Kidd .15 .40
46 Bill McCaffrey .05 .15
47 Kevin Rankin .05 .15
48 Melvin Simon .05 .15
49 Glenn Robinson .07 .20
50 Kendrick Warren .05 .15
NNO Checklist .05 .15

1995 Signature Rookies Kromax First Rounders

This 10-card standard-size set is one of three different insert sets randomly seeded in seven-card packs. The First Rounder title is at the lower left corner while the player's name is on the bottom in bright colors. The player's photo is projected in front of a wave effect. 2,500 of each card were produced. The cards are numbered with a "FR" prefix.

COMPLETE SET (10) 4.00 10.00
FR1 Donyell Marshall .60 1.50
FR2 Juwan Howard 1.00 2.50
FR3 Sharone Wright .60 1.50
FR4 Brian Grant .75 2.00
FR5 Eric Montross .60 1.50
FR6 Eddie Jones 1.25 3.00
FR7 Jalen Rose 1.25 3.00
FR8 Yinka Dare .60 1.50
FR9 B.J. Tyler .60 1.50
FR10 Charlie Ward .60 1.50

1995 Signature Rookies Kromax Flash From The Past

This 10-card standard-size set is one of three different insert sets randomly seeded in seven-card packs. Fronts feature former NBA greats in air-brushed uniforms with his name under the photo. Backs contain a player biography. The cards are numbered with a "FP" prefix.

COMPLETE SET (10) 5.00 12.00
FP1 Bob Cousy 1.00 2.50
FP2 Larry Bird 1.50 4.00
FP3 Walt Frazier .60 1.50
FP4 Rick Barry .50 1.25
FP5 Isiah Thomas .60 1.50
FP6 Tiny Archibald .50 1.25
FP7 Dave DeBusschere .60 1.50
FP8 Dave Cowens .40 1.00
FP9 Elvin Hayes .60 1.50
FP10 Kareem Abdul-Jabbar 1.00 2.50

1995 Signature Rookies Kromax Flash From The Past Signatures

All players signed 1,050 of their cards, except for Abdul-Jabbar (1,550), Bird (100), and Thomas (100). The fronts feature former NBA greats in air-brushed uniform with his name underneath. Backs contain a biography about the player pictured and on the bottom the front photo is cropped so the face of the player is shown again. Elvin Hayes (FP9) and Bob Cousy (FP1) did not sign their cards.

STATED PRINT RUNS LISTED BELOW
FP2 Larry Bird/100 125.00 200.00
FP3 Walt Frazier/1050 6.00 15.00
FP4 Rick Barry/1050 6.00 15.00
FP5 Isiah Thomas/100 15.00 40.00
FP6 Tiny Archibald/1050 6.00 15.00
FP7 Dave DeBusschere/1050 30.00 60.00
FP8 Dave Cowens/1050 6.00 15.00
FP10 Kareem Abdul-Jabbar/1550 25.00 50.00

1995 Signature Rookies Kromax Jumbos

Measuring 3 1/2" by 5", this 10-card set captures some of the 1994 NBA first round draft picks. The players pictured on the fronts stand out on brightly-colored metallic backgrounds. The production figures ("1 of 3,300") are printed in silver along the left edge, while the player's name is printed toward the bottom of the card. On a brightly neon-colored background, the backs carry a player cutout and player profile. Cards number 11 and 12 were only available through a wrapper redemption program. The values on cards numbers 1 through 10 are the same whether they are promo cards or available through the wrapper redemption program.

COMPLETE SET (12) 4.00 10.00
J1 Juwan Howard 1.00 2.50
J2 Donyell Marshall .60 1.50
J3 Sharone Wright .60 1.50
J4 Brian Grant .75 2.00
J5 Eric Montross .60 1.50
J6 Eddie Jones 1.25 3.00
J7 Jalen Rose 1.25 3.00
J8 Yinka Dare .60 1.50
J9 B.J. Tyler .60 1.50
J10 Charlie Ward .60 1.50
J11 Clifford Rozier .60 1.50
J12 Wesley Person .60 1.50

1995 Signature Rookies Kromax Signatures

Five players signed cards for Signature Rookies for inserts in Kromax boxes. The cards are listed below in alphabetical order by player's last name. Next to the players name is how many cards they signed.

1 Bill Curley/2100 1.25 3.00
2 Yinka Dare/2100 1.25 3.00
3 Eric Montross/1050 4.00 10.00
4 Wesley Person/1050 1.25 3.00
5 Sharone Wright/2100 1.25 3.00

1995 Signature Rookies Kromax Super Acrylium Promo

This standard-size promo card was issued to preview the design of the Signature Rookies Acrylium series. Sporting a protective, clear plastic covering, the fronts feature a color action cutout on a silver metallic background. The player's name is printed faintly along the left edge, while the Super Acrylium emblem adorns the lower left corner. The back has a silver cutout that is the mirror image of the front. Just 10,000 cards were produced.

1 Tim Hardaway .40 1.00

1995 Signature Rookies Kromax Super Acrylium

This five-card standard-size set is one of three insert sets randomly seeded in seven-card packs. 10,000 of each card were produced. The fronts feature the player against a plain silver background. The backs allow a collector to see the front of the card.

COMPLETE SET (5) 2.50 6.00
SA1 Scottie Pippen 1.00 2.50
SA2 Tim Hardaway .60 1.50
SA3 Charles Barkley 1.00 2.50
SA4 Dominique Wilkins .75 2.00
SA5 Patrick Ewing .75 2.00

1995 Signature Rookies Kromax Super Acrylium Signatures

STATED PRINT RUNS LISTED BELOW
SA1 Scottie Pippen/33 100.00 250.00
SA2 Tim Hardaway/1050 4.00 10.00
SA4 Dominique Wilkins/1050 6.00 15.00

1995 Signature Rookies Prime

The 1995 Signature Prime basketball set was issued in one series of 45 cards. Five-card packs included a signed card, packed in a sealed plastic case, an insert card, two regular cards and either a checklist card or mail-in offer card. There were 18 packs in each box. Borderless fronts feature the player in a full-color action shot with "Prime" printed vertically in red type on the left side. The player's name is printed in gold foil at the bottom. A full-color action shot appears on the back with the player's biography, profile, and college stats. The set is sequenced in alphabetical order.

COMPLETE SET (45) 3.00 6.00
1 Cory Alexander .10 .25
2 Jerome Allen .10 .25
3 Brent Barry .15 .40
4 Mario Bennett .10 .25
5 Travis Best .10 .25
6 Donnie Boyce .10 .25
7 Junior Burrough .10 .25
8 Jason Caffey .10 .25
9 Chris Carr .10 .25
10 Randolph Childress .10 .25
11 Mark Davis .10 .25
12 Andrew DeClercq .10 .25
13 Tyus Edney .10 .25
14 Michael Finley .30 .75
15 Sherrell Ford .10 .25
16 Kevin Garnett .75 2.00
16P Kevin Garnett PROMO 1.50 4.00
17 Alan Henderson .10 .25
18 Fred Hoiberg .10 .25
19 Jimmy King .10 .25
20 Donny Marshall .10 .25
21 Cuonzo Martin .10 .25
22 Michael McDonald .10 .25
23 Antonio McDyess .12 .30
24 Loren Meyer .10 .25
25 Lawrence Moten .10 .25
26 Ed O'Bannon .10 .25
27 Greg Ostertag .10 .25
28 Cherokee Parks .10 .25
29 Anthony Pelle .10 .25
30 Constantin Popa .10 .25
31 Theo Ratliff .15 .40
32 Bryant Reeves .10 .25
33 Don Reid .10 .25
34 Terrence Rencher .10 .25
35 Shawn Respert .10 .25
36 Lou Roe .10 .25
37 Eric Snow .10 .25
38 Damon Stoudamire .25 .60
39 Bob Sura .10 .25
40 Kurt Thomas .10 .25
41 Gary Trent .10 .25
42 David Vaughn .10 .25
43 Corliss Williamson .10 .25
44 Eric Williams .10 .25
45 George Zidek .10 .25
NNO Checklist .10 .25

1995 Signature Rookies Prime Signatures

This set represents a signed version of the 1995 SR Signature Prime series. The cards were randomly inserted into packs and each card was numbered out of 3,000. Ed O'Bannon and Jason Caffey did not sign their cards.

ONE PER PACK
STATED PRINT RUN 3,000 SERIAL #'d SETS
1 Cory Alexander 1.25 3.00
2 Jerome Allen 1.25 3.00
3 Brent Barry 2.00 5.00
4 Mario Bennett 1.25 3.00
5 Travis Best 1.25 3.00
6 Donnie Boyce 1.25 3.00
7 Junior Burrough 1.25 3.00
9 Chris Carr 1.25 3.00
10 Randolph Childress 1.25 3.00
11 Mark Davis 1.25 3.00
12 Andrew DeClercq 1.25 3.00
13 Tyus Edney 1.25 3.00
14 Michael Finley 4.00 10.00
15 Sherrell Ford 1.25 3.00
16 Kevin Garnett 15.00 40.00
17 Alan Henderson 1.25 3.00
18 Fred Hoiberg 1.25 3.00
19 Jimmy King 1.25 3.00
20 Donny Marshall 1.25 3.00
21 Cuonzo Martin 1.25 3.00
22 Michael McDonald 1.25 3.00
23 Antonio McDyess 1.50 4.00
24 Loren Meyer 1.25 3.00
25 Lawrence Moten 1.25 3.00
27 Greg Ostertag 1.25 3.00
28 Cherokee Parks 1.25 3.00
29 Anthony Pelle 1.25 3.00
30 Constantin Popa 1.25 3.00
31 Theo Ratliff 2.00 5.00
32 Bryant Reeves 1.25 3.00
33 Don Reid 1.25 3.00
34 Terrence Rencher 1.25 3.00
35 Shawn Respert 1.25 3.00
36 Lou Roe 1.25 3.00
37 Eric Snow 1.25 3.00
38 Damon Stoudamire 3.00 8.00
39 Bob Sura 1.25 3.00
40 Kurt Thomas 1.25 3.00
41 Gary Trent 1.25 3.00
42 David Vaughn 1.25 3.00
43 Corliss Williamson 1.25 3.00
44 Eric Williams 1.25 3.00
45 George Zidek 1.25 3.00

1995 Signature Rookies Prime Hoopla

This 5-card set was randomly inserted in football packs. The fronts display a color action cut-out of the player on a metallic, rainbow-colored background. The player's name and card logo is below. The word, "Hoopla" runs vertically on the left. The backs carry another cut-out of the player with his name, position, biographical information, and career summary. The set is numbered with an "H" prefix.

COMPLETE SET (5) 2.00 5.00
H1 Joe Smith .20 .50
H2 Antonio McDyess .20 .50
H3 Jerry Stackhouse .50 1.25
H4 Rasheed Wallace .50 1.25
H5 Kevin Garnett 1.25 3.00

1995 Signature Rookies Prime Hoopla Signatures

ATED PRINT RUN 500 SERIAL #'d SETS
H1 Joe Smith 4.00 10.00
H2 Antonio McDyess 8.00 20.00
H3 Jerry Stackhouse 10.00 25.00
H4 Rasheed Wallace 12.50 30.00
H5 Kevin Garnett 20.00 50.00

1995 Signature Rookies Prime Top 10

Randomly inserted in regular packs at a rate of one in 30, this 10-card standard-size set features some 1995 first round draft picks. 500 of each of the 10 cards were signed and placed in the sealed plastic containers. Borderless fronts have a full-color action shot with "TOP" printed at the top of the card and "TEN" printed at the bottom. The player's first name is printed horizontally in white type and his last name is printed in gold foil vertically underneath the first. Backs have another full-color action shot with player stats, biography and a profile. The cards are numbered with a "TT" prefix.

COMPLETE SET (10) 1.50 4.00
TT1 Joe Smith .20 .50
TT2 Antonio McDyess .20 .50
TT3 Jerry Stackhouse .50 1.25
TT4 Rasheed Wallace .50 1.25
TT5 Kevin Garnett 1.25 3.00
TT6 Bryant Reeves .15 .40
TT7 Damon Stoudamire .40 1.00
TT8 Shawn Respert .15 .40
TT9 Ed O'Bannon .15 .40
TT10 Kurt Thomas .15 .40

1995 Signature Rookies Prime Top 10 Signatures

STATED PRINT RUN 1000 SERIAL #'d SETS
TT1 Joe Smith 1.50 4.00
TT2 Antonio McDyess 5.00 12.00
TT3 Jerry Stackhouse 6.00 15.00
TT4 Rasheed Wallace 8.00 20.00
TT5 Kevin Garnett 25.00 50.00
TT6 Bryant Reeves 1.25 3.00
TT7 Damon Stoudamire 3.00 8.00
TT8 Shawn Respert 1.25 3.00
TT9 Ed O'Bannon 1.25 3.00
TT10 Kurt Thomas 1.25 3.00

1996 Signature Rookies Super Stars

COMPLETE SET (6) 3.00 8.00
SS4 Joe Smith BK .60 1.50
SS5 Jerry Stackhouse BK .75 2.00

1994 Signature Rookies Tetrad

These 120 standard-size cards feature borderless color player action shots on their fronts. The player's name appears in gold-foil lettering near the bottom. The words "1 of 45,000" appear in vertical gold-foil lettering within a simulated marble column near the left edge. The cards of this four-sport set are numbered on the back in Roman numerals and organized as follows: Football (1-40), Basketball (41-83), Baseball (84-103), and Hockey (104-118).

COMPLETE SET (120) 3.00 8.00
41 Derrick Alston .07 .20
42 Adrian Autry .07 .20
43 Damon Bailey .07 .20
44 Doremus Bennerman .07 .20
45 Melvin Booker .07 .20
46 Jevon Crudup .07 .20
47 Yinka Dare .07 .20
48 Rodney Dent .07 .20
49 Tony Dumas .07 .20
50 Dwayne Fontana .07 .20
51 Travis Ford .07 .20
52 Lawrence Funderburke .07 .20
53 Anthony Goldwire .07 .20
54 Brian Grant .15 .40
55 Kenny Harris .07 .20
56 Juwan Howard UER .15 .40
57 Askia Jones .07 .20
58 Eddie Jones .20 .50
59 Arturas Karnishovas .07 .20
60 Donyell Marshall .15 .40
61 Billy McCaffrey .15 .40
62 Jim McIlvaine .07 .20
63 Aaron McKie .07 .20
64 Greg Minor .07 .20
65 Eric Mobley .07 .20
66 Eric Montross .07 .20
67 Gaylon Nickerson .07 .20
68 Wesley Person .07 .20
69 Eric Piatkowski .15 .40
70 Kevin Rankin .07 .20
71 Shawnelle Scott .07 .20
72 Melvin Simon .07 .20
73 Dickey Simpkins .07 .20
74 Michael Smith .07 .20
75 Stevin Smith .07 .20
76 Deon Thomas .07 .20
77 Brooks Thompson .07 .20
78 B.J. Tyler .07 .20
79 Kendrick Warren .07 .20
80 Jeff Webster .07 .20
81 Monty Williams .07 .20
82 Dontonio Wingfield .07 .20
83 Sharone Wright .07 .20

1994 Signature Rookies Tetrad Autographs

Inserted one card (or trade coupon) per pack, these 117 standard-size autographed cards comprise a parallel set to the regular '94 Tetrad set. Aside from the autographs and each card's numbering out of 7,750 produced, they are identical in design to their regular issue counterparts. The cards of this four-sport set are numbered on the back in Roman numerals and organized as follows: Football (1-40), Basketball (41-83), Baseball (84-103), and Hockey (104-118). Bernard Williams (card number 11) did not sign his cards.

41 Derrick Alston 1.50 4.00
42 Adrian Autry 1.50 4.00
43 Damon Bailey 1.50 4.00
44 Doremus Bennerman 1.50 4.00
45 Melvin Booker 1.50 4.00
46 Jevon Crudup 1.50 4.00
47 Yinka Dare 1.50 4.00
48 Rodney Dent 1.50 4.00
49 Tony Dumas 1.50 4.00
50 Dwayne Fontana 1.50 4.00
51 Travis Ford 1.50 4.00
52 Lawrence Funderburke 1.50 4.00
53 Anthony Goldwire 1.50 4.00
54 Brian Grant 3.00 8.00
55 Kenny Harris 1.50 4.00
56 Juwan Howard UER 3.00 8.00
57 Askia Jones 1.50 4.00
58 Eddie Jones 4.00 10.00
59 Arturas Karnishovas 1.50 4.00
60 Donyell Marshall 2.50 6.00
61 Billy McCaffrey 1.50 4.00
62 Jim McIlvaine 1.50 4.00
63 Aaron McKie 2.50 6.00
64 Greg Minor 1.50 4.00
65 Eric Mobley 1.50 4.00
66 Eric Montross 2.00 5.00
67 Gaylon Nickerson 1.50 4.00
68 Wesley Person 2.00 5.00
69 Eric Piatkowski 2.00 5.00
70 Kevin Rankin 1.50 4.00
71 Shawnelle Scott 1.50 4.00
72 Melvin Simon 1.50 4.00
73 Dickey Simpkins 1.50 4.00
74 Michael Smith 1.50 4.00
75 Stevin Smith 1.50 4.00
76 Deon Thomas 1.50 4.00
77 Brooks Thompson 1.50 4.00
78 B.J. Tyler 1.50 4.00
79 Kendrick Warren 1.50 4.00
80 Jeff Webster 1.50 4.00
81 Monty Williams 1.50 4.00
82 Dontonio Wingfield 1.50 4.00
83 Sharone Wright 1.50 4.00

1994 Signature Rookies Tetrad Flip Cards

Randomly inserted in packs, these five standard-size two-player cards feature a borderless color action shot of one player per side. The player's name appears in gold-foil lettering near the bottom. The words "1 of 7,500" appear in vertical gold-foil lettering within a simulated marble column near the left edge. The cards are numbered on both sides.

COMPLETE SET (5) 10.00 25.00
3 Charlie Ward BK 2.00 5.00
Charlie Ward FB
4 Juwan Howard 3.00 8.00
Jalen Rose UER
5 Glenn Williams 1.25 3.00
Monty Williams UER

1994 Signature Rookies Tetrad Flip Cards Autographs

Randomly inserted in packs, this three-card set features two-player cards with a borderless color action shot of one player per side. The player's name appears in gold-foil lettering near the bottom. Each card is autographed. The cards are numbered on both sides.

AU2 Glenn/Monty Williams/275 5.00 12.00
AU3 Charlie Ward FB/BK/275 6.00 15.00

1994 Signature Rookies Tetrad Previews

Randomly inserted in Signature Rookies Football packs, these seven standard-size cards feature borderless color player action shots on their fronts. The player's name and position appear in gold-foil lettering near the bottom. The words "Promo, 1 of 10,000" appear in vertical gold-foil lettering within a simulated marble column near the left edge. On a ghosted background drawing of a Greek temple, the back carries the player's name, position, team, height and weight, and career highlights. The cards of this multisport set are numbered on the back with a "T" prefix.

COMPLETE SET (7) 1.25 3.00
T1 Eric Montross .08 .25
T5 Charlie Ward .20 .50

1994 Signature Rookies Tetrad Titans

Randomly inserted in packs, these 12 standard-size cards feature borderless color player action shots on their fronts. The player's name appears in gold-foil lettering near the bottom. The words "1 of 10,000" appear in vertical gold-foil lettering within a simulated marble column near the left edge. On a ghosted background drawing of a Greek temple, the back carries the player's name, position, team, height and weight, and career highlights. The cards of this multisport set are numbered on the back in Roman numerals.

COMPLETE SET (12) 3.00 8.00
120 Larry Bird .75 2.00
130 Isiah Thomas UER .50 1.25

1994 Signature Rookies Tetrad Titans Autographs

Randomly inserted in packs, these 12 standard-size autographed cards comprise a parallel set to the regular 1994 Tetrad Titans set. Aside from the autographs (some cards issued as redemptions in packs) and each card's numbering out of 1,050 produced (except the 2,500 signed O.J. cards), they are identical in design to their regular issue counterparts. The cards of this multisport set are numbered on the back in Roman numerals.

COMPLETE SET (12) 125.00 250.00
120 Larry Bird/1050 40.00 80.00
130 Isiah Thomas/1050 UER 6.00 15.00

1994 Signature Rookies Tetrad Top Prospects

Randomly inserted in packs, these four standard-size cards feature borderless color player action shots on their fronts. The player's name appears in gold-foil lettering near the bottom. The words "1 of 20,000" appear in vertical gold-foil lettering within a simulated marble column near the left edge. On a ghosted background drawing of a Greek temple, the back carries the player's name, biography, statistics, and career highlights. The cards of this multisport set are numbered on the back in Roman numerals.

COMPLETE SET (4) 1.00 2.50
131 Charlie Ward .30 .75

1994 Signature Rookies Tetrad Top Prospects Autographs

This four-card standard size set was randomly inserted in packs. The fronts feature borderless color player action shots with the player's name in gold-foil lettering near the bottom. The cards are autographed on the fronts. The backs carry the player's name, biography, statistics, and career highlights on a ghosted background drawing of a Greek temple. The cards are numbered on the back in Roman numerals. Other than Shante Carver, the cards are numbered out of 2,000.

131A Charlie Ward 4.00 10.00

1995 Signature Rookies Tetrad

This 76-card standard-size set features borderless fronts with color action player photos. The named player stands out on a faded background with his name printed in gold below. The backs carry an elongated color action player photo on one side while a head photo, biographical information, position, college, and career statistics round out the backs.

COMPLETE SET (76) 5.00 12.00
11 Shawn Respert .05 .15
12 Bryant Reeves .08 .25
13 Cherokee Parks .07 .20
14 Greg Ostertag .05 .15
15 Ed O'Bannon .07 .20
16 David Vaughn .05 .15
17 Gary Trent .08 .25
18 Kurt Thomas .08 .25
19 Bob Sura .08 .25
20 Damon Stoudamire .08 .25
21 Brent Barry .08 .25
22 Cory Alexander .05 .15
23 Theo Ratliff .08 .25
24 Loren Meyer .05 .15
25 George Zidek .05 .15
26 Alan Henderson .08 .25
27 Michael Finley .40 1.00
28 Randolph Childress .05 .15
29 Jason Caffey .05 .15
30 Mario Bennett .05 .15
63 Corliss Williamson .08 .25
64 Eric Williams .05 .15
65 Sherell Ford .05 .15

1995 Signature Rookies Tetrad Autographs

SIGS NUMBERED OUT OF 5000
11 Shawn Respert 1.25 3.00
12 Bryant Reeves 2.50 6.00
13 Cherokee Parks 1.50 4.00
14 Greg Ostertag 1.25 3.00
15 Ed O'Bannon 1.50 4.00
16 David Vaughn 1.25 3.00
17 Gary Trent 3.00 8.00
18 Kurt Thomas 1.25 3.00
19 Bob Sura 2.50 6.00
20 Damon Stoudamire 3.00 8.00
21 Brent Barry 1.50 4.00
22 Cory Alexander 1.25 3.00
23 Theo Ratliff 1.50 4.00
24 Loren Meyer 1.25 3.00
25 George Zidek 1.25 3.00
26 Alan Henderson 1.25 3.00
27 Michael Finley 5.00 12.00
28 Randolph Childress 1.25 3.00
29 Jason Caffey 1.25 3.00
30 Mario Bennett 1.25 3.00
63 Corliss Williamson 3.00 8.00
64 Eric Williams 1.25 3.00
65 Sherell Ford 1.25 3.00

1995 Signature Rookies Tetrad Mail-In

This five-card standard size set was available through the mail from Signature Rookies. The set highlights the 1995 first overall draft picks in basketball, football, baseball and hockey. The fronts picture color action photos blended with a fractal-swirling design. In a gold foil stamp, the players name is found vertically on the right, "Mail In" and "#1 Pick" adorn the top and bottom respectively on the left. The back has another color action photo in the upper-right corner. The rest is devoted to a player biography and statistics set on top of the same fractal-swirling design. The cards are numbered with a "P" prefix (P1-P5).

COMPLETE SET (5) 1.50 4.00
P1 Joe Smith .40 1.00
P5 Joe Smith .60 1.50
Ki-Jana Carter
Darin Erstad
Bryan Berard

1995 Signature Rookies Tetrad Previews

This five-card standard-size set was randomly inserted in SR BK autobilia packs. The fronts display borderless color action player photos. The named player stands out on a faded background with his name printed in gold below. The backs carry an elongated color action player photo on one side while a head photo, biographical information, position, college, and career statistics round out the backs.

COMPLETE SET (5) 1.00 2.50
3 Joe Smith .30 .75
4 Jerry Stackhouse .60 1.50

1995 Signature Rookies Tetrad SR Force

This 35-card standard-size set features color action player photos on the front on a white background. Pictures of one foot, the head, and one arm are set out as separate photos on the side of the main picture. The words, "SR Force," are printed in the white border at the top, while the player's name is in gold at the bottom of the picture. The backs carry the same photo as a faded background with photos of the head and parts of one leg. The player's name, position, team, biographical information, and statistics round out the back. The cards are numbered with an "F" prefix.

COMPLETE SET (35) 6.00 15.00
F21 Kevin Garnett .60 1.00
F22 Rasheed Wallace .25 .60
F23 Jerry Stackhouse .25 .60
F24 Antonio McDyess .20 .50
F25 Joe Smith .20 .50

1995 Signature Rookies Tetrad SR Force Autographs

RANDOM INSERTS IN PACKS
F21 Kevin Garnett 10.00 25.00
F22 Rasheed Wallace 5.00 12.00
F23 Jerry Stackhouse 5.00 12.00
F24 Antonio McDyess 4.00 10.00
F25 Joe Smith 3.00 8.00

1995 Signature Rookies Tetrad Titans

This five card standard-size set features borderless fronts with color player action photos on a black background. The player's name is printed at the top with the card name in gold running vertically down the side. The horizontal backs carry another player action photo on a black background with the player's name and a short personal and career summary. The player's position and team round out the back. The cards are numbered with an "T" prefix.

COMPLETE SET (5) 2.00 5.00
T2 Dennis Rodman .60 1.50
T4 Kareem Abdul-Jabbar .75 2.00

1995 Signature Rookies Tetrad Titans Autographs

T2 Dennis Rodman 15.00 40.00
T4 Kareem Abdul-Jabbar 15.00 40.00

1995 Signature Rookies Tetrad Autobilia

The 1995 Signature Rookies Tetrad Autobilia set was issued in one series with a total of 100 cards. The fronts feature a color action player cut-out on a background of a repeated action player photo with the player's name printed in a gold bar at the bottom. The words" Club Set" are printed in gold foil on the fronts as well. The backs carry two player photos with the player's name, position, biographical information, career statistics, and a player fact.

COMPLETE SET (100) 10.00 25.00
*SILVER: .4X TO 1X GOLD
1 Travis Best .30 .75
2 Junior Burrough .08 .25
3 Randolph Childress .08 .25
4 Andrew DeClercq .08 .25
5 Michael Finley .40 1.00
6 Alan Henderson .30 .75
7 Ed O'Bannon .10 .30
8 Cherokee Parks .10 .30
9 Bryant Reeves .15 .40
10 Shawn Respert .08 .25
11 Damon Stoudamire .30 .75
12 Bob Sura .30 .75
13 Scotty Thurman .08 .25
14 Gary Trent .15 .40
15 Corliss Williamson .30 .75
16 Donald Williams .08 .25
17 Eric Williams .08 .25
71 Antonio McDyess .50 1.25
73 Joe Smith .15 .40
74 Jerry Stackhouse .60 1.50
77 Kevin Garnett 1.00 2.50
78 Juwan Howard .30 .75
79 Eddie Jones .30 .75

1995 Signature Rookies Tetrad Autobilia Auto-Phonex Test

This 3-card set was issued in packs of 1995 Signature Rookies Autobilia packs. Each card follows a similar design to the base cards except for the addition of the words 'Auto-Phonex Test Issue' on the left hand side of the cardfronts. The title 'Autobilia' at the top was also replaced with the word Tetrad.

COMPLETE SET (3) 1.25 3.00
T3 Jerry Stackhouse .60 1.50

1995 Signature Rookies Tetrad Autobilia Autographed Cards

1 Travis Best 2.50 6.00
2 Junior Burrough 1.25 3.00
3 Randolph Childress 1.25 3.00
4 Andrew DeClercq 1.25 3.00
5 Michael Finley 6.00 15.00
6 Alan Henderson 3.00 8.00
7 Ed O'Bannon 1.50 4.00
8 Cherokee Parks 1.50 4.00
9 Bryant Reeves 2.50 6.00
10 Shawn Respert 1.25 3.00
11 Damon Stoudamire 3.00 8.00
12 Bob Sura 2.50 6.00
13 Scotty Thurman 1.25 3.00
14 Gary Trent 3.00 8.00
15 Corliss Williamson 3.00 8.00
16 Donald Williams 1.25 3.00
17 Eric Williams 1.25 3.00
71 Antonio McDyess 5.00 12.00
73 Joe Smith 3.00 8.00
74 Jerry Stackhouse 6.00 15.00
77 Kevin Garnett 25.00 50.00
78 Juwan Howard 3.00 8.00
79 Eddie Jones 6.00 15.00

1995 Signature Rookies Tetrad Autobilia Autographed Photos

ANNOUNCED PRINT RUN 3000
1 Travis Best 2.50 6.00
2 Junior Burrough 1.25 3.00
3 Randolph Childress 1.25 3.00
4 Andrew DeClercq 1.25 3.00
5 Michael Finley 6.00 15.00
6 Alan Henderson 1.25 3.00
7 Ed O'Bannon 1.50 4.00
8 Cherokee Parks 1.50 4.00
9 Bryant Reeves 2.50 6.00
10 Shawn Respert 1.25 3.00
11 Damon Stoudamire 3.00 8.00
12 Bob Sura 2.50 6.00
13 Scotty Thurman 1.25 3.00
14 Gary Trent 3.00 8.00
15 Corliss Williamson 3.00 8.00
16 Donald Williams 1.25 3.00
17 Eric Williams 1.25 3.00
71 Antonio McDyess 5.00 12.00
73 Joe Smith 3.00 8.00
74 Jerry Stackhouse 6.00 15.00
77 Kevin Garnett 20.00 40.00
78 Juwan Howard 3.00 8.00
79 Eddie Jones 6.00 15.00

1998 SP Top Prospects

The 1998 SP Top Prospects set was released during the 1998-99 season, and features a 62-card base set broken into tiers as follows: Base Cards (1-40), TP (41-60), and Checklists (61-62).

COMPLETE SET (62) 8.00 20.00
1 Antawn Jamison .75 2.00
2 Vince Carter 1.50 4.00
3 Michael Olowokandi .40 1.00
4 Paul Pierce 1.25 3.00
5 Korleone Young .30 .75
6 Rashard Lewis .75 2.00
7 Miles Simon .30 .75
8 Al Harrington .50 1.25
9 Robert Traylor .30 .75
10 Ansu Sesay .30 .75
11 DeMarco Johnson .30 .75
12 Earl Boykins .30 .75
13 Michael Doleac .30 .75
14 Felipe Lopez .30 .75
15 Cory Carr .20 .50
16 J.R. Henderson .30 .75
17 Michael Dickerson .30 .75
18 Jason Williams .75 2.00
19 Bonzi Wells .30 .75
20 Matt Harpring .30 .75
21 Pat Garrity .30 .75
22 Ricky Davis .50 1.25
23 Tyronn Lue .30 .75
24 Corey Benjamin .30 .75
25 Jelani McCoy .30 .75

26 Shammond Williams .30 .75
27 Toby Bailey .30 .75
28 Saddi Washington .30 .75
29 Zendon Hamilton .30 .75
30 Steve Wojciechowski .30 .75
31 Nazr Mohammed .30 .75
32 Andrae Patterson .30 .75
33 Ryan Bowen .30 .75
34 Anthony Carter .30 .75
35 Jarod Stevenson .30 .75
36 Casey Shaw .20 .50
37 Brad Miller .75 2.00
38 Charles Jones .30 .75
39 Bryce Drew .30 .75
40 Jeff Sheppard .30 .75
41 Antawn Jamison TP .40 1.00
42 Vince Carter TP .75 2.00
43 Michael Olowokandi TP .20 .50
44 Paul Pierce TP .60 1.50
45 Rashard Lewis TP .40 1.00
46 Robert Traylor TP .15 .40
47 Michael Doleac TP .15 .40
48 Felipe Lopez TP .15 .40
49 Michael Dickerson TP .15 .40
50 Jason Williams TP .40 1.00
51 Bonzi Wells TP .15 .40
52 Matt Harpring TP .15 .40
53 Ricky Davis TP .25 .60
54 Tyronn Lue TP .15 .40
55 Corey Benjamin TP .15 .40
56 Ansu Sesay TP .15 .40
57 Pat Garrity TP .15 .40
58 Shammond Williams TP .15 .40
59 Nazr Mohammed TP .15 .40
60 Bryce Drew TP .15 .40
61 Michael Olowokandi CL .20 .50
62 Antawn Jamison CL .40 1.00

1998 SP Top Prospects Carolina Heroes

Randomly inserted in packs at one in 11, this 10-card set features top draft players from North Carolina, including four Michael Jordan cards. Card backs carry a "H" prefix.

COMPLETE SET (10) 15.00 40.00
STATED ODDS 1:11
H1 Michael Jordan 4.00 10.00
H2 Michael Jordan 4.00 10.00
H3 Michael Jordan 4.00 10.00
H4 Michael Jordan 4.00 10.00
H5 Antawn Jamison 1.50 4.00
H6 Antawn Jamison 1.50 4.00
H7 Vince Carter 3.00 8.00
H8 Vince Carter 3.00 8.00
H9 Shammond Williams .60 1.50
H10 Shammond Williams .60 1.50

1998 SP Top Prospects Destination Stardom

Randomly inserted in packs at one in 23, this 20-card set focuses on the top player's from the 1998 Draft and their paths to stardom.

COMPLETE SET (20) 30.00 80.00
STATED ODDS 1:23
1 Antawn Jamison 4.00 10.00
2 Vince Carter 8.00 20.00
3 Michael Olowokandi 2.00 5.00
4 Paul Pierce 6.00 15.00
5 Rashard Lewis 4.00 10.00
6 Robert Traylor 1.50 4.00
7 Michael Doleac 1.50 4.00
8 Felipe Lopez 1.50 4.00
9 Pat Garrity 1.50 4.00
10 Michael Dickerson 1.50 4.00
11 Jason Williams 4.00 10.00
12 Bonzi Wells 1.50 4.00
13 Matt Harpring 1.50 4.00
14 Ricky Davis 2.50 6.00
15 Corey Benjamin 1.50 4.00
16 Tyronn Lue 1.50 4.00
17 Al Harrington 2.50 6.00
18 Ansu Sesay 1.50 4.00
19 Nazr Mohammed 1.50 4.00
20 Bryce Drew 1.50 4.00

1998 SP Top Prospects Phi Beta Jordan

Randomly inserted at one in two, this 23-card set featues Michael Jordan - and his days at North Carolina. Card backs carry a "J" prefix.

COMPLETE SET (23) 12.00 30.00
COMMON CARD (J1-J23) .75 2.00
STATED ODDS 1:2

1998 SP Top Prospects Vital Signs

Randomly inserted at one in 12, this 19-card set features autographs from some of the top players in the draft. The Michael Jordan autograph was numbered out of 23, and is not considered in the set price.

STATED ODDS 1:12
VINCE CARTER DOES NOT EXIST
AH Al Harrington 2.50 6.00
AJ Antawn Jamison 6.00 15.00
AS Ansu Sesay 1.50 4.00
BW Bonzi Wells 1.50 4.00
CC Cory Carr 1.00 2.50
DJ DeMarco Johnson 1.50 4.00
DO Michael Doleac 1.50 4.00
EB Earl Boykins 3.00 8.00
FL Felipe Lopez 1.50 4.00
JR J.R. Henderson 1.50 4.00
JW Jason Williams 5.00 12.00
KY Korleone Young 1.50 4.00
MD Michael Dickerson 1.50 4.00
MH Matt Harpring 1.50 4.00
MJ Michael Jordan/23 1000.00 1800.00
MO Michael Olowokandi 2.00 5.00
MS Miles Simon 1.50 4.00
PP Paul Pierce 8.00 20.00
RL Rashard Lewis 4.00 10.00
RT Robert Traylor 1.50 4.00

1999 SP Top Prospects

This 38-card set was released in August 1999, and features some of the NBA's top draft picks with each shown in his college or high school uniform. The cards were came six per pack with a suggested retail price of $4.99. Cards 8, 15, 19 and 42 were not produced due to a licensing conflict.

COMPLETE SET (38) 4.00 10.00
1 Lee Nailon .15 .40
2 A.J. Bramlett .15 .40
3 Jason Terry .40 1.00
4 Kareem Reid .15 .40
5 Melvin Levett .15 .40
6 Terrell McIntyre .15 .40
7 Trajan Langdon .15 .40
9 Chris Herren .15 .40
10 Shawnta Rogers .15 .40
11 Corey Maggette .30 .75
12 Wayne Turner .15 .40
13 Heshimu Evans .15 .40
14 Bobby Lazor .15 .40
16 Laron Profit .15 .40
17 Ron Artest .40 1.00
18 Tim James .15 .40
20 Louis Bullock .15 .40
21 William Avery .15 .40
22 Quincy Lewis .15 .40
23 Kenny Thomas .15 .40
24 Evan Eschmeyer .15 .40
25 Adrian Peterson .15 .40
26 Keith Carter .15 .40
27 Jelani Gardner .15 .40
28 Baron Davis .40 1.00
29 Jamel Thomas .15 .40
30 B.J. McKie .15 .40
31 Arthur Lee .15 .40
32 Tim Young .15 .40
33 Richard Hamilton .40 1.00
34 Calvin Booth .15 .40
35 Andre Miller .40 1.00
36 Todd MacCulloch .15 .40
37 James Posey .15 .40
38 Lenny Brown .15 .40
39 Scott Padgett .15 .40
40 Venson Hamilton .15 .40
41 Geno Carlisle .15 .40

1999 SP Top Prospects Upper Class

*UPPER CLASS: 10X TO 25X BASIC CARDS
STATED PRINT RUN 50 SERIAL #'d SETS

1999 SP Top Prospects College Legends

Inserted in packs at one in 92, this 10-card set takes a close look at some of the greatest players the college game has ever seen. Card backs contain an "L" prefix.

COMPLETE SET (10) 40.00 80.00
STATED ODDS 1:92
L1 Michael Jordan 10.00 25.00
L2 Michael Jordan 10.00 25.00
L3 Michael Jordan 10.00 25.00
L4 Larry Bird 3.00 8.00
L5 Larry Bird 3.00 8.00
L6 Larry Bird 3.00 8.00
L7 Julius Erving 2.00 5.00
L8 Julius Erving 2.00 5.00
L9 Anfernee Hardaway 2.00 5.00
L10 Anfernee Hardaway 2.00 5.00

1999 SP Top Prospects Jordan's Scrapbook

Randomly inserted in packs at one in 23, this 20-card set focuses on Michael Jordan's career at North Carolina. Card backs carry a "J" prefix.

COMPLETE SET (20) 75.00 150.00
COMMON CARD (J1-J20) 3.00 8.00
STATED ODDS 1:23

1999 SP Top Prospects MJ Flight Mechanics 101

Randomly inserted in packs at one in 4, this 28-card set focuses on 28 top draft picks and provides an introduction into the world of high-flying basketball and what Michael Jordan believes each player will bring to the league. Cards 4 and 25 do not exist. Card backs carry a "FM" prefix.

COMPLETE SET (28) 6.00 15.00
STATED ODDS 1:4
CARDS 4 AND 25 DO NOT EXIST
FM1 Jason Terry .75 2.00
FM2 Geno Carlisle .30 .75
FM3 Heshimu Evans .30 .75
FM5 Keith Carter .30 .75
FM6 Trajan Langdon .30 .75
FM7 Ron Artest .75 2.00
FM8 Kenny Thomas .30 .75
FM9 Lenny Brown .30 .75
FM10 Kareem Reid .30 .75
FM11 Shawnta Rogers .30 .75
FM12 Quincy Lewis .30 .75
FM13 Jamel Thomas .30 .75
FM14 James Posey .30 .75
FM15 Lee Nailon .30 .75
FM16 Melvin Levett .30 .75
FM17 Laron Profit .30 .75
FM18 Louis Bullock .30 .75
FM19 Evan Eschmeyer .30 .75
FM20 B.J. McKie .30 .75
FM21 A.J. Bramlett .30 .75
FM22 Wayne Turner .30 .75
FM23 Jelani Gardner .30 .75
FM24 Terrell McIntyre .30 .75
FM26 Venson Hamilton .30 .75
FM27 Andre Miller .75 2.00
FM28 Chris Herren .30 .75
FM29 Adrian Peterson .30 .75
FM30 Tim James .30 .75

1999 SP Top Prospects Vital Signs

Randomly inserted in packs at one in 4, this 39-card set features autograph cards of the league's top draft picks, as well as Michael Jordan. The Jordan cards are limited to 23. Card backs are numbered by the player's name abbreviation.

STATED ODDS 1:4
AB A.J. Bramlett 1.50 4.00
AL Arthur Lee 1.50 4.00
AM Andre Miller 4.00 10.00
AP Adrian Peterson 1.50 4.00
BD Baron Davis 4.00 10.00
BJ B.J. McKie 1.50 4.00
CH Chris Herren 1.50 4.00
DF Damon Frierson 1.50 4.00
DW Donald Watts 1.50 4.00
EE Evan Eschmeyer 1.50 4.00
GC Geno Carlisle 1.50 4.00
GL Gary Lumpkin 1.50 4.00
HE Heshimu Evans 1.50 4.00
JA Michael Jordan/23 600.00 1000.00
JG Jelani Gardner 1.50 4.00
JK Jermaine Jackson 1.50 4.00
JP James Posey 1.50 4.00
JT Jamel Thomas 1.50 4.00
KR Kareem Reid 1.50 4.00
KT Kenny Thomas 1.50 4.00
KW Kris Weems 1.50 4.00
LB Lenny Brown 1.50 4.00
LN Lee Nailon 1.50 4.00
LP Laron Profit 1.50 4.00
ML Melvin Levett 1.50 4.00
OE Obinna Ekezie 1.50 4.00
PB Pat Bradley 1.50 4.00
QL Quincy Lewis 1.50 4.00
RB Rasheed Brokenborou 1.50 4.00
RH Richard Hamilton 4.00 10.00
SP Scott Padgett 1.50 4.00
SR Shawnta Rogers 1.50 4.00
TE Jason Terry 4.00 10.00
TJ Tim James 1.50 4.00
TL Trajan Langdon 1.50 4.00
TM Terrell McIntyre 1.50 4.00
TY Tim Young 1.50 4.00
VH Venson Hamilton 1.50 4.00
WT Wayne Turner 1.50 4.00

2000 SP Top Prospects

Released in August 2000, this 50-card set features top prospects from the 2000 NBA Draft. The cards were available in five-card packs that carried a suggested retail price of $4.99. The set contains 45 base cards and five "Famous Firsts" subset cards that were individually serial numbered to 3000.

COMPLETE SET (50) 20.00 40.00
COMPLETE SET w/o SPs (45) 6.00 15.00
FF 46-50 PRINT RUN 3000 SERIAL #'d SETS
1 Kenyon Martin .60 1.50
2 Marcus Fizer .25 .60
3 Michael Redd .60 1.50
4 Desmond Mason .30 .75
5 Corey Hightower .25 .60
6 Erick Barkley .25 .60
7 A.J. Guyton .25 .60
8 Gabe Muoneke .25 .60
9 Khalid El-Amin .25 .60
10 Lavor Postell .25 .60
11 Donnell Harvey .25 .60
12 Terrance Roberson .25 .60
13 Matt Santangelo .25 .60
14 Jarrett Stephens .25 .60
15 Richie Frahm .25 .60
16 Pepe Sanchez .25 .60
17 Jason Collier .25 .60
18 Ed Cota .25 .60
19 Scoonie Penn .25 .60
20 Bootsy Thornton .25 .60
21 Eduardo Najera .25 .60
22 DerMarr Johnson .25 .60
23 Chris Carrawell .25 .60
24 Speedy Claxton .25 .60
25 Jaraan Cornell .25 .60
26 Gee Gervin .25 .60
27 Justin Love .25 .60
28 Joel Przybilla .25 .60
29 Eddie House .25 .60
30 Harold Arceneaux .25 .60
31 Johnny Hemsley .25 .60
32 Courtney Alexander .25 .60
33 Lamont Barnes .25 .60
34 Pete Mickeal .25 .60
35 Brian Cardinal .25 .60
36 Kevin Freeman .25 .60
37 Jason Hart .25 .60
38 Eddie Gill .25 .60
39 Mamadou N'Diaye .25 .60
40 Lamont Long .25 .60
41 Dan Langhi .25 .60
42 Shaheen Holloway .25 .60
43 Eric Coley .25 .60
44 JaRon Rush .25 .60
45 Stromile Swift .25 .60
46 Michael Jordan FF 8.00 20.00
47 Kobe Bryant FF 4.00 10.00
48 Kevin Garnett FF 1.50 4.00
49 Anfernee Hardaway FF 1.50 4.00
50 Kenyon Martin FF 2.50 6.00

2000 SP Top Prospects First Impressions

Randomly inserted in packs at one in five, this 38-card set features autographs of some of the top picks from the 2000 NBA Draft. A congratulatory message is on the back. The cards are numbered by the player's initials.

STATED ODDS 1:5
*GOLD: 2X TO 5X BASIC CARDS
GOLD: PRINT RUN 25 SERIAL #'d SETS
AJ A.J. Guyton 2.00 5.00
BL Bobby Lazor 2.00 5.00
CA Courtney Alexander 2.00 5.00
CC Chris Carrawell 2.00 5.00
CH Corey Hightower 2.00 5.00
CL Calvin Booth 2.00 5.00
DH Donnell Harvey 2.00 5.00
DJ DerMarr Johnson 2.00 5.00
DL Dan Langhi 2.00 5.00
DM Desmond Mason 2.50 6.00
EB Erick Barkley 2.00 5.00
EC Ed Cota 2.00 5.00
EG Eddie Gill 2.00 5.00
EH Eddie House 3.00 8.00
EN Eduardo Najera 2.00 5.00
GG Gee Gervin 2.00 5.00
HA Harold Arceneaux 2.00 5.00
HE Johnny Hemsley 2.00 5.00
JA Jason Collier 2.00 5.00
JC Jaraan Cornell 2.00 5.00
JH Jason Hart 2.00 5.00
JP Joel Przybilla 2.00 5.00
JR JaRon Rush 2.00 5.00
KD Keyon Dooling 2.00 5.00
KE Khalid El-Amin 2.00 5.00
KF Kevin Freeman 2.00 5.00
KM Kenyon Martin 6.00 15.00
LL Lamont Long 2.00 5.00
LP Lavor Postell 2.00 5.00
MF Marcus Fizer 2.00 5.00
MN Mamadou N'Diaye 2.00 5.00
MR Michael Redd 5.00 12.00
MS Matt Santangelo 2.00 5.00
PM Pete Mickeal 2.00 5.00
PS Pepe Sanchez 2.00 5.00
SC Speedy Claxton 2.00 5.00
SP Scoonie Penn 2.00 5.00
SS Stromile Swift 2.00 5.00

2000 SP Top Prospects Future Glory

Randomly inserted in packs at one in 15, this 10-card set focuses on the top draft picks who are bound for the big time. Card backs carry a "F" prefix.

COMPLETE SET (10) 5.00 12.00
STATED ODDS 1:15
F1 Scoonie Penn .60 1.50
F2 Kenyon Martin 1.50 4.00
F3 Marcus Fizer .60 1.50
F4 Chris Carrawell .60 1.50
F5 Donnell Harvey .60 1.50
F6 Erick Barkley .60 1.50
F7 A.J. Guyton .60 1.50
F8 DerMarr Johnson .60 1.50
F9 Desmond Mason .75 2.00
F10 Courtney Alexander .60 1.50

2000 SP Top Prospects Game Jerseys

Randomly inserted in packs at one in 150, this nine-card set features swatches of the players college uniforms. Card backs are numbered by the player's initials. Two autographed Game Jerseys were also inserted, numbered to 25. Those cards are not included in the set price.

STATED ODDS 1:150
CRJ Speedy Claxton 5.00 12.00
DLJ Dan Langhi 5.00 12.00
ECJ Ed Cota 5.00 12.00
JCJ Jason Collier 5.00 12.00
KFJ Kevin Freeman 5.00 12.00
KMA Kenyon Martin AU/25 75.00 150.00
KMJ Kenyon Martin 12.00 30.00
LPJ Lavor Postell 5.00 12.00
MFA Marcus Fizer AU/25 20.00 50.00
MFJ Marcus Fizer 5.00 12.00
PSJ Pepe Sanchez 5.00 12.00

2000 SP Top Prospects Honors Society

Randomly inserted in packs at one in seven, this 12-card set honors college basketball's All-American and All-Conference players. Card backs carry a "H" prefix.

COMPLETE SET (12) 5.00 12.00
STATED ODDS 1:7
H1 Kenyon Martin 1.25 3.00
H2 Marcus Fizer .50 1.25
H3 Courtney Alexander .50 1.25
H4 Chris Carrawell .50 1.25
H5 A.J. Guyton .50 1.25
H6 Desmond Mason .60 1.50
H7 Erick Barkley .50 1.25
H8 Ed Cota .50 1.25
H9 Pepe Sanchez .50 1.25
H10 DerMarr Johnson .50 1.25
H11 Scoonie Penn .50 1.25
H12 Stromile Swift .50 1.25

2000 SP Top Prospects New Wave

Randomly inserted in packs at one in three, this 20-card set features the top picks who are ready for the NBA. Card backs carry a "N" prefix.

COMPLETE SET (20) 5.00 12.00
STATED ODDS 1:3
N1 Kenyon Martin 1.00 2.50
N2 Mamadou N'Diaye .40 1.00
N3 Courtney Alexander .40 1.00
N4 Speedy Claxton .40 1.00
N5 JaRon Rush .40 1.00
N6 Pete Mickeal .40 1.00
N7 Eduardo Najera .40 1.00
N8 Erick Barkley .40 1.00
N9 Scoonie Penn .40 1.00
N10 Desmond Mason .50 1.25
N11 Chris Carrawell .40 1.00
N12 Jason Hart .40 1.00
N13 DerMarr Johnson .40 1.00
N14 Pepe Sanchez .40 1.00
N15 Jarrett Stephens .40 1.00
N16 Ed Cota .40 1.00
N17 Marcus Fizer .40 1.00
N18 A.J. Guyton .40 1.00
N19 Khalid El-Amin .40 1.00
N20 Lavor Postell .40 1.00

1990 Star Pics

This premier edition showcases sixty of college basketball's top pro prospects. The cards were issued exclusively in complete factory set boxes distributed by hobby dealers. The cards measure the standard size. The front features a color action player photo, with the player shown in his college uniform. A white border separates the picture from the surrounding "basketball" background. The player's name appears in an aqua box at the bottom. The back has a head shot of the player in the upper left corner and the card number in a red star in the upper right corner. On a tan-colored basketball court design, the back presents biography, accomplishments, and a mini-scouting report that assesses a player's strengths and weaknesses.

COMP. FACT SET (70) 3.00 6.00
1 Checklist .01 .05
2 David Robinson FLB .40 1.00
3 Antonio Davis .08 .25
4 Steve Bardo .01 .05
5 Jayson Williams .05 .15
6 Alaa Abdelnaby .01 .05
7 Trevor Wilson .01 .05
8 Dee Brown .05 .15
9 Dennis Scott .05 .15
10 Danny Ferry .05 .15
11 Stevie Thompson .01 .05
12 Anthony Bonner .01 .05
13 Keith Robinson .01 .05
14 Sean Higgins .01 .05
15 Bo Kimble .01 .05
16 David Jamerson .01 .05
17 Anthony Pullard .01 .05
18 Phil Henderson .01 .05
19 Mike Mitchell .01 .05
20 Vanderbilt Team .01 .05
21 Gary Payton .60 1.50
22 Tony Massenburg .01 .05
23 Cedric Ceballos .08 .25
24 Dwayne Schintzius .01 .05
25 Bimbo Coles .05 .15
26 Scott Williams .01 .05
27 Willie Burton .01 .05
28 Tate George .01 .05
29 Mark Stevenson .01 .05
30 UNLV Team .01 .05
31 Earl Wise .01 .05
32 Alec Kessler .01 .05
33 Les Jepsen .01 .05
34 Boo Harvey .01 .05
35 Elden Campbell .05 .15
36 Jud Buechler .01 .05
37 Loy Vaught .05 .15
38 Tyrone Hill .05 .15
39 Toni Kukoc .60 1.50
40 Jim Calhoun CO .15 .25
41 Felton Spencer .01 .05
42 Dan Godfread .01 .05
43 Derrick Coleman .08 .25
44 Terry Mills .05 .15
45 Kendall Gill .05 .15
46 A.J. English .01 .05
47 Duane Causwell .01 .05
48 Jerrod Mustaf .01 .05
49 Alan Ogg .01 .05
50 Pervis Ellison .01 .05
51 Matt Bullard .01 .05
52 Melvin Newbern .01 .05
53 Marcus Liberty .01 .05
54 Walter Palmer .01 .05
55 Negele Knight .01 .05
56 Steve Hanson .01 .05
57 Greg Foster .01 .05
58 Brian Oliver .01 .05
59 Travis Mays .01 .05
60 All-Rookie Team .05 .15
61 Steve Scheffler .01 .05
62 Chris Jackson .05 .15
63 Derek Strong .01 .05
64 David Butler .01 .05
65 Kevin Pritchard .01 .05
66 Lionel Simmons .05 .15
67 Gerald Glass .01 .05
68 Tony Harris .01 .05
69 Lance Blanks .01 .05
70 Dave Kaplan .01 .05

1990 Star Pics Medallion

COMP.FACT.SET (70) 3.00 8.00
*MEDALLIONS: .5X TO 1.25X BASE CARD HI
DISTRIBUTED IN FACTORY SET FORM
NNO Medallion special card .02 .10

1990 Star Pics Autographs

Randomly inserted in boxes, this set paralled the regular set. Each card contained the player's autograph on the front and a sticker of authenticity on the back. To ascertain values on individual cards, please refer to the multiplier in the header, coupled with the value of the base card.

*AUTOS: 15X TO 40X BASE CARD HI
STATED ODDS 1:50 FACTORY SETS

1991 Star Pics

This 73-card standard-size set was produced by Star Pics, subtitled "Pro Prospects," and features 45 of the 54 players picked in the 1991 NBA draft. The cards were issued exclusively in complete factory set boxes distributed by hobby dealers. The front features a color action photo of player in his college uniform. This picture overlays a black background with a basketball partially in view. The back has a color head shot of the player in the upper left corner and an orange border. On a two color jersey background, the back presents biographical information, accomplishments, and a mini scouting report assessing the player's strengths and weaknesses.

COMP.FACT.SET (73) 1.50 3.00
1 Draft Overview .02 .10
2 Derrick Coleman FLB .05 .15
3 Treg Lee .02 .10
4 Rich King .02 .10
5 Kenny Anderson .20 .50
6 John Crotty .05 .15
7 Mark Randall .02 .10
8 Kevin Brooks .02 .10
9 Lamont Strothers .02 .10
10 Tim Hardaway FLB .20 .50
11 Eric Murdock .05 .15
12 Melvin Cheatum .02 .10
13 Pete Chilcutt .05 .15
14 Zan Tabak .02 .10
15 Greg Anthony .05 .15
16 George Ackles .02 .10
17 Stacey Augmon .05 .15
18 Larry Johnson .30 .75
19 Alvaro Teheran .02 .10
20 Reggie Miller FLB .20 .50
21 Steve Smith .30 .75
22 Sean Green .02 .10
23 Johnny Pittman .02 .10
24 Anthony Avent .02 .10
25 Chris Gatling .05 .15
26 Mark Macon .05 .15
27 Joey Wright .02 .10
28 Von McDade .02 .10
29 Bobby Phills .05 .15
30 Larry Fleisher .02 .10
31 Luc Longley .05 .15
32 Jean Derouillere .02 .10
33 Doug Smith .02 .10
34 Chad Gallagher .02 .10
35 Marty Dow .02 .10
36 Tony Farmer .02 .10
37 John Taft .02 .10
38 Reggie Hanson .02 .10
39 Terrell Brandon .20 .50
40 Dee Brown .05 .15
41 Doug Overton .02 .10
42 Joe Wylie .02 .10
43 Myron Brown .02 .10
44 Steve Hood .02 .10
45 Randy Brown .05 .15
46 Chris Corchiani .05 .15
47 Kevin Lynch .02 .10
48 Donald Hodge .02 .10
49 LaBradford Smith .02 .10
50 Shawn Kemp FLB .20 .50
51 Brian Shorter .02 .10
52 Gary Waites .02 .10
53 Mike Iuzzolino .02 .10
54 LeRon Ellis .02 .10
55 Perry Carter .02 .10
56 Keith Hughes .02 .10
57 John Turner .02 .10
58 Marcus Kennedy .02 .10
59 Randy Ayers CO .02 .10
60 All-Rookie Team .15 .40
61 Jackie Jones .02 .10
62 Shaun Vandiver .02 .10
63 Dale Davis .20 .50
64 Jimmy Oliver .02 .10
65 Elliot Perry .05 .15
66 Jerome Harmon .02 .10
67 Darrin Chancellor .02 .10
68 Roy Fisher .02 .10
69 Rick Fox .08 .25
70 Kenny Anderson SPEC .20 .50
71 Richard Dumas .02 .10
72 Checklist .02 .10
NNO Salute/American Flag .02 .10

1991 Star Pics Medallion

SEALED SET (73) 6.00 15.00
*MEDALLION: 1X TO 2.5X BASE CARD HI

1991 Star Pics Autographs

Randomly inserted into sets, these cards featured autographs of the draft picks.

RANDOM INSERTS IN SETS
3 Treg Lee 2.00 5.00
4 Rich King 2.00 5.00
5 Kenny Anderson 5.00 12.00
6 John Crotty 2.00 5.00
7 Mark Randall 2.00 5.00
8 Kevin Brooks 2.00 5.00
9 Lamont Strothers 2.00 5.00
11 Eric Murdock 2.00 5.00
12 Melvin Cheatum 2.00 5.00
13 Pete Chilcutt 4.00 10.00
14 Zan Tabak 2.00 5.00
15 Greg Anthony 4.00 10.00
16 George Ackles 2.00 5.00
17 Stacey Augmon 4.00 10.00
18 Larry Johnson 15.00 30.00
19 Alvaro Teheran 2.00 5.00
21 Steve Smith 8.00 20.00
22 Sean Green 2.00 5.00
23 Johnny Pittman 2.00 5.00
24 Anthony Avent 2.00 5.00
25 Chris Gatling 4.00 10.00
26 Mark Macon 2.00 5.00
27 Joey Wright 2.00 5.00
28 Von McDade 2.00 5.00
29 Bobby Phills 5.00 12.00
31 Luc Longley 4.00 10.00
32 Jean Derouillere 2.00 5.00
33 Doug Smith 2.00 5.00
34 Chad Gallagher 2.00 5.00
35 Marty Dow 2.00 5.00
36 Tony Farmer 2.00 5.00
37 John Taft 2.00 5.00
38 Reggie Hanson 2.00 5.00
39 Terrell Brandon 5.00 12.00
40 Dee Brown 4.00 10.00
41 Doug Overton 2.00 5.00
42 Joe Wylie 2.00 5.00
43 Myron Brown 2.00 5.00
44 Steve Hood 2.00 5.00
45 Randy Brown 4.00 10.00
46 Chris Corchiani 4.00 10.00
47 Kevin Lynch 2.00 5.00
48 Donald Hodge 2.00 5.00
49 LaBradford Smith 2.00 5.00
50 Shawn Kemp FLB 4.00 10.00
51 Brian Shorter 2.00 5.00
52 Gary Waites 2.00 5.00
53 Mike Iuzzolino 2.00 5.00
54 LeRon Ellis 2.00 5.00
55 Perry Carter 2.00 5.00
56 Keith Hughes 2.00 5.00
57 John Turner 2.00 5.00
58 Marcus Kennedy 2.00 5.00
59 Randy Ayers CO 4.00 10.00
61 Jackie Jones 2.00 5.00
62 Shaun Vandiver 2.00 5.00
63 Dale Davis 5.00 12.00
64 Jimmy Oliver 2.00 5.00
65 Elliot Perry 4.00 10.00
66 Jerome Harmon 2.00 5.00
67 Darrin Chancellor 2.00 5.00
68 Roy Fisher 2.00 5.00
69 Rick Fox 5.00 12.00
71 Richard Dumas 2.00 5.00

1992 Star Pics

The 1992 Star Pics Pro Prospects Basketball HotPics set contains 90 standard-size cards. The set includes 47 of the 54 players selected in the 1992 NBA Draft as well as some free agents who had a chance to make NBA rosters. Special cards featured in the set include eight StarStats (10, 31, 36, 43, 74, 78, 81, 89), five Flashbacks (30, 40, 50, 60, 70), three Kid cards (33, 68, 83), and two coaches cards (5, 15). Each nine-card foil StarPak included one "Jump At The Chance" game card, with which collectors could win various prizes. The fronts display color action player photos with white borders. The player's position and name are printed vertically in the right border, with the latter in a colored stripe. The Star Pics logo in the lower right corner rounds out the card face. The backs present accomplishments, strengths, weaknesses, and biographical information. A close-up photo appears at the lower right corner inside the Star Pics logo. The unnumbered Bonus card of Steve Smith features a full-bleed color illustration by artist Rip Evans.

COMPLETE SET (90) 2.50 6.00
1 Draft Overview .01 .05
2 Bryant Stith .02 .10
3 Reggie Smith .01 .05
4 Todd Day .02 .10
5 Bob Knight CO .30 .75
6 Darren Morningstar .01 .05
7 Clarence Weatherspoon .02 .10
8 Matt Geiger .02 .10
9 Marlon Maxey .01 .05
10 Christian Laettner SS .07 .20
11 Tony Bennett .01 .05
12 Sean Rooks .01 .05
13 Tom Gugliotta .25 .60
14 Chris King .01 .05
15 Mike Krzyzewski CO .30 .75
16 Sam Mack .02 .10
17 Matt Fish .01 .05
18 Brian Davis .01 .05
19 Oliver Miller .01 .05
20 Daimon Sweet .01 .05
21 Eric Anderson .01 .05
22 Henry Williams .01 .05
23 David Johnson .01 .05
24 Duane Cooper .01 .05
25 Lucius Davis .01 .05
26 Matt Steigenga .01 .05
27 Robert Horry .07 .20
28 Brent Price .01 .05
29 Chris Smith .01 .05
30 Vlade Divac FLB .02 .10
31 Adam Keefe SS .01 .05
32 Christian Laettner .15 .40
33 LaPhonso Ellis .07 .20
34 Alex Blackwell .01 .05
35 Popeye Jones .01 .05
36 Walt Williams SS .02 .10
37 Radenko Dobras .01 .05
38 Latrell Sprewell .60 1.50
39 Isaiah Morris .01 .05
40 Horace Grant FLB .02 .10
41 Craig Upchurch .01 .05
42 Alonzo Jamison .01 .05
43 Bryant Stith SS .01 .05
44 Jon Barry .01 .05
45 Litterial Green .01 .05
46 Malik Sealy .02 .10
47 Anthony Peeler .02 .10
48 Dexter Cambridge .01 .05
49 Eric Manuel .01 .05
50 Kendall Gill FLB .02 .10
51 Hubert Davis .02 .10
52 Steve Rogers .01 .05
53 Byron Houston .01 .05
54 Randy Woods .01 .05
55 Elmer Bennett .01 .05
56 Smokey McCovery .01 .05
57 George Gilmore .01 .05
58 Predrag Danilovic .01 .05
59 John Pelphrey .01 .05
60 Dan Majerle FLB .07 .20
61 Elmore Spencer .01 .05
62 Calvin Talford .01 .05
63 David Booth .01 .05
64 Herb Jones .01 .05
65 Benford Williams .01 .05
66 Greg Dennis .01 .05
67 James McCoy .01 .05
68 Clarence Weatherspoon KID .01 .05
69 LaPhonso Ellis .07 .20
70 Sarunus Marciulionis FLB .01 .05
71 Walt Williams .07 .20
72 Lee Mayberry .01 .05
73 Doug Christie .07 .20
74 Jon Barry SS .01 .05
75 Adam Keefe .01 .05
76 Robert Werdann .01 .05
77 P.J. Brown .02 .10
78 Tom Gugliotta SS .10 .30
79 Terrell Lowery .01 .05
80 Tracy Murray .01 .05
81 Clarence Weatherspoon SS .01 .05
82 Melvin Robinson .01 .05
83 Todd Day .01 .05
84 Harold Miner .01 .05
85 Tim Burroughs .01 .05
86 Damon Patterson .01 .05
87 Corey Williams .01 .05
88 Harold Ellis .01 .05
89 LaPhonso Ellis SS .02 .10
90 Checklist .01 .05
NNO Steve Smith ART BC 1.00 2.50

1992 Star Pics Autographs

Redeemable from winning game cards, this set was a parallel to the base set. Each card featured autographs of the draft picks.

DIST.VIA MAIL FROM WINNING GAME CARDS
2 Bryant Stith 4.00 10.00
3 Reggie Smith 2.00 5.00
4 Todd Day 2.00 5.00
5 Bob Knight CO 15.00 40.00
6 Darren Morningstar 2.00 5.00
8 Matt Geiger 2.00 5.00
9 Marlon Maxey 2.00 5.00
10 Christian Laettner SS 4.00 10.00
11 Tony Bennett 2.00 5.00
12 Sean Rooks 2.00 5.00
13 Tom Gugliotta 4.00 10.00
14 Chris King 2.00 5.00
15 Mike Krzyzewski CO 75.00 150.00
16 Sam Mack 2.00 5.00
17 Matt Fish 2.00 5.00
18 Brian Davis 2.00 5.00
19 Oliver Miller 2.00 5.00
20 Daimon Sweet 2.00 5.00
21 Eric Anderson 2.00 5.00
22 Henry Williams 2.00 5.00
23 David Johnson 2.00 5.00
24 Duane Cooper 2.00 5.00
25 Lucius Davis 2.00 5.00
26 Matt Steigenga 2.00 5.00
27 Robert Horry 40.00 80.00
28 Brent Price 2.00 5.00
29 Chris Smith 2.00 5.00
30 Vlade Divac FLB 6.00 15.00
31 Adam Keefe SS 2.00 5.00
32 Christian Laettner 4.00 10.00
33 LaPhonso Ellis 4.00 10.00
34 Alex Blackwell - 2.00 5.00
35 Popeye Jones 2.00 5.00
36 Walt Williams SS 2.00 5.00
37 Radenko Dobras 2.00 5.00
38 Latrell Sprewell 15.00 40.00
39 Isaiah Morris 2.00 5.00
40 Horace Grant FLB 4.00 10.00
41 Craig Upchurch 2.00 5.00
42 Alonzo Jamison 2.00 5.00
43 Bryant Stith SS 2.00 5.00
44 Jon Barry 8.00 20.00
45 Litterial Green 2.00 5.00
46 Malik Sealy 4.00 10.00
47 Anthony Peeler 4.00 10.00
48 Dexter Cambridge 2.00 5.00
49 Eric Manuel 2.00 5.00
50 Kendall Gill FLB 4.00 10.00
51 Hubert Davis 10.00 25.00
52 Steve Rogers 2.00 5.00
53 Byron Houston 2.00 5.00
54 Randy Woods 2.00 5.00
55 Elmer Bennett 2.00 5.00
56 Smokey McCovery 2.00 5.00
57 George Gilmore 2.00 5.00
58 Predrag Danilovic 2.00 5.00
59 John Pelphrey 2.00 5.00
60 Dan Majerle FLB 5.00 12.00
61 Elmore Spencer 2.00 5.00
62 Calvin Talford 2.00 5.00
63 David Booth 2.00 5.00
64 Herb Jones 2.00 5.00
65 Benford Williams 2.00 5.00
66 Greg Dennis 2.00 5.00
67 James McCoy 2.00 5.00
68 Clarence Weatherspoon KID 4.00 10.00
69 LaPhonso Ellis 4.00 10.00
70 Sarunus Marciulionis FLB 2.00 5.00
71 Walt Williams 6.00 15.00
72 Lee Mayberry 2.00 5.00
73 Doug Christie 4.00 10.00
74 Jon Barry SS 4.00 10.00
75 Adam Keefe 5.00 12.00
76 Robert Werdann 2.00 5.00
77 P.J. Brown 4.00 10.00
78 Tom Gugliotta SS 4.00 10.00
79 Terrell Lowery 2.00 5.00
80 Tracy Murray 2.00 5.00
82 Melvin Robinson 2.00 5.00
83 Todd Day 2.00 5.00
84 Harold Miner 10.00 25.00
85 Tim Burroughs 2.00 5.00
86 Damon Patterson 2.00 5.00
87 Corey Williams 2.00 5.00
88 Harold Ellis 2.00 5.00
89 LaPhonso Ellis SS 4.00 10.00

1994-95 Superior Pix Promos

These four standard-size cards were promos for the regular edition 1994-95 Superior Pix Pro Basketball Draft Pix set. The fronts feature full-bleed color action photos, except on the left and bottom where pebble-grain stripes edge the pictures. The player's name is gold foil-stamped in the left pebble-grain stripe. The backs carry a small color player close-up in the upper left corner, and a small action shot in the lower right, along with player biography and profile.

COMPLETE SET (4) 1.50 4.00
1 Glenn Robinson .30 .75
2 Jason Kidd .75 2.00
3 Grant Hill .75 2.00
4 Eddie Jones .50 1.25

1995 Superior Pix

Formerly known as Superior Rookies, this Pro Basketball Draft Pix set consists of 80 standard-size cards. This set was released as a sub-license of Classic. Just 2,995 numbered cases were produced, with 12 boxes per case. Two authentic autographs were inserted in each box. Each case included one autographed card of Robinson or Kidd, as well as one of Mutombo, Mourning or Mashburn. The 8-card packs consist of 7 regular cards and one of 30 1st-round chrome cards (1-26, 74-77). The fronts feature full-bleed color action photos, except on the left and bottom where pebble-grain stripes edge the pictures and have the player's name. The backs carry a small color player close-up in the upper left corner, a small black-and-white player action shot in the lower right, as well as biography and player profile.

COMPLETE SET (80) 2.50 6.00
1 Glenn Robinson .12 .30
2 Jason Kidd .25 .60
3 Grant Hill .25 .60
4 Donyell Marshall .10 .25
5 Juwan Howard .15 .40
6 Sharone Wright .10 .25
7 Brian Grant .12 .30
8 Eric Montross .10 .25
9 Eddie Jones .20 .50
10 Carlos Rogers .10 .25
11 Khalid Reeves .10 .25
12 Jalen Rose .20 .50
13 Yinka Dare .10 .25
14 Eric Piatkowski .12 .30
15 Clifford Rozier .10 .25
16 Aaron McKie .10 .25
17 Eric Mobley .10 .25
18 Tony Dumas .10 .25
19 B.J. Tyler .10 .25
20 Dickey Simpkins .10 .25
21 Bill Curley .10 .25
22 Wesley Person .10 .25
23 Monty Williams .10 .25
24 Greg Minor .10 .25
25 Charlie Ward .10 .25
26 Brooks Thompson .10 .25
27 Sam Mitchell .10 .25
28 Deon Thomas .10 .25
29 Antonio Lang .10 .25
30 Howard Eisley .10 .25
31 Jamie Watson .10 .25
32 Jim McIlvaine .10 .25
33 Jervaughn Scales .10 .25

34 Kendrick Warren .10 .25
35 Melvin Simon .10 .25
36 Albert Burditt .10 .25
37 Robert Shannon .10 .25
38 Kevin Rankin .10 .25
39 Byron Starks .10 .25
40 Askia Jones .10 .25
41 Harry Moore .10 .25
42 Abdul Fox .10 .25
43 Doremus Benneman .10 .25
44 Adrian Autry .10 .25
45 Myron Walker .10 .25
46 Shawnelle Scott .10 .25
47 Tracy Webster .10 .25
48 Billy McCaffrey .10 .25
49 Arturas Karnishovas .10 .25
50 Dwayne Morton .10 .25
51 Anthony Miller .10 .25
52 Damon Bailey .10 .25
53 Lawrence Funderburke .10 .25
54 Darrin Hancock .10 .25
55 Jeff Webster .10 .25
56 Jevon Crudup .10 .25
57 Robert Churchwell .10 .25
58 Damon Key .10 .25
59 Chuck Graham .10 .25
60 Jamie Brandon .10 .25
61 Travis Ford .10 .25
62 Derrick Phelps .10 .25
63 Stevin Smith .10 .25
64 Brian Reese .10 .25
65 Kevin Salvadori .10 .25
66 Steve Woodberry .10 .25
67 Shon Tarver .10 .25
68 Joey Brown .10 .25
69 Melvin Booker .10 .25
70 Carl Ray Harris .10 .25
71 Gaylon Nickerson .10 .25
72 Trevor Ruffin .10 .25
73 Anthony Goldwire .10 .25
74 Shaquille O'Neal .40 1.00
75 Dikembe Mutombo .15 .40
76 Alonzo Mourning .20 .50
77 Jamal Mashburn .15 .40
78 Glenn Robinson .12 .30
79 Grant Hill .25 .60
80 Checklist .10 .25

1995 Superior Pix Gold

COMPLETE SET (80) 5.00 12.00
*GOLD: .75X TO 2X BASIC CARDS

1995 Superior Pix Autographs

Formerly known as Superior Rookies, this Pro Basketball Draft Pix Autograph set consists of 38 standard-size cards. The fronts feature full-bleed color action photos, except on the left and bottom where pebble-grain stripes edge the pictures and have the player's name. The signature is on the player's photo with the serial number on the bottom of the card. The backs carry a small color player close-up in the upper left corner, and a small black-and-white player action shot in the lower right, along with player biography and profile.

STATED ODDS 1:18
PRINT RUNS LISTED BELOW
POSSIBLY MORE THAN 200 O'NEALS EXIST
1 Glenn Robinson/1500 6.00 15.00
2 Jason Kidd/1500 12.00 30.00
5 Juwan Howard/1250 4.00 10.00
6 Sharone Wright/2500 .75 2.00
7 Brian Grant/3000 3.00 8.00
8 Eric Montross/2500 .75 2.00
9 Eddie Jones/3000 4.00 10.00
13 Yinka Dare/2000 .75 2.00
14 Eric Piatkowski/2500 2.00 5.00
15 Clifford Rozier/2500 .75 2.00
16 Aaron McKie/3500 .75 2.00
17 Eric Mobley/3000 .75 2.00
18 Tony Dumas/3000 .75 2.00
19 B.J. Tyler/3000 .75 2.00
20 Dickey Simpkins/2000 .75 2.00
21 Bill Curley/3000 .75 2.00
22 Wesley Person/3500 .75 2.00
23 Monty Williams/2500 .75 2.00
24 Greg Minor/2500 .75 2.00
25 Charlie Ward/2500 2.00 5.00
26 Brooks Thompson/2000 .75 2.00
28 Deon Thomas/2700 .75 2.00
30 Howard Eisley/2500 .75 2.00
32 Jim McIlvaine/2600 .75 2.00
40 Askia Jones/3600 .75 2.00
41 Harry Moore/3000 .75 2.00
44 Adrian Autry/2500 .75 2.00
46 Shawnelle Scott/4000 .75 2.00
52 Damon Bailey/3500 .75 2.00
53 Darrin Hancock/2500 .75 2.00
55 Jeff Webster/1250 .75 2.00
57 Robert Churchwell/3000 .75 2.00
61 Travis Ford/3000 .75 2.00
68 Joey Brown/3000 .75 2.00
74 Shaquille O'Neal/200 30.00 80.00
75 Dikembe Mutombo/1000 6.00 15.00
76 Alonzo Mourning/1000 10.00 25.00
77 Jamal Mashburn/1000 6.00 15.00

1995 Superior Pix Chrome

These cards were randomly inserted into packs. These standard-sized cards feature the player in their college uniform. Every player in this insert set was a first round pick in the NBA draft. There was one chrome gold card in each box. The fronts feature a player action cutout against a basketball background. The backs reads "1st round pick" against a basketball background.

COMPLETE SET (30) 4.00 10.00
*GOLD: .75X TO 2X HI COLUMN
1 Glenn Robinson .40 1.00
2 Jason Kidd .75 2.00
3 Grant Hill .75 2.00
4 Donyell Marshall .30 .75
5 Juwan Howard .50 1.25
6 Sharone Wright .30 .75
7 Brian Grant .40 1.00
8 Eric Montross .30 .75
9 Eddie Jones .60 1.50
10 Carlos Rogers .30 .75
11 Khalid Reeves .30 .75
12 Jalen Rose .60 1.50
13 Yinka Dare .30 .75
14 Eric Piatkowski .40 1.00
15 Clifford Rozier .30 .75
16 Aaron McKie .30 .75
17 Eric Mobley .30 .75
18 Tony Dumas .30 .75
19 B.J. Tyler .30 .75
20 Dickey Simpkins .30 .75
21 Bill Curley .30 .75
22 Wesley Person .30 .75
23 Monty Williams .30 .75
24 Greg Minor .30 .75
25 Charlie Ward .30 .75
26 Brooks Thompson .30 .75
27 Dikembe Mutombo .50 1.25
28 Alonzo Mourning .60 1.50
29 Jamal Mashburn .50 1.25
30 Shaquille O'Neal 1.25 3.00

1995 Superior Pix Instant Impact

This 10-card standard-size chrome standard-size set was inserted at a rate of one in every nine packs. Horizontal fronts feature the player in a box for most of the left hand side of the card. Just above the photo is the player's name. The words "Instant Impact" are at the lower right corner. The backs feature a larger version of the front photo on the left side of the card. A Glenn Robinson blank back promo was also issued.

COMPLETE SET (10) 3.00 8.00
1 Shaquille O'Neal 1.25 3.00
2 Glenn Robinson .40 1.00
2P Glenn Robinson Blank Back Promo .40 1.00
3 Jason Kidd .75 2.00
4 Grant Hill .75 2.00
5 Dikembe Mutombo .50 1.25
6 Alonzo Mourning .60 1.50
7 Jamal Mashburn .50 1.25
8 Juwan Howard .50 1.25
9 Brian Grant .40 1.00
10 Wesley Person .30 .75

1995 Superior Pix Lottery Pick

This 10-card standard-size set was inserted at a rate of one in every 36 packs. The cards are clear acetate and fronts feature the player in their college uniform with the Superior Pix logo in the upper left hand corner and the player's name on the bottom left corner of the card. Since the card is made of clear acetate, the back allows one to see what is on the front from a reverse angle.

COMPLETE SET (10) 6.00 15.00
1 Glenn Robinson 1.50 4.00
2 Jason Kidd 3.00 8.00
3 Grant Hill 3.00 8.00
4 Donyell Marshall 1.25 3.00
5 Juwan Howard 2.00 5.00
6 Sharone Wright 1.25 3.00
7 Brian Grant 1.50 4.00
8 Eric Montross 1.25 3.00
9 Eddie Jones 2.50 6.00
10 Carlos Rogers 1.25 3.00

1995 Ted Williams Promos

These standard-size card were issued to promote the 1995 Ted Williams basketball series. On a partially screened background, the front features a color action photo. Names are printed vertically in team color-coded lettering along the left edge. The back carries an advertisement for the set.

COMPLETE SET (2) 1.25 3.00
P1 Charles Barkley 1.00 2.50
P2 Jason Kidd 1.00 2.50

1995 Ted Williams

The 1995 Ted Williams Draft Pick set consists of 90 standard-size cards, featuring key 1994 draft picks and second-year standouts. 2,999 cases were produced. This set was issued as a sub-license of Classic. These cards were sold in 8-card packs, and each 24-pack box contained either one signature card or a hot pack, which had all inserts. The fronts feature the player's last name in the middle left with the Ted Williams logo in the upper left corner and a silhouette of a basketball player in the lower left side of the card. The backs feature biographical information along with collegiate statistics and a player profile. The first eighty cards are arranged in alphabetical order. The set closes with a Flashback (80-88) subset and checklist cards (89-90).

COMPLETE SET (90) 4.00 10.00
1 Derrick Alston .10 .25
2 Adrian Autry .10 .25
3 Damon Bailey .10 .25
4 Doremus Benneman .10 .25
5 Randy Blocker .10 .25
6 Melvin Booker .10 .25
7 Jamie Brandon .10 .25
8 Barry Brown UER .10 .25
9 Joey Brown UER .10 .25
10 Albert Burditt .10 .25
11 Robert Churchwell .10 .25
12 Gary Collier .10 .25
13 Jevon Crudup .10 .25
14 Bill Curley .10 .25
15 Yinka Dare .10 .25
16 Rodney Dent .10 .25
17 Tony Dumas .10 .25
18 Howard Eisley .10 .25
19 Andrei Fetisov .10 .25
20 Travis Ford .10 .25
21 Abdul Fox .10 .25
22 Lawrence Funderburke .10 .25
23 Anthony Goldwire .10 .25
24 Chuck Graham .10 .25
25 Brian Grant .12 .30
26 Thomas Hamilton .10 .25
27 Darrin Hancock .10 .25
28 Carl Ray Harris .10 .25
29 Askia Jones .10 .25
30 Eddie Jones .20 .50
31 Arturas Karnishovas .10 .25
32 Damon Key .10 .25
33 Jason Kidd .25 .60
34 Antonio Lang .10 .25
35 Donyell Marshall .10 .25
36 Billy McCaffrey .10 .25
37 Jim McIlvaine .10 .25
38 Aaron McKie .10 .25
39 Anthony Miller .10 .25
40 Greg Minor .10 .25
41 Eric Mobley .10 .25
42 Eric Montross .10 .25
43 Harry Moore .10 .25
44 Dwayne Morton .10 .25
45 Gaylon Nickerson .10 .25
46 Cornell Parker .10 .25
47 Wesley Person UER .10 .25
48 Derrick Phelps .10 .25
49 Eric Piatkowski .12 .30
50 Kevin Rankin .10 .25
51 Brian Reese .10 .25
52 Khalid Reeves .10 .25
53 Clayton Ritter .10 .25
54 Carlos Rogers .10 .25
55 Jalen Rose .20 .50
56 Clifford Rozier .10 .25
57 Kevin Salvadori .10 .25
58 Jervaughn Scales .10 .25
59 Shawnelle Scott .10 .25
60 Robert Shannon .10 .25
61 Melvin Simon .10 .25
62 Dickey Simpkins .10 .25
63 Michael Smith .10 .25
64 Stevin Smith .10 .25
65 Byron Starks .10 .25
66 Aaron Swinson .10 .25
67 Shon Tarver .10 .25
68 Deon Thomas .10 .25
69 Brooks Thompson .10 .25
70 B.J. Tyler .10 .25
71 Myron Walker .10 .25
72 Charlie Ward .10 .25
73 Kendrick Warren .10 .25
74 Jamie Watson .10 .25
75 Jeff Webster .10 .25
76 Tracy Webster .10 .25
77 Monty Williams .10 .25
78 Dontonio Wingfield .10 .25
79 Steve Woodberry .10 .25
80 Charles Barkley FLB .25 .60
81 Larry Bird FLB .40 1.00
82 Anfernee Hardaway FLB .25 .60
83 Jamal Mashburn FLB .15 .40
84 Chris Mills FB .10 .25
85 Harold Miner FB .10 .25
86 Alonzo Mourning FLB .20 .50
87 Dikembe Mutombo FB .15 .40
88 Rodney Rogers FB .10 .25
89 Checklist (1-45) .10 .25
90 Checklist (46-90) .10 .25

1995 Ted Williams Abdul Jabbar

These 9 standard-size cards were randomly inserted at a rate of one in every sixteen retail packs. The fronts feature full-bleed color action photos, with the player's name in a stripe across the bottom. On a cloudy sky background, the backs describe various highlights from his career. The cards are numbered with a "KAJ" prefix in small gold letters directly under the player's name.

COMPLETE SET (9) 2.50 6.00
COMMON KAREEM (KAJ1-KAJ9) .75 1.00

1995 Ted Williams Co-op

This 9-card standard-size set was randomly inserted at a rate of one in every twelve packs. This set spotlights both NBA superstars (active and retired) and rookies. The fronts feature the player highlighted against a dotted background. The player's name is on the left side of the card. The Ted Williams logo is in the upper left corner while the Classic logo is in the upper right corner. The back carries biography and a player photo. The cards are numbered with a "CO" prefix and are sequenced in alphabetical order.

COMPLETE SET (9) 4.00 10.00
C01 Charles Barkley .75 2.00
C02 Larry Bird 1.25 3.00
C03 Anfernee Hardaway .75 2.00
C04 Grant Hill .75 2.00
C05 Jason Kidd .75 2.00
C06 Pete Maravich .75 2.00
C07 Alonzo Mourning .60 1.50
C08 Glenn Robinson .40 1.00
C09 Checklist .40 1.00

1995 Ted Williams Constellation

Randomly inserted in foil packs, this 9-card standard-size set consists of cards from the main set as well as the insert sets. Each card sports the distinctive design of the card series to which it belongs. They differ only in their consecutive numbering C1-C9 on the back. The set is sequenced in alphabetical order.

COMPLETE SET (9) 5.00 12.00
C1 Kareem Abdul-Jabbar 1.25 3.00
C2 Charles Barkley 1.25 3.00
C3 Larry Bird 2.00 5.00
C4 Anfernee Hardaway 1.25 3.00
C5 Juwan Howard .75 2.00
C6 Jason Kidd 1.25 3.00
C7 George Mikan 1.25 3.00
C8 Alonzo Mourning 1.00 2.50
C9 Glenn Robinson .60 1.50

1995 Ted Williams Eclipse

Randomly inserted at a rate of one in every twelve packs, this 9-card standard-size set features NBA legends. The cards show the players in air-brushed professional uniforms with the word "Eclipse" in large red letters on the bottom and the player's name immediately below. The backs carry biographical information. The cards are unnumbered and checklisted below in alphabetical order.

COMPLETE SET (9) 3.00 8.00
EC1 Rick Barry .40 1.00
EC2 Larry Bird 1.25 3.00
EC3 Bob Pettit .50 1.25
EC4 Hal Greer .40 1.00
EC5 Kareem Abdul Jabbar .75 2.00
EC6 Pete Maravich .75 2.00
EC7 George Mikan .75 2.00
EC8 Dolph Schayes .50 1.25
EC9 Checklist .20 .50

1995 Ted Williams Gallery

This nine-card standard-size set was randomly inserted at a rate of one in every sixteen packs. The fronts feature a drawing of each player, with both a head-and-shoulder and an action drawing of each player. In the bottom left corner are the words "The Gallery." The backs provide biographical information about the player as well as a blurb about the player in the professional ranks. The cards are numbered with a "G" prefix in the upper left corner and are sequentially numbered at the bottom middle. The cards are sequenced in alphabetical order.

COMPLETE SET (9) 6.00 15.00
G1 Charles Barkley 1.50 4.00
G2 Larry Bird 2.50 6.00
G3 Kareem Abdul Jabbar 1.50 4.00
G4 Walt Frazier 1.00 2.50
G5 Anfernee Hardaway 1.50 4.00
G6 Jamal Mashburn 1.00 2.50
G7 Alonzo Mourning 1.25 3.00
G8 Dikembe Mutombo 1.00 2.50
G9 Checklist .20 .50

1995 Ted Williams Hardwood Legends

This 9-card standard-size set of retired basketball greats as selected by Larry Bird was randomly inserted at a rate of one in every eight regional hobby packs. This set features outstanding duos from New York (1-2), Golden State (3-4), Chicago (5-6), and Boston (7-8). The fronts feature the player in action in airbrushed uniforms while the backs feature biographical information as well as a informational blurb about the player.

COMPLETE SET (9) 1.50 4.00
HL1 Walt Frazier .40 1.00
HL2 Dave DeBusschere .40 1.00
HL3 Rick Barry .30 .75
HL4 Nate Thurmond .30 .75
HL5 Artis Gilmore .30 .75
HL6 Norm Van Lier .40 1.00
HL7 Bill Sharman .40 1.00
HL8 Jo Jo White .30 .75
HL9 Checklist .20 .50

1995 Ted Williams Royal Court

This 9-card standard-size set was randomly inserted into packs at a rate of one in every twelve packs. This set features some of Charles Barkley's favorite players. The fronts contains a full-color action photo of the player with the Ted Williams Logo in the upper left corner, the player's name in yellow lettering down the left side and a Royal Court of Charles logo in the bottom right corner. The backs present biography and on the right side a sword with the name of the player printed on it.

COMPLETE SET (9) 1.50 4.00
RC1 Anfernee Hardaway .60 1.50
RC2 Harold Miner .25 .60
RC3 Jason Kidd .60 1.50
RC4 Donyell Marshall .25 .60
RC5 Jamal Mashburn .40 1.00
RC6 Juwan Howard .40 1.00
RC7 Alonzo Mourning .50 1.25
RC8 Aaron Swinson .25 .60
RC9 Checklist .08 .25

1995 Ted Williams What's Up

This 12-card standard-size set was randomly inserted at a rate of one in every twelve packs. This set featured some of the star attractions of the 94-5 NBA Rookie Class. The fronts feature a full-bleed player photo. In the upper left corner is the Ted Williams logo while the What's Up logo is in the lower left corner of the card. The name of the player is printed in white in the bottom right corner of the card. The cards are numbered with a "WU" prefix and are sequenced in alphabetical order.

COMPLETE SET (9) 1.50 4.00
WU1 Brian Grant .40 1.00
WU2 Eric Montross .30 .75
WU3 Jason Kidd .75 2.00
WU4 Anthony Miller .30 .75
WU5 Khalid Reeves .30 .75
WU6 Carlos Rogers .30 .75
WU7 Jalen Rose .60 1.50
WU8 Charlie Ward .30 .75
WU9 Checklist .08 .25

2003-04 UD Top Prospects

Released in late July, UD Top Prospects consists of a 60-card set and features draftees from the 2003 NBA draft. Base cards place full color player action photos with a borderless top, bottom and right side along with a white border along the left that reads "Top Prospects." Card backs are green with a scale photo of the player and has the usual player stats on the back. Along with the draftees, both Kobe Bryant and Michael Jordan have appearances in this set. Also of note, UD Top Prospects marks the first live cards for the 2003 draft class, most notably, LeBron James, Carmelo Anthony and Darko Milicic. Top Prospects was packaged in 24-pack boxes where packs contained five cards and carried a suggested retail price of $3.99.

COMPLETE SET (60) 10.00 25.00
1 Michael Jordan 1.25 3.00
2 Kobe Bryant .75 2.00
3 LeBron James 3.00 8.00
4 Darko Milicic .25 .60
5 Carmelo Anthony 1.00 2.50
6 Pavel Podkolzin .30 .75
7 Maciej Lampe .20 .50
8 Zaur Pachulia .30 .75
9 Viktor Khryapa .30 .75
10 Anderson Varejao .25 .60
11 Chris Kaman .30 .75
12 Reece Gaines .20 .50
13 Sofoklis Schortsanitis .20 .50
14 Luke Ridnour .25 .60
15 Zoran Planinic .20 .50
16 Nick Collison .25 .60
17 Boris Diaw .30 .75
18 Mickael Pietrus .25 .60
19 Travis Hansen .20 .50
20 Zarko Cabarkapa .20 .50
21 Aleksandar Pavlovic .25 .60
22 David West .30 .75
23 Rick Rickert .20 .50
24 Brian Cook .20 .50
25 Josh Howard .30 .75
26 Jerome Beasley .20 .50
27 Mario Austin .30 .75
28 Brandon Hunter .20 .50
29 Joe Shipp .30 .75
30 Kyle Korver .40 1.00
31 Travis Outlaw .25 .60
32 Quentin Ross .30 .75
33 Matt Carroll .20 .50
34 Troy Bell .20 .50
35 Dahntay Jones .25 .60
36 Keith Bogans .20 .50
37 Ruben Douglas .30 .75
38 Julius Barnes .30 .75
39 Luke Walton .30 .75
40 Marquis Daniels .25 .60
41 Marcus Banks .20 .50
42 Marcus Hatten .30 .75
43 Jeff Newton .30 .75
44 Ronald Dupree .20 .50
45 James Lang .20 .50
46 Jason Gardner .30 .75
47 Jason Kapono .20 .50
48 Brett Blizzard .30 .75
49 Ebi Ere .30 .75
50 Hollis Price .30 .75
51 Steve Blake .25 .60
52 Matt Bonner .30 .75
53 Slavko Vranes .20 .50
54 Kobe Bryant .75 2.00
55 LeBron James 3.00 8.00
56 Darko Milicic .25 .60
57 Carmelo Anthony 1.00 2.50
58 Michael Jordan 1.25 3.00
59 Kobe Bryant .75 2.00
60 LeBron James 3.00 8.00
P3 LeBron James PROMO 20.00 50.00

2003-04 UD Top Prospects Gold Collection

*GOLD: 5X TO 12X BASE CARD HI
STATED PRINT RUN 100 SER.#'d SETS
3 LeBron James 100.00 250.00
55 LeBron James 100.00 250.00
60 LeBron James 100.00 250.00

2003-04 UD Top Prospects After School Specials

Randomly inserted in packs at the rate of one in 12, this 14-card set showcases full color action photography of players who made the jump from the NCAA to the NBA. Each photo is framed with a white and blue border along the top and both sides and an all gold foil border along the bottom with the player's alma mater in embossed lettering.

COMPLETE SET (14) 6.00 15.00
STATED ODDS 1:12
AS1 LeBron James 4.00 10.00
AS2 Darko Milicic .30 .75
AS3 Carmelo Anthony 1.25 3.00
AS4 Luke Ridnour .30 .75
AS5 David West .40 1.00
AS6 Travis Outlaw .30 .75
AS7 Chris Kaman .40 1.00
AS8 Marcus Banks .25 .60
AS9 Reece Gaines .25 .60
AS10 Hollis Price .40 1.00
AS11 Mario Austin .40 1.00
AS12 Nick Collison .30 .75
AS13 Travis Hansen .25 .60
AS14 Josh Howard .40 1.00

2003-04 UD Top Prospects Clashing Colors

Randomly inserted in packs, this five cards set places one player on the top next to a circular swatch of his jersey and one on the bottom. Each card is sequentially numbered to 25.

STATED PRINT RUN 25 SER.#'d SETS
CCJGJK J.Gardner/J.Kapono 10.00 25.00
CCLJCA L.James/C.Anthony 250.00 400.00
CCLWJG L.Walton/J.Gardner 12.50 30.00
CCLWJK L.Walton/J.Kapono 12.50 30.00

2003-04 UD Top Prospects Conference Call

Randomly seeded in packs at the rate of one in 12, this 14-card set places full color action photography between a top and bottom border made to look like a mesh jersey. The player's name appears along the top in gold foil, the player's NCAA conference name appears along the left edge of the card in gold, and the logo for the "Conference Call" insert set is made in embossed gold foil along the bottom of the card.

COMPLETE SET (14) 5.00 12.00
STATED ODDS 1:12
CC1 Carmelo Anthony 1.50 4.00
CC2 Luke Walton .50 1.25
CC3 Dahntay Jones .40 1.00
CC4 Brian Cook .30 .75
CC5 Chris Kaman .50 1.25
CC6 Rick Rickert .30 .75
CC7 Reece Gaines .30 .75
CC8 Hollis Price .50 1.25
CC9 Jason Gardner .50 1.25
CC10 Nick Collison .40 1.00
CC11 Troy Bell .30 .75
CC12 Mario Austin .50 1.25
CC13 Luke Ridnour .40 1.00
CC14 David West .50 1.25

2003-04 UD Top Prospects Dare to Compare Dual Autographs

Randomly inserted in packs, this six card set features top ranked draft choices paired up on each card with both player's autographs. Each card is sequentially numbered to 25.

STATED PRINT RUN 25 SER.#'d SETS
DMCA D.Milicic/C.Anthony 50.00 120.00
DMLJ D.Milicic/L.James 250.00 400.00
LJCA L.James/C.Anthony 400.00 800.00
LRLW L.Ridnour/L.Walton 20.00 50.00
MJKB M.Jordan/K.Bryant 600.00 1000.00
TFBK N.Collison/C.Anthony 50.00 120.00

2003-04 UD Top Prospects Foreign Exchange

Randomly inserted in packs at the rate of one in 24, this seven card set features players who were drafed out of foreign countries. The set utilizes a horizontal card set up with both a full-color photo of the featured player and a circular gold foil emblem which is embossed with the logo for the Foreign Exchange set.

COMPLETE SET (7) 4.00 10.00
STATED ODDS 1:24
FE1 Darko Milicic .75 2.00
FE2 Anderson Varejao .75 2.00
FE3 Sofoklis Schortsanitis .60 1.50
FE4 Pavel Podkolzin 1.00 2.50
FE5 Mickael Pietrus .75 2.00
FE6 Boris Diaw 1.00 2.50
FE7 Aleksandar Pavlovic .75 2.00

2003-04 UD Top Prospects Franchise Makers

Randomly seeded in packs, this seven card set utilizes a horizontal card design with a full color player action photo set against a colored checkered background. Each card is sequentially numbered to 25.

STATED PRINT RUN 25 SER.#'d SETS
FM1 LeBron James 150.00 300.00
FM2 Darko Milicic 6.00 15.00
FM3 Carmelo Anthony 40.00 100.00
FM4 Luke Walton 8.00 20.00
FM5 Pavel Podkolzin 8.00 20.00
FM6 Luke Ridnour 6.00 15.00
FM7 Nick Collison 6.00 15.00

2003-04 UD Top Prospects Higher Achievements

Randomly inserted in packs, this 14-card set places full color action photography on a card design that is borderless on three sides. The bottom of the card has a foil border with the set name and gold foil highlights. Each card is sequentially numbered to 50.

STATED PRINT RUN 50 SER.#'d SETS
HA1 LeBron James 60.00 150.00
HA2 Darko Milicic 5.00 12.00
HA3 Carmelo Anthony 20.00 50.00
HA4 Pavel Podkolzin 6.00 15.00
HA5 Nick Collison 5.00 12.00
HA6 Josh Howard 6.00 15.00
HA7 Chris Kaman 6.00 15.00
HA8 James Lang 4.00 10.00
HA9 Luke Walton 6.00 15.00
HA10 David West 6.00 15.00
HA11 Mario Austin 6.00 15.00
HA12 Rick Rickert 4.00 10.00
HA13 Jerome Beasley 4.00 10.00
HA14 Boris Diaw 6.00 15.00

2003-04 UD Top Prospects Mentors and Learners

Randomly inserted in packs at the rate of one in 24, this seven card set features some of the more talented draft picks paired up with either Michael Jordan or Kobe Bryant. The cards are horizontally designed and place a full color action photo of the draftee on the right and a blue-toned photo of the veteran on the left. All cards have gold foil highlights.

COMPLETE SET (7) 12.50 30.00
STATED ODDS 1:24
ML1 M.Jordan/L.James 4.00 10.00
ML2 K.Bryant/L.Ridnour 2.00 5.00
ML3 M.Jordan/C.Anthony 3.00 8.00
ML4 M.Jordan/D.Jones 2.50 5.00
ML5 K.Bryant/L.James 6.00 15.00
ML6 M.Jordan/J.Lang 2.00 5.00
ML7 M.Jordan/T.Outlaw 2.50 6.00

2003-04 UD Top Prospects Report Card

Inserted in packs, this 14-card set places a full color action photo on the left side of the horizontal design and a grading report on the players basketball skills on the right side. Each card contains gold foil highlights and is sequentially numbered to 250.

STATED PRINT RUN 250 SER.#'d SETS
RC1 LeBron James 20.00 50.00
RC2 Marcus Banks 1.00 2.50
RC3 Carmelo Anthony 5.00 12.00
RC4 David West 1.50 4.00
RC5 Nick Collison 1.25 3.00
RC6 Rick Rickert 1.00 2.50
RC7 Chris Kaman 1.50 4.00
RC8 Luke Walton 1.50 4.00
RC9 Luke Ridnour 1.25 3.00
RC10 Mickael Pietrus 1.25 3.00
RC11 Travis Outlaw 1.25 3.00
RC12 Darko Milicic 1.25 3.00
RC13 Josh Howard 1.50 4.00
RC14 Anderson Varejao 1.25 3.00

2003-04 UD Top Prospects School Colors

Inserted in packs at the rate of one in 288, this six card set features borders along the top and bottom of the horizonal design. Full color player action photos appear in the middle to the left and a jagged circular swatch of game jersey appears on the right.

STATED ODDS 1:288
SCCA Carmelo Anthony 10.00 25.00
SCJG Jason Gardner 5.00 12.00
SCJK Jason Kapono 3.00 8.00
SCLJ LeBron James 60.00 150.00
SCLW Luke Walton 5.00 12.00
SCMJ Michael Jordan SP 75.00 150.00

2003-04 UD Top Prospects Signs of Success

Randomly inserted in packs at the rate of one in 12, this 53-card set places full-color player photos along the top of the card, a "Signs of Success" logo in the middle and a silver hologram sticker on the bottom featuring the player's autograph.

STATED ODDS 1:12
SSAP Aleksandar Pavlovic 2.50 6.00
SSAV Anderson Varejao 5.00 12.00
SSBB Brett Blizzard 3.00 8.00
SSBC Brian Cook 2.00 5.00
SSBD Boris Diaw 3.00 8.00
SSBE Julius Barnes 3.00 8.00
SSCA Carmelo Anthony 25.00 60.00
SSCK Chris Kaman 3.00 8.00
SSDJ Dahntay Jones 2.50 6.00
SSDM Darko Milicic 2.50 6.00
SSEE Ebi Ere 3.00 8.00
SSHP Hollis Price 3.00 8.00
SSHU Brandon Hunter 2.00 5.00
SSJB Jerome Beasley 2.00 5.00
SSJG Jason Gardner 3.00 8.00
SSJH Josh Howard 3.00 8.00
SSJK Jason Kapono 2.00 5.00
SSJL James Lang 2.00 5.00
SSJN Jeff Newton 3.00 8.00
SSJS Joe Shipp 3.00 8.00
SSKB Keith Bogans 2.00 5.00
SSKB Kobe Bryant 100.00 200.00
SSKK Kyle Korver 4.00 10.00
SSLJ LeBron James 700.00 1000.00
SSLR Luke Ridnour 2.50 6.00
SSLW Luke Walton 3.00 8.00
SSMA Mario Austin 3.00 8.00
SSMB Marcus Banks 2.00 5.00
SSMB Matt Bonner 3.00 8.00
SSMC Matt Carroll 2.00 5.00
SSMD Marquis Daniels 2.50 6.00
SSMH Marcus Hatten 3.00 8.00
SSMJ Michael Jordan SP 350.00 600.00
SSML Maciej Lampe 2.00 5.00
SSNC Nick Collison 2.50 6.00
SSPI Mickael Pietrus 2.50 6.00
SSPP Pavel Podkozlin 3.00 8.00
SSQR Quinton Ross 3.00 8.00
SSRD Ronald Dupree 2.00 5.00
SSRD Ruben Douglas 3.00 8.00
SSRG Reece Gaines 2.00 5.00
SSRR Rick Rickert 2.00 5.00
SSSB Steve Blake 2.50 6.00
SSSS Sofoklis Schortsanitis 2.00 5.00
SSSV Slavko Vranes 2.00 5.00
SSTB Troy Bell 2.00 5.00
SSTH Travis Hansen 2.00 5.00
SSTO Travis Outlaw 2.50 6.00
SSVK Viktor Khryapa 3.00 8.00
SSWE David West 3.00 8.00
SSZA Zaur Pachulia 3.00 8.00
SSZC Zarko Cabarkapa 2.00 5.00
SSZP Zoran Planinic 2.00 5.00

1991-92 Ultimate Promo Panel

1 6-card strip 1.25 3.00

2009-10 Upper Deck Draft Edition

COMPLETE SET (69) 10.00 25.00
UNPRICED PLATINUM PRINT RUN ONE SET
1 A.J. Abrams .12 .30
2 A.J. Price .12 .30
3 Alex Ruoff .20 .50
4 Jimmy Baron SP .40 1.00
5 Alonzo Gee .12 .30
6 Garrett Temple SP .40 1.00
7 Antonio Anderson .20 .50
8 Dionte Christmas .12 .30
9 Austin Daye .12 .30
10 B.J. Mullens .12 .30
11 Ricky Rubio SP .60 1.50
12 Ryan Ayers SP .40 1.00
13 Chase Budinger .15 .40
14 Rodrigue Beaubois SP .25 .60
15 Courtney Fells .20 .50
16 Jack McClinton SP .25 .60
17 Sam Young SP .25 .60
18 Cyrus Tate .12 .30
19 Danny Green .25 .60
20 Dar Tucker .20 .50
21 Darren Collison .20 .50
22 B.J. Raymond SP .40 1.00
23 Luke Nevill SP .40 1.00
24 Derrick Brown .12 .30
25 DeMarre Carroll .15 .40
26 Dominic James .20 .50
27 Sergio Llull SP .25 .60
28 Brandon Costner .12 .30
29 Earl Clark .15 .40
30 Josh Shipp .12 .30
31 Eric Maynor .12 .30
32 Dante Cunningham SP .25 .60
33 Gerald Henderson .15 .40
34 Stephen Curry SP 8.00 20.00
35 Rasheem Barrett .12 .30
36 Lester Hudson .12 .30
37 Taj Gibson SP .40 1.00
38 Henk Norel .12 .30
39 Jon Brockman .12 .30
40 James Harden 1.00 2.50
41 James Johnson .15 .40
42 Korvotney Barber SP .40 1.00
43 Ty Lawson SP .40 1.00
44 Jeff Adrien .20 .50
45 Jeff Pendergraph .12 .30
46 Jerel McNeal .20 .50
47 Jeremy Pargo .20 .50
48 Robert Vaden .15 .40
49 Joe Ingles .15 .40
50 Micah Downs .12 .30
51 Jeff Teague .20 .50
52 Jonny Flynn .12 .30
53 Toney Douglas SP .25 .60
54 Josh Heytvelt .12 .30
55 Jrue Holiday .25 .60
56 K.C. Rivers .20 .50
57 Daniel Hackett .12 .30
58 Goran Suton SP .25 .60
59 Lee Cummard .15 .40
60 Leo Lyons .12 .30
61 Connor Atchley .12 .30
62 Tyrese Rice SP .25 .60
63 Michael Bramos .12 .30
64 Marcus Thornton SP .30 .75
65 Nando De Colo .20 .50
66 Nick Calathes .12 .30
67 Omri Casspi .15 .40
68 Wesley Matthews SP .40 1.00
B32 Tyler Hansbrough SP .30 .75
NNO Michael Jordan Rdmpt 8.00 20.00

2009-10 Upper Deck Draft Edition Blue

*BLUE/99/49: 1.25X TO 3X BASE HI
*BLUE/99/49 SP: .6X TO 1.5X BASE
*BLUE/149: .75X TO 2X BASE
*BLUE/149: .4X TO 1X BASE
*BLUE/249: .6X TO 1.5X BASE
*BLUE/249 SP: .4X TO 1X BASE
BLUE PRINT RUN 99 TO 249 SETS

2009-10 Upper Deck Draft Edition Gold

*GOLD: 4X TO 10X BASE HI
*GOLD SP: 2X TO 5X BASE HI
GOLD PRINT RUN 25 SER.#'d SETS

2009-10 Upper Deck Draft Edition Silver

*SILVER: 75X TO 2X BASE HI
*SILVER SP: .4X TO 1X BASE
SILVER PRINT RUN 299 TO 999 SETS

2009-10 Upper Deck Draft Edition Alma Mater

MPLETE SET (24) 25.00 50.00
RANDOM INSERTS IN PACKS
UNPRICED BLACK PRINT RUN ONE SET
*BLUE: .6X TO 1.5X BASE HI
BLUE PRINT RUN 99 SER.#'d SETS
AMBI Matt Biondi 1.00 2.50
AMBO Tom Bosley 1.00 2.50
AMCL Chuck Liddell 2.50 6.00
AMCP Chris Paul 1.00 2.50
AMDP Dustin Pedroia 1.25 3.00
AMFC Fred Couples 1.00 2.50
AMFI Jennie Finch 2.50 6.00
AMFT Frank Thomas 1.00 2.50
AMJF Jennie Finch 2.50 6.00
AMJO Michael Johnson 1.00 2.50
AMKB Kobe Bryant 3.00 8.00
AMKD Kevin Durant 2.00 5.00
AMKG Kevin Garnett 1.25 3.00
AMLF Lisa Fernandez 1.00 2.50
AMLJ LeBron James 3.00 8.00
AMLO Lorena Ochoa 2.50 6.00
AMMB Michael Biehn 1.00 2.50
AMMJ Michael Jordan 6.00 15.00
AMMP Michael Phelps 2.50 6.00
AMMR Matt Ryan 2.00 5.00
AMNG Natalie Gulbis 2.50 6.00
AMRC Randy Couture 2.00 5.00
AMTB Terry Bradshaw 1.00 2.50
AMTW Tiger Woods 3.00 8.00

2009-10 Upper Deck Draft Edition Alma Mater Autographs

STATED PRINT RUN 10 TO 99 SER.#'d SETS
SOME UNPRICED DUE TO SCARCITY
AMBO Tom Bosley/40 10.00 25.00
AMCL Chuck Liddell/25 100.00 200.00
AMCP Chris Paul/25 25.00 50.00
AMDP Dustin Pedroia/99 20.00 50.00
AMFC Fred Couples/99 20.00 40.00
AMFI Jennie Finch/99 20.00 40.00
AMFT Frank Thomas/25 40.00 100.00
AMJF Jennie Finch/99 20.00 40.00
AMKB Kobe Bryant/24 75.00 150.00
AMKD Kevin Durant/35 75.00 150.00
AMKG Kevin Garnett/25 60.00 120.00
AMLF Lisa Fernandez/99 10.00 25.00
AMLJ LeBron James/23 150.00 300.00
AMLO Lorena Ochoa/99 40.00 80.00
AMMB Michael Biehn/18 10.00 25.00
AMMJ Michael Jordan/23 300.00 500.00
AMMP Michael Phelps/99 150.00 300.00
AMMR Matt Ryan/25 50.00 100.00
AMNG Natalie Gulbis/11 300.00 500.00
AMRC Randy Couture/25 50.00 100.00

2009-10 Upper Deck Draft Edition Alma Mater Green

*GREEN: .75X TO 2X BASE HI
GREEN PRINT RUN 50 SER.#'d SETS
AMCL Chuck Liddell 8.00 20.00
AMMP Michael Phelps 8.00 20.00
AMNG Natalie Gulbis 30.00 60.00
AMRC Randy Couture 6.00 15.00
AMTW Tiger Woods 40.00 100.00

2009-10 Upper Deck Draft Edition Alma Mater Red

*RED: 2X TO 5X BASE HI
RED PRINT RUN 25 SER.#'d SETS
AMCL Chuck Liddell 20.00 40.00
AMMP Michael Phelps 20.00 40.00
AMNG Natalie Gulbis 50.00 100.00
AMRC Randy Couture 20.00 40.00
AMTW Tiger Woods 75.00 150.00

2009-10 Upper Deck Draft Edition Autographs

STATED PRINT RUN 149 TO 999 SER.#'d SETS
UNPRICED BLACK PRINT RUN ONE SET
*BLUE: .75X TO 2X BASE HI
BLUE PRINT RUN 25 SER.#'d SETS
UNPRICED GOLD PRINT RUN 5 SETS
*GREEN: .5X TO 1.25X BASE AU HI
GREEN PRINT RUN 49 TO 249 SER.#'d SETS
1 A.J. Abrams/399 2.00 5.00
3 Alex Ruoff/499 3.00 8.00
4 Jimmy Baron/999 3.00 8.00
5 Alonzo Gee/999 2.00 5.00
6 Garrett Temple/999 3.00 8.00
7 Antonio Anderson/999 3.00 8.00
8 Dionte Christmas/999 2.00 5.00
9 Austin Daye/499 2.00 5.00
10 B.J. Mullens/299 2.00 5.00
11 Ricky Rubio/499 20.00 50.00
12 Ryan Ayers/499 3.00 8.00
13 Chase Budinger/399 2.50 6.00
14 Rodrigue Beaubois/299 2.00 5.00
15 Courtney Fells/999 3.00 8.00
16 Jack McClinton/999 2.00 5.00
17 Sam Young/999 2.00 5.00
18 Cyrus Tate/499 2.00 5.00
19 Danny Green/399 4.00 10.00
20 Dar Tucker/399 3.00 8.00
21 Darren Collison/499 3.00 8.00
22 B.J. Raymond/999 3.00 8.00
23 Luke Nevill/399 3.00 8.00
25 DeMarre Carroll/999 2.50 6.00
26 Dominic James/549 3.00 8.00
28 Brandon Costner/399 2.00 5.00
29 Earl Clark/199 2.50 6.00
30 Josh Shipp/499 2.00 5.00
31 Eric Maynor/349 2.00 5.00
32 Dante Cunningham/899 2.00 5.00
33 Gerald Henderson/499 2.50 6.00
34 Stephen Curry/249 600.00 800.00
35 Rasheem Barrett/499 2.00 5.00

6 Lester Hudson/999 2.00 5.00
8 Henk Norel/999 2.00 5.00
9 Jon Brockman/999 2.00 5.00
0 James Harden/499 40.00 100.00
1 James Johnson/499 2.50 6.00
2 Korvotney Barber/499 3.00 8.00
Jeff Adrien/499 3.00 8.00
Jeff Pendergraph/199 2.00 5.00
Jerel McNeal 3.00 8.00
Jeremy Pargo/299 3.00 8.00
Robert Vaden/999 2.50 6.00
oe Ingles/399 2.50 6.00
Micah Downs/299 2.00 5.00
Jeff Teague/499 3.00 8.00
Jonny Flynn/499 2.00 5.00
Toney Douglas/299 2.00 5.00
Josh Heytvelt/999 2.00 5.00
Jrue Holiday/499 8.00 20.00
K.C. Rivers/499 3.00 8.00
Daniel Hackett/999 2.00 5.00
Goran Suton/299 2.00 5.00
9 Lee Cummard/399 2.50 6.00
0 Leo Lyons/999 2.00 5.00
1 Connor Atchley/999 2.00 5.00
2 Tyrese Rice/999 2.00 5.00
3 Michael Bramos/999 2.00 5.00
4 Marcus Thornton/999 2.50 6.00
6 Nick Calathes/999 2.00 5.00
7 Omri Casspi/149 2.50 6.00
8 Wesley Matthews/999 3.00 8.00

2009-10 Upper Deck Draft Edition Coaching Legends

OMPLETE SET (3) 3.00 8.00
ANDOM INSERTS IN PACKS
NPRICED BLACK PRINT RUN ONE SET
BLUE: .6X TO 1.5X BASE HI
LUE PRINT RUN 99 SER.#'d SETS
GREEN: .75X TO 2X BASE HI
GREEN PRINT RUN 50 SER.#'d SETS
RED: 1.25X TO 3X BASE HI
RED PRINT RUN 25 SER.#'d SETS
CLBD Billy Donovan 2.00 5.00
CLBK Bobby Knight 2.00 5.00
CLJT Jerry Tarkanian 1.50 4.00

2009-10 Upper Deck Draft Edition Coaching Legends Autographs

STATED PRINT RUN 25 TO 50 SER.#'d SETS
CLBD Billy Donovan/50 25.00 60.00
CLBK Bobby Knight/25 12.00 30.00
CLJT Jerry Tarkanian/50 15.00 40.00

2009-10 Upper Deck Draft Edition Draft Class

MPLETE SET (10) 10.00 25.00
APPROXIMATE ODDS 1:8
UNPRICED BLACK PRINT RUN ONE SET
BLUE: .6X TO 1.5X BASE HI
LUE PRINT RUN 99 SER.#'d SETS
GREEN: 1X TO 2.5X BASE HI
GREEN PRINT RUN 50 SER.#'d SETS
RED: 2X TO 5X BASE HI
RED PRINT RUN 25 SER.#'d SETS
D84 Olajuwon/Stockton/Jordan 5.00 12.00
D87 Robinson/Grant/Smith 2.50 6.00
D89 Armstrong/Rice/Divac 2.00 5.00
D91 Anderson/Johnson/Augmon 2.00 5.00
DARZ Budinger/Harden/Pendergraph 2.00 5.00
DCHH Hndrsn/Hrdn/Crry 8.00 20.00
DHRC Hrdn/Rbo/Crry 8.00 20.00
DMFC Mynr/Flnn/Crry 5.00 12.00
DRFC Flnn/Rbo/Crry 6.00 15.00
DTHD Hudson/Thornton/Douglas 2.00 5.00

2009-10 Upper Deck Draft Edition Draft Class Autographs

STATED PRINT RUN 15 TO 60 SER.#'d SETS
SOME UNPRICED DUE TO SCARCITY
D87 Robinson/Grant/Smith/15 30.00 80.00
D89 Amstng/Rice/Divac/15 40.00 80.00
D91 Anderson/Johnson/Augmon/15 40.00 80.00
DARZ Budinger/Harden/Pender/60 20.00 50.00
DCHH Henderson/Harden/Curry/60 200.00 400.00
DHRC Harden/Rubio/Curry/30 250.00 500.00
DMFC Maynor/Flynn/Curry/60 200.00 400.00
DRFC Flynn/Rubio/Curry/60 200.00 400.00
DTHD Hudson/Thornton/Toney/60 15.00 30.00

2009-10 Upper Deck Draft Edition School Ties

COMPLETE SET (13) 7.50 15.00
APPROXIMATE ODDS 1:8
UNPRICED BLACK PRINT RUN ONE SET
BLUE: .75X TO 2X BASE HI
BLUE PRINT RUN 99 SER.#'d SETS
GREEN: 1X TO 2.5X BASE HI
GREEN PRINT RUN 50 SER.#'d SETS
RED: 2X TO 5X BASE HI
RED PRINT RUN 25 SER.#'d SETS
STAH J.Holiday/K.Abdul-Jabbar 1.50 4.00
STAJ A.Abrams/C.Atchley 1.00 2.50
STCD S.Cassell/T.Douglas 1.00 2.50
STGB J.Pargo/M.Downs 1.00 2.50
STGS B.Sharman/T.Gibson 1.00 2.50
STHP J.Harden/J.Pendergraph 1.00 2.50
STJT L.Johnson/R.Theus 1.25 3.00
STMA J.McNeal/W.Matthews 1.00 2.50
STMT D.Carroll/L.Lyons 1.00 2.50
STPT B.Pettit/M.Thornton 1.00 2.50
STTL C.Atchley/K.Durant 1.50 4.00
STUB D.Collison/J.Shipp 1.25 3.00
STWF C.Paul/J.Johnson 1.25 3.00

2009-10 Upper Deck Draft Edition School Ties Autographs

STATED PRINT RUN 25 TO 99 SER.#'d SETS
STAH Holiday/Abdul-Jabbar/25 30.00 80.00
STAJ A.Abrams/C.Atchley/99 8.00 20.00
STCD S.Cassell/T.Douglas/25 8.00 20.00
STGB J.Pargo/M.Downs/99 8.00 20.00
STGS B.Sharman/T.Gibson/25 8.00 20.00
STHP J.Harden/J.Pendergraph/99 20.00 50.00
STJT L.Johnson/R.Theus/25 8.00 20.00
STMT D.Carroll/L.Lyons/99 8.00 20.00
STPT B.Pettit/M.Thornton/25 20.00 50.00
STTL K.Durant/C.Atchley/25 50.00 120.00
STWF C.Paul/J.Johnson/25 30.00 60.00

2009-10 Upper Deck Draft Edition Tournament Titans

COMPLETE SET (15) 10.00 25.00
APPROXIMATE ODDS 1:3
UNPRICED BLACK PRINT RUN ONE SET
*BLUE: .6X TO 1.5X BASE HI
BLUE PRINT RUN 99 SER.#'d SET
*GREEN: 1.5X TO 4X BASE HI
GREEN PRINT RUN 50 SER.#'d SETS
*RED: 2.5X TO 6X BASE HI
RED PRINT RUN 25 SER.#'d SETS
TTBW Bill Walton .60 1.50
TTCP Chris Paul .75 2.00
TTDG Darrell Griffith .40 1.00
TTDT David Thompson .50 1.25
TTEB Elgin Baylor .60 1.50
TTGR Glen Rice .50 1.25
TTHO Hakeem Olajuwon .75 2.00
TTIT Isiah Thomas .60 1.50
TTJO Michael Jordan 5.00 12.00
TTJW Jerry West .75 2.00
TTKD Kevin Durant 1.50 4.00
TTMJ Magic Johnson 1.50 4.00
TTSC Stephen Curry 10.00 25.00
TTSY Sam Young .40 1.00
TTTL Ty Lawson .60 1.50

2009-10 Upper Deck Draft Edition Tournament Titans Autographs

STATED PRINT RUN 18 TO 25 SER.#'d SETS
TTBW Bill Walton/25 12.50 30.00
TTCP Chris Paul/25 30.00 80.00
TTDG Darrell Griffith/18 20.00 40.00
TTDT David Thompson/25 12.50 30.00
TTEB Elgin Baylor/25 12.50 30.00
TTGR Glen Rice/25 30.00 60.00
TTHO Hakeem Olajuwon/25 30.00 60.00
TTIT Isiah Thomas/25 20.00 40.00
TTJO Michael Jordan/25 300.00 550.00
TTJW Jerry West/25 30.00 60.00
TTKD Kevin Durant/25 100.00 200.00
TTMJ Magic Johnson/25 30.00 80.00
TTSC Stephen Curry/25 600.00 800.00
TTSY Sam Young/25 12.50 30.00

1995 Visions Sample

This sample card was issued to herald the release of Classic's 150-card Vision series. On the fronts, the full-bleed color action photo is ghosted so that the featured player stands out. The player's name and position are stamped in purple foil. The back carries ad copy promoting the series and describing the insert sets. A tag line toward the bottom indicates that this is a sample card for promotional purposes only.
V96 Damon Stoudamire .75 2.00

1995 Visions

The 1995 Classic Basketball Visions was issued in one series totalling 100 standard-size cards. The set was issued in 5-card packs. The fronts feature a borderless color action player photo with the player's name stamped in gold foil across the picture. The word "Visions" appears in silver below the player's name. The backs carry another borderless player action color photo with the player's name, position, biographical and statistical information, and a prediction, or vision, of what will happen to the player in the coming year. The set features the following topical subsets: Clipboard (66-80), Kidd 1-On-1 (81-90) and Shaq 1-On-1 (91-100).
COMPLETE SET (100) 4.00 10.00
1 Joe Smith .15 .40
2 Antonio McDyess .15 .40
3 Jerry Stackhouse .40 1.00
4 Rasheed Wallace .40 1.00
5 Kevin Garnett 1.00 2.50
6 Damon Stoudamire .30 .75
7 Shawn Respert .12 .30
8 Ed O'Bannon .12 .30
9 Kurt Thomas .12 .30
10 Gary Trent .12 .30
11 Cherokee Parks .12 .30
12 Corliss Williamson .12 .30
13 Eric Williams .12 .30
14 Brent Barry .20 .50
15 Bob Sura .12 .30
16 Theo Ratliff .20 .50
17 Randolph Childress .12 .30
18 Jason Caffey .12 .30
19 Michael Finley .40 1.00
20 George Zidek .12 .30
21 Travis Best .12 .30
22 Loren Meyer .12 .30
23 David Vaughn .12 .30
24 Sherrell Ford .12 .30
25 Mario Bennett .12 .30
26 Greg Ostertag .12 .30
27 Cory Alexander .12 .30
28 Lou Roe .12 .30
29 Dragan Tarlac .12 .30
30 Terrence Rencher .12 .30
31 Junior Burrough .12 .30
32 Andrew DeClercq .12 .30
33 Jimmy King .12 .30
34 Lawrence Moten .12 .30
35 Frankie King .12 .30
36 Rashard Griffith .12 .30
37 Donny Marshall .12 .30
38 John Amaechi .12 .30
39 Erik Meeks .12 .30
40 Donnie Boyce .12 .30
41 Eric Snow .12 .30
42 Anthony Pelle .12 .30
43 Troy Brown .12 .30
44 George Banks .12 .30
45 Tyus Edney .12 .30
46 Mark Davis .12 .30
47 Jerome Allen .12 .30
48 Fred Hoiberg .12 .30
49 Constantin Popa .12 .30
50 Michael McDonald .12 .30
51 Chris Carr .12 .30
52 Cuonzo Martin .12 .30
53 Don Reid .12 .30
54 Shaquille O'Neal .30 .75
55 Hakeem Olajuwon .15 .40
56 Alonzo Mourning .15 .40
57 Dikembe Mutombo .12 .30
58 Jason Kidd .20 .50
59 Glenn Robinson .10 .25
60 Juwan Howard .12 .30
61 Brian Grant .10 .25
62 Eddie Jones .15 .40
63 Rebecca Lobo .20 .50
64 Clint McDaniel .12 .30
65 Scotty Thurman .12 .30
66 Joe Smith CB .07 .20
67 Jerry Stackhouse CB .20 .50
68 Rasheed Wallace CB .20 .50
69 Kevin Garnett CB .50 1.25
70 Ed O'Bannon CB .05 .15
71 Gary Trent CB .05 .15
72 Corliss Williamson CB .05 .15
73 Brent Barry CB .10 .25
74 Shaquille O'Neal CB .15 .40
75 Hakeem Olajuwon CB .07 .20
76 Jason Kidd CB .10 .25
77 Eddie Jones CB .07 .20
78 Glenn Robinson CB .05 .10
79 Brian Grant CB .05 .10
80 Rebecca Lobo CB .10 .25
81 Jerry Stackhouse KO .20 .50
82 Damon Stoudamire KO .15 .40
83 Shawn Respert KO .05 .15
84 Brent Barry KO .10 .25
85 Ed O'Bannon KO .05 .15
86 Glenn Robinson KO .05 .10
87 Randolph Childress KO .05 .15
88 Travis Best KO .05 .15
89 Eddie Jones KO .07 .20
90 Tyus Edney KO .05 .15
91 Joe Smith SO .07 .20
92 Antonio McDyess SO .07 .20
93 Rasheed Wallace SO .20 .50
94 Kevin Garnett SO .50 1.25
95 Alonzo Mourning SO .07 .20
96 Kurt Thomas SO .05 .15
97 Cherokee Parks SO .05 .15
98 Corliss Williamson SO .05 .15
99 Hakeem Olajuwon SO .07 .20
100 Shaquille O'Neal SO .15 .40

1995 Visions Effects

COMPLETE SET (100) 25.00 60.00
*EFFECTS: 1.5X TO 4X BASIC CARDS

1995 Visions Hardcourt Skills

This 15-card standard-size set was randomly inserted one to a box and was printed on 24-point grain wood card stock. The fronts feature a cut-out action player photos on a wood background with a basketball at the top and the card logo and player's name at the bottom. The cards are numbered with a "HC" prefix.
COMPLETE SET (15) 15.00 40.00
HS1 Joe Smith 1.25 3.00
HS2 Antonio McDyess 1.25 3.00
HS3 Jerry Stackhouse 3.00 8.00
HS4 Rasheed Wallace 3.00 8.00
HS5 Damon Stoudamire 2.00 5.00
HS6 Shawn Respert 1.00 2.50
HS7 Ed O'Bannon 1.00 2.50
HS8 Jimmy King 1.00 2.50
HS9 Randolph Childress 1.00 2.50
HS10 Shaquille O'Neal 2.50 6.00
HS11 Hakeem Olajuwon 1.25 3.00
HS12 Jason Kidd 1.50 4.00
HS13 Alonzo Mourning 1.25 3.00
HS14 Scottie Pippen 1.50 4.00
HS15 Glenn Robinson .75 2.00

1995 Visions Laser Art

This 10-card standard-size set was randomly inserted one every 145 packs. The cards feature a duplexed laser die-cut image on a "fabric" card stock. The fronts display a player's image with a net and basketball background. The player's name is printed in the faded blue border at the bottom. The cards are numbered with a "LA" prefix.
COMPLETE SET (10) 40.00 80.00
LA1 Shaquille O'Neal 5.00 12.00
LA2 Jason Kidd 3.00 8.00
LA3 Alonzo Mourning 2.50 6.00
LA4 Damon Stoudamire 5.00 12.00
LA5 Glenn Robinson 1.50 4.00
LA6 Joe Smith 2.50 6.00
LA7 Jerry Stackhouse 6.00 15.00
LA8 Kevin Garnett 15.00 40.00
LA9 Ed O'Bannon 2.00 5.00
LA10 Rebecca Lobo 3.00 8.00

1996 Visions

The 1996 Classic Visions set consists of 150 standard-size cards. The fronts feature full-bleed color action player photos. The player's position and name are presented in blue foil, while the Classic logo and set title "96 Visions" are stamped in gold foil. The back carries a second color photo, college statistics, biography, and a player fact.
COMPLETE SET (150) 6.00 15.00
1 Shaquille O'Neal .30 .75
2 Scottie Pippen .15 .40
3 Jason Kidd .15 .40
4 Hakeem Olajuwon .15 .40
5 Juwan Howard .15 .40
6 Alonzo Mourning .15 .40
7 Glenn Robinson .15 .40
8 Rasheed Wallace .15 .40
9 Ed O'Bannon .08 .25
10 Joe Smith .08 .25
11 Jerry Stackhouse .15 .40
12 Damon Stoudamire .08 .25
13 Cherokee Parks .08 .25
14 Gary Trent .08 .25
15 Shawn Respert .08 .25
16 Kevin Garnett .40 1.00
17 Kurt Thomas .15 .40
18 Jalen Rose .08 .25
19 Michael Finley .15 .40
20 Jason Caffey .08 .25
21 Randolph Childress .08 .25
22 Tyus Edney .08 .25
23 George Zidek .08 .25
24 Antonio McDyess .15 .40
25 Corliss Williamson .15 .40
26 Theo Ratliff .08 .25
27 Eric Williams .08 .25
28 Dikembe Mutombo .15 .40
29 Lawrence Moten .08 .25
30 Jimmy King .08 .25
31 Donyell Marshall .15 .40
32 Brian Grant .15 .40
33 Sharone Wright .08 .25
34 Eddie Jones .15 .40
35 Greg Ostertag .08 .25
36 Terrence Rencher .08 .25
37 David Vaughn .08 .25
38 Rebecca Lobo .15 .40
121 Shaquille O'Neal .30 .75
125 Scottie Pippen .15 .40
128 Jason Kidd .15 .40
131 Joe Smith .08 .25
132 Rasheed Wallace .15 .40
133 Ed O'Bannon .08 .25
134 Michael Finley .15 .40
135 Jerry Stackhouse .15 .40
136 Tyus Edney .08 .25
137 Damon Stoudamire .08 .25
138 Antonio McDyess .15 .40
139 Kevin Garnett .40 1.00
140 Corliss Williamson .15 .40
V96 Damon Stoudamire Promo .40 1.00

1996 Visions Action 21

2 Jerry Stackhouse .20 .50
3 Rasheed Wallace .15 .40

1996 Visions Basketball Update

This 10-card set was intended to update the 1995 Visions basketball draft picks 100-card set. These cards, however, were distributed exclusively as inserts in 1996 Visions multisport packs at a rate of 1:40.
COMPLETE SET (10) 6.00 15.00
U101 Shaquille O'Neal .40 1.00
U102 Jason Kidd .40 1.00
U103 Alonzo Mourning .40 1.00
U104 Damon Stoudamire .20 .50
U105 Glenn Robinson .40 1.00
U106 Joe Smith .20 .50
U107 Jerry Stackhouse .40 1.00
U108 Kevin Garnett .75 2.00
U109 Ed O'Bannon .20 .50
U110 Rebecca Lobo .40 1.00

1996 Visions Signings

The 1996 Visions Signings set consists of 100 standard-size cards. The fronts feature full-bleed color action player photos. The player's position and name are stamped in prismatic foil along with the Classic logo and set title "96 Visions Signings." This set contains standouts from five sports grouped together in this order: basketball, football, hockey, baseball and racing. Cards were distributed in six-card packs. Release date was June 1996. The main allure to this product, in addition to the conventional inserts, were autographed memorabilia redemption cards inserted one per 10 packs.
COMPLETE SET (100) 6.00 15.00
1 Shaquille O'Neal .60 1.50
2 Scottie Pippen .15 .40
3 Jason Kidd .20 .50
4 Hakeem Olajuwon .15 .40
5 Alonzo Mourning .08 .25
6 Glenn Robinson .08 .25
7 Rasheed Wallace .25 .60
8 Ed O'Bannon .08 .25
9 Joe Smith .15 .40
10 Damon Stoudamire .08 .25
11 Cherokee Parks .08 .25
12 Gary Trent .08 .25
13 Shawn Respert .08 .25
14 Kurt Thomas .08 .25
15 Michael Finley .30 .75
16 Jason Caffey .08 .25
17 Randolph Childress .08 .25
18 Tyus Edney .08 .25
19 George Zidek .08 .25
20 Antonio McDyess .20 .50
21 Corliss Williamson .08 .25
22 Theo Ratliff .08 .25
23 Eric Williams .08 .25
24 Brent Barry .08 .25
25 Lawrence Moten .08 .25
26 Bob Sura .08 .25
27 Travis Best .08 .25
28 Terrance Rencher .08 .25

1996 Visions Signings Artistry

This 10-card insert set was printed on thick 24-point stock. Cards were inserted at a rate of 1:60 Vision Signings packs.
COMPLETE SET (10) 20.00 50.00
1 Damon Stoudamire 3.00 8.00
4 Joe Smith 2.00 5.00
7 Jerry Stackhouse 3.00 8.00

1996 Visions Signings Autographs Gold

Certified autographed cards were inserted in Visions Signings packs at an overall rate of 1:12. Some players signed only the silver version while others signed both gold and silver cards. The Gold foil cards were not individually serial numbered. The quantity signed is unknown but assumed to be significantly higher than the corresponding number signed for the silver foil cards. We've listed the unnumbered cards alphabetically.
3 Cory Alexander 1.50 4.00
6 Brent Barry 2.00 5.00
9 Junior Burrough 1.50 4.00
11 Randolph Childress 1.50 4.00
19 Tyus Edney 1.50 4.00
22 Michael Finley 4.00 10.00
29 Fred Hoiberg 2.00 5.00
34 Jason Kidd 8.00 20.00
42 Lawrence Moten 1.50 4.00
43 Alonzo Mourning 6.00 15.00
46 Hakeem Olajuwon 8.00 20.00
47 Shaquille O'Neal 30.00 60.00
51 Scottie Pippen 20.00 40.00
52 Constantin Popa 1.50 4.00
53 Theo Ratliff 4.00 10.00
59 Joe Smith 4.00 10.00
62 Bob Sura 1.50 4.00
73 George Zidek 2.00 5.00

1996 Visions Signings Autographs Silver

Certified autographed cards were inserted in Visions Signings packs at an overall rate of 1:12. Some players signed only silver cards while others signed gold and silver foil cards. The Silver cards were individually serial numbered as noted below. We've listed the unnumbered cards alphabetically.
4 Cory Alexander/375 2.00 5.00
7 Brent Barry/395 2.00 5.00
12 Junior Burrough/395 2.00 5.00
14 Randolph Childress/320 2.00 5.00
22 Tyus Edney/375 2.00 5.00
26 Michael Finley/190 6.00 15.00
33 Fred Hoiberg/395 2.00 5.00
39 Jason Kidd/145 15.00 40.00
48 Lawrence Moten/170 3.00 8.00
49 Alonzo Mourning/405 10.00 25.00
52 Hakeem Olajuwon/270 15.00 40.00
53 Shaquille O'Neal/190 50.00 100.00
57 Scottie Pippen/100 30.00 80.00
58 Constantin Popa/355 2.00 5.00
59 Theo Ratliff/375 6.00 15.00
67 Joe Smith/390 3.00 8.00
70 Bob Sura/385 2.00 5.00
84 George Zidek/365 2.00 5.00

1997 Visions Signings

Score Board's follow-up to the 1996 Visions Signings debut product was released in June 1997. The second-year product had more of a memorabilia emphasis. According to Score Board, 1,700 sequentially numbered cases were produced with five cards per pack, 16 packs per box and 10 boxes per case. Each pack contains either an autographed card or an insert card. The 50-card regular set includes stars and prospects from all four major team sports. Also, one in every two packs contained a gold parallel card to the base set.
COMPLETE SET (50) 5.00 10.00
2 Hakeem Olajuwon .15 .40
3 Glenn Robinson .05 .15
8 Erick Dampier .05 .15
9 Tony Delk .05 .15
10 Steve Nash .30 .75
11 Jerry Stackhouse .15 .40
12 Lorenzen Wright .05 .15
13 Vitaly Potapenko .05 .15
14 Allen Iverson .50 1.25
15 Marcus Camby .05 .15
16 Shareef Abdur-Rahim .05 .15
17 Stephon Marbury .15 .40
18 Ray Allen .25 .60
19 Antoine Walker .15 .40
20 John Wallace .05 .15
21 Kobe Bryant .75 2.00
22 Jermaine O'Neal .08 .25
23 Clyde Drexler .15 .40
24 Scottie Pippen .15 .40
25 Rasheed Wallace .15 .40
26 Joe Smith .08 .25
27 Antonio McDyess .05 .15
28 Alonzo Mourning .05 .15

1997 Visions Signings Gold

COMPLETE SET (50) 10.00 25.00
*GOLD: .8X TO 2X BASIC CARDS
GOLD STATED ODDS 1:2

1997 Visions Signings Artistry

The cards in this 20-card set feature Score Board's "exclusive printing technology" and were inserted at a rate of 1:6 Vision Signings packs.
COMPLETE SET (20) 20.00 40.00
A2 Allen Iverson 3.00 8.00
A3 Marcus Camby 1.00 2.50
A4 Shareef Abdur-Rahim 1.00 2.50
A5 Stephon Marbury 1.00 2.50
A6 Ray Allen 2.00 5.00
A7 Antoine Walker 1.25 3.00
A8 Kobe Bryant 4.00 10.00
A9 Clyde Drexler .60 1.50
A10 Scottie Pippen .60 1.50
A11 Alonzo Mourning .60 1.50

1997 Visions Signings Artistry Autographs

These certified autographed cards feature Score Board's "exclusive printing technology" and were inserted at a rate of 1:18 packs. These 20 cards are autographed parallels of the Artistry insert set.
A2 Allen Iverson 15.00 40.00
A3 Marcus Camby 5.00 12.00
A4 Shareef Abdur-Rahim 8.00 20.00
A5 Stephon Marbury 6.00 15.00
A6 Ray Allen 10.00 25.00
A7 Antoine Walker 12.50 30.00
A8 Kobe Bryant 50.00 100.00
A9 Clyde Drexler 10.00 25.00
A10 Scottie Pippen 15.00 40.00
A11 Alonzo Mourning 8.00 20.00

1997 Visions Signings Autographs

Each 1997 Visions Signings pack contained either an autographed card or an insert card. One in six packs contain a regular autograph card. Four cards, Troy Aikman, Brett Favre, Allen Iverson, and Emmitt Smith were never issued although they appeared on early checklists. One additional key card, Tony Gonzalez, surfaced long after the manufacturer ceased operations.
1 Shareef Abdur-Rahim 4.00 10.00
3 Ray Allen 6.00 15.00
7 Dante Calabria 1.50 4.00
10 Erick Dampier 1.50 4.00
11 Tony Delk 1.50 4.00
15 Tyus Edney 1.50 4.00
16 Brian Evans 1.50 4.00
17 Derek Fisher 1.50 4.00
22 Steve Hamer 1.50 4.00
25 Othella Harrington 2.00 5.00
36 Travis Knight 1.50 4.00
39 Stephon Marbury 3.00 8.00
41 Walter McCarty 1.50 4.00
45 Vitaly Potapenko 1.50 4.00
47 Efthimis Rentzias 1.50 4.00
48 Roy Rogers 1.50 4.00
49 Malik Rose 2.00 5.00
54 Kurt Thomas 1.50 4.00
57 Antoine Walker 8.00 20.00
58 John Wallace 1.50 4.00
60 Jerome Williams 1.50 4.00
64 Lorenzen Wright 1.50 4.00

1997 Wheels Rookie Thunder

This 45-card set features color images of top rookie players silhouetted on a multi-color background with silver foil stamping and ultra gloss printed on 24 pt. paper. The backs carry player information. The set contains the following subsets: Take Two (34-39) and Young Guns (40-44).
COMPLETE SET (34) 3.00 8.00
1 Tim Duncan .60 1.50
2 Keith Van Horn .20 .50
3 Chauncey Billups .30 .75
4 Antonio Daniels .10 .25
5 Tony Battie .10 .25
6 Ron Mercer .12 .30
7 Tim Thomas .20 .50
8 Adonal Foyle .10 .25
9 Tracy McGrady .50 1.25
10 Danny Fortson .10 .25
11 Olivier Saint-Jean .10 .25
12 Austin Croshere .07 .20
13 Derek Anderson .10 .25
14 Maurice Taylor .10 .25
15 Kelvin Cato .10 .25
16 Brevin Knight .10 .25
17 Johnny Taylor .10 .25
18 Chris Anstey .10 .25
19 Scot Pollard .10 .25
20 Paul Grant .10 .25
21 Anthony Parker .10 .25
22 Ed Gray .10 .25
23 Bobby Jackson .12 .30
24 John Thomas .10 .25
25 Charles Smith .10 .25
26 Jacque Vaughn .10 .25
27 Keith Booth .10 .25
28 Serge Zwikker .10 .25
29 Charles O'Bannon .10 .25
30 Bubba Wells .10 .25
31 Kebu Stewart .10 .25
32 James Collins .10 .25
33 Eddie Elisma .10 .25
45 Checklist .10 .25

1997 Wheels Rookie Thunder Rising Storm

*STARS: 2X TO 5X BASE CARD HI

1997 Wheels Rookie Thunder Storm Front

*STARS: 2X TO 5X BASE CARD HI

1997 Wheels Rookie Thunder Ball

Randomly inserted in packs at the rate of one in 216, this 10-card set features die-cut color player images with a piece of official basketball leather embedded in a micro-ethced foil enhanced background and dual foil stamps.
T1 Tim Duncan 15.00 40.00
T2 Keith Van Horn 5.00 12.00
T3 Chauncey Billups 8.00 20.00
T4 Antonio Daniels 2.50 6.00
T5 Tony Battie 2.50 6.00
T6 Ron Mercer 3.00 8.00
T7 Tim Thomas 5.00 12.00
T8 Adonal Foyle 2.50 6.00
T9 Tracy McGrady 12.00 30.00
T10 Danny Fortson 2.50 6.00

1997 Wheels Rookie Thunder Boomers

Randomly inserted in hobby packs only at the rate of one in 28, this 10-card set features color action photos of top rookies printed on die-cut clear acrylic card stock with flame red and silver foil stamping.
COMPLETE SET (10) 12.50 30.00
TB1 Tim Duncan 6.00 15.00
TB2 Tony Battie 1.00 2.50
TB3 Tracy McGrady 5.00 12.00
TB4 Danny Fortson 1.00 2.50
TB5 Maurice Taylor 1.00 2.50
TB6 Serge Zwikker 1.00 2.50
TB7 Scot Pollard 1.00 2.50
TB8 Charles O'Bannon 1.00 2.50
TB9 Adonal Foyle 1.00 2.50
TB10 Keith Van Horn 2.00 5.00

1997 Wheels Rookie Thunder Double Trouble

Randomly inserted in packs at the rate of one in 42, this two-sided six-card set features different lifelike embossed color player images on each side with silver foil and micro-etching.
COMPLETE SET (6) 20.00 50.00
DT1 T.Duncan/K.Van Horn 10.00 25.00
DT2 C.Billups/J.Vaughn 4.00 10.00
DT3 T.McGrady/R.Mercer 6.00 15.00
DT4 B.Jackson/B.Knight 2.00 5.00
DT5 T.Duncan/T.Battie 6.00 15.00
DT6 D.Fortson/T.Thomas 3.00 8.00

1997 Wheels Rookie Thunder Lights Out

Randomly inserted in packs at the rate of one in 96, this five-card set features color images of top rookie shooters printed with phosphorescent inks that glow in the dark with bright chrome foil stamping.
COMPLETE SET (5) 12.50 30.00
LO1 Chauncey Billups 6.00 15.00
LO2 Keith Van Horn 4.00 10.00
LO3 Tim Duncan 12.00 30.00
LO4 Ron Mercer 2.50 6.00
LO5 Antonio Daniels 2.00 5.00

1997 Wheels Rookie Thunder Shooting Stars

Randomly inserted in packs at the rate of one in 11, this 10-card set features action color images of the top first-year game shooters printed on micro-etched holographic foil with foil stamping.
COMPLETE SET (10) 6.00 15.00
SS1 Chauncey Billups 2.00 5.00
SS2 Tracy McGrady 3.00 8.00
SS3 Brevin Knight .60 1.50
SS4 Austin Croshere .50 1.25
SS5 Derek Anderson .60 1.50
SS6 Jacque Vaughn .60 1.50
SS7 Bobby Jackson .75 2.00
SS8 Tim Duncan 4.00 10.00
SS9 Keith Van Horn 1.25 3.00
SS10 Ron Mercer .75 2.00

1997 Wheels Rookie Thunder Stroke Autographs

Randomly inserted in packs at the rate of one in 32, this 14-card set features color action player images with the player's signature printed on his transparent image in the background.
TS1 Tim Duncan 40.00 100.00
TS2 Keith Van Horn 4.00 10.00
TS3 Chauncey Billups 6.00 15.00
TS4 Antonio Daniels 2.00 5.00
TS5 Tony Battie 2.00 5.00
TS6 Ron Mercer 2.50 6.00
TS7 Adonal Foyle 2.00 5.00
TS8 Olivier Saint-Jean 2.00 5.00
TS9 Jacque Vaughn 2.00 5.00
TS10 Austin Croshere 1.50 4.00
TS11 Derek Anderson 2.00 5.00
TS12 Scot Pollard 2.00 5.00
TS13 Serge Zwikker 2.00 5.00
TS14 Charles O'Bannon 2.00 5.00

1997 Wheels Rookie Thunder Take Two

TT1 Ron Mercer .60 1.50
TT2 Derek Anderson .50 1.25
TT3 Scot Pollard .50 1.25
TT4 Jacque Vaughn .50 1.25
TT5 Bobby Jackson .60 1.50
TT6 John Thomas .50 1.25

1997 Wheels Rookie Thunder Young Guns

YG1 Chauncy Billups 1.50 4.00
YG2 Ron Mercer .60 1.50
YG3 Tim Thomas 1.00 2.50
YG4 Tracy McGrady 2.50 6.00
YG5 Maurice Taylor .50 1.25

1991-92 Wild Card Promos

These two standard-size cards were issued to preview the design of 1991-92 Wild Card basketball issue. Two versions of each card were produced; one was marked with and given out at the 1991 San Francisco Sports Card Expo, while the other version (without the San Francisco Sports Expo emblem) was given to dealers and also available as a random insert in Wild Card College Football foil packs. The color action player photos on the fronts are black-bordered, and colored numbers are displayed in the black border above and to the right of the picture. The backs carry a color headshot, biography, and statistics. The cards are numbered on the back with a "P" prefix. The San Francisco give-away cards are arguably less than valuable than the harder-to-obtain football foil pack insert versions.
COMPLETE SET (2) 1.00 2.50
P1 Larry Johnson .75 2.00
P2 Kenny Anderson .40 1.00

1991-92 Wild Card

The Wild Card Collegiate Basketball set contains 120 standard-size cards. One out of every 100 cards is "Wild", with a numbered stripe to indicate how many cards it can be redeemed for. There are 5, 10, 20, 50, 100, and 1,000 denominations, with the highest numbers the scarcest. Whatever the number, the card can be redeemed for that number of regular cards of the same player, after paying a redemption fee of 4.95 per order. The front design features glossy color action player photos on a black card face, with an orange frame around the picture and different color numbers in the top and right borders. The backs have different shades of purple and a color head shot, biography, and statistics.
COMPLETE SET (120) 2.50 5.00
*5/10/20 STRIPES: 2X TO 5X BASE HI
*50/100 STRIPES: 6X TO 15X BASE HI
*1000 STRIPES: 20X TO 50X BASE CARD HI
STRIPES RANDOM INSERTS IN PACKS
1 Larry Johnson No. 1 Pick .20 .50
2 LeRon Ellis .02 .10
3 Alvaro Teheran .02 .10
4 Eric Murdock .08 .25
5A Surprise Card 1 .02 .10
5B Dikembe Mutombo .30 .75
6 Anthony Avent .02 .10
7A Isiah Thomas .20 .50
7B Doug Smith .02 .10
8 Abdul Shamsid-Deen .02 .10
9 Linton Townes .02 .10
10 Joe Wylie .02 .10
11 Cozell McQueen .02 .10
12 David Benoit .08 .25
13 Rodney Monroe .02 .10
14 Dale Davis .20 .50
15 Patrick Ewing .20 .50
16 Greg Anthony .08 .25
17 Robert Pack .08 .25
18 Phil Zevenbergen .02 .10
19 Rick Fox .20 .50
20 Chris Corchiani .08 .25
21 Elliot Perry .08 .25
22 Kevin Brooks .02 .10
23 Mark Macon .08 .25
24 Larry Johnson .30 .75
25 George Ackles .02 .10
26A Surprise Card 5 .02 .10
26B Christian Laettner PROMO .20 .50
27 Andy Fields .02 .10
28 Kevin Lynch .02 .10
29 Graylin Warner .02 .10
30 James Bullock .02 .10
31 Steve Bucknall .02 .10
32 Carl Thomas .02 .10
33 Doug Overton .02 .10
34 Brian Shorter .02 .10
35 Chad Gallagher .02 .10
36 Antonio Davis .08 .25
37 Sean Green .02 .10
38 Randy Brown .08 .25
39 Richard Dumas .02 .10
40 Terrell Brandon .20 .50
41 Marty Embry .02 .10
42 Ronnie Coleman .02 .10
43 King Rice .02 .10
44 Perry Carter .02 .10
45 Andrew Gaze .02 .10
46A Surprise Card 2 .02 .10
46B Billy Owens .08 .25
47A Surprise Card 3 .02 .10
47B Stacey Augmon .08 .25
48 Jimmy Oliver .02 .10
49 Treg Lee .02 .10
50 Ricky Winslow .02 .10
51 Danny Vranes .02 .10
52 Jay Murphy .02 .10
53 Adrian Dantley .08 .25
54 Joe Arlauckas .02 .10
55 Moses Scurry .02 .10
56 Andy Toolson .02 .10
57 Ramon Rivas .02 .10
58 Charles Davis .02 .10
59 Butch Wade .02 .10
60 John Pinone .02 .10
61 Bill Wennington .08 .25
62 Walter Berry .02 .10
63 Terry Dozier .02 .10
64 Mitchell Anderson .02 .10
65 Pace Mannion .02 .10
66 Pete Myers .02 .10
67 Eddie Lee Wilkins .02 .10
68 Mark Hughes .02 .10
69 Darryl Dawkins .08 .25
70 Jay Vincent .02 .10
71 Doug Lee .02 .10
72 Russ Schoene .02 .10
73 Tim Kempton .02 .10
74 Earl Cureton .02 .10
75 Terence Stansbury .02 .10
76 Frank Kornet .02 .10
77 Bob McAdoo .20 .50
78 Haywood Workman .02 .10
79 Vinny Del Negro .08 .25
80 Harold Pressley .02 .10
81 Robert Smith .02 .10
82 Adrian Caldwell .02 .10
83 Scottie Pippen .30 .75
84 John Stockton .10 .30
85 Elwayne Campbell .02 .10
86 Chris Gatling .08 .25
87 Cedric Henderson .02 .10
88 Mike Iuzzolino .02 .10
89 Fennis Dembo .02 .10
90 Darnell Valentine .02 .10
91 Michael Brooks .02 .10
92 Marty Conlon .02 .10
93 Lamont Strothers .02 .10
94 Donald Hodge .02 .10
95 Pete Chilcutt .08 .25
96 Kenny Anderson ERR .20 .50
96B Kenny Anderson COR .20 .50
97 Ian Lockhart .02 .10
98A Surprise Card 4 .02 .10
98B Steve Smith .30 .75
99 Larry Lawrence .02 .10
100 Jerome Mincy .02 .10
101 Ben Coleman .02 .10
102 Tom Copa .02 .10
103 Demetrius Calip .02 .10
104 Myron Brown .02 .10
105 Derrick Pope .02 .10
106 Kelvin Upshaw .02 .10
107 Andrew Moten .02 .10
108 Terry Tyler .02 .10
109 Kevin Magee .02 .10
110 Tharon Mayes .02 .10
111 Perry McDonald .02 .10
112 Jose Ortiz .02 .10
113 Rick Mahorn .08 .25
114 David Butler .02 .10
115 Carl Herrera .02 .10
116 Darrell Mickens .02 .10
117 Steve Bardo .02 .10
118 Checklist 1 .02 .10
119 Checklist 2 .02 .10
120 Checklist 3 .02 .10

1991-92 Wild Card Red Hot Rookies

These cards were randomly packed in the Collegiate Basketball foil cases, and they included denomination cards. The cards measure the standard size. The front design features glossy color action player photos on a black card face, with an orange frame around the picture and different color numbers in the top and right borders. The "Red Hot Rookies" emblem in the lower left corner rounds out the card face. The backs have a color close-up photo, biography, and complete college statistics.
COMPLETE SET (10) 5.00 12.00
5/10/20 STRIPES: 1.25X TO 3X BASIC CARDS
50/100 STRIPES: 8X to 20X BASIC CARDS
1000 STRIPES: 75X TO 150X BASIC CARDS
RANDOM INSERTS IN PACKS
1 Dikembe Mutombo 1.50 4.00
2 Larry Johnson 2.00 5.00
3 Steve Smith 2.00 5.00
4 Billy Owens .50 1.25
5 Mark Macon .20 .50
6 Stacey Augmon UER .50 1.25
7 Victor Alexander .20 .50
8 Mike Iuzzolino .20 .50
9 Rick Fox .50 1.25
10 Terrell Brandon UER 1.50 4.00

1991-92 Wild Card Redemption Prototypes

This six-card standard-size was intended to preview the forthcoming Wild Card basketball set. By sending in a surprise card from the 1991-92 Wild Card Collegiate set, the collector received a cello pack consisting of a replacement card and two redemption prototype cards. The fronts feature color action player photos with white borders and colored numbers suspended in the top and right borders. The backs feature a color headshot, biography, and statistics. The cards are numbered on the back with a "P" prefix.
COMPLETE SET (6) .80 2.00
P1 LaPhonso Ellis .20 .50
P2 Adam Keefe .05 .15
P3 Robert Horry .20 .50
P4 Bryant Stith .08 .25
P5 Christian Laettner .40 1.00
P6 Malik Sealy .08 .25